BECKETT COL

GAMING ALMANAC

15TH EDITION - 2025

THE HOBBY'S MOST RELIABLE AND RELIED UPON SOURCE™

Prices in this guide reflect current retail rates determined just prior to printing. They do not reflect for-sale prices by the author, publisher, distributors, advertisers, or any card dealers associated with this guide. Every effort has been made to eliminate errors. Readers are invited to write us noting any errors which may be researched and corrected in subsequent printings. The publisher will not be held responsible for losses which may occur in the sale or purchase of cards because of information contained herein.

BECKETT is a registered trademark of BECKETT COLLECTIBLES LLC, PLANO, TEXAS
Manufactured in the United States of America | Published by Beckett Collectibles LLC

BECKETT

Beckett Collectibles LLC
2700 Summit Ave, Ste 100, Plano, TX 75074
1 (866) 287-9383 • beckett.com

First Printing ISBN: 978-1-953801-22-7

TABLE OF CONTENTS

BECKETT COLLECTIBLES
GAMING ALMANAC
15TH EDITION • 2025

EDITORIAL
Mike Payne - **Editorial Director**
Ryan Cracknell - **Hobby Editor**
Eric Knagg - **Lead Graphic Designer**

COLLECTIBLES DATA PUBLISHING
Brian Fleischer
Manager | Sr. Market Analyst
Daniel Moscoso - **Digital Studio**
Matt Bible, Jeff Camay, Steven Dalton, Justin Grunert, Rex Pastrana, Kristian Redulla, Chris Roberts, Adrian Saba, Angelou Talle, Bryl Trinidad, Sam Zimmer
Price Guide Staff

ADVERTISING
Alex Soriano - **Advertising Sales Executive**
alex@beckett.com 1.619.392.5299

BECKETT GRADING SERVICES
2700 Summit Ave, Ste 100, Plano, TX 75074
Grading Sales - www.beckett.com/contact
Mike Gardner - mgardner@beckett.com
Aram Munoz - amunoz@beckett.com
Brennan Archer - barcher@beckett.com
Kenton Bettley - kentonb@beckett.com
Mike Haburay - mhaburay@beckett.com
SHOW INFORMATION
2700 Summit Ave, Ste 100, Plano, TX 75074
lknox@Beckett.com

OPERATIONS
Alberto Chavez - **Sr. Logistics & Facilities Manager**

EDITORIAL, PRODUCTION & SALES OFFICE
2700 Summit Ave, Ste 100, Plano, TX 75074
972.991.6657 www.beckett.com

For Customer Service/Price Guide Inquiries:
Beckett Collectibles LLC
2700 Summit Ave, Ste 100, Plano, TX 75074
www.beckett.com/contact

Subscriptions, address changes, renewals, missing or damaged copies - 1.866.287.9383
Foreign inquires
subscriptions@beckett.com
Back Issues beckettmedia.com
Books, Reprints 1.469.830.3996 OPT 7
Dealer Sales 1.469.830.3996 OPT 7
dealers@beckett.com

BECKETT®

Beckett Collectibles LLC
Kevin Isaacson - **CEO**

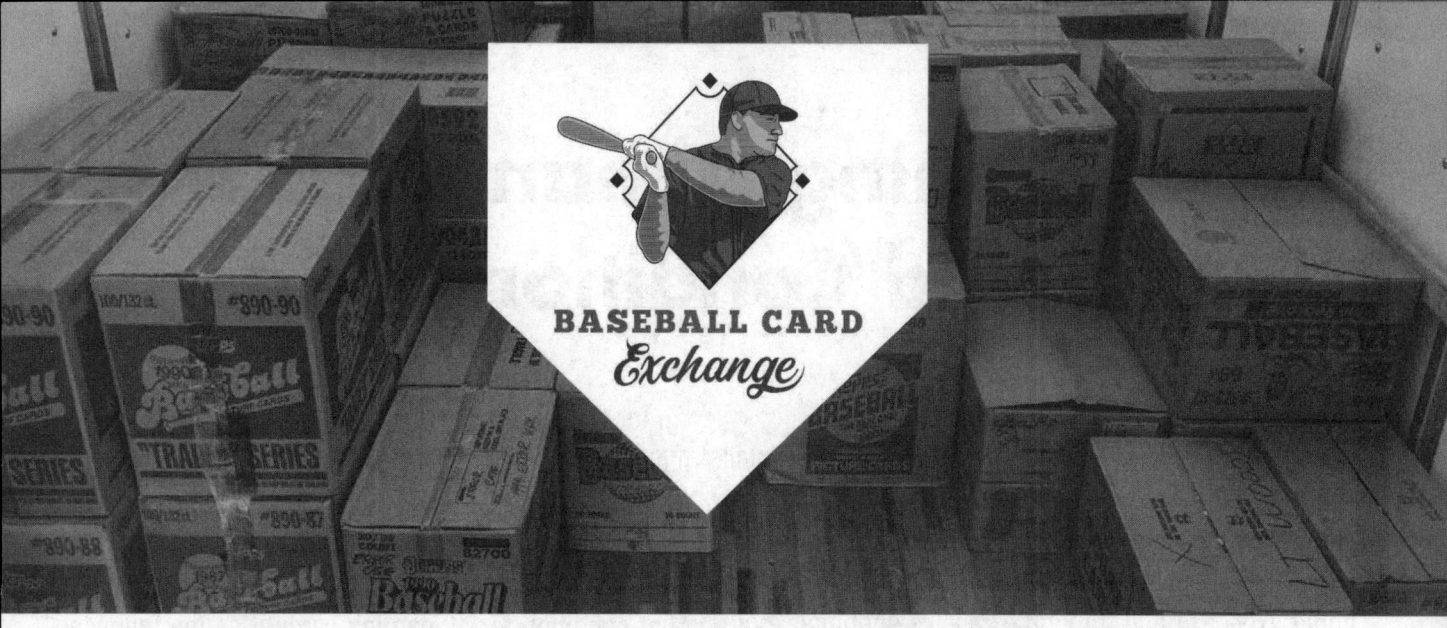

2025 Gaming Almanac How to Use and Condition Guide

WHAT THE COLUMNS MEAN

The LO and HI columns reflect a range of current retail selling prices and are listed in U.S. dollars. The HI column represents the typical full retail selling price while the LO column represents the lowest price one could expect to find through extensive shopping. Both columns represent the same condition for the card listed. Keep in mind that market conditions can change quickly, up or down, based on extreme levels of demand. The published HI and LO column prices in this particular publication are a single snapshot in time and cannot be completely accurate for every card listed.

ONLY A REFERENCE

The data and pricing information contained within this publication is intended for reference only. Beckett's goal is, and always will be, to provide the most accurate and verifiable information in the industry. However, Beckett cannot guarantee the accuracy of all data published and typographical errors periodically occur. Buyers and sellers of gaming cards should be aware of this and handle their personal transactions at their own risk. If you discover an error or misprint in this publication, please notify us via email at CRoberts@beckett.com.

MULTIPLIERS

Some parallel sets are listed with multipliers to provide values of unlisted cards. Multiplier ranges (i.e. 1X to 2X) apply only to the HI column. Example, if basic-issue card A lists for $2 to $4, and the multiplier is "1X to 2X", then the parallel version of card A or the insert card in question is valued at $4 to $8. Please note the term "basic card" used in the price guide refers to a standard regular-issue card. A "basic card" cannot be an insert or parallel card.

CARD CONDITION

The value of your card is dependent on the condition or "grade" of your card. Prices in this issue reflect the highest raw condition (i.e. not professionally graded by a third party) of the card most commonly found at shows, shops, on the internet, and right out of the pack for brand new releases. This generally means Near Mint-Mint condition for all gaming cards. Use the following chart as a guide to estimate the value of your cards in a variety of conditions using the prices found in this issue.

CARD GRADES

Mint (MT) – A card with no wear or flaws. The card has four perfect corners, 60/40 or better centering from top to bottom and from left to right, original gloss, smooth edges, and original color borders. A Mint card does not have print spots, color or focus imperfections.

Near Mint-Mint (NRMT-MT) – A card with one minor flaw. Any one of the following would lower a Mint card to Near Mint-Mint: one corner with a slight touch of wear, barely noticeable print spots, color or focus imperfections. This card must have a 60/40 or better centering in both directions, original gloss, smooth edges, and original color borders.

Near Mint (NRMT) – A card with one minor flaw. Any one of the following would lower a Mint card to Near Mint-Mint: one very slightly scuffed corner or two or four corners with slight touches of wear, 70/30 to 60/40 centering, slightly rough edges, minor print spots, color or focus imperfections. This card must have original gloss and original color borders.

Excellent-Mint (EXMT) – A card with two or three slightly worn corners with centering no worse than 80/20. The card may have no more than two of the following slightly rough edges, very slightly discolored borders, mirror print spots, color or focus imperfections. The card must have original gloss.

Excellent (EX - aka SP or Slightly Played) – A card with four slightly worn corners and centering is no worse than 80/20. The card may have a small amount of original gloss lost, rough edges, slightly discolored borders, and minor print spots, color or focus imperfections.

Very Good (VG) – A card that has been handled but not abused slightly worn corners with slight layering, slight notching on edges, a significant amount of gloss lost from the surface but no scuffing and moderate discoloration of borders. The card may have a few light creases.

Good (G), Fair (F), Poor (P) (aka HP or Heavily Played) – A well-worn, mishandled or abused card, badly worn corners, lots of scuffing, most or all original gloss missing, seriously discolored borders, moderate or heavy creasing, and one or more serious flaws. The grade of Good, Fair or Poor depends on the severity of wear and flaws. Good, Fair, or Poor cards are generally used only as fillers.

Special Note: The most widely used grades are defined here. Obviously, many cards will not perfectly match one of the definitions. Therefore, categories between the major grades known as in-between grades are used, such as Good to Very Good (G-VG), Very Good to Excellent (VG-EX), and Excellent-Mint to Near Mint (EXMT-NRMT). Such grades indicate a card with all qualities of the lower category but with at least a few qualities of the higher category.

RARITY QUICK GUIDE

***Note: Some rarities may be language exclusives. These may or may not appear within the checklists provided by Beckett. Also, these provided lists may be incomplete as companies will create new rarities with newer releases.**

DIGIMON CARD GAME
Common – C
Uncommon – U
Rare – R
Super Rare – SR
Secret Rare – SEC
Promo – P

DISNEY LORCANA
Common – – C
Uncommon – – U
Rare – – R
Super Rare – –SR
Legendary – – L
Enchanted – – E
Promo – – P

FLESH & BLOOD TCG
Common – C
Rare – R
Super Rare – SR
Majestic – M
Legendary – L
Fabled – ◆ – F

MAGIC THE GATHERING
Land – L
Common – C
Uncommon – U
Rare – R
Mythic – M
Token – T

ONE PIECE CARD GAME
Common – C
Uncommon – U
Rare – R
Super Rare – SR
Secret Rare – SEC
Leader – L
Special Card – SP
Promo – P
Treasure Rare – TR

POKÉMON
Common – ● - C
Uncommon – ◆ – U
Rare – ★ – R
Double Rare – EX or 2 Stars - RR
Rainbow Rare – White Star - R
Triple Rare – 3 Gold Stars - RRR
Ultra Rare – UR
Trainer Rare – TR
Prism Rare – PR
Amazing Rare – Rainbow A – AR
Secret Rare – ★★ I.E: 120/100 – SEC
Illustration Rare – IR
Special Illustration Rare – SIR

WEISS SCHWARZ
Trial Deck – TD
Climax Common – CC
Climax Rare – CR
Common – C
Uncommon – U
Rare – R
Double Rare – RR
Super Rare – SR
Triple Rare – RRR
Special Rare – SP
Super Special Rare – SSP
Extra Rare – XR
Over Frame Rare – OFR
KanColle Rare – RR+
Miku Rare – RR+
Wooser Rare – WR
Gigant Rare – GR
Jojo Rare – JJR
Chainsaw Man Rare – CSMR
SPYR – Spy Rare
ABR – AoButa Rare

YU-GI-OH!
Common – C
Short Print Common – SP
Super Short Print Common – SSP
Rare – R
Holofoil Rare – HFR
Super Rare – SR
Ultimate Rare – ULT
Ultra Rare – UR
Ultra Secret Rare – USCR
Secret Rare – SCR
Secret Ultra Rare – SCUR
Ghost Rare – GR
Gold Ultra Rare – GUR
Colorful Rare – CLR
Colorful Ultra Rare – CUR
Collector's Rare – CR
Extra Secret Rare – EXSCR
Prismatic Secret Rare – PSCR
Millennium Rare – MR

Starfoil Rare – SFR
Platinum Rare – PLR
Platinum Secret Rare – PLSCR
Platinum Collectors Rare – PLCR
Parallel Common – PC
Parallel Rare – PR
Super Parallel Rare – SPR
Ultra Parallel Rare – UPR
Secret Parallel Rare – SCRPR
Pharaoh's Rare – URP
Prismatic Ultimate Rare – PULTR
Starlight Rare – SLR
Quarter Century Secret Rare – QCSCR
Astral Glyph Rare – AGR
Ten Thousand Dragon Rare – TTDR

BATTLE SPIRITS SAGA
Common – C
Uncommon – UC
Rare – R
X Rare – X
Special Rare – SPR
Collaboration Rare – CR
Saga Rare – SAGA
Promo – PR

CARDFIGHT!! VANGUARD
Common – C
Rare – R
Holo Rare – H
Double Rare – RR
Triple Rare – RRR
Frame Rare – FR
Double Frame Rare – FFR
Vanguard Rare – VR
Special Vanguard Rare – SVR
Origin Rare – OR
Image Rare – IMR
Special Reprint – Re
Secret Rare – SEC
Generation Rare – GR
Special Generation Rare – SGR
Special Parallel – SP
Shaman King Rare – SKR
Lyrical Special Rare – LSR
Rummy Labyrinth Rare – RLR
Zeroth Rare – ZR
Wedding Special Parallel – WSP
Promo – P
Trial Deck – TD
Touken Ranbu Rare – TRR
Ragnarok Rare – RGR
Exclusive Rare – EX
EX Common - EXC
EX Triple Rare – EXRRR
Super Rare – SR
Token – T
Starter Deck – SD
Super Generation Rare – SGR
Vanguard Secret Rare – VSR
Over Double Rare – ORR
Lyrical Secret Rare – LSR
Legion Rare – LR
Dress Secret Rare – DSR
Z Rare – ZR

Secret Rare – SEC
Image Ride Rare - IMR
Another Secret Rare – ASR
Lyrical Special – LSP
Original Costume Rare – OCR
10th Anniversary RRR - 10th RRR
10th Anniversary SP – 10th SP
10th Anniversary SEC – 10th SEC
Serial Numbered Rare – SNR
Secret P Rare – SECP
Over Triple Rare – ORRR
World Original - WO
Bavsargra Special Rare – BSR
Special Series Rare – SSR
Secret V Rare – SECV

DRAGON BALL SUPER MASTERS
Common – C
Uncommon – UC
Rare – R
Super Rare – SR
Secret Rare – SCR
Feature Rare – FR
Special Rare – SPR
Starter Rare – ST
Promotion Rare – PR
Expansion Rare – EX
Destruction Rare – DR
Infinite Saiyan Rare – ISR
Duo Power Rare – DPR
Noble Hero Rare – NHR
Ignoble Villian Rare – IVR
Special Rare Signature – SPRS
Reboot Leader Rare – RLR
Iconic Attack Rare – IAR
Destroyer & Angel Rare – DAR
Giant Force Rare – GFR
Son Gohan Rare – SGR

DRAGON BALL SUPER FUSION WORLD
Common – C
Uncommon – U
Rare – R
Super Rare – SR
Secret Rare – SEC
Leader – L

FINAL FANTASY TCG
Common – C
Rare – R
Hero – H
Legend – L
Starter – S
Promo – PR

FORCE OF WILL TCG
Common – C
Normal – N
Rare – R
Super Rare – SR
Uncommon – U

Promo – PR
Ruler Rare – RR
Starter Exclusive – SE
Memoria – M
Marvel Rare – MRV
Sub Ruler Rare – SRR
XR – XR

METAZOO
Bronze – B
Silver – S
Gold – G

SHADOWVERSE: EVOLVE TCG
Bronze – B
Silver – S
Gold – G
Premium – PR
Legendary – L
Super Legendary – SL
Ultimate – ULT
Promo – P

STAR WARS: UNLIMITED
Common – C
Uncommon – U
Rare – R
Legendary – L
Special – S

UNIVERSUS
Common – C
Extra Rare – XR
Uncommon – U
Rare – R
Starter Exclusive – SE
Promo – P
Ultra Rare – UR
Platinum Common – PC
Platinum Rare – PR
Character Extra Rare – CHXR
Character Rare – CHR
Secret Rare – SEC
Extra Secret Rare – XSEC
Chrome Rare – CR

WIXOSS
Common – C
Rare – R
LRIG – L
LRIG Common – LC
LRIG Rare – LR
LRIG Rare Parallel - LR
Piece – PI
Super Rare – SR
Secret – SCR
Diva Rare – DiR
Ultra Rare – UR
Starter Deck – ST
Token – T
Promo – PR

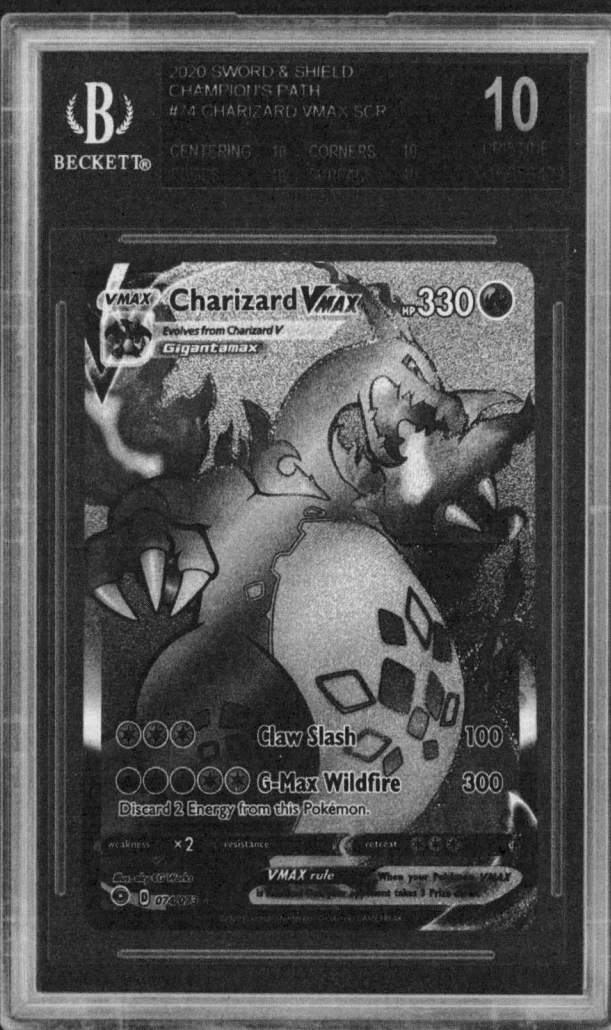

GAMING

2020 Cardfight Vanguard V Booster Set 8 Silverdust Blaze

VBT08001 Alter Ego Messiah SP	12.50	25.00
VBT08001 Alter Ego Messiah VR	2.00	4.00
VBT08002 Dragonic Overlord "The X" SP	30.00	60.00
VBT08002 Dragonic Overlord "The X" VR	6.00	12.00
VBT08003 Dragonic Blademaster "Souen" SP	12.50	25.00
VBT08003 Dragonic Blademaster "Souen" VR	2.50	5.00
VBT08004 Supreme Heavenly Battle Deity, Susanoo SP	7.50	15.00
VBT08004 Supreme Heavenly Battle Deity, Susanoo VR	1.00	2.00
VBT08005 Great Cosmic Hero, Grandgallop SP	3.00	6.00
VBT08005 Great Cosmic Hero, Grandgallop VR	.30	.75
VBT08006 Goddess of the Sun, Amaterasu RRR	4.00	8.00
VBT08006 Goddess of the Sun, Amaterasu SP	15.00	30.00
VBT08007 Goddess of Stream Waters, Ichikishima RRR	.60	1.25
VBT08007 Goddess of Stream Waters, Ichikishima SP	6.00	12.00
VBT08008 Divine Sword, Ame-no-Murakumo RRR	2.00	4.00
VBT08008 Divine Sword, Ame-no-Murakumo SP	5.00	10.00
VBT08009 Ignitroad Dragon RRR	.50	1.00
VBT08009 Ignitroad Dragon SP	7.50	15.00
VBT08010 Heat Shot Dragon RRR	.50	1.00
VBT08010 Heat Shot Dragon SP	7.50	15.00
VBT08011 Lava Flow Dragon RRR	2.50	5.00
VBT08011 Lava Flow Dragon SP	10.00	20.00
VBT08012 Black-dressed Outstanding Deity, Bladblack RRR	2.50	5.00
VBT08012 Black-dressed Outstanding Deity, Bladblack SP	25.00	50.00
VBT08013 Cosmic Hero, Grandrope RRR	1.50	3.00
VBT08013 Cosmic Hero, Grandrope SP	6.00	12.00
VBT08014 Genesis Machine Deity, Volkogode RRR	1.50	3.00
VBT08014 Genesis Machine Deity, Volkogode SP	7.50	15.00
VBT08015 Lady Fencer of Matter Transmission RRR	1.25	2.50
VBT08015 Lady Fencer of Matter Transmission SP	12.50	25.00
VBT08016 Lady Battler of the White Dwarf RRR	5.00	10.00
VBT08016 Lady Battler of the White Dwarf SP	25.00	50.00
VBT08017 Goddess of Abundant Harvest, Otogosahime RR	.25	.50
VBT08018 Diviner, Kuroikazuchi RR	.50	1.00
VBT08019 Divine Sword, Kusanagi RR	1.00	2.00
VBT08020 Torridcannon Dragon RR	1.00	2.00
VBT08021 Dragon Dancer, Faja RR	.30	.60
VBT08022 Dragon Knight, Jannat RR	.50	1.00
VBT08023 Metalborg, Sin Buster RR	.20	.40
VBT08023 Metalborg, Sin Buster SP	3.00	6.00
VBT08024 Metalborg, Ur Buster RR	.30	.60
VBT08024 Metalborg, Ur Buster SP	1.50	3.00
VBT08025 Cosmic Hero, Grandbeat RR	.30	.75
VBT08026 Screening Deletor, Idoga RR	.30	.75
VBT08027 Counterkill Strike, Gastorur RR	.50	1.00
VBT08028 Blink Messiah RR	.30	.75
VBT08029 Battle Sister, Praline R	.20	.40
VBT08030 Padparadscha Witch, GiGi R	.20	.40
VBT08031 Diviner, Yachimatahiko R	.20	.40
VBT08032 Offset Angel R	.20	.40
VBT08033 Oddness Ardor Dragon R	.20	.40
VBT08034 Dragon Knight, Ishaq R	.20	.40
VBT08035 Intense-aim Dragon R	.20	.40
VBT08036 Dragon Dancer, Soja R	.20	.40
VBT08037 Super Dimensional Robo, Daiarm R	.20	.40
VBT08038 Cosmic Hero, Grandvolver R	.20	.40
VBT08039 Dimensional Robo, Daidumper R	.20	.40
VBT08040 Dimensional Robo, Daijacker R	.20	.40
VBT08041 Dimensional Robo, Daiscooper R	.20	.40
VBT08042 White Matter, Jact R	.20	.40
VBT08043 Ditto Deletor, Baon R	.20	.40
VBT08044 Bending Solid-hit, Vanmaanen R	.20	.40
VBT08045 Hire Deletor, Farwon R	.20	.40
VBT08046 Clear Frame "Whirling Wash of Curse Cleansing" R	.20	.40
VBT08047 Sapient Angel C	.10	.20
VBT08048 Battle Maiden, Kikka C	.10	.20
VBT08049 Battle Sister, Alfenim C	.10	.20
VBT08050 Diviner, Mutou C	.10	.20
VBT08051 Director Angel C	.10	.20
VBT08052 Battle Maiden, Tsubaki C	.10	.20
VBT08053 Solar Maiden, Uzume C	.10	.20
VBT08053 Solar Maiden, Uzume SP	5.00	10.00
VBT08054 Oracle Guardian, Nike C	.10	.20
VBT08055 Battle Sister, Ginger C	.10	.20
VBT08056 Battle Sister, Tiramisu C	.10	.20
VBT08057 Battle Sister, Brioche C	1.00	2.00
VBT08058 Dragon Knight, Nizar C	.10	.20
VBT08059 Dynamelt Dragon C	.10	.20
VBT08060 Demonic Dragon Mage, Sakara C	.10	.20
VBT08061 Flame of Scorching Heat, Gibil C	.10	.20
VBT08062 Purple Gem Carbuncle C	.10	.20
VBT08063 Lizard Soldier, Conroe C	.10	.20
VBT08063 Lizard Soldier, Conroe SP	15.00	30.00
VBT08064 Angry Horn Dragon C	.10	.20
VBT08065 Demonic Dragon Mage, Rakshasa C	.10	.20
VBT08066 Toxophilite Dragon C	.10	.20
VBT08067 Mother Orb Dragon C	.10	.20
VBT08068 Super Dimensional Robo, Dairoller C	.12	.25
VBT08069 Dimensional Robo, Daiboat C	.10	.20
VBT08070 Dimensional Robo, Gofire C	.10	.20
VBT08071 Dimensional Robo, Gobiker C	.10	.20
VBT08072 Dimensional Robo, Daigyro C	.10	.20
VBT08073 Dimensional Robo, Daifalcon C	.10	.20
VBT08074 Metalborg, Blackboi C	.10	.20
VBT08074 Metalborg, Blackboi SP	7.50	15.00
VBT08075 Dimensional Robo, Dairacer C	.10	.20
VBT08076 Justice Cobalt C	.10	.20
VBT08077 Beast Fur Monster, Momomocia C	.10	.20
VBT08078 Cosmic Hero, Grandrescue C	.10	.20
VBT08079 Vast Torus, Duannulus C	.10	.20
VBT08080 Strafe Deletor, Gae C	.10	.20
VBT08081 Evil Claw of Natural Laws, Dravalclaw C	.10	.20
VBT08082 Manipulator of the Void C	.10	.20
VBT08083 Enduring Deletor, Zegrao C	.10	.20
VBT08084 Stringent Deletor, Igerma C	.10	.20
VBT08085 Ionization Master, Glubridge C	.10	.20
VBT08086 Axino Dragon C	.10	.20
VBT08087 Pulse Monk of the Quaking Foot C	.10	.20
VBT08088 Milky Way Sharp Sword, Guerg C	.10	.20
VBT08089 Juvenile Child of Virtual Particles C	.10	.20
VBT08SP19 Flowers in Vacuum, Cosmo Wreath SP	17.50	35.00
VBT08SP20 Neon Messiah SP	15.00	30.00
VBT08SP21 Quick Shield (Link Joker) SP	17.50	35.00
VBT08SP22 Wyvern Guard, Barri SP	12.50	25.00
VBT08SP24 Wyvern Strike, Doha SP	10.00	20.00
VBT08SP25 Wyvern Strike, Garan SP	12.50	25.00
VBT08SP26 Wyvernkid Ragla SP	6.00	12.00
VBT08SP27 Quick Shield (Kagero) SP	10.00	20.00
VBT08SP28 Weather Forecaster, Miss Mist SP	10.00	20.00
VBT08SP30 Quick Shield (Oracle Think Tank) SP	10.00	20.00
VBT08SP31 Diamond Ace SP	7.50	15.00
VBT08SP33 Quick Shield (Dimension Police) SP	12.50	25.00
VBT08T01 Vision T	.12	.25

2020 Cardfight Vanguard V Booster Set 9 Butterfly d'Moonlight

VBT09001 Masked Magician, Harri VR	3.00	6.00
VBT09001 Masked Magician, Harri SP	20.00	40.00
VBT09001 Masked Magician, Harri RLR	200.00	400.00
VBT09002 Vampire Princess of Night Fog, Nightrose VR	7.50	15.00
VBT09002 Vampire Princess of Night Fog, Nightrose SP	30.00	75.00
VBT09002 Vampire Princess of Night Fog, Nightrose RLR	500.00	1,000.00
VBT09003 Stealth Rogue of Revelation, Yasuie VR	.75	1.50
VBT09003 Stealth Rogue of Revelation, Yasuie SP	6.00	12.00
VBT09004 Scharhrot Vampir VR	5.00	10.00
VBT09004 Scharhrot Vampir SP	20.00	40.00
VBT09005 Silver Thorn Dragon Empress, Venus Luquier VR	2.00	4.00
VBT09005 Silver Thorn Dragon Empress, Venus Luquier SP	20.00	40.00
VBT09006 Ambush Demon Stealth Rogue, Yasuie Tenma RRR	.50	1.00
VBT09006 Ambush Demon Stealth Rogue, Yasuie Tenma SP	4.00	8.00
VBT09007 Demon Claw Stealth Rogue, Yoitogi SP	1.00	2.00
VBT09007 Demon Claw Stealth Rogue, Yoitogi RRR	.25	.50
VBT09008 Gateway Stealth Rogue, Ataka RRR	1.50	3.00
VBT09008 Gateway Stealth Rogue, Ataka SP	7.50	15.00
VBT09009 Abominable One, Gilles de Rais RRR	.50	1.00
VBT09009 Abominable One, Gilles de Rais SP	2.50	5.00
VBT09010 Succubus of Pure Love RRR	2.50	5.00
VBT09010 Succubus of Pure Love SP	15.00	30.00
VBT09011 Card Dealer, Jacqueline RRR	.60	1.25
VBT09011 Card Dealer, Jacqueline SP	6.00	12.00
VBT09012 Silver Thorn Diva, Selvia RRR	1.00	2.00
VBT09012 Silver Thorn Diva, Selvia SP	6.00	12.00
VBT09013 Masquerade Bunny RRR	3.00	6.00
VBT09013 Masquerade Bunny SP	15.00	30.00
VBT09014 Lord of the Seven Seas, Nightmist RRR	1.00	2.00
VBT09014 Lord of the Seven Seas, Nightmist SP	10.00	20.00
VBT09015 Pirate Swordsman, Colombard RRR	12.50	25.00
VBT09015 Pirate Swordsman, Colombard SP	25.00	50.00
VBT09016 Tommy the Ghostie Brothers RRR	2.50	5.00
VBT09016 Tommy the Ghostie Brothers SP	10.00	20.00
VBT09017 Dueling Dragon, ZANTETHU RR	.25	.50
VBT09018 Wisteria Flower Stealth Rogue, Takehime RR	.30	.75
VBT09019 Stealth Rogue of the Fiendish Blade, Masamura RR	.30	.60
VBT09020 Demonted Executioner RR	1.00	2.00
VBT09021 Edge in the Darkness RR	.25	.50
VBT09022 One-eyed Succubus RR	.60	1.25
VBT09023 Lore Pigeon, Pop RR	.50	1.00
VBT09024 Moonlight Melody Tamer, Betty RR	.30	.75
VBT09024 Moonlight Melody Tamer, Betty SP	2.00	4.00
VBT09025 Darkside Sword Master RR	.50	1.00
VBT09026 Thin-mist Banshee RR	.25	.50
VBT09026 Thin-mist Banshee SP	2.00	4.00
VBT09027 Seven Seas Pillager, Nightspinel RR	.50	1.00
VBT09028 Rampage Shade RR	.50	1.00
VBT09029 Stealth Rogue of Rough Skills, Masunari R	.20	.40
VBT09030 Stealth Dragon, Plumb Reimu R	.20	.40
VBT09031 Unmasked Stealth Rogue, Awazu R	.20	.40
VBT09032 Flutist Stealth Rogue, Kadotsugu R	.20	.40
VBT09033 Backward Arrester R	.25	.50
VBT09034 Ostia Heater R	.20	.40
VBT09035 Flap Fixer R	.20	.40
VBT09036 Doppel Vampir R	.20	.40
VBT09037 Stone Framer R	.20	.40
VBT09038 Deflect Sweet R	.20	.40
VBT09039 Starry Pop Dragon R	.20	.40
VBT09040 Blending Burner R	.20	.40
VBT09041 Magia Doll, Prana R	.25	.50
VBT09042 Magia Doll, Lunatec Dragon R	.25	.50
VBT09043 Silver Thorn Handlegrip, Linnea R	.20	.40
VBT09044 Nightmare Doll, Marion R	.25	.50
VBT09045 Skeleton Pirate Skipper R	.20	.40
VBT09046 Witch Doctor of Languor, Negrolazy R	.20	.40
VBT09047 Seven Seas Master Swordsman, Slash Shade R	.20	.40
VBT09048 Seven Seas Helmsman, Nightcrow R	.20	.40
VBT09049 Witch Doctor of Powdered Bone, Negrobone R	.20	.40
VBT09050 Soul Bullet Roulette R	.20	.40
VBT09051 Covert Demonic Dragon, Viamel Fudou C	.10	.20
VBT09052 Stealth Dragon, Shuratoguro C	.10	.20
VBT09053 Stealth Rogue of Intangibility, Kuninaga C	.10	.20
VBT09054 Stealth Rogue of Carnival Song, Miyagiku C	.10	.20
VBT09055 Inexhaustible Stealth Rogue, Tokitsune C	.10	.20
VBT09056 Stealth Dragon, Adoba Spike C	.10	.20
VBT09057 Stealth Beast, Moon Edge C	.10	.20
VBT09058 Stealth Fiend, Eba Wing C	.10	.20
VBT09059 Stealth Beast, Ahead Panther C	.10	.20
VBT09060 Stealth Fiend, Bamboo Fox C	.10	.20
VBT09061 Inflict Stamper C	.10	.20
VBT09062 Gravity Core Master C	.10	.20
VBT09063 Exact Frozen C	.10	.20
VBT09064 Prognos Drei C	.10	.20
VBT09065 Blemish Spire C	.15	.30
VBT09066 Tornado Genitor C	.10	.20
VBT09067 Werfleder Ordonnaz C	.10	.20
VBT09067 Werfleder Ordonnaz SP	5.00	10.00
VBT09068 Dark Knight of Nightmareland C	.10	.20
VBT09069 Pulse Taker C	.10	.20
VBT09070 Alice of Nightmareland C	.30	.60
VBT09071 Fesbright Escaper C	.10	.20
VBT09072 Flame Rowdy C	.10	.20
VBT09073 Genteel Opener C	.10	.20
VBT09074 Tempting Hoopster C	.10	.20
VBT09075 Magia Doll, Darkside Mirror Master C	.15	.30
VBT09076 Magia Doll, Flying Peryton C	.15	.30
VBT09077 Wonder Hanger C	.10	.20
VBT09078 Happiness Collector C	.10	.20
VBT09078 Happiness Collector SP	15.00	30.00
VBT09079 Silver Thorn, Barking Dragon C	.10	.20
VBT09080 Mirror Lord Surmounter C	.10	.20
VBT09081 Silver Thorn Beast Tamer, Serge C	.10	.20
VBT09082 Tender Breeder C	.10	.20
VBT09083 Parliament Shade C	.10	.20
VBT09084 Forebode Ghost Ship C	.10	.20
VBT09085 Racking Frankhini C	.10	.20
VBT09086 Night-playing Zombie C	.10	.20
VBT09087 Cyril the Ghostie C	.10	.20
VBT09088 Witch Doctor of the Seven Seas, Raistutor C	.10	.20
VBT09089 Skeleton Sea Navigator C	.10	.20
VBT09090 Undying Departed, Grenache C	.10	.20
VBT09090 Undying Departed, Grenache SP	15.00	30.00
VBT09091 Seven Seas Apprentice, Nightrunner C	.10	.20
VBT09092 Mortal Mimic C	.10	.20
VBT09093 Gunner Francette C	.10	.20
VBT09094 Good Luck Charm Banshee C	.50	1.00
VBT09SP19 Hades Hypnotist SP	12.50	25.00
VBT09SP21 Quick Shield (Pale Moon) SP	10.00	20.00
VBT09SP22 Gust Djinn SP	15.00	30.00
VBT09SP24 Quick Shield (Granblue) SP	15.00	30.00
VBT09SP25 Stealth Beast, Leaves Mirage SP	17.50	35.00
VBT09SP26 Masago Stealth Rogue, Goemon SP	10.00	20.00
VBT09SP27 Quick Shield (Murakumo) SP	15.00	30.00
VBT09SP28 Number of Terror SP	15.00	30.00
VBT09SP29 March Rabbit of Nightmareland SP	15.00	30.00
VBT09SP31 Quick Shield (Dark Irregulars) SP	20.00	40.00
VBT09SP32 Silver Thorn, Rising Dragon SP	20.00	40.00
VBT09SP33 Silver Thorn Conjurer, Romy SP	20.00	40.00
VBT09SP34 Silver Thorn Assistant, Ionela SP	12.50	25.00
VBT09T01 Treasures T	.20	.40

2020 Cardfight Vanguard V Booster Set 10 Phantom Dragon Aeon

VBT10Re01 Cherishing Knight, Branwen Re	4.00	8.00
VBT10001 Dragheart, Luard VR	4.00	8.00
VBT10001 Dragheart, Luard SP	30.00	75.00
VBT10001 Dragheart, Luard ASR	200.00	400.00
VBT10002 Phantom Blaster Overlord VR	2.00	4.00
VBT10002 Phantom Blaster Overlord SP	10.00	20.00
VBT10002 Phantom Blaster Overlord ASR	350.00	700.00
VBT10003 Emperor Dragon, Gaia Emperor VR	1.25	2.50
VBT10003 Emperor Dragon, Gaia Emperor SP	5.00	10.00
VBT10004 Exceptional Expertise, Rising Nova VR	2.00	4.00
VBT10004 Exceptional Expertise, Rising Nova SP	10.00	20.00
VBT10005 Evil Governor, Darkface Gredora VR	1.25	2.50
VBT10005 Evil Governor, Darkface Gredora SP	7.50	15.00
VBT10006 Dragdriver, Luard RRR	2.50	5.00
VBT10006 Dragdriver, Luard SP	30.00	60.00
VBT10007 Dragwizard, Morfessa RRR	3.00	6.00
VBT10007 Dragwizard, Morfessa SP	20.00	40.00
VBT10007 Dragwizard, Morfessa ASR	300.00	600.00
VBT10008 Freezing Witch, Bendi RRR	4.00	8.00
VBT10008 Freezing Witch, Bendi SP	10.00	20.00
VBT10009 True Ancient Dragon, Bladeromeus RRR	.75	1.50
VBT10009 True Ancient Dragon, Bladeromeus SP	7.50	15.00
VBT10010 Zealous Horn Dragon, Dilophopyro RRR	.75	1.50
VBT10010 Zealous Horn Dragon, Dilophopyro SP	12.50	25.00
VBT10011 Prism Bird RRR	1.50	3.00
VBT10011 Prism Bird SP	12.50	25.00
VBT10012 Adorbs Perm, Rona RRR	1.00	2.00
VBT10012 Adorbs Perm, Rona SP	4.00	8.00
VBT10013 Acrobat Verdi RRR	.75	1.50
VBT10013 Acrobat Verdi SP	4.00	8.00
VBT10014 Machining Meteorbullet RRR	.30	.60
VBT10014 Machining Meteorbullet SP	2.00	4.00
VBT10015 Despoiling Mutant, Sticky Bolas RRR	1.00	2.00
VBT10015 Despoiling Mutant, Sticky Bolas SP	4.00	8.00
VBT10016 New Face Mutant, Little Dorcas RRR	1.00	2.00
VBT10016 New Face Mutant, Little Dorcas SP	3.00	6.00
VBT10017 Dragwizard, Liafail RR	4.00	8.00
VBT10018 Dragwizard, Knies RR	.50	1.00
VBT10019 Abyssal Owl RR	4.00	8.00
VBT10020 Belial Owl RR	.50	1.00
VBT10021 True Ancient Dragon, Barreltops RR	.30	.60
VBT10022 True Ancient Dragon, Aloneros RR	.30	.60
VBT10023 Cannon Fire Dragon, Parasaulauncher RR	.30	.60
VBT10024 Spiking Cyclone RR	.30	.75
VBT10025 Ambush Dexter RR	.30	.75
VBT10025 Ambush Dexter SP	12.50	25.00
VBT10026 Liar Lips RR	.30	.75
VBT10027 Intimidating Mutant, Darkface RR	.30	.60
VBT10027 Intimidating Mutant, Darkface SP	7.50	15.00
VBT10028 Machining Scatterhorn RR	.25	.50
VBT10029 Scissor-shot Mutant, Bombscissor RR	.30	.75
VBT10030 Witch of Sculptured Group, Annelyn R	.20	.40
VBT10031 Dragwizard, Buagriu R	.20	.40
VBT10032 Hunter of Transgression, Macdobar R	.20	.40
VBT10033 Knight of Strict Order, Suels R	.20	.40
VBT10034 Slicing Dragon, Terrortherizino R	.20	.40
VBT10035 Regiment Dragon, Regiodon R	.20	.40
VBT10035 Regiment Dragon, Regiodon SP	12.50	25.00
VBT10036 Full Speed Dragon, Bluesprint R	.20	.40
VBT10036 Full Speed Dragon, Bluesprint SP	.50	1.00

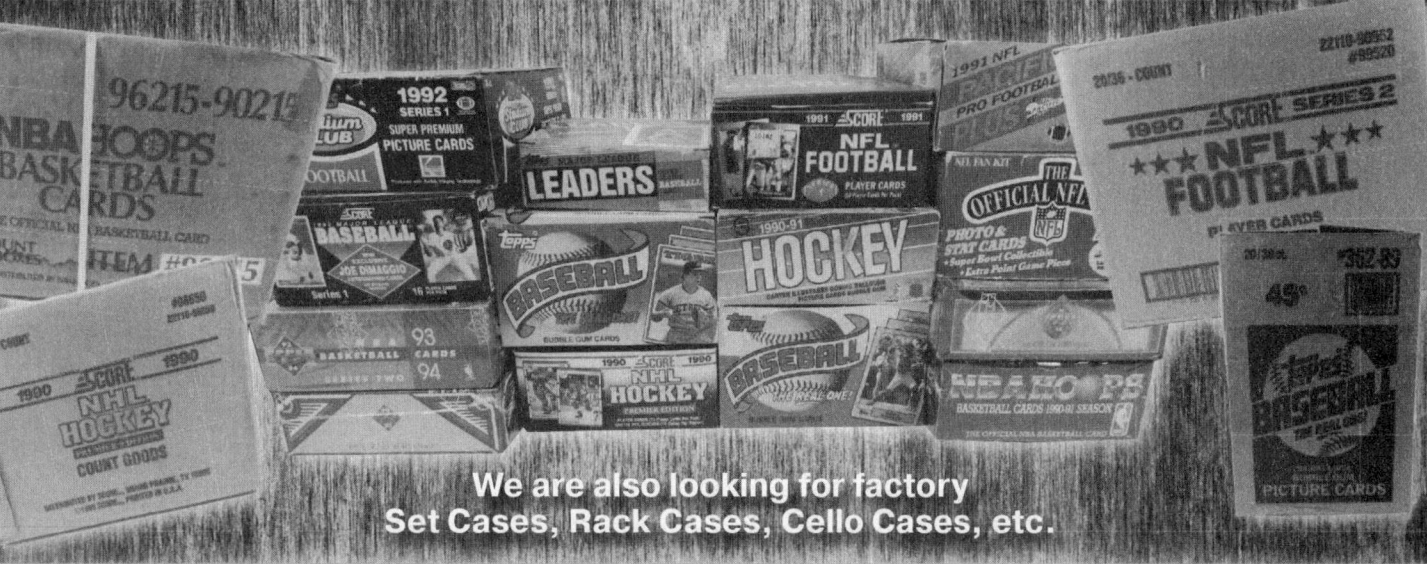

VBT10037 True Ancient Dragon, Pterafeed R	.20	.40
VBT10038 Punting Cannon R	.20	.40
VBT10039 Bullet Liner R	.20	.40
VBT10040 Breach Spurt R	.20	.40
VBT10041 Outside Rabbit R	.20	.40
VBT10042 Cheer Girl, Courtney R	.20	.40
VBT10043 Destruction Spear Mutant, Dovaspeed R	.20	.40
VBT10044 Melody Mutant, Nelnympha R	.20	.40
VBT10045 Disturbance Mutant, Morsiroro R	.20	.40
VBT10046 Cleared Breeze R	.20	.40
VBT10047 Halo of Bonds, Solidar Bangle R	.20	.40
VBT10048 Knight of Exhaustion, Ireged C	.10	.20
VBT10049 Spalbau C	.10	.20
VBT10050 Damp Hood Dragon C	.10	.20
VBT10051 Dragfighter, Meadow C	.10	.20
VBT10052 Hardship Sage, Decron C	.10	.20
VBT10053 Knight of Accomplishment, Dilaelt C	.10	.20
VBT10054 Dragprince, Rule C	.10	.20
VBT10054 Dragprince, Rule SP	17.50	35.00
VBT10055 Darkside Trumpeter C	.10	.20
VBT10056 Death Feather Eagle C	.10	.20
VBT10057 Dragwizard, Babd C	.10	.20
VBT10058 Abyss Grail C	.10	.20
VBT10059 Gunfire Dragon, Ballistic Amalga C	.10	.20
VBT10060 True Ancient Dragon, Heftstyraco C	.10	.20
VBT10061 Electric Artillery Dragon, Diplorail C	.10	.20
VBT10062 True Ancient Dragon, Albertail C	.10	.20
VBT10063 Loading Dragon, Acerocargo C	.10	.20
VBT10064 Martial Law Dragon, Compscouter C	.10	.20
VBT10065 Minimumcarno C	.10	.20
VBT10065 Minimumcarno SP	7.50	15.00
VBT10066 Savage Aggressor C	.10	.20
VBT10067 Savage Selector C	.10	.20
VBT10068 Pack Dragon, Tinyrex C	.10	.20
VBT10069 Younger Parasound C	.10	.20
VBT10070 Big Back Warlord C	.10	.20
VBT10071 Assaulting Babarias C	.10	.20
VBT10072 Defensive Evil Hater C	.10	.20
VBT10073 Meteoric Panthera C	.10	.20
VBT10074 Mecha Manager C	.10	.20
VBT10075 Mecha Referee C	.10	.20
VBT10076 Running Sniper C	.10	.20
VBT10076 Running Sniper SP	4.00	8.00
VBT10077 Killparade Mevis C	.10	.20
VBT10078 Sonic Breaker C	.10	.20
VBT10079 Cheer Girl, Pauline C	.10	.20
VBT10080 Cheer Girl, Adalaide C	.10	.20
VBT10081 Shredding Mutant, Killtrasch C	.10	.20
VBT10082 Hitting Mutant, Horde Jewel C	.10	.20
VBT10083 Beheading Mutant, Crimson Cutter C	.10	.20
VBT10084 Crag Arm Crusher C	.10	.20
VBT10085 Turbulent Signal C	.10	.20
VBT10086 Machining Cybister C	.10	.20
VBT10087 Young Mutant, Worectus C	.10	.20
VBT10087 Young Mutant, Worectus SP	7.50	15.00
VBT10088 Sharp Nail Scorpio C	.10	.20
VBT10089 Jewel Flasher C	.10	.20
VBT10090 Aflutter Drafter C	.10	.20
VBT10091 Large Snowflake Mutant, Snow Trick C	.10	.20
VBT10Re01 Cherishing Knight, Branwen SP	30.00	75.00
VBT10SP22 Phantom Blaster Dragon SP	40.00	80.00
VBT10SP23 Skull Witch, Nemain SP	50.00	100.00
VBT10SP24 Fullbau SP	20.00	40.00
VBT10SP25 Quick Shield (Shadow Paladin) SP	15.00	30.00
VBT10SP26 Archbird SP	10.00	20.00
VBT10SP30 Quick Shield (Tachikaze) SP	7.50	15.00
VBT10SP31 Cheer Girl, Marilyn SP	12.50	25.00
VBT10SP33 Quick Shield (Spike Brothers) SP	7.50	15.00
VBT10SP34 Paralyze Madonna SP	7.50	15.00
VBT10SP36 Quick Shield (Megacolony) SP	10.00	20.00
VBT10T01 Cradle T	.30	.60

2020 Cardfight Vanguard V Booster Set 11 Storm of the Blue Cavalry

VBT11001 Marine General of Heavenly Silk, Lambros VR	2.00	4.00
VBT11001 Marine General of Heavenly Silk, Lambros SP	10.00	20.00
VBT11002 Demon Stealth Dragon, Shiranui "Oboro" VR	2.50	5.00
VBT11002 Demon Stealth Dragon, Shiranui "Oboro" SP	12.50	25.00
VBT11003 Exxtreme Battler, Victor SP	12.50	25.00
VBT11003 Exxtreme Battler, Victor VR	1.00	2.00
VBT11004 Sage-saint Mentor of Black Lacquer, Isabelle SP	12.50	25.00
VBT11004 Sage-saint Mentor of Black Lacquer, Isabelle VR	1.25	2.50
VBT11005 Famous Professor, Bigbelly SP	7.50	15.00
VBT11005 Famous Professor, Bigbelly VR	.75	1.50
VBT11006 Stealth Dragon, Shiranui RRR	2.50	5.00
VBT11006 Stealth Dragon, Shiranui SP	15.00	30.00
VBT11007 Stealth Beast, Katarigitsune RRR	4.00	8.00
VBT11007 Stealth Beast, Katarigitsune SP	7.50	15.00
VBT11008 Galaxy Blaukluger RRR	2.50	5.00
VBT11008 Galaxy Blaukluger SP	17.50	35.00
VBT11009 Cool Hank RRR	2.00	4.00
VBT11009 Cool Hank SP	12.50	25.00
VBT11010 Extreme Battler, Arashid RRR	2.50	5.00
VBT11010 Extreme Battler, Arashid SP	6.00	12.00
VBT11011 One Who Surpasses the Storm, Thavas RRR	2.50	5.00
VBT11011 One Who Surpasses the Storm, Thavas SP	7.50	15.00
VBT11012 Kelpie Rider, Denis RRR	1.00	2.00
VBT11012 Kelpie Rider, Denis SP	7.50	15.00
VBT11013 Terrific Coil Dragon RRR	2.00	4.00
VBT11013 Terrific Coil Dragon SP	12.50	25.00
VBT11014 Measured Fossa RRR	.25	.50
VBT11014 Measured Fossa SP	.50	1.00
VBT11015 Lablab Dotter RRR	.50	1.00
VBT11015 Lablab Dotter SP	2.50	5.00
VBT11016 Diligent Assistant, Minibelly RRR	3.00	6.00
VBT11016 Diligent Assistant, Minibelly SP	6.00	12.00
VBT11017 Stealth Dragon, Genkai RR	.75	1.50
VBT11018 Stealth Dragon, Fuurai RR	.50	1.00
VBT11019 Stealth Dragon, Noroi RR	.50	1.00
VBT11020 Stern Blaukluger RR	.50	1.00
VBT11020 Stern Blaukluger SP	10.00	20.00
VBT11021 Extreme Battler, Dosledge RR	.50	1.00
VBT11021 Extreme Battler, Dosledge SP	12.50	25.00
VBT11022 Extreme Battler, Break-pass RR	.50	1.00
VBT11023 Kelpie Rider, Nikki RR	.50	1.00
VBT11023 Kelpie Rider, Nikki SP	12.50	25.00
VBT11024 Drifting Flow Fencer RR	.60	1.25
VBT11025 Kelpie Rider, Petros RR	.50	1.00
VBT11026 Blusher Parakeet RR	.30	.75
VBT11027 Besom Ringtail RR	.30	.60
VBT11027 Besom Ringtail SP	7.50	15.00
VBT11028 Application Researcher, Ponbelly RR	.50	1.00
VBT11029 Stealth Rogue of Incantation, Hyoue R	.20	.40
VBT11030 Stealth Rogue of Bonds, Yura R	.20	.40
VBT11031 Stealth Rogue of Cooperation, Sadamune R	.20	.40
VBT11032 Qigong Fighting Hermit, Master Torga R	.20	.40
VBT11033 Blaukluger R	.20	.40
VBT11034 Blaupanzer R	.20	.40
VBT11035 Extreme Battler, Ganbarugun R	.20	.40
VBT11036 Extreme Battler, Sosaucer R	.20	.40
VBT11037 Marine General of the Raging Tides, Hristina R	.20	.40
VBT11038 Marine General of Desperate Fight, Agias R	.20	.40
VBT11039 Bubble Ball Corporal R	.20	.40
VBT11040 Radiate Assault R	.20	.40
VBT11041 Pursuer of Perfect Circle, Flow Panther R	.20	.40
VBT11041 Pursuer of Perfect Circle, Flow Panther SP	7.50	15.00
VBT11042 Spool Merry SP	10.00	20.00
VBT11042 Spool Merry R	.20	.40
VBT11043 Clerical Kakapo R	.20	.40
VBT11044 Scoring Master, Mousetoby R	.20	.40
VBT11045 History Scientist, Bushbeck R	.20	.40
VBT11046 Illusory Spirit Manuscript, Fancyclopedia R	.20	.40
VBT11047 Stealth Beast, Zokuhihi C	.10	.20
VBT11048 Stealth Rogue of Sincerity, Mafusa C	.10	.20
VBT11049 Stealth Beast, Gyumado C	.10	.20
VBT11050 Stealth Beast, Gekihasai C	.10	.20
VBT11051 Stealth Rogue of Snake Arts, Ujihime C	.10	.20
VBT11052 Stealth Beast, Ibudanuki C	.10	.20
VBT11053 Stealth Beast, Jagunro C	.10	.20
VBT11054 Stealth Beast, Yamiyamaneko C	.10	.20
VBT11055 Stealth Dragon, Madoi C	.10	.20
VBT11055 Stealth Dragon, Madoi SP	12.50	25.00
VBT11056 Stealth Beast, Tobihiko C	.10	.20
VBT11057 Stealth Dragon, Ganbaku C	.10	.20
VBT11058 Almsgiving Stealth Rogue, Jirokichi C	.10	.20
VBT11059 Voracious Stealth Rogue, Kosode C	.10	.20
VBT11060 Visarded Ashura C	.10	.20
VBT11061 Brute the Beast C	.10	.20
VBT11062 Cutting Gyre C	.10	.20
VBT11063 Morgenrot C	.10	.20
VBT11064 Lightness Cool C	.10	.20
VBT11065 Blaujunger C	.10	.20
VBT11065 Blaujunger SP	10.00	20.00
VBT11066 Red Lightning C	.10	.20
VBT11067 Memory Bot, Aldale C	.10	.20
VBT11068 Cannon Ball C	.10	.20
VBT11069 Earnest Second C	.10	.20
VBT11070 Spout Barrage Dragon C	.10	.20
VBT11071 Steel Whip of Turbulence, George C	.10	.20
VBT11072 Kelpie Rider, Biron C	.10	.20
VBT11073 Jeweled Staff of Kingfisher Green, Elpida C	.10	.20
VBT11074 Kelpie Rider, Thodoris C	.10	.20
VBT11075 Tear Knight, Machaon C	.10	.20
VBT11076 Kelpie Rider, Mitros C	.10	.20
VBT11076 Kelpie Rider, Mitros SP	12.50	25.00
VBT11077 Blue Storm Marine General, Despina C	.10	.20
VBT11078 Loading Bullet Brave Shooter C	.10	.20
VBT11079 Dolphin Soldier of High Speed Raids C	.10	.20
VBT11080 Activate Dracokid C	.10	.20
VBT11081 Ambers Triangular C	.10	.20
VBT11082 Vacuuming Tortoise C	.10	.20
VBT11083 Burden Kangaroo C	.10	.20
VBT11084 Geological Scientist, Sigurmole C	.10	.20
VBT11085 Beginning Hyrax C	.10	.20
VBT11085 Beginning Hyrax SP	6.00	12.00
VBT11086 Ruler Chameleon C	.10	.20
VBT11087 Whimsical Idea, Kolwatta C	.10	.20
VBT11088 Castanet Donkey C	.10	.20
VBT11089 Insurance Doctor, Carebath C	.10	.20
VBT11ASR01 Blue Storm Supreme Dragon, Glory Maelstrom ASR	200.00	400.00
VBT11ASR02 Blue Storm Dragon, Maelstrom ASR	100.00	200.00
VBT11Re01 Blue Wave Soldier Senior, Beragios Re	2.50	5.00
VBT11Re01 Blue Wave Soldier Senior, Beragios SP	7.50	15.00
VBT11SP22 Emerald Shield, Paschal SP	20.00	40.00
VBT11SP24 Quick Shield (Aqua Force) SP	15.00	30.00
VBT11SP25 Stealth Dragon, Magatsu Gale SP	20.00	40.00
VBT11SP26 Stealth Beast, Mijingakure SP	12.50	25.00
VBT11SP28 Quick Shield (Nubatama) SP	12.50	25.00
VBT11SP29 Twin Blader SP	12.50	25.00
VBT11SP31 Quick Shield (Nova Grappler) SP	12.50	25.00
VBT11SP34 Cable Sheep SP	3.00	6.00
VBT11SP36 Quick Shield (Great Nature) SP	5.00	10.00
VBT11T01 Mask of Domination Token C	.10	.20

2020 Cardfight Vanguard V Booster Set 12 Divine Lightning Radiance

VSM004 Astral Plane	.15	.30
VBT12001 Black Shiver, Gavrail VR	3.00	6.00
VBT12001 Black Shiver, Gavrail SP	20.00	40.00
VBT12002 Sunrise Ray Knight, Gurguit VR	3.00	6.00
VBT12002 Sunrise Ray Knight, Gurguit SP	20.00	40.00
VBT12003 Holy Heavenly Dragon, Eosanesis Dragon VR	1.50	3.00
VBT12003 Holy Heavenly Dragon, Eosanesis Dragon SP	7.50	15.00
VBT12004 Mythic Beast, Fenrir VR	1.50	3.00
VBT12004 Mythic Beast, Fenrir SP	10.00	20.00
VBT12005 Dragonic Vanquisher "FULLBRONTO" VR	.50	1.00
VBT12005 Dragonic Vanquisher "FULLBRONTO" SP	10.00	20.00
VBT12006 Holy Seraph, Nociel RRR	1.25	2.50
VBT12006 Holy Seraph, Nociel SP	20.00	40.00
VBT12007 Black Arquerias, Japhkiel RRR	3.00	6.00
VBT12007 Black Arquerias, Japhkiel SP	15.00	30.00
VBT12008 Black Call, Nakir RRR	2.00	4.00
VBT12008 Black Call, Nakir SP	10.00	20.00
VBT12009 Oath Liberator, Aglovale RRR	5.00	10.00
VBT12009 Oath Liberator, Aglovale SP	40.00	80.00
VBT12010 Dawning Knight, Gorboduc RRR	3.00	6.00
VBT12010 Dawning Knight, Gorboduc SP	10.00	20.00
VBT12011 Cosmic Regalia, CEO Yggdrasil RRR	2.00	4.00
VBT12011 Cosmic Regalia, CEO Yggdrasil SP	30.00	75.00
VBT12012 Unappeasable Biter, Gleipnir RRR	4.00	8.00
VBT12012 Unappeasable Biter, Gleipnir SP	20.00	40.00
VBT12013 Mythic Beast, Skoll RRR	2.50	5.00
VBT12013 Mythic Beast, Skoll SP	6.00	12.00
VBT12014 Eradicator, Dragonic Descendant RRR	4.00	8.00
VBT12014 Eradicator, Dragonic Descendant SP	15.00	30.00
VBT12014 Eradicator, Dragonic Descendant ASR	100.00	200.00
VBT12015 Eradicator, Plasmacatapult Dragon RRR	1.00	2.00
VBT12015 Eradicator, Plasmacatapult Dragon SP	3.00	6.00
VBT12016 Rockclimb Dragoon RRR	.50	1.00
VBT12016 Rockclimb Dragoon SP	4.00	8.00
VBT12017 Black Observe, Hamiel RR	.75	1.50
VBT12017 Black Observe, Hamiel SP	30.00	60.00
VBT12018 Love Sniper, Nociel RR	.50	1.00
VBT12019 Black Spark, Munkar RR	.60	1.25
VBT12020 Bluish Flame Liberator, Percival RR	6.00	12.00
VBT12020 Bluish Flame Liberator, Percival SP	30.00	75.00
VBT12021 Knight of Spring's Light, Perimore RR	.60	1.25
VBT12021 Knight of Spring's Light, Perimore SP	6.00	12.00
VBT12022 Sunshine Knight, Jeffrey RR	.50	1.00
VBT12022 Sunshine Knight, Jeffrey SP	10.00	20.00
VBT12023 Scarface Lion RR	.30	.75
VBT12024 Mythical Destroyer Beast, Vanargandr RR	.50	1.00
VBT12024 Mythical Destroyer Beast, Vanargandr SP	7.50	15.00
VBT12025 Regalia of Fate, Norn RR	.50	1.00
VBT12025 Regalia of Fate, Norn SP	20.00	40.00
VBT12026 Stake Fetter, Thviti RR	.50	1.00
VBT12027 Lightning Whip Eradicator, Suhail RR	.50	1.00
VBT12028 Chain-bolt Dragoon RR	.30	.75
VBT12028 Chain-bolt Dragoon SP	12.50	25.00
VBT12029 Lightning of Triumphant Return, Reseph RR	.50	1.00
VBT12030 Black Mapping, Salaphiel R	.20	.40
VBT12031 Love Machine Gun, Nociel R	.20	.40
VBT12032 Scaling Angel R	.20	.40
VBT12033 Black Closure, Zophiel R	.20	.40
VBT12034 Battalion Lance Dragon R	.20	.40
VBT12035 Flywheel Knight, Edmund R	.20	.40
VBT12036 Knight of Benefits, Berengaria R	.20	.40
VBT12037 Converge Archer, Biscott R	.20	.40
VBT12038 White Rainbow Witch, Pyrethru R	.20	.40
VBT12039 Arcturus of Fervent Will R	.20	.40
VBT12039 Arcturus of Fervent Will SP	12.50	25.00
VBT12040 Mythic Beast, Hati R	.20	.40
VBT12040 Mythic Beast, Hati SP	7.50	15.00
VBT12041 Becrux of Stratification R	.20	.40
VBT12041 Becrux of Stratification SP	12.50	25.00
VBT12042 Eradicator, Thunderous Beat Dragon R	.20	.40
VBT12043 Eradicator, Spark Raze Dragon R	.20	.40
VBT12044 Martial Arts Dragon R	.20	.40
VBT12045 Isolation Eradicator, Nusku R	.20	.40
VBT12046 Aspirations of Limitless Power R	.20	.40
VBT12047 Buster Surgeon, Asphael C	.10	.20
VBT12048 Cleanshake Angel C	.10	.20
VBT12049 Nurse of Hold Heart C	.10	.20
VBT12050 Disinfect Angel C	.10	.20
VBT12051 Black Leash, Abdiel C	.10	.20
VBT12052 Medical Kit Angel C	.10	.20
VBT12052 Medical Kit Angel SP	7.50	15.00
VBT12053 Happy Bell, Nociel C	.10	.20
VBT12054 Critical Hit Angel C	.10	.20
VBT12055 Pinky Denturist C	.10	.20
VBT12056 Surgery Angel C	.10	.20
VBT12057 Stanching Angel C	.10	.20
VBT12058 Plenary Ray Dragon C	.10	.20
VBT12059 Holy Mage, Indulf C	.10	.20
VBT12060 Knight of Beloved Day, Cuthred C	.10	.20
VBT12061 Knight of Inspiration, Lulach C	.10	.20
VBT12062 Knight of Illumination, Muir C	.10	.20
VBT12063 Spaigal C	.10	.20
VBT12064 Knight of Early Dawn, Coel C	.10	.20
VBT12064 Knight of Early Dawn, Coel SP	12.50	25.00
VBT12065 Knight of Blue Skies, Shanak C	.10	.20
VBT12066 Player of the Holy Pipe, Gerrie C	.10	.20
VBT12067 Knight of Forceful Fight, Nalnes C	.10	.20
VBT12068 Sage Who Goes Ahead, Peyron C	.10	.20
VBT12069 Falling Star Sorcerer, Vahin C	.10	.20
VBT12070 White Phosphorus Sorcerer, Revoluta C	.10	.20
VBT12071 Source Witch, Pyxis C	.10	.20
VBT12072 Assistance Sorcerer, Comnis C	.10	.20
VBT12073 Avior of Dedication C	.10	.20
VBT12074 Incipient Long Tail C	.10	.20
VBT12074 Incipient Long Tail SP	6.00	12.00
VBT12075 Mercury of Gravitas C	.10	.20
VBT12076 Cyber Tiger C	.10	.20
VBT12077 Witch of White Emperor, Presemo C	.10	.20
VBT12078 Aesculapius of All Healing C	.10	.20
VBT12079 Djinn of Thundering Lightning Shock C	.10	.20
VBT12080 Lightning Cannon Eradicator, Corson C	.10	.20
VBT12081 Vibrocrusher Dragon C	.10	.20
VBT12082 Thundering Arm Eradicator, Ghassan C	.10	.20
VBT12083 Lightning Rifle Eradicator, Oban C	.10	.20
VBT12084 Eleckinesis Dragon C	.10	.20
VBT12085 Eradicator, Spring Light Dracokid C	.10	.20
VBT12086 Yellow Gem Carbuncle C	.10	.20
VBT12087 Dragon Dancer, Vianne C	.10	.20
VBT12088 Exorcist Mage, Lin Lin C	.10	.20
VBT12089 Dragon Dancer, Irsina C	.10	.20
VBT12ASR01 Giant Deity of Distant World, Valkerion ASR	75.00	150.00
VBT12Re01 Mighty Bolt Dragoon Re	2.50	5.00
VBT12Re01 Mighty Bolt Dragoon SP	12.50	25.00
VBT12SP25 Battle Cupid, Nociel SP	7.50	15.00
VBT12SP26 Quick Shield (Angel Feather) SP	17.50	35.00
VBT12SP28 Halo Shield, Mark SP	15.00	30.00
VBT12SP29 Quick Shield (Gold Paladin) SP	12.50	25.00
VBT12SP32 Battle Maiden, Mutsuki SP	4.00	8.00
VBT12SP33 Pan of New Style SP	5.00	10.00
VBT12SP36 Goddess of Self-sacrifice, Kushinada SP	7.50	15.00
VBT12SP37 Quick Shield (Genesis) SP	7.50	15.00
VBT12SP39 Harbinger Dracokid SP	5.00	10.00
VBT12SP40 Wyvern Guard, Guld SP	15.00	30.00
VBT12SP41 Quick Shield (Narukami) SP	17.50	35.00

2020 Cardfight Vanguard V Extra Booster Set 11 Crystal Melody

VEB11001 Crystal Pop Star, Eve LIR	6.00	12.00
VEB11001 Crystal Pop Star, Eve SP	50.00	100.00
VEB11002 Aurora Star, Coral SP	200.00	400.00
VEB11002 Aurora Star, Coral SVR	12.00	25.00
VEB11002 Aurora Star, Coral VR	4.00	8.00
VEB11003 Top Idol, Pacifica SP	75.00	150.00
VEB11003 Top Idol, Pacifica SVR	7.50	15.00
VEB11003 Top Idol, Pacifica VR	2.50	5.00
VEB11004 Top Idol, Riviere SP	200.00	400.00
VEB11004 Top Idol, Riviere SVR	25.00	50.00
VEB11004 Top Idol, Riviere VR	7.50	15.00
VEB11005 From Colorful Pastorale, Sonata RRR	.50	1.00
VEB11005 From Colorful Pastorale, Sonata SSR	30.00	60.00
VEB11006 From Colorful Pastorale, Canon RRR	.30	.75
VEB11006 From Colorful Pastorale, Canon SSR	20.00	40.00
VEB11007 From Colorful Pastorale, Serena RRR	.30	.75
VEB11007 From Colorful Pastorale, Serena SSR	20.00	40.00
VEB11008 From Colorful Pastorale, Fina RRR	.50	1.00
VEB11008 From Colorful Pastorale, Fina SSR	12.00	25.00
VEB11009 From Colorful Pastorale, Caro RRR	7.50	15.00
VEB11009 From Colorful Pastorale, Caro SSR	75.00	150.00
VEB11010 Silver Singer, Cutire RR	.20	.40
VEB11011 Shiny Star, Coral RR	4.00	8.00
VEB11012 Super Idol, Riviere RR	1.00	2.00
VEB11013 Crowning Partner, Avanne RR	.30	.75
VEB11014 Pearl Sisters, Perla RR	.20	.40
VEB11015 Pearl Sisters, Perle RR	.20	.40
VEB11016 Fresh Star, Coral RR	2.00	4.00
VEB11017 Mermaid Idol, Riviere RR	.60	1.25
VEB11018 Lavender Missy, Lapro RR	.25	.50
VEB11019 Prominent Personality, Terminer RR	.20	.40
VEB11020 Animated Rooting, Marijan R	.15	.30
VEB11021 Glaring Moon, Miera R	.15	.30
VEB11022 Refined Poiser, Urszula R	.15	.30
VEB11023 Flustered Idol, Fretta R	.15	.30
VEB11024 Scramble Red, Ellend R	.15	.30
VEB11025 Charming Make, Piaoliang R	.15	.30
VEB11026 Riddle Mysteria, Luvene R	.15	.30
VEB11027 Electro Techno, Thiko R	.15	.30
VEB11028 Topping Mascot, Serio R	.15	.30
VEB11029 Mini Mini Sparkle, Parum R	.15	.30
VEB11030 Loftiest Pier, Evge R	.15	.30
VEB11031 Intact Parasol, Enis R	.15	.30
VEB11032 Bubble Dream, Perisia C	.07	.15
VEB11033 Trouble Varidol, Pressiv C	.07	.15
VEB11034 Fleeting Memoria, Aktiana C	.07	.15
VEB11035 Ruby Sensation, Leisis C	.07	.15
VEB11036 Charging Ache, Metre C	.07	.15
VEB11037 Tide Conductor, Ekhos C	.07	.15
VEB11038 Affable Wash, Thecla C	.07	.15
VEB11039 Silent Ardor, Solda C	.07	.15
VEB11040 Mid Vocal, Eonir C	.07	.15

BECKETT
The Beckett Marketplace
Your one-stop shop for all your collecting needs.
SHOP OVER
130 Million
SPORTS, NON-SPORTS, AND GAMING CARDS.
Visit: marketplace.beckett.com
OR
SCAN HERE

VEB11041 Angelic Star, Coral C	.07	.15
VEB11042 Bermuda Triangle Cadet, Riviere C	.07	.15
VEB11043 Pure Gifter, Aliche C	.07	.15
VEB11044 Direct Sign, Pursh C	.10	.20
VEB11045 Dockin' Shooter, Pellea C	.12	.25
VEB11046 Lover Hope, Rina C	.07	.15
VEB11047 Joyful A la Carte, Irma C	.07	.15
VEB11048 Handmade Lover, Elena C	.10	.20

2020 Cardfight Vanguard V Extra Booster Set 12 Team Dragon's Vanity

VEB12001 Claret Sword Dragon SSR	100.00	200.00
VEB12001 Claret Sword Dragon SVR	15.00	30.00
VEB12001 Claret Sword Dragon VR	6.00	12.00
VEB12002 Dragonic Vanquisher SSR	100.00	200.00
VEB12002 Dragonic Vanquisher SVR	30.00	60.00
VEB12002 Dragonic Vanquisher VR	15.00	30.00
VEB12003 Last Card, Revonn SSR	75.00	150.00
VEB12003 Last Card, Revonn SVR	20.00	40.00
VEB12003 Last Card, Revonn VR	12.00	25.00
VEB12004 Morion Spear Dragon RRR	6.00	12.00
VEB12004 Morion Spear Dragon SP	20.00	40.00
VEB12005 Cherishing Knight, Branwen RRR	12.00	25.00
VEB12005 Cherishing Knight, Branwen SP	50.00	100.00
VEB12006 Voltage Horn Dragon RRR	2.50	5.00
VEB12006 Voltage Horn Dragon SP	12.00	25.00
VEB12007 Mighty Bolt Dragoon RRR	10.00	20.00
VEB12007 Mighty Bolt Dragoon SP	20.00	40.00
VEB12008 Blue Wave Marine General, Galleass RRR	3.00	6.00
VEB12008 Blue Wave Marine General, Galleass SP	15.00	30.00
VEB12009 Blue Wave Soldier Senior, Beragios RRR	7.50	15.00
VEB12009 Blue Wave Soldier Senior, Beragios SP	20.00	40.00
VEB12010 Onyx Dust Dragon RR	.75	1.50
VEB12011 Darkpride Dragon RR	.60	1.25
VEB12012 Blue Espada Dragon RR	.60	1.25
VEB12013 Jaggy Shot Dragoon RR	2.00	4.00
VEB12014 Demonic Dragon Berserker, Chatura RR	1.50	3.00
VEB12015 Dragon Dancer, Anastasia RR	.20	.40
VEB12016 Fort-vessel Dragon RR	.20	.40
VEB12017 Blue Wave Marine General, Foivos RR	3.00	6.00
VEB12018 Battle Siren, Nerissa RR	.75	1.50
VEB12019 Knight of Blind Advance, Lugaid R	.15	.30
VEB12020 Witch of Iron Chains, Ness R	.15	.30
VEB12021 Knight of Entrancement, Cailte R	.15	.30
VEB12022 Witch of Extirpation, Bheara R	.15	.30
VEB12023 Inflexible Arrow, Muorda R	.15	.30
VEB12024 Blitz-caliber Dragon R	.15	.30
VEB12025 Tactical Dagger Dragoon R	.15	.30
VEB12026 Spinous Blader Dragon R	.15	.30
VEB12027 Desert Gunner, Bhajan R	.15	.30
VEB12028 Dragon Dancer, Eluisa R	.15	.30
VEB12029 Sharpsplit Dragon R	.15	.30
VEB12030 Press Stream Dragon R	.15	.30
VEB12031 Blue Wave Shield General, Yorgos R	.15	.30
VEB12032 Blue Ward Command R	.15	.30
VEB12033 Analyze Shooter R	.15	.30
VEB12034 Knight of Insight, Bathaden C	.07	.15
VEB12035 Knight of Sudden Rage, Macmorna C	.07	.15
VEB12036 Jammer Intruder C	.07	.15
VEB12037 Knight of Machinations, Abagdo C	.07	.15
VEB12038 Defitbau C	.07	.15
VEB12039 Knight of Old Grudges, Matholuh C	.07	.15
VEB12040 Promising Knight, David C	.07	.15
VEB12041 Grim Revenger C	.07	.15
VEB12042 Darkside Trumpeter C	.07	.15
VEB12043 Howl Owl C	.07	.15
VEB12044 Abyss Healer C	.07	.15
VEB12045 Galvanic Mace Dragon C	.07	.15
VEB12046 Desert Gunner, Tengen C	.07	.15
VEB12047 Voltechshred Dragon C	.07	.15
VEB12048 Dragon Dancer, Ramolna C	.07	.15
VEB12049 Thunderlead Dragon C	.07	.15
VEB12050 Storm Strike Discharge Wyvern C	.07	.15
VEB12051 Harbinger Dracokid C	.07	.15
VEB12052 Malevolent Djinn C	.07	.15
VEB12053 Old Dragon Mage C	.07	.15
VEB12054 Dragon Dancer, Catharina C	.07	.15
VEB12055 Worm Toxin Eradicator, Seiobo C	.07	.15
VEB12056 Battle Siren, Stefana C	.07	.15
VEB12057 Tear Knight, Elmalia C	.07	.15
VEB12058 Marine General of Head Seas, Thanasis C	.07	.15
VEB12059 Talwar Assault C	.07	.15
VEB12060 Storm Rider, Banos C	.07	.15
VEB12061 Frontal Sailor C	.07	.15
VEB12062 Blue Wave Recruit, Kosty C	.07	.15
VEB12063 Supersonic Sailor C	.07	.15
VEB12064 Pyroxene Communications Sea Otter Soldier C	.07	.15
VEB12065 Outride Dracokid C	.07	.15
VEB12066 Medical Officer of the Rainbow Elixir C	.07	.15

2020 Cardfight Vanguard V Extra Booster Set 13 The Astral Force

VEB13001 Arch-aider, Malkuth-melekh SVR	25.00	50.00
VEB13001 Arch-aider, Malkuth-melekh VR	12.00	25.00
VEB13002 Origin Deity of Heavenly Light, Uranus SVR	12.00	25.00
VEB13002 Origin Deity of Heavenly Light, Uranus VR	12.00	25.00
VEB13003 Chronotiger Rebellion SVR	25.00	50.00
VEB13003 Chronotiger Rebellion VR	10.00	20.00
VEB13004 Aid-roid, Zayin RRR	3.00	6.00
VEB13004 Aid-roid, Zayin SP	20.00	40.00
VEB13005 Aid-roid, Lamedo RRR	2.50	5.00
VEB13005 Aid-roid, Lamedo SP	20.00	40.00
VEB13006 Phinomenus of the Constellations RRR	2.50	5.00
VEB13006 Phinomenus of the Constellations SP	7.50	15.00
VEB13007 Dikei of the Just Path RRR	6.00	12.00
VEB13007 Dikei of the Just Path SP	10.00	20.00
VEB13008 Chronofang Tiger RRR	3.00	6.00
VEB13008 Chronofang Tiger SP	30.00	60.00
VEB13009 Chronobite Tiger RRR	2.50	5.00
VEB13009 Chronobite Tiger SP	15.00	30.00
VEB13010 Preside Chief, Jomjael RR	.30	.75
VEB13011 Mend Scraper, Tomael RR	.25	.50
VEB13012 Amputation Angel RR	1.50	3.00
VEB13013 Sectio Angel RR	1.50	3.00
VEB13014 Blow Antler Dragon RR	.25	.50
VEB13015 Libitina of Funeral Courtship RR	.15	.30
VEB13016 Renovate Wing Dragon RR	.30	.60
VEB13017 Steam Scara, Irkab RR	10.00	20.00
VEB13018 Chronotooth Tigar RR	12.00	25.00
VEB13019 Fix Shooter, Belkeael R	.10	.20
VEB13020 Clearview Angel R	.10	.20
VEB13021 Sanitize Laser R	.10	.20
VEB13022 Wet Pack Dealer R	.10	.20
VEB13023 Auscultate Angel R	.20	.40
VEB13024 Prime Plaster R	.10	.20
VEB13025 Turning-heavens Sorcerer, Estra R	.10	.20
VEB13026 Daybreak Sorcerer, Ashwa R	.10	.20
VEB13027 Late-ripening Sorcerer, Palmeta R	.10	.20
VEB13028 Novel-around Dragon R	.10	.20
VEB13029 Steam Lynx, Gudea R	.10	.20
VEB13030 Steam Sweeper, Salgo R	.10	.20
VEB13031 Steam Maiden, Ishbie R	.12	.25
VEB13032 Steam Janitor, Gitlim R	.10	.20
VEB13033 Steam Sweeper, Kalissha R	.10	.20
VEB13034 Lucent Enforce, Taruel C	.07	.15
VEB13035 Care-mine Nurse C	.07	.15
VEB13036 Surgical Nurse C	.07	.15
VEB13037 Scissor Star Angel C	.07	.15
VEB13038 Multimedical Angel C	.07	.15
VEB13039 Service Improver C	.07	.15
VEB13040 Vantage Dresser C	.07	.15
VEB13041 Aid-roid, Resh C	.07	.15
VEB13042 Critical Hit Angel C	.07	.15
VEB13043 Hot Shot Celestial, Samyaza C	.07	.15
VEB13044 Bouquet Toss Messenger C	.07	.15
VEB13045 Sunny Smile Angel C	.07	.15
VEB13046 Conceit Boar C	.07	.15
VEB13047 All-out Dog C	.07	.15
VEB13048 Witch of Innocence, Clary C	.07	.15
VEB13049 Abundante of Riches and Honors C	.07	.15
VEB13050 Singing Dance Grace Colossus C	.07	.15
VEB13051 Steam Engineer, Shulia C	.07	.15
VEB13052 Steam Sweeper, Nalam C	.07	.15
VEB13053 Steam Reporter, Abum C	.07	.15
VEB13054 Steam Composer, Ul-kagina C	.07	.15
VEB13055 Steam Sweeper, Dodo C	.07	.15
VEB13056 Steam Fighter, Zabaia C	.07	.15
VEB13057 Underlight Meteor Colossus C	.07	.15
VEB13058 Chrono Tigar C	.07	.15
VEB13059 Steam Bomber, Digul C	.07	.15
VEB13060 Reclaim Key Dracokid C	.20	.40
VEB13061 Roly-poly Worker C	.07	.15
VEB13062 Steam Doctor, Mar-tash C	.07	.15
VEB13SSR01 Giant Deity of Distant World, Valkerion SSR	12.00	25.00
VEB13SSR02 Origin Deity of Heavenly Light, Uranus SSR	20.00	40.00
VEB13SSR03 Gleaming Lord, Uranus SSR	10.00	20.00
VEB13SSR04 Quaking Heavenly Dragon, Astraios Dragon SSR	12.00	25.00
VEB13SSR05 Phinomenus of the Constellations SSR	7.50	15.00
VEB13SSR06 Dikei of the Just Path SSR	12.00	25.00

2020 Cardfight Vanguard V Special Series 5 Festival Collection

VSS05001 Flash Shield, Iseult RR	.75	1.50
VSS05002 Weather Forecaster, Miss Mist RR	1.00	2.00
VSS05003 Battle Cupid, Nociel RR	1.50	3.00
VSS05004 Dark Shield, Mac Lir RR	5.00	10.00
VSS05005 Halo Shield, Mark RR	4.00	8.00
VSS05006 Goddess of Self-sacrifice, Kushinada RR	1.50	3.00
VSS05007 Wyvern Guard, Barri RR	3.00	6.00
VSS05008 Stealth Beast, Mijingakure RR	.75	1.50
VSS05009 Archbird RR	.50	1.00
VSS05010 Stealth Beast, Leaves Mirage RR	1.00	2.00
VSS05011 Wyvern Guard, Guld RR	5.00	10.00
VSS05012 Twin Blader RR	2.50	5.00
VSS05013 Diamond Ace RR	.60	1.25
VSS05014 Flowers in Vacuum, Cosmo Wreath RR	6.00	12.00
VSS05015 Cheer Girl, Marilyn RR	1.00	2.00
VSS05016 March Rabbit of Nightmareland RR	.60	1.25
VSS05017 Hades Hypnotist RR	5.00	10.00
VSS05018 Steam Guard, Kastilia RR	.75	1.50
VSS05019 Gust Djinn RR	.75	1.50
VSS05020 Glittery Baby, Lene RR	5.00	10.00
VSS05021 Emerald Shield, Paschal RR	3.00	6.00
VSS05022 Paralyze Madonna RR	2.00	4.00
VSS05023 Cable Sheep RR	.60	1.25
VSS05024 Maiden of Blossom Rain RR	.75	1.50
VSS05025 Knight of Truth, Gordon R	.20	.40
VSS05026 Little Sage, Marron R	.50	1.00
VSS05027 Rectangle Magus R	.50	1.00
VSS05028 Miko of Elegance, Fumino R	.30	.75
VSS05029 Crimson Impact, Metatron R	1.50	3.00
VSS05030 Underlay Celestial, Hesediel R	.25	.50
VSS05031 Black-winged Swordbreaker R	6.00	12.00
VSS05032 Skull Witch, Nemain R	20.00	40.00
VSS05033 Player of the Holy Bow, Viviane R	1.50	3.00
VSS05034 Listener of Truth, Dindrane R	.30	.60
VSS05035 Battle Maiden, Sahohime R	1.25	2.50
VSS05036 Witch of Cats, Cumin R	.30	.75
VSS05037 Flame of Hope, Aermo R	3.00	6.00
VSS05038 Sabel Dragonewt R	5.00	10.00
VSS05039 Stealth Dragon, Magatsu Gale R	2.00	4.00
VSS05040 Stealth Dragon, Togajuji R	.50	1.00
VSS05041 Ravenous Dragon, Megarex R	1.50	3.00
VSS05042 Vicious Claw Dragon, Lacraterex R	.25	.50
VSS05043 Stealth Rogue of Indignation, Meomaru R	7.50	15.00
VSS05044 Stealth Beast, Million Rat R	.20	.40
VSS05045 Dragonic Deathscythe R	.75	1.50
VSS05046 Rising Phoenix R	1.50	3.00
VSS05047 Kick Kick Typhoon R	4.00	8.00
VSS05048 Clay-doll Mechanic R	1.25	2.50
VSS05049 Platinum Ace R	.75	1.50
VSS05050 Dimensional Robo, Daibrave R	.60	1.25
VSS05051 Blast Monk of the Thundering Foot R	.50	1.00
VSS05052 Destiny Dealer R	.30	.75
VSS05053 Spike Bouncer R	1.00	2.00
VSS05054 Gyro Slinger R	.30	.75
VSS05055 Emblem Master R	3.00	6.00
VSS05056 Doreen the Thruster R	.50	1.00
VSS05057 Silver Thorn Acrobat, Leonor R	4.00	8.00
VSS05058 Purple Trapezist R	.60	1.25
VSS05059 Steam Mechanic, Nabu R	2.50	5.00
VSS05060 Quicky Quicky Worker R	1.00	2.00
VSS05061 Greed Shade R	4.00	8.00
VSS05062 Dandy Guy, Romario R	3.00	6.00
VSS05063 Choco Love Heart, Liselotte R	.60	1.25
VSS05064 Special Message, Ourora R	.25	.50
VSS05065 Coral Assault R	2.50	5.00
VSS05066 Wheel Assault R	2.00	4.00
VSS05067 Machining Mantis R	2.50	5.00
VSS05068 Machining Hornet R	.75	1.50
VSS05069 Binoculus Tiger R	1.00	2.00
VSS05070 Insurance Doctor, Womback R	.20	.40
VSS05071 Sunlight Garden's Guide R	1.25	2.50
VSS05072 Fruits Basket Elf R	.30	.75
VSS05073 Glyme C	.20	.40
VSS05074 Barcgal C	.15	.30
VSS05075 Godhawk, Ichibyoshi C	.15	.30
VSS05076 Whiteness Rabbit C	.15	.30
VSS05077 Lozenge Magus C	.20	.40
VSS05078 Aid-roid, Resh C	.15	.30
VSS05079 First Aid Celestial, Peniel C	.15	.30
VSS05080 Crisis Revenger, Fritz C	.15	.30
VSS05081 Promising Knight, David C	.15	.30
VSS05082 Fullbau C	.25	.50
VSS05083 Crimson Lion Cub, Kyrph C	.15	.30
VSS05084 Spring Breeze Messenger C	.15	.30
VSS05085 Pan of New Style C	.15	.30
VSS05086 Aiming for the Stars, Artemis C	.15	.30
VSS05087 Lizard Runner, Undeux C	.15	.30
VSS05088 Wyvernkid Ragla C	.15	.30
VSS05089 Evil Stealth Dragon, Ushimitsumaru C	.15	.30
VSS05090 Stealth Dragon, Magatsu Wind C	.15	.30
VSS05091 Dragon Egg C	.15	.30
VSS05092 Stealth Beast, Cat Devil C	.15	.30
VSS05093 Masago Stealth Rogue, Goemon C	.15	.30
VSS05094 Spark Kid Dragoon C	.15	.30
VSS05095 Harbinger Dracokid C	.15	.30
VSS05096 Barit Dracokid C	.15	.30
VSS05097 Beast Deity, White Tiger C	.15	.30
VSS05098 Sling Burster C	.15	.30
VSS05099 Tap the Hyper C	.15	.30
VSS05100 Battleraizer C	.15	.30
VSS05101 Full Moon Muscle C	.15	.30
VSS05102 Dimensional Robo, Goyusha C	.15	.30
VSS05103 Little Hero Dracokid C	.15	.30
VSS05104 Sprout Deletor, Luchi C	.15	.30
VSS05105 Starhulk, Lurli C	.20	.40
VSS05106 Neon Messiah C	.15	.30
VSS05107 Micro-hole Dracokid C	.15	.30
VSS05108 Mecha Trainer C	.15	.30
VSS05109 Vermillion Gatekeeper C	.15	.30
VSS05110 Devil in Shadow C	.20	.40
VSS05111 Entertain Messenger C	.15	.30
VSS05112 Silver Thorn Assistant, Ionela C	.30	.60
VSS05113 Primordial Dracokid C	.15	.30
VSS05114 Chrono Tigar C	.15	.30
VSS05115 Guiding Zombie C	.15	.30
VSS05116 Captain Nightkid C	.25	.50
VSS05117 Angelic Star, Coral C	.25	.50
VSS05118 Bermuda Triangle Cadet, Riviere C	.15	.30
VSS05119 Pure Gifter, Aliche C	.15	.30
VSS05120 Sonata C	.15	.30
VSS05121 Canon C	.15	.30
VSS05122 Serena C	.15	.30
VSS05123 Fina C	.15	.30
VSS05124 Caro C	.15	.30
VSS05125 Officer Cadet, Erikk C	.15	.30
VSS05126 Blue Wave Recruit, Kosty C	.15	.30
VSS05127 Blow Bubble Dracokid C	.15	.30
VSS05128 Machining Worker Ant C	.15	.30
VSS05129 Jet-ink Fox C	.15	.30
VSS05130 Blackboard Parrot C	.20	.40
VSS05131 Arboros Dragon, Ratoon C	.15	.30
VSS05132 Broccolini Musketeer, Kirah C	.15	.30

2020 Cardfight Vanguard V Special Series 5 Premium Collection 2020

VSS07001 Storm Element, Cycloned GR	3.00	6.00
VSS07002 Holy Dragon, Crystaluster Dragon RRR	15.00	30.00
VSS07002 Holy Dragon, Crystaluster Dragon SR	15.00	30.00
VSS07003 Sterling Witch, MoMo SR	6.00	12.00
VSS07003 Sterling Witch, MoMo RRR	2.00	4.00
VSS07004 Holy Seraph, Basasael RRR	1.25	2.50
VSS07004 Holy Seraph, Basasael SR	3.00	6.00
VSS07005 Dark Dragon, Chainrancor Dragon SR	7.50	15.00
VSS07005 Dark Dragon, Chainrancor Dragon RRR	5.00	10.00
VSS07006 Golden Dragon, Brambent Dragon RRR	1.00	2.00
VSS07006 Golden Dragon, Brambent Dragon SR	2.50	5.00
VSS07007 Hero Deity of the Polar Extremity, Marduk SR	4.00	8.00
VSS07007 Hero Deity of the Polar Extremity, Marduk RRR	2.00	4.00
VSS07008 Supreme Heavenly Emperor Dragon, Zanbust Dragon RRR	1.50	3.00
VSS07008 Supreme Heavenly Emperor Dragon, Zanbust Dragon SR	2.50	5.00
VSS07009 Rikudo Demonic Dragon, Jakumesso SR	1.50	3.00
VSS07009 Rikudo Demonic Dragon, Jakumesso RRR	.75	1.50
VSS07010 Destruction Tyrant, Ganturaptor SR	2.50	5.00
VSS07010 Destruction Tyrant, Ganturaptor RRR	.75	1.50
VSS07011 Ambush Demon Stealth Beast, Nue Daio SR	3.00	6.00
VSS07011 Ambush Demon Stealth Beast, Nue Daio RRR	1.25	2.50
VSS07012 Conquering Supreme Dragon, Stunverse Dragon SR	7.50	15.00
VSS07012 Conquering Supreme Dragon, Stunverse Dragon RRR	5.00	10.00
VSS07013 Uncanny Dragon King, Azhdabalk SR	5.00	10.00
VSS07013 Uncanny Dragon King, Azhdabalk RRR	.60	1.25
VSS07014 Heat Wave Beast, Geomaglass SR	6.00	12.00
VSS07014 Heat Wave Beast, Geomaglass RRR	4.00	8.00
VSS07015 Nebula Dragon, Baryoend Dragon SR	5.00	10.00
VSS07015 Nebula Dragon, Baryoend Dragon RRR	2.00	4.00
VSS07016 Great Titlist, Villain Verminous SR	1.00	2.00
VSS07016 Great Titlist, Villain Verminous RRR	.30	.75
VSS07017 Ringleader of Uproar, Gharvans SR	1.00	2.00
VSS07017 Ringleader of Uproar, Gharvans RRR	.75	1.50
VSS07018 Midair Megatrick, Yvette SR	6.00	12.00
VSS07018 Midair Megatrick, Yvette RRR	2.00	4.00
VSS07019 Interdimensional Dragon, Grogrock Dragon SR	3.00	6.00
VSS07019 Interdimensional Dragon, Grogrock Dragon RRR	1.00	2.00
VSS07020 Wight Legion Sailing Ship, Bad Bounty SR	6.00	12.00
VSS07020 Wight Legion Sailing Ship, Bad Bounty RRR	.20	.40
VSS07021 Valuable Verve, Federica SR	5.00	10.00
VSS07021 Valuable Verve, Federica RRR	.20	.40
VSS07022 Blue Storm Steel Dragon, Genbold Dragon SR	2.50	5.00
VSS07022 Blue Storm Steel Dragon, Genbold Dragon RRR	1.50	3.00
VSS07023 Pillaging Mutant Deity, Deprenor SR	1.00	2.00
VSS07023 Pillaging Mutant Deity, Deprenor RRR	.20	.40
VSS07024 Omniscience Dragon, Tciptckaam SR	1.00	2.00
VSS07024 Omniscience Dragon, Tciptckaam RRR	.30	.75
VSS07025 Entrancing Flower Princess, Sandrine SR	3.00	6.00
VSS07025 Entrancing Flower Princess, Sandrine RRR	2.00	4.00
VSS07026 Sentflare Dracokid RR	2.00	4.00
VSS07027 Celeste Witch, ToTo RR	.60	1.25
VSS07028 Augment Angel RR	.50	1.00
VSS07029 Knight of Evil Spear, Gilling RR	2.50	5.00
VSS07030 Gold Garnish Lion RR	.75	1.50
VSS07031 Ancestral Dragon of Onslaught, Mushu Fushu RR	1.50	3.00
VSS07032 Dragon Dancer, Paloma RR	1.50	3.00
VSS07033 Stealth Dragon, Eisan RR	.30	.75
VSS07034 Bombardment Dragon, Arzenewerfer RR	.30	.75
VSS07035 Stealth Fiend, Blue Andon RR	.50	1.00
VSS07036 Rumble Dagger Dracokid RR	.60	1.25
VSS07037 Kitton Pikkon RR	1.00	2.00
VSS07038 Defilement Monster, Dobluba RR	.50	1.00
VSS07039 Conditioned Child of Superatom RR	3.00	6.00
VSS07040 Cheer Girl, Lynette RR	.50	1.00
VSS07041 Pain Stinger RR	1.00	2.00
VSS07042 Convert Bunny RR	2.50	5.00
VSS07043 Steam Engineer, Apazu RR	.50	1.00
VSS07044 Chad the Ghostie RR	2.00	4.00
VSS07045 Wrapping Chorus, Trudy RR	.15	.30
VSS07046 Bumper Shooter RR	.60	1.25
VSS07047 Riddled Honey RR	.30	.60
VSS07048 Exploding Professor, Ezonoshin RR	.15	.30
VSS07049 Maiden of Polyantha RR	.50	1.00
VSS07050 Thunder Elemental, Barigiran RR	.50	1.00
VSS07051 Cloud Elemental, Mowark RR	1.00	2.00
VSS07052 Light Elemental, Mekira RR	2.50	5.00
VSS07053 Rain Elemental, Zarzan RR	.60	1.25
VSS07054 Earth Elemental, Lorock RR	.30	.75
VSS07055 Air Elemental, Bufoo RR	.15	.30
VSS07056 Heat Elemental, Huang RR	1.25	2.50
VSS07057 Tempest Sphere RR	10.00	20.00
VSS07S01 Storm Element Cycloned SGR	15.00	30.00

2020 Cardfight Vanguard V Trial Deck 10 Chronojet

VTD10001 Interdimensional Beast, Metallica Phoenix	.25	.50
VTD10002 Chronojet Dragon	.75	1.50
VTD10003 Steam Gunner, Yarlaganda	.12	.25
VTD10004 Stroboscope Dragon	.30	.75
VTD10005 Steam Fighter, Zarlab	.12	.25
VTD10006 Steam Fighter, Idena	.12	.25
VTD10007 Gears Repeater	.17	.35
VTD10008 Bearing Rover	.25	.50
VTD10009 Steam Janitor, Gitlim	.12	.25
VTD10010 Chrono Dran	.30	.60
VTD10011 Steam Bomber, Digul	.20	.40
VTD10012 Ring Ring Worker	.15	.30
VTD10013 Steam Guard, Kastilia	.20	.40
VTD10014 Luckypot Dracokid	.12	.25
VTD10015 Steam Maiden, Uluru	.30	.60
VTD10016 Power Rise Elixir	.75	1.50
VTD10TI01 Quick Shield	.30	.75

2020 Cardfight Vanguard V Trial Deck 11 Altmile

VTD11001 Blue Sky Knight, Altmile	.30	.60
VTD11002 Unite Reet Dragon	.12	.25
VTD11003 Absolute Blade Knight, Livarot	2.00	4.00
VTD11004 Knight of Magnificence, Lucus	.12	.25
VTD11005 Sage of Contemplation, Tedun	.15	.30
VTD11006 Pioneer Knight, Epaticcus	.20	.40
VTD11007 Lunar Crescent Knight, Felax	.30	.60
VTD11008 Indestructible Knight, Earina	.15	.30
VTD11009 Melodious Angel	.15	.30
VTD11010 Shining Knight, Millius	.30	.60
VTD11011 Bringer of Good Luck, Epona	.20	.40
VTD11012 Flogal	.12	.25
VTD11013 Flash Shield, Iseult	.25	.50
VTD11014 Bringer of Court's Favor, Relgla	.12	.25
VTD11015 Healing Pegasus	.15	.30
VTD11016 Power Rise Elixir	.30	.60
VTD11TI01 Quick Shield	.75	1.50

2020 Cardfight Vanguard V Trial Deck 12 Ahsha

VTD12001 Ranunculus Flower Maiden, Ahsha	.50	1.00
VTD12002 Genteel Knight, Orvell	.15	.30
VTD12003 Blossoming Maiden, Cela	.30	.60
VTD12004 Candid Maiden, Marlies	.12	.25
VTD12005 Maiden of Bot-fist	.12	.25
VTD12006 Budding Maiden, Diane	.30	.75
VTD12007 Maiden of Blue Lace	.60	1.25
VTD12008 Momosmo Peach	.15	.30
VTD12009 Amimelo Melon	.20	.40
VTD12010 Spring-Heralding Maiden, Ozu	.50	1.00
VTD12011 Night Queen Musketeer, Daniel	.15	.30
VTD12012 Chestnut Bullet	.20	.40
VTD12013 Neighborly Knight, Boris	.12	.25
VTD12014 Maiden of Blossom Rain	.30	.60
VTD12015 Fairy Light Dragon	.15	.30
VTD12016 Power Rise Elixir	.50	1.00
VTD12T01 Ahsha's Flower Fairy Token	.30	.60
VTD12T02 Plant Token	.30	.75
VTD12TI01 Quick Shield	.30	.75

2021 Cardfight Vanguard D Booster Set 1 Genesis of the Five Greats

DBT01001 Vairina Valiente RRR	4.00	8.00
DBT01001 Vairina Valiente SP	20.00	40.00
DBT01002 Heavy Artillery of Dust Storm, Eugene RRR	.30	.75
DBT01002 Heavy Artillery of Dust Storm, Eugene SP	7.50	15.00
DBT01003 Master of Gravity, Baromagnes RRR	1.25	2.50
DBT01003 Master of Gravity, Baromagnes SP	17.50	35.00
DBT01004 Diabolos Boys, Eden RRR	4.00	8.00
DBT01004 Diabolos Boys, Eden SP	15.00	30.00
DBT01005 Cardinal Deus, Orfist RRR	4.00	8.00
DBT01005 Cardinal Deus, Orfist SP	40.00	80.00
DBT01006 Aurora Battle Princess, Agarrar Rouge RRR	4.00	8.00
DBT01006 Aurora Battle Princess, Agarrar Rouge SP	20.00	40.00
DBT01007 Grand Heavenly Sword, Alden RRR	6.00	12.00
DBT01007 Grand Heavenly Sword, Alden SP	12.50	25.00
DBT01008 Hexaorb Sorceress RRR	.75	1.50
DBT01008 Hexaorb Sorceress SP	12.50	25.00
DBT01009 Mysterious Rain Spiritualist, Zorga RRR	2.00	4.00
DBT01009 Mysterious Rain Spiritualist, Zorga SP	40.00	80.00
DBT01010 Sylvan Horned Beast, Gyunosla RRR	.75	1.50
DBT01010 Sylvan Horned Beast, Gyunosla SP	7.50	15.00
DBT01011 Vairina Arcs RR	2.00	4.00
DBT01011 Vairina Arcs SP	20.00	40.00
DBT01012 Stealth Dragon, Tensha Stead RR	1.00	2.00
DBT01012 Stealth Dragon, Tensha Stead SP	7.50	15.00
DBT01013 Dragon Deity King of Resurgence, Dragveda ORR	6.00	12.00
DBT01013 Dragon Deity King of Resurgence, Dragveda SP	17.50	35.00
DBT01014 Upward Acrobat, Marjorie RR	1.25	2.50
DBT01014 Upward Acrobat, Marjorie SP	20.00	40.00
DBT01015 Steam Battler, Gungunuram RR	.50	1.00
DBT01015 Steam Battler, Gungunuram SP	10.00	20.00
DBT01016 Hades Dragon Deity of Resentment, Gallmageheld ORR	3.00	6.00
DBT01016 Hades Dragon Deity of Resentment, Gallmageheld SP	17.50	35.00
DBT01017 Hyperspeed Robo, Chevalstud RR	.75	1.50
DBT01017 Hyperspeed Robo, Chevalstud SP	6.00	12.00
DBT01018 Detonation Mutant, Bobalmine RR	2.50	5.00
DBT01018 Detonation Mutant, Bobalmine SP	12.50	25.00
DBT01019 Star Dragon Deity of Infinitude, Eldobreath ORR	6.00	12.00
DBT01019 Star Dragon Deity of Infinitude, Eldobreath SP	20.00	40.00
DBT01020 Knight of War Damage, Fosado RR	6.00	12.00
DBT01020 Knight of War Damage, Fosado SP	20.00	40.00
DBT01021 Painkiller Angel RR	.50	1.00
DBT01021 Painkiller Angel SP	5.00	10.00
DBT01022 Light Dragon Deity of Honors, Amartinoa ORR	6.00	12.00
DBT01022 Light Dragon Deity of Honors, Amartinoa SP	25.00	50.00
DBT01023 Inheritance Maiden, Hendrina RR	.30	.75
DBT01023 Inheritance Maiden, Hendrina SP	12.50	25.00
DBT01024 Spurring Maiden, Ellenia RR	.30	.75
DBT01024 Spurring Maiden, Ellenia SP	6.00	12.00
DBT01025 Source Dragon Deity of Blessings, Blessfavor ORR	5.00	10.00
DBT01025 Source Dragon Deity of Blessings, Blessfavor SP	20.00	40.00
DBT01026 Penetrate Dragon, Tribash R	.15	.30
DBT01026 Penetrate Dragon, Tribash HOLO	1.50	3.00
DBT01027 Cataclysmic Bullet of Dust Storm, Randor R	.15	.30
DBT01027 Cataclysmic Bullet of Dust Storm, Randor HOLO	.30	.60
DBT01028 Dragritter, Dabbaax R	.15	.30
DBT01029 Stealth Rogue of Strife, Fudomaru R	.15	.30
DBT01030 Dragritter, Alwalith R	.15	.30
DBT01031 Twin Buckler Dragon R	2.00	4.00
DBT01031 Twin Buckler Dragon HOLO	4.00	8.00
DBT01031 Twin Buckler Dragon SP	25.00	50.00
DBT01032 Phantasma Magician, Curtis R	25.00	.50
DBT01033 Electro Spartan R	.15	.30
DBT01033 Electro Spartan HOLO	1.25	2.50
DBT01034 Shadow Leak Magician R	.15	.30
DBT01035 Protobulb Dragon R	.60	1.25
DBT01036 Recusal Hate Dragon R	1.50	3.00
DBT01036 Recusal Hate Dragon HOLO	4.00	8.00
DBT01036 Recusal Hate Dragon SP	20.00	40.00
DBT01037 Crawl, you Insects! R	.15	.30
DBT01037 Crawl, you Insects! HOLO	.30	.60
DBT01038 Granaroad Fairtigar R	.15	.30
DBT01039 Cardinal Noid, Cubisia HOLO	.75	1.50
DBT01039 Cardinal Noid, Cubisia SP	15.00	30.00
DBT01039 Cardinal Noid, Cubisia R	.15	.30
DBT01040 Frigid Mutant, Drumler R	.15	.30
DBT01041 Fighting Dragon, Goldog Dragon R	.15	.30
DBT01042 Violate Dragon R	3.00	6.00
DBT01042 Violate Dragon SP	30.00	60.00
DBT01042 Violate Dragon HOLO	4.00	8.00
DBT01043 Hollowing Moonlit Night R	.20	.40
DBT01043 Hollowing Moonlit Night HOLO	3.00	6.00
DBT01044 Dark Strain Dragon R	.30	.60
DBT01044 Dark Strain Dragon HOLO	1.50	3.00
DBT01045 Great Snake Witch, Solaria R	.15	.30
DBT01046 Pentagleam Sorceress R	.15	.30
DBT01046 Pentagleam Sorceress HOLO	.75	1.50
DBT01047 Divine Sister, Tartine R	.15	.30
DBT01047 Divine Sister, Tartine HOLO	.30	.75
DBT01048 Divine Sister, Faciata R	.15	.30
DBT01049 Aegismare Dragon R	.15	.30
DBT01049 Aegismare Dragon SP	20.00	40.00
DBT01049 Aegismare Dragon HOLO	4.00	8.00
DBT01050 Black Tears Husk Dragon R	.15	.30
DBT01050 Black Tears Husk Dragon HOLO	.75	1.50
DBT01050 Black Tears Husk Dragon SP	12.50	25.00
DBT01051 Sylvan Horned Beast, Aleio R	.15	.30
DBT01052 Planar Prevent Dragon R	1.25	2.50
DBT01052 Planar Prevent Dragon HOLO	3.00	6.00
DBT01052 Planar Prevent Dragon SP	25.00	50.00
DBT01053 Cursed Souls Squirming in Agony R	.15	.30
DBT01054 Grief, Despair, and Rejection R	.15	.30
DBT01054 Grief, Despair, and Rejection HOLO	.60	1.25
DBT01055 Spiritual Body Condensation R	.50	1.00
DBT01055 Spiritual Body Condensation HOLO	2.50	5.00
DBT01056 Stealth Dragon, Hadou Shugen C	.12	.25
DBT01057 Stealth Rogue of Iron Blade, Oshikuni C	.12	.25
DBT01058 Dragritter, Zafar C	.12	.25
DBT01059 Extreme Dragon, Velocihazard C	.12	.25
DBT01060 Gunning of Dust Storm, Nigel C	.12	.25
DBT01060 Gunning of Dust Storm, Nigel HOLO	.30	.60
DBT01061 Stealth Fiend, Shigamanago C	.12	.25
DBT01061 Stealth Fiend, Shigamanago HOLO	.30	.75
DBT01062 Double Gun of Dust Storm, Bart C	.12	.25
DBT01062 Double Gun of Dust Storm, Bart HOLO	.30	.60
DBT01063 Contact Spark Dragon C	.75	1.50
DBT01063 Contact Spark Dragon HOLO	3.00	6.00
DBT01064 Express Dragon, Steeldilopho C	.12	.25
DBT01064 Express Dragon, Steeldilopho HOLO	.50	1.00
DBT01065 Stealth Dragon, Jaengoku C	.12	.25
DBT01065 Stealth Dragon, Jaengoku HOLO	.30	.60
DBT01066 White Light Dragon, Parasolas C	.12	.25
DBT01066 White Light Dragon, Parasolas HOLO	.60	1.25
DBT01067 Sunlight Punishment C	.12	.25
DBT01068 Burn Bright, Pure Prayers C	.12	.25
DBT01069 Selfish Engraver C	.12	.25
DBT01069 Selfish Engraver HOLO	1.25	2.50
DBT01070 Soulful Wild Master, Megan C	.12	.25
DBT01071 Eminence Jarboberos C	.12	.25
DBT01072 Steam Artist, Pithana C	.12	.25
DBT01073 Steam Detective, Uvaritt C	.12	.25
DBT01074 Direful Doll, Simone C	.12	.25
DBT01075 Deep Soniker HOLO	.60	1.25
DBT01075 Deep Soniker C	.12	.25
DBT01076 Uncanny Burning C	.12	.25
DBT01076 Uncanny Burning HOLO	.30	.60
DBT01077 Flinty Slasher C	.50	1.00
DBT01077 Flinty Slasher HOLO	3.00	6.00
DBT01078 Vital Reaver C	.12	.25
DBT01078 Vital Reaver HOLO	.30	.60
DBT01079 Hackle Hustle C	.12	.25
DBT01079 Hackle Hustle HOLO	.30	.60
DBT01080 Steam Scara, Malnigal C	.20	.40
DBT01080 Steam Scara, Malnigal HOLO	.75	1.50
DBT01081 Tartarus Beatscram C	.12	.25
DBT01082 Lightning Thief Monster, Jabattail C	.12	.25
DBT01083 Grapple External C	.12	.25
DBT01084 Cardinal Noid, Routis HOLO	.30	.75
DBT01084 Cardinal Noid, Routis SP	12.50	25.00
DBT01084 Cardinal Noid, Routis C	.12	.25
DBT01085 Electrode Monster, Adapton C	.12	.25
DBT01086 Useful Recharger C	.12	.25
DBT01087 Cardinal Fang, Phovi HOLO	.30	.60
DBT01087 Cardinal Fang, Phovi SP	10.00	20.00
DBT01087 Cardinal Fang, Phovi C	.12	.25
DBT01088 Cardinal Draco, Barbisonde HOLO	5.00	10.00
DBT01088 Cardinal Draco, Barbisonde SP	20.00	40.00
DBT01088 Cardinal Draco, Barbisonde C	.75	1.50
DBT01089 Cardinal Fang, Fulgurus C	.12	.25
DBT01089 Cardinal Fang, Fulgurus HOLO	.30	.75
DBT01090 Cardinal Draco, Abrard C	.12	.25
DBT01090 Cardinal Draco, Abrard HOLO	.50	1.00
DBT01091 Cardinal Prima, Navirem HOLO	1.00	2.00
DBT01091 Cardinal Prima, Navirem SP	12.50	25.00
DBT01091 Cardinal Prima, Navirem C	.30	.75
DBT01092 Causality Goes Crazy as I Will It C	.12	.25
DBT01093 Lightning Barrier, Emergency Deployment! C	.12	.25
DBT01094 In the Darkness Nobody Knows C	.12	.25
DBT01094 In the Darkness Nobody Knows HOLO	.30	.75
DBT01095 Actual Analyst, Kokabiel C	.20	.40
DBT01096 Divine Sister, Lepisto C	.12	.25
DBT01097 Remission Sword, Fanuel C	.12	.25
DBT01098 Divine Sister, Pastelito C	.12	.25
DBT01099 Tier Square Sorceress C	.12	.25
DBT01099 Tier Square Sorceress HOLO	.50	1.00
DBT01100 Swordsman of Heavenly Winds, Wechel C	.12	.25
DBT01101 Tri Connect Sorceress C	.12	.25
DBT01101 Tri Connect Sorceress HOLO	.30	.60
DBT01102 White Fang Witch, Disma C	.50	1.00
DBT01102 White Fang Witch, Disma HOLO	4.00	8.00
DBT01103 Knight of Raise, Airfredo C	.12	.25
DBT01103 Knight of Raise, Airfredo HOLO	.75	1.50
DBT01104 White Raven Sorcerer, Taxus C	.12	.25
DBT01104 White Raven Sorcerer, Taxus HOLO	.50	1.00
DBT01105 Cycle Ring Sorceress C	.12	.25
DBT01105 Cycle Ring Sorceress HOLO	.75	1.50
DBT01106 Swinging Sword of Judgement C	.12	.25
DBT01107 Hopeful Testudo C	.12	.25
DBT01108 Noble of Wisdom, Edgar C	.12	.25
DBT01109 Hydrolic Ram Dragon C	.12	.25
DBT01110 Gloomy Tour C	.12	.25
DBT01111 Rancor Chain HOLO	.30	.60
DBT01111 Rancor Chain SP	5.00	10.00
DBT01111 Rancor Chain C	.12	.25
DBT01112 Collusion Mutant, Admantis C	.20	.40
DBT01113 Dream Gnawing HOLO	.30	.60
DBT01113 Dream Gnawing SP	3.00	6.00
DBT01113 Dream Gnawing C	.12	.25
DBT01114 Abyss Invitation HOLO	3.00	6.00
DBT01114 Abyss Invitation SP	15.00	30.00
DBT01114 Abyss Invitation C	.30	.60
DBT01115 Lost Child of Love C	.12	.25
DBT01115 Lost Child of Love HOLO	.75	1.50
DBT01116 Grudge Hatchet C	.12	.25
DBT01116 Grudge Hatchet HOLO	.30	.60
DBT01117 Fairy of Elegy HOLO	.75	1.50
DBT01117 Fairy of Elegy SP	25.00	50.00
DBT01117 Fairy of Elegy C	.12	.25
DBT01118 Tearing Malice C	.12	.25
DBT01119 Ghost Chase C	.12	.25
DBT01120 Sealed Road C	.12	.25
DBT01DSR01 Trickstar DSR	200.00	350.00
DBT01DSR02 Chakrabarthi Divine Dragon, Nirvana DSR	100.00	200.00
DBT01T01 Shadow Army Token T	.50	1.00

2021 Cardfight Vanguard D Booster Set 2 A Brush with the Legends

DBT02001 Dragonic Overlord RRR	2.50	5.00
DBT02001 Dragonic Overlord SP	15.00	30.00
DBT02002 Vairina Erger RRR	4.00	8.00
DBT02002 Vairina Erger SP	15.00	30.00
DBT02003 Crimson Igspeller RRR	.75	1.50
DBT02003 Crimson Igspeller SP	3.00	6.00
DBT02004 Diabolos Jetbacker, Lenard SP	12.50	25.00
DBT02004 Diabolos Jetbacker, Lenard RRR	5.00	10.00
DBT02005 Cardinal Draco, Alviderd RRR	1.50	3.00
DBT02005 Cardinal Draco, Alviderd SP	12.50	25.00
DBT02006 Aurora Battle Princess, Perio Turquoise RRR	4.00	8.00
DBT02006 Aurora Battle Princess, Perio Turquoise SP	15.00	30.00
DBT02007 Heavenly Bow of Edifying Guidance, Refuerzos RRR	.50	1.00
DBT02007 Heavenly Bow of Edifying Guidance, Refuerzos SP	5.00	10.00
DBT02008 Phantom Blaster Dragon RRR	3.00	6.00
DBT02008 Phantom Blaster Dragon SP	12.50	25.00
DBT02009 Sylvan Horned Beast, Damainaru RRR	2.00	4.00
DBT02009 Sylvan Horned Beast, Damainaru SP	7.50	15.00
DBT02010 Rogue Headhunter RRR	1.00	2.00
DBT02010 Rogue Headhunter SP	7.50	15.00
DBT02011 Blaze Fist Monk, Damari RR	.25	.50
DBT02011 Blaze Fist Monk, Damari SP	1.50	3.00
DBT02012 Stealth Dragon, Togachirashi RR	4.00	8.00
DBT02012 Stealth Dragon, Togachirashi SP	7.50	15.00
DBT02013 Dragritter, Iduriss RR	.30	.60
DBT02013 Dragritter, Iduriss SP	15.00	30.00
DBT02014 Cleave Muddler RR	.25	.50
DBT02014 Cleave Muddler SP	.75	1.50
DBT02015 Legio Wild Master, Darius RR	.20	.40
DBT02015 Legio Wild Master, Darius SP	1.25	2.50
DBT02016 Diabolos Madonna, Mabel RR	.60	1.25
DBT02016 Diabolos Madonna, Mabel SP	7.50	15.00
DBT02017 Aurora Battle Princess, Derii Violet RR	.75	1.50
DBT02017 Aurora Battle Princess, Derii Violet SP	10.00	20.00
DBT02018 Cardinal Noid, Thumborino RR	1.50	3.00
DBT02018 Cardinal Noid, Thumborino SP	12.50	25.00
DBT02019 Gluttonic Monster, Malnorm RR	.25	.50
DBT02019 Gluttonic Monster, Malnorm SP	2.50	5.00
DBT02020 Soaring Dragon, Prideful Dragon RR	.30	.75
DBT02020 Soaring Dragon, Prideful Dragon SP	3.00	6.00
DBT02021 Sterilize Angel RR	.20	.40
DBT02021 Sterilize Angel SP	1.25	2.50
DBT02022 Diaglass Sorceress RR	.50	1.00
DBT02022 Diaglass Sorceress SP	5.00	10.00
DBT02023 Maiden of Deep Impression, Urjula RR	.60	1.25
DBT02023 Maiden of Deep Impression, Urjula SP	4.00	8.00
DBT02024 Regurgitation from the Underworld RR	.20	.40
DBT02024 Regurgitation from the Underworld SP	1.25	2.50
DBT02025 Wild Intelligence RR	1.00	2.00
DBT02025 Wild Intelligence SP	5.00	10.00
DBT02026 Strong Fortress Dragon, Jibrabrachio R	.15	.30
DBT02026 Strong Fortress Dragon, Jibrabrachio HOLO	.40	.80
DBT02027 Dragon Knight, Nehalem HOLO	.75	1.50
DBT02027 Dragon Knight, Nehalem R	.30	.60
DBT02027 Dragon Knight, Nehalem SP	10.00	20.00
DBT02028 Berserk Dragon HOLO	.60	1.25
DBT02028 Berserk Dragon R	.30	.75
DBT02028 Berserk Dragon SP	7.50	15.00
DBT02029 Blaze Maiden, Tanya HOLO	.30	.60
DBT02029 Blaze Maiden, Tanya R	.15	.30
DBT02030 Blaze Maiden, Parama HOLO	2.50	5.00
DBT02030 Blaze Maiden, Parama R	.15	.30
DBT02030 Blaze Maiden, Parama SP	20.00	40.00
DBT02031 Horn of Blessing HOLO	.30	.60
DBT02031 Horn of Blessing R	.15	.30
DBT02032 Time Jarate Dragon HOLO	.30	.60
DBT02032 Time Jarate Dragon R	.15	.30
DBT02033 Diabolos Edge, Grantlee HOLO	.30	.60
DBT02033 Diabolos Edge, Grantlee R	.15	.30
DBT02034 Freeze Breeze HOLO	.30	.75
DBT02034 Freeze Breeze R	.15	.30
DBT02035 Diabolos Girls, Natalia HOLO	2.00	4.00
DBT02035 Diabolos Girls, Natalia R	.75	1.50
DBT02035 Diabolos Girls, Natalia SP	12.50	25.00
DBT02036 Supernatural Extraction HOLO	.40	.80
DBT02036 Supernatural Extraction R	.15	.30
DBT02037 Hellblast Full Dive HOLO	1.00	2.00
DBT02037 Hellblast Full Dive R	.30	.75
DBT02038 Cardinal Noid, Plasteia HOLO	.30	.60
DBT02038 Cardinal Noid, Plasteia R	.15	.30
DBT02039 Cardinal Fang, Marisma R	.15	.30
DBT02039 Cardinal Fang, Marisma HOLO	.60	1.25
DBT02040 Cardinal Prima, Ecolpa HOLO	.30	.60
DBT02040 Cardinal Prima, Ecolpa R	.15	.30
DBT02041 Whimsical Machine Beast, Bugmotor HOLO	.30	.60
DBT02041 Whimsical Machine Beast, Bugmotor R	.15	.30
DBT02042 Cardinal Draco, Enpyro HOLO	2.00	4.00
DBT02042 Cardinal Draco, Enpyro R	1.25	2.50
DBT02042 Cardinal Draco, Enpyro SP	20.00	40.00
DBT02043 Moment of Securing! HOLO	.75	1.50
DBT02043 Moment of Securing! R	.30	.75
DBT02044 Exquisite Knight, Olwein HOLO	.50	1.00
DBT02044 Exquisite Knight, Olwein R	.15	.30
DBT02045 Darkness Maiden, Macha HOLO	.75	1.50
DBT02045 Darkness Maiden, Macha R	.30	.60
DBT02045 Darkness Maiden, Macha SP	7.50	15.00
DBT02046 Blaster Dark HOLO	1.25	2.50
DBT02046 Blaster Dark R	.50	1.00
DBT02046 Blaster Dark SP	15.00	30.00
DBT02047 Witch of Pandering, Brunner HOLO	1.25	2.50
DBT02047 Witch of Pandering, Brunner R	.50	1.00
DBT02048 Bard of Heavenly Song, Alpacc HOLO	3.00	6.00
DBT02048 Bard of Heavenly Song, Alpacc R	.15	.30
DBT02048 Bard of Heavenly Song, Alpacc SP	15.00	30.00
DBT02049 Form Up, O Chosen Knights HOLO	1.00	2.00
DBT02049 Form Up, O Chosen Knights R	.50	1.00
DBT02050 Sylvan Horned Beast, Elrante HOLO	.75	1.50
DBT02050 Sylvan Horned Beast, Elrante R	.25	.50
DBT02051 Fleet Swallower HOLO	.50	1.00
DBT02051 Fleet Swallower R	.15	.30
DBT02052 Fairy of Tragic Love HOLO	.30	.60
DBT02052 Fairy of Tragic Love R	.15	.30
DBT02053 Sleeve Tugging Belle HOLO	.30	.75
DBT02053 Sleeve Tugging Belle R	.15	.30

DBT02054 Frenzied Heiress HOLO .75 1.50
DBT02054 Frenzied Heiress R .60 1.25
DBT02054 Frenzied Heiress SP 10.00 20.00
DBT02055 Nectar of Sensationalism HOLO .50 1.00
DBT02055 Nectar of Sensationalism R .25 .50
DBT02056 Volcanic Gun Dragon C .12 .25
DBT02057 Crossrock Dragon C .12 .25
DBT02057 Crossrock Dragon HOLO .30 .60
DBT02058 Dragritter, Nasir C .12 .25
DBT02059 Armored Dragon, Mountcannon C .12 .25
DBT02060 Dragon Monk, Gojo C .12 .25
DBT02060 Dragon Monk, Gojo HOLO .75 1.50
DBT02060 Dragon Monk, Gojo SP 5.00 10.00
DBT02061 Stealth Dragon, Kizanreiji C .12 .25
DBT02062 Blaze Fist Monk, Enten C .12 .25
DBT02063 Blaze Maiden, Aruna C .12 .25
DBT02064 Embodiment of Armor, Bahr C .12 .25
DBT02064 Embodiment of Armor, Bahr HOLO 1.00 2.00
DBT02064 Embodiment of Armor, Bahr SP 7.50 15.00
DBT02065 Blaze Maiden, Zara C .12 .25
DBT02066 Lizard Runner, Undeux C .12 .25
DBT02066 Lizard Runner, Undeux HOLO .25 .50
DBT02066 Lizard Runner, Undeux SP 2.50 5.00
DBT02067 Flame Dragon Bomber C .12 .25
DBT02068 Prayers That Will Reach Someday C .12 .25
DBT02069 Steam Knight, Pashaltatar C .12 .25
DBT02069 Steam Knight, Pashaltatar HOLO .30 .60
DBT02070 Spiracle Splasher C .12 .25
DBT02071 Diabolos Attacker, Arwing C .12 .25
DBT02072 Unbreakable Ice Pillar, Jebinna C .12 .25
DBT02073 Steam Artist, Napir C .12 .25
DBT02074 Diabolos Madonna, Viola C .12 .25
DBT02075 Pestilent Talon C .12 .25
DBT02076 Surveillance Gear Dober C .12 .25
DBT02076 Surveillance Gear Dober HOLO .30 .60
DBT02077 Cyclone Circler C .12 .25
DBT02077 Cyclone Circler HOLO .30 .60
DBT02078 Steam Engineer, Pepelli C .12 .25
DBT02078 Steam Engineer, Pepelli HOLO .30 .60
DBT02079 Diabolos Boys, Chester C .12 .25
DBT02080 Deformed Hammer C .12 .25
DBT02081 Special Violence Yell C .12 .25
DBT02082 Cardinal Draco, Zeljio C .12 .25
DBT02083 Aurora Battle Princess, Mel Horizon C .12 .25
DBT02084 Hard Fist Dragon, Metalknuckler Dragon C .12 .25
DBT02085 Twisting Bulldoze C .12 .25
DBT02086 Cardinal Fang, Estrett C .12 .25
DBT02086 Cardinal Fang, Estrett HOLO .50 1.00
DBT02087 Aurora Battle Princess, Birett Canary C .12 .25
DBT02087 Aurora Battle Princess, Birett Canary HOLO .30 .60
DBT02088 Harmful Bite Monster, Zabokarni C .12 .25
DBT02089 Cardinal Prima, Altepo C .12 .25
DBT02090 Aurora Battle Princess, Loaded Azalee C .12 .25
DBT02091 Aurora Battle Princess, Whopper Prune C .12 .25
DBT02091 Aurora Battle Princess, Whopper Prune HOLO 1.25 2.50
DBT02092 Whirlpool Robo, Ramdrought C .12 .25
DBT02093 Explosive! Melting Heart! C .12 .25
DBT02094 Eclipsed Moonlight C .12 .25
DBT02094 Eclipsed Moonlight HOLO .60 1.25
DBT02095 Wielens Dragon C .12 .25
DBT02096 Octadevote Sorceress C .12 .25
DBT02097 Heavenly Staff of Kind Intention, Cortese C .12 .25
DBT02098 Heavenly Blade of Magnificence, Bestida C .12 .25
DBT02099 Divine Sister, Petit-four C .12 .25
DBT02100 Knight of Heavenly Collapse, Capaldo C .12 .25
DBT02100 Knight of Heavenly Collapse, Capaldo HOLO .30 .60
DBT02101 Additional Angel C .12 .25
DBT02102 Magic of Advancement, MelCoCo C .12 .25
DBT02103 Knight of Heavenly Thundering, Leedy C .12 .25
DBT02104 Blaster Javelin C .12 .25
DBT02104 Blaster Javelin HOLO .75 1.50
DBT02104 Blaster Javelin SP 6.00 12.00
DBT02105 Black Sage, Charon C .12 .25
DBT02105 Black Sage, Charon HOLO .75 1.50
DBT02105 Black Sage, Charon SP 3.00 6.00
DBT02106 Fullbau C .12 .25
DBT02106 Fullbau HOLO .30 .60
DBT02106 Fullbau SP 4.00 8.00
DBT02107 Sublime Will C .12 .25
DBT02108 Shieldfisher Dragon C .12 .25
DBT02109 Iron Anchor Resentment Dragon C .12 .25
DBT02110 Coffin Shooter C .12 .25
DBT02110 Coffin Shooter HOLO .30 .60
DBT02111 Sylvan Horned Beast, Bojalcorn C .12 .25
DBT02111 Sylvan Horned Beast, Bojalcorn HOLO .30 .60
DBT02112 Indiscriminate Shooting Mutant, Barretwasp C .12 .25
DBT02113 Roaring Pistil, Langeena C .12 .25
DBT02114 Promised Brave Shooter C .12 .25
DBT02115 Sylvan Horned Beast, Tealuf C .12 .25
DBT02116 Lady Demolish C .12 .25
DBT02117 Sylvan Horned Beast, Bilber C .12 .25
DBT02117 Sylvan Horned Beast, Bilber HOLO .30 .60
DBT02118 Sylvan Horned Beast, Croucotte C .12 .25
DBT02119 Harvesting Season C .12 .25
DBT02120 Overcoming the Unnatural Death C .12 .25
DBT02120 Overcoming the Unnatural Death HOLO .30 .60
DBT02DSR01 Diabolos, Violence Bruce DSR 125.00 250.00
DBT02DSR02 Apex Ruler, Bastion DSR 125.00 250.00

2021 Cardfight Vanguard D Booster Set 3 Advance of Intertwined Stars

DBT03001 Vairina Exspecta RRR .75 1.50
DBT03002 Howitzer of Dust Storm, Dustin RRR .30 .60
DBT03003 Avaricious Demonic Dragon, Greedon RRR 1.25 2.50
DBT03004 Diabolos Returner, Deryck RRR 1.25 2.50
DBT03005 Gravidia Nordlinger RRR 1.25 2.50
DBT03006 Cardinal Draco, Destierde RRR .30 .75
DBT03007 Unsurpassed Heavenly Impact, Ragreal RRR 1.00 2.00
DBT03008 Aspiring Magic, Cacarone RRR .50 1.00
DBT03009 Flagship Dragon, Flagburg Dragon RRR .60 1.25
DBT03010 Shadowcloak RRR 2.00 4.00
DBT03011 Stealth Dragon, Fushimachi Madoka RR 1.25 2.50
DBT03012 Blaze Maiden, Himena RR 1.25 2.50
DBT03013 Dragritter, Shihab RR .30 .75
DBT03014 Steam Mage, Ashur-da RR .30 .60
DBT03015 Diabolos Madonna, Regina RR .30 .75
DBT03016 Desire Devil, Incane RR .30 .75
DBT03017 Aurora Battle Princess, Execute Lemonun RR .30 .60
DBT03018 Gravidia Stunnel RR .50 1.00
DBT03019 Aurora Battle Princess, Tula Buganvilias RR .25 .50
DBT03020 Ease Rod Angel RR .75 1.50
DBT03021 Cloudy Heavenly Intensity, Bragard RR .20 .40
DBT03022 Revelation Magic, Totoris RR .50 1.00
DBT03023 Aggress Blue Dragon RR .50 1.00
DBT03024 Sylvan Horned Beast, Gabregg RR .50 1.00
DBT03025 Sylvan Horned Beast, Enbarr RR .30 .60
DBT03026 Blaze Fist Monk, Gyoukou R .12 .30
DBT03027 Blaze Maiden, Tressa R .12 .30
DBT03028 Steel Bullet of Dust Storm, Ethan R .12 .30
DBT03029 Twin Strike of Dust Storm, Orlando R .12 .30
DBT03030 Burning Flail Dragon R 3.00 6.00
DBT03031 Best Harvest R .12 .30
DBT03032 Diabolos Striker, Brian R .30 .60
DBT03033 Keenly Rudely R .12 .30
DBT03034 Desire Devil, Boshokku R .12 .30
DBT03035 Desire Devil, Mukka R .20 .40
DBT03036 Stem Deviate Dragon R 2.00 4.00
DBT03037 Pandemonium Tactics R .60 1.25
DBT03038 Gravidia Barringer R .12 .30
DBT03039 Aurora Battle Princess, Survey Vermillion R .12 .30
DBT03040 Cardinal Fang, Reyogia R .12 .30
DBT03041 Gravidia Orgueil R .12 .30
DBT03042 Patrol Robo, Dekarcop R 2.50 5.00
DBT03043 Beyond the Perpetual Time R .12 .30
DBT03044 Knight of Severe Punishment, Gade R .12 .30
DBT03045 Magic of Appreciation, Nanaful R .12 .30
DBT03046 Drilling Angel R .25 .50
DBT03047 Blade Feather Dragon R 3.00 6.00
DBT03048 Wish to Tomorrow R .12 .30
DBT03049 Protector Pride R .12 1.25
DBT03050 Ascendance Assault R .12 .30
DBT03051 Blooming Petal, Caryophyllus R .25 .50
DBT03052 High-rate Burst Dragon R .25 .50
DBT03053 Desiring Wild Crow R .12 .30
DBT03054 Aspiring Maiden, Alana R 3.00 6.00
DBT03055 Death-inviting Black Magic R .12 .30
DBT03056 Great Dragon, Musashido Armor C .12 .25
DBT03057 Piercing Bullet of Dust Storm, Maynard C .12 .25
DBT03058 Patrol Dragon, Scoutptero C .12 .25
DBT03059 Explosive Artillery Dragon, Brachioforce C .12 .25
DBT03060 Blaze Stick Monk, Shakune C .12 .25
DBT03061 Flare Scourge Dragon C .12 .25
DBT03062 Stun Voltech Dragon C .12 .25
DBT03063 Blaze Fist Monk, Tenji C .12 .25
DBT03064 Indirect Fire of Dust Storm, Alestor C .12 .25
DBT03065 Hunting Bullet of Dust Storm, Cedric C .12 .25
DBT03066 Deflection Pulse Dragon C .12 .25
DBT03067 Prayer of Resonating Wishes C .12 .25
DBT03068 Ambush Kill Smoke C .12 .25
DBT03069 Diabolos Charger, Nate C .12 .25
DBT03070 Desire Devil, Hystera C .12 .25
DBT03071 Diabolos Madonna, Meryl C .12 .25
DBT03072 Desire Devil, Acrats C .12 .25
DBT03073 Piercing Assistant C .12 .25
DBT03074 Metallize Erosio C .12 .25
DBT03075 Forbidden Evil Eye, Kwen Luu C .12 .25
DBT03076 Diabolos Boys, Cyril C .12 .25
DBT03077 Diabolos Girls, Belinda C .12 .25
DBT03078 Desire Devil, Gouman C .12 .25
DBT03079 Desire Devil, Yaba C .12 .25
DBT03080 Desire Devil, Taida C .12 .25
DBT03081 Geo Acceleration C .12 .25
DBT03082 Cardinal Draco, Stiljurge C .12 .25
DBT03083 Gravidia Pribram C .12 .25
DBT03084 Aurora Battle Princess, Cuff Spring C .12 .25
DBT03085 Cardinal Draco, Abstrim C .12 .25
DBT03086 Gravidia L'Aigle C .12 .25
DBT03087 Blitz Interrupter C .12 .25
DBT03088 Cardinal Fang, Cinetia C .12 .25
DBT03089 Aurora Battle Princess, Shirer Zenith C .12 .25
DBT03090 Gravidia Wells C .12 .25
DBT03091 Aurora Battle Princess, Tear Clocker C .12 .25
DBT03092 Gravidia Dellen C .12 .25
DBT03093 Refablishment Dock C .12 .25
DBT03094 Neatness Meteor Shower C .12 .25
DBT03095 Wondrous Heavenly Core, Fortid C .12 .25
DBT03096 Divine Great Magic, Milmomo C .12 .25
DBT03097 Bullseye Scope, Gaderel C .12 .25
DBT03098 Comprising Heavenly Shield, Felicida C .12 .25
DBT03099 Knight of Heavenly Bullet, Procris C .12 .25
DBT03100 Realization Magic, Kikitchu C .12 .25
DBT03101 Diffuser Angel C .12 .25
DBT03102 Knight of Heavenly Piercing, Esalta C .12 .25
DBT03103 Swordsman of Heavenly Dance, Salire C .12 .25
DBT03104 Starry Sky Magic, Maluluna C .12 .25
DBT03105 Removal Angel C .12 .25
DBT03106 Knight of Heavenly Departure, Flupp C .12 .25
DBT03107 Light Illuminating the Truth C .12 .25
DBT03108 Decay Hollow Dragon C .12 .25
DBT03109 Pulverizing Fault C .12 .25
DBT03110 Creed Assault C .12 .25
DBT03111 Sylvan Horned Beast, Rinblu C .12 .25
DBT03112 Sylvan Horned Beast, Barometz C .12 .25
DBT03113 Inroad Shooter C .12 .25
DBT03114 Sylvan Horned Beast, Molemora C .12 .25
DBT03115 Carrion Handler C .12 .25
DBT03116 Prized Trident C .25 .50
DBT03117 Sylvan Horned Beast, Hegic C .12 .25
DBT03118 Officer Cadet, Charicles C .12 .25
DBT03119 In Search of an Ideal Far Away C .12 .25
DBT03120 Darkness Hiding C .12 .25
DBT03DSR01 Sylvan Horned Beast King, Magnolia DSR 75.00 150.00
DBT03DSR02 Aurora Battle Princess, Seraph Snow DSR 125.00 250.00

2021 Cardfight Vanguard D Lyrical Booster Set 1 Lyrical Melody

DLBT01001 Earnescorrect Leader, Clarissa RRR 1.00 2.00
DLBT01002 Archangel of Twin Wings, Alestiel RRR 1.25 2.50
DLBT01003 Heartfelt Song, Loronerol RRR 1.25 2.50
DLBT01004 Prismajica, Wilista RRR .30 .75
DLBT01005 Downpouring Singer, Elkiel RRR 1.25 2.50
DLBT01006 Lovingly Watching Over, Otirie RRR .30 .75
DLBT01007 Capriccio of Circulating Star, Ingrid RRR 2.50 5.00
DLBT01008 Rondeau of Dusk Moon, Feltyroza RRR .60 1.25
DLBT01009 Overserious President, Equinoa RRR 1.50 3.00
DLBT01010 Earnescorrect Member, Evelyn RRR .60 1.25
DLBT01011 Dedicated Serenade, Eleonore RR .75 1.50
DLBT01012 Contradicting Kindness, Virginia RR .20 .40
DLBT01013 Brilliance and Elegance, Aerith RR .30 .75
DLBT01014 Unbreakable Talent, Henrietta RR .25 .50
DLBT01015 Fleeting Admiration, Baruel RR .25 .50
DLBT01016 Earnescorrect Supporter, Riona RR .50 1.00
DLBT01017 Joining Clasp, Ernesta RR 1.25 2.50
DLBT01018 Quiet Love, Elvira RR .20 .40
DLBT01019 Wings With Rainbow Glow, Erimuel RR .30 .75
DLBT01020 Spirit Recharge! Luisa RR .50 1.00
DLBT01021 Aim to be the Strongest Idol! RR .30 .75
DLBT01022 Six-Flower Fractale RR .75 1.50
DLBT01028 Lovable Dress, Rilla R .12 .30
DLBT01029 Selfie Practice, Anneliese R .30 .60
DLBT01030 Wish Granted by a Duo, Millia R .12 .30
DLBT01031 Powerful Dash, Andora R .12 .30
DLBT01032 Brainy Prayer, Bibuel R .12 .30
DLBT01033 Earnescorrect Member, Katalyn R .12 .30
DLBT01034 Shining As-is, Alestiel R .12 .30
DLBT01035 Talent of Enjoyment, Feltyrosa R .12 .30
DLBT01036 Accurate Interval, Clarissa R .12 .30
DLBT01037 Heavenly Recital, Emmael R .12 .30
DLBT01038 Blossoming Vocal, Loronerol R .12 .30
DLBT01039 Expanding World, Wilista R .12 .30
DLBT01040 Mystic Voice, Renata R .12 .30
DLBT01041 Advent Stroke, Schedael R .25 .50
DLBT01042 Sweet Tone, Kriemhild R .12 .30
DLBT01043 Precise Word Sense, Flor R .12 .30
DLBT01044 Mini-live After School, Katina R .12 .30
DLBT01045 Magnificent Timbre, Ludia R .12 .30
DLBT01046 Cloudless Heart, Miael R .12 .30
DLBT01047 Determined Cheerfulness, Sarka R .50 1.00
DLBT01048 Soapy Splash, Riviena R .30 .75
DLBT01049 Diva of Refreshing Calm, Christine R .12 .30
DLBT01050 Musical Committee, Nicolene R .12 .30
DLBT01051 Unwelcoming in Private, Desiel R .12 .30
DLBT01052 Fulfill Sweets, Anselma R .12 .30
DLBT01053 Earnescorrect Supporter, Trilby R .12 .30
DLBT01054 Blue-haired Genius, Lysius R .12 .30
DLBT01055 Truehearted Ruby R .30 .60
DLBT01056 Crimson Runway R .12 .30
DLBT01057 The Sound of Waves at Twilight R .12 .30
DLBT01058 Windy Harmonica, Tertes C .12 .25
DLBT01059 Sophisticate, Theresia C .12 .25
DLBT01060 Relaxed Conversation, Philomena C .12 .25
DLBT01061 Adoration Intensifying in Heart, Florenzia C .12 .25
DLBT01062 Positive Singing, Louche C .12 .25
DLBT01063 Active Life, Jerrie C .12 .25
DLBT01064 Midnight Lesson, Vannes C .12 .25
DLBT01065 Recorded Feelings, Romana C .12 .25
DLBT01066 Flying Away, Cheluel C .12 .25
DLBT01067 Bodyguards Captain, Marleen C .12 .25
DLBT01068 Howling Ballad, Fanael C .12 .25
DLBT01069 Friend Up, Ilda C .12 .25
DLBT01070 Longing Tied Up, Heilwig C .12 .25
DLBT01071 Loaded Sentiments, Evelina C .12 .25
DLBT01072 Charming Smile, Cecilia C .12 .25
DLBT01073 Dance Score, Ermel C .12 .25
DLBT01074 Greatest Competitive Spirit, Treyn C .12 .25
DLBT01075 Staring at Love, Tirsuel C .12 .25
DLBT01076 Laid-back Older Sister, Audrey C .12 .25
DLBT01077 Flowering Season, Rudy C .12 .25
DLBT01078 Moment of Tension, Katie C .12 .25
DLBT01079 Beautiful Day Off, Feltyrosa C .12 .25
DLBT01080 Classy Prince, Harriet C .12 .25
DLBT01081 Steady Steps, Pecoly C .12 .25
DLBT01082 Indecisive Sky, Alestiel C .12 .25
DLBT01083 Scramble Sprint, Selma C .12 .25
DLBT01084 Throbbing Search, Loronerol C .12 .25
DLBT01085 Proof of Effort, Wilista C .12 .25
DLBT01086 Fleeting Maiden, Hannerore C .12 .25
DLBT01087 Enthusiastic Lunch, Chantal C .12 .25
DLBT01088 Courage to Step Forward, Bertille C .12 .25
DLBT01089 Precise Curriculum, Libuse C .12 .25
DLBT01090 Serious Challenger, Clarissa C .12 .25
DLBT01091 Little Peace, Prael C .12 .25
DLBT01092 Little Lady, Helmina C .12 .25
DLBT01093 Reliable Senior, Aries C .12 .25
DLBT01094 Dreaming Eyes, Emmeline C .12 .25
DLBT01095 Sharing Happiness, Danael C .12 .25
DLBT01096 Appassionato, Justine C .12 .25
DLBT01097 Lively Motion that Shakes the Skies, Maribuel C .12 .25
DLBT01098 Admired Elder Sister, Feltyrosa C .12 .25
DLBT01099 For the Sake of Singing, Loronerol C .12 .25
DLBT01100 Brilliance Hiding Ore, Wilista C .12 .25
DLBT01101 Monochromic Personality, Alestiel C .12 .25
DLBT01102 Dignified Will, Clarissa C .12 .25
DLBT01103 Original Style, Elshka C .50 1.00
DLBT01104 Glutton, Nora C .60 1.25
DLBT01105 Smiling Dragon Scales, Ilze C .50 1.00
DLBT01106 Aplomb Sight, Grete C .12 .25
DLBT01107 Diligent Follower, Siguel C .12 .25
DLBT01108 Fluffy Siesta, Hilma C .12 .25
DLBT01109 Glee Singing, Tetuel C .12 .25
DLBT01110 Spiritoso, Richarda C .12 .25
DLBT01111 Running Youth, Haida C .12 .25
DLBT01112 Peaceful Garden, Anika C .12 .25
DLBT01113 Soft Light, Pruel C .30 .60
DLBT01114 Relaxed and Laid-back, Marguerite C .12 .25
DLBT01115 Cleaning Zone C .12 .25
DLBT01116 Everlasting Sapphire C .12 .25
DLBT01117 Vibrant Symphony C .12 .25
DLBT01118 Overcoming it Face to Face C .12 .25
DLBT01119 Luminescence Fountain C .12 .25
DLBT01120 Innocent Happiness C .12 .25
DLBT01023 Greatest Star, Esteranza ORR .60 1.25
DLBT01024 Mysterious Twins, Romia & Rumia ORR .60 1.25
DLBT01025 Demonic Fever, Garviera ORR .60 1.25
DLBT01026 Fantastic Fur-nale, Catrina ORR .60 1.25
DLBT01027 Blessing Diva, Grizael ORR .60 1.25

2021 Cardfight Vanguard D Start Deck 1 Yu-yu Kondo Holy Dragon

DSD01001 Chakrabarthi Divine Dragon, Nirvana .30 .60
DSD01001 Chakrabarthi Divine Dragon, Nirvana RRR 3.00 6.00
DSD01002 Blaze Maiden, Reiyu .15 .30
DSD01003 Blaze Maiden, Rino .15 .30
DSD01004 Sunrise Egg .15 .30
DSD01005 Fire Slash Dragon, Inferno Sword .15 .30
DSD01006 Vairina .15 .30
DSD01007 Iron Ball Dragon, Ankybowler .15 .30
DSD01008 Escort Stealth Dragon, Hayashi Kaze .15 .30
DSD01009 Trickstar .25 .50
DSD01010 Spiritual King of Determination, Olbaria .50 1.00
DSD01011 Blaze Maiden, Zonne .15 .30
DSD01012 Blaze Staff Monk, Cho Kuu Sha 1.50 3.00
DSD01013 Blaze Fist Monk, Nikko .15 .30
DSD01014 Blaze Maiden, Rona .25 .50
DSD01015 Sunburst Evolution .20 .40

2021 Cardfight Vanguard D Start Deck 2 Danji Momoyama Tyrant Tiger

DSD02001 Diabolos, Violence Bruce .15 .30
DSD02001 Diabolos, Violence Bruce RRR 4.00 8.00
DSD02002 Diabolos, Anger Richard .15 .30
DSD02003 Diabolos, Bad Steve .15 .30
DSD02004 Diabolos, Innocent Matt .15 .30
DSD02005 Time-fissuring Fist Colossus .15 .30
DSD02006 Icicle Ein, Aizer .15 .30
DSD02007 Steam Gunner, Brody .20 .40
DSD02008 Acrobat Presenter .15 .30
DSD02009 Psychic Prima, Miranda .15 .30
DSD02010 Spiritual King of Determination, Olbaria .30 .75
DSD02011 Diabolos Girls, Maimai .75 1.50
DSD02012 Diabolos Boys, Jake .15 .30
DSD02013 Diabolos Officer, Kilian .30 .75
DSD02014 Diabolos Girls, Arianna .15 .30
DSD02015 Brothers' Soul .60 1.25

2021 Cardfight Vanguard D Start Deck 3 Tohya Ebata Apex Ruler

DSD03001 Apex Ruler, Bastion .30 .60
DSD03001 Apex Ruler, Bastion RRR 2.50 5.00
DSD03002 Knight of Heavenly Spear, Rooks .20 .40
DSD03003 Knight of Heavenly Sword, Fort .15 .30
DSD03004 Knight of Heavenly Bows, Base .15 .30
DSD03005 Vehement Witch, Ramana .15 .30
DSD03006 Knight of Broadaxe, Rafluke .25 .50
DSD03007 Shadow Bow Archer, Lisana .15 .30

DSD03008 Platinum Wolf .15 .30
DSD03009 Lifesaving Angel, Kurabiel .15 .30
DSD03010 Spiritual King of Determination, Olbaria .30 .75
DSD03011 Knight of Heavenly Hammer, Gurgant .75 1.50
DSD03012 Knight of Heavenly Pierce, Gallus .15 .30
DSD03013 Knight of Heavenly Rend, Lif .25 .50
DSD03014 Healer of Heavenly Staff, Arshes .25 .50
DSD03015 The Hour of Holy Judgement Cometh .25 .50

2021 Cardfight Vanguard D Start Deck 4 Megumi Okura Sylvan King

DSD04001 Sylvan Horned Beast King, Magnolia .30 .60
DSD04001 Sylvan Horned Beast King, Magnolia RRR 3.00 6.00
DSD04002 Sylvan Horned Beast, Lattice .15 .30
DSD04003 Sylvan Horned Beast, Charis .15 .30
DSD04004 Sylvan Horned Beast, Lotte .15 .30
DSD04005 Seizing Slash Mutant, Bruslash .15 .30
DSD04006 Sylvan Horned Beast, Dooger .15 .30
DSD04007 Looting Petal Stomalia .15 .30
DSD04008 Knight of Friendship, Cyrus .15 .30
DSD04009 Hopeful Maiden, Alejandra .15 .30
DSD04010 Spiritual King of Determination, Olbaria .40 .80
DSD04011 Sylvan Horned Beast, Jackalope .75 1.50
DSD04012 Sylvan Horned Beast, Polatter .15 .30
DSD04013 Sylvan Horned Beast, Valin .15 .30
DSD04014 Sylvan Horned Beast, Zlatorog .15 .30
DSD04015 Call to the Beasts .15 .30

2021 Cardfight Vanguard D Start Deck 5 Tomari Seto Aurora Valkyrie

DSD05001 Aurora Battle Princess, Seraph Snow .20 .40
DSD05001 Aurora Battle Princess, Seraph Snow RRR 4.00 8.00
DSD05002 Aurora Battle Princess, Risatt Pink .15 .30
DSD05003 Aurora Battle Princess, Kyanite Blue .15 .30
DSD05004 Aurora Battle Princess, Ruby Red .15 .30
DSD05005 Alert Guard Gunner .15 .30
DSD05006 Security Patroller .15 .30
DSD05007 Jeweled Combination, Jewelion .15 .30
DSD05008 Autonomic Caution .15 .30
DSD05009 Craggy Beast, Girgrand .15 .30
DSD05010 Spiritual King of Determination, Olbaria .50 1.00
DSD05011 Aurora Battle Princess, Lourus Yellow 1.25 2.50
DSD05012 Aurora Battle Princess, Amy Orange .15 .30
DSD05013 Aurora Battle Princess, Fronte Rose .15 .30
DSD05014 Aurora Battle Princess, Treuse Green .15 .30
DSD05015 Galaxy Central Prison, Galactolus .15 .30

2021 Cardfight Vanguard D Start Deck 6 Mirei Minae Sealed Blaze Maiden

DSD06001 Sealed Blaze Maiden, Bavsargra RRR 3.00 6.00
DSD06001 Sealed Blaze Maiden, Bavsargra .30 .60
DSD06002 Sealed Blaze Dragon, Halibadra .20 .40
DSD06003 Sealed Blaze Dragon, Namorkahr .20 .40
DSD06004 Sealed Blaze Dragon, Arhinsa .15 .30
DSD06005 Sealed Blaze Dragon, Ulsalra .20 .40
DSD06006 Elecblow Dragon .15 .30
DSD06007 Sealed Blaze Dragon, Shirunga .15 .30
DSD06008 Escort Stealth Dragon, Hayashi Kaze .15 .30
DSD06009 Spiritual King of Determination, Olbaria .15 .30
DSD06010 Conduct Spark Dragon .15 .30
DSD06011 Rushing Dragon, Steel Dilopho .15 .30
DSD06012 Stealth Dragon, Jaengoku .20 .40
DSD06013 White Light Dragon, Parasolace .15 .30
DSD06014 Sealed Blaze Sword, Prithivih .15 .30
DSD06015 Sealed Blaze Shield, Swayanbuh .15 .30

2021 Cardfight Vanguard Special Series 9 Revival Collection

VSS09001EN Holy Divine Knight, Gancelot Peace Saver RRR .30 .75
VSS09002EN Holy Beast, Divine Maskkgal RRR .30 .75
VSS09002EN Holy Beast, Divine Maskkgal SP 7.50 15.00
VSS09003EN King of Knights, Alfred RRR .20 .40
VSS09004EN Favored Pupil of Light and Dark, Llew RRR .30 .60
VSS09005EN Swordsman of Light, Blaster Javelin Larousse RRR .20 .40
VSS09006EN Floral Paladin, Flogal RRR .50 1.00
VSS09007EN Encourage Angel RRR .20 .40
VSS09008EN Still Water Festival Deity, Ichikishima RRR .60 1.25
VSS09009EN Sun of Eternity, Amaterasu RRR .20 .40
VSS09009EN Sun of Eternity, Amaterasu SP 7.50 15.00
VSS09010EN Spiritual Sword of Rough Deity, Susanoo RRR .20 .40
VSS09011EN Cone Magus RRR .20 .40
VSS09012EN Higher Deity Protecting Official, Amatsu-hikone RRR .20 .40
VSS09013EN Psychic Bird RRR .20 .40
VSS09014EN Nebula Witch, Nono RRR .20 .40
VSS09015EN Fanatic Seraph, Gavrail Eden RRR .30 .75
VSS09016EN Holy Seraph, Suriel RRR .20 .40
VSS09016EN Holy Seraph, Suriel SP 6.00 12.00
VSS09017EN Black Shiver, Gavrail RRR .20 .40
VSS09018EN Black Relief, Aratoron RRR .20 .40
VSS09019EN Love Machine Gun, Nociel RRR .20 .40
VSS09020EN Battle Cupid, Nociel RRR .20 .40
VSS09021EN Surgery Angel RRR .20 .40
VSS09022EN Dragprincipal, Morfessa RRR .60 1.25
VSS09023EN Dark Dragon, Plotmaker Dragon RRR .60 1.25
VSS09023EN Dark Dragon, Plotmaker Dragon SP 10.00 20.00
VSS09024EN Dragfall, Luard RRR .50 1.00
VSS09025EN Phantom Blaster Dragon RRR .30 .60
VSS09026EN Dragsaver, Esras RRR 2.50 5.00
VSS09027EN Belial Owl RRR .75 1.50
VSS09028EN Cursed Eye Raven RRR 1.00 2.00
VSS09029EN Golden Dragon, Glorious Reigning Dragon RRR .50 1.00
VSS09030EN Master Swordsman of First Light, Gurguit Helios RRR .75 1.50
VSS09031EN Sunrise Ray Radiant Sword, Gurguit RRR .30 .75
VSS09032EN Golden Beast, Sleimy Flare RRR .50 1.00
VSS09032EN Golden Beast, Sleimy Flare SP 7.50 15.00
VSS09033EN Prominence Glare of the Azure Flames RRR .75 1.50
VSS09034EN Sunrise Ray Knight, Gurguit RRR .20 .40
VSS09035EN Ketchgal Liberator RRR .20 .40
VSS09036EN Complete Beauty, Amaruda Aphross RRR .30 .75
VSS09037EN Goddess of Seven Colors, Iris RRR .20 .40
VSS09037EN Goddess of Seven Colors, Iris SP 20.00 40.00
VSS09038EN Omniscience Regalia, Minerva RRR .20 .40
VSS09039EN Witch of Grapes, Grappa RRR .20 .40
VSS09040EN Shackle Fetter, Gelgja RRR .20 .40
VSS09041EN Witch of Oranges, Valencia RRR .20 .40
VSS09042EN Goddess of Sound Sleep, Tahro RRR .20 .40
VSS09043EN Flare General, Dumjid Valor RRR .60 1.25
VSS09044EN Flame Wing Steel Beast, Denial Griffin RRR .75 1.50
VSS09044EN Flame Wing Steel Beast, Denial Griffin SP 7.50 15.00
VSS09045EN Dragonic Overlord The TurnAbout RRR 1.25 2.50
VSS09046EN Dragonic Overlord The Destiny RRR .30 .75
VSS09047EN Dragonic Overlord The X RRR .30 .75
VSS09048EN Lizard Soldier, Bellog RRR .20 .40
VSS09049EN Inspire Yell Dragon RRR .20 .40
VSS09050EN Enma Stealth Rogue, Mujinlord RRR .25 .50
VSS09051EN Evil-eye Hades Emperor, Shiranui Mukuro RRR .20 .40
VSS09052EN Evil-eye Vidya Emperor, Shiranui Rinne RRR .50 1.00
VSS09053EN Rikudo Stealth Dragon, Gehourakan RRR .20 .40
VSS09053EN Rikudo Stealth Dragon, Gehourakan SP 20.00 40.00
VSS09054EN Stealth Dragon, Shiranui RRR .20 .40
VSS09055EN Stealth Rogue of Night Fog, Miyabi RRR .20 .40
VSS09056EN Stealth Fiend, Daruma Collapse RRR .20 .40
VSS09057EN Absolute Ruler, Gluttony Dogma RRR .25 .50
VSS09058EN Great Emperor Dragon, Gaia Dynast RRR .20 .40
VSS09059EN Cliff Authority Retainer, Blockade Ganga RRR .20 .40
VSS09059EN Cliff Authority Retainer, Blockade Ganga SP 3.00 6.00
VSS09060EN Emperor Dragon, Gaia Emperor RRR .20 .40
VSS09061EN Turbo Smilodon RRR .20 .40
VSS09062EN Sonic Noa RRR .20 .40
VSS09063EN Coelamagnum RRR .25 .50
VSS09064EN Ambush Demon Stealth Dragon, Shibarakku Viktor RRR .20 .40
VSS09065EN Dharma Deity of the Five Precepts, Yasuie Genma RRR .20 .40
VSS09066EN Ambush Demon Stealth Rogue, Shishiyuzuki RRR .20 .40
VSS09066EN Ambush Demon Stealth Rogue, Shishiyuzuki SP 3.00 6.00
VSS09067EN Covert Demonic Dragon, Aragoto Spark RRR .20 .40
VSS09068EN Stealth Dragon, Dual Weapon RRR .20 .40
VSS09069EN Stealth Rogue of Concealment, Tanba RRR .20 .40
VSS09070EN Stealth Dragon, Hiden Scroll RRR .20 .40
VSS09071EN Conquering Supreme Dragon, Dragonic Vanquisher VMAX RRR .30 .60
VSS09072EN Mystic Wisdom Creation, Brahma RRR .20 .40
VSS09073EN Sky Guardian Supreme Dragon, Bulwark Dragon RRR .30 .75
VSS09073EN Sky Guardian Supreme Dragon, Bulwark Dragon SP 6.00 12.00
VSS09074EN Dragonic Vanquisher SPARKING RRR .20 .40
VSS09075EN Fiendish Sword Eradicator, Cho-Ou RRR .20 .40
VSS09076EN Summon Lightning Dancing Princess, Anastasia RRR .20 .40
VSS09077EN Dragon Dancer, Vianne RRR .20 .40
VSS09078EN Favorite Champ, Victor RRR .30 .60
VSS09079EN Meteokaiser, Dogantitan RRR .20 .40
VSS09079EN Meteokaiser, Dogantitan SP 10.00 20.00
VSS09080EN Meteokaiser, Gundreed RRR .20 .40
VSS09081EN Zubat Battler, Victor RRR .25 .50
VSS09082EN Extreme Battler, Golshachi RRR .25 .50
VSS09083EN Bare Knuckle, Arnest RRR .20 .40
VSS09084EN Energy Girl RRR .30 .60
VSS09085EN Bravest Peak, X-gallop RRR .30 .75
VSS09086EN Gallant Incarnation, G-O-Five RRR .20 .40
VSS09087EN Oceanic Conversion, Atlantis Dolphin RRR .20 .40
VSS09087EN Oceanic Conversion, Atlantis Dolphin SP 4.00 8.00
VSS09088EN Bravest Rush, Grandgallop RRR .20 .40
VSS09089EN Dimensional Robo, Daijet RRR .20 .40
VSS09090EN Enigman Calm RRR .20 .40
VSS09091EN Operator Girl, Linka RRR .60 1.25
VSS09092EN Death Star-vader, Chaos Breaker Deluge RRR .30 .75
VSS09093EN Death Star-vader, Glueball Dragon RRR .30 .75
VSS09094EN Darkness that Lights Up Demise, Lacus Carina RRR .25 .50
VSS09095EN Large Wheel of the Cosmos, Cosmo Wreath RRR .20 .40
VSS09095EN Large Wheel of the Cosmos, Cosmo Wreath SP 12.50 25.00
VSS09096EN Star-vader, Chaos Breaker Crisis RRR .30 .60
VSS09097EN Star-vader, Freezeray Dragon RRR .50 1.00
VSS09098EN Shockwave Star-vader, Dysprosium RRR .20 .40
VSS09099EN Black Horn King, Bullpower Agrias RRR .20 .40
VSS09100EN Temerarious Cataclysmic Rogue, Hellhard Eight RRR .20 .40
VSS09101EN King of Interference, Terrible Linus RRR .20 .40
VSS09101EN King of Interference, Terrible Linus SP 7.50 15.00
VSS09102EN Exceptional Expertise, Rising Nova RRR .20 .40
VSS09103EN Jelly Beans RRR .20 .40
VSS09104EN Mecha Trainer RRR .20 .40
VSS09105EN Devil Watch RRR .20 .40
VSS09106EN Evil God Pontiff, Gastille Daimonas RRR .20 .40
VSS09107EN One who Splits Darkness, Bledermaus RRR .30 .60
VSS09108EN False Dark Wings, Agrat bat Mahlat RRR .20 .40
VSS09108EN False Dark Wings, Agrat bat Mahlat SP 7.50 15.00
VSS09109EN Scharhrot Vampir RRR .20 .40
VSS09110EN Dimension Creeper RRR .30 .75
VSS09111EN Yellow Bolt RRR .25 .50
VSS09112EN Monochrome of Nightmareland RRR .25 .50
VSS09113EN Masquerade Master, Harri RRR .30 .60
VSS09114EN Kinesis Megatrick, Coulthard RRR .20 .40
VSS09114EN Kinesis Megatrick, Coulthard SP 4.00 8.00
VSS09115EN Masked Phantom, Harri RRR .20 .40
VSS09116EN Astatic Baton Twirler RRR .20 .40
VSS09117EN Flying Peryton RRR .20 .40
VSS09118EN Purple Trapezist RRR .30 .75
VSS09119EN Prankster Girl of Mirrorland RRR .25 .50
VSS09120EN Chronodragon Gear Groovy RRR .50 1.00
VSS09121EN Bearlock RRR .20 .40
VSS09121EN Bearlock SP 10.00 20.00
VSS09122EN Interdimensional Dragon, Heteroround Dragon RRR .20 .40
VSS09123EN Chronojet Dragon G RRR .20 .40
VSS09124EN History-maker Dragon RRR .30 .60
VSS09125EN Tick Tock Worker RRR .20 .40
VSS09126EN Steam Battler, Ur-Watar RRR .20 .40
VSS09127EN Ghostie Great Emperor, Big Obadiah RRR .25 .50
VSS09128EN Great Witch Doctor of Banquets, Negrolily RRR .30 .60
VSS09128EN Great Witch Doctor of Banquets, Negrolily SP 15.00 30.00
VSS09129EN Mighty Rogue, Nightstorm RRR .20 .40
VSS09130EN Skeleton Cannoneer RRR .30 .60
VSS09131EN Samurai Spirit RRR .30 .75
VSS09132EN Undying Departed, Grenache RRR .20 .40
VSS09133EN Mick the Ghostie and Family RRR .30 .60
VSS09134EN Chouchou Popular Favor, Tirua RRR .40 .80
VSS09135EN Legendary Idol, Riviere RRR .20 .40
VSS09136EN Perfect Performance, Ange RRR .75 1.50
VSS09137EN Highest Society, Citron RRR .25 .50
VSS09137EN Highest Society, Citron SP 7.50 15.00
VSS09138EN Spirited Star, Trois RRR .20 .40
VSS09139EN Admired Sparkle, Spica RRR .20 .40
VSS09140EN Dreamer Dreamer, Kruk RRR .20 .40
VSS09141EN Marshal General of Surging Seas, Alexandros RRR .30 .60
VSS09142EN Blue Storm Deterrence Dragon, Ice Barrier Dragon RRR .20 .40
VSS09142EN Blue Storm Deterrence Dragon, Ice Barrier Dragon SP 2.50 5.00
VSS09143EN Blue Wave Armor General, Galfilia RRR .25 .50
VSS09144EN Supreme Ruler of the Storm, Thavas RRR .20 .40
VSS09145EN Tidal Assault RRR .20 .40
VSS09146EN Supersonic Sailor RRR .20 .40
VSS09147EN Dolphin Soldier of Leaping Windy Seas RRR .20 .40
VSS09148EN Lawless Mutant Deity, Obtirandus RRR .25 .50
VSS09149EN Poison Sickle Mutant Deity, Overwhelm RRR .20 .40
VSS09150EN Feather Wall Mutant Deity, Morphosian RRR .20 .40
VSS09151EN Seven Stars Mutant Deity, Relish Lady RRR .20 .40
VSS09151EN Seven Stars Mutant Deity, Relish Lady SP 7.50 15.00
VSS09152EN Evil Governor, Darkface Gredora RRR .20 .40
VSS09153EN Machining Treehopper RRR .20 .40
VSS09154EN Makeup Widow RRR .20 .40
VSS09155EN Omniscience Dragon, Balauri RRR .20 .40
VSS09156EN Cymbal Monkey RRR .20 .40
VSS09156EN Cymbal Monkey SP 2.50 5.00
VSS09157EN Sheltered Heiress, Spangled RRR .20 .40
VSS09158EN Amazing Professor, Bigbelly RRR .20 .40
VSS09159EN Talented Rhinos RRR .20 .40
VSS09160EN Crayon Tiger RRR .60 1.25
VSS09161EN Protractor Orangutan RRR .20 .40
VSS09162EN Flower Princess of Four Seasons, Velhemina RRR .20 .40
VSS09163EN Bond Protector Musketeer, Antero RRR .20 .40
VSS09163EN Bond Protector Musketeer, Antero SP 7.50 15.00
VSS09164EN Ranunculus of Searing Heart, Ahsha RRR .20 .40
VSS09165EN Pansy Musketeer, Sylvia RRR .60 1.25
VSS09166EN Maiden of Gladiolus RRR .20 .40
VSS09167EN Cherry Blossom Blizzard Maiden, Lilga RRR .20 .40
VSS09168EN Cosmos Pixy, Lizbeth RRR .20 .40

2021 Cardfight Vanguard V Extra Booster Set 15 Twinkle Melody

VEB15001 School Etoile, Olyvia SP/Swimsuit 40.00 80.00
VEB15001 School Etoile, Olyvia LIR .75 1.50
VEB15001 School Etoile, Olyvia SP 5.00 10.00
VEB15001 School Etoile, Olyvia OCR 6.00 12.00
VEB15002 Star on Stage, Plon SP/Swimsuit 50.00 100.00
VEB15002 Star on Stage, Plon VR 1.50 3.00
VEB15002 Star on Stage, Plon SP 10.00 20.00
VEB15003 Happiness Heart, Lupina SP/Swimsuit 60.00 120.00
VEB15003 Happiness Heart, Lupina VR 2.50 5.00
VEB15003 Happiness Heart, Lupina SP 10.00 20.00
VEB15003 Happiness Heart, Lupina ASR 125.00 250.00
VEB15004 Perfect Performance, Ange SP/Swimsuit 100.00 200.00
VEB15004 Perfect Performance, Ange VR 3.00 6.00
VEB15004 Perfect Performance, Ange SP 10.00 20.00
VEB15004 Perfect Performance, Ange OCR 25.00 50.00
VEB15005 PRISM-Image, Vert SP/Swimsuit 40.00 80.00
VEB15005 PRISM-Image, Vert VR 4.00 8.00
VEB15005 PRISM-Image, Vert SP 10.00 20.00
VEB15005 PRISM-Image, Vert OCR 25.00 50.00
VEB15006 Girlish Idol, Lyriquor RRR .30 .75
VEB15006 Girlish Idol, Lyriquor SP 7.50 15.00
VEB15007 Chouchou Debut Stage, Tirua SP/Swimsuit 50.00 100.00
VEB15007 Chouchou Debut Stage, Tirua RRR .75 1.50
VEB15007 Chouchou Debut Stage, Tirua SP 7.50 15.00
VEB15007 Chouchou Debut Stage, Tirua OCR 15.00 30.00
VEB15008 Sweetest Sister, Meer SP/Swimsuit 20.00 40.00
VEB15008 Sweetest Sister, Meer RRR .50 1.00
VEB15008 Sweetest Sister, Meer SP 5.00 10.00
VEB15008 Sweetest Sister, Meer OCR 7.50 15.00
VEB15009 Clear Appeal, Seredy RRR .25 .50
VEB15009 Clear Appeal, Seredy SP 2.00 4.00
VEB15010 Velvet Voice, Raindear SP/Swimsuit 100.00 200.00
VEB15010 Velvet Voice, Raindear RRR .30 .75
VEB15010 Velvet Voice, Raindear SP 7.50 15.00
VEB15010 Velvet Voice, Raindear OCR 30.00 75.00
VEB15011 Top Idol, Aqua RRR 2.00 4.00
VEB15011 Top Idol, Aqua SP 30.00 60.00
VEB15012 Mermaid Idol, Sedna RRR 2.00 4.00
VEB15012 Mermaid Idol, Sedna SP 5.00 10.00
VEB15013 Expect Rhythm, Vierra RR .20 .40
VEB15014 PRISM-Image, Rosa RR .30 .60
VEB15015 Bear Affection, Laer RR .20 .40
VEB15016 Sporty Idol, Innes RR .20 .40
VEB15017 PRISM-Image, Clear RR .30 .75
VEB15018 Mermaid Idol, Elly RR 1.25 2.50
VEB15018 Mermaid Idol, Elly SP 12.50 25.00
VEB15019 Cherished Phrase, Reina RR .50 1.00
VEB15019 Cherished Phrase, Reina SP 75.00 15.00
VEB15020 Glittery Baby, Lene RR 1.50 3.00
VEB15020 Glittery Baby, Lene SP 6.00 12.00
VEB15021 Choco Love Heart, Liselotte R .30 .75
VEB15022 Multiple Shine, Mirada R .15 .30
VEB15023 Unique Allure, Dagny R .15 .30
VEB15024 Customize Service, Maxine R .15 .30
VEB15025 Filling Reverie, Petra R .15 .30
VEB15026 Rainbow Shard, Uranie R .15 .30
VEB15027 Gleeful Mode, Tavia R .15 .30
VEB15028 Tamed Cadence, Katya R .15 .30
VEB15029 Direct Squirt, Elshe R .15 .30
VEB15030 Prudent Blue, Miep R .15 .30
VEB15031 Freshers Innovate, Rosalinda R .15 .30
VEB15032 Peppy Smile, Helga R .15 .30
VEB15033 Lyrical Veil R .15 .30
VEB15034 Consent Select, Beata C .12 .25
VEB15035 Rose Princess, Phalaina C .12 .25
VEB15036 Captivating Originality, Gerlinde C .12 .25
VEB15037 Perfectionist, Relenca C .12 .25
VEB15038 Whispering Wavelets, Miritta C .12 .25
VEB15039 Cerulean Jewelry, Phaseav C .12 .25
VEB15040 Electric Essence, Systico C .12 .25
VEB15041 Special Message, Ourora C .12 .25
VEB15042 Heart Fragrance, Liesche C .12 .25
VEB15043 Popple Empathy, Bettie C .12 .25
VEB15044 Distinguished Wink, Radka C .12 .25
VEB15045 Bermuda Triangle Cadet, Shizuku C .12 .25
VEB15045 Bermuda Triangle Cadet, Shizuku SP 5.00 10.00
VEB15046 Direct Sign, Pursh C .12 .25
VEB15047 Dockin' Shooter, Pellea C .12 .25
VEB15048 Lover Hope, Rina C .12 .25
VEB15049 Deep Crimson Surprise, Fayle C .12 .25
VEB15050 Agitato Cheer, Pipylaia C .12 .25
VEB15SP17 Quick Shield SP 2.50 5.00
VEB15T01 Meer's Present C .12 .25

2021 Cardfight Vanguard V Special Series 01 V Clan Collection Vol. 1

DVS01001 Seeker, Thing Saver Dragon RRR .50 1.00
DVS01001 Seeker, Thing Saver Dragon SP 4.00 8.00
DVS01001 Seeker, Thing Saver Dragon VSR 30.00 75.00
DVS01002 Blaster Blade Seeker RRR .60 1.25
DVS01002 Blaster Blade Seeker VSR 50.00 100.00
DVS01003 Knight of Warhammer, Augustus RRR .30 .75
DVS01004 Innocent Ray Dragon RRR 3.00 6.00
DVS01005 Laurel Knight, Sicilus RRR 2.00 4.00
DVS01006 Knight of Exemplary Sword, Lucius RRR .15 .30
DVS01007 Knight of Going Alone, Harald RRR .15 .30
DVS01008 Royal Miko of the Moon Bow, Tsukumiori RRR .25 .50
DVS01008 Royal Miko of the Moon Bow, Tsukumiori SP 2.50 5.00
DVS01009 Miko of the Round Moon, Fuyou RRR .25 .50
DVS01010 Miko of the Mirror Moon, Sae RRR .15 .30
DVS01011 Goddess of Water Dragon, Toyotamahime RRR 1.25 2.50
DVS01012 Divine Sword, Ame-no-Murakumo RRR .25 .50
DVS01013 Miko of Elegance, Fumino RRR .15 .30
DVS01014 Tetra Magus RRR .15 .30
DVS01015 Goddess of Good Luck, Fortuna RRR .25 .50
DVS01015 Goddess of Good Luck, Fortuna SP 2.00 4.00
DVS01016 Witch of Ravens, Chamomile RRR .25 .50
DVS01017 Witch of Oranges, Valencia RRR .50 1.00
DVS01018 Cornerstone Fortress, Ajax RRR 2.00 4.00
DVS01019 Mythic Beast, Skoll RRR .30 .60
DVS01020 Spiritualist Sorcerer, Croute RRR .15 .30
DVS01021 Venus Witch, Reppler RRR .30 .75
DVS01022 Seal Dragon, Blockade RRR .15 .30
DVS01022 Seal Dragon, Blockade SP 1.50 3.00
DVS01023 Seal Dragon, Corduroy RRR .15 .30
DVS01024 Seal Dragon, Kersey RRR .25 .50
DVS01025 Dragon Dancer, Nastasha RRR 2.00 4.00
DVS01026 Lava Flow Dragon RRR .60 1.25
DVS01027 Torridcannon Dragon RRR .15 .30
DVS01028 Burning Horn Dragon RRR .15 .30
DVS01029 Stealth Fiend Chief, Nura Hyouga RRR .15 .30
DVS01029 Stealth Fiend Chief, Nura Hyouga SP 2.00 4.00
DVS01030 Stealth Fiend, Flight Sickle RRR .30 .60
DVS01031 Stealth Fiend, Lady Silhouetta RRR .50 1.00
DVS01032 Covert Demonic Dragon, Kumadori Dove RRR 1.25 2.50
DVS01033 Gateway Stealth Rogue, Ataka RRR .30 .75
DVS01034 Stealth Fiend, One-Eyed Nyudo RRR .15 .30
DVS01035 Fantasy Petal Storm, Shirayuki RRR .30 .75
DVS01036 Eradicator, Vowing Sword Dragon RRR 1.00 2.00
DVS01036 Eradicator, Vowing Sword Dragon SP 6.00 12.00

DVS01037 Eradicator, Spark Rain Dragon RRR	.50	1.00
DVS01038 Eradicator, Demolition Dragon RRR	2.50	5.00
DVS01039 Blitz Knuckle Dragon RRR	.15	.30
DVS01040 Mighty Bolt Dragoon RRR	.30	.60
DVS01041 Fiendish Sword Eradicator, Cho-Ou RRR	.15	.30
DVS01042 Isolation Eradicator, Nusku RRR	.15	.30
DVS01043 Super Dimensional Robo, Daikaiser RRR	1.50	3.00
DVS01043 Super Dimensional Robo, Daikaiser SP	6.00	12.00
DVS01043 Super Dimensional Robo, Daikaiser VSR	75.00	150.00
DVS01044 Dimensional Robo, Kaizard RRR	.60	1.25
DVS01045 Dimensional Robo, Daiprop RRR	1.00	2.00
DVS01046 Ultimate Salvation Combination, Aidambulion RRR	1.50	3.00
DVS01047 Cosmic Hero, Grandrope RRR	.15	.30
DVS01048 Black-clad Top-tier Deity, Bradblack RRR	.15	.30
DVS01049 Dimensional Robo, Daiscooper RRR	.15	.30
DVS01050 Demonic Lord, Dudley Emperor RRR	.15	.30
DVS01050 Demonic Lord, Dudley Emperor SP	4.00	8.00
DVS01051 Dudley Mason RRR	.20	.40
DVS01052 Dudley Daisy RRR	.25	.50
DVS01053 Precious Cheer Girl, Cameron RRR	.50	1.00
DVS01054 Acrobat Verdi RRR	.15	.30
DVS01055 Adorbs Perm, Rona RRR	.15	.30
DVS01056 Ambush Dexter RRR	.15	.30
DVS01057 Bunny's Beast Tamer, Tilaipse RRR	.20	.40
DVS01057 Bunny's Beast Tamer, Tilaipse SP	4.00	8.00
DVS01058 Bunny's Beast Tamer Assistant, Klorina RRR	.20	.40
DVS01059 Amusing Bunny RRR	.25	.50
DVS01060 Nightmare Doll, Lindy RRR	1.50	3.00
DVS01061 Masquerade Bunny RRR	.30	.75
DVS01062 Astatic Baton Twirler RRR	.15	.30
DVS01063 Midnight Bunny RRR	.15	.30
DVS01064 Single Quiet, Refiarade RRR	.25	.50
DVS01064 Single Quiet, Refiarade SP	4.00	8.00
DVS01065 Miracle Cycle, Atrokia RRR	.25	.50
DVS01066 Reliable Faith, Lusalos RRR	.25	.50
DVS01067 Omnia Vincit Amor, Benedetta RRR	2.50	5.00
DVS01068 Mermaid Idol, Sedna RRR	.25	.50
DVS01069 Graceful Prayer, Amie RRR	.15	.30
DVS01070 Top Idol, Aqua RRR	.30	.75
DVS01071 Blue Wave Dragon, Tetra-drive Dragon RRR	.30	.75
DVS01071 Blue Wave Dragon, Tetra-drive Dragon SP	3.00	6.00
DVS01071 Blue Wave Dragon, Tetra-drive Dragon VSR	20.00	40.00
DVS01072 Blue Wave Marine General, Cuteria RRR	.30	.60
DVS01073 Blue Wave Dragon, Propulsion Dragon RRR	.50	1.00
DVS01074 Iscateo Bubble Dragon RRR	.60	1.25
DVS01075 Blue Wave Soldier Senior, Beragios RRR	.25	.50
DVS01076 Marine General of White Waves, Philogatos RRR	.15	.30
DVS01077 Terrific Coil Dragon RRR	.25	.50
DVS01078 Evil Armor General, Giraffa RRR	.25	.50
DVS01078 Evil Armor General, Giraffa SP	2.00	4.00
DVS01079 Elite Mutant, Giraffa RRR	.75	1.50
DVS01080 Pupa Mutant, Giraffa RRR	.25	.50
DVS01081 Dazzling Wings Mutant, Quinn Agria RRR	.75	1.50
DVS01082 New Face Mutant, Little Dorcas RRR	.30	.60
DVS01083 Spear-attack Mutant, Megalaralancer RRR	.15	.30
DVS01084 Cleared Breeze RRR	.15	.30

2021 Cardfight Vanguard V Special Series 02 V Clan Collection Vol. 2

DVS02001 Prophecy Celestial, Ramiel RRR	.30	.75
DVS02001 Prophecy Celestial, Ramiel SP	4.00	8.00
DVS02002 Candle Celestial, Sariel RRR	1.00	2.00
DVS02003 Spine Celestial, Jophiel RRR	.75	1.50
DVS02004 Transcendent Divider, Cassiel RRR	1.50	3.00
DVS02005 Black Call, Nakir RRR	.30	.75
DVS02006 Black Arquerias, Japhkiel RRR	.30	.75
DVS02007 Scaling Angel RRR	.15	.30
DVS02008 Revenger, Raging Form Dragon SP	12.50	25.00
DVS02008 Revenger, Raging Form Dragon RRR	2.50	5.00
DVS02008 Revenger, Raging Form Dragon VSR	75.00	150.00
DVS02009 Dark Cloak Revenger, Tartu RRR	.75	1.50
DVS02010 Dark Armor Revenger, Rinnal RRR	1.25	2.50
DVS02011 Astral Chain Dragon RRR	4.00	8.00
DVS02012 Cherishing Knight, Branwen RRR	.75	1.50
DVS02013 Dragwizard, Liafail RRR	.30	.60
DVS02014 Blaster Dark RRR	.50	1.00
DVS02015 Bluish Flame Liberator, Prominence Core RRR	.50	1.00
DVS02015 Bluish Flame Liberator, Prominence Core SP	5.00	10.00
DVS02016 Liberator of Royalty, Phallon RRR	.60	1.25
DVS02017 Fast Chase Liberator, Josephus RRR	.50	1.00
DVS02018 Clarity Wing Dragon RRR	2.50	5.00
DVS02019 Dawning Knight, Gorboduc RRR	.60	1.25
DVS02020 Knight of Strong Favors, Berengaria RRR	.15	.30
DVS02021 Oath Liberator, Aglovale RRR	1.00	2.00
DVS02022 Sword Saint of Invincibility, Daihouzan RRR	.30	.75
DVS02022 Sword Saint of Invincibility, Daihouzan SP	5.00	10.00
DVS02023 Master Swordsman of Successive Victory, Houzan RRR	.30	.60
DVS02024 Martial Artist of Laceration, Houzan RRR	.25	.50
DVS02025 Shura Stealth Dragon, Mumyoucongo RRR	1.25	2.50
DVS02026 Stealth Beast, Katarigitsune RRR	.50	1.00
DVS02027 Stealth Rogue of Invasions, Rui RRR	.15	.30
DVS02028 Stealth Dragon, Antenbrand RRR	.15	.30
DVS02029 Ancient Dragon, Spinodriver RRR	3.00	6.00
DVS02029 Ancient Dragon, Spinodriver SP	10.00	20.00
DVS02030 Ancient Dragon, Dinocrowd RRR	.50	1.00
DVS02031 Ancient Dragon, Iguanogorg RRR	.30	.75
DVS02032 Indomitable Dragon, Tenacitops RRR	1.00	2.00
DVS02033 Prism Bird RRR	.15	.30
DVS02034 Regiment Dragon, Regiodon RRR	.15	.30
DVS02035 Full Speed Dragon, Blueprint RRR	.25	.50
DVS02036 Ultimate Raizer Mega-flare RRR	.15	.30
DVS02036 Ultimate Raizer Mega-flare SP	1.50	3.00
DVS02036 Ultimate Raizer Mega-flare VSR	15.00	30.00
DVS02037 Ultimate Raizer Dual-flare RRR	.15	.30
DVS02037 Ultimate Raizer Dual-flare VSR	12.50	25.00
DVS02038 Raptoriaraizer RRR	.15	.30
DVS02039 Steel Fist Dragon, Fury All Dragon RRR	2.00	4.00
DVS02040 Extreme Battler, Arashid RRR	.50	1.00
DVS02041 Cool Hank RRR	.30	.75
DVS02042 Cat Butler RRR	.15	.30
DVS02043 Star-vader, Infinite Zero Dragon RRR	.60	1.25
DVS02043 Star-vader, Infinite Zero Dragon SP	3.00	6.00
DVS02044 Star-vader, Colony Maker RRR	.30	.75
DVS02045 Prison Gate Star-vader, Palladium RRR	.50	1.00
DVS02046 Oblivion Quasar Dragon RRR	3.00	6.00
DVS02047 Lady Battler of the White Dwarf RRR	.75	1.50
DVS02048 Nordstrom Dragon RRR	.15	.30
DVS02049 Hard Sword of Polarization, Lagranjard RRR	.25	.50
DVS02050 Blade Wing Reijy SP	3.00	6.00
DVS02050 Blade Wing Reijy RRR	.15	.30
DVS02051 Blaze Foresight RRR	.15	.30
DVS02052 Bestial Squeezer RRR	.15	.30
DVS02053 Cuticle Defender, Flavia RRR	1.50	3.00
DVS02054 Succubus of Pure Love RRR	.50	1.00
DVS02055 Demonted Executioner RRR	.15	.30
DVS02056 Werwolf Ketzer RRR	.15	.30
DVS02057 Interdimensional Dragon, Chronoscommand Dragon SP	2.50	5.00
DVS02057 Interdimensional Dragon, Chronoscommand Dragon RRR	.30	.75
DVS02057 Interdimensional Dragon, Chronoscommand Dragon VSR	30.00	75.00
DVS02058 Steam Knight, Kalibum RRR	.30	.75
DVS02059 Steam Scara, Gigi RRR	.25	.50
DVS02060 Time Tracking Dragon RRR	1.25	2.50
DVS02061 Steam Breath Dragon RRR	.20	.40
DVS02062 Steam Mechanic, Nabu RRR	.30	.75
DVS02063 Smokegear Dragon RRR	.15	.30
DVS02064 Young Pirate Noble, Pinot Noir SP	2.00	4.00
DVS02064 Young Pirate Noble, Pinot Noir RRR	.15	.30
DVS02065 Pirate Belle, Pinot Blanc RRR	.15	.30
DVS02066 Sea Strolling Banshee RRR	.75	1.50
DVS02067 Sea Cruising Banshee RRR	2.00	4.00
DVS02068 Tommy the Ghostie Brothers RRR	.25	.50
DVS02069 Pirate Swordsman, Colombard RRR	.75	1.50
DVS02070 Witch Doctor of Powdered Bone, Negrobone RRR	.30	.75
DVS02071 Honorary Professor, Chatnoir SP	2.00	4.00
DVS02071 Honorary Professor, Chatnoir RRR	.15	.30
DVS02072 Compass Lion RRR	.25	.50
DVS02073 Taping Cat RRR	.15	.30
DVS02074 Gifted Dragon, Aex Leila RRR	.75	1.50
DVS02075 Diligent Assistant, Minibelly RRR	.15	.30
DVS02076 Hammsuke's Rival, Rocket Pencil Hammdon RRR	.15	.30
DVS02077 Afflated Lemur RRR	.15	.30
DVS02078 Lycoris Musketeer, Vera SP	7.50	15.00
DVS02078 Lycoris Musketeer, Vera RRR	.75	1.50
DVS02079 Lycoris Musketeer, Saul RRR	.60	1.25
DVS02080 Water Lily Musketeer, Ruth RRR	.60	1.25
DVS02081 Qingxin Flower Maiden, Fiorenza RRR	2.00	4.00
DVS02082 Valkyrie of Reclamation, Padmini RRR	.50	1.00
DVS02083 Peony Musketeer, Martina RRR	.15	.30
DVS02084 Peony Musketeer, Toure RRR	.15	.30

2021 Cardfight Vanguard V Special Series 9 Clan Selection Plus Vol. 1

VSS09001 Sephilath-aider, Shin Malkuth-melekh RRR	.30	.75
VSS09001 Sephilath-aider, Shin Malkuth-melekh SP	7.50	15.00
VSS09002 Holy Road Angel RRR	.25	.50
VSS09003 Persistence Angel RRR	.25	.50
VSS09004 Aid-roid, Zayin RRR	.25	.50
VSS09005 Bellyful Meds Angel RRR	.50	1.00
VSS09006 Healthful Intendant RRR	.25	.50
VSS09007 Battle Cupid, Nociel RRR	.30	.60
VSS09008 Mesmerizing Witch, Fianna SP	12.50	25.00
VSS09008 Mesmerizing Witch, Fianna RRR	.30	.75
VSS09009 Witch of Reality, Femme RRR	.30	.75
VSS09010 Cold-blooded Witch, Luba RRR	.30	.60
VSS09011 Black Sage, Charon RRR	.50	1.00
VSS09012 Dead Armor Dragon RRR	.25	.50
VSS09013 Skull Witch, Nemain RRR	2.50	5.00
VSS09014 Dark Shield, Mac Lir RRR	1.00	2.00
VSS09015 Spectral Duke Dragon RRR	2.50	5.00
VSS09015 Spectral Duke Dragon SP	25.00	50.00
VSS09016 Black Dragon Knight, Vortimer RRR	.50	1.00
VSS09017 Scout of Darkness, Vortimer RRR	.50	1.00
VSS09018 Advance of the Black Chains, Kahedin RRR	.25	.50
VSS09019 Stronghold of the Black Chains, Hoel RRR	.25	.50
VSS09020 Listener of Truth, Dindrane RRR	.30	.75
VSS09021 Halo Shield, Mark RRR	.75	1.50
VSS09022 Light Battle Dragon, Gigannoblazer SP	10.00	20.00
VSS09022 Light Battle Dragon, Gigannoblazer RRR	.25	.50
VSS09023 Extortion Dragon, Spinoextort RRR	.50	1.00
VSS09024 Savage Shooter RRR	.25	.50
VSS09025 Ravenous Dragon, Megarex RRR	.25	.50
VSS09026 Clearout Dragon, Sweeperacrocanto RRR	.30	.60
VSS09027 Savage Trooper RRR	.25	.50
VSS09028 Archbird RRR	.25	.50
VSS09029 Six Flowers of Phantasms, Shirayuki SP	25.00	50.00
VSS09029 Six Flowers of Phantasms, Shirayuki RRR	.50	1.00
VSS09030 Ice Fang Princess, Tsurarahime RRR	.50	1.00
VSS09031 Apprentice Youkai, Sasameyuki RRR	.50	1.00
VSS09032 Abrupt Stealth Rogue, Ariou RRR	.30	.75
VSS09033 Stealth Fiend, Jakotsu Girl RRR	.25	.50
VSS09034 Stealth Fiend, Rainy Madame RRR	.25	.50
VSS09035 Stealth Beast, Leaves Mirage RRR	.25	.50
VSS09036 Dragonic Kaiser Vermillion THE BLOOD RRR	1.00	2.00
VSS09036 Dragonic Kaiser Vermillion THE BLOOD SP	12.50	25.00
VSS09037 Spark Arrow Dragon RRR	.75	1.50
VSS09038 Thunder Varret Dragon RRR	.50	1.00
VSS09039 Dragonic Kaiser Vermillion RRR	.25	.50
VSS09040 Bolt Pike Dragon RRR	.25	.50
VSS09041 Rising Phoenix RRR	.25	.50
VSS09042 Wyvern Guard, Guld RRR	.50	1.00
VSS09043 Star-vader, Chaos Breaker Dragon RRR	5.00	10.00
VSS09043 Star-vader, Chaos Breaker Dragon SP	75.00	150.00
VSS09044 Bisection Star-vader, Zirconium RRR	3.00	6.00
VSS09045 Star-vader, Craving Claw RRR	2.50	5.00
VSS09046 Blast Monk of the Thundering Foot RRR	.25	.50
VSS09047 Last Crust, Meranel RRR	.30	.75
VSS09048 Crunching Deletor, Baruol RRR	.60	1.25
VSS09049 Flowers in Vacuum, Cosmo Wreath RRR	1.25	2.50
VSS09050 Evil God Bishop, Gastille RRR	1.00	2.00
VSS09050 Evil God Bishop, Gastille SP	20.00	40.00
VSS09051 Poisonic Abductor RRR	.75	1.50
VSS09052 Ironheart Assassin RRR	1.25	2.50
VSS09053 Emblem Master RRR	.50	1.00
VSS09054 Phantasma Executor RRR	.25	.50
VSS09055 Variants Killertail RRR	.50	1.00
VSS09056 March Rabbit of Nightmareland RRR	.25	.50
VSS09057 Interdimensional Dragon, Time Leaper Dragon RRR	.75	1.50
VSS09057 Interdimensional Dragon, Time Leaper Dragon SP	15.00	30.00
VSS09058 Steam Gunner, Zayd RRR	.50	1.00
VSS09059 Lost Gear Dog, Eight RRR	2.50	5.00
VSS09060 Steam Scara, Irkab RRR	.75	1.50
VSS09061 Chronotooth Tigar RRR	.60	1.25
VSS09062 Steam Maiden, Ribbul RRR	3.00	6.00
VSS09063 Steam Guard, Kastilia RRR	.25	.50
VSS09064 Ghostie Leader, Beatrice SP	50.00	100.00
VSS09064 Ghostie Leader, Beatrice RRR	3.00	6.00
VSS09065 Jessie the Ghostie RRR	.50	1.00
VSS09066 Damian the Ghostie RRR	.25	.50
VSS09067 Dragon Undead, Skull Dragon RRR	.50	1.00
VSS09068 Greed Shade RRR	.50	1.00
VSS09069 Ripple Banshee RRR	.25	.50
VSS09070 Gust Djinn RRR	.25	.50
VSS09071 Worm Toxin Mutant, Venom Stinger RRR	.25	.50
VSS09071 Worm Toxin Mutant, Venom Stinger SP	15.00	30.00
VSS09072 Pincer Attack Mutant, Intrude Scissors RRR	.30	.75
VSS09073 Mutant Gentleman, High Class Moth RRR	.50	1.00
VSS09074 Machining Mantis RRR	.25	.50
VSS09075 Small Captain, Butterfly Officer RRR	.25	.50
VSS09076 Stealth Millipede RRR	.30	.75
VSS09077 Paralyze Madonna RRR	.25	.50
VSS09078 Maiden of Stand Peony SP	15.00	30.00
VSS09078 Maiden of Stand Peony RRR	.50	1.00
VSS09079 Maiden of Fall Vine RRR	.50	1.00
VSS09080 Maiden of Flower Carpet RRR	.75	1.50
VSS09081 Autumn's Turning Maiden, Rosie RRR	.25	.50
VSS09082 Maiden of Nepenthes RRR	.50	1.00
VSS09083 Fruits Basket Elf RRR	.25	.50
VSS09084 Maiden of Blossom Rain RRR	.25	.50
VSS09ASR01 Chronojet Dragon ASR	250.00	400.00

2021 Cardfight Vanguard V Special Series 10 Clan Selection Plus Vol. 2

VSS10001 Pure Heart Jewel Knight, Ashlei RRR	3.00	6.00
VSS10001 Pure Heart Jewel Knight, Ashlei SP	40.00	80.00
VSS10002 Explode Jewel Knight, Laile RRR	1.50	3.00
VSS10003 Charging Jewel Knight, Morvidus RRR	1.50	3.00
VSS10004 Diaconnect Dragon RRR	.25	.50
VSS10005 Little Sage, Marron RRR	.25	.50
VSS10006 Flourishing Knight, Edith RRR	.50	1.00
VSS10007 Flash Shield, Iseult RRR	.30	.75
VSS10008 Battle Sister, Fromage RRR	.75	1.50
VSS10008 Battle Sister, Fromage SP	30.00	60.00
VSS10009 Battle Sister, Trifle RRR	.50	1.00
VSS10010 Battle Sister, Torrijas RRR	.30	.60
VSS10011 Battle Sister, Chouquette RRR	.25	.50
VSS10012 Battle Sister, Cassata RRR	.30	.75
VSS10013 Battle Sister, Panettone RRR	.60	1.25
VSS10014 Weather Forecaster, Miss Mist RRR	.25	.50
VSS10015 Regalia of Wisdom, Angelica RRR	.75	1.50
VSS10015 Regalia of Wisdom, Angelica SP	30.00	60.00
VSS10016 Demon Exorcism Regalia, Thrud RRR	.30	.75
VSS10017 Oblation Regalia, Var RRR	.25	.50
VSS10018 Witch of Frogs, Melissa RRR	.25	.50
VSS10019 Dikei of the Just Path RRR	.25	.50
VSS10020 White Brush Witch, Artic RRR	.25	.50
VSS10021 Goddess of Self-sacrifice, Kushinada RRR	.50	1.00
VSS10022 Dauntless Drive Dragon RRR	1.50	3.00
VSS10022 Dauntless Drive Dragon SP	20.00	40.00
VSS10023 Break Breath Dragon RRR	.50	1.00
VSS10024 Dragon Knight, Heashut RRR	1.00	2.00
VSS10025 Burnrise Dragon RRR	.30	.75
VSS10026 Calamity Tower Wyvern RRR	.25	.50
VSS10027 Flame of Hope, Aermo RRR	.50	1.00
VSS10028 Wyvern Guard, Barri RRR	.30	.75
VSS10029 Evil Stealth Dragon Tasogare, Hanzo RRR	.30	.75
VSS10029 Evil Stealth Dragon Tasogare, Hanzo SP	20.00	40.00
VSS10030 Evil Stealth Dragon, Yamishibuki RRR	.30	.75
VSS10031 Evil Stealth Dragon, Kagesarashi RRR	.50	1.00
VSS10032 Evil Stealth Dragon, Zangetsu RRR	.25	.50
VSS10033 Evil Stealth Dragon, Kurogiri RRR	.25	.50
VSS10034 Stealth Rogue of the Night, Sakurafubuki RRR	.25	.50
VSS10035 Stealth Beast, Mijingakure RRR	.25	.50
VSS10036 Beast Deity, Ethics Buster RRR	.50	1.00
VSS10036 Beast Deity, Ethics Buster SP	10.00	20.00
VSS10037 Beast Deity, Typhoon Bird RRR	.25	.50
VSS10038 Beast Deity, Lift Tauros RRR	.25	.50
VSS10039 Ultra Beast Deity, Illuminal Dragon RRR	.25	.50
VSS10040 Beast Deity, Scarlet Bird RRR	.25	.50
VSS10041 Beast Deity, Glanz Dragon RRR	.25	.50
VSS10042 Twin Blader RRR	.25	.50
VSS10043 Galactic Beast, Zeal RRR	.30	.75
VSS10043 Galactic Beast, Zeal SP	15.00	30.00
VSS10044 Devourer of Planets, Zeal RRR	.30	.60
VSS10045 Eye of Destruction, Zeal RRR	.30	.75
VSS10046 Platinum Ace RRR	.25	.50
VSS10047 Twin Order RRR	2.00	4.00
VSS10048 Magical Police Quilt RRR	.25	.50
VSS10049 Diamond Ace RRR	.25	.50
VSS10050 Demonic Lord, Dudley Lucifer RRR	.30	.75
VSS10050 Demonic Lord, Dudley Lucifer SP	10.00	20.00
VSS10051 Dudley Davie RRR	.30	.60
VSS10052 Dudley William RRR	.30	.60
VSS10053 Highspeed, Brakki RRR	.25	.50
VSS10054 Commander, Garry Gannon RRR	.25	.50
VSS10055 Wonder Boy RRR	.25	.50
VSS10056 Cheer Girl, Marilyn RRR	.25	.50
VSS10057 Nightmare Doll, Chelsea RRR	.75	1.50
VSS10057 Nightmare Doll, Chelsea SP	25.00	50.00
VSS10058 Nightmare Doll, Marissa RRR	1.00	2.00
VSS10059 Nightmare Doll, Abigail RRR	1.25	2.50
VSS10060 Nightmare Doll, Alice RRR	.25	.50
VSS10061 Nightmare Doll, Carroll RRR	.25	.50
VSS10062 Amaranth Beast Tamer RRR	.25	.50
VSS10063 Hades Hypnotist RRR	.50	1.00
VSS10064 Legendary PRISM-Duo, Nectaria RRR	.50	1.00
VSS10064 Legendary PRISM-Duo, Nectaria SP	20.00	40.00
VSS10065 Noir Fixer, Hilda RRR	.30	.75
VSS10066 Innocence, Mernil RRR	.30	.75
VSS10067 Masterly Cover, Minne RRR	.25	.50
VSS10068 Rainy Tear, Stezza RRR	.25	.50
VSS10069 Equable Career, Spiana RRR	.25	.50
VSS10070 Glittery Baby, Lene RRR	.30	.75
VSS10071 Blue Wave Marshal, Valeos RRR	.60	1.25
VSS10071 Blue Wave Marshal, Valeos SP	15.00	30.00
VSS10072 Blue Wave Marine General, Galliot RRR	.25	.50
VSS10073 Blue Wave Soldier Senior, Corvette RRR	.30	.75
VSS10074 Coral Assault RRR	.25	.50
VSS10075 Blue Wave Marine General, Galleass RRR	.25	.50
VSS10076 Battle Siren, Dolcia RRR	.25	.50
VSS10077 Emerald Shield, Paschal RRR	.30	.60
VSS10078 Hammsuke's Rival, Jumbo Crayon Hammyan RRR	.30	.75
VSS10078 Hammsuke's Rival, Jumbo Crayon Hammyan SP	12.50	25.00
VSS10079 Hammsuke's Rival, Nail Pencil Hammgoro RRR	.30	.75
VSS10080 Hammsuke's Teacher, Dip Pencil Hammyuki RRR	.25	.50
VSS10081 Pencil Hero, Hammsuke RRR	.25	.50
VSS10082 Pencil Knight, Hammsuke RRR	.25	.50
VSS10083 Pencil Squire, Hammsuke RRR	.25	.50
VSS10084 Cable Sheep RRR	.25	.50
VSS10ASR01 Majesty Lord Blaster ASR	250.00	500.00

2021 Cardfight Vanguard V Title Booster 1 Bang Dream Film Live

VTB01001 Sparkly Stage, Kasumi Toyama VR	.75	1.50
VTB01001 Sparkly Stage, Kasumi Toyama SP	50.00	100.00
VTB01001 Sparkly Stage, Kasumi Toyama SSR	250.00	500.00
VTB01002 Important Friends, Ran Mitake VR	2.50	5.00
VTB01002 Important Friends, Ran Mitake SP	75.00	150.00
VTB01002 Important Friends, Ran Mitake SSR	150.00	300.00
VTB01003 Growth of Feelings, Aya Maruyama VR	2.00	4.00
VTB01003 Growth of Feelings, Aya Maruyama SP	50.00	100.00
VTB01003 Growth of Feelings, Aya Maruyama SSR	200.00	350.00
VTB01004 Blue Rose Diva, Yukina Minato VR	3.00	6.00
VTB01004 Blue Rose Diva, Yukina Minato SP	75.00	150.00
VTB01004 Blue Rose Diva, Yukina Minato SSR	350.00	700.00
VTB01005 On Stage! Kokoro Tsurumaki SSR	75.00	150.00
VTB01005 On Stage! Kokoro Tsurumaki VR	1.50	3.00
VTB01005 On Stage! Kokoro Tsurumaki SP	60.00	125.00
VTB01006 Caring for Friends, Arisa Ichigaya RRR	.30	.75
VTB01006 Caring for Friends, Arisa Ichigaya SP	75.00	150.00
VTB01006 Caring for Friends, Arisa Ichigaya SSR	100.00	200.00
VTB01007 Overly at Her Own Pace, Moca Aoba RRR	.30	.60
VTB01007 Overly at Her Own Pace, Moca Aoba SP	25.00	50.00
VTB01007 Overly at Her Own Pace, Moca Aoba SSR	150.00	300.00
VTB01008 Stoic Idol, Chisato Shirasagi RRR	.25	.50
VTB01008 Stoic Idol, Chisato Shirasagi SP	30.00	75.00
VTB01008 Stoic Idol, Chisato Shirasagi SSR	75.00	150.00
VTB01009 Unperturbed Performer, Sayo Hikawa RRR	.30	.75
VTB01009 Unperturbed Performer, Sayo Hikawa SP	40.00	80.00
VTB01009 Unperturbed Performer, Sayo Hikawa SSR	300.00	600.00
VTB01010 DJ that Brings Smiles, Michelle RRR	.30	.60
VTB01010 DJ that Brings Smiles, Michelle SP	17.50	35.00
VTB01010 DJ that Brings Smiles, Michelle SSR	25.00	50.00
VTB01011 Always Natural, Tae Hanazono RR	.25	.50
VTB01011 Always Natural, Tae Hanazono SP	25.00	50.00
VTB01011 Always Natural, Tae Hanazono SSR	100.00	200.00

VTB01012 Mood Maker, Himari Uehara RR	.25	.50
VTB01012 Mood Maker, Himari Uehara SP	20.00	40.00
VTB01012 Mood Maker, Himari Uehara SSR	25.00	50.00
VTB01013 Genius Girl, Hina Hikawa RR	.25	.50
VTB01013 Genius Girl, Hina Hikawa SP	25.00	50.00
VTB01013 Genius Girl, Hina Hikawa SSR	125.00	250.00
VTB01014 Surging Passion, Lisa Imai RR	.30	.60
VTB01014 Surging Passion, Lisa Imai SP	60.00	120.00
VTB01014 Surging Passion, Lisa Imai SSR	250.00	500.00
VTB01015 Upbeat Smile, Kanon Matsubara RR	.30	.60
VTB01015 Upbeat Smile, Kanon Matsubara SP	30.00	60.00
VTB01015 Upbeat Smile, Kanon Matsubara SSR	125.00	250.00
VTB01016 The Best Stage Made with Everyone! RR	6.00	12.00
VTB01017 Returns RR	.25	.50
VTB01018 Scarlet Sky RR	.20	.40
VTB01019 Yura-Yura Ring-Dong-Dance RR	.25	.50
VTB01020 FIRE BIRD RR	.30	.60
VTB01021 Smiling & Singing A Song RR	.25	.50
VTB01022 Brimming Ability for Action, Kasumi Toyama R	.15	.30
VTB01023 Resolute Hard Worker, Rimi Ushigome R	.15	.30
VTB01023 Resolute Hard Worker, Rimi Ushigome SP	25.00	50.00
VTB01023 Resolute Hard Worker, Rimi Ushigome SSR	75.00	150.00
VTB01024 Passionate Heart, Ran Mitake R	.15	.30
VTB01025 Figure of an Older Sister, Tomoe Udagawa R	.15	.30
VTB01025 Figure of an Older Sister, Tomoe Udagawa SP	25.00	50.00
VTB01025 Figure of an Older Sister, Tomoe Udagawa SSR	60.00	120.00
VTB01026 Fumbling Idol, Aya Maruyama R	.15	.30
VTB01027 Mechanical Drummer, Maya Yamato R	.15	.30
VTB01027 Mechanical Drummer, Maya Yamato SP	25.00	50.00
VTB01027 Mechanical Drummer, Maya Yamato SSR	200.00	350.00
VTB01028 Quiet Enthusiasm, Yukina Minato R	.15	.30
VTB01029 Little Demon, Ako Udagawa R	.15	.30
VTB01029 Little Demon, Ako Udagawa SP	12.50	25.00
VTB01029 Little Demon, Ako Udagawa SSR	25.00	50.00
VTB01030 Hurricane of Smiles!, Kokoro Tsurumaki R	.15	.30
VTB01031 Effusive Smile, Hagumi Kitazawa R	.15	.30
VTB01031 Effusive Smile, Hagumi Kitazawa SP	25.00	50.00
VTB01031 Effusive Smile, Hagumi Kitazawa SSR	30.00	60.00
VTB01032 Sparkling Star, Kasumi Toyama C	.12	.25
VTB01033 Heart-pounding Start, Kasumi Toyama C	.12	.25
VTB01034 Binds Popipa Together, Saya Yamabuki C	.12	.25
VTB01034 Binds Popipa Together, Saya Yamabuki SP	30.00	60.00
VTB01034 Binds Popipa Together, Saya Yamabuki SSR	75.00	150.00
VTB01035 Hates to Lose, Ran Mitake C	.12	.25
VTB01036 Starting as Always, Ran Mitake C	.12	.25
VTB01037 Tsugurific!, Tsugumi Hazawa C	.12	.25
VTB01037 Tsugurific!, Tsugumi Hazawa SP	7.50	15.00
VTB01037 Tsugurific!, Tsugumi Hazawa SSR	.50	1.00
VTB01038 Best Effort, Aya Maruyama C	.12	.25
VTB01039 Start of Her Dream, Aya Maruyama C	.20	.40
VTB01040 Samurai Heart, Eve Wakamiya C	.12	.25
VTB01040 Samurai Heart, Eve Wakamiya SP	25.00	50.00
VTB01040 Samurai Heart, Eve Wakamiya SSR	125.00	250.00
VTB01041 Imbuing the World, Yukina Minato C	.12	.25
VTB01042 Starting Bell, Yukina Minato C	.12	.25
VTB01043 Elegant Melody, Rinko Shirokane C	.12	.25
VTB01043 Elegant Melody, Rinko Shirokane SP	50.00	100.00
VTB01043 Elegant Melody, Rinko Shirokane SSR	125.00	250.00
VTB01044 Likes Everything!, Kokoro Tsurumaki C	.12	.25
VTB01045 Start of Her World, Kokoro Tsurumaki C	.20	.40
VTB01046 Smiling Noblesse, Kaoru Seta C	.12	.25
VTB01046 Smiling Noblesse, Kaoru Seta SP	20.00	40.00
VTB01046 Smiling Noblesse, Kaoru Seta SSR	40.00	80.00
VTB01047 Start of a Legend RAISE A SUILEN C	.12	.25
VTB01048a Sparkling Memories! C (Poppin' Party)	.12	.25
VTB01048b Sparkling Memories! C (Afterglow)	.12	.25
VTB01048c Sparkling Memories! C (Pastel Palettes)	.12	.25
VTB01048d Sparkling Memories! C (Roselia)	.12	.25
VTB01048e Sparkling Memories! C (Hello, Happy World)	.12	.25
VTB01048f Sparkling Memories! C (Raise a Suilen)	.12	.25
VTB01049a Heart-pounding Dreams! C (Poppin' Party)	.12	.25
VTB01049b Heart-pounding Dreams! C (Afterglow)	.12	.25
VTB01049c Heart-pounding Dreams! C (Pastel Palettes)	.12	.25
VTB01049d Heart-pounding Dreams! C (Roselia)	.12	.25
VTB01049e Heart-pounding Dreams! C (Hello, Happy World!)	.12	.25
VTB01049f Heart-pounding Dreams! C (Raise a Suilen)	.12	.25
VTB01050a The Greatest Live! C (Poppin' Party)	.12	.25
VTB01050b The Greatest Live! C (Afterglow)	.12	.25
VTB01050c The Greatest Live! C (Pastel Palettes)	.12	.25
VTB01050d The Greatest Live! C (Roselia)	.12	.25
VTB01050e The Greatest Live! C (Hello, Happy World)	.12	.25
VTB01050f The Greatest Live! C (Raise a Suilen)	.12	.25
VTB01051 KIZUNA MUSIC? C	.12	.25
VTB01052 Double Rainbow C	.12	.25
VTB01053 ON YOUR MARK C	.12	.25
VTB01054 Y.O.L.O!!!!! C	.12	.25
VTB01055 Kyu~Mai*Flower C	.12	.25
VTB01056 Shuwarin Dreaming C	.12	.25
VTB01057 BRAVE JEWEL C	.12	.25
VTB01058 BLACK SHOUT C	.12	.25
VTB01059 Worldwide Treasure! C	.12	.25
VTB01060 Orchestra Of Smiles! C	.12	.25
VTB01061 Phenomenal Diva LAYER SCR	1.25	2.50
VTB01061 Phenomenal Diva LAYER SP	15.00	30.00
VTB01061 Phenomenal Diva LAYER SSR	125.00	250.00
VTB01062 Bloom of Talent LOCK SCR	.50	1.00
VTB01062 Bloom of Talent LOCK SP	20.00	40.00
VTB01062 Bloom of Talent LOCK SSR	20.00	40.00
VTB01063 Mad Dog's Lament MASKING SCR	.75	1.50
VTB01063 Mad Dog's Lament MASKING SP	20.00	40.00
VTB01063 Mad Dog's Lament MASKING SSR	60.00	120.00
VTB01064 Limitless Colors PAREO SCR	1.00	2.00
VTB01064 Limitless Colors PAREO SP	40.00	80.00
VTB01064 Limitless Colors PAREO SSR	50.00	100.00
VTB01065 Most Powerful Music CHU² SCR	1.00	2.00
VTB01065 Most Powerful Music CHU² SP	30.00	75.00
VTB01065 Most Powerful Music CHU² SSR	75.00	150.00
VTB01066 EXPOSE 'Burn out!!!' SCR	1.00	2.00
VTB01067 RIOT SCR	1.00	2.00

2022 Cardfight Vanguard D Booster Set 04 Awakening of Chakrabarthi

DBT04001 Vairina Esperaridea RRR	12.50	25.00
DBT04001 Vairina Esperaridea SP	20.00	40.00
DBT04001 Vairina Esperaridea DSR	50.00	100.00
DBT04002 Chakrabarthi True Dragon, Mahar Nirvana RRR	3.00	6.00
DBT04002 Chakrabarthi True Dragon, Mahar Nirvana SP	10.00	20.00
DBT04002 Chakrabarthi True Dragon, Mahar Nirvana SSR	100.00	200.00
DBT04002 Chakrabarthi True Dragon, Mahar Nirvana DSR	30.00	60.00
DBT04003 Trickmoon RRR	4.00	8.00
DBT04003 Trickmoon SP	25.00	50.00
DBT04004 Diabolos, Unrivaled Bruce RRR	3.00	6.00
DBT04004 Diabolos, Unrivaled Bruce SP	10.00	20.00
DBT04004 Diabolos, Unrivaled Bruce SSR	75.00	150.00
DBT04005 Desire Devil, Bubetsuu RRR	3.00	6.00
DBT04005 Desire Devil, Bubetsuu SP	10.00	20.00
DBT04006 Brainwash Swirler RRR	20.00	40.00
DBT04006 Brainwash Swirler SP	40.00	80.00
DBT04007 Aurora Fierce Princess, Seraph Purelight RRR	17.50	35.00
DBT04007 Aurora Fierce Princess, Seraph Purelight SP	30.00	60.00
DBT04007 Aurora Fierce Princess, Seraph Purelight SSR	175.00	350.00
DBT04008 Cardinal Draco, Masurea RRR	.30	.60
DBT04008 Cardinal Draco, Masurea SP	2.50	5.00
DBT04009 Gravidia Bacubirito RRR	7.50	15.00
DBT04009 Gravidia Bacubirito SP	10.00	20.00
DBT04010 Apex-surpassing Sword, Bastion Prime RRR	12.50	25.00
DBT04010 Apex-surpassing Sword, Bastion Prime SP	25.00	50.00
DBT04010 Apex-surpassing Sword, Bastion Prime SSR	125.00	250.00
DBT04011 Heavenly Halberd of Solicitation, Colunvoke RRR	.50	1.00
DBT04011 Heavenly Halberd of Solicitation, Colunvoke SP	.75	1.50
DBT04012 Magic of Recurrence, Lalalita RRR	3.00	6.00
DBT04012 Magic of Recurrence, Lalalita SP	7.50	15.00
DBT04013 Sylvan Horned Beast Emperor, Magnolia Elder RRR	6.00	12.00
DBT04013 Sylvan Horned Beast Emperor, Magnolia Elder SP	12.50	25.00
DBT04013 Sylvan Horned Beast Emperor, Magnolia Elder SSR	75.00	150.00
DBT04014 Blue Artillery Dragon, Inlet Pulse Dragon RRR	15.00	30.00
DBT04014 Blue Artillery Dragon, Inlet Pulse Dragon SP	40.00	80.00
DBT04015 Roaming Prison Dragon RRR	12.50	25.00
DBT04015 Roaming Prison Dragon SP	30.00	75.00
DBT04016 Sealed Blaze Dragon, Adarla RR	.75	1.50
DBT04016 Sealed Blaze Dragon, Adarla SP	3.00	6.00
DBT04017 Twin Bullet of Dust Storm, Travis RR	1.50	3.00
DBT04017 Twin Bullet of Dust Storm, Travis SP	7.50	15.00
DBT04018 Sealed Blaze Spear, Aadhitya RR	2.50	5.00
DBT04018 Sealed Blaze Spear, Aadhitya SP	30.00	60.00
DBT04019 Desire Devil, Kenen RR	.30	.60
DBT04019 Desire Devil, Kenen SP	4.00	8.00
DBT04020 Cutting Sword Dance, Chegra RR	.30	.60
DBT04020 Cutting Sword Dance, Chegra SP	3.00	6.00
DBT04021 Diabolos Striker, Lyle RR	.30	.60
DBT04021 Diabolos Striker, Lyle SP	3.00	6.00
DBT04022 Cardinal Draco, Kharjamid RR	.30	.60
DBT04022 Cardinal Draco, Kharjamid SP	5.00	10.00
DBT04023 Gravidia Shergo RR	.30	.60
DBT04023 Gravidia Shergo SP	2.00	4.00
DBT04024 Aurora Battle Princess, Suppress Gleamer RR	1.00	2.00
DBT04024 Aurora Battle Princess, Suppress Gleamer SP	7.50	15.00
DBT04025 Twin-chain Great Magic, Totone RR	.30	.60
DBT04025 Twin-chain Great Magic, Totone SP	3.00	6.00
DBT04026 Heavenly Arrow of Sure-hit, Sparare RR	.30	.60
DBT04026 Heavenly Arrow of Sure-hit, Sparare SP	3.00	6.00
DBT04027 Armor Piercing Knight, Mugain RR	.50	1.00
DBT04027 Armor Piercing Knight, Mugain SP	3.00	6.00
DBT04028 Sylvan Horned Beast, Panthero RR	.30	.60
DBT04028 Sylvan Horned Beast, Panthero SP	4.00	8.00
DBT04029 Transferring Soul Slice Dragon RR	.30	.60
DBT04029 Transferring Soul Slice Dragon SP	3.00	6.00
DBT04030 Gather Upon Me, Ye Wandering Souls RR	.30	.60
DBT04030 Gather Upon Me, Ye Wandering Souls SP	7.50	15.00
DBT04031 Blaze Kick Monk, Koukei R	.15	.30
DBT04031 Blaze Kick Monk, Koukei H	.15	.30
DBT04032 Blaze Pole Monk, Retsuji R	.30	.75
DBT04032 Blaze Pole Monk, Retsuji H	1.00	2.00
DBT04033 Sharp Armor Dragon, Gatesfort R	.15	.30
DBT04033 Sharp Armor Dragon, Gatesfort H	.50	1.00
DBT04034 Flare Veil Dragon R	6.00	12.00
DBT04034 Flare Veil Dragon SP	60.00	125.00
DBT04035 Sealed Blaze Gun, Chandra R	.20	.40
DBT04035 Sealed Blaze Gun, Chandra H	.30	.60
DBT04035 Sealed Blaze Gun, Chandra SP	3.00	6.00
DBT04036 Sublimating Wishes R	.15	.30
DBT04036 Sublimating Wishes H	.15	.30
DBT04037 Aureate Haze Rupture R	.15	.30
DBT04037 Aureate Haze Rupture H	.30	.75
DBT04038 Desire Devil, Walzuure H	.15	.30
DBT04038 Desire Devil, Walzuure R	.15	.30
DBT04039 Sudden-turn Gear Eagle R	.15	.30
DBT04039 Sudden-turn Gear Eagle H	.30	.75
DBT04040 Diabolos Boys, Crasty R	.15	.30
DBT04040 Diabolos Boys, Crasty H	.15	.30
DBT04041 Rouse Wildmaster, Riley R	4.00	8.00
DBT04041 Rouse Wildmaster, Riley SP	75.00	150.00
DBT04042 Helheim Fervent Rage R	.15	.30
DBT04042 Helheim Fervent Rage H	.30	.75
DBT04043 Aurora Battle Princess, Taser Large R	.50	1.00
DBT04043 Aurora Battle Princess, Taser Large H	2.50	5.00
DBT04044 Cardinal Prima, Lactat R	.15	.30
DBT04044 Cardinal Prima, Lactat H	.15	.30
DBT04045 Crushing Monster, Megagrago R	.15	.30
DBT04045 Crushing Monster, Megagrago H	.15	.30
DBT04046 Ameliorate Connector R	7.50	15.00
DBT04046 Ameliorate Connector SP	75.00	150.00
DBT04047 Melt in the Darkness, its Evil Heart R	.15	.30
DBT04047 Melt in the Darkness, its Evil Heart H	.15	.30
DBT04048 Falling Hellhazard R	.50	1.00
DBT04048 Falling Hellhazard H	.75	1.50
DBT04049 Knight of Counter Spiral, Nuada R	.15	.30
DBT04049 Knight of Counter Spiral, Nuada H	.15	.30
DBT04050 Heavenly Blade of Oath, Vriend R	.15	.30
DBT04050 Heavenly Blade of Oath, Vriend H	.15	.30
DBT04051 Injection Angel R	.15	.30
DBT04051 Injection Angel H	.15	.30
DBT04052 Knight of Lonely Shadow, Finola R	.30	.75
DBT04052 Knight of Lonely Shadow, Finola H	2.00	4.00
DBT04053 Leapmya R	.15	.30
DBT04053 Leapmya H	.15	.30
DBT04054 Protection Magic, Prorobi R	3.00	6.00
DBT04054 Protection Magic, Prorobi SP	60.00	125.00
DBT04055 Sylvan Horned Beast, Girafina R	.15	.30
DBT04055 Sylvan Horned Beast, Girafina H	.15	.30
DBT04056 Heavy Strike Brave Shooter R	.15	.30
DBT04056 Heavy Strike Brave Shooter H	.15	.30
DBT04057 Sea Breeze Abduction R	.15	.30
DBT04057 Sea Breeze Abduction H	.25	.50
DBT04058 Sylvan Horned Beast, Alvan R	.15	.30
DBT04058 Sylvan Horned Beast, Alvan H	.30	.60
DBT04059 Serene Maiden, Lena R	.15	.30
DBT04059 Serene Maiden, Lena SP	75.00	150.00
DBT04060 Consuming the High-grade Sake Banned for its Sins R	.15	.30
DBT04060 Consuming the High-grade Sake Banned for its Sins H	.15	.30
DBT04061 Lightning Howl Dragon C	.07	.15
DBT04062 Sealed Blaze Dragon, Sikshanya C	.07	.15
DBT04062 Sealed Blaze Dragon, Sikshanya H	.20	.40
DBT04063 Blaze Maiden, Sonya C	.07	.15
DBT04063 Blaze Maiden, Sonya H	.30	.60
DBT04064 Stealth Dragon, Shakugan C	.07	.15
DBT04065 Lava Wire Dragon C	.07	.15
DBT04066 Throwing Bullet of Dust Storm, Ollie C	.07	.15
DBT04067 Throwing Artillery of Dust Storm, Dollie C	.07	.15
DBT04068 Blaze Maiden, Tonya C	.07	.15
DBT04068 Blaze Maiden, Tonya H	.25	.50
DBT04069 Sealed Blaze Dragon, Ihsita C	.07	.15
DBT04069 Sealed Blaze Dragon, Ihsita H	.30	.75
DBT04070 Blaze Fist Monk, Chouki C	.07	.15
DBT04071 Solitary Spiritual Treasure H	.15	.30
DBT04071 Solitary Spiritual Treasure C	.07	.15
DBT04072 Wind of Apocalypse C	.07	.15
DBT04073 Diabolos Charger, Davan C	.07	.15
DBT04074 Desire Devil, Gamettsu C	.07	.15
DBT04074 Desire Devil, Gamettsu H	.30	.75
DBT04075 Lightning Vortex-tinged Gear Eland C	.07	.15
DBT04076 Steam Performer, Lugalza C	.07	.15
DBT04076 Steam Performer, Lugalza H	.15	.30
DBT04077 Diabolos Madonna, Listh C	.07	.15
DBT04077 Diabolos Madonna, Listh H	.30	.75
DBT04078 Desire Devil, Besshii C	.07	.15
DBT04079 Violet Phantasm Butterfly, Fanju C	.07	.15
DBT04080 Steam Hunter, Nanul C	.07	.15
DBT04081 Diabolos Girls, Stephanie C	.75	1.50
DBT04082 Diabolos Jetter, Wade C	.07	.15
DBT04082 Diabolos Jetter, Wade H	.40	.80
DBT04083 Desire Devil, Yada C	.07	.15
DBT04084 Shining Selfishness C	.07	.15
DBT04084 Shining Selfishness H	.15	.30
DBT04085 Electromagnetic Monster, Elehilecity C	.07	.15
DBT04086 Aurora Battle Princess, Chasing Neer C	.07	.15
DBT04086 Aurora Battle Princess, Chasing Neer H	.25	.50
DBT04087 Cardinal Noid, Negulita C	.07	.15
DBT04087 Cardinal Noid, Negulita H	.15	.30
DBT04088 Aurora Battle Princess, Trace Jeune C	.07	.15
DBT04088 Aurora Battle Princess, Trace Jeune H	.30	.75
DBT04089 Aurora Battle Princess, Restraint Plany C	.07	.15
DBT04090 Gravidia Luluirk C	.07	.15
DBT04090 Gravidia Luluirk H	.50	1.00
DBT04091 Melting Monster, Orsidiran C	.07	.15
DBT04092 Cardinal Noid, Suprema C	.07	.15
DBT04093 Gravidia Abee C	.07	.15
DBT04093 Gravidia Abee H	.15	.30
DBT04094 Gravidia Mondieu C	.07	.15
DBT04095 Aurora Battle Princess, Riot Beeble C	.07	.15
DBT04096 Aurora Battle Princess Searching Net, Great Extraordinary Chase! C	.07	.15
DBT04097 Thundering Heavenly Slash, Getuze C	.07	.15
DBT04097 Thundering Heavenly Slash, Getuze H	.15	.30
DBT04098 Heavenly Protection Dragon, Embrace Dragon C	.07	.15
DBT04098 Heavenly Protection Dragon, Embrace Dragon H	.15	.30
DBT04099 Desire Magic, Esnono C	.07	.15
DBT04099 Desire Magic, Esnono H	.15	.30
DBT04100 Knight of Heavenly Flash, Eclesia C	.07	.15
DBT04101 Knight of Heavenly Management, Contenio C	.07	.15
DBT04102 Knight of Unnatural Death, Delbaeth C	.07	.15
DBT04103 Banner of Heavenly Salvation, Saline C	.07	.15
DBT04104 Stepmya C	.07	.15
DBT04105 Knight of Heavenly Omen, Grandiel C	.07	.15
DBT04105 Knight of Heavenly Omen, Grandiel H	.15	.30
DBT04106 Scout of Heavenly Eye, Tove C	.07	.15
DBT04107 Fortune Reading C	.07	.15
DBT04107 Fortune Reading H	.15	.30
DBT04108 Divine Protection of the Abyss Dragon C	.07	.15
DBT04109 Wicked Chef C	.07	.15
DBT04110 Corruption Usurper Dragon C	.07	.15
DBT04110 Corruption Usurper Dragon H	.60	1.25
DBT04111 Purity Maiden, Belanca C	.07	.15
DBT04112 Sylvan Horned Beast, Rhinarva C	.07	.15
DBT04112 Sylvan Horned Beast, Rhinarva H	.15	.30
DBT04113 Sylvan Horned Beast, Leuca H	.50	1.00
DBT04113 Sylvan Horned Beast, Leuca C	.07	.15
DBT04114 Darkness Diver C	.07	.15
DBT04114 Darkness Diver H	.15	.30
DBT04115 Tuning Madness C	.07	.15
DBT04116 Flourish Petal, Lathya C	.07	.15
DBT04117 Sylvan Horned Beast, Lemrea C	.07	.15
DBT04118 Let the Screams Dissolve into the Sound of the Rain C	.07	.15
DBT04118 Let the Screams Dissolve into the Sound of the Rain H	.15	.30
DBT04119 Ghost Bilk C	.07	.15
DBT04120 Advance of Great Cause C	.07	.15
DBT04SP36 Sealed Blaze Maiden, Bavsargra SP	50.00	100.00
DBT04SP37 Sealed Blaze Dragon, Halibadra SP	15.00	30.00
DBT04SP38 Sealed Blaze Dragon, Namorkahr SP	10.00	20.00
DBT04SP39 Sealed Blaze Dragon, Arhinsa SP	10.00	20.00
DBT04SP40 Sealed Blaze Sword, Prithivih SP	10.00	20.00
DBT04SP41 Sealed Blaze Shield, Swayanbuh SP	7.50	15.00
DBT04SP44 Vairina SP	5.00	10.00
DBT04SP45 Hellblast Full Dive SP	7.50	15.00
DBT04SP46 Bizarre Beast, Bagumotor SP	1.00	2.00
DBT04SP47 Shadow Army Token SP	30.00	60.00
DBT04SP48 Form up, O Chosen Knights SP	4.00	8.00
DBT04SP49 Sylvan Horned Beast, Koocy SP	2.00	4.00
DBT04SP50 Spiritual Body Condensation SP	10.00	20.00
DBT04W001EN Soul Repose Pixy, Petronella WO	2.00	4.00

2022 Cardfight Vanguard D Booster Set 05 Triumphant Return of the Brave Heroes

DBT05001 Dragonic Overlord the End 10th RRR	4.00	8.00
DBT05001 Dragonic Overlord the End 10th SP	30.00	75.00
DBT05001 Dragonic Overlord the End SP	30.00	75.00
DBT05001 Dragonic Overlord the End SCR	175.00	350.00
DBT05002 Burning Horn Dragon SP	40.00	80.00
DBT05002 Burning Horn Dragon 10th RRR	7.50	15.00
DBT05003 Phantom Blaster Overlord 10th RRR	7.50	15.00
DBT05003 Phantom Blaster Overlord 10th SP	30.00	75.00
DBT05003 Phantom Blaster Overlord SP	25.00	50.00
DBT05003 Phantom Blaster Overlord SCR	125.00	250.00
DBT05004 Majesty Lord Blaster 10th RRR	3.00	6.00
DBT05004 Majesty Lord Blaster 10th SP	20.00	40.00
DBT05004 Majesty Lord Blaster SP	15.00	30.00
DBT05005 Blaster Blade 10th RRR	7.50	15.00
DBT05005 Blaster Blade SP	25.00	50.00
DBT05005 Blaster Blade 10th SCR	100.00	200.00
DBT05006 Skull Witch, Nemain SP	25.00	50.00
DBT05006 Skull Witch, Nemain 10th RRR	15.00	30.00
DBT05007 Deepening Night, Tamayura RRR	3.00	6.00
DBT05007 Deepening Night, Tamayura SP	100.00	200.00
DBT05008 Approaching Fangs, Kheios RRR	.75	1.50
DBT05008 Approaching Fangs, Kheios SP	30.00	75.00
DBT05009 Fountain of Knowledge, Eva RRR	10.00	20.00
DBT05009 Fountain of Knowledge, Eva SP	150.00	300.00
DBT05010 One Who Walks the Path of Light, Thegrea RRR	3.00	6.00
DBT05010 One Who Walks the Path of Light, Thegrea SP	100.00	200.00
DBT05011 One Who Blooms in the Dark, Thegrea RRR	6.00	12.00
DBT05011 One Who Blooms in the Dark, Thegrea SP	125.00	250.00
DBT05012 For One's Precious Thing, Rorowa RRR	4.00	8.00
DBT05012 For One's Precious Thing, Rorowa SP	40.00	80.00
DBT05013 Dragritter Girl of Flame Blossoms, Radylina RRR	4.00	8.00
DBT05013 Dragritter Girl of Flame Blossoms, Radylina SP	50.00	100.00
DBT05014 Twin Direful Dolls, Ririmi RRR	4.00	8.00
DBT05014 Twin Direful Dolls, Ririmi SP	60.00	125.00
DBT05015 Twin Direful Dolls, Rarami RRR	4.00	8.00
DBT05015 Twin Direful Dolls, Rarami SP	30.00	75.00
DBT05016 Cool-headed Executor, Mikani RRR	3.00	6.00
DBT05016 Cool-headed Executor, Mikani SP	15.00	30.00
DBT05017 Knight of Blackness, Obscudeid RRR	10.00	20.00
DBT05017 Knight of Blackness, Obscudeid SP	75.00	150.00
DBT05018 Atrocious? Moth Girl, Maple RRR	12.50	25.00
DBT05018 Atrocious? Moth Girl, Maple SP	75.00	150.00
DBT05019 Perforate Burner Dragon RR	.30	.60
DBT05020 Stealth Fiend, Forktail RR	.30	.60
DBT05021 Acute Dragon, Eoraphas RR	.30	.60
DBT05022 Stealth Fiend, Amaviera RR	.30	.60
DBT05022 Stealth Fiend, Amaviera SP	12.50	25.00
DBT05023 Amazing Frost RR	.30	.60
DBT05024 Steam Maiden, Barni RR	.30	.60
DBT05025 Incorruptible Holy Light, Eufha RR	1.50	3.00

DBT05025 Incorruptible Holy Light, Eufha SP	12.50	25.00
DBT05026 Pantarhei Dragon RR	.30	.60
DBT05027 Lady Healer of the Creaking World RR	1.25	2.50
DBT05027 Lady Healer of the Creaking World SP	20.00	40.00
DBT05028 Experiment Successful! RR	2.50	5.00
DBT05028 Experiment Successful! SP	20.00	40.00
DBT05029 Knight of Protective Spear, Arthen RR	2.50	5.00
DBT05030 Knight of Loyalty, Bedivere RR	1.50	3.00
DBT05030 Knight of Loyalty, Bedivere SP	5.00	10.00
DBT05031 Livesaving Angel, Digriel RR	.30	.60
DBT05032 Prohibited Sight Witch, Erunmes RR	.30	.60
DBT05033 Knight of Friendship, Kay RR	1.50	3.00
DBT05033 Knight of Friendship, Kay SP	2.00	4.00
DBT05034 Invigorate Sage RR	1.50	3.00
DBT05034 Invigorate Sage SP	25.00	50.00
DBT05035 Prodpollen Rafilous RR	.30	.60
DBT05036 Adhesive Thread Monster, Actiasticky RR	1.00	2.00
DBT05037 Zypsophilia Fairy, Asher RR	.30	.60
DBT05037 Zypsophilia Fairy, Asher SP	12.50	25.00
DBT05038 Motive Stealth Rogue, Tsumugi R	.15	.30
DBT05038 Motive Stealth Rogue, Tsumugi H	.15	.30
DBT05039 Festival of Burning, Tamayura R	.15	.30
DBT05039 Festival of Burning, Tamayura H	1.00	2.00
DBT05039 Festival of Burning, Tamayura SP	15.00	30.00
DBT05040 Fleeting Shine That Lights Life R	.15	.30
DBT05040 Fleeting Shine That Lights Life H	2.00	4.00
DBT05040 Fleeting Shine That Lights Life SP	10.00	20.00
DBT05041 Quagmire of Solace, Kheios R	.15	.30
DBT05041 Quagmire of Solace, Kheios H	.15	.30
DBT05041 Quagmire of Solace, Kheios SP	5.00	10.00
DBT05042 Clumsy Assistant R	.15	.30
DBT05042 Clumsy Assistant H	.15	.30
DBT05043 Flaming Pony R	.50	1.00
DBT05043 Flaming Pony H	2.50	5.00
DBT05044 Smooth Research Progress, Eva R	.15	.30
DBT05044 Smooth Research Progress, Eva H	.15	.30
DBT05044 Smooth Research Progress, Eva SP	60.00	125.00
DBT05045 Aiding Monster, Tectien R	.50	1.00
DBT05045 Aiding Monster, Tectien H	3.00	6.00
DBT05046 Obliging Monster, Secondel R	.15	.30
DBT05046 Obliging Monster, Secondel H	.15	.30
DBT05047 Harsh Training, Thegrea R	.15	.30
DBT05047 Harsh Training, Thegrea H	1.00	2.00
DBT05047 Harsh Training, Thegrea SP	20.00	40.00
DBT05048 Knight of Spright, Freeda R	.15	.30
DBT05048 Knight of Spright, Freeda H	.30	.60
DBT05049 Blaster Dark R	.15	.30
DBT05049 Blaster Dark H	1.50	3.00
DBT05050 Energy Refill Angel R	.15	.30
DBT05050 Energy Refill Angel H	.15	.30
DBT05051 Little Sage, Marron R	.15	.30
DBT05051 Little Sage, Marron H	3.00	6.00
DBT05051 Little Sage, Marron SP	40.00	80.00
DBT05052 Bravery To Stand Against, Will to Pierce Through R	.15	.30
DBT05052 Bravery To Stand Against, Will to Pierce Through H	.75	1.50
DBT05052 Bravery To Stand Against, Will to Pierce Through SP	3.00	6.00
DBT05053 The World 3000 Years Later, Rorowa R	.15	.30
DBT05053 The World 3000 Years Later, Rorowa H	.15	.30
DBT05053 The World 3000 Years Later, Rorowa SP	12.50	25.00
DBT05054 Battle Siren, Shuzet R	.15	.30
DBT05054 Battle Siren, Shuzet H	.15	.30
DBT05055 Stepping Calyx, Salvia R	.15	.30
DBT05055 Stepping Calyx, Salvia H	.15	.30
DBT05056 Excavation Dragon, Bariodigneel H	1.25	2.50
DBT05056 Excavation Dragon, Bariodigneel C	.07	.15
DBT05057 Stealth Dragon, Hadanressou C	.07	.15
DBT05057 Stealth Dragon, Hadanressou H	.15	.30
DBT05058 Rumbling Shear Dragon C	.07	.15
DBT05058 Rumbling Shear Dragon H	.15	.30
DBT05059 In the Calm Sunlight, Tamayura C	.07	.15
DBT05059 In the Calm Sunlight, Tamayura H	.15	.30
DBT05059 In the Calm Sunlight, Tamayura SP	15.00	30.00
DBT05060 Ignite Blow Dragon C	.07	.15
DBT05060 Ignite Blow Dragon H	.15	.30
DBT05061 Nine-tailed Fox Spirit, Tamayura C	.07	.15
DBT05061 Nine-tailed Fox Spirit, Tamayura H	.15	.30
DBT05061 Nine-tailed Fox Spirit, Tamayura SP	30.00	60.00
DBT05062 Amazement Magician C	.25	.50
DBT05062 Amazement Magician H	3.00	6.00
DBT05063 Indicate Arrow Dragon C	.07	.15
DBT05063 Indicate Arrow Dragon H	.30	.60
DBT05064 Steam Reaper, Nannia C	.07	.15
DBT05064 Steam Reaper, Nannia H	.15	.30
DBT05065 In the Calm Streets, Kheios C	.07	.15
DBT05065 In the Calm Streets, Kheios H	.15	.30
DBT05065 In the Calm Streets, Kheios SP	10.00	20.00
DBT05066 One With Profound Mercy, Kheios C	.07	.15
DBT05066 One With Profound Mercy, Kheios H	.15	.30
DBT05066 One With Profound Mercy, Kheios SP	20.00	40.00
DBT05067 Heavyarmed Panzer C	.07	.15
DBT05067 Heavyarmed Panzer H	.25	.50
DBT05068 Suppression Robo, Sir Repel C	.07	.15
DBT05068 Suppression Robo, Sir Repel H	.15	.30
DBT05069 AiD 9-V C	.07	.15
DBT05069 AiD 9-V H	.15	.30
DBT05070 An Afternoon Nap Regardless of Place, Eva C	.07	.15
DBT05070 An Afternoon Nap Regardless of Place, Eva H	5.00	10.00
DBT05070 An Afternoon Nap Regardless of Place, Eva SP	50.00	100.00
DBT05071 Successor of the Variable Star C	.07	.15
DBT05071 Successor of the Variable Star H	.15	.30
DBT05072 One Who Craves Knowledge, Eva C	.07	.15
DBT05072 One Who Craves Knowledge, Eva H	.15	.30
DBT05072 One Who Craves Knowledge, Eva SP	75.00	150.00
DBT05073 Kindlight Dragon C	.07	.15
DBT05073 Kindlight Dragon H	.15	.30
DBT05074 Gigantech Beater C	.07	.15
DBT05074 Gigantech Beater H	.15	.30
DBT05075 Knight of Clearsightedness, Arvirargus C	.07	.15
DBT05075 Knight of Clearsightness, Arvirargus H	.15	.30
DBT05076 Divine Sister, Saint-Honoré C	.07	.15
DBT05076 Divine Sister, Saint-Honoré H	.15	.30
DBT05077 Knight of Fearlessness, Rediquess C	.07	.15
DBT05077 Knight of Fearlessness, Rediquess H	.15	.30
DBT05078 Ampoule Scatterer Angel C	.07	.15
DBT05078 Ampoule Scatterer Angel H	.15	.30
DBT05079 Knight of Old Animosity, Camloss C	.07	.15
DBT05079 Knight of Old Animosity, Camloss H	.30	.60
DBT05080 Orgulous Lion C	.07	.15
DBT05080 Orgulous Lion H	.15	.30
DBT05081 Beneath the Brilliant Light, Thegrea C	.07	.15
DBT05081 Beneath the Brilliant Light, Thegrea H	2.50	5.00
DBT05081 Beneath the Brilliant Light, Thegrea SP	3.00	6.00
DBT05082 Glintbreath Dragon C	.07	.15
DBT05082 Glintbreath Dragon H	.30	.60
DBT05083 Wingal Brave C	.07	.15
DBT05083 Wingal Brave H	.15	.30
DBT05083 Wingal Brave SP	30.00	60.00
DBT05084 Knight of Integrity, Thegrea C	.07	.15
DBT05084 Knight of Integrity, Thegrea H	2.50	5.00
DBT05084 Knight of Integrity, Thegrea SP	40.00	80.00
DBT05085 Rancor Spear Trooper C	.07	.15
DBT05085 Rancor Spear Trooper H	.15	.30
DBT05086 Tear Knight, Fleche C	.07	.15
DBT05086 Tear Knight, Fleche H	.15	.30
DBT05087 Wild-fire Brave Shooter C	.07	.15
DBT05087 Wild-fire Brave Shooter H	.15	.30
DBT05088 Awakening from Slumber, Rorowa C	.07	.15
DBT05088 Awakening from Slumber, Rorowa H	1.00	2.00
DBT05088 Awakening from Slumber, Rorowa SP	12.50	25.00
DBT05089 Knight of Nostalgia, Marco C	.07	.15
DBT05089 Knight of Nostalgia, Marco H	.30	.60
DBT05090 Bioroid Youth, Rorowa C	.07	.15
DBT05090 Bioroid Youth, Rorowa H	.75	1.50
DBT05090 Bioroid Youth, Rorowa SP	20.00	40.00
DBT05T01 Momokke Token T	.75	1.50
DBT05T01 Momokke Token H	1.50	3.00
DBT05T02 Plant Token T	2.00	4.00
DBT05T02 Plant Token H	.15	.30
DBT05W001EN Sensuality Elixir, Faevronia WO	7.50	15.00

2022 Cardfight Vanguard D Booster Set 06 Blazing Dragon Reborn

DBT06001 Chakrabarthi Phoenix Dragon, Nirvana Jheva RRR	12.50	25.00
DBT06001 Chakrabarthi Phoenix Dragon, Nirvana Jheva FFR	40.00	80.00
DBT06002 Brilliant Equip, Bram Vairina RRR	3.00	6.00
DBT06002 Brilliant Equip, Bram Vairina FFR	25.00	50.00
DBT06003 Jeweled Sword Equip, Garou Vairina RRR	6.00	12.00
DBT06003 Jeweled Sword Equip, Garou Vairina FFR	30.00	75.00
DBT06004 Diabolos Diver, Julian RRR	4.00	8.00
DBT06004 Diabolos Diver, Julian FFR	30.00	60.00
DBT06005 Merciless Count, Botis FFR	12.50	25.00
DBT06005 Merciless Count, Botis RRR	1.25	2.50
DBT06006 Direful Doll, Amandine RRR	4.00	8.00
DBT06006 Direful Doll, Amandine FFR	15.00	30.00
DBT06007 Galactic Hero, Unite Dianos RRR	2.50	5.00
DBT06007 Galactic Hero, Unite Dianos FFR	30.00	60.00
DBT06008 Combine Rusher RRR	12.50	25.00
DBT06008 Combine Rusher FFR	75.00	150.00
DBT06009 Galactic Hero, Direct Foriel RRR	2.50	5.00
DBT06009 Galactic Hero, Direct Foriel FFR	30.00	60.00
DBT06010 Youthberk "Skyfall Arms" RRR	12.50	25.00
DBT06010 Youthberk "Skyfall Arms" FFR	100.00	200.00
DBT06011 Youthberk "RevolForm: Gust" RRR	7.50	15.00
DBT06011 Youthberk "RevolForm: Gust" FFR	50.00	100.00
DBT06012 Knight of Fracture, Schneizal RRR	3.00	6.00
DBT06012 Knight of Fracture, Schneizal FFR	50.00	100.00
DBT06013 Grand March of Full Bloom, Lianorn RRR	6.00	12.00
DBT06013 Grand March of Full Bloom, Lianorn FFR	30.00	75.00
DBT06014 Performing Petal, Dianthe RRR	12.50	25.00
DBT06014 Performing Petal, Dianthe FFR	50.00	100.00
DBT06015 Congratulatory Performance, Sucuse RRR	.50	1.00
DBT06015 Congratulatory Performance, Sucuse FFR	7.50	15.00
DBT06016 Dragon Deity King of Resurgence, Dragveda ORR	12.50	25.00
DBT06017 Hades Dragon Deity of Resentment, Gallmageheld ORR	2.50	5.00
DBT06018 Star Dragon Deity of Infinitude, Eldobreath ORR	4.00	8.00
DBT06019 Light Dragon Deity of Honors, Amartinoa ORR	3.00	6.00
DBT06020 Source Dragon Deity of Blessings, Blesstavor ORR	6.00	12.00
DBT06021 Steel Wall Equip, Biruz Vairina RR	2.50	5.00
DBT06021 Steel Wall Equip, Biruz Vairina FR	7.50	15.00
DBT06022 Sealed Blaze Dragon, Shabda RR	.75	1.50
DBT06022 Sealed Blaze Dragon, Shabda FR	1.50	3.00
DBT06023 Flash Equip Dragon, Bramahda RR	1.25	2.50
DBT06023 Flash Equip Dragon, Bramahda FR	7.50	15.00
DBT06024 Term Fracture Dragon RR	.30	.75
DBT06024 Term Fracture Dragon FR	4.00	8.00
DBT06025 Diabolos Girls, Ivanka RR	.30	.75
DBT06025 Diabolos Girls, Ivanka FR	3.00	6.00
DBT06026 Desire Devil, Kuvisgee RR	.60	1.25
DBT06026 Desire Devil, Kuvisgee FR	.75	1.50
DBT06027 Cardinal Draco, Nuvorea RR	.75	1.50
DBT06027 Cardinal Draco, Nuvorea FR	12.50	25.00
DBT06028 Aurora Battle Princess, Crumple Orchid RR	.25	.50
DBT06028 Aurora Battle Princess, Crumple Orchid FR	.75	1.50
DBT06029 Galactic Hero, Rampart Aspida RR	.75	1.50
DBT06029 Galactic Hero, Rampart Aspida FR	1.50	3.00
DBT06030 Decisive Axe Dragon RR	.30	.60
DBT06030 Decisive Axe Dragon FR	.30	.75
DBT06031 Octaray Sorceress RR	5.00	10.00
DBT06031 Octaray Sorceress FR	12.50	25.00
DBT06032 Enucleate Angel RR	1.25	2.50
DBT06032 Enucleate Angel FR	.30	.75
DBT06033 Ensemble of Smiles, Amalie RR	.30	.75
DBT06033 Ensemble of Smiles, Amalie FR	1.75	3.50
DBT06034 Battle Siren, Theodosia RR	.30	.60
DBT06034 Battle Siren, Theodosia FR	7.50	15.00
DBT06035 In the Dim Darkness, The Frozen Resentment RR	7.50	15.00
DBT06035 In the Dim Darkness, The Frozen Resentment FR	.30	.75
DBT06036 Sword Equip Dragon, Galondight R	.15	.30
DBT06037 Wall Equip Dragon, Biruskill R	.15	.30
DBT06038 Sparkle Rejector Dragon R	1.25	2.50
DBT06039 Thoughts That Pierce Through R	.15	.30
DBT06040 Explosive Torcher R	.15	.30
DBT06041 Diabolos Madonna, Siena R	.15	.30
DBT06042 Desire Devil, Funman R	.15	.30
DBT06043 Repelled Malice Dragon R	1.25	2.50
DBT06044 Galactic Hero, Flatten Sufrey R	.50	1.00
DBT06045 Aurora Battle Princess, Detain Cycla R	.15	.30
DBT06046 Cardinal Noid, Callaphe R	.15	.30
DBT06047 Planet Wall Dragon R	1.25	2.50
DBT06048 Knight of Fierce Break, Friede R	.15	.30
DBT06049 Magic of Change, Memerul R	.15	.30
DBT06050 Palladium Zeal Dragon R	3.00	6.00
DBT06051 Departure Towards the Dawn R	.15	.30
DBT06052 Spree Vesper R	.15	.30
DBT06053 Marching Debut, Purite R	.20	.40
DBT06054 Custodial Dragon R	1.25	2.50
DBT06055 Spirits That Roam R	.15	.30
DBT06056 Fanes Powder Dragon C	.07	.15
DBT06057 Equipped Steel Dragon, Balcon C	.07	.15
DBT06058 Heat Stamping Dragon C	.07	.15
DBT06059 Snuggling Blaze Maiden, Reiyu C	.07	.15
DBT06060 Sharp Equip Dragon, Adamaros C	.07	.15
DBT06061 Blaze Maiden, Rosel C	.07	.15
DBT06062 Heart-pounding Blaze Maiden, Rino C	.07	.15
DBT06063 Surprise Egg C	.07	.15
DBT06064 Trickstar C	.07	.15
DBT06065 Blaze Duel Monk, Sougyou C	.30	.75
DBT06066 Blaze Sense Monk, Hakume C	.07	.15
DBT06067 Blaze Maiden, Arche C	.07	.15
DBT06068 Blaze Maiden, Leonie C	.30	.60
DBT06069 Holy Flames That Binds C	.07	.15
DBT06070 Phase Transition Dragon C	.07	.15
DBT06071 Diabolos Digger, Basil C	.07	.15
DBT06072 Diabolos Reverser, Diandre C	.07	.15
DBT06073 Desire Devil, Kodoku C	.07	.15
DBT06074 Diabolos Girls, Kristen C	.07	.15
DBT06075 Lively Breath Dragon C	.07	.15
DBT06076 Advanced Clock Dragon C	.07	.15
DBT06077 Steam Gunner, Ilu-shuma C	.07	.15
DBT06078 Direful Doll, Alessandra C	.30	.60
DBT06079 Galactic Hero, Wired Crossten C	.20	.40
DBT06080 Galactic Hero, Architect Percy C	.07	.15
DBT06081 Capable Helper C	.07	.15
DBT06082 Galactic Hero, Purely Agno C	.07	.15
DBT06083 Star Aggression Dragon C	.75	1.50
DBT06084 Aberrant Gleam Dragon C	.15	.30
DBT06085 Heavy Machinery Conversion, Heavy Constalion C	.07	.15
DBT06086 Alterate Sphere Dragon C	.20	.40
DBT06087 Hero Base "A.E.G.I.S." C	.20	.40
DBT06088 Quadracast Sorceress C	.07	.15
DBT06089 Divine Sister, Beignet C	.07	.15
DBT06090 Milch Weiss Schutzer C	.07	.15
DBT06091 Menacing Tiger C	.07	.15
DBT06092 Diana Digon Sorceress C	.07	.15
DBT06093 Daring Knight, Sawel C	.75	1.50
DBT06094 Operating Angel C	.12	.25
DBT06095 Merciless Buffalo C	.07	.15
DBT06096 Palpitation Angel C	.20	.40
DBT06097 Deep Green Guardian, Patoriya C	.07	.15
DBT06098 Flutter Dragon C	.07	.15
DBT06099 Recorder Raccoon C	.07	.15
DBT06100 Dual Pressure Dragon C	.60	1.25
DBT06101 Early-Summer Breeze Maiden, Willow C	.10	.20
DBT06102 Crisis Bisection C	.10	.20
DBT06103 Rhythmic Kiwi C	.10	.20
DBT06104 Happy Dreaming Festa! C	.10	.20
DBT06105 Sweetness is a Bad Dream C	.10	.20
DBT06W001EN True Arbiter Dragon of Hundred Swords, Duralvalse WO	5.00	10.00

2022 Cardfight Vanguard D Lyrical Booster Set 02 Lyrical Monasterio It's a New School Term

DLBT02001 Astesice×Live, Kairi RRR	7.50	15.00
DLBT02001 Astesice×Live, Kairi SP	15.00	30.00
DLBT02001 Astesice×Live, Kairi LSR	150.00	300.00
DLBT02002 Coming Beauty, Herminia RRR	4.00	8.00
DLBT02002 Coming Beauty, Herminia SP	10.00	20.00
DLBT02002 Coming Beauty, Herminia LSR	125.00	250.00
DLBT02003 Scintillate Rays, Ophelia RRR	30.00	60.00
DLBT02003 Scintillate Rays, Ophelia SP	50.00	100.00
DLBT02004 MiMish, Fortia RRR	3.00	6.00
DLBT02004 MiMish, Fortia SP	10.00	20.00
DLBT02004 MiMish, Fortia LSR	60.00	125.00
DLBT02005 Canon of Overlaid-spinning, Dietlinde RRR	15.00	30.00
DLBT02005 Canon of Overlaid-spinning, Dietlinde SP	60.00	125.00
DLBT02006 Privilege Potential, Phenael RRR	12.50	25.00
DLBT02006 Privilege Potential, Phenael SP	30.00	60.00
DLBT02007 Hoppin'Stellar, Melty RRR	.25	.50
DLBT02007 Hoppin'Stellar, Melty SP	1.00	2.00
DLBT02008 Mya Mya Ensemble, Nala RRR	2.00	4.00
DLBT02008 Mya Mya Ensemble, Nala SP	7.50	15.00
DLBT02009 Definite Growth, Rugena RRR	4.00	8.00
DLBT02009 Definite Growth, Rugena SP	12.50	25.00
DLBT02010 Symphonic Sky, Lyudmila SP	1.50	3.00
DLBT02010 Symphonic Sky, Lyudmila RRR	.50	1.00
DLBT02011 Sweet×Sweet RRR	.75	1.50
DLBT02011 Sweet×Sweet SP	5.00	10.00
DLBT02012 Challenge to Self, Trudie RR	.75	1.50
DLBT02012 Challenge to Self, Trudie SP	2.50	5.00
DLBT02013 Enveloping Compassion, Torquel RR	1.50	3.00
DLBT02013 Enveloping Compassion, Torquel SP	10.00	20.00
DLBT02014 Bathing Fountain, Terues RR	.50	1.00
DLBT02014 Bathing Fountain, Terues SP	10.00	20.00
DLBT02015 Detour Together, Elvi RR	.50	1.00
DLBT02015 Detour Together, Elvi SP	5.00	10.00
DLBT02016 Motivation Aplenty! Arlette RR	.30	.60
DLBT02016 Motivation Aplenty! Arlette SP	.75	1.50
DLBT02017 Along with Smiles, Geezya RR	.30	.75
DLBT02017 Along with Smiles, Geezya SP	7.50	15.00
DLBT02018 Aim for the Horizon, Piael RR	6.00	12.00
DLBT02018 Aim for the Horizon, Piael SP	15.00	30.00
DLBT02019 Grazioso Prince, Meredith RR	.30	.60
DLBT02019 Grazioso Prince, Meredith SP	7.50	15.00
DLBT02020 Sound in the Wind, Ducayla RR	2.00	4.00
DLBT02020 Sound in the Wind, Ducayla SP	2.50	5.00
DLBT02021 Beware of Overeating! Eileen RR	7.50	15.00
DLBT02021 Beware of Overeating! Eileen SP	15.00	30.00
DLBT02022 Next Step, Laplume RR	2.50	5.00
DLBT02022 Next Step, Laplume SP	10.00	20.00
DLBT02023 Spokesperson of Heavenly Voice, Herjuel RR	2.00	4.00
DLBT02023 Spokesperson of Heavenly Voice, Herjuel SP	7.50	15.00
DLBT02024 Eternally Indistinguishable Aubade, Irene RR	2.50	5.00
DLBT02024 Eternally Indistinguishable Aubade, Irene SP	7.50	15.00
DLBT02025 Burgeoning Tone, Signe RR	.50	1.00
DLBT02025 Burgeoning Tone, Signe SP	4.00	8.00
DLBT02026 Head to the Pinnacle, Katlein RR	.30	.60
DLBT02027 Hasty Panic, Floortje R	.15	.30
DLBT02028 Blessed Ray of Clear Skies, Rahsiel R	.15	.30
DLBT02029 Key to Intimacy, Cucca R	.15	.30
DLBT02030 Natural Chirp, Melria R	.15	.30
DLBT02031 Bashful Striver, Kinkee R	.15	.30
DLBT02032 Straight Gaze, Konstanze R	.15	.30
DLBT02033 Attract Peach, Ertines R	.15	.30
DLBT02033 Attract Peach, Ertines SP	2.00	4.00
DLBT02034 Elegance Moment, Loppil R	.15	.30
DLBT02035 Authentic Melody, Esmeralda R	.15	.30
DLBT02036 Pure and Proper, Yakomina R	.15	.30
DLBT02037 Cheshire Smile, Larisa R	.25	.50
DLBT02038 MiMish, Rikashenna R	.15	.30
DLBT02038 MiMish, Rikashenna SP	2.50	5.00
DLBT02039 Wings of Notables, Elnael R	.15	.30
DLBT02040 Intercommunicating Gaze, Feodora R	.15	.30
DLBT02041 Nonchalant and Composed, Ercilia R	.15	.30
DLBT02042 Wraith Embrace, Betina R	.20	.40
DLBT02043 Precious Tune, Edwige R	4.00	8.00
DLBT02043 Precious Tune, Edwige SP	40.00	80.00
DLBT02043 Precious Tune, Edwige LSR	175.00	350.00
DLBT02044 Transparent Snowy Night, Beretoi R	4.00	8.00
DLBT02044 Transparent Snowy Night, Beretoi SP	60.00	125.00
DLBT02044 Transparent Snowy Night, Beretoi LSR	150.00	300.00
DLBT02045 Snowskip, Palvi R	3.00	6.00
DLBT02045 Snowskip, Palvi SP	30.00	75.00
DLBT02045 Snowskip, Palvi LSR	125.00	250.00
DLBT02046 Fingertips that Uplift Hearts, Edelgard C	.07	.15
DLBT02047 Faithful Eye, Liliana C	.07	.15
DLBT02048 Leeway of Seniority, Altariel C	.07	.15
DLBT02049 The Flawless Me, Fiamma C	.07	.15
DLBT02050 Beating Heart, Kamila C	.07	.15
DLBT02051 Circling Lyric, Ashley C	.07	.15
DLBT02052 Permeating Kindness, Paline C	.07	.15
DLBT02053 Pouring Expectations, Ilta C	.07	.15
DLBT02054 Charmed in the Moonlit Night, Mechtild C	.07	.15
DLBT02055 Happy Tasting, Tigr C	.07	.15
DLBT02056 After School as Always, Yulia C	.07	.15
DLBT02057 Wakey World, Elisa C	.07	.15
DLBT02058 Conspicuous Anxiety, Kaadya C	.07	.15
DLBT02059 Shiny Coat, Marucia C	.07	.15
DLBT02060 Radiance Pride, Irmeli C	.07	.15
DLBT02061 Earnest Stare, Ivetta C	.07	.15
DLBT02062 Song of Salvation, Tulael C	.07	.15
DLBT02063 Delightful Encounter, Gertie C	.07	.15
DLBT02064 Sniping Eyeful, Leranje C	.07	.15

DLBT02064 Sniping Eyeful, Leranje SP 12.50 25.00
DLBT02065 Thorough Rest, Melmahr C .07 .15
DLBT02066 Fluent Style, Marijn C .07 .15
DLBT02067 MiMish, Azhachir C .07 .15
DLBT02067 MiMish, Azhachir SP 2.50 5.00
DLBT02068 Morning Routine, Aera C .07 .15
DLBT02069 Awaiting Smile, Maruel C .07 .15
DLBT02070 Cutie Topic, Rabeena C .07 .15
DLBT02070 Cutie Topic, Rabeena SP 7.50 15.00
DLBT02071 MiMish, Tubbylila C .07 .15
DLBT02071 MiMish, Tubbylila SP 10.00 20.00
DLBT02072 Wings Dancing in the Blue Skies, Antia C .50 1.00
DLBT02073 Surreal Voice, Gilberta C .20 .40
DLBT02074 Haughty Missy, Arroel C .07 .15
DLBT02075 Bouyantly Gaming, Gisele C .07 .15
DLBT02076 Hearts Connect, Rufina C .07 .15
DLBT02077 Picturesque, Luana C .07 .15
DLBT02078 Hushed Diva, Hortense C .07 .15
DLBT02079 Sigh of Relief, Fabiola C .07 .15
DLBT02080 Thoughts into Forms C .07 .15

2022 Cardfight Vanguard D Special Series 02 Festival Collection

DSS02001 Sealed Blaze Dragon, Aaushniya RRR 15.00 30.00
DSS02001 Sealed Blaze Dragon, Aaushniya SP 50.00 100.00
DSS02002 Blaze Maiden, Amelia RRR 2.50 5.00
DSS02002 Blaze Maiden, Amelia SP 15.00 30.00
DSS02003 Desire Devil, Dofund RRR 4.00 8.00
DSS02003 Desire Devil, Dofund SP 25.00 50.00
DSS02004 Diabolos Madonna, Meagan RRR 2.00 4.00
DSS02004 Diabolos Madonna, Meagan SP 30.00 75.00
DSS02005 Cardinal Dominus, Orfist Regis RRR 12.50 25.00
DSS02005 Cardinal Dominus, Orfist Regis SP 50.00 100.00
DSS02005 Cardinal Dominus, Orfist Regis SSR 300.00 600.00
DSS02006 Aurora Battle Princess, Launcher Charleen RRR .50 1.00
DSS02006 Aurora Battle Princess, Launcher Charleen SP 12.50 25.00
DSS02007 Gravidia Peters RRR .75 1.50
DSS02007 Gravidia Peters SP 7.50 15.00
DSS02008 Heavenly Command Dragon, Exalute Dragon RRR .30 .60
DSS02008 Heavenly Command Dragon, Exalute Dragon SP 4.00 8.00
DSS02009 Dead Sea Spiritualist, Grave Zorga RRR 2.50 5.00
DSS02009 Dead Sea Spiritualist, Grave Zorga SP 30.00 60.00
DSS02009 Dead Sea Spiritualist, Grave Zorga SSR 125.00 250.00
DSS02010 Sylvan Horned Beast, Armadi RRR 1.00 2.00
DSS02010 Sylvan Horned Beast, Armadi SP 7.50 15.00
DSS02011 Blaze Battle Monk, Koukan RR .20 .40
DSS02012 Sealed Blaze Dragon, Idahm RR .60 1.25
DSS02013 Sealed Blaze Dragon, Samsara RR .75 1.50
DSS02014 Blaze Covert Monk, Kageri RR .20 .40
DSS02015 Cure Flare Dracokid RR 1.50 3.00
DSS02015 Cure Flare Dracokid SP 30.00 75.00
DSS02016 Diabolos Diver, Emmett RR .20 .40
DSS02017 Diabolos Boys, Nile RR .20 .40
DSS02018 Desire Devil, Xitto RR 1.25 2.50
DSS02019 Brilliant Floral, Uania RR 2.00 4.00
DSS02019 Brilliant Floral, Uania SP 40.00 80.00
DSS02020 Cardinal Fang, Dadai RR .20 .40
DSS02021 Aurora Battle Princess, Barrage Ltra RR .50 1.00
DSS02022 Gravidia Marut RR .20 .40
DSS02023 Cardinal Principal, Regio RR .20 .40
DSS02024 Aurora Battle Princess, Horn Apricot RR .30 .60
DSS02025 Whistling Arrow of Recursion, Obifold RR 2.00 4.00
DSS02025 Whistling Arrow of Recursion, Obifold SP 30.00 75.00
DSS02026 Heavenly Judgment of Composition, Heathcourt RR .20 .40
DSS02027 Heavenly Sickle of Pulsation, Repodron RR .20 .40
DSS02028 Tetrafavor Sorceress RR .30 .60
DSS02029 Bard of the Heavenly Instrument, Lutente RR .25 .50
DSS02030 Heartiness Tear Sorceress RR 2.00 4.00
DSS02030 Heartiness Tear Sorceress SP 30.00 75.00
DSS02031 Longing Maid RR .25 .50
DSS02032 Explorer of the Grand Ravine, C. K. Sakatt RR .20 .40
DSS02033 Sylvan Horned Beast, Kamapuu RR .20 .40
DSS02034 Alchemic Hedgehog RR .75 1.50
DSS02034 Alchemic Hedgehog SP 30.00 60.00
DSS02035 Clouded Miasma RR 2.00 4.00
DSS02BSR01 Sealed Blaze Sword, Prithivih BSR 75.00 150.00
DSS02BSR02 Sealed Blaze Shield, Swayanbuh BSR 75.00 150.00
DSS02BSR03 Sealed Blaze Spear, Aadhitya BSR 125.00 250.00
DSS02BSR04 Sealed Blaze Gun, Chandra BSR 50.00 100.00
DSS02SSR01 Sealed Blaze Maiden, Bavsargra SSR 400.00 800.00

2022 Cardfight Vanguard D Title Booster 02 Record of Ragnarok

DTB05001 Unwavering Determination, Brunhilde RRR 1.25 2.50
DTB05001 Unwavering Determination, Brunhilde SSP 75.00 150.00
DTB05002 Rebellion Against the Deities, Brunhilde RRR 7.50 15.00
DTB05003 Apprentice Valkyrie, Goll RRR 4.00 8.00
DTB05004 China's Strongest Hero, Lü Bu RRR 1.25 2.50
DTB05004 China's Strongest Hero, Lü Bu SSP 50.00 100.00
DTB05005 Father of All Humanity, Adam SSP 50.00 100.00
DTB05005 Father of All Humanity, Adam RRR .75 1.50
DTB05006 History's Strongest Loser, Kojiro Sasaki RRR .75 1.50
DTB05006 History's Strongest Loser, Kojiro Sasaki SSP 30.00 75.00
DTB05007 God of Cunning, Loki RRR 3.00 6.00
DTB05008 Messenger of the Gods, Hermes RRR 3.00 6.00
DTB05009 Berserker of Thunder, Thor RRR .75 1.50
DTB05009 Berserker of Thunder, Thor SSP 50.00 100.00
DTB05010 Godfather of Cosmos, Zeus RRR .75 1.50
DTB05011 Tyrant of the Oceans, Poseidon RRR 1.50 3.00
DTB05011 Tyrant of the Oceans, Poseidon SSP 60.00 125.00
DTB05012 Ragnarok ORR .50 1.00
DTB05013 Ragnarok ORR .50 1.00
DTB05014 Most Badass & Maniacal Warrior, Lü Bu RR .50 1.00
DTB05015 The Man with the Greatest Will, Adam RR .75 1.50
DTB05016 Unrivalled, Kojiro Sasaki RR .30 .60
DTB05017 Valkyries' Fourth Sister, Randgriz RR .30 .60
DTB05018 Valkyries' Seventh Sister, Reginleif RR .30 .60
DTB05019 Valkyries' Second Sister, Hrist RR .30 .60
DTB05020 The Strongest Nordic God, Thunder God Thor RR .30 .60
DTB05021 Almighty God, Zeus RR .30 .60
DTB05022 The Most Fearsome God of Greek Myth, Poseidon RR .30 .60
DTB05023 God of War, Ares RR .30 .60
DTB05024 Passed-down Legend, Thor RR .30 .60
DTB05025 Passed-down Legend, Zeus RR .30 .60
DTB05026 Passed-down Legend, Poseidon RR .30 .60
DTB05027 Singular Counterstrike, Kojiro Sasaki R .15 .30
DTB05028 Devoting Herself, Hrist R .15 .30
DTB05029 Valkyries' Last Sister, Goll R .50 1.25
DTB05030 With its Master, Red Hare R .15 .30
DTB05031 God of Scrap and Build, Shiva R .15 .30
DTB05032 Goddess of Beauty, Aphrodite R .15 .30
DTB05033 Demise Keeper, Heimdall R .15 .30
DTB05034 Norse Supreme God, Odin R .30 .75
DTB05035 Geirrod Thors Hammer R .15 .30
DTB05036 Final Form of Zeus, Adamas R .15 .30
DTB05037 Chione Tyro Demeter R .15 .30
DTB05038 The Long-Awaited Encounter R .30 .75
DTB05039 The Long-Awaited Encounter R .30 .60
DTB05040 Rush Barely Over Heat R .20 .40
DTB05041 Rush Barely Over Heat R .20 .40
DTB05042 Penetrating Style R .25 .50
DTB05043 Penetrating Style R .25 .50
DTB05044 Premonition of Miracles, Lü Bu C .10 .20
DTB05045 Stance of Instinct, Adam C .10 .20
DTB05046 Fastest Prediction, Kojiro Sasaki C .10 .20
DTB05047 All-out Mode, Thor C .10 .20
DTB05048 Finally Facing an Equal, Thor C .10 .20
DTB05049 Thor C .10 .20
DTB05050 The Fist that Surpassed Time, Zeus C .10 .20
DTB05051 It's Me ?, Zeus C .10 .20
DTB05052 Zeus C .10 .20
DTB05053 Appeared True Character, Poseidon C .10 .20
DTB05054 You Loser, Poseidon C .10 .20
DTB05055 Poseidon C .10 .20
DTB05056 Loyal Strategist, Chen Gong Gongtai C .10 .20
DTB05057 Talking with My Brother, Liu Bei Xuande C .10 .20
DTB05058 One Who Knows the Strongest, Guan Yu Yunchang C .10 .20
DTB05059 Heart-pounding Observation, Zhang Fei Yide C .10 .20
DTB05060 Wife Driven Out of Paradise, Eve C .10 .20
DTB05061 Inspiring Eldest Son, Cain C .10 .20
DTB05062 Cheering Second Son, Abel C .10 .20
DTB05063 Dual Heavenly Style, Miyamoto Musashi C .10 .20
DTB05064 Adopted Son of Miyamoto Musashi, Miyamoto Iori C .10 .20
DTB05065 Follower, Hermes C .10 .20
DTB05066 Boiling Fighting Spirit, Shiva C .10 .20
DTB05067 Looking Intently, Aphrodite C .10 .20
DTB05068 Conquest Deity, Adamas C .10 .20
DTB05069 God of Peace, Forseti C .10 .20
DTB05070 The Strongest by Nature C .10 .20
DTB05071 Fighting Each Other is the Battle of Men C .10 .20
DTB05072 Battle of the Abyss C .10 .20
DTB05073 Heaven's Melody C .10 .20

2022 Cardfight Vanguard D Title Booster 03 Shaman King Vol. 1

DTB03001 Let's Go At Our Own Pace, Yoh Asakura RRR 6.00 12.00
DTB03002 Goddess of Victory, Anna Kyoyama RRR 4.00 8.00
DTB03003 Unwavering Heart, Tao Ren RRR .30 .75
DTB03004 Let's Go All Out! Horohoro RRR 10.00 20.00
DTB03005 With his Beloved, Faust VIII RRR .30 .75
DTB03009 By the Eternal Heavens and Earth, Tao Ren RR .30 .60
DTB03010 Big Dreams to Fulfill, Horohoro RR .30 .60
DTB03011 Necromancer, Faust VIII RR .30 .60
DTB03012 The Man with Abundant Sympathy, Wooden Sword Ryu RR .30 .60
DTB03013 Dowsing User, Lyserg RR .30 .60
DTB03014 X-LAWS, Marco RR .30 .60
DTB03015 Dreams of becoming the World's Best Comedian, Chocolove RR .30 .60
DTB03016 Warlord Serving the Tao Family, Bason RR .30 .60
DTB03017 Korpokkur, Kororo RR .30 .60
DTB03018 Beloved Wife, Eliza RR .30 .60
DTB03019 Head of Bandits, Tokageroh RR .30 .60
DTB03020 Five Grand Elemental Spirits, Spirit of Fire RR .30 .60
DTB03021 Deity of the Sun and Justice, Shamash RR .30 .60
DTB03022 Defense Deployment! Yoh Asakura R .15 .30
DTB03023 Destined Fight, Tao Ren R .15 .30
DTB03024 Initiative Victory! Horohoro R .15 .30
DTB03025 Inheriting Madness, Faust VIII R .15 .30
DTB03026 Man Who Became Big, Wooden Sword Ryu R .15 .30
DTB03027 Daoshi, Tao Jun R .15 .30
DTB03028 Officiant, Silva R .15 .30
DTB03029 Disciple of the Asakura Family, Tamao Tamamura R .15 .30
DTB03030 Man of the Stars, Hao R .15 .30
DTB03031 Head of the Tao Family, Tao En R .15 .30
DTB03032 Calcium Giant R .15 .30
DTB03033 Poppy Flower Fairy, Morphine R .15 .30
DTB03034 Archangel, Michael R .15 .30
DTB03035 Jaguar, Mic R .15 .30
DTB03036 Super! Honryohakki! R .15 .30
DTB03037 Kau Kau Priwenpe R .15 .30
DTB03038 Necromancy R .15 .30
DTB03039 In Search of Happy Place R .15 .30
DTB03040 I'll Knock You Down to Hell R .15 .30
DTB03041 Strong Foes in the Way R .15 .30
DTB03042 Hatred Towards the Tao Family, Tao Ren C .07 .15
DTB03043 Tao Ren C .07 .15
DTB03044 Korpokkur are Friends, Horohoro C .07 .15
DTB03045 Horohoro C .07 .15
DTB03046 Ominous Presence, Faust VIII C .07 .15
DTB03047 Faust VIII C .07 .15
DTB03048 Are We Doing This? Wooden Sword Ryu C .07 .15
DTB03049 Wooden Sword Ryu C .07 .15
DTB03050 Ryu's Buddies C .07 .15
DTB03051 A Dream Shared with Her Brother, Pirica C .07 .15
DTB03052 Spirit of the Strongest Horse in History, Hei-Tao C .07 .15
DTB03053 Faust House's Pet, Frankensteiny C .07 .15
DTB03054 Jiangshi, Lee Pyron C .07 .15
DTB03055 Silver Arms, Silver Wing C .07 .15
DTB03056 Silver Arms, Silver Rod C .07 .15
DTB03057 Silver Arms, Silver Tail C .07 .15
DTB03058 Silver Arms, Silver Horn C .07 .15
DTB03059 Silver Arms, Silver Shield C .07 .15
DTB03060 Love Pranks, Ponchi C .07 .15
DTB03061 Love Pranks, Conchi C .07 .15
DTB03062 Jiangshi, Shamon C .07 .15
DTB03063 Ancestor Soul of the Tao Family C .07 .15
DTB03064 Unyielding Battle, Bason C .07 .15
DTB03065 Deep Emotion! Bason C .07 .15
DTB03066 Adorable! Kororo C .07 .15
DTB03067 Cheer Up! Kororo C .07 .15
DTB03068 Will-less Strike, Eliza C .07 .15
DTB03069 Bashful? Tokageroh C .07 .15
DTB03070 Spiritualism C .07 .15
DTB03071 Combat Spells Equipped C .07 .15
DTB03072 Yuzhouzhan Luoxia C .07 .15
DTB03073 Mososo Kruppe C .07 .15
DTB03074 Emus Nokipekonr C .07 .15
DTB03075 Silva's Test C .07 .15
DTB03076 Tamao's Fortune-telling C .07 .15
DTB03077 Over Soul Da Dao Long C .07 .15
DTB03078 Homing Pendulum C .07 .15
DTB03079 Gag Wind C .07 .15
DTB03080 Wait for Me! C .07 .15
DTB03081 No Matter What Happens C .07 .15
DTB03082 Goldva's Orders C .07 .15

2022 Cardfight Vanguard P Special Series 01 P Clan Collection

DPS01001 Divine Knight of Triumph, Eulogias RRR 1.25 2.50
DPS01001 Divine Knight of Triumph, Eulogias SR 4.00 8.00
DPS01002 Happiness Gathering Dragon King SR 7.50 15.00
DPS01002 Happiness Gathering Dragon King RRR 2.50 5.00
DPS01003 Holy Seraph, Zafkiel RRR 4.00 8.00
DPS01003 Holy Seraph, Zafkiel SR 15.00 30.00
DPS01004 Dark Knight, Crow Cruach RRR 2.00 4.00
DPS01004 Dark Knight, Crow Cruach SR 12.50 25.00
DPS01005 Golden Knight of Prosperity, Idvarious RRR 1.50 3.00
DPS01005 Golden Knight of Prosperity, Idvarious SR 7.50 15.00
DPS01006 Soul-offering Heavenly Dragon, Jagdanarruga RRR 1.25 2.50
DPS01006 Soul-offering Heavenly Dragon, Jagdanarruga SR 5.00 10.00
DPS01007 Divine Dragon Knight, Barakat RRR 1.00 2.00
DPS01007 Divine Dragon Knight, Barakat SR 6.00 12.00
DPS01008 Rikudo Stealth Rogue, Yatsukalord RRR .50 1.00
DPS01008 Rikudo Stealth Rogue, Yatsukalord SR 6.00 12.00
DPS01009 Explosive Tyrant Magnate, Giganotopharaoh RRR 1.25 2.50
DPS01009 Explosive Tyrant Magnate, Giganotopharaoh SR 4.00 8.00
DPS01010 Ambush Demon Stealth Rogue, Izushiotome RRR 5.00 10.00
DPS01010 Ambush Demon Stealth Rogue, Izushiotome SR 7.50 15.00
DPS01011 Conquering Supreme Dragon, Exterminate Dragon RRR 7.50 15.00
DPS01011 Conquering Supreme Dragon, Exterminate Dragon SR 12.50 25.00
DPS01012 Fighting Emperor Dragon, Merciless Dragon RRR .75 1.50
DPS01012 Fighting Emperor Dragon, Merciless Dragon SR 5.00 10.00
DPS01013 Cosmowinger, Unibird Galaxy RRR 2.50 5.00
DPS01013 Cosmowinger, Unibird Galaxy SR 12.50 25.00
DPS01014 Nebula Dragon, Cosmic Dawn Dragon RRR 3.00 6.00
DPS01014 Nebula Dragon, Cosmic Dawn Dragon SR 12.50 25.00
DPS01015 Lawless King, Gally Gabalus RRR 2.50 5.00
DPS01015 Lawless King, Gally Gabalus SR 7.50 15.00
DPS01016 Ultimate Deep Hades Emperor, Forfax RRR 2.00 4.00
DPS01016 Ultimate Deep Hades Emperor, Forfax SR 7.50 15.00
DPS01017 Trenchant Megatrick, Leontina RRR 2.00 4.00
DPS01017 Trenchant Megatrick, Leontina SR 10.00 20.00
DPS01018 Highbrow Steam, Shlishma RRR 7.50 15.00
DPS01018 Highbrow Steam, Shlishma SR 20.00 40.00
DPS01019 Pirate King of Everlasting Darkness, Bartholomew RRR 2.00 4.00
DPS01019 Pirate King of Everlasting Darkness, Bartholomew SR 7.50 15.00
DPS01020 Radiate Ocean, Heltrauda RRR 7.50 15.00
DPS01020 Radiate Ocean, Heltrauda SR 15.00 30.00
DPS01021 Blue Furious Charge Dragon, Furiargus Dragon RRR 2.00 4.00
DPS01021 Blue Furious Charge Dragon, Furiargus Dragon SR 7.50 15.00
DPS01022 Malignant Mutant Deity, Malignantis RRR 2.50 5.00
DPS01022 Malignant Mutant Deity, Malignantis SR 7.50 15.00
DPS01023 Omniscience Dragon, Caladrius RRR .75 1.50
DPS01023 Omniscience Dragon, Caladrius SR 5.00 10.00
DPS01024 Flower Princess of Compassion, Ladislava RRR 1.00 2.00
DPS01024 Flower Princess of Compassion, Ladislava SR 10.00 20.00
DPS01025 Faithful Sacred Staff, Morgause RR 1.00 2.00
DPS01026 Octadic Reinforcer, Octagonal Magus RR .60 1.25
DPS01027 Super Mobile Hospital, Firmament Glanz RR 1.25 2.50
DPS01028 Dark Dragon, Deep Griever Dragon RR 5.00 10.00
DPS01029 Golden Dragon, Sanctified Dragon RR 1.00 2.00
DPS01030 Sky Enforcing Light Dragon, Aanavarta RR 1.00 2.00
DPS01031 Blaze Dragon Dance, Saleema RR .75 1.50
DPS01032 Rikudo Stealth Rogue, Moreilord RR .75 1.50
DPS01033 Fortress Marquis, Regalgarder RR .60 1.25
DPS01034 Ambush Demon Stealth Rogue, Aizen RR 1.25 2.50
DPS01035 Sky Guardian Supreme Dragon, Counteract Dragon RR 2.50 5.00
DPS01036 Meteokaiser, Stiffneid RR .30 .75
DPS01037 Giant Armored-Beast, Giragamelgos RR 3.00 6.00
DPS01038 Terminal Ending Darkness, Big Ripper RR .75 1.50
DPS01039 Compassion Queen, Villainess Evita RR .75 1.50
DPS01040 Rebellious Storm Princess, Niljahbis RR 1.25 2.50
DPS01041 Jester Demonic Beast, Flection Chimera RR 1.75 3.50
DPS01042 Interdimensional Dragon, History-vision Dragon RR .60 1.25
DPS01043 Diabolist Princess Singing Under the Moonlight, Oriana RR .75 1.50
DPS01044 Diva of Salvation, Lucrèce RR 2.00 4.00
DPS01045 Rebellious Heavenly Flow General, Dianera RR 1.00 2.00
DPS01046 Binding Mutant Deity, Cruwebl RR .75 1.50
DPS01047 Omniscience Dragon, Sebchet-avil RR .60 1.25
DPS01048 Flower Princess of Dedication, Robertina RR 1.00 2.00
DPS01049 Amulet Pure Eagle C .30 .60
DPS01050 Sentflare Dracokid C .50 1.00
DPS01051 Weather Girl, Cendol C .15 .30
DPS01052 Celeste Witch, ToTo C .75 1.50
DPS01053 Thundershock Angel C .15 .30
DPS01054 Augment Angel C .75 1.50
DPS01055 Dagger of Peaceful Passing, Pryderi C .25 .50
DPS01056 Knight of Evil Spear, Gillingr C 1.50 3.00
DPS01057 Player of the Holy Chord, Theodora C .50 1.00
DPS01058 Gold Garnish Lion C .75 1.50
DPS01059 Tablet Angel C .20 .40
DPS01060 Dragon Ancestral Deity of Progression, Musshussu C .50 1.00
DPS01061 Dragon Dancer, Tiqla C .75 1.50
DPS01062 Dragon Dancer, Paloma C .50 1.00
DPS01063 Stealth Dragon, Yamisaki C .20 .40
DPS01064 Stealth Dragon, Eizan C .50 1.00
DPS01065 Raid Dragon, Guerillapsittaco C .20 .40
DPS01066 Bombardment Dragon, Argenwerfer C .20 .40
DPS01067 Stealth Beast, Scratch Cat C .20 .40
DPS01068 Stealth Fiend, Bull Andon C .20 .40
DPS01069 Dragon Dancer, Paulina C .75 1.50
DPS01070 Rumble Dagger Dracokid C 1.25 2.50
DPS01071 Magnegauss 2502 C .20 .40
DPS01072 Kitton Piccon C .60 1.25
DPS01073 Quake Being, Namazooro C .20 .40
DPS01074 Impurity Monster, Daubruber C .20 .40
DPS01075 Sharp Points of Breakdown, Vandal Sharp C .20 .40
DPS01076 Hybrid Progeny of Superatoms C 1.25 2.50
DPS01077 Machinary Slotback C .20 .40
DPS01078 Cheer Girl, Lynette C .40 .80
DPS01079 Liquid Fencer C .20 .40
DPS01080 Bane Stinger C .50 1.00
DPS01081 Exotic Jerker C .25 .50
DPS01082 Convert Bunny C .75 1.50
DPS01083 Steam Gunner, Kadash C .20 .40
DPS01084 Steam Engineer, Abazu C .75 1.50
DPS01085 Wild Seas Banshee C .30 .75
DPS01086 Chad the Ghostie C .50 1.00
DPS01087 Aqua Light, Ardel C .60 1.25
DPS01088 Wrapping Chorus, Trudy C 2.00 4.00
DPS01089 Direct Strike Brave Shooter C .20 .40
DPS01090 Bumper Shooter C .75 1.50
DPS01091 Megacolony Battler F C .20 .40
DPS01092 Riddled Honey C .20 .40
DPS01093 Curious Pony C .25 .50
DPS01094 Fulmination Professor, Ezonoshin C .25 .50
DPS01095 Happy Lucky C .25 .50
DPS01096 Maiden of Polyantha C .50 1.00

2022 Cardfight Vanguard Raging Flames Against Emerald Storm

DBT07001 Flaring Cannon Equip, Baur Vairina RRR 2.50 5.00
DBT07002 Meteor Flare Dragon RRR 12.50 25.00
DBT07003 Stealth Beast, Silent Crow RRR .50 1.00
DBT07004 Heat Haze Acrobat, Miloslava RRR 4.00 8.00
DBT07005 Demonic Jewel Dragon, Drajeweled RRR 10.00 20.00
DBT07005 Demonic Jewel Dragon, Drajeweled DSR 250.00 500.00
DBT07006 Demonic Stone Dragon, Rockargour RRR 10.00 20.00
DBT07007 Blitz CEO, Welstra RRR 6.00 12.00
DBT07008 Blitz Secretary, Perphe RRR 1.25 2.50
DBT07009 Blitz Engineer, Hollio RRR 1.00 2.00
DBT07010 Unrivaled Heavenly Blade, Descorda RRR 1.00 2.00
DBT07011 Youthberk "RevolForm: Tempest" RRR 30.00 75.00
DBT07012 Knight of Rendering Flash, Cairbre RRR 15.00 30.00
DBT07013 Benevolent Maiden, Araserith RRR 1.25 2.50
DBT07014 Resonance Dragon RRR 4.00 8.00
DBT07015 Sylvan Horned Beast, Alpin RRR 7.50 15.00
DBT07016 Break Equip Dragon, Urbago RR .75 1.50
DBT07017 Assault Bullet of Dust Storm, Oswald RR .30 .60
DBT07018 Sealed Blaze Dragon, Samadhi RR 7.50 15.00
DBT07019 Lilac Rusher RR .60 1.25
DBT07020 Power Gem Dragon RR .75 1.50
DBT07021 Falcate Performer RR 7.50 15.00
DBT07022 Gravidia Aranhill RR .20 .40

DBT07023 Blitz Mechanic, Iskra RR 3.00 6.00
DBT07024 Blitz Mechanic, Schtart RR .30 .75
DBT07025 Heavenly Wings of Purity, Honnettaria RR 12.50 25.00
DBT07026 Wayward Therapy Angel RR 7.50 15.00
DBT07027 Witch of Accumulation, Sequana RR 7.50 15.00
DBT07028 Tear Knight, Aricks RR 3.00 6.00
DBT07029 Festoso Dragon RR .30 .75
DBT07030 Sylvan Horned Beast, Seroll RR 6.00 12.00
DBT07031 Striking Artillery of Dust Storm, Andrea R .15 .30
DBT07032 Assault Equip Dragon, Valsavul R .15 .30
DBT07033 Lavamane Wyvern R .15 .30
DBT07034 Twin Blades that Slice Sorrow R .15 .30
DBT07035 Attract Inverse R .15 .30
DBT07036 Reaper in the Shadows, Zeilmort R .15 .30
DBT07037 Demonic Jewel Dragon, Rystal Galer R .30 .60
DBT07038 Demonic Stone Dragon, Matelbara R .15 .30
DBT07039 Gravidia Almanon R .15 .30
DBT07040 Blitz Accounting Manager, Zoldeo R .15 .30
DBT07041 Watching Monster, Proteed R .15 .30
DBT07042 Mobile Fortress of Obliteration, Freischutz Maximum R .15 .30
DBT07043 Graceful Heavenly Flash, Hermona R .15 .30
DBT07044 Spinning Knight, Gwendolen R .15 .30
DBT07045 Divine Sister, Langue de Chat R .50 1.00
DBT07046 Divine Sister, Palmier R .15 .30
DBT07047 Sylvan Horned Beast, Tigralta R .15 .30
DBT07048 Archaeological Scientist, Anty Elter R .15 .30
DBT07049 Rousing Breath Dragon R .15 .30
DBT07050 Sympathize dB R .15 .30
DBT07051 Blaze Hook Monk, Nissha C .07 .15
DBT07052 Thundering Cannon Dragon, Salvorex C .07 .15
DBT07053 Gallant Flare Dragon C .07 .15
DBT07054 Blaze Maiden, Sienna C .07 .15
DBT07055 Beautiful Bullet of Dust Storm, Jodie C .07 .15
DBT07056 Crush Equip Dragon, Gatoyagard C .07 .15
DBT07057 Dual Electros Dragon C .07 .15
DBT07058 Dragritter, Midhat C .07 .15
DBT07059 Sky-severing Demonic Blade, Alter-slaughter C .07 .15
DBT07060 Steady Spiky C .07 .15
DBT07061 Hypno Grasper C .07 .15
DBT07062 Inhale Pit C .07 .15
DBT07063 Steam Fighter, Ziusudra C .07 .15
DBT07064 Steam Shooter, Puannum C .07 .15
DBT07065 Depletion Sabbia C .07 .15
DBT07066 Magnereversal Breaker C .07 .15
DBT07067 Erosion Demonic Monster, Nautigalbas C .07 .15
DBT07068 Blitz Top Sales, Anrig C .07 .15
DBT07069 Blitz Technology Researcher, Uber C .07 .15
DBT07070 Blitz Security, Wachten C .07 .15
DBT07071 Blitz Programmer, Strazer C .07 .15
DBT07072 Blitz Mechanic, Warton C .07 .15
DBT07073 Heavy Strike Cannon Fortress, Freischutz C .07 .15
DBT07074 Incandescent Flame Cannon, Abhasal C .07 .15
DBT07075 Silent Sorrow Dragon C .07 .15
DBT07076 Force Toll Arrow Dragon C .07 .15
DBT07077 Knight of Demolition, Maredu C .07 .15
DBT07078 Knight of Stabbing Sky, Scofiza C .07 .15
DBT07079 Dismembering Knight, Teutates C .07 .15
DBT07080 Knight of Enmity, Aine C .07 .15
DBT07081 Knight of Gale, Kyneburga C .07 .15
DBT07082 Knight of Heavenly Ringing, Sonithea C .07 .15
DBT07083 Agogik Dragon C .07 .15
DBT07084 Knight of Sincerity, Alfonso C .07 .15
DBT07085 Ferocious Hunter C .07 .15
DBT07086 Float Assault C .07 .15
DBT07087 Noblesse Frit C .07 .15
DBT07088 Billow Assault C .07 .15
DBT07089 Trigeminal Assault C .07 .15
DBT07090 Cooperative Strike Brave Shooter C .07 .15
DBT07DSR01 Chakrabarthi Phoenix Dragon, Nirvana Jheva DSR125.00 250.00
DBT07Re01 Blaze Maiden, Parama RE 5.00 10.00
DBT07Re02 Diabolos Girls, Natalia RE 4.00 8.00
DBT07Re03 Cardinal Draco, Enpyro RE 4.00 8.00
DBT07Re04 Bard of Heavenly Song, Alpacc RE 7.50 15.00
DBT07Re05 Frenzied Heiress RE 2.00 4.00
DBT07Re06 Burning Flail Dragon RE 2.00 4.00
DBT07Re07 Stem Deviate Dragon RE 3.00 6.00
DBT07Re08 Patrol Robo, Dekarcop RE 4.00 8.00
DBT07Re09 Blade Feather Dragon RE 3.00 6.00
DBT07Re10 Aspiring Maiden, Alana RE 3.00 6.00
DBT07Re11 Flare Veil Dragon RE 5.00 10.00
DBT07Re12 Rouse Wildmaster, Riley RE 7.50 15.00
DBT07Re13 Ameliorate Connector RE 7.50 15.00
DBT07Re14 Protection Magic, Prorobi RE 5.00 10.00
DBT07Re15 Serene Maiden, Lena RE 4.00 8.00
DBT07WO01EN Terrifying Wicked Dragon King, Vamfrieze WO 6.00 12.00

2022 Cardfight Vanguard V Special Series 03 V Clan Collection Vol. 3

DVS03001 Leading Jewel Knight, Salome RRR 7.50 15.00
DVS03001 Leading Jewel Knight, Salome SP 25.00 50.00
DVS03001 Leading Jewel Knight, Salome VSR 125.00 250.00
DVS03002 Dogmatize Jewel Knight, Sybill RRR 4.00 8.00
DVS03003 Fruiting Jewel Knight, Eunice RRR 6.00 12.00
DVS03004 Knight of Chivalry, Rabol RRR .25 .50
DVS03005 Absolute Blade Knight, Livarot RRR 1.00 2.00
DVS03006 Sword of Hope, Richard RRR .20 .40
DVS03007 Bringer of Dreams, Belenus RRR .20 .40
DVS03008 Benitoite Witch, YoYo RRR .50 1.00
DVS03008 Benitoite Witch, YoYo SP 7.50 15.00
DVS03009 Jade Witch, TeTe RRR .50 1.00
DVS03010 Citrine Witch, MuMu RRR .60 1.25
DVS03011 Wistaria Witch, ZoZo RRR .20 .40
DVS03012 Cobalt Witch, PuPu RRR .50 1.00
DVS03013 Seablue Witch, NiNi RRR .30 .60
DVS03014 Divine Sword, Kusanagi RRR .50 .75
DVS03015 Demise Queen, Himiko Reverse RRR .75 1.50
DVS03015 Demise Queen, Himiko Reverse SP 7.50 15.00
DVS03015 Demise Queen, Himiko Reverse VSR 60.00 125.00
DVS03016 Sunlight Goddess, Yatagarasu RRR .60 1.25
DVS03017 Apple Witch, Cider RRR 3.00 6.00
DVS03018 Strong Bow of the Starry Night, Ulixes RRR .25 .50
DVS03019 White Phosphorus Sorcerer, Revoluta RRR .20 .40
DVS03020 Unappeasable Biter, Gleipnir RRR .75 1.50
DVS03021 Stake Fetter, Thviti RRR .20 .40
DVS03022 Dauntless Dominate Dragon Reverse RRR .75 1.50
DVS03022 Dauntless Dominate Dragon Reverse SP 7.50 15.00
DVS03023 Blazing Flare Dragon RRR .75 1.50
DVS03024 Dragonic Lawkeeper RRR .25 .50
DVS03025 Dragon Dancer, Frema RRR .20 .40
DVS03026 Volantruber Dragon RRR .20 .40
DVS03027 Heatshot Dragon RRR .20 .40
DVS03028 Dragon Knight, Jannat RRR .20 .40
DVS03029 Covert Demonic Dragon, Hyakki Vogue Reverse RRR .30 .60
DVS03029 Covert Demonic Dragon, Hyakki Vogue Reverse SP 4.00 8.00
DVS03030 Platinum Blond Fox Spirit, Tamamo RRR .20 .40
DVS03031 Special Stealth Beast, Weasel Black RRR .25 .50
DVS03032 Stealth Rogue of Indignation, Meomaru RRR .25 .50
DVS03033 Stealth Rogue of Noh Masks, Awazu RRR .20 .40
DVS03034 Stealth Beast, Metamorfox RRR .20 .40
DVS03035 Stealth Rogue of the Fiendish Blade, Masamura RRR .20 .40
DVS03036 Sealed Demon Dragon, Dungaree RRR .30 .60
DVS03036 Sealed Demon Dragon, Dungaree SP 6.00 12.00
DVS03037 Exorcist Mage, Ren Ren RRR .25 .50
DVS03038 Exorcist Mage, Miu Miu RRR .30 .60
DVS03039 Jaggy Shot Dragoon RRR .20 .40
DVS03040 Dragon Dancer, Barca RRR .25 .50
DVS03041 Dragon Knight, Zubayr RRR .20 .40
DVS03042 Lightning of Triumphant Return, Reseph RRR .20 .40
DVS03043 Original Saver, Zero RRR .25 .50
DVS03043 Original Saver, Zero SP 2.00 6.00
DVS03044 Endless Float RRR .30 .75
DVS03045 Eternity Chaser RRR 1.00 2.00
DVS03046 Dimensional Robo, Daidragon RRR .20 .40
DVS03047 Toxic Monster, Gelsludge RRR .60 1.25
DVS03048 Dimensional Robo, Daibrave RRR .20 .40
DVS03049 Cosmic Hero, Grandbeat RRR .20 .40
DVS03050 Great Demon Emperor, Dudley Emperor Reverse RRR .50 1.00
DVS03050 Great Demon Emperor, Dudley Emperor Reverse SP 5.00 10.00
DVS03051 Agile Fullback RRR .60 1.25
DVS03052 Machine Gun Gloria RRR .25 .50
DVS03053 Gunburst Linebacker RRR .20 .40
DVS03054 Breach Spurt RRR .20 .40
DVS03055 Offensive Punter RRR .20 .40
DVS03056 Liar Lips RRR .20 .40
DVS03057 Silver Thorn Dragon Queen, Luquier Reverse RRR 2.50 5.00
DVS03057 Silver Thorn Dragon Queen, Luquier Reverse SP 25.00 50.00
DVS03057 Silver Thorn Dragon Queen, Luquier Reverse VSR 150.00 300.00
DVS03058 Silver Thorn Beast Tamer, Maricica RRR 1.25 2.50
DVS03059 Silver Thorn Beast Tamer, Ana RRR 1.25 2.50
DVS03060 Silver Thorn Dragon, Megalorude RRR .25 .50
DVS03061 Silver Thorn Beast Tamer, Doriane RRR .25 .50
DVS03062 Silver Thorn Handlegrip, Linnea RRR .20 .40
DVS03063 Darkside Sword Master RRR .20 .40
DVS03064 Detonate Singer, Refiarade Rock RRR .30 .75
DVS03064 Detonate Singer, Refiarade Rock SP 6.00 12.00
DVS03065 Courteous Beauty, Seria RRR 2.00 4.00
DVS03066 Sparkling Soul, Nikita RRR .50 1.00
DVS03067 Cuddle Connect, Fanessa RRR .20 .40
DVS03068 Mermaid Idol, Elly RRR .20 .40
DVS03069 Distinguished Wink, Radka RRR .20 .40
DVS03070 Cherished Phrase, Reina RRR .20 .40
DVS03071 Blue Storm Karma Dragon, Maelstrom Reverse RRR 3.00 6.00
DVS03071 Blue Storm Karma Dragon, Maelstrom Reverse SP 12.50 25.00
DVS03072 Cobalt Wave Dragon RRR .20 .40
DVS03073 Tear Knight, Valeria RRR .40 .80
DVS03074 Tidal Assault RRR .25 .50
DVS03075 Drifting Flow Fencer RRR .20 .40
DVS03076 Bubble Ball Corporal RRR .20 .40
DVS03077 Kelpie Rider, Petros RRR .20 .40
DVS03078 Martial Arts Mutant, Master Beetle RRR .30 .60
DVS03078 Martial Arts Mutant, Master Beetle SP 2.00 4.00
DVS03079 Machining Armor Beetle RRR .50 1.00
DVS03080 Brillian Blister RRR 2.50 5.00
DVS03081 Machining Black Saturn RRR .20 .40
DVS03082 Vulgar Mutant, Stamping Red RRR .30 .60
DVS03083 Machining Cybister RRR .20 .40
DVS03084 Scissor-shot Mutant, Bombscissor RRR .20 .40

2022 Cardfight Vanguard V Special Series 04 V Clan Collection Vol. 4

DVS04001 Cleanup Celestial, Ramiel Reverse SP 10.00 20.00
DVS04001 Cleanup Celestial, Ramiel Reverse RRR 2.00 4.00
DVS04002 Emergency Celestial, Danielle RRR .50 1.00
DVS04003 Nursing Celestial, Narelle RRR .50 1.00
DVS04004 Bosker Surgeon, Asphael RRR .20 .40
DVS04005 Shake Patch Angel RRR .20 .40
DVS04006 Black Mapping, Salaphiel RRR .25 .50
DVS04007 Black Spark, Munkar RRR .20 .40
DVS04008 Revenger, Raging Fall Dragon Reverse RRR 4.00 8.00
DVS04008 Revenger, Raging Fall Dragon Reverse SP 25.00 50.00
DVS04008 Revenger, Raging Fall Dragon Reverse VSR 60.00 125.00
DVS04009 Overcoming Revenger, Rukea RRR 2.50 5.00
DVS04010 Self-Control Revenger, Rakia RRR 4.00 8.00
DVS04011 Fallen Dive Eagle RRR .20 .40
DVS04012 Abyssal Owl RRR .60 1.25
DVS04013 Strict Order Knight, Liuails RRR .25 .50
DVS04014 Belial Owl RRR .20 .40
DVS04015 Salvation Lion, Grand Ezel Scissors RRR 1.25 2.50
DVS04015 Salvation Lion, Grand Ezel Scissors SP 12.50 25.00
DVS04015 Salvation Lion, Grand Ezel Scissors VSR 75.00 150.00
DVS04016 Knight of Passion, Bagdemagus RRR .30 .75
DVS04017 Sacred Twin Beast, White Lion RRR .75 1.50
DVS04018 Battlefield Storm, Sagramore RRR .60 1.25
DVS04019 Flame Wind Lion, Wonder Ezel RRR .50 1.00
DVS04020 Crimson Lion Beast, Howell RRR .20 .40
DVS04021 Scarface Lion RRR .20 .40
DVS04022 Covert Demonic Dragon, Magatsu Storm Reverse RRR .50 1.00
DVS04022 Covert Demonic Dragon, Magatsu Storm Reverse SP12.50 25.00
DVS04023 Stealth Dragon, Royale Nova RRR .25 .50
DVS04024 Stealth Dragon, Unen RRR 1.00 2.00
DVS04025 Stealth Dragon, Magatsu Gale RRR 2.50 5.00
DVS04026 Stealth Beast, Jadouneko RRR .30 .60
DVS04027 Stealth Dragon, Magatsu Breath RRR .20 .40
DVS04028 Stealth Dragon, Noroi RRR .20 .40
DVS04029 Military Dragon, Raptor Colonel RRR .75 1.50
DVS04029 Military Dragon, Raptor Colonel SP 6.00 12.00
DVS04030 Military Dragon, Raptor Captain RRR .75 1.50
DVS04031 Military Dragon, Raptor Sergeant RRR .75 1.50
DVS04032 Zealous Horn Dragon, Dilophopyro RRR .20 .40
DVS04033 Light Blade Dragon, Zandilopho RRR .20 .40
DVS04034 Vicious Claw Dragon, Laceraterex RRR .20 .40
DVS04035 Cannon Fire Dragon, Parasaulauncher RRR .20 .40
DVS04036 Deadliest Beast Deity, Ethics Buster Reverse RRR 1.00 2.00
DVS04036 Deadliest Beast Deity, Ethics Buster Reverse SP 7.50 15.00
DVS04037 Beast Deity, Brainy Papio RRR .75 1.50
DVS04038 Beast Deity, Max Beat RRR .50 1.00
DVS04039 Beast Deity, Eclair Dragon RRR .20 .40
DVS04040 Beast Deity, Black Tortoise RRR .20 .40
DVS04041 Swordbrand Gladiator RRR .20 .40
DVS04042 Extreme Battler, Break-pass RRR .20 .40
DVS04043 Star-vader, Nebula Lord Dragon RRR .75 1.50
DVS04043 Star-vader, Nebula Lord Dragon SP 4.00 8.00
DVS04044 Unrivaled Star-vader, Radon RRR .60 1.25
DVS04045 Mana Shot Star-vader, Neon RRR .50 1.00
DVS04046 Singularity Sniper RRR .20 .40
DVS04047 Aharonov Cat RRR .20 .40
DVS04048 Opener of Dark Gates RRR .20 .40
DVS04049 Blink Messiah RRR .20 .40
DVS04050 Demon World Marquis, Amon RRR 3.00 6.00
DVS04050 Demon World Marquis, Amon SP 12.50 25.00
DVS04051 Amon's Follower, Ron Geenlin RRR 2.50 5.00
DVS04052 Amon's Follower, Phu Geenlin RRR 2.00 4.00
DVS04053 Metallic-winged Cursed Princess, Rhodia RRR .20 .40
DVS04054 Dimension Creeper RRR .20 .40
DVS04055 Doreen the Thruster RRR .20 .40
DVS04056 One-eyed Succubus RRR .20 .40
DVS04057 Steam Maiden, Elul RRR 1.25 2.50
DVS04057 Steam Maiden, Elul SP 7.50 15.00
DVS04058 Steam Maiden, Alul RRR 1.00 2.00
DVS04059 Steam Maiden, Ilul RRR 2.00 4.00
DVS04060 Mellow Amusements Colossus RRR .20 .40
DVS04061 Re-innovate Wing Dragon RRR .20 .40
DVS04062 Steam Scalar, Kurunta RRR .25 .50
DVS04063 Heart Thump Worker RRR .20 .40
DVS04064 Ice Prison Hades Emperor, Cocytus Reverse RRR .25 .50
DVS04064 Ice Prison Hades Emperor, Cocytus Reverse SP 4.00 8.00
DVS04065 Witch Doctor of the Dead Sea, Negrobolt RRR .20 .40
DVS04066 Dragon Undead, Ghoul Dragon RRR .20 .40
DVS04067 Stormride Ghost Ship RRR .20 .40
DVS04068 Skeleton Sea Navigator RRR .20 .40
DVS04069 Dancing Cutlass RRR .40 .60
DVS04070 Rampage Shade RRR .25 .50
DVS04071 Battler of the Twin Brush, Polaris RRR .20 .40
DVS04071 Battler of the Twin Brush, Polaris SP 3.00 6.00
DVS04072 Guardian of Truth, Lox RRR .20 .40
DVS04073 Coiling Duckbill RRR .60 1.25
DVS04074 Ambers Triangular RRR .20 .40
DVS04075 Veteran Janitor, Siga RRR .20 .40
DVS04076 History Scholar, Bushboeckh RRR .20 .40
DVS04077 Application Researcher, Ponbelly RRR .20 .40
DVS04078 Thorn Lily Musketeer, Cecilia Reverse RRR 5.00 10.00
DVS04078 Thorn Lily Musketeer, Cecilia Reverse SP 25.00 50.00
DVS04078 Thorn Lily Musketeer, Cecilia Reverse VSR 100.00 200.00
DVS04079 Deep Green Lord, Master Wisteria RRR .25 .50
DVS04080 Cherry Blossom Musketeer, Augusto RRR .60 1.25
DVS04081 Pansy Musketeer, Sylvia RRR .30 .60
DVS04082 Anthurium Musketeer, Gastone RRR .20 .40
DVS04083 Maiden of Sweet Berry RRR .50 1.00
DVS04084 Flower Garden Maiden, Mylis RRR .20 .40

2022 Cardfight Vanguard V Special Series 05 V Clan Collection Vol. 5

DVS05001 Broken Heart Jewel Knight, Ashlei Reverse RRR 3.00 6.00
DVS05002 Banding Jewel Knight, Miranda RRR 4.00 8.00
DVS05003 Security Jewel Knight, Alwain RRR 5.00 10.00
DVS05004 Pure Heart Jewel Knight, Ashlei RRR .75 1.50
DVS05005 Explode Jewel Knight, Laile RRR .75 1.50
DVS05006 Charging Jewel Knight, Morvidus RRR .75 1.50
DVS05007 Innocent Ray Dragon RRR 1.50 3.00
DVS05008 Heretic Battle Sister, Fromage Reverse RRR 5.00 10.00
DVS05009 Battle Sister, Mocha RRR 2.00 4.00
DVS05010 Battle Sister, Cocoa RRR 2.50 5.00
DVS05011 Battle Sister, Fromage RRR .25 .50
DVS05012 Battle Sister, Trifle RRR .25 .50
DVS05013 Battle Sister, Torrijas RRR .25 .50
DVS05014 Goddess of Water Dragon, Toyotamahime RRR .75 1.50
DVS05015 Beloved Regalia, Frigg RRR 1.50 3.00
DVS05016 Regalia of Avowal, Lurilijssa RRR 2.00 4.00
DVS05017 Ordain Owl RRR .60 1.25
DVS05018 Cosmic Regalia, CEO Yggdrasil RRR .75 1.50
DVS05019 Regalia of Fate, Norn RRR .30 .75
DVS05020 Twilight Hunter, Artemis RRR .20 .40
DVS05021 Aias the Fortress RRR .75 1.50
DVS05022 Dragonic Overlord "The ?e-birth" RRR 7.50 15.00
DVS05023 Embodiment of Victory, Aleph RRR .30 .60
DVS05024 Dragon Monk, Goku RRR .30 .60
DVS05025 Dauntless Drive Dragon RRR .50 1.00
DVS05026 Break Breath Dragon RRR .50 1.00
DVS05027 Dragon Knight, Hishat RRR .75 1.50
DVS05028 Dragon Dancer, Nastasha RRR .75 1.50
DVS05029 Shikigami Master, Ryougi RRR .25 .50
DVS05030 Stealth Fiend, Fukun RRR .25 .50
DVS05031 Stealth Fiend, Taizan RRR .25 .50
DVS05032 Fantasy Petal Storm, Shirayuki RRR .25 .50
DVS05033 Stealth Fiend, Jakotsu Girl RRR .25 .50
DVS05034 Stealth Fiend, Rainy Madame RRR .25 .50
DVS05035 Covert Demonic Dragon, Kumadori Dope RRR .25 .50
DVS05036 Eradicator, Vowing Saber Dragon Reverse RRR 5.00 10.00
DVS05037 Eradicator, Sweep Command Dragon RRR 2.00 4.00
DVS05038 Armor Break Dragon RRR .30 .75
DVS05039 Eradicator, Dragonic Descendant RRR .30 .75
DVS05040 Lightning Whip Eradicator, Suheil RRR .25 .50
DVS05041 Eradicator, Spark Raze Dragon RRR .25 .50
DVS05042 Blitz Knuckle Dragon RRR .75 1.50
DVS05043 Dark Dimensional Robo, Reverse Daiyusha RRR .75 1.50
DVS05044 Enigman Storm RRR .25 .50
DVS05045 Metalborg, Mist Ghost RRR .25 .50
DVS05046 Super Dimensional Robo, Daizaurus RRR .30 .75
DVS05047 Dimensional Robo, Daidumper RRR .25 .50
DVS05048 Dimensional Robo, Daijacker RRR .25 .50
DVS05049 Ultimate Salvation Combination, Aidambulion RRR .25 .50
DVS05050 Juggernaut Maximum Maximum RRR .75 1.50
DVS05051 Sky Diver RRR .30 .75
DVS05052 Reckless Express RRR .30 .60
DVS05053 Juggernaut Maximum RRR .20 .40
DVS05054 Adorbs Perm, Rona RRR .20 .40
DVS05055 Powerback Renaldo RRR .20 .40
DVS05056 Precious Cheer Girl, Cameron RRR .30 .60
DVS05057 Sword Magician, Sarah RRR .20 .40
DVS05058 Pop Out Chimera RRR .20 .40
DVS05059 Engaging Assistant RRR .20 .40
DVS05060 Artilleryman RRR .20 .40
DVS05061 Miracle Pop, Eva RRR .20 .40
DVS05062 Tricky Assistant RRR .15 .30
DVS05063 Nightmare Doll, Lindy RRR .75 1.50
DVS05064 Duo Temptation, Reit RRR .75 1.50
DVS05065 Duo Mini Heart, Rhone RRR .75 1.50
DVS05066 Duo Pretty Horn, Ural RRR .75 1.50
DVS05067 Legendary PR?ISM-Duo, Nectaria RRR .15 .30
DVS05068 Noir Fixer, Hilda RRR .15 .30
DVS05069 Ingenuous, Mernil RRR .15 .30
DVS05070 Omnia Vincit Amor, Benedetta RRR 4.00 8.00
DVS05071 Thundering Ripple, Genovious RRR 1.25 2.50
DVS05072 Rising Ripple, Pavroth RRR .75 1.50
DVS05073 Silent Ripple, Sotirio RRR 1.00 2.00
DVS05074 Pursuit Assault RRR 3.00 6.00
DVS05075 Kelpie Rider, Denis RRR .30 .60
DVS05076 Battle Siren, Nerissa RRR 1.50 3.00
DVS05077 Escutcheo Bubble Dragon RRR .75 1.50
DVS05078 Evil Armor Sovereign, Uragiraffa Reverse RRR .50 1.00
DVS05079 Megacolony Battler S RRR .75 1.50
DVS05080 Megacolony Battler M RRR .25 .50
DVS05081 Pincer Attack Mutant, Intrude Scissors RRR .25 .50
DVS05082 Water Gang RRR .25 .50
DVS05083 Mutant Gentleman, High Class Moth RRR .25 .50
DVS05084 Faint Feather Mutant, Quinagria RRR .25 .50

2022 Cardfight Vanguard V Special Series 06 V Clan Collection Vol. 6

DVS06001 Circular Saw, Kiriel RRR .50 1.00
DVS06002 Ammunition Angel RRR .25 .50
DVS06003 Beriberi Beat Angel RRR .30 .75
DVS06004 Wild Shot Celestial, Raguel RRR .15 .30
DVS06005 Nurse of Holdheart RRR .15 .30
DVS06006 Cure Basket Angel RRR .20 .40
DVS06007 Transcendent Divider, Cassiel RRR .50 1.00
DVS06008 Revenger, Dragruler Phantom RRR .75 1.50
DVS06009 Origin Mage, Ildona RRR 10.00 20.00
DVS06010 Witch of Cursed Talisman, Etain RRR .30 .75
DVS06011 Mesmerizing Witch, Fianna RRR .20 .40
DVS06012 Witch of Reality, Femme RRR .25 .50
DVS06013 Cold-blooded Witch, Luba RRR .15 .30
DVS06014 Astral Chain Dragon RRR 2.00 4.00
DVS06015 Spectral Dupe Dragon Reverse RRR 2.50 5.00
DVS06016 Conviction Dragon, Chromejailer Dragon RRR .25 .50
DVS06017 Liberator, Holy Shine Dragon RRR 2.50 5.00

DVS06018 Spectral Duke Dragon RRR .30 .60
DVS06019 Black Dragon Knight, Vortimer RRR .30 .60
DVS06020 Scout of Darkness, Vortimer RRR .20 .40
DVS06021 Clarity Wing Dragon RRR .75 1.50
DVS06022 Evil Stealth Dragon, Magoroku ""Fugen"" RRR .30 .60
DVS06023 Evil Stealth Dragon, Kageugachi RRR .30 .75
DVS06024 Stealth Beast, Magami RRR .20 .40
DVS06025 Stealth Beast, Shishi Ressou RRR .15 .30
DVS06026 Evil Stealth Dragon, Gyokusen RRR .25 .50
DVS06027 Shura Stealth Dragon, Mumyocongo RRR .30 .60
DVS06028 Eradication Ancient Dragon, Spinodriver Reverse RRR1.25 2.50
DVS06029 Ancient Dragon, Tyrannolegend RRR .75 1.50
DVS06030 Ancient Dragon, Babyrex RRR .60 1.25
DVS06031 True Ancient Dragon, Aloneros RRR .20 .40
DVS06032 True Ancient Dragon, Heft Styraco RRR .25 .50
DVS06033 True Ancient Dragon, Pterafeed RRR .25 .50
DVS06034 Indomitable Dragon, Tenacitops RRR .30 .75
DVS06035 Strongest Beast Deity, Ethics Buster Extreme RRR .30 .75
DVS06036 War Deity, Asura Kaiser RRR .30 .75
DVS06037 Ultimate Lifeform, Cosmo Lord RRR .15 .30
DVS06038 Asura Kaiser RRR .15 .30
DVS06039 Beast Deity, Ethics Buster RRR .15 .30
DVS06040 Kick Kick Typhoon RRR .30 .75
DVS06041 Steel Fist Dragon, Frioul Dragon RRR .60 1.25
DVS06042 Star-vader, ""Omega"" Glendios RRR 1.25 2.50
DVS06043 Star-vader, Magnet Hollow RRR .50 1.00
DVS06044 Taboo Star-vader, Rubidium RRR .75 1.50
DVS06045 Star-vader, Worldline Dragon RRR .75 1.50
DVS06046 Bisection Star-vader, Zirconium RRR .50 1.00
DVS06047 Star-vader, Craving Claw RRR .50 1.00
DVS06048 Oblivion Quasar Dragon RRR .75 1.50
DVS06049 Demon Marquis, Amon Reverse RRR .30 .60
DVS06050 Amon's Follower, Soul Sucker RRR .30 .60
DVS06051 Amon's Follower, Atrocious Blow RRR .75 1.50
DVS06052 Number of Terror RRR .25 .50
DVS06053 Megarock Gigant RRR .20 .40
DVS06054 Yellow Bolt RRR .30 .60
DVS06055 Cuticle Defender, Flavia RRR .30 .75
DVS06056 Retroactive Time Maiden, Uluru RRR 2.50 5.00
DVS06057 Steam Maiden, Entarana RRR 2.50 5.00
DVS06058 Gear Cat Traveling with the Storm RRR 2.50 5.00
DVS06059 Chronojet Dragon RRR .60 1.25
DVS06060 Steam Performer, Kulm RRR .20 .40
DVS06061 Lost Gear Dog, Eight RRR 1.00 2.00
DVS06062 Time Tracking Dragon RRR .50 1.00
DVS06063 Grudgeful Spirit of the Seven Seas, Oguchi Voyage RRR.75 1.50
DVS06064 Seven Seas Sword King, Nighthaze RRR 1.50 3.00
DVS06065 King Serpent RRR .30 .60
DVS06066 Lord of the Seven Seas, Nightmist RRR .20 .40
DVS06067 Seven Seas Master Swordsman, Slash Shade RRR .20 .40
DVS06068 Sea Cruising Banshee RRR .75 1.50
DVS06069 School Punisher, Leo-pald Reverse RRR .50 1.00
DVS06070 Magic Scientist, Tester Fox RRR 1.25 2.50
DVS06071 Illusion Scientist, Researcher Fox RRR 1.25 2.50
DVS06072 Binoculus Tiger RRR .20 .40
DVS06073 Barcode Zebra RRR .20 .40
DVS06074 Monoculus Tiger RRR .20 .40
DVS06075 Gifted Dragon, Eikthlaera RRR .30 .75
DVS06076 Return of Eternity, Grajiorl Dragon RRR .30 .75
DVS06077 Eternal Stability, Grajiorl Dragon RRR .30 .75
DVS06078 Bud of Longevity, Grajiorl Dragon RRR .30 .75
DVS06079 Maiden of Fall Vine RRR .20 .40
DVS06080 Maiden of Flower Carpet RRR .25 .50
DVS06081 Pure-hearted Flower Maiden, Fiorenza RRR .75 1.50

2023 Cardfight Vanguard D Booster Set 08 Minerva Rising

DBT08001 Peak Personage Stealth Rogue, Shojodoji RRR 1.50 3.00
DBT08001 Peak Personage Stealth Rogue, Shojodoji FFR 20.00 40.00
DBT08002 Stealth Dragon, Unpreceden RRR 2.00 4.00
DBT08002 Stealth Dragon, Unpreceden FFR 15.00 30.00
DBT08003 Silver Thorn Dragon Tamer, Luquier RRR 4.00 8.00
DBT08003 Silver Thorn Dragon Tamer, Luquier FFR 30.00 75.00
DBT08003 Silver Thorn Dragon Tamer, Luquier SCR 4.00 8.00
DBT08004 Silver Thorn, Rising Dragon RRR 6.00 12.00
DBT08004 Silver Thorn, Rising Dragon FFR 75.00 150.00
DBT08005 Monster Creator, Arkhite RRR 4.00 8.00
DBT08005 Monster Creator, Arkhite FFR 50.00 100.00
DBT08006 Radio Wave Monster, Weibiros RRR 5.00 10.00
DBT08006 Radio Wave Monster, Weibiros FFR 40.00 80.00
DBT08007 Omniscience Regalia, Minerva RRR 10.00 20.00
DBT08007 Omniscience Regalia, Minerva FFR 75.00 150.00
DBT08007 Omniscience Regalia, Minerva SNR 1,000.00 2,000.00
DBT08008 Regalia of Wisdom, Angelica RRR 15.00 30.00
DBT08008 Regalia of Wisdom, Angelica FFR 60.00 125.00
DBT08009 Blue Storm Dragon, Maelstrom RRR 3.00 6.00
DBT08009 Blue Storm Dragon, Maelstrom FFR 30.00 75.00
DBT08009 Blue Storm Dragon, Maelstrom SCR 60.00 125.00
DBT08010 Tidal Assault RRR 1.50 3.00
DBT08010 Tidal Assault FFR 25.00 50.00
DBT08011 Undoubting Flame Sword, Radylina RRR 2.50 5.00
DBT08011 Undoubting Flame Sword, Radylina FFR 25.00 50.00
DBT08012 It's Showtime! Ririmi RRR 2.00 4.00
DBT08012 It's Showtime! Ririmi FFR 40.00 80.00
DBT08013 Ladies and Gentlemen! Rarami RRR 1.50 3.00
DBT08013 Ladies and Gentlemen! Rarami FFR 25.00 50.00
DBT08014 Go Ahead, Mikani RRR 20.00 40.00
DBT08014 Go Ahead, Mikani FFR 60.00 125.00
DBT08015 Greatsword of the Ferocious Black Flame, Obscudeid RRR6.0012.00
DBT08015 Greatsword of the Ferocious
Black Flame, Obscudeid FFR 75.00 150.00
DBT08016 Pink Moth Girl, Maple RRR 3.00 6.00
DBT08016 Pink Moth Girl, Maple FFR 30.00 75.00
DBT08017 Stealth Dragon, Jakumetsu Arcs RR .30 .60
DBT08017 Stealth Dragon, Jakumetsu Arcs FR 1.50 3.00
DBT08018 Staticrack Dragon RR .20 .40
DBT08018 Staticrack Dragon FR .30 .75
DBT08019 Scarlet of Fluttering Evanescent Life RR .30 .60
DBT08019 Scarlet of Fluttering Evanescent Life FR 1.50 3.00
DBT08020 Silver Thorn, Breathing Dragon RR .75 1.50
DBT08020 Silver Thorn, Breathing Dragon FR 1.25 2.50
DBT08021 Luxual Songster RR .25 .50
DBT08021 Luxual Songster FR .60 1.25
DBT08022 Song of Extolment Can Be Heard RR .30 .60
DBT08022 Song of Extolment Can Be Heard FR .50 1.00
DBT08023 Abend Robust RR 2.50 5.00
DBT08023 Abend Robust FR 4.00 8.00
DBT08024 Volcano Monster, Goukatera RR 1.25 2.50
DBT08024 Volcano Monster, Goukatera FR 2.50 5.00
DBT08025 The World is a Blue Research Lab RR 2.50 5.00
DBT08025 The World is a Blue Research Lab FR 4.00 8.00
DBT08026 Sword Saint Knight Dragon, Gramgrace RR 1.25 2.50
DBT08027 Witch of Ravens, Chamomile RR 5.00 10.00
DBT08027 Witch of Ravens, Chamomile FR 7.50 15.00
DBT08028 Turnaround Magic, Tanaluru RR 3.00 6.00
DBT08029 Dark Magenta of Blooming Hatred RR .30 .75
DBT08029 Dark Magenta of Blooming Hatred FR 2.00 4.00
DBT08030 Tear Knight, Emilios RR .20 .40
DBT08030 Tear Knight, Emilios FR .50 1.00
DBT08031 Wheel Assault RR .30 .75
DBT08031 Wheel Assault FR 2.50 5.00
DBT08032 To The Shining Stage! RR .30 .60
DBT08032 To The Shining Stage! FR 1.50 3.00
DBT08033 Gratias Gradale RR 12.50 25.00
DBT08034 Explosive Dragon, Cramstego R .15 .30
DBT08034 Explosive Dragon, Cramstego FR .50 1.00
DBT08035 Sublime Lance Dragon R .15 .30
DBT08035 Sublime Lance Dragon FR .30 .60
DBT08036 Spear Knight of Tinkling Scales, Rimuzveet R .15 .30
DBT08036 Spear Knight of Tinkling Scales, Rimuzveet FR .20 .40
DBT08037 Stealth Fiend, Koumaaun R .15 .30
DBT08037 Stealth Fiend, Koumaaun FR 1.50 3.00
DBT08038 Silver Thorn Marionette, Lilian R .15 .30
DBT08038 Silver Thorn Marionette, Lilian FR 1.50 3.00
DBT08039 Diverse Wildmaster, Onolatio R .15 .30
DBT08039 Diverse Wildmaster, Onolatio FR .30 .75
DBT08040 Brick Guardner R .15 .30
DBT08040 Brick Guardner FR .30 .75
DBT08041 Hurry and Join, Silver Thorn Servants R .15 .30
DBT08041 Hurry and Join, Silver Thorn Servants FR 3.00 6.00
DBT08042 One Who Peruses the Proto Galaxy R .15 .30
DBT08042 One Who Peruses the Proto Galaxy FR .50 1.00
DBT08043 Strahl Windhose R .15 .30
DBT08043 Strahl Windhose FR .50 1.00
DBT08044 Tornado Monster, Cycloguarde R .15 .30
DBT08044 Tornado Monster, Cycloguarde FR 2.00 4.00
DBT08045 Torrent Energy Research R .15 .30
DBT08045 Torrent Energy Research FR 4.00 8.00
DBT08046 Knight of Disruption, Diarin FR 5.00 10.00
DBT08046 Knight of Disruption, Diarin R .15 .30
DBT08047 Knight of Hammer Breaking, Sadie R .15 .30
DBT08047 Knight of Hammer Breaking, Sadie FR 1.25 2.50
DBT08048 Universal Angel R .15 .30
DBT08048 Universal Angel FR .30 .60
DBT08049 Wisdom of the Beginning to Open the World R .15 .30
DBT08049 Wisdom of the Beginning to Open the World FR 2.50 5.00
DBT08050 Shoreline Rays Dragon R .15 .30
DBT08050 Shoreline Rays Dragon FR .75 1.50
DBT08051 Ripening Dragon R .15 .30
DBT08051 Ripening Dragon FR .30 .75
DBT08052 Titan of the Azure Wave Cruise R .15 .30
DBT08052 Titan of the Azure Wave Cruise FR .30 .75
DBT08053 Judgement Maelstrom R .15 .30
DBT08053 Judgement Maelstrom FR 4.00 8.00
DBT08054 Thunderclap Dragon C .07 .15
DBT08055 World-shaper Stealth Rogue, Shojodoji C .07 .15
DBT08056 Lightning Bullet of Dust Storm, Sadiid C .07 .15
DBT08057 Vulkaan Golem C .07 .15
DBT08058 Sakura Romance Stealth Rogue, Shojodoji C .07 .15
DBT08059 Heat Breath Wyvern C .07 .15
DBT08060 Can't Quit Sake Stealth Rogue, Shojodoji C .07 .15
DBT08061 Return to Afterlife C .07 .15
DBT08062 Circulate Acrobat, Urseltje C .07 .15
DBT08063 Record Break Dragon C .07 .15
DBT08064 Enmities Dragon C .07 .15
DBT08065 Trapeze Actress C .07 .15
DBT08066 Abrupt Reaver C .07 .15
DBT08067 Silver Thorn Assistant, Irina C .07 .15
DBT08068 Dimness Fiend C .07 .15
DBT08069 Silver Thorn Assistant, Ionela C .07 .15
DBT08070 Hadron Axe Dragon C .07 .15
DBT08071 Guardian of the Slumbering, Arkhite C .07 .15
DBT08072 Fist Cannon Dragon, Dimetoria Dragon C .07 .15
DBT08073 High Flight Conversion, Silberkes C .07 .15
DBT08074 Itinerant Automaton C .07 .15
DBT08075 Monster Soul-searching, Arkhite C .07 .15
DBT08076 Cerulean Heavy Gunner C .07 .15
DBT08077 Short Rest, Arkhite C .07 .15
DBT08078 Coexistence Dragon C .07 .15
DBT08079 Relentless Dragon C .07 .15
DBT08080 Knight of Harrowing Fear, Dubthach C .07 .15
DBT08081 Witch of Frogs, Melissa C .20 .40
DBT08082 Magic of Refinement, Fufupuri C .07 .15
DBT08083 Marmors Ehre C .07 .15
DBT08084 Apple Witch, Cider C .07 .15
DBT08085 Vivid Rabbit C .07 .15
DBT08086 Full Blown Dragon C .07 .15
DBT08087 Marine General of the Whirling Wave, Leftelis C .07 .15
DBT08088 Tsunami Brave Shooter C .07 .15
DBT08089 Marine General of the Restless Tides, Algos C .07 .15
DBT08090 Signpost Fairy C .20 .40
DBT08091 Tear Knight, Theo C .07 .15
DBT08092 Fierce Attack Brave Shooter C .07 .15
DBT08093 Officer Cadet, Erikk C .07 .15
DBT08094 Looming Demise C .07 .15
DBT08095 Minacious Metamorphosis C .07 .15
DBT08096 The Start of the End C .07 .15

2023 Cardfight Vanguard D Booster Set 10 Dragon Masquerade

DBT10001 Scarlet Flame Marshal Dragon, Gandiva RRR 12.50 25.00
DBT10001 Scarlet Flame Marshal Dragon, Gandiva FFR 75.00 150.00
DBT10002 Great Flame Axe of Magnificent Scales, Calgafran RRR3.00 6.00
DBT10002 Great Flame Axe of Magnificent Scales, Calgafran FFR25.00 50.00
DBT10003 Mirror Reflection Equip, Mirrors Vairina RRR 1.50 3.00
DBT10003 Mirror Reflection Equip, Mirrors Vairina FFR 50.00 100.00
DBT10003 Mirror Reflection Equip, Mirrors Vairina SEC 75.00 150.00
DBT10004 Karmic Demonic Jewel Dragon, Drajeweled Masques RRR1.00 2.00
DBT10004 Karmic Demonic Jewel Dragon,
Drajeweled Masques FFR 25.00 50.00
DBT10004 Karmic Demonic Jewel Dragon,
Drajeweled Masques SEC 150.00 300.00
DBT10005 Xeno Almajestar, Astroea?Bico Masques RRR .75 1.50
DBT10005 Xeno Almajestar, Astroea?Bico Masques FFR 20.00 40.00
DBT10005 Xeno Almajestar, Astroea?Bico Masques SEC 125.00 250.00
DBT10006 Black Sky Thunder Quaking Queen, Leimina RRR 4.00 8.00
DBT10006 Black Sky Thunder Quaking Queen, Leimina FFR 30.00 60.00
DBT10007 Aurora Battle Princess, Penetrate Aquas RRR .50 1.00
DBT10007 Aurora Battle Princess, Penetrate Aquas FFR 25.00 50.00
DBT10008 Sickle Blade of Investigation, Habitable Zone RRR 7.50 15.00
DBT10008 Sickle Blade of Investigation, Habitable Zone FFR 50.00 100.00
DBT10009 Blue Deathster, Hanada Halfway RRR 2.00 4.00
DBT10009 Blue Deathster, Hanada Halfway FFR 30.00 60.00
DBT10010 Great Sage of Heavenly Law, Solrairon RRR .50 1.00
DBT10010 Great Sage of Heavenly Law, Solrairon FFR 20.00 40.00
DBT10011 Hexaorb Sorceress ""Aquamarine"" RRR 1.50 3.00
DBT10011 Hexaorb Sorceress ""Aquamarine"" FFR 30.00 75.00
DBT10012 Spiral Cutie Angel RRR 15.00 30.00
DBT10012 Spiral Cutie Angel FFR 75.00 150.00
DBT10013 Teasing Spiritualist, Zorga Masques RRR 1.25 2.50
DBT10013 Teasing Spiritualist, Zorga Masques FFR 30.00 75.00
DBT10013 Teasing Spiritualist, Zorga Masques SEC 200.00 400.00
DBT10014 Servitude of Funeral Procession, Lianorn Masques RRR.75 1.50
DBT10014 Servitude of Funeral Procession, Lianorn Masques FFR30.00 60.00
DBT10014 Servitude of Funeral Procession,
Lianorn Masques SEC 125.00 250.00
DBT10015 Love-binding Maiden, Margaret RRR 2.00 4.00
DBT10015 Love-binding Maiden, Margaret FFR 20.00 40.00
DBT10016 Signature Bullet of Dust Storm, Baxter RR .30 .60
DBT10016 Signature Bullet of Dust Storm, Baxter FR .50 1.00
DBT10017 Dragritter, Alfakar RR 2.50 5.00
DBT10017 Dragritter, Alfakar FR 6.00 12.00
DBT10018 Swordsman of Crimson Scales, Barnaia RR .75 1.50
DBT10018 Swordsman of Crimson Scales, Barnaia FR 2.00 4.00
DBT10019 Illuminate Equip Dragon, Graillumirror RR .30 .75
DBT10019 Illuminate Equip Dragon, Graillumirror FR 1.00 2.00
DBT10020 Diabolos Heavy Launcher, Patrick RR .30 .60
DBT10020 Diabolos Heavy Launcher, Patrick FR 1.25 2.50
DBT10021 Desire Devil, Fuujo RR .20 .40
DBT10021 Desire Devil, Fuujo FR .50 1.00
DBT10022 Dragontree Wretch, Skull Chemdah RR 7.50 15.00
DBT10022 Dragontree Wretch, Skull Chemdah FR 12.50 25.00
DBT10023 Twin Marvel Dragon RR .60 1.25
DBT10023 Twin Marvel Dragon FR 1.50 3.00
DBT10024 Solide Sturmer RR .30 .60
DBT10024 Solide Sturmer FR 1.00 2.00
DBT10025 Aurora Battle Princess, Grenade Marida RR .30 .60
DBT10025 Aurora Battle Princess, Grenade Marida FR .50 1.00
DBT10026 Hotmelt Monster, Radiabirio RR .30 .60
DBT10026 Hotmelt Monster, Radiabirio FR .30 .60
DBT10027 Cardinal Principal, Lorfield RR .30 .60
DBT10027 Cardinal Principal, Lorfield FR .30 .75
DBT10028 Dependable Pierce Dragon RR .30 .60
DBT10028 Dependable Pierce Dragon FR 1.50 3.00
DBT10029 Effulgent Wizard RR .30 .60
DBT10029 Effulgent Wizard FR 2.50 5.00
DBT10030 Sacrosanct Dragon RR .30 .60
DBT10030 Sacrosanct Dragon FR 1.00 2.00
DBT10031 Replenishment Angel RR .75 1.50
DBT10031 Replenishment Angel FR 1.50 3.00
DBT10032 Dragontree Wretch, Depth Iweleth RR 7.50 15.00
DBT10032 Dragontree Wretch, Depth Iweleth FR 12.50 25.00
DBT10033 Keel Severing RR .30 .60
DBT10033 Keel Severing FR 1.25 2.50
DBT10034 Knight of Amity, Roderick RR .30 .60
DBT10034 Knight of Amity, Roderick FR .30 .60
DBT10035 Spouting Intimacy, Amlia RR .30 .60
DBT10035 Spouting Intimacy, Amlia FR .50 1.00
DBT10036 Masque of Hydragrum RR 12.50 25.00
DBT10036 Masque of Hydragrum FR 20.00 40.00
DBT10037 Wilderness Dragon R .15 .30
DBT10037 Wilderness Dragon FR .50 1.00
DBT10038 Scarlet Flame Bow General, Rugeunt R .15 .30
DBT10038 Scarlet Flame Bow General, Rugeunt FR 2.50 5.00
DBT10039 Blaze Maiden, Hanife R .15 .30
DBT10039 Blaze Maiden, Hanife FR .30 .60
DBT10040 Scarlet Flame Bows of Demolition R .15 .30
DBT10040 Scarlet Flame Bows of Demolition FR .30 .75
DBT10041 Cranium Burner R .15 .30
DBT10041 Cranium Burner FR .75 1.50
DBT10042 Awkward Ravager R .15 .30
DBT10042 Awkward Ravager FR .25 .50
DBT10043 Desire Devil, Guhtaran R .15 .30
DBT10043 Desire Devil, Guhtaran FR .25 .50
DBT10044 Cage of Evil Stars R .15 .30
DBT10044 Cage of Evil Stars FR .30 .75
DBT10045 Thundering Fist Dragon, Jayrom Dragon R .15 .30
DBT10045 Thundering Fist Dragon, Jayrom Dragon FR .25 .50
DBT10046 Blue Deathster, Req Gewehnr R .15 .30
DBT10046 Blue Deathster, Req Gewehnr FR .75 1.50
DBT10047 Putzen Schwestern, Weepl R .15 .30
DBT10047 Putzen Schwestern, Weepl FR .75 1.50
DBT10048 Dispatch! Three Sisters of Cleaning! R .15 .30
DBT10048 Dispatch! Three Sisters of Cleaning! FR 1.25 2.50
DBT10049 Academic of Demonstration, Pyrrhic R .15 .30
DBT10049 Academic of Demonstration, Pyrrhic FR .60 1.25
DBT10050 Truncate Breath Dragon R .15 .30
DBT10050 Truncate Breath Dragon FR .75 1.50
DBT10051 Magic of Water Droplets, Utatalu R .15 .30
DBT10051 Magic of Water Droplets, Utatalu FR .30 .75
DBT10052 Trumpet of Blessing R .15 .30
DBT10052 Trumpet of Blessing FR .50 1.00
DBT10053 Sylvan Horned Beast, Labarth R .15 .30
DBT10053 Sylvan Horned Beast, Labarth FR .25 .50
DBT10054 Surging Sharp Fang R .15 .30
DBT10054 Surging Sharp Fang FR .30 .75
DBT10055 Champion of Oblivion R .15 .30
DBT10055 Champion of Oblivion FR .30 .60
DBT10056 Rousing Rasp R .15 .30
DBT10056 Rousing Rasp FR .30 .75
DBT10057 Thirstray Dragon C .07 .15
DBT10058 Equip Scrape Dragon, Drilyze C .07 .15
DBT10059 Scarlet Flame Bow General, Stirguna C .07 .15
DBT10060 Scarlet Flame Bow General, Dipanel C .07 .15
DBT10061 Strenuous Bomber Dragon C .07 .15
DBT10062 Scarlet Flame Bow Soldier, Agiredo C .07 .15
DBT10063 Scarlet Flame Bow Soldier, Bausen C .07 .15
DBT10064 Scarlet Flame Recruit, Barkish C .07 .15
DBT10065 Outstanding Demonic Swordsman, Zaleos C .07 .15
DBT10066 Steam Performer, Du-du C .07 .15
DBT10067 Steam Hunter, Zuqaqip C .07 .15
DBT10068 Brawlfeld Hydra C .07 .15
DBT10069 Giffords Ketos C .07 .15
DBT10070 Steam Launcher, Yasmah C .07 .15
DBT10071 Spooky Chirpy C .07 .15
DBT10072 Diabolos Girls, Heidi C .07 .15
DBT10073 Wohlheimer Dragon C .07 .15
DBT10074 Cardinal Noid, Grunder C .07 .15
DBT10075 Threat Fugenegator C .07 .15
DBT10076 Flight Robo, Erial Hayley C .07 .15
DBT10077 SeRVe 9-G C .07 .15
DBT10078 Putzen Schwestern, Bruush C .07 .15
DBT10079 Putzen Schwestern, Mopy C .07 .15
DBT10080 Guidance Monster, Trafficon C .07 .15
DBT10081 Euradistic Dragon C .07 .15
DBT10082 Sage of Robust, Stogron C .07 .15
DBT10083 Incisive Crow C .07 .15
DBT10084 Intriguing Academic, Intieres C .07 .15
DBT10085 Academic of Order, Olderio C .07 .15
DBT10086 Balmy Violinist C .07 .15
DBT10087 Sage of Elixir, Eliron C .07 .15
DBT10088 Sage of Horoscopy, Sron C .07 .15
DBT10089 Ascertain Dragon C .07 .15
DBT10090 Screwbullet Dragon C .07 .15
DBT10091 Sea Demon of Gluttony C .07 .15
DBT10092 Sylvan Horned Beast, Colmus C .07 .15
DBT10093 Spry Cactus C .07 .15
DBT10094 Rotating Compass C .07 .15
DBT10095 Citrusan C .07 .15
DBT10096 Deathly Silence Hunter, Lepardia C .07 .15

2023 Cardfight Vanguard D Booster Set 10 Dragon Masquerade Edition Exclusives

DBT10EX01EN Where Sakura Dance, Sakura Miko 2.00 4.00
DBT10EX02EN Elite Miko Vtuber, Sakura Miko .75 1.50
DBT10EX03EN Idol VTuber, Hoshimachi Suisei 1.00 2.00
DBT10EX04EN To Her Dream Stage, Hoshimachi Suisei 2.00 4.00
DBT10EX05EN Under a Starry Sky of Dancing Sakura, miComet .30 .75

2023 Cardfight Vanguard D Special Series 04 Stride Deckset Messiah

DSS04001EN Alter Ego Messiah	.75	1.50
DSS04001ENR Alter Ego Messiah TDR	1.50	3.00
DSS04002EN Awaking Messiah	.75	1.50
DSS04002ENR Awaking Messiah TDR	.75	1.50
DSS04003EN Asleep Messiah	15.00	30.00
DSS04004EN Neon Messiah	.75	1.50
DSS04005EN Astrolabe Dragon	.75	1.50
DSS04005ENR Astrolabe Dragon TDR	.75	1.50
DSS04006EN Kaluzar Klein	.60	1.25
DSS04006ENR Kaluzar Klein TDR	.75	1.50
DSS04007EN Arrester Messiah	.50	1.00
DSS04007ENR Arrester Messiah TDR	1.50	3.00
DSS04008EN Flowers in Vacuum, Cosmo Wreath	1.25	2.50
DSS04008ENR Flowers in Vacuum, Cosmo Wreath TDR	5.00	10.00
DSS04009EN Destiny Dealer	.60	1.25
DSS04009ENR Destiny Dealer TDR	1.25	2.50
DSS04010EN Sacrifice Messiah	.60	1.25
DSS04010ENR Sacrifice Messiah TDR	.60	1.50
DSS04011EN Herbig Claw	.60	1.25
DSS04011ENR Herbig Claw TDR	.60	1.25
DSS04012EN Star Dragon Deity of Infinitude, Eldobreath	4.00	8.00
DSS04013EN Star Agression Dragon	.50	1.00
DSS04014EN Aberrant Gleam Dragon	.25	.50
DSS04015EN Transforming Heavy Machinery, Heavy Constalion	.30	.75
DSS04016EN Alter Rate Sphere Dragon	.30	.75
DSS04017EN Genesis Dragon, Excelics Messiah	1.25	2.50
DSS04017ENR Genesis Dragon, Excelics Messiah TDR	2.50	5.00
DSS04018EN Genesis Dragon, Amnesty Messiah	1.25	2.50
DSS04018ENR Genesis Dragon, Amnesty Messiah TDR	2.50	5.00
DSS04019EN Alter Ego Messiah Crest Token	.60	1.25
DSS04019ENR Alter Ego Messiah Crest Token FOIL	7.50	15.00

2023 Cardfight Vanguard Dragontree Invasion

DBT09001EN Sealed Blaze Dragon, Kaankshati RRR	2.50	5.00
DBT09002EN Strike Equip Dragon, Stragallio RRR	3.00	6.00
DBT09003EN Dragontree Wretch, Draco Batical RRR	.75	1.50
DBT09004EN Almajestar, Astroea=Unica RRR	7.50	15.00
DBT09005EN Diabolos, "Viamance" Bruce RRR	6.00	12.00
DBT09006EN Dragontree Wretch, Demon Sheridder RRR	2.00	4.00
DBT09007EN Blue Deathster, "Skyrender" Avantgarda RRR	5.00	10.00
DBT09008EN Operate Master, Freiheit RRR	10.00	20.00
DBT09009EN Dragontree Wretch, Lloyd Akzeriyuth RRR	2.50	5.00
DBT09010EN Brave On Sky-trimmer, Rondahlia RRR	3.00	6.00
DBT09011EN Knight of Plowing, Dolbraig RRR	1.50	3.00
DBT09012EN Dragontree Wretch, Solda Saakab RRR	4.00	8.00
DBT09013EN Lavien Lord, Granfia RRR	2.00	4.00
DBT09014EN Sylvan Horned Beast, Goildoat RRR	.75	1.50
DBT09015EN Dragontree Wretch, Bist Aiyatvas RRR	7.50	15.00
DBT09016EN Dragontree of Ecliptic Decimation, Griphogila RRR	4.00	8.00
DBT09017EN Hunting Gatling of Dust Storm, Firas RR	.20	.40
DBT09018EN Pierce Equip Dragon, Halbados RR	.20	.40
DBT09019EN Desolate Spark Dragon RR	.20	.40
DBT09020EN Seal-break Dragon RR	.20	.40
DBT09021EN Kitz Peak Griffin RR	1.00	2.00
DBT09022EN Clean-sweep Dragon RR	3.00	6.00
DBT09023EN Azul Wild Flame, Frenadio RR	.20	.40
DBT09024EN Diabolos Knuckler, Jamil RR	.75	1.50
DBT09025EN Eahalten Vogel RR	.75	1.50
DBT09026EN Enlightened Age Dragon RR	.75	1.50
DBT09027EN Galactic B-Hero, Bold Salos RR	.30	.75
DBT09028EN Gravidia Claxton RR	.20	.40
DBT09029EN Decisive Heavenly Axe, Delibere RR	.30	.75
DBT09030EN Gloria Storm Dragon RR	.20	.40
DBT09031EN Resentments Dragon RR	.20	.40
DBT09032EN Knight of Vanquish Bow, Sfilt RR	.20	.40
DBT09033EN Sylvan Horned Beast, Winnsapooh RR	.20	.40
DBT09034EN Tide Line Dragon RR	2.00	4.00
DBT09035EN Ranran Orangerine RR	.50	1.00
DBT09036EN Tear Knight, Erianthe RR	.20	.40
DBT09037EN Green-scaled Flame Knight, Statol R	.15	.30
DBT09038EN Winged Dragon, Pursueptera R	.15	.30
DBT09039EN Stealth Fiend, Temarihime R	.20	.40
DBT09040EN Clad in Prayer R	.20	.40
DBT09041EN Self-aware Spring Source, Uaqua R	.15	.30
DBT09042EN Steam Scara, Zargon R	.75	1.50
DBT09043EN Direful Doll, Charmaine R	.15	.30
DBT09044EN Prison-luring Lamp R	.15	.30
DBT09045EN Lady Fencer of Quantum Regression R	.15	.30
DBT09046EN One Who Pierces Transient Causality R	.15	.30
DBT09047EN Assault Flight Carrier, Lubetzal R	.15	.30
DBT09048EN Disruption Strategy: Killshroud R	.15	.30
DBT09049EN Crystallize Dragon R	.15	.30
DBT09050EN Magic of Auspicious Signs, Tataril R	.15	.30
DBT09051EN Affectionate Harp Angel R	.15	.30
DBT09052EN Renowned Phalanx R	.15	.30
DBT09053EN Farmin' Pumpkin R	.50	1.00
DBT09054EN Burrow Mushrooms R	.75	1.50
DBT09055EN Narcissus Noble, Neeltje R	.20	.40
DBT09056EN Prolific Oranges R	.15	.30
DBT09057EN Stalwart Lance Dragon C	.07	.15
DBT09058EN Saw Equip Dragon, Chainzown C	.07	.15
DBT09059EN Sealed Blaze Dragon, Anugam C	.07	.15
DBT09060EN Hopping Bullet of Dust Storm, Hanady C	.07	.15
DBT09061EN Blaze Maiden, Addison C	.07	.15
DBT09062EN Mace Equip Dragon, Mazenalba C	.07	.15
DBT09063EN Stealth Dragon, Raspear C	.07	.15
DBT09064EN Blaze Maiden, Madison C	.07	.15
DBT09065EN Diabolos Striker, Greg C	.07	.15
DBT09066EN Rollnick Cerberus C	.07	.15
DBT09067EN Almajestar, Turan=Dyna C	.07	.15
DBT09068EN Byurakan Manticore C	.07	.15
DBT09069EN Airam Capricornus C	.07	.15
DBT09070EN Almajestar, Schwart=Sparda C	.07	.15
DBT09071EN Diabolos Girls, Trish C	.07	.15
DBT09072EN Almajestar, Pypis=Mulchie C	.07	.15
DBT09073EN Gravidia Gaoguenie C	.07	.15
DBT09074EN Blue Deathster, Sachsen Ausfuhl C	.07	.15
DBT09075EN Blue Deathster, "Heavenly Death Ray" Stelvane C	.07	.15
DBT09076EN Blue Deathster, "Dark Verdict" Findanis C	.07	.15
DBT09077EN Blue Deathster, Ruri Turning C	.07	.15
DBT09078EN Blue Deathster, Sora Period C	.07	.15
DBT09079EN Shock Strategy: Death Winds C	.07	.15
DBT09080EN Bomber Strategy: Dusting C	.07	.15
DBT09081EN Divine Sister, Amaretti C	.07	.15
DBT09082EN Destruction Dragon, Dirgeroar Dragon C	.07	.15
DBT09083EN Reverence Rush Dragon C	.07	.15
DBT09084EN Divine Sister, Cassatella C	.07	.15
DBT09085EN Cut-off Angel C	.07	.15
DBT09086EN Knight of Asepsis, Legeita C	.07	.15
DBT09087EN Knight of Heavenly Signs, Wefliese C	.07	.15
DBT09088EN Divine Sister, Spumone C	.07	.15
DBT09089EN Burst Peas C	.07	.15
DBT09090EN Burly Axe Beetle C	.07	.15
DBT09091EN Bulky Saw Stag C	.07	.15
DBT09092EN Genius Wise Wolf, Granfia C	.07	.15
DBT09093EN Sylvan Horned Beast, Lesserai C	.07	.15
DBT09094EN Future Suzerain, Granfia C	.07	.15
DBT09095EN Mouldy Shooter C	.07	.15
DBT09096EN Kind Lordling, Granfia C	.07	.15
DBT09097EN Griphosid C	.07	.15
DBT09098EN Looming Demise C	.07	.15
DBT09099EN Minacious Metamorphosis C	.07	.15
DBT09100EN The Start of the End C	.07	.15
DBT09DSR01EN Diabolos, "Viamance" Bruce DSR	75.00	150.00
DBT09DSR02EN Dragontree of Ecliptic Decimation, Griphogila DSR	60.00	125.00
DBT09FFR01EN Sealed Blaze Dragon, Kaankshati FFR	25.00	50.00
DBT09FFR02EN Strike Equip Dragon, Stragallio FFR	20.00	40.00
DBT09FFR03EN Dragontree Wretch, Draco Batical FFR	15.00	30.00
DBT09FFR04EN Almajestar, Astroea=Unica FFR	75.00	150.00
DBT09FFR05EN Diabolos, "Viamance" Bruce FFR	30.00	60.00
DBT09FFR06EN Dragontree Wretch, Demon Sheridder FFR	7.50	15.00
DBT09FFR07EN Blue Deathster, "Skyrender" Avantgarda FFR	60.00	125.00
DBT09FFR08EN Operate Master, Freiheit FFR	75.00	150.00
DBT09FFR09EN Dragontree Wretch, Lloyd Akzeriyuth FFR	25.00	50.00
DBT09FFR10EN Brave On Sky-trimmer, Rondahlia FFR	25.00	50.00
DBT09FFR11EN Knight of Plowing, Dolbraig FFR	40.00	80.00
DBT09FFR12EN Dragontree Wretch, Solda Saakab FFR	15.00	30.00
DBT09FFR13EN Lavien Lord, Granfia FFR	30.00	60.00
DBT09FFR14EN Sylvan Horned Beast, Goildoat FFR	20.00	40.00
DBT09FFR15EN Dragontree Wretch, Bist Aiyatvas FFR	25.00	50.00
DBT09FFR16EN Dragontree of Ecliptic Decimation, Griphogila FFR	25.00	50.00
DBT09FR01EN Hunting Gatling of Dust Storm, Firas FR	.25	.50
DBT09FR02EN Pierce Equip Dragon, Halbados FR	.30	.75
DBT09FR03EN Desolate Spark Dragon FR	.50	1.00
DBT09FR04EN Seal-break Dragon FR	.30	.60
DBT09FR05EN Green-scaled Flame Knight, Statol FR	.30	.60
DBT09FR06EN Winged Dragon, Pursueptera FR	.25	.50
DBT09FR07EN Stealth Fiend, Temarihime FR	1.00	2.00
DBT09FR08EN Clad in Prayer FR	1.00	2.00
DBT09FR09EN Kitz Peak Griffin FR	2.50	5.00
DBT09FR10EN Clean-sweep Dragon FR	4.00	8.00
DBT09FR11EN Azul Wild Flame, Frenadio FR	.30	.60
DBT09FR12EN Diabolos Knuckler, Jamil FR	.75	1.50
DBT09FR13EN Self-aware Spring Source, Uaqua FR	.30	.60
DBT09FR14EN Steam Scara, Zargon FR	6.00	12.00
DBT09FR15EN Direful Doll, Charmaine FR	1.50	3.00
DBT09FR16EN Prison-luring Lamp FR	.25	.50
DBT09FR17EN Eahalten Vogel FR	2.50	5.00
DBT09FR18EN Enlightened Age Dragon FR	2.00	4.00
DBT09FR19EN Galactic B-Hero, Bold Salos FR	1.00	2.00
DBT09FR20EN Gravidia Claxton FR	.30	.75
DBT09FR21EN Lady Fencer of Quantum Regression FR	.30	.60
DBT09FR22EN One Who Pierces Transient Causality FR	2.00	4.00
DBT09FR23EN Assault Flight Carrier, Lubetzal FR	2.00	4.00
DBT09FR24EN Disruption Strategy: Killshroud FR	1.25	2.50
DBT09FR25EN Decisive Heavenly Axe, Delibere FR	.75	1.50
DBT09FR26EN Gloria Storm Dragon FR	.60	1.25
DBT09FR27EN Resentments Dragon FR	.40	.80
DBT09FR28EN Knight of Vanquish Bow, Sfilt FR	.75	1.50
DBT09FR29EN Crystallize Dragon FR	.25	.50
DBT09FR30EN Magic of Auspicious Signs, Tataril FR	.50	1.00
DBT09FR31EN Affectionate Harp Angel FR	2.00	4.00
DBT09FR32EN Renowned Phalanx FR	.25	.50
DBT09FR33EN Sylvan Horned Beast, Winnsapooh FR	.40	.80
DBT09FR34EN Tide Line Dragon FR	3.00	6.00
DBT09FR35EN Ranran Orangerine FR	1.50	3.00
DBT09FR36EN Tear Knight, Erianthe FR	.30	.75
DBT09FR37EN Farmin' Pumpkin FR	4.00	8.00
DBT09FR38EN Burrow Mushrooms FR	6.00	12.00
DBT09FR39EN Narcissus Noble, Neeltje FR	.75	1.50
DBT09FR40EN Prolific Oranges FR	.50	1.00
DBT09Re01EN Stealth Dragon, Togachirashi RE	.30	.60
DBT09Re02EN Diabolos Madonna, Meagan RE	.75	1.50
DBT09Re03EN Detonation Monster, Bobalmine RE	3.00	6.00
DBT09Re04EN Painkiller Angel RE	1.25	2.50
DBT09Re05EN Spurring Maiden, Ellenia RE	.30	.60
DBT09Re06EN Trickmoon RE	6.00	12.00
DBT09Re07EN Brainwash Swirler RE	20.00	40.00
DBT09Re08EN Cardinal Draco, Masurea RE	.25	.50
DBT09Re09EN Heavenly Pike of Solicitation, Cornvoc RE	.25	.50
DBT09Re10EN Blue Artillery Dragon, Inlet Pulse Dragon RE	12.50	25.00

2023 Cardfight Vanguard Special Series 10 Premium Battle Deckset 2023

VSS10001EN Masquerade Master, Harri	.30	.60
VSS10002EN Curtain Call Announcer, Mephisto	.50	1.00
VSS10003EN Dragon Masquerade, Harri	1.50	3.00
VSS10004EN Dreamiy Axel, Milward	1.00	2.00
VSS10005EN Fancy Megatrick, Darklord Princess	12.50	25.00
VSS10006EN Midair Megatrick, Yvette	3.00	6.00
VSS10007EN Trenchant Megatrick, Leontina	.75	1.50
VSS10008EN Jester Demonic Beast, Flection Chimera	1.00	2.00
VSS10009EN Jester Demonic Dragon, Wandering Dragon	2.00	4.00
VSS10010EN Kinesis Megatrick, Coulthard	.30	.60
VSS10011EN Masked Magician, Harri	.75	1.50
VSS10012EN Starry Pop Dragon	.20	.40
VSS10013EN Tricky Assistant	.20	.40
VSS10014EN Lore Pigeon, Pop	.30	.75
VSS10015EN Magia Doll, Lunatec Dragon	.30	.60
VSS10016EN Crescent Moon Juggler	.50	1.00
VSS10017EN Dancing Princess of the Night Sky	1.50	3.00
VSS10018EN Magia Doll, Cutie Paratrooper	.30	.75
VSS10019EN Magia Doll, Darkside Mirror Master	.30	.75
VSS10020EN Magia Doll, Flying Peryton	.30	.60
VSS10021EN Masquerade Bunny	.25	.50
VSS10022EN Purple Trapezist	.30	.60
VSS10023EN Happiness Collector	.30	.75
VSS10024EN Hades Dragon Deity of Resentment, Gallmageheld	1.50	3.00
VSS10025EN Nightmare Doll, Lindy	.30	.75
VSS10026EN Hades Hypnotist	1.00	2.00
VSS10027EN Convert Bunny	.50	1.00
VSS10028EN Prankster Girl of Mirrorland	.30	.75
VSS10029EN Pirate King of the Roseate Twilight, Nightrose	1.00	2.00
VSS10030EN Eclipse Dragonhulk, Jumble Dragon	.30	.75
VSS10031EN Ghostie Great Emperor, Big Obadiah	.30	.60
VSS10032EN Ghostie Great King, Obadiah	1.00	2.00
VSS10033EN Mist Phantasm Pirate King, Nightrose	1.50	3.00
VSS10034EN Pirate King of Everlasting Darkness, Bartholomew	1.25	2.50
VSS10035EN Wight Legion Sailing Ship, Bad Bounty	6.00	12.00
VSS10036EN Diabolist of Solicitation, Negronora	4.00	8.00
VSS10037EN Diabolist Princess Singing Under the Moonlight, Oriana	.60	1.25
VSS10038EN Great Witch Doctor of Banquets, Negrolily	.25	.50
VSS10039EN Vampire Princess of Night Fog, Nightrose	3.00	6.00
VSS10040EN Dragon Undead, Skull Dragon	.30	.75
VSS10041EN Ghostie Leader, Beatrice	3.00	6.00
VSS10042EN Mighty Rogue, Nightstorm	.25	.50
VSS10043EN Greed Shade	1.00	2.00
VSS10044EN Pirate Swordsman, Colombard	.30	.60
VSS10045EN Stormride Ghost Ship	.30	.60
VSS10046EN Skeleton Cannoneer	.20	.60
VSS10047EN Sea Strolling Banshee	.20	.60
VSS10048EN Witch Doctor of Powdered Bone, Negrobone	.25	.50
VSS10049EN Dancing Cutlass	.30	.60
VSS10050EN Tommy the Ghostie Brothers	.30	.60
VSS10051EN Undying Departed, Grenache	.30	.60
VSS10052EN Source Dragon Deity of Blessings, Blesstavor	7.50	15.00
VSS10053EN Sea Cruising Banshee	.20	.60
VSS10054EN Gust Djinn	.40	.80
VSS10055EN Chad the Ghostie	.30	.60
VSS10056EN Mick the Ghostie and Family	.25	.50
VSS10057EN Quick Shield (Pale Moon)	4.00	8.00
VSS10058EN Quick Shield (Granblue)	10.00	20.00

2020 Digimon Starter Deck Cocytus Blue

ST201 Tsunomon U	.15	.30
ST202 Gomamon C	.20	.40
ST203 Gabumon U	.25	.50
ST204 Bearmon C	.10	.20
ST205 Ikkakumon C	.10	.20
ST206 Garurumon U	.50	1.00
ST207 Grizzlymon C	.30	.75
ST208 WereGarurumon R	.20	.40
ST209 Zudomon U	.15	.30
ST210 Plesiomon R	.20	.40
ST211 MetalGarurumon SR	.30	.60
ST212 Matt Ishida R	.50	1.00
ST213 Hammer Spark C	1.50	3.00
ST214 Sorrow Blue C	.10	.20
ST215 Kaiser Nail C	1.25	2.50
ST216 Cocytus Breath U	5.00	10.00

2020 Digimon Starter Deck Gaia Red

ST101 Koromon U	.25	.50
ST102 Biyomon C	.10	.20
ST103 Agumon U	1.00	2.00
ST104 Dracomon C	.10	.20
ST105 Birdramon C	.10	.20
ST106 Coredramon C	.25	.50
ST107 Greymon U	10.00	20.00
ST108 Garudamon U	.15	.30
ST109 MetalGreymon R	.20	.40
ST110 Phoenixmon R	.20	.40
ST111 WarGreymon SR	.75	1.50
ST112 Tai Kamiya R	.50	1.00
ST113 Shadow Wing C	.10	.20
ST114 Starlight Explosion C	.10	.20
ST115 Giga Destroyer C	.10	.20
ST116 Gaia Force U	.50	1.00

2020 Digimon Starter Deck Heaven's Yellow

ST301 Tokomon U	.15	.30
ST302 Salamon C	.15	.30
ST303 Tapirmon C	.10	.20
ST304 Patamon U	2.00	4.00
ST305 Angemon U	.30	.60
ST306 Gatomon C	.10	.20
ST307 Unimon C	.30	.75
ST308 MagnaAngemon R	.20	.40
ST309 Angewomon U	.60	1.25
ST310 Magnadramon R	.20	.40
ST311 Seraphimon SR	.25	.50
ST312 T.K. Takaishi R	.30	.75
ST313 Heaven's Gate C	.10	.20
ST314 Heaven's Charm C	.15	.30
ST315 Holy Flame C	1.25	3.00
ST316 Seven Heavens U	.30	.60

2020 Digimon Ver. 1.0

BT1001 Yokomon R	.20	.40
BT1002 Bebydomon U	.30	.75
BT1003 Upamon R	6.00	12.00
BT1004 Wanyamon U	.15	.30
BT1005 Kyaromon U	.15	.30
BT1006 Cupimon R	2.00	4.00
BT1007 Tanemon R	.20	.40
BT1008 Frimon U	.15	.30
BT1009 Monodramon C	.10	.20
BT1010 Agumon R	1.00	2.00
BT1010 Agumon R ALT ART	1.00	2.00
BT1011 Agumon Expert C	.10	.20
BT1012 Biyomon U	.15	.30
BT1013 Muchomon C	.10	.20
BT1014 Kokatorimon C	.10	.20
BT1015 Greymon U	.25	.50
BT1016 Tyrannomon R	.30	.75
BT1017 Birdramon U	.15	.30
BT1018 Flarerizamon C	.10	.20
BT1019 DarkTyrannomon C	.10	.20
BT1020 Groundramon U	.15	.30
BT1021 MetalGreymon U	.15	.30
BT1022 Garudamon SR	.30	.75
BT1023 SkullGreymon R	.20	.40
BT1024 MetalTyrannomon C	.10	.20
BT1025 WarGreymon SR	10.00	20.00
BT1025 WarGreymon SR ALT ART	30.00	60.00
BT1026 Breakdramon U	.15	.30
BT1027 Armadillomon C	.10	.20
BT1028 Elecmon C	.10	.20
BT1029 Gabumon R	1.00	2.00
BT1029 Gabumon R ALT ART	2.00	4.00
BT1030 Gomamon C	.10	.20
BT1031 Monmon U	.15	.30
BT1032 Frigimon C	.10	.20
BT1033 Dolphmon C	.10	.20
BT1034 Ikkakumon R	.20	.40
BT1035 Leomon U	7.50	15.00
BT1036 Garurumon U	.15	.30
BT1037 Gorillamon C	.10	.20
BT1038 Monzaemon C	.10	.20
BT1039 Cerberusmon R	.20	.40
BT1040 WereGarurumon U	.15	.30
BT1041 Zudomon SR	.75	1.50
BT1042 LoaderLiomon U	.15	.30
BT1043 SaberLeomon U	.15	.30
BT1044 MetalGarurumon SR	4.00	8.00
BT1044 MetalGarurumon SR ALT ART	12.50	25.00
BT1045 Tsukaimon C	.10	.20
BT1046 Kudamon C	.10	.20
BT1047 Tinkermon U	.15	.30
BT1048 Patamon R	.60	1.25
BT1049 Labramon U	.15	.30
BT1050 Liollmon C	.10	.20
BT1051 Reppamon C	.10	.20
BT1052 Seasarmon C	.10	.20
BT1053 Darcmon U	.15	.30
BT1054 Liamon C	.10	.20
BT1055 Angemon R	.20	.40
BT1056 Petermon U	.15	.30
BT1057 Sirenmon U	.15	.30
BT1058 Chirinmon U	.15	.30
BT1059 Piximon C	.10	.20
BT1060 MagnaAngemon SR	25.00	50.00
BT1060 MagnaAngemon SR ALT ART	30.00	75.00
BT1061 Mistymon R	.20	.40
BT1062 SlashAngemon U	.15	.30
BT1063 Seraphimon SR	2.50	5.00
BT1064 Goblimon C	.10	.20

BT1065 Mushroomon C	.10	.20
BT1066 Tentomon U	.15	.30
BT1067 Palmon U	.15	.30
BT1068 Kokuwamon C	.10	.20
BT1069 Ogremon C	.10	.20
BT1070 Kuwagamon U	.15	.30
BT1071 Vegiemon C	.10	.20
BT1072 Woodmon U	.30	.60
BT1073 Kabuterimon C	.10	.20
BT1074 Togemon R	.20	.40
BT1075 Digitamamon C	.10	.20
BT1076 MegaKabuterimon U	.15	.30
BT1077 Okuwamon C	.10	.20
BT1078 Jagamon U	.15	.30
BT1079 Lillymon R	.20	.40
BT1080 Titamon U	.15	.30
BT1081 HerculesKabuterimon SR	.50	1.00
BT1082 Rosemon SR	.50	1.00
BT1082 Rosemon SR ALT ART	4.00	8.00
BT1084 Omnimon SR	3.00	6.00
BT1084 Omnimon SR ALT ART	60.00	125.00
BT1085 Tai Kamiya R	10.00	20.00
BT1085 Tai Kamiya R ALT ART	12.50	25.00
BT1086 Matt Ishida R	1.00	2.00
BT1086 Matt Ishida R ALT ART	3.00	6.00
BT1087 T.K. Takaishi R	7.50	15.00
BT1087 T.K. Takaishi R ALT ART	12.50	25.00
BT1088 Izzy Izumi R	.20	.40
BT1088 Izzy Izumi R ALT ART	1.00	2.00
BT1089 Mimi Tachikawa R	7.50	15.00
BT1089 Mimi Tachikawa R ALT ART	12.50	25.00
BT1090 Gravity Crush C	.10	.20
BT1092 Nuclear Laser C	.10	.20
BT1093 Great Tornado C	.10	.20
BT1094 Oblivion Bird C	.10	.20
BT1096 Mad Dog Fire R	.20	.40
BT1097 Boring Storm C	.10	.20
BT1098 V-Nova Blast C	.10	.20
BT1099 Hearts Attack C	.10	.20
BT1102 Blade of the True C	.10	.20
BT1104 Golden Ripper C	.10	.20
BT1105 Blast Fire C	.10	.20
BT1106 Symphony No. 1 <Polphony> R	.20	.40
BT1108 Horn Buster C	.10	.20
BT1109 Smashed Potatoes C	.10	.20
BT1110 Flower Cannon R	.60	1.25
BT1110 Flower Cannon R ALT ART	3.00	6.00
BT1111 Giga Blaster R	.20	.40
BT1112 Dimension Scissor C	.10	.20
BT1113 Forbidden Temptation C	.10	.20
BT1114 MetalGreymon SCR	4.00	8.00
BT1114 MetalGreymon SCR ALT ART	10.00	20.00
BT1115 Veedramon SCR	3.00	6.00
BT1115 Veedramon SCR ALT ART	7.50	15.00
BT2001 Gigimon U	.15	.30
BT2002 DemiVeemon U	.15	.30
BT2003 Nyaromon U	.15	.30
BT2004 Argomon U	.60	1.25
BT2005 Kapurimon C	.10	.20
BT2006 Tsumemon R	.75	1.50
BT2007 Pagumon C	.10	.20
BT2008 Yaamon R	.20	.40
BT2009 Guilmon C	.10	.20
BT2010 Biyomon C	.10	.20
BT2011 Vorvomon C	.10	.20
BT2012 Birdramon U	.15	.30
BT2013 Growlmon U	.15	.30
BT2014 Lavorvomon C	.10	.20
BT2015 Garudamon C	.10	.20
BT2016 Lavogaritamon C	.10	.20
BT2017 WarGrowlmon R	.20	.40
BT2018 Volcanicdramon C	.10	.20
BT2019 Phoenixmon R	.20	.40
BT2020 Gallantmon SR	7.50	15.00
BT2020 Gallantmon SR ALT ART	15.00	30.00
BT2021 Veemon C	.30	.75
BT2022 Betamon C	.10	.20
BT2023 Gomamon C	.10	.20
BT2024 Seadramon C	.10	.20
BT2025 Ikkakumon C	.10	.20
BT2026 Veedramon U	.15	.30
BT2027 Zudomon U	.15	.30
BT2028 AeroVeedramon R	.50	1.00
BT2029 MegaSeadramon C	.10	.20
BT2030 MetalSeadramon R	.20	.40
BT2030 MetalSeadramon R ALT ART	.20	.40
BT2031 Vikemon U	.15	.30
BT2032 UlforceVeedramon SR	1.50	3.00
BT2032 UlforceVeedramon SR ALT ART	7.50	15.00
BT2033 Agumon C	.10	.20
BT2034 Salamon U	.75	1.50
BT2035 GeoGreymon C	.10	.20
BT2036 Gatomon U	.15	.30
BT2037 Angewomon C	.10	.20
BT2038 RizeGreymon R	.50	1.00
BT2039 Magnadramon U	.30	.75
BT2040 Ophanimon R	.20	.40
BT2041 ShineGreymon SR	.75	1.50
BT2041 ShineGreymon SR ALT ART	7.50	15.00
BT2042 Argomon C	.10	.20
BT2043 Agumon C	.10	.20
BT2044 Tyrannomon C	.10	.20
BT2045 Argomon U	.15	.30
BT2046 MetalTyrannomon R	.50	1.00
BT2047 Argomon C	.10	.20
BT2048 Cherrymon U	.15	.30
BT2049 Puppetmon R	.25	.50
BT2049 Puppetmon R ALT ART	1.00	2.00
BT2050 Argomon U	.15	.30
BT2051 RustTyrannomon SR	3.00	6.00
BT2052 Hagurumon C	.10	.20
BT2053 Keramon R	2.00	4.00
BT2054 Gotsumon U	.15	.30
BT2055 ToyAgumon C	.75	1.50
BT2056 Numemon C	.10	.20
BT2057 Greymon C	.15	.30
BT2058 Guardromon C	.10	.20
BT2059 Kurisarimon U	.75	1.50
BT2060 Megadramon U	.15	.30
BT2061 Andromon C	.10	.20
BT2062 Infermon R	.75	1.50
BT2063 MetalGreymon C	.20	.40
BT2064 HiAndromon U	.15	.30
BT2065 WarGreymon SR	.50	1.00
BT2065 WarGreymon SR ALT ART	10.00	20.00
BT2066 Machinedramon SR	.75	1.50
BT2066 Machinedramon SR ALT ART	1.00	2.00
BT2067 DemiDevimon U	.15	.30
BT2068 Impmon C	.60	1.25
BT2069 Gabumon C	.75	1.50
BT2070 Tapirmon U	.75	1.50
BT2071 Wizardmon C	.10	.20
BT2072 Vilemon C	.25	.50
BT2073 Garurumon C	.10	.20
BT2074 Devimon U	.30	.75
BT2075 Myotismon U	.15	.30
BT2076 Pumpkinmon C	.10	.20
BT2077 Kimeramon R	.20	.40
BT2078 WereGarurumon C	.10	.20
BT2079 VenomMyotismon R	.20	.40
BT2080 Piedmon SR	.60	1.25
BT2080 Piedmon SR ALT ART	3.00	6.00
BT2081 MetalGarurumon SR	.50	1.00
BT2081 MetalGarurumon SR ALT ART	5.00	10.00
BT2082 Diaboromon SR	3.00	6.00
BT2082 Diaboromon SR ALT ART	7.50	15.00
BT2083 Millenniummon SR	2.00	4.00
BT2084 Sora Takenouchi R	.20	.40
BT2084 Sora Takenouchi R ALT ART	.60	1.25
BT2085 Joe Kido R	.20	.40
BT2086 Rina Shinomiya R	.20	.40
BT2087 Kari Kamiya R	.20	.40
BT2088 Taiga R	.60	1.25
BT2089 Tai Kamiya R	.75	1.50
BT2090 Matt Ishida R	3.00	6.00
BT2091 Volcanic Flare C	.10	.20
BT2092 Radiation Blade U	.15	.30
BT2093 Shield of the Just R	.20	.40
BT2094 Arctic Blizzard C	.10	.20
BT2095 River of Power U	.15	.30
BT2096 The Ray of Victory U	.15	.30
BT2097 Lightning Paw C	.10	.20
BT2098 EDEN's Javelin U	.50	1.00
BT2099 Glorious Burst R	.20	.40
BT2100 Puppet Pummel U	.15	.30
BT2101 Cherry Blast C	.10	.20
BT2102 Terrors Cluster R	.20	.40
BT2103 Spiral Sword C	.10	.20
BT2104 Atomic Ray C	.10	.20
BT2105 Spider Shooter U	.15	.30
BT2106 Infinity Cannon R	.20	.40
BT2107 Darkness Claw U	.15	.30
BT2108 Night Raid C	.10	.20
BT2109 Heat Viper C	.10	.20
BT2110 Trump Sword R	1.00	2.00
BT2111 Beelzemon SCR	30.00	75.00
BT2111 Beelzemon SCR ALT ART	50.00	100.00
BT2112 BlackWarGreymon SCR	6.00	12.00
BT2112 BlackWarGreymon SCR ALT ART	15.00	30.00
BT3001 Poromon U	.15	.30
BT3002 DemiVeemon U	1.50	3.00
BT3003 Upamon U	.75	1.50
BT3004 Minomon U	.30	.60
BT3005 Kakkinmon U	.15	.30
BT3006 DemiMeramon U	2.00	4.00
BT3007 Agumon C	.10	.20
BT3008 Zubamon U	.15	.30
BT3009 Hawkmon C	.10	.20
BT3010 ZubaEagermon C	.10	.20
BT3011 Greymon U	.15	.30
BT3012 Aquilamon C	.10	.20
BT3013 Duramon C	.10	.20
BT3014 Silphymon R	.20	.40
BT3015 MetalGreymon R	.20	.40
BT3016 Durandamon R	.25	.50
BT3017 Valkyrimon U	.15	.30
BT3018 BlitzGreymon SR	.25	.50
BT3019 RagnaLoardmon SR	1.00	2.00
BT3019 RagnaLoardmon SR ALT ART	6.00	12.00
BT3020 Patamon C	.10	.20
BT3021 Veemon R	7.50	15.00
BT3022 Penguinmon C	.10	.20
BT3023 Angemon C	.10	.20
BT3024 Airdramon U	.15	.30
BT3025 ExVeemon R	.30	.60
BT3026 MagnaAngemon C	.10	.20
BT3027 Paildramon R	.20	.40
BT3028 Bastemon U	.15	.30
BT3029 Goldramon U	.15	.30
BT3030 Leopardmon SR	1.25	2.50
BT3030 Leopardmon SR ALT ART	4.00	8.00
BT3031 Imperialdramon Dragon Mode SR	.75	1.50
BT3031 Imperialdramon Dragon Mode SR ALT ART	4.00	8.00
BT3032 Armadillomon C	.10	.20
BT3033 Salamon R	.20	.40
BT3034 Lopmon U	.15	.30
BT3035 Gatomon C	.10	.20
BT3036 Ankylomon U	.15	.30
BT3037 Turuiemon C	.10	.20
BT3038 Antylamon C	.10	.20
BT3039 Angewomon R	.75	1.50
BT3040 Shakkoumon R	.20	.40
BT3041 Cherubimon R	.20	.40
BT3042 ClavisAngemon U	.15	.30
BT3043 Kentaurosmon SR	1.00	2.00
BT3043 Kentaurosmon SR ALT ART	4.00	8.00
BT3044 Aruraumon C	.10	.20
BT3045 Kunemon C	.10	.20
BT3046 Terriermon U	1.50	3.00
BT3047 Wormmon R	.30	.75
BT3048 Gargomon C	.10	.20
BT3049 Flymon U	.15	.30
BT3050 Stingmon R	.30	.60
BT3051 Dokugumon C	.10	.20
BT3052 Rapidmon C	.10	.20
BT3053 JewelBeemon C	.10	.20
BT3054 Blossomon C	.30	.60
BT3055 Dinobeemon R	.25	.50
BT3056 Ceresmon SR	.30	.75
BT3056 Ceresmon SR ALT ART	2.50	5.00
BT3057 MegaGargomon R	.75	1.50
BT3058 BanchoStingmon U	.15	.30
BT3059 Commandramon C	.25	.50
BT3060 Psychemon C	.10	.20
BT3061 Chuumon C	.30	.60
BT3062 Ludomon U	.15	.30
BT3063 Sukamon C	.10	.20
BT3064 TiaLudomon C	.10	.20
BT3065 Gururumon U	.15	.30
BT3066 Clockmon C	.10	.20
BT3067 Tankmon C	.10	.20
BT3068 Giromon C	.10	.20
BT3069 RaijiLudomon C	.10	.20
BT3070 Etemon R	.20	.40
BT3071 MetalMamemon R	.20	.40
BT3072 BryweLudramon R	.30	.60
BT3073 CresGarurumon SR	.50	1.00
BT3073 CresGarurumon SR ALT ART	2.00	4.00
BT3074 MetalEtemon U	.15	.30
BT3075 Craniamon SR	1.00	2.00
BT3075 Craniamon SR ALT ART	4.00	8.00
BT3076 Candlemon C	.10	.20
BT3077 Gazimon C	.75	1.50
BT3078 Shamanmon C	.10	.20
BT3079 Tsukaimon C	.10	.20
BT3080 Saberdramon C	.10	.20
BT3081 Devideramon U	.15	.30
BT3082 BlackGatomon U	.15	.30
BT3083 Meramon C	.10	.20
BT3084 Raremon R	.20	.40
BT3085 SkullMeramon C	.10	.20
BT3086 Arukenimon C	.10	.20
BT3087 Mummymon C	.10	.20
BT3088 LadyDevimon R	4.00	8.00
BT3089 Boltmon U	.15	.30
BT3090 Mastemon SR	.75	1.50
BT3090 Mastemon SR ALT ART	7.50	15.00
BT3091 Lilithmon SR	10.00	20.00
BT3091 Lilithmon SR ALT ART	30.00	60.00
BT3092 MaloMyotismon R	.25	.50
BT3093 Davis Motomiya R	12.50	25.00
BT3094 Ken Ichijoji R	.75	1.50
BT3095 Joe Kido R	.20	.40
BT3096 Mimi Tachikawa R	1.50	3.00
BT3097 A Delicate Plan U	.50	1.00
BT3098 Plasma Stake C	.10	.20
BT3099 We Have to Stop Fighting! U	.15	.30
BT3100 Death Parade Blaster C	.10	.20
BT3101 Bifrost C	.10	.20
BT3102 Code Cracking U	.15	.30
BT3103 Hidden Potential Discovered! U	.75	1.50
BT3104 Positron Laser C	.10	.20
BT3105 Breath of the Gods R	1.25	2.50
BT3106 Beast Cyclone C	.10	.20
BT3107 Looking Back on the Good Times U	.15	.30
BT3108 Dark Despair R	.20	.40
BT3109 Back for Revenge! U	.15	.30
BT3110 Necrophobia C	.10	.20
BT3111 Imperialdramon Dragon SCR	3.00	6.00
BT3111 Imperialdramon Dragon SCR ALT ART	4.00	8.00
BT3112 Omnimon Alter-S SCR	7.50	15.00
BT3112 Omnimon Alter-S SCR ALT ART	10.00	20.00

2021 Digimon Battle of Omni

BT5001U Koromon U	.75	1.50
BT5002U Tsunomon U	.15	.30
BT5003U Pickmon U	.15	.30
BT5004U Yokomon U	.15	.30
BT5005U Tsumemon U	.15	.30
BT5006U Gigimon U	.15	.30
BT5007C Agumon C	.15	.30
BT5008C Gaossmon C	.10	.20
BT5009U Shoutmon U	.15	.30
BT5010U Greymon U	.75	1.50
BT5011C Meramon C	.10	.20
BT5012C Monochromon C	.10	.20
BT5013C Triceramon C	.10	.20
BT5014R OmniShoutmon R	.20	.40
BT5015R MetalGreymon: Alterous Mode R	.30	.75
BT5016R WarGreymon R	.20	.40
BT5017U ZeigGreymon U	.15	.30
BT5018C Dorbickmon C	.10	.20
BT5020U Gabumon U	.15	.30
BT5021C Syakomon C	.10	.20
BT5022R Bulucomon R	.30	.75
BT5023C Gesomon C	.10	.20
BT5024C Garurumon C	.10	.20
BT5025C Paledramon C	.10	.20
BT5026C Coelamon C	.10	.20
BT5027C MarineDevimon C	.10	.20
BT5028U CrysPaledramon U	.15	.30
BT5029R WereGarurumon: Sagittarius Mode R	.20	.40
BT5030U Neptunemon U	.15	.30
BT5031R MetalGarurumon R	.20	.40
BT5033C Cutemon C	.10	.20
BT5034C Kotemon C	.10	.20
BT5035C Starmons C	.10	.20
BT5036R Renamon R	.30	.60
BT5037C Gladimon C	.10	.20
BT5038C Kyubimon C	.10	.20
BT5039U ShootingStarmon U	.15	.30
BT5040U SuperStarmon U	.15	.30
BT5041C Taomon C	.10	.20
BT5042C Knightmon C	.10	.20
BT5043U Jijimon U	.15	.30
BT5044R Sakuyamon R	.75	1.50
BT5046R Terriermon Assistant R	.20	.40
BT5047C Palmon C	.10	.20
BT5048C Floramon C	.10	.20
BT5049U Kiwimon U	.15	.30
BT5050C Weedmon C	.10	.20
BT5051C MoriShellmon C	.10	.20
BT5052C Garbagemon C	.10	.20
BT5053C Deramon C	.10	.20
BT5054C Piximon C	.10	.20
BT5055U BanchoLillymon U	.15	.30
BT5057U Rosemon U	.15	.30
BT5058R Argomon R	.20	.40
BT5059C Keramon C	.10	.20
BT5060U Monitamon U	.15	.30
BT5061C Commandramon C	.10	.20
BT5062C Mekanorimon C	.20	.40
BT5063C Kurisarimon C	.10	.20
BT5064C BlackGaogamon C	.10	.20
BT5065U Shademon U	.15	.30
BT5066R WaruMonzaemon R	.20	.40
BT5067U Infermon U	.15	.30
BT5068C BlackMachGaogamon C	.10	.20
BT5069R BlackWarGreymon R	.30	.60
BT5071U Guilmon U	.15	.30
BT5072U Fake Agumon Expert U	.15	.30
BT5073C Pillomon C	.10	.20
BT5074C Troopmon C	.10	.20
BT5075C Musyamon C	.10	.20
BT5076C BlackGrowlmon C	.10	.20
BT5077C Vajramon C	.10	.20
BT5078C Jokermon C	.10	.20
BT5079R BlackWarGrowlmon R	1.00	2.00
BT5080U Zanbamon U	.15	.30
BT5083R Megidramon R	.30	.75
BT5084R Diaboromon R	.20	.40
BT5088R Sora Takenouchi & Joe Kido R	1.25	2.50
BT5089R Izzy Izumi & Mimi Tachikawa R	.25	.50
BT5090R Arata Sanada R	.20	.40
BT5091R Takumi Aiba R	.25	.50
BT5092R Nokia Shiramine R	1.50	3.00
BT5093R Tai Kamiya & Matt Ishida R	.20	.40
BT5094C Rowdy Rocker C	.10	.20
BT5095U Transcendent Sword U	.15	.30
BT5096C Supreme Cannon C	.10	.20
BT5097U Absolute Blast U	.15	.30
BT5098C Meteor Shower C	.10	.20
BT5099U Spiral Masquerade U	.60	1.25

BT5100C Royal Nuts C	.10	.20
BT5101U You Can't Actually Fly? U	.15	.30
BT5102R Wisselen R	.20	.40
BT5103U A Blazing Storm of Metal! U	.15	.30
BT5104R Catastrophe Cannon R	.20	.40
BT5105C Ultimate Flare C	.10	.20
BT5106C Demonic Disaster C	.10	.20
BT5107U Revive From the Darkness! U	.15	.30
BT5108R Earth Shaker R	.20	.40
BT5109R Mega Digimon Fusion! R	.20	.40
BT5110R All Delete R	.20	.40
BT5019SR Shoutmon DX SR	.30	.75
BT5019SR Shoutmon DX SR ALT ART	5.00	10.00
BT5032SR Hexeblaumon SR	2.00	4.00
BT5045SR LordKnightmon SR	2.00	4.00
BT5056SR Rafflesimon SR	.25	.50
BT5070SR MetalGarurumon SR	.50	1.00
BT5081SR ChaosGallantmon SR	.60	1.25
BT5081SR ChaosGallantmon SR ALT ART Kenji Watanabe	3.00	6.00
BT5081SR ChaosGallantmon SR ALT ART Nakano Haito	3.00	6.00
BT5082SR Tactimon SR	.25	.50
BT5085SR Armageddemon SR	.30	.60
BT5085SR Armageddemon SR ALT ART	4.00	8.00
BT5086SR Omnimon SR	7.50	15.00
BT5086SR Omnimon SR ALT ART As'Maria	7.50	15.00
BT5086SR Omnimon SR ALT ART Nakano Haito	7.50	15.00
BT5086SR Omnimon SR ALT ART sasasi	7.50	15.00
BT5086SR Omnimon SR ALT ART Tomotake Kinoshita	12.50	25.00
BT5087SR Omnimon Zwart SR	3.00	6.00
BT5087SR Omnimon Zwart SR ALT ART As'Maria	7.50	15.00
BT5087SR Omnimon Zwart SR ALT ART Kenji Watanabe	7.50	15.00
BT5111SEC Omnimon X Anti-body SCR	7.50	15.00
BT5111SEC Omnimon X Anti-body SCR ALT ART	15.00	30.00
BT5112SEC Omnimon Zwart Defeat SCR	30.00	75.00
BT5112SEC Omnimon Zwart Defeat SCR ALT ART	40.00	80.00

2021 Digimon Classic Collection 1

EX1001U Agumon U ALT ART	10.00	20.00
EX1001U Agumon U	.15	.30
EX1002C Biyomon C ALT ART	6.00	12.00
EX1002C Biyomon C	.10	.20
EX1003U Birdramon U	.15	.30
EX1004U Greymon U	.15	.30
EX1004U Greymon U ALT ART	5.00	10.00
EX1005R Tyrannomon R	.20	.40
EX1005R Tyrannomon R ALT ART	6.00	12.00
EX1006C Garudamon C	.10	.20
EX1006C Garudamon C ALT ART	2.00	4.00
EX1007C Megadramon C	.10	.20
EX1008R MetalGreymon R	.30	.60
EX1008R MetalGreymon R ALT ART	15.00	30.00
EX1010U Phoenixmon U	.15	.30
EX1011U Gabumon U ALT ART	12.50	25.00
EX1011U Gabumon U	.15	.30
EX1012C Gomamon C ALT ART	2.50	5.00
EX1012C Gomamon C	.10	.20
EX1013R Veemon R	2.50	5.00
EX1014C ExVeemon C	.20	.40
EX1015U Garurumon U ALT ART	3.00	6.00
EX1015U Garurumon U	.15	.30
EX1016C Ikkakumon C	.10	.20
EX1017C WereGarurumon C ALT ART	3.00	6.00
EX1017C WereGarurumon C	.10	.20
EX1018C Zudomon C ALT ART	2.50	5.00
EX1018C Zudomon C	.10	.20
EX1019R Paildramon R	.20	.40
EX1019R Paildramon R ALT ART	4.00	8.00
EX1020U Plesiomon U	.15	.30
EX1023C Elecmon C	.10	.20
EX1024U Patamon U ALT ART	4.00	8.00
EX1024U Patamon U	.15	.30
EX1025C Salamon C	.10	.20
EX1026U Gatomon U ALT ART	5.00	10.00
EX1026U Gatomon U	.15	.30
EX1027R Leomon R	.20	.40
EX1028C Angemon C	.10	.20
EX1031R Seraphimon R	.20	.40
EX1032U Magnadramon U	.15	.30
EX1033C Tentomon C ALT ART	7.50	15.00
EX1033C Tentomon C	.10	.20
EX1034C Palmon C ALT ART	2.50	5.00
EX1034C Palmon C	.10	.20
EX1035U Kabuterimon U	.15	.30
EX1036C Togemon C	.10	.20
EX1037R Kuwagamon R	.20	.40
EX1037R Kuwagamon R ALT ART	5.00	10.00
EX1038C Stingmon C	.10	.20
EX1039U Lillymon U ALT ART	3.00	6.00
EX1039U Lillymon U	.15	.30
EX1040R MegaKabuterimon R ALT ART	3.00	6.00
EX1040R MegaKabuterimon R	.20	.40
EX1041U Dinobeemon U	.15	.30
EX1042U Rosemon U	.15	.30
EX1044C Keramon C	.10	.20
EX1045C Hagurumon C	.10	.20
EX1046C Kurisarimon C	.10	.20
EX1047C Guardromon C	.10	.20
EX1048C Andromon C	.10	.20
EX1049C MetalTyrannomon C	.10	.20
EX1050C MetalMamemon C	.10	.20
EX1051R Infermon R	.20	.40
EX1052U Etemon U	.15	.30
EX1053U MetalEtemon U	.15	.30
EX1054U Boltmon U	.15	.30
EX1055C Tapirmon C	.10	.20
EX1056C DemiDevimon C	.10	.20
EX1057C Wizardmon C	.10	.20
EX1058C Devimon C	.10	.20
EX1059R Ogremon R	.20	.40
EX1059R Ogremon R ALT ART	7.50	15.00
EX1060U LadyDevimon U	.15	.30
EX1061U Myotismon U	.15	.30
EX1062R SkullGreymon R	.20	.40
EX1064U Piedmon U	.15	.30
EX1066R Analog Youth R	2.00	4.00
EX1066R Analog Youth R ALT ART	40.00	80.00
EX1067R Baptism by Fire! R	.20	.40
EX1068R Ice Wall! R	.50	1.00
EX1069R Ultimate Connection! R	.20	.40
EX1070R Fight for Your Pride! R	.20	.40
EX1071R Win Rate: 60! R ALT ART	7.50	15.00
EX1071R Win Rate: 60! R	.20	.40
EX1072R Emergency Program Shutdown! R	.20	.40
EX1009SR WarGreymon SR	1.00	2.00
EX1009SR WarGreymon SR ALT ART	12.50	25.00
EX1021SR MetalGarurumon SR ALT ART	12.50	25.00
EX1021SR MetalGarurumon SR	4.00	8.00
EX1022SR Imperialdramon Dragon Mode SR	.75	1.50
EX1022SR Imperialdramon Dragon Mode SR ALT ART	10.00	20.00
EX1029SR MagnaAngemon SR ALT ART	3.00	6.00
EX1029SR MagnaAngemon SR	.30	.75
EX1030SR Angewomon SR ALT ART	.30	.60
EX1030SR Angewomon SR	.15	.30
EX1043SR HerculesKabuterimon SR ALT ART	4.00	8.00
EX1043SR HerculesKabuterimon SR	2.50	.50
EX1063SR VenomMyotismon SR	.30	.75
EX1063SR VenomMyotismon SR ALT ART	4.00	8.00
EX1065SR Diaboromon SR	1.50	3.00
EX1065SR Diaboromon SR ALT ART	12.50	25.00
EX1073SEC Machinedramon SCR	10.00	20.00
EX1073SEC Machinedramon SCR ALT ART	30.00	60.00

2021 Digimon Double Diamond

BT6001U DemiMeramon U	.25	.50
BT6001U DemiMeramon/(Box-Topper) U	2.00	4.00
BT6002U Kyaromon U	.15	.30
BT6002U Kyaromon/(Box-Topper) U	2.50	5.00
BT6003U Bibimon U	.15	.30
BT6003U Bibimon/(Box-Topper) U	.75	1.50
BT6004U Pinamon U	.15	.30
BT6004U Pinamon/(Box-Topper) U	1.50	3.00
BT6005U Pagumon U	.15	.30
BT6005U Pagumon/(Box-Topper) U	2.50	5.00
BT6006U Tsunomon U	.15	.30
BT6006U Tsunomon/(Box-Topper) U	1.00	2.00
BT6007U Agumon U	.15	.30
BT6007U Agumon U ALT ART	4.00	8.00
BT6008C Shoutmon C	.10	.20
BT6009R Huckmon R	.25	.50
BT6010U Flamemon U	.15	.30
BT6011C BaoHuckmon C	.10	.20
BT6012C Deltamon C	.10	.20
BT6013C Megadramon C	.10	.20
BT6014C Asuramon C	.10	.20
BT6015U SaviorHuckmon U	.15	.30
BT6017R MagnaKidmon R	.20	.40
BT6019U Gabumon U	.15	.30
BT6019U Gabumon U ALT ART	4.00	8.00
BT6020C Gizamon C	.10	.20
BT6021C ModokiBetamon C	.10	.20
BT6022C Strabimon C	.10	.20
BT6023C Octomon C	.10	.20
BT6024U Mojyamon U	.15	.30
BT6025C Panjyamon C	.10	.20
BT6026C Dragomon C	.10	.20
BT6027R Majiramon R	.20	.40
BT6028U Pukumon U	.15	.30
BT6031C Tinkermon C	.10	.20
BT6032C Tapirmon C	.10	.20
BT6033R Pulsemon R	.20	.40
BT6033R Pulsemon R ALT ART	3.00	6.00
BT6034U Wizardmon U	.15	.30
BT6035C Baluchimon C	.10	.20
BT6036U Mimicmon U	.15	.30
BT6037C Bulkmon C	.10	.20
BT6038C Apemon C	.10	.20
BT6039C Mammothmon C	.10	.20
BT6040C Mistymon U	.15	.30
BT6041R Manticoremon R	.20	.40
BT6042U Babamon U	.15	.30
BT6043C SkullMammothmon C	.10	.20
BT6045C Bakomon C	.10	.20
BT6046U Pomumon U	.15	.30
BT6047R Morphomon R	.20	.40
BT6047R Morphomon R ALT ART	3.00	6.00
BT6048C Parasaurmon C	.10	.20
BT6049U Arbormon U	.15	.30
BT6050C Petaldramon C	.10	.20
BT6051U Toropiamon U	.15	.30
BT6052R Entmon R	.20	.40
BT6053C Eldradimon C	.10	.20
BT6054R AncientTroymon R	.20	.40
BT6055U Junkmon U	.15	.30
BT6056C Chikurimon C	.10	.20
BT6057C ToyAgumon U	.15	.30
BT6058C Nanimon C	.10	.20
BT6059R Machmon R	.20	.40
BT6060C Deputymon C	.10	.20
BT6061C Gigadramon C	.10	.20
BT6062U Volcanomon U	.15	.30
BT6063C BigMamemon C	.10	.20
BT6065R Gundramon R	.20	.40
BT6066U PileVolcamon U	.15	.30
BT6068U Impmon U	.15	.30
BT6068U Impmon U ALT ART	30.00	75.00
BT6069C Goblimon C	.10	.20
BT6070C Elecmon C	.10	.20
BT6071C Kinkakumon C	.10	.20
BT6072R Ogremon R	.20	.40
BT6073C Ginkakumon C	.10	.20
BT6074C Boogiemon C	.10	.20
BT6075U Ginkakumon Promote U	.15	.30
BT6076C Feresmon C	.10	.20
BT6077R Rebellimon R	.20	.40
BT6079U Murmukusmon C	.10	.20
BT6080U Ornismon U	.15	.30
BT6082R Sistermon Blanc R	.30	.60
BT6082R Sistermon Blanc R ALT ART	15.00	30.00
BT6083C Eosmon C	.10	.20
BT6084R Sistermon Ciel R	.25	.50
BT6084R Sistermon Ciel R ALT ART	12.50	25.00
BT6085C Eosmon C	.30	.75
BT6087R Tai Kamiya R	.20	.40
BT6088R Matt Ishida R	.20	.40
BT6089R T.K. Takaishi & Kari Kamiya R	3.00	6.00
BT6090R Izzy Izumi & Joe Kido R	.75	1.50
BT6091R Sora Takenouchi & Mimi Tachikawa R	.20	.40
BT6092R Menoa Belluci R	.20	.40
BT6093C Judgement of the Blade C	.10	.20
BT6094R Red Reamer R	.20	.40
BT6095U Happy Bullet Showering U	.15	.30
BT6096C Forbidden Trident C	.10	.20
BT6097U Howling Memory Boost! U	.15	.30
BT6098R Raddle Star R	.20	.40
BT6099U Acid Injection U	.15	.30
BT6100C Reinforcing Memory Boost! C	.10	.20
BT6101R Wyvern's Breath R	.75	1.50
BT6102C Tropical Venom C	.10	.20
BT6103C Blasted Disaster U	.15	.30
BT6104C Parabolic Junk C	.10	.20
BT6105U Gewalt Schwarmer U	.15	.30
BT6106R Iron-Fisted Onslaught R	.50	1.00
BT6107C Glaive Memory Boost! C	.10	.20
BT6108R Underworld's Call R	.20	.40
BT6109U Fly Bullet U	.15	.30
BT6110R Cutting Edge R	.20	.40
BT6016SR Jesmon SR	1.50	3.00
BT6016SR Jesmon SR ALT ART	7.50	15.00
BT6018SR Agumon - Bond of Bravery SR	.75	1.50
BT6018SR Agumon - Bond of Bravery SR ALT ART	7.50	15.00
BT6029SR Azulongmon SR	.75	1.50
BT6030SR Gabumon - Bond of Friendship SR ALT ART	10.00	20.00
BT6030SR Gabumon - Bond of Friendship SR	.75	1.50
BT6044SR Dynasmon SR	.50	1.00
BT6044SR Dynasmon SR ALT ART	4.00	8.00
BT6064SR Mamemon SR	.20	.40
BT6064SR Mamemon SR ALT ART	2.50	5.00
BT6067SR Gankoomon SR	.30	.60
BT6067SR Gankoomon SR ALT ART	4.00	8.00
BT6078SR SkullGreymon SR	.30	.60
BT6078SR SkullGreymon SR ALT ART	3.00	6.00
BT6081SR Titamon SR	.20	.40
BT6081SR Titamon SR ALT ART	3.00	6.00
BT6086SR Eosmon SR	.30	.75
BT6086SR Eosmon SR ALT ART	4.00	8.00
BT6111SEC Alphamon SCR	15.00	30.00
BT6111SEC Alphamon SCR ALT ART	25.00	50.00
BT6112SEC BeelStarmon SCR	12.50	25.00
BT6112SEC BeelStarmon SCR ALT ART	50.00	100.00

2021 Digimon Great Legend

BT4001U Sakuttomon U	.15	.30
BT4002U Bukamon U	.15	.30
BT4003U Koromon U	.15	.30
BT4004U Budmon U	.15	.30
BT4005U Missimon U	.15	.30
BT4006U Xiaomon U	.25	.50
BT4007C Otamamon C	.10	.20
BT4008C Agumon C	.10	.20
BT4009C Flamemon C	.10	.20
BT4010C Fugamon C	.10	.20
BT4011U Agunimon U	.75	1.50
BT4011U Agunimon U ALT ART	7.50	15.00
BT4012C GeoGreymon C	.10	.20
BT4013U BurningGreymon U	.20	.40
BT4014C Vermilimon C	.10	.20
BT4015C Volcdramon C	.10	.20
BT4018U Spinomon U	.15	.30
BT4019R VictoryGreymon R	.20	.40
BT4019R VictoryGreymon R ALT ART	2.50	5.00
BT4020R ShineGreymon R	.20	.40
BT4021C Gaomon C	.10	.20
BT4022C Sangomon C	.10	.20
BT4023C Strabimon C	.25	.50
BT4024C Tobiumon C	.10	.20
BT4025U Lobomon U	.60	1.25
BT4025U Lobomon U ALT ART	10.00	20.00
BT4026C GaoGamon C	.10	.20
BT4027U KendoGarurumon U	.15	.30
BT4028U Piranimon U	.15	.30
BT4029C Gusokumon C	.10	.20
BT4031R MarinChimairamon R	.20	.40
BT4032R MachGaogamon R	.20	.40
BT4033R ZeedGarurumon R	.20	.40
BT4033R ZeedGarurumon R ALT ART	2.50	5.00
BT4034C Regalecusmon C	.10	.20
BT4036C Falcomon C	.10	.20
BT4037C Kudamon C	.10	.20
BT4038U BushiAgumon U	.30	.60
BT4039C Growlmon C	.10	.20
BT4040C Diatrymon C	.10	.20
BT4041C Meicoomon C	.10	.20
BT4042C Piddomon C	.20	.40
BT4043U Crowmon U	.15	.30
BT4044C HippoGryphonmon C	.10	.20
BT4045C Maycrackmon C	.10	.20
BT4046R WarGrowlmon R	.20	.40
BT4047U Rasielmon U	.15	.30
BT4049R Varodurumon R	.20	.40
BT4050C Liollmon C	.10	.20
BT4051C DoKunemon C	.10	.20
BT4052U Lalamon U	.15	.30
BT4053U Roachmon U	.15	.30
BT4054U Sunflowmon U	.15	.30
BT4055C Leomon C	.10	.20
BT4056C SkullScorpiomon C	.10	.20
BT4057C GrapLeomon C	.10	.20
BT4058R Orochimon R	.20	.40
BT4060U Lotosmon U	.15	.30
BT4061R BanchoLeomon R	.20	.40
BT4063R Commandramon R	1.00	2.00
BT4064U Sunarizamon U	.15	.30
BT4065C Gotsumon C	.10	.20
BT4066C Golemon C	.10	.20
BT4067U Sealsdramon U	.30	.60
BT4068U Baboongamon U	.15	.30
BT4069C Blimpmon C	.10	.20
BT4070C Meteormon C	.10	.20
BT4071C Tankdramon C	.10	.20
BT4073U BanchoGolemon U	.15	.30
BT4074R Darkdramon R	.60	1.25
BT4076C Gabumon C	.10	.20
BT4077R Ghostmon R	.20	.40
BT4078U Soundbirdmon U	.15	.30
BT4079C Labramon C	.10	.20
BT4080U Bakemon U	.15	.30
BT4081C Devimon C	.10	.20
BT4082U Dobermon U	.15	.30
BT4083C Cerberusmon C	.10	.20
BT4084C NeoDevimon C	.10	.20
BT4085C Phantomon C	.10	.20
BT4086R Cerberusmon: Werewolf Mode R	.50	1.00
BT4087U Anubismon U	.15	.30
BT4090R Chaosmon R	.30	.60
BT4090R Chaosmon R ALT ART	6.00	12.00
BT4092R Marcus Damon R	2.00	4.00
BT4093R Thomas H. Norstein R	.20	.40
BT4094R Tai Kamiya R	.20	.40
BT4095R Yoshino Fujieda R	.20	.40
BT4096R Izzy Izumi R	2.00	4.00
BT4097R Kari Kamiya R	.75	1.50
BT4098C Atomic Inferno C	.10	.20
BT4099U Heir of Dragons U	.15	.30
BT4100R Trident Revolver R	.20	.40
BT4101U I'll Drag You Into the Depths U	.15	.30
BT4102C Aqua Viper C	.10	.20
BT4103R Full Moon Blaster R	.20	.40
BT4104R Blinding Ray R	.60	1.25
BT4105U Tactical Retreat! U	.30	.60
BT4106C Purge Shine C	.10	.20
BT4107R Pollen Spray R	.20	.40
BT4108C Cyclonic Kick C	.10	.20
BT4109C Final Zubagon Punch C	.10	.20
BT4110R Dark Roar R	.20	.40
BT4111C Jack Raid C	.10	.20
BT4112R Hell's Gate R	.20	.40
BT4016SR Aldamon SR	1.00	2.00
BT4017SR RizeGreymon SR	10.00	20.00
BT4017SR RizeGreymon SR ALT ART	15.00	30.00
BT4030SR Beowolfmon SR	.75	1.50
BT4035SR MirageGaogamon SR	.20	.40
BT4035SR MirageGaogamon SR ALT ART	4.00	8.00
BT4048SR WarGreymon SR	1.00	2.00
BT4048SR WarGreymon SR ALT ART	7.50	15.00
BT4059SR Lilamon SR	.75	1.50

BT4059SR Lilamon SR ALT ART	3.00	6.00
BT4062SR Nidhoggmon SR	1.50	3.00
BT4062SR Nidhoggmon SR ALT ART	7.50	15.00
BT4072SR Gogmamon SR	.30	.75
BT4075SR Blastmon SR	.20	.40
BT4075SR Blastmon SR ALT ART	1.00	2.00
BT4088SR DanDevimon SR	.50	1.00
BT4088SR DanDevimon SR ALT ART	5.00	10.00
BT4089SR Plutomon SR	.30	.75
BT4091SR Chaosmon: Valdur Arm SR	.75	1.50
BT4113SEC AncientGreymon SCR	15.00	30.00
BT4113SEC AncientGreymon SCR ALT ART	20.00	40.00
BT4114SEC AncientGarurumon SCR	5.00	10.00
BT4114SEC AncientGarurumon SCR ALT ART	10.00	20.00
BT4115SEC Lucemon SCR	12.50	25.00
BT4115SEC Lucemon SCR ALT ART	25.00	50.00

2021 Digimon Starter Deck Gallantmon

ST116U Gaia Force U ALT ART	.25	.50
ST701U Gigimon U	.15	.30
ST702C Agumon C	.50	1.00
ST704C Biyomon C	.10	.20
ST705R Growlmon R	1.25	2.50
ST706U GeoGreymon U	.30	.60
ST707U RizeGreymon U	.15	.30
ST708R WarGrowlmon R	.20	.40
ST710R ShineGreymon R	.20	.40
ST711U Lightning Joust U	1.00	2.00
ST712C Atomic Blaster C	.30	.60
BT1009C Monodramon C ALT ART	.15	.30
BT1019C DarkTyrannomon C ALT ART	.10	.20
BT1020U Groundramon U ALT ART	.15	.30
ST703SR Guilmon SR	1.50	3.00
ST709SR Gallantmon SR	.50	1.00

2021 Digimon Starter Deck Giga Green

ST401U Motimon U	.15	.30
ST402C Floramon C	.10	.20
ST403U Tentomon U	.15	.30
ST404C Palmon C	.30	.75
ST405C Kunemon C	.10	.20
ST406C Togemon C	.10	.20
ST407C Kuwagamon C	.10	.20
ST408U Kabuterimon U	4.00	8.00
ST409C Okuwamon C	.10	.20
ST410U Lillymon U	.15	.30
ST411R MegaKabuterimon R	.75	1.50
ST412R Rosemon R	.20	.40
ST414R Izzy Izumi R	.25	.50
ST415C Needle Spray C	.20	.40
ST416U Electro Shocker U	.15	.30
ST413SR HerculesKabuterimon SR	.20	.40

2021 Digimon Starter Deck Machine Black

ST501U Kapurimon U	.15	.30
ST502C Jazamon C	.10	.20
ST503U Agumon U	.25	.50
ST504C ToyAgumon C	.10	.20
ST505C Commandramon C	1.00	2.00
ST506C Greymon C	.10	.20
ST507C Jazardmon C	.10	.20
ST508U DarkTyrannomon U	1.50	3.00
ST509U MetalGreymon U	.15	.30
ST510C MetalTyrannomon C	.10	.20
ST511R Megadramon R	1.00	2.00
ST512R Machinedramon R	.20	.40
ST514R Tai Kamiya R	.20	.40
ST515C Laser Eye C	.10	.20
ST516U Dark Side Attack U	.15	.30
ST513SR BlitzGreymon SR	.20	.40

2021 Digimon Starter Deck Ulforce Veedramon

ST213C Hammer Spark C ALT ART	1.25	2.50
ST801U DemiVeemon U	.15	.30
ST802C Gabumon C	.50	1.00
ST803C Dracomon C	.10	.20
ST805R Veedramon R	.20	.40
ST806U Coredramon U	.15	.30
ST807U Wingdramon U	.15	.30
ST808R AeroVeedramon R	.20	.40
ST809R Slayerdramon R	.20	.40
ST811U Victory Sword U	.15	.30
ST812C V-Wing Blade C	.10	.20
BT1028C Elecmon C ALT ART	.10	.20
BT1037C Gorillamon C ALT ART	.10	.20
BT1038C Monzaemon C ALT ART	.10	.20
ST804SR Veemon SR	1.25	2.50
ST810SR UlforceVeedramon SR	.20	.40

2021 Digimon Starter Deck Venemous Violet

ST601U Pagumon U	.30	.75
ST602C DemiDevimon C	.10	.20
ST603C Gabumon C	.50	1.00
ST604U Dracmon U	.15	.30
ST605C Elecmon C	.10	.20
ST606C Garurumon C	.10	.20
ST607C Youkomon C	.10	.20
ST608U Devimon U	3.00	6.00
ST609C Kyukimon C	.10	.20
ST610U SkullSatamon U	.15	.30
ST611R WereGarurumon R	.20	.40
ST612R VenomMyotismon R	.20	.40
ST614R Matt Ishida R	.20	.40
ST615C Death Claw C	.75	1.50
ST616U Nail Bone U	2.00	4.00
ST613SR CresGarurumon SR	.20	.40

2022 Digimon Digital Hazard

EX2001U Gigimon U	.15	.30
EX2001U Gigimon U ALT ART	25.00	50.00
EX2002U Xiaomon U	.15	.30
EX2003U Viximon U	.15	.30
EX2003U Viximon U ALT ART	12.50	25.00
EX2004U Gummymon U	.15	.30
EX2004U Gummymon U ALT ART	10.00	20.00
EX2005U Hopmon U	.15	.30
EX2006U Yaamon U	.15	.30
EX2006U Yaamon U ALT ART	2.50	5.00
EX2007R Mother D-Reaper R	.20	.40
EX2008R Guilmon R	.20	.40
EX2008R Guilmon R ALT ART	12.50	25.00
EX2009C Growlmon C	.10	.20
EX2010U WarGrowlmon U	.15	.30
EX2013C Labramon C	.10	.20
EX2014C IceDevimon C	.10	.20
EX2015C Seasarmon C	.10	.20
EX2016C Gorillamon C	.10	.20
EX2018R MarineAngemon R	.20	.40
EX2018R MarineAngemon R ALT ART	2.00	4.00
EX2019R Renamon R	.20	.40
EX2019R Renamon R ALT ART	12.50	25.00
EX2020C Lopmon C	.10	.20
EX2021C Kyubimon C	.10	.20
EX2022R Antylamon R	.20	.40
EX2022R Antylamon R ALT ART	3.00	6.00
EX2023U Taomon U	.15	.30
EX2025R Terriermon R	.20	.40
EX2025R Terriermon R ALT ART	7.50	15.00
EX2026C Gargomon C	.10	.20
EX2027U Rapidmon U	.15	.30
EX2028U Parasitemon U	.15	.30
EX2030U Monodramon U	.15	.30
EX2031R Guardromon R	.20	.40
EX2031R Guardromon R ALT ART	1.50	3.00
EX2032C Strikedramon C	.10	.20
EX2033C Locomon C	.10	.20
EX2034C Andromon C	.10	.20
EX2035R Cyberdramon R	.20	.40
EX2035R Cyberdramon R ALT ART	4.00	8.00
EX2036C GroundLocomon C	.10	.20
EX2037U Reapermon U	.15	.30
EX2039R Impmon R	.20	.40
EX2039R Impmon R ALT ART	.75	1.50
EX2040C Devidramon C	.10	.20
EX2041R Dobermon R	.20	.40
EX2041R Dobermon R ALT ART	6.00	12.00
EX2042C Mephistomon C	.10	.20
EX2045R Calumon R	.15	.30
EX2045R Calumon R ALT ART	10.00	20.00
EX2046C ADR-02 Searcher C	.50	1.00
EX2047C ADR-03 Pendulum Feet C	.10	.20
EX2048C ADR-04 Bubbles C	.10	.20
EX2049U ADR-01 Jeri U	.15	.30
EX2050C ADR-05 Creep Hands C	.10	.20
EX2051C ADR-07 Palates Head C	.10	.20
EX2052C ADR-06 Horn Striker C	.10	.20
EX2053C ADR-08 Optimizer C	.10	.20
EX2054C ADR-09 Gatekeeper C	.10	.20
EX2055R Reaper R	.20	.40
EX2056R Takato Matsuki R	.20	.40
EX2056R Takato Matsuki R ALT ART	25.00	50.00
EX2057U Kenta Kitagawa U	.15	.30
EX2058U Jeri Kato U	.15	.30
EX2058U Jeri Kato U ALT ART	4.00	8.00
EX2059U Shu-Chong Wong U	.15	.30
EX2060R Rika Nonaka R	.20	.40
EX2060R Rika Nonaka R ALT ART	20.00	40.00
EX2061R Henry Wong R	.20	.40
EX2061R Henry Wong R ALT ART	7.50	15.00
EX2062R Ryo Akiyama R	.20	.40
EX2062R Ryo Akiyama R ALT ART	6.00	12.00
EX2063U Kazu Shioda U	.15	.30
EX2064U Alice McCoy U	.15	.30
EX2065R Ai & Mako R	.20	.40
EX2065R Ai & Mako R ALT ART	12.50	25.00
EX2066C Offensive Plug-In A C	.10	.20
EX2067U Fire Ball U	.15	.30
EX2068C High-Speed Plug-In D C	.10	.20
EX2069U Fist of the Beast King U	.15	.30
EX2070C Digivolution Plug-In S C	.10	.20
EX2071U Death Slinger U	.15	.30
EX2072R Blue Card R	.20	.40
EX2011SR Gallantmon SR	3.00	6.00
EX2011SR Gallantmon SR ALT ART	12.50	25.00
EX2012SR Megidramon SR	.75	1.50
EX2012SR Megidramon SR ALT ART	7.50	15.00
EX2017SR Leomon SR	.30	.75
EX2017SR Leomon SR ALT ART	7.50	15.00
EX2024SR Sakuyamon SR	5.00	10.00
EX2024SR Sakuyamon SR ALT ART	25.00	50.00
EX2029SR MegaGargomon SR	.75	1.50
EX2029SR MegaGargomon SR ALT ART	5.00	10.00
EX2038SR Justimon Blitz Arm SR	.75	1.50
EX2038SR Justimon Blitz Arm SR ALT ART	7.50	15.00
EX2043SR Gulfmon SR	.20	.40
EX2043SR Gulfmon SR ALT ART	2.00	4.00
EX2044SR Beelzemon SR	1.50	3.00
EX2044SR Beelzemon SR ALT ART	25.00	50.00
EX2073SEC Gallantmon Crimson Mode SCR	30.00	60.00
EX2073SEC Gallantmon Crimson Mode SCR ALT ART	30.00	75.00
EX2074SEC Beelzemon Blast Mode SCR	25.00	50.00
EX2074SEC Beelzemon Blast Mode SCR ALT ART	30.00	75.00

2022 Digimon Draconic Roar

EX3001U Bebydomon U	.15	.30
EX3002U Missimon U	.15	.30
EX3003C Sunarizamon C	.10	.20
EX3004R Veemon R	.20	.40
EX3005U Vorvomon U	.15	.30
EX3006C Flarerizamon C	.10	.20
EX3007U Lavorvomon U	.15	.30
EX3008C Flamedramon C	.10	.20
EX3009C Volcdramon C	.10	.20
EX3010U Paildramon U	.15	.30
EX3010U Paildramon U ALT ART	2.50	5.00
EX3011R Lavogaritamon R	.20	.40
EX3014R Dorbickmon R	.20	.40
EX3014R Dorbickmon R ALT ART	5.00	10.00
EX3015C Crabmon C	.10	.20
EX3016C SnowAgumon C	.10	.20
EX3017C Ebidramon C	.10	.20
EX3018U Coredramon U	.15	.30
EX3019C Paledramon C	.10	.20
EX3020U Wingdramon U	.15	.30
EX3020U Wingdramon U ALT ART	3.00	6.00
EX3021C CrysPaledramon C	.10	.20
EX3022R MegaSeadramon R	.20	.40
EX3023U Plesiomon U	.15	.30
EX3024R Slayerdramon R	.20	.40
EX3024R Slayerdramon R ALT ART	4.00	8.00
EX3025R Azulongmon R	.20	.40
EX3025R Azulongmon R ALT ART	.75	1.50
EX3027C Agumon C	.10	.20
EX3028C Patamon C	.10	.20
EX3029C Airdramon C	.10	.20
EX3030C Gatomon C	.10	.20
EX3031U Veedramon U	.15	.30
EX3031U Veedramon U ALT ART	.60	1.25
EX3032C Majiramon C	.10	.20
EX3033R AeroVeedramon R	.20	.40
EX3034U Angewomon U	.15	.30
EX3036R Magnadramon R	.20	.40
EX3036R Magnadramon R ALT ART	3.00	6.00
EX3037U Dracomon U	.15	.30
EX3037U Dracomon U ALT ART	6.00	12.00
EX3038U Pomumon U	.15	.30
EX3039U Coredramon U	.15	.30
EX3040C Parasaurmon C	.10	.20
EX3041U Groundramon U	.15	.30
EX3041U Groundramon U ALT ART	4.00	8.00
EX3042C Toropiamon C	.10	.20
EX3043R Entmon R	.20	.40
EX3044R Breakdramon R	.20	.40
EX3044R Breakdramon R ALT ART	2.00	4.00
EX3046C Commandramon C	.10	.20
EX3047U Jazamon U	.15	.30
EX3048U Jazardmon U	.15	.30
EX3049U Sealsdramon U	.15	.30
EX3049U Sealsdramon U ALT ART	4.00	8.00
EX3050C Cyberdramon C	.10	.20
EX3051R Tankdramon R	.20	.40
EX3052R Jazarichmon R	.20	.40
EX3055R Wormmon R	.20	.40
EX3056C Guilmon C	.10	.20
EX3057C Growlmon C	.10	.20
EX3058C Shadramon C	.10	.20
EX3059C DarkTyrannomon C	.10	.20
EX3060C ExTyrannomon C	.10	.20
EX3061U Dinobeemon U	.15	.30
EX3061U Dinobeemon U ALT ART	2.50	5.00
EX3062U WarGrowlmon U	.15	.30
EX3064R Megidramon R	.20	.40
EX3064R Megidramon R ALT ART	2.00	4.00
EX3065R Hina Kurihara R	.20	.40
EX3065R Hina Kurihara R ALT ART	7.50	15.00
EX3066R Hyper Infinity Cannon R	.20	.40
EX3067U Sourai U	.15	.30
EX3068C God Flame C	.10	.20
EX3069R Trial of the Four Great Dragons R	.20	.40
EX3070R Avalon's Gate R	.20	.40
EX3071C Laser Cannon C	.10	.20
EX3072C Megiddo Flame C	.10	.20
BT3111SEC Imperialdramon: Dragon Mode SEC ALT ART	.50	1.00
EX3012SR Volcanicdramon SR	.50	1.00
EX3012SR Volcanicdramon SR ALT ART	4.00	8.00
EX3013SR Chaosdramon SR	4.00	8.00
EX3013SR Chaosdramon SR ALT ART	10.00	20.00
EX3026SR Aegisdramon SR	.30	.60
EX3026SR Aegisdramon SR ALT ART	3.00	6.00
EX3035SR Goldramon SR	.20	.40
EX3035SR Goldramon SR ALT ART	2.00	4.00
EX3045SR Hydramon SR	.50	1.00
EX3045SR Hydramon SR ALT ART	5.00	10.00
EX3053SR Metallicdramon SR	1.00	2.00
EX3053SR Metallicdramon SR ALT ART	6.00	12.00
EX3054SR Darkdramon SR	3.00	6.00
EX3054SR Darkdramon SR ALT ART	7.50	15.00
EX3063SR Imperialdramon: Dragon Mode SR	.50	1.00
EX3063SR Imperialdramon: Dragon Mode SR ALT ART	4.00	8.00
EX3073SEC Imperialdramon: Fighter Mode SEC	10.00	20.00
EX3073SEC Imperialdramon: Fighter Mode SEC ALT ART	10.00	20.00
EX3074SEC Examon SEC	15.00	30.00
EX3074SEC Examon SEC ALT ART	17.50	35.00

2022 Digimon New Awakening

BT8001U Gurimon U	.15	.30
BT8002U Hiyarimon U	.15	.30
BT8003U Frimon U	.15	.30
BT8004U Bibimon U	.15	.30
BT8005U Kyokyomon U	.15	.30
BT8006U DemiMeramon U	.15	.30
BT8007C Gazimon C	.10	.20
BT8008R Gammamon R	.20	.40
BT8008R Gammamon R ALT ART	7.50	15.00
BT8009U Hawkmon U	.15	.30
BT8009U Hawkmon U ALT ART	4.00	8.00
BT8010C Aquilamon C	.10	.20
BT8011U Cyclonemon U	.15	.30
BT8012R Flamedramon R	.25	.50
BT8012R Flamedramon R ALT ART	12.50	25.00
BT8013C BetelGammamon C	.10	.20
BT8014C SkullMeramon C	.10	.20
BT8015R Silphymon R	.20	.40
BT8016C MasterTyrannomon C	.10	.20
BT8017C UltimateBrachiomon C	.10	.20
BT8018U Marsmon U	.15	.30
BT8020C Patamon C	.10	.20
BT8021U Veemon U	.15	.30
BT8022C SnowAgumon C	.10	.20
BT8023U Submarimon U	.15	.30
BT8024C Angemon C	.10	.20
BT8025C Hookmon C	.10	.20
BT8026R Halsemon R	.20	.40
BT8026R Halsemon R ALT ART	3.00	6.00
BT8027C Scorpiomon C	.10	.20
BT8028C CaptainHookmon C	.10	.20
BT8029C Frozomon C	.10	.20
BT8030C Surfimon C	.10	.20
BT8031R FrosVelgrmon R	.20	.40
BT8033U Armadillomon U	.15	.30
BT8033U Armadillomon U ALT ART	4.00	8.00
BT8034C Elecmon C	.10	.20
BT8035C Candlemon C	.10	.20
BT8036C Ankylomon C	.10	.20
BT8037U Dinohyumon U	.15	.30
BT8040C Betsumon C	.10	.20
BT8041C Kyukimon C	.10	.20
BT8042R Shakkoumon R	.20	.40
BT8043U Cherubimon U	.15	.30
BT8044R Azulongmon R	.20	.40
BT8045C Ekakimon C	.10	.20
BT8046U Terriermon U	.15	.30
BT8047C Pulsemon C	.10	.20
BT8048U Shurimon U	.15	.30
BT8049U Namakemon U	.15	.30
BT8050C Exermon C	.10	.20
BT8051R Digmon R	.20	.40
BT8051R Digmon R ALT ART	2.50	5.00
BT8052C Drimogemon C	.10	.20
BT8053R Lighdramon R	1.25	2.50
BT8054C Pistmon C	.10	.20
BT8055R Climbmon R	.20	.40
BT8056C Spinomon C	.10	.20
BT8058R Agumon R	.20	.40
BT8059C Kokuwamon C	.10	.20
BT8060R Ryudamon R	.20	.40
BT8060R Ryudamon R ALT ART	20.00	40.00
BT8061C Thundermon C	.10	.20
BT8062U SkullKnightmon Cavalier Mode U	.15	.30
BT8063C Ginryumon C	.10	.20
BT8064C Greymon C	.10	.20
BT8065C CatchMamemon C	.10	.20
BT8066C Hisyaryumon C	.10	.20
BT8067R MetalGreymon R	.30	.60
BT8068R BanchoMamemon R	.20	.40
BT8071C Psychemon C	.10	.20
BT8072U DemiDevimon U	.15	.30
BT8073C Mushroomon C	.10	.20
BT8074C Soulmon C	.10	.20
BT8075U Kogamon U	.15	.30
BT8076C Fangmon C	.10	.20
BT8077U BlackGatomon U	.15	.30
BT8078C Karatenmon C	.10	.20
BT8079C SkullSatamon C	.10	.20

BT8080R Myotismon R	.20	.40
BT8081U Rasenmon Fury Mode U	.15	.30
BT8085R Yolei Inoue R	.20	.40
BT8085R Yolei Inoue BT R	.60	1.25
BT8086R Hiro Amanokawa R	.75	1.50
BT8087U T.K. Takaishi U	.15	.30
BT8087U T.K. Takaishi BT U	.15	.30
BT8088R Davis Motomiya & Ken Ichijoji R	.75	1.50
BT8088R Davis Motomiya & Ken Ichijoji BT R	4.00	8.00
BT8089R Cody Hida R	.20	.40
BT8089R Cody Hida BT R	2.50	5.00
BT8090U Kari Kamiya U	.15	.30
BT8090U Kari Kamiya BT U	.15	.30
BT8091R Willis R	.20	.40
BT8091R Willis BT R	.75	1.50
BT8092R Yuji Musya R	.20	.40
BT8093R Yukio Oikawa R	.20	.40
BT8094R Digimon Kaiser R	.20	.40
BT8095C Fire Rocket C	.10	.20
BT8096C Top Gun C	.10	.20
BT8097U Crimson Blaze U	.15	.30
BT8098U Innocence Blizzard U	.15	.30
BT8099R Giga Death R	.20	.40
BT8100C Disaster Blaster C	.10	.20
BT8101U Plasma Shot U	.15	.30
BT8102U Samadhi Santi U	.15	.30
BT8103C Lightning Blade C	.10	.20
BT8104U Eiseiryuoujin U	.15	.30
BT8105R Dark Gaia Force R	.20	.40
BT8106C Senbon Dokkan C	.10	.20
BT8107U Pandemonium Flame U	.15	.30
BT8108C Mist Memory Boost! C	.10	.20
BT8109R Flame Hellscythe R	.60	1.25
BT8110C Armor Texture! C	.10	.20
BT8019SR Zhuqiaomon SR	.20	.40
BT8032SR Imperialdramon Fighter Mode SR	2.50	5.00
BT8032SR Imperialdramon Fighter Mode SR ALT ART	12.50	25.00
BT8038SR Magnamon SR	6.00	12.00
BT8038SR Magnamon SR ALT ART	30.00	75.00
BT8039SR Rapidmon SR	7.50	15.00
BT8039SR Rapidmon SR ALT ART	20.00	40.00
BT8057SR Shivamon SR	.60	1.25
BT8057SR Shivamon SR ALT ART	7.50	15.00
BT8069SR Ouryumon SR	2.50	5.00
BT8069SR Ouryumon SR ALT ART	15.00	30.00
BT8070SR BlackWarGreymon SR	4.00	8.00
BT8070SR BlackWarGreymon SR ALT ART	20.00	40.00
BT8082SR Ophanimon Falldown Mode SR	3.00	6.00
BT8082SR Ophanimon Falldown Mode SR ALT ART	25.00	50.00
BT8083SR MaloMyotismon SR	.25	.50
BT8083SR MaloMyotismon SR ALT ART	5.00	10.00
BT8084SR Kimeramon SR	7.50	15.00
BT8084SR Kimeramon SR ALT ART	20.00	40.00
BT8111SEC Creepymon SCR	4.00	8.00
BT8111SEC Creepymon SCR ALT ART	12.50	25.00
BT8112SEC Imperialdramon Paladin Mode SCR	4.00	8.00
BT8112SEC Imperialdramon Paladin Mode SCR ALT ART	10.00	20.00

2022 Digimon Next Adventure

BT7001 Kapurimon U	.15	.30
BT7002 Bukamon U	.15	.30
BT7003 Pusurimon U	.15	.30
BT7004 Koromon U	.15	.30
BT7005 Dorimon U	.15	.30
BT7006 Kokomon U	.15	.30
BT7007 ToyAgumon C	.10	.20
BT7008 Flamemon R ALT ART	5.00	10.00
BT7008 Flamemon R	.20	.40
BT7009 Huckmon C	.10	.20
BT7010 Tuskmon C	.10	.20
BT7011 BurningGreymon U	.15	.30
BT7012 Brachiomon C	.10	.20
BT7013 MetalGreymon SR ALT ART	7.50	15.00
BT7013 MetalGreymon SR	.60	1.25
BT7014 Aldamon U	.15	.30
BT7015 AvengeKidmon U	.15	.30
BT7016 EmperorGreymon SR ALT ART	12.50	25.00
BT7016 EmperorGreymon SR	1.00	2.00
BT7017 Chaosdramon R	.20	.40
BT7018 Gomamon U	.15	.30
BT7019 Strabimon R ALT ART	4.00	8.00
BT7019 Strabimon R	.20	.40
BT7020 Shellmon C	.10	.20
BT7021 Kumamon C	.10	.20
BT7022 KendoGarurumon C	.10	.20
BT7023 Korikakumon C	.10	.20
BT7024 DaiPenmon U	.15	.30
BT7025 Beowolfmon U	.15	.30
BT7026 WereGarurumon SR ALT ART	4.00	8.00
BT7026 WereGarurumon SR	.25	.50
BT7027 Whamon C	.10	.20
BT7028 KingWhamon C	.10	.20
BT7029 MagnaGarurumon SR ALT ART	6.00	12.00
BT7029 MagnaGarurumon SR	1.00	2.00
BT7030 AncientMegatheriummon R	.20	.40
BT7031 Herissmon R	.20	.40
BT7031 Herissmon R ALT ART	4.00	8.00
BT7032 Pulsemon C	.10	.20
BT7033 Bulkmon C	.10	.20
BT7034 Filmon C	.10	.20
BT7035 Kazemon C	.10	.20
BT7036 Zephyrmon U	.15	.30
BT7037 Boutmon C	.10	.20
BT7038 JetSilphymon U	.15	.30
BT7039 Stefilmon U	.15	.30
BT7040 Rasenmon SR	.30	.60
BT7040 Rasenmon SR ALT ART	6.00	12.00
BT7041 Kazuchimon SR	.50	1.00
BT7041 Kazuchimon SR ALT ART	5.00	10.00
BT7042 AncientKazemon R	.20	.40
BT7043 Gotsumon C	5.00	10.00
BT7044 Betamon R	.20	.40
BT7044 Betamon R ALT ART	4.00	8.00
BT7045 Tortomon C	.10	.20
BT7046 Beetlemon U	.15	.30
BT7047 MetalKabuterimon C	.10	.20
BT7048 Monochromon C	.10	.20
BT7049 MameTyramon U	.15	.30
BT7050 Triceramon C	.10	.20
BT7051 RhinoKabuterimon U	.15	.30
BT7052 SaberLeomon C	.10	.20
BT7053 Dinorexmon R	.20	.40
BT7054 AncientBeetlemon R	.30	.75
BT7055 Ebonwumon SR	.25	.50
BT7056 Dorumon R	2.00	4.00
BT7056 Dorumon R ALT ART	30.00	75.00
BT7057 Monitamon C	.10	.20
BT7058 SkullKnightmon R	.20	.40
BT7059 DeadlyAxemon C	.10	.20
BT7060 Grumblemon C	.10	.20
BT7061 Gigasmon C	.10	.20
BT7062 Dorugamon C	.10	.20
BT7063 DarkKnightmon SR ALT ART	15.00	30.00
BT7063 DarkKnightmon SR	2.00	4.00
BT7064 DoruGreymon U	.15	.30
BT7065 Dorugoramon SR	3.00	6.00
BT7065 Dorugoramon SR ALT ART	20.00	40.00
BT7066 AncientVolcanomon R	.20	.40
BT7067 Ghostmon C	.10	.20
BT7068 Lopmon R	.20	.40
BT7068 Lopmon R ALT ART	7.50	15.00
BT7069 Eyesmon: Scatter Mode C	.15	.30
BT7070 Wendigomon C	.10	.20
BT7071 Loweemon C	.10	.20
BT7072 Eyesmon C	.10	.20
BT7073 KaiserLeomon U	.15	.30
BT7074 Antylamon C	.10	.20
BT7075 Rhihimon U	.15	.30
BT7076 Orochimon C	.10	.20
BT7077 Nidhoggmon U	.15	.30
BT7078 AncientSphinxmon R	.20	.40
BT7079 Cherubimon SR	1.00	2.00
BT7079 Cherubimon SR ALT ART	7.50	15.00
BT7080 Neemon C	.10	.20
BT7081 Bokomon C	.30	.75
BT7082 Sistermon Blanc (Awakened) R	.20	.40
BT7083 Sistermon Noir (Awakened) R	.20	.40
BT7084 Eosmon U	.15	.30
BT7085 Takuya Kanbara R	.25	.50
BT7085 Takuya Kanbara R ALT ART	1.50	3.00
BT7086 Tommy Himi R	.50	1.00
BT7086 Tommy Himi R ALT ART	2.50	5.00
BT7087 Koji Minamoto R	.20	.40
BT7087 Koji Minamoto R ALT ART	.75	1.50
BT7088 Zoe Orimoto R	1.25	2.50
BT7088 Zoe Orimoto R ALT ART	6.00	12.00
BT7089 J.P. Shibayama R	.30	.75
BT7089 J.P. Shibayama R ALT ART	2.00	4.00
BT7090 Kota Domoto R	.50	1.00
BT7091 Koichi Kimura R	.20	.40
BT7091 Koichi Kimura R ALT ART	1.00	2.00
BT7092 Flame Memory Boost! C	.10	.20
BT7093 Firedrake Strike U	.15	.30
BT7094 Giga Storm C	.10	.20
BT7095 Blue Hawaii Death C	.10	.20
BT7096 Starlight Velocity U	.15	.30
BT7097 Tidal Wave C	.10	.20
BT7098 Ultra Turbulence C	.10	.20
BT7099 Electric Rush U	.15	.30
BT7100 Qualialise Blast R	.20	.40
BT7101 Thunder Laser C	.10	.20
BT7102 Dino Memory Boost! C	.10	.20
BT7103 Mugen U	.15	.30
BT7104 Metal Cannon R	.20	.40
BT7105 Pride Memory Boost! U	.15	.30
BT7106 Brave Metal C	.10	.20
BT7107 Calling From the Darkness U	.15	.30
BT7108 Schwarz Lehrsatz C	.10	.20
BT7109 Dead or Alive R	.20	.40
BT7110 Evolution Ancient R	.20	.40
BT7111 Lucemon: Chaos Mode SCR	20.00	40.00
BT7111 Lucemon: Chaos Mode SCR ALT ART	30.00	75.00
BT7112 Susanoomon SCR	15.00	30.00
BT7112 Susanoomon SCR ALT ART	25.00	50.00

2022 Digimon Starter Deck Jesmon

ST112R Tai Kamiya R ALT ART	.25	.50
ST312R T.K. Takaishi R ALT ART	.25	.50
BT3093R Davis Motomiya R ALT ART	5.00	10.00
ST1201U Gurimon U	.15	.30
ST1202C Candlemon C	.10	.20
ST1203C Solarmon C	.10	.20
ST1204R Huckmon R	.20	.40
ST1205U Meramon R	.20	.40
ST1206C BaoHuckmon C	.10	.20
ST1207C SkullMeramon C	.10	.20
ST1208R SaviorHuckmon R	.20	.40
ST1209U Volcanomon U	.15	.30
ST1212U Sistermon Blanc U	.30	.60
ST1213U Sistermon Ciel U	.15	.30
ST1214C Aus Generics C	.10	.20
ST1215C From Master to Disciple C	.60	1.25
ST1216R Quake! Blast! Fire! Father! R	.20	.40
ST1210SR Jesmon SR	.30	.60
ST1211SR Gankoomon SR	.25	.50

2022 Digimon Starter Deck Parallel World Tactician

ST1001 Nyaromon U	.15	.30
ST1003 Lopmon C	.10	.20
ST1002C Salamon C	.10	.20
ST1005R Angewomon R	.20	.40
ST1007C Ghostmon C	.10	.20
ST1008U Tsukaimon U	.15	.30
ST1009U Witchmon U	.15	.30
ST1010C Wizardmon C	.10	.20
ST1011C Bastemon C	.10	.20
ST1012R LadyDevimon R	.20	.40
ST1013U Junomon U	.15	.30
ST1014R Chaos Degradation R	.60	1.25
ST1015U Darkness Wave U	.15	.30
ST1004SR Gatomon SR	1.50	3.00
ST1006SR Mastemon SR	.60	1.25

2022 Digimon Starter Deck Ragnaloardmon

ST614R Matt Ishida R ALT ART	.20	.40
BT3094R Ken Ichijoji R ALT ART	.20	.40
BT4096R Izzy Izumi R ALT ART	1.25	2.50
ST1301U Sakuttomon U	.15	.30
ST1302U Zubamon U	.15	.30
ST1303C ZubaEagermon C	.10	.20
ST1304U Duramon U	.15	.30
ST1307C Kotemon C	.10	.20
ST1308C Chikurimon C	.10	.20
ST1309U Ludomon U	.15	.30
ST1310C Gladimon C	.10	.20
ST1311U TiaLudomon U	.15	.30
ST1312C Knightmon C	.10	.20
ST1313R RaijiLudomon R	.20	.40
ST1314R BryweLudramon R	.20	.40
ST1315R Direct Smasher R	.20	.40
ST1316C Legend-Arms Alliance C	.10	.20
ST1305SR Durandamon SR	.25	.50
ST1306SR RagnaLoardmon SR	1.25	2.50

2022 Digimon Starter Deck Ultimate Ancient Dragon

ST901U Minomon U	.15	.30
ST902U Veemon U	.15	.30
ST903U Betamon U	.15	.30
ST904U ExVeemon U	.15	.30
ST907C KoKabuterimon C	.10	.20
ST908C Wormmon C	.10	.20
ST909U Stingmon U	.15	.30
ST910C Snimon C	.10	.20
ST911R Dinobeemon R	.20	.40
ST912C JewelBeemon C	.20	.40
ST913R GranKuwagamon R	.20	.40
ST914R Megadeath R	.50	1.00
ST915U Hell Masquerade U	.15	.30
BT1110R Flower Cannon R	.20	.40
ST905SR Paildramon SR	1.25	2.50
ST906SR Imperialdramon Dragon Mode SR	.50	1.00

2022 Digimon X Record

BT9001U Koromon U	.30	.75
BT9002U Puyoyomon U	.15	.30
BT9003U Tokomon (X Antibody) U	.15	.30
BT9004U Motimon U	.15	.30
BT9005U Tumblemon U	.15	.30
BT9006U Pagumon U	.15	.30
BT9007C Minidekachimon C	.10	.20
BT9008U Agumon (X Antibody) U	2.00	4.00
BT9008U Agumon (X Antibody) U ALT ART	40.00	80.00
BT9009U Guilmon (X Antibody) U	.30	.75
BT9010C Atamadekachimon C	.10	.20
BT9011C Growlmon (X Antibody) C	.10	.20
BT9012C Greymon (X Antibody) C	.10	.20
BT9013U OmniShoutmon (X Antibody) U	.15	.30
BT9014R WarGrowlmon (X Antibody) R	.60	1.25
BT9015R MetalGreymon (X Antibody) R	1.50	3.00
BT9018R Dinorexmon R	.20	.40
BT9019C Crabmon C	.10	.20
BT9020U Gabumon (X Antibody) U	.15	.30
BT9020U Gabumon (X Antibody) U ALT ART	12.50	25.00
BT9021R Jellymon R	.20	.40
BT9021R Jellymon R ALT ART	12.50	25.00
BT9022C Ebidramon C	.10	.20
BT9023C KausGammamon C	.10	.20
BT9024C Garurumon (X Antibody) C	.10	.20
BT9025C TeslaJellymon C	.10	.20
BT9026C Piranimon C	.10	.20
BT9027C Divermon C	.10	.20
BT9028R WereGarurumon (X Antibody) R	.20	.40
BT9029U Suijinmon U	.15	.30
BT9030C MetalPiranimon C	.10	.20
BT9032C ToyAgumon C	.10	.20
BT9033C Pillomon C	.10	.20
BT9034C Salamon (X Antibody) C	.10	.20
BT9035C Starmon C	.10	.20
BT9036C Gatomon (X Antibody) C	.10	.20
BT9037U Nefertimon U	.15	.30
BT9038U Pegasusmon U	.15	.30
BT9039C DarkSuperStarmon C	.10	.20
BT9040U Angewomon (X Antibody) U	.15	.30
BT9041R RizeGreymon (X Antibody) R	1.50	3.00
BT9042U Raijinmon U	.15	.30
BT9043R Magnadramon (X Antibody) R	.20	.40
BT9045C Elecmon C	.10	.20
BT9046U Kokuwamon (X Antibody) U	.15	.30
BT9047C Pomumon C	.10	.20
BT9048C Ninjamon C	.10	.20
BT9049C Kuwagamon (X Antibody) C	.10	.20
BT9050C Leomon (X Antibody) C	.10	.20
BT9051U Panjyamon (X Antibody) U	.15	.30
BT9052U Okuwamon (X Antibody) U	.15	.30
BT9053C Zamielmon C	.10	.20
BT9054U Fujinmon U	.15	.30
BT9056R Dinotigermon R	.20	.40
BT9057C Bearmon C	.10	.20
BT9058U Dorumon U	.15	.30
BT9059C Tapirmon C	.10	.20
BT9060C Grizzlymon C	.10	.20
BT9061C Monochromon C	.10	.20
BT9062C Raptordramon C	.10	.20
BT9063C LoaderLeomon C	.10	.20
BT9064R Grademon R	.20	.40
BT9064R Grademon R ALT ART	4.00	8.00
BT9065U Megadramon U	.15	.30
BT9066R Alphamon R	.20	.40
BT9066R Alphamon R ALT ART	17.50	35.00
BT9067R Raidenmon R	.20	.40
BT9070C Gazimon (X Antibody) C	.10	.20
BT9071U Dracmon U	.15	.30
BT9072C Salamon C	.10	.20
BT9073C Sangloupmon C	.10	.20
BT9074R Meicoomon R	.30	.60
BT9074R Meicoomon R ALT ART	7.50	15.00
BT9075U DexDorugamon U	.15	.30
BT9076C Maycrackmon: Vicious Mode C	.10	.20
BT9077C Matadormon C	.10	.20
BT9078U DexDoruGreymon U	.15	.30
BT9079R GranDracmon R	.20	.40
BT9080R Raguelmon R	.20	.40
BT9080R Raguelmon R ALT ART	3.00	6.00
BT9084R Tai Kamiya & Kari Kamiya R	2.00	4.00
BT9085R Matt Ishida & Sora Takenouchi R	.25	.50
BT9086R Kiyoshiro Higashimitarai R	.25	.50
BT9087R T.K. Takaishi & Izzy Izumi R	.20	.40
BT9088R Mimi Tachikawa & Joe Kido R	.20	.40
BT9089U Daigo Nishijima U	.15	.30
BT9090U Maki Himekawa U	.15	.30
BT9091U Meiko Mochizuki U	.15	.30
BT9092R Cool Boy R	4.00	8.00
BT9093C Flare Rock Soul C	.10	.20
BT9094U Atomic Megalo Blaster U	.15	.30
BT9095R Gaia Force ZERO R	.20	.40
BT9096C Startling Thunder C	.10	.20
BT9097R Metal Storm R	.20	.40
BT9098C Awakening of the Golden Knight C	.10	.20
BT9099R Sunrise Buster R	.30	.60
BT9100R Grandis Scissor R	.20	.40
BT9101C Ground Fang C	.10	.20
BT9102C Attack of the Heavy Mobile Digimon! C	.10	.20
BT9103C Kongou C	.10	.20
BT9104C X Digivolution! C	.10	.20
BT9105R Soul Digitalization R	.20	.40
BT9106C DeathXDigivolution! C	.10	.20
BT9107R Metal Impulse R	.20	.40
BT9108C Eye of the Gorgon C	.10	.20
BT9109U X Antibody U	2.00	4.00
BT9110U X Program U	.15	.30
BT9016SR WarGreymon (X Antibody) SR	1.25	2.50
BT9016SR WarGreymon (X Antibody) SR ALT ART	20.00	40.00
BT9017SR Gallantmon (X Antibody) SR	2.50	5.00
BT9017SR Gallantmon (X Antibody) SR ALT ART	15.00	30.00
BT9031SR MetalGarurumon (X Antibody) SR ALT ART	7.50	15.00
BT9031SR MetalGarurumon (X Antibody) SR	1.25	2.50
BT9044SR Magnamon (X Antibody) SR	3.00	6.00
BT9044SR Magnamon (X Antibody) SR ALT ART	12.50	25.00
BT9055SR GrandisKuwagamon SR	.25	.50

BT9055SR GrandisKuwagamon SR ALT ART 5.00 10.00
BT9068SR Gaiomon SR 3.00 6.00
BT9068SR Gaiomon SR ALT ART 25.00 50.00
BT9069SR Baihumon SR .60 1.25
BT9081SR DexDorugoramon SR .25 .50
BT9081SR DexDorugoramon SR ALT ART 3.00 6.00
BT9082SR Ordinemon SR 2.50 5.00
BT9082SR Ordinemon SR ALT ART 12.50 25.00
BT9083SR Omnimon: Merciful Mode SR 1.25 2.50
BT9083SR Omnimon: Merciful Mode SR ALT ART 12.50 25.00
BT9111SEC Alphamon: Ouryuken SCR 12.50 25.00
BT9111SEC Alphamon: Ouryuken SCR ALT ART 17.50 35.00
BT9112SEC DeathXmon SCR 30.00 60.00
BT9112SEC DeathXmon SCR ALT ART 40.00 80.00

2022 Digimon X Record Box Toppers

BT9001U Koromon U 4.00 8.00
BT9002U Puyoyomon U .50 1.00
BT9003U Tokomon (X Antibody) U .30 .75
BT9004U Motimon U .50 1.00
BT9005U Tumblemon U .60 1.25
BT9006U Pagumon U .50 1.00

2022 Digimon Xros Encounter

BT10001U DemiMeramon U .15 .30
BT10002U Bebydomon U .15 .30
BT10003U Pickmons U .15 .30
BT10004U Bosamon U .15 .30
BT10005U Monimon U .15 .30
BT10006U Tokomon U .15 .30
BT10007C Dondokomon C .10 .20
BT10008U Shoutmon U .25 .50
BT10009R Shoutmon X4 R .20 .40
BT10010C Asuramon C .10 .20
BT10011R Canoweissmon R .20 .40
BT10011R Canoweissmon R ALT ART 12.50 25.00
BT10012U Shoutmon X4B U .15 .30
BT10013SR Shoutmon X5 SR 1.25 2.50
BT10013SR Shoutmon X5 SR ALT ART 7.50 15.00
BT10014U PileVolcamon U .15 .30
BT10015R Shoutmon X5B R .20 .40
BT10016SR Jesmon (X Antibody) SR 2.00 4.00
BT10016SR Jesmon (X Antibody) SR ALT ART 10.00 20.00
BT10017C Bulucomon C .10 .20
BT10018C Gaossmon C .10 .20
BT10019R Greymon R .50 1.00
BT10020U Deckerdramon U .15 .30
BT10021U MailBirdramon U .15 .30
BT10022C Brachiomon C .10 .20
BT10023R Thetismon R .20 .40
BT10023R Thetismon R ALT ART 6.00 12.00
BT10024SR MetalGreymon SR 7.50 15.00
BT10024SR MetalGreymon SR ALT ART 20.00 40.00
BT10025C Cyberdramon C .10 .20
BT10026R DeckerGreymon R .20 .40
BT10026R DeckerGreymon R ALT ART 7.50 15.00
BT10027C Regalecusmon C .10 .20
BT10028U Cannondramon U .15 .30
BT10029C Starmons C .10 .20
BT10030C Tinkermon C .10 .20
BT10031C Pulsemon C .10 .20
BT10032U Renamon U .30 .60
BT10033C Shortmon C .10 .20
BT10034C Dorulumon C .10 .20
BT10035C Darcmon C .10 .20
BT10036C Kyubimon C .10 .20
BT10037C Weddinmon C .10 .20
BT10038R Sanzomon R .20 .40
BT10039U Taomon U .15 .30
BT10040R Achillesmon R .20 .40
BT10041SR Sakuyamon: Maid Mode SR 4.00 8.00
BT10041SR Sakuyamon: Maid Mode SR ALT ART 30.00 60.00
BT10042SR Venusmon SR 4.00 8.00
BT10042SR Venusmon SR ALT ART 30.00 60.00
BT10043C Mushroomon C .10 .20
BT10044R Angoramon R .20 .40
BT10044R Angoramon R ALT ART 7.50 15.00
BT10045C Kokuwamon C .10 .20
BT10046U Palmon U .30 .60
BT10047C RedVegiemon C .10 .20
BT10048U Sunflowmon C .10 .20
BT10049C Ballistamon C .10 .20
BT10050C WezenGammamon C .10 .20
BT10051C SymbareAngoramon C .10 .20
BT10052C Cherrymon C .10 .20
BT10053U Ajatarmon U .20 .40
BT10054R Lamortmon R .20 .40
BT10054R Lamortmon R ALT ART 2.00 4.00
BT10055U Gryphonmon U .15 .30
BT10056R Lotosmon R .20 .40
BT10057SR Bloomlordmon SR 3.00 6.00
BT10057SR Bloomlordmon SR ALT ART 25.00 50.00
BT10058C Monitamon C .10 .20
BT10059U Spadamon U .15 .30
BT10060R Sparrowmon R .75 1.50
BT10060R Sparrowmon R ALT ART 15.00 30.00
BT10061C SkullKnightmon: Mighty Axe Mode C .10 .20
BT10062C Golemon C .10 .20
BT10063C Hi-VisionMonitamon C .10 .20
BT10064C Gogmamon C .10 .20
BT10065C Assaultmon C .10 .20
BT10066R DarkKnightmon R .20 .40
BT10067R Justimon: Critical Arm R .20 .40
BT10068SR Gankoomon (X Antibody) SR .60 1.25
BT10068SR Gankoomon (X Antibody) SR ALT ART 7.50 15.00
BT10069SR DarkKnightmon (X Antibody) SR 1.00 2.00
BT10069SR DarkKnightmon (X Antibody) SR ALT ART 7.50 15.00
BT10070U Blastmon U .15 .30
BT10071C Gazimon C .10 .20
BT10072C Soundbirdmon C .10 .20
BT10073U ChuuChuumon U .15 .30
BT10074C Quetzalmon C .10 .20
BT10075U Damemon C .10 .20
BT10076C Troopmon C .10 .20
BT10077C MadLeomon C .10 .20
BT10078R GulusGammamon R .20 .40
BT10079C Sandiramon C .10 .20
BT10080U SkullBaluchimon U .15 .30
BT10081C Baalmon C .25 .50
BT10082U Beelzemon U .15 .30
BT10082U Beelzemon ALT ART U 4.00 8.00
BT10083SR Minervamon SR 1.00 2.00
BT10083SR Minervamon SR ALT ART 10.00 20.00
BT10084C Tactimon C .10 .20
BT10085R Sistermon Ciel R .20 .40
BT10085R Sistermon Ciel R ALT ART 10.00 20.00
BT10086SR Omnimon (X Antibody) SR .75 1.50
BT10086SR Omnimon (X Antibody) SR ALT ART 12.50 25.00
BT10087R Taiki Kudo R .20 .40
BT10088R Kiriha Aonuma R .50 1.00
BT10089R Akari Hinomoto R .20 .40
BT10090R Zenjiro Tsurugi R .20 .40
BT10091R Ruli Tsukiyono R .20 .40
BT10092R Nene Amano R .20 .40
BT10093R Yuu Amano R .20 .40
BT10094U Breaclaw U .15 .30
BT10095R Hero of the Skies! R .20 .40
BT10096C Burning Star Crusher C .10 .20
BT10097R Blazing Memory Boost! R .20 .40
BT10098C Plasma Deckerdra Launcher C .10 .20
BT10099C Healing Therapy C .10 .20
BT10100C Impulse Memory Boost! C .10 .20
BT10101U Loenkhe Adistakto U .15 .30
BT10102C Pyon Dump C .10 .20
BT10103U Gran del Sol U .15 .30
BT10104R Immortal Ruler R .20 .40
BT10105C Defense Plug-In C .10 .20
BT10106U Justice Kick U .15 .30
BT10107C Buzzing Fist C .10 .20
BT10108U Death the Cannon U .15 .30
BT10109U Reinforcement Plug-In 0 U .15 .30
BT10110U Seiken Meppa U .15 .30
BT10111SEC Shoutmon (King Version) SCR ALT ART 7.50 15.00
BT10111SEC Shoutmon (King Version) SCR 2.50 5.00
BT10112SEC Jesmon GX SCR 15.00 30.00
BT10112SEC Jesmon GX SCR ALT ART 25.00 50.00

2022 Digimon Xros Encounter Box Toppers

BT10087R Taiki Kudo R 3.00 6.00
BT10088R Kiriha Aonuma R 5.00 10.00
BT10089R Akari Hinomoto R 2.50 5.00
BT10090R Zenjiro Tsurugi R 2.00 4.00
BT10092R Nene Amano R 3.00 6.00
BT10093R Yuu Amano R 3.00 6.00

2022 Digimon Xros Encounter Pre-Release Promos

BT10001U DemiMeramon U .15 .30
BT10002U Bebydomon U .15 .30
BT10003U Pickmons U .15 .30
BT10004U Bosamon U .15 .30
BT10005U Monimon U .15 .30
BT10006U Tokomon U .15 .30
BT10008U Shoutmon U .15 .30
BT10009R Shoutmon X4 R .20 .40
BT10011R Canoweissmon R .20 .40
BT10012U Shoutmon X4B U .15 .30
BT10014U PileVolcamon U .15 .30
BT10015R Shoutmon X5B R .20 .40
BT10019R Greymon R .20 .40
BT10020U Deckerdramon U .15 .30
BT10021U MailBirdramon U .15 .30
BT10023R Thetismon R .20 .40
BT10026R DeckerGreymon R .20 .40
BT10028U Cannondramon U .15 .30
BT10032U Renamon U .15 .30
BT10038R Sanzomon R .20 .40
BT10039U Taomon U .15 .30
BT10040R Achillesmon R .20 .40
BT10044R Angoramon R .20 .40
BT10046U Palmon U .15 .30
BT10053U Ajatarmon U .15 .30
BT10054R Lamortmon R .20 .40
BT10055U Gryphonmon U .15 .30
BT10056R Lotosmon R .20 .40
BT10059U Spadamon U .15 .30
BT10060R Sparrowmon R .20 .40
BT10066R DarkKnightmon R .20 .40
BT10067R Justimon: Critical Arm R .20 .40
BT10070U Blastmon U .15 .30
BT10073U ChuuChuumon U .15 .30
BT10075U Damemon U .15 .30
BT10078R GulusGammamon R .20 .40
BT10080U SkullBaluchimon U .15 .30
BT10082U Beelzemon U .15 .30
BT10085R Sistermon Ciel R .20 .40
BT10087R Taiki Kudo R .20 .40
BT10088R Kiriha Aonuma R .20 .40
BT10089R Akari Hinomoto R .20 .40
BT10090R Zenjiro Tsurugi R .20 .40
BT10091R Ruli Tsukiyono R .20 .40
BT10092R Nene Amano R .20 .40
BT10093R Yuu Amano R .20 .40
BT10094U Breaclaw U .15 .30
BT10095R Hero of the Skies! R .20 .40
BT10097R Blazing Memory Boost! R .20 .40
BT10101U Loenkhe Adistakto U .15 .30
BT10103U Gran del Sol U .15 .30
BT10104R Immortal Ruler R .20 .40
BT10106U Justice Kick U .15 .30
BT10108U Death the Cannon U .15 .30
BT10109U Reinforcement Plug-In 0 U .15 .30
BT10110U Seiken Meppa U .15 .30

2023 Digimon Across Time

BT12001U Gigimon U .10 .20
BT12002U DemiVeemon U .12 .25
BT12003U Koromon U .07 .15
BT12004U TorikaraBallmon U .05 .10
BT12005U Kozenimon U .05 .10
BT12006U Monimon U .12 .25
BT12007C Guilmon C .07 .15
BT12008C Shoutmon C .07 .15
BT12009C Flamemon C .07 .15
BT12010C Growlmon C .07 .15
BT12011U Shoutmon (King Version) U .12 .25
BT12012U Agunimon U .15 .30
BT12013U BurningGreymon U .12 .25
BT12014C OmniShoutmon C .07 .15
BT12015R Aldamon R .20 .40
BT12016R WarGrowlmon R .15 .30
BT12017SR EmperorGreymon SR 3.00 6.00
BT12017SR EmperorGreymon SR ALT ART 12.50 25.00
BT12018SR Gallantmon SR 2.50 5.00
BT12018SR Gallantmon SR ALT ART 15.00 30.00
BT12019C Otamamon C .05 .10
BT12020C Swimmon C .05 .10
BT12021C Veemon C .12 .25
BT12022U ExVeemon U .12 .25
BT12023C Gekomon C .05 .10
BT12024U Lanamon U .12 .25
BT12025C Calmaramon C .07 .15
BT12026U ShogunGekomon U .05 .10
BT12027C Mermaimon C .05 .10
BT12028R Paildramon R .15 .30
BT12029SR UlforceVeedramon (X Antibody) SR .25 .50
BT12029SR UlforceVeedramon (X Antibody) SR ALT ART 7.50 15.00
BT12030R Imperialdramon: Dragon Mode R .15 .30
BT12031SR Imperialdramon: Fighter Mode SR 1.50 3.00
BT12031SR Imperialdramon: Fighter Mode SR ALT ART 7.50 15.00
BT12032R AncientMermaimon R .07 .15
BT12033C Pillomon C .05 .10
BT12034C Agumon C .10 .20
BT12035U Ekakimon U .07 .15
BT12036C Mikemon C .05 .10
BT12037U Opossumon U .07 .15
BT12038C GeoGreymon C .07 .15
BT12039C Gokuumon C .05 .10
BT12040C Sagomon C .05 .10
BT12041C Cho-Hakkaimon C .05 .10
BT12042R RizeGreymon R .20 .40
BT12043SR ShineGreymon SR 10.00 20.00
BT12043SR ShineGreymon SR ALT ART 30.00 75.00
BT12044U Lampmon U .05 .10
BT12045C EbiBurgamon C .05 .10
BT12046C Burgamon C .05 .10
BT12047U Wormmon U .15 .30
BT12048U Dracmon U .07 .15
BT12049C Yakiimon C .07 .15
BT12050U Stingmon U .15 .30
BT12051C Yasyamon C .05 .10
BT12052C Potamon C .05 .10
BT12053C MetallifeKuwagamon C .05 .10
BT12054C Jagamon C .05 .10
BT12055R Dinobeemon R .20 .40
BT12056R GranKuwagamon R .07 .15
BT12057SR Quartzmon SR 7.50 15.00
BT12057SR Quartzmon SR ALT ART 20.00 40.00
BT12058C Zenimon C .05 .10
BT12059C Agumon C .20 .40
BT12060C ChuuChuumon C .05 .10
BT12061C Ganemon C .05 .10
BT12062C Greymon C .15 .30
BT12063U Damemon U .12 .25
BT12064C Tuwarmon C .07 .15
BT12065U Sephirothmon U .07 .15
BT12066C Mercurymon C .07 .15
BT12067C Betsumon C .05 .10
BT12068R MetalGreymon R .60 1.25
BT12069C Footmon C .05 .10
BT12070SR WarGreymon SR 2.50 5.00
BT12070SR WarGreymon SR ALT ART 20.00 40.00
BT12071R AncientWisemon R .07 .15
BT12072SR Chaosdramon (X Antibody) SR .50 1.00
BT12073C Impmon (X Antibody) C .12 .25
BT12074U Gumdramon U .10 .20
BT12075U Psychemon U .12 .25
BT12076C Dobermon C .07 .15
BT12077U Arresterdramon U .10 .20
BT12078C Wizardmon (X Antibody) C .12 .25
BT12079C Jokermon C .05 .10
BT12080C Wisemon C .07 .15
BT12081U Astamon U .07 .15
BT12082R Baalmon (X Antibody) R .20 .40
BT12083SR Arresterdramon: Superior Mode SR 3.00 6.00
BT12083SR Arresterdramon: Superior Mode SR ALT ART 12.50 25.00
BT12084U JetMervamon U .07 .15
BT12085SR Beelzemon (X Antibody) SR 2.00 4.00
BT12085SR Beelzemon (X Antibody) SR ALT ART 15.00 30.00
BT12086R Clockmon R .12 .25
BT12087R Taiki Kudo R .15 .30
BT12087R Taiki Kudo R ALT ART 10.00 20.00
BT12088R Takuya Kanbara R .15 .30
BT12088R Takuya Kanbara R ALT ART 12.50 25.00
BT12089R Takato Matsuki R .20 .40
BT12089R Takato Matsuki R ALT ART 12.50 25.00
BT12090R Davis Motomiya R .15 .30
BT12090R Davis Motomiya R ALT ART 7.50 15.00
BT12091U Airu Suzaki U .15 .30
BT12092R Marcus Damon R .50 1.00
BT12092R Marcus Damon R ALT ART 30.00 75.00
BT12093U Ren Tobari U .05 .10
BT12094U Yuu Amano U .10 .20
BT12095R Tai Kamiya R .40 .80
BT12095R Tai Kamiya R ALT ART 25.00 50.00
BT12096R Tagiru Akashi R .15 .30
BT12096R Tagiru Akashi R ALT ART 7.50 15.00
BT12097U Ryoma Mogami U .05 .10
BT12098R Watchmaker R .12 .25
BT12099C Pyro Dragons C .07 .15
BT12100R Final Xros Blade R .07 .15
BT12101R Vee Laser R .07 .15
BT12102C Great Maelstrom C .07 .15
BT12103C Home Run Blast C .05 .10
BT12104R Shining Blast R .12 .25
BT12105C Spiking Strike C .07 .15
BT12106R Gypt Particle Cannon R .05 .10
BT12107C Laplace's Demon C .05 .10
BT12108R Super Eradication Attack R .07 .15
BT12109R Overflowing Power R .07 .15
BT12110U Seventh Full Cluster U .15 .30
BT12111SEC DarknessBagramon SEC .75 1.50
BT12111SEC DarknessBagramon SEC ALT ART 2.50 5.00
BT12111SEC DarknessBagramon SEC ALT ART B&W 50.00 100.00
BT12112SEC Shoutmon X7: Superior Mode SEC 2.50 5.00
BT12112SEC Shoutmon X7: Superior Mode SEC ALT ART 7.50 15.00
BT12112SEC Shoutmon X7: Superior Mode SEC ALT ART GOLD 75.00 150.00

2023 Digimon Across Time Box-Toppers

BT12014C OmniShoutmon C .30 .75
BT12041C Cho-Hakkaimon C .25 .50
BT12051C Yasyamon C .20 .40
BT12064C Tuwarmon C .30 .60
BT12077U Arresterdramon U 1.00 2.00
BT12081U Astamon U .30 .75

2023 Digimon Across Time Pre-Release

BT12001U Gigimon U 1.50 3.00
BT12002U DemiVeemon U 2.50 5.00
BT12003U Koromon U 7.50 15.00
BT12004U TorikaraBallmon U 1.00 2.00
BT12005U Kozenimon U 1.00 2.00
BT12006U Monimon U 7.50 15.00
BT12011U Shoutmon (King Version) U 2.50 5.00
BT12012U Agunimon U 12.50 25.00
BT12013U BurningGreymon U 10.00 20.00
BT12015R Aldamon R 2.00 4.00
BT12016R WarGrowlmon R 2.00 4.00
BT12022U ExVeemon U 7.50 15.00
BT12024U Lanamon U 12.50 25.00
BT12026U ShogunGekomon U 1.00 2.00
BT12028R Paildramon R 1.50 3.00
BT12030R Imperialdramon: Dragon Mode R 2.00 4.00
BT12032R AncientMermaimon R 1.00 2.00
BT12035U Ekakimon U 2.50 5.00
BT12037U Opossumon U 1.50 3.00
BT12042R RizeGreymon R 2.00 4.00
BT12044U Lampmon U 1.00 2.00
BT12047U Wormmon U 7.50 15.00
BT12048U Dracmon U 6.00 12.00
BT12050U Stingmon U 6.00 12.00
BT12055R Dinobeemon R 1.50 3.00
BT12056R GranKuwagamon R 1.00 2.00
BT12063U Damemon U 7.50 15.00
BT12065U Sephirothmon U 1.00 2.00
BT12068R MetalGreymon R 5.00 10.00
BT12071R AncientWisemon R 1.00 2.00
BT12074U Gumdramon U 7.50 15.00
BT12075U Psychemon U 10.00 20.00
BT12077U Arresterdramon U 3.00 6.00

BT12081U Astamon U	1.25	2.50
BT12082R Baalmon (X Antibody) R	2.50	5.00
BT12084U JetMervamon U	2.00	4.00
BT12086R Clockmon R	3.00	6.00
BT12087R Taiki Kudo R	2.50	5.00
BT12088R Takuya Kanbara R	1.50	3.00
BT12089R Takato Matsuki R	1.00	2.00
BT12090R Davis Motomiya R	1.00	2.00
BT12091U Airu Suzaki U	1.25	2.50
BT12092R Marcus Damon R	1.25	2.50
BT12093U Ren Tobari U	1.00	2.00
BT12094U Yuu Amano U	7.50	15.00
BT12095R Tai Kamiya R	.75	1.50
BT12096R Tagiru Akashi R	1.00	2.00
BT12097U Ryoma Mogami U	1.00	2.00
BT12098R Watchmaker R	3.00	6.00
BT12100R Final Xros Blade R	1.00	2.00
BT12101R Vee Laser R	1.00	2.00
BT12104R Shining Blast R	3.00	6.00
BT12106R Gypt Particle Cannon R	1.50	3.00
BT12108R Super Eradication Attack R	1.00	2.00
BT12109R Overflowing Power R	1.00	2.00
BT12110U Seventh Full Cluster U	12.50	25.00

2023 Digimon Across Time Promos

BT12001U Gigimon (Ultimate Cup) U	10.00	20.00
BT12007C Guilmon (Ultimate Cup) C	50.00	100.00
BT12010C Growlmon (Ultimate Cup) C	60.00	125.00
BT12011U Shoutmon (King Version) (2023 Regionals Finalist Exclusive) U	25.00	50.00
BT12011U Shoutmon (King Version) (2023 Regionals Participant Exclusive) U	4.00	8.00
BT12015R Aldamon (Tamer Party Special) R	.50	1.00
BT12016R WarGrowlmon (Ultimate Cup) R	125.00	250.00
BT12016R WarGrowlmon (Tamer Party Special) R	2.00	4.00
BT12018SR Gallantmon (Ultimate Cup) SR	250.00	500.00
BT12042R RizeGreymon (Tamer Party Special) R	3.00	6.00
BT12068R MetalGreymon (Tamer Party Special) R	2.50	5.00

2023 Digimon Alternative Being Booster

EX4001U Missimon U	.15	.30
EX4002U Kokomon U	.15	.30
EX4003U Tsunomon U	.15	.30
EX4004U Pinamon U	.15	.30
EX4005U Agumon U	.15	.30
EX4006C Guilmon C	.10	.20
EX4007C GeoGreymon C	.10	.20
EX4008U BlackGrowlmon U	.15	.30
EX4009R RizeGreymon R	.20	.40
EX4010U BlackWarGrowlmon U	.15	.30
EX4011R ChaosGallantmon R	.20	.40
EX4014C Gaossmon C	.10	.20
EX4015U Gaomon U	.15	.30
EX4016U Greymon U	.15	.30
EX4017C Gaogamon C	.10	.20
EX4018C MailBirdramon C	.10	.20
EX4019R MachGaogamon R	.20	.40
EX4020R MetalGreymon R	.20	.40
EX4023R Agumon Expert R	.20	.40
EX4024C Renamon C	.10	.20
EX4025C Turuiemon C	.10	.20
EX4026U Youkomon U	.15	.30
EX4027R GoldVeedramon R	.20	.40
EX4028U Doumon U	.15	.30
EX4029C Antylamon C	.10	.20
EX4031R Cherubimon R	.20	.40
EX4032C Terriermon C	.10	.20
EX4033R Terriermon Assistant R	.20	.40
EX4034C Lopmon C	.10	.20
EX4035U BlackGargomon U	.15	.30
EX4036U BlackRapidmon U	.15	.30
EX4038C Agumon C	.10	.20
EX4039C Gabumon C	.10	.20
EX4040C SkullKnightmon C	.10	.20
EX4041C DeadlyAxemon C	.10	.20
EX4042U DarkMaildramon U	.15	.30
EX4043C Garurumon C	.10	.20
EX4044C Greymon C	.10	.20
EX4045U MetalGreymon U	.15	.30
EX4046U WereGarurumon U	.15	.30
EX4047R DarkKnightmon R	.20	.40
EX4048R Gaiomon R	.20	.40
EX4050R ShadowSeraphimon R	.20	.40
EX4052C Fake Agumon Expert C	.10	.20
EX4053R Falcomon R	.20	.40
EX4054C Wendigomon C	.10	.20
EX4055C Peckmon C	.10	.20
EX4056U Crowmon U	.15	.30
EX4057C Antylamon C	.10	.20
EX4059R Cherubimon R	.20	.40
EX4061R Matt Ishida & Tai Kamiya R	.20	.40
EX4062R Kiriha Aonuma & Nene Amano R	.20	.40
EX4063R Henry Wong & Shu-Chong Wong R	.20	.40
EX4064R Keenan Crier R	.20	.40
EX4065C Trident Gaia C	.10	.20
EX4066U Adze Beast Blade and Shining Dragon Bullet U	.15	.30
EX4067C Full Metal Blaze C	.10	.20
EX4068C Heaven's Judgement C	.10	.20
EX4069U Gaia Reactor U	.15	.30
EX4070C Tarnished Hero C	.10	.20
EX4071R Ame-no-Ohabari R	.20	.40
EX4072U Digital Translator U	.15	.30
EX4072U Digital Translator U BT	.15	.30

2023 Digimon Dimensional Phase

BT2046R MetalTyrannomon R ALT ART	.20	.40
BT3077C Gazimon C ALT ART	1.50	3.00
BT3103U Hidden Potential Discovered! U ALT ART	1.25	2.50
BT4063R Commandramon R ALT ART	2.00	4.00
BT6085C Eosmon C ALT ART	1.00	2.00
BT7005U Dorimon U ALT ART	2.00	4.00
BT7036U Zephyrmon U ALT ART	1.00	2.00
BT1063SR Seraphimon SR ALT ART	.40	.80
BT11001C Yokomon C	.10	.20
BT11002C Wanyamon C	.30	.60
BT11003U Tokomon U	.07	.15
BT11004C Tanemon C	.07	.15
BT11005U Koromon U	.10	.20
BT11006C Tsunomon C	.05	.10
BT11007R Biyomon R	.25	.50
BT11008C Bearmon C	.05	.10
BT11009C Shoutmon + Star Sword C	.07	.15
BT11010C Grizzlymon C	.05	.10
BT11011U Birdramon U	.10	.20
BT11012U Shoutmon X3 U	.12	.25
BT11013C Garudamon C	.05	.10
BT11014U GrapLeomon U	.05	.10
BT11015R OmniShoutmon R	.25	.50
BT11016SR Phoenixmon SR	.50	1.00
BT11016SR Phoenixmon ALT ART SR	4.00	8.00
BT11017SR Marsmon SR	.25	.50
BT11017SR Marsmon ALT ART SR	2.00	4.00
BT11018R Shoutmon DX R	.10	.20
BT11019SR Shoutmon X7 SR	.75	1.50
BT11019SR Shoutmon X7 ALT ART SR	3.00	6.00
BT11020R Gaomon R	2.00	4.00
BT11021C SnowGoblimon C	.05	.10
BT11022U Dracomon U	.12	.25
BT11023U Veemon U	.12	.25
BT11024C Penguinmon C	.05	.10
BT11025C Gaogamon C	.07	.15
BT11026C Hyogamon C	.05	.10
BT11027U Veedramon U	.07	.15
BT11028U MachGaogamon U	.10	.20
BT11029R AeroVeedramon R	.30	.60
BT11030U MetalGreymon + Cyber Launcher U	.07	.15
BT11031R ZeigGreymon R	2.50	5.00
BT11032SR UlforceVeedramon SR	1.25	2.50
BT11032SR UlforceVeedramon ALT ART SR	12.50	25.00
BT11033SR MirageGaogamon SR	5.00	10.00
BT11033SR MirageGaogamon ALT ART SR	15.00	30.00
BT11034C Cutemon C	.05	.10
BT11035C ClearAgumon C	.05	.10
BT11036U Chuumon U	.07	.15
BT11037C Kotemon C	.05	.10
BT11038U Angemon U	.07	.15
BT11039C Centarumon C	.05	.10
BT11040U Sukamon U	.07	.15
BT11041C Etemon C	.05	.10
BT11042R Angewomon R	2.50	5.00
BT11042R Angewomon ALT ART R	20.00	40.00
BT11043R KingSukamon R	.25	.50
BT11044U MetalEtemon U	.07	.15
BT11045U ClavisAngemon U	.05	.10
BT11046U Agumon U	.10	.20
BT11047C Palmon C	.07	.15
BT11048C ModokiBetamon C	.05	.10
BT11049C Vegiemon C	.05	.10
BT11050C Ninjamon C	.05	.10
BT11051C Ogremon C	.05	.10
BT11052R Tyrannomon R	.75	1.50
BT11053C Digitamamon C	.05	.10
BT11054U Panjyamon U	.07	.15
BT11055U MetalTyrannomon U	.12	.25
BT11056SR Jijimon SR	.30	.60
BT11056SR Jijimon ALT ART SR	2.50	5.00
BT11057U Titamon U	.05	.10
BT11058R HerculesKabuterimon (X Antibody) R	.07	.15
BT11059R RustTyrannomon R	.15	.30
BT11060C Monmon C	.05	.10
BT11061C Vemmon C	.30	.60
BT11062U Agumon (X Antibody) U	.12	.25
BT11063C Geremon C	.07	.15
BT11064C Greymon (X Antibody) C	.10	.20
BT11065U Snatchmon U	.05	.10
BT11066C Tekkamon C	.05	.10
BT11067U Gigadramon U	.07	.15
BT11068R Mamemon R	1.50	3.00
BT11069R MetalGreymon (X Antibody) R	2.50	5.00
BT11070R Destromon R	.07	.15
BT11071C MusouKnightmon C	.05	.10
BT11072R Machinedramon R	.30	.60
BT11073U Justimon: Accel Arm U	.07	.15
BT11074SR BlackWarGreymon (X Antibody) SR	1.50	3.00
BT11074SR BlackWarGreymon (X Antibody) ALT ART SR	10.00	20.00
BT11075C DoKunemon C	.05	.10
BT11076U Ignitemon U	.75	1.50
BT11077U Chikurimon U	.05	.10
BT11078C Soulmon C	.05	.10
BT11079C DarkLizardmon C	.05	.10
BT11080U Devimon U	.07	.15
BT11081C MadLeomon: Armed Mode C	.07	.15
BT11082R Tuwarmon R	.15	.30
BT11083R LadyDevimon R	1.50	3.00
BT11083R LadyDevimon ALT ART R	15.00	30.00
BT11084C BlueMeramon C	.05	.10
BT11085U WaruSeadramon U	.07	.15
BT11086SR Mervamon SR	1.25	2.50
BT11086SR Mervamon ALT ART SR	10.00	20.00
BT11087R Lilithmon R	.12	.25
BT11088SR Bagramon SR	.30	.75
BT11088SR Bagramon ALT ART SR	3.00	6.00
BT11089R Akiho Rindou R	.15	.30
BT11089R Akiho Rindou ALT ART R	6.00	12.00
BT11090R Nicolai Petrov R	.15	.30
BT11090R Nicolai Petrov ALT ART R	6.00	12.00
BT11091R Taiga R	.75	1.50
BT11091R Taiga ALT ART R	6.00	12.00
BT11092R Analogman R	1.00	2.00
BT11093R Yuuya Kuga R	1.00	2.00
BT11093R Yuuya Kuga ALT ART R	7.50	15.00
BT11094SR Mirei Mikagura SR	7.50	15.00
BT11094SR Mirei Mikagura ALT ART SR	25.00	50.00
BT11095R Taiki, Kiriha, & Nene R	1.25	2.50
BT11096C Magma Bomb C	.05	.10
BT11097C Crimson Flare C	.05	.10
BT11098C Maelstrom C	.05	.10
BT11099C Ice Statue C	.07	.15
BT11100C Megalo Spark C	.05	.10
BT11101C Holy Sunshine C	.05	.10
BT11102C High Mega Blaster C	.05	.10
BT11103U Poison Powder U	.05	.10
BT11104C Buster Dive C	.05	.10
BT11105U Fusionize U	.05	.10
BT11106C Cooties Kick C	.05	.10
BT11107R Hades Force R	1.25	2.50
BT11108R DG Dimension R	.12	.25
BT11109U Astral Snatcher U	.05	.10
BT11110C Evil Squall C	.05	.10
BT11111SEC Galacticmon SCR	7.50	15.00
BT11111SEC Galacticmon ALT ART SCR	10.00	20.00
BT11112SEC Rina Shinomiya SCR	25.00	50.00
BT11112SEC Rina Shinomiya ALT ART SCR	30.00	75.00
BT2032SR UlforceVeedramon ALT ART SR	30.00	75.00
BT2051SR RustTyrannomon SR ALT ART	.25	.50
BT5032SR Hexeblaumon SR ALT ART	.50	1.00
EX1073SEC Machinedramon ALT ART SCR	75.00	150.00
ST1006SR Mastemon ALT ART SR	150.00	400.00

2023 Digimon Dimensional Phase Box-Toppers

ST103U Agumon U/(Digimon Illustration Competition Pack)	.50	1.00
ST512R Machinedramon R	.20	.40
ST608U Devimon U/(Digimon Illustration Competition Pack)	.15	.30
BT2056C Numemon C	.10	.20
BT8006R Gammamon R/(Digimon Illustration Competition Pack)	.20	.40
EX1039U Lillymon U	.15	.30
EX2025R Terriermon R	.20	.40

2023 Digimon Starter Deck Beelzemon Advanced Deck

P077 Wizardmon P ALT ART	.10	.20
P033P Sunarizamon P ALT ART	1.00	2.00
BT2068 Impmon C ALT ART	.10	.20
BT8079 SkullSatamon C ALT ART	.07	.15
EX2071 Death Slinger U ALT ART	.07	.15
ST601U Pagumon U ALT ART	.60	1.25
BT2004U Argomon U ALT ART	.50	1.00
BT4105U Tactical Retreat! U ALT ART	.20	.40
BT9109U X Antibody U ALT ART	2.50	5.00
EX2039R Impmon R ALT ART	.15	.30
ST1401U Yaamon U	.07	.15
ST1403U Candlemon U	.07	.15
ST1404C Phascomon C	.07	.15
ST1405C Porcupamon C	.07	.15
ST1406U Witchmon U	.07	.15
ST1407R Baalmon R	.07	.15
ST1411R Ai & Mako R	.07	.15
ST1412R Rival's Barrage R	2.50	5.00
ST703SR Guilmon SR ALT ART	.50	1.00
ST804SR Veemon SR ALT ART	.20	.40
BT2111SEC Beelzemon SEC ALT ART	.25	.50
ST1402SR Impmon SR	1.00	2.00
ST1408SR Beelzemon SR ALT ART	200.00	400.00
ST1408SR Beelzemon SR	.25	.50
ST1409SR BeelStarmon SR	.30	.60
ST1410SR Beelzemon: Blast Mode SR	.10	.20

2023 Digimon Starter Deck Beelzemon Advanced Deck Pre-Release

BT6068U Impmon U (April 2023 Beelzemon Special)	.15	.30
BT6068U Impmon (Beelzemon Cup Participation)	.15	.30
ST1401U Yaamon	.15	.30
ST1403U Candlemon	.15	.30
ST1404C Phascomon	.10	.20
ST1405C Porcupamon	.10	.20
ST1406U Witchmon	.15	.30
ST1407R Baalmon	.20	.40
ST1411R Ai & Mako	.20	.40
ST1412R Rival's Barrage	.20	.40

2022 Disney Lorcana D23 Expo Promos

1 Mickey Mouse - Brave Little Tailor P	600.00	1,500.00
2 Stitch - Rock Star P	600.00	1,500.00
3 Elsa - Snow Queen P	750.00	2,000.00
4 Cruella De Vil - Miserable As Usual P	600.00	1,500.00
5 Maleficent - Monstrous Dragon P	600.00	1,500.00
6 Robin Hood - Unrivaled Archer P	600.00	1,500.00
7 Captain Hook - Forceful Duelist P ERR ("When challenging")	600.00	1,500.00

2023 Disney Lorcana Disney 100 Collector Set Promos

18P1 Mickey Mouse - Friendly Face P	3.00	8.00
19P1 Elsa - Gloves Off P	12.00	30.00
20P1 Genie - Powers Unleashed P	2.00	5.00
21P1 Stitch - Abomination P	5.00	12.00
22P1 Maleficent - Uninvited P	1.50	4.00
23P1 Maui - Demigod P	3.00	8.00

2023 Disney Lorcana GamesCom Promos

12P1 Goofy - Musketeer P	50.00	120.00

2023 Disney Lorcana GenCon Promos

11P1 Mickey Mouse - Musketeer P	50.00	120.00

2023 Disney Lorcana Gift Set

*FRENCH: .4X TO 1X BASIC
*GERMAN: .4X TO 1X BASIC

5 Hades - King Of Olympus R OVERSIZED FOIL	1.50	4.00
5 Hades - King Of Olympus R FOIL	.08	.20
118 Mulan - Imperial Soldier SR FOIL	.25	.60
118 Mulan - Imperial Soldier SR OVERSIZED FOIL	1.50	4.00

2023 Disney Lorcana Rise of the Floodborn

1 Bashful - Hopeless Romantic COLD FOIL U	.25	.60
1 Bashful - Hopeless Romantic U	.08	.20
2 Christopher Robin - Adventurer R	.08	.20
2 Christopher Robin - Adventurer COLD FOIL R	.40	1.00
3 Cinderella - Ballroom Sensation COLD FOIL R	4.00	10.00
3 Cinderella - Ballroom Sensation R	2.00	5.00
4 Cobra Bubbles - Just a Social Worker R	.08	.20
4 Cobra Bubbles - Just a Social Worker COLD FOIL R	.30	.75
5 Doc - Leader of the Seven Dwarfs COLD FOIL U	1.00	2.50
5 Doc - Leader of the Seven Dwarfs U	.08	.20
6 Dopey - Always Playful COLD FOIL U	.20	.50
6 Dopey - Always Playful U	.08	.20
7 Eudora - Accomplished Seamstress COLD FOIL C	.08	.20
7 Eudora - Accomplished Seamstress C	.08	.20
8 Gaston - Baritone Bully U	.08	.20
8 Gaston - Baritone Bully COLD FOIL U	.20	.50
9 Grand Duke - Advisor to the King COLD FOIL R	.40	1.00
9 Grand Duke - Advisor to the King R	.08	.20
10 Grumpy - Bad-Tempered COLD FOIL C	.15	.40
10 Grumpy - Bad-Tempered C	.08	.20
11 Happy - Good-Natured COLD FOIL C	.15	.40
11 Happy - Good-Natured C	.08	.20
12 King Louie - Jungle VIP COLD FOIL SR	.40	1.00
12 King Louie - Jungle VIP SR	.08	.20
13 Mickey Mouse - Friendly Face COLD FOIL SR	.60	1.50
13 Mickey Mouse - Friendly Face SR	.12	.30
14 Mufasa - Betrayed Leader COLD FOIL L	20.00	50.00
14 Mufasa - Betrayed Leader L	10.00	25.00
15 Mulan - Free Spirit COLD FOIL C	.15	.40
15 Mulan - Free Spirit C	.08	.20
16 Mulan - Reflecting COLD FOIL R	.75	2.00
16 Mulan - Reflecting R	.20	.50
17 Nana - Darling Family Pet COLD FOIL U	.12	.30
17 Nana - Darling Family Pet U	.08	.20
18 Piglet - Very Small Animal COLD FOIL C	.12	.30
18 Piglet - Very Small Animal C	.08	.20
19 Rapunzel - Gifted Artist COLD FOIL U	.30	.75
19 Rapunzel - Gifted Artist U	.08	.20
20 Rapunzel - Sunshine COLD FOIL C	.20	.50
20 Rapunzel - Sunshine C	.08	.20
21 Sleepy - Nodding Off COLD FOIL C	.12	.30
21 Sleepy - Nodding Off C	.08	.20
22 Sneezy - Very Allergic COLD FOIL C	.08	.20
22 Sneezy - Very Allergic C	.08	.20
23 Snow White - Lost in the Forest COLD FOIL C	.08	.20
23 Snow White - Lost in the Forest C	.15	.40
24 Snow White - Unexpected Houseguest COLD FOIL U	.08	.20
24 Snow White - Unexpected Houseguest U	.30	.75
25 Snow White - Well Wisher COLD FOIL L	10.00	25.00
25 Snow White - Well Wisher L	2.00	5.00
26 The Queen - Commanding Presence COLD FOIL SR	.50	1.25
26 The Queen - Commanding Presence SR	.50	1.25
27 The Queen - Regal Monarch C	.30	.75
27 The Queen - Regal Monarch COLD FOIL C	.08	.20
28 Hold Still COLD FOIL C	.08	.20
28 Hold Still C	.08	.20
29 Last Stand U	.08	.20
29 Last Stand COLD FOIL U	.15	.40
30 Painting the Roses Red C	.08	.20
30 Painting the Roses Red COLD FOIL C	.15	.40
31 World's Greatest Criminal Mind R	.20	.50

31 World's Greatest Criminal Mind COLD FOIL R 1.00 2.50
32 Zero To Hero U .08 .20
32 Zero To Hero COLD FOIL U .30 .75
33 Dragon Gem R .08 .20
33 Dragon Gem COLD FOIL R .40 1.00
34 Sleepy's Flute R .40 1.00
34 Sleepy's Flute COLD FOIL R 1.50 4.00
35 Arthur - Wizard's Apprentice SR .75 2.00
35 Arthur - Wizard's Apprentice COLD FOIL SR 1.25 3.00
36 Blue Fairy - Rewarding Good Deeds COLD FOIL U .08 .20
36 Blue Fairy - Rewarding Good Deeds U .60 1.50
37 Chip the Teacup - Gentle Soul COLD FOIL C .08 .20
37 Chip the Teacup - Gentle Soul C .08 .20
38 Dr. Facilier - Savvy Opportunist COLD FOIL C .12 .30
38 Dr. Facilier - Savvy Opportunist C .08 .20
39 Elsa - Gloves Off C COR/Tree Branch Fixed) .08 .20
39 Elsa - Gloves Off COLD FOIL C COR/Tree Branch Fixed) .15 .40
40 Fairy Godmother - Here to Help COLD FOIL U .15 .40
40 Fairy Godmother - Here to Help U .08 .20
41 Fairy Godmother - Mystic Armorer L 4.00 10.00
41 Fairy Godmother - Mystic Armorer COLD FOIL L 8.00 20.00
42 Fairy Godmother - Pure Heart C .08 .20
42 Fairy Godmother - Pure Heart COLD FOIL C .15 .40
43 HeiHei - Persistent Presence COLD FOIL U .20 .50
43 HeiHei - Persistent Presence U .08 .20
44 Jiminy Cricket - Pinocchio's Conscience C .08 .20
44 Jiminy Cricket - Pinocchio's Conscience COLD FOIL C .08 .20
45 Kuzco - Wanted Llama C .08 .20
45 Kuzco - Wanted Llama COLD FOIL C .30 .75
46 Madam Mim - Fox COLD FOIL R 8.00 20.00
46 Madam Mim - Fox R 3.00 8.00
47 Madam Mim - Purple Dragon L 2.00 5.00
47 Madam Mim - Purple Dragon COLD FOIL L 6.00 15.00
48 Madam Mim - Rival of Merlin R .20 .50
48 Madam Mim - Rival of Merlin COLD FOIL R .40 1.00
49 Madam Mim - Snake COLD FOIL U 1.50 4.00
49 Madam Mim - Snake U .12 .30
50 Merlin - Crab C .08 .20
50 Merlin - Crab COLD FOIL C .40 1.00
51 Merlin - Goat COLD FOIL U 2.00 5.00
51 Merlin - Goat U .12 .30
52 Merlin - Rabbit COLD FOIL R 6.00 15.00
52 Merlin - Rabbit R 1.50 4.00
53 Merlin - Shapeshifter R .08 .20
53 Merlin - Shapeshifter COLD FOIL R .15 .40
54 Merlin - Squirrel COLD FOIL C .08 .20
54 Merlin - Squirrel C .08 .20
55 Peter Pan's Shadow - Not Sewn On SR .30 .75
55 Peter Pan's Shadow - Not Sewn On COLD FOIL SR .75 2.00
56 Pinocchio - Star Attraction COLD FOIL R 1.25 3.00
56 Pinocchio - Star Attraction R .75 2.00
57 Pinocchio - On the Run COLD FOIL U .20 .50
57 Pinocchio - On the Run U .08 .20
58 Pinocchio - Talkative Puppet COLD FOIL U .60 1.50
58 Pinocchio - Talkative Puppet U .12 .30
59 Winnie the Pooh - Hunny Wizard COLD FOIL C .20 .50
59 Winnie the Pooh - Hunny Wizard C .08 .20
60 Yzma - Scary Beyond All Reason COLD FOIL SR 1.25 3.00
60 Yzma - Scary Beyond All Reason SR .40 1.00
61 Yzma - Without Beauty Sleep COLD FOIL U .20 .50
61 Yzma - Without Beauty Sleep U .08 .20
62 Gruesome and Grim COLD FOIL R .40 1.00
62 Gruesome and Grim R .08 .20
63 I'm Stuck! COLD FOIL C .08 .20
63 I'm Stuck! C .12 .30
64 Legend of the Sword in the Stone COLD FOIL C .12 .30
64 Legend of the Sword in the Stone C .08 .20
65 Binding Contract COLD FOIL U .08 .20
65 Binding Contract U .12 .30
66 Croquet Mallet COLD FOIL C .08 .20
66 Croquet Mallet C .08 .20
67 Perplexing Signposts COLD FOIL R .30 .75
67 Perplexing Signposts R .08 .20
68 The Sorcerer's Spellbook COLD FOIL R 1.00 2.50
68 The Sorcerer's Spellbook R .50 1.25
69 Arthur - Trained Swordsman COLD FOIL C .08 .20
69 Arthur - Trained Swordsman C .12 .30
70 Beast - Relentless COLD FOIL L 10.00 25.00
70 Beast - Relentless L 3.00 8.00
71 Belle - Bookworm COLD FOIL U .08 .20
71 Belle - Bookworm U .20 .50
72 Belle - Hidden Archer COLD FOIL L 8.00 20.00
72 Belle - Hidden Archer L 3.00 8.00
73 Bucky - Squirrel Squeak Tutor COLD FOIL U .15 .40
73 Bucky - Squirrel Squeak Tutor U .50 1.25
74 Cheshire Cat - Always Grinning COLD FOIL U .20 .50
74 Cheshire Cat - Always Grinning U .08 .20
75 Cheshire Cat - From the Shadows COLD FOIL SR 1.00 2.50
75 Cheshire Cat - From the Shadows SR .20 .50
76 Daisy Duck - Secret Agent COLD FOIL U .08 .20
76 Daisy Duck - Secret Agent U .50 1.25
77 Donald Duck - Perfect Gentleman COLD FOIL U .30 .75
77 Donald Duck - Perfect Gentleman U .08 .20
78 Donald Duck - Sleepwalker COLD FOIL C .12 .30
78 Donald Duck - Sleepwalker C .08 .20
79 Dr. Facilier - Fortune Teller COLD FOIL SR .30 .75
79 Dr. Facilier - Fortune Teller SR .08 .20
80 Enchantress - Unexpected Judge COLD FOIL C .08 .20
80 Enchantress - Unexpected Judge C .15 .40
81 Flynn Rider - Confident Vagabond COLD FOIL C .20 .50
81 Flynn Rider - Confident Vagabond C .08 .20
82 Flynn Rider - His Own Biggest Fan R .40 1.00
82 Flynn Rider - His Own Biggest Fan COLD FOIL R 2.00 5.00
83 Gaston - Scheming Suitor COLD FOIL C .08 .20
83 Gaston - Scheming Suitor C .08 .20
84 Little John - Loyal Friend R .08 .20
84 Little John - Loyal Friend COLD FOIL R .25 .60
85 Lucifer - Cunning Cat COLD FOIL R .15 .40
85 Lucifer - Cunning Cat R .75 2.00
86 Pain - Underworld Imp U .08 .20
86 Pain - Underworld Imp COLD FOIL U .20 .50
87 Panic - Underworld Imp C .08 .20
87 Panic - Underworld Imp COLD FOIL C .12 .30
88 Pete - Bad Guy R .15 .40
88 Pete - Bad Guy COLD FOIL R .75 2.00
89 Prince John - Greediest of All COLD FOIL R 3.00 8.00
89 Prince John - Greediest of All R 2.00 5.00
90 Queen of Hearts - Quick-Tempered C .08 .20
90 Queen of Hearts - Quick-Tempered COLD FOIL C .12 .30
91 Ratigan - Criminal Mastermind COLD FOIL C .08 .20
91 Ratigan - Criminal Mastermind C .08 .20
92 Ray - Easygoing Firefly COLD FOIL C .15 .40
92 Ray - Easygoing Firefly C .08 .20
93 The Queen - Disguised Peddler SR .08 .20
93 The Queen - Disguised Peddler COLD FOIL SR .40 1.00
94 Tiana - True Princess COLD FOIL U .20 .50
94 Tiana - True Princess U .08 .20
95 Virana - Fang Chief C .08 .20
95 Virana - Fang Chief COLD FOIL C .08 .20
96 Bibbidi Bobbidi Boo R .25 .60
96 Bibbidi Bobbidi Boo COLD FOIL R 1.25 3.00
97 Bounce U .08 .20
97 Bounce COLD FOIL U .20 .50
98 Hypnotize COLD FOIL C .20 .50
98 Hypnotize C .08 .20
99 Improvise C .08 .20
99 Improvise COLD FOIL C .15 .40
100 Pack Tactics R .08 .20
100 Pack Tactics COLD FOIL R .40 1.00
101 Ring the Bell U .08 .20
101 Ring the Bell COLD FOIL U .25 .60
102 Ratigan's Marvelous Trap R .08 .20
102 Ratigan's Marvelous Trap COLD FOIL R .30 .75
103 Baloo - Fun-Loving Bear C .08 .20
103 Baloo - Fun-Loving Bear COLD FOIL C .08 .20
104 Boun - Precocious Entrepreneur C .08 .20
104 Boun - Precocious Entrepreneur COLD FOIL C .08 .20
105 Card Soldiers - Full Deck U .08 .20
105 Card Soldiers - Full Deck COLD FOIL U .12 .30
106 Donald Duck - Not Again! L 1.00 2.50
106 Donald Duck - Not Again! COLD FOIL L 5.00 12.00
107 Felicia - Always Hungry COLD FOIL C .15 .40
107 Felicia - Always Hungry C .08 .20
108 Fidget - Ratigan's Henchman C .08 .20
108 Fidget - Ratigan's Henchman COLD FOIL C .08 .20
109 Honest John - Not That Honest R .08 .20
109 Honest John - Not That Honest COLD FOIL R .25 .60
110 Lady Tremaine - Imperious Queen SR 1.25 3.00
110 Lady Tremaine - Imperious Queen COLD FOIL SR 3.00 8.00
111 Lady Tremaine - Overbearing Matriarch C .08 .20
111 Lady Tremaine - Overbearing Matriarch COLD FOIL C .12 .30
112 Lumiere - Hotheaded Candelabra R .08 .20
112 Lumiere - Hotheaded Candelabra COLD FOIL R .25 .60
113 Minnie Mouse - Stylish Surfer COLD FOIL U 1.00 2.50
113 Minnie Mouse - Stylish Surfer U .40 1.00
114 Minnie Mouse - Wide-Eyed Diver COLD FOIL R .25 .60
114 Minnie Mouse - Wide-Eyed Diver R .08 .20
115 Minnie Mouse - Zipping Around COLD FOIL C .08 .20
115 Minnie Mouse - Zipping Around C .08 .20
116 Mother Gothel - Withered and Wicked COLD FOIL U .40 1.00
116 Mother Gothel - Withered and Wicked U .08 .20
117 Mulan - Soldier in Training COLD FOIL C .15 .40
117 Mulan - Soldier in Training C .08 .20
118 Namaari - Nemesis COLD FOIL SR .40 1.00
118 Namaari - Nemesis SR .08 .20
119 Queen of Hearts - Impulsive Ruler COLD FOIL U 1.00 2.50
119 Queen of Hearts - Impulsive Ruler U .12 .30
120 Queen of Hearts - Sensing Weakness COLD FOIL U .50 1.25
120 Queen of Hearts - Sensing Weakness U .12 .30
121 Ratigan - Very Large Mouse COLD FOIL R .40 1.00
121 Ratigan - Very Large Mouse R .08 .20
122 Raya - Headstrong COLD FOIL C .08 .20
122 Raya - Headstrong C .08 .20
123 Raya - Leader of Heart COLD FOIL SR .40 1.00
123 Raya - Leader of Heart SR .12 .30
124 Raya - Warrior of Kumandra COLD FOIL U .15 .40
124 Raya - Warrior of Kumandra U .08 .20
125 Scar - Vicious Cheater COLD FOIL L 20.00 50.00
125 Scar - Vicious Cheater L 6.00 15.00
126 Shere Khan - Menacing Predator COLD FOIL R 1.25 3.00
126 Shere Khan - Menacing Predator R .75 2.00
127 Tigger - One of a Kind COLD FOIL C .08 .20
127 Tigger - One of a Kind C .08 .20
128 Tuk Tuk - Wrecking Ball COLD FOIL R .25 .60
128 Tuk Tuk - Wrecking Ball R .08 .20
129 Go the Distance COLD FOIL C .12 .30
129 Go the Distance C .08 .20
130 Teeth and Ambitions COLD FOIL R 2.00 5.00
130 Teeth and Ambitions R .50 1.25
131 The Most Diabolical Scheme COLD FOIL U .15 .40
131 The Most Diabolical Scheme U .08 .20
132 What Did You Call Me? COLD FOIL C .08 .20
132 What Did You Call Me? C .08 .20
133 You Can Fly! COLD FOIL U .15 .40
133 You Can Fly! U .08 .20
134 Dinner Bell COLD FOIL R .30 .75
134 Dinner Bell R .12 .30
135 Peter Pan's Dagger COLD FOIL C .08 .20
135 Peter Pan's Dagger C .08 .20
136 The Sword in the Stone COLD FOIL U .15 .40
136 The Sword in the Stone U .08 .20
137 Alice - Growing Girl COLD FOIL L 10.00 25.00
137 Alice - Growing Girl L 2.50 6.00
138 Basil - Great Mouse Detective COLD FOIL SR .40 1.00
138 Basil - Great Mouse Detective SR .08 .20
139 Basil - Of Baker Street COLD FOIL C .12 .30
139 Basil - Of Baker Street C .08 .20
140 Basil - Perceptive Investigator COLD FOIL C .08 .20
140 Basil - Perceptive Investigator C .08 .20
141 Caterpillar - Calm and Collected COLD FOIL U .20 .50
141 Caterpillar - Calm and Collected U .08 .20
142 Cogsworth - Grandfather Clock SR 2.00 5.00
142 Cogsworth - Grandfather Clock COLD FOIL SR 4.00 10.00
143 Cogsworth - Talking Clock U .08 .20
143 Cogsworth - Talking Clock COLD FOIL U .20 .50
144 Cruella De Vil - Fashionable Cruiser COLD FOIL C .12 .30
144 Cruella De Vil - Fashionable Cruiser C .08 .20
145 Cruella De Vil - Perfectly Wretched U .08 .20
145 Cruella De Vil - Perfectly Wretched COLD FOIL U .15 .40
146 Duke Weaselton - Small-Time Crook COLD FOIL C .08 .20
146 Duke Weaselton - Small-Time Crook C .08 .20
147 Gaston - Intellectual Powerhouse COLD FOIL R .25 .60
147 Gaston - Intellectual Powerhouse R .15 .40
148 Grand Pabbie - Oldest and Wisest SR .20 .50
148 Grand Pabbie - Oldest and Wisest COLD FOIL SR .75 2.00
149 Hiram Flaversham - Toymaker R 2.00 5.00
149 Hiram Flaversham - Toymaker COLD FOIL R 10.00 25.00
150 James - Role Model COLD FOIL C .08 .20
150 James - Role Model C .08 .20
151 Jasmine - Heir of Agrabah COLD FOIL C .15 .40
151 Jasmine - Heir of Agrabah C .08 .20
152 Judy Hopps - Optimistic Officer COLD FOIL U .50 1.25
152 Judy Hopps - Optimistic Officer U .08 .20
153 Mrs. Judson - Housekeeper R .08 .20
153 Mrs. Judson - Housekeeper COLD FOIL R .20 .50
154 Nick Wilde - Wily Fox COLD FOIL U .30 .75
154 Nick Wilde - Wily Fox U .08 .20
155 Noi - Orphaned Thief R .20 .50
155 Noi - Orphaned Thief COLD FOIL R .60 1.50
156 Owl - Logical Lecturer COLD FOIL C .12 .30
156 Owl - Logical Lecturer C .08 .20
157 Prince Charming - Heir to the Throne R .12 .30
157 Prince Charming - Heir to the Throne COLD FOIL R .40 1.00
158 Rabbit - Reluctant Host COLD FOIL C .08 .20
158 Rabbit - Reluctant Host C .08 .20
159 Sisu - Divine Water Dragon L 1.50 4.00
159 Sisu - Divine Water Dragon COLD FOIL L 5.00 12.00
160 The Nokk - Water Spirit C .08 .20
160 The Nokk - Water Spirit COLD FOIL C .08 .20
161 Winnie the Pooh - Having a Think COLD FOIL R 1.00 2.50
161 Winnie the Pooh - Having a Think R .08 .20
162 Falling Down the Rabbit Hole R .08 .20
162 Falling Down the Rabbit Hole COLD FOIL R .30 .75
163 Four Dozen Eggs U .08 .20
163 Four Dozen Eggs COLD FOIL U .15 .40
164 Launch U .08 .20
164 Launch COLD FOIL U .15 .40
165 Nothing to Hide C .08 .20
165 Nothing to Hide COLD FOIL C .08 .20
166 Fang Crossbow U .08 .20
166 Fang Crossbow COLD FOIL U .12 .30
167 Gumbo Pot C .08 .20
167 Gumbo Pot COLD FOIL C .12 .30
168 Maurice's Workshop R .15 .40
168 Maurice's Workshop COLD FOIL R .60 1.50
169 Pawpsicle COLD FOIL C 1.50 4.00
169 Pawpsicle C .08 .20
170 Sardine Can COLD FOIL U .20 .50
170 Sardine Can U .08 .20
171 Beast - Forbidding Recluse COLD FOIL C .12 .30
171 Beast - Forbidding Recluse C .08 .20
172 Beast - Selfless Protector COLD FOIL SR .50 1.25
172 Beast - Selfless Protector SR .12 .30
173 Beast - Tragic Hero COLD FOIL L 40.00 100.00
173 Beast - Tragic Hero L 30.00 80.00
174 Benja - Guardian of the Dragon Gem COLD FOIL C .30 .75
174 Benja - Guardian of the Dragon Gem C .08 .20
175 Chief Bogo - Respected Officer COLD FOIL R .50 1.25
175 Chief Bogo - Respected Officer R .12 .30
176 Cinderella - Knight in Training COLD FOIL C .12 .30
176 Cinderella - Knight in Training C .08 .20
177 Cinderella - Stouthearted COLD FOIL SR 4.00 10.00
177 Cinderella - Stouthearted SR 1.25 3.00
178 Donald Duck - Deep-Sea Diver COLD FOIL C .08 .20
178 Donald Duck - Deep-Sea Diver C .08 .20
179 Eli La Bouff - Big Daddy COLD FOIL U .15 .40
179 Eli La Bouff - Big Daddy U .08 .20
180 Goofy - Knight for a Day COLD FOIL R .40 1.00
180 Goofy - Knight for a Day R .15 .40
181 Hercules - Divine Hero COLD FOIL R 1.25 3.00
181 Hercules - Divine Hero R .40 1.00
182 Hercules - Hero in Training C .08 .20
182 Hercules - Hero in Training COLD FOIL C .12 .30
183 Jafar - Dreadnought COLD FOIL U 1.25 3.00
183 Jafar - Dreadnought U .20 .50
184 Jafar - Royal Vizier COLD FOIL C .20 .50
184 Jafar - Royal Vizier C .08 .20
185 Kronk - Junior Chipmunk COLD FOIL R .25 .60
185 Kronk - Junior Chipmunk R .08 .20
186 Lawrence - Jealous Manservant COLD FOIL U .15 .40
186 Lawrence - Jealous Manservant U .08 .20
187 Li Shang - Archery Instructor COLD FOIL U .25 .60
187 Li Shang - Archery Instructor U .08 .20
188 Magic Broom - Industrial Model COLD FOIL C .20 .50
188 Magic Broom - Industrial Model C .08 .20
189 Namaari - Morning Mist COLD FOIL L 5.00 12.00
189 Namaari - Morning Mist L 1.25 3.00
190 Pacha - Village Leader COLD FOIL U .15 .40
190 Pacha - Village Leader U .08 .20
191 Prince Naveen - Penniless Royal COLD FOIL C .08 .20
191 Prince Naveen - Penniless Royal C .08 .20
192 Queen of Hearts - Capricious Monarch COLD FOIL R .30 .75
192 Queen of Hearts - Capricious Monarch R .08 .20
193 Robin Hood - Capable Fighter COLD FOIL U .40 1.00
193 Robin Hood - Capable Fighter U .08 .20
194 The Huntsman - Reluctant Enforcer COLD FOIL R .30 .75
194 The Huntsman - Reluctant Enforcer R .08 .20
195 The Prince - Never Gives Up COLD FOIL U .50 1.25
195 The Prince - Never Gives Up U .08 .20
196 Tiana - Celebrating Princess COLD FOIL SR .12 .30
196 Tiana - Celebrating Princess SR .12 .30
197 Tiana - Diligent Waitress COLD FOIL C .12 .30
197 Tiana - Diligent Waitress C .08 .20
198 Charge! COLD FOIL C .08 .20
198 Charge! C .08 .20
199 Let the Storm Rage On COLD FOIL C 1.25 3.00
199 Let the Storm Rage On C .20 .50
200 Pick a Fight U .08 .20
200 Pick a Fight COLD FOIL U .20 .50
201 Strength of a Raging Fire R 3.00 8.00
201 Strength of a Raging Fire COLD FOIL R 6.00 15.00
202 Last Cannon COLD FOIL C .08 .20
202 Last Cannon C .08 .20
203 Mouse Armor U .08 .20
203 Mouse Armor COLD FOIL U .20 .50
204 Weight Set R .12 .30
204 Weight Set COLD FOIL R .50 1.25
205 Cinderella - Ballroom Sensation ENCHANTED FOIL EN 200.00 500.00
206 Snow White - Well Wisher ENCHANTED FOIL EN 100.00 250.00
207 Arthur - Wizard's Apprentice ENCHANTED FOIL EN 50.00 120.00
208 Madam Mim - Purple Dragon ENCHANTED FOIL EN 50.00 120.00
209 Pete - Bad Guy ENCHANTED FOIL EN 40.00 100.00
210 Beast - Relentless ENCHANTED FOIL EN 60.00 150.00
211 Lady Tremaine - Imperious Queen ENCHANTED FOIL EN 50.00 120.00
212 Shere Khan - Menacing Predator ENCHANTED FOIL EN 60.00 150.00
213 Alice - Growing Girl ENCHANTED FOIL EN 150.00 400.00
214 Sisu - Divine Water Dragon ENCHANTED FOIL EN 75.00 200.00
215 Hercules - Divine Hero ENCHANTED FOIL EN 50.00 120.00
216 Namaari - Morning Mist ENCHANTED FOIL EN 50.00 120.00
NNO Minnie Mouse - Wide-Eyed Diver Puzzle Insert (Bottom Left) .08 .20
NNO Minnie Mouse - Wide-Eyed Diver Puzzle Insert (Bottom Right) .08 .20
NNO Minnie Mouse - Wide-Eyed Diver Puzzle Insert (Top Left) .08 .20
NNO Minnie Mouse - Wide-Eyed Diver Puzzle Insert (Top Right) .08 .20

2023 Disney Lorcana The First Chapter

1 Ariel - On Human Legs U .08 .20
1 Ariel - On Human Legs COLD FOIL U .25 .60
2 Ariel - Spectacular Singer SR 2.50 6.00
2 Ariel - Spectacular Singer COLD FOIL SR 8.00 20.00
3 Cinderella - Gentle and Kind U .08 .20
3 Cinderella - Gentle and Kind COLD FOIL U .25 .60
4 Goofy - Musketeer U .08 .20
4 Goofy - Musketeer COLD FOIL U .30 .75
5 Hades - King of Olympus R .15 .40
5 Hades - King of Olympus COLD FOIL R .20 .50
6 Hades - Lord of the Underworld R .15 .40
6 Hades - Lord of the Underworld COLD FOIL R 1.50 4.00
7 Heihei - Boat Snack C COR/("to another chosen") .08 .20
7 Heihei - Boat Snack COLD FOIL C COR/("to another chosen") .20 .50
8 Lefou - Bumbler U .08 .20
8 Lefou - Bumbler COLD FOIL U .20 .50
9 Lilo - Making a Wish R 1.00 2.50
9 Lilo - Making a Wish COLD FOIL R 2.50 6.00
10 Maximus - Palace Horse SR .15 .40
10 Maximus - Palace Horse COLD FOIL SR 1.00 2.50
11 Maximus - Relentless Pursuer U .08 .20
11 Maximus - Relentless Pursuer COLD FOIL U .20 .50
12 Mickey Mouse - True Friend U .08 .20
12 Mickey Mouse - True Friend COLD FOIL U .40 1.00
13 Minnie Mouse - Beloved Princess C .08 .20
13 Minnie Mouse - Beloved Princess COLD FOIL C .12 .30
14 Moana - Of Motunui R .20 .50
14 Moana - Of Motunui COLD FOIL R .30 .75

15 Mr. Smee - Loyal First Mate C	.08	.20
15 Mr. Smee - Loyal First Mate COLD FOIL C	.12	.30
16 Prince Phillip - Dragonslayer U	.08	.20
16 Prince Phillip - Dragonslayer COLD FOIL U	.20	.50
17 Pumbaa - Friendly Warthog C	.08	.20
17 Pumbaa - Friendly Warthog COLD FOIL C	.15	.40
18 Rapunzel - Gifted with Healing L	25.00	60.00
18 Rapunzel - Gifted with Healing COLD FOIL L	40.00	100.00
19 Sebastian - Court Composer C	.08	.20
19 Sebastian - Court Composer COLD FOIL C	.12	.30
20 Simba - Protective Cub C	.15	.40
20 Simba - Protective Cub COLD FOIL C	.50	1.25
21 Stitch - Carefree Surfer L	5.00	12.00
21 Stitch - Carefree Surfer COLD FOIL L	25.00	60.00
22 Stitch - New Dog C	.08	.20
22 Stitch - New Dog COLD FOIL C	.40	1.00
23 Stitch - Rock Star SR	2.00	5.00
23 Stitch - Rock Star COLD FOIL SR	4.00	10.00
24 Timon - Grub Rustler C	.08	.20
24 Timon - Grub Rustler COLD FOIL C	.12	.30
25 Be Our Guest U	.08	.20
25 Be Our Guest COLD FOIL U	.40	1.00
26 Control Your Temper! C	.08	.20
26 Control Your Temper! COLD FOIL C	.12	.30
27 Hakuna Matata C	.08	.20
27 Hakuna Matata COLD FOIL C	.12	.30
28 Healing Glow C	.08	.20
28 Healing Glow COLD FOIL C	.12	.30
29 Just in Time R	.12	.30
29 Just in Time COLD FOIL R	.60	1.50
30 Part of Your World R	.08	.20
30 Part of Your World COLD FOIL R	1.00	2.50
31 You Have Forgotten Me U	.08	.20
31 You Have Forgotten Me COLD FOIL U	.60	1.50
32 Dinglehopper C	.08	.20
32 Dinglehopper COLD FOIL C	.12	.30
33 Lantern R	.50	1.25
33 Lantern COLD FOIL R	2.00	5.00
34 Ursula's Shell Necklace R	.12	.30
34 Ursula's Shell Necklace COLD FOIL R	.60	1.50
35 Anna - Heir to Arendelle U	.08	.20
35 Anna - Heir to Arendelle COLD FOIL U	.25	.60
36 Archimedes - Highly Educated Owl C	.08	.20
36 Archimedes - Highly Educated Owl COLD FOIL C	.20	.50
37 Dr. Facilier - Agent Provocateur R	.08	.20
37 Dr. Facilier - Agent Provocateur COLD FOIL R	.75	2.00
38 Dr. Facilier - Charlatan C	.08	.20
38 Dr. Facilier - Charlatan COLD FOIL C	.15	.40
39 Dr. Facilier - Remarkable Gentleman R	.12	.30
39 Dr. Facilier - Remarkable Gentleman COLD FOIL R	.60	1.50
40 Elsa - Queen Regent C	.08	.20
40 Elsa - Queen Regent COLD FOIL C	.20	.50
41 Elsa - Snow Queen U	.08	.20
41 Elsa - Snow Queen COLD FOIL U	.75	2.00
42 Elsa - Spirit of Winter L	5.00	12.00
42 Elsa - Spirit of Winter COLD FOIL L	20.00	50.00
43 Flotsam - Ursula's Spy R	.08	.20
43 Flotsam - Ursula's Spy COLD FOIL R	.60	1.50
44 Jafar - Keeper of Secrets R	.20	.50
44 Jafar - Keeper of Secrets COLD FOIL R	1.00	2.50
45 Jafar - Wicked Sorcerer C	.08	.20
45 Jafar - Wicked Sorcerer COLD FOIL C	.20	.50
46 Jetsam - Ursula's Spy C	.15	.40
46 Jetsam - Ursula's Spy COLD FOIL C	.08	.20
47 Magic Broom - Bucket Brigade C	.08	.20
47 Magic Broom - Bucket Brigade COLD FOIL C	.30	.75
48 Maleficent - Biding Her Time R	1.00	2.50
48 Maleficent - Biding Her Time COLD FOIL R	2.50	6.00
49 Maleficent - Sorceress C	.12	.30
49 Maleficent - Sorceress COLD FOIL C	.50	1.25
50 Marshmallow - Persistant Guardian SR	.12	.30
50 Marshmallow - Persistant Guardian COLD FOIL SR	.60	1.50
51 Mickey Mouse - Wayward Sorcerer SR	.75	2.00
51 Mickey Mouse - Wayward Sorcerer COLD FOIL SR	1.00	2.50
52 Olaf - Friendly Snowman U	.08	.20
52 Olaf - Friendly Snowman COLD FOIL U	1.00	2.50
53 Pascal - Repunzel's Companion U	.08	.20
53 Pascal - Repunzel's Companion COLD FOIL U	1.25	3.00
54 Rafiki - Mysterious Sage U	.08	.20
54 Rafiki - Mysterious Sage COLD FOIL U	.40	1.00
55 Sven - Official Ice Deliverer U	.08	.20
55 Sven - Official Ice Deliverer COLD FOIL U	.20	.50
56 The Queen - Wicked and Vain SR	.20	.50
56 The Queen - Wicked and Vain COLD FOIL SR	.60	1.50
57 The Wardrobe - Belle's Confidant C	.08	.20
57 The Wardrobe - Belle's Confidant COLD FOIL C	.12	.30
58 Tinker Bell - Peter Pan's Ally C	.08	.20
58 Tinker Bell - Peter Pan's Ally COLD FOIL C	.15	.40
59 Ursula - Power Hungry L	2.00	5.00
59 Ursula - Power Hungry COLD FOIL L	10.00	25.00
60 Yzma - Alchemist C	.08	.20
60 Yzma - Alchemist COLD FOIL C	.12	.30
61 Zeus - God of Lightning R	.15	.40
61 Zeus - God of Lightning COLD FOIL R	.60	1.50
62 Befuddle U COR/(Return chosen""	.15	.40
62 Befuddle COLD FOIL U COR/(Return chosen""	.75	2.00
63 Freeze C	.08	.20
63 Freeze COLD FOIL C	.15	.40
64 Friends on the Other Side C	.20	.50
64 Friends on the Other Side COLD FOIL C	2.00	5.00
65 Reflection U	.08	.20
65 Reflection COLD FOIL U	.25	.60
66 Magic Mirror R	.12	.30
66 Magic Mirror COLD FOIL R	.60	1.50
67 Ursula's Cauldron U	.08	.20
67 Ursula's Cauldron COLD FOIL U	.30	.75
68 White Rabbit's Pocket Watch R	.15	.40
68 White Rabbit's Pocket Watch COLD FOIL R	.50	1.25
69 Aladdin - Prince Ali C	.08	.20
69 Aladdin - Prince Ali COLD FOIL C	.15	.40
70 Beast - Wolfsbane L	1.00	2.50
70 Beast - Wolfsbane COLD FOIL L	8.00	20.00
71 Cheshire Cat - Not All There U	.15	.40
71 Cheshire Cat - Not All There COLD FOIL U	.50	1.25
72 Cruella de Vil - Miserable as Usual R	.08	.20
72 Cruella de Vil - Miserable as Usual COLD FOIL R	.15	.40
73 Duke of Weselton - Opportunistic Official C	.08	.20
73 Duke of Weselton - Opportunistic Official COLD FOIL C	.08	.20
74 Flynn Rider - Charming Rogue U	.75	2.00
74 Flynn Rider - Charming Rogue COLD FOIL U	2.00	5.00
75 Genie - On the Job SR	.20	.50
75 Genie - On the Job COLD FOIL SR	1.00	2.50
76 Genie - Powers Unleashed R	.08	.20
76 Genie - Powers Unleashed COLD FOIL R	.50	1.25
77 Genie - The Ever Impressive C	.08	.20
77 Genie - The Ever Impressive COLD FOIL C	.12	.30
78 Hans - Scheming Prince R	.20	.50
78 Hans - Scheming Prince COLD FOIL R	.60	1.50
79 Horace - No-Good Scoundrel C	.08	.20
79 Horace - No-Good Scoundrel COLD FOIL C	.08	.20
80 Iago - Loud-Mouthed Parrot R	.08	.20
80 Iago - Loud-Mouthed Parrot COLD FOIL R	.40	1.00
81 Jasper - Common Crook U	.08	.20
81 Jasper - Common Crook COLD FOIL U	.20	.50
82 John Silver - Alien Pirate L	1.25	3.00
82 John Silver - Alien Pirate COLD FOIL L	8.00	20.00
83 Jumba Jookiba - Renegade Scientist U	.08	.20
83 Jumba Jookiba - Renegade Scientist COLD FOIL U	.20	.50
84 Kuzco - Temperamental Emperor R	.25	.60
84 Kuzco - Temperamental Emperor COLD FOIL R	1.25	3.00
85 Lady Tremaine - Wicked Stepmother R	.12	.30
85 Lady Tremaine - Wicked Stepmoster COLD FOIL R	.75	2.00
86 Mad Hatter - Gracious Host U	.08	.20
86 Mad Hatter - Gracious Host COLD FOIL U	.25	.60
87 Megara - Pulling the Strings C	.08	.20
87 Megara - Pulling the Strings COLD FOIL C	.15	.40
88 Mickey Mouse - Artful Rogue SR	.20	.50
88 Mickey Mouse - Artful Rogue COLD FOIL SR	.75	2.00
89 Mickey Mouse - Steamboat Pilot C	.08	.20
89 Mickey Mouse - Steamboat Pilot COLD FOIL C	.20	.50
90 Mother Gothel - Selfish Manipulator SR	.20	.50
90 Mother Gothel - Selfish Manipulator COLD FOIL SR	1.00	2.50
91 Peter Pan - Never Landing C	.08	.20
91 Peter Pan - Never Landing COLD FOIL C	.08	.20
92 Tamatoa - Drab Little Crab U	.08	.20
92 Tamatoa - Drab Little Crab COLD FOIL U	.30	.75
93 Tinker Bell - Most Helpful C	.08	.20
93 Tinker Bell - Most Helpful COLD FOIL C	.20	.50
94 Do It Again! R	.08	.20
94 Do It Again! COLD FOIL R	.60	1.50
95 Mother Knows Best U	.08	.20
95 Mother Knows Best COLD FOIL U	1.00	2.50
96 Stampede C	.08	.20
96 Stampede COLD FOIL C	.15	.40
97 Steal From The Rich R	.08	.20
97 Steal From The Rich COLD FOIL R	.40	1.00
98 Sudden Chill C	.08	.20
98 Sudden Chill COLD FOIL C	.50	1.25
99 The Beast is Mine! U	.08	.20
99 The Beast is Mine! COLD FOIL U	.20	.50
100 Vicious Betrayal C	.08	.20
100 Vicious Betrayal COLD FOIL C	.12	.30
101 Dr. Facilier's Cards U	.08	.20
101 Dr. Facilier's Cards COLD FOIL U	.25	.60
102 Stolen Scimitar C	.08	.20
102 Stolen Scimitar COLD FOIL C	.08	.20
103 Abu - Mischievous Monkey C	.08	.20
103 Abu - Mischievous Monkey COLD FOIL C	.12	.30
104 Aladdin - Heroic Outlaw SR	.30	.75
104 Aladdin - Heroic Outlaw COLD FOIL SR	.25	.60
105 Aladdin - Street Rat C	.08	.20
105 Aladdin - Street Rat COLD FOIL C	.12	.30
106 Captain - Colonel's Lieutenant U	.08	.20
106 Captain - Colonel's Lieutenant COLD FOIL U	.20	.50
107 Captain Hook - Ruthless Pirate R	.08	.20
107 Captain Hook - Ruthless Pirate COLD FOIL R	.40	1.00
108 Donald Duck - Boisterous Fowl U	.08	.20
108 Donald Duck - Boisterous Fowl COLD FOIL U	.25	.60
109 Elsa - Ice Surfer C	.08	.20
109 Elsa - Ice Surfer COLD FOIL C	.20	.50
110 Gaston - Arrogant Hunter C	.08	.20
110 Gaston - Arrogant Hunter COLD FOIL C	.20	.50
111 Goofy - Daredevil C	.08	.20
111 Goofy - Daredevil COLD FOIL C	.12	.30
112 Lefou - Instigator R	.20	.50
112 Lefou - Instigator COLD FOIL R	1.00	2.50
113 Maleficent - Monstrous Dragon L	20.00	50.00
113 Maleficent - Monstrous Dragon COLD FOIL L	40.00	100.00
114 Maui - Hero to All R	6.00	15.00
114 Maui - Hero to All COLD FOIL R	10.00	25.00
115 Mickey Mouse - Brave Little Tailor L	2.50	6.00
115 Mickey Mouse - Brave Little Tailor COLD FOIL L	30.00	80.00
116 Minnie Mouse - Always Classy C	.08	.20
116 Minnie Mouse - Always Classy COLD FOIL C	.40	1.00
117 Moana - Chosen by the Ocean U	.08	.20
117 Moana - Chosen by the Ocean COLD FOIL U	.20	.50
118 Mulan - Imperial Soldier SR	.08	.20
118 Mulan - Imperial Soldier COLD FOIL SR	.25	.60
119 Peter Pan - Fearless Fighter C	.08	.20
119 Peter Pan - Fearless Fighter COLD FOIL C	.12	.30
120 Pongo - Ol' Rascal C	.08	.20
120 Pongo - Ol' Rascal COLD FOIL C	.20	.50
121 Rapunzel - Letting Down Her Hair U	.08	.20
121 Rapunzel - Letting Down Her Hair COLD FOIL U	.20	.50
122 Scar - Fiery Usurper C	.08	.20
122 Scar - Fiery Usurper COLD FOIL C	.15	.40
123 Scar - Shameless Firebrand R	.08	.20
123 Scar - Shameless Firebrand COLD FOIL R	.60	1.50
124 Sergeant Tibbs - Courageous Cat C	.08	.20
124 Sergeant Tibbs - Courageous Cat COLD FOIL C	.15	.40
125 Stitch - Abomination R	.12	.30
125 Stitch - Abomination COLD FOIL R	.60	1.50
126 Te Ka - The Burning One SR	.08	.20
126 Te Ka - The Burning One COLD FOIL SR	.60	1.50
127 Tigger - Wonderful Thing U	.08	.20
127 Tigger - Wonderful Thing COLD FOIL U	.50	1.25
128 Be Prepared R	4.00	10.00
128 Be Prepared COLD FOIL R	10.00	25.00
129 Cut to the Chase U	.08	.20
129 Cut to the Chase COLD FOIL U	.15	.40
130 Dragon Fire U	.08	.20
130 Dragon Fire COLD FOIL U	.50	1.25
131 Fan the Flames U	.08	.20
131 Fan the Flames COLD FOIL U	.25	.60
132 He's Got A Sword! C	.08	.20
132 He's Got A Sword! COLD FOIL C	.12	.30
133 Tangle C	.08	.20
133 Tangle COLD FOIL C	.12	.30
134 Poisoned Apple R	.08	.20
134 Poisoned Apple COLD FOIL R	.60	1.50
135 Shield of Virtue U	.08	.20
135 Shield of Virtue COLD FOIL U	.40	1.00
136 Sword of Truth R	.12	.30
136 Sword of Truth COLD FOIL R	.50	1.25
137 Ariel - Whoseit Collector R	.20	.50
137 Ariel - Whoseit Collector COLD FOIL R	1.50	4.00
138 Aurora - Briar Rose C	.08	.20
138 Aurora - Briar Rose COLD FOIL C	.15	.40
139 Aurora - Dreaming Guardian SR	.25	.60
139 Aurora - Dreaming Guardian COLD FOIL SR	.30	.75
140 Aurora - Regal Princess U	.08	.20
140 Aurora - Regal Princess COLD FOIL U	.25	.60
141 Belle - Inventive Engineer U	.08	.20
141 Belle - Inventive Engineer COLD FOIL U	.25	.60
142 Belle - Strange but Special L	12.00	30.00
142 Belle - Strange but Special COLD FOIL L	30.00	80.00
143 Chief Tui - Respected Leader U COR/(""to another chosen"")	.08	.20
143 Chief Tui - Respected Leader COLD FOIL U COR/(""to another chosen"")	.20	.50
144 Donald Duck - Strutting His Stuff C	.08	.20
144 Donald Duck - Strutting His Stuff COLD FOIL C	.08	.20
145 Flounder - Voice of Reason C	.08	.20
145 Flounder - Voice of Reason COLD FOIL C	.15	.40
146 Gramma Tala - Storyteller U	.12	.30
146 Gramma Tala - Storyteller COLD FOIL U	1.00	2.50
147 Hades - Infernal Schemer L	4.00	10.00
147 Hades - Infernal Schemer COLD FOIL L	20.00	50.00
148 Jasmine - Disguised C	.08	.20
148 Jasmine - Disguised COLD FOIL C	.20	.50
149 Jasmine - Queen of Agrabah R	.40	1.00
149 Jasmine - Queen of Agrabah COLD FOIL R	1.25	3.00
150 Maleficent - Sinister Visitor C	.08	.20
150 Maleficent - Sinister Visitor COLD FOIL C	.12	.30
151 Maleficent - Univited R	.12	.30
151 Maleficent - Univited COLD FOIL R	.60	1.50
152 Maurice - World-Famous Inventor R	.15	.40
152 Maurice - World-Famous Inventor COLD FOIL R	.60	1.50
153 Merlin - Self-Appointed Mentor C COR/(""to another chosen"")	.08	.20
153 Merlin - Self- Appointed Mentor COLD FOIL C COR/(""to another chosen"")	.20	.50
154 Mickey Mouse - Detective C	.08	.20
154 Mickey Mouse - Detective COLD FOIL C	.25	.60
155 Mufasa - King of the Pride Lands C	.08	.20
155 Mufasa - King of the Pride Lands COLD FOIL C	.12	.30
156 Philoctetes - Trainer of Heroes C COR/(""to another chosen"")	.08	.20
156 Philoctetes - Trainer of Heroes COLD FOIL C COR/(""to another chosen"")	.15	.40
157 Robin Hood - Unrivaled Archer SR	.15	.40
157 Robin Hood - Unrivaled Archer COLD FOIL SR	1.25	3.00
158 Scar - Mastermind R	.08	.20
158 Scar - Mastermind COLD FOIL R	.50	1.25
159 Tamatoa - So Shiny! SR	5.00	12.00
159 Tamatoa - So Shiny! COLD FOIL SR	8.00	20.00
160 Triton - The Sea King U	.08	.20
160 Triton - The Sea King COLD FOIL U	.20	.50
161 Develop Your Brain C	.08	.20
161 Develop Your Brain COLD FOIL C	.50	1.25
162 If It's Not Baroque R	.08	.20
162 If It's Not Baroque COLD FOIL R	.50	1.25
163 Let It Go R	1.00	2.50
163 Let It Go COLD FOIL R	2.00	5.00
164 One Jump Ahead U	.12	.30
164 One Jump Ahead COLD FOIL U	4.00	10.00
165 Work Together C COR/(""Pacha""	.08	.20
165 Work Together COLD FOIL C COR/(""Pacha""	.15	.40
166 Coconut Basket U	.08	.20
166 Coconut Basket COLD FOIL U	.20	.50
167 Eye of the Fates U	.08	.20
167 Eye of the Fates COLD FOIL U	.40	1.00
168 Fishbone Quill R	5.00	12.00
168 Fishbone Quill COLD FOIL R	8.00	20.00
169 Magic Golden Flower C	.08	.20
169 Magic Golden Flower COLD FOIL C	.15	.40
170 Scepter of Arendelle U	.08	.20
170 Scepter of Arendelle COLD FOIL U	.25	.60
171 Aladdin - Cornered Swordsman C	.08	.20
171 Aladdin - Cornered Swordsman COLD FOIL C	.08	.20
172 Beast - Hardheaded U	.08	.20
172 Beast - Hardheaded COLD FOIL U	.25	.60
173 Captain Hook - Captain of the Jolly Roger R	.15	.40
173 Captain Hook - Captain of the Jolly Roger COLD FOIL R	.75	2.00
174 Captain Hook - Forceful Duelist C	.08	.20
174 Captain Hook - Forceful Duelist COLD FOIL C	.75	2.00
175 Captain Hook - Thinking a Happy Thought R	.20	.50
175 Captain Hook - Thinking a Happy Thought COLD FOIL R	1.00	2.50
176 Cerberus - Three-Headed Dog C	.08	.20
176 Cerberus - Three-Headed Dog COLD FOIL C	.12	.30
177 Donald Duck - Musketeer U	.08	.20
177 Donald Duck - Musketeer COLD FOIL U	.25	.60
178 Gantu - Galatic Federation Captain L	.75	2.00
178 Gantu - Galatic Federation Captain COLD FOIL L	6.00	15.00
179 Goons - Maleficent's Underlings C	.08	.20
179 Goons - Maleficent's Underlings COLD FOIL C	.15	.40
180 Hans - Thirteenth in Line SR	.25	.60
180 Hans - Thirteenth in Line COLD FOIL SR	1.00	2.50
181 Hercules - True Hero C	.08	.20
181 Hercules - True Hero COLD FOIL C	.12	.30
182 Kristoff - Official Ice Master C	.08	.20
182 Kristoff - Official Ice Master COLD FOIL C	.12	.30
183 Kronk - Right-Hand Man U	.08	.20
183 Kronk - Right-Hand Man COLD FOIL U	.20	.50
184 Lilo - Galactic Hero C	.08	.20
184 Lilo - Galactic Hero COLD FOIL C	.15	.40
185 Maui - Demigod R	.08	.20
185 Maui - Demigod COLD FOIL R	.50	1.25
186 Mickey Mouse - Musketeer R	.20	.50
186 Mickey Mouse - Musketeer COLD FOIL R	1.00	2.50
187 Prince Eric - Dashing and Brave C	.08	.20
187 Prince Eric - Dashing and Brave COLD FOIL C	.20	.50
188 Simba - Future King C	.08	.20
188 Simba - Future King COLD FOIL C	.25	.60
189 Simba - Returned King R	.08	.20
189 Simba - Returned King COLD FOIL R	.20	.50
190 Simba - Rightful Heir U	.08	.20
190 Simba - Rightful Heir COLD FOIL U	.20	.50
191 Starkey - Hook's Henchman U	.08	.20
191 Starkey - Hook's Henchman COLD FOIL U	.20	.50
192 Te Ka - Heartless L	1.00	2.50
192 Te Ka - Heartless COLD FOIL L	10.00	25.00
193 Tinker Bell - Giant Fairy SR	4.00	10.00
193 Tinker Bell - Giant Fairy COLD FOIL SR	8.00	20.00
194 Tinker Bell - Tiny Tactician C	.08	.20
194 Tinker Bell - Tiny Tactician COLD FOIL C	.25	.60
195 A Whole New World SR	6.00	15.00
195 A Whole New World COLD FOIL SR	10.00	25.00
196 Break C	.08	.20
196 Break COLD FOIL C	.12	.30
197 Fire the Cannons! C	.08	.20
197 Fire the Cannons! COLD FOIL C	.25	.60
198 Grab Your Sword R	1.00	2.50
198 Grab Your Sword COLD FOIL R	4.00	10.00
199 Ransack U	.08	.20
199 Ransack COLD FOIL U	.25	.60
200 Smash U	.08	.20
200 Smash COLD FOIL U	1.00	2.50
201 Beast's Mirror C	.08	.20
201 Beast's Mirror COLD FOIL C	.15	.40
202 Frying Pan U	.08	.20
202 Frying Pan COLD FOIL U	.20	.50
203 Musketeer Tabard R	.12	.30
203 Musketeer Tabard COLD FOIL R	.75	2.00
204 Plasma Blaster R	.08	.20
204 Plasma Blaster COLD FOIL R	.50	1.25
205 Hades - King of Olympus ENCHANTED FOIL E	75.00	200.00
206 Stitch - Carefree Surfer ENCHANTED FOIL E	200.00	500.00
207 Elsa - Spirit of Winter ENCHANTED FOIL E	600.00	1,500.00
208 Mickey Mouse - Wayward Sorcerer ENCHANTED FOIL E	150.00	400.00
209 Genie - On the Job ENCHANTED FOIL E	75.00	200.00
210 Mickey Mouse - Artful Rogue ENCHANTED FOIL E	75.00	200.00
211 Aladdin - Heroic Outlaw ENCHANTED FOIL E	100.00	250.00
212 Maui - Hero to All ENCHANTED FOIL E	100.00	250.00
213 Aurora - Dreaming Guardian ENCHANTED FOIL E	150.00	400.00

214 Belle - Strange but Special ENCHANTED FOIL E 200.00 500.00
215 Simba - Returned King ENCHANTED FOIL
E ERR/("When challenging") 100.00 250.00
216 Tinker Bell - Giant Fairy ENCHANTED FOIL E 200.00 500.00
NNO Mickey Mouse - Brave Little Tailor Puzzle Insert (Bottom Left) .08 .20
NNO Mickey Mouse - Brave Little Tailor Puzzle Insert (Bottom Right) .08 .20
NNO Mickey Mouse - Brave Little Tailor Puzzle Insert (Top Left) .08 .20
NNO Mickey Mouse - Brave Little Tailor Puzzle Insert (Top Right) .08 .20

2024 Disney Lorcana Into The Inklands

1 Baloo - von Bruinwald XIII COLD FOIL R .60 1.50
1 Baloo - von Bruinwald XIII R .20 .50
2 Bernard - Brand-New Agent R .08 .20
2 Bernard - Brand-New Agent COLD FOIL R .20 .50
3 Chernabog - Evildoer COLD FOIL SR 1.25 3.00
3 Chernabog - Evildoer SR .25 .60
5 Joshua Sweet - The Doctor COLD FOIL C .08 .20
5 Joshua Sweet - The Doctor C .08 .20
6 Kida - Atlantean COLD FOIL C .25 .60
6 Kida - Atlantean C .08 .20
7 Kida - Protector of Atlantis COLD FOIL L 6.00 15.00
7 Kida - Protector of Atlantis L 5.00 12.00
8 Lucky - The 15th Puppy COLD FOIL R .50 1.25
8 Lucky - The 15th Puppy R .08 .20
9 Minnie Mouse - Musical Artist R .08 .20
9 Minnie Mouse - Musical Artist COLD FOIL R .30 .75
10 Miss Bianca - Rescue Aid Society Agent C .08 .20
10 Miss Bianca - Rescue Aid Society Agent COLD FOIL C .12 .30
11 Mr. Snoops - Inept Businessman COLD FOIL C .08 .20
11 Mr. Snoops - Inept Businessman C .08 .20
12 Nani - Protective Sister U .08 .20
12 Nani - Protective Sister COLD FOIL U .20 .50
13 Orville - Ace Pilot COLD FOIL C .08 .20
13 Orville - Ace Pilot C .08 .20
14 Patch - Intimidating Pup C .20 .50
14 Patch - Intimidating Pup COLD FOIL C .08 .20
15 Perdita - Devoted Mother COLD FOIL L 8.00 20.00
15 Perdita - Devoted Mother L 4.00 10.00
16 Piglet - Pooh Pirate Captain COLD FOIL SR 1.50 4.00
16 Piglet - Pooh Pirate Captain SR .75 2.00
17 Pluto - Determined Defender COLD FOIL R .50 1.25
17 Pluto - Determined Defender R .12 .30
18 Pluto - Friendly Pooch COLD FOIL U .50 1.25
18 Pluto - Friendly Pooch U .08 .20
19 Pongo - Determined Father SR .15 .40
19 Pongo - Determined Father COLD FOIL SR .25 .60
20 Queen of Hearts - Wonderland Empress COLD FOIL U .15 .40
20 Queen of Hearts - Wonderland Empress U .08 .20
21 Rolly - Hungry Pup U .08 .20
21 Rolly - Hungry Pup COLD FOIL U .12 .30
22 Tinker Bell - Generous Fairy COLD FOIL U .08 .20
22 Tinker Bell - Generous Fairy U .20 .50
23 Wendy Darling - Talented Sailor U .08 .20
23 Wendy Darling - Talented Sailor COLD FOIL U .12 .30
24 99 Puppies COLD FOIL U .20 .50
24 99 Puppies U .08 .20
25 Boss's Orders COLD FOIL C .08 .20
25 Boss's Orders C .08 .20
26 Heal What Has Been Hurt C .08 .20
26 Heal What Has Been Hurt COLD FOIL C .15 .40
27 Quick Patch C .08 .20
27 Quick Patch COLD FOIL C .08 .20
28 The Bare Necessities R .60 1.50
28 The Bare Necessities COLD FOIL R 2.00 5.00
29 Cleansing Rainwater C .08 .20
29 Cleansing Rainwater COLD FOIL C .08 .20
30 Heart of Atlantis R .08 .20
30 Heart of Atlantis COLD FOIL R .30 .75
31 Wildcat's Wrench COLD FOIL U .08 .20
31 Wildcat's Wrench U .08 .20
32 Never Land - Mermaid Lagoon C .08 .20
32 Never Land - Mermaid Lagoon COLD FOIL C .12 .30
33 Pride Lands - Pride Rock R .25 .60
33 Pride Lands - Pride Rock COLD FOIL R 1.25 3.00
34 Tiana's Palace - Jazz Restaurant U .08 .20
34 Tiana's Palace - Jazz Restaurant COLD FOIL U .12 .30
35 Alice - Tea Alchemist SR .12 .30
35 Alice - Tea Alchemist COLD FOIL SR .50 1.25
36 Chernabog's Followers - Creatures of Evil U .25 .60
36 Chernabog's Followers - Creatures of Evil COLD FOIL U 1.50 4.00
37 Diablo - Faithful Familiar C .08 .20
37 Diablo - Faithful Pet COLD FOIL C .08 .20
38 Genie - Supportive Friend SR .15 .40
38 Genie - Supportive Friend COLD FOIL SR .60 1.50
39 Hydros - Ice Titan U .08 .20
39 Hydros - Ice Titan COLD FOIL U .15 .40
40 Iago - Pretty Polly COLD FOIL C .08 .20
40 Iago - Pretty Polly C .08 .20
41 Jafar - Lamp Thief U .08 .20
41 Jafar - Lamp Thief COLD FOIL U .20 .50
42 Jafar - Striking Illusionist L 5.00 12.00
42 Jafar - Striking Illusionist COLD FOIL L 10.00 25.00
43 Lena Darkwing - Rebellious Teenager C .08 .20
43 Lena Sabrewing - Rebellious Teenager COLD FOIL C .08 .20
44 Magic Broom - Dancing Duster U .08 .20
44 Magic Broom - Dancing Duster COLD FOIL U .25 .60
45 Magic Broom - Swift Cleaner C .08 .20
45 Magic Broom - Swift Cleaner COLD FOIL C .20 .50
46 Magic Broom - The Big Sweeper C .08 .20
46 Magic Broom - The Big Sweeper COLD FOIL C .20 .50
47 Magic Carpet - Flying Rug C .08 .20
47 Magic Carpet - Flying Rug COLD FOIL C .08 .20
48 Magica De Spell - Ambitious Witch C .08 .20
48 Magica De Spell - Ambitious Witch COLD FOIL C .08 .20
49 Magica De Spell - The Midas Touch SR .08 .20
49 Magica De Spell - The Midas Touch COLD FOIL SR .50 1.25
4a Dalmatian Puppy - Tail Wagger COLD FOIL C .50 1.25
4a Dalmatian Puppy - Tail Wagger C .40 1.00
4b Dalmatian Puppy - Tail Wagger COLD FOIL C .50 1.25
4b Dalmatian Puppy - Tail Wagger C .40 1.00
4c Dalmatian Puppy - Tail Wagger COLD FOIL C .50 1.25
4c Dalmatian Puppy - Tail Wagger C .40 1.00
4d Dalmatian Puppy - Tail Wagger COLD FOIL C .50 1.25
4d Dalmatian Puppy - Tail Wagger C .40 1.00
4e Dalmatian Puppy - Tail Wagger COLD FOIL C .50 1.25
4e Dalmatian Puppy - Tail Wagger C .40 1.00
50 Magica De Spell - Thieving Sorceress U .08 .20
50 Magica De Spell - Thieving Sorceress COLD FOIL U .12 .30
51 Maleficent - Mistress of All Evil L 2.00 5.00
51 Maleficent - Mistress of All Evil COLD FOIL L 4.00 10.00
52 Mama Odie - Voice of Wisdom U .08 .20
52 Mama Odie - Voice of Wisdom COLD FOIL U .12 .30
53 Pua - Potbellied Buddy C .08 .20
53 Pua - Potbellied Buddy COLD FOIL C .08 .20
54 Rafiki - Mystical Fighter R 1.00 2.50
54 Rafiki - Mystical Fighter COLD FOIL R 2.50 6.00
55 Stratos - Tornado Titan R .12 .30
55 Stratos - Tornado Titan COLD FOIL R .40 1.00
56 The Firebird - Force of Destruction C .08 .20
56 The Firebird - Force of Destruction COLD FOIL C .12 .30
57 The Queen - Hateful Rival C .08 .20
57 The Queen - Hateful Rival COLD FOIL C .08 .20
58 Treasure Guardian - Protector of the Cave R .08 .20
58 Treasure Guardian - Protector of the Cave COLD FOIL R .30 .75
59 Ursula - Sea Witch R .08 .20
59 Ursula - Sea Witch COLD FOIL R .25 .60
60 Bestow A Gift C .08 .20
60 Bestow a Gift COLD FOIL C .08 .20
61 It Calls Me U .08 .20
61 It Calls Me COLD FOIL U .15 .40
62 Last-Ditch Effort COLD FOIL U .12 .30
62 Last-Ditch Effort U .08 .20
63 The Boss is on a Roll COLD FOIL R .60 1.50
63 The Boss is on a Roll R .20 .50
64 The Lamp COLD FOIL R .25 .60
64 The Lamp R .08 .20
65 The Sorcerer's Hat COLD FOIL R .40 1.00
65 The Sorcerer's Hat R .12 .30
66 Forbidden Mountain - Maleficent's Castle COLD FOIL C .08 .20
66 Forbidden Mountain - Maleficent's Castle C .08 .20
67 The Queen's Castle - Mirror Chamber COLD FOIL R 4.00 10.00
67 The Queen's Castle - Mirror Chamber R 3.00 8.00
68 The Sorcerer's Tower - Wondrous Workspace COLD FOIL U .50 1.25
68 The Sorcerer's Tower - Wondrous Workplace U .08 .20
69 Cubby - Mighty Lost Boy COLD FOIL C .08 .20
69 Cubby - Mighty Lost Boy C .08 .20
70 Cursed Merfolk - Ursula's Handiwork COLD FOIL R 4.00 10.00
70 Cursed Merfolk - Ursula's Handiwork R 2.00 5.00
71 Don Karnage - Prince of Pirates COLD FOIL C .08 .20
71 Don Karnage - Prince of Pirates C .08 .20
72 Flotsam - Riffraff COLD FOIL C .08 .20
72 Flotsam - Riffraff C .08 .20
73 Friar Tuck - Priest of Nottingham COLD FOIL U .20 .50
73 Friar Tuck - Priest of Nottingham U .08 .20
74 Helga Sinclair - Femme Fatale COLD FOIL SR .50 1.25
74 Helga Sinclair - Femme Fatale SR .12 .30
75 Helga Sinclair - Vengeful Partner COLD FOIL R .20 .50
75 Helga Sinclair - Vengeful Partner R .08 .20
76 Jetsam - Riffraff COLD FOIL C .08 .20
76 Jetsam - Riffraff C .08 .20
77 Kit Cloudkicker - Tough Guy COLD FOIL U .25 .60
77 Kit Cloudkicker - Tough Guy U .08 .20
78 Lyle Tiberius Rourke - Cunning Mercenary COLD FOIL SR .50 1.25
78 Lyle Tiberius Rourke - Cunning Mercenary SR .12 .30
79 Milo Thatch - Clever Cartographer COLD FOIL C .08 .20
79 Milo Thatch - Clever Cartographer C .08 .20
80 Milo Thatch - King of Atlantis COLD FOIL L 2.00 5.00
80 Milo Thatch - King of Atlantis L 1.00 2.50
81 Morph - Space Goo COLD FOIL R 3.00 8.00
81 Morph - Space Goo R 1.00 2.50
82 Peter Pan - Lost Boy Leader R .08 .20
82 Peter Pan - Lost Boy Leader COLD FOIL R .08 .20
83 Prince John - Phony King COLD FOIL U .15 .40
83 Prince John - Phony King U .08 .20
84 Robin Hood - Daydreamer R .08 .20
84 Robin Hood - Daydreamer COLD FOIL R .50 1.25
85 Shenzi - Hyena Pack Leader COLD FOIL SR .40 1.00
85 Shenzi - Hyena Pack Leader SR .08 .20
86 Sir Hiss - Aggravating Asp C .08 .20
86 Sir Hiss - Aggravating Asp COLD FOIL C .08 .20
87 Skippy - Energetic Rabbit COLD FOIL C .08 .20
87 Skippy - Energetic Rabbit C .08 .20
88 Starkey - Devious Pirate U .08 .20
88 Starkey - Devious Pirate COLD FOIL U .08 .20
89 Stitch - Covert Agent COLD FOIL R .20 .50
89 Stitch - Covert Agent R .08 .20
90 Ursula - Deceiver U .20 .50
90 Ursula - Deceiver COLD FOIL U 2.00 5.00
91 Ursula - Deceiver of All COLD FOIL L ERR/("Storyborn") 25.00 60.00
91 Ursula - Deceiver of All L ERR/("Storyborn") 20.00 50.00
92 Wildcat - Mechanic COLD FOIL U .20 .50
92 Wildcat - Mechanic U .08 .20
93 Zazu - Steward of the Pride Lands C .08 .20
93 Zazu - Steward of the Pride Lands COLD FOIL C .08 .20
94 Has Set My Heaaaaaaart . . . COLD FOIL U .15 .40
94 Has Set My Heaaaaaaart . . . U .08 .20
95 I Will Find My Way C .08 .20
95 I Will Find My Way COLD FOIL C .08 .20
96 Strike a Good Match COLD FOIL C .15 .40
96 Strike A Good Match C .08 .20
97 Airfoil C .08 .20
97 Airfoil COLD FOIL C .08 .20
98 Robin's Bow COLD FOIL U .15 .40
98 Robin's Bow U .08 .20
99 Starlight Vial COLD FOIL R .20 .50
99 Starlight Vial R .08 .20
100 De Vil Manor - Cruella's Estate C .08 .20
100 De Vil Manor - Cruella's Estate COLD FOIL C .08 .20
101 Fang - River City R .12 .30
101 Fang - River City COLD FOIL R .30 .75
102 Kuzco's Palace - Home of the Emperor U .08 .20
102 Kuzco's Palace - Home of the Emperor COLD FOIL U .12 .30
103 Ariel - Adventurous Collector SR .15 .40
103 Ariel - Adventurous Collector COLD FOIL SR .50 1.25
104 Billy Bones - Keeper of the Map C .08 .20
104 Billy Bones - Keeper of the Map COLD FOIL C .08 .20
105 Captain Hook - Master Swordsman R .08 .20
105 Captain Hook - Master Swordsman COLD FOIL R .40 1.00
106 Della Duck - Unstoppable Mum C .08 .20
106 Della Duck - Unstoppable Mom COLD FOIL C .08 .20
107 HeiHei - Accidental Explorer U .08 .20
107 HeiHei - Accidental Explorer COLD FOIL U .30 .75
108 Hydra - Deadly Serpent L 1.00 2.50
108 Hydra - Deadly Serpent COLD FOIL L 3.00 8.00
109 Jim Hawkins - Space Traveler L 4.00 10.00
109 Jim Hawkins - Space Traveler COLD FOIL L 8.00 20.00
110 Jim Hawkins - Thrill Seeker C .08 .20
110 Jim Hawkins - Thrill Seeker COLD FOIL C .08 .20
111 Kakamora - Menacing Sailor C .08 .20
111 Kakamora - Menacing Sailor COLD FOIL C .08 .20
112 Madame Medusa - The Boss SR 2.50 6.00
112 Madame Medusa - The Boss COLD FOIL SR 10.00 25.00
113 Maui - Soaring Demigod U .08 .20
113 Maui - Soaring Demigod COLD FOIL U .12 .30
114 Maui - Whale R .08 .20
114 Maui - Whale COLD FOIL R .20 .50
115 Milo Thatch - Spirited Scholar C .08 .20
115 Milo Thatch - Spirited Scholar COLD FOIL C .08 .20
116 Moana - Born Leader R .08 .20
116 Moana - Born Leader COLD FOIL R .12 .30
117 Moana - Undeterred Voyager C .08 .20
117 Moana - Undeterred Voyager COLD FOIL C .08 .20
118 Nutsy - Vulture Henchman C .08 .20
118 Nutsy - Vulture Henchman COLD FOIL C .08 .20
119 Peter Pan - Never Land Hero C .08 .20
119 Peter Pan - Never Land Hero COLD FOIL C .08 .20
120 Peter Pan - Pirate's Bane R .08 .20
120 Peter Pan - Pirate's Bane COLD FOIL R .25 .60
121 Prince Eric - Expert Helmsman SR .20 .50
121 Prince Eric - Expert Helmsman COLD FOIL SR 1.00 2.50
122 Scroop - Backstabber U .08 .20
122 Scroop - Backstabber COLD FOIL U .12 .30
123 Simba - Scrappy Cub R .15 .40
123 Simba - Scrappy Cub COLD FOIL R .60 1.50
124 Slightly - Lost Boy U .08 .20
124 Slightly - Lost Boy COLD FOIL U .08 .20
125 Stitch - Little Rocket C .08 .20
125 Stitch - Little Rocket COLD FOIL C .15 .40
126 Trigger - Not-So-Sharp Shooter U .08 .20
126 Trigger - Not-So-Sharp Shooter COLD FOIL U .15 .40
127 Webby Vanderquack - Enthusiastic Duck C .08 .20
127 Webby Vanderquack - Enthusiastic Duck COLD FOIL C .08 .20
128 Divebomb U .08 .20
128 Divebomb COLD FOIL U .12 .30
129 I've Got A Dream U .08 .20
129 I've Got a Dream COLD FOIL U .12 .30
130 On Your Feet! Now! R .08 .20
130 On Your Feet! Now! COLD FOIL R .20 .50
131 Voyage C .08 .20
131 Voyage COLD FOIL C .08 .20
132 Maui's Fish Hook R .12 .30
132 Maui's Fish Hook COLD FOIL R 1.00 2.50
133 Sumerian Talisman U .08 .20
133 Sumerian Talisman COLD FOIL U .20 .50
134 Agrabah - Marketplace C .08 .20
134 Agrabah - Marketplace COLD FOIL C .12 .30
135 Jolly Roger - Hook's Ship U .08 .20
135 Jolly Roger - Hook's Ship COLD FOIL U .20 .50
136 RLS Legacy - Solar Galleon R 1.00 2.50
136 RLS Legacy - Solar Galleon COLD FOIL R .20 .50
137 Audrey Ramirez - The Engineer R .25 .60
137 Audrey Ramirez - The Engineer COLD FOIL R .08 .20
138 Captain Amelia - First in Command C .08 .20
138 Captain Amelia - First in Command COLD FOIL C .08 .20
139 Dewey - Showy Nephew U .08 .20
139 Dewey - Showy Nephew COLD FOIL U .12 .30
140 Flintheart Glomgold - Lone Cheater COLD FOIL U .08 .20
140 Flintheart Glomgold - Lone Cheater U .08 .20
141 Genie - Cramped in the Lamp COLD FOIL U .08 .20
141 Genie - Cramped in the Lamp U .15 .40
142 Gramma Tala - Keeper of Ancient Stories COLD FOIL C .08 .20
142 Gramma Tala - Keeper of Ancient Stories C .20 .50
143 Gramma Tala - Spirit of the Ocean COLD FOIL L 1.50 4.00
143 Gramma Tala - Spirit of the Ocean L 3.00 8.00
144 Gyro Gearloose - Gadget Whiz COLD FOIL R .15 .40
144 Gyro Gearloose - Gadget Whiz R .08 .20
145 Huey - Savvy Nephew COLD FOIL R .25 .60
145 Huey - Savvy Nephew R .08 .20
146 King Louie - Bandleader COLD FOIL C .08 .20
146 King Louie - Bandleader C .08 .20
147 Kit Cloudkicker - Navigator COLD FOIL U .08 .20
147 Kit Cloudkicker - Navigator U .15 .40
148 Kit Cloudkicker - Spunky Bear Cub COLD FOIL C .08 .20
148 Kit Cloudkicker - Spunky Bear Cub C .12 .30
149 Louie - Chill Nephew COLD FOIL C .08 .20
149 Louie - Chill Nephew C .08 .20
150 Maid Marian - Delightful Dreamer COLD FOIL C .08 .20
150 Maid Marian - Delightful Dreamer C .08 .20
151 Mama Odie - Mystical Maven COLD FOIL R .30 .75
151 Mama Odie - Mystical Maven R .08 .20
152 Pluto - Mickey's Clever Friend COLD FOIL C .08 .20
152 Pluto - Mickey's Clever Friend C .08 .20
153 Rufus - Orphanage Cat COLD FOIL C .08 .20
153 Rufus - Orphanage Cat C .08 .20
154 Scrooge McDuck - Richest Duck in the World COLD FOIL SR .20 .50
154 Scrooge McDuck - Richest Duck in the World SR .08 .20
155 Scrooge McDuck - Uncle Moneybags COLD FOIL U .20 .50
155 Scrooge McDuck - Uncle Moneybags U .08 .20
156 The Queen - Mirror Seeker COLD FOIL U .15 .40
156 The Queen - Mirror Seeker U .08 .20
157 Tinker Bell - Very Clever Fairy COLD FOIL SR .20 .50
157 Tinker Bell - Very Clever Fairy SR .08 .20
158 Wendy Darling - Authority on Peter Pan COLD FOIL SR .30 .75
158 Wendy Darling - Authority on Peter Pan SR .08 .20
159 Distract COLD FOIL C .08 .20
159 Distract C .08 .20
160 Friend Like Me COLD FOIL R .25 .60
160 Friend Like Me R .08 .20
161 How Far I'll Go COLD FOIL U .40 1.00
161 How Far I'll Go U .08 .20
162 Repair COLD FOIL C .08 .20
162 Repair C .08 .20
163 Aurelian Gyrosensor COLD FOIL R .25 .60
163 Aurelian Gyrosensor R .08 .20
164 Heart of Te Fiti COLD FOIL R .40 1.00
164 Heart of Te Fiti R .08 .20
165 Lucky Dime COLD FOIL L 8.00 20.00
165 Lucky Dime L 8.00 20.00
166 Scrooge's Top Hat COLD FOIL U .12 .30
166 Scrooge's Top Hat U .08 .20
167 Vault Door COLD FOIL C .08 .20
167 Vault Door C .08 .20
168 Belle's House - Maurice's Workshop COLD FOIL R .30 .75
168 Belle's House - Maurice's Workshop R .08 .20
169 McDuck Manor - Scrooge's Mansion COLD FOIL C .20 .50
169 McDuck Manor - Scrooge's Mansion C .08 .20
170 Motunui - Island Paradise COLD FOIL U .25 .60
170 Motunui - Island Paradise U .08 .20
171 Chief Tui - Proud of Motunui COLD FOIL C .08 .20
171 Chief Tui - Proud of Motunui C .08 .20
172 Eeyore - Overstuffed Donkey COLD FOIL C .15 .40
172 Eeyore - Overstuffed Donkey C .08 .20
173 Gustav the Giant - Terror of the Kingdom COLD FOIL R .20 .50
173 Gustav the Giant - Terror of the Kingdom R .08 .20
174 Hades - Hotheaded Ruler COLD FOIL R .30 .75
174 Hades - Hotheaded Ruler R .12 .30
175 Helga Sinclair - Right-Hand Woman COLD FOIL C .08 .20
175 Helga Sinclair - Right-Hand Woman C .08 .20
176 John Silver - Greedy Treasure Seeker COLD FOIL R .50 1.25
176 John Silver - Greedy Treasure Seeker R .20 .50
177 Kida - Royal Warrior COLD FOIL C .12 .30
177 Kida - Royal Warrior C .08 .20
178 Little John - Resourceful Outlaw SR .15 .40
178 Little John - Resourceful Outlaw COLD FOIL SR .40 1.00
179 Little John - Robin's Pal U .08 .20
179 Little John - Robin's Pal COLD FOIL U .15 .40
180 Lythos - Rock Titan U .08 .20
180 Lythos - Rock Titan COLD FOIL U .20 .50
181 Mickey Mouse - Stalwart Explorer C .08 .20
181 Mickey Mouse - Stalwart Explorer COLD FOIL C .08 .20
182 Mickey Mouse - Trumpeter L 1.25 3.00
182 Mickey Mouse - Trumpeter COLD FOIL L 3.00 8.00
183 Minnie Mouse - Funky Spelunker C .08 .20
183 Minnie Mouse - Funky Spelunker COLD FOIL C .08 .20
184 Mr Smee - Bumbling Mate U .15 .40
184 Mr. Smee - Bumbling Mate COLD FOIL U 1.50 4.00
185 Mufasa - Champion of the Pride Lands R .08 .20
185 Mufasa - Champion of the Pride Lands COLD FOIL R .20 .50
186 Nala - Fierce Friend U .08 .20
186 Nala - Fierce Friend COLD FOIL U .12 .30
187 Pyros - Lava Titan R .12 .30
187 Pyros - Lava Titan COLD FOIL R .40 1.00
188 Razoul - Palace Guard C .08 .20

2024 Disney Lorcana Into The Inklands

188 Razoul - Palace Guard COLD FOIL C .08 .20
189 Robin Hood - Beloved Outlaw C .08 .20
189 Robin Hood - Beloved Outlaw COLD FOIL C .60 1.50
190 Robin Hood - Champion of Sherwood L 25.00 60.00
190 Robin Hood - Champion of Sherwood COLD FOIL L 25.00 60.00
191 Sheriff Of Nottingham - Corrupt Official SR .08 .20
191 Sheriff of Nottingham - Corrupt Official COLD FOIL SR .50 1.25
192 Simba - Fighting Prince SR .15 .40
192 Simba - Fighting Prince COLD FOIL SR .60 1.50
193 Simba - Rightful King U .08 .20
193 Simba - Rightful King COLD FOIL U .15 .40
194 Thaddeus E. Klang - Metallic Leader U .08 .20
194 Thaddeus E. Klang - Metallic Leader COLD FOIL U .15 .40
195 And Then Along Came Zeus R 2.00 5.00
195 And Then Along Came Zeus COLD FOIL R 3.00 8.00
196 Ba-Boom! C .08 .20
196 Ba-Boom! COLD FOIL C .20 .50
197 Olympus Would Be That Way C .08 .20
197 Olympus Would Be That Way COLD FOIL C .08 .20
198 Rise of the Titans U .12 .30
198 Rise of the Titans COLD FOIL U .50 1.25
199 Captain Hook's Rapier U .08 .20
199 Captain Hook's Rapier COLD FOIL U .20 .50
200 Gizmosuit C .08 .20
200 Gizmosuit COLD FOIL C .08 .20
201 Map of Treasure Planet R .08 .20
201 Map of Treasure Planet COLD FOIL R .30 .75
202 Maui's Place of Exile - Hidden Island R .12 .30
202 Maui's Place of Exile - Hidden Island COLD FOIL R .40 1.00
203 Nottingham - Prince John's Castle C .08 .20
203 Nottingham - Prince John's Castle COLD FOIL C .08 .20
204 The Bayou - Mysterious Swamp U .08 .20
204 The Bayou - Mysterious Swamp COLD FOIL U .20 .50
205 Chernabog - Evildoer ENCHANTED FOIL E 75.00 200.00
206 Kida - Protector of Atlantis ENCHANTED FOIL E 75.00 200.00
207 Pride Lands - Pride Rock ENCHANTED FOIL E 40.00 100.00
208 Jafar - Striking Illusionist ENCHANTED FOIL E 100.00 250.00
209 Maleficent - Mistress of All Evil ENCHANTED FOIL E 75.00 200.00
210 The Sorcerer's Hat ENCHANTED FOIL E 50.00 120.00
211 Morph - Space Goo ENCHANTED FOIL E 100.00 250.00
212 Ursula - Deceiver of All ENCHANTED FOIL E ERR/((Storyborn") 200.00 500.00
213 Kuzco's Palace - Home of the Emperor ENCHANTED FOIL E 30.00 80.00
214 Captain Hook - Master Swordsman ENCHANTED FOIL E 50.00 120.00
215 Peter Pan - Pirate's Bane ENCHANTED FOIL E COR/("Peter Pan.) 75.00 200.00
215 Peter Pan - Pirate's Bane ENCHANTED FOIL E ERR/("Peter Pan).) 200.00 500.00
216 RLS Legacy - Solar Galleon ENCHANTED FOIL E 30.00 80.00
217 Gramma Tala - Spirit of the Ocean ENCHANTED FOIL E 40.00 100.00
218 Scrooge McDuck - Richest Duck in the World ENCHANTED FOIL E 75.00 200.00
219 Belle's House - Maurice's Workshop ENCHANTED FOIL E 40.00 100.00
220 Mickey Mouse - Trumpeter ENCHANTED FOIL E 75.00 200.00
221 Robin Hood - Champion of Sherwood ENCHANTED FOIL E 100.00 250.00
222 And Then Along Came Zeus ENCHANTED FOIL E 75.00 200.00

2024 Disney Lorcana Into The Inklands Gift Set

89 Stitch - Covert Agent OVERSIZED R 1.25 3.00
157 Tinker Bell - Very Clever Fairy OVERSIZED SR 1.25 3.00

2024 Disney Lorcana Promos

30P1 Stitch - Rock Star P/(Into The Inklands Championship Prize) 300.00 800.00
39P1 Scrooge McDuck - Uncle Moneybags P 12.00 30.00
40P1 Flotsam and Jetsam - Entangling Eels P 15.00 40.00

2024 Disney Lorcana Ursula's Return

1 Agustin Madrigal - Clumsy Dad C .08 .20
1 Agustin Madrigal - Clumsy Dad COLD FOIL C .08 .20
2 Alma Madrigal - Matriarch of the Family COLD FOIL R .40 1.00
2 Alma Madrigal - Matriarch of the Family R .20 .50
3 Ariel - Singing Mermaid R .15 .40
3 Ariel - Singing Mermaid COLD FOIL R .75 2.00
4 Cinderella - Melody Weaver COLD FOIL L 4.00 10.00
4 Cinderella - Melody Weaver L 2.00 5.00
5 Cogsworth - Majordomo C .08 .20
5 Cogsworth - Majordomo COLD FOIL C .08 .20
6 Daisy Duck - Lovely Lady COLD FOIL U .15 .40
6 Daisy Duck - Lovely Lady U .08 .20
7 Daisy Duck - Musketeer Spy C .08 .20
7 Daisy Duck - Musketeer Spy COLD FOIL C .20 .50
8 Donald Duck - Musketeer Soldier COLD FOIL U .25 .60
8 Donald Duck - Musketeer Soldier U .08 .20
9 Felix Madrigal - Fun-Loving Family Man U .08 .20
9 Felix Madrigal - Fun-Loving Family Man COLD FOIL U .08 .20
10 Gaston - Despicable Dealer COLD FOIL S 1.00 2.50
10 Gaston - Despicable Dealer S .25 .60
11 Golden Harp - Enchanter of the Land R .08 .20
11 Golden Harp - Enchanter of the Land COLD FOIL R .30 .75
12 Goofy - Musketeer Swordsman COLD FOIL R .20 .50
12 Goofy - Musketeer Swordsman R .08 .20
13 Julieta Madrigal - Excellent Cook U .08 .20
13 Julieta Madrigal - Excellent Cook COLD FOIL U .40 1.00
14 Max - Loyal Sheepdog C .08 .20
14 Max - Loyal Sheepdog COLD FOIL C .08 .20
15 Mickey Mouse - Leader of the Band U .08 .20
15 Mickey Mouse - Leader of the Band COLD FOIL U .15 .40
16 Mickey Mouse - Musketeer Captain L 2.00 5.00
16 Mickey Mouse - Musketeer Captain COLD FOIL L 4.00 10.00
17 Minnie Mouse - Musketeer Champion S .20 .50
17 Minnie Mouse - Musketeer Champion COLD FOIL S .60 1.50
18 Mirabel Madrigal - Gift of the Family S .08 .20
18 Mirabel Madrigal - Gift of the Family COLD FOIL S .20 .50
19 Mirabel Madrigal - Prophecy Finder C .08 .20
19 Mirabel Madrigal - Prophecy Finder COLD FOIL C .08 .20
20 Pluto - Rescue Dog C .08 .20
20 Pluto - Rescue Dog COLD FOIL C .08 .20
21 Prince Eric - Seafaring Prince C .08 .20
21 Prince Eric - Seafaring Prince COLD FOIL C .08 .20
22 Prince Eric - Ursula's Groom U .08 .20
22 Prince Eric - Ursula's Groom COLD FOIL U .25 .60
23 Stitch - Alien Dancer COLD FOIL C .15 .40
23 Stitch - Alien Dancer C .08 .20
24 Ursula - Eric's Bride R .25 .60
24 Ursula - Eric's Bride COLD FOIL R 1.00 2.50
25 Ursula - Vanessa COLD FOIL C .25 .60
25 Ursula - Vanessa C .08 .20
26 Bruno's Return U .08 .20
26 Bruno's Return COLD FOIL U .15 .40
27 First Aid COLD FOIL C .08 .20
27 First Aid C .08 .20
28 Look at this Family R .20 .50
28 Look at this Family COLD FOIL R .75 2.00
29 Lost in the Woods COLD FOIL U .12 .30
29 Lost in the Woods U .08 .20
30 Sign the Scroll U .08 .20
30 Sign the Scroll COLD FOIL U .12 .30
31 Miracle Candle COLD FOIL R .30 .75
31 Miracle Candle R .08 .20
32 Record Player C .08 .20
32 Record Player COLD FOIL C .15 .40
33 Atlantica - Concert Hall COLD FOIL C .08 .20
33 Atlantica - Concert Hall C .08 .20
34 The Underworld - River Styx R .08 .20
34 The Underworld - River Styx COLD FOIL R .30 .75
35 Antonio Madrigal - Animal Expert COLD FOIL U .12 .30
35 Antonio Madrigal - Animal Expert U .08 .20
36 Belle - Accomplished Mystic S .20 .50
36 Belle - Accomplished Mystic COLD FOIL S .75 2.00
37 Belle - Untrained Mystic COLD FOIL C .20 .50
37 Belle - Untrained Mystic C .08 .20
38 Bruno Madrigal - Out of the Shadows R .08 .20
38 Bruno Madrigal - Out of the Shadows COLD FOIL R .15 .40
39 Bruno Madrigal - Undetected Uncle COLD FOIL S 1.00 2.50
39 Bruno Madrigal - Undetected Uncle S .60 1.50
40 Camilo - Madrigal Prankster U .08 .20
40 Camilo - Madrigal Prankster COLD FOIL U .15 .40
41 Dolores Madrigal - Easy Listener COLD FOIL C .08 .20
41 Dolores Madrigal - Easy Listener C .08 .20
42 Elsa - Storm Chaser R .08 .20
42 Elsa - Storm Chaser COLD FOIL R .30 .75
43 Flotsam - Ursula's "Baby" COLD FOIL U .12 .30
43 Flotsam - Ursula's "Baby" U .08 .20
44 Flotsam & Jetsam - Entangling Eels U .08 .20
44 Flotsam & Jetsam - Entangling Eels COLD FOIL U .12 .30
45 Isabela Madrigal - Golden Child COLD FOIL R 1.25 3.00
45 Isabela Madrigal - Golden Child R .25 .60
46 Jetsam - Ursula's "Baby" C .08 .20
46 Jetsam - Ursula's "Baby" COLD FOIL C .08 .20
47 Luisa Madrigal - Magically Strong One COLD FOIL C .08 .20
47 Luisa Madrigal - Magically Strong One C .08 .20
48 Magic Broom - Illuminary Keeper C .08 .20
48 Magic Broom - Illuminary Keeper COLD FOIL C .40 1.00
49 Magic Broom - Life Filled Sweeper COLD FOIL C .15 .40
49 Magic Broom - Life Filled Sweeper C .08 .20
50 Magical Maid - Feather Duster U .08 .20
50 Magical Maid - Feather Duster COLD FOIL U .15 .40
51 Marshmallow - Terrifying Snowman COLD FOIL U .12 .30
51 Marshmallow - Terrifying Snowman U .08 .20
52 Mrs. Potts - Enchanted Teapot COLD FOIL R .20 .50
52 Mrs. Potts - Enchanted Teapot R .08 .20
53 Pepa Madrigal - Weather Maker COLD FOIL R .25 .60
53 Pepa Madrigal - Weather Maker R .08 .20
54 Peter Pan - Shadow Finder COLD FOIL S 1.00 2.50
54 Peter Pan - Shadow Finder S .20 .50
55 Pico - Helpful Toucan COLD FOIL C .08 .20
55 Pico - Helpful Toucan C .08 .20
56 Tick-Tock - Ever-Present Pursuer COLD FOIL C .08 .20
56 Tick-Tock - Ever-Present Pursuer C .08 .20
57 Ursula - Mad Sea Witch COLD FOIL U .25 .60
57 Ursula - Mad Sea Witch U .08 .20
58 Ursula - Sea Witch Queen COLD FOIL L 10.00 25.00
58 Ursula - Sea Witch Queen L 6.00 15.00
59 Yen Sid - Powerful Sorcerer COLD FOIL L 10.00 25.00
59 Yen Sid - Powerful Sorcerer L 6.00 15.00
60 Poor Unfortunate Souls C .08 .20
60 Poor Unfortunate Souls COLD FOIL C .12 .30
61 Second Star to the Right R .20 .50
61 Second Star to the Right COLD FOIL R .40 1.00
62 Swing Into Action C .08 .20
62 Swing Into Action COLD FOIL C .08 .20
63 Ursula's Plan U .08 .20
63 Ursula's Plan COLD FOIL U .20 .50
64 Mystical Rose R .08 .20
64 Mystical Rose COLD FOIL R .30 .75
65 Rose Lantern C .08 .20
65 Rose Lantern COLD FOIL C .08 .20
66 Triton's Trident U .08 .20
66 Triton's Trident COLD FOIL U .08 .20
67 Casa Madrigal - Casita C .08 .20
67 Casa Madrigal - Casita COLD FOIL C .12 .30
68 Ursula's Lair - Eye of the Storm R .12 .30
68 Ursula's Lair - Eye of the Storm COLD FOIL R .40 1.00
69 Cri-Kee - Lucky Cricket R .25 .60
69 Cri-Kee - Lucky Cricket COLD FOIL R 1.25 3.00
70 Diablo - Devoted Herald L 30.00 80.00
70 Diablo - Devoted Herald COLD FOIL L 40.00 100.00
71 Diablo - Maleficent's Spy C .08 .20
71 Diablo - Maleficent's Spy COLD FOIL C .50 1.25
72 Gunther - Interior Designer C .08 .20
72 Gunther - Interior Designer COLD FOIL C .08 .20
73 Gus - Champion of Cheese C .08 .20
73 Gus - Champion of Cheese COLD FOIL C .08 .20
74 Hades - Double Dealer L 1.50 4.00
74 Hades - Double Dealer COLD FOIL L 4.00 10.00
75 HeiHei - Clumsy Rooster U .08 .20
75 HeiHei - Clumsy Rooster COLD FOIL U .40 1.00
76 Hera - Queen of the Gods R .12 .30
76 Hera - Queen of the Gods COLD FOIL R .30 .75
77 Jaq - Connoisseur of Climbing C .08 .20
77 Jaq - Connoisseur of Climbing COLD FOIL C .12 .30
78 Jasmine - Desert Warrior R .12 .30
78 Jasmine - Desert Warrior COLD FOIL R .50 1.25
79 Megara - Captivating Cynic C .08 .20
79 Megara - Captivating Cynic COLD FOIL C .08 .20
80 Megara - Liberated One U .08 .20
80 Megara - Liberated One COLD FOIL U .25 .60
81 Pain - Immortal Sidekick U .08 .20
81 Pain - Immortal Sidekick COLD FOIL U .20 .50
82 Panic - Immortal Sidekick U .08 .20
82 Panic - Immortal Sidekick COLD FOIL U .12 .30
83 Pegasus - Cloud Racer U .15 .40
83 Pegasus - Cloud Racer COLD FOIL U 1.50 4.00
84 Pegasus - Gift for Hercules C .08 .20
84 Pegasus - Gift for Hercules COLD FOIL C .75 2.00
85 Pete - Born to Cheat S .08 .20
85 Pete - Born to Cheat COLD FOIL S .40 1.00
86 Pete - Rotten Guy U .08 .20
86 Pete - Rotten Guy COLD FOIL U .12 .30
87 Prince Phillip - Slayer of Enemies S .12 .30
87 Prince Phillip - Slayer of Enemies COLD FOIL S .50 1.25
88 Prince Phillip - Warden of the Woods R .08 .20
88 Prince Phillip - Warden of the Woods COLD FOIL R .30 .75
89 The Fates - Only One Eye C .08 .20
89 The Fates - Only One Eye COLD FOIL C .08 .20
90 The Muses - Proclaimers of Heroes R .15 .40
90 The Muses - Proclaimers of Heroes COLD FOIL R 1.25 3.00
91 Tor - Florist C .08 .20
91 Tor - Florist COLD FOIL C .08 .20
92 Zeus - Mr. Lightning Bolts S .15 .40
92 Zeus - Mr. Lightning Bolts COLD FOIL S .50 1.25
93 Dodge! C .08 .20
93 Dodge! COLD FOIL C .12 .30
94 Make the Potion C .08 .20
94 Make the Potion COLD FOIL C .12 .30
95 Under the Sea R .20 .50
95 Under the Sea COLD FOIL R 1.25 3.00
96 Ursula's Trickery U .08 .20
96 Ursula's Trickery COLD FOIL U .15 .40
97 We Don't Talk About Bruno R 1.00 2.50
97 We Don't Talk About Bruno COLD FOIL R 2.00 5.00
98 Hidden Inkcaster C .08 .20
98 Hidden Inkcaster COLD FOIL C .15 .40
99 Signed Contract U .08 .20
99 Signed Contract COLD FOIL U .20 .50
100 Vision Slab U .08 .20
100 Vision Slab COLD FOIL U .20 .50
101 Hidden Cove - Tranquil Haven COLD FOIL C .15 .40
101 Hidden Cove - Tranquil Haven C .08 .20
102 Ursula's Garden - Full of the Unfortunate R .12 .30
102 Ursula's Garden - Full of the Unfortunate COLD FOIL R .30 .75
103 Beast - Wounded COLD FOIL U .50 1.25
103 Beast - Wounded U .08 .20
104 Benja - Bold Uniter C .08 .20
104 Benja - Bold Uniter COLD FOIL C .08 .20
105 Fa Zhou - Mulan's Father COLD FOIL C .08 .20
105 Fa Zhou - Mulan's Father C .08 .20
106 Flynn Rider - Frenemy S 2.50 6.00
106 Flynn Rider - Frenemy COLD FOIL S 5.00 12.00
107 Goofy - Super Goof COLD FOIL R 2.50 6.00
107 Goofy - Super Goof R .60 1.50
108 Hercules - Clumsy Kid C .08 .20
108 Hercules - Clumsy Kid COLD FOIL C .12 .30
109 Hercules - Daring Demigod COLD FOIL U .25 .60
109 Hercules - Daring Demigod U .08 .20
110 Khan - Beloved Steed U .08 .20
110 Khan - Beloved Steed COLD FOIL U .08 .20
111 Li Shang - General's Son COLD FOIL C .08 .20
111 Li Shang - General's Son C .08 .20
112 Li Shang - Valorous General U .08 .20
112 Li Shang - Valorous General COLD FOIL U .15 .40
113 Lumiere - Fiery Friend COLD FOIL R 1.00 2.50
113 Lumiere - Fiery Friend R .25 .60
114 Mulan - Elite Archer L 4.00 10.00
114 Mulan - Elite Archer COLD FOIL L 8.00 20.00
115 Mulan - Enemy of Entanglement COLD FOIL U .25 .60
115 Mulan - Enemy of Entanglement U .08 .20
116 Mulan - Injured Soldier C .08 .20
116 Mulan - Injured Soldier COLD FOIL C .25 .60
117 Namaari - Heir of Fang COLD FOIL R .25 .60
117 Namaari - Heir of Fang R .08 .20
118 Nessus - River Guardian U .08 .20
118 Nessus - River Guardian COLD FOIL U .12 .30
119 Noi - Acrobatic Baby COLD FOIL S .30 .75
119 Noi - Acrobatic Baby S .08 .20
120 Pegasus - Flying Steed C .08 .20
120 Pegasus - Flying Steed COLD FOIL C .15 .40
121 Raya - Fierce Protector COLD FOIL S .50 1.25
121 Raya - Fierce Protector S .08 .20
122 Raya - Guardian of the Dragon Gem C .08 .20
122 Raya - Guardian of the Dragon Gem COLD FOIL C .08 .20
123 Sisu - Daring Visitor COLD FOIL U 1.25 3.00
123 Sisu - Daring Visitor U .08 .20
124 Sisu - Emboldened Warrior R 2.00 5.00
124 Sisu - Emboldened Warrior COLD FOIL R 5.00 12.00
125 Sisu - Responsible Sister COLD FOIL L 20.00 50.00
125 Sisu - Responsible Sister L 12.00 30.00
126 Tong - Survivor C .08 .20
126 Tong - Survivor COLD FOIL C .12 .30
127 Tuk Tuk - Lively Partner COLD FOIL R .60 1.50
127 Tuk Tuk - Lively Partner R .12 .30
128 A Pirate's Life U .08 .20
128 A Pirate's Life COLD FOIL U .20 .50
129 Be King Undisputed COLD FOIL R 2.00 5.00
129 Be King Undisputed R .50 1.25
130 Brawl COLD FOIL C 1.00 2.50
130 Brawl C .08 .20
131 Imperial Proclamation COLD FOIL R .50 1.25
131 Imperial Proclamation R .12 .30
132 Medallion Weights COLD FOIL U .20 .50
132 Medallion Weights U .08 .20
133 The Plank COLD FOIL C .12 .30
133 The Plank C .08 .20
134 Vitalisphere COLD FOIL C .20 .50
134 Vitalisphere C .08 .20
135 Snuggly Duckling - Disreputable Pub COLD FOIL R .40 1.00
135 Snuggly Duckling - Disreputable Pub R .15 .40
136 Training Grounds - Impossible Pillar COLD FOIL C .08 .20
136 Training Grounds - Impossible Pillar C .08 .20
137 Anna - Braving the Storm COLD FOIL C .12 .30
137 Anna - Braving the Storm C .08 .20
138 Anna - True-Hearted S .20 .50
138 Anna - True-Hearted COLD FOIL S .60 1.50
139 Ariel - Treasure Collector S .75 2.00
139 Ariel - Treasure Collector COLD FOIL S 2.50 6.00
140 Aurora - Lore Guardian S .25 .60
140 Aurora - Lore Guardian COLD FOIL S 1.00 2.50
141 Aurora - Tranquil Princess C .08 .20
141 Aurora - Tranquil Princess COLD FOIL C .12 .30
142 Dang Hu - Talon Chief R .08 .20
142 Dang Hu - Talon Chief COLD FOIL R .20 .50
143 Fa Li - Mulan's Mother C .08 .20
143 Fa Li - Mulan's Mother COLD FOIL C .08 .20
144 Flounder - Collector's Companion U .08 .20
144 Flounder - Collector's Companion COLD FOIL U .15 .40
145 Hades - Meticulous Planner U .08 .20
145 Hades - Meticulous Planner COLD FOIL U .12 .30
146 Hans - Noble Scoundrel C .08 .20
146 Hans - Noble Scoundrel COLD FOIL C .08 .20
147 Iduna - Caring Mother U .08 .20
147 Iduna - Caring Mother COLD FOIL U .12 .30
148 John Silver - Horrors of the Empire R .08 .20
148 John Silver - Horrors of the Empire COLD FOIL R .20 .50
149 Olaf - Carrot Enthusiast U .08 .20
149 Olaf - Carrot Enthusiast COLD FOIL U .25 .60
150 Olaf - Trusting Companion C .08 .20
150 Olaf - Trusting Companion COLD FOIL C .12 .30
151 Pascal - Inquisitive Pet C .08 .20
151 Pascal - Inquisitive Pet COLD FOIL C .12 .30
152 Prince Phillip - Gallant Defender R .08 .20
152 Prince Phillip - Gallant Defender COLD FOIL R .20 .50
153 Rapunzel - Appreciative Artist R .08 .20
153 Rapunzel - Appreciative Artist COLD FOIL R .30 .75
154 Scuttle - Expert on Humans U .15 .40
154 Scuttle - Expert on Humans COLD FOIL U 2.00 5.00
155 Sisu - Wise Friend U .08 .20
155 Sisu - Wise Friend COLD FOIL U .20 .50
156 The Queen - Diviner L 2.00 5.00
156 The Queen - Diviner COLD FOIL L 4.00 10.00
157 Transformed Chef - Castle Stove C .08 .20
157 Transformed Chef - Castle Stove COLD FOIL C .08 .20
158 Triton - Champion of Atlantica L 1.00 2.50
158 Triton - Champion of Atlantica COLD FOIL L 2.50 6.00
159 Triton - Discerning King R .15 .40
159 Triton - Discerning King COLD FOIL R .60 1.50
160 Triton - Young Prince U .08 .20
160 Triton - Young Prince COLD FOIL U .20 .50
161 Tuk Tuk - Curious Partner C .08 .20
161 Tuk Tuk - Curious Partner COLD FOIL C .12 .30
162 Dig a Little Deeper U .08 .20
162 Dig a Little Deeper COLD FOIL U .20 .50

163 Glean C	.08	.20
163 Glean COLD FOIL C	.12	.30
164 Seldom All They Seem C	.08	.20
164 Seldom All They Seem COLD FOIL C	.08	.20
165 Treasures Untold R	.12	.30
165 Treasures Untold COLD FOIL R	.40	1.00
166 Field of Ice R	.08	.20
166 Field of Ice COLD FOIL R	.30	.75
167 Great Stone Dragon U	.08	.20
167 Great Stone Dragon COLD FOIL U	.25	.60
168 Ice Block C	.08	.20
168 Ice Block COLD FOIL C	.60	1.50
169 Ariel's Grotto - A Secret Place R	.08	.20
169 Ariel's Grotto - A Secret Place COLD FOIL R	.30	.75
170 Winter Camp - Medical Tent C	.08	.20
170 Winter Camp - Medical Tent COLD FOIL C	.08	.20
171 Aladdin - Brave Rescuer U	.08	.20
171 Aladdin - Brave Rescuer COLD FOIL U	1.00	2.50
172 Aladdin - Resolute Swordsman C	.08	.20
172 Aladdin - Resolute Swordsman COLD FOIL C	.08	.20
173 Arges - The Cyclops C	.08	.20
173 Arges - The Cyclops COLD FOIL C	.08	.20
174 Ariel - Determined Mermaid C	.08	.20
174 Ariel - Determined Mermaid COLD FOIL C	.20	.50
175 Ariel - Sonic Warrior S	.60	1.50
175 Ariel - Sonic Warrior COLD FOIL S	2.50	6.00
176 Beast - Thick-Skinned C	.08	.20
176 Beast - Thick-Skinned COLD FOIL C	.12	.30
177 Chi-Fu - Imperial Advisor U	.08	.20
177 Chi-Fu - Imperial Advisor COLD FOIL U	.15	.40
178 Chien-Po - Imperial Soldier C	.08	.20
178 Chien-Po - Imperial Soldier COLD FOIL C	.08	.20
179 Donald Duck - Buccaneer COLD FOIL L	3.00	8.00
179 Donald Duck - Buccaneer L	1.50	4.00
180 Hercules - Beloved Hero R	.12	.30
180 Hercules - Beloved Hero COLD FOIL R	.25	.60
181 LeFou - Opportunistic Flunky COLD FOIL R	.50	1.25
181 LeFou - Opportunistic Flunky R	.08	.20
182 Li Shang - Imperial Captain U	.08	.20
182 Li Shang - Imperial Captain COLD FOIL U	.15	.40
183 Ling - Imperial Soldier COLD FOIL U	.12	.30
183 Ling - Imperial Soldier U	.08	.20
184 Luisa Madrigal - Rock of the Family C	.08	.20
184 Luisa Madrigal - Rock of the Family COLD FOIL C	.08	.20
185 Magic Broom - Aerial Cleaner COLD FOIL C	.25	.60
185 Magic Broom - Aerial Cleaner C	.08	.20
186 Magic Broom - Brigade Captain S	.30	.75
186 Magic Broom - Brigade Captain COLD FOIL S	.75	2.00
187 Mickey Mouse - Playful Sorcerer COLD FOIL R	1.50	4.00
187 Mickey Mouse - Playful Sorcerer R	.60	1.50
188 Mickey Mouse - Standard Bearer C	.08	.20
188 Mickey Mouse - Standard Bearer COLD FOIL C	.08	.20
189 Mulan - Armored Fighter COLD FOIL U	.15	.40
189 Mulan - Armored Fighter U	.08	.20
190 Philoctetes - No-Nonsense Instructor R	.50	1.25
190 Philoctetes - No-Nonsense Instructor COLD FOIL R	1.50	4.00
191 Piglet - Sturdy Swordsman COLD FOIL L	4.00	10.00
191 Piglet - Sturdy Swordsman L	1.25	3.00
192 Rajah - Royal Protector R	.08	.20
192 Rajah - Royal Protector COLD FOIL R	.15	.40
193 Raya - Unstoppable Force COLD FOIL S	.50	1.25
193 Raya - Unstoppable Force S	.12	.30
194 Yao - Imperial Soldier C	.08	.20
194 Yao - Imperial Soldier COLD FOIL C	.08	.20
195 Avalanche COLD FOIL U	.25	.60
195 Avalanche U	.08	.20
196 I Find 'em, I Flatten 'em U	.08	.20
196 I Find 'em, I Flatten 'em COLD FOIL U	.25	.60
197 One Last Hope COLD FOIL R	.30	.75
197 One Last Hope R	.08	.20
198 The Mob Song U	.08	.20
198 The Mob Song COLD FOIL U	.15	.40
199 Triton's Decree COLD FOIL C	.12	.30
199 Triton's Decree C	.08	.20
200 Fortisphere C	.08	.20
200 Fortisphere COLD FOIL C	.60	1.50
201 Imperial Bow COLD FOIL U	.20	.50
201 Imperial Bow U	.08	.20
202 RLS Legacy's Cannon R	.08	.20
202 RLS Legacy's Cannon COLD FOIL R	.30	.75
203 The Wall - Border Fortress COLD FOIL R	.30	.75
203 The Wall - Border Fortress R	.08	.20
204 Thebes - The Big Olive C	.08	.20
204 Thebes - The Big Olive COLD FOIL C	.08	.20
205 Cinderella - Melody Weaver ENCHANTED FOIL E	100.00	250.00
206 Minnie Mouse - Musketeer Champion ENCHANTED FOIL E	75.00	200.00
207 Look at this Family ENCHANTED FOIL E	50.00	120.00
208 Ursula - Sea Witch Queen ENCHANTED FOIL E	100.00	250.00
209 Yen Sid - Powerful Sorcerer ENCHANTED FOIL E	75.00	200.00
210 Second Star to the Right ENCHANTED FOIL E	50.00	120.00
211 Diablo - Devoted Herald ENCHANTED FOIL E	150.00	400.00
212 Jasmine - Desert Warrior ENCHANTED FOIL E	60.00	150.00
213 We Don't Talk About Bruno ENCHANTED FOIL E	60.00	150.00
214 Goofy - Super Goof ENCHANTED FOIL E	75.00	200.00
215 Sisu - Empowered Sibling ENCHANTED FOIL E	100.00	250.00
216 Snuggly Duckling - Disreputable Pub ENCHANTED FOIL E	30.00	80.00
217 Anna - True-Hearted ENCHANTED FOIL E	100.00	250.00
218 The Queen - Diviner ENCHANTED FOIL E	60.00	150.00
219 Ariel's Grotto - A Secret Place ENCHANTED FOIL E	30.00	80.00
220 Ariel - Sonic Warrior ENCHANTED FOIL E	200.00	500.00
221 Piglet - Sturdy Swordsman ENCHANTED FOIL E	75.00	200.00
222 The Wall - Border Fortress ENCHANTED FOIL E	30.00	80.00
2024 Disney Lorcana Ursula's Return Illumineers Quest		
223 Yen Sid - Powerful Sorcerer L	10.00	25.00
224 Mulan - Elite Archer L	8.00	20.00
225 Mickey Mouse - Playful Sorcerer R	6.00	15.00
223 Piglet - Pooh Pirate Captain R	4.00	10.00
NNO Ursula - Ruler of Lorcana OVERSIZED	3.00	8.00
2024 Disney Lorcana Challenge Event Promos		
1C1 Dragon Fire P/(Participation Prize)	60.00	150.00
2C1 Let It Go P/(Top 128 Prize)	500.00	1,200.00
3C1 Cinderella - Stouthearted P/(Top 64 Prize)	150.00	400.00
4C1 Rapunzel - Gifted with Healing P/(Top 32 Prize)	125.00	300.00
2020 Dragon Ball Super Draft Box 5 Divine Multiverse		
DB2001 SSB Kaio-Ken Son Goku, Concentrated Destruction SR	30.00	60.00
DB2002 Ultra Instinct Son Goku, Monumental Presence SR	5.00	10.00
DB2003 Tien Shinhan, Unwavering Anchor C	.12	.25
DB2004 Piccolo, Namekian Fortification C	.12	.25
DB2005 Android 17, Rebel Reinforcements R	1.25	2.50
DB2006 Majin Buu, Cheerful Demon C	.12	.25
DB2007 Frieza, Imperial Inspiration SR	1.50	3.00
DB2008 Frieza, Double-Edged Sword C	.12	.25
DB2009 Worthy Warrior Kefla U	.15	.30
DB2010 Anato, Gentle Supremacy R	.20	.40
DB2011 Ganos, Bird of Prey SR	.75	1.50
DB2012 Ganos C	.12	.25
DB2013 Kuru, Proud Supremacy C	.12	.25
DB2014 Caway C	.12	.25
DB2015 Dercori, the Unstoppable Shadow U	.15	.30
DB2016 Feral Strike Shosa U	.15	.30
DB2017 Monna, the Confidence Booster U	.15	.30
DB2018 Burly Brawler Nink C	.12	.25
DB2019 Majora, Unseeing Aid U	.15	.30
DB2020 Mirage Maker Shantza R	1.00	2.00
DB2021 Stealth Silhouette Gamisaras U	.15	.30
DB2022 Damon, Might of Many C	.12	.25
DB2023 Jiren, the All-Seeing R	4.00	8.00
DB2024 Kunshi, Threaded Manipulation R	.20	.40
DB2025 Bear Hug Tupper C	.12	.25
DB2026 Pride Collective Zoiray C	.12	.25
DB2027 Pride Collective Cocotte U	.15	.30
DB2028 Pride Collective Kettol R	.20	.40
DB2029 Flight of the Grand Eagle SR	3.00	6.00
DB2030 Ultrasonic Exchange R	.20	.40
DB2031 Universe 4, Assemble! U	.30	.75
DB2032 Mystic Talismans C	.12	.25
DB2033 Meditation C	.12	.25
DB2034 Master Roshi, Maximum Muscle R	1.25	2.50
DB2035 Master Roshi, Still Got It C	.12	.25
DB2036 Android 17, Turning the Tide R	7.50	15.00
DB2037 Android 18, Neverending Energy R	2.50	5.00
DB2038 Energetic Outburst Kale U	.15	.30
DB2039 Energetic Frenzy Kefla R	7.50	15.00
DB2040 Hit, Deadly Vanguard SR	12.50	25.00
DB2041 Frost, Chaotic Burst U	.15	.30
DB2042 Dr. Rota, Unknown Potential U	.60	1.25
DB2043 Pirina, Namekian Ambush U	.15	.30
DB2044 Saonel, Namekian Ensnarement C	.12	.25
DB2045 Fuwa, Strategic Supremacy U	.15	.30
DB2046 Obuni, Afterimage Slash SR	6.00	12.00
DB2047 Zium, Lucky Air Raid R	.20	.40
DB2048 Lilibeu, Wings of Fortune C	.12	.25
DB2049 Jirasen, Graceful Wager U	.15	.30
DB2050 Murichim, Brave Bruiser U	.50	1.00
DB2051 Lilibeu, Exploitative Flight C	.12	.25
DB2052 Jirasen, Fortuitous Flurry C	.12	.25
DB2053 Murisarm, Manipulative Blow C	.12	.25
DB2054 Mechiorp, Bobbing and Weaving U	1.00	2.00
DB2055 Napapa C	.12	.25
DB2056 Rubalt C	.12	.25
DB2057 Jilcol, High Stakes Guardian C	.12	.25
DB2058 Gowasu, Manipulative Supremacy C	.12	.25
DB2059 Dyspo, Sonic Subversion SR	1.50	3.00
DB2060 Agu, Virtuous Supremacy U	.15	.30
DB2061 Great Priest, Herald of Deliverance SR	3.00	6.00
DB2062 Dirty Burst SR	10.00	20.00
DB2063 Internal Energy Shift R	.60	1.25
DB2064 Universe 10, Assemble! C	.12	.25
DB2065 Son Goku, Spirited Contender U	.15	.30
DB2066 Son Goku, Evening the Odds R	.20	.40
DB2067 Krillin, Destructo Disc Unleashed U	.15	.30
DB2068 Ribrianne, Avatar of Affection SR	7.50	15.00
DB2069 Ribrianne, Punishing Passion SR	4.00	8.00
DB2070 Ribrianne, Boundless Heart U	.15	.30
DB2071 Brianne De Chateau, Dazzling Maiden R	.75	1.50
DB2072 Kakunsa, Beastly Maiden SR	10.00	20.00
DB2073 Kakunsa, Maiden Might C	.12	.25
DB2074 Sanka Ku, Maiden Dominance C	.12	.25
DB2075 Rozie, Maiden Cunning U	.15	.30
DB2076 Rozie, Maiden's Scorn C	.12	.25
DB2077 Su Roas, Maiden Augment C	.12	.25
DB2078 Zirloin, Maiden Supporter SR	6.00	12.00
DB2079 Zirloin, Love's Guardian C	.12	.25
DB2080 Zarbuto, Maiden Avenger C	.12	.25
DB2081 Zarbuto, Heroic Stance C	.12	.25
DB2082 Rabanra, Maiden Devotee R	1.25	2.50
DB2083 Rabanra, Love's Guardian C	.12	.25
DB2084 Jimeze C	.12	.25
DB2085 Vikal C	.12	.25
DB2086 Prum, Reflective Fighter C	.12	.25
DB2087 Hermilla, Pinpoint Accuracy C	.12	.25
DB2088 Pell, Confident Supremacy U	.15	.30
DB2089 Ganos, Aerial Assault U	.15	.30
DB2090 Ogma, Compassionate Supremacy R	1.00	2.00
DB2091 Toppo, Righteous Reprisal U	.15	.30
DB2092 Hasty Dispatch Dyspo R	4.00	8.00
DB2093 Pretty Black Hole SR	2.50	5.00
DB2094 Heart Arrow of Love R	2.00	4.00
DB2095 Universe 2, Assemble! R	.75	1.50
DB2096 Heavy Light Shatter Burst U	.15	.30
DB2097 Big Amour C	.75	1.50
DB2098 Cabba C	.12	.25
DB2099 Cabba, Saiyan Invigoration U	.15	.30
DB2100 Caulifla, Saiyan Invalidation U	.15	.30
DB2101 Caulifla C	.12	.25
DB2102 Kale, Uncontrollable Rage U	.15	.30
DB2103 Kale the Mischievous C	.12	.25
DB2104 Hit, the Revoker R	.60	1.25
DB2105 Raw Power Botamo C	.12	.25
DB2106 Metal Volley Magetta C	.12	.25
DB2107 Ille, Dignified Supremacy R	.20	.40
DB2108 Bergamo, Ferocious Roar SR	10.00	20.00
DB2109 Bergamo, Lupine Predator R	2.50	5.00
DB2110 Gigantic Crusher Bergamo U	.15	.30
DB2111 Basil, Fatal Rampage SR	5.00	10.00
DB2112 Basil, the Impervious C	.12	.25
DB2113 Venomous Fist Lavender SR	3.00	6.00
DB2114 Lavender, Universe 9 Agent C	.12	.25
DB2115 Amphibious Assault Comfrey R	.20	.40
DB2116 Roselle, Wings of Universe 9 U	.15	.30
DB2117 Oregano the Webslinger C	.12	.25
DB2118 Hyssop the Frozen Titan C	.12	.25
DB2119 Chappil the Iron Drake U	2.00	4.00
DB2120 Sorrel, the Cottontailed Warrior C	.12	.25
DB2121 Feline Force Hop U	.15	.30
DB2122 Roh, Brash Supremacy U	.15	.30
DB2123 Jiren, Army of One SR	4.00	8.00
DB2124 Toppo, Justice Forsaken R	.60	1.25
DB2125 Khai, Righteous Supremity C	.12	.25
DB2126 Giant Ball SR	12.50	25.00
DB2127 Universe 9, Assemble! R	1.00	2.00
DB2128 Justice Crush R	.20	.40
DB2129 Ice Lance U	.15	.30
DB2130 Triangle Danger Beam C	.12	.25
DB2131 Son Goku, Strength of Legends SR	7.50	15.00
DB2132 Saiyan Shield Son Gohan R	2.00	4.00
DB2133 Vegeta, Strength of Legends R	2.50	5.00
DB2134 Enraged Eminence Vegeta R	.75	1.50
DB2135 Dynamic Blow Vegeta C	.12	.25
DB2136 Shin, Noble Supremacy R	1.50	3.00
DB2137 Anilaza, the Towering Atrocity SR	1.00	2.00
DB2138 Impregnable Fortress Anilaza C	.12	.25
DB2139 Paparoni, Brilliant Inventor U	.15	.30
DB2140 Secret Technique Paparoni U	.15	.30
DB2141 Koichiarator, Menacing Assassin U	.15	.30
DB2142 Koichiarator, the Ultimate Robot Fusion C	.12	.25
DB2143 Koitsukai, Mechanical Courage SR	30.00	60.00
DB2144 Panchia, Robo Warrior C	.12	.25
DB2145 Bionic Battler Bollarator C	.12	.25
DB2146 Katopesla, Envoy of Justice R	4.00	8.00
DB2147 Katopesla, Righteous Fury U	.60	1.25
DB2148 Katopesla, Sonic Justice U	.60	1.25
DB2149 Katopesla, Universe 3 Policeman C	.12	.25
DB2150 Narirama C	.12	.25
DB2151 Nigrisshi, from the Shadows U	.15	.30
DB2152 The Preecho C	.12	.25
DB2153 Viara, Everlasting Assault R	.20	.40
DB2154 Majikayo, the Shapeshifter U	.15	.30
DB2155 Eyre, Intellectual Supremacy C	.12	.25
DB2156 Jiren, Survival of the Fittest R	5.00	10.00
DB2157 Vuon, the Righteous C	.12	.25
DB2158 Kahseral, the Righteous C	.12	.25
DB2159 Protector of the People SR	.75	1.50
DB2160 Not Even a Scratch R	2.50	5.00
DB2161 Universe 3, Assemble! U	.15	.30
DB2162 Bollarator's Elastic Strike! U	.15	.30
DB2163 The Final Mission C	.12	.25
DB2164 Phantom Fist R	.50	1.00
DB2165 Sleepy Boy Technique U	.50	1.00
DB2166 Arack & Cucatail, Universe 5 Destroyer & Angel DAR	5.00	10.00
DB2167 Liquir & Korun, Universe 8 Destroyer & Angel DAR	12.50	25.00
DB2168 Iwne & Awamo, Universe 1 Destroyer & Angel DAR	4.00	8.00
DB2169 Geene & Martinne, Universe 12 Destroyer & Angel DAR	7.50	15.00
DB2170 Quitela & Conic, Universe 4 Destroyer & Angel DAR	3.00	6.00
DB2171 Sidra & Mohito, Universe 9 Destroyer & Angel DAR	4.00	8.00
DB2172 Mosco & Kampari, Universe 3 Destroyer & Angel DAR	2.50	5.00
DB2173 Rumsshi & Kusu, Universe 10 Destroyer & Angel DAR	7.50	15.00
DB2174 Beerus & Whis, Universe 7 Destroyer & Angel DAR	12.50	25.00
DB2175 Champa & Vados, Universe 6 Destroyer & Angel DAR	4.00	8.00
DB2176 Heles & Sawar, Universe 2 Destroyer & Angel DAR	5.00	10.00
DB2177 Belmod & Marcarita, Universe 11 Destroyer & Angel DAR	3.00	6.00
2020 Dragon Ball Super Draft Box 6 Giant Force		
DB3001 Master Roshi, Potential Unleashed U	.50	1.00
DB3002 Son Goku, Off to Defeat King Piccolo SR	1.00	2.00
DB3003 Son Goku, Nimbus Master SR	12.50	25.00
DB3004 Bulma, a Heartfelt Wish C	.12	.25
DB3005 Yamcha, Eye for an Eye U	.25	.50
DB3006 Tien Shinhan, Eye for an Eye U	.15	.30
DB3007 Master Roshi C	.12	.25
DB3008 Master Shen C	.12	.25
DB3009 Mutaito C	.12	.25
DB3010 Kami, Lord of the Lookout R	.20	.40
DB3011 Pilaf, King Piccolo's Underling C	.12	.25
DB3012 Shu, King Piccolo's Underling C	.12	.25
DB3013 Mai, King Piccolo's Underling U	1.25	2.50
DB3014 King Piccolo, 5 Seconds to Eradication R	.30	.60
DB3015 King Piccolo, the New Ruler SR	40.00	80.00
DB3016 King Piccolo, Yearning for Youth C	.12	.25
DB3017 Tambourine, Demon Clan Warrior C	.12	.25
DB3018 Piano, Demon Clan Warrior C	.12	.25
DB3019 Cymbal, Demon Clan Warrior C	.12	.25
DB3020 Drum, Demon Clan Warrior C	.12	.25
DB3021 Piccolo Jr., the King's Return U	.15	.30
DB3022 Korin Tower's Secret Medicine R	.50	1.00
DB3023 Strength Through Survival C	.12	.25
DB3024 The Final Blow SR	1.50	3.00
DB3025 Tien Shinhan's Mafuba C	.12	.25
DB3026 Saibaimen, Infinite Swarm U	.15	.30
DB3027 Bardock, Great Ape Assault SR	10.00	20.00
DB3028 Bardock, the Final Spark U	.15	.30
DB3029 Bardock C	.12	.25
DB3030 King Vegeta, Great Ape Assault C	.12	.25
DB3031 King Vegeta, the Distrustful SR	.60	1.25
DB3032 Vegeta, Young Elite C	.12	.25
DB3033 Tora, Great Ape Assault R	.20	.40
DB3034 Tora, Bardock's Crewmate C	.12	.25
DB3035 Fasha, Great Ape Assault U	.15	.30
DB3036 Fasha, Bardock's Crewmate C	.12	.25
DB3037 Shugesh, Great Ape Assault U	.15	.30
DB3038 Shugesh, Bardock's Crewmate C	.12	.25
DB3039 Borgos, Great Ape Assault C	.12	.25
DB3040 Borgos, Bardock's Crewmate U	.30	.75
DB3041 Toolo C	.12	.25
DB3042 Nappa, Promising Youth C	.12	.25
DB3043 Nappa C	.12	.25
DB3044 Chilled, Greatest Pirate in the Cosmos SR	6.00	12.00
DB3045 Pirate Guard Tobi C	.12	.25
DB3046 Pirate Guard Cabira C	.12	.25
DB3047 Riot Javelin SR	2.00	4.00
DB3048 Flame Bullet C	.12	.25
DB3049 Intersecting Fates R	1.00	2.00
DB3050 Downfall of Pride R	.20	.40
DB3051 Trunks, the Last Hope U	.20	.40
DB3052 SS3 Son Goku, Fist of Fortitude SR	2.50	5.00
DB3053 Son Goku, Power to Protect R	.20	.40
DB3054 Super Saiyan Son Goku C	.12	.25
DB3055 Son Gohan, Hidden Might SR	12.50	25.00
DB3056 Son Gohan C	.12	.25
DB3057 Son Goten, Reckless Ability U	.15	.30
DB3058 Son Goten, Boundless Curiosity C	.12	.25
DB3059 Vegeta, Protecting His Loved Ones U	.75	1.50
DB3060 Trunks C	.12	.25
DB3061 Trunks, Wielder of the Legendary Blade C	.12	.25
DB3062 Trunks, Legacy of a Hero C	.12	.25
DB3063 SS3 Gotenks, Full Throttle C	.12	.25
DB3064 Gotenks, Reckless Ability C	.12	.25
DB3065 Great Saiyaman 2, Budding Hero SR	15.00	30.00
DB3066 Tapion, Hero of Legend C	.12	.25
DB3067 Tapion, Unsealed Hero C	.12	.25
DB3068 Minotia, Unsealed Hero C	.12	.25
DB3069 Hirudegarn, Phantasmic Evolution SR	6.00	12.00
DB3070 Hirudegarn, Phantasmic Revival R	.20	.40
DB3071 Hirudegarn, the Phantom Limbs U	.30	.60
DB3072 Hoi, Hidden Ambition U	.15	.30
DB3073 The Brave Sword R	.20	.40
DB3074 Sealed Music Box C	.12	.25
DB3075 Wrath of the Dragon C	.12	.25
DB3076 Crushing Despair C	.12	.25
DB3077 Son Gohan & Hire-Dragon, New Pals U	.25	.50
DB3078 Son Goku, Smashing Limits C	.12	.25
DB3079 Son Goku, Relentless Assault U	.15	.30
DB3080 Son Gohan, the Battle Begins U	.15	.30
DB3081 Son Gohan & Hire-Dragon, Peacekeepers C	.12	.25
DB3082 Piccolo, the Brilliant Rogue C	.12	.25
DB3083 Piccolo C	.12	.25
DB3084 Krillin, Going All-Out C	.12	.25
DB3085 Krillin, Protector of the People C	.12	.25
DB3086 Yajirobe C	.12	.25
DB3087 Hire-Dragon, a Fated Meeting C	.12	.25
DB3088 Hire-Dragon, a Kind Friend SR	2.00	4.00
DB3089 Chi-Chi, Melee Matriarch U	.15	.30
DB3090 Bulma, the Power of Science C	.12	.25
DB3091 Lord Slug, Power Overwhelming U	.15	.30
DB3092 Lord Slug, Super Namekian SR	10.00	20.00
DB3093 Lord Slug, Evil Invader R	.20	.40
DB3094 Angila, the Graceful Warrior SR	2.00	4.00

DB3095 Wings, the Gargantuan Warrior C .12 .25
DB3096 Medamatcha, the Miniscule Warrior C .12 .25
DB3097 Zeiun C .12 .25
DB3098 Kakuja, Lord Slug's Scientist C .12 .25
DB3099 To Save the Earth C .12 .25
DB3100 Whistled Melody R .20 .40
DB3101 Tyrannical Blow R .30 .60
DB3102 Super Namekian Might SR 1.50 3.00
DB3103 Towa, Dark Demon Realm Scientist SR 10.00 20.00
DB3104 Son Goku C .12 .25
DB3105 Son Gohan, Changing History U 1.25 2.50
DB3106 Son Goten, Changing History C .12 .25
DB3107 Vegeta C .12 .25
DB3108 Trunks, Changing History U .15 .30
DB3109 Demon God Demigra, True Power Unleashed SR 30.00 75.00
DB3110 Demon God Demigra, Destroyer of History U .15 .30
DB3111 Demigra, Demon Realm Sorcerer U .15 .30
DB3112 Boiling Burg C .12 .25
DB3113 True Power Unleashed C .12 .25
DB3114 Super Dragon Flash C .12 .25
DB3115 Piccolo Jr., Eradicator of Peace SR 25.00 50.00
DB3116 Son Goku, Unwavering Conviction R .30 .60
DB3117 Korin, the Cat Sage U .15 .30
DB3118 Bardock, Legend's Origin SR 2.50 5.00
DB3119 Imparted Wishes Tora R .20 .40
DB3120 Gine, the Loving Saiyan U .20 .40
DB3121 King Piccolo, the Exterminator SR .75 1.50
DB3122 Son Goku, Plan for Victory R .20 .40
DB3123 Yajirobe, a New Ally U .15 .30
DB3124 Hirudegarn, the Reoccurring Nightmare SR 3.00 6.00
DB3125 Tapion, Fate of a Hero R .75 1.50
DB3126 Vegeta, Villain-Turned-Protector U .15 .30
DB3127 Kakarot, Fate's Dawning U .15 .30
DB3128 Final Heat Phalanx R .20 .40
DB3129 Explosive Demon Wave SR 1.00 2.00
DB3130 Lord Slug, Youth Regained SR 1.25 2.50
DB3131 Angila, the Invader R .25 .50
DB3132 Oolong, the Cowardly U .15 .30
DB3133 Piccolo Jr., Giant Force GFR 10.00 20.00
DB3134 Lord Slug, Giant Force GFR 1.50 3.00
DB3135 King Piccolo, Giant Force GFR .75 1.50
DB3136 Raditz, Giant Force GFR 7.50 15.00
DB3137 Bardock, Giant Force GFR 1.50 3.00
DB3138 King Vegeta, Giant Force GFR 1.25 2.50
DB3139 Hirudegarn, Giant Force GFR 2.00 4.00
DB3140 Bio-Broly, Giant Force GFR 2.00 4.00
DB3141 Cell, Giant Force GFR 1.00 2.00
DB3142 Meta-Cooler Core, Giant Force GFR 1.50 3.00
DB3143 Porunga, Giant Force GFR .75 1.50
DB3144 Bergamo, Giant Force GFR 2.00 4.00

2020 Dragon Ball Super Expansion Deck 9 Saiyan Surge

EX0901 Son Goku, Nimbus Voyager ER .25 .50
EX0902 Vegeta, Time for Vacation ER .25 .50
EX0903 Super Saiyan Son Goku // SSG Son Goku, Surge of Divinity ER .30 .75
EX0904 Son Gohan & Videl, Power Couple ER .30 .75
EX0905 Son Goten & Trunks, Back to Back ER .25 .50
EX0906 Almighty Resistance ER .30 .60

2020 Dragon Ball Super Expansion Deck 10 Namekian Surge

EX1001 Heavy Kick Krillin ER .25 .50
EX1002 Master Roshi, Kamehameha Origins ER .75 1.50
EX1003 Piccolo // Son Gohan & Piccolo, Surge of Consciousness ER .25 .50
EX1004 Kaio-Ken Son Goku Returns ER .25 .50
EX1005 Dr. Uiro, Cybernetic Rebirth ER .50 1.00
EX1006 Hidden Potential ER .25 .50

2020 Dragon Ball Super Expansion Deck 11 Universe 7 Unison

EX1101 Vegeta // Vegeta, Candidate of Destruction .20 .40
EX1102 Gotenks, Unison of Rage .60 1.25
EX1103 Whis, Destruction's Conductor .20 .40
EX1104 Beerus, Wrath of the Gods .15 .30
EX1105 Android 17, High Alert .15 .30
EX1106 Frieza, Fair-Weather Fiend 1.50 3.00
EX1107 Omen of Awakening 1.00 2.00

2020 Dragon Ball Super Expansion Deck 12 Universe 11 Unison

EX1201 Toppo // Toppo, Candidate of Destruction .20 .40
EX1202 Vegeta, Unison of Fury 5.00 10.00
EX1203 Belmod, the Self-Indulgent .20 .40
EX1204 Marcarita, Tutor of Power .15 .30
EX1205 Dyspo, the Flashstriker .15 .30
EX1206 Kahseral, the Slashstriker .15 .30
EX1207 Spirit Fist .15 .30

2020 Dragon Ball Super Expansion Deck 13 Special Anniversary Set

EX1301 Frost, for the Clan .15 .30
EX1302 Jiren, Legend of Universe 11 1.25 2.50
EX1303 Son Goku, Resolve Renewed .25 .50
EX1304 Vegeta, Resolve Renewed .30 .75
EX1305 Vegito, Resolve Combined .30 .60
EX1306 Frieza, Irate Emperor .15 .30
EX1307 Planet Vegeta's Final Moments .15 .30
EX1308 Janemba, Wicked Agent of Destruction .30 .75
EX1309 Turles, Chaotic Agent of Destruction .30 .60
EX1310 Janemba, Raging Incarnation of Evil .20 .40
EX1311 Combo Attack Janemba .20 .40
EX1312 Restoration .15 .30
EX1313 Vegeta, Resolute Agent of Destruction .60 1.25
EX1314 Gokule, the Legendary Fusion Warrior .15 .30
EX1315 Son Goten & Trunks, Faultless Youth .30 .60
EX1316 Gotenks, the Grim Reaper of Justice .15 .30
EX1317 Cheelai & Lemo, the Bandits .15 .30
EX1318 Broly, Invincible Agent of Destruction .15 .30
EX1319 Lord Slug, Mighty Agent of Destruction .25 .50
EX1320 Android 13, Exterminating Agent of Destruction .15 .30
EX1321 Allied Reinforcements .15 .30
EX1322 King Vegeta, Royal Pride .15 .30
EX1323 Great Ape Bardock, Might of the Resistance .20 .40
EX1324 Boujack, Galactic Disruptor .15 .30
EX1325 Violent Rush Zangya .15 .30
EX1326 Garlic Jr., Immortal Agent of Destruction .15 .30
EX1327 The Agents of Destruction Strike Back .25 .50
EX1328 Full Moon .15 .30
EX1329 Babidi, Leader of the Agents of Destruction // Majin Buu, Leader of the Agents of Destruction 4.00 8.00
EX1330 Son Goku Jr. & Vegeta Jr., Saiyan Scions .60 1.25
EX1331 Son Goku & Android 8, Bonds of Battle .15 .30
EX1332 Hatchhyack, Vengeful Agent of Destruction .60 1.25
EX1333 Hatchhyack, Mad With Hate .15 .30
EX1334 Max Power Kamehameha 1.25 2.50
EX1335 Violent Rush Boujack 1.00 2.00
EX1336 Super 17, Hell's Ultimate Weapon .20 .40

2020 Dragon Ball Super Expansion Deck 14 Battle Advanced

EX1401 Ultimate Shenron, Dimensional Wishmaster .50 1.00
EX1402 Trunks, Power to Save the Future .25 .50
EX1403 Ginyu Force, the Showstoppers .20 .40
EX1404 Son Goten & Trunks, Super Saiyan Tag Team .20 .40
EX1405 Towa, Rewriting History .60 1.25

2020 Dragon Ball Super Expansion Deck 15 Battle Enhanced

EX1501 Gogeta, Time for Payback .30 .75
EX1502 Vegeta, Protector of the Earth .25 .50
EX1503 Majin Buu, Malice Distilled .25 .50
EX1504 Garlic Jr., Immortal Avenger .25 .50
EX1505 Mira, Dimensional Superpower .25 .50

2020 Dragon Ball Super Rise of the Unison Warrior

BT10001 Yamcha // Yamcha, Supersonic Warrior U .15 .30
BT10002 Pilaf // Pilaf, Shu, and Mai Assemble! C .12 .25
BT10003 Vegito, Unison of Might SPR 4.00 8.00
BT10003 Vegito, Unison of Might SR 1.25 2.50
BT10004 Syn Shenron, Unison of Calamity SPR 2.00 4.00
BT10004 Syn Shenron, Unison of Calamity SR 2.00 4.00
BT10005 Vegeta, Elite Unison U .15 .30
BT10006 Son Goku, Savagery Awakened U .15 .30
BT10007 Son Goku, Bursting with Energy R .20 .40
BT10008 Yamcha, Merciless Barrage SPR 7.50 15.00
BT10008 Yamcha, Merciless Barrage SR 5.00 10.00
BT10009 Yamcha, the Desert Hyena R .20 .40
BT10010 Master Roshi, Martial Virtuoso U .15 .30
BT10011 Bulma the Bunny Girl SR 10.00 20.00
BT10012 Bulma, Out Adventuring U .25 .50
BT10013 Chi-Chi, Ox-King's Daughter C .12 .25
BT10014 Innocent Princess Chi-Chi C .12 .25
BT10015 Oolong, the Many-Faced C .12 .25
BT10016 Oolong, Goku's Pal R .20 .40
BT10017 Puar, Yamcha's Sidekick C .12 .25
BT10018 Ox-King C .12 .25
BT10019 Pilaf, Plotting World Domination C .12 .25
BT10020 Pilaf, Dragon Ball Chaser C .12 .25
BT10021 Shu, Pilaf's Admirer C .12 .25
BT10022 Shu, Dragon Ball Chaser C .12 .25
BT10023 Mai, the Gang's Femme Fatale C .12 .25
BT10024 Mai, Dragon Ball Chaser C .12 .25
BT10025 Pilaf Machine, the Master Bot U .15 .30
BT10026 Pilaf Machine, Ostrich Form R .20 .40
BT10027 Mercenary Tao, Unequaled Assassin U .20 .40
BT10028 Pilaf's Castle C .12 .25
BT10029 Pilaf Missile R .20 .40
BT10030 Wolf Fang Fist SR 10.00 20.00
BT10031 Trunks // SS2 Trunks, Envoy of Justice C .12 .25
BT10032 Fused Zamasu // Fused Zamasu, Divine Ruinbringer U .15 .30
BT10033 SS Gotenks, Absolute Unison SR 1.25 2.50
BT10034 Supreme Kai of Time, Unison of History U .15 .30
BT10035 Zen-Oh, Cosmic Unison SPR 6.00 12.00
BT10035 Zen-Oh, Cosmic Unison SR 3.00 6.00
BT10036 SSB Son Goku, Hope for Victory U .15 .30
BT10037 Son Goku C .12 .25
BT10038 Son Goku, Warrior That Crossed Time C .12 .25
BT10039 Son Gohan, Accelerated Slam C .12 .25
BT10040 SSB Vegeta, Blaze of Passion U .15 .30
BT10041 Vegeta, Savior of the Future C .12 .25
BT10042 Vegeta, Warrior That Crossed Time C .12 .25
BT10043 SS2 Trunks, for a Brighter Future U .15 .30
BT10044 SS Trunks, God-Sealing Technique SPR 15.00 30.00
BT10044 SS Trunks, God-Sealing Technique SR 12.50 25.00
BT10045 SSB Vegito, Paralyzing Prowess R 1.00 2.00
BT10046 Vegito, Infinite Radiance U .15 .30
BT10047 Bulma, Master Scientist C .12 .25
BT10048 Mai, Bulwark of the Future C .12 .25
BT10049 Respectful Master Gowasu C .12 .25
BT10050 Goku Black Rose, Lofty Aspirations R .20 .40
BT10051 Goku Black, Future Decimator R .30 .60
BT10052 Fused Zamasu, the Divine Immortal R .20 .40
BT10053 Fused Zamasu, Advocate for Evil C .12 .25
BT10054 Zamasu, Cosmic Traitor C .12 .25
BT10055 Zen-Oh, Edge of Space U .15 .30
BT10056 Final Hope Slash SR 2.50 5.00
BT10057 God-Slicing Black Kamehameha R .20 .40
BT10058 Tragedy Overground C .12 .25
BT10059 Absolute Confidence C .12 .25
BT10060 Son Goku // Ferocious Strike SS Son Goku U .15 .30
BT10061 Ginyu // Ginyu, New Leader of the Force C .12 .25
BT10062 SS Bardock, Paternal Unison SPR 4.00 8.00
BT10062 SS Bardock, Paternal Unison SR 2.50 5.00
BT10063 Golden Frieza, Unison of Malice SR 1.25 2.50
BT10064 Demigra, Unison of Sorcery U .60 1.25
BT10065 SS Son Goku, Pride of the Saiyans R .20 .40
BT10066 Intensive Training Son Goku R .20 .40
BT10067 Son Gohan, Potential Unlocked U .15 .30
BT10068 Vegeta, the Lone Prince C .12 .25
BT10069 Ultimate Power Piccolo C .12 .25
BT10070 Krillin, Potential Unlocked R .20 .40
BT10071 Bulma, Life on Namek C .12 .25
BT10072 Frieza, Cosmic Horror U .15 .30
BT10073 Frieza, Terrifying Transformation U .15 .30
BT10074 Frieza C .12 .25
BT10075 Frieza, Charismatic Villain SPR 15.00 30.00
BT10075 Frieza, Charismatic Villain SR 12.50 25.00
BT10076 Ginyu, Backbone of the Force C .12 .25
BT10077 Ginyu the Bodysnatcher C .12 .25
BT10078 Recoome the Musclehead U .15 .30
BT10079 Jeice, Second in Command C .12 .25
BT10080 Burter, Fastest in the Universe C .12 .25
BT10081 Guldo, Psycho Psychic C .12 .25
BT10082 Dodoria, Brimming with Power R .20 .40
BT10083 Dodoria the Cold-Blooded C .12 .25
BT10084 Zarbon, Victory Over Beauty C .12 .25
BT10085 Zarbon the Gorgeous U .15 .30
BT10086 Frieza, Dark Infestation R .20 .40
BT10087 Frieza the Power Monger C .12 .25
BT10088 Dormant Potential Unleashed SR 20.00 40.00
BT10089 Blue Impulse C .12 .25
BT10090 Dark Death Ball R .20 .40
BT10091 One-Star Ball, Parasitic Darkness U .15 .30
BT10092 Gotenks // SS Gotenks, Display of Mastery C .12 .25
BT10093 Syn Shenron // Syn Shenron, Negative Energy Overflow U .15 .30
BT10094 SS Broly, Legendary Unison U .15 .30
BT10095 SS Gogeta, Dynamic Unison SPR 4.00 8.00
BT10095 SS Gogeta, Dynamic Unison SR 2.50 5.00
BT10096 Mechikabura, Plotting Revival SR 2.00 4.00
BT10097 Son Goku, Absolute Annihilation R 1.50 3.00
BT10098 Technique Chain Son Goku C .12 .25
BT10099 Son Goku, Adventure into the Unknown U .15 .30
BT10100 Counterblast Son Gohan U .15 .30
BT10101 Son Goten, Flash of Brilliance C .12 .25
BT10102 Son Goten the Eager U .15 .30
BT10103 Pan the Earnest C .12 .25
BT10104 Pan C .12 .25
BT10105 Vegeta, Prideful Transformation SPR 7.50 15.00
BT10105 Vegeta, Prideful Transformation SR 6.00 12.00
BT10106 Vegeta, Earthbound Pride C .12 .25
BT10107 Vegeta the Impregnable C .12 .25
BT10108 Trunks, Flash of Brilliance C .12 .25
BT10109 Trunks the Eager U .15 .30
BT10110 Gotenks, Going All-Out SPR 4.00 8.00
BT10110 Gotenks, Going All-Out SR 1.00 2.00
BT10111 Gotenks, Overwhelming Might U .15 .30
BT10112 Gotenks, the Power of Fusion R .20 .40
BT10113 Bulma, Devoted Supporter R .20 .40
BT10114 Giru, the Dragon Ball Discoverer C .12 .25
BT10115 Syn Shenron, Destruction Incarnate R 1.00 2.00
BT10116 Syn Shenron, Shadow Dragon Leader U .15 .30
BT10117 Haze Shenron, Venomous Mist R .75 1.50
BT10118 Haze Shenron, the Poisonmancer C .12 .25
BT10119 Negative Energy One-Star Ball C .12 .25
BT10120 Negative Energy Two-Star Ball C .12 .25
BT10121 Dark Dragon-Slaying Bullet R .20 .40
BT10122 Burning Kanehameha C .12 .25
BT10123 Released from Evil SR 4.00 8.00
BT10124 Two-Star Ball, Parasitic Darkness C .12 .25
BT10125 Shenron, Unison of Rescue SR 4.00 8.00
BT10126 Majin Buu, Wickedness Incarnate R 1.00 2.00
BT10127 Bardock the Resolute U .50 1.00
BT10128 Son Goku, Power of Legend U .50 1.00
BT10129 Vegeta, Demonstration of Might C .12 .25
BT10130 Trunks, Elite Descendant C .12 .25
BT10131 Vegeks, Burning Impact Unleashed C .12 .25
BT10132 Vegeks, Spacetime Synthesis R 1.00 2.00
BT10133 Demigra, the Sinister Sorcerer C .12 .25
BT10134 Mira, Explosion of Energy C .12 .25
BT10135 Mira, Faithful Servant U .15 .30
BT10136 Towa, Twisted Sister SR 2.00 4.00
BT10137 Towa, Secret Maneuver C .12 .25
BT10138 Gravy, the Dark Sorcerer U .15 .30
BT10139 Putine, the Dark Sorcerer U 1.00 2.00
BT10140 Secret Identity Masked Saiyan R 2.50 5.00
BT10141 Mechikabura, the Broken Seal SR 6.00 12.00
BT10142 Burning Impact R .20 .40
BT10143 Time Bullet U .15 .30
BT10144 Vegeta & Trunks, No Holds Barred R .20 .40
BT10145 Son Goku & Hit, Supreme Alliance R 2.00 4.00
BT10146 Vegeta & Bulma, Joined by Fate R .20 .40
BT10147 Son Gohan & Piccolo, Skills Sharpened R .50 1.00
BT10148 Son Goku, Rival Seeker SR 2.00 4.00
BT10149 Frieza, Colossal Dynamo U .15 .30
BT10150 Cell, the Dark Parasite SR 5.00 10.00
BT10151 Jiren, Alien Power U .15 .30
BT10152 Great Ape Masked Saiyan, Primal Carnage SCR 75.00 150.00
BT10153 SS3 Gotenks, Blazing Fusion SCR 75.00 150.00
BT10154 SS4 Gogeta, Peerless Fusion SCR 150.00 300.00

2020 Dragon Ball Super Starter Deck Clan Collusion

SD1301 Frieza//Last Resort Frieza .25 .50
SD1302 Frieza: Xeno, Darkness Overflowing .50 1.00
SD1302 Frieza: Xeno, Darkness Overflowing (gold stamp) .30 .75
SD1303 Ginyu, Frieza's Greatest Soldier .20 .40
SD1304 Zarbon, Frieza's Right-Hand Man .20 .40
SD1305 Dodoria, Frieza's Devoted Servant .20 .40

2020 Dragon Ball Super Starter Deck Instinct Surpassed

SD1101 Son Goku // Ultra Instinct Son Goku, Hero of Universe 7 6.00 12.00
SD1102 Friendly Rival Frieza 1.00 2.00
SD1103 Ultra Instinct Son Goku, Universal Impulse 1.50 3.00
SD1103 Ultra Instinct Son Goku, Universal Impulse (gold stamped) 4.00 8.00
SD1104 SSB Vegeta, Steadfast Ally 1.50 3.00
SD1105 We're in This Together! 1.00 2.00

2020 Dragon Ball Super Starter Deck Saiyan Wonder

SD1401 Vegeta: Xeno & Trunks Xeno// Vegeks, the Unsung Fusion Hero .50 1.00
SD1402 SS Gotenks, Fusion of Friendship 1.25 2.50
SD1402 SS Gotenks, Fusion of Friendship (gold stamp) .75 1.50
SD1403 Time Agent Vegeta .60 1.25
SD1404 Time Agent Trunks .75 1.50
SD1405 Supreme Kai of Time, Guardian of Spacetime 1.25 2.50

2020 Dragon Ball Super Starter Deck Spirit of Potara

SD1201 Vegito//SSB Vegito, Godhood Transcended 1.00 2.00
SD1202 Gogeta, Pursuit of Power 2.50 5.00
SD1202 Gogeta, Pursuit of Power (gold stamp) 1.50 3.00
SD1203 SSB Son Goku, Tenacious Warrior .30 .60
SD1204 SSB Vegeta, Heroic Warrior .30 .60
SD1205 SS Trunks, Architect of Peace .30 .60

2020 Dragon Ball Super Universal Onslaught

BT9001 Frieza // Frieza, the Planet Wrecker C .12 .25
BT9002 Cooler // Cooler, Revenge Transformed U .15 .30
BT9003 Frieza, No Introductions C .12 .25
BT9004 Clan Commander Frieza R .20 .40
BT9005 Frieza, Death's Embrace SR 7.50 15.00
BT9006 King Cold, Imminent Invasion U .15 .30
BT9007 Meta-Cooler, Metallic Genesis C .12 .25
BT9008 Meta-Cooler, Titanic Glare U .15 .30
BT9009 Chilled, Pirate's Bounty U .15 .30
BT9010 Son Gohan, Swift Reinforcement C .12 .25
BT9011 SS Vegeta, Blast Barrage C .12 .25
BT9012 Tien Shinhan, Spirit Vanisher C .12 .25
BT9013 Android 17, Spirit Vanisher C .12 .25
BT9014 Full-Power Frost C .12 .25
BT9015 Chaos Beam Frost C .12 .25
BT9016 Frost, Before the Storm C .12 .25
BT9017 Cease to Exist R .20 .40
BT9018 We Are Universe 7 U .15 .30
BT9019 Thought I Was Finished? C .12 .25
BT9020 You're Mine! C .12 .25
BT9021 Android 17 // Android 17, Universal Guardian C .12 .25
BT9022 Frieza, Unending Onslaught U .15 .30
BT9023 Combo Attack Cooler R .20 .40
BT9024 King Cold, Astral Tyrant C .12 .25
BT9025 Chilled, Intergalactic Marauder U .15 .30
BT9026 Ultra Instinct Son Goku, Battle Mastery C .12 .25
BT9027 Frieza, Undying Emperor U .15 .30
BT9028 Krillin, Battle Mastery C .12 .25
BT9029 Piccolo, Namekian C .12 .25
BT9030 Master Roshi C .12 .25
BT9031 Android 18, Steadfast Technique C .12 .25
BT9032 Majin Buu, Innocent Trickster U .15 .30
BT9033 Whis, Tournament Spectator C .12 .25
BT9034 Kale, Universe 6 Protector C .12 .25
BT9035 Chaos Beam Volley C .12 .25
BT9036 Barrier of Hope R .20 .40
BT9037 Tournament of Power Arena U .50 1.00
BT9038 Android 20 // Androids 20, 17, & 18, Bionic Renaissance C .12 .25
BT9039 Cell, Android Absorber U .15 .30
BT9040 Cell Jr., Minions Unleashed C .12 .25
BT9041 Android 19, Energy Fiend C .12 .25
BT9042 Android 18, Covert Combatant C .12 .25

BT9043 Android 16, Prototype Power U .15 .30
BT9044 Android 13, Red Ribbon Raider C .12 .25
BT9045 Quick Sweep Android 17 C .12 .25
BT9046 Toppo, Gaze of Justice U .15 .30
BT9047 Cocotte, Technique Unleashed C .12 .25
BT9048 Zoiray, Justice Spin C .12 .25
BT9049 Avian Assault Ganos C .12 .25
BT9050 Belmod, Double Devastation U 1.00 2.00
BT9051 Artificial Impact R .30 .60
BT9052 Flash Bomber U .15 .30
BT9053 Jiren // Full-Power Jiren, the Unstoppable C .12 .25
BT9054 Android 20, Mastermind Architect R .20 .40
BT9055 Android 18, Under Your Skin C .12 .25
BT9056 Android 17, Titan Toppler C .12 .25
BT9057 Android 14, Stoic Fist C .12 .25
BT9058 Android 15, Vicious Vendetta R .20 .40
BT9059 Hell Fighter 17, the Neutralizer U .15 .30
BT9060 Jiren, Righteous Leader U .15 .30
BT9061 Binary Blade Kahseral U .15 .30
BT9062 Caulifla, the Time Has Come C .12 .25
BT9063 Kunshi, Threaded Energy C .12 .25
BT9064 Vuon, Dynamite Blaster C .12 .25
BT9065 Trio De Dangers, Mark of the Wolves C .12 .25
BT9066 Marcarita, Adorable Assailant U .15 .30
BT9067 Justice Blast R .20 .40
BT9068 Light Bullet C .12 .25
BT9069 Mind Expansion U .15 .30
BT9070 Bibidi // Majin Buu, One with Nothingness C .12 .25
BT9071 Dabura, Darkness Perfected R .50 1.00
BT9072 Yakon, Light Devourer C .12 .25
BT9073 Pui Pui, Devious Disruptor U .15 .30
BT9074 Spopovich & Yamu C .12 .25
BT9075 Babidi, Unrepentant Sorcerer U .15 .30
BT9076 Bibidi, Primeval Conjurer C .20 .40
BT9077 Majin Buu, Supreme Evil SR 1.50 3.00
BT9078 Majin Buu, Unparalleled Absorption C .12 .25
BT9079 Majin Buu, Hybrid Absorption C .12 .25
BT9080 Majin Buu, Steadfast Absorption U .15 .30
BT9081 Majin Buu, Supreme Absorption C .12 .25
BT9082 Majin Buu, Ghastly Rampage SR 2.00 4.00
BT9083 Demonic Scream Majin Buu C .12 .25
BT9084 Majin Buu, Virtuous Demon C .12 .25
BT9085 Capricious Onslaught U .15 .30
BT9086 Demonic Absorption R .20 .40
BT9087 Petrification U .60 1.25
BT9088 Divine Favor C .12 .25
BT9089 Unexpected Recovery C .12 .25
BT9090 Nappa, Demolition Man C .75 1.50
BT9090 Nappa, Demolition Man SPR 20.00 40.00
BT9091 Zamasu, Sacred Disbelief C 1.00 2.00
BT9091 Zamasu, Sacred Disbelief SPR 25.00 50.00
BT9092 Celestial Union Kefla R .20 .40
BT9093 Hit, in Cold Blood SR .75 1.50
BT9094 SS4 Son Goku, Saiyan Lineage R .20 .40
BT9095 Super Baby 2, Malignant Force U .15 .30
BT9096 Whis, Celestial Moderator C .12 .25
BT9096 Whis, Celestial Moderator SPR 7.50 15.00
BT9097 SS Son Goku, Another Chance R .20 .40
BT9098 Android 16, Imperfect Assassin U .15 .30
BT9099 Android 18, Bionic Blitz C .12 .25
BT9099 Android 18, Bionic Blitz SPR 15.00 30.00
BT9100 Son Goku // Ultra Instinct Son Goku, Limits Surpassed U .15 .30
BT9101 Full-Power Frieza, 100-Percent Overdrive SPR 12.50 25.00
BT9101 Full-Power Frieza, 100-Percent Overdrive SR 4.00 8.00
BT9102 Mech Frieza, Energy Blight R .75 1.50
BT9103 Cooler, Tyrannical Assault SR 7.50 15.00
BT9103 Cooler, Tyrannical Assault SPR 20.00 40.00
BT9104 Ultra Instinct Son Goku, Energy Explosion SR 5.00 10.00
BT9105 SSB Vegeta, Inspired Technique SR 6.00 12.00
BT9106 Golden Frieza, Sovereign Technique R .20 .40
BT9107 Beerus, Divine Obliterator C .12 .25
BT9107 Beerus, Divine Obliterator SPR 25.00 50.00
BT9108 Tyranny's Cost C .12 .25
BT9109 Emperor's Death Beam R .30 .75
BT9110 Royal Condemnation SPR 15.00 30.00
BT9110 Royal Condemnation SR 4.00 8.00
BT9111 Catastrophic Blow SR 3.00 6.00
BT9112 Cell // Cell, Perfection Surpassed U .15 .30
BT9113 Cell, Unthinkable Perfection SR 2.00 4.00
BT9113 Cell, Unthinkable Perfection SPR 7.50 15.00
BT9114 Cell, Devourer of the Masses U .15 .30
BT9115 Dr. Gero, Progenitor of Terror C .25 .50
BT9115 Dr. Gero, Progenitor of Terror SPR 12.50 25.00
BT9116 Android 13, Adamantine Avenger SR 2.00 4.00
BT9117 Super 17, Hell's Storm Unleashed SR 3.00 6.00
BT9118 Super 17, Total Exclipse C .12 .25
BT9119 Jiren, Strength in Silence SR 2.50 5.00
BT9120 Toppo, Mortality Surpassed SR 2.50 5.00
BT9121 Dyspo, Unprecedented Speed SR 1.25 2.50
BT9122 Ribrianne, Massive Love R .20 .40
BT9123 Anilaza, the Soaring Colossus R .75 1.50
BT9124 Cell Games Arena C .12 .25
BT9125 Hit // Assassin Hit Returns RLR 2.00 4.00
BT9126 Beerus // Beerus, God of Destruction Returns RLR 2.00 4.00
BT9127 Son Goku // Heightened Evolution SS3
Son Goku Returns RLR 6.00 12.00
BT9128 Son Gohan // Father-Son Kamehameha
Goku & Gohan Return RLR 5.00 10.00
BT9129 Meta-Cooler // Nucleus of Evil Meta-Cooler
Core Returns RLR 1.00 2.00
BT9130 Frieza's Death Ball IAR 5.00 10.00
BT9131 Ultra Instinct Goku's Kamehameha IAR 12.50 25.00
BT9132 Cell's Earth-Destroying Kamehameha IAR 6.00 12.00
BT9133 Vegeta's Final Flash IAR 7.50 15.00
BT9134 Majin Buu's Human Extinction Attack IAR 5.00 10.00
BT9135 Black Smoke Dragon, Eternal Evil SCR 75.00 150.00
BT9136 Son Goku & Vegeta Apex of Power SCR 750.00 1,500.00
BT9137 Cell Xeno, Unspeakable Abomination SCR 250.00 500.00

2020 Dragon Ball Super Vermilion Bloodline

BT11001 Gogeta // SSB Gogeta, Prophet of Demise C .12 .25
BT11002 Broly // Broly, the Awakened Demon U .15 .30
BT11003 Gotenks, Earth-Shattering Might SPR 2.50 5.00
BT11003 Gotenks, Earth-Shattering Might SR 1.25 2.50
BT11004 Kale, Savage Berserker R .20 .40
BT11005 Raditz, Saiyan Youth R 5.00 10.00
BT11006 SSB Son Goku, Technique Unchained U .15 .30
BT11007 Son Goku C .12 .25
BT11008 Son Goku, Saiyan Youth U .15 .30
BT11009 SSB Vegeta, Technique Unchained U .15 .30
BT11010 Vegeta C .12 .25
BT11011 Vegeta, Saiyan Youth C .12 .25
BT11012 SSB Gogeta, Technique Unchained SPR 20.00 40.00
BT11012 SSB Gogeta, Technique Unchained SR 6.00 12.00
BT11013 Gogeta, Fusion of the Gods R .20 .40
BT11014 SS Broly, Unlimited Power SR 5.00 10.00
BT11015 SS Broly, Combat Evolution R .75 1.50
BT11016 Broly, Power of the Great Ape R .50 1.00
BT11017 Broly, Bonafide Saiyan U .15 .30
BT11018 Broly, Saiyan Youth U .15 .30
BT11019 Ba, Broly's First Friend C .12 .25
BT11020 Goliamite, Beast of the Planet Vampa C .12 .25
BT11021 Paragus, Oath of Vengeance C .12 .25
BT11022 Paragus, New Ambitions C .12 .25
BT11023 Cheelai, Trusted Friend C .12 .25
BT11024 Lemo, Trusted Friend C .12 .25
BT11025 Bardock, Strategic Mind SR 2.50 5.00
BT11026 Nappa, Elite Warrior C .12 .25
BT11027 Seven-Star Ball, Parasitic Darkness C .12 .25
BT11028 Planet Vampa R .20 .40
BT11029 Birth of a Super Warrior U .15 .30
BT11030 Violent Rays SR 20.00 40.00
BT11031 Baby // Baby, Spirit of the Tuffles C .12 .25
BT11032 Vegeta // SS4 Vegeta, Ultimate Evolution U .15 .30
BT11033 Baby, the Unknown Parasite SR 10.00 20.00
BT11034 SS4 Son Goku, Protector of the Earth SPR 7.50 15.00
BT11034 SS4 Son Goku, Protector of the Earth SR 2.00 4.00
BT11035 Son Gohan, Baby's Minion R 1.25 2.50
BT11036 Son Goten, Baby's Minion U .15 .30
BT11037 Bulma, Baby's Minion U .15 .30
BT11038 Bulla, Baby's Minion R .20 .40
BT11039 Uub C .12 .25
BT11040 Uub, Power of Hope U .15 .30
BT11041 Mr. Buu C .12 .25
BT11042 Baby, Golden Avenger SR 10.00 20.00
BT11043 Baby, the Saiyan Slayer R .20 .40
BT11044 Baby, Artificial Lifeform C .12 .25
BT11045 Baby, Diabolic Parasite C .12 .25
BT11046 Baby, the Body Snatcher C .12 .25
BT11047 Baby, Successor of the Tuffle King C .12 .25
BT11048 Dr. Myuu, Creator of the Machine Mutants C .12 .25
BT11049 SS4 Son Goku, Energy Annihilator R .20 .40
BT11050 SS3 Son Goku, Overflowing Spirit SR .75 1.50
BT11051 Son Goku, Shadow Dragon Suppressor C .60 1.25
BT11052 SS4 Vegeta, Rise of the Super Warrior SPR 6.00 12.00
BT11052 SS4 Vegeta, Rise of the Super Warrior SR 2.50 5.00
BT11053 Vegeta, Ready to Rumble R 1.00 2.00
BT11054 Vegeta, Disciplined Warrior R 4.00 8.00
BT11055 Bulma, Wife of the Prince U .15 .30
BT11056 Gotenks, Return of the Reaper of Justice U .15 .30
BT11057 Super Blutz Wave Generator C .12 .25
BT11058 Planet Tuffle C .12 .25
BT11059 Golden Revenge U .15 .30
BT11060 Final Shine Attack C .12 .25
BT11061 Gotenks // Gotenks, Extravagant Assault C .12 .25
BT11062 Vegeta & Babidi // Babidi & Prince of Destruction
Vegeta, Mightiest Majin U .15 .30
BT11063 SS3 Vegito, Peerless Warrior R .75 1.50
BT11064 Dark Broly, Overwhelming Evil SPR 5.00 10.00
BT11064 Dark Broly, Overwhelming Evil SR 3.00 6.00
BT11065 Great Saiyaman, Vanquisher of Villainy R .20 .40
BT11066 Prince of Destruction Vegeta, Prideful Warrior SPR 12.50 25.00
BT11066 Prince of Destruction Vegeta, Prideful Warrior SR 1.25 2.50
BT11067 Prince of Destruction Vegeta, Life and Death U .15 .30
BT11068 Mighty Strike Prince of Destruction Vegeta R .20 .40
BT11069 Videl, a Hero's Daughter U .15 .30
BT11070 Majin Buu, Ghastly Energy C .12 .25
BT11071 Babidi, Evil Mindsnatcher U .15 .30
BT11072 Bibidi, Creator of Majin Buu C .12 .25
BT11073 Dabura, King of the Demon Realm C .12 .25
BT11074 SS3 Son Goku, to New Extremes U .15 .30
BT11075 Super Saiyan Son Goku C .12 .25
BT11076 Son Gohan (Green) C .12 .25
BT11077 Son Gohan, Here to Help C .12 .25
BT11078 Son Goten, Bonds of Friendship C .12 .25
BT11079 Trunks, Bonds of Friendship C .12 .25
BT11080 SS Gotenks, Friendship Fusion U .15 .30
BT11081 SS3 Gotenks, All-Out Assault SR 2.00 4.00
BT11082 Majin Buu, Looking for a Fight C .12 .25
BT11083 Majin Buu, Royal Absorption SR 4.00 8.00
BT11084 Majin Buu, Dark Parasite R .20 .40
BT11085 Demon God Dabura, Dark Dominion U .15 .30
BT11086 Dabura, Dark Gambit R .20 .40
BT11087 Three-Star Ball, Parasitic Darkness C .12 .25
BT11088 The Majin Quickening C .12 .25
BT11089 Final Explosion R .20 .40
BT11090 Buu Buu Volleyball U .15 .30
BT11091 Son Gohan // Son Gohan & Hire-Dragon,
Boundless Friendship U .15 .30
BT11092 Garlic Jr. // Garlic Jr., the Immortal Demon C .12 .25
BT11093 Son Goku, Forever in Our Memories R .20 .40
BT11094 Baby, Resolute Avenger SPR 2.00 4.00
BT11094 Baby, Resolute Avenger SR 1.00 2.00
BT11095 Son Gohan & Hire-Dragon, Flying High U .15 .30
BT11096 Son Gohan (Yellow) C .12 .25
BT11097 Krillin, Moments Before Comeback R 3.00 6.00
BT11098 Piccolo, a Bad Omen C .12 .25
BT11099 Piccolo, Demonic Transformation SR .60 1.25
BT11100 Yamcha, Demonic Transformation C .12 .25
BT11101 Master Roshi, Demonic Transformation C .12 .25
BT11102 Bulma, Demonic Transformation C .12 .25
BT11103 Hire-Dragon C .12 .25
BT11104 Garlic Jr., Overlord of the Dead Zone SPR 2.00 4.00
BT11104 Garlic Jr., Overlord of the Dead Zone SR .60 1.25
BT11105 Garlic Jr., Commander of the Demon Clan U .15 .30
BT11106 Gassyu of the Demonic Elite Four C .12 .25
BT11107 Vinegar of the Demonic Elite Four U .15 .30
BT11108 Tardo of the Demonic Elite Four C .12 .25
BT11109 Zoldo of the Demonic Elite Four C .12 .25
BT11110 Exceptional Ability Pan U .15 .30
BT11111 Eis Shenron, the Diabolic R .20 .40
BT11112 Eis Shenron, the Cryomancer SR 4.00 8.00
BT11113 Super Naturon Shenron, Pan Absorbed R .20 .40
BT11114 Naturon Shenron, the Terramancer U .15 .30
BT11115 Three-Star Ball, Negative Energy Overflow U .15 .30
BT11116 Seven-Star Ball, Negative Energy Overflow U .15 .30
BT11117 Super Water of the Gods C .12 .25
BT11118 Energy Field C .12 .25
BT11119 Makyo Star R .20 .40
BT11120 Super Ice Ray R .20 .40
BT11121 Son Goku // SS4 Son Goku, Guardian of History C .12 .25
BT11122 Dark Broly & Paragus // Dark Broly & Paragus,
the Corrupted U .15 .30
BT11123 SS4 Son Gohan, Beyond the Ultimate SPR 3.00 6.00
BT11123 SS4 Son Gohan, Beyond the Ultimate SR 2.50 5.00
BT11124 SS4 Vegeta, Supreme Saiyan Power SR 2.00 4.00
BT11125 SS Broly, the Rampaging Monstrosity R .20 .40
BT11126 SS4 Son Goku, Conqueror of Evil SR 2.00 4.00
BT11127 SS3 Son Goku, Man on a Mission R 2.50 5.00
BT11128 SS Son Goku, Time Patrol Elite C .12 .25
BT11129 SS3 Vegeta, Unstoppable Evolution R .20 .40
BT11130 SS Vegeta, the Prince Strikes Back R .30 .75
BT11131 SS4 Bardock, Combat Instincts SPR 3.00 6.00
BT11131 SS4 Bardock, Combat Instincts SR 1.00 2.00
BT11132 SS Bardock, the Tenacious R .75 1.50
BT11133 Dark Broly, Demon Realm Ravager R .20 .40
BT11134 Dark Broly, Uncontrollable Berserker SR 7.50 15.00
BT11135 Dark Broly, the New Masked Saiyan U .15 .30
BT11136 Paragus, Towa's Subordinate U .15 .30
BT11137 Ultimate Transformation Mira C .12 .25
BT11138 Mira, Arcane Overflow C .12 .25
BT11139 Towa, Union of Magic and Science U .15 .30
BT11140 Towa, Dark Aura Deluge U .15 .30
BT11141 Putine C .12 .25
BT11142 Gravy C .12 .25
BT11143 Shun Shun, Haru Haru's Sister C .12 .25
BT11144 Haru Haru, Shun Shun's Sister C .12 .25
BT11145 Psi Devilman, Exploding With Evil C .12 .25
BT11146 Great Devilman, Demonic Trickster C .12 .25
BT11147 Broly, Savage Push U .30 .60
BT11148 Rebellion Hammer U .15 .30
BT11149 Dark Power Absorption C .12 .25
BT11150 Darkness Blast Stinger C .12 .25
BT11151 Instant Transmission 10x Kamehameha U .15 .30
BT11152 SS4 Broly, the Great Destroyer SCR 200.00 400.00
BT11153 Baby Hatchhyack, Saiyan Destroyer SCR 200.00 400.00
BT11154 Vegito, Warrior From Another Dimension SCR 100.00 200.00

2021 Dragon Ball Super Battle Evolution Booster

P062 Scrambling Assault Son Goten P .30 .75
EB101 Nappa // Nappa & Saibaimen, the First Invaders C .12 .25
EB102 Yamcha, Wolf Fang Pitching Fistball U .15 .30
EB103 Launch, Inspiring Support C .12 .25
EB104 Vegeta, the Executioner C .12 .25
EB105 Nappa, Testing the Opposition R .20 .40
EB106 Saibaiman, Infinite Assault C .30 .75
EB107 Vegeta, Royal Evolution SR 2.50 5.00
EB108 Golden Frieza, the Perished C .12 .25
EB109 Vegeta the 3rd, Lineage's Beginning R .20 .40
EB110 Unexpected Casualties C .12 .25
EB111 Testing the Opposition C .12 .25
EB112 Android 16 // Android 16, Bottomless Inferno C .12 .25
EB113 Super Android 13, Neverending Bloodlust U .15 .30
EB114 Tora, Keeper of the Red Armband C .20 .40
EB115 Majin Buu, Revitalizing Absorption SR 1.50 3.00
EB116 Majin Buu, Tide-Turning Absorption U .15 .30
EB117 Borgamo, Unstoppable Colossus R .20 .40
EB118 Gine, Heroic Support SR 1.00 2.00
EB119 Android 17, Restrained Support C .12 .25
EB120 Android 18, Let the Battle Begin U .50 1.00
EB121 Android 16, For His Mother C .12 .25
EB122 Chilled's Army Reinforcements C .30 .60
EB123 Assault of the Great Apes C .12 .25
EB124 Tien Shinhan // Tien Shinhan, Mysterious Technique C .12 .25
EB125 Launch, the Wild One U .15 .30
EB126 Son Goku, the Long-Awaited Rematch R .30 .75
EB127 Tien Shinhan, the Long-Awaited Rematch R .50 1.00
EB128 Chiaotzu, Unwanted Reunion C .12 .25
EB129 Mercenary Tao, Overflowing Confidence C .12 .25
EB130 Broly, the Swift Berserker U .30 .60
EB131 Broly, the Tamed Beast C .12 .25
EB132 Ribrianne, the Power of Support U .15 .30
EB133 Ribrianne, Pretty Cannon Unleashed U .15 .30
EB134 Kakunsa, Feral Fury SR 1.50 3.00
EB135 Rozie, Blast Manipulator SR 7.50 15.00
EB136 Goku's Solar Flare C .12 .25
EB137 Homicidal Clones C .12 .25
EB138 Android 13, Android 14, & Android 15 // Android 13,
the Unstoppable C .12 .25
EB139 Super 17, Energy Absorber U .15 .30
EB140 Android 14, the Mission Begins C .12 .25
EB141 Android 15, the Mission Begins C .12 .25
EB142 Mecha Frieza, Full Assault C .12 .25
EB143 SS3 Son Goku, Even Further Beyond SR 6.00 12.00
EB144 Kaio-Ken Son Goku, a Heavy Toll U .15 .30
EB145 Pan, the Courageous Youth SR 2.50 5.00
EB146 Death Blaster R .20 .40
EB147 Your Worst Nightmare U .15 .30
EB148 Frieza Army Reinforcements C .12 .25
EB149 Bulma // Bulma, Life of a Heroine C .12 .25
EB150 Bulma, Inspiring Support C .12 .25
EB151 Son Goku, the Path to Power SR 4.00 8.00
EB152 Android 8, Helping a Friend C .12 .25
EB153 Katopesla, Modular Mastery C .12 .25
EB154 Towa, the Next Move C .12 .25
EB155 Playtime's Over! R .50 1.00
EB156 King Vegeta, the Insubordinate R .20 .40
EB157 Vegeta, Unyielding Pride U .15 .30
EB158 Nappa, Break Cannon Unleashed R .20 .40
EB159 SS Bardock, Neverending Vengeance U .15 .30
EB160 Trio De Dangers, Fierce Trinity SR 2.00 4.00
EB161 Sorrel & Hop, Fiends of Universe 9 C .12 .25
EB162 Android 17 & Android 18, Siblings Revived SR 1.50 3.00
EB163 Android 16, Steadfast Ally R .20 .40
EB164 Android 16, Steadfast Comeback SR 2.00 4.00
EB165 Super Android 13, Cores of the Trio R .30 .75
EB166 Android 13, the Mission Begins SR 4.00 8.00
EB167 Android 14 & Android 15, Target Acquired R .20 .40
EB168 Heroines' Lineage SCR 60.00 120.00
SD604 Ultimate Fusion Gogeta SCR .25 .50
SD804 Defending Father Paragus SCR .75 1.50
SD805 Cheelai, Frieza Force Soldier SCR .25 .50
XD208 Android 21, A Bad Omen SCR .30 .75
BT1014 Saiyan Cabba C .12 .25
BT1025 Vados's Assistance C .20 .40
BT1027 Cabba's Awakening C .12 .25
BT1053 Senzu Bean C .75 1.50
BT1076 Broly, Dawn of the Rampage C .12 .25
BT1089 Avenging Frieza C .12 .25
BT1090 Mecha-Frieza, The Returning Terror U .15 .30
BT1101 Zarbon, The Emperor's Attendant C .12 .25
BT1109 Frieza's Call C .12 .25
BT3062 Trunks, Bridge to the Future C .12 .25
BT3070 Dawn of Terror, Android 13 U .15 .30
BT3104 Flying Nimbus C .30 .60
BT3120 Haru Haru, Attacker Majin C .12 .25
BT4012 Intensifying Power Trunks U .15 .30
BT4048 Newfound Power Son Gohan U .15 .30
BT4091 Adoptive Father Son Gohan C .12 .25
BT6089 Fearless Assault Krillin C .12 .25
BT6114 Bonds of Friendship Android 8 C .12 .25
BT6119 Eighter Aid C .12 .25
BT7068 Saibaimen, Endless Explosions C .12 .25
BT7103 Trunks, Time Regulator C .12 .25
BT9057 Android 14, Stoic Fist C .12 .25
BT9065 Trio De Dangers, Mark of the Wolves C .12 .25
DB1002 SS Vegeta, Exploiting Weakness SR 3.00 6.00
DB1027 Master Roshi, Universe 7 United U .15 .30
DB1040 Desperate Measures C .12 .25
DB1056 SS Rose Goku Black, a Delicate Plan R .20 .40
DB1065 Pan, Natural Fighter U .15 .30
DB1086 Remote Serious Bomb U .15 .30
DB1100 Bardock, Father and Son DPR .50 1.00
DB2003 Tien Shinhan, Unwavering Anchor C .12 .25
DB2004 Piccolo, Namekian Fortification C .12 .25
DB2005 Android 17, Rebel Reinforcements R .20 .40
DB2031 Universe 4, Assemble! U .15 .30
DB2042 Dr. Rota, Unknown Potential U .15 .30
DB2046 Obuni, Afterimage Slash SR 3.00 6.00
DB2054 Mechiorp, Bobbing and Weaving U .15 .30
DB2069 Ribrianne, Punishing Passion SR 5.00 10.00
DB2073 Kakunsa, Maiden Might C .60 1.25

DB2081 Zarbuto, Heroic Stance C .12 .25
DB2111 Basil, Fatal Rampage SR 2.00 4.00
DB2122 Roh, Brash Supremacy U .15 .30
DB2127 Universe 9, Assemble! R .20 .40
DB2147 Katopesla, Righteous Fury U .15 .30
DB2148 Katopesla, Sonic Justice U .15 .30
DB2149 Katopesla, Universe 3 Policeman C .25 .50
TB1034 Universe 9 Supreme Kai Roh C .12 .25
TB1042 Universe 9 Striker Oregano C .12 .25
TB1049 Shining Blaster C .12 .25
TB1072 Maiden Charge C .12 .25
TB2012 Hidden Power, East Supreme Kai U .15 .30
TB3033 Dream the Future C .12 .25

2021 Dragon Ball Super Cross Spirits

BT14001 Son Gohan // Son Gohan, the Power of Duty C .12 .25
BT14002 Jiren // Jiren, Blind Destruction U .15 .30
BT14003 Frieza, Unlikely Savior U .15 .30
BT14004 Toppo, Force of Obliteration SR 1.00 2.00
BT14004 Toppo, Force of Obliteration SPR 4.00 8.00
BT14005 Son Goku, Divine Presence SR 10.00 20.00
BT14006 Super Saiyan Son Goku C .12 .25
BT14007 Son Gohan, Ultimate Essence SR 2.50 5.00
BT14007 Son Gohan, Ultimate Essence SPR 6.00 12.00
BT14008 Piccolo C .12 .25
BT14009 Krillin, Universe 7 Challenger C .12 .25
BT14010 Tien Shinhan, Universe 7 Challenger C .12 .25
BT14011 Master Roshi, Universe 7 Challenger C .12 .25
BT14012 Android 17, Universe 7 Challenger U .15 .30
BT14013 Android 18, Universe 7 Challenger R .60 1.25
BT14014 Jiren, Zenith of Power SR 7.50 15.00
BT14015 Jiren, Surge of Strength R .50 1.00
BT14016 Jiren, Devastating Might R .30 .60
BT14017 Jiren, Thirst for Power U .15 .30
BT14018 Jiren, the Avenger U .15 .30
BT14019 Dyspo, Thwarting the Enemy R .25 .50
BT14020 Vuon, Warrior of Universe 11 C .12 .25
BT14021 Kunshi, Warrior of Universe 11 C .12 .25
BT14022 Tupper, Warrior of Universe 11 U .15 .30
BT14023 Zoiray, Warrior of Universe 11 C .12 .25
BT14024 Cocotte, Warrior of Universe 11 R .60 1.25
BT14025 Kettol, Warrior of Universe 11 R .75 1.50
BT14026 Kahseral, Warrior of Universe 11 C .12 .25
BT14027 Teamwork of Universe 7 U .15 .30
BT14028 Exchange of Power C .12 .25
BT14029 Difference of Status SR 4.00 8.00
BT14030 Source of Power C .12 .25
BT14031 Trunks // Trunks, the Hero's Successor U .15 .30
BT14032 Hirudegarn // Hirudegarn, the Calamity Revived C .12 .25
BT14033 Tapion, the Hero Revived SR .75 1.50
BT14033 Tapion, the Hero Revived SPR 2.50 5.00
BT14034 Hoi, Bringer of Calamity U .15 .30
BT14035 SS3 Son Goku, Calamity Conqueror R .50 1.00
BT14036 Super Saiyan Son Goku C .12 .25
BT14037 Son Goku, Calamity Challenger SR 3.00 6.00
BT14038 Son Gohan, Calamity Challenger C .12 .25
BT14039 Great Saiyaman, Combo of Justice U .15 .30
BT14040 Great Saiyaman, Call of a Hero C .12 .25
BT14041 SS Son Goten, Fully-Powered Fusion C .75 1.50
BT14042 Son Goten, Calamity Challenger C .12 .25
BT14043 SS Vegeta, Thwarting the Enemy R .50 1.00
BT14044 SS Trunks, Fully-Powered Fusion C .12 .25
BT14045 Trunks, Calamity Challenger SR .75 1.50
BT14046 SS3 Gotenks, Calamity Challenger R .20 .40
BT14047 SS3 Gotenks, Combo of Justice R .60 1.25
BT14048 Great Saiyaman 2, Combo of Justice U .15 .30
BT14049 Tapion, Hero of the Calamity C .12 .25
BT14050 Tapion, Calamity Challenger SR 2.00 4.00
BT14050 Tapion, Calamity Challenger SPR 6.00 12.00
BT14051 Tapion C .12 .25
BT14052 Minotia, Calamity Challenger U .15 .30
BT14053 Minotai, the Hero's Sibling C .12 .25
BT14054 Hirudegarn, Calamity Complete R .20 .40
BT14055 Hirudegarn, Catastrophic Combination U .15 .30
BT14056 Hirudegarn, Catastrophic Comeback R .20 .40
BT14057 Foreboding Music Box C .12 .25
BT14058 The Coming Calamity C .25 .50
BT14059 Tapion's Sword U .15 .30
BT14060 An Unlikely Protector C .12 .25
BT14061 Videl // Videl, the Town's Heroine C .12 .25
BT14062 Majin Buu // Majin Buu, Unadulterated Might U .15 .30
BT14063 Great Saiyaman, the Mysterious Hero SR 1.50 3.00
BT14063 Great Saiyaman, the Mysterious Hero SPR 2.50 5.00
BT14064 Babidi, Wicked Mentor U .15 .30
BT14065 SS Son Gohan, Glimpsing Potential R .30 .60
BT14066 Krillin, a Brief Return C .12 .25
BT14067 Videl, With All Her Strength SR 1.50 3.00
BT14067 Videl, With All Her Strength SPR 3.00 6.00
BT14068 Videl C .12 .25
BT14069 Videl C .12 .25
BT14070 Android 18, Ready for a Fight R .20 .40
BT14071 Son Goku, Spirit Bomb Unleashed SR 4.00 8.00
BT14072 Son Goku, Majin Exterminator C .12 .25
BT14073 SS Vegeta, Majin Exterminator C .12 .25
BT14074 Son Gohan, Majin Exterminator R .30 .60
BT14075 Hercule, Majin Exterminator R .50 1.00
BT14076 Majin Buu, Unadulterated Destruction SR 3.00 6.00
BT14077 Majin Buu, Ultimate Despair SR 2.00 4.00
BT14078 Majin Buu, Mighty Absorption U .15 .30
BT14079 Majin Buu, Brilliant Absorption U .15 .30
BT14080 Majin Buu, the Neverending Absorber C .12 .25
BT14081 Majin Buu, Absorption Scheme C .12 .25
BT14082 Majin Buu, Unadulterated Malice R 3.00 6.00
BT14083 Majin Buu, Thwarting the Enemy R .60 1.25
BT14084 Broly, Berserker of Frieza's Army U .15 .30
BT14085 Defender of Justice C .12 .25
BT14086 Heart of a Maiden U .15 .30
BT14087 Power Beyond Super Saiyan 2 C .12 .25
BT14088 Diabolical Blow C .12 .25
BT14089 Commemorative Photo C .12 .25
BT14090 Wicked Mimicry U .15 .30
BT14091 Son Goku // SS4 Son Goku, Returned from Hell U .15 .30
BT14092 Super 17 // Super 17, Emissary of Hell C .12 .25
BT14093 Android 18, Defender of Heroes SR 2.00 4.00
BT14093 Android 18, Defender of Heroes SPR 5.00 10.00
BT14094 Android 20 & Dr. Myuu, Hellish Accomplices SR 3.00 6.00
BT14095 SS4 Son Goku, the Brawler R .30 .75
BT14096 Self-Restraint SS Son Goku R .30 .75
BT14097 Son Goku, Return of the Dragon Fist SR 7.50 15.00
BT14098 Son Gohan, the Brawler U .15 .30
BT14099 SS Son Goten, the Brawler C .12 .25
BT14100 Pan, the Brawler U .15 .30
BT14101 Vegeta, the Brawler C .12 .25
BT14102 Vegeta (BT14-102) C .12 .25
BT14103 Trunks, the Brawler C .12 .25
BT14104 Piccolo, the Gate Opener C .12 .25
BT14105 Krillin, the Brawler R .20 .40
BT14106 Great Saiyaman 2 C .12 .25
BT14107 Android 17, Conceding to Union U .15 .30
BT14108 Android 17, Mechanical Charity C .12 .25
BT14109 Android 17, Thwarting the Enemy R .30 .60
BT14110 Hell Fighter 17, Conceding to Union U .15 .30
BT14111 Hell Fighter 17, Mechanical Charity C .12 .25
BT14112 Super 17, Powers Combined R .20 .40
BT14113 Super 17, Hellish Amalgamation U .15 .30
BT14114 Super 17, Prepping for Union C .12 .25
BT14115 Dr. Myuu, Returned from the Beyond C .12 .25
BT14116 Opening the Gates of Hell SR .75 1.50
BT14116 Opening the Gates of Hell SPR 3.00 6.00
BT14117 Watchman's Strike C .12 .25
BT14118 A Trip to Hell R .50 1.00
BT14119 Awakened Attack U .15 .30
BT14120 A Fated Meeting C .12 .25
BT14121 Syn Shenron // Syn Shenron, Resonance of Shadow U .15 .30
BT14122 SS4 Bardock, Spirit Resonance SR 2.00 4.00
BT14122 SS4 Bardock, Spirit Resonance SPR 5.00 10.00
BT14123 Towa, Resonance of Shadow U .15 .30
BT14124 Kibito Kai, Opening Strike U .15 .30
BT14125 SS4 Son Goku, Prepping for Fusion U .15 .30
BT14126 Son Goku C .12 .25
BT14127 SS4 Vegeta, Prepping for Fusion U .15 .30
BT14128 Vegeta C .12 .25
BT14129 SS4 Gogeta, Thwarting the Dark Empire SR 5.00 10.00
BT14129 SS4 Gogeta, Thwarting the Dark Empire SPR 15.00 30.00
BT14130 Robelu, Meticulous Investigator C .12 .25
BT14131 Syn Shenron, Negative Energy Explosion R .30 .75
BT14132 Syn Shenron, Power of Darkness R .30 .75
BT14133 Haze Shenron, Negative Energy Explosion C .12 .25
BT14134 Haze Shenron, Power of Darkness C .12 .25
BT14135 Oceanus Shenron, Negative Energy Explosion SR 20.00 40.00
BT14136 Oceanus Shenron, Power of Darkness R .50 1.00
BT14137 Naturon Shenron, Negative Energy Explosion U .15 .30
BT14138 Naturon Shenron, Power of Darkness C .12 .25
BT14139 Negative Energy Explosion C .12 .25
BT14140 Ultimate Dark Dragon-Slaying Bullet SR 12.50 25.00
BT14141 Ultimate Dragon Quake C .12 .25
BT14142 Ultimate Whirlwind Spin C .12 .25
BT14143 Ultimate Dragon Tackle U .15 .30
BT14144 Vegeta, Devastating Alliance C .12 .25
BT14145 Saibaimen, Faithful to the End U .15 .30
BT14146 Hit, Flawless Attacker R .20 .40
BT14147 Beerus, Unceasing Rage U .15 .30
BT14148 Son Gohan & Krillin, Buying Time U .15 .30
BT14149 Android 16, Limiter Disengaged SR 1.50 3.00
BT14150 King Cold, Gathering the Clan R .20 .40
BT14151 Android 13, Cybernetic Onslaught R .20 .40
BT14152 SS Son Goku & Frieza, Miraculous Conclusion SCR 300.00 600.00
BT14153 Majin Buu, Kibito Kai Absorbed SCR 125.00 250.00
BT14154 Super 17, Sibling Absorbed SCR 75.00 150.00

2021 Dragon Ball Super Expansion Deck 16 Ultimate Deck

EX1601 Towa // Towa & Mechikabura, Dark Conjurers .50 1.00
EX1602 Dark Shenron, Tyrannical Savior .50 1.00
EX1603 Dark Broly, Unbridled Destruction 2.00 4.00
EX1604 Dark Broly, the Shadow Warrior .50 1.00
EX1605 Janemba, the Shadow Warrior .30 .60
EX1606 Frieza, the Shadow Warrior .30 .60
EX1607 Majin Buu, the Shadow Warrior 1.00 2.00
EX1608 Lord Slug, the Shadow Warrior .30 .60
EX1609 Dark Dragon Balls .30 .75
EX1610 Lord Slug, Unbridled Might .30 .60

2021 Dragon Ball Super Expansion Deck 17 Saiyan Boost

EX1701 SS Son Goku, Spirit Boost Striker .30 .75
EX1702 Bardock, Spirit Boost Avenger .30 .75
EX1703 SS Bardock, Spirit Resonance .25 .50
EX1704 Hunt of the Demon God .30 .60
EX1705 Android 17, Ki Channeler .25 .50

2021 Dragon Ball Super Expansion Deck 18 Namekian Boost

EX1801 Piccolo, Spirit Boost Defender .50 1.00
EX1802 Son Gohan, Spirit Boost Vindicator .30 .75
EX1803 Trunks, Spirit Resonance .25 .50
EX1804 Sword Dance of the Demon God .30 .75
EX1805 Boujack, Pinpoint Onslaught 1.00 2.00

2021 Dragon Ball Super Saiyan Showdown

BT15001 Son Goten // SS Son Goten, Kamehameha Miracle U .15 .30
BT15002 Broly // SS Broly, Demon's Second Coming U .15 .30
BT15003 SS Son Gohan, Kamehameha Miracle U .15 .30
BT15004 Dark Broly, Resonant Obliteration SR 1.00 2.00
BT15005 Raditz, On Guard R .20 .40
BT15006 Training Buddy Bubbles C .12 .25
BT15007 SS Son Goku, Kamehameha Miracle R .20 .40
BT15008 SS Son Gohan, Opposing the Demon C .12 .25
BT15009 Speed Rush Son Gohan C .12 .25
BT15010 SS Son Goten, Opposing the Demon C .12 .25
BT15011 Son Goten, Journey's Beginning C .12 .25
BT15012 Trunks C .12 .25
BT15013 Trunks, Journey's Beginning U .15 .30
BT15014 Quick Assist Krillin C .12 .25
BT15015 Videl, Opposing the Demon R .20 .40
BT15016 Videl, Encountering Danger SPR 6.00 12.00
BT15016 Videl, Encountering Danger SR 4.00 8.00
BT15017 Coco, Dedicated to the Village C .12 .25
BT15018 Natade Village Monster C .12 .25
BT15019 SS Broly, Brutality Beyond Measure SPR 2.00 4.00
BT15019 SS Broly, Brutality Beyond Measure SR .60 1.25
BT15020 SS Broly, Finishing the Job U .15 .30
BT15021 SS Broly, Awakened Attacker U .15 .30
BT15022 Broly, Slumbering Demon C .12 .25
BT15023 The Demon Cometh R .20 .40
BT15024 Natade Village Ritual C .12 .25
BT15025 The Demon Awakens C .12 .25
BT15026 Monstrous Encounter C .12 .25
BT15027 Demonic Blitz U .15 .30
BT15028 Demonic Barrier U .15 .30
BT15029 Demonic Playtime R .20 .40
BT15030 Gigantic Meteor SR .75 1.50
BT15031 Cabba // SS Cabba, Proud Volley U .15 .30
BT15032 Kale // Kale, Demon of Universe 6 U .15 .30
BT15033 Hit, Battlefield Manipulator SPR 4.00 8.00
BT15033 Hit, Battlefield Manipulator SR 2.50 5.00
BT15034 SS Caulifla, Spirited Striker U .15 .30
BT15035 Champa, Right on Time C .12 .25
BT15036 Vados, Right on Time R .20 .40
BT15037 SS Cabba, Proud Zenith SR 1.00 2.00
BT15038 SS Cabba, Universe 6 Combination U .15 .30
BT15039 Cabba, Saiyan Pride U .15 .30
BT15040 SS Caulifla, Rapid Riposte C .12 .25
BT15041 SS2 Caulifla, Universe 6 Combination C .12 .25
BT15042 Kale, Rampaging Demon SR 6.00 12.00
BT15043 SS Kale, Universe 6 Combination R .20 .40
BT15044 Kale, Ready to Fuse U .15 .30
BT15045 Hit, On Guard C .12 .25
BT15046 Hit, Universe 6 Combination C .12 .25
BT15047 SS Kefla, Unending Evolution R .20 .40
BT15048 Kefla, Universe 6 Fusion Warrior R .20 .40
BT15049 Botamo C .12 .25
BT15050 Magetta C .12 .25
BT15051 Full-Power Frost, Embodied Might U .15 .30
BT15052 Frost, Universal Deception C .12 .25
BT15053 Frost, Evolutionary Milestone C .12 .25
BT15054 Dr. Rota, Power's Draw C .12 .25
BT15055 Saonel, Universe 6 Combination C .12 .25
BT15056 Pirina, Universe 6 Combination C .12 .25
BT15057 Universe 6, Assemble! R .20 .40
BT15058 A Sister's Determination SR .75 1.50
BT15059 Universe 6 Combination R .20 .40
BT15060 Mentor's Rescue C .12 .25
BT15061 Son Goku // Son Goku, Destined Confrontation U .15 .30
BT15062 Vegeta // Vegeta, Destined Confrontation U .15 .30
BT15063 King Vegeta, Invasion's Command SPR 2.00 4.00
BT15063 King Vegeta, Invasion's Command SR .60 1.25
BT15064 Krillin, Staunch Defender U .15 .30
BT15065 Raditz, Requesting Reinforcements U .15 .30
BT15066 Kaio-Ken Son Goku, Decisive Battle SPR 1.50 3.00
BT15066 Kaio-Ken Son Goku, Decisive Battle SR .50 1.00
BT15067 Kaio-Ken Son Goku, Maximum Gains C .12 .25
BT15068 Kaio-Ken Son Goku, Confronting Invasion C .12 .25
BT15069 Training Goals Son Goku R .20 .40
BT15070 Son Gohan, Simian Revenge U .15 .30
BT15071 Son Gohan, Confronting Invasion R .20 .40
BT15072 Son Gohan, Rageful Fury C .12 .25
BT15073 Great Ape Vegeta, Embodied Might C .12 .25
BT15074 Vegeta, Preparing to Invade C .12 .25
BT15075 Vegeta, Elite Resolve SR 2.00 4.00
BT15076 Piccolo, Confronting Invasion C .12 .25
BT15077 Yamcha, Confronting Invasion C .12 .25
BT15078 Tien Shinhan, Confronting Invasion U .15 .30
BT15079 Chiaotzu, Confronting Invasion R .20 .40
BT15080 Yajirobe, Confronting Invasion R .20 .40
BT15081 North Kai, Master's Guidance U .15 .30
BT15082 North Kai C .12 .25
BT15083 Training Buddy Gregory U .15 .30
BT15084 Nappa, the Intimidator R .20 .40
BT15085 Nappa, on Guard R .20 .40
BT15086 Saibaiman, Unison Sapper C .12 .25
BT15087 Plains Monster C .12 .25
BT15088 King Kai's Planet C .12 .25
BT15089 King Kai's Training C .12 .25
BT15090 Vegeta's Power Ball C .12 .25
BT15091 Son Gohan // Great Ape Son Gohan, Saiyan Impulse U .15 .30
BT15092 Turles // Turles, Accursed Power U .15 .30
BT15093 Kaio-Ken Son Goku, Reclaiming Hope R .20 .40
BT15094 Tree of Might, Divine Roots C .12 .25
BT15095 Son Goku, A Gift from the Earth SR 1.25 2.50
BT15096 Son Goku, Steadfast Assistance SR 10.00 20.00
BT15097 Son Gohan, the Misadventure U .15 .30
BT15098 Son Gohan & Hire-Dragon, Best Buds C .12 .25
BT15099 Krillin, Battle at the Tree C .12 .25
BT15100 Piccolo, Battle at the Tree SR .50 1.00
BT15101 Tien Shinhan & Chiaotzu, Battle at the Tree R .20 .40
BT15102 Yamcha, Battle at the Tree U .15 .30
BT15103 Hire-Dragon, Battle at the Tree C .12 .25
BT15104 Hire-Dragon C .12 .25
BT15105 Wilderness Monster C .12 .25
BT15106 Turles, Great Ape Manipulator R .20 .40
BT15107 Turles, All Too Easy SR 6.00 12.00
BT15108 Turles, Power of the Tree C .12 .25
BT15109 Amond, Power of the Tree C .12 .25
BT15110 Daiz, Power of the Tree R .20 .40
BT15111 Cacao, Power of the Tree R .20 .40
BT15112 Rasin, Power of the Tree U .15 .30
BT15113 Lakasei, Power of the Tree U .15 .30
BT15114 Forest Fire C .12 .25
BT15115 Nature's Revival C .12 .25
BT15116 Hire-Dragon's Home C .12 .25
BT15117 Scout U .15 .30
BT15118 Turles's Power Ball C .12 .25
BT15119 Forbidden Power SPR 4.00 8.00
BT15119 Forbidden Power SR 2.50 5.00
BT15120 Blessing of the Tree of Might C .12 .25
BT15121 Fin // Fin, Apocalyptic Absorption U .15 .30
BT15122 Skill Hunter Majin Buu U .15 .30
BT15123 Demon God Dabura, Skill Hunter C .12 .25
BT15124 Dabura, Demonic Defender C .12 .25
BT15125 Skill Hunter Towa U .15 .30
BT15126 Towa, Calling the Hordes C .12 .25
BT15127 Fin, the All-Absorbing R .20 .40
BT15128 Fin, Coercion Incarnate SR 4.00 8.00
BT15129 Fin, Unison Absorber C .12 .25
BT15130 Omega Shenron, Ultimate Darkness SR .75 1.50
BT15131 Omega Shenron, Darkness Absorbed R .20 .40
BT15132 Eis Shenron, Negative Energy Explosion C .12 .25
BT15133 Eis Shenron, Power of Darkness R .20 .40
BT15134 Nuova Shenron, Power of Darkness SR .75 1.50
BT15135 Nuova Shenron, Negative Energy Explosion U .15 .30
BT15136 Rage Shenron, Power of Darkness U .15 .30
BT15137 Rage Shenron, Negative Energy Explosion U .15 .30
BT15138 Absorption of Doom R .20 .40
BT15139 Ultimate Minus Energy Power Ball SPR 1.50 3.00
BT15139 Ultimate Minus Energy Power Ball SR 1.00 2.00
BT15140 Ultimate Ice Ray C .12 .25
BT15141 Ultimate Flame Shot R .20 .40
BT15142 Ultimate Electric Slime C .12 .25
BT15143 Vegeta, Omnipotent Elite SPR 2.00 4.00
BT15143 Vegeta, Omnipotent Elite SR .60 1.25
BT15144 SS Broly, Annihilation Personified R .20 .40
BT15145 Great Ape Raditz, Might Unleashed U .15 .30
BT15146 SSG Son Goku & Hit, Temporary Truce R .20 .40
BT15147 Vegeta & Cabba, Lessons Learned U .15 .30
BT15148 SS2 Kefla, Lightning Speed SPR 4.00 8.00
BT15148 SS2 Kefla, Lightning Speed SR 2.00 4.00
BT15149 Rasin & Lakasei, Twin Teamwork C .12 .25
BT15150 Turles, Dark Power Unleashed R .20 .40
BT15151 Turles, Dominance at Hand SR .75 1.50
BT15152 SS4: The Vermilion Saiyans SCR 75.00 150.00
BT15153 The Wicked Saiyans SCR 75.00 150.00
BT15154 The Radiant Saiyans SCR 50.00 100.00
BT15155 Pan, Time Patrol Maiden SCR 150.00 300.00

2021 Dragon Ball Super Special Anniversary Set

BT1005 Furthering Destruction Champa ALT ART U .75 1.50
BT5073 Infernal Villainy Cell ALT ART C .30 .60
BT5112 Dark Power Black Masked Saiyan ALT ART U .20 .40
BT6117 Four-Star Ball ALT ART R .20 .40
DB1064 Great Ape Son Goku, Saiyan Instincts ALT ART SR 1.50 3.00
DB2036 Android 17, Turning the Tide ALT ART R .30 .60
DB2040 Hit, Deadly Vanguard ALT ART R .20 .40
DB3109 Demon God Demigra, True Power Unleashed ALT ART SR .30 .60
EX1901 Bulma, to Incite a Sneeze EX .12 .25
EX1902 Quick Growing Saibaimen EX .07 .15
EX1903 SS Son Goku, Might in the Making EX .12 .25
EX1904 SS Vegeta, Might in the Making EX .12 .25
EX1905 King Cold, Blessing of the Clan EX .07 .15
EX1906 Zamasu, Teamwork Undying EX .15 .30
EX1907 Shugesh, Power of Unity EX .10 .20
EX1908 Goku Black, Works Undone EX .15 .30
EX1909 Veku, Might in the Making EX .07 .15
EX1910 Lord Slug, Conqueror's Claim EX .07 .15

EX1911 Broly, Saiyan Instinct EX	.07	.15
EX1912 Broly, Omen of Evolution EX	.15	.30
EX1913 Encountering the Unknown EX	.07	.15
EX1914 Cheelai and Lemo, Allied Assistance EX	.07	.15
EX1915 Bardock, Resurrected Lineage EX	.10	.20
EX1916 Meta-Cooler, Maddening Multiplication EX	.07	.15
EX1917 Ginyu, Former Galactic Elite EX	.12	.25
EX1918 God of Destruction Toppo, Skillbreaker EX	.10	.20
EX1919 Swift Rescue Dyspo EX	.07	.15
EX1920 Bardock // SS4 Bardock, Prismatic Striker EX	2.00	4.00
EX1921 SS4 Broly, Prismatic Burst EX	.25	.50
EX1922 SS4 Gogeta, Prismatic Burst EX	.30	.60
EX1923 Supreme Kai of Time, Prism Bringer EX	.12	.25
EX1924 SS4's Call EX	.15	.30
EX1925 SS4 Bardock, Prismatic Burst EX	.25	.50
EX1926 SS4 Bardock, Prismatic Aegis EX	.25	.50
EX1927 SS Rose Goku Black, Epochal Schemer EX	.20	.40
EX1928 SS4 Vegeta, Prismatic Burst EX	.30	.60
EX1929 SS4 Vegeta, Prismatic Aegis EX	.30	.60
EX1930 Full Power Broly, Impulsive Destroyer EX	.15	.30
EX1931 SS Broly, Reckless Pursuit EX	.15	.30
EX1932 Skillsteal Cheelai EX	.15	.30
EX1933 SS4 Son Gohan, Prismatic Burst EX	.25	.50
EX1934 SS4 Son Gohan, Prismatic Aegis EX	.25	.50
EX1935 SS4 Son Goku, Prismatic Burst EX	.25	.50
EX1936 SS4 Son Goku, Prismatic Aegis EX	.25	.50
TB2011 Heroic Duo Videl ALT ART C	.07	.15
BT11005 Raditz, Saiyan Youth ALT ART R	.75	1.50
BT11054 Vegeta, Disciplined Warrior ALT ART R	.75	1.50
BT11065 Great Saiyaman, Vanquisher of Villainy ALT ART R	.75	1.50
BT11097 Krillin, Moments Before Comeback ALT ART R	1.00	2.00
BT11130 SS Vegeta, the Prince Strikes Back ALT ART R	3.00	6.00

2021 Dragon Ball Super Starter Deck Darkness Reborn

SD1601 Masked Saiyan // SS3 Bardock, Reborn from Darkness	1.50	3.00
SD1602 Dark Masked King, Spirit Resonance	2.00	4.00
SD1603 Dark Broly, Spirit Boost Berserker	2.00	4.00
SD1604 Masked Saiyan, Spirit Boost Enigma	2.00	4.00
SD1605 Black Masked Saiyan, Spirit Boost Minion	2.00	4.00

2021 Dragon Ball Super Starter Deck Pride of the Saiyans

SD1501 Vegeta // SSB Vegeta, Spirit Boost Elite	1.25	2.50
SD1502 SS Cabba, Spirit Resonance	2.50	5.00
SD1503 Son Goku, Spirit Boost Warrior	2.50	5.00
SD1504 Surprise Attack Son Gohan	2.50	5.00
SD1505 Surprise Attack SSB Vegeta	2.50	5.00

2021 Dragon Ball Super Supreme Rivalry

BT13001 Bardock // SS Bardock, the Legend Awakened U	.15	.30
BT13002 King Vegeta // King Vegeta, Head of the Saiyan Rebellion C	.12	.25
BT13003 Masked Saiyan, Avenger from Another Dimension U	.15	.30
BT13004 Black Masked Saiyan, Brawler from Another Dimension SR	2.00	4.00
BT13005 Bardock, Pride of a Low-Class Warrior R	.30	.60
BT13006 Chain Attack Tora C	.12	.25
BT13007 Chain Attack Fasha U	.15	.30
BT13008 Chain Attack Shugesh U	.15	.30
BT13009 Chain Attack Borgos C	.12	.25
BT13010 SS Bardock, Super Saiyan Enlightenment SR	2.00	4.00
BT13011 King Piccolo, the Next Step to Youth C	.12	.25
BT13012 SS Son Goku, the Legend Personified SR	2.50	5.00
BT13013 Son Goten C	.12	.25
BT13014 Trunks C	.12	.25
BT13015 Son Gohan, Saiyan Combo R	.20	.40
BT13016 Gine, at Her Husband's Side R	.20	.40
BT13017 SSB Son Goku, at Full Power R	.20	.40
BT13018 SSG Son Goku, to the Next Level U	.15	.30
BT13019 Son Goku, Hope of the Saiyans C	.12	.25
BT13020 King Vegeta, Hidden Ambitions SR	.75	1.50
BT13020 King Vegeta, Hidden Ambitions SPR	2.00	4.00
BT13021 SSB Vegeta, at Full Power R	.50	1.00
BT13022 SSG Vegeta, to the Next Level U	.15	.30
BT13023 Vegeta, the Young Invader C	.12	.25
BT13024 SS Broly, Brawn Amplified U	.15	.30
BT13025 SS Broly, Unchained Might U	.15	.30
BT13026 Broly, the Young Invader C	.12	.25
BT13027 Invasion of Bardock's Crew R	.20	.40
BT13028 Young Invader C	.12	.25
BT13029 A Sudden Escape C	.12	.25
BT13030 King Vegeta's Imposing Presence SR	4.00	8.00
BT13030 King Vegeta's Imposing Presence SPR	6.00	12.00
BT13031 Son Gohan // SS2 Son Gohan, Pushed to the brink U	.15	.30
BT13032 Boujack // Boujack, Subjugator Unbound C	.12	.25
BT13033 Pan & Giru, Energy Fortification U	.15	.30
BT13034 Majin Buu, Assault of the Agents of Destruction SR	7.50	15.00
BT13034 Majin Buu, Assault of the Agents of Destruction SPR	10.00	20.00
BT13035 Son Goku, Dad to the Rescue U	.15	.30
BT13036 SS2 Son Gohan, Astonishing Strike SR	4.00	8.00
BT13036 SS2 Son Gohan, Astonishing Strike SPR	12.50	25.00
BT13037 Super Saiyan Son Gohan C	.12	.25
BT13038 Son Gohan, Unbelievable Might C	.12	.25
BT13039 SS Vegeta, Saiyan Tenacity R	.20	.40
BT13040 Vegeta, Energy Fortification U	.15	.30
BT13041 Super Saiyan Trunks C	.12	.25
BT13042 Trunks, Unbelievable Might SR	1.25	2.50
BT13043 Krillin, Energy Fortification C	.12	.25
BT13044 Yamcha, Hope Abandoned U	.15	.30
BT13045 Tien Shinhan, Energy Fortification C	.12	.25
BT13046 Boujack, On a Rampage SR	6.00	12.00
BT13047 Boujack, the Evildoer R	.30	.75
BT13048 Gokua, the Evildoer C	.12	.25
BT13049 Gokua, the Calamity R	.20	.40
BT13050 Zangya, the Evildoer C	.12	.25
BT13051 Zangya, the Savage R	.20	.40
BT13052 Bido, the Evildoer U	.15	.30
BT13053 Bido, the Cruel R	.20	.40
BT13054 Bujin, the Evildoer R	.20	.40
BT13055 Bujin, the Commando U	.15	.30
BT13056 Son Goku, Hellish Throwdown C	.12	.25
BT13057 SS Trunks, Defender From Another Dimension C	.12	.25
BT13058 Full Power Unleashed C	.12	.25
BT13059 The Champ to the Rescue! C	.12	.25
BT13060 Galactic Buster SR	12.50	25.00
BT13061 King Cold // King Cold, Ruler of the Galactic Dynasty U	.15	.30
BT13062 Chilled // Chilled, the Pillager C	.12	.25
BT13063 Frieza, Invader from Another Dimension SR	.60	1.25
BT13063 Frieza, Invader from Another Dimension SPR	1.25	2.50
BT13064 King Vegeta, Umbral Invader U	.15	.30
BT13065 Chilled, Let the Battle Begin SR	.60	1.25
BT13066 Chilled, Space Pirate Captain C	.12	.25
BT13067 Tobi, the Besieger C	.12	.25
BT13068 Tobi, Feigned Greeting R	.20	.40
BT13069 Cabira, the Besieger C	.12	.25
BT13070 Cabira, Feigned Greeting U	.15	.30
BT13071 Son Goku, Allies in the Heart SR	.50	1.00
BT13072 Wings, Supporting the Master's Wish C	.12	.25
BT13073 Cooler, Effortless Strike SR	2.00	4.00
BT13073 Cooler, Effortless Strike SPR	4.00	8.00
BT13074 Cooler, Vicious Ambush C	.12	.25
BT13075 Babidi, Bewitching Domination R	.20	.40
BT13076 Golden Frieza, Pinnacle of the Clan R	.50	1.00
BT13077 Frieza, Revived and Reviled R	.50	1.00
BT13078 Frieza, Demolisher of Planet Vegeta U	.15	.30
BT13079 Cheelai C	.12	.25
BT13080 Berryblue, Frieza's Advisor U	.15	.30
BT13081 Kikono C	.12	.25
BT13082 King Cold, Supreme Ruler U	.15	.30
BT13083 Invasion of Chilled's Army C	.12	.25
BT13084 King Cold's Dynasty C	.12	.25
BT13085 A New Ruler C	.12	.25
BT13086 Anticipated Onslaught R	.20	.40
BT13087 Terrified Realization U	.15	.30
BT13088 Unstoppable Invasion C	.12	.25
BT13089 Chilled Army Assault R	.20	.40
BT13090 Royal Supremacy R	.50	1.00
BT13091 Son Gohan // SS Son Gohan, Hope of the Resistance C	.12	.25
BT13092 Android 17 & Android 18 // Android 17 & Android 18, Harbingers of Calamity U	.15	.30
BT13093 SS Trunks, Altering the Future SR	1.00	2.00
BT13093 SS Trunks, Altering the Future SPR	2.50	5.00
BT13094 Android 13, Robotic Unity U	.15	.30
BT13095 SS Son Goku, Trusted Ally U	.15	.30
BT13096 SS Son Goku, the Hero Returns C	.12	.25
BT13097 SS Son Gohan, Desperate Last Stand C	.12	.25
BT13098 Son Gohan, Trusted Ally R	.25	.50
BT13099 Son Gohan, Warrior of Hope U	.15	.30
BT13100 SS Vegeta, Trusted Ally U	.15	.30
BT13101 Trunks, Might Born of Hope SR	4.00	8.00
BT13102 SS Trunks, to Change the Future U	.15	.30
BT13103 Trunks, Warrior of Hope C	.12	.25
BT13104 Piccolo, Trusted Ally C	.12	.25
BT13105 Bulma, Hope for a Better Future R	.20	.40
BT13106 Android 17 & Android 18, Bringers of the Apocalypse SR	1.25	2.50
BT13107 Android 17 & Android 18, Demonic Duo R	.20	.40
BT13108 Android 17 C	.12	.25
BT13109 Android 17, Sibling Strike U	.15	.30
BT13110 Android 18 C	.12	.25
BT13111 Android 18, Sibling Strike U	.15	.30
BT13112 Android 16, Going All Out C	.12	.25
BT13113 Android 16, Mechanical Partner R	.25	.50
BT13114 Android 19, Bionic Punisher Unleashed R	.20	.40
BT13115 Android 20, Mechanical Patriarch C	.12	.25
BT13116 Android 20, Skill Absorber C	.12	.25
BT13117 Furious Awakening C	.12	.25
BT13118 The Future's in Your Hands C	.12	.25
BT13119 Assault of the Androids R	.20	.40
BT13120 The Power of a Super Saiyan SR	7.50	15.00
BT13120 The Power of a Super Saiyan SPR	10.00	20.00
BT13121 Supreme Kai of Time // Supreme Kai of Time, the Chronokeeper C	.12	.25
BT13122 Mechikabura // Dark King Mechikabura, Restored to the Throne U	.15	.30
BT13123 Demigra, Momentary Ally SR	1.00	2.00
BT13123 Demigra, Momentary Ally SPR	3.00	6.00
BT13124 Black Smoke Dragon, Offering of Destruction U	.15	.30
BT13125 SS3 Bardock, Breaking Free From the Mask SR	.60	1.25
BT13126 SS4 Son Goku, Thwarting the Dark Empire C	.12	.25
BT13127 Son Goten, Thwarting the Dark Empire U	.15	.30
BT13128 Son Goten, Fusion Renewed C	.12	.25
BT13129 Son Goten, Time Patrol's Charity C	.12	.25
BT13130 SS4 Vegeta, Thwarting the Dark Empire R	.50	1.00
BT13131 Trunks, Thwarting the Dark Empire U	.15	.30
BT13132 Trunks, Fusion Renewed C	.12	.25
BT13133 SS Gotenks, Surging Strike U	.15	.30
BT13134 Gotenks, Fusion Renewed C	.12	.25
BT13135 Supreme Kai of Time, Time Labyrinth Unleashed SR	3.00	6.00
BT13135 Supreme Kai of Time, Time Labyrinth Unleashed SPR	6.00	12.00
BT13136 Dark Droly, the Vindicator C	.12	.25
BT13137 Dabura, Ritual at Hand C	.12	.25
BT13138 Demon God Towa, Ritual at Hand R	.30	.60
BT13139 Demon God Towa, Offering of the Dark Dragon Balls C	.12	.25
BT13140 Demon God Putine, Ritual at Hand R	.30	.60
BT13141 Demon God Gravy, Ritual at Hand C	.12	.25
BT13142 Dark King Mechikabura, Power Restored SR	2.00	4.00
BT13143 Mechikabura, Ritual at Hand R	.30	.60
BT13144 Shroom, Ritual at Hand U	.15	.30
BT13145 Salsa, Ritual at Hand U	.15	.30
BT13146 King Vegeta, a Kingdom Lost SR	6.00	12.00
BT13147 Dark Masked King, Pursuit of Power C	.12	.25
BT13148 Dark Shenron, Wicked Wishmaster C	.12	.25
BT13149 Yearning for the Dark Dragon Balls C	.12	.25
BT13150 Clash of the Masked Warriors R	.20	.40
BT13151 Darkness Judgment R	.25	.50
BT13152 Syn Shenron, Corrupted by the Darkness SCR	100.00	200.00
BT13153 SS3 Gohanks, Interdimensional Warrior SCR	75.00	150.00
BT13154 Robelu, Demigra's Secretary SCR	75.00	150.00

2021 Dragon Ball Super Vicious Rejuvenation

BT12001 Launch // Launch, Nothing to Sneeze At C	.12	.25
BT12002 King Piccolo // King Piccolo, Demonic Rejuvenation U	.15	.30
BT12003 Bulma, Secret Supporter U	.15	.30
BT12004 Piccolo Jr., Descendant of the King SPR	12.50	25.00
BT12004 Piccolo Jr., Descendant of the King SR	10.00	20.00
BT12005 Son Goku, Eye for an Eye SPR	3.00	6.00
BT12005 Son Goku, Eye for an Eye SR	.60	1.25
BT12006 Son Goku, Ready for Anything C	.12	.25
BT12007 Krillin, Dearest Friend C	.12	.25
BT12008 Yamcha, Righteous Onslaught C	.12	.25
BT12009 Tien Shinhan, Ready for Anything C	.12	.25
BT12010 Master Roshi, Ready for Anything C	.12	.25
BT12011 Bulma, Confident Friend U	.15	.30
BT12012 Launch, Brown County's Most Wanted R	.20	.40
BT12013 Launch, the Pure-Hearted SR	4.00	8.00
BT12014 Pilaf, the Gang's All Here! C	.12	.25
BT12015 Shu C	.12	.25
BT12016 Mai C	.12	.25
BT12017 King Piccolo, Evil Dictator SR	.75	1.50
BT12018 King Piccolo, Time to Fight R	.20	.40
BT12019 King Piccolo, Dragon Ball Obsession U	.15	.30
BT12020 Tambourine, Reign of Terror U	.15	.30
BT12021 Cymbal, Reign of Terror C	.12	.25
BT12022 Drum, Reign of Terror C	.12	.25
BT12023 Piano, Reign of Terror R	.20	.40
BT12024 Master Roshi's Mafuba R	.20	.40
BT12025 Attack of the Demon Clan R	.20	.40
BT12026 Achoo! U	.15	.30
BT12027 Paikuhan // Paikuhan, Penetrating Strike U	.15	.30
BT12028 Janemba // Janemba, Demonic Dynasty C	.12	.25
BT12029 Frieza & Cell, a Match Made in Hell SPR	3.00	6.00
BT12029 Frieza & Cell, a Match Made in Hell SR	1.25	2.50
BT12030 Majin Buu, Dimensional Intervention U	.15	.30
BT12031 Son Goku, Heavy Hitter U	.15	.30
BT12032 Son Goku, Fusion Synergy U	.15	.30
BT12033 Great Saiyaman, Punisher of Evil R	.75	1.50
BT12034 Son Goten, Battling the Forces of Evil C	.12	.25
BT12035 Vegeta, Sentinel from Hell U	.15	.30
BT12036 Vegeta, Fusion Synergy C	.12	.25
BT12037 Trunks, Battling the Forces of Evil U	.15	.30
BT12038 Gogeta, Godspeed Demolisher SR	2.00	4.00
BT12039 Gogeta, the Demon Destroyer R	.30	.60
BT12040 Veku, Making Excuses C	.12	.25
BT12041 Gotenks, Battling the Forces of Evil SR	3.00	6.00
BT12042 Paikuhan, Stalling for Time R	.20	.40
BT12043 Paikuhan, Flawless Technique C	.12	.25
BT12044 Paikuhan, Supporting His Comrades U	.15	.30
BT12045 Janemba, Bewitching Blow SPR	4.00	8.00
BT12045 Janemba, Bewitching Blow SR	3.00	6.00
BT12046 Janemba (A) C	.12	.25
BT12047 Janemba (B) C	.12	.25
BT12048 Janemba, Enchanted Transformation R	.20	.40
BT12049 Saike Demon, the Careless C	.12	.25
BT12050 Janemba, Rampaging Demon U	.25	.50
BT12051 Janemba, Dark Parasite R	2.00	4.00
BT12052 Five-Star Ball, Parasitic Darkness C	.12	.25
BT12053 West Galaxy Revival R	.20	.40
BT12054 Soul Cleansing Machine C	.12	.25
BT12055 Lord Slug // Lord Slug, Rejuvenated Invader C	.12	.25
BT12056 Turles // Turles, Fiendish Force U	.15	.30
BT12057 King Piccolo, Dimensional Conqueror SPR	2.50	5.00
BT12057 King Piccolo, Dimensional Conqueror SR	.60	1.25
BT12058 Raditz, Invader From Afar U	.15	.30
BT12059 Lord Slug, Monstrous Muscle SR	.75	1.50
BT12060 Lord Slug, Thwarter of Plans SR	.75	1.50
BT12061 Lord Slug, Conqueror Restored R	.20	.40
BT12062 Angila, Invader of Earth U	.15	.30
BT12063 Medamatcha, Invader of Earth R	.20	.40
BT12064 Wings, Invader of Earth R	.20	.40
BT12065 Zeiun C	.12	.25
BT12066 Kakuja C	.12	.25
BT12067 Gyoshu, Invader of Earth U	.15	.30
BT12068 Turles, Cosmic Rogue SPR	2.00	4.00
BT12068 Turles, Cosmic Rogue SR	1.00	2.00
BT12069 Turles, Crusher Corps Commander U	.15	.30
BT12070 Turles, Invader of Earth SR	2.50	5.00
BT12071 Amond, Invader of Earth C	.12	.25
BT12072 Daiz, Invader of Earth C	.12	.25
BT12073 Cacao, Invader of Earth C	.12	.25
BT12074 Rasin, Invader of Earth C	.12	.25
BT12075 Lakasei, Invader of Earth C	.12	.25
BT12076 Lord Slug, Out of Control U	.75	1.50
BT12077 Lord Slug, Dark Parasite R	2.00	4.00
BT12078 Turles, Chaotic Rampage U	.15	.30
BT12079 Turles, Dark Parasite R	.50	1.00
BT12080 Four-Star Ball, Parasitic Darkness C	.12	.25
BT12081 Six-Star Ball, Parasitic Darkness C	.12	.25
BT12082 The Tree of Might C	.12	.25
BT12083 Fruit of the Tree of Might R	.30	.75
BT12084 Kill Driver U	.15	.30
BT12085 Whis // Whis, Godly Mentor C	.12	.25
BT12086 Frieza // Frieza, Resurrected U	.15	.30
BT12087 Vados, Cosmic Aide U	.15	.30
BT12088 Ginyu, a New Transformation SPR	1.00	2.00
BT12088 Ginyu, a New Transformation SR	.50	1.00
BT12089 Son Goku, Deity's Disciple R	.20	.40
BT12090 Son Goku C	.12	.25
BT12091 Son Gohan, Stalling for Time C	.12	.25
BT12092 Vegeta, Deity's Disciple R	.20	.40
BT12093 Vegeta C	.12	.25
BT12094 Piccolo, Precision Strikes C	.12	.25
BT12095 Krillin, Making a Comeback C	.12	.25
BT12096 Master Roshi, Body of Steel C	.12	.25
BT12097 Bulma, Sending Out an SOS R	.20	.40
BT12098 Beerus, in Awe of the Golden Emperor R	.20	.40
BT12099 Whis, a Helping Hand SR	1.50	3.00
BT12100 Frieza, Divine Transformation SR	1.50	3.00
BT12101 Frieza, Trained at Last R	.20	.40
BT12102 Frieza, the Onslaught Begins U	.15	.30
BT12103 Frieza, Same Stuff Different Day C	.12	.25
BT12104 Sorbet, Commander of Frieza's Forces U	.15	.30
BT12105 Ginyu, One Last Body Change R	.20	.40
BT12106 Tagoma, Cold as Ice U	.15	.30
BT12107 Shisami, Frieza Force Elite U	.15	.30
BT12108 Omega Shenron, Allies Absorbed SPR	3.00	6.00
BT12108 Omega Shenron, Allies Absorbed SR	1.50	3.00
BT12109 Nuova Shenron, Flame Shot Unleashed SR	2.50	5.00
BT12110 Nuova Shenron, the Pyromancer U	.15	.30
BT12111 Rage Shenron, Electricity Absorbed C	.12	.25
BT12112 Rage Shenron, the Electromancer C	.12	.25
BT12113 Oceanus Shenron, the Anemancer SR	4.00	8.00
BT12114 Oceanus Shenron, Swift Spirals C	.12	.25
BT12115 Negative Energy Four-Star Ball C	.12	.25
BT12116 Negative Energy Five-Star Ball C	.12	.25
BT12117 Negative Energy Six-Star Ball C	.12	.25
BT12118 Spatial Transmission U	.15	.30
BT12119 Burning Spin U	.15	.30
BT12120 Dragon Thunder R	.20	.40
BT12121 Cutting-Edge Recovery Device C	.12	.25
BT12122 Son Goku & Vegeta // Gogeta, Fateful Fusion U	.15	.30
BT12123 Shroom & Salsa // Shroom & Salsa, Might of the Demon Gods C	.12	.25
BT12124 Paikuhan, Savior from Another Time SPR	2.50	5.00
BT12124 Paikuhan, Savior from Another Time SR	1.50	3.00
BT12125 Dabura, Dimensional Meddler U	.15	.30
BT12126 Towa, Dimensional Meddler C	.12	.25
BT12127 Son Goku, Catastrophic Premonition U	.15	.30
BT12128 Son Goku, True Fighting Spirit C	.50	1.00
BT12129 SS3 Son Gohan, Marvelous Might C	.12	.25
BT12130 Son Gohan, Catastrophic Premonition C	.12	.25
BT12131 Son Gohan, Brainy Backup C	.12	.25
BT12132 Vegeta, Catastrophic Premonition U	.15	.30
BT12133 Vegeta, True Fighting Spirit C	.12	.25
BT12134 SS3 Trunks, Marvelous Might C	.12	.25
BT12135 Trunks, Catastrophic Premonition C	.12	.25
BT12136 SS3 Gogeta, Marvelous Might SPR	6.00	12.00
BT12136 SS3 Gogeta, Marvelous Might SR	2.00	4.00
BT12137 Gogeta, Fearless Fusion R	2.50	5.00
BT12138 Gohanks, Marvelous Might R	.20	.40
BT12139 Gohanks, Master-Student Union R	.20	.40
BT12140 Dark Masked King, Devilish Dominator SR	7.50	15.00
BT12141 Towa, Dimensional Convoker U	.15	.30
BT12142 Chain Attack Gravy U	.15	.30
BT12143 Chain Attack Putine U	.15	.30
BT12144 Mechikabura, the King's Summons SR	1.25	2.50
BT12145 Shroom, a New Demon God R	.20	.40
BT12146 Shroom C	.12	.25
BT12147 Salsa, a New Demon God R	.20	.40
BT12148 Salsa C	.12	.25
BT12149 Temptation of the Mask R	.20	.40
BT12150 Dark King's Flash C	.12	.25
BT12151 Explosive Barrage Slash C	.12	.25
BT12152 Super Paikuhan, Might Manifested SCR	75.00	150.00
BT12153 Majin Buu, Incarnation of Demonic Evil SCR	100.00	200.00
BT12154 Supreme Kai of Time, Spacetime Unraveler SCR	200.00	400.00

2022 Dragon Ball Super 5th Anniversary

P211 Super Saiyan God Son Goku // SSGSS Son Goku, Soul Striker Reborn RE P	.15	.30
P337 Zamasu, the Eliminator RE P	.60	1.25
P360 Vegeta // SSG Vegeta, Crimson Warrior RE P	.12	.25
P398 Majin Buu, Tricky Nemesis RE P	.10	.20
EB126 Son Goku, the Long-Awaited Rematch RE R	.10	.20

BT3123 Hyper Evolution Super Saiyan 4 Son Goku SCR PE 7.50 15.00
BT3123 Hyper Evolution Super Saiyan 4 Son Goku SCR 12.50 25.00
BT6125 Broly, Ultimate Agent of Destruction SCR PE 12.50 25.00
BT6125 Broly, Ultimate Agent of Destruction SCR 20.00 40.00
BT7072 Hidden Power of the Saiyans RE U .12 .25
BT9076 Bibidi, Primeval Conjurer RE C .10 .20
BT9101 Full-Power Frieza, 100% Overdrive RE SR .15 .30
BT9111 Catastrophic Blow RE SR .15 .30
DB2030 Ultrasonic Exchange RE R .12 .25
EX2101 Hit, Ready to Brawl EX .75 1.50
EX2102 Pilaf, Mechanized Partnership EX .07 .15
EX2103 Android 18, With Reckless Abandon EX .12 .25
EX2104 SS Rose Goku Black, Mortals Become EX 2.00 4.00
EX2105 Majin Buu, Reshaping Regeneration EX .07 .15
EX2106 Bulma, Fighting for Vegeta EX .10 .20
EX2107 Frieza, Before the Fall EX .12 .25
EX2108 Ginyu, a Captain's Responsibility EX .15 .30
EX2109 Prince of Destruction Vegeta, Proud Defiance EX .07 .10
EX2110 Son Gohan, In Earth's Defense EX .12 .25
EX2111 Dyspo, Hyperspeed Strike EX .10 .20
EX2112 SS3 Gotenks, Invincible Fists EX .30 .60
EX2113 Hatchhyack, Saiyan Exterminator EX .15 .30
EX2114 Putine, Schemes Most Wicked EX .07 .10
EX2115 Masked Saiyan, Belligerent Warrior EX .60 1.25
EX2116 Chilled, Ruling Through Fear EX .12 .25
EX2117 Piccolo, Three Moves Ahead EX .30 .75
EX2118 Cell, Unending Despair EX .12 .25
EX2119 SSB Vegito, a New Look EX .20 .40
EX2120 SS Gogeta, Facing Fierce Foes EX .30 .60
EX2121 Ultra Instinct Son Goku, Unthinking Onslaught EX .30 .60
EX2122 Janemba, New Depths of Evil EX .07 .15
EX2123 Whis, From on High EX .20 .40
EX2124 SS Caulifla, Tenacious Spirit EX .07 .15
EX2125 Majin Buu, the Insatiable EX .07 .10
EX2126 SS Son Goku, Awakened by Rage EX .20 .40
EX2127 SS Vegito, Ready When You Are EX .75 1.50
EX2128 Fused Zamasu, Righteous Iniquity EX .75 1.50
EX2129 SS Son Gohan, Come What May EX .20 .40
EX2130 Frieza, Just a WarmUp EX .07 .10
EX2131 SS3 Broly, Surpassing Legend EX .15 .30
EX2132 SS Son Goku, For the Mission EX .07 .15
EX2133 Towa, Unpredictable Offense EX .10 .20
EX2134 SS Broly, the Demon Revived EX .25 .50
EX2135 Super Baby 1, Parasitic Comeuppance EX .20 .40
EX2136 Hit, Pursuing Improvement EX .12 .25
SD1401 Vegeta: Xeno & Trunks Xeno // Vegeks, the Unsung Fusion Hero RE R .12 .25
BT11028 Planet Vampa RE R .12 .25
BT11058 Planet Tuffle RE C .10 .20
BT11064 Dark Broly, Overwhelming Evil RE SR .12 .25
BT11088 The Majin Quickening RE C .10 .20
BT11091 Son Gohan // Son Gohan & Hire-Dragon, Boundless Friendship RE U .12 .25
BT11122 Dark Broly & Paragus // Dark Broly & Paragus, the Corrupted RE U .12 .25
BT11133 Dark Broly, Demon Realm Ravager RE R .15 .30
BT11134 Dark Broly, Uncontrollable Berserker RE SR .15 .30
BT11135 Dark Broly, the New Masked Saiyan RE U .15 .30
BT11153 Baby Hatchhyack, Saiyan Destroyer SCR PE 7.50 15.00
BT11153 Baby Hatchhyack, Saiyan Destroyer SCR 10.00 20.00
BT12082 The Tree of Might RE C .10 .20
BT12128 Son Goku, True Fighting Spirit RE C .15 .30
BT13028 Young Invaders RE C .12 .25
BT13060 Galactic Buster RE SR .15 .30
BT13124 Black Smoke Dragon, Offering of Destruction RE U .12 .25
BT13139 Demon God Towa, Offering of the Dark Dragon Balls RE C .12 .25
BT14061 Videl // Videl, the Town's Heroine RE C .12 .25
BT14087 Power Beyond Super Saiyan 2 RE C .07 .15
BT14140 Ultimate Dark Dragon-Slaying Bullet RE SR .12 .25
BT15057 Universe 6, Assemble! RE R .07 .15
BT15066 Kaio-Ken Son Goku, Decisive Battle RE SR .15 .30
BT15068 Kaio-Ken Son Goku, Confronting Invasion RE C .12 .25
BT15069 Training Goals Son Goku RE R .12 .25
BT15088 King Kai's Planet RE C .12 .25
BT15089 King Kai's Training RE C .12 .25
BT16098 Dabura // Demon God Dabura, Diabolical Awakening RE U .07 .15

2022 Dragon Ball Super Collector's Selection Vol. 2

P211 Super Saiyan God Son Goku // SSGSS Son Goku, Soul Striker Reborn 6.00 12.00
P219 SS2 Trunks, Heroic Prospect 2.00 4.00
P263 Masked Saiyan, Brainwashed No More 2.00 4.00
P276 Son Goku & Vegeta, Saiyan Synergy 10.00 20.00
P286 SS3 Gogeta, Martial Melee 2.00 4.00
P331 Mecha Frieza, Robotic Riposte 20.00 40.00
BT9090 Nappa, Demolition Man 1.50 3.00
BT9091 Zamasu, Sacred Disbelief 4.00 8.00
BT9096 Whis, Celestial Moderator 1.00 2.00
BT9099 Android 18, Bionic Blitz 7.50 15.00
BT9107 Beerus, Divine Obliterator 7.50 15.00
BT9115 Dr. Gero, Progenitor of Terror .60 1.25
DB2039 Energetic Frenzy Kefla 1.25 2.50
DB3003 Son Goku, Nimbus Master 1.25 2.50
TB1052 Son Goku, Hope of Universe 7 2.50 5.00
BT10075 Frieza, Charismatic Villain 6.00 12.00
BT11030 Violent Rays 5.00 10.00
BT12013 Launch, the Pure-Hearted 3.00 6.00

2022 Dragon Ball Super Dawn of the Z-Legends

BT1111 SSB Kaio-Ken Son Goku, United Divinity SCR 75.00 150.00
BT18001 Son Goku & Vegeta/SS4 Son Goku & SS4 Vegeta, In It Together U .10 .20
BT18002 One-Star Ball/Syn Shenron, Despair Made Manifest U .07 .12
BT18003 SS4 Gogeta, the Ultimate Fusion U .07 .15
BT18004 Omega Shenron, Merciless Negativity U .07 .12
BT18005 Rush Attack SSB Vegeta SR 1.25 2.50
BT18006 SS4 Gogeta, Power's Connection SPR 4.00 8.00
BT18006 SS4 Gogeta, Power's Connection SR 7.50 15.00
BT18007 Omega Shenron, Assimilating Evil R .12 .25
BT18008 Great Ape Son Goku, the Aggressor C .15 .30
BT18009 Pan, United Emotion R .40 .80
BT18010 SS4 Son Goku, Rivalry United U .25 .50
BT18011 SS4 Son Goku, Digging Deep R .25 .50
BT18012 SS4 Son Goku, Preparing to Brawl C .10 .20
BT18013 SS Son Goku C .07 .12
BT18014 Pan C .07 .12
BT18015 SS4 Vegeta, Rivalry United U .15 .30
BT18016 SS4 Vegeta, Searching for Rivals R .25 .50
BT18017 SS4 Vegeta, Preparing to Brawl C .10 .20
BT18018 Vegeta, Lone Saiyan Warrior U .12 .25
BT18019 SS4 Gogeta, Triumphant Together SPR 1.00 2.00
BT18019 SS4 Gogeta, Triumphant Together SR 2.00 4.00
BT18020 Omega Shenron, Unfeeling Retribution SPR .75 1.50
BT18020 Omega Shenron, Unfeeling Retribution SR 2.50 5.00
BT18021 Syn Shenron, Dread Destroyer R .20 .40
BT18022 Haze Shenron, Gathering Evil C .07 .15
BT18023 Eis Shenron, Reanimating Evil C .07 .15
BT18024 Nuova Shenron, Tenacious Evil U .12 .25
BT18025 Rage Shenron, Impenetrable Evil R .17 .35
BT18026 Oceanus Shenron, Assembling Evil C .07 .15
BT18027 Super Naturon Shenron, Congregating Evil C .07 .10
BT18028 Minus Energy Power Ball C .07 .15
BT18029 Cracked Dragon Ball C .12 .25
BT18030 Son Goku/Son Goku, Another World Fighter U .07 .10
BT18031 Paikuhan/Paikuhan, West Galaxy Warrior U .07 .12
BT18032 Paikuhan, Depthless Skill U .07 .12
BT18033 SS Son Goku, Awakened Onslaught R .25 .50
BT18034 Cell, Awakening of the Created R 2.50 5.00
BT18035 Vegeta, Another World Warrior C .07 .10
BT18036 Super Paikuhan, True Master R .12 .25
BT18037 SS Son Goku, Another World Blitz SPR .75 1.50
BT18037 SS Son Goku, Another World Blitz SR 2.00 4.00
BT18038 SS Son Goku Vs. Paikuhan, Dead Heat SPR .20 .40
BT18038 SS Son Goku Vs. Paikuhan, Dead Heat SR .75 1.50
BT18039 North Kai, Here to Cheer U .07 .10
BT18040 Paikuhan, Another World Champ SPR .10 .20
BT18040 Paikuhan, Another World Champ SR .30 .60
BT18041 Paikuhan, Testing the Opposition R .10 .20
BT18042 Paikuhan, Glimpse of Might C .07 .10
BT18043 Mijorin, North Galaxy Warrior U .07 .10
BT18044 Sarta, North Galaxy Warrior R .07 .10
BT18045 Olibu, North Galaxy Warrior R .07 .15
BT18046 South Kai C .07 .10
BT18047 West Kai, Impending Crash C .07 .10
BT18048 East Kai C .07 .10
BT18049 Grand Kai, Grandest of All U .07 .12
BT18050 Frieza, Hellish Hellraiser C .07 .10
BT18051 Cell, Hellish Hellraiser C .07 .10
BT18052 Beerus, the Visitor U .10 .20
BT18053 Whis, the Visitor C .07 .10
BT18054 SSB Son Goku, Help from the Past C .07 .15
BT18055 SSB Vegeta, Help from the Past C .10 .20
BT18056 Angel Halo C .07 .10
BT18057 Thunder Flash U .07 .10
BT18058 Another World Budokai Finals C .07 .10
BT18059 Master Roshi/Son Goku, Krillin, Yamcha, & Master Roshi, Reunited U .12 .25
BT18060 King Piccolo/King Piccolo, World Conquest Awaits U .07 .10
BT18061 Piccolo Jr., Vengeful Awakening U .07 .15
BT18062 Son Goku, Krillin, & Yamcha, Turtle School Inheritors R .10 .20
BT18063 Frieza, Resurrected Ambition R 3.00 6.00
BT18064 Yurin, Crane School Witchcraft Master C .07 .15
BT18065 Piccolo, Guardian of Earth SPR 2.00 4.00
BT18065 Piccolo, Guardian of Earth SR 3.00 6.00
BT18066 Son Goku, Training's Beginning C .07 .15
BT18067 Krillin, Training's Beginning C .07 .15
BT18068 Yamcha, Training's Beginning C .07 .15
BT18069 Son Goku, Fated Rival SPR 10.00 20.00
BT18069 Son Goku, Fated Rival SR 6.00 12.00
BT18070 Son Goku, Skills Improved U .10 .20
BT18071 Krillin, Skills Improved R .12 .25
BT18072 Yamcha, Skills Improved U .07 .15
BT18073 Tien Shinhan, Head-To-Head U .07 .10
BT18074 Chiaotzu C .07 .10
BT18075 Chi-Chi, Promise Fulfilled C .07 .15
BT18076 Piccolo Jr., Fated Rival SPR 3.00 6.00
BT18076 Piccolo Jr., Fated Rival SR 1.25 2.50
BT18077 Pilaf, Shu, & Mai, Madcap Miscalculation C .07 .10
BT18078 King Piccolo, Newly Youthful Conqueror R .12 .25
BT18079 King Piccolo, Seal Undone R .17 .35
BT18080 Tambourine, Demonic Subordinate C .07 .15
BT18081 Cymbal, Demonic Subordinate C .07 .15
BT18082 Drum, Demonic Subordinate U .07 .15
BT18083 Piano, Faithful Aide C .07 .10
BT18084 Piccolo Jr., Vengeance Reborn U .07 .10
BT18085 SS Son Goten & SS Trunks, Unfurled Potential C .12 .25
BT18086 SS Gotenks, Beyond Serious R .25 .50
BT18087 Master Roshi's Training C .07 .15
BT18088 A Demon Is Born C .07 .10
BT18089 Bardock's Crew/Bardock, Inherited Will U .07 .15
BT18090 Piccolo/Piccolo, Facing New Foes U .07 .12
BT18091 Bardock, Saiyan Determination U .07 .15
BT18092 Son Gohan, Facing New Foes R .30 .60
BT18093 SSB Son Goku, Evolved Defender SR .75 1.50
BT18094 Gine, for the Sake of Family C .10 .20
BT18095 Pan, Facing New Foes R .17 .35
BT18096 Great Ape Son Goku, Instincts Unleashed R .40 .80
BT18097 Bulma, Searching for Adventure C .10 .20
BT18098 Great Ape Tora, Saiyan Potential R .17 .35
BT18099 Tora, Feelings Bequeathed C .07 .15
BT18100 Great Ape Fasha C .07 .12
BT18101 Fasha, Feelings Bequeathed C .07 .15
BT18102 Great Ape Shugesh, Saiyan Potential U .15 .30
BT18103 Shugesh, Feelings Bequeathed C .07 .15
BT18104 Great Ape Borgos, Saiyan Potential U .12 .25
BT18105 Borgos, Feelings Bequeathed C .07 .15
BT18106 Great Ape Bardock, Saiyan Potential R .20 .40
BT18107 Bardock, Inherited Might SPR .75 1.50
BT18107 Bardock, Inherited Might SR .17 .35
BT18108 Bardock, Crew Leader C .07 .15
BT18109 Son Gohan, Flash of Brilliance SPR 1.00 2.00
BT18109 Son Gohan, Flash of Brilliance SR .75 1.50
BT18110 SS Son Gohan, Guardian of Earth R .15 .30
BT18111 Son Gohan, Parental Love U .07 .15
BT18112 Son Goten, Growing Up Fast C .07 .10
BT18113 Pan, Inherited Bloodline SPR 1.25 2.50
BT18113 Pan, Inherited Bloodline SR 1.00 2.00
BT18114 Pan, Growing Up Fast U .10 .20
BT18115 Piccolo, Namekian Pride C .07 .15
BT18116 Piccolo, Heart of a Teacher C .07 .15
BT18117 Trunks, Growing Up Fast U .07 .15
BT18118 Bulma C .07 .10
BT18119 Gone but Not Forgotten C .07 .15
BT18120 A Saiyan's Willpower C .07 .10
BT18121 For the Sake of Family C .07 .10
BT18122 Shroom & Salsa/Demon God Shroom & Salsa, Deadly Genius U .07 .10
BT18123 Demon God Shroom & Demon God Salsa, Imminent Annihilation U .07 .15
BT18124 Demon God Demigra, Begrudging Ally R .15 .30
BT18125 Demon God Putine & Demon God Gravy, Treacherous Intel C .10 .20
BT18126 SS Bardock C .07 .15
BT18127 Supreme Kai of Time, Final Battle at Hand C .07 .10
BT18128 Dark Broly, Heartless Berserker C .25 .50
BT18129 Dark King Mechikabura, Imminent Annihilation R .15 .30
BT18130 Dark King Mechikabura, Final Battle at Hand C .07 .15
BT18131 Demon God Shroom, Demonic Invitation R .12 .25
BT18132 Demon God Shroom, Dark King's Vanguard U .07 .15
BT18133 Demon God Shroom & Demon God Salsa, Unending Nightmare SR .20 .40
BT18134 Demon God Salsa, Stormclad R .10 .20
BT18135 Demon God Salsa, Dark King's Vanguard U .07 .15
BT18136 Demon God Salsa, Dark Combination U .07 .15
BT18137 King Vegeta C .07 .10
BT18138 Reaper's Cunning C .07 .15
BT18139 Genius's Craft C .07 .15
BT18140 Begrudging Allies C .07 .15
BT18141 Cooler, Calculated Warrior R .15 .30
BT18142 Son Goku, Power Untold U .10 .20
BT18143 SS4 Gogeta, Indomitable Might SPR 2.50 5.00
BT18143 SS4 Gogeta, Indomitable Might SR 4.00 8.00
BT18144 Android 18, Measureless Strength SPR 4.00 8.00
BT18144 Android 18, Measureless Strength SR 7.50 15.00
BT18145 Hirudegarn, Accursed Destroyer SR .40 .80
BT18146 Bardock, Saiyan Warrior R .10 .20
BT18147 SS4 Vegito, A Light in the Dark SCR 75.00 150.00
BT18148 Bardock, Origin of the Legend GDR 750.00 1,500.00
BT18148 Bardock, Origin of the Legend SCR 30.00 75.00

2022 Dragon Ball Super Dawn of the Z-Legends Pre-Release

BT18001 Son Goku & Vegeta/SS4 Son Goku & SS4 Vegeta, In It Together U .15 .30
BT18002 One-Star Ball/Syn Shenron, Despair Made Manifest U .15 .30
BT18003 SS4 Gogeta, the Ultimate Fusion U .15 .30
BT18004 Omega Shenron, Merciless Negativity U .15 .30
BT18007 Omega Shenron, Assimilating Evil R .20 .40
BT18009 Pan, United Emotion R .20 .40
BT18010 SS4 Son Goku, Rivalry United U .15 .30
BT18011 SS4 Son Goku, Digging Deep R .20 .40
BT18015 SS4 Vegeta, Rivalry United U .15 .30
BT18016 SS4 Vegeta, Searching for Rivals R .20 .40
BT18018 Vegeta, Lone Saiyan Warrior U .15 .30
BT18021 Syn Shenron, Dread Destroyer R .20 .40
BT18024 Nuova Shenron, Tenacious Evil U .15 .30
BT18025 Rage Shenron, Impenetrable Evil R .20 .40
BT18030 Son Goku/Son Goku, Another World Fighter U .15 .30
BT18031 Paikuhan/Paikuhan, West Galaxy Warrior U .15 .30
BT18032 Paikuhan, Depthless Skill U .15 .30
BT18033 SS Son Goku, Awakened Onslaught R .20 .40
BT18034 Cell, Awakening of the Created R .20 .40
BT18036 Super Paikuhan, True Master R .20 .40
BT18039 North Kai, Here to Cheer U .15 .30
BT18041 Paikuhan, Testing the Opposition R .20 .40
BT18043 Mijorin, North Galaxy Warrior U .15 .30
BT18044 Sarta, North Galaxy Warrior R .20 .40
BT18045 Olibu, North Galaxy Warrior R .20 .40
BT18049 Grand Kai, Grandest of All U .15 .30
BT18052 Beerus, the Visitor U .15 .30
BT18057 Thunder Flash U .15 .30
BT18059 Master Roshi/Son Goku, Krillin, Yamcha, & Master Roshi, Reunited U .15 .30
BT18060 King Piccolo/King Piccolo, World Conquest Awaits U .15 .30
BT18061 Piccolo Jr., Vengeful Awakening U .15 .30
BT18062 Son Goku, Krillin, & Yamcha, Turtle School Inheritors R .20 .40
BT18063 Frieza, Resurrected Ambition R .20 .40
BT18070 Son Goku, Skills Improved U .15 .30
BT18071 Krillin, Skills Improved R .20 .40
BT18072 Yamcha, Skills Improved U .15 .30
BT18073 Tien Shinhan, Head-To-Head U .15 .30
BT18078 King Piccolo, Newly Youthful Conqueror R .20 .40
BT18079 King Piccolo, Seal Undone R .20 .40
BT18082 Drum, Demonic Subordinate U .15 .30
BT18084 Piccolo Jr., Vengeance Reborn U .15 .30
BT18086 SS Gotenks, Beyond Serious R .20 .40
BT18089 Bardock's Crew/Bardock, Inherited Will U .15 .30
BT18090 Piccolo/Piccolo, Facing New Foes U .15 .30
BT18091 Bardock, Saiyan Determination U .15 .30
BT18092 Son Gohan, Facing New Foes R .20 .40
BT18095 Pan, Facing New Foes R .20 .40
BT18096 Great Ape Son Goku, Instincts Unleashed R .20 .40
BT18098 Great Ape Tora, Saiyan Potential R .20 .40
BT18102 Great Ape Shugesh, Saiyan Potential U .15 .30
BT18104 Great Ape Borgos, Saiyan Potential U .15 .30
BT18106 Great Ape Bardock, Saiyan Potential R .20 .40
BT18110 SS Son Gohan, Guardian of Earth R .20 .40
BT18111 Son Gohan, Parental Love U .15 .30
BT18114 Pan, Growing Up Fast U .15 .30
BT18117 Trunks, Growing Up Fast U .15 .30
BT18122 Shroom & Salsa/Demon God Shroom & Salsa, Deadly Genius U .15 .30
BT18123 Demon God Shroom & Demon God Salsa, Imminent Annihilation U .15 .30
BT18124 Demon God Demigra, Begrudging Ally R .20 .40
BT18129 Dark King Mechikabura, Imminent Annihilation R .20 .40
BT18131 Demon God Shroom, Demonic Invitation R .20 .40
BT18132 Demon God Shroom, Dark King's Vanguard U .15 .30
BT18134 Demon God Salsa, Stormclad R .20 .40
BT18135 Demon God Salsa, Dark King's Vanguard U .15 .30
BT18136 Demon God Salsa, Dark Combination U .15 .30
BT18141 Cooler, Calculated Warrior R .20 .40
BT18142 Son Goku, Power Untold U .15 .30
BT18146 Bardock, Saiyan Warrior R .20 .40

2022 Dragon Ball Super Expansion Deck Box Set 20 Ultimate Deck

EB137 Homicidal Clones C .30 .75
XD302 Cell, Genetic Consumption STR .07 .15
XD304 Android 17, Impending Crisis FOIL C .07 .15
XD309 Cell, Perfection Misspent STR .12 .25
XD310 Cell, Perfection Reclaimed STR .10 .20
BT2084 Perfect Force Cell SR .20 .40
BT5075 Shocking Death Ball FOIL C .12 .25
BT9099 Android 18, Bionic Blitz C .15 .30
EX2001 Cell // Cell, Return of the Ultimate Lifeform XR .20 .40
EX2002 Dr. Gero, Evil's Activation XR .12 .25
EX2003 Android 17, Absorption Imminent XR .15 .30
EX2004 Android 17 & Android 18, Absorption Imminent XR .15 .30
EX2005 Android 18, Absorption Imminent XR .15 .30
EX2006 Cell, Startling Assimilation XR .20 .40
EX2007 Cell, Absorption Onslaught XR .15 .30
EX2008 Wretched Regeneration XR .25 .50
EX2009 Cell, Unending Torrent XR .20 .40
EX2010 Cell, Dawn of Despair XR .15 .30
BT10075 Frieza, Charismatic Villain FOIL SR .75 1.50
BT11063 SS3 Vegito, Peerless Warrior FOIL R .15 .30

2022 Dragon Ball Super Fighter's Ambition

BT19001 Son Goku & Vegeta & Trunks // SS Son Goku, SS Vegeta, & SS Trunks, the Ultimate Team U .07 .15
BT19002 Gero's Supercomputer // Android 13, Terror's Inception U .07 .15
BT19003 SS Son Goku, United Onslaught U .07 .15
BT19004 Android 13, Nightmarish Combination U .07 .15
BT19005 Son Gohan, at the Ready U .10 .20
BT19006 Android 14 & Android 15, Team-Up Terrors R .15 .30
BT19007 Mercenary Tao, Villainous Threat C .07 .15
BT19008 SS Son Goku, Spirit Bomb Absorbed SPR 2.50 5.00
BT19008 SS Son Goku, Spirit Bomb Absorbed SR .30 .60
BT19009 SS Son Goku, Evolved Offensive R .15 .30
BT19010 Son Goku, at the Ready C .10 .20
BT19011 SS Son Goku, SS Vegeta, & SS Trunks, Triple Combination SPR 10.00 20.00
BT19011 SS Son Goku, SS Vegeta, & SS Trunks, Triple Combination SR 4.00 8.00
BT19012 Son Gohan C .07 .10
BT19013 SS Vegeta, Evolved Offensive R .12 .25
BT19014 Vegeta, at the Ready C .07 .15
BT19015 SS Trunks, Evolved Offensive R .10 .20
BT19016 Trunks, at the Ready C .07 .15
BT19017 Piccolo, at the Ready R .12 .25
BT19018 Krillin, at the Ready U .10 .20

BT19019 Android 13, Total Annihilator SR .25 .50
BT19019 Android 13, Total Annihilator SPR .75 1.50
BT19020 Android 13, Villainous Threat C .10 .20
BT19021 Android 13, Uninvited Guest R .25 .50
BT19022 Android 14, Uninvited Guest U .12 .25
BT19023 Android 14, Mechanical Assailant C .07 .15
BT19024 Android 15, Uninvited Guest U .10 .20
BT19025 Android 15, Mechanical Assailant C .07 .15
BT19026 Android 17, Finally Freed R .15 .30
BT19027 Android 18 C .07 .15
BT19028 Android 20, Inherited Evil U .15 .30
BT19029 SS Broly, Returning Villainous Threat C .07 .15
BT19030 Spirit Bomb Unleashed C .07 .15
BT19031 S.S. Deadly Bomber C .07 .15
BT19032 Forgotten Capsules C .07 .15
BT19033 Android Assault C .07 .15
BT19034 Son Gohan // Son Gohan, Former Glory Regained U .10 .20
BT19035 Son Goten & Trunks // Gotenks, Fusion Hiccup U .07 .10
BT19036 Beerus, Airy Annihilator SR 5.00 10.00
BT19037 Son Goku, Stronger Together SR .75 1.50
BT19038 Vegeta, Stronger Together R .15 .30
BT19039 Son Goten, Tournament Competitor C .07 .10
BT19040 Trunks, Tournament Competitor C .07 .15
BT19041 Boujack, Villainous threat C .07 .15
BT19042 Janemba, Villainous Threat C .10 .20
BT19043 Hirudegarn, Villainous threat C .07 .15
BT19044 Red Ribbon Robot, Villainous threat C .07 .15
BT19045 Son Goku, Interplanitary Training U .12 .25
BT19046 Son Goku C .07 .10
BT19047 Son Goku, Daily Diligence U .07 .15
BT19048 Son Goku & Vegeta, Immortal Rivalry SPR 6.00 12.00
BT19048 Son Goku & Vegeta, Immortal Rivalry SR .75 1.50
BT19049 Son Gohan, Power Unshackled R .75 1.50
BT19050 SS Son Gohan, Wrathful Awakening U .10 .20
BT19051 SS Son Gohan C .07 .10
BT19052 Son Goten, Fast Improving C .07 .10
BT19053 Son Goten, Tenacious Tag-Team U .07 .10
BT19054 Son Goten, Developing Teamwork U .07 .15
BT19055 Pan, Glimpse of Talent C .12 .25
BT19056 Vegeta, Interplanetary Training R .20 .40
BT19057 Vegeta, Daily Diligence C .07 .15
BT19058 Trunks, Tenacious Tag-Team U .07 .15
BT19059 Trunks, Developing Teamwork U .10 .20
BT19060 Gotenks, Reckless Rush R .07 .15
BT19061 Piccolo, the Infiltrator SR 7.50 15.00
BT19062 Android 18, Here to Assist C .07 .10
BT19063 Gamma 1, New Hero R .12 .25
BT19064 Gamma 2, New Hero R .12 .25
BT19065 Decisive Strike R .30 .60
BT19066 A Wild Fighter Is Born R .07 .15
BT19067 Veku // Gogeta, Fusion Complete U .07 .15
BT19068 Broly // Broly, the Ultimate Saiyan U .07 .10
BT19069 SSB Gogeta, Supreme Fusion U .07 .15
BT19070 SS Broly, Awakened Might U .07 .15
BT19071 Jiren, the Immovable SR 2.50 5.00
BT19072 Bulma, a Humble Wish R .12 .25
BT19073 Cheelai, Dependable Friend R .12 .25
BT19074 Lemo, Dependable Friend R .12 .25
BT19075 Turles, Villainous Threat C .07 .15
BT19076 Bio-Broly, Villainous Threat C .07 .15
BT19077 SSG Son Goku, Crimson Impact U .12 .25
BT19078 SS Son Goku, All-Out Evolution C .07 .15
BT19079 Son Goku, Limbering Up C .10 .20
BT19080 SSB Son Goku & SSB Vegeta, Team Attack R .15 .30
BT19081 SSG Vegeta, Crimson Impact U .12 .25
BT19082 SS Vegeta, All-Out Evolution C .10 .20
BT19083 Vegeta, Limbering Up C .10 .20
BT19084 SSB Gogeta, Limits Broken SR .75 1.50
BT19084 SSB Gogeta, Limits Broken SPR 2.50 5.00
BT19085 SS Gogeta, Facing the Ultimate R .15 .30
BT19086 Gogeta, Battle's Beginning U .15 .30
BT19087 Piccolo C .07 .15
BT19088 SS Broly, Full Power Frenzy SR .40 .80
BT19088 SS Broly, Full Power Frenzy SPR 7.50 15.00
BT19089 SS Broly, Villainous Threat C .07 .15
BT19090 Broly, Bestial Rage U .10 .20
BT19091 Paragus, Issuing Orders C .07 .15
BT19092 Whis's Capriciousness C .10 .20
BT19093 Cheelai's Aid C .07 .15
BT19094 Control Ring's Restraint U .10 .20
BT19095 Training with Ba R .25 .50
BT19096 Out of Control Power R .25 .50
BT19097 Cunning Murder C .07 .15
BT19098 True Power Awakened SR .60 1.25
BT19098 True Power Awakened SPR 7.50 15.00
BT19099 Wishing to End the Battle U .10 .20
BT19100 Lord Slug // Lord Slug, in His Prime U .07 .10
BT19101 Piccolo // Piccolo, Yet Unseen Power U .10 .20
BT19102 Lord Slug, Colossal Conqueror U .07 .15
BT19103 Piccolo, Power Unyielding U .07 .15
BT19104 Angila, Defensive Prowess R .12 .25
BT19105 Krillin, Trusty Assistance C .07 .15
BT19106 Shenron, Granter of Wishes R .20 .40
BT19107 Guru, For All Namekians C .07 .15
BT19108 Son Gohan & Piccolo, Training's Beginnings R .20 .40
BT19109 Son Gohan & Piccolo, Desperate Defense C .07 .15
BT19110 Piccolo, Moon Destroyer C .07 .15
BT19111 Garlic Jr., Villainous Threat C .07 .15
BT19112 Lord Slug, Colossal Destroyer SPR .50 1.00
BT19112 Lord Slug, Colossal Destroyer SR .10 .20
BT19113 Lord Slug, Cruel Overlord R .12 .25
BT19114 Lord Slug, Villainous Threat C .07 .15
BT19115 Lord Slug, Craving for Youth SR .25 .50
BT19116 Angila, Restricting Options C .07 .15
BT19117 Angila, Lord Slug's Henchman U .07 .15
BT19118 Medamatcha, Body Splitter C .07 .15
BT19119 Medamatcha, Lord Slug's Henchman U .07 .15
BT19120 Wings, Lord Slug's Henchman U .10 .20
BT19121 Zeiun C .10 .20
BT19122 Kakuja, Scientist of Lord Slug U .07 .15
BT19123 Gyoshu, Scientist of Lord Slug U .07 .15
BT19124 Son Gohan & Piccolo, Master-Student Bond C .07 .10
BT19125 Piccolo, Mentor's Rage R .12 .25
BT19126 Golden Frieza, Villainous Threat C .10 .20
BT19127 Son Gohan & Piccolo, Moment's Respite C .07 .15
BT19128 Son Gohan & Piccolo, Full-Power Training SR .30 .60
BT19129 Son Gohan & Piccolo, Master-Student Combination SR .25 .50
BT19130 Pan, Remarkable Improvement C .07 .15
BT19131 Piccolo, New Evolution R .15 .30
BT19132 Cling to Life C .07 .10
BT19133 Gohan Whistles C .07 .10
BT19134 Son Goku, Power of Friendship R .10 .20
BT19135 Bulma, First Ally U .07 .15
BT19136 Android 8, Kindhearted Friend R .10 .20
BT19137 King Gurumes, Villainous Threat C .07 .15
BT19138 Lucifer, Villainous Threat C .07 .15
BT19139 Broly, Villainous Threat C .07 .15
BT19140 Black Smoke Dragon, Accumulated Negativity SR 10.00 20.00
BT19141 Black Masked Saiyan, Assassin from the Darkness SPR 2.50 5.00
BT19141 Black Masked Saiyan, Assassin from the Darkness SR .40 .80
BT19142 Cooler, Villainous Threat C .07 .15
BT19143 Beerus, Villainous Threat C .07 .15
BT19144 Dr. Uiro, Villainous Threat C .07 .15
BT19145 Son Gohan & Piccolo, Heroic Team SPR 15.00 30.00
BT19145 Son Gohan & Piccolo, Heroic Team SR 1.00 2.00
BT19146 Meta-Cooler, Villainous Threat C .07 .15
BT19147 Son Gohan, Hostile Saiyan Encounter SGR 7.50 15.00
BT19148 Son Gohan, Dependable Young Fighter SGR 2.50 5.00
BT19149 Son Gohan, Facing the Android Terror SGR 7.50 15.00
BT19150 Son Gohan, Latent Power Unleashed SGR 12.50 25.00
BT19151 Son Gohan, Power Reclaimed SGR 15.00 30.00
BT19152 Son Gohan, Beyond the Ultimate SCR 175.00 350.00
BT19153 Cell Max, Deliverer of Despair SCR 75.00 150.00
BT19154 Evil Saiyan, Malice Made Flesh SCR 100.00 200.00

2022 Dragon Ball Super Mythic Booster

P019 Ginyu, The Reliable Captain C .07 .15
P055 Dark Temptation Towa C .10 .20
P056 Supreme Kai of Time, Light's Guide C .07 .10
P059 Ultimate Form Son Goku C .07 .15
P063 Glory-Obsessed Prince of Destruction Vegeta C .07 .15
P065 Vegito, Super Warrior Reborn C .07 .15
P067 Bardock, Fully Unleashed C .07 .15
P068 Broly // Broly, Legend's Dawning C .07 .15
P069 Son Goku & Vegeta // Miracle Strike Gogeta C .07 .15
P082 Revived Ravager Vegeta C .07 .15
P128 Trunks, a Helping Blast C .07 .10
P169 Saiyan Technique Great Ape Vegeta C .07 .10
P172 Android 18, Full of Rage C .07 .10
P179 Son Goten, Awakening the Beast C .10 .20
P181 Broly // Broly, Surge of Brutality U .15 .30
P184 Kefla // Kefla, Surge of Ferocity U .10 .20
P185 Kefla, Everlasting Light C .12 .25
P198 Son Goku, Instincts Surpassed U .07 .15
P201 Frieza, Mutable Menace U .07 .10
P204 Bardock, Surge of Inspiration U .15 .30
P205 Broly, Swift Executioner U .07 .15
P206 SS Rose Goku Black, Divine Prosperity U .15 .30
P207 Whis, Ethereal Guidance U .15 .30
P209 Cooler, Clan Avenger U .07 .15
P210 Android 18, Perfection's Prey U .07 .15
P219 SS2 Trunks, Heroic Prospect R .12 .25
P223 Zarbon, Cosmic Elite U .10 .20
P244 Piccolo, Savior from Beyond C .07 .15
P248 Broly, Astonishing Potential R .07 .15
P260 Surprise Attack Naturon Shenron U .07 .15
P261 SS4 Bardock, Fighting Against Fate R .10 .20
P262 SS4 Son Goku, Beyond All Limits R .20 .40
P263 Masked Saiyan, Brainwashed No More R .07 .15
P274 Launch, Feminine Wiles R .10 .20
P308 SS3 Gogeta, Thwarting the Dark Empire R .15 .30
SD203 Unbreakable Super Saiyan Son Goku C .07 .10
SD205 Chain Attack Trunks C .07 .15
XD304 Android 17, Impending Crisis C .07 .15
BT1053 Senzu Bean C .30 .75
BT2064 Mafuba C .07 .10
BT5023 Afterimage Technique C .10 .20
BT5050 Dimension Magic C .15 .30
BT5075 Shocking Death Ball C .07 .15
BT5101 Time Magic C .10 .20
BT5115 Power Burst C .10 .20
BT5117 Dragon Ball C .10 .20
BT8104 Super Kamehameha C .07 .15
BT8136 SS4 Vegeta, Peak of Primitive Power SCR 3.00 6.00
BT9103 Cooler, Tyrannical Assault SR .15 .30
BT9137 Cell Xeno, Unspeakable Abomination SCR 10.00 20.00
DB1014 Toppo, Righteous Aid C .10 .20
DB1057 Fused Zamasu, Deity's Wrath SR .30 .60
DB1079 Final Spirit Cannon U .07 .10
DB2001 SSB Kaio-Ken Son Goku, Concentrated Destruction SR .75 1.50
DB2062 Dirty Burst SR 1.25 2.50
DB2126 Giant Ball SR .10 .20
DB2143 Koitsukai, Mechanical Courage SR .60 1.25
DB3003 Son Goku, Nimbus Master SR .15 .30
EX0401 SS Gogeta, Acrobatic Warrior C .07 .15
EX0403 SSB Gogeta, Resonant Explosion U .07 .15
SD1002 SS3 Son Goku, the Last Straw C .07 .10
TB3045 Cheelai, the Beautiful R .07 .15
TB3051 Vegeta, Striving to be the Best R .10 .20

2022 Dragon Ball Super Mythic Booster Gold Foil Stamped

P019 Ginyu, The Reliable Captain C .07 .15
P055 Dark Temptation Towa C .30 .60
P056 Supreme Kai of Time, Light's Guide C .12 .25
P059 Ultimate Form Son Goku C .30 .75
P063 Glory-Obsessed Prince of Destruction Vegeta C .30 .60
P065 Vegito, Super Warrior Reborn C .12 .25
P067 Bardock, Fully Unleashed C .20 .40
P068 Broly // Broly, Legend's Dawning C .25 .50
P069 Son Goku & Vegeta // Miracle Strike Gogeta C .75 1.50
P082 Revived Ravager Vegeta C .30 .75
P128 Trunks, a Helping Blast C .12 .25
P169 Saiyan Technique Great Ape Vegeta C .12 .25
P172 Android 18, Full of Rage C .20 .40
P179 Son Goten, Awakening the Beast C .07 .10
P181 Broly // Broly, Surge of Brutality U .50 1.00
P184 Kefla // Kefla, Surge of Ferocity U .25 .50
P185 Kefla, Everlasting Light C .20 .40
P198 Son Goku, Instincts Surpassed U 1.25 2.50
P201 Frieza, Mutable Menace U .20 .40
P204 Bardock, Surge of Inspiration U .20 .40
P205 Broly, Swift Executioner U .30 .75
P206 SS Rose Goku Black, Divine Prosperity U .75 1.50
P207 Whis, Ethereal Guidance U .25 .50
P209 Cooler, Clan Avenger U .30 .60
P210 Android 18, Perfection's Prey U .30 .60
P219 SS2 Trunks, Heroic Prospect R .40 .80
P223 Zarbon, Cosmic Elite U .40 .80
P244 Piccolo, Savior from Beyond C .25 .50
P248 Broly, Astonishing Potential R .25 .50
P260 Surprise Attack Naturon Shenron U .15 .30
P261 SS4 Bardock, Fighting Against Fate R .30 .60
P262 SS4 Son Goku, Beyond All Limits R 1.25 2.50
P263 Masked Saiyan, Brainwashed No More R .25 .50
P274 Launch, Feminine Wiles R .25 .50
P308 SS3 Gogeta, Thwarting the Dark Empire R .30 .60
SD203 Unbreakable Super Saiyan Son Goku C .60 1.25
SD205 Chain Attack Trunks C .25 .50
XD304 Android 17, Impending Crisis C .25 .50
BT1053 Senzu Bean C 7.50 15.00
BT2064 Mafuba C .30 .60
BT5023 Afterimage Technique C .75 1.50
BT5050 Dimension Magic C 2.50 5.00
BT5075 Shocking Death Ball C .30 .75
BT5101 Time Magic C .50 1.00
BT5115 Power Burst C .30 .75
BT5117 Dragon Ball C 1.00 2.00
BT8104 Super Kamehameha C .75 1.50
BT8136 SS4 Vegeta, Peak of Primitive Power SCR 15.00 30.00
BT9103 Cooler, Tyrannical Assault SR .30 .75
BT9137 Cell Xeno, Unspeakable Abomination SCR 20.00 40.00
DB1014 Toppo, Righteous Aid C .75 1.50
DB1057 Fused Zamasu, Deity's Wrath SR .75 1.50
DB1079 Final Spirit Cannon U .12 .25
DB2001 SSB Kaio-Ken Son Goku, Concentrated Destruction SR 1.00 2.00
DB2062 Dirty Burst SR 2.00 4.00
DB2126 Giant Ball SR .30 .60
DB2143 Koitsukai, Mechanical Courage SR 1.25 2.50
DB3003 Son Goku, Nimbus Master SR .25 .50
EX0401 SS Gogeta, Acrobatic Warrior C .75 1.50
EX0403 SSB Gogeta, Resonant Explosion U .75 1.50
SD1002 SS3 Son Goku, the Last Straw C .20 .40
TB3045 Cheelai, the Beautiful R .12 .25
TB3051 Vegeta, Striving to be the Best R .15 .30

2022 Dragon Ball Super Realm of the Gods

BT16001 Son Goku // Son Goku, Supreme Warrior U .10 .20
BT16002 Great Priest // Great Priest, Commander of Angels U .07 .15
BT16003 Golden Frieza & Android 17, Determined Tag Team U .07 .15
BT16004 Super Shenron, Universal Revival U .07 .15
BT16005 Son Goku, Ultra Mastery SPR 2.50 5.00
BT16005 Son Goku, Ultra Mastery SR .50 1.00
BT16006 Son Goku, Sign of Mastery R .25 .50
BT16007 Son Goku C .07 .15
BT16008 Android 17, for the Universe's Survival SR .75 1.50
BT16009 Android 17, Heeding the Call C .10 .20
BT16010 Golden Frieza, for the Universe's Survival U .12 .25
BT16011 Frieza, Universe 7 Combination U .20 .40
BT16012 SSB Vegeta, for the Universe's Survival R .15 .30
BT16013 Vegeta C .07 .15
BT16014 SS Son Goku, the Interceptor C .07 .15
BT16015 SS Vegeta, the Pursuer C .07 .15
BT16016 Spectate C .07 .15
BT16017 Erase a Universe C .07 .15
BT16018 Realm of the Gods - Ultra Instinct R .25 .50
BT16018 Realm of the Gods - Ultra Instinct SPR 2.50 5.00
BT16019 Universe 7 Unified U .07 .15
BT16020 Son Goku // SSG Son Goku, Crimson Warrior U .10 .20
BT16021 Whis // Whis, Invitation to Battle U .07 .15
BT16022 SSG Vegeta, Silent Strike SR .25 .50
BT16023 Great Priest, Invitation to Battle U .07 .15
BT16024 SSG Son Goku, Miraculous Transformation SPR 3.00 6.00
BT16024 SSG Son Goku, Miraculous Transformation SR 1.25 2.50
BT16025 Son Goku, Harnessed Power C .07 .15
BT16026 Son Gohan, the Interceptor C .07 .15
BT16027 Son Gohan, Harnessed Power C .07 .10
BT16028 SS Son Goten, the Interceptor R .10 .20
BT16029 Son Goten, Harnessed Power R .07 .10
BT16030 SS Vegeta, the Interceptor C .15 .30
BT16031 Vegeta, Harnessed Power C .07 .15
BT16032 SS Trunks, the Interceptor R .10 .20
BT16033 Trunks, Harnessed Power R .07 .10
BT16034 Videl, the Interceptor U .07 .15
BT16035 Videl, Harnessed Power U .20 .40
BT16036 Beerus, Ruthless Pursuer SR .40 .80
BT16037 Beerus, Aesthetic of Annihilation C .07 .15
BT16038 Beerus, Belligerent God C .07 .15
BT16039 Whis, Beerus's Backup C .07 .15
BT16040 Whis, Rejuvenating Support U .07 .15
BT16041 Moginan C .07 .15
BT16042 Planet Mogina Monster C .07 .15
BT16043 Carefree Playtime U .07 .10
BT16044 The Legend of SSG C .07 .10
BT16045 Realm of the Gods - Beerus Destroys R 2.50 5.00
BT16045 Realm of the Gods - Beerus Destroys SPR 6.00 12.00
BT16046 Beerus // Beerus, Victory at All Costs U .07 .15
BT16047 Champa // Champa, Victory at All Costs U .07 .15
BT16048 Whis, Pre-Fight Preparations U .10 .20
BT16049 Vados, Pre-Fight Preparations U .07 .15
BT16050 SSB Kaio-Ken Son Goku, Might's Calling SR 1.25 2.50
BT16051 SS Son Goku, to Battle Universe 6 U .10 .20
BT16052 SSB Vegeta, Lost Kingdom's Pride SPR 1.50 3.00
BT16052 SSB Vegeta, Lost Kingdom's Pride SR .50 1.00
BT16053 SS Vegeta, to Battle Universe 6 C .07 .10
BT16054 Piccolo, to Battle Universe 6 C .07 .10
BT16055 Majin Buu, to Battle Universe 6 U .15 .30
BT16056 Monaka, Universe 7's Ace C .07 .15
BT16057 Whis C .07 .15
BT16058 Vados C .07 .15
BT16059 SS Cabba, Wrathful Evolution U .07 .10
BT16060 Cabba, to Battle Universe 7 C .07 .10
BT16061 Hit, Assassin's Strike SPR 1.50 3.00
BT16061 Hit, Assassin's Strike SR .25 .50
BT16062 Hit, to Battle Universe 7 U .12 .25
BT16063 Botamo, to Battle Universe 7 C .07 .10
BT16064 Magetta, to Battle Universe 7 C .07 .15
BT16065 Frost, to Battle Universe 7 C .07 .10
BT16066 Referee, Introducing the Fighters C .07 .10
BT16067 Sibling Squabble R .07 .15
BT16068 The Nameless Planet C .07 .10
BT16069 Realm of the Gods - Champa Destroys R .20 .40
BT16069 Realm of the Gods - Champa Destroys SPR 1.25 2.50
BT16070 Damage Negation R .07 .15
BT16071 Trunks // SSB Vegeta & SS Trunks, Father-Son Onslaught U .07 .15
BT16072 Zamasu // SS Rose Goku Black, Wishes Fulfilled U .12 .25
BT16073 Mai, Opposing the Divine U .07 .15
BT16074 Rumsshi, Universe 10 Supporter U .10 .20
BT16075 SSB Son Goku, Future on the Line C .07 .15
BT16076 Son Goku, Facing Goku Black U .12 .25
BT16077 SSB Vegeta, Future on the Line R .25 .50
BT16078 SSB Vegeta, Fatherly Assistance U .12 .25
BT16079 Vegeta, Father-Son Teamwork C .10 .20
BT16080 SSB Vegeta & SS Trunks, Father-Son Bonds SPR 1.25 2.50
BT16080 SSB Vegeta & SS Trunks, Father-Son Bonds SR .30 .60
BT16081 SS2 Trunks, Future on the Line R .30 .60
BT16082 SS Trunks C .07 .15
BT16083 Trunks, Father-Son Teamwork C .10 .20
BT16084 Bulma, Future on the Line U .15 .30
BT16085 Yajirobe C .07 .15
BT16086 Gowasu, the Careless C .12 .25
BT16087 SS Rose Goku Black, Future on the Line SR .75 1.50
BT16088 Goku Black, Surpassing Time itself R .07 .15
BT16089 Zamasu, Self-Supported U .12 .25
BT16090 Zamasu, Plotting Eradication C .07 .15
BT16091 Zamasu, Mortal Loathing C .10 .20
BT16092 Realm of the Gods - Black Kamehameha R 1.50 3.00
BT16092 Realm of the Gods - Black Kamehameha SPR 7.50 15.00
BT16093 Coercion C .07 .15
BT16094 Body Steal C .07 .15
BT16095 United in Will C .07 .15
BT16096 Shadows Aligned C .07 .15
BT16097 Trunks // SSG Trunks, Crimson Warrior U .10 .20
BT16098 Dabura // Demon God Dabura, Diabolical Awakening U .07 .10
BT16099 Supreme Kai of Time, Opposing the Empire U .12 .25
BT16100 Dark King Mechikabura, Might Inconceivable SR .10 .20
BT16101 Son Goku, Challenging a Demon God C .10 .20
BT16102 Son Gohan C .07 .10
BT16103 Son Gohan, Challenging a Demon God R .20 .40
BT16104 Son Goten, Challenging a Demon God R .15 .30
BT16105 Pan, Challenging a Demon God R .25 .50
BT16106 Vegeta C .07 .10
BT16107 SSG Trunks, Power Awakened SPR 7.50 15.00

BT16107 SSG Trunks, Power Awakened SR	4.00	8.00
BT16108 SS3 Trunks, Challenging a Demon God R	.25	.50
BT16109 Trunks, Duty of the Time Patrol U	.12	.25
BT16110 Demigra, Challenging a Demon God C	.07	.15
BT16111 Robelu, Challenging a Demon God C	.07	.15
BT16112 Demon God Dabura, Umbral Might C	.07	.10
BT16113 Dabura, Annihilation at Hand U	.07	.10
BT16114 Mira, Unwavering Loyalty U	.07	.15
BT16115 Demon God Towa, Umbral Might SR	.20	.40
BT16116 Towa, Annihilation at Hand C	.07	.15
BT16117 Demon God Putine, Umbral Might SR	.75	1.50
BT16118 Putine, Annihilation at Hand C	.07	.15
BT16119 Demon God Gravy, Umbral Might C	.07	.10
BT16120 Gravy, Annihilation at Hand C	.07	.15
BT16121 Fin, Evolutionary Premonition C	.07	.15
BT16122 Birth of the Crimson Hero R	.10	.20
BT16123 Attack of the Dark Empire C	.07	.15
BT16124 Support of the Dark Empire C	1.25	2.50
BT16125 Realm of the Gods - Crimson Hero's Strike R	.15	.30
BT16125 Realm of the Gods - Crimson Hero's Strike SPR	1.25	2.50
BT16126 Cucatail, Angel of Universe 5 R	.10	.20
BT16127 Korun, Angel of Universe 8 C	.07	.15
BT16128 Beerus, Combative Impulse R	.20	.40
BT16129 Fused Zamasu, Exterminating Force SR	.50	1.00
BT16130 Fused Zamasu, Divine Condemnation R	.15	.30
BT16131 Whis, Calling to Order SPR	1.00	2.00
BT16131 Whis, Calling to Order SR	.25	.50
BT16132 Awamo, Angel of Universe 1 R	.10	.20
BT16133 Martinne, Angel of Universe 12 C	.07	.10
BT16134 Conic, Angel of Universe 4 C	.07	.15
BT16135 Mohito, Angel of Universe 9€	.07	.15
BT16136 Frost, by Any Means Necessary R	.12	.25
BT16137 Frost, Coming to Blows R	.12	.25
BT16138 Kampari, Angel of Universe 3 C	.07	.15
BT16139 Kusu, Angel of Universe 10 SPR	4.00	8.00
BT16139 Kusu, Angel of Universe 10 SR	2.00	4.00
BT16140 Whis, Angel of Universe 7 R	.20	.40
BT16141 Vados, Angel of the Universe 6 U	.07	.15
BT16142 SS Gogeta, Holding Nothing Back U	.10	.20
BT16143 Sawar, Angel of Universe 2 C	.07	.15
BT16144 Marcarita, Angel of Universe 11 SPR	1.00	2.00
BT16144 Marcarita, Angel of Universe 11 SR	.30	.60
BT16145 SS4 Vegeta, Ready to Strike R	.20	.40
BT16146 SS4 Son Goku, Ready to Strike R	.15	.30
BT16147 SSB Vegeta, Unbridled Power GDR	1,500.00	3,000.00
BT16147 SSB Vegeta, Unbridled Power SCR	125.00	250.00
BT16148 Super Mira, Diabolical Fusion SCR	10.00	20.00
BT16149 Supreme Kai of Time, Brainwashed SCR	20.00	40.00

2022 Dragon Ball Super Realm of the Gods Pre-Release

BT16001 Son Goku // Son Goku, Supreme Warrior U	.15	.30
BT16002 Great Priest // Great Priest, Commander of Angels U	.15	.30
BT16003 Golden Frieza & Android 17, Determined Tag Team U	.15	.30
BT16004 Super Shenron, Universal Revival U	.15	.30
BT16006 Son Goku, Sign of Mastery R	.20	.40
BT16010 Golden Frieza, for the Universe's Survival U	.15	.30
BT16011 Frieza, Universe 7 Combination U	.15	.30
BT16012 SSB Vegeta, for the Universe's Survival R	.20	.40
BT16018 Realm of the Gods - Ultra Instinct R	.20	.40
BT16019 Universe 7 Unified U	.15	.30
BT16020 Son Goku // SSG Son Goku, Crimson Warrior U	.15	.30
BT16021 Whis // Whis, Invitation to Battle U	.15	.30
BT16023 Great Priest, Invitation to Battle U	.15	.30
BT16028 SS Son Goten, the Interceptor R	.20	.40
BT16029 Son Goten, Harnessed Power R	.20	.40
BT16032 SS Trunks, the Interceptor R	.20	.40
BT16033 Trunks, Harnessed Power R	.20	.40
BT16034 Videl, the Interceptor U	.15	.30
BT16035 Videl, Harnessed Power U	.15	.30
BT16040 Whis, Rejuvenating Support U	.15	.30
BT16043 Carefree Playtime U	.15	.30
BT16045 Realm of the Gods - Beerus Destroys R	.20	.40
BT16046 Beerus // Beerus, Victory at All Costs U	.15	.30
BT16047 Champa // Champa, Victory at All Costs U	.15	.30
BT16048 Whis, Pre-Fight Preparations U	.15	.30
BT16049 Vados, Pre-Fight Preparations U	.15	.30
BT16051 SS Son Goku, to Battle Universe 6 U	.15	.30
BT16055 Majin Buu, to Battle Universe 6 U	.15	.30
BT16059 SS Cabba, Wrathful Evolution U	.15	.30
BT16062 Hit, to Battle Universe 7 U	.15	.30
BT16067 Sibling Squabble R	.20	.40
BT16069 Realm of the Gods - Champa Destroys R	.20	.40
BT16070 Damage Negation R	.20	.40
BT16071 Trunks // SSB Vegeta & SS Trunks, Father-Son Onslaught U	.15	.30
BT16072 Zamasu // SS Rose Goku Black, Wishes Fulfilled U	.15	.30
BT16073 Mai, Opposing the Divine U	.15	.30
BT16074 Rumsshi, Universe 10 Supporter U	.15	.30
BT16076 Son Goku, Facing Goku Black U	.15	.30
BT16077 SSB Vegeta, Future on the Line R	.20	.40
BT16078 SSB Vegeta, Fatherly Assistance U	.15	.30
BT16081 SS2 Trunks, Future on the Line R	.20	.40
BT16084 Bulma, Future on the Line U	.15	.30
BT16088 Goku Black, Surpassing Time itself R	.20	.40
BT16089 Zamasu, Self-Supported U	.15	.30
BT16092 Realm of the Gods - Black Kamehameha R	.20	.40
BT16097 Trunks // SSG Trunks, Crimson Warrior U	.15	.30
BT16098 Dabura // Demon God Dabura, Diabolical Awakening U	.15	.30
BT16099 Supreme Kai of Time, Opposing the Empire U	.15	.30
BT16103 Son Gohan, Challenging a Demon God R	.20	.40
BT16104 Son Goten, Challenging a Demon God R	.20	.40
BT16105 Pan, Challenging a Demon God R	.20	.40
BT16108 SS3 Trunks, Challenging a Demon God R	.20	.40
BT16109 Trunks, Duty of the Time Patrol U	.15	.30
BT16113 Dabura, Annihilation at Hand U	.15	.30
BT16114 Mira, Unwavering Loyalty U	.15	.30
BT16122 Birth of the Crimson Hero R	.20	.40
BT16125 Realm of the Gods - Crimson Hero's Strike R	.20	.40
BT16126 Cucatail, Angel of Universe 5 R	.20	.40
BT16128 Beerus, Combative Impulse R	.20	.40
BT16130 Fused Zamasu, Divine Condemnation R	.20	.40
BT16132 Awamo, Angel of Universe 1 R	.20	.40
BT16136 Frost, by Any Means Necessary R	.20	.40
BT16137 Frost, Coming to Blows R	.20	.40
BT16140 Whis, Angel of Universe 7 R	.20	.40
BT16141 Vados, Angel of the Universe 6 U	.15	.30
BT16142 SS Gogeta, Holding Nothing Back U	.15	.30
BT16145 SS4 Vegeta, Ready to Strike R	.20	.40
BT16146 SS4 Son Goku, Ready to Strike R	.20	.40

2022 Dragon Ball Super Starter Deck Blue Fusion

SD1801 Trunks // SS2 Trunks, Envoy of Justice Returns FOIL	.30	.60
SD1802 SSB Vegito, Godly Spirit FOIL	6.00	12.00
SD1803 SSB Vegeta, Committed to Victory	.25	.50
SD1804 SSB Son Goku, Hope for the Future	.60	1.25
SD1805 SS2 Trunks, Hopeful Strike	.25	.50

2022 Dragon Ball Super Starter Deck Green Fusion

SD1901 Gotenks // SS3 Gotenks, Extravagant Assault Returns FOIL	.30	.60
SD1902 SS3 Gotenks, Warrior's Growth FOIL	.40	.80
SD1903 SS3 Gogeta, Carefree Combatant	.50	1.00
SD1904 SS3 Gotenks, Ultimate Rookie	.40	.80
SD1905 Gotenks, Fusion Confusion	.75	1.50

2022 Dragon Ball Super Starter Deck Red Rage

SD1701 Pan // Pan, Ready to Fight Returns FOIL	.17	.35
SD1702 SS4 Son Goku, Defender of Life FOIL	4.00	8.00
SD1703 Son Gohan, the Awakened	.30	.75
SD1704 SS4 Son Goku, Senses Returned	.50	1.00
SD1705 Pan, Wisher of Miracles	.30	.75

2022 Dragon Ball Super Starter Deck Yellow Transformation

SD2001 Son Goku // Uncontrollable Great Ape Son Goku Returns FOIL	.25	.50
SD2002 Son Goku, Growing Up Fast FOIL	.30	.60
SD2003 Bulma, Stalwart Adventurer	.75	1.50
SD2004 Son Goku, to Lands Unknown	.30	.60
SD2005 Yamcha, Dastardly Bandit	.25	.50

2022 Dragon Ball Super Theme Selection History of Goku

BT9131 Ultra Instinct Goku's Kamehameha IAR	7.50	15.00
DB1021 Ultra Instinct Son Goku, the Unstoppable SR	1.00	2.00
DB1040 Desperate Measures C	1.25	2.50
DB3022 Korin Tower's Secret Medicine R	.30	.60
DB3116 Son Goku, Unwavering Conviction R	.30	.60
DB3127 Kakarot, Fate's Dawning U	.40	.80
BT10060 Son Goku // Ferocious Strike SS Son Goku U	.60	1.25
BT10065 SS Son Goku, Pride of the Saiyans R	.50	1.00
BT10066 Intensive Training Son Goku R	.25	.50
BT11034 SS4 Son Goku, Protector of the Earth SR	.75	1.50
BT11074 SS3 Son Goku, to New Extremes U	.30	.75
BT11093 Son Goku, Forever in Our Memories R	.25	.50
BT13012 SS Son Goku, the Legend Personified SR	2.00	4.00
BT13071 Son Goku, Allies in the Heart SR	.30	.75
BT14029 Difference of Status SR	.75	1.50

2022 Dragon Ball Super Theme Selection History of Vegeta

EB107 Vegeta, Royal Evolution SR	.50	1.00
BT9133 Vegeta's Final Flash IAR	2.50	5.00
DB1002 SS Vegeta, Exploiting Weakness SR	.30	.75
DB2133 Vegeta, Strength of Legends R	.30	.60
DB2159 Protector of the People SR	1.25	2.50
DB3126 Vegeta, Villain-Turned-Protector U	.25	.50
EX1202 Vegeta, Unison of Fury XR	.75	1.50
BT10041 Vegeta, Savior of the Future C	1.00	2.00
BT10068 Vegeta, the Lone Prince C	.30	.75
BT10088 Dormant Potential Unleashed SR	7.50	15.00
BT10105 Vegeta, Prideful Transformation SR	.75	1.50
BT11032 Vegeta // SS4 Vegeta, Ultimate Evolution U	.30	.75
BT11052 SS4 Vegeta, Rise of the Super Warrior SR	1.25	2.50
BT11053 Vegeta, Ready to Rumble R	.75	1.50
BT11066 Prince of Destruction Vegeta, Prideful Warrior SR	.75	1.50

2022 Dragon Ball Super Ultimate Squad

BT17001 Son Goku/Son Goku, Pan, and Trunks, Space Adventurers U	.07	.15
BT17002 Dr. Myuu & General Rilldo/Dr. Myuu & Hyper Meta-Rilldo, Rulers of Planet-2 U	.07	.10
BT17003 Spaceship, Vessel of Hope U	.12	.25
BT17004 Baby, Juvenile Parasite SR	2.00	4.00
BT17005 Infinite Multiplication Meta-Cooler C	.07	.15
BT17006 SS Son Goku, Soaring Through Space R	.15	.30
BT17007 Son Goku, Battle on Planet M-2 U	.12	.25
BT17008 Son Goku, Adventure's Advent C	.15	.30
BT17009 SS Son Goku, Pan, and SS Trunks, Galactic Explorers SPR	2.00	4.00
BT17009 SS Son Goku, Pan, and SS Trunks, Galactic Explorers SR	.60	1.25
BT17010 Pan, Soaring Through Space SR	.30	.60
BT17011 Pan, Adventure's Advent R	.12	.25
BT17012 SS Trunks, Soaring Through Space R	.15	.30
BT17013 Trunks, Battle on Planet M-2 C	.10	.20
BT17014 Trunks, Adventure's Advent C	.10	.20
BT17015 Giru, Travel Support U	.07	.15
BT17016 Luud, Stunning Power C	.07	.10
BT17017 Meta-Rilldo, Ascended General R	.10	.20
BT17018 Hyper Meta-Rilldo, Combined Power R	.12	.25
BT17019 General Rilldo, Battle on Planet M-2 C	.07	.10
BT17020 General Rilldo, Combination Ready C	.07	.10
BT17021 Super Sigma, Combining Warrior R	.12	.25
BT17022 Super Sigma C	.07	.10
BT17023 Nezi, Combination Ready U	.07	.10
BT17024 Bizu, Combination Ready C	.10	.20
BT17025 Ribet, Combination Ready U	.12	.25
BT17026 Vegeta C	.10	.20
BT17027 Ba, Friend From Planet Vampa C	.07	.10
BT17028 Mechanized Planet C	.07	.10
BT17029 Clash on Planet M-2 C	.07	.15
BT17030 Setting Forth to Space C	.07	.15
BT17031 Commander Red/Red Ribbon Robot, Seeking World Conquest U	.07	.15
BT17032 Gamma 1 & Gamma 2/Gamma 1 & Gamma 2, Newfound Foes U	.07	.15
BT17033 Android 17 & Android 18, Teaming Up SPR	2.50	5.00
BT17033 Android 17 & Android 18, Teaming Up SR	.75	1.50
BT17034 Dr. Gero, Abominable Creator U	.07	.15
BT17035 Mercenary Tao, Expert Assassin C	.07	.10
BT17036 Commander Red, Hidden Ambitions SR	.20	.40
BT17037 Commander Red, Red Ribbon Unifier R	.12	.25
BT17038 Red Ribbon Robot, Colossal Power R	.12	.25
BT17039 General Blue, Red Ribbon Officer U	.07	.15
BT17040 General Blue, Ever Loyal C	.10	.20
BT17041 General White, Red Ribbon Officer C	.07	.15
BT17042 Colonel Violet C	.07	.10
BT17043 Major Metallitron, Red Ribbon Officer C	.07	.15
BT17044 Android 8, Kindhearted Machine U	.15	.30
BT17045 Android 8, For His Friends C	.07	.15
BT17046 Android 17, Rebellious Will U	.15	.30
BT17047 Android 18, Rebellious Will U	.12	.25
BT17048 Android 16, Hidden Power R	.12	.25
BT17049 Cell, the Ultimate Bio-Android SPR	3.00	6.00
BT17049 Cell, the Ultimate Bio-Android SR	.75	1.50
BT17050 Android 19, Energy Absorber C	.10	.20
BT17051 Android 20, Energy Absorber C	.07	.15
BT17052 Android 13, Inorganic Horror R	.12	.25
BT17053 Android 14, Inorganic Horror R	.15	.30
BT17054 Android 14 & Android 15, the Ravagers R	.15	.30
BT17055 Android 15, Inorganic Horror C	.07	.15
BT17056 Red Ribbon Army, Assemble! C	.07	.15
BT17057 Sacrificial Strike C	.07	.10
BT17058 Results of Research C	.07	.10
BT17059 Cooler/Cooler, Galactic Dynasty U	.07	.15
BT17060 Meta-Cooler/Meta-Cooler Core, Unlimited Power U	.07	.15
BT17061 Frieza, Galactic Dynasty SP	1.25	2.50
BT17061 Frieza, Galactic Dynasty SR	.40	.80
BT17062 Salza, Cooler's Armored Squadron R	.15	.30
BT17063 Dore, Cooler's Armored Squadron R	.15	.30
BT17064 Neiz, Cooler's Armored Squadron R	.20	.40
BT17065 Mecha Frieza, Back From the Abyss U	.07	.15
BT17066 Golden Frieza, Newfound Might SR	1.00	2.00
BT17067 Piccolo, First Fusion R	.12	.25
BT17068 Cooler, Sibling Cruelty SPR	2.00	4.00
BT17068 Cooler, Sibling Cruelty SR	.30	.75
BT17069 Cooler, Mightiest Sibling in Space C	.10	.20
BT17070 Cooler, On Watch U	.07	.15
BT17071 Cooler C	.07	.15
BT17072 Meta-Cooler, Multiplying Threat C	.07	.10
BT17073 Infinite Multiplication Meta-Cooler C	.25	.50
BT17074 Cyclopian Guard C	.12	.25
BT17075 Cyclopian Guard, Mass-Production Model C	.07	.15
BT17076 Piccolo, Fusing With Kami U	.07	.15
BT17077 Piccolo, Fusing Further R	.12	.25
BT17078 Cooler's Armored Squadron C	.07	.15
BT17079 Big Gete Star, Nightmarish Regeneration C	.07	.15
BT17080 A Hopeless Sight C	.07	.10
BT17081 Son Goku/SS Son Goku, Fearless Fighter U	.07	.15
BT17082 Piccolo/Piccolo, Supreme Power U	.07	.15
BT17083 SS2 Son Gohan, Z Fighter SPR	10.00	20.00
BT17083 SS2 Son Gohan, Z Fighter SR	2.50	5.00
BT17084 SS Vegeta, Z Fighter SR	.30	.75
BT17085 Piccolo, Z Fighter R	.15	.30
BT17086 Krillin, Z Fighter R	.12	.25
BT17087 Yamcha, Z Fighter U	.12	.25
BT17088 Tien Shinhan, Z Fighter U	.07	.15
BT17089 Dende Guardian's Destiny C	.07	.15
BT17090 Piccolo, with Nail's Might U	.07	.15
BT17091 Piccolo, Ready to Fuse R	.15	.30
BT17092 Nail, the Protector C	.07	.15
BT17093 SS Son Goku, Final Sacrifice SPR	.50	1.00
BT17093 SS Son Goku, Final Sacrifice SR	1.25	2.50
BT17094 Son Goku, Returning to Earth U	.10	.20
BT17095 SS Son Gohan, Furious Training R	.15	.30
BT17096 SS Son Gohan, Inherited Will U	.10	.20
BT17097 SS Trunks, Super Warrior C	.07	.15
BT17098 Trunks, From the Future C	.07	.15
BT17099 Piccolo, Fusion's Resolve R	.15	.30
BT17100 Kami, Guardian of Earth C	.07	.10
BT17101 Saonel C	.07	.15
BT17102 Saonel, Burdens Shouldered C	.07	.10
BT17103 Pirina C	.07	.15
BT17104 Pirina, Burdens Shouldered C	.07	.15
BT17105 Infinite Multiplication Meta-Cooler C	.15	.30
BT17106 Weight on One's Shoulders C	.07	.15
BT17107 The Z Fighters at the Cell Games C	.07	.15
BT17108 The World Champion Strikes C	.07	.15
BT17109 Instant Kamehameha C	.07	.10
BT17110 Towa/Demon God Towa, Dark Leader U	.07	.15
BT17111 Super Mira, Overflowing Power SPR	1.25	2.50
BT17111 Super Mira, Overflowing Power SR	.30	.60
BT17112 Demon God Dabura, Imperial Warrior C	.07	.10
BT17113 Super Mira, Imperial Warrior U	.07	.15
BT17114 Super Mira, Preparing to Fight U	.07	.15
BT17115 Demon God Towa, Furious Onslaught SPR	1.25	2.50
BT17115 Demon God Towa, Furious Onslaught SR	.25	.50
BT17116 Demon God Towa, Imperial Warrior U	.07	.15
BT17117 Demon God Towa, Preparing to Fight R	.12	.25
BT17118 Demon God Gravy, Imperial Warrior U	.10	.20
BT17119 Demon God Putine, Imperial Warrior R	.15	.30
BT17120 Demon God Putine, Preparing to Fight R	.15	.30
BT17121 Mechikabura, Dark Ruler C	.10	.20
BT17122 Supreme Kai of Time, Fallen Deity C	.07	.10
BT17123 Demon God Shroom, Imperial Warrior R	.12	.25
BT17124 Demon God Shroom, Preparing to Fight C	.07	.10
BT17125 Demon God Salsa, Imperial Warrior R	.15	.30
BT17126 Demon God Salsa, Preparing to Fight C	.07	.10
BT17127 Fin C	.07	.15
BT17128 Fin, Preparing to Fight C	.07	.10
BT17129 Invasion of the Dark Empire C	.07	.15
BT17130 Further Evolution C	.07	.10
BT17131 Lightning Sentence C	.07	.10
BT17132 Vegeta, Proud Warrior SPR	2.00	4.00
BT17132 Vegeta, Proud Warrior U	.12	.25
BT17133 SS2 Kefla, Super Fusion SPR	.75	1.50
BT17133 SS2 Kefla, Super Fusion U	.12	.25
BT17134 Beerus, Motivated Destruction SPR	.50	1.00
BT17134 Beerus, Motivated Destruction U	4.00	8.00
BT17135 Android 17 & Android-18, Limitless Energy SR	1.25	2.50
BT17136 Android 17 & Android 18, Team-Up Attack SPR	2.50	5.00
BT17136 Android 17 & Android 18, Team-Up Attack U	.12	.25
BT17137 Android 13, Frenzied Warrior U	.10	.20
BT17138 SSG Son Goku, Magnificent Might SPR	1.25	2.50
BT17138 SSG Son Goku, Magnificent Might U	.10	.20
BT17139 Piccolo, Fusing With Nail R	.12	.25
BT17140 Meta-Cooler, Newfound Foe R	.12	.25
BT17141 Meta-Cooler, Enhanced Menace SR	.25	.50
BT17142 Meta-Cooler Core, the Collective R	.15	.30
BT17143 Meta-Cooler Core, Energy Source C	.07	.10
BT17144 Piccolo, Fused With Kami SR	.30	.60
BT17145 Cell Abominable Power SR	.25	.50
BT17146 Cell, the Awakened SPR	1.25	2.50
BT17146 Cell, the Awakened U	.12	.25
BT17147 Invader's Vow SCR	12.50	25.00
BT17148 Piccolo & Son Gohan, Newfound Might SCR	100.00	200.00
BT17149 Oath of Z SCR	30.00	75.00

2022 Dragon Ball Super Ultimate Squad Pre-Release

BT17001 Son Goku // Son Goku, Pan, and Trunks, Space Adventurers U	.15	.30
BT17002 Dr. Myuu & General Rilldo // Dr. Myuu & Hyper Meta-Rilldo, Rulers of Planet-2 U	.15	.30
BT17003 Spaceship, Vessel of Hope U	.15	.30
BT17006 SS Son Goku, Soaring Through Space R	.20	.40
BT17007 Son Goku, Battle on Planet M-2 U	.15	.30
BT17011 Pan, Adventure's Advent R	.20	.40
BT17012 SS Trunks, Soaring Through Space R	.20	.40
BT17015 Giru, Travel Support U	.15	.30
BT17017 Meta-Rilldo, Ascended General R	.20	.40
BT17018 Hyper Meta-Rilldo, Combined Power R	.20	.40
BT17021 Super Sigma, Combining Warrior R	.20	.40
BT17023 Nezi, Combination Ready U	.15	.30
BT17025 Ribet, Combination Ready U	.15	.30
BT17031 Commander Red // Red Ribbon Robot, Seeking World Conquest U	.15	.30
BT17032 Gamma 1 & Gamma 2 // Gamma 1 & Gamma 2, Newfound Foes U	.15	.30
BT17034 Dr. Gero, Abominable Creator U	.15	.30
BT17037 Commander Red, Red Ribbon Unifier R	.20	.40
BT17038 Red Ribbon Robot, Colossal Power R	.20	.40
BT17039 General Blue, Red Ribbon Officer U	.15	.30
BT17044 Android 8, Kindhearted Machine U	.15	.30
BT17046 Android 17, Rebellious Will U	.15	.30
BT17047 Android 18, Rebellious Will U	.15	.30
BT17048 Android 16, Hidden Power R	.20	.40
BT17052 Android 13, Inorganic Horror R	.20	.40
BT17053 Android 14, Inorganic Horror R	.20	.40
BT17054 Android 14 & Android 15, the Ravagers R	.20	.40
BT17059 Cooler // Cooler, Galactic Dynasty U	.15	.30
BT17060 Meta-Cooler // Meta-Cooler Core, Unlimited Power U	.15	.30
BT17062 Salza, Cooler's Armored Squadron R	.20	.40
BT17063 Dore, Cooler's Armored Squadron R	.20	.40
BT17064 Neiz, Cooler's Armored Squadron R	.20	.40
BT17065 Mecha Frieza, Back From the Abyss U	.15	.30

BT17067 Piccolo, First Fusion R	.20	.40
BT17070 Cooler, On Watch U	.15	.30
BT17076 Piccolo, Fusing With Kami U	.15	.30
BT17077 Piccolo, Fusing Further R	.20	.40
BT17081 Son Goku // SS Son Goku, Fearless Fighter U	.15	.30
BT17082 Piccolo // Piccolo, Supreme Power U	.15	.30
BT17085 Piccolo, Z Fighter R	.20	.40
BT17086 Krillin, Z Fighter R	.20	.40
BT17087 Yamcha, Z Fighter U	.15	.30
BT17088 Tien Shinhan, Z Fighter U	.15	.30
BT17090 Piccolo, with Nail's Might U	.15	.30
BT17091 Piccolo, Ready to Fuse R	.20	.40
BT17094 Son Goku, Returning to Earth U	.15	.30
BT17095 SS Son Gohan, Furious Training R	.20	.40
BT17096 SS Son Gohan, Inherited Will U	.15	.30
BT17099 Piccolo, Fusion's Resolve R	.20	.40
BT17110 Towa // Demon God Towa, Dark Leader U	.15	.30
BT17113 Super Mira, Imperial Warrior U	.15	.30
BT17114 Super Mira, Preparing to Fight U	.15	.30
BT17116 Demon God Towa, Imperial Warrior U	.15	.30
BT17117 Demon God Towa, Preparing to Fight R	.20	.40
BT17118 Demon God Gravy, Imperial Warrior U	.15	.30
BT17119 Demon God Putine, Imperial Warrior R	.20	.40
BT17120 Demon God Putine, Preparing to Fight R	.20	.40
BT17123 Demon God Shroom, Imperial Warrior R	.20	.40
BT17125 Demon God Salsa, Imperial Warrior R	.20	.40
BT17132 Vegeta, Proud Warrior U	.15	.30
BT17133 SS2 Kefla, Super Fusion U	.15	.30
BT17134 Beerus, Motivated Destruction U	.15	.30
BT17136 Android 17 & Android 18, Team-Up Attack U	.15	.30
BT17137 Android 13, Frenzied Warrior U	.15	.30
BT17138 SSG Son Goku, Magnificent Might U	.15	.30
BT17139 Piccolo, Fusing With Nail R	.20	.40
BT17140 Meta-Cooler, Newfound Foe R	.20	.40
BT17142 Meta-Cooler Core, the Collective R	.20	.40
BT17146 Cell, the Awakened U	.15	.30

2023 Dragon Ball Super Expansion Deck Box Set 22 Ultimate Deck

EB122 Chilled's Army Reinforcements RE C	.25	.50
BT1053 Senzu Bean RE C	.30	.60
BT2058 Infinite Force Fused Zamasu RE SR	.20	.40
BT5050 Dimension Magic RE C	.30	.75
EX2201 Goku Black/SS Rose Goku Black, the Beginning of the Return to Despair EX	2.00	4.00
EX2201 Goku Black/SS Rose Goku Black, the Beginning of the Return to Despair EX GOLD STAMP	12.50	25.00
EX2202 SS Rose Goku Black, Dark Purple Sickle EX	.75	1.50
EX2202 SS Rose Goku Black, Dark Purple Sickle EX GOLD STAMP	6.00	12.00
EX2203 Zamasu, Serving Justice EX	.30	.60
EX2203 Zamasu, Serving Justice EX GOLD STAMP	4.00	8.00
EX2204 SS Rose Goku Black, Serving Justice EX	.30	.60
EX2204 SS Rose Goku Black, Serving Justice EX GOLD STAMP	6.00	12.00
EX2205 Fused Zamasu, Striving for Perfect Order EX	.75	1.50
EX2206 Fused Zamasu, the Power of the Gods is Complete EX	.30	.75
EX2207 SS Rose Goku Black, Shining Illusion EX	.50	1.00
EX2208 SS Rose Goku Black, Justice of Destruction EX	1.50	3.00
EX2209 SS Rose Goku Black, Close Combat EX	.50	1.00
EX2210 Goku Black, Fake Protagonist EX	.25	.50
EX2211 Gowasu, Easygoing Watcher EX	.30	.60
EX2212 Zuno, Convergence of Knowledge EX	.60	1.25
EX2213 Breaking a Taboo EX	.25	.50
BT10049 Respectful Master Gowasu RE C	.15	.30
BT10050 Goku Black Rose, Lofty Aspirations RE R	.20	.40
BT10052 Fused Zamasu, the Divine Immortal RE R	.20	.40
BT10053 Fused Zamasu, Advocate for Evil RE C	.20	.40
BT10058 Tragedy Overground RE C	.12	.25
BT15042 Kale, Rampaging Demon RE SR	.30	.75

2023 Dragon Ball Super Power Absorbed

BT20001 Android 17/Warriors of Universe 7, United as One U	.15	.30
BT20002 Paparoni/Warriors of Universe 3, United as One U	.07	.15
BT20003 SSG Son Goku, Rapidfire Response U	.12	.25
BT20003 SSG Son Goku, Rapidfire Response U GOLD STAMP	5.00	10.00
BT20003 SSG Son Goku, Rapidfire Response U FOIL	1.25	2.50
BT20004 Son Gohan, Daring Onslaught R	.12	.25
BT20004 Son Gohan, Daring Onslaught R GOLD STAMP	3.00	6.00
BT20004 Son Gohan, Daring Onslaught R FOIL	1.50	3.00
BT20005 Android 17, Impeccable Defense R	.10	.20
BT20005 Android 17, Impeccable Defense R GOLD STAMP	3.00	6.00
BT20005 Android 17, Impeccable Defense R FOIL	1.25	2.50
BT20006 Anilaza, Dimension Bender R	.07	.15
BT20007 Koichiarator, the Masterwork U	.07	.15
BT20008 SSG Son Goku C	.07	.15
BT20009 Frieza, Pride of an Emperor U	.10	.20
BT20010 Android 18, Selfless Savior R	.12	.25
BT20010 Android 18, Selfless Savior R GOLD STAMP	7.50	15.00
BT20010 Android 18, Selfless Savior R FOIL	1.25	2.50
BT20011 Anilaza, Universe 3's Ultimate Weapon SPR	.50	1.00
BT20011 Anilaza, Universe 3's Ultimate Weapon SR	.12	.25
BT20012 Koichiarator, Plan X Activation R	.10	.20
BT20013 Paparoni, the Brains of Universe 3 R	.12	.25
BT20014 Koitsukai, Team Attacker C	.07	.15
BT20015 Koitsukai, Warrior of Universe 3 R	.10	.20
BT20016 Panchia, Team Attacker C	.07	.15
BT20017 Panchia, Warrior of Universe 3 C	.07	.15
BT20018 Bollarator, Team Attacker C	.07	.15
BT20019 Bollarator, Warrior of Universe 3 C	.07	.15
BT20020 Narirama, Mechanical Tactician U	.07	.15
BT20021 Viara C	.07	.15
BT20022 Paparoni's Tactical Orders C	.07	.15
BT20023 Android 18/Android 18, Impenetrable Rushdown U	.12	.25
BT20024 Android 21/Android 21, the Nature of Evil U	.10	.20
BT20025 Android 18, Accel Dance U	.12	.25
BT20026 Krillin, Accel Dance U	.10	.20
BT20027 Android 17, Accel Dance U	.10	.20
BT20028 Android 21, in the Name of Hunger SR	1.25	2.50
BT20028 Android 21, in the Name of Hunger SR GOLD STAMP	12.50	25.00
BT20028 Android 21, in the Name of Hunger SR FOIL	2.00	4.00
BT20029 Android 21, in the Name of Peace R	.15	.30
BT20029 Android 21, in the Name of Peace R GOLD STAMP	10.00	20.00
BT20029 Android 21, in the Name of Peace R FOIL	2.00	4.00
BT20030 Android 18, Krillin, and Maron, Family United R	.12	.25
BT20031 SSB Son Goku, Beyond Full Power C	.07	.15
BT20031 SSB Son Goku, Beyond Full Power C GOLD STAMP	2.00	4.00
BT20031 SSB Son Goku, Beyond Full Power C FOIL	1.00	2.00
BT20032 SSB Vegeta, Beyond Full Power R	.12	.25
BT20032 SSB Vegeta, Beyond Full Power R GOLD STAMP	6.00	12.00
BT20032 SSB Vegeta, Beyond Full Power R FOIL	1.00	2.00
BT20033 Android 17, Calm Judgement C	.10	.20
BT20033 Android 17, Calm Judgement C GOLD STAMP	7.50	15.00
BT20033 Android 17, Calm Judgement C FOIL	1.25	2.50
BT20034 SSB Gogeta, Blistering Barrage C	.07	.15
BT20034 SSB Gogeta, Blistering Barrage C GOLD STAMP	4.00	8.00
BT20034 SSB Gogeta, Blistering Barrage C FOIL	1.25	2.50
BT20035 SS Vegeta C	.07	.15
BT20036 Krillin, Powers Expanded R	.12	.25
BT20037 Krillin, Defensive Battler C	.10	.20
BT20038 Krillin, Absolute Guard U	.10	.20
BT20039 Krillin, Gearing Up for Battle C	.12	.25
BT20040 Bulma, Helpful Cheer C	.10	.20
BT20041 Android 18, Energy Wave SPR	1.25	2.50
BT20041 Android 18, Energy Wave SR	.25	.50
BT20042 Android 18, Gearing Up for Battle C	.10	.20
BT20042 Android 18, Gearing Up for Battle C GOLD STAMP	4.00	8.00
BT20042 Android 18, Gearing Up for Battle C FOIL	1.25	2.50
BT20043 Android 18 & Krillin, Future Spun By Battle SPR	.75	1.50
BT20043 Android 18 & Krillin, Future Spun By Battle SR	.25	.50
BT20044 Android 17, Emergency Defense R	.12	.25
BT20045 Android 17, Supporting His Sister R	.12	.25
BT20045 Android 17, Supporting His Sister R GOLD STAMP	3.00	6.00
BT20045 Android 17, Supporting His Sister R FOIL	1.00	2.00
BT20046 Android 21, Wavering Will U	.10	.20
BT20046 Android 21, Wavering Will U GOLD STAMP	25.00	50.00
BT20046 Android 21, Wavering Will U FOIL	2.50	5.00
BT20047 Android 21, Total Audacity R	.25	.50
BT20048 Android 21, Mandatory Gathering C	2.50	5.00
BT20048 Android 21, Mandatory Gathering C GOLD STAMP	20.00	40.00
BT20048 Android 21, Mandatory Gathering C FOIL	.10	.20
BT20049 Frieza, Common Enemy C	.07	.15
BT20050 Cell, Common Enemy C	.07	.15
BT20051 Android 16 C	.07	.15
BT20052 Krillin Helping His Family U	.10	.20
BT20052 Krillin Helping His Family U FOIL	3.00	6.00
BT20053 Unstoppable Technique C	.07	.15
BT20053 Unstoppable Technique C GOLD STAMP	12.50	25.00
BT20053 Unstoppable Technique C FOIL	2.00	4.00
BT20054 Son Goku/SS4 Son Goku, Betting It All U	.07	.15
BT20055 Android 20 & Dr. Myuu/Hell Fighter 17, Plans in Motion U	.07	.15
BT20056 Son Goku, Full-Strength Kamehameha U	.10	.20
BT20057 Super 17, Ready to Absorb U	.10	.20
BT20058 Super 17, Bound by Blood U	.07	.15
BT20059 Super 17, Diabolical Union U	.07	.15
BT20060 Son Goku, Golden Dragon Fist R	.07	.15
BT20061 Android 18, Wrathful Strike R	.10	.20
BT20062 SS4 Son Goku, Stygian Journey R	.12	.25
BT20062 SS4 Son Goku, Stygian Journey R GOLD STAMP	4.00	8.00
BT20062 SS4 Son Goku, Stygian Journey R FOIL	1.00	2.00
BT20063 SS4 Son Goku, to Hell and Back U	.07	.15
BT20063 SS4 Son Goku, to Hell and Back U GOLD STAMP	4.00	8.00
BT20063 SS4 Son Goku, to Hell and Back U FOIL	.75	1.50
BT20064 Son Goku & Android 18, Vital Teamwork SPR	1.25	2.50
BT20064 Son Goku & Android 18, Vital Teamwork SR	.30	.75
BT20065 Son Gohan, Spirit of Resistance C	.10	.20
BT20065 Son Gohan, Spirit of Resistance C GOLD STAMP	3.00	6.00
BT20065 Son Gohan, Spirit of Resistance C FOIL	1.25	2.50
BT20066 Son Goten, Spirit of Resistance C	.10	.20
BT20067 Pan, Spirit of Resistance U	.07	.15
BT20068 SS Vegeta, Spirit of Resistance R	.12	.25
BT20068 SS Vegeta, Spirit of Resistance R GOLD STAMP	3.00	6.00
BT20068 SS Vegeta, Spirit of Resistance R FOIL	1.25	2.50
BT20069 Trunks, Spirit of Resistance C	.07	.15
BT20070 Uub C	.07	.15
BT20071 Android 18, for the Sake of Family C	.10	.20
BT20071 Android 18, for the Sake of Family C FOIL	1.25	2.50
BT20072 Android 17, Brainwashed Fighter C	.10	.20
BT20072 Android 17, Brainwashed Fighter C GOLD STAMP	2.50	5.00
BT20072 Android 17, Brainwashed Fighter C FOIL	.75	1.50
BT20073 Super 17, Onyx Lightning SPR	.75	1.50
BT20073 Super 17, Onyx Lightning SR	.25	.50
BT20074 Super 17, Hell's Avenger R	.12	.25
BT20074 Super 17, Hell's Avenger R GOLD STAMP	5.00	10.00
BT20074 Super 17, Hell's Avenger R FOIL	1.25	2.50
BT20075 Hell Fighter 17, Calculated Cruelty C	.10	.20
BT20075 Hell Fighter 17, Calculated Cruelty C GOLD STAMP	3.00	6.00
BT20075 Hell Fighter 17, Calculated Cruelty C FOIL	1.00	2.00
BT20076 Hell Fighter 17, the Brainwasher C	.07	.15
BT20077 Android 17 & Hell Fighter 17, Synchronized SPR	.75	1.50
BT20077 Android 17 & Hell Fighter 17, Synchronized SR	.15	.30
BT20078 Android 20, Vengeful Alliance C	.07	.15
BT20079 Dr. Myuu, Vengeful Alliance C	.07	.15
BT20080 Android 18, Powerful Quarry C	.07	.15
BT20081 Cell, Powerful Quarry C	.07	.15
BT20082 Goku's Kamehameha Deflection R	1.00	2.00
BT20083 Ki Energy Absorb C	.07	.15
BT20083 Ki Energy Absorb C GOLD STAMP	1.00	2.00
BT20083 Ki Energy Absorb C FOIL	1.25	2.50
BT20084 SS Vegito/Son Goku & Vegeta, Path to Victory U	.10	.20
BT20085 Majin Buu/Majin Buu, Absorption Complete U	.12	.25
BT20086 SS Son Goku, Majin Showdown U	.12	.25
BT20087 Son Goku, Spirit Bomb Hope R	.10	.20
BT20088 Majin Buu, Apocalyptic Awakening U	.12	.25
BT20089 Hercule, Rallying Hope U	.12	.25
BT20090 Majin Buu, Two Hearts U	.10	.20
BT20091 Majin Buu, Heart of Evil C	.12	.25
BT20092 Majin Buu, Heart of Good C	.07	.15
BT20093 Dabura C	.07	.15
BT20094 Babidi, Behind it All C	.07	.15
BT20095 SS3 Son Goku, Universe at Stake SPR	6.00	12.00
BT20095 SS3 Son Goku, Universe at Stake SR	1.00	2.00
BT20095 SS3 Son Goku, Universe at Stake SR HOLO	1,500.00	3,000.00
BT20096 SS Son Goku & SS Vegeta, Ultimate Duo R	3.00	6.00
BT20096 SS Son Goku & SS Vegeta, Ultimate Duo R GOLD STAMP	20.00	40.00
BT20096 SS Son Goku & SS Vegeta, Ultimate Duo R FOIL	7.50	15.00
BT20097 SS Vegeta, Indomitable Spirit C	.10	.20
BT20097 SS Vegeta, Indomitable Spirit C GOLD STAMP	5.00	10.00
BT20097 SS Vegeta, Indomitable Spirit C FOIL	1.25	2.50
BT20098 Vegeta, Buying Time R	.15	.30
BT20099 SS Vegito, Overwhelming Might SPR	10.00	20.00
BT20099 SS Vegito, Overwhelming Might SR	6.00	12.00
BT20100 Vegito, Unexpected Separation U	.12	.25
BT20100 Vegito, Unexpected Separation U GOLD STAMP	2.00	4.00
BT20100 Vegito, Unexpected Separation U FOIL	.75	1.50
BT20101 Hercule, Expecting the Unexpected C	.07	.15
BT20102 Dende, Laying the Foundation C	.07	.15
BT20103 Kibito Kai, Potara on Display C	.12	.25
BT20104 Majin Buu, Vile Onslaught SPR	4.00	8.00
BT20104 Majin Buu, Vile Onslaught SR	.75	1.50
BT20105 Majin Buu, Budding Evil C	.07	.15
BT20106 Majin Buu, Power Manifest SR	.25	.50
BT20107 Majin Buu, Talent Manifest U	.10	.20
BT20108 Majin Buu, Intelligence Manifest C	.12	.25
BT20109 Majin Buu, Nightmarish Glimpse C	.10	.20
BT20110 Majin Buu, Desperate Defiance C	.07	.15
BT20111 Majin Buu, the Innocent C	.12	.25
BT20112 Spirit Bomb C	.07	.15
BT20113 Shocking Regeneration C	.07	.15
BT20114 Evil Saiyan/Cumber, Maddening Force U	.10	.20
BT20115 SS Cumber, Battle Frenzy U	.12	.25
BT20116 Fu, Assembling the Strong U	.12	.25
BT20117 Cumber, Captive Fighter C	.12	.25
BT20118 Fu, All According to Plan R	.15	.30
BT20119 Dende & Porunga, the Third Wish C	.12	.25
BT20120 Great Priest, Declaration of Annihilation C	.07	.15
BT20121 SS Son Goku, Berserk Instincts SPR	1.00	2.00
BT20121 SS Son Goku, Berserk Instincts SR	2.50	5.00
BT20122 SS4 Son Goku, Otherworldly Infiltrator R	.15	.30
BT20122 SS4 Son Goku, Otherworldly Infiltrator R GOLD STAMP	3.00	6.00
BT20122 SS4 Son Goku, Otherworldly Infiltrator R FOIL	2.00	4.00
BT20123 Vegeta, Against All Odds R	.25	.50
BT20123 Vegeta, Against All Odds R GOLD STAMP	7.50	15.00
BT20123 Vegeta, Against All Odds R FOIL	1.50	3.00
BT20124 Trunks, Prisoner From the Future C	.10	.20
BT20124 Trunks, Prisoner From the Future C FOIL	3.00	6.00
BT20125 SSB Vegito, Supreme Gleaming R	.12	.25
BT20125 SSB Vegito, Supreme Gleaming R GOLD STAMP	7.50	15.00
BT20125 SSB Vegito, Supreme Gleaming R FOIL	1.50	3.00
BT20126 Mai, Ace in the Hole C	.10	.20
BT20127 Cooler, Evolution's Premonition C	.10	.20
BT20128 Evil Saiyan, Thirsting for Battle C	.12	.25
BT20129 Evil Saiyan, Incipient Malice U	.12	.25
BT20130 SS Cumber, Berserker Barrage SPR	3.00	6.00
BT20130 SS Cumber, Berserker Barrage SR	1.25	2.50
BT20131 Cumber, Furious Frenzy R	.60	1.25
BT20131 Cumber, Furious Frenzy R GOLD STAMP	10.00	20.00
BT20131 Cumber, Furious Frenzy R FOIL	2.50	5.00
BT20132 Cumber C	.12	.25
BT20133 Fu, Scheming Overlord U	.12	.25
BT20134 Explosion of Malice C	.10	.20
BT20135 Prison Planet C	.12	.25
BT20136 Evil Aura Overflow U	.12	.25
BT20137 SS Vegeta, Immediate Response R	.15	.30
BT20138 Son Gohan, Strength of Conviction SR	.25	.50
BT20138 Son Gohan, Strength of Conviction SR GOLD STAMP	7.50	15.00
BT20138 Son Gohan, Strength of Conviction SR FOIL	1.50	3.00
BT20139 Android 17, The Move that Turns the Tide SPR	.75	1.50
BT20139 Android 17, The Move that Turns the Tide SR	.25	.50
BT20140 Universe 7, Powers Combined SPR	2.00	4.00
BT20140 Universe 7, Powers Combined SR	.50	1.00
BT20141 Deadly Clash U	.12	.25
BT20141 Deadly Clash U GOLD STAMP	2.50	5.00
BT20141 Deadly Clash U FOIL	1.50	3.00
BT20142 Nappa, Full-scale Attack R	.15	.30
BT20143 Android 21, Ceaseless Despair SPR	3.00	6.00
BT20143 Android 21, Ceaseless Despair SR	1.00	2.00
BT20144 Android 21, Bewitching Battler U	.10	.20
BT20144 Android 21, Bewitching Battler U GOLD STAMP	7.50	15.00
BT20144 Android 21, Bewitching Battler U FOIL	1.00	2.00
BT20145 Android 21, Full-Power Counter SPR	5.00	10.00
BT20145 Android 21, Full-Power Counter SR	2.00	4.00
BT20146 SS2 Kefla, Warming Up C	.10	.20
BT20147 You Are Number One SCR	30.00	75.00
BT20147 You Are Number One SCR ALT ART	300.00	600.00
BT20148 Golden Cooler, Radiant Pride SCR ALT ART	300.00	750.00
BT20148 Golden Cooler, Radiant Pride SCR	75.00	150.00
BT20149 Android 21, Transcendental Predator SCR	75.00	150.00
BT20149 Android 21, Transcendental Predator SCR ALT ART	600.00	1,200.00

2023 Dragon Ball Super Power Absorbed Pre-Release

BT20001 Android 17/Warriors of Universe 7, United as One U	7.50	15.00
BT20002 Paparoni/Warriors of Universe 3, United as One U	1.25	2.50
BT20003 SSG Son Goku, Rapidfire Response U	.75	1.50
BT20004 Son Gohan, Daring Onslaught R	.40	.80
BT20005 Android 17, Impeccable Defense R	.25	.50
BT20006 Anilaza, Dimension Bender R	.25	.50
BT20007 Koichiarator, the Masterwork U	.50	1.00
BT20009 Frieza, Pride of an Emperor U	.30	.75
BT20010 Android 18, Selfless Savior R	.50	1.00
BT20012 Koichiarator, Plan X Activation R	.60	1.25
BT20013 Paparoni, the Brains of Universe 3 R	.25	.50
BT20015 Koitsukai, Warrior of Universe 3 R	.30	.75
BT20020 Narirama, Mechanical Tactician U	.75	1.50
BT20023 Android 18/Android 18, Impenetrable Rushdown U	2.50	5.00
BT20024 Android 21/Android 21, the Nature of Evil U	7.50	15.00
BT20025 Android 18, Accel Dance U	2.00	4.00
BT20026 Krillin, Accel Dance U	6.00	12.00
BT20027 Android 17, Accel Dance U	4.00	8.00
BT20029 Android 21, in the Name of Peace R	.75	1.50
BT20030 Android 18, Krillin, and Maron, Family United R	1.25	2.50
BT20032 SSB Vegeta, Beyond Full Power R	.40	.80
BT20036 Krillin, Powers Expanded R	1.50	3.00
BT20038 Krillin, Absolute Guard U	.75	1.50
BT20044 Android 17, Emergency Defense R	.75	1.50
BT20045 Android 17, Supporting His Sister R	.75	1.50
BT20046 Android 21, Wavering Will U	1.25	2.50
BT20047 Android 21, Total Audacity R	7.50	15.00
BT20052 Krillin Helping His Family U	.50	1.00
BT20054 Son Goku/SS4 Son Goku, Betting It All U	7.50	15.00
BT20055 Android 20 & Dr. Myuu/Hell Fighter 17, Plans in Motion U	2.50	5.00
BT20056 Son Goku, Full-Strength Kamehameha U	.75	1.50
BT20057 Super 17, Ready to Absorb U	1.25	2.50
BT20058 Super 17, Bound by Blood U	1.50	3.00
BT20059 Super 17, Diabolical Union U	1.25	2.50
BT20060 Son Goku, Golden Dragon Fist R	.30	.60
BT20061 Android 18, Wrathful Strike R	1.00	2.00
BT20062 SS4 Son Goku, Stygian Journey R	.30	.75
BT20063 SS4 Son Goku, to Hell and Back U	.30	.60
BT20067 Pan, Spirit of Resistance U	.30	.60
BT20068 SS Vegeta, Spirit of Resistance R	.30	.60
BT20074 Super 17, Hell's Avenger R	.30	.60
BT20082 Goku's Kamehameha Deflection R	3.00	6.00
BT20084 SS Vegito/Son Goku & Vegeta, Path to Victory U	7.50	15.00
BT20085 Majin Buu/Majin Buu, Absorption Complete U	2.00	4.00
BT20086 SS Son Goku, Majin Showdown U	1.50	3.00
BT20087 Son Goku, Spirit Bomb Hope R	1.00	2.00
BT20088 Majin Buu, Apocalyptic Awakening U	2.50	5.00
BT20089 Hercule, Rallying Hope U	1.25	2.50
BT20090 Majin Buu, Two Hearts U	2.00	4.00
BT20096 SS Son Goku & SS Vegeta, Ultimate Duo R	3.00	6.00
BT20098 Vegeta, Buying Time R	1.00	2.00
BT20100 Vegito, Unexpected Separation U	.50	1.00
BT20107 Majin Buu, Talent Manifest U	2.00	4.00
BT20114 Evil Saiyan/Cumber, Maddening Force U	3.00	6.00
BT20115 SS Cumber, Battle Frenzy U	2.00	4.00
BT20116 Fu, Assembling the Strong U	2.50	5.00
BT20118 Fu, All According to Plan R	1.25	2.50
BT20122 SS4 Son Goku, Otherworldly Infiltrator R	1.00	2.00
BT20123 Vegeta, Against All Odds R	.75	1.50
BT20125 SSB Vegito, Supreme Gleaming R	.40	.80
BT20129 Evil Saiyan, Incipient Malice U	1.25	2.50
BT20131 Cumber, Furious Frenzy R	1.00	2.00
BT20133 Fu, Scheming Overlord U	1.50	3.00
BT20136 Evil Aura Overflow U	.50	1.00
BT20137 SS Vegeta, Immediate Response R	1.25	2.50
BT20141 Deadly Clash U	1.00	2.00
BT20142 Nappa, Full-scale Attack R	.40	.80
BT20144 Android 21, Bewitching Battler U	1.00	2.00

2023 Dragon Ball Super Starter Deck Proud Warrior

SD2201 Vegeta/SS Vegeta, Fighting Instincts	.75	1.50
SD2202 Prince of Destruction Vegeta, Emotions Unleashed	1.00	2.00
SD2203 SS2 Son Goku, Overflowing Aura	.30	.60
SD2204 Majin Buu, Despair's Revival	.30	.75
SD2205 SS2 Son Goku, Destined Battle	1.50	3.00
SD2206 Prince of Destruction Vegeta, Destined Battle	2.00	4.00
SD2207 Trunks, Rambunctious Son	.30	.75

2023 Dragon Ball Super Starter Deck Ultimate Awakened Power

SD2101 Son Gohan/Son Gohan, Command of Universe 7	1.00	2.00
SD2102 Piccolo, Master-Student Technique	.30	.60
SD2103 Frieza, Unexpected Assistance	.25	.50
SD2104 Son Gohan, Master-Student Technique	.75	1.50

SD2105 Piccolo, Piercing Flash .30 .60
SD2106 Krillin, Clever Fighter .75 1.50
SD2107 Android 18, Perfect Teamwork .75 1.50

2023 Dragon Ball Super Wild Resurgence

BT21001 Son Goku/Son Goku, for the Sake of Family U .12 .25
BT21002 Garlic Jr./Garlic Jr., Immortal Being U .07 .15
BT21003 Son Goku, Full Power and Full Blast U .07 .15
BT21004 Piccolo, Unleashed Power U .07 .15
BT21005 Garlic Jr., Absorbing All U .07 .15
BT21006 Garlic Jr., Destruction and Revenge U .07 .15
BT21007 Garlic Jr., Child of Evil U .07 .15
BT21008 Son Goku, Overwhelming Power SPR .75 1.50
BT21008 Son Goku, Overwhelming Power SR .40 .80
BT21009 Son Goku, Enduring Fury R .12 .25
BT21010 Son Goku, Daily Training R .10 .20
BT21011 Son Goku & Piccolo, Arch-Rivals Fighting Together SPR2.00 4.00
BT21011 Son Goku & Piccolo, Arch-Rivals Fighting Together SR1.00 2.00
BT21012 Son Gohan, Awakened Hidden Power C .07 .15
BT21013 Piccolo, Plentiful Strength C .07 .15
BT21014 Piccolo, Prideful Strength R .12 .25
BT21015 Piccolo, Opposing Strength U .07 .15
BT21016 Krillin C .07 .10
BT21017 Krillin, Desperate Straits C .07 .15
BT21018 Krillin, Student Bonds C .07 .15
BT21019 Master Roshi C .07 .15
BT21020 Bulma, Talented Youth C .07 .15
BT21021 Chi-Chi, Protecting Mother C .07 .15
BT21022 Ox-King, Grandfather of Son Gohan C .07 .15
BT21023 Garlic Jr., Invitation to Eternal Darkness SPR .75 1.50
BT21023 Garlic Jr., Invitation to Eternal Darkness SR .20 .40
BT21024 Garlic Jr., Eternal Life SPR .20 .40
BT21024 Garlic Jr., Eternal Life SR .75 1.50
BT21025 Garlic Jr., Dark Ambitions C .07 .15
BT21026 Ginger, Two Sword Technique R .10 .20
BT21027 Ginger, Malevolent Henchman C .07 .15
BT21028 Sansyo, Giant Fighting Spirit R .10 .20
BT21029 Sansyo, Malevolent Henchman C .07 .15
BT21030 Nikky, One Sword Technique R .15 .30
BT21031 Nikky, Malevolent Henchman C .07 .15
BT21032 Power Pole R .20 .40
BT21033 Garlic Jr.'s Ambition C .07 .15
BT21034 Uub/Uub & Mr. Buu, Resonating Spirits U .10 .20
BT21035 Baby/Baby, Awakening With a Grudge U .07 .15
BT21036 Uub, Fusion of Two Spirits U .07 .15
BT21037 Baby, Finishing Revenge U .07 .15
BT21038 Uub, Holder of Majin Power U .07 .15
BT21039 Mr. Buu, Majin Defender U .07 .15
BT21040 Baby, Parasitizing Complete U .07 .15
BT21041 Baby, Parasitic Premonition U .07 .15
BT21042 SS3 Son Goku, Warrior Savior C .07 .15
BT21043 Son Goten, Domination Complete C .07 .15
BT21044 Pan C .07 .10
BT21045 Pan, Brave Defense C .07 .15
BT21046 Vegeta, Disturbing Harbinger C .07 .15
BT21047 Vegeta, Tempered Body C .07 .15
BT21048 Trunks, Domination Complete R .12 .25
BT21049 Bulla, Domination Complete R .12 .25
BT21050 Bulma, Domination Complete C .07 .15
BT21051 Uub, Focused Full-Strength Blow SPR 4.00 8.00
BT21051 Uub, Focused Full-Strength Blow SR 1.50 3.00
BT21052 Uub, Body Resistance SPR 2.00 4.00
BT21052 Uub, Body Resistance SR .30 .75
BT21053 Uub, Intercepting Kamehameha R .12 .25
BT21054 Uub, Warrior Left on Earth R .20 .40
BT21055 Uub, Standing Up to a Threat U .07 .15
BT21056 Hercule, Earth's Champion C .07 .10
BT21057 Hercule, Friend's Defense C .07 .15
BT21058 Mr. Buu, For Friendship C .07 .15
BT21059 Mr. Buu, In Disguise C .07 .15
BT21060 Baby, Shining Gold Evil Lifeform SPR 3.00 6.00
BT21060 Baby, Shining Gold Evil Lifeform SR 1.00 2.00
BT21061 Baby, Anti-Saiyan Murder Weapon R .20 .40
BT21062 Baby, Bitter Revenge on Saiyans SPR 2.50 5.00
BT21062 Baby, Bitter Revenge on Saiyans SR .75 1.50
BT21063 Baby, A Quiet Beginning C .07 .15
BT21064 Dr. Myuu C .07 .10
BT21065 Full Strength Absorption R .12 .25
BT21066 Universal Tuffleization Plan C .07 .15
BT21067 Son Gohan/SS Son Gohan,
The Results of Fatherly Training U .07 .15
BT21068 Cell/Cell, The Greatest Threat to Mankind U .07 .15
BT21069 SS2 Son Gohan, Trigger to Fierce Rage C .07 .15
BT21070 Cell, Perfect Resurrection U .07 .15
BT21071 Cell, Waiting Impatiently U .07 .15
BT21072 Cell, About to Explode U .07 .15
BT21073 SS Son Goku, Assisting His Son R .25 .50
BT21074 Android 16, Final Wish U .07 .15
BT21075 Cell, Greedy Absorption U .07 .15
BT21076 SS Son Goku, Decision Made SPR 3.00 6.00
BT21076 SS Son Goku, Decision Made SR 1.25 2.50
BT21077 SS Son Goku, Believing in His Son R .15 .30
BT21078 SS Son Goku, Showing the Results of Training R .20 .40
BT21079 SS Son Goku & SS2 Son Gohan,
Father-Son Solidarity SPR 12.50 25.00
BT21079 SS Son Goku & SS2 Son Gohan, Father-Son Solidarity SR3.00 6.00
BT21080 SS Son Gohan, Showing the Results of Training R .50 1.00
BT21081 SS Vegeta, Arrogance C .07 .15
BT21082 SS Trunks, Mysterious Future Warrior C .07 .15
BT21083 Piccolo C .07 .15
BT21084 Krillin, Battle Support C .07 .15
BT21085 Hercule, Cheater U .07 .10
BT21086 Android 17, Encroaching Hand of Evil C .07 .15
BT21087 Android 18, Encroaching Hand of Evil C .07 .15
BT21088 Cell, Pursuit of Despair SPR 1.25 2.50
BT21088 Cell, Pursuit of Despair SR .40 .80
BT21089 Cell, Giving in to Despair C .07 .15
BT21090 Cell, Saiyan Absorption R .07 .15
BT21091 Cell, Namekian Absorption C .07 .15
BT21092 Cell, Preparing a Plan C .07 .15
BT21093 Cell, Chrysalis Form C .07 .15
BT21094 Cell, Birth Omen C .07 .15
BT21095 Spy Robot, Collecting Cells C .07 .15
BT21096 Hyperbolic Time Chamber C .07 .15
BT21097 Unceasing Awakened Rage SR 7.50 15.00
BT21098 Cell's Full-Power Kamehameha R .15 .30
BT21099 Gingertown C .07 .15
BT21100 SSB Son Goku/SSB Vegeta, God-Level Power U .07 .15
BT21101 Frieza/Frieza, The Emperor Who Swore Revenge U .07 .15
BT21102 Golden Frieza, Shining Emperor R .12 .25
BT21103 SSB Son Goku, Finishing Blow R .20 .40
BT21104 Whis, Time Regression U .07 .15
BT21105 Sorbet, Emperor's Subject U .07 .15
BT21106 Tagoma, Emperor's Subject U .07 .15
BT21107 SSB Son Goku, Unceasing Progress R .12 .25
BT21108 SS Son Goku, Waiting To See C .07 .15
BT21109 Son Goku, Trial Run C .07 .15
BT21110 SSB Son Goku & SSB Vegeta, Rivalry SPR 4.00 8.00
BT21110 SSB Son Goku & SSB Vegeta, Rivalry SR 1.25 2.50
BT21111 SSB Son Goku VS Golden Frieza, Spirit Clash SPR 7.50 15.00
BT21111 SSB Son Goku VS Golden Frieza, Spirit Clash SR 1.50 3.00
BT21112 SSB Vegeta, Unceasing Progress U .07 .15
BT21113 Vegeta, Trial Run C .07 .15
BT21114 Vegeta, Waiting To See C .07 .15
BT21115 Piccolo, A Bad Feeling C .07 .15
BT21116 Krillin, Remembering Terror C .07 .10
BT21117 Master Roshi C .07 .15
BT21118 Bulma, Making a Wish C .07 .15
BT21119 Jaco, A Dangerous Signal C .07 .15
BT21120 Golden Frieza, Evolved Emperor SPR 1.50 3.00
BT21120 Golden Frieza, Evolved Emperor SR .30 .75
BT21121 Frieza, Waiting To See R .12 .25
BT21122 Frieza, Limitless Raw Power U .07 .15
BT21123 Frieza, Overflowing With Confidence U .07 .15
BT21124 Frieza, Coldhearted Behavior C .07 .15
BT21125 Frieza, Bitter Scream R .15 .30
BT21126 Sorbet, Pursuing Deepest Desires C .07 .15
BT21127 Sorbet, Devoted Support C .07 .15
BT21128 Tagoma, Pursuing Deepest Desires C .07 .15
BT21129 Tagoma C .07 .15
BT21130 Shisami, Pursuing Deepest Desires U .07 .15
BT21131 Training With Whis C .07 .15
BT21132 The Return of the Army of Terror SR 1.50 3.00
BT21133 SGG Trunks, Guiding Light U .07 .15
BT21134 SGG Trunks, Sealing Power R .20 .40
BT21135 Supreme Kai of Time, Releasing Time Power C .10 .20
BT21136 Mira, Creator Absorption R .30 .75
BT21137 Towa, Combo Attack U .07 .15
BT21138 Towa, Rebuilding the Demon Realm C .07 .15
BT21139 Dark King Mechikabura, Ruler of the Demon Realm R .15 .30
BT21140 Shroom, Violent Majin Assault U .07 .15
BT21141 Salsa, Violent Majin Assault C .07 .15
BT21142 Whis, Angel's Teachings SR .75 1.50
BT21143 Beerus, Judge of Ruin SR .25 .50
BT21144 Android 16, Companion for Desperation R .10 .20
BT21145 Cell, Ultimate Lifeform of Despair R .15 .30
BT21146 Cell, Longing for Perfection R .15 .30
BT21147 Shenron, the Eternal Dragon SCR 75.00 150.00
BT21148 Son Goku, Peace Resolution GDR 1,000.00 2,000.00
BT21148 Son Goku, Peace Resolution SCR 100.00 200.00
BT21149 Dark King Mechikabura, Last Judgement SCR 25.00 50.00

2018 Final Fantasy Opus V

5001C Red Mage C .07 .15
5002R Ayame R .10 .20
5003C Ifrit C .07 .15
5004R Caius R .10 .20
5005R Gadot R .10 .20
5006R Carla R .10 .20
5007H Royal Ripeness H .15 .30
5008R Grenade R .10 .20
5009C Black Mage C .07 .15
5010C Manasvin Warmech C .07 .15
5011H Vermilion Bird l'Cie Zhuyu H .15 .30
5012H Vermilion Bird l'Cie Caetuna H .15 .30
5013C Warrior C .07 .15
5014C Warrior C .07 .15
5015H Tellah H .15 .30
5016C Fighter C .07 .15
5017C Ninja C .07 .15
5018L Palom L .30 .60
5019L Phoenix L 7.50 15.00
5020R Volker R .10 .20
5021R Mutsuki R .10 .20
5022C Parivir C .07 .15
5023C Ryid C .07 .15
5024H Luneth H .15 .30
5025H Aloeidai H .15 .30
5026C Vayne C .07 .15
5027R Unei R .10 .20
5028C Arcanist C .07 .15
5029L Orphan L 2.00 4.00
5030C Scholar C .07 .15
5031H Edward H .75 1.50
5032H Glasya Labolas H .15 .30
5033R Gumbah R .10 .20
5034C Gesper C .07 .15
5035C Conjurer C .07 .15
5036L The Emperor L .50 1.00
5037R Zeid R .10 .20
5038C Arithmetician C .07 .15
5039R Cid Raines R .10 .20
5040C Thaumaturge C .07 .15
5041R Snow R .10 .20
5042C Trickster C .07 .15
5043R Hurdy R .10 .20
5044C Mateus, the Corrupt C .07 .15
5045H Barnabas H .15 .30
5046R Buccaboo R .10 .20
5047C Mystic Knight C .07 .15
5048H Lugae H .15 .30
5049C Asura C .07 .15
5050H Adelle H 1.00 2.00
5051R Aria (TYPE-0) R .10 .20
5052H Arc H .15 .30
5053R Echo R .10 .20
5054C Ranger C .07 .15
5055C Thief C .07 .15
5056H Cid Pollendina H .15 .30
5057C White Mage C .07 .15
5058C Elementalist C .07 .15
5059R Semih Lafihna R .10 .20
5060C Chocobo C .07 .15
5061C Chocobo Knight C .07 .15
5062L Diabolos L 10.00 20.00
5063H Deathgaze H .15 .30
5064R Nanaa Mihgo R .10 .20
5065C Ninja C .07 .15
5066R Penelo R .10 .20
5067R Miounne R .10 .20
5068L Y'shtola L 7.50 15.00
5069H Luso H .15 .30
5070C Reks C .07 .15
5071R Leyak R .10 .20
5072C Spiceacilian C .07 .15
5073R Heretical Knight Garland R .10 .20
5074H Ingus H .50 1.00
5075L Wol L 12.00 25.00
5076C Botanist C .07 .15
5077H Carbuncle H .15 .30
5078R Gabranth R .10 .20
5079H Calbrena H .15 .30
5080R Grav'iton R .10 .20
5081C Cockatrice C .07 .15
5082C Miner C .07 .15
5083C PSICOM Enforcer C .07 .15
5084C PSICOM Warden C .07 .15
5085R Sarah (MOBIUS) R .10 .20
5086L Cecil L 7.50 15.00
5087R Doga R .10 .20
5088C Flandit C .07 .15
5089C Berserker C .07 .15
5090R Hill Gigas R .10 .20
5091H Star Sibyl H .60 1.25
5092C Master Monk C .07 .15
5093C Mog (MOBIUS) C .07 .15
5094R Momodi R .10 .20
5095H Yang H .15 .30
5096C Lanista C .07 .15
5097C Red Mage C .07 .15
5098C Assassin C .07 .15
5099H Illua H 1.25 2.50
5100H Odin H .30 .75
5101H Twilight Odin H .15 .30
5102C Scholar C .07 .15
5103R Cid of Clan Gully R .10 .20
5104R Khalia Chival R .10 .20
5105R Quon R .10 .20
5106R Black Knight R .10 .20
5107H Thancred H .50 1.00
5108L Zemus L 4.00 8.00
5109R Destin R .10 .20
5110C Bunkerbeast C .07 .15
5111R Trion R .10 .20
5112R Naghi R .10 .20
5113C Ravager C .07 .15
5114C Cannoneer C .07 .15
5115C Dark Knight C .07 .15
5116H Lightning H .15 .30
5117C Ramuh C .07 .15
5118L Ramza L 2.50 5.00
5119C Dragoon C .07 .15
5120C Louisoix C .07 .15
5121R Andoria R .10 .20
5122R Vossler R .10 .20
5123H Aria (III) H .15 .30
5124H Ozma H .15 .30
5125C Ondore C .07 .15
5126L Cloud of Darkness L 7.50 15.00
5127R Curilla R .10 .20
5128R Claidie R .10 .20
5129C Schrodinger C .07 .15
5130R Tonberry R .10 .20
5131C Arcanist C .07 .15
5132R Baderon R .10 .20
5133H Bismarck H 1.00 2.00
5134R Celestia R .10 .20
5135L Porom L 3.00 6.00
5136C Flintlock C .07 .15
5137C Green Mage C .07 .15
5138C Moogle Knight C .07 .15
5139C Leviathan C .07 .15
5140C Fisher C .07 .15
5141H Refia H .75 1.50
5142H Rosa H .15 .30
5143C Orator C .07 .15
5144C Orator C .07 .15
5145L Vaan L .75 1.50
5146H Wol H .15 .30
5147L Eald'narche L .60 1.25
5148H Kam'lanaut H .30 .75
5149S Amodar S .50 1.00
5150S Noel S .50 1.00
5151S Lebreau S .30 .60
5152S Serah S .75 1.50
5153S Mog (XIII-2) S .30 .60
5154S Yeul S .50 1.00
5155S Vaan S .30 .60
5156S Balthier S .60 1.25
5157S Fran S .60 1.25
5158S Yda S .30 .60
5159S Papalymo S .30 .60
5160S Minfilia S .30 .60
5161S Alisaie S .30 .75
5162S Alphinaud S .50 1.00
5163S Urianger S 1.00 2.00
5164S Ashe S .30 .60
5165S Larsa S .30 .60
5166S Rasler S 1.25 2.50

2021 Final Fantasy Crystal Dominion

C001 Crystal Token C 1.00 2.50
C002 Crystal Token C 1.00 2.50
15001R Ifrita H .10 .25
15002C Sky Warrior C .01 .08
15003C Sky Samurai C .08 .20
15004C Edgar C .05 .12
15005R Guy R .10 .25
15006H Cyan H .15 .40
15007C Samurai C .05 .12
15008C Shadow EX C .08 .20
15009C Bahamut C .08 .20
15010R Vargas R .08 .20
15011L Palom L 2.50 6.00
15012H Faris H .10 .25
15013L Firion L .75 2.00
15014H Brynhildr EX H .60 1.50
15015R Bwagi R .04 .10
15016C Bomb C .04 .10
15017H Machina H .20 .50
15018C Sabin C .05 .12
15019C Josef C .05 .12
15020R Rinok R .05 .12
15021R General Leo R .08 .20
15022C Amidatelion C .08 .20
15023R Werei R .10 .25
15024R Orphan EX R .05 .12
15025C Scholar C .04 .10
15026C Kazusa C .04 .10
15027R The Emperor R .04 .10
15028H Gogo H 1.25 3.00
15029R Zalera H .15 .40
15030H Shiva EX H .40 1.00
15031C Shiva C .05 .12
15032C Cid Raines C .04 .10
15033C Jumbo Flan C .04 .10
15034R Snow R .04 .10
15035H Setzer H .20 .50
15036H Celes H 1.25 3.00
15037L Terra L 2.50 6.00
15038C Knight C .04 .10
15039C Mime C .04 .10
15040C Larzos C .04 .10
15041l Lightning L 5.00 12.00
15042R Locke EX R .12 .30
15043R Alexander R .08 .20
15044L Vaan L 1.50 4.00
15045H Edge H .20 .50
15046C Dancer C .04 .10
15047R Kytes R .05 .12
15048L Kain EX L 2.00 5.00
15049C Garchimacera C .04 .10
15050C Gigantuar C .04 .10
15051C Shikaree G C .05 .12

15052C Chocobo C	.08	.20
15053H Diabolos H	.12	.30
15054R Nono R	.05	.12
15055H Bartz EX H	.20	.50
15056R Filo R	.10	.25
15057R Maria R	.05	.12
15058C Dragoon C	.05	.12
15059C Llyud C	.04	.10
15060R Leon R	.08	.20
15061H Lehko Habhoka H	.12	.30
15062C Rem C	.04	.10
15063C Romaa Mihgo C	.05	.12
15064C Vanille C	.04	.10
15065C Scholar C	.05	.12
15066C Galuf C	.04	.10
15067R Gijuk R	.08	.20
15068R Gilgamesh R	.05	.12
15069C Cu Sith C	.05	.12
15070R Cait Sith (XI) EX R	.05	.12
15071H Kefka EX H	.10	.25
15072R Cid Sophiar R	.08	.20
15073H Cecil H	.10	.25
15074C Zombie C	.08	.20
15075R Titan EX R	.08	.20
15076C Titan C	.04	.10
15077H Dadaluma H	.10	.25
15078C Berserker C	.04	.10
15079R Ba'Gamnan R	.04	.10
15080C Geomancer C	.10	.25
15081C Firion C	.01	.08
15082H Hecatoncheir H	2.00	5.00
15083L Rydia L	10.00	25.00
15084L Robel-Akbel L	2.50	6.00
15085R Aquila EX R	.05	.12
15086R Axis R	.10	.25
15087C Aranea C	.05	.12
15088H Vayne H	.10	.25
15089C Sky Soldier C	.05	.12
15090H Odin H	.15	.40
15091C Thunder Drake C	.04	.10
15092C Sonitus C	.04	.10
15093R Tredd R	.08	.20
15094L Nyx L	2.00	5.00
15095C Ninja C	.05	.12
15096C Noel C	.04	.10
15097H Feolthanos H	.10	.25
15098C Pelna C	.08	.20
15099C Magitek Armor C	.05	.12
15100R Ragelise EX R	.04	.10
15101R Ramuh R	.10	.25
15102H Lilisette H	.15	.40
15103R Regis R	.08	.20
15104L Lady Lilith L	4.00	10.00
15105C Remora C	.04	.10
15106C Atomos C	.05	.12
15107H Umaro H	.15	.40
15108C Dancer C	.05	.12
15109R Ultros R	.08	.20
15110C Gau EX C	.10	.25
15111C Keiss C	.10	.25
15112R Shinryu Celestia R	.04	.10
15113C Strago C	.04	.10
15115C Hilda EX C	.05	.12
15115H Penelo L	.20	.50
15117R Famfrit R	.05	.12
15118C Blue Wyrm C	.10	.25
15119L Porom L	12.00	30.00
15120H Mind Flayer H	.50	1.25
15121R Mayakov H	.05	.12
15122L Mog (VI) L	.75	2.00
15123C Oracle C	.04	.10
15124H Relm H	.30	.75
15125R Lunafreya R	.08	.20
15126R Lenna R	.10	.25
15127H Ace H	.12	.30
15128L Noctis L	2.00	5.00
15129L Ardyn L	.60	1.50
15130H Nox Suzaku H	.10	.25
15131S Wedge S	.30	.75
15132S Jessie S	.40	1.00
15133S Barret S	.40	1.00
15134S Biggs S	.50	1.25
15135S Tseng S	.30	.75
15136S President Shinra EX S	3.00	8.00
15137S Rude S	.25	.60
15138S Reno S	.25	.60
15139S Cloud S	.60	1.50
15140S Rufus S	.60	1.50

2021 Final Fantasy Opus XIII Crystal Radiance

13001R Irvine R	.08	.20
13002L Akstar L	2.00	5.00
13003C Imaginary Soldier C	.05	.12
13004C Clavat C	.08	.20
13005C Black Mage C	.05	.12
13006C Xande C	.08	.20
13007R Cinque R	.10	.25
13008R Vermilion Bird l'Cie Caetuna R	.05	.12
13009H Selphie H	.15	.40
13010C Onion Knight (FFT) C	.05	.12
13011C Iron Giant C	.08	.20
13012H Bahamut EX H	.20	.50
13013C Palom C	.05	.12
13014R Larkeicus R	.10	.25
13015C Luneth C	.10	.25
13016H Rubicante H	.15	.40
13017H Rain H	.25	.60
13018H Quistis C	.10	.25
13019C Coeurl C	.05	.12
13020C Kurasame C	.05	.12
13021R Shiva EX R	.10	.25
13022H Cid Randell H	10.00	25.00
13023R Charlotte R	2.50	6.00
13024R Squall R	.10	.25
13025C Onion Knight (FFT) C	.05	.12
13026C Tellah EX C	.05	.12
13027C Time Mage C	.05	.12
13028L Physalis L	2.50	6.00
13029C Counterfeit Wraith C	.08	.20
13030C Yuke C	.05	.12
13031R Laguna R	.10	.25
13032H Rinoa H	.40	1.00
13033R Levnato R	.05	.12
13034H Remedi H	.25	.60
13035C Arc C	.08	.20
13036R Eight R	.10	.25
13037C Ochu C	.08	.20
13038H Cid Haze H	.10	.25
13039C Cid Pollendina EX C	.05	.12
13040L Shara L	1.00	2.50
13041C White Mage C	.05	.12
13042C White Mage C	.05	.12
13043C Stiltzkin C	.10	.25
13044C Selkie C	.05	.12
13045R Dryad EX R	.05	.12
13046R Pavlov R	.10	.25
13047H Barbariccia H	1.25	3.00
13048H Balthier H	1.25	3.00
13049C Counterfeit Youth C	.08	.20
13050R Mid R	.10	.25
13051R Mog (FFBE) R	.10	.25
13052C Abyss Worm C	.08	.20
13053R Alexander EX R	.10	.25
13054C Lady of Antiquity C	.10	.25
13055C Ingus C	.08	.20
13056R Vanille R	.08	.20
13057H Graff H	.20	.50
13058C Sherlotta C	.08	.20
13059H Scarmiglione H	.15	.40
13060R Cecil R	.08	.20
13061C Hugh Yurg C	.05	.12
13062H Bhunivelze H	.15	.40
13063C Monk C	.08	.20
13064R Yang R	.10	.25
13065R Rydia R	.10	.25
13066C Lilty C	.04	.10
13067L Leo L	.30	.75
13068C Alchemist C	.05	.12
13069C Red Mage C	.05	.12
13070C Delusory Warlock C	.10	.25
13072R Odin EX R	.60	1.50
13073H Kain H	.20	.50
13074C Clavat C	.08	.20
13075R Sakura R	.10	.25
13076R Jake R	.08	.20
13077C Zemus C	.08	.20
13078C Propagator C	.08	.20
13079L Behemoth K L	10.00	25.00
13080C Marach C	.05	.12
13081H Lightning H	.40	1.00
13082C Rapha C	.05	.12
13083H Lid H	.25	.60
13084C Dragoon C	.10	.25
13085R Lumina R	.12	.30
13086R Agrias EX R	.20	.50
13087C Delusory Knight C	.08	.20
13088H Elle H	.25	.60
13089C Oilboyle C	.05	.12
13090L Ovelia L	4.00	10.00
13091H Cagnazzo H	1.25	3.00
13092C Sage C	.05	.12
13093H Sara H	3.00	8.00
13094C Simon C	.05	.12
13095C Tonogiri C	.04	.10
13096R Nichol R	.08	.20
13097C Viking C	.08	.20
13098R Fina R	.10	.25
13099C Yuke C	.04	.10
13100R Leviathan EX R	.50	1.25
13101R Luka R	.10	.25
13102C Refia C	.05	.12
13103L Materia L	1.50	4.00
13104L Spiritus L	1.00	2.50
13105R Lasswell R	.10	.25
13106H Onion Knight H	.20	.50
13107C Cater C	.05	.12
13108L Llednar L	1.00	2.50
13109R Hope R	.10	.25
13110H Unei H	.10	.25
13111C Delita C	.10	.25
13112L White Tiger l'Cie Nimbus L	2.50	6.00
13113R Gudon R	.10	.25
13114H Kunshira H	.25	.60
13115L Golbez EX L	1.50	4.00
13116C Lightning C	.08	.20
13117R Wol R	.10	.25
13118C Sarah (MOBIUS) C	.10	.25
13119L Sophie L	8.00	20.00
13120H Doga H	.20	.50
13121R Ramza R	.10	.25
13122H Aldore Emperor H	.12	.30
13123L Nine L	2.00	5.00
13124C Noel C	.08	.20
13125R Yuzuki R	.75	2.00
13126C Ultimecia C	.08	.20
13127H Chime H	.15	.40
13128L Celestia L	4.00	10.00
13129S Philia S	1.00	2.50
13130S Ran'jit S	.40	1.00
13131S Emet-Selch S	.75	2.00
13132S Titania S	.25	.60
13133S The Crystal Exarch S	.40	1.00
13134S Y'shtola S	1.00	2.50
13135S Urianger EX S	10.00	25.00
13136S Thancred S	4.00	10.00
13137S Innocence S	.30	.75
13138S The Oracle of Light S	3.00	8.00
13071R/2101H Exdeath R	.05	.12

2021 Final Fantasy Opus XIV Crystal Abyss

14001C Amalj'aa C	.08	.20
14002R Ifrita EX R	.10	.25
14003R Illua R	.10	.25
14004C Warrior of Light C	.05	.12
14005C Oelde Leonis C	.04	.10
14006R Ifrit, Lord of the Inferno EX R	.15	.40
14007L Garland L	10.00	25.00
14008C Caius C	.05	.12
14009R Gabranth R	.10	.25
14010H Gutsco H	.30	.75
14011H Susano, Lord of the Revel H	.60	1.50
14012C Kojin C	.08	.20
14013C Koboldroid Yang C	.05	.12
14014C Samurai C	.08	.20
14015R Zenos R	.15	.40
14016C Geomancer C	.05	.12
14017H Mom Bomb H	.15	.40
14018C Maliris (IX) C	.05	.12
14019R Red XIII R	.12	.30
14020R Ysayle R	.10	.25
14021H Valfodr H	.12	.30
14022H Kam'lanaut H	.12	.30
14023L Gilgamesh (FFBE) L	20.00	50.00
14024C Bard C	.04	.10
14025C Kuja C	.08	.20
14026R Kefka EX R	.10	.25
14027R The Emperor R	.08	.20
14028C Goblin C	.05	.12
14029R Shivalry EX R	.10	.25
14030C Serah C	.05	.12
14031R Good King Moggle Mog XII R	.10	.25
14032R Proto fal'Cie Adam R	.10	.25
14033C Devout C	.08	.20
14034C Time Mage C	.08	.20
14035C Don Corneo C	.05	.12
14036L Shiva, Lady of Frost L	1.50	4.00
14037C Moogle (XIV) C	.05	.12
14038H Lugae H	.25	.60
14039R Adelle R	.08	.20
14040C Abquhbah C	.08	.20
14041C Ixali C	.10	.25
14042L Bismarck, Lord of the Mists L	2.00	5.00
14043C Cactuaroni C	.05	.12
14044C White Mage C	.05	.12
14045H Sin H	.30	.75
14046C Sniper C	.04	.10
14047R Choco/Mog EX R	.10	.25
14048C Tiamat (IX) C	.05	.12
14049H Typhon H	.60	1.50
14050R Naja Salaheem R	.08	.20
14051C Vanu Vanu C	.05	.12
14052C Fran C	.08	.20
14053R Mjrn R	.10	.25
14054R Jote EX R	.10	.25
14055C Lezaford C	.04	.10
14056R Garuda, Lady of the Vortex R	.10	.25
14057H Rosa H	4.00	10.00
14058C Dark Knight C	.05	.12
14059R Wol R	.10	.25
14060R Carbuncle EX R	.10	.25
14061H Calbrena H	.10	.25
14062L Titan, Lord of Crags L	5.00	12.00
14063C Chichu C	.10	.25
14064R Kitone EX R	.12	.30
14065L Cloud L	4.00	10.00
14066C Kobold C	.08	.20
14067H Shantotto H	.30	.75
14068C Dark Elf C	.10	.25
14069R Noctis R	.08	.20
14070R Ba'Gamnan C	.04	.10
14071C Paladin C	.05	.12
14072R Hojo R	.05	.12
14073R Muraga Fennes R	.05	.12
14074C Monk C	.08	.20
14075H Mont Leonis H	.20	.50
14076C Lich (IX) C	.05	.12
14077C Ovjang C	.05	.12
14078H Trap Door H	.15	.40
14079R Aphmau R	.04	.10
14080R Exdeath R	.10	.25
14081C Puppetmaster C	.05	.12
14082C Gnath C	.08	.20
14083C Fachan C	.05	.12
14084C Schuzelt C	.04	.10
14085C Sylph (XIV) C	.05	.12
14086R Heidegger R	.10	.25
14087L Ravana, Savior of the Gnath L	4.00	10.00
14088C Mnejing C	.05	.12
14089C Ewen C	.05	.12
14090R Ramuh, Lord of Levin R	.10	.25
14091R Ramuh EX R	.10	.25
14092C Dragoon C	.10	.25
14093H Luso EX H	.12	.30
14094R Ravus R	.08	.20
14095H Roche H	1.25	3.00
14096C Blue Mage C	.05	.12
14097C Ananta C	.10	.25
14098R Ultimecia R	.10	.25
14099C Eiko C	.08	.20
14100H Octomammoth H	.40	1.00
14101R Ultros R	.10	.25
14102L Leviathan, Lord of the Whorl L	2.00	5.00
14103R Quina R	.08	.20
14104C Kraken (IX) C	.05	.12
14105C Corsair C	.04	.10
14106H Golbez H	.30	.75
14107C Sahagin (XIV) C	.08	.20
14108H Jecht H	.20	.50
14109C Steiner C	.05	.12
14110C Tonberry C	.10	.25
14111R Lakshmi, Lady of Bliss R	.15	.40
14112L Larsa EX L	1.50	4.00
14113R Leviathan EX R	.75	2.00
14114R Luzaf R	.10	.25
14115L Shinryu L	4.00	10.00
14116H Macherie H	.30	.75
14117L Omega L	1.00	2.50
14118H Sterne Leonis H	.25	.60
14119C Ardyn C	.08	.20
14120H Tifa H	8.00	20.00
14121L Barret L	6.00	15.00
14122L Al-Cid L	4.00	10.00
14123C Sephiroth C	.10	.25
14124H Zeromus H	2.50	6.00
14125L Vaan L	4.00	10.00
14126C Aerith C	.08	.20
14127H Zidane H	.50	1.25
14128H Prishe H	.50	1.25
14129H Gessho H	.20	.50
14130H Cloud of Darkness H	.10	.25

2022 Final Fantasy Emissaries of Light

C003 Crystal Token (Earth) C	1.50	4.00
C004 Crystal Token (Water) C	1.00	2.50
16001R Vaan R	.08	.20
16002H Ace EX H	.10	.25
16003C Elbis EX C	.05	.12
16004C Onion Knight C	.04	.10
16005C Cloud C	.08	.20
16006C Crimson Hound C	.04	.10
16007R Black Waltz 2 R	.08	.20
16008C Black Mage C	.04	.10
16009C Samurai C	.05	.12
16010H Djinn H	.15	.40
16011L Squall L	8.00	20.00
16012R Suzaku EX R	.04	.10
16013H Sol H	.15	.40
16014R Delita R	.08	.20
16015H Morrow H	.12	.30
16016C Bahamut C	.08	.20
16017R Ramza R	.10	.25
16018C Lilty C	.05	.12
16019R Luneth R	.10	.25
16020L Luso L	.60	1.50
16021C Rain EX C	.04	.10
16022R Erwin R	.05	.12
16023R Agrias H	.40	1.00
16024H Vincent H	.10	.25
16025C Bard C	.04	.10
16026L Cloud of Darkness L	.30	.75
16027C Black Waltz 1 C	.05	.12
16028C Shiva C	.08	.20
16029R Shelke R	.05	.12

16030L Shantotto L	4.00	10.00
16031R Scarlet R	.05	.12
16032H Serah H	.10	.25
16033C Celes EX C	.04	.10
16034C DG Sniper C	.05	.12
16035C YKT-63 C	.04	.10
16036C Devout C	.04	.10
16037R Babus R	.04	.10
16038H Byblos H	1.00	2.50
16039C Heavy Armored Soldier EX C	.05	.12
16040R Mustadio R	.05	.12
16041C Yunalesca C	.08	.20
16042R Lasswell C	.08	.20
16043H Atomos H	2.00	5.00
16044L Wol L	1.00	2.50
16045C Gargoyle C	.04	.10
16046C Chocobo Chick (VII) C	.05	.12
16047R Sherlotta EX R	.10	.25
16048H Zidane H	.50	1.25
16049R Seiryu EX R	.05	.12
16050H Ceodore H	.12	.30
16051L Cecil L	8.00	20.00
16052C Selkie C	.04	.10
16053H King Tycoon H	.12	.30
16054C Chocobo C	.05	.12
16055C Chocobo Sam C	.05	.12
16056R Fat Chocobo R	.08	.20
16057C Ninja C	.04	.10
16058R Fina R	.08	.20
16059C Pecciotta EX C	.04	.10
16060C Madam M EX C	.05	.12
16061R Yuri R	.05	.12
16062C Lexa C	.05	.12
16063R Rosa R	.04	.10
16064C Dark Knight C	.04	.10
16065C Amber EX C	.05	.12
16066R Heretical Knight Garland R	.10	.25
16067L Aerith L	1.00	2.50
16068C Eiko C	.04	.10
16069C Ciaran C	.01	.08
16070L Kirin L	1.00	2.50
16071C Gladiator C	.04	.10
16072C Beastmaster C	.04	.10
16073C Benjamin C	.01	.08
16074C Cactuar C	.08	.20
16075R Shinju R	.10	.25
16076R Sophie R	.08	.20
16077R Terra R	.08	.20
16078C Demonolith C	.04	.10
16079H Hades H	.10	.25
16080H Madam Edel H	.50	1.25
16081R Mira R	.08	.20
16082H Mont Leonis H	.10	.25
16083H Layle H	.12	.30
16084R Ieslie R	.10	.25
16085C Assassin C	.04	.10
16086C Ixion C	.08	.20
16087C Puppetmaster C	.04	.10
16088L Black Waltz 3 L	1.00	2.50
16089H Zack H	.12	.30
16090R Seymour R	.10	.25
16091C Chadley C	.05	.12
16092C Noel EX C	.05	.12
16093R Noctis R	.10	.25
16094C Palmer C	.05	.12
16095H Vivi EX H	.12	.30
16096R Byakko EX R	.04	.10
16097H Hyoh H	.20	.50
16098H Spectral Keeper H	.20	.50
16099C Merald C	.05	.12
16100L Y'shtola L	2.50	6.00
16101C Yuke C	.04	.10
16102R Lann R	.05	.12
16103C Larva C	.04	.10
16104R Reeve R	.10	.25
16105R Reynn R	.08	.20
16106R Andrea Rhodea R	.05	.12
16107R Ezel R	.10	.25
16108C Kimahri C	.05	.12
16109C Kyrie EX C	.05	.12
16110C Clavat C	.04	.10
16111R Genbu EX R	.04	.10
16112C Corsair C	.04	.10
16113C Sahagin C	.05	.12
16114C White Mage C	.05	.12
16115H Sarah (MOBIUS) H	.12	.30
16116L Tidus L	4.00	10.00
16117H Tros H	1.50	4.00
16118C Fiona EX C	.05	.12
16119H Fusoya H	.15	.40
16120C Firion C	.04	.10
16121R Vesvia EX R	.08	.20
16122R Marche R	.04	.10
16123L Meia L	.50	1.25
16124H Lightning H	.60	1.50
16125C Leviathan C	.05	.12
16126R Leo R	.04	.10
16127L Warrior of Light L	.50	1.25
16128H Bartz H	.15	.40
16129L Chaos L	10.00	25.00
16130H Twintania H	.10	.25
16131S Jecht EX S	.25	.60
16132S Bahamut S	.20	.50
16133S Braska S	.50	1.25
16134S Yuna S	.20	.50
16135S Lulu S	2.50	6.00
16136S Auron S	.40	1.00
16137S Rikku EX S	.40	1.00
16138S Wakka S	.30	.75
16139S Tidus EX S	.50	1.25
16140S Sin S	.20	.50

2022 Final Fantasy Rebellion's Call

17001H Adelard H	.25	.60
17002L Edgar L	5.00	12.00
17003C Elfe EX C	.10	.25
17004C Garland C	.04	.10
17005C King C	.01	.08
17006R Gosetsu R	.10	.25
17007C Goblin C	.08	.20
17008H Samurai H	.20	.50
17009C Samurai C	.08	.20
17010C Scott C	.05	.12
17011R Zenos R	.10	.25
17012R Tifa EX R	.10	.25
17013C Berserker C	.04	.10
17014R Bahamut R	.10	.25
17015H Jet Bahamut H	.10	.25
17016L Hien L	6.00	15.00
17017H Sabin H	.30	.75
17018C Mystic Knight C	.05	.12
17019R Marilith R	.08	.20
17020R Montblanc R	.04	.10
17021C Red XIII C	.08	.20
17022H Umaro H	.12	.30
17023H Scholar H	.10	.25
17024C Supersoldier C	.04	.10
17025C Edward C	.08	.20
17026H Khury Wezette H	.10	.25
17027R Shiva R	.08	.20
17028C Calautidon C	.05	.12
17029L Xezat L	.60	1.50
17030H Setzer H	.10	.25
17031L Serah L	1.00	2.50
17032C Terra C	.08	.20
17033C Time Mage C	.05	.12
17034R Hurdy R	.05	.12
17035R Garnet Bahamut R	.08	.20
17036R Amber Bahamut R	.10	.25
17037C Harley C	.10	.25
17038R White Tiger l'Cie Qun'mi R	.10	.25
17039C Fencer C	.04	.10
17040C Mog (XIII-2) C	.05	.12
17041C Yotsuyu EX C	.05	.12
17042R Legendary Turk R	.10	.25
17043H Dancer H	.20	.50
17044R Onion Knight R	.10	.25
17045R Gargas R	.05	.12
17046C Ranger C	.04	.10
17047L Kelger L	1.25	3.00
17048C Thief C	.05	.12
17049C Cid Pollendina C	.08	.20
17050C Cecil EX C	.04	.10
17051C Seven C	.05	.12
17052H Dario Hourne H	.12	.30
17053R Chocobo EX R	.20	.50
17054R Tiamat EX R	.05	.12
17055H Typhon H	.15	.40
17056L Noel L	.60	1.50
17057H Penelo H	.12	.30
17058R Fuhito R	.05	.12
17059L Hope C	.04	.10
17060C Yagudo C	.05	.12
17061C Archer C	.04	.10
17062C Ricard C	.04	.10
17063R Luso R	.10	.25
17064C Ursula C	.05	.12
17065H Arciela H	.40	1.00
17066C Cardian C	.05	.12
17067C Gabranth C	.05	.12
17068R Duke Snakeheart R	.10	.25
17069C Warrior C	.05	.12
17070R Titan R	.08	.20
17071R Dorando R	.10	.25
17072H Baron Guardsman H	.12	.30
17073C Seeping Brie C	.05	.12
17074L Prishe L	.60	1.50
17075C Maat C	.04	.10
17076H Matoya (I) H	.20	.50
17077C Monk C	.08	.20
17078R The Night Dancer R	.04	.10
17079L Shadow Lord L	2.00	5.00
17080R Ewen EX R	.05	.12
17081H Lyse H	.20	.50
17082R Lich R	.08	.20
17083C Rydia C	.05	.12
17084C Lorenzo C	.04	.10
17085R Ovjang & Mnejing R	.08	.20
17086H Red Mage H	.20	.50
17087H Aphmau H	.12	.30
17088R Alisaie R	.08	.20
17089C Arecia Al-Rashia C	.04	.10
17090R Ixion R	.12	.30
17091L Exdeath L	4.00	10.00
17092R Owe R	.08	.20
17093C Orc C	.05	.12
17094C Cid of Clan Gully EX C	.08	.20
17095C Quon C	.05	.12
17096H Man in Black H	.75	2.00
17097H Salire H	.15	.40
17098R Cissnei R	.10	.25
17099C Jack C	.04	.10
17100C Knight C	.04	.10
17101C Knight C	.05	.12
17102L Hooded Man L	2.00	5.00
17103R Yugiri EX R	.10	.25
17104C Learte C	.05	.12
17105C Dragoon C	.08	.20
17106C Blue Mage C	.05	.12
17107R Alphinaud R	.10	.25
17108C Andoria C	.04	.10
17109R Cuchulainn EX R	.05	.12
17110C Quadav C	.05	.12
17111C Chemist C	.04	.10
17112R Kraken EX R	.08	.20
17113L Glaciela Wezette L	12.00	30.00
17114C Curilla C	.08	.20
17115R Maquis the Phantasm R	.08	.20
17116C Gordon C	.05	.12
17117C Zazan C	.04	.10
17118R Alys the Ensorceled R	.10	.25
17119C White Mage C	.05	.12
17120H Princess Sarah H	.10	.25
17121H Frimelda EX H	.12	.30
17122C Miranda C	.05	.12
17123L Minwu L	.75	2.00
17124H Mog (VI) H	.15	.40
17125R Ramada R	.08	.20
17126H Rursan Reaver H	.12	.30
17127H Engelbert H	.15	.40
17128L Maria L	.30	.75
17129H Vinera Fennes H	.15	.40
17130L The Emperor L	.30	.75
17131S Kain ST	.25	.60
17132S Zemus ST	.15	.40
17133S Scarmiglione ST	.40	1.00
17134S Baigan EX ST	.20	.50
17135S Edge ST	.30	.75
17136S Kain EX ST	.30	.75
17137S Rydia ST	1.00	2.50
17138S Rosa ST	1.50	4.00
17139S Cecil ST	.50	1.25
17140S Golbez ST	.50	1.25

2022 Final Fantasy Resurgence of Power

C006 Crystal Token C	1.00	2.50
18001C Achuka C	.01	.08
18002C False Stalwart C	.01	.08
18003C Machinist C	.01	.08
18004R Cleome R	.04	.10
18005C Salamander C	.05	.12
18006C Zell C	.05	.12
18007C Selphie EX C	.05	.12
18008H Two-Headed Dragon H	.12	.30
18009H Tidus H	.10	.25
18010C Berserker C	.01	.08
18011R Paine EX R	.04	.10
18012L Faris L	4.00	10.00
18013R Fang R	.10	.25
18014R Meeth EX R	.08	.20
18015R Ramza R	.10	.25
18016C Lulu C	.04	.10
18017R Rain R	.05	.12
18018R Alhanalem R	.04	.10
18019R Weiss R	.10	.25
18020R Quistis C	.04	.10
18021R Cu Chaspel EX R	.01	.08
18022C Black Mage C	.05	.12
18023H Krysta H	.12	.30
18024C Shiva C	.04	.10
18025C Chime C	.04	.10
18026L Teodor L	1.25	3.00
18027C Nooj C	.01	.08
18028C Nero EX C	.05	.12
18029R Hein R	.04	.10
18030H Physalis H	.20	.50
18031C Rune Fencer C	.04	.10
18032C Phantasmal Girl C	.01	.08
18033R Yuna R	.05	.12
18034R Lasswell R	.05	.12
18035R Arc EX R	.04	.10
18036R Iris R	.05	.12
18037C Delusory Dragoon C	.01	.08
18038C Kytes C	.04	.10
18039C Ranger C	.08	.20
18040H Cerberus H	.15	.40
18041C Colkhab C	.04	.10
18042C Zhijie C	.04	.10
18043C Thief C	.04	.10
18044R Sherlotta C	.04	.10
18045C Dryad C	.05	.12
18046R Gnash R	.04	.10
18047H Bartz H	.20	.50
18048R Poppy R	.05	.12
18049R Yuri R	.04	.10
18050L Yuffie L	12.00	30.00
18051C Leafkin C	.04	.10
18052H Ahriman H	.12	.30
18053C Delusory Knight C	.04	.10
18054L Galuf L	1.50	4.00
18055R Krile EX R	.08	.20
18056C Cait Sith (XI) C	.04	.10
18057C Kolka C	.05	.12
18058R Serafie R	.04	.10
18059R Tama R	.05	.12
18060H Daisy H	.10	.25
18061R Tilika R	.05	.12
18062R Nayo R	.05	.12
18063C Hashmal C	.04	.10
18064C Geomancer C	.04	.10
18065C Polk C	.05	.12
18066C Beastmaster C	.01	.08
18067C Yumcax C	.05	.12
18068R Rikku R	.05	.12
18069C Red Mage C	.04	.10
18070C Aphmau C	.04	.10
18071R August R	.04	.10
18072C Kam'lanaut C	.04	.10
18073H Garuda (III) H	.10	.25
18074L Gilgamesh L	2.00	5.00
18075R Seifer R	.04	.10
18076C Cid Kramer C	.05	.12
18077R Cid Sophiar EX R	.05	.12
18078R Cindy R	.08	.20
18079R Fujin R	.05	.12
18080C Hurkan C	.04	.10
18081H Melusine H	.20	.50
18082C Imitation Despot C	.04	.10
18083R Raijin R	.05	.12
18084C Ramuh C	.04	.10
18085C Dragoon C	.04	.10
18086H Ashe EX H	.30	.75
18087C False Hero C	.01	.08
18088R Ingrid R	.04	.10
18089H Echidna H	.30	.75
18090R Kalmia R	.05	.12
18091R Cloud of Darkness R	.04	.10
18092C Tchakka C	.05	.12
18093R Nerine R	.05	.12
18094C Geomancer C	.04	.10
18095C Rune Fencer C	.01	.08
18096C Leviathan C	.08	.20
18097R Rinoa R	.04	.10
18098R Lunafreya R	.08	.20
18099C Leo EX C	.04	.10
18100L Lenna L	1.00	2.50
18101C Lenne C	.04	.10
18102C Wakka EX C	.05	.12
18103H Elena (FFBE) H	.15	.40
18104H Squall H	.15	.40
18105H Ultimecia H	.12	.30
18106H Sol (FFBE) H	.10	.25
18107L Akstar L	4.00	10.00
18108H Caius H	.08	.20
18109C Snow C	.04	.10
18110H Xande H	.10	.25
18111L Basch L	4.00	10.00
18112C Leon C	.04	.10
18113H Cid Haze H	.15	.40
18114C Maria C	.04	.10
18115L Melvien L	.30	.75
18116L Sephiroth L	10.00	25.00
18117H Lightning H	.75	2.00
18118C Laguna C	.04	.10
18119C Chelinka C	.04	.10
18120H Tifa H	.30	.75
18121L Fran L	1.00	2.50
18122H Vanille H	.20	.50
18123L Sonon EX L	.50	1.25
18124C Billy Bob C	.04	.10
18125H Onion Knight H	.15	.40
18126L Lightning L	2.00	5.00
18127C Lilisette C	.04	.10
18128H Arciela H	.15	.40
18129C Jecht C	.04	.10
18130L Firion L	1.25	3.00
18131S Iedolas S	1.25	3.00
18132S Ravus S	.15	.40
18133S Ignis S	.50	1.25
18134S Prompto S	.50	1.25
18135S Gladiolus S	.75	2.00
18136S Titan S	.50	1.25
18137S Aranea EX S	4.00	10.00

18138S Glauca S	.30	.75
18139S Noctis EX S	1.25	3.00
18140S Ardyn S	.60	1.50

2023 Final Fantasy Beyond Destiny

14102L Leviathan, Lord of the Whorl FULL ART L	4.00	10.00
21001R Ward EX R	.10	.25
21002R Edgar R	.10	.25
21003R Flameserpent General Gadalar R	.08	.20
21004L Cyan L	4.00	10.00
21005C Black Mage C	.05	.12
21006C Samurai C	.05	.12
21007L Shadow L	.50	1.25
21008R Vermilion Bird l'Cie R	.08	.20
21009C Warrior C	.05	.12
21010H Taivas H	.60	1.50
21011H Neon H	.12	.30
21012H Bahamut H	.30	.75
21013H Feolthanos H	.15	.40
21014C Bomb C	.05	.12
21015R Marilith R	.08	.20
21016C Mutsuki C	.05	.12
21017C Monk C	.05	.12
21018R Rain R	.10	.25
21019C Reynn C	.05	.12
21020C Lehftia C	.05	.12
21021C Red Mage C	.08	.20
21022H Astos H	.12	.30
21023L Ultimecia L	2.50	6.00
21024C Scholar C	.05	.12
21025R Kiros R	.08	.20
21026C Bard C	.08	.20
21027L Griever L	4.00	10.00
21028H Shiva H	.50	1.25
21029R Squall R	.08	.20
21030C Snow C	.05	.12
21031H Setzer H	.25	.60
21032R Terra R	.10	.25
21033R The Girl Who Forgot Her Name R	.10	.25
21034C Fomor C	.05	.12
21035C Minwu C	.05	.12
21036H Y'shtola FULL ART H	2.50	6.00
21036H Y'shtola H	.30	.75
21037C Reaper C	.08	.20
21038R Rinoa R	.08	.20
21039C Lufenian C	.08	.20
21040R Rursan Arbiter R	.08	.20
21041C Evil Weapon C	.05	.12
21042H Vaan H	.12	.30
21043C Viera C	.05	.12
21044C Dancer C	.05	.12
21045C Princess Gobli C	.05	.12
21046C Cid (II) C	.05	.12
21047C Summoner C	.05	.12
21048L Princess Sarah L	.50	1.25
21049R Sarah (MOBIUS) R	.10	.25
21050H Sophia (SOPFFO) H	.15	.40
21051R Tiamat R	.10	.25
21052R Niini R	.08	.20
21053L Balthier L	1.25	3.00
21054H Pandemonium H	.12	.30
21055H Penelo H	.15	.40
21056R Galeserpent General Najelith R	.05	.12
21057R Fran R	.10	.25
21058C Machina C	.05	.12
21059C Dragoon C	.05	.12
21060R Rikku EX R	.08	.20
21061H Ursula H	.12	.30
21062H Ash H	.15	.40
21063C Dark Knight C	.04	.10
21064L Ingus EX L	4.00	10.00
21065R Onion Knight R	.08	.20
21066C Guy C	.01	.08
21067R Galuf R	.10	.25
21068C Qiqirn C	.05	.12
21069C Krile C	.05	.12
21070C White Mage C	.08	.20
21071H Titan H	.20	.50
21072H Tulien H	.15	.40
21073R Stoneserpent General Zazarg R	.08	.20
21074L Neo Exdeath L	3.00	8.00
21075R Haveh R	.10	.25
21076C White Tiger l'Cie Qun'mi C	.05	.12
21077C Monk C	.05	.12
21078C Ram C	.05	.12
21079R Lich R	.08	.20
21080R Runda R	.08	.20
21081L Irvine L	15.00	40.00
21082C Red Mage C	.05	.12
21083H Ace H	.12	.30
21084H Odin H	.25	.60
21085H Emperor Gestah H	.20	.50
21086C Gunbreaker C	.05	.12
21087C Machinist C	.04	.10
21088C Gilgamesh C	.05	.12
21089R Queen R	.10	.25
21090R Cloud R	.10	.25
21091C Black Knight C	.05	.12
21092R Man in Black R	.10	.25
21093L Xande L	2.00	5.00
21094C Shantotto C	.05	.12
21095C Trey EX C	.05	.12
21096R Nine R	.08	.20
21097R Neilikka R	.10	.25
21098R Palom EX R	.08	.20
21099H Firion H	.25	.60
21100C Dragoon C	.05	.12
21101C Ashe C	.05	.12
21102L Gau L	2.50	6.00
21103R Kraken R	.08	.20
21104C Sage C	.08	.20
21105C Sahagin C	.05	.12
21106H Jed H	.12	.30
21107R Springserpent General Mihli Aliapoh R	.10	.25
21108R Ceodore R	.08	.20
21109C Astrologian C	.05	.12
21110C Desch C	.04	.10
21111C Paladin C	.05	.12
21112C Ninja C	.05	.12
21113R Bikke R	.08	.20
21114L Faris L	2.50	6.00
21115C Larsa C	.05	.12
21116H Leviathan H	.20	.50
21117R Rhus R	.08	.20
21118H Leila H	.20	.50
21119H Lenna H	2.50	6.00
21120R Refia R	.05	.12
21121L Warrior of Light L	10.00	25.00
21122H Skyserpent General Rughadjee H	2.00	5.00
21123H Darkness Manif H	.15	.40
21124L Jack Garland L	1.50	4.00
21125S Onion Knight S	.50	1.25
21126S Cloud EX S	.60	1.50
21127S Firion S	.10	.25
21128S Shantotto S	.30	.75
21129S Terra S	.60	1.50
21130S Noctis S	.20	.50
21131S Warrior of Light S	.40	1.00
21132S Cecil S	.12	.30
21133S Tidus EX	.60	1.50
21134S Bartz S	1.00	2.50

2023 Final Fantasy Beyond Destiny Premium Foil

14102L Leviathan, Lord of the Whorl L FULL ART RE	25.00	60.00
15011L Palom P FULL ART RE	10.00	25.00
15119L Porom P FULL ART RE	20.00	50.00
21001R Ward EX R	8.00	20.00
21001R Ward EX R FULL ART	.50	1.25
21002R Edgar R	.60	1.50
21003R Flameserpent General Gadalar R	.25	.60
21004L Cyan L	5.00	12.00
21005C Black Mage C	.30	.75
21006C Samurai C	.60	1.50
21007L Shadow L	1.25	3.00
21007L Shadow L FULL ART	8.00	20.00
21008R Vermilion Bird l'Cie R	.60	1.50
21009C Warrior C	.40	1.00
21010H Taivas H	1.25	3.00
21011H Neon H	.30	.75
21012H Bahamut H	1.00	2.50
21013H Feolthanos H	.40	1.00
21014C Bomb C	.30	.75
21015R Marilith R	.20	.50
21016C Mutsuki C	.25	.60
21016C Mutsuki C FULL ART	3.00	8.00
21017C Monk C	.60	1.50
21017C Monk C FULL ART	2.50	6.00
21018R Rain R	.75	2.00
21019C Reynn C	.15	.40
21020C Lehftia C	.60	1.50
21021C Red Mage C	.25	.60
21021C Red Mage C FULL ART	8.00	20.00
21022H Astos H	.50	1.25
21023L Ultimecia L	3.00	8.00
21023L Ultimecia L FULL ART	20.00	50.00
21024C Scholar C	.60	1.50
21025R Kiros R	.25	.60
21025R Kiros R FULL ART	4.00	10.00
21026C Bard C	.25	.60
21027L Griever L	5.00	12.00
21028H Shiva H	.75	2.00
21028H Shiva H FULL ART	15.00	40.00
21029R Squall R	.20	.50
21030C Snow C	.60	1.50
21031H Setzer H	.40	1.00
21032R Terra R	.60	1.50
21033R The Girl Who Forgot Her Name R	.60	1.50
21033R The Girl Who Forgot Her Name R FULL ART	10.00	25.00
21034C Fomor C	.50	1.25
21035C Minwu C	.30	.75
21036H Y'shtola H	.60	1.50
21036H Y'shtola H FULL ART	15.00	40.00
21037C Reaper C	.25	.60
21038R Rinoa R	.30	.75
21039C Lufenian C	.75	2.00
21040R Rursan Arbiter R	.30	.75
21041C Evil Weapon C	.40	1.00
21042H Vaan H	.20	.50
21042H Vaan H FULL ART	6.00	15.00
21043C Viera C	.60	1.50
21044C Dancer C	.30	.75
21045C Princess Gobli C	.50	1.25
21046C Cid (II) C	.20	.50
21047C Summoner C	.30	.75
21048L Princess Sarah L	.60	1.50
21049R Sarah (MOBIUS) R	.25	.60
21050H Sophia (SOPFFO) H	.30	.75
21051R Tiamat R	.20	.50
21052R Niini R	.20	.50
21053L Balthier L	2.00	5.00
21053L Balthier L FULL ART	8.00	20.00
21054H Pandemonium H	.20	.50
21055H Penelo H	.30	.75
21055H Penelo H FULL ART	10.00	25.00
21056R Galeserpent General Najelith R	.20	.50
21057R Fran R	.50	1.25
21058C Machina C	.30	.75
21059C Dragoon C	.50	1.25
21060R Rikku EX R	.50	1.25
21061H Ursula H	.20	.50
21061H Ursula H FULL ART	12.00	30.00
21062H Ash H	1.50	4.00
21063C Dark Knight C	.25	.60
21064L Ingus EX L	3.00	8.00
21064L Ingus EX L FULL ART	12.00	30.00
21065R Onion Knight R	.15	.40
21066C Guy C	.10	.25
21067R Galuf R	.25	.60
21068C Qiqirn C	.40	1.00
21069C Krile C	.30	.75
21070C White Mage C	.15	.40
21071H Titan H	5.00	12.00
21071H Titan H FULL ART	.50	1.25
21072H Tulien H	1.00	2.50
21073R Stoneserpent General Zazarg R	.30	.75
21074L Neo Exdeath L	5.00	12.00
21075R Haveh R	.30	.75
21076C White Tiger l'Cie Qun'mi C	.50	1.25
21076C White Tiger l'Cie Qun'mi C FULL ART	2.00	5.00
21077C Monk C	.25	.60
21078C Ram C	.40	1.00
21079R Lich R	.30	.75
21081L Irvine L	12.00	30.00
21081L Irvine L FULL ART	30.00	80.00
21082C Red Mage C	.40	1.00
21083H Ace H	.60	1.50
21084H Odin H	1.25	3.00
21085H Emperor Gestah H	1.25	3.00
21086C Gunbreaker C	.50	1.25
21087C Machinist C	.30	.75
21088C Gilgamesh C	.50	1.25
21089R Queen R	.40	1.00
21090R Cloud R	.25	.60
21091C Black Knight C	.20	.50
21091C Black Knight C FULL ART	2.00	5.00
21092R Man in Black R	.50	1.25
21093L Xande L	3.00	8.00
21094C Shantotto C	.20	.50
21095C Trey EX C	.50	1.25
21096R Nine R	.40	1.00
21097R Neilikka R	.12	.30
21098R Palom EX R	.40	1.00
21099H Firion H	.40	1.00
21100C Dragoon C	.30	.75
21101C Ashe C	.20	.50
21102L Gau L	3.00	8.00
21103R Kraken R	.15	.40
21104C Sage C	.50	1.25
21105C Sahagin C	.30	.75
21106H Jed H	.20	.50
21107R Springserpent General Mihli Aliapoh R	.30	.75
21108R Ceodore R	.10	.25
21108R Ceodore R FULL ART	3.00	8.00
21109C Astrologian C	.60	1.50
21110C Desch C FULL ART	1.25	3.00
21111C Paladin C	.50	1.25
21112C Ninja C	.25	.60
21113R Bikke R	.75	2.00
21114L Faris L	3.00	8.00
21115C Larsa C	1.00	2.50
21116H Leviathan H	.75	2.00
21116H Leviathan H FULL ART	4.00	10.00
21118H Leila H	.50	1.25
21118H Leila H FULL ART	12.00	30.00
21119H Lenna H	4.00	10.00
21120R Refia R	.08	.20
21121L Warrior of Light L	10.00	25.00
21122H Skyserpent General Rughadjee H	4.00	10.00
21123H Darkness Manif H	.40	1.00
21124L Jack Garland L	2.50	6.00
21124L Jack Garland L SPECIAL	200.00	500.00
21125S Onion Knight S	1.25	3.00
21126S Cloud EX S	1.00	2.50
21127S Firion S	.60	1.50
21128S Shantotto S	.60	1.50
21129S Terra S	2.50	6.00
21130S Noctis S	.50	1.25
21131S Warrior of Light S	1.50	4.00
21132S Cecil S	.75	2.00
21133S Tidus EX	1.25	3.00
21134S Bartz S	.75	2.00
21134S Bartz S FULL ART	4.00	10.00

2023 Final Fantasy Dawn of Heroes

20001R Ardyn R	.10	.25
20002H Auron H	.20	.50
20003H Ifrit H	.25	.60
20004C Warrior of Light C	.05	.12
20005C Garland EX C	.04	.10
20006C Blacksmith C	.05	.12
20007L The Demon L	10.00	25.00
20008H Kefka H	.12	.30
20009L Zack L	4.00	10.00
20011R Jecht R	.08	.20
20012C Goldsmith C	.05	.12
20013C Culinarian C	.08	.20
20014C Tifa R	.15	.40
20015C Morrow EX C	.05	.12
20016R Barret EX R	.08	.20
20017R Palom R	.08	.20
20018H Phoinix H	.12	.30
20019C Hedgehog Pie C	.05	.12
20020C Montblanc C	.05	.12
20021R Red XIII R	.08	.20
20022C Alhanalem C	.04	.10
20023C Armourer C	.08	.20
20024H Calbrena R	.10	.25
20025C Juggler C	.05	.12
20026C Edward EX C	.04	.10
20027C Genesis C	.05	.12
20028R Cissnei R	.10	.25
20029C Jihl Nabaat C	.01	.08
20030R Setzer R	.08	.20
20031R Celes R	.08	.20
20032C SOLDIER: 3rd Class C	.05	.12
20033C Cerulean Drake C	.05	.12
20034R Terra R	.08	.20
20036H Number 24 H	.12	.30
20037H Mateus (FFTA) H	.20	.50
20038H wicked Mask H	.10	.25
20039R Rude R	.10	.25
20040L Rufus L	15.00	40.00
20041R Reno R	.10	.25
20042L Locke EX L	2.50	6.00
20043R Brother R	.08	.20
20044L Edge L	1.00	2.50
20045C Botanist C	.05	.12
20046C Ghost (VII) C	.04	.10
20047H Jenova Dreamweaver H	.10	.25
20048R Stiltzkin R	.05	.12
20049R Chelinka R	.05	.12
20050C Chocobo C	.08	.20
20051H Fat Chocobo H	.20	.50
20052C Gnash C	.05	.12
20053H Number 128 H	.20	.50
20054R Nono EX R	.08	.20
20055C Prompto C	.05	.12
20056H Bel Dat H	.20	.50
20057L The Goddess L	1.50	4.00
20058C Melphie C	.08	.20
20059C Carpenter C	.08	.20
20060R Yuri L	.05	.12
20061C Yuffie C	.08	.20
20062R Ritz R	.04	.10
20064C Arkasodara C	.05	.12
20065H Antlion (IV) H	.10	.25
20066R Ignis R	.10	.25
20067R Itaina R	.08	.20
20068R Aerith R	.08	.20
20069H Chaos H	.12	.30
20070C Leatherworker C	.08	.20
20071C Ciaran C	.04	.10
20072C Gigas (FFCC) C	.08	.20
20073C Kimahri C	.05	.12
20074C Miner C	.08	.20
20075L Cecil R	5.00	12.00
20076C Sonon C	.04	.10
20077L Tifa L	2.50	6.00
20078H Noctis H	.20	.50
20080R Fake R	.08	.20
20081H Fenrir H	.15	.40
20082C Mira EX C	.08	.20
20083R The Magus Sisters (XIV) R	.05	.12
20084R Leo R	.05	.12
20085C Assassin C	.04	.10
20086H Alisaie H	.25	.60
20087R Angeal R	.05	.12
20088L Estinien L	12.00	30.00
20089C Kadaj C	.04	.10
20090H G'raha Tia H	2.00	5.00
20091C Illusionist C	.04	.10
20092R The Emperor R	.05	.12
20093H Shadow Dragon H	.15	.40
20094R Cor R	.08	.20
20095C Weaver C	.05	.12

20096C Johnny C	.05	.12
20097C Sephiroth C	.08	.20
20098R Chadley R	.08	.20
20100R Fusoya EX R	.05	.12
20101C Behemoth C	.04	.10
20102L Mira L	1.00	2.50
20103H Ramuh H	.75	2.00
20104R Ramza R	.08	.20
20105C Reeve EX C	.05	.12
20106R Alphinaud R	.05	.12
20107H Urianger H	.15	.40
20108C O'aka EX C	.05	.12
20109H Cecil H	.20	.50
20110H Hippokampos H	.15	.40
20111C Blugu C	.04	.10
20112C Frimelda C	.01	.08
20113R Porom R	.04	.10
20114L The Fiend L	4.00	10.00
20115R Mist R	.05	.12
20116R Meliadoul R	.05	.12
20117L Yuna L	1.50	4.00
20118H Unicorn H	.20	.50
20120C Fisher C	.05	.12
20121C Lunafreya C	.05	.12
20122R Leslie R	.05	.12
20123C Loporrit C	.05	.12
20124C Alchemist C	.08	.20
20125R Rosa R	.05	.12
20126C Wakka C	.04	.10
20127L Shinryu L	15.00	40.00
20128H Materia H	.12	.30
20129H Spiritus H	.20	.50
20130L Zenos L	.50	1.25
20010C15007C Samurai C	.05	.12
20035C15038C Knight C	.04	.10
20063C15058C Dragoon C	.05	.12
20079C15080C Geomancer C	.04	.10
20099C15095C Ninja C	.05	.12
20119C15123C Oracle C	.05	.12

2023 Final Fantasy From Nightmares

14011H Susano, Lord of the Revel (January 2023) P	.20	.50
19001R Ifrit R	.08	.20
19002L Ace L	.50	1.25
19003R Edgar R	.08	.20
19004R Kukki-Chebukki R	.05	.12
19005C Sazh C	.05	.12
19006C Tifa C	.08	.20
19007C Dajh EX C	.04	.10
19008R Buffasaur R	.08	.20
19009C Bomb C	.04	.10
19010H Sabin H	.15	.40
19011C Miyu C	.04	.10
19012C Monk C	.04	.10
19013C Lilty C	.01	.08
19014C Luneth C	.05	.12
19015R Ruby Weapon R	.10	.25
19016H Laragorn H	.12	.30
19017R Leon R	.05	.12
19018R Waltrill R	.04	.10
19019R Vincent R	.10	.25
19020H Umaro H	.12	.30
19021C Cloud of Darkness C	.05	.12
19022R Shiva R	.10	.25
19023C Snow C	.05	.12
19024L Sarah (MOBIUS) L	1.00	2.50
19-025R Sephiroth R	.10	.25
19026H Curlax H	.10	.25
19027R Chocobo Eater R	.08	.20
19028C Terra EX C	.05	.12
19029C Tohno C	.08	.20
19030R Norschtalen R	.04	.10
19031C Flan C	.04	.10
19032C Yuke C	.04	.10
19033C Lean C	.04	.10
19034C Nu Mou C	.04	.10
19035R Alexander R	.08	.20
19036L Vayne L	.50	1.25
19037R Wol R	.04	.10
19038R Evrae R	.10	.25
19039R Emerald Weapon R	.08	.20
19040C Thief C	.05	.12
19041H Cid Highwind H	.15	.40
19042C White Mage C	.04	.10
19043C Zu C	.04	.10
19044R Sarah (MOBIUS) R	.08	.20
19045H Sophie H	.10	.25
19046C Buddy C	.05	.12
19047C Gramps EX C	.04	.10
19048C Bartz C	.01	.08
19049R Makki-Chebukki R	.08	.20
19050C Matoya C	.05	.12
19051C Rikku C	.08	.20
19052C Undead Princess C	.05	.12
19053C Vanille C	.04	.10
19054C Vincent C	.05	.12
19055R Eiko R	.04	.10
19056C Graff C	.04	.10
19057L Kefka L	.50	1.25
19058R Jenova SYNTHESIS R	.08	.20
19059R Aster Protoflorian R	.04	.10
19060C Animist C	.04	.10
19061H Doga H	.05	.12
19062R Nacht EX R	.08	.20
19063H Barret H	.10	.25
19064R Fenrir R	.08	.20
19065C The Deathlord C	.05	.12
19066C Behemoth C	.08	.20
19067C Monk C	.04	.10
19068R Rydia R	.08	.20
19069R Emperor (FFL) R	.10	.25
19070C Edge C	.04	.10
19071C Elgo EX C	.04	.10
19072C Eald'narche C	.01	.08
19073C Kain C	.08	.20
19074C Scholar C	.04	.10
19075C Chimera C	.08	.20
19076R Kuja EX R	.05	.12
19077L Golbez L	.50	1.25
19078C Jinnai C	.04	.10
19079H Moebius H	.12	.30
19080R Vivi R	.08	.20
19081R Behemoth R	.08	.20
19082H Lightning H	.15	.40
19083R Ramuh R	.05	.12
19084R Ricard R	.08	.20
19085C Dragoon C	.04	.10
19086R Ashe EX R	.10	.25
19087R Wol R	.05	.12
19088C Aerith C	.05	.12
19089H Gau H	.12	.30
19090C Clavat C	.04	.10
19091R Sapphire Weapon R	.08	.20
19092C White Mage C	.05	.12
19093H Strago EX H	.15	.40
19094R Sanctuary Keeper R	.08	.20
19095C Sophia C	.01	.08
19096C Tidus EX C	.04	.10
19097C Tonberry C	.05	.12
19098C Yuna C	.08	.20
19099R Josef R	.05	.12
19100C Larsa C	.04	.10
19101R Leviathan R	.08	.20
19102L Refia L	4.00	10.00
19103H Tidus EX H	.12	.30
19104H Madeen H	.20	.50
19105H Ark H	.20	.50
19106H Sin H	.10	.25
19107C Vaan EX C	.04	.10
19108L Zidane L	3.00	8.00
19109H Cherukiki H	.10	.25
19110H The Emperor H	.20	.50
19111L Prishe L	.75	2.00
19112C Larkeicus C	.04	.10
19113C Gilgamesh C	.04	.10
19114L Cloud L	2.00	5.00
19115H Veriaulde H	.08	.20
19116C Paine C	.05	.12
19117H Hilda H	.10	.25
19118L Yuna L	.30	.75
19119L Unei L	5.00	12.00
19120C Garnet C	.05	.12
19121H Meia H	.10	.25
19122C Zack EX C	.05	.12
19123H Anima H	.12	.30
19124L Y'shtola L	10.00	25.00
19125H Mog (VI) H	.25	.60
19126C Shadow Lord C	.04	.10
19127L Relm L	.60	1.50
19128L Warrior of Light L	20.00	50.00
19129S Vanille EX ST	1.00	2.50
19130S Bahamut ST	.60	1.50
19131S Fang ST	.50	1.25
19132S Snow ST	.60	1.50
19133S Serah EX ST	.50	1.25
19134S Mog (XIII-2) ST	.30	.75
19135S Cid Raines ST	.50	1.25
19136S Noel ST	.60	1.50
19137S Hope ST	.60	1.50
19138S Lightning ST	1.00	2.50

2024 Final Fantasy Hidden Hope

22001R Auron R	.10	.25
22002C Red Mage C	.08	.20
22003R Ayame R	.10	.25
22004H Angeal H	.25	.60
22005R Ignacio R	.12	.30
22006H Garland EX H	.25	.60
22007C Carla C	.05	.12
22008C Clavat C	.05	.12
22009H Jecht H	.25	.60
22010L Selphie L	3.00	8.00
22011C Warrior C	.05	.12
22012C Foulander C	.10	.25
22013C Machina C	.05	.12
22014R Belias, the Gigas R	.08	.20
22015C Meeth C	.10	.25
22016H Minwu (FFBE) H	.25	.60
22017C Lilyth C	.08	.20
22018R Luartha R	.10	.25
22019C Ice Bomb C	.10	.25
22020R Vallaide R	.10	.25
22021R Emina R	.10	.25
22022R Quistis R	.10	.25
22023C Bard C	.08	.20
22024L Kurasame L	.60	1.50
22025C Cloud of Darkness C	.08	.20
22026C Seymour EX C	.05	.12
22027R Shiva R	.10	.25
22028H Cissnei H	.20	.50
22029R Jihl Nabaat EX R	.10	.25
22030C Shinryu Celestia C	.05	.12
22031H Squall H	.50	1.25
22032L Sephiroth L	2.50	6.00
22033C Time Mage C	.05	.12
22034H Medusa H	.25	.60
22035C Yuke C	.10	.25
22036C Rinoa C	.08	.20
22037R Alexander R	.12	.30
22038C Wol C	.05	.12
22039C Epiornis C	.08	.20
22040H Enkidu H	.30	.75
22041C Kain C	.08	.20
22042C Ranger C	.08	.20
22043C Clavat C	.05	.12
22044R Cid (FFBE) R	.10	.25
22045C Sosha C	.08	.20
22046R Chelinka R	.10	.25
22047L Dorgan L	.75	2.00
22048H Nanaa Mihgo H	.40	1.00
22048H Nanaa Mihgo FULL ART	8.00	20.00
22049H Bartz H	.25	.60
22050C Geomancer C	.05	.12
22051R Hope R	.12	.30
22052H Helena Leonis H	.20	.50
22053C Lilisette EX C	.05	.12
22054R Reddas R	.10	.25
22055H Vossler EX H	.20	.50
22056R Exdeath EX R	.12	.30
22057R Carbuncle R	.10	.25
22058H Qator Bashtar H	.30	.75
22059C Gabranth C	.05	.12
22060H Ghido H	.40	1.00
22061L Gilgamesh L	1.50	4.00
22062R Glaive EX R	.10	.25
22063C Sand Worm C	.05	.12
22064C G Assassin C	.08	.20
22065R Sieghard R	.10	.25
22066C Summoner C	.05	.12
22067L Nacht L	2.50	6.00
22068R Prishe R	.10	.25
22069C Baelo C	.05	.12
22070C Ramza C	.05	.12
22071C Lich C	.08	.20
22072C Lilty C	.05	.12
22073L Ultimecia L	4.00	10.00
22074R Alba EX R	.10	.25
22075H Edea H	.50	1.25
22076R Odin R	.10	.25
22077H Garuda (III) H	.20	.50
22078C Sice C	.05	.12
22079L Seifer L	8.00	20.00
22080C Selkie C	.08	.20
22081R Diana R	.10	.25
22082C Drace C	.10	.25
22083C Ninja C	.05	.12
22084R Fujin R	.10	.25
22085C Moth Slasher C	.08	.20
22086C Yaag Rosch C	.05	.12
22087R Raijin R	.10	.25
22088C Rygdea C	.10	.25
22089C Dragoon C	.08	.20
22090H Lulu H	.40	1.00
22091C Blue Mage C	.05	.12
22092C Agrias C	.05	.12
22093R Anima (X) R	.10	.25
22094C Vaan C	.05	.12
22095H Warrior of Light EX H	.40	1.00
22096C Clavat C	.05	.12
22097L Curilla L	4.00	10.00
22098H Siren (V) H	.30	.75
22099R Severo R	.10	.25
22100R Chime R	.12	.30
22101C Paladin C	.08	.20
22102C Piranha C	.05	.12
22103C Faris C	.05	.12
22104R Folka R	.10	.25
22105H Miwa H	.25	.60
22106R Yuna R	.10	.25
22107C Yuni C	.08	.20
22108H Lenna H	.40	1.00
22109H Eden H	.40	1.00
22110L Citra L	.75	2.00
22111L Raegen L	1.25	3.00
22112R Zack LB R	.12	.30
22113L Mont Leonis LB L	2.50	6.00
22114H Viktora LB H	.60	1.50
22115R Serjes LB R	.12	.30
22116L Ace LB L	2.00	5.00
22117R Yuri LB R	.12	.30
22118H Shantotto LB H	.50	1.25
22119R Maat LB R	.15	.40
22120H Cloud LB H	1.25	3.00
22121R Lightning LB R	.12	.30
22122L Tidus LB L	10.00	25.00
22123R Leo LB R	.15	.40
22124H Little Leela LB H	2.00	5.00

2024 Final Fantasy Hidden Hope Premium Foil

4064L Fat Chocobo L	10.00	25.00
16129L Chaos FULL ART L	15.00	40.00
18116L Sephiroth FULL ART L	20.00	50.00
22001R Auron R	.75	2.00
22002C Red Mage C	.12	.30
22003R Ayame R	.20	.50
22004H Angeal H	.60	1.50
22004H Angeal FULL ART H	10.00	25.00
22005R Ignacio R	.20	.50
22006H Garland EX H	1.00	2.50
22007C Carla C	.25	.60
22008C Clavat C	.12	.30
22009H Jecht H	1.00	2.50
22010L Selphie L	5.00	12.00
22010L Selphie FULL ART L	20.00	50.00
22011C Warrior C	.15	.40
22012C Foulander C	.10	.25
22013C Machina C	.20	.50
22013C Machina FULL ART C	3.00	8.00
22014R Belias, the Gigas R	.75	2.00
22015C Meeth C	.20	.50
22016H Minwu (FFBE) H	1.25	3.00
22017C Lilyth C	.30	.75
22018R Luartha R	.50	1.25
22019C Ice Bomb C	.20	.50
22020R Vallaide R	.25	.60
22021R Emina R	.75	2.00
22022R Quistis FULL ART R	.30	.75
22022R Quistis R	15.00	40.00
22023C Bard C	.12	.30
22024L Kurasame L	1.50	4.00
22025C Cloud of Darkness C	.12	.30
22026C Seymour EX C	.20	.50
22027R Shiva R	.30	.75
22027R Shiva FULL ART R	6.00	15.00
22028H Cissnei H	.60	1.50
22028H Cissnei FULL ART H	12.00	30.00
22029R Jihl Nabaat EX R	.25	.60
22029R Jihl Nabaat EX FULL ART R	4.00	10.00
22030C Shinryu Celestia C	.15	.40
22031H Squall H	1.00	2.50
22031H Squall FULL ART H	20.00	50.00
22032L Sephiroth L	4.00	10.00
22032L Sephiroth FULL ART L	400.00	1,000.00
22032L Sephiroth FULL ART SIGNATURE L	20.00	50.00
22033C Time Mage C	.12	.30
22034H Medusa H	.25	.60
22035C Yuke C	.15	.40
22036C Rinoa C	1.00	2.50
22036C Rinoa FULL ART C	20.00	50.00
22037R Alexander R	.20	.50
22037R Alexander FULL ART R	5.00	12.00
22038C Wol C	.20	.50
22039C Epiornis C	.12	.30
22040H Enkidu H	.60	1.50
22040H Enkidu FULL ART H	3.00	8.00
22041C Kain C	.15	.40
22041C Kain FULL ART C	8.00	20.00
22042C Ranger C	.15	.40
22043C Clavat C	.20	.50
22044R Cid (FFBE) R	.25	.60
22045C Sosha C	.25	.60
22046R Chelinka R	.20	.50
22047L Dorgan L	2.00	5.00
22047L Dorgann FULL ART L	5.00	12.00
22048H Nanaa Mihgo H	1.00	2.50
22048H Nanaa Mihgo FULL ART H	10.00	25.00
22049H Bartz H	.60	1.50
22050C Geomancer C	.10	.25
22051R Hope R	.20	.50
22052H Helena Leonis H	1.00	2.50
22053C Lilisette EX C	.20	.50
22054R Reddas R	.20	.50
22054R Reddas FULL ART R	3.00	8.00
22055H Vossler EX H	.40	1.00
22055H Vossler EX FULL ART H	6.00	15.00
22056R Exdeath EX R	.25	.60
22057R Carbuncle R	.25	.60
22058H Qator Bashtar H	1.00	2.50
22059C Gabranth C	.12	.30
22060H Ghido H	.75	2.00
22060H Ghido FULL ART H	6.00	15.00
22061L Gilgamesh L	2.50	6.00
22061L Gilgamesh FULL ART L	10.00	25.00
22062R Glaive EX R	.20	.50
22062R Glaive EX FULL ART R	5.00	12.00

22063C Sand Worm C	.15	.40
22064C G Assassin C	.15	.40
22065R Sieghard R	.20	.50
22066C Summoner C	.20	.50
22067L Nacht L	4.00	10.00
22068R Prishe R	.20	.50
22069C Baelo C	.25	.60
22070C Ramza C	.15	.40
22071C Lich C	.15	.40
22072C Lilty C	.12	.30
22073L Ultimecia L	5.00	12.00
22074R Alba EX R	.25	.60
22074R Alba EX FULL ART R	12.00	30.00
22075H Edea FULL ART H	25.00	60.00
22075H Edea H	1.50	4.00
22076R Odin R	.25	.60
22077H Garuda (III) H	1.00	2.50
22078C Sice C	.15	.40
22079L Seifer L	8.00	20.00
22079L Seifer FULL ART L	25.00	60.00
22080C Selkie C	.12	.30
22081R Diana R	.25	.60
22081R Diana FULL ART R	10.00	25.00
22082C Drace C	.20	.50
22082C Drace FULL ART C	6.00	15.00
22083C Ninja C	.12	.30
22084R Fujin R	.50	1.25
22085C Moth Slasher C	.15	.40
22086C Yaag Rosch C	.12	.30
22086C Yaag Rosch FULL ART C	2.50	6.00
22087R Raijin R	.60	1.50
22088C Rygdea C	.12	.30
22088C Rygdea FULL ART C	3.00	8.00
22089C Dragoon C	.20	.50
22090H Lulu H	.75	2.00
22090H Lulu FULL ART H	40.00	100.00
22091C Blue Mage C	.15	.40
22092C Agrias C	.20	.50
22093R Anima (X) R	1.25	3.00
22094C Vaan C	.25	.60
22095H Warrior of Light EX H	.60	1.50
22096C Clavat C	.12	.30
22097L Curilla L	3.00	8.00
22097L Curilla FULL ART L	15.00	40.00
22098H Siren (V) H	1.00	2.50
22099R Severo R	.25	.60
22100R Chime R	.25	.60
22101C Paladin C	.12	.30
22102C Piranha C	.15	.40
22103C Faris C	.15	.40
22104R Folka R	.30	.75
22105H Miwa H	.75	2.00
22106R Yuna R	1.25	3.00
22107C Yuni C	.20	.50
22108H Lenna H	1.00	2.50
22109H Eden H	1.00	2.50
22110L Citra L	3.00	8.00
22111L Raegen L	3.00	8.00
22112R Zack LB R	2.50	6.00
22113L Mont Leonis LB L	5.00	12.00
22114H Viktora LB H	2.00	5.00
22115R Serjes LB R	2.00	5.00
22116L Ace LB L	4.00	10.00
22117R Yuri LB R	.40	1.00
22118H Shantotto LB H	1.50	4.00
22119R Maat LB R	1.25	3.00
22120H Cloud LB H	1.50	4.00
22121R Lightning LB R	1.25	3.00
22122L Tidus LB L	12.00	30.00
22123R Leo LB R	2.00	5.00
22124H Little Leela LB H	3.00	8.00

2019 Flesh and Blood Welcome to Rathe Alpha

WTR000 Heart of Fyendal F	15,000.00	30,000.00
WTR004 Scabskin Leathers L	2,000.00	4,000.00
WTR005 Barkbone Strapping C	1.25	2.50
WTR006 Alpha Rampage M	20.00	40.00
WTR007 Bloodrush Bellow M	20.00	40.00
WTR008 Reckless Swing SR	7.50	15.00
WTR009 Sand Sketched Plan SR	6.00	12.00
WTR010 Bone Head Barrier SR	4.00	8.00
WTR011 Breakneck Battery (red) R	1.00	2.00
WTR012 Breakneck Battery (yellow) R	.75	1.50
WTR013 Breakneck Battery (blue) R	.75	1.50
WTR014 Savage Feast (red) R	1.50	3.00
WTR015 Savage Feast (yellow) R	.75	1.50
WTR016 Savage Feast (blue) R	.75	1.50
WTR017 Barraging Beatdown (red) R	2.50	5.00
WTR018 Barraging Beatdown (yellow) R	1.25	2.50
WTR019 Barraging Beatdown (blue) R	2.00	4.00
WTR020 Savage Swing (red) C	.30	.75
WTR021 Savage Swing (yellow) C	.30	.75
WTR022 Savage Swing (blue) C	.30	.60
WTR023 Pack Hunt (red) C	.50	1.00
WTR024 Pack Hunt (yellow) C	.30	.75
WTR025 Pack Hunt (blue) C	.30	.75
WTR026 Smash Instinct (red) C	.50	1.00
WTR027 Smash Instinct (yellow) C	.30	.60
WTR028 Smash Instinct (blue) C	.30	.60
WTR029 Wrecker Romp (red) C	.60	1.25
WTR030 Wrecker Romp (yellow) C	.30	.75
WTR031 Wrecker Romp (blue) C	.25	.50
WTR032 Awakening Bellow (red) C	.25	.50
WTR033 Awakening Bellow (yellow) C	.30	.60
WTR034 Awakening Bellow (blue) C	.40	.80
WTR035 Primeval Bellow (red) C	.60	1.25
WTR036 Primeval Bellow (yellow) C	.50	1.00
WTR037 Primeval Bellow (blue) C	.50	1.00
WTR041 Tectonic Plating L	2,000.00	4,000.00
WTR042 Helm of Isen's Peak C	2.50	5.00
WTR043 Crippling Crush M	30.00	60.00
WTR044 Spinal Crush M	30.00	60.00
WTR045 Cranial Crush SR	7.50	15.00
WTR046 Forged for War SR	5.00	10.00
WTR047 Show Time! SR	7.50	15.00
WTR048 Disable (red) R	4.00	8.00
WTR049 Disable (yellow) R	1.00	2.00
WTR050 Disable (blue) R	1.00	2.00
WTR051 Staunch Response (red) R	2.00	4.00
WTR052 Staunch Response (yellow) R	.75	1.50
WTR053 Staunch Response (blue) R	.75	1.50
WTR054 Blessing of Deliverance (red) R	3.00	6.00
WTR055 Blessing of Deliverance (yellow) R	.75	1.50
WTR056 Blessing of Deliverance (blue) R	1.00	2.00
WTR057 Buckling Blow (red) C	.50	1.00
WTR058 Buckling Blow (yellow) C	.30	.60
WTR059 Buckling Blow (blue) C	.30	.75
WTR060 Cartilage Crush (red) C	.50	1.00
WTR061 Cartilage Crush (yellow) C	.30	.75
WTR062 Cartilage Crush (blue) C	.50	1.00
WTR063 Crush Confidence (red) C	.50	1.00
WTR064 Crush Confidence (yellow) C	.30	.60
WTR065 Crush Confidence (blue) C	.20	.40
WTR066 Debilitate (red) C	.40	.80
WTR067 Debilitate (yellow) C	.30	.75
WTR068 Debilitate (blue) C	.25	.50
WTR069 Emerging Power (red) C	.30	.75
WTR070 Emerging Power (yellow) C	.30	.60
WTR071 Emerging Power (blue) C	.30	.60
WTR072 Stonewall Confidence (red) C	.60	1.25
WTR073 Stonewall Confidence (yellow) C	.50	1.00
WTR074 Stonewall Confidence (blue) C	.25	.50
WTR079 Mask of Momentum L	3,000.00	6,000.00
WTR080 Breaking Scales C	.75	1.50
WTR081 Lord of Wind M	25.00	50.00
WTR082 Ancestral Empowerment M	20.00	40.00
WTR083 Mugenshi: RELEASE SR	7.50	15.00
WTR084 Hurricane Technique SR	6.00	12.00
WTR085 Pounding Gale SR	12.50	25.00
WTR086 Fluster Fist (red) R	3.00	6.00
WTR087 Fluster Fist (yellow) R	.75	1.50
WTR088 Fluster Fist (blue) R	.60	1.25
WTR089 Blackout Kick (red) R	1.00	2.00
WTR090 Blackout Kick (yellow) R	.75	1.50
WTR091 Blackout Kick (blue) R	.75	1.50
WTR092 Flic Flak (red) R	2.00	4.00
WTR093 Flic Flak (yellow) R	1.00	2.00
WTR094 Flic Flak (blue) R	.75	1.50
WTR095 Open the Center (red) C	.60	1.25
WTR096 Open the Center (yellow) C	.30	.60
WTR097 Open the Center (blue) C	.50	1.00
WTR098 Head Jab (red) C	.75	1.50
WTR099 Head Jab (yellow) C	.30	.75
WTR100 Head Jab (blue) C	.30	.60
WTR101 Leg Tap (red) C	1.00	2.00
WTR102 Leg Tap (yellow) C	.30	.60
WTR103 Leg Tap (blue) C	.25	.50
WTR104 Rising Knee Thrust (red) C	.75	1.50
WTR105 Rising Knee Thrust (yellow) C	.20	.40
WTR106 Rising Knee Thrust (blue) C	.50	1.00
WTR107 Surging Strike (red) C	.75	1.50
WTR108 Surging Strike (yellow) C	.30	.60
WTR109 Surging Strike (blue) C	.30	.75
WTR110 Whelming Gustwave (red) C	1.00	2.00
WTR111 Whelming Gustwave (yellow) C	.30	.60
WTR112 Whelming Gustwave (blue) C	.60	1.25
WTR115 Dawnblade T	1.00	2.00
WTR116 Braveforge Bracers L	2,000.00	4,000.00
WTR117 Refraction Bolters C	2.00	4.00
WTR118 Glint the Quicksilver M	25.00	50.00
WTR119 Steelblade Supremacy M	30.00	60.00
WTR120 Rout SR	7.50	15.00
WTR121 Singing Steelblade SR	10.00	20.00
WTR122 Ironsong Determination SR	10.00	20.00
WTR123 Overpower (red) R	1.00	2.00
WTR124 Overpower (yellow) R	.75	1.50
WTR125 Overpower (blue) R	1.00	2.00
WTR126 Steelblade Shunt (red) R	3.00	6.00
WTR127 Steelblade Shunt (yellow) R	1.00	2.00
WTR128 Steelblade Shunt (blue) R	.75	1.50
WTR129 Warrior's Valor (red) R	3.00	6.00
WTR130 Warrior's Valor (yellow) R	.75	1.50
WTR131 Warrior's Valor (blue) R	1.25	2.50
WTR132 Ironsong Response (red) C	.30	.60
WTR133 Ironsong Response (yellow) C	.25	.50
WTR134 Ironsong Response (blue) C	.25	.50
WTR135 Biting Blade (red) C	3.00	6.00
WTR136 Biting Blade (yellow) C	.30	.75
WTR137 Biting Blade (blue) C	.50	1.00
WTR138 Stroke of Foresight (red) C	.75	1.50
WTR139 Stroke of Foresight (yellow) C	.30	.60
WTR140 Stroke of Foresight (blue) C	.30	.60
WTR141 Sharpen Steel (red) C	.50	1.00
WTR142 Sharpen Steel (yellow) C	.25	.50
WTR143 Sharpen Steel (blue) C	.30	.75
WTR144 Driving Blade (red) C	.50	1.00
WTR145 Driving Blade (yellow) C	.30	.75
WTR146 Driving Blade (blue) C	.50	1.00
WTR147 Nature's Path Pilgrimage (red) C	.50	1.00
WTR148 Nature's Path Pilgrimage (yellow) C	.30	.75
WTR149 Nature's Path Pilgrimage (blue) C	.50	1.00
WTR150 Fyendal's Spring Tunic L	3,000.00	6,000.00
WTR151 Hope Merchant's Hood C	1.00	2.00
WTR152 Heartened Cross Strap C	1.25	2.50
WTR153 Goliath Gauntlet C	1.00	2.00
WTR154 Snapdragon Scalers C	2.50	5.00
WTR155 Ironrot Helm C	2.00	4.00
WTR156 Ironrot Plate C	2.00	4.00
WTR157 Ironrot Gauntlet C	1.50	3.00
WTR158 Ironrot Legs C	1.25	2.50
WTR159 Enlightened Strike M	125.00	250.00
WTR160 Tome of Fyendal M	75.00	150.00
WTR161 Last Ditch Effort SR	5.00	10.00
WTR162 Crazy Brew SR	7.50	15.00
WTR163 Remembrance SR	20.00	40.00
WTR164 Drone of Brutality (red) R	2.50	5.00
WTR165 Drone of Brutality (yellow) R	2.00	4.00
WTR166 Drone of Brutality (blue) R	1.25	2.50
WTR167 Snatch (red) R	7.50	15.00
WTR168 Snatch (yellow) R	.75	1.50
WTR169 Snatch (blue) R	1.50	3.00
WTR170 Energy Potion R	2.50	5.00
WTR171 Potion of Strength R	7.50	15.00
WTR172 Timesnap Potion R	2.00	4.00
WTR173 Sigil of Solace (red) R	7.50	15.00
WTR174 Sigil of Solace (yellow) R	1.50	3.00
WTR175 Sigil of Solace (blue) R	.75	1.50
WTR176 Barraging Brawnhide (red) C	.30	.60
WTR177 Barraging Brawnhide (yellow) C	.75	1.50
WTR178 Barraging Brawnhide (blue) C	.20	.40
WTR179 Demolition Crew (red) C	.60	1.25
WTR180 Demolition Crew (yellow) C	.50	1.00
WTR181 Demolition Crew (blue) C	.30	.75
WTR182 Flock of the Feather Walkers (red) C	4.00	8.00
WTR183 Flock of the Feather Walkers (yellow) C	.50	1.00
WTR184 Flock of the Feather Walkers (blue) C	.50	1.00
WTR185 Nimble Strike (red) C	.75	1.50
WTR186 Nimble Strike (yellow) C	.30	.75
WTR187 Nimble Strike (blue) C	.30	.60
WTR188 Raging Onslaught (red) C	.50	1.00
WTR189 Raging Onslaught (yellow) C	.30	.75
WTR190 Raging Onslaught (blue) C	.30	.60
WTR191 Scar for a Scar (red) C	.50	1.00
WTR192 Scar for a Scar (yellow) C	.20	.40
WTR193 Scar for a Scar (blue) C	.30	.75
WTR194 Scour the Battlescape (red) C	3.00	6.00
WTR195 Scour the Battlescape (yellow) C	.30	.75
WTR196 Scour the Battlescape (blue) C	.25	.50
WTR197 Regurgitating Slog (red) C	.50	1.00
WTR198 Regurgitating Slog (yellow) C	.50	1.00
WTR199 Regurgitating Slog (blue) C	.20	.40
WTR200 Wounded Bull (red) C	.60	1.25
WTR201 Wounded Bull (yellow) C	.50	1.00
WTR202 Wounded Bull (blue) C	.30	.75
WTR203 Wounding Blow (red) C	.50	1.00
WTR204 Wounding Blow (yellow) C	.50	1.00
WTR205 Wounding Blow (blue) C	.50	1.00
WTR206 Pummel (red) C	6.00	12.00
WTR207 Pummel (yellow) C	4.00	8.00
WTR208 Pummel (blue) C	2.00	4.00
WTR209 Razor Reflex (red) C	3.00	6.00
WTR210 Razor Reflex (yellow) C	.60	1.25
WTR211 Razor Reflex (blue) C	.60	1.25
WTR212 Unmovable (red) C	7.50	15.00
WTR213 Unmovable (yellow) C	2.50	5.00
WTR214 Unmovable (blue) C	.50	1.00
WTR215 Sink Below (red) C	4.00	8.00
WTR216 Sink Below (yellow) C	1.50	3.00
WTR217 Sink Below (blue) C	.75	1.50
WTR218 Nimblism (red) C	.75	1.50
WTR219 Nimblism (yellow) C	.30	.75
WTR220 Nimblism (blue) C	.25	.50
WTR221 Sloggism (red) C	.75	1.50
WTR222 Sloggism (yellow) C	.50	1.00
WTR223 Sloggism (blue) C	.50	1.00
WTR224 Cracked Bauble T	7.50	15.00

2019 Flesh and Blood Welcome to Rathe Alpha Foil

WTR005 Barkbone Strapping C	150.00	300.00
WTR006 Alpha Rampage M	200.00	400.00
WTR007 Bloodrush Bellow M	250.00	500.00
WTR008 Reckless Swing SR	50.00	100.00
WTR009 Sand Sketched Plan SR	75.00	150.00
WTR010 Bone Head Barrier SR	100.00	200.00
WTR011 Breakneck Battery (red) R	15.00	30.00
WTR012 Breakneck Battery (yellow) R	12.50	25.00
WTR013 Breakneck Battery (blue) R	10.00	20.00
WTR014 Savage Feast (red) R	30.00	60.00
WTR015 Savage Feast (yellow) R	10.00	20.00
WTR016 Savage Feast (blue) R	7.50	15.00
WTR017 Barraging Beatdown (red) R	30.00	60.00
WTR018 Barraging Beatdown (yellow) R	60.00	125.00
WTR019 Barraging Beatdown (blue) R	40.00	80.00
WTR020 Savage Swing (red) C	3.00	6.00
WTR021 Savage Swing (yellow) C	2.00	4.00
WTR022 Savage Swing (blue) C	4.00	8.00
WTR023 Pack Hunt (red) C	6.00	12.00
WTR024 Pack Hunt (yellow) C	1.50	3.00
WTR025 Pack Hunt (blue) C	3.00	6.00
WTR026 Smash Instinct (red) C	4.00	8.00
WTR027 Smash Instinct (yellow) C	3.00	6.00
WTR028 Smash Instinct (blue) C	2.50	5.00
WTR029 Wrecker Romp (red) C	4.00	8.00
WTR030 Wrecker Romp (yellow) C	4.00	8.00
WTR031 Wrecker Romp (blue) C	3.00	6.00
WTR032 Awakening Bellow (red) C	4.00	8.00
WTR033 Awakening Bellow (yellow) C	3.00	6.00
WTR034 Awakening Bellow (blue) C	2.00	4.00
WTR035 Primeval Bellow (red) C	6.00	12.00
WTR036 Primeval Bellow (yellow) C	4.00	8.00
WTR037 Primeval Bellow (blue) C	4.00	8.00
WTR042 Helm of Isen's Peak C	400.00	800.00
WTR043 Crippling Crush M	300.00	750.00
WTR044 Spinal Crush M	1,000.00	2,000.00
WTR045 Cranial Crush SR	50.00	100.00
WTR046 Forged for War SR	50.00	100.00
WTR047 Show Time! SR	125.00	250.00
WTR048 Disable (red) R	7.50	15.00
WTR049 Disable (yellow) R	7.50	15.00
WTR050 Disable (blue) R	7.50	15.00
WTR051 Staunch Response (red) R	20.00	40.00
WTR052 Staunch Response (yellow) R	10.00	20.00
WTR053 Staunch Response (blue) R	10.00	20.00
WTR054 Blessing of Deliverance (red) R	20.00	40.00
WTR055 Blessing of Deliverance (yellow) R	10.00	20.00
WTR056 Blessing of Deliverance (blue) R	10.00	20.00
WTR057 Buckling Blow (red) C	4.00	8.00
WTR058 Buckling Blow (yellow) C	4.00	8.00
WTR059 Buckling Blow (blue) C	3.00	6.00
WTR060 Cartilage Crush (red) C	6.00	12.00
WTR061 Cartilage Crush (yellow) C	2.00	4.00
WTR062 Cartilage Crush (blue) C	3.00	6.00
WTR063 Crush Confidence (red) C	6.00	12.00
WTR064 Crush Confidence (yellow) C	4.00	8.00
WTR065 Crush Confidence (blue) C	6.00	12.00
WTR066 Debilitate (red) C	2.50	5.00
WTR067 Debilitate (yellow) C	2.00	4.00
WTR068 Debilitate (blue) C	4.00	8.00
WTR069 Emerging Power (red) C	3.00	6.00
WTR070 Emerging Power (yellow) C	2.00	4.00
WTR071 Emerging Power (blue) C	1.50	3.00
WTR072 Stonewall Confidence (red) C	5.00	10.00
WTR073 Stonewall Confidence (yellow) C	3.00	6.00
WTR074 Stonewall Confidence (blue) C	3.00	6.00
WTR080 Breaking Scales C	300.00	600.00
WTR081 Lord of Wind M	200.00	400.00
WTR082 Ancestral Empowerment M	1,000.00	2,000.00
WTR083 Mugenshi: RELEASE SR	40.00	80.00
WTR084 Hurricane Technique SR	60.00	125.00
WTR085 Pounding Gale SR	60.00	125.00
WTR086 Fluster Fist (red) R	15.00	30.00
WTR087 Fluster Fist (yellow) R	7.50	15.00
WTR088 Fluster Fist (blue) R	4.00	8.00
WTR089 Blackout Kick (red) R	15.00	30.00
WTR090 Blackout Kick (yellow) R	10.00	20.00
WTR091 Blackout Kick (blue) R	7.50	15.00
WTR092 Flic Flak (red) R	20.00	40.00
WTR093 Flic Flak (yellow) R	30.00	75.00
WTR094 Flic Flak (blue) R	30.00	60.00
WTR095 Open the Center (red) C	6.00	12.00
WTR096 Open the Center (yellow) C	5.00	10.00
WTR097 Open the Center (blue) C	7.50	15.00
WTR098 Head Jab (red) C	20.00	40.00
WTR099 Head Jab (yellow) C	2.50	5.00
WTR100 Head Jab (blue) C	3.00	6.00
WTR101 Leg Tap (red) C	7.50	15.00
WTR102 Leg Tap (yellow) C	3.00	6.00
WTR103 Leg Tap (blue) C	6.00	12.00
WTR104 Rising Knee Thrust (red) C	5.00	10.00
WTR105 Rising Knee Thrust (yellow) C	2.00	4.00
WTR106 Rising Knee Thrust (blue) C	6.00	12.00
WTR107 Surging Strike (red) C	7.50	15.00
WTR108 Surging Strike (yellow) C	6.00	12.00
WTR109 Surging Strike (blue) C	2.00	4.00
WTR110 Whelming Gustwave (red) C	7.50	15.00
WTR111 Whelming Gustwave (yellow) C	2.50	5.00
WTR112 Whelming Gustwave (blue) C	4.00	8.00
WTR117 Refraction Bolters C	500.00	1,000.00
WTR118 Glint the Quicksilver M	750.00	1,500.00
WTR119 Steelblade Supremacy M	750.00	1,500.00
WTR120 Rout SR	50.00	100.00
WTR121 Singing Steelblade SR	200.00	400.00
WTR122 Ironsong Determination SR	75.00	150.00

WTR123 Overpower (red) R	20.00	40.00
WTR124 Overpower (yellow) R	30.00	60.00
WTR125 Overpower (blue) R	15.00	30.00
WTR126 Steelblade Shunt (red) R	30.00	75.00
WTR127 Steelblade Shunt (yellow) R	7.50	15.00
WTR128 Steelblade Shunt (blue) R	7.50	15.00
WTR129 Warrior's Valor (red) R	12.50	25.00
WTR130 Warrior's Valor (yellow) R	6.00	12.00
WTR131 Warrior's Valor (blue) R	7.50	15.00
WTR132 Ironsong Response (red) C	4.00	8.00
WTR133 Ironsong Response (yellow) C	2.00	4.00
WTR134 Ironsong Response (blue) C	2.50	5.00
WTR135 Biting Blade (red) C	7.50	15.00
WTR136 Biting Blade (yellow) C	2.00	4.00
WTR137 Biting Blade (blue) C	2.50	5.00
WTR138 Stroke of Foresight (red) C	4.00	8.00
WTR139 Stroke of Foresight (yellow) C	5.00	10.00
WTR140 Stroke of Foresight (blue) C	4.00	8.00
WTR141 Sharpen Steel (red) C	5.00	10.00
WTR142 Sharpen Steel (yellow) C	2.50	5.00
WTR143 Sharpen Steel (blue) C	3.00	6.00
WTR144 Driving Blade (red) C	7.50	15.00
WTR145 Driving Blade (yellow) C	2.00	4.00
WTR146 Driving Blade (blue) C	3.00	6.00
WTR147 Nature's Path Pilgrimage (red) C	7.50	15.00
WTR148 Nature's Path Pilgrimage (yellow) C	4.00	8.00
WTR149 Nature's Path Pilgrimage (blue) C	2.00	4.00
WTR151 Hope Merchant's Hood C	250.00	500.00
WTR152 Heartened Cross Strap C	250.00	500.00
WTR153 Goliath Gauntlet C	250.00	500.00
WTR154 Snapdragon Scalers C	500.00	1,000.00
WTR155 Ironrot Helm C	150.00	300.00
WTR156 Ironrot Plate C	250.00	500.00
WTR157 Ironrot Gauntlet C	200.00	400.00
WTR158 Ironrot Legs C	150.00	300.00
WTR159 Enlightened Strike M	30.00	75.00
WTR160 Tome of Fyendal M	750.00	1,500.00
WTR161 Last Ditch Effort SR	60.00	125.00
WTR162 Crazy Brew SR	100.00	200.00
WTR163 Remembrance SR	100.00	200.00
WTR164 Drone of Brutality (red) R	30.00	60.00
WTR165 Drone of Brutality (yellow) R	12.50	25.00
WTR166 Drone of Brutality (blue) R	10.00	20.00
WTR167 Snatch (red) R	30.00	75.00
WTR168 Snatch (yellow) R	10.00	20.00
WTR169 Snatch (blue) R	12.50	25.00
WTR170 Energy Potion R	40.00	80.00
WTR171 Potion of Strength R	300.00	600.00
WTR172 Timesnap Potion R	30.00	60.00
WTR173 Sigil of Solace (red) R	50.00	100.00
WTR174 Sigil of Solace (yellow) R	12.50	25.00
WTR175 Sigil of Solace (blue) R	7.50	15.00
WTR176 Barraging Brawnhide (red) C	3.00	6.00
WTR177 Barraging Brawnhide (yellow) C	4.00	8.00
WTR178 Barraging Brawnhide (blue) C	2.50	5.00
WTR179 Demolition Crew (red) C	2.50	5.00
WTR180 Demolition Crew (yellow) C	4.00	8.00
WTR181 Demolition Crew (blue) C	5.00	10.00
WTR182 Flock of the Feather Walkers (red) C	30.00	60.00
WTR183 Flock of the Feather Walkers (yellow) C	3.00	6.00
WTR184 Flock of the Feather Walkers (blue) C	7.50	15.00
WTR185 Nimble Strike (red) C	4.00	8.00
WTR186 Nimble Strike (yellow) C	3.00	6.00
WTR187 Nimble Strike (blue) C	2.00	4.00
WTR188 Raging Onslaught (red) C	4.00	8.00
WTR189 Raging Onslaught (yellow) C	3.00	6.00
WTR190 Raging Onslaught (blue) C	4.00	8.00
WTR191 Scar for a Scar (red) C	3.00	6.00
WTR192 Scar for a Scar (yellow) C	2.50	5.00
WTR193 Scar for a Scar (blue) C	2.50	5.00
WTR194 Scour the Battlescape (red) C	25.00	50.00
WTR195 Scour the Battlescape (yellow) C	7.50	15.00
WTR196 Scour the Battlescape (blue) C	6.00	12.00
WTR197 Regurgitating Slog (red) C	3.00	6.00
WTR198 Regurgitating Slog (yellow) C	2.50	5.00
WTR199 Regurgitating Slog (blue) C	3.00	6.00
WTR200 Wounded Bull (red) C	7.50	15.00
WTR201 Wounded Bull (yellow) C	2.00	4.00
WTR202 Wounded Bull (blue) C	3.00	6.00
WTR203 Wounding Blow (red) C	3.00	6.00
WTR204 Wounding Blow (yellow) C	4.00	8.00
WTR205 Wounding Blow (blue) C	3.00	6.00
WTR206 Pummel (red) C	30.00	60.00
WTR207 Pummel (yellow) C	10.00	20.00
WTR208 Pummel (blue) C	12.50	25.00
WTR209 Razor Reflex (red) C	75.00	150.00
WTR210 Razor Reflex (yellow) C	5.00	10.00
WTR211 Razor Reflex (blue) C	12.50	25.00
WTR212 Unmovable (red) C	40.00	80.00
WTR213 Unmovable (yellow) C	10.00	20.00
WTR214 Unmovable (blue) C	4.00	8.00
WTR215 Sink Below (red) C	25.00	50.00
WTR216 Sink Below (yellow) C	7.50	15.00
WTR217 Sink Below (blue) C	6.00	12.00
WTR218 Nimblism (red) C	20.00	40.00
WTR219 Nimblism (yellow) C	2.50	5.00
WTR220 Nimblism (blue) C	4.00	.80
WTR221 Sloggism (red) C	7.50	15.00
WTR222 Sloggism (yellow) C	6.00	12.00
WTR223 Sloggism (blue) C	6.00	12.00

2020 Flesh and Blood Arcane Rising 1st Edition

ARC000 Eye of Ophidia F	750.00	1,500.00
ARC001 Dash, Inventor Extraordinaire T	.30	.75
ARC002 Dash T	.30	.75
ARC003 Teklo Plasma Pistol T	.30	.75
ARC004 Teklo Foundry Heart L	1,000.00	2,000.00
ARC005 Achilles Accelerator C	.75	1.50
ARC006 High Octane M	15.00	30.00
ARC007 Teklo Core M	20.00	40.00
ARC008 Maximum Velocity SR	3.00	6.00
ARC009 Spark of Genius SR	10.00	20.00
ARC010 Induction Chamber SR	5.00	10.00
ARC011 Pedal to the Metal (red) R	.75	1.50
ARC012 Pedal to the Metal (yellow) R	.75	1.50
ARC013 Pedal to the Metal (blue) R	.30	.60
ARC014 Pour the Mold (red) R	.50	1.00
ARC015 Pour the Mold (yellow) R	.50	1.00
ARC016 Pour the Mold (blue) R	.75	1.50
ARC017 Aether Sink R	.50	1.00
ARC018 Cognition Nodes R	.60	1.25
ARC019 Convection Amplifier R	.75	1.50
ARC020 Over Loop (red) C	.15	.30
ARC021 Over Loop (yellow) C	.30	.75
ARC022 Over Loop (blue) C	.25	.50
ARC023 Throttle (red) C	.50	1.00
ARC024 Throttle (yellow) C	.60	1.25
ARC025 Throttle (blue) C	.30	.75
ARC026 Zero to Sixty (red) C	.50	1.00
ARC027 Zero to Sixty (yellow) C	.30	.75
ARC028 Zero to Sixty (blue) C	.50	1.00
ARC029 Zipper Hit (red) C	.40	.80
ARC030 Zipper Hit (yellow) C	.25	.50
ARC031 Zipper Hit (blue) C	.40	.80
ARC032 Locked and Loaded (red) C	.30	.75
ARC033 Locked and Loaded (yellow) C	.20	.40
ARC034 Locked and Loaded (blue) C	.30	.75
ARC035 Dissipation Shield C	.20	.40
ARC036 Hyper Driver C	.15	.30
ARC037 Optekal Monocle C	.20	.40
ARC038 Azalea, Ace in the Hole T	.30	.75
ARC039 Azalea T	.30	.75
ARC040 Death Dealer T	.30	.75
ARC041 Skullbone Crosswrap L	750.00	1,500.00
ARC042 Bull's Eye Bracers C	.50	1.00
ARC043 Red in the Ledger M	12.50	25.00
ARC044 Three of a Kind M	20.00	40.00
ARC045 Endless Arrow SR	7.50	15.00
ARC046 Nock the Deathwhistle SR	6.00	12.00
ARC047 Rapid Fire SR	4.00	8.00
ARC048 Take Cover (red) R	.75	1.50
ARC049 Take Cover (yellow) R	.60	1.25
ARC050 Take Cover (blue) R	.60	1.25
ARC051 Silver the Tip (red) R	.30	.75
ARC052 Silver the Tip (yellow) R	.40	.80
ARC053 Silver the Tip (blue) R	.50	1.00
ARC054 Take Aim (red) R	.75	1.50
ARC055 Take Aim (yellow) R	.75	1.50
ARC056 Take Aim (blue) R	.60	1.25
ARC057 Head Shot (red) R	.15	.30
ARC058 Head Shot (yellow) R	.30	.75
ARC059 Head Shot (blue) R	.40	.80
ARC060 Hamstring Shot (red)	.20	.40
ARC061 Hamstring Shot (yellow)	.30	.60
ARC062 Hamstring Shot (blue)	.50	1.00
ARC063 Ridge Rider Shot (red) C	.25	.50
ARC064 Ridge Rider Shot (yellow) C	.30	.75
ARC065 Ridge Rider Shot (blue) C	.20	.40
ARC066 Salvage Shot (red) C	.20	.40
ARC067 Salvage Shot (yellow) C	.15	.30
ARC068 Salvage Shot (blue) C	.50	1.00
ARC069 Searing Shot (red) C	.15	.30
ARC070 Searing Shot (yellow) C	.15	.30
ARC071 Searing Shot (blue) C	.20	.40
ARC072 Sic 'Em Shot (red) C	.15	.30
ARC073 Sic 'Em Shot (yellow) C	.15	.30
ARC074 Sic 'Em Shot (blue) C	.15	.30
ARC077 Nebula Blade T	.30	.75
ARC078 Grasp of the Arknight L	2,000.00	4,000.00
ARC079 Crown of Dichotomy C	1.00	2.00
ARC080 Arknight Ascendancy M	12.50	25.00
ARC081 Mordred Tide M	15.00	30.00
ARC082 Ninth Blade of the Blood Oath SR	4.00	8.00
ARC083 Become the Arknight SR	7.50	15.00
ARC084 Tome of the Arknight SR	7.50	15.00
ARC085 Spellblade Assault (red) R	.50	1.00
ARC086 Spellblade Assault (yellow) R	.75	1.50
ARC087 Spellblade Assault (blue) R	.60	1.25
ARC088 Reduce to Runechant (red) R	.75	1.50
ARC089 Reduce to Runechant (yellow) R	.50	1.00
ARC090 Reduce to Runechant (blue) R	.30	.75
ARC091 Oath of the Arknight (red) R	.75	1.50
ARC092 Oath of the Arknight (yellow) R	.75	1.50
ARC093 Oath of the Arknight (blue) R	.50	1.00
ARC094 Amplify the Arknight (red) C	.60	.80
ARC095 Amplify the Arknight (yellow) C	.15	.30
ARC096 Amplify the Arknight (blue)	.25	.50
ARC097 Drawn to the Dark Dimension (red) C	.15	.30
ARC098 Drawn to the Dark Dimension (yellow) C	.30	.60
ARC099 Drawn to the Dark Dimension (blue) C	.30	.75
ARC100 Rune Flash (red) C	.30	.60
ARC101 Rune Flash (yellow) C	.30	.60
ARC102 Rune Flash (blue) C	.30	.75
ARC103 Spellblade Strike (red) C	.20	.40
ARC104 Spellblade Strike (yellow) C	.20	.40
ARC105 Spellblade Strike (blue) C	.30	.75
ARC106 Bloodspill Invocation (red) C	.20	.40
ARC107 Bloodspill Invocation (yellow) C	.25	.50
ARC108 Bloodspill Invocation (blue) C	.15	.30
ARC109 Read the Runes (red) C	.30	.60
ARC110 Read the Runes (yellow) C	.50	1.00
ARC111 Read the Runes (blue) C	.25	.50
ARC113 Kano, Dracai of Aether T	.30	.75
ARC114 Kano T	.30	.75
ARC115 Crucible of Aetherweave T	.30	.75
ARC116 Storm Striders L	1,000.00	2,000.00
ARC117 Robe of Rapture C	.50	1.00
ARC118 Blazing Aether M	12.50	25.00
ARC119 Sonic Boom M	25.00	50.00
ARC120 Forked Lightning SR	4.00	8.00
ARC121 Lesson in Lava SR	7.50	15.00
ARC122 Tome of Aetherwind SR	7.50	15.00
ARC123 Absorb in Aether (red) R	.75	1.50
ARC124 Absorb in Aether (yellow) R	1.00	2.00
ARC125 Absorb in Aether (blue) R	1.00	2.00
ARC126 Aether Spindle (red) R	.60	1.25
ARC127 Aether Spindle (yellow) R	.50	1.00
ARC128 Aether Spindle (blue) R	1.00	2.00
ARC129 Stir the Aetherwinds (red) R	.60	1.25
ARC130 Stir the Aetherwinds (yellow) R	.75	1.50
ARC131 Stir the Aetherwinds (blue) R	1.00	2.00
ARC132 Aether Flare (red) C	.25	.50
ARC133 Aether Flare (yellow) C	.25	.50
ARC134 Aether Flare (blue) C	.25	.50
ARC135 Index (red) C	.25	.50
ARC136 Index (yellow) C	.20	.40
ARC137 Index (blue) C	.20	.40
ARC138 Reverberate (red) C	.15	.30
ARC139 Reverberate (yellow) C	.20	.40
ARC140 Reverberate (blue) C	.25	.50
ARC141 Scalding Rain (red) C	.15	.30
ARC142 Scalding Rain (yellow) C	.15	.30
ARC143 Scalding Rain (blue) C	.30	.75
ARC144 Zap (red) C	.12	.25
ARC145 Zap (yellow) C	.20	.40
ARC146 Zap (blue) C	.30	.75
ARC147 Voltic Bolt (red) C	.30	.75
ARC148 Voltic Bolt (yellow) C	.15	.30
ARC149 Voltic Bolt (blue) C	.40	.80
ARC150 Arcanite Skullcap L	2,500.00	5,000.00
ARC151 Talismanic Lens C	.50	1.00
ARC152 Vest of the First Fist C	.15	.30
ARC153 Bracers of Belief C	.50	1.00
ARC154 Mage Master Boots C	.50	1.00
ARC155 Nullrune Hood C	1.00	2.00
ARC156 Nullrune Robe C	1.50	3.00
ARC157 Nullrune Gloves C	3.00	6.00
ARC158 Nullrune Boots C	1.50	3.00
ARC159 Command and Conquer M	125.00	250.00
ARC160 Art of War M	60.00	125.00
ARC161 Pursuit of Knowledge SR	4.00	8.00
ARC162 Chains of Eminence SR	6.00	12.00
ARC163 Rusted Relic SR	2.50	5.00
ARC164 Life for a Life (red) R	2.00	4.00
ARC165 Life for a Life (yellow) R	.75	1.50
ARC166 Life for a Life (blue) R	.60	1.25
ARC167 Enchanting Melody (red) R	.30	.75
ARC168 Enchanting Melody (yellow) R	.50	1.00
ARC169 Enchanting Melody (blue) R	.75	1.50
ARC170 Plunder Run (red) R	6.00	12.00
ARC171 Plunder Run (yellow) R	1.50	3.00
ARC172 Plunder Run (blue) R	2.50	5.00
ARC173 Eirina's Prayer (red) R	1.00	2.00
ARC174 Eirina's Prayer (yellow) R	.75	1.50
ARC175 Eirina's Prayer (blue) R	.75	1.50
ARC176 Back Alley Breakline (red) C	.20	.40
ARC177 Back Alley Breakline (yellow) C	.15	.30
ARC178 Back Alley Breakline (blue) C	.20	.40
ARC179 Cadaverous Contraband (red) C	.30	.75
ARC180 Cadaverous Contraband (yellow) C	.20	.40
ARC181 Cadaverous Contraband (blue) C	.20	.40
ARC182 Fervent Forerunner (red) C	.30	.75
ARC183 Fervent Forerunner (yellow) C	.30	.75
ARC184 Fervent Forerunner (blue) C	.50	1.00
ARC185 Moon Wish (red) C	.30	.60
ARC186 Moon Wish (yellow) C	.25	.50
ARC187 Moon Wish (blue) C	.30	.60
ARC188 Push the Point (red) C	.60	1.25
ARC189 Push the Point (yellow) C	.30	.60
ARC190 Push the Point (blue) C	.40	.80
ARC191 Ravenous Rabble (red) C	.75	1.50
ARC192 Ravenous Rabble (yellow) C	.50	1.00
ARC193 Ravenous Rabble (blue) C	.30	.60
ARC194 Rifting (red) C	.50	1.00
ARC195 Rifting (yellow) C	.50	1.00
ARC196 Rifting (blue) C	.30	.75
ARC197 Vigor Rush (red) C	.50	1.00
ARC198 Vigor Rush (yellow) C	.30	.75
ARC199 Vigor Rush (blue) C	.40	.80
ARC200 Fate Foreseen (red) C	3.00	6.00
ARC201 Fate Foreseen (yellow) C	.60	1.25
ARC202 Fate Foreseen (blue) C	.15	.30
ARC203 Come to Fight (red) C	.40	.80
ARC204 Come to Fight (yellow) C	.20	.40
ARC205 Come to Fight (blue) C	.25	.50
ARC206 Force Sight (red) C	.20	.40
ARC207 Force Sight (yellow) C	.20	.40
ARC208 Force Sight (blue) C	.20	.40
ARC209 Lead the Charge (red) C	.75	1.50
ARC210 Lead the Charge (yellow) C	.75	1.50
ARC211 Lead the Charge (blue) C	.75	1.50
ARC212 Sun Kiss (red) C	.50	1.00
ARC213 Sun Kiss (yellow) C	.30	.75
ARC214 Sun Kiss (blue) C	.30	.60
ARC215 Whisper of the Oracle (red) C	.50	1.00
ARC216 Whisper of the Oracle (yellow) C	.30	.75
ARC217 Whisper of the Oracle (blue) C	.50	1.00
ARC218 Cracked Bauble T	6.00	12.00

2020 Flesh and Blood Arcane Rising 1st Edition Foil

ARC005 Achilles Accelerator C	500.00	1,000.00
ARC006 High Octane M	300.00	600.00
ARC007 Teklo Core M	150.00	300.00
ARC008 Maximum Velocity SR	.60	125.00
ARC009 Spark of Genius SR	40.00	80.00
ARC010 Induction Chamber SR	125.00	250.00
ARC011 Pedal to the Metal (red) R	7.50	15.00
ARC012 Pedal to the Metal (yellow) R	5.00	10.00
ARC013 Pedal to the Metal (blue) R	5.00	10.00
ARC014 Pour the Mold (red) R	15.00	30.00
ARC015 Pour the Mold (yellow) R	12.50	25.00
ARC016 Pour the Mold (blue) R	15.00	30.00
ARC017 Aether Sink R	2.50	5.00
ARC018 Cognition Nodes R	12.50	25.00
ARC019 Convection Amplifier R	12.50	25.00
ARC020 Over Loop (red) C	7.50	15.00
ARC021 Over Loop (yellow) C	2.50	5.00
ARC022 Over Loop (blue) C	6.00	12.00
ARC023 Throttle (red) C	6.00	12.00
ARC024 Throttle (yellow) C	4.00	8.00
ARC025 Throttle (blue) C	7.50	15.00
ARC026 Zero to Sixty (red) C	20.00	40.00
ARC027 Zero to Sixty (yellow) C	7.50	15.00
ARC028 Zero to Sixty (blue) C	12.50	25.00
ARC029 Zipper Hit (red) C	7.50	15.00
ARC030 Zipper Hit (yellow) C	12.50	25.00
ARC031 Zipper Hit (blue) C	12.50	25.00
ARC032 Locked and Loaded (red) C	4.00	8.00
ARC033 Locked and Loaded (yellow) C	3.00	6.00
ARC034 Locked and Loaded (blue) C	4.00	8.00
ARC035 Dissipation Shield C	6.00	12.00
ARC036 Hyper Driver C	4.00	8.00
ARC037 Optekal Monocle C	2.00	4.00
ARC042 Bull's Eye Bracers C	250.00	500.00
ARC043 Red in the Ledger M	250.00	500.00
ARC044 Three of a Kind M	30.00	75.00
ARC045 Endless Arrow SR	50.00	100.00
ARC046 Nock the Deathwhistle SR	50.00	100.00
ARC047 Rapid Fire SR	40.00	80.00
ARC048 Take Cover (red) R	10.00	20.00
ARC049 Take Cover (yellow) R	7.50	15.00
ARC050 Take Cover (blue) R	7.50	15.00
ARC051 Silver the Tip (red) R	10.00	20.00
ARC052 Silver the Tip (yellow) R	4.00	8.00
ARC053 Silver the Tip (blue) R	10.00	20.00
ARC054 Take Aim (red) R	20.00	40.00
ARC055 Take Aim (yellow) R	7.50	15.00
ARC056 Take Aim (blue) R	3.00	6.00
ARC057 Head Shot (red) R	4.00	8.00
ARC058 Head Shot (yellow) R	5.00	10.00
ARC059 Head Shot (blue) R	5.00	10.00
ARC060 Hamstring Shot (red)	4.00	8.00
ARC061 Hamstring Shot (yellow)	7.50	15.00
ARC062 Hamstring Shot (blue)	4.00	8.00
ARC063 Ridge Rider Shot (red) C	2.00	4.00
ARC064 Ridge Rider Shot (yellow) C	3.00	6.00
ARC065 Ridge Rider Shot (blue) C	6.00	12.00
ARC066 Salvage Shot (red) C	4.00	8.00
ARC067 Salvage Shot (yellow) C	6.00	12.00
ARC068 Salvage Shot (blue) C	1.00	2.00
ARC069 Searing Shot (red) C	12.50	25.00
ARC070 Searing Shot (yellow) C	3.00	6.00
ARC071 Searing Shot (blue) C	2.00	4.00
ARC072 Sic 'Em Shot (red) C	3.00	6.00
ARC073 Sic 'Em Shot (yellow) C	2.50	5.00
ARC074 Sic 'Em Shot (blue) C	2.50	5.00
ARC079 Crown of Dichotomy C	250.00	500.00
ARC080 Arknight Ascendancy M	6,000.00	12,000.00
ARC081 Mordred Tide M	200.00	400.00
ARC082 Ninth Blade of the Blood Oath SR	75.00	150.00
ARC083 Become the Arknight SR	75.00	150.00

ARC084 Tome of the Arknight SR	30.00	75.00
ARC085 Spellblade Assault (red) R	15.00	30.00
ARC086 Spellblade Assault (yellow) R	10.00	20.00
ARC087 Spellblade Assault (blue) R	10.00	20.00
ARC088 Reduce to Runechant (red) R	7.50	15.00
ARC089 Reduce to Runechant (yellow) R	10.00	20.00
ARC090 Reduce to Runechant (blue) R	12.50	25.00
ARC091 Oath of the Arknight (red) R	12.50	25.00
ARC092 Oath of the Arknight (yellow) R	75.00	150.00
ARC093 Oath of the Arknight (blue) R	12.50	25.00
ARC094 Amplify the Arknight (red) C	4.00	8.00
ARC095 Amplify the Arknight (yellow) C	5.00	10.00
ARC096 Amplify the Arknight (blue)	3.00	6.00
ARC097 Drawn to the Dark Dimension (red) C	3.00	6.00
ARC098 Drawn to the Dark Dimension (yellow) C	2.50	5.00
ARC099 Drawn to the Dark Dimension (blue) C	3.00	6.00
ARC100 Rune Flash (red) C	4.00	8.00
ARC101 Rune Flash (yellow) C	3.00	6.00
ARC102 Rune Flash (blue) C	2.50	5.00
ARC103 Spellblade Strike (red) C	7.50	15.00
ARC104 Spellblade Strike (yellow) C	2.50	5.00
ARC105 Spellblade Strike (blue) C	3.00	6.00
ARC106 Bloodspill Invocation (red) C	4.00	8.00
ARC107 Bloodspill Invocation (yellow) C	4.00	8.00
ARC108 Bloodspill Invocation (blue) C	2.00	4.00
ARC109 Read the Runes (red) C	7.50	15.00
ARC110 Read the Runes (yellow) C	4.00	8.00
ARC111 Read the Runes (blue) C	4.00	8.00
ARC117 Robe of Rapture C	125.00	250.00
ARC118 Blazing Aether M	250.00	500.00
ARC119 Sonic Boom M	750.00	1,500.00
ARC120 Forked Lightning SR	50.00	100.00
ARC121 Lesson in Lava SR	50.00	100.00
ARC122 Tome of Aetherwind SR	30.00	75.00
ARC123 Absorb in Aether (red) R	.75	1.50
ARC124 Absorb in Aether (yellow) R	7.50	15.00
ARC125 Absorb in Aether (blue) R	10.00	20.00
ARC126 Aether Spindle (red) R	10.00	20.00
ARC127 Aether Spindle (yellow) R	7.50	15.00
ARC128 Aether Spindle (blue) R	12.50	25.00
ARC129 Stir the Aetherwinds (red) R	10.00	20.00
ARC130 Stir the Aetherwinds (yellow) R	10.00	20.00
ARC131 Stir the Aetherwinds (blue) R	10.00	20.00
ARC132 Aether Flare (red) C	5.00	10.00
ARC133 Aether Flare (yellow) C	2.50	5.00
ARC134 Aether Flare (blue) C	2.50	5.00
ARC135 Index (red) C	2.50	5.00
ARC136 Index (yellow) C	2.50	5.00
ARC137 Index (blue) C	2.50	5.00
ARC138 Reverberate (red) C	5.00	10.00
ARC139 Reverberate (yellow) C	4.00	8.00
ARC140 Reverberate (blue) C	2.50	5.00
ARC141 Scalding Rain (red) C	5.00	10.00
ARC142 Scalding Rain (yellow) C	2.00	4.00
ARC143 Scalding Rain (blue) C	5.00	10.00
ARC144 Zap (red) C	1.50	3.00
ARC145 Zap (yellow) C	2.50	5.00
ARC146 Zap (blue) C	4.00	8.00
ARC147 Voltic Bolt (red) C	2.50	5.00
ARC148 Voltic Bolt (yellow) C	2.00	4.00
ARC149 Voltic Bolt (blue) C	3.00	6.00
ARC151 Talismanic Lens C	200.00	400.00
ARC152 Vest of the First Fist C	.15	.30
ARC153 Bracers of Belief C	300.00	600.00
ARC154 Mage Master Boots C	200.00	400.00
ARC155 Nullrune Hood C	150.00	300.00
ARC156 Nullrune Robe C	250.00	500.00
ARC157 Nullrune Gloves C	300.00	600.00
ARC158 Nullrune Boots C	300.00	600.00
ARC159 Command and Conquer M	3,000.00	6,000.00
ARC160 Art of War M	500.00	1,000.00
ARC161 Pursuit of Knowledge SR	7.50	15.00
ARC162 Chains of Eminence SR	50.00	100.00
ARC163 Rusted Relic SR	20.00	40.00
ARC164 Life for a Life (red) R	20.00	40.00
ARC165 Life for a Life (yellow) R	4.00	8.00
ARC166 Life for a Life (blue) R	7.50	15.00
ARC167 Enchanting Melody (red) R	4.00	8.00
ARC168 Enchanting Melody (yellow) R	12.50	25.00
ARC169 Enchanting Melody (blue) R	4.00	8.00
ARC170 Plunder Run (red) R	15.00	30.00
ARC171 Plunder Run (yellow) R	7.50	15.00
ARC172 Plunder Run (blue) R	12.50	25.00
ARC173 Eirina's Prayer (red) R	7.50	15.00
ARC174 Eirina's Prayer (yellow) R	4.00	8.00
ARC175 Eirina's Prayer (blue) R	5.00	10.00
ARC176 Back Alley Breakline (red) C	4.00	8.00
ARC177 Back Alley Breakline (yellow) C	3.00	6.00
ARC178 Back Alley Breakline (blue) C	1.25	2.50
ARC179 Cadaverous Contraband (red) C	7.50	15.00
ARC180 Cadaverous Contraband (yellow) C	6.00	12.00
ARC181 Cadaverous Contraband (blue) C	2.00	4.00
ARC182 Fervent Forerunner (red) C	1.25	2.50
ARC183 Fervent Forerunner (yellow) C	3.00	6.00
ARC184 Fervent Forerunner (blue) C	2.00	4.00
ARC185 Moon Wish (red) C	7.50	15.00
ARC186 Moon Wish (yellow) C	2.50	5.00
ARC187 Moon Wish (blue) C	4.00	8.00
ARC188 Push the Point (red) C	.75	1.50
ARC189 Push the Point (yellow) C	2.00	4.00
ARC190 Push the Point (blue) C	2.00	4.00
ARC191 Ravenous Rabble (red) C	7.50	15.00
ARC192 Ravenous Rabble (yellow) C	6.00	12.00
ARC193 Ravenous Rabble (blue) C	3.00	6.00
ARC194 Rifting (red) C	4.00	8.00
ARC195 Rifting (yellow) C	2.00	4.00
ARC196 Rifting (blue) C	4.00	8.00
ARC197 Vigor Rush (red) C	1.50	3.00
ARC198 Vigor Rush (yellow) C	1.50	3.00
ARC199 Vigor Rush (blue) C	2.00	4.00
ARC200 Fate Foreseen (red) C	60.00	125.00
ARC201 Fate Foreseen (yellow) C	5.00	10.00
ARC202 Fate Foreseen (blue) C	6.00	12.00
ARC203 Come to Fight (red) C	4.00	8.00
ARC204 Come to Fight (yellow) C	2.00	4.00
ARC205 Come to Fight (blue) C	3.00	6.00
ARC206 Force Sight (red) C	2.50	5.00
ARC207 Force Sight (yellow) C	2.00	4.00
ARC208 Force Sight (blue) C	2.00	4.00
ARC209 Lead the Charge (red) C	7.50	15.00
ARC210 Lead the Charge (yellow) C	10.00	20.00
ARC211 Lead the Charge (blue) C	7.50	15.00
ARC212 Sun Kiss (red) C	4.00	8.00
ARC213 Sun Kiss (yellow) C	2.00	4.00
ARC214 Sun Kiss (blue) C	2.50	5.00
ARC215 Whisper of the Oracle (red) C	10.00	20.00
ARC216 Whisper of the Oracle (yellow) C	4.00	8.00
ARC217 Whisper of the Oracle (blue) C	10.00	20.00

2020 Flesh and Blood Crucible of War 1st Edition

CRU000 Arknight Shard F	2,500.00	5,000.00
CRU001 Rhinar, Reckless Rampage T	.75	1.50
CRU002 Kayo, Berserker Runt R	.15	.30
CRU003 Romping Club T	.50	1.00
CRU004 Mandible Claw R	1.25	2.50
CRU005 Mandible Claw (Reverse) R	1.00	2.00
CRU006 Skullhorn M	10.00	20.00
CRU007 Beast Within M	5.00	10.00
CRU008 Massacre M	3.00	6.00
CRU009 Argh... Smash! M	1.50	3.00
CRU010 Barraging Big Horn (Red) R	.15	.30
CRU011 Barraging Big Horn (Yellow) R	.15	.30
CRU012 Barraging Big Horn (Blue) R	.25	.50
CRU013 Predatory Assault (Red) C	.25	.50
CRU014 Predatory Assault (Yellow) C	.15	.30
CRU015 Predatory Assault (Blue) C	.10	.20
CRU016 Riled Up (Red) C	.10	.20
CRU017 Riled Up (Yellow) C	.25	.50
CRU018 Riled Up (Blue) C	.10	.20
CRU019 Swing Fist, Think Later (Red) C	.10	.20
CRU020 Swing Fist, Think Later (Yellow) C	.15	.30
CRU021 Swing Fist, Think Later (Blue) C	.10	.20
CRU022 Bravo, Showstopper T	.60	1.25
CRU023 Anothos T	.50	1.00
CRU024 Sledge of Anvilheim R	1.50	3.00
CRU025 Crater Fist M	25.00	50.00
CRU026 Mangle M	2.00	4.00
CRU027 Righteous Cleansing M	4.00	8.00
CRU028 Stamp Authority M	4.00	8.00
CRU029 Towering Titan (Red) R	.15	.30
CRU030 Towering Titan (Yellow) R	.15	.30
CRU031 Towering Titan (Blue) R	.75	1.50
CRU032 Crush the Weak (Red) C	.12	.25
CRU033 Crush the Weak (Yellow) C	.12	.25
CRU034 Crush the Weak (Blue) C	.30	.60
CRU035 Chokeslam (Red) C	.10	.20
CRU036 Chokeslam (Yellow) C	.15	.30
CRU037 Chokeslam (Blue) C	.30	.75
CRU038 Emerging Dominance (Red) C	.10	.20
CRU039 Emerging Dominance (Yellow) C	.12	.25
CRU040 Emerging Dominance (Blue) C	.10	.20
CRU041 Blessing of Serenity (Red) C	.12	.25
CRU042 Blessing of Serenity (Yellow) C	.07	.15
CRU043 Blessing of Serenity (Blue) C	.07	.15
CRU044 Seismic Surge T	7.50	15.00
CRU045 Katsu, the Wanderer T	.75	1.50
CRU046 Ira, Crimson Haze C	.25	.50
CRU047 Benji, the Piercing Wind R	1.25	2.50
CRU048 Harmonized Kodachi T	2.50	5.00
CRU049 Harmonized Kodachi (Reverse) R	.60	1.25
CRU050 Edge of Autumn R	.20	.40
CRU051 Zephyr Needle R	.20	.40
CRU052 Zephyr Needle (Reverse) R	.50	1.00
CRU053 Breeze Rider Boots M	20.00	40.00
CRU054 Find Center M	7.50	15.00
CRU055 Flood of Force M	4.00	8.00
CRU056 Heron's Flight M	2.50	5.00
CRU057 Crane Dance (Red) R	.12	.25
CRU058 Crane Dance (Yellow) R	.15	.30
CRU059 Crane Dance (Blue) R	.30	.75
CRU060 Rushing River (Red) R	.25	.50
CRU061 Rushing River (Yellow) R	.15	.30
CRU062 Rushing River (Blue) R	.25	.50
CRU063 Flying Kick (Red) C	.10	.20
CRU064 Flying Kick (Yellow) C	.07	.15
CRU065 Flying Kick (Blue) C	.07	.15
CRU066 Soulbead Strike (Red) C	1.00	2.00
CRU067 Soulbead Strike (Yellow) C	.10	.20
CRU068 Soulbead Strike (Blue) C	.30	.60
CRU069 Torrent of Tempo (Red) C	.50	1.00
CRU070 Torrent of Tempo (Yellow) C	.12	.25
CRU071 Torrent of Tempo (Blue) C	.07	.15
CRU072 Bittering Thorns C	.12	.25
CRU073 Salt the Wound C	.12	.25
CRU074 Whirling Mist Blossom C	.12	.25
CRU075 Dorinthea Ironsong T	.50	1.00
CRU075 Zen State R	.25	.50
CRU077 Kassai, Cintari Sellsword R	.75	1.50
CRU078 Dawnblade T	.75	1.50
CRU079 Cintari Saber R	.75	1.50
CRU080 Cintari Saber (Reverse) R	1.00	2.00
CRU081 Courage of Bladehold M	30.00	60.00
CRU082 Twinning Blade M	6.00	12.00
CRU082 Twinning Blade (Extended Art) M	750.00	1,500.00
CRU083 Unified Decree M	.75	1.50
CRU084 Spoils of War M	10.00	20.00
CRU085 Dauntless (Red) R	.25	.50
CRU086 Dauntless (Yellow) R	.25	.50
CRU087 Dauntless (Blue) R	.15	.30
CRU088 Out for Blood (Red) C	.75	1.50
CRU089 Out for Blood (Yellow) C	.15	.30
CRU090 Out for Blood (Blue) C	.20	.40
CRU091 Hit and Run (Red) C	.15	.30
CRU092 Hit and Run (Yellow) C	.15	.30
CRU093 Hit and Run (Blue) C	.15	.30
CRU094 Push Forward (Red) C	.20	.40
CRU095 Push Forward (Yellow) C	.07	.15
CRU096 Push Forward (Blue) C	.12	.25
CRU097 Shiyana, Diamond Gemini L	1,500.00	3,000.00
CRU098 Dash, Inventor Extraordinaire T	.30	.75
CRU099 Data Doll MKII R	.75	1.50
CRU100 Teklo Plasma Pistol T	2.50	5.00
CRU101 Plasma Barrel Shot R	1.00	2.00
CRU102 Viziertronic Model i M	15.00	30.00
CRU103 Meganetic Shockwave M	3.00	6.00
CRU104 Absorption Dome M	2.00	4.00
CRU105 Plasma Purifier M	4.00	8.00
CRU106 High Speed Impact (Red) R	.50	1.00
CRU107 High Speed Impact (Yellow) R	.20	.40
CRU108 High Speed Impact (Blue) R	.75	1.50
CRU109 Combustible Courier (Red) C	.30	.60
CRU110 Combustible Courier (Yellow) C	.10	.20
CRU111 Combustible Courier (Blue) C	1.00	2.00
CRU112 Overblast (Red) C	.15	.30
CRU113 Overblast (Yellow) C	.12	.25
CRU114 Overblast (Blue) C	.25	.50
CRU115 Teklovossen's Workshop (Red) C	.12	.25
CRU116 Teklovossen's Workshop (Yellow) C	.12	.25
CRU117 Teklovossen's Workshop (Blue) C	.12	.25
CRU118 Kavdaen, Trader of Skins R	.75	1.50
CRU119 Azalea, Ace in the Hole T	.20	.40
CRU120 Death Dealer T	.75	1.50
CRU121 Red Liner R	1.50	3.00
CRU122 Perch Grapplers M	25.00	50.00
CRU123 Remorseless M	15.00	30.00
CRU124 Poison the Tips M	2.50	5.00
CRU125 Feign Death M	1.25	2.50
CRU126 Tripwire Trap R	.20	.40
CRU127 Pitfall Trap R	.30	.60
CRU128 Rockslide Trap R	.20	.40
CRU129 Pathing Helix (Red) C	.30	.60
CRU130 Pathing Helix (Yellow) C	.12	.25
CRU131 Pathing Helix (Blue) C	.12	.25
CRU132 Sleep Dart (Red) C	.25	.50
CRU133 Sleep Dart (Yellow) C	.15	.30
CRU134 Sleep Dart (Blue) C	.15	.30
CRU135 Increase the Tension (Red) C	.30	.75
CRU136 Increase the Tension (Yellow) C	.12	.25
CRU137 Increase the Tension (Blue) C	.07	.15
CRU138 Viserai, Rune Blood T	.75	1.50
CRU139 Nebula Blade T	4.00	8.00
CRU140 Reaping Blade R	1.50	3.00
CRU141 Bloodsheath Skeleta M	20.00	40.00
CRU142 Dread Triptych M	10.00	20.00
CRU143 Rattle Bones M	7.50	15.00
CRU144 Runeblood Barrier M	2.00	4.00
CRU145 Mauvrion Skies (Red) R	.25	.50
CRU146 Mauvrion Skies (Yellow) R	.40	.80
CRU147 Mauvrion Skies (Blue) R	.50	.40
CRU148 Consuming Volition (Red) C	.15	.30
CRU149 Consuming Volition (Yellow) C	.15	.30
CRU150 Consuming Volition (Blue) C	.12	.25
CRU151 Meat and Greet (Red) C	.75	1.50
CRU152 Meat and Greet (Yellow) C	.10	.20
CRU153 Meat and Greet (Blue) C	.30	.75
CRU154 Sutcliffe's Research Notes (Red) C	.12	.25
CRU155 Sutcliffe's Research Notes (Yellow) C	.10	.20
CRU156 Sutcliffe's Research Notes (Blue) C	.10	.20
CRU157 Runechant T	1.00	2.00
CRU158 Kano, Dracai of Aether T	1.00	2.00
CRU159 Crucible of Aetherweave T	.75	1.50
CRU160 Aether Conduit R	.75	.40
CRU161 Metacarpus Node M	20.00	40.00
CRU162 Chain Lightning M	3.00	6.00
CRU163 Gaze the Ages M	15.00	30.00
CRU164 Aetherize M	3.00	6.00
CRU165 Cindering Foresight (Red) R	.20	.40
CRU166 Cindering Foresight (Yellow) R	.15	.30
CRU167 Cindering Foresight (Blue) R	.25	.50
CRU168 Foreboding Bolt (Red) C	.12	.25
CRU169 Foreboding Bolt (Yellow) C	.12	.25
CRU170 Foreboding Bolt (Blue) C	.25	.50
CRU171 Rousing Aether (Red) C	.15	.30
CRU172 Rousing Aether (Yellow) C	.15	.30
CRU173 Rousing Aether (Blue) C	.15	.30
CRU174 Snapback (Red) C	.75	1.50
CRU175 Snapback (Yellow) C	.10	.20
CRU176 Snapback (Blue) C	.25	.50
CRU177 Talishar, the Lost Prince R	.25	.50
CRU178 Fyendal's Spring Tunic L	150.00	300.00
CRU179 Gambler's Gloves M	75.00	150.00
CRU180 Coax a Commotion M	4.00	8.00
CRU181 Gorganian Tome M	20.00	40.00
CRU182 Snag M	4.00	8.00
CRU183 Promise of Plenty (Red) R	.15	.30
CRU184 Promise of Plenty (Yellow) R	.15	.30
CRU185 Promise of Plenty (Blue) R	.30	.60
CRU186 Lunging Press R	.20	.40
CRU188 Cash In R	1.50	3.00
CRU189 Reinforce the Line (Red) R	.20	.40
CRU190 Reinforce the Line (Yellow) R	.10	.20
CRU191 Reinforce the Line (Blue) R	.10	.20
CRU192 Brutal Assault (Red) C	.12	.25
CRU193 Brutal Assault (Yellow) C	.10	.20
CRU194 Brutal Assault (Blue) C	.12	.25
CRU196 Quicken T	3.00	6.00
CRU197 Copper C	.20	.40

2020 Flesh and Blood Crucible of War 1st Edition Foil

CRU002 Kayo, Berserker Runt R	10.00	20.00
CRU004 Mandible Claw R	100.00	200.00
CRU005 Mandible Claw (Reverse) R	100.00	200.00
CRU006 Skullhorn M	200.00	400.00
CRU007 Beast Within M	20.00	40.00
CRU008 Massacre M	10.00	20.00
CRU009 Argh... Smash! M	6.00	12.00
CRU010 Barraging Big Horn (Red) R	1.25	2.50
CRU011 Barraging Big Horn (Yellow) R	2.00	4.00
CRU012 Barraging Big Horn (Blue) R	.75	1.50
CRU013 Predatory Assault (Red) C	.30	.60
CRU014 Predatory Assault (Yellow) C	.20	.40
CRU015 Predatory Assault (Blue) C	.20	.40
CRU016 Riled Up (Red) C	.30	.60
CRU017 Riled Up (Yellow) C	.50	1.00
CRU018 Riled Up (Blue) C	.50	1.00
CRU019 Swing Fist, Think Later (Red) C	.40	.80
CRU020 Swing Fist, Think Later (Yellow) C	.25	.50
CRU021 Swing Fist, Think Later (Blue) C	.30	.75
CRU024 Sledge of Anvilheim R	100.00	200.00
CRU025 Crater Fist M	250.00	500.00
CRU026 Mangle M	12.50	25.00
CRU027 Righteous Cleansing M	20.00	40.00
CRU028 Stamp Authority M	25.00	50.00
CRU029 Towering Titan (Red) R	2.50	5.00
CRU030 Towering Titan (Yellow) R	.60	1.25
CRU031 Towering Titan (Blue) R	2.50	5.00
CRU032 Crush the Weak (Red) C	.50	1.00
CRU033 Crush the Weak (Yellow) C	.20	.40
CRU034 Crush the Weak (Blue) C	2.50	5.00
CRU035 Chokeslam (Red) C	.30	.75
CRU036 Chokeslam (Yellow) C	.50	1.00
CRU037 Chokeslam (Blue) C	.50	1.00
CRU038 Emerging Dominance (Red) C	.50	1.00
CRU039 Emerging Dominance (Yellow) C	.30	.75
CRU040 Emerging Dominance (Blue) C	.75	1.50
CRU041 Blessing of Serenity (Red) C	.30	.60
CRU042 Blessing of Serenity (Yellow) C	.30	.75
CRU043 Blessing of Serenity (Blue) C	.30	.75
CRU046 Ira, Crimson Haze C	6.00	12.00
CRU047 Benji, the Piercing Wind R	12.50	25.00
CRU049 Harmonized Kodachi (Reverse) R	100.00	200.00
CRU050 Edge of Autumn R	75.00	150.00
CRU051 Zephyr Needle R	60.00	125.00
CRU052 Zephyr Needle (Reverse) R	75.00	150.00
CRU053 Breeze Rider Boots M	250.00	500.00
CRU054 Find Center M	15.00	30.00
CRU055 Flood of Force M	7.50	15.00
CRU056 Heron's Flight M	10.00	20.00
CRU057 Crane Dance (Red) R	1.00	2.00
CRU058 Crane Dance (Yellow) R	1.00	2.00
CRU059 Crane Dance (Blue) R	4.00	8.00
CRU060 Rushing River (Red) R	1.50	3.00
CRU061 Rushing River (Yellow) R	1.25	2.50
CRU062 Rushing River (Blue) R	3.00	6.00
CRU063 Flying Kick (Red) C	3.00	6.00
CRU064 Flying Kick (Yellow) C	.60	1.25
CRU065 Flying Kick (Blue) C	.50	1.00
CRU066 Soulbead Strike (Red) C	3.00	6.00
CRU067 Soulbead Strike (Yellow) C	.30	.75
CRU068 Soulbead Strike (Blue) C	1.00	2.00
CRU069 Torrent of Tempo (Red) C	2.50	5.00
CRU070 Torrent of Tempo (Yellow) C	.15	1.00
CRU071 Torrent of Tempo (Blue) C	1.00	2.00

CRU072 Bittering Thorns C	.30	.60
CRU073 Salt the Wound C	1.00	2.00
CRU074 Whirling Mist Blossom C	2.50	5.00
CRU075 Zen State R	4.00	8.00
CRU077 Kassai, Cintari Sellsword R	25.00	50.00
CRU079 Cintari Saber R	125.00	250.00
CRU080 Cintari Saber (Reverse) R	125.00	250.00
CRU081 Courage of Bladehold M	400.00	800.00
CRU082 Twinning Blade M	40.00	80.00
CRU083 Unified Decree M	6.00	12.00
CRU084 Spoils of War M	30.00	60.00
CRU085 Dauntless (Red) R	.75	1.50
CRU086 Dauntless (Yellow) R	.75	1.50
CRU087 Dauntless (Blue) R	1.25	2.50
CRU088 Out for Blood (Red) C	4.00	8.00
CRU089 Out for Blood (Yellow) C	.40	.80
CRU090 Out for Blood (Blue) C	.75	1.50
CRU091 Hit and Run (Red) C	.15	.30
CRU092 Hit and Run (Yellow) C	.15	.30
CRU093 Hit and Run (Blue) C	.15	.30
CRU094 Push Forward (Red) C	.75	1.50
CRU095 Push Forward (Yellow) C	.75	1.50
CRU096 Push Forward (Blue) C	3.00	6.00
CRU099 Data Doll MKII R	10.00	20.00
CRU101 Plasma Barrel Shot R	75.00	150.00
CRU102 Viziertronic Model i M	250.00	500.00
CRU103 Meganetic Shockwave M	10.00	20.00
CRU104 Absorbtion Dome M	7.50	15.00
CRU105 Plasma Purifier M	10.00	20.00
CRU106 High Speed Impact (Red) R	4.00	8.00
CRU107 High Speed Impact (Yellow) R	1.25	2.50
CRU108 High Speed Impact (Blue) R	4.00	8.00
CRU109 Combustible Courier (Red) C	2.00	4.00
CRU110 Combustible Courier (Yellow) C	.75	1.50
CRU111 Combustible Courier (Blue) C	2.50	5.00
CRU112 Overblast (Red) C	1.00	2.00
CRU113 Overblast (Yellow) C	.75	1.50
CRU114 Overblast (Blue) C	.75	1.50
CRU115 Teklovossen's Workshop (Red) C	.75	1.50
CRU116 Teklovossen's Workshop (Yellow) C	.40	.80
CRU117 Teklovossen's Workshop (Blue) C	.75	1.50
CRU118 Kavdaen, Trader of Skins R	10.00	20.00
CRU121 Red Liner R	60.00	125.00
CRU122 Perch Grapplers M	250.00	500.00
CRU123 Remorseless M	40.00	80.00
CRU124 Poison the Tips M	15.00	30.00
CRU125 Feign Death M	12.50	25.00
CRU126 Tripwire Trap R	2.00	4.00
CRU127 Pitfall Trap R	1.25	2.50
CRU128 Rockslide Trap R	.60	1.25
CRU129 Pathing Helix (Red) C	3.00	6.00
CRU130 Pathing Helix (Yellow) C	.50	1.00
CRU131 Pathing Helix (Blue) C	.50	1.00
CRU132 Sleep Dart (Red) C	4.00	8.00
CRU133 Sleep Dart (Yellow) C	2.50	5.00
CRU134 Sleep Dart (Blue) C	1.50	3.00
CRU135 Increase the Tension (Red) C	2.50	5.00
CRU136 Increase the Tension (Yellow) C	.50	1.00
CRU137 Increase the Tension (Blue) C	.30	.75
CRU140 Reaping Blade R	100.00	200.00
CRU141 Bloodsheath Skeleta M	300.00	750.00
CRU142 Dread Triptych M	25.00	50.00
CRU143 Rattle Bones M	10.00	20.00
CRU144 Runeblood Barrier M	10.00	20.00
CRU145 Mauvrion Skies (Red) R	4.00	8.00
CRU146 Mauvrion Skies (Yellow) R	4.00	8.00
CRU147 Mauvrion Skies (Blue) R	.20	.40
CRU148 Consuming Volition (Red) C	2.00	4.00
CRU149 Consuming Volition (Yellow) C	.50	1.00
CRU150 Consuming Volition (Blue) C	.30	.75
CRU151 Meat and Greet (Red) C	3.00	6.00
CRU152 Meat and Greet (Yellow) C	.75	1.50
CRU153 Meat and Greet (Blue) C	2.00	4.00
CRU154 Sutcliffe's Research Notes (Red) C	.50	1.00
CRU155 Sutcliffe's Research Notes (Yellow) C	.15	.30
CRU156 Sutcliffe's Research Notes (Blue) C	.15	.30
CRU160 Aether Conduit R	40.00	80.00
CRU161 Metacarpus Node M	300.00	600.00
CRU162 Chain Lightning M	15.00	30.00
CRU163 Gaze the Ages M	3.00	6.00
CRU164 Aetherize M	12.50	25.00
CRU165 Cindering Foresight (Red) R	1.50	3.00
CRU166 Cindering Foresight (Yellow) R	1.25	2.50
CRU167 Cindering Foresight (Blue) R	1.50	3.00
CRU168 Foreboding Bolt (Red) C	.30	.75
CRU169 Foreboding Bolt (Yellow) C	.25	.50
CRU170 Foreboding Bolt (Blue) C	1.50	3.00
CRU171 Rousing Aether (Red) C	.50	1.00
CRU172 Rousing Aether (Yellow) C	1.25	2.50
CRU173 Rousing Aether (Blue) C	.40	.80
CRU174 Snapback (Red) C	4.00	8.00
CRU175 Snapback (Yellow) C	1.50	3.00
CRU176 Snapback (Blue) C	2.50	5.00
CRU177 Talishar, the Lost Prince R	75.00	150.00
CRU179 Gambler's Gloves M	25.00	50.00
CRU180 Coax a Commotion M	30.00	60.00
CRU181 Gorganian Tome M	150.00	300.00
CRU182 Snag M	12.50	25.00
CRU183 Promise of Plenty (Red) R	.75	1.50
CRU184 Promise of Plenty (Yellow) R	.60	1.25
CRU185 Promise of Plenty (Blue) R	.75	1.50
CRU186 Lunging Press R	4.00	8.00
CRU187 Springboard Somersault R	4.00	8.00
CRU188 Cash In R	10.00	20.00
CRU189 Reinforce the Line (Red) R	.75	1.50
CRU190 Reinforce the Line (Yellow) R	.60	1.25
CRU191 Reinforce the Line (Blue) R	.75	1.50
CRU192 Brutal Assault (Red) C	.30	.60
CRU193 Brutal Assault (Yellow) C	.50	1.00
CRU194 Brutal Assault (Blue) C	.30	.75
CRU197 Copper C	5.00	10.00

2020 Flesh and Blood Hero Deck Bravo

BVO001 Bravo, Showstopper C	.15	.30
BVO003 Anothos C	.15	.30
BVO004 Helm of Isen's Peak C	.15	.30
BVO005 Ironrot Plate C	.15	.30
BVO006 Goliath Gauntlet C	.15	.30
BVO007 Ironrot Legs C	.15	.30
BVO008 Buckling Blow (Red) C	.15	.30
BVO009 Cartilage Crush (Red) C	.15	.30
BVO010 Debilitate (Red) C	.15	.30
BVO011 Disable (Red) R	.15	.40
BVO012 Emerging Power (Red) C	.15	.30
BVO013 Debilitate (Yellow) C	.15	.30
BVO014 Emerging Power (Yellow) C	.15	.30
BVO015 Springboard Somersault C	.15	.30
BVO016 Buckling Blow (Blue) C	.15	.30
BVO017 Cartilage Crush (Blue) C	.15	.30
BVO018 Crush Confidence (Blue) C	.15	.30
BVO019 Disable (Blue) R	.15	.40
BVO020 Staunch Response (Blue) R	.15	.40
BVO021 Blessing of Deliverance (Blue) R	.15	.40
BVO022 Stonewall Confidence (Blue) C	.15	.30
BVO023 Barraging Brawnhide (Blue) C	.15	.30
BVO024 Raging Onslaught (Blue) C	.15	.30
BVO025 Drone of Brutality (Blue) R	.15	.40
BVO026 Wounded Bull (Blue) R	.15	.40
BVO027 Pummel (Blue) C	.15	.30
BVO028 Potion of Strength R	.15	.40
BVO029 Sloggism (Blue) C	.15	.30

2020 Flesh and Blood Hero Deck Dorinthea

TEA001 Dorinthea Ironsong C	.15	.30
TEA003 Dawnblade C	.15	.30
TEA004 Hope Merchant's Hood C	.15	.30
TEA005 Ironrot Plate C	.15	.30
TEA006 Ironrot Gauntlet C	.15	.30
TEA007 Refraction Bolters C	.15	.30
TEA008 Biting Blade (Red) C	.15	.30
TEA009 Stroke of Foresight (Red) C	.15	.30
TEA010 Overpower (Red) R	.20	.40
TEA011 Steelblade Shunt (Red) R	.20	.40
TEA012 Driving Blade (Red) C	.15	.30
TEA013 Nature's Path Pilgrimage (Red) C	.15	.30
TEA014 Sharpen Steel (Red) C	.15	.30
TEA015 Wounding Blow (Red) C	.15	.30
TEA016 Razor Reflex (Red) C	.15	.30
TEA017 Stroke of Foresight (Yellow) C	.15	.30
TEA018 Warrior's Valor (Yellow) R	.20	.40
TEA019 Springboard Somersault C	.15	.30
TEA020 Biting Blade (Blue) C	.15	.30
TEA021 Ironsong Response (Blue) C	.15	.30
TEA022 Driving Blade (Blue) C	.15	.30
TEA023 Nature's Path Pilgrimage (Blue) C	.15	.30
TEA024 Sharpen Steel (Blue) C	.15	.30
TEA025 Warrior's Valor (Blue) R	.20	.40
TEA026 Flock of the Feather Walkers (Blue) C	.15	.30
TEA027 Scour the Battlescape (Blue) C	.15	.30
TEA028 Energy Potion R	.20	.40
TEA029 Sigil of Solace (Blue) R	.20	.40

2020 Flesh and Blood Hero Deck Katsu

KSU001 Katsu, the Wanderer C	.15	.30
KSU003 Harmonized Kodachi C	.15	.30
KSU003 Harmonized Kodachi (Reverse) C	.15	.30
KSU005 Ironrot Helm C	.15	.30
KSU006 Heartened Cross Strap C	.15	.30
KSU007 Breaking Scales C	.15	.30
KSU008 Ironrot Legs C	.15	.30
KSU009 Blackout Kick (Red) R	.20	.40
KSU010 Fluster Fist (Red) R	.20	.40
KSU011 Head Jab (Red) C	.15	.30
KSU012 Leg Tap (Red) C	.15	.30
KSU013 Open the Center (Red) C	.15	.30
KSU014 Rising Knee Thrust (Red) C	.15	.30
KSU015 Surging Strike (Red) C	.15	.30
KSU016 Whelming Gustwave (Red) C	.15	.30
KSU017 Scar for a Scar (Red) C	.15	.30
KSU018 Leg Tap (Yellow) C	.15	.30
KSU019 Rising Knee Thrust (Yellow) C	.15	.30
KSU020 Surging Strike (Yellow) C	.15	.30
KSU021 Springboard Somersault C	.15	.30
KSU022 Fluster Fist (Blue) R	.20	.40
KSU023 Head Jab (Blue) C	.15	.30
KSU024 Whelming Gustwave (Blue) C	.15	.30
KSU025 Flic Flak (Blue) R	.20	.40
KSU026 Scour the Battlescape (Blue) C	.15	.30
KSU027 Wounding Blow (Blue) C	.15	.30
KSU028 Lunging Press C	.15	.30
KSU029 Energy Potion R	.20	.40
KSU030 Sigil of Solace (Blue) R	.20	.40

2020 Flesh and Blood Hero Deck Rhinar

RNR001 Rhinar, Reckless Rampage C	.15	.30
RNR003 Romping Club C	.15	.30
RNR004 Ironrot Helm C	.15	.30
RNR005 Barkbone Strapping C	.15	.30
RNR006 Ironrot Gauntlet C	.15	.30
RNR007 Snapdragon Scalers C	.15	.30
RNR008 Breakneck Battery (Red) R	.20	.40
RNR009 Pack Hunt (Red) C	.15	.30
RNR010 Savage Feast (Red) R	.20	.40
RNR011 Savage Swing (Red) C	.15	.30
RNR012 Smash Instinct (Red) C	.15	.30
RNR013 Wrecker Romp (Red) C	.15	.30
RNR014 Awakening Bellow (Red) C	.15	.30
RNR015 Drone of Brutality (Red) R	.20	.40
RNR016 Savage Swing (Yellow) C	.15	.30
RNR017 Smash Instinct (Yellow) C	.15	.30
RNR018 Barraging Beatdown (Yellow) R	.20	.40
RNR019 Barraging Brawnhide (Yellow) C	.15	.30
RNR020 Raging Onslaught (Yellow) C	.15	.30
RNR021 Wounded Bull (Yellow) C	.15	.30
RNR022 Springboard Somersault C	.15	.30
RNR023 Wrecker Romp (Blue) C	.15	.30
RNR024 Awakening Bellow (Blue) C	.15	.30
RNR025 Barraging Beatdown (Blue) R	.20	.40
RNR026 Primeval Bellow (Blue) C	.15	.30
RNR027 Flock of the Feather Walkers (Blue) C	.15	.30
RNR028 Scour the Battlescape (Blue) C	.15	.30
RNR029 Timesnap Potion R	.20	.40
RNR030 Sigil of Solace (Blue) R	.20	.40

2021 Flesh and Blood Monarch Blitz Deck Boltyn

BOL001 Boltyn R	3.00	.40
BOL002 Minerva Themis M	6.00	12.00
BOL003 Hatchet of Body C	.15	.30
BOL004 Hatchet of Mind C	.15	.30
BOL005 Halo of Illumination C	.15	.30
BOL006 Spell Fray Cloak C	.15	.30
BOL007 Gallantry Gold C	.15	.30
BOL008 Snapdragon Scalers C	.15	.30
BOL009 V of the Vanguard R	.30	.40
BOL010 Battlefield Blitz R	.30	.40
BOL011 Bolt of Courage (Red) C	.15	.30
BOL012 Courageous Steelhand C	.15	.30
BOL013 Cross the Line (Red) C	.15	.30
BOL014 Engulfing Light (Red) C	.15	.30
BOL015 Express Lightning (Red) C	.15	.30
BOL016 Take Flight (Red) C	.15	.30
BOL017 Valiant Thrust R	.30	.40
BOL018 Courageous Steelhand (Yellow) C	.15	.30
BOL019 Cross the Line (Yellow) C	.15	.30
BOL020 Express Lightning (Yellow) C	.15	.30
BOL021 Take Flight (Yellow) C	.15	.30
BOL022 Bolt of Courage (Blue) C	.15	.30
BOL023 Engulfing Light (Blue) C	.15	.30
BOL024 Invigorating Light (Red) R	.30	.40
BOL025 Rising Solartide (Red) C	.15	.30
BOL026 Rising Solartide (Yellow) C	.15	.30
BOL027 Illuminate (Blue) C	.15	.30
BOL028 Seek Enlightenment (Blue) C	.15	.30
BOL029 Dusk Path Pilgrimage (Red) R	.30	.40
BOL030 Push Forward (Red) C	.15	.30

2021 Flesh and Blood Monarch Blitz Deck Chane

CHN001 Chane R	.50	.40
CHN002 Lord Sutcliffe MR	4.00	8.00
CHN003 Galaxxi Black R	.50	.40
CHN004 Ebon Fold C	.15	.30
CHN005 Aether Ironweave C	.15	.30
CHN006 Spell Fray Gloves C	.15	.30
CHN007 Snapdragon Scalers C	.15	.30
CHN008 Soul Reaping R	.50	.40
CHN009 Bounding Demigon (Red) C	.15	.30
CHN010 Piercing Shadow Vise (Red) C	.15	.30
CHN011 Rift Bind (Red) C	.15	.30
CHN012 Rifted Torment (Red) C	.15	.30
CHN013 Rip Through Reality (Red) C	.15	.30
CHN014 Seeds of Agony (Red) C	.15	.30
CHN015 Unhallowed Rites (Red) R	.50	.40
CHN016 Seeds of Agony (Yellow) C	.15	.30
CHN017 Seeping Shadows (Yellow) R	.50	.40
CHN018 Piercing Shadow Vise (Blue) C	.15	.30
CHN019 Rift Bind (Blue) C	.15	.30
CHN020 Rifted Torment (Blue) C	.15	.30
CHN021 Ghostly Visit (Red) C	.15	.30
CHN022 Howl from Beyond (Red) R	.50	.40
CHN023 Lunartide Plunderer (Yellow) C	.15	.30
CHN024 Spew Shadow (Yellow) C	.15	.30
CHN025 Consuming Volition (Red) C	.15	.30
CHN026 Vexing Malice (Red) R	.50	.40
CHN027 Arcanic Crackle (Blue) C	.15	.30
CHN028 Warmonger's Recital (Red) C	.15	.30
CHN029 Warmongers Recital (Yellow) C	.15	.30
CHN030 Soul Shackle T	.75	1.50

2021 Flesh and Blood Monarch Blitz Deck Levia

LEV001 Levia R	2.00	.40
LEV002 Lady Barthimont MR	6.00	12.00
LEV003 Ravenous Meataxe C	.15	.30
LEV004 Ebon Fold C	.15	.30
LEV005 Spell Fray Cloak C	.15	.30
LEV006 Goliath Gauntlet C	.15	.30
LEV007 Hooves of the Shadowbeast C	.15	.30
LEV008 Soul Harvest R	.50	.40
LEV009 Boneyard Marauder (Red) C	.15	.30
LEV010 Deadwood Rumbler (Red) C	.15	.30
LEV011 Dread Screamer (Red) C	.15	.30
LEV012 Endless Maw (Red) R	.50	.40
LEV013 Graveling Growl (Red) C	.15	.30
LEV014 Hungering Slaughterbeast (Red) C	.15	.30
LEV015 Unworldly Bellow (Red) C	.15	.30
LEV016 Writhing Beast Hulk (Red) R	.50	.40
LEV017 Hungering Slaughterbeast (Yellow) C	.15	.30
LEV018 Boneyard Marauder (Blue) C	.15	.30
LEV019 Convulsions from the Bellows of Hell (Blue) R	.50	.40
LEV020 Deadwood Rumbler (Blue) C	.15	.30
LEV021 Dread Screamer (Blue) C	.15	.30
LEV022 Unworldly Bellow (Blue) C	.15	.30
LEV023 Consuming Aftermath (Red) R	.50	.40
LEV024 Lunartide Plunderer (Yellow) C	.15	.30
LEV025 Blood Tribute (Blue) C	.15	.30
LEV026 Smash with Big Tree (Red) C	.15	.30
LEV027 Smash with Big Tree (Yellow) C	.15	.30
LEV028 Rally the Rearguard (Red) C	.15	.30
LEV029 Rally the Rearguard (Blue) C	.15	.30

2021 Flesh and Blood Monarch Blitz Deck Prism

PSM001 Prism R	.20	.40
PSM002 The Librarian MR	5.00	10.00
PSM003 Iris of Reality C	.15	.30
PSM004 Halo of Illumination C	.15	.30
PSM005 Heartened Cross Strap C	.15	.30
PSM006 Dream Weavers C	.15	.30
PSM007 Spell Fray Leggings R	.20	.40
PSM008 Herald of Judgment R	.20	.40
PSM009 Herald of Protection (Red) C	.15	.30
PSM010 Herald of Ravages (Red) C	.15	.30
PSM011 Herald of Rebirth (Red) C	.15	.30
PSM012 Herald of Tenacity (Red) C	.15	.30
PSM013 Wartune Herald (Red) C	.15	.30
PSM014 Merciful Retribution R	.20	.40
PSM015 Ode to Wrath R	.20	.40
PSM016 Herald of Protection (Blue) C	.15	.30
PSM017 Herald of Ravages (Blue) C	.15	.30
PSM018 Herald of Rebirth (Blue) C	.15	.30
PSM019 Herald of Tenacity (Blue) C	.15	.30
PSM020 Wartune Herald (Blue) C	.15	.30
PSM021 Illuminate (Red) C	.15	.30
PSM022 Seek Enlightenment (Red) C	.15	.30
PSM023 Rising Solartide (Yellow) C	.15	.30
PSM024 Illuminate (Blue) C	.15	.30
PSM025 Phantasmify (Red) R	.20	.40
PSM026 Prismatic Shield (Red) R	.20	.40
PSM027 Enigma Chimera (Yellow) C	.15	.30
PSM028 Enigma Chimera (Blue) C	.15	.30
PSM029 Spears of Surreality (Blue) C	.15	.30
PSM030 Spectral Shield T	.50	1.00

2021 Flesh and Blood Monarch 1st Edition

MON000 Great Library of Solana F	500.00	1,000.00
MON003 Luminaris M	3.00	6.00
MON004 Herald of Erudition M	3.00	6.00
MON005 Arc Light Sentinel M	.75	1.50
MON006 Genesis M	2.50	5.00
MON007 Herald of Judgment R	.25	.50
MON008 Herald of Triumph (Red) R	.30	.75
MON009 Herald of Triumph (Yellow) R	.75	1.50
MON010 Herald of Triumph (Blue) R	.75	1.50
MON011 Parable of Humility R	.30	.75
MON012 Merciful Retribution R	.30	.75
MON013 Ode to Wrath R	.30	.75
MON014 Herald of Protection (Red) C	.12	.25
MON015 Herald of Protection (Yellow) C	.12	.25
MON016 Herald of Protection (Blue) C	.12	.25
MON017 Herald of Ravages (Red) C	.07	.15
MON018 Herald of Ravages (Yellow) C	.07	.15
MON019 Herald of Ravages (Blue) C	.07	.15
MON020 Herald of Rebirth (Red) C	.07	.15
MON021 Herald of Rebirth (Yellow) C	.07	.15
MON022 Herald of Rebirth (Blue) C	.07	.15
MON023 Herald of Tenacity (Red) C	.07	.15
MON024 Herald of Tenacity (Yellow) C	.07	.15
MON025 Herald of Tenacity (Blue) C	.07	.15
MON026 Wartune Herald (Red) C	.07	.15
MON027 Wartune Herald (Yellow) C	.07	.15
MON028 Wartune Herald (Blue) C	.07	.15

MON031 Raydn, Duskbane M	.75	1.50
MON032 Bolting Blade M	.75	1.50
MON033 Beacon of Victory M	.75	1.50
MON034 Lumina Ascension M	.60	1.25
MON035 V of the Vanguard R	.20	.40
MON036 Battlefield Blitz (Red) R	.25	.50
MON037 Battlefield Blitz (Yellow) R	.15	.30
MON038 Battlefield Blitz (Blue) R	.20	.40
MON039 Valiant Thrust (Red) R	.20	.40
MON040 Valiant Thrust (Yellow) R	.20	.40
MON041 Valiant Thrust (Blue) R	.20	.40
MON042 Bolt of Courage (Red) C	.07	.15
MON043 Bolt of Courage (Yellow) C	.15	.30
MON044 Bolt of Courage (Blue) C	.07	.15
MON045 Cross the Line (Red) C	.07	.15
MON046 Cross the Line (Yellow) C	.07	.15
MON047 Cross the Line (Blue) C	.07	.15
MON048 Engulfing Light (Red) C	.07	.15
MON049 Engulfing Light (Yellow) C	.07	.15
MON050 Engulfing Light (Blue) C	.07	.15
MON051 Express Lightning (Red) C	.07	.15
MON052 Express Lightning (Yellow) C	.07	.15
MON053 Express Lightning (Blue) C	.07	.15
MON054 Take Flight (Red) C	.07	.15
MON055 Take Flight (Yellow) C	.07	.15
MON056 Take Flight (Blue) C	.07	.15
MON057 Courageous Steelhand (Red) C	.07	.15
MON058 Courageous Steelhand (Yellow) C	.07	.15
MON059 Courageous Steelhand (Blue) C	.07	.15
MON060 Vestige of Sol L	100.00	200.00
MON061 Halo of Illumination C	.15	.30
MON062 Celestial Cataclysm M	4.00	8.00
MON063 Soul Shield M	5.00	10.00
MON064 Soul Food M	.30	.75
MON065 Tome of Divinity M	.75	1.50
MON066 Invigorating Light (Red) R	.12	.25
MON067 Invigorating Light (Yellow) R	.12	.25
MON068 Invigorating Light (Blue) R	.07	.15
MON069 Glisten (Red) R	.12	.25
MON070 Glisten (Yellow) R	.20	.40
MON071 Glisten (Blue) R	.10	.20
MON072 Illuminate (Red) C	.07	.15
MON073 Illuminate (Yellow) C	.07	.15
MON074 Illuminate (Blue) C	.07	.15
MON075 Impenetrable Belief (Red) C	.07	.15
MON076 Impenetrable Belief (Yellow) C	.07	.15
MON077 Impenetrable Belief (Blue) C	.07	.15
MON078 Rising Solartide (Red) C	.07	.15
MON079 Rising Solartide (Yellow) C	.07	.15
MON080 Rising Solartide (Blue) C	.07	.15
MON081 Seek Enlightenment (Red) C	.07	.15
MON082 Seek Enlightenment (Yellow) C	.07	.15
MON083 Seek Enlightenment (Blue) C	.07	.15
MON084 Blinding Beam (Red) C	.07	.15
MON085 Blinding Beam (Yellow) C	.07	.15
MON086 Blinding Beam (Blue) C	.07	.15
MON087 Ray of Hope C	.07	.15
MON089 Phantasmal Footsteps L	200.00	400.00
MON090 Dream Weavers C	.07	.15
MON091 Phantasmaclasm M	1.50	3.00
MON092 Prismatic Shield (Red) R	.50	1.00
MON093 Prismatic Shield (Yellow) R	.15	.30
MON094 Prismatic Shield (Blue) R	.15	.30
MON095 Phantasmify (Red) R	.12	.25
MON096 Phantasmify (Yellow) R	.15	.30
MON097 Phantasmify (Blue) R	.20	.40
MON098 Enigma Chimera (Red) C	.07	.15
MON099 Enigma Chimera (Yellow) C	.07	.15
MON100 Enigma Chimera (Blue) C	.07	.15
MON101 Spears of Surreality (Red) C	.12	.25
MON102 Spears of Surreality (Yellow) C	.07	.15
MON103 Spears of Surreality (Blue) C	.07	.15
MON107 Valiant Dynamo L	125.00	250.00
MON108 Gallantry Gold C	.07	.15
MON109 Spill Blood M	1.25	2.50
MON110 Dusk Path Pilgrimage (Red) R	.15	.30
MON111 Dusk Path Pilgrimage (Yellow) R	.12	.25
MON112 Dusk Path Pilgrimage (Blue) R	.10	.20
MON113 Plow Through (Red) R	.30	.75
MON114 Plow Through (Yellow) R	.12	.25
MON115 Plow Through (Blue) R	.12	.25
MON116 Second Swing (Red) C	.07	.15
MON117 Second Swing (Yellow) C	.07	.15
MON118 Second Swing (Blue) C	.07	.15
MON121 Hexagore, the Death Hydra M	.50	1.00
MON122 Hooves of the Shadowbeast C	.07	.15
MON123 Deep Rooted Evil M	.30	.75
MON124 Mark of the Beast M	.60	1.25
MON125 Shadow of Blasmophet M	.30	.75
MON126 Endless Maw (Red) R	.25	.50
MON127 Endless Maw (Yellow) R	.10	.20
MON128 Endless Maw (Blue) R	.07	.15
MON129 Writhing Beast Hulk (Red) R	.20	.40
MON130 Writhing Beast Hulk (Yellow) R	.07	.15
MON131 Writhing Beast Hulk (Blue) R	.07	.15
MON132 Convulsions from the Bellows of Hell (Red) R	.12	.25
MON133 Convulsions from the Bellows of Hell (Yellow) R	.10	.20
MON134 Convulsions from the Bellows of Hell (Blue) R	.20	.40

MON135 Boneyard Marauder (Red) C	.07	.15
MON136 Boneyard Marauder (Yellow) C	.07	.15
MON137 Boneyard Marauder (Blue) C	.07	.15
MON138 Deadwood Rumbler (Red) C	.07	.15
MON139 Deadwood Rumbler (Yellow) C	.07	.15
MON140 Deadwood Rumbler (Blue) C	.07	.15
MON141 Dread Screamer (Red) C	.07	.15
MON142 Dread Screamer (Yellow) C	.07	.15
MON143 Dread Screamer (Blue) C	.07	.15
MON144 Graveling Growl (Red) C	.07	.15
MON145 Graveling Growl (Yellow) C	.07	.15
MON146 Graveling Growl (Blue) C	.07	.15
MON147 Hungering Slaughterbeast (Red) C	.07	.15
MON148 Hungering Slaughterbeast (Yellow) C	.07	.15
MON149 Hungering Slaughterbeast (Blue) C	.07	.15
MON150 Unworldy Bellow (Red) C	.07	.15
MON151 Unworldy Bellow (Yellow) C	.07	.15
MON152 Unworldy Bellow (Blue) C	.07	.15
MON156 Shadow of Ursur M	1.25	2.50
MON157 Dimenxxional Crossroads M	.30	.60
MON158 Invert Existence M	1.00	2.00
MON159 Unhallowed Rites (Red) R	.30	.60
MON160 Unhallowed Rites (Yellow) R	.10	.20
MON161 Unhallowed Rites (Blue) R	.20	.40
MON162 Dimenxxional Gateway (Red) R	.20	.40
MON163 Dimenxxional Gateway (Yellow) R	.20	.40
MON164 Dimenxxional Gateway (Blue) R	.20	.40
MON165 Seeping Shadows (Red) R	.12	.25
MON166 Seeping Shadows (Yellow) R	.15	.30
MON167 Seeping Shadows (Blue) R	.20	.40
MON168 Bounding Demigon (Red) C	.10	.20
MON169 Bounding Demigon (Yellow) C	.07	.15
MON170 Bounding Demigon (Blue) C	.10	.20
MON171 Piercing Shadow Vise (Red) C	.07	.15
MON172 Piercing Shadow Vise (Yellow) C	.07	.15
MON173 Piercing Shadow Vise (Blue) C	.07	.15
MON174 Rift Bind (Red) C	.07	.15
MON175 Rift Bind (Yellow) C	.07	.15
MON176 Rift Bind (Blue) C	.07	.15
MON177 Rifted Torment (Red) C	.07	.15
MON178 Rifted Torment (Yellow) C	.07	.15
MON179 Rifted Torment (Blue) C	.07	.15
MON180 Rip Through Reality (Red) C	.07	.15
MON181 Rip Through Reality (Yellow) C	.07	.15
MON182 Rip Through Reality (Blue) C	.07	.15
MON183 Seeds of Agony (Red) C	.07	.15
MON184 Seeds of Agony (Yellow) C	.07	.15
MON185 Seeds of Agony (Blue) C	.07	.15
MON187 Carrion Husk L	150.00	300.00
MON188 Ebon Fold C	.07	.15
MON189 Doomsday L	50.00	100.00
MON190 Eclipse L	30.00	75.00
MON191 Mutated Mass M	.30	.75
MON192 Guardian of the Shadowrealm M	.60	1.25
MON193 Shadow Puppetry M	3.00	6.00
MON194 Tome of Torment M	.75	1.50
MON195 Consuming Aftermath (Red) R	.07	.15
MON196 Consuming Aftermath (Yellow) R	.07	.15
MON197 Consuming Aftermath (Blue) R	.07	.15
MON198 Soul Harvest R	.07	.15
MON199 Soul Reaping R	.10	.20
MON200 Howl from Beyond (Red) R	.50	1.00
MON201 Howl from Beyond (Yellow) R	.30	.60
MON202 Howl from Beyond (Blue) R	.12	.25
MON203 Ghostly Visit (Red) C	.12	.25
MON204 Ghostly Visit (Yellow) C	.07	.15
MON205 Ghostly Visit (Blue) C	.07	.15
MON206 Lunartide Plunderer (Red) C	.07	.15
MON207 Lunartide Plunderer (Yellow) C	.07	.15
MON208 Lunartide Plunderer (Blue) C	.07	.15
MON209 Void Wraith (Red) C	.07	.15
MON210 Void Wraith (Yellow) C	.07	.15
MON211 Void Wraith (Blue) C	.07	.15
MON212 Spew Shadow (Red) C	.07	.15
MON213 Spew Shadow (Yellow) C	.07	.15
MON214 Spew Shadow (Blue) C	.07	.15
MON215 Blood Tribute (Red) C	.07	.15
MON216 Blood Tribute (Yellow) C	.07	.15
MON217 Blood Tribute (Blue) C	.12	.25
MON218 Eclipse Existence C	.07	.15
MON222 Tear Limb from Limb M	.75	1.50
MON223 Pulping (Red) R	.50	1.00
MON224 Pulping (Yellow) R	.12	.25
MON225 Pulping (Blue) R	.10	.20
MON226 Smash with a Big Tree (Red) C	.07	.15
MON227 Smash with a Big Tree (Yellow) C	.10	.20
MON228 Smash with a Big Tree (Blue) C	.07	.15
MON229 Dread Scythe M	.30	.75
MON230 Aether Ironweave C	.07	.15
MON231 Sonata Arcanix M	4.00	8.00
MON232 Vexing Malice (Red) R	.20	.40
MON233 Vexing Malice (Yellow) R	.20	.40
MON234 Vexing Malice (Blue) R	.75	1.50
MON235 Arcanic Crackle (Red) C	.07	.15
MON236 Arcanic Crackle (Yellow) C	.07	.15
MON237 Arcanic Crackle (Blue) C	.07	.15
MON238 Blood Drop Brocade C	.07	.15
MON239 Stubby Hammerers C	.12	.25

MON240 Time Skippers C	.07	.15
MON241 Ironhide Helm C	.10	.20
MON242 Ironhide Plate C	.07	.15
MON243 Ironhide Gauntlet C	.10	.20
MON244 Ironhide Legs C	.07	.15
MON245 Exude Confidence M	3.00	6.00
MON246 Nourishing Emptiness M	3.00	6.00
MON247 Rouse the Ancients M	3.00	6.00
MON248 Out Muscle (Red) R	.15	.30
MON249 Out Muscle (Yellow) R	.07	.15
MON250 Out Muscle (Blue) R	.10	.20
MON251 Seek Horizon (Red) R	.15	.30
MON252 Seek Horizon (Yellow) R	.12	.25
MON253 Seek Horizon (Blue) R	.10	.20
MON254 Tremor of iArathael (Red) R	.15	.30
MON255 Tremor of iArathael (Yellow) R	.10	.20
MON256 Tremor of iArathael (Blue) R	.20	.40
MON257 Rise Above (Red) R	.15	.30
MON258 Rise Above (Yellow) R	.20	.40
MON259 Rise Above (Blue) R	.10	.20
MON260 Captain's Call (Red) R	.20	.40
MON261 Captain's Call (Yellow) R	.75	1.50
MON262 Captain's Call (Blue) R	.75	1.50
MON263 Adrenaline Rush (Red) C	.07	.15
MON264 Adrenaline Rush (Yellow) C	.07	.15
MON265 Adrenaline Rush (Blue) C	.07	.15
MON266 Belittle (Red) C	.15	.30
MON267 Belittle (Yellow) C	.07	.15
MON268 Belittle (Blue) C	.07	.15
MON269 Brandish (Red) C	.07	.15
MON270 Brandish (Yellow) C	.07	.15
MON271 Brandish (Blue) C	.07	.15
MON272 Frontline Scout (Red) C	.07	.15
MON273 Frontline Scout (Yellow) C	.07	.15
MON274 Frontline Scout (Blue) C	.07	.15
MON275 Overload (Red) C	.07	.15
MON276 Overload (Yellow) C	.07	.15
MON277 Overload (Blue) C	.07	.15
MON278 Pound for Pound (Red) C	.07	.15
MON279 Pound for Pound (Yellow) C	.07	.15
MON280 Pound for Pound (Blue) C	.07	.15
MON281 Rally the Rearguard (Red) C	.07	.15
MON282 Rally the Rearguard (Yellow) C	.07	.15
MON283 Rally the Rearguard (Blue) C	.07	.15
MON284 Stony Wootenhog (Red) C	.07	.15
MON285 Stony Wootenhog (Yellow) C	.07	.15
MON286 Stony Wootenhog (Blue) C	.07	.15
MON287 Surging Militia (Red) C	.07	.15
MON288 Surging Militia (Yellow) C	.07	.15
MON289 Surging Militia (Blue) C	.07	.15
MON290 Yinti Yanti (Red) C	.07	.15
MON291 Yinti Yanti (Yellow) C	.07	.15
MON292 Yinti Yanti (Blue) C	.07	.15
MON293 Zealous Belting (Red) C	.12	.25
MON294 Zealous Belting (Yellow) C	.12	.25
MON295 Zealous Belting (Blue) C	.07	.15
MON296 Minnowism (Red) C	.15	.30
MON297 Minnowism (Yellow) C	.07	.15
MON298 Minnowism (Blue) C	.15	.30
MON299 Warmongers Recital (Red) C	.07	.15
MON300 Warmongers Recital (Yellow) C	.07	.15
MON301 Warmongers Recital (Blue) C	.07	.15
MON302 Talisman of Dousing C	.15	.30
MON303 Memorial Ground (Red) C	.07	.15
MON304 Memorial Ground (Yellow) C	.12	.25
MON305 Memorial Ground (Blue) C	.07	.15
MON306 Cracked Bauble T	.30	.75

2021 Flesh and Blood Tales of Aria 1st Edition

ELE000 Korshem, Crossroad of Elements F	150.00	300.00
ELE003 Winter's Wail M	2.00	4.00
ELE004 Endless Winter M	1.00	2.00
ELE005 Oaken Old M	.60	1.25
ELE006 Awakening M	.50	1.00
ELE007 Biting Gale (Red) R	.10	.20
ELE008 Biting Gale (Yellow) R	.10	.20
ELE009 Biting Gale (Blue) R	.12	.25
ELE010 Turn Timber (Red) R	.10	.20
ELE011 Turn Timber (Yellow) R	.10	.20
ELE012 Turn Timber (Blue) R	.07	.15
ELE013 Entangle (Red) C	.07	.15
ELE014 Entangle (Yellow) C	.07	.15
ELE015 Entangle (Blue) C	.07	.15
ELE016 Glacial Footsteps (Red) C	.07	.15
ELE017 Glacial Footsteps (Yellow) C	.07	.15
ELE018 Glacial Footsteps (Blue) C	.07	.15
ELE019 Mulch (Red) C	.07	.15
ELE020 Mulch (Yellow) C	.07	.15
ELE021 Mulch (Blue) C	.07	.15
ELE022 Snow Under (Red) C	.07	.15
ELE023 Snow Under (Yellow) C	.07	.15
ELE024 Snow Under (Blue) C	.07	.15
ELE025 Emerging Avalanche (Red) C	.07	.15
ELE026 Emerging Avalanche (Yellow) C	.07	.15
ELE027 Emerging Avalanche (Blue) C	.15	.30
ELE028 Strength of Sequoia (Red) C	.07	.15
ELE029 Strength of Sequoia (Yellow) C	.07	.15
ELE030 Strength of Sequoia (Blue) C	.07	.15

ELE034 Voltaire, Strike Twice M	1.50	3.00
ELE035 Frost Lock M	.75	1.50
ELE036 Light it Up M	.60	1.25
ELE037 Ice Storm M	.30	.75
ELE038 Cold Wave (Red) R	.15	.30
ELE039 Cold Wave (Yellow) R	.20	.40
ELE040 Cold Wave (Blue) R	.10	.20
ELE041 Snap Shot (Red) R	.10	.20
ELE042 Snap Shot (Yellow) R	.12	.25
ELE043 Snap Shot (Blue) R	.10	.20
ELE044 Blizzard Bolt (Red) C	.07	.15
ELE045 Blizzard Bolt (Yellow) C	.07	.15
ELE046 Blizzard Bolt (Blue) C	.07	.15
ELE047 Buzz Bolt (Red) C	.07	.30
ELE048 Buzz Bolt (Yellow) C	.07	.15
ELE049 Buzz Bolt (Blue) C	.07	.15
ELE050 Chilling Icevein (Red) C	.07	.15
ELE051 Chilling Icevein (Yellow) C	.07	.15
ELE052 Chilling Icevein (Blue) C	.07	.15
ELE053 Dazzling Crescendo (Red) C	.07	.15
ELE054 Dazzling Crescendo (Yellow) C	.10	.20
ELE055 Dazzling Crescendo (Blue) C	.10	.20
ELE056 Flake Out (Red) C	.07	.15
ELE057 Flake Out (Yellow) C	.07	.15
ELE058 Flake Out (Blue) C	.07	.15
ELE059 Frazzle (Red) C	.07	.15
ELE060 Frazzle (Yellow) C	.07	.15
ELE061 Frazzle (Blue) C	.07	.15
ELE064 Blossoming Spellblade M	.30	.60
ELE065 Flicker Wisp M	.25	.50
ELE066 Force of Nature M	.60	1.25
ELE067 Explosive Growth (Red) R	.10	.20
ELE068 Explosive Growth (Yellow) R	.07	.15
ELE069 Explosive Growth (Blue) R	.20	.40
ELE070 Rites of Lightning (Red) R	.07	.15
ELE071 Rites of Lightning (Yellow) R	.07	.15
ELE072 Rites of Lightning (Blue) R	.07	.15
ELE073 Arcanic Shockwave (Red) C	.07	.15
ELE074 Arcanic Shockwave (Yellow) C	.07	.15
ELE075 Arcanic Shockwave (Blue) C	.07	.15
ELE076 Vela Flash (Red) C	.07	.15
ELE077 Vela Flash (Blue) C	.07	.15
ELE078 Vela Flash (Yellow) C	.07	.15
ELE079 Rites of Replenishment (Red) C	.07	.15
ELE080 Rites of Replenishment (Yellow) C	.07	.15
ELE081 Rites of Replenishment (Blue) C	.07	.15
ELE082 Stir the Wildwood (Red) C	.07	.15
ELE083 Stir the Wildwood (Yellow) C	.07	.15
ELE084 Stir the Wildwood (Blue) C	.07	.15
ELE085 Bramble Spark (Red) C	.07	.15
ELE086 Bramble Spark (Yellow) C	.07	.15
ELE087 Bramble Spark (Blue) C	.07	.15
ELE088 Inspire Lightning (Red) C	.07	.15
ELE089 Inspire Lightning (Yellow) C	.07	.15
ELE090 Inspire Lightning (Blue) C	.07	.15
ELE091 Fulminate M	.30	.60
ELE092 Flashfreeze M	.25	.50
ELE093 Exposed to the Elements M	.50	1.00
ELE094 Entwine Earth (Red) C	.07	.15
ELE095 Entwine Earth (Yellow) C	.07	.15
ELE096 Entwine Earth (Blue) C	.10	.20
ELE097 Entwine Ice (Red) C	.07	.15
ELE098 Entwine Ice (Yellow) C	.07	.15
ELE099 Entwine Ice (Blue) C	.07	.15
ELE100 Entwine Lightning (Red) C	.07	.15
ELE101 Entwine Lightning (Yellow) C	.07	.15
ELE102 Entwine Lightning (Blue) C	.07	.15
ELE103 Invigorate (Red) C	.07	.15
ELE104 Invigorate (Yellow) C	.07	.15
ELE105 Invigorate (Blue) C	.07	.15
ELE106 Rejuvenate (Red) C	.07	.15
ELE107 Rejuvenate (Yellow) C	.07	.15
ELE108 Rejuvenate (Blue) C	.07	.15
ELE112 Pulse of Volthaven M	3.00	6.00
ELE113 Pulse of Candlehold M	2.50	5.00
ELE114 Pulse of Isenloft M	2.00	4.00
ELE115 Crown of Seeds L	100.00	200.00
ELE116 Plume of Evergrowth C	.07	.15
ELE117 Channel Mount Heroic M	1.00	2.00
ELE118 Tome of Harvests M	1.25	2.50
ELE119 Evergreen (Red) R	.10	.20
ELE120 Evergreen (Yellow) R	.10	.20
ELE121 Evergreen (Blue) R	.07	.15
ELE122 Weave Earth (Red) R	.07	.15
ELE123 Weave Earth (Yellow) R	.07	.15
ELE124 Weave Earth (Blue) R	.10	.20
ELE125 Summerwood Shelter (Red) R	.10	.20
ELE126 Summerwood Shelter (Yellow) R	.07	.15
ELE127 Summerwood Shelter (Blue) R	.07	.15
ELE128 Autumn's Touch (Red) C	.07	.15
ELE129 Autumn's Touch (Yellow) C	.07	.15
ELE130 Autumn's Touch (Blue) C	.10	.20
ELE131 Break Ground (Red) C	.07	.15
ELE132 Break Ground (Yellow) C	.07	.15
ELE133 Break Ground (Blue) C	.07	.15
ELE134 Burgeoning (Red) C	.07	.15
ELE135 Burgeoning (Yellow) C	.07	.15
ELE136 Burgeoning (Blue) C	.07	.15

ELE137 Earthlore Surge (Red) C	.07	.15
ELE138 Earthlore Surge (Yellow) C	.07	.15
ELE139 Earthlore Surge (Blue) C	.07	.15
ELE140 Sow Tomorrow (Red) C	.07	.15
ELE141 Sow Tomorrow (Yellow) C	.07	.15
ELE142 Sow Tomorrow (Blue) C	.07	.15
ELE143 Amulet of Earth C	.75	.15
ELE144 Heart of Ice L	125.00	250.00
ELE145 Coat of Frost C	.07	.15
ELE146 Channel Lake Frigid M	12.50	25.00
ELE146 Channel Lake Frigid M ALT ART	100.00	200.00
ELE147 Blizzard M	7.50	15.00
ELE148 Frost Fang (Red) R	.12	.25
ELE149 Frost Fang (Yellow) R	.10	.20
ELE150 Frost Fang (Blue) R	.10	.20
ELE151 Ice Quake (Red) R	.20	.40
ELE152 Ice Quake (Yellow) R	.15	.30
ELE153 Ice Quake (Blue) R	.20	.40
ELE154 Weave Ice (Red) R	.10	.20
ELE155 Weave Ice (Yellow) R	.10	.20
ELE156 Weave Ice (Blue) R	.10	.20
ELE157 Icy Encounter (Red) C	.07	.15
ELE158 Icy Encounter (Yellow) C	.07	.15
ELE160 Winter's Grasp (Red) C	.07	.15
ELE161 Winter's Grasp (Yellow) C	.07	.15
ELE162 Winter's Grasp (Blue) C	.07	.15
ELE163 Chill to the Bone (Red) C	.07	.15
ELE164 Chill to the Bone (Yellow) C	.07	.15
ELE165 Chill to the Bone (Blue) C	.07	.15
ELE166 Polar Blast (Red) C	.07	.15
ELE167 Polar Blast (Yellow) C	.07	.15
ELE168 Polar Blast (Blue) C	.07	.15
ELE169 Winters Bite (Red) C	.07	.15
ELE170 Winters Bite (Yellow) C	.07	.15
ELE171 Winters Bite (Blue) C	.15	.30
ELE172 Amulet of Ice C	.12	.25
ELE173 Shock Charmers L	75.00	150.00
ELE174 Mark of Lightning C	.07	.15
ELE175 Channel Thunder Steppe M	.25	.50
ELE176 Blink M	.75	1.50
ELE177 Flash (Red) R	.10	.20
ELE178 Flash (Yellow) R	.10	.20
ELE179 Flash (Blue) R	.10	.20
ELE180 Weave Lightning (Red) R	.12	.25
ELE181 Weave Lightning (Yellow) R	.12	.25
ELE182 Weave Lightning (Blue) R	.07	.15
ELE183 Lightning Press (Red) R	.60	1.25
ELE184 Lightning Press (Yellow) R	.12	.25
ELE185 Lightning Press (Blue) R	.07	.15
ELE186 Ball Lightning (Red) C	.07	.15
ELE187 Ball Lightning (Yellow) C	.07	.15
ELE188 Ball Lightning (Blue) C	.07	.15
ELE189 Lightning Surge (Red) C	.10	.20
ELE190 Lightning Surge (Yellow) C	.07	.15
ELE191 Lightning Surge (Blue) C	.07	.15
ELE192 Heaven's Claws (Red) C	.07	.15
ELE193 Heaven's Claws (Yellow) C	.07	.15
ELE194 Heaven's Claws (Blue) C	.07	.15
ELE195 Shock Striker (Red) C	.07	.15
ELE196 Shock Striker (Yellow) C	.07	.15
ELE197 Shock Striker (Blue) C	.07	.15
ELE198 Electrify (Red) C	.60	1.25
ELE199 Electrify (Yellow) C	.07	.15
ELE200 Electrify (Blue) C	.07	.15
ELE201 Amulet of Lightning C	.07	.15
ELE203 Rampart of the Ram's Head L	100.00	200.00
ELE204 Rotten Old Buckler C	.07	.15
ELE205 Tear Asunder M	1.25	2.50
ELE206 Embolden (Red) R	.07	.15
ELE207 Embolden (Yellow) R	.10	.20
ELE208 Embolden (Blue) R	.10	.20
ELE209 Thump (Red) C	.07	.15
ELE210 Thump (Yellow) C	.07	.15
ELE211 Thump (Blue) C	.07	.15
ELE213 New Horizon L	125.00	250.00
ELE214 Honing Hood C	.07	.15
ELE215 Seek and Destroy M	.50	1.00
ELE216 Bolt'n Shot (Red) R	.30	.60
ELE217 Bolt'n Shot (Yellow) R	.15	.30
ELE218 Bolt'n Shot (Blue) R	.12	.25
ELE219 Over Flex (Red) C	.07	.15
ELE220 Over Flex (Yellow) C	.07	.15
ELE221 Over Flex (Blue) C	.07	.15
ELE223 Duskblade M	.60	1.25
ELE224 Spellbound Creepers L	100.00	200.00
ELE225 Sutcliffe's Suede Hides C	.10	.20
ELE226 Sting of Sorcery M	.60	1.25
ELE227 Sigil of Suffering (Red) R	.15	.30
ELE228 Sigil of Suffering (Yellow) R	.07	.15
ELE229 Sigil of Suffering (Blue) R	.07	.15
ELE230 Singeing Spellblade (Red) R	.07	.15
ELE231 Singeing Spellblade (Yellow) R	.07	.15
ELE232 Singeing Spellblade (Blue) R	.07	.15
ELE233 Ragamuffin's Hat C	.07	.15
ELE234 Deep Blue C	.07	.15
ELE235 Cracker Jax C	.07	.15
ELE236 Runaways C	.07	.15

2022 Flesh and Blood Dynasty

DYN000 Command and Conquer F	300.00	750.00
DYN001 Emperor, Dracai of Aesir L	30.00	75.00
DYN001 Emperor, Dracai of Aesir MVR	600.00	1,200.00
DYN002 Dust from the Golden Plains M	.30	.60
DYN003 Dust from the Red Desert M	.60	1.25
DYN004 Dust from the Shadow Crypts M	.30	.75
DYN005 Rok M	.50	1.00
DYN005 Rok MVR	40.00	80.00
DYN006 Beaten Trackers R	.15	.30
DYN007 Savage Beatdown M	.75	1.50
DYN008 Skull Crack M	1.50	3.00
DYN009 Berserk M	.75	1.50
DYN010 Reincarnate (Red) R	.10	.20
DYN011 Reincarnate (Yellow) R	.12	.25
DYN012 Reincarnate (Blue) R	.07	.15
DYN013 Blessing of Savagery (Red) R	.07	.15
DYN014 Blessing of Savagery (Yellow) R	.07	.15
DYN015 Blessing of Savagery (Blue) R	.07	.15
DYN016 Madcap Charger (Red) C	.07	.15
DYN017 Madcap Charger (Yellow) C	.07	.15
DYN018 Madcap Charger (Blue) C	.07	.15
DYN019 Madcap Muscle (Red) C	.07	.15
DYN020 Madcap Muscle (Yellow) C	.07	.15
DYN021 Madcap Muscle (Blue) C	.07	.15
DYN022 Rumble Grunting (Red) C	.10	.20
DYN023 Rumble Grunting (Yellow) C	.07	.15
DYN024 Rumble Grunting (Blue) C	.07	.15
DYN025 Yoji, Royal Protector M	.30	.75
DYN026 Seasoned Saviour M	.40	.80
DYN026 Seasoned Saviour MVR	25.00	50.00
DYN027 Steelbraid Buckler R	.12	.25
DYN028 Buckle M	2.50	5.00
DYN029 Never Yield M	.30	.75
DYN030 Shield Bash (Red) R	.07	.15
DYN031 Shield Bash (Yellow) R	.07	.15
DYN032 Shield Bash (Blue) R	.07	.15
DYN033 Blessing of Patience (Red) R	.07	.15
DYN034 Blessing of Patience (Yellow) R	.05	.10
DYN035 Blessing of Patience (Blue) R	.05	.10
DYN036 Shield Wall (Red) C	.07	.15
DYN037 Shield Wall (Yellow) C	.05	.10
DYN038 Shield Wall (Blue) C	.07	.15
DYN039 Reinforce Steel (Red) C	.07	.15
DYN040 Reinforce Steel (Yellow) C	.05	.10
DYN041 Reinforce Steel (Blue) C	.07	.15
DYN042 Withstand (Red) C	.07	.15
DYN043 Withstand (Yellow) C	.07	.15
DYN044 Withstand (Blue) C	.07	.15
DYN045 Blazen Yoroi M	.75	1.50
DYN045 Blazen Yoroi MVR	30.00	60.00
DYN046 Tearing Shuko R	.07	.15
DYN047 Tiger Swipe M	.50	1.00
DYN048 Mindstate of Tiger M	.40	.80
DYN049 Roar of the Tiger M	.60	1.25
DYN050 Flex Claws (Red) R	.07	.15
DYN051 Flex Claws (Yellow) R	.07	.15
DYN052 Flex Claws (Blue) R	.07	.15
DYN053 Blessing of Qi (Red) R	.07	.15
DYN054 Blessing of Qi (Yellow) R	.05	.10
DYN055 Blessing of Qi (Blue) R	.07	.15
DYN056 Pouncing Qi (Red) C	.07	.15
DYN057 Pouncing Qi (Yellow) C	.07	.15
DYN058 Pouncing Qi (Blue) C	.07	.15
DYN059 Qi Unleashed (Red) C	.07	.15
DYN060 Qi Unleashed (Yellow) C	.07	.15
DYN061 Qi Unleashed (Blue) C	.07	.15
DYN062 Predatory Streak (Red) C	.07	.15
DYN063 Predatory Streak (Yellow) C	.07	.15
DYN064 Predatory Streak (Blue) C	.07	.15
DYN065 Crouching Tiger C	.10	.20
DYN065 Crouching Tiger MVR	15.00	30.00
DYN066 Spirit of Eirina L	30.00	75.00
DYN067 Jubeel, Spellbane M	.75	1.50
DYN068 Merciless Battleaxe M	.60	1.25
DYN068 Merciless Battleaxe M	30.00	75.00
DYN069 Quicksilver Dagger (DYN069) R	.10	.20
DYN070 Quicksilver Dagger (DYN070) R	.05	.10
DYN071 Cleave M	.30	.75
DYN072 Ironsong Pride M	1.25	2.50
DYN072 Ironsong Pride (Extended Art) M	30.00	60.00
DYN073 Blessing of Steel (Red) R	.07	.15
DYN074 Blessing of Steel (Yellow) R	.07	.15
DYN075 Blessing of Steel (Blue) R	.07	.15
DYN076 Precision Press (Red) R	.07	.15
DYN077 Precision Press (Yellow) R	.07	.15
DYN078 Precision Press (Blue) R	.15	.30
DYN079 Puncture (Red) R	.10	.20
DYN080 Puncture (Yellow) R	.07	.15
DYN081 Puncture (Blue) R	.07	.15
DYN082 Felling Swing (Red) C	.07	.15
DYN083 Felling Swing (Yellow) C	.07	.15
DYN084 Felling Swing (Blue) C	.07	.15
DYN085 Visit the Imperial Forge (Red) C	.07	.15
DYN086 Visit the Imperial Forge (Yellow) C	.07	.15
DYN087 Visit the Imperial Forge (Blue) C	.07	.15
DYN088 Hanabi Blaster M	1.00	2.00
DYN088 Hanabi Blaster MVR	75.00	150.00

DYN089 Galvanic Bender MVR	.12	.25
DYN090 Pulsewave Harpoon M	2.50	5.00
DYN091 Bios Update M	.75	1.50
DYN092 Construct Nitro Mechanoid // Nitro Mechanoid M	12.50	25.00
DYN092 Construct Nitro Mechanoid // Nitro Mechanoid MVR	75.00	150.00
DYN093 Plasma Mainline M	1.25	2.50
DYN094 Powder Keg M	.60	1.25
DYN095 Scramble Pulse (Red) R	.10	.20
DYN096 Scramble Pulse (Yellow) R	.07	.15
DYN097 Scramble Pulse (Blue) R	.07	.15
DYN098 Blessing of Ingenuity (Red) R	.07	.15
DYN099 Blessing of Ingenuity (Yellow) R	.07	.15
DYN100 Blessing of Ingenuity (Blue) R	.05	.10
DYN101 Crankshaft (Red) C	.07	.15
DYN102 Crankshaft (Yellow) C	.07	.15
DYN103 Crankshaft (Blue) C	.07	.15
DYN104 Jump Start (Red) C	.07	.15
DYN105 Jump Start (Yellow) C	.07	.15
DYN106 Jump Start (Blue) C	.07	.15
DYN107 Urgent Delivery (Red) C	.07	.15
DYN108 Urgent Delivery (Yellow) C	.05	.10
DYN109 Urgent Delivery (Blue) C	.07	.15
DYN110 Hyper Driver (Red) C	.07	.15
DYN111 Hyper Driver (Yellow) C	.07	.15
DYN112 Hyper Driver (Blue) C	.07	.15
DYN113 Arakni, Huntsman M	.20	.40
DYN114 Arakni R	.10	.20
DYN115 Spider's Bite (115) R	.10	.20
DYN116 Spider's Bite (116) R	.40	.80
DYN117 Blacktek Whisperers L	125.00	250.00
DYN118 Mask of Perdition M	3.00	6.00
DYN119 Eradicate M	2.00	4.00
DYN120 Leave No Witnesses M	5.00	10.00
DYN121 Regicide M	.15	.30
DYN121 Regicide M EX ART	7.50	15.00
DYN122 Surgical Extraction M	10.00	20.00
DYN123 Pay Day M	.30	.75
DYN124 Plunder the Poor (Red) R	.15	.30
DYN125 Plunder the Poor (Yellow) R	.07	.15
DYN126 Plunder the Poor (Blue) R	.10	.20
DYN127 Rob the Rich (Red) R	.12	.25
DYN128 Rob the Rich (Yellow) R	.07	.15
DYN129 Rob the Rich (Blue) R	.12	.25
DYN130 Shred (Red) R	.25	.50
DYN131 Shred (Yellow) R	.30	.60
DYN132 Shred (Blue) R	.25	.50
DYN133 Annihilate the Armed (Red) C	.10	.20
DYN134 Annihilate the Armed (Yellow) C	.07	.15
DYN135 Annihilate the Armed (Blue) C	.07	.15
DYN136 Fleece the Frail (Red) C	.07	.15
DYN137 Fleece the Frail (Yellow) C	.05	.10
DYN138 Fleece the Frail (Blue) C	.07	.15
DYN139 Nix the Nimble (Red) C	.07	.15
DYN140 Nix the Nimble (Yellow) C	.05	.10
DYN141 Nix the Nimble (Blue) C	.05	.10
DYN142 Sack the Shifty (Red) C	.07	.15
DYN143 Sack the Shifty (Yellow) C	.07	.15
DYN144 Sack the Shifty (Blue) C	.07	.15
DYN145 Slay the Scholars (Red) C	.07	.15
DYN146 Slay the Scholars (Yellow) C	.05	.10
DYN147 Slay the Scholars (Blue) C	.07	.15
DYN148 Cut to the Chase (Red) C	.07	.15
DYN149 Cut to the Chase (Yellow) C	.07	.15
DYN150 Cut to the Chase (Blue) C	.07	.15
DYN151 Sandscour Greatbow M	.75	1.50
DYN151 Sandscour Greatbow MVR	75.00	150.00
DYN152 Hornet's Sting R	.10	.20
DYN153 Heat Seeker R	1.25	2.50
DYN154 Immobilizing Shot M	1.25	2.50
DYN155 Dead Eye M	1.25	2.50
DYN156 Dead Eye R	.50	1.00
DYN156 Drill Shot (Red) R	.07	.15
DYN157 Drill Shot (Yellow) R	.12	.25
DYN158 Drill Shot (Blue) R	.07	.15
DYN159 Blessing of Focus (Red) R	.07	.15
DYN160 Blessing of Focus (Yellow) R	.12	.25
DYN161 Blessing of Focus (Blue) R	.10	.20
DYN162 Hemorrhage Bore (Red) R	.05	.10
DYN163 Hemorrhage Bore (Yellow) R	.07	.15
DYN164 Hemorrhage Bore (Blue) R	.07	.15
DYN165 Long Shot (Red) C	.07	.15
DYN166 Long Shot (Yellow) C	.07	.15
DYN167 Long Shot (Blue) C	.07	.15
DYN168 Point the Tip (Red) C	.07	.15
DYN169 Point the Tip (Yellow) C	.07	.15
DYN170 Point the Tip (Blue) C	.40	.80
DYN171 Amethyst Tiara M	30.00	75.00
DYN171 Amethyst Tiara MVR	.10	.20
DYN172 Annals of Sutcliffe R	.60	1.25
DYN173 Cryptic Crossing M	.25	.50
DYN174 Diabolic Ultimatum M	.75	1.50
DYN175 Looming Doom M	20.00	40.00
DYN176 Deathly Duet (Red) R	.12	.25
DYN177 Deathly Duet (Yellow) R	.07	.15
DYN178 Deathly Duet (Blue) R	.12	.25
DYN179 Blessing of Occult (Red) R	.07	.15
DYN180 Blessing of Occult (Yellow) R	.07	.15
DYN181 Blessing of Occult (Blue) R	.05	.10

DYN182 Aether Slash (Red) C	.07	.15
DYN183 Aether Slash (Yellow) C	.05	.10
DYN184 Aether Slash (Blue) C	.05	.10
DYN185 Runic Reaping (Red) C	.07	.15
DYN186 Runic Reaping (Yellow) C	.05	.10
DYN187 Runic Reaping (Blue) C	.05	.10
DYN188 Sky Fire Lanterns (Red) C	.07	.15
DYN189 Sky Fire Lanterns (Yellow) C	.05	.10
DYN190 Sky Fire Lanterns (Blue) C	.05	.10
DYN191 Runechant C	.07	.15
DYN192 Surgent Aethertide M	.40	.80
DYN192 Surgent Aethertide MVR	30.00	75.00
DYN193 Seerstone R	.07	.15
DYN194 Mind Warp M	.50	1.00
DYN195 Swell Tidings M	1.00	2.00
DYN196 Brainstorm M	.15	.30
DYN197 Aether Quickening (Red) R	.12	.25
DYN198 Aether Quickening (Yellow) R	.07	.15
DYN199 Aether Quickening (Blue) R	.12	.25
DYN200 Blessing of Aether (Red) R	.07	.15
DYN201 Blessing of Aether (Yellow) R	.05	.10
DYN202 Blessing of Aether (Blue) R	.07	.15
DYN203 Prognosticate (Red) C	.07	.15
DYN204 Prognosticate (Yellow) C	.07	.15
DYN205 Prognosticate (Blue) C	.07	.15
DYN206 Sap (Red) C	.07	.15
DYN207 Sap (Yellow) C	.07	.15
DYN208 Sap (Blue) C	.07	.15
DYN209 Tempest Aurora (Red) C	.07	.15
DYN210 Tempest Aurora (Yellow) C	.07	.15
DYN211 Tempest Aurora (Blue) C	.07	.15
DYN212 Invoke Suraya // Suraya, Archangel of Knowledge L	75.00	150.00
DYN212 Invoke Suraya // Suraya, Archangel of Knowledge MVR	250.00	500.00
DYN213 Celestial Kimono MVR	75.00	150.00
DYN213 Celestial Kimono M	.60	1.25
DYN214 Wave of Reality R	.15	.30
DYN215 Phantasmal Symbiosis M	.75	1.50
DYN216 Spectral Procession M	.20	.40
DYN217 Tome of Aeo M	.30	.60
DYN218 Blessing of Spirits (Red) R	.07	.15
DYN219 Blessing of Spirits (Yellow) R	.07	.15
DYN220 Blessing of Spirits (Blue) R	.07	.15
DYN221 Tranquil Passing (Red) R	.07	.15
DYN222 Tranquil Passing (Yellow) R	.07	.15
DYN223 Tranquil Passing (Blue) R	.07	.15
DYN224 Spectral Prowler (Red) C	.07	.15
DYN225 Spectral Prowler (Yellow) C	.07	.15
DYN226 Spectral Prowler (Blue) C	.07	.15
DYN227 Spectral Rider (Red) C	.07	.15
DYN228 Spectral Rider (Yellow) C	.07	.15
DYN229 Spectral Rider (Blue) C	.07	.15
DYN230 Water Glow Lanterns (Red) C	.07	.15
DYN231 Water Glow Lanterns (Yellow) C	.07	.15
DYN232 Water Glow Lanterns (Blue) C	.05	.10
DYN233 Spectral Shield C	.07	.15
DYN234 Crown of Dominion L	40.00	80.00
DYN234 Crown of Dominion MVR	125.00	250.00
DYN235 Ornate Tessen R	.10	.20
DYN236 Spell Fray Tiara R	.10	.20
DYN237 Spell Fray Cloak R	.10	.20
DYN238 Spell Fray Gloves R	.10	.20
DYN239 Spell Fray Leggings R	.07	.15
DYN240 Imperial Edict M	.75	1.50
DYN241 Imperial Ledger M	.40	.80
DYN242 Imperial Warhorn M	.75	1.50
DYN243 Gold C	.15	.30
DYN244 Ponder C	.07	.15
DYN245 Silver C	.07	.15
DYN246 Spellbane Aegis C	.07	.15

2022 Flesh and Blood Everfest 1st Edition

EVR000 Grandeur of Valahai F	150.00	300.00
EVR001 Skull Crushers M	.50	1.00
EVR002 Swing Big M	5.00	10.00
EVR003 Ready to Roll M	.30	.75
EVR004 Rolling Thunder M	.40	.80
EVR005 High Roller (Red) R	.15	.30
EVR006 High Roller (Yellow) R	.15	.30
EVR007 High Roller (Blue) R	.15	.30
EVR008 Bare Fangs (Red) C	.12	.25
EVR009 Bare Fangs (Yellow) C	.12	.25
EVR010 Bare Fangs (Blue) C	.12	.25
EVR011 Wild Ride (Red) C	.12	.25
EVR012 Wild Ride (Yellow) C	.12	.25
EVR013 Wild Ride (Blue) C	.12	.25
EVR014 Bad Beats (Red) C	.12	.25
EVR015 Bad Beats (Yellow) C	.12	.25
EVR016 Bad Beats (Blue) C	.12	.25
EVR017 Bravo, Star of the Show M	.25	.50
EVR018 Stalagmite, Bastion of Isenloft L	50.00	100.00
EVR019 Valda Brightaxe M	.25	.50
EVR020 Earthlore Bounty M	1.25	2.50
EVR020 Earthlore Bounty EX ART M	25.00	50.00
EVR021 Pulverize M	2.50	5.00
EVR021 Pulverize EX ART M	60.00	125.00
EVR022 Imposing Visage M	.50	1.00
EVR023 Nerves of Steel M	.30	.75
EVR024 Thunder Quake (Red) R	.15	.30

EVR024 Thunder Quake (Red) EX ART R	.15	.30
EVR025 Thunder Quake (Yellow) R	.15	.30
EVR025 Thunder Quake (Yellow) EX ART R	.15	.30
EVR026 Thunder Quake (Blue) R	.15	.30
EVR026 Thunder Quake (Blue) EX ART R	.15	.30
EVR027 Macho Grande (Red) C	.12	.25
EVR028 Macho Grande (Yellow) C	.12	.25
EVR029 Macho Grande (Blue) C	.12	.25
EVR030 Seismic Stir (Red) C	.12	.25
EVR031 Seismic Stir (Yellow) C	.12	.25
EVR032 Seismic Stir (Blue) C	.12	.25
EVR033 Steadfast (Red) C	.12	.25
EVR034 Steadfast (Yellow) C	.12	.25
EVR035 Steadfast (Blue) C	.12	.25
EVR036 Seismic Surge T	.15	.30
EVR037 Mask of the Pouncing Lynx M	3.00	6.00
EVR038 Break Tide M	1.25	2.50
EVR039 Spring Tidings M	.75	1.50
EVR040 Winds of Eternity M	5.00	10.00
EVR040 Winds of Eternity EX ART M	75.00	150.00
EVR041 Hundred Winds (Red) R	.15	.30
EVR041 Hundred Winds (Red) EX ART R	.15	.30
EVR042 Hundred Winds (Yellow) R	.15	.30
EVR042 Hundred Winds (Yellow) EX ART R	.15	.30
EVR043 Hundred Winds (Blue) R	.15	.30
EVR043 Hundred Winds (Blue) EX ART R	.15	.30
EVR044 Ride the Tailwind (Red) C	.12	.25
EVR045 Ride the Tailwind (Yellow) C	.12	.25
EVR046 Ride the Tailwind (Blue) C	.12	.25
EVR047 Twin Twisters (Red) C	.12	.25
EVR048 Twin Twisters (Yellow) C	.12	.25
EVR049 Twin Twisters (Blue) C	.12	.25
EVR050 Wax On (Red) C	.12	.25
EVR051 Wax On (Yellow) C	.12	.25
EVR052 Wax On (Blue) C	.12	.25
EVR053 Helm of Sharp Eye M	1.00	2.00
EVR054 Shatter M	.30	.75
EVR055 Blood on Her Hands M	1.25	2.50
EVR056 Oath of Steel M	.75	1.50
EVR057 Slice and Dice (Red) R	.15	.30
EVR057 Slice and Dice (Red) EX ART R	.15	.30
EVR058 Slice and Dice (Yellow) R	.15	.30
EVR058 Slice and Dice (Yellow) EX ART R	.15	.30
EVR059 Slice and Dice (Blue) R	.15	.30
EVR059 Slice and Dice (Blue) EX ART R	.15	.30
EVR060 Blade Runner (Red) C	.12	.25
EVR061 Blade Runner (Yellow) C	.12	.25
EVR062 Blade Runner (Blue) C	.12	.25
EVR063 In the Swing (Red) C	.12	.25
EVR064 In the Swing (Yellow) C	.12	.25
EVR065 In the Swing (Blue) C	.12	.25
EVR066 Outland Skirmish (Red) C	.12	.25
EVR067 Outland Skirmish (Yellow) C	.12	.25
EVR068 Outland Skirmish (Blue) C	.12	.25
EVR069 Dissolution Sphere M	.50	1.00
EVR070 Micro-processor M	.30	.75
EVR071 Signal Jammer M	.60	1.25
EVR072 Teklo Pounder M	1.00	2.00
EVR073 T-Bone (Red) R	.15	.30
EVR074 T-Bone (Yellow) R	.15	.30
EVR075 T-Bone (Blue) R	.15	.30
EVR076 Payload (Red) C	.12	.25
EVR077 Payload (Yellow) C	.12	.25
EVR078 Payload (Blue) C	.12	.25
EVR079 Zoom In (Red) C	.12	.25
EVR080 Zoom In (Yellow) C	.12	.25
EVR081 Zoom In (Blue) C	.12	.25
EVR082 Rotary Ram (Red) C	.12	.25
EVR083 Rotary Ram (Yellow) C	.12	.25
EVR084 Rotary Ram (Blue) C	.12	.25
EVR085 Genis Wotchuneed M	.25	.50
EVR086 Silver Palms L	25.00	50.00
EVR087 Dreadbore M	.30	.75
EVR088 Battering Bolt M	1.50	3.00
EVR089 Tri-shot M	.75	1.50
EVR090 Rain Razors M	3.00	6.00
EVR091 Release the Tension (Red) R	.15	.30
EVR092 Release the Tension (Yellow) R	.15	.30
EVR093 Release the Tension (Blue) R	.15	.30
EVR094 Fatigue Shot (Red) C	.12	.25
EVR095 Fatigue Shot (Yellow) C	.12	.25
EVR096 Fatigue Shot (Blue) C	.12	.25
EVR097 Timidity Point (Red) C	.12	.25
EVR098 Timidity Point (Yellow) C	.12	.25
EVR099 Timidity Point (Blue) C	.12	.25
EVR100 Read the Glide Path (Red) C	.12	.25
EVR101 Read the Glide Path (Yellow) C	.12	.25
EVR102 Read the Glide Path (Blue) C	.12	.25
EVR103 Vexing Quillhand M	2.00	4.00
EVR104 Runic Reclamation M	2.00	4.00
EVR105 Swarming Gloomveil M	7.50	15.00
EVR106 Revel in Runeblood M	7.50	15.00
EVR107 Runeblood Incantation (Red) R	.15	.30
EVR107 Runeblood Incantation (Red) EX ART R	.15	.30
EVR108 Runeblood Incantation (Yellow) R	.15	.30
EVR108 Runeblood Incantation (Yellow) EX ART R	.15	.30
EVR109 Runeblood Incantation (Blue) R	.15	.30
EVR109 Runeblood Incantation (Blue) EX ART R	.15	.30

EVR110 Drowning Dire (Red) C	.12	.25
EVR111 Drowning Dire (Yellow) C	.12	.25
EVR112 Drowning Dire (Blue) C	.12	.25
EVR113 Reek of Corruption (Red) C	.12	.25
EVR114 Reek of Corruption (Yellow) C	.12	.25
EVR115 Reek of Corruption (Blue) C	.12	.25
EVR116 Shrill of Skullform (Red) C	.12	.25
EVR117 Shrill of Skullform (Yellow) C	.12	.25
EVR118 Shrill of Skullform (Blue) C	.12	.25
EVR119 Runechant T	.15	.30
EVR120 Iyslander M	.30	.75
EVR121 Kraken's Aethervein M	.50	1.00
EVR122 Sigil of Parapets M	.50	1.00
EVR123 Aether Wildfire M	2.50	5.00
EVR123 Aether Wildfire M EXT ART	75.00	150.00
EVR124 Scour M	1.25	2.50
EVR125 Emeritus Scolding (Red) R	.15	.30
EVR126 Emeritus Scolding (Yellow) R	.15	.30
EVR127 Emeritus Scolding (Blue) R	.15	.30
EVR128 Pry (Red) C	.12	.25
EVR129 Pry (Yellow) C	.12	.25
EVR130 Pry (Blue) C	.12	.25
EVR131 Pyroglyphic Protection (Red) C	.12	.25
EVR132 Pyroglyphic Protection (Yellow) C	.12	.25
EVR133 Pyroglyphic Protection (Blue) C	.12	.25
EVR134 Timekeeper's Whim (Red) C	.12	.25
EVR135 Timekeeper's Whim (Yellow) C	.12	.25
EVR136 Timekeeper's Whim (Blue) C	.12	.25
EVR137 Crown of Reflection M	.75	1.50
EVR138 Fractal Replication M	3.00	6.00
EVR139 Miraging Metamorph M	4.00	8.00
EVR140 Shimmers of Silver M	3.00	6.00
EVR141 Haze Bending R	.15	.30
EVR142 Passing Mirage R	.15	.30
EVR143 Pierce Reality R	.15	.30
EVR144 Coalescence Mirage (Red) C	.12	.25
EVR145 Coalescence Mirage (Yellow) C	.12	.25
EVR146 Coalescence Mirage (Blue) C	.12	.25
EVR147 Phantasmal Haze (Red) C	.12	.25
EVR148 Phantasmal Haze (Yellow) C	.12	.25
EVR149 Phantasmal Haze (Blue) C	.12	.25
EVR150 Veiled Intentions (Red) C	.12	.25
EVR151 Veiled Intentions (Yellow) C	.12	.25
EVR152 Veiled Intentions (Blue) C	.12	.25
EVR153 Spectral Shield T	.15	.30
EVR154 Arcanite Skullcap L	50.00	100.00
EVR155 Arcane Lantern R	.15	.30
EVR156 Bingo M	.60	1.25
EVR157 Firebreathing M	1.00	2.00
EVR158 Cash Out M	.30	.75
EVR159 Knick Knack Bric-a-brac M	.30	.75
EVR159 Knick Knack Bric-a-brac EX ART M	30.00	60.00
EVR160 This Round's on Me M	5.00	10.00
EVR161 Life of the Party (Red) R	.15	.30
EVR162 Life of the Party (Yellow) R	.15	.30
EVR163 Life of the Party (Blue) R	.15	.30
EVR164 High Striker (Red) R	.15	.30
EVR164 High Striker (Red) EX ART R	.15	.30
EVR165 High Striker (Yellow) EX ART R	.15	.30
EVR165 High Striker (Yellow) R	.15	.30
EVR166 High Striker (Blue) R	.15	.30
EVR166 High Striker (Blue) EX ART R	.15	.30
EVR167 Pick a Card, Any Card (Red) R	.15	.30
EVR167 Pick a Card, Any Card (Red) EX ART R	.15	.30
EVR168 Pick a Card, Any Card (Yellow) R	.15	.30
EVR168 Pick a Card, Any Card (Yellow) EX ART R	.15	.30
EVR169 Pick a Card, Any Card (Blue) R	.15	.30
EVR169 Pick a Card, Any Card (Blue) EX ART R	.15	.30
EVR170 Smashing Good Time (Red) R	.15	.30
EVR171 Smashing Good Time (Yellow) R	.15	.30
EVR172 Smashing Good Time (Blue) R	.15	.30
EVR173 Even Bigger Than That (Red) R	.15	.30
EVR174 Even Bigger Than That (Yellow) R	.15	.30
EVR175 Even Bigger Than That (Blue) R	.15	.30
EVR176 Amulet of Assertiveness R	.15	.30
EVR177 Amulet of Echoes R	.15	.30
EVR178 Amulet of Havencall R	.15	.30
EVR179 Amulet of Ignition R	.15	.30
EVR180 Amulet of Intervention R	.15	.30
EVR181 Amulet of Oblation R	.15	.30
EVR182 Clarity Potion R	.15	.30
EVR183 Healing Potion R	.15	.30
EVR184 Potion of Seeing R	.15	.30
EVR185 Potion of Deja Vu R	.15	.30
EVR186 Potion of Ironhide R	.15	.30
EVR187 Potion of Luck R	.15	.30
EVR188 Talisman of Balance R	.15	.30
EVR189 Talisman of Cremation R	.15	.30
EVR190 Talisman of Featherfoot R	.15	.30
EVR191 Talisman of Recompense R	.15	.30
EVR192 Talisman of Tithes R	.15	.30
EVR193 Talisman of Warfare R	.15	.30
EVR194 Copper C	.12	.25
EVR195 Silver C	.12	.25
EVR196 Quicken T	.15	.30
EVR197 Frostbite T	.15	.30

2022 Flesh and Blood Everfest 1st Edition Foil

EVR001 Skull Crushers M	7.50	15.00
EVR002 Swing Big M	7.50	15.00
EVR003 Ready to Roll M	.75	1.50
EVR004 Rolling Thunder M	.75	1.50
EVR005 High Roller (Red) R	.15	.30
EVR006 High Roller (Yellow) R	.15	.30
EVR007 High Roller (Blue) R	.15	.30
EVR008 Bare Fangs (Red) C	.12	.25
EVR009 Bare Fangs (Yellow) C	.12	.25
EVR010 Bare Fangs (Blue) C	.12	.25
EVR011 Wild Ride (Red) C	.12	.25
EVR012 Wild Ride (Yellow) C	.12	.25
EVR013 Wild Ride (Blue) C	.12	.25
EVR014 Bad Beats (Red) C	.12	.25
EVR015 Bad Beats (Yellow) C	.12	.25
EVR016 Bad Beats (Blue) C	.12	.25
EVR017 Bravo, Star of the Show M	40.00	80.00
EVR019 Valda Brightaxe M	.75	1.50
EVR020 Earthlore Bounty M	30.00	75.00
EVR021 Pulverize M	4.00	8.00
EVR022 Imposing Visage M	2.50	5.00
EVR023 Nerves of Steel M	2.00	4.00
EVR024 Thunder Quake (Red) R	.15	.30
EVR025 Thunder Quake (Yellow) R	.15	.30
EVR026 Thunder Quake (Blue) R	.15	.30
EVR027 Macho Grande (Red) C	.12	.25
EVR028 Macho Grande (Yellow) C	.12	.25
EVR029 Macho Grande (Blue) C	.12	.25
EVR030 Seismic Stir (Red) C	.12	.25
EVR031 Seismic Stir (Yellow) C	.12	.25
EVR032 Seismic Stir (Blue) C	.12	.25
EVR033 Steadfast (Red) C	.12	.25
EVR034 Steadfast (Yellow) C	.12	.25
EVR035 Steadfast (Blue) C	.12	.25
EVR037 Mask of the Pouncing Lynx M	15.00	30.00
EVR038 Break Tide M	3.00	6.00
EVR039 Spring Tidings M	2.50	5.00
EVR040 Winds of Eternity M	7.50	15.00
EVR041 Hundred Winds (Red) R	.15	.30
EVR042 Hundred Winds (Yellow) R	.15	.30
EVR043 Hundred Winds (Blue) R	.15	.30
EVR044 Ride the Tailwind (Red) C	.12	.25
EVR045 Ride the Tailwind (Yellow) C	.12	.25
EVR046 Ride the Tailwind (Blue) C	.12	.25
EVR047 Twin Twisters (Red) C	.12	.25
EVR048 Twin Twisters (Yellow) C	.12	.25
EVR049 Twin Twisters (Blue) C	.12	.25
EVR050 Wax On (Red) C	.12	.25
EVR051 Wax On (Yellow) C	.12	.25
EVR052 Wax On (Blue) C	.12	.25
EVR053 Helm of Sharp Eye M	10.00	20.00
EVR054 Shatter M	1.00	2.00
EVR055 Blood on Her Hands M	3.00	6.00
EVR056 Oath of Steel M	2.00	4.00
EVR057 Slice and Dice (Red) R	.15	.30
EVR058 Slice and Dice (Yellow) R	.15	.30
EVR059 Slice and Dice (Blue) R	.15	.30
EVR060 Blade Runner (Red) C	.12	.25
EVR061 Blade Runner (Yellow) C	.12	.25
EVR062 Blade Runner (Blue) C	.12	.25
EVR063 In the Swing (Red) C	.12	.25
EVR064 In the Swing (Yellow) C	.12	.25
EVR065 In the Swing (Blue) C	.12	.25
EVR066 Outland Skirmish (Red) C	.12	.25
EVR067 Outland Skirmish (Yellow) C	.12	.25
EVR068 Outland Skirmish (Blue) C	.12	.25
EVR069 Dissolution Sphere M	1.50	3.00
EVR070 Micro-processor M	2.00	4.00
EVR071 Signal Jammer M	1.50	3.00
EVR072 Teklo Pounder M	3.00	6.00
EVR073 T-Bone (Red) R	.15	.30
EVR074 T-Bone (Yellow) R	.15	.30
EVR075 T-Bone (Blue) R	.15	.30
EVR076 Payload (Red) C	.12	.25
EVR077 Payload (Yellow) C	.12	.25
EVR078 Payload (Blue) C	.12	.25
EVR079 Zoom In (Red) C	.12	.25
EVR080 Zoom In (Yellow) C	.12	.25
EVR081 Zoom In (Blue) C	.12	.25
EVR082 Rotary Ram (Red) C	.12	.25
EVR083 Rotary Ram (Yellow) C	.12	.25
EVR084 Rotary Ram (Blue) C	.12	.25
EVR085 Genis Wotchuneed M	1.00	2.00
EVR087 Dreadbore M	10.00	20.00
EVR088 Battering Bolt M	3.00	6.00
EVR089 Tri-shot M	1.50	3.00
EVR090 Rain Razors M	7.50	15.00
EVR091 Release the Tension (Red) R	.15	.30
EVR092 Release the Tension (Yellow) R	.15	.30
EVR093 Release the Tension (Blue) R	.15	.30
EVR094 Fatigue Shot (Red) C	.12	.25
EVR095 Fatigue Shot (Yellow) C	.12	.25
EVR096 Fatigue Shot (Blue) C	.12	.25
EVR097 Timidity Point (Red) C	.12	.25
EVR098 Timidity Point (Yellow) C	.12	.25

EVR099 Timidity Point (Blue) C	.12	.25
EVR100 Read the Glide Path (Red) C	.12	.25
EVR101 Read the Glide Path (Yellow) C	.12	.25
EVR102 Read the Glide Path (Blue) C	.12	.25
EVR103 Vexing Quillhand M	12.50	25.00
EVR104 Runic Reclamation M	4.00	8.00
EVR105 Swarming Gloomveil M	15.00	30.00
EVR106 Revel in Runeblood M	12.50	25.00
EVR107 Runeblood Incantation (Red) R	.15	.30
EVR108 Runeblood Incantation (Yellow) R	.15	.30
EVR109 Runeblood Incantation (Blue) R	.15	.30
EVR110 Drowning Dire (Red) C	.12	.25
EVR111 Drowning Dire (Yellow) C	.12	.25
EVR112 Drowning Dire (Blue) C	.12	.25
EVR113 Reek of Corruption (Red) C	.12	.25
EVR114 Reek of Corruption (Yellow) C	.12	.25
EVR115 Reek of Corruption (Blue) C	.12	.25
EVR116 Shrill of Skullform (Red) C	.12	.25
EVR117 Shrill of Skullform (Yellow) C	.12	.25
EVR118 Shrill of Skullform (Blue) C	.12	.25
EVR120 Iyslander M	2.00	4.00
EVR121 Kraken's Aethervein M	25.00	50.00
EVR122 Sigil of Parapets M	2.50	5.00
EVR123 Aether Wildfire M	7.50	15.00
EVR124 Scour M	3.00	6.00
EVR125 Emeritus Scolding (Red) R	.15	.30
EVR126 Emeritus Scolding (Yellow) R	.15	.30
EVR127 Emeritus Scolding (Blue) R	.15	.30
EVR128 Pry (Red) C	.12	.25
EVR129 Pry (Yellow) C	.12	.25
EVR130 Pry (Blue) C	.12	.25
EVR131 Pyroglyphic Protection (Red) C	.12	.25
EVR132 Pyroglyphic Protection (Yellow) C	.12	.25
EVR133 Pyroglyphic Protection (Blue) C	.12	.25
EVR134 Timekeeper's Whim (Red) C	.12	.25
EVR135 Timekeeper's Whim (Yellow) C	.12	.25
EVR136 Timekeeper's Whim (Blue) C	.12	.25
EVR137 Crown of Reflection M	20.00	40.00
EVR138 Fractal Replication M	12.50	25.00
EVR139 Miraging Metamorph M	10.00	20.00
EVR140 Shimmers of Silver M	10.00	20.00
EVR141 Haze Bending R	.15	.30
EVR142 Passing Mirage R	.15	.30
EVR143 Pierce Reality R	.15	.30
EVR144 Coalescence Mirage (Red) C	.12	.25
EVR145 Coalescence Mirage (Yellow) C	.12	.25
EVR146 Coalescence Mirage (Blue) C	.12	.25
EVR147 Phantasmal Haze (Red) C	.12	.25
EVR148 Phantasmal Haze (Yellow) C	.12	.25
EVR149 Phantasmal Haze (Blue) C	.12	.25
EVR150 Veiled Intentions (Red) C	.12	.25
EVR151 Veiled Intentions (Yellow) C	.12	.25
EVR152 Veiled Intentions (Blue) C	.12	.25
EVR155 Arcane Lantern R	.15	.30
EVR156 Bingo M	2.50	5.00
EVR157 Firebreathing M	4.00	8.00
EVR158 Cash Out M	1.50	3.00
EVR159 Knick Knack Bric-a-brac M	3.00	6.00
EVR160 This Round's on Me M	7.50	15.00
EVR161 Life of the Party (Red) R	.15	.30
EVR162 Life of the Party (Yellow) R	.15	.30
EVR163 Life of the Party (Blue) R	.15	.30
EVR164 High Striker (Red) R	.15	.30
EVR165 High Striker (Yellow) R	.15	.30
EVR166 High Striker (Blue) R	.15	.30
EVR167 Pick a Card, Any Card (Red) R	.15	.30
EVR168 Pick a Card, Any Card (Yellow) R	.15	.30
EVR169 Pick a Card, Any Card (Blue) R	.15	.30
EVR170 Smashing Good Time (Red) R	.15	.30
EVR171 Smashing Good Time (Yellow) R	.15	.30
EVR172 Smashing Good Time (Blue) R	.15	.30
EVR173 Even Bigger Than That (Red) R	.15	.30
EVR174 Even Bigger Than That (Yellow) R	.15	.30
EVR175 Even Bigger Than That (Blue) R	.15	.30
EVR176 Amulet of Assertiveness R	.15	.30
EVR177 Amulet of Echoes R	.15	.30
EVR178 Amulet of Havencall R	.15	.30
EVR179 Amulet of Ignition R	.15	.30
EVR180 Amulet of Intervention R	.15	.30
EVR181 Amulet of Oblation R	.15	.30
EVR182 Clarity Potion R	.15	.30
EVR183 Healing Potion R	.15	.30
EVR184 Potion of Seeing R	.15	.30
EVR185 Potion of Deja Vu R	.15	.30
EVR186 Potion of Ironhide R	.15	.30
EVR187 Potion of Luck R	.15	.30
EVR188 Talisman of Balance R	.15	.30
EVR189 Talisman of Cremation R	.15	.30
EVR190 Talisman of Featherfoot R	.15	.30
EVR191 Talisman of Recompense R	.15	.30
EVR192 Talisman of Tithes R	.15	.30
EVR193 Talisman of Warfare R	.15	.30
EVR194 Copper C	.12	.25
EVR195 Silver C	.12	.25

2022 Flesh and Blood History Pack Vol. 1

1HP001 Rhinar, Reckless Rampage C	.12	.25
1HP002 Rhinar T	.30	.60
1HP003 Kayo, Berserker Runt R	.30	.75
1HP004 Mandible Claw R	.20	.40
1HP005 Mandible Claw R	.50	1.00
1HP006 Romping Club C	.25	.50
1HP007 Scabskin Leathers L	25.00	50.00
1HP008 Barkbone Strapping C	.10	.20
1HP009 Skullhorn M	5.00	10.00
1HP010 Alpha Rampage M	.30	.60
1HP011 Beast Within M	3.00	6.00
1HP012 Massacre M	1.25	2.50
1HP013 Reckless Swing M	.75	1.50
1HP014 Bloodrush Bellow M	1.50	3.00
1HP015 Sand Sketched Plan M	.40	.80
1HP016 Breakneck Battery (Red) R	.10	.20
1HP017 Breakneck Battery (Yellow) R	.10	.20
1HP018 Breakneck Battery (Blue) R	.10	.20
1HP019 Savage Feast (Red) R	.15	.30
1HP020 Savage Feast (Yellow) R	.07	.15
1HP021 Savage Feast (Blue) R	.07	.15
1HP022 Barraging Beatdown (Red) R	.15	.30
1HP023 Barraging Beatdown (Yellow) R	.15	.30
1HP024 Barraging Beatdown (Blue) R	.15	.30
1HP025 Pack Hunt (Red) C	.12	.25
1HP026 Pack Hunt (Yellow) C	.17	.35
1HP027 Pack Hunt (Blue) C	.17	.35
1HP028 Riled Up (Red) C	.12	.25
1HP029 Riled Up (Yellow) C	.12	.25
1HP030 Riled Up (Blue) C	.17	.35
1HP031 Savage Swing (Red) C	.10	.20
1HP032 Savage Swing (Yellow) C	.15	.30
1HP033 Savage Swing (Blue) C	.17	.35
1HP034 Smash Instinct (Red) C	.07	.15
1HP035 Smash Instinct (Yellow) C	.10	.20
1HP036 Smash Instinct (Blue) C	.17	.35
1HP037 Wrecker Romp (Red) C	.07	.15
1HP038 Wrecker Romp (Yellow) C	.07	.15
1HP039 Wrecker Romp (Blue) C	.15	.30
1HP040 Primeval Bellow (Red) C	.07	.15
1HP041 Primeval Bellow (Yellow) C	.40	.80
1HP042 Primeval Bellow (Blue) C	.10	.20
1HP043 Bravo, Showstopper T	.30	.60
1HP044 Bravo T	.30	.60
1HP045 Anothos C	.30	.75
1HP046 Sledge of Anvilheim R	.20	.40
1HP047 Tectonic Plating L	30.00	60.00
1HP048 Helm of Isen's Peak C	.15	.30
1HP049 Crater Fist M	7.50	15.00
1HP050 Crippling Crush M	1.00	2.00
1HP051 Mangle M	.60	1.25
1HP052 Righteous Cleansing M	.60	1.25
1HP053 Spinal Crush M	2.00	4.00
1HP054 Show Time! M	.75	1.50
1HP055 Disable (Red) R	.15	.30
1HP056 Disable (Yellow) R	.25	.50
1HP057 Disable (Blue) R	.20	.40
1HP058 Staunch Response (Red) R	.15	.30
1HP059 Staunch Response (Yellow) R	.15	.30
1HP060 Staunch Response (Blue) R	.25	.50
1HP061 Blessing of Deliverance (Red) R	.20	.40
1HP062 Blessing of Deliverance (Yellow) R	.10	.20
1HP063 Blessing of Deliverance (Blue) R	.15	.30
1HP064 Towering Titan (Red) R	.10	.20
1HP065 Towering Titan (Yellow) R	.07	.15
1HP066 Towering Titan (Blue) R	.25	.50
1HP067 Cartilage Crush (Red) C	.15	.30
1HP068 Cartilage Crush (Yellow) C	.10	.20
1HP069 Cartilage Crush (Blue) C	.10	.20
1HP070 Chokeslam (Red) C	.15	.30
1HP071 Chokeslam (Yellow) C	.15	.30
1HP072 Chokeslam (Blue) C	.15	.30
1HP073 Crush Confidence (Red) C	.20	.40
1HP074 Crush Confidence (Yellow) C	.07	.15
1HP075 Crush Confidence (Blue) C	.20	.40
1HP076 Debilitate (Red) C	.12	.25
1HP077 Debilitate (Yellow) C	.17	.35
1HP078 Debilitate (Blue) C	.15	.30
1HP079 Emerging Dominance (Red) C	.20	.40
1HP080 Emerging Dominance (Yellow) C	.17	.35
1HP081 Emerging Dominance (Blue) C	.20	.40
1HP082 Stonewall Confidence (Red) C	.17	.35
1HP083 Stonewall Confidence (Yellow) C	.17	.35
1HP084 Stonewall Confidence (Blue) C	.07	.15
1HP085 Seismic Surge C	.40	.80
1HP086 Katsu, the Wanderer C	.30	.60
1HP087 Katsu C	.30	.75
1HP088 Benji, the Piercing Wind R	.50	1.00
1HP089 Ira, Crimson Haze C	.30	.60
1HP090 Edge of Autumn R	.12	.25
1HP091 Harmonized Kodachi C	.40	.80
1HP092 Harmonized Kodachi C	.50	1.00
1HP093 Zephyr Needle R	.30	.60
1HP094 Zephyr Needle R	.20	.40
1HP095 Mask of Momentum L	50.00	100.00
1HP096 Breaking Scales C	.12	.25
1HP097 Breeze Rider Boots M	3.00	6.00
1HP098 Find Center M	1.00	2.00
1HP099 Flood of Force M	.50	1.00
1HP100 Heron's Flight M	.25	.50
1HP101 Lord of Wind M	.75	1.50
1HP102 Mugenshi: RELEASE M	.75	1.50
1HP103 Ancestral Empowerment M	3.00	6.00
1HP104 Blackout Kick (Red) R	.15	.30
1HP105 Blackout Kick (Yellow) R	.12	.25
1HP106 Blackout Kick (Blue) R	.15	.30
1HP107 Crane Dance (Red) R	.12	.25
1HP108 Crane Dance (Yellow) R	.12	.25
1HP109 Crane Dance (Blue) R	.17	.35
1HP110 Rushing River (Red) R	.15	.30
1HP111 Rushing River (Yellow) R	.12	.25
1HP112 Rushing River (Blue) R	.15	.30
1HP113 Flic Flak (Red) R	.15	.30
1HP114 Flic Flak (Yellow) R	.15	.30
1HP115 Flic Flak (Blue) R	.12	.25
1HP116 Leg Tap (Red) C	.12	.25
1HP117 Leg Tap (Yellow) C	.07	.15
1HP118 Leg Tap (Blue) C	.10	.20
1HP119 Rising Knee Thrust (Red) C	.07	.15
1HP120 Rising Knee Thrust (Yellow) C	.10	.20
1HP121 Rising Knee Thrust (Blue) C	.07	.15
1HP122 Soulbead Strike (Red) C	.17	.35
1HP123 Soulbead Strike (Yellow) C	.10	.20
1HP124 Soulbead Strike (Blue) C	.20	.40
1HP125 Surging Strike (Red) C	.12	.25
1HP126 Surging Strike (Yellow) C	.10	.20
1HP127 Surging Strike (Blue) C	.07	.15
1HP128 Torrent of Tempo (Red) C	.10	.20
1HP129 Torrent of Tempo (Yellow) C	.10	.20
1HP130 Torrent of Tempo (Blue) C	.07	.15
1HP131 Whelming Gustwave (Red) C	.10	.20
1HP132 Whelming Gustwave (Yellow) C	.10	.20
1HP133 Whelming Gustwave (Blue) C	.12	.25
1HP134 Bittering Thorns C	.10	.20
1HP135 Salt the Wound C	.30	.60
1HP136 Whirling Mist Blossom C	.07	.15
1HP137 Zen State C	.20	.40
1HP138 Dorinthea Ironsong C	.75	1.50
1HP139 Dorinthea C	.50	1.00
1HP140 Kassai, Cintari Sellsword R	.50	1.00
1HP141 Cintari Saber R	.20	.40
1HP142 Cintari Saber R	.50	1.00
1HP143 Dawnblade C	.75	1.50
1HP144 Braveforge Bracers L	30.00	60.00
1HP145 Refraction Bolters C	.12	.25
1HP146 Courage of Bladehold M	15.00	30.00
1HP147 Glint the Quicksilver M	2.50	5.00
1HP148 Rout M	.60	1.25
1HP149 Singing Steelblade M	.75	1.50
1HP150 Twinning Blade M	2.00	4.00
1HP151 Spoils of War M	5.00	10.00
1HP152 Steelblade Supremacy M	1.25	2.50
1HP153 Overpower (Red) R	.17	.35
1HP154 Overpower (Yellow) R	.07	.15
1HP155 Overpower (Blue) R	.15	.30
1HP156 Steelblade Shunt (Red) R	.12	.25
1HP157 Steelblade Shunt (Yellow) R	.15	.30
1HP158 Steelblade Shunt (Blue) R	.12	.25
1HP159 Warrior's Valor (Red) R	.15	.30
1HP160 Warrior's Valor (Yellow) R	.12	.25
1HP161 Warrior's Valor (Blue) R	.20	.40
1HP162 Ironsong Response (Red) C	.07	.15
1HP163 Ironsong Response (Yellow) C	.07	.15
1HP164 Ironsong Response (Blue) C	.07	.15
1HP165 Out for Blood (Red) C	.15	.30
1HP166 Out for Blood (Yellow) C	.07	.15
1HP167 Out for Blood (Blue) C	.10	.20
1HP168 Stroke of Foresight (Red) C	.12	.25
1HP169 Stroke of Foresight (Yellow) C	.07	.15
1HP170 Stroke of Foresight (Blue) C	.07	.15
1HP171 Driving Blade (Red) C	.07	.15
1HP172 Driving Blade (Yellow) C	.07	.15
1HP173 Driving Blade (Blue) C	.10	.20
1HP174 Hit and Run (Red) C	.20	.40
1HP175 Hit and Run (Yellow) C	.15	.30
1HP176 Hit and Run (Blue) C	.20	.40
1HP177 Nature's Path Pilgrimage (Red) C	.07	.15
1HP178 Nature's Path Pilgrimage (Yellow) C	.17	.35
1HP179 Nature's Path Pilgrimage (Blue) C	.17	.35
1HP180 Dash, Inventor Extraordinaire C	.60	1.25
1HP181 Dash C	1.00	2.00
1HP182 Data Doll MKII R	.30	.60
1HP183 Plasma Barrel Shot R	.60	1.25
1HP184 Teklo Plasma Pistol C	.75	1.50
1HP185 Teklo Foundry Heart L	50.00	100.00
1HP186 Achilles Accelerator C	.17	.35
1HP187 Viziertronic Model i M	7.50	15.00
1HP188 High Octane M	3.00	6.00
1HP189 Induction Chamber M	.75	1.50
1HP190 Plasma Purifier M	2.00	4.00
1HP191 Spark of Genius M	2.00	4.00
1HP192 Teklo Core M	4.00	8.00
1HP193 High Speed Impact (Red) R	.30	.75
1HP194 High Speed Impact (Yellow) R	.20	.40
1HP195 High Speed Impact (Blue) R	.50	1.00
1HP196 Pedal to the Metal (Red) R	.15	.30
1HP197 Pedal to the Metal (Yellow) R	.25	.50
1HP198 Pedal to the Metal (Blue) R	.20	.40
1HP199 Aether Sink R	.10	.20
1HP200 Cognition Nodes R	.12	.25
1HP201 Convection Amplifier R	.07	.15
1HP202 Combustible Courier (Red) C	.15	.30
1HP203 Combustible Courier (Yellow) C	.15	.30
1HP204 Combustible Courier (Blue) C	.15	.30
1HP205 Over Loop (Red) C	.07	.15
1HP206 Over Loop (Yellow) C	.07	.15
1HP207 Over Loop (Blue) C	.07	.15
1HP208 Throttle (Red) C	.10	.20
1HP209 Throttle (Yellow) C	.07	.15
1HP210 Throttle (Blue) C	.10	.20
1HP211 Zero to Sixty (Red) C	.10	.20
1HP212 Zero to Sixty (Yellow) C	.10	.20
1HP213 Zero to Sixty (Blue) C	.12	.25
1HP214 Zipper Hit (Red) C	.07	.15
1HP215 Zipper Hit (Yellow) C	.07	.15
1HP216 Zipper Hit (Blue) C	.12	.25
1HP217 Dissipation Shield C	.07	.15
1HP218 Hyper Driver C	.07	.15
1HP219 Optekal Monocle C	.10	.20
1HP220 Kavdaen, Trader of Skins R	.40	.80
1HP221 Azalea, Ace in the Hole C	.30	.60
1HP222 Azalea C	.50	1.00
1HP223 Death Dealer C	.75	1.50
1HP224 Red Liner R	.25	.50
1HP225 Skullbone Crosswrap L	60.00	125.00
1HP226 Bull's Eye Bracers C	.12	.25
1HP227 Perch Grapplers M	7.50	15.00
1HP228 Endless Arrow M	3.00	6.00
1HP229 Red in the Ledger M	4.00	8.00
1HP230 Remorseless M	10.00	20.00
1HP231 Nock the Deathwhistle M	2.50	5.00
1HP232 Three of a Kind M	4.00	8.00
1HP233 Feign Death M	.40	.80
1HP234 Take Cover (Red) R	.30	.60
1HP235 Take Cover (Yellow) R	.15	.30
1HP236 Take Cover (Blue) R	.15	.30
1HP237 Take Aim (Red) R	.20	.40
1HP238 Take Aim (Yellow) R	.12	.25
1HP239 Take Aim (Blue) R	.10	.20
1HP240 Head Shot (Red) C	.07	.15
1HP241 Head Shot (Yellow) C	.07	.15
1HP242 Head Shot (Blue) C	.12	.25
1HP243 Ridge Rider Shot (Red) C	.10	.20
1HP244 Ridge Rider Shot (Yellow) C	.07	.15
1HP245 Ridge Rider Shot (Blue) C	.07	.15
1HP246 Salvage Shot (Red) C	.07	.15
1HP247 Salvage Shot (Yellow) C	.07	.15
1HP248 Salvage Shot (Blue) C	.07	.15
1HP249 Searing Shot (Red) C	.10	.20
1HP250 Searing Shot (Yellow) C	.07	.15
1HP251 Searing Shot (Blue) C	.12	.25
1HP252 Sic 'Em Shot (Red) C	.10	.20
1HP253 Sic 'Em Shot (Yellow) C	.10	.20
1HP254 Sic 'Em Shot (Blue) C	.07	.15
1HP255 Sleep Dart (Red) C	.15	.30
1HP256 Sleep Dart (Yellow) C	.07	.15
1HP257 Sleep Dart (Blue) C	.15	.30
1HP258 Viserai, Rune Blood C	.30	.75
1HP259 Viserai C	.30	.75
1HP260 Nebula Blade C	.50	1.00
1HP261 Reaping Blade R	.20	.40
1HP262 Grasp of the Arknight L	50.00	100.00
1HP263 Crown of Dichotomy C	.12	.25
1HP264 Bloodsheath Skeleta M	.75	1.50
1HP265 Arknight Ascendancy M	.50	1.00
1HP266 Dread Triptych M	.75	1.50
1HP267 Become the Arknight M	.75	1.50
1HP268 Mordred Tide M	2.50	5.00
1HP269 Runeblood Barrier M	.25	.50
1HP270 Spellblade Assault (Red) R	.15	.30
1HP271 Spellblade Assault (Yellow) R	.20	.40
1HP272 Spellblade Assault (Blue) R	.12	.25
1HP273 Reduce to Runechant (Red) R	.25	.50
1HP274 Reduce to Runechant (Yellow) R	.15	.30
1HP275 Reduce to Runechant (Blue) R	.25	.50
1HP276 Mauvrion Skies (Red) R	.25	.50
1HP277 Mauvrion Skies (Yellow) R	.30	.60
1HP278 Mauvrion Skies (Blue) R	.60	1.25
1HP279 Oath of the Arknight (Red) R	.15	.30
1HP280 Oath of the Arknight (Yellow) R	.15	.30
1HP281 Oath of the Arknight (Blue) R	.15	.30
1HP282 Amplify the Arknight (Red) C	.15	.30
1HP283 Amplify the Arknight (Yellow) C	.17	.35
1HP284 Amplify the Arknight (Blue) C	.15	.30
1HP285 Meat and Greet (Red) C	.15	.30
1HP286 Meat and Greet (Yellow) C	.25	.50
1HP287 Meat and Greet (Blue) C	.20	.40
1HP288 Rune Flash (Red) C	.12	.25
1HP289 Rune Flash (Yellow) C	.40	.80
1HP290 Rune Flash (Blue) C	.30	.60
1HP291 Bloodspill Invocation (Red) C	.17	.35
1HP292 Bloodspill Invocation (Yellow) C	.15	.30
1HP293 Bloodspill Invocation (Blue) C	.25	.50
1HP294 Read the Runes (Red) C	.12	.25
1HP295 Read the Runes (Yellow) C	.20	.40
1HP296 Read the Runes (Blue) C	.30	.75
1HP297 Sutcliffe's Research Notes (Red) C	.30	.60
1HP298 Sutcliffe's Research Notes (Yellow) C	.30	.75
1HP299 Sutcliffe's Research Notes (Blue) C	.30	.60
1HP300 Runechant C	.25	.50
1HP301 Kano, Dracai of Aether C	.30	.60
1HP302 Kano C	.50	1.00
1HP303 Crucible of Aetherweave C	.50	1.00
1HP304 Aether Conduit R	.10	.20
1HP305 Storm Striders L	60.00	125.00
1HP306 Robe of Rapture C	.15	.30
1HP307 Metacarpus Node M	4.00	8.00
1HP308 Blazing Aether M	1.25	2.50
1HP309 Chain Lightning M	.40	.80
1HP310 Forked Lightning M	.30	.75
1HP311 Lesson in Lava M	.75	1.50
1HP312 Sonic Boom M	1.25	2.50
1HP313 Tome of Aetherwind M	.75	1.50
1HP314 Aether Spindle (Red) R	.25	.50
1HP315 Aether Spindle (Yellow) R	.07	.15
1HP316 Aether Spindle (Blue) R	.15	.30
1HP317 Cindering Foresight (Red) R	.12	.25
1HP318 Cindering Foresight (Yellow) R	.10	.20
1HP319 Cindering Foresight (Blue) R	.12	.25
1HP320 Stir the Aetherwinds (Red) R	.20	.40
1HP321 Stir the Aetherwinds (Yellow) R	.20	.40
1HP322 Stir the Aetherwinds (Blue) R	.20	.40
1HP323 Aether Flare (Red) C	.12	.25
1HP324 Aether Flare (Yellow) C	.10	.20
1HP325 Aether Flare (Blue) C	.12	.25
1HP326 Reverberate (Red) C	.15	.30
1HP327 Reverberate (Yellow) C	.17	.35
1HP328 Reverberate (Blue) C	.15	.30
1HP329 Scalding Rain (Red) C	.07	.15
1HP330 Scalding Rain (Yellow) C	.17	.35
1HP331 Scalding Rain (Blue) C	.12	.25
1HP332 Snapback (Red) C	.12	.25
1HP333 Snapback (Yellow) C	.12	.25
1HP334 Snapback (Blue) C	.17	.35
1HP335 Voltic Bolt (Red) C	.15	.30
1HP336 Voltic Bolt (Yellow) C	.17	.35
1HP337 Voltic Bolt (Blue) C	.15	.30
1HP338 Zap (Red) C	.15	.30
1HP339 Zap (Yellow) C	.17	.35
1HP340 Zap (Blue) C	.12	.25
1HP341 Fyendal's Spring Tunic L	125.00	250.00
1HP342 Ironrot Helm C	.12	.25
1HP343 Ironrot Plate C	.15	.30
1HP344 Ironrot Gauntlet C	.15	.30
1HP345 Ironrot Legs C	.15	.30
1HP346 Nullrune Hood C	.30	.75
1HP347 Nullrune Robe C	.30	.60
1HP348 Nullrune Gloves C	.50	1.00
1HP349 Nullrune Boots C	.30	.60
1HP350 Hope Merchant's Hood C	.15	.30
1HP351 Heartened Cross Strap C	.15	.30
1HP352 Goliath Gauntlet C	.15	.30
1HP353 Snapdragon Scalers C	.20	.40
1HP354 Talismanic Lens C	.20	.40
1HP355 Bracers of Belief C	.07	.15
1HP356 Vest of the First Fist C	.15	.30
1HP357 Mage Master Boots C	.25	.50
1HP358 Gambler's Gloves M	6.00	12.00
1HP359 Coax a Commotion M	1.00	2.00
1HP360 Command and Conquer M	50.00	100.00
1HP361 Enlightened Strike M	20.00	40.00
1HP362 Last Ditch Effort M	.30	.60
1HP363 Crazy Brew M	.30	.60
1HP364 Gorganian Tome M	3.00	6.00
1HP365 Tome of Fyendal M	3.00	6.00
1HP366 Art of War M	25.00	50.00
1HP367 Talishar, the Lost Prince R	.30	.75
1HP368 Life for a Life (Red) R	.15	.30
1HP369 Life for a Life (Yellow) R	.10	.20
1HP370 Life for a Life (Blue) R	.12	.25
1HP371 Snatch (Red) R	.75	1.50
1HP372 Snatch (Yellow) R	.07	.15
1HP373 Snatch (Blue) R	.20	.40
1HP374 Springboard Somersault R	.20	.40
1HP375 Enchanting Melody (Red) R	.15	.30
1HP376 Enchanting Melody (Yellow) R	.10	.20
1HP377 Enchanting Melody (Blue) R	.12	.25
1HP378 Plunder Run (Red) R	.40	.80
1HP379 Plunder Run (Yellow) R	.25	.50
1HP380 Plunder Run (Blue) R	.15	.30
1HP381 Energy Potion R	1.00	2.00
1HP382 Potion of Strength R	.30	.75
1HP383 Timesnap Potion R	.40	.80
1HP384 Eirina's Prayer (Red) R	.15	.30
1HP385 Eirina's Prayer (Yellow) R	.07	.15
1HP386 Eirina's Prayer (Blue) R	.07	.15
1HP387 Sigil of Solace (Red) R	.75	1.50
1HP388 Sigil of Solace (Yellow) R	.07	.15
1HP389 Sigil of Solace (Blue) R	.07	.15
1HP390 Flock of the Feather Walkers (Red) C	.10	.20

1HP391 Flock of the Feather Walkers (Yellow) C	.07	.15
1HP392 Flock of the Feather Walkers (Blue) C	.12	.25
1HP393 Ravenous Rabble (Red) C	.75	1.50
1HP394 Ravenous Rabble (Yellow) C	.07	.15
1HP395 Ravenous Rabble (Blue) C	.07	.15
1HP396 Scar for a Scar (Red) C	.20	.40
1HP397 Scar for a Scar (Yellow) C	.17	.35
1HP398 Scar for a Scar (Blue) C	.17	.35
1HP399 Pummel (Red) C	.20	.40
1HP400 Pummel (Yellow) C	.12	.25
1HP401 Pummel (Blue) C	.12	.25
1HP402 Razor Reflex (Red) C	.30	.60
1HP403 Razor Reflex (Yellow) C	.10	.20
1HP404 Razor Reflex (Blue) C	.07	.15
1HP405 Fate Foreseen (Red) C	.60	1.25
1HP406 Fate Foreseen (Yellow) C	.12	.25
1HP407 Fate Foreseen (Blue) C	.12	.25
1HP408 Sink Below (Red) C	.75	1.50
1HP409 Sink Below (Yellow) C	.20	.40
1HP410 Sink Below (Blue) C	.15	.30
1HP411 Unmovable (Red) C	.25	.50
1HP412 Unmovable (Yellow) C	.15	.30
1HP413 Unmovable (Blue) C	.15	.30
1HP414 Come to Fight (Red) C	.07	.15
1HP415 Come to Fight (Yellow) C	.10	.20
1HP416 Come to Fight (Blue) C	.10	.20
1HP417 Nimblism (Red) C	.15	.30
1HP418 Nimblism (Yellow) C	.07	.15
1HP419 Nimblism (Blue) C	.07	.15
1HP420 Sloggism (Red) C	.07	.15
1HP421 Sloggism (Yellow) C	.07	.15
1HP422 Sloggism (Blue) C	.07	.15
1HP423 Whisper of the Oracle (Red) C	.15	.30
1HP424 Whisper of the Oracle (Yellow) C	.15	.30
1HP425 Whisper of the Oracle (Blue) C	.15	.30
1HP426 Copper C	.15	.30
1HP427 Quicken C	.10	.20

2022 Flesh and Blood Uprising

UPR000 Blood of the Dracai F	200.00	400.00
UPR001 Dromai, Ash Artist/UPR002 Dromai T	.15	.30
UPR002 Dromai/UPR165 Waning Moon T	.15	.30
UPR004 Silken Form C	.12	.25
UPR005 Burn Them All M	1.25	2.50
UPR006 Invoke Dracona Optimai/Dracona Optimai M	2.50	5.00
UPR006 Invoke Dracona Optimai/Dracona Optimai MVR	75.00	150.00
UPR007 Invoke Tomeltai/Tomeltai M	5.00	10.00
UPR007 Invoke Tomeltai/Tomeltai MVR	100.00	200.00
UPR008 Invoke Dominia/Dominia M	4.00	8.00
UPR008 Invoke Dominia/Dominia MVR	75.00	150.00
UPR009 Invoke Azvolai/Azvolai MVR	20.00	40.00
UPR009 Invoke Azvolai/Azvolai R	.15	.30
UPR010 Invoke Cromai/Cromai MVR	20.00	40.00
UPR010 Invoke Cromai/Cromai R	.15	.30
UPR011 Invoke Kyloria/Kyloria MVR	25.00	50.00
UPR011 Invoke Kyloria/Kyloria R	.15	.30
UPR012 Invoke Miragai/Miragai MVR	20.00	40.00
UPR012 Invoke Miragai/Miragai R	.15	.30
UPR013 Invoke Nekria/Nekria MVR	15.00	30.00
UPR013 Invoke Nekria/Nekria R	.15	.30
UPR014 Invoke Ouvia/Ouvia MVR	20.00	40.00
UPR014 Invoke Ouvia/Ouvia R	.15	.30
UPR015 Invoke Themai/Themai MVR	20.00	40.00
UPR015 Invoke Themai/Themai R	.15	.30
UPR016 Invoke Vynserakai/Vynserakai MVR	15.00	30.00
UPR016 Invoke Vynserakai/Vynserakai R	.15	.30
UPR017 Invoke Yendurai/Yendurai R	.15	.30
UPR017 Invoke Yendurai/Yendurai MVR	20.00	40.00
UPR018 Billowing Mirage (Red) C	.12	.25
UPR019 Billowing Mirage (Yellow) C	.12	.25
UPR020 Billowing Mirage (Blue) C	.12	.25
UPR021 Dunebreaker Cenipai (Red) C	.12	.25
UPR022 Dunebreaker Cenipai (Yellow) C	.12	.25
UPR023 Dunebreaker Cenipai (Blue) C	.12	.25
UPR024 Dustup (Red) C	.12	.25
UPR025 Dustup (Yellow) C	.12	.25
UPR026 Dustup (Blue) C	.12	.25
UPR027 Embermaw Cenipai (Red) C	.12	.25
UPR028 Embermaw Cenipai (Yellow) C	.12	.25
UPR029 Embermaw Cenipai (Blue) C	.12	.25
UPR030 Sweeping Blow (Red) C	.12	.25
UPR031 Sweeping Blow (Yellow) C	.12	.25
UPR032 Sweeping Blow (Blue) C	.12	.25
UPR033 Rake the Embers (Red) C	.12	.25
UPR034 Rake the Embers (Yellow) C	.12	.25
UPR035 Rake the Embers (Blue) C	.12	.25
UPR036 Skittering Sands (Red) C	.12	.25
UPR037 Skittering Sands (Yellow) C	.12	.25
UPR038 Skittering Sands (Blue) C	.12	.25
UPR039 Sand Cover (Red) C	.12	.25
UPR040 Sand Cover (Yellow) C	.12	.25
UPR041 Sand Cover (Blue) C	.12	.25
UPR042 Aether Ashwing C	.12	.25
UPR042 Aether Ashwing/UPR043 Ash T	.15	.30
UPR043 Ash C	.12	.25
UPR043 Ash/Aether Ashwing MVR	75.00	150.00
UPR044 Fai, Rising Rebellion/UPR045 Fai T	.15	.30
UPR045 Fai/UPR003 Storm of Sandikai T	.15	.30
UPR047 Heat Wave C	.12	.25

UPR048 Phoenix Form M	2.50	5.00
UPR048 Phoenix Form M EXT ART	25.00	50.00
UPR049 Spreading Flames M	4.00	8.00
UPR050 Combustion Point M	.50	1.00
UPR051 Engulfing Flamewave (Red) R	.15	.30
UPR052 Engulfing Flamewave (Yellow) R	.15	.30
UPR053 Engulfing Flamewave (Blue) R	.15	.30
UPR054 Mounting Anger (Red) R	.15	.30
UPR055 Mounting Anger (Yellow) R	.15	.30
UPR056 Mounting Anger (Blue) R	.15	.30
UPR057 Rise From the Ashes (Red) R	.15	.30
UPR058 Rise from the Ashes (Yellow) R	.15	.30
UPR059 Rise from the Ashes (Blue) R	.15	.30
UPR060 Brand with Cinderclaw (Red) C	.12	.25
UPR061 Brand with Cinderclaw (Yellow) C	.12	.25
UPR062 Brand with Cinderclaw (Blue) C	.12	.25
UPR063 Cinderskin Devotion (Red) C	.12	.25
UPR064 Cinderskin Devotion (Yellow) C	.12	.25
UPR065 Cinderskin Devotion (Blue) C	.12	.25
UPR066 Dust Runner Outlaw (Red) C	.12	.25
UPR067 Dust Runner Outlaw (Yellow) C	.12	.25
UPR068 Dust Runner Outlaw (Blue) C	.12	.25
UPR069 Lava Vein Loyalty (Red) C	.12	.25
UPR070 Lava Vein Loyalty (Yellow) C	.12	.25
UPR071 Lava Vein Loyalty (Blue) C	.12	.25
UPR072 Rebellious Rush (Red) C	.12	.25
UPR073 Rebellious Rush (Yellow) C	.12	.25
UPR074 Rebellious Rush (Blue) C	.12	.25
UPR075 Rising Resentment (Red) C	.12	.25
UPR076 Rising Resentment (Yellow) C	.12	.25
UPR077 Rising Resentment (Blue) C	.12	.25
UPR078 Ronin Renegade (Red) C	.12	.25
UPR079 Ronin Renegade (Yellow) C	.12	.25
UPR080 Ronin Renegade (Blue) C	.12	.25
UPR081 Soaring Strike (Red) C	.12	.25
UPR082 Soaring Strike (Yellow) C	.12	.25
UPR083 Soaring Strike (Blue) C	.12	.25
UPR084 Flamescale Furnace L	125.00	250.00
UPR085 Sash of Sandikai C	.12	.25
UPR086 Thaw M	3.00	6.00
UPR087 Liquefy M	.50	1.00
UPR088 Uprising M	2.00	4.00
UPR089 Tome of Firebrand M	2.00	4.00
UPR090 Red Hot R	.15	.30
UPR091 Rise Up R	.15	.30
UPR092 Blaze Headlong C	.12	.25
UPR093 Breaking Point C	.12	.25
UPR094 Burn Away C	.12	.25
UPR095 Flameborn Retribution C	.12	.25
UPR096 Flamecall Awakening C	.12	.25
UPR096 Flamecall Awakening C EXT ART	.12	.25
UPR097 Inflame C	.12	.25
UPR097 Inflame C EXT ART	.12	.25
UPR098 Lava Burst C	.12	.25
UPR099 Searing Touch C	.12	.25
UPR100 Stoke the Flames C	.12	.25
UPR100 Stoke the Flames C EXT ART	.12	.25
UPR101 Phoenix Flame MVR	25.00	50.00
UPR101 Phoenix Flame T	.15	.30
UPR102 Iyslander, Stormbind/UPR103 Iyslander T	.15	.30
UPR103 Iyslander MVR	75.00	150.00
UPR103 Iyslander/UPR046 Searing Emberblade T	.15	.30
UPR104 Encase M	.75	1.50
UPR105 Freezing Point M	1.25	2.50
UPR106 Sigil of Permafrost (Red) R	.15	.30
UPR107 Sigil of Permafrost (Yellow) R	.15	.30
UPR108 Sigil of Permafrost (Blue) R	.15	.30
UPR109 Ice Eternal R	.15	.30
UPR110 Succumb to Winter (Red) R	.15	.30
UPR111 Succumb to Winter (Yellow) R	.15	.30
UPR112 Succumb to Winter (Blue) R	.15	.30
UPR113 Aether Icevein (Red) C	.12	.25
UPR114 Aether Icevein (Yellow) C	.12	.25
UPR115 Aether Icevein (Blue) C	.12	.25
UPR116 Brain Freeze (Red) C	.12	.25
UPR117 Brain Freeze (Yellow) C	.12	.25
UPR118 Brain Freeze (Blue) C	.12	.25
UPR119 Icebind (Red) C	.12	.25
UPR120 Icebind (Yellow) C	.12	.25
UPR121 Icebind (Blue) C	.12	.25
UPR122 Polar Cap (Red) C	.12	.25
UPR123 Polar Cap (Yellow) C	.12	.25
UPR124 Polar Cap (Blue) C	.12	.25
UPR125 Conduit of Frostburn C	.12	.25
UPR126 Frost Hex M	2.00	4.00
UPR127 Aether Hail (Red) C	.12	.25
UPR128 Aether Hail (Yellow) C	.12	.25
UPR129 Aether Hail (Blue) C	.12	.25
UPR130 Frosting (Red) C	.12	.25
UPR131 Frosting (Yellow) C	.12	.25
UPR132 Frosting (Blue) C	.12	.25
UPR133 Ice Bolt (Red) C	.12	.25
UPR134 Ice Bolt (Yellow) C	.12	.25
UPR135 Ice Bolt (Blue) C	.12	.25
UPR136 Coronet Peak L	60.00	125.00
UPR137 Glacial Horns C	.12	.25
UPR138 Channel the Bleak Expanse M	1.00	2.00
UPR139 Hypothermia M	2.50	5.00

UPR140 Insidious Chill M	2.50	5.00
UPR141 Isenhowl Weathervane (Red) R	.15	.30
UPR142 Isenhowl Weathervane (Yellow) R	.15	.30
UPR143 Isenhowl Weathervane (Blue) R	.15	.30
UPR144 Arctic Incarceration (Red) C	.12	.25
UPR145 Arctic Incarceration (Yellow) C	.12	.25
UPR146 Arctic Incarceration (Blue) C	.12	.25
UPR147 Cold Snap (Red) C	.12	.25
UPR148 Cold Snap (Yellow) C	.12	.25
UPR149 Cold Snap (Blue) C	.12	.25
UPR150 Frostbite/UPR183 Helio's Mitre T	.15	.30
UPR151 Ghostly Touch L	75.00	150.00
UPR152 Silent Stilettos C	.12	.25
UPR153 Frightmare M	.30	.75
UPR154 Semblance M	.50	1.00
UPR155 Transmogrify (Red) R	.15	.30
UPR156 Transmogrify (Yellow) R	.15	.30
UPR157 Transmogrify (Blue) R	.15	.30
UPR158 Tiger Stripe Shuko L	75.00	150.00
UPR159 Tide Flippers C	.12	.25
UPR160 Double Strike M	2.50	5.00
UPR161 Take the Tempo M	1.25	2.50
UPR162 Rapid Reflex (Red) R	.15	.30
UPR163 Rapid Reflex (Yellow) R	.15	.30
UPR164 Rapid Reflex (Blue) R	.15	.30
UPR166 Alluvion Constellas L	75.00	150.00
UPR167 Spellfire Cloak R	.15	.30
UPR168 Tome of Duplicity M	.50	1.00
UPR169 Rewind M	.60	1.25
UPR169 Rewind M ALT ART	30.00	60.00
UPR170 Dampen (Red) R	.15	.30
UPR171 Dampen (Yellow) R	.15	.30
UPR172 Dampen (Blue) R	.15	.30
UPR173 Aether Dart (Red) C	.12	.25
UPR174 Aether Dart (Yellow) C	.12	.25
UPR175 Aether Dart (Blue) C	.12	.25
UPR176 Read the Ripples (Red) C	.12	.25
UPR177 Read the Ripples (Yellow) C	.12	.25
UPR178 Read the Ripples (Blue) C	.12	.25
UPR179 Singe (Red) C	.12	.25
UPR180 Singe (Yellow) C	.12	.25
UPR181 Singe (Blue) C	.12	.25
UPR182 Crown of Providence L	150.00	300.00
UPR183 Helio's Mitre C	.12	.25
UPR184 Quelling Robe C	.12	.25
UPR185 Quelling Sleeves C	.12	.25
UPR186 Quelling Slippers C	.12	.25
UPR187 Erase Face M	15.00	30.00
UPR188 Vipox M	.75	1.50
UPR189 That All You Got? M	3.00	6.00
UPR190 Fog Down M	.50	1.00
UPR191 Flex (Red) R	.15	.30
UPR192 Flex (Yellow) R	.15	.30
UPR193 Flex (Blue) R	.15	.30
UPR194 Fyendal's Fighting Spirit (Red) R	.15	.30
UPR195 Fyendal's Fighting Spirit (Yellow) R	.15	.30
UPR196 Fyendal's Fighting Spirit (Blue) R	.15	.30
UPR197 Sift (Red) R	.15	.30
UPR198 Sift (Yellow) R	.15	.30
UPR199 Sift (Blue) R	.15	.30
UPR200 Strategic Planning (Red) R	.15	.30
UPR201 Strategic Planning (Yellow) R	.15	.30
UPR202 Strategic Planning (Blue) R	.15	.30
UPR203 Brothers in Arms (Red) C	.12	.25
UPR204 Brothers in Arms (Yellow) C	.12	.25
UPR205 Brothers in Arms (Blue) C	.12	.25
UPR206 Critical Strike (Red) C	.12	.25
UPR207 Critical Strike (Yellow) C	.12	.25
UPR208 Critical Strike (Blue) C	.12	.25
UPR209 Scar for a Scar (Red) C	.12	.25
UPR210 Scar for a Scar (Yellow) C	.12	.25
UPR211 Scar for a Scar (Blue) C	.12	.25
UPR212 Trade In (Red) C	.12	.25
UPR213 Trade In (Yellow) C	.12	.25
UPR214 Trade In (Blue) C	.12	.25
UPR215 Healing Balm (Red) C	.12	.25
UPR216 Healing Balm (Yellow) C	.12	.25
UPR217 Healing Balm (Blue) C	.12	.25
UPR218 Sigil of Protection (Red) C	.12	.25
UPR219 Sigil of Protection (Yellow) C	.12	.25
UPR220 Sigil of Protection (Blue) C	.12	.25
UPR221 Oasis Respite (Red) C	.12	.25
UPR222 Oasis Respite (Yellow) C	.12	.25
UPR223 Oasis Respite (Blue) C	.12	.25
UPR224 Cracked Bauble T	.15	.30
UPR225 Dragons of Legend Invocation Placeholder Card T	.15	.30

2022 Flesh and Blood Uprising Foil

UPR001 Dromai, Ash Artist/UPR002 Dromai T	.15	.30
UPR002 Dromai/UPR165 Waning Moon T	.15	.30
UPR004 Silken Form C	.12	.25
UPR009 Invoke Azvolai/Azvolai R	.15	.30
UPR010 Invoke Cromai/Cromai R	.15	.30
UPR011 Invoke Kyloria/Kyloria R	.15	.30
UPR012 Invoke Miragai/Miragai R	.15	.30
UPR013 Invoke Nekria/Nekria R	.15	.30
UPR014 Invoke Ouvia/Ouvia R	.15	.30
UPR015 Invoke Themai/Themai R	.15	.30
UPR016 Invoke Vynserakai/Vynserakai R	.15	.30
UPR017 Invoke Yendurai/Yendurai MVR	.15	.30
UPR018 Billowing Mirage (Red) C	.12	.25
UPR019 Billowing Mirage (Yellow) C	.12	.25
UPR020 Billowing Mirage (Blue) C	.12	.25
UPR021 Dunebreaker Cenipai (Red) C	.12	.25
UPR022 Dunebreaker Cenipai (Yellow) C	.12	.25
UPR023 Dunebreaker Cenipai (Blue) C	.12	.25
UPR024 Dustup (Red) C	.12	.25
UPR025 Dustup (Yellow) C	.12	.25
UPR026 Dustup (Blue) C	.12	.25
UPR027 Embermaw Cenipai (Red) C	.12	.25
UPR028 Embermaw Cenipai (Yellow) C	.12	.25
UPR029 Embermaw Cenipai (Blue) C	.12	.25
UPR030 Sweeping Blow (Red) C	.12	.25
UPR031 Sweeping Blow (Yellow) C	.12	.25
UPR032 Sweeping Blow (Blue) C	.12	.25
UPR033 Rake the Embers (Red) C	.12	.25
UPR034 Rake the Embers (Yellow) C	.12	.25
UPR035 Rake the Embers (Blue) C	.12	.25
UPR036 Skittering Sands (Red) C	.12	.25
UPR037 Skittering Sands (Yellow) C	.12	.25
UPR038 Skittering Sands (Blue) C	.12	.25
UPR039 Sand Cover (Red) C	.12	.25
UPR040 Sand Cover (Yellow) C	.12	.25
UPR041 Sand Cover (Blue) C	.12	.25
UPR042 Aether Ashwing/UPR043 Ash T	.12	.25
UPR042 Aether Ashwing C	.15	.30
UPR043 Ash/Aether Ashwing MVR	.12	.25
UPR044 Fai, Rising Rebellion/UPR045 Fai T	.15	.30
UPR045 Fai/UPR003 Storm of Sandikai T	.15	.30
UPR047 Heat Wave C	.12	.25
UPR051 Engulfing Flamewave (Red) R	.15	.30
UPR052 Engulfing Flamewave (Yellow) R	.15	.30
UPR053 Engulfing Flamewave (Blue) R	.15	.30
UPR054 Mounting Anger (Red) R	.15	.30
UPR055 Mounting Anger (Yellow) R	.15	.30
UPR056 Mounting Anger (Blue) R	.15	.30
UPR057 Rise From the Ashes (Red) R	.15	.30
UPR058 Rise from the Ashes (Yellow) R	.15	.30
UPR059 Rise from the Ashes (Blue) R	.15	.30
UPR060 Brand with Cinderclaw (Red) C	.12	.25
UPR061 Brand with Cinderclaw (Yellow) C	.12	.25
UPR062 Brand with Cinderclaw (Blue) C	.12	.25
UPR063 Cinderskin Devotion (Red) C	.12	.25
UPR064 Cinderskin Devotion (Yellow) C	.12	.25
UPR065 Cinderskin Devotion (Blue) C	.12	.25
UPR066 Dust Runner Outlaw (Red) C	.12	.25
UPR067 Dust Runner Outlaw (Yellow) C	.12	.25
UPR068 Dust Runner Outlaw (Blue) C	.12	.25
UPR069 Lava Vein Loyalty (Red) C	.12	.25
UPR070 Lava Vein Loyalty (Yellow) C	.12	.25
UPR071 Lava Vein Loyalty (Blue) C	.12	.25
UPR072 Rebellious Rush (Red) C	.12	.25
UPR073 Rebellious Rush (Yellow) C	.12	.25
UPR074 Rebellious Rush (Blue) C	.12	.25
UPR075 Rising Resentment (Red) C	.12	.25
UPR076 Rising Resentment (Yellow) C	.12	.25
UPR077 Rising Resentment (Blue) C	.12	.25
UPR078 Ronin Renegade (Red) C	.12	.25
UPR079 Ronin Renegade (Yellow) C	.12	.25
UPR080 Ronin Renegade (Blue) C	.12	.25
UPR081 Soaring Strike (Red) C	.12	.25
UPR082 Soaring Strike (Yellow) C	.12	.25
UPR083 Soaring Strike (Blue) C	.12	.25
UPR085 Sash of Sandikai C	.12	.25
UPR090 Red Hot R	.15	.30
UPR091 Rise Up R	.15	.30
UPR092 Blaze Headlong C	.12	.25
UPR093 Breaking Point C	.12	.25
UPR094 Burn Away C	.12	.25
UPR095 Flameborn Retribution C	.12	.25
UPR096 Flamecall Awakening C EXT ART	.12	.25
UPR096 Flamecall Awakening C	.12	.25
UPR097 Inflame C EXT ART	.12	.25
UPR097 Inflame C	.12	.25
UPR098 Lava Burst C	.12	.25
UPR099 Searing Touch C	.12	.25
UPR100 Stoke the Flames C EXT ART	.12	.25
UPR100 Stoke the Flames C	.12	.25
UPR101 Phoenix Flame MVR	.15	.30
UPR102 Iyslander, Stormbind/UPR103 Iyslander T	.15	.30
UPR103 Iyslander MVR	.15	.30
UPR106 Sigil of Permafrost (Red) R	.15	.30
UPR107 Sigil of Permafrost (Yellow) R	.15	.30
UPR108 Sigil of Permafrost (Blue) R	.15	.30
UPR109 Ice Eternal R	.15	.30
UPR110 Succumb to Winter (Red) R	.15	.30
UPR111 Succumb to Winter (Yellow) R	.15	.30
UPR112 Succumb to Winter (Blue) R	.15	.30
UPR113 Aether Icevein (Red) C	.12	.25
UPR114 Aether Icevein (Yellow) C	.12	.25
UPR115 Aether Icevein (Blue) C	.12	.25
UPR116 Brain Freeze (Red) C	.12	.25
UPR117 Brain Freeze (Yellow) C	.12	.25
UPR118 Brain Freeze (Blue) C	.12	.25
UPR119 Icebind (Red) C	.12	.25
UPR120 Icebind (Yellow) C	.12	.25
UPR121 Icebind (Blue) C	.12	.25

UPR122 Polar Cap (Red) C	.12	.25
UPR123 Polar Cap (Yellow) C	.12	.25
UPR124 Polar Cap (Blue) C	.12	.25
UPR125 Conduit of Frostburn C	.12	.25
UPR127 Aether Hail (Red) C	.12	.25
UPR128 Aether Hail (Yellow) C	.12	.25
UPR129 Aether Hail (Blue) C	.12	.25
UPR130 Frosting (Red) C	.12	.25
UPR131 Frosting (Yellow) C	.12	.25
UPR132 Frosting (Blue) C	.12	.25
UPR133 Ice Bolt (Red) C	.12	.25
UPR134 Ice Bolt (Yellow) C	.12	.25
UPR135 Ice Bolt (Blue) C	.12	.25
UPR137 Glacial Horns C	.12	.25
UPR141 Isenhowl Weathervane (Red) R	.15	.30
UPR142 Isenhowl Weathervane (Yellow) R	.15	.30
UPR143 Isenhowl Weathervane (Blue) R	.15	.30
UPR144 Arctic Incarceration (Red) C	.12	.25
UPR145 Arctic Incarceration (Yellow) C	.12	.25
UPR146 Arctic Incarceration (Blue) C	.12	.25
UPR147 Cold Snap (Red) C	.12	.25
UPR148 Cold Snap (Yellow) C	.12	.25
UPR149 Cold Snap (Blue) C	.12	.25
UPR150 Frostbite/UPR183 Helio's Mitre T	.15	.30
UPR152 Silent Stilettos C	.12	.25
UPR155 Transmogrify (Red) R	.15	.30
UPR156 Transmogrify (Yellow) R	.15	.30
UPR157 Transmogrify (Blue) R	.15	.30
UPR159 Tide Flippers C	.12	.25
UPR162 Rapid Reflex (Red) R	.15	.30
UPR163 Rapid Reflex (Yellow) R	.15	.30
UPR164 Rapid Reflex (Blue) R	.15	.30
UPR167 Spellfire Cloak R	.15	.30
UPR170 Dampen (Red) R	.15	.30
UPR171 Dampen (Yellow) R	.15	.30
UPR172 Dampen (Blue) R	.15	.30
UPR173 Aether Dart (Red) C	.12	.25
UPR174 Aether Dart (Yellow) C	.12	.25
UPR175 Aether Dart (Blue) C	.12	.25
UPR176 Read the Ripples (Red) C	.12	.25
UPR177 Read the Ripples (Yellow) C	.12	.25
UPR178 Read the Ripples (Blue) C	.12	.25
UPR179 Singe (Red) C	.12	.25
UPR180 Singe (Yellow) C	.12	.25
UPR181 Singe (Blue) C	.12	.25
UPR183 Helio's Mitre C	.12	.25
UPR184 Quelling Robe C	.12	.25
UPR185 Quelling Sleeves C	.12	.25
UPR186 Quelling Slippers C	.12	.25
UPR191 Flex (Red) R	.15	.30
UPR192 Flex (Yellow) R	.15	.30
UPR193 Flex (Blue) R	.15	.30
UPR194 Fyendal's Fighting Spirit (Red) R	.15	.30
UPR195 Fyendal's Fighting Spirit (Yellow) R	.15	.30
UPR196 Fyendal's Fighting Spirit (Blue) R	.15	.30
UPR197 Sift (Red) R	.15	.30
UPR198 Sift (Yellow) R	.15	.30
UPR199 Sift (Blue) R	.15	.30
UPR200 Strategic Planning (Red) R	.15	.30
UPR201 Strategic Planning (Yellow) R	.15	.30
UPR202 Strategic Planning (Blue) R	.15	.30
UPR203 Brothers in Arms (Red) C	.12	.25
UPR204 Brothers in Arms (Yellow) C	.12	.25
UPR205 Brothers in Arms (Blue) C	.12	.25
UPR206 Critical Strike (Red) C	.12	.25
UPR207 Critical Strike (Yellow) C	.12	.25
UPR208 Critical Strike (Blue) C	.12	.25
UPR209 Scar for a Scar (Red) C	.12	.25
UPR210 Scar for a Scar (Yellow) C	.12	.25
UPR211 Scar for a Scar (Blue) C	.12	.25
UPR212 Trade In (Red) C	.12	.25
UPR213 Trade In (Yellow) C	.12	.25
UPR214 Trade In (Blue) C	.12	.25
UPR215 Healing Balm (Red) C	.12	.25
UPR216 Healing Balm (Yellow) C	.12	.25
UPR217 Healing Balm (Blue) C	.12	.25
UPR218 Sigil of Protection (Red) C	.12	.25
UPR219 Sigil of Protection (Yellow) C	.12	.25
UPR220 Sigil of Protection (Blue) C	.12	.25
UPR221 Oasis Respite (Red) C	.12	.25
UPR222 Oasis Respite (Yellow) C	.12	.25
UPR223 Oasis Respite (Blue) C	.12	.25
UPR224 Cracked Bauble T	.15	.30
UPR225 Dragons of Legend Invocation Placeholder Card T	.15	.30

2023 Flesh and Blood Outsiders

OUT000 Plague Hive F	175.00	350.00
OUT001 Uzuri, Switchblade T	.15	.30
OUT002 Uzuri T	.15	.30
OUT003 Arakni, Solitary Confinement T	.15	.30
OUT004 Spider's Bite T	.15	.30
OUT005 Nerve Scalpel M	3.00	6.00
OUT006 Nerve Scalpel M	3.00	6.00
OUT007 Orbitoclast M	2.50	5.00
OUT008 Orbitoclast M	2.50	5.00
OUT009 Scale Peeler M	2.00	4.00
OUT010 Scale Peeler M	2.00	4.00
OUT011 Redback Shroud L	75.00	150.00
OUT011 Redback Shroud L FULL ART	125.00	250.00
OUT012 Infiltrate M	.75	1.50
OUT013 Shake Down M	4.00	8.00
OUT014 Spreading Plague M	.75	1.50
OUT015 Back Stab (Red) R	.15	.30
OUT016 Back Stab (Yellow) R	.15	.30
OUT017 Back Stab (Blue) R	.15	.30
OUT018 Sneak Attack (Red) R	.15	.30
OUT019 Sneak Attack (Yellow) R	.15	.30
OUT020 Sneak Attack (Blue) R	.15	.30
OUT021 Spike with Bloodrot (Red) R	.15	.30
OUT022 Spike with Frailty R	.15	.30
OUT023 Spike with Inertia R	.15	.30
OUT024 Infect (Red) C	.12	.25
OUT025 Infect (Yellow) C	.12	.25
OUT026 Infect (Blue) C	.12	.25
OUT027 Isolate (Red) C	.12	.25
OUT028 Isolate (Yellow) C	.12	.25
OUT029 Isolate (Blue) C	.12	.25
OUT030 Malign (Red) C	.12	.25
OUT031 Malign (Yellow) C	.12	.25
OUT032 Malign (Blue) C	.12	.25
OUT033 Prowl (Red) C	.12	.25
OUT034 Prowl (Yellow) C	.12	.25
OUT035 Prowl (Blue) C	.12	.25
OUT036 Sedate (Red) C	.12	.25
OUT037 Sedate (Yellow) C	.12	.25
OUT038 Sedate (Blue) C	.12	.25
OUT039 Wither (Red) C	.12	.25
OUT040 Wither (Yellow) C	.12	.25
OUT041 Wither (Blue) C	.12	.25
OUT042 Razor's Edge (Red) C	.12	.25
OUT043 Razor's Edge (Yellow) C	.12	.25
OUT044 Razor's Edge (Blue) C	.12	.25
OUT045 Katsu, the Wanderer T	.40	.80
OUT046 Katsu T	.15	.30
OUT047 Benji, the Piercing Wind T	.15	.30
OUT048 Harmonized Kodachi T	.15	.30
OUT049 Mask of Many Faces C	.12	.25
OUT050 Cyclone Roundhouse M	.20	.40
OUT051 Dishonor M	2.50	5.00
OUT052 Head Leads the Tail M	.30	.60
OUT053 Wander With Purpose M	.50	1.00
OUT054 Silverwind Shuriken M	.25	.50
OUT055 Visit the Floating Dojo M	.75	1.50
OUT056 Bonds of Ancestry (Red) R	.15	.30
OUT057 Bonds of Ancestry (Yellow) R	.15	.30
OUT058 Bonds of Ancestry (Blue) R	.15	.30
OUT059 Recoil (Red) R	.15	.30
OUT060 Recoil (Yellow) R	.15	.30
OUT061 Recoil (Blue) R	.15	.30
OUT062 Spinning Wheel Kick (Red) R	.15	.30
OUT063 Spinning Wheel Kick (Yellow) R	.15	.30
OUT064 Spinning Wheel Kick (Blue) R	.15	.30
OUT065 Back Heel Kick (Red) C	.12	.25
OUT066 Back Heel Kick (Yellow) C	.12	.25
OUT067 Back Heel Kick (Blue) C	.12	.25
OUT068 Be Like Water (Red) C	.12	.25
OUT069 Be Like Water (Yellow) C	.12	.25
OUT070 Be Like Water (Blue) C	.12	.25
OUT071 Deadly Duo (Red) C	.12	.25
OUT072 Deadly Duo (Yellow) C	.12	.25
OUT073 Deadly Duo (Blue) C	.12	.25
OUT074 Descendent Gustwave (Red) C	.12	.25
OUT075 Descendent Gustwave (Yellow) C	.12	.25
OUT076 Descendent Gustwave (Blue) C	.12	.25
OUT077 Head Jab (Red) C	.12	.25
OUT078 Head Jab (Yellow) C	.12	.25
OUT079 Head Jab (Blue) C	.12	.25
OUT080 One-Two Punch (Red) C	.12	.25
OUT081 One-Two Punch (Yellow) C	.12	.25
OUT082 One-Two Punch (Blue) C	.12	.25
OUT083 Surging Strike (Red) C	.12	.25
OUT084 Surging Strike (Yellow) C	.12	.25
OUT085 Surging Strike (Blue) C	.12	.25
OUT086 Twin Twisters (Red) C	.12	.25
OUT087 Twin Twisters (Yellow) C	.12	.25
OUT088 Twin Twisters (Blue) C	.12	.25
OUT089 Azalea, Ace in the Hole T	.15	.30
OUT090 Azalea T	.15	.30
OUT091 Riptide, Lurker of the Deep T	.15	.30
OUT092 Riptide T	.15	.30
OUT093 Barbed Castaway T	.15	.30
OUT094 Trench of Sunken Treasure L	40.00	80.00
OUT094 Trench of Sunken Treasure L FULL ART	125.00	250.00
OUT095 Quiver of Abyssal Depths L	30.00	75.00
OUT096 Quiver of Rustling Leaves M	1.00	2.00
OUT097 Crow's Nest T	.15	.30
OUT098 Driftwood Quiver T	.15	.30
OUT099 Wayfinder's Crest C	.12	.25
OUT100 Amplifying Arrow M	.50	1.00
OUT101 Barbed Undertow M	1.25	2.50
OUT102 Buzzsaw Trap M	2.50	5.00
OUT103 Collapsing Trap M	2.50	5.00
OUT104 Spike Pit Trap M	1.50	3.00
OUT105 Melting Point M	1.50	3.00
OUT106 Boulder Trap (Yellow) R	.15	.30
OUT107 Pendulum Trap (Yellow) R	.15	.30
OUT108 Tarpit Trap (Yellow) R	.15	.30
OUT109 Fletch a Red Tail (Red) R	.15	.30
OUT110 Fletch a Yellow Tail (Yellow) R	.15	.30
OUT111 Fletch a Blue Tail (Blue) R	.15	.30
OUT112 Lace with Bloodrot (Red) R	.20	.40
OUT113 Lace with Frailty (Red) R	.15	.30
OUT114 Lace with Inertia (Red) R	.15	.30
OUT115 Falcon Wing (Red) C	.12	.25
OUT116 Falcon Wing (Yellow) C	.12	.25
OUT117 Falcon Wing (Blue) C	.12	.25
OUT118 Infecting Shot (Red) C	.12	.25
OUT119 Infecting Shot (Yellow) C	.12	.25
OUT120 Infecting Shot (Blue) C	.12	.25
OUT121 Murkmire Grapnel (Red) C	.12	.25
OUT122 Murkmire Grapnel (Yellow) C	.12	.25
OUT123 Murkmire Grapnel (Blue) C	.12	.25
OUT124 Sedation Shot (Red) C	.12	.25
OUT125 Sedation Shot (Yellow) C	.12	.25
OUT126 Sedation Shot (Blue) C	.12	.25
OUT127 Skybound Shot (Red) C	.12	.25
OUT128 Skybound Shot (Yellow) C	.12	.25
OUT129 Skybound Shot (Blue) C	.12	.25
OUT130 Spire Sniping (Red) C	.12	.25
OUT131 Spire Sniping (Yellow) C	.12	.25
OUT132 Spire Sniping (Blue) C	.12	.25
OUT133 Widowmaker (Red) C	.12	.25
OUT134 Widowmaker (Yellow) C	.12	.25
OUT135 Widowmaker (Blue) C	.12	.25
OUT136 Withering Shot (Red) C	.12	.25
OUT137 Withering Shot (Yellow) C	.12	.25
OUT138 Withering Shot (Blue) C	.12	.25
OUT139 Flick Knives L	75.00	150.00
OUT140 Mask of Shifting Perspectives C	.12	.25
OUT141 Blade Cuff C	.12	.25
OUT142 Stab Wound M	.75	1.50
OUT143 Concealed Blade M	4.00	8.00
OUT144 Knives Out M	.50	1.00
OUT145 Bleed Out (Red) R	.15	.30
OUT146 Bleed Out (Yellow) R	.15	.30
OUT147 Bleed Out (Blue) R	.15	.30
OUT148 Hurl (Red) R	.15	.30
OUT149 Hurl (Yellow) R	.15	.30
OUT150 Hurl (Blue) R	.15	.30
OUT151 Plunge (Red) C	.12	.25
OUT152 Plunge (Yellow) C	.12	.25
OUT153 Plunge (Blue) C	.12	.25
OUT154 Short and Sharp (Red) C	.12	.25
OUT155 Short and Sharp (Yellow) C	.12	.25
OUT156 Short and Sharp (Blue) C	.12	.25
OUT157 Mask of Malicious Manifestations C	.12	.25
OUT158 Toxic Tips C	.12	.25
OUT159 Codex of Bloodrot M	3.00	6.00
OUT159 Codex of Bloodrot MVR	125.00	250.00
OUT160 Codex of Frailty M	30.00	60.00
OUT160 Codex of Frailty MVR	200.00	400.00
OUT161 Codex of Inertia M	3.00	6.00
OUT161 Codex of Inertia MVR	100.00	200.00
OUT162 Death Touch (Red) R	.25	.50
OUT163 Death Touch (Yellow) R	.15	.30
OUT164 Death Touch (Blue) R	.15	.30
OUT165 Toxicity (Red) R	.15	.30
OUT166 Toxicity (Yellow) R	.15	.30
OUT167 Toxicity (Blue) R	.15	.30
OUT168 Virulent Touch (Red) C	.12	.25
OUT169 Virulent Touch (Yellow) C	.12	.25
OUT170 Virulent Touch (Blue) C	.12	.25
OUT171 Bloodrot Trap (Red) C	.12	.25
OUT172 Frailty Trap (Red) C	.12	.25
OUT173 Inertia Trap (Red) C	.12	.25
OUT174 Vambrace of Determination L	75.00	150.00
OUT175 Seeker's Hood C	.12	.25
OUT176 Seeker's Gilet C	.12	.25
OUT177 Seeker's Mitts C	.12	.25
OUT178 Seeker's Leggings C	.12	.25
OUT179 Silken Gi C	.12	.25
OUT180 Threadbare Tunic C	.12	.25
OUT181 Fisticuffs C	.12	.25
OUT182 Fleet Foot Sandals C	.12	.25
OUT183 Amnesia M	2.00	4.00
OUT184 Down and Dirty M	7.50	15.00
OUT185 Give and Take M	4.00	8.00
OUT186 Gore Belching M	.30	.75
OUT187 Burdens of the Past M	.75	1.50
OUT188 Premeditate M	15.00	30.00
OUT189 Humble (Red) R	.15	.30
OUT190 Humble (Yellow) R	.15	.30
OUT191 Humble (Blue) R	.15	.30
OUT192 Infectious Host (Red) R	.15	.30
OUT193 Infectious Host (Yellow) R	.15	.30
OUT194 Infectious Host (Blue) R	.15	.30
OUT195 Looking for a Scrap (Red) R	.15	.30
OUT196 Looking for a Scrap (Yellow) R	.15	.30
OUT197 Looking for a Scrap (Blue) R	.15	.30
OUT198 Wreck Havoc (Red) R	.15	.30
OUT199 Wreck Havoc (Yellow) R	.15	.30
OUT200 Wreck Havoc (Blue) R	.15	.30
OUT201 Cut Down to Size (Red) C	.12	.25
OUT202 Cut Down to Size (Yellow) C	.12	.25
OUT203 Cut Down to Size (Blue) C	.12	.25
OUT204 Destructive Deliberation (Red) C	.12	.25
OUT205 Destructive Deliberation (Yellow) C	.12	.25
OUT206 Destructive Deliberation (Blue) C	.12	.25
OUT207 Feisty Locals (Red) C	.12	.25
OUT208 Feisty Locals (Yellow) C	.12	.25
OUT209 Feisty Locals (Blue) C	.12	.25
OUT210 Freewheeling Renegades (Red) C	.12	.25
OUT211 Freewheeling Renegades (Yellow) C	.12	.25
OUT212 Freewheeling Renegades (Blue) C	.12	.25
OUT213 Ravenous Rabble (Red) C	.12	.25
OUT214 Ravenous Rabble (Yellow) C	.12	.25
OUT215 Ravenous Rabble (Blue) C	.12	.25
OUT216 Seek Horizon (Red) C	.12	.25
OUT217 Seek Horizon (Yellow) C	.12	.25
OUT218 Seek Horizon (Blue) C	.12	.25
OUT219 Spring Load (Red) C	.12	.25
OUT220 Spring Load (Yellow) C	.12	.25
OUT221 Spring Load (Blue) C	.12	.25
OUT222 Come to Fight (Red) C	.12	.25
OUT223 Come to Fight (Yellow) C	.12	.25
OUT224 Come to Fight (Blue) C	.12	.25
OUT225 Scout the Periphery (Red) C	.12	.25
OUT226 Scout the Periphery (Yellow) C	.12	.25
OUT227 Scout the Periphery (Blue) C	.12	.25
OUT228 Brush Off (Red) C	.12	.25
OUT229 Brush Off (Yellow) C	.12	.25
OUT230 Brush Off (Blue) C	.12	.25
OUT231 Peace of Mind (Red) C	.12	.25
OUT232 Peace of Mind (Yellow) C	.12	.25
OUT233 Peace of Mind (Blue) C	.12	.25
OUT234 Bloodrot Pox T	.15	.30
OUT235 Frailty T	.15	.30
OUT236 Inertia T	.15	.30
OUT237 Ponder T	.15	.30
OUT238 Cracked Bauble T	.15	.30

2023 Flesh and Blood Outsiders Blitz Deck Arakni

ARA001 Arakni, Solitary Confinement C	.12	.25
ARA002 Spider's Bite C	.12	.25
ARA003 Mask of Malicious Manifestations C	.12	.25
ARA004 Blossom of Spring C	.12	.25
ARA005 Toxic Tips C	.12	.25
ARA006 Snapdragon Scalers C	.75	1.50
ARA007 Hurl (Red) R	.75	1.50
ARA008 Infect (Red) C	.30	.75
ARA009 Isolate (Red) C	.12	.25
ARA010 Malign (Red) C	.12	.25
ARA011 Prowl (Red) C	.12	.25
ARA012 Sedate (Red) C	.12	.25
ARA013 Wither (Red) C	.12	.25
ARA014 Virulent Touch (Red) C	.12	.25
ARA015 Spring Load (Red) C	.12	.25
ARA016 Razor's Edge (Red) C	.12	.25
ARA017 Short and Sharp (Red) C	.12	.25
ARA018 Spike with Bloodrot R	.25	.50
ARA019 Bloodrot Trap C	.30	.60
ARA020 Infect (Yellow) C	.12	.25
ARA021 Prowl (Yellow) C	.12	.25
ARA022 Infect (Blue) C	.20	.40
ARA023 Prowl (Blue) C	.12	.25
ARA024 Sedate (Blue) C	.25	.50
ARA025 Wither (Blue) C	.12	.25
ARA026 Razor's Edge (Blue) C	.12	.25
ARA027 Bloodrot Pox T	.15	.30
ARA028 Frailty T	.15	.30
ARA029 Inertia T	.15	.30

2023 Flesh and Blood Outsiders Blitz Deck Azalea

AZL001 Azalea C	.12	.25
AZL002 Barbed Castaway C	.12	.25
AZL003 Crow's Nest C	.12	.25
AZL004 Wayfinder's Crest C	.12	.25
AZL005 Threadbare Tunic C	.12	.25
AZL006 Bracers of Belief C	.12	.25
AZL007 Ironrot Legs C	.12	.25
AZL008 Falcon Wing (Red) C	.12	.25
AZL009 Infecting Shot (Red) C	.12	.25
AZL010 Murkmire Grapnel (Red) C	.12	.25
AZL011 Salvage Shot (Red) C	.12	.25
AZL012 Sedation Shot (Red) C	.12	.25
AZL013 Skybound Shot (Red) C	.12	.25
AZL014 Spire Sniping (Red) C	.12	.25
AZL015 Widowmaker (Red) C	.12	.25
AZL016 Withering Shot (Red) C	.12	.25
AZL017 Ravenous Rabble (Red) C	.12	.25
AZL018 Seek Horizon (Red) C	.12	.25
AZL019 Fletch a Red Tail (Red) R	.15	.30
AZL020 Scout the Periphery (Red) C	.12	.25
AZL021 Sedation Shot (Yellow) C	.12	.25
AZL022 Spire Sniping (Yellow) C	.12	.25
AZL023 Falcon Wing (Blue) C	.12	.25

AZL024 Sedation Shot (Blue) C	.12	.25
AZL025 Spire Sniping (Blue) C	.12	.25
AZL026 Scout the Periphery (Blue) C	.12	.25
AZL027 Toxicity (Blue) R	.30	.60
AZL028 Bloodrot Pox T	.15	.30
AZL029 Frailty T	.15	.30
AZL030 Inertia T	.15	.30

2023 Flesh and Blood Outsiders Blitz Deck Benji

BEN001 Benji, the Piercing Wind C	.12	.25
BEN002 Harmonized Kodachi C	.12	.25
BEN003 Mask of Shifting Perspectives C	.12	.25
BEN004 Silken Gi C	.12	.25
BEN005 Fisticuffs C	.12	.25
BEN006 Fleet Foot Sandals C	.12	.25
BEN007 Bleed Out (Red) R	.15	.30
BEN008 Back Heel Kick (Red) C	.12	.25
BEN009 Twin Twisters (Red) C	.12	.25
BEN010 Head Jab (Red) C	.12	.25
BEN011 Feisty Locals (Red) C	.12	.25
BEN012 Spring Load (Red) C	.12	.25
BEN013 Short and Sharp (Red) C	.12	.25
BEN014 Back Heel Kick (Yellow) C	.12	.25
BEN015 Twin Twisters (Yellow) C	.12	.25
BEN016 One-Two Punch (Yellow) C	.12	.25
BEN017 Head Jab (Yellow) C	.12	.25
BEN018 Be Like Water (Yellow) C	.12	.25
BEN019 Plunge (Yellow) C	.12	.25
BEN020 Salt the Wound (Yellow) C	.30	.60
BEN021 Be Like Water (Blue) C	.12	.25
BEN022 One-Two Punch (Blue) C	.12	.25
BEN023 Recoil (Blue) R	.30	.60
BEN024 Head Jab (Blue) C	.12	.25
BEN025 Soulbead Strike (Blue) C	.12	.25
BEN026 Lunging Press C	.25	.50

2023 Flesh and Blood Outsiders Blitz Deck Katsu

KAT001 Katsu C	.12	.25
KAT002 Harmonized Kodachi C	.75	1.50
KAT003 Mask of Many Faces C	.12	.25
KAT004 Blossom of Spring C	.75	1.50
KAT005 Fisticuffs C	.12	.25
KAT006 Quelling Slippers C	.12	.25
KAT007 Bonds of Ancestry (Red) R	.30	.75
KAT008 Descendent Gustwave (Red) C	.12	.25
KAT009 Whelming Gustwave (Red) C	.12	.25
KAT010 Surging Strike (Red) C	.12	.25
KAT011 Fluster Fist (Red) R	.15	.30
KAT012 Open the Center (Red) C	.12	.25
KAT013 Head Jab (Red) C	.12	.25
KAT014 Be Like Water (Red) C	.30	.75
KAT015 Scar for a Scar (Red) C	.12	.25
KAT016 One-Two Punch (Yellow) C	.12	.25
KAT017 Head Jab (Yellow) C	.12	.25
KAT018 Descendent Gustwave (Yellow) C	.12	.25
KAT019 Surging Strike (Yellow) C	.12	.25
KAT020 Be Like Water (Yellow) C	.12	.25
KAT021 One-Two Punch (Blue) C	.12	.25
KAT022 Head Jab (Blue) C	.12	.25
KAT023 Whelming Gustwave (Blue) C	.12	.25
KAT024 Surging Strike (Blue) C	.12	.25
KAT025 Be Like Water (Blue) C	.12	.25
KAT026 Lunging Press C	.12	.25

2023 Flesh and Blood Outsiders Blitz Deck Riptide

RIP001 Riptide C	.12	.25
RIP002 Barbed Castaway C	.12	.25
RIP003 Driftwood Quiver C	.12	.25
RIP004 Mask of Malicious Manifestations C	.12	.25
RIP005 Threadbare Tunic C	.12	.25
RIP006 Toxic Tips C	.12	.25
RIP007 Ironrot Legs C	.12	.25
RIP008 Bloodrot Trap (Red) C	.12	.25
RIP009 Frailty Trap (Red) C	.30	.75
RIP010 Inertia Trap (Red) C	.12	.25
RIP011 Boulder Trap (Yellow) R	.15	.30
RIP012 Pendulum Trap (Yellow) R	.15	.30
RIP013 Tarpit Trap (Yellow) R	.15	.30
RIP014 Falcon Wing (Red) C	.12	.25
RIP015 Hemorrhage Bore (Red) C	.12	.25
RIP016 Murkmire Grapnel (Red) C	.12	.25
RIP017 Salvage Shot (Red) C	.12	.25
RIP018 Searing Shot (Red) C	.12	.25
RIP019 Sedation Shot (Red) C	.12	.25
RIP020 Withering Shot (Red) C	.12	.25
RIP021 Ravenous Rabble (Red) C	.12	.25
RIP022 Increase the Tension (Red) C	.30	.75
RIP023 Scout the Periphery (Red) C	.12	.25
RIP024 Falcon Wing (Yellow) C	.12	.25
RIP025 Infecting Shot (Yellow) C	.12	.25
RIP026 Murkmire Grapnel (Yellow) C	.12	.25
RIP027 Scout the Periphery (Yellow) C	.12	.25
RIP028 Bloodrot Pox C	.12	.25
RIP029 Frailty T	.15	.30
RIP030 Inertia T	.15	.30

2023 Flesh and Blood Outsiders Blitz Deck Uzuri

UZU001 Uzuri C	.50	1.00
UZU002 Spider's Bite C	.17	.35
UZU003 Mask of Shifting Perspectives C	.12	.25
UZU004 Quelling Robe C	.12	.25
UZU005 Fisticuffs C	.75	1.50
UZU006 Ironhide Legs C	.75	1.50
UZU007 Sneak Attack (Red) R	.15	.30
UZU008 Death Touch (Red) R	.25	.50
UZU009 Cut Down to Size (Red) C	.30	.75
UZU010 Demolition Crew (Red) C	.12	.25
UZU011 Destructive Deliberation (Red) C	.12	.25
UZU012 Humble (Red) R	.15	.30
UZU013 Infect (Red) C	.17	.35
UZU014 Isolate (Red) C	.17	.35
UZU015 Sedate (Red) C	.12	.25
UZU016 Peace of Mind (Red) C	.12	.25
UZU017 Infect (Yellow) C	.12	.25
UZU018 Isolate (Yellow) C	.30	.60
UZU019 Sedate (Yellow) C	.12	.25
UZU020 Wither (Yellow) C	.12	.25
UZU021 Infect (Blue) C	.20	.40
UZU022 Isolate (Blue) C	.20	.40
UZU023 Prowl (Blue) C	.12	.25
UZU024 Sedate (Blue) C	.30	.75
UZU025 Wither (Blue) C	.12	.25
UZU026 Razor's Edge (Blue) C	.12	.25
UZU027 Unmovable (Blue) C	.20	.40
UZU028 Bloodrot Pox T	.15	.30
UZU029 Frailty T	.15	.30
UZU030 Inertia T	.75	1.50
UZU031 Ponder T	.15	.30

2020 Force of Will Alice Origin II

AO2001 Bai Hu, the Sacred Beast N	.12	.25
AO2002 Secret Duel in the Moonlight SR	3.00	6.00
AO2003 Zhu Que, the Sacred Beast N	.12	.25
AO2004 A Present from Machina N	.12	.25
AO2005 All Consuming Suspicion N	.12	.25
AO2006 Buster Rifle R	.20	.40
AO2007 Caller of Gorgons R	.30	.75
AO2008 Euryale, the Dark Eye of Blindness N	.12	.25
AO2009 Foresee N	.12	.25
AO2010 Gear Golem, the Magical Soldier (Stranger) SR	.30	.60
AO2011 Leginus, the City of Science R	.20	.40
AO2012 Linked Battle Robot SR	1.00	2.00
AO2013 Medusa, the Dead Eye of Petrification N	.15	.30
AO2014 Mirage Golem (Stranger) R	.25	.50
AO2015 Shangri-La, the Paradise on the Ocean N	.12	.25
AO2016 Shion, the Sorrowful Songstress SR	.75	1.50
AO2017 Stheno, the Evil Eye of Temptaion N	.12	.25
AO2018 Suppression Order R	.30	.60
AO2019 The Betrayer Returns R	.60	1.25
AO2020 Twin Robots N	.15	.30
AO2021 Ultimate Shield R	.30	.60
AO2022 Underwater Robot N	.12	.25
AO2023 Xuan Wu, the Sacred Beast N	.12	.25
AO2024 Athenia, the Wind Master (Stranger) R	.30	.75
AO2025 Don't Cheat! SR	2.50	5.00
AO2026 Pricia's Call to Action N	.12	.25
AO2027 Qing Long, the Sacred Beast N	.12	.25
AO2028 Ratatoskr, the Spirit Beast of Yggdrasil N	.12	.25
AO2029 Rushing Boar R	4.00	8.00
AO2030 Secret Hot Spring of Sissei SR	12.50	25.00
AO2031 Sissei, the Ancient Forest N	.12	.25
AO2032 Sprout of Treasure Tree (Stranger) SR	.75	1.50
AO2033 World Tree Spider R	.30	.75
AO2034 Brutal Majin R	.25	.50
AO2035 Dance of the Shadows N	.12	.25
AO2036 Laboratory of Forbidden Acts R	.75	1.50
AO2037 Aura of the Sacred Sword SR	1.00	2.00
AO2038 Awakening of Ambition SR	.75	1.50
AO2039 Burning Rush! R	3.00	6.00
AO2040 Chronos, the Master of Labyrinth (Stranger) SR	.50	1.00
AO2041 Communication Robot N	.12	.25
AO2042 Elemental of the Demon Sword R	.30	.60
AO2043 Forbidden Summoning SR	.75	1.50
AO2044 Forest Bear R	.30	.60
AO2045 Huanglong SR	3.00	6.00
AO2046 Mariabella SR	1.50	3.00
AO2047 Mariabella's Recycling Robot SR	.60	1.25
AO2048 Marybell Type Zero SR	4.00	8.00
AO2049 Nameless Knight R	1.50	3.00
AO2050 Royal Palace Guardian Mage, Freya (Stranger) SR	.50	1.00
AO2051 Sniper Robot R	.15	.30
AO2052 Super Beast Burning Rush! SR	2.00	4.00
AO2053 The Determination of the Machine Lord SR	2.50	5.00
AO2054 The Tune-up of Marybell R	.20	.40
AO2055 Wanderer in the Nightmare Land SR	1.50	3.00
AO2056 Clockwork Soldiers N	.12	.25
AO2057 Healing Gimmick (Stranger) R	.25	.50
AO2058 Leginus, the Mechanical City N	.12	.25
AO2059 Machine Lab of Leginus N	.12	.25
AO2060 Mariabella's Work N	.12	.25
AO2061 Remote Control Beast N	.12	.25
AO2062 Remote Control Golem N	.12	.25
AO2063 Attoractia's Memoria N	.50	1.00
AO2064 Magic Stone of Deep Wood N	.30	.60

2020 Force of Will Alice Origin II Life Points

Life010 Machina	.15	.30
Life011 Machina	.15	.30
Life012 Machina	.15	.30
Life013 Pricia	.15	.30
Life014 Pricia	.15	.30
Life015 Pricia	.15	.30
Life016 Valentina	.15	.30
Life017 Valentina	.15	.30
Life018 Valentina	.15	.30

2020 Force of Will Alice Origin II Magic Stones

A02MS001 Darkness Magic Stone	.15	.30
A02MS002 Darkness Magic Stone	.15	.30
A02MS003 Fire Magic Stone	.15	.30
A02MS004 Fire Magic Stone	.15	.30
A02MS005 Light Magic Stone	.15	.30
A02MS006 Light Magic Stone	.15	.30
A02MS007 Water Magic Stone	.15	.30
A02MS008 Water Magic Stone	.15	.30
A02MS009 Wind Magic Stone	.15	.30
A02MS010 Wind Magic Stone	.15	.30

2020 Force of Will Alice Origin II Will Coins

Coin014 Taegrus Pearlshine	.15	.30
Coin015 Kirik Rerik	.20	.40
Coin016 Shaela	.15	.30
Coin017 Gill	.15	.30
Coin018 Reiya	.15	.30
Coin019 Pandora	.15	.30
Coin020 Faerur Letoliel	.15	.30
Coin021 Frayla	.15	.30
Coin022 Welser	.15	.30
Coin023 Ayu	.15	.30
Coin024 Almul	.15	.30
Coin025 Scheherazade	.15	.30
Coin026 Nyarlathotep	.15	.30
Coin027 The Time Spinning Witch	.15	.30
Coin028 Fiethsing	.15	.30
Coin029 Valentina	.15	.30
Coin030 Pricia	.15	.30
Coin031 Machina	.20	.40

2020 Force of Will Alice Origin III

AO3001 Accel, the White Gale Eagle R	.30	.60
AO3002 Accel's Reconnaissance N	.20	.40
AO3003 Apollon, the God of Light (Stranger) R	.15	.30
AO3004 Ares, the Knight God Emperor (Stranger) R	.20	.40
AO3005 Celestial Wing Seraph N	.15	.30
AO3006 Crystallization N	.15	.30
AO3007 Dignified Seraph N	.15	.30
AO3008 Give Wings N	.12	.25
AO3009 Heavenly Garden of Armalla N	.12	.25
AO3010 Herald of the Winged Lord N	.12	.25
AO3011 Knight of the White Hill N	.12	.25
AO3012 Michael, the Archangel (Stranger) R	.25	.50
AO3013 Mourning Angel N	.20	.40
AO3014 Pier, the Godspeed Archer SR	1.50	3.00
AO3015 Rabbit of Moonlit Nights N	.12	.25
AO3016 Release N	.12	.25
AO3017 Wingman of Armalla N	.12	.25
AO3018 Crime and Punishment N	.12	.25
AO3019 Gatekeeeper of Vell-Savaria N	.15	.30
AO3020 Red Illusionary Dragon of Passion SR	.30	.75
AO3021 Red Illusionary Hero N	.12	.25
AO3022 Reflect's Summoning N	.12	.25
AO3023 Shuren, the King of Supremacy (Stranger) N	.20	.40
AO3024 Snow White, the Valkyrie of Passion N	.12	.25
AO3025 Spirit of Passion N	.12	.25
AO3026 Ushuah, the Flame Samurai Swordman (Stranger) R	.30	.60
AO3027 Alice's Castling N	.20	.40
AO3028 Antorite, the Guardian of Deep Blue (Stranger) N	.15	.30
AO3029 Blue Illusionary Dragon of Calmness SR	.20	.40
AO3030 Blue Illusionary Hero N	.15	.30
AO3031 Refrain's Summoning N	.12	.25
AO3032 Riina, the Girl with Nothing N	.12	.25
AO3033 Spirit of Calmness N	.20	.40
AO3034 Wall of Ideas N	.12	.25
AO3035 Faurecia's Journey N	.25	.50
AO3036 Frigg, the Goddess of Abundance (Stranger) SR	.20	.40
AO3037 Morgiana, the Wise Servant N	.12	.25
AO3038 Perceval, the Flying Knight R	.30	.75
AO3039 Arthur, the Dead Lord of Vengeance N	.15	.30
AO3040 Black Wizard (Stranger) N	.15	.30
AO3041 Blood of the Mikage N	.15	.30
AO3042 Fallen Angelic Destroyer, Lucifer N	.15	.30
AO3043 Grave Robbers N	.12	.25
AO3044 Knight of Sigurd N	.12	.25
AO3045 Laurier, the Twilight Witch (Stranger) R	.20	.40
AO3046 Mikage Reiya SR	7.50	15.00
AO3047 Moan of the Dead N	.15	.30
AO3048 Necromancy of the Undead Lord N	.15	.30
AO3049 Niflheim, the Realm of the Dead N	.12	.25
AO3050 Priestess of the Black City N	.12	.25
AO3051 Residents of the Black City N	.12	.25
AO3052 Soulhunt N	.12	.25
AO3053 Soulless Soldier N	.12	.25
AO3054 Vampire's Staff N	.12	.25
AO3055 A Part of True Power SR	3.00	6.00
AO3056 Angel of Healing N	.25	.50
AO3057 Artemis, the Goddess of Hunt (Stranger) SR	.60	1.25
AO3058 Awakening of the Undead Lord SR	.60	1.25
AO3059 Awakening of the Winged Lord SR	2.00	4.00
AO3060 Between Passion and Calmness SR	.50	1.00
AO3061 Butterfly Effect R	.20	.40
AO3062 Cathedral of Armalla N	.12	.25
AO3063 Change the Heart SR	1.00	2.00
AO3064 Charlotte, the Sleeping Girl in the Castle R	.50	1.00
AO3065 Deathscythe SR	2.00	4.00
AO3066 Earthly Flash R	.30	.75
AO3067 Faurecia, the Virtuous Vampire SR	2.00	4.00
AO3068 Faust, the Promising Warrior (Stranger) SR	.20	.40
AO3069 Gloria's Round Table N	.12	.25
AO3070 Griphon, Racing Across Darkness N	.12	.25
AO3071 Heavenly Flash SR	.30	.60
AO3072 Jabberwock, the Chaotic Disaster (Stranger) R	.25	.50
AO3073 Magna's Angel N	.15	.30
AO3074 Mikage Seijuro R	.30	.75
AO3075 Mikage Seijuro's Game of Dreams R	.30	.75
AO3076 Milcell, the Clairvoyant Guide R	.25	.50
AO3077 Pricia, Pursuant of Exploding Flame N	.15	.30
AO3078 Resistance of the Twelve Protective Deities R	.75	1.50
AO3079 Sacred Beast of Artemis SR	.30	.75
AO3080 Scheherazade, the Teller of Heroic Epics SR	.25	.50
AO3081 Scheherazade's Heroic Epic R	1.00	2.00
AO3082 Sigurd, the Covenant King R	.50	1.00
AO3083 Spiral of Potential and Convergence N	.12	.25
AO3084 The End of Friendship N	.12	.25
AO3085 The Last Secret Sword R	2.00	4.00
AO3086 Will-o'-the-Wisp (Stranger) R	.20	.40
AO3087 Wings of the Archangel SR	1.50	3.00
AO3088 Wounded Black Dragon N	.12	.25
AO3089 Attoractia's Memoria N	1.25	2.50
AO3090 Magic Stone of Black Silence R	2.00	4.00
AO3091 Magic Stone of Gusting Skies R	1.25	2.50
AO3092 Magic Stone of Hearth's Core R	.75	1.50

2020 Force of Will Alice Origin III Life Points

LIFE019 Arla	.15	.30
LIFE020 Arla (Heavenly Flash)	.15	.30
LIFE021 Arla (Awakening of the Winged Lord)	.15	.30
LIFE022 Reflect/Refrain	.15	.30
LIFE023 Reflect/Refrain (Between Passion and Calmness)	.15	.30
LIFE024 Reflect/Refrain (Spiral of Potential and Convergence)	.15	.30
LIFE025 Rezzard	.15	.30
LIFE026 Rezzard (Awakening of the Undead Lord)	.15	.30
LIFE027 Rezzard (The End of Friendship)	.15	.30

2020 Force of Will Alice Origin III Magic Stones

AO3MS001 Darkness	.15	.30
AO3MS002 Darkness	.15	.30
AO3MS003 Fire	.15	.30
AO3MS004 Fire	.15	.30
AO3MS005 Light	.15	.30
AO3MS006 Light	.15	.30
AO3MS007 Water	.15	.30
AO3MS008 Water	.15	.30
AO3MS009 Wind	.15	.30
AO3MS010 Wind	.15	.30

2020 Force of Will Alice Origin III Will Coins

COIN032 Arla/Arla J	.20	.40
COIN033 Reflect/Refrain	.20	.40
COIN034 Rezzard/Rezzard J	.30	.60

2020 Force of Will Alice Origin IV Prologue of Attoractia

PofA001 Intimidation N	.12	.25
PofA002 King of Kings R	.20	.40
PofA003 Lenneth's Wish N	.12	.25
PofA004 Mage Jack N	.12	.25
PofA005 Return of the Soul R	.20	.40
PofA006 Richesse, the Swordsman (Stranger) N	.12	.25
PofA007 Schrödinger's Cry N	.12	.25
PofA008 Summoning Art of Magna R	.20	.40
PofA009 The Road to the Sacred Queen N	.12	.25
PofA010 The Road to the Winged Lord N	.12	.25
PofA011 Three of a Kind R	.20	.40
PofA012 Tsukuyomi Noble N	.12	.25
PofA013 Valkyrie, the Weaver of Destiny (Stranger) N	.12	.25
PofA014 White Wolf N	.12	.25
PofA015 Wizard of Vell-Savaria N	.12	.25
PofA016 Workshop Assistant Researcher N	.12	.25
PofA017 Yggdrasil's Grace R	.20	.40
PofA018 Agni, the Pyre War God (Stranger) N	.12	.25
PofA019 Alisaris, Minion of Lapis SR	.30	.60
PofA020 Athena, Titan of Revenge N	5.00	10.00
PofA021 Blaze Tornado N	.12	.25
PofA022 Hino Kagutsuchino Mikoto, the Flaming God of Fate (Stranger) N	.12	.25
PofA023 Magical Arrow N	.12	.25
PofA024 Ouroboros, the Snake of Reincarnation N	.12	.25
PofA025 Phoenix, the Flame of the World N	.12	.25
PofA026 Reflect's Rushing In N	.12	.25
PofA027 Swordmaster of Exploding Flame N	.12	.25
PofA028 Sylvia's Burning Flame R	.20	.40
PofA029 The Road to the Flame King N	.12	.25

PofA030 Gentleman Lightning Caller N	.12	.25
PofA031 Mariabella's Active Decoy N	.12	.25
PofA032 Princess of Dragon Palace (Stranger) N	.12	.25
PofA033 Random Walk N	.12	.25
PofA034 Refrain's Getting Out N	.12	.25
PofA035 The Road to the Machine Lord N	.12	.25
PofA036 The Road to the Princess of Love N	.12	.25
PofA037 Amphisbaena, the Two-Headed Dragon (Stranger) N	.12	.25
PofA038 Behemoth SR	.30	.60
PofA039 The Road to the Beast Queen N	.12	.25
PofA040 A Meeting in the Darkest Night N	.20	.40
PofA041 Anubis, the Guardian of Throne (Stranger) N	.12	.25
PofA042 Berserker of the Black Moon N	.12	.25
PofA043 Bizarre Zombie N	.12	.25
PofA044 Black Moonlight N	.12	.25
PofA045 Black Moon Ray N	.12	.25
PofA046 Black Rabbit N	.12	.25
PofA047 Black Wolf N	.12	.25
PofA048 Blazer, Minion of Lapis R	.20	.40
PofA049 Blazer's Art of Slaughter N	.12	.25
PofA050 Collapsing World N	.12	.25
PofA051 Curse of Caduceus N	.12	.25
PofA052 Dark Alice's Smile N	.12	.25
PofA053 Dark Summoning SR	.25	.50
PofA054 Demon of the Black Moon N	.12	.25
PofA055 Demon of the Black Moon, Lilith N	.12	.25
PofA056 Distortion of the Phenomenon R	.20	.40
PofA057 End of the World SR	.50	1.00
PofA058 Izanami, the Sealed Terror N	.12	.25
PofA059 Jeanne d'Arc, Heroine of Shadow R	.20	.40
PofA060 Lapis' Dark Storm N	.12	.25
PofA061 Lenneth, the Dark Priestess MVR	1.25	2.50
PofA062 Magician of Outland N	.12	.25
PofA063 Mimic N	.12	.25
PofA064 Mind Break N	.12	.25
PofA065 Miria, the Fallen Vampire R	.20	.40
PofA066 One Pair N	.12	.25
PofA067 Perceval, the Holy Grail of the Black Moon R	.20	.40
PofA068 Pitch Black Moon N	.12	.25
PofA069 Pitch Black Minion N	.12	.25
PofA070 Save the Queen R	.20	.40
PofA071 Shadow Doppelganger N	.12	.25
PofA072 Shadow Strike N	.12	.25
PofA073 Shadow X N	.12	.25
PofA074 Summoning of a Minion N	.12	.25
PofA075 The Road to the Undead Lord N	.12	.25
PofA076 The Scorn of Dark Alice N	.12	.25
PofA077 True Black Ribbon N	.12	.25
PofA078 Vicious Scarecrow N	.12	.25
PofA079 World Ender SR	.75	1.50
PofA080 Adombrali SR	.25	.50
PofA081 Alice's World of Madness N	.30	.60
PofA082 Attack Stance N	.12	.25
PofA083 Avatar of Strangers SR	.30	.75
PofA084 Bounty Hunter of Leginus N	.12	.25
PofA085 Cage of Mother Goose R	.20	.40
PofA086 Dark Gaming Hall N	.12	.25
PofA087 Defense Stance N	.12	.25
PofA088 Disappearing Power R	.20	.40
PofA089 Exorcist of Certo N	.12	.25
PofA090 Fafnir (Stranger) N	.12	.25
PofA091 Faithless Summoner N	.12	.25
PofA092 Grand Cross Reincarnation MVR	1.50	3.00
PofA093 Hades R	.20	.40
PofA094 Hoenir, the Bishop God (Stranger) N	.12	.25
PofA095 Leviathan R	.20	.40
PofA096 Mad Pyromancer N	.12	.25
PofA097 Magic Stance N	.12	.25
PofA098 Magic Storing Golem N	.12	.25
PofA099 Magician of Vell-Sevaria N	.12	.25
PofA100 Necromancer N	.12	.25
PofA101 Nidhogg R	.20	.40
PofA102 Nightmare Knight SR	.60	1.25
PofA103 Paratrooper of Leginus N	.12	.25
PofA104 Royal Straight Flush SR	.75	1.50
PofA105 Schrödinger MVR	7.50	15.00
PofA106 Shadow Swordmaster SR	.25	.50
PofA107 Skycrusher N	.12	.25
PofA108 Soul Dealer N	.12	.25
PofA109 Swordsman of Otherworld N	.12	.25
PofA110 Sylvia, Minion of Lapis SR	.30	.75
PofA111 The Final Stance SR	.75	1.50
PofA112 The Origin of the Seven Lands MVR	1.00	2.00
PofA113 The World of Dark Alice SR	.60	1.25
PofA114 Titania R	.20	.40
PofA115 Unknown Mother Goose SR	2.50	5.00
PofA116 Vell-Savaria, Field of the Final Battle R	.20	.40
PofA117 Veteran Warrior of Valhalla N	.12	.25
PofA118 Zain, the Warrior of Condemnation (Stranger) N	.12	.25
PofA119 Ziz R	.20	.40
PofA120 Genesis SR	.75	1.50
PofA121 Yggdrasil, Heroic Spirit of the World Tree MVR	5.00	10.00
PofA122 Black Moon's Memoria N	.12	.25
PofA123 Magic Stone of Heaven's Rift R	.20	.40
PofA124 Ruler's Memoria N	.12	.25

2020 Force of Will Alice Origin IV Prologue of Attoractia Full Art Foil

PofA001 Intimidation N	.75	1.50
PofA002 King of Kings R	.30	.60
PofA003 Lenneth's Wish N	.12	.25
PofA004 Mage Jack N	1.50	3.00
PofA005 Return of the Soul R	.20	.40
PofA006 Richesse, the Swordsman (Stranger) N	.30	.75
PofA007 Schrödinger's Cry N	12.50	25.00
PofA008 Summoning Art of Magna R	.20	.40
PofA009 The Road to the Sacred Queen N	4.00	8.00
PofA010 The Road to the Winged Lord N	.50	1.00
PofA011 Three of a Kind R	.30	.75
PofA012 Tsukuyomi Noble N	.12	.25
PofA013 Valkyrie, the Weaver of Destiny (Stranger) N	2.00	4.00
PofA014 White Wolf N	.75	1.50
PofA015 Wizard of Vell-Sevaria N	.12	.25
PofA016 Workshop Assistant Researcher N	.12	.25
PofA017 Yggdrasil's Grace R	.50	1.00
PofA018 Agni, the Pyre War God (Stranger) N	.12	.25
PofA019 Alisaris, Minion of Lapis SR	.25	.50
PofA020 Athena, Titan of Revenge N	5.00	10.00
PofA021 Blaze Tornado N	.75	1.50
PofA022 Hino Kagutsuchino Mikoto, the Flaming God of Fate (Stranger) N	1.00	2.00
PofA023 Magical Arrow N	.75	1.50
PofA024 Ouroboros, the Snake of Reincarnation N	.60	1.25
PofA025 Phoenix, the Flame of the World N	.30	.75
PofA026 Reflect's Rushing In N	.12	.25
PofA027 Swordmaster of Exploding Flame N	1.50	3.00
PofA028 Sylvia's Burning Flame R	1.50	3.00
PofA029 The Road to the Flame King N	.50	1.00
PofA030 Gentleman Lightning Caller N	1.25	2.50
PofA031 Mariabella's Active Decoy N	.12	.25
PofA032 Princess of Dragon Palace (Stranger) N	2.50	5.00
PofA033 Random Walk N	.12	.25
PofA034 Refrain's Getting Out N	.12	.25
PofA035 The Road to the Machine Lord N	.75	1.50
PofA036 The Road to the Princess of Love N	.60	1.25
PofA037 Amphisbaena, the Two-Headed Dragon (Stranger) N	.12	.25
PofA038 Behemoth SR	.50	1.00
PofA039 The Road to the Beast Queen N	1.50	3.00
PofA040 A Meeting in the Darkest Night N	.50	1.00
PofA041 Anubis, the Guardian of Throne (Stranger) N	.12	.25
PofA042 Berserker of the Black Moon N	.12	.25
PofA043 Bizarre Zombie N	5.00	10.00
PofA044 Black Moonlight N	.60	1.25
PofA045 Black Moon Ray N	4.00	8.00
PofA046 Black Rabbit N	.12	.25
PofA047 Black Wolf N	.12	.25
PofA048 Blazer, Minion of Lapis R	.30	.60
PofA049 Blazer's Art of Slaughter N	.12	.25
PofA050 Collapsing World N	.12	.25
PofA051 Curse of Caduceus N	2.00	4.00
PofA052 Dark Alice's Smile N	.12	.25
PofA053 Dark Summoning SR	.30	.75
PofA054 Demon of the Black Moon N	.12	.25
PofA055 Demon of the Black Moon, Lilith N	.12	.25
PofA056 Distortion of the Phenomenon R	.20	.40
PofA057 End of the World SR	.75	1.50
PofA058 Izanami, the Sealed Terror N	.12	.25
PofA059 Jeanne d'Arc, Heroine of Shadow R	1.25	2.50
PofA060 Lapis' Dark Storm N	.12	.25
PofA061 Lenneth, the Dark Priestess MVR	5.00	10.00
PofA062 Magician of Outland N	.12	.25
PofA063 Mimic N	.12	.25
PofA064 Mind Break N	.12	.25
PofA065 Miria, the Fallen Vampire R	1.25	2.50
PofA066 One Pair N	.12	.25
PofA067 Perceval, the Holy Grail of the Black Moon R	.50	1.00
PofA068 Pitch Black Moon N	.12	.25
PofA069 Pitch Black Minion N	.12	.25
PofA070 Save the Queen R	.25	.50
PofA071 Shadow Doppelganger N	1.00	2.00
PofA072 Shadow Strike N	.12	.25
PofA073 Shadow X N	7.50	15.00
PofA074 Summoning of a Minion N	.75	1.50
PofA075 The Road to the Undead Lord N	5.00	10.00
PofA076 The Scorn of Dark Alice N	.12	.25
PofA077 True Black Ribbon N	.75	1.50
PofA078 Vicious Scarecrow N	.12	.25
PofA079 World Ender SR	2.50	5.00
PofA080 Adombrali SR	.75	1.50
PofA081 Alice's World of Madness N	.12	.25
PofA082 Attack Stance N	.12	.25
PofA084 Bounty Hunter of Leginus N	.12	.25
PofA085 Cage of Mother Goose R	.20	.40
PofA086 Dark Gaming Hall N	.50	1.00
PofA087 Defense Stance N	2.50	5.00
PofA088 Disappearing Power R	.25	.50
PofA089 Exorcist of Certo N	.12	.25
PofA090 Fafnir (Stranger) N	.75	1.50
PofA091 Faithless Summoner N	2.00	4.00
PofA092 Grand Cross Reincarnation MVR	1.25	2.50
PofA093 Hades R	.20	.40
PofA094 Hoenir, the Bishop God (Stranger) N	.20	.40
PofA095 Leviathan R	.25	.50
PofA096 Mad Pyromancer N	.25	.50
PofA097 Magic Stance N	1.50	3.00
PofA098 Magic Storing Golem N	.30	.75
PofA099 Magician of Vell-Sevaria N	1.25	2.50
PofA100 Necromancer N	3.00	6.00
PofA101 Nidhogg R	.20	.40
PofA102 Nightmare Knight SR	.75	1.50
PofA103 Paratrooper of Leginus N	.12	.25
PofA104 Royal Straight Flush SR	3.00	6.00
PofA105 Schrödinger MVR	7.50	15.00
PofA106 Shadow Swordmaster SR	.75	1.50
PofA107 Skycrusher N	.12	.25
PofA108 Soul Dealer N	.60	1.25
PofA109 Swordsman of Otherworld N	.12	.25
PofA110 Sylvia, Minion of Lapis SR	2.50	5.00
PofA111 The Final Stance SR	.60	1.25
PofA112 The Origin of the Seven Lands MVR	1.50	3.00
PofA113 The World of Dark Alice SR	3.00	6.00
PofA114 Titania R	.30	.75
PofA115 Unknown Mother Goose SR	2.50	5.00
PofA116 Vell-Savaria, Field of the Final Battle R	.20	.40
PofA117 Veteran Warrior of Valhalla N	.12	.25
PofA118 Zain, the Warrior of Condemnation (Stranger) N	.12	.25
PofA119 Ziz R	.30	.75
PofA120 Genesis SR	1.25	2.50
PofA121 Yggdrasil, Heroic Spirit of the World Tree MVR	7.50	15.00
PofA122 Black Moon's Memoria N	.30	.75
PofA123 Magic Stone of Heaven's Rift R	1.00	2.00
PofA124 Ruler's Memoria N	1.50	3.00

2020 Force of Will Alice Origin IV Prologue of Attoractia Life Points

LFIE027 Gill Lapis	.15	.30
LFIE028 Dark Alice	.15	.30
LFIE029 Magna	.15	.30
LFIE030 The Road to the Machine Lord	.15	.30
LFIE031 The Road to the Princess of Love	.15	.30
LFIE032 The Road to the Beast Queen	.15	.30
LFIE033 The Road to the Flame King	.15	.30
LFIE034 The Road to the Winged Lord	.15	.30
LFIE035 The Road to the Undead Lord	.15	.30

2020 Force of Will Alice Origin IV Prologue of Attoractia Magic Stones

POFAMS001 Darkness	1.00	2.00
POFAMS002 Fire	.75	1.50
POFAMS003 Light	.75	1.50
POFAMS004 Water	.30	.60
POFAMS005 Wind	.25	.50

2020 Force of Will Alice Origin IV Prologue of Attoractia Will Coins

COIN035 Gill Lapis	.20	.40
COIN036 Dark Alice	.20	.40
COIN037 Magna	.20	.40

2020 Force of Will The Epic of the Dragon Lord

EDL001 Dispelling Stone N	.12	.25
EDL002 Endless Starlight, the Star Sword SR	.30	.75
EDL003 Exorcist Mage at the Academy R	2.00	4.00
EDL004 Flute, Captive Dragonoid Child // Group of Comets SR	7.50	15.00
EDL005 Grace of the Star N	.15	.30
EDL006 Light Servant of Ragnarok N	.12	.25
EDL007 Magic Bird N	.20	.40
EDL008 Magic Crest of Light N	.12	.25
EDL010 Pilgrim of the Star N	.12	.25
EDL011 Reiya, Spawn of the Star // Twinkle of the Star MVR	5.00	10.00
EDL012 Silmeria, Summoner of Spirits // Dance of Spirits R	.60	1.25
EDL013 Spirit of Light N	.12	.25
EDL014 Spirit of the Star N	1.25	2.50
EDL015 Star Dragon SR	.50	1.00
EDL016 Starlit Canopy R	.20	.40
EDL017 The Hidden History - ""Oborozuki"" N	.12	.25
EDL018 The Showdown with Ragnarok N	.12	.25
EDL019 Twinkling Dragon N	.12	.25
EDL020 Arle, the Seven-Tailed Fox // Arle's Flame MVR	3.00	6.00
EDL021 Burning Rabbit Dash R	.30	.75
EDL022 Chasing Dragon N	.15	.30
EDL023 Claw of the Dragonoid N	.15	.30
EDL024 Contract with the Fox God N	.15	.30
EDL025 Cook at the Academy N	.12	.25
EDL026 Fire Servant of Ragnarok N	.15	.30
EDL027 Groundsplitter Rabbit // Split Heaven and Earth SR	1.00	2.00
EDL028 Hoelle Pig // Food Supply N	.20	.40
EDL029 Hunting Dragon SR	.25	.50
EDL030 Injured Fox N	.12	.25
EDL032 Lilias's Mentor R	.50	1.00
EDL033 Lilias's Strike N	.15	.30
EDL034 Magic Crest of Fire N	.12	.25
EDL035 Shrine of the Dragonoids N	.12	.25
EDL036 Spirit of Scorched Bales SR	.30	.75
EDL037 The Hidden History - ""Lilias"" N	.12	.25
EDL038 Thunder Wolf // Thunder R	.75	1.50
EDL039 Academy Guard of Lykeion N	.15	.30
EDL040 Appraisal of Treasures N	.12	.25
EDL041 Chelina, Sorceress of Sending Back // Send Back R	.30	.60
EDL042 Crown of the Ancient King N	.15	.30
EDL043 Endless Purse N	.15	.30
EDL044 Insatiable Desire for Treasure N	.12	.25
EDL045 Jewel of the Panda King SR	.75	1.50
EDL046 Kiki, Selesta's Partner // Kiki's Exploration MVR	5.00	10.00
EDL047 Magic Crest of Water N	.12	.25
EDL048 Mermaid's Thunder Parasol R	.60	1.25
EDL049 Mirage, Fantasy Guide // Foresee SR	2.50	5.00
EDL051 Skycover Squirrel N	.12	.25
EDL052 The Hidden History - ""Selesta"" N	.12	.25
EDL053 The Library of Lykeion N	.12	.25
EDL054 Water Servant of Ragnarok N	.15	.30
EDL055 Water Spirit of the Lamp R	.30	.75
EDL056 Waterfront Frog N	.12	.25
EDL057 Wise Dragon SR	.25	.50
EDL058 Altesing, Mischievous Boy // A Glimpse of the Prodigy MVR	4.00	8.00
EDL059 Altesing's Secret Hideout N	.20	.40
EDL060 Elixir, Crest Researcher // Research Results SR	.50	1.00
EDL061 Elixir's Love N	.15	.30
EDL062 Lykeion, the Magic Academy R	.30	.75
EDL063 Magic Crest of Wind N	.12	.25
EDL064 Magical Dragon SR	.75	1.50
EDL065 Magical Wind Arrow N	.12	.25
EDL066 Monstrous Rush SR	.30	.60
EDL067 Perpetual Student at the Academy N	.12	.25
EDL068 Spirit of Magic R	.20	.40
EDL069 Spirit of the Soil // Loamy Soil R	.20	.40
EDL070 Stormy Sky N	.12	.25
EDL071 Student at the Academy N	.12	.25
EDL072 The Grimoire of the Seven Luminaries N	.12	.25
EDL073 Unceasing Wind N	.12	.25
EDL075 Wind of the Star N	.12	.25
EDL076 Wind Servant of Ragnarok N	.15	.30
EDL077 Abhorrent Revival N	.12	.25
EDL078 Arm of the Demon N	.15	.30
EDL079 Bone Dragon SR	1.00	2.00
EDL080 Darkness Servant of Ragnarok N	.20	.40
EDL081 Frightened Villager N	.12	.25
EDL082 Gravekeeper at the Academy N	.15	.30
EDL083 Interdimensional Graveyard R	.25	.50
EDL084 Isolated Demon of Revenge R	.30	.75
EDL085 Lonely Vampire N	.20	.40
EDL086 Lord of the Undead // Deadly Dive R	.50	1.00
EDL087 Magic Crest of Darkness N	.12	.25
EDL089 Ominous Moon, the Lunar Sword SR	.30	.60
EDL090 Reaper Knight // Endless Night N	.12	.25
EDL091 The Battle comes to an end, and then... N	.75	1.50
EDL092 The Elegant Mikage Sisters // Eternal Recurrence SR	1.00	2.00
EDL093 The Hidden History - ""Mikage"" N	.12	.25
EDL094 Tsuiya, Cursed Spawn of the Star // Curse of Ragnarok MVR	12.50	25.00
EDL095 Tsuiya's Darkness N	.12	.25
EDL096 Ragnarok, Invading Dragon Lord R	7.50	15.00
EDL097 Epic Stone of the Blood R	.30	.75
EDL098 Epic Stone of the Dragon R	.30	.60
EDL099 Epic Stone of the Elements R	.30	.60
EDL100 Epic Stone of the Star R	.20	.40
EDL101 Epic Stone of the Treasure R	.25	.50
EDL009 JR Oborozuki, Star Sword Visionary R	20.00	40.00
EDL009 JR Oborozuki, Star Sword Visionary ALT ART R	30.00	75.00
EDL031 JR Lilias, Last Descendant of Dragonoids R	12.50	25.00
EDL050 JR Selesta, Treasure Hunter R	12.50	25.00
EDL074 JR Welser, the Progenitor of Magic R	12.50	25.00
EDL088 JR Mikage Seijuro, Interdimensional Messenger R	2.50	5.00

2020 Force of Will The Epic of the Dragon Lord Will Coins

EDLCoin001 Oborozuki	.20	.40
EDLCoin002 Lilias	.20	.40
EDLCoin003 Selesta	.20	.40
EDLCoin004 Welser	.20	.40
EDLCoin005 Mikage Seijuro	.20	.40
EDLCoin006 Ragnarok	.20	.40

2020 Force of Will Ghost in the Shell SAC 2045

GITS2045001 Acrobatic Shot N	.12	.25
GITS2045002 Ada Byron N	.12	.25
GITS2045003 Android Harlot N	.12	.25
GITS2045004 Aramaki & Togusa SR	1.50	3.00
GITS2045005 Aramaki, An Executive of the Public Security R	.20	.40
GITS2045006 Armed Suit R	.20	.40
GITS2045007 Armored Car N	.12	.25
GITS2045008 Batou SR	.50	1.00
GITS2045009 Batou & Ishikawa N	.12	.25
GITS2045010 Batou & Motoko SR	1.25	2.50
GITS2045011 Batou & Saito SR	1.00	2.00
GITS2045012 Batou & Stan SR	1.00	2.00
GITS2045013 Batou & Togusa SR	1.00	2.00
GITS2045014 Batou, a Mercenary Crew N	.12	.25
GITS2045015 Batou, the Ranger R	.20	.40
GITS2045016 Blackhawk N	.12	.25
GITS2045017 Borma R	.20	.40
GITS2045018 Buggy N	.12	.25
GITS2045019 Civilian with Business Spirit N	.12	.25
GITS2045020 Cyber Interface N	.12	.25
GITS2045021 Delta-Cyborged Army N	.12	.25
GITS2045022 Evasive Action N	.12	.25
GITS2045023 Gary Harts N	.12	.25
GITS2045024 Gaze with Curiosity N	.12	.25
GITS2045025 Ghost Meeting N	.12	.25
GITS2045026 Hacker with a Brief N	.12	.25
GITS2045027 Head Mounted Display N	.12	.25
GITS2045028 Infiltration Reconnaissance N	.12	.25
GITS2045029 Ishikawa & Motoko R	.20	.40
GITS2045030 Ishikawa, the Experienced Crew N	.12	.25

GITS2045031 John Smith N .12 .25
GITS2045032 Jumping N .12 .25
GITS2045033 Kurisu Otomo Tello N .12 .25
GITS2045034 Kusanagi Motoko, Boarding Tachikoma SR .75 1.50
GITS2045035 Kusanagi Motoko, in Formal Wear SR 1.50 3.00
GITS2045036 Kusanagi Motoko, the Captain of Mercenary N .12 .25
GITS2045037 Kusanagi Motoko, the Major SR 7.50 15.00
GITS2045038 Laying Down of Arms N .12 .25
GITS2045039 Maid Robot N .12 .25
GITS2045040 Nomads N .12 .25
GITS2045041 Onslaught N .12 .25
GITS2045042 Patrick Huge N .12 .25
GITS2045043 Paz R .20 .40
GITS2045044 Presidential Order N .12 .25
GITS2045045 Purin Esaki, an Investigator SR 2.50 5.00
GITS2045046 Purin Esaki, the Girl in Love SR 3.00 6.00
GITS2045047 Raydist N .12 .25
GITS2045048 Roundhouse Kick N .12 .25
GITS2045049 Saito & Stan N .12 .25
GITS2045050 Saito, Boarding Tachikoma N .12 .25
GITS2045051 Saito, in Relax N .12 .25
GITS2045052 Saito, the Skilled Sniper R .20 .40
GITS2045053 Saito, the Sniper SR 1.00 2.00
GITS2045054 Sanji Yaguchi N .12 .25
GITS2045055 Secret Agent N .12 .25
GITS2045056 Security Robot N .12 .25
GITS2045057 SP N .12 .25
GITS2045058 Spider-Type Drone N .12 .25
GITS2045059 Stan, the Good Helper R .20 .40
GITS2045060 Stan, the Noob N .12 .25
GITS2045061 Stealth Drone N .12 .25
GITS2045062 Tachikoma A R .20 .40
GITS2045063 Tachikoma B R .20 .40
GITS2045064 The President of Obsidian Inc. N .12 .25
GITS2045065 Togusa N .12 .25
GITS2045066 Togusa, in the Secret Order R .20 .40
GITS2045067 Togusa, the Competent Investigator SR 5.00 10.00
GITS2045068 Top Secret Document N .12 .25
GITS2045069 Truck N .12 .25
GITS2045070 Wasp-Type Drone N .12 .25
GITS2045071 Watchdog Robot N .12 .25
GITS2045072 Wired Anchor N .12 .25
GITS2045073 Worldwide Default R .20 .40
GITS2045074 Edwards Air Force Base R .20 .40
GITS2045075 Home Ministry R .20 .40
GITS2045076 NSA Headquarters R .20 .40
GITS2045077 Prime Minister's Office R .20 .40
GITS2045078 Section 9 New Headquarters R .20 .40
GITS2045079 Kusanagi Motoko, Boarding Tachikoma SCR 100.00 200.00
GITS2045080 Kusanagi Motoko, the Major SCR 75.00 150.00

2020 Force of Will Starter Deck Alice Origin II

SDAO2001 Barust, the Machine God of Conflagration (Stranger) .75 1.50
SDAO2002 Blue Wizard (Stranger) 1.50 3.00
SDAO2003 Charm of the Princess .12 .25
SDAO2004 Cinderella, the Valkyrie of Glass .12 .25
SDAO2005 Perceval, the Charmed Knight .75 1.50
SDAO2006 Triton, the Prince of Ocean (Stranger) .25 .50
SDAO2007 Valentina's Zealot .12 .25
SDAO2008 Afanc, the Phantom Beast .12 .25
SDAO2009 Deep Green Magician, Liz (Stranger) .75 1.50
SDAO2010 Friendly Seeking Mole .15 .30
SDAO2011 Green Wizard (Stranger) .30 .75
SDAO2012 Herald of the Beast Lady .12 .25
SDAO2013 Pricia's Encouragement .20 .40
SDAO2014 Rapid Growth .12 .25
SDAO2015 Sprinting Wolf .12 .25
SDAO2016 Yggnitsvay, the Guardian of Green Branch (Stranger) .75 1.50
SDAO2017 Loki, the Ancient Demon Lord (Stranger) .50 1.00
SDAO2018 Awakening of the Beast Queen .15 .30
SDAO2019 Claw of the Sacred Beast .30 .75
SDAO2020 El Chifon, the Pet Dragon of the Lord of the Seas .30 .60
SDAO2021 Eureka, the Puppet Lord of the Seas .25 .50
SDAO2022 Freya, the Goddess of Full Moon (Stranger) .50 1.00
SDAO2023 Guardian of Outland (Stranger) .30 .60
SDAO2024 Lovers' Lock .30 .60
SDAO2025 Magna's Guardian Beast .30 .75
SDAO2026 Masked Prince .15 .30
SDAO2027 Morrigan, the Goddess of Tragic Love (Stranger) .50 1.00
SDAO2028 Pricia 1.50 3.00
SDAO2029 Space-Time Anomaly .12 .25
SDAO2030 The Princess of Love Takes Control .30 .60
SDAO2031 Valentina 4.00 8.00
SDAO2032 World Tree Fox .15 .30
SDAO2033 Attoractia's Memoria .75 1.50
SDAO2034 Magic Stone of Blasting Waves .75 1.50
SDAO2035 Magic Stone of Dark Depth .75 1.50
SDAO2036 Water Magic Stone .12 .25
SDAO2037 Wind Magic Stone .12 .25

2020 Force of Will Starter Deck Ghost in the Shell SAC 2045

GITS2045SD001 Aramaki .75 1.50
GITS2045SD002 Batou & Kusanagi Motoko .60 1.25
GITS2045SD003 Batou, the Motoko's Buddy .20 .40
GITS2045SD004 Bombarding .50 1.00
GITS2045SD005 Ishikawa, the Competent Supporter .15 .30
GITS2045SD006 Kusanagi Motoko, in Body Suit .75 1.50
GITS2045SD007 Kusanagi Motoko, in Relax .75 1.50
GITS2045SD008 Optical Camouflage 3.00 6.00
GITS2045SD009 Purin Esaki, the Elite .20 .40
GITS2045SD010 Stan, a Former Army Infantry .15 .30
GITS2045SD011 Tachikoma C .15 .30
GITS2045SD012 Beverly Hills .20 .40
GITS2045SD013 Gated Town .30 .60
GITS2045SD014 Palm Springs .15 .30

2021 Force of Will Assault into the Demonic World

ADW001 Charlotte, Future of the Sacred Spirit SR .30 .75
ADW002 Charlotte's Light Transformation Magic R .25 .50
ADW004 Excalibur Reincarnation N .12 .25
ADW005 Excalibur Revolution SR .50 1.00
ADW006 Giant of the Sacred Spirit N .12 .25
ADW007 Glowing Tree of Valhalla R .20 .40
ADW008 Guidance N .12 .25
ADW009 Hero of Compassion N .12 .25
ADW010 Hero of Courage N .12 .25
ADW011 Hero of Might N .12 .25
ADW012 Manifestation of the Sacred Spirit N .15 .30
ADW013 Schrodinger, White Cat MVR 2.50 5.00
ADW014 Schrodinger's Call N .12 .25
ADW015 White Garden N .15 .30
ADW016 Atomic Bahamut MVR 3.00 6.00
ADW017 Atomic Fairy N .12 .25
ADW018 Atomic Fusion N .12 .25
ADW019 Atomic Reactor N .12 .25
ADW020 Atomic Turbulence SR 1.00 2.00
ADW021 Firestorm N .12 .25
ADW022 Gradius N .20 .40
ADW023 Improved Burning Robot R .30 .75
ADW024 Oil Demon N .12 .25
ADW025 Oil Pond N .12 .25
ADW026 Shining Heart, Scorching Hero R .20 .40
ADW027 The Mysteries of Milest N .15 .30
ADW028 The Witch of Quenched Fire N .15 .30
ADW029 Tiny Violet SR 7.50 15.00
ADW031 Bogus Meditation N .12 .25
ADW032 Dolly, Olivia's Electric Dolphin MVR 7.50 15.00
ADW033 Everfrost N .12 .25
ADW034 Fish Drive R .20 .40
ADW035 Fish of the Demonic World N .20 .40
ADW036 Hero of Water N .12 .25
ADW037 Improved Healing Robot N .20 .40
ADW038 Lightning Rod Mermaid N .15 .30
ADW040 Permafrost N .12 .25
ADW041 Surging Lightning N .12 .25
ADW042 Tera Thunderfish SR .75 1.50
ADW043 The Mysteries of Moojdart N .12 .25
ADW044 The Thunder Empress's Strike SR .75 1.50
ADW045 The Witch of Melting Ice R .20 .40
ADW046 Absorbing Knowledge R .20 .40
ADW047 Avenger of Amadeus SR .50 1.00
ADW049 Eternal Wind N .12 .25
ADW050 Eyes of the Avenger N .12 .25
ADW051 Guardian Dragon of the Kingdom R .75 1.50
ADW052 Heart of the Avenger N .15 .30
ADW053 Hero of Wind N .12 .25
ADW054 Limbs of the Avenger N .12 .25
ADW055 Number Four, Anti-Magic N .15 .30
ADW056 Plains of Raging Winds N .12 .25
ADW057 Spark of Life SR .50 1.00
ADW058 Starving Beast N .12 .25
ADW059 The Witch of Unblowing Wind N .12 .25
ADW060 Witch With A Pointy Hat MVR 4.00 8.00
ADW061 Bloodlord R .20 .40
ADW062 Darklord R .15 .30
ADW063 Fallen Angel of Terminus MVR 1.25 2.50
ADW064 Hero of Darkness N .12 .25
ADW065 Mapmaker of the Demonic World N .15 .30
ADW066 Necronomicon Barrier SR 2.50 5.00
ADW067 Residents of the Demonic World N .20 .40
ADW068 Swamp of Sorrows N .20 .40
ADW069 Temple of the Dead N .12 .25
ADW070 The First Layer of the Demonic World N .12 .25
ADW071 The Mysteries of Grusbalesta N .15 .30
ADW072 The Witch of the Fallen Kingdom SR 10.00 20.00
ADW073 Void N .20 .40
ADW074 Wind of the Demonic World N .12 .25
ADW076 Aegis N .12 .25
ADW077 Amadeus, Fallen Kingdom SR .50 1.00
ADW078 Brave Force R .20 .40
ADW079 Call from the Depths N .12 .25
ADW080 Dark Prominence SR .75 1.50
ADW081 Fallen Angel of Hatred R .20 .40
ADW082 Fallen Angel of the Paradise N .12 .25
ADW083 Hero of the Sacred Spirit N .12 .25
ADW084 Lenneth, Heroic Goddes of Guidance SR 1.50 3.00
ADW085 Lightning Passion R .30 .60
ADW086 Magical Loveliness N .20 .40
ADW087 Number Seven, Anti-Magic N .20 .40
ADW088 Number Thirteen, Anti-Magic SR 7.50 15.00
ADW089 Pulsing Thunder SR .50 1.00
ADW090 Scorching Mountain Trail R .20 .40
ADW091 Sparkle Fish N .12 .25
ADW092 The Forest of Darkness N .12 .25
ADW093 The Mysteries of Almerius N .20 .40
ADW094 The Mysteries of Zero R .20 .40
ADW095 The Paradise of Fallen Angels N .12 .25
ADW096 Magic Stone of Atoms N .30 .60
ADW097 Magic Stone of Guidance N .30 .60
ADW098 Magic Stone of Knowledge N .75 1.50
ADW099 Magic Stone of the Kingdom N .25 .50
ADW100 Magic Stone of Tides N .30 .60
ADW101 Darkness Magic Stone .12 .25
ADW102 Fire Magic Stone .12 .25
ADW103 Light Magic Stone .12 .25
ADW104 Water Magic Stone .15 .30
ADW105 Wind Magic Stone .15 .30
ADW003 JR Excalibur Genesis // Faria, Swordmaster of Creation JR3.00 6.00
ADW030 JR Violet, Atomic Automaton JR 7.50 15.00
ADW039 JR Olivia, Thunder Empress R 4.00 8.00
ADW048 JR Brad, Immortal Sage R .75 1.50
ADW075 JR Wolfgang, Guide of the Demonic World JR 3.00 6.00

2021 Force of Will Assault into the Demonic World Life Points

1 1000 .15 .30
2 500 .15 .30
3 100 .15 .30
4 1000 .15 .30
5 500 .15 .30
6 100 .15 .30
7 1000 .15 .30
8 500 .15 .30
9 100 .15 .30
10 1000 .15 .30
11 500 .15 .30
12 100 .15 .30
13 1000 .15 .30
14 500 .15 .30
15 100 .15 .30

2021 Force of Will Assault into the Demonic World Will Coins

1 Coin .15 .30
2 Coin .15 .30
3 Coin .15 .30
4 Coin .15 .30
5 Coin .15 .30

2021 Force of Will Game of Gods

GOG001 Artillerist of Faith NR .20 .40
GOG002 Brunhild, Sign of Faith SR 1.50 3.00
GOG003 Choir of the Valkyries NR .12 .25
GOG004 Hegel, Giant of the Dark Sun R .50 1.00
GOG005 Kara, Swift Valkyrie NR .12 .25
GOG006 Keep the Faith! NR .12 .25
GOG007 Light Mage of Ma'at NR .12 .25
GOG008 Misteltein, Dark Sword Saint MVR 4.00 8.00
GOG009 Odin Enters the Game of Gods SR 1.00 2.00
GOG010 Odin's Intimidation NR .12 .25
GOG011 Praying Valkyrie NR .15 .30
GOG012 Randgrid R .30 .75
GOG013 Repeating Faith Revival NR .12 .25
GOG014 Soldier of Minerva NR .12 .25
GOG015 The Holy Sword of Misteltein R .30 .75
GOG016 Wind of Asgard R .30 .75
GOG017 Ambushing Scorpion NR .20 .40
GOG018 Barbatos, Aspiring Ascendant R .25 .50
GOG019 Cthulhu's Intimidation NR .20 .40
GOG020 Explosive Withdrawal NR .15 .30
GOG021 Flame Soldier of Ma'at NR .12 .25
GOG022 Flaming Salamander NR .15 .30
GOG023 Isis, Heat of the Sand SR 2.50 5.00
GOG024 Magic Stone Dance of Chaos SR 3.00 6.00
GOG025 Melua, Mage of Ma'at R .75 1.50
GOG026 Phantasmal Ascendant NR 1.50 3.00
GOG027 Rebirth of Flaming Disaster R .75 1.50
GOG028 Red Flame NR .25 .50
GOG029 Red Riding Hood, Crimson Wolf MVR 6.00 12.00
GOG030 Spirit of Ma'at NR .15 .30
GOG031 Sudden Manifestation of Power NR .15 .30
GOG032 This Means War! R .75 1.50
GOG033 Fairy of Trickery NR 1.50 3.00
GOG034 Fenrir R .50 1.00
GOG035 Garmheld MVR 2.00 4.00
GOG036 Giants, Advance! NR .12 .25
GOG037 Loki Enters the Game of Gods R 2.00 4.00
GOG038 Loki's Curse NR .15 .30
GOG039 Loki's Deception SR 2.00 4.00
GOG040 Masked Giant of Trickery NR .12 .25
GOG041 Roar of the Underground Giant NR .15 .30
GOG042 Skidbladnir, Magical Sailing Ship R .20 .40
GOG043 Underground Giant NR .12 .25
GOG044 Volmol, Snake of Knowledge SR 1.00 2.00
GOG045 Water Mage of Ma'at NR .12 .25
GOG046 And War It Shall Be! NR .15 .30
GOG047 Fiethsing, 100 Years of Wizardry MVR 7.50 15.00
GOG048 Gale of the Moon NR 1.50 3.00
GOG049 Galileo, Polymath R .50 1.00
GOG050 Hanzo, Ninja of the Moon SR 1.50 3.00
GOG051 Kaguya Enters the Game of Gods SR .50 1.00
GOG052 Kaguya's Moonwatching NR .12 .25
GOG053 Kotaro, Ninja of Silence R .75 1.50
GOG054 Mimi Tribe Spectator NR .12 .25
GOG055 Moon Rabbit Spectator NR .12 .25
GOG056 Ninja of Silence NR .12 .25
GOG057 Rabbit Ninja R .60 1.25
GOG058 Wind Knight of Ma'at R .30 .75
GOG059 Wind Moon NR .15 .30
GOG060 Call of Darkness NR .15 .30
GOG061 Dark Mage of Ma'at NR .12 .25
GOG062 Dark Sun SR .50 1.00
GOG063 Falling from Fate NR .12 .25
GOG064 Night Moon NR .12 .25
GOG065 Phantasmal Scarlet SR .60 1.25
GOG066 Schmel, Giant of Distrust SR 2.50 5.00
GOG067 Soulstealing Valkyrie NR .15 .30
GOG068 Arena Expansion: Asgard R .25 .50
GOG069 Arena Expansion: Eien no Tsuki no Miyako R .60 1.25
GOG070 Arena Expansion: R'lyeh R .75 1.50
GOG071 Arena Expansion: Utgard R 1.50 3.00
GOG072 Calamity Shield NR .15 .30
GOG073 Demon Beast of Hellfire NR .20 .40
GOG074 Dogra Magra SR 1.00 2.00
GOG075 Double Bind NR .12 .25
GOG076 Gungnir, Magic Spear of Devotion SR .50 1.00
GOG077 Huginn and Muninn R .25 .50
GOG078 Kaguya, God of Cats and the Moon JR 7.50 15.00
GOG079 Loki, Master of Trickery JR 7.50 15.00
GOG080 Loki's Strategy SR 2.00 4.00
GOG081 Nyarlathotep, Game Master JR 7.50 15.00
GOG082 Odin, God of War JR 1.25 2.50
GOG083 Odin's Gloom NR .12 .25
GOG084 Seal of Wind and Water NR .20 .40
GOG085 Teachings of the Moon SR .60 1.25
GOG086 Ma'at, World of Duels and Ascendants MVR 2.00 4.00
GOG087 The Tales' Magic Stone R .30 .75
GOG088 The Villains' Magic Stone R .40 .80
GOG089 Darkness Magic Stone .12 .25
GOG090 Fire Magic Stone .12 .25
GOG091 Light Magic Stone .12 .25
GOG092 Water Magic Stone .12 .25
GOG093 Wind Magic Stone .12 .25

2021 Force of Will Game of Gods Life Points

LIFE001 Life Point .20 .40
LIFE002 Life Point .20 .40
LIFE003 Life Point .20 .40
LIFE004 Life Point .20 .40
LIFE005 Life Point .20 .40
LIFE006 Life Point .20 .40
LIFE007 Life Point .20 .40
LIFE008 Life Point .20 .40
LIFE009 Life Point .20 .40
LIFE010 Life Point .20 .40

2021 Force of Will Game of Gods Will Coins

COIN001 Kaguya .30 .75
COIN002 Loki .25 .50
COIN003 Nyarlathotep .30 .60
COIN004 Odin .20 .40

2021 Force of Will The Magic Stone War Zero

MSW001 A Duet of Light N .15 .30
MSW003 Chiffon, Spirit of Guidance SR .25 .50
MSW004 Gathering of the Six Sages N .12 .25
MSW005 Guardian Wizard N .12 .25
MSW006 Gullwing, Dragon Spirit SR 1.00 2.00
MSW007 Messenger From The Spirit Village N .12 .25
MSW008 Princess Kaguya // Flying Bamboo MVR 2.50 5.00
MSW009 Rapunzel, The Long-Haired Princess N .12 .25
MSW010 Rush of Spirits N .12 .25
MSW011 Spirit of Hope N .12 .25
MSW012 Spirit Ring N .12 .25
MSW013 Spirit Village R .20 .40
MSW014 The Awakening of Almerius SR .75 1.50
MSW015 The Awakening of Zero R .50 1.00
MSW016 The Beginning of a Fairy Tale N .15 .30
MSW017 Tinker Bell, the Spirit // Rain of Light R .30 .75
MSW019 A Duet of Fire N .20 .40
MSW020 Cane of the Salamander N .15 .30
MSW021 Desperate Aid N .12 .25
MSW022 Elfina, Spirit of Trials SR .75 1.50
MSW023 Fairy Tale Resistance Force N .12 .25
MSW024 Fountain of Trials R .50 1.00
MSW025 Infinite Matchsticks N 1.25 2.50
MSW027 Salamander, the Spirit of Fire // Ghostflame R .25 .50
MSW028 Shaman of the Spirit Village N .12 .25
MSW029 Snow White of the Red Apple // Apple Avenger MVR 1.00 2.00
MSW030 Snow White's Fire Dwarves N .12 .25
MSW031 Spirit of the Fiery Stone N .12 .25
MSW032 The Awakening of Milest SR .50 1.00
MSW033 The Little Explosive Match Girl SR .25 .50
MSW034 A Duet of Water N .15 .30
MSW035 Cinderella, Freed from the Ashes // Rampaging Pumpkin Carriage MVR .50 1.00
MSW036 Fairy Tale Rabbit N .12 .25
MSW037 Fiola, Spirit of Oblivion SR 5.00 10.00
MSW038 Fountain of the Oblivion Moon N .12 .25
MSW039 Illusionary Flower of Sorrow N .12 .25
MSW040 Illusionary Mermaid N .12 .25
MSW041 Illusionary Snow N .12 .25
MSW043 Neverend, Fairy Tale Dragon SR 3.00 6.00
MSW044 Neverend's Roar N .12 .25
MSW045 Purplemist, the Fantasy Dragon // Moon Incarnation R .20 .40

MSW046 Spirit of Knowledge N .12 .25
MSW047 The Awakening of Moojdart SR .50 1.00
MSW048 Three-Eyed Fortune Teller R .30 .60
MSW049 A Blank Page N .15 .30
MSW050 A Duet of Wind N .15 .30
MSW051 An Ancestor's Portrait N .12 .25
MSW052 Fairy Tale Moon R .30 .60
MSW054 Glinda, the Fairy N .12 .25
MSW055 Little Red, Fairy Tale of Air // Wind of Gods R .50 1.00
MSW056 Magic Beanstalk N .12 .25
MSW057 Magic Stone Bird R .20 .40
MSW058 Magic Stone Devotee N .12 .25
MSW059 Scheherazade, Weaver of Fairy Tales SR 1.50 3.00
MSW060 The Awakening of Fiethsing SR 2.00 4.00
MSW061 The Hidden History - ""The Magic Stone War"" N .12 .25
MSW062 The Release of the Fairy Tales N .15 .30
MSW063 Trish, Spirit of Autumn Wind SR .50 1.00
MSW064 Welser, Master of the Six Sages // His Last Lecture MVR4.00 8.00
MSW065 Wind Stone Shot N .12 .25
MSW066 A Duet of Darkness N .20 .40
MSW067 A World Invaded N .12 .25
MSW068 Abdul Alhazred, Poet of Madness // Dark Pulse R 1.00 2.00
MSW069 Assault from the Demonic World N .12 .25
MSW070 Awakening of the Magic Stones N .12 .25
MSW071 Darksphere, Spirit of Dark Night SR .50 1.00
MSW072 Extraction Wizard R .30 .75
MSW074 Lilias Petal // Awakening of the Nine-Tailed Fox MVR 1.00 2.00
MSW075 One-Tailed Fox N .12 .25
MSW076 Secluded Fox Village R .25 .50
MSW077 Sparkling Boon of the Magic Stones N .12 .25
MSW078 Spirit of Regret N .12 .25
MSW079 Student at the Institute N .15 .30
MSW080 The Awakening of Grusbalesta SR .50 1.00
MSW081 The Transformed N .12 .25
MSW082 Ultra Magic Stone Golem SR 1.50 3.00
MSW083 A Sacrifice of Words and Memories R .15 .30
MSW084 Azathoth, Manifestation of Death SR .75 1.50
MSW085 Deeper Ones R 1.50 3.00
MSW086 Hastur, Messenger of Madness R .50 1.00
MSW087 Magic Stone Research Institute R 1.00 2.00
MSW088 Minphia, Storytelling Girl R .50 1.00
MSW089 Necronomicon, Book of Outer World R .50 1.00
MSW090 Nyarlathotep, Bringer of War SR .75 1.50
MSW091 Satan's Phantasmal Body // Flame of Outer World R .75 1.50
MSW092 Shub-Niggurath, Gatekeeper of Outer World R .75 1.50
MSW093 Spirits of Fire and Water N .12 .25
MSW094 Symphony of the Two Great Dragons R .20 .40
MSW095 The Magic of Trust and Love N .12 .25
MSW096 Umr at-Tawil, Keymaster of Outer World R 1.00 2.00
MSW098 Wolfgang's Apocalypse R .30 .60
MSW099 Yog-Sothoth, True Hunger SR 1.50 3.00
MSW100 Moonbreeze's Memoria N .12 .25
MSW101 The Magic Stone of the Demonic World R 1.25 2.50
MSW102 The Magic Stone of the Six Sages R 20.00 40.00
MSW103 Darkness Magic Stone .12 .25
MSW104 Fire Magic Stone .12 .25
MSW105 Light Magic Stone .12 .25
MSW106 Water Magic Stone .12 .25
MSW107 Wind Magic Stone .12 .25
MSW002JR Almerius R 7.50 15.00
MSW018JR Zero, Apprentice Sage R 5.00 10.00
MSW026JR Milest R 7.50 15.00
MSW042JR Moojdart JR 25.00 50.00
MSW053JR Fiethsing JR .20 .40
MSW073JR Grusbalesta JR .20 .40
MSW097RR Wolfgang, Exiled Demon Prince JR 20.00 40.00

2021 Force of Will The Magic Stone War Zero Life Points

1 Rush of Spirits .15 .30
2 The Awakening of Almerius .15 .30
3 A Duet of Light (Almerius) .15 .30
4 Gathering of the Six Sages .15 .30
5 The Awakening of Zero .15 .30
6 A Duet of Light (Zero) .15 .30
7 A Sacrifice of Words and Memories (Milest) .15 .30
8 The Magic of Trust and Love (Milest) .15 .30
9 The Awakening of Milest .15 .30
10 A Duet of Water (Moojdart) .15 .30
11 The Magic of Trust and Love (Moojdart) .15 .30
12 The Awakening of Moojdart .15 .30
13 A Duet of Wind (Fiethsing) .15 .30
14 Wind Stone Shot .15 .30
15 The Awakening of Fiethsing .15 .30
16 A Duet of Darkness (Grusbalesta) .15 .30
17 Magic Stone Research Institute .15 .30
18 The Awakening of Grusbalesta .15 .30
19 Nyarlathotep, Bringer of War .15 .30
20 Yog-Sothoth, True Hunger .15 .30
21 Azathoth, Manifestation of Death .15 .30

2021 Force of Will The Magic Stone War Zero Will Coins

1 Almerius .20 .40
2 Zero .25 .50
3 Milest .20 .40
4 Moojdart .30 .60
5 Fiethsing .30 .60
6 Grusbalesta .30 .60
7 Wolfgang .20 .40

2021 Force of Will Rebirth of Legend

ROL001 Abel, Top Two of the Light Palace R .20 .40
ROL002 Eldorado Pearlshine R .25 .50
ROL003 Grimm and Pandora SR .25 .50
ROL004 Lars, Sacred King SR .50 1.00
ROL005 Lumia, Princess of Rebirth // Wings of Light and Darkness MVR 7.50 15.00
ROL006 Cain, Top Two of the Light Palace R .20 .40
ROL007 Kirik's Training Grounds R .20 .40
ROL008 Magna // God's Breath MVR .30 .75
ROL009 Shakti, Mercenary Queen SR .30 .75
ROL010 Sylvia Lilias SR 1.00 2.00
ROL011 Flute, Shion's Attendant R .75 1.50
ROL012 Lunya, Master Guide SR .75 1.50
ROL013 Mariabella, Sincere Engineer // Heart-to-Heart Talk MVR10.00 20.00
ROL014 Selesta's Tremendous Treasure Trove R .20 .40
ROL015 Valentina, Owner of the Theater SR .25 .50
ROL016 Faurecia, Lady-In Attoractia R .20 .40
ROL017 Melfee, Traveling Sorceress R .30 .60
ROL018 Pricia, Seeker of Friends // Pricia's Big Show MVR 7.50 15.00
ROL019 Rezzard, Attoractia's Leading Doctor SR .30 .60
ROL020 Yggdrasil, Top Tourist Destination SR .50 1.00
ROL021 Abdul Alhazred, The Possessed R .20 .40
ROL022 Alvarez, True Demon Castle R .20 .40
ROL023 Dracula, Reborn Vampire // The Jewel of Darkness MVR4.00 8.00
ROL024 Frayla, Dark Huntress SR .75 1.50
ROL025 Ragnarok's Fiery Stone SR 2.00 4.00

2021 Force of Will The Seventh

TST001 Avatar of the Will of Amadeus R .75 1.50
TST002 Belial's Hymn N .12 .25
TST003 Belial's Messenger N .12 .25
TST004 Charlotte, Inheritor of the Seventh Power MVR 2.00 4.00
TST005 Choir of Fallen Angels R .75 1.50
TST006 Cradle of Fleeting Hope N .20 .40
TST007 Hand of the Void N .12 .25
TST008 Hunting Angel R .50 1.00
TST009 Prideful Rule R .75 1.50
TST010 Revealing the Power of Salvation N .12 .25
TST011 The Graveyard of Amadeus N .15 .30
TST012 The Seventh Boon: Amadeus, Holy Spear SR .30 .75
TST013 Cradle of Scorching Heat N .12 .25
TST014 Demon of Explosions N .12 .25
TST015 Envious Dragon R .30 .60
TST016 Fallen Angel of the Chasm R .30 .60
TST017 Flame of Oblivion N .15 .30
TST018 Prideful Fire N .12 .25
TST019 Raging Ogre N .15 .30
TST020 Swarming Cthulhu N .15 .30
TST021 The Second Boon: Tachyon, Holy Atom R .25 .50
TST022 Violet, Flame of Providence Distortion SR .30 .75
TST023 A Voice from the Void N .12 .25
TST024 Alecto, Unstoppable Fury SR .20 .40
TST025 Cradle of Biting Frost N .12 .25
TST026 Guide to the Center of the Demonic World N .20 .40
TST027 Mermaid of the Despairing Voice R .30 .75
TST028 Phantasmal Friend N .15 .30
TST029 Prideful Mermaid N .12 .25
TST030 Sky Ruler of the Demonic World R .30 .60
TST031 Tears of Corruption R .50 1.00
TST032 The Fifth Boon: Lightning Bolt, Bow R .20 .40
TST033 Wall of Terror N .15 .30
TST034 Agrade, Giant Pig R .15 .30
TST035 Attendant of Asmodeus N .12 .25
TST036 Brad, Masked Mage SR .75 1.50
TST037 Carlina's Storm R .30 .75
TST038 Cradle of Silent Earth N .12 .25
TST039 Pointy Hat's Camouflage N .12 .25
TST040 Prideful Mage N .20 .40
TST041 Starving Dragon N .15 .30
TST042 Table Manners N .12 .25
TST043 The Third Boon: Persona, Magic Mask R .50 1.00
TST045 Asmodeus' Demon R .30 .60
TST046 Asmodeus' Enchantment SR 1.00 2.00
TST047 Astema's Wrath N .12 .25
TST048 Banquet Demon R .15 .30
TST049 Belial's Favor N .12 .25
TST050 Black Rain N .15 .30
TST051 Castle of Asmodeus N .12 .25
TST052 Corpse Eater Dragon N .15 .30
TST053 Cradle of Crippling Despair N .15 .30
TST055 Fallen Angel of Black Tears R .60 1.25
TST056 Fallen Angel of Dusk N .12 .25
TST058 Invisible Terror N .12 .25
TST059 Marching of The Dead R .50 1.00
TST060 Selective Decapitation N .12 .25
TST061 The Fourth Boon: Last Regrets, Black Tears SR .75 1.50
TST062 Tisiphone, Avenging Fury SR .60 1.25
TST063 Vercilius, Rebel Against Satan MVR 4.00 8.00
TST064 Acheron, River of The Dead R .15 .30
TST065 Angel of False Glory MVR .75 1.50
TST066 Angel of False Life R .60 1.25
TST068 Astema's Cerberus R .60 1.25
TST069 Astema's Fury SR 1.00 2.00
TST071 Beatrice's Curse N .12 .25
TST072 Beatrice's Imagination SR .50 1.00
TST074 Belial's Rule SR 1.25 2.50
TST076 Carlina's Hunting SR .20 .40
TST077 Castle of Astema N .20 .40
TST078 Castle of Beatrice N .15 .30
TST079 Castle of Belial N .20 .40
TST080 Castle of Carlina N .25 .50
TST081 Demon of Pride and Greed R .20 .40
TST082 Fallen Angel of The Mark N .15 .30
TST083 Faria, Igniter of Holy Fire SR .75 1.50
TST084 Geryon MVR 7.50 15.00
TST085 Imaginary Dagon N .12 .25
TST086 Inferno MVR 1.00 2.00
TST087 Megaera, Jealous Fury SR .30 .75
TST088 Olivia, Skysplitting Thunderbolt SR .25 .50
TST089 The First Boon: Excalibur Cassius, Sword R .60 1.25
TST090 The Gate in The Center of The Demonic World R .20 .40
TST091 The Mimicking Beast N .12 .25
TST092 The Sixth Boon: Requiem, Jewel R .30 .75
TST093 Wolfgang, Prince of Amadeus SR .30 .60
TST095 Amadeus, Holy Crystal R .30 .75
TST096 Erythropia, Blood Stone R .75 1.50
TST097 Imaginary Satan, Magic Crystal R 7.50 1.50
TST044JR Asmodeus JR 4.00 8.00
TST054JR Dante, Fallen Angel JR 7.50 15.00
TST067JR Astema JR 7.50 15.00
TST070JR Beatrice JR 5.00 10.00
TST073JR Belial JR 7.50 15.00
TST075JR Carlina JR 12.50 25.00
TST094RR Satan R 10.00 20.00

2021 Force of Will Starter Deck Tales

DSD001 Barbatos, Aspiring Ascendant .12 .25
DSD002 Cthulhu's Intimidation .12 .25
DSD003 Flame Soldier of Ma'at .12 .25
DSD004 Flaming Salamander .12 .25
DSD005 Lovecraft, Dragon of Chaos .60 1.50
DSD006 Phantasmal Ascendant .20 .40
DSD007 Red Flame .12 .25
DSD008 Red Wine and Bread 1.00 2.00
DSD009 Spirit of Ma'at .12 .25
DSD010 Sudden Manifestation of Power .12 .25
DSD011 Nyarlathotep, Game Master 3.00 6.00
DSD023 Fire Magic Stone .12 .25

2021 Force of Will Starter Deck Villains

DSD012 Artillerist of Faith .15 .30
DSD013 Choir of the Valkyries .15 .30
DSD014 Geri and Freki, Greedy Wolves .15 .30
DSD015 Kara, Swift Valkyrie .20 .40
DSD016 Keep the Faith! .15 .30
DSD017 Praying Valkyrie .15 .30
DSD018 Randgrid .15 .30
DSD019 Repeating Faith Revival .15 .30
DSD020 Soldier of Minerva .15 .30
DSD021 The Holy Shield of Misteltein .15 .30
DSD022 Odin, God of War .15 .30
DSD024 Light Magic Stone .15 .30

2022 Force of Will 10th Anniversary Ruler Collection

RCS001RR Grimm, the Fairy Tale Prince JR 2.00 4.00
RCS002JR Pandora Box/Light JR 1.50 3.00
RCS003JR Pandora Box/Dark JR 1.50 3.00
RCS004JR Little Red Riding Hood/Wolf Girl JR 6.00 12.00
RCS005JR Snow White/Bloody Sn.White JR 1.50 3.00
RCS006JR Nameless Girl/Jeanne d'Arc JR 5.00 10.00
RCS007JR Seer of the Blue Moon/Kaguya JR 1.50 3.00
RCS008JR Christie/Helsing JR 1.50 3.00
RCS009JR Puss in Boots/D'Artagnan JR 1.50 3.00
RCS010JR Alucard/Dracula JR 7.50 15.00
RCS011JR Sacred Princess/Lumia JR 4.00 8.00
RCS012JR Falltgold/Bahamut JR 2.50 5.00
RCS013JR Alice in Wonderland/Drifter in the World JR 7.50 15.00
RCS014JR Crimson Girl/Little Red JR 7.50 15.00
RCS015JR Ebony Prophet/Abdul Alhazred JR 2.50 5.00
RCS016JR Pandora/Grimmia JR 1.50 3.00
RCS017JR Apostle of Creation/Cain JR 2.50 5.00
RCS018JR Moon Princess/Kaguya JR 2.00 4.00
RCS019JR Liberator of Wind/Scheherazade JR 3.00 6.00
RCS020JR Fiend of Dark Pyre/Nyarlathotep JR 4.00 8.00
RCS021JR Arla Winged Lord/Hegemon of the Sky JR 1.50 3.00
RCS022JR Faria Sacred Queen/Ruler of God Sword JR 2.00 4.00
RCS023RR Melgis Flame King/One Charmed by Demon Sword JR1.50 3.00
RCS024JR Valentina/Ruler of Paradise JR 2.50 5.00
RCS025JR Pricia Beast Lady/Commander of Sacred Beasts JR 7.50 15.00
RCS026JR Rezzard Undead Lord/Desecrating Vampire JR 1.50 3.00
RCS027JR Machina Machine Lord/Mechanical Emperor JR 1.50 3.00
RCS028JR Alice Girl in Looking Glass/Saint of Healing JR 1.50 3.00
RCS029JR Alice Girl in Looking Glass/Valkyrie of Fairy Tales JR 1.50 3.00
RCS030JR Blazer Gill Rabus JR 1.50 3.00
RCS031JR Alice Girl of the Lake/Fairy Queen JR 3.00 6.00
RCS032JR Sylvia Gill Palarilias JR 1.50 3.00
RCS033JR Valentina Plotting Lord of Seas
Overlord of Seven Lands JR 1.50 3.00
RCS034JR Reflect Child of Potential/Child of Convergence JR 7.50 15.00
RCS035JR Girl in Twilight Garb/Dark Alice JR 7.50 15.00
RCS036JR Friend from Another World, Kaguya/Moonlit Savior JR7.50 15.00
RCS037JR The Observer/Alisaris JR 1.50 3.00
RCS038JR Songstress of Shangri-La/Shion JR 1.50 3.00
RCS039RR Yggdrasil, the World Tree JR 1.50 3.00
RCS040JR Gill Lapis/Primogenitor JR 1.50 3.00
RCS041JR Memoria of the Seven Lands/Faria JR 1.50 3.00
RCS042JR Memoria of the Seven Lands/Melgis JR 1.50 3.00
RCS043JR Memoria of the Seven Lands/Machina JR 1.50 3.00
RCS044JR Memoria of the Seven Lands/Arla JR 1.50 3.00
RCS045JR Memoria of the Seven Lands/Rezzard JR 1.50 3.00
RCS046JR Zero, Six Sage of Light/Master of Magic Saber JR 12.50 25.00
RCS047JR Mars Fortuneteller of Fire Star
Dark Commander of Fire JR 1.50 3.00
RCS048JR Charlotte, Determined Girl/Mage of Sacred Spirit JR 1.50 3.00
RCS049JR Monkey King/Sun Wukong JR 1.50 3.00
RCS050JR Umr at-Tawil/Yog-Sothoth JR 1.50 3.00
RCS051JR Glorius/Faria JR 5.00 10.00
RCS052JR Valentina/Released Terror JR 1.50 3.00
RCS053JR Lilias Petal/Nine-Tailed Fox JR 1.50 3.00
RCS054JR Lumia Fated Rebirth/Saint of Crimson Lotus JR 20.00 40.00
RCS055JR Sol Hierophant of Helio Star
Dark Commander of Steam JR 1.50 3.00
RCS056JR Gill Alhama'at/Ebon Dragon Emperor
He Who Grasps All JR 1.50 3.00
RCS057JR Gill Lapis Conqueror of Attoractia
Rebel of Darkest Fires JR 1.50 3.00
RCS058JR Kaguya Tears of Moon/Millennium Princess JR 1.50 3.00
RCS059JR Millium Successor of the Dragon Crest/Sacred Dragon JR1.50 3.00
RCS060JR Pricia True Beastmaster/Rein.Maiden of Flame JR 7.50 15.00
RCS061JR Book of Light/Re-Earth JR 1.50 3.00
RCS062JR Swordsman of Fire/Adelbert JR 1.50 3.00
RCS063JR Dragon Shrine Maiden/Flute JR 6.00 12.00
RCS064RR Yggdrasil, Malefic Verdant Tree JR 1.50 3.00
RCS065JR Book of Dark/Lapistory JR 1.50 3.00
RCS066JR Pandora/Guardian of Sacred Temple JR 1.50 3.00
RCS067JR Faerur Letoliel/King of Wind JR 1.50 3.00
RCS068JR Frayla/Revolutionist JR 1.50 3.00
RCS069JR Taegrus Pearlshine/Lord of the Mountain JR 1.50 3.00
RCS070JR Welser Archmage/King of Demons JR 17.50 35.00
RCS071JR Ayu Lunar Swordswoman/Shaman Swordswoman JR12.50 25.00
RCS072JR Gill/Gifted Conjurer JR 1.50 3.00
RCS073JR Princess of Fleeting Hope/Aimul JR 1.50 3.00
RCS074JR Kirik Rerik/Draconic Warrior JR 1.50 3.00
RCS075JR Shaela/Mermaid Princess JR 7.50 15.00
RCS076JR Speaker of Eternal Night/Scheherazade JR 1.50 3.00
RCS077JR Dusk Girl/Scarlet Crimson Beast JR 1.50 3.00
RCS078JR Time Spinning Witch/Time Spinning Witch/Kaguya JR1.50 3.00
RCS079JR Ciel/Phantom Wind Fiethsing JR 1.50 3.00
RCS080JR Reiya, Fourth Daughter of Mikage JR 12.50 25.00
RCS081JR Lenneth, Priestess of Vell-Savaria JR 7.50 15.00
RCS082JR Machina JR 1.50 3.00
RCS083JR Arla JR 1.50 3.00
RCS084RR Reflect/Refrain JR 1.50 3.00
RCS085JR Rezzard JR 1.50 3.00
RCS086JR Gill Lapis JR 1.50 3.00
RCS087JR Dark Alice JR 25.00 50.00
RCS088JR Magna, the Creator of Regalia JR 1.50 3.00
RCS089JR Oborozuki, Star Sword Visionary JR 1.50 3.00
RCS090JR Lilias, Last Descendant of Dragonoids JR 1.50 3.00
RCS091JR Selesta, Treasure Hunter JR 1.50 3.00
RCS092JR Welser, the Progenitor of Magic JR 1.50 3.00
RCS093JR Mikage Seijuro, Interdimensional Messenger JR 1.50 3.00
RCS094RR Ragnarok, Invading Dragon Lord JR 7.50 15.00
RCS095JR Almerius JR 7.50 15.00
RCS096JR Zero, Apprentice Sage JR 1.50 3.00
RCS097JR Milest JR 1.50 3.00
RCS098JR Moojdart JR 15.00 30.00
RCS099JR Fiethsing JR 1.50 3.00
RCS100JR Grusbalesta JR 1.50 3.00
RCS101RR Wolfgang, Exiled Demon Prince JR 7.50 15.00
RCS102JR Excalibur Genesis/Faria JR 1.50 3.00
RCS103JR Violet, Atomic Automaton JR 5.00 10.00
RCS104JR Olivia, Thunder Empress JR 1.50 3.00
RCS105JR Brad, Immortal Sage JR 1.50 3.00
RCS106JR Wolfgang, Guide of the Demonic World JR 1.50 3.00
RCS107JR Asmodeus JR 7.50 15.00
RCS108JR Dante, Fallen Angel JR 7.50 15.00
RCS109JR Astema JR 7.50 15.00
RCS110JR Beatrice JR 6.00 12.00
RCS111JR Belial JR 1.50 3.00
RCS112JR Carlina JR 10.00 20.00
RCS113RR Satan JR 10.00 20.00
RCS114JR Millium, Prince of Light Palace
Voice of New Generation JR 1.50 3.00
RCS115JR Lunya Wolf Girl/Nyarlathotep JR 3.00 6.00
RCS116JR Mercurius, Wizard of Water Star
Dark Commander of Ice JR 3.00 6.00
RCS117JR Fiethsing, Six Sage of Wind
Master Magus of Holy Wind JR 7.50 15.00
RCS118JR Ally of the Black Moon/Mikage Seijuro JR 1.50 3.00
RCS119JR Gill Alhama'at He Who Controls the Taboo
Treasonous Emperor JR 1.50 3.00
RCS120JR Atom Seikhart/Shimmering Rabbit JR 7.50 15.00
RCS121JR Brunhild/Caller of Spirits JR 7.50 15.00
RCS122JR Fu Xi/King of Kunlun JR 1.50 3.00
RCS123JR Isis/Isis Hundred Weapon Master JR 1.50 3.00
RCS124JR Arthur/Arthur, King of Machines JR 1.50 3.00
RCS125JR Loki/Loki, the Witch of Chaos JR 10.00 20.00
RCS126JR Chamimi/Chamimi, Guardian of the Sacred Bow JR 1.50 3.00
RCS127JR Hanzo/Hanzo, Chief of the Kouga JR 1.50 3.00
RCS128JR Lich/Lich, the Saint of Death JR 1.50 3.00
RCS129JR Lucifer/Lucifer, Fallen Angel of Sorrow JR 1.50 3.00

RCS130JR Faria JR	1.50	3.00
RCS131JR Melgis JR	1.50	3.00
RCS132JR Pricia JR	7.50	15.00
RCS133RR Valentina JR	4.00	8.00
RCS134JR Guardian/Avatar of Light Magic Stones JR	4.00	8.00
RCS135JR Guardian/Avatar of Fire Magic Stones JR	1.50	3.00
RCS136JR Guardian/Avatar of Water Magic Stones JR	1.50	3.00
RCS137JR Guardian/Avatar of Wind Magic Stones JR	1.50	3.00
RCS138JR Guardian/Avatar of Darkness Magic Stones JR	1.50	3.00
RCS139JR Pricia Friend to the Animals/Champion of Yggdrasil JR	30.00	60.00
RCS140JR Alice Ally of Fairies/Paladin of Unwavering Hope JR	1.50	3.00
RCS141JR Acolyte of the Abyss/Alisaris JR	1.50	3.00
RCS142JR Vlad Tepes JR	1.50	3.00

2022 Force of Will A New World Emerges

NWE001N Angelic Battle Barrier N	1.00	2.00
NWE002N Bird of Solari N	.12	.25
NWE003RR Child of the Light Moon RUR	7.50	15.00
NWE004R First Regrets R	1.25	2.50
NWE005N Inquisitor of the Solaris Order N	.12	.25
NWE006SR Jeanne, Light Punisher of the Solaris Order SR	.50	1.00
NWE007N Judgmental Recovery N	.12	.25
NWE008N Phantasmal March Hare N	.12	.25
NWE009SR Raymond, Member of the Twelve Sacred Knights SR	2.50	5.00
NWE010R The King's Dragon R	.75	1.50
NWE011N Warhorse N	.50	1.00
NWE012SR Cecilia, Fire Punisher of the Solaris Order SR	.75	1.50
NWE013RR Child of the Fire Moon RUR	7.50	15.00
NWE014N Dragon of Solari N	.12	.25
NWE015R Gresia, Heretic of Solari R	.20	.40
NWE016N Head Shot N	.12	.25
NWE017SR Leowulf, Undefeated Warrior SR	1.00	2.00
NWE018N Magic Stone Researcher N	.12	.25
NWE019N Pillar of Flame N	.12	.25
NWE020N Purging Flames N	.12	.25
NWE021R Sprinting Steward R	1.25	2.50
NWE022N Supporter of the Rebellion N	.12	.25
NWE023R Charge of the Fairy Tale King R	.50	1.00
NWE024RR Child of the Water Moon RUR	3.00	6.00
NWE025N Confronting Eins N	.12	.25
NWE026N Justice Barrier N	.12	.25
NWE027SR Mikey, Jack of All Trades SR	4.00	8.00
NWE028N Mikey's Enormous Task N	.12	.25
NWE029N Moon Researcher N	.25	.50
NWE030N Phantasmal Dormouse N	.12	.25
NWE031SR Phantom of the Water Moon SR	1.00	2.00
NWE032N Shark of Solari N	.12	.25
NWE033RR Child of the Wind Moon RUR	3.00	6.00
NWE034R Deathspeaker Monk R	.20	.40
NWE035N Emergency Takeoff N	.12	.25
NWE036R Justice Hurricane R	.20	.40
NWE037SR Justice Punch SR	1.50	3.00
NWE038R Justice's Missile Pod R	.75	1.50
NWE039N Justice's Recon Drone N	.12	.25
NWE040N Misty Isle, Island of the Mumu Tribe N	.12	.25
NWE041N Mumu Tribe of Misty Isle N	.12	.25
NWE042N Ritual of the Mumu Tribe N	.12	.25
NWE043N Sacred Burial N	.30	.75
NWE044SR Sacred Tree of the Paramita of the Dead SR	.75	1.50
NWE045N Squirrel of Solari N	.20	.40
NWE046N Adventurer of Narrow Valley N	.12	.25
NWE047N All In N	.12	.25
NWE048SR Alpha, Owner of the Underground Fighting Arena SR	2.00	4.00
NWE049N Bat of Solari N	.25	.50
NWE050R Beros, Alpha's Watchdog R	.20	.40
NWE051RR Child of the Darkness Moon RUR	4.00	8.00
NWE052R Death Glare R	2.50	5.00
NWE053N Demon Bet Collector N	.20	.40
NWE054SR Hero Reincarnation SR	1.00	2.00
NWE055N Lore of Tsukuyomi N	.30	.60
NWE056N VIP Seats N	.25	.50
NWE057RR Aristella, Twin Prince RUR	12.50	25.00
NWE058RR Asuka, Gravekeeper of Tsukuyomi RUR	10.00	20.00
NWE059N Captain of the Heresy Hunt N	.12	.25
NWE060JR Fairy Tale King/Contract of the Water Moon RUR	3.00	6.00
NWE061N Daily Research N	.20	.40
NWE062JR Messiah/Decree of Absolution RUR	10.00	20.00
NWE063N Engineer of Eternal N	.25	.50
NWE064N Eternal, Artificial Archipelago N	.20	.40
NWE065JR Berserker/Extract of the Fire Moon RUR	5.00	10.00
NWE066RR Falchion, Solitary Scientist RUR	6.00	12.00
NWE067N Fistfighter of the Underground Fighting Arena N	.12	.25
NWE068RR Justice/Grandfather's Research Project RUR	2.50	5.00
NWE069MR Judgment of Solari MVR	4.00	8.00
NWE070RR Mika, Saint of the Solaris Order RUR	3.00	6.00
NWE071MR Muumuu, Servant of Falchion MVR	1.25	2.50
NWE072JR End of Night/Night of the Legendary Vampire RUR	6.00	12.00
NWE073N Night of the Phantom Moon N	.12	.25
NWE074N Painful Blow N	.12	.25
NWE075N Paramita of the Dead N	.12	.25
NWE076N Perfect Coordination N	.12	.25
NWE077N Phantasmal Mad Hatter N	.12	.25
NWE078MR Revenant MVR	6.00	12.00
NWE079MR Sealed One-Eyed Dragon MVR	10.00	20.00
NWE080N Silence of a Dark Night N	.12	.25
NWE081N Solari, Religious Nation N	.12	.25
NWE082JR Excalibur Chronogear/The Flight of the Holy Sword MVR	30.00	75.00
NWE083N The Great Wall of the Twelve Sacred Knights N	.30	.60
NWE084N Underground Fighting Arena in Narrow Valley N	.12	.25
NWE085RR Viga, Steadfast Steward RUR	7.50	15.00
NWE086N Zombie Returning from the Paramita of the Dead N	.30	.75
NWE087N Attack Trooper of Eins N	.12	.25
NWE088N Chronopawns N	.12	.25
NWE089N Defense Trooper of Eins N	.12	.25
NWE090RR Eins RUR	6.00	12.00
NWE091N Gearsification N	.20	.40
NWE092N Gearsification Facility of Solaris N	.20	.40
NWE093N Light of Solaris N	.12	.25
NWE094N Outer Space N	.25	.50
NWE095N Prototype Magi Trooper N	.30	.60
NWE096N Rain of Comets N	.12	.25
NWE097N Satellite Shield of Solaris N	.12	.25
NWE098JR Laevateinn Chronogear/The Flight of the Demon Sword RUR	25.00	50.00
NWE099SR The Three Wise Men SR	.75	1.50
NWE100SR Typhon, Asteroid Cluster SR	1.75	3.50
NWESEC1JR Fairy Tale King SCR	30.00	75.00
NWESEC2JR Messiah SCR	50.00	100.00
NWESEC3JR Berserker SCR	30.00	75.00
NWESEC4JR Justice SCR	30.00	75.00
NWESEC5JR End of Night SCR	30.00	75.00

2022 Force of Will Game of Gods Reloaded

GRL001 A Flashing Smile N	.20	.40
GRL002 A Fragment of Omniscient Power N	.20	.40
GRL003 Alice Enters the Game of Gods SR	3.00	6.00
GRL004 Alice's Fantastic Trick N	.15	.30
GRL005 Atom in the World of Duels R	1.50	3.00
GRL006 Ayu, Multidimensional Wanderer MVR	7.50	15.00
GRL007 Ayu's Little Friend N	.20	.40
GRL008 Charlotte, Chasing Light SR	3.00	6.00
GRL009 Deep Blue Soldier N	.20	.40
GRL010 Delphinius, Whale Hero R	2.00	4.00
GRL011 Fairy of Ma'at N	.15	.30
GRL012 Phantom Beastmaster of Ma'at N	.20	.40
GRL013 Strategy Meeting N	.15	.30
GRL014 Tea Party before the Decisive Duel R	3.00	6.00
GRL015 The Three Tea Party Members R	2.00	4.00
GRL016 Agni, God of Rampaging Flames SR	4.00	8.00
GRL017 Dedicated Duel N	.20	.40
GRL018 Hellfire of the Demonic World N	.30	.75
GRL019 Nyarlathotep Doll N	.30	.60
GRL020 Pricia, Dangerous Duelist SR	3.00	6.00
GRL021 Rogue Spectator N	.20	.40
GRL022 Shiva's Flame Aura N	.20	.40
GRL023 Tiny Dragon of Ma'at N	.20	.40
GRL024 Violet and Mariabella, Chasing Fire SR	2.50	5.00
GRL025 Arthur, Space-Time Knight R	2.00	4.00
GRL026 Crawler from Between the Cracks of Time N	.30	.60
GRL027 DeLorius, Space-Time Vehicle R	2.00	4.00
GRL028 Deus Ex Machina Enters the Game of Gods SR	3.00	6.00
GRL029 Falling into the Cracks of Time N	.15	.30
GRL030 Guinevere, Space-Time Watcher SR	2.50	5.00
GRL031 Knowledge from the Future N	.12	.30
GRL032 Lancelot, Space-Time Knight R	1.00	2.00
GRL033 Mass-Produced Knight of the Round Table N	.30	.60
GRL034 Setting the Stage for Providence N	.20	.40
GRL035 Space-Time Mage of Ma'at N	.20	.40
GRL036 Titor, Emissary from the Future MVR	6.00	12.00
GRL037 Titor's Gimmick N	.20	.40
GRL038 Unity of the Machine Knights N	.15	.30
GRL039 Back to Nature N	.20	.40
GRL040 Chamimi, Divine Power MVR	7.50	15.00
GRL041 Dinner Time N	.30	.60
GRL042 Giant Bird of Ma'at N	.20	.40
GRL043 Magellanica, Mimi Tribe Giant R	1.50	3.00
GRL044 Mimi Tribe Brave N	.20	.40
GRL045 Mimi Tribe Chef N	.15	.30
GRL046 Mimi Tribe Warrior N	.15	.30
GRL047 Rudra, God of Rampaging Winds SR	4.00	8.00
GRL048 Shiva Enters the Game of Gods SR	4.00	8.00
GRL049 Shiva's Encouragement N	.20	.40
GRL050 Shiva's Wind Aura N	.20	.40
GRL051 Sniper Shot R	1.00	2.00
GRL052 The Three Beast Warriors R	1.00	2.00
GRL053 Trishula R	1.25	2.50
GRL054 Amadeus, Beloved Fallen Angel MVR	7.50	15.00
GRL055 Chimeric Beast of Ma'at N	.15	.30
GRL056 Count Dracula R	3.00	6.00
GRL057 Dante Enters the Game of Gods SR	6.00	12.00
GRL058 Dante's Dark Wave N	.25	.50
GRL059 Dark Charlotte, Alternative SR	6.00	12.00
GRL060 Dark Sphere of Asmodeus N	.20	.40
GRL061 Defeated Arena Fighters N	.15	.30
GRL062 Excalibur Fallen R	1.50	3.00
GRL063 Fallen Angel in the Arena N	.15	.30
GRL064 Lucifer, Defeated One-Wing R	1.25	2.50
GRL065 The Tears of Amadeus N	.20	.40
GRL066 The World of Amadeus R	1.50	3.00
GRL067 Alice, Tales of Creation JR	15.00	30.00
GRL068 Arena Expansion: Demonic World R	2.50	5.00
GRL069 Arena Expansion: Linorsphairia R	1.50	3.00
GRL070 Arena Expansion: Mimi Tribe Festival R	1.00	2.00
GRL071 Arena Expansion: Sky Round v2.0 R	1.25	2.50
GRL072 Dante, Seven Deadly Sins JR	10.00	20.00
GRL073 Dark Alice in Ma'at MVR	12.50	25.00
GRL074 Dark Sphere of Astema N	.20	.40
GRL075 Dark Sphere of Beatrice N	.25	.50
GRL076 Dark Sphere of Belial N	.20	.40
GRL077 Dark Sphere of Carlina N	.20	.40
GRL078 Deus Ex Machina, God from Future Dimension JR	7.50	15.00
GRL079 Knight of Knights SR	2.50	5.00
GRL080 Rigveda SR	3.00	6.00
GRL081 Shiva, Providence of Nature JR	12.50	25.00
GRL082 Shoot the Mimi N	.15	.30
GRL083 Tales of Phantasia SR	5.00	10.00
GRL084 The Light of the Unknown N	.15	.30
GRL085 The Power of Zeus N	.20	.40
GRL086 The Seven Deadly Sins SR	3.00	6.00
GRL087 Vergilius, Chasing Darkness R	3.00	6.00
GRL088 Darkness Magic Stone NR	.12	.25
GRL089 Fire Magic Stone NR	.12	.25
GRL090 Light Magic Stone NR	.20	.40
GRL091 Water Magic Stone NR	.12	.25
GRL092 Wind Magic Stone NR	.12	.25

2022 Force of Will Game of Gods Reloaded Life Points

GRVLife001 Life Point	.30	.60
GRVLife002 Life Point	.30	.60
GRVLife003 Life Point	.30	.60
GRVLife004 Life Point	.30	.60
GRVLife005 Life Point	.30	.60
GRVLife006 Life Point	.30	.60
GRVLife007 Life Point	.30	.60
GRVLife008 Life Point	.30	.60
GRVLife009 Life Point	.30	.60
GRVLife010 Life Point	.30	.60
GRVLife011 Life Point	.30	.60
GRVLife012 Life Point	.30	.60

2022 Force of Will Game of Gods Reloaded Will Coins

GRVCoin001 Alice, Tales of Creation	.60	1.25
GRVCoin002 Dante, Seven Deadly Sins	.50	1.00
GRVCoin003 Deus Ex Machina, God from Future Dimension	.50	1.00
GRVCoin004 Shiva, Providence of Nature	.50	1.00

2022 Force of Will Game of Gods Revolution

GRV001 Apollon, the Third Olympian R	.50	1.00
GRV002 Regalia Beast N	.30	.60
GRV003 Roskva N	.25	.50
GRV004 The Essence of Alice's Power N	.15	.30
GRV005 The Essence of Odin's Power N	.30	.60
GRV006 The Light of Zeus N	.15	.30
GRV007 Thialfi N	.25	.50
GRV008 Thor, Reincarnated God of Thunder SR	.75	1.50
GRV009 Thor's Hammer R	.30	.75
GRV010 Zeus Enters the Game of Gods SR	2.50	5.00
GRV011 Apostle of Dragon Flame N	.20	.40
GRV012 Conclave at Dragon Mountain N	.15	.30
GRV013 Daji, Mass Produced Queen R	1.00	2.00
GRV014 Dragon Crystal R	.75	1.50
GRV015 Dragon Flame Enters the Game of Gods SR	3.00	6.00
GRV016 Hestia, the Sixth Olympian R	.50	1.00
GRV017 Increase Dragon Power! N	.30	.60
GRV018 Mechanized Armored Dragon N	.30	.75
GRV019 Mechanized Blade Dragon N	.30	.75
GRV020 Mechanized Flame Soldier N	.30	.60
GRV021 Pang Tong, Awakening Phoenix SR	1.25	2.50
GRV022 The Essence of Dragon Flame's Power N	.20	.40
GRV023 The Essence of Nyarlathotep's Power N	.15	.30
GRV024 The Fire of Zeus N	.30	.60
GRV025 Tiger and Dragon, Giant Futuristic Weapon SR	1.50	3.00
GRV026 Zhuge Liang, Perfect Strategist MVR	2.50	5.00
GRV027 Einsberg, Mechanized Invasion Leader MVR	3.00	6.00
GRV028 Mechanical Engineer of Ma'at N	.20	.40
GRV029 Mechanization R	.50	1.00
GRV030 Mechanized Fenrir SR	2.00	4.00
GRV031 Mechanized Water Soldier N	.15	.30
GRV032 Poseidon, the Second Olympian R	.50	1.00
GRV033 Terminator Drone N	.20	.40
GRV034 The Essence of Deus Ex Machina's Power N	.20	.40
GRV035 The Essence of Loki's Power N	.15	.30
GRV036 The Water of Zeus N	.30	.75
GRV037 Zweihunter, Mechanized Round Table Destroyer SR	2.00	4.00
GRV038 Algernon, Wise Observer SR	2.50	5.00
GRV039 Artemis, the Fifth Olympian R	.75	1.50
GRV040 Dreiwing, Mechanized Wind of Destruction R	2.00	4.00
GRV041 I Alone Am the World-Honored One N	.25	.50
GRV042 Shaka, Shiva's Successor SR	2.00	4.00
GRV043 Spirit of Growth N	.25	.50
GRV044 The Essence of Kaguya's Power N	.30	.60
GRV045 The Essence of Shiva's Power N	.15	.30
GRV046 The Wind of Zeus N	.30	.60
GRV047 Tree of Growth N	.30	.60
GRV048 Arena Expansion: Mount Othrys R	2.50	5.00
GRV049 Athenia Enters the Game of Gods SR	2.50	5.00
GRV050 Decay of the Machines R	1.00	2.00
GRV051 Echidna, Mechanized Monster R	3.00	6.00
GRV052 Gill Lapis, Vampire Guardian SR	2.00	4.00
GRV053 Hades, the Fourth Olympian R	1.50	3.00
GRV054 Lich, Immortal Saint R	.75	1.50
GRV055 Mechanized Children of Chronos N	.30	.40
GRV056 Mechanized Children of Gaia N	.15	.30
GRV057 Mikage Shinjuro SR	2.50	5.00
GRV058 Necromancer of Ma'at N	.20	.40
GRV059 Oborozuki, Vampire Astrologer MVR	7.50	15.00
GRV060 Spirit of Decay N	.20	.40
GRV061 The Darkness of Zeus N	.30	.75
GRV062 The Essence of Athenia's Power N	.20	.40
GRV063 The Essence of Dante's Power N	.20	.40
GRV064 Themis, Mechanized God of Law N	.30	.60
GRV065 Tree of Decay N	.30	.75
GRV066 Typhon's Antibodies N	1.50	3.00
GRV067 Typhon's Blood N	2.00	4.00
GRV068 Typhon's Cells R	1.50	3.00
GRV069 Typhon's Heart MVR	7.50	15.00
GRV070 Typhon's Wave of Terror N	.25	.50
GRV071 Aphrodite, the Tenth Olympian N	.20	.40
GRV072 Arena Expansion: Flourishing Bone Field R	.25	.50
GRV073 Arena Expansion: Mount Olympus R	.75	1.50
GRV074 Arena Expansion: Valley of the Dragons R	.75	1.50
GRV075 Ares, the Eighth Olympian N	.30	.60
GRV076 Athena, the Seventh Olympian N	.30	.75
GRV077 Athenia JR	12.50	25.00
GRV078 Death and Rebirth SR	6.00	12.00
GRV079 Dragon Flame JR	10.00	20.00
GRV080 Hera, the Ninth Olympian N	.25	.50
GRV081 Magna and Lenneth, the Twelfth Olympian MVR	5.00	10.00
GRV082 Persephone, the Eleventh Olympian N	.30	.75
GRV083 Supercalifragilisticexpialidocious Flame SR	5.00	10.00
GRV084 The Thunder of Zeus N	.15	.30
GRV085 Typhon, the Infinite Monster JR	25.00	50.00
GRV086 Typhonomachy, the Final Duel SR	1.50	3.00
GRV087 Zeus, the First Olympian JR	15.00	30.00
GRV088 Magic Stone of Infinity R	1.25	2.50
GRV089 The One Magic Stone R	2.00	4.00
GRV090 Darkness Magic Stone NR	.12	.25
GRV091 Fire Magic Stone NR	.12	.25
GRV092 Light Magic Stone NR	.12	.25
GRV093 Water Magic Stone NR	.12	.25
GRV094 Wind Magic Stone NR	.12	.25

2022 Force of Will Game of Gods Revolution Life Points

GRVLife001 Athenia Enters the Game of Gods	.50	1.00
GRVLife002 Death and Rebirth	.50	1.00
GRVLife003 Decay of the Machines	.50	1.00
GRVLife004 Dragon Flame Enters the Game of Gods	.50	1.00
GRVLife005 Supercalifragilisticexpialidocious	.50	1.00
GRVLife006 Increase Dragon Power!	.50	1.00
GRVLife007 Typhon's Wave of Terror	.50	1.00
GRVLife008 Typhon's Heart	.50	1.00
GRVLife009 Typhon's Cells	.50	1.00
GRVLife010 Zeus Enters the Game of Gods	.50	1.00
GRVLife011 Typhonomachy, the Final Duel	.50	1.00
GRVLife012 The Thunder of Zeus	.50	1.00

2022 Force of Will Game of Gods Revolution Will Coins

GRVCoin001 Athenia	.75	1.50
GRVCoin002 Dragon Flame	.75	1.50
GRVCoin003 Typhon, the Infinite Monster	.75	1.50
GRVCoin004 Zeus, the First Olympian	.75	1.50

2023 Force of Will Crimson Moon's Battleground

CMB000XR Crimson Moon's Battleground XR	5.00	10.00
CMB001RR Aristella, Ascendant Prince of the Crimson Moon RUR	4.00	8.00
CMB002JR Ascending to the Crimson Moon/Red Eyes RUR	7.50	15.00
CMB003N Battle Wolf of the Crimson Moon N	.30	.60
CMB004N Curse of Magog N	.30	.75
CMB005SR Light Curtain SR	3.00	6.00
CMB006R Light Palace, Phantasmal Moon Castle R	1.00	2.00
CMB007N Lingering Scent of Fairies N	.30	.75
CMB008N Mumu Tribe Researcher N	.30	.60
CMB009N Rabbit of the Crimson Moon N	.30	.60
CMB010SR Rumsfeld, Member of the Twelve Sacred Knights SR	2.50	5.00
CMB011R Spirits of the Crimson Moon R	.30	.75
CMB012N The End of the False Savior N	.30	.60
CMB013N The Last Believer N	.30	.75
CMB014MR Tinker Bell, Spirit of the Light Trials MVR	5.00	10.00
CMB015JR Armament Refinement/Elektra: Dragon Form RUR	5.00	10.00
CMB016N Armed Dog N	.30	.60
CMB017R Armed Dragon R	.30	.75
CMB018N Armed Weasel N	.30	.60
CMB019N Blade Dance N	.30	.60
CMB020SR Chevaleresse's Tears SR	3.00	6.00
CMB021N Gears Eater N	.30	.60
CMB022N Glorious Little Moon N	.30	.60
CMB023R Immortal Little Moon N	.60	1.25
CMB024MR Lone Wolf of the Crimson Moon MVR	4.00	8.00
CMB025SR Ryzenn, Fiery Clown SR	1.50	3.00
CMB026N The End of the War N	.30	.60
CMB027N Whispering of the Clown N	.30	.60
CMB028N Aspiring Diva N	.75	1.50
CMB029R Crystal Barrier R	.75	1.50
CMB030N Cyclone Emerges! N	.30	.60
CMB031R Cyclone, New Hero of Eternal R	.75	1.50
CMB032N Exploration Mission to the Crimson Moon N	.30	.60
CMB033SR Falchion, Designer of the Reunion SR	2.00	4.00
CMB034N Guardian of Eternal N	.30	.60
CMB035N Hologram of the Crimson Moon N	.30	.75
CMB036SR Last Movement SR	2.50	5.00
CMB037R Lasting Spirits of the Crimson Moon R	.30	.60
CMB038N Observing the Crimson Moon N	.30	.60
CMB039SR Ray Aznable, Reunion's Navigator SR	2.50	5.00

CMB040N Reunion's Head Chef N .30 .60
CMB041MR Brad, Amnesic Immortal MVR 7.50 15.00
CMB042SR Conflict of Memory and Soul SR 4.00 8.00
CMB043SR Garfie, Administrator of the Great Dimension Library SR2.50 5.00
CMB044N Garfie's Rejection N .30 .60
CMB045R Great Dimension Library R .75 1.50
CMB046N Inheritance of Magical Power N .30 .60
CMB047N Magic Stumblebug N .30 .60
CMB048N Rainbow Spirit N .30 .60
CMB049N Recalling Wind N .30 .60
CMB050R Reflect and Refrain, Guardian Twins of Coccon R .75 1.50
CMB051N Stone Monument of the Sage N .30 .60
CMB052R The Explosion of Magog R 2.00 4.00
CMB053N Topographer of Eternal N .30 .60
CMB054JR Armament Upgrade/Elektra: Horror Form RUR 3.00 6.00
CMB055N Black Rust Wolf N .30 .60
CMB056N Blade Shower N .30 .60
CMB057MR Carmilla, Armed Vampire MVR 3.00 6.00
CMB058N Curse of the Clown N .30 .60
CMB059R Cursed Cocoon R .75 1.50
CMB060N Cursed Warlord N .30 .60
CMB061N Demon of the Crimson Moon N .30 .60
CMB062SR Inntel, Dark Clown SR 3.00 6.00
CMB063N Roamer of the Crimson Moon N .30 .60
CMB064SR Roar of Dark Blessing SR 3.00 6.00
CMB065N Rotting Slime N .30 .60
CMB066N Sword Saint's Insight N .30 .60
CMB067RR Elektra, Armament Apex RUR 5.00 10.00
CMB068RR Reunion, Moon Battleship RUR 3.00 6.00
CMB069SR Ark's Descenders SR 2.50 5.00
CMB070SR Ark's Gears Grail SR 4.00 8.00
CMB071JR Attack Order/Genocider RUR 5.00 10.00
CMB072N Cowrie of Gears N .30 .75
CMB073JR Defense Order/Prisoner RUR 3.00 6.00
CMB074RR Imitation: Abel RUR 4.00 8.00
CMB075RR Imitation: Cain RUR 4.00 8.00
CMB076RR Imitation: Eve RUR 4.00 8.00
CMB077R Jeweled Branch of Gears R .75 1.50
CMB078N Jewels on Gears' Neck N .50 1.00
CMB079SR Minions of Tsuki-Hime SR 2.50 5.00
CMB080SR Moon Dust Revolution SR 1.25 2.50
CMB081JR Recapture Order/Queen RUR 3.00 6.00
CMB082N Robe of Fire-Gears N .30 .60
CMB083N Stone Bowl of Gears N .30 .60
CMB084MR Tsuki-Hime, Gears Princess of the Moon MVR 6.00 12.00
CMB085SRR Bow and Arrows SRR 1.50 3.00
CMB086SRR Chain-Sickle SRR 2.50 5.00
CMB087SRR Flame Earrings SRR 2.50 5.00
CMB088SRR Longsword SRR 2.50 5.00
CMB089SRR Rapier SRR 2.50 5.00
CMB090SRR Devil Spear SRR 2.50 5.00
CMB091SRR Dragon Armor of the God of War SRR 2.50 5.00
CMB092SRR Amulet Orb SRR 2.50 5.00
CMB093SRR Battle Flag SRR 2.50 5.00
CMB094SRR Headband SRR 2.50 5.00
CMB095SRR Rough Magic Stone SRR 3.00 6.00
CMB096SRR War Horn SRR 3.00 6.00
CMB097SRR Cursed Sword SRR 3.00 6.00
CMB098SRR Horror, Armor of the God of Death SRR 3.00 6.00
CMB099 Light Magic Stone .30 .75
CMB100 Fire Magic Stone .30 .75
CMB101 Water Magic Stone .30 .75
CMB102 Wind Magic Stone .30 .75
CMB103 Darkness Magic Stone .30 .75

2023 Force of Will Heroes' Contract Pack

HCP001JR The Flight of the Holy Sword/Excalibur Chronogear RUR12.5025.00
HCP002JR Decree of Absolution/Messiah RUR 7.50 15.00
HCP002JR The Flight of the Demon Sword
Laevateinn Chronogear RUR 7.50 15.00
HCP003JR Extract of the Fire Moon/Berserker RUR 7.50 15.00
HCP005JR Grandfather's Research Project/Justice RUR 7.50 15.00
HCP006JR Launch of Megiddo/Mover of Worlds RUR 7.50 15.00
HCP007JR Memory of Worlds/Recorder of Worlds RUR 10.00 20.00
HCP008JR Divine Lightning/Predator RUR 10.00 20.00
HCP009JR Metamorphosis/Dendrobium RUR 6.00 12.00
HCP010JR Rocket Dive/Pink Spider RUR 7.50 15.00
HCP011JR Soul Absorption/The Ethereal King RUR 7.50 15.00
HCP012JR Twin Deathscythe, Severing Scythe
Deathscythe Chronogear RUR 7.50 15.00

2023 Force of Will The War of the Suns

TWS001RR Actor Drei, Savior Child RUR 3.00 6.00
TWS002R Age of Famine R 1.00 2.00
TWS003N Angel of the False Savior N .20 .40
TWS004RR Child of Famine RUR 2.50 5.00
TWS005N Famished Wolf N .20 .40
TWS006N Followers of the False Savior N .20 .40
TWS007R Guidance of the False Savior R 1.25 2.50
TWS008SR Jeanne, Famished Punisher of the Solaris Order SR 1.25 2.50
TWS009N Locusts from Paradise N .20 .40
TWS010R Olgaria, Member of the Twelve Sacred Knights R 2.00 4.00
TWS011N Olgaria's Last Epistle N .20 .40
TWS012N Photon Drive N .20 .40
TWS013N Prevalence of Famishment N .30 .75
TWS014N Rains of Saints N .20 .40
TWS015SR Replicant: Aimul SR 3.00 6.00
TWS016MR Startail, Dragon from Outer Space MVR 4.00 8.00
TWS017JR Summon the Wolf of Famine! // Artemis Chronogear RUR7.5015.00
TWS018R Age of War R 1.00 2.00
TWS019N Arms Dealer of Solari N .20 .40
TWS020SR Cecilia, Warring Punisher of the Solaris Order SR 1.25 2.50
TWS021R Charge of Infinite Blades R 1.25 2.50
TWS022RR Chevaleresse Acht, Thousand Blades RUR 4.00 8.00
TWS023N Chevaleresse's Hatred N .20 .40
TWS024RR Child of War RUR 2.50 5.00
TWS025N Flighter of the Underground Fighting Arena N .30 .75
TWS026N Hymn of Triumph N .20 .40
TWS027N Necromancy of Cursed Spirits N .30 .60
TWS028MR Raging Messiah MVR 4.00 8.00
TWS029SR Replicant: Scarlet SR 2.00 4.00
TWS030N Scarlet's Explosion N .25 .50
TWS031N Spirit in Dis N .30 .75
TWS032JR Summon the Charger of War! // Ifrit
Glass Chronogear RUR 7.50 15.00
TWS033R Warring Dragon R .60 1.25
TWS034N Warring Mercenary N .20 .40
TWS035R Age of Reign R 1.00 2.00
TWS036RR Child of Reign RUR 2.50 5.00
TWS037N Constriction of Reign N .25 .50
TWS038SR Dissonance of Reign SR 1.00 2.00
TWS039N Dolce N .20 .40
TWS040N Einsatz N .25 .50
TWS041N Forbidden Malus N .20 .40
TWS042MR Little Maria, Archaic Legacy MVR 3.00 6.00
TWS043R Melody of Reign R 1.00 2.00
TWS044R Mifa, Serenade's Agent R 1.00 2.00
TWS045N Mysterious Snake N .25 .50
TWS046N Paradise Lost N .25 .50
TWS047SR Rain of Serpents SR 2.00 4.00
TWS048RR Serenade Vier, Tragic Diva RUR 2.00 4.00
TWS049N Serpent of Temptation N .20 .40
TWS050N Sonic Siren N .20 .40
TWS051JR Summon the Serpent of Reign! // Gleipnir
Chronogear RUR 4.00 8.00
TWS052N Aggressor from the Future N .20 .40
TWS053RR Child of Eclipse RUR 3.00 6.00
TWS054R Eternal, Assaulted Archipelago R .75 1.50
TWS055N Generate Replicant N .20 .40
TWS056N Growing Egg N .20 .40
TWS057N Keeper of Dynamics N .20 .40
TWS058N Keeper of Static N .20 .40
TWS059SR Magog, Artificial Eclipse SR 1.25 2.50
TWS060N Overwhelming Difference of Power N .20 .40
TWS061SR Replicant: Scheherazade SR 1.00 2.00
TWS062R Shelley, Olgaria's Partner Bird R 1.25 2.50
TWS063R The Descent of Ulga R 1.25 2.50
TWS064N The End of the Book N .20 .40
TWS065JR The Sword of Progression // Genesis Chronogear RUR7.50 15.00
TWS066R The Sword of Regression R 1.00 2.00
TWS067RR Ulga, Eclipser RUR 4.00 8.00
TWS068N Wings of Genesis N .20 .40
TWS069R Age of Death R 1.00 2.00
TWS070R Alpha, Money Zombie of the Decayed Arena R .75 1.50
TWS071N Assistant of Dark Feather N .50 1.00
TWS072SR Blessing of Dark Feather SR 1.25 3.00
TWS073RR Child of Death RUR .25 .50
TWS074N Corrosion of Dark Feather N .30 .60
TWS075N Dark Scorpion of Blessing N .30 .75
TWS076RR Deathwing Funf, Dark Feather RUR 2.50 5.00
TWS077N Dragon of Magog N .30 .75
TWS078MR Imaginary God of the Fallen MVR 3.00 6.00
TWS079N Laboratory of Blessing N .30 .75
TWS080R Leowulf, Undead Warrior R .75 1.50
TWS081N Perished Punisher N .30 .75
TWS082N Pillar of Graveflame N .25 .50
TWS083SR Sprout of the Treasure Tree of Magog SR 2.00 4.00
TWS084JR Summon the Dragon of Death! // Unknown
Mother Goose Chronogear RUR 7.50 15.00
TWS085N Thought Conversion N 2.00 4.00
TWS086SR Aristella's World Conference SR .75 1.50
TWS087SR Civil War in Solari SR .60 1.25
TWS088N Emergency Barrier of the Wanderer Twins N .30 .60
TWS089N Excavation of a Legacy N .30 .75
TWS090N Ki Lua: Fossil Girl in the City** N .50 1.25
TWS091SR Maamuu, Restoration King of the Mumu Tribe SR .75 1.50
TWS092JR Repairing the Deathscythe //
Deathscythe Rebooted RUR 7.50 15.00
TWS093N Spy Mission N .50 1.00
TWS094SR The End of the Undefeated Legend SR 3.00 6.00
TWS095N The Ethereal King and The Dragon of Death N .25 .50
TWS096R Magic Stone of Famine R 1.25 2.50
TWS097R Magic Stone of War R 2.00 4.00
TWS098R Magic Stone of Reign R 2.50 5.00
TWS099R Magic Stone of Progress R 1.50 3.00
TWS100R Magic Stone of Death R 1.25 2.50
TWS101R Magic Stone of Eclipse R 1.50 3.00
TWSSEC1JR Summon the Wolf of Famine!
Artemis Chronogear SCR 15.00 30.00
TWSSEC2JR Summon the Charger of War!/I
frit Glass Chronogear SCR 40.00 80.00
TWSSEC3JR Summon the Serpent of Reign!
Gleipnir Chronogear SCR 7.50 15.00
TWSSEC4JR The Sword of Progression/Genesis Chronogear SCR60.00125.00
TWSSEC5JR Summon the Dragon of Death!
Unknown Mother Goose Chronogear SCR 10.00 20.00
TWSSEC6JR Repairing the Deathscythe/Deathscythe Rebooted SCR15.0030.00

2023 Force of Will The War of the Suns Will Coins

TWSCoin001 Actor Drei 1.00 2.00
TWSCoin002 Chevaleresse 1.00 2.00
TWSCoin003 Serenade Vier 1.00 2.00
TWSCoin004 Ulga 1.00 2.00
TWSCoin005 Deathwing Funf 1.00 2.00

2020 MetaZoo Cryptid Nation Christmas Promos

1 Santa Claus R 600.00 1,200.00
2 Santa's Bag R 150.00 300.00
3 Abominable Snowman R 400.00 800.00
4 Gingerbread Man R 200.00 400.00
5 North Pole 125.00 250.00
6 New Year's New Beginnings R 150.00 300.00

2020 MetaZoo Cryptid Nation Halloween Pack

1 Headless Horseman R 500.00 1,000.00
2 Wendigo R 250.00 500.00
3 Treat-No-Trick U 200.00 400.00
4 Fright Night U 200.00 400.00
5 Beastie Bash U 150.00 300.00

2020 MetaZoo Cryptid Nation Sample Set

1 Aura Battery R 300.00 600.00
2 Aura Generator R 200.00 400.00
3 Aura Potion C 125.00 250.00
4 Babe The Blue Ox R 750.00 1,500.00
5 Batsquatch C 75.00 150.00
6 Bigfoot R 1,000.00 2,000.00
7 Billdad C 75.00 150.00
8 Bloodlust R 500.00 1,000.00
9 Boohag C 150.00 300.00
10 Book of Shadows U 200.00 400.00
11 Broom C 150.00 300.00
12 Bunny Man C 150.00 300.00
13 Cactus Cat C 75.00 150.00
14 Chaos Crystal R 2,000.00 4,000.00
15 Chupacabra R 1,000.00 2,000.00
16 Cosmic Aura C 125.00 250.00
17 Crawfordsville Monster R 300.00 600.00
18 Cumberland Dragon R 1,500.00 3,000.00
19 Dark Aura C 150.00 300.00
20 Dark Crystal R 300.00 600.00
21 Death Beam R 250.00 500.00
22 Dingbelle R 200.00 400.00
23 Dover Demon R 250.00 500.00
24 Dragon's Breath R 400.00 800.00
25 Dual Permafrost U 100.00 200.00
26 Earth Aura C 200.00 400.00
27 Eternal Snowflake R 250.00 500.00
28 Exorcist's Nail C 125.00 250.00
29 Fire Aura C 125.00 250.00
30 Fireball C 125.00 250.00
31 Fire Elemental R 750.00 1,500.00
32 Fire Trap U 75.00 150.00
33 Flatwoods Monster R 250.00 500.00
34 Forest Aura C 75.00 150.00
35 Forest God's Amber R 200.00 400.00
36 Fountain Of Youth R 600.00 1,200.00
37 Fresno Nightcrawlers R 300.00 600.00
38 Frost Aura C 100.00 200.00
39 Funeral Mountain Terrashot C 125.00 250.00
40 Gee-Gee Bird C 200.00 400.00
41 Ghost Train R 600.00 1,200.00
42 Giant Salamander C 300.00 600.00
43 Giant Space Brains R 400.00 800.00
44 Grim Reaper R 500.00 1,000.00
45 Growth R 600.00 1,200.00
46 Health Potion C 100.00 200.00
46 Headless Horseman R 1,500.00 3,000.00
48 Hodag R 300.00 600.00
49 Hopkinsville Goblin R 750.00 1,500.00
50 Indrid Cold R 1,000.00 2,000.00
51 Jackalope C 150.00 300.00
52 Jersey Devil R 750.00 1,500.00
53 Johnny Appleseed C 200.00 400.00
54 Kentucky Hellhound U 300.00 600.00
55 Kushtaka R 1,000.00 2,000.00
56 Light Aura C 200.00 400.00
57 Lightning Aura C 150.00 300.00
58 Lightning Bolt C 150.00 300.00
59 Lightning Crystal R 400.00 800.00
60 Loveland Frogman R 2,500.00 5,000.00
61 Matlox C 100.00 200.00
62 Men In Black R 1,000.00 2,000.00
63 Metal Man Of Alabama R 250.00 500.00
64 Minnesota Iceman U 150.00 300.00
65 Mothman R 1,000.00 2,000.00
66 Nain Rouge C 200.00 400.00
67 Napa Rebobs C 75.00 150.00
68 Old Saybrook Blockheads R 300.00 750.00
69 Ozark Howler U 200.00 400.00
70 Paul Bunyan R 1,500.00 3,000.00
71 Piasa Bird R 1,250.00 2,500.00
72 Pope Lick Monster U 300.00 600.00
73 Pukwudgie C 150.00 300.00
74 Quezalcoatlus R 750.00 1,500.00
75 Razored Leaf C 75.00 150.00
76 River Dinos C 125.00 250.00
77 Rubberado C 150.00 300.00
78 Sam Sinclair R 2,500.00 5,000.00
79 Sewer Alligator C 100.00 200.00
80 Shock Aura U 150.00 300.00
81 Sin Hole Sam R 200.00 400.00
82 Squonk U 200.00 400.00
83 The Char Man U 125.00 250.00
84 Thorned Whip U 150.00 300.00
85 Tizheruk R 200.00 400.00
86 Tripodero C 125.00 250.00
87 Twin Meteor U 300.00 600.00
88 UFO R 1,500.00 3,000.00
89 Van Meter Visitor R 500.00 1,000.00
90 Walking Sam R 1,000.00 2,000.00
91 Water Aura C 100.00 200.00
92 White Thang C 125.00 250.00
93 Wendigo R 2,000.00 4,000.00

2021 MetaZoo Cryptid Nation 1st Edition

1 Chupacabra R 12.50 25.00
2 Jersey Devil R 20.00 40.00
3 Mothman R 200.00 400.00
4 Bigfoot R 30.00 60.00
5 Hodag R 15.00 30.00
6 Lizard Man of Scape Ore Swamp R 10.00 20.00
7 Snallygaster R 6.00 12.00
8 Uncle Sam R 20.00 40.00
9 Walking Sam R 7.50 15.00
10 Chessie R 20.00 40.00
11 Loveland Frogman R 30.00 75.00
12 Besat of Busco R 6.00 12.00
13 Flatwoods Monster R 7.50 15.00
14 Fresno Nightcrawlers R 7.50 15.00
15 Sinkhole Sam R 7.50 15.00
16 Slide-Rock Bolter R 6.00 12.00
17 Piasa Bird R 25.00 50.00
18 Babe the Blue Ox R 12.50 25.00
19 Tizheruk R 12.50 25.00
20 Sam Sinclair R 40.00 80.00
21 Metal Man of Alabama R 10.00 20.00
22 Quetzalcoatlus R 20.00 40.00
23 Death Beam R 25.00 50.00
24 Growth R 30.00 40.00
25 Powerup Red R 25.00 50.00
26 Phoenix Rain R 20.00 40.00
27 Silver Bullet R 20.00 40.00
28 Ghost Train R 25.00 50.00
29 Blood Ruby R 6.00 12.00
30 Forest God's Amber R 7.50 15.00
31 Chaos Crystal R 60.00 125.00
32 Black Hole Shard R 7.50 15.00
33 Earth's Core R 6.00 12.00
34 Unending Fire Crystal R 7.50 15.00
35 Eternal Snowflake R 6.00 12.00
36 Holy Gem R 7.50 15.00
37 Lightning Glass R 6.00 12.00
38 Medium's Third Eye R 7.50 15.00
39 Mermaid Scales R 6.00 12.00
40 Black Cat U .50 1.00
41 Salem's Witches U .50 1.00
42 Batsquatch C 1.25 2.50
43 Bunny Man C .25 .50
44 Chibi Mothman C 1.00 2.00
45 Killer Clown C 1.25 2.50
46 Shadow People C 1.25 2.50
47 Crossroads U .75 1.50
48 Gluttony U 1.25 2.50
49 Necromancy C .75 1.50
50 Book of Shadows U 1.00 2.00
51 Broom C 1.25 2.50
52 The Skeletons' Lanterns C .50 1.00
53 Hide Behind U .30 .60
54 Hoop Snake U 1.50 3.00
55 Squonk U 1.00 2.00
56 Gumberoo C 1.25 2.50
57 Joint Snake C 1.00 2.00
58 River Dinos C .75 1.50
59 Rumptifusel C .30 .75
60 Sliver Cat C .30 .75
61 Wapaloosie C 1.50 3.00
62 Powerup Green U 1.50 3.00
63 Thorned Whip U .30 .75
64 Poison Arrow C .50 1.00
65 Sam's 4-Leaf Clover C 1.50 3.00
66 White Thang C .25 .50
67 Balancing Beam U .50 1.00
68 Powerup Blue U 1.25 2.50
69 Scatterscot U .75 1.50
70 Antidote C .25 .50
71 Bookmark C 1.00 2.00
72 Catnap C .30 .75
73 Pass Trap C .50 1.00
74 Chaos Potion C 1.50 3.00

75 Luck Potion U 1.00 2.00
76 Enfield Monster U .30 .60
77 Moon-Eyed People C .25 .50
78 Space Penguins C .75 1.50
79 Alien Astronaut C .25 .50
80 Proton Beam U 1.00 2.00
81 Transfiguration U .75 1.50
82 Antimagic Field C .60 1.25
83 Funeral Mountain Terrashot U 1.25 2.50
84 Cactus Cat C 1.25 2.50
85 Matlox C .75 1.50
86 Tripodero C 1.00 2.00
87 Rock Rain U 1.00 2.00
88 Stoneskin U .30 .75
89 Earthquake U 1.25 2.50
90 Kentucky Hellbound U 1.50 3.00
91 Giant Salamander C .30 .60
92 Lava Bear C 1.50 3.00
93 Dragon's Breath U .75 1.50
94 Fire Trap U .75 1.50
95 Exploding Mine C 1.25 2.50
96 Fireball C .75 1.50
97 Gee-Gee Bird C .75 1.50
98 Snow Snake C .75 1.50
99 Snow Wasset C .25 .50
100 Frozen People C 1.00 2.00
101 Ice Spell U 2.00 4.00
102 Ice Storm U .75 1.50
103 Icy Path U 1.00 2.00
104 Menehune U 1.25 2.50
105 Miracle Touch U .75 1.50
106 Retribution U .75 1.50
107 Lightbeam U 1.25 2.50
108 Sam's EMF Device C .75 1.50
109 Sam's Rabbit Foot C .25 .50
110 Health Potion C .60 1.25
111 Chibi Quetza U .75 1.50
112 Grounding U .30 .60
113 Haste C 1.50 3.00
114 Lightning Bolt C 1.50 3.00
115 Paralyze C 1.25 2.50
116 Shock Aura U .30 .60
117 Lightning in a Bottle U .30 .60
118 Huggin' Molly U 1.50 3.00
119 The Spookster U .75 1.50
120 Ghost Deer C .75 1.50
121 Old Green Eyes C 1.00 2.00
122 Morpheus U .50 1.00
123 Pyrokinetic Blast C .75 1.50
124 Telekinesis C .50 1.00
125 Lake Worth Monster C 1.25 2.50
126 Sewer Alligator C .60 1.25
127 Fog of War U 1.50 3.00
128 Invisibility U 1.00 2.00
129 Reflection C .75 1.50
130 Water Gun C .75 1.50
131 Dark Aura C .60 1.25
132 Forest Aura C .60 1.25
133 Cosmic Aura C 1.00 2.00
134 Earth Aura C .60 1.25
135 Flame Aura C .60 1.25
136 Frost Aura C .60 1.25
137 Light Aura C .75 1.50
138 Lightning Aura C .50 1.00
139 Spirit Aura C .50 1.00
140 Water Aura C .60 1.25
141 Meteor Shower 2.50 5.00
142 Stars 1.50 3.00
143 Nighttime 1.00 2.00
144 Desert .75 1.50
145 Ground .75 1.50
147 Mountain 1.50 3.00
148 Snowing 1.00 2.00
149 Winter .75 1.50
150 Daytime .75 1.50
151 Lightning Storm 1.25 2.50
152 Farm 1.25 2.50
153 Suburban 2.00 4.00
154 City 1.50 3.00
155 Lake .75 1.50
156 Ocean .75 1.50
157 Raining 1.50 3.00
158 River C 1.25 2.50
159 Island 1.00 2.00

2021 MetaZoo Cryptid Nation 1st Edition Christmas Promos

1 Prism Beam Tree Topper 1.25 2.50
2 Eternal Snowflake Snowball .75 1.50
3 Snowman .60 1.25
4 Dingbelle on the Shelf 1.50 3.00
5 Mistletoe .75 1.50
6 New Year's Celebrations 2.00 4.00

2021 MetaZoo Cryptid Nation 1st Edition Halloween Promos

1 Chaos Crystal Crunch 2.50 5.00
2 Piasa Bird's Peach Rings 3.00 6.00
3 Headless Horseman's Pumpkin Gummies 2.50 5.00
4 Kinderhook Krackle Bar 2.00 4.00
5 Ludwig's Lemondrops 1.50 3.00

2021 MetaZoo Cryptid Nation 1st Edition Pin Club Mystery Collection

1a Mothman 12.50 25.00
2a Piasa Bird 3.00 6.00
3a Babe the Blue Ox 2.50 5.00
4 Jersey Devil 3.00 6.00
5 Flatwoods Monster 2.50 5.00
6 Joint Snake 2.50 5.00
7 Bigfoot 4.00 8.00
8 Sinkhole Sam 3.00 6.00
9 Sewer Alligator 3.00 6.00
10 Squonk 2.00 4.00

2021 MetaZoo Cryptid Nation 1st Edition Theme Deck Alpha Iceman

1 Alpha Minnesota Iceman R 2.50 5.00
2 Kushtaka R 1.25 2.50
3 Minnesota Iceman U 1.25 2.50
4 Gee-Gee Bird C 1.00 2.00
5 White Thang C 1.25 2.50
6 Icy Path U 1.50 3.00
7 Slow U .50 1.00
8 Bookmark C 1.00 2.00
9 Eternal Snowflake R 1.50 3.00
10 Chaos Crystal R 5.00 10.00
11 Snowing .50 1.00
12 Frost Aura .75 1.50

2021 MetaZoo Cryptid Nation 1st Edition Theme Deck Dingbelle Ring Leader

2 Dingbelle C 1.25 2.50
3 Ball Lightning C 1.00 2.00
4 Terror Bird C .50 1.00
5 Lightning Bolt C 1.00 2.00
6 Haste C 1.50 3.00
7 Distraction C 1.00 2.00
8 Bookmark C 1.00 2.00
9 Lightning Glass R 3.00 6.00
10 Chaos Crystal R 2.00 4.00
11 Lightning Storm 1.25 2.50
12 Lightning Aura .50 1.00

2021 MetaZoo Cryptid Nation 1st Edition Theme Deck Hopkinsville Goblin King

1 Hopkinsville Goblin King R 4.00 8.00
2 Hopkinsville Goblin U .75 1.50
3 Boohag C 1.00 2.00
4 Bunny Man C 2.00 4.00
5 Death Beam U 4.00 8.00
6 Bog U 1.50 3.00
7 Necromancy C 3.00 6.00
8 Bookmark C 1.00 2.00
9 Blood Ruby R 2.00 4.00
10 Chaos Crystal R 4.00 8.00
11 Nighttime 4.00 8.00
12 Dark Aura C 1.00 2.00

2021 MetaZoo Cryptid Nation 1st Edition Theme Deck Pukwudgie Chieftain

1 Pukwudgie Chieftain R 1.50 3.00
2 Pukwudgie C 1.00 2.00
3 Agropelter C 1.00 2.00
4 Mantis Man C 1.00 2.00
5 Roperite C 3.00 6.00
6 Thorned Whip U 2.00 4.00
7 Razored Leaf C 1.00 2.00
8 Bookmark C 1.00 2.00
9 Forest God's Amber R 1.50 3.00
10 Chaos Crystal R 5.00 10.00
11 Forest 5.00 10.00
12 Forest Aura .50 1.00

2021 MetaZoo Cryptid Nation 1st Edition Theme Deck Salamander Queen

1 Salamander Queen R 4.00 8.00
2 Giant Salamander C 1.00 2.00
3 Fire Elemental C 1.50 3.00
4 The Char Man C 2.00 4.00
5 Spontaneous Combustion C 2.00 4.00
6 Fire Enchant C .50 1.00
7 Fireball C 3.00 6.00
8 Bookmark C 1.00 2.00
10 Chaos Crystal R 7.50 15.00
11 Desert 2.50 5.00
12 Flame Aura C 3.00 6.00

2021 MetaZoo Cryptid Nation 2nd Edition

1 Chupacabra G .30 .75
2 Jersey Devil G .60 1.25
3 Mothman G 15.00 30.00
4 Bigfoot G 1.00 2.00
5 Hodag G .50 1.00
6 Lizard Man of Scape Ore Swamp G .50 1.00
7 Snallygaster G .30 .75
8 Uncle Sam G 2.50 5.00
0 Walking Sam G 1.25 2.50
10 Chessie G 1.50 3.00
11 Loveland Frogman G 5.00 10.00
12 Beast of Busco G .25 .50
13 Flatwoods Monster G .25 .50
14 Fresno Nightcrawlers G 1.25 2.50
15 Sinkhole Sam G .30 .60
16 Slide-Rock Bolter G .50 1.00
17 Piasa Bird G 1.25 2.50
18 Babe the Blue Ox G .50 1.00
19 Tizheruk G .60 1.25
20 Sam Sinclair G 4.00 8.00
21 Metal Man of Alabama G 1.00 2.00
22 Quetzalcoatlus G 7.50 15.00
23 Death Beam G 2.50 5.00
24 Growth G 3.00 6.00
25 Powerup Red G 10.00 20.00
26 Phoenix Rain G 4.00 8.00
27 Silver Bullet G 3.00 6.00
28 Ghost Train G 3.00 6.00
29 Blood Ruby G 1.25 2.50
30 Forest God's Amber G 1.00 2.00
31 Chaos Crystal G 3.00 6.00
32 Black Hole Shard G 1.25 2.50
33 Earth's Core G .60 1.25
34 Unending Fire Crystal G .75 1.50
35 Eternal Snowflake G 1.50 3.00
36 Holy Gem G 1.50 3.00
37 Lightning Glass G 1.50 3.00
38 Medium's Third Eye G 2.50 5.00
39 Mermaid Scales G .75 1.50
40 Black Cat S .15 .30
41 Salem's Witches S .15 .30
42 Batsquatch B .12 .25
43 Bunny Man B .12 .25
44 Chibi Mothman B .12 .25
45 Killer Clown B .12 .25
46 Shadow People B .12 .25
47 Crossroads S .15 .30
48 Gluttony S .15 .30
49 Necromancy B .12 .25
50 Book of Shadows S .15 .30
51 Broom B .12 .25
52 The Skeletons' Lanterns B .12 .25
53 Hide Behind S .15 .30
54 Hoop Snake S .15 .30
55 Squonk S .15 .30
56 Gumberoo B .12 .25
57 Joint Snake B .12 .25
58 River Dinos B .12 .25
59 Rumptifusel B .12 .25
60 Sliver Cat B .12 .25
61 Wapaloosie B .12 .25
62 Powerup Green S .15 .30
63 Thorned Whip S .15 .30
64 Poison Arrow B .12 .25
65 Sam's 4-Leaf Clover B .12 .25
66 White Thang B .12 .25
67 Balancing Beam S .15 .30
68 Powerup Blue S .15 .30
69 Scattershot S .15 .30
70 Antidote B .12 .25
71 Bookmark B .12 .25
72 Catnap B .12 .25
73 Pass Trap B .12 .25
74 Chaos Potion B .12 .25
75 Luck Potion S .15 .30
76 Enfield Monster S .15 .30
77 Moon-Eyed People B .12 .25
78 Space Penguins B .12 .25
79 Alien Astronaut B .12 .25
80 Proton Beam S .15 .30
81 Transfiguration S .15 .30
82 Antimagic Field B .12 .25
83 Funeral Mountain Terrashot S .15 .30
84 Cactus Cat B .12 .25
85 Matlox B .12 .25
86 Tripodero B .12 .25
87 Rock Rain S .15 .30
88 Stoneskin S .15 .30
89 Earthquake S .15 .30
90 Kentucky Hellhound S .25 .50
91 Giant Salamander B .12 .25
92 Lava Bear B .12 .25
93 Dragon's Breath S .15 .30
94 Fire Trap S .15 .30
95 Exploding Mine B .12 .25
96 Fireball B .12 .25
97 Gee-Gee Bird B .12 .25
98 Snow Snake B .12 .25
99 Snow Wasset B .12 .25
100 Frozen People B .12 .25
101 Ice Spell S .15 .30
102 Ice Storm S .15 .30
103 Icy Path S .15 .30
104 Menehune S .15 .30
105 Miracle Touch S .15 .30
106 Retribution S .15 .30
107 Lightbeam S .15 .30
108 Sam's EMF Device B .12 .25
109 Sam's Rabbit Foot B .12 .25
110 Health Potion B .12 .25
111 Chibi Quetza S .15 .30
112 Grounding S .15 .30
113 Haste B .12 .25
114 Lightning Bolt B .12 .25
115 Paralyze B .12 .25
116 Shock Aura S .15 .30
117 Lightning in a Bottle S .50 1.00
118 Huggin' Molly S .15 .30
119 The Spookster S .15 .30
120 Ghost Deer B .12 .25
121 Old Green Eyes B .12 .25
122 Morpheus S .15 .30
123 Pyrokinetic Blast B .15 .30
124 Telekinesis B .25 .50
125 Lake Worth Monster B .20 .40
126 Sewer Alligator B .25 .50
127 Fog of War S .15 .30
128 Invisibility S .20 .40
129 Reflection B .12 .25
130 Water Gun B .12 .25
131 Dark Aura B .12 .25
132 Forest Aura B .12 .25
134 Earth Aura B .12 .25
135 Flame Aura B .12 .25
136 Frost Aura B .12 .25
137 Light Aura B .12 .25
138 Lightning Aura B .12 .25
139 Spirit Aura B .12 .25
140 Water Aura NR .12 .25
141 Meteor Shower NR .20 .40
142 Stars NR .12 .25
143 Nighttime NR .12 .25
144 Desert NR .20 .40
145 Ground NR .12 .25
146 Forest B .15 .30
147 Mountain NR .15 .30
148 Snowing NR .20 .40
149 Winter NR .15 .30
150 Daytime NR .12 .25
151 Lightning Storm NR .12 .25
152 Farm NR .15 .30
153 Suburban NR .12 .25
154 City NR .20 .40
155 Lake NR .12 .25
156 Ocean NR .12 .25
157 Raining NR .12 .25
158 River NR .12 .25
159 Island NR .12 .25

2021 MetaZoo Cryptid Nation 2nd Edition Box-Toppers

1 Meteor Shower 7.50 15.00
2 Raining 7.50 15.00
3 Stars 7.50 15.00
4 Nighttime 10.00 20.00
5 Ground 7.50 15.00
6 Mountain 7.50 15.00
7 Snowing 7.50 15.00
8 Lightning Storm 10.00 20.00
9 City 7.50 15.00
10 Ocean 7.50 15.00
NNO Blue Ink SCR/159* 1,000.00 2,000.00

2021 MetaZoo Cryptid Nation 2nd Edition Christmas Promos

1 Santa Claus 5.00 10.00
2 Santa's Bag 2.50 5.00
3 Abominable Snowman 4.00 8.00
4 Gingerbread Man 2.00 4.00
5 North Pole 3.00 6.00
6 New Year's New Beginnings 30.00 60.00

2021 MetaZoo Cryptid Nation 2nd Edition Halloween Promos

1 Headless Horseman 15.00 30.00
2 Wendigo 12.50 25.00
3 Treat-No-Trick 3.00 6.00
4 Fright Night 7.50 15.00
5 Beastie Bash 4.00 8.00

2021 MetaZoo Cryptid Nation Box Promos

1 Cryptid Nation R 4.00 8.00
2 Mothman R 5.00 10.00

2021 MetaZoo Cryptid Nation Kickstarter Edition

1 Chupacabra R 20.00 40.00
2 Jersey Devil R 25.00 50.00
3 Mothman R 150.00 300.00
4 Bigfoot R 75.00 150.00
5 Hodag R 75.00 150.00
6 Lizard Man of Scape Ore Swamp R 30.00 75.00
7 Snallygaster R 15.00 30.00
8 Uncle Sam R 125.00 250.00
9 Walking Sam R 50.00 100.00
10 Chessie R 30.00 75.00

11 Loveland Frogman R	175.00	350.00
12 Besat of Busco R	50.00	100.00
13 Flatwoods Monster R	20.00	40.00
14 Fresno Nightcrawlers R	25.00	50.00
15 Sinkhole Sam R	10.00	20.00
16 Slide-Rock Bolter R	30.00	75.00
17 Piasa Bird R	30.00	75.00
18 Babe the Blue Ox R	100.00	200.00
19 Tizheruk R	50.00	100.00
20 Sam Sinclair R	250.00	500.00
21 Metal Man of Alabama R	30.00	75.00
22 Quetzalcoatlus R	50.00	100.00
23 Death Beam R	150.00	300.00
24 Growth R	125.00	250.00
25 Powerup Red R	75.00	150.00
26 Phoenix Rain R	75.00	150.00
28 Ghost Train R	75.00	150.00
29 Blood Ruby R	30.00	75.00
30 Forest God's Amber R	30.00	60.00
31 Chaos Crystal R	300.00	600.00
32 Black Hole Shard R	15.00	30.00
33 Earth's Core R	20.00	40.00
34 Unending Fire Crystal R	60.00	125.00
35 Eternal Snowflake R	60.00	120.00
36 Holy Gem R	50.00	100.00
37 Lightning Glass R	12.50	25.00
38 Medium's Third Eye R	75.00	150.00
39 Mermaid Scales R	50.00	100.00
40 Black Cat U	2.50	5.00
41 Salem's Witches U	4.00	8.00
42 Batsquatch C	3.00	6.00
43 Bunny Man C	3.00	6.00
44 Chibi Mothman C	2.50	5.00
45 Killer Clown C	3.00	6.00
46 Shadow People C	1.50	3.00
47 Crossroads U	3.00	6.00
48 Gluttony U	2.00	4.00
49 Necromancy C	1.50	3.00
50 Book of Shadows U	2.00	4.00
51 Broom C	2.00	4.00
52 The Skeletons' Lanterns C	2.50	5.00
53 Hide Behind U	2.50	5.00
54 Hoop Snake U	2.00	4.00
55 Squonk U	2.00	4.00
56 Gumberoo C	3.00	6.00
57 Joint Snake C	2.00	4.00
58 River Dinos C	1.50	3.00
59 Rumptifusel C	1.50	3.00
60 Sliver Cat C	1.50	3.00
61 Wapaloosie C	1.50	3.00
62 Powerup Green U	2.00	4.00
63 Thorned Whip U	2.00	4.00
64 Poison Arrow C	1.50	3.00
65 Sam's 4-Leaf Clover C	1.50	3.00
66 White Thang C	1.50	3.00
67 Balancing Beam U	2.50	5.00
68 Powerup Blue U	2.00	4.00
69 Scatterscot U	2.00	4.00
70 Antidote C	1.50	3.00
71 Bookmark C	2.50	5.00
72 Catnap C	2.00	4.00
73 Pass Trap C	1.50	3.00
74 Chaos Potion C	3.00	6.00
75 Luck Potion U	4.00	8.00
76 Enfield Monster U	2.50	5.00
77 Moon-Eyed People C	1.50	3.00
78 Space Penguins C	3.00	6.00
79 Alien Astronaut C	2.50	5.00
80 Proton Beam U	2.00	4.00
81 Transfiguration U	2.00	4.00
82 Antimagic Field C	2.00	4.00
83 Funeral Mountain Terrashot U	2.00	4.00
84 Cactus Cat C	2.00	4.00
85 Matlox C	2.00	4.00
86 Tripodero C	1.50	3.00
87 Rock Rain U	2.00	4.00
88 Stoneskin U	2.50	5.00
89 Earthquake U	2.50	5.00
90 Kentucky Hellbound U	3.00	6.00
91 Giant Salamander C	2.50	5.00
92 Lava Bear C	2.00	4.00
93 Dragon's Breath U	3.00	6.00
94 Fire Trap U	2.00	4.00
95 Exploding Mine C	1.50	3.00
96 Fireball C	1.50	3.00
97 Gee-Gee Bird C	2.00	4.00
98 Snow Snake C	2.50	5.00
99 Snow Wasset C	2.50	5.00
100 Frozen People C	3.00	6.00
101 Ice Spell U	2.00	4.00
102 Ice Storm U	2.00	4.00
103 Icy Path U	2.50	5.00
104 Menehune U	2.50	5.00
105 Miracle Touch U	2.00	4.00
106 Retribution U	2.00	4.00
107 Lightbeam U	2.00	4.00
108 Sam's EMF Device C	1.50	3.00
109 Sam's Rabbit Foot C	1.50	3.00
110 Health Potion C	4.00	8.00
111 Chibi Quetza U	2.00	4.00
112 Grounding U	2.50	5.00
113 Haste C	2.50	5.00
114 Lightning Bolt C	2.50	5.00
115 Paralyze C	1.50	3.00
116 Shock Aura U	2.00	4.00
117 Lightning in a Bottle U	2.50	5.00
118 Huggin' Molly U	3.00	6.00
119 The Spookster U	2.00	4.00
120 Ghost Deer C	2.50	5.00
121 Old Green Eyes C	2.00	4.00
122 Morpheus U	3.00	6.00
123 Pyrokinetic Blast C	2.50	5.00
124 Telekinesis C	3.00	6.00
125 Lake Worth Monster C	3.00	6.00
126 Sewer Alligator C	1.50	3.00
127 Fog of War U	4.00	8.00
128 Invisibility U	3.00	6.00
129 Reflection C	1.50	3.00
130 Water Gun C	1.50	3.00
131 Dark Aura C	10.00	20.00
132 Forest Aura C	7.50	15.00
133 Cosmic Aura C	5.00	10.00
134 Earth Aura C	6.00	12.00
135 Flame Aura C	7.50	15.00
136 Frost Aura C	4.00	8.00
137 Light Aura C	7.50	15.00
138 Lightning Aura C	6.00	12.00
139 Spirit Aura C	6.00	12.00
140 Water Aura C	1.50	3.00
141 Meteor Shower	5.00	10.00
142 Stars	25.00	50.00
143 Nighttime	7.50	15.00
144 Desert	12.50	25.00
145 Ground	5.00	10.00
146 Forest	5.00	10.00
147 Mountain	7.50	15.00
148 Snowing	3.00	6.00
150 Daytime	4.00	8.00
151 Lightning Storm	10.00	20.00
152 Farm	17.50	35.00
153 Suburban	12.50	25.00
154 City	12.50	25.00
156 Ocean	7.50	15.00
157 Raining	7.50	15.00
158 River C	7.50	15.00
159 Island	10.00	20.00

2021 MetaZoo Cryptid Nation Nightfall 1st Edition

1 Grim Reaper G	.50	1.00
2 Headless Horseman G	.50	1.00
3 Indrid Cold G	.75	1.50
4 Mothman G	1.00	2.00
5 Wendigo G	.75	1.50
6 Guardian Angel G	.30	.75
7 Adam Ackler G	.20	.40
8 Dark Watchers G	.20	.40
9 Frank Shaw's Gargoyle G	.20	.40
10 Grafton Monster G	.20	.40
11 Headless Coal Miner G	1.00	2.00
12 Momo G	.20	.40
13 Wood Devil of Coos Country G	.20	.40
14 Jack Frost G	.30	.60
15 Thunderbird G	1.00	2.00
16 Bell Witch G	.20	.40
17 The Red Ghost G	.20	.40
18 Oklahoma Octopus G	.20	.40
19 Divine Covenant G	.30	.60
20 Prism Beam G	.20	.40
21 Righteous Reckoning G	.60	1.25
22 Borne From The Earth G	.50	1.00
23 Abduction G	.20	.40
24 Boil Over G	.20	.40
25 Alaskan Vortex G	.20	.40
26 Lightning Split G	.20	.40
27 Flood The Earth G	2.00	4.00
28 River Of Time G	1.50	3.00
29 Potion Seller G	.20	.40
30 Stalactites G	.30	.60
31 Hell's Gate G	.25	.50
32 Hope Diamond G	.30	.75
33 Obsidian Obelisk G	.20	.40
34 Twin Meteor G	.50	1.00
35 Old Book's Crying Tree G	.25	.50
36 Permafrost G	.20	.40
37 Lightning Alley G	.20	.40
38 Boogeyman S	.15	.30
39 Dover Demon S	.15	.30
40 The Werewolf Of Defiance S	.15	.30
41 Vampire Mercy Brown S	.20	.40
42 Beast of Bladenboro B	.12	.25
43 Cabbagetown Tunnel Monster B	.12	.25
44 Ludwig B	.12	.25
45 Napa Rebobs B	.50	1.00
46 Bloodlust S	.15	.30
47 Sinister Shadows S	.15	.30
48 Zombie Apocalypse S	.15	.30
49 Nightmare B	.12	.25
50 Imprisonment B	.12	.25
51 Smokey Spirits B	1.25	2.50
52 Headless Nun S	.15	.30
53 Belled Buzzard B	.12	.25
54 Light Elemental B	.15	.30
55 Banish S	.15	.30
56 Destroy Evil S	.15	.30
57 Holy Eyes S	.15	.30
58 Blessed B	.12	.25
59 Sam's Holy Water B	.12	.25
60 Water To Wine B	.12	.25
61 Crystallized Light S	.15	.30
62 Trinity Amulet B	.12	.25
63 Destroy Terra S	.15	.30
64 Feign Death S	.15	.30
65 Index S	.30	.60
66 Absorb Aura B	.30	.75
67 Aura Prowess B	.12	.25
68 Destroy Aura B	.12	.25
69 Land Tax NR	.15	.30
70 Tribal Warcry B	.15	.30
71 Tribe Tirade B	.15	.30
72 Boost Aura S	.15	.30
73 Caster Center, MD S	.15	.30
74 The Purple Blob Of Philadelphia S	.15	.30
75 Veggieman S	.15	.30
76 Air Rods B	.12	.25
77 Crazy Critter of Bald Mountain B	.12	.25
78 Kinderhook Blob B	.12	.25
79 Cosmic Warp B	.12	.25
80 Brain In A Jar S	.15	.30
81 Murphysboro Mud Monster S	.15	.30
82 Teihiihan B	.12	.25
83 Tuttle Bottoms Monster B	.20	.40
84 Wunk B	.12	.25
85 Earth's Binding S	.15	.30
86 Excavation B	.12	.25
87 Graveyard's Mud S	.15	.30
88 Feu Follet B	.12	.25
89 Teakettler B	.12	.25
90 Jack-O-Lantern Bomb S	.20	.40
91 Unholy Fire S	.15	.30
92 Pyre B	.12	.25
93 Smokescreen B	.12	.25
94 Bubbling Brew S	.15	.30
95 Arkansas Snipe B	.12	.25
96 Axehandle Hound B	.12	.25
97 Lufferlang B	.12	.25
98 Bursting Spiderlings S	.15	.30
99 Jack-O-Lantern B	.12	.25
100 Nightshade S	.30	.60
101 Exquisite Stew S	.15	.30
102 Qalupalik S	.15	.30
103 A-Mi-Kuk B	.12	.25
104 Iliamna Lake Monster B	.20	.50
105 Great Blizzard S	.15	.30
106 Frostbite B	.12	.25
107 Iceberg B	.12	.25
108 Copy Cup S	.15	.30
109 Poltergeist B	.12	.25
110 The Colombia River Sand Squink B	.20	.40
111 Simultaneous Bioluminescence S	.15	.30
112 Witch's Lightning S	.15	.30
113 Static Wand B	.12	.25
114 Spooky Kite S	.15	.30
115 Dark Lightning Orb B	.12	.25
116 Specter Moose S	.15	.30
117 Black-Eyed Children B	.12	.25
118 Familiar B	.12	.25
119 Robert The Doll S	.15	.30
120 Halloween Ghost Sheet B	.12	.25
121 Possession B	.12	.25
122 Unlucky Potion S	.15	.30
123 Bloody Bones S	.15	.30
124 The Bandage Man Of Cannon Beach B	.20	.40
125 Wallowa Lake Crustacean B	.12	.25
126 Water Baby Of Massacre Rock B	.12	.25
127 Dampen S	.15	.30
128 Torrential River S	.20	.40
129 Mermaid's Shimmer B	.12	.25
130 Dark Aura B	.12	.25
131 Light Aura B	.12	.25
132 Cosmic Aura B	.12	.25
133 Earth Aura B	.12	.25
134 Flame Aura B	.12	.25
135 Forest Aura B	.12	.25
136 Frost Aura B	.12	.25
137 Lightning Aura B	.12	.25
138 Spirit Aura S	.15	.30
139 Water Aura NR	.15	.30
140 Meteor Shower NR	.15	.30
141 Stars NR	.25	.50
142 Nighttime NR	.30	.75
143 Full Moon NR	.15	.30
144 Desert NR	.15	.30
145 Ground NR	.15	.30
146 Swamp NR	.30	.60
147 Forest NR	.15	.30
148 Mountain NR	.30	.75
149 Snowing NR	.20	.40
150 Winter NR	.15	.30
151 Dawn NR	.75	1.50
152 Daytime NR	.15	.30
153 Dusk NR	.15	.30
154 Lightning Storm NR	.25	.50
155 Farm NR	.15	.30
156 Suburban NR	.30	.60
157 City NR	.15	.30
158 Fog NR	.30	.60
159 Lake NR	.15	.30
160 Ocean NR	.15	.30
161 Raining NR	.30	.75
162 River NR	.25	.50
163 Island NR	.15	.30

2021 MetaZoo Cryptid Nation Nightfall 1st Edition Pin Club Mystery Collection

1 Mothman	12.50	25.00
2 Wendigo	7.50	15.00
3 Headless Horseman	4.00	8.00
3 Teakettler	3.00	6.00
5 Kinderhook Blob	2.00	4.00
6 Adam Ackler	2.00	4.00
7 The Red Ghost	1.25	2.50
8 Momo	1.50	3.00
9 Indrid Cold	2.50	5.00
10 Crazy Critter of Bald Mountain	1.00	2.00
11 Wood Devil of Coos County	2.50	5.00
12 Flying Manta Ray	2.50	5.00
13 Poltergeist	1.50	3.00
14 A-Mi-Kuk	1.50	3.00
15 Feu Follet	1.00	2.00
1A4 Headless Horseman ALT ART	10.00	20.00
3A4 Wendigo ALT ART	60.00	125.00

2021 MetaZoo Cryptid Nation Nightfall Theme Deck Elder Matlox

1 Elder Matlox	.75	1.50
2 Grafton Monster	.25	.50
3 Matlox	.15	.30
4 Murphysboro Mud Monster	.15	.30
5 Teihiihan	.15	.30
6 Earth's Binding	.15	.30
7 Rock Rain	.30	.75
8 Powerup Red	4.00	8.00
9 Bookmark	.25	.50
10 Borne from the Earth	1.00	2.00
11 Index	.50	1.00
12 New Beginnings	1.25	2.50
13 Graveyard Mud	.25	.50
14 Ground	.15	.30
15 Mountain	.15	.30
16 Earth Aura	.15	.30

2021 MetaZoo Cryptid Nation Nightfall Theme Deck Flying Manta Ray

1 Flying Manta Ray	2.00	4.00
2 Chessie	1.25	2.50
3 The Bandage Man of Cannon Beach	.15	.30
4 Bloody Bones	.20	.40
5 Wallowa Lake Crustacean	.50	1.00
6 Water Baby of Massacre Rock	.50	1.00
7 Dampen	.50	1.00
8 Flood the Earth	1.25	2.50
9 Mermaid's Shimmer	.25	.50
10 Torrential River	.15	.30
11 New Beginnings	1.25	2.50
12 Mermaid's Scales	.75	1.50
13 Lake	.15	.30
14 River	.50	1.00
15 Water Aura	.15	.30

2021 MetaZoo Cryptid Nation Nightfall Theme Deck Reptoid Ruler

1 Reptoid Ruler	7.50	15.00
2 Flatwoods Monster	1.50	3.00
3 Air Rods	.15	.30
4 Kinderhook Blob	.30	.75
5 Space Penguins	.40	.80
6 Abduction	.25	.50
7 Powerup Red	4.00	8.00
8 Bookmark	.25	.50
9 New Beginnings	2.50	5.00
10 Tribal Warcry	.30	.75
11 Stars	.30	.60
12 Cosmic Aura	.25	.50

2021 MetaZoo Cryptid Nation Nightfall Theme Deck Stikini Owl

1 Stikini Owl	1.50	3.00
2 Black-Eyed Children	.20	.40
3 Familiar	.15	.30
4 Specter Moose	.15	.30
5 The Spookster	.25	.50
6 Morpheus	.30	.60
7 Possession	.25	.50

8 Powerup Red	4.00	8.00
9 Bookmark	.25	.50
10 New Beginnings	1.50	3.00
11 Unlucky Potion	.50	1.00
12 Nighttime	.30	.75
13 Spirit Aura	.15	.30

2021 MetaZoo Cryptid Nation Nightfall Theme Deck The Ghost Marshall

1 The Ghost Marshall	1.50	3.00
2 Headless Nun	.15	.30
3 Light Elemental	.15	.30
4 Banish	.50	1.00
5 Prism Beam	.15	.30
6 Bookmark	.30	.60
7 Index	.50	1.00
8 New Beginnings	1.00	2.00
9 Silver Bullet	.30	.75
10 Lightning in a Bottle	.75	1.50
11 Light Aura	.15	.30

2022 MetaZoo Cryptid Nation Nightfall ReVive Skateboard Promos

1 Babe the Blue Ox G/150*	75.00	150.00
2 Bigfoot G/300*	30.00	75.00
3 Hodag G/300*	50.00	100.00
4 Jersey Devil G/300*	50.00	100.00
5 Loveland Frogman G/150*	150.00	300.00
6 Metal Man of Alabama G/300*	20.00	40.00
7 Mothman G/50*	600.00	1,200.00
8 Piasa Bird G/300*	100.00	200.00
9 Sam Sinclair G/150*	30.00	75.00

2022 MetaZoo Cryptid Nation Seance 1st Edition

1 Edgar Cayce G	.30	.60
2 Lady of the Lake G	.30	.60
3 Walking Sam G	30.00	60.00
4 Wingoc G	.30	.75
5 Basket Ogress G	.30	.60
6 Chasse-Galerie G	.30	.60
7 Sentry Box Devil G	.60	1.25
8 Callopode G	.30	.60
9 Brown Mountain Lights G	.30	.60
10 Cisco Grove Entities G	.30	.60
11 Black Aggie G	.30	.60
12 Humpledumple G	.30	.60
13 Casey Jones G	.30	.60
14 Ghosts of the Sloss Furnaces G	.30	.60
15 Sheepsquatch G	15.00	30.00
16 Alaskan Ice Monster G	.30	.60
17 Glacial Demon G	.40	.80
18 Lady Luck G	30.00	75.00
19 Copenhagen Devil G	.30	.60
20 Splinter Cat G	.30	.60
21 Manchac Swamp Sunken Skeletons G	.40	.80
22 Shawnahooc G	.50	1.00
23 Cursed Contract G	40.00	80.00
24 Spirit Storm G	.30	.60
25 Satanic Panic! G	30.00	75.00
26 Embedding The Soul G	30.00	75.00
27 Chains of Old Scratch G	40.00	80.00
28 Planchette G	.30	.60
29 Frost Shield G	.30	.60
30 Medium's Crystal Eye G	.30	.60
31 Reaper's Crown G	.50	1.00
32 Houdini's Hat G	.30	.60
33 Space Rock Dagger G	.30	.60
34 Sunken Gravestones of Manchac G	.50	1.00
35 Jagged Peaks Orb G	.30	.60
36 Calcified Dunes Orb G	.30	.60
37 Hidden Grove Orb G	.30	.60
38 Natural Chaos Orb G	.30	.60
39 Heat Lightning Orb G	.30	.60
40 Possessed Aura G	125.00	250.00
41 Black Dog Of The Hanging Hills S	.12	.25
42 Hag of Detroit S	.12	.25
43 Sackabilly S	.12	.25
44 Dark Fortune S	.12	.25
45 Permanent Possession S	.12	.25
46 Fetish Artifact S	.12	.25
47 D.C. the Demon Cat B	.10	.20
48 Drowned Pianist B	.10	.20
49 Not Deer B	.10	.20
50 Clairvoyance B	.10	.20
51 Ectoplasm B	.10	.20
52 The Hierophant B	.10	.20
53 Talking Board B	.20	.40
54 The Gargoyle S	.12	.25
55 All Hallows' Eve S	.12	.25
56 Death S	.12	.25
57 Blood Grimoire S	.12	.25
58 Chibi Salem's Witches B	.10	.20
59 Green Thing B	.10	.20
60 Stickman of Clark County B	.10	.20
61 Third Eye Man B	.10	.20
62 Black Mass B	.25	.50
63 Boojum B	.10	.20
64 Temperance B	.10	.20
65 Magic Scarecrow B	.10	.20
66 Sam's Cryptid Cam B	.10	.20
67 Colorado Springs Elf B	.10	.20
68 Kissie Bug B	.10	.20
69 Materialize B	.10	.20
70 Dybbik Box B	.10	.20
71 Sam's Backpack B	.10	.20
72 Bay Rum B	.10	.20
73 Black Helicopter S	.12	.25
74 Martian Bees S	.12	.25
75 Element 115 S	.12	.25
76 Mince Pie Martian B	.10	.20
77 The Betz Sphere B	.30	.75
78 Solar Bathing Ritual B	.10	.20
79 The Moon B	.20	.40
80 Dimension in a Bottle B	.10	.20
81 Cement Worm S	.12	.25
82 Tommyknocker S	.12	.25
83 The World B	.10	.20
84 Giraffe Possum B	.10	.20
85 Rocky Mountain Barking Spider B	.10	.20
86 Tomb Effigy B	.20	.40
87 Cairn B	.20	.40
88 Fireship of Baie Des Chaleurs S	.12	.25
89 Demonic Evocation S	.12	.25
90 Wheel of Fortune S	.12	.25
91 Burned Cross Ghost B	.10	.20
92 Scorched Pages B	.40	.80
93 Burning Effigies B	.25	.50
94 Scry by Fire B	.10	.20
95 Orange Eyes S	.12	.25
96 Tailybones S	.12	.25
97 Ghost Forest S	.12	.25
98 Goofus Bird B	.10	.20
99 Wazooey Man B	.10	.20
100 Whintosser B	.25	.50
101 The Lovers B	.10	.20
102 Witch's Blight B	.20	.40
103 Chibi Babe the Blue Ox S	.12	.25
104 Ice Worm S	.12	.25
105 The Hermit S	.12	.25
106 Alaskan Platypus B	.10	.20
107 Snow Ghost B	.10	.20
108 Sky Burial B	.10	.20
109 Sam's Scarf B	.10	.20
110 Bolt of Life S	.12	.25
111 Disbanding Energy S	.12	.25
112 Token Plasm Pool S	.12	.25
113 Bourgeoisie Birds B	.10	.20
114 EVP B	.10	.20
115 Static Attraction B	.10	.20
116 Ectoplasmic Sludge B	.10	.20
117 The Kind Ghost S	.12	.25
118 The Empress S	.12	.25
119 The Fool S	.12	.25
120 Scroll of Spirit Control S	.12	.25
121 Habitat B	.10	.20
122 Locked Contract B	.10	.20
123 Appendix B	.20	.40
124 Token Potion B	.20	.40
125 Phantom Steamboat of the Tombigbee S	.12	.25
126 Spiteful Mermaid of Pyramid Lake S	.12	.25
127 The Tower S	.12	.25
128 Boathound B	.10	.20
129 Seashell Divination B	.10	.20
130 Spontaneous Voyage B	.10	.20
131 Circle of Sea Salt B	.10	.20
132 Spirit Aura B	.10	.20
133 Dark Aura B	.10	.20
134 Light Aura B	.10	.20
135 Cosmic Aura B	.10	.20
136 Earth Aura B	.10	.20
137 Flame Aura B	.10	.20
138 Forest Aura B	.10	.20
139 Frost Aura B	.10	.20
140 Lightning Aura B	.10	.20
141 Water Aura B	.10	.20
142 Meteor Shower NR	.10	.20
143 Stars NR	.10	.20
144 Trick-or-Treat Town (Nighttime) NR	.50	1.00
145 Harvest Moon (Full Moon) NR	.10	.20
146 Desert NR	.10	.20
147 Ground NR	.10	.20
148 Witch's Cabin (Swamp) NR	.20	.40
149 Forest NR	.10	.20
150 Mountain NR	.10	.20
151 Snowing NR	.10	.20
152 Winter NR	.10	.20
153 Dawn NR	.10	.20
154 Daytime NR	.10	.20
155 Christmas Eve (Dusk) NR	.10	.20
156 Lightning Storm NR	.10	.20
157 Pumpkin Town (Farm) NR	1.25	2.50
158 Bonaventure Cemetery (Suburban) NR	.15	.30
159 City of Spirits (City) NR	.20	.40
160 Vile Vapors (Fog) NR	.25	.50
161 Lake NR	.10	.20
162 Ocean NR	.20	.40
163 Raining NR	.12	.25
164 River NR	.12	.25
165 Island NR	.50	1.00

2022 MetaZoo Cryptid Nation UFO 1st Edition

1 Flatwoods Monster G	10.00	20.00
2 Men in Black G	.25	.50
3 UFO G	2.50	5.00
4 Van Meter Visitor G	.25	.50
5 Gargantuan Gliders G	.12	.25
6 The Levelland Rocket G	.20	.40
7 Wakinyan G	.12	.25
8 Hat Man G	.12	.25
9 Lechuza G	.20	.40
10 Griddlegreaser Pete G	4.00	8.00
11 Houston Batman G	.10	.20
12 Mountain Boomer G	.12	.25
13 Proctor Valley Monster G	.12	.25
14 Mini T-Rex G	7.50	15.00
15 Pamola G	.25	.50
16 Foo Fighters G	.10	.20
17 Cryptid Busters G	.12	.25
18 Ogua G	.10	.20
19 Supernatural Black Hole G	.30	.75
20 Dragons Rise G	.07	.15
21 Evil Wins G	.07	.15
22 Forest Friends G	.07	.15
23 Sparky Slushy G	.15	.30
24 Water Submergence G	.07	.15
25 Spirit Infusion Suit G	.12	.25
26 Caster Gun G	.10	.20
27 Infinite Power G	.10	.20
28 Dark Shard Meteorite G	.12	.25
29 Static Snow Stone G	.12	.25
30 Burning Spirit Imprint G	.12	.25
31 Glistening Beachrock G	.10	.20
32 Opalescent Moss G	.12	.25
33 Pocket Dimension Orb G	.12	.25
34 Omen Street Orb G	.07	.15
35 Sunset Finality Orb G	.07	.15
36 Frozen Rain Orb G	.07	.15
37 Iridescent Orb G	.07	.15
38 Drowned Sea Orb G	.07	.15
39 Magic Engineers Oil G	.10	.20
40 Neutrality Totality Aura G	30.00	60.00
41 Alien Bigfoot S	.07	.15
42 Crawfordsville Monster S	.10	.20
43 Giant Space Brains S	.07	.15
44 The Haddock Goblin S	.07	.15
45 Bookmark Blue S	.07	.15
46 Crop Circles S	.07	.15
47 Breakfast Aliens B	.10	.20
48 Grays B	.20	.40
49 Old Saybrooks Blockheads B	.07	.15
50 Riverside Monster B	.10	.20
51 Roswell Recreation B	.07	.15
52 Terraforming B	.07	.15
53 Laser Beam Gun Upgrade B	.10	.20
54 Blue Jet Strike S	.07	.15
55 Call of the Storm S	.10	.20
56 Static Hault S	.07	.15
57 Polybius S	.30	.75
58 Tin Foil Hat S	.07	.15
59 Speedemon B	.07	.15
60 The Seven Thunders B	.12	.25
61 Cosmic Lightning Cyclone B	.07	.15
62 Lightning Spark B	.07	.15
63 Tin Foil Suit B	.10	.20
64 Jolt in a Jug B	.10	.20
65 Energy Being S	.07	.15
66 White Stag S	.10	.20
67 Resurrection from the Afterlife S	.12	.25
68 Spirit's Shadow S	.07	.15
69 Headless Cannoneer B	.10	.20
70 Lady in Red G	.07	.15
71 Phantom Kangaroo B	.07	.15
72 Dozing Off G	.07	.10
73 Stargate Project B	.10	.20
74 Unwanted Guests B	.07	.15
75 The Green Fireballs S	.20	.40
76 Blighted Embers S	.10	.20
77 Flare Up S	.12	.25
78 Felixtowe Fire Demon B	.07	.10
79 Sky Snake B	.10	.20
80 Burn Out B	.07	.15
81 Coming in Hot! B	.07	.15
82 Merging Flames B	.12	.25
83 Casa Blanca Entities S	.10	.20
84 Dusk's Omen S	.10	.20
85 Reaper's Scythe S	.10	.20
86 Carmel Area Creature B	.10	.20
87 Grunch Road Monster B	.07	.15
88 Rougarou B	.12	.25
89 Wolf Among Sheep B	.07	.15
90 Gowrow S	.07	.15
91 San Pedro Mountains Mummy S	.07	.15
92 Arid Drought S	.07	.10
93 Crocodingo B	.07	.10
94 [illegible]	.07	.15
95 Boulder Bash B	.10	.20
96 Earth Shattering Quake B	.07	.15
97 Accordianteater S	.07	.15
98 Whirling Whimpus S	.07	.15
99 Bask in the Sunlight NR	.07	.15
100 Forest Elemental B	.07	.15
101 Johnny Appleseed B	.07	.15
102 Robo Flowers B	.10	.20
103 Invigorate B	.07	.10
104 Kodiak Dinosaur S	.12	.25
105 The Monster of Partridge Creek S	.12	.25
106 Frost Ring S	.12	.25
107 Sabertooth Tiger B	.10	.20
108 Trapspringer B	.07	.15
109 Avalanche B	.07	.15
110 Thunder and Ice B	.15	.30
111 Lubbock Lights S	.07	.15
112 Eye for an Eye S	.10	.20
113 Dwarf Star S	.07	.15
114 Hidden Templars B	.12	.25
115 Peace Offering B	.07	.15
116 Sam's Trusty Baseball Bat B	.07	.15
117 Time Machine Blueprints B	.10	.20
118 Mysterious Disappearance S	.07	.15
119 Hull Spell S	.20	.40
120 Token Corrosion S	.12	.25
121 Mike the Headless Chicken B	.12	.25
122 Gravity Shift B	.07	.15
123 Intergalactic Space Council B	.10	.20
124 Devoid Potion B	.07	.15
125 Giant Squid S	.12	.25
126 USO S	.10	.20
127 Aqua Pura S	.07	.15
128 Black Demon B	.07	.15
129 Charles Mill Lake Monster B	.12	.25
130 Rising Tides B	.07	.15
131 The Ocean Calls B	.12	.25
132 Cosmic Aura B	.07	.15
133 Lightning Aura B	.07	.15
134 Spirit Aura B	.07	.15
135 Flame Aura B	.07	.15
136 Dark Aura B	.07	.15
137 Earth Aura B	.07	.15
138 Forest Aura B	.10	.20
139 Frost Aura B	.07	.15
140 Light Aura B	.07	.15
141 Water Aura B	.07	.10
142 Meteor Shower NR	.12	.25
143 Planetary Alignment (Stars) NR	.15	.30
144 Nighttime NR	.25	.50
145 Blood Moon (Full Moon) NR	.12	.25
146 Area 51 (Desert) NR	.10	.20
147 A Lucky View (Ground) NR	.10	.20
148 Radioactive Swamp (Swamp) NR	.15	.30
149 Forest NR	.07	.15
150 Mountain NR	.12	.25
151 Snowing NR	.12	.25
152 Chilling Winter (Winter) NR	.15	.30
153 Daybreak (Dawn) NR	.10	.20
154 Bright Skies (Daytime) NR	.10	.20
155 Sunset (Dusk) NR	.07	.15
156 Lightning Storm NR	.12	.25
157 Farm NR	.10	.20
158 Suburban NR	.10	.20
159 City NR	.07	.15
160 Fearful Fog (Fog) NR	.12	.25
161 Skipping Lake (Lake) NR	.12	.25
162 Ocean NR	.20	.40
163 Raining NR	.07	.15
164 Rushing River (River) NR	.20	.40
165 Island NR	.10	.20

2022 MetaZoo Cryptid Nation UFO 1st Edition Blister Pack Promos

NNO UFO	1.25	2.50
NNO Foo Fighters	1.25	2.50
NNO Wakinyan	1.00	2.00
NNO Mini T-Rex	1.25	2.50

2022 MetaZoo Cryptid Nation UFO 1st Edition Event Promos

NNO Billiwhack Monster HOLO/(SDCC Exclusive)	20.00	40.00
NNO Release Event Medal	4.00	8.00

2022 MetaZoo Cryptid Nation UFO 1st Edition Release Deck 1

1 Beast of Bray Road HOLO G	2.00	4.00
2 The Werewolf of Defiance S	.50	1.00
3 Breakfast Aliens B	.75	1.50
4 Rougarou B	.75	1.50
5 Roswell Recreation B	.40	.80
6 Patient Insight B	.50	1.00
7 Next Chapter B	.75	1.50
8 Meteor Shower NR	.50	1.00
9 Cosmic Aura B	.75	1.50
10 Dark Aura B	.75	1.50

2022 MetaZoo Cryptid Nation UFO 1st Edition Release Deck 2

1 Alaskan Triangle Alien HOLO G 2.00 4.00
2 The Monster of Patridge Creek S .75 1.50
3 Sabertooth Tiger B .75 1.50
4 Speedemon B .75 1.50
5 Ice Storm S .75 1.50
6 Patient Insight B .60 1.25
7 Next Chapter B .60 1.25
8 Snowing NR .75 1.50
9 Lightning Aura B .75 1.50
10 Frost Aura B .75 1.50

2022 MetaZoo Cryptid Nation UFO 1st Edition Release Deck 3

1 Blue Mist HOLO G 5.00 10.00
2 The Green Fireballs S .40 .80
3 Felixstowe Fire Demon B .60 1.25
4 Ghost Deer B .40 .80
5 Dozing Off B .60 1.25
6 Patient Insight B .40 .80
7 Next Chapter B .75 1.50
8 Forest NR .75 1.50
9 Flame Aura B .75 1.50
10 Spirit Aura B .50 1.00

2022 MetaZoo Cryptid Nation UFO 1st Edition Release Deck 4

1 Falcon Lake UFO HOLO G 2.50 5.00
2 Accordianteater S .75 1.50
3 Lubbock Lights S .75 1.50
4 Hidden Templars G .75 1.50
5 Eye for an Eye S .75 1.50
6 Light Ward B .50 1.00
8 Next Chapter B .60 1.25
9 Dawn NR .75 1.50
10 Forest Aura B .75 1.50
11 Light Aura B .75 1.50

2022 MetaZoo Cryptid Nation UFO 1st Edition Release Deck 5

1 Caddy HOLO G 6.00 12.00
5 Excavation B .50 1.00
7 Patient Insight B .40 .80
8 Next Chapter B .40 .80

2022 MetaZoo Cryptid Nation UFO 1st Edition Spellbook Promo

NNO UFO! .50 1.00

2022 MetaZoo Cryptid Nation UFO 1st Edition Tribal Deck Black Knight

1 Black Knight Satellite HOLO G 1.50 3.00
2 Alien Bigfoot S .30 .60
3 El Verde Entity S .30 .75
4 Breakfast Aliens B .30 .75
5 Grays B .30 .60
6 The Haddock Goblin S .30 .60
7 Bookmark Blue S .30 .75
8 Roswell Recreation B .25 .50
9 Terraforming B .25 .50
10 Next Chapter B .50 1.00
11 Patient Insight B .75 1.50
12 Meteor Shower NR .30 .75
13 Planetary Alignment Stars NR .30 .60
14 Cosmic Aura B .30 .60

2022 MetaZoo Cryptid Nation UFO 1st Edition Tribal Deck Forest Elemental Queen

1 Forest Elemental Queen HOLO G 2.00 4.00
2 Accordianteater S .25 .50
3 Arkansas Snipe B .30 .60
4 Forest Elemental B .25 .50
5 Invigorate G .30 .60
6 Next Chapter B .50 1.00
7 Patient Insight B .75 1.50
8 Forest NR .10 .20
9 Forest Aura B .25 .50

2022 MetaZoo Cryptid Nation UFO 1st Edition Tribal Deck Gaubancex

1 Guabancex HOLO G .75 1.50
2 Speed Demon B .25 .50
3 The Seven Thunders B .20 .40
4 Blue Jet Strike S .30 .60
5 Call of the Storm S .25 .50
6 Cosmic Lightning Cyclone B .30 .60
7 Lightning Bolt B .25 .50
8 Next Chapter B .50 1.00
9 Patient Insight B .75 1.50
10 Lightning Storm NR .30 .75
11 Lightning Aura B .20 .40

2022 MetaZoo Cryptid Nation UFO 1st Edition Tribal Deck Genoskwa

1 Genoskwa HOLO G 1.50 3.00
2 Gowrow S .25 .50
3 San Pedros Mountain Mummy S .20 .40
4 Crocodingo B .25 .50
5 Sherman Beasts B .30 .60
6 Boulder Bash B .25 .50
7 Earth Shattering Quake B .20 .40
8 Ready the Defender B .25 .50
9 Next Chapter B .50 1.00
10 Patient Insight B .75 1.50
11 A Lucky View Ground NR .30 .75
12 Mountain NR .30 .60
13 Earth Aura B .20 .40

2022 MetaZoo Cryptid Nation UFO 1st Edition Tribal Deck The Tombstone Monster

1 Tombstone Monster HOLO G 1.00 2.00
2 The Green Fireballs S .30 .75
3 Feu Follet B .50 1.00
4 Sky Snake B .30 .60
5 Burn Out B .30 .75
6 Merging Flames B .30 .60
7 Next Chapter B .50 1.00
8 Patient Insight B .75 1.50
9 Area 51 Desert NR .30 .75
10 Nighttime NR .30 .75
11 Flame Aura B .20 .40

2022 MetaZoo Cryptid Nation Wilderness 1st Edition

1 Bigfoot G 4.00 8.00
2 Chibi Bigfoot G .20 .40
3 Cumberland Dragon G .30 .75
4 Jackalope G .25 .50
5 Rose Robinson G .50 1.00
6 Green Clawed Monster G .20 .40
7 Mishipeshu G 10.00 20.00
8 Rocky G .20 .40
9 Snoligoster G .30 .75
10 Stone Man G 6.00 12.00
11 The Pink Mess of Goose Creek Lagoon G .30 .60
12 Dragon of Oconto Falls G 7.50 15.00
13 Golden Bear G .30 .60
14 Atmospheric Jellyfish G .20 .40
15 Pascagoula River Aliens G .20 .40
16 Awful G 3.00 6.00
17 Iowa Dragon G .20 .40
18 Old Man Winter G .30 .75
19 Woolly Mammoth G .30 .60
20 Snipe G 15.00 30.00
21 Big Bird G .20 .40
22 Wampus Cat G .30 .60
23 Black Dog G .20 .40
24 Golden Haired Girl G .20 .40
25 Germinate G .20 .40
26 Hateful Demise G .20 .40
27 Seafood BBQ G .50 1.00
28 Turbo Charge G .50 1.00
29 Fountain of Youth G .30 .60
30 Token Sitter G .20 .40
31 Living Earth Sigil G .20 .40
32 Starlight Sigil G .20 .40
33 Midnight Lake Sigil G .20 .40
34 Frozen Spirit Sigil G .20 .40
35 Scorching Rod Sigil G .20 .40
36 Megalodon Tooth G .25 .50
37 Petrified Wood G .30 .75
38 Starlight Bloom G .20 .40
39 Kindling Sparkroot G .20 .40
40 Haunted Tundra G .20 .40
41 Prism Aura G 50.00 100.00
42 Chibi Cumberland Dragon S .25 .50
43 Chibi Jackalope S .25 .50
44 Hugag S .12 .25
45 Skunk Ape S .12 .25
46 Billdad B .10 .20
47 Billiwhack Monster B .10 .20
48 Glastonbury Glawakus B .10 .20
49 Mogollon Monster B .10 .20
50 Ohio Grassman B .15 .30
51 Rubberado B .10 .20
52 Restricting Roots S .25 .50
53 Hiding in Thickets B .10 .20
54 Idaho Potatoes B .10 .20
55 Whitey S .12 .25
56 Beavershark B .10 .20
57 Dublin Lake Monster B .10 .20
58 River Mermaid B .10 .20
59 Armored Scales S .12 .25
60 Carnal Edge S .12 .25
61 Sixth Sense S .12 .25
62 Sudden Camouflage S .12 .25
63 Tidal Pull B .10 .20
64 Pearl of Desire B .10 .20
65 Toxic Water B .20 .40
66 John Henry S .12 .25
67 Stone-Eating Gyascutus S .12 .25
68 Honey Island Swamp Monster B .10 .20
69 Peninsula Python B .10 .20
70 Selbyville Swamp Monster B .10 .20
71 The Great Earthquake S .12 .25
72 Jeering Rocks B .10 .20
73 Primordial Ooze B .10 .20
74 Ready the Defender B .10 .20
75 Boulder of Power S .12 .25
76 Weeping Black Angel S .12 .25
77 Unicorn B .10 .20
78 Aurora Borealis S .12 .25
79 Save the Holy S .12 .25
80 Artifact Barrier B .10 .20
81 Light Ward B .10 .20
82 Stone of Protection B .10 .20
83 El Verde Entity S .12 .25
84 Cumberland Spaceman B .10 .20
85 Lizard People B .10 .20
86 Medford Shmoos B .10 .20
87 Beam Up S .12 .25
88 Mind Probe S .25 .50
89 Alien Intelligence B .10 .20
90 Ozark Howler S .12 .25
91 Pope Lick Monster S .12 .25
92 Banshee of the Badlands B .10 .20
93 Spearfinger B .10 .20
94 White Screamer B .10 .20
95 Terrify S .12 .25
96 Bloodstained B .10 .20
97 Joe Magarac S .12 .25
98 Explosive Rabbit B .10 .20
99 Spring Heeled Jack B .10 .20
100 Heat Wave S .25 .50
101 Wildfire S .12 .25
102 Explosion! B .10 .20
103 Flare Shot B .10 .20
104 Janet and Rosetta Van de Voort S .20 .40
105 Friendly Snowman B .10 .20
106 Frost Elemental B .20 .40
107 Fur Bearing Trout B .10 .20
108 Shatter Ice S .20 .40
109 Winter's Wrath S .20 .40
110 Frost Shot B .10 .20
111 Phantom Car S .25 .50
112 Mad Gasser of Mattoon B .10 .20
113 Radioactive Hornets B .10 .20
114 E.M.P. S .12 .25
115 Lightning Strikes Twice B .10 .20
116 Shockburn B .10 .20
117 Power Cell S .30 .75
118 Spectrum Shift S .12 .25
119 Survival Insitincts S .12 .25
120 Void Spell S .12 .25
121 Powerup Purple B .10 .20
122 Shovel B .10 .20
123 Anti-Potion Potion B .10 .20
124 Camouflage Potion B .10 .20
125 Deer Woman S .12 .25
126 Nightmarchers S .12 .25
127 Spook Light B .10 .20
128 The Phantom Jogger of Canyon Hill B .10 .20
129 Spirit Veil S .12 .25
130 Curse B .20 .40
131 Rest in Peace B .10 .20
132 Forest Aura B .10 .20
133 Water Aura B .10 .20
134 Earth Aura B .10 .20
135 Light Aura B .10 .20
136 Cosmic Aura B .10 .20
137 Dark Aura B .10 .20
138 Flame Aura B .10 .20
139 Frost Aura B .10 .20
140 Lightning Aura B .10 .20
141 Spirit Aura B .10 .20
142 Cosmic Rain (Meteors Shower) .10 .20
143 Stars .10 .20
144 Quiet Night (Nighttime) .10 .20
145 Full Moon .10 .20
146 Desert .10 .20
147 Ground .10 .20
148 Swamp .10 .20
149 Grand National Park (Forest) .10 .20
150 Big Tall Mountain (Mountain) .10 .20
151 White Out (Snowing) .10 .20
152 Winter .10 .20
153 Dawn .10 .20
154 Daytime .10 .20
155 Dusk .10 .20
156 Stunning Storm (Lightning Storm) .10 .20
157 Abandoned Silo (Farm) .10 .20
158 Chibi Playground (Suburban) .10 .20
159 Overgrown City (City) .10 .20
160 Fog .10 .20
161 Lake .10 .20
162 Open Waters (Ocean) .10 .20
163 Replenishing Showers (Raining) .10 .20
164 River .10 .20
165 Tiny Island (Island) .10 .20

2022 MetaZoo Cryptid Nation Wilderness Fan Art Blister Pack

1 Altamaha-Ha G 15.00 30.00
2 Bloody Mary G 30.00 60.00
3 Crosswick Monster G 25.00 50.00
4 White Death G 12.50 25.00
5 Gallinipper S 5.00 10.00
6 Little Green Men S 7.50 15.00
7 Mole Person S 6.00 12.00
8 St. Elmo's Fire S 6.00 12.00
9 Menehune's Hammer S 7.50 15.00
10 Tesla's Coil S 10.00 20.00
11 Cosmic Aura S 2.50 5.00
12 Dark Aura S 3.00 6.00
13 Earth Aura S 2.50 5.00
14 Flame Aura S 4.00 8.00
15 Forest Aura S 3.00 6.00
16 Frost Aura S 2.00 4.00
17 Light Aura S 4.00 8.00
18 Lightning Aura S 4.00 8.00
19 Spirit Aura S 2.50 5.00
20 Water Aura S 4.00 8.00
NNO Bookmark G 6.00 12.00

2022 MetaZoo Cryptid Nation Wilderness MagiCast April Fool's Box

1 Chaos G 3.00 6.00
2 Metamic G 3.00 6.00
3 Mothman G 6.00 12.00
4 Moth Man G 4.00 8.00
5 April Fool's G 20.00 40.00
6 4th Wall G 3.00 6.00
7 Metapoo Medal G 12.50 25.00
8 Unrefined Chaos Crystal G 3.00 6.00

2022 MetaZoo Cryptid Nation Wilderness Release Event Deck Fouke Monster

1 Fouke Monster .75 1.50
2 Honey Island Swamp Monster .30 .75
3 Peninsula Python .30 .60
4 Selbyville Swamp Monster .20 .40
5 Biliwhack Monster .25 .50
6 Mogollon Monster .30 .60
7 Survival Instincts .25 .50
8 Bookmark .25 .50
9 New Beginnings .75 1.50
10 Lightning in a Bottle .50 1.00
11 Swamp .30 .75
12 Earth Aura .30 .75
13 Forest Aura .30 .60

2022 MetaZoo Cryptid Nation Wilderness Release Event Deck Lake Chelan Monster

1 Lake Chelan Monster 1.00 2.00
2 Ozark Howler .20 .40
3 Whitey .25 .50
4 Banshee of the Badlands .15 .30
5 Dublin Lake Monster .20 .40
6 Tidal Pull .25 .50
7 Survival Instincts .25 .50
8 New Beginnings .75 1.50
9 Bookmark .25 .50
10 Smokey Spirits 1.00 2.00
11 Full Moon .30 .75
12 Dark Aura .30 .75
13 Water Aura .30 .75

2022 MetaZoo Cryptid Nation Wilderness Release Event Deck Pale-Faced Lightning

1 Pale-Faced Lightning .75 1.50
2 Ball Lightning 1.00 2.00
3 Explosive Rabbit .20 .40
4 Spring Heeled Jack .15 .30
5 Lightning Strikes Twice .25 .50
6 Shockburn .20 .40
7 Explosion .20 .40
8 Bookmark .25 .50
9 New Beginnings .75 1.50
10 Lightning in a Bottle .60 1.25
11 Desert .20 .40
12 Lightning Aura .20 .40
13 Flame Aura .30 .75

2022 MetaZoo Cryptid Nation Wilderness Release Event Deck Star Person

1 Star Person 1.50 3.00
2 Cumberland Spaceman .75 1.50
3 Medford Shmoos .50 1.00
4 Unicorn .30 .75
5 Transfiguration .20 .40
6 Alien Intelligence .75 1.50
7 Bookmark .25 .50
8 New Beginnings .75 1.50
9 Stone of Protection .15 .30
10 Stars .30 .75
11 Daytime .30 .60
12 Cosmic Aura .30 .60
13 Light Aura .30 .60

2022 MetaZoo Cryptid Nation Wilderness Release Event Deck Tagriasuit

1 Tagriasuit	.75	1.50
2 Janet and Rosetta Van de Voort	.50	1.00
3 Nightmarchers	.20	.40
4 Familiar	.50	1.00
5 Spook Light	.75	1.50
6 Curse	.30	.60
7 Frost Shot	.50	1.00
8 Bookmark	.25	.50
9 New Beginnings	.75	1.50
10 Fog	.20	.40
11 Spirit Aura	.30	.75
12 Frost Aura	.15	.30

2022 MetaZoo Cryptid Nation Wilderness Theme Deck Alpha Gator

1 Alpha Gator	1.25	2.50
2 Rocky	.25	.50
3 Sewer Alligator	.20	.40
4 Powerup Red	3.00	6.00
5 Armored Scales	.30	.75
6 Carnal Edge	.30	.75
7 Tidal Pull	.60	1.25
8 Bookmark	.25	.50
9 New Beginnings	.75	1.50
10 Lightning in a Bottle	.50	1.00
11 Overgrown City	.25	.50
12 Water Aura	.15	.30

2022 MetaZoo Cryptid Nation Wilderness Theme Deck Father Time

1 Father Time	1.00	2.00
2 Golden Bear	.30	.60
3 Unicorn	.15	.30
4 Powerup Red	3.00	6.00
5 Water to Wine	.60	1.25
6 Light Ward	.20	.40
7 Stone of Protection	.25	.50
8 Bookmark	.25	.50
9 New Beginnings	.75	1.50
10 Daytime Terra	.30	.60
11 Light Aura	.15	.30

2022 MetaZoo Cryptid Nation Wilderness Theme Deck Ijiraq

1 Ijiraq	1.00	2.00
2 Woolly Mammoth	.25	.50
3 Janet and Rosetta Van de Voort	.30	.60
4 Friendly Snowman	.30	.60
5 Alaskan Vortex	.30	.75
6 Powerup Red	3.00	6.00
7 Shatter Ice	.60	1.25
8 Winter's Wrath	.50	1.00
9 Frost Shot	.15	.30
10 Bookmark	.25	.50
11 New Beginnings	.75	1.50
12 White Out (Snowing)	.40	.80
13 Winter	.50	1.00
14 Frost Aura	.15	.30

2022 MetaZoo Cryptid Nation Wilderness Theme Deck Nita Black Bearer

1 Nita, Black Bearer	.75	1.50
2 Wampus Cat	.30	.75
3 Joe Magarac	.30	.75
4 Explosive Rabbit	.25	.50
5 Powerup Red	3.00	6.00
6 Unholy Fire	.50	1.00
7 Wildfire	.30	.60
8 Explosion!	.50	1.00
9 Flare Shot	.50	1.00
10 Bookmark	.25	.50
11 New Beginnings	.75	1.50
12 Lightning in a Bottle	.50	1.00
13 Abandoned Silo (Farm)	.50	1.00
14 Flame Aura	.15	.30

2022 MetaZoo Cryptid Nation Wilderness Theme Deck Paul Bunyan

1 Paul Bunyan	1.50	3.00
2 Ohio Grassman	.20	.40
3 Billiwhack Monster	.20	.40
4 Skunk Ape	.20	.40
5 Growth	3.00	6.00
6 Powerup Red	3.00	6.00
7 Hiding in Thickets	.20	.40
8 Bookmark	.25	.50
9 New Beginnings	.75	1.50
10 Lightning in a Bottle	.50	1.00
11 Grand National Park (Forest)	.20	.40
12 Forest Aura	.15	.30

2022 MetaZoo Cryptid Nation Wilderness Valentine's Day Holiday Box

1 Chibi Bunnyman G	3.00	6.00
2 Chibi Enfield Monster S	2.50	5.00
3 Chibi Grim Reaper G	4.00	8.00
4 Chibi Growth S	7.50	15.00
5 Chibi Guardian Angel S	2.50	5.00
6 Chibi Loveland Frogman G	12.50	25.00
7 Chibi Menehune S	2.50	5.00
8 Chibi Momo S	2.50	5.00
9 Chibi Parade G	4.00	8.00
10 Chibi Piasa Bird S	4.00	8.00
11 Chibi Squonk S	2.50	5.00
12 Chibi Unicorn S	2.50	5.00

2022 MetaZoo Hiroquest 2.0 Amazon Music

1 Stars Robot G	1.50	3.00
2 Death G	7.50	15.00
3 Ziri G	3.00	6.00
4 Cement Worm G	1.50	3.00
5 Extant Group G	1.50	3.00
6 Tom the Zombie G	2.00	4.00
7 Kong G	3.00	6.00
8 Nobody G	.75	1.50
9 Perfect G	.75	1.50
10 Robotic Demon G	1.50	3.00
11 Mini T-Rex G	3.00	6.00
12 Webby G	1.00	2.00
13 Alaskan Ice Monster G	1.00	2.00
14 Chi Chi G	1.50	3.00
15 Pamola G	2.50	5.00
16 Copenhagen Devil G	1.50	3.00
17 Wakinyan G	2.00	4.00
18 Goth Holly G	.75	1.50
19 Hiro G	3.00	6.00
20 AI Reconstruction G	1.25	3.00
21 Stop the World G	1.50	3.00
22 Counterfeit Pullet Ring G	1.50	3.00
23 Hiro's Cape G	1.25	2.50
24 Diasos Pullet Ring G	1.25	2.50
25 Russian Roulette G	1.50	3.00
26 Whistle Raver Backpack G	1.50	3.00
27 Black Dog of Hanging Hills G	1.50	3.00
28 Bait Robbers G	1.25	2.50
29 Fog Hog G	1.50	3.00
30 Giant Squid G	1.50	3.00
31 Love Brains G	.75	1.50
32 Ogua G	2.00	4.00
33 Sea Sorcerer G	2.50	5.00
34 Cosmic Aura G	2.50	5.00
35 Earth Aura G	4.00	8.00
36 Flame Aura G	4.00	8.00
37 Forest Aura G	6.00	12.00
38 Lightning Aura G	2.00	4.00

2022 MetaZoo Hiroquest 2.0 Apple Music

1 Stars Robot G	1.50	3.00
2 Death G	4.00	8.00
3 Ziri G	2.00	4.00
4 Cement Worm G	1.50	3.00
5 Extant Group G	1.50	3.00
6 Tom the Zombie G	1.50	3.00
7 Kong G	10.00	20.00
8 Nobody G	.75	1.50
9 Perfect G	1.50	3.00
10 Robotic Demon G	1.50	3.00
11 Mini T-Rex G	2.50	5.00
12 Webby G	2.50	5.00
13 Alaskan Ice Monster G	2.00	4.00
14 Chi Chi G	1.00	2.00
15 Pamola G	2.00	4.00
16 Copenhagen Devil G	2.50	5.00
17 Wakinyan G	2.50	5.00
18 Goth Holly G	1.50	3.00
19 Hiro G	.75	1.50
20 AI Reconstruction G	2.50	5.00
21 Stop the World G	2.00	4.00
22 Counterfeit Pullet Ring G	1.50	3.00
23 Hiro's Cape G	3.00	6.00
24 Diasos Pullet Ring G	2.50	5.00
25 Russian Roulette G	1.50	3.00
26 Whistle Raver Backpack G	2.00	4.00
27 Black Dog of Hanging Hills G	1.25	2.50
28 Bait Robbers G	1.50	3.00
29 Fog Hog G	2.50	5.00
30 Giant Squid G	1.50	3.00
31 Love Brains G	.75	1.50
32 Ogua G	2.00	4.00
33 Sea Sorcerer G	1.50	3.00
34 Cosmic Aura G	2.50	5.00
35 Earth Aura G	3.00	6.00
36 Flame Aura G	7.50	15.00
37 Forest Aura G	6.00	12.00
38 Lightning Aura G	2.00	4.00

2022 MetaZoo Hiroquest 2.0 Spotify

1 Stars Robot G	5.00	10.00
2 Death G	3.00	6.00
3 Ziri G	3.00	6.00
4 Cement Worm G	3.00	6.00
5 Extant Group G	1.00	2.00
6 Tom the Zombie G	2.00	4.00
7 Kong G	2.50	5.00
8 Nobody G	1.00	2.00
9 Perfect G	2.00	4.00
10 Robotic Demon G	4.00	8.00
11 Mini T-Rex G	2.00	4.00
12 Webby G	1.00	2.00
13 Alaskan Ice Monster G	1.50	3.00
14 Chi Chi G	.75	1.50
15 Pamola G	1.00	2.00
16 Copenhagen Devil G	2.00	4.00
17 Wakinyan G	2.50	5.00
18 Goth Holly G	2.00	4.00
19 Hiro G	5.00	10.00
20 AI Reconstruction G	1.00	2.00
21 Stop the World G	2.00	4.00
22 Counterfeit Pullet Ring G	1.50	3.00
23 Hiro's Cape G	1.50	3.00
24 Diasos Pullet Ring G	2.50	5.00
25 Russian Roulette G	1.25	2.50
26 Whistle Raver Backpack G	1.50	3.00
27 Black Dog of Hanging Hills G	.50	1.00
28 Bait Robbers G	.50	1.00
29 Fog Hog G	1.50	3.00
30 Giant Squid G	1.00	2.00
31 Love Brains G	.75	1.50
32 Ogua G	2.00	4.00
33 Sea Sorcerer G	1.50	3.00
34 Cosmic Aura G	2.50	5.00
35 Earth Aura G	6.00	12.00
36 Flame Aura G	4.00	8.00
37 Forest Aura G	4.00	8.00
38 Lightning Aura G	2.00	4.00

2022 MetaZoo Hiroquest 2.0 YouTube Steve Aoki

1 Stars Robot G	1.50	3.00
2 Death G	5.00	10.00
3 Ziri G	1.00	2.00
4 Cement Worm G	1.50	3.00
5 Extant Group G	1.25	2.50
6 Tom the Zombie G	1.50	3.00
7 Kong G	2.50	5.00
8 Nobody G	2.50	5.00
9 Perfect G	2.00	4.00
10 Robotic Demon G	2.00	4.00
11 Mini T-Rex G	2.50	5.00
12 Webby G	1.00	2.00
13 Alaskan Ice Monster G	1.00	2.00
14 Chi Chi G	1.50	3.00
15 Pamola G	1.00	2.00
16 Copenhagen Devil G	2.50	5.00
17 Wakinyan G	1.00	2.00
18 Goth Holly G	2.50	5.00
19 Hiro G	10.00	20.00
20 AI Reconstruction G	2.00	4.00
21 Stop the World G	1.50	3.00
22 Counterfeit Pullet Ring G	2.00	4.00
23 Hiro's Cape G	1.50	3.00
24 Diasos Pullet Ring G	2.50	5.00
25 Russian Roulette G	1.25	2.50
26 Whistle Raver Backpack G	5.00	10.00
27 Black Dog of Hanging Hills G	2.00	4.00
28 Bait Robbers G	2.00	4.00
29 Fog Hog G	2.00	4.00
30 Giant Squid G	1.00	2.00
31 Love Brains G	.75	1.50
32 Ogua G	2.00	4.00
33 Sea Sorcerer G	1.25	2.50
34 Cosmic Aura G	2.50	5.00
35 Earth Aura G	3.00	6.00
36 Flame Aura G	7.50	15.00
37 Forest Aura G	4.00	8.00
38 Lightning Aura G	3.00	6.00

2023 MetaZoo 30th Anniversary Reprint Edition

1 Crawling Sam G	7.50	15.00
2 Gumberoo G	6.00	12.00
3 Lizard People G	10.00	20.00
4 Love Land Frog Man G	7.50	15.00
5 MetaZoo 30th Anniversary Celebration G	20.00	40.00
6 All Hallows' Eve G	5.00	10.00
7 Flood the Sky G	12.50	25.00
8 Invisible Ink G	15.00	30.00
9 Melted Path G	10.00	20.00
10 New Year Same Shenanigans G	10.00	20.00
11 Concave Decagon Aura G	15.00	30.00
12 Eternal Ice Cube G	4.00	8.00
13 Fungible Token G	4.00	8.00
14 Neverstating Fire Crystal G	3.00	6.00
15 Sam's Cryptid Cam G	10.00	20.00
16 Thunder Glass G	4.00	8.00

2023 MetaZoo Cryptid Nation Native 1st Edition

1 Achiyalabopa G	.30	.75
2 Djieien G	25.00	50.00
3 Dzoavits G	.30	.60
4 Piasa Bird G	75.00	150.00
5 Amaguq G	.30	.60
6 Nanook G	.30	.60
7 Negafook G	.30	.60
8 Atabey G	25.00	50.00
9 Ogopogo G	.30	.60
10 Chibi Wendigo G	.60	1.25
11 Wendigo G	50.00	100.00
12 Winalagalis G	30.00	60.00
13 Rainbow Crow G	.30	.60
14 The Uktena G	30.00	60.00
15 Boinayel G	.50	1.00
16 Maromu G	.75	1.50
17 Agojo So'Jo, the Big Star G	.30	.60
18 Asintmah G	.30	.60
19 Caribou Mother G	.30	.60
20 Skookum G	17.50	35.00
21 Ahayuta, War Twins G	12.50	25.00
22 Haietlik G	17.50	35.00
23 Raven Mocker G	.40	.80
24 Tsohanoai G	20.00	40.00
25 White Bison G	.75	1.50
26 Seismic Shockwaves G	.75	1.50
27 Winter Solstice G	.30	.60
28 Rainmaking G	.30	.75
29 Falling Stars of Ask-wee-da-eed G	.30	.60
30 Birth of the Sun G	.40	.80
31 Ghost Dance G	.40	.80
32 Giant's Blood G	.30	.60
33 Pot of Stagnation G	.30	.60
34 Igloo G	.75	1.50
35 Squash Blossom Necklace G	.30	.60
36 The Jewel of the Uktena G	.30	.60
37 Battle Rug of Piasa Bird and Quetzalcoatlus G	.30	.75
38 Medicine Stick G	.30	.60
39 Dreamcatcher G	.30	.75
40 Frozen Cairn Fusion Aura G	50.00	100.00
41 Fulgurite Fusion Aura G	50.00	100.00
42 Magma Fusion Aura G	75.00	150.00
43 Meteoric Fusion Aura G	30.00	60.00
44 Rainbow Quartz Fusion Aura G	40.00	80.00
45 Sacrificial Stone Fusion Aura G	50.00	100.00
46 Sylvan Mud Fusion Aura G	60.00	125.00
47 Unearthly Stratum Fusion Aura G	50.00	100.00
48 Vadose Fusion Aura G	60.00	125.00
49 Ankkiyyini S	.20	.40
50 Nun'Yunu'Wi S	.20	.40
51 Odziozo S	.20	.40
52 Behemoth Stampede S	.20	.40
53 The Matlox Cave S	.20	.40
54 Battle Rug of Matlox and Elder Matlox S	.20	.40
55 Haakapainizi B	.25	.50
56 Jogah, Drum Dancers B	.25	.50
57 Mannegishi B	.25	.50
58 Volcano Woman B	.25	.50
59 Grounded Chieftain B	.25	.50
60 Rise of Turtle Island B	.25	.50
61 Sand Paint Shield B	.25	.50
62 Sinkhole Sam Tapestry B	.25	.50
63 Koguhpuk S	.30	.75
64 Mhuwe S	.30	.60
65 Turn Into Snow S	.20	.40
66 Ice Fishing S	.25	.50
67 Nootaikok B	.25	.50
68 Pal-Rai-Yuk B	.15	.30
69 Caribou Kindness B	.15	.30
70 Prepare for the Hunt B	.15	.30
71 Kakivak B	.25	.50
72 Pamola Effigy B	.15	.30
73 Asiaq S	.20	.40
74 Miniwashitu S	.20	.40
75 Sedna, Mother of the Deep S	.20	.40
76 Sudden Rainfall S	.20	.40
77 Akhlut B	.15	.30
78 Kumugwe, the Copper-Maker B	.15	.30
79 Maxinuxw Ascension B	.15	.30
80 Save the Ogopogo! B	.15	.30
81 Water Spirit Offerings B	.15	.30
82 Rain Mask B	.15	.30
83 Aipaloovik S	.20	.40
84 Iktomi S	.20	.40
85 Charnel House Visit S	.20	.40
86 Awakkule B	.15	.30
87 Tupilaq B	.15	.30
88 Caw of the Raven Mocker B	.15	.30
89 Taboo B	.15	.30
90 Booger Mask B	.15	.30
91 Issitoq S	.20	.40
92 Yokahu, the Sleeping Giant S	.75	1.50
93 Horned Snake Statue S	.20	.40
94 Chibi Uktena B	.15	.30
95 Chipiapoos, the Ghost Rabbit B	.15	.30
96 Dismantled Creations B	.40	.80

97 Powwow B	.15	.30
98 Medicine Wheel B	.30	.75
99 Alignak S	.20	.40
100 Ask-wee-da-eed S	.20	.40
101 The Skidi Pawnee Star Chart S	.20	.40
102 Canotila B	.15	.30
103 Vision Quest B	.30	.75
104 Battle Rug of Flatwoods and Slide-Rock B	.15	.30
105 Peyote B	.15	.30
106 Ababinili S	.50	1.00
107 Ani Hyuntikwalaski S	.20	.40
108 Sun Dance S	.20	.40
109 Loowit B	.25	.50
110 Wi B	.25	.50
111 Sacred Fire B	.25	.50
112 Piasa Claw B	.25	.50
113 Gather the Gluttonous Gopher S	.20	.40
114 Death Cap Mushroom S	.20	.40
115 Stiff-Legged Bear B	.30	.75
116 Yehasuri B	.30	.75
117 Surrounded By Wolves B	.15	.30
118 Green Corn Ceremony Basket B	.15	.30
119 He-No S	.20	.40
120 Drumming Circle S	.20	.40
121 Gathering of the Seven Thunders S	.20	.40
122 Transform Into Thunderbird S	.20	.40
123 Awanyu B	.15	.30
124 Dreams of Thunder Beings B	.15	.30
125 Lightning-Striked Wooden Armor B	.15	.30
126 Thunderbird Totem Pole B	.50	1.00
127 Azeban S	.20	.40
128 Crow Mother S	.20	.40
129 Panti' S	.20	.40
130 Cabinet of Skulls S	.20	.40
131 Chepi B	.15	.30
132 Channel Spirit Animals B	.15	.30
133 Ghost Sickness B	.15	.30
134 Hunting Tactics S	.20	.40
135 Oral Tradition S	.20	.40
136 Tomahawk S	1.00	2.00
137 Medicine Bag B	.15	.30
138 Token Pot B	.15	.30
139 Bottle of Hoof Glue B	.15	.30
140 Powdered Turquoise B	1.25	2.50
141 Earth Aura B	.15	.30
142 Frost Aura B	.15	.30
143 Water Aura B	.15	.30
144 Dark Aura B	.15	.30
145 Light Aura B	.15	.30
146 Cosmic Aura B	.15	.30
147 Flame Aura B	.15	.30
148 Forest Aura B	.15	.30
149 Lightning Aura B	.15	.30
150 Spirit Aura B	.15	.30
151 Pool of Stars (Meteor Shower) NR	.30	.60
152 Stars NR	.30	.60
153 Night Strike (Nighttime) NR	.30	.75
154 Hunting Moon (Full Moon) NR	.10	.20
155 Desert NR	.10	.20
156 Steep Cliffs (Ground) NR	.10	.20
157 Swamp NR	.10	.20
158 Forest NR	.10	.20
159 Colossal Claim (Mountain) NR	.50	1.00
160 Blinding Blizzard (Snowing) NR	.10	.20
161 Winter NR	.10	.20
162 Dawn NR	.10	.20
163 Daytime NR	.10	.20
164 Dusk NR	.10	.20
165 Lightning Storm NR	.75	1.50
166 Farm NR	.10	.20
167 Suburban NR	.10	.20
168 City NR	.10	.20
169 Fog NR	.10	.20
170 Yokahu's Lake View (Lake) NR	.10	.20
171 Ocean NR	.10	.20
172 Unending Rainfall (Raining) NR	.40	.80
173 River NR	.10	.20
174 Island NR	.10	.20

2023 MetaZoo Cryptid Nation Native Gala-Stamped Edition

49 Ankkiyyini S	.12	.25
50 Nun'Yunu'Wi S	.12	.25
51 Odziozo S	.12	.25
52 Behemoth Stampede S	.12	.25
53 The Matlox Cave S	.12	.25
54 Battle Rug of Matlox and Elder Matlox S	.12	.25
63 Koguhpuk S	.12	.25
64 Mhuwe S	.12	.25
65 Turn Into Snow S	.12	.25
66 Ice Fishing S	.12	.25
73 Asiaq S	.12	.25
74 Miniwashitu S	.12	.25
75 Sedna, Mother of the Deep S	.12	.25
76 Sudden Rainfall S	.12	.25
83 Aipaloovik S	.12	.25
84 Iktomi S	.12	.25
85 Charnel House Visit S	.12	.25
91 Issitoq S	.12	.25
92 Yokahu, the Sleeping Giant S	.12	.25
93 Horned Snake Statue S	.12	.25
99 Alignak S	.12	.25
100 Ask-wee-da-eed S	.12	.25
101 The Skidi Pawnee Star Chart S	.12	.25
106 Ababinili S	.12	.25
107 Ani Hyuntikwalaski S	.12	.25
108 Sun Dance S	.12	.25
113 Gather the Gluttonous Gopher S	.12	.25
114 Death Cap Mushroom S	.12	.25
119 He-No S	.12	.25
120 Drumming Circle S	.12	.25
121 Gathering of the Seven Thunders S	.12	.25
122 Transform Into Thunderbird S	.12	.25
127 Azeban S	.12	.25
128 Crow Mother S	.12	.25
129 Panti' S	.12	.25
130 Cabinet of Skulls S	.12	.25
134 Hunting Tactics S	.12	.25
135 Oral Tradition S	.12	.25
136 Tomahawk S	.12	.25
151 Pool of Stars (Meteor Shower) NR	.10	.20
152 Stars NR	.10	.20
153 Night Strike (Nighttime) NR	.10	.20
154 Hunting Moon (Full Moon) NR	.10	.20
155 Desert NR	.10	.20
156 Steep Cliffs (Ground) NR	.10	.20
157 Swamp NR	.10	.20
158 Forest NR	.10	.20
159 Colossal Claim (Mountain) NR	.10	.20
160 Blinding Blizzard (Snowing) NR	.10	.20
161 Winter NR	.10	.20
162 Dawn NR	.10	.20
163 Daytime NR	.10	.20
164 Dusk NR	.10	.20
165 Lightning Storm NR	.10	.20
166 Farm NR	.10	.20
167 Suburban NR	.10	.20
168 City NR	.10	.20
169 Fog NR	.10	.20
170 Yokahu's Lake View (Lake) NR	.10	.20
171 Ocean NR	.10	.20
172 Unending Rainfall (Raining) NR	.10	.20
173 River NR	.10	.20
174 Island NR	.10	.20

2023 MetaZoo Hello Kitty Promos

NNO Badtz-Maru G	50.00	100.00
NNO Chococat G	100.00	200.00
NNO Cinnamoroll G	40.00	80.00
NNO Hello Kitty G	125.00	250.00
NNO Keroppi G	60.00	125.00
NNO Kuromi G	75.00	150.00
NNO My Melody G	50.00	100.00
NNO Pompompurin G	40.00	80.00

2022-24 One Piece Promos

P007 Monkey.D.Luffy P/(Tournament Pack Vol. 1)	2.50	6.00
P008 Yamato P/(Tournament Pack Vol. 1)	.60	1.50
P009 Trafalgar Law P/(Tournament Pack Vol. 1)	1.00	2.50
P010 Kaido P/(Tournament Pack Vol. 1)	1.50	4.00
P011 Uta P/(Film Red Promotion Exclusive)	.40	1.00
P012 Jellyfish Pirates P/(Film Red Promotion Exclusive)	.40	1.00
P013 Gordon P/(Film Red Promotion Exclusive)	6.00	15.00
P014 Koby P/(Film Red Promotion Exclusive)	.25	.60
P015 Sunny-Kun P/(Film Red Promotion Exclusive)	6.00	15.00
P016 Shanks P/(Film Red Promotion Exclusive)	.30	.60
P017 Trafalgar Law P/(Film Red Promotion Exclusive)	.40	1.00
P018 Bartolomeo P/(Film Red Promotion Exclusive)	.75	.30
P019 Bepo P/(Film Red Promotion Exclusive)	.50	1.25
P020 Helmeppo P/(Film Red Promotion Exclusive)	.40	1.00
P021 Benn.Beckman P/(Film Red Promotion Exclusive)	.20	.50
P022 Monkey.D.Luffy P/(Film Red Promotion Exclusive)	.75	2.00
P023 Yasopp P/(Film Red Promotion Exclusive)	.40	1.00
P024 I'm Gonna Be the King of the Pirates!! P (Pirates Party Card Vol. 1)	10.00	25.00
P028 Portgas.D.Ace P/(Event Pack Vol. 1)	8.00	20.00
P029 Bartolomeo P/(Event Pack Vol. 1)	40.00	100.00
P030 Jinbe P/(Event Pack Vol. 1)	50.00	120.00
P031 Uta P/(Event Pack Vol. 1)	12.00	30.00
P032 Sengoku P/(Event Pack Vol. 1)	6.00	15.00
P033 Monkey.D.Luffy P/(Event Pack Vol. 2)	40.00	100.00
P034 Sanji P/(Event Pack Vol.2, Asia Special Prize February Standard Battle)	25.00	60.00
P035 Monkey.D.Luffy P/(Pirate Party Vol.3, Prize March Meet-Up Event)	1.50	4.00

2022 One Piece Romance Dawn

OP01001 Roronoa Zoro L	.10	.25
OP01001 Roronoa Zoro ALT ART L	100.00	250.00
OP01002 Trafalgar Law L/""play 1...""	.10	.25
OP01002 Trafalgar Law L/""play up to 1...""	.10	.25
OP01002 Trafalgar Law ALT ART L/""play 1...""	75.00	200.00
OP01002 Trafalgar Law ALT ART L/""play up to 1...""	75.00	200.00
OP01003 Monkey.D.Luffy L/""Set 1...""	.12	.30
OP01003 Monkey.D.Luffy L/""Set up to 1...""	.12	.30
OP01003 Monkey.D.Luffy ALT ART L/""Set 1...""	30.00	80.00
OP01003 Monkey.D.Luffy ALT ART L/""Set up to 1...""	30.00	80.00
OP01004 Usopp R	.12	.30
OP01005 Uta R/""Add 1...""	.12	.30
OP01005 Uta R/""Add up to 1...""	.12	.30
OP01006 Otama UC/""Give 1...""	1.25	3.00
OP01006 Otama UC/""Give up to 1...""	1.25	3.00
OP01007 Caribou C/""K.O. 1...""	.08	.20
OP01007 Caribou C/""K.O. up to 1...""	.08	.20
OP01008 Cavendish C	.08	.20
OP01008 Cavendish ALT ART C/(Box Topper)	.20	.50
OP01009 Carrot C	.08	.20
OP01010 Komachiyo C	.08	.20
OP01011 Gordon UC	.08	.20
OP01012 Sai C	.08	.20
OP01013 Sanji R	.08	.20
OP01013 Sanji ALT ART R	10.00	25.00
OP01014 Jinbe UC/""Play 1...""	.12	.25
OP01014 Jinbe UC/""Play up to 1...""	.12	.25
OP01015 Tony Tony.Chopper UC/""Add 1...""	.12	.25
OP01015 Tony Tony.Chopper UC/""Add up to 1...""	.12	.25
OP01016 Nami R/""reveal up to 1 {Straw Hat...""	.75	2.00
OP01016 Nami R/""reveal 1 {Straw Hat...""	.75	2.00
OP01016 Nami ALT ART R/""reveal 1 {Straw Hat...""	75.00	200.00
OP01016 Nami ALT ART R/""reveal up to 1 {Straw Hat...""	75.00	200.00
OP01017 Nico Robin R/""K.O. 1...""	.50	1.25
OP01017 Nico Robin R/""K.O. up to 1...""	.50	1.25
OP01018 Hajrudin C	.08	.20
OP01019 Bartolomeo C	.08	.20
OP01020 Hyogoro C/""Character: Your Leader...""	.08	.20
OP01020 Hyogoro C/""Character: Up to 1 of your Leader...""	.08	.20
OP01021 Franky UC	.12	.25
OP01022 Brook UC	.08	.20
OP01023 Marco C	.08	.20
OP01024 Monkey.D.Luffy SR	.40	1.00
OP01024 Monkey.D.Luffy ALT ART SR	12.00	30.00
OP01025 Roronoa Zoro SR	8.00	20.00
OP01025 Roronoa Zoro ALT ART SR CORR	40.00	100.00
OP01025 Roronoa Zoro ALT ART SR ERR/ Wave 1 Holo Color Wheel)	40.00	100.00
OP01026 Gum-Gum Fire-Fist Pistol Red Hawk R/""[Counter] Your Leader...""	.30	.75
OP01026 Gum-Gum Fire-Fist Pistol Red Hawk R ""[Counter] Up to 1 of your Leader...""	.30	.75
OP01027 Round Table C/""Give 1...""	.08	.20
OP01027 Round Table C/""Give up to 1...""	.08	.20
OP01028 Green Star Rafflesia C/""Give 1...""	.08	.20
OP01028 Green Star Rafflesia C/""Give up to 1...""	.08	.20
OP01029 Radical Beam!! UC/""[Counter] Your Leader...""	.25	.60
OP01029 Radical Beam!! UC/""[Counter] Up to 1 of your Leader...""	.25	.60
OP01030 In Two Years!! At the Sabaody Archipelago!! UC/""reveal 1 {Straw Hat...""	.08	.20
OP01030 In Two Years!! At the Sabaody Archipelago!! UC/""reveal up to 1 {Straw Hat...""	.08	.20
OP01031 Kouzuki Oden L	.10	.25
OP01031 Kouzuki Oden ALT ART L	20.00	50.00
OP01032 Ashura Doji UC	.12	.25
OP01033 Izo UC/""[On Play] Rest up to 1...""	.20	.50
OP01033 Izo UC/""[On Play] Rest 1...""	.20	.50
OP01034 Inuarashi C/""Set 1...""	.08	.20
OP01034 Inuarashi C/""Set up to 1...""	.08	.20
OP01034 Inuarashi ALT ART C/(Box Topper/""Set 1..."")	.30	.75
OP01034 Inuarashi ALT ART C/(Box Topper/""Set up to 1..."")	.30	.75
OP01035 Okiku R/""[Once Per Turn] Rest up to 1...""	.20	.50
OP01035 Okiku R/""[Once Per Turn] Rest 1...""	.20	.50
OP01036 Otsuru C	.08	.20
OP01037 Kawamatsu C	.08	.20
OP01038 Kanjuro C/""K.O. up to 1...""	.08	.20
OP01038 Kanjuro C/""K.O. 1...""	.08	.20
OP01039 Killer UC	.15	.40
OP01040 Kin'emon SR/""play 1...""	.12	.30
OP01040 Kin'emon SR/""play up to 1...""	.12	.30
OP01040 Kin'emon ALT ART SR/""play 1...""	3.00	8.00
OP01040 Kin'emon ALT ART SR/""play up to 1...""	3.00	8.00
OP01041 Kouzuki Momonosuke R ""reveal up to 1 {Land of Wano...""	.08	.20
OP01041 Kouzuki Momonosuke R/""reveal 1 {Land of Wano...""	.08	.20
OP01042 Komurasaki UC/""set up to 1...""	.12	.25
OP01042 Komurasaki UC/""set 1...""	.12	.25
OP01043 Shinobu C	.08	.20
OP01044 Shachi C/""play up to 1...""	.08	.20
OP01044 Shachi C/""play 1...""	.08	.20
OP01045 Jean Bart C	.08	.20
OP01046 Denjiro R	.15	.30
OP01047 Trafalgar Law SR/""return 1 Character...""	6.00	15.00
OP01047 Trafalgar Law SR/""return 1 of your Characters...""	6.00	15.00
OP01047 Trafalgar Law ALT ART SR/""return 1 Character...""	30.00	80.00
OP01047 Trafalgar Law ALT ART SR ""return 1 of your Characters...""	30.00	80.00
OP01048 Nekomamushi C/""[On Play] Rest 1...""	.08	.20
OP01048 Nekomamushi C/""[On Play] Rest up to 1...""	.08	.20
OP01048 Nekomamushi ALT ART C/(Box Topper ""[On Play] Rest 1..."")	.75	2.00
OP01048 Nekomamushi ALT ART C/(Box Topper ""[On Play] Rest up to 1..."")	.75	2.00
OP01049 Bepo R/""[When Attacking] Play up to 1...""	.15	.30
OP01049 Bepo R/""[When Attacking] Play 1...""	.15	.30
OP01050 Penguin C/""play up to 1...""	.08	.20
OP01050 Penguin C/""play 1...""	.08	.20
OP01051 Eustass""Captain""Kid SR/""cannot attack any Character...""	.75	2.00
OP01051 Eustass""Captain""Kid SR/""cannot attack any card other than...""	.75	2.00
OP01051 Eustass""Captain""Kid ALT ART SR ""cannot attack any Character...""	8.00	20.00
OP01051 Eustass""Captain""Kid ALT ART SR/ ""cannot attack any card other than...""	8.00	20.00
OP01052 Raizo UC	.10	.25
OP01053 Wire C	.08	.20
OP01054 X. Drake R/""[On Play] K.O. up to 1...""	.12	.30
OP01054 X. Drake R/""[On Play] K.O. 1...""	.12	.30
OP01055 You Can Be My Samurai!! C	.08	.20
OP01056 Demon Face UC/""[Main] K.O. up to 2...""	.08	.20
OP01056 Demon Face UC/""[Main] K.O. 2...""	.08	.20
OP01057 Paradise Waterfall UC/""[Counter] Up to 1 of your Leader...""	.25	.60
OP01057 Paradise Waterfall UC/""[Counter] Your Leader...""	.25	.60
OP01058 Punk Gibson R/""[Counter] Up to 1 of your Leader...""	2.00	5.00
OP01058 Punk Gibson R/""[Counter] Your Leader...""	2.00	5.00
OP01059 BE-BENG!! C/""Set up to 1 of your...""	.08	.20
OP01059 BE-BENG!! C/""Set 1 of your...""	.08	.20
OP01060 Donquixote Doflamingo L	.12	.30
OP01060 Donquixote Doflamingo ALT ART L	40.00	100.00
OP01061 Kaido L/""add 1 card...""	.10	.25
OP01061 Kaido L/""add up to 1 DON!!...""	.10	.25
OP01061 Kaido ALT ART L/""add 1 card...""	25.00	60.00
OP01061 Kaido ALT ART L/""add up to 1 DON!!...""	25.00	60.00
OP01062 Crocodile L	.08	.20
OP01062 Crocodile ALT ART L	25.00	60.00
OP01063 Arlong UC/""place up to 1 card...""	.12	.25
OP01063 Arlong UC/""place 1 card...""	.12	.25
OP01064 Alvida C/(""Return 1 of your..."")	.10	.20
OP01064 Alvida C/(""Return up to 1 of your..."")	.10	.20
OP01064 Alvida ALT ART C/(Box Topper/""Return 1 of your..."")	3.00	8.00
OP01064 Alvida ALT ART C/(Box Topper ""Return up to 1 of your..."")	3.00	8.00
OP01065 Vergo C	.08	.20
OP01066 Krieg C	.08	.20
OP01067 Crocodile SR	.15	.40
OP01067 Crocodile ALT ART SR	8.00	20.00
OP01068 Gecko Moria R	.08	.20
OP01069 Caesar Clown R/""[On K.O.] Play up to 1...""	.15	.30
OP01069 Caesar Clown R/""[On K.O.] Play 1...""	.15	.30
OP01070 Dracule Mihawk SR/""[On Play] Place 1...""	3.00	8.00
OP01070 Dracule Mihawk SR/""[On Play] Place up to 1...""	3.00	8.00
OP01070 Dracule Mihawk ALT ART SR/""[On Play] Place 1...""	20.00	50.00
OP01070 Dracule Mihawk ALT ART SR/""[On Play] Place up to 1...""	20.00	50.00
OP01071 Jinbe R/""[On Play] Place up to 1...""	.08	.20
OP01071 Jinbe R/""[On Play] Place 1...""	.08	.20
OP01072 Smiley C	.08	.20
OP01073 Donquixote Doflamingo R	.40	1.00
OP01073 Donquixote Doflamingo ALT ART R	15.00	40.00
OP01074 Bartholomew Kuma R/""[On K.O.] Play up to 1...""	.15	.40
OP01074 Bartholomew Kuma R/""[On K.O.] Play 1...""	.15	.40
OP01075 Pacifista C	.15	.40
OP01076 Bellamy C	.08	.20
OP01077 Perona ALT ART UC/(Box Topper)	6.00	15.00
OP01077 Perona UC	.20	.50
OP01078 Boa Hancock SR	2.50	6.00
OP01078 Boa Hancock ALT ART SR	30.00	80.00
OP01079 Ms. All Sunday R/""add up to 1 Event...""	.12	.30
OP01079 Ms. All Sunday R/""add 1 Event...""	.12	.30
OP01080 Miss Doublefinger (Zala) C	.08	.20
OP01081 Mocha C	.08	.20
OP01082 Monet C	.08	.20
OP01083 Mr. 1 (Daz. Bonez) UC	.10	.25
OP01084 Mr. 2 Bon Kurei (Bentham) UC/""deck; reveal up to 1...""	.10	.25
OP01084 Mr. 2 Bon Kurei (Bentham) UC/""deck; reveal 1...""	.10	.25
OP01085 Mr. 3 (Galdino) UC/""select up to 1 of...""	.10	.25
OP01085 Mr. 3 (Galdino) UC/""select 1 of...""	.10	.25
OP01086 Overheat R/""[Counter] Up to 1 of your Leader...""	.60	1.50
OP01086 Overheat R/""[Counter] Your Leader...""	.60	1.50
OP01087 Officer Agents C/""[Counter] Play up to 1...""	.08	.20
OP01087 Officer Agents C/""[Counter] Play 1...""	.08	.20
OP01088 Desert Spada UC/""[Counter] Up to 1 of your Leader...""	.15	.40
OP01088 Desert Spada UC/""[Counter] Your Leader...""	.15	.40
OP01089 Crescent Cutlass C/return up to 1...""	.08	.20
OP01089 Crescent Cutlass C/return 1...""	.08	.20
OP01090 Baroque Works UC/""deck; reveal up to 1...""	.10	.25
OP01090 Baroque Works UC/""deck; reveal 1...""	.10	.25
OP01091 King L	.08	.20
OP01091 King ALT ART L	15.00	40.00
OP01092 Urashima C	.08	.20
OP01093 Ulti R/""Add 1 card...""	.15	.40
OP01093 Ulti R/""Add up to 1 DON!!...""	.15	.40
OP01093 Ulti ALT ART R/""Add 1 card...""	6.00	15.00
OP01093 Ulti ALT ART R/""Add up to 1 DON!!...""	6.00	15.00
OP01094 Kaido SR	.30	.75
OP01094 Kaido ALT ART SR	8.00	20.00
OP01095 Kyoshirou UC	.10	.25
OP01096 King SR/""K.O. 1 of your...""	.25	.60
OP01096 King SR/""K.O. up to 1 of your...""	.25	.60
OP01096 King ALT ART SR/""K.O. 1 of your...""	8.00	20.00
OP01096 King ALT ART SR/""K.O. up to 1 of your...""	8.00	20.00
OP01097 Queen R/""Give 1 of your...""	.12	.30
OP01097 Queen R/""Then, give 1 of your...""	.12	.30
OP01097 Queen ALT ART R/""Give 1 of your...""	2.50	6.00
OP01097 Queen ALT ART R/""Then, give 1 of your...""	2.50	6.00
OP01098 Kurozumi Orochi UC/""[On Play] Reveal 1...""	.10	.25

OP01098 Kurozumi Orochi UC/""[On Play] Reveal up to 1...""	.10	.25
OP01099 Kurozumi Semimaru C	.08	.20
OP01100 Kurozumi Higurashi C	.08	.20
OP01101 Sasaki UC/""Add 1 card from...""	.15	.40
OP01101 Sasaki UC/""Add up to 1 DON!!...""	.15	.40
OP01102 Jack R	.12	.30
OP01102 Jack ALT ART R	2.50	6.00
OP01103 Scratchmen Apoo C	.08	.20
OP01104 Speed C	.08	.20
OP01105 Bao Huang C	.08	.20
OP01106 Basil Hawkins UC/""[On Play] Add 1...""	.10	.25
OP01106 Basil Hawkins UC/""[On Play] Add up to 1 DON!!...""	.10	.25
OP01107 Babanuki C	.08	.20
OP01108 Hitokiri Kamazo UC/""K.O. 1 of your...""	.10	.25
OP01108 Hitokiri Kamazo UC/""K.O. up to 1 of your...""	.10	.25
OP01109 Who's Who UC	.10	.25
OP01109 Who's Who ALT ART UC/(Box Topper)	.20	.50
OP01110 Fukurokuju C	.08	.20
OP01111 Black Maria R	.08	.20
OP01112 Page One R	.08	.20
OP01113 Holedem C/""Add 1 card...""	.08	.20
OP01113 Holedem C/""Add up to 1 DON!!...""	.08	.20
OP01114 X. Drake R	.15	.40
OP01115 Elephant's Marchoo C/""K.O. one of your...""	.08	.20
OP01115 Elephant's Marchoo C/""K.O. up to 1 of your...""	.08	.20
OP01116 Artificial Devil Fruit Smile UC/""play 1...""	.10	.25
OP01116 Artificial Devil Fruit Smile UC/""play up to 1...""	.10	.25
OP01117 Sheep's Horn C/""Rest 1 of your...""	.08	.20
OP01117 Sheep's Horn C/""Rest up to 1 of your...""	.08	.20
OP01118 Ulti-Mortar UC/""Your Leader or...""	.10	.25
OP01118 Ulti-Mortar UC/""Up to 1 of your Leader...""	.10	.25
OP01119 Thunder Bagua R/""[Counter] Your Leader...]""	.40	1.00
OP01119 Thunder Bagua R/""[Counter] Up to 1 of your Leader...]""	.40	1.00
OP01120 Shanks SEC	6.00	15.00
OP01120 Shanks ALT ART SEC	10.00	25.00
OP01120 Shanks MANGA ART SEC	300.00	800.00
OP01121 Yamato SEC	6.00	15.00
OP01121 Yamato ALT ART SEC	20.00	50.00

2022 One Piece Starter Deck Animal Kingdom Pirates

ST04001 Kaido L	.25	.50
ST04002 Ulti C	.10	.20
ST04003 Kaido SR	.30	.75
ST04004 King SR	1.00	2.00
ST04005 Queen C	5.00	10.00
ST04006 Sasaki C	.10	.20
ST04007 Sheepshead C	.10	.20
ST04008 Jack C	.10	.20
ST04009 Ginrummy C	.10	.20
ST04010 Who's.Who C	.10	.20
ST04011 Black Maria C	.10	.20
ST04012 Page One C	.10	.20
ST04013 X.Drake C	.10	.20
ST04014 Lead Performer ""Disaster"" C	.10	.20
ST04015 Brachio Bomber C	.10	.20
ST04016 Blast Breath C	.10	.20
ST04017 Onigashima Island C	.10	.20

2022 One Piece Starter Deck Straw Hat Crew

ST01001 Monkey.D.Luffy L	.50	1.00
ST01002 Usopp C	.10	.20
ST01003 Karoo C	.10	.20
ST01004 Sanji C	.10	.20
ST01005 Jinbe C	.10	.20
ST01006 Tony Tony.Chopper C	.20	.40
ST01007 Nami C	.15	.30
ST01008 Nico Robin C	.10	.20
ST01009 Nefeltari Vivi C	.10	.20
ST01010 Franky C	.10	.20
ST01011 Brook C	2.00	4.00
ST01012 Monkey.D.Luffy SR	2.50	5.00
ST01013 Roronoa Zoro SR	.60	1.25
ST01014 Guard Point C	4.00	8.00
ST01015 Gum-Gum Jet Pistol C	.10	.20
ST01016 Diable Jambe C	.12	.25
ST01017 Thousand Sunny C	.10	.20

2022 One Piece Starter Deck The Seven Warlords of the Sea

ST03001 Crocodile L	.15	.30
ST03002 Edward Weevil C	.10	.20
ST03003 Crocodile SR	.20	.40
ST03004 Gecko Moria C	.20	.40
ST03005 Dracule Mihawk C	5.00	10.00
ST03006 Jinbe C	.10	.20
ST03007 Sentomaru C	.17	.35
ST03008 Trafalgar Law C	.30	.75
ST03009 Donquixote Doflamingo SR	.30	.60
ST03010 Bartholomew Kuma C	.10	.20
ST03011 Buggy C	.10	.20
ST03012 Pacifista C	.10	.20
ST03013 Boa Hancock C	.10	.20
ST03014 Marshall.D.Teach C	.20	.40
ST03015 Sables C	.10	.20
ST03016 Thrust Pad Cannon C	.10	.20
ST03017 Love-Love Mellow C	6.00	12.00

2022 One Piece Starter Deck Worst Generation

ST02001 Eustass ""Captain"" Kid L	2.50	5.00
ST02002 Vito C	.10	.20
ST02003 Urouge C	.10	.20
ST02004 Capone ""Gang"" Bege C	.60	1.25
ST02005 Killer C	.12	.25
ST02006 Koby C	.10	.20
ST02007 Jewelry Bonney C	.60	1.25
ST02008 Scratchmen Apoo C	.20	.40
ST02009 Trafalgar Law SR	2.00	4.00
ST02010 Basil Hawkins C	.75	1.50
ST02011 Heat C	.10	.20
ST02012 Bepo C	.10	.20
ST02013 Eustass ""Captain"" Kid SR/""Set this card as...""	1.00	2.00
ST02013 Eustass ""Captain"" Kid SR/""Set this Character as...""	1.00	2.00
ST02014 X.Drake C	.10	.20
ST02015 Scalpel C	.10	.20
ST02016 Repel C	.10	.20
ST02017 Straw Sword C	.10	.20

2023 One Piece Awakening of the New Era

OP01016 Nami ALT ART SP	60.00	150.00
OP01121 Yamato ALT ART SP	40.00	100.00
OP03092 Rob Lucci ALT ART SP	15.00	40.00
OP04044 Kaido ALT ART SP	25.00	60.00
OP05001 Sabo L	.10	.25
OP05001 Sabo ALT ART L	10.00	25.00
OP05002 Belo Betty L	.08	.20
OP05002 Belo Betty ALT ART L	10.00	25.00
OP05003 Inazuma U	.08	.20
OP05004 Emporio.Ivankov U	.10	.25
OP05005 Karasu R	.15	.40
OP05006 Koala SR	.60	1.50
OP05006 Koala ALT ART SR	6.00	15.00
OP05007 Sabo SR	.25	.60
OP05007 Sabo ALT ART SR	2.00	5.00
OP05008 Chaka U	.08	.20
OP05010 Nico Robin U	.12	.30
OP05012 Hack C	.10	.25
OP05015 Belo Betty R	.12	.30
OP05015 Belo Betty ALT ART R	6.00	15.00
OP05016 Morley R	.08	.20
OP05017 Lindbergh R	.20	.50
OP05018 Emporio Energy Hormone C	.08	.20
OP05019 Fire Fist R	.12	.30
OP05020 Four Thousand-Brick Fist U	.08	.20
OP05021 Revolutionary Army HQ U	.08	.20
OP05022 Donquixote Rosinante L	.08	.20
OP05022 Donquixote Rosinante ALT ART L	10.00	25.00
OP05026 Sarquiss C	.08	.20
OP05027 Trafalgar Law U	.08	.20
OP05029 Donquixote Doflamingo U	.08	.20
OP05030 Donquixote Rosinante R	1.00	2.50
OP05032 Pica SR	.10	.25
OP05032 Pica ALT ART SR	1.50	4.00
OP05033 Baby 5 C	.08	.20
OP05034 Baby 5 R	.50	1.25
OP05034 Baby 5 ALT ART R	12.00	30.00
OP05035 Bellamy C	.08	.20
OP05036 Monet U	.10	.25
OP05037 Because the Side of Justice Will Be Whichever Side Wins!! R	.20	.50
OP05039 Stick-Stickem Meteora U	.08	.20
OP05040 Birdcage C	.08	.20
OP05041 Sakazuki L	.10	.25
OP05041 Sakazuki ALT ART L	15.00	40.00
OP05042 Issho R	.08	.20
OP05043 Ulti SR	.25	.60
OP05043 Ulti ALT ART SR	3.00	8.00
OP05047 Basil Hawkins C	.08	.20
OP05050 Hina R	.10	.25
OP05051 Borsalino SR	.20	.50
OP05051 Borsalino ALT ART SR	2.50	6.00
OP05054 Monkey.D.Garp U	.10	.25
OP05055 X.Drake R	.10	.25
OP05055 X.Drake ALT ART R	2.50	6.00
OP05057 Hound Blaze R	.10	.25
OP05059 Let Us Begin the World of Violence!!! U	.08	.20
OP05060 Monkey.D.Luffy L	.10	.25
OP05060 Monkey.D.Luffy ALT ART L	20.00	50.00
OP05061 Uso-Hachi U	.10	.25
OP05062 O-Nami U	.10	.25
OP05063 O-Robi C	.08	.20
OP05064 Killer R	.10	.25
OP05067 Zoro-Juurou R	.30	.75
OP05067 Zoro-Juurou ALT ART R	15.00	40.00
OP05068 Chopa-Emon C	.08	.20
OP05069 Trafalgar Law SR	.25	.60
OP05069 Trafalgar Law ALT ART SR	600.00	1,500.00
OP05069 Trafalgar Law MANGA ART SR	3.00	8.00
OP05070 Fra-Nosuke U	.10	.25
OP05071 Bepo R	.08	.20
OP05072 Hone-Kichi C	.08	.20
OP05073 Miss Doublefinger(Zala) U	.20	.50
OP05074 Eustass""Captain""Kid SR	3.00	8.00
OP05074 Eustass""Captain""Kid ALT ART SR	20.00	50.00
OP05074 Eustass""Captain""Kid MANGA ART SR	500.00	1,200.00
OP05075 Mr.1(Daz.Bonez) C	.08	.20
OP05076 When You're at Sea You Fight against Pirates!! R	.10	.25
OP05078 Punk Rotten U	.08	.20
OP05079 Viola U	.08	.20
OP05081 One-Legged Toy Soldier U	.12	.30
OP05082 Shirahoshi R	.10	.25
OP05086 Nefeltari Vivi R	.08	.20
OP05088 Mansherry R	.08	.20
OP05088 Mansherry ALT ART R	4.00	10.00
OP05090 Riku Doldo III C	.08	.20
OP05091 Rebecca SR	2.50	6.00
OP05091 Rebecca ALT ART SR	20.00	50.00
OP05093 Rob Lucci SR	1.25	3.00
OP05093 Rob Lucci ALT ART SR	25.00	60.00
OP05098 Enel L	.10	.25
OP05098 Enel ALT ART L	40.00	100.00
OP05100 Enel SR	.50	1.25
OP05100 Enel ALT ART SR	6.00	15.00
OP05100 Enel ALT ART SP	40.00	100.00
OP05101 Ohm R	.12	.30
OP05102 Gedatsu R	.30	.75
OP05102 Gedatsu ALT ART R	10.00	25.00
OP05104 Conis U	.08	.20
OP05105 Satori R	.30	.75
OP05106 Shura R	.10	.25
OP05108 Nola C	.08	.20
OP05114 El Thor U	.10	.25
OP05115 Two-Hundred Million Volts Amaru R	.25	.60
OP05117 Upper Yard U	.08	.20
OP05118 Kaido SEC	6.00	15.00
OP05118 Kaido ALT ART SEC	12.00	30.00
OP05119 Monkey.D.Luffy SEC	5.00	12.00
OP05119 Monkey.D.Luffy ALT ART SEC	20.00	50.00
OP05119 Monkey.D.Luffy MANGA ART SEC	2,500.00	6,000.00
ST01012 Monkey.D.Luffy SIGNED SP (1st Anniversary Special Card)	1,000.00	2,500.00
ST01012 Monkey.D.Luffy/(1st Anniversary Special Card)	6.00	15.00

2023 One Piece Kingdoms of Intrigue

OP01047 Trafalgar Law ALT ART SP	40.00	100.00
OP01078 Boa Hancock ALT ART SP	50.00	120.00
OP02004 Edward.Newgate ALT ART SP	25.00	60.00
OP02085 Magellan ALT ART SP	30.00	80.00
OP02099 Sakazuki ALT ART SP	20.00	50.00
OP04001 Nefeltari Vivi L	.08	.20
OP04001 Nefeltari Vivi ALT ART L	25.00	60.00
OP04002 Igaram R	.08	.20
OP04003 Usopp UC	.08	.20
OP04004 Karoo C	.08	.20
OP04005 Kung Fu Dugong C	.08	.20
OP04006 Koza UC	.08	.20
OP04007 Sanji C	.08	.20
OP04008 Chaka R	.08	.20
OP04009 Super Spot-Billed Duck Troops UC	.08	.20
OP04010 Tony Tony.Chopper C	.08	.20
OP04011 Nami C	.08	.20
OP04012 Nefeltari Cobra C	.08	.20
OP04013 Pell SR	.20	.50
OP04013 Pell ALT ART SR	4.00	10.00
OP04014 Monkey.D.Luffy UC	.08	.20
OP04015 Roronoa Zoro R	.08	.20
OP04016 Bad Manners Kick Course R	.08	.20
OP04017 Happiness Punch C	.08	.20
OP04018 Enchanting Vertigo Dance UC	.08	.20
OP04019 Donquixote Doflamingo L	.08	.20
OP04019 Donquixote Doflamingo ALT ART L	30.00	80.00
OP04020 Issho L	.08	.20
OP04020 Issho ALT ART L	12.00	30.00
OP04021 Viola C	.08	.20
OP04022 Eric UC	.08	.20
OP04023 Kuro C	.08	.20
OP04024 Sugar SR	.60	1.50
OP04024 Sugar ALT ART SR	8.00	20.00
OP04025 Giolla C	.08	.20
OP04026 Senor Pink R	.08	.20
OP04027 Daddy Masterson C	.08	.20
OP04028 Diamante R	.08	.20
OP04028 Diamante ALT ART R	5.00	12.00
OP04029 Dellinger C	.08	.20
OP04030 Trebol R	.08	.20
OP04030 Trebol ALT ART R	2.50	6.00
OP04031 Donquixote Doflamingo SR	.75	2.00
OP04031 Donquixote Doflamingo ALT ART SR	12.00	30.00
OP04032 Baby 5 UC	.08	.20
OP04033 Machvise UC	.08	.20
OP04034 Lao G UC	.08	.20
OP04035 Spiderweb R	.15	.40
OP04036 Donquixote Family C	.08	.20
OP04037 Flapping Thread UC	.08	.20
OP04038 The Weak Do Not Have the Right to Choose How They Die!!! C	.08	.20
OP04039 Rebecca L	.08	.20
OP04039 Rebecca ALT ART L	40.00	100.00
OP04040 Queen L	.08	.20
OP04040 Queen ALT ART L	15.00	40.00
OP04041 Apis C	.08	.20
OP04042 Ipponmatsu C	.08	.20
OP04043 Ulti R	.08	.20
OP04044 Kaido SR	.60	1.50
OP04044 Kaido ALT ART SR	10.00	25.00
OP04045 King R	.08	.20
OP04046 Queen UC	.08	.20
OP04047 Ice Oni C	.08	.20
OP04048 Sasaki UC	.08	.20
OP04049 Jack UC	.08	.20
OP04050 Mr. Hanger C	.08	.20
OP04051 Who's Who R	.08	.20
OP04051 Who's Who ALT ART R	6.00	15.00
OP04052 Black Maria UC	.08	.20
OP04053 Page One UC	.08	.20
OP04054 Rokki C	.08	.20
OP04055 Plague Rounds C	.08	.20
OP04056 Gum Gum Red Roc R	.40	1.00
OP04057 Dragon Twister Demolition Breath UC	.08	.20
OP04058 Crocodile L	.08	.20
OP04058 Crocodile ALT ART L	15.00	40.00
OP04059 Iceburg UC	.08	.20
OP04060 Crocodile SR	.25	.60
OP04060 Crocodile ALT ART SR	5.00	12.00
OP04061 Tom C	.08	.20
OP04062 Banana Gator C	.08	.20
OP04063 Franky R	.08	.20
OP04064 Miss All Sunday SR	2.00	5.00
OP04064 Miss All Sunday ALT ART SR	15.00	40.00
OP04065 Miss.Goldenweek(Marianne) C	.08	.20
OP04066 Miss Valentine (Mikita) R	.08	.20
OP04067 Miss.Merry Christmas(Drophy) C	.08	.20
OP04068 Yokozuna C	.08	.20
OP04069 Mr. 2 Bon Clay (Bentham) UC	.08	.20
OP04070 Mr. 3 (Galdino) UC	.08	.20
OP04071 Mr. 4 (Babe) UC	.08	.20
OP04072 Mr. 5 (Gem) R	.08	.20
OP04072 Mr. 5 (Gem) ALT ART R	2.00	5.00
OP04073 Mr. 13 & Miss Friday C	.08	.20
OP04074 Colors Trap R	.08	.20
OP04075 Nez Palm Cannon UC	.08	.20
OP04076 Weakness... Is an Unforgivable Sin. C	.08	.20
OP04077 Ideo C	.08	.20
OP04078 Oimo & Kashii C	.08	.20
OP04079 Orlumbus C	.08	.20
OP04080 Gyats UC	.08	.20
OP04081 Cavendish R	.08	.20
OP04082 Kyros R	.12	.30
OP04082 Kyros ALT ART R	6.00	15.00
OP04083 Sabo SR	4.00	10.00
OP04083 Sabo ALT ART SR	20.00	50.00
OP04083 Sabo MANGA ART SR	250.00	600.00
OP04084 Stussy C	.08	.20
OP04085 Suleiman UC	.08	.20
OP04086 Chinjao C	.08	.20
OP04087 Trafalgar Law C	.08	.20
OP04088 Hajrudin UC	.08	.20
OP04089 Bartolomeo R	.30	.75
OP04090 Monkey.D.Luffy SR	1.00	2.50
OP04090 Monkey.D.Luffy ALT ART SR	12.00	30.00
OP04091 Leo UC	.08	.20
OP04092 Rebecca R	.20	.50
OP04093 Gum-Gum King Kong Gun UC	.08	.20
OP04094 Trueno Bastardo R	.08	.20
OP04095 Barrier!! C	.08	.20
OP04096 Corrida Colosseum C	.08	.20
OP04097 Otama C	.08	.20
OP04098 Toko UC	.08	.20
OP04099 Olin R	.08	.20
OP04100 Capone ""Gang"" Bege R	.50	1.25
OP04100 Capone ""Gang"" Bege ALT ART R	15.00	40.00
OP04101 Carmel C	.08	.20
OP04102 Kin'emon R	.08	.20
OP04103 Kouzuki Hiyori UC	.08	.20
OP04104 Sanji SR	3.00	8.00
OP04104 Sanji ALT ART SR	20.00	50.00
OP04105 Charlotte Amande R	.08	.20
OP04106 Charlotte Bavarois C	.08	.20
OP04107 Charlotte Perospero C	.08	.20
OP04108 Charlotte Moscato UC	.08	.20
OP04109 Tonoyasu C	.08	.20
OP04110 Pound C	.08	.20
OP04111 Hera U	.08	.20
OP04112 Yamato SR	4.00	10.00
OP04112 Yamato ALT ART SR	40.00	100.00
OP04113 Rabiyan C	.08	.20
OP04114 Randolph C	.08	.20
OP04115 Gun Modoki C	.08	.20
OP04116 Diable Jambe Joue Shot U	.08	.20
OP04117 Heavenly Fire R	.08	.20
OP04118 Nefeltari Vivi SEC	2.00	5.00
OP04118 Nefeltari Vivi ALT ART SEC	12.00	30.00
OP04119 Donquixote Rosinante SEC	2.00	5.00
OP04119 Donquixote Rosinante ALT ART SEC	8.00	20.00

2023 One Piece Paramount War

OP02001 Edward.Newgate L	.15	.30
OP02001 Edward.Newgate ALT ART L	75.00	150.00
OP02002 Monkey.D.Garp L/""Leader or 1 of...""	.12	.25
OP02002 Monkey.D.Garp L/""Leader or any of...""	.12	.25
OP02002 Monkey.D.Garp ALT ART L/""Leader or 1 of...""	40.00	80.00
OP02002 Monkey.D.Garp ALT ART L/""Leader or any of...""	40.00	80.00

OP02003 Atmos C	.10	.20
OP02004 Edward.Newgate SR	7.50	15.00
OP02004 Edward.Newgate ALT ART SR	30.00	75.00
OP02005 Curly.Dadan UC	.30	.60
OP02006 Kingdew C	.10	.20
OP02007 Thatch C	.10	.20
OP02008 Jozu R	1.00	2.00
OP02009 Squard UC	.12	.25
OP02009 Squard ALT ART UC/(Box Topper)	.75	1.50
OP02010 Dogura C	.10	.20
OP02011 Vista R	1.00	2.00
OP02012 Blenheim C	.10	.20
OP02013 Portgas.D.Ace SR	4.00	8.00
OP02013 Portgas.D.Ace ALT ART SR	30.00	75.00
OP02013 Portgas.D.Ace MANGA ART SR	500.00	1,000.00
OP02014 Whitey Bay UC	.12	.25
OP02015 Makino UC	.60	1.25
OP02016 Magura C	.10	.20
OP02017 Masked Deuce R	.15	.30
OP02017 Masked Deuce ALT ART R	4.00	8.00
OP02018 Marco R	2.00	4.00
OP02018 Marco ALT ART R	30.00	75.00
OP02019 Rakuyo UC	.12	.25
OP02020 LittleOars Jr. C	.10	.20
OP02021 Seaquake R	.25	.50
OP02022 Whitebear Pirates UC	.30	.75
OP02023 You May Be a Fool…but I Still Love You C	.10	.20
OP02024 Moby Dick C	.10	.20
OP02025 Kin'emon L	.12	.25
OP02025 Kin'emon ALT ART L	30.00	75.00
OP02026 Sanji L	.12	.25
OP02026 Sanji ALT ART L	30.00	60.00
OP02027 Inuarashi UC	.12	.25
OP02028 Usopp C	.10	.20
OP02029 Carrot R	.15	.30
OP02030 Kouzuki Oden SR	.75	1.50
OP02030 Kouzuki Oden ALT ART SR	10.00	20.00
OP02031 Kouzuki Toki UC	.12	.25
OP02031 Kouzuki Toki ALT ART UC/(Box Topper)	2.50	5.00
OP02032 Shishilian UC	.12	.25
OP02033 Jinbe C	.10	.20
OP02034 Tony Tony.Chopper UC	.15	.30
OP02035 Trafalgar Law C	.10	.20
OP02036 Nami SR	3.00	6.00
OP02036 Nami ALT ART SR	30.00	60.00
OP02037 Nico Robin UC	.12	.25
OP02038 Nekomamushi C	.10	.20
OP02039 Franky C	.10	.20
OP02040 Brook R	.20	.40
OP02041 Monkey.D.Luffy R	.25	.50
OP02041 Monkey.D.Luffy ALT ART R	20.00	40.00
OP02042 Yamato R	.20	.40
OP02043 Roronoa Zoro C	.10	.20
OP02044 Wanda C	.10	.20
OP02045 Three Sword Style Oni Girl C	.10	.20
OP02046 Diable Jambe Venaison Shoot UC	.12	.25
OP02047 Paradise Totsuka R	.15	.30
OP02048 Land of Wano C	.10	.20
OP02049 Emporio.Ivankov L	.15	.30
OP02049 Emporio.Ivankov ALT ART L	30.00	60.00
OP02050 Inazuma R	.15	.30
OP02051 Emporio.Ivankov SR	.60	1.25
OP02051 Emporio.Ivankov ALT ART SR	7.50	15.00
OP02052 Cabaji C	.10	.20
OP02053 Crocodile C	.10	.20
OP02054 Gecko Moria C	.10	.20
OP02055 Dracule Mihawk C	.10	.20
OP02056 Donquixote Doflamingo UC	.12	.25
OP02057 Bartholomew Kuma UC	.12	.25
OP02058 Buggy R	.25	.50
OP02058 Buggy ALT ART R	10.00	20.00
OP02059 Boa Hancock UC	.12	.25
OP02059 Boa Hancock ALT ART UC/(Box Topper)	1.50	3.00
OP02060 Mohji C	.10	.20
OP02061 Morley UC	.12	.25
OP02062 Monkey.D.Luffy SR	.75	1.50
OP02062 Monkey.D.Luffy ALT ART SR	12.50	25.00
OP02063 Mr.1 (Daz.Bonez) UC	.12	.25
OP02064 Mr.2.Bon.Kurei (Bentham) R	.15	.30
OP02065 Mr.3 (Galdino) R	.15	.30
OP02066 Impel Down All Stars C	.10	.20
OP02067 Arabesque Brick Fist UC	.12	.25
OP02068 Gum-Gum Rain R	.15	.30
OP02069 DEATH WINK C	.10	.20
OP02070 New Kama Land C	.10	.20
OP02071 Magellan L/""DON!! card on your field...""	.12	.25
OP02071 Magellan L/""DON!! card on the field...""	.12	.25
OP02071 Magellan ALT ART L/""DON!! card on your field...""	30.00	60.00
OP02071 Magellan ALT ART L/""DON!! card on the field...""	30.00	60.00
OP02072 Zephyr L	.12	.25
OP02072 Zephyr ALT ART L	25.00	50.00
OP02073 Little Sadi R	.15	.30
OP02073 Little Sadi ALT ART R	10.00	20.00
OP02074 Saldeath C	.10	.20
OP02075 Shiki R	.15	.30
OP02076 Shiryu R	.15	.30
OP02077 Solitaire C	.10	.20
OP02078 Daifugo UC	.12	.25
OP02079 Douglas Bullet UC	.12	.25
OP02080 Dobon C	.10	.20
OP02081 Domino C	.10	.20
OP02082 Byrnndi World UC	.12	.25
OP02083 Hannyabal R	.15	.30
OP02084 Blugori C	.10	.20
OP02085 Magellan SR	1.50	3.00
OP02085 Magellan ALT ART SR	10.00	20.00
OP02086 Minokoala UC	.12	.25
OP02086 Minokoala ALT ART UC/(Box Topper)	2.00	4.00
OP02087 Minotaur UC	.12	.25
OP02088 Sphinx C	.10	.20
OP02089 Judgment of Hell R	.50	1.00
OP02090 Hydra UC	.12	.25
OP02091 Venom Road C	.10	.20
OP02092 Impel Down C	.10	.20
OP02093 Smoker L	.15	.30
OP02093 Smoker ALT ART L	50.00	100.00
OP02094 Isuka UC	.12	.25
OP02095 Onigumo UC	.12	.25
OP02096 Kuzan SR	3.00	6.00
OP02096 Kuzan ALT ART SR	20.00	40.00
OP02097 Komille C	.10	.20
OP02098 Koby R	.50	1.00
OP02099 Sakazuki SR	4.00	8.00
OP02099 Sakazuki ALT ART SR	25.00	50.00
OP02100 Jango C	.10	.20
OP02101 Strawberry C	.10	.20
OP02102 Smoker R	.15	.30
OP02103 Sengoku R	.15	.30
OP02104 Sentomaru C	.10	.20
OP02105 Tashigi C	.10	.20
OP02105 Tashigi ALT ART C/(Box Topper)	1.00	2.00
OP02106 Tsuru UC	.30	.75
OP02107 Doberman C	.10	.20
OP02108 Donquixote Rosinante C	.10	.20
OP02108 Donquixote Rosinante ALT ART C/(Box Topper)	3.00	6.00
OP02109 Jaguar.D.Saul C	.10	.20
OP02110 Hina R	.15	.30
OP02111 Fullbody C	.10	.20
OP02112 Bell-mere UC	.12	.25
OP02113 Helmeppo UC	.12	.25
OP02114 Borsalino SR	7.50	15.00
OP02114 Borsalino ALT ART SR	30.00	60.00
OP02115 Monkey.D.Garp R	.30	.60
OP02115 Monkey.D.Garp ALT ART R	17.50	35.00
OP02116 Yamakaji C	.10	.20
OP02117 Ice Age UC	.12	.25
OP02118 Yasakani Sacred Jewel C	.10	.20
OP02119 Meteor Volcano R	.20	.40
OP02120 Uta SEC	3.00	6.00
OP02120 Uta ALT ART SEC	15.00	30.00
OP02121 Kuzan SEC	12.50	25.00
OP02121 Kuzan ALT ART SEC	25.00	50.00

2023 One Piece Pillars of Strength

OP01051 Eustass ""Captain"" Kid ALT ART SP	20.00	40.00
OP03001 Portgas.D.Ace L	.15	.30
OP03001 Portgas.D.Ace ALT ART L	75.00	150.00
OP03002 Adio UC	.12	.25
OP03003 Izo R	.50	1.00
OP03004 Curiel C	.10	.20
OP03005 Thatch UC	.12	.25
OP03006 Speed Jil C	.10	.20
OP03007 Namule C	.10	.20
OP03008 Buggy UC	.25	.50
OP03009 Haruta C	.10	.20
OP03010 Fossa C	.10	.20
OP03011 Blamenco UC	.12	.25
OP03012 Marshall.D.Teach R	.15	.30
OP03013 Marco SR	12.50	25.00
OP03013 Marco ALT ART SR	30.00	75.00
OP03014 Monkey.D.Garp UC	.12	.25
OP03015 Lim UC	.12	.25
OP03016 Flame Emperor R	.20	.40
OP03017 Cross Fire UC	.12	.25
OP03018 Fire Fist R	.30	.60
OP03018 Fire Fist ALT ART R	17.50	35.00
OP03019 Fiery Doll C	.10	.20
OP03020 Striker C	.10	.20
OP03021 Kuro ALT ART L	25.00	50.00
OP03021 Kuro L	.12	.25
OP03022 Arlong L	.12	.25
OP03022 Arlong ALT ART L	25.00	50.00
OP03023 Alvida C	.10	.20
OP03024 Gin R	.15	.30
OP03024 Gin ALT ART R	7.50	15.00
OP03025 Krieg SR	.60	1.25
OP03025 Krieg ALT ART SR	7.50	15.00
OP03026 Kuroobi UC	.12	.25
OP03027 Sham C	.10	.20
OP03028 Jango R	.15	.30
OP03029 Chew UC	.12	.25
OP03030 Nami R	.15	.30
OP03031 Pearl C	.10	.20
OP03032 Buggy C	.10	.20
OP03033 Hatchan UC	.12	.25
OP03034 Buchi UC	.12	.25
OP03035 Momoo C	.10	.20
OP03036 Out-of-the-Bag C	.10	.20
OP03037 Tooth Attack C	.10	.20
OP03038 Deathly Poison Gas Bomb MH5	.15	.30
OP03039 One Two Jango UC	.12	.25
OP03040 Nami L	.20	.40
OP03040 Nami ALT ART L	75.00	150.00
OP03041 Usopp SR	.60	1.25
OP03041 Usopp ALT ART SR	6.00	12.00
OP03042 Usopp Pirates C	.10	.20
OP03043 Gaimon C	.10	.20
OP03044 Kaya R	.30	.75
OP03045 Carne UC	.12	.25
OP03046 Genzo C	.10	.20
OP03047 Zeff R/""and trash 2...""	.15	.30
OP03047 Zeff R/""and you may trash 2...""	.15	.30
OP03047 Zeff ALT ART R/""and trash 2...""	10.00	20.00
OP03047 Zeff ALT ART R/""and you may trash 2...""	10.00	20.00
OP03048 Nojiko UC	.15	.30
OP03049 Patty UC	.12	.25
OP03050 Boodle UC	.12	.25
OP03051 Bell-mere R	.15	.30
OP03052 Merry C	.10	.20
OP03053 Yosaku and Johnny C	.10	.20
OP03054 Usopp's Rubber Band of Doom!!! C/""and trash 1...""	.10	.20
OP03054 Usopp's Rubber Band of Doom!!! C ""and you may trash 1...""	.10	.20
OP03055 Gum-Gum Giant Gavel C	.10	.20
OP03056 Sanji's Pilaf UC	1.25	2.50
OP03057 Three Thousand Worlds R	.50	1.00
OP03058 Iceburg L	.12	.25
OP03058 Iceburg ALT ART L	25.00	50.00
OP03059 Kaku UC	.12	.25
OP03060 Kalifa UC	.12	.25
OP03061 Kiwi & Mozu C	.10	.20
OP03062 Kokoro R	.15	.30
OP03063 Zambai UC	.12	.25
OP03064 Tilestone C	.10	.20
OP03065 Chimney & Gombe C	.10	.20
OP03066 Paulie SR	.30	.60
OP03066 Paulie ALT ART SR	5.00	10.00
OP03067 Peepley Lulu UC	.12	.25
OP03068 Minozebra C	.10	.20
OP03069 Minorhinoceros C	.10	.20
OP03070 Monkey.D.Luffy R	.15	.30
OP03071 Rob Lucci R	.15	.30
OP03072 Gum-Gum Jet Gatling R	.15	.30
OP03073 Hull Dismantling Slash C	.10	.20
OP03074 Top Knot UC	.12	.25
OP03075 Galley-La Company C	.10	.20
OP03076 Rob Lucci L	.15	.30
OP03076 Rob Lucci ALT ART L	60.00	125.00
OP03077 Charlotte Linlin L	.12	.25
OP03077 Charlotte Linlin ALT ART L	30.00	60.00
OP03078 Issho SR	2.00	4.00
OP03078 Issho ALT ART SR	20.00	40.00
OP03079 Vergo UC	.12	.25
OP03080 Kaku SR	1.25	2.50
OP03080 Kaku ALT ART SR	12.50	25.00
OP03081 Kalifa R	.25	.50
OP03081 Kalifa ALT ART R	30.00	60.00
OP03082 Kumadori C	.12	.25
OP03083 Corgy C	.10	.20
OP03084 Jerry C	.10	.20
OP03085 Jabra C	.10	.20
OP03086 Spandam ALT ART R	10.00	20.00
OP03086 Spandam R	.20	.40
OP03087 Nero C	.10	.20
OP03088 Fukurou UC	.20	.40
OP03089 Brannew R	.15	.30
OP03090 Blueno R	.15	.30
OP03091 Helmeppo C	.10	.20
OP03092 Rob Lucci SR	.60	1.25
OP03092 Rob Lucci ALT ART SR	10.00	20.00
OP03093 Wanze UC	.12	.25
OP03094 Air Door UC	.17	.35
OP03095 Soap Sheep C	.10	.20
OP03096 Tempest Kick Sky Slicer UC	.12	.25
OP03097 Six King Pistol R	.15	.30
OP03098 Enies Lobby C	.10	.20
OP03099 Charlotte Katakuri L	.15	.30
OP03099 Charlotte Katakuri ALT ART L	100.00	200.00
OP03100 Kingbaum C	.10	.20
OP03101 Camie C	.10	.20
OP03102 Sanji R	.60	1.25
OP03103 Bobbin the Disposer C	.10	.20
OP03104 Shirley UC	.12	.25
OP03105 Charlotte Oven UC	.12	.25
OP03106 Charlotte Opera C	.10	.20
OP03107 Charlotte Garrett C	.10	.20
OP03108 Charlotte Cracker SR	3.00	6.00
OP03108 Charlotte Cracker ALT ART SR	30.00	60.00
OP03109 Charlotte Chiffon C	.10	.20
OP03110 Charlotte Smoothie R	.15	.30
OP03111 Charlotte Praline C	.10	.20
OP03112 Charlotte Pudding R	.20	.40
OP03112 Charlotte Pudding ALT ART R	40.00	80.00
OP03113 Charlotte Perospero SR	7.50	15.00
OP03113 Charlotte Perospero ALT ART SR	30.00	60.00
OP03114 Charlotte Linlin SR	6.00	12.00
OP03114 Charlotte Linlin ALT ART SR	30.00	60.00
OP03115 Streusen R	.60	1.25
OP03116 Shirahoshi UC	.12	.25
OP03117 Napoleon UC	.12	.25
OP03118 Ikoku Sovereignty UC	.40	.80
OP03119 Buzz Cut Mochi R	.15	.30
OP03120 Tropical Torment C	.10	.20
OP03121 Thunder Bolt C	.10	.20
OP03122 Sogeking SEC	7.50	15.00
OP03122 Sogeking ALT ART SEC	12.50	25.00
OP03122 Sogeking MANGA ART SEC	300.00	750.00
OP03123 Charlotte Katakuri SEC	30.00	60.00
OP03123 Charlotte Katakuri ALT ART SEC	50.00	100.00
ST01012 Monkey.D.Luffy ALT ART SP	50.00	100.00
ST03009 Donquixote Doflamingo ALT ART SP	17.50	35.00
ST04003 Kaido ALT ART SP	20.00	40.00

2023 One Piece Starter Deck Absolute Justice

ST06001 Sakazuki L	.25	.50
ST06002 Koby C	.10	.20
ST06003 Jango C	.10	.20
ST06004 Smoker SR	.75	1.50
ST06005 Sengoku C	.10	.20
ST06006 Tashigi C	.20	.40
ST06007 Tsuru C	.12	.25
ST06008 Hina C	.12	.25
ST06009 Fullbody C	.10	.20
ST06010 Helmeppo C	.10	.20
ST06011 Momonga C	.10	.20
ST06012 Monkey.D.Garp SR	.75	1.50
ST06013 T-Bone C	.10	.20
ST06014 Shockwave C	4.00	8.00
ST06015 Great Eruption C	.30	.75
ST06016 White Out C	.10	.20
ST06017 Navy HQ C	.10	.20

2023 One Piece Starter Deck Big Mom Pirates

ST07001 Charlotte Linlin L	.75	1.50
ST07002 Charlotte Anana C	.10	.20
ST07003 Charlotte Katakuri SR	1.75	3.50
ST07004 Charlotte Snack C	.10	.20
ST07005 Charlotte Daifuku C	.40	.80
ST07006 Charlotte Flampe C	.10	.20
ST07007 Charlotte Brulee C	3.00	6.00
ST07008 Charlotte Pudding C	.30	.75
ST07009 Charlotte Mont-d'Or C	.10	.20
ST07010 Charlotte Linlin SR	4.00	8.00
ST07011 Zeus C	1.00	2.00
ST07012 Baron Tamago C	.10	.20
ST07013 Prometheus C	.60	1.25
ST07014 Pekoms C	.10	.20
ST07015 Soul Pocus C	.50	1.00
ST07016 Power Mochi C	.12	.25
ST07017 Queen Mama Chanter C	.12	.25

2023 One Piece Starter Deck Film Edition

ST05001 Shanks L	.20	.40
ST05002 Ain C	.10	.20
ST05003 Ann C	.10	.20
ST05004 Uta SR	4.00	8.00
ST05005 Carina C	.15	.30
ST05006 Gild Tesoro C	1.50	3.00
ST05007 Gordon C	.10	.20
ST05008 Shiki C	.20	.40
ST05009 Scarlet C	.10	.20
ST05010 Zephyr C	.20	.40
ST05011 Douglas Bullet SR	.60	1.25
ST05012 Baccarat C	.10	.20
ST05013 Bins C	.10	.20
ST05014 Buena Festa C	.20	.40
ST05015 Dr. Indigo C	.10	.20
ST05016 Lion's Threat Imperial Earth Bind C	.25	.50
ST05017 Union Armada C	.10	.20

2023 One Piece Starter Deck 9 Yamato

ST09001 Yamato L	.50	1.25
ST09003 Ulti C	.10	.25
ST09005 Kouzuki Oden SR	.40	1.00
ST09007 Shinobu C	.10	.25
ST09010 Portgas.D.Ace SR	.25	.60
ST09011 Monkey.D.Luffy C	.08	.20
ST09012 Yamato C	.15	.40
ST09013 Yamato C	.08	.20
ST09014 Narikabura Arrow C	1.00	2.50
ST09015 Thunder Bagua C	.10	.25

2023 One Piece Starter Deck 10 Ultimate Deck The Three Captains

OP01016 Nami ALT ART R	5.00	12.00
OP01025 Roronoa Zoro ALT ART SR	.20	.50
ST10001 Trafalgar Law L	5.00	12.00
ST10002 Monkey.D.Luffy L	.20	.50
ST10003 Eustass""Captain""Kid L	15.00	40.00
ST10004 Sanji C	.10	.25
ST10005 Jinbe C	2.50	6.00

ST10006 Monkey.D.Luffy SR	.12	.30
ST10007 Killer C	2.00	5.00
ST10009 Jean Bart C	.20	.50
ST10010 Trafalgar Law SR	.10	.25
ST10011 Heat C	3.00	8.00
ST10012 Bepo C	.30	.75
ST10013 Eustass""Captain""Kid SR	2.50	6.00
ST10014 Wire C	.08	.20
ST10015 GumGum Giant Sumo Slap C	.50	1.25
ST10016 GumGum Kong Gatling C	.10	.25
ST10017 Punk Vise C	.10	.25

2024 One Piece 500 Years in the Future

NNO DON!! Card ALT ART	.20	.50
NNO DON!! Card (Trafalgar Law, Eustass Kid and Monkey.D.Luffy) (Double Pack Set Vol. 4)	2.00	5.00
NNO DON!! Card (Boa Hancock) (Double Pack Set Vol. 4)	4.00	10.00
OP01035 Okiku FOIL SP	12.00	30.00
OP01073 Donquixote Doflamingo FOIL SP	40.00	100.00
OP03003 Izo FOIL SP	25.00	60.00
OP03078 Issho FOIL SP	25.00	60.00
OP05074 Eustass""Captain""Kid FOIL SP	40.00	100.00
OP06101 O-Nami FOIL SP	75.00	200.00
OP07001 Monkey.D.Dragon L	.08	.20
OP07001 Monkey.D.Dragon ALT ART FOIL L	12.00	30.00
OP07002 Ain FOIL R	.08	.20
OP07005 Carina FOIL R	.10	.25
OP07005 Carina ALT ART FOIL R	4.00	10.00
OP07006 Sterry C	.08	.20
OP07009 Dogura & Magura C	.08	.20
OP07010 Baccarat FOIL R	.10	.25
OP07011 Bluejam C	.08	.20
OP07012 Porchemy C	.08	.20
OP07013 Masked Deuce U	.08	.20
OP07015 Monkey.D.Dragon FOIL SR	.60	1.50
OP07015 Monkey.D.Dragon ALT ART FOIL SR	8.00	20.00
OP07016 Galaxy Wink FOIL R	.08	.20
OP07017 Dragon Breath U	.08	.20
OP07019 Jewelry Bonney L	.10	.25
OP07019 Jewelry Bonney ALT ART FOIL L	50.00	120.00
OP07021 Urouge FOIL R	.15	.40
OP07022 Otama FOIL R	.20	.50
OP07022 Otama ALT ART FOIL R	10.00	25.00
OP07023 Caribou U	.08	.20
OP07026 Jewelry Bonney FOIL SR	1.25	3.00
OP07026 Jewelry Bonney ALT ART FOIL SR	15.00	40.00
OP07028 Scratchmen Apoo C	.08	.20
OP07029 Basil Hawkins FOIL SR	2.00	5.00
OP07029 Basil Hawkins ALT ART FOIL SR	20.00	50.00
OP07031 Bartolomeo U	.10	.25
OP07032 Fisher Tiger FOIL R	.08	.20
OP07033 Monkey.D.Luffy U	.08	.20
OP07034 Roronoa Zoro U	.08	.20
OP07035 Karmic Punishment C	.08	.20
OP07036 Demonic Aura Nine-Sword Style Asura Demon Nine Flash FOIL R	.10	.25
OP07037 More Pizza!! U	.08	.20
OP07038 Boa Hancock L	.12	.30
OP07038 Boa Hancock ALT ART FOIL L	50.00	120.00
OP07040 Crocodile U	.12	.30
OP07041 Gloriosa (Grandma Nyon) U	.08	.20
OP07045 Jinbe ALT ART FOIL SR	20.00	50.00
OP07045 Jinbe FOIL SR	2.00	5.00
OP07046 Sengoku FOIL R	.20	.50
OP07046 Sengoku ALT ART FOIL R	8.00	20.00
OP07047 Trafalgar Law FOIL R	.30	.75
OP07047 Trafalgar Law ALT ART FOIL R	12.00	30.00
OP07048 Donquixote Doflamingo U	.10	.25
OP07051 Boa Hancock FOIL SR	2.50	6.00
OP07051 Boa Hancock ALT ART FOIL SR	25.00	60.00
OP07051 Boa Hancock MANGA ART	600.00	1,500.00
OP07053 Portgas.D.Ace FOIL R	.12	.30
OP07054 Marguerite FOIL R	.10	.25
OP07055 Snake Dance C	.08	.20
OP07056 Slave Arrow U	.08	.20
OP07057 Perfume Femur FOIL R	.15	.40
OP07059 Foxy L	.08	.20
OP07059 Foxy ALT ART FOIL L	12.00	30.00
OP07060 Itomimizu U	.08	.20
OP07064 Sanji FOIL SR	4.00	10.00
OP07064 Sanji ALT ART FOIL SR	20.00	50.00
OP07065 Gina U	.10	.25
OP07066 Tony Tony.Chopper FOIL R	.10	.25
OP07068 Hamburg U	.08	.20
OP07070 Big Bun U	.08	.20
OP07071 Foxy FOIL R	.10	.25
OP07071 Foxy ALT ART FOIL R	5.00	12.00
OP07072 Porche FOIL SR	.30	.75
OP07072 Porche ALT ART FOIL SR	6.00	15.00
OP07073 Monkey.D.Luffy FOIL R	.08	.20
OP07075 Slow-Slow Beam U	.08	.20
OP07077 We're Going to Claim the One Piece!!! FOIL R	.15	.40
OP07079 Rob Lucci L	.10	.25
OP07079 Rob Lucci ALT ART FOIL L	40.00	100.00
OP07080 Kaku FOIL R	.08	.20
OP07083 Gecko Moria U	.08	.20
OP07085 Stussy FOIL SR	.50	1.25
OP07085 Stussy ALT ART FOIL SR	10.00	25.00
OP07088 Hattori U	.08	.20
OP07091 Monkey.D.Luffy FOIL R	.10	.25
OP07092 Joseph U	.08	.20
OP07093 Rob Lucci FOIL R	.08	.20
OP07094 Shave U	.08	.20
OP07096 Tempest Kick FOIL R	.40	1.00
OP07097 Vegapunk L	.08	.20
OP07097 Vegapunk ALT ART FOIL L	20.00	50.00
OP07098 Atlas U	.08	.20
OP07101 Shaka U	.10	.25
OP07104 Nico Robin U	.10	.25
OP07105 Pythagoras U	.10	.25
OP07107 Franky FOIL R	.20	.50
OP07107 Franky ALT ART FOIL R	12.00	30.00
OP07109 Monkey.D.Luffy FOIL SR	5.00	12.00
OP07109 Monkey.D.Luffy ALT ART FOIL SR	30.00	80.00
OP07111 Lilith FOIL SR	.50	1.25
OP07111 Lilith ALT ART FOIL SR	8.00	20.00
OP07112 Lucy FOIL R	.08	.20
OP07113 Roronoa Zoro U	.10	.25
OP07114 He Possesses the World's Most Brilliant Mind U	.08	.20
OP07115 I Re-Quasar Helllp!! C	.08	.20
OP07116 Blaze Slice FOIL R	.10	.25
OP07118 Sabo FOIL SEC	10.00	25.00
OP07118 Sabo ALT ART FOIL SEC	25.00	60.00
OP07119 Portgas.D.Ace FOIL SEC	25.00	60.00
OP07119 Portgas.D.Ace ALT ART FOIL SEC	40.00	100.00
ST10010 Trafalgar Law FOIL TR	30.00	80.00

2024 One Piece Memorial Collection

EB01001 Kouzuki Oden L	.10	.25
EB01001 Kouzuki Oden ALT ART L	12.00	30.00
EB01002 Izo R	.12	.30
EB01003 Kid & Killer R	2.00	5.00
EB01003 Kid & Killer ALT ART R	25.00	60.00
EB01006 Tony Tony.Chopper SR	3.00	8.00
EB01006 Tony Tony.Chopper ALT ART SR	12.00	30.00
EB01006 Tony Tony.Chopper MANGA ART SR	400.00	1,000.00
EB01007 Yamato C	.08	.20
EB01008 LittleOars Jr. R	.08	.20
EB01010 There's No Way You Could Defeat Me!! R	.08	.20
EB01012 Cavendish SR	10.00	25.00
EB01012 Cavendish ALT ART SR	20.00	50.00
EB01013 Kouzuki Hiyori R	.50	1.25
EB01013 Kouzuki Hiyori ALT ART R	12.00	30.00
EB01014 Sanji R	.30	.75
EB01015 Scratchmen Apoo R	.40	1.00
EB01017 Blueno C	.08	.20
EB01018 Mountain God C	.08	.20
EB01019 Off-White R	.10	.25
EB01021 Hannyabal L	.10	.25
EB01021 Hannyabal ALT ART L	6.00	15.00
EB01022 Inazuma SR	.50	1.25
EB01022 Inazuma ALT ART SR	4.00	10.00
EB01023 Edward Weevil R	.20	.50
EB01027 Mr.1(Daz.Bonez) R	.08	.20
EB01027 Mr.1(Daz.Bonez) ALT ART R	2.00	5.00
EB01028 Gum-Gum Champion Rifle R	.10	.25
EB01031 Kalifa R	.10	.25
EB01031 Kalifa ALT ART R	2.00	5.00
EB01033 Blueno R	.08	.20
EB01034 Ms. Wednesday SR	.50	1.25
EB01034 Ms. Wednesday ALT ART SR	6.00	15.00
EB01039 Conquerer of Three Worlds Ragnaraku R	.10	.25
EB01040 Kyros ALT ART L	8.00	20.00
EB01040 Kyros L	.10	.25
EB01042 Scarlet R	.10	.25
EB01043 Spandine R	.20	.50
EB01046 Brook SR	6.00	15.00
EB01046 Brook ALT ART SR	20.00	50.00
EB01048 Laboon SR	.50	1.25
EB01048 Laboon ALT ART SR	8.00	20.00
EB01049 T-Bone R	.10	.25
EB01049 T-Bone ALT ART R	3.00	8.00
EB01051 Finger Pistol R	.10	.25
EB01052 Viola SR	1.25	3.00
EB01052 Viola ALT ART SR	6.00	15.00
EB01054 Gan.Fall R	.08	.20
EB01056 Charlotte Flampe R	2.00	5.00
EB01056 Charlotte Flampe ALT ART R	20.00	50.00
EB01057 Shirahoshi SR	1.50	4.00
EB01057 Shirahoshi ALT ART SR	6.00	15.00
EB01059 Kingdom Come R	.25	.60
EB01060 Did Someone Say...Kami? C	.08	.20
EB01061 Mr.2.Bon.Kurei(Bentham) SEC	20.00	50.00
EB01061 Mr.2.Bon.Kurei(Bentham) ALT ART SEC	50.00	120.00

2024 One Piece Starter Deck 11 Uta

ST11001 Uta L	.40	1.00
ST11002 Uta SR	1.50	4.00
ST11003 Backlight C	.25	.60
ST11004 New Genesis SR	.40	1.00
ST11005 I'm invincible C	.08	.20

2024 One Piece Starter Deck 12 Zoro and Sanji

ST12001 Roronoa Zoro & Sanji L	.25	.60
ST12003 Dracule Mihawk SR	3.00	8.00
ST12005 Perona C	.08	.20
ST12007 Rika C	.08	.20
ST12008 Roronoa Zoro C	.12	.30
ST12010 Emporio.Ivankov SR	.20	.50
ST12011 Sanji C	.10	.25
ST12012 Charlotte Pudding C	.10	.25
ST12013 Zeff C	.08	.20
ST12014 Duval C	.50	1.25
ST12016 Lion Strike C	.08	.20
ST12017 Plastic Surgery Shot C	.08	.20

2024 One Piece Starter Deck 13 The Three Brothers Ultra Deck

ST13001 Sabo L	.15	.40
ST13001 Sabo ALT ART L	5.00	12.00
ST13002 Portgas.D.Ace L	.20	.50
ST13002 Portgas.D.Ace ALT ART L	5.00	12.00
ST13003 Monkey.D.Luffy L	.20	.50
ST13003 Monkey.D.Luffy ALT ART L	15.00	40.00
ST13004 Edward.Newgate C	.10	.25
ST13004 Edward.Newgate ALT ART C	2.50	6.00
ST13005 Emporio.Ivankov R	.12	.30
ST13005 Emporio.Ivankov ALT ART R	2.00	5.00
ST13006 Curly.Dadan ALT ART C	.20	.50
ST13007 Sabo C	.10	.25
ST13007 Sabo ALT ART C	3.00	8.00
ST13008 Sabo SR	.30	.75
ST13008 Sabo ALT ART SR	2.50	6.00
ST13009 Shanks C	.08	.20
ST13009 Shanks ALT ART C	.50	1.25
ST13010 Portgas.D.Ace C	.10	.25
ST13010 Portgas.D.Ace ALT ART C	4.00	10.00
ST13011 Portgas.D.Ace SR	3.00	8.00
ST13011 Portgas.D.Ace ALT ART SR	15.00	40.00
ST13012 Makino C	.10	.25
ST13012 Makino ALT ART C	1.25	3.00
ST13013 Monkey.D.Garp ALT ART SR	8.00	20.00
ST13013 Monkey.D.Garp SR	.60	1.50
ST13014 Monkey.D.Luffy C	.10	.25
ST13014 Monkey.D.Luffy ALT ART C	4.00	10.00
ST13015 Monkey.D.Luffy SR	.60	1.50
ST13015 Monkey.D.Luffy ALT ART SR	10.00	25.00
ST13016 Yamato C	.10	.25
ST13016 Yamato ALT ART C	1.50	4.00
ST13017 Flame Dragon King C	.20	.50
ST13019 The Three Brothers' Bond C	.10	.25

2024 One Piece Wings of the Captain

NNO DON!! Card ALT ART	.25	.60
NNO DON!! Card (Ivankov & Sanji)/(Double Pack Set Vol. 3)	.75	2.00
NNO DON!! Card (Mihawk & Zoro)/(Double Pack Set Vol. 3)	1.50	4.00
OP03008 Buggy FOIL SP	40.00	100.00
OP03114 Charlotte Linlin FOIL SP	40.00	100.00
OP04024 Sugar FOIL SP	20.00	50.00
OP04064 Ms. All Sunday FOIL SP	60.00	150.00
OP05051 Borsalino FOIL SP	10.00	25.00
OP05091 Rebecca FOIL SP	75.00	200.00
OP06001 Uta ALT ART L	12.00	30.00
OP06001 Uta L	.10	.25
OP06003 Emporio.Ivankov U	.10	.25
OP06007 Shanks ALT ART SR	8.00	20.00
OP06007 Shanks SR	.50	1.25
OP06009 Shuraiya ALT ART SR	10.00	25.00
OP06009 Shuraiya SR	1.00	2.50
OP06013 Monkey.D.Luffy ALT ART R	3.00	8.00
OP06013 Monkey.D.Luffy R	.10	.25
OP06016 Raise Max U	.20	.50
OP06018 Gum-Gum King Kong Gatling R	.10	.25
OP06019 Blue Dragon Seal Water Stream U	.10	.25
OP06020 Hody Jones ALT ART L	8.00	20.00
OP06021 Perona ALT ART L	40.00	100.00
OP06021 Perona L	.08	.20
OP06022 Yamato ALT ART L	50.00	120.00
OP06022 Yamato L	.10	.25
OP06023 Arlong R	.10	.25
OP06025 Camie ALT ART R	2.50	6.00
OP06025 Camie R	.08	.20
OP06033 Vander Decken IX R	.08	.20
OP06035 Hody Jones ALT ART SR	12.00	30.00
OP06035 Hody Jones SR	4.00	10.00
OP06036 Ryuma R	.20	.50
OP06038 The Billion-fold World Trichiliocosm U	.08	.20
OP06039 You Ain't Even Worth Killing Time!! R	.10	.25
OP06041 The Ark Noah C	.08	.20
OP06042 Vinsmoke Reiju L	.08	.20
OP06042 Vinsmoke Reiju ALT ART L	25.00	60.00
OP06043 Aramaki SR	.10	.25
OP06043 Aramaki ALT ART SR	2.00	5.00
OP06044 Gion U	.08	.20
OP06047 Charlotte Pudding R	.25	.60
OP06050 Tashigi R	.10	.25
OP06050 Tashigi ALT ART R	3.00	8.00
OP06051 Tsuru R	.10	.25
OP06057 But I Will Never Doubt a Woman's Tears!!!! C	.08	.20
OP06058 Gravity Blade Raging Tiger R	.30	.75
OP06059 White Snake U	.10	.25
OP06060 Vinsmoke Ichiji C	.08	.20
OP06061 Vinsmoke Ichiji R	.15	.40
OP06061 Vinsmoke Ichiji ALT ART R	5.00	12.00
OP06062 Vinsmoke Judge ALT ART SR	2.50	6.00
OP06062 Vinsmoke Judge SR	.15	.40
OP06063 Vinsmoke Sora U	.10	.25
OP06065 Vinsmoke Niji R	.15	.40
OP06067 Vinsmoke Yonji R	.20	.50
OP06068 Vinsmoke Reiju C	.10	.25
OP06069 Vinsmoke Reiju SR	4.00	10.00
OP06069 Vinsmoke Reiju ALT ART SR	40.00	100.00
OP06071 Gild Tesoro U	.08	.20
OP06073 Shiki U	.08	.20
OP06074 Zephyr (Navy) R	.10	.25
OP06076 Hitokiri Kamazo U	.10	.25
OP06077 Black Bug R	.10	.25
OP06078 GERMA 66 U	.10	.25
OP06080 Gecko Moria L	.08	.20
OP06080 Gecko Moria ALT ART L	20.00	50.00
OP06081 Absalom ALT ART R	5.00	12.00
OP06081 Absalom R	.10	.25
OP06086 Gecko Moria ALT ART SR	50.00	120.00
OP06086 Gecko Moria SR	10.00	25.00
OP06090 Dr. Hogback R	.12	.30
OP06091 Victoria Cindry U	.10	.25
OP06092 Brook R	.10	.25
OP06093 Perona ALT ART SR	25.00	60.00
OP06093 Perona SR	1.00	2.50
OP06097 Negative Hollow R	.10	.25
OP06100 Inuarashi U	.08	.20
OP06101 O-Nami ALT ART R	20.00	50.00
OP06101 O-Nami R	.15	.40
OP06104 Kikunojo R	.50	1.25
OP06106 Kouzuki Hiyori ALT ART SR	25.00	60.00
OP06106 Kouzuki Hiyori SR	8.00	20.00
OP06107 Kouzuki Momonosuke ALT ART SR	8.00	20.00
OP06107 Kouzuki Momonosuke SR	.50	1.25
OP06110 Nekomamushi U	.20	.50
OP06115 You're the One Who Should Disappear. R	.75	2.00
OP06116 Reject R	.10	.25
OP06118 Roronoa Zoro ALT ART SEC	40.00	100.00
OP06118 Roronoa Zoro MANGA ART SEC	500.00	1,200.00
OP06118 Roronoa Zoro SEC	15.00	40.00
OP06119 Sanji ALT ART SEC	20.00	50.00
OP06119 Sanji SEC	6.00	15.00

2016 Weiss Schwarz Disgaea

DGENS03E003 Devil Buster Adell R	.20	.40
DGENS03E004 Prinny XTerminators Leader Fuka R	.20	.40
DGENS03E005 Mystery Angel Sicily R	.20	.40
DGENS03E006 Beliefs of a Maiden Fuka R	.20	.40
DGENS03E007 Overlord Mao R	.20	.40
DGENS03E008 Asuka Cranekicker R	.20	.40
DGENS03E009 Younger Sister Aura Sicily U	.12	.25
DGENS03E010 Death Emizel U	.12	.25
DGENS03E011 Kyoko Needleworker U	.12	.25
DGENS03E012 Childhood Friend Raspberyl U	.12	.25
DGENS03E013 Fallen Angel Flonne U	.12	.25
DGENS03E014 Salvatore the Magnificent U	.12	.25
DGENS03E015 Legendary Chief Graduate Beryl U	.12	.25
DGENS03E016 Overlord Laharl U	.12	.25
DGENS03E017 Netherworld Honor Student Mao C	.10	.20
DGENS03E018 Big Sis Fuka C	.10	.20
DGENS03E019 Pampered Child Emizel C	.10	.20
DGENS03E020 Special Assassination Task Force Leader Emizel C	.10	.20
DGENS03E021 Girl in a Prinny Cap Fuka C	.10	.20
DGENS03E022 Like a Picnic Sicily C	.10	.20
DGENS03E023 Overlords Spot Sicily C	.10	.20
DGENS03E024 Middle Schooler Who Fell to Hades Fuka C	.10	.20
DGENS03E025 Netherworld President Jr Emizel C	.10	.20
DGENS03E026 Package from Celestia Sicily C	.10	.20
DGENS03E027 Adell and Rozalin C	.10	.20
DGENS03E028 President Raspberyl C	.10	.20
DGENS03E029 Overlord Sicily C	.10	.20
DGENS03E030 Mao and Raspberyl C	.10	.20
DGENS03E031 Delinquent Student Raspberyl C	.10	.20
DGENS03E032 Sexy Demon Wish Hanako C	.10	.20
DGENS03E033 Majin Etna C	.10	.20
DGENS03E034 Geoffrey C	.10	.20
DGENS03E035 Battle Maniac Adell C	.10	.20
DGENS03E036 Overthrow God of All Overlords U	.12	.25
DGENS03E037 Strongest Overlord U	.12	.25
DGENS03E038 Important Allies U	.12	.25
DGENS03E039 Battle Arena Begins C	.10	.20
DGENS03E040 And trust this CR	.20	.40
DGENS03E041 Prinny Wars CR	.20	.40
DGENS03E042 To my lab CC	.15	.30
DGENS03E043 And have become legend CC	.15	.30
DGENS03E044 Vow of the Phoenix CC	.15	.30
DGENS03E045 Birth of a New Overlord CC	.15	.30
DGENS03E049 Evangelist of Love Flonne R	.20	.40
DGENS03E050 Thief Angel Artina R	.20	.40
DGENS03E051 Archangel Flonne R	.20	.40
DGENS03E052 Cute Little Demon Etna R	.20	.40
DGENS03E053 Awakened Angel Pure Flonne R	.20	.40
DGENS03E054 Pringer X R	.20	.40
DGENS03E055 Big Sis Prinny R	.20	.40
DGENS03E056 Laharl and Etna R	.20	.40
DGENS03E057 Super Alloy Great Flonzor X U	.12	.25
DGENS03E058 Young Etna U	.12	.25
DGENS03E059 Angel Trainee Flonne U	.12	.25
DGENS03E060 Ordinary Cleric U	.12	.25
DGENS03E061 Petty Thief U	.12	.25
DGENS03E062 Flonne the Love Maniac U	.12	.25

DGENS03E063 Supreme Overlord Baal U .12 .25
DGENS03E064 Nurse Altina C .10 .20
DGENS03E065 Judge Nemo C .10 .20
DGENS03E066 NiceBodied Etna C .10 .20
DGENS03E067 Mystery Demon Xenolith C .10 .20
DGENS03E068 Player 2 Etna C .10 .20
DGENS03E069 Samurai Legend C .10 .20
DGENS03E070 Trespasser from Celestia Artina C .10 .20
DGENS03E071 Unkind Demon Etna C .10 .20
DGENS03E072 Elusive Artina C .10 .20
DGENS03E073 Outofcontrol Artifact Xenolith C .10 .20
DGENS03E074 Dumbfounded Etna C .10 .20
DGENS03E075 Prinny Squad C .10 .20
DGENS03E076 Genius Magic Knight C .10 .20
DGENS03E077 Etna and Flonne C .10 .20
DGENS03E078 Space Detective Guardian Flonne C .10 .20
DGENS03E079 Helplessly Useless Archer C .10 .20
DGENS03E080 Seraph Lamington C .10 .20
DGENS03E081 Winged Slayer R .20 .40
DGENS03E082 They are all mine U .12 .25
DGENS03E083 Conspiracy of the School Board U .12 .25
DGENS03E084 Bow Revival C .10 .20
DGENS03E085 Supreme Overlord Girl CR .20 .40
DGENS03E086 Siblings Conversation CR .20 .40
DGENS03E087 Even a Demon Needs Love CC .15 .30
DGENS03E088 Assassin from Celestia CC .15 .30
DGENS03E089 Demon and Angel Bond CC .15 .30
DGENS03E092 Power of Sardines Valvatorez R .20 .40
DGENS03E093 Werewolf Butler Fenrich R .20 .40
DGENS03E094 Reborn Krichevskoy R .20 .40
DGENS03E095 Dominating Presence of Netherworld Laharl R .20 .40
DGENS03E096 Tyrant Valvatorez R .20 .40
DGENS03E097 Likes Superhero Shows Flonne R .20 .40
DGENS03E098 Supreme Overlord Laharl R .20 .40
DGENS03E099 Former Angel Flonne R .20 .40
DGENS03E100 Dark AdonisMidBoss R .20 .40
DGENS03E101 Caretaker of Prinnies Fenrich U .12 .25
DGENS03E102 Trainer of Prinnies Valvatorez U .12 .25
DGENS03E103 Selfcentered Overlord Laharl U .12 .25
DGENS03E104 Absolute Loyalty Fenrich U .12 .25
DGENS03E105 Sharp Criticism Etna U .12 .25
DGENS03E106 Rebel Against God Valvatorez U .12 .25
DGENS03E107 Master Big Star U .12 .25
DGENS03E108 Fake Laharl U .12 .25
DGENS03E109 Vyers the Dark Adonis MidBoss U .12 .25
DGENS03E110 Prince Laharl of the Netherworld U .12 .25
DGENS03E111 Defender of Earth Kurtis U .12 .25
DGENS03E112 Overlord Laharl and his Vassal Etna C .10 .20
DGENS03E113 Busty Girl Laharl C .10 .20
DGENS03E114 Overlords Dignity Laharl C .10 .20
DGENS03E115 Sadistic Etna C .10 .20
DGENS03E116 My Lords Advisor Fenrich C .10 .20
DGENS03E117 New Overlord Laharl C .10 .20
DGENS03E118 Demon Girl Etna the Ultimate Beauty C .10 .20
DGENS03E119 Demon Awaiting Instructions Barbara C .10 .20
DGENS03E120 Strongest In the World Etna C .10 .20
DGENS03E121 Elite Red Mage C .10 .20
DGENS03E122 Super Robot Thursday C .10 .20
DGENS03E123 Captain Gordon Defender of Earth C .10 .20
DGENS03E124 Jennifer Defender of Earths Assistant C .10 .20
DGENS03E125 Dissection Experiment U .12 .25
DGENS03E126 The Dark Assembly U .12 .25
DGENS03E127 Back Together C .10 .20
DGENS03E128 Coming Up Next C .10 .20
DGENS03E129 King of the Earth CC .15 .30
DGENS03E130 Overlord Passing Through CC .15 .30
DGENS03E131 Vow of the Moon CC .15 .30
DGENS03E135 Final Boss Training Desco R .20 .40
DGENS03E136 DingDongDitches Axel R .20 .40
DGENS03E137 62nd Netherworld President Axel U .12 .25
DGENS03E138 Fancy Dreamy Desco U .12 .25
DGENS03E139 Raspberyl and Sapphire U .12 .25
DGENS03E140 Almaz Von Almandine Adamant U .12 .25
DGENS03E141 Secretive Teacher Mr. Champloo U .12 .25
DGENS03E142 Sheltered Lady Rozalin U .12 .25
DGENS03E143 Obstinate Rozalin U .12 .25
DGENS03E144 Girl Ninja Yukimaru U .12 .25
DGENS03E145 Unusual Frog Tink U .12 .25
DGENS03E146 Rozalin and Sapphire U .12 .25
DGENS03E147 Killing Machine Sapphire U .12 .25
DGENS03E148 Overlords Daughter Rozalin U .12 .25
DGENS03E149 Master of the Forbidden Chamber Desco C .10 .20
DGENS03E150 Hades Warden Axel C .10 .20
DGENS03E151 Perfect Version DES X C .10 .20
DGENS03E152 Robust Princess Sapphire C .10 .20
DGENS03E153 Rozalins Servant Taro C .10 .20
DGENS03E154 Hero Almaz C .10 .20
DGENS03E155 Dark Hero Axel C .10 .20
DGENS03E156 Super Hero Aurum C .10 .20
DGENS03E157 Home Economics Teacher Mr. Champloo C .10 .20
DGENS03E158 Cell Phone U .12 .25
DGENS03E159 Broadcast Incident U .12 .25
DGENS03E160 Pudding Mountain U .12 .25
DGENS03E161 Dark Hero C .10 .20
DGENS03E162 Newlywed Queen CR .20 .40
DGENS03E163 Final Weapon Appears CR .20 .40
DGENS03E164 Overlord Summon CC .15 .30
DGENS03E165 Overlord Almaz CC .15 .30

2016 Weiss Schwarz Extra Booster NISEKOI False Love

NKWE22E01 Unrivaled Beauty Chitoge R .20 .40
NKWE22E02 Pajama Party Chitoge R .20 .40
NKWE22E02SP Pajama Party Chitoge SP 60.00 120.00
NKWE22E03 Magical Gorilla Chitoge C .10 .20
NKWE22E04 To and From School Raku C .10 .20
NKWE22E05 New Life Chitoge C .10 .20
NKWE22E06 Great Style Chitoge C .10 .20
NKWE22E07 But Its All About You C .10 .20
NKWE22E08 Neighbor Haru R .20 .40
NKWE22E09 New Life Haru R .20 .40
NKWE22E10 Tsugumyaa R .20 .40
NKWE22E11 Swimsuit Haru R .20 .40
NKWE22E12 Pajama Party Haru R .20 .40
NKWE22E12SP Pajama Party Haru SP 75.00 150.00
NKWE22E13 New Life Seishiro C .10 .20
NKWE22E14 Harus Friend Fuu C .10 .20
NKWE22E15 Clue Haru C .10 .20
NKWE22E16 Paula McCoy C .10 .20
NKWE22E17 From Here On Seishiro C .10 .20
NKWE22E18 Haru Onodera C .10 .20
NKWE22E19 Beehives White Fang Paula C .10 .20
NKWE22E20 Someday My Prince Will C .10 .20
NKWE22E21 Magical Police Marika R .20 .40
NKWE22E22 Marikas Dress Look C .10 .20
NKWE22E23 New Life Marika C .10 .20
NKWE22E24 Draw of the Shop Haru R .20 .40
NKWE22E25 Freshman Haru R .20 .40
NKWE22E26 Magical Patissiere Kosaki R .20 .40
NKWE22E27 Pajama Party Kosaki R .20 .40
NKWE22E27SP Pajama Party Kosaki SP 75.00 150.00
NKWE22E28 Sisters Taking a Bath Kosaki C .10 .20
NKWE22E29 Rurin C .10 .20
NKWE22E30 Fuus Prank Haru C .10 .20
NKWE22E31 Sisters Taking a Bath Haru C .10 .20
NKWE22E32 110000 Miracle Kosaki C .10 .20
NKWE22E33 New Life Kosaki C .10 .20
NKWE22E34 Head Tilt Haru C .10 .20
NKWE22E35 New Life Ruri C .10 .20
NKWE22E36 Contract Concluded C .10 .20

2016 Weiss Schwarz Extra Booster NISEKOI False Love Parallel Foil

NKWE22E01 Unrivaled Beauty Chitoge R .20 .40
NKWE22E02 Pajama Party Chitoge R .20 .40
NKWE22E03 Magical Gorilla Chitoge C .10 .20
NKWE22E04 To and From School Raku C .10 .20
NKWE22E05 New Life Chitoge C .10 .20
NKWE22E06 Great Style Chitoge C .10 .20
NKWE22E07 But Its All About You C .10 .20
NKWE22E08 Neighbor Haru R .20 .40
NKWE22E09 New Life Haru R .20 .40
NKWE22E10 Tsugumyaa R .20 .40
NKWE22E11 Swimsuit Haru R .20 .40
NKWE22E12 Pajama Party Haru R .20 .40
NKWE22E13 New Life Seishiro C .10 .20
NKWE22E14 Harus Friend Fuu C .10 .20
NKWE22E15 Clue Haru C .10 .20
NKWE22E16 Paula McCoy C .10 .20
NKWE22E17 From Here On Seishiro C .10 .20
NKWE22E18 Haru Onodera C .10 .20
NKWE22E19 Beehives White Fang Paula C .10 .20
NKWE22E20 Someday My Prince Will C .10 .20
NKWE22E21 Magical Police Marika R .20 .40
NKWE22E22 Marikas Dress Look C .10 .20
NKWE22E23 New Life Marika C .10 .20
NKWE22E24 Draw of the Shop Haru R .20 .40
NKWE22E25 Freshman Haru R .20 .40
NKWE22E26 Magical Patissiere Kosaki R .20 .40
NKWE22E27 Pajama Party Kosaki R .20 .40
NKWE22E28 Sisters Taking a Bath Kosaki C .10 .20
NKWE22E29 Rurin C .10 .20
NKWE22E30 Fuus Prank Haru C .10 .20
NKWE22E31 Sisters Taking a Bath Haru C .10 .20
NKWE22E32 110000 Miracle Kosaki C .10 .20
NKWE22E33 New Life Kosaki C .10 .20
NKWE22E34 Head Tilt Haru C .10 .20
NKWE22E35 New Life Ruri C .10 .20
NKWE22E36 Contract Concluded C .10 .20

2016 Weiss Schwarz Extra Booster Sword Art Online II Vol 2

SAOSE26E01 Asuna Joins a Party R .20 .40
SAOSE26E02 Vestige of an Elder Sister Asuna R .20 .40
SAOSE26E03 Restful Stroll Asuna C .10 .20
SAOSE26E04 Childhood Asuna C .10 .20
SAOSE26E05 Berserk Healer Asuna C .10 .20
SAOSE26E06 Demise of Zekken C .10 .20
SAOSE26E07 Undefeated Super Swordsman Yuuki R .20 .40
SAOSE26E08 Sword Skill Lore Yuuki R .20 .40
SAOSE26E09 Sleeping Knights Talken Nori Jun R .20 .40
SAOSE26E10 Zekken Yuuki R .20 .40
SAOSE26E11 Memories That Were Fun Yuuki R .20 .40
SAOSE26E12 Yuukis Raised Antenna C .10 .20
SAOSE26E13 Sleeping Knights Yuuki C .10 .20
SAOSE26E14 Simultaneous Attack Leafa C .10 .20
SAOSE26E15 Time Limit Leafa C .10 .20
SAOSE26E16 Imp Girl Yuuki C .10 .20
SAOSE26E17 Innocent and Uninhibited Yuuki C .10 .20
SAOSE26E18 Asuna Yuuki C .10 .20
SAOSE26E19 Sleeping Knights Siune Tecchi C .10 .20
SAOSE26E20 Mothers Rosario C .10 .20
SAOSE26E21 Braves of 27th floor C .10 .20
SAOSE26E22 Strong and Stouthearted Lisbeth R .20 .40
SAOSE26E23 Trusted Skills Lisbeth R .20 .40
SAOSE26E24 Sinister GlintDeath Gun C .10 .20
SAOSE26E25 Fluffy on the Head Silica C .10 .20
SAOSE26E26 Battle Stance Silica C .10 .20
SAOSE26E27 SAO Survivor Kirito R .20 .40
SAOSE26E28 Brains of the Party Yui R .20 .40
SAOSE26E29 Getting the Holy Sword Kirito R .20 .40
SAOSE26E30 Wildcat Girl Sinon C .10 .20
SAOSE26E31 Challenging Many Kirito C .10 .20
SAOSE26E32 Providing Information Yui C .10 .20
SAOSE26E33 In the Face of Death Kirito Sinon C .10 .20
SAOSE26E34 Cait Sith Archer Sinon C .10 .20
SAOSE26E35 Skill Connect Kirito C .10 .20
SAOSE26E36 Quest to Get Excalibur C .10 .20

2016 Weiss Schwarz Extra Booster Sword Art Online II Vol 2 Parallel Foil

SAOSE26E01 Asuna Joins a Party R .20 .40
SAOSE26E02 Vestige of an Elder Sister Asuna R .20 .40
SAOSE26E03 Restful Stroll Asuna C .10 .20
SAOSE26E04 Childhood Asuna C .10 .20
SAOSE26E05 Berserk Healer Asuna C .10 .20
SAOSE26E06 Demise of Zekken C .10 .20
SAOSE26E07 Undefeated Super Swordsman Yuuki R .20 .40
SAOSE26E08 Sword Skill Lore Yuuki R .20 .40
SAOSE26E09 Sleeping Knights Talken Nori Jun R .20 .40
SAOSE26E10 Zekken Yuuki R .20 .40
SAOSE26E11 Memories That Were Fun Yuuki R .20 .40
SAOSE26E12 Yuukis Raised Antenna C .10 .20
SAOSE26E13 Sleeping Knights Yuuki C .10 .20
SAOSE26E14 Simultaneous Attack Leafa C .10 .20
SAOSE26E15 Time Limit Leafa C .10 .20
SAOSE26E16 Imp Girl Yuuki C .10 .20
SAOSE26E17 Innocent and Uninhibited Yuuki C .10 .20
SAOSE26E18 Asuna Yuuki C .10 .20
SAOSE26E19 Sleeping Knights Siune Tecchi C .10 .20
SAOSE26E20 Mothers Rosario C .10 .20
SAOSE26E21 Braves of 27th floor C .10 .20
SAOSE26E22 Strong and Stouthearted Lisbeth R .20 .40
SAOSE26E23 Trusted Skills Lisbeth R .20 .40
SAOSE26E24 Sinister GlintDeath Gun C .10 .20
SAOSE26E25 Fluffy on the Head Silica C .10 .20
SAOSE26E26 Battle Stance Silica C .10 .20
SAOSE26E27 SAO Survivor Kirito R .20 .40
SAOSE26E28 Brains of the Party Yui R .20 .40
SAOSE26E29 Getting the Holy Sword Kirito R .20 .40
SAOSE26E30 Wildcat Girl Sinon C .10 .20
SAOSE26E31 Challenging Many Kirito C .10 .20
SAOSE26E32 Providing Information Yui C .10 .20
SAOSE26E33 In the Face of Death Kirito Sinon C .10 .20
SAOSE26E34 Cait Sith Archer Sinon C .10 .20
SAOSE26E35 Skill Connect Kirito C .10 .20
SAOSE26E36 Quest to Get Excalibur C .10 .20

2016 Weiss Schwarz Fate kaleid liner PRISMA ILLYA

PIENS04E003 Sweets Battle Outbreak Kuro R .20 .40
PIENS04E004 Temporary Retreat Kuro R .20 .40
PIENS04E005 Another Illya Kuro R .20 .40
PIENS04E006 Flame Burst sevenfold Luvia R .20 .40
PIENS04E007 Miracle Kuro R .20 .40
PIENS04E008 Gale Burst fivefold Rin R .20 .40
PIENS04E009 Kaleido Ruby Rin U .12 .25
PIENS04E010 Luvia in Regular Clothes U .12 .25
PIENS04E011 Kuro All Ready for Gym U .12 .25
PIENS04E012 A Maids Job Rin U .12 .25
PIENS04E013 In a Pinch Kuro U .12 .25
PIENS04E014 Rin in Uniform C .10 .20
PIENS04E015 Former Master Rin C .10 .20
PIENS04E016 Former Master Luvia C .10 .20
PIENS04E017 Shared Pain Kuro C .10 .20
PIENS04E018 Homurabara Academy Student Kuro C .10 .20
PIENS04E019 Domineering Princess Luvia C .10 .20
PIENS04E020 School Nursing Karen C .10 .20
PIENS04E021 Kaleido Sapphire Luvia C .10 .20
PIENS04E022 Top Candidate of Clock Tower Rin C .10 .20
PIENS04E023 Sealing Designation Enforcer Bazett C .10 .20
PIENS04E024 Luvia in Uniform C .10 .20
PIENS04E025 Mana Resupply CC .15 .30
PIENS04E026 Behind the Lies and Strong Front CC .15 .30
PIENS04E033 In a Pinch Illya R .20 .40
PIENS04E034 Magical Stick Ruby R .20 .40
PIENS04E035 A Maids Job Miyu R .20 .40
PIENS04E036 Coincidence Miyu R .20 .40
PIENS04E037 Kaleido Magical Girl Illya R .20 .40
PIENS04E038 Perfect Superhuman Miyu R .20 .40
PIENS04E039 Maid Outfit Miyu R .20 .40
PIENS04E040 Swimsuit Illya and Miyu R .20 .40
PIENS04E041 Dreamy Girl Illya R .20 .40
PIENS04E042 Big Bath at Luvias Mansion Miyu R .20 .40
PIENS04E043 To Protect Daily Life Illya R .20 .40
PIENS04E044 Practicing Magic Illya U .12 .25
PIENS04E045 Worst Luck Illya U .12 .25
PIENS04E046 Big Bro Shirou U .12 .25
PIENS04E047 Kaleido Magical Girl Miyu U .12 .25
PIENS04E048 Promise Illya U .12 .25
PIENS04E049 Sudden Transfer Student Miyu U .12 .25
PIENS04E050 Normal Girl Illya U .12 .25
PIENS04E051 Homurabara Academy Student Miyu U .12 .25
PIENS04E052 Mission Failed Miyu U .12 .25
PIENS04E053 Cooking is Love Illya U .12 .25
PIENS04E054 Illya Being Toyed Around With U .12 .25
PIENS04E055 Sign of Closeness Leys U .12 .25
PIENS04E056 Mama Irisviel U .12 .25
PIENS04E057 Magical Stick Sapphire U .12 .25
PIENS04E058 Trainer Sella U .12 .25
PIENS04E059 At the End of the Night Illya U .12 .25
PIENS04E060 Realistic Miyu U .12 .25
PIENS04E061 Friend Illya and Miyu U .12 .25
PIENS04E062 Magical Sapphire C .10 .20
PIENS04E063 Einzbern Family Sella and Leys C .10 .20
PIENS04E064 Classmate Mimi C .10 .20
PIENS04E065 Mamas Intuition Irisviel C .10 .20
PIENS04E066 Miyu in Regular Clothes C .10 .20
PIENS04E067 Classmate Suzuka C .10 .20
PIENS04E068 Magical Ruby C .10 .20
PIENS04E069 Belief Miyu C .10 .20
PIENS04E070 After School with Friends Illya C .10 .20
PIENS04E071 After School with Friends Miyu C .10 .20
PIENS04E072 Guided Fate Illya C .10 .20
PIENS04E073 Homeroom Teacher Taiga C .10 .20
PIENS04E074 Saber Install Miyu C .10 .20
PIENS04E075 Illya in Pajamas C .10 .20
PIENS04E076 Classmate Tatsuko C .10 .20
PIENS04E077 Lovestruck Miyu C .10 .20
PIENS04E078 Big Bath at Luvias Mansion Illya C .10 .20
PIENS04E079 Classmate Nanaki C .10 .20
PIENS04E080 Another Magical Girl Miyu C .10 .20
PIENS04E081 Class Card Saber CR .25 .50
PIENS04E082 Another Me CR .25 .50
PIENS04E083 Birth of A Magical Girl CC .15 .30
PIENS04E084 Class Card Archer CC .15 .30
PIENS04E085 Class Card Lancer CC .15 .30
PIENS04E086 Class Card Rider CC .15 .30

2016 Weiss Schwarz Fate/Stay Night Unlimited Blade Works Vol. 2

FSS36E001 Trace On Shirou RR 7.50 15.00
FSS36E001R Trace On Shirou RRR 12.00 25.00
FSS36E002 Excalibur Saber RR 7.50 15.00
FSS36E002SP Excalibur Saber SP 60.00 120.00
FSS36E003 Unlimited Blade Works Shirou RR 4.00 8.00
FSS36E003R Unlimited Blade Works Shirou RRR 10.00 20.00
FSS36E004 Summoning with a Command Seal Shirou R .20 .40
FSS36E004S Summoning with a Command Seal Shirou SR 4.00 8.00
FSS36E005 Contract Concluded Saber R .20 .40
FSS36E006 Kings Self-esteem Gilgamesh R .20 .40
FSS36E007 Tough Strength Saber R .20 .40
FSS36E007S Tough Strength Saber SR 5.00 10.00
FSS36E008 Gate of Babylon Gilgamesh R .20 .40
FSS36E008S Gate of Babylon Gilgamesh SR 2.50 5.00
FSS36E009 Serious Assault Shirou R .20 .40
FSS36E010 Non-intersecting Ideals Shirou & Archer U .12 .25
FSS36E011 Divine Construct Saber U .12 .25
FSS36E012 Pure White Dress Saber U .12 .25
FSS36E013 Top Servant Saber U .12 .25
FSS36E014 Using a Command Seal Shirou U .12 .25
FSS36E015 Furious Punch Shirou U .12 .25
FSS36E016 Defeats End Gilgamesh C .10 .20
FSS36E017 A Battle of Legend Gilgamesh C .10 .20
FSS36E018 Greatest Natural Enemy Gilgamesh C .10 .20
FSS36E019 Endless Blades Gilgamesh C .10 .20
FSS36E020 Highest Class Noble Phantasm Gilgamesh C .10 .20
FSS36E021 Dauntless Heart Shirou C .10 .20
FSS36E022 New Contract Saber C .10 .20
FSS36E023 Neat and Tidy Appearance Saber C .10 .20
FSS36E024 Challenging a King Gilgamesh C .10 .20
FSS36E025 Ultimate Slash Saber C .10 .20
FSS36E026 Signal to Counterattack U .12 .25
FSS36E027 Idealisms End U .12 .25
FSS36E028 Unlimited Blade Works CR .20 .40
FSS36E028S Unlimited Blade Works SR 7.50 15.00
FSS36E029 Gate of Babylon CC .15 .30
FSS36E030 Excalibur CC .15 .30
FSS36E031 Battle Mode Rider RR 3.00 6.00
FSS36E031R Battle Mode Rider RRR 7.50 15.00
FSS36E032 Dedicated Junior Sakura R .20 .40
FSS36E033 Cold and Ruthless Rider R .20 .40
FSS36E034 Gae Bolg Lancer R .20 .40
FSS36E034S Gae Bolg Lancer SR 2.00 4.00
FSS36E035 Gae-Bolg Lancer U .12 .25
FSS36E036 Deadly Strike Lancer U .12 .25
FSS36E037 Quiet Personality Sakura U .12 .25
FSS36E038 Battle Continues Lancer C .10 .20
FSS36E039 Self-defense Class Luvia C .10 .20
FSS36E040 Complex Emotions Sakura C .10 .20
FSS36E041 Uneasiness in the Heart Sakura C .10 .20
FSS36E042 United Battlefront Lancer C .10 .20
FSS36E043 Invading the Base Shinji C .10 .20
FSS36E044 Shaken U .12 .25
FSS36E045 Last Farewell U .12 .25
FSS36E046 Gae Bolg CC .15 .30
FSS36E047 Daily Visits CC .15 .30

FSS36E048 Invitation to London Rin RR	7.50	15.00
FSS36E048SP Invitation to London Rin SP	60.00	120.00
FSS36E049 Idealisms Despair Archer RR	1.00	2.00
FSS36E049SP Idealisms Despair Archer SP	25.00	50.00
FSS36E050 Lord and Retainer Rin & Archer RR	12.00	25.00
FSS36E050R Lord and Retainer Rin & Archer RRR	15.00	30.00
FSS36E051 Super First-rate Mage Rin R	.20	.40
FSS36E051R Super First-rate Mage Rin RRR	4.00	8.00
FSS36E052 Successor of Tohsaka Rin R	.20	.40
FSS36E053 Counterattack Barrage Archer R	.20	.40
FSS36E054 Caladbolg ? Archer R	.20	.40
FSS36E055 Fire Support Archer R	.20	.40
FSS36E056 Beautiful and Smart Honor Student Rin R	.20	.40
FSS36E057 Dual-wielding Archer R	.20	.40
FSS36E057S Dual-wielding Archer SR	2.50	5.00
FSS36E058 Ideal Existence Archer U	.12	.25
FSS36E059 Jewel Magic Rin U	.12	.25
FSS36E060 Complex Emotions Rin U	.12	.25
FSS36E061 Further Pursuit Archer U	.12	.25
FSS36E062 End of Fight Archer U	.12	.25
FSS36E063 Full Power Pitch Rin U	.12	.25
FSS36E064 Time to Part Ways Rin C	.10	.20
FSS36E065 Center Breakthrough Rin C	.10	.20
FSS36E066 In the Conflict Archer C	.10	.20
FSS36E067 Caladbolg ? Archer U	.12	.25
FSS36E068 Conclusion to the Fight U	.12	.25
FSS36E069 Rho Aias CR	.20	.40
FSS36E069S Rho Aias SR	4.00	8.00
FSS36E070 Last Words CR	.20	.40
FSS36E071 Mischievous Smile CC	.15	.30
FSS36E072 Snow Fairy Illya RR	3.00	6.00
FSS36E072SP Snow Fairy Illya SP	30.00	75.00
FSS36E073 Signal to Commence Battle Illya R	.20	.40
FSS36E073S Signal to Commence Battle Illya SR	5.00	10.00
FSS36E074 Mage from the Age of Myths Caster R	.20	.40
FSS36E075 Mage of Tragedy Caster R	.20	.40
FSS36E076 Relationship of Trust Illya & Berserker R	.20	.40
FSS36E076R Relationship of Trust Illya & Berserker RRR	4.00	8.00
FSS36E077 Strong Bond Illya U	.12	.25
FSS36E078 Strongest Warrior Berserker U	.12	.25
FSS36E079 Confronting a King Illya U	.12	.25
FSS36E080 A Battle of Legend Illya U	.12	.25
FSS36E081 Strong Will Berserker U	.12	.25
FSS36E082 Further Attack Souichirou Kuzuki C	.10	.20
FSS36E083 Great Magic Caster C	.10	.20
FSS36E084 Magic Duel Caster C	.10	.20
FSS36E085 Swallow Reversal Assassin C	.10	.20
FSS36E086 Repeated Pursuit Souichirou Kuzuki C	.10	.20
FSS36E087 A Short Rest Illya C	.10	.20
FSS36E088 Sturdy Servant Berserker C	.10	.20
FSS36E089 Fictional Heroic Spirit Assassin C	.10	.20
FSS36E090 Middle of the Final Test Illya C	.10	.20
FSS36E091 Fulfilling the Wish Souichirou Kuzuki C	.10	.20
FSS36E092 A Visitor Illya C	.10	.20
FSS36E093 Priest of Fuyuki Church Kirei C	.10	.20
FSS36E094 Reverberation of Defeat Assassin C	.10	.20
FSS36E095 Encounter on a Rainy Day U	.12	.25
FSS36E096 Berserkers Will U	.12	.25
FSS36E097 Encounter and Bond CR	.20	.40
FSS36E098 Official Contract CC	.15	.30
FSS36E099 Granted Wish CC	.15	.30
FSS36E100 Swallow Reversal CC	.15	.30

2016 Weiss Schwarz Love Live DX Vol 2

LLENW02E001 Maid Outfit us R	.20	.40
LLENW02E001auR Maid Outfit us R	.20	.40
LLENW02E001buR Maid Outfit us R	.20	.40
LLENW02E001cuR Maid Outfit us R	.20	.40
LLENW02E001duR Maid Outfit us R	.20	.40
LLENW02E001euR Maid Outfit us R	.20	.40
LLENW02E001fuR Maid Outfit us R	.20	.40
LLENW02E001guR Maid Outfit us R	.20	.40
LLENW02E001huR Maid Outfit us R	.20	.40
LLENW02E001iuR Maid Outfit us R	.20	.40
LLENW02E002 Tea Time Kotori Hanayo U	.12	.25
LLENW02E003 Leader of us Honoka C	.10	.20
LLENW02E004 Summer Festival Date Eli Ayase RR	7.50	15.00
LLENW02E004SP Summer Festival Date Eli Ayase SP	75.00	150.00
LLENW02E005 Angelic Angel Nozomi Tojo RR	4.00	8.00
LLENW02E006 Summer Festival Date Nico Yazawa RR	4.00	8.00
LLENW02E006SP Summer Festival Date Nico Yazawa SP	75.00	150.00
LLENW02E007 Angelic Angel Eli Ayase RR	1.00	2.00
LLENW02E008 Summer Festival Date Nozomi Tojo RR	4.00	8.00
LLENW02E008SP Summer Festival Date Nozomi Tojo SP	75.00	150.00
LLENW02E009 We Are A Single Light Nico Yazawa RR	12.00	25.00
LLENW02E010 Dressed Up Nozomi Tojo R	.20	.40
LLENW02E010R Dressed Up Nozomi Tojo RRR	5.00	10.00
LLENW02E011 Angelic Angel Nico Yazawa R	.20	.40
LLENW02E012 Sweets Fairy Nozomi Tojo R	.20	.40
LLENW02E012S Sweets Fairy Nozomi Tojo SR	4.00	8.00
LLENW02E013 Sweets Fairy Nico Yazawa R	.20	.40
LLENW02E013S Sweets Fairy Nico Yazawa SR	4.00	8.00
LLENW02E014 Dressed Up Eli Ayase R	.20	.40
LLENW02E014R Dressed Up Eli Ayase RRR	7.50	15.00
LLENW02E015 Heartbeat Eli Ayase R	.20	.40
LLENW02E016 Heartbeat Nozomi Tojo R	.20	.40
LLENW02E017 Sweets Fairy Eli Ayase R	.20	.40
LLENW02E017S Sweets Fairy Eli Ayase SR	4.00	8.00
LLENW02E018 Dressed Up Nico Yazawa R	.20	.40
LLENW02E018R Dressed Up Nico Yazawa RRR	10.00	20.00
LLENW02E019 Taking Care of Nails Nico U	.12	.25
LLENW02E020 Apple Candy and You Eli Ayase U	.12	.25
LLENW02E021 Great Summer Break Nico Yazawa U	.12	.25
LLENW02E022 Someday from Here On Maki Nico Rin U	.12	.25
LLENW02E023 Snack Time Nozomi Nico U	.12	.25
LLENW02E024 Christmas Date Nico Yazawa U	.12	.25
LLENW02E025 Festival Girl Nozomi Tojo U	.12	.25
LLENW02E026 Christmas Date Nozomi Tojo U	.12	.25
LLENW02E027 A Present for You Eli Ayase U	.12	.25
LLENW02E028 Secret Gift U	.12	.25
LLENW02E029 Happiest Girl U	.12	.25
LLENW02E030 Lucky New Year U	.12	.25
LLENW02E031 Your Special Santa Nozomi Tojo C	.10	.20
LLENW02E032 New Years Treat Nico Yazawa C	.10	.20
LLENW02E033 Autumn With Books Eli Ayase C	.10	.20
LLENW02E034 Chinese Vampire Nozomi Tojo C	.10	.20
LLENW02E035 Marching Girl Eli Ayase C	.10	.20
LLENW02E036 Western Girl Nico Yazawa C	.10	.20
LLENW02E037 Doll Festival Nico Yazawa C	.10	.20
LLENW02E038 Student of Otonokizaka High Alisa C	.10	.20
LLENW02E039 Sunny Day Song Eli Ayase C	.10	.20
LLENW02E040 Light Umbrella Eli Ayase C	.10	.20
LLENW02E041 Shrine Maiden Outfit Nozomi Tojo C	.10	.20
LLENW02E042 Sunny Day Song Alisa Ayase C	.10	.20
LLENW02E043 Good Girl Christmas Nico Yazawa C	.10	.20
LLENW02E044 School Matters Eli C	.10	.20
LLENW02E045 Special Stew Eli Ayase C	.10	.20
LLENW02E046 Homely Idol Nico Yazawa C	.10	.20
LLENW02E047 Christmas Date Eli Ayase C	.10	.20
LLENW02E048 Full Course of Luck Nozomi Tojo C	.10	.20
LLENW02E049 Sunny Day Song Nico Yazawa C	.10	.20
LLENW02E050 Sunny Day Song Nozomi Tojo C	.10	.20
LLENW02E051 Hug Attack Nozomi Tojo C	.10	.20
LLENW02E052 A Piece of Chocolate R	.20	.40
LLENW02E053 Special Chocolate R	.20	.40
LLENW02E054a We Are A Single Light R	.20	.40
LLENW02E054aSP We Are A Single Light SP	30.00	55.00
LLENW02E054b We Are A Single Light R	.20	.40
LLENW02E054bSP We Are A Single Light SP	25.00	50.00
LLENW02E054c We Are A Single Light R	.20	.40
LLENW02E054cSP We Are A Single Light SP	30.00	60.00
LLENW02E055 Happy Valentine C	.10	.20
LLENW02E056 Heartbeat C	.10	.20
LLENW02E057 Angelic Angel C	.10	.20
LLENW02E058 We Are A Single Light Kotori Minami RR	4.00	8.00
LLENW02E059 Angelic Angel Umi Sonoda RR	4.00	8.00
LLENW02E060 Summer Festival Date Kotori Minami RR	1.25	2.50
LLENW02E060SP Summer Festival Date Kotori Minami SP	50.00	100.00
LLENW02E061 Summer Festival Date Honoka Kosaka RR	4.00	8.00
LLENW02E061SP Summer Festival Date Honoka Kosaka SP	50.00	100.00
LLENW02E062 Summer Festival Date Umi Sonoda RR	4.00	8.00
LLENW02E062SP Summer Festival Date Umi Sonoda SP	75.00	150.00
LLENW02E063 Sunny Day Song Honoka Kosaka RR	4.00	8.00
LLENW02E064 Dressed Up Honoka Kosaka R	.20	.40
LLENW02E064R Dressed Up Honoka Kosaka RRR	10.00	20.00
LLENW02E065 Sweets Fairy Kotori Minami R	.20	.40
LLENW02E065S Sweets Fairy Kotori Minami SR	4.00	8.00
LLENW02E066 Dressed Up Kotori Minami R	.20	.40
LLENW02E066R Dressed Up Kotori Minami RRR	6.00	12.00
LLENW02E067 Dressed Up Umi Sonoda R	.20	.40
LLENW02E067R Dressed Up Umi Sonoda RRR	5.00	10.00
LLENW02E068 Sweets Fairy Umi Sonoda R	.20	.40
LLENW02E068S Sweets Fairy Umi Sonoda SR	4.00	8.00
LLENW02E069 Sweets Fairy Honoka Kosaka R	.20	.40
LLENW02E069S Sweets Fairy Honoka Kosaka SR	4.00	8.00
LLENW02E070 Sunny Day Song Umi Sonoda R	.20	.40
LLENW02E071 Angelic Angel Honoka Kosaka R	.20	.40
LLENW02E072 Angelic Angel Kotori Minami R	.20	.40
LLENW02E073 The First Step Honoka U	.12	.25
LLENW02E074 Everyones Festival Honoka Kosaka U	.12	.25
LLENW02E075 Christmas Date Kotori Minami U	.12	.25
LLENW02E076 Pure Night Umi Sonoda U	.12	.25
LLENW02E077 Lets go slowly Honoka Kosaka U	.12	.25
LLENW02E078 Cool Evening Breeze Kotori Minami U	.12	.25
LLENW02E079 Christmas Date Umi Sonoda U	.12	.25
LLENW02E080 Christmas Date Honoka Kosaka U	.12	.25
LLENW02E081 Happy New Year? U	.12	.25
LLENW02E082 New Years Dream U	.12	.25
LLENW02E083 Yearly Greetings U	.12	.25
LLENW02E084 Maid Outfit Umi C	.10	.20
LLENW02E085 Snow Lady Umi Sonoda C	.10	.20
LLENW02E086 White Christmas Kotori Minami C	.10	.20
LLENW02E087 Taisho Era Girl Honoka Kosaka C	.10	.20
LLENW02E088 Snowy Night Umi Sonoda C	.10	.20
LLENW02E089 Cotton Kimono Umi Sonoda C	.10	.20
LLENW02E090 In Practice Umi Sonoda C	.10	.20
LLENW02E091 Sunny Day Song Kotori Minami C	.10	.20
LLENW02E092 Sunny Day Song Yukiho Kosaka C	.10	.20
LLENW02E093 Student of Otonokizaka High Yukiho C	.10	.20
LLENW02E094 Sunny Day Song Tsubasa Kira C	.10	.20
LLENW02E095 Sunny Day Song Erena Todo C	.10	.20
LLENW02E096 Sunny Day Song Anju Yuki C	.10	.20
LLENW02E097 Future Style Honoka Kosaka C	.10	.20
LLENW02E098 Angel Nurse Kotori Minami C	.10	.20
LLENW02E099 Blissful Snacks Honoka Kosaka C	.10	.20
LLENW02E100 Candle Night Honoka Kosaka C	.10	.20
LLENW02E101 Angel Nurse Kotori Minami C	.10	.20
LLENW02E102 Bird Watching Kotori Minami C	.10	.20
LLENW02E103 Future Style Umi Sonoda C	.10	.20
LLENW02E104 Homuras Star Honoka Kosaka C	.10	.20
LLENW02E105 Hiking Honoka Kosaka C	.10	.20
LLENW02E106 Female Singer C	.10	.20
LLENW02E107 Swimsuit Kotori C	.10	.20
LLENW02E108 Thankful Feast Umi Sonoda C	.10	.20
LLENW02E109 Open Wide Kotori Minami C	.10	.20
LLENW02E110 Find Your Answer C	.10	.20
LLENW02E111 Secret Desire R	.20	.40
LLENW02E112a We Are A Single Light R	.20	.40
LLENW02E112aSP We Are A Single Light SP	25.00	45.00
LLENW02E112b We Are A Single Light R	.20	.40
LLENW02E112bSP We Are A Single Light SP	25.00	50.00
LLENW02E112c We Are A Single Light R	.20	.40
LLENW02E112cSP We Are A Single Light SP	30.00	55.00
LLENW02E113 Lots o Animals C	.10	.20
LLENW02E114 Sweet and Smooth C	.10	.20
LLENW02E115 Future Style C	.10	.20
LLENW02E116 Sunny Day Song C	.10	.20
LLENW02E117 Summer Festival Date Maki Nishikino RR	10.00	20.00
LLENW02E117SP Summer Festival Date Maki Nishikino SP	75.00	150.00
LLENW02E118 Hello Count the Stars Rin Hoshizora RR	4.00	8.00
LLENW02E119 We Are A Single Light Maki Nishikino RR	12.00	25.00
LLENW02E120 Summer Festival Date Rin Hoshizora RR	1.00	2.00
LLENW02E120SP Summer Festival Date Rin Hoshizora SP	30.00	55.00
LLENW02E121 Summer Festival Date Hanayo Koizumi RR	4.00	8.00
LLENW02E121SP Summer Festival Date Hanayo Koizumi SP	30.00	60.00
LLENW02E122 Angelic Angel Hanayo Koizumi RR	1.25	2.50
LLENW02E123 Sweets Fairy Hanayo Koizumi R	.20	.40
LLENW02E123R Sweets Fairy Hanayo Koizumi SR	4.00	8.00
LLENW02E124 Sweets Fairy Rin Hoshizora R	.20	.40
LLENW02E124R Sweets Fairy Rin Hoshizora SR	4.00	8.00
LLENW02E125 Sunny Day Song Hanayo Koizumi R	.20	.40
LLENW02E126 Dressed Up Rin Hoshizora R	.20	.40
LLENW02E126R Dressed Up Rin Hoshizora RRR	4.00	8.00
LLENW02E127 Angelic Angel Maki Nishikino R	.20	.40
LLENW02E128 Dressed Up Hanayo Koizumi R	.20	.40
LLENW02E128R Dressed Up Hanayo Koizumi RRR	4.00	8.00
LLENW02E129 Sweets Fairy Maki Nishikino R	.20	.40
LLENW02E129S Sweets Fairy Maki Nishikino SR	4.00	8.00
LLENW02E130 Angelic Angel Rin Hoshizora R	.20	.40
LLENW02E131 Dressed Up Maki Nishikino R	.20	.40
LLENW02E131R Dressed Up Maki Nishikino RRR	12.00	25.00
LLENW02E132 Secret Expression Maki U	.12	.25
LLENW02E133 Melody Played Maki U	.12	.25
LLENW02E134 In the Middle of Recording Rin Hanayo U	.12	.25
LLENW02E135 Christmas Date Hanayo Koizumi U	.12	.25
LLENW02E136 Bon Dance Rin Hoshizora U	.12	.25
LLENW02E137 Goldfish Scooper Maki Nishikino U	.12	.25
LLENW02E138 Christmas Date Rin Hoshizora U	.12	.25
LLENW02E139 Night StallHopping Hanayo Koizumi U	.12	.25
LLENW02E140 Christmas Date Maki Nishikino U	.12	.25
LLENW02E141 Alpaca U	.12	.25
LLENW02E142 Finest Once a Year U	.12	.25
LLENW02E143 Mochi is Rice Too U	.12	.25
LLENW02E144 365 Happy Days U	.12	.25
LLENW02E145 Gothic Girl Maki Nishikino C	.10	.20
LLENW02E146 Princess Kaguya Rin Hoshizora C	.10	.20
LLENW02E147 Elven Ties Hanayo Koizumi C	.10	.20
LLENW02E148 Lets Skate Together Hanayo Koizumi C	.10	.20
LLENW02E149 Christmas Carol Maki Nishikino C	.10	.20
LLENW02E150 Scattering Beans Maki Nishikino C	.10	.20
LLENW02E151 Sunny Day Song Rin Hoshizora C	.10	.20
LLENW02E152 A Service for You Maki Nishikino C	.10	.20
LLENW02E153 Christmas Bells Rin Hoshizora C	.10	.20
LLENW02E154 Secret Recipes Maki Nishikino C	.10	.20
LLENW02E155 My Christmas Treat Hanayo Koizumi C	.10	.20
LLENW02E156 Fluffy Alpaca C	.10	.20
LLENW02E157 Homemade Ramen Rin Hoshizora C	.10	.20
LLENW02E158 Snow Sprite Rin Hoshizora C	.10	.20
LLENW02E159 Sunny Day Song Maki Nishikino C	.10	.20
LLENW02E160 View the Full Moon Rin Hoshizora C	.10	.20
LLENW02E161 Healing Menu Hanayo Koizumi C	.10	.20
LLENW02E162 Clam Hunting Hanayo Koizumi C	.10	.20
LLENW02E163 Hello Count the Stars Hanayo Koizumi R	.20	.40
LLENW02E164 Romantic Valentine R	.20	.40
LLENW02E165a We Are A Single Light R	.20	.40
LLENW02E165aSP We Are A Single Light SP	25.00	45.00
LLENW02E165b We Are A Single Light R	.20	.40
LLENW02E165bSP We Are A Single Light SP	50.00	100.00
LLENW02E165c We Are A Single Light R	.20	.40
LLENW02E165cSP We Are A Single Light SP	20.00	40.00
LLENW02E166 Rins Secret C	.10	.20
LLENW02E167 Makis Secret C	.10	.20
LLENW02E168 Hello Count the Stars C	.10	.20
LLENW02E169 Time for Home Economics C	.10	.20

2016 Weiss Schwarz NISEMONOGATARI

NMS24E003 The Way Back Shinobu Oshino R	.20	.40
NMS24E004 Blessing of the Moon Shinobu Oshino R	.20	.40
NMS24E005 Words of Courage Mayoi Hachikuji R	.20	.40
NMS24E006 Serious Mode Shinobu Oshino R	.20	.40
NMS24E007 Sake of Cooperation Shinobu Oshino U	.12	.25
NMS24E008 Primp and Proper Nadeko Sengoku U	.12	.25
NMS24E009 Vampires Dignity Shinobu Oshino U	.12	.25
NMS24E010 Resident of the Shadows Shinobu Oshino U	.12	.25
NMS24E011 Flower Garden Shinobu Oshino U	.12	.25
NMS24E012 Sudden Attack Koyomi Araragi C	.10	.20
NMS24E013 Shinobu Oshino in the Shadows C	.10	.20
NMS24E014 First Visitor Nadeko Sengoku C	.10	.20
NMS24E015 Shinobu Oshino in a Good Mood C	.10	.20
NMS24E016 Blond with Gold Eyes Shinobu Oshino C	.10	.20
NMS24E017 Being Bashful Mayoi Hachikuji C	.10	.20
NMS24E018 Ritual One Level Higher U	.12	.25
NMS24E019 Encounter in the Ruins CR	.25	.50
NMS24E020 Welcome CC	.15	.30
NMS24E023 Combat Role Karen Araragi R	.20	.40
NMS24E024 Benefactors Advice Tsubasa Hanekawa R	.20	.40
NMS24E025 Girl Who Was Given a Bee Karen Araragi R	.20	.40
NMS24E026 Someone to Protect Hitagi Senjyogahara R	.20	.40
NMS24E027 Wreathefire Bee Karen Araragi R	.20	.40
NMS24E028 Bigger of the Sisters Karen Araragi U	.12	.25
NMS24E029 Fake Deishu Kaiki U	.12	.25
NMS24E030 Sharp Intuition Hitagi Senjyogahara U	.12	.25
NMS24E031 Brushing Teeth Karen Araragi U	.12	.25
NMS24E032 Lighthearted Karen Araragi U	.12	.25
NMS24E033 Playing With Cards Suruga Kanbaru U	.12	.25
NMS24E034 A Morning Sight Karen Araragi U	.12	.25
NMS24E035 Tutor Tsubasa Hanekawa C	.10	.20
NMS24E036 Pride of an Elder Brother Koyomi Araragi C	.10	.20
NMS24E037 Celebrity of Tsuganoki 2nd Middle School Karen Araragi C	.10	.20
NMS24E038 What is Justice Karen Araragi C	.10	.20
NMS24E039 Family Bond Karen Araragi C	.10	.20
NMS24E040 Innocence Suruga Kanbaru C	.10	.20
NMS24E041 Mischievous Nature Tsubasa Hanekawa C	.10	.20
NMS24E042 Teeth Brushing Time CR	.25	.50
NMS24E043 Sandy Beach for Two CC	.15	.30
NMS24E044 Girl Who Knows Anything CC	.15	.30
NMS24E045 KAREN Bee CC	.15	.30
NMS24E048 Farewell to the Past Hitagi Senjyogahara R	.20	.40
NMS24E049 Phoenix Tsukihi Araragi R	.20	.40
NMS24E050 Sense of Liberation Suruga Kanbaru R	.20	.40
NMS24E051 Celebrity of Tsuganoki 2nd Middle School Tsukihi Araragi R	.20	.40
NMS24E052 Usual Parting Mayoi Hachikuji R	.20	.40
NMS24E053 Promise Exchange Mayoi Hachikuji U	.12	.25
NMS24E054 Accelerator Suruga Kanbaru U	.12	.25
NMS24E055 Matters of Younger Sisters Koyomi Araragi U	.12	.25
NMS24E056 Fire Sisters Tsukihi Araragi U	.12	.25
NMS24E057 Advisor Role Tsukihi Araragi U	.12	.25
NMS24E058 Passionate Personality Tsukihi Araragi U	.12	.25
NMS24E059 Loves Kimono Tsukihi Araragi C	.10	.20
NMS24E060 Smaller of the Sisters Tsukihi Araragi C	.10	.20
NMS24E061 Tea Ceremony Club Tsukihi Araragi C	.10	.20
NMS24E062 A Morning Sight Tsukihi Araragi C	.10	.20
NMS24E063 Unexpected Words Hitagi Senjyogahara C	.10	.20
NMS24E064 Secret Conversation Mayoi Hachikuji C	.10	.20
NMS24E065 Pervert Suruga Kanbaru C	.10	.20
NMS24E066 Usual Occurrence U	.12	.25
NMS24E067 TSUKIHI Phoenix CR	.25	.50
NMS24E068 I flubbed it CC	.15	.30
NMS24E069 Handling Memories CC	.15	.30
NMS24E070 Platinum Mad CC	.15	.30
NMS24E072 Hairband Nadeko Sengoku R	.20	.40
NMS24E073 Sisters Helper Tsubasa Hanekawa U	.12	.25
NMS24E074 Shikigami Yotsugi Ononoki U	.12	.25
NMS24E075 Unlimited Rulebook Yotsugi Ononoki C	.10	.20
NMS24E076 Way Back Tsubasa Hanekawa C	.10	.20
NMS24E077 Playing Together Nadeko Sengoku C	.10	.20
NMS24E078 Onmyoji Yozuru Kagenui C	.10	.20
NMS24E079 Losers Bravado U	.12	.25
NMS24E080 Family Matters CC	.15	.30

2016 Weiss Schwarz Extra Booster The Melancholy of Haruhi Suzumiya

SYWE09E01 Kyon and Koizumi C	.10	.20
SYWE09E02 Koizumi Talking About the Stars C	.10	.20
SYWE09E03 Kyon Looking Up at the Night Sky C	.10	.20
SYWE09E04 5th Grade Elementary Student Kyons Sister C	.10	.20
SYWE09E05 Mikuru Wishing Upon the Stars R	.20	.40
SYWE09E06 Time Travel Kyon and Mikuru R	.20	.40
SYWE09E07 Encounter with Mikuru MikuruAdult R	.20	.40
SYWE09E08 Energetic Senior Tsuruya C	.10	.20
SYWE09E09 Mikuru Working Parttime C	.10	.20
SYWE09E10 Flower Viewing Mikuru C	.10	.20
SYWE09E11 Cicada Capturing Competition Mikuru C	.10	.20
SYWE09E12 Guiding Role C	.10	.20
SYWE09E13 Super Director Haruhi R	.20	.40
SYWE09E14 Flower Viewing Haruhi R	.20	.40
SYWE09E15 Bamboo Leaf Rhapsody Haruhi R	.20	.40
SYWE09E16 Girl Who Will Change the World Haruhi C	.10	.20
SYWE09E17 Swimsuit Haruhi C	.10	.20
SYWE09E18 Haruhi at a Summer Festival C	.10	.20
SYWE09E19a Endless Eight C	.10	.20
SYWE09E19b Endless Eight C	.10	.20
SYWE09E19c Endless Eight C	.10	.20
SYWE09E19d Endless Eight C	.10	.20
SYWE09E19e Endless Eight C	.10	.20
SYWE09E19f Endless Eight C	.10	.20
SYWE09E19g Endless Eight C	.10	.20
SYWE09E19h Endless Eight C	.10	.20
SYWE09E20 I am here C	.10	.20
SYWE09E21 End of Summer C	.10	.20

SYWE09E22 Observer Nagato R .20 .40
SYWE09E23 Mage Nagato and Shamisen R .20 .40
SYWE09E24 Nagato at a Summer Festival R .20 .40
SYWE09E25 Standby Mode Nagato C .10 .20
SYWE09E26 Flower Viewing Nagato C .10 .20
SYWE09E27 Night with Two Weeks Left C .10 .20

2017 Weiss Schwarz Accel World

AWS18E006 Maiden in Love Kuroyukihime R .20 .40
AWS18E007 Challenging a Formidable Foe Silver Crow R .20 .40
AWS18E008 Pure Desire to Monopolize Kuroyukihime R .20 .40
AWS18E009 Black Lotus R .20 .40
AWS18E010 Black Lotus Facing a Crossroad Duel U .12 .25
AWS18E011 Amateur Burst Linker Silver Crow U .12 .25
AWS18E012 Black KingBlack Lotus U .12 .25
AWS18E013 Twilight Promise Kuroyukihime U .12 .25
AWS18E014 Real Strength Kuroyukihime U .12 .25
AWS18E015 To the Unexplored Heights of Mankind Haruyuki U .12 .25
AWS18E016 The Boy Who Wanted Wings Haruyuki C .10 .20
AWS18E017 Pink Pig Haruyuki C .10 .20
AWS18E018 Kings Return Black Lotus C .10 .20
AWS18E019 School Madonna Kuroyukihime C .10 .20
AWS18E020 Bullied Kid Haruyuki C .10 .20
AWS18E021 Enormous Klutz Haruyuki C .10 .20
AWS18E022 Silver Wings Silver Crow C .10 .20
AWS18E023 Pony Tail Kuroyukihime C .10 .20
AWS18E024 Impeding Wall Haruyuki C .10 .20
AWS18E025 Betrayal U .12 .25
AWS18E026 Gale Thruster U .12 .25
AWS18E027 The Heart That Yearns for the Sky CR .25 .50
AWS18E028 A Feeling Never Felt Before CC .15 .30
AWS18E029 Death By Piercing CC .15 .30
AWS18E030 Knight of theBlack King CC .15 .30
AWS18E033 Nonchalant Talk Chiyuri R .20 .40
AWS18E034 Apology Ice Cream Chiyuri R .20 .40
AWS18E035 Optimistic Lime Bell R .20 .40
AWS18E036 Taking Care of Friends Chiyuri R .20 .40
AWS18E037 Chiyuri Kurashima R .20 .40
AWS18E038 Lime Bell U .12 .25
AWS18E039 Seiji Nomi U .12 .25
AWS18E040 Ash Roller U .12 .25
AWS18E041 Dusk Taker U .12 .25
AWS18E042 Betrayer Lime Bell U .12 .25
AWS18E043 Younger Days Chiyuri C .10 .20
AWS18E044 Suspicious Gaze Chiyuri C .10 .20
AWS18E045 Silver Cat Chiyuri C .10 .20
AWS18E046 Bright and Cheerful Chiyuri C .10 .20
AWS18E047 Manly Skull Mask Ash Roller C .10 .20
AWS18E048 Sunny Smile Chiyuri C .10 .20
AWS18E049 Lovable Charm Chiyuri C .10 .20
AWS18E050 Good Rival Ash Roller C .10 .20
AWS18E051 Pyro Dealer U .12 .25
AWS18E052 Choir Chime U .12 .25
AWS18E053 Chiyuris Tears CR .25 .50
AWS18E054 Citron Call CC .15 .30
AWS18E055 Demonic Commandeer CC .15 .30
AWS18E058 Emotional Scarlet Rain R .20 .40
AWS18E059 Cute Cousin Niko R .20 .40
AWS18E060 Rain and Leopard R .20 .40
AWS18E061 Immobile FortressScarlet Rain R .20 .40
AWS18E062 Red KingScarlet Rain R .20 .40
AWS18E063 Niko Staying Over U .12 .25
AWS18E064 Heart Race in the Bath Niko U .12 .25
AWS18E065 Angel Mode Niko U .12 .25
AWS18E066 Darkness of the Heart Silver Crow U .12 .25
AWS18E067 Strongest Name C.K U .12 .25
AWS18E068 Crimson Kingbolt C .10 .20
AWS18E069 Maid of Nerima Pard C .10 .20
AWS18E070 Megumi Wakamiya C .10 .20
AWS18E071 Bloody Storm Scarlet Rain C .10 .20
AWS18E072 Close Friend Going Out of control Scarlet Rain C .10 .20
AWS18E073 5th Generation Chrome Disaster C .10 .20
AWS18E074 Prominences Top Niko and Pard C .10 .20
AWS18E075 Peak of Impudence Niko C .10 .20
AWS18E076 Invincible U .12 .25
AWS18E077 Armor of Calamity U .12 .25
AWS18E078 Hailstorm Domination CR .25 .50
AWS18E079 Black Repercussions CC .15 .30
AWS18E080 Judgment Blow CC .15 .30
AWS18E083 Calm Smile Fuko R .20 .40
AWS18E084 Cyan Pile R .20 .40
AWS18E085 Fuko Kurasaki R .20 .40
AWS18E086 Former Ally Sky Raker U .12 .25
AWS18E087 Reliable Partner Cyan Pile U .12 .25
AWS18E088 Intelligent and Cute Fuko U .12 .25
AWS18E089 Ashs Teacher Sky Raker U .12 .25
AWS18E090 Mana Itosu C .10 .20
AWS18E091 New Ally Takumu C .10 .20
AWS18E092 Bouncer Aqua Current C .10 .20
AWS18E093 Ruka Asato C .10 .20
AWS18E094 Glasses Character Takumu C .10 .20
AWS18E095 Unlimited Field Cyan Pile C .10 .20
AWS18E096 Silent Beauty Aqua Current C .10 .20
AWS18E097 Pile Driver U .12 .25
AWS18E098 Forced Transition U .12 .25
AWS18E099 Incarnation CR .25 .50
AWS18E100 Lightning Cyan Spike CC .15 .30

2017 Weiss Schwarz Accel World Infinite Burst

AWS43E003 Vacillating Memories, Kuroyukihime R .20 .40
AWS43E004 Summer Festival, Kuroyukihime R .20 .40
AWS43E005 Silver Crow R .20 .40
AWS43E006 Dress Fluttering in the Wind, Kuroyukihime R .20 .40
AWS43E007 Rousing Battlecry, Kuroyukihime R .20 .40
AWS43E008 Lotus of Black Death Black Lotus R .20 .40
AWS43E009 Looking Flushed After a Bath, Kuroyukihime U .12 .25
AWS43E010 Beacon of Counterattack, Black Lotus U .12 .25
AWS43E011 Unforeseen Circumstances, Kuroyukihime U .12 .25
AWS43E012 Uneasy Feeling, Kuroyukihime U .12 .25
AWS43E013 Bad at Cooking, Kuroyukihime U .12 .25
AWS43E014 A Scene in the Summer, Kuroyukihime U .12 .25
AWS43E015 Will of Opposition, Haruyuki U .12 .25
AWS43E016 Silver Crow Embracing the Monarch U .12 .25
AWS43E017 Acrimonious Advice, Metatron C .10 .20
AWS43E018 Waking from Siesta, Kuroyukihime C .10 .20
AWS43E019C Yellow Radio C .10 .20
AWS43E020 Promised Reward, Kuroyukihime C .10 .20
AWS43E021 Armed to the Teeth, Haruyuki C .10 .20
AWS43E022 Reasonable Acceleration, Haruyuki C .10 .20
AWS43E023 Acting on Volition, Black Lotus C .10 .20
AWS43E024 Nurturing Counsel, Kuroyukihime C .10 .20
AWS43E025 3D Icon U .12 .25
AWS43E026 Incident at the Summer Festival C .10 .20
AWS43E027 Nega Nebulas CLR .25 .50
AWS43E028 Dual Flight CC .15 .30
AWS43E029 Vorpal Strike CC .15 .30
AWS43E032 Quiet Love, Rin R .20 .40
AWS43E033 Watch Witch Lime Bell R .20 .40
AWS43E034 Green Grande R .20 .40
AWS43E035 One Who Never Looks Back, Ash Roller R .20 .40
AWS43E036 Humming, Lime Bell U .12 .25
AWS43E037 Cat-like Behavior, Chiyuri U .12 .25
AWS43E038 Traversing Through the Black Cloud, Lime Bell U .12 .25
AWS43E039 Nyx & Risa U .12 .25
AWS43E040 Goddess of Night, Nyx U .12 .25
AWS43E041 Hometown Is Shibuya, Ash Roller C .10 .20
AWS43E042 Disc-shaped Enemy C .10 .20
AWS43E043 White Duel Avatar C .10 .20
AWS43E044 Nox Core C .10 .20
AWS43E045 Summer Festival, Rin C .10 .20
AWS43E046 Summer Festival, Chiyuri C .10 .20
AWS43E047 Nemesis & Thanatos C .10 .20
AWS43E048 Strategy Meeting, Chiyuri C .10 .20
AWS43E049 Famous Healer Skill U .12 .25
AWS43E050 Return to Reality C .10 .20
AWS43E051 Special Exception for a Childhood Friend CLR .25 .50
AWS43E052 Citron Call CC .15 .30
AWS43E053 Older Brother's Punishment CC .15 .30
AWS43E056 Driving, Scarlet Rain R .20 .40
AWS43E057 Summer Festival, Utai R .20 .40
AWS43E058 Calming Sight, Niko & Pado R .20 .40
AWS43E059 Winter's Day Niko R .20 .40
AWS43E060 A Scene in the Summer, Pado R .20 .40
AWS43E061 Competitive, Scarlet Rain R .20 .40
AWS43E062 Battle at the Jingu, Ardor Maiden U .12 .25
AWS43E063 Executing the Plan, Blood Leopard U .12 .25
AWS43E064 Bloody Kitty Blood Leopard U .12 .25
AWS43E065 Matsunoki Elementary School, Utai U .12 .25
AWS43E066 Cool Vibe, Pado U .12 .25
AWS43E067 Armor Up Command, Scarlet Rain U .12 .25
AWS43E068 Enforced Logout, Niko C .10 .20
AWS43E069 Chatterbox, Niko C .10 .20
AWS43E070 Cooking with a Smile, Niko C .10 .20
AWS43E071 Stable Person, Utai C .10 .20
AWS43E072 In the Heat of Battle, Utai C .10 .20
AWS43E073 Foothold U .12 .25
AWS43E074 Dangerous Driving C .10 .20
AWS43E075 Having Fun in the Summer CLR .25 .50
AWS43E076 Heat Blast Saturation CC .15 .30
AWS43E077 Flame Torrents CC .15 .30
AWS43E080 Girl Who Aimed for the Skies, Fuko R .20 .40
AWS43E081 Akira Himi R .20 .40
AWS43E082 Summer Festival, Fuko R .20 .40
AWS43E083 Traversing Through the Black Cloud, Sky Raker R .20 .40
AWS43E084 Blue Knight U .12 .25
AWS43E085 Aquamatic Aqua Current U .12 .25
AWS43E086 Changing Clothes, Fuko U .12 .25
AWS43E087 Nega Nebulas Submaster, Fuko U .12 .25
AWS43E088 Melee Combat Form, Aqua Current U .12 .25
AWS43E089 Summer Festival, Akira C .10 .20
AWS43E090 Purple Thorn C .10 .20
AWS43E091 Strategist Position, Takumu C .10 .20
AWS43E092 Cyan Pile Becoming a Shield C .10 .20
AWS43E093 Birds of a Feather, Takumu & Haruyuki C .10 .20
AWS43E094 Battle at the Jingu, Sky Raker C .10 .20
AWS43E095 Perforation Ability, Cyan Pile C .10 .20
AWS43E096 Marker of Mortification U .12 .25
AWS43E097 Gale Thruster C .10 .20
AWS43E098 Summer Night's Slumber CLR .25 .50
AWS43E099 Combination? CC .15 .30
AWS43E100 Lightning Cyan Spike CC .15 .30

2017 Weiss Schwarz Attack on Titan Vol. 2

AOTS50E001 To Seize Freedom Armin RR .10 .20
AOTS50E001SP To Seize Freedom Armin SP .10 .20
AOTS50E002 My Fate to Bear Eren RR .10 .20
AOTS50E002SP My Fate to Bear Eren SP .10 .20
AOTS50E003 Crimson Fighting Spirit Eren RR .10 .20
AOTS50E003R Crimson Fighting Spirit Eren RRR .10 .20
AOTS50E004 Single Ray of Light Armin R .20 .40
AOTS50E004S Single Ray of Light Armin SR .10 .20
AOTS50E005 Keen Mind Armin R .20 .40
AOTS50E006 To Seize Freedom Eren R .20 .40
AOTS50E006S To Seize Freedom Eren SR .10 .20
AOTS50E007 Until the Dying Breath Armin R .20 .40
AOTS50E008 Single Ray of Light Eren Titan R .20 .40
AOTS50E009 Relief Eren U .12 .25
AOTS50E010 Cleanup Eren U .12 .25
AOTS50E011 Born in Ragako Conny U .12 .25
AOTS50E012 Steady Advance Eren Titan U .12 .25
AOTS50E013a Memory of that Day Annie U .12 .25
AOTS50E013b Memory of that Day Annie U .12 .25
AOTS50E014 Whimsical Days Eren C .10 .20
AOTS50E015 Recovering Eren Armin C .10 .20
AOTS50E016 Until the Dying Breath Conny C .10 .20
AOTS50E017a Revenge Hannes C .10 .20
AOTS50E017b Revenge Hannes C .10 .20
AOTS50E018 Captured Eren C .10 .20
AOTS50E019 Sunset on Your Back Eren Titan C .10 .20
AOTS50E020 Anti Titan Device Omni Directional Mobility Gear U .12 .25
AOTS50E021 Coordinate U .12 .25
AOTS50E022 Outcry CR .20 .40
AOTS50E022R Outcry RRR .10 .20
AOTS50E023a Yell of Rage CC .15 .30
AOTS50E023b Yell of Rage CC .15 .30
AOTS50E024 Close Combat CC .15 .30
AOTS50E024S Close Combat SR .10 .20
AOTS50E025 Silent Fury Levi RR .10 .20
AOTS50E025SP Silent Fury Levi SP .10 .20
AOTS50E026 To Seize Freedom Hange RR .10 .20
AOTS50E026SP To Seize Freedom Hange SP .10 .20
AOTS50E027 Until the Dying Breath Hange R .20 .40
AOTS50E028 Until the Dying Breath Erwin R .20 .40
AOTS50E029 Single Ray of Light Levi R .20 .40
AOTS50E029S Single Ray of Light Levi SR .10 .20
AOTS50E030 Until the Dying Breath Levi R .20 .40
AOTS50E031 To Seize Freedom Levi R .20 .40
AOTS50E031S To Seize Freedom Levi SR .10 .20
AOTS50E032 Pastor Nick U .12 .25
AOTS50E033 Confirming the Unknown Hanji U .12 .25
AOTS50E034 To Seize Freedom Erwin U .12 .25
AOTS50E035 Cleanup Levi U .12 .25
AOTS50E036 Sunset on Your Back Levi U .12 .25
AOTS50E037 Communication Hange U .12 .25
AOTS50E038 The Fate of Mankinds Survival Erwin C .10 .20
AOTS50E039a Veteran Scout Nanaba C .10 .20
AOTS50E039b Veteran Scout Nanaba C .10 .20
AOTS50E040a Veteran Scout Gelgar C .10 .20
AOTS50E040b Veteran Scout Gelgar C .10 .20
AOTS50E041 Moblit C .10 .20
AOTS50E042 What Happens Henceforth Hange C .10 .20
AOTS50E043 A Definite Step Hange C .10 .20
AOTS50E044 What Happens Henceforth Levi C .10 .20
AOTS50E045a Until the Dying Breath Miche C .10 .20
AOTS50E045b Until the Dying Breath Miche C .10 .20
AOTS50E046 A Request or an Order U .12 .25
AOTS50E047 Repose U .12 .25
AOTS50E048 Blade that Rends Despair CR .20 .40
AOTS50E048R Blade that Rends Despair RRR .10 .20
AOTS50E049a Revolutionists CC .15 .30
AOTS50E049b Revolutionists CC .15 .30
AOTS50E050a Standby for Full Scale Assault CC .15 .30
AOTS50E050b Standby for Full Scale Assault CC .15 .30
AOTS50E051 Goddess Smile Christa RR .10 .20
AOTS50E051SP Goddess Smile Christa SP .10 .20
AOTS50E052 Embraced Memories Mikasa RR .10 .20
AOTS50E052SP Embraced Memories Mikasa SP .10 .20
AOTS50E053 To Seize Freedom Sasha RR .10 .20
AOTS50E053SP To Seize Freedom Sasha SP .10 .20
AOTS50E054 Single Ray of Light Mikasa R .20 .40
AOTS50E054S Single Ray of Light Mikasa SR .10 .20
AOTS50E055 Insatiable Hunger Sasha R .20 .40
AOTS50E056 Brief Respite Christa R .20 .40
AOTS50E057 Sunset on Your Back Mikasa R .20 .40
AOTS50E058 Until the Dying Breath Sasha R .20 .40
AOTS50E058S Until the Dying Breath Sasha SR .10 .20
AOTS50E059 To Seize Freedom Mikasa R .20 .40
AOTS50E059R To Seize Freedom Mikasa RRR .10 .20
AOTS50E060 Until the Dying Breath Christa R .20 .40
AOTS50E060R Until the Dying Breath Christa RRR .10 .20
AOTS50E061 Recovering Eren Mikasa U .12 .25
AOTS50E062 Piercing Terror Sasha U .12 .25
AOTS50E063 Fine as Is Christa U .12 .25
AOTS50E064a Hidden Truth Ymir U .12 .25
AOTS50E064b Hidden Truth Ymir U .12 .25
AOTS50E065 Until the Dying Breath Bertholdt U .12 .25
AOTS50E066 Hidden Truth Bertholdt U .12 .25
AOTS50E067 Born in Dauper Sasha U .12 .25
AOTS50E068 Hidden Truth Reiner U .12 .25
AOTS50E069 The Smile I Want to Protect Christa C .10 .20
AOTS50E070 Until the Dying Breath Jean C .10 .20
AOTS50E071 Soldier and Warrior Reiner C .10 .20
AOTS50E072 Dispossession Bertholdt C .10 .20
AOTS50E073 Until the Dying Breath Ymir C .10 .20
AOTS50E074 Until the Dying Breath Reiner C .10 .20
AOTS50E075 Until the Dying Breath Mikasa C .10 .20
AOTS50E076 Safekeeping Sasha C .10 .20
AOTS50E077 To Seize Freedom Jean C .10 .20
AOTS50E078 Relief Mikasa C .10 .20
AOTS50E079 Noble Bloodline Christa C .10 .20
AOTS50E080 The Goddess U .12 .25
AOTS50E081 Murderous Glare U .12 .25
AOTS50E082 My Real Name CR .20 .40
AOTS50E082S My Real Name SR .10 .20
AOTS50E083 Thank You CC .15 .30
AOTS50E083R Thank You RRR .10 .20
AOTS50E084a Run CC .15 .30
AOTS50E084b Run CC .15 .30
AOTS50E085 Strength Assessment Beast Titan R .20 .40
AOTS50E086 Beast Titan R .20 .40
AOTS50E086S Beast Titan SR .10 .20
AOTS50E087 Resurgence Armored Titan R .20 .40
AOTS50E087S Resurgence Armored Titan SR .10 .20
AOTS50E088a Pursuit Titan U .12 .25
AOTS50E088b Pursuit Titan U .12 .25
AOTS50E088c Pursuit Titan U .12 .25
AOTS50E088d Pursuit Titan U .12 .25
AOTS50E089 Multiple Decisive Battles Colossal Titan U .12 .25
AOTS50E090a Ymir Titan U .12 .25
AOTS50E090b Ymir Titan U .12 .25
AOTS50E091 Enemy of Humanity Colossal Titan U .12 .25
AOTS50E092 Nemesis Titan C .10 .20
AOTS50E093 Incomprehensible Titan C .10 .20
AOTS50E094 Until the Goal is Accomplished Armored Titan C .10 .20
AOTS50E095a Predation Titan C .10 .20
AOTS50E095b Predation Titan C .10 .20
AOTS50E095c Predation Titan C .10 .20
AOTS50E095d Predation Titan C .10 .20
AOTS50E096 All surpassing Existence Colossal Titan C .10 .20
AOTS50E097 Confrontation Armored Titan C .10 .20
AOTS50E098 In the Wall U .12 .25
AOTS50E099a Sentience CR .20 .40
AOTS50E099b Sentience CR .20 .40
AOTS50E100a Duel CC .15 .30
AOTS50E100b Duel CC .15 .30
AOTS50E101 Mischievous Battle Chimi Armin PR .10 .20
AOTS50E102 Mischievous Battle Chimi Eren PR .10 .20
AOTS50E103 Mischievous Battle Chimi Mikasa PR .10 .20
AOTS50E104 Mischievous Battle Chimi Colossal Titan PR .10 .20
AOTS50PE01 Indomitable Will Eren PR .10 .20

2017 Weiss Schwarz BanG Dream

BDW47E001 Glitter Green Nanana Wanibe R .20 .40
BDW47E002 Glitter Green Hinako Nijikki R .20 .40
BDW47E003 Glitter Green Rii Uzawa R .20 .40
BDW47E004 Glitter Green Yuri Ushigome R .20 .40
BDW47E005 Hinako Nijikki U .12 .25
BDW47E006 Friend of Saya Natsuki U .12 .25
BDW47E007 Gentle Stare Yuri U .12 .25
BDW47E008 On the Stage Rii U .12 .25
BDW47E009 Student Council President Nanana U .12 .25
BDW47E010 Yuri Ushigome C .10 .20
BDW47E011 Senior of Kasumi and Gang Hinako C .10 .20
BDW47E012 Reliable Elder Sister Yuri C .10 .20
BDW47E013 Together with Debeko Rii C .10 .20
BDW47E014 On Keyboards Nanana C .10 .20
BDW47E015 Club Show Yuri C .10 .20
BDW47E016 Rii Uzawa C .10 .20
BDW47E017 Nanana Wanibe C .10 .20
BDW47E018 Our Stage CR .25 .50
BDW47E019 Moment Between Sisters CC .15 .30
BDW47E026 StarrinPARTY Saya Yamabuki R .20 .40
BDW47E027 First Feeling of Heart Race Kasumi R .20 .40
BDW47E028 Live House at Sunset Rimi R .20 .40
BDW47E029 Twinkle Star Kasumi R .20 .40
BDW47E030 Melancholic Awakening Rimi R .20 .40
BDW47E031 Happy Halloween Kasumi R .20 .40
BDW47E032 Heart pounding Stage Rimi R .20 .40
BDW47E033 High School Girl Saya R .20 .40
BDW47E034 Caring for Friends Saya R .20 .40
BDW47E035 In the Sunlight Forest Saya R .20 .40
BDW47E036 StarrinPARTY Kasumi Toyama R .20 .40
BDW47E037 StarrinPARTY Rimi Ushigome R .20 .40
BDW47E038 Suggestion Rimi U .12 .25
BDW47E039 Under the Night Sky Kasumi U .12 .25
BDW47E040 Asuka Toyama U .12 .25
BDW47E041 Girl Band Mecca Kasumi U .12 .25
BDW47E042 A New Start Saya U .12 .25
BDW47E043 Good at Housework Saya U .12 .25
BDW47E044 Emotions Gushing Out Saya U .12 .25
BDW47E045 Midsummer Beachside Saya and Rimi U .12 .25
BDW47E046 Discovering Sparkles Rimi U .12 .25
BDW47E047 Choco Cornet Song Rimi U .12 .25
BDW47E048 SprinPARTY Saya Yamabuki U .12 .25
BDW47E049 Good Morning Kasumi U .12 .25
BDW47E050 Satisfied Kasumi U .12 .25
BDW47E051 A Scene at Sunset Rimi U .12 .25
BDW47E052 Club Show Saya C .10 .20

BDW47E053 Shy Girl Rimi C .10 .20
BDW47E054 Weirdo Kasumi C .10 .20
BDW47E055 Caring for Elder Sister Asuka C .10 .20
BDW47E056 Morning Events Rimi C .10 .20
BDW47E057 Club Show Kasumi C .10 .20
BDW47E058 Wrapped in Curtains Rimi C .10 .20
BDW47E059 Self introduction Saya C .10 .20
BDW47E060 Invitation Saya C .10 .20
BDW47E061 SprinPARTY Rimi Ushigome C .10 .20
BDW47E062 Trading Parts of Their Lunch Kasumi C .10 .20
BDW47E063 A Scene in the Morning Saya C .10 .20
BDW47E064 Club Show Rimi C .10 .20
BDW47E065 Saya Handing Over Choco Cornets C .10 .20
BDW47E066 Kasumis Younger Sister Asuka C .10 .20
BDW47E067 First Live Kasumi C .10 .20
BDW47E068 Real Feelings Saya C .10 .20
BDW47E069 SprinPARTY Kasumi Toyama C .10 .20
BDW47E070 One Day Manager Kasumi C .10 .20
BDW47E071 Something in the Warehouse U .12 .25
BDW47E072 Under the Night Sky U .12 .25
BDW47E073 Letter from Kasumi U .12 .25
BDW47E074 STAR BEAT CR .25 .50
BDW47E075 Exchanged Promise CR .25 .50
BDW47E076 Twinkle Twinkle Little Star CC .15 .30
BDW47E077 A Big Step CC .15 .30
BDW47E078 Aspired Stage CC .15 .30
BDW47E079 Gentle Elder Sis CC .15 .30
BDW47E080 We Are PoppinParty CC .15 .30
BDW47E085 Way Home Arisa R .20 .40
BDW47E086 A Scene in the Morning Tae R .20 .40
BDW47E087 SprinPARTY Tae Hanazono R .20 .40
BDW47E088 Bonsai Girl Arisa R .20 .40
BDW47E089 Club Show Tae R .20 .40
BDW47E090 Arisa Trying Not to Laugh R .20 .40
BDW47E091 StarrinPARTY Arisa Ichigaya R .20 .40
BDW47E092 StarrinPARTY Tae Hanazono R .20 .40
BDW47E093 Lunch Break Tae U .12 .25
BDW47E094 SprinPARTY Arisa Ichigaya U .12 .25
BDW47E095 SPACE Owner Shizen Tsuzuki U .12 .25
BDW47E096 Full of Sparkles Arisa U .12 .25
BDW47E097 First Live Arisa U .12 .25
BDW47E098 Part Time Job at SPACE Tae U .12 .25
BDW47E099 Club Show Arisa U .12 .25
BDW47E100 Tsundere Arisa U .12 .25
BDW47E101 Well prepared Tae U .12 .25
BDW47E102 Explosive Summer Tae and Arisa and Kasumi U .12 .25
BDW47E103 Remedial Classroom Tae C .10 .20
BDW47E104 High School Girl Tae C .10 .20
BDW47E105 Happy Halloween Arisa C .10 .20
BDW47E106 Heart pounding Feeling Tae C .10 .20
BDW47E107 Bewitching Omelet Arisa C .10 .20
BDW47E108 Yesterdays Events Arisa C .10 .20
BDW47E109 Childhood Tae C .10 .20
BDW47E110 High School Student Arisa C .10 .20
BDW47E111 First Live Tae C .10 .20
BDW47E112 Boggy Arisa C .10 .20
BDW47E113 Panicking Arisa C .10 .20
BDW47E114 That Irritating Girl U .12 .25
BDW47E115 Hearing a Guitar for the First Time U .12 .25
BDW47E116 Heart Pounding Star CR .25 .50
BDW47E117 Moved With Everyone CC .15 .30
BDW47E118 Real Intentions CC .15 .30
BDW47E119 Arisa Selling Off Tonegawa CC .15 .30
BDW47E120 PoppinParty First LIVE CC .15 .30

2017 Weiss Schwarz Extra Booster KanColle Fleet in the Deep Sea Sighted

KCSE28E04 Ne class Heavy Cruiser R .20 .40
KCSE28E05 Midway Princess in the Deep Sea R .20 .40
KCSE28E06 Aircraft Carrier Ogre in the Deep Sea R .20 .40
KCSE28E07 Armored Aircraft Carrier Ogre in the Deep Sea R .20 .40
KCSE28E08 Armored Aircraft Carrier Princess in the Deep Sea R .20 .40
KCSE28E09 Airfield Princess in the Deep Sea R .20 .40
KCSE28E10 Tsu class Light Cruiser U .12 .25
KCSE28E11 Ni Class Destroyer U .12 .25
KCSE28E12 Port Hydro Ogre in the Deep Sea U .12 .25
KCSE28E13 Aircraft Carrier Hydro Ogre in the Deep Sea U .12 .25
KCSE28E14 Aircraft Carrier Princess in the Deep Sea U .12 .25
KCSE28E15 Berserker Mode Port Princess in the Deep Sea C .10 .20
KCSE28E16 Floating Fortress C .10 .20
KCSE28E17 I class Destroyer C .10 .20
KCSE28E18 So class Submarine C .10 .20
KCSE28E19 Chi class Torpedo Cruiser C .10 .20
KCSE28E20 Ru class Battleship C .10 .20
KCSE28E21 Port Princess in the Deep Sea C .10 .20
KCSE28E22 Final Mode Midway Princess in the Deep Sea C .10 .20
KCSE28E23 Sink CC .15 .30
KCSE28E24 Nothing you dont understand anything at all CC .15 .30
KCSE28E25 I told you its hopeless CC .15 .30
KCSE28E29 Southern Battle Princess in the Deep Sea R .20 .40
KCSE28E30 Southern Ogre in the Deep Sea R .20 .40
KCSE28E31 Anchorage Princess in the Deep Sea R .20 .40
KCSE28E32 Seaplane Carrier Princess in the Deep Sea R .20 .40
KCSE28E33 Isolated Island Ogre in the Deep Sea R .20 .40
KCSE28E34 Air Defense Princess in the Deep Sea R .20 .40
KCSE28E35 Wa class Supply Ship U .12 .25
KCSE28E36 Ka class Submarine U .12 .25
KCSE28E37 Light Cruiser Ogre in the Deep Sea U .12 .25
KCSE28E38 Nu class Light Aircraft Carrier U .12 .25
KCSE28E39 Re class Battleship U .12 .25
KCSE28E40 Battleship Princess in the Deep Sea U .12 .25
KCSE28E41 Destroyer Princess in the Deep Sea C .10 .20
KCSE28E42 Ri class Heavy Cruiser C .10 .20
KCSE28E43 Ha class Destroyer C .10 .20
KCSE28E44 Ho class Light Cruiser C .10 .20
KCSE28E45 Ta class Battleship C .10 .20
KCSE28E46 Southern Battle Ogre in the Deep Sea C .10 .20
KCSE28E47 Anchorage Hydro Ogre in the Deep Sea C .10 .20
KCSE28E48 Fall CC .15 .30
KCSE28E49 Please sink CC .15 .30
KCSE28E50 Hehehe Does it hurt CC .15 .30

2017 Weiss Schwarz Konosuba God's Blessing on This Wonderful World

KSW49E003 Kazuma R .20 .40
KSW49E004 Shameful Abuse Darkness R .20 .40
KSW49E005 Lots of Anxiety Kazuma R .20 .40
KSW49E006 Bonafide Pervert Darkness R .20 .40
KSW49E007 Special Talent is Fantasizing Darkness R .20 .40
KSW49E008 Skill Lecture Chris R .20 .40
KSW49E009 Decide What They Were Worth on My Own Chris U .12 .25
KSW49E010 Successful Rescue Darkness U .12 .25
KSW49E011 Imperial Capital Prosecutor Sena U .12 .25
KSW49E012 Luna U .12 .25
KSW49E013 Standing Tall With Arms Wide Open Darkness U .12 .25
KSW49E014 Something That Must Be Protected Darkness U .12 .25
KSW49E015 Please Use Me As A Shield Darkness U .12 .25
KSW49E016 Create Water Kazuma C .10 .20
KSW49E017 Invitation to Learn Skill Chris C .10 .20
KSW49E018 Model Knight Darkness C .10 .20
KSW49E019 Ruffian C .10 .20
KSW49E020 Mitsurugi C .10 .20
KSW49E021 Adventurer Kazuma C .10 .20
KSW49E022 Finished Learning A Skill Kazuma C .10 .20
KSW49E023 Danger Perception Darkness C .10 .20
KSW49E024 Charge Attack Darkness C .10 .20
KSW49E025 Seems Happy Darkness C .10 .20
KSW49E026 Steal Kazuma C .10 .20
KSW49E027 Gathering Ideas Chris C .10 .20
KSW49E028 Freeze U .12 .25
KSW49E029 Tremble With Pleasure U .12 .25
KSW49E030 Thief Skill CR .25 .50
KSW49E031 Charging Power CC .15 .30
KSW49E032 Masochistic Crusader CC .15 .30
KSW49E033 Shaming By the Devil Kings Army CC .15 .30
KSW49E037 Board Game Megumin R .20 .40
KSW49E038 Knowledge of Learning A Skill Megumin R .20 .40
KSW49E039 Polite Yunyun R .20 .40
KSW49E040 Nuisance Megumin R .20 .40
KSW49E041 Pouring Tea Wiz R .20 .40
KSW49E042 Nice Explosion Megumin R .20 .40
KSW49E043 Cant Say It Straight Yunyun R .20 .40
KSW49E044 Concurrent Strike Wiz R .20 .40
KSW49E045 Highly skilled Arch Wizard Wiz U .12 .25
KSW49E046 Involving Megumin Yunyun U .12 .25
KSW49E047 Shaken Megumin U .12 .25
KSW49E048 Awfully Reserved Today Megumin U .12 .25
KSW49E049 Town Celebrity Wiz U .12 .25
KSW49E050 Fear of Dolls Megumin U .12 .25
KSW49E051 Calling for Teacher Megumin U .12 .25
KSW49E052 Insufficient Magic Wiz C .10 .20
KSW49E053 Professor C .10 .20
KSW49E054 Marbled Red Crab Megumin C .10 .20
KSW49E055 Insistence Megumin C .10 .20
KSW49E056 Giant Toad C .10 .20
KSW49E057 Cabbage C .10 .20
KSW49E058 Dark Purple Smoke Verdia C .10 .20
KSW49E059 Spell Casting Megumin C .10 .20
KSW49E060 Gentle Lich Wiz C .10 .20
KSW49E061 My Name is Yunyun C .10 .20
KSW49E062 Long term Contract Negotiation Megumin C .10 .20
KSW49E063 Rookie Succubus C .10 .20
KSW49E064 Keeps Firing Explosion Magic Every Single Day U .12 .25
KSW49E065 Drain Touch U .12 .25
KSW49E066 Destroyer Alert U .12 .25
KSW49E067 Real Explosion Magic CR .25 .50
KSW49E068 Megumins Rival CR .25 .50
KSW49E069 Explosion Magic CC .15 .30
KSW49E070 Sending Spirits Home CC .15 .30
KSW49E074 Gentle Goddess Eris R .20 .40
KSW49E075 Significance of Killing Snow Sprites? Aqua R .20 .40
KSW49E076 Gentle Smile Eris R .20 .40
KSW49E077 Sacred Create Water Aqua R .20 .40
KSW49E078 Sacred Turn Undead Aqua R .20 .40
KSW49E079 Being Shy Eris R .20 .40
KSW49E080 Covered in Snot Aqua U .12 .25
KSW49E081 Full of Smiles Aqua U .12 .25
KSW49E082 Flattering Aqua U .12 .25
KSW49E083 In Deep Sleep Aqua U .12 .25
KSW49E084 Provoking Style Aqua U .12 .25
KSW49E085 Providing Magic Aqua U .12 .25
KSW49E086 Going All Out Aqua U .12 .25
KSW49E087 Adventure About to Begin Aqua C .10 .20
KSW49E088 Goddess In Charge of Backwater Eris C .10 .20
KSW49E089 Quest Clear Aqua C .10 .20
KSW49E090 Real Goddess Aqua C .10 .20
KSW49E091 Natures Beauty Aqua C .10 .20
KSW49E092 Head of the Axis Sect Aqua C .10 .20
KSW49E093 Demand for Apology Aqua C .10 .20
KSW49E094 Tasty Way to Drink Aqua C .10 .20
KSW49E095 Stunned Aqua C .10 .20
KSW49E096 God Blow U .12 .25
KSW49E097 Senpai Appears U .12 .25
KSW49E098 Resurrection CR .25 .50
KSW49E099 Revival CC .15 .30
KSW49E100 Sacred Break Spell CC .15 .30

2017 Weiss Schwarz Love Live Sunshine

LSSW45E005 Koini Naritai AQUARIUM Ruby Kurosawa R .20 .40
LSSW45E006 Hanamaru Kunikida R .20 .40
LSSW45E007 Yoshiko Tsushima R .20 .40
LSSW45E008 Koini Naritai AQUARIUM Yoshiko Tsushima R .20 .40
LSSW45E009 Ruby Kurosawa R .20 .40
LSSW45E010 Long awaited New Comer Yoshiko Tsushima U .12 .25
LSSW45E011 Yohane samas Little Demon No4 Ruby Kurosawa U .12 .25
LSSW45E012 Tokyo Coordinate Ruby Kurosawa U .12 .25
LSSW45E013 Normal Clothes Hanamaru Kunikida U .12 .25
LSSW45E014 Fallen Angel Mode Release Yoshiko Tsushima U .12 .25
LSSW45E015 Special Friend Ruby Kurosawa U .12 .25
LSSW45E016 Special Friend Hanamaru Kunikida U .12 .25
LSSW45E017 Girl Going to School Yoshiko Tsushima U .12 .25
LSSW45E018 My Retreat Hanamaru Kunikida U .12 .25
LSSW45E019 Wearing a Smile with Sadness Yoshiko Tsushima C .10 .20
LSSW45E020 Tokyo Coordinate Hanamaru Kunikida C .10 .20
LSSW45E021 Club Application Form Ruby Kurosawa C .10 .20
LSSW45E022 Polite Bow Hanamaru Kunikida C .10 .20
LSSW45E023 Favorite School Idol Ruby Kurosawa C .10 .20
LSSW45E024 Fallen Angel Yohanes Demon Eyes Yoshiko Tsushima C .10 .20
LSSW45E025 Morning Escape Yoshiko Tsushima C .10 .20
LSSW45E026 Live Invitation Ruby Kurosawa C .10 .20
LSSW45E027 Actually an Angel Hanamaru Kunikida C .10 .20
LSSW45E028 The Smiles of Pretty Girls C .10 .20
LSSW45E029 Little Demon Summoning C .10 .20
LSSW45E030 Aozora Jumping Heart Hanamaru CR .25 .50
LSSW45E031 Make Our Dreams Come True CC .15 .30
LSSW45E032 We Want to Shine Hanamaru and Ruby and Yoshiko CC .15 .30
LSSW45E033 Your Favorite Self CC .15 .30
LSSW45E037 Koini Naritai AQUARIUM You Watanabe R .20 .40
LSSW45E038 Riko Sakurauchi R .20 .40
LSSW45E039 You Watanabe R .20 .40
LSSW45E040 Chika Takami R .20 .40
LSSW45E041 Koini Naritai AQUARIUM Chika Takami R .20 .40
LSSW45E042 Koini Naritai AQUARIUM Riko Sakurauchi R .20 .40
LSSW45E043 A Wonderful Thing Chika Takami U .12 .25
LSSW45E044 Cute Salute You Watanabe U .12 .25
LSSW45E045 High Dive You Watanabe U .12 .25
LSSW45E046 A Maidens Excitement Riko Sakurauchi U .12 .25
LSSW45E047 Daisuki Dattara Daijoubu Chika Takami U .12 .25
LSSW45E048 Whats Good About Uchiura Chika Takami U .12 .25
LSSW45E049 Silence Retuns to the Sandy Beach Riko Sakurauchi U .12 .25
LSSW45E050 Yume no Tobira Riko Sakurauchi U .12 .25
LSSW45E051 Disappearance of the Subject You Watanabe U .12 .25
LSSW45E052 A Wonderful Thing Riko Sakurauchi C .10 .20
LSSW45E053 Normal Girl Chika Takami C .10 .20
LSSW45E054 Ill Start from Here Chika Takami C .10 .20
LSSW45E055 Daisuki Dattara Daijoubu Riko Sakurauchi C .10 .20
LSSW45E056 Aye Aye You Watanabe C .10 .20
LSSW45E057 Daisuki Dattara Daijoubu You Watanabe C .10 .20
LSSW45E058 Lets All Walk Together You Watanabe C .10 .20
LSSW45E059 Sparkling Shine Chika Takami C .10 .20
LSSW45E060 Live Invitation Riko Sakurauchi C .10 .20
LSSW45E061 Honest Words C .10 .20
LSSW45E062 Niceoodles C .10 .20
LSSW45E063 Aozora Jumping Heart Chika CR .25 .50
LSSW45E064 Aozora Jumping Heart You CC .15 .30
LSSW45E065 We Want to Shine You and Chika and Riko CC .15 .30
LSSW45E066 Outstretched Hand CC .15 .30
LSSW45E070 Dia Kurosawa R .20 .40
LSSW45E071 Koini Naritai AQUARIUM Mari Ohara R .20 .40
LSSW45E072 Kanan Matsuura R .20 .40
LSSW45E073 Koini Naritai AQUARIUM Kanan Matsuura R .20 .40
LSSW45E074 Koini Naritai AQUARIUM Dia Kurosawa R .20 .40
LSSW45E075 Mari Ohara R .20 .40
LSSW45E076 Approved Mari Ohara U .12 .25
LSSW45E077 Capture Stance Kanan Matsuura U .12 .25
LSSW45E078 Gentle Smile Dia Kurosawa U .12 .25
LSSW45E079 Tokyo Chance Kanan Matsuura U .12 .25
LSSW45E080 Friendly Sisters Dia Kurosawa U .12 .25
LSSW45E081 Expectations and Insecurities Mari Ohara U .12 .25
LSSW45E082 New Chairman Mari Ohara U .12 .25
LSSW45E083 Looking Ahead Kanan Matsuura U .12 .25
LSSW45E084 Beautiful Dance Dia Kurosawa U .12 .25
LSSW45E085 Unconveyed Feelings Mari Ohara C .10 .20
LSSW45E086 Confrontation at the Beach Kanan Matsuura C .10 .20
LSSW45E087 Dear Sister Dia Kurosawa C .10 .20
LSSW45E088 Favorite School Idol Dia Kurosawa C .10 .20
LSSW45E089 View from the Helicopter Mari Ohara C .10 .20
LSSW45E090 Hug Kanan Matsuura C .10 .20
LSSW45E091 First Live Kanan Matsuura C .10 .20
LSSW45E092 Unnoticed Feelings Mari Ohara C .10 .20
LSSW45E093 Firm Refusal Dia Kurosawa C .10 .20
LSSW45E094 Lost Time U .12 .25
LSSW45E095 The Truth Beind the Name C .10 .20
LSSW45E096 Aozora Jumping Heart Kanan CR .25 .50
LSSW45E097 We Want to Shine Mari and Kanan and Dia CC .15 .30
LSSW45E098 Two Favorite People CC .15 .30
LSSW45E099 Conveyed Feelings CC .15 .30
LSSW45E100 We Want to Shine Aqours CC .15 .30

2017 Weiss Schwarz Sword Art Online Re Edit

SAOS47E001 Asuna Invites to Party R .20 .40
SAOS47E002 Lightning FlashAsuna R .20 .40
SAOS47E003 Asunas Commanding Strength R .20 .40
SAOS47E004 Beacon of Hope Asuna R .20 .40
SAOS47E005 Asuna Lays on the Sofa U .12 .25
SAOS47E006 Asunas Married Life U .12 .25
SAOS47E006R Asunas Married Life R .20 .40
SAOS47E007 Vice Commander Asuna U .12 .25
SAOS47E008 Asuna Joins a Party U .12 .25
SAOS47E009 Lead GroupAsuna U .12 .25
SAOS47E010 Asunas Quiet Time U .12 .25
SAOS47E011 Vestige of an Elder Sister Asuna U .12 .25
SAOS47E012 Restful Stroll Asuna C .10 .20
SAOS47E013 Childhood Asuna C .10 .20
SAOS47E014 ALO Days Asuna C .10 .20
SAOS47E015 Asuna Takes Shelter C .10 .20
SAOS47E016 Autumn Walk Asuna C .10 .20
SAOS47E017 Asuna Putting Herself in the Front Lines C .10 .20
SAOS47E018 Asuna Replies to a Proposal C .10 .20
SAOS47E019 Berserk Healer Asuna C .10 .20
SAOS47E020 Asuna Yuuki C .10 .20
SAOS47E021 Asuna Changes Clothes C .10 .20
SAOS47E022 Self sacrifice U .12 .25
SAOS47E023 Demise of Zekken CR .25 .50
SAOS47E024 Star Splash CC .15 .30
SAOS47E025 On Top of the World Tree CC .15 .30
SAOS47E026 Undefeated Super Swordsman Yuuki R .20 .40
SAOS47E027 Sleeping Knights Talken and Nori and Jun R .20 .40
SAOS47E029 Leafas Pure Wish R .20 .40
SAOS47E030 Virtual and Reality Leafa and Suguha R .20 .40
SAOS47E031 Yuukis Raised Antenna U .12 .25
SAOS47E032 Sword Skill Lore Yuuki U .12 .25
SAOS47E033 Reliable Guide Leafa U .12 .25
SAOS47E034 Time Limit Leafa U .12 .25
SAOS47E035 Imp Girl Yuuki U .12 .25
SAOS47E036 Sibling Moment Suguha U .12 .25
SAOS47E037 Memories That Were Fun Yuuki U .12 .25
SAOS47E038 Simultaneous Attack Leafa C .10 .20
SAOS47E039 Speedholic Leafa C .10 .20
SAOS47E040 SylphGirl Leafa C .10 .20
SAOS47E041 Gathering Materials Leafa C .10 .20
SAOS47E042 Innocent and Uninhibited Yuuki C .10 .20
SAOS47E043 Sleeping Knights Yuuki C .10 .20
SAOS47E044 Asuna and Yuuki C .10 .20
SAOS47E045 Tutor Suguha C .10 .20
SAOS47E046 Sleeping Knights Siune and Tecchi C .10 .20
SAOS47E047 Recons Courage U .12 .25
SAOS47E048 Mothers Rosario CR .25 .50
SAOS47E049 Fairy Dance CC .15 .30
SAOS47E050 Braves of 27th floor CC .15 .30
SAOS47E052 Strong and Stout hearted Lisbeth R .20 .40
SAOS47E053 Trusted Skills Lisbeth R .20 .40
SAOS47E054 Lisbeth Changes Clothes R .20 .40
SAOS47E055 Like a Younger Sister Silica R .20 .40
SAOS47E056 Lisbeths Professional Pride U .12 .25
SAOS47E057 Silica Looking Up At the Sky U .12 .25
SAOS47E058 Silicas Unyielding Trust U .12 .25
SAOS47E059 Unknown Identity Death Gun U .12 .25
SAOS47E060 Cait Sith Girl Silica C .10 .20
SAOS47E061 Searching Lisbeth C .10 .20
SAOS47E062 Sterben Death Gun C .10 .20
SAOS47E063 Light hearted Talk Kyoji C .10 .20
SAOS47E064 Shoichi Shinkawa C .10 .20
SAOS47E065 Familiar Pina C .10 .20
SAOS47E066 Sinister GlintDeath Gun C .10 .20
SAOS47E067 Fluffy on the Head Silica C .10 .20
SAOS47E068 Lisbeths Determined Confession C .10 .20
SAOS47E069 Excessive Obsession Kyoji C .10 .20
SAOS47E070 Battle Stance Silica C .10 .20
SAOS47E071 Lisbeths Shining Smile C .10 .20
SAOS47E072 Demonic Sword Gram U .12 .25
SAOS47E073 Seeking Warmth CR .25 .50
SAOS47E074 Pinas Resurrection CC .15 .30
SAOS47E075 Fateful Estoc Wielder CC .15 .30
SAOS47E077 Temporary Alliance Kirito R .20 .40
SAOS47E078 Temporary Alliance Sinon R .20 .40
SAOS47E079 Machine of Ice Sinon R .20 .40
SAOS47E080 Getting the Holy Sword Kirito R .20 .40
SAOS47E081 Demon of Dual wielding Kirito R .20 .40
SAOS47E082 SAO Survivor Kirito U .12 .25
SAOS47E083 In the Sunlight Forest Sinon U .12 .25
SAOS47E084 Choice to Fight Kirito U .12 .25
SAOS47E085 In the Face of Death Kirito and Sinon U .12 .25
SAOS47E086 Strong Existence Sinon U .12 .25
SAOS47E087 Kirito Discovers a Unique Skill U .12 .25
SAOS47E088 Black Swordsman Kirito U .12 .25
SAOS47E089 Blade User Klein C .10 .20
SAOS47E090 Brains of the Party Yui C .10 .20
SAOS47E091 Challenging Many Kirito C .10 .20
SAOS47E092 Providing Information Yui C .10 .20
SAOS47E093 Kiritos Strong Bond C .10 .20
SAOS47E094 Angry Sinon C .10 .20

SAOS47E095 Kiritos Natural Gentleness C .10 .20
SAOS47E096 Skill Connect Kirito C .10 .20
SAOS47E097 Late Self introduction U .12 .25
SAOS47E098 Phantom Bullet CR .25 .50
SAOS47E099 Dual wieldingUser CC .15 .30
SAOS47E100 Quest to Get Excalibur CC .15 .30
SAOS47E103 Comforting Moment Asuna U .12 .25
SAOS47E104 Agile Start Asuna U .12 .25
SAOS47E105 Quest to Get Excalibur CC .15 .30
SAOS47E109 Adventure with Everyone Silica U .12 .25
SAOS47E110 After Party Keiko U .12 .25
SAOS47E111 Rika Delighted at the Meeting U .12 .25
SAOS47E113 After the Battle Kirito R .20 .40
SAOS47E114 Determination with Life on the Line Kirito R .20 .40
SAOS47E115 Adventure with Everyone Yui U .12 .25
SAOS47E116 Frightened Eyes Sinon U .12 .25
SAOS47E117 Intense Spirit Klein U .12 .25
SAOS47E118 Dicey Cafe Gilbert U .12 .25
SAOS47E119 Adventure with Everyone Sinon U .12 .25

2017 Weiss Schwarz Sword Art Online The Movie Ordinal Scale

SAOS51E004R Park Date, Asuna R .20 .40
SAOS51E005R Kirito's Love, Asuna R .20 .40
SAOS51E006R Snack Time, Asuna R .20 .40
SAOS51E007R Lightning Flash Asuna & Black Swordsman Kirito R.20 .40
SAOS51E008U Link Strike Asuna U .12 .25
SAOS51E009U Long-Awaited Promised Day, Asuna U .12 .25
SAOS51E010U Promise in your Heart, Asuna & Kirito U .12 .25
SAOS51E011U Today's MVP, Asuna U .12 .25
SAOS51E012C Seductive Shore, Asuna C .10 .20
SAOS51E013C Taking On the Boss Battle, Asuna C .10 .20
SAOS51E014C Important Habit, Asuna C .10 .20
SAOS51E015C Thrusting Gale, Asuna C .10 .20
SAOS51E016C Prepared for Battle, Asuna C .10 .20
SAOS51E017C Genius Game Designer Kayaba C .10 .20
SAOS51E018U Sudden Whisper U .12 .25
SAOS51E019CR Mother's Rosario CLR .25 .50
SAOS51E020CC Enduring Emotions CC .15 .30
SAOS51E023R Kendo Boot Camp, Suguha R .20 .40
SAOS51E024R Swimsuit Suguha R .20 .40
SAOS51E025R AR Idol Yuna R .20 .40
SAOS51E026R Profound Communication, Yuna R .20 .40
SAOS51E027R Inviting Provocation, Eiji R .20 .40
SAOS51E028R Vexation of Being Absent, Leafa R .20 .40
SAOS51E029U Instantaneous Movement, Eiji U .12 .25
SAOS51E030U Fragment of Memory, Yuna U .12 .25
SAOS51E031U Confident Profile, Eiji U .12 .25
SAOS51E032U Knights of the Blood Oath Nautilus U .12 .25
SAOS51E033U Augma Developer, Shigemura U .12 .25
SAOS51E034U Special Stage, Yuna U .12 .25
SAOS51E035U An Incarnate of the Radius U .12 .25
SAOS51E036C Mysterious Young Swordsman, Eiji C .10 .20
SAOS51E037C A Lonely Toast, Eiji C .10 .20
SAOS51E038C Really Loves Singing, Yuna C .10 .20
SAOS51E039C In the Midst of Loud Cheering, Yuna C .10 .20
SAOS51E040C Toto Institute of Technology Professor, Shigemura C.10 .20
SAOS51E041C The Smile I Wanted to Protect, Yuna C .10 .20
SAOS51E042C Magic Attack, Leafa C .10 .20
SAOS51E043C Stable Sister, Leafa C .10 .20
SAOS51E044R Opposition by the Shield R .20 .40
SAOS51E045U Ordinal Scale U .12 .25
SAOS51E046U The Complete SAO Incident Records U .12 .25
SAOS51E047CR The Giant Stage of Dreams CLR .25 .50
SAOS51E048CC Ordinal Number 2 CC .15 .30
SAOS51E049CC White Holy Tree CC .15 .30
SAOS51E050CC Assistance From the Fairies CC .15 .30
SAOS51E053R On Stage, Silica R .20 .40
SAOS51E054R Refreshing Personality, Lisbeth R .20 .40
SAOS51E055R Lively Post-Lessons, Rika R .20 .40
SAOS51E056R Silica On Guard R .20 .40
SAOS51E057R Link Strike Lisbeth R .20 .40
SAOS51E058U Close Call, Silica U .12 .25
SAOS51E059U Beacon of Counterattack, Lisbeth U .12 .25
SAOS51E060U Surging Raid, Silica U .12 .25
SAOS51E061C Taking On the Boss Battle, Lisbeth C .10 .20
SAOS51E062C Stunned Keiko C .10 .20
SAOS51E063C Buoyant Behavior, Silica C .10 .20
SAOS51E064C Taking On the Boss Battle, Silica C .10 .20
SAOS51E065C Stunned Rika C .10 .20
SAOS51E066C Rhapsodic Lisbeth C .10 .20
SAOS51E067U Cheerful Singing U .12 .25
SAOS51E068U Former Formidable Foe U .12 .25
SAOS51E069CR Experienced Multiplayer CLR .25 .50
SAOS51E070CC Heinous Trap CC .15 .30
SAOS51E074R In Doubt, Sinon R .20 .40
SAOS51E075R SAO Survivor Asuna & Kazuto R .20 .40
SAOS51E076R Reliable Reinforcement, Sinon R .20 .40
SAOS51E077R AR Battle, Kirito R .20 .40
SAOS51E078R Welcome Assistance, Yui R .20 .40
SAOS51E079R Full of Vigor, Yui R .20 .40
SAOS51E080U Asuna's Love, Kirito U .12 .25
SAOS51E081U Kazuto Can't Get Used to AR U .12 .25
SAOS51E082U Fawning Klein U .12 .25
SAOS51E083U Snack Time, Yui U .12 .25
SAOS51E084U Link Strike Agil U .12 .25
SAOS51E085U Data Collection, Yui U .12 .25
SAOS51E086U Cuddling Couple, Kazuto & Asuna U .12 .25
SAOS51E087C Sweating From a Tough Fight, Agil C .10 .20
SAOS51E088C Angry Confrontation, Kirito C .10 .20
SAOS51E089C Drive of An Angry God, Kirito C .10 .20
SAOS51E090C Kirito Seeking a Lead C .10 .20
SAOS51E091C Gentle Expression, Kirito C .10 .20
SAOS51E092C Cool Confutation, Sinon C .10 .20
SAOS51E093C Urgent Participation in Battle, Klein C .10 .20
SAOS51E094C Somehow Seeming Lonely, Kazuto C .10 .20
SAOS51E095U Investigation Report U .12 .25
SAOS51E096U Ordinal Number 1 U .12 .25
SAOS51E097CR Black Swordsman Once More CLR .25 .50
SAOS51E098CC Dependable Marksmanship CC .15 .30
SAOS51E099CC Sorry to Keep You Waiting! CC .15 .30
SAOS51E100CC Perpetuation of the Promise CC .15 .30

2018 Weiss Schwarz Bang Dream Girls Band Party

BDW54E004R Everybody, On Three! Hagumi Kitazawa R .20 .40
BDW54E005R Confession of Love Misaki Okusawa R .20 .40
BDW54E006R Make the World Smile! Kokoro Tsurumaki R .20 .40
BDW54E007R First Step Kanon Matsubara R .20 .40
BDW54E008U Onstage Hagumi Kitazawa U .12 .25
BDW54E009U Onstage Kanon Matsubara U .12 .25
BDW54E010U Onstage Kokoro Tsurumaki U .12 .25
BDW54E011U Yes, I'm Michelle! Misaki Okusawa U .12 .25
BDW54E012U Onstage Kaoru Seta U .12 .25
BDW54E013C Captive Princess Kanon Matsubara C .10 .20
BDW54E014C Twin Problems Hina Hikawa C .10 .20
BDW54E015C Invincible Hero Kokoro Tsurumaki C .10 .20
BDW54E016C My First Drums Maya Yamato C .10 .20
BDW54E017C Michelle's Secret Misaki Okusawa C .10 .20
BDW54E018C Onstage Misaki Okusawa C .10 .20
BDW54E019C Cute Detective Hagumi Kitazawa C .10 .20
BDW54E020C Catch Me If You Can Kaoru Seta C .10 .20
BDW54E021U Michelle Stickers U .12 .25
BDW54E022CR Thief! Stop! CLR .25 .50
BDW54E023CC Orchestra Of Smiles! CC .15 .30
BDW54E024CC Hello, Happy Phantom Thief! CC .15 .30
BDW54E025CC Samurai Help Each Other CC .15 .30
BDW54E028R Glasses Off Maya Yamato R .20 .40
BDW54E029R Pajama Patient Tomoe Udagawa R .20 .40
BDW54E030R Swimming Trio Himari Uehara R .20 .40
BDW54E031R Always Starting Tsugumi Hazawa R .20 .40
BDW54E032R Proof I'm Here Ran Mitake R .20 .40
BDW54E033U Sunset Memory Moca Aoba U .12 .25
BDW54E034U Onstage Aya Maruyama U .12 .25
BDW54E035U Onstage Tomoe Udagawa U .12 .25
BDW54E036U Act, Don't Think! Tsugumi Hazawa U .12 .25
BDW54E037U Present For You Himari Uehara U .12 .25
BDW54E038U No Hesitation Ran Mitake U .12 .25
BDW54E039C Onstage Ran Mitake C .10 .20
BDW54E040C Onstage Tsugumi Hazawa C .10 .20
BDW54E041C Onstage Himari Uehara C .10 .20
BDW54E042C Onstage Moca Aoba C .10 .20
BDW54E043C Tanabata Clerk Aya Maryuama C .10 .20
BDW54E044C Mysterious Charm Himari Uehara C .10 .20
BDW54E045C Hard Strike Tomoe Udagawa C .10 .20
BDW54E046U Hard Being Honest U .12 .25
BDW54E047CR Enthusiastic Cry CLR .25 .50
BDW54E048CC That is How I Roll! CC .15 .30
BDW54E049CC Let's Start a Band! CC .15 .30
BDW54E050CC Shuwarin Dreaming CC .15 .30
BDW54E054R Secret Pose Aya Maruyama R .20 .40
BDW54E055R Theme Park Fun! Kasumi Toyama R .20 .40
BDW54E055SSR Theme Park Fun! Kasumi Toyama R .20 .40
BDW54E056R Place Of Purity Chisato Shirasagi R .20 .40
BDW54E057R Bride For A Day Saya Yamabuki R .20 .40
BDW54E058U Matching Scrunchies Saya Yamabuki U .12 .25
BDW54E059U Onstage Rimi Ushigome U .12 .25
BDW54E060C Onstage Saya Yamabuki C .10 .20
BDW54E061C Time for Chocolate Cornets Rimi Ushigome C .10 .20
BDW54E062C Onstage Kasumi Toyama C .10 .20
BDW54E063C Onstage Chisato Shirasagi C .10 .20
BDW54E064U Something in the Warehouse U .12 .25
BDW54E065U Buns For Luck U .12 .25
BDW54E066CR STAR BEAT! CLR .25 .50
BDW54E067CR The One I Admire CLR .25 .50
BDW54E068CC Chocolate Cornet Love CC .15 .30
BDW54E071R Shared Happiness Tae Hanazono R .20 .40
BDW54E072R Four In The Cafeteria Yukina Minato R .20 .40
BDW54E073R Indispensable Lisa Imai R .20 .40
BDW54E074R Private Nurse Ako Udagawa R .20 .40
BDW54E075R Tanabata Pair Sayo Hikawa R .20 .40
BDW54E076R Cute Friends Arisa Ichigaya R .20 .40
BDW54E077R Unknown Presence Hina Hikawa R .20 .40
BDW54E078U Selected Swimsuit Rinko Shirokane U .12 .25
BDW54E079U Reliable Companion Arisa Ichigaya U .12 .25
BDW54E080U Prepared Diva Yukina Minato U .12 .25
BDW54E081U Good Sound Sayo Hikawa U .12 .25
BDW54E082U Perfect Smile Chisato Shirasagi U .12 .25
BDW54E083U Silver Fairy Eve Wakamiya U .12 .25
BDW54E084U Little Demon Ako Udagawa U .12 .25
BDW54E085U Our Song Tae Hanazono U .12 .25
BDW54E086U Dazzling Sunshine Lisa Imai U .12 .25
BDW54E087U Onstage Maya Yamato U .12 .25
BDW54E088U Onstage Hina Hikawa U .12 .25
BDW54E089C Connected Pair Lisa Imai C .10 .20
BDW54E090C Pajama Party Tae Hanazono C .10 .20
BDW54E091C Aimed Journey Chisato Shirasagi C .10 .20
BDW54E092C Onstage Eve Wakamiya C .10 .20
BDW54E093C Sincere Ambition Ako Udagawa C .10 .20
BDW54E094C Onstage Arisa Ichigaya C .10 .20
BDW54E095C What Should I...? Rinko Shirokane C .10 .20
BDW54E096C Onstage Tae Hanazono C .10 .20
BDW54E097C Twin Problems Sayo Hikawa C .10 .20
BDW54E098CR Intense Shout CLR .25 .50
BDW54E099CC Always With You CC .15 .30
BDW54E100CC Under The Blossoming Sakura CC .15 .30

2018 Weiss Schwarz Fate-Apocrypha

APOS53E004R Faraway Promise Ruler R .20 .40
APOS53E005R Master's Qualifications Sieg R .20 .40
APOS53E006R Adjudicator Ruler R .20 .40
APOS53E007R La Pucelle Ruler R .20 .40
APOS53E008R Depraved Dragon Fafnir R .20 .40
APOS53E009U Return to the Greater Grail Ruler U .12 .25
APOS53E010U Great Holy Grail War Sieg U .12 .25
APOS53E011U With My Command Spell Ruler U .12 .25
APOS53E012U Hero Possession Sieg U .12 .25
APOS53E013U Lord El-Melloi II U .12 .25
APOS53E014U Legend of Dracula Dracula U .12 .25
APOS53E015C Gilles de Rais C .10 .20
APOS53E016C King of Knights Altria C .10 .20
APOS53E017C To the Hanging Gardens Ruler C .10 .20
APOS53E018C Laetitia C .10 .20
APOS53E019C Apocrypha Sieg C .10 .20
APOS53E020C Dead Count Shapeshifter Sieg C .10 .20
APOS53E021C The Me in the Mirror Ruler C .10 .20
APOS53E022U The Greater Grail U .12 .25
APOS53E023CR Luminosite Eternelle CLR .25 .50
APOS53E024CC Speaking To My Reflection CC .15 .30
APOS53E025CC Blasted Tree (Yellow) CC .15 .30
APOS53E029R Secret of Pedigree Saber of Red R .20 .40
APOS53E030R Humanity's Salvation Shirou Kotomine R .20 .40
APOS53E031R Promised Rematch Lancer of Red R .20 .40
APOS53E032R Blessing of Immortality Rider of Red R .20 .40
APOS53E033R Duel Rider of Red R .20 .40
APOS53E034R Before the Throne Assassin of Red R .20 .40
APOS53E035R Knight of the Round Table Saber of Red R .20 .40
APOS53E036R Apocrypha Shirou R .20 .40
APOS53E037R Demonic Beast Strength Archer of Red R .20 .40
APOS53E038U Overflowing Interest Caster of Red U .12 .25
APOS53E039U Bewitching Smile Assassin of Red U .12 .25
APOS53E040U Quick Judgment Saber of Red U .12 .25
APOS53E041U Kairi Shishigou U .12 .25
APOS53E042U Command Spell Saber of Red U .12 .25
APOS53E043U Gold Armor Lancer of Red U .12 .25
APOS53E044U Transformation Archer of Red U .12 .25
APOS53E045U Empress Assassin of Red U .12 .25
APOS53E046C Tauropolos Archer of Red C .10 .20
APOS53E047C With My Command Spell Kairi Shishigou C .10 .20
APOS53E048C Crying Warmonger Berserker of Red C .10 .20
APOS53E049C In the Gardens Assassin of Red C .10 .20
APOS53E050C Realization of the Goal Shirou C .10 .20
APOS53E051C Huntress Archer of Red C .10 .20
APOS53E052C Playwright Caster of Red C .10 .20
APOS53E053C Defense Lancer of Red C .10 .20
APOS53E054C In the Gardens Shirou C .10 .20
APOS53E055C Rebel Berserker of Red C .10 .20
APOS53E056C Promised Feast Saber of Red C .10 .20
APOS53E057aU Two Cigarettes U .12 .25
APOS53E057bU Two Cigarettes U .12 .25
APOS53E058U Miike Tenta U .12 .25
APOS53E059CR Clarent CLR .25 .50
APOS53E060CR Hanging Gardens of Babylon CLR .25 .50
APOS53E061CC Vermillion Peal CC .15 .30
APOS53E062CC Conflict of Desires CC .15 .30
APOS53E067R Battle Ready Berserker of Black R .20 .40
APOS53E068R Savagery Assassin of Black R .20 .40
APOS53E069R Fiore Forvedge Yggdmillennia R .20 .40
APOS53E070R Growl Berserker of Black R .20 .40
APOS53E071R Duel Archer of Black R .20 .40
APOS53E072R King of Capital Punishment Lancer of Black R .20 .40
APOS53E073R Before the Duel Rider of Black R .20 .40
APOS53E074R Divine Blade Saber of Black R .20 .40
APOS53E075U Reika Rikudou U .12 .25
APOS53E076U Heroic Spirit Saber of Black U .12 .25
APOS53E077U Poison Mist Assassin of Black U .12 .25
APOS53E078U The Twelve Paladins Rider of Black U .12 .25
APOS53E079U Gordes Musik Yggdmillennia U .12 .25
APOS53E080U Deep Satisfaction Berserker of Black U .12 .25
APOS53E081U Golem Keter Malkuth U .12 .25
APOS53E082U Caules Forvedge Yggdmillennia U .12 .25
APOS53E083U Twice Overlapping Assassin of Black U .12 .25
APOS53E084C Mage Caster of Black C .10 .20
APOS53E085C Relieved Expression Rider of Black C .10 .20
APOS53E086C Bowman Archer of Black C .10 .20
APOS53E087C Transfiguration Lancer of Black C .10 .20
APOS53E088C On the Phone Assassin of Black C .10 .20
APOS53E089C Roche Frain Yggdmillennia C .10 .20
APOS53E090C Homunculus C .10 .20
APOS53E091C Bridal Chest Berserker of Black C .10 .20
APOS53E092C Inherited Heart Saber of Black C .10 .20
APOS53E093C Darnic Prestone Yggdmillennia C .10 .20
APOS53E094C Celenike Icecolle Yggdmillennia C .10 .20
APOS53E095U La Black Luna U .12 .25
APOS53E096U Entrusted Shield U .12 .25
APOS53E097CC Master's Command CC .15 .30
APOS53E098CR Blasted Tree (Blue) CLR .25 .50
APOS53E099CC Balmung CC .15 .30
APOS53E100CC Maria the Ripper CC .15 .30

2018 Weiss Schwarz Gurren Lagann

GLS52E005 Team Super Galaxy DAI-GURREN, Yoko R .20 .40
GLS52E006 Kid & Iraak R .20 .40
GLS52E007 King Kittan R .20 .40
GLS52E008 Warrior Brimming With Life Experience, Makken R .20 .40
GLS52E009 Sniper Yoko R .20 .40
GLS52E010 Zorthy R .20 .40
GLS52E011 Science Bureau Chief, Leeron R .20 .40
GLS52E012 Chief Advisor's Secretary, Kinon U .12 .25
GLS52E013 Aretenborough U .12 .25
GLS52E014 Setting Off from Adai Village, Rossiu U .12 .25
GLS52E015 If You Doubt Yourself, Kamina U .12 .25
GLS52E016 Jorgun & Balinbow U .12 .25
GLS52E017 Dreadnaught Captain, Dayakka U .12 .25
GLS52E018 Make the Impossible Possible! Kamina U .12 .25
GLS52E019 Special Lesson, Yomako U .12 .25
GLS52E020 The Black Siblings, Kinon & Kiyoh & Kiyal C .10 .20
GLS52E021 I Have to Know-! Kiyal & Kiyoh C .10 .20
GLS52E022 Yomako's Students, Maosha & Nakim C .10 .20
GLS52E023 Girls' Feelings, Leeron C .10 .20
GLS52E024 New Supreme Commander of the New Government, Rossiu C .10 .20
GLS52E025 Reliable Mechanic, Leyte C .10 .20
GLS52E026 Masculinity Is About Fighting Spirit! Kamina C .10 .20
GLS52E027 The Black Siblings, Kittan C .10 .20
GLS52E028 New Teacher, Yomako C .10 .20
GLS52E029 Team DAI-GURREN Flag U .12 .25
GLS52E030 Later, Buddy CLR .25 .50
GLS52E031 For the Sake of Precious Children CC .15 .30
GLS52E032 So This Is the Power of the Spiral, Huh...? CC .15 .30
GLS52E035 Human Eradication Forces Far East Theater Commander, Viral R .20 .40
GLS52E036 Team DAI-GURREN's Head Cook, Nia R .20 .40
GLS52E037 Spiral King's Supreme General, Cytomander the Swift R.20 .40
GLS52E038 Believing Heart, Nia R .20 .40
GLS52E039 Lazengann R .20 .40
GLS52E040 The Spiral King, Lordgenome R .20 .40
GLS52E041 Elusive Old Coco U .12 .25
GLS52E042 My Feelings, Nia U .12 .25
GLS52E043 Tyrant of Teppelin, Lordgenome U .12 .25
GLS52E044 Destined Duel, Enkidu U .12 .25
GLS52E045 Mobile Fortress Gunmen, Dai-Gunzan U .12 .25
GLS52E046 Special Seat of an Ex-Rival, Viral U .12 .25
GLS52E047 First Swimsuit, Nia C .10 .20
GLS52E048 Spiral King's Supreme General, Thymilph the Raging Wave C .10 .20
GLS52E049 Two Faces, Enki C .10 .20
GLS52E050 Bio-Computer Lordgenome Head C .10 .20
GLS52E051 Mystery Monstrous Mecha, Gunmen C .10 .20
GLS52E052 Spiral King's Supreme General, Adiane the Elegant C .10 .20
GLS52E053 Obstructive Viral C .10 .20
GLS52E054 Spiral King's Supreme General, Guame the Immovable C.10 .20
GLS52E055 Spiral Energy U .12 .25
GLS52E056 That's What... I Was Waiting For!! U .12 .25
GLS52E057 Destiny Combining, GURREN LAGANN CLR .25 .50
GLS52E058 This Time, It Really Is Over... CC .15 .30
GLS52E059 Lord of the Beastmen CC .15 .30
GLS52E064 A Proper Member of Team DAI-GURREN, Boota R .20 .40
GLS52E065 Drill Power, LAGANN R .20 .40
GLS52E066 Strong Will, Simon R .20 .40
GLS52E067 Team Super Galaxy DAI-GURREN's Leader, Simon R .20 .40
GLS52E068 GURREN LAGANN R .20 .40
GLS52E069 Super Galaxy DAI-GURREN R .20 .40
GLS52E070 Super Galaxy GURREN LAGANN R .20 .40
GLS52E071 Supreme Commander of the New Government, Simon U.12 .25
GLS52E072 DAI-GURREN U .12 .25
GLS52E073 Evolution By Spiral Power, Boota U .12 .25
GLS52E074 Piercing Sentiments, Simon & Nia U .12 .25
GLS52E075 Kamina's Partner, Simon U .12 .25
GLS52E076 ARCH-GURREN LAGANN U .12 .25
GLS52E077 Grapearl (For Gimmy's & Darry's Dedicated Use) C .10 .20
GLS52E078 LAGANN IMPACT! C .10 .20
GLS52E079 Mass-Production Model, Grapearl C .10 .20
GLS52E080 Berserk Simon C .10 .20
GLS52E081 Ace of the New Government Defense Squadron, Gimmy C .10 .20
GLS52E082 First Rate Marksman, Darry C .10 .20
GLS52E083 ARC-GURREN C .10 .20
GLS52E084 Core Drill U .12 .25
GLS52E085 GIGA DRILL BREAK U .12 .25
GLS52E086 On My Back, In My Heart, CLR .25 .50
GLS52E087 Dueling with the Moon CC .15 .30
GLS52E088 My Drill Is the Drill That Creates the Heavens!!!! CC .15 .30
GLS52E089 That's the Team DAI-GURREN Way!! CC .15 .30
GLS52E090 Messenger Nia R .20 .40
GLS52E091 Ultimate Universal Diablo, Granzeboma R .20 .40
GLS52E092 Anti-Spiral Race U .12 .25
GLS52E093 Ashtanga Class U .12 .25
GLS52E094 Mugann C .10 .20
GLS52E095 Advanced Class Mugann C .10 .20
GLS52E096 Ku-Mugann C .10 .20
GLS52E097 Kyo-Mugann C .10 .20

GLS52E098 Death Spiral Machine U	.12	.25
GLS52E099 The Conclusion of Evolution is Universal Destruction-- CLR	.25	.50
GLS52E100 Humanity Extermination System CC	.15	.30

2018 Weiss Schwarz KanColle Arrival Reinforcement Fleets from Europe

KCS42E003R During the Festival, Urakaze R	.20	.40
KCS42E004R Taiho-class Armored Aircraft Carrier, Taiho R	.20	.40
KCS42E005R 1st Shokaku-class Aircraft Carrier, Shokaku Kai-II R	.20	.40
KCS42E006R 2nd Shokaku-class Aircraft Carrier, Zuikaku Kai-II R	.20	.40
KCS42E007R 1st Shokaku-class Armored Aircraft Carrier, Shokaku Kai-II Type.Kou R	.20	.40
KCS42E008R 2nd Shokaku-class Armored Aircraft Carrier, Zuikaku Kai-II Type.Kou R	.20	.40
KCS42E009U 3rd Yugumo-class Destroyer, Kazagumo U	.12	.25
KCS42E010U 16th Kagero-class Destroyer, Arashi U	.12	.25
KCS42E011U 17th Kagero-class Destroyer, Hagikaze U	.12	.25
KCS42E012U 14th Yugumo-class Destroyer, Okinami U	.12	.25
KCS42E013U 3rd Unryu-class Aircraft Carrier, Katsuragi U	.12	.25
KCS42E014U 2nd Akizuki-class Destroyer, Teruzuki U	.12	.25
KCS42E015U 15th Kagero-class Destroyer, Nowaki U	.12	.25
KCS42E016U Delicious Season, Isokaze U	.12	.25
KCS42E017C 6th Yugumo-class Destroyer, Takanami C	.10	.20
KCS42E018C 16th Yugumo-class destroyer, Asashimo C	.10	.20
KCS42E019C 2nd Unryu-class Aircraft Carrier, Amagi Kai C	.10	.20
KCS42E020C 6th Yugumo-class Destroyer, Takanami Kai C	.10	.20
KCS42E021C During the Festival, Hamakaze C	.10	.20
KCS42E022C 16th Yugumo-class Destroyer, Asashimo Kai C	.10	.20
KCS42E023C 3rd Unryu-class Aircraft Carrier, Katsuragi Kai C	.10	.20
KCS42E024C 4th Akizuki-class Destroyer, Hatsuzuki C	.10	.20
KCS42E025U Hishi Mochi U	.12	.25
KCS42E026CR 1st Task Force, heading out! CLR	.25	.50
KCS42E027CC Let me show you the true power of a re-modelled Hiryu-class!! CC	.15	.30
KCS42E028CC Main guns, get ready for aerial combat! CC	.15	.30
KCS42E029CC Sis, leave this to me CC	.15	.30
KCS42E032R 1st Bismarck-class Battleship, Bismarck R	.20	.40
KCS42E033R U-boat IXC-class Submarine, U-511 R	.20	.40
KCS42E034R 1st Graf Zeppelin-class Aircraft Carrier, Graf Zeppelin Kai R	.20	.40
KCS42E035R Ro-number Submarine, Ro-500 R	.20	.40
KCS42E036R 3rd Admiral Hipper-class Heavy Cruiser, Prinz Eugen Kai R	.20	.40
KCS42E037U 3rd Z1-class Destroyer, Z3 U	.12	.25
KCS42E038U During the Festival, Jintsu Kai-II U	.12	.25
KCS42E039U 3rd Takao-class Heavy Cruiser, Maya Kai-II U	.12	.25
KCS42E040U 1st Bismarck-class Battleship, Bismarck zwei U	.12	.25
KCS42E041U 1st Akatsuki-class Destroyer, Akatsuki Kai-II U	.12	.25
KCS42E042U 1st Z1-class Destroyer, Z1 zwei U	.12	.25
KCS42E043C 1st Z1-class Destroyer, Z1 C	.10	.20
KCS42E044C 1st Furutaka-class Heavy Cruiser, Furutaka Kai-II C	.10	.20
KCS42E045C 4th Takao-class Heavy Cruiser, Chokai Kai-II C	.10	.20
KCS42E046C 7th Ayanami-class Destroyer, Oboro Kai C	.10	.20
KCS42E047C 10th Ayanami-class Destroyer, Ushio Kai-II C	.10	.20
KCS42E048C A Midsummer Moment, Akebono C	.10	.20
KCS42E049C 3rd Z1-class Destroyer, Z3 zwei C	.10	.20
KCS42E050C 4th Hatsuharu-class Destroyer, Hatsushimo Kai-II C	.10	.20
KCS42E051C 1st Bismarck-class Battleship, Bismarck Kai C	.10	.20
KCS42E052C 2nd Furutaka-class Heavy Cruiser, Kako Kai-II C	.10	.20
KCS42E053C 1st Graf Zeppelin-class Aircraft Carrier, Graf Zeppelin C	.10	.20
KCS42E054U Class S Type.Kou Medal U	.12	.25
KCS42E055CR Fleet warfare... I can hardly wait! CLR	.25	.50
KCS42E056CC Aim carefully...... Feuer! CC	.15	.30
KCS42E057CC Ro-number Submarine, heading out! CC	.15	.30
KCS42E061R 2nd Kazahaya-class Transport Ship, Hayasui R	.20	.40
KCS42E062R Akitsushima-class Seaplane Tender, Akitsushima R	.20	.40
KCS42E063R 6th Nagara-class Light Cruiser, Abukuma Kai-II R	.20	.40
KCS42E064R 1st Fuso-class Aircraft Battleship, Fuso Kai-II R	.20	.40
KCS42E065R 2nd Fuso-class Aircraft Battleship, Yamashiro Kai-II R	.20	.40
KCS42E066U 1st Katori-class Training Cruiser, Katori U	.12	.25
KCS42E067U 2nd Kazahaya-class Transport Ship, Hayasui Kai U	.12	.25
KCS42E068C 1st Mutsuki-class Destroyer, Mutsuki Kai-II C	.10	.20
KCS42E069C 2nd Mutsuki-class Destroyer, Kisaragi Kai-II C	.10	.20
KCS42E070C 5th Fubuki-class Destroyer, Murakumo Kai-II C	.10	.20
KCS42E071C Mizuho-class Seaplane Tender, Mizuho C	.10	.20
KCS42E072U Offshore Supply U	.12	.25
KCS42E073CR Marine Escort Corp Flagship Kashima, anchors aweigh CLR	.25	.50
KCS42E074CC I think I've found it! CC	.15	.30
KCS42E076R 9th Shiratsuyu-class Destroyer, Kawakaze R	.20	.40
KCS42E077R A Midsummer Moment, Littorio R	.20	.40
KCS42E078R 3rd Maestrale-class Destroyer, Libeccio R	.20	.40
KCS42E079R Interlude of the Rain, Murasame Kai R	.20	.40
KCS42E080U 6th Asashio-class Destroyer, Yamagumo U	.12	.25
KCS42E081U 1st Zara-class Heavy Cruiser, Zara U	.12	.25
KCS42E082U 3rd Myoko-class Heavy Cruiser, Asahigara Kai-II U	.12	.25
KCS42E083U 10th Asashio-class Destroyer, Kasumi Kai-II U	.12	.25
KCS42E084U 10th Asashio-class Destroyer, Kasumi Kai-II-Otsu U	.12	.25
KCS42E085U 2nd Myoko-class Heavy Cruiser, Nachi Kai-II U	.12	.25
KCS42E086U 2nd Vittorio Veneto-class Battleship, Littorio U	.12	.25
KCS42E087U 4th Vittorio Veneto-class Battleship, Roma Kai U	.12	.25
KCS42E088C 1st Shoho-class Light Aircraft Carrier, Shoho Kai C	.10	.20
KCS42E089C Happy Halloween Roma C	.10	.20
KCS42E090C Happy Halloween Libeccio C	.10	.20
KCS42E091C 5th Asashio-class Destroyer, Asagumo Kai C	.10	.20
KCS42E092C 6th Asashio-class Destroyer, Yamagumo Kai C	.10	.20
KCS42E093C 5th Shiratsuyu-class Destroyer, Harusame Kai C	.10	.20
KCS42E094C 7th Shiratsuyu-class Destroyer, Umikaze C	.10	.20
KCS42E095C 4th Vittorio Veneto-class Battleship, Roma C	.10	.20
KCS42E096C A Midsummer Moment, Yudachi Kai-II C	.10	.20
KCS42E097U Combat Rations U	.12	.25
KCS42E098CR Let me show you Italia's true power! CLR	.25	.50
KCS42E099CC Kasumi, anchors aweigh! Please follow me! CC	.15	.30
KCS42E100CC I'm going all out, follow me! CC	.15	.30

2018 Weiss Schwarz Konosuba God's Blessing on This Wonderful World 2

KSW55E005R Snipe Kazuma R	.20	.40
KSW55E006R Decoy Kazuma R	.20	.40
KSW55E007R Precious Item Chris R	.20	.40
KSW55E008R Sightseeing in Arcanretia Darkness R	.20	.40
KSW55E009R Swimsuit Darkness R	.20	.40
KSW55E010R Herald Darkness R	.20	.40
KSW55E011R Power of the Mask Darkness R	.20	.40
KSW55E012R Setting Out Kazuma R	.20	.40
KSW55E013U Patriarch's Poise Darkness' Father U	.12	.25
KSW55E014U Cross-Examination Sena U	.12	.25
KSW55E015U Aristocrat Daughter Darkness U	.12	.25
KSW55E016U Rock-Paper-Scissors Master Kazuma U	.12	.25
KSW55E017U A New Quest Kazuma U	.12	.25
KSW55E018U Sending Off Ruffian U	.12	.25
KSW55E019U Dead-On Accuracy Darkness U	.12	.25
KSW55E020U Iron Will Darkness U	.12	.25
KSW55E021C Impromptu Butler Kazuma C	.10	.20
KSW55E022C Third Witness Clemea & Fio C	.10	.20
KSW55E023C Catharsis Coachman C	.10	.20
KSW55E024C In Ecstasy Darkness C	.10	.20
KSW55E025C Dignified Darkness C	.10	.20
KSW55E026C Second Generation Vanir C	.10	.20
KSW55E027C Masked Demon Vanir C	.10	.20
KSW55E028C First Witness Chris C	.10	.20
KSW55E029C Second Witness Mitsurugi C	.10	.20
KSW55E030C Freeze Kazuma C	.10	.20
KSW55E031C Embarrassed Sena C	.10	.20
KSW55E032U Aristocratic Insignia U	.12	.25
KSW55E033U Lurk Skill U	.12	.25
KSW55E034U Lie-Detecting Device U	.12	.25
KSW55E035U Chicken Race U	.12	.25
KSW55E036CR Subduing Even My Heart...... CLR	.25	.50
KSW55E037CC First Incitation CC	.15	.30
KSW55E038CC To the Next Adventure! CC	.15	.30
KSW55E039CC Unparalled Deleterious Desire CC	.15	.30
KSW55E040CC Return It to Me!! CC	.15	.30
KSW55E045R Having a Nightmare Wiz R	.20	.40
KSW55E046R Elated Wiz R	.20	.40
KSW55E047R Chomp Chomp Megumin R	.20	.40
KSW55E048R Ambush Yunyun R	.20	.40
KSW55E049R Brightening Eyes Megumin R	.20	.40
KSW55E050R Tad Bit Shy Yunyun R	.20	.40
KSW55E051R Setting Out Megumin R	.20	.40
KSW55E052R Eternal Rival Yunyun R	.20	.40
KSW55E053R Powered-Up Explosion Magic Megumin R	.20	.40
KSW55E054U Consecutive Victories Megumin U	.12	.25
KSW55E055U Chommusuke U	.12	.25
KSW55E056U Radiant Smile Megumin U	.12	.25
KSW55E057U Taken Aback Yunyun U	.12	.25
KSW55E058U General Store Shopkeeper Wiz U	.12	.25
KSW55E059U Developmental Challenge Yunyun U	.12	.25
KSW55E060U Lonely Birthday Yunyun U	.12	.25
KSW55E061U Deadly Poison Slime Hans U	.12	.25
KSW55E062U Nice Assist Wiz U	.12	.25
KSW55E063C Hans C	.10	.20
KSW55E064C Maxed-Out Motivation Yunyun C	.10	.20
KSW55E065C Challenge Accepted Megumin C	.10	.20
KSW55E066C Reminiscent Reunion Wiz C	.10	.20
KSW55E067C Insufficient Magic Power Megumin C	.10	.20
KSW55E068C Coming with Gifts Yunyun C	.10	.20
KSW55E069C Out of the Bath Wiz C	.10	.20
KSW55E070C Objection! Megumin C	.10	.20
KSW55E071C In the Dream Wiz C	.10	.20
KSW55E072C Power of a Demon Army General Wiz C	.10	.20
KSW55E073C The Rival Makes Her Appearance Yunyun C	.10	.20
KSW55E074U Friendship Crystal U	.12	.25
KSW55E075CR New Explosion Magic CLR	.25	.50
KSW55E076CR Light of Saber! CLR	.25	.50
KSW55E077CC In the Bath CC	.15	.30
KSW55E078CC Cursed Crystal Prison! CC	.15	.30
KSW55E081R Swimsuit Eris R	.20	.40
KSW55E082R Soul Salvation Aqua R	.20	.40
KSW55E083R Real Magic Power is Down to Luck Too Aqua R	.20	.40
KSW55E084R Swimsuit Aqua R	.20	.40
KSW55E085R Furious Fist Aqua R	.20	.40
KSW55E086U Decoy Aqua U	.12	.25
KSW55E087U Our Little Secret Here Eris U	.12	.25
KSW55E088U Who I Really Am Aqua U	.12	.25
KSW55E089aC Swarmed on the Street Axis Church Devotee A C	.10	.20
KSW55E089bC Swarmed on the Street Axis Church Devotee B C	.10	.20
KSW55E089cC Swarmed on the Street Axis Church Devotee C C	.10	.20
KSW55E089dC Swarmed on the Street Axis Church Devotee D C	.10	.20
KSW55E090C Carefree Maid Aqua C	.10	.20
KSW55E091C Purification Aqua C	.10	.20
KSW55E092C Sweet Smile Axis Church Devotee C	.10	.20
KSW55E093C Bewildered Eris C	.10	.20
KSW55E094C Tipsy Aqua C	.10	.20
KSW55E095U The Power of Purification U	.12	.25
KSW55E096U Seizure of Private Property U	.12	.25
KSW55E097U Axis Church Creed U	.12	.25
KSW55E098CR In the Name of the Goddess CLR	.25	.50
KSW55E099CC Goddess' Fury CC	.15	.30
KSW55E100CC Well Then, See You CC	.15	.30

2018 Weiss Schwarz Love Live Sunshine

LSSWE27E04R Do Your Rubesty Ruby Kurosawa R	.20	.40
LSSWE27E05R Mijuku DREAMER Hanamaru Kunikida R	.20	.40
LSSWE27E06R Mijuku DREAMER Ruby Kurosawa R	.20	.40
LSSWE27E07R Mijuku DREAMER Yoshiko Tsushima R	.20	.40
LSSWE27E08U Aim to Shine Hanamaru Kunikida U	.12	.25
LSSWE27E09U My Dear Sister Ruby Kurosawa U	.12	.25
LSSWE27E10U Tears of a Fallen Angel Yoshiko Tsushima U	.12	.25
LSSWE27E11U Today's Ultimate Ragnarok Yoshiko Tsushima U	.12	.25
LSSWE27E12U Together with Everyone Hanamaru Kunikida U	.12	.25
LSSWE27E13C Aim to Shine Yoshiko Tsushima C	.10	.20
LSSWE27E14C Aim to Shine Ruby Kurosawa C	.10	.20
LSSWE27E15C Encountering the Future Hanamaru Kunikida C	.10	.20
LSSWE27E16C Th-This is a PC! C	.10	.20
LSSWE27E17C MIRAI TICKET (Yellow) C	.10	.20
LSSWE27E18C Mijuku DREAMER (Yellow) C	.10	.20
LSSWE27E22R Mijuku DREAMER You Watanabe R	.20	.40
LSSWE27E23R Mijuku DREAMER Chika Takami R	.20	.40
LSSWE27E24R Aim to Shine You Watanabe R	.20	.40
LSSWE27E25R Mijuku DREAMER Riko Sakurauchi R	.20	.40
LSSWE27E26U Aim to Shine Chika Takami U	.12	.25
LSSWE27E27U Shining All Together You Watanabe U	.12	.25
LSSWE27E28U From Zero to One! Riko Sakurauchi U	.12	.25
LSSWE27E29C From Zero to One! Chika Takami C	.10	.20
LSSWE27E30C Aim to Shine Riko Sakurauchi C	.10	.20
LSSWE27E31C From Zero to One! You Watanabe C	.10	.20
LSSWE27E32C Pool Cleaning You Watanabe C	.10	.20
LSSWE27E33C Something Precious Chika Takami C	.10	.20
LSSWE27E34U Shining Much Brighter Than Anyone Could Alone U	.12	.25
LSSWE27E35C Mijuku DREAMER (Red) C	.10	.20
LSSWE27E36C Feelings, Become One! C	.10	.20
LSSWE27E40R Mijuku DREAMER Dia Kurosawa R	.20	.40
LSSWE27E41R Mijuku DREAMER Kanan Matsuura R	.20	.40
LSSWE27E42R Aim to Shine Dia Kurosawa R	.20	.40
LSSWE27E43R Mijuku DREAMER Mari Ohara R	.20	.40
LSSWE27E44U GLAMorous Swimsuit Figure Kanan Matsuura U	.12	.25
LSSWE27E45U Aim to Shine Mari Ohara U	.12	.25
LSSWE27E46U Welcome to Aqours! Dia Kurosawa U	.12	.25
LSSWE27E47C Reminiscent Hug Kanan Matsuura C	.10	.20
LSSWE27E48C Escaping Reality Dia Kurosawa C	.10	.20
LSSWE27E49C My Best Friend Mari Ohara C	.10	.20
LSSWE27E50C Aim to Shine Kanan Matsuura C	.10	.20
LSSWE27E51C Stewshine Mari Ohara C	.10	.20
LSSWE27E52U Thinking For the Other U	.12	.25
LSSWE27E53C MIRAI TICKET (Blue) C	.10	.20
LSSWE27E54C Mijuku DREAMER (Blue) C	.10	.20

2018 Weiss Schwarz Love Live Sunshine Foil

LSSWE27E04R Do Your Rubesty Ruby Kurosawa R	.20	.40
LSSWE27E05R Mijuku DREAMER Hanamaru Kunikida R	.20	.40
LSSWE27E06R Mijuku DREAMER Ruby Kurosawa R	.20	.40
LSSWE27E07R Mijuku DREAMER Yoshiko Tsushima R	.20	.40
LSSWE27E08U Aim to Shine Hanamaru Kunikida U	.12	.25
LSSWE27E09U My Dear Sister Ruby Kurosawa U	.12	.25
LSSWE27E10U Tears of a Fallen Angel Yoshiko Tsushima U	.12	.25
LSSWE27E11U Today's Ultimate Ragnarok Yoshiko Tsushima U	.12	.25
LSSWE27E12U Together with Everyone Hanamaru Kunikida U	.12	.25
LSSWE27E13C Aim to Shine Yoshiko Tsushima C	.10	.20
LSSWE27E14C Aim to Shine Ruby Kurosawa C	.10	.20
LSSWE27E15C Encountering the Future Hanamaru Kunikida C	.10	.20
LSSWE27E16C Th-This is a PC! C	.10	.20
LSSWE27E17C MIRAI TICKET (Yellow) C	.10	.20
LSSWE27E18C Mijuku DREAMER (Yellow) C	.10	.20
LSSWE27E22R Mijuku DREAMER You Watanabe R	.20	.40
LSSWE27E23R Mijuku DREAMER Chika Takami R	.20	.40
LSSWE27E24R Aim to Shine You Watanabe R	.20	.40
LSSWE27E25R Mijuku DREAMER Riko Sakurauchi R	.20	.40
LSSWE27E26U Aim to Shine Chika Takami U	.12	.25
LSSWE27E27U Shining All Together You Watanabe U	.12	.25
LSSWE27E28U From Zero to One! Riko Sakurauchi U	.12	.25
LSSWE27E29C From Zero to One! Chika Takami C	.10	.20
LSSWE27E30C Aim to Shine Riko Sakurauchi C	.10	.20
LSSWE27E31C From Zero to One! You Watanabe C	.10	.20
LSSWE27E32C Pool Cleaning You Watanabe C	.10	.20
LSSWE27E33C Something Precious Chika Takami C	.10	.20
LSSWE27E34U Shining Much Brighter Than Anyone Could Alone U	.12	.25
LSSWE27E35C Mijuku DREAMER (Red) C	.10	.20
LSSWE27E36C Feelings, Become One! C	.10	.20
LSSWE27E40R Mijuku DREAMER Dia Kurosawa R	.20	.40
LSSWE27E41R Mijuku DREAMER Kanan Matsuura R	.20	.40
LSSWE27E42R Aim to Shine Dia Kurosawa R	.20	.40
LSSWE27E43R Mijuku DREAMER Mari Ohara R	.20	.40
LSSWE27E44U GLAMorous Swimsuit Figure Kanan Matsuura U	.12	.25
LSSWE27E45U Aim to Shine Mari Ohara U	.12	.25
LSSWE27E46U Welcome to Aqours! Dia Kurosawa U	.12	.25
LSSWE27E47C Reminiscent Hug Kanan Matsuura C	.10	.20
LSSWE27E48C Escaping Reality Dia Kurosawa C	.10	.20
LSSWE27E49C My Best Friend Mari Ohara C	.10	.20
LSSWE27E50C Aim to Shine Kanan Matsuura C	.10	.20
LSSWE27E51C Stewshine Mari Ohara C	.10	.20
LSSWE27E52U Thinking For the Other U	.12	.25
LSSWE27E53C MIRAI TICKET (Blue) C	.10	.20
LSSWE27E54C Mijuku DREAMER (Blue) C	.10	.20

2018 Weiss Schwarz Persona 5

P5/S45-E001 Protagonist as JOKER & Arsene RR	5.00	10.00
P5/S45-E001SP Protagonist as JOKER & Arsene SP	30.00	60.00
P5/S45-E002 Ryuji as SKULL: All-out Attack RR	5.00	10.00
P5/S45-E002SP Ryuji as SKULL: All-out Attack SP	30.00	60.00
P5/S45-E003 Protagonist: The Will of Rebellion R	.20	.40
P5/S45-E003S Protagonist: The Will of Rebellion SR	7.50	15.00
P5/S45-E004 Ryuji as SKULL: The Phantom Vanguard R	.20	.40
P5/S45-E004S Ryuji as SKULL: The Phantom Vanguard SR	7.50	15.00
P5/S45-E005 Ryuji Sakamoto R	.20	.40
P5/S45-E005S Ryuji Sakamoto SR	7.50	15.00
P5/S45-E006 Protagonist as JOKER: All-out Attack R	.20	.40
P5/S45-E006S Protagonist as JOKER: All-out Attack SR	7.50	15.00
P5/S45-E007 Ryuji as SKULL & Captain Kidd R	.20	.40
P5/S45-E008 Ryuji as SKULL: A Big Smile U	.12	.25
P5/S45-E009 Protagonist: Leblanc's Troublesome Guest U	.12	.25
P5/S45-E010 Akechi: The New Detective Prince U	.12	.25
P5/S45-E011 Ryuji: It's a Deal U	.12	.25
P5/S45-E012 Protagonist: Prisoner of Fate U	.12	.25
P5/S45-E013 Swimsuit Ryuji C	.10	.20
P5/S45-E014 Goro Akechi C	.10	.20
P5/S45-E015 Swimsuit Protagonist C	.10	.20
P5/S45-E016 Protagonist as JOKER: Thief Clad in Black C	.10	.20
P5/S45-E017 Protagonist as JOKER: Lurking in the Dark C	.10	.20
P5/S45-E018 Ryuji as SKULL: The Fight Is On C	.10	.20
P5/S45-E019 Yuuki Mishima C	.10	.20
P5/S45-E020 Akechi: The High-School Detective C	.10	.20
P5/S45-E021 Calling Card U	.12	.25
P5/S45-E022 Wild Talk U	.12	.25
P5/S45-E023 THE SHOW'S OVER CR	.20	.40
P5/S45-E023R THE SHOW'S OVER RRR	7.50	15.00
P5/S45-E024 FREAKiN' BoRiNG CC	.15	.30
P5/S45-E024R FREAKiN' BoRiNG RRR	7.50	15.00
P5/S45-E025 Yo, I'm Ready... CC	.15	.30
P5/S45-E026 Makoto as QUEEN & Johanna RR	5.00	10.00
P5/S45-E026SP Makoto as QUEEN & Johanna SP	30.00	60.00
P5/S45-E027 Haru as NOIR & Milady RR	5.00	10.00
P5/S45-E027SP Haru as NOIR & Milady SP	30.00	60.00
P5/S45-E028 Makoto as QUEEN: The Phantom Tactician R	.20	.40
P5/S45-E028S Makoto as QUEEN: The Phantom Tactician SR	7.50	15.00
P5/S45-E029 Haru Okumura R	.20	.40
P5/S45-E029S Haru Okumura SR	7.50	15.00
P5/S45-E030 Swimsuit Makoto R	.20	.40
P5/S45-E031 Makoto Niijima R	.20	.40
P5/S45-E031S Makoto Niijima SR	7.50	15.00
P5/S45-E032 Haru as NOIR: All-out Attack R	.20	.40
P5/S45-E032S Haru as NOIR: All-out Attack SR	7.50	15.00
P5/S45-E033 Sadayo Kawakami U	.12	.25
P5/S45-E034 Toranosuke Yoshida U	.12	.25
P5/S45-E035 Haru as NOIR: The Mysterious Beauty Thief U	.12	.25
P5/S45-E036 Makoto as QUEEN: All-out Attack U	.12	.25
P5/S45-E037 Haru as NOIR: The Phantom Lady U	.12	.25
P5/S45-E038 Makoto as QUEEN: Miss Post-Apocalyptic Raider U	.12	.25
P5/S45-E039 Sae Niijima C	.10	.20
P5/S45-E040 Prosecutor Sae C	.10	.20
P5/S45-E041 Haru: It's a Deal C	.10	.20
P5/S45-E042 Makoto: It's a Deal C	.10	.20
P5/S45-E043 Haru: A Life on Rails C	.10	.20
P5/S45-E044 Chihaya Mifune C	.10	.20
P5/S45-E045 Ichiko Ohya C	.10	.20
P5/S45-E046 Calling Card U	.12	.25
P5/S45-E047 Metaverse Navigator C	.10	.20
P5/S45-E048 Tanaka's Shady Commodities C	.10	.20
P5/S45-E049 Adieu. CR	.20	.40
P5/S45-E049R Adieu. RRR	.12	.25
P5/S45-E050 JUSTICE HAS PREVAILED. CC	.10	.20
P5/S45-E050R JUSTICE HAS PREVAILED. RRR	7.50	15.00
P5/S45-E051 Morgana as MONA & Zorro RR	5.00	10.00
P5/S45-E051SP Morgana as MONA & Zorro SP	30.00	60.00
P5/S45-E052 Ann as PANTHER: All-out Attack RR	5.00	10.00
P5/S45-E052SP Ann as PANTHER: All-out Attack SP	30.00	60.00
P5/S45-E053 Ann as PANTHER: The Talented(?) Phantom Actress R	.20	.40
P5/S45-E053S Ann as PANTHER: The Talented(?) Phantom Actress SR	7.50	15.00
P5/S45-E054 Morgana as MONA: The Phantom Guide R	.20	.40
P5/S45-E054S Morgana as MONA: The Phantom Guide SR	7.50	15.00
P5/S45-E055 Ann as PANTHER & Carmen R	.20	.40
P5/S45-E055S Ann as PANTHER & Carmen SR	7.50	15.00
P5/S45-E056 Morgana as MONA: All-out Attack R	.20	.40
P5/S45-E056S Morgana as MONA: All-out Attack SR	7.50	15.00
P5/S45-E057 Ann Takamaki R	.20	.40
P5/S45-E058 Shinya Oda U	.12	.25
P5/S45-E059 Ann as PANTHER: Quiet Rage U	.12	.25
P5/S45-E060 Ann: It's a Deal U	.12	.25
P5/S45-E061 Morgana as MONA: It's a Deal U	.12	.25
P5/S45-E062 Ann as PANTHER: Determination U	.12	.25
P5/S45-E063 Morgana Car U	.12	.25
P5/S45-E064 Hifumi Togo C	.10	.20
P5/S45-E065 Morgana as MONA: Earnest Affection C	.10	.20
P5/S45-E066 Munehisa Iwai C	.10	.20
P5/S45-E067 Swimsuit Ann C	.10	.20
P5/S45-E068 Morgana as MONA: Identity Unknown C	.10	.20
P5/S45-E069 Morgana as MONA: For the Sake of the Team C	.10	.20
P5/S45-E070 Calling Card U	.12	.25
P5/S45-E071 Mementos C	.10	.20
P5/S45-E072 omg!! We are SO awesome CR	.20	.40
P5/S45-E072R omg!! We are SO awesome RRR	7.50	15.00
P5/S45-E073 For My Best Friend CC	.15	.30

P5/S45-E074 MISSION ACCOMPLISHED CC	.15	.30
P5/S45-E074R MISSION ACCOMPLISHED RRR	7.50	15.00
P5/S45-E075 Where I Belong CC	.15	.30
P5/S45-E076 Futaba as ORACLE: Navigation Duty RR	5.00	10.00
P5/S45-E076SP Futaba as ORACLE: Navigation Duty SP	30.00	60.00
P5/S45-E077 Yusuke as FOX & Goemon RR	5.00	10.00
P5/S45-E077SP Yusuke as FOX & Goemon SP	30.00	60.00
P5/S45-E078 Caroline R	.20	.40
P5/S45-E078S Caroline SR	7.50	15.00
P5/S45-E079 Futaba Sakura R	.20	.40
P5/S45-E079S Futaba Sakura SR	7.50	15.00
P5/S45-E080 Yusuke as FOX: The Phantom Artist R	.20	.40
P5/S45-E081 Futaba as ORACLE & Necronomicon R	.20	.40
P5/S45-E081S Futaba as ORACLE & Necronomicon SR	7.50	15.00
P5/S45-E082 Yusuke Kitagawa R	.20	.40
P5/S45-E082S Yusuke Kitagawa SR	7.50	15.00
P5/S45-E083 Justine U	.12	.25
P5/S45-E084 Swimsuit Futaba U	.12	.25
P5/S45-E085 Igor: Imposer of Rehabilitation U	.12	.25
P5/S45-E086 Futaba as ORACLE: The Phantom Hacker U	.12	.25
P5/S45-E087 Tae Takemi U	.12	.25
P5/S45-E088 Sojiro Sakura C	.10	.20
P5/S45-E089 Yusuke: First Encounter C	.10	.20
P5/S45-E090 Yusuke: It's a Deal C	.10	.20
P5/S45-E091 Futaba: It's a Deal C	.10	.20
P5/S45-E092 Futaba: Hacking in Session C	.10	.20
P5/S45-E093 Yusuke: Card Duplication C	.10	.20
P5/S45-E094 Igor: Master of the Velvet Room C	.10	.20
P5/S45-E095 Yusuke as FOX: All-out Attack C	.10	.20
P5/S45-E096 Calling Card U	.12	.25
P5/S45-E097 Execution U	.12	.25
P5/S45-E098 Velvet Room C	.10	.20
P5/S45-E099 IT WAS FUN WHILE IT LASTED, GOODBYE. CR	.20	.40
P5/S45-E099R IT WAS FUN WHILE IT LASTED, GOODBYE. RRR	7.50	15.00
P5/S45-E100 I'll Never Forgive Them! CC	.15	.30
P5/S45-E100R I'll Never Forgive Them! RRR	7.50	15.00
P5/S45-E101 Protagonist as JOKER: Phantom Thief of Hearts PR	2.50	5.00
P5/S45-E102 Ryuji: Phantom Thief of Hearts PR	2.50	5.00
P5/S45-E103 Ann: Phantom Thief of Hearts PR	2.50	5.00
P5/S45-E104 Morgana as MONA: Phantom Thief of Hearts PR	2.50	5.00
P5/S45-E105 Yusuke: Phantom Thief of Hearts PR	2.50	5.00
P5/S45-E106 Makoto: Phantom Thief of Hearts PR	2.50	5.00
P5/S45-E107 Futaba: Phantom Thief of Hearts PR	2.50	5.00
P5/S45-E108 Haru: Phantom Thief of Hearts PR	2.50	5.00
P5/S45-E109 Protagonist as JOKER: Destiny Awaits PR	2.50	5.00

2018 Weiss Schwarz Re Zero Starting Life in Another World

RZS46E002R Former Sword Saint, Theresia R	.20	.40
RZS46E003R Head of House Karsten, Crusch R	.20	.40
RZS46E004R Young Swordsman, Wilhelm R	.20	.40
RZS46E005R Declaration of War, Felt R	.20	.40
RZS46E006R The Greatest Knight, Julius R	.20	.40
RZS46E007R Sword Saint, Reinhard R	.20	.40
RZS46E008U Expert Negotiator, Anastasia U	.12	.25
RZS46E009U Healer, Felix U	.12	.25
RZS46E010U White Whale Hunt, Crusch U	.12	.25
RZS46E011U Felt's Knight, Reinhard U	.12	.25
RZS46E012U Old Man Rom U	.12	.25
RZS46E013U Pride of the Slums, Felt U	.12	.25
RZS46E014U Wilhelm van Astrea U	.12	.25
RZS46E015U Unseen Hand, Petelgeuse U	.12	.25
RZS46E016C Sloth Sin Archbishop, Petelgeuse C	.10	.20
RZS46E017C Thankful Feelings, Felt C	.10	.20
RZS46E018C Fang of Iron Vice-Captain, Mimi C	.10	.20
RZS46E019C Fang of Iron Vice-Captain, Hetaro C	.10	.20
RZS46E020C Priscilla's Knight, Aldebaran C	.10	.20
RZS46E021C Royal Election Candidate, Anastasia C	.10	.20
RZS46E022C Royal Election Candidate, Priscilla C	.10	.20
RZS46E023C Negotiating An Alliance, Crusch C	.10	.20
RZS46E024C Airs of a Queen, Priscilla C	.10	.20
RZS46E025C Bowel Hunter, Elsa C	.10	.20
RZS46E026C Fang of Iron Captain, Ricardo C	.10	.20
RZS46E027aU Royal Election A U	.12	.25
RZS46E027bU Royal Election B U	.12	.25
RZS46E027cU Royal Election C U	.12	.25
RZS46E027dU Royal Election D U	.12	.25
RZS46E027eU Royal Election E U	.12	.25
RZS46E028CR Mistral Maiden CLR	.25	.50
RZS46E029CC Hundred Man Sword Strike CC	.15	.30
RZS46E033R Clairvoyance, Ram R	.20	.40
RZS46E034R The Maid Saw! Ram R	.20	.40
RZS46E035R Canopy-Piercing Sunlight, Rem & Ram R	.20	.40
RZS46E036R Sunset Knoll, Beatrice R	.20	.40
RZS46E037R Forbidden Library Warden, Beatrice R	.20	.40
RZS46E038R Bathtime! Rem & Ram R	.20	.40
RZS46E039U With Puck, Subaru U	.12	.25
RZS46E040U Court Sorcerer, Roswaal U	.12	.25
RZS46E041U Forbidden Library Librarian, Beatrice U	.12	.25
RZS46E042U Oni Prodigy, Ram U	.12	.25
RZS46E043U With Puck, Beatrice U	.12	.25
RZS46E044U Self-Praise, Ram U	.12	.25
RZS46E045C Sticking with Bubby, Beatrice C	.10	.20
RZS46E046C Innocent Child, Petra C	.10	.20
RZS46E047C Door Crossing, Beatrice C	.10	.20
RZS46E048C Sulking Beatrice C	.10	.20
RZS46E049C A Flower in Each Arm, Ram C	.10	.20
RZS46E050C Challenging Another World, Subaru C	.10	.20
RZS46E051C Sister's Avenger, Ram C	.10	.20
RZS46E052C Margrave Roswaal C	.10	.20
RZS46E053U Forbidden Library U	.12	.25
RZS46E054CR Subaru Natsuki's Decoy Tactic CLR	.25	.50
RZS46E055CC As the Older Sister CC	.15	.30
RZS46E056CC Mana Drain CC	.15	.30
RZS46E057CC Breaking the Curse CC	.15	.30
RZS46E062R Angel's Smile, Emilia R	.20	.40
RZS46E063R Happy Daydream, Rem R	.20	.40
RZS46E064R Pure Maiden, Emilia R	.20	.40
RZS46E065R Unconditional Trust, Rem R	.20	.40
RZS46E066R Bathtime! Emilia R	.20	.40
RZS46E067R Demon's Demeanor, Rem R	.20	.40
RZS46E068R Subaru Natsuki R	.20	.40
RZS46E069R Modest Request, Rem R	.20	.40
RZS46E069RRRR Modest Request, Rem R	.20	.40
RZS46E070U In Uniforms, Rem & Ram U	.12	.25
RZS46E071U Stunned, Emilia U	.12	.25
RZS46E072U Talking About the Future Smiling, Rem U	.12	.25
RZS46E073U Talking About the Future Smiling, Subaru U	.12	.25
RZS46E074U Gaze of Admiration, Rem U	.12	.25
RZS46E075U Great Spirit, Puck U	.12	.25
RZS46E076U Midnight Visit, Rem U	.12	.25
RZS46E077U Peaceful Life, Emilia U	.12	.25
RZS46E078U Smug Look, Emilia U	.12	.25
RZS46E079U Dim Light Seen With Those Eyes, Rem U	.12	.25
RZS46E080U Intense Ire, Puck U	.12	.25
RZS46E081C Capital's Fruit Seller, Kadomon C	.10	.20
RZS46E082C Fated Encounter, Subaru C	.10	.20
RZS46E083C Ground Dragon, Patrasche C	.10	.20
RZS46E084C In My Hero's Arms, Rem C	.10	.20
RZS46E085C In a Corner of This Dark World, Emilia C	.10	.20
RZS46E086C Fire Spirit, Puck C	.10	.20
RZS46E087C A Morning Moment, Emilia C	.10	.20
RZS46E088C A Flower in Each Arm, Rem C	.10	.20
RZS46E089C Masterly Maid, Rem C	.10	.20
RZS46E090C Two Riding A Ground Dragon, Rem C	.10	.20
RZS46E091C Merchant, Otto C	.10	.20
RZS46E092C Gentle Disparagement, Emilia C	.10	.20
RZS46E093C Anxious Emilia C	.10	.20
RZS46E094U Return by Death U	.12	.25
RZS46E095CR Oni's Smile CLR	.25	.50
RZS46E096CR Starting Life in Another World CLR	.25	.50
RZS46E097CC A Boy's Fantasy CC	.15	.30
RZS46E098CC Demon's True Form CC	.15	.30
RZS46E099CC Wishing CC	.15	.30
RZS46E100CC Like A Demon CC	.15	.30

2019 Weiss Schwarz Bang Dream Girls Band Party Multi Live

BDENW03003R Perfect Nutrition! Hagumi Kitazawa R	.20	.40
BDENW03004R A Nice Change Kanon Matsubara R	.20	.40
BDENW03005R Love's Light Wings Kaoru Seta R	.20	.40
BDENW03006R Worries, Be Gone! Kokoro Tsurumaki R	.20	.40
BDENW03007R A Happy Revolution! Kokoro Tsurumaki R	.20	.40
BDENW03008R What's Important to Me Misaki Okusawa R	.20	.40
BDENW03009U The Magic of Smiles Kanon Matsubara U	.12	.25
BDENW03010U I Want to Help Kanon Matsubara U	.12	.25
BDENW03011U The Magic of Smiles Misaki Okusawa U	.12	.25
BDENW03012U This, Too, is Fleeting Kaoru Seta U	.12	.25
BDENW03013U Sakura Michelle Misaki Okusawa U	.12	.25
BDENW03014C Everything In Moderation Misaki Okusawa C	.10	.20
BDENW03015C A Sparkling Stage Hina Hikawa C	.10	.20
BDENW03016C Fired Up! Hagumi Kitazawa C	.10	.20
BDENW03017C Gentle Girl Kanon Matsubara C	.10	.20
BDENW03018C Smile Captain Hagumi Kitazawa C	.10	.20
BDENW03019C The Magic of Smiles Kaoru Seta C	.10	.20
BDENW03020C Rumored Prince Kaoru Seta C	.10	.20
BDENW03021C Hanasakigawa Dimension Kokoro Tsurumaki C	.10	.20
BDENW03022U Reppin' Hello, Happy World! U	.12	.25
BDENW03023CR Orchestra Of Smiles! CLR	.25	.50
BDENW03024CC Surpise Show Downtown! CC	.15	.30
BDENW03025CC Source of Happiness CC	.15	.30
BDENW03026CC The Magic of Smiles CC	.15	.30
BDENW03031R Stand Firm! Tsugumi Hazawa R	.20	.40
BDENW03032R Please Explain! Tomoe Udagawa R	.20	.40
BDENW03033R Rock and Glow Tsugumi Hazawa R	.20	.40
BDENW03034R Full Support Aya Maruyama R	.20	.40
BDENW03035R Rock and Glow Ran Mitake R	.20	.40
BDENW03036R Legend of the Seven Mysteries- Moca Aoba R	.20	.40
BDENW03037R A Sparkling Stage Eve Wakamiya R	.20	.40
BDENW03038U We're Rooting For You! Eve Wakamiya U	.12	.25
BDENW03039U Childhood Friends Moca Aoba U	.12	.25
BDENW03040U Rock and Glow Tomoe Udagawa U	.12	.25
BDENW03041U The Spooky Scare-Case Tomoe Udagawa U	.12	.25
BDENW03042U A Sparkling Stage Maya Yamato U	.12	.25
BDENW03043U Rock and Glow Himari Uehara U	.12	.25
BDENW03044U Sister Figure Tomoe Udagawa U	.12	.25
BDENW03045U Familiar Tune Himari Uehara U	.12	.25
BDENW03046U It's Not like I'm Scared! Ran Mitake U	.12	.25
BDENW03047C Tsugu the Fearless Tsugumi Hazawa C	.10	.20
BDENW03048C Otaku Drummer Maya Yamato C	.10	.20
BDENW03049C Leader Of The Group! Himari Uehara C	.10	.20
BDENW03050C Iron Smile Chisato Shirasagi C	.10	.20
BDENW03051C Cool Friends Ran Mitake C	.10	.20
BDENW03052C My Own Pace Moca Aoba C	.10	.20
BDENW03053C Everyone's Support Tsugumi Hazawa C	.10	.20
BDENW03054C Rock and Glow Moca Aoba C	.10	.20
BDENW03055U Important Tanzaku U	.12	.25
BDENW03056U Fifty-Fifty Fear U	.12	.25
BDENW03057CR Shuwarin Dreaming CLR	.25	.50
BDENW03058CR That Is How I Roll! CLR	.25	.50
BDENW03059CC Autumn Moon Festival CC	.15	.30
BDENW03060CC Haneoka's Seven Mysteries CC	.15	.30
BDENW03061CC Same as Always, After All CC	.15	.30
BDENW03062CC Rock and Glow CC	.15	.30
BDENW03065R Excellent Performance Maya Yamato R	.20	.40
BDENW03066R Feelings to be Conveyed Saya Yamabuki R	.20	.40
BDENW03067R A Sparkling Stage Aya Maruyama R	.20	.40
BDENW03068R Into The Greatest Stage! Kasumi Toyoma R	.20	.40
BDENW03069R If I Could Be Myself... Chisato Shirasagi R	.20	.40
BDENW03070U Backstage Hina Hikawa U	.12	.25
BDENW03071U Saya's Confession Saya & Kasumi U	.12	.25
BDENW03072U Queen Of Hearts Chisato Shirasagi U	.12	.25
BDENW03073U Bushido! Eve Wakamiya U	.12	.25
BDENW03074U Poppin'Colors! Saya Yamabuki U	.12	.25
BDENW03075U Poppin'Colors! Rimi Ushigome U	.12	.25
BDENW03076C Pretty In Pink Aya Maruyama C	.10	.20
BDENW03077C Reckless! Kasumi Toyama C	.10	.20
BDENW03078C I Love Chocolate Rimi Ushigome C	.10	.20
BDENW03079C Poppin'Colors! Kasumi Toyama C	.10	.20
BDENW03080C Moved To Tears Maya Yamato C	.10	.20
BDENW03081C Everybody's Sister Saya Yamabuki C	.10	.20
BDENW03082C Genius Girl Hina Hikawa C	.10	.20
BDENW03083C Now I'm Nervous Rimi Ushigome C	.10	.20
BDENW03084C Spirit Of Bushido Eve Wakamiya C	.10	.20
BDENW03085C Many Mementos Saya Yamabuki C	.10	.20
BDENW03086CR Double Rainbow CLR	.25	.50
BDENW03087CC My Confidante CC	.15	.30
BDENW03088CC Taste of Fall! CC	.15	.30
BDENW03089CC Poppin'Colors! CC	.15	.30
BDENW03092R A Favor I Will Never Forget Tae Hanazono R	.20	.40
BDENW03093R Blue Roses in Harmony Sayo Hikawa R	.20	.40
BDENW03094R Poppin'Colors! Tae Hanazono R	.20	.40
BDENW03095R All That I Hear Rinko Shirokane R	.20	.40
BDENW03096R Blue Roses in Harmony Ako Udagawa R	.20	.40
BDENW03097R Onstage Yukina Minato R	.20	.40
BDENW03098R Trace of Effort Lisa Imai R	.20	.40
BDENW03099R Will Definitely Take It Arisa Ichigaya R	.20	.40
BDENW03100U Angel's Smile Ako Udagawa U	.12	.25
BDENW03101U Onstage Rinko Shirokane U	.12	.25
BDENW03102U A Notebook With All My Heart Arisa Ichigaya U	.12	.25
BDENW03103U Blue Roses in Harmony Lisa Imai U	.12	.25
BDENW03104U Mood Maker Lisa Imai U	.12	.25
BDENW03105U A Sparkling Stage Chisato Shirasagi U	.12	.25
BDENW03106U Bands Are About Support Kasumi & Tae U	.12	.25
BDENW03107U Blue Roses in Harmony Rinko Shirokane U	.12	.25
BDENW03108U Hard Worker Sayo Hikawa U	.12	.25
BDENW03109C Lone-Wolf Songstress Yukina Minato C	.10	.20
BDENW03110C Poppin'Colors! Arisa Ichigaya C	.10	.20
BDENW03111C Blue Roses in Harmony Yukina Minato C	.10	.20
BDENW03112C I Don't Like Crowds Rinko Shirokane C	.10	.20
BDENW03113C Natural Beauty Tae Hanazono C	.10	.20
BDENW03114C Onstage Ako Udagawa C	.10	.20
BDENW03115C Onstage Sayo Hikawa C	.10	.20
BDENW03116C World Class Faker Arisa Ichigaya C	.10	.20
BDENW03117C Onstage Lisa Imai C	.10	.20
BDENW03118C The Coolest Drummer! Ako Udagawa C	.10	.20
BDENW03119U Midafternoon Hamburger Patty U	.12	.25
BDENW03120U Phone-Shy U	.12	.25
BDENW03121CR Zeit CLR	.25	.50
BDENW03122CC 1st Live Show Pre-Party CC	.15	.30
BDENW03123CC What a Fun Song! CC	.15	.30
BDENW03124CC Looking Up at the Starry Sky CC	.15	.30
BDENW03125CC A Sparkling Stage CC	.15	.30
BDENW03126CC Blue Roses in Harmony CC	.15	.30

2019 Weiss Schwarz BanG Dream! Girls Band Party! Vol.2

BDW63E004R For the Smiles! Hagumi Kitazawa R	.20	.40
BDW63E005R With Everyone's Help Kanon Matsubara R	.20	.40
BDW63E006R I Am Me Kaoru Seta R	.20	.40
BDW63E007R What an Idol Is Maya Yamato R	.20	.40
BDW63E008R Happy Adventure Kokoro Tsurumaki R	.20	.40
BDW63E009U I'm a Human, You Know Hagumi Kitazawa U	.12	.25
BDW63E010U Heave, Ho? Heave, Ho! Aya Maruyama U	.12	.25
BDW63E011U Can You Comprehend Kaoru Seta U	.12	.25
BDW63E012U To Become More Admired Eve Wakamiya U	.12	.25
BDW63E013U Getting Dizzy... Kanon Matsubara U	.12	.25
BDW63E014U Keep Running Until the End Misaki Okusawa U	.12	.25
BDW63E015C Rendezvous of Smiles Kokoro Tsurumaki C	.10	.20
BDW63E016C Tea Ceremony Excellence Kanon Matsubara C	.10	.20
BDW63E017C A Penguin? A Bear? Misaki Okusawa C	.10	.20
BDW63E018C Rules of Being an Idol Chisato Shirasagi C	.10	.20
BDW63E019C Grand Adventure! Hagumi Kitazawa C	.10	.20
BDW63E020C Fragrance of a Caffe Latte Kaoru Seta C	.10	.20
BDW63E021C I Love Fluffy Mascots! Kokoro Tsurumaki C	.10	.20
BDW63E022U Message from Michelle U	.12	.25
BDW63E023U Moment in the Sun U	.12	.25
BDW63E024CR An Idol that Inspires CLR	.25	.50
BDW63E025CR Glistening Sun CLR	.25	.50
BDW63E026CC A Forced Dance CC	.15	.30
BDW63E029R Our Sunset Tomoe Udagawa R	.20	.40
BDW63E030R By Your Side Moca Aoba R	.20	.40
BDW63E031R Noticing Change Tsugumi Hazawa R	.20	.40
BDW63E032U Moderation is Key! Tsugumi Hazawa U	.12	.25
BDW63E033U Sign of Youth Tomoe Udagawa U	.12	.25
BDW63E034U I'll Hold Them Off! Moca Aoba U	.12	.25
BDW63E035U It's So Hot... Ran Mitake U	.12	.25
BDW63E036U We're Here! Himari Uehara U	.12	.25
BDW63E037C The Modest Idol Maya Yamato C	.10	.20
BDW63E038C Always Being Ourselves Ran Mitake C	.10	.20
BDW63E039C My Own Kind of Good Himari Uehara C	.10	.20
BDW63E040C Longtime Childhood Friend Tomoe Udagawa C	.10	.20
BDW63E041C A Little Bit of Growth? Moca Aoba C	.10	.20
BDW63E042C Forgetting Something Important Tsugumi Hazawa C	.10	.20
BDW63E043C Poppin' & Happy Ran Mitake C	.10	.20
BDW63E044U An Eternal Sunset U	.12	.25
BDW63E045C The Dessert Instructor C	.10	.20
BDW63E046CR A Leader's Proposal CLR	.25	.50
BDW63E047CC Ever-Changing Sky CC	.15	.30
BDW63E048CC A Quick Detour CC	.15	.30
BDW63E052R Day Off with Chocolate Rimi Ushigome R	.20	.40
BDW63E053R Hina's Request Hina Hikawa R	.20	.40
BDW63E054R Enthusiastic Huddle Kasumi Toyama R	.20	.40
BDW63E055R Aya Maruyama, The Idol! Aya Maruyama R	.20	.40
BDW63E056U CiRCLE Storage Expedition Saya Yamabuki U	.12	.25
BDW63E057U Self-Taught Survival Maya Yamato U	.12	.25
BDW63E058U I'm Me Hina Hikawa U	.12	.25
BDW63E059U In a Place as Big as This...?! Rimi Ushigome U	.12	.25
BDW63E060C Important Moment Saya Yamabuki C	.10	.20
BDW63E061C Important Opportunity Hina Hikawa C	.10	.20
BDW63E062C Call for Courage Rimi Ushigome C	.10	.20
BDW63E063C Origami Fun Kasumi Toyama C	.10	.20
BDW63E064C Like That! Kasumi Toyama C	.10	.20
BDW63E065C First Time Latte Art Aya Maruyama C	.10	.20
BDW63E066U Our Beginnings U	.12	.25
BDW63E067U My Bushido! U	.12	.25
BDW63E068CR A Sparkly Smile CLR	.25	.50
BDW63E069CC Let's Sing CC	.15	.30
BDW63E070CC Serious Survivor CC	.15	.30
BDW63E071CC The One and Only Me CC	.15	.30
BDW63E074R Secret Spot Arisa Ichigawa R	.20	.40
BDW63E075R Teatime with the Band Ako Udagawa R	.20	.40
BDW63E076R I'll Stay Up This Time Chisato Shirasagi R	.20	.40
BDW63E077R Sharing Something with You Eve Wakamiya R	.20	.40
BDW63E078R This Time, I Will Sayo Hikawa R	.20	.40
BDW63E079R Seeing Rabbits Tae Hanazono R	.20	.40
BDW63E080R Tears Overflowing Yukina Minato R	.20	.40
BDW63E081R Determined Cries Rinko Shirokane R	.20	.40
BDW63E082U A Real Challenge Lisa Imai U	.12	.25
BDW63E083U ... H-Hello? Rinko Shirokane U	.12	.25
BDW63E084U Ugh, Seriously...? Arisa Ichigaya U	.12	.25
BDW63E085U The Coolest in the World! Ako Udagawa U	.12	.25
BDW63E086U No Way Except Forward Tae Hanazono U	.12	.25
BDW63E087U Dense Cookies Sayo Hikawa U	.12	.25
BDW63E088C Serious Mind Eve Wakamiya C	.10	.20
BDW63E089C My First Pair of Cat Ears Yukina Minato C	.10	.20
BDW63E090C Bunny Strategy Tae Hanazono C	.10	.20
BDW63E091C Ice Cream In Summer Sayo Hikawa C	.10	.20
BDW63E092C Protective Gaze Yukina Minato C	.10	.20
BDW63E093C Quietly Worrying Rinko Shirokane C	.10	.20
BDW63E094C Arisa In Wonderland Arisa Ichigaya C	.10	.20
BDW63E095C A Crucial Member Lisa Imai C	.10	.20
BDW63E096C Relaxing With Friends Ako Udagawa C	.10	.20
BDW63E097U Teardrops and Rainfall U	.12	.25
BDW63E098U Lisa-like Lyrics U	.12	.25
BDW63E099CR Temporary Club Member CLR	.25	.50
BDW63E100CC Making Cookies CC	.15	.30

2019 Weiss Schwarz Batman Ninja

BNJSX01004R Joker: Joke's On You! R	.20	.40
BNJSX01005R Joker: Happy-Go-Lucky R	.20	.40
BNJSX01006R Joker: Primal Pleasures R	.20	.40
BNJSX01007R Poison Ivy: Turning the Tables R	.20	.40
BNJSX01008R Joker: Tricks up the Sleeve R	.20	.40
BNJSX01009R Deathstroke Castle R	.20	.40
BNJSX01010R Joker: Nemesis R	.20	.40
BNJSX01011R Joker Balloon R	.20	.40
BNJSX01012R Poison Ivy R	.20	.40
BNJSX01013U Penguin: Weaponized Wagasa U	.12	.25
BNJSX01014U Deathstroke U	.12	.25
BNJSX01015U Two-Face: Coxswained by the Coin U	.12	.25
BNJSX01016U Lord Joker U	.12	.25
BNJSX01017U Joker: Stealing the Limelight U	.12	.25
BNJSX01018U Joker: Sadistic U	.12	.25
BNJSX01019C Poison Ivy Castle C	.10	.20
BNJSX01020C Bane C	.10	.20
BNJSX01021C Joker: Samurai Swordfight C	.10	.20
BNJSX01022C Joker: Battle on the Big Boat C	.10	.20
BNJSX01023C Penguin Castle C	.10	.20
BNJSX01024C Joker: Amnesia? C	.10	.20
BNJSX01025C Penguin C	.10	.20
BNJSX01026C Deathstroke: Power Struggle C	.10	.20
BNJSX01027C Two-Face Castle C	.10	.20
BNJSX01028U Unyielding Fortitude U	.12	.25
BNJSX01029U Rock and a Hard Place U	.12	.25
BNJSX01030U Efflorescence U	.12	.25
BNJSX01031U Exploding Barrel U	.12	.25
BNJSX01032CR Maniacal Feudal Lord CLR	.25	.50
BNJSX01033CC Fusion of the Felons CC	.15	.30
BNJSX01034CC Vivification CC	.15	.30
BNJSX01035CC Coin Toss CC	.15	.30
BNJSX01039R Harley Quinn: Status Report R	.20	.40
BNJSX01040R Alfred R	.20	.40
BNJSX01041R Robin R	.20	.40
BNJSX01042R Harley Quinn: Battle on the Big Boat R	.20	.40
BNJSX01043R Red Hood: Tea Ceremony R	.20	.40

BNJSX01044R Harley Quinn: Mighty Hammer R .20 .40
BNJSX01045U Red Hood: Rooted Rancor U .12 .25
BNJSX01046U Giant Monkey U .12 .25
BNJSX01047U Harley Quinn: Party in the Clouds U .12 .25
BNJSX01048C Alfred: Dutiful Butler C .10 .20
BNJSX01049C Monkey Horde C .10 .20
BNJSX01050C Robin: Reluctant Adieu C .10 .20
BNJSX01051C Red Robin C .10 .20
BNJSX01052C Harley Quinn: Amnesia? C .10 .20
BNJSX01053C Red Robin: Battle on the Big Boat C .10 .20
BNJSX01054C Harley Quinn: Doctor Quinzel C .10 .20
BNJSX01055C Red Robin: Tea Ceremony C .10 .20
BNJSX01056C Harley Quinn: Bombs Away! C .10 .20
BNJSX01057U Monkey Flute U .12 .25
BNJSX01058U It Was a Disguise! U .12 .25
BNJSX01059CR Trigger Happy CLR .25 .50
BNJSX01060CC Bat Swarm CC .15 .30
BNJSX01061CC Delirious Damsel CC .15 .30
BNJSX01062CC Gunslinger CC .15 .30
BNJSX01067R Batman: Missionary Disguise R .20 .40
BNJSX01068R Catwoman: Sly Deal R .20 .40
BNJSX01069R Batman: Information Extraction R .20 .40
BNJSX01070R Eian: Bat Clan Leader R .20 .40
BNJSX01071R Catwoman: Catfight R .20 .40
BNJSX01072R Batman: Blast From the Past R .20 .40
BNJSX01073R Catwoman: Unimpressed R .20 .40
BNJSX01074R Batman: Batmobile R .20 .40
BNJSX01075U Batman: Ancient Grappling Hook U .12 .25
BNJSX01076U Nightwing: Tea Ceremony U .12 .25
BNJSX01077U Gorilla Grood: Assembling the Pieces U .12 .25
BNJSX01078aU Bat Clan of Hida A U .12 .25
BNJSX01078bU Bat Clan of Hida B U .12 .25
BNJSX01078cU Bat Clan of Hida C U .12 .25
BNJSX01078dU Bat Clan of Hida D U .12 .25
BNJSX01079U Catwoman: Back to the Present U .12 .25
BNJSX01080U Batman: The Final Showdown U .12 .25
BNJSX01081U Catwoman: Beguiling Maiden U .12 .25
BNJSX01082U Batman: Batcycle U .12 .25
BNJSX01083U Gorilla Grodd: Battle on the Big Boat U .12 .25
BNJSX01084U Batman: Batwing U .12 .25
BNJSX01085C Batman: Sinking Ship C .10 .20
BNJSX01086C Catwoman: Battle on the Big Boat C .10 .20
BNJSX01087C Gorilla Grodd: Decoy C .10 .20
BNJSX01088C Eian: Battle on the Big Boat C .10 .20
BNJSX01089C Nightwing: Coordinated Assault C .10 .20
BNJSX01090C Armored Batman C .10 .20
BNJSX01091C Batman: Charitable Dealings C .10 .20
BNJSX01092C Batman: Infiltration C .10 .20
BNJSX01093C Catwoman: Surprise! C .10 .20
BNJSX01094C Nightwing C .10 .20
BNJSX01095U Donning the Mask U .12 .25
BNJSX01096U Quake Engine U .12 .25
BNJSX01097CR The Dark Knight CLR .25 .50
BNJSX01098CR Your Opponent's Right Here! CLR .25 .50
BNJSX01099CC Anachronistic Gadgetry CC .15 .30
BNJSX01100CC Elusive Kitty C .10 .20

2019 Weiss Schwarz Batman Ninja Trial Deck

BNJSX01T07TD All-Out Attack CC .15 .30

2019 Weiss Schwarz Cardcaptor Sakura Clear Card

CCSWX01005R Sakura: Sudden Showers R .15 .40
CCSWX01006R Sakura: Whipping Up a Storm R .20 .40
CCSWX01007R Sakura: Dexterous R .20 .40
CCSWX01008R Sakura: Not Very Effective R .20 .40
CCSWX01009R Sakura Kinomoto R .20 .40
CCSWX01010R Sakura: Lost in the Labyrinth R .20 .40
CCSWX01011R Toya: Concerned Big Brother R .20 .40
CCSWX01012U Cardcaptor Sakura: GRAVITATION U .12 .25
CCSWX01013U Tomoyo: Ever Ready U .12 .25
CCSWX01014aU Sakura: Middle School Life A U .12 .25
CCSWX01014bU Sakura: Middle School Life B U .12 .25
CCSWX01014cU Sakura: Middle School Life C U .12 .25
CCSWX01014dU Sakura: Middle School Life D U .12 .25
CCSWX01015aU Toya: Mean Big Brother A U .12 .25
CCSWX01015bU Toya: Mean Big Brother B U .12 .25
CCSWX01016U Sonomi Daidouji U .12 .25
CCSWX01017U Rika Sasaki U .12 .25
CCSWX01018C Takashi Yamazaki C .10 .20
CCSWX01019aC Kinomoto Family A C .10 .20
CCSWX01019bC Kinomoto Family B C .10 .20
CCSWX01019cC Kinomoto Family C C .10 .20
CCSWX01020C Akiho: Flower Viewing C .10 .20
CCSWX01021C Naoko: Flower Viewing C .10 .20
CCSWX01022C Sakura: Flower Viewing C .10 .20
CCSWX01023C Tomoyo: Flower Viewing C .10 .20
CCSWX01024C Chiharu Mihara C .10 .20
CCSWX01025C Syaoran: Flower Viewing C .10 .20
CCSWX01026C Sakura: Elemetary School Play C .10 .20
CCSWX01027U Speaking of Which... U .12 .25
CCSWX01028U Rare Cheesecake Recipe U .12 .25
CCSWX01029U Clear Card: GALE U .12 .25
CCSWX01030CR Lunch Break CLR .25 .50
CCSWX01031CC Flower Viewing CC .15 .30
CCSWX01032CC Release! GALE! CC .15 .30
CCSWX01035R Sakura: Pure White Dress R .20 .40
CCSWX01036R Sakura: Stunned R .20 .40
CCSWX01037R Syaoran: Sword Summoning R .20 .40
CCSWX01038U Syaoran & Sakura U .12 .25
CCSWX01039U Meiling Li U .12 .25
CCSWX01040U Sakura: Aquarium Date U .12 .25
CCSWX01041U Syaoran: Aquarium Date U .12 .25
CCSWX01042U Sakura: Befriending the Card U .12 .25
CCSWX01043U Syaoran U .12 .25
CCSWX01044C Sakura: Not a Polyglot C .10 .20
CCSWX01045C Syaoran: Beloved Bento C .10 .20
CCSWX01046C Nakuru Akizuki C .10 .20
CCSWX01047C Eriol Hiiragizawa C .10 .20
CCSWX01048C Cardcaptor Sakura: FLIGHT C .10 .20
CCSWX01049C Spinny C .10 .20
CCSWX01050C Syaoran: Ice God, Come Forth! C .10 .20
CCSWX01051C Kaho Mizuki C .10 .20
CCSWX01052U Treasured Teddy U .12 .25
CCSWX01053U Clear Card: RECORD U .12 .25
CCSWX01054CR Release! RECORD! CLR .25 .50
CCSWX01055CC Intertwining Hearts CC .15 .30
CCSWX01056CC Fire God, Come Forth! CC .15 .30
CCSWX01059R Tomoyo R .20 .40
CCSWX01060R Sakura: Slip of the Tongue R .20 .40
CCSWX01061R Tomoyo: Best Friend R .20 .40
CCSWX01062R Kero: Insatiable Hunger R .20 .40
CCSWX01063R Cardcaptor Sakura: LUCID R .20 .40
CCSWX01064R Kero: Beast Mode R .20 .40
CCSWX01065U Sakura: Invisible Books U .12 .25
CCSWX01066U Sakura: In the Torrential Flame U .12 .25
CCSWX01067U Tomoyo: Carefree Camerawoman U .12 .25
CCSWX01068C Sakura: Deja Vu C .10 .20
CCSWX01069C Kero: Plushie Mode C .10 .20
CCSWX01070C Sakura: Caught Off-Guard C .10 .20
CCSWX01071C Sakura: Irresistible Pull C .10 .20
CCSWX01072U Secure! U .12 .25
CCSWX01073U Clear Card: REFLECT U .12 .25
CCSWX01074CR Release! REFLECT! CLR .25 .50
CCSWX01075CC Hunger Overwhelming CC .15 .30
CCSWX01076CC Dress Designer's Delight CC .15 .30
CCSWX01079R Sakura: Abashed R .20 .40
CCSWX01080R Akiho: Just Visiting R .20 .40
CCSWX01081R Yue R .20 .40
CCSWX01082R Yukito: Just Visiting R .20 .40
CCSWX01083R Sakura: Choices, Choices R .20 .40
CCSWX01084R Yukito: Dual Identity R .20 .40
CCSWX01085U Yukito & Toya U .12 .25
CCSWX01086U Sakura: Lunch Break U .12 .25
CCSWX01087U Akiho: New Transfer Student U .12 .25
CCSWX01088U Sakura: Hospitable U .12 .25
CCSWX01089C Cardcaptor Sakura: AQUA C .10 .20
CCSWX01090C Kaito: Warm Invitation C .10 .20
CCSWX01091C Momo C .10 .20
CCSWX01092C Sakura: A New Key C .10 .20
CCSWX01093C Sakura: Topsy-Turvy C .10 .20
CCSWX01094C Yuna D. Kaito C .10 .20
CCSWX01095C Kaito & Akiho C .10 .20
CCSWX01096U Clear Card: SIEGE U .12 .25
CCSWX01097U Mysterious Hooded Figure U .12 .25
CCSWX01098CR Release! SIEGE! CLR .25 .50
CCSWX01099CC Otherworldly Encounter CC .15 .30
CCSWX01100CC Birds of a Feather CC .15 .30

2019 Weiss Schwarz Fate-stay Night Heaven's Feel

FSS64E003R Entrusted Arm of Archer, Shirou R .20 .40
FSS64E004R Reaching for the Grail, Saber R .20 .40
FSS64E005R Sword Shrouded by Wind, Saber R .20 .40
FSS64E006U Blushing, Shirou U .12 .25
FSS64E007U Savage King of Heroes, Gilgamesh U .12 .25
FSS64E008U As a Master, Shirou U .12 .25
FSS64E009U Rain Shirou U .12 .25
FSS64E010U Injury's Status, Shirou U .12 .25
FSS64E011U What I Can Do, Shirou U .12 .25
FSS64E012U Entrusted, Shirou U .12 .25
FSS64E013C Friendly Teacher, Taiga C .10 .20
FSS64E014C Foreign Acquaintance? Saber C .10 .20
FSS64E015C Student Council President, Issei C .10 .20
FSS64E016C Strong Sense of Justice, Shirou C .10 .20
FSS64E017C Archery Club President, Ayako C .10 .20
FSS64E018C Golden Benevolence, Gilgamesh C .10 .20
FSS64E019C Smile Lit by Sunrise, Saber C .10 .20
FSS64E020R A Servant's Power Sealed Within R .20 .40
FSS64E021CR Strike Air CLR .25 .50
FSS64E022CC Solitary Return CC .15 .30
FSS64E027R Rider Attacking R .20 .40
FSS64E028R Peaceful Morning, Sakura R .20 .40
FSS64E029R Distortion of Daily Life, Sakura R .20 .40
FSS64E030R Flexible Physique, Rider R .20 .40
FSS64E031R FLUFFY, Sakura R .20 .40
FSS64E032R Protection from Arrows Lancer R .20 .40
FSS64E033R Enchanting Beauty, Rider R .20 .40
FSS64E034U Sakura Waiting to Return Together U .12 .25
FSS64E035U Agonizing Decision, Shinji U .12 .25
FSS64E036U True Intentions, Rider U .12 .25
FSS64E037U Master's Capability, Rider U .12 .25
FSS64E038U Rain Sakura U .12 .25
FSS64E039U Anti-Heroic Knight, Rider U .12 .25
FSS64E040U Final Command Spell, Sakura U .12 .25
FSS64E041U Ulster's Hero, Lancer U .12 .25
FSS64E042C First-Time Substitute Master, Shinji C .10 .20
FSS64E043C Study Mode, Sakura C .10 .20
FSS64E044C Helping Out at the Emiya Household, Sakura C .10 .20
FSS64E045C Battle-Hungry Smile, Lancer C .10 .20
FSS64E046C Servant Chase Lancer C .10 .20
FSS64E047C Monstrous Strength Rider C .10 .20
FSS64E048C Warrior with Backbone, Lancer C .10 .20
FSS64E049C Having a Nightmare, Sakura C .10 .20
FSS64E050C Mysterious Knight, Rider C .10 .20
FSS64E051U Spellbook of Fake Authority U .12 .25
FSS64E052CR Storytime CLR .25 .50
FSS64E053CR Mystic Eyes of Petrification CLR .25 .50
FSS64E054CC I'm starved! CC .15 .30
FSS64E055CC Fate-Changing Blow CC .15 .30
FSS64E059R Variety of Fighting Styles, Archer R .20 .40
FSS64E060R Dreamt of Moment, Rin R .20 .40
FSS64E061R Black Shadow R .20 .40
FSS64E062R Awkward Relationship, Rin R .20 .40
FSS64E063R HEROIC, Rin & Archer R .20 .40
FSS64E064R Overwhelming Strength, Saber Alter R .20 .40
FSS64E065R Straightforward Sense of Justice, Rin R .20 .40
FSS64E066U Shocked Expression, Rin U .12 .25
FSS64E067U Standing By in the Rain, Archer U .12 .25
FSS64E068U Decisive Judgement, Archer U .12 .25
FSS64E069U Stellar Offense and Defense, Saber Alter U .12 .25
FSS64E070C Beauty Feigning Innocence, Rin C .10 .20
FSS64E071C Revealed Face, Saber Alter C .10 .20
FSS64E072C Battle Stance, Archer C .10 .20
FSS64E073C Knight Clothed in Black, Saber Alter C .10 .20
FSS64E074C Offering Protection, Rin C .10 .20
FSS64E075C Pair of Swords, Archer C .10 .20
FSS64E076C Making Plans, Rin C .10 .20
FSS64E077U Sakura's Ribbon U .12 .25
FSS64E078U Shadow that Engulfs Heroic Spirits U .12 .25
FSS64E079CR Distance Separating the Two CLR .25 .50
FSS64E080CC Ultimate Choice CC .15 .30
FSS64E081CC Excalibur Morgan CC .15 .30
FSS64E083R Dirty Tactics, True Assasin R .20 .40
FSS64E084R One of Many Faces, Illyasviel R .20 .40
FSS64E085R Mad Warrior's Howl, Berserker R .20 .40
FSS64E086R Fearless Smile, Illyasviel R .20 .40
FSS64E087R Valorous Warrior, Berserker R .20 .40
FSS64E088U Rule Breaker, Caster U .12 .25
FSS64E089U Spectating the Battle, Illyasviel U .12 .25
FSS64E090U Tenacious, Berserker U .12 .25
FSS64E091U One of Three Great Families, Illyasviel U .12 .25
FSS64E092C Unsettling Warning, Illyasviel C .10 .20
FSS64E093C Easygoing Swordsman, Assassin C .10 .20
FSS64E094C 5th Holy Grail War's Overseer Kirei C .10 .20
FSS64E095C Masked Hitman, True Assassin C .10 .20
FSS64E096C Fierce Presence, Berserker C .10 .20
FSS64E097U Kotomine's Meal U .12 .25
FSS64E098CC Cutthroat Battle CC .15 .30
FSS64E099CC Winter's Lorelei CC .15 .30
FSS64E100CC Zabaniya CC .15 .30

2019 Weiss Schwarz Gun Gale Online

GGOS59E004R Affiliated Girls' High School Rhythmic Gymnastics Club, Shiori R .20 .40
GGOS59E005R Interested in VR, Karen R .20 .40
GGOS59E006R Affiliated Girls' High School Rhythmic Gymnastics Club Leader, Saki R .20 .40
GGOS59E007R Question About Chances of Winning, LLENN R .20 .40
GGOS59E008R Craving for Sweets Too! Saki & Milana R .20 .40
GGOS59E009R Taking Every Last Ounce of Courage, LLENN R .20 .40
GGOS59E010R Boss of SHINC, Eva R .20 .40
GGOS59E011U SHINC, Sophie U .12 .25
GGOS59E012U Narrow Escape from Death, LLENN U .12 .25
GGOS59E013U Affiliated Girls' High School Rhythmic Gymnastics Club, Milana U .12 .25
GGOS59E014U Thoroughness of Small, LLENN U .12 .25
GGOS59E015U Hunch of a Reunion, Karen U .12 .25
GGOS59E016U SHINC, Roza U .12 .25
GGOS59E017U SHINC, Toma U .12 .25
GGOS59E018U Lurking in a Suitcase LLENN U .12 .25
GGOS59E019C Poncho Style, LLENN C .10 .20
GGOS59E020C SHINC, Tanya C .10 .20
GGOS59E021C Last Battle, LLENN C .10 .20
GGOS59E022C Affiliated Girls' High School Rhythmic Gymnastics Club, Moe C .10 .20
GGOS59E023C All Set! LLENN C .10 .20
GGOS59E024C SHINC, Anna C .10 .20
GGOS59E025C Affiliated Girls' High School Rhythmic Gymnastics Club, Risa C .10 .20
GGOS59E026C Operation Sweets, Eva C .10 .20
GGOS59E027C Affiliated Girls' High School Rhythmic Gymnastics Club, Kana C .10 .20
GGOS59E028C Slip into Pink, LLENN C .10 .20
GGOS59E029U Plasma Grenade U .12 .25
GGOS59E030U Degtyaryov Anti-Tank Rifle U .12 .25
GGOS59E031CR Word of Honor CLR .25 .50
GGOS59E032CC Course of the Last Battle CC .15 .30
GGOS59E033CC Operation Sweets A Major Success! CC .15 .30
GGOS59E034CC Serious Battle CC .15 .30
GGOS59E039R Beautiful Beloved Weapon, Fukaziroh R .20 .40
GGOS59E040R Beloved Weapons Don't Betray LLENN R .20 .40
GGOS59E041R Bold Tactic, Fukaziroh R .20 .40
GGOS59E042R Super Haphazard, LLENN R .20 .40
GGOS59E043R Tough Partner, Fukaziroh R .20 .40
GGOS59E044R Feeling of Uneasiness, LLENN R .20 .40
GGOS59E045R Best Tactic Up Their Sleeves, Fukaziroh R .20 .40
GGOS59E046R Lively Assault, LLENN R .20 .40
GGOS59E047U Altruist, Clarence U .12 .25
GGOS59E048U Bond with P-chan, LLENN U .12 .25
GGOS59E049U Keeping In Check At Gunpoint, Fukaziroh U .12 .25
GGOS59E050U Supporting Fire, Fukaziroh U .12 .25
GGOS59E051U Ability of a Champion, LLENN U .12 .25
GGOS59E052C Magazines & A Kiss, LLENN U .12 .25
GGOS59E053C LLENN Piling Up Experience C .10 .20
GGOS59E054C Way To Fight With a Petite Figure, LLENN C .10 .20
GGOS59E055C Hidden Blade, Fukaziroh C .10 .20
GGOS59E056C Ice Cream Before Battle, Miyu C .10 .20
GGOS59E057C Searching for Comrades, Karen C .10 .20
GGOS59E058C With My Beloved Weapons, Fukaziroh C .10 .20
GGOS59E059C Pinpoint Induction, LLENN C .10 .20
GGOS59E060C Helper from ALO, Fukaziroh C .10 .20
GGOS59E061C Real Life Close Friends, Karen & Miyu C .10 .20
GGOS59E062U Chatting P-chan U .12 .25
GGOS59E063U Multiple Grenade Launcher U .12 .25
GGOS59E064U Emergency Med Kit U .12 .25
GGOS59E065CR Don't Underestimate A Fairy! CLR .25 .50
GGOS59E066CR Even By Gnawing Through The Throat CLR .25 .50
GGOS59E067CC How Adorable... CC .15 .30
GGOS59E068CC Cut! Kick! CC .15 .30
GGOS59E072R Excellent Combat Skill, M R .20 .40
GGOS59E073R In Coma, Pitohui R .20 .40
GGOS59E074R Superb Geographical Sense, M R .20 .40
GGOS59E075R Look of a Sadist, Pitohui R .20 .40
GGOS59E076R Setting the Stage, M R .20 .40
GGOS59E077R Gun Enthusiast, Pitohui R .20 .40
GGOS59E078R Origin of Name, M R .20 .40
GGOS59E079U Boring Tactic, Pitohui U .12 .25
GGOS59E080U Declaration of War, Pitohui U .12 .25
GGOS59E081U Dissatisfied Pitohui U .12 .25
GGOS59E082U Leader of MMTM, David U .12 .25
GGOS59E083U Being Outnumbered? Pitohui U .12 .25
GGOS59E084U Marksmanship, M U .12 .25
GGOS59E085C Imminent Death, M C .10 .20
GGOS59E086C Real World Circumstances, Goushi C .10 .20
GGOS59E087C Purging the Traitor, Pitohui C .10 .20
GGOS59E088C Machine Guns are FUN! ZEMAL C .10 .20
GGOS59E089C KKHC Bright Flower, Shirley C .10 .20
GGOS59E090C Fathomed Act, Elza C .10 .20
GGOS59E091C Fright & Betrayal, M C .10 .20
GGOS59E092C Excessive Excitement, Pitohui C .10 .20
GGOS59E093C Incensed Pitohui C .10 .20
GGOS59E094U Satellite Scan U .12 .25
GGOS59E095U Muramasa F9 U .12 .25
GGOS59E096U Shield of M U .12 .25
GGOS59E097CR Resurrection of the Devil CLR .25 .50
GGOS59E098CC Pleasure in Massacre CC .15 .30
GGOS59E099CC Strategy of the Cautious Type CC .15 .30
GGOS59E100CC A Love at the Risk of One's Life CC .15 .30

2019 Weiss Schwarz No Game No Life

NGLS58E004R Rebirthed World, Sora R .20 .40
NGLS58E005R Detected Deceit, Sora R .20 .40
NGLS58E006R Existence-Robbing Game, Sora R .20 .40
NGLS58E007R Cold Reading, Sora R .20 .40
NGLS58E008U First Move, Sora U .12 .25
NGLS58E009U Election Battle Winner, Sora U .12 .25
NGLS58E010U Adolescent Sora U .12 .25
NGLS58E011U Declaration of War, Sora U .12 .25
NGLS58E012C Communication Error, Sora C .10 .20
NGLS58E013C Divulging the Trick, Sora C .10 .20
NGLS58E014C Creator of Disboard, Tet C .10 .20
NGLS58E015C Objection! Sora C .10 .20
NGLS58E016C Memory Sharing, Sora C .10 .20
NGLS58E017U Rock-Paper-Scissors U .12 .25
NGLS58E018U BLANK Doesn't Know Defeat U .12 .25
NGLS58E019CR Overthrowing A God CLR .25 .50
NGLS58E020CC Checkmate CC .15 .30
NGLS58E021CC Super Healthy Space CC .15 .30
NGLS58E025R Innocent, Izuna R .20 .40
NGLS58E026R Tantrum, Kurami R .20 .40
NGLS58E027R Ino Hatsuse R .20 .40
NGLS58E028R Cool Character, Kurami R .20 .40
NGLS58E029R Eastern Federation Ambassador, Izuna R .20 .40
NGLS58E030R Precious Presence, Fil R .20 .40
NGLS58E031U Limits of Endurance, Kurami U .12 .25
NGLS58E032U Grudge of Antiquity, Fil U .12 .25
NGLS58E033U Warbeasts' Representative, Shrine Priestess U .12 .25
NGLS58E034U Little Warbeast Girl, Izuna U .12 .25
NGLS58E035U Bathing, Kurami U .12 .25
NGLS58E036U Power Beyond Physical Limits, Izuna U .12 .25
NGLS58E037U Inherently Innocent, Izuna U .12 .25
NGLS58E038U Obsession With Victory, Izuna U .12 .25
NGLS58E039U Unrelenting Assault, Izuna U .12 .25
NGLS58E040C Humanity's Potential, Fil U .12 .25
NGLS58E041C Superior Magic User, Fil C .10 .20
NGLS58E042C Memory Sharing, Kurami C .10 .20
NGLS58E043C Elf Conspirator, Fil C .10 .20
NGLS58E044C Adolescent Kurami C .10 .20
NGLS58E045C Humanity's Potential, Kurami C .10 .20
NGLS58E046U Peas in a Pod U .12 .25
NGLS58E047CR The Promise Long Ago CLR .25 .50
NGLS58E048CC The Final Piece CC .15 .30
NGLS58E049CC Docile Reaction CC .15 .30
NGLS58E050CC Blood Destruction CC .15 .30

NGLS58E053R Commonsensical Hard Worker, Steph R .20 .40
NGLS58E054R Knowledge Esteeming Race, Jibril R .20 .40
NGLS58E055R Only One Game, Jibril R .20 .40
NGLS58E056R Pride of Power, Jibril R .20 .40
NGLS58E057R A Gift from the Former King, Steph R .20 .40
NGLS58E058R Chief of Elkia's Domestic Affairs, Steph R .20 .40
NGLS58E059U True Form of the Game, Jibril U .12 .25
NGLS58E060U Eureka! Steph U .12 .25
NGLS58E061U Former King's Granddaughter, Steph U .12 .25
NGLS58E062U Former Council of 18 Wings, Jibril U .12 .25
NGLS58E063U Euphoric Mood, Steph U .12 .25
NGLS58E064U Overflowing Self-Confidence, Jibril U .12 .25
NGLS58E065C Destroyed Steph C .10 .20
NGLS58E066C Unstoppable Love, Steph C .10 .20
NGLS58E067C Immense Curiosity, Jibril C .10 .20
NGLS58E068C Memories of Bygone Days, Jibril C .10 .20
NGLS58E069C Lacking Presence, Steph C .10 .20
NGLS58E070C Flugel in the Library, Jibril C .10 .20
NGLS58E071C Loyalty and Devotion, Jibril C .10 .20
NGLS58E072C Form of the Defeated, Steph C .10 .20
NGLS58E073R Materialization Word Chain R .20 .40
NGLS58E074U Key of Hope U .12 .25
NGLS58E075U The Man Ridiculed as a Foolish King U .12 .25
NGLS58E076CR Expert at Getting Mixed In CLR .25 .50
NGLS58E077CC All of the Trust in Humanity CC .15 .30
NGLS58E078CC True Power of Flugels CC .15 .30
NGLS58E079CC That Thing Called Death CC .15 .30
NGLS58E082R Prodigy of Ingenuity, Shiro R .20 .40
NGLS58E083R Only We Can Know, Shiro R .20 .40
NGLS58E084R The Ten Pledges, Tet R .20 .40
NGLS58E085R Adolescent War God, Shiro R .20 .40
NGLS58E086R Rebirthed World, Shiro R .20 .40
NGLS58E087U Word Chain Battle, Shiro U .12 .25
NGLS58E088U Alone in the Morning, Shiro U .12 .25
NGLS58E089U Sudden Surprise Strike, Shiro U .12 .25
NGLS58E090C What's This? Shiro C .10 .20
NGLS58E091C Reunion with Brother, Shiro C .10 .20
NGLS58E092C Psyche Breakdown, Shiro C .10 .20
NGLS58E093C Boring Challenge, Shiro C .10 .20
NGLS58E094C Adolescent Shiro C .10 .20
NGLS58E095C Trophy, Shiro C .10 .20
NGLS58E096U Intrinsic Genius U .12 .25
NGLS58E097C Accelerated Alacrity C .10 .20
NGLS58E098CR Welcome, Gamer CLR .25 .50
NGLS58E099CC Affection-Loaded Piece CC .15 .30
NGLS58E100CC Promise Between the Two CC .15 .30

2019 Weiss Schwarz Rascal Does Not Dream of Bunny Girl Senpai

SBYW64E003 Pent-Up Feelings, Nodoka Toyohama R .20 .40
SBYW64E004 Talented Individual, Mai Sakurajima R .20 .40
SBYW64E005 Surfaced Feelings, Mai Sakurajima R .20 .40
SBYW64E006 Sunset Sky, Mai Sakurajima R .20 .40
SBYW64E007 Brother Complex, Kaede Azusagawa R .20 .40
SBYW64E008 Longing and Respect, Nodoka Toyohama R .20 .40
SBYW64E009 Indoors Preference, Kaede Azusagawa U .12 .25
SBYW64E010 First Steps, Kaede Azusagawa U .12 .25
SBYW64E011 Sisterly Thoughts, Nodoka Toyohama U .12 .25
SBYW64E012 Press Interview, Mai Sakurajima U .12 .25
SBYW64E013 A Strong Impact, Mai Sakurajima U .12 .25
SBYW64E014 Awkward Kindness, Sakuta Azusagawa C .10 .20
SBYW64E015 Complex Feelings, Mai Sakurajima C .10 .20
SBYW64E016 Embarassed, Mai Sakurajima C .10 .20
SBYW64E017 Secret of Lost Memories, Mai Sakurajima C .10 .20
SBYW64E018 Crisis as a Sister, Kaede Azusagawa C .10 .20
SBYW64E019 Announcer, Fumika Nanjo C .10 .20
SBYW64E020 Courage to Move On, Kaede Azusagawa C .10 .20
SBYW64E021 Panda Pajamas U .12 .25
SBYW64E022 Secret Treasure U .12 .25
SBYW64E023 A Shot to the Heart CC .15 .30
SBYW64E024 Sister Panic CC .15 .30
SBYW64E025 The Kaede Quest CLR .25 .50
SBYW64E027 Observation Theory, Rio Futaba R .20 .40
SBYW64E028 Clear Blue Skies, Tomoe Koga R .20 .40
SBYW64E029 Phantom Elder Sister, Shoko Makinohara R .20 .40
SBYW64E030 Sunset Sky, Shoko Makinohara R .20 .40
SBYW64E031 Sunset Sky, Rio Futaba R .20 .40
SBYW64E032 Cool and Collected, Rio Futaba R .20 .40
SBYW64E033 Swimsuit, Tomoe Koga R .20 .40
SBYW64E034 Sudden Reunion, Tomoe Koga U .12 .25
SBYW64E035 Laplace's Demon, Tomoe Koga U .12 .25
SBYW64E036 Indirectly Showing Off, Tomoe Koga U .12 .25
SBYW64E037 Scathing Words, Rio Futaba U .12 .25
SBYW64E038 What Lies Ahead, Rio Futaba U .12 .25
SBYW64E039 Lost, Sakuta Azusagawa C .10 .20
SBYW64E040 Two of Myself, Rio Futaba C .10 .20
SBYW64E041 Honest Opinion, Shoko Makinohara C .10 .20
SBYW64E042 Home Visit, Shoko Makinohara C .10 .20
SBYW64E043 Parting in the Rain, Sakuta Azusagawa C .10 .20
SBYW64E044 Memories That Remain, Shoko Makinohara C .10 .20
SBYW64E045 Visiting the Sick, Tomoe Koga C .10 .20
SBYW64E046 First Love's Reason U .12 .25
SBYW64E047 Looping World U .12 .25
SBYW64E048 All the Lies I Have for You CLR .25 .50
SBYW64E049 Shrewd Brainiac CC .15 .30
SBYW64E050 Amongst the Pain in the Rain CC .15 .30
SBYW64E054 Sunset Sky, Nodoka Toyohama R .20 .40
SBYW64E055 Girl Who Loves Her Big Brother, Kaede Azusagawa R .20 .40
SBYW64E056 Welcoming With Nasuno, Kaede Azusagawa R .20 .40
SBYW64E057 Schooling High School Idol, Nodoka Toyohama R .20 .40
SBYW64E058 Self-Loathing, Nodoka Toyohama U .12 .25
SBYW64E059 Paper-Thin Existence, Mai Sakurajima U .12 .25
SBYW64E060 Present? Kaede Azusagawa U .12 .25
SBYW64E061 As a Lover, Mai Sakurajima U .12 .25
SBYW64E062 Rascal, Sakuta Azusagawa U .12 .25
SBYW64E063 Runaway, Nodoka Toyohama U .12 .25
SBYW64E064 Secret of Lost Memories, Nodoka Toyohama C .10 .20
SBYW64E065 Emotions Escalating Quickly, Mai Sakurajima C .10 .20
SBYW64E066 An Adult's Charm, Mai Sakurajima C .10 .20
SBYW64E067 Change of Clothes, Kaede Azusagawa C .10 .20
SBYW64E068 Fluffy Breakfast, Kaede Azusagawa C .10 .20
SBYW64E069 On Set, Mai Sakurajima C .10 .20
SBYW64E070 Confidence to Face Tomorrow, Kaede Azusagawa C .10 .20
SBYW64E071 Scars U .12 .25
SBYW64E072 Feelings That Bind U .12 .25
SBYW64E073 The World Without You CLR .25 .50
SBYW64E074 A Sparkling Stage CC .15 .30
SBYW64E075 Together With Nasuno CC .15 .30
SBYW64E080 Unspoken Significance, Shoko Makinohara R .20 .40
SBYW64E081 Love's Frustrations, Rio Futaba R .20 .40
SBYW64E082 Sunset Sky, Tomoe Koga R .20 .40
SBYW64E083 Wholesome Middle School Student, Shoko Makinohara R .20 .40
SBYW64E084 Study Session, Shoko Makinohara U .12 .25
SBYW64E085 Corrupt Gaze, Tomoe Koga U .12 .25
SBYW64E086 Seized Present, Tomoe Koga U .12 .25
SBYW64E087 Basketball Club, Yuma Kunimi U .12 .25
SBYW64E088 Classmate, Saki Kamisato U .12 .25
SBYW64E089 Together with Hayate, Shoko Makinohara U .12 .25
SBYW64E090 Protective Shadow, Rio Futaba C .10 .20
SBYW64E091 Study Session, Rio Futaba C .10 .20
SBYW64E092 Back From Shopping, Rio Futaba C .10 .20
SBYW64E093 Unconditional Support, Shoko Makinohara C .10 .20
SBYW64E094 Roundabout Solution, Sakuta Azusagawa C .10 .20
SBYW64E095 Responding Unenthusiastically, Rio Futaba C .10 .20
SBYW64E096 Mind-Reader? Tomoe Koga C .10 .20
SBYW64E097 Nasuno and Hayate U .12 .25
SBYW64E098 Adolescence Paradox CLR .25 .50
SBYW64E099 Returning World, Unreturned Feelings CC .15 .30
SBYW64E100 Blue-Filled Vision CC .15 .30

2019 Weiss Schwarz Re Zero Starting Life in Another World Vol.2

RZS55E003R Bullish Personality, Felt R .20 .40
RZS55E004R Value of the Insignia, Felt R .20 .40
RZS55E005R Unacceptable Situation, Felt R .20 .40
RZS55E006R Petelgeuse Romanee-Conti R .20 .40
RZS55E007U Posture in the Face of Enemy, Felt U .12 .25
RZS55E008U Unseen Hand U .12 .25
RZS55E009U Professional Fur Craftsman, Subaru U .12 .25
RZS55E010U Unseen Threat, Petelgeuse U .12 .25
RZS55E011U Cool Gesture, Reinhard U .12 .25
RZS55E012U Reunion at the Royal Castle, Reinhard U .12 .25
RZS55E013U Stout-Hearted Young Lady, Felt U .12 .25
RZS55E014C United Trust, Julius C .10 .20
RZS55E015C Ten Fingers C .10 .20
RZS55E016C Beauty Dressed as a Man, Crusch C .10 .20
RZS55E017C Royal Guard Knight, Ferris C .10 .20
RZS55E018C Moment of Joy, Ferris C .10 .20
RZS55E019C Face the Crisis, Wilhelm C .10 .20
RZS55E020C Fearless Smile, Petelgeuse C .10 .20
RZS55E021C Shout of Victory, Crusch C .10 .20
RZS55E022U Rental Goa U .12 .25
RZS55E023CR I'll Do Your Royal Election CLR .25 .50
RZS55E024CC Proof of Love CC .15 .30
RZS55E025CC Sword Strike CC .15 .30
RZS55E029R Sister's Crisis, Ram R .20 .40
RZS55E030R Studies, Ram R .20 .40
RZS55E031R Maid Sisters, Rem & Ram R .20 .40
RZS55E032R Fond of Bubby, Beatrice R .20 .40
RZS55E033R Feeling Irritated, Beatrice R .20 .40
RZS55E034R Look of Amazement, Ram R .20 .40
RZS55E035R Unexpected Mischief, Beatrice R .20 .40
RZS55E036U Demure Reply, Ram U .12 .25
RZS55E037U Frightened Ram U .12 .25
RZS55E038U Assassin from Roswaal Mansion, Ram U .12 .25
RZS55E039U Witch's Scent, Beatrice U .12 .25
RZS55E040U Pouting Beatrice U .12 .25
RZS55E041U Gaze of Contempt, Ram U .12 .25
RZS55E042C Anxious Ram C .10 .20
RZS55E043C Confrontation with Roswaal, Beatrice C .10 .20
RZS55E044C Naked Companionship, Roswaal C .10 .20
RZS55E045C The Twin Maids, Ram C .10 .20
RZS55E046C Stamping Feet Beatrice C .10 .20
RZS55E047C Just Out of the Bath Subaru C .10 .20
RZS55E048C Drill-Hairstyled Girl, Beatrice C .10 .20
RZS55E049C Oni's Blood Relative, Ram C .10 .20
RZS55E050U Source of The Curse U .12 .25
RZS55E051U Forbidden Library U .12 .25
RZS55E052CR Proud of Own Cooking CLR .25 .50
RZS55E053CC Invasion of Witch Cult CC .15 .30
RZS55E054CC Pronouncement of Remaining Life CC .15 .30
RZS55E055CC Secret Private Chamber CC .15 .30
RZS55E061R I'll Teach You Emilia R .20 .40
RZS55E062R Chomp Chomp Puck R .20 .40
RZS55E063R Honest Smile, Rem R .20 .40
RZS55E064R Going to School in a Hurry, Rem R .20 .40
RZS55E065R The Happy Roswaal Mansion Family, Emilia R .20 .40
RZS55E066R Charming Servants, Ram & Rem R .20 .40
RZS55E067R Gentle Appearance, Emilia R .20 .40
RZS55E068R Beloved's Guidance, Rem R .20 .40
RZS55E069R Furious Questioning, Emilia R .20 .40
RZS55E070R Steadfast Principles, Emilia R .20 .40
RZS55E071R The Happy Roswaal Mansion Family, Rem R .20 .40
RZS55E071SSR The Happy Roswaal Mansion Family, Rem R .20 .40
RZS55E072U Working with Subaru, Rem U .12 .25
RZS55E073U Second Morning Emilia U .12 .25
RZS55E074U About the Future, Rem U .12 .25
RZS55E075U Emilia Protecting Felt U .12 .25
RZS55E076U Mad Demon's Strike, Rem U .12 .25
RZS55E077U Capable of Anything, Rem U .12 .25
RZS55E078U White Whale Hunt, Rem U .12 .25
RZS55E079U Farewell, Emilia U .12 .25
RZS55E080U United Trust, Subaru U .12 .25
RZS55E081U Posture of Urgency, Rem U .12 .25
RZS55E082C Oni's Blood Relative, Rem C .10 .20
RZS55E083C Flooding Tears, Emilia C .10 .20
RZS55E084C Megamorph, Puck C .10 .20
RZS55E085C Sudden Departure, Rem C .10 .20
RZS55E086C Unexpected Switching, Emilia C .10 .20
RZS55E087C Kind Elder Sister, Emilia C .10 .20
RZS55E088C Downhearted, Rem C .10 .20
RZS55E089C Lap Pillow Rem C .10 .20
RZS55E090C Frightened Rem C .10 .20
RZS55E091C Magic Analysis, Emilia C .10 .20
RZS55E092C Seemingly Sad Look, Emilia C .10 .20
RZS55E093C The Twin Maids, Rem C .10 .20
RZS55E094U Metia U .12 .25
RZS55E095U Memory of Atonement U .12 .25
RZS55E096CR Just the Two of Us Occasionally CLR .25 .50
RZS55E097CR World's No.1 Hero CLR .25 .50
RZS55E098CC Delightful Special Treatment CC .15 .30
RZS55E099CC Defying Despair CC .15 .30
RZS55E100CC Shocking Scene CC .15 .30

2019 Weiss Schwarz Revue Starlight

RSLS56E004R My Own Shine, Nana Daiba R .20 .40
RSLS56E005R Full of Fighting Spirit, Futaba Isurugi R .20 .40
RSLS56E006R My Own Shine, Kaoruko Hanayagi R .20 .40
RSLS56E007R No Other Friend, Futaba & Kaoruko R .20 .40
RSLS56E008R Good at Cooking, Nana Daiba R .20 .40
RSLS56E009R Truth Behind Words, Kaoruko Hanayagi R .20 .40
RSLS56E010R My Own Shine, Futaba Isurugi R .20 .40
RSLS56E011U Brimming with Confidence, Kaoruko Hanayagi U .12 .25
RSLS56E012U Confrontation of Companion, Futaba Isurugi U .12 .25
RSLS56E013U Bright Stage, Nana Daiba U .12 .25
RSLS56E014U Leotard Futaba Isurugi U .12 .25
RSLS56E015U Leotard Kaoruko Hanayagi U .12 .25
RSLS56E016U Pointed Sword, Nana Daiba U .12 .25
RSLS56E017U Eternal Stage, Nana Daiba U .12 .25
RSLS56E018C Pajama Party, Nana Daiba C .10 .20
RSLS56E019C Friend's Flight, Futaba Isurugi C .10 .20
RSLS56E020C Giraffe C .10 .20
RSLS56E021C To Be the Very Best, Kaoruko Hanayagi C .10 .20
RSLS56E022C Bana-nice! Nana Daiba C .10 .20
RSLS56E023C Center of Attention, Kaoruko Hanayagi C .10 .20
RSLS56E024C Spectating, Futaba Isurugi C .10 .20
RSLS56E025C Precious Memories, Nana Daiba C .10 .20
RSLS56E026C Spectating, Kaoruko Hanayagi C .10 .20
RSLS56E027C Arguing, Futaba Isurugi C .10 .20
RSLS56E028C Enrollment Invitation, Futaba Isurugi C .10 .20
RSLS56E029U Stubborn Spat U .12 .25
RSLS56E030U After-Party Photo U .12 .25
RSLS56E031CR My Best Self CLR .25 .50
RSLS56E032CC Closest to You CC .15 .30
RSLS56E033CC Night of the Star Festival CC .15 .30
RSLS56E038R Leotard Karen & Hikari R .20 .40
RSLS56E039R Our Own Stage, Mahiru Tsuyuzaki R .20 .40
RSLS56E040R My Own Shine, Hikari Kagura R .20 .40
RSLS56E041R Outstretched Hand, Karen Aijo R .20 .40
RSLS56E042R Two Become One, Karen & Hikari R .20 .40
RSLS56E043R Rebirthed Shine Hikari Kagura R .20 .40
RSLS56E044R Sudden Closeness, Karen & Mahiru R .20 .40
RSLS56E045R Encore, Karen Aijo R .20 .40
RSLS56E046R My Own Shine, Mahiru Tsuyuzaki R .20 .40
RSLS56E047U Time to Relax, Hikari Kagura U .12 .25
RSLS56E048U Stage Girl's Summer, Hikari Kagura U .12 .25
RSLS56E049U Tag, Karen Aijo U .12 .25
RSLS56E050U Begin Cleanup! Mahiru Tsuyuzaki U .12 .25
RSLS56E051U Last Day of Auditions, Hikari Kagura U .12 .25
RSLS56E052U Awaking Mahiru Tsuyuzaki U .12 .25
RSLS56E053U New Chapter, Karen Aijo U .12 .25
RSLS56E054U Hallway-Protecting Goddess, Mahiru Tsuyuzaki U .12 .25
RSLS56E055C Tag, Mahiru Tsuyuzaki C .10 .20
RSLS56E056C New Roommate, Karen Aijo C .10 .20
RSLS56E057C Life in London, Hikari Kagura C .10 .20
RSLS56E058C The Promised Tower Karen Aijo C .10 .20
RSLS56E059C New Roommate, Mahiru Tsuyuzaki C .10 .20
RSLS56E060C Our Promise, Hikari Kagura C .10 .20
RSLS56E061C New Chapter, Hikari Kagura C .10 .20
RSLS56E062U Unexpected Return at Dawn U .12 .25
RSLS56E063CR Towards the Light CLR .25 .50
RSLS56E064CR The Stage Continues Nonetheless CLR .25 .50
RSLS56E065CC Where the Shine Is CC .15 .30
RSLS56E069R My Own Shine, Claudine Saijo R .20 .40
RSLS56E070R Pajama Party, Maya Tendo R .20 .40
RSLS56E071R My Own Shine, Maya Tendo R .20 .40
RSLS56E072R My Own Shine, Junna Hoshimi R .20 .40
RSLS56E073R Ready to Challenge the Stage, Claudine Saijo R .20 .40
RSLS56E074R Prim and Proper Rep, Junna Hoshimi R .20 .40
RSLS56E075U Achieving the Highest Star, Junna Hoshimi U .12 .25
RSLS56E076U Stage Girl's Summer, Claudine Saijo U .12 .25
RSLS56E077U Revue Duet, Maya Tendo U .12 .25
RSLS56E078U Leotard Junna & Mahiru U .12 .25
RSLS56E079U The Next Starlight, Maya Tendo U .12 .25
RSLS56E080U Secret of the Best, Maya Tendo U .12 .25
RSLS56E081U Revenge, Junna Hoshimi U .12 .25
RSLS56E082U Pajama Party, Claudine Saijo U .12 .25
RSLS56E083C Precious Memories, Junna Hoshimi C .10 .20
RSLS56E084C 99th Seisho Festival Maya Tendo C .10 .20
RSLS56E085C Unreachable Existence, Maya Tendo C .10 .20
RSLS56E086C 99th Seisho Festival Claudine Saijo C .10 .20
RSLS56E087C The Next Starlight, Claudine Saijo C .10 .20
RSLS56E088C Excessive Self-Practice, Junna Hoshimi C .10 .20
RSLS56E089C Oversleeping Claudine Saijo C .10 .20
RSLS56E090C Stage Girl's Summer, Junna Hoshimi C .10 .20
RSLS56E091C Top Star Seat, Maya Tendo C .10 .20
RSLS56E092C Chronic Stage Fright? Claudine Saijo C .10 .20
RSLS56E093U As For Us U .12 .25
RSLS56E094U I'll Seize My Own Star!! U .12 .25
RSLS56E095CR The Show Must Go On CLR .25 .50
RSLS56E096CC To Greater Heights CC .15 .30
RSLS56E097CC Leading Role of Fate CC .15 .30
RSLS56E098CC Top Star CC .15 .30
RSLS56E099CC Reprise CC .15 .30
RSLS56E100CC Revue Starlight CC .15 .30

2020 Weiss Schwarz Adventure Time

ATWX02001RR Finn the Human & Jake the Dog RR 15.00 30.00
ATWX02001SSR Finn the Human & Jake the Dog SR 50.00 100.00
ATWX02002RR Finn the Human RR 1.25 2.50
ATWX02002SPSP Finn the Human SP 75.00 150.00
ATWX02003RR Finn: Heroic Pose RR 5.00 10.00
ATWX02003SSR Finn: Heroic Pose SR 20.00 40.00
ATWX02004RR Jake the Dog RR 3.00 6.00
ATWX02004SPSP Jake the Dog SP 125.00 250.00
ATWX02005RR Jake: Mocking Imitation RR .75 1.50
ATWX02005SSR Jake: Mocking Imitation SR 25.00 50.00
ATWX02006R Finn: Trusty Weapon R .25 .50
ATWX02007R Finn: What Was Missing R .25 .50
ATWX02008R Finn: Demonic Disguise R .25 .50
ATWX02009R Jake: Demonic Disguise R .25 .50
ATWX02010R Jake: Infected R .25 .50
ATWX02010SSR Jake: Infected SR 10.00 20.00
ATWX02011R Cake the Cat R .25 .50
ATWX02012R Flame Princess R .25 .50
ATWX02013U Finn & Jake: Working as a Team U .15 .30
ATWX02014U Finn: Prince Hotbod U .15 .30
ATWX02015U Jake: Finding His Buddy a New Love Interest U .15 .30
ATWX02016U Jake: What Was Missing U .15 .30
ATWX02017U BMO: Buttons Pushed U .15 .30
ATWX02018U BMO: Professor Pants U .15 .30
ATWX02019U Billy the Hero U .20 .40
ATWX02020U Fionna the Human U .15 .30
ATWX02021U Joshua & Margaret U .15 .30
ATWX02022C Finn: Protected from the Cold C .12 .25
ATWX02023C Finn: Fireproof Suit C .12 .25
ATWX02024C Finn: Filled with Chaotic Evil C .12 .25
ATWX02025C Jake: Gold-Crazed C .12 .25
ATWX02026C Jake: Fireproof Suit C .12 .25
ATWX02027C Jake: Randy Butternubs C .12 .25
ATWX02028C BMO: Noire C .12 .25
ATWX02029C BMO: Beating Himself at His Own Game C .12 .25
ATWX02030C N.E.P.T.R. C .12 .25
ATWX02031C Super Freak C .12 .25
ATWX02032U Demon Blood Sword U .15 .30
ATWX02033U Scarlet, the Golden Sword of Battle U .15 .30
ATWX02034C Card Wars! C .12 .25
ATWX02035CR The Call of Adventure CLR .20 .40
ATWX02035RRRR The Call of Adventure RRR 50.00 100.00
ATWX02036CR His Hero CLR .20 .40
ATWX02036RRRR His Hero RRR 7.50 15.00
ATWX02037CC A Tough Case to Crack CC .15 .30
ATWX02038CC The Creeps! CC .10 .20
ATWX02039CC Escape from Ice Kingdom CC .10 .20
ATWX02040RR Princess Bubblegum RR 7.50 15.00
ATWX02040SPSP Princess Bubblegum SP 125.00 250.00
ATWX02041RR Princess Bubblegum: Sending Off on a Quest RR 1.00 2.00
ATWX02041SSR Princess Bubblegum: Sending Off on a Quest SR 25.00 50.00
ATWX02042RR Marceline the Vampire Queen RR 3.00 6.00
ATWX02042SPSP Marceline the Vampire Queen SP 200.00 400.00
ATWX02043RR Marceline: I Remember You RR 12.50 25.00
ATWX02043SSR Marceline: I Remember You SR 40.00 80.00
ATWX02044R Princess Bubblegum: Possessed R .25 .50
ATWX02045R Princess Bubblegum: Beauty and Brains R .25 .50
ATWX02045SSR Princess Bubblegum: Beauty and Brains SR 20.00 40.00
ATWX02046R Princess Bubblegum: Lady Quietbottom R .25 .50
ATWX02047R Marceline: Monstrous R .25 .50
ATWX02048R Marceline: What Was Missing R .25 .50
ATWX02048SSR Marceline: What Was Missing SR 7.50 15.00
ATWX02049R Wildberry Princess R .25 .50
ATWX02050R Lady Rainicorn R .25 .50
ATWX02050SSR Lady Rainicorn SR 25.00 50.00
ATWX02051U Princess Bubblegum: What Was Missing U .15 .30
ATWX02052U Marceline: With Hambo U .15 .30
ATWX02053U Marceline: Filled with Chaotic Evil U .15 .30

ATWX02054U Teenaged Marceline U .15 .30
ATWX02055U Slime Princess U .15 .30
ATWX02056U Lady Rainicorn: Afraid for Her Love U .15 .30
ATWX02057U Lord Monochromicorn U .15 .30
ATWX02058U Marshall Lee U .15 .30
ATWX02059U Prince Gumball U .15 .30
ATWX02060C Princess Bubblegum: Reconstituted C .12 .25
ATWX02061C Princess Bubblegum: Infected C .12 .25
ATWX02062C Marceline: Sanguine Form C .12 .25
ATWX02063C Hot Dog Princess C .12 .25
ATWX02064C Lumpy Space Princess C .12 .25
ATWX02065C Muscle Princess C .12 .25
ATWX02066C Skeleton Princess C .12 .25
ATWX02067C Turtle Princess C .12 .25
ATWX02068C Bob & Ethel Rainicorn C .12 .25
ATWX02069R Remember You R .25 .50
ATWX02070C The Nightosphere Amulet C .12 .25
ATWX02071CR My Best Friends In The World CLR .20 .40
ATWX02071RRRR My Best Friends In The World RRR 20.00 40.00
ATWX02072CR Science! CLR .20 .40
ATWX02072RRRR Science! RRR 30.00 60.00
ATWX02073CC Fry Song CC .10 .20
ATWX02073RRRR Fry Song RRR 12.50 25.00
ATWX02074CC Captured! CC .10 .20
ATWX02075RR Ice King: The King of Ice RR .50 1.00
ATWX02075SSR Ice King: The King of Ice SR 7.50 15.00
ATWX02076R Ice King R .25 .50
ATWX02076SSR Ice King SR 7.50 15.00
ATWX02077R Ice King: I Remember You R .25 .50
ATWX02077SSR Ice King: I Remember You SR 20.00 40.00
ATWX02078R The Lich R .25 .50
ATWX02078SSR The Lich SR 15.00 30.00
ATWX02079R Hunson Abadeer R .25 .50
ATWX02079SSR Hunson Abadeer SR 6.00 12.00
ATWX02080R Hunson Abadeer: Chaotic Evil R .25 .50
ATWX02081R Kitten R .25 .50
ATWX02081SSR Kitten SR 30.00 60.00
ATWX02082R Ice King: Nice King? R .25 .50
ATWX02083U Ice King: Past Self U .15 .30
ATWX02084SSR Gunter SR 30.00 75.00
ATWX02084U Gunter U .15 .30
ATWX02085U The Lich: Possessing Billy U .15 .30
ATWX02086U Earl of Lemongrab U .15 .30
ATWX02087U Ice Queen U .15 .30
ATWX02088U Magic Man U .15 .30
ATWX02089U Ricardio the Heart Guy U .15 .30
ATWX02090C Gunter: Demonic Wishing Eye C .12 .25
ATWX02091C Gunter: Giant Penguin Monster C .12 .25
ATWX02092C The Lich: Possessing Snail C .12 .25
ATWX02093C Princess Monster Wife C .12 .25
ATWX02094C King of Mars C .12 .25
ATWX02095U Demonic Wishing Eye U .15 .30
ATWX02096C The Ice King's Schemes C .12 .25
ATWX02097C Unlocking the Enchiridion C .12 .25
ATWX02098CR Prisoners of Love CLR .20 .40
ATWX02099CC Ruler of the Nightosphere CC .10 .20
ATWX02100CC Ultimate Evil CC .10 .20
ATWX02100RRRR Ultimate Evil RRR 30.00 75.00
ATWX02101PR Finn: Let's Play! P 1.00 2.00
ATWX02102PR Jake: Let's Play! P .75 1.50
ATWX02103PR Princess Bubblegum: Let's Play! P .50 1.00
ATWX02104PR Marceline: Let's Play! P 3.00 6.00

2020 Weiss Schwarz Adventure Time Trial Deck

ATWX02T01TD Finn: Home Remedy .15 .30
ATWX02T02TD Finn: Pledge of Ultimate Responsibility .30 .75
ATWX02T03TD Jake: Don't Roast Them! 1.00 2.00
ATWX02T04RRRR BMO: Movie Filming Time RRR 30.00 60.00
ATWX02T04TD BMO: Movie Filming Time .60 1.25
ATWX02T05TD Finn & Jake: Gauntlet Dock Cleared! .75 1.50
ATWX02T06TD Jake: No Longer Pure .50 1.00
ATWX02T07TD Finn: Daily Diligence .30 .60
ATWX02T08TD BMO: Doing Strange Things When Nobody's Around .30 .60
ATWX02T09SPaSP Finn & Jake: Heroes of Ooo A SP 150.00 300.00
ATWX02T09SPbSP Finn & Jake: Heroes of Ooo B SP 200.00 400.00
ATWX02T09SSR Finn & Jake: Heroes of Ooo SR 2.50 5.00
ATWX02T09TD Finn & Jake: Heroes of Ooo 2.00 4.00
ATWX02T10TD Vampire Kick .50 1.00
ATWX02T11TD Imagination Hyperdrive .75 1.50
ATWX02T12RRRR Princess Bubblegum: Casual RRR 10.00 20.00
ATWX02T12TD Princess Bubblegum: Casual .50 1.00
ATWX02T13SSR Princess Bubblegum: Stately Gown SR 3.00 6.00
ATWX02T13TD Princess Bubblegum: Stately Gown 1.25 2.50
ATWX02T14TD Emerald Princess .75 1.50
ATWX02T15RRRR Marceline: Vampiric Tendencies RRR 100.00 200.00
ATWX02T15TD Marceline: Vampiric Tendencies 2.50 5.00
ATWX02T16TD Engagement Ring Princess 1.00 2.00
ATWX02T17TD Lady Rainicorn: Universally Understood 1.00 2.00
ATWX02T18TD Marceline: Fond of Pranks .20 .40
ATWX02T19TD Don't Eat Those .20 .40
ATWX02T20TD Whistling Choir Deathmatch Championship Practice 1.50 3.00

2020 Weiss Schwarz BanG Dream! Vol.2

BDW73E003R For the Sake of Smiles, Kokoro Tsurumaki R .25 .50
BDW73E004R Music of Smiles Misaki Okusawa R .25 .50
BDW73E005R Music of Smiles Kaoru Seta R .25 .50
BDW73E006R Turning Trembles into Strength, Aya Maruyama R .25 .50
BDW73E007 An Enticing Invitation, Kaoru Seta U .15 .30
BDW73E008U Engine On! Misaki Okusawa U .15 .30
BDW73E009U Sincere Feelings, Eve Wakamiya U .15 .30
BDW73E010U Music of Smiles Kanon Matsubara U .15 .30
BDW73E011C No Sense of Direction, Kanon Matsubara C .12 .25
BDW73E012C Determined Challenge, Hagumi Kitazawa C .12 .25
BDW73E013C Usual Catchphrase, Kokoro Tsurumaki C .12 .25
BDW73E014U After-school Strategy Meeting U .15 .30
BDW73E015CR Smile in the Night Sky CLR .20 .40
BDW73E016CC Tonight, When the Stars Shine CC .10 .20
BDW73E021R Our Music Tomoe Udagawa R .25 .50
BDW73E022R Our Music Moca Aoba R .25 .50
BDW73E023R Interweaving Music Eve Wakamiya R .25 .50
BDW73E024R Supreme Music MASKING R .25 .50
BDW73E025R Desperate Invitation, LOCK R .25 .50
BDW73E026R Overwhelming Vocal Ability, LAYER R .25 .50
BDW73E027R Our Music Himari Uehara R .25 .50
BDW73E028U RAISE YOUR HANDS, LOCK U .15 .30
BDW73E029U RAISE YOUR HANDS, LAYER U .15 .30
BDW73E030U My Own Pace, Moca Aoba U .15 .30
BDW73E031U Blunt Kindness, MASKING U .15 .30
BDW73E032U Unchanging Bonds, Ran Mitake U .15 .30
BDW73E033U Hard Worker, Tsugumi Hazawa U .15 .30
BDW73E034C Usual Cheers, Himari Uehara C .12 .25
BDW73E035C Exceptional Ability to Take Action, Hina Hikawa C .12 .25
BDW73E036C Freshmen, LOCK & Asuka C .12 .25
BDW73E037C Shining Admiration, LOCK C .12 .25
BDW73E038C Handling Difficult Demands, LOCK C .12 .25
BDW73E039C Powerful Eyes, Ran Mitake C .12 .25
BDW73E040C Full of Spirit, Tomoe Udagawa C .12 .25
BDW73E041C RAISE YOUR HANDS, MASKING C .12 .25
BDW73E042C Request, Aya Maruyama C .12 .25
BDW73E043C Childhood Promise, LAYER C .12 .25
BDW73E044C Mad Dog, MASKING C .12 .25
BDW73E045U An Eternal Sunset U .15 .30
BDW73E046CR Promise From Before CLR .20 .40
BDW73E047CR Our Melody CLR .20 .40
BDW73E048CC The View on That Day CC .10 .20
BDW73E051R Music of Bonds Saya Yamabuki R .25 .50
BDW73E052R Music of Bonds Rimi Ushigome R .25 .50
BDW73E053R Time for Our Live! Kasumi Toyama R .25 .50
BDW73E054U Pounding Heart, Rimi Ushigome U .15 .30
BDW73E055U All Together, Chisato Shirasagi U .15 .30
BDW73E056U Interweaving Music Maya Yamato U .15 .30
BDW73E057C New Sticks, Saya Yamabuki C .12 .25
BDW73E058C Practice Interval, Kasumi Toyama C .12 .25
BDW73E059C Hype! Saya Yamabuki C .12 .25
BDW73E060C Teary Eyes, Rimi Ushigome C .12 .25
BDW73E061U Overlapping Palms U .15 .30
BDW73E062U Enthusiastic Huddle U .15 .30
BDW73E063CC Melody of Bonds CC .10 .20
BDW73E064CR Interweaving Melodies CLR .20 .40
BDW73E069R Here is Where I Belong, Tae Hanazono R .25 .50
BDW73E070R Supreme Music CHU² R .25 .50
BDW73E071R Unwavering Music Ako Udagawa R .25 .50
BDW73E072R Competent Producer, CHU² R .25 .50
BDW73E073R Supreme Music PAREO R .25 .50
BDW73E074R Interweaving Music Chisato Shirasagi R .25 .50
BDW73E075R Quiet Passion, Yukina Minato R .25 .50
BDW73E076R Unwavering Music Lisa Imai R .25 .50
BDW73E077U Watching Over Nearby, Lisa Imai U .15 .30
BDW73E078U Cheerful Smile, PAREO U .15 .30
BDW73E079U Unwavering Music Rinko Shirokane U .15 .30
BDW73E080U Music of Bonds Arisa Ichigaya U .15 .30
BDW73E081U Playing a Melody, Tae Hanazono U .15 .30
BDW73E082U Festive Mood CHU² U .15 .30
BDW73E083U Cool and Collected, Sayo Hikawa U .15 .30
BDW73E084U Embarassing Feelings, Arisa Ichigaya U .15 .30
BDW73E085C Courage Little by Little, Rinko Shirokane C .12 .25
BDW73E086C RAISE YOUR HANDS, CHU² C .12 .25
BDW73E087C Turning Individuality into Strength, Maya Yamato C .12 .25
BDW73E088C Beginning of a Legend, PAREO C .12 .25
BDW73E089C Puzzled, Arisa Ichigaya C .12 .25
BDW73E090C More Power, Ako Udagawa C .12 .25
BDW73E091C Real Feelings Behind Harsh Words, Yukina Minato C .12 .25
BDW73E092C RAISE YOUR HANDS, PAREO C .12 .25
BDW73E093C Throbbing, Tae Hanazono C .12 .25
BDW73E094U Aiming for the Top as Five U .15 .30
BDW73E095U Yes!! You Guys Are the Best!! U .15 .30
BDW73E096CR Jumpin' Girls! CLR .20 .40
BDW73E097CR Unwavering Melody CLR .20 .40
BDW73E098CC Supreme Melody CC .10 .20
BDW73E099CC After the Rain CC .10 .20
BDW73E100CC School Festival CC .10 .20

2020 Weiss Schwarz Fujimi Fantasia Bunko

F35W65E034 Reason for Being Solitary, Ouka C .12 .25
FabW65E025 Acting Manager's Aide, Isuzu RR .75 1.50
FabW65E025S Acting Manager's Aide, Isuzu SR 15.00 30.00
FabW65E026 First Princess of Maple Land, Latifah R .25 .50
FabW65E026S First Princess of Maple Land, Latifah SR 10.00 20.00
FabW65E029 Fairy of Water, Muse U .15 .30
FabW65E032 First Time at a School Festival, Isuzu & Latifah U .15 .30
FabW65E036 The Four Girls of Elementario, Muse/Salama/Sylphy/Kobory C .12 .25
FabW65E040 Welcome to Amagi Brilliant Park! CC .10 .20
FabW65E040R Welcome to Amagi Brilliant Park! RRR 5.00 10.00
FddW65E043 Girl of Healing, Asia RR 15.00 30.00
FddW65E043SP Girl of Healing, Asia SP 300.00 600.00
FddW65E044 Red-Haired Ruin Princess, Rias R .25 .50
FddW65E044S Red-Haired Ruin Princess, Rias SR 250.00 500.00
FddW65E048 The Ultimate S, Akeno R 12.50 25.00
FddW65E048S The Ultimate S, Akeno SR 300.00 600.00
FddW65E049 Reward Time, Rias R 10.00 20.00
FddW65E049S Reward Time, Rias SR 200.00 400.00
FddW65E052 Devilish Smile, Rias R .25 .50
FddW65E052FBR Devilish Smile, Rias FBR 1,500.00 3,000.00
FddW65E054 Cross-Dressing Half-Vampire, Gasper U .15 .30
FddW65E056 Quiet White Cat, Koneko U .15 .30
FddW65E059 Silver-Haired Former Valkyrie, Rossweisse U .15 .30
FddW65E060 Master-and-Servant Relationship, Rias & Issei C .12 .25
FddW65E062 Gigantis Dragon's Contractor, Asia C .12 .25
FddW65E064 Holy Sword User, Xenovia C .12 .25
FddW65E065 Swift Sword Skills, Yuuto C .12 .25
FddW65E068 Believing in the Same Dream U .15 .30
FddW65E071 First Friend CC .10 .20
FddW65E071R First Friend RRR 30.00 60.00
FdlW65E074 Insane and Beautiful Nightmare, Kurumi RR 20.00 40.00
FdlW65E074SP Insane and Beautiful Nightmare, Kurumi SP 750.00 1,500.00
FdlW65E076 White-Winged Angel, Origami R 6.00 12.00
FdlW65E076S White-Winged Angel, Origami SR 150.00 300.00
FdlW65E077 Elegant Clockwork, Kurumi R .25 .50
FdlW65E077FBR Elegant Clockwork, Kurumi FBR 600.00 1,200.00
FdlW65E080 Pure Princess, Touka R .25 .50
FdlW65E080S Pure Princess, Touka SR 12.50 25.00
FdlW65E083 Ifrit of Burning Affection, Kotori U .15 .30
FdlW65E086 Timid Hermit, Yoshino U .15 .30
FdlW65E088 Diva of Temptation, Miku U .15 .30
FdlW65E091 Berserk of the Whirlwind, Kaguya & Yuzuru C .12 .25
FdlW65E093 Savior of the Girls' Minds, Shidou C .12 .25
FdlW65E094 Saddled with the Past, Origami C .12 .25
FdlW65E099 Demon King's Love U .15 .30
FdlW65E101 Journey to the Afterlife CLR .20 .40
FdlW65E101R Journey to the Afterlife RRR 30.00 60.00
FdlW65E103 Attack of Steel CC .10 .20
FdyW65E035 Journey to Find Relics of a Legendary Hero, Ryner & Ferris C .12 .25
FfpW65E023 High School Girl from Jindai High, Kaname RR 1.00 2.00
FfpW65E023S High School Girl from Jindai High, Kaname SR 2.50 5.00
FfpW65E028 Tuatha de Danaan's Captain, Teresa R .25 .50
FfpW65E028S Tuatha de Danaan's Captain, Teresa SR 10.00 20.00
FfpW65E030 Call Sign Urzu-7, Sousuke U .15 .30
FfpW65E031 ARX-8 Laevatein U .15 .30
FfpW65E041 Beginning of the Battle CC .10 .20
FfpW65E041R Beginning of the Battle RRR 6.00 12.00
FhcW65E090 Coffin-Carrying Wizard, Chaika C .12 .25
FiiW65E072 Sibling Affection, Suzuka RR 3.00 6.00
FiiW65E072S Sibling Affection, Suzuka SR 20.00 40.00
FiiW65E082 Towano Chikai's Rival, Mai R .25 .50
FiiW65E082S Towano Chikai's Rival, Mai SR 40.00 80.00
FiiW65E085 Interview for Valentine? Suzuka U .15 .30
FiiW65E087 Blushing Younger Sister, Suzuka U .15 .30
FiiW65E096 Illustrator from United Kingdom, Ahegao W Peace Sensei C .12 .25
FiiW65E105 Love Story of the Princess CLR .20 .40
FiiW65E105R Love Story of the Princess RRR 12.50 25.00
FkmW65E095 Magical Cannon Swordsman-in-Training, Misora C .12 .25
FksW65E015 Ice Witch, Aliceliese C .12 .25
FkzW65E002 Tsundere Magical Arms Girl, Haruna RR .75 1.50
FkzW65E002SP Tsundere Magical Arms Girl, Haruna SP 250.00 500.00
FkzW65E003 Silver-Haired Necromancer, Eu R .25 .50
FkzW65E003FBR Silver-Haired Necromancer, Eu FBR 300.00 750.00
FkzW65E005 Many Different Festivals, Eu R .25 .50
FkzW65E006 Vampire Ninja, Sera R .25 .50
FkzW65E006S Vampire Ninja, Sera SR 60.00 125.00
FkzW65E007 Healthy Outdoorsy Girl, Tomonori R .25 .50
FkzW65E007S Healthy Outdoorsy Girl, Tomonori SR 30.00 75.00
FkzW65E008 Broken Heart Magnum, Haruna U .15 .30
FkzW65E011 Ideal Way to Awake, Sera U .15 .30
FkzW65E012 Wide-Open Shirt, Eu U .15 .30
FkzW65E014 Top Student of the Academic Year, Taeko C .12 .25
FkzW65E016 Creepy in a Cute Way, Ayumu C .12 .25
FkzW65E018 Dual-Personality Vampire Ninja, Saras C .12 .25
FkzW65E019 No Coming in Between U .15 .30
FkzW65E020 Absurd Daily Life CR .60 1.25
FkzW65E020R Absurd Daily Life RRR 15.00 30.00
FkzW65E021 Solid Situation Panic CC .10 .20
FmrW65E024 Devoted Magician, Yuna RR .60 1.25
FmrW65E024S Devoted Magician, Yuna SR 6.00 12.00
FmrW65E027 Master of Swordsmanship, Rin R .25 .50
FmrW65E027S Master of Swordsmanship, Rin SR 3.00 6.00
FmrW65E033 Noble Young Woman, Kuriko U .15 .30
FmrW65E038 Hidden Qualities, Kazuki C .12 .25
FmrW65E039 Secrets Inherited from Mother to Child CR .20 .40
FmrW65E039R Secrets Inherited from Mother to Child RRR 3.00 6.00
FosW65E037 Hero's Mom, Mamako C .12 .25
FoyW65E001 Nation Unified by Force, Nobuna RR 1.00 2.00
FoyW65E001S Nation Unified by Force, Nobuna SR 7.50 15.00
FoyW65E004 Frail Exorcist, Hanbei R .25 .50
FoyW65E004S Frail Exorcist, Hanbei SR 3.00 6.00
FoyW65E009 Queen of Zipang, Nobuna U .15 .30
FoyW65E010 Turbulent Times, Nobuna U .15 .30
FoyW65E013 Center of the Universe, Masamune C .12 .25
FoyW65E022 One Who Fulfils Ambitions CC .10 .20
FoyW65E022R One Who Fulfils Ambitions RRR 3.00 6.00
FraW65E073 Inherited Magic Talent, Sistine RR 6.00 12.00
FraW65E073SP Inherited Magic Talent, Sistine SP 250.00 500.00
FraW65E075 Gentle Smile, Rumia R .25 .50
FraW65E075S Gentle Smile, Rumia SR 60.00 125.00
FraW65E078 Under One Roof, Rumia & Sistine R .25 .50
FraW65E079 Unique Mage Corps Member, Re=L R .25 .50
FraW65E079S Unique Mage Corps Member, Re=L SR 6.00 12.00
FraW65E081 Kindness and Strength, Rumia R 4.00 8.00
FraW65E081FBR Kindness and Strength, Rumia FBR 150.00 300.00
FraW65E084 Instantaneous Decision, Glenn U .15 .30
FraW65E089 Pure White Dress, Sistine U .15 .30
FraW65E092 Twinkling of the Star, Albert C .12 .25
FraW65E097 Messing Around, Rumia & Sistine C .12 .25
FraW65E098 The Greatest Mage of the Continent, Celica C .12 .25
FraW65E100 Black Magic of Destruction U .15 .30
FraW65E102 Eden of Everlasting Summer CR .20 .40
FraW65E102R Eden of Everlasting Summer RRR 12.50 25.00
FraW65E104 Not Wanting to Lose Precious Things CLR .20 .40
FsiW65E042 Hekiyou Academy Student Council Treasurer, Mafuyu RR 1.00 2.00
FsiW65E042SP Hekiyou Academy Student Council Treasurer, Mafuyu SP 125.00 250.00
FsiW65E045 Hekiyou Academy Student Council President, Kurimu R .25 .50
FsiW65E045S Hekiyou Academy Student Council President, Kurimu SR 25.00 50.00
FsiW65E047 Absolute God, Kurimu R .25 .50
FsiW65E047S Absolute God, Kurimu SR 15.00 30.00
FsiW65E050 Hekiyou Academy Student Council Vice President, Minatsu R .25 .50
FsiW65E050S Hekiyou Academy Student Council Vice President, Minatsu SR 7.50 15.00
FsiW65E051 Hekiyou Academy Student Council Secretary, Chizuru R .25 .50
FsiW65E051FBR Hekiyou Academy Student Council Secretary, Chizuru FBR 250.00 500.00
FsiW65E053 Tsundere Maid, Minatsu U .15 .30
FsiW65E055 Ungraspable Beauty, Chizuru U .15 .30
FsiW65E057 Naivete, Kurimu U .15 .30
FsiW65E058 Pretty Face and Fair-Skinned, Mafuyu U .15 .30
FsiW65E061 Hekiyou Academy Student Council Vice President, Ken C .12 .25
FsiW65E063 Otaku Girl, Mafuyu C .12 .25
FsiW65E066 Fragrance of Yuri, Chizuru C .12 .25
FsiW65E067 Dazzling, Minatsu C .12 .25
FsiW65E069 In Slumber CLR .20 .40
FsiW65E069R In Slumber RRR 7.50 15.00
FsiW65E070 Irreplaceable Daily Life CC .10 .20
FsiW65E070R Irreplaceable Daily Life RRR 20.00 40.00
FslW65E046 Genius Mage & Swordswoman, Lina R .25 .50
FtrW65E017 Fulfilled Promise, Natsume & Harutora C .12 .25

2020 Weiss Schwarz Fujimi Fantasia Bunko Trial Deck

FabW65TE07 Duty of the Two, Isuzu & Seiya TD .30 .75
FabW65TE08 Maple Kitchen, Latifah TD .25 .50
FddW65TE09R High-Class Charms, Rias RRR 300.00 600.00
FddW65TE09 High-Class Charms, Rias TD 4.00 8.00
FddW65TE10S Occult Research Club Head, Rias SR 15.00 30.00
FddW65TE10 Occult Research Club Head, Rias TD 3.00 6.00
FddW65TE13 A Voice Heard TD 3.00 6.00
FdlW65TE16SP Mysterious Girl, Touka SP 400.00 800.00
FdlW65TE16 Mysterious Girl, Touka TD 4.00 8.00
FdlW65TE17 A Cute Side, Kurumi TD 6.00 12.00
FfpW65TE02 Stand by Me Always, Sousuke & Kaname TD .30 .60
FiiW65TE15 Mai & Ahegao W Peace Sensei in Uniform TD 1.25 2.50
FiiW65TE19 Dangerous Younger Sister, Suzuka TD .25 .50
FkzW65TE01 Troubled Expression, Eu .60 1.25
FkzW65TE05R Year Refrain's Rising Class, Haruna RRR 30.00 60.00
FkzW65TE05 Year Refrain's Rising Class, Haruna .30 .75
FmrW65TE04 Heart Magic, Yuna 1.00 2.00
FoyW65TE03 Burdened, Nobuna .30 .75
FoyW65TE06R Head of the Oda Family, Nobuna RRR 30.00 75.00
FoyW65TE06 Head of the Oda Family, Nobuna .30 .75
FraW65TE18S Mind Made Up, Sistine SR 3.00 6.00
FraW65TE18 Mind Made Up, Sistine .75 1.50
FraW65TE20 Silver Key .30 .75
FsiW65TE11SP Ringing Declaration, Kurimu SP 200.00 400.00
FsiW65TE11 Ringing Declaration, Kurimu .30 .75
FsiW65TE12 I Am Echo of Death .30 .60
FsiW65TE14 Student Council's Discretion .30 .75

2020 Weiss Schwarz Goblin Slayer

GBSS63E001RR Pride of an Elf, High Elf Archer RR 3.00 6.00
GBSS63E001SSR Pride of an Elf, High Elf Archer SR 20.00 40.00
GBSS63E002RR Natural Adventurer, High Elf Archer RR 3.00 6.00
GBSS63E002SPSP Natural Adventurer, High Elf Archer SP 125.00 250.00
GBSS63E003R Envy for the Unknown, High Elf Archer R .25 .50
GBSS63E003SSR Envy for the Unknown, High Elf Archer SR 7.50 15.00
GBSS63E004R Inquiry About a Warrior, High Elf Archer R .25 .50
GBSS63E004SSR Inquiry About a Warrior, High Elf Archer SR 4.00 8.00
GBSS63E005R Generous Heavy Drinker, Dwarf Shaman R .25 .50
GBSS63E006R Sure-Hit Strike, High Elf Archer R .25 .50
GBSS63E007R Rapid Firing of Pebbles, Dwarf Shaman R .25 .50
GBSS63E008R Banisher of Heresy, Lizard Priest R .25 .50
GBSS63E009U Battle Stance, Lizard Priest U .15 .30
GBSS63E010U Exploding! High Elf Archer U .15 .30
GBSS63E011U Rear Support, High Elf Archer U .15 .30
GBSS63E012U Eye of a Veteran Fighter, Dwarf Shaman U .15 .30
GBSS63E013C Overwhelming Interest, High Elf Archer C .12 .25
GBSS63E014C Miracle from Ancestors, Lizard Priest C .12 .25
GBSS63E015C Spirited Dreams, Dwarf Shaman C .12 .25

GBSS63E016C Effective Words, High Elf Archer C	.12	.25
GBSS63E017C Cherished Flavor, Lizard Priest C	.12	.25
GBSS63E018C Promise to Oneself, High Elf Archer C	.12	.25
GBSS63E019C Final Battle, Female Sage C	.12	.25
GBSS63E020C Final Battle, Female Swordmaster C	.12	.25
GBSS63E021C Soldier from Dragon Bones, Dragon Tooth Warrior C	.12	.25
GBSS63E022C Final Battle, Female Hero C	.12	.25
GBSS63E023C Dragon Bones U	.15	.30
GBSS63E024C Dice U	.15	.30
GBSS63E025CR Colorful Adventures CLR	.20	.40
GBSS63E025RRRR Colorful Adventures RRR	5.00	10.00
GBSS63E026CC Faith Entrusted to the Bow CC	.10	.20
GBSS63E027CC Friends to Battle Alongside With CC	.10	.20
GBSS63E027RRRR Friends to Battle Alongside With RRR	2.50	5.00
GBSS63E028RR Energetic Childhood Friend, Cow Girl RR	4.00	8.00
GBSS63E028SPSP Energetic Childhood Friend, Cow Girl SP	30.00	75.00
GBSS63E029RR Precise Battle Tactics, Goblin Slayer RR	20.00	40.00
GBSS63E029SSR Precise Battle Tactics, Goblin Slayer SR	30.00	75.00
GBSS63E030RR Iron Shadow of Annihilation, Goblin Slayer RR	2.50	5.00
GBSS63E030SPSP Iron Shadow of Annihilation, Goblin Slayer SP	100.00	200.00
GBSS63E031R True Bonds, Goblin Slayer R	2.50	5.00
GBSS63E032R Bewitching Demeanor, Witch R	.25	.50
GBSS63E033R Enchanting Looks, Witch R	.25	.50
GBSS63E033SSR Enchanting Looks, Witch SR	10.00	20.00
GBSS63E034R Burdened by Fate, Goblin Slayer R	3.00	6.00
GBSS63E034SSR Burdened by Fate, Goblin Slayer SR	30.00	75.00
GBSS63E035R Bursting with Vigor, Cow Girl R	.25	.50
GBSS63E035SSR Bursting with Vigor, Cow Girl SR	20.00	40.00
GBSS63E036U Unbending Will, Cow Girl U	.15	.30
GBSS63E037U A Moment of Peace, Cow Girl U	.15	.30
GBSS63E038U Predetermined Outcome, Goblin Slayer U	1.50	3.00
GBSS63E039U A Little Kindness, Witch U	.15	.30
GBSS63E040U Gleaming Dagger, Goblin Slayer U	.15	.30
GBSS63E041U Where the Two Belong, Cow Girl U	.15	.30
GBSS63E042U Hunting Big Game, Spearman U	.15	.30
GBSS63E043U Unyielding Stance, Goblin Slayer U	.15	.30
GBSS63E044C Sleep Spell, Witch C	.12	.25
GBSS63E045C Strange Request, Witch C	.12	.25
GBSS63E046C Man of Few Words, Goblin Slayer C	.12	.25
GBSS63E047C Under the Starry Sky, Cow Girl C	.12	.25
GBSS63E048C Flickering Fire Arrow, Goblin Slayer C	.12	.25
GBSS63E049C Flash of Silver, Goblin Slayer C	.12	.25
GBSS63E050C Great Health, Cow Girl C	.12	.25
GBSS63E051C Most Stubborn Frontline, Spearman C	.12	.25
GBSS63E052R Gate Scroll R	.25	.50
GBSS63E053U Torch U	.15	.30
GBSS63E054U Canary U	.15	.30
GBSS63E055U Duffel Bag U	.15	.30
GBSS63E056CR Last Breath CLR	.20	.40
GBSS63E056RRRR Last Breath RRR	5.00	10.00
GBSS63E057CC Battle with One's Life at Stake CC	.10	.20
GBSS63E057RRRR Battle with One's Life at Stake RRR	30.00	75.00
GBSS63E058CC Brand New Morning CC	.10	.20
GBSS63E058RRRR Brand New Morning RRR	30.00	75.00
GBSS63E059CC Secret XXXX CC	.10	.20
GBSS63E060RR Guild's Poster Girl, Guild Girl RR	.30	.75
GBSS63E060SSR Guild's Poster Girl, Guild Girl SR	6.00	12.00
GBSS63E061RR Kind Acolyte, Priestess RR	5.00	10.00
GBSS63E061SSR Kind Acolyte, Priestess SR	15.00	30.00
GBSS63E062RR Beloved Archbishop, Sword Maiden RR	6.00	12.00
GBSS63E062SPSP Beloved Archbishop, Sword Maiden SP	200.00	400.00
GBSS63E063RR Passionate Yearning, Sword Maiden RR	7.50	15.00
GBSS63E063SSR Passionate Yearning, Sword Maiden SR	60.00	125.00
GBSS63E064RR Pure Aide, Priestess RR	10.00	20.00
GBSS63E064SPSP Pure Aide, Priestess SP	200.00	400.00
GBSS63E065R Personal Special Reward, Priestess R	.25	.50
GBSS63E066R Everyday Anticipation, Guild Girl R	.25	.50
GBSS63E066SSR Everyday Anticipation, Guild Girl SR	12.50	25.00
GBSS63E067R Cherubic Smile, Priestess R	.25	.50
GBSS63E067SSR Cherubic Smile, Priestess SR	2.50	5.00
GBSS63E068R Clear Gaze, Priestess R	.50	1.00
GBSS63E068SSR Clear Gaze, Priestess SR	7.50	15.00
GBSS63E069R Translucent Skin, Sword Maiden R	.25	.50
GBSS63E070R Innocent Virgin, Priestess R	.25	.50
GBSS63E070SSR Innocent Virgin, Priestess SR	30.00	75.00
GBSS63E071R Inevitable Gathering, Priestess R	.25	.50
GBSS63E072R Figure of Tranquility, Sword Maiden R	.75	1.50
GBSS63E072SSR Figure of Tranquility, Sword Maiden SR	30.00	75.00
GBSS63E073R Utmost Assistance, Guild Girl R	.25	.50
GBSS63E074R Heart's Truth, Sword Maiden R	.25	.50
GBSS63E075U Super Rare Shot! Guild Girl U	.15	.30
GBSS63E076U Welcome to the City of Water, Sword Maiden U	.15	.30
GBSS63E077U For the Future, Guild Girl U	.15	.30
GBSS63E078U Profound Reason, Priestess U	.15	.30
GBSS63E079U Ardent Request, Sword Maiden U	.15	.30
GBSS63E080U Sulking Priestess U	.15	.30
GBSS63E081U Professional Smile, Guild Girl U	.15	.30
GBSS63E082U Always Together, Priestess U	.15	.30
GBSS63E083U What is a Discussion? Priestess U	.15	.30
GBSS63E084C Quick-Witted Decision, Priestess C	.12	.25
GBSS63E085C Hoping to Repay, Apprentice Cleric C	.12	.25
GBSS63E086C Ultimate Miracle, Sword Maiden C	.12	.25
GBSS63E087C Little Considerations, Priestess C	.12	.25
GBSS63E088C Sweet Encounter, Priestess C	.12	.25
GBSS63E089C Feelings of Appreciation, Priestess C	.12	.25
GBSS63E090C Morning After Resurrection, Sword Maiden C	.12	.25
GBSS63E091C Lie-Detecting Gaze, Examiner C	.12	.25
GBSS63E092C Hitting Guild Girl's Weakness C	.12	.25
GBSS63E093C A New Experience, Greenhorn Warrior C	.12	.25
GBSS63E094U Obsidian Rank U	.15	.30
GBSS63E095U Resurrection U	.15	.30
GBSS63E096CR A Woman Swayed CR	.20	.40
GBSS63E096RRRR A Woman Swayed RRR	2.00	4.00
GBSS63E097CR Extensive Divine Protection CLR	.75	1.50
GBSS63E097RRRR Extensive Divine Protection RRR	30.00	75.00
GBSS63E098CC Guide to Salvation CC	.10	.20
GBSS63E099CC Ice Creme Shock! CC	.10	.20
GBSS63E100CC Here for the Adventurers, Here for You. CC	.10	.20
GBSS63E100RRRR Here for the Adventurers, Here for You. RRR	.75	1.50
GBSW63E101PR An Ordinary Piece, High Elf Archer P	2.00	4.00
GBSW63E102PR An Ordinary Piece, Cow Girl P	25.00	50.00
GBSW63E103PR An Ordinary Piece, Goblin Slayer P	2.50	5.00
GBSW63E104PR An Ordinary Piece, Priestess P	1.25	2.50
GBSW63E105PR An Ordinary Piece, Guild Girl P	.60	1.25

2020 Weiss Schwarz Goblin Slayer Trial Deck

GBSS63TE01TD Brave Girl, Cow Girl	.30	.60
GBSS63TE02TD Concealed Tactics, Goblin Slayer	.30	.60
GBSS63TE03SSR He Who Slays Goblins, Goblin Slayer SR	.75	1.50
GBSS63TE03TD He Who Slays Goblins, Goblin Slayer	.30	.75
GBSS63TE04TD Quiet Consideration, Goblin Slayer	.30	.60
GBSS63TE05TD Merciless Actions, Goblin Slayer	.30	.60
GBSS63TE06TD Like a Parent, Goblin Slayer	.30	.60
GBSS63TE07TD Masked Figure's Name, Goblin Slayer	2.50	5.00
GBSS63TE08TD Torch	2.00	4.00
GBSS63TE09RRRR Rhythmical Extermination RRR	6.00	12.00
GBSS63TE09TD Rhythmical Extermination	.30	.60
GBSS63TE10TD Charge!	.30	.60
GBSS63TE11RRRR Unnoticed Beauty, Guild Girl RRR	15.00	30.00
GBSS63TE11TD Unnoticed Beauty, Guild Girl	.30	.75
GBSS63TE12TD One's Own Will, Priestess	.30	.75
GBSS63TE13SPSP Earth Mother's Disciple, Priestess SP	125.00	250.00
GBSS63TE13SSR Earth Mother's Disciple, Priestess SR	2.50	5.00
GBSS63TE13TD Earth Mother's Disciple, Priestess	2.00	4.00
GBSS63TE14TD Adventurer, Female Mage	.30	.60
GBSS63TE15TD Adventurer, Swordsman	.30	.60
GBSS63TE16TD Adventurer, Female Martial Artist	.30	.60
GBSS63TE17TD Flame's Source, Priestess	.30	.75
GBSS63TE18TD Like a Child, Priestess	.30	.60
GBSS63TE19TD Light That Exposes Chaos, Priestess	.30	.60
GBSS63TE20RRRR Merciful, Priestess RRR	150.00	300.00
GBSS63TE20TD Merciful, Priestess	1.25	2.50
GBSS63TE21TD Unanswered Prayers	.30	.75

2020 Weiss Schwarz JoJo's Bizarre Adventure Golden Wind

JJS66E001 Seeker of Truth, Giorno RR	15.00	30.00
JJS66E002 Path Within the Darkness, Mista RR	2.00	4.00
JJS66E002SP Path Within the Darkness, Mista SP	150.00	300.00
JJS66E003 The Path Ahead, Giorno RR	1.00	2.00
JJS66E003SP The Path Ahead, Giorno SP	125.00	250.00
JJS66E004 Final Form, G.W.R RR	6.00	12.00
JJS66E005 Embodiment of Justice, Giorno R	.25	.50
JJS66E006 Simmering Fury, Fugo R	.50	1.00
JJS66E006SP Simmering Fury, Fugo SP	75.00	150.00
JJS66E007 The One Chosen by Fate, Giorno R	.30	.75
JJS66E007J The One Chosen by Fate, Giorno JJR	12.50	25.00
JJS66E008 Heavy Gunshots, Mista R	.25	.50
JJS66E009 Angry Lunatic Tendencies, Fugo U	.15	.30
JJS66E010 Closing in on Death, Mista U	.15	.30
JJS66E011J Harbinger of Hope, Polnareff JJR	12.50	25.00
JJS66E011U Harbinger of Hope, Polnareff U	.15	.30
JJS66E012 Bizarre Investigation Request, Koichi & Reverb Act 3 U	.20	.40
JJS66E012J Bizarre Investigation Request, Koichi & Reverb Act 3 JJR	15.00	30.00
JJS66E013 Abundance of Life, G.W U	.30	.60
JJS66E014a 6 Together as 1, S.B A U	.60	1.25
JJS66E014b 6 Together as 1, S.B B U	.60	1.25
JJS66E014c 6 Together as 1, S.B C U	.60	1.25
JJS66E014d 6 Together as 1, S.B D U	.60	1.25
JJS66E014e 6 Together as 1, S.B E U	.60	1.25
JJS66E014f 6 Together as 1, S.B F U	1.25	2.50
JJS66E015 Savage Smoke, P.S U	.15	.30
JJS66E016 Smoke of Death, Fugo U	.15	.30
JJS66E016J Smoke of Death, Fugo JJR	15.00	30.00
JJS66E017 Silent Dance, C.R C	.12	.25
JJS66E018 A New Power, G.W C	.12	.25
JJS66E019 Determination of Life, Giorno C	.12	.25
JJS66E020 A New Power, Giorno C	.12	.25
JJS66E021 Unexpected Clean Freak, P.S C	.12	.25
JJS66E022 Determined Stand, S.B C	.12	.25
JJS66E023 Ladybug Brooch C	.12	.25
JJS66E024 The Arrow of Hope C	.12	.25
JJS66E025 The World's Truth CLR	.75	1.50
JJS66E025J The World's Truth JJR	25.00	50.00
JJS66E026 The Path to Resolution CC	.10	.20
JJS66E026J The Path to Resolution JJR	25.00	50.00
JJS66E027 Rampant Death CC	.10	.20
JJS66E027J Rampant Death JJR	10.00	20.00
JJS66E028 Fear of Shrinking, Formaggio & T.F R	.30	.75
JJS66E028J Fear of Shrinking, Formaggio & T.F JJR	30.00	60.00
JJS66E029 Crucial Compatibility Check, Melone & Bh R	.30	.60
JJS66E029J Crucial Compatibility Check, Melone & Bh JJR	7.50	15.00
JJS66E030 Grand Teachings, Prosciutto R	1.50	3.00
JJS66E030J Grand Teachings, Prosciutto JJR	25.00	50.00
JJS66E031 Grand Teachings, Pesci & F.M R	3.00	6.00
JJS66E031J Grand Teachings, Pesci & F.M JJR	30.00	60.00
JJS66E032 Freezing World, Ghiaccio & W.I R	.25	.50
JJS66E033 Flipped World, Illuso & M.M R	.25	.50
JJS66E033J Flipped World, Illuso & M.M JJR	7.50	15.00
JJS66E034 Unavoidable Assassination, Risotto R	.30	.75
JJS66E034J Unavoidable Assassination, Risotto JJR	15.00	30.00
JJS66E035 Man in the Mirror, Illuso U	.15	.30
JJS66E036 Conception of the Two, Bh U	.15	.30
JJS66E037 A Traitor's Dignity, Risotto & Mt U	.15	.30
JJS66E038 Resourceful Assassin, Formaggio U	.15	.30
JJS66E039 Significance of Resolution, Prosciutto & T.D U	.25	.50
JJS66E040 Mammoni, Pesci & F.M C	.12	.25
JJS66E041 Targeting the Hidden Treasure, Zucchero & T.M C	.12	.25
JJS66E041J Targeting the Hidden Treasure, Zucchero & T.M JJR	7.50	15.00
JJS66E042 Targeting the Hidden Treasure, Sale & A&C C	.12	.25
JJS66E042J Targeting the Hidden Treasure, Sale & A&C JJR	10.00	20.00
JJS66E043 Gently Weeps, Ghiaccio & W.I.G.W C	.12	.25
JJS66E044 The Disappearance of Sorbet and Gelato C	.12	.25
JJS66E045 Controller of Magnetism CLR	.20	.40
JJS66E045J Controller of Magnetism JJR	7.50	15.00
JJS66E046 Grand Death CC	.20	.40
JJS66E046J Grand Death JJR	30.00	60.00
JJS66E047 Remnant of the Past, Diavolo RR	.50	1.00
JJS66E048 Erased World, E.C RR	2.50	5.00
JJS66E048J Erased World, E.C JJR	40.00	80.00
JJS66E049 Predator of the Waters, Cr R	.30	.60
JJS66E049J Predator of the Waters, Cr JJR	20.00	40.00
JJS66E050 Movements in the Future, Doppio & Eu R	2.00	4.00
JJS66E051 Spinner of Lies, T.M R	.75	1.50
JJS66E051J Spinner of Lies, T.M JJR	7.50	15.00
JJS66E052 Sowing Seeds of Despair, Cioccolata & G.T R	.60	1.25
JJS66E052J Sowing Seeds of Despair, Cioccolata & G.T JJR	12.50	25.00
JJS66E053 Pride of a King, Diavolo R	.25	.50
JJS66E054 He Who Sinks Into the Ground, Secco & Sa R	.25	.50
JJS66E054J He Who Sinks Into the Ground, Secco & Sa JJR	12.50	25.00
JJS66E055 Tyrant Residing in Jail, Polpo U	.15	.30
JJS66E056 10 Hours Ago, Pericolo U	.15	.30
JJS66E057 Harmonized Teamwork, Tiziano U	.15	.30
JJS66E058 Harmonized Teamwork, Squalo U	.15	.30
JJS66E059 Restless Pursuer, N.C U	.15	.30
JJS66E059J Restless Pursuer, N.C JJR	30.00	60.00
JJS66E060 Leaky Eye Luca C	.12	.25
JJS66E061 Eternal Ruler, E.C C	.12	.25
JJS66E062 Treat Time, Cioccolata C	.12	.25
JJS66E063 Split Personality, Diavolo C	.12	.25
JJS66E064 Split Personality, Doppio C	.12	.25
JJS66E065 Revenge of the Dead, Carne C	.12	.25
JJS66E066 Treat Time, Secco & Sa C	.12	.25
JJS66E067 Observer From the Shadows, S.S C	.12	.25
JJS66E067J Observer From the Shadows, S.S JJR	25.00	50.00
JJS66E068 Miraculous Public Telephone U	.15	.30
JJS66E069 Polpo's Entry Test U	.15	.30
JJS66E070 Eternal Ruler CLR	.30	.60
JJS66E070J Eternal Ruler JJR	15.00	30.00
JJS66E071 10 Seconds Into the Future CC	.10	.20
JJS66E071J 10 Seconds Into the Future JJR	25.00	50.00
JJS66E072 Cioccolata and Secco CC	.10	.20
JJS66E072J Cioccolata and Secco JJR	12.50	25.00
JJS66E073 Guiding Fate, Trish RR	6.00	12.00
JJS66E073SP Guiding Fate, Trish SPR	300.00	600.00
JJS66E074 Noble Resolutions, Bucciarati RR	1.00	2.00
JJS66E074SP Noble Resolutions, Bucciarati SP	200.00	400.00
JJS66E075 Soul's Will, Bucciarati RR	10.00	20.00
JJS66E075SSP Soul's Will, Bucciarati SSP	250.00	500.00
JJS66E076 Replaying the Past, Abbacchio RR	.60	1.25
JJS66E076SP Replaying the Past, Abbacchio SP	200.00	400.00
JJS66E077 Beacon Dispelling the Darkness, Bucciarati R	.60	1.25
JJS66E077J Beacon Dispelling the Darkness, Bucciarati JJR	25.00	50.00
JJS66E078 Choosing His Own Path, Narancia R	.30	.75
JJS66E078SP Choosing His Own Path, Narancia SP	100.00	200.00
JJS66E079 Awakened Power, Trish R	.30	.75
JJS66E079J Awakened Power, Trish JJR	40.00	80.00
JJS66E080 Pursuer of Information, Abbacchio R	.25	.50
JJS66E080J Pursuer of Information, Abbacchio JJR	25.00	50.00
JJS66E081 Aerial Hunter, Narancia R	.30	.75
JJS66E081J Aerial Hunter, Narancia JJR	30.00	60.00
JJS66E082 Determination to Uncover Truth, M.J U	.15	.30
JJS66E083 Awakened Power, S.L U	.15	.30
JJS66E084 The One Who Opens, Z.M U	.15	.30
JJS66E085 Indestructible Flexibility, S.L U	.15	.30
JJS66E086 Rebelling Against Fate, Bucciarati U	.15	.30
JJS66E087 Rebelling, Trish U	.15	.30
JJS66E088 Agile Aeroplane, L.B C	.12	.25
JJS66E089 The Right Path, Bucciarati C	.12	.25
JJS66E090 Transforming Path, Z.M C	.12	.25
JJS66E091 Overwhelming Mental Strength, Narancia C	.12	.25
JJS66E092 Heart of Justice, Abbacchio C	.12	.25
JJS66E093 Destructive Tempest, L.B C	.12	.25
JJS66E094 Playback Investigation, M.J C	.12	.25
JJS66E095 Key to the Safe Vehicle U	.15	.30
JJS66E096 Room in the Turtle U	.15	.30
JJS66E097 The Sound of Farewell CLR	.60	1.25
JJS66E097J The Sound of Farewell JJR	20.00	40.00
JJS66E098 Determination to Awaken CC	.10	.20
JJS66E099 Under the Falling Sky CC	.15	.30
JJS66E099J Under the Falling Sky JJR	7.50	15.00
JJS66E100 Unflinching Spirit CC	.10	.20
JJS66E100J Unflinching Spirit JJR	20.00	40.00
JJS66E101PR Pioneer of Fate, Mista P	2.00	4.00
JJS66E102PR Pioneer of Fate, Giorno P	7.50	15.00
JJS66E103PR Pioneer of Fate, Fugo P	2.00	4.00
JJS66E104PR Pioneer of Fate, Narancia P	1.50	3.00
JJS66E105PR Pioneer of Fate, Bucciarati P	2.00	4.00
JJS66E106PR Pioneer of Fate, Abbacchio P	2.00	4.00
JJS66E107PR Pioneer of Fate, Trish P	3.00	6.00

2020 Weiss Schwarz JoJo's Bizarre Adventure Golden Wind Trial Deck Plus

JJS66TE01 Bad at Studying, Narancia TD	.25	.50
JJS66TE02 Kind Teacher, Fugo TD	.75	1.50
JJS66TE03 Gang Newcomer, Giorno TD	3.00	6.00
JJS66TE03SP Gang Newcomer, Giorno SP	300.00	600.00
JJS66TE04 Hazing the Newcomer, Abbacchio TD	.30	.75
JJS66TE05 Accurate Shot, Mista TD	2.00	4.00
JJS66TE06 Golden Experience, G.W TD	1.25	2.50
JJS66TE06S Golden Experience, G.W SR	2.00	4.00
JJS66TE07 Golden Intentions, Giorno TD	.75	1.50
JJS66TE07S Golden Intentions, Giorno SR	2.00	4.00
JJS66TE08 Overflowing Life Force TD	.15	.30
JJS66TE09 Golden Experience TD	.15	.30
JJS66TE09J Golden Experience JJR	30.00	75.00
JJS66TE10 Last Bullet TD	.25	.50
JJS66TE11 Readiness to Die, Bucciarati TD	.30	.60
JJS66TE12 Interest in the Newcomer, Abbacchio TD	.15	.30
JJS66TE13 Icebreaker, Mista TD	.25	.50
JJS66TE14 Sudden Fury, Fugo TD	.25	.50
JJS66TE15 Z.M TD	.60	1.25
JJS66TE16 Pure and Innocent, Narancia TD	.25	.50
JJS66TE17 Unseen Attack, Bucciarati TD	.25	.50
JJS66TE18 Sudden Attack, Bucciarati TD	.25	.50
JJS66TE19 Future Comrade, Giorno TD	.25	.50
JJS66TE20 Permitted to Join TD	.25	.50

2020 Weiss Schwarz Konosuba God's Blessing on This Wonderful World Legend of Crimson

KSW76E001RR Endurance Is My Forte Darkness RR	5.00	10.00
KSW76E001SPSP Endurance Is My Forte Darkness SP	150.00	300.00
KSW76E002RR Musclebrained Crusader Darkness RR	1.50	3.00
KSW76E002SSR Musclebrained Crusader Darkness SR	12.50	25.00
KSW76E003R A Break in the Forest Darkness R	.30	.60
KSW76E004R Beauty in a Yukata Darkness R	6.00	12.00
KSW76E005R Important Friend Kazuma R	.25	.50
KSW76E006R Shivering from Disparagement Darkness R	.25	.50
KSW76E006SSR Shivering from Disparagement Darkness SR	6.00	12.00
KSW76E007R Fireworks Display Kazuma R	.25	.50
KSW76E008R Fierce Battle Vanir R	.25	.50
KSW76E008SSR Fierce Battle Vanir SR	3.00	6.00
KSW76E009R My Popular Phase is Here! Kazuma R	.25	.50
KSW76E009SSR My Popular Phase is Here! Kazuma SR	2.50	5.00
KSW76E010U S-Rank Luck Kazuma U	.15	.30
KSW76E011U Dumbfounded Darkness U	.15	.30
KSW76E012U Sightseeing in the Crimson Demon Village! Darkness U	.15	.30
KSW76E013U Straightforward Confession Kazuma U	.15	.30
KSW76E014U Welcome Vanir U	.15	.30
KSW76E015U Sought-After Paradise Kazuma U	.15	.30
KSW76E016U Blocking the Way Darkness U	.15	.30
KSW76E017C To the Crimson Demon Village! Kazuma C	.12	.25
KSW76E018C Mind-Reading Demon Vanir C	.12	.25
KSW76E019C Vigorous Assertion Kazuma C	.12	.25
KSW76E020C Scope Set! Kazuma C	.12	.25
KSW76E021C Bold Bluff Kazuma C	.12	.25
KSW76E022C Sole Redeeming Feature Darkness C	.12	.25
KSW76E023C To the Crimson Demon Village! Darkness C	.12	.25
KSW76E024U Up Up Down Down Left Right Left Right! There you go! U	.15	.30
KSW76E025CR M-My Defensive Strength? CLR	.20	.40
KSW76E025RRRR M-My Defensive Strength? RRR	4.00	8.00
KSW76E026CC Orc Invasion! CC	.10	.20
KSW76E027CC Thumbs Up! CC	.10	.20
KSW76E028RR Faith in Comrades Yunyun RR	1.00	2.00
KSW76E028SPSP Faith in Comrades Yunyun SP	125.00	250.00
KSW76E029RR To the Crimson Demon Village! Megumin & Yunyun RR	4.00	8.00
KSW76E029SSR To the Crimson Demon Village! Megumin & Yunyun SR	20.00	40.00
KSW76E030RR To the Crimson Demon Village! Wiz RR	1.00	2.00
KSW76E031RR Sentiments Toward Explosion Magic Megumin RR	10.00	20.00
KSW76E032RR Greatest Mage Yunyun RR	10.00	20.00
KSW76E032SSPSSP Greatest Mage Yunyun SSP	500.00	1,000.00
KSW76E033RR Foremost Mage Megumin RR	1.50	3.00
KSW76E033SSPSSP Foremost Mage Megumin SSP	300.00	600.00
KSW76E034R Watching Over Gently Yunyun R	.25	.50
KSW76E034SSR Watching Over Gently Yunyun SR	1.00	2.00
KSW76E035R Master of Explosion Magic Someday Megumin R	.25	.50
KSW76E035SSR Master of Explosion Magic Someday Megumin SR	6.00	12.00
KSW76E036R Shy Yunyun R	.25	.50
KSW76E036SSR Shy Yunyun SR	60.00	125.00
KSW76E037R Chewing Komekko R	.25	.50
KSW76E037SSR Chewing Komekko SR	1.00	2.00
KSW76E038R Against the Mage Killer Wiz R	.25	.50
KSW76E039R When Push Comes to Shove Megumin R	.25	.50
KSW76E039SSR When Push Comes to Shove Megumin SR	1.25	2.50
KSW76E040R Embarassed Laugh Megumin R	.25	.50
KSW76E040SSR Embarassed Laugh Megumin SR	30.00	75.00

KSW76E041R Reunited After a Long Time Wiz R .25 .50
KSW76E041SSR Reunited After a Long Time Wiz SR 1.00 2.00
KSW76E042R Signature Statement Yunyun R .25 .50
KSW76E042SSR Signature Statement Yunyun SR 2.50 5.00
KSW76E043R Convenient Transportation Magic Wiz R .25 .50
KSW76E044U Breaking Out in Cold Sweat Yunyun U .15 .30
KSW76E045U I Am Called Funifura U .15 .30
KSW76E046U Sightseeing in the Crimson
Demon Village! Megumin U .15 .30
KSW76E047aU Expert Self-Introduction Crimson Demon A U .25 .50
KSW76E047bU Expert Self-Introduction Crimson Demon B U .25 .50
KSW76E047cU Expert Self-Introduction Crimson Demon C U .25 .50
KSW76E047dU Expert Self-Introduction Crimson Demon D U .25 .50
KSW76E048U Loading Up with Magic Power Wiz U .15 .30
KSW76E049U Unreasonable Demand Megumin U .15 .30
KSW76E050U Unyielding Spirit of Rivalry Megumin U .15 .30
KSW76E051U Fierce Battle Wiz U .15 .30
KSW76E052U Important Friend Megumin U .15 .30
KSW76E053U Party Member? Yunyun U .15 .30
KSW76E054U Supportive Cover Yuiyui U .15 .30
KSW76E055U Receiving Guests Komekko U .15 .30
KSW76E056U Today's Explosion Magic Megumin U .15 .30
KSW76E057C Beauty in a Yukata Megumin C .12 .25
KSW76E058C Megumin & Komekko C .12 .25
KSW76E059C Hyoizaburo & Yuiyui C .12 .25
KSW76E060C I Am Called Arue C .12 .25
KSW76E061C I Am Called Dodonko C .12 .25
KSW76E062C Freezing Magic Wiz C .12 .25
KSW76E063C Extreme Misunderstanding Yunyun C .12 .25
KSW76E064C Devious Younger Sister Komekko C .12 .25
KSW76E065C Do-or-Die Confession Yunyun C .12 .25
KSW76E066C Confrontation on the Cliff Yunyun C .12 .25
KSW76E067C Suggestive Megumin C .12 .25
KSW76E068C Beauty in a Yukata Yunyun C .12 .25
KSW76E069C Overflowing Magic Power Yunyun C .12 .25
KSW76E070U Forbidden Weapon U .15 .30
KSW76E071CR Teasing CLR .50 1.00
KSW76E071RRRR Teasing RRR 25.00 50.00
KSW76E072CR Linked Palms CLR .25 .50
KSW76E072RRRR Linked Palms RRR 10.00 20.00
KSW76E073CC Clap of Thunder CC .10 .20
KSW76E074CC Homecoming and Welcome Greetings CC .10 .20
KSW76E075CC An Explosion A Day CC .10 .20
KSW76E076RR Giving Full Support Aqua RR 1.25 2.50
KSW76E076SPSP Giving Full Support Aqua SP 150.00 300.00
KSW76E077RR To the Crimson Demon Village! Aqua RR 3.00 6.00
KSW76E077SSR To the Crimson Demon Village! Aqua SR 15.00 30.00
KSW76E078R Occasionally Goddess-Like Aqua R .25 .50
KSW76E078SSR Occasionally Goddess-Like Aqua SR 2.00 4.00
KSW76E079R Sightseeing in the Crimson Demon Village! Aqua R .25 .50
KSW76E079SSR Sightseeing in the
Crimson Demon Village! Aqua SR 1.50 3.00
KSW76E080R Result of Synthesis and Modification Sylvia R .25 .50
KSW76E081R Required Quality of Adventurer Life Aqua R .25 .50
KSW76E081SSR Required Quality of Adventurer Life Aqua SR 5.00 10.00
KSW76E082R Synthesis With the Mage Killer Sylvia R .25 .50
KSW76E083U Cunning Idea Aqua U .15 .30
KSW76E084U Women and Men's Feelings Sylvia U .15 .30
KSW76E085U Devil King Army General Sylvia U .15 .30
KSW76E086U Supportive Magic Aqua U .15 .30
KSW76E087U Droopy Temptation Sylvia U .15 .30
KSW76E088C Beauty in a Yukata Aqua C .12 .25
KSW76E089C Surprise Blow Aqua C .12 .25
KSW76E090C Chasing Down Sylvia C .12 .25
KSW76E091C Composed Retreat Sylvia C .12 .25
KSW76E092C Close to Tears Aqua C .12 .25
KSW76E093C Burn to Nothingness Sylvia C .12 .25
KSW76E094C Menacing Pose Aqua C .12 .25
KSW76E095C Discerning Eyes Sylvia C .12 .25
KSW76E096U Devil King Army Invades! U .15 .30
KSW76E097CR Protection of a Goddess CLR .30 .75
KSW76E097RRRR Protection of a Goddess RRR 4.00 8.00
KSW76E098CC Quest Failed CC .10 .20
KSW76E099CC Invasion of the Crimson Demon Village CC .10 .20
KSW76E099RRRR Invasion of the Crimson Demon Village RRR 3.00 6.00
KSW76E100CC Because Something Is! CC .10 .20
KSW76E101PR A Knight's Duty Darkness P .50 1.00
KSW76E102PR Mattress at Home Megumin P .30 .75
KSW76E103PR Appearance of the Main Star Yunyun P .75 1.50
KSW76E104PR Magical Academy Field Trip Aqua P .25 .50

2020 Weiss Schwarz Mob Psycho 100

MOBSX02001RR Arataka Reigen RR 2.50 5.00
MOBSX02001SPSP Arataka Reigen SP 100.00 200.00
MOBSX02002RR Reigen: Empathy RR .50 1.00
MOBSX02002SSR Reigen: Empathy SR 3.00 6.00
MOBSX02003RR Teruki Hanazawa RR .40 .80
MOBSX02003SPSP Teruki Hanazawa SP 50.00 100.00
MOBSX02004RR Teruki: Challenged Beliefs RR 1.00 2.00
MOBSX02004SSR Teruki: Challenged Beliefs SR 7.50 15.00
MOBSX02005R Reigen: Calling for Reinforcements R .25 .50
MOBSX02006R Teruki: Awakening Lab R .25 .50
MOBSX02007R Reigen: Life Advice R .25 .50
MOBSX02007SSR Reigen: Life Advice SR 3.00 6.00
MOBSX02008R Reigen: Searching for a Tsuchinoko R .25 .50
MOBSX02008SSR Reigen: Searching for a Tsuchinoko SR 4.00 8.00
MOBSX02009U Teruki: Delinquent U .15 .30
MOBSX02010U Teruki: On a Rescue Mission U .15 .30
MOBSX02011C Reigen: Adult Tactics C .12 .25
MOBSX02012C Teruki: A Close Shave C .12 .25
MOBSX02013C Reigen: Creepy Warning C .12 .25
MOBSX02014C Takeshi Hoshino C .12 .25
MOBSX02015C Rei Kurosaki C .12 .25
MOBSX02016C Go Asahi C .12 .25
MOBSX02017C Daichi Shiratori C .12 .25
MOBSX02018C Kaito Shiratori C .12 .25
MOBSX02019U Wig U .15 .30
MOBSX02020U Takoyaki U .15 .30
MOBSX02021CR A Huge Accident CLR .20 .40
MOBSX02021RRRR A Huge Accident RRR 7.50 15.00
MOBSX02022CR It's Okay to Run Away! CLR .20 .40
MOBSX02022RRRR It's Okay to Run Away! RRR 7.50 15.00
MOBSX02023CC Ultimate Technique: Esper Kick! CC .10 .20
MOBSX02024RR Dimple RR 2.50 5.00
MOBSX02024SPSP Dimple SP 60.00 125.00
MOBSX02025R Dimple: (LOL) Cult Leader R .25 .50
MOBSX02025SSR Dimple: (LOL) Cult Leader SR 2.00 4.00
MOBSX02026R Tome: Desperate for a New Member R .25 .50
MOBSX02026SSR Tome: Desperate for a New Member SR .75 1.50
MOBSX02027R Dimple: High-Level Evil Spirit R .25 .50
MOBSX02028R Chocolate-chan R .25 .50
MOBSX02029R Dimple: Output Assistant R .25 .50
MOBSX02030U Ichi Mezato U .15 .30
MOBSX02031U Tsubomi: Childhood Memories U .15 .30
MOBSX02032U Dimple: Innocent Introduction U .15 .30
MOBSX02033U Cookie-chan U .15 .30
MOBSX02034U Gum-chan U .15 .30
MOBSX02035U Candy-chan U .15 .30
MOBSX02036C Shirihiko Saruta C .12 .25
MOBSX02037C Mameta Inukawa C .12 .25
MOBSX02038C Haruto Kijibayashi C .12 .25
MOBSX02039C Scent-Ghoul C .12 .25
MOBSX02040C Dimple: Super Smug C .12 .25
MOBSX02041C Dimple: Possessing a Claw Minion C .12 .25
MOBSX02042C Caramel-chan C .12 .25
MOBSX02043C (LOL) Cult Member C .12 .25
MOBSX02044U (LOL) Mask U .15 .30
MOBSX02045U Psycho Helmet Cult Flyer U .15 .30
MOBSX02046CC What a Wonderful Smile! CC .10 .20
MOBSX02046RRRR What a Wonderful Smile! RRR 1.50 3.00
MOBSX02047CC Get a Clue! CC .10 .20
MOBSX02048CC What!? CC .10 .20
MOBSX02049RR Sho: Inspection RR 1.00 2.00
MOBSX02049SSR Sho: Inspection SR 3.00 6.00
MOBSX02050R Ishiguro R .25 .50
MOBSX02050SSR Ishiguro SR 2.50 5.00
MOBSX02051R Matsuo R .25 .50
MOBSX02051SSR Matsuo SR 1.00 2.00
MOBSX02052R Muto R .25 .50
MOBSX02053R Mukai R .25 .50
MOBSX02054U Yusuke Sakurai U .15 .30
MOBSX02055U Matsuo: Ritual Completion U .15 .30
MOBSX02056U Muraki: Having to Face Reality U .15 .30
MOBSX02057U Miyagawa U .15 .30
MOBSX02058U Yusuke: Having to Face Reality U .15 .30
MOBSX02059C Takeuchi C .12 .25
MOBSX02060C Tsuchiya C .12 .25
MOBSX02061C Terada C .12 .25
MOBSX02062C Megumu Koyama C .12 .25
MOBSX02063C Muraki C .12 .25
MOBSX02064C Takeuchi: Serious Mode C .12 .25
MOBSX02065C Matsuo's Poison Jar C .12 .25
MOBSX02066CC Claw Organization CC .10 .20
MOBSX02067CC Matsuo's Petshop of Horrors CC .10 .20
MOBSX02067RRRR Matsuo's Petshop of Horrors RRR 2.00 4.00
MOBSX02068RR Shigeo MOB Kageyama RR 4.00 8.00
MOBSX02068SPSP Shigeo MOB Kageyama SP 60.00 125.00
MOBSX02070RR Ritsu Kageyama RR 4.00 8.00
MOBSX02070SPSP Ritsu Kageyama SP 60.00 125.00
MOBSX02071RR Ritsu: Psychic Powers RR .30 .75
MOBSX02071SSR Ritsu: Psychic Powers SR 3.00 6.00
MOBSX02072R Musashi Goda R .25 .50
MOBSX02072SSR Musashi Goda SR 2.50 5.00
MOBSX02073R Ritsu: Concentrating R .25 .50
MOBSX02073SSR Ritsu: Concentrating SR 2.50 5.00
MOBSX02074R MOB: Puppy Love R .25 .50
MOBSX02074SSR MOB: Puppy Love SR 5.00 10.00
MOBSX02075R Ritsu: Guilty Conscience R .25 .50
MOBSX02075SSR Ritsu: Guilty Conscience SR 2.50 5.00
MOBSX02076R MOB: Searching for a Tsuchinoko R .25 .50
MOBSX02076SSR MOB: Searching for a Tsuchinoko SR 4.00 8.00
MOBSX02077R Ritsu: Fateful Meeting R .25 .50
MOBSX02077SSR Ritsu: Fateful Meeting SR 4.00 8.00
MOBSX02078R MOB: Childhood Memories R .25 .50
MOBSX02079R MOB: Gratitude Towards His Master R .25 .50
MOBSX02080U MOB: Together With Ritsu U .15 .30
MOBSX02081U Ritsu: Newfound Powers U .15 .30
MOBSX02082U Hikaru Tokugawa U .15 .30
MOBSX02083U Shinji Kamuro U .15 .30
MOBSX02084U Jun Sagawa U .15 .30
MOBSX02085U Hiroshi Kumagawa U .15 .30
MOBSX02086SSR Onigawara: Body Building Club SR 2.00 4.00
MOBSX02086U Onigawara: Body Building Club U .15 .30
MOBSX02087U Ritsu: Falling From Grace U .15 .30
MOBSX02088U MOB: Part-Time Job U .15 .30
MOBSX02089U Ritsu: Childhood Memories U .15 .30
MOBSX02090C Hideki Yamamura C .12 .25
MOBSX02091C Ryohei Shimura C .12 .25
MOBSX02092C Ritsu: Together with MOB C .12 .25
MOBSX02093C MOB: Club Activities C .12 .25
MOBSX02094C Ritsu: Awakening Lab C .12 .25
MOBSX02095aR Explosion Counter A R 6.00 12.00
MOBSX02095bR Explosion Counter B R 7.50 15.00
MOBSX02096U Spoon U .15 .30
MOBSX02097CR Together With These Guys... CLR .20 .40
MOBSX02097RRRR Together With These Guys... RRR 2.50 5.00
MOBSX02098CC Corruption and Guilt CC .10 .20
MOBSX02099CC Urgent Club Mission CC .10 .20
MOBSX02100CR 100% CLR .30 .60
MOBSX02100RRRR 100% RRR 6.00 12.00
MOBSX02101PR Petit Reigen P 12.50 25.00
MOBSX02102PR Petit Teruki P .60 1.25
MOBSX02103PR Petit Dimple P 2.00 4.00
MOBSX02104PR Petit Ritsu P .50 1.00
MOBSX02105PR Petit MOB P 4.00 8.00

2020 Weiss Schwarz Mob Psycho 100 Trial Deck

MOBSX02T01TD Reigen: Crossdressing .20 .40
MOBSX02T02RRRR Reigen: Banishing Salt Punch! RRR 1.50 3.00
MOBSX02T02TD Reigen: Banishing Salt Punch! .30 .75
MOBSX02T03SSR Reigen: Accepting a Client's Request SR 1.00 2.00
MOBSX02T03TD Reigen: Accepting a Client's Request .50 1.00
MOBSX02T04TD Reigen: Salt Splash! .20 .40
MOBSX02T05TD Reigen: Letting His Disciple Work .20 .40
MOBSX02T06TD Tome Kurata .20 .40
MOBSX02T07TD Ceiling Crasher .20 .40
MOBSX02T08TD Boss .20 .40
MOBSX02T09TD Tsubomi .20 .40
MOBSX02T10TD Club Recruitment (Green) .20 .40
MOBSX02T11SPSP MOB: Natural Psychic SP 200.00 400.00
MOBSX02T11TD MOB: Natural Psychic 2.00 4.00
MOBSX02T12TD Mr. Kageyama: Dinnertime .20 .40
MOBSX02T13RRRR Ritsu: Dinnertime RRR 20.00 40.00
MOBSX02T13TD Ritsu: Dinnertime .25 .50
MOBSX02T14TD Mrs. Kageyama: Dinnertime .20 .40
MOBSX02T15TD Goda: New Clubroom .20 .40
MOBSX02T16SSR MOB: Psychic Powers SR 2.00 4.00
MOBSX02T16TD MOB: Psychic Powers .75 1.50
MOBSX02T17TD Tenga Onigawara .20 .40
MOBSX02T18TD MOB: Crossdressing .20 .40
MOBSX02T19TD Part-Time Pay .30 .60
MOBSX02T20RRRR Fulfilling a Client's Request RRR 10.00 20.00
MOBSX02T20TD Fulfilling a Client's Request .30 .75
MOBSX02T21TD Club Recruitment (Blue) .20 .40

2020 Weiss Schwarz Nazarick Tomb of the Undead

OVLS62E001 Beautiful Princess, Nabe RR 5.00 10.00
OVLS62E001SP Beautiful Princess, Nabe GOLD SIGNATURE SP 200.00 400.00
OVLS62E002 Hero of Heroes, Momon RR .60 1.25
OVLS62E002SP Hero of Heroes, Momon GOLD SIGNATURE SP 750.00 1,500.00
OVLS62E003 Entomancer, Entoma R .25 .50
OVLS62E004 Nazarick's Maid Intern, Tuare R .25 .50
OVLS62E004S Nazarick's Maid Intern, Tuare SR 4.00 8.00
OVLS62E005 Commending Humans, Momon R .25 .50
OVLS62E006 Tuare's Rescue Operation, Sebas R .25 .50
OVLS62E006S Tuare's Rescue Operation, Sebas SR .50 1.00
OVLS62E007 Nazarick's Values, Nabe R .25 .50
OVLS62E007S Nazarick's Values, Nabe SR .50 1.00
OVLS62E008 Demon King, Jaldabaoth R .25 .50
OVLS62E008S Demon King, Jaldabaoth SR .60 1.25
OVLS62E009 Infiltration of the Capital, Shalltear U .15 .30
OVLS62E010 Undefeated Warrior, Momon U .15 .30
OVLS62E011 Ingenious Demon, Demiurge U .15 .30
OVLS62E012 Cold Reaction, Nabe U .15 .30
OVLS62E013 Details of Operation Gehenna, Demiurge U .15 .30
OVLS62E014 Where Happiness Is, Tuare C .12 .25
OVLS62E015 Dissolution Vessel, Solution C .12 .25
OVLS62E016 Djungarian Hamster? Hamsuke C .12 .25
OVLS62E017 Bug-Loving Maid, Entoma C .12 .25
OVLS62E018 Embodiment of Justice, Sebas C .12 .25
OVLS62E019 Stupefied, Nabe C .12 .25
OVLS62E020 Subjugation of the Wise King of the Forest, Momon C .12 .25
OVLS62E021 Kiss of Happiness U .15 .30
OVLS62E022 Wise King of the Forest U .15 .30
OVLS62E023 The Curtains Rise on a Legend CLR .30 .60
OVLS62E023R The Curtains Rise on a Legend RRR 6.00 12.00
OVLS62E024 Operation Gehenna CC .10 .20
OVLS62E024R Operation Gehenna RRR .75 1.50
OVLS62E025 Butler of Steel CC .10 .20
OVLS62E025R Butler of Steel RRR 3.00 6.00
OVLS62E026 Master of Great Tomb of Nazarick, Ainz RR 1.00 2.00
OVLS62E026S Master of Great Tomb of Nazarick, Ainz SR 7.50 15.00
OVLS62E027 Unreliable Nature Manipulator, Mare RR 3.00 6.00
OVLS62E027SP Unreliable Nature Manipulator,
Mare GOLD SIGNATURE SP 75.00 150.00
OVLS62E028 Boundless Obsessive Love, Albedo RR 1.25 2.50
OVLS62E028SP Boundless Obsessive Love,
Albedo GOLD SIGNATURE SP 750.00 1,500.00
OVLS62E029 Energetic Beast Tamer, Aura RR .75 1.50
OVLS62E029SP Energetic Beast Tamer,
Aura GOLD SIGNATURE SP 75.00 150.00
OVLS62E030 Emotion Inhibition, Ainz R .25 .50
OVLS62E031 Protector of the Treasury, Pandora's Actor R .25 .50
OVLS62E031S Protector of the Treasury, Pandora's Actor SR .50 1.00
OVLS62E032 Death Knight R .25 .50
OVLS62E032S Death Knight SR 2.00 4.00
OVLS62E033 A Woman's Battle, Albedo R .25 .50
OVLS62E033S A Woman's Battle, Albedo SR 7.50 15.00
OVLS62E034 Remains of a Dark Past, Pandora's Actor U .15 .30
OVLS62E035 Precious Watch, Aura U .15 .30
OVLS62E036 A Ring of Reward, Mare U .15 .30
OVLS62E037 Allure of Position of Uncle, Cocytus U .15 .30
OVLS62E038 Ecstatic Respect and Affection, Albedo U .15 .30
OVLS62E039 Absolute Loyalty, Demiurge U .15 .30
OVLS62E040 Elder Sister of the Battle Maids, Yuri U .15 .30
OVLS62E041 Assault Maid, CZ2128 Delta C .12 .25
OVLS62E042 Command Mantra, Demiurge C .12 .25
OVLS62E043 Sadist with a Smile, Lupusregina C .12 .25
OVLS62E044 Financial Management, Ainz C .12 .25
OVLS62E045 Oval Battle Maid, Narberal C .12 .25
OVLS62E046 As a Warrior, Cocytus C .12 .25
OVLS62E047 Freezing Spell R .25 .50
OVLS62E048 Benevolent Pure White Demon CLR .20 .40
OVLS62E048R Benevolent Pure White Demon RRR 15.00 30.00
OVLS62E049 A Woman's Nature CC .10 .20
OVLS62E049R A Woman's Nature RRR 10.00 20.00
OVLS62E050 Floor Guardian Twins CC .10 .20
OVLS62E050R Floor Guardian Twins RRR 2.50 5.00
OVLS62E051 Crimson Red Battle Maiden, Shalltear RR 7.50 15.00
OVLS62E051SP Crimson Red Battle Maiden,
Shalltear GOLD SIGNATURE SP 150.00 300.00
OVLS62E052 Infinite Loyalty, Albedo RR 7.50 15.00
OVLS62E052S Infinite Loyalty, Albedo SR 30.00 75.00
OVLS62E053 Overlord, Ainz RR .50 1.00
OVLS62E053SP Overlord, Ainz GOLD SIGNATURE SP 150.00 300.00
OVLS62E054 Strongest Magic Caster, Ainz R .25 .50
OVLS62E054S Strongest Magic Caster, Ainz SR 10.00 20.00
OVLS62E055 Defender of the Throne, Albedo R .25 .50
OVLS62E055S Defender of the Throne, Albedo SR 30.00 75.00
OVLS62E056 Cute Blunder, Albedo R .25 .50
OVLS62E057 Ability of a Floor Guardian, Shalltear R .25 .50
OVLS62E057S Ability of a Floor Guardian, Shalltear SR 5.00 10.00
OVLS62E058 8th Floor Guardian, Victim U .15 .30
OVLS62E059 Vampire Bride U .15 .30
OVLS62E060 Reason for the Handicap, Ainz U .15 .30
OVLS62E061 A Woman's Battle, Shalltear U .15 .30
OVLS62E062 True Vampire Ancestor, Shalltear U .15 .30
OVLS62E063 4th Floor Guardian, Gargantua U .15 .30
OVLS62E064 Leader of Pleiades, Sebas C .12 .25
OVLS62E065 Assistant Butler, Eclair C .12 .25
OVLS62E066 Nature of a Floor Guardian, Albedo C .12 .25
OVLS62E067 True Power, Ainz C .12 .25
OVLS62E068 Crazed Bloodlust, Shalltear C .12 .25
OVLS62E069 Resurrection Ritual, Ainz C .12 .25
OVLS62E070 Diversionary Tactics, Sebas C .12 .25
OVLS62E071 Shooting Star R .30 .75
OVLS62E072 Fallen Down U .15 .30
OVLS62E073 Grasp Heart CLR .20 .40
OVLS62E073R Grasp Heart RRR 2.50 5.00
OVLS62E074 Shalltear's Resurrection CC .10 .20
OVLS62E074R Shalltear's Resurrection RRR 15.00 30.00
OVLS62E075 Pipette Lance CC .10 .20
OVLS62E075R Pipette Lance RRR 5.00 10.00
OVLS62E076 Blue Rose Evileye RR 1.00 2.00
OVLS62E076SP Blue Rose Evileye GOLD SIGNATURE SP 75.00 150.00
OVLS62E077 The Golden Princess, Renner R .25 .50
OVLS62E077SP The Golden Princess, Renner
GOLD SIGNATURE SP 200.00 400.00
OVLS62E078 A Maiden's Heart, Evileye R .25 .50
OVLS62E079 White-Scaled Beauty, Crusch R .25 .50
OVLS62E079S White-Scaled Beauty, Crusch SR 2.00 4.00
OVLS62E080 Blue Rose Lakyus R .25 .50
OVLS62E080S Blue Rose Lakyus SR 2.00 4.00
OVLS62E081 Honorable Warrior, Cocytus R .25 .50
OVLS62E081S Honorable Warrior, Cocytus SR 3.00 6.00
OVLS62E082 A New Legend, Momon R .30 .75
OVLS62E082S A New Legend, Momon SR 3.00 6.00
OVLS62E083 Battle to Protect a Kingdom, Momon U .15 .30
OVLS62E084 Grotesque Hydra, Rororo U .15 .30
OVLS62E085 Strongest Lizardman Warrior, Zaryusu U .15 .30
OVLS62E086 Invisibility Magic, Evileye U .15 .30
OVLS62E087 Kingdom's Head Warrior, Gazef U .15 .30
OVLS62E088 Blue Rose Tina C .12 .25
OVLS62E089 Extreme Love, Renner C .12 .25
OVLS62E090 Blue Rose Tia C .12 .25
OVLS62E091 Green Claw Cheftian Shasuryu C .12 .25
OVLS62E092 Struggles of the Untalented, Climb C .12 .25
OVLS62E093 Brain C .12 .25
OVLS62E094 Blue Rose Gagaran C .12 .25
OVLS62E095 Berserker with a Giant Fist, Zenberu C .12 .25
OVLS62E096 Frost Pain U .15 .30
OVLS62E097 Adamantite-Class Adventurer U .15 .30
OVLS62E098 5th Tier Magic Caster CLR .30 .60
OVLS62E098R 5th Tier Magic Caster RRR 6.00 12.00
OVLS62E099 Raven Black Hero CC .10 .20
OVLS62E099R Raven Black Hero RRR 1.50 3.00
OVLS62E100 Ruler of the Frozen Lake CC .10 .20
OVLS62E100R Ruler of the Frozen Lake RRR 2.50 5.00
OVLS62E101PR Nazarick's Loyal Retainer, Demiurge P 1.25 2.50
OVLS62E102PR Unique Speech Mannerisms, Shalltear P 2.00 4.00
OVLS62E103PR To the Most Beloved One, Albedo P 12.50 25.00
OVLS62E104PR Supreme in a Weapons Battle, Cocytus P .50 1.00

OVLS62E105PR Bashful Effeminate Boy, Mare P .75 1.50
OVLS62E106PR Breath of Mental Manipulation, Aura P 6.00 12.00

2020 Weiss Schwarz Nazarick Tomb of the Undead Trial Deck

OVLS62TE01 6th Floor Guardian, Mare TD .20 .40
OVLS62TE02 6th Floor Guardian, Aura TD .20 .40
OVLS62TE03 Scheming Demon, Demiurge TD .20 .40
OVLS62TE04 Lunchtime, Aura TD .20 .40
OVLS62TE05 Innocent Insult, Mare TD .20 .40
OVLS62TE06 Butler of Great Tomb of Nazarick, Sebas TD .20 .40
OVLS62TE07 7th Floor Guardian, Demiurge TD .20 .40
OVLS62TE08 5th Floor Guardian, Cocytus TD 1.50 3.00
OVLS62TE09SP Endless Devotion, Albedo GOLD SIGNATURE SP 1,000.00 2,000.00
OVLS62TE09 Endless Devotion, Albedo TD 2.00 4.00
OVLS62TE10 Loyalty Ritual TD .20 .40
OVLS62TE11 The End and the Beginning, Momonga TD .20 .40
OVLS62TE12R Overseer of Floor Guardians, Albedo RRR 150.00 300.00
OVLS62TE12 Overseer of Floor Guardians, Albedo TD .30 .60
OVLS62TE13 1st to 3rd Floor Guardian, Shalltear TD 1.25 2.50
OVLS62TE14R Benevolent Overlord, Ainz RRR 6.00 12.00
OVLS62TE14 Benevolent Overlord, Ainz TD .20 .40
OVLS62TE15 The End and the Beginning, Albedo TD .20 .40
OVLS62TE16R Crimson Red Tyrant, Shalltear RRR 30.00 60.00
OVLS62TE16 Crimson Red Tyrant, Shalltear TD .20 .40
OVLS62TE17SP Ruler of Death, Ainz GOLD SIGNATURE SP 300.00 600.00
OVLS62TE17S Ruler of Death, Ainz SR 2.00 4.00
OVLS62TE17 Ruler of Death, Ainz TD 1.00 2.00
OVLS62TE18 Ring of Ainz Ooal Gown TD .20 .40
OVLS62TE19S The Curtain Closes SR 1.25 2.50
OVLS62TE19 The Curtain Closes TD .20 .40
OVLS62TE20 Staff of Ainz Ooal Gown TD .20 .40

2020 Weiss Schwarz Re ZERO Starting Life in Another World Memory Snow

RZS68E001 Snow Bunny R .25 .50
RZS68E002 Aim for New York? Petra R .25 .50
RZS68E003 Snow Bunny and Petra R .25 .50
RZS68E003S Snow Bunny and Petra SR 3.00 6.00
RZS68E004 Memory Snow Subaru R .25 .50
RZS68E004SP Memory Snow Subaru SP 75.00 150.00
RZS68E005 Aim for New York? Dine U .15 .30
RZS68E006 Aim for New York? Lucas U .15 .30
RZS68E007 Girl from Village Irlam, Petra U .15 .30
RZS68E008 Delicious Reward, Petra C .12 .25
RZS68E009 Aim for New York? Mildo C .12 .25
RZS68E010 Another World-Style? Incitement, Subaru C .12 .25
RZS68E011 Flying Assault Form of the Ultra-Firepower Weapon S-NO BUN-E C .12 .25
RZS68E012 First Wild and Crazy Snow Festival CC .10 .20
RZS68E013 Out-of-Season Snow Festival CC .10 .20
RZS68E013R Out-of-Season Snow Festival RRR 3.00 6.00
RZS68E014 Memory Snow Ram & Rem RR 4.00 8.00
RZS68E014S Memory Snow Ram & Rem SR 20.00 40.00
RZS68E015 God's Vantage Point, Ram RR 1.00 2.00
RZS68E015SP God's Vantage Point, Ram SP 200.00 400.00
RZS68E016 Memory Snow Beatrice RR .50 1.00
RZS68E016SP Memory Snow Beatrice SP 150.00 300.00
RZS68E017 Heavy Drinker, Ram RR .30 .75
RZS68E017S Heavy Drinker, Ram SR 20.00 40.00
RZS68E018 Beatrice Trying Her Best Alone R .25 .50
RZS68E018S Beatrice Trying Her Best Alone SR 3.00 6.00
RZS68E019 Ram With a Weakness to Cold R .25 .50
RZS68E019S Ram With a Weakness to Cold SR 4.00 8.00
RZS68E020 Ram Holding Her Breath R .50 1.00
RZS68E021 Unexpectedly Low Rating, Ram R .25 .50
RZS68E021S Unexpectedly Low Rating, Ram SR 5.00 10.00
RZS68E022 Delightful Banquet, Ram R .25 .50
RZS68E023 Subaru Shining Under the Night Sky R .25 .50
RZS68E024 Actually Having Fun? Beatrice R .25 .50
RZS68E025 Super Artist, Ram R .30 .75
RZS68E025S Super Artist, Ram SR 12.50 25.00
RZS68E026 Magnificent Subawaal Sculpture R .25 .50
RZS68E026S Magnificent Subawaal Sculpture SR 3.00 6.00
RZS68E027 Cold Surprise Attack, Beatrice U .15 .30
RZS68E028 Magic-Release Season Strategy Meeting, Beatrice U .15 .30
RZS68E029 Slight Omen, Roswaal U .15 .30
RZS68E030 Presented by Me! Subaru U .15 .30
RZS68E031 Scornful Gaze, Ram U .15 .30
RZS68E032 Expectedly Cold, Beatrice U .15 .30
RZS68E033 Harsher Than Usual, Ram U .15 .30
RZS68E034 Dinner Drink, Roswaal U .15 .30
RZS68E035 A Day to Remember, Ram U .15 .30
RZS68E036 Memory Snow Roswaal U .15 .30
RZS68E037 Ram Being a Wet Blanket U .15 .30
RZS68E038 Taking Care of the Drunkards, Ram C .12 .25
RZS68E039 Busy, Beatrice C .12 .25
RZS68E040 Abnormal Weather? Subaru C .12 .25
RZS68E041 Banquet's Corner, Beatrice C .12 .25
RZS68E042 Judge, Roswaal C .12 .25
RZS68E043 Slight Change, Ram C .12 .25
RZS68E044 Precious Alcohol, Ram C .12 .25
RZS68E045 Bored Spectator, Beatrice C .12 .25
RZS68E046 Madly in Love With Bubby, Beatrice C .12 .25
RZS68E047 Strong Enemy, Roswaal C .12 .25
RZS68E048 Tranquil Reception U .15 .30
RZS68E049 Daily Duties CLR .20 .40
RZS68E049R Daily Duties RRR 3.00 6.00
RZS68E050 Participating in the Snow Festival! CLR .20 .40
RZS68E050R Participating in the Snow Festival! RRR 1.50 3.00
RZS68E051 Expectant Gazes CC .10 .20
RZS68E051R Expectant Gazes RRR 3.00 6.00
RZS68E052CC Not a Bad Day CC .10 .20
RZS68E053 Secret Flower Garden, Emilia RR 2.50 5.00
RZS68E053S Secret Flower Garden, Emilia SR 30.00 75.00
RZS68E054 Leave Everything to Me, Rem RR 10.00 20.00
RZS68E054SP Leave Everything to Me, Rem SP 100.00 200.00
RZS68E055 That's Not It, Rem RR 3.00 6.00
RZS68E055S That's Not It, Rem SR 7.50 15.00
RZS68E056 The World Reflected in Her Eyes, Emilia RR 4.00 8.00
RZS68E056S The World Reflected in Her Eyes, Emilia SR 10.00 20.00
RZS68E057 Memory Snow Emilia RR 2.00 4.00
RZS68E057SP Memory Snow Emilia SP 125.00 250.00
RZS68E058 Delightful Banquet, Rem RR 2.50 5.00
RZS68E058S Delightful Banquet, Rem SR 15.00 30.00
RZS68E059 Dream-Like Scenery, Rem & Emilia R .25 .50
RZS68E060 I Worked Hard! Rem R 1.50 3.00
RZS68E061 About the Future, Puck R .25 .50
RZS68E061S About the Future, Puck SR 1.25 2.50
RZS68E062 No Cheating, Emilia R .25 .50
RZS68E062S No Cheating, Emilia SR 7.50 15.00
RZS68E063 Unsettling Declaration, Rem R .25 .50
RZS68E064 Recognition-Hindering Robe, Emilia R .25 .50
RZS68E064S Recognition-Hindering Robe, Emilia SR 10.00 20.00
RZS68E065 Magic-Release Season Strategy Meeting, Emilia R .25 .50
RZS68E066 Date-Day Morning, Emilia R .50 1.00
RZS68E067 Combination of Ideals, Rem R .25 .50
RZS68E067S Combination of Ideals, Rem SR 2.50 5.00
RZS68E068 Satisfying Conclusion, Puck U .15 .30
RZS68E069 Delightful Banquet, Emilia U .15 .30
RZS68E070 Great Spirit Attack, Puck U .15 .30
RZS68E071 Internet Literacy? Emilia U .15 .30
RZS68E072 Concaved Puck U .15 .30
RZS68E073 Earnest Admiration, Rem U .15 .30
RZS68E074 Madly in Love With Puck, Emilia U .15 .30
RZS68E075 Hot Springs Operation, Subaru U .15 .30
RZS68E076 Magic-Release Season Strategy Meeting, Puck U .15 .30
RZS68E077 Aloof Emilia U .15 .30
RZS68E078 Speaking in Riddles, Puck U .15 .30
RZS68E079 Drunk Emilia C .12 .25
RZS68E080 Secret Mission, Subaru C .12 .25
RZS68E081 Highly Considerate, Puck C .12 .25
RZS68E082 Slight Change, Rem C .12 .25
RZS68E083 Can't Get Enough of This, Subaru C .12 .25
RZS68E084 Emilia Working Hard C .12 .25
RZS68E085 Magic-Release Season Strategy Meeting, Rem C .12 .25
RZS68E086 Winter Clothing, Rem C .12 .25
RZS68E087 Unsatisfied With the Grading, Emilia C .12 .25
RZS68E088 Releasing Mana, Puck C .12 .25
RZS68E089 The One Who Did the Work, Rem C .12 .25
RZS68E090 Secret Flower Garden, Subaru C .12 .25
RZS68E091 Imploring Gaze, Rem C .12 .25
RZS68E092 Drunk Rem C .12 .25
RZS68E093 Horrific Mayonnaise Human U .15 .30
RZS68E094 Avant-Garde Sculpture U .15 .30
RZS68E095 Peaceful Moment CLR .20 .40
RZS68E095R Peaceful Moment RRR 7.50 15.00
RZS68E096 It's All Subaru's Fault CLR .20 .40
RZS68E096R It's All Subaru's Fault RRR 15.00 30.00
RZS68E097 Praise me! Praise me! Aura CC .10 .20
RZS68E097R Praise me! Praise me! Aura RRR 12.50 25.00
RZS68E098 It's Magic-Release Season! CC .10 .20
RZS68E098R It's Magic-Release Season! RRR 1.25 2.50
RZS68E099 First Experience With Alcohol CC .10 .20
RZS68E100 Arrival of the Next Morning CC .10 .20
RZS68E101PR Dot Ram (Memory Snow) P 20.00 40.00
RZS68E102PR Dot Beatrice (Memory Snow) P .60 1.25
RZS68E103PR Dot Rem (Memory Snow) P 1.50 3.00
RZS68E104PR Dot Emilia & Puck (Memory Snow) P 1.00 2.00

2020 Weiss Schwarz Sword Art Online Alicization

SAOS65E001RR To the Cave in the North, Alice RR 12.50 25.00
SAOS65E001SPSP To the Cave in the North, Alice SP 250.00 500.00
SAOS65E002RR Resolution to Break Away, Alice RR 12.50 25.00
SAOS65E002SSR Resolution to Break Away, Alice SR 15.00 30.00
SAOS65E003RR If You Want My Answer Asuna RR 5.00 10.00
SAOS65E004RR Brilliant Female Knight, Alice RR 15.00 30.00
SAOS65E004SPSP Brilliant Female Knight, Alice SP 75.00 150.00
SAOS65E005R Party in Full Swing, Selka R .25 .50
SAOS65E006R Lifeline Chains, Alice R .25 .50
SAOS65E006SSR Lifeline Chains, Alice SR 10.00 20.00
SAOS65E007R How About Something Sweet? Asuna R .25 .50
SAOS65E008R Cooking with the Sacred Arts, Alice R .50 1.00
SAOS65E008SSR Cooking with the Sacred Arts, Alice SR 12.50 25.00
SAOS65E009R Glittering Osmanthus, Alice R 2.00 4.00
SAOS65E009SSR Glittering Osmanthus, Alice SR 12.50 25.00
SAOS65E010U Information About the Virtual World, Asuna U .30 .60
SAOS65E011U Sore Loser, Alice U .15 .30
SAOS65E012U Incident of a Certain Summer, Alice U .15 .30
SAOS65E013U Memories of a Younger Sister, Alice U .30 .60
SAOS65E014C An Unexpected Welcome, Alice C .12 .25
SAOS65E015C Dauntless Perfect Control Art, Alice C .12 .25
SAOS65E016C Confrontation with PK Squadron, Asuna C .12 .25
SAOS65E017C Fighting with Minions, Alice C .12 .25
SAOS65E018C Feelings Towards Older Sister, Selka C .12 .25
SAOS65E019C Girl to Be Saved, Alice C .12 .25
SAOS65E020C Ocean Turtle Asuna C .12 .25
SAOS65E021U Godsend U .15 .30
SAOS65E022U Sergeant First Class Natsuki Aki U .15 .30
SAOS65E023CR Osmanthus Sword CLR .75 1.50
SAOS65E023RRRR Osmanthus Sword RRR 15.00 30.00
SAOS65E024CC Declaration of Independence CC .10 .20
SAOS65E024RRRR Declaration of Independence RRR 15.00 30.00
SAOS65E025CC To Where You Are CC .10 .20
SAOS65E026RR With Pride Cardinal RR 2.00 4.00
SAOS65E026SSR With Pride Cardinal SR 7.50 15.00
SAOS65E027R Spending a Day Off, Sortiliena R .25 .50
SAOS65E028R Fight Between Bitter Enemies, Cardinal R .25 .50
SAOS65E028SSR Fight Between Bitter Enemies, Cardinal SR 1.25 2.50
SAOS65E029R Girls of Age, Ronie & Tiese R .25 .50
SAOS65E029SSR Girls of Age, Ronie & Tiese SR 25.00 50.00
SAOS65E030R Perfect Control Art Cardinal R .25 .50
SAOS65E031R The Sage of the Library Cardinal R .75 1.50
SAOS65E031SSR The Sage of the Library Cardinal SR 7.50 15.00
SAOS65E032R The Legendary Hero Bercouli Synthesis One R .25 .50
SAOS65E033U The Girl Called Lyserith, Cardinal U .15 .30
SAOS65E034U Sister-In-Training Fizel Synthesis Twenty-Nine U .15 .30
SAOS65E035U Appeal to the Integrity Knight, Tiese & Ronie U .25 .50
SAOS65E036U Heroic Warrior, Bercouli U .20 .40
SAOS65E037U Page Tiese U .15 .30
SAOS65E038U Serlut Style User, Sortiliena U .15 .30
SAOS65E039U Detestable Face Fanatio U .15 .30
SAOS65E040C The Crimson Knight Deusolbert Synthesis Seven C .12 .25
SAOS65E041C Page Ronie C .12 .25
SAOS65E042C Sister-In-Training Linel Synthesis Twenty-Eight C .12 .25
SAOS65E043C Violet-Haired Suave Man Eldrie Synthesis Thirty-One C .12 .25
SAOS65E044C Information About the Virtual World, Leafa C .12 .25
SAOS65E045C The Relentless Knight Fanatio Synthesis Two C .12 .25
SAOS65E046C Knight on Flying Dragon, Deulsolbert C .12 .25
SAOS65E047C Swordsman's Pride Volo C .12 .25
SAOS65E048U Cardinal's Dagger U .15 .30
SAOS65E049CR What It Means to Be Human CLR .30 .75
SAOS65E049RRRR What It Means to Be Human RRR 5.00 10.00
SAOS65E050CC Conclusion After 200 Years CC .10 .20
SAOS65E051CC Bercouli and the Northern White Dragon CC .10 .20
SAOS65E052RR Pontifex of the Axiom Church Administrator RR 4.00 8.00
SAOS65E052SSR Pontifex of the Axiom Church Administrator SR 15.00 30.00
SAOS65E053R Sacred Arts Researcher Quinella R .25 .50
SAOS65E053SSR Sacred Arts Researcher Quinella SR 3.00 6.00
SAOS65E054R Preparation for the Load Test, Administrator R .25 .50
SAOS65E054SSR Preparation for the Load Test, Administrator SR 20.00 40.00
SAOS65E055R Brutal Lightning Attack, Administrator R .25 .50
SAOS65E056R Sweet Temptation, Administrator R .60 1.25
SAOS65E056SSR Sweet Temptation, Administrator SR 5.00 10.00
SAOS65E057R Ruler Administrator R .25 .50
SAOS65E057SSR Ruler Administrator SR 4.00 8.00
SAOS65E058U Confrontation with PK Squadron, Lisbeth U .15 .30
SAOS65E059U Sword Skill Administrator U .15 .30
SAOS65E060U Endless Thirst to Rule Quinella U .15 .30
SAOS65E061C Unexpected Limit, Administrator C .12 .25
SAOS65E062C Your Eminence, Prime Senator Chudelkin C .12 .25
SAOS65E063C Information About the Virtual World, Silica C .12 .25
SAOS65E064C Sword Automaton Sword Golem C .12 .25
SAOS65E065U Piety Module U .20 .40
SAOS65E066C Memory Crystal C .12 .25
SAOS65E067CC Ruler of the Human Realm CC .20 .40
SAOS65E067RRRR Ruler of the Human Realm RRR 30.00 75.00
SAOS65E068CR Temptation into Eternal Stasis CLR .20 .40
SAOS65E069RR Eugeo's Partner Kirito RR 10.00 20.00
SAOS65E069SPSP Eugeo's Partner Kirito SP 150.00 300.00
SAOS65E070RR Roommate of a Free Spirit, Eugeo RR 6.00 12.00
SAOS65E070SSR Roommate of a Free Spirit, Eugeo SR 20.00 40.00
SAOS65E071RR Kirito's Partner Eugeo RR 15.00 30.00
SAOS65E071SPSP Kirito's Partner Eugeo SP 150.00 300.00
SAOS65E072RR Night-Sky-Colored Hero, Kirito RR 7.50 15.00
SAOS65E072SSR Night-Sky-Colored Hero, Kirito SR 40.00 80.00
SAOS65E073R Repayment for Lunch, Kirito R .25 .50
SAOS65E073SSR Repayment for Lunch, Kirito SR 6.00 12.00
SAOS65E074R Power of Meaning Kirito R .50 1.00
SAOS65E075R Body into Sword, Eugeo R 4.00 8.00
SAOS65E076R Light from Sacred Arts, Eugeo R .50 1.00
SAOS65E077R Taboo and Justice, Eugeo R .30 .75
SAOS65E078R Eternal Ice and the Rose Eugeo R .50 1.00
SAOS65E078SSR Eternal Ice and the Rose Eugeo SR 4.00 8.00
SAOS65E079U Searching for Papa, Yui U .25 .50
SAOS65E080U To the Cave in the North, Kirito U .25 .50
SAOS65E081U Seventh-Generation Carver, Eugeo U .25 .50
SAOS65E082U Confrontation with PK Squadron, Kirito U .25 .50
SAOS65E083U Swordsman's Pride Kirito U .25 .50
SAOS65E084U Information About the Virtual World, Sinon U .25 .50
SAOS65E085U Truce Kirito U .20 .40
SAOS65E086U Departure from Rulid Village, Kirito U .20 .40
SAOS65E087U Spurring on a Best Friend, Eugeo U .20 .40
SAOS65E088C To the Cave in the North, Eugeo C .20 .40
SAOS65E089C Zephilia Buds, Kirito C .12 .25
SAOS65E090C Former Appearance, Kirito C .12 .25
SAOS65E091C Confrontation with PK Squadron, Sinon C .12 .25
SAOS65E092C The 32nd Knight Eugeo Synthesis Thirty-Two C .12 .25
SAOS65E093C Suspicious Part-Time Job? Kazuto C .12 .25
SAOS65E094C Someone Else's Sword Skill, Eugeo C .12 .25
SAOS65E095U Charlotte's Assist U .15 .30
SAOS65E096C The Demon Tree Gigas Cedar C .12 .25
SAOS65E097CR Red Rose Sword CLR .50 1.00
SAOS65E097RRRR Red Rose Sword RRR 30.00 75.00
SAOS65E098CC Night-Sky Blade CC .20 .40
SAOS65E098RRRR Night-Sky Blade RRR 6.00 12.00
SAOS65E099CC Blue Rose Sword CC .20 .40
SAOS65E099RRRR Blue Rose Sword RRR 30.00 60.00
SAOS65E100CC Stay Cool CC .10 .20
SAOS65E101PR Glitter of the Water's Surface, Asuna P 25.00 50.00
SAOS65E102PR Glitter of the Water's Surface, Alice P 6.00 12.00
SAOS65E103PR How a Noble Should Be, Tiese & Ronie P 6.00 12.00
SAOS65E104PR The Other Pontifex Cardinal P 3.00 6.00
SAOS65E105PR Willowy Body, Administrator P 12.50 25.00
SAOS65E106PR Glitter of the Water's Surface, Eugeo & Kirito P 30.00 60.00

2020 Weiss Schwarz Sword Art Online Alicization Trial Deck

SAOS65TE01TD Memories That Shouldn't Exist Alice .15 .30
SAOS65TE02SSR Dazzling Gold, Alice SR 1.00 2.00
SAOS65TE02TD Dazzling Gold, Alice .15 .30
SAOS65TE03TD Seeking Ice, Alice .15 .30
SAOS65TE04TD Hard Worker, Selka .15 .30
SAOS65TE05RRRR The Osmanthus Knight Alice Synthesis Thirty RRR 30.00 75.00
SAOS65TE05TD The Osmanthus Knight Alice Synthesis Thirty .15 .30
SAOS65TE06SPSP Female Childhood Friend Alice SP 200.00 400.00
SAOS65TE06TD Female Childhood Friend Alice .15 .30
SAOS65TE07TD Crime Committed by Fingertips .15 .30
SAOS65TE08TD Right Hand Self to Left .15 .30
SAOS65TE09TD Somber Expression, Eugeo .15 .30
SAOS65TE10TD Seeking Ice, Kirito .30 .60
SAOS65TE11SSR Primary Trainee Eugeo & Kirito SR 1.00 2.00
SAOS65TE11TD Primary Trainee Eugeo & Kirito .50 1.00
SAOS65TE12TD Carver of the Giant Tree Kirito .50 1.00
SAOS65TE13TD Lunch Time, Eugeo .15 .30
SAOS65TE14SPSP Fate Beginning to Change, Eugeo SP .15 .30
SAOS65TE14TD Fate Beginning to Change, Eugeo .15 .30
SAOS65TE15TD Memories That Shouldn't Exist Eugeo .15 .30
SAOS65TE16TD Carver of the Giant Tree Eugeo .30 .75
SAOS65TE17RRRR Lost Child of Vecta Kirito RRR 12.50 25.00
SAOS65TE17TD Lost Child of Vecta Kirito .50 1.00
SAOS65TE18TD Stacia Window .50 1.00
SAOS65TE19RRRR Adventure of the Past RRR 20.00 40.00
SAOS65TE19TD Adventure of the Past .20 .40

2020 Weiss Schwarz That Time I Got Reincarnated As a Slime

TSKS70E001RR After the Battle, Rimuru RR 10.00 20.00
TSKS70E001SECSEC After the Battle, Rimuru SCR 300.00 600.00
TSKS70E002RR Successor, Rimuru RR 3.00 6.00
TSKS70E003RR Achieving Vindication, Shion RR 10.00 20.00
TSKS70E004R Cutting Down in One Blow, Hakurou R .25 .50
TSKS70E005R Feeling of Respect, Eren R 1.50 3.00
TSKS70E006R Caretaker of the Great Forest Treyni R .50 1.00
TSKS70E007R Samurai Shion R .75 1.50
TSKS70E008R Mighty Warrior, Shion R .50 1.00
TSKS70E008SSR Mighty Warrior, Shion SR 20.00 40.00
TSKS70E009R Shared Journey, Rimuru R .50 1.00
TSKS70E009SSR Shared Journey, Rimuru SR 4.00 8.00
TSKS70E010R Mysterious Demon, Cromwell R .50 1.00
TSKS70E010SSR Mysterious Demon, Cromwell SR 1.50 3.00
TSKS70E011R Orc Disaster Geld R .30 .75
TSKS70E012U Orc Lord Geld U .15 .30
TSKS70E013U Elemental Colossus U .15 .30
TSKS70E014U Demon Lord Ramiris U 1.50 3.00
TSKS70E015U Instructor Hakurou U .15 .30
TSKS70E016U Master, Hakurou U .15 .30
TSKS70E017U Hero King Gazel U .15 .30
TSKS70E018C Cunning Majin, Gelmud C .12 .25
TSKS70E019C Orcs C .12 .25
TSKS70E020C Expert Blacksmith, Kaijin C .12 .25
TSKS70E021C Grandmaster Yuuki C .12 .25
TSKS70E022C Orc General C .12 .25
TSKS70E023C Troublemakers Kaval & Eren & Gido C .12 .25
TSKS70E024C Successor of Orc Disaster's Dying Wishes, Geld C .12 .25
TSKS70E025C Fierce Rivalry, Shion C .12 .25
TSKS70E026U Shion's Home Cooking U .15 .30
TSKS70E027C Weapons Made in Tempest C .12 .25
TSKS70E028CR Meguru Mono CLR .30 .75
TSKS70E028RRRR Meguru Mono RRR 1.50 3.00
TSKS70E029CC Overwhelming Blow CC .10 .20
TSKS70E029RRRR Overwhelming Blow RRR 1.25 2.50
TSKS70E030CC Death March Dance CC .10 .20
TSKS70E031RR Tribe's Princess, Shuna RR 3.00 6.00
TSKS70E032RR Child on the Inside? Milim RR 10.00 20.00
TSKS70E032SSR Child on the Inside? Milim SR 30.00 60.00
TSKS70E033RR Dragonoid Milim RR 3.00 6.00
TSKS70E034RR Power of a Kijin, Benimaru RR 1.00 2.00
TSKS70E034SSR Power of a Kijin, Benimaru SR 6.00 12.00
TSKS70E035R A Blow from Above, Rimuru R 7.50 15.00
TSKS70E036R Loss of Fighting Spirit, Milim R .60 1.25
TSKS70E037R Shared Journey, Shizu R .25 .50
TSKS70E037SSR Shared Journey, Shizu SR 7.50 15.00
TSKS70E038R Imperial Wrath, Milim R .25 .50
TSKS70E038SSR Imperial Wrath, Milim SR 7.50 15.00
TSKS70E039R Glare, Rimuru R .50 1.00
TSKS70E040R For Everyone's Sake, Shuna R 2.00 4.00
TSKS70E040SSR For Everyone's Sake, Shuna SR 12.50 25.00
TSKS70E041R Pursuit, Milim R .50 1.00
TSKS70E041SSR Pursuit, Milim SR 7.50 15.00
TSKS70E042U Daily Training, Benimaru U .15 .30

TSKS70E043U Swordsmith Kurobe U .15 .30
TSKS70E044U Everyone's Teacher, Rimuru U .15 .30
TSKS70E045U Honed Senses, Kurobe U .15 .30
TSKS70E046U Shrine Maiden Princess Shuna U .15 .30
TSKS70E047U Ifrit's Manifestation, Shizu U .15 .30
TSKS70E048U Highest-Ranked Flame Spirit Ifrit U .15 .30
TSKS70E049C Strong Will, Benimaru C .12 .25
TSKS70E050C Radiant Smile, Milim C .12 .25
TSKS70E051C Which One Do You Choose? Rimuru C .12 .25
TSKS70E052C A Break at the Hot Springs, Milim C .12 .25
TSKS70E053C Black Lightning Rimuru C .12 .25
TSKS70E054C Taking Care Together, Shizu C .12 .25
TSKS70E055C Fierce Rivalry, Shuna C .12 .25
TSKS70E056C Samurai General Benimaru C .12 .25
TSKS70E057U Declaration of Being Besties! U .15 .30
TSKS70E058U Flare Circle U .15 .30
TSKS70E059CR A Way of Saying Hello CLR .25 .50
TSKS70E059RRRR A Way of Saying Hello RRR 5.00 10.00
TSKS70E060CR New Power CLR .30 .75
TSKS70E060RRRR New Power RRR 4.00 8.00
TSKS70E061CC Power of a Demon Lord CC .15 .30
TSKS70E062CC A Scenery to Be Shared CC .15 .30
TSKS70E063CC Awoken Impulse CC .15 .30
TSKS70E064RR Head of the Monsters, Rimuru RR 7.50 15.00
TSKS70E065RR Conqueror of Flames Shizu RR 7.50 15.00
TSKS70E066RR Memories of Japan, Shizu RR 6.00 12.00
TSKS70E066SSR Memories of Japan, Shizu SR 30.00 75.00
TSKS70E067R Request at the Kingdom of Filtwood, Shizu R 7.50 15.00
TSKS70E067SSR Request at the Kingdom of Filtwood, Shizu SR 7.50 15.00
TSKS70E068R Partner Sharing Body and Soul, Rimuru R .30 .75
TSKS70E068SSR Partner Sharing Body and Soul, Rimuru SR 6.00 12.00
TSKS70E069R Power to Protect Comrades, Rimuru R .60 1.25
TSKS70E070R Intimidation Ranga R .50 1.00
TSKS70E070SSR Intimidation Ranga SR 1.50 3.00
TSKS70E071R Inherited Wishes, Rimuru R .30 .75
TSKS70E072R Secret Strategy, Rimuru R .20 .40
TSKS70E072SSR Secret Strategy, Rimuru SR 2.50 5.00
TSKS70E073R Quiet Anger, Souei R .50 1.00
TSKS70E073SSR Quiet Anger, Souei SR 1.00 2.00
TSKS70E074U Auto-Battle Mode Rimuru U .15 .30
TSKS70E075SSR Last Journey, Shizu SR 12.50 25.00
TSKS70E075U Last Journey, Shizu U .50 1.00
TSKS70E076U Sensible Rigur U .15 .30
TSKS70E077U All to Oneself, Chloe U .50 1.00
TSKS70E078U Creating Potions! Rimuru U .30 .60
TSKS70E079U Spy Souei U .15 .30
TSKS70E080U Sticky Steel Thread Rimuru U .15 .30
TSKS70E081U Attendance Check, Rimuru U .25 .50
TSKS70E082U The One Who Devours All, Rimuru U .15 .30
TSKS70E083U Power of a Hero, Shizu U .15 .30
TSKS70E084U Execution of Duty, Souei U .15 .30
TSKS70E085C Into the Midst of Battle, Ranga C .12 .25
TSKS70E086C New Subordinate, Soka C .12 .25
TSKS70E087C Vortex Crash Gabiru C .12 .25
TSKS70E088C Clone, Souei C .12 .25
TSKS70E089C Desperate Battle, Gobta C .12 .25
TSKS70E090C Name Overwritten, Gabiru C .12 .25
TSKS70E091C Chloe & Alice & Kenya & Ryota & Gale C .12 .25
TSKS70E092C A Break at the Hot Springs, Rimuru C .12 .25
TSKS70E093C Rigurd Shock Rigurd C .12 .25
TSKS70E094C Shadow Movement Ranga C .12 .25
TSKS70E095SSR Anti-Magic Mask SR 2.50 5.00
TSKS70E095U Anti-Magic Mask U .15 .30
TSKS70E096C Unique Skill Great Sage C .12 .25
TSKS70E097CR Legendary Hero CLR .30 .75
TSKS70E097RRRR Legendary Hero RRR 20.00 40.00
TSKS70E098CC A Trap Laid Out CC .15 .30
TSKS70E099CC Last-Ditch Effort CC .15 .30
TSKS70E099RRRR Last-Ditch Effort RRR 1.50 3.00
TSKS70E100CC Squaring off Against a Spirit CC .10 .20
TSKS70E101PR Life Amongst Bountiful Valleys, Rimuru P 2.00 4.00
TSKS70E102PR A Break at the Hot Springs, Shion P 4.00 8.00
TSKS70E103PR Splendid Transformation! Milim P 2.50 5.00
TSKS70E104PR A Break at the Hot Springs, Shuna P 1.25 2.50
TSKS70E105PR Everyone's Teacher, Shizu P 1.00 2.00

2020 Weiss Schwarz That Time I Got Reincarnated As a Slime Trial Deck

TSKS70TE01SPSP Rimuru Tempest SP .20 .40
TSKS70TE01TD Rimuru Tempest 12.50 25.00
TSKS70TE02TD Soon-to-be Sage, Mikami Satoru .20 .40
TSKS70TE03TD Bonds of Friendship, Veldora .20 .40
TSKS70TE04SSR Reincarnated From Another World, Rimuru SR 2.50 5.00
TSKS70TE04TD Reincarnated From Another World, Rimuru .20 .40
TSKS70TE05TD Free Union Adventurer Gido .20 .40
TSKS70TE06TD Free Union Adventurer Kaval .20 .40
TSKS70TE07TD Free Union Adventurer Eren .20 .40
TSKS70TE08RRRR Predator Rimuru RRR 30.00 60.00
TSKS70TE08TD Predator Rimuru 1.00 2.00
TSKS70TE09SSR Naming SR 2.50 5.00
TSKS70TE09TD Naming .20 .40
TSKS70TE10TD Promises and Gratitude .20 .40
TSKS70TE11RRRR Looking for Party Members, Shizu RRR 10.00 20.00
TSKS70TE11TD Looking for Party Members, Shizu .20 .40
TSKS70TE12TD Water BladeRimuru .20 .40
TSKS70TE13TD Muscles Everywhere, Rigurd .20 .40
TSKS70TE14TD Solitary Path, Shizu .20 .40
TSKS70TE15TD Summoning Tempest Wolves! Gobta .20 .40
TSKS70TE16RRRR Heart of Loyalty, Ranga RRR 7.50 15.00
TSKS70TE16TD Heart of Loyalty, Ranga .20 .40
TSKS70TE17TD Bonds of Friendship, Rimuru .20 .40
TSKS70TF18SPSP Gushing Flames, Shizu SP 400.00 800.00
TSKS70TE18TD Gushing Flames, Shizu .30 .75
TSKS70TE19TD Anti-Magic Mask 4.00 8.00
TSKS70TE20TD Fated One .20 .40

2021 Weiss Schwarz Bofuri I Don't Want to Get Hurt So I'll Max Out My Defense

BFRS78E001RR Battle Craftswoman, Iz RR 15.00 30.00
BFRS78E001SPSP Battle Craftswoman, Iz SP 125.00 250.00
BFRS78E002RR Loving Sacrifice, Maple RR 7.50 15.00
BFRS78E002SECSEC Loving Sacrifice, Maple SCR 300.00 600.00
BFRS78E003RR Giant Killing, May & Yui RR 4.00 8.00
BFRS78E003SPaSP Giant Killing, May & Yui A SP 150.00 300.00
BFRS78E003SPbSP Giant Killing, May & Yui B SP 125.00 250.00
BFRS78E004R Moment Between the Two, Maple R 1.00 2.00
BFRS78E004SSR Moment Between the Two, Maple SR 7.50 15.00
BFRS78E005R Newbie Players, May & Yui R .75 1.50
BFRS78E005SSR Newbie Players, May & Yui SR 12.50 25.00
BFRS78E006R Endless Exploration, Iz R .30 .75
BFRS78E006SSR Endless Exploration, Iz SR 1.00 2.00
BFRS78E007R Guild Master, Maple R .30 .75
BFRS78E008R Battle-Ready Force, May R .75 1.50
BFRS78E008SSR Battle-Ready Force, May SR 7.50 15.00
BFRS78E009R Battle-Ready Force, Yui R .50 1.00
BFRS78E009SSR Battle-Ready Force, Yui SR 7.50 15.00
BFRS78E010R Snow White, Maple R .75 1.50
BFRS78E010SSR Snow White, Maple SR 7.50 15.00
BFRS78E011U Swimsuit, Yui U .15 .30
BFRS78E012U Third Place in the Event, Maple U .15 .30
BFRS78E013U Swimsuit, May U .15 .30
BFRS78E014U Solid Fighting Style, Kuromu U .15 .30
BFRS78E015U Twin Younger Sister, Yui U .15 .30
BFRS78E016U Unbalanced, Maple U .15 .30
BFRS78E017U Twin Elder Sister, May U .15 .30
BFRS78E018U Alchemist's Long Coat, Iz U .15 .30
BFRS78E019C One of the Twins, May C .12 .25
BFRS78E020C Mature Response, Iz C .12 .25
BFRS78E021C One of the Twins, Yui C .12 .25
BFRS78E022C Counter, Maple C .12 .25
BFRS78E023C Maxing Out, May C .12 .25
BFRS78E024C Maxing Out,Yui C .12 .25
BFRS78E025C Bloodstained Plate, Kuromu C .12 .25
BFRS78E026U Unexpected Bonus U .15 .30
BFRS78E027CR Loving Sacrifice CLR .25 .50
BFRS78E027RRRR Loving Sacrifice RRR 12.50 25.00
BFRS78E028CC Maple Tree CC .12 .25
BFRS78E029CC Destroyer CC .12 .25
BFRS78E029RRRR Destroyer RRR 3.00 6.00
BFRS78E030CC Iz's Workshop CC .12 .25
BFRS78E031RR Multi-Colored, Sally RR 12.50 25.00
BFRS78E031SPSP Multi-Colored, Sally SP 250.00 500.00
BFRS78E032RR Longsword, Kasumi RR .50 1.00
BFRS78E032SPSP Longsword, Kasumi SP 75.00 150.00
BFRS78E033R Event Bonus, Kasumi R .25 .50
BFRS78E033SSR Event Bonus, Kasumi SR 2.00 4.00
BFRS78E034R Strongest Newbie, Maple R .30 .75
BFRS78E034SSR Strongest Newbie, Maple SR 6.00 12.00
BFRS78E035R Event Bonus, Maple R .30 .75
BFRS78E035SSR Event Bonus, Maple SR 2.50 5.00
BFRS78E036R Event Bonus, Sally R .30 .75
BFRS78E036SSR Event Bonus, Sally SR 2.50 5.00
BFRS78E037R A Wild Adventure, Maple & Sally R .30 .75
BFRS78E037SSR A Wild Adventure, Maple & Sally SR 3.00 6.00
BFRS78E038R Rumored Player in Blue, Sally R .30 .60
BFRS78E038SSR Rumored Player in Blue, Sally SR 2.50 5.00
BFRS78E039U Super Speed, Sally U .50 1.00
BFRS78E040U Hibernate and Awaken, Maple U .15 .30
BFRS78E041U Awaken, Syrup U .15 .30
BFRS78E042U Guardian Angel, Maple U .15 .30
BFRS78E043U Multi-Colored Bloom, Kasumi U .15 .30
BFRS78E044C Newbie Adventurer, Maple C .12 .25
BFRS78E045C Real Skills, Sally C .12 .25
BFRS78E046aC Shadow Clone, Sally A C .12 .25
BFRS78E046bC Shadow Clone, Sally B C .12 .25
BFRS78E047C Collecting Medals, Maple C .12 .25
BFRS78E048C Relaxation, Maple C .12 .25
BFRS78E049C Too Early, Kasumi C .12 .25
BFRS78E050C Relaxation, Sally C .12 .25
BFRS78E051C Cloudless Azure Skies, Kasumi C .12 .25
BFRS78E052U Wooly U .15 .30
BFRS78E053CR No Longer Normal CLR .20 .40
BFRS78E053RRRR No Longer Normal RRR 2.00 4.00
BFRS78E054CC Azure Gleam of Her Eyes CC .12 .25
BFRS78E055CC When in Trouble, Eating Could Be a Solution CC .12 .25
BFRS78E056RR Two Faces Within, Mii RR 1.25 2.50
BFRS78E056SPSP Two Faces Within, Mii SP 125.00 250.00
BFRS78E057RR Walking Fortress, Maple RR .75 1.50
BFRS78E057SSR Walking Fortress, Maple SR 7.50 15.00
BFRS78E058RR Saint Misery RR 4.00 8.00
BFRS78E058SPSP Saint Misery SP 125.00 250.00
BFRS78E059R Securing a Crucial Position, Maple R .25 .50
BFRS78E060R Flare Accel, Mii R .75 1.50
BFRS78E060SSR Flare Accel, Mii SR 7.50 15.00
BFRS78E061R Change in Strategy, Misery R .25 .50
BFRS78E062R Chomping Down, Maple R .75 1.50
BFRS78E062SSR Chomping Down, Maple SR 3.00 6.00
BFRS78E063R Atrocity, Maple R .30 .60
BFRS78E063SSR Atrocity, Maple SR 10.00 20.00
BFRS78E064R Flame Emperor, Mii R .25 .50
BFRS78E064SSR Flame Emperor, Mii SR 4.00 8.00
BFRS78E065U Markus the Trapper U .15 .30
BFRS78E066U Shin the Split-Sword U .15 .30
BFRS78E067U Each One's Roles, Misery U .15 .30
BFRS78E068U No Damage, Maple U .15 .30
BFRS78E069U Entrusted Lives, Mii U .15 .30
BFRS78E070U Armor of the Black Rose, Maple U .15 .30
BFRS78E071C Guild Master, Mii C .12 .25
BFRS78E072C Prison of Flame, Mii C .12 .25
BFRS78E073C Stout Guardian, Maple C .12 .25
BFRS78E074C [Hydra] Maple C .12 .25
BFRS78E075C Unique Series C .12 .25
BFRS78E076CR Showdown Between Guild Masters CLR .30 .60
BFRS78E076RRRR Showdown Between Guild Masters RRR 7.50 15.00
BFRS78E077CC Boss Monster CC .12 .25
BFRS78E077RRRR Boss Monster RRR 3.00 6.00
BFRS78E078CC Guild Master of Flame Emperors CC .12 .25
BFRS78E078RRRR Guild Master of Flame Emperors RRR 4.00 8.00
BFRS78E079RR Multi-Chant, Frederica RR 3.00 6.00
BFRS78E079SPSP Multi-Chant, Frederica SP 60.00 125.00
BFRS78E080RR Moment Between the Two, Sally RR 2.00 4.00
BFRS78E080SSR Moment Between the Two, Sally SR 15.00 30.00
BFRS78E081RR Young Genius, Kanade RR 7.50 15.00
BFRS78E081SPSP Young Genius, Kanade SP 75.00 150.00
BFRS78E082RR Machine God, Maple RR 4.00 8.00
BFRS78E082SPSP Machine God, Maple SP 200.00 400.00
BFRS78E083R Information Warfare, Sally R .25 .50
BFRS78E083SSR Information Warfare, Sally SR 15.00 30.00
BFRS78E084R Maxing Out, Sally R .25 .50
BFRS78E084SSR Maxing Out, Sally SR 3.00 6.00
BFRS78E085R Multi-Colored, Kanade R .25 .50
BFRS78E085SSR Multi-Colored, Kanade SR 3.00 6.00
BFRS78E086R Versatile, Frederica R .25 .50
BFRS78E086SSR Versatile, Frederica SR 6.00 12.00
BFRS78E087R Shield and Buckler, Maple & Sally R 3.00 6.00
BFRS78E088R Information Warfare, Frederica R .30 .60
BFRS78E088SSR Information Warfare, Frederica SR 6.00 12.00
BFRS78E089R Best Friends, Maple & Sally R .30 .60
BFRS78E089SSR Best Friends, Maple & Sally SR 5.00 10.00
BFRS78E090U Berserk, Drag U .15 .30
BFRS78E091U Tranquil Waters, Maple U .15 .30
BFRS78E092U Spell Slash, Kanade U .15 .30
BFRS78E093U Awaken, Oboro U .15 .30
BFRS78E094U Devour, Maple U .15 .30
BFRS78E095U Guild Master, Payne U .15 .30
BFRS78E096U Oceanic Coat, Sally U .15 .30
BFRS78E097C Super Speed, Dread C .12 .25
BFRS78E098C Fake Skill, Sally C .12 .25
BFRS78E099C Curiosity, Maple C .12 .25
BFRS78E100C Hex, Maple C .12 .25
BFRS78E101C Hibernate and Awaken, Sally C .12 .25
BFRS78E102C Winning Formula, Maple C .12 .25
BFRS78E103C For the Win, Kanade C .12 .25
BFRS78E104C Maxing Out, Maple C .12 .25
BFRS78E105C Sword Dance, Sally C .12 .25
BFRS78E106U Spell Slash U .15 .30
BFRS78E107CR [Deploy] Left Arm CLR .25 .50
BFRS78E107RRRR [Deploy] Left Arm RRR 3.00 6.00
BFRS78E108CC Never-Ending Sunset Area CC .12 .25
BFRS78E108RRRR Never-Ending Sunset Area RRR 7.50 15.00
BFRS78E109CC Duel System CC .12 .25
BFRS78E110CC Akashic Record CC .12 .25
BFRS78E111PR Fun Times, Maple P 7.50 1.50
BFRS78E112PR Giving Thanks, Kasumi P 10.00 20.00
BFRS78E113PR Charisma, Mii P 1.00 2.00
BFRS78E114PR New Equipment, Sally P .75 1.50

2021 Weiss Schwarz Bofuri I Don't Want to Get Hurt So I'll Max Out My Defense Trial Deck

BFRS78TE01SPSP Face of the Game, Maple SP 300.00 600.00
BFRS78TE01TD Face of the Game, Maple .75 1.50
BFRS78TE02TD Conqueror, Yui .20 .40
BFRS78TE03TD Conqueror, May .20 .40
BFRS78TE04TD Superb Memory, Kanade .20 .40
BFRS78TE05TD Brotherly Figure, Kuromu .20 .40
BFRS78TE06RRRR Assertive, Yui RRR 6.00 12.00
BFRS78TE06TD Assertive, Yui .20 .40
BFRS78TE07RRRR Worrier, May RRR 2.00 4.00
BFRS78TE07TD Worrier, May .20 .40
BFRS78TE08SSR Replica of the Dark Night, Maple SR .75 1.50
BFRS78TE08TD Replica of the Dark Night, Maple .20 .40
BFRS78TE09TD The Curtains Rise On Maxing Out .20 .40
BFRS78TE10TD Non-Stressful Adventure .20 .40
BFRS78TE11TD Consistently Flawless, Risa Shiromine .20 .40
BFRS78TE12SSR Cool and Collected, Kasumi SR .75 1.50
BFRS78TE12TD Cool and Collected, Kasumi .50 1.00
BFRS78TE13TD Focused, Sally .20 .40
BFRS78TE14TD Imposing and Majestic, Kasumi .20 .40
BFRS78TE15TD I Don't Want to Get Hurt, Kaede Honjo .20 .40
BFRS78TE16TD Passion for Crafting, Iz .20 .40
BFRS78TE17TD Supportive Role, Iz .75 1.50
BFRS78TE18SPSP Marble Muffler, Sally SP 250.00 500.00
BFRS78TE18TD Marble Muffler, Sally 2.00 4.00
BFRS78TE19TD Quest Activated .20 .40
BFRS78TE20RRRR Path to the Second Level RRR 3.00 6.00
BFRS78TE20TD Path to the Second Level .20 .40

2021 Weiss Schwarz Booster Pack Fate-Grand Order Absolute Demonic Front Babylonia

FGOS75E001RR New Being Created by the Gods, Kingu RR 1.50 3.00
FGOS75E001SPSP New Being Created by the Gods, Kingu SP 75.00 150.00
FGOS75E002RR Acquiring Freedom, Ereshkigal RR 3.00 6.00
FGOS75E002SSR Acquiring Freedom, Ereshkigal SR 7.50 15.00
FGOS75E003R Pledge Severed, Ereshkigal R .30 .75
FGOS75E004R Absolute Tactics, Kingu R .25 .50
FGOS75E005R Head-On Fight, Quetzalcoatl R .25 .50
FGOS75E005SSR Head-On Fight, Quetzalcoatl SR 4.00 8.00
FGOS75E006R Observing the State of Battle, Kingu R .25 .50
FGOS75E007R The Goddess of Revenge, Gorgon R .25 .50
FGOS75E007SSR The Goddess of Revenge, Gorgon SR 2.50 5.00
FGOS75E008U Coldhearted Eyes, Kingu U .15 .30
FGOS75E009U Irritated Outcry, Gorgon U .15 .30
FGOS75E010U The Great Bird of the Sun, Quetzalcoatl U .15 .30
FGOS75E011U Resolve to Persist, Ereshkigal U .15 .30
FGOS75E012C Seated in the Temple, Quetzalcoatl C .12 .25
FGOS75E013C Proud Warrior of the Jungle, Jaguar Warrior C .12 .25
FGOS75E014C Imminent Threat, Gorgon C .12 .25
FGOS75E015C For the Sake of the Plan, Kingu C .12 .25
FGOS75E016C Frantic Retort! Ereshkigal C .12 .25
FGOS75E017C Act of Madness, Gorgon C .12 .25
FGOS75E018C Virtuous Terror, Quetzalcoatl C .12 .25
FGOS75E019U Terrorizing Gaze U .15 .30
FGOS75E020U Fierce Attack U .15 .30
FGOS75E021CC Emerged Fault CC .12 .25
FGOS75E021RRRR Emerged Fault RRR 2.00 4.00
FGOS75E022CC Enormous Size and Strength CC .12 .25
FGOS75E023CC Thrilling Fight CC .12 .25
FGOS75E024CC Dignity of a Goddess CC .12 .25
FGOS75E025RR No Buts! Ishtar RR 6.00 12.00
FGOS75E025SSR No Buts! Ishtar SR 30.00 75.00
FGOS75E026RR King Who Leads the People, Gilgamesh RR .75 1.50
FGOS75E026SSR King Who Leads the People, Gilgamesh SR 7.50 15.00
FGOS75E027RR Time for the Final Battle, Gilgamesh RR 2.50 5.00
FGOS75E027SPSP Time for the Final Battle, Gilgamesh SP 100.00 200.00
FGOS75E028R The High Priestess of Uruk, Siduri R .25 .50
FGOS75E029R Brimming with Power, Ana R .25 .50
FGOS75E029SSR Brimming with Power, Ana SR 3.00 6.00
FGOS75E030R Battle Where Sand Clouds Whirl, Gilgamesh R .25 .50
FGOS75E030SSR Battle Where Sand Clouds Whirl, Gilgamesh SR 2.50 5.00
FGOS75E031R Wise King's Orders, Gilgamesh R .25 .50
FGOS75E032R All That Was Wished For, Kingu R .25 .50
FGOS75E032SSR All That Was Wished For, Kingu SR 1.00 2.00
FGOS75E033R Grand Caster, Merlin R .25 .50
FGOS75E033SSR Grand Caster, Merlin SR 12.50 25.00
FGOS75E034U Wise King Seated on the Throne, Gilgamesh U .15 .30
FGOS75E035U Halving With a Single Stroke, Gilgamesh U .15 .30
FGOS75E036U Dreamlike Existence, Merlin U .15 .30
FGOS75E037U Seething Fighting Spirit, Quetzalcoatl U .15 .30
FGOS75E038U Writhing in Conflict, Ishtar U .15 .30
FGOS75E039C Time to Part, Ana C .12 .25
FGOS75E040C All-Out Seriousness, Jaguar Warrior C .12 .25
FGOS75E041C Souvenir for the Travelers, Gilgamesh C .12 .25
FGOS75E042C Delicious Meal, Ana C .12 .25
FGOS75E043C Sudden Visit, Gilgamesh C .12 .25
FGOS75E044C Return of the King, Siduri C .12 .25
FGOS75E045C Wise King Returned From the Underworld, Gilgamesh C .12 .25
FGOS75E046U Wise King's Holy Grail U .15 .30
FGOS75E047U Operation Marduk Blitz U .15 .30
FGOS75E048U Awakening To... U .15 .30
FGOS75E049CR The Will of Uruk to Continue Fighting CLR .20 .40
FGOS75E049RRRR The Will of Uruk to Continue Fighting RRR 7.50 15.00
FGOS75E050CC Recollections Through Battle CC .12 .25
FGOS75E050RRRR Recollections Through Battle RRR 4.00 8.00
FGOS75E051CC She Actually Loves It? CC .12 .25
FGOS75E052RR The Mistress of the Underworld, Ereshkigal RR 4.00 8.00
FGOS75E052SPSP The Mistress of the Underworld, Ereshkigal SP 300.00 600.00
FGOS75E053RR Goddess Who Rules Over Venus, Ishtar RR 10.00 20.00
FGOS75E053SPSP Goddess Who Rules Over Venus, Ishtar SP 400.00 800.00
FGOS75E054R Goddess-Style Contract, Ishtar R .60 1.25
FGOS75E055R Splendid Appearance, Ereshkigal R .25 .50
FGOS75E055SSR Splendid Appearance, Ereshkigal SR 10.00 20.00
FGOS75E056R Reassuring Ally, Ishtar R 1.00 2.00
FGOS75E056SSR Reassuring Ally, Ishtar SR 40.00 80.00
FGOS75E057R Bringing the Underworld Beneath Uruk! Ereshkigal R .60 1.25
FGOS75E057SSR Bringing the Underworld Beneath Uruk! Ereshkigal SR 7.50 15.00
FGOS75E058R Steady Accumulation, Ereshkigal R .25 .50
FGOS75E059R Firing a Shot at a God, Ishtar R .25 .50
FGOS75E059SSR Firing a Shot at a God, Ishtar SR 20.00 40.00
FGOS75E060U Granting Special Rights, Ereshkigal U .15 .30
FGOS75E061U Fused Consciousness, Ishtar U .15 .30
FGOS75E062U Intense Mid-Air Battle, Ishtar U .15 .30
FGOS75E063U Careful Aim, Ishtar U .15 .30
FGOS75E064U Expectant Gaze, Ereshkigal U .15 .30
FGOS75E065C Great Warrior, Benkei C .12 .25
FGOS75E066C Battle in the Underworld, Ereshkigal C .12 .25
FGOS75E067C Triumphant Expression, Ishtar C .12 .25
FGOS75E068C The Spartan King, Leonidas I C .12 .25
FGOS75E069C Storied Hero, Ushiwakamaru C .12 .25

FGOS75E070C Self-Reflection, Ishtar C	.12	.25
FGOS75E071C Gifted in Warfare, Ushiwakamaru C	.12	.25
FGOS75E072U Bribing a Goddess U	.15	.30
FGOS75E073CR Together With Bloomed Flowers in the Underworld CLR	.60	1.25
FGOS75E073RRRR Together With Bloomed Flowers in the Underworld RRR	30.00	60.00
FGOS75E074CR Final Battle With Mother (Ereshkigal) CLR	.30	.75
FGOS75E074RRRR Final Battle With Mother (Ereshkigal) RRR	10.00	20.00
FGOS75E075CC Final Battle With Mother (Ishtar) CC	.15	.30
FGOS75E075RRRR Final Battle With Mother (Ishtar) RRR	5.00	10.00
FGOS75E076RR Towards the Final Singularity, Mash RR	7.50	15.00
FGOS75E076SPSP Towards the Final Singularity, Mash SP	300.00	600.00
FGOS75E077RR Trust in Her Master, Mash Kyrielight RR	3.00	6.00
FGOS75E078RR Shared Journey, Mash RR	7.50	15.00
FGOS75E078SECSEC Shared Journey, Mash SCR	300.00	600.00
FGOS75E079R Battle With a Strong Enemy, Mash R	.25	.50
FGOS75E079SSR Battle With a Strong Enemy, Mash SR	12.50	25.00
FGOS75E080R Coordination with Comrades, Mash R	.25	.50
FGOS75E080SSR Coordination with Comrades, Mash SR	2.50	5.00
FGOS75E081R Special Honorary Advisor of Chaldea's Tech Division, Leonardo da Vinci R	.30	.60
FGOS75E081SSR Special Honorary Advisor of Chaldea's Tech Division, Leonardo da Vinci SR	7.50	15.00
FGOS75E082R Raising Her Shield, Mash R	.30	.75
FGOS75E083R Attack by a Formidable Enemy, Fujimaru & Mash R	.30	.60
FGOS75E084SSR Resilient Heart, Romani Archaman SR	2.00	4.00
FGOS75E084U Resilient Heart, Romani Archaman U	.15	.30
FGOS75E085U Enticing Words, Fujimaru U	.30	.60
FGOS75E086U Short Break, Mash U	.15	.30
FGOS75E087U Shuddering Genius, Da Vinci U	.25	.50
FGOS75E088U Supporting Comrades, Mash U	.25	.50
FGOS75E089C Unfortunate Reality, Da Vinci C	.12	.25
FGOS75E090C Rescue From a Crisis, Fou C	.12	.25
FGOS75E091C Loss of Observational Waves, Da Vinci & Romani C	.12	.25
FGOS75E092C Integrated Offense and Defense, Mash C	.12	.25
FGOS75E093C Exchange of Sarcasm, Romani C	.12	.25
FGOS75E094C Valiantly Breaking Through, Fujimaru Ritsuka C	.12	.25
FGOS75E095C Tears of Relief, Mash C	.12	.25
FGOS75E096U Proof of a Master, Command Seals U	.15	.30
FGOS75E097U Entrusted Shield U	.15	.30
FGOS75E098CR Belief in Her Choice CLR	.30	.60
FGOS75E098RRRR Belief in Her Choice RRR	7.50	15.00
FGOS75E099CC Chaldea Support CC	.12	.25
FGOS75E100CC Path to the Conclusion CC	.12	.25
FGOS75E101PR SD Mash P	6.00	12.00
FGOS75E102PR SD Gilgamesh P	10.00	20.00
FGOS75E103PR SD Kingu P	.50	1.00
FGOS75E104PR SD Ishtar P	3.00	6.00
FGOS75E105PR SD Ereshkigal P	3.00	6.00

2021 Weiss Schwarz Booster Pack Fate-Grand Order Absolute Demonic Front Babylonia Trial Deck

FGOS75TE01RRRR The Wise King of Uruk, Gilgamesh RRR	30.00	60.00
FGOS75TE01TD The Wise King of Uruk, Gilgamesh	.15	.30
FGOS75TE02RRRR The Goddess of Fertility and War, Ishtar RRR	25.00	50.00
FGOS75TE02TD The Goddess of Fertility and War, Ishtar	.15	.30
FGOS75TE03TD Mysterious Servant Enkidu	.15	.30
FGOS75TE04TD Forest of Schemes, Kingu	.15	.30
FGOS75TE05TD The Mage of Flowers, Merlin	.15	.30
FGOS75TE06TD Girl Who Shoulders a Heavy Destiny, Ana	.15	.30
FGOS75TE07TD The One Who Has Seen Everything, Gilgamesh	2.00	4.00
FGOS75TE08TD Power of a Goddess, Ishtar	.50	1.00
FGOS75TE09TD Wise King's Ascertainment	.15	.30
FGOS75TE10TD Rage-Filled Attack	.15	.30
FGOS75TE11TD Time to Display Strength, Fujimaru	.15	.30
FGOS75TE12SPSP Firm Courage, Mash SP	.15	.30
FGOS75TE12TD Firm Courage, Mash	.75	1.50
FGOS75TE13TD Acting Director of Chaldea, Romani	.15	.30
FGOS75TE14TD Mankind's Last Master, Fujimaru	.15	.30
FGOS75TE15RRRR The Universal Genius, Da Vinci RRR	4.00	8.00
FGOS75TE15TD The Universal Genius, Da Vinci	.20	.40
FGOS75TE16TD Time to Display Strength, Mash	.15	.30
FGOS75TE17TD Perfect Proof of Existence, Da Vinci	.15	.30
FGOS75TE18SSR Shield Maiden, Mash SR	1.00	2.00
FGOS75TE18TD Shield Maiden, Mash	.60	1.25
FGOS75TE19TD Round Table Deployment	.30	.75
FGOS75TE20SSR Instant Offense and Defense SR	1.50	3.00
FGOS75TE20TD Instant Offense and Defense	.30	.60

2021 Weiss Schwarz Date A Bullet

DALWE33E001OFROFR Nightmare or Queen Kurumi OFR	30.00	75.00
DALWE33E001RR Nightmare or Queen Kurumi RR	6.00	12.00
DALWE33E002OFROFR Girl Entwined With Nightmares, Kurumi OFR	30.00	60.00
DALWE33E002RR Girl Entwined With Nightmares, Kurumi RR	2.00	4.00
DALWE33E003RR Spirit in Black, Kurumi RR	2.00	4.00
DALWE33E004RR Zafkiel Kurumi RR	2.00	4.00
DALWE33E004SPSP Zafkiel Kurumi SP	300.00	750.00
DALWE33E005R Holding at Gun Point, Kurumi R	.25	.50
DALWE33E006R Visitor, Kurumi R	.25	.50
DALWE33E007R Difference in Status, Kurumi R	.25	.50
DALWE33E008R Original Appearance, Hibiki R	.25	.50
DALWE33E009R Imperturbable, Kurumi R	.25	.50
DALWE33E010R Logical Judgement, Kurumi R	.25	.50
DALWE33E011R A New Story, Kurumi & Hibiki R	.25	.50
DALWE33E012U Aleph Kurumi U	.15	.30
DALWE33E013U Fight Between Equals, Kurumi U	.15	.30
DALWE33E014U Precise Firing, Kurumi U	.15	.30
DALWE33E015U Brief Truce, Hibiki U	.15	.30
DALWE33E016C Unfading Memories, Kurumi C	.12	.25
DALWE33E017C In Recollections, Hibiki C	.12	.25
DALWE33E018C No Questions Asked, Kurumi C	.12	.25
DALWE33E019C Carrying a White Cat, Kurumi C	.12	.25
DALWE33E020C Trade, Kurumi C	.12	.25
DALWE33E021C Penetrating Bullet, Kurumi C	.12	.25
DALWE33E022C Shadow That Should Not Exist, Kurumi C	.12	.25
DALWE33E023U Released Chains U	.15	.30
DALWE33E024R Confrontation of Black and White R	.25	.50
DALWE33E024SPSP Confrontation of Black and White SP	125.00	250.00
DALWE33E025C Zafkiel C	.12	.25
DALWE33E026RR Spirit in White, Queen RR	.50	1.00
DALWE33E027RR Lucifugus Queen RR	.50	1.00
DALWE33E027SPSP Lucifugus Queen SP	150.00	300.00
DALWE33E028R Declaration of War, Queen R	.25	.50
DALWE33E029R Predetermined Conclusion, Queen R	.25	.50
DALWE33E030R Sinking White Shadow, Queen R	.25	.50
DALWE33E031U Doll Master Pannier U	.15	.30
DALWE33E032U Blissful Days, Sawa U	.15	.30
DALWE33E033U Kunoichi, Yui U	.15	.30
DALWE33E034U Holding at Gun Point, Queen U	.15	.30
DALWE33E035U Unfading Memories, Sawa U	.15	.30
DALWE33E036U Repelling Bullets, Queen U	.15	.30
DALWE33E037U In Recollections, Tsang U	.15	.30
DALWE33E038C Moznaim Queen C	.12	.25
DALWE33E039C Traces of a Best Friend, Queen C	.12	.25
DALWE33E040C Fatal Move, Queen C	.12	.25
DALWE33E041C In Recollections, Isami C	.12	.25
DALWE33E042C White Space, Queen C	.12	.25
DALWE33E043C True Swordsmanship, Isami C	.12	.25
DALWE33E044C In Recollections, Pannier C	.12	.25
DALWE33E045C Lonely World, Queen C	.12	.25
DALWE33E046C Overwhelming Difference, Queen C	.12	.25
DALWE33E047C In Recollections, Yui C	.12	.25
DALWE33E048C Battle Stance, Tsang C	.12	.25
DALWE33E049R Clashing Emotions R	.25	.50
DALWE33E049SPSP Clashing Emotions SP	60.00	125.00
DALWE33E050C Lucifugus C	.12	.25

2021 Weiss Schwarz Date-A-Live

DALW79E001RR Frenzied Nightmare Kurumi RR	2.50	5.00
DALW79E001SPSP Frenzied Nightmare Kurumi SP	100.00	200.00
DALW79E002RR Reliable Little Sister, Kotori RR	6.00	12.00
DALW79E002SPSP Reliable Little Sister, Kotori SP	75.00	150.00
DALW79E003RR Kurumi Tokisaki RR	2.50	5.00
DALW79E003SSR Kurumi Tokisaki SR	12.50	25.00
DALW79E004R Transfer Student, Kurumi R	.25	.50
DALW79E004SSR Transfer Student, Kurumi SR	3.00	6.00
DALW79E005R Time-Eating Castle Kurumi R	.25	.50
DALW79E005SR Time-Eating Castle Kurumi SR	6.00	12.00
DALW79E006R Swimsuit, Kurumi R	.25	.50
DALW79E006SSR Swimsuit, Kurumi SR	20.00	40.00
DALW79E007R To Save Spirits, Kotori R	.25	.50
DALW79E007SSR To Save Spirits, Kotori SR	2.50	5.00
DALW79E008R Under the Azure Skies, Kurumi R	.25	.50
DALW79E008SSR Under the Azure Skies, Kurumi SR	2.50	5.00
DALW79E009U Restraining Oneself, Kotori U	.15	.30
DALW79E010U Shido Itsuka U	.25	.50
DALW79E011U Your Choices, Everyone! Kotori U	.15	.30
DALW79E012U Under the Azure Skies, Kotori U	.15	.30
DALW79E013U The Me From That Time Kurumi U	.15	.30
DALW79E014U Proactive Approach, Kurumi U	.15	.30
DALW79E015C Seemingly-Happy Expression, Kotori C	.12	.25
DALW79E016C Day After the Date, Kurumi C	.12	.25
DALW79E017C Questioning Gaze, Kotori C	.12	.25
DALW79E018aC Clone, Kurumi A C	.12	.25
DALW79E018bC Clone, Kurumi B C	.12	.25
DALW79E019C Enjoying the Amusement Park, Kotori C	.12	.25
DALW79E020C Proposing a Break, Kannazuki C	.12	.25
DALW79E021C Words of Bravado, Kotori C	.12	.25
DALW79E022U My Little Shido (Yellow) U	.60	1.25
DALW79E023CR With Candy in One Hand CLR	.25	.50
DALW79E023RRRR With Candy in One Hand RRR	6.00	12.00
DALW79E024CC Special Existence CC	.12	.25
DALW79E024RRRR Special Existence RRR	2.00	4.00
DALW79E025CC Obstructing Existence CC	.12	.25
DALW79E026RR Mysterious Classmate, Origami RR	.30	.75
DALW79E026SPSP Mysterious Classmate, Origami SP	40.00	80.00
DALW79E027RR Yoshino & Yoshinon RR	.25	.50
DALW79E027SSR Yoshino & Yoshinon SR	2.50	5.00
DALW79E028R Swimsuit, Yoshino R	.25	.50
DALW79E029R Returning to School, Origami R	.25	.50
DALW79E030R Swimsuit, Origami R	.25	.50
DALW79E031R Yoshino Missing Her Yoshinon R	.25	.50
DALW79E032R Battle Stance, Origami R	.25	.50
DALW79E032SSR Battle Stance, Origami SR	2.00	4.00
DALW79E033U Visiting the Sick, Yoshino U	.15	.30
DALW79E034U Happy Incoming Message, Origami U	.15	.30
DALW79E035U Reason for Wanting Time Together, Yoshino U	.15	.30
DALW79E036U Mana Takamiya U	.15	.30
DALW79E037U Unexpected Meeting in Town, Origami U	.15	.30
DALW79E038U Angel Manifestation, Yoshino U	.15	.30
DALW79E039C Prompt Judgement, Origami C	.12	.25
DALW79E040C Gathering Information, Origami C	.12	.25
DALW79E041C Shido Pinned Down C	.12	.25
DALW79E042C Sensing Danger, Yoshino C	.12	.25
DALW79E043C Date Support, Yoshino C	.12	.25
DALW79E044C Exchanging Conditions, Origami C	.12	.25
DALW79E045C Halving With a Single Stroke, Kusakabe C	.12	.25
DALW79E046C Choosing a Swimsuit, Yoshino C	.12	.25
DALW79E047U Basic Realizer U	.15	.30
DALW79E048CR Freezing Earth CLR	.20	.40
DALW79E048RRRR Freezing Earth RRR	1.00	2.00
DALW79E049CC Apology From a Super Genius CC	.12	.25
DALW79E050CC Large Tears CC	.12	.25
DALW79E051RR Kotori Itsuka RR	2.00	4.00
DALW79E051SSR Kotori Itsuka SR	6.00	12.00
DALW79E052RR Dignified Appearance, Tohka RR	1.50	3.00
DALW79E052SPSP Dignified Appearance, Tohka SP	75.00	150.00
DALW79E053RR Terrible Spirit Kurumi RR	7.50	15.00
DALW79E053SECSEC Terrible Spirit Kurumi SCR	400.00	800.00
DALW79E054R Swimsuit, Kotori R	.25	.50
DALW79E055R Power to Turn Back Time, Kurumi R	.25	.50
DALW79E055SSR Power to Turn Back Time, Kurumi SR	3.00	6.00
DALW79E056R A Spring Moment, Tohka R	.25	.50
DALW79E056SSR A Spring Moment, Tohka SR	2.50	5.00
DALW79E057R Tohka Yatogami R	.25	.50
DALW79E057SSR Tohka Yatogami SR	5.00	10.00
DALW79E058R Expression of Killing Intent, Kotori R	.25	.50
DALW79E059R Efreet Kotori R	.25	.50
DALW79E059SSR Efreet Kotori SR	2.50	5.00
DALW79E060U Strong Emotions, Tohka U	.15	.30
DALW79E061U Cruel Reality, Tohka U	.15	.30
DALW79E062U Descent of Calamity, Tohka U	.15	.30
DALW79E063C Analyst of Ratatoskr, Reine C	.12	.25
DALW79E064C Power to Stop Time, Kurumi C	.12	.25
DALW79E065C Wavering Heart, Kurumi C	.12	.25
DALW79E066C A Pity, Kurumi C	.12	.25
DALW79E067C Surveillance at the Bun Shop? Kotori C	.12	.25
DALW79E068C Meeting up for a Date, Tohka C	.12	.25
DALW79E069C Great Interest, Kurumi C	.12	.25
DALW79E070C Cornered, Kurumi C	.12	.25
DALW79E071U What About This? Course U	.15	.30
DALW79E072U Practicing Hitting on the Teacher U	.15	.30
DALW79E073CR Fearless Smile CLR	.50	1.00
DALW79E073RRRR Fearless Smile RRR	15.00	30.00
DALW79E074CC Brunt of Fury CC	.12	.25
DALW79E075CC Flames Which Pierce Through Time CC	.12	.25
DALW79E076RR Rainy Girl Yoshino RR	.30	.75
DALW79E076SPSP Rainy Girl Yoshino SP	50.00	100.00
DALW79E077RR Important Promise, Tohka RR	.30	.75
DALW79E077SECSEC Important Promise, Tohka SCR	300.00	600.00
DALW79E078R Enjoying the Amusement Park, Shido R	.25	.50
DALW79E079R For the Sky and the Sword Tohka R	.25	.50
DALW79E079SSR For the Sky and the Sword Tohka SR	10.00	20.00
DALW79E080R Lonely Eyes, Yoshino R	.25	.50
DALW79E080SSR Lonely Eyes, Yoshino SR	.75	1.50
DALW79E081R Naive and Innocent Girl, Tohka R	.25	.50
DALW79E081SSR Naive and Innocent Girl, Tohka SR	1.50	3.00
DALW79E082R Sullen Rain Yoshino R	.25	.50
DALW79E082SSR Sullen Rain Yoshino SR	1.00	2.00
DALW79E083R Origami Tobiichi R	.25	.50
DALW79E083SSR Origami Tobiichi SR	3.00	6.00
DALW79E084U Unexpected Meeting in Town, Tohka U	.15	.30
DALW79E085U A Spring Moment, Origami U	.15	.30
DALW79E086U School Uniform, Tohka U	.25	.50
DALW79E087U Long Range Shot, Origami U	.15	.30
DALW79E088U A Spring Moment, Yoshino U	.15	.30
DALW79E089U Battle to Protect, Tohka U	.15	.30
DALW79E090U Intensifying Battlefield? Origami U	.15	.30
DALW79E091U Under the Azure Skies, Tohka U	.30	.60
DALW79E092C Out of the Bath, Origami C	.12	.25
DALW79E093C Spirit Barrier, Tohka C	.12	.25
DALW79E094C Sulking, Tohka C	.12	.25
DALW79E095C Under the Azure Skies, Yoshino C	.12	.25
DALW79E096C Swimsuit, Tohka C	.12	.25
DALW79E097U Draw Back in Disgust U	.15	.30
DALW79E098CR In This Town Basked in Sunset CLR	.20	.40
DALW79E098RRRR In This Town Basked in Sunset RRR	1.00	2.00
DALW79E099CC Delicious Date CC	.12	.25
DALW79E099RRRR Delicious Date RRR	1.25	2.50
DALW79E100CC Revenge for 5 Years Ago CC	.12	.25
DALW79E100RRRR Revenge for 5 Years Ago RRR	1.00	2.00
DALW79E101PR Trying On, Kurumi P	7.50	15.00
DALW79E102PR Confirmation of Feelings, Kotori P	.60	1.25
DALW79E103PR Within the Frozen Barrier, Yoshino P	1.00	2.00
DALW79E104PR Complex Feelings, Tohka P	.30	.75
DALW79E105PR Meeting up for a Date, Origami P	1.00	2.00

2021 Weiss Schwarz Date-A-Live Trial Deck

DALW79TE01TD Yesterday's Incident, Shido	.20	.40
DALW79TE02TD Worst Awakening Method, Kotori	.20	.40
DALW79TE03SPSP Confrontation With Humans, Tohka SP	250.00	500.00
DALW79TE03TD Confrontation With Humans, Tohka	12.50	25.00
DALW79TE04TD Meeting up for a Date, Kurumi	.20	.40
DALW79TE05TD Commander of Ratatoskr, Kotori	.50	1.00
DALW79TE06SSR Engraving Despair, Kurumi SR	2.00	4.00
DALW79TE06TD Engraving Despair, Kurumi	.30	.75
DALW79TE07TD Date Day, Tohka	.20	.40
DALW79TE08RRRR Maximum Support, Kotori RRR	12.50	25.00
DALW79TE08TD Maximum Support, Kotori	.75	1.50
DALW79TE09TD Overwhelming Emotions, Kurumi	.60	1.25
DALW79TE10SSR Hostile, Tohka SR	2.00	4.00
DALW79TE10TD Hostile, Tohka	1.50	3.00
DALW79TE11RRRR Us RRR	15.00	30.00
DALW79TE11TD Us	.20	.40
DALW79TE12TD Abrupt Greeting, Origami	.20	.40
DALW79TE13RRRR Fearful Yoshino RRR	7.50	15.00
DALW79TE13TD Fearful Yoshino	.20	.40
DALW79TE14TD Stopped by the Doctor, Yoshino	.50	1.00
DALW79TE15TD Strange Conversation, Origami	.50	1.00
DALW79TE16TD Cool? Yoshino	.30	.60
DALW79TE17SPSP Confrontation With Spirits, Origami SP	125.00	250.00
DALW79TE17TD Confrontation With Spirits, Origami	.75	1.50
DALW79TE18TD My Little Shido (Blue)	.25	.50
DALW79TE19TD Battle Begins	.20	.40
DALW79TE20TD Searching for Yoshinon	.20	.40

2021 Weiss Schwarz Extra Booster Re ZERO Starting Life in Another World The Frozen Bond

RZSE35E01RR Girl Imprisoned in Ice, Emilia RR	.60	1.25
RZSE35E02RR Resisting Against Fate, Puck RR	3.00	6.00
RZSE35E02SP Resisting Against Fate, Puck SP	50.00	100.00
RZSE35E03RR The Frozen Bond Puck & Emilia RR	.75	1.50
RZSE35E04RR Contractor and Spirit, Emilia & Puck RR	4.00	8.00
RZSE35E04SP Contractor and Spirit, Emilia & Puck SP	200.00	400.00
RZSE35E05RR Believe That Time Will Come, Puck RR	7.50	15.00
RZSE35E06R Contract With a Lesser Spirit, Emilia R	.25	.50
RZSE35E07R Sliding Action! Emilia R	.25	.50
RZSE35E08R Puck Joking Around R	.25	.50
RZSE35E09R Exploring the Forest, Emilia R	.25	.50
RZSE35E10R Your Father Puck R	.25	.50
RZSE35E11R Emilia All Alone R	.25	.50
RZSE35E12R Mana Release, Emilia R	.25	.50
RZSE35E13R Caring Disposition, Emilia R	.25	.50
RZSE35E14R Just Emilia R	.25	.50
RZSE35E15R Desperate Resistance, Emilia R	.25	.50
RZSE35E16R Star Beastification Puck R	.25	.50
RZSE35E17U Strengthened Bond, Emilia U	.15	.30
RZSE35E18U Mining Shiny Stones, Emilia U	.15	.30
RZSE35E19U Encounter Between the Two, Emilia U	.15	.30
RZSE35E20U One With Power, Puck U	.15	.30
RZSE35E21U Call My Name Puck U	.15	.30
RZSE35E22U Punishment Time, Puck U	.15	.30
RZSE35E23C Invitation to the Outside, Puck C	.12	.25
RZSE35E24C Exploring the Forest, Puck C	.12	.25
RZSE35E25C Emilia Reminiscing the Past C	.12	.25
RZSE35E26C Visiting the Village, Emilia C	.12	.25
RZSE35E27C Unsettling Premonition, Puck C	.12	.25
RZSE35E28C In the Present With Everyone, Emilia C	.12	.25
RZSE35E29C Unreasonable Censure, Emilia C	.12	.25
RZSE35E30C Always By Your Side Puck C	.12	.25
RZSE35E31C Balance Between Oath and Contract, Puck C	.12	.25
RZSE35E32C Life in the Forest, Emilia C	.12	.25
RZSE35E33C Considerate Warning, Emilia C	.12	.25
RZSE35E34C Surging Rage, Puck C	.12	.25
RZSE35E35C Emilia Basked in Sunset C	.12	.25
RZSE35E36C Feelings Toward Emilia, Puck C	.12	.25
RZSE35E37U Ice Blooms U	.15	.30
RZSE35E38U Shiny Stone U	.15	.30
RZSE35E39U Sacred Dialogue U	.15	.30
RZSE35E40U The Road Ahead for the Two U	.15	.30
RZSE35E41C Encounter Between the Two C	.12	.25
RZSE35E42C Clash Between Spirits C	.12	.25
RZSE35E43R Ram in a Hakama R	.25	.50
RZSE35E43SP Ram in a Hakama SP	150.00	300.00
RZSE35E44U Bandits in the Forest, Chap U	.15	.30
RZSE35E45U Mediator Melaquera U	.15	.30
RZSE35E46C Black Water C	.12	.25
RZSE35E47C Great Four Melaquera C	.12	.25
RZSE35E48C Avenger, Chap C	.12	.25
RZSE35E49U All-Consuming Flames U	.15	.30
RZSE35E50RR Rem in a Hakama RR	1.50	3.00
RZSE35E50SP Rem in a Hakama SP	250.00	500.00

2021 Weiss Schwarz Fate-stay Night Heaven's Feel Vol. 2

FSS77E001RR Pristine Beauty, Saber RR	.75	1.50
FSS77E001SSR Pristine Beauty, Saber SR	20.00	40.00
FSS77E002RR Trigger Off, Shirou RR	.25	.50
FSS77E002SPSP Trigger Off, Shirou SP	30.00	75.00
FSS77E003RR Oath of the Sword, Saber RR	1.00	2.00
FSS77E003SPSP Oath of the Sword, Saber SP	125.00	250.00
FSS77E004R Entrusted Arm, Shirou R	.25	.50
FSS77E004SSR Entrusted Arm, Shirou SR	1.00	2.00
FSS77E005R 8th Heroic Spirit, Gilgamesh R	.25	.50
FSS77E006R Battle With Mages, Saber R	.25	.50
FSS77E006SSR Battle With Mages, Saber SR	2.00	4.00
FSS77E007U Special Existence Shirou U	.15	.30
FSS77E008U Using All Her Strength, Saber U	.15	.30
FSS77E009C What Lies Beyond the Resolution, Shirou C	.12	.25
FSS77E010C Furious, Gilgamesh C	.12	.25
FSS77E011C Preparing for Battle, Shirou C	.12	.25
FSS77E012C Continuing to Advance, Shirou C	.12	.25
FSS77E013U Rho Aias U	.15	.30
FSS77E014CR Excalibur CLR	.20	.40
FSS77E014RRRR Excalibur RRR	4.00	8.00
FSS77E015CC Battle of Determination CC	.12	.25
FSS77E015RRRR Battle of Determination RRR	2.00	4.00
FSS77E016CC Rule Breaker CC	.12	.25
FSS77E016RRRR Rule Breaker RRR	.60	1.25
FSS77E017RR spring song Sakura RR	.60	1.25
FSS77E017SECSEC spring song Sakura SCR	125.00	250.00

FSS77E018RR Keeping to Her Convictions, Rider RR	2.50	5.00
FSS77E018SPSP Keeping to Her Convictions, Rider SP	100.00	200.00
FSS77E019R Strategizing Against A Strong Enemy, Shirou & Rider R	.25	.50
FSS77E019SSR Strategizing Against A Strong Enemy, Shirou & Rider SR	2.00	4.00
FSS77E020R For Her Master, Rider R	.25	.50
FSS77E020SSR For Her Master, Rider SR	5.00	10.00
FSS77E021R Cloud-Concealed Moon, Sakura R	.25	.50
FSS77E021SSR Cloud-Concealed Moon, Sakura SR	3.00	6.00
FSS77E022R Bellerophon, Rider R	.25	.50
FSS77E022SSR Bellerophon, Rider SR	1.25	2.50
FSS77E023R Blissful Days, Sakura R	.25	.50
FSS77E023SSR Blissful Days, Sakura SR	3.00	6.00
FSS77E024R Beyond the Gaze, Rider R	.25	.50
FSS77E024SSR Beyond the Gaze, Rider SR	7.50	15.00
FSS77E025U Creeping Insanity, Sakura U	.15	.30
FSS77E026U Continuing Rainfall, Sakura U	.15	.30
FSS77E027U Towards His Gaze, Lancer U	.15	.30
FSS77E028U Blissful Days, Rider U	.15	.30
FSS77E029U Execution of Orders, Rider U	.15	.30
FSS77E030U Curse of the Mystic Eyes, Rider U	.15	.30
FSS77E031C Assault, Rider C	.12	.25
FSS77E032C Battle on Top a Vehicle, Lancer C	.12	.25
FSS77E033C Indignant, Shinji C	.12	.25
FSS77E034C Intruding, Rider C	.12	.25
FSS77E035C Overflowing Words, Sakura C	.12	.25
FSS77E036C Moment Between the Two, Sakura C	.12	.25
FSS77E037C A Small Wish, Sakura C	.12	.25
FSS77E038U Duplicate Key to the Emiya Household U	.15	.30
FSS77E039CC Bellerophon CC	.12	.25
FSS77E040CC Important Person and Something to Protect CC	.12	.25
FSS77E041RR Wielder of the Jeweled Sword, Rin RR	2.00	4.00
FSS77E041SSR Wielder of the Jeweled Sword, Rin SR	10.00	20.00
FSS77E042RR Resolution to Fight, Rin RR	1.00	2.00
FSS77E042SPSP Resolution to Fight, Rin SP	125.00	250.00
FSS77E043RR Makiri's Grail, Sakura RR	6.00	12.00
FSS77E043SPSP Makiri's Grail, Sakura SP	200.00	400.00
FSS77E044RR Onyx Beauty, Saber Alter RR	.30	.75
FSS77E044SPSP Onyx Beauty, Saber Alter SPR	100.00	200.00
FSS77E045R Battle in the Rain, Rin R	.25	.50
FSS77E045SSR Battle in the Rain, Rin SR	2.50	5.00
FSS77E046R Towards the Battle, Rin R	.25	.50
FSS77E047R Sharing Intel, Rin R	.25	.50
FSS77E047SSR Sharing Intel, Rin SR	4.00	8.00
FSS77E048R Flowing Tears, Sakura R	.25	.50
FSS77E048SSR Flowing Tears, Sakura SR	2.00	4.00
FSS77E049R Special Feelings, Sakura R	.25	.50
FSS77E049SSR Special Feelings, Sakura SR	2.50	5.00
FSS77E050R Standing Guard, Saber Alter R	.25	.50
FSS77E050SSR Standing Guard, Saber Alter SR	1.25	2.50
FSS77E051R Temporary Coalition, Rin R	.25	.50
FSS77E051SSR Temporary Coalition, Rin SR	3.00	6.00
FSS77E052U She Who Has Accepted the Shadow, Sakura U	.15	.30
FSS77E053U Smiling, Saber Alter U	.15	.30
FSS77E054U Cold Attitude, Rin U	.15	.30
FSS77E055U Black-Armored Knight, Saber Alter U	.15	.30
FSS77E056U Overwhelming Power, Sakura U	.15	.30
FSS77E057U Bowman's Guidance, Archer U	.15	.30
FSS77E058U Cool and Collected, Rin U	.15	.30
FSS77E059U Jealous, Sakura U	.15	.30
FSS77E060U Corrupted Mad Warrior, Berserker U	.15	.30
FSS77E061C Enchanting Smile, Sakura C	.12	.25
FSS77E062C Lecture, Rin C	.12	.25
FSS77E063C Harsh Words, Rin C	.12	.25
FSS77E064C Tiny Shadow People C	.12	.25
FSS77E065C Yielding Her Heart, Sakura C	.12	.25
FSS77E066C Full Picture of the Basement, Archer C	.12	.25
FSS77E067C Jewel Defense Magic, Rin C	.12	.25
FSS77E068C Roaring, Berserker C	.12	.25
FSS77E069C Corrupted Knight, Saber Alter C	.12	.25
FSS77E070C Bluffing Smile, Rin C	.12	.25
FSS77E071U Fluttering Shadow U	.15	.30
FSS77E072U Jeweled Sword Zelretch U	.15	.30
FSS77E073CR Mystic Code Zelretch CLR	.20	.40
FSS77E073RRRR Mystic Code Zelretch RRR	7.50	15.00
FSS77E074CR Deep Love CLR	.20	.40
FSS77E074RRRR Deep Love RRR	10.00	20.00
FSS77E075CC Rediscovered Kindness CC	.12	.25
FSS77E076CC Inverted Light CC	.12	.25
FSS77E077CC Sisters' Relationship CC	.12	.25
FSS77E078RR Dress of Heaven, Illya RR	.50	1.00
FSS77E078SPSP Dress of Heaven, Illya SP	60.00	125.00
FSS77E079R Silver Thread Alchemy Elgen Lied, Illya R	.25	.50
FSS77E079SSR Silver Thread Alchemy Elgen Lied, Illya SR	15.00	30.00
FSS77E080R Sending Off, Illya R	.25	.50
FSS77E081R Strategic Retreat, True Assassin R	.25	.50
FSS77E082R Enemy Assault at Night, Caster R	.25	.50
FSS77E083R Self-Deprecating Smile, Illya R	.25	.50
FSS77E084R Solitary Existence, Kirei Kotomine R	.25	.50
FSS77E084SSR Solitary Existence, Kirei Kotomine SR	.75	1.50
FSS77E085U Top Mage, Caster U	.15	.30
FSS77E086U Insane Mage, Zouken U	.15	.30
FSS77E087U Purifying Light, Kirei U	.15	.30
FSS77E088U Vigor, Berserker U	.15	.30
FSS77E089U Battle in the Ruined Church, Kirei U	.15	.30
FSS77E090U Elusive Girl Illya U	.15	.30
FSS77E091C War Cry, Berserker C	.12	.25
FSS77E092C Escaping, Kirei & Illya C	.12	.25
FSS77E093C Where It Leads, Illya C	.12	.25
FSS77E094C Simple Question, Illya C	.12	.25
FSS77E095C Commemorative Photograph, Souichiro C	.12	.25
FSS77E096C Waiting, Illya C	.12	.25
FSS77E097C Requesting Freedom, True Assassin C	.12	.25
FSS77E098U Baptism Rite U	.15	.30
FSS77E099CR Heaven's Feel CLR	.20	.40
FSS77E099RRRR Heaven's Feel RRR	4.00	8.00
FSS77E100CC Impeding Wall CC	.12	.25
FSS77E101PR Staking All of Himself, Shirou P	.60	1.25
FSS77E102PR After the Battle, Sakura P	.50	1.00
FSS77E103PR Continuing to Believe, Rider P	.75	1.50
FSS77E104PR As an Elder Sister, Rin P	.60	1.25

2021 Weiss Schwarz Kaguya-sama Love Is War

KGLS79E001RR Supreme Bliss, Chika RR	12.50	25.00
KGLS79E001SPSP Supreme Bliss, Chika SP	250.00	500.00
KGLS79E002RR Serious Showdown Between Geniuses, Chika RR	1.25	2.50
KGLS79E002SPSP Serious Showdown Between Geniuses, Chika SP	75.00	150.00
KGLS79E003R Critical Hit, Chika R	.25	.50
KGLS79E003SSR Critical Hit, Chika SR	2.50	5.00
KGLS79E004R Shameful, Chika R	.25	.50
KGLS79E005R Fireworks Display, Yu R	.30	.60
KGLS79E005SSR Fireworks Display, Yu SR	4.00	8.00
KGLS79E006R Consumer, Chika R	.25	.50
KGLS79E006SSR Consumer, Chika SR	2.00	4.00
KGLS79E007U Escaping From Reality, Yu U	.15	.30
KGLS79E008U Tank-Class, Chika U	.15	.30
KGLS79E009U God of Thunder, Chika U	.15	.30
KGLS79E010U Additional Blow, Yu U	.15	.30
KGLS79E011U Seasonal Uniform Change, Chika U	.15	.30
KGLS79E012U Flustered, Chika U	.15	.30
KGLS79E013C Happiness Tax, Yu C	.12	.25
KGLS79E014C Meddling, Chika C	.12	.25
KGLS79E015C Chika Having Faraway Thoughts C	.12	.25
KGLS79E016C Full Throttle! Yu C	.12	.25
KGLS79E017C Unstoppable Yu C	.12	.25
KGLS79E018KRKR Love Detective KR	60.00	125.00
KGLS79E018R Love Detective R	.50	1.00
KGLS79E019C Shut Up, You Moron! C	.12	.25
KGLS79E020C Marked Deck C	.12	.25
KGLS79E021CR Yo! Man CLR	.20	.40
KGLS79E021KRKR Yo! Man KR	25.00	50.00
KGLS79E022CC Ramen Connoisseur CC	.12	.25
KGLS79E022RRRR Ramen Connoisseur RRR	2.00	4.00
KGLS79E023CC Broken Brakes CC	.12	.25
KGLS79E023RRRR Broken Brakes RRR	.75	1.50
KGLS79E024RR Serious Showdown Between Geniuses, Kei RR	10.00	20.00
KGLS79E024SPSP Serious Showdown Between Geniuses, Kei SP	100.00	200.00
KGLS79E025RR Love Detective, Chika RR	1.00	2.00
KGLS79E025SSR Love Detective, Chika SR	3.00	6.00
KGLS79E026RR Persisting Conviction, Miyuki RR	2.50	5.00
KGLS79E026SPSP Persisting Conviction, Miyuki SP	75.00	150.00
KGLS79E027R Flag? Chika R	.25	.50
KGLS79E028R Pressure of the Top Seat, Miyuki R	.25	.50
KGLS79E028SSR Pressure of the Top Seat, Miyuki SR	2.00	4.00
KGLS79E029R Psychological Test, Chika R	.25	.50
KGLS79E029SSR Psychological Test, Chika SR	2.50	5.00
KGLS79E030R A Certain Summer Day, Kei R	.25	.50
KGLS79E030SSR A Certain Summer Day, Kei SR	7.50	15.00
KGLS79E031U Overflowing Smiles, Kei U	.25	.50
KGLS79E032SSR Fireworks Display, Chika SR	.75	1.50
KGLS79E032U Fireworks Display, Chika U	.15	.30
KGLS79E033U Twisted Product of the Times, Miyuki U	.15	.30
KGLS79E034U His Mother!? Chika U	.15	.30
KGLS79E035U Hawaii Vacation, Chika U	.15	.30
KGLS79E036U A Man's Dignity, Miyuki U	.15	.30
KGLS79E037C Hello, Way of the Sword! Chika C	.12	.25
KGLS79E038C Marked Deck, Chika C	.12	.25
KGLS79E039C Bribery, Chika C	.12	.25
KGLS79E040C Miyuki Taken Aback C	.12	.25
KGLS79E041C Miyuki Watching Over C	.12	.25
KGLS79E042C Head Tilt Kei C	.12	.25
KGLS79E043C Hello, Way of the Sword Back! Kei C	.20	.40
KGLS79E044KRKR That's It! KR	15.00	30.00
KGLS79E044R That's It! R	.25	.50
KGLS79E045U Spartan Training U	.15	.30
KGLS79E046CC Rebelling Against Society CC	.12	.25
KGLS79E046RRRR Rebelling Against Society RRR	2.50	5.00
KGLS79E047CC President's Pride CC	.12	.25
KGLS79E047RRRR President's Pride RRR	1.00	2.00
KGLS79E048CC Get Better at Making Conversation CC	.12	.25
KGLS79E048RRRR Get Better at Making Conversation RRR	.60	1.25
KGLS79E049RR Skill Miss Innocent, Kaguya (Miss Innocent: Feigning Ignorance) RR	.75	1.50
KGLS79E049SSR Skill Miss Innocent, Kaguya (Miss Innocent: Feigning Ignorance) SR	6.00	12.00
KGLS79E050RR Serious Showdown Between Geniuses, Kaguya RR	7.50	15.00
KGLS79E050SPSP Serious Showdown Between Geniuses, Kaguya SP	400.00	800.00
KGLS79E051R Trembling, Kaguya R	.25	.50
KGLS79E051SSR Trembling, Kaguya SR	7.50	15.00
KGLS79E052R Panic, Kaguya R	.25	.50
KGLS79E053R In the Corridor at Dusk, Kaguya R	.25	.50
KGLS79E053SSR In the Corridor at Dusk, Kaguya SR	25.00	50.00
KGLS79E054R Hopeless at I.T., Kaguya R	.50	1.00
KGLS79E055R Fireworks Display, Miyuki R	.25	.50
KGLS79E055SSR Fireworks Display, Miyuki SR	1.00	2.00
KGLS79E056U 20 Questions Kaguya U	.15	.30
KGLS79E057U Bluff, Kaguya U	.15	.30
KGLS79E058U Dignified Appearance, Kaguya U	.15	.30
KGLS79E059U Flurried, Miyuki U	.15	.30
KGLS79E060U Skill A Maiden's Tears, Kaguya (A Maiden's Tears: Deception) U	.15	.30
KGLS79E061U Mission Accomplished, Kaguya U	.15	.30
KGLS79E062C As a Brother, Miyuki C	.12	.25
KGLS79E063C Wall-Down, Miyuki C	.12	.25
KGLS79E064C Romantic Advice, Nagisa C	.12	.25
KGLS79E065C Smartphone Debut, Miyuki C	.12	.25
KGLS79E066C Confess Your Love! Kaguya C	.12	.25
KGLS79E067C Weakness, Kaguya C	.12	.25
KGLS79E068KRKR A Romantic Battle of the Brains KR	20.00	40.00
KGLS79E068R A Romantic Battle of the Brains R	.25	.50
KGLS79E069U No Longer Friends U	.15	.30
KGLS79E070CR Exchange Party Aftermath CLR	.30	.60
KGLS79E070SECaSEC Exchange Party Aftermath A SCR	125.00	250.00
KGLS79E070SECbSEC Exchange Party Aftermath B SCR	100.00	200.00
KGLS79E071CR Now We're Even CLR	.20	.40
KGLS79E071KRKR Now We're Even KR	75.00	150.00
KGLS79E072CC I Can't Hear the Fireworks CC	.12	.25
KGLS79E072RRRR I Can't Hear the Fireworks RRR	2.50	5.00
KGLS79E073RR Miraculous Compatibility, Kaguya (Miraculous Compatibility: Marriage) RR	1.00	2.00
KGLS79E073SPSP Miraculous Compatibility, Kaguya (Miraculous Compatibility: Marriage) SP	150.00	300.00
KGLS79E074RR Subservient Relationship, Ai RR	.50	1.00
KGLS79E074SSR Subservient Relationship, Ai SR	4.00	8.00
KGLS79E075RR Serious Showdown Between Geniuses, Ai RR	.75	1.50
KGLS79E075SPSP Serious Showdown Between Geniuses, Ai SP	100.00	200.00
KGLS79E076R First Phone Call, Kaguya R	.25	.50
KGLS79E076SSR First Phone Call, Kaguya SR	.75	1.50
KGLS79E077R Ai Bestowing Courage R	.25	.50
KGLS79E077SSR Ai Bestowing Courage SR	15.00	30.00
KGLS79E078R Bewitching Pose Kaguya R	.25	.50
KGLS79E078SSR Bewitching Pose Kaguya SR	6.00	12.00
KGLS79E079R At the School Gates, Ai R	.25	.50
KGLS79E080R Smart Proposal, Kaguya R	.25	.50
KGLS79E081U Reminder, Herthaka U	.15	.30
KGLS79E082U Fearless Smile, Kaguya U	.15	.30
KGLS79E083U Thumbs Up! Ai U	.15	.30
KGLS79E084U Outcasted, Maki U	.15	.30
KGLS79E085U Envious Gazes, Karen & Erika U	.15	.30
KGLS79E086U About a Friend, Kaguya U	.15	.30
KGLS79E087U Psychological Test, Kaguya U	.15	.30
KGLS79E088U Smithee A. Herthaka U	.15	.30
KGLS79E089C Kaguya in a Yukata C	.12	.25
KGLS79E090C Unusual Morning, Ai C	.12	.25
KGLS79E091C Flying Ace, Kaguya C	.12	.25
KGLS79E092C Unusual Morning, Kaguya C	.12	.25
KGLS79E093C Ai Giving a Vague Answer C	.12	.25
KGLS79E094C After School, Ai C	.12	.25
KGLS79E095C Reluctant Summons, Ai C	.12	.25
KGLS79E096C Playful Spirit, Kaguya C	.12	.25
KGLS79E097KRKR Incident of the Century KR	25.00	50.00
KGLS79E097R Incident of the Century R	.25	.50
KGLS79E098CR Brief Respite CLR	.20	.40
KGLS79E098KRKR Brief Respite KR	20.00	40.00
KGLS79E099CC A Rainy Day CC	.12	.25
KGLS79E099RRRR A Rainy Day RRR	1.25	2.50
KGLS79E100CC Delightful and Embarrassing First Mail CC	.12	.25
KGLS79E100RRRR Delightful and Embarrassing First Mail RRR	2.00	4.00
KGLS79E101PR Full of Smiles, Chika P	.60	1.25
KGLS79E102PR Kei Looking Around P	.50	1.00
KGLS79E103PR Full Sprint, Kaguya P	12.50	25.00
KGLS79E104PR Sideways Peace Sign, Ai P	.75	1.50

2021 Weiss Schwarz Kaguya-sama Love Is War Trial Deck

KGLS79TE01TD Romantic Advice, Yu	.15	.30
KGLS79TE02TD Student Council President, Miyuki	.15	.30
KGLS79TE03TD The Birdie from Tottori, Chika	.15	.30
KGLS79TE04TD Secretary, Chika	.15	.30
KGLS79TE05TD Romantic Advice, Miyuki	.15	.30
KGLS79TE06TD Tabletop Games Club, Chika	.15	.30
KGLS79TE07RRRR At That Age, Chika RRR	7.50	15.00
KGLS79TE07TD At That Age, Chika	.60	1.25
KGLS79TE08TD Student Council Pair	.15	.30
KGLS79TE09TD Shuchiin's Student Council	.15	.30
KGLS79TE10TD Ai Sitting at the Bedside	.15	.30
KGLS79TE11TD Kaguya in a Great Mood	.15	.30
KGLS79TE12RRRR Valet, Ai RRR	7.50	15.00
KGLS79TE12TD Valet, Ai	.50	1.00
KGLS79TE13SSR Uncertainty and Expectations, Kaguya SR	.60	1.25
KGLS79TE13TD Uncertainty and Expectations, Kaguya	.15	.30
KGLS79TE14TD Scene Inspection, Ai	.15	.30
KGLS79TE15TD Picking Out Clothes, Ai	.15	.30
KGLS79TE16RRRR Shirogane's Lineage? Kei RRR	7.50	15.00
KGLS79TE16TD Shirogane's Lineage? Kei	.15	.30
KGLS79TE17SPSP Vice President, Kaguya SP	250.00	500.00
KGLS79TE17TD Vice President, Kaguya	2.00	4.00
KGLS79TE18TD A Romantic Battle of the Brains (Blue)	.50	1.00
KGLS79TE19SSR Blessed Me SR	.75	1.50
KGLS79TE19TD Blessed Me	.15	.30

2021 Weiss Schwarz Magia Record Puella Magi Madoka Magica Side Story Anime

MRW80E001RR Comrades of Mikazuki Villa, Tsuruno RR	12.50	25.00
MRW80E001SPSP Comrades of Mikazuki Villa, Tsuruno SP	300.00	600.00
MRW80E002RR Comrades of Mikazuki Villa, Felicia RR	12.50	25.00
MRW80E002SPSP Comrades of Mikazuki Villa, Felicia SP	150.00	300.00
MRW80E003RR Comrades of Mikazuki Villa, Iroha RR	3.00	6.00
MRW80E003SPSP Comrades of Mikazuki Villa, Iroha SP	125.00	250.00
MRW80E004R Raring to Go, Felicia R	.25	.50
MRW80E004SSR Raring to Go, Felicia SR	12.50	25.00
MRW80E005R Everyone's Own Feelings, Iroha R	.25	.50
MRW80E006R Pursuing the Truth of Rumors, Iroha R	.25	.50
MRW80E006SSR Pursuing the Truth of Rumors, Iroha SR	2.00	4.00
MRW80E007R Ui Tamaki R	.30	.60
MRW80E008R Everyone's Own Feelings, Sana R	.25	.50
MRW80E008SSR Everyone's Own Feelings, Sana SR	1.00	2.00
MRW80E009R Precious Memories, Sana R	.25	.50
MRW80E009SSR Precious Memories, Sana SR	2.00	4.00
MRW80E010R Rumor of the Saint of Kamihama, Mami R	.25	.50
MRW80E010SSR Rumor of the Saint of Kamihama, Mami SR	3.00	6.00
MRW80E011U Advice on a Present, Iroha U	.15	.30
MRW80E012U Invitation to Hang Out, Tsuruno U	.15	.30
MRW80E013U Tsuruno Investigating the Rumors U	.15	.30
MRW80E014U Search for Her Sister, Iroha U	.15	.30
MRW80E015U Magical Girl from Mitakihara City, Mami U	.15	.30
MRW80E016U Iroha's Doppel U	.15	.30
MRW80E017C Let's Go Home Together! Iroha C	.12	.25
MRW80E018C Heartfelt Thanks, Sana C	.12	.25
MRW80E019C Unsettling Self-Introduction, Mami C	.12	.25
MRW80E020C Mercenary's Reward, Felicia C	.12	.25
MRW80E021C Return From a Delivery, Tsuruno C	.12	.25
MRW80E022C Imprisoned Girl, Sana C	.12	.25
MRW80E023C Magical Girl Transformation, Felicia C	.12	.25
MRW80E024U Mercenary Business U	.15	.30
MRW80E025CR To Cure Her Younger Sister's Disease CLR	.30	.75
MRW80E025RRRR To Cure Her Younger Sister's Disease RRR	15.00	30.00
MRW80E026CC Welcome to Banbanzai CC	.12	.25
MRW80E027CC Reason for Becoming a Magical Girl CC	.12	.25
MRW80E027RRRR Reason for Becoming a Magical Girl RRR	25.00	50.00
MRW80E028CC A Step Towards the Future CC	.12	.25
MRW80E029RR In an Apron, Yachiyo RR	.75	1.50
MRW80E029SSR In an Apron, Yachiyo SR	6.00	12.00
MRW80E030RR Comrades of Mikazuki Villa, Sana RR	2.50	5.00
MRW80E030SPSP Comrades of Mikazuki Villa, Sana SP	60.00	125.00
MRW80E031R Pursuing the Truth of Rumors, Yachiyo R	.25	.50
MRW80E031SSR Pursuing the Truth of Rumors, Yachiyo SR	3.00	6.00
MRW80E032R Iroha & Madoka R	.25	.50
MRW80E032SSR Iroha & Madoka SR	1.25	2.50
MRW80E033R Well-Coordinated Sisters, Tsukasa R	.25	.50
MRW80E034R Well-Coordinated Sisters, Tsukuyo R	.25	.50
MRW80E035R Wealth of Battle Experience, Yachiyo R	.25	.50
MRW80E036R Alina Gray R	.25	.50
MRW80E036SSR Alina Gray SR	4.00	8.00
MRW80E037U A World with Just Me Sana U	.15	.30
MRW80E038U Where I Belong, Sana U	.15	.30
MRW80E039U Nemu Hiiragi U	.15	.30
MRW80E040U A Bout of Chess, Sana U	.15	.30
MRW80E041C Reminiscing, Yachiyo C	.12	.25
MRW80E042C Sudden Attack, Alina C	.12	.25
MRW80E043C Using Her New Year's Money, Sana C	.12	.25
MRW80E044C Return Gift of Gratitude, Sana C	.12	.25
MRW80E045C Caution Against the Unknown, Yachiyo C	.12	.25
MRW80E046U Seance Shrine U	.15	.30
MRW80E047CR You'll Compensate Me, Right? CC	.25	.50
MRW80E047RRRR You'll Compensate Me, Right? RRR	2.50	5.00
MRW80E048CC Encounter With A New Enemy CC	.12	.25
MRW80E048RRRR Encounter With a New Enemy RRR	2.00	4.00
MRW80E049CC Sisters' Entertaining Performance CC	.12	.25
MRW80E050RR Pursuing the Truth of Rumors, Momoko RR	1.00	2.00
MRW80E050SPSP Pursuing the Truth of Rumors, Momoko SP	75.00	150.00
MRW80E051RR Pursuing the Truth of Rumors, Kaede RR	.30	.75
MRW80E051SPSP Pursuing the Truth of Rumors, Kaede SP	30.00	75.00
MRW80E052RR Pursuing the Truth of Rumors, Rena RR	.75	1.50
MRW80E052SPSP Pursuing the Truth of Rumors, Rena SP	40.00	80.00
MRW80E053R Shop's Poster Girl, Tsuruno R	.30	.75
MRW80E053SSR Shop's Poster Girl, Tsuruno SR	3.00	6.00
MRW80E054R Touka Satomi R	.25	.50
MRW80E054SSR Touka Satomi SR	4.00	8.00
MRW80E055R Everyone's Own Feelings, Rena R	.25	.50
MRW80E056R Everyone's Own Feelings, Tsuruno R	.25	.50
MRW80E056SSR Everyone's Own Feelings, Tsuruno SR	2.00	4.00
MRW80E057R Kaede's Doppel R	.25	.50
MRW80E058U Usual Squabble, Rena U	.15	.30
MRW80E059U Getting Fired Up! Tsuruno U	.15	.30
MRW80E060U Kamihama City Recon, Kyoko U	.15	.30
MRW80E061U Everyone's Own Feelings, Kaede U	.15	.30
MRW80E062U Wings of the Magius, Mifuyu U	.15	.30
MRW80E063U Mightiest Magical Girl, Tsuruno U	.15	.30
MRW80E064U Everyone's Own Feelings, Momoko U	.15	.30
MRW80E065C Coincidence on the Rooftop, Rena C	.12	.25
MRW80E066C Regarding Artistic Skills, Kaede C	.12	.25
MRW80E067C Precise Advice, Momoko C	.12	.25
MRW80E068C Black Feather C	.12	.25
MRW80E069C Advice for Her Comrades, Tsuruno C	.12	.25
MRW80E070C Sudden Assistance, Kyoko C	.12	.25
MRW80E071C Small Kyubey C	.12	.25
MRW80E072C Magical Girl Transformation, Momoko C	.12	.25

MRW80E073C Magical Girl Service, Tsuruno C	.12	.25
MRW80E074U Chinese Restaurant Banbanzai U	.15	.30
MRW80E075U Lucky Owl Water U	.15	.30
MRW80E076CR Connect CLR	.20	.40
MRW80E076RRRR Connect RRR	2.00	4.00
MRW80E077CC Composure of the Mightiest CC	.12	.25
MRW80E077RRRR Composure of the Mightiest RRR	2.00	4.00
MRW80E078RR Frolicking Iroha RR	5.00	10.00
MRW80E078SSR Frolicking Iroha SR	20.00	40.00
MRW80E079RR Comrades of Mikazuki Villa, Yachiyo RR	1.00	2.00
MRW80E079SPSP Comrades of Mikazuki Villa, Yachiyo SP	60.00	125.00
MRW80E080R The One She Wanted to See, Yachiyo R	.25	.50
MRW80E081R Serious Gaze, Iroha R	.25	.50
MRW80E081SSR Serious Gaze, Iroha SR	2.00	4.00
MRW80E082R Everyone's Own Feelings, Felicia R	.30	.75
MRW80E082SSR Everyone's Own Feelings, Felicia SR	2.00	4.00
MRW80E083R Everyone's Own Feelings, Yachiyo R	.25	.50
MRW80E083SSR Everyone's Own Feelings, Yachiyo SR	2.50	5.00
MRW80E084U I'll Do Anything Felicia U	.15	.30
MRW80E085U Meal Invitation, Yachiyo U	.15	.30
MRW80E086U At Her Part-Time Job, Felicia U	.15	.30
MRW80E087U The Importance of Points, Yachiyo U	.15	.30
MRW80E088U Towards the Uwasa, Iroha U	.15	.30
MRW80E089U Certain Memories, Iroha U	.15	.30
MRW80E090C Magical Girl from Mitakihara City, Sayaka C	.12	.25
MRW80E091C Coordinator, Mitama C	.12	.25
MRW80E092C East Territory, Felicia C	.12	.25
MRW80E093C Battle at the Memory Museum, Sayaka C	.12	.25
MRW80E094C Things Good Friends Do, Yachiyo C	.12	.25
MRW80E095C Reason for the Fight, Felicia C	.12	.25
MRW80E096C Unbelievably Good Luck, Felicia C	.12	.25
MRW80E097U New Roommate U	.15	.30
MRW80E098CR Compensation for a Wish CLR	.30	.60
MRW80E098RRRR Compensation for a Wish RRR	2.00	4.00
MRW80E099CC Apprehensive Reunion CC	.12	.25
MRW80E100CC Recalling the Past CC	.12	.25
MRW80E100RRRR Recalling the Past RRR	1.00	2.00
MRW80E101PR Reunion on the Bridge, Iroha P	1.25	2.50
MRW80E102PR Encounter on the Bridge, Yachiyo P	1.00	2.00
MRW80E103PR Advice on a Present, Tsuruno P	.30	.75
MRW80E104PR Glutton, Felicia P	.30	.75
MRW80E105PR Sudden Designation, Sana P	.25	.50

2021 Weiss Schwarz Magia Record Puella Magi Madoka Magica Side Story Anime Trial Deck

MRW80TE01RRRR Making Up, Kaede RRR	7.50	15.00
MRW80TE01TD Making Up, Kaede	.20	.40
MRW80TE02TD Looking for the Chain Witch, Rena	.20	.40
MRW80TE03TD Helping Each Other, Momoko	.20	.40
MRW80TE04TD Reunion, Rena	.20	.40
MRW80TE05TD Way Home in the Dusk, Momoko	.30	.75
MRW80TE06TD Reunion, Kaede	.20	.40
MRW80TE07TD Kaede Chased by a Witch	.20	.40
MRW80TE08TD Making Up, Rena	.20	.40
MRW80TE09RRRR One Who Unifies the Members, Momoko RRR	12.50	25.00
MRW80TE09TD One Who Unifies the Members, Momoko	.30	.60
MRW80TE10TD Friendship Ending Staircase	.30	.60
MRW80TE11TD Kamihama Trio	.20	.40
MRW80TE12SSR Self-Introduction, Iroha SR	2.00	4.00
MRW80TE12TD Self-Introduction, Iroha	.20	.40
MRW80TE13TD Assistance in a Predicament, Yachiyo	.25	.50
MRW80TE14SPSP Veteran Magical Girl, Yachiyo SP	250.00	500.00
MRW80TE14TD Veteran Magical Girl, Yachiyo	.30	.75
MRW80TE15RRRR Decision on the Rooftop, Iroha RRR	25.00	50.00
MRW80TE15TD Decision on the Rooftop, Iroha	.20	.40
MRW80TE16TD Short Break, Iroha	.25	.50
MRW80TE17TD Kamihama West Territory, Yachiyo	.30	.60
MRW80TE18SPSP That Rumor About the Magical Girls Iroha SP	150.00	300.00
MRW80TE18TD That Rumor About the Magical Girls Iroha	.30	.75
MRW80TE19SSR Wish SR	1.50	3.00
MRW80TE19TD Wish	.20	.40
MRW80TE20TD Girl Who Chases Rumors	.30	.75

2021 Weiss Schwarz Magia Record Puella Magi Madoka Magica Side Story Mobile

MRW59E001RR Things to Protect, Sana RR	1.25	2.50
MRW59E001SPSP Things to Protect, Sana SP	75.00	150.00
MRW59E002RR A New Story, Mami RR	1.00	2.00
MRW59E002SSR A New Story, Mami SR	6.00	12.00
MRW59E003RR Mercenary's Battle Style, Felicia RR	10.00	20.00
MRW59E003SPSP Mercenary's Battle Style, Felicia SP	150.00	300.00
MRW59E004RR Throne of the Strongest, Tsuruno RR	2.50	5.00
MRW59E004SPSP Throne of the Strongest, Tsuruno SP	75.00	150.00
MRW59E005R Reliable Upperclassman, Mami R	.30	.75
MRW59E006R Onward to the Light! Tsuruno R	.30	.60
MRW59E007R Memories of Hatred Felicia R	.30	.60
MRW59E008R Recovery and Resolve Sana R	.30	.60
MRW59E009R Kokoro Awane R	.30	.60
MRW59E010U Masara Kagami U	.15	.30
MRW59E011U Melissa de Vignolles U	.15	.30
MRW59E012U Ayaka Mariko U	.15	.30
MRW59E013U A Shower of Light Felicia & Sana U	.15	.30
MRW59E014U The Maiden's Resolve Darc U	.15	.30
MRW59E015U Battle Stance, Mami U	.15	.30
MRW59E016C Felicia Mitsuki C	.12	.25
MRW59E017C Magical Girl VS Series? Holy Mami C	.12	.25
MRW59E018C Meiyui Chun C	.12	.25
MRW59E019C Sana Futaba C	.12	.25
MRW59E020C Sasara Minagi C	.12	.25
MRW59E021C Saintly Descent Holy Mami C	.12	.25
MRW59E022C Tsuruno Yui C	.12	.25
MRW59E023C Asuka Tatsuki C	.12	.25
MRW59E024C Memories from the Farm C	.12	.25
MRW59E025U Back Alley Pal U	.15	.30
MRW59E026U How's It Taste? U	.15	.30
MRW59E027CR I'm Even the Mightiest at Hoops! CLR	.20	.40
MRW59E027RRR I'm Even the Mightiest at Hoops! RRR	3.00	6.00
MRW59E028CC Perfectly Imbalanced CC	.15	.30
MRW59E029CC It's a Holiday! Nap All You Like CC	.15	.30
MRW59E030CC Invisible Girl After School CC	.15	.30
MRW59E031RR As Long as We Are Together, Homura RR	7.50	15.00
MRW59E031SPSP As Long as We Are Together, Homura SP	125.00	250.00
MRW59E032RR Offering a Hand, Madoka RR	2.50	5.00
MRW59E032SPSP Offering a Hand, Madoka SP	125.00	250.00
MRW59E033R A New Story, Madoka R	.25	.50
MRW59E033SSR A New Story, Madoka SR	4.00	8.00
MRW59E034R Sworn Promise Homura R	1.00	2.00
MRW59E035R Konoha Shizumi R	.25	.50
MRW59E036R Tsukuyo Amane R	.25	.50
MRW59E037R Qualities of a Magical Girl, Madoka R	.25	.50
MRW59E038R A New Story, Homura R	.25	.50
MRW59E038SSR A New Story, Homura SR	10.00	20.00
MRW59E039U Unwavering Light Madoka U	.15	.30
MRW59E040U Nanaka Tokiwa U	.15	.30
MRW59E041U Ayame Mikuri U	.15	.30
MRW59E042U Attitude Toward Art Alina U	.15	.30
MRW59E043U Tsukasa Amane U	.15	.30
MRW59E044C Natsuki Utsuho C	.12	.25
MRW59E045C This Year's Fortune Madoka & Homura C	.12	.25
MRW59E046C Kanoko Yayoi C	.12	.25
MRW59E047C Emiri Kisaki C	.12	.25
MRW59E048C Kako Natsume C	.12	.25
MRW59E049C Hazuki Yusa C	.12	.25
MRW59E050C Konomi Haruna C	.12	.25
MRW59E051C Hinano Miyako C	.12	.25
MRW59E052U Madoka's Notebook U	.15	.30
MRW59E053U I Want to Be Able to Protect Her U	.15	.30
MRW59E054CR Another Hope CLR	.20	.40
MRW59E054RRR Another Hope RRR	4.00	8.00
MRW59E055CC Non-Stop Training CC	.12	.25
MRW59E056CC Those Days are Gone CC	.12	.25
MRW59E057RR A New Story, Kyoko RR	.75	1.50
MRW59E057SSR A New Story, Kyoko SR	5.00	10.00
MRW59E058R Novice Magical Girl, Kaede R	.25	.50
MRW59E058SSR Novice Magical Girl, Kaede SR	1.25	2.50
MRW59E059R Swinging Her Sword, Momoko R	.25	.50
MRW59E059SSR Swinging Her Sword, Momoko SR	1.00	2.00
MRW59E060R Battle in Sync Momoko & Kaede & Rena R	.25	.50
MRW59E060SSR Battle in Sync Momoko & Kaede & Rena SR	1.00	2.00
MRW59E061R Confirmation of Feelings, Rena R	.25	.50
MRW59E061SSR Confirmation of Feelings, Rena SR	3.00	6.00
MRW59E062R The Hunt Begins Momoko & Kaede & Rena R	.30	.60
MRW59E063R Ren Isuzu R	.25	.50
MRW59E064U Karin Misono U	.15	.30
MRW59E065U Manaka Kurumi U	.15	.30
MRW59E066U Single Point Breakthrough, Kyoko U	.15	.30
MRW59E067U Unfaltering Conviction Kyoko U	.15	.30
MRW59E068C Team Leader, Momoko C	.12	.25
MRW59E069C Unable to be Honest, Rena C	.12	.25
MRW59E070C Shizuku Hozumi C	.12	.25
MRW59E071C Aimi Eri C	.12	.25
MRW59E072C For the Members, Kaede C	.12	.25
MRW59E073C Rika Ayano C	.12	.25
MRW59E074U Antithetical Existence U	.15	.30
MRW59E075CC Let's Eat Together! CC	.12	.25
MRW59E076CC Here With You CC	.12	.25
MRW59E077RR Battle Alongside Friends, Yachiyo RR	2.50	5.00
MRW59E077SPSP Battle Alongside Friends, Yachiyo SP	250.00	500.00
MRW59E078RR Guide to the Future, Iroha RR	.30	.75
MRW59E078SPSP Guide to the Future, Iroha SP	60.00	125.00
MRW59E079RR A New Story, Sayaka RR	6.00	12.00
MRW59E079SSR A New Story, Sayaka SR	30.00	75.00
MRW59E080R Preemptive Strike, Yachiyo R	.25	.50
MRW59E081R I Won't Stray Iroha R	.25	.50
MRW59E081SSR I Won't Stray Iroha SR	1.50	3.00
MRW59E082R Providing Cover, Iroha R	.25	.50
MRW59E083R Kazumi R	.25	.50
MRW59E084R Past and Future Yachiyo R	.25	.50
MRW59E084SSR Past and Future Yachiyo SR	2.00	4.00
MRW59E085U Loyalty Towards Oriko, Kirika U	.15	.30
MRW59E086U Enforced Justice, Oriko U	.15	.30
MRW59E087U My Favorite Kimono Yachiyo U	.15	.30
MRW59E088U Her Hope Within, Iroha U	.15	.30
MRW59E089U Emergency Reinforcement, Sayaka U	.15	.30
MRW59E090U Magical Girl Confrontation, Yachiyo U	.15	.30
MRW59E091C Young Magical Girl, Yuma C	.12	.25
MRW59E092C Clear Summer Colors Yachiyo & Iroha C	.12	.25
MRW59E093C Kaoru Maki C	.30	.75
MRW59E094C Umika Misaki C	.12	.25
MRW59E095C For The Ones I Love Sayaka C	.12	.25
MRW59E096C Akira Shinobu C	.12	.25
MRW59E097U Detailed Recipe U	.15	.30
MRW59E098CR Connections CLR	.20	.40
MRW59E098RRRR Connections RRR	1.25	2.50
MRW59E099CR Kamihama City's Magical Girl CLR	.20	.40
MRW59E099RRRR Kamihama City's Magical Girl RRR	3.00	6.00
MRW59E100CC The Flavor of Drama! CC	.12	.25
MRW59E101PR Petit Tsuruno P	.30	.75
MRW59E102PR Petit Felicia P	.30	.75
MRW59E103PR Petit Sana P	.50	1.00
MRW59E104PR Petit Iroha P	.30	.60
MRW59E105PR Petit Yachiyo P	.30	.60

2021 Weiss Schwarz Magia Record Puella Magi Madoka Magica Side Story Mobile Trial Deck

MRW59TE01RRRR Kaede Akino RRR	30.00	75.00
MRW59TE01TD Kaede Akino	.15	.30
MRW59TE02TD My First Homemade Chocolate Ren	.15	.30
MRW59TE03TD Surrounded by White Wings Kaede	.15	.30
MRW59TE04RRRR Teamwork on Our First Meeting Momoko & Iroha RRR	60.00	125.00
MRW59TE04TD Teamwork on Our First Meeting Momoko & Iroha	.15	.30
MRW59TE05SSR Momoko Togame SR	.50	1.00
MRW59TE05TD Momoko Togame	.15	.30
MRW59TE06TD It's Not Like I Was Waiting Rena	.15	.30
MRW59TE07TD Love Smells Like This Rika	.15	.30
MRW59TE08RRRR Rena Minami RRR	30.00	75.00
MRW59TE08TD Rena Minami	.15	.30
MRW59TE09TD PPPH! Perfect Cheers!	.15	.30
MRW59TE10SPSP Our Story Starts Here Iroha SP	150.00	300.00
MRW59TE10TD Our Story Starts Here Iroha	.50	1.00
MRW59TE11RRRR Yachiyo Nanami RRR	7.50	15.00
MRW59TE11TD Yachiyo Nanami	.15	.30
MRW59TE12TD As a Fashion Model Yachiyo	.15	.30
MRW59TE13TD Kirika Kure	.15	.30
MRW59TE14TD Yuma Chitose	.15	.30
MRW59TE15TD Iroha Starting Out	.15	.30
MRW59TE16TD Oriko Mikuni	.15	.30
MRW59TE17SSR Iroha Tamaki SR	.60	1.25
MRW59TE17TD Iroha Tamaki	.30	.75
MRW59TE18TD Tea for Three	.15	.30
MRW59TE19TD The Magical Girls' New Story	.15	.30
MRW59TE20TD Believe in Your Memories	.15	.30

2021 Weiss Schwarz Marvel Collection

MARS89001 Star-Lord MR	100.00	200.00
MARS89001 Star-Lord RR	2.50	5.00
MARS89002 Hulk AVGR	250.00	500.00
MARS89002 Hulk RR	2.50	5.00
MARS89003 Thor AVGR	200.00	400.00
MARS89003 Thor RR	3.00	6.00
MARS89004 Mantis MR	30.00	75.00
MARS89004 Mantis R	1.50	3.00
MARS89005 Groot MR	30.00	75.00
MARS89005 Groot R	1.50	3.00
MARS89006 Hulk MR	50.00	100.00
MARS89006 Hulk R	1.50	3.00
MARS89007 Rocket MR	60.00	125.00
MARS89007 Rocket R	1.25	2.50
MARS89008 Thor MR	50.00	100.00
MARS89008 Thor R	1.50	3.00
MARS89009 Drax MR	25.00	60.00
MARS89009 Drax R	1.25	2.50
MARS89010 Gamora MR	30.00	75.00
MARS89010 Gamora R	2.00	4.00
MARS89011 Thor SR	15.00	30.00
MARS89011 Thor U	1.00	2.00
MARS89012 Loki SR	12.50	25.00
MARS89012 Loki U	1.00	2.00
MARS89013 Baby Groot SR	10.00	20.00
MARS89013 Baby Groot U	.75	1.50
MARS89014 Drax SR	12.50	25.00
MARS89014 Drax U	.50	1.00
MARS89015 Mantis SR	7.50	15.00
MARS89015 Mantis U	.50	1.00
MARS89016 Gamora U	1.25	2.50
MARS89016 Gamora SR	12.50	25.00
MARS89017 Hulk SR	15.00	30.00
MARS89017 Hulk U	1.00	2.00
MARS89018 Rocket SR	10.00	20.00
MARS89018 Rocket U	.50	1.00
MARS89019 Star-Lord SR	12.50	25.00
MARS89019 Star-Lord U	1.25	2.50
MARS89020 Nebula C	.30	.75
MARS89021 Thor C	.60	1.25
MARS89022 Yondu C	.30	.75
MARS89023 Loki C	.50	1.00
MARS89024 Hulk C	.60	1.25
MARS89025 Mjolnir C	.50	1.00
MARS89026 Thor RRR	10.00	20.00
MARS89026 Thor CR	.60	1.50
MARS89027 Hulk RRR	15.00	30.00
MARS89027 Hulk CR	.60	1.50
MARS89028 Guardians of the Galaxy CC	.60	1.25
MARS89029 Star-Lord CC	.60	1.25
MARS89030 Black Widow AVGR	250.00	500.00
MARS89030 Black Widow RR	2.00	4.00
MARS89031 Spider-Man MR	200.00	400.00
MARS89031 Spider-Man RR	7.50	15.00
MARS89032 Iron Man AVGR	1,000.00	2,000.00
MARS89032 Iron Man RR	6.00	12.00
MARS89033 Captain Marvel MR	125.00	250.00
MARS89033 Captain Marvel RR	4.00	8.00
MARS89034 Thanos MR	75.00	150.00
MARS89034 Thanos RR	4.00	8.00
MARS89035 Black Panther MR	125.00	250.00
MARS89035 Black Panther R	2.00	4.00
MARS89036 Iron Man MR	125.00	250.00
MARS89036 Iron Man R	2.50	5.00
MARS89037 War Machine MR	75.00	150.00
MARS89037 War Machine R	1.25	3.00
MARS89038 Doctor Strange MR	60.00	125.00
MARS89038 Doctor Strange R	2.00	4.00
MARS89039 Vision MR	60.00	125.00
MARS89039 Vision R	1.25	2.50
MARS89040 Thanos SR	12.50	25.00
MARS89040 Thanos R	2.50	5.00
MARS89041 Spider-Man SR	50.00	100.00
MARS89041 Spider-Man R	4.00	8.00
MARS89042 Black Widow MR	50.00	100.00
MARS89042 Black Widow R	2.00	4.00
MARS89043 Vision SR	3.00	6.00
MARS89043 Vision U	.60	1.50
MARS89044 Ghost-Spider SR	40.00	80.00
MARS89044 Ghost-Spider U	2.50	5.00
MARS89045 Thanos U	2.00	4.00
MARS89046 Black Widow SR	7.50	15.00
MARS89046 Black Widow U	1.50	3.00
MARS89047 Doctor Strange SR	10.00	20.00
MARS89047 Doctor Strange U	1.25	2.50
MARS89048 Captain Marvel SR	10.00	20.00
MARS89048 Captain Marvel U	1.50	3.00
MARS89049 Black Panther SR	12.50	25.00
MARS89049 Black Panther U	1.50	3.00
MARS89050 War Machine SR	10.00	20.00
MARS89050 War Machine U	1.00	2.00
MARS89051 Spider-Man U	3.00	6.00
MARS89052 Iron Man SR	25.00	50.00
MARS89052 Iron Man U	1.50	3.00
MARS89053 Vision C	.75	1.50
MARS89054 War Machine C	.30	.75
MARS89055 Spider-Man C	1.50	3.00
MARS89056 Ultron C	.50	1.00
MARS89057 Shuri C	.30	.75
MARS89058 Red Skull C	.30	.75
MARS89059 Okoye C	.30	.75
MARS89060 Ghost-Spider C	1.50	3.00
MARS89061 Black Panther C	1.25	2.50
MARS89062 Iron Man C	1.00	2.00
MARS89063 Black Widow C	.60	1.25
MARS89064 Doctor Strange C	.60	1.25
MARS89065 Spider-Man C	1.50	3.00
MARS89066 Iron Man C	1.00	2.00
MARS89067 Infinity Gauntlet C	1.25	2.50
MARS89068 Iron Man RRR	10.00	20.00
MARS89068 Iron Man CR	.75	1.50
MARS89069 Black Widow RRR	6.00	12.00
MARS89069 Black Widow CR	.60	1.25
MARS89070 Thanos RRR	12.50	25.00
MARS89070 Thanos CC	1.00	2.00
MARS89071 Captain Marvel CC	1.00	2.00
MARS89072 Spider-Man RRR	15.00	30.00
MARS89072 Spider-Man CC	1.25	2.50
MARS89073 Hawkeye AVGR	75.00	150.00
MARS89073 Hawkeye RR	2.00	4.00
MARS89074 Captain America AVGR	300.00	750.00
MARS89074 Captain America RR	4.00	8.00
MARS89075 Hawkeye MR	30.00	60.00
MARS89075 Hawkeye R	1.25	2.50
MARS89076 Falcon MR	30.00	60.00
MARS89076 Falcon R	1.50	3.00
MARS89077 Scarlet Witch MR	125.00	250.00
MARS89077 Scarlet Witch R	2.00	4.00
MARS89078 Wasp MR	60.00	125.00
MARS89078 Wasp R	1.25	2.50
MARS89079 Ant-Man MR	75.00	150.00
MARS89079 Ant-Man R	1.25	2.50
MARS89080 Winter Soldier MR	50.00	100.00
MARS89080 Winter Soldier R	1.00	2.00
MARS89081 Captain America MR	125.00	250.00
MARS89081 Captain America R	1.50	3.00
MARS89082 Nick Fury U	1.00	2.00
MARS89083 Ant-Man SR	6.00	12.00
MARS89083 Ant-Man U	.75	1.50
MARS89084 Captain America SR	12.50	25.00
MARS89084 Captain America U	1.50	3.00
MARS89085 Wasp SR	7.50	15.00
MARS89085 Wasp U	.60	1.25
MARS89086 Scarlet Witch SR	30.00	60.00
MARS89086 Scarlet Witch U	1.00	2.00
MARS89087 Venom SR	50.00	100.00
MARS89087 Venom U	2.00	4.00
MARS89088 Falcon SR	10.00	20.00
MARS89088 Falcon U	.60	1.25
MARS89089 Winter Soldier SR	5.00	10.00
MARS89089 Winter Soldier U	.60	1.25
MARS89090 Hawkeye SR	7.50	15.00
MARS89090 Hawkeye U	.60	1.25
MARS89091 Vulture C	.30	.75
MARS89092 Nick Fury C	.50	1.00
MARS89093 Venom C	1.50	3.00

MARS89094 Captain America C	1.00	2.00
MARS89095 Carnage C	2.00	4.00
MARS89096 Hawkeye C	.30	.75
MARS89097 Avengers Assemble C	1.25	2.50
MARS89098 Hawkeye RRR	4.00	8.00
MARS89098 Hawkeye CR	.50	1.00
MARS89099 Captain America RRR	20.00	40.00
MARS89099 Captain America CR	1.00	2.00
MARS89100 Avengers CC	1.50	3.00

2021 Weiss Schwarz Marvel Collection Trial Deck

MARS89T01 Thor	1.25	2.50
MARS89T02 Hulk	1.25	2.50
MARS89T03 Thor	1.25	2.50
MARS89T03 Thor SP	150.00	300.00
MARS89T04 Hulk	1.25	2.50
MARS89T05 Thor	1.25	2.50
MARS89T06 Hulk	1.25	2.50
MARS89T06 Hulk RRR	25.00	50.00
MARS89T07 Thor	1.25	2.50
MARS89T08 Black Widow	1.00	2.00
MARS89T09 Iron Man	1.50	3.00
MARS89T10 Black Widow	1.00	2.00
MARS89T10 Black Widow RRR	40.00	80.00
MARS89T11 Black Widow	1.00	2.00
MARS89T12 Iron Man	1.50	3.00
MARS89T13 Iron Man	1.50	3.00
MARS89T13 Iron Man SR	5.00	10.00
MARS89T13 Iron Man SP	300.00	600.00
MARS89T14 Iron Man SR	5.00	10.00
MARS89T14 Iron Man	1.50	3.00
MARS89T15 Hawkeye RRR	20.00	40.00
MARS89T15 Hawkeye	1.00	2.00
MARS89T16 Hawkeye	1.00	2.00
MARS89T17 Captain America SP	500.00	1,000.00
MARS89T17 Captain America	1.25	2.50
MARS89T18 Captain America	1.25	2.50
MARS89T19 Hawkeye	1.00	2.00
MARS89T20 Captain America	1.25	2.50
MARS89T21 Captain America	1.25	2.50

2021 Weiss Schwarz The Quintessential Quintuplets

5HYW83E001RR+ Unstoppable Feelings, Ichika Nakano RR+	7.50	15.00
5HYW83E001SSPSSP Unstoppable Feelings, Ichika Nakano SSP	400.00	800.00
5HYW83E002RR In a Yukata, Ichika Nakano RR	.25	.50
5HYW83E002SPSP In a Yukata, Ichika Nakano SP	40.00	80.00
5HYW83E003HYRHYR The Quintessential Quintuplets, Ichika Nakano HYR	125.00	250.00
5HYW83E003RR The Quintessential Quintuplets, Ichika Nakano RR	1.00	2.00
5HYW83E004R Onwards to the School Camp! Yotsuba Nakano R	.25	.50
5HYW83E004SSR Onwards to the School Camp! Yotsuba Nakano SR	2.00	4.00
5HYW83E005R Habit of Undressing, Ichika Nakano R	.25	.50
5HYW83E005SSR Habit of Undressing, Ichika Nakano SR	2.50	5.00
5HYW83E006R One Step Forward, Ichika Nakano R	.25	.50
5HYW83E006SSR One Step Forward, Ichika Nakano SR	4.00	8.00
5HYW83E007R Intimate Sisters, Ichika Nakano R	.25	.50
5HYW83E007SSR Intimate Sisters, Ichika Nakano SR	4.00	8.00
5HYW83E008R Overflowing Charm, Ichika Nakano R	.25	.50
5HYW83E008SSR Overflowing Charm, Ichika Nakano SR	4.00	8.00
5HYW83E009R Test of Courage, Yotsuba Nakano R	.25	.50
5HYW83E009SSR Test of Courage, Yotsuba Nakano SR	1.00	2.00
5HYW83E010R Yotsuba Check, Yotsuba Nakano R	.25	.50
5HYW83E010SSR Yotsuba Check, Yotsuba Nakano SR	1.50	3.00
5HYW83E011R In a Jersey, Yotsuba Nakano R	.25	.50
5HYW83E011SSR In a Jersey, Yotsuba Nakano SR	1.00	2.00
5HYW83E012U Working Towards a Goal, Ichika Nakano U	.15	.30
5HYW83E013U Will It Look Good? Yotsuba Nakano U	.15	.30
5HYW83E014U In a Yukata, Yotsuba Nakano U	.15	.30
5HYW83E015U For Her Dream, Ichika Nakano U	.15	.30
5HYW83E016U Owner of the Mess, Ichika Nakano U	.15	.30
5HYW83E017U Overnight Study Session, Ichika Nakano U	.15	.30
5HYW83E018U Making Curry, Ichika Nakano U	.15	.30
5HYW83E019C Test Preparation, Futaro Uesugi C	.12	.25
5HYW83E020C Test Preparation, Ichika Nakano C	.12	.25
5HYW83E021C Operation Doppelganger, Futaro Uesugi C	.12	.25
5HYW83E022C Trembling in Fear, Yotsuba Nakano C	.12	.25
5HYW83E023C Shocking Truth, Yotsuba Nakano C	.12	.25
5HYW83E024C Mock Trial C	.12	.25
5HYW83E025CR Surprise Approach CR	.20	.40
5HYW83E025RRRR Surprise Approach RRR	20.00	40.00
5HYW83E026CC Blossom in the Dark of Night CC	.12	.25
5HYW83E026RRRR Blossom in the Dark of Night RRR	3.00	6.00
5HYW83E027CC Impersonating Ghosts CC	.12	.25
5HYW83E028RR+ Variety of Charms, Yotsuba Nakano RR+	2.00	4.00
5HYW83E028SSPSSP Variety of Charms, Yotsuba Nakano SSP	250.00	500.00
5HYW83E029HYRHYR The Quintessential Quintuplets, Yotsuba Nakano HYR	125.00	250.00
5HYW83E029RR The Quintessential Quintuplets, Yotsuba Nakano RR	.50	1.00
5HYW83E030RR Beyond Her Gaze, Miku Nakano RR	.30	.75
5HYW83E030SPSP Beyond Her Gaze, Miku Nakano SP	50.00	100.00
5HYW83E031RR Sparkling Smile, Yotsuba Nakano RR	.50	1.00
5HYW83E031SPSP Sparkling Smile, Yotsuba Nakano SP	50.00	100.00
5HYW83E032R Honor Student? Yotsuba Nakano R	.25	.50
5HYW83E032SSR Honor Student? Yotsuba Nakano SR	2.50	5.00
5HYW83E033R Worst Timing, Itsuki Nakano R	.25	.50
5HYW83E033SSR Worst Timing, Itsuki Nakano SR	6.00	12.00
5HYW83E034R By Your Side, Miku Nakano R	.25	.50
5HYW83E034SSR By Your Side, Miku Nakano SR	1.50	3.00
5HYW83E035R Intimate Sisters, Yotsuba Nakano R	.25	.50
5HYW83E035SSR Intimate Sisters, Yotsuba Nakano SR	4.00	8.00
5HYW83E036R Scorning Eyes, Miku Nakano R	.25	.50
5HYW83E036SSR Scorning Eyes, Miku Nakano SR	1.25	2.50
5HYW83E037R Awkward Atmosphere, Itsuki Nakano R	.25	.50
5HYW83E037SSR Awkward Atmosphere, Itsuki Nakano SR	1.00	2.00
5HYW83E038U Each and Everyone's Strengths, Yotsuba Nakano U	.15	.30
5HYW83E039U Honest and Positive, Yotsuba Nakano U	.15	.30
5HYW83E040U Impassioned Defense, Yotsuba Nakano U	.15	.30
5HYW83E041U Scene in the Morning, Yotsuba Nakano U	.15	.30
5HYW83E042U Sengoku Quiz, Miku Nakano U	.15	.30
5HYW83E043U After Much Deliberation, Yotsuba Nakano U	.15	.30
5HYW83E044U Fresh Start, Itsuki Nakano U	.15	.30
5HYW83E045U Which Test? Yotsuba Nakano U	.15	.30
5HYW83E046C Inside the Igloo, Miku Nakano C	.12	.25
5HYW83E047C Operation Doppelganger, Miku Nakano C	.12	.25
5HYW83E048C Operation Doppelganger, Itsuki Nakano C	.12	.25
5HYW83E049C Together With Raiha, Yotsuba Nakano C	.12	.25
5HYW83E050C Studying in Advance, Itsuki Nakano C	.12	.25
5HYW83E051C Best Value School Lunch, Futaro Uesugi C	.12	.25
5HYW83E052C Questioning Gaze, Futaro Uesugi C	.12	.25
5HYW83E053C Progressing Alone, Itsuki Nakano C	.12	.25
5HYW83E054C Chauffeured to School, Itsuki Nakano C	.12	.25
5HYW83E055C Filling in Answers, Miku Nakano C	.12	.25
5HYW83E056C Questioning Gaze, Yotsuba Nakano C	.12	.25
5HYW83E057C Reason for Trying Hard, Itsuki Nakano C	.12	.25
5HYW83E058C Fan of Sengoku Warlords, Miku Nakano C	.12	.25
5HYW83E059U Album of Memories U	.15	.30
5HYW83E060CR Carefree Smile CR	.20	.40
5HYW83E060RRRR Carefree Smile RRR	4.00	8.00
5HYW83E061CC Like Sisters CC	.12	.25
5HYW83E061RRRR Like Sisters RRR	1.25	2.50
5HYW83E062CC Making Up Starts With Lies CC	.12	.25
5HYW83E062RRRR Making Up Starts With Lies RRR	2.00	4.00
5HYW83E063CC Words She Couldn't Say Before CC	.12	.25
5HYW83E064RR+ In a Yukata, Itsuki Nakano RR+	5.00	10.00
5HYW83E064SSPSSP In a Yukata, Itsuki Nakano SSP	250.00	500.00
5HYW83E065HYRHYR The Quintessential Quintuplets, Itsuki Nakano HYR	100.00	200.00
5HYW83E065RR The Quintessential Quintuplets, Itsuki Nakano RR	1.00	2.00
5HYW83E066HYRHYR The Quintessential Quintuplets, Nino Nakano HYR	250.00	500.00
5HYW83E066RR The Quintessential Quintuplets, Nino Nakano RR	1.00	2.00
5HYW83E067RR Kind Gaze, Itsuki Nakano RR	.25	.50
5HYW83E067SPSP Kind Gaze, Itsuki Nakano SP	330.00	75.00
5HYW83E068R At That Age, Nino Nakano R	.25	.50
5HYW83E068SSR At That Age, Nino Nakano SR	2.50	5.00
5HYW83E069R In Pajamas, Itsuki Nakano R	.25	.50
5HYW83E069SSR In Pajamas, Itsuki Nakano SR	2.50	5.00
5HYW83E070R Knowing the Circumstances, Itsuki Nakano R	.25	.50
5HYW83E070SSR Knowing the Circumstances, Itsuki Nakano SR	2.00	4.00
5HYW83E071R Under the Moonlight, Nino Nakano R	.25	.50
5HYW83E071SSR Under the Moonlight, Nino Nakano SR	7.50	15.00
5HYW83E072R Intimate Sisters, Itsuki Nakano R	.25	.50
5HYW83E072SSR Intimate Sisters, Itsuki Nakano SR	3.00	6.00
5HYW83E073R Belligerent, Itsuki Nakano R	.25	.50
5HYW83E073SSR Belligerent, Itsuki Nakano SR	2.00	4.00
5HYW83E074R Unknown Truth, Ichika Nakano R	.25	.50
5HYW83E074SSR Unknown Truth, Ichika Nakano SR	2.00	4.00
5HYW83E075R Intimate Sisters, Nino Nakano R	.25	.50
5HYW83E075SSR Intimate Sisters, Nino Nakano SR	7.50	15.00
5HYW83E076R In a Santa Suit, Ichika Nakano R	.25	.50
5HYW83E076SSR In a Santa Suit, Ichika Nakano SR	4.00	8.00
5HYW83E077U Drawing Back, Ichika Nakano U	.15	.30
5HYW83E078U Method to Feel Better, Itsuki Nakano U	.15	.30
5HYW83E079U As an Elder Sister, Ichika Nakano U	.15	.30
5HYW83E080U Operation Doppelganger, Ichika Nakano U	.15	.30
5HYW83E081U Honest Apology, Nino Nakano U	.15	.30
5HYW83E082U Hostility, Nino Nakano U	.15	.30
5HYW83E083U Unable to Be Honest, Itsuki Nakano U	.15	.30
5HYW83E084U Top of the Cohort, Futaro Uesugi U	.15	.30
5HYW83E085U Calm Reaction, Ichika Nakano U	.15	.30
5HYW83E086C Seeking Confirmation, Itsuki Nakano C	.12	.25
5HYW83E087C Commuting to School, Futaro Uesugi C	.12	.25
5HYW83E088C Extended Helping Hand, Nino Nakano C	.12	.25
5HYW83E089C Vaguely Familiar Term, Nino Nakano C	.12	.25
5HYW83E090C All Five Together, Itsuki Nakano C	.12	.25
5HYW83E091C Surprise Attack, Ichika Nakano C	.12	.25
5HYW83E092C Drenched, Ichika Nakano C	.12	.25
5HYW83E093C Resting, Nino Nakano C	.12	.25
5HYW83E094C Taking a Photo Sticker Together, Itsuki Nakano C	.12	.25
5HYW83E095C Breakfast, Nino Nakano C	.12	.25
5HYW83E096C In the Forest, Futaro Uesugi C	.12	.25
5HYW83E097C In the Forest, Nino Nakano C	.12	.25
5HYW83E098C Commuting to School, Itsuki Nakano C	.12	.25
5HYW83E099U Quintuplets Game U	.15	.30
5HYW83E100U Important Charm U	.15	.30
5HYW83E101CR Blossoming Smile CR	.20	.40
5HYW83E101RRRR Blossoming Smile RRR	7.50	15.00
5HYW83E102CC Moonlit Invitation CC	.12	.25
5HYW83E102RRRR Moonlit Invitation RRR	7.50	15.00
5HYW83E103CC Under the Winter Stars CC	.12	.25
5HYW83E104CC Source of Discomfort CC	.12	.25
5HYW83E105RR+ Sensitive and Straightforward, Nino Nakano RR+	2.50	5.00
5HYW83E105SSPSSP Sensitive and Straightforward, Nino Nakano SSP	450.00	900.00
5HYW83E106RR+ A Step Forward, Miku Nakano RR+	7.50	15.00
5HYW83E106SSPSSP A Step Forward, Miku Nakano SSP	500.00	1,000.00
5HYW83E107RR Fresh From a Bath, Nino Nakano RR	2.00	4.00
5HYW83E107SPSP Fresh From a Bath, Nino Nakano SP	125.00	250.00
5HYW83E108HYRHYR The Quintessential Quintuplets, Miku Nakano HYR	.50	1.00
5HYW83E108RR The Quintessential Quintuplets, Miku Nakano RR	150.00	300.00
5HYW83E109R Operation Doppelganger, Nino Nakano R	.25	.50
5HYW83E109SSR Operation Doppelganger, Nino Nakano SR	4.00	8.00
5HYW83E110R In a Jersey, Miku Nakano R	.25	.50
5HYW83E110SSR In a Jersey, Miku Nakano SR	4.00	8.00
5HYW83E111R Secret Ingredient, Miku Nakano R	.25	.50
5HYW83E111SSR Secret Ingredient, Miku Nakano SR	3.00	6.00
5HYW83E112R Heartfelt, Miku Nakano R	.25	.50
5HYW83E112SSR Heartfelt, Miku Nakano SR	7.50	15.00
5HYW83E113R Firm Resolve, Nino Nakano R	.25	.50
5HYW83E113SSR Firm Resolve, Nino Nakano SR	3.00	6.00
5HYW83E114R In a Santa Suit, Nino Nakano R	.25	.50
5HYW83E114SSR In a Santa Suit, Nino Nakano SR	10.00	20.00
5HYW83E115R Intimate Sisters, Miku Nakano R	.25	.50
5HYW83E115SSR Intimate Sisters, Miku Nakano SR	10.00	20.00
5HYW83E116U In a Yukata, Nino Nakano U	.15	.30
5HYW83E117U In a Yukata, Miku Nakano U	.15	.30
5HYW83E118U Broad Smile, Miku Nakano U	.15	.30
5HYW83E119U Showing Off, Futaro Uesugi U	.15	.30
5HYW83E120U Things to Be Said, Miku Nakano U	.15	.30
5HYW83E121U Why So Guarded? Nino Nakano U	.15	.30
5HYW83E122U Unexpected Response, Miku Nakano U	.15	.30
5HYW83E123C Confrontation, Futaro Uesugi C	.12	.25
5HYW83E123C Worst Timing, Miku Nakano C	.12	.25
5HYW83E124C Confrontation, Miku Nakano C	.12	.25
5HYW83E126C Waiting for Someone, Nino Nakano C	.12	.25
5HYW83E127C Sleeping Pills, Nino Nakano C	.12	.25
5HYW83E128C Following After, Futaro Uesugi C	.12	.25
5HYW83E129C Shopping After School, Nino Nakano C	.12	.25
5HYW83E130C How Do You Really Feel? Miku Nakano C	.12	.25
5HYW83E131U Headphone U	.15	.30
5HYW83E132CR A White Lie CR	.20	.40
5HYW83E132RRRR A White Lie RRR	5.00	10.00
5HYW83E133CR Opening up the Way CR	.20	.40
5HYW83E133RRRR Opening up the Way RRR	15.00	30.00
5HYW83E134CC Let's Be Fair CC	.12	.25
5HYW83E134RRRR Let's Be Fair RRR	10.00	20.00
5HYW83E135CC Picking an Outfit Seriously CC	.12	.25

2021 Weiss Schwarz The Quintessential Quintuplets Trial Deck

5HYW83TE01TD The Two Alone in the Shed, Ichika Nakano	.12	.25
5HYW83TE02TD Mid-Terms Exam Report, Ichika Nakano	.12	.25
5HYW83TE03TD Short-Cut Hairstyle, Ichika Nakano	2.00	4.00
5HYW83TE04TD Eldest of the Quintuplets, Ichika Nakano	.15	.30
5HYW83TE05TD A Day of Turbulent Events, Ichika Nakano	.12	.25
5HYW83TE06TD Air of Maturity, Ichika Nakano	.07	.15
5HYW83TE07TDRRRR Sitting by a Small Fire, Ichika Nakano RRR	.75	1.50
5HYW83TE07TD Sitting by a Small Fire, Ichika Nakano	.25	.50
5HYW83TE08TD Escape, Ichika Nakano	.07	.15
5HYW83TE09TD Dozing, Ichika Nakano	.07	.15
5HYW83TE10TDRRRR Going Home After School, Ichika Nakano RRR	.75	1.50
5HYW83TE10TD Going Home After School, Ichika Nakano	.10	.20
5HYW83TE11TD Surprise Attack	.12	.25
5HYW83TE12TDRRRR Rewarding Those Who Make an Effort RRR	.30	.75
5HYW83TE12TD Rewarding Those Who Make an Effort	.12	.25
5HYW83TE13TD Stranded in a Snowstorm, Ichika Nakano	.12	.25
5HYW83TE14TD Loathe of Studying, Ichika Nakano	.12	.25
5HYW83TE15TD Acting Practice, Ichika Nakano	.12	.25
5HYW83TE16TD That Day at Sunset, Ichika Nakano	.07	.15
5HYW83TE17TD Talking About Love, Ichika Nakano	.12	.25
5HYW83TE18TD Quintuplets Lined Up (Red)	.12	.25
5HYW83TE19TD Social Butterfly, Nino Nakano	.12	.25
5HYW83TE20TD Blossoming Fireworks, Nino Nakano	.10	.20
5HYW83TE21TD Chilly Reception, Nino Nakano	.12	.25
5HYW83TE22TD Good at Cooking, Nino Nakano	.20	.40
5HYW83TE23TD Participating Mid-Game, Nino Nakano	.20	.40
5HYW83TE24TD Separated and Lost, Nino Nakano	1.00	2.00
5HYW83TE25TD Second of the Quintuplets, Nino Nakano	.25	.50
5HYW83TE26TD Secret Within the Student Handbook	.10	.20
5HYW83TE27TDRRRR Full Feminine Power! RRR	.60	1.25
5HYW83TE27TD Full Feminine Power!	.20	.40
5HYW83TE28TD Hidden Kindness, Nino Nakano	.20	.40
5HYW83TE29TD Informed About the Departure, Nino Nakano	.20	.40
5HYW83TE30TD Tsundere, Nino Nakano	.25	.50
5HYW83TE31TDRRRR Important Charm, Nino Nakano RRR	.75	1.50
5HYW83TE31TD Important Charm, Nino Nakano	.60	1.25
5HYW83TE32TD Criticizing Words, Nino Nakano	.12	.25
5HYW83TE33TD Scornful Gaze, Nino Nakano	.12	.25
5HYW83TE34TD Fight Between Sisters, Nino Nakano	.12	.25
5HYW83TE35TDRRRR Obstructing Barrier, Nino Nakano RRR	1.00	2.00
5HYW83TE35TD Obstructing Barrier, Nino Nakano	.25	.50
5HYW83TE36TD Quintuplets Lined Up (Blue)	.10	.20
5HYW83TE37TD Blossoming Fireworks, Miku Nakano	.12	.25
5HYW83TE38TD Ideal Image, Miku Nakano	.20	.40
5HYW83TE39TD Fight Between Sisters, Miku Nakano	.07	.15
5HYW83TE40TD Words She Couldn't Say, Miku Nakano	.07	.15
5HYW83TE41TD Guarded, Miku Nakano	.20	.40
5HYW83TE42TD Quintuplets Lined Up (Green)	.12	.25
5HYW83TE43TD Summer Festival, Miku Nakano	.12	.25
5HYW83TE44TD In Return, Miku Nakano	.12	.25
5HYW83TE45TD Third of the Quintuplets, Miku Nakano	1.50	3.00
5HYW83TE46TD Burglar? Miku Nakano	.12	.25
5HYW83TE47TDRRRR Detected Discomfort, Miku Nakano RRR	.75	1.50
5HYW83TE47TD Detected Discomfort, Miku Nakano	.75	1.50
5HYW83TE48TDRRRR New Student, Miku Nakano RRR	.75	1.50
5HYW83TE48TD New Student, Miku Nakano	.20	.40
5HYW83TE49TD Warlord Shiritori, Miku Nakano	.12	.25
5HYW83TE50TD Unexpectedly Fast Learner, Miku Nakano	.07	.15
5HYW83TE51TD A Maiden's Heart, Miku Nakano	.15	.30
5HYW83TE52TD Headphone Girl, Miku Nakano	7.50	15.00
5HYW83TE53TD Matcha Soda	.12	.25
5HYW83TE54TDRRRR Swift as the Wind RRR	.75	1.50
5HYW83TE54TD Swift as the Wind	.25	.50
5HYW83TE55TD Yotsuba Question, Yotsuba Nakano	.25	.50
5HYW83TE56TD Face of Her Sisters, Yotsuba Nakano	.25	.50
5HYW83TE57TD Blossoming Fireworks, Yotsuba Nakano	.20	.40
5HYW83TE58TD Missing Line, Yotsuba Nakano	.12	.25
5HYW83TE59TD Invitation to the Slopes, Yotsuba Nakano	.15	.30
5HYW83TE60TD Role of a Ghost, Yotsuba Nakano	.15	.30
5HYW83TE61TD Playing Tag, Yotsuba Nakano	.20	.40
5HYW83TE62TD Quintuplets Lined Up (Yellow)	.12	.25
5HYW83TE63TD Ribbon Girl, Yotsuba Nakano	.40	.80
5HYW83TE64TD The Two Left Behind, Yotsuba Nakano	.20	.40
5HYW83TE65TD Wood-Splitting, Yotsuba Nakano	.15	.30
5HYW83TE66TDRRRR Assisting Player, Yotsuba Nakano RRR	.75	1.50
5HYW83TE66TD Assisting Player, Yotsuba Nakano	.30	.75
5HYW83TE67TD Fourth of the Quintuplets, Yotsuba Nakano	3.00	6.00
5HYW83TE68TD An Acceptable Answer, Yotsuba Nakano	.20	.40
5HYW83TE69TD Teacher For the Day, Yotsuba Nakano	.07	.15
5HYW83TE70TDRRRR Prepping for the Camp, Yotsuba Nakano RRR	.50	1.00
5HYW83TE70TD Prepping for the Camp, Yotsuba Nakano	.30	.75
5HYW83TE71TD Checkered Ribbon	.30	.60
5HYW83TE72TDRRRR Fake Confession RRR	2.50	5.00
5HYW83TE72TD Fake Confession	2.50	5.00
5HYW83TE73TD Glutton, Itsuki Nakano	.12	.25
5HYW83TE74TD Bad With Ghosts, Itsuki Nakano	.12	.25
5HYW83TE75TD When Push Comes to Shove, Itsuki Nakano	1.00	2.00
5HYW83TE76TD Rumor, Itsuki Nakano	.07	.15
5HYW83TE77TD Bold Move, Itsuki Nakano	.12	.25
5HYW83TE78TD Overly Unnatural Declaration, Itsuki Nakano	.12	.25
5HYW83TE79TD Among the Crowd, Itsuki Nakano	.12	.25
5HYW83TE80TD Quintuplets Lined Up (Green)	.20	.40
5HYW83TE81TD Discord, Itsuki Nakano	.20	.40
5HYW83TE82TDRRRR Awkward Personality, Itsuki Nakano RRR	.50	1.00
5HYW83TE82TD Awkward Personality, Itsuki Nakano	.40	.80
5HYW83TE83TD Escorting Home, Itsuki Nakano	.12	.25
5HYW83TE84TDRRRR Table-Sharing Acquaintances, Itsuki Nakano RRR	2.50	5.00
5HYW83TE84TD Table-Sharing Acquaintances, Itsuki Nakano	1.00	2.00
5HYW83TE85TD Youngest of the Quintuplets, Itsuki Nakano	.25	.50
5HYW83TE86TD Choosing a Book, Itsuki Nakano	.12	.25
5HYW83TE87TD Blossoming Fireworks, Itsuki Nakano	.12	.25
5HYW83TE88TD Earnest Girl, Itsuki Nakano	.25	.50
5HYW83TE89TD Unacceptable Reality	.12	.25
5HYW83TE90TDRRRR Being Obstinate RRR	.75	1.50
5HYW83TE90TD Being Obstinate	.25	.50

2021 Weiss Schwarz RWBY

RWBYWX03001RR Yang Xiao Long RR	2.50	5.00
RWBYWX03001SPSP Yang Xiao Long SP	150.00	300.00
RWBYWX03002RR Jaune: School Dance RR	.50	1.00
RWBYWX03002SSR Jaune: School Dance SR	2.50	5.00
RWBYWX03003R Sun Wukong R	.25	.50
RWBYWX03003SSR Sun Wukong SR	5.00	10.00
RWBYWX03004R Jaune Arc R	.25	.50
RWBYWX03004SSR Jaune Arc SR	2.50	5.00
RWBYWX03005R Yang: Vytal Festival R	.25	.50
RWBYWX03005RBRRBR Yang: Vytal Festival RBR	50.00	100.00
RWBYWX03006U Neon Katt U	.15	.30
RWBYWX03007U Uniform Jaune U	.15	.30
RWBYWX03008U Yang: Framed U	.15	.30
RWBYWX03009U Uniform Yang U	.15	.30
RWBYWX03010U Taiyang Xiao Long U	.15	.30
RWBYWX03011U Yang: Warm Welcome U	.15	.30
RWBYWX03012U Glynda Goodwitch U	.15	.30
RWBYWX03013C Arslan Altan C	.12	.25
RWBYWX03014C Brawnz Ni C	.12	.25
RWBYWX03015C Sun: Vytal Festival C	.12	.25
RWBYWX03016U A Childhood Memory U	.15	.30
RWBYWX03017CR School Dance CR	.20	.40
RWBYWX03017RRRR School Dance RRR	1.50	3.00
RWBYWX03018CC Falling Into a Trap CC	.12	.25
RWBYWX03018RRRR Falling Into a Trap RRR	4.00	8.00
RWBYWX03019CC Team SSSN CC	.12	.25
RWBYWX03020RR Lie Ren RR	.60	1.25
RWBYWX03020SSR Lie Ren SR	3.00	6.00
RWBYWX03021R Emerald Sustrai R	.25	.50
RWBYWX03021SSR Emerald Sustrai SR	2.50	5.00
RWBYWX03022R Ozpin R	.25	.50
RWBYWX03022SSR Ozpin SR	3.00	6.00
RWBYWX03023R Penny Polendina R	.25	.50
RWBYWX03024U Oobleck: Field Trip U	.15	.30
RWBYWX03025U Ren: Winning Advice U	.15	.30
RWBYWX03026U Uniform Ren U	.15	.30
RWBYWX03027U Ozpin: Fighting Off Cinder U	.15	.30
RWBYWX03028C Roy Stallion C	.12	.25
RWBYWX03029C Sage Ayana C	.12	.25
RWBYWX03030C Yatsuhashi Daichi C	.12	.25
RWBYWX03031C Bartholomew Oobleck C	.12	.25
RWBYWX03032C Flynt Coal C	.12	.25
RWBYWX03033C Coco Adel C	.12	.25

RWBYWX03034C Emerald & Mercury: Infiltrating Beacon Academy C .12 .25
RWBYWX03035C Emerald: Scouted C .12 .25
RWBYWX03036C Reese Chloris C .12 .25
RWBYWX03037C Cardin Winchester C .12 .25
RWBYWX03038U Beacon Academy U .15 .30
RWBYWX03039CC Military Weapon CC .12 .25
RWBYWX03040CC Defending the School CC .12 .25
RWBYWX03041RR Pyrrha: Fall Maiden's Vessel Candidate RR 6.00 12.00
RWBYWX03041SECSEC Pyrrha: Fall Maiden's Vessel Candidate SCR 75.00 150.00
RWBYWX03042RR Nora Valkyrie RR 2.50 5.00
RWBYWX03042SSR Nora Valkyrie SR 12.50 25.00
RWBYWX03043RR Cinder: Complete Maiden Powers RR .75 1.50
RWBYWX03043SSR Cinder: Complete Maiden Powers SR 7.50 15.00
RWBYWX03044RR Ruby Rose RR 3.00 6.00
RWBYWX03044SPSP Ruby Rose SP 150.00 300.00
RWBYWX03045RR Salem RR .50 1.00
RWBYWX03046R Raven Branwen R .25 .50
RWBYWX03046SSR Raven Branwen SR 2.50 5.00
RWBYWX03047R Adam Taurus R .25 .50
RWBYWX03047SSR Adam Taurus SR 2.00 4.00
RWBYWX03048R Amber: Fall Maiden R .25 .50
RWBYWX03048SSR Amber: Fall Maiden SR 6.00 12.00
RWBYWX03049R Zwei R .25 .50
RWBYWX03049SSR Zwei SR 6.00 12.00
RWBYWX03050R Qrow Branwen R .25 .50
RWBYWX03050SSR Qrow Branwen SR 7.50 15.00
RWBYWX03051R Cinder: Infiltrating Beacon Academy R .25 .50
RWBYWX03051SSR Cinder: Infiltrating Beacon Academy SR 4.00 8.00
RWBYWX03052R Ruby: Embarking on a New Journey R .25 .50
RWBYWX03053R Pyrrha Nikos R .25 .50
RWBYWX03053SSR Pyrrha Nikos SR 7.50 15.00
RWBYWX03054R Ruby: Vytal Festival R .25 .50
RWBYWX03054RBRRBR Ruby: Vytal Festival RBR 60.00 125.00
RWBYWX03055U Cinder: Scouting U .15 .30
RWBYWX03056U Ruby: Life-Changing Scene U .15 .30
RWBYWX03057U Cinder: Leading a Grimm Invasion U .15 .30
RWBYWX03058U Uniform Pyrrha U .15 .30
RWBYWX03059U Uniform Ruby U .15 .30
RWBYWX03060U Uniform Nora U .15 .30
RWBYWX03061C Qrow: Priorities C .12 .25
RWBYWX03062C Scarlet David C .12 .25
RWBYWX03063C Nadir Shiko C .12 .25
RWBYWX03064C May Zedong C .12 .25
RWBYWX03065C Fox Alistair C .12 .25
RWBYWX03066C Junior Xiong C .12 .25
RWBYWX03067C Nora: Winning Advice C .12 .25
RWBYWX03068C Peter Port C .12 .25
RWBYWX03069C Velvet Scarlatina C .12 .25
RWBYWX03070U Salem's Glove U .15 .30
RWBYWX03071U Maidens U .15 .30
RWBYWX03072CR Ruby's Awakening CR .20 .40
RWBYWX03072RRRR Ruby's Awakening RRR 15.00 30.00
RWBYWX03073CR Fall Maiden's Downfall CR .20 .40
RWBYWX03073RRRR Fall Maiden's Downfall RRR 3.00 6.00
RWBYWX03074CC A Kiss to Remember By CC .12 .25
RWBYWX03074RRRR A Kiss to Remember By RRR 7.50 15.00
RWBYWX03075CC Grimm Invasion CC .12 .25
RWBYWX03076RR Weiss Schnee RR .75 1.50
RWBYWX03076SPSP Weiss Schnee SP 100.00 200.00
RWBYWX03077RR Blake Belladonna RR 4.00 8.00
RWBYWX03077SPSP Blake Belladonna SP 125.00 250.00
RWBYWX03078R Roman Torchwick R .25 .50
RWBYWX03078SSR Roman Torchwick SR 2.00 4.00
RWBYWX03079R James Ironwood R .25 .50
RWBYWX03079SSR James Ironwood SR 7.50 15.00
RWBYWX03080R Mercury Black R .25 .50
RWBYWX03080SSR Mercury Black SR 2.00 4.00
RWBYWX03081R Winter Schnee R .25 .50
RWBYWX03081SSR Winter Schnee SR 3.00 6.00
RWBYWX03082R Weiss: Summoning R .25 .50
RWBYWX03082RBRRBR Weiss: Summoning RBR 30.00 75.00
RWBYWX03083R Neopolitan R .30 .75
RWBYWX03083SSR Neopolitan SR 12.50 25.00
RWBYWX03084R Blake: Going Undercover R .25 .50
RWBYWX03084RBRRBR Blake: Going Undercover RBR 40.00 80.00
RWBYWX03085U Weiss: Focusing U .15 .30
RWBYWX03086U Blake: Focusing Her Sights U .15 .30
RWBYWX03087SSR Neptune Vasilias SR 2.50 5.00
RWBYWX03087U Neptune Vasilias U .15 .30
RWBYWX03088U Jacques Schnee U .15 .30
RWBYWX03089U Mercury: Scouted U .15 .30
RWBYWX03090U James: Half-Cyborg U .15 .30
RWBYWX03091C Uniform Blake C .12 .25
RWBYWX03092C Neptune: Vytal Festival C .12 .25
RWBYWX03093C Shopkeep C .12 .25
RWBYWX03094C Nolan Porfirio C .12 .25
RWBYWX03095C Bolin Hori C .12 .25
RWBYWX03096C Uniform Weiss C .12 .25
RWBYWX03097U Dust U .15 .30
RWBYWX03098CR Team RWBY CR .20 .40
RWBYWX03098RRRR Team RWBY RRR 7.50 15.00
RWBYWX03099CC Activist Childhood CC .12 .25
RWBYWX03100CC Hijacking the Control Ship CC .12 .25

2021 Weiss Schwarz RWBY Trial Deck

RWBYWX03T01TDRRRR Ruby: Running RRR 15.00 30.00
RWBYWX03T01TD Ruby: Running 1.50 3.00
RWBYWX03T02TD Yang: Free-Falling .20 .40
RWBYWX03T03TD Pyrrha: Lending a Helping Hand .20 .40
RWBYWX03T04TDSPSP Ruby: Huntress Wannabe SP 250.00 500.00
RWBYWX03T04TD Ruby: Huntress Wannabe .50 1.00
RWBYWX03T05TD Jaune: Having His Aura Unlocked .20 .40
RWBYWX03T06TD Glynda: Huntress to the Rescue .20 .40
RWBYWX03T07TDSSR Ruby: Teamwork SR .75 1.50
RWBYWX03T07TD Ruby: Teamwork .20 .40
RWBYWX03T08TD Ren: Hunted .25 .50
RWBYWX03T09TD Nora: Free-Falling .20 .40
RWBYWX03T10TD Pyrrha: Spectating .20 .40
RWBYWX03T11TDRRRR Yang: Enraged RRR 15.00 30.00
RWBYWX03T11TD Yang: Enraged .20 .40
RWBYWX03T12TD Initiation Relic .75 1.50
RWBYWX03T13TDSSR Initiation SR .20 .40
RWBYWX03T13TD Initiation .20 .40
RWBYWX03T14TDRRRR Blake: Bookworm RRR 20.00 40.00
RWBYWX03T14TD Blake: Bookworm .20 .40
RWBYWX03T15TD Ozpin: Monitoring .20 .40
RWBYWX03T16TD Roman: Towards a Heist .20 .40
RWBYWX03T17TD Weiss: Teamwork .25 .50
RWBYWX03T18TD Blake: Battle Stance .20 .40
RWBYWX03T19TDSPSP Weiss: Battle Stance SP 200.00 400.00
RWBYWX03T19TD Weiss: Battle Stance .25 .50
RWBYWX03T20TD Assignment of Teams .20 .40

2021 Weiss Schwarz The Seven Deadly Sins

SDSSX03001RR Meliodas: Important Things RR 2.50 5.00
SDSSX03001SP Meliodas: Important Things SP 125.00 250.00
SDSSX03002RR Elizabeth: Druid Priestess RR 2.00 4.00
SDSSX03002SP Elizabeth: Druid Priestess SP 200.00 400.00
SDSSX03003RR Meliodas: To the Rescue RR 2.50 5.00
SDSSX03004R Arthur: Confident R .25 .50
SDSSX03004SSR Arthur: Confident SR 1.00 2.00
SDSSX03005R Meliodas: Hypnotized R .25 .50
SDSSX03006R Hawk: Passion for Scraps R .25 .50
SDSSX03006SP Hawk: Passion for Scraps SP 75.00 150.00
SDSSX03007R Elizabeth: Breaking the Spell R .25 .50
SDSSX03008R Elizabeth: Sacrificing Herself R .25 .50
SDSSX03008SSR Elizabeth: Sacrificing Herself SR 5.00 10.00
SDSSX03009R Meliodas: Ultimate Blow R .25 .50
SDSSX03009SSR Meliodas: Ultimate Blow SR 2.00 4.00
SDSSX03010U Elizabeth: Courage and Determination U .15 .30
SDSSX03011U Elizabeth: Instant Answer U .15 .30
SDSSX03012U Meliodas: Unrepentant U .15 .30
SDSSX03013U Arthur: Provoking the Enemy U .15 .30
SDSSX03014U Elizabeth: New Dress U .15 .30
SDSSX03015U Hawk: Confusion U .15 .30
SDSSX03016U Elizabeth: Options for Disguise U .15 .30
SDSSX03017C Hawk: Mode of Transportation C .12 .25
SDSSX03018C Elizabeth: Backup Plan C .12 .25
SDSSX03019C Meliodas: Reunion C .12 .25
SDSSX03020C Hawk: Traveling Peddler C .12 .25
SDSSX03021C Meliodas: Mysterious Marks C .12 .25
SDSSX03022aU Wanted Poster A U .75 1.50
SDSSX03022bU Wanted Poster B U .75 1.50
SDSSX03022cU Wanted Poster C U .75 1.50
SDSSX03022dU Wanted Poster D U .75 1.50
SDSSX03022eU Wanted Poster E U .75 1.50
SDSSX03022fU Wanted Poster F U .75 1.50
SDSSX03022gU Wanted Poster G U .75 1.50
SDSSX03023CR Full Counter CLR .20 .40
SDSSX03023RRRR Full Counter RRR 10.00 20.00
SDSSX03024CC Incredible Power CC .12 .25
SDSSX03025RR Gilthunder: Magic Words RR 2.50 5.00
SDSSX03026RR Diane: Cheerful RR 2.50 5.00
SDSSX03026SP Diane: Cheerful SP 150.00 300.00
SDSSX03027RR King: Wielder of Chastiefol RR .50 1.00
SDSSX03027SSR King: Wielder of Chastiefol SR 4.00 8.00
SDSSX03028R King & Oslo: Away From the Bustle R .25 .50
SDSSX03029R King: For a Special Someone R .25 .50
SDSSX03029SP King: For a Special Someone SP 75.00 150.00
SDSSX03030R Diane: Childhood R .25 .50
SDSSX03030SSR Diane: Childhood SR 1.25 2.50
SDSSX03031R Diane: Twirling Her Hair R .25 .50
SDSSX03032R Gilthunder: Smile of Relief R .25 .50
SDSSX03032SSR Gilthunder: Smile of Relief SR .75 1.50
SDSSX03033R Diane: Wielder of Gideon R .25 .50
SDSSX03033SSR Diane: Wielder of Gideon SR 4.00 8.00
SDSSX03034U Diane: Hypnotized U .15 .30
SDSSX03035U King: Unrecognizable U .15 .30
SDSSX03036U Diane: Convincing Threat U .15 .30
SDSSX03037U King: Incident of the Past U .15 .30
SDSSX03038U Gilthunder: Negative Little Gil U .15 .30
SDSSX03039C Helbram: Actual Form C .12 .25
SDSSX03040C Margaret: Sacrificing Herself C .12 .25
SDSSX03041C Diane: Tough Giant C .12 .25
SDSSX03042C King: Breakdown C .12 .25
SDSSX03043C Veronica: Sacrificing Herself C .12 .25
SDSSX03044C Griamore: Loyal Bodyguard C .12 .25
SDSSX03045C Helbram: Last Request to a Friend C .12 .25
SDSSX03046C Bartra: Benevolent Ruler C .12 .25
SDSSX03047C Diane: Cowering C .12 .25
SDSSX03048C King: Presentable Appearance C .12 .25
SDSSX03049U Goddess Amber U .15 .30
SDSSX03050CR Last Minute Save CLR .20 .40
SDSSX03050RRRR Last Minute Save RRR .75 1.50
SDSSX03051CC Broken Curse CC .12 .25
SDSSX03052CC Versatile Weapon CC .12 .25
SDSSX03053RR Merlin: Surprise Reveal RR 2.50 5.00
SDSSX03054RR Ban: For a Special Someone RR .75 1.50
SDSSX03054SP Ban: For a Special Someone SP 200.00 400.00
SDSSX03055RR Elaine: Facing a Demon RR 1.00 2.00
SDSSX03056R Ban: Ready to Kill R .25 .50
SDSSX03056SSR Ban: Ready to Kill SR .60 1.25
SDSSX03057R Elaine: Guarding the Spring R .25 .50
SDSSX03057SSR Elaine: Guarding the Spring SR 7.50 15.00
SDSSX03058R Gowther: Holding His Head Up R .25 .50
SDSSX03059R Gowther: Mind Manipulator R .25 .50
SDSSX03059SSR Gowther: Mind Manipulator SR 1.25 2.50
SDSSX03060R Gowther: True Identity R .25 .50
SDSSX03061R Merlin: Joining the Party R .25 .50
SDSSX03062R Gowther: Wielder of Harlit R .25 .50
SDSSX03062SSR Gowther: Wielder of Harlit SR 1.00 2.00
SDSSX03063R Merlin: Superior Skills R .25 .50
SDSSX03063SSR Merlin: Superior Skills SR 1.50 3.00
SDSSX03064U Ban: Fresh Out of Prison U .15 .30
SDSSX03065U Merlin: Hooded Magician U .15 .30
SDSSX03066SSR Ban: Rage SR 2.50 5.00
SDSSX03066U Ban: Rage U .15 .30
SDSSX03067U Gowther: Sinister Shadow U .15 .30
SDSSX03068U Ban: Facing a Demon U .15 .30
SDSSX03069C Armor Giant C .12 .25
SDSSX03070C Gowther: Unassuming Disguise C .12 .25
SDSSX03071C Ban: Reunion C .12 .25
SDSSX03072C Ban: Striking a Deal C .12 .25
SDSSX03073C Elaine: Left Behind C .12 .25
SDSSX03074C Gowther: Forcibly Silenced C .12 .25
SDSSX03075C Trumpet of Cernunnos C .12 .25
SDSSX03076CR Fountain of Youth CLR .20 .40
SDSSX03076RRRR Fountain of Youth RRR 7.50 15.00
SDSSX03077CC Putting an End CC .12 .25
SDSSX03078RR Hendrickson: No Longer Human RR .25 .50
SDSSX03078SSR Hendrickson: No Longer Human SR 3.00 6.00
SDSSX03079R Hendrickson: Grand Master R .25 .50
SDSSX03080R Guila: Switching Sides R .25 .50
SDSSX03081R Howzer: Switching Sides R .25 .50
SDSSX03082U Howzer: Attracted U .15 .30
SDSSX03083U Dreyfus: Repenting U .15 .30
SDSSX03084SSR Guila: Spending Time at Home SR 1.00 2.00
SDSSX03084U Guila: Spending Time at Home U .15 .30
SDSSX03085SSR Jericho: Hungry for Revenge SR 2.50 5.00
SDSSX03085U Jericho: Hungry for Revenge U .15 .30
SDSSX03086U Dale: Final Moments U .15 .30
SDSSX03087U Jericho: Dressed Up U .15 .30
SDSSX03088U Slader: Focused on the Job U .15 .30
SDSSX03089U Guila: Aggressive Request U .15 .30
SDSSX03090U Howzer: At the Fighting Festival U .15 .30
SDSSX03091U Guila: Unbothered U .15 .30
SDSSX03092C Howzer: Smile of Relief C .12 .25
SDSSX03093C Vivian: Mildly Threatening Words C .12 .25
SDSSX03094C Zeal: Doted Younger Brother C .12 .25
SDSSX03095C Dreyfus: Grand Master C .12 .25
SDSSX03096C Hendrickson: Tables Turned C .12 .25
SDSSX03097C Jericho: Embarassing State C .12 .25
SDSSX03098C Demon Blood C .12 .25
SDSSX03099CR Forbidden Power CLR .20 .40
SDSSX03099RRRR Forbidden Power RRR 2.00 4.00
SDSSX03100CC New Partnership CC .12 .25
SDSSX03101PR SD Meliodas P .60 1.25
SDSSX03102PR SD Elizabeth P 1.00 2.00
SDSSX03103PR SD Diane P 1.00 2.00
SDSSX03104PR SD King P .50 1.00
SDSSX03105PR SD Ban P .50 1.00

2021 Weiss Schwarz The Seven Deadly Sins Trial Deck

SDSSX03T01TD Elizabeth: Unconscious .20 .40
SDSSX03T02RRRR Meliodas: Clever Feint RRR 6.00 12.00
SDSSX03T02TD Meliodas: Clever Feint .20 .40
SDSSX03T03SSR Elizabeth: Newbie Waitress SR 1.00 2.00
SDSSX03T03TD Elizabeth: Newbie Waitress .25 .50
SDSSX03T04TD Hawk Mama .20 .40
SDSSX03T05TD Meliodas: Owner of the Boar Hat .20 .40
SDSSX03T06TD Hawk: Wound Treatment .20 .40
SDSSX03T07TD Elizabeth: Memories .20 .40
SDSSX03T08TD Meliodas: Self-Introduction .20 .40
SDSSX03T09TD Meliodas: Casual Rejection .20 .40
SDSSX03T10TD Hawk: In the Rust Knight's Armor .20 .40
SDSSX03T11SP Elizabeth: Searching for the Sins SP 200.00 400.00
SDSSX03T11TD Elizabeth: Searching for the Sins .20 .40
SDSSX03T12RRRR Catching the Spear RRR 15.00 30.00
SDSSX03T12TD Catching the Spear .20 .40
SDSSX03T13TD Diane: Sleeping .20 .40
SDSSX03T14TD Gilthunder: Ruthless .20 .40
SDSSX03T15SSR Diane: Favorite Food SR .50 1.00
SDSSX03T15TD Diane: Favorite Food .20 .40
SDSSX03T16TD Gilthunder: Eager for Revenge .20 .40
SDSSX03T17TD Diane: Ending the Battle .20 .40
SDSSX03T18TD Holy Knight's Sword .20 .40
SDSSX03T19TD Raging With Jealousy .20 .40
SDSSX03T20RRRR Testing the Ground RRR 7.50 15.00
SDSSX03T20TD Testing the Ground .20 .40

2021 Weiss Schwarz Sword Art Online Alicization Vol. 2

SAOS80E001RR Together With a Memory, Asuna & Yuuki RR 1.25 2.50
SAOS80E001SSR Together With a Memory, Asuna & Yuuki SR 7.50 15.00
SAOS80E002OFROFR Where the Soul Is, Alice OFR 40.00 80.00
SAOS80E002RR Where the Soul Is, Alice RR .75 1.50
SAOS80E003RR Joint Battle, Asuna & Alice RR 1.50 3.00
SAOS80E003SSR Joint Battle, Asuna & Alice SR 7.50 15.00
SAOS80E004RR Unbending Fighting Spirit, Asuna RR 1.00 2.00
SAOS80E004SPSP Unbending Fighting Spirit, Asuna SP 125.00 250.00
SAOS80E005RR Priestess of Light Alice RR 2.00 4.00
SAOS80E005SPSP Priestess of Light Alice SP 75.00 150.00
SAOS80E006R Splitting Sound of the Sword, Alice R .25 .50
SAOS80E006SSR Splitting Sound of the Sword, Alice SR 3.00 6.00
SAOS80E007R Charming Figure, Alice R .25 .50
SAOS80E007SSR Charming Figure, Alice SR 10.00 20.00
SAOS80E008R Street Pin-up, Asuna & Alice R .25 .50
SAOS80E008SSR Street Pin-up, Asuna & Alice SR 7.50 15.00
SAOS80E009R Are These Two Rivals? Asuna & Alice R .25 .50
SAOS80E009SSR Are These Two Rivals? Asuna & Alice SR 4.00 8.00
SAOS80E010R Goddess of Creation Stacia Asuna R .25 .50
SAOS80E010SSR Goddess of Creation Stacia Asuna SR 7.50 15.00
SAOS80E011R Uneasy Night, Alice R .25 .50
SAOS80E011SSR Uneasy Night, Alice SR 3.00 6.00
SAOS80E012U To Kirito's Side, Asuna U .15 .30
SAOS80E013U Time to Part, Alice U .15 .30
SAOS80E014U Her Hometown's Skies, Alice U .15 .30
SAOS80E015U Endless Summer by the Beach, Alice & Asuna U 2.50 5.00
SAOS80E016U Oceanic Resource Exploration & Research Institution, Rinko U .15 .30
SAOS80E017U Sisters' Private Time, Selka & Alice U .15 .30
SAOS80E018U As Long as I Can Wield a Sword Alice U .15 .30
SAOS80E019U Alice on a Summer Day U .15 .30
SAOS80E020C Asuna on a Summer Day C .12 .25
SAOS80E021C Niemon C .12 .25
SAOS80E022C Genius Engineer, Higa C .12 .25
SAOS80E023C Lieutenant Colonel of the Ground Self-Defense Force, Kikuoka C .12 .25
SAOS80E024C Unlimited Landscape Alteration Asuna C .12 .25
SAOS80E025C Beyond Time, Asuna C .12 .25
SAOS80E026C Memories Will Never Vanish Asuna C .12 .25
SAOS80E027C Assure Me Asuna C .12 .25
SAOS80E028U Cloned Soul U .15 .30
SAOS80E029CR Our Memories Are Here CR .20 .40
SAOS80E029RRRR Our Memories Are Here RRR 3.00 6.00
SAOS80E030CR Mother's Rosario CR .20 .40
SAOS80E030OFROFR Mother's Rosario OFR 60.00 125.00
SAOS80E031CC New World CC .12 .25
SAOS80E031RRRR New World RRR 3.00 6.00
SAOS80E032CC A God or Something Else? CC .12 .25
SAOS80E033RR As His Little Sister, Leafa RR .60 1.25
SAOS80E033SPSP As His Little Sister, Leafa SP 40.00 80.00
SAOS80E034R Integrity Knight, Eldrie R .25 .50
SAOS80E035R Reliable Juniors, Tiese & Ronie R .25 .50
SAOS80E035SSR Reliable Juniors, Tiese & Ronie SR 2.00 4.00
SAOS80E036R Unexpected Reinforcements, Yuna & Eiji R .25 .50
SAOS80E036SSR Unexpected Reinforcements, Yuna & Eiji SR 2.00 4.00
SAOS80E037R Earth Goddess Terraria Leafa R .25 .50
SAOS80E037SSR Earth Goddess Terraria Leafa SR 3.00 6.00
SAOS80E038R Commander of the Integrity Knights, Bercouli R .25 .50
SAOS80E038SSR Commander of the Integrity Knights, Bercouli SR .75 1.50
SAOS80E039U No Discrimination, Leafa U .15 .30
SAOS80E040U Lively Smile, Ronie U .15 .30
SAOS80E041U Miraculous Wish, Tiese U .15 .30
SAOS80E042U Integrity Knight, Linel U .15 .30
SAOS80E043U Integrity Knight, Fizel U .15 .30
SAOS80E044U Manly Leader, Bercouli U .15 .30
SAOS80E045U Vice Commander of the Integrity Knights, Fanatio U .15 .30
SAOS80E046C Integrity Knight, Renly C .12 .25
SAOS80E047aC Overlapping Traces, Yuna (A) C .12 .25
SAOS80E047bC Overlapping Traces, Yuna (B) C .12 .25
SAOS80E048C Integrity Knight, Sheyta C .12 .25
SAOS80E049aC Revived Imposing Appearance, Eiji (A) C .12 .25
SAOS80E049bC Revived Imposing Appearance, Eiji (B) C .12 .25
SAOS80E050C Unlimited Automatic Regeneration Leafa C .12 .25
SAOS80E051C Pajama Party, Sortiliena C .12 .25
SAOS80E052C Full of Spirit, Leafa C .12 .25
SAOS80E053C Integrity Knight, Deusolbert C .12 .25
SAOS80E054CC Evil Should Be Slashed CC .12 .25
SAOS80E054RRRR Evil Should Be Slashed RRR 2.50 5.00
SAOS80E055CC The Time-Splitting Sword Uragiri CC .12 .25
SAOS80E055RRRR The Time-Splitting Sword Uragiri RRR .60 1.25
SAOS80E056R Administrator Living On in Memories R .25 .50
SAOS80E057R Affiliated With the Dark Knights, Lipia R .25 .50
SAOS80E058R Dark God Vecta R .25 .50
SAOS80E059R Incarnation of Nihilism, Gabriel R .25 .50
SAOS80E059SSR Incarnation of Nihilism, Gabriel SR .50 1.00
SAOS80E060U Persuasion to Convert, Lisbeth U .15 .30
SAOS80E061U Agitator of the Opposition, Vassago U .15 .30
SAOS80E062U PoH U .15 .30
SAOS80E063U Chance Meeting, Subtilizer U .15 .30
SAOS80E064C Commander of the Dark Knights, Shasta C .12 .25
SAOS80E065C Chief of the Orcs, Lilpilin C .12 .25
SAOS80E066C Swarm of Red Copper, Dark Knights C .12 .25
SAOS80E067C Convert Silica C .12 .25
SAOS80E068C Black Mages Guild Leader, Dee Eye Ell C .12 .25
SAOS80E069C Champion of the Pugilists Guild, Iskahn C .12 .25
SAOS80E070U Maximum-Acceleration Phase U .15 .30

SAOS80E071CC Blade of Nihilism CC .12 .25
SAOS80E071RRRR Blade of Nihilism RRR 1.50 3.00
SAOS80E072CC Preaching of Hatred CC .12 .25
SAOS80E072RRRR Preaching of Hatred RRR 2.00 4.00
SAOS80E073RR Time to Rise Up, Kirito RR 3.00 6.00
SAOS80E073SPSP Time to Rise Up, Kirito SP 60.00 125.00
SAOS80E074OFROFR Night-Sky-Clad Hero, Kirito OFR 75.00 150.00
SAOS80E074RR Night-Sky-Clad Hero, Kirito RR 2.00 4.00
SAOS80E075RR Aincrad Style Eugeo RR 2.50 5.00
SAOS80E075SPSP Aincrad Style Eugeo SP 30.00 60.00
SAOS80E076RR Light That Penetrates Darkness Sinon RR .75 1.50
SAOS80E076SPSP Light That Penetrates Darkness Sinon SP 75.00 150.00
SAOS80E077R Reliable Cover From the Back, Kirito R .25 .50
SAOS80E078R Release Recollection Eugeo R .25 .50
SAOS80E078SSR Release Recollection Eugeo SR 2.00 4.00
SAOS80E079R Sun Goddess Solus Sinon R .25 .50
SAOS80E079SSR Sun Goddess Solus Sinon SR 3.00 6.00
SAOS80E080R Return to the Real World, Kazuto R .25 .50
SAOS80E081R The Last Piece, Eugeo R .25 .50
SAOS80E081SSR The Last Piece, Eugeo SR 2.50 5.00
SAOS80E082R Time for Revenge, Sinon R .25 .50
SAOS80E082SSR Time for Revenge, Sinon SR 7.50 15.00
SAOS80E083R Starburst Stream Kirito R .25 .50
SAOS80E083SSR Starburst Stream Kirito SR 2.00 4.00
SAOS80E084U Beyond Time, Kirito U .15 .30
SAOS80E085U Efforts Towards the Convert, Yui U .15 .30
SAOS80E086U What Certainly Remains, Eugeo U .15 .30
SAOS80E087SSR Fair and Square, Kirito SR 2.00 4.00
SAOS80E087U Fair and Square, Kirito U .15 .30
SAOS80E088U Something Important, Kirito U .15 .30
SAOS80E089U Wide-Range Annihilation Attack Sinon U .15 .30
SAOS80E090C Utmost Concentration, Sinon C .12 .25
SAOS80E091C Convert Agil C .12 .25
SAOS80E092C Shattered Self-Image, Kirito C .12 .25
SAOS80E093C Convert Klein C .12 .25
SAOS80E094C Together With a Memory, Kirito & Eugeo C .12 .25
SAOS80E095C Revisiting Underworld, Kirito C .12 .25
SAOS80E096SSR War of Underworld SR 4.00 8.00
SAOS80E096U War of Underworld U .15 .30
SAOS80E097CR Night Sky Enveloping the World CR .20 .40
SAOS80E097RRRR Night Sky Enveloping the World RRR 7.50 15.00
SAOS80E098CR Ultima Ratio Hecate II CR .20 .40
SAOS80E098RRRR Ultima Ratio Hecate II RRR 6.00 12.00
SAOS80E099CC Healing Heart CC .12 .25
SAOS80E100CC Rainbow-Colored Waves CC .12 .25
SAOS80E101PR Making Sweet Desserts, Alice P .50 1.00
SAOS80E102PR Making Sweet Desserts, Asuna P .50 1.00
SAOS80E103PR Eat Up, Kirito P .50 1.00
SAOS80E104PR Eat Up, Eugeo P .50 1.00

2021 Weiss Schwarz That Time I Got Reincarnated As a Slime Vol. 2

TSKS82E001RR For My Comrades, Rimuru RR .50 1.00
TSKS82E001SSR For My Comrades, Rimuru SR 5.00 10.00
TSKS82E002RR Decapitating Demon Blade Shion RR .75 1.50
TSKS82E002SPSP Decapitating Demon Blade Shion SP 150.00 300.00
TSKS82E003RR Inherited Form, Rimuru RR .60 1.25
TSKS82E003SPSP Inherited Form, Rimuru SP 75.00 150.00
TSKS82E004R Case Complete, Rimuru R .25 .50
TSKS82E004SSR Case Complete, Rimuru SR .75 1.50
TSKS82E005R This Belongs to Me! Shion R .25 .50
TSKS82E005SSR This Belongs to Me! Shion SR 4.00 8.00
TSKS82E006R Drawn-Out Battle, Rimuru R .25 .50
TSKS82E007R Savant, Hakurou R .25 .50
TSKS82E008R Secretary and Bodyguard, Shion R .30 .60
TSKS82E009R Cool Beauty, Shion R .25 .50
TSKS82E010U Great Sword Wielder, Shion U .15 .30
TSKS82E011U Icicle Lance Eren U .15 .30
TSKS82E012U Flash, Hakurou U .15 .30
TSKS82E013U Reproach, Rimuru U .15 .30
TSKS82E014U Misunderstanding, Rimuru U .15 .30
TSKS82E015U Magnificent Swordwork, Hakurou U .15 .30
TSKS82E016C 3 Rules, Rimuru C .12 .25
TSKS82E017C Prankster, Ramiris C .12 .25
TSKS82E018C Threat to Survival, Rimuru C .12 .25
TSKS82E019C Unsettling Atmosphere, Shion C .12 .25
TSKS82E020C Simple Task Before Dinner, Hakurou C .12 .25
TSKS82E021C Promise? Shion C .12 .25
TSKS82E022C Capable Lady, Shion C .12 .25
TSKS82E023C Basking in Sunset, Geld C .12 .25
TSKS82E024U First Friend U .15 .30
TSKS82E025U Sleep Mode U .15 .30
TSKS82E026CR Decapitating Demon Blade CR .20 .40
TSKS82E026RRRR Decapitating Demon Blade RRR 2.50 5.00
TSKS82E027CR Nameless Story CR .20 .40
TSKS82E027RRRR Nameless Story RRR 4.00 8.00
TSKS82E028CC Reliable Existence CC .12 .25
TSKS82E029RR It's Delicious! Milim RR 7.50 15.00
TSKS82E029SPSP It's Delicious! Milim SP 125.00 250.00
TSKS82E030RR Swept Along, Rimuru RR 3.00 6.00
TSKS82E030SSP+SSP+ Swept Along, Rimuru SSP 150.00 300.00
TSKS82E031RR Full of Smiles, Shuna RR 3.00 6.00
TSKS82E031SPSP Full of Smiles, Shuna SP 100.00 200.00
TSKS82E032RR Drago Buster Milim RR 5.00 10.00
TSKS82E032SSR Drago Buster Milim SR 12.50 25.00
TSKS82E033R Meditating? Milim R .25 .50
TSKS82E033SSR Meditating? Milim SR 6.00 12.00
TSKS82E034R Destroyer Milim R .25 .50
TSKS82E034SSR Destroyer Milim SR 4.00 8.00
TSKS82E035R Towards the Dwelling of Spirits, Rimuru R .25 .50
TSKS82E035SSR Towards the Dwelling of Spirits, Rimuru SR 1.50 3.00
TSKS82E036R In a Meeting, Shuna R .25 .50
TSKS82E036SSR In a Meeting, Shuna SR 4.00 8.00
TSKS82E037R Sweet Beauty, Shuna R .25 .50
TSKS82E037SSR Sweet Beauty, Shuna SR 2.00 4.00
TSKS82E038R Warm Welcome, Rimuru R .25 .50
TSKS82E038SSR Warm Welcome, Rimuru SR .50 1.25
TSKS82E039R Leave It to Me! Milim R .25 .50
TSKS82E039SSR Leave It to Me! Milim SR 4.00 8.00
TSKS82E040R I Can't Hear You? Rimuru R .25 .50
TSKS82E040SSR I Can't Hear You? Rimuru SR .50 1.00
TSKS82E041R Benimaru Breaking the Enemy's Formation R .25 .50
TSKS82E042U Battle in the Goblin's Village, Rimuru U .15 .30
TSKS82E043U Multi-Talented, Shuna U .15 .30
TSKS82E044U Skillful Consumption, Shizu U .15 .30
TSKS82E045U Shuna Watching Over U .15 .30
TSKS82E046U Mature Tastes, Rimuru U .15 .30
TSKS82E047U Great Mood, Benimaru U .15 .30
TSKS82E048U Capable Lady, Shuna U .15 .30
TSKS82E049U Awaited Chance to Shine, Milim U .15 .30
TSKS82E050U Victory Celebration, Benimaru U .15 .30
TSKS82E051U Taunting the Kids, Rimuru U .15 .30
TSKS82E052U Cute Request, Milim U .15 .30
TSKS82E053C Victory Celebration, Kurobe C .12 .25
TSKS82E054C Aren't We Besties? Rimuru C .12 .25
TSKS82E055C Strategy Meeting, Shuna C .12 .25
TSKS82E056C Great Victory! Milim C .12 .25
TSKS82E057C Great Haul! Milim C .12 .25
TSKS82E058C Summoning Call, Benimaru C .12 .25
TSKS82E059C What That Body Harbors, Shizu C .12 .25
TSKS82E060C Of Course We're Besties! Milim C .12 .25
TSKS82E061C Distressed, Shuna C .12 .25
TSKS82E062C Rimuru Sealing an Agreement C .12 .25
TSKS82E063R Drago Buster R .60 1.25
TSKS82E064C Calamity-Class Charybdis C .12 .25
TSKS82E065CR A Historical Moment CR .25 .50
TSKS82E065RRRR A Historical Moment RRR 5.00 10.00
TSKS82E066CR Recently Learned Restraint CR .20 .40
TSKS82E066RRRR Recently Learned Restraint RRR 12.50 25.00
TSKS82E067CC Delightful Cheek-Rubbing CC .12 .25
TSKS82E068CC I Want to Fight More! CC .12 .25
TSKS82E069RR User of Ifrit, Shizu RR .75 1.50
TSKS82E069SPSP User of Ifrit, Shizu SP 125.00 250.00
TSKS82E070RR Triumphant Return, Rimuru RR .60 1.25
TSKS82E070SSP+SSP+ Triumphant Return, Rimuru SSP 150.00 300.00
TSKS82E071RR Shizu Resolutely Facing Off RR .30 .75
TSKS82E071SSR Shizu Resolutely Facing Off SR .75 1.50
TSKS82E072R Rimuru Fresh From a Bath R .25 .50
TSKS82E072SSR Rimuru Fresh From a Bath SR .50 1.00
TSKS82E073R Mock Battle, Chloe R .25 .50
TSKS82E074R Destined Person, Shizu R .25 .50
TSKS82E074SSR Destined Person, Shizu SR .50 10.00
TSKS82E075R Tempest Star Wolf Ranga R .25 .50
TSKS82E076R Always by Your Side, Shizu R .25 .50
TSKS82E076SSR Always by Your Side, Shizu SR .75 1.50
TSKS82E077R Shadow in the Darkness, Souei R .25 .50
TSKS82E078U Cool and Collected, Souei U .15 .30
TSKS82E079U Solemn Expression, Rimuru U .15 .30
TSKS82E080U Final Push, Rimuru U .15 .30
TSKS82E081U Temporary Retreat, Gobta U .15 .30
TSKS82E082U Taking a Break, Rimuru U .15 .30
TSKS82E083U Truth of the Tale, Shizu U .15 .30
TSKS82E084U When Push Comes to Shove, Gobta U .15 .30
TSKS82E085U Chance to Perform, Ranga U .15 .30
TSKS82E086C To Survive, Souei C .12 .25
TSKS82E087C Combination With Gobta, Tempest Wolf C .12 .25
TSKS82E088C Within a Blissful Dream, Shizu C .12 .25
TSKS82E089C Thirst for Revenge, Phobio C .12 .25
TSKS82E090C Loyal Subordinate, Soka C .12 .25
TSKS82E091C Victory Celebration, Souei C .12 .25
TSKS82E092C Beastmaster Carrion C .12 .25
TSKS82E093C Precise Instructions, Gabiru C .12 .25
TSKS82E094U Fruits of Wisdom U .15 .30
TSKS82E095C Coincidental Meeting With the Future C .12 .25
TSKS82E096CC Conqueror of Flames CC .12 .25
TSKS82E096CC Conqueror of Flames RRR .75 1.50
TSKS82E097CC I'm Not a Bad Slime! CC .12 .25
TSKS82E097RRRR I'm Not a Bad Slime! RRR 1.50 3.00
TSKS82E098CC Shadow Squad CC .12 .25
TSKS82E099CC Great Combination! CC .12 .25
TSKS82E100CC Orc Lord Strategy Meeting CC .12 .25
TSKS82E101PR Petit Shion P 1.25 2.50
TSKS82E102PR Petit Rimuru P .75 1.50
TSKS82E103PR Petit Milim P 1.25 2.50
TSKS82E104PR Petit Shuna P .60 1.25
TSKS82E105PR Petit Shizu P 1.50 3.00
TSKS82E106PR Anti-Magic Mask P 4.00 8.00

2022 Weiss Schwarz Attack on Titan Final Season

AOTSX04001RR Armin: Lending a Hand RR .75 1.50
AOTSX04001SSPSSP Armin: Lending a Hand SSP 75.00 150.00
AOTSX04002RR Eren: Determined RR 1.00 2.00
AOTSX04002SSPSSP Eren: Determined SSP 150.00 300.00
AOTSX04003RR Eren Titan: Declaration of War RR .75 1.50
AOTSX04003SECSEC Eren Titan: Declaration of War SCR 50.00 100.00
AOTSX04004R Colossal Titan: Painful Sight from Above R .20 .40
AOTSX04004TTRTTR Colossal Titan: Painful Sight from Above TTR20.0040.00
AOTSX04005R Eren Titan: Alternative Plan R .15 .30
AOTSX04005TTRTTR Eren Titan: Alternative Plan TTR 25.00 50.00
AOTSX04006R Eren: Embarking on a Different Path R .25 .50
AOTSX04006SSR Eren: Embarking on a Different Path SR 1.50 3.00
AOTSX04007R Conny: Strengthened Resolve R .07 .15
AOTSX04007SSR Conny: Strengthened Resolve SR .40 .80
AOTSX04008R Floch: Smug Face R .07 .15
AOTSX04009U Conny: Taken Aback U .05 .10
AOTSX04010U Colossal Titan: Facing a Foreign Land U .07 .15
AOTSX04011U Armin: Exiting the Titan U .10 .20
AOTSX04012U Eren: Conversation at Sunset U .10 .20
AOTSX04013U Floch: Leading the Jaegerists U .07 .15
AOTSX04014U Armin: Fight Among Friends U .05 .10
AOTSX04015C Armin: Conversation at Sunset C .05 .10
AOTSX04016C Dot Pyxis C .05 .10
AOTSX04017C Conny: Providing Support C .10 .20
AOTSX04018C Conny: Conversation at Sunset C .05 .10
AOTSX04019C Eren: Advancing C .07 .15
AOTSX04020U New Omni Directional Mobility Gear U .10 .20
AOTSX04021U Anti-Marleyan Volunteers U .05 .10
AOTSX04022CR Declaration of War CR .20 .40
AOTSX04022TTRTTR Declaration of War TTR 30.00 75.00
AOTSX04023CC Jaegerists CC .05 .10
AOTSX04024CC A Rare Confession CC .07 .15
AOTSX04024RRRR A Rare Confession RRR .50 1.00
AOTSX04025CC Old Friends CC .05 .10
AOTSX04025RRRR Old Friends RRR .30 .60
AOTSX04026RR Levi: Merciless Assault RR 7.50 15.00
AOTSX04026SSPSSP Levi: Merciless Assault SSP 200.00 400.00
AOTSX04027RR Falco: Turning Point RR .15 .30
AOTSX04027SSR Falco: Turning Point SR .40 .80
AOTSX04028RR Gabi: Fatal Shot RR .25 .50
AOTSX04028SSR Gabi: Fatal Shot SR 1.50 3.00
AOTSX04029R Hange: Growing Suspicions R .07 .15
AOTSX04029SSR Hange: Growing Suspicions SR .75 1.50
AOTSX04030R Gabi: Involuntary Witness R .07 .15
AOTSX04030SSR Gabi: Involuntary Witness SR .50 1.00
AOTSX04031R Hange: Scout Regiment Commanding Officer R .12 .25
AOTSX04031SSR Hange: Scout Regiment Commanding Officer SR.60 1.25
AOTSX04032R Levi: Keeping Watch R .07 .15
AOTSX04032SSR Levi: Keeping Watch SR .30 .60
AOTSX04033R Levi: Drawing Boundaries R .07 .15
AOTSX04033SSR Levi: Drawing Boundaries SR .25 .50
AOTSX04034R Levi: Deep Grudge R .12 .25
AOTSX04034SSR Levi: Deep Grudge SR 1.00 2.00
AOTSX04035U Hange: Introduction to New Technology U .07 .15
AOTSX04036U Eren: Mr. Kruger U .05 .10
AOTSX04037U Gabi: On the Run U .10 .20
AOTSX04038U Falco: On the Run U .07 .15
AOTSX04039SSR Falco: Involuntary Witness SR .25 .50
AOTSX04039U Falco: Involuntary Witness U .12 .25
AOTSX04040C Theo Magath C .05 .10
AOTSX04041C Falco: Running Errands C .05 .10
AOTSX04042C Colt Grice C .07 .15
AOTSX04043C Gabi: War Hero C .05 .10
AOTSX04044U Azumabito U .05 .10
AOTSX04045CR Deep Grudge CR .12 .25
AOTSX04045RRRR Deep Grudge RRR 1.00 2.00
AOTSX04046CC Entering the Enemy Airship CC .05 .10
AOTSX04046RRRR Entering the Enemy Airship RRR .50 1.00
AOTSX04047RR Mikasa: Recovery Mission RR 1.25 2.50
AOTSX04047SSPSSP Mikasa: Recovery Mission SSP 200.00 400.00
AOTSX04048RR Sasha: "Wandering the Forest" RR .25 .50
AOTSX04048SSR Sasha: "Wandering the Forest" SR 2.50 5.00
AOTSX04049R Historia: Political Meeting R .20 .40
AOTSX04049SSR Historia: Political Meeting SR 2.00 4.00
AOTSX04050R Jean: Overseeing the Celebrations R .12 .25
AOTSX04051R Sasha: High Praise R .20 .40
AOTSX04051SSR Sasha: High Praise SR 1.00 2.00
AOTSX04052R Jean: Strengthened Resolve R .10 .20
AOTSX04052SSR Jean: Strengthened Resolve SR .40 .80
AOTSX04053R Jean: Covering Fire R .07 .15
AOTSX04053SSR Jean: Covering Fire SR .75 1.50
AOTSX04054U Mikasa: Conversation at Sunset U .05 .10
AOTSX04055U Jean: Conversation at Sunset U .05 .10
AOTSX04056U Mikasa: Providing Support U .10 .20
AOTSX04057U Mikasa: Mourning U .07 .15
AOTSX04058C Artur Braus C .07 .15
AOTSX04059C Kaya: Murderous Rage C .05 .10
AOTSX04060C Kaya: Delivering Lunch C .05 .10
AOTSX04061C Historia: Expecting C .05 .10
AOTSX04062C Sasha: Conversation at Sunset C .10 .20
AOTSX04063U Crest Mark U .05 .10
AOTSX04064U Spiked Wine U .05 .10
AOTSX04065CR Fatal Wound CR .15 .30
AOTSX04065RRRR Fatal Wound RRR 2.50 5.00
AOTSX04066CC Perfect Timing CC .12 .25
AOTSX04066RRRR Perfect Timing RRR 4.00 8.00
AOTSX04067RR Zeke: Succeeding the Beast Titan RR .40 .80
AOTSX04067SSR Zeke: Succeeding the Beast Titan SR 1.25 2.50
AOTSX04068RR Reiner: Haunted by His Own Advice RR .60 1.25
AOTSX04068SSPSSP Reiner: Haunted by His Own Advice SSP 75.00 150.00
AOTSX04069R Cart Titan: Providing Cover R .12 .25
AOTSX04069TTRTTR Cart Titan: Providing Cover TTR 10.00 20.00
AOTSX04070R Reiner: Trying to Give Up R .10 .20
AOTSX04070SSR Reiner: Trying to Give Up SR .30 .60
AOTSX04071R Beast Titan: Supreme Artillery R .25 .50
AOTSX04071TTRTTR Beast Titan: Supreme Artillery TTR 30.00 60.00
AOTSX04072R Jaw Titan: Retaking of the Founding Titan R .12 .25
AOTSX04072TTRTTR Jaw Titan: Retaking of the Founding Titan TTR20.0040.00
AOTSX04073R Armored Titan: Show of Resistance R .25 .50
AOTSX04073TTRTTR Armored Titan: Show of Resistance TTR 30.00 60.00
AOTSX04074R Zeke: Reliable Marleyan Warrior R .12 .25
AOTSX04075U Porco: Growing Unease U .12 .25
AOTSX04076U Pieck: Mediator U .12 .25
AOTSX04077U War Hammer Titan: Variety of Weapons U .07 .15
AOTSX04078TTRTTR War Hammer Titan: Facing the Usurper TTR15.00 30.00
AOTSX04078U War Hammer Titan: Facing the Usurper U .05 .10
AOTSX04079SSR Reiner: Past Shadows SR .75 1.50
AOTSX04079U Reiner: Past Shadows U .12 .25
AOTSX04080C Lara Tybur C .05 .10
AOTSX04081C Willy Tybur C .12 .25
AOTSX04082C Jaw Titan: Sharp Teeth C .07 .15
AOTSX04083C Tom Ksaver C .05 .10
AOTSX04084C Porco: Taken Aback C .20 .40
AOTSX04085C Pieck: Pointing Out the Enemy C .07 .15
AOTSX04086C Zeke: Whistleblower C .05 .10
AOTSX04087C Armored Titan: Marley Mid-East War C .07 .15
AOTSX04088C Cart Titan: Fending Off C .07 .15
AOTSX04089C Reiner: Overseeing the Celebrations C .07 .15
AOTSX04090C Porco: Harsh Words C .12 .25
AOTSX04091C Pieck: Trusted by Her Squad C .07 .15
AOTSX04092C Zeke: Scream C .10 .20
AOTSX04093C Beast Titan: Marley Mid-East War C .05 .10
AOTSX04094U The Panzer Unit U .05 .10
AOTSX04095U Baseball U .05 .10
AOTSX04096U Ready to End U .07 .15
AOTSX04097CR Facing Off CR .15 .30
AOTSX04097TTRTTR Facing Off TTR 15.00 30.00
AOTSX04098CC Reunion CC .10 .20
AOTSX04098RRRR Reunion RRR 1.00 2.00
AOTSX04099CC Spinal Fluid Activation CC .10 .20
AOTSX04100CC Sharp Teeth CC .07 .15
AOTSX04101PR Chimi Eren: Branching Paths P .25 .50
AOTSX04102PR Chimi Armin: Branching Paths P .20 .40
AOTSX04103PR Chimi Levi: Branching Paths P .20 .40
AOTSX04104PR Chimi Gabi P .12 .25
AOTSX04105PR Chimi Falco P .25 .50
AOTSX04106PR Chimi Mikasa: Branching Paths P .20 .40
AOTSX04107PR Chimi Reiner P .20 .40
AOTSX04108PR Armin: Optimistic P .12 .25
AOTSX04108SPR Armin: Optimistic P FOIL .20 .40
AOTSX04109PR Eren: Asking for Advice P .20 .40
AOTSX04109SPR Eren: Asking for Advice P FOIL 1.25 2.50
AOTSX04110PR Eren Titan: Welcoming Foreigners P .20 .40
AOTSX04110SPR Eren Titan: Welcoming Foreigners P FOIL .75 1.50
AOTSX04111PR Erwin: Receiving a Promise P .12 .25
AOTSX04111SPR Erwin: Receiving a Promise P FOIL .25 .50
AOTSX04112PR Levi: Making a Promise P .20 .40
AOTSX04112SPR Levi: Making a Promise P FOIL 1.25 2.50
AOTSX04113PR Mikasa: Hopeful P .60 1.25
AOTSX04113SPR Mikasa: Hopeful P FOIL 1.25 2.50
AOTSX04114PR Reiner: Giving Advice P .20 .40
AOTSX04114SPR Reiner: Giving Advice P FOIL .75 1.50
AOTSX04115PR Historia: Political Pawn P .15 .30
AOTSX04115SPR Historia: Political Pawn P FOIL .20 .40
AOTSX04116PR Ymir: Titan Inheritance Ritual P .25 .50
AOTSX04116SPR Ymir: Titan Inheritance Ritual P FOIL .30 .75
AOTSX04117PR Bertholdt: Reserved Thoughts P .07 .15
AOTSX04117SPR Bertholdt: Reserved Thoughts P FOIL .12 .25

2022 Weiss Schwarz Attack on Titan Final Season Trial Deck

AOTSX04T01TD Colt: Ferrying to Safety .25 .50
AOTSX04T02SSR Eren: Undercover SR .40 .80
AOTSX04T02TD Eren: Undercover P .50 1.00
AOTSX04T03SPSP Gabi Braun SP 75.00 150.00
AOTSX04T03TD Gabi Braun .25 .50
AOTSX04T04SPSP Falco Grice SP 75.00 150.00
AOTSX04T04TD Falco Grice .12 .25
AOTSX04T05RRRR Falco: Warrior Candidate RRR 2.00 4.00
AOTSX04T05TD Falco: Warrior Candidate .07 .15
AOTSX04T06TD Zofia: Warrior Candidate .10 .20
AOTSX04T07TD Udo: Warrior Candidate .10 .20
AOTSX04T08RRRR Gabi: Warrior Candidate RRR 2.00 4.00
AOTSX04T08TD Gabi: Warrior Candidate .15 .30
AOTSX04T09TD Eldian Armband .07 .15
AOTSX04T10RRRR War Heroine RRR 1.25 2.50
AOTSX04T10TD War Heroine .07 .15
AOTSX04T11TD Zeke: Warrior Candidate .15 .30
AOTSX04T12TD Pieck: Warrior Candidate .12 .25
AOTSX04T13TD Annie: Warrior Candidate .07 .15
AOTSX04T14TD Marcel: Warrior Candidate .07 .15
AOTSX04T15TD Reiner: Warrior Candidate .07 .15
AOTSX04T16TD Jaw Titan: Marley Mid-East War .15 .30
AOTSX04T17TD Bertholdt: Warrior Candidate .10 .20
AOTSX04T18TD Cart Titan: Marley Mid-East War .07 .15
AOTSX04T19SSR Reiner: Man on a Mission SR .30 .75
AOTSX04T19TD Reiner: Man on a Mission .15 .30
AOTSX04T20TD Raining Titans .10 .20

2022 Weiss Schwarz Fate Grand Order The Movie Divine Realm of the Round Table Camelot

FGOS87E001RR Bearer of the Holy Lance, The Lion King RR 3.00 6.00
FGOS87E001SPSP Bearer of the Holy Lance, The Lion King SP125.00 250.00
FGOS87E002R Divine Spirit, The Lion King R .20 .40
FGOS87E002SSR Divine Spirit, The Lion King SR 1.25 2.50
FGOS87E003R Aide to the Lion King, Agravain R .25 .50
FGOS87E003RTRRTR Aide to the Lion King, Agravain RTR 20.00 40.00
FGOS87E004R Unwavering Loyalty, Gawain & The Lion King R .25 .50
FGOS87E004SSR Unwavering Loyalty, Gawain & The Lion King SR3.00 6.00
FGOS87E005R Knight of Sorrow, Tristan R .25 .50
FGOS87E006R As Long as the Sun Shines, Gawain R .20 .40
FGOS87E006RTRRTR As Long as the Sun Shines, Gawain RTR 7.50 15.00
FGOS87E007R In the Name of the King of Storms, The Lion King R.20 .40
FGOS87E007SSR In the Name of the King of Storms, The Lion King SR 2.00 4.00
FGOS87E008R Blessed Rampage, Mordred R .25 .50
FGOS87E008RTRRTR Blessed Rampage, Mordred RTR 50.00 100.00
FGOS87E009U Reduced to a Monster, Tristan U .15 .30
FGOS87E010SSR Monster With the Heart of a Beast, Tristan SR .50 1.00
FGOS87E010U Monster With the Heart of a Beast, Tristan U .15 .30
FGOS87E011U King Who Governs the Holy City, The Lion King U .12 .25
FGOS87E012U Knight of Iron, Agravain U .12 .25
FGOS87E013SSR Agravain of Iron SR .25 .50
FGOS87E013U Agravain of Iron U .07 .15
FGOS87E014SSR Raider Knight, Mordred SR 1.00 2.00
FGOS87E014U Raider Knight, Mordred U .20 .40
FGOS87E015C Crumbling Tower at the Ends of the World, Agravain C .07 .15
FGOS87E016C Knight of Treachery, Mordred C .07 .15
FGOS87E017C Nightless Holy Punishment, Gawain C .10 .20
FGOS87E018C Return of the Sacred Sword, The Lion King C .10 .20
FGOS87E019C The Mercy of Buddha, Mordred C .10 .20
FGOS87E020C Setting Sun, Gawain C .12 .25
FGOS87E021C Reversed Fairy Strings User, Tristan C .07 .15
FGOS87E022C Knight of the Sun, Gawain C .10 .20
FGOS87E023U The Ritual of Holy Selection U .20 .40
FGOS87E024CR Rhongomyniad CR .25 .50
FGOS87E024RRRR Rhongomyniad RRR 10.00 20.00
FGOS87E025CC Excalibur Galatine CC .10 .20
FGOS87E025RRRR Excalibur Galatine RRR 1.25 2.50
FGOS87E026CC Clarent Blood Arthur CC .10 .20
FGOS87E027CC Failnaught CC .12 .25
FGOS87E028RR Ancient Queen of the Heavens, Nitocris RR .25 .50
FGOS87E028SPSP Ancient Queen of the Heavens, Nitocris SP 50.00 100.00
FGOS87E029RR Bonze Traveling the Wastelands, Xuanzang Sanzang RR .30 .75
FGOS87E029SPSP Bonze Traveling the Wastelands, Xuanzang Sanzang SP 40.00 80.00
FGOS87E030RR The Sun King, Ozymandias RR .30 .75
FGOS87E030SPSP The Sun King, Ozymandias SP 40.00 80.00
FGOS87E031R Rescue of the World, Ozymandias R .20 .40
FGOS87E031SSR Rescue of the World, Ozymandias SR .75 1.50
FGOS87E032R The Mercy of Buddha, Xuanzang Sanzang R .25 .50
FGOS87E032SSR The Mercy of Buddha, Xuanzang Sanzang SR 1.00 2.00
FGOS87E033R As a Pharaoh, Nitocris R .20 .40
FGOS87E033SSR As a Pharaoh, Nitocris SR 1.25 2.50
FGOS87E034R The God King, Ozymandias R .20 .40
FGOS87E034SSR The God King, Ozymandias SR 1.00 2.00
FGOS87E035R Compassionate Mage Queen, Nitocris R .20 .40
FGOS87E035SSR Compassionate Mage Queen, Nitocris SR .75 1.50
FGOS87E036U Influence of the Mage Queen, Nitocris U .15 .30
FGOS87E037U Where Justice Is, Xuanzang Sanzang U .20 .40
FGOS87E038U Magnanimous Like the Sun, Ozymandias U .12 .25
FGOS87E039U Condition for the Alliance, Ozymandias U .20 .40
FGOS87E040U Body Outside Body, Xuanzang Sanzang U .10 .20
FGOS87E041U Guardian of the Egyptian Region, Nitocris U .15 .30
FGOS87E042C Provocative Gaze, Nitocris C .12 .25
FGOS87E043C Joining Up With Counterattack Forces, Xuanzang Sanzang C .07 .15
FGOS87E044C King Among Kings, Ozymandias C .10 .20
FGOS87E045C Confrontation Against the Strong, Xuanzang Sanzang C .12 .25
FGOS87E046C Pharaoh's Divine Authority, Ozymandias C .07 .15
FGOS87E047C Delivery of an Unneeded Item, Nitocris C .07 .15
FGOS87E048U The Sun King's Holy Grail U .15 .30
FGOS87E049CR Ramesseum Tentyris CR .20 .40
FGOS87E049RRRR Ramesseum Tentyris RRR 2.00 4.00
FGOS87E050CC To the Land of Eternity CC .07 .15
FGOS87E051CC Five Elements Mountain Buddha Palm CC .12 .25
FGOS87E051RRRR Five Elements Mountain Buddha Palm RRR 2.00 4.00
FGOS87E052RR Girl of Poison, Hassan of the Serenity RR .75 1.50
FGOS87E052SPSP Girl of Poison, Hassan of the Serenity SP 75.00 150.00
FGOS87E053RR Radiant Agateram, Bedivere RR 1.50 3.00
FGOS87E053SPSP Radiant Agateram, Bedivere SP 75.00 150.00
FGOS87E054RR Silver Knight of Violet, Bedivere RR .30 .75
FGOS87E054SR Silver Knight of Violet, Bedivere SR 1.25 2.50
FGOS87E055R Night Before the Decisive Battle, Hassan of the Serenity R .20 .40
FGOS87E056R Loyal Knight, Bedivere R .20 .40
FGOS87E056SSR Loyal Knight, Bedivere SR 1.50 3.00
FGOS87E057R Replica, Bedivere R .20 .40
FGOS87E058R Arrow of All His Strength, Arash R .15 .30
FGOS87E058SSR Arrow of All His Strength, Arash SR .30 .60
FGOS87E059R Independent Knight, Lancelot R .15 .30
FGOS87E059RTRRTR Independent Knight, Lancelot RTR 5.00 10.00
FGOS87E060R First Hassan-i Sabbah ""Old Man of the Mountain"" R.12 .25
FGOS87E060SSR First Hassan-i Sabbah ""Old Man of the Mountain"" SR .30 .75
FGOS87E061U Arash Kamangir U .15 .30
FGOS87E062U Grand Assassin ""Old Man of the Mountain"" U .10 .20
FGOS87E063SSR The Way of a Round Table Knight, Lancelot SR .30 .75
FGOS87E063U The Way of a Round Table Knight, Lancelot U .12 .25
FGOS87E064U Dance of Pale Death, Hassan of the Serenity U .20 .40
FGOS87E065U Confrontation Against the Strong, Lancelot U .12 .25
FGOS87E066U Return of the Sacred Sword, Bedivere U .25 .50
FGOS87E067C Zabaniya, Hassan of the Serenity C .07 .15
FGOS87E068C Journey for Somebody's Sake, Bedivere C .15 .30
FGOS87E069C Original Law, Hassan of the Cursed Arm C .15 .30
FGOS87E070C Great Hero of Persia, Arash C .12 .25
FGOS87E071C Setting Sun, Bedivere C .10 .20
FGOS87E072C Proud Assassin, Hassan of the Cursed Arm C .07 .15
FGOS87E073C Reality of the Sacred Lance, Bedivere C .12 .25
FGOS87E074C Fierce Knight of the Lake, Lancelot C .12 .25
FGOS87E075U Evening Bell U .12 .25
FGOS87E076U Exploration of the Sixth Singularity U .15 .30
FGOS87E077CR Switch On - Agateram CR .30 .60
FGOS87E077RRRR Switch On - Agateram RRR 10.00 20.00
FGOS87E078CC Lancelot of the Light of the Lake CC .12 .25
FGOS87E078RRRR Lancelot of the Light of the Lake RRR 2.50 5.00
FGOS87E079CC Stella CC .12 .25
FGOS87E079RRRR Stella RRR .75 1.50
FGOS87E080RR With This Flesh and Bone, Mash Kyrielight RR .50 1.00
FGOS87E080SSR With This Flesh and Bone, Mash Kyrielight SR2.00 4.00
FGOS87E081RR Great Genius, Leonardo da Vinci RR .25 .50
FGOS87E081SSR Great Genius, Leonardo da Vinci SR 1.50 3.00
FGOS87E082RR Knight of the Sacred Shield, Mash Kyrielight RR .25 .50
FGOS87E082SPSP Knight of the Sacred Shield, Mash Kyrielight SP 50.00 100.00
FGOS87E083R Rousing Resolution, Mash Kyrielight R .20 .40
FGOS87E084R Qualified to Know Her Origins, Mash Kyrielight R .15 .30
FGOS87E084SSR Qualified to Know Her Origins, Mash Kyrielight SR1.25 2.50
FGOS87E085R Indestructible Genius, Leonardo da Vinci R .20 .40
FGOS87E086R The Way of a Round Table Knight, Mash Kyrielight R.15 .30
FGOS87E086SSR The Way of a Round Table Knight, Mash Kyrielight SR .75 1.50
FGOS87E087U Ci Vediamo, Leonardo da Vinci U .07 .15
FGOS87E088U Reason for the Good Mood, Leonardo da Vinci U .15 .30
FGOS87E089U Journey for Somebody's Sake, Ritsuka Fujimaru U.12 .25
FGOS87E090U Heroic Spirit Within Me, Mash Kyrielight U .12 .25
FGOS87E091U Truth of the Holy Selection, Leonardo da Vinci U .10 .20
FGOS87E092C Journey for Somebody's Sake, Mash Kyrielight C .07 .15
FGOS87E093C Chaldea's Master, Ritsuka Fujimaru C .07 .15
FGOS87E094C Entrusted With Goodness, Mash Kyrielight C .12 .25
FGOS87E095C Truth of the Holy Selection, Mash Kyrielight C .07 .15
FGOS87E096C Turn for a Genius, Leonardo da Vinci C .07 .15
FGOS87E097C Whereabouts of the Holy Grail, Romani Archaman C.12 .25
FGOS87E098U Goodness of Humans U .15 .30
FGOS87E099CR Lord Camelot CR .15 .30
FGOS87E099RRRR Lord Camelot RRR 2.50 5.00
FGOS87E100CC Worth Tagging Along CC .10 .20

2022 Weiss Schwarz Hololive Production

HOLW91E001 Towards the Future Together, Natsuiro Matsuri RR 4.00 8.00
HOLW91E001SSP Towards the Future Together, Natsuiro Matsuri SSP 250.00 500.00
HOLW91E002 Towards the Future Together, Inugami Korone RR 1.50 3.00
HOLW91E002SSP Towards the Future Together, Inugami Korone SSP 500.00 1,000.00
HOLW91E003 Towards the Future Together, Tsunomaki Watame RR.50 1.00
HOLW91E003SSP Towards the Future Together, Tsunomaki Watame SSP 300.00 600.00
HOLW91E004 Towards the Future Together, Kiryu Coco RR .60 1.25
HOLW91E004SSP Towards the Future Together, Kiryu Coco SSP 500.00 1,000.00
HOLW91E005 Towards the Future Together, Shiranui Flare R .30 .60
HOLW91E005SSP Towards the Future Together, Shiranui Flare SSP 300.00 600.00
HOLW91E006 Protection Racketch, Kiryu Coco R .30 .60
HOLW91E006SP Protection Racketch, Kiryu Coco SP 100.00 200.00
HOLW91E007 Freshly Drawn Korone, Inugami Korone R .30 .75
HOLW91E007SP Freshly Drawn Korone, Inugami Korone SP 75.00 150.00
HOLW91E008 Tsunomaki Art, Tsunomaki Watame R .25 .50
HOLW91E008SP Tsunomaki Art, Tsunomaki Watame SP 75.00 150.00
HOLW91E009 Festival Drawings, Natsuiro Matsuri R .30 .60
HOLW91E009SP Festival Drawings, Natsuiro Matsuri SP 50.00 100.00
HOLW91E010 Towards the Future Together, Oozora Subaru R .30 .60
HOLW91E010SSP Towards the Future Together, Oozora Subaru SSP 500.00 1,000.00
HOLW91E011 Towards the Future Together, Yozora Mel R .20 .40
HOLW91E011SSP Towards the Future Together, Yozora Mel SSP125.00 250.00
HOLW91E012S Shiranui Flare SR 2.50 5.00
HOLW91E012 Shiranui Flare U .15 .30
HOLW91E013S Yozora Mel SR 2.50 5.00
HOLW91E013 Yozora Mel U .15 .30
HOLW91E014S Natsuiro Matsuri SR .75 1.50
HOLW91E014 Natsuiro Matsuri U .15 .30
HOLW91E015S Tsunomaki Watame SR .60 1.25
HOLW91E015 Tsunomaki Watame U .15 .30
HOLW91E016SP Protein The Subaru, Oozora Subaru SP 75.00 150.00
HOLW91E016 Protein The Subaru, Oozora Subaru U .50 1.00
HOLW91E017S Kiryu Coco SR 2.50 5.00
HOLW91E017 Kiryu Coco U .15 .30
HOLW91E018SP Mel Art, Yozora Mel SP 30.00 75.00
HOLW91E018 Mel Art, Yozora Mel U .15 .30
HOLW91E019SP Shiranuillust, Shiranui Flare SP 40.00 80.00
HOLW91E019 Shiranuillust, Shiranui Flare U .25 .50
HOLW91E020S Inugami Korone SR 2.00 4.00
HOLW91E020 Inugami Korone U .15 .30
HOLW91E021 Acerola Replenishment, Yozora Mel C .15 .30
HOLW91E021S Acerola Replenishment, Yozora Mel SR 1.25 2.50
HOLW91E022 Successfully Pranked! Oozora Subaru C .15 .30
HOLW91E022S Successfully Pranked! Oozora Subaru SR .75 1.50
HOLW91E023 Brimming With Interest, Tsunomaki Watame C .15 .30
HOLW91E023S Brimming With Interest, Tsunomaki Watame SR .75 1.50
HOLW91E024 Feeling Like a Baby, Natsuiro Matsuri C .15 .30
HOLW91E024S Feeling Like a Baby, Natsuiro Matsuri SR 1.25 2.50
HOLW91E025 Dramatic Scene in the Office, Kiryu Coco C .20 .40
HOLW91E025S Dramatic Scene in the Office, Kiryu Coco SR 2.00 4.00
HOLW91E026 Cat Police, Inugami Korone C .15 .30
HOLW91E026S Cat Police, Inugami Korone SR 1.00 2.00
HOLW91E027 Fanatical Over Hiyoko, Shiranui Flare C .15 .30
HOLW91E027S Fanatical Over Hiyoko, Shiranui Flare SR 1.00 2.00
HOLW91E028 Oozora Subaru C .15 .30
HOLW91E028S Oozora Subaru SR .60 1.50
HOLW91E029 Bouquet R .25 .50
HOLW91E029S Bouquet SR 1.50 3.00
HOLW91E030 Welcome to the Kiryu Club CR .15 .30
HOLW91E030R Welcome to the Kiryu Club RRR 5.00 10.00
HOLW91E031 Fruit Tart of Happiness CC .30 .75
HOLW91E031R Fruit Tart of Happiness RRR 3.00 6.00
HOLW91E032 Summer Memory CC .15 .30
HOLW91E032R Summer Memory RRR 1.50 3.00
HOLW91E033 A Summer Love CC .15 .30
HOLW91E033R A Summer Love RRR 1.00 2.00
HOLW91E034 Towards the Future Together, Uruha Rushia RR .30 .60
HOLW91E034SSP Towards the Future Together, Uruha Rushia SSP 500.00 1,000.00
HOLW91E035 Towards the Future Together, Shirakami Fubuki RR2.50 5.00
HOLW91E035SSP Towards the Future Together, Shirakami Fubuki SSP 600.00 1,200.00
HOLW91E036 Towards the Future Together, Nekomata Okayu RR .50 1.00
HOLW91E036SSP Towards the Future Together, Nekomata Okayu SSP 400.00 800.00
HOLW91E037 Towards the Future Together, Tokino Sora RR .25 .50
HOLW91E037SSP Towards the Future Together, Tokino Sora SSP250.00500.00
HOLW91E038 Artkayu, Nekomata Okayu R .15 .30
HOLW91E038SP Artkayu, Nekomata Okayu SP 50.00 100.00
HOLW91E039 Sketcromancer, Uruha Rushia R .15 .30
HOLW91E039SP Sketcromancer, Uruha Rushia SP 75.00 150.00
HOLW91E040 Towards the Future Together, Himemori Luna R .15 .30
HOLW91E040SSP Towards the Future Together, Himemori Luna SSP 250.00 500.00
HOLW91E041 Towards the Future Together, Ookami Mio R .15 .30
HOLW91E041SSP Towards the Future Together, Ookami Mio SSP300.00600.00
HOLW91E042 Towards the Future Together, AkiRose R .15 .30
HOLW91E042SSP Towards the Future Together, AkiRose SSP 200.00 400.00
HOLW91E043 Towards the Future Together, Tokoyami Towa R .15 .30
HOLW91E043SSP Towards the Future Together, Tokoyami Towa SSP 400.00 800.00
HOLW91E044 Sora Art, Tokino Sora R .15 .30
HOLW91E044SP Sora Art, Tokino Sora SP 30.00 75.00
HOLW91E045 Drawing Fubuki, Shirakami Fubuki R .25 .50
HOLW91E045SP Drawing Fubuki, Shirakami Fubuki SP 75.00 150.00
HOLW91E046 Towards the Future Together, Amane Kanata R .20 .40
HOLW91E046SSP Towards the Future Together, Amane Kanata SSP 200.00 400.00
HOLW91E047SP ARO Art, Aki Rose SP 30.00 60.00
HOLW91E047 ARO Art, Aki Rose U .15 .30
HOLW91E048S Shirakami Fubuki SR 1.50 3.00
HOLW91E048 Shirakami Fubuki U .15 .30
HOLW91E049S Tokino Sora SR 3.00 6.00
HOLW91E049 Tokino Sora U .30 .60
HOLW91E050SP Kanatart, Amane Kanata SP 30.00 75.00
HOLW91E050 Kanatart, Amane Kanata U .30 .60
HOLW91E051S Uruha Rushia SR 30.00 75.00
HOLW91E051 Uruha Rushia U .30 .60
HOLW91E052SP Lunart, Himemori Luna SP 30.00 75.00
HOLW91E052 Lunart, Himemori Luna U .30 .75
HOLW91E053S Amane Kanata SR 1.00 2.00
HOLW91E053 Amane Kanata U .15 .30
HOLW91E054S Nekomata Okayu SR 1.25 2.50
HOLW91E054 Nekomata Okayu U .25 .50
HOLW91E055SP Mioon Art, Ookami Mio SP 50.00 100.00
HOLW91E055 Mioon Art, Ookami Mio U .30 .75
HOLW91E056SP TOWART, Tokoyami Towa SP 75.00 150.00
HOLW91E056 TOWART, Tokoyami Towa U .20 .40
HOLW91E057S Himemori Luna SR .75 1.50
HOLW91E057 Himemori Luna U .25 .50
HOLW91E058 Simple Question, Tokoyami Towa C .15 .30
HOLW91E058S Simple Question, Tokoyami Towa SR 2.50 5.00
HOLW91E059 In an Interview, Tokino Sora C .15 .30
HOLW91E059S In an Interview, Tokino Sora SR 1.00 2.00
HOLW91E060 Juggling-in-Charge, Ookami Mio C .20 .40
HOLW91E060S Juggling-in-Charge, Ookami Mio SR .75 1.50
HOLW91E061 Fully Pwepared! Himemori Luna C .15 .30
HOLW91E061S Fully Pwepared! Himemori Luna SR .60 1.25
HOLW91E062 Which Is The Real One? Amane Kanata C .15 .30
HOLW91E062S Which Is The Real One? Amane Kanata SR 1.25 2.50
HOLW91E063 Hikoboshi? Shirakami Fubuki C .25 .50
HOLW91E063S Hikoboshi? Shirakami Fubuki SR .30 .60
HOLW91E064 Violent Cat-Making, Aki Rose C .15 .30
HOLW91E064S Violent Cat-Making, Aki Rose SR .60 1.50
HOLW91E065 Ookami Mio C .15 .30
HOLW91E065S Ookami Mio SR 1.00 2.00
HOLW91E066 Tokoyami Towa C .15 .30
HOLW91E066S Tokoyami Towa SR .60 1.25
HOLW91E067 Aki Rosenthal C .15 .30
HOLW91E067S Aki Rosenthal SR 2.00 4.00
HOLW91E068 The Strongest Greeting, Uruha Rushia C .15 .30
HOLW91E068S The Strongest Greeting, Uruha Rushia SR .50 1.00
HOLW91E069 Office's Revival? Nekomata Okayu C .15 .30
HOLW91E069S Office's Revival? Nekomata Okayu SR .75 1.50
HOLW91E070 Together in an Expanding World C .15 .30
HOLW91E070S Together in an Expanding World SR .75 1.50
HOLW91E071 Wanna Try Touching My Secret Tumtum? CC .25 .50
HOLW91E071R Wanna Try Touching My Secret Tumtum? RRR 7.50 15.00
HOLW91E072 Aozora No Symphony CC .15 .30
HOLW91E072R Aozora No Symphony RRR 3.00 6.00
HOLW91E073 Devilish Eyes CC .15 .30
HOLW91E073R Devilish Eyes RRR 2.50 5.00
HOLW91E074 Towards the Future Together, Akai Haato RR .30 .75
HOLW91E074SSP Towards the Future Together, Akai Haato SSP150.00 300.00
HOLW91E075 Towards the Future Together, Sakura Miko RR .30 .75
HOLW91E075SSP Towards the Future Together, Sakura Miko SSP300.00600.00
HOLW91E076 Towards the Future Together, Houshou Marine RR 6.00 12.00
HOLW91E076SSP Towards the Future Together, Houshou Marine SSP 750.00 1,500.00
HOLW91E077 Towards the Future Together, Yuzuki Choco R .50 1.00
HOLW91E077SSP Towards the Future Together, Yuzuki Choco SSP 250.00 500.00
HOLW91E078 HAATO Art, Akai Haato R .15 .30
HOLW91E078SP HAATO Art, Akai Haato SP 30.00 75.00
HOLW91E079 Marines Treasure, Houshou Marine R .15 .30
HOLW91E079SP Marines Treasure, Houshou Marine SP 75.00 150.00
HOLW91E080 Towards the Future Together, Robocosan R .15 .30
HOLW91E080SSP Towards the Future Together, Robocosan SSP200.00 400.00
HOLW91E081 miko_Art, Sakura Miko R .30 .60
HOLW91E081SP miko_Art, Sakura Miko SP 30.00 60.00
HOLW91E082 Towards the Future Together, Nakiri Ayame R .15 .30
HOLW91E082SSP Towards the Future Together, Nakiri Ayame SSP 400.00 800.00
HOLW91E083 Towards the Future Together, Omaru Polka R .25 .50
HOLW91E083SSP Towards the Future Together, Omaru Polka SSP 250.00 500.00
HOLW91E084 Towards the Future Together, Momosuzu Nene R .15 .30
HOLW91E084SSP Towards the Future Together, Momosuzu Nene SSP 250.00 500.00
HOLW91E085S Omaru Polka SR .50 1.00
HOLW91E085 Omaru Polka U .15 .30
HOLW91E086S Momosuzu Nene SR 1.00 2.00
HOLW91E086 Momosuzu Nene U .15 .30
HOLW91E087SP Artmaru, Omaru Polka SP 30.00 75.00
HOLW91E087 Artmaru, Omaru Polka U .15 .30
HOLW91E088S Robocosan SR .75 1.50
HOLW91E088 Robocosan U .20 .40
HOLW91E089SP Chocolart, Yuzuki Choco SP 60.00 125.00
HOLW91E089 Chocolart, Yuzuki Choco U .20 .40
HOLW91E090SP Nakiri Art Scrolls, Nakiri Ayame SP 75.00 150.00
HOLW91E090 Nakiri Art Scrolls, Nakiri Ayame U .20 .40
HOLW91E091SP Nenes Album, Momosuzu Nene SP 50.00 100.00
HOLW91E091 Nenes Album, Momosuzu Nene U .20 .40
HOLW91E092S Sakura Miko SR 3.00 6.00
HOLW91E092 Sakura Miko U .15 .30
HOLW91E093SP Roboco Art, Robocosan SP 25.00 50.00
HOLW91E093 Roboco Art, Robocosan U .15 .30
HOLW91E094S Houshou Marine SR 2.00 4.00
HOLW91E094 Houshou Marine U .20 .40
HOLW91E095S Yuzuki Choco SR 1.00 2.00
HOLW91E095 Yuzuki Choco U .15 .30
HOLW91E096S Akai Haato SR 1.00 2.00
HOLW91E096 Akai Haato U .15 .30
HOLW91E097 Wish Upon a Star, Yuzuki Choco C .15 .30
HOLW91E097S Wish Upon a Star, Yuzuki Choco SR 1.00 2.00
HOLW91E098 Believer of Spring, Momosuzu Nene C .15 .30
HOLW91E098S Believer of Spring, Momosuzu Nene SR 1.50 3.00
HOLW91E099 Crafting Weapons, Houshou Marine C .15 .30
HOLW91E099S Crafting Weapons, Houshou Marine SR 1.50 3.00
HOLW91E100 Perfect Measures Taken! Robocosan C .25 .50
HOLW91E100S Perfect Measures Taken! Robocosan SR 1.50 3.00
HOLW91E101 Kawayo, Nakiri Ayame C .15 .30
HOLW91E101S Kawayo, Nakiri Ayame SR .75 1.50
HOLW91E102 Nakiri Ayame C .15 .30
HOLW91E102S Nakiri Ayame SR 1.25 2.50
HOLW91E103 Absent-Minded, Sakura Miko C .15 .30
HOLW91E103S Absent-Minded, Sakura Miko SR .75 1.50
HOLW91E104 Revenge, Omaru Polka C .15 .30
HOLW91E104S Revenge, Omaru Polka SR 3.00 6.00
HOLW91E105 Haachama Beam, Akai Haato C .15 .30
HOLW91E105S Haachama Beam, Akai Haato SR 3.00 6.00
HOLW91E106 Beyond the Stage With You C .15 .30
HOLW91E106S Beyond the Stage With You SR 2.00 4.00
HOLW91E107 Meeting With 35P CR .30 .60
HOLW91E107R Meeting With 35P RRR 2.50 5.00
HOLW91E108 Enchanting Gaze CR .30 .60
HOLW91E108R Enchanting Gaze RRR 10.00 20.00
HOLW91E109 Towards the Dream Stage CC .15 .30
HOLW91E109R Towards the Dream Stage RRR 2.00 4.00
HOLW91E110 Present From the Devilish Santa CC .15 .30
HOLW91E110R Present From the Devilish Santa RRR 2.00 4.00
HOLW91E111 To Senpai With Love CC .15 .30

HOLW91E111R To Senpai With Love RRR 1.50 3.00
HOLW91E112 Towards the Future Together, Usada Pekora RR 1.00 2.00
HOLW91E112SSP Towards the Future Together, Usada Pekora SSP 300.00 750.00
HOLW91E113 Towards the Future Together, Hoshimachi Suisei RR4.00 8.00
HOLW91E113SSP Towards the Future Together, Hoshimachi Suisei SSP 600.00 1,200.00
HOLW91E114 Towards the Future Together, Shirogane Noel RR .25 .50
HOLW91E114SSP Towards the Future Together, Shirogane Noel SSP 500.00 1,000.00
HOLW91E115 Towards the Future Together, Minato Aqua RR .30 .75
HOLW91E115SSP Towards the Future Together, Minato Aqua SSP300.00600.00
HOLW91E116 Towards the Future Together, Murasaki Shion RR .15 .30
HOLW91E116SSP Towards the Future Together, Murasaki Shion SSP 200.00 400.00
HOLW91E117 Towards the Future Together, Yukihana Lamy R .20 .40
HOLW91E117SSP Towards the Future Together, Yukihana Lamy SSP 300.00 750.00
HOLW91E118 Hoshimachi Gallery, Hoshimachi Suisei R .20 .40
HOLW91E118SP Hoshimachi Gallery, Hoshimachi Suisei SP 200.00 400.00
HOLW91E119 Noelart, Shirogane Noel R .15 .30
HOLW91E119SP Noelart, Shirogane Noel SP 75.00 150.00
HOLW91E120 Aquart, Minato Aqua R .20 .40
HOLW91E120SP Aquart, Minato Aqua SP 30.00 75.00
HOLW91E121 Towards the Future Together, Shishiro Botan R .20 .40
HOLW91E121SSP Towards the Future Together, Shishiro Botan SSP 200.00 400.00
HOLW91E122 Pekorart, Usada Pekora R .15 .30
HOLW91E122SP Pekorart, Usada Pekora SP 100.00 200.00
HOLW91E123S Hoshimachi Suisei SR 3.00 6.00
HOLW91E123 Hoshimachi Suisei U .15 .30
HOLW91E124SP Shishirart, Shishiro Botan SP 40.00 80.00
HOLW91E124 Shishirart, Shishiro Botan U .15 .30
HOLW91E125S Minato Aqua SR 1.25 2.50
HOLW91E125 Minato Aqua U .15 .30
HOLW91E126SP Lamy Art, Yukihana Lamy SP 60.00 125.00
HOLW91E126 Lamy Art, Yukihana Lamy U .15 .30
HOLW91E127SP Shion Drawings, Murasaki Shion SP 30.00 75.00
HOLW91E127 Shion Drawings, Murasaki Shion U .15 .30
HOLW91E128S Usada Pekora SR 2.00 4.00
HOLW91E128 Usada Pekora U .15 .30
HOLW91E129S Shirogane Noel SR 4.00 8.00
HOLW91E129 Shirogane Noel U .15 .30
HOLW91E130S Murasaki Shion SR 1.50 3.00
HOLW91E130 Murasaki Shion U .15 .30
HOLW91E131 Yamada Hermione, Minato Aqua C .50 1.00
HOLW91E131S Yamada Hermione, Minato Aqua SR 7.50 15.00
HOLW91E132 An Expert's Power, Murasaki Shion C .15 .30
HOLW91E132S An Expert's Power, Murasaki Shion SR .75 1.50
HOLW91E133 Shy, Usada Pekora C .15 .30
HOLW91E133S Shy, Usada Pekora SR 1.00 2.00
HOLW91E134 Stunned, Shirogane Noel C .15 .30
HOLW91E134S Stunned, Shirogane Noel SR .75 1.50
HOLW91E135 Morning Rays, Shishiro Botan C .20 .40
HOLW91E135S Morning Rays, Shishiro Botan SR 3.00 6.00
HOLW91E136 My Alcohol! Yukihana Lamy C .15 .30
HOLW91E136S My Alcohol! Yukihana Lamy SR .75 1.50
HOLW91E137 Shishiro Botan C .15 .30
HOLW91E137S Shishiro Botan SR 1.25 2.50
HOLW91E138 Hoshimachi Suisei Who Grants Wishes C .20 .40
HOLW91E138S Hoshimachi Suisei Who Grants Wishes SR 2.50 5.00
HOLW91E139 Yukihana Lamy C .15 .30
HOLW91E139S Yukihana Lamy SR 1.00 2.00
HOLW91E140 Spending Time With Everyone CR .25 .50
HOLW91E140R Spending Time With Everyone RRR 4.00 8.00
HOLW91E141 Gaming on a Day Off CR .15 .30
HOLW91E141R Gaming on a Day Off RRR 4.00 8.00
HOLW91E142 Peaceful Moment CC .25 .50
HOLW91E142R Peaceful Moment RRR 3.00 6.00
HOLW91E143 Shion's Birthday CC .15 .30
HOLW91E143R Shion's Birthday RRR 1.00 2.00
HOLW91E144 Together With Danchou CC .15 .30
HOLW91E144R Together With Danchou RRR 5.00 10.00

2022 Weiss Schwarz Is It Wrong to Try to Pick Up Girls in a Dungeon

DDMS88E001 Exploring the Dungeon, Lili RR .30 .75
DDMS88E001SP Exploring the Dungeon, Lili SP 30.00 75.00
DDMS88E002 Reason for Her Strength, Ais RR .25 .50
DDMS88E002S Reason for Her Strength, Ais SR .75 1.50
DDMS88E003 [Sword Princess] Ais RR 3.00 6.00
DDMS88E003SP [Sword Princess] Ais SP 150.00 300.00
DDMS88E004 Encounter by the River, Ais & Hestia R 1.25 2.50
DDMS88E004S Encounter by the River, Ais & Hestia SR 12.50 25.00
DDMS88E005 Victory Feast, Tiona R .20 .40
DDMS88E006 Victory Feast, Tione R .10 .20
DDMS88E007 Rivals, Hestia & Lili R .12 .25
DDMS88E007S Rivals, Hestia & Lili SR 1.50 3.00
DDMS88E008 Cue for the Feast, Loki R .10 .20
DDMS88E009 Supporter, Lili R .20 .40
DDMS88E009S Supporter, Lili SR .60 1.25
DDMS88E010 Expedition to the Lower Levels, Finn U .12 .25
DDMS88E011 Foul-Mouthed Werewolf, Bete U .07 .15
DDMS88E012 Senior Mage, Riveria U .07 .15
DDMS88E013 Unstoppable Words, Lili U .12 .25
DDMS88E014 Moment Between the Two, Ais U .12 .25
DDMS88E015 End of Special Training, Ais C .07 .15
DDMS88E016 Lure of Alcohol, Loki C .05 .10
DDMS88E017 Returning From an Expedition, Tione C .05 .10
DDMS88E018 Transformation Magic, Lili C .05 .10
DDMS88E019 Fairy Tale, Tiona C .05 .10
DDMS88E020 Linked Wishes, Lili C .05 .10
DDMS88E021 Veteran Adventurer, Gareth C .05 .10
DDMS88E022 All Fired Up, Bete C .05 .10
DDMS88E023 Compensating With a Lap Pillow, Ais C .10 .20
DDMS88E024 Battle Practice CR .12 .25
DDMS88E024R Battle Practice RRR 2.50 5.00
DDMS88E025 Expedition to the Lower Levels CC .10 .20
DDMS88E026 One More Time CC .10 .20
DDMS88E026R One More Time RRR 1.00 2.00
DDMS88E027 City-Savvy Maiden, Syr RR .25 .50
DDMS88E027SP City-Savvy Maiden, Syr SP 30.00 75.00
DDMS88E028 Gale, Ryu RR .40 .80
DDMS88E028SP Gale, Ryu SP 75.00 150.00
DDMS88E029 Cunning Appeal, Syr R .10 .20
DDMS88E029S Cunning Appeal, Syr SR .75 1.50
DDMS88E030 A Man's Dream, Hermes R .15 .30
DDMS88E031 Past Sins, Ryu R .15 .30
DDMS88E031S Past Sins, Ryu SR 1.00 2.00
DDMS88E032 Unusual Interest, Syr R .12 .25
DDMS88E032S Unusual Interest, Syr SR .75 1.50
DDMS88E033 Ex-Adventurer, Ryu R .12 .25
DDMS88E033S Ex-Adventurer, Ryu SR 1.00 2.00
DDMS88E034 Sharing Potions, Miach U .07 .15
DDMS88E035 Perseus Asfi U .07 .15
DDMS88E036 Celebration, Syr U .05 .10
DDMS88E037 Mysterious Backup, Ryu U .10 .20
DDMS88E038 Chance Meeting in the Back Alley, Ryu C .07 .15
DDMS88E039 Owner of Hostess of Fertility, Mia C .05 .10
DDMS88E040 Owner of Hostess of Fertility, Syr C .05 .10
DDMS88E041 Owner of Hostess of Fertility, Ryu C .05 .10
DDMS88E042 Having It Hard, Asfi C .05 .10
DDMS88E043 Today's Lunch Box, Syr C .05 .10
DDMS88E044 Birth of a Hero, Hermes C .05 .10
DDMS88E045 Grimoire U .05 .10
DDMS88E046 [Luminous Wind] CR .12 .25
DDMS88E046R [Luminous Wind] RRR 2.50 5.00
DDMS88E047 Love Is Blind CC .07 .15
DDMS88E047R Love Is Blind RRR 1.25 2.50
DDMS88E048 First Adventure, Bell RR 3.00 6.00
DDMS88E048S First Adventure, Bell SR 7.50 15.00
DDMS88E049 Argonaut, Bell RR .30 .75
DDMS88E049SP Argonaut, Bell SP 50.00 100.00
DDMS88E050 The Story Begins Here, Bell & Hestia R .15 .30
DDMS88E050S The Story Begins Here, Bell & Hestia SR 2.50 5.00
DDMS88E051 Turf War, Welf R .20 .40
DDMS88E052 Cursed Clan, Welf R .12 .25
DDMS88E052S Cursed Clan, Welf SR .20 .40
DDMS88E053 Little Rookie Bell R .20 .40
DDMS88E053S Little Rookie Bell SR 1.50 3.00
DDMS88E054 Adventurer, Bell R .15 .30
DDMS88E054S Adventurer, Bell SR .75 1.50
DDMS88E055 Qualifications of a Hero, Bell U .25 .50
DDMS88E056 Message, Hephaistos U .05 .10
DDMS88E057 [God of the Masses] Ganesha U .12 .25
DDMS88E058 Meeting Up for a Date, Bell U .12 .25
DDMS88E059 A Blacksmith's Resolve, Welf U .07 .15
DDMS88E060 Present Self, Bell C .07 .15
DDMS88E061 Goddess of Beauty, Freya C .05 .10
DDMS88E062 Wavering Heart, Welf C .05 .10
DDMS88E063 Aiming for Greater Heights, Bell C .12 .25
DDMS88E064 Encouraging Words, Bell C .10 .20
DDMS88E065 Trials of an Adventurer, Ottarl C .05 .10
DDMS88E066 Anti-Magic Fire, Welf C .12 .25
DDMS88E067 Ushiwakamaru U .12 .25
DDMS88E068 Fire Bolt U .20 .40
DDMS88E069 Pyonkichi U .25 .50
DDMS88E070 Crozzo's Magic Sword U .07 .15
DDMS88E071 The Heroic Shot CR .15 .30
DDMS88E071R The Heroic Shot RRR 1.25 2.50
DDMS88E072 Unyielding Feelings CC .12 .25
DDMS88E072R Unyielding Feelings RRR 7.50 15.00
DDMS88E073 [Familia Myth] CC .10 .20
DDMS88E074 A Blacksmith's Obstinance CC .07 .15
DDMS88E075 Human Activity, Hestia RR 4.00 8.00
DDMS88E075SSR Human Activity, Hestia SR 10.00 20.00
DDMS88E076 Advisor of the Labyrinth's Exploration, Eina RR .30 .60
DDMS88E076SP Advisor of the Labyrinth's Exploration, Eina SP30.00 60.00
DDMS88E077 Proof of Trust, Hestia RR 7.50 15.00
DDMS88E077SP Proof of Trust, Hestia SP 200.00 400.00
DDMS88E078 Goddess's Judgment, Hestia R .15 .30
DDMS88E078S Goddess's Judgment, Hestia SR 2.00 4.00
DDMS88E079 Balance Between Friends, Mikoto R .10 .20
DDMS88E079S Balance Between Friends, Mikoto SR .40 .80
DDMS88E080 Guild Receptionist, Eina R .07 .15
DDMS88E080S Guild Receptionist, Eina SR .40 .80
DDMS88E081 Gift From Goddess, Hestia R .12 .25
DDMS88E081S Gift From Goddess, Hestia SR .75 1.50
DDMS88E082 Receptionist's Day Off, Eina R .10 .20
DDMS88E082S Receptionist's Day Off, Eina SR .60 1.25
DDMS88E083 Loli Goddess, Hestia R 1.25 2.50
DDMS88E083S Loli Goddess, Hestia SR 12.50 25.00
DDMS88E084 Case's Conclusion, Eina U .15 .30
DDMS88E085 Role of Sending Off, Takemikazuchi U .07 .15
DDMS88E086 Gravity Cage, Mikoto U .07 .15
DDMS88E087 Belief in His Victory, Hestia U .07 .15
DDMS88E088 Meeting Up for a Date, Hestia U .10 .20
DDMS88E089 Present of Croquettes, Hestia U .12 .25
DDMS88E090 Pursuit of Truth, Eina C .07 .15
DDMS88E091 Part-Time Job on the Side, Hestia C .12 .25
DDMS88E092 Support Role, Chigusa C .15 .30
DDMS88E093 Drunken Goddess, Hestia C .12 .25
DDMS88E094 A Man's Obstinance, Ouka C .07 .15
DDMS88E095 Hestia Knife U .25 .50
DDMS88E096 Eina's Present U .07 .15
DDMS88E097 Magic Stone U .07 .15
DDMS88E098 I Shall Make You Win CR .25 .50
DDMS88E098R I Shall Make You Win RRR 17.50 35.00
DDMS88E099 Paradise in Heaven CC .12 .25
DDMS88E099R Paradise in Heaven RRR 25.00 50.00
DDMS88E100 [Futsu-no-Mitama] CC .07 .15

2022 Weiss Schwarz Is It Wrong to Try to Pick Up Girls in a Dungeon Trial Deck

DDMS88TE01 Chienthrope? Girl, Lili TD .15 .30
DDMS88TE02SP First Class Adventurer, Ais SP 150.00 300.00
DDMS88TE02 First Class Adventurer, Ais TD .60 1.25
DDMS88TE03 Blacksmith Master, Welf TD .12 .25
DDMS88TE04R Shy Maiden, Lili RRR 2.00 4.00
DDMS88TE04 Shy Maiden, Lili TD .12 .25
DDMS88TE05R Encounter in the Dungeon, Ais RRR 2.50 5.00
DDMS88TE05 Encounter in the Dungeon, Ais TD .25 .50
DDMS88TE06 Monster Feria, Ais TD .20 .40
DDMS88TE07 Vow of Atonement, Lili TD .20 .40
DDMS88TE08 Hestia Familia TD .20 .40
DDMS88TE09 Start of a Day, Hestia TD .20 .40
DDMS88TE10R Moment in Labyrinth City, Hestia RRR 5.00 10.00
DDMS88TE10 Moment in Labyrinth City, Hestia TD .25 .50
DDMS88TE11 Towards His Aspiration, Bell TD .12 .25
DDMS88TE12S Familia of Just Two People, Hestia SR .30 .75
DDMS88TE12 Familia of Just Two People, Hestia TD .15 .30
DDMS88TE13 Trying to Pick Up Girls, Bell TD .20 .40
DDMS88TE14 Flattery Can Do Wonders, Bell TD .15 .30
DDMS88TE15R Moment in Labyrinth City, Bell RRR .75 1.50
DDMS88TE15 Moment in Labyrinth City, Bell TD .25 .50
DDMS88TE16SP Goddess, Hestia SP 200.00 400.00
DDMS88TE16 Goddess, Hestia TD .25 .50
DDMS88TE17 Status Update TD .30 .75
DDMS88TE18 Next Stage TD .12 .25
DDMS88TE19R A God's Role RRR .25 .50
DDMS88TE19 A God's Role TD .12 .25

2022 Weiss Schwarz Miss Kobayashi's Dragon Maid

KMDW96E001 Trusting Relations With Dragons, Miss Kobayashi RR7.5015.00
KMDW96E001SSP Trusting Relations With Dragons, Miss Kobayashi SSP 100.00 200.00
KMDW96E002 Bridging Humans and Dragons, Tohru & Miss Kobayashi RR 2.00 4.00
KMDW96E002MDR Bridging Humans and Dragons, Tohru & Miss Kobayashi MDR 12.50 25.00
KMDW96E003 Perfect Maid, Tohru RR 2.50 5.00
KMDW96E003SSP Perfect Maid, Tohru SSP 200.00 400.00
KMDW96E004MDRMDR Go Go Choro-gons! Tohru MDR 4.00 8.00
KMDW96E004R Go Go Choro-gons! Tohru R .20 .40
KMDW96E005OFROFR School Swimsuits, Perfect Pool Weather! Miss Kobayashi OFR 40.00 80.00
KMDW96E005R School Swimsuits, Perfect Pool Weather! Miss Kobayashi R .75 1.50
KMDW96E006MDRMDR Bedtime, Kanna MDR 2.50 5.00
KMDW96E006R Bedtime, Kanna R .10 .20
KMDW96E007MDRMDR Hindering Recognition, Tohru MDR 2.50 5.00
KMDW96E007R Hindering Recognition, Tohru R .25 .50
KMDW96E008MDRMDR Go Go Choro-gons! Kanna MDR 2.50 5.00
KMDW96E008R Go Go Choro-gons! Kanna R .15 .30
KMDW96E009MDRMDR Beachside Invitation, Kanna MDR 3.00 6.00
KMDW96E009U Beachside Invitation, Kanna U .20 .40
KMDW96E010U Loves Pranks, Kanna U .10 .20
KMDW96E011U Choro-gon Breath, Miss Kobayashi U .12 .25
KMDW96E012U Chaos Faction, Tohru U .12 .25
KMDW96E013U Unknown to Fear, Kanna U .10 .20
KMDW96E014MDRMDR Vow of Love, Tohru MDR 2.00 4.00
KMDW96E014U Vow of Love, Tohru U .12 .25
KMDW96E015MDRMDR Leave the Cooking to Me! Tohru MDR 2.50 5.00
KMDW96E015U Leave the Cooking to Me! Tohru U .12 .25
KMDW96E016C Usual Daily Life, Tohru C .07 .15
KMDW96E017C Yearning for a Human Life, Kanna C .07 .15
KMDW96E018C First Meeting, Tohru C .07 .15
KMDW96E019C Method to Gain Energy, Kanna C .07 .15
KMDW96E019MDRMDR Method to Gain Energy, Kanna MDR 1.50 3.00
KMDW96E020C Wings of Love, Tohru C .07 .15
KMDW96E021C Elementary School Student, Kanna C .07 .15
KMDW96E022MDRMDR Discussion of Maids MDR 2.50 5.00
KMDW96E022U Discussion of Maids U .10 .20
KMDW96E023CR Words She Wanted to Convey CR 12.50 25.00
KMDW96E023MDRMDR Words She Wanted to Convey MDR .25 .50
KMDW96E024CC Playful Age CC .07 .15
KMDW96E025CC Spreading of Wings CC .20 .40
KMDW96E026OFROFR School Swimsuits, Perfect Pool Weather! Tohru OFR 100.00 200.00
KMDW96E026RR School Swimsuits, Perfect Pool Weather! Tohru RR7.5015.00
KMDW96E027MDRMDR Choro-gon Breath, Iruru MDR 25.00 50.00
KMDW96E027RR Choro-gon Breath, Iruru RR 4.00 8.00
KMDW96E028MDRMDR Doll of Memories, Iruru MDR 1.25 2.50
KMDW96E028R Doll of Memories, Iruru R .15 .30
KMDW96E029OFROFR Awakening, Tohru OFR 30.00 60.00
KMDW96E029R Awakening, Tohru R .30 .60
KMDW96E030MDRMDR At Loggerheads, Tohru & Elma MDR 2.50 5.00
KMDW96E030R At Loggerheads, Tohru & Elma R .12 .25
KMDW96E031MDRMDR Of Age Duo, Iruru & Taketo Aida MDR 1.50 3.00
KMDW96E031R Of Age Duo, Iruru & Taketo Aida R .20 .40
KMDW96E032MDRMDR Otaku Alliance, Fafnir & Makoto Takiya MDR 1.00 2.00
KMDW96E032R Otaku Alliance, Fafnir & Makoto Takiya R .15 .30
KMDW96E033MDRMDR Shut-in Being Serious, Fafnir MDR 1.25 2.50
KMDW96E033R Shut-in Being Serious, Fafnir R .12 .25
KMDW96E034MDRMDR Choro-gon Breath, Tohru MDR 25.00 50.00
KMDW96E034R Choro-gon Breath, Tohru R .20 .40
KMDW96E035MDRMDR Favorite Clothes, Tohru MDR 2.50 5.00
KMDW96E035U Favorite Clothes, Tohru U .12 .25
KMDW96E036MDRMDR Dragon Maid, Tohru MDR 3.00 6.00
KMDW96E036U Dragon Maid, Tohru U .12 .25
KMDW96E037U Preparations for a Deadly Battle, Fafnir U .10 .20
KMDW96E038MDRMDR Extremist of the Chaos Faction, Iruru MDR1.25 2.50
KMDW96E038U Extremist of the Chaos Faction, Iruru U .10 .20
KMDW96E039U Particular Person, Miss Kobayashi U .12 .25
KMDW96E040MDRMDR Colleague, Makoto Takiya MDR .75 1.50
KMDW96E040U Colleague, Makoto Takiya U .07 .15
KMDW96E041C New Decision, Fafnir C .07 .15
KMDW96E042C Beyond Species, Miss Kobayashi C .07 .15
KMDW96E043C Childhood Memories, Iruru C .07 .15
KMDW96E043MDRMDR Childhood Memories, Iruru MDR 7.50 15.00
KMDW96E044C Underlying Face, Makoto Takiya C .07 .15
KMDW96E045C Conspiring, Tohru C .07 .15
KMDW96E046C Molting" Tohru C .12 .25
KMDW96E046MDRMDR Molting" Tohru MDR 1.25 2.50
KMDW96E047C Temporary Farewell, Fafnir C .07 .15
KMDW96E048C Keeping the Town's Peace, Tohru C .07 .15
KMDW96E049MDRMDR Search for a Present MDR 2.00 4.00
KMDW96E049U Search for a Present U .10 .20
KMDW96E050CR Search for Treasure CR .20 .40
KMDW96E050OFROFR Search for Treasure OFR 40.00 80.00
KMDW96E051CC A Dragon's Reserve Power CC .12 .25
KMDW96E051MDRMDR A Dragon's Reserve Power MDR 7.50 15.00
KMDW96E052CC Serious Showdown Between Otaku CC .07 .15
KMDW96E052MDRMDR Serious Showdown Between Otaku MDR1.00 2.00
KMDW96E053MDRMDR Trip on a Day Off, Tohru & Kanna & Miss Kobayashi MDR 6.00 12.00
KMDW96E053RR Trip on a Day Off, Tohru & Kanna & Miss Kobayashi RR .75 1.50
KMDW96E054RR Prank-Loving Young Dragon, Kanna RR .60 1.25
KMDW96E054SPSSP Prank-Loving Young Dragon, Kanna SSP125.00250.00
KMDW96E055OFROFR School Swimsuits, Perfect Pool Weather! Kanna OFR 20.00 40.00
KMDW96E055RR School Swimsuits, Perfect Pool Weather! Kanna RR .75 1.50
KMDW96E056OFROFR Awakening, Kanna OFR 20.00 40.00
KMDW96E056R Awakening, Kanna R .40 .80
KMDW96E057MDRMDR Go Go Choro-gons! Iruru MDR 2.50 5.00
KMDW96E057R Go Go Choro-gons! Iruru R .15 .30
KMDW96E058MDRMDR Crying Aloud, Riko Saikawa MDR 2.00 4.00
KMDW96E058R Crying Aloud, Riko Saikawa R .15 .30
KMDW96E059MDRMDR Choro-gon Breath, Kanna MDR 3.00 6.00
KMDW96E059R Choro-gon Breath, Kanna R .25 .50
KMDW96E060MDRMDR Always Together, Kanna & Riko Saikawa MDR 1.50 3.00
KMDW96E060R Always Together, Kanna & Riko Saikawa R .20 .40
KMDW96E061U Sinister Scheme, Kanna U .10 .20
KMDW96E062U First Time Having Such Feelings, Iruru U .10 .20
KMDW96E063MDRMDR Beginning a New Life, Miss Kobayashi MDR 2.50 5.00
KMDW96E063U Beginning a New Life, Miss Kobayashi U .15 .30
KMDW96E064MDRMDR Co-Existing With Humans, Iruru MDR 2.00 4.00
KMDW96E064U Co-Existing With Humans, Iruru U .10 .20
KMDW96E065U Friends Forever, Riko Saikawa U .10 .20
KMDW96E066U Adolescent High School Student, Taketo Aida U .12 .25
KMDW96E067C Chosen Place to Belong, Kanna C .07 .15
KMDW96E068C Lazy Member of Chaos Faction, Iruru C .07 .15
KMDW96E069C Each Other's Feelings, Miss Kobayashi C .07 .15
KMDW96E070C New Faction! Kanna C .07 .15
KMDW96E071C Young Dragon, Kanna C .07 .15
KMDW96E072C Conversation With Humans, Iruru C .07 .15
KMDW96E073MDRMDR Pranking With Whole Being MDR 1.25 2.50
KMDW96E073U Pranking With Whole Being U .10 .20
KMDW96E074CR Surprise Reveal CR 20.00 40.00
KMDW96E074OFROFR Surprise Reveal OFR .60 1.25
KMDW96E075CC Towards Where Everyone Awaits CC .07 .15
KMDW96E075MDRMDR Towards Where Everyone Awaits MDR 2.00 4.00
KMDW96E076CC Budding Feelings CC .07 .15
KMDW96E077MDRMDR Choro-gon Breath, Lucoa MDR 30.00 75.00
KMDW96E077RR Choro-gon Breath, Lucoa RR 1.25 2.50
KMDW96E078OFROFR Awakening, Elma OFR 30.00 60.00
KMDW96E078RR Awakening, Elma RR 1.25 2.50
KMDW96E079MDRMDR Choro-gon Breath, Elma MDR 7.50 15.00
KMDW96E079R Choro-gon Breath, Elma R .20 .40
KMDW96E080MDRMDR Go Go Choro-gons! Lucoa MDR 4.00 8.00
KMDW96E080R Go Go Choro-gons! Lucoa R .20 .40
KMDW96E081MDRMDR Stimulating Daily Life, Lucoa & Shouta Magatsuchi MDR 3.00 6.00
KMDW96E081R Stimulating Daily Life, Lucoa & Shouta Magatsuchi R .25 .50
KMDW96E082MDRMDR Go Go Choro-gons! Elma MDR 4.00 8.00
KMDW96E082R Go Go Choro-gons! Elma R .25 .50

KMDW96E083MDRMDR Demonic Embrace, Lucoa MDR 4.00 8.00
KMDW96E083R Demonic Embrace, Lucoa R .30 .75
KMDW96E084MDRMDR Voluptuous Body, Lucoa MDR 12.50 25.00
KMDW96E084U Voluptuous Body, Lucoa U .12 .25
KMDW96E085MDRMDR Loves Sweets, Elma MDR 2.50 5.00
KMDW96E085U Loves Sweets, Elma U .12 .25
KMDW96E086MDRMDR Predator, Elma MDR 2.50 5.00
KMDW96E086U Predator, Elma U .12 .25
KMDW96E087MDRMDR Sweet Proposal, Miss Kobayashi MDR 1.25 2.50
KMDW96E087U Sweet Proposal, Miss Kobayashi U .07 .15
KMDW96E088U Gigantic Winged Dragon, Lucoa U .10 .20
KMDW96E089U Talent for Magic, Shouta Magatsuchi U .12 .25
KMDW96E090C Maid Experience, Lucoa C .07 .15
KMDW96E090MDRMDR Maid Experience, Lucoa MDR 3.00 6.00
KMDW96E091C As a Master, Shouta Magatsuchi C .07 .15
KMDW96E092C Hidden Potential, Elma C .07 .15
KMDW96E093C Ex-God, Lucoa C .07 .15
KMDW96E094C Wavering Beliefs, Elma C .07 .15
KMDW96E095C New Hire, Elma C .07 .15
KMDW96E096C Actions in the Face of Death, Miss Kobayashi C .07 .15
KMDW96E097C Unlimited Appetite C .07 .15
KMDW96E097MDRMDR Unlimited Appetite MDR 7.50 15.00
KMDW96E098CR Confession of a Harmony Faction Member CR .15 .30
KMDW96E098MDRMDR Confession
of a Harmony Faction Member MDR 4.00 8.00
KMDW96E099CC Battle With the Strong CC .07 .15
KMDW96E100CC Failed Summoning? CC .15 .30
KMDW96E100MDRMDR Failed Summoning? MDR 10.00 20.00
KMDW96E101PR Leave Performing to Me, Tohru P .40 .80
KMDW96E101SPR Leave Performing to Me, Tohru FOIL P 2.00 4.00
KMDW96E102PR A Human's Resolve, Miss Kobayashi P .30 .60
KMDW96E102SPR A Human's Resolve, Miss Kobayashi FOIL P 1.25 2.50
KMDW96E103PR Impatient, Kanna P .30 .75
KMDW96E103SPR Impatient, Kanna FOIL P .30 .75
KMDW96E104PR World She Never Knew Of, Iruru P 1.00 2.00
KMDW96E104SPR World She Never Knew Of, Iruru FOIL P 1.50 3.00

2022 Weiss Schwarz Miss Kobayashi's Dragon Maid Trial Deck

KMDW96TE01RRRR Heart-Pounding Part-Time Job, Iruru RRR .75 1.50
KMDW96TE01TD Heart-Pounding Part-Time Job, Iruru .07 .15
KMDW96TE02RRRR Cheering for Love, Kanna RRR 1.00 2.00
KMDW96TE02TD Cheering for Love, Kanna .07 .15
KMDW96TE03SPSSP Poolside Temptation, Tohru SSP 300.00 750.00
KMDW96TE03TD Poolside Temptation, Tohru .50 1.00
KMDW96TE04RRRR Eating off the Ground, Kanna RRR .50 1.00
KMDW96TE04TD Eating off the Ground, Kanna .07 .15
KMDW96TE05OFROFR Self-Proclaimed Best Maid, Tohru OFR 15.00 30.00
KMDW96TE05TD Self-Proclaimed Best Maid, Tohru .07 .15
KMDW96TE06RRRR Onset of Puberty, Iruru RRR 1.50 3.00
KMDW96TE06TD Onset of Puberty, Iruru .07 .15
KMDW96TE07RRRR Modeling, Lucoa RRR 2.50 5.00
KMDW96TE07TD Modeling, Lucoa .10 .20
KMDW96TE08SSR A Maid Just for You, Tohru SR .15 .30
KMDW96TE08TD A Maid Just for You, Tohru .07 .15
KMDW96TE09OFROFR Peeking Back
in Japanese Clothes, Kanna OFR 12.50 25.00
KMDW96TE09TD Peeking Back in Japanese Clothes, Kanna .07 .15
KMDW96TE10RRRR Making the Best Memories RRR .07 .15
KMDW96TE10TD Making the Best Memories 4.00 8.00
KMDW96TE11RRRR The Scenery Together With You RRR .50 1.00
KMDW96TE11TD The Scenery Together With You .07 .15
KMDW96TE12RRRR Blissful Times, Miss Kobayashi RRR .75 1.50
KMDW96TE12TD Blissful Times, Miss Kobayashi .07 .15
KMDW96TE13RRRR Peaceful Daily Life, Miss Kobayashi RRR .75 1.50
KMDW96TE13TD Peaceful Daily Life, Miss Kobayashi .07 .15
KMDW96TE14RRRR Priestess of the Sea, Elma RRR .75 1.50
KMDW96TE14TD Priestess of the Sea, Elma .07 .15
KMDW96TE15RRRR First Time Using a Computer, Elma RRR .30 .75
KMDW96TE15TD First Time Using a Computer, Elma .07 .15
KMDW96TE16RRRR For the Sake of Friends, Miss Kobayashi RRR.50 1.00
KMDW96TE16TD For the Sake of Friends, Miss Kobayashi .07 .15
KMDW96TE17RRRR Participating! Fafnir RRR .75 1.50
KMDW96TE17TD Participating! Fafnir .07 .15
KMDW96TE18RRRR Harmony Faction, Elma RRR 1.50 3.00
KMDW96TE18TD Harmony Faction, Elma .07 .15
KMDW96TE19RRRR High-Five of Trust RRR .75 1.50
KMDW96TE19TD High-Five of Trust .07 .15
KMDW96TE20RRRR Busy Shopping RRR .75 1.50
KMDW96TE20TD Busy Shopping .07 .15

2022 Weiss Schwarz Mushoku Tensei Jobless Reincarnation

MTIS83E001 Talent for Magic Rudeus RR 12.50 25.00
MTIS83E001SP Talent for Magic Rudeus SP 100.00 200.00
MTIS83E002 Living Earnestly Rudeus RR .50 1.00
MTIS83E002SSP Living Earnestly Rudeus SSP 125.00 250.00
MTIS83E003 In the Sunlight Rudeus R .25 .50
MTIS83E003S In the Sunlight Rudeus SR 2.00 4.00
MTIS83E004 Adventurer Party Dead End Rudeus R .25 .50
MTIS83E005 Daily Growth Rudeus R .25 .50
MTIS83E005S Daily Growth Rudeus SR 3.00 6.00
MTIS83E006 Words of Encouragement Rudeus R .25 .50
MTIS83E007 Life's Starting Line Rudeus R .25 .50
MTIS83E007S Life's Starting Line Rudeus SR 4.00 8.00
MTIS83E008 Courageous Young Man Rudeus U .15 .30
MTIS83E009 Just a Child Rudeus U .15 .30
MTIS83E010 Talented Swordsman Paul U .15 .30
MTIS83E011 Friends Rudeus C .12 .25
MTIS83E012 Unraveling Heart Lilia C .12 .25
MTIS83E013 Offering a Hand Rudeus C .12 .25
MTIS83E014 Aisha & Norn C .12 .25
MTIS83E015 Blessed With Life Zenith C .12 .25
MTIS83E016 Holy Relic U .25 .50
MTIS83E017a Figure Making U .15 .30
MTIS83E017b Figure Making U .15 .30
MTIS83E017c Figure Making U .15 .30
MTIS83E018 Man-God U .15 .30
MTIS83E019 Aqua Heartia CR .20 .40
MTIS83E019R Aqua Heartia RRR 1.00 2.00
MTIS83E020 Little Magician CC .12 .25
MTIS83E020R Little Magician RRR 1.50 3.00
MTIS83E021 Smile to Be Protected Sylphiette RR .75 1.50
MTIS83E021SSP Smile to Be Protected Sylphiette SSP 125.00 250.00
MTIS83E022 Pure and Innocent Heart Sylphiette RR .50 1.00
MTIS83E022SP Pure and Innocent Heart Sylphiette SP 75.00 150.00
MTIS83E023 Warrior of Superd Race Ruijerd RR .75 1.50
MTIS83E023 Warrior of Superd Race Ruijerd SR 2.00 4.00
MTIS83E024 Angel's Haven Sylphiette R .25 .50
MTIS83E024S Angel's Haven Sylphiette SR 4.00 8.00
MTIS83E025 Eye on the Forehead Ruijerd R .25 .50
MTIS83E025S Eye on the Forehead Ruijerd SR 3.00 6.00
MTIS83E026 Adventurer Party Dead End Ruijerd R .25 .50
MTIS83E027 Tomboyish Childhood Friend Sylphiette R .25 .50
MTIS83E027S Tomboyish Childhood Friend Sylphiette SR 4.00 8.00
MTIS83E028 Battle Stance Ruijerd R .25 .50
MTIS83E028S Battle Stance Ruijerd SR 2.50 5.00
MTIS83E029 Quarter-Elf Girl Sylphiette R .25 .50
MTIS83E029S Quarter-Elf Girl Sylphiette SR 2.00 4.00
MTIS83E030 Pretty Boy? Sylphiette U .15 .30
MTIS83E031 Adventurer's Guild Receptionist U .15 .30
MTIS83E032a Tokurabu Toughs U .15 .30
MTIS83E032b Tokurabu Toughs U .15 .30
MTIS83E032c Tokurabu Toughs U .15 .30
MTIS83E033a P Hunter U .15 .30
MTIS83E033b P Hunter U .15 .30
MTIS83E034 Magic Practice Sylphiette U .15 .30
MTIS83E035 Sparkly Eyes Sylphiette U .15 .30
MTIS83E036 Feared Race Ruijerd C .12 .25
MTIS83E037 Nokopara C .12 .25
MTIS83E038 Overflowing Tears Sylphiette C .12 .25
MTIS83E039 Alone Time for Two Sylphiette C .12 .25
MTIS83E040 Friends Sylphiette C .12 .25
MTIS83E041 Intense Outrage Ruijerd C .12 .25
MTIS83E042 Studying with Rudy Sylphiette C .12 .25
MTIS83E043 In the Sunlight Sylphiette C .12 .25
MTIS83E044 Wounded Pride Ruijerd C .12 .25
MTIS83E045 Superd's Soul U .15 .30
MTIS83E046 Sylph U .15 .30
MTIS83E047 The Smile You Gave CR .20 .40
MTIS83E047R The Smile You Gave RRR 2.50 5.00
MTIS83E048 Dead End CC .12 .25
MTIS83E048R Dead End RRR 2.00 4.00
MTIS83E049 Future Magician CC .12 .25
MTIS83E050 Children and Warriors CC .12 .25
MTIS83E051 Swordsman of Beauty Eris RR .30 .75
MTIS83E051SSP Swordsman of Beauty Eris SSP 200.00 400.00
MTIS83E052 Violent Tsundere Young Lady Eris RR 6.00 12.00
MTIS83E052SP Violent Tsundere Young Lady Eris SP 200.00 400.00
MTIS83E053 Strong Swordswoman Ghislaine RR 6.00 12.00
MTIS83E053SSP Strong Swordswoman Ghislaine SSP 250.00 500.00
MTIS83E054 Seductive Invitation Eris R .25 .50
MTIS83E054S Seductive Invitation Eris SR 30.00 75.00
MTIS83E055 Swordsmanship Coach Ghislaine R .25 .50
MTIS83E055S Swordsmanship Coach Ghislaine SR 7.50 15.00
MTIS83E056 Sword God Style Ghislaine R .25 .50
MTIS83E056S Sword God Style Ghislaine SR 2.00 4.00
MTIS83E057 Strong Body Ghislaine R .25 .50
MTIS83E057SP Strong Body Ghislaine SP 125.00 250.00
MTIS83E058 Boreas Family's Daughter Eris R .25 .50
MTIS83E058S Boreas Family's Daughter Eris SR 6.00 12.00
MTIS83E059 Hidden Strength Eris R .25 .50
MTIS83E059S Hidden Strength Eris SR 5.00 10.00
MTIS83E060 Adventurer Party Dead End Eris U .15 .30
MTIS83E061 Angelic Sleeping Face Eris U .15 .30
MTIS83E062 Magic Practice Eris U .15 .30
MTIS83E063 Boreas Family's Bodyguard Ghislaine SR 3.00 6.00
MTIS83E063 Boreas Family's Bodyguard Ghislaine U .15 .30
MTIS83E064 Beast Race Ghislaine U .15 .30
MTIS83E065 Philip Boreas Greyrat U .15 .30
MTIS83E066 Sauros Boreas Greyrat U .15 .30
MTIS83E067a Beast Race Maids of the Boreas Family C .12 .25
MTIS83E067b Beast Race Maids of the Boreas Family C .12 .25
MTIS83E067c Beast Race Maids of the Boreas Family C .12 .25
MTIS83E068 Hilda Boreas Greyrat C .12 .25
MTIS83E069 Study Time Eris C .12 .25
MTIS83E070 Magic Practice Ghislaine C .12 .25
MTIS83E071 Penetrating Gaze Eris C .12 .25
MTIS83E072 What Lies Beyond Effort Eris C .12 .25
MTIS83E073 Fine Feathers Make Fine Birds Eris C .12 .25
MTIS83E074 Insolence Eris C .12 .25
MTIS83E075 Fangs of the Black Wolf U .15 .30
MTIS83E076 You Can't Buy Dere With Money! U .15 .30
MTIS83E077 Eris's Request CR .30 .60
MTIS83E077R Eris's Request RRR 25.00 50.00
MTIS83E078 Right Demon Eye CC .12 .25
MTIS83E078R Right Demon Eye RRR 15.00 30.00
MTIS83E079 Special CC .12 .25
MTIS83E080 Sword King Ghislaine CC .12 .25
MTIS83E081 Things I Can Give You Roxy RR 7.50 15.00
MTIS83E081SP Things I Can Give You Roxy SP 200.00 400.00
MTIS83E082 Warm Gaze Roxy RR 1.00 2.00
MTIS83E082SSP Warm Gaze Roxy SSP 300.00 600.00
MTIS83E083 Audible Gasps Roxy R .25 .50
MTIS83E084 Future Guide Roxy R .25 .50
MTIS83E084S Future Guide Roxy SR 6.00 12.00
MTIS83E085 Culinary Class Roxy R .25 .50
MTIS83E086 In the Sunlight Roxy R .25 .50
MTIS83E086S In the Sunlight Roxy SR 10.00 20.00
MTIS83E087 Migurd Race Magician Roxy R .25 .50
MTIS83E087S Migurd Race Magician Roxy SR 10.00 20.00
MTIS83E088 Composing a Letter Roxy U .15 .30
MTIS83E089 Almanfi the Radiant U .15 .30
MTIS83E090 Pax Shirone U .15 .30
MTIS83E091 Rudy's Home Tutor Roxy U .15 .30
MTIS83E092 Kishirika Kishirisu U .15 .30
MTIS83E093 Mischievous Smile Roxy C .12 .25
MTIS83E094 Rokari Migurdia C .12 .25
MTIS83E095 Rowin Migurdia C .12 .25
MTIS83E096 Orsted C .12 .25
MTIS83E097 Cringe Roxy C .12 .25
MTIS83E098 Amulet of Migurd Race U .25 .50
MTIS83E099 Blessing CR .20 .40
MTIS83E099R Blessing RRR 7.50 15.00
MTIS83E100 Cumulonimbus CC .12 .25
MTIS83E100R Cumulonimbus RRR 2.50 5.00

2022 Weiss Schwarz Mushoku Tensei Jobless Reincarnation Trial Deck

MTIS83TE01TD Good Wife, Wise Mother Zenith .15 .30
MTIS83TE02TD Graduation Exam Rudeus .60 1.25
MTIS83TE02TDRRRR Graduation Exam Rudeus RRR 15.00 30.00
MTIS83TE03TD Paul Greyrat .15 .30
MTIS83TE04TD Zenith Greyrat .30 .60
MTIS83TE05TD Lilia Greyrat .60 1.25
MTIS83TE06TD Jobless Reincarnation Rudeus .60 1.50
MTIS83TE06TDSPSP Jobless Reincarnation Rudeus SP 100.00 200.00
MTIS83TE07TD The Beginning of a New Life Rudeus .15 .30
MTIS83TE08TD Magic Practice Rudeus .15 .30
MTIS83TE09TD Sword Training Paul .15 .30
MTIS83TE10TD Chant Rudeus .15 .30
MTIS83TE10TDSSR Chant Rudeus SR 1.25 2.50
MTIS83TE11TD Previous Life's Trauma .15 .30
MTIS83TE12TD From Master to Disciple .15 .30
MTIS83TE12TDSSR From Master to Disciple SR 2.00 4.00
MTIS83TE13TD Amidst the Passing Days .15 .30
MTIS83TE14TD Loli, Scornful Eyes, Unfriendly Roxy .60 1.25
MTIS83TE14TDSSP Loli, Scornful Eyes, Unfriendly Roxy SP 750.00 1,500.00
MTIS83TE15TD Demon Race Roxy .60 1.25
MTIS83TE16TD Depressed Feelings Roxy .15 .30
MTIS83TE17TD Welcome Party Roxy .15 .30
MTIS83TE17TDRRRR Welcome Party Roxy RRR 7.50 15.00
MTIS83TE18TD Unexpected Failure Roxy .15 .30
MTIS83TE19TD Chant Roxy .60 1.25
MTIS83TE19TDRRRR Chant Roxy RRR 15.00 30.00
MTIS83TE20TD Little Master .15 .30

2022 Weiss Schwarz Rascal Does Not Dream of a Dreaming Girl

SBYW77E001RR Time and Memories, Mai Sakurajima RR .40 .80
SBYW77E001SSR Time and Memories, Mai Sakurajima SR 4.00 8.00
SBYW77E002RR Respective Choices, Mai Sakurajima RR .75 1.50
SBYW77E002SPSP Respective Choices, Mai Sakurajima SP 100.00 200.00
SBYW77E003RR Christmas Present, Nodoka Toyohama RR .75 1.50
SBYW77E003SPSP Christmas Present, Nodoka Toyohama SP 50.00 100.00
SBYW77E004R Together With Big Brother, Kaede Azusagawa R .12 .25
SBYW77E004SSR Together With Big Brother, Kaede Azusagawa SR1.25 2.50
SBYW77E005R Reunion Beyond Time, Mai Sakurajima R .12 .25
SBYW77E005SSR Reunion Beyond Time, Mai Sakurajima SR 1.00 2.00
SBYW77E006R Everlasting Summer Date, Mai Sakurajima R .12 .25
SBYW77E006SSR Everlasting Summer Date, Mai Sakurajima SR2.50 5.00
SBYW77E007R Relaxation Time, Mai Sakurajima R .15 .30
SBYW77E007SSR Relaxation Time, Mai Sakurajima SR 3.00 6.00
SBYW77E008U Resolute Statement, Mai Sakurajima U .20 .40
SBYW77E009U Close Sisters, Nodoka Toyohama U .10 .20
SBYW77E010U Close Sisters, Mai Sakurajima U .12 .25
SBYW77E011U Compromise, Mai Sakurajima U .07 .15
SBYW77E012aU Crossroads, Sakuta Azusagawa (a) U .07 .15
SBYW77E012bU Crossroads, Sakuta Azusagawa (b) U .07 .15
SBYW77E013U Evasion of the Accident, Sakuta Azusagawa U .07 .15
SBYW77E014C Going Home Together, Mai Sakurajima C .07 .15
SBYW77E015C Best Part About Winter, Kaede Azusagawa C .25 .50
SBYW77E016C Younger Sister's Warning, Nodoka Toyohama C .07 .15
SBYW77E017C Preparing Dinner, Mai Sakurajima C .07 .15
SBYW77E018C Call from Dad, Kaede Azusagawa C .07 .15
SBYW77E019U Numerous Memories U .07 .15
SBYW77E020U Seeking Help U .10 .20
SBYW77E021CR Person to Make Happy CR .12 .25
SBYW77E021RRRR Person to Make Happy RRR 4.00 8.00
SBYW77E022CC Small Gig! CC .07 .15
SBYW77E022RRRR Small Gig! RRR 2.50 5.00
SBYW77E023CC Unsettling Atmosphere CC .07 .15
SBYW77E024RR Little Devil's Troubles, Tomoe Koga RR .20 .40
SBYW77E024SPSP Little Devil's Troubles, Tomoe Koga SP 30.00 60.00
SBYW77E025RR Time and Memories, Shoko Makinohara RR .15 .30
SBYW77E025SSR Time and Memories, Shoko Makinohara SR 1.50 3.00
SBYW77E026R Visiting the Sick, Rio Futaba R .10 .20
SBYW77E027R Coincidental Alignment, Shoko Makinohara R .25 .50
SBYW77E028R Intermediation via Phone, Rio Futaba R .10 .20
SBYW77E028SSR Intermediation via Phone, Rio Futaba SR .75 1.50
SBYW77E029R My Theory"" Rio Futaba R .10 .20
SBYW77E029SSR My Theory"" Rio Futaba SR .75 1.50
SBYW77E030R Yearned-For Wedding Dress, Shoko Makinohara R.12 .25
SBYW77E030SSR Yearned-For Wedding
Dress, Shoko Makinohara SR 1.50 3.00
SBYW77E031R Usual Conversational Exchange, Rio Futaba R .12 .25
SBYW77E031SSR Usual Conversational Exchange, Rio Futaba SR.75 1.50
SBYW77E032U Cohabiting, Shoko Makinohara U .07 .15
SBYW77E033U Incident in a Dream, Tomoe Koga U .07 .15
SBYW77E034U Expression of Relief, Rio Futaba U .07 .15
SBYW77E035U Which Senpai Are You?"" Tomoe Koga U .07 .15
SBYW77E036U Arrival at the Destination! Shoko Makinohara U .07 .15
SBYW77E037C Unexpected Destination, Sakuta Azusagawa C .07 .15
SBYW77E038C Favorite Phrases, Shoko Makinohara C .07 .15
SBYW77E039C What I Want to Write Now"" Shoko Makinohara C .07 .15
SBYW77E040C Encounter at the Hospital, Shoko Makinohara C .07 .15
SBYW77E041C Sudden Change in Condition, Sakuta Azusagawa C.07 .15
SBYW77E042C Sudden Change in Condition, Shoko Makinohara C.07 .15
SBYW77E043C Cleaning, Shoko Makinohara C .07 .15
SBYW77E044C Incident in a Dream, Rio Futaba C .07 .15
SBYW77E045C Reason for Existence, Shoko Makinohara C .07 .15
SBYW77E046U December/24/ U .07 .15
SBYW77E047CC Returning Phrase CC .07 .15
SBYW77E048CC Impossible Phenomenon CC .07 .15
SBYW77E049CC Seaside Wedding Venue CC .07 .15
SBYW77E050RR Strange Incidents, Mai Sakurajima RR .75 1.50
SBYW77E050SECSEC Strange Incidents, Mai Sakurajima SCR300.00 750.00
SBYW77E051RR Taking a New Step, Kaede Azusagawa RR .12 .25
SBYW77E051SPSP Taking a New Step, Kaede Azusagawa SP 30.00 60.00
SBYW77E052R Precious Younger Sister, Kaede Azusagawa R .15 .30
SBYW77E052SSR Precious Younger Sister, Kaede Azusagawa SR1.25 2.50
SBYW77E053R Santa Claus Duo, Mai Sakurajima R .12 .25
SBYW77E053SSR Santa Claus Duo, Mai Sakurajima SR 2.50 5.00
SBYW77E054R Cohabiting, Mai Sakurajima R .12 .25
SBYW77E055R Santa Claus Duo, Nodoka Toyohama R .12 .25
SBYW77E055SSR Santa Claus Duo, Nodoka Toyohama SR 1.50 3.00
SBYW77E056R In a Swimsuit, Mai Sakurajima R .15 .30
SBYW77E056SSR In a Swimsuit, Mai Sakurajima SR 7.50 15.00
SBYW77E057U Date Invitation, Mai Sakurajima U .07 .15
SBYW77E058U Alone in the Dressing Room, Mai Sakurajima U .07 .15
SBYW77E059U Satisfaction Check, Mai Sakurajima U .07 .15
SBYW77E060U Retreating From the Bloodbath, Kaede Azusagawa U.07 .15
SBYW77E061U Unpleasant Prying, Mai Sakurajima U .07 .15
SBYW77E062C Bitter Decision, Sakuta Azusagawa C .07 .15
SBYW77E063C Incident in a Dream, Nodoka Toyohama C .12 .25
SBYW77E064C Visiting the Sick, Mai Sakurajima C .07 .15
SBYW77E065C Strange Incidents, Sakuta Azusagawa C .07 .15
SBYW77E066C Incident in a Dream, Mai Sakurajima C .10 .20
SBYW77E067C Running Away From Home, Nodoka Toyohama C .07 .15
SBYW77E068U Organ Donor Card U .07 .15
SBYW77E069CC Good Morning Kiss CC .07 .15
SBYW77E069RRRR Good Morning Kiss RRR .40 .80
SBYW77E070CC The Truth Revealed CC .07 .15
SBYW77E071CC Just the Three of Them CC .07 .15
SBYW77E072RR Respective Choices, Shoko Makinohara RR .25 .50
SBYW77E072SPSP Respective Choices, Shoko Makinohara SP50.00 100.00
SBYW77E073RR Reliable Friend, Rio Futaba RR .20 .40
SBYW77E074RR Irreplaceable Existence, Shoko Makinohara RR .60 1.25
SBYW77E075R Future Dreams, Shoko Makinohara R .10 .20
SBYW77E075SSR Future Dreams, Shoko Makinohara SR 1.25 2.50
SBYW77E076R Special Existence, Shoko Makinohara R .10 .20
SBYW77E076SSR Special Existence, Shoko Makinohara SR 1.50 3.00
SBYW77E077R Sudden Confession, Shoko Makinohara R .10 .20
SBYW77E077SSR Sudden Confession, Shoko Makinohara SR .25 .50
SBYW77E078R Date Invitation, Shoko Makinohara R .07 .15
SBYW77E079R Theory on the Wound, Rio Futaba R .12 .25
SBYW77E080R Reasons for Attraction, Shoko Makinohara R .12 .25
SBYW77E080SSR Reasons for Attraction, Shoko Makinohara SR1.00 2.00
SBYW77E081R Date Plans, Tomoe Koga R .12 .25
SBYW77E081SSR Date Plans, Tomoe Koga SR 1.00 2.00
SBYW77E082U Nostalgic Topic, Shoko Makinohara U .12 .25
SBYW77E083U Contents of the Printout, Rio Futaba U .07 .15
SBYW77E084U Wedding Dress Try-On, Shoko Makinohara U .07 .15
SBYW77E085U To Return to the Present, Shoko Makinohara U .07 .15
SBYW77E086U Homework Left Undone, Shoko Makinohara U .15 .30
SBYW77E087U Unraveling the Superstring Theory"" Rio Futaba U.12 .25
SBYW77E088C Quantum Entanglement"" Tomoe Koga C .07 .15
SBYW77E089C Checking the Printout, Sakuta Azusagawa C .07 .15
SBYW77E090C Ordinary Days, Rio Futaba C .10 .20
SBYW77E091C Bathing Hayate, Shoko Makinohara C .07 .15
SBYW77E092C Quantum Entanglement"" Sakuta Azusagawa C .25 .50
SBYW77E093C Usual Conversational Exchange, Tomoe Koga C .07 .15
SBYW77E094C Incident in a Dream, Shoko Makinohara C .07 .15
SBYW77E095C Worrying Over a Friend, Yuma Kunimi C .07 .15
SBYW77E096aU Future Plans (a) U .07 .15
SBYW77E096bU Future Plans (b) U .07 .15
SBYW77E097U Marking Homework U .07 .15
SBYW77E098CR Complicated State of Mind CR .10 .20
SBYW77E098RRRR Complicated State of Mind RRR 2.50 5.00
SBYW77E099CR Memory of First Love CR .07 .15
SBYW77E099RRRR Memory of First Love RRR 1.25 2.50
SBYW77E100CR The Future They Finally Reached CR .10 .20
SBYW77E100RRRR The Future They Finally Reached RRR 2.00 4.00
SBYW77E101PR Chibi Nodoka P .20 .40
SBYW77E101SPR Chibi Nodoka P FOIL 2.50 5.00

SBYW77E102PR Chibi Tomoe P .25 .50
SBYW77E102SPR Chibi Tomoe P FOIL 2.50 5.00
SBYW77E103PR Chibi Mai P 1.25 2.50
SBYW77E103SPR Chibi Mai P FOIL 2.50 5.00
SBYW77E104PR Chibi Kaede P .25 .50
SBYW77E104SPR Chibi Kaede P FOIL 2.50 5.00
SBYW77E105PR Chibi Shoko P .30 .75
SBYW77E105SPR Chibi Shoko P FOIL 2.00 4.00
SBYW77E106PR Chibi Futaba P .25 .50
SBYW77E106SPR Chibi Futaba P FOIL 1.25 2.50

2022 Weiss Schwarz Rent-A-Girlfriend

KNKW86E001RR Ex-Girlfriend, Mami RR 1.25 2.50
KNKW86E001SSPSSP Ex-Girlfriend, Mami SSP 200.00 400.00
KNKW86E002RR Mami Nanami RR .60 1.25
KNKW86E002SPSP Mami Nanami SP 100.00 200.00
KNKW86E003R Memories Between the Two, Mami R .25 .50
KNKW86E003SSR Memories Between the Two, Mami SR 25.00 50.00
KNKW86E004R Centimeter, Mami R .25 .50
KNKW86E004SSR Centimeter, Mami SR 1.50 3.00
KNKW86E005R Equally Bad, Mami R .25 .50
KNKW86E005SSR Equally Bad, Mami SR 2.00 4.00
KNKW86E006R Done With Love, Mami R .25 .50
KNKW86E006SSR Done With Love, Mami SR 1.50 3.00
KNKW86E007U Through a Viewfinder, Mami U .15 .30
KNKW86E008U Annoying... Mami U .15 .30
KNKW86E009U As an Ex-Girlfriend, Mami U .15 .30
KNKW86E010C First Girlfriend, Mami C .12 .25
KNKW86E011C Bungee Jump of Confession, Mami C .12 .25
KNKW86E012C Fated One Mami C .12 .25
KNKW86E013C Usual Dynamic, Mami C .12 .25
KNKW86E014C Casual Greeting, Mami C .12 .25
KNKW86E015C Broken Promise, Mami C .12 .25
KNKW86E016U Could You Stop? U .15 .30
KNKW86E017CR Compared to When We Were Dating CR .20 .40
KNKW86E017RRRR Compared to When We Were Dating RRR 4.00 8.00
KNKW86E018CC Let's Date CC .12 .25
KNKW86E019RR Ruka Sarashina RR 2.50 5.00
KNKW86E019SPSP Ruka Sarashina SP 100.00 200.00
KNKW86E020RR Sumi Sakurasawa RR .60 1.25
KNKW86E020SPSP Sumi Sakurasawa SP 75.00 150.00
KNKW86E021RR Treasured Moment, Chizuru RR .60 1.25
KNKW86E021SSR Treasured Moment, Chizuru SR 10.00 20.00
KNKW86E022R Fantasy Date, Chizuru R .25 .50
KNKW86E022SSR Fantasy Date, Chizuru SR 4.00 8.00
KNKW86E023R Centimeter, Sumi R .25 .50
KNKW86E023SSR Centimeter, Sumi SR 2.50 5.00
KNKW86E024R Challenging for the First Time, Sumi R .25 .50
KNKW86E024SSR Challenging for the First Time, Sumi SR 2.00 4.00
KNKW86E025R While I'm Your Girlfriend, Chizuru R .25 .50
KNKW86E025SSR While I'm Your Girlfriend, Chizuru SR 5.00 10.00
KNKW86E026R About Kazuya, Mami R .25 .50
KNKW86E026SSR About Kazuya, Mami SR 2.00 4.00
KNKW86E027R Waiting Impatiently, Sumi R .25 .50
KNKW86E027SSR Waiting Impatiently, Sumi SR 1.25 2.50
KNKW86E028R Secret Date, Ruka R .25 .50
KNKW86E029U Serious Gaze, Chizuru U .15 .30
KNKW86E030U Practicing Smiling, Sumi U .15 .30
KNKW86E031U Relaxing Through Exercise, Sumi U .15 .30
KNKW86E032U Let's Not Mami U .15 .30
KNKW86E033U Offering a Bite, Sumi U .15 .30
KNKW86E034C Not a Kiss, Chizuru C .12 .25
KNKW86E035C Bungee Jump of Confession, Sumi C .12 .25
KNKW86E036C Important Conversation, Ruka C .12 .25
KNKW86E037C Balcony at 9pm, Chizuru C .12 .25
KNKW86E038C Realizing the Truth, Mami C .12 .25
KNKW86E039C Confused, Sumi C .12 .25
KNKW86E040C Calling Out Accurately, Ruka C .12 .25
KNKW86E041C Straw Hat, Chizuru C .12 .25
KNKW86E042C Are You an Idiot!? Chizuru C .12 .25
KNKW86E043U Embarrassed Maiden U .15 .30
KNKW86E044CC Proof of Lovers CC .12 .25
KNKW86E045CC Problem Between the Two CC .12 .25
KNKW86E045RRRR Problem Between the Two RRR 1.50 3.00
KNKW86E046CC Look Here, Kazuya! CC .12 .25
KNKW86E047CC Towards Her Goal CC .12 .25
KNKW86E047RRRR Towards Her Goal RRR 3.00 6.00
KNKW86E048CC Surprisingly Resilient? CC .12 .25
KNKW86E049RR Shy Girlfriend, Sumi RR 1.50 3.00
KNKW86E049SSPSSP Shy Girlfriend, Sumi SSP 200.00 400.00
KNKW86E050RR Chizuru Mizuhara RR 1.00 2.00
KNKW86E050SPSP Chizuru Mizuhara SP 125.00 250.00
KNKW86E051RR Everyone's Girlfriend, Chizuru RR 2.00 4.00
KNKW86E051SSPSSP Everyone's Girlfriend, Chizuru SSP 750.00 1,500.00
KNKW86E052R Non-Refundable Feelings, Chizuru R .25 .50
KNKW86E053R Filling the Hole in the Heart, Chizuru R .25 .50
KNKW86E053SSR Filling the Hole in the Heart, Chizuru SR 3.00 6.00
KNKW86E054R Clearing Things Up, Chizuru R .25 .50
KNKW86E055R Morning Routine, Sumi R .25 .50
KNKW86E055SSR Morning Routine, Sumi SR 10.00 20.00
KNKW86E056R You're the One Chizuru R .25 .50
KNKW86E056SSR You're the One Chizuru SR 3.00 6.00
KNKW86E057R High-End Specs, Sumi R .25 .50
KNKW86E057SSR High-End Specs, Sumi SR 2.50 5.00
KNKW86E058U Bungee Jump of Confession, Chizuru U .15 .30
KNKW86E059U Merry Christmas, Chizuru U .15 .30
KNKW86E060U One Question Chizuru U .15 .30
KNKW86E061U First Date, Chizuru U .15 .30
KNKW86E062U Sudden Visitor, Chizuru U .15 .30
KNKW86E063U Nerves of Steel, Chizuru U .15 .30
KNKW86E064U Step by Step, Sumi U .15 .30
KNKW86E065C Overly Shy Sumi C .12 .25
KNKW86E066C Lucky Lecher, Chizuru C .12 .25
KNKW86E067C Bowling, Sumi C .12 .25
KNKW86E068C Happy New Year, Chizuru C .12 .25
KNKW86E069C Meeting at the Station, Chizuru C .12 .25
KNKW86E070C An Opportunity To Take, Chizuru C .12 .25
KNKW86E071C Sea and Girlfriend, Chizuru C .12 .25
KNKW86E072U Um... Do You Mind? U .15 .30
KNKW86E073U This Month's #1 U .15 .30
KNKW86E074CR An Apology Present CR .20 .40
KNKW86E074RRRR An Apology Present RRR 6.00 12.00
KNKW86E075CR Routine Walk CR .20 .40
KNKW86E075RRRR Routine Walk RRR 5.00 10.00
KNKW86E076CC Each Other's Feelings CC .12 .25
KNKW86E076RRRR Each Other's Feelings RRR 7.50 15.00
KNKW86E077RR Bouldering Date, Ruka RR 1.50 3.00
KNKW86E077SSR Bouldering Date, Ruka SR 12.50 25.00
KNKW86E078RR I'm an Adult Ruka RR .25 .50
KNKW86E078SSPSSP I'm an Adult Ruka SSP 200.00 400.00
KNKW86E079R At Least a Trial Run, Ruka R .25 .50
KNKW86E079SSR At Least a Trial Run, Ruka SR 1.50 3.00
KNKW86E080R Cheater!! Ruka R .25 .50
KNKW86E081R What Do You Think? Ruka R .25 .50
KNKW86E081SSR What Do You Think? Ruka SR 5.00 10.00
KNKW86E082R Say Ahh Ruka R .25 .50
KNKW86E082SSR Say Ahh Ruka SR 4.00 8.00
KNKW86E083R I'm the Girlfriend, Ruka R .25 .50
KNKW86E083SSR I'm the Girlfriend, Ruka SR 7.50 15.00
KNKW86E084U Hugs Ruka U .15 .30
KNKW86E085U We Finally Meet, Ruka U .15 .30
KNKW86E086U Girlfriend and Girlfriend, Ruka U .15 .30
KNKW86E087U Why Are You Here!? Ruka U .15 .30
KNKW86E088U Friend's Girlfriend, Ruka U .15 .30
KNKW86E089U Is There Something in This Room? Ruka U .15 .30
KNKW86E090U Come Along Blindfolded Ruka U .15 .30
KNKW86E091C Bungee Jump of Confession, Ruka C .12 .25
KNKW86E092C Happy New Year, Ruka C .12 .25
KNKW86E093C I Can't Take it! Ruka C .12 .25
KNKW86E094C The Real Me, Ruka C .12 .25
KNKW86E095C My Position, Ruka C .12 .25
KNKW86E096C A Move in a Battle of Endurance, Ruka C .12 .25
KNKW86E097U Just a Little More U .15 .30
KNKW86E098U Shut Up and Come Along! U .15 .30
KNKW86E099CR I am Fully Prepared!!! CR .25 .50
KNKW86E099RRRR I am Fully Prepared!!! RRR 6.00 12.00
KNKW86E100CC Increased Heartrate CC .12 .25
KNKW86E100RRRR Increased Heartrate RRR 6.00 12.00

2022 Weiss Schwarz Rent-A-Girlfriend Trial Deck

KNKW86TE01TD Coincidental Reunion, Mami .20 .40
KNKW86TE02TD Chilly Gaze, Mami .20 .40
KNKW86TE03SSR Original Appearance, Ruka SR .75 1.50
KNKW86TE03TD Original Appearance, Ruka .20 .40
KNKW86TE04TD Waiting Impatiently, Ruka .20 .40
KNKW86TE05TD Suspicious Gaze, Ruka .20 .40
KNKW86TE06TD Parting Words, Ruka .20 .40
KNKW86TE07RRRR Mysterious Cute Girl, Ruka RRR 6.00 12.00
KNKW86TE07TD Mysterious Cute Girl, Ruka .20 .40
KNKW86TE08RRRR Unexpected Words, Mami RRR 7.50 15.00
KNKW86TE08TD Unexpected Words, Mami .20 .40
KNKW86TE09RRRR Through a Viewfinder, Sumi RRR 7.50 15.00
KNKW86TE09TD Through a Viewfinder, Sumi .20 .40
KNKW86TE10TD Please Go Out With Me!! .20 .40
KNKW86TE11TD Subtle Distance, Kazuya .20 .40
KNKW86TE12TD The Start of Chaos, Chizuru .20 .40
KNKW86TE13TD Beyond Reach, Kazuya .20 .40
KNKW86TE14SPSP Rental Girlfriend, Chizuru SP 250.00 500.00
KNKW86TE14TD Rental Girlfriend, Chizuru .75 1.50
KNKW86TE15SSR Ideal Lover, Chizuru SR .75 1.50
KNKW86TE15TD Ideal Lover, Chizuru .60 1.25
KNKW86TE16TD Subtle Distance, Chizuru .20 .40
KNKW86TE17TD Girlfriend's Late Arrival, Chizuru .30 .75
KNKW86TE18TD Not a Word to Anyone! .20 .40
KNKW86TE19TD Girlfriend Mode .20 .40

2022 Weiss Schwarz Saekano How to Raise a Boring Girlfriend

SHSW56E001RR Qualities of a Maiden, Eriri RR .15 .30
SHSW56E001SPSP Qualities of a Maiden, Eriri SP 30.00 75.00
SHSW56E002RR Tomoya's Beloved Disciple, Izumi RR .10 .20
SHSW56E002SPSP Tomoya's Beloved Disciple, Izumi SP 20.00 40.00
SHSW56E003RR Tsundere Trope Childhood Friend, Eriri RR .10 .20
SHSW56E003SSR Tsundere Trope Childhood Friend, Eriri SR 5.00 10.00
SHSW56E004R Nostalgic Memory, Eriri R 4.00 8.00
SHSW56E005R Unexpected Gift, Izumi R 1.25 2.50
SHSW56E005SSR Unexpected Gift, Izumi SR 10.00 20.00
SHSW56E006R What Separates the Two, Eriri R .20 .40
SHSW56E006SSR What Separates the Two, Eriri SR 3.00 6.00
SHSW56E007R blessing software, Eriri R .12 .25
SHSW56E008R Confronting the Past, Eriri R .12 .25
SHSW56E009R The Morning of the Battle, Izumi R .10 .20
SHSW56E010R Fancy Wave, Izumi R .12 .25
SHSW56E011R Flustered, Eriri R .07 .15
SHSW56E012U Critiquing the Proposal, Eriri U .07 .15
SHSW56E013U Overflowing Talent, Izumi U .12 .25
SHSW56E014U Training Camp With Everyone, Eriri U .10 .20
SHSW56E015U Prince of Otaku, Tomoya U .07 .15
SHSW56E016C Strong Fixation, Izumi C .07 .15
SHSW56E017C Who She Admired, Izumi C .07 .15
SHSW56E018C In a Tracksuit and Glasses, Eriri C .07 .15
SHSW56E019C Little Sister Trope Kouhai, Izumi C .07 .15
SHSW56E020C Event Disguise, Eriri C .15 .30
SHSW56E021C Sold Out for the First Time, Izumi C .07 .15
SHSW56E022C Staring, Eriri C .07 .15
SHSW56E023C Middle Schooler Led Astray, Izumi C .07 .15
SHSW56E024U Tomoya's Proposal (24) U .07 .15
SHSW56E025U Little Love Rhapsody U .07 .15
SHSW56E026U Eri Kashiwagi's LLR Autograph Board U .07 .15
SHSW56E027CR A Separate Route After 8 Years CR .10 .20
SHSW56E027RRRR A Separate Route After 8 Years RRR .50 1.00
SHSW56E028CC Cheap Knockoff Childhood Friends CC .07 .15
SHSW56E029CC Enemy? Ally? Or a New Character? CC .07 .15
SHSW56E029RRRR Enemy? Ally? Or a New Character? RRR 1.25 2.50
SHSW56E030CC Reliable Helpers CC .07 .15
SHSW56E031RR Reliable Senior, Utaha RR .75 1.50
SHSW56E031SSR Reliable Senior, Utaha SR 3.00 6.00
SHSW56E032RR Ideal Girl, Megumi RR .50 1.00
SHSW56E032SPSP Ideal Girl, Megumi SP 60.00 125.00
SHSW56E033R Invading the Battlefield, Eriri R .12 .25
SHSW56E034R Unnecessary Concern, Megumi R .15 .30
SHSW56E035R No Flags Raised, Megumi R .12 .25
SHSW56E035SSR No Flags Raised, Megumi SR 2.50 5.00
SHSW56E036R Dark Side of Creators, Utaha R .12 .25
SHSW56E037R blessing software, Megumi R .15 .30
SHSW56E038R Faint Presence, Megumi R .12 .25
SHSW56E038SSR Faint Presence, Megumi SR 4.00 8.00
SHSW56E039U Vain Resistance, Eriri U .07 .15
SHSW56E040U Image Change, Megumi U .12 .25
SHSW56E041U Mysterious Intimidation, Megumi U .07 .15
SHSW56E042U Anger Voltage, Eriri U .07 .15
SHSW56E043U Insufficient Facial Expressions, Megumi U .07 .15
SHSW56E044U Advice From a Senpai, Utaha U .10 .20
SHSW56E045C Sudden Revelation, Tomoya C .07 .15
SHSW56E046C Costume Design, Eriri C .07 .15
SHSW56E047C Acting Director, Utaha C .07 .15
SHSW56E048C Mad Expression, Megumi C .07 .15
SHSW56E049C Unexpected Words, Megumi C .07 .15
SHSW56E050C Watching a Live Concert Together, Megumi C .07 .15
SHSW56E051C Sense of Rivalry, Eriri C .07 .15
SHSW56E052U Pulling an All-Nighter to Game U .60 1.25
SHSW56E053CR How to Raise a Boring Girlfriend CR .15 .30
SHSW56E053RRRR How to Raise a Boring Girlfriend RRR 10.00 20.00
SHSW56E054CC Cost of Pulling an All-Nighter CC .07 .15
SHSW56E055CC Being Serious in Creating Games CC .07 .15
SHSW56E056RR The Night Together, Utaha RR 7.50 15.00
SHSW56E056SSR The Night Together, Utaha SR 20.00 40.00
SHSW56E057RR Tale About Achieving a Dream, Megumi RR .50 1.00
SHSW56E057SSR Tale About Achieving a Dream, Megumi SR 2.50 5.00
SHSW56E058RR Variety of Outfits, Megumi RR 1.50 3.00
SHSW56E058SSR Variety of Outfits, Megumi SR 4.00 8.00
SHSW56E059RR Pride of Creators, Utaha RR .60 1.25
SHSW56E059SPSP Pride of Creators, Utaha SP 60.00 125.00
SHSW56E059SPSP Pride of Creators, Utaha SP/10 50.00 100.00
SHSW56E060R Victory Through Persistence, Utaha R .15 .30
SHSW56E061R Vulgar Incitement, Utaha R .12 .25
SHSW56E062R Beginning of a Long Night, Utaha R .12 .25
SHSW56E063R The Battle at Rokutenba Mall, Megumi R .15 .30
SHSW56E064R blessing software, Utaha R .12 .25
SHSW56E064SSR blessing software, Utaha SR 1.00 2.00
SHSW56E065U First Autograph Event, Utaha U .15 .30
SHSW56E066U Sharp Tongue Trope Senpai, Utaha U .10 .20
SHSW56E067U Critiquing the Proposal, Utaha U .12 .25
SHSW56E068U Smug Decision, Tomoya U .10 .20
SHSW56E069U Utako Kasumi's Editor, Sonoko U .12 .25
SHSW56E070C Unconcealable Hostility, Utaha C .10 .20
SHSW56E071C Exposing Her Embarrassment, Megumi C .07 .15
SHSW56E072C The Peak of Confusion, Utaha C .07 .15
SHSW56E073C The Morning Together, Utaha C .07 .15
SHSW56E074C Training Camp With Everyone, Utaha C .07 .15
SHSW56E075C Closing the Distance, Megumi C .07 .15
SHSW56E076U Fading Highlight U .12 .25
SHSW56E077U Tomoya's Proposal (77) U .12 .25
SHSW56E078CR Choices During the Night Together CR .12 .25
SHSW56E078RRRR Choices During the Night Together RRR 2.50 5.00
SHSW56E079CC Metronome in Love CC .12 .25
SHSW56E080CC Passed-By Date Event CC .07 .15
SHSW56E080RRRR Passed-By Date Event RRR 1.25 2.50
SHSW56E081RR icy tail, Michiru RR .75 1.50
SHSW56E081SPSP icy tail, Michiru SP 30.00 60.00
SHSW56E082R Unwavering Dream, Michiru R .07 .15
SHSW56E083R Childhood Friends From Birth, Michiru R .07 .15
SHSW56E083SSR Childhood Friends From Birth, Michiru SP 1.25 2.50
SHSW56E084R Live Costume, Michiru R .15 .30
SHSW56E084SSR Live Costume, Michiru SP .75 1.50
SHSW56E085U Live Costume, Tokino R .07 .15
SHSW56E086U Training Camp With Everyone, Michiru U .10 .20
SHSW56E087U Cool Boy, Tomoya U .12 .25
SHSW56E088U icy tail, Ranko U .10 .20
SHSW56E089U icy tail, Echika U .12 .25
SHSW56E090U blessing software, Michiru U .12 .25
SHSW56E091C Delightful Surprise, Michiru C .07 .15
SHSW56E092C Shocking Truth, Michiru C .12 .25
SHSW56E093C icy tail, Tokino C .12 .25
SHSW56E094C Nostalgic Memory, Michiru C .07 .15
SHSW56E095C Live Costume, Echika C .07 .15
SHSW56E096C Promise Made at the Lake, Michiru C .07 .15
SHSW56E097C Live Costume, Ranko C .12 .25
SHSW56E098U The Truth of icy tail U .10 .20
SHSW56E099CR icy tail CR .12 .25
SHSW56E099RRRR Icy tail RRR 2.50 5.00
SHSW56E100CC Memories of a Faint Love CC .07 .15
SHSW56E101PR Nendoroid Plus, Eriri P 1.25 2.50
SHSW56E101SPR Nendoroid Plus, Eriri FOIL P .60 1.25
SHSW56E102PR Nendoroid Plus, Izumi P .07 .15
SHSW56E102SPR Nendoroid Plus, Izumi FOIL P 2.00 4.00
SHSW56E103PR Nendoroid Plus, Megumi P 1.50 3.00
SHSW56E103SPR Nendoroid Plus, Megumi FOIL P .30 .75
SHSW56E104PR Nendoroid Plus, Utaha P 1.50 3.00
SHSW56E104SPR Nendoroid Plus, Utaha FOIL P 2.00 4.00
SHSW56E105PR Nendoroid Plus, Michiru P .75 1.50
SHSW56E105SPR Nendoroid Plus, Michiru FOIL P .20 .40
SHSW56PE06PR Flat Position, Megumi P .30 .60
SHSW56PE07PR Stealthy Classmate, Megumi P 5.00 10.00

2022 Weiss Schwarz Saekano How to Raise a Boring Girlfriend Trial Deck

SHSW56TE01TD Closet Otaku, Eriri .05 .10
SHSW56TE02TD Annoyed, Eriri .07 .15
SHSW56TE03TD At Loggerheads, Eriri .05 .10
SHSW56TE04RRRR Main Heroine In-Charge, Megumi RRR 50.00 100.00
SHSW56TE04SSR Main Heroine In-Charge, Megumi SP 1.25 3.00
SHSW56TE04TD Main Heroine In-Charge, Megumi .12 .25
SHSW56TE05TD The Day It All Begins, Tomoya .05 .10
SHSW56TE06TD Moved to Tears, Tomoya .07 .15
SHSW56TE07TD Encouragement, Megumi .07 .15
SHSW56TE08TD Staring Daggers, Eriri .07 .15
SHSW56TE09RRRR Illustration In-Charge, Eriri RRR 30.00 60.00
SHSW56TE09TD Illustration In-Charge, Eriri .10 .20
SHSW56TE10TD Face to Face With Destiny .07 .15
SHSW56TE11TD Super-Popular Illustrator, Eri Kashiwagi .05 .10
SHSW56TE12TD Slope Where They First Met, Megumi .07 .15
SHSW56TE13SPSP Fated Encounter? Megumi SR 60.00 125.00
SHSW56TE13TD Fated Encounter? Megumi .07 .15
SHSW56TE14TD Irresponsible and Carefree Attitude, Megumi .12 .25
SHSW56TE15TD Cold Stare, Utaha .07 .15
SHSW56TE16TD At Loggerheads, Utaha .05 .10
SHSW56TE17TD Bewilderment and Desolateness, Utaha .05 .10
SHSW56TE18RRRR Scenario Writing In-Charge, Utaha RRR 25.00 50.00
SHSW56TE18SSR Scenario Writing In-Charge, Utaha SP .20 .40
SHSW56TE18TD Scenario Writing In-Charge, Utaha .12 .25
SHSW56TE19TD Waiting in Vain .07 .15
SHSW56TE20TD High School Author, Utako Kasumi .05 .10

2022 Weiss Schwarz Star Wars Comeback Edition

SWS49001RR Escape from the First Order Finn RR 2.00 5.00
SWS49001RRRR Escape from the First Order Fin RRR FOIL 3.00 6.00
SWS49002RR Smuggler Han Solo RR 5.00 12.00
SWS49002SPSP Smuggler Han Solo SP FOIL 75.00 200.00
SWS49003reRR Secret Mission Leia RR 6.00 15.00
SWS49003SreSR Secret Mission Leia SR FOIL 12.50 30.00
SWS49004R Lightsaber in hand Finn R 1.50 4.00
SWS49005reR Rogue Han Solo R 5.00 12.00
SWS49005SreSR Rogue Han Solo SR FOIL 15.00 40.00
SWS49006R Han Solo R 2.00 5.00
SWS49007R Captain of the Millennium Falcon Han Solo R 2.00 5.00
SWS49007SSR Captain of the Millennium Falcon Han Solo SR FOIL2.00 5.00
SWS49008R New name Fin R 1.50 4.00
SWS49008SSR New name Fin SR FOIL 3.00 8.00
SWS49009R Starfighter Pilot Poe R 1.50 4.00
SWS49010reR Wookie Roar Chewbacca R 4.00 10.00
SWS49011U Force Lineage Leia U 2.00 5.00
SWS49012U Turn the tables Chewbacca U 2.00 5.00
SWS49013U Maz Kanata U 1.50 4.00
SWS49014U Rescue Chewbacca U 1.50 4.00
SWS49015U Ewoks U 1.50 4.00
SWS49016U Lando Calrissian U 1.50 4.00
SWS49017U Reunion Po U 1.50 4.00
SWS49018C Thoughts for my son Han Solo & Leia C 1.50 4.00
SWS49019C Wicket C 1.50 4.00
SWS49020C Nine Nan C 1.50 4.00
SWS49021C Robot C 1.50 4.00
SWS49022C Back and forth battle Han Solo C 1.50 4.00
SWS49023C Princess Leia C 1.50 4.00
SWS49024C Rescue Operation Han Solo C 1.50 4.00
SWS49025C Wookie Chewbacca C 1.50 4.00
SWS49026C Admiral Ackbar C 1.50 4.00
SWS49027U Jakku U 1.50 4.00
SWS49028U Dejarik Holochess U 1.50 4.00
SWS49029C X-wing starfighter C 1.50 4.00
SWS49030C Millennium Falcon C 1.50 4.00
SWS49031CR Mission! CR 1.50 4.00
SWS49031SWRSWR Mission! SWR FOIL 15.00 40.00
SWS49032reCC Medal Ceremony CC 1.50 4.00
SWS49032SWRreSWR Medal Ceremony SWR FOIL 40.00 100.00

SWS49032SWReSWR Medal Ceremony SWR	20.00	50.00
SWS49033CC I can do this! CC	1.50	4.00
SWS49034CC Brilliant battle CC	1.50	4.00
SWS49035RR Bushi's True Identity Leia RR	3.00	8.00
SWS49035RRRR Bushi's True Identity Leia RRR FOIL	6.00	15.00
SWS49036R Jabba the Hut R	3.00	8.00
SWS49037R Boba Fett R	1.50	4.00
SWS49038U Message and Gift Java U	1.50	4.00
SWS49039U Bib Fortuna U	1.50	4.00
SWS49040U Desert Crime King Jabba U	1.50	4.00
SWS49041U Combat Professional Boba Fett U	1.50	4.00
SWS49042C Gamorrian C	1.50	4.00
SWS49043C Hidden Mission R2-D2 C	1.50	4.00
SWS49044C Anchor platform C	1.50	4.00
SWS49045aC Max Revo Band C	1.50	4.00
SWS49045bC Max Revo Band C	1.50	4.00
SWS49045cC Max Revo Band C	1.50	4.00
SWS49046C New Rice Flipping System C-3PO C	1.50	4.00
SWS49047C Tiger Observation Land C	1.50	4.00
SWS49048U Cantina Band U	1.50	4.00
SWS49049U Carbon Freezing U	1.50	4.00
SWS49050C The Sarlacc Pit C	1.50	4.00
SWS49051CC Jabba's Palace CC	1.50	4.00
SWS49052CC Bounty hunter CC	1.50	4.00
SWS49053RR Reunion and Death Struggle Darth Vader RR	5.00	12.00
SWS49053RRRR Reunion and Deadly Fight Darth Vader RRR FOIL	15.00	40.00
SWS49054reRR Kylo Ren RR	5.00	12.00
SWS49054RreRRR Kylo Ren RRR FOIL	6.00	15.00
SWS49054RrReRRR Kylo Ren RRR FOIL	15.00	40.00
SWS49055reRR Dark Lord of the Sith Darth Vader RR	15.00	40.00
SWS49055SPreSP Dark Lord of the Sith Darth Vader SP FOIL	150.00	400.00
SWS49056R Dark Side Darth Vader R	5.00	12.00
SWS49056RRRR Dark Side Darth Vader RRR FOIL	12.00	30.00
SWS49057R Mask Removed Kylo Ren R	3.00	6.00
SWS49057SSR Mask Removed Kylo Ren SR FOIL	6.00	12.00
SWS49058R Commander of Darkness Kylo Ren R	2.00	5.00
SWS49059R Rush Darth Vader R	2.00	5.00
SWS49060reR The Evil One Darth Vader R	4.00	10.00
SWS49060SreSR The Evil One Darth Vader SR FOIL	10.00	25.00
SWS49061R Supreme Leader Snoke R	1.50	4.00
SWS49062R Emperor R	1.50	4.00
SWS49063SSR Stormtrooper SR FOIL	4.00	10.00
SWS49063U Stormtrooper U	1.50	4.00
SWS49064U Captain Phasma U	1.50	4.00
SWS49065U Skillful Pilot Darth Vader U	1.50	4.00
SWS49066U Persistence to compete Kylo Ren U	1.50	4.00
SWS49067U General Hux U	1.50	4.00
SWS49068U Overconfidence is prohibited Darth Vader U	1.50	4.00
SWS49069U Heir to the Will Kylo Ren U	1.50	4.00
SWS49070C FN-2187 Stormtrooper C	1.50	4.00
SWS49071C Many Soldiers Stormtrooper C	1.50	4.00
SWS49072C First Order Stormtrooper C	1.50	4.00
SWS49073C Admiral Piet C	1.50	4.00
SWS49074C Grand Moff Wilhuff Tarkin C	1.50	4.00
SWS49075reC New vanguard Stormtrooper C	1.50	4.00
SWS49076C Scout Trooper C	1.50	4.00
SWS49076SSR Scout Trooper SR FOIL	5.00	12.00
SWS49077C Dark Menace Darth Vader C	1.50	4.00
SWS49078C Ruler of Dark Side Emperor C	1.50	4.00
SWS49079U Star Destroyer U	1.50	4.00
SWS49080U The Dark Side U	1.50	4.00
SWS49081U Death Star U	1.50	4.00
SWS49082C Lightsaber Duel C	1.50	4.00
SWS49083reCR I am your father. CR	3.00	8.00
SWS49083SWReSWR I am your father. SWR	75.00	200.00
SWS49083SWRreSWR I am your father. SWR FOIL	60.00	150.00
SWS49084CC You are beaten. CC	1.50	4.00
SWS49085CC Show me CC	1.50	4.00
SWS49085SWRSWR Show me SWR	12.00	30.00
SWS49085SWRSWR Show me SWR FOIL	10.00	25.00
SWS49086CC Starkiller CC	1.50	4.00
SWS49087RR R2-D2 RR	25.00	60.00
SWS49087RRRR R2-D2 RRR FOIL	25.00	60.00
SWS49088reRR Awakening Rey RR	5.00	10.00
SWS49088SPreSP Awakening Rey SP FOIL	40.00	100.00
SWS49089reRR Young man chasing his dreams Luke RR	10.00	25.00
SWS49089SPreSP Young man chasing his dreams Luke SP FOIL	75.00	200.00
SWS49090R Jedi Training Luke R	3.00	8.00
SWS49090SSR Jedi Training Luke SR FOIL	4.00	10.00
SWS49091R Qualities of a Pilot Ray R	2.00	5.00
SWS49091RRRR Pilot Qualities Ray RRR FOIL	5.00	12.00
SWS49092R Courageous Supporter C-3PO R	1.50	4.00
SWS49093R Astromech Droid R2-D2 R	1.50	4.00
SWS49093SSR Astromech Droid R2-D2 SR FOIL	4.00	10.00
SWS49094reR Moment of Counterattack Luke R	4.00	10.00
SWS49095R Yoda R	1.50	4.00
SWS49095SSR Yoda SR FOIL	4.00	8.00
SWS49096R Teachings of the Sage Obi-Wan R	1.50	4.00
SWS49097R Fateful Encounter Luke R	2.00	5.00
SWS49097RRRR Fate Encounter Luke RRR FOIL	6.00	15.00
SWS49098U Desert Recluse Ben Kenobi U	1.50	4.00
SWS49099U Long-awaited good news R2-D2 U	1.50	4.00
SWS49100reU Lovable partner C-3PO U	1.50	4.00
SWS49101U Obi-Wan Kenobi U	1.50	4.00
SWS49102U Jedi Master Luke U	1.50	4.00
SWS49103SSR Premonition of Friendship BB-8 SR FOIL	4.00	10.00
SWS49103U Premonition of Friendship BB-8 U	1.50	4.00
SWS49104reC Jedi Master Yoda C	4.00	10.00
SWS49105C Jedi Knight Luke C	1.50	4.00
SWS49106C Buddy BB-8 C	1.50	4.00
SWS49107C Light Side Luke C	1.50	4.00
SWS49108C Luke Skywalker C	1.50	4.00
SWS49109C C-3PO C	1.50	4.00
SWS49110C Sudden Attack Luke C	1.50	4.00
SWS49111C Shooting Skill Rey C	1.50	4.00
SWS49112C Jedi Master Obi-Wan C	1.50	4.00
SWS49113reU Lightsaber U	1.50	4.00
SWS49114reU Lightsaber U	2.50	6.00
SWS49115U AT-AT U	1.50	4.00
SWS49116C Rey's Speeder C	1.50	4.00
SWS49117CR A New Hope CR	1.50	4.00
SWS49117SWRSWR A New Hope SWR	15.00	40.00
SWS49118CR The Force Awakens CR	2.00	5.00
SWS49118SWRSWR The Force Awakens SWR	12.00	30.00
SWS49118SWRSWR The Force Awakens SWR FOIL	6.00	15.00
SWS49119CC Great Mentor CC	2.00	5.00
SWS49120reCC Return of the Jedi CC	2.50	6.00

2022 Weiss Schwarz Star Wars Comeback Edition Trial Deck

SWS49T01TD The Leftover Jacket Fin	1.50	4.00
SWS49T02TD Hero Han Solo	1.50	4.00
SWS49T03TD Captive Pilot Poe	1.50	4.00
SWS49T04TD Invasion of the Resistance Poe	1.50	4.00
SWS49T05TD Relentless Pursuit Finn	1.50	4.00
SWS49T06TD With a New Determination Han Solo	1.50	4.00
SWS49T07TD With a New Determination Chewbacca	1.50	4.00
SWS49T08TD Deadly Combat in the Forest	1.50	4.00
SWS49T09RRRR The Adventure Begins Rey RRR FOIL	6.00	15.00
SWS49T09TD The Adventure Begins Ray	1.50	4.00
SWS49T10TD Lower Sun Tekka	1.50	4.00
SWS49T11TD To the Land of Jakku BB-8	1.50	4.00
SWS49T12TD Reunion C-3PO	1.50	4.00
SWS49T13RRRR Long sleep R2-D2 RRR FOIL	12.00	30.00
SWS49T13TD Long sleep R2-D2	1.50	4.00
SWS49T14reTD For a modest meal Ray	2.50	6.00
SWS49T15TD Days of Garbage Collection Rey	1.50	4.00
SWS49T16SSR Existence to Protect Rey SR FOIL	4.00	10.00
SWS49T16TD Existence to be protected Rey	1.50	4.00
SWS49T17TD BB unit	1.50	4.00
SWS49T18reTD Escape from Jakku	2.50	6.00
SWS49T19SPSP Those who have the force SP FOIL	25.00	60.00
SWS49T19TD One with Force	2.50	6.00

2022 Weiss Schwarz The Quintessential Quintuplets 2

5HYW90E001OFROFR As an Actress, Ichika Nakano OFR	100.00	200.00
5HYW90E001RR As an Actress, Ichika Nakano RR	2.00	4.00
5HYW90E002RR Awkward Love, Ichika Nakano RR	.20	.40
5HYW90E002SPSSP Awkward Love, Ichika Nakano SSP	100.00	200.00
5HYW90E003R Tutor of the Quintuplets, Futaro Uesugi R	.07	.15
5HYW90E003SSR Tutor of the Quintuplets, Futaro Uesugi SR	1.00	2.00
5HYW90E004HYRHYR Pure Wish, Yotsuba Nakano HYR	30.00	60.00
5HYW90E004R Pure Wish, Yotsuba Nakano R	.12	.25
5HYW90E005HYRHYR Pure Wish, Ichika Nakano HYR	30.00	75.00
5HYW90E005R Pure Wish, Ichika Nakano R	.12	.25
5HYW90E006R Good Actress, Ichika Nakano R	.07	.15
5HYW90E006SSR Good Actress, Ichika Nakano SR	.75	1.50
5HYW90E007R In School Uniform, Ichika Nakano R	.10	.20
5HYW90E007SSR In School Uniform, Ichika Nakano SR	2.00	4.00
5HYW90E008R Always Prioritizing Others, Yotsuba Nakano R	.12	.25
5HYW90E008SSR Always Prioritizing Others, Yotsuba Nakano SR	2.00	4.00
5HYW90E009SSR Rooftop of Memories, Ichika Nakano SR	.40	.80
5HYW90E009U Rooftop of Memories, Ichika Nakano U	.05	.10
5HYW90E010SSR New Year, Yotsuba Nakano SR	1.00	2.00
5HYW90E010U New Year, Yotsuba Nakano U	.10	.20
5HYW90E011SSR Spur-of-the-Moment Reply, Ichika Nakano SR	1.00	2.00
5HYW90E011U Spur-of-the-Moment Reply, Ichika Nakano U	.05	.10
5HYW90E012SSR Cheerful Girl, Yotsuba Nakano SR	.60	1.25
5HYW90E012U Cheerful Girl, Yotsuba Nakano U	.07	.15
5HYW90E013SSR What An Elder Sister Can Do, Ichika Nakano SR	.40	.80
5HYW90E013U What An Elder Sister Can Do, Ichika Nakano U	.05	.10
5HYW90E014C Rena C	.05	.10
5HYW90E014SSR Rena SR	.75	1.50
5HYW90E015C New Year, Ichika Nakano C	.10	.20
5HYW90E015SSR New Year, Ichika Nakano SR	1.25	2.50
5HYW90E016C Preparations for the School Trip, Yotsuba Nakano C	.05	.10
5HYW90E016SSR Preparations for the School Trip, Yotsuba Nakano SR	.40	.80
5HYW90E017C Overconfidence and Carelessness, Ichika Nakano C	.10	.20
5HYW90E017SSR Overconfidence and Carelessness, Ichika Nakano SR	1.75	3.50
5HYW90E018C Irreplaceable Bond, Yotsuba Nakano C	.05	.10
5HYW90E018SSR Irreplaceable Bond, Yotsuba Nakano SR	.75	1.50
5HYW90E019SSR Disguise With Glasses SR	.75	1.50
5HYW90E019U Disguise With Glasses U	.07	.15
5HYW90E020CR A Single Lie CR	.10	.20
5HYW90E020RRRR A Single Lie RRR	1.25	2.50
5HYW90E021CC Intensifying Love CC	.10	.20
5HYW90E021OFROFR Intensifying Love OFR	15.00	30.00
5HYW90E022OFROFR Active Lifestyle, Yotsuba Nakano OFR	20.00	40.00
5HYW90E022RR Active Lifestyle, Yotsuba Nakano RR	.25	.50
5HYW90E023RR What She Yearned For, Yotsuba Nakano RR	.20	.40
5HYW90E023SSPSSP What She Yearned For, Yotsuba Nakano SSP	75.00	150.00
5HYW90E024R Mood Maker, Yotsuba Nakano R	.12	.25
5HYW90E024SSR Mood Maker, Yotsuba Nakano SR	1.50	3.00
5HYW90E025R What I Can Do, Yotsuba Nakano R	.10	.20
5HYW90E025SSR What I Can Do, Yotsuba Nakano SR	.75	1.50
5HYW90E026R New Year, Itsuki Nakano R	.20	.40
5HYW90E026SSR New Year, Itsuki Nakano SR	5.00	10.00
5HYW90E027HYRHYR Pure Wish, Miku Nakano HYR	40.00	80.00
5HYW90E027R Pure Wish, Miku Nakano R	.07	.15
5HYW90E028SSR Conversation With Dad, Itsuki Nakano SR	.75	1.50
5HYW90E028U Conversation With Dad, Itsuki Nakano U	.07	.15
5HYW90E029SSR Like Cats and Dogs, Miku Nakano SR	.75	1.50
5HYW90E029U Like Cats and Dogs, Miku Nakano U	.07	.15
5HYW90E030SSR Dense, Itsuki Nakano SR	.30	.75
5HYW90E030U Dense, Itsuki Nakano U	.07	.15
5HYW90E031SSR Unexpected Gift, Miku Nakano SR	.40	.80
5HYW90E031U Unexpected Gift, Miku Nakano U	.05	.10
5HYW90E032SSR Class Representative, Yotsuba Nakano SR	.75	1.50
5HYW90E032U Class Representative, Yotsuba Nakano U	.12	.25
5HYW90E033SSR Sisterly Love, Yotsuba Nakano SR	.75	1.50
5HYW90E033U Sisterly Love, Yotsuba Nakano U	.05	.10
5HYW90E034SSR Intensive Training, Miku Nakano SR	.75	1.50
5HYW90E034U Intensive Training, Miku Nakano U	.05	.10
5HYW90E035SSR Awkwardness Between the Two, Itsuki Nakano SR	.30	.75
5HYW90E035U Awkwardness Between the Two, Itsuki Nakano U	.05	.10
5HYW90E036C Gifting, Itsuki Nakano C	.05	.10
5HYW90E036SSR Gifting, Itsuki Nakano SR	.60	1.25
5HYW90E037C At a Loss, Yotsuba Nakano C	.05	.10
5HYW90E037SSR At a Loss, Yotsuba Nakano SR	.75	1.50
5HYW90E038C Awkward Atmosphere, Yotsuba Nakano C	.07	.15
5HYW90E038SSR Awkward Atmosphere, Yotsuba Nakano SR	.40	.80
5HYW90E039C Reward for Meritorious Deeds, Yotsuba Nakano C	.07	.15
5HYW90E039SSR Reward for Meritorious Deeds, Yotsuba Nakano SR	.75	1.50
5HYW90E040C On the Search, Miku Nakano C	.05	.10
5HYW90E040SSR On the Search, Miku Nakano SR	.50	1.00
5HYW90E041C Running, Yotsuba Nakano C	.10	.20
5HYW90E041SSR Running, Yotsuba Nakano SR	.50	1.00
5HYW90E042C Irreplaceable Bond, Miku Nakano C	.05	.10
5HYW90E042SSR Irreplaceable Bond, Miku Nakano SR	.75	1.50
5HYW90E043C Irreplaceable Bond, Itsuki Nakano C	.05	.10
5HYW90E043SSR Irreplaceable Bond, Itsuki Nakano SR	1.00	2.00
5HYW90E044SSR Flashcards SR	.75	1.50
5HYW90E044U Flashcards U	.07	.15
5HYW90E045SSR Five Cranes in Return SR	.40	.80
5HYW90E045U Five Cranes in Return U	.05	.10
5HYW90E046CR The World As She Leaps CR	.20	.40
5HYW90E046OFROFR The World As She Leaps OFR	12.50	25.00
5HYW90E047CC A New Choice CC	.05	.10
5HYW90E047RRRR A New Choice RRR	.75	1.50
5HYW90E048CC Memories of the Quintuplets CC	.05	.10
5HYW90E048RRRR Memories of the Quintuplets RRR	4.00	8.00
5HYW90E049OFROFR Gentle and Sincere, Itsuki Nakano OFR	30.00	75.00
5HYW90E049RR Gentle and Sincere, Itsuki Nakano RR	.30	.75
5HYW90E050RR Budding Trust, Itsuki Nakano RR	2.00	4.00
5HYW90E050SSPSSP Budding Trust, Itsuki Nakano SSP	200.00	400.00
5HYW90E051OFROFR Wholehearted Maiden, Nino Nakano OFR	75.00	150.00
5HYW90E051RR Wholehearted Maiden, Nino Nakano RR	1.75	3.50
5HYW90E052RR Love Taking Off, Nino Nakano RR	2.50	5.00
5HYW90E052SSPSSP Love Taking Off, Nino Nakano SSP	400.00	800.00
5HYW90E053R Daily Routine, Nino Nakano R	.25	.50
5HYW90E053SSR Daily Routine, Nino Nakano SR	12.50	25.00
5HYW90E054HYRHYR Pure Wish, Itsuki Nakano HYR	75.00	150.00
5HYW90E054R Pure Wish, Itsuki Nakano R	.75	1.50
5HYW90E055R Towards Her Dream, Itsuki Nakano R	.12	.25
5HYW90E055SSR Towards Her Dream, Itsuki Nakano SR	1.75	3.50
5HYW90E056R Secretly Making an Effort, Ichika Nakano R	.12	.25
5HYW90E056SSR Secretly Making an Effort, Ichika Nakano SR	7.50	15.00
5HYW90E057R Frank Words, Nino Nakano R	.12	.25
5HYW90E057SSR Frank Words, Nino Nakano SR	7.50	15.00
5HYW90E058HYRHYR Pure Wish, Nino Nakano HYR	30.00	60.00
5HYW90E058R Pure Wish, Nino Nakano R	.07	.15
5HYW90E059R Someone Who'll Fall For You, Nino Nakano R	.12	.25
5HYW90E059SSR Someone Who'll Fall For You, Nino Nakano SR	2.50	5.00
5HYW90E060R On a Moonlit Night, Itsuki Nakano R	.10	.20
5HYW90E060SSR On a Moonlit Night, Itsuki Nakano SR	5.00	10.00
5HYW90E061SSR Dozing Off, Ichika Nakano SR	4.00	8.00
5HYW90E061U Dozing Off, Ichika Nakano U	.15	.30
5HYW90E062SSR Reckless, Nino Nakano SR	.75	1.50
5HYW90E062U Reckless, Nino Nakano U	.07	.15
5HYW90E063SSR Good Relations, Itsuki Nakano SR	.75	1.50
5HYW90E063U Good Relations, Itsuki Nakano U	.07	.15
5HYW90E064SSR Rampaging, Itsuki Nakano SR	.75	1.50
5HYW90E064U Rampaging, Itsuki Nakano U	.05	.10
5HYW90E065C Echoing, Itsuki Nakano C	.05	.10
5HYW90E065SSR Echoing, Itsuki Nakano SR	.75	1.50
5HYW90E066C Patissier Outfit, Nino Nakano C	.05	.10
5HYW90E066SSR Patissier Outfit, Nino Nakano SR	1.00	2.00
5HYW90E067C Bath Time, Ichika Nakano C	.05	.10
5HYW90E067SSR Bath Time, Ichika Nakano SR	.75	1.50
5HYW90E068C Monthly Death Anniversary, Itsuki Nakano C	.05	.10
5HYW90E068SSR Monthly Death Anniversary, Itsuki Nakano SR	1.00	2.00
5HYW90E069C Mother in Her Memories, Itsuki Nakano C	.07	.15
5HYW90E069SSR Mother in Her Memories, Itsuki Nakano SR	4.00	8.00
5HYW90E070C Parting Words, Nino Nakano C	.10	.20
5HYW90E070SSR Parting Words, Nino Nakano SR	4.00	8.00
5HYW90E071C New Year, Nino Nakano C	.05	.10
5HYW90E071SSR New Year, Nino Nakano SR	1.25	2.50
5HYW90E072C Wanting to Atone, Ichika Nakano C	.05	.10
5HYW90E072SSR Wanting to Atone, Ichika Nakano SR	.60	1.25
5HYW90E073C Fantasizing, Ichika Nakano C	.10	.20
5HYW90E073SSR Fantasizing, Ichika Nakano SR	1.75	3.50
5HYW90E074C Irreplaceable Bond, Ichika Nakano C	.05	.10
5HYW90E074SSR Irreplaceable Bond, Ichika Nakano SR	1.50	3.00
5HYW90E075R Bell of Vows R	.05	.10
5HYW90E075SSR Bell of Vows SR	.75	1.50
5HYW90E076SSR Codeword SR	15.00	30.00
5HYW90E076U Codeword U	.10	.20
5HYW90E077SSR Runaway Train of Love SR	1.25	2.50
5HYW90E077U Runaway Train of Love U	.07	.15
5HYW90E078CR Straightforward Feelings CR	.30	.75
5HYW90E078OFROFR Straightforward Feelings OFR	75.00	150.00
5HYW90E079CR Visiting Her Mother's Grave CR	.25	.50
5HYW90E079OFROFR Visiting Her Mother's Grave OFR	50.00	100.00
5HYW90E080CC Unstoppable Feelings CC	.12	.25
5HYW90E080RRRR Unstoppable Feelings RRR	7.50	15.00
5HYW90E081CC Under the Moonlight CC	.07	.15
5HYW90E081RRRR Under the Moonlight RRR	2.50	5.00
5HYW90E082OFROFR Devoted Feelings, Miku Nakano OFR	30.00	75.00
5HYW90E082RR Devoted Feelings, Miku Nakano RR	.25	.50
5HYW90E083RR Confession of Love, Miku Nakano RR	.15	.30
5HYW90E083SSPSSP Confession of Love, Miku Nakano SSP	150.00	300.00
5HYW90E084R In a Kimono, Miku Nakano R	.07	.15
5HYW90E084SSR In a Kimono, Miku Nakano SR	1.75	3.50
5HYW90E085R Inherent Kindness, Miku Nakano R	.07	.15
5HYW90E085SSR Inherent Kindness, Miku Nakano SR	1.50	3.00
5HYW90E086R Love's Vexations, Miku Nakano R	.07	.15
5HYW90E086SSR Love's Vexations, Miku Nakano SR	4.00	8.00
5HYW90E087SSR School Trip, Nino Nakano SR	.60	1.25
5HYW90E087U School Trip, Nino Nakano U	.07	.15
5HYW90E088SSR Head Start on Gifting, Nino Nakano SR	1.00	2.00
5HYW90E088U Head Start on Gifting, Nino Nakano U	.05	.10
5HYW90E089SSR Sudden Approach, Nino Nakano SR	6.00	12.00
5HYW90E089U Sudden Approach, Nino Nakano U	.05	.10
5HYW90E090SSR Coincidental Encounter? Miku Nakano SR	1.25	2.50
5HYW90E090U Coincidental Encounter? Miku Nakano U	.10	.20
5HYW90E091C Part-Time Job Interview, Miku Nakano C	.05	.10
5HYW90E091SSR Part-Time Job Interview, Miku Nakano SR	.60	1.25
5HYW90E092C New Year, Miku Nakano C	.07	.15
5HYW90E092SSR New Year, Miku Nakano SR	2.00	4.00
5HYW90E093C Tea Break on the Sofa, Miku Nakano C	.05	.10
5HYW90E093SSR Tea Break on the Sofa, Miku Nakano SR	.75	1.50
5HYW90E094C Cheering From the Sidelines, Nino Nakano C	.05	.10
5HYW90E094SSR Cheering From the Sidelines, Nino Nakano SR	.75	1.50
5HYW90E095C Shopping, Nino Nakano C	.05	.10
5HYW90E095SSR Shopping, Nino Nakano SR	.75	1.50
5HYW90E096C Irreplaceable Bond, Nino Nakano C	.05	.10
5HYW90E096SSR Irreplaceable Bond, Nino Nakano SR	1.25	2.50
5HYW90E097SSR Headphone SR	1.75	3.50
5HYW90E097U Headphone U	.07	.15
5HYW90E098SSR Secret Confession SR	1.25	2.50
5HYW90E098U Secret Confession U	.07	.15
5HYW90E099CR What She Loves CR	.07	.15
5HYW90E099OFROFR What She Loves OFR	12.50	25.00
5HYW90E100CC Wholehearted Feelings CC	.05	.10
5HYW90E100RRRR Wholehearted Feelings RRR	1.50	3.00
5HYW90E101PR Rent, Ichika Nakano P	.15	.30
5HYW90E102PR Loss of Privacy, Nino Nakano P	.15	.30
5HYW90E103PR Baffled Gaze, Miku Nakano P	.15	.30
5HYW90E104PR Great at Sports, Yotsuba Nakano P	.12	.25
5HYW90E105PR Crossed Boundary, Itsuki Nakano P	7.50	15.00

2022 Weiss Schwarz The Seven Deadly Sins Revival of the Commandments

SDSSX05001RR Elizabeth: Trust in the Promise RR	7.50	15.00
SDSSX05001SPSP Elizabeth: Trust in the Promise SP	200.00	400.00
SDSSX05002RR Hawk: Pride of a Hero RR	.75	1.50
SDSSX05002SPSP Hawk: Pride of a Hero SP	75.00	150.00
SDSSX05003RR Meliodas: Wielder of Lostvayne RR	4.00	8.00
SDSSX05003SSR Meliodas: Wielder of Lostvayne SR	20.00	40.00
SDSSX05004RR Escanor: Arrogant and Powerful RR	10.00	20.00
SDSSX05004SPSP Escanor: Arrogant and Powerful SP	250.00	500.00
SDSSX05005R Escanor: Wielder of Rhitta R	.30	.60
SDSSX05005SSR Escanor: Wielder of Rhitta SR	10.00	20.00
SDSSX05006R Meliodas: Fulfilling His Promise R	.50	1.00
SDSSX05006SPSP Meliodas: Fulfilling His Promise SP	125.00	250.00
SDSSX05007R Escanor: Master of the Tavern R	4.00	8.00
SDSSX05008R Elizabeth: Strong Heart R	.25	.50
SDSSX05008SSR Elizabeth: Strong Heart SR	3.00	6.00
SDSSX05009R Meliodas: Overcoming His Past R	.50	1.00
SDSSX05009SSR Meliodas: Overcoming His Past SR	5.00	10.00
SDSSX05010R Meliodas: Internal Strife R	.40	.80
SDSSX05011SSR Hawk: Transpork SR	2.50	5.00
SDSSX05011U Hawk: Transpork U	.12	.25
SDSSX05012DSRDSR Meliodas: The Dragon Sin of Wrath DSR	40.00	80.00
SDSSX05012U Meliodas: The Dragon Sin of Wrath U	.25	.50
SDSSX05013U Hawk Mama: Casually Saving the Day U	.15	.30
SDSSX05014U Escanor: Flashback U	.20	.40
SDSSX05015U Nanashi: Mysterious Swordsman U	.20	.40
SDSSX05016DSRDSR Escanor: The Lion Sin of Pride DSR	30.00	75.00
SDSSX05016U Escanor: The Lion Sin of Pride U	.20	.40
SDSSX05017U Elizabeth: New Power U	.20	.40
SDSSX05018C Druid Chief Zaneri C	.12	.25
SDSSX05019C Druid Chief Jenna C	.07	.15
SDSSX05020C Liz: Happier Times C	.07	.15
SDSSX05021C Elizabeth: Emotional Support C	.15	.30
SDSSX05022C Elizabeth: Through Thick and Thin C	.20	.40
SDSSX05023C Arthur: Monster Cat Companion C	.12	.25
SDSSX05024C Meliodas: Mid-Match Squabble C	.12	.25
SDSSX05025C Arthur: Tearful Apology C	.07	.15
SDSSX05026C Balor's Magical Eye C	.07	.15

SDSSX05027CR The Trial CR .25 .50
SDSSX05027RRRR The Trial RRR 7.50 15.00
SDSSX05028CC A World Without You CC .15 .30
SDSSX05029CC Master of the Sun CC .15 .30
SDSSX05030RR Diane: Importance of Memories RR 1.25 2.50
SDSSX05030SPSP Diane: Importance of Memories SP 125.00 250.00
SDSSX05031RR King: Greedy RR .50 1.00
SDSSX05031SPSP King: Greedy SP 75.00 150.00
SDSSX05032R Deldry: Love Manipulator R .30 .60
SDSSX05033R Deathpierce: Realization R .25 .50
SDSSX05034R Griamore: Reverted to a Child R .25 .50
SDSSX05035R King: Protective R .25 .50
SDSSX05035SSR King: Protective SR 1.25 2.50
SDSSX05036R Diane: Believing in Her Friends R .30 .60
SDSSX05037R Gilthunder: Training Buddies R .30 .60
SDSSX05037SSR Gilthunder: Training Buddies SR 3.00 6.00
SDSSX05038U Gerheade: Matter-of-Factly U .12 .25
SDSSX05039SSR Helbram: Adviser in the Helmet SR 2.50 5.00
SDSSX05039U Helbram: Adviser in the Helmet U .15 .30
SDSSX05040DSRDSR King: The Grizzly Sin of Sloth DSR 10.00 20.00
SDSSX05040U King: The Grizzly Sin of Sloth U .15 .30
SDSSX05041SSR Diane: Learning to Dance SR 1.50 3.00
SDSSX05041U Diane: Learning to Dance U .20 .40
SDSSX05042SSR Matrona: Warrior Chief SR 2.50 5.00
SDSSX05042U Matrona: Warrior Chief U .15 .30
SDSSX05043DSRDSR Diane: The Serpent Sin of Envy DSR 30.00 75.00
SDSSX05043U Diane: The Serpent Sin of Envy U .15 .30
SDSSX05044C Arden: Draining Enemies C .07 .15
SDSSX05046C Diane: Retaliating C .12 .25
SDSSX05047C Gilthunder: Second Thoughts C .07 .15
SDSSX05048C King: Internal Strife C .15 .30
SDSSX05049C Denzel: Demon Clan Researcher C .20 .40
SDSSX05050C King: Protecting the Forest C .25 .50
SDSSX05051C Waillo: Seeking Marriage C .07 .15
SDSSX05052U Fairy King's Forest U .20 .40
SDSSX05053CR True Spirit Spear Chastiefol CR .20 .40
SDSSX05053RRRR True Spirit Spear Chastiefol RRR 2.00 4.00
SDSSX05054CC Friends CC .12 .25
SDSSX05055CC Summoning a Goddess CC .12 .25
SDSSX05056RR Gowther: Fighting It Out RR .75 1.50
SDSSX05056SSR Gowther: Fighting It Out SR 2.50 5.00
SDSSX05057RR Merlin: True Identity RR .75 1.50
SDSSX05057SSR Merlin: True Identity SR 2.50 5.00
SDSSX05058RR Ban: Facing Off RR .75 1.50
SDSSX05058SSR Ban: Facing Off SR 1.25 2.50
SDSSX05059R Gowther: Reflecting R .25 .50
SDSSX05060R Merlin: Handy Ability R .40 .80
SDSSX05061R Merlin: Miscalculation R .20 .40
SDSSX05062R Ban: Mid-Match Squabble R .30 .75
SDSSX05063R Elaine: Capable Saint R .25 .50
SDSSX05063SSR Elaine: Capable Saint SR 2.00 4.00
SDSSX05064R Merlin: Wielder of Aldan R .75 1.50
SDSSX05064SSR Merlin: Wielder of Aldan SR 5.00 10.00
SDSSX05065SSR Zhivago: Taking Under His Wing SR .75 1.50
SDSSX05065U Zhivago: Taking Under His Wing U .12 .25
SDSSX05066U Elaine: Revived U .75 1.50
SDSSX05067U Elaine: Coming to Her Senses U .15 .30
SDSSX05068DSRDSR Gowther: The Goat Sin of Lust DSR 12.50 25.00
SDSSX05068U Gowther: The Goat Sin of Lust U .15 .30
SDSSX05069DSRDSR Ban: The Fox Sin of Greed DSR 30.00 60.00
SDSSX05069U Ban: The Fox Sin of Greed U .20 .40
SDSSX05070DSRDSR Merlin: The Boar Sin of Gluttony DSR 20.00 40.00
SDSSX05070U Merlin: The Boar Sin of Gluttony U .12 .25
SDSSX05071C Ban: To Save a Friend C .07 .15
SDSSX05072C Merlin: Recruitment C .10 .20
SDSSX05073C Zhivago & Ban: A Final Reunion C .07 .15
SDSSX05074C Gowther: Original Form C .12 .25
SDSSX05075C Ban: Rough Childhood C .07 .15
SDSSX05077U Delicious Meat U .12 .25
SDSSX05078CR Back From the Dead CR .20 .40
SDSSX05078RRRR Back From the Dead RRR 5.00 10.00
SDSSX05079CC Caught In a Trap CC .10 .20
SDSSX05080CC Striking Fear CC .12 .25
SDSSX05081RR Zeldris of the Ten Commandments RR .75 1.50
SDSSX05081SSR Zeldris of the Ten Commandments SR 4.00 8.00
SDSSX05082R Jericho: Passionate R .25 .50
SDSSX05082SSR Jericho: Passionate SR 2.00 4.00
SDSSX05083R Hendrickson: Usual Self R .30 .60
SDSSX05083SSR Hendrickson: Usual Self SR 1.25 2.50
SDSSX05084R Gustaf: Desperate Attempt R .12 .25
SDSSX05085R Gloxinia & Drole: Reasons for Switching R .30 .75
SDSSX05086R Howzer: Training Buddies R .20 .40
SDSSX05086SSR Howzer: Training Buddies SR 2.50 5.00
SDSSX05087R Gloxinia of the Ten Commandments R .25 .50
SDSSX05087SSR Gloxinia of the Ten Commandments SR 4.00 8.00
SDSSX05088SSR Drole of the Ten Commandments SR 2.50 5.00
SDSSX05088U Drole of the Ten Commandments U .15 .30
SDSSX05089SSR Fraudrin of the Ten Commandments SR 6.00 12.00
SDSSX05089U Fraudrin of the Ten Commandments U .15 .30
SDSSX05090SSR Galland of the Ten Commandments SR 4.00 8.00
SDSSX05090U Galland of the Ten Commandments U .15 .30
SDSSX05091SSR Derieri of the Ten Commandments SR 6.00 12.00
SDSSX05091U Derieri of the Ten Commandments U .15 .30
SDSSX05092SSR Grayroad of the Ten Commandments SR 3.00 6.00
SDSSX05092U Grayroad of the Ten Commandments U .15 .30
SDSSX05093SSR Monspeet of the Ten Commandments SR 5.00 10.00
SDSSX05093U Monspeet of the Ten Commandments U .15 .30
SDSSX05094U Jericho: Following Behind U .15 .30
SDSSX05095SSR Melascula of the Ten Commandments SR 7.50 15.00
SDSSX05095U Melascula of the Ten Commandments U .15 .30
SDSSX05096SSR Estarossa of the Ten Commandments SR 4.00 8.00
SDSSX05096U Estarossa of the Ten Commandments U .15 .30
SDSSX05097SSR Dreyfus: Usual Self SR 1.50 3.00
SDSSX05097U Dreyfus: Usual Self U .25 .50
SDSSX05098C Monspeet & Derieri: Taken Aback C .12 .25
SDSSX05099C Dreyfus: Unfortunate Investigation C .07 .15
SDSSX05100C Slader: Pledging Loyalty C .10 .20
SDSSX05101C Vivian: Disguised as Gilfrost C .10 .20
SDSSX05102C Grayroad & Fraudrin: Upper Hand C .12 .25
SDSSX05103C Zeldris & Estarossa: In the Heat of Battle C .12 .25
SDSSX05104C Zaratras: Heading to the Capital C .07 .15
SDSSX05105C Galland & Melascula: Drinking C .10 .20
SDSSX05107U Flyer Distributors U .12 .25
SDSSX05108CR Ten Commandments CR .15 .30
SDSSX05108RRRR Ten Commandments RRR 7.50 15.00
SDSSX05109CC Death-Trap Maze CC .10 .20
SDSSX05110CC Galland Game! CC .10 .20
SDSSX05111PR Petit Meliodas: New Chapter .75 1.50
SDSSX05111SPR Petit Meliodas: New Chapter FOIL 5.00 10.00
SDSSX05112PR Petit Elizabeth: New Chapter 2.00 4.00
SDSSX05112SPR Petit Elizabeth: New Chapter FOIL 5.00 10.00
SDSSX05113PR Petit Escanor: New Chapter .50 1.00
SDSSX05113SPR Petit Escanor: New Chapter FOIL 5.00 10.00
SDSSX05114PR Petit Diane: New Chapter 1.25 2.50
SDSSX05114SPR Petit Diane: New Chapter FOIL 5.00 10.00
SDSSX05115PR Petit King: New Chapter .60 1.25
SDSSX05115SPR Petit King: New Chapter FOIL 5.00 10.00
SDSSX05116PR Petit Ban: New Chapter 1.00 2.00
SDSSX05116SPR Petit Ban: New Chapter FOIL 4.00 8.00
SDSSX05117PR Petit Gowther: New Chapter .75 1.50
SDSSX05117SPR Petit Gowther: New Chapter FOIL 4.00 8.00
SDSSX05118PR Petit Merlin: New Chapter .75 1.50
SDSSX05118SPR Petit Merlin: New Chapter FOIL 6.00 12.00

2022 Weiss Schwarz Tokyo Revengers

TRVS92E001RR A Future Where You're Saved, Takemichi & Hina RR.75 1.50
TRVS92E001TRVTRV A Future Where You're
Saved, Takemichi & Hina TRV 50.00 100.00
TRVS92E002RR Special Person, Hina RR 3.00 6.00
TRVS92E002SSPSSP Special Person, Hina SSP 250.00 500.00
TRVS92E003RR Thanks for the Courage, Takemichi RR .75 1.50
TRVS92E004R Special Person, Emma R 1.25 2.50
TRVS92E005R Festival, Draken & Mikey R .30 .75
TRVS92E005SSR Festival, Draken & Mikey SR 2.00 4.00
TRVS92E006R Changing the Tides of Battle, Draken R .12 .25
TRVS92E006SSR Changing the Tides of Battle, Draken SR 1.50 3.00
TRVS92E007R No Matter How Many Times I Fail, Takemichi R .25 .50
TRVS92E008R Kid's Meal, Mikey R 4.00 8.00
TRVS92E008SSR Kid's Meal, Mikey SR 20.00 40.00
TRVS92E009U Having It the Hardest, Mikey U .15 .30
TRVS92E010U Hooked on the Occult, Naoto U .12 .25
TRVS92E011U Birthday Present, Emma & Draken U .15 .30
TRVS92E012TRVTRV You Always Turn Up Suddenly, Hina TRV 25.00 50.00
TRVS92E012U You Always Turn Up Suddenly, Hina U .10 .20
TRVS92E013U Successful Surgery, Hina & Emma U .12 .25
TRVS92E015U Please Save Everyone, Akkun U .12 .25
TRVS92E016U Friends Starting Today, Takemichi & Mikey U .12 .25
TRVS92E017SSR Caring Towards Comrades, Akkun SR 1.25 2.50
TRVS92E018SSR Trigger, Naoto SR .75 1.50
TRVS92E018U Trigger, Naoto U .25 .50
TRVS92E019C Mood Maker, Yamagishi C .05 .10
TRVS92E020C Shampoo Hat, Draken C .07 .15
TRVS92E021C Childhood Friend, Takuya C .07 .15
TRVS92E023C Preoccupied with Perversions, Makoto C .07 .15
TRVS92E024C Reason Behind His Maturity, Draken C .07 .15
TRVS92E025C Cheerful Tone, Hina C .07 .15
TRVS92E027C Impatient to Be an Adult, Emma C .05 .10
TRVS92E028U Clover Necklace U .15 .30
TRVS92E029CR First Kiss CR .20 .40
TRVS92E029RRRR First Kiss RRR 1.50 3.00
TRVS92E030CR Time Leap CR .20 .40
TRVS92E030RRRR Time Leap RRR 1.50 3.00
TRVS92E031CC Hope It Goes Well CC .12 .25
TRVS92E032CC Mizo Middle Five CC .12 .25
TRVS92E033RR Light of the 1st Division, Chifuyu RR .60 1.25
TRVS92E033SSPSSP Light of the 1st Division, Chifuyu SSP 50.00 100.00
TRVS92E034RR Way of the Delinquent, Draken RR 1.00 2.00
TRVS92E034TRVTRV Way of the Delinquent, Draken TRV 60.00 125.00
TRVS92E035RR New Era for Delinquents, Mikey RR 2.00 4.00
TRVS92E035SSPSSP New Era for Delinquents, Mikey SSP 300.00 600.00
TRVS92E036RR Everyday Lives, Mikey & Draken RR .60 1.25
TRVS92E036TRVTRV Everyday Lives, Mikey & Draken TRV 75.00 150.00
TRVS92E037R My Treasure, Baji R 3.00 6.00
TRVS92E037TRVTRV My Treasure, Baji TRV 75.00 150.00
TRVS92E038R Older Brother Figure, Mitsuya R .40 .80
TRVS92E038SSR Older Brother Figure, Mitsuya SR 2.00 4.00
TRVS92E039R Just a Scratch, Baji R .20 .40
TRVS92E039SSR Just a Scratch, Baji SR 2.00 4.00
TRVS92E040R Draken & Mikey & Takemichi R .60 1.25
TRVS92E040SSR Draken & Mikey & Takemichi SR 4.00 8.00
TRVS92E041R Let's Split Halves, Baji & Chifuyu R .15 .30
TRVS92E042R See? There's No One! Mikey R .10 .20
TRVS92E042TRVTRV See? There's No One! Mikey TRV 60.00 125.00
TRVS92E043R Commander, Mikey R .25 .50
TRVS92E043SSR Commander, Mikey SR 2.50 5.00
TRVS92E044R Can't Promise It, Chifuyu & Baji R .15 .30
TRVS92E045R Can't Hit Ya, Chifuyu R .10 .20
TRVS92E045SSR Can't Hit Ya, Chifuyu SR .75 1.50
TRVS92E046R I'm Never Going to Back Down! Takemichi R .07 .15
TRVS92E047R The Only Way is Attacking, Draken R .25 .50
TRVS92E048R Unwavering Loyalty, Chifuyu R .50 1.00
TRVS92E048SSR Unwavering Loyalty, Chifuyu SR 2.00 4.00
TRVS92E049SSR 5th Division Captain, Mucho SR 1.50 3.00
TRVS92E049U 5th Division Captain, Mucho U .15 .30
TRVS92E050U Becoming a Man That's Fitting, Takemichi U .30 .75
TRVS92E051SSR Sin and Punishment, Hanma SR 1.25 2.50
TRVS92E051U Sin and Punishment, Hanma U .12 .25
TRVS92E052SSR 3rd Division Vice-Captain, Peh-yan SR 3.00 6.00
TRVS92E052U 3rd Division Vice-Captain, Peh-yan U .30 .60
TRVS92E053U Most Important Thing, Baji U .30 .75
TRVS92E054SSR Man Shrouded in Mystery, Kisaki SR 1.25 2.50
TRVS92E054U Man Shrouded in Mystery, Kisaki U .12 .25
TRVS92E055U Reason for Not Turning Back, Takemichi U .20 .40
TRVS92E056SSR Last Wishes, Takemichi & Chifuyu SR 1.25 2.50
TRVS92E056U Last Wishes, Takemichi & Chifuyu U .12 .25
TRVS92E057SSR No One's Losing, Mikey SR 1.25 2.50
TRVS92E057U No One's Losing, Mikey U .15 .30
TRVS92E058SSR 3rd Division Captain, Pah-chin SR 3.00 6.00
TRVS92E058U 3rd Division Captain, Pah-chin U .50 1.00
TRVS92E059SSR 4th Division Captain, Smiley SR 2.50 5.00
TRVS92E059U 4th Division Captain, Smiley U .15 .30
TRVS92E060C Strongest Man, Mikey C .07 .15
TRVS92E061C Most Important Thing, Kazutora C .07 .15
TRVS92E062C Revenge, Takemichi C .25 .50
TRVS92E063C 3rd Division Captain, Kisaki C .07 .15
TRVS92E064C 2nd Division Captain, Mitsuya C .12 .25
TRVS92E065C The Enemy In Front of You, Chifuyu C .15 .30
TRVS92E066C Temporary In-Charge, Hanma C .15 .30
TRVS92E067C The Heart Can't Keep Up, Mikey C .10 .20
TRVS92E068C Handicrafts Club Leader, Mitsuya C .05 .10
TRVS92E069C Concluding the Gamble on a Fight, Draken C .07 .15
TRVS92E070C Allegiance Test, Baji C .20 .40
TRVS92E071C Apologize Properly, Mitsuya C .15 .30
TRVS92E072U Kick Like a Nuclear Warhead U .12 .25
TRVS92E073CR The Heart That Cares for Others CR .20 .40
TRVS92E073RRRR The Heart That Cares for Others RRR 3.00 6.00
TRVS92E074CR New Era for Delinquents CR .15 .30
TRVS92E074RRRR New Era for Delinquents RRR 7.50 15.00
TRVS92E075CC The First Person I Wanted to Follow CC .20 .40
TRVS92E075RRRR The First Person I Wanted to Follow RRR 6.00 12.00
TRVS92E076CC My Hero CC .12 .25
TRVS92E077CC Captain of the Bodyguard Squad CC 1.25 2.50
TRVS92E078RR Founding Member, Baji RR .75 1.50
TRVS92E078SSPSSP Founding Member, Baji SSP 75.00 150.00
TRVS92E079RR Founding Member, Mitsuya RR .25 .50
TRVS92E079SSPSSP Founding Member, Mitsuya SSP 75.00 150.00
TRVS92E080RR Founding Member, Kazutora RR .30 .75
TRVS92E081R Bloody Halloween, Kazutora & Mikey R .40 .80
TRVS92E081SSR Bloody Halloween, Kazutora & Mikey SR 2.50 5.00
TRVS92E082R Draken & Mitsuya R .07 .15
TRVS92E083R Founding Member, Mikey R .25 .50
TRVS92E083SSR Founding Member, Mikey SR 1.50 3.00
TRVS92E084R Together 'Til the End, Baji & Kazutora R .12 .25
TRVS92E085R Our Everything, Baji R 1.25 2.50
TRVS92E085SSR Our Everything, Baji SR 10.00 20.00
TRVS92E086U Bodyguard Squad, Mitsuya U .75 1.50
TRVS92E087U Seventh Elementary, Mikey U 1.50 3.00
TRVS92E088SSR Founding Member, Draken SR 1.25 2.50
TRVS92E088U Founding Member, Draken U .12 .25
TRVS92E089U To Become a Hero, Kazutora U .20 .40
TRVS92E092C Race to the Shrine, Mitsuya C .07 .15
TRVS92E094C King of the World, Mikey C .07 .15
TRVS92E097U Amulet From That Day U .20 .40
TRVS92E098CC I'll Forgive You CC .12 .25
TRVS92E098RRRR I'll Forgive You RRR .75 1.50
TRVS92E099CC A Team Where Each Person Protects Everyone CC.20 .40
TRVS92E099RRRR A Team Where Each
Person Protects Everyone RRR 1.50 3.00
TRVS92E100CC We'll Entrust Our Everything to You CC .25 .50
TRVS92E100RRRR We'll Entrust Our Everything to You RRR 4.00 8.00
TRVS92E101PR 1st Division Captain, Takemichi P .07 .15
TRVS92E101SPR 1st Division Captain, Takemichi FOIL P .15 .30
TRVS92E102PR I'll Protect It, Chifuyu P .30 .60
TRVS92E102SPR I'll Protect It, Chifuyu FOIL P .20 .40
TRVS92E103SPR Special Attack Unit, Baji FOIL P .10 .20
TRVS92E104SPR Childish Side, Mikey FOIL P .05 .10
TRVS92E105SPR Vice-Commander, Draken FOIL P .07 .15
TRVS92E106SPR Bringing Everyone Together, Mitsuya FOIL P .10 .20

2022 Weiss Schwarz Tokyo Revengers Trial Deck

TRVS92TE01TD Wrecked, Chifuyu .12 .25
TRVS92TE02SPSP I'll Protect You, Hinata SP 150.00 300.00
TRVS92TE02SSR I'll Protect You, Hinata SR 3.00 6.00
TRVS92TE02TD I'll Protect You, Hinata 2.50 5.00
TRVS92TE03SSR Fight Me One-On-One, Takemichi SR .30 .75
TRVS92TE03TD Fight Me One-On-One, Takemichi .20 .40
TRVS92TE04RRRR Unfathomable Woman's Mind, Emma RRR 12.50 30.00
TRVS92TE04TD Unfathomable Woman's Mind, Emma .10 .20
TRVS92TE05TD Man of the Times, Takemichi .75 1.50
TRVS92TE06TD To Save His Sister, Naoto .12 .25
TRVS92TE07TD First Time Using Polite Speech, Chifuyu .12 .25
TRVS92TE08TD The Moment He Thought I'm Dead .20 .40
TRVS92TE09TD Promise to Take Over the World .20 .40
TRVS92TE10TD Gathering at Musashi Shrine .10 .20
TRVS92TE11TD Commander's Right-Hand Man, Draken .12 .25
TRVS92TE12TD Everyone'll Understand, Mitsuya .10 .20
TRVS92TE13TD Flag Wielder, Pah-chin .10 .20
TRVS92TE14TD Special Attack Unit, Kazutora .12 .25
TRVS92TE15TD Race to the Shrine, Baji .10 .20
TRVS92TE16TD Path Towards a Dream, Mikey .12 .25
TRVS92TE17TD 1st Division Captain, Baji .12 .25
TRVS92TE18RRRR Changing the Tides of Battle Alone, Draken RRR7.50 15.00
TRVS92TE18TD Changing the Tides of Battle Alone, Draken .12 .25
TRVS92TE19RRRR Take Good Care of Her, Mikey RRR 30.00 75.00
TRVS92TE19TD Take Good Care of Her, Mikey .12 .25
TRVS92TE20TD You Should Come Along Too .12 .25

2023 Weiss Schwarz Arifureta From Commonplace to World's Strongest

ARIS103E001 Talented Healer, Kaori RR 5.00 12.00
ARIS103E001SP Talented Healer, Kaori FOIL SP 100.00 250.00
ARIS103E002 Tremendous Power, Yue RR 1.00 2.50
ARIS103E002SP Tremendous Power, Yue FOIL SP 250.00 600.00
ARIS103E003 Adorable Maids, Yue & Myu & Kaori R .10 .25
ARIS103E004 Summer Beach, Yue R 1.00 2.50
ARIS103E004S Summer Beach, Yue FOIL SR 8.00 20.00
ARIS103E005 Composure of a Wife, Yue R .60 1.50
ARIS103E005S Composure of a Wife, Yue FOIL SR 12.00 30.00
ARIS103E006 Reason for Falling in Love, Kaori U .10 .25
ARIS103E007 Peaceful Morning, Kaori U .10 .25
ARIS103E008 Swimsuit Yue U .12 .30
ARIS103E009 Coaxing, Yue U .12 .30
ARIS103E010 Newfound Power, Kaori U .15 .40
ARIS103E011 Late Night Visitation, Kaori C .08 .20
ARIS103E012 The Girl Who Can't Die, Yue C .12 .30
ARIS103E013 Spirit Magic, Yue C .10 .25
ARIS103E014 God's Apostle, Noint C .10 .25
ARIS103E015 Battle Practice, Yue C .10 .25
ARIS103E016 Gravitic Magic R .10 .25
ARIS103E016S Gravitic Magic FOIL SR 1.50 4.00
ARIS103E017 The Golden Vampire Princess CR .60 1.50
ARIS103E017R The Golden Vampire Princess FOIL RRR 8.00 20.00
ARIS103E018 Aftertaste of a Kiss CC .50 1.25
ARIS103E019 Endearing Girl, Myu RR .60 1.50
ARIS103E019SP Endearing Girl, Myu FOIL SP 40.00 100.00
ARIS103E020 Full Power, Shea RR .20 .50
ARIS103E020SP Full Power, Shea FOIL SP 50.00 120.00
ARIS103E021 Towards the New World, Tio RR 1.00 2.50
ARIS103E021SP Towards the New World, Tio FOIL SP 150.00 400.00
ARIS103E022 Butt Up! Rabbit Time! Shea R .50 1.25
ARIS103E023 Body Strengthening, Shea R .10 .25
ARIS103E023S Body Strengthening, Shea FOIL SR 5.00 12.00
ARIS103E024 [Guardian] Tio R .12 .30
ARIS103E024S [Guardian] Tio FOIL SR 1.00 2.50
ARIS103E025 Pain Conversion, Tio R .12 .30
ARIS103E026 To Be Acknowledged, Shea R .12 .30
ARIS103E026S To Be Acknowledged, Shea FOIL SR 4.00 10.00
ARIS103E027 Reward Date, Shea U .12 .30
ARIS103E028 Swimsuit Tio U .10 .25
ARIS103E029 Swimsuit Myu U .10 .25
ARIS103E030 Graceful Beauty, Remia U .12 .30
ARIS103E031 Conquering Grand Gruen Volcano, Tio U .10 .25
ARIS103E032 Full of Curiosity, Myu U .10 .25
ARIS103E033 Big Pervert, Tio U .10 .25
ARIS103E034 Practicing Magic, Myu C .08 .20
ARIS103E035 Promise With the Haulia Tribe, Hajime C .08 .20
ARIS103E036 [Synergist] Hajime C .10 .25
ARIS103E037 Conquering the Great Reisen Labyrinth, Hajime C .08 .20
ARIS103E038 Conquering the Great Reisen Labyrinth, Shea C .10 .25
ARIS103E039 [Astrologist] Shea C .10 .25
ARIS103E040 Swimsuit Shea C .10 .25
ARIS103E041 Conquering the Great Orcus Labyrinth, Hajime C .08 .20
ARIS103E042 Kicking Away a Dragon's Rear U .10 .25
ARIS103E043 I'm Just a Girl with Bunny Ears! CR .30 .75
ARIS103E043R I'm Just a Girl with Bunny Ears! FOIL RRR 1.25 3.00
ARIS103E044 True Form of the Black Dragon CC .50 1.25
ARIS103E044R True Form of the Black Dragon FOIL RRR 2.00 5.00
ARIS103E045 New Sensation CC .15 .40
ARIS103E046 Unwavering Beliefs, Hajime RR 6.00 15.00
ARIS103E046SP Unwavering Beliefs, Hajime FOIL SP 100.00 250.00
ARIS103E047 Together Always, Yue RR 2.00 5.00
ARIS103E047S Together Always, Yue FOIL SR 10.00 25.00
ARIS103E048 Intelligent Side, Tio R .10 .25
ARIS103E048S Intelligent Side, Tio FOIL SR 2.00 5.00
ARIS103E049 Artifact, Hajime R .15 .40
ARIS103E049S Artifact, Hajime FOIL SR 1.00 2.50
ARIS103E050 Personal Story, Yue R .10 .25
ARIS103E050S Personal Story, Yue FOIL SR 1.25 3.00
ARIS103E051 Place of Belonging Found, Yue R .10 .25
ARIS103E051S Place of Belonging Found, Yue FOIL SR 2.00 5.00
ARIS103E052 Irregular, Hajime R .12 .30
ARIS103E052S Irregular, Hajime FOIL SR .60 1.50
ARIS103E053 One Who Crawled Out From the Abyss, Hajime R .20 .50
ARIS103E053S One Who Crawled Out
From the Abyss, Hajime FOIL SR 2.00 5.00
ARIS103E054 Commonplace Job, Hajime U .12 .30
ARIS103E055 Record of the Labyrinth, Yue U .12 .30
ARIS103E056 Girl Who Was Sealed Away, Yue U .12 .30
ARIS103E057 Nice Shot, Hajime U .12 .30
ARIS103E058 Prepared to Intercept, Tio U .10 .25
ARIS103E059 Ingested Power, Hajime U .10 .25
ARIS103E060 Conquest Achieved, Yue U .10 .25
ARIS103E061 Covered in Monster Skin, Yue C .08 .20
ARIS103E062 Deadly Battle in the Deep, Hajime C .08 .20
ARIS103E063 Deadly Battle in the Deep, Yue C .10 .25

ARIS103E064 Yue Providing Care C	.10	.25
ARIS103E065 Being Ignored Like This…, Tio C	.08	.20
ARIS103E066 Enjoying the Taste, Tio C	.08	.20
ARIS103E067 Ring From the Treasury U	.10	.25
ARIS103E068 Proposal? CC	.30	.75
ARIS103E068R Proposal? FOIL RRR	5.00	12.00
ARIS103E069 Final Battle at the Divine Mountain CC	.12	.30
ARIS103E070 The Best at Being the Worst CC	.30	.75
ARIS103E070R The Best at Being the Worst FOIL RRR	2.50	6.00
ARIS103E071 Resolve to Battle, Shizuku RR	.25	.60
ARIS103E071SP Resolve to Battle, Shizuku FOIL SP	40.00	100.00
ARIS103E072 Protective Teacher, Aiko RR	.40	1.00
ARIS103E072SP Protective Teacher, Aiko FOIL SP	20.00	50.00
ARIS103E073 A Wholesome Meeting, Shea RR	.25	.60
ARIS103E073S A Wholesome Meeting, Shea FOIL SR	10.00	25.00
ARIS103E074 Love Rivals, Kaori & Yue R	.10	.25
ARIS103E074S Love Rivals, Kaori & Yue SR	2.00	5.00
ARIS103E075 Conquering the Sunken Ruins of Melusine, Kaori R	.10	.25
ARIS103E076 Sexy Bikini, Yue & Shea R	.15	.40
ARIS103E077 Emotions Welling Up, Aiko R	.10	.25
ARIS103E077S Emotions Welling Up, Aiko FOIL SR	1.00	2.50
ARIS103E078 Summer Beach, Shea R	.12	.30
ARIS103E078S Summer Beach, Shea FOIL SR	10.00	25.00
ARIS103E079 [Priest] Kaori R	.12	.30
ARIS103E079S [Priest] Kaori FOIL SR	2.00	5.00
ARIS103E080 [Swordsman] Shizuku R	.15	.40
ARIS103E080S [Swordsman] Shizuku FOIL SR	1.25	3.00
ARIS103E081 [Farmer] Aiko U	.20	.50
ARIS103E082 Worthless Rabbit, Shea U	.12	.30
ARIS103E083 [Hero] Kouki U	.10	.25
ARIS103E084 Yaegashi-Ryu Swordsmanship, Shizuku U	.60	1.50
ARIS103E084S Yaegashi-Ryu Swordsmanship, Shizuku SR	.08	.20
ARIS103E085 Firm Resolve, Kaori U	.10	.25
ARIS103E086 Tending the Wounded, Kaori U	.10	.25
ARIS103E087 Self-Practice, Shizuku C	.10	.25
ARIS103E088 All Over, Kaori C	.08	.20
ARIS103E089 Return to the Royal Palace, Shizuku C	.08	.20
ARIS103E090 Swimsuit Kaori C	.08	.20
ARIS103E091 Defending the Royal Capital, Shea C	.10	.25
ARIS103E092 Princess Liliana C	.10	.25
ARIS103E093 For Humanity, Shizuku C	.10	.25
ARIS103E094 The Final Blow, Shea C	.10	.25
ARIS103E095 Goddess of Abundance, Aiko C	.08	.20
ARIS103E096 Saving a Life C	.10	.25
ARIS103E097 Bequeathed Sword CR	.30	.75
ARIS103E097R Bequeathed Sword RRR	2.00	5.00
ARIS103E098 Once in a Lifetime Request CR	.30	.75
ARIS103E098R Once in a Lifetime Request FOIL RRR	2.50	6.00
ARIS103E099 Duties of a Priest CC	.25	.60
ARIS103E100 Benevolence CC	.15	.40
ARIS103E100R Benevolence FOIL RRR	.75	2.00

2023 Weiss Schwarz Arifureta From Commonplace to World's Strongest Promos

ARIS103E101 Clothing Exchange Party, Yue PR	.60	1.50
ARIS103E101S Clothing Exchange Party, Yue FOIL PR	3.00	8.00
ARIS103E102 Clothing Exchange Party, Shea PR	.75	2.00
ARIS103E102S Clothing Exchange Party, Shea FOIL PR	3.00	8.00
ARIS103E103 Clothing Exchange Party, Myu PR	.60	1.50
ARIS103E103S Clothing Exchange Party, Myu FOIL PR	4.00	10.00
ARIS103E104 Clothing Exchange Party, Tio PR	.60	1.50
ARIS103E104S Clothing Exchange Party, Tio FOIL PR	2.50	6.00
ARIS103E105 Clothing Exchange Party, Kaori PR	.60	1.50
ARIS103E105S Clothing Exchange Party, Kaori FOIL PR	3.00	8.00
ARIS103PE02 Bathtime, Yue PR	.25	.60
ARIS103PE03 Winning, Shea FOIL PR	5.00	12.00

2023 Weiss Schwarz Arifureta From Commonplace to World's Strongest Trial Deck

ARIS103TE01 Fresh Out the Bath, Kaori TD	.10	.25
ARIS103TE01R Fresh Out the Bath, Kaori FOIL RRR	1.50	4.00
ARIS103TE02 Special Lover, Yue TD	.20	.50
ARIS103TE02SP Special Lover, Yue FOIL SP	500.00	1,200.00
ARIS103TE03 Compassionate Girl, Kaori TD	.20	.50
ARIS103TE03R Compassionate Girl, Kaori FOIL RRR	3.00	8.00
ARIS103TE04 Strongest Duo, Yue & Hajime TD	.20	.50
ARIS103TE04R Strongest Duo, Yue & Hajime RRR	1.00	2.50
ARIS103TE04S Strongest Duo, Yue & Hajime FOIL SR	.20	.50
ARIS103TE05 Suggestion Half in Jest, Kaori TD	.10	.25
ARIS103TE05R Suggestion Half in Jest, Kaori FOIL RRR	.50	1.25
ARIS103TE06 Bad With Heat, Yue TD	.10	.25
ARIS103TE06R Bad With Heat, Yue FOIL RRR	1.25	3.00
ARIS103TE07 The Last Vampire, Yue TD	.15	.40
ARIS103TE07R The Last Vampire, Yue FOIL RRR	2.50	6.00
ARIS103TE08 At the Bottom of the Abyss TD	.15	.40
ARIS103TE08R At the Bottom of the Abyss FOIL RRR	5.00	12.00
ARIS103TE09 Conveying Sentiments TD	.15	.40
ARIS103TE09R Conveying Sentiments FOIL RRR	2.00	5.00
ARIS103TE10 Merfolk Girl, My TD	.12	.30
ARIS103TE10R Merfolk Girl, Myu FOIL RRR	1.50	4.00
ARIS103TE11 Bad With Heat, Hajime TD	.10	.25
ARIS103TE11R Bad With Heat, Hajime FOIL RRR	.40	1.00
ARIS103TE12 Important Friend, Shea TD	.20	.50
ARIS103TE12SP Important Friend, Shea FOIL SP	150.00	400.00
ARIS103TE13 Honorable Dragonborn, Tio TD	.12	.30
ARIS103TE13R Honorable Dragonborn, Tio FOIL RRR	2.00	5.00
ARIS103TE14 Important Friend, Tio TD	.12	.30
ARIS103TE14SP Important Friend, Tio FOIL SP	125.00	300.00
ARIS103TE15 Wanting That Pleasure Once More, Tio TD	.12	.30
ARIS103TE15R Wanting That Pleasure Once More, Tio FOIL RRR	2.50	6.00
ARIS103TE16 Showing Off Her Strength, Shea TD	.10	.25
ARIS103TE16R Showing Off Her Strength, Shea FOIL RRR	2.00	5.00
ARIS103TE17 Brave Rabbitman, Shea TD	.15	.40
ARIS103TE17R Brave Rabbitman, Shea FOIL RRR	25.00	60.00
ARIS103TE18 Well Then, Let's Go! TD	.20	.50
ARIS103TE18R Well Then, Let's Go! FOIL RRR	8.00	20.00
ARIS103TE19 A New Journey TD	.12	.30
ARIS103TE19R A New Journey FOIL RRR	1.25	3.00

2023 Weiss Schwarz Avatar The Last Airbender

ATLAWX04001 Aang: The Last Airbender RR	.50	1.25
ATLAWX04001SP Aang: The Last Airbender SP	20.00	50.00
ATLAWX04002 Aang: Master of All Elements RR	.40	1.00
ATLAWX04002SEC Aang: Master of All Elements SEC	300.00	800.00
ATLAWX04003 Aang: Blending In R	.08	.20
ATLAWX04003S Aang: Blending In SR	.75	2.00
ATLAWX04004 Lion Turtle U	.10	.25
ATLAWX04005 Appa: Flying Bison U	.10	.25
ATLAWX04005S Appa: Flying Bison SR	2.00	5.00
ATLAWX04006 Appa & Momo: Samurai Battle U	.08	.20
ATLAWX04007 Aang: Learning Avatar State U	.20	.50
ATLAWX04007S Aang: Learning Avatar State SR	10.00	25.00
ATLAWX04008 Aang: Missing Companion U	.08	.20
ATLAWX04008ATR Aang: Missing Companion ATR	10.00	25.00
ATLAWX04009 Aang: The Importance of Forgiveness U	.08	.20
ATLAWX04010 Koh: The Face Stealer C	.08	.20
ATLAWX04011 Aang & Katara: Expressing Affection C	.08	.20
ATLAWX04012 Ember Island Players: Casting Horrors C	.08	.20
ATLAWX04013 Momo: Winged Lemur C	.10	.25
ATLAWX04013S Momo: Winged Lemur SR	8.00	20.00
ATLAWX04018 Yip-Yip! U	.08	.20
ATLAWX04020 Energy Bending CR	.10	.25
ATLAWX04020R Energy Bending RRR	1.25	3.00
ATLAWX04021 Struck Down CR	.10	.25
ATLAWX04021R Struck Down RRR	.30	.75
ATLAWX04022 Reunion With the Group CC	.08	.20
ATLAWX04023 Toph: Wanted RR	4.00	10.00
ATLAWX04023S Toph: Wanted SR	8.00	20.00
ATLAWX04024 Toph: The Blind Bandit RR	4.00	10.00
ATLAWX04024SP Toph: The Blind Bandit SP	40.00	100.00
ATLAWX04025 Toph: Stopping Library From Sinking R	.10	.25
ATLAWX04025S Toph: Stopping Library From Sinking SR	.60	1.50
ATLAWX04026 Suki: Kiyoshi Warrior R	.15	.40
ATLAWX04026S Suki: Kiyoshi Warrior SR	6.00	15.00
ATLAWX04027 Toph & Aang: Earthbending Lessons R	.10	.25
ATLAWX04027S Toph & Aang: Earthbending Lessons SR	1.00	2.50
ATLAWX04028 Toph: High Society R	.10	.25
ATLAWX04028S Toph: High Society SR	1.25	3.00
ATLAWX04029 Toph: Metalbending R	.10	.25
ATLAWX04029ATR Toph: Metalbending ATR	15.00	40.00
ATLAWX04030 Aang: Protecting Ba Sing Se U	.08	.20
ATLAWX04031 Toph: Childhood U	.08	.20
ATLAWX04032 Suki: Coming to the Rescue U	.10	.25
ATLAWX04034 Xin Fu & Master Yu: Trapped by Metal U	.08	.20
ATLAWX04035 Toph: Sleep Deprived U	.10	.25
ATLAWX04036 Toph: Prankster U	.10	.25
ATLAWX04037 Long Feng: Grand Secretariat U	.08	.20
ATLAWX04038 Bumi: An Old Friend C	.08	.20
ATLAWX04039 Ember Island Players: Played by a Man C	.08	.20
ATLAWX04040a Joo Dee: Welcome to Ba Sing Se C	.08	.20
ATLAWX04040b Joo Dee: Welcome to Ba Sing Se C	.08	.20
ATLAWX04040c Joo Dee: Welcome to Ba Sing Se C	.08	.20
ATLAWX04043 Toph: Melon Lord C	.08	.20
ATLAWX04044 There's No War in Ba Sing Se U	.08	.20
ATLAWX04045 Skillful Display CR	2.00	5.00
ATLAWX04045R Skillful Display RRR	5.00	12.00
ATLAWX04046 Invention of Metalbending CC	.08	.20
ATLAWX04046R Invention of Metalbending RRR	2.00	5.00
ATLAWX04048 Zuko: Crossroads RR	.25	.60
ATLAWX04048SP Zuko: Crossroads SP	25.00	60.00
ATLAWX04049 Zuko: For Honor RR	.40	1.00
ATLAWX04049SEC Zuko: For Honor SEC	125.00	300.00
ATLAWX04050 Azula: Verge of Insanity RR	1.25	3.00
ATLAWX04050S Azula: Verge of Insanity SR	20.00	50.00
ATLAWX04051 Zuko: Tea Server R	.15	.40
ATLAWX04051S Zuko: Tea Server SR	3.00	8.00
ATLAWX04052 Zuko & Iroh: Forgiveness R	.10	.25
ATLAWX04052S Zuko & Iroh: Forgiveness SR	1.25	3.00
ATLAWX04053 Iroh: Tea Server R	.10	.25
ATLAWX04053S Iroh: Tea Server SR	2.50	6.00
ATLAWX04054 Azula: Talented Sister R	.10	.25
ATLAWX04054ATR Azula: Talented Sister ATR	40.00	100.00
ATLAWX04055 Mai: Moody R	.10	.25
ATLAWX04055ATR Mai: Moody ATR	12.00	30.00
ATLAWX04056 Zuko: On the Run R	.10	.25
ATLAWX04056ATR Zuko: On the Run ATR	15.00	40.00
ATLAWX04057 Ty Lee: Popular R	.50	1.25
ATLAWX04057ATR Ty Lee: Popular ATR	25.00	60.00
ATLAWX04058 Iroh: The Dragon of the West R	.10	.25
ATLAWX04058S Iroh: The Dragon of the West SR	2.00	5.00
ATLAWX04059 Zuko & Aang: The Dancing Dragon R	.12	.30
ATLAWX04059S Zuko & Aang: The Dancing Dragon SR	3.00	8.00
ATLAWX04060 Ty Lee: Betrayal U	.10	.25
ATLAWX04061 Lord Ozai U	.08	.20
ATLAWX04062 Iroh: Order of the White Lotus U	.08	.20
ATLAWX04063 Zuko: Near the Campfire U	.10	.25
ATLAWX04064 Zuko: Redirecting Lightning U	.08	.20
ATLAWX04065 Iroh: Buffed U	.08	.20
ATLAWX04066 Azula: Sinister Scheme U	.10	.25
ATLAWX04067 Aang: Firebending Misfire C	.08	.20
ATLAWX04070 Ember Island Players: Scar On the Wrong Side C	.08	.20
ATLAWX04073a Tea Wisdom U	.08	.20
ATLAWX04073b Tea Wisdom U	.08	.20
ATLAWX04074 Siblings' Agni Kai CR	3.00	8.00
ATLAWX04074R Siblings' Agni Kai RRR	10.00	25.00
ATLAWX04075 Colors of Fire CR	.25	.60
ATLAWX04075R Colors of Fire RRR	4.00	10.00
ATLAWX04077 Sokka: Warrior of the Southern Water Tribe RR	.12	.30
ATLAWX04077SP Sokka: Warrior of the Southern Water Tribe SP	20.00	50.00
ATLAWX04078 Katara: Desire to Help RR	.25	.60
ATLAWX04078SP Katara: Desire to Help SP	25.00	60.00
ATLAWX04079 Katara: Saving Aang RR	.08	.20
ATLAWX04079S Katara: Saving Aang SR	1.00	2.50
ATLAWX04080 Katara: Quick Thinker R	.10	.25
ATLAWX04080ATR Katara: Quick Thinker ATR	10.00	25.00
ATLAWX04081 Katara: No Chance Given R	.10	.25
ATLAWX04081S Katara: No Chance Given SR	.75	2.00
ATLAWX04082 Sokka: Offering Different Perspectives R	1.00	2.50
ATLAWX04082ATR Sokka: Offering Different Perspectives ATR	25.00	60.00
ATLAWX04083 Katara: Experienced Fighter R	.10	.25
ATLAWX04083S Katara: Experienced Fighter SR	.60	1.50
ATLAWX04084 Katara: Vengeful R	.10	.25
ATLAWX04084S Katara: Vengeful SR	2.50	6.00
ATLAWX04085 Sokka: Cactus Juice R	.10	.25
ATLAWX04085S Sokka: Cactus Juice SR	1.25	3.00
ATLAWX04086 Katara & Aang: Reciprocated Feelings R	.10	.25
ATLAWX04086S Katara & Aang: Reciprocated Feelings SR	.50	1.25
ATLAWX04087 Sokka: Warm Welcome U	.10	.25
ATLAWX04087S Sokka: Warm Welcome SR	.75	2.00
ATLAWX04088 Tui & La U	.08	.20
ATLAWX04089 Aang: Attacking With Water C	.10	.25
ATLAWX04092 Ember Island Players: Melodramatic C	.08	.20
ATLAWX04097 Healing Lessons U	.08	.20
ATLAWX04098 Spirit Water CR	.12	.30
ATLAWX04098R Spirit Water RRR	.50	1.25
ATLAWX04099 Space Sword CC	.08	.20
ATLAWX04100 Frozen in Action CC	.08	.20
ATLAWX04101 Chibi Aang PR	.25	.60
ATLAWX04101S Chibi Aang FOIL PR	5.00	12.00
ATLAWX04102 Chibi Toph PR	.20	.50
ATLAWX04102S Chibi Toph FOIL PR	4.00	10.00
ATLAWX04103 Chibi Zuko PR	.15	.40
ATLAWX04104S Chibi Zuko FOIL PR	2.50	6.00
ATLAWX04105 Chibi Sokka PR	.25	.60
ATLAWX04105S Chibi Sokka FOIL PR	3.00	8.00
ATLAWX04106 Aang & Momo: Relaxing PR	.20	.50
ATLAWX04106 Chibi Katara PR	5.00	12.00
ATLAWX04106S Aang & Momo: Relaxing FOIL PR	.75	2.00
ATLAWX04106S Chibi Katara FOIL PR	1.25	3.00
ATLAWX04107 Toph: Spa Day PR	1.25	3.00
ATLAWX04107S Toph: Spa Day FOIL PR	2.00	5.00
ATLAWX04108 Iroh: Lightning PR	.60	1.50
ATLAWX04108S Iroh: Lightning FOIL PR	2.00	5.00
ATLAWX04109 Zuko & Mai: In Their Own World PR	.50	1.25
ATLAWX04109S Zuko & Mai: In Their Own World FOIL PR	.60	1.50
ATLAWX04110 Katara: Confrontation PR	.60	1.50
ATLAWX04110S Katara: Confrontation FOIL P	.50	1.25

2023 Weiss Schwarz Avatar The Last Airbender Promos

ATLAWX04P01 Zuko: Empathy PR	2.50	6.00
ATLAWX04P04 Team Avatar PR	10.00	25.00

2023 Weiss Schwarz Avatar The Last Airbender Trial Deck

ATLAWX04T01 Zuko: Trapped in a Cave TD	.10	.25
ATLAWX04T02S Aang & Zuko: Unexpected Cooperation SR	.60	1.50
ATLAWX04T02 Aang & Zuko: Unexpected Cooperation TD	.50	1.25
ATLAWX04T03 Aang: Trapped in a Cave TD	.10	.25
ATLAWX04T04R Zuko: Agni Kai RRR	5.00	12.00
ATLAWX04T04 Zuko: Agni Kai TD	.10	.25
ATLAWX04T05 Iroh: Stern Warning TD	.10	.25
ATLAWX04T06 Iroh: Fatherly Figure TD	.10	.25
ATLAWX04T07 Admiral Zhao: Killing the Moon Spirit TD	.10	.25
ATLAWX04T08 Stuck in a Blizzard TD	.10	.25
ATLAWX04T09 Katara: New Necklace TD	.15	.40
ATLAWX04T10 Sokka: Ship Steering TD	.10	.25
ATLAWX04T11 Katara & Sokka: Siblings TD	.12	.30
ATLAWX04T12S Aang: The Boy Trapped In Ice SR	.20	.50
ATLAWX04T12 Aang: The Boy Trapped In Ice TD	.20	.50
ATLAWX04T13 Yue: Moon Spirit TD	.12	.30
ATLAWX04T14 Jet & Freedom Fighters TD	.12	.30
ATLAWX04T15 Sokka: First Love TD	.10	.25
ATLAWX04T16SP Aang: Avatar State SP	50.00	120.00
ATLAWX04T16 Aang: Avatar State TD	.15	.40
ATLAWX04T17R Katara: Protecting Aang RRR	4.00	10.00
ATLAWX04T17 Katara: Protecting Aang TD	.10	.25
ATLAWX04T18 Katara's Necklace TD	.10	.25
ATLAWX04T19R Fury of the Ocean Spirit RRR	4.00	10.00
ATLAWX04T19 Fury of the Ocean Spirit TD	.12	.30

2023 Weiss Schwarz Azur Lane

AZLS102E001 Unicorn RR	2.50	6.00
AZLS102E001SP Unicorn SP FOIL	100.00	250.00
AZLS102E002 Jean Bart RR	.60	1.50
AZLS102E002SP Jean Bart SP FOIL	125.00	300.00
AZLS102E003 Belfast RR	.50	1.25
AZLS102E004 Cheshire RR	.50	1.25
AZLS102E004SP Cheshire SP FOIL	125.00	300.00
AZLS102E005 Sheffield R	.10	.25
AZLS102E005SP Sheffield SP FOIL	30.00	80.00
AZLS102E006 Ying Swei R	.10	.25
AZLS102E006SP Ying Swei SP FOIL	40.00	100.00
AZLS102E007 Formidable R	.10	.25
AZLS102E007SP Formidable SP FOIL	200.00	500.00
AZLS102E008 Sirius R	.10	.25
AZLS102E008SP Sirius SP FOIL	100.00	250.00
AZLS102E009 Drake R	.10	.25
AZLS102E009SP Drake SP FOIL	200.00	500.00
AZLS102E010 Perseus R	.10	.25
AZLS102E010SP Perseus SP FOIL	125.00	300.00
AZLS102E011 Le Malin R	.08	.20
AZLS102E011SP Le Malin SP FOIL	40.00	100.00
AZLS102E012 Rodney U	.08	.20
AZLS102E012S Rodney SR FOIL	4.00	10.00
AZLS102E013 Cygnet U	.08	.20
AZLS102E013S Cygnet SR FOIL	1.00	2.50
AZLS102E014 Ajax U	.08	.20
AZLS102E014S Ajax SR FOIL	3.00	8.00
AZLS102E015S Ark Royal SR FOIL	1.50	4.00
AZLS102E016 Chao Ho U	.08	.20
AZLS102E016S Chao Ho SR FOIL	1.25	3.00
AZLS102E017 Prince of Wales U	.08	.20
AZLS102E017S Prince of Wales SR FOIL	6.00	15.00
AZLS102E018 Saint Louis U	.10	.25
AZLS102E018SP Saint Louis SP FOIL	75.00	200.00
AZLS102E019 Neptune U	.10	.25
AZLS102E019S Neptune SR FOIL	1.25	3.00
AZLS102E020 Jervis U	.10	.25
AZLS102E020S Jervis SR FOIL	1.25	3.00
AZLS102E021 Queen Elizabeth U	.08	.20
AZLS102E021S Queen Elizabeth SR FOIL	1.25	3.00
AZLS102E022 Richelieu U	.10	.25
AZLS102E022SP Richelieu SP FOIL	125.00	300.00
AZLS102E023 Monarch U	.10	.25
AZLS102E023S Monarch SR FOIL	4.00	10.00
AZLS102E024 Howe U	.10	.25
AZLS102E024S Howe SR FOIL	1.25	3.00
AZLS102E025S Erebus SR FOIL	.60	1.50
AZLS102E026 Glorious C	.08	.20
AZLS102E026S Glorious SR FOIL	4.00	10.00
AZLS102E027S Hood SR FOIL	3.00	8.00
AZLS102E028 Black Prince C	.08	.20
AZLS102E028S Black Prince SR FOIL	5.00	12.00
AZLS102E029 Swiftsure C	.08	.20
AZLS102E029S Swiftsure SR FOIL	4.00	10.00
AZLS102E030 Universal Bulin R	.08	.20
AZLS102E030S Universal Bulin SR FOIL	.40	1.00
AZLS102E031 Maid Squad's Service CR	.15	.40
AZLS102E031R Maid Squad's Service RRR FOIL	4.00	10.00
AZLS102E032 Owner's Favorites? CR	.12	.30
AZLS102E032R Owner's Favorites? RRR FOIL	1.50	4.00
AZLS102E033 Afternoon Tea CC	.08	.20
AZLS102E033R Afternoon Tea RRR FOIL	1.25	3.00
AZLS102E034 Knight Princesses' Fantasy CC	.08	.20
AZLS102E034R Knight Princesses' Fantasy RRR FOIL	.60	1.50
AZLS102E035 All Too Reliable Side of Her CC	.08	.20
AZLS102E035R All Too Reliable Side of Her RRR FOIL	.60	1.50
AZLS102E036 Shimakaze RR	.20	.50
AZLS102E036SP Shimakaze SP FOIL	50.00	120.00
AZLS102E037 Nagato RR	5.00	12.00
AZLS102E037SEC Nagato SEC FOIL	200.00	500.00
AZLS102E038 Shinano RR	1.50	4.00
AZLS102E038SP Shinano SP FOIL	300.00	800.00
AZLS102E039 Taihou R	.75	2.00
AZLS102E039SP Taihou SP FOIL	250.00	600.00
AZLS102E040 Amagi R	.08	.20
AZLS102E040SP Amagi SP FOIL	150.00	400.00
AZLS102E041 Hanazuki R	.10	.25
AZLS102E041SP Hanazuki SP FOIL	50.00	120.00
AZLS102E042 Kashino R	.12	.30
AZLS102E042SP Kashino SP FOIL	200.00	500.00
AZLS102E043 Noshiro R	.08	.20
AZLS102E043SP Noshiro SP FOIL	50.00	120.00
AZLS102E044 Ibuki R	.10	.25
AZLS102E044SP Ibuki SP FOIL	75.00	200.00
AZLS102E045 Hakuryuu R	.12	.30
AZLS102E045SP Hakuryuu SP FOIL	50.00	120.00
AZLS102E046 Azuma R	.12	.30
AZLS102E046SP Azuma SP FOIL	125.00	300.00
AZLS102E047 Katsuragi U	.10	.25
AZLS102E047S Katsuragi SR FOIL	.75	2.00
AZLS102E048 Asashio U	.08	.20
AZLS102E048S Asashio SR FOIL	.75	2.00
AZLS102E049 I-168 U	.08	.20
AZLS102E049S I-168 SR FOIL	1.00	2.50

AZLS102E050 Kasumi U .08 .20
AZLS102E050S Kasumi SR FOIL 1.50 4.00
AZLS102E051 Yuudachi U .10 .25
AZLS102E051SP Yuudachi SP FOIL 40.00 100.00
AZLS102E052 Kitakaze U .10 .25
AZLS102E052S Kitakaze SR FOIL 1.00 2.50
AZLS102E053 Yukikaze U .08 .20
AZLS102E053SP Yukikaze SP FOIL 40.00 100.00
AZLS102E054 Suruga U .08 .20
AZLS102E054S Suruga SR FOIL .75 2.00
AZLS102E055 Kii U .10 .25
AZLS102E055S Kii SR FOIL 12.00 30.00
AZLS102E056 Fusou C .20 .50
AZLS102E056S Fusou SR FOIL 20.00 50.00
AZLS102E057 Mutsu C .08 .20
AZLS102E057S Mutsu SR FOIL .75 2.00
AZLS102E058 Naganami C .08 .20
AZLS102E058S Naganami SR FOIL 2.00 5.00
AZLS102E059S Agano SR FOIL 2.00 5.00
AZLS102E060S Fubuki SR FOIL .50 1.25
AZLS102E061 Yamashiro C .20 .50
AZLS102E061S Yamashiro SR FOIL 20.00 50.00
AZLS102E062 Souryuu C .08 .20
AZLS102E062S Souryuu SR FOIL 6.00 15.00
AZLS102E063 Hiryuu C .08 .20
AZLS102E063S Hiryuu SR FOIL 8.00 20.00
AZLS102E064S Kinu SR FOIL .75 2.00
AZLS102E065S I-19 SR FOIL 1.50 4.00
AZLS102E066 Shoukaku C .10 .25
AZLS102E066S Shoukaku SR FOIL 4.00 10.00
AZLS102E067 Zuikaku C .10 .25
AZLS102E067S Zuikaku SR FOIL 4.00 10.00
AZLS102E068 Bombing Ships U .08 .20
AZLS102E068S Bombing Ships SR FOIL .75 2.00
AZLS102E069 Ephemeral Dream U .15 .40
AZLS102E069R Ephemeral Dream RRR FOIL 4.00 10.00
AZLS102E070 Upon the Shimmering Blue CC .10 .25
AZLS102E070R Upon the Shimmering Blue RRR FOIL 2.00 5.00
AZLS102E071 Phoenix's Spring Song CC .12 .30
AZLS102E071R Phoenix's Spring Song RRR FOIL 8.00 20.00
AZLS102E072 Frank Cynic CC .10 .25
AZLS102E072R Frank Cynic RRR FOIL 2.00 5.00
AZLS102E073 Zara RR .25 .60
AZLS102E073SP Zara SP FOIL 400.00 1,000.00
AZLS102E074 August von Parseval RR .75 2.00
AZLS102E074SP August von Parseval SP FOIL 250.00 600.00
AZLS102E075 Roon RR 1.25 3.00
AZLS102E075SP Roon SP FOIL 150.00 400.00
AZLS102E076 Friedrich der Grosse RR .50 1.25
AZLS102E076SEC Friedrich der Grosse SEC FOIL 300.00 800.00
AZLS102E077 Peter Strasser R .10 .25
AZLS102E077SP Peter Strasser SP FOIL 60.00 150.00
AZLS102E078 Ulrich von Hutten R .10 .25
AZLS102E078SP Ulrich von Hutten SP FOIL 60.00 150.00
AZLS102E079 Libeccio R .08 .20
AZLS102E079SP Libeccio SP FOIL 40.00 100.00
AZLS102E080 Admiral Graf Spee R .10 .25
AZLS102E080S Admiral Graf Spee SR FOIL 5.00 12.00
AZLS102E081 U-110 U .10 .25
AZLS102E081S U-110 SR FOIL 1.50 4.00
AZLS102E082 Elbing U .10 .25
AZLS102E082S Elbing SR FOIL 4.00 10.00
AZLS102E083 Vittorio Veneto U .10 .25
AZLS102E083SP Vittorio Veneto SP FOIL 100.00 250.00
AZLS102E084 Odin U .10 .25
AZLS102E084S Odin SR FOIL 3.00 8.00
AZLS102E085 Aquila U .10 .25
AZLS102E085SP Aquila SP FOIL 100.00 250.00
AZLS102E086 Agir U .10 .25
AZLS102E086S Agir SR FOIL 15.00 40.00
AZLS102E087 Deutschland U .08 .20
AZLS102E087S Deutschland SR FOIL 10.00 25.00
AZLS102E088 Graf Zeppelin U .10 .25
AZLS102E088S Graf Zeppelin SR FOIL 8.00 20.00
AZLS102E089S Z46 SR FOIL 1.25 3.00
AZLS102E090 Emden C .10 .25
AZLS102E090S Emden SR FOIL 2.00 5.00
AZLS102E091 Seydlitz C .08 .20
AZLS102E091S Seydlitz SR FOIL 1.25 3.00
AZLS102E092 U-47 C .10 .25
AZLS102E092S U-47 SR FOIL 3.00 8.00
AZLS102E093S Wisdom Cubes SR FOIL .60 1.50
AZLS102E094 Witches' Banquet? CR .20 .50
AZLS102E094R Witches' Banquet? RRR FOIL 5.00 12.00
AZLS102E095 Rhapsodie of Darkness CR .10 .25
AZLS102E095R Rhapsodie of Darkness RRR FOIL 1.00 2.50
AZLS102E096 Daily Lives Filled With Influence CC .08 .20
AZLS102E096R Daily Lives Filled With Influence RRR FOIL 1.00 2.50
AZLS102E097 Until the End This Time CC .10 .25
AZLS102E097R Until the End This Time RRR FOIL 5.00 12.00
AZLS102E098R Iron Blood Wings RRR FOIL 1.00 2.50
AZLS102E099 Pamiat' Merkuria RR .12 .30
AZLS102E099SP Pamiat' Merkuria SP FOIL 50.00 120.00
AZLS102E100 Cleveland RR 8.00 20.00
AZLS102E100SEC Cleveland SEC FOIL 150.00 400.00
AZLS102E101 Bremerton RR .60 1.50
AZLS102E102 New Jersey RR 4.00 10.00
AZLS102E102SP New Jersey SP FOIL 600.00 1,500.00
AZLS102E103 Eldridge R .08 .20
AZLS102E103SP Eldridge SP FOIL 30.00 80.00
AZLS102E104S Nicholas SR FOIL .60 1.50
AZLS102E105 Reno R .10 .25
AZLS102E105S Reno SR FOIL 8.00 20.00
AZLS102E106 Independence R .10 .25
AZLS102E106S Independence SR FOIL 2.50 6.00
AZLS102E107 Massachusetts R .10 .25
AZLS102E107S Massachusetts SR FOIL 8.00 20.00
AZLS102E108 Shangri-La R .10 .25
AZLS102E108S Shangri-La SR FOIL 1.00 2.50
AZLS102E109 Georgia R .10 .25
AZLS102E109S Georgia SR FOIL 1.25 3.00
AZLS102E110 Essex R .10 .25
AZLS102E110SP Essex SP FOIL 75.00 200.00
AZLS102E111 Kronshtadt R .25 .60
AZLS102E111SP Kronshtadt SP FOIL 75.00 200.00
AZLS102E112 Tashkent U .08 .20
AZLS102E112S Tashkent SR FOIL .50 1.25
AZLS102E113 Bataan U .08 .20
AZLS102E113S Bataan SR FOIL 1.50 4.00
AZLS102E114 Sovetskaya Rossiya U .12 .30
AZLS102E114SP Sovetskaya Rossiya SP FOIL 60.00 150.00
AZLS102E115 Ingraham U .08 .20
AZLS102E115S Ingraham SR FOIL .60 1.50
AZLS102E116 Ticonderoga U .12 .30
AZLS102E116S Ticonderoga SR FOIL 5.00 12.00
AZLS102E117 St. Louis U .10 .25
AZLS102E117S St. Louis SR FOIL 5.00 12.00
AZLS102E118 San Francisco U .10 .25
AZLS102E118S San Francisco SR FOIL 2.00 5.00
AZLS102E119 Allen M. Sumner U .10 .25
AZLS102E119S Allen M. Sumner SR FOIL 1.25 3.00
AZLS102E120 Washington U .10 .25
AZLS102E120S Washington SR FOIL 5.00 12.00
AZLS102E121S Cavalla SR FOIL .60 1.50
AZLS102E122S Bache SR FOIL 2.50 6.00
AZLS102E123S Concord SR FOIL 2.00 5.00
AZLS102E124 Marblehead C .08 .20
AZLS102E124S Marblehead SR FOIL 2.00 5.00
AZLS102E125S Casablanca SR FOIL 5.00 12.00
AZLS102E126S Princeton SR FOIL 4.00 10.00
AZLS102E127S Vincennes SR FOIL .50 1.25
AZLS102E128S Cassin SR FOIL .75 2.00
AZLS102E129 Albacore C .08 .20
AZLS102E129S Albacore SR FOIL 5.00 12.00
AZLS102E130S Honolulu SR FOIL 6.00 15.00
AZLS102E131 Boise C .08 .20
AZLS102E131S Boise SR FOIL 3.00 8.00
AZLS102E132S Bailey SR FOIL .50 1.25
AZLS102E133 Birmingham C .08 .20
AZLS102E133S Birmingham SR FOIL 2.00 5.00
AZLS102E134S Portland SR FOIL .75 2.00
AZLS102E135S Stephen Potter SR FOIL 2.50 6.00
AZLS102E136 Meowfficer U .08 .20
AZLS102E136S Meowfficer SR FOIL 1.00 2.50
AZLS102E137 After-School Ace CR .10 .25
AZLS102E137R After-School Ace RRR FOIL 4.00 10.00
AZLS102E138 You Like This, Right? CC .10 .25
AZLS102E138R You Like This, Right? RRR FOIL 8.00 20.00
AZLS102E139 Observer of the Sky and Sea CC .08 .20
AZLS102E139R Observer of the Sky and Sea RRR FOIL .75 2.00
AZLS102E140 What a Spoiled Child You Are… CC .10 .25
AZLS102E140R What a Spoiled Child You Are… RRR FOIL 4.00 10.00

2023 Weiss Schwarz Azur Lane Promos

AZLS102E141 Maid Squad's Service P .40 1.00
AZLS102E142 Owner's Favorites? P .40 1.00
AZLS102E143 Afternoon Tea P .20 .50
AZLS102E144 Knight Princesses' Fantasy P .20 .50
AZLS102E145 All Too Reliable Side of Her P .25 .60
AZLS102E146 Ephemeral Dream P .40 1.00
AZLS102E147 Upon the Shimmering Blue P .20 .50
AZLS102E148 Phoenix's Spring Song P .60 1.50
AZLS102E149 Frank Cynic P .20 .50
AZLS102E150 Witches' Banquet? P .60 1.50
AZLS102E151 Rhapsodie of Darkness P .30 .75
AZLS102E152 Daily Lives Filled With Influence P .40 1.00
AZLS102E153 Until the End This Time P .30 .75
AZLS102E154 Iron Blood Wings P .30 .75
AZLS102E155 After-School Ace P .50 1.25
AZLS102E156 You Like This, Right? P .40 1.00
AZLS102E157 Observer of the Sky and Sea P .40 1.00
AZLS102E158 What a Spoiled Child You Are... P .40 1.00
AZLS102PE01 Javelin & Z23 & Ayanami & Laffey P .15 .40
AZLS102PE02 Akagi & Kaga P 1.25 3.00
AZLS102PE03 New Year's Greetings, Shoukaku P .25 .60

2023 Weiss Schwarz Azur Lane Trial Deck

AZLS102TE01 Helena TD .08 .20
AZLS102TE01R Helena RRR FOIL 2.50 6.00
AZLS102TE02R Benson RRR FOIL 1.50 4.00
AZLS102TE03 Minneapolis TD .10 .25
AZLS102TE03R Minneapolis RRR FOIL 2.50 6.00
AZLS102TE04R Craven RRR FOIL 2.00 5.00
AZLS102TE05 Hammann TD .08 .20
AZLS102TE05R Hammann RRR FOIL 2.50 6.00
AZLS102TE06 Laffey TD .20 .50
AZLS102TE06S Laffey SR FOIL .15 .40
AZLS102TE06SP Laffey SP FOIL 200.00 500.00
AZLS102TE07 North Carolina TD .10 .25
AZLS102TE07R North Carolina RRR FOIL 10.00 25.00
AZLS102TE08 San Diego TD .10 .25
AZLS102TE08SP San Diego SP FOIL 50.00 120.00
AZLS102TE09 Baltimore TD 1.00 2.50
AZLS102TE09SP Baltimore SP FOIL 300.00 800.00
AZLS102TE10 Gridley TD .10 .25
AZLS102TE10R Gridley RRR FOIL .75 2.00
AZLS102TE11 Long Island TD .12 .30
AZLS102TE11R Long Island RRR FOIL 1.50 4.00
AZLS102TE12 South Dakota TD .15 .40
AZLS102TE12R South Dakota RRR FOIL 12.00 30.00
AZLS102TE13 Hornet TD .08 .20
AZLS102TE13R Hornet RRR FOIL 2.00 5.00
AZLS102TE14 Saratoga TD .08 .20
AZLS102TE14R Saratoga RRR FOIL 1.00 2.50
AZLS102TE15 Yorktown TD .10 .25
AZLS102TE15R Yorktown RRR FOIL 1.50 4.00
AZLS102TE16 Enterprise TD .12 .30
AZLS102TE17 Eagle Union TD .10 .25
AZLS102TE17R Eagle Union RRR FOIL 1.00 2.50
AZLS102TE18 Hanging Out With the Teacher TD .10 .25
AZLS102TE18R Hanging Out With the Teacher RRR FOIL 4.00 10.00
AZLS102TE19 Grey Ghost TD .10 .25
AZLS102TE19R Grey Ghost RRR FOIL 6.00 15.00
AZLS102TE20 Holy Night of Love and Peace TD .10 .25
AZLS102TE20R Holy Night of Love and Peace RRR FOIL 2.00 5.00
AZLS102TE21 Glasgow TD .10 .25
AZLS102TE21R Glasgow RRR FOIL 1.50 4.00
AZLS102TE22 Hermione TD .10 .25
AZLS102TE22R Hermione RRR FOIL 6.00 15.00
AZLS102TE23 Amazon TD .08 .20
AZLS102TE23R Amazon RRR FOIL 2.00 5.00
AZLS102TE24 Icarus TD .10 .25
AZLS102TE24R Icarus RRR FOIL 10.00 25.00
AZLS102TE25 Eskimo TD .10 .25
AZLS102TE25R Eskimo RRR FOIL 2.00 5.00
AZLS102TE26 Javelin TD .12 .30
AZLS102TE26S Javelin SR FOIL .15 .40
AZLS102TE26SP Javelin SP FOIL 200.00 500.00
AZLS102TE27 York TD .10 .25
AZLS102TE27R York RRR FOIL 2.00 5.00
AZLS102TE28 Aurora TD .08 .20
AZLS102TE28R Aurora RRR FOIL 1.00 2.50
AZLS102TE29 Warspite TD .10 .25
AZLS102TE29SP Warspite SP FOIL 100.00 250.00
AZLS102TE30 Dido TD .15 .40
AZLS102TE31 Newcastle TD .10 .25
AZLS102TE31R Newcastle RRR FOIL 2.00 5.00
AZLS102TE32 Centaur TD .12 .30
AZLS102TE32R Centaur RRR FOIL 5.00 12.00
AZLS102TE33 Duke of York TD .10 .25
AZLS102TE33R Duke of York RRR FOIL 4.00 10.00
AZLS102TE34 Nelson TD .10 .25
AZLS102TE34R Nelson RRR FOIL 10.00 25.00
AZLS102TE35 Illustrious TD .12 .30
AZLS102TE35SP Illustrious SP FOIL 200.00 500.00
AZLS102TE36 Victorious TD .12 .30
AZLS102TE36R Victorious RRR FOIL 12.00 30.00
AZLS102TE37 Royal Navy TD .10 .25
AZLS102TE37R Royal Navy RRR FOIL 2.00 5.00
AZLS102TE38 Royal Navy Ships TD .10 .25
AZLS102TE38R Royal Navy Ships RRR FOIL 3.00 8.00
AZLS102TE39 Never-Ending Tea Party TD .10 .25
AZLS102TE39R Never-Ending Tea Party RRR FOIL 5.00 12.00
AZLS102TE40 To the Proud You TD .12 .30
AZLS102TE40R To the Proud You RRR FOIL 2.50 6.00
AZLS102TE41 Kawakaze TD .10 .25
AZLS102TE41R Kawakaze RRR FOIL 2.00 5.00
AZLS102TE42 Hibiki TD .10 .25
AZLS102TE42R Hibiki RRR FOIL 1.25 3.00
AZLS102TE43 Isuzu TD .10 .25
AZLS102TE43R Isuzu RRR FOIL 1.50 4.00
AZLS102TE44 Akashi TD .20 .50
AZLS102TE45 Suzutsuki TD .10 .25
AZLS102TE45R Suzutsuki RRR FOIL 2.00 5.00
AZLS102TE46 Takao TD .20 .50
AZLS102TE46SP Takao SP FOIL 150.00 400.00
AZLS102TE47 Inazuma TD .10 .25
AZLS102TE47R Inazuma RRR FOIL 4.00 10.00
AZLS102TE48 Yoizuki TD .10 .25
AZLS102TE48R Yoizuki RRR FOIL 2.50 6.00
AZLS102TE49 Shigure TD .10 .25
AZLS102TE49R Shigure RRR FOIL 2.00 5.00
AZLS102TE50 Ayanami TD .12 .30
AZLS102TE50S Ayanami SR FOIL .20 .50
AZLS102TE50SP Ayanami SP FOIL 250.00 600.00
AZLS102TE51 Nagara TD .10 .25
AZLS102TE51R Nagara RRR FOIL 2.00 5.00
AZLS102TE52 Atago TD .12 .30
AZLS102TE52R Atago RRR FOIL 6.00 15.00
AZLS102TE53 Hiei TD .10 .25
AZLS102TE53R Hiei RRR FOIL 4.00 10.00
AZLS102TE54 Kongou TD .10 .25
AZLS102TE54R Kongou RRR FOIL 2.50 6.00
AZLS102TE55 Akagi TD .20 .50
AZLS102TE55SP Akagi SP FOIL 200.00 500.00
AZLS102TE56 Kaga TD .20 .50
AZLS102TE56R Kaga RRR FOIL 10.00 25.00
AZLS102TE57 Sakura Empire TD .10 .25
AZLS102TE57R Sakura Empire RRR FOIL .60 1.50
AZLS102TE58 Four Sisters of Kongou TD .10 .25
AZLS102TE58R Four Sisters of Kongou RRR FOIL 1.50 4.00
AZLS102TE59 Sentiments and Fireworks TD .20 .50
AZLS102TE59R Sentiments and Fireworks RRR FOIL 1.25 3.00
AZLS102TE60 Snack Time TD .10 .25
AZLS102TE60R Snack Time RRR FOIL 2.50 6.00
AZLS102TE61 Z1 TD .10 .25
AZLS102TE61R Z1 RRR FOIL 1.00 2.50
AZLS102TE62 Admiral Hipper TD .10 .25
AZLS102TE62R Admiral Hipper RRR FOIL 1.25 3.00
AZLS102TE63 Z23 TD .20 .50
AZLS102TE63S Z23 SR FOIL .10 .25
AZLS102TE63SP Z23 SP FOIL 125.00 300.00
AZLS102TE64 Z24 TD .15 .40
AZLS102TE64R Z24 RRR FOIL 3.00 8.00
AZLS102TE65 Nurnberg TD .10 .25
AZLS102TE65R Nurnberg RRR FOIL 2.50 6.00
AZLS102TE66 Leipzig TD .10 .25
AZLS102TE66R Leipzig RRR FOIL 1.25 3.00
AZLS102TE67 U-96 TD .40 1.00
AZLS102TE67SP U-96 SP FOIL 100.00 250.00
AZLS102TE68 Elbe TD .20 .50
AZLS102TE68R Elbe RRR FOIL 4.00 10.00
AZLS102TE69 U-556 TD .10 .25
AZLS102TE69R U-556 RRR FOIL .50 1.25
AZLS102TE70 Prinz Eugen TD .10 .25
AZLS102TE70SP Prinz Eugen SP FOIL 500.00 1,200.00
AZLS102TE71 Z2 TD .10 .25
AZLS102TE71R Z2 RRR FOIL 1.00 2.50
AZLS102TE72 Prinz Adalbert TD .25 .60
AZLS102TE72R Prinz Adalbert RRR FOIL 15.00 40.00
AZLS102TE73 Weser TD .10 .25
AZLS102TE73R Weser RRR FOIL 4.00 10.00
AZLS102TE74 Prinz Heinrich TD .10 .25
AZLS102TE74R Prinz Heinrich RRR FOIL 10.00 25.00
AZLS102TE75 Tirpitz TD .15 .40
AZLS102TE75R Tirpitz RRR FOIL 4.00 10.00
AZLS102TE76 Bismarck TD .60 1.50
AZLS102TE76SP Bismarck SP FOIL 300.00 800.00
AZLS102TE77 Iron Blood TD .10 .25
AZLS102TE77R Iron Blood RRR FOIL 1.50 4.00
AZLS102TE78 Army of Bonds TD .10 .25
AZLS102TE78R Army of Bonds RRR FOIL .75 2.00
AZLS102TE79 The Charisma of Black Iron TD .50 1.25
AZLS102TE79R The Charisma of Black Iron RRR FOIL 5.00 12.00
AZLS102TE80 Naive Scheme TD 1.50 4.00
AZLS102TE80R Naive Scheme RRR FOIL .10 .25

2023 Weiss Schwarz The Fruit of Grisaia

GRIS72E001RR Baking Diligently! Makina RR 2.00 4.00
GRIS72E001SPSP Baking Diligently! Makina SP 75.00 150.00
GRIS72E002RR Towards the Shimmering Sea, Michiru RR 2.50 5.00
GRIS72E002SPSP Towards the Shimmering Sea, Michiru SP 100.00 200.00
GRIS72E003RR The Fruit in God's Grasp, Kazuki RR 2.50 5.00
GRIS72E004R Farewell and Promise, Kazuki R 2.00 4.00
GRIS72E004SSR Farewell and Promise, Kazuki SR 12.50 25.00
GRIS72E005R Afterschool Sunset, Makina R .30 .60
GRIS72E005SSR Afterschool Sunset, Makina SR 3.00 6.00
GRIS72E006R Together with Meowmel, Michiru R .30 .75
GRIS72E006SSR Together with Meowmel, Michiru SR 4.00 8.00
GRIS72E007R Fruit of Remorse, Michiru R .30 .75
GRIS72E008R Fruit of Remorse, Makina R .25 .50
GRIS72E008SSR Fruit of Remorse, Makina SR 4.00 8.00
GRIS72E009U Summer Festival Sniper, Makina U .12 .25
GRIS72E010U Atop the Hill Facing the Sea, Michiru U .20 .40
GRIS72E011U Superb Team, Makina & Sachi U .30 .60
GRIS72E012U "Ichigaya" JB U .20 .40
GRIS72E013U Annoying Tsundere, Michiru U .20 .40
GRIS72E014U A Summer Memory, Amane & Makina U .20 .40
GRIS72E015U "Swimsuit" Michiru U .25 .50
GRIS72E016C The Meaning of a "Kiss", Michiru U .12 .25
GRIS72E017C Overwhelming Difference in Skill, Yuuji C .07 .15
GRIS72E018C An Abrupt Visit, JB C .07 .15
GRIS72E019C Pretend Lover, Michiru C .10 .20
GRIS72E020C Riding Tandem, Makina & Yuuji C .05 .10
GRIS72E021C Naive and Innocent, Makina C .05 .10
GRIS72E022C I'm Not a Child, Makina C .07 .15
GRIS72E023U Feeding U .75 1.50
GRIS72E024U Fresh-Fish Superman Tunafish Man U .20 .40
GRIS72E025CR Dangerous Air Mattress CR .30 .75
GRIS72E025RRRR Dangerous Air Mattress RRR 30.00 60.00
GRIS72E026CC Full-Scale Combat Training CC .12 .25
GRIS72E026RRRR Full-Scale Combat Training RRR 4.00 8.00
GRIS72E027CC Sleepy Eyes CC .12 .25

GRIS72E027RRRR Sleepy Eyes RRR 7.50 15.00
GRIS72E028RR Derived Answer, Yuuji RR 1.00 2.00
GRIS72E029R Lone Wolf Disposition, Yumiko R .30 .60
GRIS72E030R During the Peaceful Days, Kazuki R .30 .75
GRIS72E030SSR During the Peaceful Days, Kazuki SR 4.00 8.00
GRIS72E031R Innocent Heart, Makina R .30 .60
GRIS72E031SSR Innocent Heart, Makina SR 5.00 10.00
GRIS72E032R Assertive Stance, Amane R .30 .75
GRIS72E032SSR Assertive Stance, Amane SR 4.00 8.00
GRIS72E033U Afterschool Sunset, Yumiko U .20 .40
GRIS72E034U Blazing Clutches, Makina U .12 .25
GRIS72E035U During the Peaceful Days, Amane U .20 .40
GRIS72E036U Psychology Test, Kazuki U .30 .75
GRIS72E037U Yuuji Kazami U .12 .25
GRIS72E038U Will to Confront, Yumiko U .20 .40
GRIS72E039U The Worst Outcome, Makina U .12 .25
GRIS72E040U Raison d'Etre, Yumiko U .25 .50
GRIS72E041C Withering Heart, Makina U .15 .30
GRIS72E042C Overly Caring Wife, Amane U .05 .10
GRIS72E043C Angelic Howl, Amane U .07 .15
GRIS72E044U Dere For Me U .12 .25
GRIS72E045C Amane-chan's Beauty School C .07 .15
GRIS72E046CR Thundering Roar Under the Bridge CR .20 .40
GRIS72E046RRRR Thundering Roar Under the Bridge RRR 2.50 5.00
GRIS72E047CC Ticket to Heaven CC .12 .25
GRIS72E047RRRR Ticket to Heaven RRR 4.00 8.00
GRIS72E048CC Clinging Wish CC .12 .25
GRIS72E049RR Embracing Affection, Amane RR 2.00 4.00
GRIS72E049SPSP Embracing Affection, Amane SP 150.00 300.00
GRIS72E050RR Well-Loved Maid, Sachi RR 4.00 8.00
GRIS72E050SPSP Well-Loved Maid, Sachi SP 125.00 250.00
GRIS72E051RR Fruit of Remorse, Amane RR 1.00 2.00
GRIS72E051SSR Fruit of Remorse, Amane SR 3.00 6.00
GRIS72E052R Fruit of Remorse, Sachi R .40 .80
GRIS72E052SSR Fruit of Remorse, Sachi SR 2.50 5.00
GRIS72E053R Never-Ending Punishment, Amane R .30 .75
GRIS72E053SSR Never-Ending Punishment, Amane SR 5.00 10.00
GRIS72E054R Embarrassed Smile, Amane R .30 .75
GRIS72E054SSR Embarrassed Smile, Amane SR 5.00 10.00
GRIS72E055R Skilled and Witty Honor Student, Sachi R .75 1.50
GRIS72E055SSR Skilled and Witty Honor Student, Sachi SR 5.00 10.00
GRIS72E056R Suggestive Big Sister, Amane R .30 .75
GRIS72E056SSR Suggestive Big Sister, Amane SR 7.50 15.00
GRIS72E057R Blissful Days, Sachi R .30 .75
GRIS72E057SSR Blissful Days, Sachi SR 5.00 10.00
GRIS72E058R Afterschool Sunset, Amane R .30 .60
GRIS72E058SSR Afterschool Sunset, Amane SR 2.50 5.00
GRIS72E059R Afterschool Sunset, Michiru R .30 .75
GRIS72E059SSR Afterschool Sunset, Michiru SR 2.50 5.00
GRIS72E060U Guitarist, Amane U .20 .40
GRIS72E061U Never-Ending Tunnel, Michiru U .20 .40
GRIS72E062U Spirit to Serve, Sachi U .20 .40
GRIS72E063U Natural Born Tsundere, Michiru U .15 .30
GRIS72E064U The Girls of an Enclosed Garden U .12 .25
GRIS72E065U Always With You, Amane & Yuuji U .12 .25
GRIS72E066C Class Representative, Sachi C .15 .30
GRIS72E067C Descending Sunset, Yuuji & Sachi C .10 .20
GRIS72E068C Rules to Stay Human, Kazuki C .20 .40
GRIS72E069C Wanting to Be Loved, Amane C .20 .40
GRIS72E070C Admiration for Sharks, Sachi C .07 .15
GRIS72E071C Childhood Memories, Sachi C .12 .25
GRIS72E072C Early Arrival, Michiru C .07 .15
GRIS72E073U Charlie U .20 .40
GRIS72E074C Cooking With Sacchin U .30 .75
GRIS72E075CR Night of the Summer Festival CR .30 .75
GRIS72E075RRRR Night of the Summer Festival RRR 6.00 12.00
GRIS72E076CC Pleading Outcry CC .20 .40
GRIS72E076RRRR Pleading Outcry RRR 3.00 6.00
GRIS72E077CC Sunny Park CC .30 .60
GRIS72E077RRRR Sunny Park RRR 12.50 25.00
GRIS72E078RR Genius in Name and Reality, Kazuki RR 3.00 6.00
GRIS72E078SSR Genius in Name and Reality, Kazuki SR 25.00 50.00
GRIS72E079RR Fruit of Remorse, Yumiko RR 2.00 4.00
GRIS72E079SSR Fruit of Remorse, Yumiko SR 12.50 25.00
GRIS72E080RR Je vous suis attache, Yumiko RR 4.00 8.00
GRIS72E080SPSP Je vous suis attache, Yumiko SP 200.00 400.00
GRIS72E081R Shadow Extending in Twilight, Yumiko R .30 .60
GRIS72E081SSR Shadow Extending in Twilight, Yumiko SR 2.00 4.00
GRIS72E082R Speeding, Yuuji R .30 .60
GRIS72E082SSR Speeding, Yuuji SR 2.50 5.00
GRIS72E083R Ephemeral Girl, Yumiko R .30 .75
GRIS72E083SSR Ephemeral Girl, Yumiko SR 6.00 12.00
GRIS72E084R Kuudere, Yumiko R .30 .60
GRIS72E084SSR Kuudere, Yumiko SR 2.50 5.00
GRIS72E085R Omnipotent, Kazuki R .30 .60
GRIS72E085SSR Omnipotent, Kazuki SR 2.50 5.00
GRIS72E086U Youthful Looks, Chizuru U .30 .75
GRIS72E087U Afterschool Sunset, Sachi U .15 .30
GRIS72E088C "Promise" Sachi C .20 .40
GRIS72E089C A Summer Memory, Yumiko C .20 .40
GRIS72E090C Surprise Attack, Yumiko & Yuuji C .20 .40
GRIS72E091C Principal, Chizuru C .25 .50
GRIS72E092C My Own Will, Sachi C .10 .20
GRIS72E093C Little Expectation, Yumiko C .05 .10
GRIS72E094C Confession From the Past, Sachi C .07 .15
GRIS72E095C Throbbing Heartbeat, Yumiko C .07 .15
GRIS72E096SSR Turn Around And There's Sachi SR 5.00 10.00
GRIS72E096U Turn Around And There's Sachi U .20 .40
GRIS72E097CR L'oiseau bleu CR .75 1.50
GRIS72E097RRRR L'oiseau bleu RRR 25.00 50.00
GRIS72E098CC Kiss in the Middle of the Night CC .12 .25
GRIS72E098RRRR Kiss in the Middle of the Night RRR 3.00 6.00
GRIS72E099CC Facing the Future CC .10 .20
GRIS72E100CC Crazy Apple CC .15 .30
GRIS72E100RRRR Crazy Apple RRR 6.00 12.00
GRIS72E101PR Heartbreaking Resolve, Yumiko P 1.50 3.00
GRIS72E102PR Two Taking a Bath, Amane P 1.50 3.00
GRIS72E102SPR Two Taking a Bath, Amane P FOIL 10.00 20.00
GRIS72E103PR A New Beginning, Michiru P 1.50 3.00
GRIS72E103SPR A New Beginning, Michiru P FOIL 7.50 15.00
GRIS72E104PR Napping, Sachi P .75 1.50
GRIS72E104SPR Napping, Sachi P FOIL 7.50 15.00
GRIS72E105PR Awkward Gratitude, Makina P 1.50 3.00

2023 Weiss Schwarz The Fruit of Grisaia Trial Deck

GRIS72TE01TD Her Uneasy Daily Life, Yumiko .25 .50
GRIS72TE02TD Reliable Bodyguard, Yuuji .75 1.50
GRIS72TE03TD Sisterly Relationship, Makina .30 .75
GRIS72TE04RRRR Makina Irisu RRR 10.00 20.00
GRIS72TE04TD Makina Irisu .12 .25
GRIS72TE05SSR Yumiko Sakaki SR .30 .75
GRIS72TE05TD Yumiko Sakaki .12 .25
GRIS72TE06TD Spoiled Child, Makina .30 .60
GRIS72TE07SPSP Sheltered Young Lady, Yumiko SP 175.00 350.00
GRIS72TE07TD Sheltered Young Lady, Yumiko .75 1.50
GRIS72TE08TD Parent-Teacher Conference .25 .50
GRIS72TE09TD Sleeping Like A Cat .30 .75
GRIS72TE10RRRR Sachi Komine RRR 2.50 5.00
GRIS72TE10TD Sachi Komine .30 .75
GRIS72TE11TD Important Practice, Michiru .30 .75
GRIS72TE12TD Sisterly Relationship, Amane .30 .75
GRIS72TE13SPSP Love at First Sight, Amane SP 200.00 400.00
GRIS72TE13TD Love at First Sight, Amane .30 .75
GRIS72TE14TD Together at the Sea, Sachi .25 .50
GRIS72TE15TD Insignificant Worries, Michiru .30 .75
GRIS72TE16RRRR Michiru Matsushima RRR 2.50 5.00
GRIS72TE16TD Michiru Matsushima .30 .75
GRIS72TE17TD Winner's Reward, Sachi .12 .25
GRIS72TE18SSR Amane Suou SR .30 .75
GRIS72TE18TD Amane Suou .12 .25
GRIS72TE19TD Cicada Sisters .60 1.25
GRIS72TE20TD Surprise Party .75 1.50

2023 Weiss Schwarz Guilty Gear - Strive-

GGSTSX06001 Nagoriyuki: Vampire Samurai RR 1.00 2.50
GGSTSX06001SP Nagoriyuki: Vampire Samurai SP 12.00 30.00
GGSTSX06002 May: Cheerful Pirate RR 2.00 5.00
GGSTSX06002OFR May: Cheerful Pirate OFR 50.00 120.00
GGSTSX06003 May: First Mate of Jellyfish Pirates R .25 .60
GGSTSX06003SP May: First Mate of Jellyfish Pirates SP 30.00 80.00
GGSTSX06004 Goldlewis: Secretary of Defense R .30 .75
GGSTSX06004SP Goldlewis: Secretary of Defense SP 20.00 50.00
GGSTSX06005 Chipp: Ninja President R .50 1.25
GGSTSX06005SP Chipp: Ninja President SP 20.00 50.00
GGSTSX06006 Leo: Second King of Illyria R .40 1.00
GGSTSX06006SP Leo: Second King of Illyria SP 8.00 20.00
GGSTSX06007 Nagoriyuki: Wasureyuki R .50 1.25
GGSTSX06007S Nagoriyuki: Wasureyuki SR .60 1.50
GGSTSX06009 Leo: Overworked King U .12 .30
GGSTSX06009S Leo: Overworked King SR .60 1.50
GGSTSX06010 Nagoriyuki: Nightless U .20 .50
GGSTSX06011 Goldlewis: Coffin Wielder U .15 .40
GGSTSX06011S Goldlewis: Coffin Wielder SR 1.00 2.50
GGSTSX06012 Chipp: Incredible Memory U .20 .50
GGSTSX06012S Chipp: Incredible Memory SR .75 2.00
GGSTSX06013S May: Spunky Girl SR 1.50 4.00
GGSTSX06015 Chipp: Calm and Collected Ninja C .15 .40
GGSTSX06019 Goldlewis: Wall of Protection C .15 .40
GGSTSX06021S Rude Awakening SR .60 1.50
GGSTSX06022S Presidential Meeting SR 1.25 3.00
GGSTSX06023C Clash of Immortals CC .25 .60
GGSTSX06024R Jellyfish Pirates CR .50 1.25
GGSTSX06024RR Jellyfish Pirates RRR 2.50 6.00
GGSTSX06025C Overdrive: Down With the System CC .20 .50
GGSTSX06026 Ramlethal: Brigadier of Illyria RR 15.00 40.00
GGSTSX06026OFR Ramlethal: Brigadier of Illyria OFR 125.00 300.00
GGSTSX06027 Millia: Master Assassin RR 1.00 2.50
GGSTSX06027SP Millia: Master Assassin SP 25.00 60.00
GGSTSX06028 Giovanna: Special Operations Unit Officer RR 8.00 20.00
GGSTSX06028SP Giovanna: Special Operations Unit Officer SP 60.00 150.00
GGSTSX06029 Potemkin: Proud Soldier of Zepp R .50 1.25
GGSTSX06029SP Potemkin: Proud Soldier of Zepp SP 20.00 50.00
GGSTSX06030 Giovanna: Ventania R .40 1.00
GGSTSX06030S Giovanna: Ventania SR 2.00 5.00
GGSTSX06031 Zato=1: Dead Man Walking R .30 .75
GGSTSX06031SP Zato=1: Dead Man Walking SP 8.00 20.00
GGSTSX06032 Millia: Winger R .50 1.25
GGSTSX06032S Millia: Winger SR .75 2.00
GGSTSX06033 Ramlethal Valentine R .50 1.25
GGSTSX06033SP Ramlethal Valentine SP 100.00 250.00
GGSTSX06034 Giovanna: Possessing Rei U .12 .30
GGSTSX06035 Millia: Impending Doom U .20 .50
GGSTSX06036 Zato=1: Cursed Entity U .15 .40
GGSTSX06036S Zato=1: Cursed Entity SR 1.25 3.00
GGSTSX06037 Vernon: World Changer U .15 .40
GGSTSX06038 Lucifero: Ramlethal's Familiar U .12 .30
GGSTSX06038S Lucifero: Ramlethal's Familiar SR 10.00 25.00
GGSTSX06039 Potemkin: Heavenly Potemkin Buster U .12 .30
GGSTSX06039S Potemkin: Heavenly Potemkin Buster SR 1.50 4.00
GGSTSX06040 Zato=1: Shadow Wielder C .12 .30
GGSTSX06043 Millia: Bureau Director C .15 .40
GGSTSX06044 Zato=1: Bureau Administrator C .12 .30
GGSTSX06047b Shocking Revelation U .12 .30
GGSTSX06047c Shocking Revelation U .15 .40
GGSTSX06047S Shocking Revelation SR 1.25 3.00
GGSTSX06048 Overdrive: Calvados CR 2.50 6.00
GGSTSX06049 Overdrive: Winger CR .40 1.00
GGSTSX06049R Overdrive: Winger RRR 1.00 2.50
GGSTSX06051 I-No: Time Travelling Musician RR 8.00 20.00
GGSTSX06051SP I-No: Time Travelling Musician SP 50.00 120.00
GGSTSX06052 Baiken: Avenging Swordswoman RR 4.00 10.00
GGSTSX06052SP Baiken: Avenging Swordswoman SP 125.00 300.00
GGSTSX06053 Sol: Savior of the World RR 4.00 10.00
GGSTSX06053SEC Sol: Savior of the World SEC 150.00 400.00
GGSTSX06054 Anji: Fan Dancer R .12 .30
GGSTSX06054SP Anji: Fan Dancer SP 6.00 15.00
GGSTSX06055 Baiken: Samurai Slasher R .40 1.00
GGSTSX06055S Baiken: Samurai Slasher SR 3.00 8.00
GGSTSX06056 Sol: Hastily Summoned R .30 .75
GGSTSX06056S Sol: Hastily Summoned SR 1.50 4.00
GGSTSX06057 Jack-O' Valentine R .40 1.00
GGSTSX06057SP Jack-O' Valentine SP 60.00 150.00
GGSTSX06058 Axl: Time Manipulator R .25 .60
GGSTSX06058SP Axl: Time Manipulator SP 20.00 50.00
GGSTSX06059 I-No: Crushing Power R .40 1.00
GGSTSX06059S I-No: Crushing Power SR 2.00 5.00
GGSTSX06060 Jack-O': By His Side U .12 .30
GGSTSX06061 Sol: Prototype Gear U .12 .30
GGSTSX06061S Sol: Prototype Gear SR 2.00 5.00
GGSTSX06062 Axl: Unfair Way of Life U .12 .30
GGSTSX06062S Axl: Unfair Way of Life SR .50 1.25
GGSTSX06064S Anji: Charismatic Dance SR 1.50 4.00
GGSTSX06066 Jack-O': Forever Elysion Driver U .20 .50
GGSTSX06066S Jack-O': Forever Elysion Driver SR 5.00 12.00
GGSTSX06067 Jack-O': Right to Save the World C .20 .50
GGSTSX06072 Baiken: Campfire Conversation C .12 .30
GGSTSX06073 Anji & Baiken: Common Understanding C .12 .30
GGSTSX06075 Outrage MK.II R .50 1.25
GGSTSX06075S Outrage MK.II SR 2.00 5.00
GGSTSX06076 Removing the Corruption U .15 .40
GGSTSX06076S Removing the Corruption SR 2.00 5.00
GGSTSX06077 Resolve of Steel CR .50 1.25
GGSTSX06078 0 Possible CR .50 1.25
GGSTSX06078RR 0 Possible RRR 2.50 6.00
GGSTSX06079 Overdrive: Forever Elysion Driver CC .50 1.25
GGSTSX06080 Freedom CC .15 .40
GGSTSX06081 Ky: Sword of Justice RR 4.00 10.00
GGSTSX06081OFR Ky: Sword of Justice OFR 50.00 120.00
GGSTSX06082 Faust: Nutty Doctor RR 2.00 5.00
GGSTSX06082SP Faust: Nutty Doctor SP 40.00 100.00
GGSTSX06083 Happy Chaos: Unpredictable Menace R .25 .60
GGSTSX06083SP Happy Chaos: Unpredictable Menace SP 20.00 50.00
GGSTSX06084 Faust: Beginning Operation R .40 1.00
GGSTSX06084S Faust: Beginning Operation SR 2.00 5.00
GGSTSX06085 Testament: Beautiful Gear R .50 1.25
GGSTSX06085SP Testament: Beautiful Gear SP 40.00 100.00
GGSTSX06086 Ky: Mighty King R .40 1.00
GGSTSX06086SP Ky: Mighty King SP 15.00 40.00
GGSTSX06087 Ky: Blood of Juno U .12 .30
GGSTSX06087S Ky: Blood of Juno SR 2.50 6.00
GGSTSX06088 Testament: Elegant Grim Reaper U .20 .50
GGSTSX06088S Testament: Elegant Grim Reaper SR 3.00 8.00
GGSTSX06089 Faust: Bone-Crushing Excitement U .25 .60
GGSTSX06091 Happy Chaos: Tome of Origin U .12 .30
GGSTSX06091S Happy Chaos: Tome of Origin SR .60 1.50
GGSTSX06096 Sibling Succubi of Testament C .15 .40
GGSTSX06097 Dragon Install R .30 .75
GGSTSX06097S Dragon Install SR 2.00 5.00
GGSTSX06098S No Answer SR .60 1.50
GGSTSX06099 Overdrive: Ride the Lightning CR .50 1.25
GGSTSX06099RR Overdrive: Ride the Lightning RRR 3.00 8.00

2023 Weiss Schwarz Guilty Gear - Strive- Promos

GGSTSX06101 SD May & Faust PR 2.50 6.00
GGSTSX06101S SD May & Faust FOIL PR 4.00 10.00
GGSTSX06102 SD Anji & Chipp PR .60 1.50
GGSTSX06102S SD Anji & Chipp FOIL PR 4.00 10.00
GGSTSX06103 SD Nagoriyuki & Potemkin PR 2.50 6.00
GGSTSX06104 SD Giovanna & Goldlewis PR 2.50 6.00
GGSTSX06104S SD Giovanna & Goldlewis FOIL PR 8.00 20.00
GGSTSX06105 SD Millia & Zato=1 PR 1.25 3.00
GGSTSX06105S SD Millia & Zato=1 FOIL PR 3.00 8.00
GGSTSX06106 SD Ramlethal & Baiken PR 4.00 10.00
GGSTSX06106S SD Ramlethal & Baiken FOIL PR 10.00 25.00
GGSTSX06107 SD Sol, Jack-O' & Axl PR 2.00 5.00
GGSTSX06107S SD Sol, Jack-O' & Axl FOIL PR 6.00 15.00
GGSTSX06108 SD I-No & Happy Chaos PR 3.00 8.00
GGSTSX06108S SD I-No & Happy Chaos FOIL PR 5.00 12.00
GGSTSX06109 SD Ky & Leo PR 1.25 3.00
GGSTSX06109S SD Ky & Leo FOIL PR 3.00 8.00
GGSTSX06110 SD Testament PR 4.00 10.00
GGSTSX06110S SD Testament FOIL PR .75 2.00
GGSTSX06P01 GUILTY GEAR -STRIVE- PR 2.50 6.00
GGSTSX06P02 Bridget: New Purpose PR 50.00 120.00
GGSTSX06P03 Sol: Brash Warrior PR .75 2.00
GGSTSX06P05 Ky: Solemn Blade PR 6.00 15.00
GGSTSX06P06 May: Anchor of the Crew PR 4.00 10.00

2023 Weiss Schwarz Guilty Gear - Strive- Trial Deck

GGSTSX06T01 I-No: Malicious Intent TD 2.50 6.00
GGSTSX06T01RR I-No: Malicious Intent RRR .50 1.25
GGSTSX06T02 Sol: Left Behind TD .50 1.25
GGSTSX06T03 Anji & Chipp: Observing From Afar TD 2.00 5.00
GGSTSX06T04 Jack-O' & Aria: Between Existences TD 20.00 50.00
GGSTSX06T05 Sol: Bounty Hunter TD .50 1.25
GGSTSX06T05S Sol: Bounty Hunter SR .50 1.25
GGSTSX06T05SP Sol: Bounty Hunter SP 2.00 5.00
GGSTSX06T06 I-No: Staff Interview TD 3.00 8.00
GGSTSX06T07 Axl: Something Amiss TD 2.00 5.00
GGSTSX06T07RR Axl: Something Amiss RRR .50 1.25
GGSTSX06T08 Jack-O': Bounty Hunter TD .50 1.25
GGSTSX06T08RR Jack-O': Bounty Hunter RRR .50 1.25
GGSTSX06T09 Sol: Greatest Rival TD .50 1.25
GGSTSX06T10 Birthday Memories TD .40 1.00
GGSTSX06T11 Overdrive: Dragon Install TD .50 1.25
GGSTSX06T12 Dangerous Duo TD .50 1.25
GGSTSX06T13 Happy Chaos: Gunslinger TD .50 1.25
GGSTSX06T14 Ky: First King of Illyria TD .60 1.50
GGSTSX06T15 Asuka: Gear Maker TD 1.50 4.00
GGSTSX06T17 Ky: Rapid Escalation TD 40.00 100.00
GGSTSX06T17S Ky: Rapid Escalation SR .50 1.25
GGSTSX06T18 Ky: Greatest Rival TD .50 1.25
GGSTSX06T18OFR Ky: Greatest Rival OFR .50 1.25

2023 Weiss Schwarz Hololive Production Premium Booster

HOL/WE36-E01N Wishing for a Future With You, La+ Darknesss .12 .25
HOL/WE36-E02N Wishing for a Future With You, Oozora Subaru .12 .25
HOL/WE36-E03N Wishing for a Future With You, Inugami Korone .12 .25
HOL/WE36-E04N Wishing for a Future With You, Hakui Koyori .12 .25
HOL/WE36-E05N Wishing for a Future With You, Kazama Iroha .12 .25
HOL/WE36-E06N Wishing for a Future With You, Shiranui Flare .12 .25
HOL/WE36-E07N Wishing for a Future With You, Watson Amelia .12 .25
HOL/WE36-E08N Wishing for a Future With You, Yozora Mel .12 .25
HOL/WE36-E09N Wishing for a Future With You, Amane Kanata .12 .25
HOL/WE36-E10N Wishing for a Future With You, Tsunomaki Watame .12 .25
HOL/WE36-E11N Wishing for a Future With You, Takanashi Kiara .12 .25
HOL/WE36-E12N Wishing for a Future With You, Natsuiro Matsuri .12 .25
HOL/WE36-E13N Wishing for a Future With You, Mori Calliope .12 .25
HOL/WE36-E14N Wishing for a Future With You, Uruha Rushia .12 .25
HOL/WE36-E15N Wishing for a Future With You, Hakos Baelz .12 .25
HOL/WE36-E16N Wishing for a Future With You, Tokoyami Towa .12 .25
HOL/WE36-E17N Wishing for a Future With You, Tokino Sora .12 .25
HOL/WE36-E18N Wishing for a Future With You, Ayunda Risu .12 .25
HOL/WE36-E19N Wishing for a Future With You, Shirakami Fubuki .12 .25
HOL/WE36-E20N Wishing for a Future With You, Pavolia Reine .12 .25
HOL/WE36-E21N Wishing for a Future With You, Ookami Mio .12 .25
HOL/WE36-E22N Wishing for a Future With You, Ceres Fauna .12 .25
HOL/WE36-E23N Wishing for a Future With You, Himemori Luna .12 .25
HOL/WE36-E24N Wishing for a Future With You, Aki Rosenthal .12 .25
HOL/WE36-E25N Wishing for a Future With You, Airani Iofifteen .12 .25
HOL/WE36-E26N Wishing for a Future With You, IRyS .12 .25
HOL/WE36-E27N Wishing for a Future With You, Nekomata Okayu .12 .25
HOL/WE36-E28N Wishing for a Future With You, AZKi .12 .25
HOL/WE36-E29N Wishing for a Future With You, Yuzuki Choco .12 .25
HOL/WE36-E30N Wishing for a Future With You, Kureiji Ollie .12 .25
HOL/WE36-E31N Wishing for a Future With You, Sakamata Chloe .12 .25
HOL/WE36-E32N Wishing for a Future With You, Sakura Miko .12 .25
HOL/WE36-E33N Wishing for a Future With You, Omaru Polka .12 .25
HOL/WE36-E34N Wishing for a Future With You, Momosuzu Nene .12 .25
HOL/WE36-E35N Wishing for a Future With You, Houshou Marine .12 .25
HOL/WE36-E36N Wishing for a Future With You, Robocosan .12 .25
HOL/WE36-E37N Wishing for a Future With You, Nakiri Ayame .12 .25
HOL/WE36-E38N Wishing for a Future With You, Anya Melfissa .12 .25
HOL/WE36-E39N Wishing for a Future With You, Takane Lui .12 .25
HOL/WE36-E40N Wishing for a Future With You, Akai Haato .12 .25
HOL/WE36-E41N Wishing for a Future With You, Ninomae Ina'nis .12 .25
HOL/WE36-E42N Wishing for a Future With You, Moona Hoshinova .12 .25
HOL/WE36-E43N Wishing for a Future With You, Shirogane Noel .12 .25
HOL/WE36-E44N Wishing for a Future With You, Yukihana Lamy .12 .25
HOL/WE36-E45N Wishing for a Future With You, Shishiro Botan .12 .25
HOL/WE36-E46N Wishing for a Future With You, Ouro Kronii .12 .25
HOL/WE36-E47N Wishing for a Future With You, Murasaki Shion .12 .25
HOL/WE36-E48N Wishing for a Future With You, Nanashi Mumei .12 .25
HOL/WE36-E49N Wishing for a Future With You, Minato Aqua .12 .25
HOL/WE36-E50N Wishing for a Future With You, Usada Pekora .12 .25
HOL/WE36-E51N Wishing for a Future With You, Gawr Gura .12 .25
HOL/WE36-E52N Wishing for a Future With You, Tsukumo Sana .12 .25
HOL/WE36-E53N Wishing for a Future With You, Hoshimachi Suisei .12 .25

2023 Weiss Schwarz Hololive Production Vol. 2

HOLW104E001 Aquarium Date for Two Amane Kanata RR 5.00 12.00
HOLW104E001S Aquarium Date for Two Amane Kanata SR 5.00 12.00

HOLW104E002 A Step Towards the Future Mori Calliope RR 5.00 12.00
HOLW104E002S A Step Towards the Future Mori Calliope SR 12.00 30.00
HOLW104E002SP A Step Towards the Future Mori Calliope SP 75.00 200.00
HOLW104E003 Summer Memories Oozora Subaru RR .10 .25
HOLW104E003S Summer Memories Oozora Subaru SR 1.50 4.00
HOLW104E003SSP Summer Memories Oozora Subaru SSP 125.00 300.00
HOLW104E004 A Step Towards the Future Laplace Darknesss RR .30 .75
HOLW104E004S A Step Towards the Future Laplace Darknesss SR2.50 6.00
HOLW104E004SSP A Step Towards the
Future Laplace Darknesss SP 40.00 100.00
HOLW104E005 Chew the Night Sky Yozora Mel R .10 .25
HOLW104E005S Chew the Night Sky Yozora Mel SR .75 2.00
HOLW104E005SSP Chew the Night Sky Yozora Mel SSP 100.00 250.00
HOLW104E006 Handmade Charm Kazema Iroha R .20 .50
HOLW104E006S Handmade Charm Kazema Iroha SR 4.00 10.00
HOLW104E006SSP Handmade Charm Kazema Iroha SSP 200.00 500.00
HOLW104E007 The Princess Tea Party Natsuiro Matsuri R .10 .25
HOLW104E007S The Princess Tea Party Natsuiro Matsuri SR .50 1.25
HOLW104E008 Great Detective Watson Amelia R .15 .40
HOLW104E008S Great Detective Watson Amelia SR 2.50 6.00
HOLW104E008SSP Great Detective Watson Amelia SSP 250.00 600.00
HOLW104E009 A Cozy Time With You Tsunomaki Watame R .10 .25
HOLW104E009S A Cozy Time With You Tsunomaki Watame SR 1.00 2.50
HOLW104E010 Pride of the Phoenix Takanashi Kiara R .10 .25
HOLW104E010S Pride of the Phoenix Takanashi Kiara SR 1.50 4.00
HOLW104E010SSP Pride of the Phoenix Takanashi Kiara SSP 200.00 500.00
HOLW104E011 Morning Greetings Inugami Korone R .10 .25
HOLW104E011S Morning Greetings Inugami Korone SR 1.00 2.50
HOLW104E011SSP Morning Greetings Inugami Korone SSP 150.00 400.00
HOLW104E012 Always By Your Side Hakui Koyori R .10 .25
HOLW104E012S Always By Your Side Hakui Koyori SR 1.25 3.00
HOLW104E013 An Elfs Tea Party Shiranui Flare R .10 .25
HOLW104E013S An Elfs Tea Party Shiranui Flare SR 1.50 4.00
HOLW104E014 A Step Towards the Future Inugami Korone U .10 .25
HOLW104E014S A Step Towards the Future Inugami Korone SR .75 2.00
HOLW104E014SP A Step Towards the Future Inugami Korone SP40.00 100.00
HOLW104E015 One Step Towards the Future Shiranui Flare U .08 .20
HOLW104E015S One Step Towards the Future Shiranui Flare SR .40 1.00
HOLW104E015SP One Step Towards the Future Shiranui Flare SP25.00 60.00
HOLW104E016 A Step Towards the Future Amane Kanata U .08 .20
HOLW104E016S A Step Towards the Future Amane Kanata SR 1.25 3.00
HOLW104E017 A Step Towards the Future Tsunomaki Watame U .08 .20
HOLW104E017S A Step Towards the Future Tsunomaki Watame SR.60 1.50
HOLW104E017SP A Step Towards the Future Tsunomaki Watame SP20.0050.00
HOLW104E018 A Step Towards the Future Oozora Subaru U .08 .20
HOLW104E018S A Step Towards the Future Oozora Subaru SR .75 2.00
HOLW104E018SP A Step Towards the Future Oozora Subaru SP20.00 50.00
HOLW104E019 A Step Towards the Future Natsuiro Matsuri U .08 .20
HOLW104E019S A Step Towards the Future Natsuiro Matsuri SR .60 1.50
HOLW104E019SP A Step Towards the Future Natsuiro Matsuri SP12.00 30.00
HOLW104E020 Hunting Fried Chicken Laplace Darknesss U .08 .20
HOLW104E020S Hunting Fried Chicken Laplace Darknesss SR .50 1.25
HOLW104E021 A Step Towards the Future Yozora Mel U .08 .20
HOLW104E021S A Step Towards the Future Yozora Mel SR .50 1.25
HOLW104E021SP A Step Towards the Future Yozora Mel SP 20.00 50.00
HOLW104E022 A Step Towards the Future Hakui Koyori U .08 .20
HOLW104E022S A Step Towards the Future Hakui Koyori SR 1.25 3.00
HOLW104E022SP A Step Towards the Future Hakui Koyori SP 25.00 60.00
HOLW104E023 A Step Towards the Future Kazama Iroha U .08 .20
HOLW104E023S A Step Towards the Future Kazama Iroha SR 1.00 2.50
HOLW104E023SP A Step Towards the Future Kazama Iroha SP 40.00 100.00
HOLW104E024 A Step Towards the Future Watson Amelia U .15 .40
HOLW104E024S A Step Towards the Future Watson Amelia SR 8.00 20.00
HOLW104E024SP A Step Towards the Future Watson Amelia SP60.00 150.00
HOLW104E025S Tree of Fried Chicken Laplace Darknesss SR 1.00 2.50
HOLW104E026S A Step Towards the Future Takanashi Kiara SR 1.00 2.50
HOLW104E026SP A Step Towards the Future Takanashi Kiara SP40.00 100.00
HOLW104E027S Famous Producer? Tsunomaki Watame SR .50 1.25
HOLW104E028S Property Search Yozora Mel SR .50 1.25
HOLW104E029S Counterattack Shiranui Flare SR .50 1.25
HOLW104E030 One-to-One Fight Kazama Iroha C .10 .25
HOLW104E030S One-to-One Fight Kazama Iroha SR 4.00 10.00
HOLW104E031 Search for the Treasure Box Inugami Korone C .08 .20
HOLW104E031S Search for the Treasure Box Inugami Korone SR .30 .75
HOLW104E032S Are You Feeling Fine? Natsuiro Matsuri SR .60 1.50
HOLW104E033 Research Result Hakui Koyori C .08 .20
HOLW104E033S Research Result Hakui Koyori SR 1.00 2.50
HOLW104E034S Beyond the Universe Oozora Subaru SR .50 1.25
HOLW104E035S Things in This World Are
Too Fragile Amane Kanata SR .60 1.50
HOLW104E036 #SecretSocietyholoX U .08 .20
HOLW104E036S #SecretSocietyholoX SR 2.50 6.00
HOLW104E037 Your Mori CR .12 .30
HOLW104E037R Your Mori RRR 6.00 15.00
HOLW104E038 Sun, Shining CC .10 .25
HOLW104E038R Sun, Shining RRR 2.50 6.00
HOLW104E039R Both Hands Full of Happiness RRR 2.00 5.00
HOLW104E040 Relaxing by the Pool Ookami Mio RR 8.00 20.00
HOLW104E040S Relaxing by the Pool Ookami Mio SR 10.00 25.00
HOLW104E040SSP Relaxing by the Pool Ookami Mio SSP 200.00 500.00
HOLW104E041 Moments of Relaxation IRyS RR .25 .60
HOLW104E041S Moments of Relaxation IRyS SR 3.00 8.00
HOLW104E042 Clad in Pure White Tokoyami Towa RR .20 .50
HOLW104E042S Clad in Pure White Tokoyami Towa SR 4.00 10.00
HOLW104E043 Fluttering Cherry Blossoms
in the Spring Sky Tokino Sora R .10 .25
HOLW104E043S Fluttering Cherry Blossoms
in the Spring Sky Tokino Sora SR 1.00 2.50
HOLW104E043SSP Fluttering Cherry Blossoms
in the Spring Sky Tokino Sora SSP 125.00 300.00
HOLW104E044 A Step Towards the Future Ceres Fauna R .10 .25
HOLW104E044S A Step Towards the Future Ceres Fauna SR 1.50 4.00
HOLW104E044SP A Step Towards the Future Ceres Fauna SP 50.00 120.00
HOLW104E045 Sorry for the Intrusion! Nekomata Okayu R .10 .25
HOLW104E045S Sorry for the Intrusion! Nekomata Okayu SR 2.50 6.00
HOLW104E046 A Step Towards the Future Hakos Baelz R .10 .25
HOLW104E046S A Step Towards the Future Hakos Baelz SR 1.00 2.50
HOLW104E046SP A Step Towards the Future Hakos Baelz SP 100.00 250.00
HOLW104E047 Flower Field and a Dancer AkiRose R .10 .25
HOLW104E047S Flower Field and a Dancer AkiRose SR 1.00 2.50
HOLW104E048 With You in a Land Glowing Red Shirakami Fubuki R.10 .25
HOLW104E048S With You in a Land Glowing
Red Shirakami Fubuki SR 2.50 6.00
HOLW104E048SSP With You in a Land Glowing
Red Shirakami Fubuki SSP 400.00 1,000.00
HOLW104E049 Embarrassed Princess Himemori Luna R .10 .25
HOLW104E049S Embarrassed Princess Himemori Luna SR 1.00 2.50
HOLW104E050 A Step Towards the Future Himemori Luna U .08 .20
HOLW104E050S A Step Towards the Future Himemori Luna SR .75 2.00
HOLW104E050SP A Step Towards the Future Himemori Luna SP20.00 50.00
HOLW104E051 A Step Towards the Future Nekomata Okayu U .08 .20
HOLW104E051S A Step Towards the Future Nekomata Okayu SR 1.25 3.00
HOLW104E051SP A Step Towards the Future Nekomata Okayu SP20.00 50.00
HOLW104E052 A Step Towards the Future Tokino Sora U .08 .20
HOLW104E052S A Step Towards the Future Tokino Sora SR .40 1.00
HOLW104E052SP A Step Towards the Future Tokino Sora SP 20.00 50.00
HOLW104E053 A Step Towards the Future Ookami Mio U .08 .20
HOLW104E053S A Step Towards the Future Ookami Mio SR .50 1.25
HOLW104E053SP A Step Towards the Future Ookami Mio SP 30.00 80.00
HOLW104E054 A Step Towards the Future Tokoyami Towa U .08 .20
HOLW104E054S A Step Towards the Future Tokoyami Towa SR .75 2.00
HOLW104E054SP A Step Towards the Future Tokoyami Towa SP25.00 60.00
HOLW104E055 A Step Towards the Future Shirakami Fubuki U .10 .25
HOLW104E055S A Step Towards the Future Shirakami Fubuki SR .75 2.00
HOLW104E055SP A Step Towards the Future Shirakami Fubuki SP20.00 50.00
HOLW104E056S A Step Towards the Future AkiRose SR .60 1.50
HOLW104E056SP A Step Towards the Future AkiRose SP 12.00 30.00
HOLW104E057 Professor of Manners Tokoyami Towa C .10 .25
HOLW104E057S Professor of Manners Tokoyami Towa SR 1.50 4.00
HOLW104E058 Vampire Hunter Shirakami Fubuki C .08 .20
HOLW104E058S Vampire Hunter Shirakami Fubuki SR .40 1.00
HOLW104E059S Asset Management AkiRose SR .50 1.25
HOLW104E060S Fishing for the
Pond's Boss Monster Ookami Mio SR .40 1.00
HOLW104E061 Hide and Seek Himemori Luna C .08 .20
HOLW104E061S Hide and Seek Himemori Luna SR .75 2.00
HOLW104E062S Pressure From a Senior Tokino Sora SR .40 1.00
HOLW104E063 Riceball Bartender Nekomata Okayu C .08 .20
HOLW104E063S Riceball Bartender Nekomata Okayu SR .50 1.25
HOLW104E064S A Step Towards the Future IRyS SR .50 1.25
HOLW104E064SP A Step Towards the Future IRyS SP 50.00 120.00
HOLW104E065 Waking Up Together CR .08 .20
HOLW104E065R Waking Up Together RRR 8.00 20.00
HOLW104E066 Keeper of Nature CC .08 .20
HOLW104E066R Keeper of Nature RRR 4.00 10.00
HOLW104E067 Thank Chew! CC .08 .20
HOLW104E067R Thank Chew! RRR 5.00 12.00
HOLW104E068 Shirakami's Secret Base CC .10 .25
HOLW104E068R Shirakami's Secret Base RRR 3.00 8.00
HOLW104E069 Encore Just for Two Omaru Polka RR .40 1.00
HOLW104E069S Encore Just for Two Omaru Polka SR 2.50 6.00
HOLW104E070 A Step Towards the Future Sakamata Chloe RR .40 1.00
HOLW104E070S A Step Towards the Future Sakamata Chloe SR 2.50 6.00
HOLW104E070SP A Step Towards the Future Sakamata Chloe SP40.00 100.00
HOLW104E071 Demon Pop Nakiri Ayame RR .30 .75
HOLW104E071S Demon Pop Nakiri Ayame SR 2.50 6.00
HOLW104E072 A Step Towards the Future Kureiji Ollie RR .12 .30
HOLW104E072S A Step Towards the Future Kureiji Ollie SR 2.00 5.00
HOLW104E072SP A Step Towards the Future Kureiji Ollie SP 30.00 80.00
HOLW104E073 Sweet Girlfriend Robocosan R .08 .20
HOLW104E073S Sweet Girlfriend Robocosan SR 1.00 2.50
HOLW104E074 Time Just for Two of Us... Pavolia Reine R 1.25 3.00
HOLW104E074S Time Just for Two of Us... Pavolia Reine SR 10.00 25.00
HOLW104E074SSP Time Just for Two of Us... Pavolia Reine SSP250.00600.00
HOLW104E075 Valentine for You Yuzuki Choco R .10 .25
HOLW104E075S Valentine for You Yuzuki Choco SR 1.50 4.00
HOLW104E076 Peach-Colored Angel Akai Haato R .08 .20
HOLW104E076S Peach-Colored Angel Akai Haato SR .75 2.00
HOLW104E077 Shelter in a Shared Umbrella Takane Lui R .10 .25
HOLW104E077S Shelter in a Shared Umbrella Takane Lui SR 4.00 10.00
HOLW104E078 Reminiscence Anya Melfissa R .10 .25
HOLW104E078S Reminiscence Anya Melfissa SR .75 2.00
HOLW104E078SSP Reminiscence Anya Melfissa SSP 100.00 250.00
HOLW104E079 Event at Home? Momosuzu Nene R .12 .30
HOLW104E079S Event at Home? Momosuzu Nene SR 1.00 2.50
HOLW104E079SSP Event at Home? Momosuzu Nene SSP 100.00 250.00
HOLW104E080 Half-Awake Gaze Sakura Miko R .10 .25
HOLW104E080S Half-Awake Gaze Sakura Miko SR 1.25 3.00
HOLW104E081 After Playing in the Sea... Houshou Marine R .12 .30
HOLW104E081S After Playing in the Sea... Houshou Marine SR12.00 30.00
HOLW104E082 Together With You at the Beachside Town AZKi R .10 .25
HOLW104E082S Together With You at the Beachside Town AZKi SR3.00 8.00
HOLW104E082SSP Together With You
at the Beachside Town AZKi SSP 200.00 500.00
HOLW104E083 A Step Towards the Future Nakiri Ayame U .10 .25
HOLW104E083S A Step Towards the Future Nakiri Ayame SR .60 1.50
HOLW104E083SP A Step Towards the Future Nakiri Ayame SP 25.00 60.00
HOLW104E084 A Step Towards the Future Yuzuki Choco U .08 .20
HOLW104E084S A Step Towards the Future Yuzuki Choco SR .40 1.00
HOLW104E084SP A Step Towards the Future Yuzuki Choco SP 25.00 60.00
HOLW104E085 Spreading the Word Sakamata Chloe U .08 .20
HOLW104E085S Spreading the Word Sakamata Chloe SR 1.50 4.00
HOLW104E086 A Step Towards the Future AZKi U .12 .30
HOLW104E086S A Step Towards the Future AZKi SR 5.00 12.00
HOLW104E086SP A Step Towards the Future AZKi SP 40.00 100.00
HOLW104E087 A Step Towards the Future Akai Haato U .08 .20
HOLW104E087S A Step Towards the Future Akai Haato SR .40 1.00
HOLW104E087SP A Step Towards the Future Akai Haato SP 15.00 40.00
HOLW104E088 A Step Towards the Future Pavolia Reine U .10 .25
HOLW104E088S A Step Towards the Future Pavolia Reine SR 1.25 3.00
HOLW104E088SP A Step Towards the Future Pavolia Reine SP 40.00 100.00
HOLW104E089 A Step Towards the Future Sakura Miko U .08 .20
HOLW104E089S A Step Towards the Future Sakura Miko SR .50 1.25
HOLW104E089SP A Step Towards the Future Sakura Miko SP 40.00 100.00
HOLW104E090 A Step Towards the Future Houshou Marine U .08 .20
HOLW104E090S A Step Towards the Future Houshou Marine SR .50 1.25
HOLW104E090SP A Step Towards the Future Houshou Marine SP40.00 100.00
HOLW104E091 A Step Towards the Future Omaru Polka U .10 .25
HOLW104E091S A Step Towards the Future Omaru Polka SR 2.00 5.00
HOLW104E091SP A Step Towards the Future Omaru Polka SP 40.00 100.00
HOLW104E092 A Step Towards the Future Takane Lui U .08 .20
HOLW104E092S A Step Towards the Future Takane Lui SR 1.00 2.50
HOLW104E092SP A Step Towards the Future Takane Lui SP 20.00 50.00
HOLW104E093 A Step Towards the Future Robocosan U .08 .20
HOLW104E093S A Step Towards the Future Robocosan SR 1.00 2.50
HOLW104E093SP A Step Towards the Future Robocosan SP 15.00 40.00
HOLW104E094 A Step Towards the Future Momosuzu Nene U .08 .20
HOLW104E094S A Step Towards the Future Momosuzu Nene SR .60 1.50
HOLW104E094SP A Step Towards the Future Momosuzu Nene SP25.00 60.00
HOLW104E095 Arachnotrainer Akai Haato C .08 .20
HOLW104E095S Arachnotrainer Akai Haato SR .60 1.50
HOLW104E096S NeneRose Momosuzu Nene SR .25 .60
HOLW104E097S Sushi to Reconsider Humanity Omaru Polka SR .60 1.50
HOLW104E098S Fishing for the Pond's
Boss Monster Sakura Miko SR .50 1.25
HOLW104E099 Boss Nakiri Ayame C .08 .20
HOLW104E099S Boss Nakiri Ayame SR .20 .50
HOLW104E100S I'll Be Your Opponent! Robocosan SR .50 1.25
HOLW104E101S Methods for Success Takane Lui SR .50 1.25
HOLW104E102 Invincible Nurse Yuzuki Choco C .10 .25
HOLW104E102S Invincible Nurse Yuzuki Choco SR .75 2.00
HOLW104E103 Apology Conference Sakamata Chloe C .08 .20
HOLW104E103S Apology Conference Sakamata Chloe SR .60 1.50
HOLW104E104S Apology Conference Houshou Marine SR .75 2.00
HOLW104E105 A Step Towards the Future Anya Melfissa C .08 .20
HOLW104E105S A Step Towards the Future Anya Melfissa SR .60 1.50
HOLW104E105SP A Step Towards the Future Anya Melfissa SP 25.00 60.00
HOLW104E106 Only Two of Us at the Beach CR .10 .25
HOLW104E106R Only Two of Us at the Beach RRR 5.00 12.00
HOLW104E107 Meanwhile, in Another World… CR .10 .25
HOLW104E107R Meanwhile, in Another World… RRR 1.25 3.00
HOLW104E108 REPEAT THiS LiFE WiTH U CC .15 .40
HOLW104E108R REPEAT THiS LiFE WiTH U RRR 8.00 20.00
HOLW104E109 A Gelato For You CC .10 .25
HOLW104E109R A Gelato For You RRR 2.50 6.00
HOLW104E110 City Lights and the Winter Streets Yukihana Lamy RR4.0010.00
HOLW104E110S City Lights and the Winter
Streets Yukihana Lamy SR 10.00 25.00
HOLW104E110SSP City Lights and the Winter
Streets Yukihana Lamy SSP 200.00 500.00
HOLW104E111 Birthday Date Moona Hoshinova RR .30 .75
HOLW104E111S Birthday Date Moona Hoshinova SR 1.50 4.00
HOLW104E112 Catgirl Mode Murasaki Shion RR .12 .30
HOLW104E112S Catgirl Mode Murasaki Shion SR .50 1.25
HOLW104E113 A Step Towards the Future Gawr Gura RR 6.00 15.00
HOLW104E113S A Step Towards the Future Gawr Gura SR 10.00 25.00
HOLW104E113SP A Step Towards the Future Gawr Gura SP 150.00 400.00
HOLW104E114 A Step Towards the Future Ayunda Risu RR .10 .25
HOLW104E114S A Step Towards the Future Ayunda Risu SR 1.00 2.50
HOLW104E114SP A Step Towards the Future Ayunda Risu SP 25.00 60.00
HOLW104E115 Wild Rabbit's Rest Day Usada Pekora R .10 .25
HOLW104E115S Wild Rabbit's Rest Day Usada Pekora SR 2.00 5.00
HOLW104E116 Ina & Takogram Ninomae Ina'nis R 2.00 5.00
HOLW104E116S Ina & Takogram Ninomae Ina'nis SR 12.00 30.00
HOLW104E117 Taking a Bath With You Shirogane Noel R .10 .25
HOLW104E117S Taking a Bath With You Shirogane Noel SR 8.00 20.00
HOLW104E118 Lining up the Pillows Side by Side Ouro Kronii R .12 .30
HOLW104E118S Lining up the Pillows Side by Side Ouro Kronii SR4.00 10.00
HOLW104E118SSP Lining up the Pillows
Side by Side Ouro Kronii SSP 300.00 800.00
HOLW104E119 Pastel Rapper Minato Aqua R .12 .30
HOLW104E119S Pastel Rapper Minato Aqua SR 2.00 5.00
HOLW104E120 A Step Towards the Future Nanashi Mumei R .10 .25
HOLW104E120S A Step Towards the Future Nanashi Mumei SR 1.50 4.00
HOLW104E120SP A Step Towards the Future Nanashi Mumei SP75.00 200.00
HOLW104E121 Backstreet Lion Shishiro Botan R .10 .25
HOLW104E121S Backstreet Lion Shishiro Botan SR .75 2.00
HOLW104E122 At My Home… Airani Iofifteen R .10 .25
HOLW104E122S At My Home… Airani Iofifteen SR 1.00 2.50
HOLW104E123 STELLAR into the GALAXY Hoshimachi Suisei R .25 .60
HOLW104E123S STELLAR into the GALAXY Hoshimachi Suisei SR12.0030.00
HOLW104E124S A Step Towards the Future Yukihana Lamy SR .60 1.50
HOLW104E125 A Step Towards the Future Ouro Kronii U .08 .20
HOLW104E125S A Step Towards the Future Ouro Kronii SR .75 2.00
HOLW104E125SP A Step Towards the Future Ouro Kronii SP 50.00 120.00
HOLW104E126 A Step Towards the Future Shirogane Noel U .08 .20
HOLW104E126S A Step Towards the Future Shirogane Noel SR .60 1.50
HOLW104E126SP A Step Towards the Future Shirogane Noel SP20.00 50.00
HOLW104E127 A Step Towards the Future Moona Hoshinova U .08 .20
HOLW104E127S A Step Towards the Future Moona Hoshinova SR.50 1.25
HOLW104E127SP A Step Towards the Future Moona Hoshinova SP25.00 60.00
HOLW104E128 A Step Towards the Future Murasaki Shion U .10 .25
HOLW104E128S A Step Towards the Future Murasaki Shion SR .50 1.25
HOLW104E128SP A Step Towards the Future Murasaki Shion SP20.00 50.00
HOLW104E129 A Step Towards the Future Shishiro Botan U .08 .20
HOLW104E129S A Step Towards the Future Shishiro Botan SR 1.00 2.50
HOLW104E129SP A Step Towards the Future Shishiro Botan SP40.00 100.00
HOLW104E130 A Step Towards the Future Usada Pekora U .10 .25
HOLW104E130S A Step Towards the Future Usada Pekora SR .75 2.00
HOLW104E130SP A Step Towards the Future Usada Pekora SP 20.00 50.00
HOLW104E131 A Step Towards the Future Hoshimachi Suisei U .08 .20
HOLW104E131S A Step Towards the Future Hoshimachi Suisei SR1.50 4.00
HOLW104E131SP A Step Towards the
Future Hoshimachi Suisei SP 50.00 120.00
HOLW104E132 A Step Towards the Future Minato Aqua U .08 .20
HOLW104E132S A Step Towards the Future Minato Aqua SR 1.50 4.00
HOLW104E132SP A Step Towards the Future Minato Aqua SP 25.00 60.00
HOLW104E133S Dig Here, Arf! Minato Aqua SR .25 .60
HOLW104E134S A Step Towards the Future Airani Iofifteen SR 1.00 2.50
HOLW104E134SP A Step Towards the Future Airani Iofifteen SP12.00 30.00
HOLW104E135S Reticent Sushi Chef Hoshimachi Suisei SR 1.25 3.00
HOLW104E136S Beyond the Rules Shishiro Botan SR .60 1.50
HOLW104E137 Magical Power of Chocolate Usada Pekora C .08 .20
HOLW104E137S Magical Power of Chocolate Usada Pekora SR .40 1.00
HOLW104E138 The Last Supper Murasaki Shion C .10 .25
HOLW104E138S The Last Supper Murasaki Shion SR .25 .60
HOLW104E139 A Step Towards the Future Ninomae Ina'nis C .10 .25
HOLW104E139S A Step Towards the Future Ninomae Ina'nis SR 5.00 12.00
HOLW104E139SP A Step Towards the Future Ninomae Ina'nis SP50.00 120.00
HOLW104E140S Slight Changes Yukihana Lamy SR .75 2.00
HOLW104E141S Musclebrain Stretches Shirogane Noel SR .40 1.00
HOLW104E142 Midsummer Sun CR .15 .40
HOLW104E142R Midsummer Sun RRR 12.00 30.00
HOLW104E143 Magic Lesson CC 1.25 3.00
HOLW104E143R Magic Lesson RRR .08 .20
HOLW104E144R On the Twilight Hill RRR 5.00 12.00
HOLW104E145 COMET CC .10 .25
HOLW104E145R COMET RRR 10.00 25.00

2023 Weiss Schwarz Hololive Production Vol. 2 Promos

HOLW104E146 Sun, Shining PR .25 .60
HOLW104E147 Both Hands Full of Happiness PR .20 .50
HOLW104E148 Your Mori PR .30 .75
HOLW104E149 Shirakami's Secret Base PR .50 1.25
HOLW104E150 Waking Up Together PR .50 1.25
HOLW104E151 Keeper of Nature PR .30 .75
HOLW104E152 Thank Chew! PR .20 .50
HOLW104E153 REPEAT THiS LiFE WiTH U PR .40 1.00
HOLW104E154 A Gelato For You PR .20 .50
HOLW104E155 Only Two of Us at the Beach PR .50 1.25
HOLW104E156 Meanwhile, in Another World… PR .20 .50
HOLW104E157 COMET PR .40 1.00
HOLW104E158 Magic Lesson PR .15 .40
HOLW104E159 Midsummer Sun PR .60 1.50
HOLW104E160 On the Twilight Hill PR .25 .60
HOLW104EP02 Before It Melts Away IRyS PR .10 .25

2023 Weiss Schwarz Nazarick: Tomb of the Undead Vol. 2

OVLS99E001 Nazarick's Greatest Strategist, Demiurge RR .12 .30
OVLS99E001SP Nazarick's Greatest Strategist, Demiurge SP 20.00 50.00
OVLS99E002 True Capability, Narberal RR .12 .30
OVLS99E002SP True Capability, Narberal SP 30.00 80.00
OVLS99E003S The Founding of the Sorcerer Kingdom, Demiurge SR.60 1.50
OVLS99E004S Human Interactions, Lupusregina SR .20 .50
OVLS99E005S Beautiful Adventurer, Nabe SR .60 1.50
OVLS99E006S The Founding of the Sorcerer Kingdom, Shalltear SR2.00 5.00
OVLS99E007S Confronting Despair, Shalltear SR .50 1.25
OVLS99E008 Gazing at the Intruder, CZ U .10 .25
OVLS99E009 Confirming the Operation, Shalltear U .10 .25
OVLS99E010 Initiation for Visitors, Demiurge U .08 .20
OVLS99E011 Easy Victory, Lupusregina U .08 .20
OVLS99E012 Naked Companionship, Demiurge U .08 .20
OVLS99E013 A Demand for an Exchange, Momon U .10 .25
OVLS99E015 Seductive Battle Maid, Solution C .10 .25
OVLS99E020 Prompt Apology, Narberal C .10 .25
OVLS99E021 A Reward of an Encyclopedia U .08 .20
OVLS99E022 The Operation's True Intent CR .12 .30
OVLS99E022R The Operation's True Intent RRR 1.00 2.50
OVLS99E023R Cruel Nature RRR .50 1.25
OVLS99E024 An Escape's End CC .10 .25
OVLS99E024R An Escape's End RRR 1.00 2.50
OVLS99E025 Throne of the Founding Declaration, Albedo RR .15 .40
OVLS99E025SEC Throne of the Founding
Declaration, Albedo SEC 500.00 1,200.00
OVLS99E026 Dark Elf Beast Tamer, Aura RR 3.00 8.00
OVLS99E026SP Dark Elf Beast Tamer, Aura SP 60.00 150.00
OVLS99E027 Timid Floor Guardian, Mare RR .15 .40
OVLS99E027SP Timid Floor Guardian, Mare SP 20.00 50.00
OVLS99E028 Sorcerer King, Ainz RR 2.00 5.00
OVLS99E028SP Sorcerer King, Ainz SP 100.00 250.00
OVLS99E029S Throne of the Founding Declaration, Mare SR .60 1.50

OVLS99E030 Discussion About the Future, Demiurge R .12 .30
OVLS99E030S Discussion About the Future, Demiurge SR 1.00 2.50
OVLS99E031 Delightful Words, Albedo R .08 .20
OVLS99E031S Delightful Words, Albedo SR .60 1.50
OVLS99E032 A Return Gift from ShubNiggurath, Ainz R .12 .30
OVLS99E032S A Return Gift from ShubNiggurath, Ainz SR 4.00 10.00
OVLS99E033S The Founding of the Sorcerer Kingdom, Aura SR 1.00 2.50
OVLS99E034 Unexpected Outcome, Ainz U .25 .60
OVLS99E035 A Moment of Relaxation, Mare U .08 .20
OVLS99E036 Blade to Strike Rebels, Albedo U .10 .25
OVLS99E037 Escaping Laughter, Albedo U .10 .25
OVLS99E038 Hypocritical Master, Ainz U .15 .40
OVLS99E039 Deputy Leader of the Pleiades, Yuri U .20 .50
OVLS99E047 Black Little Goats R .20 .50
OVLS99E047S Black Little Goats SR 6.00 15.00
OVLS99E048 War Bicon Lord U .10 .25
OVLS99E049 Ia ShubNiggurath CR .50 1.25
OVLS99E049R Ia ShubNiggurath RRR 6.00 15.00
OVLS99E050 Emissary to the Empire CC .08 .20
OVLS99E050R Emissary to the Empire RRR .50 1.25
OVLS99E051 Protector of the King CC .10 .25
OVLS99E051R Protector of the King RRR .60 1.50
OVLS99E052 Sentiments Toward Subordinates, Ainz RR 1.00 2.50
OVLS99E052SEC Sentiments Toward Subordinates, Ainz SEC 200.00 500.00
OVLS99E053 Petite and Beautiful Vampire, Shalltear RR 2.00 5.00
OVLS99E053SP Petite and Beautiful Vampire, Shalltear SP 125.00 300.00
OVLS99E054 Dedicated Love for the Lord, Albedo RR .20 .50
OVLS99E054SP Dedicated Love for the Lord, Albedo SP 150.00 400.00
OVLS99E055 Deathbringer, Ainz R .08 .20
OVLS99E055S Deathbringer, Ainz SR .25 .60
OVLS99E056 Cornerlady, Albedo R .12 .30
OVLS99E056S Cornerlady, Albedo SR 1.25 3.00
OVLS99E057S The Founding of the Sorcerer Kingdom, Sebas SR 1.25 3.00
OVLS99E058 Summoning Cavalry Beast, Albedo R .08 .20
OVLS99E058S Summoning Cavalry Beast, Albedo SR .50 1.25
OVLS99E059 The Founding of the Sorcerer Kingdom, Ainz R .08 .20
OVLS99E059S The Founding of the Sorcerer Kingdom, Ainz SR .75 2.00
OVLS99E060 The Surprising Truth, Shalltear R .08 .20
OVLS99E060S The Surprising Truth, Shalltear SR .60 1.50
OVLS99E061 Praises to the Lord, Shalltear U .20 .50
OVLS99E062 Newlywed Roleplay, Albedo U .12 .30
OVLS99E063 Intent of the Operation, Albedo U .10 .25
OVLS99E067 ColdBlooded Pursuer, Shalltear C .08 .20
OVLS99E068 A Fight in the Spa, Ainz C .08 .20
OVLS99E070 Idle Talk in the Audience, Shalltear C .08 .20
OVLS99E071 Sentiments Out of Control U .10 .25
OVLS99E072 True Death U .08 .20
OVLS99E073 Unsuppressible Feelings CR .20 .50
OVLS99E073R Unsuppressible Feelings RRR 4.00 10.00
OVLS99E074 Punishment by Humiliation CC .20 .50
OVLS99E074R Punishment by Humiliation RRR 8.00 20.00
OVLS99E075 The Sorcerer Kingdom of Ainz Ooal Gown CC .10 .25
OVLS99E075R The Sorcerer Kingdom of Ainz Ooal Gown RRR 2.00 5.00
OVLS99E076 FourArm Warrior, Cocytus RR .20 .50
OVLS99E076SP FourArm Warrior, Cocytus SP 20.00 50.00
OVLS99E077 The Founding of the Sorcerer Kingdom, Cocytus R .10 .25
OVLS99E077S The Founding of the Sorcerer Kingdom, Cocytus SR 1.25 3.00
OVLS99E078 Petite Magic Caster, Evileye R .08 .20
OVLS99E078S Petite Magic Caster, Evileye SR 1.00 2.50
OVLS99E080 A Leader's Resolution, Enri R .10 .25
OVLS99E080S A Leader's Resolution, Enri SR 2.50 6.00
OVLS99E081 Reluctant Parting, Evileye R .08 .20
OVLS99E082 Moving Forward Hand in Hand, Enri U .10 .25
OVLS99E083 Gruelling Battle, Evileye U .08 .20
OVLS99E084 Words of Appreciation, Cocytus U .12 .30
OVLS99E085 Sentiments Towards the Villagers, Jugem U .10 .25
OVLS99E086 Goblin Elite Guards U .20 .50
OVLS99E087 Bloody Emperor, Jircniv U .08 .20
OVLS99E090 Goblin Military Band C .10 .25
OVLS99E097 Horn of the Goblin General U .10 .25
OVLS99E098 Forgotten Feelings CR .12 .30
OVLS99E098R Forgotten Feelings RRR .50 1.25
OVLS99E099 Last Resort CC .10 .25
OVLS99E099R Last Resort RRR .60 1.50
OVLS99E100 Male Floor Guardian's Break CC .10 .25
OVLS99E100R Male Floor Guardian's Break RRR .40 1.00
OVLS99E101 Affirmative Demiurge P .10 .25
OVLS99E101S Affirmative Demiurge P FOIL 3.00 8.00
OVLS99E102 The Pursuit Begins, Shalltear P .12 .30
OVLS99E102S The Pursuit Begins, Shalltear P FOIL 2.50 6.00
OVLS99E103 Reading Time, Mare P .20 .50
OVLS99E103S Reading Time, Mare P FOIL 1.00 2.50
OVLS99E104 Brimming with Confidence, Aura P 2.50 6.00
OVLS99E104S Brimming with Confidence, Aura P FOIL 8.00 20.00
OVLS99E105 Floor Guardian of the 5th Floor, Cocytus P .12 .30
OVLS99E105S Floor Guardian of the 5th Floor, Cocytus P FOIL 2.00 5.00
OVLS99E106 Everlasting Devotion, Albedo P .25 .60
OVLS99E106S Everlasting Devotion, Albedo P FOIL 2.00 5.00
OVLS99E107 Time Halt, Ainz P .20 .50
OVLS99E107S Time Halt, Ainz P FOIL 3.00 8.00
OVLS99PE01 Hidden Feelings, Albedo P .15 .40
OVLS99PE02 Deepening Love, Albedo P .50 1.25

2023 Weiss Schwarz Revue Starlight - Re LIVE-

RSLS69E001 Phantom Nana Daiba RR .60 1.50
RSLS69E002 Pandora Misora Kano RR 1.25 3.00
RSLS69E003 Cinderella Lalafin Nonomiya RR .50 1.25
RSLS69E003SP Cinderella Lalafin Nonomiya SP 12.00 30.00
RSLS69E004 Greenhorn Captain Aruru Otsuki RR .50 1.25
RSLS69E004SP Greenhorn Captain Aruru Otsuki SP 40.00 100.00
RSLS69E005 Holiday Felicitations! Tsukasa Ebisu R .25 .60
RSLS69E006 Knight of the Sun Nation Nana Daiba R .50 1.25
RSLS69E006S Knight of the Sun Nation Nana Daiba SR 1.25 3.00
RSLS69E008 Pirate Queen Shizuha Kocho R .50 1.25
RSLS69E009 Pirate Queen's Bodyguard Lalafin Nonomiya R .50 1.25
RSLS69E009S Pirate Queen's Bodyguard Lalafin Nonomiya SR .50 1.25
RSLS69E010 Puss in Boots Futaba Isurugi R .25 .60
RSLS69E011 Jack-o-Lantern Shizuha Kocho R .12 .30
RSLS69E011S Jack-o-Lantern Shizuha Kocho SR .50 1.25
RSLS69E012 Empress of the Digital World Shizuha Kocho U .10 .25
RSLS69E013 Serious Practice Misora & Shizuha U .10 .25
RSLS69E014 Found an Egg! Tsukasa & Misora U .10 .25
RSLS69E015 You Haven't Changed a Bit Futaba & Kaoruko U .50 1.25
RSLS69E016 Fairy Godmother Aruru Otsuki U .10 .25
RSLS69E016S Fairy Godmother Aruru Otsuki SR .50 1.25
RSLS69E017 Sunlit Milk Break Lalafin Nonomiya U .10 .25
RSLS69E018 Ample Athletic Ability Misora Kano U .10 .25
RSLS69E019 A Surprising Skill Tsukasa Ebisu C .10 .25
RSLS69E020 New Stage, Aruru Otsuki C .10 .25
RSLS69E021 Thorough Maintenance Futaba Isurugi C .12 .30
RSLS69E022 Black Lion Nation General Kaoruko Hanayagi C .12 .30
RSLS69E023 Greenhorn Helmsman Misora Kano C .12 .30
RSLS69E024 The Allure of Annitsu Kaoruko Hanayagi C .12 .30
RSLS69E026 Veteran Pirate Tsukasa Ebisu C .12 .30
RSLS69E027 So Many Frogs to Choose From Nana Daiba C .20 .50
RSLS69E028 Friends at the Aquarium U .10 .25
RSLS69E029 The Riches of the World Belong to Us CR .12 .30
RSLS69E029R The Riches of the World Belong to Us RRR .50 1.25
RSLS69E030 Banana's Strawberry Sweets CC .10 .25
RSLS69E030R Banana's Strawberry Sweets RRR .50 1.25
RSLS69E031 The New Cinderella: Champion of Justice! CC .12 .30
RSLS69E031R The New Cinderella: Champion of Justice! RRR .50 1.25
RSLS69E032 Trendy Snacks CC .10 .25
RSLS69E032R Trendy Snacks RRR .60 1.50
RSLS69E033 Yoshitsune Minamoto Yuyuko Tanaka RR .50 1.25
RSLS69E034 Winged Tengu Ichie Otonashi RR .40 1.00
RSLS69E035 Ghost Patrol Squad Deputy Captain Tamao Tomoe RR .50 1.25
RSLS69E036 Benzaiten Fumi Yumeoji R .40 1.00
RSLS69E037 Not a Late Riser, Just a Night Owl Yuyuko Tanaka SP .25 .60
RSLS69E038 Yagyu Jubei Rui Akikaze R .75 2.00
RSLS69E039 Ghost Patrol Squad Captain Ichie Otonashi R .75 2.00
RSLS69E039S Ghost Patrol Squad Captain Ichie Otonashi SR 1.50 4.00
RSLS69E041 Cherry Blossoms in the Bento Tamao & Fumi U .10 .25
RSLS69E041S Cherry Blossoms in the Bento Tamao & Fumi SR 1.25 3.00
RSLS69E042 The Idol of the Room Yuyuko & Ichie U .12 .30
RSLS69E045S Ghost Patrol Squad Member Rui Akikaze SR .25 .60
RSLS69E046 Ghost Patrol Squad Member Yuyuko Tanaka U .10 .25
RSLS69E047 Tengu's Handiwork Ichie Otonashi C .12 .30
RSLS69E049 Balancing the Budget Fumi Yumeoji C .12 .30
RSLS69E051R Keepers of the Peace RRR 1.25 3.00
RSLS69E052 Martial and Dramatic Arts CC .12 .30
RSLS69E052R Martial and Dramatic Arts RRR 1.25 3.00
RSLS69E053 The Hotpot Master CC .10 .25
RSLS69E053R The Hotpot Master RRR .30 .75
RSLS69E054 New Stage, Karen Aijo RR .50 1.25
RSLS69E055 Musketeer Athos Hikari Kagura RR 1.00 2.50
RSLS69E055SP Musketeer Athos Hikari Kagura SP 75.00 200.00
RSLS69E056 Surprise Chocolate Hikari & Karen R .25 .60
RSLS69E056S Surprise Chocolate Hikari & Karen SR .40 1.00
RSLS69E057 Musketeer d'Artagnan Karen Aijo R .50 1.25
RSLS69E057S Musketeer d'Artagnan Karen Aijo SR 2.00 5.00
RSLS69E058 New Stage, Hikari Kagura R .30 .75
RSLS69E058S New Stage, Hikari Kagura SR .40 1.00
RSLS69E059 Musketeer Porthos Mahiru Tsuyuzaki R .25 .60
RSLS69E059SP Musketeer Porthos Mahiru Tsuyuzaki SP 60.00 150.00
RSLS69E060 Knight of the Black Lion Nation Hikari Kagura U .12 .30
RSLS69E061 Knight of the Sun Nation Karen Aijo U .10 .25
RSLS69E062 Knight of the Sun Nation Mahiru Tsuyuzaki U .10 .25
RSLS69E066 Until the Others Arrive Karen & Mahiru U .12 .30
RSLS69E067 A Moment in the Living Room U .10 .25
RSLS69E068 Recharging the Jellyfish Meter CR .10 .25
RSLS69E068R Recharging the Jellyfish Meter RRR .50 1.25
RSLS69E069 A Sunny Day for Laundry CC .25 .60
RSLS69E069R A Sunny Day for Laundry RRR 1.50 4.00
RSLS69E070 Earth Goddess Yachiyo Tsuruhime RR .75 2.00
RSLS69E070SP Earth Goddess Yachiyo Tsuruhime SP 30.00 80.00
RSLS69E071 Belle Shiori Yumeoji RR .50 1.25
RSLS69E072 New Stage, Akira Yukishiro RR 1.00 2.50
RSLS69E073 Aladdin Claudine Saijo R .40 1.00
RSLS69E074 Lu Bu Mei Fan Liu R .40 1.00
RSLS69E075 Heracles Michiru Otori R .25 .60
RSLS69E076 Celestial Goddess Akira Yukishiro R .60 1.50
RSLS69E076S Celestial Goddess Akira Yukishiro SR 1.00 2.50
RSLS69E077 Idle Banter for Two Yachiyo & Mei Fan R .25 .60
RSLS69E077S Idle Banter for Two Yachiyo & Mei Fan SR 2.00 5.00
RSLS69E078 Musketeer Aramis Hoshimi Junna R .50 1.25
RSLS69E078SP Musketeer Aramis Hoshimi Junna SP 40.00 100.00
RSLS69E079 Sun Nation General Maya Tendo R .25 .60
RSLS69E080 Choosing a Frame Carefully Hoshimi Junna U .10 .25
RSLS69E081 Water Goddess Michiru Otori U .10 .25
RSLS69E082 Knight of the Black Lion Nation Claudine Saijo U .10 .25
RSLS69E083 Wind Goddess Shiori Yumeoji U .10 .25
RSLS69E084 This'll Make You Feel Better Michiru Otori U .12 .30
RSLS69E085 Diaochan Yachiyo Tsuruhime U .12 .30
RSLS69E086 Sweet Days Junna & Nana C .12 .30
RSLS69E089 Knight of the Black Lion Nation Hoshimi Junna C .12 .30
RSLS69E090 Looking Fresh in the Mirror Shiori Yumeoji C .10 .25
RSLS69E091 Genie of the Lamp Maya Tendo C .12 .30
RSLS69E092 Fire Goddess Mei Fan Liu C .12 .30
RSLS69E093 Beast Akira Yukishiro C .20 .50
RSLS69E094 Smirking Behind the Pillar Yachiyo Tsuruhime C .12 .30
RSLS69E095 Flexible Girl from China Mei Fan Liu C .12 .30
RSLS69E096C The Opera House Expert Claudine Saijo C .20 .50
RSLS69E097 You Need Friends for Clothes Shopping U .12 .30
RSLS69E098 Platinum on Ice CR .12 .30
RSLS69E098R Platinum on Ice RRR .50 1.25
RSLS69E099 Glittering Fish Tanks, Glittering Eyes CC .10 .25
RSLS69E099R Glittering Fish Tanks, Glittering Eyes RRR .50 1.25
RSLS69E100 A Fan-tea-stic Tasting CC .20 .50
RSLS69E100R A Fan-tea-stic Tasting RRR .50 1.25

2023 Weiss Schwarz Revue Starlight - Re LIVE- Promos

RSLS69E101 Sweet but Dangerous** Aruru Otsuki PR .50 1.25
RSLS69E101S Sweet but Dangerous** Aruru Otsuki FOIL PR .40 1.00
RSLS69E102 A Green Thumb's Delight** Tamao Tomoe PR .25 .60
RSLS69E102S A Green Thumb's Delight** Tamao Tomoe FOIL PR .25 .60
RSLS69E103 Trying Out the Mask** Karen Aijo PR .50 1.25
RSLS69E104 Siegfeld General Hospital** Akira Yukishiro PR .60 1.50
RSLS69E104S Siegfeld General Hospital** Akira Yukishiro FOIL PR .50 1.25
RSLS69PE01 Witch Twins Unite!** Aruru Otsuki PR .12 .30
RSLS69PE02 Testing Luck in the New Year** Tamao Tomoe PR 3.00 8.00

2023 Weiss Schwarz Revue Starlight The Movie

RSLS98E001 Towards the Stage Beyond the Rerun, Nana Daiba RR 2.00 5.00
RSLS98E001SP Towards the Stage Beyond the Rerun, Nana Daiba SP 75.00 200.00
RSLS98E002 Path Adorned with Cherry Blossoms, Kaoruko Hanayagi RR 1.50 4.00
RSLS98E003 Stage Girl of the Silver Screen, Nana Daiba R .50 1.25
RSLS98E003S Stage Girl of the Silver Screen, Nana Daiba SR 2.00 5.00
RSLS98E004 Stage Girl of the Silver Screen, Kaoruko Hanayagi R .30 .75
RSLS98E004S Stage Girl of the Silver Screen, Kaoruko Hanayagi SR 2.00 5.00
RSLS98E005 Our Future Destination, Kaoruko Hanayagi R .25 .60
RSLS98E005S Our Future Destination, Kaoruko Hanayagi SR 4.00 10.00
RSLS98E006 Hunting Revue, Nana Daiba R .25 .60
RSLS98E006S Hunting Revue, Nana Daiba SR 1.25 3.00
RSLS98E007 Our Future Destination, Nana Daiba R .20 .50
RSLS98E007S Our Future Destination, Nana Daiba SR 2.00 5.00
RSLS98E008 Selfish Highway, Kaoruko Hanayagi R .25 .60
RSLS98E008S Selfish Highway, Kaoruko Hanayagi SR 1.00 2.50
RSLS98E010 The One Mesmerized by the Stage Girls, Giraffe .10 .25
RSLS98E011 Dancing Sword, Nana Daiba U .12 .30
RSLS98E011S Dancing Sword, Nana Daiba SR 1.00 2.50
RSLS98E012 Breaking Off Ties, Kaoruko Hanayagi U .15 .40
RSLS98E013S Resentment Revue, Kaoruko Hanayagi SR .75 2.00
RSLS98E014 It's All for Me? Kaoruko Hanayagi C .12 .30
RSLS98E015 Now Is the Time to Descend From the Tower, Nana Daiba .08 .20
RSLS98E017 Her Real Self, Kaoruko Hanayagi C .25 .60
RSLS98E019 Reminiscence, Nana Daiba C .12 .30
RSLS98E021 Annihilation Revue CR .20 .50
RSLS98E021SCC Annihilation Revue SCC 25.00 60.00
RSLS98E022 Waiting for You CC .25 .60
RSLS98E022SCC Waiting for You SCC 2.50 6.00
RSLS98E023SCC Blooming Rage SCC 5.00 12.00
RSLS98E024 To Live Her Life on Stage, Mahiru Tsuyuzaki RR 8.00 20.00
RSLS98E024SP To Live Her Life on Stage, Mahiru Tsuyuzaki SP 60.00 150.00
RSLS98E025 Green Glow, Junna Hoshimi RR .50 1.25
RSLS98E026 Hunting Revue, Junna Hoshimi R .25 .60
RSLS98E027 Stage Girl of the Silver Screen, Junna Hoshimi R .50 1.25
RSLS98E027S Stage Girl of the Silver Screen, Junna Hoshimi SR 2.50 6.00
RSLS98E028 Our Future Destination, Junna Hoshimi R .20 .50
RSLS98E028S Our Future Destination, Junna Hoshimi SR 1.50 4.00
RSLS98E029 Our Future Destination, Mahiru Tsuyuzaki R .25 .60
RSLS98E029S Our Future Destination, Mahiru Tsuyuzaki SR 1.50 4.00
RSLS98E030 Stage Girl of the Silver Screen, Mahiru Tsuyuzaki R .20 .50
RSLS98E030S Stage Girl of the Silver Screen, Mahiru Tsuyuzaki SR 2.00 5.00
RSLS98E031 If You Won't Act on Stage, Mahiru Tsuyuzaki R .20 .50
RSLS98E031S If You Won't Act on Stage, Mahiru Tsuyuzaki SR .50 1.25
RSLS98E032 You're on the Stage With Me, Right? Mahiru Tsuyuzaki U .08 .20
RSLS98E032S You're on the Stage With Me, Right? Mahiru Tsuyuzaki SR .75 2.00
RSLS98E035S Her Own Words, Junna Hoshimi SR 1.25 3.00
RSLS98E036 Still an Unfinished Script, Junna Hoshimi C .20 .50
RSLS98E037 Someday on a New Stage, Junna Hoshimi C .15 .40
RSLS98E038 Cheering On, Mahiru Tsuyuzaki C .08 .20
RSLS98E039 Aiming for the Gold Medal, Mahiru Tsuyuzaki C .08 .20
RSLS98E040 For the Field Trip, Mahiru Tsuyuzaki C .08 .20
RSLS98E043 Specially Made Gold Medal U .08 .20
RSLS98E044 A Stage Where I'm the Protagonist CR .20 .50
RSLS98E044SCC A Stage Where I'm the Protagonist SCC 6.00 15.00
RSLS98E045 Our Stage CC .08 .20
RSLS98E045SCC Our Stage SCC 5.00 12.00
RSLS98E046 Co-star Revue CC .08 .20
RSLS98E046SCC Co-star Revue SCC 5.00 12.00
RSLS98E047 Path Adorned with Cherry Blossoms, Futaba Isurugi DR 1.25 3.00
RSLS98E047SP Path Adorned with Cherry Blossoms, Futaba Isurugi SP 40.00 100.00
RSLS98E048 You and I Together, Claudine Saijo DR .30 .75
RSLS98E049 Next Stage and Next Role, Karen Aijo DR 2.50 6.00
RSLS98E049SEC Next Stage and Next Role, Karen Aijo SEC 125.00 300.00
RSLS98E050 Stage Girl of the Silver Screen, Claudine Saijo R .25 .60
RSLS98E050S Stage Girl of the Silver Screen, Claudine Saijo SR 2.00 5.00
RSLS98E051 [RIVAL] Claudine Saijo R .20 .50
RSLS98E051S [RIVAL] Claudine Saijo SR 2.00 5.00
RSLS98E052 Selfish Highway, Futaba Isurugi R .40 1.00
RSLS98E052S Selfish Highway, Futaba Isurugi SR 4.00 10.00
RSLS98E053 Stage Girl of the Silver Screen, Karen Aijo R .30 .75
RSLS98E053S Stage Girl of the Silver Screen, Karen Aijo SR 1.50 4.00
RSLS98E054 Reunion, Karen Aijo R .25 .60
RSLS98E054S Reunion, Karen Aijo SR 4.00 10.00
RSLS98E055 Stage Girl of the Silver Screen, Futaba Isurugi R .20 .50
RSLS98E055S Stage Girl of the Silver Screen, Futaba Isurugi SR 1.50 4.00
RSLS98E056 Our Future Destination, Futaba Isurugi R .25 .60
RSLS98E056S Our Future Destination, Futaba Isurugi SR 1.50 4.00
RSLS98E057 Our Future Destination, Claudine Saijo R .25 .60
RSLS98E057S Our Future Destination, Claudine Saijo SR 1.50 4.00
RSLS98E058 Our Future Destination, Karen Aijo R .25 .60
RSLS98E058S Our Future Destination, Karen Aijo SR 1.50 4.00
RSLS98E059S The Last Line, Karen Aijo SR 1.00 2.50
RSLS98E060 Gambling Den, Claudine Saijo U .20 .50
RSLS98E061 Greetings, Karen Aijo U .20 .50
RSLS98E063 The Devil's Sweet Talk, Claudine Saijo U .15 .40
RSLS98E063S The Devil's Sweet Talk, Claudine Saijo SR 2.50 6.00
RSLS98E064 Interrupting, Futaba Isurugi U .20 .50
RSLS98E064S Interrupting, Futaba Isurugi SR 2.50 6.00
RSLS98E066 Everyone's Future Path, Claudine Saijo C .12 .30
RSLS98E067 Skills on the Board, Claudine Saijo C .12 .30
RSLS98E068 Why? Futaba Isurugi C .10 .25
RSLS98E069 Seeking Understanding, Futaba Isurugi C .08 .20
RSLS98E072 Day Before the Field Trip, Futaba Isurugi C .08 .20
RSLS98E074 Train of the Reborn U .20 .50
RSLS98E075 I Am Reborn CR .30 .75
RSLS98E075SCC I Am Reborn SCC 20.00 50.00
RSLS98E076 Making You Wait CC .15 .40
RSLS98E077 A Beautiful Conclusion CC .10 .25
RSLS98E077SCC A Beautiful Conclusion SCC 8.00 20.00
RSLS98E078 Our Future Destination, Hikari Kagura RR 2.00 5.00
RSLS98E078S Our Future Destination, Hikari Kagura SR 6.00 15.00
RSLS98E079 See You, Hikari Kagura RR 1.25 3.00
RSLS98E079SEC See You, Hikari Kagura SEC 75.00 200.00
RSLS98E080 You and I Together, Maya Tendo RR .40 1.00
RSLS98E081 Stage Girl of the Silver Screen, Hikari Kagura R .20 .50
RSLS98E081S Stage Girl of the Silver Screen, Hikari Kagura SR .40 1.00
RSLS98E082 Our Future Destination, Maya Tendo R 1.25 3.00
RSLS98E082S Our Future Destination, Maya Tendo SR 15.00 40.00
RSLS98E083 Stage Girl of the Silver Screen, Maya Tendo R .25 .60
RSLS98E083S Stage Girl of the Silver Screen, Maya Tendo SR 1.50 4.00
RSLS98E084 Vessel of the Gods That Reflects Infinity, Maya Tendo R .30 .75
RSLS98E084S Vessel of the Gods That Reflects Infinity, Maya Tendo SR 4.00 10.00
RSLS98E085 Reunion, Hikari Kagura R .25 .60
RSLS98E085S Reunion, Hikari Kagura SR 1.25 3.00
RSLS98E086 Natural Disposition on the Board, Maya Tendo U .20 .50
RSLS98E087 Time of Farewell, Hikari Kagura U .20 .50
RSLS98E087S Time of Farewell, Hikari Kagura SR .50 1.25
RSLS98E088 [RIVAL] Maya Tendo U .20 .50
RSLS98E088S [RIVAL] Maya Tendo SR 3.00 8.00
RSLS98E089 Aiming for the Gold Medal, Hikari Kagura U .10 .25
RSLS98E090 Gazing at the Faraway Sea, Hikari Kagura C .15 .40
RSLS98E092 Greetings, Hikari Kagura C .12 .30
RSLS98E095 Run! Hikari Kagura C .08 .20
RSLS98E096 Soul Revue U .20 .50
RSLS98E097 Ripe Tomato U .20 .50
RSLS98E098 Final Act, And... CR .30 .75
RSLS98E098SCC Final Act, And... SCC 25.00 60.00
RSLS98E099 Because It's You, My All Can Be... CR .25 .60
RSLS98E099SCC Because It's You, My All Can Be... SCC 8.00 20.00
RSLS98E100 Let's Meet Again on This Stage CC .08 .20

2023 Weiss Schwarz Revue Starlight The Movie Promo

RSLS98E101 Pop-up Stage Girl, Karen Aijo PR 5.00 12.00
RSLS98E102 Pop-up Stage Girl, Hikari Kagura PR 1.00 2.50
RSLS98E103 Pop-up Stage Girl, Mahiru Tsuyuzaki PR 1.00 2.50
RSLS98E104 Pop-up Stage Girl, Claudine Saijo PR 1.00 2.50
RSLS98E105 Pop-up Stage Girl, Maya Tendo PR 1.00 2.50
RSLS98E107 Pop-up Stage Girl, Nana Daiba PR .75 2.00
RSLS98E108 Pop-up Stage Girl, Kaoruko Hanayagi PR 1.00 2.50
RSLS98PE02 Ticket to the Stage of Destiny, Hikari Kagura PR 2.00 5.00

2023 Weiss Schwarz The Quintessential Quintuplets Movie

5HYW101E001OFROFR Unparalleled Beauty, Ichika Nakano OFR 40.00 80.00
5HYW101E001RR Unparalleled Beauty, Ichika Nakano RR .75 1.50
5HYW101E002RR Irrepressible Feelings, Ichika Nakano RR .75 1.50
5HYW101E002SSPSSP Irrepressible Feelings, Ichika Nakano SSP 150.00 300.00
5HYW101E003R Relaxing in a Yukata, Ichika Nakano R .30 .60
5HYW101E003SSR Relaxing in a Yukata, Ichika Nakano SR 4.00 8.00
5HYW101E004HYRHYR Flowers of Gratitude, Yotsuba Nakano HYR 30.00 75.00
5HYW101E004R Flowers of Gratitude, Yotsuba Nakano R .75 1.50
5HYW101E005R Beside You, Yotsuba Nakano R .50 1.00
5HYW101E005SSR Beside You, Yotsuba Nakano SR 6.00 12.00
5HYW101E006R Guts of the Eldest Sister, Ichika Nakano R .20 .40
5HYW101E006SSR Guts of the Eldest Sister, Ichika Nakano SR 2.00 4.00
5HYW101E007R The Answer He Chose, Futaro Uesugi R .20 .40
5HYW101E007SSR The Answer He Chose, Futaro Uesugi SR .75 1.50
5HYW101E008R Quintuplicate Trails, Ichika Nakano R .30 .60
5HYW101E008SSR Quintuplicate Trails, Ichika Nakano SR 4.00 8.00

5HYW101E009SSR Established Actress, Ichika Nakano SR 2.50 5.00
5HYW101E009U Established Actress, Ichika Nakano U .10 .20
5HYW101E010SSR Sneaking Into the School Festival, Ichika Nakano SR 2.00 4.00
5HYW101E010U Sneaking Into the School Festival, Ichika Nakano U.12 .25
5HYW101E011SSR Our Resolve, Yotsuba Nakano SR .75 1.50
5HYW101E011U Our Resolve, Yotsuba Nakano U .10 .20
5HYW101E012SSR Unexpected Meeting, Yotsuba Nakano SR 1.50 3.00
5HYW101E012U Unexpected Meeting, Yotsuba Nakano U .07 .15
5HYW101E013C Good at Trapping People, Ichika Nakano C .07 .15
5HYW101E013SSR Good at Trapping People, Ichika Nakano SR 1.50 3.00
5HYW101E014C Growth, Ichika Nakano C .07 .15
5HYW101E014SSR Growth, Ichika Nakano SR 1.25 2.50
5HYW101E015C Surprise Marriage Proposal, Yotsuba Nakano C .07 .15
5HYW101E015SSR Surprise Marriage Proposal, Yotsuba Nakano SR1.25 2.50
5HYW101E016C Forever as Five, Ichika & Nino & Miku & Yotsuba & Itsuki C .10 .20
5HYW101E016SSR Forever as Five, Ichika & Nino & Miku & Yotsuba & Itsuki SR 12.50 25.00
5HYW101E017C Quintuplets in Swimsuits, Ichika & Nino & Miku & Yotsuba & Itsuki C .05 .10
5HYW101E017SSR Quintuplets in Swimsuits, Ichika & Nino & Miku & Yotsuba & Itsuki SR 7.50 15.00
5HYW101E018C First Date, Yotusba Nakano C .10 .20
5HYW101E018SSR First Date, Yotsuba Nakano SR 5.00 10.00
5HYW101E019C Reminiscing, Ichika Nakano C .05 .10
5HYW101E019SSR Reminiscing, Ichika Nakano SR 1.25 2.50
5HYW101E020C Treasuring Her Honest Feelings C .10 .20
5HYW101E020SSR Treasuring Her Honest Feelings SR 2.50 5.00
5HYW101E021CR Bold Answer-Checking Method CR .15 .30
5HYW101E021OFROFR Bold Answer-Checking Method OFR 75.00 150.00
5HYW101E022CC Acting Performance of an Actress CC .07 .15
5HYW101E022RRRR Acting Performance of an Actress RRR 2.00 4.00
5HYW101E023CC As Five Now and In the Future CC .07 .15
5HYW101E023RRRR As Five Now and In the Future RRR 2.00 4.00
5HYW101E024OFROFR Unparalleled Beauty, Yotsuba Nakano OFR75.00150.00
5HYW101E024RR Unparalleled Beauty, Yotsuba Nakano RR 1.00 2.00
5HYW101E025RR Special** Yotsuba Nakano RR 1.25 2.50
5HYW101E025SSPSSP Special** Yotsuba Nakano SSP 125.00 250.00
5HYW101E026R My Memory With You, Yotsuba Nakano R .60 1.25
5HYW101E026SSR My Memory With You, Yotsuba Nakano SR 1.25 2.50
5HYW101E027HYRHYR Flowers of Gratitude, Miku Nakano HYR75.00 150.00
5HYW101E027R Flowers of Gratitude, Miku Nakano R .40 .80
5HYW101E028R Quintuplicate Trails, Itsuki Nakano R .60 1.25
5HYW101E028SSR Quintuplicate Trails, Itsuki Nakano SR 12.50 25.00
5HYW101E029R Quintuplicate Trails, Yotsuba Nakano R .50 1.00
5HYW101E029SSR Quintuplicate Trails, Yotsuba Nakano SR 5.00 10.00
5HYW101E030SSR Outstanding Physical Ability, Yotsuba Nakano SR1.25 2.50
5HYW101E030U Outstanding Physical Ability, Yotsuba Nakano U .07 .15
5HYW101E031SSR Our Resolve, Itsuki Nakano SR 4.00 8.00
5HYW101E031U Our Resolve, Itsuki Nakano U .10 .20
5HYW101E032SSR At Work, Yotsuba Nakano SR 1.00 2.00
5HYW101E032U At Work, Yotsuba Nakano U .12 .25
5HYW101E033SSR In a Costume, Yotsuba Nakano SR 3.00 6.00
5HYW101E033U In a Costume, Yotsuba Nakano U .12 .25
5HYW101E034SSR What She Wanted to Convey, Miku Nakano SR1.25 2.50
5HYW101E034U What She Wanted to Convey, Miku Nakano U .07 .15
5HYW101E035SSR Watchful Gaze, Itsuki Nakano SR 5.00 10.00
5HYW101E035U Watchful Gaze, Itsuki Nakano U .12 .25
5HYW101E036SSR Fulfillment of Her Dream, Miku Nakano SR 2.00 4.00
5HYW101E036U Fulfillment of Her Dream, Miku Nakano U .07 .15
5HYW101E037SSR Fruits of Labor, Itsuki Nakano SR 3.00 6.00
5HYW101E037U Fruits of Labor, Itsuki Nakano U .15 .30
5HYW101E038C Checking Out the Competition? Miku Nakano C .07 .15
5HYW101E038SSR Checking Out the Competition? Miku Nakano SR1.50 3.00
5HYW101E039C End of Her Escape, Yotsuba Nakano C .05 .10
5HYW101E039SSR End of Her Escape, Yotsuba Nakano SR 1.50 3.00
5HYW101E040C Being Diligent After School, Itsuki Nakano C .07 .15
5HYW101E040SSR Being Diligent After School, Itsuki Nakano SR1.50 3.00
5HYW101E041C Sneaking Around Isn't Bad Either? Yotsuba Nakano C .05 .10
5HYW101E041SSR Sneaking Around Isn't Bad Either? Yotsuba Nakano SR .75 1.50
5HYW101E042C First Day's After Party, Yotsuba Nakano C .05 .10
5HYW101E042SSR First Day's After Party, Yotsuba Nakano SR 1.50 3.00
5HYW101E043C Believing in ""Like"", Miku Nakano C .05 .10
5HYW101E043S(SR) Believing in ""Like"", Miku Nakano SR 1.25 2.50
5HYW101E044C Delightful Present, Itsuki Nakano C .05 .10
5HYW101E044SSR Delightful Present, Itsuki Nakano SR 2.50 5.00
5HYW101E045C Sensing Her Growth, Miku Nakano C .07 .15
5HYW101E045SSR Sensing Her Growth, Miku Nakano SR 2.00 4.00
5HYW101E046R Last Quintuplets Game R .25 .50
5HYW101E046SSR Last Quintuplets Game SR 1.25 2.50
5HYW101E047SSR Reason For Transferring Schools SR 5.00 10.00
5HYW101E047U Reason For Transferring Schools U .05 .10
5HYW101E048CR Feelings Void of Lies CR .17 .35
5HYW101E048OFROFR Feelings Void of Lies OFR 25.00 50.00
5HYW101E049CC Parting With a Memory CC .12 .25
5HYW101E049RRRR Parting With a Memory RRR 4.00 8.00
5HYW101E050OFROFR Unparalleled Beauty, Itsuki Nakano OFR50.00 100.00
5HYW101E050RR Unparalleled Beauty, Itsuki Nakano RR 2.00 4.00
5HYW101E051RR Unchanging Feelings, Nino Nakano RR 7.50 15.00
5HYW101E051SSPSSP Unchanging Feelings, Nino Nakano SSP250.00500.00
5HYW101E052OFROFR Unparalleled Beauty, Nino Nakano OFR75.00 150.00
5HYW101E052RR Unparalleled Beauty, Nino Nakano RR 1.00 2.00
5HYW101E053RR Realized Feelings, Itsuki Nakano RR 6.00 12.00
5HYW101E053SSPSSP Realized Feelings, Itsuki Nakano SSP 300.00 750.00
5HYW101E054HYRHYR Flowers of Gratitude, Ichika Nakano HYR125.00250.00
5HYW101E054R Flowers of Gratitude, Ichika Nakano R .60 1.25
5HYW101E055HYRHYR Flowers of Gratitude, Itsuki Nakano HYR125.00250.00
5HYW101E055R Flowers of Gratitude, Itsuki Nakano R .30 .75
5HYW101E056R Recreation, Nino Nakano R .60 1.25
5HYW101E056SSR Recreation, Nino Nakano SR 7.50 15.00
5HYW101E057R Continuous Pursuit of Ideals, Itsuki Nakano R .60 1.25
5HYW101E057SSR Continuous Pursuit of Ideals, Itsuki Nakano SR7.50 15.00
5HYW101E058R Great Love, Nino Nakano R .50 1.00
5HYW101E058SSR Great Love, Nino Nakano SR 6.00 12.00
5HYW101E059R Studying in Glasses, Itsuki Nakano R .50 1.00
5HYW101E059SSR Studying in Glasses, Itsuki Nakano SR 7.50 15.00
5HYW101E060SSR Food Made With Love, Nino Nakano SR 2.50 5.00
5HYW101E060U Food Made With Love, Nino Nakano U .07 .15
5HYW101E061SSR Hearty Appetite? Itsuki Nakano SR 7.50 15.00
5HYW101E061U Hearty Appetite? Itsuki Nakano U .15 .30
5HYW101E062SSR Our Resolve, Ichika Nakano SR 2.00 4.00
5HYW101E062U Our Resolve, Ichika Nakano U .12 .25
5HYW101E063SSR Soft Gaze, Ichika Nakano SR 1.50 3.00
5HYW101E063U Soft Gaze, Ichika Nakano U .15 .30
5HYW101E064SSR Her Own Volition, Itsuki Nakano SR 1.25 2.50
5HYW101E064U Her Own Volition, Itsuki Nakano U .07 .15
5HYW101E065SSR Up-And-Coming Actress, Ichika Nakano SR 7.50 15.00
5HYW101E065U Up-And-Coming Actress, Ichika Nakano U .10 .20
5HYW101E066SSR Our Resolve, Nino Nakano SR .75 1.50
5HYW101E066U Our Resolve, Nino Nakano U .10 .20
5HYW101E067C Gentle Teasing, Ichika Nakano C .07 .15
5HYW101E067SSR Gentle Teasing, Ichika Nakano SR 1.50 3.00
5HYW101E068C Secluded Incident, Itsuki Nakano C .05 .10
5HYW101E069C School Festival, Itsuki Nakano C .05 .10
5HYW101E069SSR School Festival, Itsuki Nakano SR 1.25 2.50
5HYW101E070C Reason for the Outfit, Nino Nakano C .05 .10
5HYW101E070SSR Reason for the Outfit, Nino Nakano SR 1.00 2.00
5HYW101E071C Successful Actress, Ichika Nakano C .05 .10
5HYW101E071SSR Successful Actress, Ichika Nakano SR 1.25 2.50
5HYW101E072C Competing in Closeness, Itsuki Nakano C .05 .10
5HYW101E072SSR Competing in Closeness, Itsuki Nakano SR 1.25 2.50
5HYW101E073SSR Playing a Prank by Acting SR 1.25 2.50
5HYW101E073U Playing a Prank by Acting U .07 .15
5HYW101E074CR Stealthy Strong Attack CR .25 .50
5HYW101E074OFROFR Stealthy Strong Attack OFR 75.00 150.00
5HYW101E075CR Ideal Image of a Teacher CR .30 .60
5HYW101E075OFROFR Ideal Image of a Teacher OFR 75.00 150.00
5HYW101E076CC Re-enacting the Encounter CC .07 .15
5HYW101E077CC Declaration of War Over Love CC .07 .15
5HYW101E077RRRR Declaration of War Over Love RRR 2.00 4.00
5HYW101E078OFROFR Unparalleled Beauty, Miku Nakano OFR75.00 150.00
5HYW101E078RR Unparalleled Beauty, Miku Nakano RR .75 1.50
5HYW101E079RR What She Wants to Do, Miku Nakano RR .75 1.50
5HYW101E079SSPSSP What She Wants to Do, Miku Nakano SSP 200.00 400.00
5HYW101E080R Harbored Feelings, Miku Nakano R .20 .40
5HYW101E080SSR Harbored Feelings, Miku Nakano SR 10.00 20.00
5HYW101E081HYRHYR Flowers of Gratitude, Nino Nakano HYR125.00 250.00
5HYW101E081R Flowers of Gratitude, Nino Nakano R .40 .80
5HYW101E082R Quintuplicate Trails, Miku Nakano R .20 .40
5HYW101E082SSR Quintuplicate Trails, Miku Nakano SR 6.00 12.00
5HYW101E083R Our Resolve, Miku Nakano R .20 .40
5HYW101E083SSR Our Resolve, Miku Nakano SR 1.50 3.00
5HYW101E084R Quintuplicate Trails, Nino Nakano R .30 .75
5HYW101E084SSR Quintuplicate Trails, Nino Nakano SR 10.00 20.00
5HYW101E085SSR Looking Out for Her Elder Sister, Nino Nakano SR 1.25 2.50
5HYW101E085U Looking Out for Her Elder Sister, Nino Nakano U .10 .20
5HYW101E086SSR Confession? Miku Nakano SR 1.25 2.50
5HYW101E086U Confession? Miku Nakano U .10 .20
5HYW101E087SSR A Self She Could Like, Miku Nakano SR 3.00 6.00
5HYW101E087U A Self She Could Like, Miku Nakano U .15 .30
5HYW101E088SSR Aquarium Date, Miku Nakano SR 1.50 3.00
5HYW101E088U Aquarium Date, Miku Nakano U .10 .20
5HYW101E089SSR Secretly Being Helped, Nino Nakano SR 1.00 2.00
5HYW101E089U Secretly Being Helped, Nino Nakano U .12 .25
5HYW101E090SSR Takoyaki Faction, Nino Nakano SR 4.00 8.00
5HYW101E090U Takoyaki Faction, Nino Nakano U .10 .20
5HYW101E091SSR Reading on a Bench, Miku Nakano SR 4.00 8.00
5HYW101E091U Reading on a Bench, Miku Nakano U .10 .20
5HYW101E092C Rooftop Discussion, Nino Nakano C .05 .10
5HYW101E092SSR Rooftop Discussion, Nino Nakano SR 1.50 3.00
5HYW101E093C Gratitude Towards Her Father, Nino Nakano C .10 .20
5HYW101E093SSR Gratitude Towards Her Father, Nino Nakano SR.75 1.50
5HYW101E094C Rivalry, Nino Nakano C .07 .15
5HYW101E094SSR Rivalry, Nino Nakano SR 1.25 2.50
5HYW101E095C Love Vacation, Nino Nakano C .05 .10
5HYW101E095SSR Love Vacation, Nino Nakano SR 2.50 5.00
5HYW101E096C Operation Substitute? Miku Nakano C .05 .10
5HYW101E096SSR Operation Substitute? Miku Nakano SR 1.00 2.00
5HYW101E097C Nice Idea C .07 .15
5HYW101E097SSR Nice Idea SR 2.50 5.00
5HYW101E098C Riding Tandem C .05 .10
5HYW101E098SSR Riding Tandem SR 1.25 2.50
5HYW101E099CR Not Holding Back CR .12 .25
5HYW101E099OFROFR Not Holding Back OFR 30.00 75.00
5HYW101E100CC Dream to Achieve CC .07 .15
5HYW101E100RRRR Dream to Achieve RRR 2.50 5.00
5HYW101E101 The Quintuplets After 5 Years, Ichika Nakano P 1.00 2.00
5HYW101E102 The Quintuplets After 5 Years, Yotsuba Nakano P2.50 5.00
5HYW101E102S The Quintuplets After 5 Years, Yotsuba Nakano P FOIL 2.50 5.00
5HYW101E103 The Quintuplets After 5 Years, Nino Nakano P 1.25 2.50
5HYW101E103S The Quintuplets After 5 Years, Nino Nakano P FOIL3.00 6.00
5HYW101E104 The Quintuplets After 5 Years, Itsuki Nakano P 1.50 3.00
5HYW101E105 The Quintuplets After 5 Years, Miku Nakano P 2.50 5.00
5HYW101E105S The Quintuplets After 5 Years, Miku Nakano P FOIL2.00 4.00

2023 Weiss Schwarz Saekano How to Raise a Boring Girlfriend Flat

SHSW71E001RR Overcoming Barriers, Eriri RR 2.50 5.00
SHSW71E001SSR Overcoming Barriers, Eriri SR 3.00 6.00
SHSW71E002RR A New Everyday, Utaha & Eriri RR 1.25 2.50
SHSW71E002SSR A New Everyday, Utaha & Eriri SR 3.00 6.00
SHSW71E003RR Illustrator Battle, Izumi RR 2.50 5.00
SHSW71E003SPSP Illustrator Battle, Izumi SP 40.00 80.00
SHSW71E004R Reason for Being in a Slump, Eriri R .30 .60
SHSW71E005R Provocation by the Pool, Izumi R .30 .60
SHSW71E005SSR Provocation by the Pool, Izumi SR 2.50 5.00
SHSW71E006R An Answer to the Autograph Board, Izumi R .30 .60
SHSW71E007R A New Beginning, Izumi R .30 .60
SHSW71E007SSR A New Beginning, Izumi SR 2.00 4.00
SHSW71E008R Cropped View, Eriri R .25 .50
SHSW71E008SSR Cropped View, Eriri SR 2.50 5.00
SHSW71E009R Parting Gift, Eriri R .75 1.50
SHSW71E009SSR Parting Gift, Eriri SR 3.00 6.00
SHSW71E011U Shift in Attitude, Eriri U .12 .25
SHSW71E013U Time to Make a Decision, Tomoya U .12 .25
SHSW71E014U Absolute Commitment, Eriri U .20 .40
SHSW71E016U Forced Interruption, Eriri U .15 .30
SHSW71E017U The Emotional Childhood Friend Ending, Eriri U .12 .25
SHSW71E018U After the Drinking Bout, Akane U .12 .25
SHSW71E029CR And the Rivals Will Challenge God CR .12 .25
SHSW71E029RRRR And the Rivals Will Challenge God RRR 2.50 5.00
SHSW71E031CC Confronting Determination CC .10 .20
SHSW71E031RRRR Confronting Determination RRR 2.50 5.00
SHSW71E032CC Alluring Kouhai Body CC .10 .15
SHSW71E033RR Betrayal and Farewell, Utaha RR 7.50 15.00
SHSW71E033SSR Betrayal and Farewell, Utaha SR 25.00 50.00
SHSW71E034RR Growth and Departure, Eriri RR 2.00 4.00
SHSW71E034SPSP Growth and Departure, Eriri SP 30.00 75.00
SHSW71E035RR Wavering Sentiments, Megumi RR 7.50 15.00
SHSW71E036R First-Time Feelings, Megumi R .75 1.50
SHSW71E036SSR First-Time Feelings, Megumi SR 10.00 20.00
SHSW71E037R Developing Duo, Megumi R .25 .50
SHSW71E037SSR Developing Duo, Megumi SR 5.00 10.00
SHSW71E038R Fueled by Defeat, Eriri R .75 1.50
SHSW71E039R Before Bed, Megumi R 1.25 2.50
SHSW71E040R Unexpected Enthusiasm, Megumi R .25 .50
SHSW71E041R Rewarding Scene, Megumi R .25 .50
SHSW71E041SSR Rewarding Scene, Megumi SR 7.50 15.00
SHSW71E044U Seeking Treasure, Megumi U .15 .30
SHSW71E045U Barriers to Overcome, Eriri U .12 .25
SHSW71E047C Rematch at Rokutenba Mall, Megumi C .10 .15
SHSW71E051U Disappearing Highlights Once Again U .15 .30
SHSW71E052C Time to Make a Decision C .10 .15
SHSW71E053CR The Girl Who Didn't Break the Flag CR .30 .75
SHSW71E053RRRR The Girl Who Didn't Break the Flag RRR 12.50 25.00
SHSW71E054CC A Different Gift CC .10 .15
SHSW71E055RR Girlfriend Who's Not Monotonous, Megumi RR2.50 5.00
SHSW71E055SSR Girlfriend Who's Not Monotonous, Megumi SR7.50 15.00
SHSW71E056RR A New Story, Megumi RR 7.50 15.00
SHSW71E056SPSP A New Story, Megumi SP 250.00 500.00
SHSW71E057RR A New Option, Utaha RR 2.50 5.00
SHSW71E057SPSP A New Option, Utaha SP 100.00 200.00
SHSW71E058R Squandered Spendings, Utaha R .30 .60
SHSW71E058SSR Squandered Spendings, Utaha SR 7.50 15.00
SHSW71E059R Determined Duo, Utaha R .30 .60
SHSW71E059SSR Determined Duo, Utaha SR 4.00 8.00
SHSW71E060R Negotiation Between Boy and Girl, Utaha R .75 1.50
SHSW71E061R Explosion of Emotion, Megumi R 1.00 2.00
SHSW71E063R Morning of the Festival, Megumi R .25 .50
SHSW71E064U Refrain, Megumi U .10 .15
SHSW71E066U Developing Relationship, Megumi U .12 .25
SHSW71E067U Feelings of Detestation, Utaha U .15 .30
SHSW71E068U Immoral Senpai, Utaha U .12 .25
SHSW71E072C What She Wanted, Megumi C .10 .15
SHSW71E073C After the Festival, Megumi C .10 .15
SHSW71E077U A Collaborative Work U .12 .25
SHSW71E079CR New Route of Two Nights and Three Days CR .12 .25
SHSW71E079RRRR New Route of Two Nights and Three Days RRR4.00 8.00
SHSW71E080CC Restart and Start a New Game CC .20 .40
SHSW71E080RRRR Restart and Start a New Game RRR 20.00 40.00
SHSW71E081CC His First Girl CC .10 .20
SHSW71E083RR Game Development Training Camp, Michiru RR2.50 5.00
SHSW71E083SPSP Game Development Training Camp, Michiru SP40.0080.00
SHSW71E084R Late-Night Invitation? Michiru R .30 .60
SHSW71E085R Band's Future in Crisis, Tokino & Echika & Ranko R.25 .50
SHSW71E086R Morning of the Festival, Michiru R .25 .50
SHSW71E086SSR Morning of the Festival, Michiru SR 2.50 5.00
SHSW71E087R Childhood Friend by the Pool, Michiru R .25 .50
SHSW71E087SSR Childhood Friend by the Pool, Michiru SR 4.00 8.00
SHSW71E088U Unexpected Reinforcement? Michiru U .15 .30
SHSW71E089U Assisting All Night, Ranko U .20 .40
SHSW71E090U Assisting All Night, Echiko U .20 .40
SHSW71E091U Assisting All Night, Tokino U .20 .40
SHSW71E092U Appealing Presence, Michiru U .12 .25
SHSW71E093C Scapegoat, Michiru C .10 .20
SHSW71E094C Reversal Move, Tomoya C .30 .75
SHSW71E095C Uncontrollable Crowd, Michiru C .10 .15
SHSW71E096C Misunderstanding and Punishment, Michiru C .30 .75
SHSW71E097C Realization of an Outmaneuver, Michiru C .10 .15
SHSW71E098U Reveal of New Songs U .20 .40
SHSW71E099CR Childhood Friend by the Pool CR .20 .40
SHSW71E099RRRR Childhood Friend by the Pool RRR 6.00 12.00
SHSW71E100CC Fall In, icy tail! CC .15 .30
SHSW71E101SPR A New Start, Izumi P FOIL 12.50 25.00
SHSW71E103PR A New Start, Megumi P 7.50 15.00
SHSW71E103SPR A New Start, Megumi P FOIL 12.50 25.00
SHSW71E104PR A New Start, Utaha P 7.50 15.00

2023 Weiss Schwarz Sword Art Online Animation 10th Anniversary

SAOS100E001RR Informant Argo the Rat RR 1.00 2.00
SAOS100E001SPSP Informant Argo the Rat SPR 75.00 150.00
SAOS100E002RR Longing Osmanthus, Alice RR 1.00 2.00
SAOS100E002SPSP Longing Osmanthus, Alice SPR 125.00 250.00
SAOS100E003RR A Thousand-Year Journey, Asuna RR 2.00 4.00
SAOS100E003SPSP A Thousand-Year Journey, Asuna SPR 500.00 1,000.00
SAOS100E004R Unbreakable Hope, Asuna R .12 .25
SAOS100E004SSR Unbreakable Hope, Asuna SR 1.50 3.00
SAOS100E005R Newbie Gamer, Asuna R .60 1.25
SAOS100E005SSR Newbie Gamer, Asuna SR 12.50 25.00
SAOS100E006R Shout Echoing Across the Battlefield, Alice R .30 .75
SAOS100E006SSR Shout Echoing Across the Battlefield, Alice SR20.00 40.00
SAOS100E007R Together With You, Asuna R .15 .30
SAOS100E007SSR Together With You, Asuna SR 2.00 4.00
SAOS100E008R Piling Up Emotions, Asuna & Kirito R .25 .50
SAOS100E008SSR Piling Up Emotions, Asuna & Kirito SR 3.00 6.00
SAOS100E009R Rising Expectations, Argo R .30 .75
SAOS100E009SSR Rising Expectations, Argo SR 2.00 4.00
SAOS100E010SSR Asuna's Commanding Strength SR 1.50 3.00
SAOS100E010U Asuna's Commanding Strength U .15 .30
SAOS100E011SSR Straight Path, Alice SR 12.50 25.00
SAOS100E011U Straight Path, Alice U .25 .50
SAOS100E012SSR Self-Sacrificing, Alice SR 1.00 2.00
SAOS100E012U Self-Sacrificing, Alice U .15 .30
SAOS100E013SSR Moment of Healing, Asuna SR 25.00 50.00
SAOS100E013U Moment of Healing, Asuna U .20 .40
SAOS100E014SSR Into the Light, Alice & Eugeo SR .75 1.50
SAOS100E014U Into the Light, Alice & Eugeo U .15 .30
SAOS100E015C Game Master, Kayaba C .07 .15
SAOS100E015SSR Game Master, Kayaba SR .60 1.25
SAOS100E016C Aria of a Starless Night Asuna C .10 .20
SAOS100E016SSR Aria of a Starless Night Asuna SR 1.25 2.50
SAOS100E017C A New Promise, Asuna C .07 .15
SAOS100E017SSR A New Promise, Asuna SR 1.25 2.50
SAOS100E018C [Aria of a Starless Night] Asuna C .07 .15
SAOS100E018SSR [Aria of a Starless Night] Asuna SR 1.25 2.50
SAOS100E019C Battle Stance, Asuna C .10 .20
SAOS100E019SSR Battle Stance, Asuna SR 1.50 3.00
SAOS100E020R Game of Life or Death R .15 .30
SAOS100E020SECSEC Game of Life or Death SEC 200.00 400.00
SAOS100E021SSR Floating Castle Aincrad SR 25.00 50.00
SAOS100E021U Floating Castle Aincrad U .15 .30
SAOS100E022CC Guardian of Human Realm CC .30 .60
SAOS100E022RRRR Guardian of Human Realm RRR 20.00 40.00
SAOS100E023CC Reliable Information CC .20 .40
SAOS100E023RRRR Reliable Information RRR 3.00 6.00
SAOS100E024CC The World of Swords CC .10 .20
SAOS100E024RRRR The World of Swords RRR 3.00 6.00
SAOS100E025RR Bond Between Siblings, Leafa RR 4.00 8.00
SAOS100E025SPSP Bond Between Siblings, Leafa SPR 175.00 350.00
SAOS100E026RR Mother's Rosario Yuuki RR .25 .50
SAOS100E026SPSP Mother's Rosario Yuuki SPR 100.00 200.00
SAOS100E027RR Towards Tomorrow Together, Mito RR .15 .30
SAOS100E027SPSP Towards Tomorrow Together, Mito SPR 125.00 250.00
SAOS100E028R [Aria of a Starless Night] Misumi R .25 .50
SAOS100E028SSR [Aria of a Starless Night] Misumi SR 3.00 6.00
SAOS100E029R Undefeated Super Swordsman, Yuuki R .20 .40
SAOS100E029SSR Undefeated Super Swordsman, Yuuki SR 1.25 2.50
SAOS100E030R Maidens of the Holy Night R .20 .40
SAOS100E030SSR Maidens of the Holy Night SR 2.50 5.00
SAOS100E031R Beta Tester, Mito R .15 .30
SAOS100E031SSR Beta Tester, Mito SR 2.00 4.00
SAOS100E032R Promise to Protect, Mito R .15 .30
SAOS100E032SSR Promise to Protect, Mito SR 2.50 5.00
SAOS100E033R Bewitching Smile, Yuna R .15 .30
SAOS100E033SSR Bewitching Smile, Yuna SR 2.50 5.00
SAOS100E034SSR After School Together, Misumi & Asuna SR .40 .80
SAOS100E034U After School Together, Misumi & Asuna U .10 .20
SAOS100E035SSR The Real Songstress, Yuna SR 2.00 4.00
SAOS100E035U The Real Songstress, Yuna U .15 .30
SAOS100E036SSR Innocent Smile, Yuuki SR 1.50 3.00
SAOS100E036U Innocent Smile, Yuuki U .15 .30
SAOS100E037SSR In a Party Dress, Sortiliena SR 2.50 5.00
SAOS100E037U In a Party Dress, Sortiliena U .12 .25
SAOS100E038SSR Internal Conflict, Yuuki SR 1.00 2.00
SAOS100E038U Internal Conflict, Yuuki U .20 .40
SAOS100E039SSR The Best Parts of the Game, Mito SR .75 1.50
SAOS100E039U The Best Parts of the Game, Mito U .12 .25
SAOS100E040SSR Refreshed Feelings, Fanatio SR .75 1.50
SAOS100E040U Refreshed Feelings, Fanatio U .12 .25
SAOS100E041SSR Entrusted Hopes, Cardinal SR .30 .75
SAOS100E041U Entrusted Hopes, Cardinal U .12 .25
SAOS100E042SSR Leafa's Pure Wish SR 2.50 5.00

SAOS100E042U Leafa's Pure Wish U .15 .30
SAOS100E043C Great Fortune! Suguha C .07 .15
SAOS100E043SSR Great Fortune! Suguha SR 1.25 2.50
SAOS100E044C Deep Regrets, Mito C .20 .40
SAOS100E044SSR Deep Regrets, Mito SR .75 1.50
SAOS100E045C Until We Meet Again, Yuuki & Asuna C .12 .25
SAOS100E045SSR Until We Meet Again, Yuuki & Asuna SR 2.00 4.00
SAOS100E046C Leveling Up Together, Mito C .07 .15
SAOS100E046SSR Leveling Up Together, Mito SR .40 .80
SAOS100E047C Relaxed Time, Misumi C .10 .20
SAOS100E047SSR Relaxed Time, Misumi SR 3.00 6.00
SAOS100E048C Wielder of Time-Splitting Sword, Bercouli C .07 .15
SAOS100E048SSR Wielder of Time-Splitting Sword, Bercouli SR .50 1.00
SAOS100E049C Misumi Tozawa C .12 .25
SAOS100E049SSR Misumi Tozawa SR .25 .50
SAOS100E050C Unyielding, Leafa C .07 .15
SAOS100E050SSR Unyielding, Leafa SR 2.50 5.00
SAOS100E051C Assistants, Ronie & Tiese C .15 .30
SAOS100E051SSR Assistants, Ronie & Tiese SR 1.25 2.50
SAOS100E052C Conquering Floor 1's Boss, Mito C .12 .25
SAOS100E052SSR Conquering Floor 1's Boss, Mito SR 1.00 2.00
SAOS100E053SSR Inherited Sword Technique SR .60 1.25
SAOS100E053U Inherited Sword Technique U .12 .25
SAOS100E054CR Mother's Rosario CR .15 .30
SAOS100E054CR Mother's Rosario CR 6.00 12.00
SAOS100E055CR Final Push CR .15 .30
SAOS100E055RRRR Final Push RRR 7.50 15.00
SAOS100E056CC Happy Christmas! CC .07 .15
SAOS100E056RRRR Happy Christmas! RRR 7.50 15.00
SAOS100E057CC Promise at Dusk CC .15 .30
SAOS100E057RRRR Promise at Dusk RRR 2.50 5.00
SAOS100E058CC Ephemeral Memories CC .10 .20
SAOS100E058RRRR Ephemeral Memories RRR 12.50 25.00
SAOS100E059RR Always Friendly, Silica RR .75 1.50
SAOS100E059SPSP Always Friendly, Silica SPR 175.00 350.00
SAOS100E060R Like a Younger Sister, Silica R .20 .40
SAOS100E060SSR Like a Younger Sister, Silica SR 3.00 6.00
SAOS100E061R Mace User, Lisbeth R .15 .30
SAOS100E061SSR Mace User, Lisbeth SR .60 1.25
SAOS100E062R Top Class Blacksmith, Lisbeth R .25 .50
SAOS100E062SPSP Top Class Blacksmith, Lisbeth SPR 75.00 150.00
SAOS100E063SSR Cute Mischief, Silica SR 4.00 8.00
SAOS100E063U Cute Mischief, Silica U .15 .30
SAOS100E064SSR Irrepairable, Lisbeth SR .50 1.00
SAOS100E064U Irrepairable, Lisbeth U .15 .30
SAOS100E065SSR Spring Blooms, Rika & Suguha & Keiko SR 2.50 5.00
SAOS100E065U Spring Blooms, Rika & Suguha & Keiko U .12 .25
SAOS100E066SSR Death Gun Alongside Fear SR 1.00 2.00
SAOS100E066U Death Gun Alongside Fear U .12 .25
SAOS100E067SSR Yearning, Silica & Lisbeth SR 1.50 3.00
SAOS100E067U Yearning, Silica & Lisbeth U .15 .30
SAOS100E068C Mysterious Smile, Administrator C .10 .20
SAOS100E068SSR Mysterious Smile, Administrator SR 6.00 12.00
SAOS100E069C He Who Seeks, Steals, and Robs, Gabriel C .07 .15
SAOS100E069SSR He Who Seeks, Steals, and Robs, Gabriel SR .40 .80
SAOS100E070C Silica's Gratitude C .10 .20
SAOS100E070SSR Silica's Gratitude SR .75 1.50
SAOS100E071C Heart's Warmth, Asuna & Lisbeth C .10 .20
SAOS100E071SSR Heart's Warmth, Asuna & Lisbeth SR 7.50 15.00
SAOS100E072C Twisted Love, Vassago C .07 .15
SAOS100E072SSR Twisted Love, Vassago SR .40 .80
SAOS100E073CR Hill of Memories CR .30 .60
SAOS100E073RRRR Hill of Memories RRR 10.00 20.00
SAOS100E074CC Awakened Feelings CC .30 .75
SAOS100E074RRRR Awakened Feelings RRR .40 .80
SAOS100E075RR Flower Crown of Happiness, Yui RR .25 .50
SAOS100E075SPSP Flower Crown of Happiness, Yui SPR 40.00 80.00
SAOS100E076RR GGO's Strongest Sniper, Sinon RR .25 .50
SAOS100E076SPSP GGO's Strongest Sniper, Sinon SPR 150.00 300.00
SAOS100E077RR The Power of Divine Authority, Kirito RR .50 1.00
SAOS100E077SPSP The Power of Divine Authority, Kirito SPR 75.00 150.00
SAOS100E078R Aria of a Starless Night Kirito R .20 .40
SAOS100E078SSR Aria of a Starless Night Kirito SR 1.25 2.50
SAOS100E079R Stay Cool Eugeo R .10 .20
SAOS100E079SPSP Stay Cool Eugeo SPR 50.00 100.00
SAOS100E080R 2.5 Years of Memories, Eugeo R .20 .40
SAOS100E080SSR 2.5 Years of Memories, Eugeo SR .75 1.50
SAOS100E081R Familial Love, Asuna & Yui R .20 .40
SAOS100E081SSR Familial Love, Asuna & Yui SR .75 1.50
SAOS100E082R Unlimited Flight Ability Sinon R .12 .25
SAOS100E082SSR Unlimited Flight Ability Sinon SR 1.25 2.50
SAOS100E083SSR Moonlit Night Swordsmen, Asuna & Kirito SR2.00 4.00
SAOS100E083U Moonlit Night Swordsmen, Asuna & Kirito U .10 .20
SAOS100E084SSR Memory Fragment, Kirito SR .75 1.50
SAOS100E084U Memory Fragment, Kirito U .15 .30
SAOS100E085SSR Valuable Strength, Kirito SR 1.00 2.00
SAOS100E085U Valuable Strength, Kirito U .20 .40
SAOS100E086SSR Bullet of Determination, Sinon SR 2.00 4.00
SAOS100E086U Bullet of Determination, Sinon U .12 .25
SAOS100E087SSR [Aria of a Starless Night] Kazuto SR .75 1.50
SAOS100E087U [Aria of a Starless Night] Kazuto U .10 .20
SAOS100E088SSR In a Bad Mood, Shino SR 2.50 5.00
SAOS100E088U In a Bad Mood, Shino U .12 .25
SAOS100E089C Black Swordsman Kirito C .15 .30
SAOS100E089SSR Black Swordsman Kirito SR 1.25 2.50
SAOS100E090C Ordinal Scale Silica & Asuna & Kirito C .12 .25
SAOS100E090SSR Ordinal Scale Silica & Asuna & Kirito SR 2.00 4.00
SAOS100E091C Assault Team, Agil C .12 .25
SAOS100E091SSR Assault Team, Agil SR .40 .80
SAOS100E092C Giving Advice, Sinon C .12 .25
SAOS100E092SSR Giving Advice, Sinon SR .75 1.50
SAOS100E093C Even if It's a Trap, Klein C .12 .25
SAOS100E094C Happy Family, Asuna & Yui C .12 .25
SAOS100E095C For the World He Loves, Eugeo C .12 .25
SAOS100E096C Coat of Midnight Kirito C .12 .25
SAOS100E097R Alicization R .30 .60
SAOS100E098U SYSTEM ALERT U .15 .30
SAOS100E099CR Night-Sky Blade CR .30 .75
SAOS100E100CC Cold-Hearted Sniper CC .12 .25

2023 Weiss Schwarz That Time I Got Reincarnated as a Slime Vol.3

TSKS101E001 Pride of a Secretary, Shion RR .20 .50
TSKS101E001SP Pride of a Secretary, Shion FOIL SP 50.00 120.00
TSKS101E002 All-Piercing Light, Rimuru RR .40 1.00
TSKS101E002SP All-Piercing Light, Rimuru FOIL SP 50.00 120.00
TSKS101E003 Heart-Pounding Cooking, Shion R .10 .25
TSKS101E003S Heart-Pounding Cooking, Shion SR 2.50 6.00
TSKS101E004 A 3.14 Percent Hope, Rimuru R .10 .25
TSKS101E004S A 3.14 Percent Hope, Rimuru SR 1.25 3.00
TSKS101E005 Loyal Servant, Diablo R .10 .25
TSKS101E005S Loyal Servant, Diablo SR 2.00 5.00
TSKS101E006 In a Dire Situation, Shion R .10 .25
TSKS101E006S In a Dire Situation, Shion SR 1.00 2.50
TSKS101E007 Battle-Hungry, Shion R .12 .30
TSKS101E007S Battle-Hungry, Shion SR 8.00 20.00
TSKS101E008 Cornered, Rimuru U .10 .25
TSKS101E008S Cornered, Rimuru SR .60 1.50
TSKS101E009 Irrevocable Regret, Rimuru U .08 .20
TSKS101E009S Irrevocable Regret, Rimuru SR .40 1.00
TSKS101E010 She Who Entrusts Hope, Eren U .08 .20
TSKS101E011 Unrelenting Sharpness, Hakurou U .12 .30
TSKS101E011S Unrelenting Sharpness, Hakurou SR .60 1.50
TSKS101E013 Having a Meal, Ramiris U .10 .25
TSKS101E013S Having a Meal, Ramiris SR .75 2.00
TSKS101E014 Sudden Assault, Shion U .12 .30
TSKS101E016S Overflowing Charisma, Diablo SR .75 2.00
TSKS101E017 Spoiled Child, Shion C .08 .20
TSKS101E021 Daily Life Gone Up in Flames U .10 .25
TSKS101E022 Shower of Light Under Clear Skies CR .12 .30
TSKS101E022R Shower of Light Under Clear Skies FOIL RRR 2.00 5.00
TSKS101E023 Culinary Genius CC .08 .20
TSKS101E024 The Joy of Being a Servant CC .10 .25
TSKS101E025 Delightfully Embarrassed, Rimuru RR .12 .30
TSKS101E025S Delightfully Embarrassed, Rimuru SR .60 1.50
TSKS101E026 A Seal Released, Veldora RR .12 .30
TSKS101E026SP A Seal Released, Veldora FOIL SP 40.00 100.00
TSKS101E027 Heart-Pounding Introduction, Veldora R .10 .25
TSKS101E027S Heart-Pounding Introduction, Veldora SR .50 1.25
TSKS101E028 Magnificent Transformation, Luminus R .75 2.00
TSKS101E028 Magnificent Transformation, Luminus SR .10 .25
TSKS101E029S Friendship Transcending Time, Rimuru SR .50 1.25
TSKS101E030 Firm Friendship, Veldora R .10 .25
TSKS101E030S Firm Friendship, Veldora SR .50 1.25
TSKS101E031 Calm and Collected Swordswoman, Hinata R .10 .25
TSKS101E031S Calm and Collected Swordswoman, Hinata SR 1.25 3.00
TSKS101E032 High Tension! Veldora U .10 .25
TSKS101E033 Vessel for a Friend, Rimuru U .20 .50
TSKS101E033S Vessel for a Friend, Rimuru SR 1.25 3.00
TSKS101E034 Friendship Transcending Time, Veldora SR .60 1.50
TSKS101E034 Friendship Transcending Time, Veldora U .10 .25
TSKS101E035 Hidden Talent, Veldora C .10 .25
TSKS101E036 Unexpected Help, Rimuru C .08 .20
TSKS101E037 Sudden Intrusion, Veldora C .08 .20
TSKS101E038 Crazy About Manga, Veldora C .08 .20
TSKS101E039 On the Defense, Rimuru C .10 .25
TSKS101E040 Sworn Friend Declaration! U .10 .25
TSKS101E041 Ultimate Skill Raphael U .10 .25
TSKS101E042 Meeting After 2 Years CR .12 .30
TSKS101E042R Meeting After 2 Years FOIL RRR 1.50 4.00
TSKS101E043 A Secret Strategy of the Distressed CC .10 .25
TSKS101E044 Mercy in Pink, Shuna RR 4.00 10.00
TSKS101E044SP Mercy in Pink, Shuna FOIL SP 75.00 200.00
TSKS101E045 Power Out of This World, Milim RR 1.25 3.00
TSKS101E045SP Power Out of This World, Milim FOIL SP 100.00 250.00
TSKS101E046 Calamity-Destroying Black Flame, Benimaru RR .25 .60
TSKS101E046SP Calamity-Destroying Black Flame,
Benimaru FOIL SP 40.00 100.00
TSKS101E047 Newbie Demon Lord, Rimuru RR .30 .75
TSKS101E047SEC Newbie Demon Lord, Rimuru FOIL SEC 100.00 250.00
TSKS101E048 According to Strategy, Milim R .15 .40
TSKS101E048S According to Strategy, Milim SR 6.00 15.00
TSKS101E049 Awakening of a True Demon Lord, Rimuru R .12 .30
TSKS101E049S Awakening of a True Demon Lord, Rimuru SR 1.00 2.50
TSKS101E050 A New Journey, Rimuru R .10 .25
TSKS101E050S A New Journey, Rimuru SR 1.00 2.50
TSKS101E051 A Sudden Request, Shuna R .10 .25
TSKS101E051S A Sudden Request, Shuna SR 2.50 6.00
TSKS101E052 Quiet Anger, Shuna R .25 .60
TSKS101E052S Quiet Anger, Shuna SR 12.00 30.00
TSKS101E053 Pressured Decision, Milim R .12 .30
TSKS101E053S Pressured Decision, Milim SR 1.25 3.00
TSKS101E054 To the Strong, Benimaru R .30 .75
TSKS101E054S To the Strong, Benimaru SR 10.00 25.00
TSKS101E055 At a Boastful Age, Milim U .10 .25
TSKS101E056 A Little Forgetful, Milim U .10 .25
TSKS101E056S A Little Forgetful, Milim SR 2.00 5.00
TSKS101E057 A Goal to Achieve, Leon U .08 .20
TSKS101E058 Conclusion to Enmity, Rimuru U .10 .25
TSKS101E058S Conclusion to Enmity, Rimuru SR .50 1.25
TSKS101E059 Primordial Demon Lord, Guy U .08 .20
TSKS101E060 Moment of Affirmation, Rimuru C .08 .20
TSKS101E061 Seductive Beauty, Frey C .08 .20
TSKS101E062 A Fight to Become the Demon Lord, Rimuru C .10 .25
TSKS101E063 Leader of the Delegation, Benimaru C .10 .25
TSKS101E069 Preparations for a Counterattack, Shuna C .12 .30
TSKS101E070 A 3.14 Miracle U .10 .25
TSKS101E070S A 3.14 Miracle SR .75 2.00
TSKS101E071 Octagram U .10 .25
TSKS101E072 A Miraculous Spirit Restoration Secret Art CR .25 .60
TSKS101E072R A Miraculous Spirit Restoration Secret Art FOIL RRR2.50 6.00
TSKS101E073 A Glimpse of Her Seriousness CC .10 .25
TSKS101E074 Black Flame That Illuminates Darkness CC .10 .25
TSKS101E074R Black Flame That Illuminates Darkness FOIL RRR2.00 5.00
TSKS101E075 Insuppressible Anger CC .08 .20
TSKS101E076 For a World to Live In With a Smile, Rimuru RR .60 1.50
TSKS101E076SEC For a World to Live In
With a Smile, Rimuru FOIL SEC 300.00 800.00
TSKS101E077 A Throbbing That Signals Freedom, Mjurran RR 3.00 8.00
TSKS101E077SP A Throbbing That Signals
Freedom, Mjurran FOIL SP 100.00 250.00
TSKS101E078 A Treasured Place to Return To, Soei R .15 .40
TSKS101E078S A Treasured Place to Return To, Soei SR 1.25 3.00
TSKS101E079 Operation Dress-Up, Rimuru R .12 .30
TSKS101E079S Operation Dress-Up, Rimuru SR .50 1.25
TSKS101E080 Ardent Relationship, Youm & Mjurran R .12 .30
TSKS101E080S Ardent Relationship, Youm & Mjurran SR 8.00 20.00
TSKS101E081 Bodyguard in the Shadow, Ranga R .12 .30
TSKS101E081S Bodyguard in the Shadow, Ranga SR .50 1.25
TSKS101E082 To His Dear Friends, Rimuru R .12 .30
TSKS101E082S To His Dear Friends, Rimuru SR .25 .60
TSKS101E083 Competent Right-Hand Woman, Soka U .10 .25
TSKS101E083S Competent Right-Hand Woman, Soka SR 1.00 2.50
TSKS101E084 Unsurpassable Difference in Power, Carrion U .10 .25
TSKS101E085 Onwards to Paradise! Rimuru U .10 .25
TSKS101E086 News of Distress, Soei U .12 .30
TSKS101E087 Signs of a Greed-Fueled Disaster, Rimuru U .10 .25
TSKS101E088S A Unique Fighting Style, Gobta SR .25 .60
TSKS101E090 Captive Wizard, Mjurran C .10 .25
TSKS101E091 A Scene in His Daily Life, Ranga C .10 .25
TSKS101E093 Dependable Leader of the Hiryu, Gabiru C .10 .25
TSKS101E096 Expanding Friendship, Rimuru C .10 .25
TSKS101E097 Barrier Between Hope and Disaster U .10 .25
TSKS101E098 Everlasting Words of Love CR .30 .75
TSKS101E098R Everlasting Words of Love FOIL RRR 25.00 60.00
TSKS101E099 To the Friends Awaiting His Return CC .08 .20
TSKS101E099R To the Friends Awaiting His Return FOIL RRR 1.25 3.00

2023 Weiss Schwarz That Time I Got Reincarnated as a Slime Vol.3 Promos

TSKS101E101 Capable Secretary? Shion PR .40 1.00
TSKS101E102 Unnecessary Statement, Veldora PR .60 1.50
TSKS101E102S Unnecessary Statement, Veldora FOIL PR 1.50 4.00
TSKS101E103 Request for a Try-on, Shuna PR .50 1.25
TSKS101E103S Request for a Try-on, Shuna FOIL PR .50 1.25
TSKS101E104 Full of Liveliness, Milim PR .50 1.25
TSKS101E104S Full of Liveliness, Milim FOIL PR 2.50 6.00
TSKS101E105 Achieving Victory With Everyone, Rimuru PR .50 1.25
TSKS101E105S Achieving Victory With Everyone, Rimuru FOIL PR.75 2.00
TSKS101PE02 The Children's Reliable Teacher, Rimuru PR 1.50 4.00

2024 Weiss Schwarz BanG Dream! Girls Band Party! Countdown Collection Premium Booster

BDWE42E001 Admiring My Sister, Hina Hikawa N .12 .30
BDWE42E001BDR Admiring My Sister, Hina Hikawa BDR 3.00 8.00
BDWE42E002 And the Croquettes, Hagumi Kitazawa N .20 .50
BDWE42E003 Full of Energy, Hagumi Kitazawa N .40 1.00
BDWE42E003BDR Full of Energy, Hagumi Kitazawa BDR 2.50 6.00
BDWE42E004 As the Six of Us, Misaki Okusawa N .25 .60
BDWE42E004BDR As the Six of Us, Misaki Okusawa BDR .50 1.25
BDWE42E005BDR On My Path Towards True Bushido,
Eve Wakamiya BDR 3.00 8.00
BDWE42E006 Deliver Smiles, Kokoro Tsurumaki N .12 .30
BDWE42E006BDR Deliver Smiles, Kokoro Tsurumaki BDR 2.50 6.00
BDWE42E006SP Deliver Smiles, Kokoro Tsurumaki SP 60.00 150.00
BDWE42E007 Make Everyone Smile, Kokoro Tsurumaki N .25 .60
BDWE42E007BDR Make Everyone Smile, Kokoro Tsurumaki BDR2.00 5.00
BDWE42E008 A Shared Fate, Kaoru Seta N .75 2.00
BDWE42E008BDR A Shared Fate, Kaoru Seta BDR 2.50 6.00
BDWE42E009 Normal Teenager Life, Nanami Hiromachi N .12 .30
BDWE42E009BDR Normal Teenager Life, Nanami Hiromachi BDR2.00 5.00
BDWE42E010 A Cute Idol, Aya Maruyama N .30 .75
BDWE42E010BDR A Cute Idol, Aya Maruyama BDR 1.50 4.00
BDWE42E011 Popular Girl Online, Toko Kirigaya N .25 .60
BDWE42E011BDR Popular Girl Online, Toko Kirigaya BDR 2.50 6.00
BDWE42E012BDR Looking for Fun Things, Kokoro Tsurumaki BDR2.00 5.00
BDWE42E013 Loaded With Fun, Hagumi Kitazawa N .20 .50
BDWE42E013BDR Loaded With Fun, Hagumi Kitazawa BDR 1.50 4.00
BDWE42E014 Wacha-Mocha Panic, Kanon Matsubara N .50 1.25
BDWE42E014BDR Wacha-Mocha Panic, Kanon Matsubara BDR 2.00 5.00
BDWE42E015BDR The Band's Charm, Toko Kirigaya BDR 2.00 5.00
BDWE42E016 Whether Normal or Not, Nanami Hiromachi N .50 1.25
BDWE42E016BDR Whether Normal or Not, Nanami Hiromachi BDR3.00 8.00
BDWE42E017 That Courage, Kanon Matsubara N .12 .30
BDWE42E017BDR That Courage, Kanon Matsubara BDR .50 1.25
BDWE42E018 With the Other Me, Misaki Okusawa N .40 1.00
BDWE42E018BDR With the Other Me, Misaki Okusawa BDR 1.25 3.00
BDWE42E019 Sweat of Effort, Misaki Okusawa N 1.00 2.50
BDWE42E019BDR Sweat of Effort, Misaki Okusawa BDR 2.50 6.00
BDWE42E019SP Sweat of Effort, Misaki Okusawa SP 125.00 300.00
BDWE42E020BDR Colorful Decorations, Eve Wakamiya BDR 2.50 6.00
BDWE42E021 All the World's a Stage, Kaoru Seta N .12 .30
BDWE42E021BDR All the World's a Stage, Kaoru Seta BDR 3.00 8.00
BDWE42E022 A Place of Happiness, Kanon Matsubara N .12 .30
BDWE42E022BDR A Place of Happiness, Kanon Matsubara BDR .50 1.25
BDWE42E023BDR Tsukinomori's Charismatic
Student, Toko Kirigaya BDR 1.00 2.50
BDWE42E023SP Tsukinomori's Charismatic
Student, Toko Kirigaya SP 30.00 80.00
BDWE42E024 Actor Who Continues Performing, Kaoru Seta N .40 1.00
BDWE42E024BDR Actor Who Continues
Performing, Kaoru Seta BDR 2.00 5.00
BDWE42E025BDR A Scene of Daily Life, Aya Maruyama BDR 1.50 4.00
BDWE42E026BDR A Fun Performance, Nanami Hiromachi BDR 2.50 6.00
BDWE42E027 Heartwarming Cafe, Tomoe Udagawa N .50 1.25
BDWE42E027BDR Heartwarming Cafe, Tomoe Udagawa BDR 2.00 5.00
BDWE42E028BDR An Idol's Job, Maya Yamato BDR 3.00 8.00
BDWE42E028SP An Idol's Job, Maya Yamato SP 60.00 150.00
BDWE42E029 Always Giving It Her All, LOCK N .12 .30
BDWE42E029BDR Always Giving It Her All, LOCK BDR .60 1.50
BDWE42E030 One Step at a Time, Ran Mitake N 1.00 2.50
BDWE42E030BDR One Step at a Time, Ran Mitake BDR 3.00 8.00
BDWE42E031 Star Fairy, Moca Aoba N .12 .30
BDWE42E031BDR Star Fairy, Moca Aoba BDR .60 1.50
BDWE42E032 Sweet Time, Himari Uehara N .25 .60
BDWE42E032BDR Sweet Time, Himari Uehara BDR 4.00 10.00
BDWE42E033 Hey, Hey, Hoh-! Himari Uehara N .40 1.00
BDWE42E033BDR Hey, Hey, Hoh-! Himari Uehara BDR 3.00 8.00
BDWE42E034 An Unusual Maid, Tomoe Udagawa N .50 1.25
BDWE42E034BDR An Unusual Maid, Tomoe Udagawa BDR 2.00 5.00
BDWE42E035 Tsugurific, Tsugumi Hazawa N .20 .50
BDWE42E035BDR Tsugurific, Tsugumi Hazawa BDR 2.50 6.00
BDWE42E036BDR Repaint, LAYER BDR 1.00 2.50
BDWE42E037 Where She Feels at Ease, MASKING N .20 .50
BDWE42E037BDR Where She Feels at Ease, MASKING BDR 2.00 5.00
BDWE42E038 Beloved for the Strangeness, Hina Hikawa N .25 .60
BDWE42E038SP Beloved for the Strangeness, Hina Hikawa SP100.00 250.00
BDWE42E039 Sound of Heat, LAYER N .25 .60
BDWE42E039BDR Sound of Heat, LAYER BDR 2.50 6.00
BDWE42E040 The Greatest Stage, LOCK N .12 .30
BDWE42E040BDR The Greatest Stage, LOCK BDR 2.50 6.00
BDWE42E041 Full-Power Switch, LOCK N .30 .75
BDWE42E041BDR Full-Power Switch, LOCK BDR 2.50 6.00
BDWE42E042 Aspiring to Be Cool, Tomoe Udagawa N .30 .75
BDWE42E042BDR Aspiring to Be Cool, Tomoe Udagawa BDR 2.50 6.00
BDWE42E043BDR Together Forever, Tsugumi Hazawa BDR 2.50 6.00
BDWE42E044 A Bright Smile, Himari Uehara N .50 1.25
BDWE42E044BDR A Bright Smile, Himari Uehara BDR 2.50 6.00
BDWE42E045 A Helping Hand, Moca Aoba N .20 .50
BDWE42E046 Powerful Singing, LAYER N .20 .50
BDWE42E046BDR Powerful Singing, LAYER BDR 2.00 5.00
BDWE42E047 Incredible Performance, MASKING N .30 .75
BDWE42E047BDR Incredible Performance, MASKING BDR 2.00 5.00
BDWE42E048 Band Organizer, Tsugumi Hazawa N .12 .30
BDWE42E048BDR Band Organizer, Tsugumi Hazawa BDR 1.00 2.50
BDWE42E049 Changing Times, Ran Mitake N .50 1.25
BDWE42E049BDR Changing Times, Ran Mitake BDR 1.50 4.00
BDWE42E050 Passionate Performance, MASKING N .15 .40
BDWE42E050BDR Passionate Performance, MASKING BDR 1.25 3.00
BDWE42E051 The Same as Always, Ran Mitake N .30 .75
BDWE42E051BDR The Same as Always, Ran Mitake BDR 2.00 5.00
BDWE42E052 Continuing Performance, Moca Aoba N .50 1.25
BDWE42E052BDR Continuing Performance, Moca Aoba BDR 2.50 6.00
BDWE42E053 Congratulatory Bouquet, Kasumi Toyama N .50 1.25
BDWE42E053BDR Congratulatory Bouquet, Kasumi Toyama BDR2.00 5.00
BDWE42E053SP Congratulatory Bouquet, Kasumi Toyama SP 125.00 300.00
BDWE42E054BDR Armful of Happiness, Rimi Ushigome BDR 2.50 6.00
BDWE42E055 That Which Lies in Her Hands, Kasumi Toyama N .40 1.00
BDWE42E055BDR That Which Lies in Her Hands,
Kasumi Toyama BDR 3.00 8.00
BDWE42E056 Story of Unfolding Dreams, Kasumi Toyama N 2.00 5.00
BDWE42E056BDR Story of Unfolding Dreams, Kasumi Toyama BDR8.00 20.00
BDWE42E057 Appearance of an Actress, Chisato Shirasagi N .40 1.00
BDWE42E057BDR Appearance of an Actress, Chisato Shirasagi BDR.50 1.25
BDWE42E058 Overflowing Enthusiasm, Saya Yamabuki N .40 1.00
BDWE42E058BDR Overflowing Enthusiasm, Saya Yamabuki BDR2.50 6.00
BDWE42E059 A Stage of Blessings, Rimi Ushigome N .12 .30
BDWE42E059BDR A Stage of Blessings, Rimi Ushigome BDR 1.25 3.00
BDWE42E060 Summer Uniform, Saya Yamabuki N .20 .50
BDWE42E060BDR Summer Uniform, Saya Yamabuki BDR 2.50 6.00
BDWE42E061 Dreamlike Scenery, Rimi Ushigome N .50 1.25

BDWE42E061BDR Dreamlike Scenery, Rimi Ushigome BDR 3.00 8.00
BDWE42E062 Like the Sun, Saya Yamabuki N .40 1.00
BDWE42E062BDR Like the Sun, Saya Yamabuki BDR 2.50 6.00
BDWE42E062SP Like the Sun, Saya Yamabuki SP 150.00 400.00
BDWE42E063 My Way of Being an Idol, Chisato Shirasagi N .50 1.25
BDWE42E063BDR My Way of Being an Idol, Chisato Shirasagi BDR1.50 4.00
BDWE42E063SP My Way of Being an Idol, Chisato Shirasagi SP75.00 200.00
BDWE42E064 Fluffy Bunny, Tae Hanazono N .50 1.25
BDWE42E064BDR Fluffy Bunny, Tae Hanazono BDR 2.00 5.00
BDWE42E065 Scenery of Everyday Life, Sayo Hikawa N .50 1.25
BDWE42E065BDR Scenery of Everyday Life, Sayo Hikawa BDR 1.25 3.00
BDWE42E066 The Coolest Drummer in the World, Ako Udagawa N.15 .40
BDWE42E066BDR The Coolest Drummer in the World,
Ako Udagawa BDR 2.00 5.00
BDWE42E066SP The Coolest Drummer in the World,
Ako Udagawa SP 60.00 150.00
BDWE42E067 My Feelings Towards Music, Rui Yashio N .12 .30
BDWE42E067BDR My Feelings Towards Music, Rui Yashio BDR 2.00 5.00
BDWE42E068 The Real Me, Maya Yamato N .15 .40
BDWE42E068BDR The Real Me, Maya Yamato BDR 3.00 8.00
BDWE42E069 Passionate About Music, Yukina Minato N 3.00 8.00
BDWE42E069BDR Passionate About Music, Yukina Minato BDR 5.00 12.00
BDWE42E070 All the Time Spent Is Important, Rinko Shirokane N .50 1.25
BDWE42E071 Not Used to the Dress, Rinko Shirokane N 2.00 5.00
BDWE42E071BDR Not Used to the Dress, Rinko Shirokane BDR 2.50 6.00
BDWE42E071SP Not Used to the Dress, Rinko Shirokane SP 125.00 300.00
BDWE42E072 Bloody la Vie en Rose, Mashiro Kurata N .50 1.25
BDWE42E072BDR Bloody la Vie en Rose, Mashiro Kurata BDR 1.50 4.00
BDWE42E073 Loves Jerky, CHU2 N .40 1.00
BDWE42E073BDR Loves Jerky, CHU2 BDR 1.50 4.00
BDWE42E074 Natural in Front of Camera, Aya Maruyama N .12 .30
BDWE42E074BDR Natural in Front of Camera, Aya Maruyama BDR.60 1.50
BDWE42E074SP Natural in Front of Camera, Aya Maruyama SP125.00 300.00
BDWE42E075 Songstress of the Blue Rose, Yukina Minato N 5.00 12.00
BDWE42E075BDR Songstress of the Blue Rose, Yukina Minato BDR15.0040.00
BDWE42E075SP Songstress of the Blue Rose, Yukina Minato SP150.00400.00
BDWE42E076 Daily Efforts, Lisa Imai N .50 1.25
BDWE42E076BDR Daily Efforts, Lisa Imai BDR 2.50 6.00
BDWE42E077 As the Little Sister, Ako Udagawa N .30 .75
BDWE42E077BDR As the Little Sister, Ako Udagawa BDR 2.50 6.00
BDWE42E078 Path to a Dream, Chisato Shirasagi N .30 .75
BDWE42E078BDR Path to a Dream, Chisato Shirasagi BDR .60 1.50
BDWE42E079 Confident Hard Worker, Tsukushi Futaba N 2.00 5.00
BDWE42E079BDR Confident Hard Worker, Tsukushi Futaba BDR 5.00 12.00
BDWE42E080BDR Outcome of Prioritizing Emotion, Rui Yashio BDR2.50 6.00
BDWE42E080SP Outcome of Prioritizing Emotion, Rui Yashio SP75.00 200.00
BDWE42E081 Commitment to Cuteness, PAREO N 1.50 4.00
BDWE42E081BDR Commitment to Cuteness, PAREO BDR 4.00 10.00
BDWE42E082 An Honest Smile, Arisa Ichigaya N .40 1.00
BDWE42E082BDR An Honest Smile, Arisa Ichigaya BDR .60 1.50
BDWE42E083 The Path Chosen Again, Rui Yashio N .12 .30
BDWE42E083BDR The Path Chosen Again, Rui Yashio BDR 2.50 6.00
BDWE42E084 Embracing Ideals, Lisa Imai N .30 .75
BDWE42E084BDR Embracing Ideals, Lisa Imai BDR 2.50 6.00
BDWE42E085BDR Research on Coolness, Ako Udagawa BDR 2.00 5.00
BDWE42E086BDR Good Example for
Everyone, Tsukushi Futaba BDR 2.00 5.00
BDWE42E087 Love for Rabbits, Tae Hanazono N .50 1.25
BDWE42E087BDR Love for Rabbits, Tae Hanazono BDR 3.00 8.00
BDWE42E087SP Love for Rabbits, Tae Hanazono SP 100.00 250.00
BDWE42E088BDR Striving to Be Positive, Rinko Shirokane BDR 2.50 6.00
BDWE42E089 Facing the Camera, Arisa Ichigaya N .30 .75
BDWE42E089BDR Facing the Camera, Arisa Ichigaya BDR 1.00 2.50
BDWE42E090 My Daydreams, Mashiro Kurata N 1.50 4.00
BDWE42E090BDR My Daydreams, Mashiro Kurata BDR 2.00 5.00
BDWE42E091 Rising Power Levels, PAREO N .12 .30
BDWE42E091BDR Rising Power Levels, PAREO BDR 2.50 6.00
BDWE42E092 Moves at Her Own Pace, Tae Hanazono N .15 .40
BDWE42E092BDR Moves at Her Own Pace, Tae Hanazono BDR 2.00 5.00
BDWE42E093 Overflowing With Feelings, Eve Wakamiya N .12 .30
BDWE42E093BDR Overflowing With Feelings, Eve Wakamiya BDR3.00 8.00
BDWE42E093SP Overflowing With Feelings, Eve Wakamiya SP 75.00 200.00
BDWE42E094 To Hold One's Head High, Tsukushi Futaba N .12 .30
BDWE42E094BDR To Hold One's Head High, Tsukushi Futaba BDR.75 2.00
BDWE42E095 Prepared to Fully Devote Oneself, Yukina Minato N .40 1.00
BDWE42E095BDR Prepared to Fully Devote
Oneself, Yukina Minato BDR 2.50 6.00
BDWE42E096 To Stand Side by Side, Sayo Hikawa N .40 1.00
BDWE42E096BDR To Stand Side by Side, Sayo Hikawa BDR 2.50 6.00
BDWE42E097 My Idol Path, Maya Yamato N .12 .30
BDWE42E097BDR My Idol Path, Maya Yamato BDR 3.00 8.00
BDWE42E098 Adorable Makeover, PAREO N .40 1.00
BDWE42E098BDR Adorable Makeover, PAREO BDR 2.50 6.00
BDWE42E099BDR Even if It Rains, Sayo Hikawa BDR 2.50 6.00
BDWE42E100 Even an Ordinary Girl Like Me, Mashiro Kurata N .50 1.25
BDWE42E100BDR Even an Ordinary Girl
Like Me, Mashiro Kurata BDR 2.50 6.00
BDWE42E101 The Greatest Music, CHU2 N 2.00 5.00
BDWE42E101BDR The Greatest Music, CHU2 BDR 6.00 15.00
BDWE42E102BDR Totally Boppin'! Hina Hikawa BDR 1.50 4.00
BDWE42E103 Always by Your Side, Lisa Imai N 1.50 4.00
BDWE42E103BDR Always by Your Side, Lisa Imai BDR 8.00 20.00
BDWE42E103SP Always by Your Side, Lisa Imai SP 200.00 500.00
BDWE42E104 Waterside Rest Area N 5.00 12.00
BDWE42E104BDR Waterside Rest Area BDR 20.00 50.00
BDWE42E105 Change the World With Sound N .50 1.25
BDWE42E105BDR Change the World With Sound BDR 2.50 6.00

2024 Weiss Schwarz BanG Dream! Girls Band Party! Countdown Collection Premium Booster Promos

BDWE42PE13 To the Next Stage** Kasumi Toyama PR 2.50 6.00
BDWE42PE14 To the Next Stage** Ran Mitake PR 2.50 6.00
BDWE42PE15 To the Next Stage** Aya Maruyama PR 3.00 8.00
BDWE42PE16 To the Next Stage** Yukina Minato PR 5.00 12.00
BDWE42PE17 To the Next Stage** Kokoro Tsurumaki PR 2.50 6.00
BDWE42PE18 To the Next Stage** Mashiro Kurata PR 2.50 6.00
BDWE42PE19 To the Next Stage** LAYER PR 2.50 6.00
BDWE42PE20 MyGO!!!!!** Tomori Takamatsu PR 3.00 8.00
BDWE42PE21 MyGO!!!!!** Anon Chihaya PR 3.00 8.00
BDWE42PE22 MyGO!!!!!** Rana Kaname PR 3.00 8.00
BDWE42PE23 MyGO!!!!!** Soyo Nagasaki PR 2.00 5.00
BDWE42PE24 MyGO!!!!!** Taki Shiina PR 3.00 8.00

2024 Weiss Schwarz BanG Dream! MyGO!!!!! Trial Deck Plus

BDWE42TE01 In the Sound of Moving Forward** Soyo Nagasaki TD1.25 3.00
BDWE42TE02 In the Sound of Moving Forward** Anon Chihaya TD3.00 8.00
BDWE42TE04 Hesitating Without Hesitation** Anon Chihaya TD125.00 300.00
BDWE42TE05 Live With Our Voice** Anon Chihaya TD 4.00 10.00
BDWE42TE05R Live With Our Voice** Anon Chihaya RRR .30 .75
BDWE42TE06 Hesitating Without Hesitation** Soyo Nagasaki TD100.00250.00
BDWE42TE06SP Hesitating Without Hesitation** Soyo Nagasaki SP.30 .75
BDWE42TE07 Embrace the Moment TD 5.00 12.00
BDWE42TE08 Hesitating Without Hesitation** Taki Shiina TD 60.00 150.00
BDWE42TE08SP Hesitating Without Hesitation** Taki Shiina SP .30 .75
BDWE42TE09 Live With Our Voice** Tomori Takamatsu TD 1.50 4.00
BDWE42TE09R Live With Our Voice** Tomori Takamatsu RRR .40 1.00
BDWE42TE10 Hesitating Without Hesitation** Rana Kaname TD125.00 300.00
BDWE42TE10SP Hesitating Without Hesitation** Rana Kaname SP.30 .75
BDWE42TE11 In the Sound of Moving Forward** Rana Kaname TD3.00 8.00
BDWE42TE11R In the Sound of Moving
Forward** Rana Kaname RRR .30 .75
BDWE42TE12 Live With Our Voice** Taki Shiina TD 2.00 5.00
BDWE42TE13 In the Sound of Moving Forward** Taki Shiina TD 2.50 6.00
BDWE42TE13R In the Sound of Moving Forward** Taki Shiina RRR.30 .75
BDWE42TE14 In the Sound of Moving
Forward** Tomori Takamatsu TD 1.00 2.50
BDWE42TE14S In the Sound of Moving
Forward** Tomori Takamatsu SR .30 .75
BDWE42TE15 Live With Our Voice** Rana Kaname TD 2.50 6.00
BDWE42TE17 Silhouette Dance TD 4.00 10.00
BDWE42TE17R Silhouette Dance RRR .40 1.00
BDWE42TE18 We Are Shouting Here TD 8.00 20.00

2024 Weiss Schwarz BOCCHI THE ROCK!

BTRW107E001 Let's Become Rock Stars! Nijika Ijichi RR 6.00 15.00
BTRW107E002 Bocchi-chan**, Hitori Gotoh RR 125.00 300.00
BTRW107E002KBR Bocchi-chan**, Hitori Gotoh KBR 6.00 15.00
BTRW107E003 Affirmation for the Future, Nijika Ijichi RR 2.50 6.00
BTRW107E004 Sentiments Towards Starry, Nijika Ijichi RR 1.50 4.00
BTRW107E004SSP Sentiments Towards Starry, Nijika Ijichi SSP200.00 500.00
BTRW107E005 Overlapping Sounds, Kessoku Band R .50 1.25
BTRW107E005S Overlapping Sounds, Kessoku Band SR 4.00 10.00
BTRW107E006 Nijika's Summer Vacation, Nijika Ijichi R .50 1.25
BTRW107E006S Nijika's Summer Vacation, Nijika Ijichi SR 2.50 6.00
BTRW107E007 Seaside Scenery, Hitori Gotoh R .50 1.25
BTRW107E008 See You Tomorrow, Hitori Gotoh R .50 1.25
BTRW107E008S See You Tomorrow, Hitori Gotoh SR 2.50 6.00
BTRW107E009 Collapse, Nijika Ijichi R .50 1.25
BTRW107E009S Collapse, Nijika Ijichi SR 2.50 6.00
BTRW107E010 Overly Hospitable Maid, Nijika Ijichi R .50 1.25
BTRW107E010S Overly Hospitable Maid, Nijika Ijichi SR 2.00 5.00
BTRW107E011 Can't Tell You! Nijika Ijichi R .50 1.25
BTRW107E012 Look Into Their Eyes and Smile, Hitori Gotoh U .08 .20
BTRW107E012S Look Into Their Eyes and Smile, Hitori Gotoh SR2.00 5.00
BTRW107E013 Growth? Hitori Gotoh U .15 .40
BTRW107E013S Growth? Hitori Gotoh SR 2.00 5.00
BTRW107E017 Real Dream, Nijika Ijichi U .20 .50
BTRW107E017S Real Dream, Nijika Ijichi SR 2.50 6.00
BTRW107E018 Blunt Attitude, Ryo Yamada U .15 .40
BTRW107E019 Steeped White, Hitori Gotoh U .20 .50
BTRW107E019S Steeped White, Hitori Gotoh SR 2.50 6.00
BTRW107E022 Urgent Member Recruitment, Nijika Ijichi C .12 .30
BTRW107E022S Urgent Member Recruitment, Nijika Ijichi SR 2.00 5.00
BTRW107E024 Ryo's Summer Vacation, Ryo Yamada C .08 .20
BTRW107E025 Astonished, Ryo Yamada C .20 .50
BTRW107E025S Astonished, Ryo Yamada SR 2.50 6.00
BTRW107E026 Watching Over, Seika Ijichi C .08 .20
BTRW107E028 Forgotten Cuteness, Hitori Gotoh C .20 .50
BTRW107E028S Forgotten Cuteness, Hitori Gotoh SR 2.00 5.00
BTRW107E030S Ripe Mangoes SR 3.00 8.00
BTRW107E031a I Am An Extrovert! C .12 .30
BTRW107E032OFR Light Shone Upon Their Path CR 2.50 6.00
BTRW107E033 Beyond Their Budokan Performance CC .15 .40
BTRW107E034 Melancholic Scream at the Future CC .20 .50
BTRW107E034R Melancholic Scream at the Future RRR 2.00 5.00
BTRW107E036 Let's Become Rock Stars! Ikuyo Kita RR 2.00 5.00
BTRW107E037 Let's Become Rock Stars! Ryo Yamada RR 2.00 5.00
BTRW107E037SSP Let's Become Rock Stars! Ryo Yamada SSP200.00 500.00
BTRW107E038 Sticking By Her Music, Ryo Yamada RR 2.00 5.00
BTRW107E038SSP Sticking By Her Music, Ryo Yamada SSP 400.00 1,000.00
BTRW107E039 Wellspring of Confidence, Ryo Yamada R .50 1.25
BTRW107E039SR Wellspring of Confidence, Ryo Yamada SR 2.50 6.00
BTRW107E040 Side-By-Side, Kessoku Band R .50 1.25
BTRW107E040S Side-By-Side, Kessoku Band SR 2.00 5.00
BTRW107E041 Mop-Top Hairstyle, Ryo Yamada R .60 1.50
BTRW107E042 Unimpressed Expression, Nijika Ijichi R .50 1.25
BTRW107E042S Unimpressed Expression, Nijika Ijichi SR 2.00 5.00
BTRW107E043 Hidden Name, Ikuyo Kita R .50 1.25
BTRW107E043S Hidden Name, Ikuyo Kita SR 3.00 8.00
BTRW107E044 Converting Bass to Cash, Ryo Yamada R .50 1.25
BTRW107E044S Converting Bass to Cash, Ryo Yamada SR 12.00 30.00
BTRW107E045 Fate of the Poor, Ryo Yamada R .50 1.25
BTRW107E045KBR Fate of the Poor, Ryo Yamada KBR 12.00 30.00
BTRW107E046 Issta-Worthy Shot, Ikuyo Kita U .15 .40
BTRW107E048 Serving With a Smile, Nijika Ijichi U .20 .50
BTRW107E048KBR Serving With a Smile, Nijika Ijichi KBR 12.00 30.00
BTRW107E049 Cross-Dressing Butler, Ryo Yamada U .20 .50
BTRW107E049S Cross-Dressing Butler, Ryo Yamada SR 2.50 6.00
BTRW107E051S Ikuyo's Summer Vacation, Ikuyo Kita SR 2.00 5.00
BTRW107E052 Nailing the Superficial Stuff, Nijika Ijichi U .15 .40
BTRW107E052S Nailing the Superficial Stuff, Nijika Ijichi SR 2.50 6.00
BTRW107E053S Let's Take ProPhos! Nijika Ijichi SR 3.00 8.00
BTRW107E056S Despite Being Jerked Around, Ikuyo Kita SR 2.50 6.00
BTRW107E057 Perfect Service, Ikuyo Kita C .08 .20
BTRW107E058 Gaze Just Like Her Sister, Nijika Ijichi C 1.50 4.00
BTRW107E060 Drunk Gifted Bassist, Kikuri Hiroi C .20 .50
BTRW107E060S Drunk Gifted Bassist, Kikuri Hiroi SR 2.50 6.00
BTRW107E062S In High Spirits Under the Sun! SR 2.00 5.00
BTRW107E063 Non-Stop Drinking C .08 .20
BTRW107E063S Non-Stop Drinking SR 2.50 6.00
BTRW107E064 My Own Color CR .50 1.25
BTRW107E064OFR My Own Color OFR 20.00 50.00
BTRW107E066R Preparing for Their Performance RRR 2.50 6.00
BTRW107E067 Heart-Fluttering Encounter CC .15 .40
BTRW107E068 True Face of Guitarhero, Hitori Gotoh RR 4.00 10.00
BTRW107E068SSP True Face of Guitarhero, Hitori Gotoh SSP 600.00 1,500.00
BTRW107E069 Admiration for the Extraordinary, Ikuyo Kita RR 2.00 5.00
BTRW107E069SSP Admiration for the
Extraordinary, Ikuyo Kita SSP 500.00 1,200.00
BTRW107E070 Let's Become Rock Stars! Hitori Gotoh RR 2.50 6.00
BTRW107E071 Desperate Ad-Lib, Hitori Gotoh R .50 1.25
BTRW107E071KBR Desperate Ad-Lib, Hitori Gotoh KBR 20.00 50.00
BTRW107E072 With 4 of Us! Kessoku Band R .50 1.25
BTRW107E072S With 4 of Us! Kessoku Band SR 2.50 6.00
BTRW107E073 Ecstatic After Praises, Hitori Gotoh R .50 1.25
BTRW107E073S Ecstatic After Praises, Hitori Gotoh SR 8.00 20.00
BTRW107E074 No Cooperation! No Life! Hitori Gotoh R .50 1.25
BTRW107E074S No Cooperation! No Life! Hitori Gotoh SR 3.00 8.00
BTRW107E075 Way Home in Sunset, Ikuyo Kita R .60 1.50
BTRW107E076 Stroke of Growth, Ikuyo Kita R .50 1.25
BTRW107E076S Stroke of Growth, Ikuyo Kita SR 2.50 6.00
BTRW107E077 Bragged Too Much, Hitori Gotoh U .20 .50
BTRW107E077S Bragged Too Much, Hitori Gotoh SR 3.00 8.00
BTRW107E078KBR Spell For Deliciousness, Ikuyo Kita KBR 15.00 40.00
BTRW107E079 Limit Break, Ikuyo Kita U .12 .30
BTRW107E079KBR Limit Break, Ikuyo Kita KBR .08 .20
BTRW107E080 Where the Tickets Go, Hitori Gotoh U .08 .20
BTRW107E080S Where the Tickets Go, Hitori Gotoh SR .08 .20
BTRW107E081 Reminiscent Guitar Girl, Hitori Gotoh U .08 .20
BTRW107E081KBR Reminiscent Guitar Girl, Hitori Gotoh KBR .08 .20
BTRW107E082 Plankton Gotoh, Hitori Gotoh U .08 .20
BTRW107E082KBR Plankton Gotoh, Hitori Gotoh KBR .08 .20
BTRW107E083 Orthodox Maid, Ikuyo Kita U .08 .20
BTRW107E083S Orthodox Maid, Ikuyo Kita SR 2.00 5.00
BTRW107E084 Just Imagine Ikuyo Kita U .12 .30
BTRW107E085 What? Hitori Gotoh U .15 .40
BTRW107E085S What? Hitori Gotoh SR 2.50 6.00
BTRW107E086 Attention-Seeking Monster, Hitori Gotoh U .15 .40
BTRW107E086S Attention-Seeking Monster, Hitori Gotoh SR 8.00 20.00
BTRW107E091 Wanting Everyone to Know, Ikuyo Kita C .12 .30
BTRW107E092 Futari Gotoh C .12 .30
BTRW107E092S Futari Gotoh SR 10.00 25.00
BTRW107E093S Extroverted Aura, Ikuyo Kita SR 2.50 6.00
BTRW107E094S Surging Power, Hitori Gotoh SR 3.00 8.00
BTRW107E095a Disgraceful History R .50 1.25
BTRW107E095b Disgraceful History R .50 1.25
BTRW107E095S Disgraceful History SR 2.50 6.00
BTRW107E096a Disgraceful History R .40 1.00
BTRW107E096b Disgraceful History R .50 1.25
BTRW107E096S Disgraceful History SR 6.00 15.00
BTRW107E097 Breakthrough Overdrive CR .40 1.00
BTRW107E097OFR Breakthrough Overdrive OFR 25.00 60.00
BTRW107E098 8 Tremolos of Growth and Trust CR .30 .75
BTRW107E099 Performance of Her Dreams CC .15 .40
BTRW107E099R Performance of Her Dreams RRR 10.00 25.00

2024 Weiss Schwarz BOCCHI THE ROCK! Promos

BTRW107E101 Energetic, Nijika Ijichi PR 1.00 2.50
BTRW107E102 Mysterious, Ryo Yamada PR 1.00 2.50
BTRW107E103 Extremely Shy, Hitori Gotoh PR 1.25 3.00
BTRW107E104 Social Media Master, Ikuyo Kita PR 1.00 2.50
BTRW107PE01 Lonely Girl Who Loves the Guitar, Hitori Gotoh PR2.00 5.00

2024 Weiss Schwarz BOCCHI THE ROCK! Trial Deck

BTRW107TE01R Nijika Ijichi RRR 5.00 12.00
BTRW107TE02 One Who Keeps the Band Together, Nijika Ijichi TD.50 1.25
BTRW107TE04 Lead Guitarist, Hitori Gotoh TD .50 1.25
BTRW107TE04R Lead Guitarist, Hitori Gotoh RRR 5.00 12.00
BTRW107TE06R Talk About Favorite Music-- Nijika Ijichi RRR 1.50 4.00
BTRW107TE08R Cool and Aloof, Ryo Yamada RRR 4.00 10.00
BTRW107TE09R Ryo Yamada RRR 4.00 10.00
BTRW107TE10R Band Name "Kessoku Band" RRR 2.00 5.00
BTRW107TE11 Longed-For Band Activities TD .50 1.25
BTRW107TE11R Longed-For Band Activities RRR 3.00 8.00
BTRW107TE11SP Longed-For Band Activities SP 60.00 150.00
BTRW107TE12 First Picture Taken With Everyone TD .50 1.25
BTRW107TE12R First Picture Taken With Everyone RRR 2.00 5.00
BTRW107TE14S Hitori Gotoh SP 100.00 250.00
BTRW107TE14S Hitori Gotoh SR 2.50 6.00
BTRW107TE15 Extrovert, Ikuyo Kita TD .50 1.25
BTRW107TE18R Ikuyo Kita RRR 5.00 12.00
BTRW107TE19 New Nickname, Hitori Gotoh TD .50 1.25

2024 Weiss Schwarz Chainsaw Man

CSMS96E001 Blood Fiend, Power RR .50 1.25
CSMS96E001SP Blood Fiend, Power FOIL SP 75.00 200.00
CSMS96E002 Public Safety Devil
Extermination Special Division 4, Power RR .60 1.50
CSMS96E002S Public Safety Devil
Extermination Special Division 4, Power FOIL SR 2.50 6.00
CSMS96E003R The Devil Hunter
Feared by Devils, Chainsaw Man RR .40 1.00
CSMS96E004 Always Together, Pochita R .12 .30
CSMS96E004SP Always Together, Pochita SP 40.00 100.00
CSMS96E005OFR Leader of Special Division 4, Makima FOIL OFR8.00 20.00
CSMS96E006S Promise with a Fiend, Power FOIL SR .75 2.00
CSMS96E007OFR Start of the Battle, Denji OFR 2.50 6.00
CSMS96E008OFR Angelic Temptation, Power FOIL OFR 10.00 25.00
CSMS96E009S Request From a Superior, Makima FOIL SR 1.25 3.00
CSMS96E010 After a Fierce Battle, Denji U .15 .40
CSMS96E012 That's an Indirect Kiss! Denji U .15 .40
CSMS96E013 Scuffle, Chainsaw Man U .12 .30
CSMS96E015 New Objective, Denji U .60 1.50
CSMS96E015S New Objective, Denji FOIL SR .12 .30
CSMS96E016 Battle of Wits, Power U .12 .30
CSMS96E016S Battle of Wits, Power FOIL SR .75 2.00
CSMS96E017 Newcomer Welcome Party, Denji C .12 .30
CSMS96E018 Sudden Resignation, Makima C .12 .30
CSMS96E022 Slice of Everyday Life, Power C .12 .30
CSMS96E024 Rowdy Life U .15 .40
CSMS96E025OFR Blood-Soaked Declaration of War FOIL OFR 8.00 20.00
CSMS96E025R Blood-Soaked Declaration of War CR .15 .40
CSMS96E026RRR Fiend's Everyday Life FOIL RRR 2.50 6.00
CSMS96E027C Fiend Going Berserk CC .12 .30
CSMS96E027RRR Fiend Going Berserk FOIL RRR 1.25 3.00
CSMS96E028R Devil Hunter, Himeno RR 1.50 4.00
CSMS96E028SP Devil Hunter, Himeno FOIL SP 100.00 250.00
CSMS96E029R Public Safety Devil
Extermination Special Division 4, Aki Hayakawa RR 4.00 10.00
CSMS96E029S Public Safety Devil Extermination Special
Division 4, Aki Hayakawa FOIL SR 10.00 25.00
CSMS96E030 Devil Hunter, Kobeni R .50 1.25
CSMS96E030SP Devil Hunter, Kobeni SP 75.00 200.00
CSMS96E031 Newcomer Welcome Party, Kobeni R .12 .30
CSMS96E031S Newcomer Welcome Party, Kobeni FOIL SR .60 1.50
CSMS96E032SP Devil Hunter, Kishibe SP 20.00 50.00
CSMS96E033OFR Contract with the Fox Devil,
Aki Hayakawa FOIL OFR 6.00 15.00
CSMS96E034 Invitation to Smoke, Himeno R .12 .30
CSMS96E034S Invitation to Smoke, Himeno FOIL SR .60 1.50
CSMS96E035SP Bearing the Heart of a Devil, Samurai Sword SP25.00 60.00
CSMS96E036S Senior Devil Hunter, Himeno FOIL SR 1.25 3.00
CSMS96E037 Last Cigarette, Himeno U .15 .40
CSMS96E038 Sudden Assault, Kobeni U .15 .40
CSMS96E038S Sudden Assault, Kobeni FOIL SR .75 2.00
CSMS96E039 Contract with the Snake Devil, Sawatari U .12 .30
CSMS96E040 Public Safety Devil Extermination
Special Division 4 Captain, Kishibe U .15 .40
CSMS96E041 Manic, Kobeni U .12 .30
CSMS96E043 Sliced in Half, Samurai Sword U .12 .30
CSMS96E043S Sliced in Half, Samurai Sword FOIL SR .60 1.50
CSMS96E047 After the Newcomer Welcome Party, Himeno C .12 .30
CSMS96E049 Really Timid, Kobeni C .12 .30
CSMS96E050 Flesh of the Gun Devil U .12 .30
CSMS96E051 Resolute Unsheathing CR .20 .50
CSMS96E051R Resolute Unsheathing FOIL RRR 6.00 15.00
CSMS96E052OFR Strike From a Katana OFR 2.50 6.00
CSMS96E053R Living Like in a Dream, Denji RR .50 1.25
CSMS96E054CSMR First Taste, Makima CSMR 500.00 1,200.00
CSMS96E054R First Taste, Makima RR 6.00 15.00
CSMS96E055R Public Safety Devil Extermination
Special Division 4, Makima RR .40 1.00
CSMS96E055S Public Safety Devil Extermination
Special Division 4, Makima FOIL SR 2.00 5.00
CSMS96E056S Expressing Resolve, Denji SR .60 1.50
CSMS96E057S Devil Covered in Blood, Chainsaw Man FOIL SR .75 2.00
CSMS96E058S Devil Hunter, Makima FOIL SR 1.50 4.00
CSMS96E059S What a Pitiful Home-- Power FOIL SR .50 1.25
CSMS96E060S Bearing the Heart of a Devil, Chainsaw Man FOIL SR.60 1.50
CSMS96E061 Sudden Confession, Makima U .15 .40

CSMS96E062 After a Fierce Battle, Power U .12 .30
CSMS96E063 Childlike Fiend, Power U .12 .30
CSMS96E064 Directly Under the Chief Cabinet Secretary, Makima U .12 .30
CSMS96E065 Sound of a Loser, Denji U .12 .30
CSMS96E068 I Wasn't Shot, Makima C .12 .30
CSMS96E069 Change in Partner, Denji C .12 .30
CSMS96E073 Assault on the Bullet Train, Makima C .12 .30
CSMS96E075 First Indirect Kiss U .12 .30
CSMS96E076OFR Hidden Strength FOIL OFR .12 .30
CSMS96E076R Hidden Strength CR 12.00 30.00
CSMS96E077C Concealed Ability CC .12 .30
CSMS96E077R Concealed Ability FOIL RRR 4.00 10.00
CSMS96E078C Special Request CC .20 .50
CSMS96E079C Best Contest Ever CC .12 .30
CSMS96E080R Watchdog of Special Division 4, Aki Hayakawa RR .12 .30
CSMS96E080SP Watchdog of Special Division 4,
Aki Hayakawa FOIL SP 40.00 100.00
CSMS96E081R Public Safety Devil Extermination
Special Division 4, Himeno RR .20 .50
CSMS96E081S Public Safety Devil Extermination
Special Division 4, Himeno FOIL SR 1.00 2.50
CSMS96E082S Devil Hunter, Aki Hayakawa FOIL SR .75 2.00
CSMS96E083 Revenge, Aki Hayakawa R .25 .60
CSMS96E083S Revenge, Aki Hayakawa FOIL SR 3.00 8.00
CSMS96E084 First Cigarette, Himeno R 5.00 12.00
CSMS96E085 Forming an Alliance, Himeno U .20 .50
CSMS96E086 Break Time, Himeno U 4.00 10.00
CSMS96E086S Break Time, Himeno FOIL SR .15 .40
CSMS96E088 Morning Routine, Aki Hayakawa U .12 .30
CSMS96E089 Last Cigarette, Aki Hayakawa U .60 1.50
CSMS96E090 Requiem to Heaven, Aki Hayakawa U .12 .30
CSMS96E091 Scene at the Hotel, Aki Hayakawa C .12 .30
CSMS96E092 Request for Devil Extermination, Himeno C .12 .30
CSMS96E093 Honest Question, Himeno C .12 .30
CSMS96E097 Easy Revenge! R .50 1.25
CSMS96E097S Easy Revenge! FOIL SR 5.00 12.00
CSMS96E098R Starting Point of Devil Hunting CR .15 .40
CSMS96E098R Starting Point of Devil Hunting RRR .50 1.25
CSMS96E099C Ghost's Right Hand CC .12 .30
CSMS96E099R Ghost's Right Hand FOIL RRR .60 1.50
CSMS96E100R Secret Alliance FOIL RRR 6.00 15.00

2024 Weiss Schwarz Chainsaw Man Promos

CSMS96E101 Gaze of Attraction, Power PR 1.00 2.50
CSMS96E101S Gaze of Attraction, Power FOIL PR 5.00 12.00
CSMS96E102 After the Newcomer Welcome Party, Denji PR .60 1.50
CSMS96E102S After the Newcomer Welcome Party, Denji FOIL PR 5.00 12.00
CSMS96E103 Intoxicated, Himeno PR .50 1.25
CSMS96E103S Intoxicated, Himeno FOIL PR 5.00 12.00
CSMS96E104 After the Newcomer Welcome Party, Makima PR .60 1.50
CSMS96E104S After the Newcomer Welcome
Party, Makima FOIL PR 5.00 12.00
CSMS96E105 Daily Life After a Fierce Battle, Aki Hayakawa PR .60 1.50
CSMS96E105S Daily Life After a Fierce Battle,
Aki Hayakawa FOIL PR 4.00 10.00
CSMS96PE01 Chainsaw Man PR 1.25 3.00
CSMS96PE02 Public Safety Devil Extermination
Special Division 4, Denji PR 1.25 3.00

2024 Weiss Schwarz Chainsaw Man Trial Deck

CSMS96TE01 Belief for the Job, Aki Hayakawa TD .60 1.50
CSMS96TE01R Belief for the Job, Aki Hayakawa FOIL RRR .20 .50
CSMS96TE02 Devil Hunter, Power TD 1.50 4.00
CSMS96TE02SSP Devil Hunter, Power SSP 300.00 800.00
CSMS96TE03 Chainsaw Devil, Pochita TD .40 1.00
CSMS96TE03R Chainsaw Devil, Pochita FOIL RRR 3.00 8.00
CSMS96TE04 Type of Person She Likes? Makima TD .30 .75
CSMS96TE04R Type of Person She Likes? Makima RRR 1.50 4.00
CSMS96TE05 Scent of Blood, Power TD .40 1.00
CSMS96TE05R Scent of Blood, Power FOIL RRR 5.00 12.00
CSMS96TE06 Devils' Names, Makima TD .20 .50
CSMS96TE06R Devils' Names, Makima RRR 1.00 2.50
CSMS96TE07 Resolve Towards the Job, Aki Hayakawa TD .12 .30
CSMS96TE07R Resolve Towards the Job, Aki Hayakawa FOIL RRR 1.25 3.00
CSMS96TE08 Best Toast TD .40 1.00
CSMS96TE08R Best Toast FOIL RRR 1.25 3.00
CSMS96TE09 Dog and Owner TD .15 .40
CSMS96TE09R Dog and Owner RRR 1.25 3.00
CSMS96TE10 First Meeting, Power TD .30 .75
CSMS96TE10R First Meeting, Power FOIL RRR 2.50 6.00
CSMS96TE11 Mysterious Scent, Makima TD .60 1.50
CSMS96TE11R Mysterious Scent, Makima RRR 2.50 6.00
CSMS96TE12 Devil With an Electric Chainsaw, Chainsaw Man TD .20 .50
CSMS96TE12R Devil With an Electric Chainsaw,
Chainsaw Man FOIL RRR 1.00 2.50
CSMS96TE13 Devil Hunter, Denji TD .25 .60
CSMS96TE13S Devil Hunter, Denji FOIL SR .25 .60
CSMS96TE13SSP Devil Hunter, Denji SSP 75.00 200.00
CSMS96TE14 Aiming for the Vitals, Denji TD .25 .60
CSMS96TE14R Aiming for the Vitals, Denji RRR .75 2.00
CSMS96TE15 Serious Motive, Makima TD .25 .60
CSMS96TE15R Serious Motive, Makima RRR 2.50 6.00
CSMS96TE16 Heart's Secret, Denji TD .40 1.00
CSMS96TE16R Heart's Secret, Denji FOIL RRR 2.50 6.00
CSMS96TE17 Devil Hunting Devils, Chainsaw Man TD .60 1.50
CSMS96TE17OFR Devil Hunting Devils, Chainsaw Man OFR 30.00 80.00
CSMS96TE18 How Foolish! Power TD 1.00 2.50
CSMS96TE18R How Foolish! Power FOIL RRR 4.00 10.00
CSMS96TE19 Forming a Contract in the Trash Bin TD .25 .60
CSMS96TE19OFR Forming a Contract in the Trash Bin OFR 12.00 30.00
CSMS96TE20 Roar of a Devil TD .30 .75
CSMS96TE20R Roar of a Devil RRR 1.50 4.00

2024 Weiss Schwarz Lycoris Recoil Promos

LRCW105E101 Photoshoot, Kurumi PR 1.50 4.00
LRCW105E101S Photoshoot, Kurumi FOIL PR 2.50 6.00
LRCW105E102 Member of LycoReco, Kurumi PR 1.50 4.00
LRCW105E102S Member of LycoReco, Kurumi FOIL PR 2.50 6.00
LRCW105E103 Photoshoot, Chisato PR 1.50 4.00
LRCW105E103S Photoshoot, Chisato FOIL PR 5.00 12.00
LRCW105E104 Delightful Present PR 1.50 4.00
LRCW105E105 Sailor Uniform Takina PR 2.00 5.00
LRCW105E105S Sailor Uniform Takina FOIL PR 8.00 20.00
LRCW105E106 Guitarist, Takina PR 1.50 4.00
LRCW105E106S Guitarist, Takina FOIL PR 8.00 20.00
LRCW105PE03 Reason to Act, Chisato PR 1.50 4.00

2024 Weiss Schwarz Lycoris Recoil Trial Deck

LRCW105TE01 Let's Hang Out, Chisato TD 2.00 5.00
LRCW105TE02 Send Off, Mizuki TD 1.25 3.00
LRCW105TE02R Send Off, Mizuki RRR 2.50 6.00
LRCW105TE03 Cafe LycoReco in Hawaii, Mizuki TD 1.00 2.50
LRCW105TE03R Cafe LycoReco in Hawaii, Mizuki RRR 4.00 10.00
LRCW105TE04 My Way of Life, Chisato TD 1.00 2.50
LRCW105TE04R My Way of Life, Chisato RRR 4.00 10.00
LRCW105TE05 Particular About Coffee, Mika TD 1.00 2.50
LRCW105TE05R Particular About Coffee, Mika RRR 2.50 6.00
LRCW105TE06 Living Together, Chisato TD 1.25 3.00
LRCW105TE06R Living Together, Chisato RRR 6.00 15.00
LRCW105TE07 Deliciously and Enjoyably, Chisato TD 1.00 2.50
LRCW105TE07R Deliciously and Enjoyably, Chisato RRR 2.00 5.00
LRCW105TE08 Hawaiian Camouflage, Chisato TD 1.00 2.50
LRCW105TE08R Hawaiian Camouflage, Chisato RRR 3.00 8.00
LRCW105TE09 Proof of Alan Children TD 1.00 2.50
LRCW105TE10 Soundless Heartbeat TD .50 1.25
LRCW105TE10R Soundless Heartbeat RRR 3.00 8.00
LRCW105TE11 Good Change, Takina TD 2.00 5.00
LRCW105TE11R Good Change, Takina RRR 4.00 10.00
LRCW105TE12 Cohabiting, Takina TD 1.25 3.00
LRCW105TE12R Cohabiting, Takina RRR 3.00 8.00
LRCW105TE13 Mysterious Hacker, Kurumi TD 1.50 4.00
LRCW105TE13R Mysterious Hacker, Kurumi RRR 6.00 15.00
LRCW105TE14 Let's Hang Out, Takina TD 1.00 2.50
LRCW105TE14SP Let's Hang Out, Takina SP 50.00 120.00
LRCW105TE15 To Save Her Comrades, Kurumi TD 1.00 2.50
LRCW105TE15R To Save Her Comrades, Kurumi RRR 3.00 8.00
LRCW105TE16 To Save Her Comrades, Takina TD 1.00 2.50
LRCW105TE17 Lycoris, Takina & Chisato TD 1.00 2.50
LRCW105TE17R Lycoris, Takina & Chisato RRR 8.00 20.00
LRCW105TE17S Lycoris, Takina & Chisato SR 1.00 2.50
LRCW105TE18 Long-Awaited Reunion, Takina TD .75 2.00
LRCW105TE18R Long-Awaited Reunion, Takina RRR 6.00 15.00
LRCW105TE19 Combining Strengths TD 1.00 2.50
LRCW105TE19R Combining Strengths RRR 6.00 15.00
LRCW105TE20 Job That Helps People in Need TD .50 1.25
LRCW105TE20R Job That Helps People in Need RRR 1.25 3.00

2024 Weiss Schwarz Saekano the Movie: Finale

SHSW98E004 Dressed Up, Eriri R .50 1.25
SHSW98E004S Dressed Up, Eriri SR 2.50 6.00
SHSW98E005 Sincere Emotions, Eriri R .50 1.25
SHSW98E007 Earnest Emotions, Izumi R .30 .75
SHSW98E007S Earnest Emotions, Izumi SR .50 1.25
SHSW98E009 Unfading Youth Graffiti, Izumi R .30 .75
SHSW98E010 Last Spurt, Izumi U .12 .30
SHSW98E012 Unfading Youth Graffiti, Tomoya U .15 .40
SHSW98E016 Gathered Again, Izumi U .12 .30
SHSW98E017 Watching a Live Concert, Eriri U .12 .30
SHSW98E018 A Maiden's Sharp Instinct, Izumi U .12 .30
SHSW98E019 Working on Edits, Izumi C .12 .30
SHSW98E022 Together Someday, Eriri C .12 .30
SHSW98E023 A Face Deep in Thought, Izumi C .12 .30
SHSW98E026 After-Concert Party, Izumi C .12 .30
SHSW98E028 Did You Like Me 10 Years Ago? CR .50 1.25
SHSW98E028R Did You Like Me 10 Years Ago? RRR 1.25 3.00
SHSW98E030 Dream-Spun Sketch CC .12 .30
SHSW98E030R Dream-Spun Sketch RRR 2.50 6.00
SHSW98E031 World's Happiest Main Heroine, Megumi RR 2.50 6.00
SHSW98E061 Gym Time, Megumi RR 2.50 6.00
SHSW98E061S Gym Time, Megumi SR 5.00 12.00
SHSW98E062 Path You Chose To Walk, Megumi RR 1.50 4.00
SHSW98E062S Path You Chose To Walk, Megumi SR 2.50 6.00
SHSW98E063 World's Happiest Author, Utaha RR .50 1.25
SHSW98E064 Hanging Out Together, Utaha RR 1.50 4.00
SHSW98E065 Unfading Youth Graffiti, Utaha R .50 1.25
SHSW98E066 Unwavering Feelings, Utaha R .50 1.25
SHSW98E066S Unwavering Feelings, Utaha SR 1.50 4.00
SHSW98E067 Racing Heartbeat Overlap, Megumi R .40 1.00
SHSW98E067S Racing Heartbeat Overlap, Megumi SR 2.50 6.00
SHSW98E068 Dressed Up, Megumi R .60 1.50
SHSW98E068S Dressed Up, Megumi SR 2.00 5.00
SHSW98E069 Dressed Up, Utaha R .50 1.25
SHSW98E069S Dressed Up, Utaha SR .75 2.00
SHSW98E070 Gathered Again, Utaha R .50 1.25
SHSW98E071 Gathered Again, Tomoya U .12 .30
SHSW98E073 Meeting For Two, Megumi U .15 .40
SHSW98E076 Smile of Relief, Utaha C .12 .30
SHSW98E081 After Negotiation U .12 .30
SHSW98E082 It Was Exactly What I Wanted CR .50 1.25
SHSW98E082R It Was Exactly What I Wanted RRR 4.00 10.00
SHSW98E083 He's Definitely Fallen For Us CR .50 1.25
SHSW98E083R He's Definitely Fallen For Us RRR 2.50 6.00
SHSW98E084R Closing The Distance Between Us RRR 4.00 10.00
SHSW98E001 Hanging Out Together, Eriri RR 1.25 3.00
SHSW98E002 Hanging Out Together, Izumi RR 1.25 3.00
SHSW98E003 World's Happiest Illustrator, Eriri RR .75 2.00
SHSW98E032 Hanging Out Together, Megumi RR 1.25 3.00
SHSW98E033 Painted Future, Eriri R .50 1.25
SHSW98E034 A Maiden's Melancholy, Megumi R .60 1.50
SHSW98E034S A Maiden's Melancholy, Megumi SR 2.00 5.00
SHSW98E035 Unfading Youth Graffiti, Megumi R .40 1.00
SHSW98E036 Graduation Day, Megumi R .40 1.00
SHSW98E037 Connected Future, Utaha R .50 1.25
SHSW98E037S Connected Future, Utaha SR 2.50 6.00
SHSW98E038 Straightforward Emotions, Megumi R .50 1.25
SHSW98E038S Straightforward Emotions, Megumi SR 3.00 8.00
SHSW98E039 Graduation Day, Eriri R .25 .60
SHSW98E040 Waiting For Her Date, Megumi U .12 .30
SHSW98E041 After-Concert Party, Utaha U .12 .30
SHSW98E043 Sakura-Colored Wind, Megumi U .12 .30
SHSW98E044 Parting Words, Megumi U .15 .40
SHSW98E045 Gathered Again, Megumi U .12 .30
SHSW98E046 Inexcusable, Eriri C .12 .30
SHSW98E048 After-Concert Party, Megumi C .12 .30
SHSW98E054 Great Helper, Utaha C .12 .30
SHSW98E055 Rubbishly Cute Storyline U .15 .40
SHSW98E056 Happy Birthday MEGUMI U .15 .40
SHSW98E057 A Main Heroine For You Only CR .50 1.25
SHSW98E057R A Main Heroine For You Only RRR 4.00 10.00
SHSW98E058 He Will Continue to Chase After Us From Now On CC .12 .30
SHSW98E058R He Will Continue to Chase
After Us From Now On RRR 1.00 2.50
SHSW98E059 Because We're Best Friends CC .12 .30
SHSW98E060 Best Incident CC .12 .30
SHSW98E085 How To Raise A Boring Girlfriend Finale CC .12 .30
SHSW98E085R How To Raise A Boring Girlfriend Finale RRR .50 1.25
SHSW98E086 Hanging Out Together, Michiru RR 1.25 3.00
SHSW98E087 Emotions in Her Music, Michiru R .50 1.25
SHSW98E088 Composing Till the Night, Michiru R .60 1.50
SHSW98E089 Unfading Youth Graffiti, Michiru R .50 1.25
SHSW98E090 After-Concert Party, Tokino U .12 .30
SHSW98E091 Gathered Again, Michiru U .12 .30
SHSW98E092 After-Concert Party, Ranko U .12 .30
SHSW98E093 After-Concert Party, Echika U .15 .40
SHSW98E095 Surprise Visit, Michiru C .12 .30
SHSW98E096 Disorderly Sleeping Position, Michiru C .12 .30
SHSW98E098 Good-Willed Impulse, Michiru C .15 .40
SHSW98E099 Busy Preparations U .15 .40
SHSW98E100 First Solo Concert CC .15 .40

2024 Weiss Schwarz Saekano the Movie: Finale Promos

SHSW98E101S Happy Life, Eriri PR 2.50 6.00
SHSW98E102 Happy Life, Izumi PR 1.00 2.50
SHSW98E102S Happy Life, Izumi PR 2.00 5.00
SHSW98E103 Happy Life, Megumi PR 4.00 10.00
SHSW98E103S Happy Life, Megumi PR 6.00 15.00
SHSW98E104 Happy Life, Utaha PR 1.25 3.00
SHSW98E104S Happy Life, Utaha PR 3.00 8.00
SHSW98E105 Happy Life, Michiru PR 5.00 12.00
SHSW98E105S Happy Life, Michiru PR 2.00 5.00
SHSW98PE04 Cat-Eared Beauty, Megumi PR 1.25 3.00
SHSW98PE05 Cat-Eared Beauty, Eriri PR .30 .75
SHSW98PE06 Diary With You, Megumi PR 1.25 3.00

2024 Weiss Schwarz SPY x FAMILY

SPYS106E001R Telepath Girl, Anya RR 8.00 20.00
SPYS106E001SP Telepath Girl, Anya SP 100.00 250.00
SPYS106E002R Matching Keychain, Becky RR .50 1.25
SPYS106E002SP Matching Keychain, Becky SP 30.00 80.00
SPYS106E003R Matching Keychain, Anya RR 2.00 5.00
SPYS106E003SEC Matching Keychain, Anya SEC 200.00 500.00
SPYS106E004S Daughter of the Blackbell Family,
Becky Blackbell SR .50 1.25
SPYS106E005S Good Mood, Anya SR 1.00 2.50
SPYS106E006S Shocked, Anya SR 1.00 2.50
SPYS106E007S First Stella, Anya SR .60 1.50
SPYS106E008SPY Student of Eden College,
Anya Forger SPYR 10.00 25.00
SPYS106E009SPY Classmates, Anya & Damian SPYR 3.00 8.00
SPYS106E011S Second Son of the Desmond Family,
Damian Desmond SR .50 1.25
SPYS106E022SPY Killer Punch Trained by a Mother SPYR 12.00 30.00
SPYS106E025 Together on an Outing CR .30 .75
SPYS106E025R Together on an Outing RRR 2.50 6.00
SPYS106E026SPY Tearful Apology SPYR 3.00 8.00
SPYS106E027R Sudden Heart-Throbbing RRR .50 1.25
SPYS106E028R Kind Smile, Loid RR .50 1.25
SPYS106E028SEC Kind Smile, Loid SEC 125.00 300.00
SPYS106E029R Smiling, Yor RR .25 .60
SPYS106E029SEC Smiling, Yor SEC 200.00 500.00
SPYS106E030R Family Full of Secrets, Loid & Anya & Yor RR .60 1.50
SPYS106E030SPY Family Full of Secrets, Loid &
Anya & Yor SPYR 15.00 40.00
SPYS106E031S On an Outing, Yor SR .75 2.00
SPYS106E032S Bond Forger SR 1.00 2.50
SPYS106E033S Smiling Anya SR 1.00 2.50
SPYS106E034S Perfect Father, Loid SR .75 2.00
SPYS106E035 Lively Daughter, Anya R .15 .40
SPYS106E035SPY Lively Daughter, Anya SPYR 50.00 120.00
SPYS106E036S Kind-Hearted Mother, Yor SR 1.50 4.00
SPYS106E037SPY Father and Daughter, Loid & Anya SPYR 12.00 30.00
SPYS106E041S Mother-Daughter Tie, Anya & Yor SR .75 2.00
SPYS106E043S Excited Feeling, Anya SR 1.00 2.50
SPYS106E044S Precious Family, Anya & Bond SR 1.00 2.50
SPYS106E052SPY Incident at the Bar, Loid & Yor SPYR 8.00 20.00
SPYS106E054SPY Moment of Acceptance SPYR 8.00 20.00
SPYS106E055 Vows Alongside an Explosion CR .12 .30
SPYS106E055SPY Vows Alongside an Explosion SPYR 8.00 20.00
SPYS106E056R In the Midst of Dancing Petals RRR 1.25 3.00
SPYS106E057R Family Celebration RRR 1.25 3.00
SPYS106E058R Extremely Skilled Assassin, Yor RR 5.00 12.00
SPYS106E058SPY Extremely Skilled Assassin, Yor SPYR 60.00 150.00
SPYS106E059R Thorn Princess**, Yor RR .60 1.50
SPYS106E059SP Thorn Princess**, Yor SP 150.00 400.00
SPYS106E060S Assassin From Garden, Yor Forger SR 1.50 4.00
SPYS106E061S Second Lieutenant in the State
Security Service, Yuri Briar SR .25 .60
SPYS106E062 Black Dress, Yor R .12 .30
SPYS106E062SPY Black Dress, Yor SPYR 20.00 50.00
SPYS106E063S Lying on Petals, Yor SR .75 2.00
SPYS106E064S Assassination Technique User, Yor SR 1.00 2.50
SPYS106E076 Wife of The Forgers CR .12 .30
SPYS106E076R Wife of The Forgers RRR 2.50 6.00
SPYS106E077R Killing Time RRR 1.25 3.00
SPYS106E078R Thorn Princess** RRR 1.00 2.50
SPYS106E079 Nightfall**, Fiona Frost RR 6.00 15.00
SPYS106E079SP Nightfall**, Fiona Frost SP 75.00 200.00
SPYS106E080R Agent **Twilight** RR .75 2.00
SPYS106E080SP Agent **Twilight** SP 60.00 150.00
SPYS106E081SP Handler, Sylvia Sherwood SP 20.00 50.00
SPYS106E082 Hospital Staff, Fiona R .25 .60
SPYS106E082S Hospital Staff, Fiona SR 5.00 12.00
SPYS106E083S Meeting with the Target, Loid Forger SR .50 1.25
SPYS106E084SPY Brilliant Spy From **WISE**, **Twilight** SPYR 4.00 10.00
SPYS106E085S Stylish Agent, **Twilight** SR 1.00 2.50
SPYS106E086 Bullet Signifying the End, **Twilight** U 12.00 30.00
SPYS106E086SPY Bullet Signifying the End, **Twilight** SPYR .12 .30
SPYS106E098SPY Accomplishing Missions in Style SPYR 12.00 30.00
SPYS106E099R Silent Passion in Her Heart RRR 6.00 15.00
SPYS106E100R For the Sake of a Better World RRR .60 1.50
SPYS106TE05SP Telepath, Anya SP 100.00 250.00
SPYS106TE14SP Cool Agent, **Twilight** SP 100.00 250.00
SPYS106TE21R Hero Who Saves the Princess RRR 2.00 5.00

2024 Weiss Schwarz SPY x FAMILY Promos

SPYS106E101 Smirk, Anya PR .60 1.50
SPYS106E101S Smirk, Anya FOIL PR 3.00 8.00
SPYS106E102 Morning Moment, Yor PR 1.50 4.00
SPYS106E102S Morning Moment, Yor FOIL PR 3.00 8.00
SPYS106E103 Serious Expression, Anya PR .60 1.50
SPYS106E103S Serious Expression, Anya FOIL PR 1.00 2.50
SPYS106E104 Standing Up, Loid PR .50 1.25
SPYS106E104S Standing Up, Loid FOIL PR 2.00 5.00
SPYS106E105 Kicking Up, Yor PR 1.25 3.00
SPYS106E105S Kicking Up, Yor FOIL PR 4.00 10.00
SPYS106E106 On the Phone With Allies, Loid PR .75 2.00
SPYS106E106S On the Phone With Allies, Loid FOIL PR 1.50 4.00
SPYS106PE01 Together With Penguin, Anya PR 1.50 4.00
SPYS106PE01M Together With Penguin, Anya MEISTER PR 4.00 10.00
SPYS106PE01S Together With Penguin, Anya FOIL PR 6.00 15.00
SPYS106PE02 Family Full of Secrets, Loid & Anya & Yor PR 4.00 10.00

2024 Weiss Schwarz SPY x FAMILY Trial Deck

SPYS106TE01 Happy Bond TD .12 .30
SPYS106TE01R Happy Bond RRR 1.50 4.00
SPYS106TE02R In the Toilet, Bond RRR 2.00 5.00
SPYS106TE03R Sitting, Anya RRR 2.00 5.00
SPYS106TE04 Okey-Dokey, Anya TD .15 .40
SPYS106TE04R Okey-Dokey, Anya RRR 2.50 6.00
SPYS106TE06 Promise, Anya TD .12 .30
SPYS106TE06R Promise, Anya RRR 1.00 2.50
SPYS106TE07 Nerve-Racking Interview, Anya TD .12 .30
SPYS106TE07R Nerve-Racking Interview, Anya RRR 2.00 5.00
SPYS106TE08 Operation Strix TD .15 .40
SPYS106TE08R Operation Strix RRR 2.50 6.00
SPYS106TE09 Fun Times TD .12 .30
SPYS106TE09R Fun Times RRR 2.00 5.00
SPYS106TE10 Seeking a Daughter, **Twilight** TD .12 .30
SPYS106TE10R Seeking a Daughter, **Twilight** RRR 1.00 2.50

SPYS106TE11 Full of Motivation, Yor TD .15 .40
SPYS106TE11R Full of Motivation, Yor RRR 2.50 6.00
SPYS106TE12 Assassin, Yor TD 1.50 4.00
SPYS106TE12SP Assassin, Yor SP 250.00 600.00
SPYS106TE13 Moment at Home, Loid TD .12 .30
SPYS106TE13R Moment at Home, Loid RRR 2.50 6.00
SPYS106TE14 Cool Agent, "Twilight" TD .20 .50
SPYS106TE15 Exchange Under Moonlight, Loid TD .15 .40
SPYS106TE15R Exchange Under Moonlight, Loid RRR 1.50 4.00
SPYS106TE16 Entrance Examination, Yor TD .20 .50
SPYS106TE16R Entrance Examination, Yor RRR 8.00 20.00
SPYS106TE17 For The Sake of Peace, Loid TD .15 .40
SPYS106TE17R For The Sake of Peace, Loid RRR 1.50 4.00
SPYS106TE18 Favor, Yor TD .12 .30
SPYS106TE18R Favor, Yor RRR 2.00 5.00
SPYS106TE19 Fake Family, Loid & Anya & Yor TD .15 .40
SPYS106TE19S Fake Family, Loid & Anya & Yor SR .75 2.00
SPYS106TE19SP Fake Family, Loid & Anya & Yor SP 125.00 300.00
SPYS106TE20 Family Full of Secrets TD .15 .40
SPYS106TE20R Family Full of Secrets RRR 8.00 20.00
SPYS106TE21 Hero Who Saves the Princess TD .15 .40

2021 WIXOSS WXDi-D01 Diva Debut Deck Ancient Surprise

WXDi-D01-001 At =Noll=, the Opened Gate 2.00 4.00
WXDi-D01-002 At =Elt=, the Opened Gate .30 .75
WXDi-D01-003 At =Två=, the Opened Gate .40 .80
WXDi-D01-004 At =Tre=, the Opened Gate .25 .50
WXDi-D01-005 Tawil =Noll=, Awakened One .75 1.50
WXDi-D01-006 Tawil =Screech= .75 1.50
WXDi-D01-007 Tawil =Rainbow= .50 1.00
WXDi-D01-008 Umr =Noll=, Key to Salvation 1.25 2.50
WXDi-D01-009 Umr =Draw= 1.25 2.50
WXDi-D01-010 Umr =Down= .75 1.50
WXDi-D01-011 Harmonic Call .50 1.00
WXDi-D01-012 Camelopar, Natural Planet .20 .40
WXDi-D01-013 Sen no Rikyu, Jade General .15 .30
WXDi-D01-014 Zwei =Slow Loris= .20 .40
WXDi-D01-015 Tobiel, Full Armed 1.25 2.50
WXDi-D01-016 Assylen, Natural Crystal .20 .40
WXDi-D01-017 Atalanta, Jade Angel .20 .40
WXDi-D01-018 Water Buffalo, Phantom Aquatic Beast .20 .40
WXDi-D01-019 Koalala, Phantom Terra Beast .20 .40
WXDi-D01-020 Servant ? .20 .40
WXDi-D01-021 Polygenesis .20 .40

2021 WIXOSS WXDi-D02 Diva Debut Deck Nijisanji ver. Sanbaka

WXDi-D02-01LAT Lize, Level 0 .75 1.50
WXDi-D02-02L [Center] Lize, Level 1 .50 1.00
WXDi-D02-03L [Center] Lize, Level 2 .50 1.00
WXDi-D02-04L [Center] Lize, Level 3 .75 1.50
WXDi-D02-05LAT Ange, Level 0 2.50 5.00
WXDi-D02-06LT [Assist] Ange, Level 1 3.00 6.00
WXDi-D02-07LT [Assist] Ange, Level 2 2.50 5.00
WXDi-D02-08LAT Toko, Level 0 2.50 5.00
WXDi-D02-09LA [Assist] Toko, Level 1 .30 .75
WXDi-D02-10LA [Assist] Toko, Level 2 .50 1.00
WXDi-D02-19LAT Samba Carnival 1.25 2.50
WXDi-D02-20 Chihiro Yuki, Code 2434 .30 .75
WXDi-D02-21 Ichigo Ushimi, Code 2434 .20 .40
WXDi-D02-22 Morinaka Kazaki, Code 2434 .20 .40
WXDi-D02-23 Era Otogibara, Code 2434 .30 .75
WXDi-D02-24 Kaede Higuchi, Code 2434 .60 1.25
WXDi-D02-25 Rin Shizuka, Code 2434 .60 1.25
WXDi-D02-26 Sara Hoshikawa, Code 2434 .30 .60
WXDi-D02-27 Mao Matsukai, Code 2434 .20 .40
WXDi-D02-28 Servant ? .30 .75
WXDi-D02-29 Wonder Land .60 1.25

2021 WIXOSS WXDi-D03 Diva Debut Deck No Limit

WXDi-D03-001 Hirana, a Spark of Hope 2.00 4.00
WXDi-D03-002 Hirana, a Dream of a Miracle .75 1.50
WXDi-D03-003 Hirana, a Glimpse of the Truth .50 1.00
WXDi-D03-004 Hirana, a Step Towards the Top .75 1.50
WXDi-D03-005 Akino, Bound for the Future 1.50 3.00
WXDi-D03-006 Akino*Rock 2.00 4.00
WXDi-D03-007 Akino*Paper 1.25 2.50
WXDi-D03-008 Rei, On the Wings of Tomorrow 2.00 4.00
WXDi-D03-009 Rei*Flash Blade .60 1.25
WXDi-D03-010 Rei*Empty Blade .75 1.50
WXDi-D03-011 Glory Grow .50 1.00
WXDi-D03-012 Romail, Lightly Armed .30 .75
WXDi-D03-013 Lancelot, Crimson General .75 1.50
WXDi-D03-014 Volcanic, Natural Crystal .30 .60
WXDi-D03-015 Kagutsuchi, Crimson Angel .25 .50
WXDi-D03-016 Letti, Heavy Armed .10 .20
WXDi-D03-017 Adamanthia, Natural Crystal .20 .40
WXDi-D03-018 Bronze, Natural Crystal .10 .20
WXDi-D03-019 Silvana, Natural Crystal .20 .40
WXDi-D03-020 Servant ? .50 1.00
WXDi-D03-021 Deafening Inferno 2.00 4.00

2021 WIXOSS WXDi-D04 Diva Debut Deck Card Jockey

WXDi-D04-001 MC LION - Standby 1.50 3.00
WXDi-D04-002 MC LION - 1st Verse .50 1.00
WXDi-D04-003 MC LION - 2nd Verse .75 1.50
WXDi-D04-004 MC LION - 3rd Verse 1.00 2.00
WXDi-D04-005 DJ LOVIT - Standby 1.50 3.00
WXDi-D04-006 DJ LOVIT - SCRATCH 1.25 2.50
WXDi-D04-007 DJ LOVIT - MIX .60 1.25
WXDi-D04-008 VJ WOLF - Standby 1.25 2.50
WXDi-D04-009 VJ WOLF - CUE .75 1.50
WXDi-D04-010 VJ WOLF - SYNC 1.25 2.50
WXDi-D04-011 Endless Punchline .75 1.50
WXDi-D04-012 F - Lite, Code: Art .40 .80
WXDi-D04-013 Michael, Blessed Angel .75 1.50
WXDi-D04-014 Amazoness, Jade General .50 1.00
WXDi-D04-015 Athena, Blessed Angel .60 1.25
WXDi-D04-016 Chandelier, Code: Art .60 1.25
WXDi-D04-017 Flopsy, Phantom Terra Beast .75 1.50
WXDi-D04-018 Triomphe, Code: Maze .50 1.00
WXDi-D04-019 Babel, Code: Maze .20 .40
WXDi-D04-020 Servant ? .30 .60
WXDi-D04-021 Good Dig .30 .75

2021 WIXOSS WXDi-D05 Diva Debut Deck Uchu No Hajimari

WXDi-D05-001 Newborn Dr. Tamago .60 1.25
WXDi-D05-002 Let's Go! Dr. Tamago .30 .75
WXDi-D05-003 You Can Do It! Dr. Tamago 1.50 3.00
WXDi-D05-004 Never Give Up! Dr. Tamago 1.00 2.00
WXDi-D05-005 Newborn Nova 3.00 6.00
WXDi-D05-006 Nova =Dirty= .30 .75
WXDi-D05-007 Nova =Chopper= .50 1.00
WXDi-D05-008 Newborn Bang 2.00 4.00
WXDi-D05-009 Bang =Crescendo= .75 1.50
WXDi-D05-010 Bang =Repeat= .75 1.50
WXDi-D05-011 Hanpanai?Destruction .50 1.00
WXDi-D05-012 Sharkspeare, Azure Evil .50 1.00
WXDi-D05-013 Curson, Blessed Evil .50 1.00
WXDi-D05-014 Carmilla Screw, Azure Evil .50 1.00
WXDi-D05-015 Captain Hook, Azure Evil .30 .75
WXDi-D05-016 Shimpachi, Azure General .30 .75
WXDi-D05-017 Giacobinids, Natural Planet .60 1.25
WXDi-D05-018 Procyon A, Natural Planet .30 .60
WXDi-D05-019 Sirius, Natural Planet .50 1.00
WXDi-D05-020 Servant ? .30 .75
WXDi-D05-021 RANDOM DRAIN 3.00 6.00

2021 WIXOSS WXDi-D06 Diva Debut Deck Diagram

WXDi-D06-001 Muzica START 1.00 2.00
WXDi-D06-002 Muzica, Vogue 1 1.50 3.00
WXDi-D06-003 Muzica, Vogue 2 .75 1.50
WXDi-D06-004 Muzica, Vogue 3 .50 1.00
WXDi-D06-005 Madoka START 2.00 4.00
WXDi-D06-006 Madoka//Float 2.50 5.00
WXDi-D06-007 Madoka//Dub .50 1.00
WXDi-D06-008 Sanga START 2.50 5.00
WXDi-D06-009 Sanga//Aerial 2.50 5.00
WXDi-D06-010 Sanga//Shake .30 .75
WXDi-D06-011 Salvage the Future .75 1.50
WXDi-D06-012 Noboribetsu, Code: Maze .30 .75
WXDi-D06-013 He, Natural Element .75 1.50
WXDi-D06-014 Gaap, Doomed Angel .20 .40
WXDi-D06-015 Ge, Natural Element .20 .40
WXDi-D06-016 Aconis Type: Drei .15 .30
WXDi-D06-017 Anna Mirage, Doomed Evil 2.00 4.00
WXDi-D06-018 Green Gas Type: Eins .50 1.00
WXDi-D06-019 Tick - Tock, Azure Doomed Evil .15 .30
WXDi-D06-020 Servant ? .20 .40
WXDi-D06-021 Enervating Melody .20 .40

2021 WIXOSS WXDi-P01 Glowing Diva

WXDiD03002SEN Hirana, a Dream of a Miracle SCR 4.00 8.00
WXDiD03003SEN Hirana, a Glimpse of the Truth SCR 5.00 10.00
WXDiD03004DEN Hirana, a Step Towards the Top DIR 40.00 80.00
WXDiD03004SEN Hirana, a Step Towards the Top SCR 2.50 5.00
WXDiD04002SEN MC LION - 1st Verse SCR 2.50 5.00
WXDiD04003SEN MC LION - 2nd Verse SCR 5.00 10.00
WXDiD04004SEN MC LION - 3rd Verse SCR 4.00 8.00
WXDiD04011DEN Endless Punchline DIR 25.00 50.00
WXDiD05002SEN Let's Go! Dr. Tamago SCR 1.50 3.00
WXDiD05003SEN You Can Do It! Dr. Tamago SCR 2.50 5.00
WXDiD05004DEN Never Give Up! Dr. Tamago DIR 30.00 75.00
WXDiD05004SEN Never Give Up! Dr. Tamago SCR 1.25 2.50
WXDiD05011DEN Hanpanai Destruction DIR 30.00 75.00
WXDiD06002SEN Muzica, Vogue 1 SCR 3.00 6.00
WXDiD06003SEN Muzica, Vogue 2 SCR 2.00 4.00
WXDiD06004DEN Muzica, Vogue 3 DIR 20.00 40.00
WXDiD06004SEN Muzica, Vogue 3 SCR 2.00 4.00
WXDiD06011DEN Salvage the Future DIR 25.00 50.00
WXDiP01001EN Go to the Top! PI 1.25 2.50
WXDiP01002EN Silent Assassin PI .20 .40
WXDiP01003EN Great! Re - ver - sal! PI .15 .30
WXDiP01004EN Code: L/O PI .15 .30
WXDiP01005EN Nightmare Step PI .30 .75
WXDiP01006EN Never Surrender PI .50 1.00
WXDiP01007EN Tap Down Tap PI .40 .80
WXDiP01008EN Kyururi Kyururira PI .75 1.50
WXDiP01009EN Akino*Thumbs Up! L .20 .40
WXDiP01010EN Akino*Peace! L .25 .50
WXDiP01011EN Akino*Bye - Bye! L .20 .40
WXDiP01012EN Rei*Lunar Blossom L .15 .30
WXDiP01013EN Rei*Absolute Zero L .15 .30
WXDiP01014EN Rei*Rending Blade L .12 .25
WXDiP01015EN DJ LOVIT - SCRATCHx2 L .07 .15
WXDiP01016EN DJ LOVIT - BEATJUG L .07 .15
WXDiP01017EN DJ LOVIT - CROSSFADE L .10 .20
WXDiP01018EN VJ WOLF - LASER L .07 .15
WXDiP01019EN VJ WOLF - STREAM L .10 .20
WXDiP01020EN VJ WOLF - MIRAGE L .15 .30
WXDiP01021EN Nova =Mute= L .15 .30
WXDiP01022EN Nova =Slash= L .12 .25
WXDiP01023EN Nova =Supernova= L .15 .30
WXDiP01024EN Bang =Pianissimo= L .15 .30
WXDiP01025EN Bang =Da Capo= L .15 .30
WXDiP01026EN Bang =Big Bang= L .15 .30
WXDiP01027EN Madoka//Slide L .10 .20
WXDiP01028EN Madoka//Break L .07 .15
WXDiP01029EN Madoka//Clap L .20 .40
WXDiP01030EN Sanga//Swing L .10 .20
WXDiP01031EN Sanga//Strike L .10 .20
WXDiP01032EN Sanga//Parallel L .12 .25
WXDiP01033EN Arcgwyn, Blessed Angel Queen SR 4.00 8.00
WXDiP01034EN Libra, Natural Planet Queen SR .30 .75
WXDiP01035EN PRJ - MAP, Code: Heart SR 7.50 15.00
WXDiP01036EN Nobunaga, Crimson General Queen SR 6.00 12.00
WXDiP01037EN Rose Quartz, Natural Crystal Brilliance SR 3.00 6.00
WXDiP01038EN Fenrir, Azure Evil Queen SR 7.50 15.00
WXDiP01039EN Saturne, Natural Planet Queen SR .75 1.50
WXDiP01040EN Robin Hood, Jade General Queen SR .30 .75
WXDiP01041EN Quin, Code: Labyrinth SR .60 1.25
WXDiP01042EN Osagitsune, Phantom Terra Beast God SR 4.00 8.00
WXDiP01043EN Dark Energie, Full Armed SR 4.00 8.00
WXDiP01044EN Lanling Type: Drei SR 1.25 2.50
WXDiP01045EN Haniel, Blessed Angel R .30 .75
WXDiP01046EN Zhao Yun, Blessed General R 2.50 5.00
WXDiP01047EN Andras, Blessed Evil C .10 .20
WXDiP01048EN Alphard, Natural Planet C .07 .15
WXDiP01049EN Ma Chao, Blessed General R .25 .50
WXDiP01050EN Bow, High Armed C .15 .30
WXDiP01051EN Salangidae, Phantom Aquatic Beast C .07 .15
WXDiP01052EN Stand Up R .12 .25
WXDiP01053EN Sita, Crimson Angel C .07 .15
WXDiP01054EN Yue Fei, Crimson General R .10 .20
WXDiP01055EN Amethystal, Natural Crystal C .07 .15
WXDiP01056EN C2H2, Natural Element R .07 .15
WXDiP01057EN Rama, Crimson Angel C .07 .15
WXDiP01058EN Shokudai - kiri, High Armed R .12 .25
WXDiP01059EN Carina, Natural Planet C .07 .15
WXDiP01060EN Resonating Sound of Destruction R .10 .20
WXDiP01061EN Charon, Azure Angel C .07 .15
WXDiP01062EN Bradamante, Azure General R .20 .40
WXDiP01063EN Antila, Natural Planet R .10 .20
WXDiP01064EN Regalecus, Phantom Aquatic Beast C .07 .15
WXDiP01065EN Cocytus, Azure Angel C .10 .20
WXDiP01066EN Focalor, Azure Evil C .75 1.50
WXDiP01067EN Coelacanth, Phantom Aquatic Beast R .07 .15
WXDiP01068EN Trouble R .12 .25
WXDiP01069EN Garmr, Jade Angel C .12 .25
WXDiP01070EN Maid Marian, Jade General R .07 .15
WXDiP01071EN Vassago, Jade Evil R .15 .30
WXDiP01072EN Hyakkoko, Phantom Terra Beast C .07 .15
WXDiP01073EN Skadi, Jade Angel C .12 .25
WXDiP01074EN Pavo, Natural Planet R .07 .15
WXDiP01075EN Kiyosumi, Code: Maze C .07 .15
WXDiP01076EN Musuzaku, Phantom Terra Beast C .07 .15
WXDiP01077EN Great Snake R .07 .15
WXDiP01078EN Azrael, Doomed Angel R .12 .25
WXDiP01079EN Sgathaich, Doomed General R .10 .20
WXDiP01080EN Baal, Doomed Evil C .07 .15
WXDiP01081EN Fragarach, Lightly Armed C .07 .15
WXDiP01082EN Horologium, Natural Planet C .07 .15
WXDiP01083EN Paimon, Doomed Evil C .07 .15
WXDiP01084EN Gram, High Armed C .10 .20
WXDiP01085EN Dagger Type: Zwei R .07 .15
WXDiP01086EN Corvus, Natural Planet C .07 .15
WXDiP01087EN Kawasaki, Code: Maze R .12 .25
WXDiP01088EN Under Attractive R .12 .25
WXDiP01089EN Percival, Blessed Crimson General C .10 .20
WXDiP01090EN Gawain, Blessed Crimson General C .10 .20
WXDiP01091EN Procyon A, Natural Planet C .07 .15
WXDiP01092EN Sirius, Natural Planet C .12 .25
WXDiP01093EN Triomphe, Code: Maze C .07 .15
WXDiP01094EN Babel, Code: Maze C .07 .15
WXDiP01095EN Imp, Azure Doomed Evil C .07 .15
WXDiP01096EN Tick - Tock, Azure Doomed Evil C .07 .15
WXDiP01097EN Green Gas Type: Eins C .07 .15
WXDiP01098EN Cobra Type: Zwei C .07 .15
WXDiP01099EN Servant # C .07 .15

2022 WIXOSS WXDi-D07 Top Diva Deck DXM

WXDiD07001EN Ex Zero .75 1.50
WXDiD07002EN Ex One .50 1.00
WXDiD07003EN Ex Two .60 1.25
WXDiD07004EN Ex Three .75 1.50
WXDiD07005EN Deus Zero .75 1.50
WXDiD07006EN Deus Drive .30 .75
WXDiD07007EN Deus Shield .50 1.00
WXDiD07008EN Machina Zero .75 1.50
WXDiD07009EN Machina Wing Slash 2.00 4.00
WXDiD07010EN Machina Smash .75 1.50
WXDiD07011EN TRIGGER OF VICTORY .75 1.50
WXDiD07012EN Chime of the Blessed Key 1.00 2.00
WXDiD07013EN Cargo, Code: Ride .25 .50
WXDiD07014EN Baphomet, Doomed Evil .75 1.50
WXDiD07015EN Lancelot, Crimson General .75 1.50
WXDiD07016EN Musca, Natural Planet .20 .40
WXDiD07017EN Gull - Wing, Code: Accel .20 .40
WXDiD07018EN Devil Stinger, Phantom Aquatic Beast .25 .50
WXDiD07019EN Obelisk, Code: Anti .25 .50
WXDiD07020EN Eckesachs, Lightly Armed .25 .50
WXDiD07021EN Servant # .75 1.50
WXDiD07022EN Burning Calamity .20 .40

2022 WIXOSS WXDi-D08 Diva Debut White Hope

WXDiD08001 Tamayorihime, New Moon Miko .75 1.50
WXDiD08002 Tamayorihime, Crescent Moon Miko .75 1.50
WXDiD08003 Tamayorihime, Half Moon Miko .75 1.50
WXDiD08004 Tamayorihime, Musical Moon Miko 6.00 12.00
WXDiD08005 Hanayo, Zero .75 1.50
WXDiD08006 Hanayo, Camellia .75 1.50
WXDiD08007 Hanayo, Orchid .75 1.50
WXDiD08008 Midoriko, Battle Girl .75 1.50
WXDiD08009 Midoriko, Gemmation .75 1.50
WXDiD08010 Midoriko, Reinforcement .75 1.50
WXDiD08011 Go to the Top! .75 1.50
WXDiD08012 Burning Curiosity .75 1.50
WXDiD08013 Aglaea, Blessed Angel .17 .35
WXDiD08014 Haniel, Blessed Angel .50 1.00
WXDiD08015 Romail, Lightly Armed .30 .75
WXDiD08016 Michael, Blessed Angel .30 .60
WXDiD08017 Bow, High Armed .30 .60
WXDiD08018 Athena, Blessed Angel .30 .60
WXDiD08019 Arc Athena, Holy Angel .30 .60
WXDiD08020 Letti, Heavy Armed .30 .60
WXDiD08021 Servant .40 .80
WXDiD08022 Get Big Bible .30 .75
WXDiD08023 Arcgwyn, Blessed Angel Queen 7.50 15.00

2022 WIXOSS WXDi-P02 Changing Diva

WXDiP02001 Illusions and Lightning PI .30 .75
WXDiP02002 ITTEN - TOPPA PI .25 .50
WXDiP02003 Azure Black GAIA PI .30 .75
WXDiP02004 Heaven's Door PI .30 .75
WXDiP02005 Zeno Cluster PI 10.00 20.00
WXDiP02006 End of the Turn PI .75 1.50
WXDiP02007 Akino, Bound for Dreams L .12 .25
WXDiP02007S Akino, Bound for Dreams SCR 4.00 8.00
WXDiP02008 Akino, Bound for Brightness L .12 .25
WXDiP02008S Akino, Bound for Brightness SCR 7.50 15.00
WXDiP02009 Akino, Bound for Valor L .12 .25
WXDiP02009D Akino, Bound for Valor DIR 40.00 80.00
WXDiP02009S Akino, Bound for Valor SCR 3.00 6.00
WXDiP02010 Hirana On - Stage L .12 .25
WXDiP02011 Hirana Glowing L .12 .25
WXDiP02012 Hirana Honest and Earnest L .12 .25
WXDiP02013 Hirana Power On L .12 .25
WXDiP02014 DJ LOVIT - 1st Verse L .20 .40
WXDiP02014S DJ LOVIT - 1st Verse SCR 1.50 3.00
WXDiP02015 DJ LOVIT - 2nd Verse L .12 .25
WXDiP02015S DJ LOVIT - 2nd Verse SCR 4.00 8.00
WXDiP02016 DJ LOVIT - 3rd Verse L .12 .25
WXDiP02016D DJ LOVIT - 3rd Verse DIR 10.00 20.00
WXDiP02016S DJ LOVIT - 3rd Verse SCR 4.00 8.00
WXDiP02017 MC LION - DIG L .12 .25
WXDiP02018 MC LION - STANDUP L .12 .25
WXDiP02019 MC LION - DISRESPECT L .12 .25
WXDiP02020 MC LION - DOPE L .12 .25
WXDiP02021 Bang, Singer of Melodies L .12 .25
WXDiP02021S Bang, Singer of Melodies SCR 1.50 3.00
WXDiP02022 Bang, Front and Center L .12 .25
WXDiP02022S Bang, Front and Center SCR 3.00 6.00
WXDiP02023 Bang, Read to Fight L .12 .25
WXDiP02023D Bang, Read to Fight DIR 25.00 50.00
WXDiP02023S Bang, Read to Fight SCR 1.25 2.50
WXDiP02024 Tamago =Double Stroke Roll= L .12 .25
WXDiP02025 Tamago =Beating= L .12 .25
WXDiP02026 Tamago =Jet Stick= L .12 .25
WXDiP02027 Tamago =Drumroll= L .12 .25
WXDiP02028 Madoka, Vogue 1 L .12 .25
WXDiP02028S Madoka, Vogue 1 SCR 3.00 6.00
WXDiP02029 Madoka, Vogue 2 L .12 .25
WXDiP02029S Madoka, Vogue 2 SCR 4.00 8.00
WXDiP02030 Madoka, Vogue 3 L .12 .25
WXDiP02030D Madoka, Vogue 3 DIR 20.00 40.00
WXDiP02030S Madoka, Vogue 3 SCR 1.50 3.00
WXDiP02031 Muzica//Dolphin L .20 .40
WXDiP02032 Muzica//Power Move L .12 .25
WXDiP02033 Muzica//Splits L .12 .25
WXDiP02034 Muzica//Groovy L .12 .25
WXDiP02035 Yaekiri, Full Armed SR 1.00 2.00
WXDiP02036 Casseopeia, Natural Planet Queen SR 1.50 3.00
WXDiP02037 Daji, Crimson Evil Queen SR 2.00 4.00
WXDiP02038 Phoenix, Natural Planet Queen SR 2.50 5.00
WXDiP02039 Buffalo, Phantom Terra Beast God SR 2.00 4.00
WXDiP02040 Amabie, Azure Angel Queen SR 1.00 2.00
WXDiP02041 Royal Blue, Natural Crystal Brilliance SR 3.00 6.00
WXDiP02042 ZrO2, Natural Element Queen SR 12.50 25.00
WXDiP02043 Influen D Type: Drei SR .75 1.50

WXDiP02044 Gauche Agnese, Natural Planet Queen SR .75 1.50
WXDiP02045 Valkyrie, Doomed Angel Queen SR .40 .80
WXDiP02046 Phalaris, Code: Ancients SR 17.50 35.00
WXDiP02047 Pele, Blessed Angel R .20 .40
WXDiP02048 Kogitsunemaru, Lightly Armed C .12 .25
WXDiP02049 Totorisa, Code: Maze C .12 .25
WXDiP02050 Circe, Blessed Angel C .12 .25
WXDiP02051 Circinus, Natural Planet C .12 .25
WXDiP02052 Symphorce, Code: Maze C .12 .25
WXDiP02053 Dekasanbashi, Code: Maze R .20 .40
WXDiP02054 White Betta, Phantom Aquatic Beast C .12 .25
WXDiP02055 A Shade of Bravery R .20 .40
WXDiP02056 Kamuy - huci, Crimson Angel C .12 .25
WXDiP02057 Zepar, Crimson Evil R .20 .40
WXDiP02058 Mensah, Natural Planet R .20 .40
WXDiP02059 Nuncha, High Armed C .12 .25
WXDiP02060 S - Tove, Code: Art C .12 .25
WXDiP02061 Hamster, Phantom Terra Beast C .12 .25
WXDiP02062 Boudica, Crimson General C .12 .25
WXDiP02063 In Perfect Harmony R .20 .40
WXDiP02064 Heqet, Azure Angel C .12 .25
WXDiP02065 Snow Myu, Code: Maze R .50 1.00
WXDiP02066 Hassi, Phantom Aquatic Beast C .12 .25
WXDiP02067 Gaghiel, Azure Angel C .12 .25
WXDiP02068 Hijikata, Azure General R .20 .40
WXDiP02069 Dorado, Natural Planet C .12 .25
WXDiP02070 Con Aqua, Master Trickster C .12 .25
WXDiP02071 Spinning Harmony R .20 .40
WXDiP02072 Kamapua'a, Jade Angel C .12 .25
WXDiP02073 Ophiuchus, Natural Planet C .12 .25
WXDiP02074 Parajulis, Phantom Aquatic Beast C .12 .25
WXDiP02075 Sitri, Jade Evil C .12 .25
WXDiP02076 Cicuta Virosa Type: Zwei C .12 .25
WXDiP02077 Palustre, Phantom Aquatic Beast R .20 .40
WXDiP02078 Fujisapa, Code: Maze C .12 .25
WXDiP02079 Fennec, Phantom Terra Beast R .20 .40
WXDiP02080 Heterophony R .20 .40
WXDiP02081 Nyx, Doomed Angel C .12 .25
WXDiP02082 Gamigin, Doomed Evil C .12 .25
WXDiP02083 Mo, Natural Element C .12 .25
WXDiP02084 Erebus, Doomed Angel C .12 .25
WXDiP02085 Chen Gong, Doomed General C .12 .25
WXDiP02086 Agares, Doomed Evil R .20 .40
WXDiP02087 Tucana, Natural Planet C .12 .25
WXDiP02088 E - Fone, Code: Art R .20 .40
WXDiP02089 Search Light R .20 .40
WXDiP02090 Bronze, Natural Crystal C .12 .25
WXDiP02091 Silvana, Natural Crystal C .12 .25
WXDiP02092 Pandada, Phantom Terra Beast C .12 .25
WXDiP02093 Koalala, Phantom Terra Beast C .12 .25
WXDiP02094 Water Buffalo, Phantom Aquatic Beast C .12 .25
WXDiP02095 Tree Froggy, Phantom Aquatic Beast C .12 .25
WXDiP02096 Servant # C .20 .40

2022 WIXOSS WXDi-P03 Standup Diva

WXDiP03001 SONG OF WIXOSS PI .75 1.50
WXDiP03002 G-G-G PI .30 .75
WXDiP03003 Apex Warriors PI .50 1.00
WXDiP03004 LIFE LOOP RESPECTS PI .30 .60
WXDiP03005 RHAPSODY PARTY PI .40 .80
WXDiP03006 Burning Curiosity PI 3.00 6.00
WXDiP03007 Rei, On the Wings of Truth SCR 5.00 10.00
WXDiP03007 Rei, On the Wings of Truth L .12 .25
WXDiP03008 Rei, On the Wings of Azure Sky SCR 4.00 8.00
WXDiP03008 Rei, On the Wings of Azure Sky L .12 .25
WXDiP03009 Rei, On the Wings of Supremacy DiR 75.00 150.00
WXDiP03009 Rei, On the Wings of Supremacy L .20 .40
WXDiP03010 Akino Clap L .20 .40
WXDiP03011 Hirana Kaboom L .25 .50
WXDiP03012 Hirana Stamp L .12 .25
WXDiP03013 Rei Divine Majesty L .12 .25
WXDiP03014 VJ WOLF - 1st Verse L .12 .25
WXDiP03014 VJ WOLF - 1st Verse SCR 3.00 6.00
WXDiP03015 VJ WOLF - 2nd Verse SCR 2.00 4.00
WXDiP03015 VJ WOLF - 2nd Verse L .12 .25
WXDiP03016 VJ WOLF - 3rd Verse L .25 .50
WXDiP03016 VJ WOLF - 3rd Verse DiR 30.00 75.00
WXDiP03017 MC LION - BUILD UP L .12 .25
WXDiP03018 MC LION - DROP L .12 .25
WXDiP03019 DJ LOVIT - RE: EDIT L .12 .25
WXDiP03020 VJ WOLF - REVERB L .12 .25
WXDiP03021 Nova, Prelude L .12 .25
WXDiP03021 Nova, Prelude SCR 6.00 12.00
WXDiP03022 Nova, Fighting Spirit SCR 4.00 8.00
WXDiP03022 Nova, Fighting Spirit L .12 .25
WXDiP03023 Nova, Skyfeather L .12 .25
WXDiP03023 Nova, Skyfeather DiR 60.00 125.00
WXDiP03024 Nova =Outro= L .12 .25
WXDiP03025 Tamago =Cymbal Roll= L .12 .25
WXDiP03026 Tamago =Accents= L .12 .25
WXDiP03027 Bang =Solo= L .12 .25
WXDiP03028 Sanga, Vogue 1 L .12 .25
WXDiP03028 Sanga, Vogue 1 SCR 2.50 5.00
WXDiP03029 Sanga, Vogue 2 SCR 1.50 3.00
WXDiP03029 Sanga, Vogue 2 L .12 .25
WXDiP03030 Sanga, Vogue 3 L .12 .25
WXDiP03030 Sanga, Vogue 3 DiR 25.00 50.00
WXDiP03031 Madoka//Arrangement L .12 .25
WXDiP03032 Sanga//Reboot L .12 .25
WXDiP03033 Muzica//Stomping L .12 .25
WXDiP03034 Muzica//Power Bomb L .12 .25
WXDiP03035 Koumei, Blessed General Queen SR 5.00 10.00
WXDiP03036 P - Nlight, Code: Heart SR 12.50 25.00
WXDiP03037 Blue Whaleen, Aquatic Phantom Queen SR 2.00 4.00
WXDiP03038 Zeusias, Crimson Angel Queen SR 2.00 4.00
WXDiP03039 Cocco Lupico, Phantom Beast Deity SR .75 1.50
WXDiP03040 Waffle Ice, Code: Order SR 2.50 5.00
WXDiP03041 Firefly Squid, Aquatic Phantom Deity SR 7.50 15.00
WXDiP03042 Demeter, Jade Angel Queen SR 1.00 2.00
WXDiP03043 Giroppon, Code: Labyrinth SR .75 1.50
WXDiP03044 Saber Tiger, Phantom Beast Deity SR 1.25 2.50
WXDiP03045 Ereshkigal, Doomed Evil Queen SR 1.50 3.00
WXDiP03046 Ac, Natural Element Queen SR 1.00 2.00
WXDiP03047 Aglaea, Blessed Angel C .12 .25
WXDiP03048 Aquiel, Blessed Evil R .20 .40
WXDiP03049 Typo, Natural Planet C .12 .25
WXDiP03050 Ishikirimaru, High Armed C .12 .25
WXDiP03051 R - Mlight, Code: Art C .12 .25
WXDiP03052 Elena, Code: Anti R .30 .60
WXDiP03053 Himejijo, Code: Maze C .25 .50
WXDiP03054 Miracle Draw R .30 .75
WXDiP03055 Bifrons, Crimson Evil R .20 .40
WXDiP03056 Rubellite, Natural Crystal R .20 .40
WXDiP03057 Truck Mixer, Code: Ride C .12 .25
WXDiP03058 Iris, Crimson Angel C .12 .25
WXDiP03059 Globaeia, Natural Planet C .12 .25
WXDiP03060 Tengu Zaru, Phantom Terra Beast R .30 .75
WXDiP03061 B - Lanket, Code: Art R .20 .40
WXDiP03062 Mandrill, Phantom Terra Beast C .12 .25
WXDiP03063 Eternal Influence R .30 .60
WXDiP03064 Audomula, Azure Angel R .20 .40
WXDiP03065 Ronove, Azure Evil C .12 .25
WXDiP03066 Hydras, Natural Planet C .12 .25
WXDiP03067 Apatite, Natural Crystal R .20 .40
WXDiP03068 Primora, Code: Maze C .12 .25
WXDiP03069 Tobijei, Phantom Aquatic Beast C .12 .25
WXDiP03070 Lu Xun, Azure General R .20 .40
WXDiP03071 Lapis Lazuli, Natural Crystal C .12 .25
WXDiP03072 THRILLING R .30 .75
WXDiP03073 Wutugu, Jade General C .12 .25
WXDiP03074 Marai, Jade Beauty R .50 1.00
WXDiP03075 Orangutan, Phantom Terra Beast C .12 .25
WXDiP03076 Churin, Natural Plant R 1.00 2.00
WXDiP03077 Akufuku, Code: Maze C .30 .60
WXDiP03078 Octodon, Phantom Terra Beast C .12 .25
WXDiP03079 Solenostomus, Phantom Aquatic Beast C .12 .25
WXDiP03080 Affection R .20 .40
WXDiP03081 Reticulum, Natural Planet C .12 .25
WXDiP03082 Pa, Natural Element C .30 .60
WXDiP03083 U - Selessbo, Code: Art R .20 .40
WXDiP03084 Sabnock, Doomed Angel C .12 .25
WXDiP03085 Luca, Doomed Evil R .20 .40
WXDiP03086 Tyrfing, High Armed C .12 .25
WXDiP03087 Izo, Doomed General R .20 .40
WXDiP03088 Telescopium, Natural Planet C .12 .25
WXDiP03089 Reticle Digger R .20 .40
WXDiP03090 Procyon A, Natural Planet C .12 .25
WXDiP03091 Sirius, Natural Planet C .12 .25
WXDiP03092 Triomphe, Code: Maze C .12 .25
WXDiP03093 Babel, Code: Maze C .12 .25
WXDiP03094 Green Gas Type: Eins C .12 .25
WXDiP03095 Cobra Type: Zwei C .20 .40
WXDiP03096 Servant C .12 .25

2022 WIXOSS WXDi-P04 Vertex Diva

WXDD07003 Ex Two SCR 5.00 10.00
WXDiD07002 Ex One SCR 5.00 10.00
WXDiD07004 Ex Three DiR 150.00 300.00
WXDiD07004 Ex Three SCR 5.00 10.00
WXDiP04001 White Heaven PI .75 1.50
WXDiP04002 World Reverse PI .30 .75
WXDiP04003 Summer Live Blues PI .60 1.25
WXDiP04004 DEATH DECK PI 1.00 2.00
WXDiP04005 Innocent Battle PI .30 .60
WXDiP04006 DEVIL'S CARNIVAL PI .30 .75
WXDiP04007 Akino, Advancing Towards Tomorrow L .50 1.00
WXDiP04007 Akino, Advancing Towards Tomorrow DiR 100.00 200.00
WXDiP04007 Akino, Advancing Towards Tomorrow SCR 7.50 15.00
WXDiP04008 MC LION 3rd Verse-ALT SCR 5.00 10.00
WXDiP04008 MC LION 3rd Verse-ALT DiR 175.00 350.00
WXDiP04008 MC LION 3rd Verse-ALT L .12 .25
WXDiP04009 Dr. Tamago, Nonstop L .12 .25
WXDiP04009 Dr. Tamago, Nonstop SCR 6.00 12.00
WXDiP04010 Madoka, Vogue 3-EX SCR 6.00 12.00
WXDiP04010 Madoka, Vogue 3-EX DiR 75.00 150.00
WXDiP04010 Madoka, Vogue 3-EX L .12 .25
WXDiP04011 Deus One L .12 .25
WXDiP04011 Deus One SCR 7.50 15.00
WXDiP04012 Deus Two L .30 .60
WXDiP04012 Deus Two SCR 7.50 15.00
WXDiP04013 Deus Three L .12 .25
WXDiP04013 Deus Three DiR 125.00 250.00
WXDiP04013 Deus Three SCR 7.50 15.00
WXDiP04014 Machina One L .30 .75
WXDiP04014 Machina One SCR 6.00 12.00
WXDiP04015 Machina Two L .30 .60
WXDiP04015 Machina Two SCR 6.00 12.00
WXDiP04016 Machina Three L .12 .25
WXDiP04016 Machina Three DiR 125.00 250.00
WXDiP04016 Machina Three SCR 4.00 8.00
WXDiP04017 Ex Gazer L .30 .60
WXDiP04018 Ex Echo L .25 .50
WXDiP04019 Ex Crossbeam L .30 .60
WXDiP04020 Ex Crossfire L .30 .60
WXDiP04021 Ex Stepout L .30 .75
WXDiP04022 Deus Recovery L .30 .75
WXDiP04023 Deus Limited L .20 .40
WXDiP04024 Deus Digger L .30 .75
WXDiP04025 Machina Seeds L .25 .50
WXDiP04026 Machina Repair L .30 .75
WXDiP04027 Machina Bind L .30 .75
WXDiP04028 At =Tre=, Opened Door L .30 .75
WXDiP04028 At =Tre=, Opened Door DiR 75.00 150.00
WXDiP04028 At =Tre=, Opened Door SCR 12.50 25.00
WXDiP04029 Tawil =Hangout= L .30 .60
WXDiP04030 Umr =Outsider= L .30 .60
WXDiP04031 At =Eject= L .30 .75
WXDiP04032 Exia, Blessed Angel Queen SR 15.00 30.00
WXDiP04033 Douman, Blessed Evil Queen SR .40 .80
WXDiP04034 Kintoki, Crimson General Queen SR 10.00 20.00
WXDiP04035 Alexandrite, Natural Pyroxene SR 2.00 4.00
WXDiP04036 Columbus, Azure General Queen SR .75 1.50
WXDiP04037 Orion, Natural Planet Queen SR 2.00 4.00
WXDiP04038 Code Labyrinth Notre Dame SR 7.50 15.00
WXDiP04039 Newton, Jade Wisdom Queen SR .30 .75
WXDiP04040 Ibaraki-Douji, Jade Evil Queen SR .75 1.50
WXDiP04041 Muramasa, Full Armed SR .60 1.25
WXDiP04042 Code Ancients Steampunk SR 7.50 15.00
WXDiP04043 Dragon Maid, Phantom Dragon Queen SR 5.00 10.00
WXDiP04044 Lepus, Natural Planet C .30 .60
WXDiP04045 Code Art R Inglight R .30 .75
WXDiP04046 Lemon Tetra, Water Phantom C .12 .25
WXDiP04047 Isis, Blessed Angel C .25 .50
WXDiP04048 Wei Yan, Blessed General R .30 .60
WXDiP04049 Code Maze Antnest C .12 .25
WXDiP04050 Huang Zhong, Blessed General C .12 .25
WXDiP04051 Rhongomyniad, Full Armed R .20 .40
WXDiP04052 Rebirth Return R .20 .40
WXDiP04053 Garasha, Crimson General C .12 .25
WXDiP04054 Iwatooshi, Lightly Armed C .12 .25
WXDiP04055 Cuélepe, Phantom Dragon C .12 .25
WXDiP04056 Corgi, Phantom Beast R .20 .40
WXDiP04057 Bedivere, Crimson General R .30 .75
WXDiP04058 Morax, Crimson Evil C .12 .25
WXDiP04059 Code Art Y Akitori Machine C .12 .25
WXDiP04060 Bathin, Crimson Evil C .12 .25
WXDiP04061 Cancer, Natural Planet R .25 .50
WXDiP04062 Roaring Thunder in Broad Daylight R .30 .75
WXDiP04063 Norma, Natural Planet C .12 .25
WXDiP04064 Ga, Natural Element C .12 .25
WXDiP04065 Plankton, Natural Bacteria C .12 .25
WXDiP04066 Bruno, Azure General R .30 .60
WXDiP04067 Team Palette, Azure Beauty R .20 .40
WXDiP04067 Team Palette, Azure Beauty R ALT ART 2.50 5.00
WXDiP04068 Halphas, Azure Evil C .12 .25
WXDiP04069 Glasya, Azure Evil C .12 .25
WXDiP04070 EXCHANGE R .30 .60
WXDiP04071 Sátyros, Jade Angel C .12 .25
WXDiP04072 Takaoni, First Play R .20 .40
WXDiP04073 Tasmanian, Phantom Beast C .12 .25
WXDiP04074 Mulu, Jade General R .25 .50
WXDiP04075 Leraje, Jade Evil C .12 .25
WXDiP04076 American Bullfrog, Water Phantom C .12 .25
WXDiP04077 Zeruel, Jade Angel R .25 .50
WXDiP04078 Code Eat Caesar C .12 .25
WXDiP04079 Strong Spear R .20 .40
WXDiP04080 Ipetam, Lightly Armed C .25 .50
WXDiP04081 Longhorn Beetle, Phantom Insect C .12 .25
WXDiP04082 Brutus, Doomed General R .30 .60
WXDiP04083 Zwei-Fire Ant C .12 .25
WXDiP04084 Code Anti Dogu R .20 .40
WXDiP04085 Code Art W Inecellar C .12 .25
WXDiP04086 Black Pack R .25 .50
WXDiP04087 Zagan, Blessed Crimson Evil C .12 .25
WXDiP04088 Orias, Blessed Crimson Evil C .12 .25
WXDiP04089 Eckesachs, Lightly Armed C .12 .25
WXDiP04090 Sansetsukon, High Armed C .12 .25
WXDiP04091 Raphae, Doomed Jade Angel C .12 .25
WXDiP04092 Aizen, Doomed Jade Angel C .12 .25
WXDiP04093 Servant C .12 .25
WXDiP04094 Rapid Accumulation R .20 .40

2022 WIXOSS WXDi-P05 Curiosity Diva

WXDiP05001 RED ZONE PI 1.00 2.00
WXDiP05002 DANCE IN THE LANCE PI 1.00 2.00
WXDiP05003 Machina Guardian Dragon PI 2.50 5.00
WXDiP05004 Paradise Universe PI 1.25 2.50
WXDiP05005 Don't STOP! PI .75 1.50
WXDiP05006 Eternal Immortal Kyurukyurun DiR 125.00 250.00
WXDiP05006 Eternal Immortal Kyurukyurun PI .75 1.50
WXDiP05007 Hirana, a Step Towards the Glimmer L .30 .60
WXDiP05007 Hirana, a Step Towards the Glimmer SCR 7.50 15.00
WXDiP05007 Hirana, a Step Towards the Glimmer DIR 100.00 200.00
WXDiP05008 VJ WOLF - 3rd Verse - ALT L .30 .60
WXDiP05008 VJ WOLF - 3rd Verse - ALT SCR 5.00 10.00
WXDiP05008 VJ WOLF - 3rd Verse - ALT DIR 100.00 200.00
WXDiP05009 Nova, Destiny Imperial L .30 .60
WXDiP05009 Nova, Destiny Imperial SCR 4.00 8.00
WXDiP05009 Nova, Destiny Imperial DIR 100.00 200.00
WXDiP05010 Muzica, Vogue 3 - EX L .12 .25
WXDiP05010 Muzica, Vogue 3 - EX SCR 4.00 8.00
WXDiP05010 Muzica, Vogue 3 - EX DIR 100.00 200.00
WXDiP05011 Mikomiko Zero L .25 .50
WXDiP05012 Mikomiko One L .20 .40
WXDiP05012 Mikomiko One SCR 4.00 8.00
WXDiP05013 Mikomiko Two L .20 .40
WXDiP05013 Mikomiko Two SCR 5.00 10.00
WXDiP05014 Mikomiko Three L .30 .75
WXDiP05014 Mikomiko Three SCR 7.50 15.00
WXDiP05015 Tawil =Tre=, Heralding One L .30 .60
WXDiP05015 Tawil =Tre=, Heralding One SCR 3.00 6.00
WXDiP05016 Umr =Tre=, Key to Uproar L .25 .50
WXDiP05016 Umr =Tre=, Key to Uproar SCR 4.00 8.00
WXDiP05016 Umr =Tre=, Key to Uproar DIR 75.00 150.00
WXDiP05017 Ex Trap L .25 .50
WXDiP05018 Deus Thunder L .25 .50
WXDiP05019 Machina Nebula L .25 .50
WXDiP05020 Yukayuka Zero L .20 .40
WXDiP05021 Yukayuka Pon L .20 .40
WXDiP05022 Yukayuka Zubaan L .20 .40
WXDiP05023 Yukayuka BooBoo L .20 .40
WXDiP05024 Yukayuka Zubaba L .20 .40
WXDiP05025 Yukayuka Piihyara L .20 .40
WXDiP05026 Mahomaho Zero L .20 .40
WXDiP05027 Mahomaho Jajaan L .20 .40
WXDiP05028 Mahomaho Zugagaan L .20 .40
WXDiP05029 Mahomaho Dogaan L .20 .40
WXDiP05030 Mahomaho Zudodon L .20 .40
WXDiP05031 Mahomaho Been L .20 .40
WXDiP05032 Gae Bolg, Full Armed SR 10.00 20.00
WXDiP05033 Tamamozen, Phantom Spirit Queen SR 4.00 8.00
WXDiP05034 Hyahha, Code: Accel SR .75 1.50
WXDiP05035 Draco, Natural Planet Queen SR 2.50 5.00
WXDiP05036 Diabride, Natural Engagement Crystal SR 15.00 30.00
WXDiP05037 Hameln, Master Trickster SR 3.00 6.00
WXDiP05038 H2O, Natural Element Queen SR 12.50 25.00
WXDiP05039 Honeyto Ice, Code: Order SR 2.50 5.00
WXDiP05040 Gaia, Jade Angel Queen SR 1.00 2.00
WXDiP05041 Tiger, Roaring Cannon SR .60 1.25
WXDiP05042 Eclipse, Natural Planet Queen SR 3.00 6.00
WXDiP05043 M - Odem, Code: Heart SR 2.00 4.00
WXDiP05044 Tokiyuki, Blessed General C .12 .25
WXDiP05045 Yaekori, Lightly Armed R .20 .40
WXDiP05046 S - Unbed, Code: Art C .12 .25
WXDiP05047 Crius, Blessed Angel R .20 .40
WXDiP05048 Lynx, Natural Planet C .12 .25
WXDiP05049 Luvdabi, Code: Maze C .12 .25
WXDiP05050 Bigfoot, Code: Anti C .12 .25
WXDiP05051 Mathdrill, Blessed Wisdom R .25 .50
WXDiP05052 Get Bolg R .30 .60
WXDiP05053 Hemera, Crimson Angel C .12 .25
WXDiP05054 Heihachiro, Crimson General C .12 .25
WXDiP05055 Buffa, Phantom Beast R .20 .40
WXDiP05056 Nabeno - Tsuna, Crimson General R .40 .80
WXDiP05057 Decarabia, Crimson Evil C .12 .25
WXDiP05058 Jasper, Natural Crystal C .12 .25
WXDiP05059 R - Unning, Code: Art C .12 .25
WXDiP05060 Apocalypse Drift R .25 .50
WXDiP05061 Manomin, Azure Evil C .12 .25
WXDiP05062 Benitoite, Natural Crystal C .12 .25
WXDiP05063 CZ, Natural Element R .30 .60
WXDiP05064 Hauynite, Natural Crystal R .30 .60
WXDiP05065 Muscari, Natural Plant C .12 .25
WXDiP05066 Anahaze, Phantom Aquatic Beast C .12 .25
WXDiP05067 H2, Natural Element C .12 .25
WXDiP05068 HAMELN STEP R .25 .50
WXDiP05069 Little John, Jade General R .25 .50
WXDiP05070 William Tell, Jade General C .12 .25
WXDiP05071 Tocho, Code: Maze C .12 .25
WXDiP05072 Orthrus, Jade Evil C .12 .25
WXDiP05073 Nettle Type: Zwei C .12 .25
WXDiP05074 Passionflower, Natural Plant R .20 .40
WXDiP05075 Polypterus, Water Phantom C .12 .25
WXDiP05076 Chameleon, Phantom Beast R .25 .50
WXDiP05077 Edenify R .25 .50
WXDiP05078 Walkure, Doomed Angel R .25 .50
WXDiP05079 Malphas, Doomed Evil R .25 .50
WXDiP05080 Timer Bomb, Natural Erupting Planet C .12 .25
WXDiP05081 Caesar, Wicked General R .30 .75
WXDiP05082 Typhon, Doomed Evil C .12 .25
WXDiP05083 Buckler, High Armed C .12 .25
WXDiP05084 BP, Natural Element C .12 .25
WXDiP05085 Tartarus, Doomed Angel C .12 .25
WXDiP05086 Moon Bites R .30 .60
WXDiP05087 Mastema, Blessed Doomed Angel C .12 .25
WXDiP05088 Uriel, Blessed Doomed Angel C .12 .25
WXDiP05089 Yorishige, Blessed Azure General C .12 .25
WXDiP05090 Touta, Blessed Azure General C .12 .25
WXDiP05091 Se, Natural Element C .12 .25
WXDiP05092 I, Natural Element C .12 .25
WXDiP05093 Servant C .30 .60
WXDiP05094 Hirana, a Step Towards the Top SCR 17.50 35.00
WXDiP05TK01A [Hastalyk] .20 .40

2022 WIXOSS WXDi-P06 Welcome Back Diva Selector

WXDiP06 Yuzuki 75.00 150.00

WXDiD08002R Tamayorihime, Crescent Moon Miko LR	10.00	20.00
WXDiD08003R Tamayorihime, Half Moon Miko LR	6.00	12.00
WXDiD08004U Tamayorihime, Musical Moon Miko LR	10.00	20.00
WXDiP06001 Entwined Supremacy LR	.40	.80
WXDiP06002 Peeping Future LR	.40	.80
WXDiP06003 Miasma Labyrinth LR	.75	1.50
WXDiP06003 Miasma Labyrinth LRP	50.00	100.00
WXDiP06004 Innocent One - Piece LRP	25.00	50.00
WXDiP06004 Innocent One - Piece LR	.50	1.00
WXDiP06005 Green Bigs LR	.25	.50
WXDiP06005 Green Bigs LRP	25.00	50.00
WXDiP06006 Garden of Singularity LRP	50.00	100.00
WXDiP06006 Garden of Singularity LR	.30	.60
WXDiP06007 Rei, On the Wings of Radiance LR	2.50	6.00
WXDiP06007 Rei, On the Wings of Radiance UR	175.00	350.00
WXDiP06007 Rei, On the Wings of Radiance LC	.30	.75
WXDiP06008 DJ LOVIT - 3rd Verse - ALT LRP	12.50	25.00
WXDiP06008 DJ LOVIT - 3rd Verse - ALT LR	3.00	6.00
WXDiP06008 DJ LOVIT - 3rd Verse - ALT LC	.30	.75
WXDiP06008 DJ LOVIT - 3rd Verse - ALT UR	125.00	250.00
WXDiP06009 Bang, Making a Miracle LR	4.00	8.00
WXDiP06009 Bang, Making a Miracle LRP	12.50	25.00
WXDiP06009 Bang, Making a Miracle LC	.30	.75
WXDiP06010 Sanga, Vogue 3 - EX LRP	30.00	60.00
WXDiP06010 Sanga, Vogue 3 - EX LR	1.25	2.50
WXDiP06010 Sanga, Vogue 3 - EX LC	.40	.80
WXDiP06011 Yuzuki Three, Blazing Fire Chant LR	3.00	6.00
WXDiP06011 Yuzuki Three, Blazing Fire Chant LC	.30	.75
WXDiP06012 Code Piruluk xi LRP	125.00	250.00
WXDiP06012 Code Piruluk xi LR	7.50	15.00
WXDiP06012 Code Piruluk xi LC	.30	.60
WXDiP06013 Urith, Maniacal Enma LR	7.50	15.00
WXDiP06013 Urith, Maniacal Enma LRP	75.00	150.00
WXDiP06013 Urith, Maniacal Enma LC	.30	.75
WXDiP06014 Yuzuki Zero LC	.25	.50
WXDiP06015 Yuzuki One, Blazing Chant LC	.30	.60
WXDiP06015 Yuzuki One, Blazing Chant LR	2.50	5.00
WXDiP06016 Yuzuki Two, Blazing Chant LR	4.00	8.00
WXDiP06016 Yuzuki Two, Blazing Chant LC	.30	.60
WXDiP06017 Code Piruluk LC	.25	.50
WXDiP06018 Code Piruluk K LC	.30	.60
WXDiP06018 Code Piruluk K LR	6.00	12.00
WXDiP06019 Code Piruluk M LC	.25	.50
WXDiP06019 Code Piruluk M LR	2.50	5.00
WXDiP06020 Urith, Enma LC	.30	.60
WXDiP06021 Urith, Burning Enma LC	.30	.60
WXDiP06021 Urith, Burning Enma LR	4.00	8.00
WXDiP06022 Urith, Fatal Enma LC	.30	.60
WXDiP06022 Urith, Fatal Enma LR	7.50	15.00
WXDiP06023 Yukayuka Dojaan LC	.30	.60
WXDiP06024 Mahomaho Zuun LC	.30	.60
WXDiP06025 Hanayo, Sakura LC	.30	.60
WXDiP06026 Hanayo, Pomegranate LC	.40	.80
WXDiP06027 Hanayo, Gentian LC	.30	.60
WXDiP06028 Midoriko, Rainspear LC	.30	.60
WXDiP06029 Midoriko, Half - Moon LC	.30	.60
WXDiP06030 Midoriko, Repair LC	.30	.60
WXDiP06031 Remember//Memoria, Code: Heart SR	12.50	25.00
WXDiP06032 Osiris, Code: Ancients SRP	30.00	75.00
WXDiP06032 Osiris, Code: Ancients SR	1.25	2.50
WXDiP06033 Coela, Aquatic Phantom Queen SRP	50.00	100.00
WXDiP06033 Coela, Aquatic Phantom Queen SR	3.00	6.00
WXDiP06034 Cu Chulainn, Crimson General Queen SRP	25.00	50.00
WXDiP06034 Cu Chulainn, Crimson General Queen SR	.75	1.50
WXDiP06035 Shiva, Crimson Evil Queen SRP	20.00	40.00
WXDiP06035 Shiva, Crimson Evil Queen SR	.25	.50
WXDiP06036 Blue Adamas, Natural Pyroxene SRP	20.00	40.00
WXDiP06036 Blue Adamas, Natural Pyroxene SR	.30	.75
WXDiP06037 Eldora//Memoria, Aquatic Phantom Queen SRP	25.00	50.00
WXDiP06037 Eldora//Memoria, Aquatic Phantom Queen SR	.25	.50
WXDiP06038 Ann//Memoria, Jade Beauty Queen SRP	50.00	100.00
WXDiP06038 Ann//Memoria, Jade Beauty Queen SR	.30	.75
WXDiP06039 Lavender, Natural Plant Queen SRP	20.00	40.00
WXDiP06039 Lavender, Natural Plant Queen SR	.30	.75
WXDiP06040 Tama//Memoria, Doomed Angel Queen SRP	75.00	150.00
WXDiP06040 Tama//Memoria, Doomed Angel Queen SR	12.50	25.00
WXDiP06041 Lucifer, Doomed Evil Queen SRP	30.00	60.00
WXDiP06041 Lucifer, Doomed Evil Queen SR	2.50	5.00
WXDiP06042 Iona//Memoria, Code: Ancients SRP	75.00	150.00
WXDiP06042 Iona//Memoria, Code: Ancients SR	.75	1.50
WXDiP06043 Martiel, Blessed Angel C	.12	.25
WXDiP06044 Sashe//Memoria, Natural Planet R	.12	.25
WXDiP06045 Yuki//Memoria, Code: Maze R	.30	.75
WXDiP06046 Round, Blessed General C	.07	.15
WXDiP06047 Succu, Blessed Evil C	.12	.25
WXDiP06048 Ose, Blessed Evil C	.12	.25
WXDiP06049 Mikagami, High Armed C	.25	.50
WXDiP06050 Get Remember R	.40	.80
WXDiP06051 Imoko, Crimson General C	.20	.40
WXDiP06052 Ariton, Crimson Evil R	.25	.50
WXDiP06053 Bonya, Lightly Armed C	.12	.25
WXDiP06054 E - Lectro Bike, Code: Art C	.12	.25
WXDiP06055 Aphrodite, Crimson Angel R	.20	.40
WXDiP06056 Tristan, Crimson General C	.12	.25
WXDiP06057 Lalaru//Memoria, Code: Art R	.40	.80
WXDiP06058 Beiar, Phantom Burning Beast C	.12	.25
WXDiP06059 E - Lectrobike Revealed R	.07	.15
WXDiP06060 Saniel, Azure Angel C	.12	.25
WXDiP06061 Soui//Memoria, Azure General R	.12	.25
WXDiP06062 Futase//Memoria, Azure Beauty R	.20	.40
WXDiP06063 Jack Frost, Azure Evil C	.12	.25
WXDiP06064 Delphinus, Natural Planet C	.12	.25
WXDiP06065 Iolite, Natural Crystal C	.20	.40
WXDiP06066 Milulun//Memoria, Natural Element R	.30	.60
WXDiP06067 Okatotoki, Natural Plant C	.12	.25
WXDiP06068 DISCOVERY R	.07	.15
WXDiP06069 Orobas, Jade Evil R	.12	.25
WXDiP06070 Monkey Bars, First Playground C	.07	.15
WXDiP06071 Capricorn, Natural Planet C	.12	.25
WXDiP06072 Pony, Phantom Terra Beast C	.07	.15
WXDiP06073 Sukunabikona, Jade Angel R	.20	.40
WXDiP06074 Hanuman, Jade Angel C	.12	.25
WXDiP06075 Aiyai//Memoria, Second Play R	.30	.75
WXDiP06076 Chelydridae, Phantom Aquatic Beast C	.12	.25
WXDiP06077 Encounter R	.20	.40
WXDiP06078 Karasawa, Doomed General C	.12	.25
WXDiP06079 Hanare//Memoria, Type: Eins R	.25	.50
WXDiP06080 D - Humidifier, Code: Art C	.12	.25
WXDiP06081 Vial, Type: Zwei C	.30	.60
WXDiP06082 Microscopium, Natural Planet C	.12	.25
WXDiP06083 Tyranno, Phantom Black Dragon C	.12	.25
WXDiP06084 Myu//Memoria, Phantom Insect R	.30	.60
WXDiP06085 Once Salvage R	.20	.40
WXDiP06086 Sea Star, Phantom Aquatic Beast C	.12	.25
WXDiP06087 Bargibanti, Phantom Aquatic Beast C	.12	.25
WXDiP06088 Canes Vena, Natural Planet C	.20	.40
WXDiP06089 Serpens, Natural Planet C	.12	.25
WXDiP06090 Tc, Natural Element C	.12	.25
WXDiP06091 Te, Natural Element C	.07	.15
WXDiP06092 Servant C	.12	.25

2023 WIXOSS WXDi-P08 Spread Diva

WXDiP08007EN Yukayuka Threee LC	.12	.25
WXDiP08007REN Yukayuka Threee LR	.12	.25
WXDiP08008EN Eldora X Mark v LC	.12	.25
WXDiP08008REN Eldora X Mark v LR	.12	.25
WXDiP08009EN Ann III, Maiden of Mettle LC	.12	.25
WXDiP08009REN Ann III, Maiden of Mettle LR	.12	.25
WXDiP08010EN Iona, Triangle/Maiden LC	.12	.25
WXDiP08010REN Iona, Triangle/Maiden LR	.12	.25
WXDiP08011EN Yukayuka One LC	.12	.25
WXDiP08011REN Yukayuka One LR	.12	.25
WXDiP08012EN Yukayuka Two LC	.12	.25
WXDiP08012REN Yukayuka Two LR	.12	.25
WXDiP08013EN Eldora X Mark 0 LC	.12	.25
WXDiP08013PEN Eldora X Mark 0 LC FOIL	.12	.25
WXDiP08014EN Eldora X Mark I LC	.12	.25
WXDiP08014REN Eldora X Mark I LR	.12	.25
WXDiP08015EN Eldora X Mark II LC	.12	.25
WXDiP08015REN Eldora X Mark II LR	.12	.25
WXDiP08016EN Ann, Marvel of Miracles LC	.12	.25
WXDiP08016PEN Ann, Marvel of Miracles LC FOIL	.12	.25
WXDiP08017EN Ann I, Icon of Innovation LC	.12	.25
WXDiP08017REN Ann I, Icon of Innovation LR	.12	.25
WXDiP08018EN Ann II, Boon of Brilliance LC	.12	.25
WXDiP08018REN Ann II, Boon of Brilliance LR	.12	.25
WXDiP08019EN Iona, Zero/Maiden LC	.12	.25
WXDiP08019PEN Iona, Zero/Maiden LC FOIL	.12	.25
WXDiP08020EN Iona, Nepto/Maiden LC	.12	.25
WXDiP08020REN Iona, Nepto/Maiden LR	.12	.25
WXDiP08021EN Iona, Uranus/Maiden LC	.12	.25
WXDiP08021REN Iona, Uranus/Maiden LR	.12	.25
WXDiP08022EN Tama Loud Voice LC	.12	.25
WXDiP08022PEN Tama Loud Voice LC FOIL	.12	.25
WXDiP08023EN Tama Bible LC	.12	.25
WXDiP08023PEN Tama Bible LC FOIL	.12	.25
WXDiP08024EN Tama Shield LC	.12	.25
WXDiP08024PEN Tama Shield LC FOIL	.12	.25
WXDiP08025EN Tama Boundary LC	.12	.25
WXDiP08025PEN Tama Boundary LC FOIL	.12	.25
WXDiP08026EN Tama Aura LC	.12	.25
WXDiP08026PEN Tama Aura LC FOIL	.12	.25
WXDiP08027EN Ril, Flash LC	.12	.25
WXDiP08027PEN Ril, Flash LC FOIL	.12	.25
WXDiP08028EN Ril, Flame Dance LC	.12	.25
WXDiP08028PEN Ril, Flame Dance LC FOIL	.12	.25
WXDiP08029EN Ril, Drawn Sword LC	.12	.25
WXDiP08029PEN Ril, Drawn Sword LC FOIL	.12	.25
WXDiP08030EN Ril, in Prayer LC	.12	.25
WXDiP08030PEN Ril, in Prayer LC FOIL	.12	.25
WXDiP08031EN Ril, Inspiration LC	.12	.25
WXDiP08031PEN Ril, Inspiration LC FOIL	.12	.25
WXDiP08032EN Piruluk / Draw LC	.12	.25
WXDiP08032PEN Piruluk / Draw LC FOIL	.12	.25
WXDiP08033EN Piruluk / Snipe LC	.12	.25
WXDiP08033PEN Piruluk / Snipe LC FOIL	.12	.25
WXDiP08034EN Piruluk / Don't Escape LC	.12	.25
WXDiP08034PEN Piruluk / Don't Escape LC FOIL	.12	.25
WXDiP08035EN Piruluk / Don't Move LC	.12	.25
WXDiP08035PEN Piruluk / Don't Move LC FOIL	.12	.25
WXDiP08036EN Piruluk / Peeping Analyze LC	.12	.25
WXDiP08036PEN Piruluk / Peeping Analyze LC FOIL	.12	.25
WXDiP08049EN Chisel, Blessed Beauty C	.12	.25
WXDiP08049PEN Chisel, Blessed Beauty C FOIL	.12	.25
WXDiP08050EN Proto Energe, Lightly Armed C	.12	.25
WXDiP08050PEN Proto Energe, Lightly Armed C FOIL	.12	.25
WXDiP08051EN Akino//Memoria, Aquatic Phantom R	.20	.40
WXDiP08051PEN Akino//Memoria, Aquatic Phantom R FOIL	.20	.40
WXDiP08052EN Flash Cards, Blessed Mind C	.12	.25
WXDiP08052PEN Flash Cards, Blessed Mind C FOIL	.12	.25
WXDiP08053EN Nova//Memoria, Natural Planet R	.20	.40
WXDiP08053PEN Nova//Memoria, Natural Planet R FOIL	.20	.40
WXDiP08054EN Hestia, Blessed Angel C	.12	.25
WXDiP08054PEN Hestia, Blessed Angel C FOIL	.12	.25
WXDiP08055EN Over Pursuit R	.20	.40
WXDiP08055PEN Over Pursuit R FOIL	.20	.40
WXDiP08056EN P - tato Fryer, Code: Art C	.12	.25
WXDiP08056PEN P - tato Fryer, Code: Art C FOIL	.12	.25
WXDiP08057EN Yuzuki//Memoria, Phantom Dragon R	.20	.40
WXDiP08057PEN Yuzuki//Memoria, Phantom Dragon R FOIL	.20	.40
WXDiP08058EN Tawil//Memoria, Crimson Evil R	.20	.40
WXDiP08058PEN Tawil//Memoria, Crimson Evil R FOIL	.20	.40
WXDiP08059EN Garnet, Natural Dancing Stone C	.12	.25
WXDiP08059PEN Garnet, Natural Dancing Stone C FOIL	.12	.25
WXDiP08060EN Launchan, Roaring Gun C	.12	.25
WXDiP08060PEN Launchan, Roaring Gun C FOIL	.12	.25
WXDiP08061EN Arcadian Resonance C	.12	.25
WXDiP08061PEN Arcadian Resonance C FOIL	.12	.25
WXDiP08062EN Umr//Memoria, Code: Maze R	.20	.40
WXDiP08062PEN Umr//Memoria, Code: Maze R FOIL	.20	.40
WXDiP08063EN Piruluk//Memoria, Code: Art R	.20	.40
WXDiP08063PEN Piruluk//Memoria, Code: Art R FOIL	.20	.40
WXDiP08064EN Kanaloa, Azure Angel C	.12	.25
WXDiP08064PEN Kanaloa, Azure Angel C FOIL	.12	.25
WXDiP08065EN Rei//Memoria, Natural Crystal R	.20	.40
WXDiP08065PEN Rei//Memoria, Natural Crystal R FOIL	.20	.40
WXDiP08066EN VO, Natural Element C	.12	.25
WXDiP08066PEN VO, Natural Element C FOIL	.12	.25
WXDiP08067EN Saprolegnia, Natural Pale Bacteria C	.12	.25
WXDiP08067PEN Saprolegnia, Natural Pale Bacteria C FOIL	.12	.25
WXDiP08068EN FAILURE C	.12	.25
WXDiP08068PEN FAILURE C FOIL	.12	.25
WXDiP08069EN Bang//Memoria, Jade Evil R	.20	.40
WXDiP08069PEN Bang//Memoria, Jade Evil R FOIL	.20	.40
WXDiP08070EN Kebab, Code Eat C	.12	.25
WXDiP08070PEN Kebab, Code Eat C FOIL	.12	.25
WXDiP08071EN Hibiscus, Natural Dancing Plant C	.12	.25
WXDiP08071PEN Hibiscus, Natural Dancing Plant C FOIL	.12	.25
WXDiP08072EN Midoriko//Memoria, Phantom Beast R	.20	.40
WXDiP08072PEN Midoriko//Memoria, Phantom Beast R FOIL	.20	.40
WXDiP08073EN Mammo, Phantom Terra Beast C	.12	.25
WXDiP08073PEN Mammo, Phantom Terra Beast C FOIL	.12	.25
WXDiP08074EN Fabricate C	.12	.25
WXDiP08074PEN Fabricate C FOIL	.12	.25
WXDiP08075EN Wight, Doomed Evil C	.12	.25
WXDiP08075PEN Wight, Doomed Evil C FOIL	.12	.25
WXDiP08076EN Dumbbell, Lightly Armed C	.12	.25
WXDiP08076PEN Dumbbell, Lightly Armed C FOIL	.12	.25
WXDiP08077EN S - Kycat, Code: Art R	.20	.40
WXDiP08077PEN S - Kycat, Code: Art R FOIL	.20	.40
WXDiP08078EN Senbero, Doomed Evil C	.12	.25
WXDiP08078PEN Senbero, Doomed Evil C FOIL	.12	.25
WXDiP08079EN Mamushi Type: Zwei R	.20	.40
WXDiP08079PEN Mamushi Type: Zwei R FOIL	.20	.40
WXDiP08080EN Habble, Natural Planet C	.12	.25
WXDiP08080PEN Habble, Natural Planet C FOIL	.12	.25
WXDiP08081EN Inside Devils R	.20	.40
WXDiP08081PEN Inside Devils R FOIL	.20	.40
WXDiP08082EN Servant # C	.12	.25
WXDiP08082PEN Servant # C FOIL	.12	.25

2023 WIXOSS WXDi-P07 Welcome Back Diva Lostorage

WXDiP07001 Sparkling Memories LR	1.25	2.50
WXDiP07002 ENERGY DOOR LR	.50	1.00
WXDiP07003 True Honesty LR	.75	1.50
WXDiP07003P True Honesty LRP	50.00	100.00
WXDiP07004 Can't Stop Pretty! LR	1.25	2.50
WXDiP07005 Instantaneous Explosion LR	.60	1.25
WXDiP07006 Take Off! WIXOSS Robo! LR	1.00	2.00
WXDiP07007 Mahomaho Three LR	125.00	250.00
WXDiP07007 Mahomaho Three UR	3.00	6.00
WXDiP07007 Mahomaho Threee LC	.30	.60
WXDiP07007P Mahomaho Threee LRP	30.00	60.00
WXDiP07008 Ril, Memory of Martial Dancing UR	17.50	35.00
WXDiP07008 Ril, Memory of Martial Dancing LR	175.00	350.00
WXDiP07008 Ril, Memory of Martial Dancing LC	.75	1.50
WXDiP07008P Ril, Memory of Martial Dancing LRP	75.00	150.00
WXDiP07009 Dona SUN LR	175.00	350.00
WXDiP07009 Dona SUN UR	6.00	12.00
WXDiP07009 Dona SUN LC	.30	.75
WXDiP07010 Digital Aya! III UR	10.00	20.00
WXDiP07010 Digital Aya! III LR	200.00	400.00
WXDiP07010 Digital Aya! III LC	.75	1.50
WXDiP07011 Mahomaho One LC	.30	.60
WXDiP07011R Mahomaho One LR	4.00	8.00
WXDiP07012 Mahomaho Two LC	.30	.75
WXDiP07012R Mahomaho Two LR	10.00	20.00
WXDiP07013 Ril, Memory of Innocence LC	.60	1.25
WXDiP07014 Ril, Memory of Seeking Change LC	.75	1.50
WXDiP07014R Ril, Memory of Seeking Change LR	3.00	6.00
WXDiP07015 Ril, Memory of Flickering LC	.75	1.50
WXDiP07015R Ril, Memory of Flickering LR	4.00	8.00
WXDiP07016 Dona START LC	.75	1.50
WXDiP07017 Dona FIRST++ LC	.30	.75
WXDiP07017R Dona FIRST++ LR	1.50	3.00
WXDiP07018 Dona SECOND LC	.25	.50
WXDiP07018R Dona SECOND LR	2.50	5.00
WXDiP07019 Aya! 0 LC	.40	.80
WXDiP07020 Beep Boop Aya! I LC	.40	.80
WXDiP07020R Beep Boop Aya! I LR	7.50	15.00
WXDiP07021 Great Aya! II LC	.60	1.25
WXDiP07021R Great Aya! II LR	4.00	8.00
WXDiP07022 Mikomiko Gacchan LC	.75	1.50
WXDiP07023 Mikomiko Kirakkira LC	.20	.40
WXDiP07024 Mikomiko Bashiin LC	.25	.50
WXDiP07025 Mikomiko Zubashaan LC	.75	1.50
WXDiP07026 Mikomiko Bye - Bye LC	.75	1.50
WXDiP07027 Mel - Ready LC	1.25	2.50
WXDiP07028 Mel Burst LC	.30	.60
WXDiP07029 Mel Revise LC	.75	1.50
WXDiP07030 Mel Invisible LC	1.25	2.50
WXDiP07031 Mel Overrun LC	1.00	2.00
WXDiP07032 Mel Present LC	.50	1.00
WXDiP07033 Nanashi, Part Zero LC	.50	1.00
WXDiP07034 Nanashi Scattering LC	.50	1.00
WXDiP07035 Nanashi Search LC	.50	1.00
WXDiP07036 Nanashi Purification LC	.60	1.25
WXDiP07037 Nanashi Locking LC	.60	1.25
WXDiP07038 Nanashi Selection LC	1.25	2.50
WXDiP07039 Yukime//Memoria, Blessed Warlord SR	2.50	5.00
WXDiP07039P Yukime//Memoria, Blessed Warlord SRP	30.00	75.00
WXDiP07040 Pegasus, Natural Planet Queen SR	1.25	2.50
WXDiP07040P Pegasus, Natural Planet Queen SRP	75.00	150.00
WXDiP07041 Carnival//Memoria, Galactic Queen SR	3.00	6.00
WXDiP07041P Carnival//Memoria, Galactic Queen SRP	125.00	250.00
WXDiP07042 Thoroughbred, Phantom Beast Deity SR	1.25	2.50
WXDiP07043 Brynhildr, Azure Angel Queen SR	3.00	6.00
WXDiP07044 Allos Piruluk//Memoria, Great Insect SR	3.00	6.00
WXDiP07044P Allos Piruluk//Memoria, Great Insect SRP	75.00	150.00
WXDiP07045 Mama//Memoria, Jade Wisdom Queen SR	1.00	2.00
WXDiP07046 Drei =Patra= SR	1.50	3.00
WXDiP07046P Drei =Patra= SRP	20.00	40.00
WXDiP07047 Guzuko//Memoria, Tragic Party Queen SR	2.50	5.00
WXDiP07048 A - To Massager, Code: Heart SR	.75	1.50
WXDiP07048P A - To Massager, Code: Heart SRP	20.00	40.00
WXDiP07049 Liwat//Memoria, Lucent Angel Queen SR	3.00	6.00
WXDiP07049P Liwat//Memoria, Lucent Angel Queen SRP	75.00	150.00
WXDiP07050 Mugen//Memoria SR	3.00	6.00
WXDiP07050P Mugen//Memoria SRP	100.00	200.00
WXDiP07051 Yagyu, Blessed General C	.12	.25
WXDiP07052 Haity//Memoria, Blessed Evil R	.25	.50
WXDiP07053 D Ispenser, Code: Art C	.15	.30
WXDiP07054 Tawil//Memoria, Blessed Angel R	.30	.60
WXDiP07055 Mohayhä, Blessed General C	.10	.20
WXDiP07056 Picture Frame, Blessed Beauty C	.12	.25
WXDiP07057 Eel, Phantom Aquatic White Beast C	.12	.25
WXDiP07058 Karaten, Phantom Spirit R	.25	.50
WXDiP07059 Serve Color R	.25	.50
WXDiP07060 Hyperion, Crimson Angel C	.12	.25
WXDiP07061 Fornax, Natural Planet R	.25	.50
WXDiP07062 Ruriru, Lonely Natural Crystal C	.12	.25
WXDiP07063 Bardiche, High Armed C	.12	.25
WXDiP07064 Diorta, Natural Planet C	.12	.25
WXDiP07065 Layla//Memoria, Code: Ride R	.25	.50
WXDiP07066 Buggy Car, Code: Ride C	.12	.25
WXDiP07067 Gilgamej, Crimson General R	.30	.60
WXDiP07068 Legend of the Mask R	.25	.50
WXDiP07069 Scylla, Azure Evil R	.20	.40
WXDiP07070 Kyanite, Natural Crystal C	.15	.30
WXDiP07071 Hyacinth, Natural Plant C	.12	.25
WXDiP07072 Caeneus, Azure Angel C	.12	.25
WXDiP07073 In, Natural Element C	.12	.25
WXDiP07074 Wisteria Flower, Natural Plant C	.15	.30
WXDiP07075 Ryuujou, Code Palace R	.30	.60
WXDiP07076 Honeytra, Master Trickster R	.25	.50
WXDiP07077 RECOVERY R	.20	.40
WXDiP07078 Geronimo, Jade General C	.12	.25
WXDiP07079 Ein =Green Lucbor= R	.25	.50
WXDiP07080 Tuna Mayo, Code Eat C	.12	.25
WXDiP07081 Centurion, Explosive Gun C	.12	.25
WXDiP07082 Colt, Natural Planet R	.25	.50
WXDiP07083 Lacerta, Natural Planet C	.12	.25
WXDiP07084 Race Course, Code: Maze C	.15	.30
WXDiP07085 Nightile, Jade Wisdom R	.25	.50
WXDiP07086 Calculation R	.25	.50
WXDiP07087 Berenice, Natural Planet C	.10	.20
WXDiP07088 Shoukokabi, Natural Oil Bacteria C	.10	.20
WXDiP07089 Umr//Memoria, Code: Anti R	.25	.50
WXDiP07090 Thanatos, Doomed Angel C	.15	.30
WXDiP07091 Agravain, Doomed General C	.12	.25
WXDiP07092 Alfou//Memoria, Doomed Evil R	.40	.80
WXDiP07093 Sayuragi, Doomed Evil R	.25	.50
WXDiP07094 Lilith, Doomed Evil C	.12	.25
WXDiP07095 Black Memory R	.25	.50
WXDiP07096 Origami, Blessed Jade Beauty C	.10	.20
WXDiP07097 Surrelis, Blessed Jade Beauty C	.12	.25
WXDiP07098 C Repe Maker, Code: Art C	.12	.25
WXDiP07099 T Akoyaki Pan, Code: Art C	.10	.20
WXDiP07100 Servant C	.50	1.00
WXDiP07101 Mikomiko Zero RE	.20	.40
WXDiP07102 Mahomaho Zero RE	.20	.40

MAGIC: THE GATHERING

1993 Magic The Gathering Alpha

NNO Air Elemental U	150.00	300.00
NNO Ancestral Recall R	10,000.00	20,000.00
NNO Animate Artifact U	150.00	300.00
NNO Animate Dead U	500.00	1,000.00
NNO Animate Wall R	400.00	800.00
NNO Ankh of Mishra R	750.00	1,500.00
NNO Armageddon R	750.00	1,500.00
NNO Aspect of Wolf R	1,250.00	2,500.00
NNO Bad Moon R	1,250.00	2,500.00
NNO Badlands R	3,000.00	7,500.00
NNO Balance R	2,000.00	4,000.00
NNO Basalt Monolith U	175.00	350.00
NNO Bayou R	3,000.00	6,000.00
NNO Benalish Hero C	40.00	80.00
NNO Berserk U	600.00	1,200.00
NNO Birds of Paradise R	3,000.00	6,000.00
NNO Black Knight U	300.00	600.00
NNO Black Lotus R	30,000.00	75,000.00
NNO Black Vise U	500.00	1,000.00
NNO Black Ward U	50.00	100.00
NNO Blaze of Glory R	1,000.00	2,000.00
NNO Blessing R	200.00	400.00
NNO Blue Elemental Blast C	50.00	100.00
NNO Blue Ward U	30.00	75.00
NNO Bog Wraith U	75.00	150.00
NNO Braingeyser R	3,000.00	6,000.00
NNO Burrowing U	30.00	75.00
NNO Camouflage U	75.00	150.00
NNO Castle U	100.00	200.00
NNO Celestial Prism U	60.00	125.00
NNO Channel U	400.00	800.00
NNO Chaos Orb R	7,500.00	15,000.00
NNO Chaoslace R	400.00	800.00
NNO Circle of Protection Blue C	15.00	30.00
NNO Circle of Protection Green C	15.00	30.00
NNO Circle of Protection Red C	30.00	60.00
NNO Circle of Protection White C	17.50	35.00
NNO Clockwork Beast R	500.00	1,000.00
NNO Clone U	175.00	350.00
NNO Cockatrice R	750.00	1,500.00
NNO Consecrate Land U	40.00	80.00
NNO Conservator U	60.00	125.00
NNO Contract from Below R	750.00	1,500.00
NNO Control Magic U	300.00	600.00
NNO Conversion U	50.00	100.00
NNO Copper Tablet U	150.00	300.00
NNO Copy Artifact R	3,000.00	6,000.00
NNO Counterspell U	1,250.00	2,500.00
NNO Craw Wurm C	30.00	60.00
NNO Creature Bond C	17.50	35.00
NNO Crusade R	500.00	1,000.00
NNO Crystal Rod U	100.00	200.00
NNO Cursed Land U	100.00	200.00
NNO Cyclopean Tomb R	1,250.00	2,500.00
NNO Dark Ritual C	150.00	300.00
NNO Darkpact R	1,000.00	2,000.00
NNO Death Ward C	20.00	40.00
NNO Deathgrip U	100.00	200.00
NNO Deathlace R	400.00	800.00
NNO Demonic Attorney R	1,000.00	2,000.00
NNO Demonic Hordes R	1,000.00	2,000.00
NNO Demonic Tutor U	1,250.00	2,500.00
NNO Dingus Egg R	400.00	800.00
NNO Disenchant C	100.00	200.00
NNO Disintegrate C	60.00	125.00
NNO Disrupting Scepter R	500.00	1,000.00
NNO Dragon Whelp U	400.00	800.00
NNO Drain Life C	125.00	250.00
NNO Drain Power R	400.00	800.00
NNO Drudge Skeletons C	40.00	80.00
NNO Dwarven Demolition Team U	75.00	150.00
NNO Dwarven Warriors C	15.00	30.00
NNO Earth Elemental U	75.00	150.00
NNO Earthbind C	125.00	250.00
NNO Earthquake R	1,500.00	3,000.00
NNO Elvish Archers R	750.00	1,500.00
NNO Evil Presence U	100.00	200.00
NNO False Orders C	25.00	50.00
NNO Farmstead R	400.00	800.00
NNO Fastbond R	750.00	1,500.00
NNO Fear C	30.00	60.00
NNO Feedback U	75.00	150.00
NNO Fire Elemental U	150.00	300.00
NNO Fireball C	125.00	250.00
NNO Firebreathing C	25.00	50.00
NNO Flashfires U	50.00	100.00
NNO Flight C	15.00	30.00
NNO Fog C	30.00	75.00
NNO Force of Nature R	1,250.00	2,500.00
NNO Forcefield R	1,000.00	2,000.00
NNO Forest v1 L	25.00	50.00
NNO Forest v2 L	40.00	80.00
NNO Fork R	4,000.00	8,000.00
NNO Frozen Shade C	30.00	60.00
NNO Fungusaur R	400.00	800.00
NNO Gaea's Liege R	400.00	800.00
NNO Gauntlet of Might R	1,500.00	3,000.00
NNO Giant Growth C	100.00	200.00
NNO Giant Spider C	30.00	60.00
NNO Glasses of Urza U	100.00	200.00
NNO Gloom U	100.00	200.00
NNO Goblin Balloon Brigade U	175.00	350.00
NNO Goblin King R	1,750.00	3,500.00
NNO Granite Gargoyle R	1,750.00	3,500.00
NNO Gray Ogre C	17.50	35.00
NNO Green Ward U	40.00	80.00
NNO Grizzly Bears C	50.00	100.00
NNO Guardian Angel C	25.00	50.00
NNO Healing Salve C	30.00	60.00
NNO Helm of Chatzuk R	500.00	1,000.00
NNO Hill Giant C	17.50	35.00
NNO Holy Armor C	30.00	75.00
NNO Holy Strength C	25.00	50.00
NNO Howl from Beyond C	17.50	35.00
NNO Howling Mine R	1,750.00	3,500.00
NNO Hurloon Minotaur C	17.50	35.00
NNO Hurricane U	125.00	250.00
NNO Hypnotic Specter U	300.00	600.00
NNO Ice Storm U	200.00	400.00
NNO Icy Manipulator U	750.00	1,500.00
NNO Illusionary Mask R	750.00	1,500.00
NNO Instill Energy U	100.00	200.00
NNO Invisibility C	25.00	50.00
NNO Iron Star U	150.00	300.00
NNO Ironclaw Orcs C	25.00	50.00
NNO Ironroot Treefolk C	30.00	60.00
NNO Island Sanctuary R	75.00	150.00
NNO Island v1 L	60.00	125.00
NNO Island v2 L	50.00	100.00
NNO Ivory Cup U	50.00	100.00
NNO Jade Monolith R	3,000.00	7,500.00
NNO Jade Statue U	250.00	500.00
NNO Jayemdae Tome R	2,500.00	5,000.00
NNO Juggernaut U	400.00	800.00
NNO Jump C	25.00	50.00
NNO Karma U	100.00	200.00
NNO Keldon Warlord U	175.00	350.00
NNO Kormus Bell R	1,250.00	2,500.00
NNO Kudzu R	600.00	1,200.00
NNO Lance U	125.00	250.00
NNO Ley Druid U	50.00	100.00
NNO Library of Leng U	75.00	150.00
NNO Lich R	1,500.00	3,000.00
NNO Lifeforce U	60.00	125.00
NNO Lifelace R	150.00	300.00
NNO Lifetap U	75.00	150.00
NNO Lightning Bolt C	750.00	1,500.00
NNO Living Artifact R	300.00	600.00
NNO Living Lands R	600.00	1,200.00
NNO Living Wall U	125.00	250.00
NNO Llanowar Elves C	250.00	500.00
NNO Lord of Atlantis R	750.00	1,500.00
NNO Lord of the Pit R	750.00	1,500.00
NNO Lure U	100.00	200.00
NNO Magical Hack R	250.00	500.00
NNO Mahamoti Djinn R	3,000.00	7,500.00
NNO Mana Flare R	750.00	1,500.00
NNO Mana Short R	400.00	800.00
NNO Mana Vault R	3,000.00	6,000.00
NNO Manabarbs R	400.00	800.00
NNO Meekstone R	1,500.00	3,000.00
NNO Merfolk of the Pearl Trident C	40.00	80.00
NNO Mesa Pegasus C	25.00	50.00
NNO Mind Twist R	2,000.00	4,000.00
NNO Mons's Goblin Raiders C	30.00	60.00
NNO Mountain v1 L	30.00	75.00
NNO Mountain v2 L	30.00	75.00
NNO Mox Emerald R	6,000.00	12,000.00
NNO Mox Jet R	7,500.00	15,000.00
NNO Mox Pearl R	6,000.00	12,000.00
NNO Mox Ruby R	10,000.00	20,000.00
NNO Mox Sapphire R	10,000.00	20,000.00
NNO Natural Selection R	750.00	1,500.00
NNO Nether Shadow R	750.00	1,500.00
NNO Nettling Imp U	60.00	125.00
NNO Nevinyrral's Disk R	1,250.00	2,500.00
NNO Nightmare R	1,750.00	3,500.00
NNO Northern Paladin R	1,000.00	2,000.00
NNO Obsianus Golem U	75.00	150.00
NNO Orcish Artillery U	400.00	800.00
NNO Orcish Oriflamme U	750.00	1,500.00
NNO Paralyze C	30.00	75.00
NNO Pearled Unicorn C	25.00	50.00
NNO Personal Incarnation R	750.00	1,500.00
NNO Pestilence C	50.00	100.00
NNO Phantasmal Forces U	100.00	200.00
NNO Phantasmal Terrain C	17.50	35.00
NNO Phantom Monster U	75.00	150.00
NNO Pirate Ship R	250.00	500.00
NNO Plague Rats C	50.00	100.00
NNO Plains v1 L	30.00	60.00
NNO Plains v2 L	30.00	60.00
NNO Plateau R	3,000.00	7,500.00
NNO Power Leak C	25.00	50.00
NNO Power Sink C	30.00	75.00
NNO Power Surge R	300.00	600.00
NNO Prodigal Sorcerer C	50.00	100.00
NNO Psionic Blast U	300.00	600.00
NNO Psychic Venom C	40.00	80.00
NNO Purelace R	200.00	400.00
NNO Raging River R	1,250.00	2,500.00
NNO Raise Dead C	50.00	100.00
NNO Red Elemental Blast C	125.00	250.00
NNO Red Ward U	30.00	75.00
NNO Regeneration C	25.00	50.00
NNO Regrowth U	250.00	500.00
NNO Resurrection U	75.00	150.00
NNO Reverse Damage R	250.00	500.00
NNO Righteousness R	300.00	600.00
NNO Roc of Kher Ridges R	750.00	1,500.00
NNO Rock Hydra R	750.00	1,500.00
NNO Rod of Ruin U	60.00	125.00
NNO Royal Assassin R	400.00	800.00
NNO Sacrifice U	100.00	200.00
NNO Samite Healer C	25.00	50.00
NNO Savannah Lions R	3,000.00	7,500.00
NNO Savannah R	1,750.00	3,500.00
NNO Scathe Zombies C	17.50	35.00
NNO Scavenging Ghoul U	75.00	150.00
NNO Scrubland R	7,500.00	15,000.00
NNO Scryb Sprites C	30.00	75.00
NNO Sea Serpent C	25.00	50.00
NNO Sedge Troll R	6,000.00	12,000.00
NNO Sengir Vampire U	750.00	1,500.00
NNO Serra Angel U	750.00	1,500.00
NNO Shanodin Dryads C	17.50	35.00
NNO Shatter C	40.00	80.00
NNO Shivan Dragon R	7,500.00	15,000.00
NNO Simulacrum U	125.00	250.00
NNO Sinkhole C	125.00	250.00
NNO Siren's Call U	50.00	100.00
NNO Sleight of Mind R	500.00	1,000.00
NNO Smoke R	500.00	1,000.00
NNO Sol Ring U	1,500.00	3,000.00
NNO Soul Net U	75.00	150.00
NNO Spell Blast C	25.00	50.00
NNO Stasis R	1,750.00	3,500.00
NNO Steal Artifact U	100.00	200.00
NNO Stone Giant U	60.00	125.00
NNO Stone Rain C	60.00	125.00
NNO Stream of Life C	20.00	40.00
NNO Sunglasses of Urza R	750.00	1,500.00
NNO Swamp v1 L	30.00	75.00
NNO Swamp v2 L	30.00	75.00
NNO Swords to Plowshares U	4,000.00	8,000.00
NNO Taiga R	1,750.00	3,500.00
NNO Terror C	75.00	150.00
NNO The Hive R	1,000.00	2,000.00
NNO Thicket Basilisk U	175.00	350.00
NNO Thoughtlace R	400.00	800.00
NNO Throne of Bone U	75.00	150.00
NNO Timber Wolves R	600.00	1,200.00
NNO Time Vault R	5,000.00	10,000.00
NNO Time Walk R	7,500.00	15,000.00
NNO Timetwister R	7,500.00	15,000.00
NNO Tranquility C	30.00	60.00
NNO Tropical Island R	7,500.00	15,000.00
NNO Tsunami U	100.00	200.00
NNO Tundra R	6,000.00	12,000.00
NNO Tunnel U	75.00	150.00
NNO Twiddle C	60.00	125.00
NNO Two-Headed Giant of Foriys R	1,000.00	2,000.00
NNO Underground Sea R	10,000.00	20,000.00
NNO Unholy Strength C	50.00	100.00
NNO Unsummon C	40.00	80.00
NNO Uthden Troll U	100.00	200.00
NNO Verduran Enchantress R	1,250.00	2,500.00
NNO Vesuvan Doppelganger R	400.00	800.00
NNO Veteran Bodyguard R	750.00	1,500.00
NNO Volcanic Eruption R	1,000.00	2,000.00
NNO Wall of Air U	125.00	250.00
NNO Wall of Bone U	100.00	200.00
NNO Wall of Brambles U	125.00	250.00
NNO Wall of Fire U	60.00	125.00
NNO Wall of Ice U	75.00	150.00
NNO Wall of Stone U	60.00	125.00
NNO Wall of Swords U	75.00	150.00
NNO Wall of Water U	75.00	150.00
NNO Wall of Wood C	17.50	35.00
NNO Wanderlust U	75.00	150.00
NNO War Mammoth C	30.00	60.00
NNO Warp Artifact R	300.00	600.00
NNO Water Elemental U	75.00	150.00
NNO Weakness C	30.00	75.00
NNO Web R	150.00	300.00
NNO Wheel of Fortune R	4,000.00	8,000.00
NNO White Knight U	300.00	600.00
NNO White Ward U	30.00	75.00
NNO Wild Growth C	40.00	80.00
NNO Will-O'-The-Wisp R	400.00	800.00
NNO Winter Orb R	1,750.00	3,500.00
NNO Wooden Sphere U	75.00	150.00
NNO Word of Command R	1,750.00	3,500.00
NNO Wrath of God R	600.00	1,200.00
NNO Zombie Master R	500.00	1,000.00

1993 Magic The Gathering Arabian Nights

1 Abu Jafar U3	25.00	50.00
2a Army of Allah (dark 1) C3	12.50	25.00
2b Army of Allah (light 1) C1	25.00	50.00
3 Camel C5	6.00	12.00
4 Eye for an Eye U3	17.50	35.00
5 Jihad U2	125.00	250.00
6 King Suleiman U2	150.00	300.00
7a Moorish Cavalry (dark 2) C4	5.00	10.00
7b Moorish Cavalry (light 2) C1	7.50	15.00
8a Piety (dark 1) C3	3.00	6.00
8b Piety (light 1) C1	7.50	15.00
9 Repentant Blacksmith U2	40.00	80.00
10 Shahrazad U2	300.00	750.00
11a War Elephant (dark 3) C3	5.00	10.00
11b War Elephant (light 3) C1	15.00	30.00
12 Dandan C4	12.50	25.00
13a Fishliver Oil (dark 1) C3	3.00	6.00
13b Fishliver Oil (light 1) C1	10.00	20.00
14 Flying Men C5	7.50	15.00
15a Giant Tortoise (dark 1) C3	4.00	8.00
15b Giant Tortoise (light 1) C1	10.00	20.00
16 Island Fish Jasconius U2	30.00	75.00
17 Merchant Ship U3	30.00	75.00
18 Old Man of the Sea U2	250.00	500.00
19a Serendib Djinn U2	125.00	250.00
19b Serendib Efreet U2	400.00	800.00
21 Sindbad U3	25.00	50.00
21a Desert C11	7.50	15.00
21b Desert (mirage variant) C11	12.50	25.00
22 Unstable Mutation C5	4.00	8.00
23 Cuombajj Witches C4	7.50	15.00
24 El-Hajjaj U2	150.00	300.00
25a Erg Raiders (dark 1) C3	3.00	6.00
25b Erg Raiders (light 1) C2	5.00	10.00
26 Guardian Beast U2	750.00	1,500.00
27a Hasran Ogress (dark mana) C3	3.00	6.00
27b Hasran Ogress (light mana) C2	4.00	8.00
28 Junun Efreet U2	60.00	125.00
29 Juzam Djinn U2	1,000.00	4,000.00
30 Khabal Ghoul U3	125.00	250.00
31a Oubliette (dark 1) C2	15.00	30.00
31b Oubliette (light 1) C2	17.50	35.00
32 Sorceress Queen U3	75.00	150.00
33a Stone-Throwing Devils (dark mana) C3	4.00	8.00
33b Stone-Throwing Devils (light mana) C1	4.00	8.00
34 Aladdin U2	30.00	75.00
35 Ali Baba U3	17.50	35.00
36 Ali from Cairo U2	250.00	500.00
37a Bird Maiden (dark 1) C2	6.00	12.00
37b Bird Maiden (light 1) C2	7.50	15.00
38 Desert Nomads C4	5.00	10.00
39 Hurr Jackal C4	3.00	6.00
40 Kird Ape C5	7.50	15.00
41 Magnetic Mountain U3	12.50	25.00
42 Mijae Djinn U2	30.00	75.00
43a Rukh Egg (dark 3) C3	12.50	25.00
43b Rukh Egg (light 3) C1	17.50	35.00
44 Ydwen Efreet U2	75.00	150.00
45 Cyclone U3	12.50	25.00
46 Desert Twister U3	30.00	60.00
47 Drop of Honey U2	300.00	750.00
48 Erhnam Djinn U2	200.00	400.00
49 Ghazban Ogre C4	3.00	6.00
50 Ifh-Biff Efreet U2	125.00	250.00
51 Metamorphosis C4	3.00	6.00
52a Nafs Asp (dark 1) C3	4.00	8.00
52b Nafs Asp (light 1) C2	4.00	8.00
53 Sandstorm C4	3.00	6.00
54 Singing Tree U2	200.00	400.00
55a Wyluli Wolf (dark 1) C4	7.50	15.00
55b Wyluli Wolf (light 1) C1	25.00	50.00
56 Aladdin's Lamp U2	50.00	100.00
57 Aladdin's Ring U2	50.00	100.00
58 Bottle of Suleiman U2	40.00	80.00
59 Brass Man U3	30.00	75.00
60 City in a Bottle U2	300.00	600.00
61 Dancing Scimitar U2	30.00	75.00
62 Ebony Horse U2	25.00	50.00
63 Flying Carpet U3	25.00	50.00
64 Jandor's Ring U2	30.00	60.00
65 Jandor's Saddlebags U2	30.00	75.00
66 Jeweled Bird U3	25.00	50.00
67 Pyramids U2	100.00	200.00
68 Ring of Maruf U2	75.00	150.00
69 Sandals of Abdallah U3	50.00	100.00
70 Bazaar of Baghdad U3	1,500.00	3,000.00
71 City of Brass U3	300.00	750.00
73 Diamond Valley U2	750.00	1,500.00
74 Elephant Graveyard U2	30.00	75.00
75 Island of Wak-Wak U2	250.00	500.00
76 Library of Alexandria U3	1,250.00	2,500.00
77 Mountain C1	150.00	300.00
78 Oasis U4	25.00	50.00

1993 Magic The Gathering Beta

NNO Air Elemental U	40.00	80.00
NNO Ancestral Recall R	5,000.00	12,000.00
NNO Animate Artifact U	12.50	25.00
NNO Animate Dead U	200.00	400.00
NNO Animate Wall R	125.00	250.00
NNO Ankh of Mishra R	250.00	500.00
NNO Armageddon R	600.00	1,200.00
NNO Aspect of Wolf R	250.00	500.00

NNO Bad Moon R	150.00	300.00
NNO Badlands R	1,250.00	2,500.00
NNO Balance R	1,500.00	3,000.00
NNO Basalt Monolith U	150.00	300.00
NNO Bayou R	2,000.00	4,000.00
NNO Benalish Hero C	7.50	15.00
NNO Berserk U	250.00	500.00
NNO Birds of Paradise R	1,500.00	3,000.00
NNO Black Knight U	100.00	200.00
NNO Black Lotus R	30,000.00	60,000.00
NNO Black Vise U	125.00	250.00
NNO Black Ward U	12.50	25.00
NNO Blaze of Glory R	300.00	750.00
NNO Blessing R	100.00	200.00
NNO Blue Elemental Blast C	50.00	100.00
NNO Blue Ward U	7.50	15.00
NNO Bog Wraith U	17.50	35.00
NNO Braingeyser R	750.00	1,500.00
NNO Burrowing U	12.50	25.00
NNO Camouflage U	25.00	50.00
NNO Castle U	10.00	20.00
NNO Celestial Prism U	10.00	20.00
NNO Channel U	50.00	100.00
NNO Chaos Orb R	2,500.00	5,000.00
NNO Chaoslace R	60.00	125.00
NNO Circle of Protection Black C	10.00	20.00
NNO Circle of Protection Blue C	5.00	10.00
NNO Circle of Protection Green C	5.00	10.00
NNO Circle of Protection Red C	12.50	25.00
NNO Circle of Protection White C	6.00	12.00
NNO Clockwork Beast R	150.00	300.00
NNO Clone U	75.00	150.00
NNO Cockatrice R	250.00	500.00
NNO Consecrate Land U	17.50	35.00
NNO Conservator U	15.00	30.00
NNO Contract from Below R	500.00	1,000.00
NNO Control Magic U	75.00	150.00
NNO Conversion U	10.00	20.00
NNO Copper Tablet U	75.00	150.00
NNO Copy Artifact R	1,000.00	2,000.00
NNO Counterspell U	750.00	1,500.00
NNO Craw Wurm C	12.50	25.00
NNO Creature Bond C	7.50	15.00
NNO Crusade R	300.00	750.00
NNO Crystal Rod U	25.00	50.00
NNO Cursed Land U	10.00	20.00
NNO Cyclopean Tomb R	250.00	500.00
NNO Dark Ritual C	100.00	200.00
NNO Darkpact R	175.00	350.00
NNO Death Ward C	4.00	8.00
NNO Deathgrip U	20.00	40.00
NNO Deathlace R	30.00	60.00
NNO Demonic Attorney R	200.00	400.00
NNO Demonic Hordes R	250.00	500.00
NNO Demonic Tutor U	600.00	1,200.00
NNO Dingus Egg R	125.00	250.00
NNO Disenchant C	30.00	75.00
NNO Disintegrate C	12.50	25.00
NNO Disrupting Scepter R	150.00	300.00
NNO Dragon Whelp U	60.00	125.00
NNO Drain Life C	12.50	25.00
NNO Drain Power R	75.00	150.00
NNO Drudge Skeletons C	10.00	20.00
NNO Dwarven Demolition Team U	17.50	35.00
NNO Dwarven Warriors C	7.50	15.00
NNO Earth Elemental U	15.00	30.00
NNO Earthbind C	40.00	80.00
NNO Earthquake R	300.00	600.00
NNO Elvish Archers R	300.00	600.00
NNO Evil Presence U	25.00	50.00
NNO False Orders C	7.50	15.00
NNO Farmstead R	75.00	150.00
NNO Fastbond R	750.00	1,500.00
NNO Fear C	6.00	12.00
NNO Feedback U	12.50	25.00
NNO Fire Elemental U	75.00	150.00
NNO Fireball C	60.00	125.00
NNO Firebreathing C	7.50	15.00
NNO Flashfires U	30.00	75.00
NNO Flight C	4.00	8.00
NNO Fog C	12.50	25.00
NNO Force of Nature R	400.00	800.00
NNO Forcefield R	750.00	1,500.00
NNO Forest v1 L	12.50	25.00
NNO Forest v2 L	20.00	40.00
NNO Forest v3 L	25.00	50.00
NNO Fork R	500.00	1,000.00
NNO Frozen Shade C	7.50	15.00
NNO Fungusaur R	175.00	350.00
NNO Gaea's Liege R	150.00	300.00
NNO Gauntlet of Might R	750.00	1,500.00
NNO Giant Growth C	20.00	40.00
NNO Giant Spider C	12.50	25.00
NNO Glasses of Urza U	75.00	150.00
NNO Gloom U	40.00	80.00
NNO Goblin Balloon Brigade U	40.00	80.00
NNO Goblin King R	300.00	750.00
NNO Granite Gargoyle R	250.00	500.00
NNO Gray Ogre C	7.50	15.00

NNO Green Ward U	10.00	20.00
NNO Grizzly Bears C	12.50	25.00
NNO Guardian Angel C	7.50	15.00
NNO Healing Salve C	5.00	10.00
NNO Helm of Chatzuk R	200.00	400.00
NNO Hill Giant C	7.50	15.00
NNO Holy Armor C	7.50	15.00
NNO Holy Strength C	6.00	12.00
NNO Howl from Beyond C	7.50	15.00
NNO Howling Mine R	750.00	1,500.00
NNO Hurloon Minotaur C	7.50	15.00
NNO Hurricane U	30.00	75.00
NNO Hypnotic Specter U	300.00	600.00
NNO Ice Storm U	100.00	200.00
NNO Icy Manipulator U	400.00	800.00
NNO Illusionary Mask R	600.00	1,200.00
NNO Instill Energy U	50.00	100.00
NNO Invisibility C	10.00	20.00
NNO Iron Star U	12.50	25.00
NNO Ironclaw Orcs C	7.50	15.00
NNO Ironroot Treefolk C	5.00	10.00
NNO Island Sanctuary R	150.00	300.00
NNO Island v1 L	17.50	35.00
NNO Island v2 L	25.00	50.00
NNO Island v3 L	25.00	50.00
NNO Ivory Cup U	12.50	25.00
NNO Jade Monolith R	100.00	200.00
NNO Jade Statue U	50.00	100.00
NNO Jayemdae Tome R	750.00	1,500.00
NNO Juggernaut U	125.00	250.00
NNO Jump C	5.00	10.00
NNO Karma U	25.00	50.00
NNO Keldon Warlord U	30.00	60.00
NNO Kormus Bell R	250.00	500.00
NNO Kudzu R	175.00	350.00
NNO Lance U	12.50	25.00
NNO Ley Druid U	15.00	30.00
NNO Library of Leng U	60.00	125.00
NNO Lich R	400.00	800.00
NNO Lifeforce U	17.50	35.00
NNO Lifelace R	60.00	125.00
NNO Lifetap U	15.00	30.00
NNO Lightning Bolt C	250.00	500.00
NNO Living Artifact R	60.00	125.00
NNO Living Lands R	100.00	200.00
NNO Living Wall U	30.00	60.00
NNO Llanowar Elves C	75.00	150.00
NNO Lord of Atlantis R	250.00	500.00
NNO Lord of the Pit R	400.00	800.00
NNO Lure U	17.50	35.00
NNO Magical Hack R	125.00	250.00
NNO Mahamoti Djinn R	750.00	1,500.00
NNO Mana Flare R	300.00	600.00
NNO Mana Short R	250.00	500.00
NNO Mana Vault R	1,000.00	2,000.00
NNO Manabarbs R	175.00	350.00
NNO Meekstone R	250.00	500.00
NNO Merfolk of the Pearl Trident C	7.50	15.00
NNO Mesa Pegasus C	10.00	20.00
NNO Mind Twist R	750.00	1,500.00
NNO Mons's Goblin Raiders C	12.50	25.00
NNO Mountain v1 L	10.00	20.00
NNO Mountain v2 L	17.50	35.00
NNO Mountain v3 L	17.50	35.00
NNO Mox Emerald R	7,500.00	15,000.00
NNO Mox Jet R	7,500.00	15,000.00
NNO Mox Pearl R	3,000.00	7,500.00
NNO Mox Ruby R	7,500.00	15,000.00
NNO Mox Sapphire R	3,000.00	6,000.00
NNO Natural Selection R	200.00	400.00
NNO Nether Shadow R	200.00	400.00
NNO Nettling Imp U	75.00	150.00
NNO Nevinyrral's Disk R	750.00	1,500.00
NNO Nightmare R	300.00	600.00
NNO Northern Paladin R	175.00	350.00
NNO Obsianus Golem U	25.00	50.00
NNO Orcish Artillery U	15.00	30.00
NNO Orcish Oriflamme U	12.50	25.00
NNO Paralyze C	10.00	20.00
NNO Pearled Unicorn C	6.00	12.00
NNO Personal Incarnation R	150.00	300.00
NNO Pestilence C	15.00	30.00
NNO Phantasmal Forces U	20.00	40.00
NNO Phantasmal Terrain C	7.50	15.00
NNO Phantom Monster U	30.00	60.00
NNO Pirate Ship R	150.00	300.00
NNO Plague Rats C	10.00	20.00
NNO Plains v1 L	17.50	35.00
NNO Plains v2 L	12.50	25.00
NNO Plains v3 L	12.50	25.00
NNO Plateau R	1,250.00	2,500.00
NNO Power Leak C	6.00	12.00
NNO Power Sink C	12.50	25.00
NNO Power Surge R	150.00	300.00
NNO Prodigal Sorcerer C	15.00	30.00
NNO Psionic Blast U	125.00	250.00
NNO Psychic Venom C	10.00	20.00
NNO Purelace R	60.00	125.00
NNO Raging River R	200.00	400.00

NNO Raise Dead C	7.50	15.00
NNO Red Elemental Blast C	75.00	150.00
NNO Red Ward U	12.50	25.00
NNO Regeneration C	7.50	15.00
NNO Regrowth U	75.00	150.00
NNO Resurrection U	12.50	25.00
NNO Reverse Damage R	75.00	150.00
NNO Righteousness R	125.00	250.00
NNO Roc of Kher Ridges R	175.00	350.00
NNO Rock Hydra R	150.00	300.00
NNO Rod of Ruin U	17.50	35.00
NNO Royal Assassin R	600.00	1,200.00
NNO Sacrifice U	75.00	150.00
NNO Samite Healer C	7.50	15.00
NNO Savannah Lions R	1,750.00	3,500.00
NNO Savannah R	750.00	1,500.00
NNO Scathe Zombies C	7.50	15.00
NNO Scavenging Ghoul U	17.50	35.00
NNO Scrubland R	1,750.00	3,500.00
NNO Scryb Sprites C	10.00	20.00
NNO Sea Serpent C	7.50	15.00
NNO Sedge Troll R	300.00	600.00
NNO Sengir Vampire U	150.00	300.00
NNO Serra Angel U	300.00	600.00
NNO Shanodin Dryads C	7.50	15.00
NNO Shatter C	12.50	25.00
NNO Shivan Dragon R	2,500.00	5,000.00
NNO Simulacrum U	17.50	35.00
NNO Sinkhole C	75.00	150.00
NNO Siren's Call U	17.50	35.00
NNO Sleight of Mind R	125.00	250.00
NNO Smoke R	125.00	250.00
NNO Sol Ring U	750.00	1,500.00
NNO Soul Net U	20.00	40.00
NNO Spell Blast C	7.50	15.00
NNO Stasis R	600.00	1,200.00
NNO Steal Artifact U	25.00	50.00
NNO Stone Giant U	15.00	30.00
NNO Stone Rain C	15.00	30.00
NNO Stream of Life C	7.50	15.00
NNO Sunglasses of Urza R	75.00	150.00
NNO Swamp v1 L	15.00	30.00
NNO Swamp v2 L	17.50	35.00
NNO Swamp v3 L	25.00	50.00
NNO Swords to Plowshares U	500.00	1,000.00
NNO Taiga R	3,000.00	6,000.00
NNO Terror C	17.50	35.00
NNO The Hive R	250.00	500.00
NNO Thicket Basilisk U	15.00	30.00
NNO Thoughtlace R	125.00	250.00
NNO Throne of Bone U	12.50	25.00
NNO Timber Wolves R	200.00	400.00
NNO Time Vault R	2,000.00	4,000.00
NNO Time Walk R	4,000.00	10,000.00
NNO Timetwister R	10,000.00	20,000.00
NNO Tranquility C	17.50	35.00
NNO Tropical Island R	2,500.00	5,000.00
NNO Tsunami U	25.00	50.00
NNO Tundra R	2,500.00	5,000.00
NNO Tunnel U	15.00	30.00
NNO Twiddle C	17.50	35.00
NNO Two-Headed Giant of Foriys R	200.00	400.00
NNO Underground Sea R	4,000.00	8,000.00
NNO Unholy Strength C	12.50	25.00
NNO Unsummon C	10.00	20.00
NNO Uthden Troll U	25.00	50.00
NNO Verduran Enchantress R	750.00	1,500.00
NNO Vesuvan Doppelganger R	1,250.00	2,500.00
NNO Veteran Bodyguard R	250.00	500.00
NNO Volcanic Eruption R	125.00	250.00
NNO Volcanic Island R	10,000.00	20,000.00
NNO Wall of Air U	25.00	50.00
NNO Wall of Bone U	17.50	35.00
NNO Wall of Brambles U	15.00	30.00
NNO Wall of Fire U	12.50	25.00
NNO Wall of Ice U	17.50	35.00
NNO Wall of Stone U	15.00	30.00
NNO Wall of Swords U	25.00	50.00
NNO Wall of Water U	15.00	30.00
NNO Wall of Wood C	6.00	12.00
NNO Wanderlust U	12.50	25.00
NNO War Mammoth C	10.00	20.00
NNO Warp Artifact R	100.00	200.00
NNO Water Elemental U	12.50	25.00
NNO Weakness C	7.50	15.00
NNO Web R	100.00	200.00
NNO Wheel of Fortune R	2,000.00	4,000.00
NNO White Knight U	75.00	150.00
NNO White Ward U	10.00	20.00
NNO Wild Growth C	30.00	60.00
NNO Will-O'-The-Wisp R	200.00	400.00
NNO Winter Orb R	750.00	1,500.00
NNO Wooden Sphere U	10.00	20.00
NNO Word of Command R	300.00	750.00
NNO Wrath of God R	750.00	1,500.00
NNO Zombie Master R	150.00	300.00

1993 Magic The Gathering Collector's Edition

1 Animate Wall R	4.00	8.00
2 Armageddon R	25.00	50.00
3 Balance R	30.00	75.00
4 Benalish Hero C	2.00	4.00
5 Black Ward U	1.50	3.00
6 Blaze of Glory R	15.00	30.00
7 Blessing R	4.00	8.00
8 Blue Ward U	2.50	5.00
9 Castle U	2.50	5.00
10 Circle of Protection Black C	1.50	3.00
11 Circle of Protection Blue C	1.50	3.00
12 Circle of Protection Green C	1.50	3.00
13 Circle of Protection Red C	2.00	4.00
14 Circle of Protection White C	2.00	4.00
15 Consecrate Land U	2.50	5.00
16 Conversion U	1.25	2.50
17 Crusade R	10.00	20.00
18 Death Ward C	1.50	3.00
19 Disenchant C	12.50	25.00
20 Farmstead R	3.00	6.00
21 Green Ward U	1.75	3.50
22 Guardian Angel C	1.50	3.00
23 Healing Salve C	2.50	5.00
24 Holy Armor C	1.25	2.50
25 Holy Strength C	1.50	3.00
26 Island Sanctuary R	7.50	15.00
27 Karma U	3.00	6.00
28 Lance U	1.50	3.00
29 Mesa Pegasus C	2.50	5.00
30 Northern Paladin R	4.00	8.00
31 Pearled Unicorn C	1.50	3.00
32 Personal Incarnation R	7.50	15.00
33 Purelace R	3.00	6.00
34 Red Ward U	1.50	3.00
35 Resurrection U	2.00	4.00
36 Reverse Damage R	4.00	8.00
37 Righteousness R	4.00	8.00
38 Samite Healer C	2.00	4.00
39 Savannah Lions R	150.00	300.00
40 Serra Angel U	50.00	100.00
41 Swords to Plowshares U	40.00	80.00
42 Veteran Bodyguard R	7.50	15.00
43 Wall of Swords U	2.50	5.00
44 White Knight U	7.50	15.00
45 White Ward U	1.75	3.50
46 Wrath of God R	30.00	75.00
47 Air Elemental U	3.00	6.00
48 Ancestral Recall R	600.00	1,200.00
49 Animate Artifact U	2.50	5.00
50 Blue Elemental Blast C	4.00	8.00
51 Braingeyser R	30.00	60.00
52 Clone U	5.00	10.00
53 Control Magic U	4.00	8.00
54 Copy Artifact R	60.00	125.00
55 Counterspell U	30.00	75.00
56 Creature Bond C	1.50	3.00
57 Drain Power R	4.00	8.00
58 Feedback U	1.50	3.00
59 Flight C	1.75	3.50
60 Invisibility C	1.25	2.50
61 Jump C	1.25	2.50
62 Lifetap U	2.50	5.00
63 Lord of Atlantis R	12.50	25.00
64 Magical Hack R	7.50	15.00
65 Mahamoti Djinn R	17.50	35.00
66 Mana Short R	12.50	25.00
67 Merfolk of the Pearl Trident C	7.50	15.00
68 Phantasmal Forces U	5.00	10.00
69 Phantasmal Terrain C	1.75	3.50
70 Phantom Monster U	2.00	4.00
71 Pirate Ship R	10.00	20.00
72 Power Leak C	1.75	3.50
73 Power Sink C	2.50	5.00
74 Prodigal Sorcerer C	2.50	5.00
75 Psionic Blast U	30.00	60.00
76 Psychic Venom C	2.50	5.00
77 Sea Serpent C	1.50	3.00
78 Siren's Call U	3.00	6.00
79 Sleight of Mind R	5.00	10.00
80 Spell Blast C	1.50	3.00
81 Stasis R	17.50	35.00
82 Steal Artifact U	2.50	5.00
83 Thoughtlace R	2.00	4.00
84 Time Walk R	400.00	800.00
85 Timetwister R	1,250.00	2,500.00
86 Twiddle C	4.00	8.00
87 Unsummon C	3.00	6.00
88 Vesuvan Doppelganger R	40.00	80.00
89 Volcanic Eruption R	4.00	8.00
90 Wall of Air U	2.00	4.00
91 Wall of Water U	2.50	5.00
92 Water Elemental U	2.00	4.00
93 Animate Dead U	15.00	30.00
94 Bad Moon R	12.50	25.00
95 Black Knight U	7.50	15.00
96 Bog Wraith U	2.50	5.00
97 Contract from Below R	12.50	25.00
98 Cursed Land U	2.00	4.00
99 Dark Ritual C	25.00	50.00
100 Darkpact R	15.00	30.00
101 Deathgrip U	2.50	5.00
102 Deathlace R	3.00	6.00
103 Demonic Attorney R	10.00	20.00
104 Demonic Hordes R	10.00	20.00
105 Demonic Tutor U	75.00	150.00
106 Drain Life C	2.50	5.00
107 Drudge Skeletons C	1.75	3.50
108 Evil Presence U	1.50	3.00
109 Fear C	1.75	3.50
110 Frozen Shade C	1.50	3.00
111 Gloom U	4.00	8.00
112 Howl from Beyond C	1.50	3.00
113 Hypnotic Specter U	30.00	75.00
114 Lich R	40.00	80.00
115 Lord of the Pit R	10.00	20.00
116 Mind Twist R	17.50	35.00
117 Nether Shadow R	7.50	15.00
118 Nettling Imp U	3.00	6.00
119 Nightmare R	15.00	30.00
120 Paralyze C	1.75	3.50
121 Pestilence C	2.50	5.00
122 Plague Rats C	2.50	5.00
123 Raise Dead C	2.00	4.00
124 Royal Assassin R	30.00	60.00
125 Sacrifice U	6.00	12.00
126 Scathe Zombies C	2.50	5.00
127 Scavenging Ghoul U	1.75	3.50
128 Sengir Vampire U	12.50	25.00
129 Simulacrum U	2.50	5.00
130 Sinkhole C	17.50	35.00
131 Terror C	7.50	15.00
132 Unholy Strength C	4.00	8.00
133 Wall of Bone U	2.50	5.00
134 Warp Artifact R	4.00	8.00
135 Weakness C	12.50	25.00
136 Will-O'-The-Wisp R	10.00	20.00
137 Word of Command R	75.00	150.00
138 Zombie Master R	10.00	20.00
139 Burrowing U	1.50	3.00
140 Chaoslace R	3.00	6.00
141 Disintegrate C	2.00	4.00
142 Dragon Whelp U	7.50	15.00
143 Dwarven Demolition Team U	2.50	5.00
144 Dwarven Warriors C	1.50	3.00
145 Earth Elemental U	2.50	5.00
146 Earthbind C	17.50	35.00
147 Earthquake R	10.00	20.00
148 False Orders C	2.50	5.00
149 Fire Elemental U	3.00	6.00
150 Fireball C	10.00	20.00
151 Firebreathing C	1.25	2.50
152 Flashfires U	2.50	5.00
153 Fork R	25.00	50.00
154 Goblin Balloon Brigade U	5.00	10.00
155 Goblin King R	12.50	25.00
156 Granite Gargoyle R	12.50	25.00
157 Gray Ogre C	1.25	2.50
158 Hill Giant C	1.75	3.50
159 Hurloon Minotaur C	2.00	4.00
160 Ironclaw Orcs C	2.00	4.00
161 Keldon Warlord U	4.00	8.00
162 Lightning Bolt C	75.00	150.00
163 Mana Flare R	12.50	25.00
164 Manabarbs R	3.00	6.00
165 Mons's Goblin Raiders C	2.50	5.00
166 Orcish Artillery U	2.50	5.00
167 Orcish Oriflamme U	1.75	3.50
168 Power Surge R	3.00	6.00
169 Raging River R	50.00	100.00
170 Red Elemental Blast C	6.00	12.00
171 Roc of Kher Ridges R	7.50	15.00
172 Rock Hydra R	12.50	25.00
173 Sedge Troll R	25.00	50.00
174 Shatter C	3.00	6.00
175 Shivan Dragon R	100.00	200.00
176 Smoke R	5.00	10.00
177 Stone Giant U	2.00	4.00
178 Stone Rain C	7.50	15.00
179 Tunnel U	2.50	5.00
180 Two-Headed Giant of Foriys R	25.00	50.00
181 Uthden Troll U	2.50	5.00
182 Wall of Fire U	3.00	6.00
183 Wall of Stone U	2.50	5.00
184 Wheel of Fortune R	150.00	300.00
185 Aspect of Wolf R	7.50	15.00
186 Berserk U	60.00	125.00
187 Birds of Paradise R	75.00	150.00
188 Camouflage U	3.00	6.00
189 Channel U	4.00	8.00
190 Cockatrice R	4.00	8.00
191 Craw Wurm C	4.00	8.00
192 Elvish Archers R	7.50	15.00
193 Fastbond R	15.00	30.00
194 Fog C	2.00	4.00
195 Force of Nature R	12.50	25.00

196 Fungusaur R	6.00	12.00
197 Gaea's Liege R	3.00	6.00
198 Giant Growth C	7.50	15.00
199 Giant Spider C	2.50	5.00
200 Grizzly Bears C	2.50	5.00
201 Hurricane U	3.00	6.00
202 Ice Storm U	25.00	50.00
203 Instill Energy U	5.00	10.00
204 Ironroot Treefolk C	2.50	5.00
205 Kudzu R	4.00	8.00
206 Ley Druid U	2.50	5.00
207 Lifeforce U	2.00	4.00
208 Lifelace R	3.00	6.00
209 Living Artifact R	2.50	5.00
210 Living Lands R	3.00	6.00
211 Llanowar Elves C	17.50	35.00
212 Lure U	2.00	4.00
213 Natural Selection R	25.00	50.00
214 Regeneration C	2.50	5.00
215 Regrowth U	10.00	20.00
216 Scryb Sprites C	3.00	6.00
217 Shanodin Dryads C	1.75	3.50
218 Stream of Life C	2.50	5.00
219 Thicket Basilisk U	3.00	6.00
220 Timber Wolves R	5.00	10.00
221 Tranquility C	2.50	5.00
222 Tsunami U	3.00	6.00
223 Verduran Enchantress R	12.50	25.00
224 Wall of Brambles U	2.50	5.00
225 Wall of Ice U	3.00	6.00
226 Wall of Wood C	2.00	4.00
227 Wanderlust U	2.00	4.00
228 War Mammoth C	2.50	5.00
229 Web R	4.00	8.00
230 Wild Growth C	5.00	10.00
231 Ankh of Mishra R	25.00	50.00
232 Basalt Monolith U	10.00	20.00
233 Black Lotus R	3,000.00	7,500.00
234 Black Vise U	12.50	25.00
235 Celestial Prism U	1.75	3.50
236 Chaos Orb R	250.00	500.00
237 Clockwork Beast R	7.50	15.00
238 Conservator U	2.00	4.00
239 Copper Tablet U	10.00	20.00
240 Crystal Rod U	1.75	3.50
241 Cyclopean Tomb R	30.00	60.00
242 Dingus Egg R	4.00	8.00
243 Disrupting Scepter R	7.50	15.00
244 Forcefield R	125.00	250.00
245 Gauntlet of Might R	125.00	250.00
246 Glasses of Urza U	2.00	4.00
247 Helm of Chatzuk R	2.50	5.00
248 Howling Mine R	30.00	60.00
249 Icy Manipulator U	50.00	100.00
250 Illusionary Mask R	25.00	50.00
251 Iron Star U	2.50	5.00
252 Ivory Cup U	1.50	3.00
253 Jade Monolith R	4.00	8.00
254 Jade Statue U	7.50	15.00
255 Jayemdae Tome R	30.00	60.00
256 Juggernaut U	5.00	10.00
257 Kormus Bell R	3.00	6.00
258 Library of Leng U	7.50	15.00
259 Living Wall U	3.00	6.00
260 Mana Vault R	60.00	125.00
261 Meekstone R	10.00	20.00
262 Mox Emerald R	400.00	800.00
263 Mox Jet R	400.00	800.00
264 Mox Pearl R	400.00	800.00
265 Mox Ruby R	750.00	1,500.00
266 Mox Sapphire R	400.00	800.00
267 Nevinyrral's Disk R	25.00	50.00
268 Obsianus Golem U	2.00	4.00
269 Rod of Ruin U	2.00	4.00
270 Sol Ring U	75.00	150.00
271 Soul Net U	1.50	3.00
272 Sunglasses of Urza R	7.50	15.00
273 The Hive R	6.00	12.00
274 Throne of Bone U	2.50	5.00
275 Time Vault R	200.00	400.00
276 Winter Orb R	30.00	75.00
277 Wooden Sphere U	2.50	5.00
278 Badlands R	175.00	350.00
279 Bayou R	150.00	300.00
280 Plateau R	175.00	350.00
281 Savannah R	30.00	75.00
282 Scrubland R	175.00	350.00
283 Taiga R	200.00	400.00
284 Tropical Island R	300.00	600.00
285 Tundra R	200.00	400.00
286 Underground Sea R	300.00	600.00
287 Volcanic Island R	300.00	600.00
288 Plains v1 L	2.00	4.00
289 Plains v2 L	2.50	5.00
290 Plains v3 L	2.50	5.00
291 Island v1 L	4.00	8.00
292 Island v2 L	4.00	8.00
293 Island v3 L	3.00	6.00
294 Swamp v1 L	2.50	5.00
295 Swamp v2 L	3.00	6.00
296 Swamp v3 L	3.00	6.00
297 Mountain v1 L	2.00	4.00
298 Mountain v2 L	2.50	5.00
299 Mountain v3 L	2.50	5.00
300 Forest v1 L	3.00	6.00
301 Forest v2 L	2.00	4.00
302 Forest v3 L	2.50	5.00

1993 Magic The Gathering Unlimited

NNO Air Elemental U	4.00	10.00
NNO Ancestral Recall R	2,000.00	5,000.00
NNO Animate Artifact U	4.00	10.00
NNO Animate Dead U	15.00	40.00
NNO Animate Wall R	10.00	25.00
NNO Ankh of Mishra R	40.00	100.00
NNO Armageddon R	75.00	200.00
NNO Aspect of Wolf R	8.00	20.00
NNO Bad Moon R	25.00	60.00
NNO Badlands R	300.00	800.00
NNO Balance R	40.00	100.00
NNO Basalt Monolith U	8.00	20.00
NNO Bayou R	400.00	1,000.00
NNO Benalish Hero C	.60	1.50
NNO Berserk U	40.00	100.00
NNO Birds of Paradise R	100.00	250.00
NNO Black Knight U	10.00	25.00
NNO Black Lotus R	10,000.00	25,000.00
NNO Black Vise U	10.00	25.00
NNO Black Ward U	1.25	3.00
NNO Blaze of Glory R	25.00	60.00
NNO Blessing R	10.00	25.00
NNO Blue Elemental Blast C	2.50	6.00
NNO Blue Ward U	1.25	3.00
NNO Bog Wraith U	1.50	4.00
NNO Braingeyser R	50.00	120.00
NNO Burrowing U	1.25	3.00
NNO Camouflage U	2.50	6.00
NNO Castle U	1.50	4.00
NNO Celestial Prism U	1.25	3.00
NNO Channel U	2.00	5.00
NNO Chaos Orb R	600.00	1,500.00
NNO Chaoslace R	5.00	12.00
NNO Circle of Protection Black C	.60	1.50
NNO Circle of Protection Blue C	.60	1.50
NNO Circle of Protection Green C	.40	1.00
NNO Circle of Protection Red C	.60	1.50
NNO Circle of Protection White C	.40	1.00
NNO Clockwork Beast R	10.00	25.00
NNO Clone U	2.50	6.00
NNO Cockatrice R	15.00	40.00
NNO Consecrate Land U	1.00	2.50
NNO Conservator U	1.25	3.00
NNO Contract from Below R	20.00	50.00
NNO Control Magic U	8.00	20.00
NNO Conversion U	1.00	2.50
NNO Copper Tablet U	15.00	40.00
NNO Copy Artifact R	100.00	250.00
NNO Counterspell U	30.00	80.00
NNO Craw Wurm C	.75	2.00
NNO Creature Bond C	.20	.50
NNO Crusade R	.08	.20
NNO Crystal Rod U	1.25	3.00
NNO Cursed Land U	2.00	5.00
NNO Cyclopean Tomb R	50.00	120.00
NNO Dark Ritual C	6.00	15.00
NNO Darkpact R	20.00	50.00
NNO Death Ward C	.40	1.00
NNO Deathgrip U	2.00	5.00
NNO Deathlace R	8.00	20.00
NNO Demonic Attorney R	12.00	30.00
NNO Demonic Hordes R	30.00	80.00
NNO Demonic Tutor U	30.00	80.00
NNO Dingus Egg R	12.00	30.00
NNO Disenchant C	2.50	6.00
NNO Disintegrate C	1.25	3.00
NNO Disrupting Scepter R	20.00	50.00
NNO Dragon Whelp U	4.00	10.00
NNO Drain Life C	1.50	4.00
NNO Drain Power R	10.00	25.00
NNO Drudge Skeletons C	1.00	2.50
NNO Dwarven Demolition Team U	2.00	5.00
NNO Dwarven Warriors C	.50	1.25
NNO Earth Elemental U	2.00	5.00
NNO Earthbind C	4.00	10.00
NNO Earthquake R	25.00	60.00
NNO Elvish Archers R	25.00	60.00
NNO Evil Presence U	1.50	4.00
NNO False Orders C	1.00	2.50
NNO Farmstead R	10.00	25.00
NNO Fastbond R	30.00	80.00
NNO Fear C	.50	1.25
NNO Feedback U	1.25	3.00
NNO Fire Elemental U	2.00	5.00
NNO Fireball C	1.50	4.00
NNO Firebreathing C	.50	1.25
NNO Flashfires U	2.00	5.00
NNO Flight C	.40	1.00
NNO Fog C	.60	1.50
NNO Force of Nature R	20.00	50.00
NNO Forcefield R	200.00	500.00
NNO Forest v1 L	1.25	3.00
NNO Forest v2 L	1.50	4.00
NNO Forest v3 L	1.50	4.00
NNO Fork R	50.00	120.00
NNO Frozen Shade C	.60	1.50
NNO Fungusaur R	10.00	25.00
NNO Gaea's Liege R	12.00	30.00
NNO Gauntlet of Might R	250.00	600.00
NNO Giant Growth C	1.50	4.00
NNO Giant Spider C	.60	1.50
NNO Glasses of Urza U	2.50	6.00
NNO Gloom U	5.00	12.00
NNO Goblin Balloon Brigade U	5.00	12.00
NNO Goblin King R	30.00	80.00
NNO Granite Gargoyle R	40.00	100.00
NNO Gray Ogre C	.50	1.25
NNO Green Ward U	1.25	3.00
NNO Grizzly Bears C	.75	2.00
NNO Guardian Angel C	.50	1.25
NNO Healing Salve C	.50	1.25
NNO Helm of Chatzuk R	6.00	15.00
NNO Hill Giant C	.40	1.00
NNO Holy Armor C	.40	1.00
NNO Holy Strength C	.60	1.50
NNO Howl from Beyond C	.60	1.50
NNO Howling Mine R	40.00	100.00
NNO Hurloon Minotaur C	.40	1.00
NNO Hurricane U	6.00	15.00
NNO Hypnotic Specter U	20.00	50.00
NNO Ice Storm U	40.00	100.00
NNO Icy Manipulator U	50.00	120.00
NNO Illusionary Mask R	40.00	100.00
NNO Instill Energy U	2.50	6.00
NNO Invisibility C	1.00	2.50
NNO Iron Star U	1.00	2.50
NNO Ironclaw Orcs C	.75	2.00
NNO Ironroot Treefolk C	.60	1.50
NNO Island Sanctuary R	20.00	50.00
NNO Island v1 L	2.00	5.00
NNO Island v2 L	2.00	5.00
NNO Island v3 L	3.00	8.00
NNO Ivory Cup U	1.50	4.00
NNO Jade Monolith R	6.00	15.00
NNO Jade Statue U	10.00	25.00
NNO Jayemdae Tome R	100.00	250.00
NNO Juggernaut U	8.00	20.00
NNO Jump C	.40	1.00
NNO Karma U	1.50	4.00
NNO Keldon Warlord U	2.00	5.00
NNO Kormus Bell R	15.00	40.00
NNO Kudzu R	12.00	30.00
NNO Lance U	1.00	2.50
NNO Ley Druid U	1.25	3.00
NNO Library of Leng U	5.00	12.00
NNO Lich R	75.00	200.00
NNO Lifeforce U	2.00	5.00
NNO Lifelace R	6.00	15.00
NNO Lifetap U	1.00	2.50
NNO Lightning Bolt C	12.00	30.00
NNO Living Artifact R	6.00	15.00
NNO Living Lands R	10.00	25.00
NNO Living Wall U	2.00	5.00
NNO Llanowar Elves C	5.00	12.00
NNO Lord of Atlantis R	30.00	80.00
NNO Lord of the Pit R	15.00	40.00
NNO Lure U	2.50	6.00
NNO Magical Hack R	12.00	30.00
NNO Mahamoti Djinn R	40.00	100.00
NNO Mana Flare R	20.00	50.00
NNO Mana Short R	15.00	40.00
NNO Mana Vault R	100.00	250.00
NNO Manabarbs R	12.00	30.00
NNO Meekstone R	15.00	40.00
NNO Merfolk of the Pearl Trident C	.60	1.50
NNO Mesa Pegasus C	.75	2.00
NNO Mind Twist R	50.00	120.00
NNO Mons's Goblin Raiders C	.60	1.50
NNO Mountain v1 L	2.00	5.00
NNO Mountain v2 L	1.50	4.00
NNO Mountain v3 L	1.50	4.00
NNO Mox Emerald R	1,200.00	3,000.00
NNO Mox Jet R	2,000.00	5,000.00
NNO Mox Pearl R	1,500.00	4,000.00
NNO Mox Ruby R	1,200.00	3,000.00
NNO Mox Sapphire R	2,000.00	5,000.00
NNO Natural Selection R	40.00	100.00
NNO Nether Shadow R	20.00	50.00
NNO Nettling Imp U	2.50	6.00
NNO Nevinyrral's Disk R	75.00	200.00
NNO Nightmare R	50.00	120.00
NNO Northern Paladin R	20.00	50.00
NNO Obsianus Golem U	1.25	3.00
NNO Orcish Artillery U	2.00	5.00
NNO Orcish Oriflamme U	1.50	4.00
NNO Paralyze C	.75	2.00
NNO Pearled Unicorn C	.50	1.25
NNO Personal Incarnation R	10.00	25.00
NNO Pestilence C	1.00	2.50
NNO Phantasmal Forces U	2.00	5.00
NNO Phantasmal Terrain C	.50	1.25
NNO Phantom Monster U	2.00	5.00
NNO Pirate Ship R	12.00	30.00
NNO Plague Rats C	1.00	2.50
NNO Plains v1 L	1.50	4.00
NNO Plains v2 L	1.50	4.00
NNO Plains v3 L	1.50	4.00
NNO Plateau R	300.00	800.00
NNO Power Leak C	.40	1.00
NNO Power Sink C	1.00	2.50
NNO Power Surge R	8.00	20.00
NNO Prodigal Sorcerer C	1.00	2.50
NNO Psionic Blast U	30.00	80.00
NNO Psychic Venom C	.50	1.25
NNO Purelace R	4.00	10.00
NNO Raging River R	60.00	150.00
NNO Raise Dead C	.60	1.50
NNO Red Elemental Blast C	4.00	10.00
NNO Red Ward U	1.25	3.00
NNO Regeneration C	.40	1.00
NNO Regrowth U	6.00	15.00
NNO Resurrection U	2.00	5.00
NNO Reverse Damage R	8.00	20.00
NNO Righteousness R	10.00	25.00
NNO Roc of Kher Ridges R	12.00	30.00
NNO Rock Hydra R	20.00	50.00
NNO Rod of Ruin U	1.50	4.00
NNO Royal Assassin R	40.00	100.00
NNO Sacrifice U	6.00	15.00
NNO Samite Healer C	.50	1.25
NNO Savannah Lions R	100.00	250.00
NNO Savannah R	300.00	800.00
NNO Scathe Zombies C	.75	2.00
NNO Scavenging Ghoul U	1.00	2.50
NNO Scrubland R	300.00	800.00
NNO Scryb Sprites C	.75	2.00
NNO Sea Serpent C	.50	1.25
NNO Sedge Troll R	60.00	150.00
NNO Sengir Vampire U	12.00	30.00
NNO Serra Angel U	30.00	80.00
NNO Shanodin Dryads C	.50	1.25
NNO Shatter C	1.50	4.00
NNO Shivan Dragon R	100.00	250.00
NNO Simulacrum U	2.00	5.00
NNO Sinkhole C	12.00	30.00
NNO Siren's Call U	2.00	5.00
NNO Sleight of Mind R	15.00	40.00
NNO Smoke R	12.00	30.00
NNO Sol Ring U	30.00	80.00
NNO Soul Net U	1.00	2.50
NNO Spell Blast C	.40	1.00
NNO Stasis R	40.00	100.00
NNO Steal Artifact U	1.50	4.00
NNO Stone Giant U	1.25	3.00
NNO Stone Rain C	1.50	4.00
NNO Stream of Life C	.50	1.25
NNO Sunglasses of Urza R	12.00	30.00
NNO Swamp v1 L	2.00	5.00
NNO Swamp v2 L	2.00	5.00
NNO Swamp v3 L	1.00	2.50
NNO Swords to Plowshares U	25.00	60.00
NNO Taiga R	200.00	500.00
NNO Terror C	2.50	6.00
NNO The Hive R	10.00	25.00
NNO Thicket Basilisk U	2.50	6.00
NNO Thoughtlace R	5.00	12.00
NNO Throne of Bone U	1.25	3.00
NNO Timber Wolves R	15.00	40.00
NNO Time Vault R	500.00	1,200.00
NNO Time Walk R	1,200.00	3,000.00
NNO Timetwister R	2,500.00	6,000.00
NNO Tranquility C	.75	2.00
NNO Tropical Island R	400.00	1,000.00
NNO Tsunami U	4.00	10.00
NNO Tundra R	500.00	1,200.00
NNO Tunnel U	1.00	2.50
NNO Twiddle C	1.00	2.50
NNO Two-Headed Giant of Foriys R	30.00	80.00
NNO Underground Sea R	600.00	1,500.00
NNO Unholy Strength C	1.50	4.00
NNO Unsummon C	.60	1.50
NNO Uthden Troll U	2.50	6.00
NNO Verduran Enchantress R	20.00	50.00
NNO Vesuvan Doppelganger R	60.00	150.00
NNO Veteran Bodyguard R	20.00	50.00
NNO Volcanic Eruption R	20.00	50.00
NNO Volcanic Island R	600.00	1,500.00
NNO Wall of Air U	2.00	5.00
NNO Wall of Bone U	1.25	3.00
NNO Wall of Brambles U	1.25	3.00
NNO Wall of Fire U	1.00	2.50
NNO Wall of Ice U	2.00	5.00
NNO Wall of Stone U	.60	1.50
NNO Wall of Swords U	2.00	5.00
NNO Wall of Water U	1.50	4.00
NNO Wall of Wood C	.30	.75
NNO Wanderlust U	1.50	4.00
NNO War Mammoth C	.40	1.00
NNO Warp Artifact R	10.00	25.00
NNO Water Elemental U	1.50	4.00
NNO Weakness C	.60	1.50
NNO Web R	10.00	25.00
NNO Wheel of Fortune R	200.00	500.00
NNO White Knight U	8.00	20.00
NNO White Ward U	1.00	2.50
NNO Wild Growth C	1.25	3.00
NNO Will-O'-The-Wisp R	30.00	80.00
NNO Winter Orb R	50.00	120.00
NNO Wooden Sphere U	2.00	5.00
NNO Word of Command R	125.00	300.00
NNO Wrath of God R	60.00	150.00
NNO Zombie Master R	25.00	60.00

1994 Magic The Gathering Antiquities

1 Argivian Archaeologist U1	100.00	200.00
2 Argivian Blacksmith C4	.75	1.50
3 Artifact Ward C4:W:	.50	1.00
4 Circle of Protection Artifacts U3	2.00	4.00
5 Damping Field U3	7.50	15.00
6 Martyrs of Korlis U3	5.00	10.00
7 Reverse Polarity C4	.50	1.00
8 Drafna's Restoration C4	3.00	6.00
9 Energy Flux U3	25.00	50.00
10 Hurkyl's Recall R	30.00	60.00
11 Power Artifact U3	150.00	300.00
12 Reconstruction C4	1.25	2.50
13 Sage of Lat-Nam C4	.75	1.50
14 Transmute Artifact U3	200.00	400.00
15 Artifact Possession C4	1.25	2.50
16 Gate to Phyrexia U3	50.00	100.00
17 Haunting Wind U3	20.00	40.00
18 Phyrexian Gremlins C4	1.00	2.00
19 Priest of Yawgmoth C4	1.00	2.00
20 Xenic Poltergeist U3	1.50	3.00
21 Yawgmoth Demon U3	6.00	12.00
22 Artifact Blast C4	.75	1.50
23 Atog C4	2.00	4.00
24 Detonate U3	2.00	4.00
25 Dwarven Weaponsmith U3	1.50	3.00
26 Goblin Artisans U3	5.00	10.00
27 Orcish Mechanics C4	1.25	2.50
28 Shatterstorm U1	20.00	40.00
29 Argothian Pixies C4	1.50	3.00
30 Argothian Treefolk C4	.75	1.50
31 Citanul Druid U3	15.00	30.00
32 Crumble C4	.50	1.00
33 Gaea's Avenger U1	40.00	80.00
34 Powerleech U3	20.00	40.00
35 Titania's Song U3	3.00	6.00
36 Amulet of Kroog C4	1.50	3.00
37 Armageddon Clock U2	6.00	12.00
38 Ashnod's Altar U2	30.00	60.00
39 Ashnod's Battle Gear U2	2.50	5.00
40 Ashnod's Transmogrant U3	2.00	4.00
41 Battering Ram C4	.50	1.00
42 Bronze Tablet U1	7.50	15.00
43 Candelabra of Tawnos U1	700.00	1,400.00
44 Clay Statue C4	1.00	2.00
45 Clockwork Avian R	5.00	10.00
46 Colossus of Sardia R	20.00	40.00
47 Coral Helm R	5.00	10.00
48 Cursed Rack C1	3.00	6.00
49 Dragon Engine C4	1.00	2.00
50 Feldon's Cane C1	4.00	8.00
51 Golgothian Sylex R	40.00	80.00
52 Grapeshot Catapult C4	.50	1.00
53 Ivory Tower U3	3.00	6.00
54 Jalum Tome U2	6.00	12.00
55 Mightstone U3	12.50	25.00
56 Millstone U3	6.00	12.00
57 Mishra's War Machine R	6.00	12.00
58 Obelisk of Undoing R	6.00	12.00
59 Onulet U3	2.50	5.00
60 Ornithopter C4	1.50	3.00
61 Primal Clay U3	2.00	4.00
62 Rakalite U3	1.25	2.50
63 Rocket Launcher U3	1.50	3.00
64 Shapeshifter U1	6.00	12.00
65 Staff of Zegon C4	.60	1.25
66 Su-Chi U3	75.00	150.00
67 Tablet of Epityr C4	.50	1.00
68 Tawnos's Coffin U1	125.00	250.00
69 Tawnos's Wand U3	1.50	3.00
70 Tawnos's Weaponry U3	1.50	3.00
71 Tetravus U1	30.00	60.00
72 The Rack U3	7.50	15.00
73 Triskelion U1	50.00	100.00
74 Urza's Avenger U1	6.00	12.00
75 Urza's Chalice C4	1.25	2.50
76 Urza's Miter U1	20.00	40.00
77 Wall of Spears U3	1.50	3.00

78 Weakstone U3	6.00	12.00
79 Yotian Soldier C4	.60	1.25
80a Mishra's Factory, autumn U1	60.00	120.00
80b Mishra's Factory, spring C1	20.00	40.00
80c Mishra's Factory, summer U1	50.00	100.00
80d Mishra's Factory, winter U1	250.00	400.00
81 Mishra's Workshop U1	1,500.00	3,000.00
82a Strip Mine, horizon, even stripe U1	40.00	80.00
82b Strip Mine, horizon, uneven stripe U1	50.00	100.00
82c Strip Mine, no horizon C1	45.00	100.00
82d Strip Mine, small tower in forest U1	50.00	100.00
83a Urza's Mine, clawed sphere C2	4.00	8.00
83b Urza's Mine, mouth C1	6.00	12.00
83c Urza's Mine, pulley C1	7.50	15.00
83d Urza's Mine, tower C2	4.00	8.00
84a Urza's Power Plant, bug C2	4.00	8.00
84b Urza's Power Plant, columns C1	7.50	15.00
84c Urza's Power Plant, rock in pot C1	5.00	10.00
84d Urza's Power Plant, sphere C2	4.00	8.00
85a Urza's Tower, forest C2	5.00	10.00
85b Urza's Tower, mountains C1	7.50	15.00
85c Urza's Tower, plains C1	7.50	15.00
85d Urza's Tower, shore C1	7.50	15.00

1994 Magic The Gathering The Dark

1 Angry Mob U2	1.25	2.50
2 Blood of the Martyr U2	.50	1.00
3 Brainwash C3	.20	.40
4 Cleansing U1	10.00	20.00
5 Dust to Dust C3	.50	1.00
6 Exorcist U1	12.50	25.00
7 Fasting U2	.30	.75
8 Festival C3	.20	.40
9 Fire and Brimstone U2	.50	1.00
10 Holy Light C3	.50	1.00
11 Knights of Thorn U1	7.50	15.00
12 Martyr's Cry U1	15.00	30.00
13 Miracle Worker C3	.20	.40
14 Morale C3	.20	.40
15 Pikemen C3	1.00	2.00
16 Preacher U1	50.00	100.00
17 Squire C3	.20	.40
18 Tivadar's Crusade U2	1.50	3.00
19 Witch Hunter U1	7.50	15.00
20 Amnesia U2	2.00	4.00
21 Apprentice Wizard U1	5.00	10.00
22 Dance of Many U1	6.00	12.00
23 Deep Water C3	.20	.40
24 Drowned C3	.15	.30
25 Electric Eel U2	.75	1.50
26 Erosion C3	.15	.30
27 Flood U2	.75	1.50
28 Ghost Ship C3	.20	.40
29 Giant Shark C3	.20	.40
30 Leviathan U1	6.00	12.00
31 Mana Vortex U1	30.00	60.00
32 Merfolk Assassin U2	1.00	2.00
33 Mind Bomb U1	3.00	6.00
34 Psychic Allergy U1	4.00	8.00
35 Riptide C3	.25	.50
36 Sunken City C3	.20	.40
37 Tangle Kelp U2	.50	1.00
38 Water Wurm C3	.15	.30
39 Ashes to Ashes C3	.50	1.00
40 Banshee U2	1.00	2.00
41 Bog Imp C3	.15	.30
42 Bog Rats C3	.15	.30
43 Curse Artifact U2	.60	1.25
44 Eater of the Dead U2	6.00	12.00
45 Frankenstein's Monster U1	15.00	30.00
46 Grave Robbers U1	10.00	20.00
47 Inquisition C3	.20	.40
48 Marsh Gas C3	.30	.60
49 Murk Dwellers C3	.20	.40
50 Nameless Race U1	6.00	12.00
51 Rag Man U1	2.50	5.00
52 Season of the Witch U1	30.00	60.00
53 The Fallen U2	1.25	2.50
54 Uncle Istvan U2	1.50	3.00
55 Word of Binding C3	.15	.30
56 Worms of the Earth U1	10.00	20.00
57 Ball Lightning U1	30.00	75.00
58 Blood Moon U1	50.00	100.00
59 Brothers of Fire U2	.50	1.00
60 Cave People U2	.50	1.00
61 Eternal Flame U1	7.50	15.00
62 Fire Drake U2	.60	1.25
63 Fissure C3	.20	.40
64 Goblin Caves C3	.50	1.00
65 Goblin Digging Team C3	.20	.40
66 Goblin Hero C3	.20	.40
67 Goblin Rock Sled C3	.15	.30
68 Goblin Shrine C3	.15	.30
69 Goblin Wizard U1	75.00	150.00
70 Goblins of the Flarg C3	.20	.40
71 Inferno U1	5.00	10.00
72 Mana Clash U1	5.00	10.00
73 Orc General U2	.75	1.50
74 Sisters of the Flame U2	.12	.25
75 Carnivorous Plant C3	.20	.40
76 Elves of Deep Shadow U2	12.50	25.00
77 Gaea's Touch C3	2.00	4.00
78 Hidden Path U1	10.00	20.00
79 Land Leeches C3	.15	.30
80 Lurker U1	7.50	15.00
81 Marsh Viper C3	.20	.40
82 Niall Silvain U1	6.00	12.00
83 People of the Woods U2	.75	1.50
84 Savaen Elves C3	.20	.40
85 Scarwood Bandits U1	10.00	20.00
86 Scarwood Hag U2	.30	.60
87 Scavenger Folk C3	.20	.40
88 Spitting Slug U2	.60	1.25
89 Tracker U1	7.50	15.00
90 Venom C3	.15	.30
91 Whippoorwill U2	.75	1.50
92 Wormwood Treefolk U1	6.00	12.00
93 Marsh Goblins C3/	.20	.40
94 Scarwood Goblins C3/	.20	.40
95 Dark Heart of the Wood C3	.20	.40
96 Barl's Cage U1	7.50	15.00
97 Bone Flute U2	.30	.60
98 Book of Rass U2	1.50	3.00
99 Coal Golem U2	.50	1.00
100 Dark Sphere U2	2.50	5.00
101 Diabolic Machine U2	.20	.40
102 Fellwar Stone U2	10.00	20.00
103 Fountain of Youth U2	2.00	4.00
104 Living Armor U2	.50	1.00
105 Necropolis U2	2.00	4.00
106 Reflecting Mirror U2	1.50	3.00
107 Runesword U2	.60	1.25
108 Scarecrow U2	2.50	5.00
109 Skull of Orm U2	1.00	2.00
110 Standing Stones U2	.50	1.00
111 Stone Calendar U1	25.00	50.00
112 Tormod's Crypt U2	6.00	12.00
113 Tower of Coireall U2	.30	.75
114 Wand of Ith U2	1.50	3.00
115 War Barge U2	.60	1.25
116 City of Shadows U1	50.00	100.00
117 Maze of Ith C1	30.00	60.00
118 Safe Haven U1	6.00	12.00
119 Sorrow's Path U1	7.50	15.00

1994 Magic The Gathering Fallen Empires

1a Combat Medic v1 C1	.10	.20
1b Combat Medic v2 C1	.10	.20
1c Combat Medic v3 C1	.10	.20
1d Combat Medic v4 C1	.10	.20
2 Farrel's Mantle U3	.10	.20
3a Farrel's Zealot v1 C1	.10	.20
3b Farrel's Zealot v2 C1	.10	.20
3c Farrel's Zealot v3 C1	.10	.20
4 Farrelite Priest U3	.10	.20
5 Hand of Justice U1	2.00	4.00
6 Heroism U3	.10	.20
7a Icatian Infantry v1 C1	.10	.20
7b Icatian Infantry v2 C1	.10	.20
7c Icatian Infantry v3 C1	.10	.20
7d Icatian Infantry v4 C1	.10	.20
8a Icatian Javelineers v1 C1	.10	.20
8b Icatian Javelineers v2 C1	.10	.20
8c Icatian Javelineers v3 C1	.10	.20
9 Icatian Lieutenant U1	.75	1.50
10a Icatian Moneychanger v1 C1	.10	.20
10b Icatian Moneychanger v2 C1	.10	.20
10c Icatian Moneychanger v3 C1	.10	.20
11 Icatian Phalanx U3	.12	.25
12 Icatian Priest U3	.10	.20
13a Icatian Scout v1 C1	.10	.20
13b Icatian Scout v2 C1	.10	.20
13c Icatian Scout v3 C1	.10	.20
13d Icatian Scout v4 C1	.10	.20
14 Icatian Skirmishers U1	.60	1.25
15 Icatian Town U1	.20	.40
16a Order of Leitbur v1 C1	.12	.25
16b Order of Leitbur v2 C1	.12	.25
16c Order of Leitbur v3 C1	.12	.25
17 Deep Spawn U3	.15	.30
18a High Tide v1 C1	1.50	3.00
18b High Tide v2 C1	.50	1.00
18c High Tide v3 C1	.50	1.00
19a Homarid v1 C1	.10	.20
19b Homarid v2 C1	.10	.20
19c Homarid v3 C1	.10	.20
19d Homarid v4 C1	.10	.20
20 Homarid Shaman U1	1.00	2.00
21 Homarid Spawning Bed U3	.15	.30
22a Homarid Warrior v1 C1	.10	.20
22b Homarid Warrior v2 C1	.10	.20
22c Homarid Warrior v3 C1	.10	.20
23a Merseine v1 C1	.10	.20
23b Merseine v2 C1	.10	.20
23c Merseine v3 C1	.10	.20
23d Merseine v4 C1	.10	.20
24 River Merfolk U1	1.00	2.00
25 Seasinger U3	.15	.30
26 Svyelunite Priest U3	.10	.20
27a Tidal Flats v1 C1	.10	.20
27b Tidal Flats v2 C1	.10	.20
27c Tidal Flats v3 C1	.10	.20
28 Tidal Influence U3	.12	.25
29 Vodalian Knights U1	.75	1.50
30a Vodalian Mage v1 C1	.10	.20
30b Vodalian Mage v2 C1	.10	.20
30c Vodalian Mage v3 C1	.10	.20
31a Vodalian Soldiers v1 C1	.10	.20
31b Vodalian Soldiers v2 C1	.10	.20
31c Vodalian Soldiers v3 C1	.10	.20
31d Vodalian Soldiers v4 C1	.10	.20
32 Vodalian War Machine U1	1.50	3.00
33a Armor Thrull v1 C1	.10	.20
33b Armor Thrull v4 C1	.10	.20
33c Armor Thrull v3 C1	.10	.20
33d Armor Thrull v4 C1	.20	.40
34a Basal Thrull v1 C1	.10	.20
34b Basal Thrull v2 C1	.10	.20
34c Basal Thrull v3 C1	.10	.20
34d Basal Thrull v4 C1	.10	.20
35 Breeding Pit U3	.10	.20
36 Derelor U1	.30	.60
37 Ebon Praetor U1	3.00	6.00
38a Hymn to Tourach v1 C1	.30	.60
38b Hymn to Tourach v2 C1	.50	1.00
38c Hymn to Tourach v3 C1	.30	.60
38d Hymn to Tourach v4 C1	.60	1.25
39a Initiates of the Ebon Hand v1 C1	.10	.20
39b Initiates of the Ebon Hand v2 C1	.10	.20
39c Initiates of the Ebon Hand v3 C1	.10	.20
40a Mindstab Thrull v1 C1	.10	.20
40b Mindstab Thrull v2 C1	.10	.20
40c Mindstab Thrull v3 C1	.10	.20
41a Necrite v1 C1	.10	.20
41b Necrite v2 C1	.10	.20
41c Necrite v3 C1	.10	.20
42a Order of the Ebon Hand v1 C1	.12	.25
42b Order of the Ebon Hand v2 C1	.12	.25
42c Order of the Ebon Hand v3 C1	.12	.25
43 Soul Exchange U3	.20	.40
44 Thrull Champion U1	4.00	8.00
45 Thrull Retainer U3	.20	.40
46 Thrull Wizard U3	.15	.30
47 Tourach's Chant U3	.12	.25
48 Tourach's Gate U1	1.25	2.50
49a Brassclaw Orcs v1 C1	.10	.20
49b Brassclaw Orcs v2 C1	.10	.20
49c Brassclaw Orcs v3 C1	.10	.20
49d Brassclaw Orcs v4 C1	.10	.20
50 Dwarven Armorer U1	1.50	3.00
51 Dwarven Catapult U3	.12	.25
52 Dwarven Lieutenant U3	.15	.30
53a Dwarven Soldier v1 C1	.10	.20
53b Dwarven Soldier v2 C1	.10	.20
53c Dwarven Soldier v3 C1	.10	.20
54a Goblin Chirurgeon v1 C1	.20	.40
54b Goblin Chirurgeon v2 C1	.20	.40
54c Goblin Chirurgeon v3 C1	.75	1.50
55 Goblin Flotilla U1	.75	1.50
56a Goblin Grenade v1 C1	.20	.40
56b Goblin Grenade v2 C1	.20	.40
56c Goblin Grenade v3 C1	.30	.60
57 Goblin Kites U3	.10	.20
58a Goblin War Drums v1 C1	.10	.20
58b Goblin War Drums v2 C1	.10	.20
58c Goblin War Drums v3 C1	.10	.20
58d Goblin War Drums v4 C1	.10	.20
59 Goblin Warrens U1	1.00	2.00
60 Orcish Captain U3	.15	.30
61a Orcish Spy v1 C1	.10	.20
61b Orcish Spy v2 C1	.10	.20
61c Orcish Spy v3 C1	.10	.20
62a Orcish Veteran v1 C1	.12	.25
62b Orcish Veteran v2 C1	.10	.20
62c Orcish Veteran v3 C1	.10	.20
62d Orcish Veteran v4 C1	.10	.20
63 Orgg U1	.20	.40
64 Raiding Party U3	.12	.25
65a Elven Fortress v1 C1	.10	.20
65b Elven Fortress v2 C1	.10	.20
65c Elven Fortress v3 C1	.10	.20
65d Elven Fortress v4 C1	.10	.20
66 Elvish Farmer U1	3.00	6.00
67a Elvish Hunter v1 C1	.12	.25
67b Elvish Hunter v2 C1	.10	.20
67c Elvish Hunter v3 C1	.10	.20
68a Elvish Scout v1 C1	.10	.20
68b Elvish Scout v2 C1	.10	.20
68c Elvish Scout v3 C1	.10	.20
69 Feral Thallid U3	.10	.20
70 Fungal Bloom U1	1.50	3.00
71a Night Soil v1 C1	.10	.20
71b Night Soil v2 C1	.10	.20
71c Night Soil v3 C1	.10	.20
72a Spore Cloud v1 C1	.12	.25
72b Spore Cloud v2 C1	.12	.25
72c Spore Cloud v3 C1	.12	.25
73 Spore Flower U3	.25	.50
74a Thallid v1 C1	.10	.20
74b Thallid v2 C1	.10	.20
74c Thallid v3 C1	.10	.20
74d Thallid v4 C1	.10	.20
75 Thallid Devourer U3	.25	.50
76 Thelon's Chant U3	.10	.20
77 Thelon's Curse U1	2.00	4.00
78 Thelonite Druid U3	.20	.40
79 Thelonite Monk U1	1.50	3.00
80a Thorn Thallid v1 C1	.12	.25
80b Thorn Thallid v2 C1	.12	.25
80c Thorn Thallid v3 C1	.12	.25
80d Thorn Thallid v4 C1	.12	.25
81 Aeolipile U1	1.50	3.00
82 Balm of Restoration U1	1.00	2.00
83 Conch Horn U1	7.50	15.00
84 Delif's Cone C1	.10	.20
85 Delif's Cube U1	1.50	3.00
86 Draconian Cylix U1	1.50	3.00
87 Elven Lyre U1	1.00	2.00
88 Implements of Sacrifice U1	2.50	5.00
89 Ring of Renewal U1	1.50	3.00
90 Spirit Shield U1	1.00	2.00
91 Zelyon Sword U1	5.00	10.00
92 Bottomless Vault U1	1.00	2.00
93 Dwarven Hold U1	1.00	2.00
94 Dwarven Ruins U2	.30	.60
95 Ebon Stronghold U2	.30	.60
96 Havenwood Battleground U2	.15	.30
97 Hollow Trees U1	.60	1.25
98 Icatian Store U1	.50	1.00
99 Rainbow Vale U1	10.00	20.00
100 Ruins of Trokair U2	.15	.30
101 Sand Silos U1	.60	1.25
102 Svyelunite Temple U2	.15	.30

1994 Magic The Gathering Legends

1 Akron Legionnaire R1	6.00	12.00
2 Alabaster Potion C2	.75	1.50
3 Amrou Kithkin C2	.50	1.00
4 Angelic Voices R1	10.00	20.00
5 Cleanse R1	150.00	300.00
6 Clergy of the Holy Nimbus C2	.50	1.00
7 D'Avenant Archer C2	.50	1.00
8 Divine Intervention R1	75.00	150.00
9 Divine Offering C2	.60	1.25
10 Divine Transformation R1	10.00	20.00
11 Elder Land Wurm R1	6.00	12.00
12 Enchanted Being C1	.30	.75
13 Equinox C1	1.00	2.00
14 Fortified Area U1	1.25	2.50
15 Glyph of Life C2	.30	.75
16 Great Defender U1	1.50	3.00
17 Great Wall U1	1.00	2.00
18 Greater Realm of Preservation U1	4.00	8.00
19 Heaven's Gate U1	10.00	20.00
20 Holy Day C1	.75	1.50
21 Indestructible Aura C2	.30	.75
22 Infinite Authority R1	12.50	25.00
23 Ivory Guardians U1	1.00	2.00
24 Keepers of the Faith C2	.30	.75
25 Kismet U1	7.50	15.00
26 Land Tax U1	50.00	100.00
27 Lifeblood R1	25.00	50.00
28 Moat R1	600.00	1,200.00
29 Osai Vultures C1	.30	.75
30 Petra Sphinx R1	7.50	15.00
31 Presence of the Master U1	10.00	20.00
32 Rapid Fire R1	15.00	30.00
33 Remove Enchantments C1	2.00	4.00
34 Righteous Avengers U1	1.25	2.50
35 Seeker U1	1.00	2.00
36 Shield Wall U1	1.00	2.00
37 Spirit Link U1	10.00	20.00
38 Spiritual Sanctuary R1	10.00	20.00
39 Thunder Spirit R1	75.00	150.00
40 Tundra Wolves C2	.60	1.25
41 Visions U1	2.50	5.00
42 Wall of Caltrops C1	.60	1.25
43 Wall of Light U1	3.00	6.00
44 Acid Rain R1	60.00	120.00
45 Anti-Magic Aura C1	.50	1.00
46 Azure Drake U1	6.00	12.00
47 Backfire U1	1.50	3.00
48 Boomerang C2	.75	1.50
49 Brine Hag U1	2.50	5.00
50 Devouring Deep C2	.50	1.00
51 Dream Coat U1	3.00	6.00
52 Elder Spawn R1	20.00	40.00
53 Enchantment Alteration C1	.30	.75
54 Energy Tap C2	.75	1.50
55 Field of Dreams R1	75.00	150.00
56 Flash Counter C2	.50	1.00
57 Flash Flood C2	.30	.75
58 Force Spike C2	1.00	2.00
59 Gaseous Form C1	.30	.75
60 Glyph of Delusion C1	.30	.75
61 In the Eye of Chaos R1	125.00	250.00
62 Invoke Prejudice R1	300.00	600.00
63 Juxtapose R1	15.00	30.00
64 Land Equilibrium R1	125.00	250.00
65 Mana Drain U1	200.00	400.00
66 Part Water U1	1.50	3.00
67 Psionic Entity R1	4.00	8.00
68 Psychic Purge C1	1.50	3.00
69 Puppet Master U1	1.50	3.00
70 Recall R1	50.00	100.00
71 Relic Bind U1	1.50	3.00
72 Remove Soul C2	.50	1.00
73 Reset U1	25.00	50.00
74 Reverberation R1	25.00	50.00
75 Sea Kings' Blessing U1	3.00	6.00
76 Segovian Leviathan U1	1.50	3.00
77 Silhouette U1	1.50	3.00
78 Spectral Cloak U1	3.00	6.00
79 Telekinesis R1	40.00	80.00
80 Teleport R1	6.00	12.00
81 Time Elemental R1	15.00	30.00
82 Undertow U1	1.25	2.50
83 Venarian Gold C1	.50	1.00
84 Wall of Vapor C2	.30	.75
85 Wall of Wonder U1	2.00	4.00
86 Zephyr Falcon C2	.50	1.00
87 Abomination U1	1.50	3.00
88 All Hallow's Eve R1	300.00	500.00
89 Blight U1	5.00	10.00
90 Carrion Ants R1	6.00	12.00
91 Chains of Mephistopheles R1	600.00	1,200.00
92 Cosmic Horror R1	7.50	15.00
93 Cyclopean Mummy C2	.50	1.00
94 Darkness C1	6.00	12.00
95 Demonic Torment U1	3.00	6.00
96 Evil Eye of Orms-By-Gore U1	4.00	8.00
97 Fallen Angel U1	7.50	15.00
98 Ghosts of the Damned C2	.30	.75
99 Giant Slug C2	.30	.75
100 Glyph of Doom C2	.30	.75
101 Greed R1	40.00	80.00
102 Headless Horseman C1	.50	1.00
103 Hell Swarm C1	.30	.75
104 Hell's Caretaker R1	25.00	50.00
105 Hellfire R1	100.00	200.00
106 Horror of Horrors U1	2.00	4.00
107 Imprison R1	100.00	200.00
108 Infernal Medusa U1	3.00	6.00
109 Jovial Evil R1	30.00	60.00
110 Lesser Werewolf U1	4.00	8.00
111 Lost Soul C2	.30	.75
112 Mold Demon R1	20.00	40.00
113 Nether Void R1	500.00	1,000.00
114 Pit Scorpion C2	.30	.75
115 Quagmire U1	1.00	2.00
116 Shimian Night Stalker U1	1.50	3.00
117 Spirit Shackle C1	.30	.75
118 Syphon Soul C2	.30	.75
119 Takklemaggot U1	1.50	3.00
120 The Abyss R1	750.00	1,500.00
121 The Wretched R1	15.00	30.00
122 Touch of Darkness U1	2.00	4.00
123 Transmutation C1	.30	.75
124 Underworld Dreams U1	40.00	80.00
125 Vampire Bats C2	.50	1.00
126 Walking Dead C1	3.00	6.00
127 Wall of Putrid Flesh U1	1.50	3.00
128 Wall of Shadows C2	.30	.75
129 Wall of Tombstones U1	2.50	5.00
130 Active Volcano C2	.75	1.50
131 Aerathi Berserker U1	1.50	3.00
132 Backdraft U1	1.00	2.00
133 Beasts of Bogardan U1	1.50	3.00
134 Blazing Effigy C2	.50	1.00
135 Blood Lust U1	6.00	12.00
136 Caverns of Despair R1	50.00	100.00
137 Chain Lightning C2	10.00	20.00
138 Crevasse U1	1.00	2.00
139 Crimson Kobolds C2	2.00	4.00
140 Crimson Manticore R1	6.00	12.00
141 Crookshank Kobolds C2	2.50	5.00
142 Disharmony R1	40.00	80.00
143 Dwarven Song U1	2.00	4.00
144 Eternal Warrior U1	1.50	3.00
145 Falling Star R1	40.00	200.00
146 Feint C1	2.00	4.00
147 Firestorm Phoenix R1	30.00	60.00
148 Frost Giant U1	2.50	5.00
149 Giant Strength C2	.50	1.00
150 Glyph of Destruction C2	.50	1.00
151 Gravity Sphere R1	75.00	150.00
152 Hyperion Blacksmith U1	2.00	4.00
153 Immolation C1	.50	1.00
154 Kobold Drill Sergeant U1	7.50	15.00
155 Kobold Overlord R1	50.00	100.00
156 Kobold Taskmaster U1	5.00	10.00
157 Kobolds of Kher Keep C2	7.50	15.00

158 Land's Edge R1	25.00	50.00
159 Mountain Yeti U1	2.00	4.00
160 Primordial Ooze U1	1.50	3.00
161 Pyrotechnics C2	.50	1.00
162 Quarum Trench Gnomes R1	12.50	25.00
163 Raging Bull C1	.30	.75
164 Spinal Villain R1	40.00	80.00
165 Storm World R1	40.00	80.00
166 Tempest Efreet R1	12.50	25.00
167 The Brute C1	.50	1.00
168 Wall of Dust U1	1.00	2.00
169 Wall of Earth C2	.30	.75
170 Wall of Heat C1	.30	.75
171 Wall of Opposition R1	7.50	15.00
172 Winds of Change U1	20.00	40.00
173 Aisling Leprechaun C1	.75	1.50
174 Arboria U1	10.00	20.00
175 Avoid Fate C1	3.00	6.00
176 Barbary Apes C1	.50	1.00
177 Cat Warriors C2	.50	1.00
178 Cocoon U1	1.00	2.00
179 Concordant Crossroads R1	100.00	200.00
180 Craw Giant U1	2.50	5.00
181 Deadfall U1	1.00	2.00
182 Durkwood Boars C2	.50	1.00
183 Elven Riders R1	6.00	12.00
184 Emerald Dragonfly C2	.30	.75
185 Eureka R1	350.00	700.00
186 Fire Sprites C2	.50	1.00
187 Floral Spuzzem U1	1.50	3.00
188 Giant Turtle C2	.30	.75
189 Glyph of Reincarnation C1	.50	1.00
190 Hornet Cobra C2	.30	.75
191 Ichneumon Druid U1	5.00	10.00
192 Killer Bees R1	25.00	50.00
193 Living Plane R1	250.00	500.00
194 Master of the Hunt R1	25.00	50.00
195 Moss Monster C2	.30	.75
196 Pixie Queen R1	60.00	120.00
197 Pradesh Gypsies U1	25.00	50.00
198 Rabid Wombat U1	3.00	6.00
199 Radjan Spirit U1	1.50	3.00
200 Rebirth R1	6.00	12.00
201 Reincarnation U1	5.00	10.00
202 Revelation R1	12.50	25.00
203 Rust C2	.30	.75
204 Shelkin Brownie C1	.50	1.00
205 Storm Seeker U1	7.50	15.00
206 Subdue C1	.50	1.00
207 Sylvan Library U1	100.00	200.00
208 Sylvan Paradise U1	5.00	10.00
209 Typhoon R1	15.00	30.00
210 Untamed Wilds U1	4.00	8.00
211 Whirling Dervish U1	10.00	20.00
212 Willow Satyr R1	60.00	125.00
213 Winter Blast R1	12.50	25.00
214 Wolverine Pack C2	.50	1.00
215 Wood Elemental R1	20.00	40.00
216 Adun Oakenshield R1	75.00	150.00
217 Angus Mackenzie R1	175.00	350.00
218 Arcades Sabboth R1	30.00	60.00
219 Axelrod Gunnarson R1	7.50	15.00
220 Ayesha Tanaka R1	10.00	20.00
221 Barktooth Warbeard U1	2.50	5.00
222 Bartel Runeaxe R1	40.00	80.00
223 Boris Devilboon R1	25.00	50.00
224 Chromium R1	30.00	60.00
225 Dakkon Blackblade R1	75.00	150.00
226 Gabriel Angelfire R1	25.00	50.00
227 Gosta Dirk R1	25.00	50.00
228 Gwendlyn Di Corci R1	200.00	400.00
229 Halfdane R1	30.00	60.00
230 Hazezon Tamar R1	150.00	300.00
231 Hunding Gjornersen U1	2.00	4.00
232 Jacques le Vert R1	25.00	50.00
233 Jasmine Boreal U1	3.00	6.00
234 Jedit Ojanen U1	2.50	5.00
235 Jerrard of the Closed Fist U1	2.50	5.00
236 Johan R1	12.50	25.00
237 Kasimir the Lone Wolf U1	2.00	4.00
238 Kei Takahashi R1	6.00	12.00
239 Lady Caleria R1	30.00	60.00
240 Lady Evangela R1	50.00	100.00
241 Lady Orca U1	2.00	4.00
242 Livonya Silone R1	50.00	100.00
243 Lord Magnus U1	3.00	6.00
244 Marhault Elsdragon U1	2.00	4.00
245 Nebuchadnezzar R1	40.00	80.00
246 Nicol Bolas R1	60.00	120.00
247 Palladia-Mors R1	25.00	50.00
248 Pavel Maliki U1	1.50	3.00
249 Princess Lucrezia U1	2.00	4.00
250 Ragnar R1	30.00	60.00
251 Ramirez DePietro U1	5.00	10.00
252 Ramses Overdark R1	50.00	100.00
253 Rasputin Dreamweaver R1	75.00	150.00
254 Riven Turnbull U1	2.50	5.00
255 Rohgahh of Kher Keep R1	50.00	100.00
256 Rubinia Soulsinger R1	12.50	25.00
257 Sir Shandlar of Eberyn U1	2.00	4.00
258 Sivitri Scarzam U1	2.00	4.00
259 Sol'kanar the Swamp King R1	30.00	60.00
260 Stangg R1	25.00	50.00
261 Sunastian Falconer U1	2.00	4.00
262 Tetsuo Umezawa R1	75.00	150.00
263 The Lady of the Mountain U1	3.00	6.00
264 Tobias Andrion U1	1.00	2.00
265 Tor Wauki U1	1.50	3.00
266 Torsten Von Ursus U1	2.00	4.00
267 Tuknir Deathlock R1	15.00	30.00
268 Ur-Drago R1	20.00	40.00
269 Vaevictis Asmadi R1	30.00	60.00
270 Xira Arien R1	20.00	40.00
271 Al-abara's Carpet R1	35.00	75.00
272 Alchor's Tomb R1	15.00	30.00
273 Arena of the Ancients R1	12.50	25.00
274 Black Mana Battery U1	3.00	6.00
275 Blue Mana Battery U1	1.50	3.00
276 Bronze Horse R1	6.00	12.00
277 Forethought Amulet R1	15.00	30.00
278 Gauntlets of Chaos R1	7.50	15.00
279 Green Mana Battery U1	1.50	3.00
280 Horn of Deafening R1	6.00	12.00
281 Knowledge Vault R1	25.00	50.00
282 Kry Shield U1	1.25	2.50
283 Life Chisel U2	1.50	3.00
284 Life Matrix R1	30.00	60.00
285 Mana Matrix R1	50.00	100.00
286 Marble Priest U1	2.00	4.00
287 Mirror Universe R1	200.00	400.00
288 North Star R1	50.00	100.00
289 Nova Pentacle R1	30.00	60.00
290 Planar Gate R1	40.00	80.00
291 Red Mana Battery U1	2.50	5.00
292 Relic Barrier U2	7.50	15.00
293 Ring of Immortals R1	30.00	60.00
294 Sentinel R1	5.00	10.00
295 Serpent Generator R1	7.50	15.00
296 Sword of the Ages R1	60.00	120.00
297 Triassic Egg R1	12.50	25.00
298 Voodoo Doll R1	7.50	15.00
299 White Mana Battery U1	1.50	3.00
300 Adventurers' Guildhouse U1	12.50	25.00
301 Cathedral of Serra U1	7.50	15.00
302 Hammerheim U2	5.00	10.00
303 Karakas U2	30.00	60.00
304 Mountain Stronghold U1	3.00	6.00
305 Pendelhaven U2	12.50	25.00
306 Seafarers Quay U2	3.00	6.00
307 The Tabernacle at Pendrell Vale R1	2,000.00	4,000.00
308 Tolaria U2	5.00	10.00
309 Unholy Citadel U2	4.00	8.00
310 Urborg U2	15.00	30.00

1994 Magic The Gathering Revised Edition

1 Animate Wall R	.50	1.00
2 Armageddon R	7.50	15.00
3 Balance R	4.00	8.00
4 Benalish Hero C	.15	.30
5 Black Ward U	.20	.40
6 Blessing R	1.00	2.00
7 Blue Ward U	.15	.30
8 Castle U	.20	.40
9 Circle of Protection Black C	.15	.30
10 Circle of Protection Blue C	.15	.30
11 Circle of Protection Green C	.15	.30
12 Circle of Protection Red C	.15	.30
13 Circle of Protection White C	.15	.30
14 Conversion U	.15	.30
15 Crusade R	1.50	3.00
16 Death Ward C	.15	.30
17 Disenchant C	.20	.40
18 Eye for an Eye R	.75	1.50
19 Farmstead R	5.00	10.00
20 Green Ward U	.15	.30
21 Guardian Angel C	.15	.30
22 Healing Salve C	.15	.30
23 Holy Armor C	.15	.30
24 Holy Strength C	.15	.30
25 Island Sanctuary R	3.00	6.00
26 Karma U	.20	.40
27 Lance U	.15	.30
28 Mesa Pegasus C	.15	.30
29 Northern Paladin R	2.00	4.00
30 Pearled Unicorn C	.15	.30
31 Personal Incarnation R	.60	1.25
32 Purelace R	.30	.60
33 Red Ward U	.15	.30
34 Resurrection U	.20	.40
35 Reverse Damage R	2.00	4.00
36 Reverse Polarity U	.20	.40
37 Righteousness R	3.00	6.00
38 Samite Healer C	.15	.30
39 Savannah Lions R	5.00	10.00
40 Serra Angel U	4.00	8.00
41 Swords to Plowshares U	3.00	6.00
42 Veteran Bodyguard R	4.00	8.00
43 Wall of Swords U	.15	.30
44 White Knight U	.75	1.50
45 White Ward U	.15	.30
46 Wrath of God R	15.00	30.00
47 Air Elemental U	.20	.40
48 Animate Artifact U	.15	.30
49 Blue Elemental Blast C	.15	.30
50 Braingeyser R	30.00	75.00
51 Clone U	1.00	2.00
52 Control Magic U	1.00	2.00
53 Copy Artifact R	75.00	150.00
54 Counterspell U	3.00	6.00
55 Creature Bond C	.15	.30
56 Drain Power R	2.50	5.00
57 Energy Flux U	.20	.40
58 Feedback U	.15	.30
59 Flight C	.15	.30
60 Hurkyl's Recall R	2.00	4.00
61 Island Fish Jasconius R	.30	.75
62 Jump C	.15	.30
63 Lifetap U	.15	.30
64 Lord of Atlantis R	4.00	8.00
65 Magical Hack R	.75	1.50
66 Mahamoti Djinn R	5.00	10.00
67 Mana Short R	3.00	6.00
68 Merfolk of the Pearl Trident C	.15	.30
69 Phantasmal Forces U	.15	.30
70 Phantasmal Terrain C	.15	.30
71 Phantom Monster U	.15	.30
72 Pirate Ship R	.50	1.00
73 Power Leak C	.15	.30
74 Power Sink C	.15	.30
75 Prodigal Sorcerer C	.15	.30
76 Psychic Venom C	.15	.30
77 Reconstruction C	.15	.30
78 Sea Serpent C	.15	.30
79 Serendib Efreet R	7.50	15.00
80 Siren's Call U	.15	.30
81 Sleight of Mind R	.75	1.50
82 Spell Blast C	.15	.30
83 Stasis R	6.00	12.00
84 Steal Artifact U	.20	.40
85 Thoughtlace R	.30	.60
86 Unstable Mutation C	.20	.40
87 Unsummon C	.20	.40
88 Vesuvan Doppelganger R	50.00	100.00
89 Volcanic Eruption R	.60	1.25
90 Wall of Air U	.15	.30
91 Wall of Water U	.15	.30
92 Water Elemental U	.15	.30
93 Animate Dead U	2.00	4.00
94 Bad Moon R	6.00	12.00
95 Black Knight U	1.00	2.00
96 Bog Wraith U	.20	.40
97 Contract from Below R	7.50	15.00
98 Cursed Land U	.20	.40
99 Dark Ritual C	.60	1.25
100 Darkpact R	4.00	8.00
101 Deathgrip U	.15	.30
102 Deathlace R	.30	.75
103 Demonic Attorney R	4.00	8.00
104 Demonic Hordes R	15.00	30.00
105 Demonic Tutor U	30.00	75.00
106 Drain Life C	.15	.30
107 Drudge Skeletons C	.15	.30
108 El-Hajjaj R	.50	1.00
109 Erg Raiders C	.15	.30
110 Evil Presence U	.20	.40
111 Fear C	.15	.30
112 Frozen Shade C	.15	.30
113 Gloom U	.20	.40
114 Howl from Beyond C	.15	.30
115 Hypnotic Specter U	2.50	5.00
116 Lord of the Pit R	4.00	8.00
117 Mind Twist R	5.00	10.00
118 Nether Shadow R	2.00	4.00
119 Nettling Imp U	.50	1.00
120 Nightmare R	6.00	12.00
121 Paralyze C	.15	.30
122 Pestilence C	.20	.40
123 Plague Rats C	.15	.30
124 Raise Dead C	.15	.30
125 Royal Assassin R	7.50	15.00
126 Sacrifice U	2.00	4.00
127 Scathe Zombies C	.15	.30
128 Scavenging Ghoul U	.15	.30
129 Sengir Vampire U	2.00	4.00
130 Simulacrum U	.20	.40
131 Sorceress Queen R	6.00	12.00
132 Terror C	.15	.30
133 Unholy Strength C	.20	.40
134 Wall of Bone U	.15	.30
135 Warp Artifact R	.30	.75
136 Weakness C	.15	.30
137 Will-O'-The-Wisp R	5.00	10.00
138 Zombie Master R	6.00	12.00
139 Atog C	.20	.40
140 Burrowing U	.15	.30
141 Chaoslace R	.30	.60
142 Disintegrate C	.15	.30
143 Dragon Whelp U	.30	.60
144 Dwarven Warriors C	.15	.30
145 Dwarven Weaponsmith U	.20	.40
146 Earth Elemental U	.15	.30
147 Earthbind C	.20	.40
148 Earthquake R	1.50	3.00
149 Fire Elemental U	.30	.60
150 Fireball C	.30	.60
151 Firebreathing C	.15	.30
152 Flashfires U	.15	.30
153 Fork R	60.00	120.00
154 Goblin Balloon Brigade U	.30	.60
155 Goblin King R	5.00	10.00
156 Granite Gargoyle R	5.00	10.00
157 Gray Ogre C	.15	.30
158 Hill Giant C	.15	.30
159 Hurloon Minotaur C	.15	.30
160 Keldon Warlord U	.25	.50
161 Kird Ape C	.20	.40
162 Lightning Bolt C	2.00	4.00
163 Magnetic Mountain R	.50	1.00
164 Mana Flare R	7.50	15.00
165 Manabarbs R	1.00	2.00
166 Mijae Djinn R	1.50	3.00
167 Mons's Goblin Raiders C	.15	.30
168 Orcish Artillery U	.20	.40
169 Orcish Oriflamme U	.15	.30
170 Power Surge R	1.50	3.00
171 Red Elemental Blast C	1.00	2.00
172 Roc of Kher Ridges R	6.00	12.00
173 Rock Hydra R	7.50	15.00
174 Sedge Troll R	6.00	12.00
175 Shatter C	.15	.30
176 Shatterstorm U	.30	.75
177 Shivan Dragon R	15.00	30.00
178 Smoke R	3.00	6.00
179 Stone Giant U	.15	.30
180 Stone Rain C	.15	.30
181 Tunnel U	.15	.30
182 Uthden Troll U	.20	.40
183 Wall of Fire U	.15	.30
184 Wall of Stone U	.15	.30
185 Wheel of Fortune R	350.00	700.00
186 Aspect of Wolf R	1.25	2.50
187 Birds of Paradise R	20.00	40.00
188 Channel U	.15	.30
189 Cockatrice R	2.50	5.00
190 Craw Wurm C	.15	.30
191 Crumble U	.20	.40
192 Desert Twister U	.20	.40
193 Elvish Archers R	2.00	4.00
194 Fastbond R	30.00	75.00
195 Fog C	.15	.30
196 Force of Nature R	5.00	10.00
197 Fungusaur R	.60	1.25
198 Gaea's Liege R	1.50	3.00
199 Giant Growth C	.15	.30
200 Giant Spider C	.15	.30
201 Grizzly Bears C	.15	.30
202 Hurricane U	.25	.50
203 Instill Energy U	1.50	3.00
204 Ironroot Treefolk C	.15	.30
205 Kudzu R	6.00	12.00
206 Ley Druid U	.15	.30
207 Lifeforce U	.20	.40
208 Lifelace R	.50	1.00
209 Living Artifact R	.50	1.00
210 Living Lands R	.50	1.00
211 Llanowar Elves C	.30	.60
212 Lure U	.20	.40
213 Regeneration C	.15	.30
214 Regrowth U	.75	1.50
215 Scryb Sprites C	.15	.30
216 Shanodin Dryads C	.15	.30
217 Stream of Life C	.15	.30
218 Thicket Basilisk U	.20	.40
219 Timber Wolves R	.60	1.25
220 Titania's Song R	.60	1.25
221 Tranquility C	.15	.30
222 Tsunami U	.20	.40
223 Verduran Enchantress R	2.50	5.00
224 Wall of Brambles U	.15	.30
225 Wall of Ice U	.50	1.00
226 Wall of Wood C	.15	.30
227 Wanderlust U	.15	.30
228 War Mammoth C	.15	.30
229 Web R	.75	1.50
230 Wild Growth C	.20	.40
231 Aladdin's Lamp R	.60	1.25
232 Aladdin's Ring R	.30	.75
233 Ankh of Mishra R	3.00	6.00
234 Armageddon Clock R	.30	.75
235 Basalt Monolith U	2.00	4.00
236 Black Vise U	.75	1.50
237 Bottle of Suleiman R	.50	1.00
238 Brass Man U	.20	.40
239 Celestial Prism U	.20	.40
240 Clockwork Beast R	.30	.60
241 Conservator U	.15	.30
242 Crystal Rod U	.15	.30
243 Dancing Scimitar R	.50	1.00
244 Dingus Egg R	1.00	2.00
245 Disrupting Scepter R	1.25	2.50
246 Dragon Engine R	.50	1.00
247 Ebony Horse R	.30	.60
248 Flying Carpet R	.30	.75
249 Glasses of Urza U	.25	.50
250 Helm of Chatzuk R	.30	.75
251 Howling Mine R	7.50	15.00
252 Iron Star U	.15	.30
253 Ivory Cup U	.15	.30
254 Ivory Tower R	7.50	15.00
255 Jade Monolith R	.30	.75
256 Jandor's Ring R	.30	.60
257 Jandor's Saddlebags R	.75	1.50
258 Jayemdae Tome R	3.00	6.00
259 Juggernaut U	.75	1.50
260 Kormus Bell R	1.25	2.50
261 Library of Leng U	1.00	2.00
262 Living Wall U	.30	.60
263 Mana Vault R	50.00	100.00
264 Meekstone R	4.00	8.00
265 Millstone R	2.50	5.00
266 Mishra's War Machine R	.30	.75
267 Nevinyrral's Disk R	7.50	15.00
268 Obsianus Golem U	.20	.40
269 Onulet R	.30	.60
270 Ornithopter U	.25	.50
271 Primal Clay R	.50	1.00
272 Rocket Launcher R	.60	1.25
273 Rod of Ruin U	.15	.30
274 Sol Ring U	15.00	30.00
275 Soul Net U	.15	.30
276 Sunglasses of Urza R	1.00	2.00
277 The Hive R	.75	1.50
278 The Rack U	1.00	2.00
279 Throne of Bone U	.20	.40
280 Winter Orb R	25.00	50.00
281 Wooden Sphere U	.15	.30
282 Badlands R	225.00	450.00
283 Bayou R	250.00	500.00
284 Plateau R	200.00	350.00
285 Savannah R	200.00	350.00
286 Scrubland R	200.00	400.00
287 Taiga R	250.00	400.00
288 Tropical Island R	500.00	1,000.00
289 Tundra R	400.00	700.00
290 Underground Sea R	600.00	1,200.00
291 Volcanic Island R	500.00	1,000.00
292 Plains v1 L	.25	.50
293 Plains v2 L	.25	.50
294 Plains v3 L	.25	.50
295 Island v1 L	.30	.60
296 Island v2 L	.30	.60
297 Island v3 L	.30	.60
298 Swamp v1 L	.25	.50
299 Swamp v2 L	.25	.50
300 Swamp v3 L	.25	.50
301 Mountain v1 L	.25	.50
302 Mountain v2 L	.25	.50
303 Mountain v3 L	.25	.50
304 Forest v1 L	.25	.50
305 Forest v2 L	.25	.50
306 Forest v3 L	.25	.50

1994 Magic The Gathering Summer Edition

1 Animate Wall R	800.00	1,000.00
2 Armageddon R	1,750.00	2,000.00
3 Balance R	2,000.00	2,500.00
4 Benalish Hero C	120.00	250.00
5 Black Ward U	100.00	200.00
6 Blessing R	750.00	950.00
7 Blue Ward U	150.00	300.00
8 Castle U	120.00	250.00
9 Circle of Protection Black C	150.00	300.00
10 Circle of Protection Blue C	100.00	200.00
11 Circle of Protection Green C	100.00	200.00
12 Circle of Protection Red C	300.00	450.00
13 Circle of Protection White C	100.00	200.00
14 Conversion U	150.00	300.00
15 Crusade R	1,000.00	1,250.00
16 Death Ward C	120.00	250.00
17 Disenchant C	400.00	600.00
18 Eye for an Eye R	850.00	1,100.00
19 Farmstead R	800.00	1,000.00
20 Green Ward U	120.00	250.00
21 Guardian Angel C	100.00	200.00
22 Healing Salve C	100.00	200.00
23 Holy Armor C	100.00	200.00
24 Holy Strength C	100.00	200.00
25 Island Sanctuary R	700.00	900.00
26 Karma U	150.00	300.00
27 Lance U	120.00	250.00

28 Mesa Pegasus C	100.00	200.00
29 Northern Paladin R	550.00	800.00
30 Pearled Unicorn C	100.00	200.00
31 Personal Incarnation R	800.00	1,000.00
32 Purelace R	950.00	1,200.00
33 Red Ward U	150.00	300.00
34 Resurrection U	350.00	500.00
35 Reverse Damage R	800.00	1,000.00
36 Reverse Polarity U	150.00	300.00
37 Righteousness R	800.00	1,000.00
38 Samite Healer C	100.00	200.00
39 Savannah Lions R	1,550.00	1,900.00
40 Serra Angel U	2,000.00	2,500.00
41 Swords to Plowshares U	1,750.00	2,000.00
42 Veteran Bodyguard R	800.00	1,000.00
43 Wall of Swords U	150.00	300.00
44 White Knight U	350.00	500.00
45 White Ward U	150.00	300.00
46 Wrath of God R	2,500.00	3,000.00
47 Air Elemental U	250.00	400.00
48 Animate Artifact U	150.00	300.00
49 Blue Elemental Blast C	100.00	200.00
50 Braingeyser R	1,750.00	2,000.00
51 Clone U	550.00	800.00
52 Control Magic U	550.00	800.00
53 Copy Artifact R	950.00	1,200.00
54 Counterspell U	1,850.00	2,200.00
55 Creature Bond C	80.00	150.00
56 Drain Power R	550.00	800.00
57 Energy Flux U	150.00	300.00
58 Feedback U	150.00	300.00
59 Flight C	80.00	150.00
60 Hurkyl's Recall R	1,750.00	2,000.00
61 Island Fish Jasconius R	800.00	1,000.00
62 Jump C	80.00	150.00
63 Lifetap U	150.00	300.00
64 Lord of Atlantis R	1,400.00	1,600.00
65 Magical Hack R	800.00	1,000.00
66 Mahamoti Djinn R	1,300.00	1,500.00
67 Mana Short R	1,300.00	1,500.00
68 Merfolk of the Pearl Trident C	100.00	200.00
69 Phantasmal Forces U	150.00	300.00
70 Phantasmal Terrain C	80.00	150.00
71 Phantom Monster U	120.00	250.00
72 Pirate Ship R	800.00	1,000.00
73 Power Leak C	80.00	150.00
74 Power Sink C	80.00	150.00
75 Prodigal Sorcerer C	100.00	200.00
76 Psychic Venom C	100.00	200.00
77 Reconstruction C	100.00	200.00
78 Sea Serpent C	80.00	150.00
79 Serendib Efreet R	9,000.00	12,000.00
80 Siren's Call U	150.00	300.00
81 Sleight of Mind R	550.00	800.00
82 Spell Blast C	100.00	200.00
83 Stasis R	1,450.00	1,700.00
84 Steal Artifact U	150.00	300.00
85 Thoughtlace R	800.00	1,000.00
86 Unstable Mutation C	100.00	200.00
87 Unsummon C	150.00	300.00
88 Vesuvan Doppelganger R	2,500.00	3,000.00
89 Volcanic Eruption R	800.00	1,000.00
90 Wall of Air U	150.00	300.00
91 Wall of Water U	150.00	300.00
92 Water Elemental U	150.00	300.00
93 Animate Dead U	400.00	600.00
94 Bad Moon R	850.00	1,100.00
95 Black Knight U	400.00	600.00
96 Bog Wraith U	120.00	250.00
97 Contract from Below R	1,400.00	1,600.00
98 Cursed Land U	150.00	300.00
99 Dark Ritual C	800.00	1,000.00
100 Darkpact R	550.00	800.00
101 Deathgrip U	150.00	300.00
102 Deathlace R	800.00	1,000.00
103 Demonic Attorney R	750.00	950.00
104 Demonic Hordes R	1,400.00	1,600.00
105 Demonic Tutor U	2,700.00	3,400.00
106 Drain Life C	350.00	500.00
107 Drudge Skeletons C	100.00	200.00
108 El-Hajjaj R	550.00	800.00
109 Erg Raiders C	100.00	200.00
110 Evil Presence U	150.00	300.00
111 Fear C	100.00	200.00
112 Frozen Shade C	100.00	200.00
113 Gloom U	250.00	400.00
114 Howl from Beyond C	100.00	200.00
115 Hypnotic Specter U	1,100.00	1,300.00
116 Lord of the Pit R	1,400.00	1,600.00
117 Mind Twist R	4,100.00	4,500.00
118 Nether Shadow R	950.00	1,200.00
119 Nettling Imp U	120.00	250.00
120 Nightmare R	1,450.00	1,750.00
121 Paralyze C	100.00	200.00
122 Pestilence C	100.00	200.00
123 Plague Rats C	100.00	200.00
124 Raise Dead C	100.00	200.00
125 Royal Assassin R	1,800.00	2,100.00
126 Sacrifice U	150.00	300.00
127 Scathe Zombies C	100.00	200.00
128 Scavenging Ghoul U	150.00	300.00
129 Sengir Vampire U	700.00	900.00
130 Simulacrum U	150.00	300.00
131 Sorceress Queen R	550.00	800.00
132 Terror C	350.00	500.00
133 Unholy Strength C	150.00	300.00
134 Wall of Bone U	150.00	300.00
135 Warp Artifact R	550.00	800.00
136 Weakness C	100.00	200.00
137 Will-O'-The-Wisp R	1,300.00	1,500.00
138 Zombie Master R	800.00	1,000.00
139 Atog C	100.00	200.00
140 Burrowing U	100.00	200.00
141 Chaoslace R	550.00	800.00
142 Disintegrate C	250.00	400.00
143 Dragon Whelp U	250.00	400.00
144 Dwarven Warriors C	100.00	200.00
145 Dwarven Weaponsmith U	100.00	200.00
146 Earth Elemental U	120.00	250.00
147 Earthbind C	80.00	150.00
148 Earthquake R	850.00	1,100.00
149 Fire Elemental U	120.00	250.00
150 Fireball C	250.00	400.00
151 Firebreathing C	80.00	150.00
152 Flashfires U	120.00	250.00
153 Fork R	2,000.00	2,500.00
154 Goblin Balloon Brigade U	150.00	300.00
155 Goblin King R	950.00	1,200.00
156 Granite Gargoyle R	700.00	900.00
157 Gray Ogre C	100.00	200.00
158 Hill Giant C	80.00	150.00
159 Hurloon Minotaur C	100.00	200.00
160 Keldon Warlord U	150.00	300.00
161 Kird Ape C	450.00	700.00
162 Lightning Bolt C	800.00	1,000.00
163 Magnetic Mountain R	800.00	1,000.00
164 Mana Flare R	1,300.00	1,500.00
165 Manabarbs R	550.00	800.00
166 Mijae Djinn R	550.00	800.00
167 Mons's Goblin Raiders C	100.00	200.00
168 Orcish Artillery U	150.00	300.00
169 Orcish Oriflamme U	200.00	350.00
170 Power Surge R	550.00	800.00
171 Red Elemental Blast C	550.00	800.00
172 Roc of Kher Ridges R	800.00	1,000.00
173 Rock Hydra R	800.00	1,000.00
174 Sedge Troll R	550.00	800.00
175 Shatter C	100.00	200.00
176 Shatterstorm U	350.00	500.00
177 Shivan Dragon R	5,400.00	6,000.00
179 Stone Giant U	150.00	300.00
180 Stone Rain C	350.00	500.00
181 Tunnel U	150.00	300.00
182 Uthden Troll U	150.00	300.00
183 Wall of Fire U	150.00	300.00
184 Wall of Stone U	150.00	300.00
185 Wheel of Fortune R	2,500.00	3,000.00
186 Aspect of Wolf R	550.00	800.00
187 Birds of Paradise R	3,300.00	3,800.00
188 Channel U	550.00	800.00
189 Cockatrice R	800.00	1,000.00
190 Craw Wurm C	120.00	250.00
191 Crumble U	200.00	350.00
192 Desert Twister U	150.00	300.00
193 Elvish Archers R	800.00	1,000.00
194 Fastbond R	1,900.00	2,300.00
195 Fog C	80.00	150.00
196 Force of Nature R	950.00	1,200.00
197 Fungusaur R	450.00	700.00
198 Gaea's Liege R	450.00	700.00
199 Giant Growth C	250.00	400.00
200 Giant Spider C	80.00	150.00
201 Grizzly Bears C	100.00	200.00
202 Hurricane U	6,500.00	8,000.00
203 Instill Energy U	150.00	300.00
204 Ironroot Treefolk C	80.00	150.00
205 Kudzu R	350.00	500.00
206 Ley Druid U	150.00	300.00
207 Lifeforce U	120.00	250.00
208 Lifelace R	800.00	1,000.00
209 Living Artifact R	800.00	1,000.00
210 Living Lands R	800.00	1,000.00
211 Llanowar Elves C	550.00	800.00
212 Lure U	150.00	300.00
213 Regeneration C	100.00	200.00
214 Regrowth U	1,450.00	1,750.00
215 Scryb Sprites C	80.00	150.00
216 Shanodin Dryads C	100.00	200.00
217 Stream of Life C	100.00	200.00
218 Thicket Basilisk U	150.00	300.00
219 Timber Wolves R	800.00	1,000.00
220 Titania's Song R	800.00	1,000.00
221 Tranquility C	100.00	200.00
222 Tsunami U	150.00	300.00
223 Verduran Enchantress R	800.00	1,000.00
224 Wall of Brambles U	150.00	300.00
225 Wall of Ice U	150.00	300.00
226 Wall of Wood C	100.00	200.00
227 Wanderlust U	150.00	300.00
228 War Mammoth C	100.00	200.00
229 Web R	350.00	500.00
230 Wild Growth C	150.00	300.00
231 Aladdin's Lamp R	800.00	1,000.00
232 Aladdin's Ring R	800.00	1,000.00
233 Ankh of Mishra R	950.00	1,200.00
234 Armageddon Clock R	550.00	800.00
235 Basalt Monolith U	500.00	750.00
236 Black Vise U	1,450.00	1,700.00
237 Bottle of Suleiman R	800.00	1,000.00
238 Brass Man U	150.00	300.00
239 Celestial Prism U	120.00	250.00
240 Clockwork Beast R	850.00	1,100.00
241 Conservator U	100.00	200.00
242 Crystal Rod U	200.00	350.00
243 Dancing Scimitar R	800.00	1,000.00
244 Dingus Egg R	700.00	900.00
245 Disrupting Scepter R	800.00	1,000.00
246 Dragon Engine R	950.00	1,200.00
246 Smoke R	550.00	800.00
247 Ebony Horse R	800.00	1,000.00
247 Sol Ring U	2,350.00	2,800.00
248 Flying Carpet R	550.00	800.00
249 Glasses of Urza U	120.00	250.00
250 Helm of Chatzuk R	550.00	800.00
251 Howling Mine R	1,200.00	1,400.00
252 Iron Star U	150.00	300.00
253 Ivory Cup U	150.00	300.00
254 Ivory Tower R	950.00	1,200.00
255 Jade Monolith R	950.00	1,200.00
256 Jandor's Ring R	950.00	1,200.00
257 Jandor's Saddlebags R	950.00	1,200.00
258 Jayemdae Tome R	950.00	1,200.00
259 Juggernaut U	250.00	400.00
260 Kormus Bell R	550.00	800.00
261 Library of Leng U	120.00	250.00
262 Living Wall U	120.00	250.00
262 Mana Vault R	4,600.00	5,000.00
264 Meekstone R	550.00	800.00
265 Millstone R	1,200.00	1,400.00
266 Mishra's War Machine R	800.00	1,000.00
267 Nevinyrral's Disk R	1,500.00	1,800.00
268 Obsianus Golem U	150.00	300.00
269 Onulet R	850.00	1,100.00
270 Ornithopter U	350.00	500.00
271 Primal Clay R	800.00	1,000.00
272 Rocket Launcher R	550.00	800.00
273 Rod of Ruin U	120.00	250.00
275 Soul Net U	150.00	300.00
276 Sunglasses of Urza R	550.00	800.00
277 The Hive R	300.00	450.00
278 The Rack U	80.00	1,000.00
279 Throne of Bone U	150.00	300.00
280 Winter Orb R	1,300.00	1,500.00
281 Wooden Sphere U	150.00	300.00
282 Badlands R	2,500.00	3,000.00
283 Bayou R	2,350.00	2,800.00
284 Plateau R	2,600.00	3,200.00
285 Savannah R	2,600.00	3,200.00
286 Scrubland R	2,500.00	3,000.00
287 Taiga R	2,350.00	2,800.00
288 Tropical Island R	3,600.00	4,000.00
289 Tundra R	4,100.00	4,500.00
290 Underground Sea R	7,500.00	10,000.00
291 Volcanic Island R	6,000.00	6,500.00
292 Plains v1 L	250.00	400.00
293 Plains v2 L	250.00	400.00
294 Plains v3 L	250.00	400.00
295 Island v1 L	400.00	600.00
296 Island v2 L	400.00	600.00
297 Island v3 L	400.00	600.00
298 Swamp v1 L	300.00	450.00
299 Swamp v2 L	300.00	450.00
300 Swamp v3 L	300.00	450.00
301 Mountain v1 L	200.00	350.00
302 Mountain v2 L	200.00	350.00
303 Mountain v3 L	200.00	350.00
304 Forest v1 L	250.00	400.00
305 Forest v2 L	250.00	400.00
306 Forest v3 L	250.00	400.00

1995 Magic The Gathering 4th Edition

NNO Alabaster Potion C	.10	.20
NNO Amrou Kithkin C	.07	.15
NNO Angry Mob U	.12	.25
NNO Animate Wall R	.20	.40
NNO Armageddon R	2.50	5.00
NNO Balance R	1.00	2.00
NNO Benalish Hero C	.07	.15
NNO Black Ward U	.10	.20
NNO Blessing R	.25	.50
NNO Blue Ward U	.10	.20
NNO Brainwash C	.07	.15
NNO Castle U	.10	.20
NNO Circle of Protection Artifacts U	.15	.30
NNO Circle of Protection Black C	.07	.15
NNO Circle of Protection Blue C	.07	.15
NNO Circle of Protection Green C	.07	.15
NNO Circle of Protection Red C	.07	.15
NNO Circle of Protection White C	.07	.15
NNO Conversion U	.10	.20
NNO Crusade R	1.25	2.50
NNO Death Ward C	.07	.15
NNO Disenchant C	.10	.20
NNO Divine Transformation U	.15	.30
NNO Elder Land Wurm R	.20	.40
NNO Eye for an Eye R	.20	.40
NNO Fortified Area C	.07	.15
NNO Green Ward U	.10	.20
NNO Healing Salve C	.07	.15
NNO Holy Armor C	.07	.15
NNO Holy Strength C	.07	.15
NNO Island Sanctuary R	2.50	5.00
NNO Karma U	.10	.20
NNO Kismet U	.60	1.25
NNO Land Tax R	25.00	50.00
NNO Mesa Pegasus C	.07	.15
NNO Morale C	.07	.15
NNO Northern Paladin R	.30	.60
NNO Osai Vultures U	.10	.20
NNO Pearled Unicorn C	.07	.15
NNO Personal Incarnation R	.25	.50
NNO Piety C	.07	.15
NNO Pikemen C	.07	.15
NNO Purelace R	.20	.40
NNO Red Ward U	.12	.25
NNO Reverse Damage R	.25	.50
NNO Righteousness R	.30	.60
NNO Samite Healer C	.07	.15
NNO Savannah Lions R	1.50	3.00
NNO Seeker C	.07	.15
NNO Serra Angel U	1.50	3.00
NNO Spirit Link U	.50	1.00
NNO Swords to Plowshares U	2.50	5.00
NNO Tundra Wolves C	.07	.15
NNO Visions U	.12	.25
NNO Wall of Swords U	.10	.20
NNO White Knight U	.20	.40
NNO White Ward U	.10	.20
NNO Wrath of God R	5.00	10.00
NNO Air Elemental U	.10	.20
NNO Animate Artifact U	.12	.25
NNO Apprentice Wizard C	.12	.25
NNO Backfire U	.15	.30
NNO Blue Elemental Blast C	.10	.20
NNO Control Magic U	.50	1.00
NNO Counterspell U	1.50	3.00
NNO Creature Bond C	.07	.15
NNO Drain Power R	.75	1.50
NNO Energy Flux U	.12	.25
NNO Energy Tap C	.15	.30
NNO Erosion C	.07	.15
NNO Feedback U	.10	.20
NNO Flight C	.07	.15
NNO Flood C	.07	.15
NNO Gaseous Form C	.07	.15
NNO Ghost Ship U	.10	.20
NNO Giant Tortoise C	.07	.15
NNO Hurkyl's Recall R	1.25	2.50
NNO Island Fish Jasconius R	.15	.30
NNO Jump C	.07	.15
NNO Leviathan R	.25	.50
NNO Lifetap U	.10	.20
NNO Lord of Atlantis R	2.00	4.00
NNO Magical Hack R	.25	.50
NNO Mahamoti Djinn R	.30	.60
NNO Mana Short R	1.25	2.50
NNO Merfolk of the Pearl Trident C	.07	.15
NNO Mind Bomb U	.12	.25
NNO Phantasmal Forces U	.10	.20
NNO Phantasmal Terrain C	.07	.15
NNO Phantom Monster U	.10	.20
NNO Pirate Ship R	.20	.40
NNO Power Leak C	.07	.15
NNO Power Sink C	.07	.15
NNO Prodigal Sorcerer C	.07	.15
NNO Psionic Entity R	.20	.40
NNO Psychic Venom C	.07	.15
NNO Relic Bind R	.20	.40
NNO Sea Serpent C	.07	.15
NNO Segovian Leviathan U	.10	.20
NNO Sindbad U	.10	.20
NNO Siren's Call U	.10	.20
NNO Sleight of Mind R	.15	.30
NNO Spell Blast C	.07	.15
NNO Stasis R	4.00	8.00
NNO Steal Artifact U	.10	.20
NNO Sunken City C	.07	.15
NNO Thoughtlace R	.20	.40
NNO Time Elemental R	.25	.50
NNO Twiddle C	.15	.30
NNO Unstable Mutation C	.07	.15
NNO Unsummon C	.07	.15
NNO Volcanic Eruption R	.15	.30
NNO Wall of Air U	.10	.20
NNO Wall of Water U	.10	.20
NNO Water Elemental U	.20	.40
NNO Zephyr Falcon C	.07	.15
NNO Abomination U	.15	.30
NNO Animate Dead U	2.00	4.00
NNO Ashes to Ashes U	.25	.50
NNO Bad Moon R	1.50	3.00
NNO Black Knight U	.20	.40
NNO Blight U	.15	.30
NNO Bog Imp C	.07	.15
NNO Bog Wraith U	.12	.25
NNO Carrion Ants U	.10	.20
NNO Cosmic Horror R	.20	.40
NNO Cursed Land U	.10	.20
NNO Cyclopean Mummy C	.07	.15
NNO Dark Ritual C	.07	.15
NNO Deathgrip U	.15	.30
NNO Deathlace R	.15	.30
NNO Drain Life C	.10	.20
NNO Drudge Skeletons C	.07	.15
NNO El-Hajjaj R	.20	.40
NNO Erg Raiders C	.07	.15
NNO Evil Presence U	.12	.25
NNO Fear C	.07	.15
NNO Frozen Shade C	.07	.15
NNO Gloom U	.12	.25
NNO Greed R	2.00	4.00
NNO Howl from Beyond C	.07	.15
NNO Hypnotic Specter U	1.25	2.50
NNO Junun Efreet U	.10	.20
NNO Lord of the Pit R	.50	1.00
NNO Lost Soul C	.07	.15
NNO Marsh Gas C	.07	.15
NNO Mind Twist R	5.00	10.00
NNO Murk Dwellers C	.07	.15
NNO Nether Shadow R	1.00	2.00
NNO Nightmare R	.75	1.50
NNO Paralyze C	.07	.15
NNO Pestilence C	.15	.30
NNO Pit Scorpion C	.07	.15
NNO Plague Rats C	.07	.15
NNO Rag Man R	.20	.40
NNO Raise Dead C	.07	.15
NNO Royal Assassin R	2.50	5.00
NNO Scathe Zombies C	.07	.15
NNO Scavenging Ghoul U	.10	.20
NNO Sengir Vampire U	.25	.50
NNO Simulacrum U	.15	.30
NNO Sorceress Queen R	.50	1.00
NNO Spirit Shackle U	.10	.20
NNO Terror C	.10	.20
NNO Uncle Istvan U	.10	.20
NNO Unholy Strength C	.07	.15
NNO Vampire Bats C	.07	.15
NNO Wall of Bone U	.10	.20
NNO Warp Artifact R	.20	.40
NNO Weakness C	.07	.15
NNO Will-O'-The-Wisp R	2.00	4.00
NNO Word of Binding C	.07	.15
NNO Xenic Poltergeist R	.20	.40
NNO Zombie Master R	3.00	6.00
NNO Ali Baba U	.12	.25
NNO Ball Lightning R	2.00	4.00
NNO Bird Maiden C	.07	.15
NNO Blood Lust C	.10	.20
NNO Brothers of Fire C	.07	.15
NNO Burrowing U	.10	.20
NNO Cave People U	.10	.20
NNO Chaoslace R	.15	.30
NNO Crimson Manticore R	.15	.30
NNO Detonate U	.10	.20
NNO Disintegrate C	.07	.15
NNO Dragon Whelp U	.12	.25
NNO Dwarven Warriors C	.07	.15
NNO Earth Elemental U	.12	.25
NNO Earthquake R	.50	1.00
NNO Eternal Warrior C	.07	.15
NNO Fire Elemental U	.10	.20
NNO Fireball C	.07	.15
NNO Firebreathing C	.07	.15
NNO Fissure C	.07	.15
NNO Flashfires U	.10	.20
NNO Giant Strength C	.07	.15
NNO Goblin Balloon Brigade U	.10	.20
NNO Goblin King R	2.00	4.00
NNO Goblin Rock Sled C	.07	.15
NNO Gray Ogre C	.07	.15
NNO Hill Giant C	.07	.15
NNO Hurloon Minotaur C	.10	.20
NNO Hurr Jackal R	.20	.40
NNO Immolation C	.07	.15
NNO Inferno R	.25	.50
NNO Ironclaw Orcs C	.07	.15
NNO Keldon Warlord U	.10	.20
NNO Lightning Bolt C	1.50	3.00
NNO Magnetic Mountain R	.25	.50
NNO Mana Clash R	.30	.60
NNO Mana Flare R	7.50	15.00
NNO Manabarbs R	.50	1.00
NNO Mons's Goblin Raiders C	.07	.15

NNO Orcish Artillery U	.10	.20
NNO Orcish Oriflamme U	.10	.20
NNO Power Surge R	.50	1.00
NNO Pyrotechnics U	.10	.20
NNO Red Elemental Blast C	1.00	2.00
NNO Shatter C	.07	.15
NNO Shivan Dragon R	4.00	8.00
NNO Sisters of the Flame C	.07	.15
NNO Smoke R	2.00	4.00
NNO Stone Giant U	.10	.20
NNO Stone Rain C	.07	.15
NNO Tempest Efreet R	.20	.40
NNO The Brute C	.07	.15
NNO Tunnel U	.10	.20
NNO Uthden Troll U	.10	.20
NNO Wall of Dust U	.10	.20
NNO Wall of Fire U	.10	.20
NNO Wall of Stone U	.10	.20
NNO Winds of Change R	10.00	20.00
NNO Aspect of Wolf R	.30	.60
NNO Birds of Paradise R	7.50	15.00
NNO Carnivorous Plant C	.07	.15
NNO Channel U	.12	.25
NNO Cockatrice R	.25	.50
NNO Craw Wurm C	.07	.15
NNO Crumble U	.10	.20
NNO Desert Twister U	.10	.20
NNO Durkwood Boars C	.07	.15
NNO Elven Riders U	.10	.20
NNO Elvish Archers R	.30	.60
NNO Fog C	.12	.25
NNO Force of Nature R	.60	1.25
NNO Fungusaur R	.20	.40
NNO Gaea's Liege R	.20	.40
NNO Giant Growth C	.07	.15
NNO Giant Spider C	.07	.15
NNO Grizzly Bears C	.07	.15
NNO Hurricane U	.12	.25
NNO Instill Energy U	.30	.75
NNO Ironroot Treefolk C	.07	.15
NNO Killer Bees U	.10	.20
NNO Land Leeches C	.07	.15
NNO Ley Druid U	.10	.20
NNO Lifeforce U	.12	.25
NNO Lifelace R	.25	.50
NNO Living Artifact R	.25	.50
NNO Living Lands R	.20	.40
NNO Llanowar Elves C	.15	.30
NNO Lure U	.10	.20
NNO Marsh Viper C	.07	.15
NNO Nafs Asp C	.15	.30
NNO Pradesh Gypsies C	2.50	5.00
NNO Radjan Spirit U	.10	.20
NNO Rebirth R	.20	.40
NNO Regeneration C	.07	.15
NNO Sandstorm C	.07	.15
NNO Scryb Sprites C	.07	.15
NNO Shanodin Dryads C	.07	.15
NNO Stream of Life C	.07	.15
NNO Sylvan Library R	30.00	60.00
NNO Thicket Basilisk U	.10	.20
NNO Timber Wolves R	.20	.40
NNO Titania's Song R	.20	.40
NNO Tranquility C	.10	.20
NNO Tsunami U	.10	.20
NNO Untamed Wilds U	.12	.25
NNO Venom C	.07	.15
NNO Verduran Enchantress R	.30	.60
NNO Wall of Brambles U	.10	.20
NNO Wall of Ice U	.50	1.00
NNO Wall of Wood C	.07	.15
NNO Wanderlust U	.10	.20
NNO War Mammoth C	.07	.15
NNO Web R	.20	.40
NNO Whirling Dervish U	.10	.20
NNO Wild Growth C	.20	.40
NNO Winter Blast U	.10	.20
NNO Aladdin's Lamp R	.20	.40
NNO Aladdin's Ring R	.20	.40
NNO Amulet of Kroog C	.07	.15
NNO Ankh of Mishra R	1.50	3.00
NNO Armageddon Clock R	.20	.40
NNO Ashnod's Battle Gear U	.10	.20
NNO Battering Ram C	.07	.15
NNO Black Mana Battery R	.30	.60
NNO Black Vise U	.30	.75
NNO Blue Mana Battery R	.25	.50
NNO Bottle of Suleiman R	.20	.40
NNO Brass Man U	.10	.20
NNO Bronze Tablet R	.20	.40
NNO Celestial Prism U	.10	.20
NNO Clay Statue C	.07	.15
NNO Clockwork Avian R	.20	.40
NNO Clockwork Beast R	.20	.40
NNO Colossus of Sardia R	.25	.50
NNO Conservator U	.10	.20
NNO Coral Helm R	.15	.30
NNO Crystal Rod U	.10	.20
NNO Cursed Rack U	.15	.30
NNO Dancing Scimitar R	.20	.40
NNO Diabolic Machine U	.10	.20
NNO Dingus Egg R	.30	.75
NNO Disrupting Scepter R	.20	.40
NNO Dragon Engine R	.15	.30
NNO Ebony Horse R	.15	.30
NNO Fellwar Stone U	3.00	6.00
NNO Flying Carpet R	.20	.40
NNO Glasses of Urza U	.20	.40
NNO Grapeshot Catapult C	.07	.15
NNO Green Mana Battery R	.30	.60
NNO Helm of Chatzuk R	.20	.40
NNO Howling Mine R	3.00	6.00
NNO Iron Star U	.10	.20
NNO Ivory Cup U	.10	.20
NNO Ivory Tower R	.30	.75
NNO Jade Monolith R	.20	.40
NNO Jandor's Saddlebags R	.30	.60
NNO Jayemdae Tome R	.20	.40
NNO Kormus Bell R	.30	.60
NNO Library of Leng U	1.00	2.00
NNO Mana Vault R	30.00	75.00
NNO Meekstone R	3.00	6.00
NNO Millstone R	.25	.50
NNO Mishra's War Machine R	.20	.40
NNO Nevinyrral's Disk R	2.00	4.00
NNO Obsianus Golem U	.10	.20
NNO Onulet R	.20	.40
NNO Ornithopter U	.20	.40
NNO Primal Clay R	.20	.40
NNO Red Mana Battery R	.25	.50
NNO Rod of Ruin U	.10	.20
NNO Shapeshifter U	.12	.25
NNO Soul Net U	.10	.20
NNO Sunglasses of Urza R	.20	.40
NNO Tawnos's Wand U	.10	.20
NNO Tawnos's Weaponry U	.10	.20
NNO Tetravus R	.30	.75
NNO The Hive R	.25	.50
NNO The Rack U	1.00	2.00
NNO Throne of Bone U	.10	.20
NNO Triskelion R	2.00	4.00
NNO Urza's Avenger R	.30	.60
NNO Wall of Spears C	.07	.15
NNO White Mana Battery R	.25	.50
NNO Winter Orb R	10.00	20.00
NNO Wooden Sphere U	.10	.20
NNO Yotian Soldier C	.07	.15
NNO Mishra's Factory U	2.00	4.00
NNO Oasis U	.15	.30
NNO Strip Mine U	10.00	20.00
NNO Plains v2 L	.20	.40
NNO Plains v2 L	.20	.40
NNO Plains v3 L	.20	.40
NNO Island v1 L	.25	.50
NNO Island v2 L	.25	.50
NNO Island v3 L	.25	.50
NNO Swamp v1 L	.20	.40
NNO Swamp v2 L	.20	.40
NNO Swamp v3 L	.20	.40
NNO Mountain v1 L	.20	.40
NNO Mountain v2 L	.20	.40
NNO Mountain v3 L	.20	.40
NNO Forest v1 L	.15	.30
NNO Forest v2 L	.15	.30
NNO Forest v3 L	.15	.30

1995 Magic The Gathering Chronicles

1 Abu Ja'far U3	.12	.25
2 Akron Legionnaire U1	.12	.25
3 Angelic Voices U1	.25	.50
4 Blood of the Martyr U3	.12	.25
5 D'Avenant Archer C3	.12	.25
6 Divine Offering C3	.12	.25
7 Indestructible Aura C3	.12	.25
8 Ivory Guardians U3	.12	.25
9 Keepers of the Faith C3	.12	.25
10 Petra Sphinx U1	.12	.25
11 Repentant Blacksmith C3	.12	.25
12 Shield Wall U3	.12	.25
13 War Elephant C3	.12	.25
14 Witch Hunter U3	.12	.25
15 Azure Drake U3	.12	.25
16 Boomerang C3	.12	.25
17 Dance of Many U1	.12	.25
18 Dandan C3	.12	.25
19 Enchantment Alteration U3	.12	.25
20 Fishliver Oil C3	.12	.25
21 Flash Flood C3	.12	.25
22 Juxtapose U1	.12	.25
23 Puppet Master U3	.12	.25
24 Recall U3	.12	.25
25 Remove Soul C3	.12	.25
26 Teleport U1	.12	.25
27 Wall of Vapor C3	.12	.25
28 Wall of Wonder U3	.12	.25
29 Banshee U3	.12	.25
30 Bog Rats C3	.12	.25
31 Cuombajj Witches C3	.25	.50
32 Fallen Angel U3	.12	.25
33 Giant Slug U3	.12	.25
34 Hasran Ogress C3	.12	.25
35 Hell's Caretaker C3	1.25	2.50
36 Shimian Night Stalker U1	.12	.25
37 Takklemaggot U3	.12	.25
38 The Fallen U3	.12	.25
39 The Wretched C3	.20	.40
40 Transmutation C3	.12	.25
41 Wall of Shadows U1	.12	.25
42 Yawgmoth Demon U1	.12	.25
43 Active Volcano C3	.12	.25
44 Aladdin U1	.12	.25
45 Beasts of Bogardan U3	.12	.25
46 Blood Moon U1	20.00	40.00
47 Fire Drake U3	.12	.25
48 Goblin Artisans U3	.12	.25
49 Goblin Digging Team C3	.12	.25
50 Goblin Shrine C3	.12	.25
51 Goblins of the Flarg C3	.12	.25
52 Lands Edge U1	.12	.25
53 Mountain Yeti C3	.12	.25
54 Primordial Ooze U3	.12	.25
55 Wall of Heat C3	.12	.25
56 Wall of Opposition U3	.12	.25
57 Argothian Pixies C3	.12	.25
58 Cat Warriors C3	.12	.25
59 Cocoon U3	.12	.25
60 Concordant Crossroads U1	4.00	8.00
61 Craw Giant U3	.12	.25
62 Cyclone U1	.12	.25
63 Emerald Dragonfly C3	.12	.25
64 Erhnam Djinn U3	.12	.25
65 Ghazban Ogre C3	.12	.25
66 Metamorphosis C3	.12	.25
67 Rabid Wombat U3	.12	.25
68 Revelation U1	.12	.25
69 Scavenger Folk C3	.12	.25
70 Storm Seeker U3	.12	.25
71 Arcades Sabboth U1/:W:/:B:	.25	.50
72 Axelrod Gunnarson U1/	.12	.25
73 Ayesha Tanaka U1/:B:	.12	.25
74 Chromium U1/:B:/	.30	.60
75 Dakkon Blackblade U1/:B:/	.30	.60
76 Gabriel Angelfire U1/:W:	.20	.40
77 Johan U1/:W:	.20	.40
78 Kei Takahashi C1/:W:	.12	.25
79 Marhault Elsdragon C1	.12	.25
80 Nebuchadnezzar U1/	.12	.25
81 Nicol Bolas U1//	.75	1.50
82 Palladia-Mors U1/:W:	.25	.50
83 Rubinia Soulsinger U1/:W:/:B:	.12	.25
84 Sivitri Scarzam C1/	.12	.25
85 Sol'kanar the Swamp King U1//	.12	.25
86 Stangg U1	.12	.25
87 Tobias Andrion C1/:B:	.12	.25
88 Tor Wauki C1/	.12	.25
89 Vaevictis Asmadi U1/	.30	.60
90 Xira Arien U1/	.25	.50
91 Arena of the Ancients U1	.30	.60
92 Ashnod's Altar C2	.75	1.50
93 Ashnod's Transmogrant C2	.12	.25
94 Barl's Cage U1	.12	.25
95 Book of Rass U1	.12	.25
96 Bronze Horse U1	.12	.25
97 Feldon's Cane C2	.12	.25
98 Fountain of Youth C2	.12	.25
99 Gauntlets of Chaos U1	.12	.25
100 Horn of Deafening U1	.12	.25
101 Jalum Tome U1	.12	.25
102 Jeweled Bird U1	.12	.25
103 Living Armor C2	.12	.25
104 Obelisk of Undoing U1	.12	.25
105 Rakalite U1	.12	.25
106 Runesword C2	.12	.25
107 Sentinel U1	.20	.40
108 Serpent Generator U1	.25	.50
109 Tormod's Crypt C2	.25	.50
110 Triassic Egg U1	.12	.25
111 Voodoo Doll U1	.12	.25
112 City of Brass U1	2.00	4.00
113 Safe Haven U1	.12	.25
114 Urza's Mine v4 C1	.75	1.50
114 Urza's Mine v4 C1	.75	1.50
114 Urza's Mine v3 C1	.75	1.50
114 Urza's Mine v3 C1	.75	1.50
115 Urza's Power Plant v4 C1	.75	1.50
115 Urza's Power Plant v4 C1	.75	1.50
115 Urza's Power Plant v3 C1	.75	1.50
115 Urza's Power Plant v3 C1	.75	1.50
116 Urza's Tower v4 C1	.75	1.50
116 Urza's Tower v4 C1	.75	1.50
116 Urza's Tower v3 C1	.75	1.50
116 Urza's Tower v3 C1	.75	1.50

1995 Magic The Gathering Homelands

1 Abbey Gargoyles U3	.12	.25
2 Abbey Matron v1 C2	.12	.25
3 Abbey Matron v2 C2	.12	.25
3 Aysen Bureaucrats v1 C2	.12	.25
3 Aysen Bureaucrats v2 C2	.12	.25
4 Aysen Crusader U1	.40	.80
5 Aysen Highway U1	.12	.25
6 Beast Walkers U1	.12	.25
7 Death Speakers U3	.12	.25
8 Hazduhr the Abbot U1	.12	.25
9 Leeches U1	4.00	8.00
10 Mesa Falcon v1 C2	.12	.25
10 Mesa Falcon v2 C2	.12	.25
11 Prophecy C1	.12	.25
12 Rashka the Slayer U3	.12	.25
13 Samite Alchemist v1 C2	.12	.25
13 Samite Alchemist v2 C2	.12	.25
14 Serra Aviary U1	3.00	6.00
15 Serra Bestiary C1	.12	.25
16 Serra Inquisitors U3	.12	.25
17 Serra Paladin C1	.12	.25
18 Soraya the Falconer U1	2.50	5.00
19 Trade Caravan v2 C2	.12	.25
19 Trade Caravan v1 C2	.12	.25
20 Truce U1	.12	.25
21 Aether Storm U3	.12	.25
22 Baki's Curse U1	.12	.25
23 Chain Stasis U1	3.00	6.00
24 Coral Reef C1	.12	.25
25 Dark Maze v1 C2	.40	.80
25 Dark Maze v2 C2	.12	.25
26 Forget U1	.12	.25
27 Giant Albatross v1 C2	.12	.25
27 Giant Albatross v2 C2	.12	.25
28 Giant Oyster U3	.12	.25
29 Jinx C1	.12	.25
30 Labyrinth Minotaur v1 C2	.12	.25
30 Labyrinth Minotaur v2 C2	.12	.25
31 Marjhan U1	.12	.25
32 Memory Lapse v1 C2	.12	.25
32 Memory Lapse v2 C2	.12	.25
33 Merchant Scroll C1	5.00	10.00
34 Mystic Decree U1	4.00	8.00
35 Narwhal U1	2.50	5.00
36 Reef Pirates v1 C2	.12	.25
36 Reef Pirates v2 C2	.12	.25
37 Reveka, Wizard Savant U1	3.00	6.00
38 Sea Sprite U3	.12	.25
39 Sea Troll U3	.12	.25
40 Wall of Kelp U1	6.00	12.00
41 Baron Sengir U1	10.00	20.00
42 Black Carriage U1	.12	.25
43 Broken Visage U1	.12	.25
44 Cemetery Gate v1 C2	.40	.80
44 Cemetery Gate v2 C2	.40	.80
45 Drudge Spell U3	.12	.25
46 Dry Spell v1 C2	.40	.80
46 Dry Spell v2 C2	.40	.80
47 Feast of the Unicorn v1 C2	.40	.80
47 Feast of the Unicorn v2 C2	.40	.80
48 Funeral March C1	.12	.25
49 Ghost Hounds U3	.12	.25
50 Grandmother Sengir U1	1.00	2.00
51 Greater Werewolf C1	.12	.25
52 Headstone C1	.12	.25
53 Ihsan's Shade U3	.12	.25
54 Irini Sengir U3	.12	.25
55 Koskun Falls U1	7.50	15.00
56 Sengir Autocrat U1	.12	.25
57 Sengir Bats v1 C2	.12	.25
57 Sengir Bats v2 C2	.12	.25
58 Timmerian Fiends U1	.50	1.00
59 Torture v1 C2	.40	.80
59 Torture v2 C2	.40	.80
60 Veldrane of Sengir U1	.60	1.25
61 Aliban's Tower v1 C2	.12	.25
61 Aliban's Tower v2 C2	.12	.25
62 Ambush C1	.12	.25
63 Ambush Party v1 C2	.12	.25
63 Ambush Party v2 C2	.12	.25
64 An-Zerrin Ruins U1	5.00	10.00
65 Anaba Ancestor U1	.40	.80
66 Anaba Bodyguard v1 C2	.12	.25
66 Anaba Bodyguard v2 C2	.12	.25
67 Anaba Shaman v1 C2	.12	.25
67 Anaba Shaman v2 C2	.12	.25
68 Anaba Spirit Crafter U1	4.00	8.00
69 Chandler C1	.12	.25
70 Dwarven Pony U1	1.50	3.00
71 Dwarven Sea Clan U1	.12	.25
72 Dwarven Trader v1 C2	.12	.25
72 Dwarven Trader v2 C2	.12	.25
73 Eron the Relentless U3	.12	.25
74 Evaporate U3	.12	.25
75 Heart Wolf U1	1.00	2.00
76 Ironclaw Curse U1	.12	.25
77 Joven C1	.12	.25
78 Orcish Mine U3	.12	.25
79 Retribution U3	.12	.25
80 Winter Sky U1	2.00	4.00
81 An-Havva Constable U1	.12	.25
82 An-Havva Inn U3	.12	.25
83 Autumn Willow U1	.40	.80
84 Carapace v1 C2	.12	.25
84 Carapace v2 C2	.12	.25
85 Daughter of Autumn U1	.12	.25
86 Faerie Noble U1	3.00	6.00
87 Folk of An-Havva v1 C2	.12	.25
87 Folk of An-Havva v2 C2	.12	.25
88 Hungry Mist v1 C2	.40	.80
88 Hungry Mist v2 C2	.40	.80
89 Joven's Ferrets C1	.12	.25
90 Leaping Lizard C1	.12	.25
91 Mammoth Harness U1	.12	.25
92 Primal Order U1	1.25	2.50
93 Renewal C1	.12	.25
94 Root Spider U3	.12	.25
95 Roots U3	.12	.25
96 Rysorian Badger U1	1.00	2.00
97 Shrink v1 C2	.12	.25
97 Shrink v2 C2	.12	.25
98 Spectral Bears U3	.12	.25
99 Willow Faerie v1 C2	.50	1.00
99 Willow Faerie v2 C2	.50	1.00
100 Willow Priestess U1	7.50	15.00
101 Apocalypse Chime U1	2.50	5.00
102 Clockwork Gnomes C1	.12	.25
103 Clockwork Steed C1	.12	.25
104 Clockwork Swarm C1	.12	.25
105 Didgeridoo U1	15.00	30.00
106 Ebony Rhino C1	.12	.25
107 Feroz's Ban U1	.12	.25
108 Joven's Tools U3	.12	.25
109 Roterothopter C1	.12	.25
110 Serrated Arrows C1	.12	.25
111 An-Havva Township U3	.12	.25
112 Aysen Abbey U3	.12	.25
113 Castle Sengir U3	.12	.25
114 Koskun Keep U3	.12	.25
115 Wizards School U3	.12	.25

1995 Magic The Gathering Ice Age

1 Adarkar Unicorn C	.07	.15
2 Arctic Foxes C	.07	.15
3 Arenson's Aura C	.07	.15
4 Armor of Faith C	.07	.15
5 Battle Cry U	.12	.25
6 Black Scarab U	.12	.25
7 Blessed Wine C	.07	.15
8 Blinking Spirit R	.25	.50
9 Blue Scarab U	.15	.30
10 Call to Arms R	1.25	2.50
11 Caribou Range R	.25	.50
12 Circle of Protection Black C	.07	.15
13 Circle of Protection Blue C	.07	.15
14 Circle of Protection Green C	.07	.15
15 Circle of Protection Red C	.07	.15
16 Circle of Protection White C	.07	.15
17 Cold Snap U	.12	.25
18 Cooperation C	.07	.15
19 Death Ward C	.07	.15
20 Disenchant C	.07	.15
21 Drought U	.20	.40
22 Elvish Healer C	.07	.15
23 Enduring Renewal R	2.00	4.00
24 Energy Storm R	5.00	10.00
25 Formation R	1.50	3.00
26 Fylgja C	.07	.15
27 General Jarkeld R	3.00	6.00
28 Green Scarab U	.15	.30
29 Hallowed Ground U	.15	.30
30 Heal C	.07	.15
31 Hipparion U	.10	.20
32 Justice U	.10	.20
33 Kelsinko Ranger C	.07	.15
34 Kjeldoran Elite Guard U	.10	.20
35 Kjeldoran Guard C	.07	.15
36 Kjeldoran Knight R	1.00	2.00
37 Kjeldoran Phalanx R	1.00	2.00
38 Kjeldoran Royal Guard R	.25	.50
39 Kjeldoran Skycaptain U	.10	.20
40 Kjeldoran Skyknight C	.07	.15
41 Kjeldoran Warrior C	.07	.15
42 Lightning Blow R	1.50	3.00
43 Lost Order of Jarkeld R	.25	.50
44 Mercenaries R	1.00	2.00
45 Order of the Sacred Torch R	.60	1.25
46 Order of the White Shield U	.15	.30
47 Prismatic Ward C	.07	.15
48 Rally C	.07	.15
49 Red Scarab U	.12	.25
50 Sacred Boon U	.10	.20
51 Seraph R	.50	1.00
52 Shield Bearer C	.07	.15

53 Snow Hound U	.20	.40
54 Swords to Plowshares U	3.00	6.00
55 Warning C	.07	.15
56 White Scarab U	.20	.40
57 Arnjlot's Ascent C	.07	.15
58 Balduvian Conjurer U	.15	.30
59 Balduvian Shaman C	.07	.15
60 Binding Grasp U	.10	.20
61 Brainstorm C	.75	1.50
62 Breath of Dreams U	.12	.25
63 Clairvoyance C	.12	.25
64 Counterspell C	1.25	2.50
65 Deflection R	.15	.30
66 Dreams of the Dead U	.12	.25
67 Enervate C	.07	.15
68 Errant Minion C	.07	.15
69 Essence Flare C	.07	.15
70 Force Void U	.20	.40
71 Glacial Wall U	.15	.30
72 Hydroblast C	.30	.75
73 Iceberg U	.15	.30
74 Icy Prison R	.25	.50
75 Illusionary Forces C	.07	.15
76 Illusionary Presence R	1.50	3.00
77 Illusionary Terrain U	.12	.25
78 Illusionary Wall C	.07	.15
79 Illusions of Grandeur R	10.00	20.00
80 Infuse C	.07	.15
81 Krovikan Sorcerer C	.07	.15
82 Magus of the Unseen R	.50	1.00
83 Mesmeric Trance R	1.50	3.00
84 Mistfolk C	.07	.15
85 Musician R	3.00	6.00
86 Mystic Might R	1.25	2.50
87 Mystic Remora C	5.00	10.00
88 Phantasmal Mount U	.10	.20
89 Polar Kraken R	4.00	8.00
90 Portent C	.20	.40
91 Power Sink C	.07	.15
92 Ray of Command C	.07	.15
93 Ray of Erasure C	.07	.15
94 Reality Twist R	3.00	6.00
95 Sea Spirit U	.10	.20
96 Shyft R	.20	.40
97 Sibilant Spirit R	.20	.40
98 Silver Erne U	.10	.20
99 Sleight of Mind U	.10	.20
100 Snow Devil C	.07	.15
101 Snowfall C	.07	.15
102 Soldevi Machinist U	.12	.25
103 Soul Barrier U	.60	1.25
104 Thunder Wall U	.10	.20
105 Updraft U	.12	.25
106 Wind Spirit U	.10	.20
107 Winter's Chill R	7.50	15.00
108 Word of Undoing C	.07	.15
109 Wrath of Marit Lage R	.20	.40
110 Zur's Weirding R	.75	1.50
111 Zuran Enchanter C	.07	.15
112 Zuran Spellcaster C	.12	.25
113 Abyssal Specter U	.10	.20
114 Ashen Ghoul U	.15	.30
115 Brine Shaman C	.10	.20
116 Burnt Offering C	.25	.50
117 Cloak of Confusion C	.07	.15
118 Dance of the Dead U	5.00	10.00
119 Dark Banishing C	.07	.15
120 Dark Ritual C	.50	1.00
121 Demonic Consultation U	12.50	25.00
122 Dread Wight R	.25	.50
123 Drift of the Dead U	.12	.25
124 Fear C	.07	.15
125 Flow of Maggots R	1.00	2.00
126 Foul Familiar C	.07	.15
127 Gangrenous Zombies C	.12	.25
128 Gaze of Pain C	.07	.15
129 Gravebind R	2.00	4.00
130 Hecatomb R	.50	1.00
131 Hoar Shade C	.07	.15
132 Howl from Beyond C	.07	.15
133 Hyalopterous Lemure U	.12	.25
134 Icequake U	.50	1.00
135 Infernal Darkness R	2.50	5.00
136 Infernal Denizen R	2.00	4.00
137 Kjeldoran Dead C	.07	.15
138 Knight of Stromgald U	.15	.30
139 Krovikan Elementalist U	.10	.20
140 Krovikan Fetish C	.07	.15
141 Krovikan Vampire U	.20	.40
142 Legions of Lim-Dul C	.07	.15
143 Leshrac's Rite U	.10	.20
144 Leshrac's Sigil U	.20	.40
145 Lim-Dul's Cohort C	.07	.15
146 Lim-Dul's Hex U	.15	.30
147 Mind Ravel C	.07	.15
148 Mind Warp U	.10	.20
149 Mind Whip R	.30	.60
150 Minion of Leshrac R	.75	1.50
151 Minion of Tevesh Szat R	1.25	2.50
152 Mole Worms U	.10	.20
153 Moor Fiend C	.07	.15
154 Necropotence R	25.00	50.00
155 Norritt C	.07	.15
156 Oath of Lim-Dul R	.30	.60
157 Pestilence Rats C	.15	.30
158 Pox R	7.50	15.00
159 Seizures C	.07	.15
160 Songs of the Damned C	.30	.75
161 Soul Burn C	.07	.15
162 Soul Kiss C	.07	.15
163 Spoils of Evil R	6.00	12.00
164 Spoils of War R	2.00	4.00
165 Stench of Evil U	.10	.20
166 Stromgald Cabal R	.25	.50
167 Touch of Death C	.07	.15
168 Withering Wisps U	.20	.40
169 Aggression U	.15	.30
170 Anarchy U	.25	.50
171 Avalanche U	.10	.20
172 Balduvian Barbarians C	.07	.15
173 Balduvian Hydra R	2.00	4.00
174 Barbarian Guides C	.07	.15
175 Battle Frenzy C	.07	.15
176 Bone Shaman C	.07	.15
177 Brand of Ill Omen R	2.00	4.00
178 Chaos Lord R	.30	.60
179 Chaos Moon R	.30	.75
180 Conquer U	.12	.25
181 Curse of Marit Lage R	.30	.60
182 Dwarven Armory R	.20	.40
183 Errantry C	.07	.15
184 Flame Spirit U	.10	.20
185 Flare C	.07	.15
186 Game of Chaos R	1.50	3.00
187 Glacial Crevasses R	6.00	12.00
188 Goblin Mutant U	.10	.20
189 Goblin Sappers C	.07	.15
190 Goblin Ski Patrol C	.07	.15
191 Goblin Snowman U	.20	.40
192 Grizzled Wolverine C	.07	.15
193 Imposing Visage C	.07	.15
194 Incinerate C	.12	.25
195 Jokulhaups R	4.00	8.00
196 Karplusan Giant U	.10	.20
197 Karplusan Yeti R	.25	.50
198 Lava Burst C	.07	.15
199 Marton Stromgald R	12.50	25.00
200 Melee U	.10	.20
201 Melting U	.12	.25
202 Meteor Shower C	.07	.15
203 Mountain Goat C	.07	.15
204 Mudslide R	6.00	12.00
205 Orcish Cannoneers U	.12	.25
206 Orcish Conscripts C	.07	.15
207 Orcish Farmer C	.07	.15
208 Orcish Healer U	.10	.20
209 Orcish Librarian R	.25	.50
210 Orcish Lumberjack C	.20	.40
211 Orcish Squatters R	.25	.50
212 Panic C	.15	.30
213 Pyroblast C	1.50	3.00
214 Pyroclasm U	.30	.60
215 Sabretooth Tiger C	.07	.15
216 Shatter C	.07	.15
217 Stone Rain C	.07	.15
218 Stone Spirit U	.10	.20
219 Stonehands C	.07	.15
220 Tor Giant C	.07	.15
221 Total War R	.30	.75
222 Vertigo U	.10	.20
223 Wall of Lava U	.12	.25
224 Word of Blasting U	.10	.20
225 Aurochs C	.07	.15
226 Balduvian Bears C	.20	.40
227 Blizzard R	4.00	8.00
228 Brown Ouphe C	.07	.15
229 Chub Toad C	.07	.15
230 Dire Wolves C	.07	.15
231 Earthlore C	.07	.15
232 Elder Druid R	.25	.50
233 Essence Filter C	.07	.15
234 Fanatical Fever U	.10	.20
235 Folk of the Pines C	.07	.15
236 Forbidden Lore R	.25	.50
237 Forgotten Lore U	.20	.40
238 Foxfire C	.07	.15
239 Freyalise Supplicant U	.10	.20
240 Freyalise's Charm U	.10	.20
241 Freyalise's Winds R	.30	.60
242 Fyndhorn Brownie C	.07	.15
243 Fyndhorn Elder U	.10	.20
244 Fyndhorn Elves C	.50	1.00
245 Fyndhorn Pollen R	1.50	3.00
246 Giant Growth C	.07	.15
247 Gorilla Pack C	.07	.15
248 Hot Springs R	1.25	2.50
249 Hurricane U	.15	.30
250 Johtull Wurm U	.10	.20
251 Juniper Order Druid C	.07	.15
252 Lhurgoyf R	1.00	2.00
253 Lure U	.10	.20
254 Maddening Wind U	.10	.20
255 Nature's Lore U	3.00	6.00
256 Pale Bears R	2.00	4.00
257 Pygmy Allosaurus R	.30	.75
258 Pyknite C	.07	.15
259 Regeneration C	.07	.15
260 Rime Dryad C	.07	.15
261 Ritual of Subdual R	2.50	5.00
262 Scaled Wurm C	.07	.15
263 Shambling Strider C	.07	.15
264 Snowblind R	2.00	4.00
265 Stampede R	.25	.50
266 Stunted Growth R	.30	.75
267 Tarpan C	.10	.20
268 Thermokarst U	.30	.75
269 Thoughtleech U	.10	.20
270 Tinder Wall C	.20	.40
271 Touch of Vitae U	.20	.40
272 Trailblazer R	1.50	3.00
273 Venomous Breath U	.10	.20
274 Wall of Pine Needles U	.12	.25
275 Whiteout U	.20	.40
276 Wiitigo R	.25	.50
277 Wild Growth C	.25	.50
278 Woolly Mammoths C	.07	.15
279 Woolly Spider C	.07	.15
280 Yavimaya Gnats U	.12	.25
281 Altar of Bone R/:W:	7.50	15.00
282 Centaur Archer U	.10	.20
283 Chromatic Armor R/:B:	2.00	4.00
284 Diabolic Vision U/	.20	.40
285 Earthlink R/	2.50	5.00
286 Elemental Augury R//	.30	.75
287 Essence Vortex U/	.20	.40
288 Fiery Justice R/:W:	.30	.60
289 Fire Covenant U/	4.00	8.00
290 Flooded Woodlands R/	.75	1.50
291 Fumarole U/	.12	.25
292 Ghostly Flame R/	.25	.50
293 Giant Trap Door Spider U	.12	.25
294 Glaciers R/:B:	.20	.40
295 Hymn of Rebirth U/:W:	.15	.30
296 Kjeldoran Frostbeast U/:W:	.10	.20
297 Merieke Ri Berit R/:B:/	1.25	2.50
298 Monsoon R	.30	.60
299 Mountain Titan R/	.15	.30
300 Reclamation R/:W:	.30	.75
301 Skeleton Ship R/	6.00	12.00
302 Spectral Shield U/:B:	.10	.20
303 Storm Spirit R/:W:/:B:	2.00	4.00
304 Stormbind R	.30	.75
305 Wings of Aesthir U/:B:	.12	.25
306 Adarkar Sentinel U	.10	.20
307 Aegis of the Meek R	2.00	4.00
308 Amulet of Quoz R	2.50	5.00
309 Arcum's Sleigh U	.12	.25
310 Arcum's Weathervane U	.12	.25
311 Arcum's Whistle U	.12	.25
312 Barbed Sextant C	.15	.30
313 Baton of Morale U	.15	.30
314 Celestial Sword R	.25	.50
315 Crown of the Ages R	.30	.60
316 Despotic Scepter R	.60	1.25
317 Elkin Bottle R	.20	.40
318 Fyndhorn Bow U	.10	.20
319 Goblin Lyre R	.20	.40
320 Hematite Talisman U	.12	.25
321 Ice Cauldron R	5.00	10.00
322 Icy Manipulator U	.50	1.00
323 Infinite Hourglass R	.20	.40
324 Jester's Cap R	10.00	20.00
325 Jester's Mask R	10.00	20.00
326 Jeweled Amulet U	2.00	4.00
327 Lapis Lazuli Talisman U	.15	.30
328 Malachite Talisman U	.20	.40
329 Nacre Talisman U	.20	.40
330 Naked Singularity R	.75	1.50
331 Onyx Talisman U	.10	.20
332 Pentagram of the Ages R	.20	.40
333 Pit Trap U	.10	.20
334 Runed Arch R	.20	.40
335 Shield of the Ages U	.12	.25
336 Skull Catapult U	.10	.20
337 Snow Fortress R	.30	.75
338 Soldevi Golem R	1.25	2.50
339 Soldevi Simulacrum U	.10	.20
340 Staff of the Ages R	.20	.40
341 Sunstone U	2.00	4.00
342 Time Bomb R	.30	.60
343 Urza's Bauble U	2.00	4.00
344 Vexing Arcanix R	.25	.50
345 Vibrating Sphere R	.25	.50
346 Walking Wall U	.12	.25
347 Wall of Shields U	.15	.30
348 War Chariot U	.10	.20
349 Whalebone Glider U	.10	.20
350 Zuran Orb U	2.50	5.00
351 Adarkar Wastes R	6.00	12.00
352 Brushland R	5.00	10.00
353 Glacial Chasm U	2.50	5.00
354 Halls of Mist R	6.00	12.00
355 Ice Floe U	.15	.30
356 Karplusan Forest R	4.00	8.00
357 Land Cap R	2.00	4.00
358 Lava Tubes R	2.00	4.00
359 River Delta R	2.50	5.00
360 Sulfurous Springs R	10.00	20.00
361 Timberline Ridge R	2.00	4.00
362 Underground River R	7.50	15.00
363 Veldt R	2.50	5.00
364 Plains v1 L	.30	.60
365 Plains v2 L	.20	.40
366 Plains v3 L	.25	.50
367 Snow-Covered Plains L	1.00	2.00
368 Island v1 L	.25	.50
369 Island v2 L	.25	.50
370 Island v3 L	.25	.50
371 Snow-Covered Island L	2.00	4.00
372 Snow-Covered Swamp L	1.50	3.00
373 Swamp v1 L	.50	1.00
374 Swamp v2 L	.30	.60
375 Swamp v3 L	.30	.60
376 Mountain v1 L	.30	.75
377 Mountain v2 L	.30	.75
378 Mountain v3 L	.30	.75
379 Snow-Covered Mountain L	1.00	2.00
380 Forest v1 L	.60	1.25
381 Forest v2 L	.50	1.00
382 Forest v3 L	.30	.60
383 Snow-Covered Forest L	1.50	3.00

1996 Magic The Gathering Alliances

1 Carrier Pigeons v1 C	.07	.15
1 Carrier Pigeons v2 C	.07	.15
2 Errand of Duty v1 C	.07	.15
2 Errand of Duty v2 C	.07	.15
3 Exile R	1.25	2.50
4 Inheritance U	.25	.50
5 Ivory Gargoyle R	1.50	3.00
6 Juniper Order Advocate U	.10	.20
7 Kjeldoran Escort v1 C	.07	.15
7 Kjeldoran Escort v2 C	.07	.15
8 Kjeldoran Home Guard U	.10	.20
9 Kjeldoran Pride v1 C	.07	.15
9 Kjeldoran Pride v2 C	.07	.15
10 Martyrdom v1 C	.07	.15
10 Martyrdom v2 C	.07	.15
11 Noble Steeds v1 C	.07	.15
11 Noble Steeds v2 C	.07	.15
12 Reinforcements v1 C	.07	.15
12 Reinforcements v2 C	.07	.15
13 Reprisal v1 C	.07	.15
13 Reprisal v2 C	.07	.15
14 Royal Decree R	2.00	4.00
15 Royal Herbalist v1 C	.07	.15
15 Royal Herbalist v2 C	.07	.15
16 Scars of the Veteran U	.10	.20
17 Seasoned Tactician U	.10	.20
18 Sustaining Spirit R	4.00	8.00
19 Sworn Defender R	2.00	4.00
20 Unlikely Alliance U	.10	.20
21 Wild Aesthir v1 C	.07	.15
21 Wild Aesthir v2 C	.07	.15
22 Arcane Denial v1 C	.50	1.00
22 Arcane Denial v2 C	.07	.15
23 Awesome Presence v1 C	.07	.15
23 Awesome Presence v2 C	.07	.15
24 Benthic Explorers v1 C	.07	.15
24 Benthic Explorers v2 C	.07	.15
25 Browse U	.10	.20
26 Diminishing Returns R	.30	.75
27 False Demise v1 C	.07	.15
27 False Demise v2 C	.07	.15
28 Force of Will U	100.00	200.00
29 Foresight v1 C	.15	.30
29 Foresight v2 C	.07	.15
30 Lat-Nam's Legacy v1 C	.07	.15
30 Lat-Nam's Legacy v2 C	.07	.15
31 Library of Lat-Nam R	.25	.50
32 Phantasmal Sphere R	2.00	4.00
33 Soldevi Heretic v1 C	.07	.15
33 Soldevi Heretic v2 C	.07	.15
34 Soldevi Sage v1 C	.07	.15
34 Soldevi Sage v2 C	.07	.15
35 Spiny Starfish U	.15	.30
36 Storm Crow v1 C	.07	.15
36 Storm Crow v2 C	.07	.15
37 Storm Elemental U	.10	.20
38 Suffocation U	.10	.20
39 Thought Lash R	15.00	30.00
40 Tidal Control R	4.00	8.00
41 Viscerid Armor v1 C	.07	.15
41 Viscerid Armor v2 C	.07	.15
42 Viscerid Drone U	.10	.20
43 Balduvian Dead U	.10	.20
44 Casting of Bones v1 C	.07	.15
44 Casting of Bones v2 C	.07	.15
45 Contagion U	.30	.75
46 Diseased Vermin U	.10	.20
47 Dystopia R	7.50	15.00
48 Fatal Lore R	3.00	6.00
49 Feast or Famine v1 C	.07	.15
49 Feast or Famine v2 C	.07	.15
50 Fevered Strength v1 C	.07	.15
50 Fevered Strength v2 C	.07	.15
51 Insidious Bookworms v1 C	.07	.15
51 Insidious Bookworms v2 C	.07	.15
52 Keeper of Tresserhorn R	2.00	4.00
53 Krovikan Horror R	4.00	8.00
54 Krovikan Plague U	.10	.20
55 Lim-Dul's High Guard v1 C	.07	.15
55 Lim-Dul's High Guard v2 C	.07	.15
56 Misinformation U	.15	.30
57 Phantasmal Fiend v1 C	.07	.15
57 Phantasmal Fiend v2 C	.07	.15
58 Phyrexian Boon v1 C	.07	.15
58 Phyrexian Boon v2 C	.07	.15
59 Ritual of the Machine R	10.00	20.00
60 Soldevi Adnate v1 C	.50	1.00
60 Soldevi Adnate v2 C	.30	.75
61 Stench of Decay v1 C	.07	.15
61 Stench of Decay v2 C	.07	.15
62 Stromgald Spy U	.10	.20
63 Swamp Mosquito v1 C	.07	.15
63 Swamp Mosquito v2 C	.07	.15
64 Agent of Stromgald v1 C	.07	.15
64 Agent of Stromgald v2 C	.07	.15
65 Balduvian Horde R	1.50	3.00
66 Balduvian War-Makers v1 C	.07	.15
66 Balduvian War-Makers v2 C	.07	.15
67 Bestial Fury v1 C	.07	.15
67 Bestial Fury v2 C	.07	.15
68 Burnout U	1.00	2.00
69 Chaos Harlequin R	2.00	4.00
70 Death Spark U	.15	.30
71 Enslaved Scout v1 C	.07	.15
71 Enslaved Scout v2 C	.07	.15
72 Gorilla Shaman v2 C	.30	.75
73 Gorilla Shaman v1 C	.50	1.00
73 Gorilla War Cry v2 C	.07	.15
73 Gorilla War Cry v1 C	.12	.25
74 Guerrilla Tactics v1 C	.07	.15
74 Guerrilla Tactics v2 C	.07	.15
75 Omen of Fire R	4.00	8.00
76 Pillage U	.50	1.00
77 Primitive Justice U	.10	.20
78 Pyrokinesis U	.20	.40
79 Rogue Skycaptain R	1.25	2.50
80 Soldier of Fortune U	.15	.30
81 Storm Shaman v1 C	.07	.15
81 Storm Shaman v2 C	.07	.15
82 Varchild's Crusader v1 C	.07	.15
82 Varchild's Crusader v2 C	.07	.15
83 Varchild's War-Riders R	7.50	15.00
84 Veteran's Voice v1 C	.07	.15
84 Veteran's Voice v2 C	.07	.15
85 Bounty of the Hunt U	.10	.20
86 Deadly Insect v1 C	.07	.15
86 Deadly Insect v2 C	.07	.15
87 Elvish Bard U	.10	.20
88 Elvish Ranger v1 C	1.25	2.50
88 Elvish Ranger v2 C	.07	.15
89 Elvish Spirit Guide U	10.00	20.00
90 Fyndhorn Druid v1 C	.07	.15
90 Fyndhorn Druid v2 C	.07	.15
91 Gargantuan Gorilla R	1.50	3.00
92 Gift of the Woods v1 C	.07	.15
92 Gift of the Woods v2 C	.07	.15
93 Gorilla Berserkers v1 C	.07	.15
93 Gorilla Berserkers v2 C	.07	.15
94 Gorilla Chieftain v1 C	.07	.15
94 Gorilla Chieftain v2 C	.07	.15
95 Hail Storm U	.10	.20
96 Kaysa R	10.00	20.00
97 Nature's Chosen U	1.00	2.00
98 Nature's Wrath R	5.00	10.00
99 Splintering Wind R	1.25	2.50
100 Taste of Paradise v1 C	.07	.15
100 Taste of Paradise v2 C	.07	.15
101 Tornado R	1.50	3.00
102 Undergrowth v1 C	.07	.15
102 Undergrowth v2 C	.07	.15
103 Whip Vine v1 C	.07	.15
103 Whip Vine v2 C	.07	.15
104 Yavimaya Ancients v1 C	.07	.15
104 Yavimaya Ancients v2 C	.07	.15
105 Yavimaya Ants U	.10	.20
106 Energy Arc U/:B:	.15	.30
107 Lim-Dul's Vault U/	4.00	8.00
108 Lim-Dul's Paladin U/	.10	.20
109 Surge of Strength U	.10	.20
110 Nature's Blessing U/:W:	.10	.20
111 Wandering Mage R/	2.50	5.00

112 Lord of Tresserhorn R//	7.50	15.00
113 Misfortune R/	2.50	5.00
114 Winter's Night R/:W:	6.00	12.00
115 Pheldagrif R/:W:/:B:	15.00	30.00
116 Aesthir Glider v1 C	.10	.20
116 Aesthir Glider v2 C	.10	.20
117 Ashnod's Cylix R	2.00	4.00
118 Astrolabe v1 C	.10	.20
118 Astrolabe v2 C	.10	.20
119 Floodwater Dam R	2.00	4.00
120 Gustha's Scepter R	6.00	12.00
121 Helm of Obedience R	50.00	100.00
122 Lodestone Bauble R	7.50	15.00
123 Mishra's Groundbreaker U	.10	.20
124 Mystic Compass U	.10	.20
125 Phyrexian Devourer R	12.50	25.00
126 Phyrexian Portal R	4.00	8.00
127 Phyrexian War Beast v1 C	.10	.20
127 Phyrexian War Beast v2 C	.10	.20
128 Scarab of the Unseen U	.10	.20
129 Shield Sphere U	3.00	6.00
130 Sol Grail U	.10	.20
131 Soldevi Digger R	4.00	8.00
132 Soldevi Sentry v1 C :A:	.15	.30
132 Soldevi Sentry v2 C :A:	.10	.20
133 Soldevi Steam Beast v1 C	.10	.20
133 Soldevi Steam Beast v2 C	.10	.20
134 Storm Cauldron R	1.50	3.00
135 Urza's Engine U	.10	.20
136 Whirling Catapult U	.10	.20
137 Balduvian Trading Post R	7.50	15.00
138 Heart of Yavimaya R	10.00	20.00
139 Kjeldoran Outpost R	20.00	40.00
140 Lake of the Dead R	100.00	200.00
141 School of the Unseen U	.15	.30
142 Sheltered Valley R	7.50	15.00
143 Soldevi Excavations R	20.00	40.00
144 Thawing Glaciers R	30.00	60.00

1996 Magic The Gathering Mirage

1 Afterlife U	.10	.20
2 Alarum C	.07	.15
3 Auspicious Ancestor R	7.50	15.00
4 Benevolent Unicorn C	.07	.15
5 Blinding Light U	.10	.20
6 Celestial Dawn R	1.00	2.00
7 Civic Guildmage C	.07	.15
8 Dazzling Beauty C	.07	.15
9 Disempower C	.07	.15
10 Disenchant C	.07	.15
11 Divine Offering C	.07	.15
12 Divine Retribution R	2.00	4.00
13 Ekundu Griffin C	.07	.15
14 Enlightened Tutor U	30.00	60.00
15 Ethereal Champion R	.20	.40
16 Favorable Destiny U	.10	.20
17 Femeref Healer C	.07	.15
18 Femeref Knight C	.07	.15
19 Femeref Scouts C	.07	.15
20 Healing Salve C	.07	.15
21 Illumination U	4.00	8.00
22 Iron Tusk Elephant U	.10	.20
23 Ivory Charm C	.07	.15
24 Jabari's Influence R	4.00	8.00
25 Mangara's Blessing U	.10	.20
26 Mangara's Equity U	.10	.20
27 Melesse Spirit U	.10	.20
28 Mtenda Griffin U	.10	.20
29 Mtenda Herder C	.07	.15
30 Noble Elephant C	.07	.15
31 Null Chamber R	3.00	6.00
32 Pacifism C	.07	.15
33 Pearl Dragon R	.30	.75
34 Prismatic Circle C	.07	.15
35 Rashida Scalebane R	2.50	5.00
36 Ritual of Steel C	.07	.15
37 Sacred Mesa R	.30	.75
38 Shadowbane U	.10	.20
39 Sidar Jabari R	1.50	3.00
40 Soul Echo R	2.00	4.00
41 Spectral Guardian R	4.00	8.00
42 Sunweb R	.30	.60
43 Teremko Griffin C	.07	.15
44 Unyaro Griffin U	.10	.20
45 Vigilant Martyr U	.20	.40
46 Wall of Resistance C	.07	.15
47 Ward of Lights C	.07	.15
48 Yare R	2.50	5.00
49 Zhalfirin Commander U	.10	.20
50 Zhalfirin Knight C	.07	.15
51 Zuberi, Golden Feather R	5.00	10.00
52 Ancestral Memories R	.30	.60
53 Azimaet Drake C	.07	.15
54 Bay Falcon C	.07	.15
55 Bazaar of Wonders R	6.00	12.00
56 Boomerang C	.07	.15
57 Cerulean Wyvern U	.10	.20
58 Cloak of Invisibility C	.07	.15
59 Coral Fighters U	.10	.20
60 Daring Apprentice R	.30	.60
61 Dissipate U	.30	.60
62 Dream Cache C	.07	.15
63 Dream Fighter C	.07	.15
64 Energy Vortex R	4.00	8.00
65 Ether Well U	.10	.20
66 Flash R	1.25	2.50
67 Floodgate U	.10	.20
68 Hakim, Loreweaver R	3.00	6.00
69 Harmattan Efreet U	.10	.20
70 Jolt C	.07	.15
71 Kukemssa Pirates R	7.50	15.00
72 Kukemssa Serpent C	.07	.15
73 Meddle U	.10	.20
74 Memory Lapse C	.07	.15
75 Merfolk Raiders C	.07	.15
76 Merfolk Seer C	.07	.15
77 Mind Bend U	.15	.30
78 Mind Harness U	.15	.30
79 Mist Dragon R	3.00	6.00
80 Mystical Tutor U	12.50	25.00
81 Political Trickery R	1.00	2.00
82 Polymorph R	.60	1.25
83 Power Sink C	.07	.15
84 Prismatic Lace R	4.00	8.00
85 Psychic Transfer R	.20	.40
86 Ray of Command C	.07	.15
87 Reality Ripple C	.15	.30
88 Sandbar Crocodile C	.07	.15
89 Sapphire Charm C	.07	.15
90 Sea Scryer C	.12	.25
91 Shaper Guildmage C	.07	.15
92 Shimmer R	6.00	12.00
93 Soar C	.07	.15
94 Suq'Ata Firewalker U	.20	.40
95 Taniwha R	4.00	8.00
96 Teferi's Curse C	.07	.15
97 Teferi's Drake C	.07	.15
98 Teferi's Imp R	3.00	6.00
99 Thirst C	.07	.15
100 Tidal Wave U	.10	.20
101 Vaporous Djinn U	.10	.20
102 Wave Elemental U	.12	.25
103 Abyssal Hunter R	.20	.40
104 Ashen Powder R	.50	1.00
105 Barbed-Back Wurm U	.10	.20
106 Binding Agony C	.07	.15
107 Blighted Shaman U	.10	.20
108 Bone Harvest C	.07	.15
109 Breathstealer C	.07	.15
110 Cadaverous Knight C	.07	.15
111 Carrion R	6.00	12.00
112 Catacomb Dragon R	10.00	20.00
113 Choking Sands C	.07	.15
114 Crypt Cobra U	.15	.30
115 Dark Banishing C	.07	.15
116 Dark Ritual C	.30	.75
117 Dirtwater Wraith C	.07	.15
118 Drain Life C	.07	.15
119 Dread Specter U	.10	.20
120 Ebony Charm C	.07	.15
121 Enfeeblement C	.07	.15
122 Feral Shadow C	.07	.15
123 Fetid Horror C	.07	.15
124 Forbidden Crypt R	.30	.75
125 Forsaken Wastes R	7.50	15.00
126 Grave Servitude C	.07	.15
127 Gravebane Zombie C	.07	.15
128 Harbinger of Night R	6.00	12.00
129 Infernal Contract R	.60	1.25
130 Kaervek's Hex U	.10	.20
131 Mire Shade U	.10	.20
132 Nocturnal Raid U	.10	.20
133 Painful Memories U	.10	.20
134 Phyrexian Tribute R	4.00	8.00
135 Purraj of Urborg R	7.50	15.00
136 Ravenous Vampire U	.10	.20
137 Reign of Terror U	.10	.20
138 Restless Dead C	.07	.15
139 Sewer Rats C	.07	.15
140 Shadow Guildmage C	.07	.15
141 Shallow Grave R	30.00	60.00
142 Shauku, Endbringer R	6.00	12.00
143 Skulking Ghost C	.07	.15
144 Soul Rend U	.10	.20
145 Soulshriek C	.07	.15
146 Spirit of the Night R	10.00	20.00
147 Stupor U	.20	.40
148 Tainted Specter R	1.50	3.00
149 Tombstone Stairwell R	10.00	20.00
150 Urborg Panther C	.07	.15
151 Wall of Corpses C	.07	.15
152 Withering Boon U	3.00	6.00
153 Zombie Mob U	.10	.20
154 Agility C	.07	.15
155 Aleatory U	.30	.60
156 Armorer Guildmage C	.07	.15
157 Barreling Attack R	1.00	2.00
158 Blind Fury U	.10	.20
159 Blistering Barrier C	.07	.15
160 Builder's Bane C	.07	.15
161 Burning Palm Efreet U	.10	.20
162 Burning Shield Askari C	.07	.15
163 Chaos Charm C	.07	.15
164 Chaosphere R	6.00	12.00
165 Cinder Cloud U	.10	.20
166 Consuming Ferocity U	.10	.20
167 Crimson Hellkite R	.60	1.25
168 Crimson Roc U	.10	.20
169 Dwarven Miner U	3.00	6.00
170 Dwarven Nomad C	.15	.30
171 Ekundu Cyclops C	.07	.15
172 Emberwilde Djinn R	1.25	2.50
173 Final Fortune R	20.00	40.00
174 Firebreathing C	.07	.15
175 Flame Elemental U	.10	.20
176 Flare C	.07	.15
177 Goblin Elite Infantry C	.07	.15
178 Goblin Scouts U	.15	.30
179 Goblin Soothsayer U	.25	.50
180 Goblin Tinkerer C	.07	.15
181 Hammer of Bogardan R	1.00	2.00
182 Hivis of the Scale R	1.25	2.50
183 Illicit Auction R	1.00	2.00
184 Incinerate C	.07	.15
185 Kaervek's Torch C	.07	.15
186 Lightning Reflexes C	.07	.15
187 Pyric Salamander C	.07	.15
188 Raging Spirit C	.07	.15
189 Reckless Embermage R	.25	.50
190 Reign of Chaos U	.10	.20
191 Searing Spear Askari C	.07	.15
192 Sirocco U	.15	.30
193 Spitting Earth C	.07	.15
194 Stone Rain C	.07	.15
195 Subterranean Spirit R	2.00	4.00
196 Talruum Minotaur C	.07	.15
197 Telim'Tor R	2.00	4.00
198 Telim'Tor's Edict R	3.00	6.00
199 Torrent of Lava R	1.00	2.00
200 Viashino Warrior C	.07	.15
201 Volcanic Dragon R	.30	.75
202 Volcanic Geyser U	.15	.30
203 Wildfire Emissary U	.10	.20
204 Zirilan of the Claw R	10.00	20.00
205 Afiya Grove R	2.50	5.00
206 Armor of Thorns C	.07	.15
207 Barbed Foliage U	.10	.20
208 Brushwagg R	2.50	5.00
209 Canopy Dragon R	2.00	4.00
210 Crash of Rhinos C	.07	.15
211 Cycle of Life R	1.00	2.00
212 Decomposition U	.10	.20
213 Early Harvest R	1.50	3.00
214 Fallow Earth U	.10	.20
215 Femeref Archers U	.10	.20
216 Fog C	.07	.15
217 Foratog U	.10	.20
218 Giant Mantis C	.07	.15
219 Gibbering Hyenas C	.07	.15
220 Granger Guildmage C	.07	.15
221 Hall of Gemstone R	25.00	50.00
222 Jolrael's Centaur C	.07	.15
223 Jungle Patrol R	3.00	6.00
224 Jungle Wurm C	.07	.15
225 Karoo Meerkat U	.10	.20
226 Locust Swarm U	.10	.20
227 Lure of Prey R	7.50	15.00
228 Maro R	.25	.50
229 Mindbender Spores R	1.00	2.00
230 Mtenda Lion C	.07	.15
231 Natural Balance R	7.50	15.00
232 Nettletooth Djinn U	.10	.20
233 Preferred Selection R	2.00	4.00
234 Quirion Elves C	.15	.30
235 Rampant Growth C	.60	1.25
236 Regeneration C	.07	.15
237 Roots of Life U	.15	.30
238 Sabertooth Cobra C	.15	.30
239 Sandstorm C	.07	.15
240 Seedling Charm C	.07	.15
241 Seeds of Innocence R	10.00	20.00
242 Serene Heart C	.07	.15
243 Stalking Tiger C	.07	.15
244 Superior Numbers U	.10	.20
245 Tranquil Domain C	.07	.15
246 Tropical Storm U	.10	.20
247 Uktabi Faerie C	.07	.15
248 Uktabi Wildcats R	.30	.60
249 Unseen Walker U	.10	.20
250 Unyaro Bee Sting U	.10	.20
251 Village Elder C	.07	.15
252 Waiting in the Weeds R	.60	1.25
253 Wall of Roots C	.20	.40
254 Wild Elephant C	.07	.15
255 Worldly Tutor U	20.00	40.00
256 Asmira, Holy Avenger R/:W:	6.00	12.00
257 Benthic Djinn R/	1.50	3.00
258 Cadaverous Bloom R	12.50	25.00
259 Circle of Despair R/	5.00	10.00
260 Delirium U/	.30	.60
261 Discordant Spirit R/	1.25	2.50
262 Emberwilde Caliph R/	1.25	2.50
263 Energy Bolt R/:W:	2.50	5.00
264 Frenetic Efreet R/	7.50	15.00
265 Grim Feast R	7.50	15.00
266 Harbor Guardian U/:B:	.10	.20
267 Haunting Apparition U/	.10	.20
268 Hazerider Drake U/:B:	.10	.20
269 Jungle Troll U	.10	.20
270 Kaervek's Purge U/	.10	.20
271 Leering Gargoyle R/:B:	1.50	3.00
272 Malignant Growth R/:B:	.75	1.50
273 Phyrexian Purge R/	7.50	15.00
274 Prismatic Boon U/:B:	.10	.20
275 Purgatory R/	6.00	12.00
276 Radiant Essence U/:W:	.10	.20
277 Reflect Damage R/:W:	1.50	3.00
278 Reparations R/:B:	7.50	15.00
279 Rock Basilisk R	1.25	2.50
280 Savage Twister U	.15	.30
281 Sawback Manticore R	1.00	2.00
282 Sealed Fate U/	.12	.25
283 Shauku's Minion U/	.10	.20
284 Spatial Binding U/	.10	.20
285 Unfulfilled Desires R/	10.00	20.00
286 Vitalizing Cascade U/:W:	.25	.50
287 Warping Wurm R/:B:	1.00	2.00
288 Wellspring R/:W:	3.00	6.00
289 Windreaper Falcon U	.10	.20
290 Zebra Unicorn U/:W:	.25	.50
291 Acidic Dagger R	1.25	2.50
292 Amber Prison R	.30	.75
293 Amulet of Unmaking R	2.50	5.00
294 Basalt Golem U	.10	.20
295 Bone Mask R	2.50	5.00
296 Charcoal Diamond U	.10	.20
297 Chariot of the Sun U	.10	.20
298 Crystal Golem U	.10	.20
299 Cursed Totem R	20.00	40.00
300 Elixir of Vitality U	.10	.20
301 Ersatz Gnomes U	.10	.20
302 Fire Diamond U	1.25	2.50
303 Grinning Totem R	.60	1.25
304 Horrible Hordes U	.10	.20
305 Igneous Golem U	.10	.20
306 Lead Golem U	.10	.20
307 Lion's Eye Diamond R	300.00	600.00
308 Mana Prism U	.10	.20
309 Mangara's Tome R	10.00	20.00
310 Marble Diamond U	.75	1.50
311 Misers' Cage R	2.50	5.00
312 Moss Diamond U	.15	.30
313 Patagia Golem U	.10	.20
314 Paupers' Cage R	1.50	3.00
315 Phyrexian Dreadnought R	60.00	125.00
316 Phyrexian Vault U	.10	.20
317 Razor Pendulum R	1.25	2.50
318 Sand Golem U	.10	.20
319 Sky Diamond U	1.00	2.00
320 Teeka's Dragon R	6.00	12.00
321 Telim'Tor's Darts U	.10	.20
322 Unerring Sling U	.10	.20
323 Ventifact Bottle R	2.00	4.00
324 Bad River U	2.50	5.00
325 Crystal Vein U	1.50	3.00
326 Flood Plain U	1.25	2.50
327 Grasslands U	1.00	2.00
328 Mountain Valley U	1.50	3.00
329 Rocky Tar Pit U	.75	1.50
330 Teferi's Isle R	12.50	25.00
331 Plains L	.30	.75
332 Plains L	.30	.75
333 Plains L	.30	.75
334 Plains L	.30	.75
335 Island L	.30	.60
336 Island L	.30	.60
337 Island L	.30	.60
338 Island L	.30	.60
339 Swamp L	.50	1.00
340 Swamp L	1.25	2.50
341 Swamp L	.50	1.00
342 Swamp L	1.00	2.00
343 Mountain L	.50	1.00
344 Mountain L	.30	.60
345 Mountain L	.30	.60
346 Mountain L	1.25	2.50
347 Forest L	.30	.75
348 Forest L	.25	.50
349 Forest L	1.00	2.00
350 Forest L	.30	.60

1997 Magic The Gathering 5th Edition

1 Abbey Gargoyles U	.10	.20
2 Akron Legionnaire R	.20	.40
3 Alabaster Potion C	.07	.15
4 Angry Mob U	.10	.20
5 Animate Wall R	.20	.40
6 Arenson's Aura U	.12	.25
7 Armageddon R	3.00	6.00
8 Armor of Faith C	.07	.15
9 Aysen Bureaucrats C	.07	.15
10 Benalish Hero C	.07	.15
11 Blessed Wine C	.07	.15
12 Blinking Spirit R	.20	.40
13 Brainwash C	.07	.15
14 Caribou Range R	.25	.50
15 Castle U	.10	.20
16 Circle of Protection Artifacts U	.10	.20
17 Circle of Protection Black C	.07	.15
18 Circle of Protection Blue C	.07	.15
19 Circle of Protection Green C	.07	.15
20 Circle of Protection Red C	.07	.15
21 Circle of Protection White C	.07	.15
22 Crusade R	1.00	2.00
23 D'Avenant Archer C	.07	.15
24 Death Speakers C	.07	.15
25 Death Ward C	.07	.15
26 Disenchant C	.07	.15
27 Divine Offering C	.07	.15
28 Divine Transformation U	.10	.20
29 Dust to Dust U	.30	.60
30 Eye for an Eye R	.25	.50
31 Greater Realm of Preservation U	.15	.30
32 Heal C	.07	.15
33 Healing Salve C	.07	.15
34 Hipparion C	.07	.15
35 Holy Strength C	.07	.15
36 Icatian Phalanx U	.10	.20
37 Icatian Scout C	.07	.15
38 Icatian Town R	.20	.40
39 Island Sanctuary R	3.00	6.00
40 Ivory Guardians U	.10	.20
41 Justice U	.10	.20
42 Karma U	.10	.20
43 Kismet U	.60	1.25
44 Kjeldoran Royal Guard R	.20	.40
45 Kjeldoran Skycaptain U	.10	.20
46 Mesa Falcon C	.10	.20
47 Mesa Pegasus C	.07	.15
48 Order of the Sacred Torch R	.30	.75
49 Order of the White Shield U	.10	.20
50 Pearled Unicorn C	.07	.15
51 Personal Incarnation R	.20	.40
52 Pikemen C	.07	.15
53 Prismatic Ward C	.07	.15
54 Repentant Blacksmith C	.07	.15
55 Reverse Damage R	.25	.50
56 Righteousness R	.20	.40
57 Sacred Boon U	.10	.20
58 Samite Healer C	.07	.15
59 Seraph R	.50	1.00
60 Serra Bestiary U	.10	.20
61 Serra Paladin U	.10	.20
62 Shield Bearer C	.07	.15
63 Shield Wall C	.07	.15
64 Spirit Link U	.30	.60
65 Truce R	.60	1.25
66 Tundra Wolves C	.07	.15
67 Wall of Swords U	.10	.20
68 White Knight U	.12	.25
69 Wrath of God R	4.00	8.00
70 Aether Storm U	.20	.40
71 Air Elemental U	.10	.20
72 Anti-Magic Aura U	.12	.25
73 Azure Drake U	.10	.20
74 Binding Grasp U	.10	.20
75 Boomerang C	.07	.15
76 Brainstorm C	.60	1.25
77 Counterspell C	1.00	2.00
78 Dance of Many R	2.50	5.00
79 Dandan C	.07	.15
80 Dark Maze C	.07	.15
81 Deflection R	.25	.50
82 Drain Power R	1.50	3.00
83 Energy Flux U	.20	.40
84 Enervate C	.07	.15
85 Feedback U	.12	.25
86 Flight C	.07	.15
87 Flood C	.07	.15
88 Force Spike C	.15	.30
89 Forget R	.20	.40
90 Gaseous Form C	.07	.15
91 Glacial Wall U	.15	.30
92 Homarid Warrior C	.07	.15
93 Hurkyl's Recall R	2.00	4.00
94 Hydroblast U	.50	1.00
95 Juxtapose R	.20	.40
96 Krovikan Sorcerer C	.07	.15

97 Labyrinth Minotaur C	.07	.15
98 Leviathan R	.20	.40
99 Lifetap U	.10	.20
100 Lord of Atlantis R	2.50	5.00
101 Magical Hack R	.25	.50
102 Magus of the Unseen R	.30	.75
103 Memory Lapse C	.10	.20
104 Merfolk of the Pearl Trident C	.07	.15
105 Mind Bomb U	.10	.20
106 Phantasmal Forces U	.10	.20
107 Phantasmal Terrain C	.07	.15
108 Phantom Monster U	.10	.20
109 Pirate Ship R	.20	.40
110 Portent C	.20	.40
111 Power Sink U	.10	.20
112 Prodigal Sorcerer C	.07	.15
113 Psychic Venom C	.07	.15
114 Ray of Command C	.07	.15
115 Recall R	.30	.75
116 Reef Pirates C	.07	.15
117 Remove Soul C	.07	.15
118 Sea Serpent C	.07	.15
119 Sea Spirit U	.10	.20
120 Sea Sprite U	.20	.40
121 Seasinger U	.20	.40
122 Segovian Leviathan U	.10	.20
123 Sibilant Spirit R	.20	.40
124 Sleight of Mind R	.20	.40
125 Soul Barrier C	.30	.60
126 Spell Blast C	.07	.15
127 Stasis R	4.00	8.00
128 Steal Artifact U	.10	.20
129 Time Elemental R	.25	.50
130 Twiddle C	.15	.30
131 Unstable Mutation C	.07	.15
132 Unsummon C	.07	.15
133 Updraft C	.10	.20
134 Vodalian Soldiers C	.07	.15
135 Wall of Air U	.10	.20
136 Wind Spirit U	.10	.20
137 Zephyr Falcon C	.07	.15
138 Zur's Weirding R	.30	.75
139 Abyssal Specter U	.12	.25
140 Animate Dead U	3.00	6.00
141 Ashes to Ashes U	.75	1.50
142 Bad Moon R	1.25	2.50
143 Black Knight U	.25	.50
144 Blight U	.25	.50
145 Bog Imp C	.07	.15
146 Bog Rats C	.07	.15
147 Bog Wraith U	.10	.20
148 Breeding Pit U	.15	.30
149 Broken Visage R	.20	.40
150 Carrion Ants U	.12	.25
151 Cloak of Confusion C	.07	.15
152 Cursed Land U	.10	.20
153 Dark Ritual C	.30	.75
154 Deathgrip U	.20	.40
155 Derelor R	.20	.40
156 Drain Life C	.12	.25
157 Drudge Skeletons C	.07	.15
158 Erg Raiders C	.07	.15
159 Evil Eye of Orms-by-Gore U	.10	.20
160 Evil Presence U	.12	.25
161 Fallen Angel U	.15	.30
162 Fear C	.07	.15
163 Frozen Shade C	.07	.15
164 Funeral March C	.07	.15
165 Gloom U	.10	.20
166 Greater Werewolf U	.10	.20
167 Hecatomb R	.25	.50
168 Howl from Beyond C	.07	.15
169 Initiates of the Ebon Hand C	.07	.15
170 Kjeldoran Dead C	.07	.15
171 Knight of Stromgald U	.10	.20
172 Krovikan Fetish C	.07	.15
173 Leshrac's Rite U	.10	.20
174 Lord of the Pit R	.30	.75
175 Lost Soul C	.07	.15
176 Mind Ravel C	.07	.15
177 Mind Warp U	.10	.20
178 Mindstab Thrull C	.07	.15
179 Mole Worms U	.10	.20
180 Murk Dwellers C	.07	.15
181 Necrite C	.07	.15
182 Necropotence R	25.00	50.00
183 Nether Shadow R	1.00	2.00
184 Nightmare R	.60	1.25
185 Paralyze C	.12	.25
186 Pestilence C	.25	.50
187 Pit Scorpion C	.07	.15
188 Plague Rats C	.07	.15
189 Pox R	10.00	20.00
190 Rag Man R	.30	.60
191 Raise Dead C	.07	.15
192 Scathe Zombies C	.07	.15
193 Sengir Autocrat R	.30	.60
194 Sorceress Queen R	.75	1.50
195 Stromgald Cabal R	.25	.50

196 Terror C	.07	.15
197 The Wretched R	.25	.50
198 Thrull Retainer U	.10	.20
199 Torture C	.07	.15
200 Touch of Death C	.07	.15
201 Unholy Strength C	.07	.15
202 Vampire Bats C	.07	.15
203 Wall of Bone U	.10	.20
204 Warp Artifact R	.20	.40
205 Weakness C	.07	.15
206 Xenic Poltergeist R	.25	.50
207 Zombie Master R	4.00	8.00
208 Ambush Party C	.07	.15
209 Atog U	.25	.50
210 Ball Lightning R	2.00	4.00
211 Bird Maiden C	.07	.15
212 Blood Lust C	.07	.15
213 Brassclaw Orcs C	.07	.15
214 Brothers of Fire C	.07	.15
215 Cave People U	.10	.20
216 Conquer U	.10	.20
217 Crimson Manticore R	.20	.40
218 Detonate U	.10	.20
219 Disintegrate C	.07	.15
220 Dwarven Catapult U	.10	.20
221 Dwarven Soldier C	.07	.15
222 Dwarven Warriors C	.07	.15
223 Earthquake R	.60	1.25
224 Errantry C	.07	.15
225 Eternal Warrior C	.07	.15
226 Fire Drake U	.10	.20
227 Fireball C	.10	.20
228 Firebreathing C	.10	.20
229 Flame Spirit U	.10	.20
230 Flare C	.07	.15
231 Flashfires U	.10	.20
232 Game of Chaos R	2.00	4.00
2.33E+02 Giant Strength C	.07	.15
2.34E+02 Goblin Digging Team C	.07	.15
2.35E+02 Goblin Hero C	.07	.15
2.36E+02 Goblin King R	2.50	5.00
2.37E+02 Goblin War Drums C	.20	.40
2.38E+02 Goblin Warrens R	.75	1.50
2.39E+02 Hill Giant C	.07	.15
2.40E+02 Hurloon Minotaur C	.07	.15
241 Imposing Visage C	.07	.15
242 Incinerate C	.07	.15
243 Inferno R	.25	.50
244 Ironclaw Curse R	.20	.40
245 Ironclaw Orcs C	.07	.15
246 Jokulhaups R	2.50	5.00
247 Keldon Warlord U	.10	.20
248 Mana Clash R	.30	.60
249 Mana Flare R	7.50	15.00
250 Manabarbs R	.30	.75
251 Mons's Goblin Raiders C	.07	.15
252 Mountain Goat C	.07	.15
253 Orcish Artillery U	.10	.20
254 Orcish Captain U	.15	.30
255 Orcish Conscripts C	.07	.15
256 Orcish Farmer C	.07	.15
257 Orcish Oriflamme U	.10	.20
258 Orcish Squatters R	.20	.40
259 Orgg R	.20	.40
260 Panic C	.20	.40
261 Primordial Ooze U	.10	.20
262 Pyroblast U	2.50	5.00
263 Pyrotechnics U	.10	.20
264 Sabretooth Tiger C	.07	.15
265 Shatter C	.07	.15
266 Shatterstorm U	.30	.60
267 Shivan Dragon R	5.00	10.00
268 Smoke R	3.00	6.00
269 Stone Giant U	.10	.20
270 Stone Rain C	.07	.15
271 Stone Spirit U	.10	.20
272 The Brute C	.07	.15
273 Wall of Fire U	.10	.20
274 Wall of Stone U	.10	.20
275 Winds of Change R	10.00	20.00
276 Word of Blasting U	.10	.20
277 An-Havva Constable R	.20	.40
278 Aspect of Wolf R	.30	.60
279 Aurochs C	.07	.15
280 Birds of Paradise R	7.50	15.00
281 Carapace C	.15	.30
282 Cat Warriors C	.07	.15
283 Chub Toad C	.07	.15
284 Cockatrice R	.20	.40
285 Craw Giant U	.10	.20
286 Craw Wurm C	.10	.20
287 Crumble U	.10	.20
288 Desert Twister U	.10	.20
289 Durkwood Boars C	.07	.15
290 Elder Druid R	.25	.50
291 Elven Riders U	.12	.25
292 Elvish Archers R	.30	.60
293 Fog C	.07	.15
294 Force of Nature R	.25	.50

295 Foxfire C	.07	.15
296 Fungusaur R	.25	.50
297 Fyndhorn Elder U	.12	.25
298 Ghazban Ogre C	.07	.15
299 Giant Growth C	.07	.15
300 Giant Spider C	.07	.15
301 Grizzly Bears C	.07	.15
302 Hungry Mist C	.07	.15
303 Hurricane U	.15	.30
304 Instill Energy U	1.25	2.50
305 Ironroot Treefolk C	.12	.25
306 Johtull Wurm U	.10	.20
307 Killer Bees U	.20	.40
308 Ley Druid C	.07	.15
309 Lhurgoyf R	.30	.60
310 Lifeforce U	.15	.30
311 Living Artifact R	.20	.40
312 Living Lands R	.20	.40
313 Llanowar Elves C	.20	.40
314 Lure U	.10	.20
315 Marsh Viper C	.07	.15
316 Nature's Lore C	4.00	8.00
317 Pradesh Gypsies C	.07	.15
318 Primal Order R	1.50	3.00
319 Rabid Wombat U	.10	.20
320 Radjan Spirit U	.10	.20
321 Regeneration C	.07	.15
322 Scaled Wurm C	.07	.15
323 Scavenger Folk C	.07	.15
324 Scryb Sprites C	.07	.15
325 Shanodin Dryads C	.07	.15
326 Shrink C	.07	.15
327 Stampede R	.25	.50
328 Stream of Life C	.07	.15
329 Sylvan Library R	25.00	50.00
330 Tarpan C	.07	.15
331 Thicket Basilisk U	.10	.20
332 Titania's Song R	.25	.50
333 Tranquility C	.07	.15
334 Tsunami U	.15	.30
335 Untamed Wilds U	.10	.20
336 Venom C	.07	.15
337 Verduran Enchantress R	2.00	4.00
338 Wall of Brambles U	.10	.20
339 Wanderlust U	.20	.40
340 War Mammoth C	.07	.15
341 Whirling Dervish U	.12	.25
342 Wild Growth C	.20	.40
343 Winter Blast U	.15	.30
344 Wolverine Pack U	.10	.20
345 Wyluli Wolf R	.30	.60
346 Aladdin's Ring R	.20	.40
347 Amulet of Kroog C	.07	.15
348 Ankh of Mishra R	4.00	8.00
349 Ashnod's Altar U	6.00	12.00
350 Ashnod's Transmogrant C	.12	.25
351 Barbed Sextant C	.15	.30
352 Barl's Cage R	.25	.50
353 Battering Ram C	.07	.15
354 Bottle of Suleiman R	.25	.50
355 Clay Statue C	.07	.15
356 Clockwork Beast R	.20	.40
357 Clockwork Steed U	.25	.50
358 Colossus of Sardia R	.30	.60
359 Coral Helm R	.20	.40
360 Crown of the Ages R	.20	.40
361 Crystal Rod U	.10	.20
362 Dancing Scimitar R	.25	.50
363 Diabolic Machine U	.10	.20
364 Dingus Egg R	.25	.50
365 Disrupting Scepter R	.20	.40
366 Dragon Engine R	.20	.40
367 Elkin Bottle R	.20	.40
368 Feldon's Cane U	.25	.50
369 Fellwar Stone U	4.00	8.00
370 Feroz's Ban R	.20	.40
371 Flying Carpet R	.20	.40
372 Fountain of Youth U	.10	.20
373 Gauntlets of Chaos R	.20	.40
374 Glasses of Urza U	.20	.40
375 Grapeshot Catapult C	.07	.15
376 Helm of Chatzuk R	.25	.50
377 Howling Mine R	3.00	6.00
378 Infinite Hourglass R	.25	.50
379 Iron Star U	.10	.20
380 Ivory Cup U	.10	.20
381 Jade Monolith R	.25	.50
382 Jalum Tome R	.20	.40
383 Jandor's Saddlebags R	.30	.60
384 Jayemdae Tome R	.25	.50
385 Jester's Cap R	3.00	6.00
386 Joven's Tools U	.10	.20
387 Library of Leng U	1.25	2.50
388 Mana Vault R	40.00	80.00
389 Meekstone R	3.00	6.00
390 Millstone R	.25	.50
391 Nevinyrral's Disk R	2.50	5.00
392 Obelisk of Undoing R	.25	.50
393 Ornithopter U	.30	.60

394 Pentagram of the Ages R	.20	.40
395 Primal Clay R	.20	.40
396 Rod of Ruin U	.10	.20
397 Serpent Generator R	.30	.75
398 Shapeshifter U	.10	.20
399 Skull Catapult U	.10	.20
400 Soul Net U	.10	.20
401 Tawnos's Weaponry U	.10	.20
402 The Hive R	.20	.40
403 Throne of Bone U	.10	.20
404 Time Bomb R	.25	.50
405 Urza's Avenger R	.25	.50
406 Urza's Bauble U	2.00	4.00
407 Wall of Spears C	.07	.15
408 Winter Orb R	10.00	20.00
409 Wooden Sphere U	.10	.20
410 Adarkar Wastes R	6.00	12.00
411 Bottomless Vault R	1.00	2.00
412 Brushland R	3.00	6.00
413 City of Brass R	10.00	20.00
414 Dwarven Hold R	.75	1.50
415 Dwarven Ruins U	.20	.40
416 Ebon Stronghold U	.15	.30
417 Havenwood Battleground U	.10	.20
418 Hollow Trees R	1.00	2.00
419 Icatian Store R	.60	1.25
420 Ice Floe U	.20	.40
421 Karplusan Forest R	3.00	6.00
422 Ruins of Trokair U	.10	.20
423 Sand Silos R	.50	1.00
424 Sulfurous Springs R	6.00	12.00
425 Svyelunite Temple U	.10	.20
426 Underground River R	6.00	12.00
427 Urza's Mine C	.75	1.50
428 Urza's Power Plant C	.75	1.50
429 Urza's Tower C	.75	1.50
430 Plains L	.07	.15
431 Plains L	.07	.15
432 Plains L	.07	.15
433 Plains L	.07	.15
434 Island L	.07	.15
435 Island L	.07	.15
436 Island L	.07	.15
437 Island L	.07	.15
438 Swamp L	.07	.15
439 Swamp L	.07	.15
440 Swamp L	.07	.15
441 Swamp L	.07	.15
442 Mountain L	.07	.15
443 Mountain L	.07	.15
444 Mountain L	.07	.15
445 Mountain L	.07	.15
446 Forest L	.07	.15
447 Forest L	.07	.15
448 Forest L	.07	.15
449 Forest L	.07	.15

1997 Magic The Gathering Portal

1 Alabaster Dragon R	1.25	2.50
2 Angelic Blessing C	.07	.15
3 Archangel R	.60	1.25
4 Ardent Militia U	.10	.20
5 Armageddon R	5.00	10.00
6 Armored Pegasus C	.07	.15
7 Blessed Reversal R	.30	.60
8 Blinding Light R	.30	.60
9 Border Guard C	.07	.15
10 Breath of Life C	.30	.60
11 Charging Paladin U	.15	.30
12 Defiant Stand U	.10	.20
13 Devoted Hero C	.07	.15
14 False Peace C	.07	.15
15 Fleet-Footed Monk C	.20	.40
16 Foot Soldiers C	.07	.15
17 Gift of Estates R	6.00	12.00
18 Harsh Justice R	3.00	6.00
19 Keen-Eyed Archers C	.07	.15
20 Knight Errant C	.07	.15
21 Path of Peace C	.07	.15
22 Regal Unicorn C	.12	.25
23 Renewing Dawn U	.15	.30
24 Sacred Knight C	.07	.15
25 Sacred Nectar C	.07	.15
26 Seasoned Marshal U	.10	.20
27 Spiritual Guardian R	.75	1.50
28 Spotted Griffin C	.07	.15
29 Starlight U	.20	.40
30 Starlit Angel U	.50	1.00
31 Steadfastness C	.07	.15
32 Stern Marshal R	.20	.40
33 Temporary Truce R	2.50	5.00
34 Valorous Charge U	.10	.20
35 Venerable Monk U	.10	.20
36 Vengeance U	.10	.20
37 Wall of Swords U	.20	.40
38 Warrior's Charge v1 C	.07	.15
38 Warrior's Charge v2 C	.07	.15
39 Wrath of God R	7.50	15.00

40 Ancestral Memories R	.30	.75
41 Balance of Power R	.30	.75
42 Baleful Stare U	.10	.20
43 Capricious Sorcerer R	.50	1.00
44 Cloak of Feathers C	1.25	2.50
45 Cloud Dragon R	2.00	4.00
46 Cloud Pirates C	1.00	2.00
47 Cloud Spirit U	.12	.25
48 Command of Unsummoning U	.10	.20
49 Coral Eel C	.07	.15
50 Cruel Fate R	.40	.80
51 Deep-Sea Serpent U	.15	.30
52 Djinn of the Lamp R	.30	.75
53 Deja Vu C	.07	.15
54 Exhaustion R	.75	1.50
55 Flux U	.30	.60
56 Giant Octopus C	.07	.15
57 Horned Turtle C	.07	.15
58 Ingenious Thief U	.10	.20
59 Man-o'-War U	.30	.60
60 Merfolk of the Pearl Trident C	.07	.15
61 Mystic Denial U	.10	.20
62 Omen C	.07	.15
63 Owl Familiar C	.50	1.00
64 Personal Tutor U	50.00	100.00
65 Phantom Warrior R	.30	.60
66 Prosperity R	2.50	5.00
67 Snapping Drake C	.07	.15
68 Sorcerous Sight C	1.00	2.00
69 Storm Crow C	.20	.40
70 Symbol of Unsummoning C	.07	.15
71 Taunt R	.30	.75
72 Theft of Dreams U	.20	.40
73 Thing from the Deep R	.60	1.25
74 Tidal Surge C	.07	.15
75 Time Ebb C	.07	.15
76 Touch of Brilliance C	.07	.15
77 Wind Drake C	.07	.15
78 Withering Gaze U	.15	.30
79 Arrogant Vampire U	.20	.40
80 Assassin's Blade U	.25	.50
81 Bog Imp C	.07	.15
82 Bog Raiders C	.07	.15
83 Bog Wraith U	.10	.20
84 Charging Bandits U	.10	.20
85 Craven Knight C	.07	.15
86 Cruel Bargain R	6.00	12.00
87 Cruel Tutor R	25.00	50.00
88 Dread Charge R	.30	.75
89 Dread Reaper R	.30	.60
90 Dry Spell U	.10	.20
91 Ebon Dragon R	2.50	5.00
92 Endless Cockroaches R	1.25	2.50
93 Feral Shadow C	.07	.15
94 Final Strike R	.60	1.25
95 Gravedigger U	.10	.20
96 Hand of Death v1 C	.07	.15
96 Hand of Death v2 C	.07	.15
97 Howling Fury C	.07	.15
98 King's Assassin R	2.00	4.00
99 Mercenary Knight R	2.00	4.00
100 Mind Knives C	.07	.15
101 Mind Rot C	.07	.15
102 Muck Rats C	.07	.15
103 Nature's Ruin U	.30	.75
104 Noxious Toad U	.75	1.50
105 Python C	.07	.15
106 Rain of Tears U	.30	.75
107 Raise Dead C	.07	.15
108 Serpent Assassin R	1.25	2.50
109 Serpent Warrior C	.07	.15
110 Skeletal Crocodile C	.07	.15
111 Skeletal Snake C	.07	.15
112 Soul Shred C	.07	.15
113 Undying Beast C	.07	.15
114 Vampiric Feast U	.10	.20
115 Vampiric Touch C	.07	.15
116 Virtue's Ruin U	.60	1.25
117 Wicked Pact R	1.00	2.00
118 Blaze v1 U	.10	.20
118 Blaze v2 U	.10	.20
119 Boiling Seas U	.50	1.00
120 Burning Cloak C	.07	.15
121 Craven Giant C	.07	.15
122 Desert Drake U	.10	.20
123 Devastation R	12.50	25.00
124 Earthquake R	.75	1.50
125 Fire Dragon R	3.00	6.00
126 Fire Imp U	.10	.20
127 Fire Snake C	.07	.15
128 Fire Tempest R	.60	1.25
129 Flashfires U	.10	.20
130 Forked Lightning R	.60	1.25
131 Goblin Bully C	.07	.15
132 Highland Giant C	.07	.15
133 Hill Giant C	.07	.15
134 Hulking Cyclops U	.10	.20
135 Hulking Goblin C	.07	.15
136 Last Chance R	50.00	100.00

137 Lava Axe C	.07	.15
138 Lava Flow U	.20	.40
139 Lizard Warrior C	.07	.15
140 Minotaur Warrior C	.07	.15
141 Mountain Goat U	.10	.20
142 Pillaging Horde R	.30	.75
143 Pyroclasm R	2.00	4.00
144 Raging Cougar C	.15	.30
145 Raging Goblin v1 C	.07	.15
145 Raging Goblin v2 C	.07	.15
146 Raging Minotaur C	.20	.40
147 Rain of Salt U	.25	.50
148 Scorching Spear C	.07	.15
149 Scorching Winds U	.20	.40
150 Spitting Earth C	.07	.15
151 Stone Rain C	.20	.40
152 Thundermare R	.60	1.25
153 Volcanic Dragon R	.75	1.50
154 Volcanic Hammer C	.07	.15
155 Wall of Granite U	.20	.40
156 Winds of Change R	20.00	40.00
157 Alluring Scent R	.50	1.00
158 Anaconda v1 U	.10	.20
158 Anaconda v2 U	.10	.20
159 Bee Sting U	.15	.30
160 Bull Hippo U	.10	.20
161 Charging Rhino R	.25	.50
162 Deep Wood U	.15	.30
163 Elite Cat Warrior v1 C	.07	.15
163 Elite Cat Warrior v2 C	.07	.15
164 Elven Cache C	.07	.15
165 Elvish Ranger C	.07	.15
166 Fruition C	.25	.50
167 Giant Spider C	.07	.15
168 Gorilla Warrior C	.07	.15
169 Grizzly Bears C	.07	.15
170 Hurricane R	.50	1.00
171 Jungle Lion C	.30	.75
172 Mobilize C	10.00	20.00
173 Monstrous Growth v1 C	.07	.15
173 Monstrous Growth v2 C	.07	.15
174 Moon Sprite U	.25	.50
175 Natural Order R	25.00	50.00
176 Natural Spring U	.10	.20
177 Nature's Cloak R	.60	1.25
178 Nature's Lore C	4.00	8.00
179 Needle Storm U	.10	.20
180 Panther Warriors C	.07	.15
181 Plant Elemental U	.10	.20
182 Primeval Force R	.30	.60
183 Redwood Treefolk C	.07	.15
184 Rowan Treefolk C	.07	.15
185 Spined Wurm C	.07	.15
186 Stalking Tiger C	.07	.15
187 Summer Bloom R	2.50	5.00
188 Sylvan Tutor R	40.00	80.00
189 Thundering Wurm R	.60	1.25
190 Treetop Defense R	.40	.80
191 Untamed Wilds U	.10	.20
192 Whiptail Wurm U	.15	.30
193 Willow Dryad C	.20	.40
194 Winter's Grasp U	.30	.60
195 Wood Elves R	7.50	15.00
196 Plains L	.07	.15
196 Plains L	.07	.15
196 Plains L	.07	.15
196 Plains L	.07	.15
200 Island L	.07	.15
200 Island L	.07	.15
200 Island L	.07	.15
200 Island L	.07	.15
204 Swamp L	.07	.15
204 Swamp L	.07	.15
204 Swamp L	.07	.15
204 Swamp L	.07	.15
208 Mountain L	.07	.15
208 Mountain L	.07	.15
208 Mountain L	.07	.15
208 Mountain L	.07	.15
212 Forest L	.07	.15
212 Forest L	.07	.15
212 Forest L	.07	.15
212 Forest L	.07	.15

1997 Magic The Gathering Tempest

1 Advance Scout C	.07	.15
2 Angelic Protector U	.10	.20
3 Anoint C	.07	.15
4 Armor Sliver U	.10	.20
5 Armored Pegasus C	.07	.15
6 Auratog R	.30	.75
7 Avenging Angel R	6.00	12.00
8 Circle of Protection Black C	.07	.15
9 Circle of Protection Blue C	.07	.15
10 Circle of Protection Green C	.07	.15
11 Circle of Protection Red C	.07	.15
12 Circle of Protection Shadow C	.07	.15
13 Circle of Protection White C	.07	.15
14 Clergy en-Vec C	.07	.15
15 Cloudchaser Eagle C	.07	.15
16 Disenchant C	.07	.15
17 Elite Javelineer C	.07	.15
18 Field of Souls R	.30	.75
19 Flickering Ward U	2.50	5.00
20 Gallantry U	.10	.20
21 Gerrard's Battle Cry R	.30	.75
22 Hanna's Custody R	1.00	2.00
23 Hero's Resolve C	.07	.15
24 Humility R	50.00	100.00
25 Invulnerability U	.30	.75
26 Knight of Dawn U	.10	.20
27 Light of Day U	.15	.30
28 Marble Titan R	1.50	3.00
29 Master Decoy C	.07	.15
30 Mounted Archers C	.07	.15
31 Oracle en-Vec R	.30	.60
32 Orim's Prayer U	.30	.60
33 Orim, Samite Healer R	5.00	10.00
34 Pacifism C	.07	.15
35 Pegasus Refuge R	.25	.50
36 Quickening Licid U	.10	.20
37 Repentance U	.10	.20
38 Sacred Guide R	.75	1.50
39 Safeguard R	.25	.50
40 Serene Offering U	.10	.20
41 Soltari Crusader U	.15	.30
42 Soltari Emissary R	.30	.60
43 Soltari Foot Soldier C	.12	.25
44 Soltari Lancer C	.07	.15
45 Soltari Monk U	.25	.50
46 Soltari Priest U	.10	.20
47 Soltari Trooper C	.07	.15
48 Spirit Mirror R	.60	1.25
49 Staunch Defenders U	.10	.20
50 Talon Sliver C	.30	.75
51 Warmth U	.10	.20
52 Winds of Rath R	1.25	2.50
53 Worthy Cause U	.30	.60
54 Benthic Behemoth R	.30	.75
55 Capsize C	1.00	2.00
56 Chill U	.20	.40
57 Counterspell C	1.25	2.50
58 Dismiss U	.10	.20
59 Dream Cache C	.07	.15
60 Duplicity R	.20	.40
61 Ertai's Meddling R	1.00	2.00
62 Escaped Shapeshifter R	3.00	6.00
63 Fighting Drake U	.10	.20
64 Fylamarid U	.10	.20
65 Gaseous Form C	.07	.15
66 Giant Crab C	.07	.15
67 Horned Turtle C	.07	.15
68 Insight U	2.00	4.00
69 Interdict U	.20	.40
70 Intuition R	100.00	200.00
71 Legacy's Allure U	.30	.75
72 Legerdemain U	.15	.30
73 Mana Severance R	6.00	12.00
74 Manta Riders C	.07	.15
75 Mawcor R	.20	.40
76 Meditate R	12.50	25.00
77 Mnemonic Sliver U	.20	.40
78 Power Sink C	.07	.15
79 Precognition R	.25	.50
80 Propaganda U	3.00	6.00
81 Rootwater Diver U	.15	.30
82 Rootwater Hunter C	.07	.15
83 Rootwater Matriarch R	.25	.50
84 Rootwater Shaman R	.30	.75
85 Sea Monster C	.07	.15
86 Shadow Rift C	.75	1.50
87 Shimmering Wings C	.07	.15
88 Skyshroud Condor U	.10	.20
89 Spell Blast C	.07	.15
90 Steal Enchantment U	2.00	4.00
91 Stinging Licid U	.10	.20
92 Thalakos Dreamsower U	.10	.20
93 Thalakos Mistfolk C	.07	.15
94 Thalakos Seer C	.20	.40
95 Thalakos Sentry C	.07	.15
96 Time Ebb C	.07	.15
97 Time Warp R	15.00	30.00
98 Tradewind Rider R	6.00	12.00
99 Twitch C	.07	.15
100 Unstable Shapeshifter R	.30	.75
101 Volrath's Curse C	.07	.15
102 Whim of Volrath R	25.00	50.00
103 Whispers of the Muse U	.20	.40
104 Wind Dancer U	.10	.20
105 Wind Drake C	.07	.15
106 Winged Sliver C	.50	1.00
107 Abandon Hope U	.10	.20
108 Bellowing Fiend R	.20	.40
109 Blood Pet C	.20	.40
110 Bounty Hunter R	4.00	8.00
111 Carrionette R	.25	.50
112 Clot Sliver C	.20	.40
113 Coercion C	.07	.15
114 Coffin Queen R	5.00	10.00
115 Commander Greven il-Vec R	6.00	12.00
116 Corpse Dance R	25.00	50.00
117 Dark Banishing C	.07	.15
118 Dark Ritual C	.30	.75
119 Darkling Stalker C	.07	.15
120 Dauthi Embrace U	2.00	4.00
121 Dauthi Ghoul U	.25	.50
122 Dauthi Horror C	.07	.15
123 Dauthi Marauder C	.07	.15
124 Dauthi Mercenary U	.15	.30
125 Dauthi Mindripper U	.15	.30
126 Dauthi Slayer C	.07	.15
127 Death Pits of Rath R	.75	1.50
128 Diabolic Edict C	.20	.40
129 Disturbed Burial C	.12	.25
130 Dread of Night U	.30	.60
131 Dregs of Sorrow R	.30	.75
132 Endless Scream C	.12	.25
133 Enfeeblement C	.07	.15
134 Evincar's Justice C	.15	.30
135 Extinction R	.60	1.25
136 Fevered Convulsions R	.50	1.00
137 Gravedigger C	.07	.15
138 Imps' Taunt U	.10	.20
139 Kezzerdrix R	.20	.40
140 Knight of Dusk U	.15	.30
141 Leeching Licid U	.10	.20
142 Living Death R	6.00	12.00
143 Maddening Imp R	2.00	4.00
144 Marsh Lurker C	.07	.15
145 Mindwhip Sliver U	.20	.40
146 Minion of the Wastes R	.30	.60
147 Perish U	.20	.40
148 Pit Imp C	.07	.15
149 Rain of Tears U	.15	.30
150 Rats of Rath C	.07	.15
151 Reanimate U	7.50	15.00
152 Reckless Spite U	.10	.20
153 Sadistic Glee C	.07	.15
154 Sarcomancy R	6.00	12.00
155 Screeching Harpy U	.10	.20
156 Servant of Volrath C	.07	.15
157 Skyshroud Vampire U	.10	.20
158 Souldrinker U	.10	.20
159 Spinal Graft C	.07	.15
160 Aftershock C	.15	.30
161 Ancient Runes U	.10	.20
162 Apocalypse R	15.00	30.00
163 Barbed Sliver U	.10	.20
164 Blood Frenzy C	.07	.15
165 Boil U	4.00	8.00
166 Canyon Drake R	.20	.40
167 Canyon Wildcat C	.07	.15
168 Chaotic Goo R	2.00	4.00
169 Crown of Flames C	.07	.15
170 Deadshot R	.20	.40
171 Enraging Licid U	.10	.20
172 Firefly U	.10	.20
173 Fireslinger C	.07	.15
174 Flowstone Giant C	.07	.15
175 Flowstone Salamander U	.10	.20
176 Flowstone Wyvern R	.20	.40
177 Furnace of Rath R	4.00	8.00
178 Giant Strength C	.07	.15
179 Goblin Bombardment U	4.00	8.00
180 Hand to Hand R	.20	.40
181 Havoc U	.10	.20
182 Heart Sliver C	.75	1.50
183 Jackal Pup U	.10	.20
184 Kindle C	.07	.15
185 Lightning Blast C	.07	.15
186 Lightning Elemental C	.07	.15
187 Lowland Giant C	.07	.15
188 Magmasaur R	.30	.60
189 Mogg Conscripts C	.15	.30
190 Mogg Fanatic C	.15	.30
191 Mogg Raider C	.15	.30
192 Mogg Squad U	.10	.20
193 No Quarter R	.20	.40
194 Opportunist U	.10	.20
195 Pallimud R	.25	.50
196 Rathi Dragon R	.30	.75
197 Renegade Warlord U	.10	.20
198 Rolling Thunder C	.15	.30
199 Sandstone Warrior C	.07	.15
200 Scorched Earth R	.30	.60
201 Searing Touch U	.10	.20
202 Shadowstorm U	.10	.20
203 Shatter C	.07	.15
204 Shocker R	.60	1.25
205 Starke of Rath R	1.00	2.00
206 Stone Rain C	.07	.15
207 Stun C	.07	.15
208 Sudden Impact U	.10	.20
209 Tahngarth's Rage U	.20	.40
210 Tooth and Claw R	.20	.40
211 Wall of Diffusion C	.07	.15
212 Wild Wurm U	.10	.20
213 Aluren R	50.00	100.00
214 Apes of Rath U	.10	.20
215 Bayou Dragonfly C	.07	.15
216 Broken Fall C	.07	.15
217 Canopy Spider C	.07	.15
218 Charging Rhino U	.10	.20
219 Choke U	2.50	5.00
220 Crazed Armodon R	.30	.60
221 Dirtcowl Wurm R	.50	1.00
222 Earthcraft R	100.00	200.00
223 Eladamri's Vineyard R	10.00	20.00
224 Eladamri, Lord of Leaves R	10.00	20.00
225 Elven Warhounds R	.30	.75
226 Elvish Fury C	.07	.15
227 Flailing Drake U	.10	.20
228 Frog Tongue C	.07	.15
229 Fugitive Druid R	.20	.40
230 Harrow U	.30	.60
231 Heartwood Dryad C	.07	.15
232 Heartwood Giant R	.20	.40
233 Heartwood Treefolk U	.15	.30
234 Horned Sliver U	4.00	8.00
235 Krakilin U	.15	.30
236 Mirri's Guile R	25.00	50.00
237 Mongrel Pack R	1.50	3.00
238 Muscle Sliver C	.60	1.25
239 Natural Spring C	.07	.15
240 Nature's Revolt R	1.00	2.00
241 Needle Storm U	.10	.20
242 Nurturing Licid U	.10	.20
243 Overrun U	.10	.20
244 Pincher Beetles C	.07	.15
245 Rampant Growth C	.60	1.25
246 Reality Anchor C	.07	.15
247 Reap U	2.00	4.00
248 Recycle R	7.50	15.00
249 Respite C	.15	.30
250 Root Maze R	4.00	8.00
251 Rootbreaker Wurm C	.07	.15
252 Rootwalla C	.07	.15
253 Scragnoth U	.10	.20
254 Seeker of Skybreak C	.75	1.50
255 Skyshroud Elf C	.12	.25
256 Skyshroud Ranger C	.30	.60
257 Skyshroud Troll C	.07	.15
258 Spike Drone C	.07	.15
259 Storm Front U	.15	.30
260 Trained Armodon C	.07	.15
261 Tranquility C	.07	.15
262 Trumpeting Armodon U	.10	.20
263 Verdant Force R	1.25	2.50
264 Verdigris U	.10	.20
265 Winter's Grasp U	.20	.40
266 Dracoplasm R/	.30	.60
267 Lobotomy U/	.10	.20
268 Ranger en-Vec U/:W:	.10	.20
269 Segmented Wurm U	.10	.20
270 Selenia, Dark Angel R/	10.00	20.00
271 Sky Spirit U/:B:	.10	.20
272 Soltari Guerrillas R/:W:	.40	.80
273 Spontaneous Combustion U/	.10	.20
274 Vhati il-Dal R	1.25	2.50
275 Wood Sage R/:B:	.25	.50
276 Altar of Dementia R	7.50	15.00
277 Booby Trap R	.30	.60
278 Bottle Gnomes U	.20	.40
279 Coiled Tinviper C	.07	.15
280 Cold Storage R	1.50	3.00
281 Cursed Scroll R	20.00	40.00
282 Echo Chamber R	.20	.40
283 Emerald Medallion R	10.00	20.00
284 Emmessi Tome R	.25	.50
285 Energizer R	.25	.50
286 Essence Bottle U	.10	.20
287 Excavator U	.10	.20
288 Flowstone Sculpture R	.20	.40
289 Fool's Tome R	.20	.40
290 Grindstone R	20.00	40.00
291 Helm of Possession R	4.00	8.00
292 Jet Medallion R	30.00	60.00
293 Jinxed Idol R	.50	1.00
294 Lotus Petal C	7.50	15.00
295 Magnetic Web R	.25	.50
296 Manakin C	.20	.40
297 Metallic Sliver C	.15	.30
298 Mogg Cannon U	.10	.20
299 Patchwork Gnomes U	.10	.20
300 Pearl Medallion R	12.50	25.00
301 Phyrexian Grimoire R	.20	.40
302 Phyrexian Hulk U	.10	.20
303 Phyrexian Splicer U	.15	.30
304 Puppet Strings U	.10	.20
305 Ruby Medallion R	20.00	40.00
306 Sapphire Medallion R	30.00	60.00
307 Scalding Tongs R	.25	.50
308 Scroll Rack R	30.00	60.00
309 Squee's Toy C	.12	.25
310 Static Orb R	12.50	25.00
311 Telethopter U	.10	.20
312 Thumbscrews R	.20	.40
313 Torture Chamber R	.20	.40
314 Watchdog U	.20	.40
315 Ancient Tomb U	30.00	60.00
316 Caldera Lake R	1.00	2.00
317 Cinder Marsh U	.15	.30
318 Ghost Town U	2.50	5.00
319 Maze of Shadows U	.10	.20
320 Mogg Hollows U	.10	.20
321 Pine Barrens R	1.00	2.00
322 Reflecting Pool R	20.00	40.00
323 Rootwater Depths U	.10	.20
324 Salt Flats R	.75	1.50
325 Scabland R	.60	1.25
326 Skyshroud Forest R	.75	1.50
327 Stalking Stones U	.15	.30
328 Thalakos Lowlands U	.10	.20
329 Vec Townships U	.10	.20
330 Wasteland U	25.00	50.00
331 Plains L	.07	.15
332 Plains L	.07	.15
333 Plains L	.07	.15
334 Plains L	.07	.15
335 Island L	.07	.15
336 Island L	.07	.15
337 Island L	.07	.15
338 Island L	.07	.15
339 Swamp L	.07	.15
340 Swamp L	.07	.15
341 Swamp L	.07	.15
342 Swamp L	.07	.15
343 Mountain L	.07	.15
344 Mountain L	.07	.15
345 Mountain L	.07	.15
346 Mountain L	.07	.15
347 Forest L	.07	.15
348 Forest L	.07	.15
349 Forest L	.07	.15
350 Forest L	.07	.15

1997 Magic The Gathering Vanguard

1 Ashnod R	10.00	20.00
2 Barrin R	6.00	12.00
3 Crovax R	7.50	15.00
4 Eladamri R	7.50	15.00
5 Ertai R	1.50	3.00
6 Gerrard R	1.25	2.50
7 Gix R	50.00	100.00
8 Greven il-Vec R	2.50	5.00
9 Hanna R	6.00	12.00
10 Karn R	5.00	10.00
11 Lyna R	15.00	30.00
12 Maraxus R	.75	1.50
13 Mirri R	3.00	6.00
14 Mishra R	6.00	12.00
15 Multani R	2.00	4.00
16 Oracle R	25.00	50.00
17 Orim R	7.50	15.00
18 Rofellos R	7.50	15.00
19 Selenia R	25.00	50.00
20 Serra R	10.00	20.00
21 Sidar Kondo R	7.50	15.00
22 Sisay R	2.50	5.00
23 Sliver Queen, Brood Mother R	60.00	125.00
24 Squee R	5.00	10.00
25 Starke R	3.00	6.00
26 Tahngarth R	.75	1.50
27 Takara R	1.25	2.50
28 Tawnos R	5.00	10.00
29 Titania R	50.00	100.00
30 Urza R	15.00	30.00
31 Volrath R	7.50	15.00
32 Xantcha R	20.00	40.00

1997 Magic The Gathering Visions

1 Archangel R	.30	.60
2 Daraja Griffin U	.10	.20
3 Equipoise R	12.50	25.00
4 Eye of Singularity R	3.00	6.00
5 Freewind Falcon C	.10	.20
6 Gossamer Chains C	.12	.25
7 Honorable Passage U	.10	.20
8 Hope Charm C	.07	.15
9 Infantry Veteran C	.07	.15
10 Jamuraan Lion C	.07	.15
11 Knight of Valor C	.07	.15
12 Longbow Archer U	.10	.20
13 Miraculous Recovery U	.12	.25
14 Parapet C	.07	.15
15 Peace Talks U	.12	.25
16 Relic Ward U	.10	.20
17 Remedy C	.07	.15
18 Resistance Fighter C	.07	.15

19 Retribution of the Meek R	10.00	20.00
20 Righteous Aura C	.10	.20
21 Sun Clasp C	.07	.15
22 Teferi's Honor Guard U	.10	.20
23 Tithe R	30.00	60.00
24 Warrior's Honor C	.07	.15
25 Zhalfirin Crusader R	2.00	4.00
26 Betrayal C	.10	.20
27 Breezekeeper C	.07	.15
28 Chronatog R	3.00	6.00
29 Cloud Elemental C	.07	.15
30 Desertion R	3.00	6.00
31 Dream Tides U	.50	1.00
32 Flooded Shoreline R	2.50	5.00
33 Foreshadow U	.10	.20
34 Impulse C	.30	.60
35 Inspiration C	.07	.15
36 Knight of the Mists C	.07	.15
37 Man-o'-War C	.07	.15
38 Mystic Veil C	.07	.15
39 Ovinomancer U	.10	.20
40 Prosperity U	1.25	2.50
41 Rainbow Efreet R	4.00	8.00
42 Shimmering Efreet U	.10	.20
43 Shrieking Drake C	.50	1.00
44 Teferi's Realm R	4.00	8.00
45 Three Wishes R	10.00	20.00
46 Time and Tide U	.10	.20
47 Undo C	.07	.15
48 Vanishing C	.25	.50
49 Vision Charm C	.12	.25
50 Waterspout Djinn U	.10	.20
51 Aku Djinn R	4.00	8.00
52 Blanket of Night U	.30	.75
53 Brood of Cockroaches U	.20	.40
54 Coercion C	.07	.15
55 Crypt Rats C	.20	.40
56 Dark Privilege C	.15	.30
57 Death Watch C	.07	.15
58 Desolation U	4.00	8.00
59 Fallen Askari C	.07	.15
60 Forbidden Ritual R	4.00	8.00
61 Funeral Charm C	.15	.30
62 Infernal Harvest C	.07	.15
63 Kaervek's Spite R	3.00	6.00
64 Necromancy U	10.00	20.00
65 Necrosavant R	.25	.50
66 Nekrataal U	.20	.40
67 Pillar Tombs of Aku R	2.50	5.00
68 Python C	.07	.15
69 Suq'Ata Assassin U	.12	.25
70 Tar Pit Warrior C	.07	.15
71 Urborg Mindsucker C	.07	.15
72 Vampiric Tutor R	40.00	80.00
73 Vampirism U	.12	.25
74 Wake of Vultures C	.07	.15
75 Wicked Reward C	.07	.15
76 Bogardan Phoenix R	1.50	3.00
77 Dwarven Vigilantes C	.07	.15
78 Elkin Lair R	3.00	6.00
79 Fireblast C	1.00	2.00
80 Goblin Recruiter U	3.00	6.00
81 Goblin Swine-Rider C	.07	.15
82 Hearth Charm C	.07	.15
83 Heat Wave U	.10	.20
84 Hulking Cyclops U	.07	.15
85 Keeper of Kookus C	.07	.15
86 Kookus R	1.25	2.50
87 Lightning Cloud R	4.00	8.00
88 Mob Mentality U	.12	.25
89 Ogre Enforcer R	1.25	2.50
90 Raging Gorilla C	.07	.15
91 Relentless Assault R	1.50	3.00
92 Rock Slide C	.07	.15
93 Solfatara C	.07	.15
94 Song of Blood C	.07	.15
95 Spitting Drake U	.10	.20
96 Suq'Ata Lancer C	.07	.15
97 Talruum Champion C	.07	.15
98 Talruum Piper U	.12	.25
99 Tremor C	.07	.15
100 Viashino Sandstalker U	.25	.50
101 Bull Elephant C	.07	.15
102 City of Solitude R	30.00	60.00
103 Creeping Mold U	.12	.25
104 Elephant Grass U	1.50	3.00
105 Elven Cache C	.07	.15
106 Emerald Charm C	.20	.40
107 Feral Instinct C	.07	.15
108 Giant Caterpillar C	.07	.15
109 Katabatic Winds R	2.50	5.00
110 King Cheetah C	.07	.15
111 Kyscu Drake U	.10	.20
112 Lichenthrope R	1.50	3.00
113 Mortal Wound C	.07	.15
114 Natural Order R	25.00	50.00
115 Panther Warriors C	.07	.15
116 Quirion Druid R	6.00	12.00
117 Quirion Ranger C	3.00	6.00
118 River Boa C	.12	.25
119 Rowen R	.25	.50
120 Spider Climb C	.07	.15
121 Stampeding Wildebeests U	.12	.25
122 Summer Bloom U	1.25	2.50
123 Uktabi Orangutan U	.20	.40
124 Warthog C	.07	.15
125 Wind Shear U	.10	.20
126 Army Ants U/	.20	.40
127 Breathstealer's Crypt R/	7.50	15.00
128 Corrosion R/	2.50	5.00
129 Femeref Enchantress R/:W:	12.50	25.00
130 Firestorm Hellkite R/	1.25	2.50
131 Guiding Spirit R/:B:	3.00	6.00
132 Mundungu U/	.15	.30
133 Pygmy Hippo R/:B:	12.50	25.00
134 Righteous War R/	6.00	12.00
135 Scalebane's Elite U/:W:	.10	.20
136 Simoon U	.12	.25
137 Squandered Resources R	20.00	40.00
138 Suleiman's Legacy R/:W:	10.00	20.00
139 Tempest Drake U/:B:	.10	.20
140 Viashivan Dragon R	2.50	5.00
141 Anvil of Bogardan R	50.00	100.00
142 Brass Talon Chimera U	.12	.25
143 Diamond Kaleidoscope R	6.00	12.00
144 Dragon Mask U	.10	.20
145 Helm of Awakening U	3.00	6.00
146 Iron-Heart Chimera U	.12	.25
147 Juju Bubble U	.10	.20
148 Lead-Belly Chimera U	.10	.20
149 Magma Mine U	.10	.20
150 Matopi Golem U	.12	.25
151 Phyrexian Marauder R	3.00	6.00
152 Phyrexian Walker C	1.00	2.00
153 Sands of Time R	6.00	12.00
154 Sisay's Ring C	.30	.75
155 Snake Basket R	1.00	2.00
156 Teferi's Puzzle Box R	4.00	8.00
157 Tin-Wing Chimera U	.10	.20
158 Triangle of War R	3.00	6.00
159 Wand of Denial R	.25	.50
160 Coral Atoll U	.50	1.00
161 Dormant Volcano U	.20	.40
162 Everglades U	.30	.60
163 Griffin Canyon R	10.00	20.00
164 Jungle Basin U	.20	.40
165 Karoo U	.30	.60
166 Quicksand U	.20	.40
167 Undiscovered Paradise R	20.00	40.00

1997 Magic The Gathering Weatherlight

1 Abeyance R	15.00	30.00
2 Alabaster Dragon R	.50	1.00
3 Alms C	.07	.15
4 Angelic Renewal C	.20	.40
5 Ardent Militia C	.07	.15
6 Argivian Find U	1.00	2.00
7 Aura of Silence U	2.50	5.00
8 Benalish Infantry C	.07	.15
9 Benalish Knight C	.07	.15
10 Benalish Missionary C	.07	.15
11 Debt of Loyalty R	20.00	40.00
12 Duskrider Falcon C	.12	.25
13 Empyrial Armor C	.15	.30
14 Foriysian Brigade U	.10	.20
15 Gerrard's Wisdom U	.12	.25
16 Guided Strike C	.07	.15
17 Heavy Ballista C	.07	.15
18 Inner Sanctum R	6.00	12.00
19 Kithkin Armor C	.07	.15
20 Master of Arms U	.10	.20
21 Mistmoon Griffin U	.20	.40
22 Peacekeeper R	25.00	50.00
23 Revered Unicorn U	.15	.30
24 Serenity R	1.50	3.00
25 Serra's Blessing U	.30	.75
26 Soul Shepherd C	.07	.15
27 Southern Paladin R	.30	.75
28 Tariff R	.30	.60
29 Volunteer Reserves U	.12	.25
30 Abduction U	.20	.40
31 Abjure C	.25	.50
32 Ancestral Knowledge R	10.00	20.00
33 Apathy C	.07	.15
34 Argivian Restoration U	.20	.40
35 Avizoa R	1.25	2.50
36 Cloud Djinn U	.10	.20
37 Disrupt C	.15	.30
38 Ertai's Familiar R	3.00	6.00
39 Flux C	.20	.40
40 Fog Elemental C	.07	.15
41 Mana Chains C	.12	.25
42 Manta Ray C	.07	.15
43 Merfolk Traders C	.07	.15
44 Noble Benefactor U	.30	.60
45 Ophidian C	.07	.15
46 Paradigm Shift R	15.00	30.00
47 Pendrell Mists R	15.00	30.00
48 Phantom Warrior U	.12	.25
49 Phantom Wings C	.07	.15
50 Psychic Vortex R	10.00	20.00
51 Relearn U	.30	.75
52 Sage Owl C	.12	.25
53 Teferi's Veil U	2.00	4.00
54 Timid Drake U	.10	.20
55 Tolarian Drake C	.07	.15
56 Tolarian Entrancer R	6.00	12.00
57 Tolarian Serpent R	2.50	5.00
58 Vodalian Illusionist U	.30	.75
59 Abyssal Gatekeeper C	.20	.40
60 Agonizing Memories U	.10	.20
61 Barrow Ghoul C	.07	.15
62 Bone Dancer R	7.50	15.00
63 Buried Alive U	3.00	6.00
64 Circling Vultures U	.12	.25
65 Coils of the Medusa C	.07	.15
66 Doomsday R	7.50	15.00
67 Fatal Blow C	.10	.20
68 Festering Evil U	.15	.30
69 Fledgling Djinn C	.07	.15
70 Gallowbraid R	2.00	4.00
71 Haunting Misery C	.12	.25
72 Hidden Horror U	.07	.15
73 Infernal Tribute R	7.50	15.00
74 Mischievous Poltergeist U	.20	.40
75 Morinfen R	2.00	4.00
76 Necratog U	.12	.25
77 Odylic Wraith U	.10	.20
78 Razortooth Rats C	.07	.15
79 Shadow Rider C	.07	.15
80 Shattered Crypt C	.07	.15
81 Spinning Darkness C	.15	.30
82 Strands of Night U	.50	1.00
83 Tendrils of Despair C	.07	.15
84 Urborg Justice R	7.50	15.00
85 Urborg Stalker R	3.00	6.00
86 Wave of Terror R	2.50	5.00
87 Zombie Scavengers C	.07	.15
88 Aether Flash U	.30	.75
89 Betrothed of Fire C	.07	.15
90 Bloodrock Cyclops C	.07	.15
91 Bogardan Firefiend C	.07	.15
92 Boiling Blood C	.20	.40
93 Cinder Giant U	.12	.25
94 Cinder Wall C	.07	.15
95 Cone of Flame U	.10	.20
96 Desperate Gambit U	.25	.50
97 Dwarven Berserker C	.15	.30
98 Dwarven Thaumaturgist R	6.00	12.00
99 Fervor R	2.50	5.00
100 Fire Whip C	.10	.20
101 Firestorm R	15.00	30.00
102 Fit of Rage C	.07	.15
103 Goblin Bomb R	7.50	15.00
104 Goblin Grenadiers U	.25	.50
105 Goblin Vandal C	.12	.25
106 Heart of Bogardan R	2.50	5.00
107 Heat Stroke R	7.50	15.00
108 Hurloon Shaman U	.25	.50
109 Lava Hounds U	.10	.20
110 Lava Storm C	.07	.15
111 Maraxus of Keld R	5.00	10.00
112 Orcish Settlers U	.30	.75
113 Roc Hatchling U	.10	.20
114 Sawtooth Ogre C	.07	.15
115 Thunderbolt C	.07	.15
116 Thundermare R	.75	1.50
117 Aboroth R	6.00	12.00
118 Arctic Wolves U	.10	.20
119 Barishi U	.12	.25
120 Blossoming Wreath C	.07	.15
121 Briar Shield C	.07	.15
122 Call of the Wild R	.30	.75
123 Choking Vines C	.12	.25
124 Dense Foliage R	.60	1.25
125 Downdraft U	.10	.20
126 Fallow Wurm U	.10	.20
127 Familiar Ground U	.15	.30
128 Fungus Elemental R	4.00	8.00
129 Gaea's Blessing U	.30	.75
130 Harvest Wurm C	.12	.25
131 Liege of the Hollows R	7.50	15.00
132 Llanowar Behemoth U	.10	.20
133 Llanowar Druid C	.20	.40
134 Llanowar Sentinel C	.10	.20
135 Mwonvuli Ooze R	1.00	2.00
136 Nature's Kiss C	.07	.15
137 Nature's Resurgence R	.25	.50
138 Redwood Treefolk C	.07	.15
139 Rogue Elephant C	.12	.25
140 Striped Bears C	.20	.40
141 Sylvan Hierophant U	.12	.25
142 Tranquil Grove R	2.00	4.00
143 Uktabi Efreet C	.07	.15
144 Veteran Explorer U	.25	.50
145 Vitalize C	2.00	4.00
146 Bubble Matrix R	10.00	20.00
147 Bosium Strip R	7.50	15.00
148 Chimeric Sphere U	.12	.25
149 Dingus Staff U	.30	.75
150 Jabari's Banner U	.12	.25
151 Jangling Automaton C	.07	.15
152 Mana Web R	20.00	40.00
153 Mind Stone C	1.25	2.50
154 Null Rod R	75.00	150.00
155 Phyrexian Furnace U	.30	.60
156 Serrated Biskelion U	.25	.50
157 Steel Golem U	.50	1.00
158 Straw Golem U	.10	.20
159 Thran Forge U	.15	.30
160 Thran Tome R	3.00	6.00
161 Touchstone U	.10	.20
162 Well of Knowledge R	6.00	12.00
163 Xanthic Statue R	1.50	3.00
164 Gemstone Mine U	5.00	10.00
165 Lotus Vale R	30.00	75.00
166 Scorched Ruins R	30.00	75.00
167 Winding Canyons R	30.00	60.00

1998 Magic The Gathering Exodus

1 Allay C	.10	.20
2 Angelic Blessing C	.07	.15
3 Cataclysm R	6.00	12.00
4 Charging Paladin C	.07	.15
5 Convalescence R	.20	.40
6 Exalted Dragon R	5.00	10.00
7 High Ground U	.12	.25
8 Keeper of the Light U	.12	.25
9 Kor Chant C	.07	.15
10 Limited Resources R	2.50	5.00
11 Oath of Lieges R	4.00	8.00
12 Paladin en-Vec R	.75	1.50
13 Peace of Mind U	.12	.25
14 Pegasus Stampede U	.12	.25
15 Penance U	.60	1.25
16 Reaping the Rewards C	.07	.15
17 Reconnaissance U	4.00	8.00
18 Shackles C	.07	.15
19 Shield Mate C	.07	.15
20 Soltari Visionary C	.15	.30
21 Soul Warden C	.60	1.25
22 Standing Troops C	.07	.15
23 Treasure Hunter U	.15	.30
24 Wall of Nets R	2.50	5.00
25 Welkin Hawk C	.07	.15
26 Zealots en-Dal U	.12	.25
27 Aether Tide C	.07	.15
28 Cunning C	.07	.15
29 Curiosity U	.30	.75
30 Dominating Licid R	7.50	15.00
31 Ephemeron R	.20	.40
32 Equilibrium R	4.00	8.00
33 Ertai, Wizard Adept R	25.00	50.00
34 Fade Away C	.30	.75
35 Forbid U	1.25	2.50
36 Keeper of the Mind U	.12	.25
37 Killer Whale U	.12	.25
38 Mana Breach U	2.00	4.00
39 Merfolk Looter C	.07	.15
40 Mind Over Matter R	50.00	100.00
41 Mirozel U	.12	.25
42 Oath of Scholars R	.20	.40
43 Robe of Mirrors C	.12	.25
44 Rootwater Mystic C	.07	.15
45 School of Piranha C	.07	.15
46 Scrivener U	.12	.25
47 Thalakos Drifters R	.20	.40
48 Thalakos Scout C	.07	.15
49 Theft of Dreams C	.07	.15
50 Treasure Trove U	.12	.25
51 Wayward Soul C	.07	.15
52 Whiptongue Frog C	.07	.15
53 Carnophage C	.15	.30
54 Cat Burglar C	.07	.15
55 Culling the Weak C	5.00	10.00
56 Cursed Flesh C	.07	.15
57 Dauthi Cutthroat U	.12	.25
58 Dauthi Jackal C	.12	.25
59 Dauthi Warlord U	.15	.30
60 Death's Duet C	.07	.15
61 Entropic Specter R	.25	.50
62 Fugue U	.12	.25
63 Grollub C	.07	.15
64 Hatred R	20.00	40.00
65 Keeper of the Dead U	.12	.25
66 Mind Maggots U	.12	.25
67 Nausea C	.07	.15
68 Necrologia U	.75	1.50
69 Oath of Ghouls R	12.50	25.00
70 Pit Spawn R	.40	.80
71 Plaguebearer R	.50	1.00
72 Recurring Nightmare R	40.00	80.00
73 Scare Tactics C	.07	.15
74 Slaughter U	.25	.50
75 Spike Cannibal U	.15	.30
76 Thrull Surgeon C	.07	.15
77 Vampire Hounds C	.07	.15
78 Volrath's Dungeon R	.25	.50
79 Anarchist C	.10	.20
80 Cinder Crawler C	.07	.15
81 Dizzying Gaze C	.07	.15
82 Fighting Chance R	.75	1.50
83 Flowstone Flood U	.12	.25
84 Furnace Brood C	.07	.15
85 Keeper of the Flame U	.12	.25
86 Mage il-Vec C	.07	.15
87 Maniacal Rage C	.07	.15
88 Mogg Assassin U	1.00	2.00
89 Monstrous Hound R	.20	.40
90 Oath of Mages R	.20	.40
91 Ogre Shaman R	.20	.40
92 Onslaught C	.07	.15
93 Pandemonium R	1.50	3.00
94 Paroxysm U	.12	.25
95 Price of Progress U	2.00	4.00
96 Raging Goblin C	.07	.15
97 Ravenous Baboons R	.30	.75
98 Reckless Ogre C	.07	.15
99 Sabertooth Wyvern U	.12	.25
100 Scalding Salamander U	.12	.25
101 Seismic Assault R	1.00	2.00
102 Shattering Pulse C	.12	.25
103 Sonic Burst C	.07	.15
104 Spellshock U	3.00	6.00
105 Avenging Druid C	.10	.20
106 Bequeathal C	.15	.30
107 Cartographer U	.12	.25
108 Crashing Boars U	.12	.25
109 Elven Palisade U	.12	.25
110 Elvish Berserker C	.07	.15
111 Jackalope Herd C	.07	.15
112 Keeper of the Beasts U	.12	.25
113 Manabond R	4.00	8.00
114 Mirri, Cat Warrior R	2.00	4.00
115 Oath of Druids R	10.00	20.00
116 Plated Rootwalla C	.07	.15
117 Predatory Hunger C	.20	.40
118 Pygmy Troll C	.07	.15
119 Rabid Wolverines C	.07	.15
120 Reclaim C	.07	.15
121 Resuscitate U	.12	.25
122 Rootwater Alligator C	.07	.15
123 Skyshroud Elite U	.12	.25
124 Skyshroud War Beast R	.30	.60
125 Song of Serenity U	.12	.25
126 Spike Hatcher R	.20	.40
127 Spike Rogue U	.12	.25
128 Spike Weaver R	5.00	10.00
129 Survival of the Fittest R	150.00	300.00
130 Wood Elves C	.75	1.50
131 Coat of Arms R	10.00	20.00
132 Erratic Portal R	5.00	10.00
133 Medicine Bag U	.20	.40
134 Memory Crystal R	.75	1.50
135 Mindless Automaton R	.30	.60
136 Null Brooch R	2.00	4.00
137 Skyshaper U	.12	.25
138 Spellbook U	1.50	3.00
139 Sphere of Resistance R	15.00	30.00
140 Thopter Squadron R	.60	1.25
141 Transmogrifying Licid U	.15	.30
142 Workhorse R	3.00	6.00
143 City of Traitors R	150.00	300.00

1998 Magic The Gathering Judge Gift Rewards

1 Lightning Bolt R	600.00	1,200.00
2 Stroke of Genius R	30.00	60.00
3 Gaea's Cradle R	1,750.00	3,500.00

1998 Magic The Gathering Portal Second Age

1 Alaborn Cavalier U	.12	.25
2 Alaborn Grenadier C	.15	.30
3 Alaborn Musketeer C	.15	.30
4 Alaborn Trooper C	.07	.15
5 Alaborn Veteran R	.50	1.00
6 Alaborn Zealot U	.75	1.50
7 Angel of Fury R	1.50	3.00
8 Angel of Mercy U	.12	.25
9 Angelic Blessing C	.07	.15
10 Angelic Wall C	.15	.30
11 Archangel R	2.00	4.00
12 Armageddon R	3.00	6.00
13 Armored Griffin U	.12	.25
14 Bargain U	.50	1.00
15 Breath of Life C	.25	.50
16 Festival of Trokin C	.30	.75
17 Just Fate R	.50	1.00
18 Path of Peace C	.07	.15
19 Rally the Troops U	.25	.50
20 Righteous Charge C	.07	.15
21 Righteous Fury R	2.50	5.00

22 Steam Catapult R	2.50	5.00
23 Temple Acolyte C	.12	.25
24 Temple Elder U	.12	.25
25 Town Sentry C	.12	.25
26 Trokin High Guard C	.15	.30
27 Vengeance U	.12	.25
28 Volunteer Militia C	.07	.15
29 Warrior's Stand U	.12	.25
30 Wild Griffin C	.07	.15
31 Air Elemental U	.12	.25
32 Apprentice Sorcerer U	.30	.60
33 Armored Galleon U	.50	1.00
34 Coastal Wizard R	2.50	5.00
35 Denizen of the Deep R	1.50	3.00
36 Deja Vu C	.12	.25
37 Exhaustion R	1.00	2.00
38 Extinguish C	.07	.15
39 Eye Spy U	.12	.25
40 False Summoning C	.25	.50
41 Mystic Denial U	.12	.25
42 Piracy R	15.00	30.00
43 Remove U	.12	.25
44 Screeching Drake C	.20	.40
45 Sea Drake U	2.50	5.00
46 Sleight of Hand C	3.00	6.00
47 Steam Frigate C	.15	.30
48 Talas Air Ship C	.07	.15
49 Talas Explorer C	.20	.40
50 Talas Merchant C	.07	.15
51 Talas Researcher R	1.00	2.00
52 Talas Scout C	.15	.30
53 Talas Warrior R	6.00	12.00
54 Temporal Manipulation R	30.00	60.00
55 Theft of Dreams U	.12	.25
56 Tidal Surge C	.07	.15
57 Time Ebb C	.07	.15
58 Touch of Brilliance C	.07	.15
59 Undo U	.12	.25
60 Wind Sail C	.07	.15
61 Abyssal Nightstalker U	.15	.30
62 Ancient Craving R	2.00	4.00
63 Bloodcurdling Scream U	.20	.40
64 Brutal Nightstalker U	.12	.25
65 Chorus of Woe C	.07	.15
66 Coercion U	.12	.25
67 Cruel Edict C	.07	.15
68 Dakmor Bat C	.12	.25
69 Dakmor Plague U	.30	.60
70 Dakmor Scorpion C	.07	.15
71 Dakmor Sorceress R	3.00	6.00
72 Dark Offering U	.12	.25
73 Foul Spirit U	.25	.50
74 Hand of Death C	.07	.15
75 Hidden Horror R	.75	1.50
76 Kiss of Death U	.12	.25
77 Lurking Nightstalker C	.07	.15
78 Mind Rot C	.07	.15
79 Moaning Spirit C	.07	.15
80 Muck Rats C	.15	.30
81 Nightstalker Engine R	.20	.40
82 Predatory Nightstalker U	6.00	12.00
83 Prowling Nightstalker C	.07	.15
84 Raiding Nightstalker C	.07	.15
85 Rain of Daggers R	3.00	6.00
86 Raise Dead C	.07	.15
87 Ravenous Rats C	.30	.75
88 Return of the Nightstalkers R	.30	.60
89 Swarm of Rats C	1.00	2.00
90 Vampiric Spirit R	.75	1.50
91 Blaze U	.20	.40
92 Brimstone Dragon R	2.50	5.00
93 Cunning Giant R	1.00	2.00
94 Earthquake R	1.50	3.00
95 Goblin Cavaliers C	.07	.15
96 Goblin Firestarter U	.30	.75
97 Goblin General R	4.00	8.00
98 Goblin Glider C	.07	.15
99 Goblin Lore U	2.50	5.00
100 Goblin Matron U	1.25	2.50
101 Goblin Mountaineer C	.07	.15
102 Goblin Piker C	.07	.15
103 Goblin Raider C	.07	.15
104 Goblin War Cry U	1.50	3.00
105 Goblin War Strike C	1.25	2.50
106 Jagged Lightning U	.12	.25
107 Lava Axe C	.07	.15
108 Magma Giant R	.50	1.00
109 Obsidian Giant U	.12	.25
110 Ogre Arsonist U	.50	1.00
111 Ogre Berserker C	.07	.15
112 Ogre Taskmaster U	.15	.30
113 Ogre Warrior C	.07	.15
114 Raging Goblin C	.07	.15
115 Relentless Assault R	2.00	4.00
116 Spitting Earth C	.07	.15
117 Stone Rain C	.30	.75
118 Tremor C	.15	.30
119 Volcanic Hammer C	.20	.40

120 Wildfire R	1.00	2.00
121 Alluring Scent R	.60	1.25
122 Barbtooth Wurm C	.15	.30
123 Bear Cub C	1.00	2.00
124 Bee Sting U	.12	.25
125 Deathcoil Wurm R	4.00	8.00
126 Deep Wood U	.12	.25
127 Golden Bear C	2.00	4.00
128 Harmony of Nature U	1.25	2.50
129 Hurricane R	.50	1.00
130 Ironhoof Ox U	.12	.25
131 Lone Wolf U	.12	.25
132 Lynx C	.30	.60
133 Monstrous Growth C	.15	.30
134 Natural Spring C	.07	.15
135 Nature's Lore C	4.00	8.00
136 Norwood Archers C	.30	.60
137 Norwood Priestess R	50.00	100.00
138 Norwood Ranger C	.07	.15
139 Norwood Riders C	.30	.60
140 Norwood Warrior C	.20	.40
141 Plated Wurm C	.07	.15
142 Razorclaw Bear R	30.00	60.00
143 Renewing Touch U	1.50	3.00
144 River Bear U	3.00	6.00
145 Salvage C	6.00	12.00
146 Sylvan Basilisk R	.50	1.00
147 Sylvan Yeti R	.75	1.50
148 Tree Monkey C	.20	.40
149 Untamed Wilds U	.15	.30
150 Wild Ox U	.12	.25
151 Plains L	.07	.15
152 Plains L	.07	.15
153 Plains L	.07	.15
154 Island L	.07	.15
155 Island L	.07	.15
156 Island L	.07	.15
157 Swamp L	.07	.15
158 Swamp L	.07	.15
159 Swamp L	.07	.15
160 Mountain L	.07	.15
161 Mountain L	.07	.15
162 Mountain L	.07	.15
163 Forest L	.07	.15
164 Forest L	.07	.15
165 Forest L	.07	.15

1998 Magic The Gathering Stronghold

1 Bandage C	.15	.30
2 Calming Licid U	.12	.25
3 Change of Heart C	.07	.15
4 Contemplation U	.12	.25
5 Conviction C	.07	.15
6 Hidden Retreat R	.25	.50
7 Honor Guard C	.07	.15
8 Lancers en-Kor U	.12	.25
9 Nomads en-Kor C	.15	.30
10 Pursuit of Knowledge R	1.00	2.00
11 Rolling Stones R	1.00	2.00
12 Sacred Ground R	.30	.75
13 Samite Blessing C	.07	.15
14 Scapegoat U	.25	.50
15 Shaman en-Kor R	.60	1.25
16 Skyshroud Falcon C	.07	.15
17 Smite C	.07	.15
18 Soltari Champion R	1.00	2.00
19 Spirit en-Kor C	.07	.15
20 Temper U	.12	.25
21 Venerable Monk C	.07	.15
22 Wall of Essence U	.20	.40
23 Warrior en-Kor U	.12	.25
24 Warrior Angel R	.25	.50
25 Youthful Knight C	.07	.15
26 Cloud Spirit C	.07	.15
27 Contempt C	.07	.15
28 Dream Halls R	40.00	80.00
29 Dream Prowler C	.07	.15
30 Evacuation R	4.00	8.00
31 Gliding Licid U	.12	.25
32 Hammerhead Shark C	.07	.15
33 Hesitation U	.20	.40
34 Intruder Alarm R	4.00	8.00
35 Leap C	1.00	2.00
36 Mana Leak C	.30	.60
37 Mask of the Mimic U	.30	.75
38 Mind Games C	.30	.60
39 Ransack U	.12	.25
40 Rebound U	.12	.25
41 Reins of Power R	1.50	3.00
42 Sift C	.07	.15
43 Silver Wyvern R	3.00	6.00
44 Spindrift Drake C	.07	.15
45 Thalakos Deceiver R	2.00	4.00
46 Tidal Surge C	.07	.15
47 Tidal Warrior C	.07	.15
48 Volrath's Shapeshifter R	10.00	20.00
49 Walking Dream U	.12	.25
50 Wall of Tears U	.50	1.00
51 Bottomless Pit U	4.00	8.00
52 Brush With Death C	.07	.15
53 Cannibalize C	.07	.15
54 Corrupting Licid U	.12	.25
55 Crovax, the Cursed R	6.00	12.00
56 Dauthi Trapper U	.20	.40
57 Death Stroke C	.07	.15
58 Dungeon Shade C	.07	.15
59 Foul Imp C	.07	.15
60 Grave Pact R	20.00	40.00
61 Lab Rats C	.07	.15
62 Megrim U	.25	.50
63 Mind Peel U	.12	.25
64 Mindwarper R	.20	.40
65 Morgue Thrull C	.07	.15
66 Mortuary R	2.00	4.00
67 Rabid Rats C	.07	.15
68 Revenant R	.25	.50
69 Serpent Warrior C	.07	.15
70 Skeleton Scavengers R	.20	.40
71 Stronghold Assassin R	.50	1.00
72 Stronghold Taskmaster U	.12	.25
73 Torment C	.07	.15
74 Tortured Existence C	.07	.15
75 Wall of Souls U	.30	.60
76 Amok R	.20	.40
77 Convulsing Licid U	.12	.25
78 Craven Giant C	.07	.15
79 Duct Crawler C	.07	.15
80 Fanning the Flames U	.15	.30
81 Flame Wave U	.12	.25
82 Fling C	.07	.15
83 Flowstone Blade C	.07	.15
84 Flowstone Hellion U	.12	.25
85 Flowstone Mauler R	.25	.50
86 Flowstone Shambler C	.07	.15
87 Furnace Spirit C	.07	.15
88 Heat of Battle U	.12	.25
89 Invasion Plans R	.60	1.25
90 Mob Justice C	.30	.60
91 Mogg Bombers C	.07	.15
92 Mogg Flunkies C	.07	.15
93 Mogg Infestation R	4.00	8.00
94 Mogg Maniac U	.60	1.25
95 Ruination R	5.00	10.00
96 Seething Anger C	.12	.25
97 Shard Phoenix R	.20	.40
98 Shock C	.07	.15
99 Spitting Hydra R	.20	.40
100 Wall of Razors U	.20	.40
101 Awakening R	5.00	10.00
102 Burgeoning R	15.00	30.00
103 Cardassid R	.25	.50
104 Constant Mists U	5.00	10.00
105 Crossbow Ambush C	.07	.15
106 Elven Rite U	.12	.25
107 Endangered Armodon C	.07	.15
108 Hermit Druid R	12.50	25.00
109 Lowland Basilisk C	.07	.15
110 Mulch C	.12	.25
111 Overgrowth C	.20	.40
112 Primal Rage U	1.50	3.00
113 Provoke C	.07	.15
114 Skyshroud Archer C	.07	.15
115 Skyshroud Troopers C	.07	.15
116 Spike Breeder R	.20	.40
117 Spike Colony C	.07	.15
118 Spike Feeder U	.75	1.50
119 Spike Soldier U	.12	.25
120 Spike Worker C	.07	.15
121 Spined Wurm C	.07	.15
122 Tempting Licid U	.15	.30
123 Verdant Touch R	.20	.40
124 Volrath's Gardens R	.20	.40
125 Wall of Blossoms U	.75	1.50
126 Acidic Sliver U/	.25	.50
127 Crystalline Sliver U/:B:	5.00	10.00
128 Hibernation Sliver U/	2.00	4.00
129 Sliver Queen R/:B://	250.00	500.00
130 Spined Sliver U	.20	.40
131 Victual Sliver U/:W:	.20	.40
132 Bullwhip U	.12	.25
133 Ensnaring Bridge R	15.00	30.00
134 Heartstone U	2.50	5.00
135 Horn of Greed R	7.50	15.00
136 Hornet Cannon U	.12	.25
137 Jinxed Ring R	.30	.75
138 Mox Diamond R	300.00	600.00
139 Portcullis R	.75	1.50
140 Shifting Wall U	.50	1.00
141 Sword of the Chosen R	1.00	2.00
142 Volrath's Laboratory R	.30	.75
143 Volrath's Stronghold R	100.00	200.00

1998 Magic The Gathering Unglued

1 Charm School U	.25	.50
2 Double Dip C	.07	.15
2 The Cheese Stands Alone R	1.25	2.50
4 Get a Life U	.15	.30
5 I'm Rubber, You're Glue R	.60	1.25
6 Knight of the Hokey Pokey C	.12	.25
7 Lexivore U	.15	.30
8 Look at Me, I'm the DCI R	.50	1.00
9 Mesa Chicken C	.10	.20
10 Miss Demeanor U	.20	.40
11 Once More with Feeling R	.75	1.50
12 Prismatic Wardrobe C	.10	.20
13 Sex Appeal C	.10	.20
14 Bureaucracy R	.50	1.00
15 Censorship U	.75	1.50
16 Checks and Balances U	.15	.30
17 Chicken a la King R	.75	1.50
18 Clam Session C	.07	.15
19 Clambassadors C	.07	.15
20 Clam-I-Am C	.07	.15
21 Common Courtesy U	.30	.60
22 Denied! C	.07	.15
23 Double Take C	.07	.15
24 Fowl Play C	.07	.15
25 Free-for-All R	.75	1.50
26 Psychic Network R	.50	1.00
27 Sorry U	.15	.30
28 Big Furry Monster-L R	10.00	20.00
29 Big Furry Monster-R R	10.00	20.00
30 Deadhead C	.07	.15
31 Double Cross C	.07	.15
32 Handcuffs U	.30	.75
33 Infernal Spawn of Evil R	1.25	2.50
34 Jumbo Imp U	.15	.30
35 Organ Harvest C	.15	.30
36 Ow R	.50	1.00
37 Poultrygeist C	.10	.20
38 Temp of the Damned C	.10	.20
39 Volrath's Motion Sensor U	.25	.50
40 Burning Cinder Fury of Crimson Chaos Fire R.50		1.00
41 Chicken Egg C	.12	.25
42 Double Deal C	.07	.15
43 Goblin Bookie C	.12	.25
44 Goblin Bowling Team C	.12	.25
45 Goblin Tutor U	.50	1.00
46 Hurloon Wrangler C	.07	.15
47 Jalum Grifter R	.40	.80
48 Krazy Kow C	.07	.15
49 Landfill R	.25	.50
50 Ricochet U	.20	.40
51 Spark Fiend R	.30	.75
52 Strategy, Schmategy R	2.50	5.00
53 The Ultimate Nightmare of Wizards of the Coast Customer Service U	.25	.50
54 Cardboard Carapace R	.75	1.50
55 Double Play C	.07	.15
56 Elvish Impersonators C	.07	.15
57 Flock of Rabid Sheep U	.25	.50
58 Free-Range Chicken C	.10	.20
59 Gerrymandering U	.20	.40
60 Ghazban Ogress C	.10	.20
61 Growth Spurt C	.07	.15
62 Gus C	.07	.15
63 Hungry Hungry Heifer U	.15	.30
64 Incoming! R	.75	1.50
65 Mine, Mine, Mine! R	.75	1.50
66 Squirrel Farm R	1.00	2.00
67 Team Spirit C	.10	.20
68 Timmy, Power Gamer R	1.00	2.00
69 Ashnod's Coupon R	3.00	6.00
70 Blacker Lotus R	20.00	40.00
71 Bronze Calendar U	.20	.40
72 Chaos Confetti C	.75	1.50
73 Clay Pigeon U	.20	.40
74 Giant Fan R	.50	1.00
75 Jack-in-the-Mox R	2.00	4.00
76 Jester's Sombrero R	.30	.60
77 Mirror Mirror R	.75	1.50
78 Paper Tiger C	.50	1.00
79 Rock Lobster C	.60	1.25
80 Scissors Lizard C	.50	1.00
81 Spatula of the Ages U	.15	.30
82 Urza's Contact Lenses U	.25	.50
83 Urza's Science Fair Project U	.25	.50
84 Plains C	2.50	5.00
85 Island C	5.00	10.00
86 Swamp C	3.00	6.00
87 Mountain C	4.00	8.00
88 Forest C	6.00	12.00

1998 Magic The Gathering Unglued Tokens

1 Pegasus	.30	.75
2 Soldier	1.00	2.00
3 Zombie	5.00	10.00
4 Goblin	2.00	4.00
5 Sheep	.75	1.50
6 Squirrel	4.00	8.00

1998 Magic The Gathering Urza's Saga

1 Absolute Grace U	.30	.60
2 Absolute Law U	.25	.50
3 Angelic Chorus R	1.50	3.00
4 Angelic Page C	.07	.15
5 Brilliant Halo C	.07	.15
6 Catastrophe R	3.00	6.00
7 Clear U	.20	.40
8 Congregate C	.07	.15
9 Defensive Formation U	.15	.30
10 Disciple of Grace C	.07	.15
11 Disciple of Law C	.07	.15
12 Disenchant C	.07	.15
13 Elite Archers R	.20	.40
14 Faith Healer R	.75	1.50
15 Glorious Anthem R	1.25	2.50
16 Healing Salve C	.07	.15
17 Herald of Serra R	10.00	20.00
18 Humble U	.12	.25
19 Intrepid Hero R	.60	1.25
20 Monk Idealist U	.12	.25
21 Monk Realist C	.07	.15
22 Opal Acrolith U	.12	.25
23 Opal Archangel R	5.00	10.00
24 Opal Caryatid C	.07	.15
25 Opal Gargoyle C	.07	.15
26 Opal Titan R	.20	.40
27 Pacifism C	.07	.15
28 Pariah R	1.50	3.00
29 Path of Peace C	.07	.15
30 Pegasus Charger C	.07	.15
31 Planar Birth R	2.50	5.00
32 Presence of the Master U	.12	.25
33 Redeem U	.12	.25
34 Remembrance R	3.00	6.00
35 Rune of Protection Artifacts U	.12	.25
36 Rune of Protection Black C	.07	.15
37 Rune of Protection Blue C	.07	.15
38 Rune of Protection Green C	.07	.15
39 Rune of Protection Lands R	.20	.40
40 Rune of Protection Red C	.07	.15
41 Rune of Protection White C	.15	.30
42 Sanctum Custodian C	.07	.15
43 Sanctum Guardian U	.12	.25
44 Seasoned Marshal U	.12	.25
45 Serra Avatar R	1.50	3.00
46 Serra Zealot C	.07	.15
47 Serra's Embrace U	.12	.25
48 Serra's Hymn U	.12	.25
49 Serra's Liturgy R	.30	.60
50 Shimmering Barrier U	.12	.25
51 Silent Attendant C	.07	.15
52 Songstitcher U	.12	.25
53 Soul Sculptor R	.30	.75
54 Voice of Grace U	.12	.25
55 Voice of Law U	.15	.30
56 Waylay U	.12	.25
57 Worship R	2.00	4.00
58 Academy Researchers U	.12	.25
59 Annul C	.12	.25
60 Arcane Laboratory U	1.50	3.00
61 Attunement R	2.50	5.00
62 Back to Basics R	12.50	25.00
63 Barrin, Master Wizard R	40.00	80.00
64 Catalog C	.07	.15
65 Cloak of Mists C	.07	.15
66 Confiscate U	.20	.40
67 Coral Merfolk C	.07	.15
68 Curfew C	.07	.15
69 Disruptive Student C	.25	.50
70 Douse U	.20	.40
71 Drifting Djinn R	.25	.50
72 Enchantment Alteration U	.12	.25
73 Energy Field R	2.50	5.00
74 Exhaustion U	.20	.40
75 Fog Bank U	.25	.50
76 Gilded Drake R	200.00	400.00
77 Great Whale R	25.00	50.00
78 Hermetic Study C	.07	.15
79 Hibernation U	.12	.25
80 Horseshoe Crab C	.07	.15
81 Imaginary Pet R	.20	.40
82 Launch C	.07	.15
83 Lilting Refrain U	.20	.40
84 Lingering Mirage U	.12	.25
85 Morphling R	20.00	40.00
86 Pendrell Drake C	.07	.15
87 Pendrell Flux C	.07	.15
88 Peregrine Drake U	2.50	5.00
89 Power Sink C	.07	.15
90 Power Taint C	.07	.15
91 Recantation R	.20	.40
92 Rescind C	.07	.15
93 Rewind C	.20	.40
94 Sandbar Merfolk C	.07	.15
95 Sandbar Serpent U	.12	.25
96 Show and Tell R	12.50	25.00
97 Somnophore R	.20	.40
98 Spire Owl C	.15	.30
99 Stern Proctor U	.12	.25
100 Stroke of Genius R	5.00	10.00
101 Sunder R	6.00	12.00

102 Telepathy U .40 .80
103 Time Spiral R 150.00 300.00
104 Tolarian Winds C .30 .75
105 Turnabout U 4.00 8.00
106 Veil of Birds C .07 .15
107 Veiled Apparition U .12 .25
108 Veiled Crocodile R .20 .40
109 Veiled Sentry U .12 .25
110 Veiled Serpent C .07 .15
111 Windfall U 2.50 5.00
112 Wizard Mentor C .07 .15
113 Zephid R 5.00 10.00
114 Zephid's Embrace U .12 .25
115 Abyssal Horror R .20 .40
116 Befoul C .07 .15
117 Bereavement U .12 .25
118 Blood Vassal C .07 .15
119 Bog Raiders C .07 .15
120 Breach C .07 .15
121 Cackling Fiend C .07 .15
122 Carrion Beetles C .07 .15
123 Contamination R 30.00 60.00
124 Corrupt C .07 .15
125 Crazed Skirge U .12 .25
126 Dark Hatchling R .20 .40
127 Dark Ritual C .60 1.25
128 Darkest Hour R 3.00 6.00
129 Despondency C .07 .15
130 Diabolic Servitude U .12 .25
131 Discordant Dirge R .25 .50
132 Duress C .60 1.25
133 Eastern Paladin R .20 .40
134 Exhume C .75 1.50
135 Expunge C .07 .15
136 Flesh Reaver U .12 .25
137 Hollow Dogs C .07 .15
138 Ill-Gotten Gains R .50 1.00
139 Looming Shade C .07 .15
140 Lurking Evil R .20 .40
141 Mana Leech U .12 .25
142 No Rest for the Wicked U .50 1.00
143 Oppression R 30.00 60.00
144 Order of Yawgmoth U .12 .25
145 Parasitic Bond U .12 .25
146 Persecute R .60 1.25
147 Pestilence C .20 .40
148 Phyrexian Ghoul C .07 .15
149 Planar Void U .75 1.50
150 Priest of Gix U .75 1.50
151 Rain of Filth U 3.00 6.00
152 Ravenous Skirge C .07 .15
153 Reclusive Wight U .12 .25
154 Reprocess R 1.25 2.50
155 Sanguine Guard U .12 .25
156 Sicken C .07 .15
157 Skirge Familiar U 3.00 6.00
158 Skittering Skirge C .07 .15
159 Sleeper Agent R 1.00 2.00
160 Spined Fluke U .12 .25
161 Tainted Aether R 10.00 20.00
162 Unnerve C .07 .15
163 Unworthy Dead C .07 .15
164 Vampiric Embrace U .12 .25
165 Vebulid R .20 .40
166 Victimize U 1.25 2.50
167 Vile Requiem U .12 .25
168 Western Paladin R .30 .75
169 Witch Engine R .20 .40
170 Yawgmoth's Edict U .12 .25
171 Yawgmoth's Will R 200.00 400.00
172 Acidic Soil U 1.50 3.00
173 Antagonism R .25 .50
174 Arc Lightning C .07 .15
175 Bedlam R 2.50 5.00
176 Brand R 4.00 8.00
177 Bravado C .07 .15
178 Bulwark R .20 .40
179 Crater Hellion R .25 .50
180 Destructive Urge U .15 .30
181 Disorder U .12 .25
182 Dromosaur C .07 .15
183 Electryte R .20 .40
184 Falter C .07 .15
185 Fault Line R 2.00 4.00
186 Fiery Mantle C .07 .15
187 Fire Ants U .12 .25
188 Gamble R 15.00 30.00
189 Goblin Cadets U .20 .40
190 Goblin Lackey U 10.00 20.00
191 Goblin Matron C .30 .75
192 Goblin Offensive U 1.50 3.00
193 Goblin Patrol C .07 .15
194 Goblin Raider C .07 .15
195 Goblin Spelunkers C .07 .15
196 Goblin War Buggy C .07 .15
197 Guma U .12 .25
198 Headlong Rush C .07 .15
199 Heat Ray C .07 .15
200 Jagged Lightning U .12 .25
201 Lay Waste C .07 .15
202 Lightning Dragon R 7.50 15.00
203 Meltdown U .30 .75
204 Okk R .20 .40
205 Outmaneuver U .20 .40
206 Rain of Salt U .12 .25
207 Raze C .15 .30
208 Reflexes C .07 .15
209 Retromancer C .07 .15
210 Rumbling Crescendo R .30 .60
211 Scald U .12 .25
212 Scoria Wurm R .25 .50
213 Scrap C .07 .15
214 Shivan Hellkite R .60 1.25
214 Shivan Hellkite R .60 1.25
216 Shiv's Embrace U .12 .25
217 Shower of Sparks C .07 .15
218 Sneak Attack R 20.00 40.00
219 Steam Blast U .12 .25
220 Sulfuric Vapors R .20 .40
221 Thundering Giant U .12 .25
222 Torch Song U .12 .25
223 Viashino Outrider C .07 .15
224 Viashino Runner C .07 .15
225 Viashino Sandswimmer R .20 .40
226 Viashino Weaponsmith C .07 .15
227 Vug Lizard U .12 .25
228 Wildfire R .50 1.00
229 Abundance R 2.00 4.00
230 Acridian C .07 .15
231 Albino Troll U .12 .25
232 Anaconda U .12 .25
233 Argothian Elder U 2.50 5.00
234 Argothian Enchantress R 15.00 30.00
235 Argothian Swine C .07 .15
236 Argothian Wurm R 5.00 10.00
237 Blanchwood Armor U .12 .25
238 Blanchwood Treefolk C .07 .15
239 Bull Hippo U .12 .25
240 Carpet of Flowers U 15.00 30.00
241 Cave Tiger C .07 .15
242 Child of Gaea R .25 .50
243 Citanul Centaurs R 2.00 4.00
244 Citanul Hierophants R 2.00 4.00
245 Cradle Guard U .12 .25
246 Crosswinds U .12 .25
247 Elvish Herder C .07 .15
248 Elvish Lyrist C .07 .15
249 Endless Wurm R .50 1.00
250 Exploration R 20.00 40.00
251 Fecundity U .30 .75
252 Fertile Ground C .20 .40
253 Fortitude C .07 .15
254 Gaea's Bounty C .30 .60
255 Gaea's Embrace U .12 .25
256 Gorilla Warrior C .07 .15
257 Greater Good R 6.00 12.00
258 Greener Pastures R .25 .50
259 Hawkeater Moth U .12 .25
260 Hidden Ancients U .12 .25
261 Hidden Guerrillas U .12 .25
262 Hidden Herd R .20 .40
263 Hidden Predators R .25 .50
264 Hidden Spider C .07 .15
265 Hidden Stag R .20 .40
266 Hush C .07 .15
267 Lull C .07 .15
268 Midsummer Revel R .20 .40
269 Pouncing Jaguar C .07 .15
270 Priest of Titania C 7.50 15.00
271 Rejuvenate C .07 .15
272 Retaliation U .12 .25
273 Sporogenesis R 1.25 2.50
274 Spreading Algae U .12 .25
275 Symbiosis C .07 .15
276 Titania's Boon U .12 .25
277 Titania's Chosen U .15 .30
278 Treefolk Seedlings U .12 .25
279 Treetop Rangers C .07 .15
280 Venomous Fangs C .07 .15
281 Vernal Bloom R 4.00 8.00
282 War Dance U .12 .25
283 Whirlwind R .30 .60
284 Wild Dogs C .07 .15
285 Winding Wurm C .07 .15
286 Barrin's Codex R .25 .50
287 Cathodion U .12 .25
288 Chimeric Staff R .20 .40
289 Citanul Flute R 1.50 3.00
290 Claws of Gix U .30 .60
291 Copper Gnomes R 1.00 2.00
292 Crystal Chimes U 1.00 2.00
293 Dragon Blood U .12 .25
294 Endoskeleton U .12 .25
295 Fluctuator R 3.00 6.00
296 Grafted Skullcap R .50 1.00
297 Hopping Automaton U .12 .25
298 Karn Silver Golem R 25.00 50.00
299 Lifeline R 40.00 80.00
300 Lotus Blossom R 4.00 8.00
301 Metrognome R .20 .40
302 Mishras Helix R 1.00 2.00
303 Mobile Fort U .12 .25
304 Noetic Scales R 4.00 8.00
305 Phyrexian Colossus R .30 .75
306 Phyrexian Processor R 3.00 6.00
307 Pit Trap U .12 .25
308 Purging Scythe R .20 .40
309 Smokestack R 15.00 30.00
310 Temporal Aperture R 15.00 30.00
311 Thran Turbine U 1.00 2.00
312 Umbilicus R 1.25 2.50
313 Urzas Armor U .20 .40
314 Voltaic Key U 1.50 3.00
315 Wall of Junk U 1.00 2.00
316 Whetstone R .25 .50
317 Wirecat U .12 .25
318 Worn Powerstone U 1.50 3.00
319 Blasted Landscape U 1.00 2.00
320 Drifting Meadow C .07 .15
321 Gaea's Cradle R 600.00 1,200.00
322 Phyrexian Tower R 20.00 40.00
323 Polluted Mire C .07 .15
324 Remote Isle C .15 .30
325 Serra's Sanctum R 200.00 400.00
326 Shivan Gorge R 2.50 5.00
327 Slippery Karst C .15 .30
328 Smoldering Crater C .12 .25
329 Thran Quarry R 4.00 8.00
330 Tolarian Academy R 125.00 250.00
331 Plains L .07 .15
332 Plains L .07 .15
333 Plains L .07 .15
334 Plains L .07 .15
335 Island L .07 .15
336 Island L .07 .15
337 Island L .07 .15
338 Island L .07 .15
339 Swamp L .07 .15
340 Swamp L .07 .15
341 Swamp L .07 .15
342 Swamp L .07 .15
343 Mountain L .07 .15
344 Mountain L .07 .15
345 Mountain L .07 .15
346 Mountain L .07 .15
347 Forest L .07 .15
348 Forest L .07 .15
349 Forest L .07 .15
350 Forest L .07 .15

1999 Magic The Gathering Battle Royale Box Set

1 Abyssal Specter U .30 .75
2 Advance Scout C .30 .60
3 Air Elemental U .20 .40
4 Angelic Page C .25 .50
5 Arc Lightning C .25 .50
6 Argothian Elder U 1.25 2.50
7 Armored Pegasus C .20 .40
8 Azure Drake U .20 .40
9 Blinking Spirit R .25 .50
10 Broken Fall C .30 .75
11 Cackling Fiend C .30 .60
12 Catastrophe R 2.50 5.00
13 Cinder Marsh U .25 .50
14 Control Magic U .75 1.50
15 Counterspell C 1.50 3.00
16 Crazed Skirge U .20 .40
17 Curfew C .40 .80
18 Dark Ritual C .75 1.50
19 Dirtcowl Wurm C 1.25 2.50
20 Disenchant R .25 .50
21 Disruptive Student C .50 1.00
22 Drifting Meadow C .20 .40
23 Elvish Lyrist U .20 .40
24 Exhume C 2.50 5.00
25 Fecundity U .75 1.50
26 Fertile Ground C .75 1.50
27 Fire Ants U .30 .60
28 Flood C .30 .60
29 Giant Growth C .25 .50
30 Gorilla Warrior C .20 .40
31 Healing Salve C .25 .50
32 Heat Ray C .20 .40
33 Hurricane U .25 .50
34 Infantry Veteran C .20 .40
35 Land Tax U 20.00 40.00
36 Lhurgoyf R .30 .60
37 Lightning Elemental C .20 .40
38 Living Death R 4.00 8.00
39 Llanowar Elves C 1.00 2.00
40 Man-o'-War C .20 .40
41 Mana Leak C .25 .50
42 Maniacal Rage C 1.00 2.00
43 Manta Riders C .20 .40
44 Master Decoy C .20 .40
45 Mogg Hollows U .25 .50
46 Nekrataal U .25 .50
47 Opportunity U .25 .50
48 Pacifism C .25 .50
49 Pestilence U .30 .75
50 Phyrexian Ghoul C .30 .75
51 Pincher Beetles C .20 .40
52 Plated Rootwalla C .20 .40
53 Polluted Mire C .30 .60
54 Prodigal Sorcerer C .75 1.50
55 Raging Goblin C .30 .60
56 Ray of Command C .30 .75
57 Reanimate U 10.00 20.00
58 Remote Isle C .75 1.50
59 River Boa U .30 .60
60 Rolling Thunder C .30 .75
61 Sadistic Glee C .50 1.00
62 Sanctum Custodian C .20 .40
63 Sanctum Guardian U .20 .40
64 Sandstorm C .20 .40
65 Scaled Wurm C .20 .40
66 Scryb Sprites C .20 .40
67 Seasoned Marshal U .20 .40
68 Seeker of Skybreak C .75 1.50
69 Sengir Vampire U .30 .75
70 Sewer Rats C .60 1.25
71 Shower of Sparks C .20 .40
72 Skyshroud Elite U .30 .75
73 Slippery Karst C .25 .50
74 Soltari Foot Soldier C 1.00 2.00
75 Songstitcher U .20 .40
76 Soul Warden C 2.00 4.00
77 Spike Colony C .20 .40
78 Spike Feeder U .75 1.50
79 Spike Weaver R 3.00 6.00
80 Spike Worker C .20 .40
81 Steam Blast U .25 .50
82 Subversion R 1.25 2.50
83 Sun Clasp C .25 .50
84 Swords to Plowshares U 2.00 4.00
85 Symbiosis C .20 .40
86 Syphon Soul C .30 .60
87 Terror C .20 .40
88 Thalakos Lowlands U .30 .60
89 Tranquility C .30 .60
90 Trumpeting Armodon U .20 .40
91 Unnerve C .40 .80
92 Uthden Troll U .25 .50
93 Vec Townships U .30 .60
94 Village Elder C .25 .50
95 Wall of Heat C .20 .40
96 Weakness C .20 .40
97 Wildfire Emissary U .20 .40
98 Wind Drake C .30 .60
99 Windfall U 4.00 8.00
100 Wrath of God R 3.00 6.00
101 Forest L 1.25 2.50
102 Forest L 1.50 3.00
103 Forest L .60 1.25
104 Forest L .75 1.50
105 Forest L .30 .75
106 Forest L 2.00 4.00
107 Forest L 3.00 6.00
108 Forest L 1.50 3.00
109 Forest L .60 1.25
110 Island L 1.00 2.00
111 Island L .75 1.50
112 Island L .75 1.50
113 Island L 4.00 8.00
114 Island L .50 1.00
115 Mountain L .75 1.50
116 Mountain L .75 1.50
117 Mountain L .30 .75
118 Mountain L 1.00 2.00
119 Mountain L .60 1.25
120 Mountain L 1.50 3.00
121 Mountain L 1.00 2.00
122 Mountain L .75 1.50
123 Mountain L 12.50 25.00
124 Plains L 2.00 4.00
125 Plains L 1.50 3.00
126 Plains L .75 1.50
127 Plains L .75 1.50
128 Plains L .75 1.50
129 Plains L 2.00 4.00
130 Plains L .75 1.50
131 Plains L .75 1.50
132 Plains L .75 1.50
133 Swamp L .75 1.50
134 Swamp L .75 1.50
135 Swamp L .75 1.50
136 Swamp L .40 .80

1999 Magic The Gathering Classic Sixth Edition

1 Animate Wall R .25 .50
2 Archangel R .30 .60
3 Ardent Militia U .12 .25
4 Armageddon R 3.00 6.00
5 Armored Pegasus C .07 .15
6 Castle U .12 .25
7 Celestial Dawn R 1.00 2.00
8 Circle of Protection Black C .07 .15
9 Circle of Protection Blue C .07 .15
10 Circle of Protection Green C .07 .15
11 Circle of Protection Red C .07 .15
12 Circle of Protection White C .07 .15
13 Crusade R 10.00 20.00
14 D'Avenant Archer C .07 .15
15 Daraja Griffin U .12 .25
16 Disenchant C .07 .15
17 Divine Transformation U .12 .25
18 Ekundu Griffin C .07 .15
19 Enlightened Tutor U 25.00 50.00
20 Ethereal Champion R .25 .50
21 Exile R .75 1.50
22 Healing Salve C .07 .15
23 Heavy Ballista U .12 .25
24 Hero's Resolve C .07 .15
25 Icatian Town R .20 .40
26 Infantry Veteran C .07 .15
27 Kismet U 1.00 2.00
28 Kjeldoran Royal Guard R .20 .40
29 Light of Day U .15 .30
30 Longbow Archer U .12 .25
31 Mesa Falcon C .07 .15
32 Order of the Sacred Torch R .30 .60
33 Pacifism C .07 .15
34 Pearl Dragon R .30 .60
35 Regal Unicorn C .07 .15
36 Remedy C .07 .15
37 Reprisal U .12 .25
38 Resistance Fighter C .07 .15
39 Reverse Damage R .30 .60
40 Samite Healer C .07 .15
41 Serenity R 1.00 2.00
42 Serra's Blessing U .30 .75
43 Spirit Link U .25 .50
44 Standing Troops C .07 .15
45 Staunch Defenders U .12 .25
46 Sunweb R .20 .40
47 Tariff R .25 .50
48 Tundra Wolves C .07 .15
49 Unyaro Griffin U .12 .25
50 Venerable Monk C .07 .15
51 Wall of Swords U .12 .25
52 Warmth U .12 .25
53 Warrior's Honor C .07 .15
54 Wrath of God R 4.00 8.00
55 Abduction U .25 .50
56 Air Elemental U .12 .25
57 Ancestral Memories R .25 .50
58 Boomerang C .07 .15
59 Browse U .12 .25
60 Chill U .15 .30
61 Counterspell C 1.00 2.00
62 Daring Apprentice R .25 .50
63 Deflection R .20 .40
64 Desertion R 2.50 5.00
65 Diminishing Returns R .50 1.00
66 Dream Cache C .07 .15
67 Flash R 1.50 3.00
68 Flight C .07 .15
69 Fog Elemental C .07 .15
70 Forget R .25 .50
71 Gaseous Form C .07 .15
72 Glacial Wall U .12 .25
73 Harmattan Efreet U .12 .25
74 Horned Turtle C .07 .15
75 Insight U 2.50 5.00
76 Inspiration C .07 .15
77 Juxtapose R .20 .40
78 Library of Lat-Nam R .25 .50
79 Lord of Atlantis R 3.00 6.00
80 Mana Short R 1.00 2.00
81 Memory Lapse C .07 .15
82 Merfolk of the Pearl Trident C .07 .15
83 Mystical Tutor U 12.50 25.00
84 Phantasmal Terrain C .07 .15
85 Phantom Warrior U .12 .25
86 Polymorph R 1.00 2.00
87 Power Sink U .12 .25
88 Prodigal Sorcerer C .07 .15
89 Prosperity U 1.00 2.00
90 Psychic Transfer R .20 .40
91 Psychic Venom C .07 .15
92 Recall R .30 .60
93 Relearn U .12 .25
94 Remove Soul C .07 .15
95 Sage Owl C .07 .15
96 Sea Monster C .07 .15
97 Segovian Leviathan U .12 .25
98 Sibilant Spirit R .20 .40
99 Soldevi Sage U .12 .25
100 Spell Blast C .07 .15
101 Storm Crow C .07 .15
102 Tidal Surge C .07 .15
103 Unsummon C .07 .15
104 Vodalian Soldiers C .07 .15

105 Wall of Air U	.12	.25
106 Wind Drake C	.07	.15
107 Wind Spirit U	.12	.25
108 Zur's Weirding R	.30	.60
109 Abyssal Hunter R	.25	.50
110 Abyssal Specter U	.12	.25
111 Agonizing Memories U	.12	.25
112 Ashen Powder R	.50	1.00
113 Blight U	.25	.50
114 Blighted Shaman U	.12	.25
115 Blood Pet C	.20	.40
116 Bog Imp C	.07	.15
117 Bog Rats C	.07	.15
118 Bog Wraith U	.12	.25
119 Coercion C	.07	.15
120 Derelor R	.20	.40
121 Doomsday R	10.00	20.00
122 Dread of Night U	.25	.50
123 Drudge Skeletons C	.07	.15
124 Dry Spell C	.07	.15
125 Enfeeblement C	.07	.15
126 Evil Eye of Orms-by-Gore U	.12	.25
127 Fallen Angel R	.25	.50
128 Fatal Blow C	.07	.15
129 Fear C	.07	.15
130 Feast of the Unicorn C	.07	.15
131 Feral Shadow C	.07	.15
132 Forbidden Crypt R	.30	.60
133 Gravebane Zombie U	.12	.25
134 Gravedigger C	.07	.15
135 Greed R	2.50	5.00
136 Hecatomb R	.20	.40
137 Hidden Horror U	.12	.25
138 Howl from Beyond C	.07	.15
139 Infernal Contract R	.30	.75
140 Kjeldoran Dead C	.07	.15
141 Leshrac's Rite U	.12	.25
142 Lost Soul C	.07	.15
143 Mind Warp U	.12	.25
144 Mischievous Poltergeist U	.12	.25
145 Necrosavant R	.20	.40
146 Nightmare R	.50	1.00
147 Painful Memories C	.07	.15
148 Perish U	.12	.25
149 Pestilence U	.30	.60
150 Python C	.07	.15
151 Rag Man R	.20	.40
152 Raise Dead C	.07	.15
153 Razortooth Rats C	.07	.15
154 Scathe Zombies C	.07	.15
155 Sengir Autocrat R	.30	.60
156 Strands of Night U	.30	.60
157 Stromgald Cabal R	.25	.50
158 Stupor U	.12	.25
159 Syphon Soul C	.07	.15
160 Terror C	.07	.15
161 Vampiric Tutor R	40.00	80.00
162 Zombie Master R	5.00	10.00
163 Aether Flash U	.40	.80
164 Anaba Bodyguard C	.07	.15
165 Anaba Shaman C	.07	.15
166 Balduvian Barbarians C	.07	.15
167 Balduvian Horde R	.25	.50
168 Blaze U	.12	.25
169 Boil U	2.50	5.00
170 Burrowing U	.12	.25
171 Conquer U	.12	.25
172 Crimson Hellkite R	.50	1.00
173 Earthquake R	.50	1.00
174 Fervor R	3.00	6.00
175 Final Fortune R	15.00	30.00
176 Fire Elemental U	.12	.25
177 Firebreathing C	.07	.15
178 Fit of Rage C	.07	.15
179 Flame Spirit C	.07	.15
180 Flashfires U	.12	.25
181 Giant Strength C	.07	.15
182 Goblin Digging Team C	.07	.15
183 Goblin Elite Infantry C	.07	.15
184 Goblin Hero C	.07	.15
185 Goblin King R	2.50	5.00
186 Goblin Recruiter U	5.00	10.00
187 Goblin Warrens R	1.00	2.00
188 Hammer of Bogardan R	.20	.40
189 Hulking Cyclops U	.12	.25
190 Illicit Auction R	1.00	2.00
191 Inferno R	.20	.40
192 Jokulhaups R	3.00	6.00
193 Lightning Blast C	.07	.15
194 Manabarbs R	.30	.60
195 Mountain Goat C	.07	.15
196 Orcish Artillery U	.12	.25
197 Orcish Oriflamme U	.12	.25
198 Pillage U	.12	.25
199 Pyrotechnics C	.07	.15
200 Raging Goblin C	.07	.15
201 Reckless Embermage R	.20	.40
202 Relentless Assault R	1.50	3.00
203 Sabretooth Tiger C	.07	.15
204 Shatter C	.07	.15
205 Shatterstorm R	.50	1.00
206 Shock C	.07	.15
207 Spitting Drake U	.12	.25
208 Spitting Earth C	.07	.15
209 Stone Rain C	.07	.15
210 Talruum Minotaur C	.07	.15
211 Tremor C	.07	.15
212 Vertigo U	.12	.25
213 Viashino Warrior C	.07	.15
214 Volcanic Dragon R	.25	.50
215 Volcanic Geyser U	.12	.25
216 Wall of Fire U	.12	.25
217 Birds of Paradise R	12.50	25.00
218 Call of the Wild R	.25	.50
219 Cat Warriors C	.07	.15
220 Creeping Mold U	.12	.25
221 Dense Foliage R	.50	1.00
222 Early Harvest R	1.00	2.00
223 Elder Druid R	.25	.50
224 Elven Cache C	.07	.15
225 Elven Riders U	.12	.25
226 Elvish Archers R	.25	.50
227 Fallow Earth U	.12	.25
228 Familiar Ground U	.12	.25
229 Femeref Archers U	.12	.25
230 Fog C	.07	.15
231 Fyndhorn Brownie C	.07	.15
232 Fyndhorn Elder U	.12	.25
233 Giant Growth C	.07	.15
234 Giant Spider C	.07	.15
235 Gorilla Chieftain C	.07	.15
236 Grizzly Bears C	.07	.15
237 Hurricane R	.25	.50
238 Living Lands R	.20	.40
239 Llanowar Elves C	.20	.40
240 Lure U	.12	.25
241 Maro R	.20	.40
242 Nature's Resurgence R	.20	.40
243 Panther Warriors C	.07	.15
244 Pradesh Gypsies C	.07	.15
245 Radjan Spirit U	.12	.25
246 Rampant Growth C	.60	1.25
247 Redwood Treefolk C	.07	.15
248 Regeneration C	.07	.15
249 River Boa U	.12	.25
250 Rowen R	.25	.50
251 Scaled Wurm C	.07	.15
252 Shanodin Dryads C	.07	.15
253 Stalking Tiger C	.07	.15
254 Stream of Life C	.07	.15
255 Summer Bloom U	1.25	2.50
256 Thicket Basilisk U	.12	.25
257 Trained Armodon C	.07	.15
258 Tranquil Grove R	1.50	3.00
259 Tranquility C	.07	.15
260 Uktabi Orangutan U	.12	.25
261 Uktabi Wildcats R	.25	.50
262 Unseen Walker U	.12	.25
263 Untamed Wilds U	.12	.25
264 Verduran Enchantress R	1.50	3.00
265 Vitalize C	2.50	5.00
266 Waiting in the Weeds R	.30	.75
267 Warthog U	.12	.25
268 Wild Growth C	.20	.40
269 Worldly Tutor U	15.00	30.00
270 Wyluli Wolf R	.25	.50
271 Aladdin's Ring R	.20	.40
272 Amber Prison R	.25	.50
273 Ankh of Mishra R	5.00	10.00
274 Ashnod's Altar U	5.00	10.00
275 Bottle of Suleiman R	.25	.50
276 Charcoal Diamond U	1.25	2.50
277 Crystal Rod U	.12	.25
278 Cursed Totem R	15.00	30.00
279 Dancing Scimitar R	.20	.40
280 Dingus Egg R	.30	.60
281 Disrupting Scepter R	.25	.50
282 Dragon Engine R	.20	.40
283 Dragon Mask U	.12	.25
284 Fire Diamond U	1.50	3.00
285 Flying Carpet R	.20	.40
286 Fountain of Youth U	.12	.25
287 Glasses of Urza U	.12	.25
288 Grinning Totem R	.30	.60
289 Howling Mine R	3.00	6.00
290 Iron Star U	.12	.25
291 Ivory Cup U	.12	.25
292 Jade Monolith R	.25	.50
293 Jalum Tome R	.25	.50
294 Jayemdae Tome R	.20	.40
295 Lead Golem U	.12	.25
296 Mana Prism U	.12	.25
297 Marble Diamond U	.75	1.50
298 Meekstone R	4.00	8.00
299 Millstone R	.25	.50
300 Moss Diamond U	.12	.25
301 Mystic Compass U	.12	.25
302 Obsianus Golem U	.12	.25
303 Ornithopter U	.20	.40
304 Patagia Golem U	.12	.25
305 Pentagram of the Ages R	.25	.50
306 Phyrexian Vault U	.12	.25
307 Primal Clay R	.20	.40
308 Rod of Ruin U	.12	.25
309 Skull Catapult U	.12	.25
310 Sky Diamond U	1.25	2.50
311 Snake Basket R	1.00	2.00
312 Soul Net U	.12	.25
313 Storm Cauldron R	2.00	4.00
314 Teferi's Puzzle Box R	4.00	8.00
315 The Hive R	.20	.40
316 Throne of Bone U	.12	.25
317 Wand of Denial R	.25	.50
318 Wooden Sphere U	.12	.25
319 Adarkar Wastes R	7.50	15.00
320 Brushland R	4.00	8.00
321 City of Brass R	12.50	25.00
322 Crystal Vein U	1.50	3.00
323 Dwarven Ruins U	.12	.25
324 Ebon Stronghold U	.12	.25
325 Havenwood Battleground U	.12	.25
326 Karplusan Forest R	3.00	6.00
327 Ruins of Trokair U	.12	.25
328 Sulfurous Springs R	6.00	12.00
329 Svyelunite Temple U	.12	.25
330 Underground River R	6.00	12.00
331 Plains L	.07	.15
332 Plains L	.07	.15
333 Plains L	.07	.15
334 Plains L	.07	.15
335 Island L	.07	.15
336 Island L	.07	.15
337 Island L	.07	.15
338 Island L	.07	.15
339 Swamp L	.07	.15
340 Swamp L	.07	.15
341 Swamp L	.07	.15
342 Swamp L	.07	.15
343 Mountain L	.07	.15
344 Mountain L	.07	.15
345 Mountain L	.07	.15
346 Mountain L	.07	.15
347 Forest L	.07	.15
348 Forest L	.07	.15
349 Forest L	.07	.15
350 Forest L	.07	.15

1999 Magic The Gathering Judge Gift Rewards

1 Memory Lapse R	20.00	40.00

1999 Magic The Gathering Junior Super Series

1 Thran Quarry R	30.00	75.00
2 Serra Avatar R	75.00	150.00
3 Lord of Atlantis R	40.00	80.00
4 Crusade R	75.00	150.00
5 Elvish Lyrist R	6.00	12.00
6 City of Brass R	300.00	600.00
7 Volcanic Hammer R	6.00	12.00
8 Giant Growth R	2.50	5.00
9 Two-Headed Dragon R	7.50	15.00
10 Slith Firewalker R	7.50	15.00
11 Royal Assassin R	30.00	60.00
12 Sakura-Tribe Elder R	15.00	30.00
13 Shard Phoenix R	7.50	15.00
14 Soltari Priest R	4.00	8.00
15 Whirling Dervish R	5.00	10.00
16 Glorious Anthem R	12.50	25.00
17 Elvish Champion R	30.00	75.00
18 Mad Auntie R	15.00	30.00

1999 Magic The Gathering Mercadian Masques

1 Afterlife U	.12	.25
2 Alabaster Wall C	.07	.15
3 Armistice R	.20	.40
4 Arrest U	.12	.25
5 Ballista Squad U	.12	.25
6 Charm Peddler C	.07	.15
7 Charmed Griffin U	.12	.25
8 Cho-Arrim Alchemist R	.20	.40
9 Cho-Arrim Bruiser R	.20	.40
10 Cho-Arrim Legate U	.12	.25
11 Cho-Manno, Revolutionary R	.30	.60
12 Cho-Manno's Blessing C	.30	.60
13 Common Cause R	.20	.40
14 Cornered Market R	.30	.60
15 Crackdown R	5.00	10.00
16 Crossbow Infantry C	.07	.15
17 Devout Witness C	.07	.15
18 Disenchant C	.07	.15
19 Fountain Watch R	5.00	10.00
20 Fresh Volunteers C	.07	.15
21 Honor the Fallen R	.50	1.00
22 Ignoble Soldier U	.12	.25
23 Inviolability C	.07	.15
24 Ivory Mask R	.60	1.25
25 Jhovall Queen R	.25	.50
26 Jhovall Rider U	.12	.25
27 Last Breath U	.12	.25
28 Moment of Silence C	.12	.25
29 Moonlit Wake U	.12	.25
30 Muzzle C	.07	.15
31 Nightwind Glider C	.12	.25
32 Noble Purpose U	.20	.40
33 Orim's Cure C	.12	.25
34 Pious Warrior C	.07	.15
35 Ramosian Captain U	.12	.25
36 Ramosian Commander U	.12	.25
37 Ramosian Lieutenant C	.12	.25
38 Ramosian Rally C	.12	.25
39 Ramosian Sergeant C	.12	.25
40 Ramosian Sky Marshal R	.20	.40
41 Rappelling Scouts R	.20	.40
42 Renounce U	.12	.25
43 Revered Elder C	.07	.15
44 Reverent Mantra R	.60	1.25
45 Righteous Aura U	.12	.25
46 Righteous Indignation U	.12	.25
47 Security Detail R	.20	.40
48 Soothing Balm C	.07	.15
49 Spiritual Focus R	.25	.50
50 Steadfast Guard C	.07	.15
51 Story Circle U	.30	.60
52 Task Force C	.07	.15
53 Thermal Glider C	.07	.15
54 Tonic Peddler U	.12	.25
55 Trap Runner U	.12	.25
56 Wave of Reckoning R	2.00	4.00
57 Wishmonger U	.12	.25
58 Aerial Caravan R	.20	.40
59 Balloon Peddler C	.07	.15
60 Blockade Runner C	.07	.15
61 Brainstorm C	.75	1.50
62 Bribery R	15.00	30.00
63 Buoyancy C	.07	.15
64 Chambered Nautilus U	.12	.25
65 Chameleon Spirit U	.12	.25
66 Charisma R	2.50	5.00
67 Cloud Sprite C	.07	.15
68 Coastal Piracy U	2.50	5.00
69 Counterspell C	1.25	2.50
70 Cowardice R	.30	.60
71 Customs Depot U	.12	.25
72 Darting Merfolk C	.07	.15
73 Dehydration C	.07	.15
74 Diplomatic Escort U	.12	.25
75 Diplomatic Immunity C	.60	1.25
76 Drake Hatchling C	.07	.15
77 Embargo R	.75	1.50
78 Energy Flux U	.12	.25
79 Extravagant Spirit R	.20	.40
80 False Demise U	.12	.25
81 Glowing Anemone U	.12	.25
82 Gush C	.50	1.00
83 High Seas U	.12	.25
84 Hoodwink C	.07	.15
85 Indentured Djinn U	.20	.40
86 Karn's Touch R	.20	.40
87 Misdirection R	3.00	6.00
88 Misstep C	.07	.15
89 Overtaker R	.25	.50
90 Port Inspector C	.07	.15
91 Rishadan Airship C	.12	.25
92 Rishadan Brigand R	1.25	2.50
93 Rishadan Cutpurse C	.12	.25
94 Rishadan Footpad U	.50	1.00
95 Sailmonger U	.12	.25
96 Sand Squid R	.25	.50
97 Saprazzan Bailiff R	.20	.40
98 Saprazzan Breaker U	.12	.25
99 Saprazzan Heir R	.60	1.25
100 Saprazzan Legate U	.12	.25
101 Saprazzan Outrigger C	.07	.15
102 Saprazzan Raider C	.07	.15
103 Shoving Match U	.12	.25
104 Soothsaying U	1.50	3.00
105 Squeeze R	.25	.50
106 Statecraft R	2.00	4.00
107 Stinging Barrier C	.07	.15
108 Thwart U	.50	1.00
109 Tidal Bore C	.07	.15
110 Tidal Kraken R	.60	1.25
111 Timid Drake U	.12	.25
112 Trade Routes R	5.00	10.00
113 War Tax U	.60	1.25
114 Waterfront Bouncer C	.07	.15
115 Alley Grifters C	.07	.15
116 Black Market R	5.00	10.00
117 Bog Smugglers C	.12	.25
118 Bog Witch C	.15	.30
119 Cackling Witch U	.12	.25
120 Cateran Brute C	.07	.15
121 Cateran Enforcer U	.12	.25
122 Cateran Kidnappers U	.12	.25
123 Cateran Overlord R	.25	.50
124 Cateran Persuader C	.07	.15
125 Cateran Slaver R	.25	.50
126 Cateran Summons U	.25	.50
127 Conspiracy R	3.00	6.00
128 Corrupt Official R	.20	.40
129 Dark Ritual C	.75	1.50
130 Deathgazer U	.12	.25
131 Deepwood Ghoul C	.07	.15
132 Deepwood Legate U	.12	.25
133 Delraich R	.30	.75
134 Enslaved Horror U	.12	.25
135 Extortion R	.20	.40
136 Forced March R	.50	1.00
137 Ghoul's Feast U	.12	.25
138 Haunted Crossroads U	1.00	2.00
139 Highway Robber C	.07	.15
140 Instigator R	.20	.40
141 Insubordination C	.07	.15
142 Intimidation U	.15	.30
143 Larceny U	.15	.30
144 Liability R	.25	.50
145 Maggot Therapy C	.07	.15
146 Midnight Ritual R	.20	.40
147 Misshapen Fiend C	.07	.15
148 Molting Harpy U	.12	.25
149 Nether Spirit R	1.00	2.00
150 Notorious Assassin R	.25	.50
151 Pretender's Claim U	.12	.25
152 Primeval Shambler U	.12	.25
153 Putrefaction U	.12	.25
154 Quagmire Lamprey U	.12	.25
155 Rain of Tears U	.12	.25
156 Rampart Crawler C	.07	.15
157 Rouse C	.07	.15
158 Scandalmonger U	.12	.25
159 Sever Soul C	.07	.15
160 Silent Assassin R	.25	.50
161 Skulking Fugitive C	.07	.15
162 Snuff Out C	2.00	4.00
163 Soul Channeling C	.15	.30
164 Specter's Wail C	.07	.15
165 Strongarm Thug U	.12	.25
166 Thrashing Wumpus R	.30	.60
167 Undertaker C	.07	.15
168 Unmask R	7.50	15.00
169 Unnatural Hunger R	.25	.50
170 Vendetta C	.07	.15
171 Wall of Distortion C	.07	.15
172 Arms Dealer U	.15	.30
173 Battle Rampart C	.07	.15
174 Battle Squadron R	.20	.40
175 Blaster Mage C	.07	.15
176 Blood Hound R	.25	.50
177 Blood Oath R	.25	.50
178 Brawl R	.20	.40
179 Cave Sense C	.07	.15
180 Cave-In R	.50	1.00
181 Cavern Crawler C	.07	.15
182 Ceremonial Guard C	.07	.15
183 Cinder Elemental U	.12	.25
184 Close Quarters U	.12	.25
185 Crag Saurian R	.20	.40
186 Crash C	.07	.15
187 Flailing Manticore R	.20	.40
188 Flailing Ogre U	.12	.25
189 Flailing Soldier C	.07	.15
190 Flaming Sword C	.07	.15
191 Furious Assault C	.07	.15
192 Gerrard's Irregulars C	.07	.15
193 Hammer Mage U	.50	1.00
194 Hired Giant U	.12	.25
195 Kris Mage C	.07	.15
196 Kyren Glider C	.07	.15
197 Kyren Legate U	.12	.25
198 Kyren Negotiations U	2.50	5.00
199 Kyren Sniper C	.07	.15
200 Lava Runner R	.25	.50
201 Lightning Hounds C	.07	.15
202 Lithophage R	.20	.40
203 Lunge C	.07	.15
204 Magistrate's Veto U	.12	.25
205 Mercadia's Downfall U	.75	1.50
206 Ogre Taskmaster U	.12	.25
207 Pulverize R	.50	1.00
208 Puppet's Verdict R	2.50	5.00
209 Robber Fly U	.12	.25
210 Rock Badger U	.12	.25
211 Seismic Mage R	.25	.50
212 Shock Troops C	.07	.15
213 Sizzle C	.07	.15
214 Squee, Goblin Nabob R	3.00	6.00
215 Stone Rain C	.07	.15
216 Tectonic Break R	2.00	4.00
217 Territorial Dispute R	.20	.40

218 Thieves' Auction R	2.00	4.00
219 Thunderclap C	.07	.15
220 Tremor C	.07	.15
221 Two-Headed Dragon R	.75	1.50
222 Uphill Battle U	.12	.25
223 Volcanic Wind U	.12	.25
224 War Cadence U	.30	.60
225 Warmonger U	.12	.25
226 Warpath U	.12	.25
227 Wild Jhovall C	.07	.15
228 Word of Blasting U	.12	.25
229 Ancestral Mask C	.60	1.25
230 Bifurcate R	.25	.50
231 Boa Constrictor U	.12	.25
232 Briar Patch U	.12	.25
233 Caller of the Hunt R	.30	.75
234 Caustic Wasps U	.12	.25
235 Clear the Land R	.25	.50
236 Collective Unconscious R	2.50	5.00
237 Dawnstrider R	1.25	2.50
238 Deadly Insect C	.07	.15
239 Deepwood Drummer C	.07	.15
240 Deepwood Elder R	.25	.50
241 Deepwood Tantiv U	.12	.25
242 Deepwood Wolverine C	.07	.15
243 Desert Twister U	.12	.25
244 Erithizon R	.20	.40
245 Ferocity C	.07	.15
246 Food Chain R	30.00	75.00
247 Foster R	.25	.50
248 Game Preserve R	.20	.40
249 Giant Caterpillar C	.07	.15
250 Groundskeeper U	.12	.25
251 Horned Troll C	.07	.15
252 Howling Wolf C	.07	.15
253 Hunted Wumpus U	.12	.25
254 Invigorate C	.15	.30
255 Land Grant C	.30	.75
256 Ley Line U	.12	.25
257 Lumbering Satyr U	.12	.25
258 Lure U	.12	.25
259 Megatherium R	.20	.40
260 Natural Affinity R	.60	1.25
261 Pangosaur R	.25	.50
262 Revive U	.12	.25
263 Rushwood Dryad C	.15	.30
264 Rushwood Elemental R	.50	1.00
265 Rushwood Herbalist C	.07	.15
266 Rushwood Legate U	.12	.25
267 Saber Ants U	.20	.40
268 Sacred Prey C	.07	.15
269 Silverglade Elemental C	.07	.15
270 Silverglade Pathfinder U	.15	.30
271 Snake Pit U	.25	.50
272 Snorting Gahr C	.07	.15
273 Spidersilk Armor C	1.00	2.00
274 Spontaneous Generation R	.60	1.25
275 Squall C	.07	.15
276 Squallmonger U	.12	.25
277 Stamina U	.12	.25
278 Sustenance U	.12	.25
279 Tiger Claws C	.07	.15
280 Tranquility C	.07	.15
281 Venomous Breath U	.12	.25
282 Venomous Dragonfly C	.07	.15
283 Vernal Equinox R	1.50	3.00
284 Vine Dryad R	.30	.60
285 Vine Trellis C	.15	.30
286 Assembly Hall R	.20	.40
287 Barbed Wire U	.12	.25
288 Bargaining Table R	.25	.50
289 Credit Voucher U	.60	1.25
290 Crenellated Wall U	.25	.50
291 Crooked Scales R	1.00	2.00
292 Crumbling Sanctuary R	.25	.50
293 Distorting Lens R	.30	.60
294 Eye of Ramos R	1.25	2.50
295 General's Regalia R	.20	.40
296 Heart of Ramos R	1.25	2.50
297 Henge Guardian U	.12	.25
298 Horn of Plenty R	.25	.50
299 Horn of Ramos R	.25	.50
300 Iron Lance U	.12	.25
301 Jeweled Torque U	.12	.25
302 Kyren Archive R	.20	.40
303 Kyren Toy R	.25	.50
304 Magistrate's Scepter R	1.00	2.00
305 Mercadian Atlas R	.25	.50
306 Mercadian Lift R	.20	.40
307 Monkey Cage R	.25	.50
308 Panacea U	.12	.25
309 Power Matrix R	4.00	8.00
310 Puffer Extract U	.12	.25
311 Rishadan Pawnshop R	.25	.50
312 Skull of Ramos R	1.00	2.00
313 Tooth of Ramos R	.30	.60
314 Toymaker U	.12	.25
315 Worry Beads R	.20	.40
316 Dust Bowl R	7.50	15.00
317 Fountain of Cho U	.20	.40
318 Henge of Ramos U	.12	.25
319 Hickory Woodlot C	.15	.30
320 High Market R	3.00	6.00
321 Mercadian Bazaar U	.20	.40
322 Peat Bog C	.50	1.00
323 Remote Farm C	.12	.25
324 Rishadan Port R	25.00	50.00
325 Rushwood Grove U	.20	.40
326 Sandstone Needle C	.20	.40
327 Saprazzan Cove U	.30	.75
328 Saprazzan Skerry C	.25	.50
329 Subterranean Hangar U	.12	.25
330 Tower of the Magistrate R	2.50	5.00
331 Plains L	.07	.15
332 Plains L	.07	.15
333 Plains L	.07	.15
334 Plains L	.07	.15
335 Island L	.07	.15
336 Island L	.07	.15
337 Island L	.07	.15
338 Island L	.07	.15
339 Swamp L	.07	.15
340 Swamp L	.07	.15
341 Swamp L	.07	.15
342 Swamp L	.07	.15
343 Mountain L	.07	.15
344 Mountain L	.07	.15
345 Mountain L	.07	.15
346 Mountain L	.07	.15
347 Forest L	.07	.15
348 Forest L	.07	.15
349 Forest L	.07	.15
350 Forest L	.07	.15

1999 Magic The Gathering Portal Three Kingdoms

1 Alert Shu Infantry U	15.00	30.00
2 Eightfold Maze R	25.00	50.00
3 Empty City Ruse U	15.00	30.00
4 False Defeat C	12.50	25.00
5 Flanking Troops U	2.00	4.00
6 Guan Yu, Sainted Warrior R	25.00	50.00
7 Guan Yu's 1,000-Li March R	20.00	40.00
8 Huang Zhong, Shu General R	15.00	30.00
9 Kongming, "Sleeping Dragon" R	20.00	40.00
10 Kongming's Contraptions R	25.00	50.00
11 Liu Bei, Lord of Shu R	12.50	25.00
12 Loyal Retainers U	30.00	75.00
13 Misfortune's Gain C	1.25	2.50
14 Pang Tong, "Young Phoenix" R	15.00	30.00
15 Peach Garden Oath U	5.00	10.00
16 Rally the Troops U	10.00	20.00
17 Ravages of War R	125.00	250.00
18 Riding Red Hare C	6.00	12.00
19 Shu Cavalry C	3.00	6.00
20 Shu Defender C	1.50	3.00
21 Shu Elite Companions U	3.00	6.00
22 Shu Elite Infantry C	1.25	2.50
23 Shu Farmer C	1.25	2.50
24 Shu Foot Soldiers C	1.25	2.50
25 Shu General U	5.00	10.00
26 Shu Grain Caravan C	1.25	2.50
27 Shu Soldier-Farmers U	3.00	6.00
28 Vengeance U	7.50	15.00
29 Virtuous Charge C	1.25	2.50
30 Volunteer Militia C	1.25	2.50
31 Warrior's Stand U	7.50	15.00
32 Zhang Fei, Fierce Warrior R	50.00	100.00
33 Zhao Zilong, Tiger General R	30.00	75.00
34 Balance of Power R	30.00	60.00
35 Borrowing 100,000 Arrows U	5.00	10.00
36 Brilliant Plan U	2.00	4.00
37 Broken Dam C	6.00	12.00
38 Capture of Jingzhou R	150.00	300.00
39 Champion's Victory U	7.50	15.00
40 Council of Advisors U	5.00	10.00
41 Counterintelligence U	5.00	10.00
42 Exhaustion R	7.50	15.00
43 Extinguish C	1.25	2.50
44 Forced Retreat C	2.50	5.00
45 Lady Sun R	50.00	100.00
46 Lu Meng, Wu General R	30.00	75.00
47 Lu Su, Wu Advisor R	20.00	40.00
48 Lu Xun, Scholar General R	15.00	30.00
49 Mystic Denial U	7.50	15.00
50 Preemptive Strike C	2.00	4.00
51 Red Cliffs Armada U	2.50	5.00
52 Sage's Knowledge C	4.00	8.00
53 Strategic Planning U	20.00	40.00
54 Straw Soldiers C	10.00	20.00
55 Sun Ce, Young Conqueror R	30.00	75.00
56 Sun Quan, Lord of Wu R	20.00	40.00
57 Wu Admiral U	2.50	5.00
58 Wu Elite Cavalry C	2.00	4.00
59 Wu Infantry C	2.00	4.00
60 Wu Light Cavalry C	3.00	6.00
61 Wu Longbowman U	2.00	4.00
62 Wu Scout C	3.00	6.00
63 Wu Spy U	7.50	15.00
64 Wu Warship C	3.00	6.00
65 Zhou Yu, Chief Commander R	30.00	60.00
66 Zhuge Jin, Wu Strategist R	25.00	50.00
67 Ambition's Cost R	20.00	40.00
68 Cao Cao, Lord of Wei R	20.00	40.00
69 Cao Ren, Wei Commander R	40.00	80.00
70 Coercion U	1.50	3.00
71 Corrupt Court Official U	15.00	30.00
72 Cunning Advisor U	7.50	15.00
73 Deception C	1.50	3.00
74 Desperate Charge U	10.00	20.00
75 Famine U	15.00	30.00
76 Ghostly Visit C	4.00	8.00
77 Imperial Edict C	1.50	3.00
78 Imperial Seal R	400.00	800.00
79 Overwhelming Forces R	30.00	75.00
80 Poison Arrow U	12.50	25.00
81 Return to Battle C	3.00	6.00
82 Sima Yi, Wei Field Marshal R	12.50	25.00
83 Stolen Grain U	5.00	10.00
84 Stone Catapult R	30.00	60.00
85 Wei Ambush Force C	2.00	4.00
86 Wei Assassins U	4.00	8.00
87 Wei Elite Companions U	2.50	5.00
88 Wei Infantry C	1.25	2.50
89 Wei Night Raiders U	10.00	20.00
90 Wei Scout C	2.50	5.00
91 Wei Strike Force C	4.00	8.00
92 Xiahou Dun, the One-Eyed R	75.00	150.00
93 Xun Yu, Wei Advisor R	30.00	60.00
94 Young Wei Recruits C	1.25	2.50
95 Zhang He, Wei General R	30.00	75.00
96 Zhang Liao, Hero of Hefei R	30.00	60.00
97 Zodiac Pig U	15.00	30.00
98 Zodiac Rat C	12.50	25.00
99 Zodiac Snake C	4.00	8.00
100 Barbarian General U	7.50	15.00
101 Barbarian Horde C	3.00	6.00
102 Blaze U	6.00	12.00
103 Burning Fields C	5.00	10.00
104 Burning of Xinye R	30.00	60.00
105 Control of the Court U	20.00	40.00
106 Corrupt Eunuchs U	10.00	20.00
107 Desert Sandstorm C	10.00	20.00
108 Diaochan, Artful Beauty R	30.00	75.00
109 Dong Zhou, the Tyrant R	50.00	100.00
110 Eunuchs' Intrigues U	15.00	30.00
111 Fire Ambush C	3.00	6.00
112 Fire Bowman U	6.00	12.00
113 Imperial Recruiter U	100.00	200.00
114 Independent Troops C	1.50	3.00
115 Lu Bu, Master-at-Arms R	20.00	40.00
116 Ma Chao, Western Warrior R	30.00	60.00
117 Mountain Bandit C	5.00	10.00
118 Ravaging Horde U	7.50	15.00
119 Relentless Assault R	30.00	60.00
120 Renegade Troops U	1.50	3.00
121 Rockslide Ambush U	6.00	12.00
122 Rolling Earthquake R	50.00	100.00
123 Stone Rain C	2.50	5.00
124 Warrior's Oath R	150.00	300.00
125 Yellow Scarves Cavalry C	5.00	10.00
126 Yellow Scarves General R	25.00	50.00
127 Yellow Scarves Troops C	1.25	2.50
128 Yuan Shao, the Indecisive R	100.00	200.00
129 Yuan Shao's Infantry U	5.00	10.00
130 Zodiac Dog C	12.50	25.00
131 Zodiac Dragon R	250.00	500.00
132 Zodiac Goat C	3.00	6.00
133 Borrowing the East Wind R	25.00	50.00
134 False Mourning U	12.50	25.00
135 Forest Bear C	20.00	40.00
136 Heavy Fog U	7.50	15.00
137 Hua Tuo, Honored Physician R	20.00	40.00
138 Hunting Cheetah U	25.00	50.00
139 Lady Zhurong, Warrior Queen R	75.00	150.00
140 Lone Wolf U	12.50	25.00
141 Marshaling the Troops R	15.00	30.00
142 Meng Huo, Barbarian King R	30.00	75.00
143 Meng Huo's Horde C	1.25	2.50
144 Riding the Dilu Horse R	125.00	250.00
145 Slashing Tiger R	15.00	30.00
146 Southern Elephant C	3.00	6.00
147 Spoils of Victory U	6.00	12.00
148 Spring of Eternal Peace C	5.00	10.00
149 Stalking Tiger C	4.00	8.00
150 Taoist Hermit U	7.50	15.00
151 Taoist Mystic R	12.50	25.00
152 Taunting Challenge R	30.00	60.00
153 Three Visits C	50.00	100.00
154 Trained Cheetah U	6.00	12.00
155 Trained Jackal C	6.00	12.00
156 Trip Wire U	6.00	12.00
157 Wielding the Green Dragon C	10.00	20.00
158 Wolf Pack R	50.00	100.00
159 Zodiac Horse U	20.00	40.00
160 Zodiac Monkey C	4.00	8.00
161 Zodiac Ox U	30.00	60.00
162 Zodiac Rabbit C	7.50	15.00
163 Zodiac Rooster C	12.50	25.00
164 Zodiac Tiger U	25.00	50.00
165 Zuo Ci, the Mocking Sage R	30.00	60.00
166 Plains L	1.25	2.50
167 Plains L	1.25	2.50
168 Plains L	1.25	2.50
169 Island L	2.00	4.00
170 Island L	2.00	4.00
171 Island L	2.00	4.00
172 Swamp L	2.00	4.00
173 Swamp L	7.50	15.00
174 Swamp L	1.50	3.00
175 Mountain L	7.50	15.00
176 Mountain L	15.00	30.00
177 Mountain L	15.00	30.00
178 Forest L	2.00	4.00
179 Forest L	4.00	8.00
180 Forest L	2.00	4.00

1999 Magic The Gathering Starter

1 Angel of Light U	1.50	3.00
2 Angel of Mercy U	.30	.75
3 Angelic Blessing C	.07	.15
4 Archangel R	.50	1.00
5 Ardent Militia U	.20	.40
6 Armageddon R	3.00	6.00
7 Bargain U	.50	1.00
8 Blinding Light R	.50	1.00
9 Border Guard C	.15	.30
10 Breath of Life U	.25	.50
11 Champion Lancer R	1.50	3.00
12 Charging Paladin U	.15	.30
13 Devoted Hero C	.07	.15
14 Devout Monk C	.07	.15
15 Eager Cadet C	.12	.25
16 False Peace U	.15	.30
17 Foot Soldiers C	.07	.15
18 Gerrard's Wisdom R	.50	1.00
19 Knight Errant C	.07	.15
20 Loyal Sentry R	1.00	2.00
21 Path of Peace C	.07	.15
22 Righteous Charge U	.25	.50
23 Righteous Fury R	2.50	5.00
24 Royal Falcon C	.15	.30
25 Royal Trooper U	.20	.40
26 Sacred Nectar C	.07	.15
27 Steadfastness C	.07	.15
28 Venerable Monk C	.07	.15
29 Vengeance U	.15	.30
30 Veteran Cavalier U	.30	.60
31 Wild Griffin C	.07	.15
32 Air Elemental U	.15	.30
33 Coral Eel C	.07	.15
34 Counterspell U	1.50	3.00
35 Denizen of the Deep R	1.00	2.00
36 Exhaustion U	.15	.30
37 Extinguish C	.07	.15
38 Eye Spy U	.15	.30
39 Giant Octopus C	.07	.15
40 Ingenious Thief C	.07	.15
41 Man-o'-War U	.60	1.25
42 Merfolk of the Pearl Trident C	.07	.15
43 Owl Familiar U	.30	.60
44 Phantom Warrior R	.50	1.00
45 Piracy R	20.00	40.00
46 Psychic Transfer R	.30	.60
47 Ransack R	.25	.50
48 Relearn U	.30	.60
49 Remove Soul C	.07	.15
50 Sea Eagle C	.07	.15
51 Sleight of Hand C	1.00	2.00
52 Snapping Drake C	.07	.15
53 Storm Crow C	.30	.60
54 Tidings U	1.00	2.00
55 Time Ebb C	.07	.15
56 Time Warp R	12.50	25.00
57 Touch of Brilliance C	.07	.15
58 Undo U	.20	.40
59 Vizzerdrix R	.25	.50
60 Water Elemental U	.15	.30
61 Wind Drake C	.07	.15
62 Wind Sail U	.15	.30
63 Abyssal Horror R	.30	.75
64 Ancient Craving R	.75	1.50
65 Bog Imp C	.07	.15
66 Bog Raiders C	.07	.15
67 Bog Wraith U	.15	.30
68 Chorus of Woe C	.15	.30
69 Coercion U	.15	.30
70 Dakmor Ghoul U	.75	1.50
71 Dakmor Lancer R	.30	.60
72 Dakmor Plague U	.25	.50
73 Dakmor Scorpion C	.07	.15
74 Dakmor Sorceress R	5.00	10.00
75 Dark Offering U	.20	.40
76 Dread Reaper R	.60	1.25
77 Feral Shadow C	.12	.25
78 Gravedigger U	.15	.30
79 Grim Tutor R	75.00	150.00
80 Hand of Death C	.07	.15
81 Hollow Dogs C	.07	.15
82 Howling Fury U	.20	.40
83 Mind Rot C	.07	.15
84 Muck Rats C	.07	.15
85 Raise Dead C	.07	.15
86 Ravenous Rats U	.20	.40
87 Scathe Zombies C	.07	.15
88 Serpent Warrior C	.07	.15
89 Shrieking Specter U	.50	1.00
90 Soul Feast U	.15	.30
91 Stream of Acid U	2.00	4.00
92 Wicked Pact R	.50	1.00
93 Cinder Storm U	.60	1.25
94 Devastation R	10.00	20.00
95 Earth Elemental U	.15	.30
96 Fire Elemental U	.15	.30
97 Fire Tempest R	.75	1.50
98 Goblin Cavaliers C	.07	.15
99 Goblin Chariot C	.07	.15
100 Goblin Commando U	.75	1.50
101 Goblin General U	3.00	6.00
102 Goblin Glider U	.15	.30
103 Goblin Hero C	.20	.40
104 Goblin Lore U	2.50	5.00
105 Goblin Mountaineer C	.07	.15
106 Goblin Settler U	20.00	40.00
107 Hulking Goblin C	.07	.15
108 Hulking Ogre U	.15	.30
109 Jagged Lightning U	.15	.30
110 Last Chance R	30.00	75.00
111 Lava Axe C	.07	.15
112 Mons's Goblin Raiders C	.15	.30
113 Ogre Warrior C	.15	.30
114 Raging Goblin C	.07	.15
115 Relentless Assault R	1.50	3.00
116 Scorching Spear C	.07	.15
117 Spitting Earth U	.15	.30
118 Stone Rain C	.17	.35
119 Thunder Dragon R	6.00	12.00
120 Trained Orgg R	.25	.50
121 Tremor C	.07	.15
122 Volcanic Dragon R	.30	.60
123 Volcanic Hammer C	.07	.15
124 Alluring Scent R	.50	1.00
125 Barbtooth Wurm C	.15	.30
126 Bull Hippo U	.15	.30
127 Durkwood Boars C	.07	.15
128 Gorilla Warrior C	.07	.15
129 Grizzly Bears C	.07	.15
130 Lone Wolf C	.07	.15
131 Lynx U	.30	.60
132 Monstrous Growth C	.07	.15
133 Moon Sprite U	.15	.30
134 Natural Spring U	.15	.30
135 Nature's Cloak R	.60	1.25
136 Nature's Lore C	3.00	6.00
137 Norwood Archers C	.15	.30
138 Norwood Ranger C	.07	.15
139 Pride of Lions U	.30	.75
140 Renewing Touch U	2.00	4.00
141 Silverback Ape U	.50	1.00
142 Southern Elephant C	.15	.30
143 Squall C	.07	.15
144 Summer Bloom R	2.00	4.00
145 Sylvan Basilisk R	1.00	2.00
146 Sylvan Yeti R	.50	1.00
147 Thorn Elemental R	.50	1.00
148 Untamed Wilds U	.25	.50
149 Whiptail Wurm U	.15	.30
150 Whirlwind R	.50	1.00
151 Wild Ox U	.15	.30
152 Willow Elf C	.15	.30
153 Wood Elves U	2.50	5.00
154 Plains L	.07	.15
155 Plains L	.07	.15
156 Plains L	.07	.15
157 Plains L	.07	.15
158 Island L	.07	.15
159 Island L	.07	.15
160 Island L	.07	.15
161 Island L	.07	.15
162 Swamp L	.07	.15
163 Swamp L	.07	.15
164 Swamp L	.07	.15
165 Swamp L	.07	.15
166 Mountain L	.07	.15
167 Mountain L	.07	.15
168 Mountain L	.07	.15
169 Mountain L	.07	.15
170 Forest L	.07	.15
171 Forest L	.07	.15
172 Forest L	.07	.15
173 Forest L	.07	.15

1999 Magic The Gathering Urza's Destiny

1 Academy Rector R	75.00	150.00
2 Archery Training U	.12	.25
3 Capashen Knight C	.07	.15
4 Capashen Standard C	.07	.15
5 Capashen Templar C	.07	.15
6 False Prophet R	.75	1.50
7 Fend Off C	.07	.15
8 Field Surgeon C	.07	.15
9 Flicker R	.75	1.50
10 Jasmine Seer U	.12	.25
11 Mask of Law and Grace C	.15	.30
12 Master Healer R	.20	.40
13 Opalescence R	15.00	30.00
14 Reliquary Monk C	.07	.15
15 Replenish R	60.00	125.00
16 Sanctimony U	.12	.25
17 Scent of Jasmine C	.07	.15
18 Scour U	.12	.25
19 Serra Advocate U	.12	.25
20 Solidarity C	.15	.30
21 Tethered Griffin R	.30	.60
22 Tormented Angel C	.07	.15
23 Voice of Duty U	.12	.25
24 Voice of Reason U	.12	.25
25 Wall of Glare C	.50	1.00
26 Aura Thief R	6.00	12.00
27 Blizzard Elemental R	.25	.50
28 Brine Seer U	.12	.25
29 Bubbling Beebles C	.07	.15
30 Disappear U	.12	.25
31 Donate R	12.50	25.00
32 Fatigue C	.07	.15
33 Fledgling Osprey C	.07	.15
34 Illuminated Wings C	.07	.15
35 Iridescent Drake U	.12	.25
36 Kingfisher C	.07	.15
37 Mental Discipline C	.07	.15
38 Metathran Elite U	.12	.25
39 Metathran Soldier C	.07	.15
40 Opposition R	7.50	15.00
41 Private Research U	.12	.25
42 Quash U	.12	.25
43 Rayne, Academy Chancellor R	1.50	3.00
44 Rescue C	.07	.15
45 Scent of Brine C	.07	.15
46 Sigil of Sleep C	.20	.40
47 Telepathic Spies C	.07	.15
48 Temporal Adept R	.30	.75
49 Thieving Magpie U	.12	.25
50 Treachery R	50.00	100.00
51 Apprentice Necromancer R	1.00	2.00
52 Attrition R	6.00	12.00
53 Body Snatcher R	1.00	2.00
54 Bubbling Muck C	1.50	3.00
55 Carnival of Souls R	12.50	25.00
56 Chime of Night C	.07	.15
57 Disease Carriers C	.07	.15
58 Dying Wail C	.07	.15
59 Encroach U	.12	.25
60 Eradicate U	.12	.25
61 Festering Wound U	.15	.30
62 Lurking Jackals U	.12	.25
63 Nightshade Seer U	.12	.25
64 Phyrexian Monitor C	.07	.15
65 Phyrexian Negator R	10.00	20.00
66 Plague Dogs U	.12	.25
67 Rapid Decay R	.25	.50
68 Ravenous Rats C	.07	.15
69 Scent of Nightshade C	.07	.15
70 Skittering Horror C	.07	.15
71 Slinking Skirge C	.07	.15
72 Soul Feast U	.12	.25
73 Squirming Mass C	.07	.15
74 Twisted Experiment C	.07	.15
75 Yawgmoth's Bargain R	15.00	30.00
76 Aether Sting U	.15	.30
77 Bloodshot Cyclops R	.25	.50
78 Cinder Seer U	.12	.25
79 Colos Yearling C	.07	.15
80 Covetous Dragon R	6.00	12.00
81 Flame Jet C	.07	.15
82 Goblin Berserker U	.12	.25
83 Goblin Festival R	.30	.75
84 Goblin Gardener C	.07	.15
85 Goblin Marshal R	.60	1.25
86 Goblin Masons C	.07	.15
87 Hulking Ogre C	.07	.15
88 Impatience R	.25	.50
89 Incendiary U	.12	.25
90 Keldon Champion U	.12	.25
91 Keldon Vandals C	.07	.15
92 Landslide U	.12	.25
93 Mark of Fury C	.15	.30
94 Reckless Abandon C	.15	.30
95 Repercussion R	15.00	30.00
96 Scent of Cinder C	.07	.15
97 Sowing Salt U	.12	.25
98 Trumpet Blast C	.07	.15
99 Wake of Destruction R	1.50	3.00
100 Wild Colos C	.07	.15
101 Ancient Silverback R	.20	.40
102 Compost U	2.00	4.00
103 Elvish Lookout C	.07	.15
104 Elvish Piper R	4.00	8.00
105 Emperor Crocodile R	.20	.40
106 Gamekeeper U	.12	.25
107 Goliath Beetle C	.07	.15
108 Heart Warden C	.15	.30
109 Hunting Moa U	.12	.25
110 Ivy Seer U	.12	.25
111 Magnify C	.12	.25
112 Marker Beetles C	.07	.15
113 Momentum U	.12	.25
114 Multani's Decree C	.07	.15
115 Pattern of Rebirth R	2.00	4.00
116 Plated Spider C	.07	.15
117 Plow Under R	1.50	3.00
118 Rofellos, Llanowar Emissary R	40.00	80.00
119 Rofellos's Gift C	.07	.15
120 Scent of Ivy C	.07	.15
121 Splinter U	.25	.50
122 Taunting Elf C	.07	.15
123 Thorn Elemental R	.30	.60
124 Yavimaya Elder C	.25	.50
125 Yavimaya Enchantress U	.12	.25
126 Braidwood Cup U	.12	.25
127 Braidwood Sextant U	.12	.25
128 Brass Secretary U	.12	.25
129 Caltrops U	.25	.50
130 Extruder U	.12	.25
131 Fodder Cannon U	.12	.25
132 Junk Diver R	1.25	2.50
133 Mantis Engine U	.12	.25
134 Masticore R	12.50	25.00
135 Metalworker R	100.00	200.00
136 Powder Keg R	12.50	25.00
137 Scrying Glass R	.20	.40
138 Storage Matrix R	2.50	5.00
139 Thran Dynamo U	2.50	5.00
140 Thran Foundry U	.12	.25
141 Thran Golem R	.25	.50
142 Urzas Incubator R	20.00	40.00
143 Yavimaya Hollow R	75.00	150.00

1999 Magic The Gathering Urza's Legacy

1 Angelic Curator C	.07	.15
2 Blessed Reversal R	.20	.40
3 Burst of Energy C	.07	.15
4 Cessation C	.07	.15
5 Defender of Law C	.07	.15
6 Devout Harpist C	.07	.15
7 Erase C	.07	.15
8 Expendable Troops C	.07	.15
9 Hope and Glory U	.12	.25
10 Iron Will C	.07	.15
11 Karmic Guide R	6.00	12.00
12 Knighthood U	.12	.25
13 Martyr's Cause U	.75	1.50
14 Mother of Runes U	4.00	8.00
15 Opal Avenger R	.20	.40
16 Opal Champion C	.07	.15
17 Peace and Quiet U	.12	.25
18 Planar Collapse R	1.00	2.00
19 Purify R	.20	.40
20 Radiant, Archangel R	1.25	2.25
21 Radiant's Dragoons U	.12	.25
22 Radiant's Judgment C	.15	.30
23 Sustainer of the Realm U	.12	.25
24 Tragic Poet C	.07	.15
25 Anthroplasm R	.20	.40
26 Archivist R	.20	.40
27 Aura Flux C	.07	.15
28 Bouncing Beebles C	.07	.15
29 Cloud of Faeries C	2.00	4.00
30 Delusions of Mediocrity R	.30	.60
31 Fleeting Image R	.20	.40
32 Frantic Search C	.60	1.25
33 Intervene C	.15	.30
34 King Crab U	.12	.25
35 Levitation U	.12	.25
36 Miscalculation C	.25	.50
37 Opportunity U	.12	.25
38 Palinchron R	60.00	125.00
39 Raven Familiar U	.12	.25
40 Rebuild U	.25	.50
41 Second Chance R	7.50	15.00
42 Slow Motion C	.07	.15
43 Snap C	1.25	2.50
44 Thornwind Faeries C	.07	.15
45 Tinker U	1.25	2.50
46 Vigilant Drake C	.07	.15
47 Walking Sponge U	.12	.25
48 Weatherseed Faeries C	.07	.15
49 Bone Shredder U	.20	.40
50 Brink of Madness R	.20	.40
51 Engineered Plague U	.20	.40
52 Eviscerator R	.20	.40
53 Fog of Gnats C	.75	1.50
54 Giant Cockroach C	.07	.15
55 Lurking Skirge R	.20	.40
56 No Mercy R	25.00	50.00
57 Ostracize C	.07	.15
58 Phyrexian Broodlings C	.07	.15
59 Phyrexian Debaser C	.07	.15
60 Phyrexian Defiler U	.12	.25
61 Phyrexian Denouncer C	.07	.15
62 Phyrexian Plaguelord R	.25	.50
63 Phyrexian Reclamation U	2.50	5.00
64 Plague Beetle C	.07	.15
65 Rank and File U	.12	.25
66 Sick and Tired C	.07	.15
67 Sleeper's Guile C	.07	.15
68 Subversion R	1.00	2.00
69 Swat C	.07	.15
70 Tethered Skirge U	.12	.25
71 Treacherous Link U	.12	.25
72 Unearth C	.60	1.25
73 About Face C	.07	.15
74 Avalanche Riders U	.12	.25
75 Defender of Chaos C	.07	.15
76 Ghitu Fire-Eater U	.12	.25
77 Ghitu Slinger C	.07	.15
78 Ghitu War Cry U	.12	.25
79 Goblin Medics C	.07	.15
80 Goblin Welder R	7.50	15.00
81 Granite Grip C	.07	.15
82 Impending Disaster R	1.00	2.00
83 Last-Ditch Effort U	.25	.50
84 Lava Axe C	.07	.15
85 Molten Hydra R	.25	.50
86 Parch C	.07	.15
87 Pygmy Pyrosaur C	.07	.15
88 Pyromancy R	.25	.50
89 Rack and Ruin U	.12	.25
90 Rivalry R	.20	.40
91 Shivan Phoenix R	.25	.50
92 Sluggishness C	.07	.15
93 Viashino Bey C	.07	.15
94 Viashino Cutthroat U	.12	.25
95 Viashino Heretic U	.75	1.50
96 Viashino Sandscout C	.07	.15
97 Bloated Toad U	.12	.25
98 Crop Rotation C	.75	1.50
99 Darkwatch Elves U	.12	.25
100 Defense of the Heart R	10.00	20.00
101 Deranged Hermit R	30.00	60.00
102 Gang of Elk U	.12	.25
103 Harmonic Convergence U	.12	.25
104 Hidden Gibbons R	.25	.50
105 Lone Wolf U	.12	.25
106 Might of Oaks R	2.00	4.00
107 Multani, Maro-Sorcerer R	15.00	30.00
108 Multani's Acolyte C	.07	.15
109 Multani's Presence U	.12	.25
110 Rancor C	.07	.15
111 Repopulate C	.07	.15
112 Silk Net C	.07	.15
113 Simian Grunts C	.07	.15
114 Treefolk Mystic C	.07	.15
115 Weatherseed Elf C	.07	.15
116 Weatherseed Treefolk R	4.00	8.00
117 Wing Snare U	.12	.25
118 Yavimaya Granger C	.20	.40
119 Yavimaya Scion C	.07	.15
120 Yavimaya Wurm C	.07	.15
121 Angel's Trumpet U	.50	1.00
122 Beast of Burden R	.20	.40
123 Crawlspace R	7.50	15.00
124 Damping Engine R	.30	.75
125 Defense Grid R	12.50	25.00
126 Grim Monolith R	250.00	500.00
127 Iron Maiden R	1.25	2.50
128 Jhoira's Toolbox U	.15	.30
129 Memory Jar R	50.00	100.00
130 Quicksilver Amulet R	5.00	10.00
131 Ring of Gix R	6.00	12.00
132 Scrapheap R	.25	.50
133 Thran Lens R	.30	.75
134 Thran War Machine U	.12	.25
135 Thran Weaponry R	.20	.40
136 Ticking Gnomes U	.12	.25
137 Urza's Blueprints R	.25	.50
138 Wheel of Torture R	1.00	2.00
139 Faerie Conclave U	.75	1.50
140 Forbidding Watchtower U	.25	.50
141 Ghitu Encampment U	.15	.30
142 Spawning Pool U	.15	.30
143 Treetop Village U	.50	1.00

1999 Magic The Gathering World Championship

1 Balduvian Horde R	2.00	4.00

1999 Magic The Gathering WOTC Online Store

1 Serra Angel R	30.00	60.00

2000 Magic The Gathering Invasion

1 Alabaster Leech R	.25	.50
2 Angel of Mercy U	.10	.20
3 Ardent Soldier C	.07	.15
4 Atalya, Samite Master R	.50	1.00
5 Benalish Emissary U	.10	.20
6 Benalish Heralds U	.10	.20
7 Benalish Lancer C	.07	.15
8 Benalish Trapper C	.07	.15
9 Blinding Light U	.10	.20
10 Capashen Unicorn C	.12	.25
11 Crimson Acolyte C	.15	.30
12 Crusading Knight R	.50	1.00
13 Death or Glory R	.30	.60
14 Dismantling Blow C	.07	.15
15 Divine Presence R	.75	1.50
16 Fight or Flight R	.30	.60
17 Glimmering Angel C	.07	.15
18 Global Ruin R	.30	.60
19 Harsh Judgment R	.25	.50
20 Holy Day C	.15	.30
21 Liberate U	.25	.50
22 Obsidian Acolyte C	.15	.30
23 Orim's Touch C	.07	.15
24 Pledge of Loyalty U	.10	.20
25 Prison Barricade C	.07	.15
26 Protective Sphere C	.07	.15
27 Pure Reflection R	.30	.60
28 Rampant Elephant C	.07	.15
29 Razorfoot Griffin C	.07	.15
30 Restrain C	.07	.15
31 Reviving Dose C	.07	.15
32 Rewards of Diversity U	.10	.20
33 Reya Dawnbringer R	1.50	3.00
34 Rout R	1.00	2.00
35 Ruham Djinn U	.10	.20
36 Samite Ministration U	.10	.20
37 Shackles C	.07	.15
38 Spirit of Resistance R	1.25	2.50
39 Spirit Weaver U	.10	.20
40 Strength of Unity C	.07	.15
41 Sunscape Apprentice C	.07	.15
42 Sunscape Master R	.25	.50
43 Teferi's Care U	.10	.20
44 Wayfaring Giant U	.10	.20
45 Winnow R	.20	.40
46 Barrin's Unmaking C	.07	.15
47 Blind Seer R	.30	.75
48 Breaking Wave R	.60	1.25
49 Collective Restraint R	7.50	15.00
50 Crystal Spray R	.25	.50
51 Disrupt U	.10	.20
52 Distorting Wake R	.30	.60
53 Dream Thrush C	.07	.15
54 Empress Galina R	12.50	25.00
55 Essence Leak U	.10	.20
56 Exclude C	.15	.30
57 Fact or Fiction U	2.00	4.00
58 Faerie Squadron C	.07	.15
59 Mana Maze R	3.00	6.00
60 Manipulate Fate U	.75	1.50
61 Metathran Aerostat R	.25	.50
62 Metathran Transport U	.10	.20
63 Metathran Zombie C	.07	.15
64 Opt C	.50	1.00
65 Phantasmal Terrain C	.07	.15
66 Probe C	.07	.15
67 Prohibit C	.15	.30
68 Psychic Battle R	1.00	2.00
69 Rainbow Crow U	.10	.20
70 Repulse C	.07	.15
71 Sapphire Leech R	.25	.50
72 Shimmering Wings C	.07	.15
73 Shoreline Raider C	.07	.15
74 Sky Weaver U	.10	.20
75 Stormscape Apprentice C	.07	.15
76 Stormscape Master R	.25	.50
77 Sway of Illusion U	.10	.20
78 Teferi's Response R	.75	1.50
79 Temporal Distortion R	.25	.50
80 Tidal Visionary C	.07	.15
81 Tolarian Emissary U	.10	.20
82 Tower Drake C	.07	.15
83 Traveler's Cloak C	.07	.15
84 Vodalian Hypnotist U	.10	.20
85 Vodalian Merchant C	.07	.15
86 Vodalian Serpent C	.07	.15
87 Wash Out U	1.00	2.00
88 Well-Laid Plans R	.25	.50
89 Worldly Counsel C	.07	.15
90 Zanam Djinn U	.10	.20
91 Addle U	.10	.20
92 Agonizing Demise C	.07	.15
93 Andradite Leech R	.25	.50
94 Annihilate U	.10	.20
95 Bog Initiate C	.07	.15
96 Cremate U	.10	.20
97 Crypt Angel R	.75	1.50
98 Cursed Flesh C	.07	.15
99 Defiling Tears U	.10	.20
100 Desperate Research R	.25	.50
101 Devouring Strossus R	.30	.60
102 Do or Die R	3.00	6.00
103 Dredge U	.10	.20
104 Duskwalker C	.07	.15
105 Exotic Curse C	.07	.15
106 Firescreamer C	.07	.15
107 Goham Djinn U	.10	.20
108 Hate Weaver U	.10	.20
109 Hypnotic Cloud C	.07	.15
110 Marauding Knight R	.30	.60
111 Mourning C	.07	.15
112 Nightscape Apprentice C	.07	.15
113 Nightscape Master R	.30	.60
114 Phyrexian Battleflies C	.07	.15
115 Phyrexian Delver R	1.25	2.50
116 Phyrexian Infiltrator R	.25	.50
117 Phyrexian Reaper C	.07	.15
118 Phyrexian Slayer C	.07	.15
119 Plague Spitter U	.75	1.50
120 Ravenous Rats C	.12	.25
121 Reckless Spite U	.10	.20
122 Recover C	.07	.15
123 Scavenged Weaponry C	.07	.15
124 Soul Burn C	.20	.40
125 Spreading Plague R	3.00	6.00
126 Tainted Well C	.07	.15
127 Trench Wurm U	.10	.20
128 Tsabo's Assassin R	.25	.50
129 Tsabo's Decree R	.60	1.25
130 Twilight's Call R	.75	1.50
131 Urborg Emissary U	.10	.20
132 Urborg Phantom C	.07	.15
133 Urborg Shambler U	.10	.20
134 Urborg Skeleton C	.07	.15
135 Yawgmoth's Agenda R	.30	.60
136 Ancient Kavu C	.07	.15
137 Bend or Break R	.30	.75
138 Breath of Darigaaz U	.10	.20
139 Callous Giant R	.25	.50
140 Chaotic Strike U	.50	1.00
141 Collapsing Borders R	.25	.50
142 Crown of Flames C	.07	.15
143 Firebrand Ranger U	.10	.20
144 Ghitu Fire R	.25	.50
145 Goblin Spy U	.10	.20
146 Halam Djinn U	.10	.20
147 Hooded Kavu C	.07	.15
148 Kavu Aggressor C	.07	.15
149 Kavu Monarch R	.25	.50
150 Kavu Runner U	.10	.20
151 Kavu Scout C	.07	.15
152 Lightning Dart U	.10	.20
153 Loafing Giant R	.25	.50
154 Mages' Contest R	3.00	6.00
155 Maniacal Rage C	.07	.15
156 Obliterate R	3.00	6.00
157 Overload C	.07	.15
158 Pouncing Kavu C	.07	.15
159 Rage Weaver U	.10	.20
160 Rogue Kavu C	.07	.15
161 Ruby Leech R	.20	.40
162 Savage Offensive C	.07	.15
163 Scarred Puma C	.07	.15
164 Scorching Lava C	.07	.15
165 Searing Rays U	.10	.20
166 Shivan Emissary U	.10	.20
167 Shivan Harvest U	.75	1.50
168 Skittish Kavu U	.10	.20
169 Skizzik R	.30	.60
170 Slimy Kavu C	.07	.15
171 Stand or Fall R	.25	.50
172 Stun C	.07	.15
173 Tectonic Instability R	7.50	15.00
174 Thunderscape Apprentice C	.07	.15
175 Thunderscape Master R	.25	.50
176 Tribal Flames C	.07	.15
177 Turf Wound C	.07	.15
178 Urza's Rage R	.60	1.25
179 Viashino Grappler C	.07	.15
180 Zap C	.07	.15
181 Aggressive Urge C	.07	.15
182 Bind R	.75	1.50
183 Blurred Mongoose R	.25	.50
184 Canopy Surge U	.10	.20
185 Elfhame Sanctuary U	.30	.60
186 Elvish Champion R	20.00	40.00

187 Explosive Growth C .07 .15
188 Fertile Ground C .12 .25
189 Harrow C .20 .40
190 Jade Leech R .25 .50
191 Kavu Chameleon U .10 .20
192 Kavu Climber C .07 .15
193 Kavu Lair R .60 1.25
194 Kavu Titan R .75 1.50
195 Llanowar Cavalry C .07 .15
196 Llanowar Elite C .07 .15
197 Llanowar Vanguard C .07 .15
198 Might Weaver U .10 .20
199 Molimo, Maro-Sorcerer R .30 .60
200 Nomadic Elf C .07 .15
201 Pincer Spider C .07 .15
202 Pulse of Llanowar U .10 .20
203 Quirion Elves C .15 .30
204 Quirion Sentinel C .07 .15
205 Quirion Trailblazer C .12 .25
206 Restock R .30 .60
207 Rooting Kavu U .10 .20
208 Saproling Infestation R .30 .60
209 Saproling Symbiosis R 5.00 10.00
210 Scouting Trek U .30 .75
211 Serpentine Kavu C .07 .15
212 Sulam Djinn U .10 .20
213 Tangle U 1.50 3.00
214 Thicket Elemental R .25 .50
215 Thornscape Apprentice C .07 .15
216 Thornscape Master R .25 .50
217 Tranquility C .07 .15
218 Treefolk Healer U .10 .20
219 Utopia Tree R 1.25 2.50
220 Verdeloth the Ancient R 1.25 2.50
221 Verduran Emissary U .10 .20
222 Vigorous Charge C .07 .15
223 Wallop U .10 .20
224 Wandering Stream C .07 .15
225 Whip Silk C .07 .15
226 Absorb R 4.00 8.00
227 Aether Rift R .30 .60
228 Angelic Shield U .10 .20
229 Armadillo Cloak C .30 .60
230 Armored Guardian R .30 .60
231 Artifact Mutation R 1.50 3.00
232 Aura Mutation R 1.50 3.00
233 Aura Shards U 7.50 15.00
234 Backlash U .60 1.25
235 Barrin's Spite R .30 .60
236 Blazing Specter R .50 1.00
237 Captain Sisay R 10.00 20.00
238 Cauldron Dance U .20 .40
239 Charging Troll U .10 .20
240 Cinder Shade U .10 .20
241 Coalition Victory R .50 1.00
242 Crosis, the Purger R 2.50 5.00
243 Darigaaz, the Igniter R .60 1.25
244 Dromar, the Banisher R 2.50 5.00
245 Dueling Grounds R 4.00 8.00
246 Fires of Yavimaya U .25 .50
247 Frenzied Tilling C .07 .15
248 Galina's Knight C .07 .15
249 Hanna, Ship's Navigator R 1.50 3.00
250 Heroes' Reunion U .10 .20
251 Horned Cheetah U .10 .20
252 Hunting Kavu U .10 .20
253 Kangee, Aerie Keeper R 2.00 4.00
254 Llanowar Knight C .07 .15
255 Lobotomy U .10 .20
256 Meteor Storm R .25 .50
257 Noble Panther R .20 .40
258 Ordered Migration U .10 .20
259 Overabundance R 6.00 12.00
260 Plague Spores C .07 .15
261 Pyre Zombie R .25 .50
262 Raging Kavu R .30 .60
263 Reckless Assault R .25 .50
264 Recoil C .12 .25
265 Reviving Vapors U .10 .20
266 Riptide Crab U .10 .20
267 Rith, the Awakener R 1.00 2.00
268 Sabertooth Nishoba R .20 .40
269 Samite Archer U .10 .20
270 Seer's Vision U .15 .30
271 Shivan Zombie C .07 .15
272 Simoon U .10 .20
273 Sleeper's Robe U .10 .20
274 Slinking Serpent U .10 .20
275 Smoldering Tar U .10 .20
276 Spinal Embrace R .25 .50
277 Stalking Assassin R .25 .50
278 Sterling Grove U 10.00 20.00
279 Teferi's Moat R .60 1.25
280 Treva, the Renewer R .75 1.50
281 Tsabo Tavoc R 1.00 2.00
282 Undermine R 2.00 4.00
283 Urborg Drake U .10 .20
284 Vicious Kavu U .10 .20
285 Vile Consumption R .60 1.25
286 Vodalian Zombie C .12 .25
287 Void R .30 .60
288 Voracious Cobra U .10 .20
289 Wings of Hope C .07 .15
290 Yavimaya Barbarian C .07 .15
291 Yavimaya Kavu U .10 .20
292 Stand/Deliver U .10 .20
293 Spite/Malice U .10 .20
294 Pain/Suffering U .10 .20
295 Assault/Battery U .10 .20
296 Wax/Wane U .10 .20
297 Alloy Golem U .10 .20
298 Bloodstone Cameo U .10 .20
299 Chromatic Sphere U 1.25 2.50
300 Crosis's Attendant U .10 .20
301 Darigaaz's Attendant U .10 .20
302 Drake-Skull Cameo U .10 .20
303 Dromar's Attendant U .10 .20
304 Juntu Stakes R .30 .75
305 Lotus Guardian R .30 .60
306 Phyrexian Altar R 50.00 100.00
307 Phyrexian Lens R .25 .50
308 Planar Portal R 2.50 5.00
309 Power Armor U .10 .20
310 Rith's Attendant U .10 .20
311 Seashell Cameo U .10 .20
312 Sparring Golem U .10 .20
313 Tek R .30 .60
314 Tigereye Cameo U .10 .20
315 Treva's Attendant U .10 .20
316 Troll-Horn Cameo U .10 .20
317 Tsabo's Web R 3.00 6.00
318 Urza's Filter R 3.00 6.00
319 Ancient Spring C .07 .15
320 Archaeological Dig U .20 .40
321 Coastal Tower U .30 .60
322 Elfhame Palace U .10 .20
323 Geothermal Crevice C .15 .30
324 Irrigation Ditch C .07 .15
325 Keldon Necropolis R .30 .60
326 Salt Marsh U .30 .75
327 Shivan Oasis U .10 .20
328 Sulfur Vent C .07 .15
329 Tinder Farm C .07 .15
330 Urborg Volcano U .20 .40
331 Plains L .07 .15
332 Plains L .07 .15
333 Plains L .07 .15
334 Plains L .07 .15
335 Island L .07 .15
336 Island L .07 .15
337 Island L .07 .15
338 Island L .07 .15
339 Swamp L .07 .15
340 Swamp L .07 .15
341 Swamp L .07 .15
342 Swamp L .07 .15
343 Mountain L .07 .15
344 Mountain L .07 .15
345 Mountain L .07 .15
346 Mountain L .07 .15
347 Forest L .07 .15
348 Forest L .07 .15
349 Forest L .07 .15
350 Forest L .07 .15

2000 Magic The Gathering Judge Gift Rewards

1 Counterspell R 60.00 125.00
2 Vampiric Tutor R 175.00 350.00

2000 Magic The Gathering Nemesis

1 Angelic Favor U .10 .20
2 Avenger en-Dal R .15 .30
3 Blinding Angel R 2.00 4.00
4 Chieftain en-Dal U .10 .20
5 Defender en-Vec C .07 .15
6 Defiant Falcon C .07 .15
7 Defiant Vanguard U .10 .20
8 Fanatical Devotion C 1.50 3.00
9 Lashknife C .07 .15
10 Lawbringer C .07 .15
11 Lightbringer C .07 .15
12 Lin Sivvi, Defiant Hero R 1.50 3.00
13 Netter en-Dal C .07 .15
14 Noble Stand U .10 .20
15 Off Balance C .07 .15
16 Oracle's Attendants R .15 .30
17 Parallax Wave R 3.00 6.00
18 Seal of Cleansing C .15 .30
19 Silkenfist Fighter C .07 .15
20 Silkenfist Order U .10 .20
21 Sivvi's Ruse U .10 .20
22 Sivvi's Valor R .20 .40
23 Spiritual Asylum R .60 1.25
24 Topple C .07 .15
25 Voice of Truth U .10 .20
26 Accumulated Knowledge C .15 .30
27 Aether Barrier R 1.50 3.00
28 Air Bladder C .07 .15
29 Cloudskate C .07 .15
30 Daze C .75 1.50
31 Dominate U .10 .20
32 Ensnare U .10 .20
33 Infiltrate C .07 .15
34 Jolting Merfolk U .10 .20
35 Oraxid C .12 .25
36 Pale Moon R .15 .30
37 Parallax Tide R 1.50 3.00
38 Rising Waters R 1.50 3.00
39 Rootwater Commando C .07 .15
40 Rootwater Thief R 2.50 5.00
41 Seahunter R 3.00 6.00
42 Seal of Removal C .25 .50
43 Sliptide Serpent R .15 .30
44 Sneaky Homunculus C .07 .15
45 Stronghold Biologist U .10 .20
46 Stronghold Machinist U .10 .20
47 Stronghold Zeppelin U .10 .20
48 Submerge U 5.00 10.00
49 Trickster Mage C .07 .15
50 Wandering Eye C .07 .15
51 Ascendant Evincar R .75 1.50
52 Battlefield Percher U .10 .20
53 Belbe's Percher C .07 .15
54 Carrion Wall U .10 .20
55 Dark Triumph U .10 .20
56 Death Pit Offering R .20 .40
57 Divining Witch R 2.50 5.00
58 Massacre U .30 .60
59 Mind Slash U .50 1.00
60 Mind Swords C .15 .30
61 Murderous Betrayal R .15 .30
62 Parallax Dementia C .07 .15
63 Parallax Nexus R .15 .30
64 Phyrexian Driver C .07 .15
65 Phyrexian Prowler U .10 .20
66 Plague Witch C .07 .15
67 Rathi Assassin R .15 .30
68 Rathi Fiend U .10 .20
69 Rathi Intimidator C .07 .15
70 Seal of Doom C .07 .15
71 Spineless Thug C .07 .15
72 Spiteful Bully C .07 .15
73 Stronghold Discipline C .07 .15
74 Vicious Hunger C .07 .15
75 Volrath the Fallen R .50 1.00
76 Ancient Hydra U .10 .20
77 Arc Mage U .10 .20
78 Bola Warrior C .07 .15
79 Downhill Charge C .15 .30
80 Flame Rift C .25 .50
81 Flowstone Crusher C .07 .15
82 Flowstone Overseer R .15 .30
83 Flowstone Slide R .15 .30
84 Flowstone Strike C .07 .15
85 Flowstone Surge U .10 .20
86 Flowstone Wall C .07 .15
87 Laccolith Grunt C .07 .15
88 Laccolith Rig C .07 .15
89 Laccolith Titan R .15 .30
90 Laccolith Warrior U .10 .20
91 Laccolith Whelp C .07 .15
92 Mana Cache R .50 1.00
93 Mogg Alarm U .10 .20
94 Mogg Salvage U .75 1.50
95 Mogg Toady C .07 .15
96 Moggcatcher R 7.50 15.00
97 Rupture U .10 .20
98 Seal of Fire C .30 .60
99 Shrieking Mogg R .20 .40
100 Stronghold Gambit R .60 1.25
101 Animate Land U .10 .20
102 Blastoderm C .07 .15
103 Coiling Woodworm U .10 .20
104 Fog Patch C .07 .15
105 Harvest Mage C .07 .15
106 Mossdog C .07 .15
107 Nesting Wurm U .10 .20
108 Overlaid Terrain R .20 .40
109 Pack Hunt R .25 .50
110 Refreshing Rain U .10 .20
111 Reverent Silence C .20 .40
112 Rhox R .20 .40
113 Saproling Burst R .75 1.50
114 Saproling Cluster R .15 .30
115 Seal of Strength C .07 .15
116 Skyshroud Behemoth R 1.50 3.00
117 Skyshroud Claim C 1.50 3.00
118 Skyshroud Cutter C .07 .15
119 Skyshroud Poacher R 15.00 30.00
120 Skyshroud Ridgeback C .07 .15
121 Skyshroud Sentinel C .07 .15
122 Stampede Driver U .10 .20
123 Treetop Bracers C .07 .15
124 Wild Mammoth U .10 .20
125 Woodripper U .10 .20
126 Belbe's Armor U .10 .20
127 Belbe's Portal R 1.50 3.00
128 Complex Automaton R .15 .30
129 Eye of Yawgmoth R .15 .30
130 Flint Golem U .10 .20
131 Flowstone Armor U .10 .20
132 Flowstone Thopter U .10 .20
133 Kill Switch R .25 .50
134 Parallax Inhibitor R .15 .30
135 Predator, Flagship R .50 1.00
136 Rackling U .10 .20
137 Rejuvenation Chamber U .10 .20
138 Rusting Golem U .10 .20
139 Tangle Wire R 12.50 25.00
140 Viseling U .10 .20
141 Kor Haven R 7.50 15.00
142 Rath's Edge R .20 .40
143 Terrain Generator U 3.00 6.00

2000 Magic The Gathering Prophecy

1 Abolish U .20 .40
2 Aura Fracture C .07 .15
3 Avatar of Hope R .30 .75
4 Blessed Wind R .20 .40
5 Celestial Convergence R .75 1.50
6 Diving Griffin C .07 .15
7 Entangler U .50 1.00
8 Excise C .07 .15
9 Flowering Field U .10 .20
10 Glittering Lion U .10 .20
11 Glittering Lynx C .07 .15
12 Jeweled Spirit R .15 .30
13 Mageta the Lion R .75 1.50
14 Mageta's Boon C .07 .15
15 Mercenary Informer R .15 .30
16 Mine Bearer C .07 .15
17 Mirror Strike U .15 .30
18 Reveille Squad U .15 .30
19 Rhystic Circle C .07 .15
20 Rhystic Shield C .07 .15
21 Samite Sanctuary R .15 .30
22 Sheltering Prayers R .15 .30
23 Shield Dancer U .10 .20
24 Soul Charmer C .07 .15
25 Sword Dancer U .10 .20
26 Trenching Steed C .07 .15
27 Troubled Healer C .07 .15
28 Alexi, Zephyr Mage R .30 .75
29 Alexi's Cloak C .20 .40
30 Avatar of Will R .30 .75
31 Coastal Hornclaw C .07 .15
32 Denying Wind R .30 .60
33 Excavation U .15 .30
34 Foil U .25 .50
35 Gulf Squid C .07 .15
36 Hazy Homunculus C .07 .15
37 Heightened Awareness R .20 .40
38 Mana Vapors U .15 .30
39 Overburden R 7.50 15.00
40 Psychic Theft R .15 .30
41 Quicksilver Wall U .10 .20
42 Rethink C .07 .15
43 Rhystic Deluge C .07 .15
44 Rhystic Scrying U .10 .20
45 Rhystic Study C 25.00 50.00
46 Ribbon Snake C .07 .15
47 Shrouded Serpent R .15 .30
48 Spiketail Drake U .10 .20
49 Spiketail Hatchling C .07 .15
50 Stormwatch Eagle C .07 .15
51 Sunken Field U .20 .40
52 Troublesome Spirit R .15 .30
53 Windscouter U .10 .20
54 Withdraw C .07 .15
55 Agent of Shauku C .07 .15
56 Avatar of Woe R 2.00 4.00
57 Bog Elemental R .15 .30
58 Bog Glider C .07 .15
59 Chilling Apparition U .10 .20
60 Coffin Puppets R .15 .30
61 Death Charmer C .07 .15
62 Despoil C .07 .15
63 Endbringer's Revel U .10 .20
64 Fen Stalker C .07 .15
65 Flay C .07 .15
66 Greel, Mind Raker R .25 .50
67 Greel's Caress C .07 .15
68 Infernal Genesis R .25 .50
69 Nakaya Shade U .10 .20
70 Noxious Field U .10 .20
71 Outbreak U .10 .20
72 Pit Raptor U .10 .20
73 Plague Fiend C .07 .15
74 Plague Wind R 1.50 3.00
75 Rebel Informer R .15 .30
76 Rhystic Syphon U .10 .20
77 Rhystic Tutor R 1.25 2.50
78 Soul Strings C .07 .15
79 Steal Strength C .07 .15
80 Wall of Vipers U .10 .20
81 Whipstitched Zombie C .07 .15
82 Avatar of Fury R .30 .75
83 Barbed Field U .10 .20
84 Branded Brawlers C .07 .15
85 Brutal Suppression U .10 .20
86 Citadel of Pain U 4.00 8.00
87 Devastate C .07 .15
88 Fault Riders C .07 .15
89 Fickle Efreet R .20 .40
90 Flameshot U .10 .20
91 Inflame C .07 .15
92 Keldon Arsonist U .10 .20
93 Keldon Berserker C .07 .15
94 Keldon Firebombers R 2.00 4.00
95 Latulla, Keldon Overseer R .20 .40
96 Latulla's Orders C .07 .15
97 Lesser Gargadon U .10 .20
98 Panic Attack C .07 .15
99 Rhystic Lightning C .07 .15
100 Ridgeline Rager C .07 .15
101 Scoria Cat U .10 .20
102 Search for Survivors R .15 .30
103 Searing Wind R .30 .75
104 Spur Grappler C .07 .15
105 Task Mage Assembly R .15 .30
106 Veteran Brawlers R .15 .30
107 Whip Sergeant U .10 .20
108 Zerapa Minotaur C .07 .15
109 Avatar of Might R .30 .75
110 Calming Verse C .50 1.00
111 Darba U .10 .20
112 Dual Nature R .50 1.00
113 Elephant Resurgence R .15 .30
114 Forgotten Harvest R .20 .40
115 Jolrael, Empress of Beasts R .75 1.50
116 Jolrael's Favor C .07 .15
117 Living Terrain U .10 .20
118 Marsh Boa C .07 .15
119 Mungha Wurm R .15 .30
120 Pygmy Razorback C .07 .15
121 Rib Cage Spider C .07 .15
122 Root Cage U .10 .20
123 Silt Crawler C .07 .15
124 Snag U .10 .20
125 Spitting Spider U .10 .20
126 Spore Frog C .20 .40
127 Squirrel Wrangler R 1.25 2.50
128 Thresher Beast C .07 .15
129 Thrive C .07 .15
130 Verdant Field U .10 .20
131 Vintara Elephant C .07 .15
132 Vintara Snapper U .10 .20
133 Vitalizing Wind R .20 .40
134 Wild Might C .07 .15
135 Wing Storm U .10 .20
136 Chimeric Idol U .10 .20
137 Copper-Leaf Angel R .30 .75
138 Hollow Warrior U .10 .20
139 Keldon Battlewagon R .15 .30
140 Well of Discovery R .15 .30
141 Well of Life U .10 .20
142 Rhystic Cave U .15 .30
143 Wintermoon Mesa R .15 .30

2000 Magic The Gathering Starter

1 Angelic Blessing C .15 .30
3 Breath of Life U .10 .20
5 Eager Cadet C .07 .15
7 Knight Errant C .07 .15
8 Royal Falcon C .07 .15
11 Wild Griffin C .07 .15
14 Giant Octopus C .07 .15
18 Sea Eagle C .07 .15
19 Time Ebb C .07 .15
20 Vizzerdrix R .50 1.00
25 Hand of Death C .07 .15
31 Lava Axe C .07 .15
32 Mons's Goblin Raiders C .07 .15
33 Ogre Warrior C .07 .15
37 Trained Orgg R .50 1.00
38 Durkwood Boars C .07 .15
41 Monstrous Growth C .07 .15
42 Moon Sprite U .10 .20
43 Rhox R .75 1.50
45 Willow Elf C .07 .15

2001 Magic The Gathering Apocalypse

1 Angelfire Crusader C .07 .15
2 Coalition Flag U .12 .25
3 Coalition Honor Guard C .07 .15
4 Dega Disciple C .07 .15
5 Dega Sanctuary U .12 .25
6 Degavolver R .15 .30
7 Diversionary Tactics U .12 .25
8 Divine Light C .07 .15

9 Enlistment Officer U	.12	.25
10 False Dawn R	.15	.30
11 Gerrard Capashen R	.25	.50
12 Haunted Angel U	.12	.25
13 Helionaut C	.07	.15
14 Manacles of Decay C	.07	.15
15 Orim's Thunder C	.07	.15
16 Shield of Duty and Reason C	.07	.15
17 Spectral Lynx R	.15	.30
18 Standard Bearer C	.50	1.00
19 Ceta Disciple C	.07	.15
20 Ceta Sanctuary U	.12	.25
21 Cetavolver R	.15	.30
22 Coastal Drake C	.07	.15
23 Evasive Action U	.12	.25
24 Ice Cave R	.30	.60
25 Index C	.07	.15
26 Jaded Response C	.07	.15
27 Jilt C	.12	.25
28 Living Airship C	.07	.15
29 Reef Shaman C	.07	.15
30 Shimmering Mirage C	.07	.15
31 Tidal Courier U	.12	.25
32 Unnatural Selection R	4.00	8.00
33 Vodalian Mystic U	.12	.25
34 Whirlpool Drake U	.30	.60
35 Whirlpool Rider C	.30	.60
36 Whirlpool Warrior R	2.50	5.00
37 Dead Ringers C	.07	.15
38 Desolation Angel R	.75	1.50
39 Foul Presence U	.12	.25
40 Grave Defiler U	.12	.25
41 Last Caress C	.07	.15
42 Mind Extraction C	.07	.15
43 Mournful Zombie C	.07	.15
44 Necra Disciple C	.07	.15
45 Necra Sanctuary U	.12	.25
46 Necravolver R	.15	.30
47 Phyrexian Arena R	20.00	40.00
48 Phyrexian Gargantua U	.12	.25
49 Phyrexian Rager C	.07	.15
50 Planar Despair R	.15	.30
51 Quagmire Druid C	.07	.15
52 Suppress U	.12	.25
53 Urborg Uprising C	.07	.15
54 Zombie Boa C	.07	.15
55 Bloodfire Colossus R	.15	.30
56 Bloodfire Dwarf C	.07	.15
57 Bloodfire Infusion C	.07	.15
58 Bloodfire Kavu U	.12	.25
59 Desolation Giant R	.15	.30
60 Dwarven Landslide C	.07	.15
61 Dwarven Patrol U	.12	.25
62 Goblin Ringleader U	.75	1.50
63 Illuminate U	.12	.25
64 Kavu Glider C	.07	.15
65 Minotaur Tactician C	.07	.15
66 Raka Disciple C	.07	.15
67 Raka Sanctuary U	.12	.25
68 Rakavolver R	.15	.30
69 Smash C	.07	.15
70 Tahngarth's Glare C	.07	.15
71 Tundra Kavu C	.07	.15
72 Wild Research R	1.50	3.00
73 Ana Disciple C	.07	.15
74 Ana Sanctuary U	.12	.25
75 Anavolver R	.15	.30
76 Bog Gnarr C	.07	.15
77 Gaea's Balance U	.12	.25
78 Glade Gnarr C	.07	.15
79 Kavu Howler U	.12	.25
80 Kavu Mauler R	.15	.30
81 Lay of the Land C	.07	.15
82 Penumbra Bobcat C	.07	.15
83 Penumbra Kavu U	.12	.25
84 Penumbra Wurm R	.15	.30
85 Savage Gorilla C	.07	.15
86 Strength of Night C	.07	.15
87 Sylvan Messenger U	.15	.30
88 Symbiotic Deployment R	.15	.30
89 Tranquil Path C	.07	.15
90 Urborg Elf C	.12	.25
91 Aether Mutation U	.12	.25
92 Captain's Maneuver U	.12	.25
93 Consume Strength C	.07	.15
94 Cromat R	1.50	3.00
95 Death Grasp R	.25	.50
96 Death Mutation U	.20	.40
97 Ebony Treefolk U	.12	.25
98 Fervent Charge R	.30	.75
99 Flowstone Charger U	.12	.25
100 Fungal Shambler R	.15	.30
101 Gaea's Skyfolk C	.07	.15
102 Gerrard's Verdict U	.20	.40
103 Goblin Legionnaire C	.07	.15
104 Goblin Trenches R	.15	.30
105 Guided Passage R	1.00	2.00
106 Jungle Barrier U	.12	.25
107 Last Stand R	.15	.30
108 Lightning Angel R	.50	1.00
109 Llanowar Dead C	.07	.15
110 Martyrs' Tomb U	.12	.25
111 Minotaur Illusionist U	.12	.25
112 Mystic Snake R	.75	1.50
113 Overgrown Estate R	.15	.30
114 Pernicious Deed R	7.50	15.00
115 Powerstone Minefield R	.30	.60
116 Prophetic Bolt R	.15	.30
117 Putrid Warrior C	.07	.15
118 Quicksilver Dagger C	.07	.15
119 Razorfin Hunter C	.07	.15
120 Soul Link C	.07	.15
121 Spiritmonger R	.75	1.50
122 Squee's Embrace C	.07	.15
123 Squee's Revenge U	.50	1.00
124 Suffocating Blast R	.15	.30
125 Temporal Spring C	.15	.30
126 Vindicate R	7.50	15.00
127 Yavimaya's Embrace R	.15	.30
128 Fire/Ice U	.30	.60
129 Illusion/Reality U	.12	.25
130 Life/Death U	1.00	2.00
131 Night/Day U	.12	.25
132 Order/Chaos U	.12	.25
133 Brass Herald U	.50	1.00
134 Dodecapod U	.12	.25
135 Dragon Arch U	2.00	4.00
136 Emblazoned Golem U	.12	.25
137 Legacy Weapon R	3.00	6.00
138 Mask of Intolerance R	.15	.30
139 Battlefield Forge R	4.00	8.00
140 Caves of Koilos R	3.00	6.00
141 Llanowar Wastes R	10.00	20.00
142 Shivan Reef R	5.00	10.00
143 Yavimaya Coast R	7.50	15.00

2001 Magic The Gathering Judge Gift Rewards

1 Ball Lightning R	12.50	25.00
2 Oath of Druids R	20.00	40.00

2001 Magic The Gathering Odyssey

1 Aegis of Honor R	.60	1.25
2 Ancestral Tribute R	.20	.40
3 Angelic Wall C	.07	.15
4 Animal Boneyard U	.12	.25
5 Auramancer C	.07	.15
6 Aven Archer U	.12	.25
7 Aven Cloudchaser C	.07	.15
8 Aven Flock C	.07	.15
9 Aven Shrine R	.20	.40
10 Balancing Act R	.30	.60
11 Beloved Chaplain U	.12	.25
12 Blessed Orator U	.12	.25
13 Cantivore R	.20	.40
14 Cease-Fire C	.07	.15
15 Confessor C	.07	.15
16 Dedicated Martyr C	.07	.15
17 Delaying Shield R	4.00	8.00
18 Devoted Caretaker R	1.25	2.50
19 Divine Sacrament R	1.25	2.50
20 Dogged Hunter R	.20	.40
21 Earnest Fellowship R	.60	1.25
22 Embolden C	.07	.15
23 Gallantry U	.12	.25
24 Graceful Antelope R	.20	.40
25 Hallowed Healer C	.07	.15
26 Karmic Justice R	7.50	15.00
27 Kirtar's Desire C	.07	.15
28 Kirtar's Wrath R	.20	.40
29 Lieutenant Kirtar R	1.25	2.50
30 Life Burst C	.07	.15
31 Luminous Guardian U	.12	.25
32 Master Apothecary R	.60	1.25
33 Mystic Crusader R	.20	.40
34 Mystic Penitent U	.12	.25
35 Mystic Visionary C	.07	.15
36 Mystic Zealot C	.07	.15
37 Nomad Decoy U	.12	.25
38 Patrol Hound C	.07	.15
39 Pianna, Nomad Captain R	.30	.75
40 Pilgrim of Justice C	.07	.15
41 Pilgrim of Virtue C	.07	.15
42 Ray of Distortion C	.07	.15
43 Resilient Wanderer U	.12	.25
44 Sacred Rites C	.07	.15
45 Second Thoughts C	.07	.15
46 Shelter C	.07	.15
47 Soulcatcher U	.12	.25
48 Sphere of Duty U	.12	.25
49 Sphere of Grace U	.12	.25
50 Sphere of Law U	.12	.25
51 Sphere of Reason U	.12	.25
52 Sphere of Truth U	.12	.25
53 Spiritualize U	.12	.25
54 Tattoo Ward U	.12	.25
55 Testament of Faith U	.12	.25
56 Tireless Tribe C	.07	.15
57 Wayward Angel R	.30	.60
58 Aboshan, Cephalid Emperor R	.50	1.00
59 Aboshan's Desire C	.07	.15
60 Aether Burst C	.07	.15
61 Amugaba R	.20	.40
62 Aura Graft U	.12	.25
63 Aven Fisher C	.07	.15
64 Aven Smokeweaver U	.12	.25
65 Aven Windreader C	.07	.15
66 Balshan Beguiler U	.12	.25
67 Balshan Griffin U	.12	.25
68 Bamboozle U	.12	.25
69 Battle of Wits R	.20	.40
70 Careful Study C	1.50	3.00
71 Cephalid Broker U	.12	.25
72 Cephalid Looter C	.07	.15
73 Cephalid Retainer R	.20	.40
74 Cephalid Scout C	.07	.15
75 Cephalid Shrine R	.20	.40
76 Chamber of Manipulation U	1.25	2.50
77 Cognivore R	.20	.40
78 Concentrate U	.12	.25
79 Cultural Exchange R	3.00	6.00
80 Deluge U	.12	.25
81 Dematerialize C	.07	.15
82 Divert R	.50	1.00
83 Dreamwinder C	.07	.15
84 Escape Artist C	.07	.15
85 Extract R	7.50	15.00
86 Fervent Denial U	.20	.40
87 Immobilizing Ink C	.07	.15
88 Laquatus's Creativity U	.25	.50
89 Patron Wizard R	7.50	15.00
90 Pedantic Learning R	.20	.40
91 Peek C	.20	.40
92 Persuasion R	.20	.40
93 Phantom Whelp C	.07	.15
94 Predict U	.30	.60
95 Psionic Gift C	.07	.15
96 Pulsating Illusion U	.12	.25
97 Puppeteer U	.12	.25
98 Repel C	.07	.15
99 Rites of Refusal C	.07	.15
100 Scrivener C	.07	.15
101 Shifty Doppelganger R	.30	.75
102 Standstill U	3.00	6.00
103 Syncopate C	.07	.15
104 Think Tank U	.12	.25
105 Thought Devourer R	.20	.40
106 Thought Eater U	.12	.25
107 Thought Nibbler C	.07	.15
108 Time Stretch R	12.50	25.00
109 Touch of Invisibility C	.07	.15
110 Traumatize R	2.50	5.00
111 Treetop Sentinel U	.12	.25
112 Unifying Theory R	.20	.40
113 Upheaval R	2.00	4.00
114 Words of Wisdom C	.07	.15
115 Afflict C	.07	.15
116 Bloodcurdler R	.20	.40
117 Braids, Cabal Minion R	.50	1.00
118 Buried Alive U	3.00	6.00
119 Cabal Inquisitor C	.07	.15
120 Cabal Patriarch R	.20	.40
121 Cabal Shrine R	.20	.40
122 Caustic Tar U	.12	.25
123 Childhood Horror U	.12	.25
124 Coffin Purge C	.07	.15
125 Crypt Creeper C	.07	.15
126 Cursed Monstrosity R	.20	.40
127 Decaying Soil R	.20	.40
128 Decompose U	.12	.25
129 Diabolic Tutor U	2.00	4.00
130 Dirty Wererat C	.07	.15
131 Dusk Imp C	.07	.15
132 Entomb R	20.00	40.00
133 Execute U	.12	.25
134 Face of Fear U	.12	.25
135 Famished Ghoul U	.12	.25
136 Filthy Cur C	.07	.15
137 Fledgling Imp C	.07	.15
138 Frightcrawler C	.07	.15
139 Ghastly Demise C	.20	.40
140 Gravedigger C	.07	.15
141 Gravestorm R	1.00	2.00
142 Haunting Echoes R	.30	.60
143 Hint of Insanity R	.20	.40
144 Infected Vermin U	.20	.40
145 Innocent Blood C	.07	.15
146 Last Rites C	.07	.15
147 Malevolent Awakening U	.12	.25
148 Mind Burst C	.07	.15
149 Mindslicer R	20.00	40.00
150 Morbid Hunger C	.07	.15
151 Morgue Theft C	.07	.15
152 Mortivore R	1.00	2.00
153 Nefarious Lich R	.75	1.50
154 Overeager Apprentice C	.07	.15
155 Painbringer U	.12	.25
156 Patriarch's Desire C	.07	.15
157 Repentant Vampire R	.20	.40
158 Rotting Giant U	.12	.25
159 Sadistic Hypnotist U	1.00	2.00
160 Screams of the Damned U	.12	.25
161 Skeletal Scrying U	.12	.25
162 Skull Fracture U	.12	.25
163 Stalking Bloodsucker R	.20	.40
164 Tainted Pact R	60.00	120.00
165 Tombfire R	.20	.40
166 Traveling Plague R	.20	.40
167 Whispering Shade C	.07	.15
168 Zombie Assassin C	.07	.15
169 Zombie Cannibal C	.07	.15
170 Zombie Infestation U	.30	.75
171 Zombify U	.20	.40
172 Acceptable Losses C	.07	.15
173 Anarchist C	.07	.15
174 Ashen Firebeast R	.20	.40
175 Barbarian Lunatic C	.07	.15
176 Bash to Bits U	.12	.25
177 Battle Strain U	.12	.25
178 Blazing Salvo C	.07	.15
179 Bomb Squad R	1.50	3.00
180 Burning Sands R	2.00	4.00
181 Chainflinger C	.07	.15
182 Chance Encounter R	12.50	25.00
183 Demolish U	.12	.25
184 Demoralize C	.07	.15
185 Dwarven Grunt C	.07	.15
186 Dwarven Recruiter U	5.00	10.00
187 Dwarven Shrine R	.20	.40
188 Dwarven Strike Force U	.12	.25
189 Earth Rift C	.07	.15
190 Ember Beast C	.07	.15
191 Engulfing Flames U	.12	.25
192 Epicenter R	1.00	2.00
193 Firebolt C	.07	.15
194 Flame Burst C	.07	.15
195 Frenetic Ogre U	.12	.25
196 Halberdier C	.07	.15
197 Impulsive Maneuvers R	3.00	6.00
198 Kamahl, Pit Fighter R	.20	.40
199 Kamahl's Desire C	.07	.15
200 Lava Blister U	.30	.60
201 Liquid Fire U	.12	.25
202 Mad Dog C	.07	.15
203 Magma Vein U	.12	.25
204 Magnivore R	.20	.40
205 Mine Layer R	6.00	12.00
206 Minotaur Explorer U	.12	.25
207 Molten Influence R	1.00	2.00
208 Mudhole R	.20	.40
209 Need for Speed R	.75	1.50
210 Obstinate Familiar R	.50	1.00
211 Pardic Firecat C	.07	.15
212 Pardic Miner R	.75	1.50
213 Pardic Swordsmith C	.07	.15
214 Price of Glory U	7.50	15.00
215 Reckless Charge C	.07	.15
216 Recoup U	.15	.30
217 Rites of Initiation C	.07	.15
218 Savage Firecat R	.20	.40
219 Scorching Missile C	.07	.15
220 Seize the Day R	4.00	8.00
221 Shower of Coals U	.12	.25
222 Spark Mage U	.50	1.00
223 Steam Vines U	.12	.25
224 Thermal Blast C	.07	.15
225 Tremble C	.07	.15
226 Volcanic Spray U	.12	.25
227 Volley of Boulders R	.20	.40
228 Whipkeeper U	.20	.40
229 Bearscape R	2.50	5.00
230 Beast Attack U	.12	.25
231 Call of the Herd R	.50	1.00
232 Cartographer C	.07	.15
233 Chatter of the Squirrel C	.07	.15
234 Chlorophant R	.50	1.00
235 Crashing Centaur U	.12	.25
236 Deep Reconnaissance U	.12	.25
237 Diligent Farmhand C	.60	1.25
238 Druid Lyrist C	.07	.15
239 Druid's Call U	5.00	10.00
240 Elephant Ambush C	.07	.15
241 Gorilla Titan U	.12	.25
242 Ground Seal R	.75	1.50
243 Holistic Wisdom R	1.00	2.00
244 Howling Gale U	.12	.25
245 Ivy Elemental R	.20	.40
246 Krosan Archer C	.07	.15
247 Krosan Avenger C	.07	.15
248 Krosan Beast R	4.00	8.00
249 Leaf Dancer C	.07	.15
250 Metamorphic Wurm U	.12	.25
251 Moment's Peace C	1.00	2.00
252 Muscle Burst C	.07	.15
253 Nantuko Disciple C	.07	.15
254 Nantuko Elder U	.12	.25
255 Nantuko Mentor R	.20	.40
256 Nantuko Shrine R	.75	1.50
257 New Frontiers R	2.50	5.00
258 Nimble Mongoose U	.25	.50
259 Nut Collector R	15.00	30.00
260 Overrun U	.20	.40
261 Piper's Melody U	.12	.25
262 Primal Frenzy C	.07	.15
263 Rabid Elephant C	.07	.15
264 Refresh C	.07	.15
265 Rites of Spring C	.07	.15
266 Roar of the Wurm U	.12	.25
267 Seton, Krosan Protector R	1.25	2.50
268 Seton's Desire C	.07	.15
269 Simplify C	.07	.15
270 Skyshooter U	.12	.25
271 Spellbane Centaur R	.20	.40
272 Springing Tiger C	.07	.15
273 Squirrel Mob R	7.50	15.00
274 Squirrel Nest U	.75	1.50
275 Still Life U	.12	.25
276 Stone-Tongue Basilisk R	.20	.40
277 Sylvan Might U	.12	.25
278 Terravore R	1.25	2.50
279 Twigwalker U	.12	.25
280 Verdant Succession R	.20	.40
281 Vivify U	.12	.25
282 Werebear C	.20	.40
283 Wild Mongrel C	.15	.30
284 Woodland Druid C	.07	.15
285 Zoologist R	.30	.75
286 Atogatog R	.75	1.50
287 Decimate R	2.50	5.00
288 Iridescent Angel R	.75	1.50
289 Lithatog U	.12	.25
290 Mystic Enforcer R	.20	.40
291 Phantatog U	.12	.25
292 Psychatog U	.30	.60
293 Sarcatog U	.12	.25
294 Shadowmage Infiltrator R	1.25	2.50
295 Thaumatog U	.12	.25
296 Vampiric Dragon R	.75	1.50
297 Catalyst Stone R	.75	1.50
298 Charmed Pendant R	.30	.60
299 Darkwater Egg U	.12	.25
300 Junk Golem R	.20	.40
301 Limestone Golem U	.12	.25
302 Millikin U	1.00	2.00
303 Mirari R	1.00	2.00
304 Mossfire Egg U	.12	.25
305 Otarian Juggernaut R	.20	.40
306 Patchwork Gnomes U	.12	.25
307 Sandstone Deadfall U	.12	.25
308 Shadowblood Egg U	.12	.25
309 Skycloud Egg U	.20	.40
310 Steamclaw U	.12	.25
311 Sungrass Egg U	.12	.25
312 Abandoned Outpost C	.07	.15
313 Barbarian Ring U	.50	1.00
314 Bog Wreckage C	.07	.15
315 Cabal Pit U	.12	.25
316 Centaur Garden U	.12	.25
317 Cephalid Coliseum U	5.00	10.00
318 Crystal Quarry R	5.00	10.00
319 Darkwater Catacombs R	2.00	4.00
320 Deserted Temple R	50.00	100.00
321 Mossfire Valley R	2.50	5.00
322 Nomad Stadium U	.20	.40
323 Petrified Field R	4.00	8.00
324 Ravaged Highlands C	.07	.15
325 Seafloor Debris C	.07	.15
326 Shadowblood Ridge R	2.50	5.00
327 Skycloud Expanse R	3.00	6.00
328 Sungrass Prairie R	1.00	2.00
329 Tarnished Citadel R	20.00	40.00
330 Timberland Ruins C	.07	.15
331 Plains v1 L	.07	.15
332 Plains v2 L	.07	.15
333 Plains v3 L	.07	.15
334 Plains v4 L	.07	.15
335 Island v1 L	.07	.15
336 Island v2 L	.07	.15
337 Island v3 L	.07	.15
338 Island v4 L	.07	.15
339 Swamp v1 L	.07	.15
340 Swamp v2 L	.07	.15
341 Swamp v3 L	.07	.15
342 Swamp v4 L	.07	.15
343 Mountain v1 L	.07	.15
344 Mountain v2 L	.07	.15
345 Mountain v3 L	.07	.15
346 Mountain v4 L	.07	.15
347 Forest v1 L	.07	.15
348 Forest v2 L	.07	.15

349 Forest v3 L	.07	.15
350 Forest v4 L	.07	.15

2001 Magic The Gathering Planeshift

1 Aura Blast C	.07	.15
2 Aurora Griffin C	.07	.15
3 Disciple of Kangee C	.07	.15
4 Dominaria's Judgment R	.20	.40
5 Guard Dogs U	.12	.25
6 Heroic Defiance C	.07	.15
7 Hobble C	.07	.15
8 Honorable Scout C	.07	.15
9 Lashknife Barrier U	.12	.25
10 March of Souls R	.60	1.25
11 Orim's Chant R	12.50	25.00
12 Planeswalker's Mirth R	.20	.40
13 Pollen Remedy C	.07	.15
14 Samite Elder R	.20	.40
15 Samite Pilgrim C	.07	.15
16 Sunscape Battlemage U	.12	.25
17 Sunscape Familiar C	1.00	2.00
18 Surprise Deployment U	.12	.25
19 Voice of All U	.20	.40
20 Allied Strategies U	.12	.25
21 Arctic Merfolk C	.07	.15
22 Confound C	.07	.15
23 Dralnu's Pet R	.20	.40
24 Ertai's Trickery U	.12	.25
25 Escape Routes C	.07	.15
26 Gainsay U	.12	.25
27 Hunting Drake C	.07	.15
28 Planar Overlay R	.20	.40
29 Planeswalker's Mischief R	.20	.40
30 Rushing River C	.15	.30
31 Sea Snidd C	.07	.15
32 Shifting Sky U	.12	.25
33 Sisay's Ingenuity C	.07	.15
34 Sleeping Potion C	.07	.15
35 Stormscape Battlemage U	.12	.25
36 Stormscape Familiar C	.15	.30
37 Sunken Hope R	.20	.40
38 Waterspout Elemental R	.20	.40
39 Bog Down C	.07	.15
40 Dark Suspicions R	.25	.50
41 Death Bomb C	.07	.15
42 Diabolic Intent R	25.00	50.00
43 Exotic Disease U	.12	.25
44 Lord of the Undead R	7.50	15.00
45 Maggot Carrier C	.07	.15
46 Morgue Toad C	.07	.15
47 Nightscape Battlemage U	.12	.25
48 Nightscape Familiar C	.30	.60
49 Noxious Vapors U	.12	.25
50 Phyrexian Bloodstock C	.07	.15
51 Phyrexian Scuta R	.50	1.00
52 Planeswalker's Scorn R	.20	.40
53 Shriek of Dread C	.12	.25
54 Sinister Strength C	.07	.15
55 Slay U	.12	.25
56 Volcano Imp C	.07	.15
57 Warped Devotion U	.12	.25
58 Caldera Kavu C	.07	.15
59 Deadapult R	.20	.40
60 Flametongue Kavu U	.25	.50
61 Goblin Game R	1.25	2.50
62 Implode U	.12	.25
63 Insolence C	.07	.15
64 Kavu Recluse C	.07	.15
65 Keldon Mantle C	.07	.15
66 Magma Burst C	.07	.15
67 Mire Kavu C	.07	.15
68 Mogg Jailer U	.12	.25
69 Mogg Sentry R	.20	.40
70 Planeswalker's Fury R	.20	.40
71 Singe C	.07	.15
72 Slingshot Goblin C	.07	.15
73 Strafe U	.12	.25
74a Tahngarth, Talruum Hero R	.75	1.50
74b Tahngarth, Talruum Hero R ALT ART	25.00	50.00
75 Thunderscape Battlemage U	.12	.25
76 Thunderscape Familiar C	.07	.15
77 Alpha Kavu U	.12	.25
78 Amphibious Kavu C	.07	.15
79 Falling Timber C	.07	.15
80 Gaea's Herald R	1.50	3.00
81 Gaea's Might C	.07	.15
82 Magnigoth Treefolk R	.20	.40
83 Mirrorwood Treefolk U	.12	.25
84 Multani's Harmony U	.12	.25
85 Nemata, Grove Guardian R	3.00	6.00
86 Planeswalker's Favor R	.20	.40
87 Primal Growth C	.60	1.25
88 Pygmy Kavu C	.07	.15
89 Quirion Dryad R	.20	.40
90 Quirion Explorer C	.07	.15
91 Root Greevil C	.07	.15
92 Skyshroud Blessing U	.12	.25
93 Stone Kavu C	.07	.15
94 Thornscape Battlemage U	.12	.25
95 Thornscape Familiar C	.07	.15
96 Ancient Spider R	.20	.40
97 Cavern Harpy C	.20	.40
98 Cloud Cover R	1.25	2.50
99 Crosis's Charm U	.30	.75
100 Darigaaz's Charm U	.12	.25
101 Daring Leap C	.07	.15
102 Destructive Flow R	.30	.75
103 Doomsday Specter R	.50	1.00
104 Dralnu's Crusade R	.50	1.00
105 Dromar's Charm U	.15	.30
106 Eladamri's Call R	5.00	10.00
107a Ertai, the Corrupted R	2.50	5.00
108 Fleetfoot Panther U	.30	.60
109 Gerrard's Command C	.07	.15
110 Horned Kavu C	.07	.15
111 Hull Breach C	.75	1.50
112 Keldon Twilight R	.20	.40
113 Lava Zombie C	.07	.15
114 Malicious Advice C	.07	.15
115 Marsh Crocodile U	.12	.25
116 Meddling Mage R	5.00	10.00
117 Natural Emergence R	.20	.40
118 Phyrexian Tyranny R	4.00	8.00
119 Questing Phelddagrif R	.75	1.50
120 Radiant Kavu R	.20	.40
121 Razing Snidd U	.12	.25
122 Rith's Charm U	.12	.25
123 Sawtooth Loon U	.12	.25
124 Shivan Wurm R	.75	1.50
125 Silver Drake C	.07	.15
126 Sparkcaster U	.12	.25
127 Steel Leaf Paladin C	.07	.15
128 Terminate C	.60	1.25
129 Treva's Charm U	.15	.30
130 Urza's Guilt R	.30	.75
131 Draco R	2.50	5.00
132 Mana Cylix U	.12	.25
133a Skyship Weatherlight R	1.50	3.00
134 Star Compass U	1.25	2.50
135 Stratadon U	.12	.25
136 Crosis's Catacombs U	1.50	3.00
137 Darigaaz's Caldera U	1.00	2.00
138 Dromar's Cavern U	.60	1.25
139 Forsaken City R	1.00	2.00
140 Meteor Crater R	2.50	5.00
141 Rith's Grove U	.50	1.00
142 Terminal Moraine U	.75	1.50
143 Treva's Ruins U	1.00	2.00

2001 Magic The Gathering Seventh Edition

1 Angelic Page C	.07	.15
2 Ardent Militia U	.12	.25
3 Blessed Reversal R	.15	.30
4 Breath of Life U	.20	.40
5 Castle U	.15	.30
6 Circle of Protection Black C	.07	.15
7 Circle of Protection Blue C	.07	.15
8 Circle of Protection Green C	.07	.15
9 Circle of Protection Red C	.15	.30
10 Circle of Protection White C	.07	.15
11 Cloudchaser Eagle C	.07	.15
12 Crossbow Infantry C	.07	.15
13 Disenchant C	.07	.15
14 Eager Cadet C	.07	.15
15 Elite Archers R	.15	.30
16 Gerrard's Wisdom U	.12	.25
17 Glorious Anthem R	.60	1.25
18 Healing Salve C	.07	.15
19 Heavy Ballista U	.12	.25
20 Holy Strength C	.07	.15
21 Honor Guard C	.07	.15
22 Intrepid Hero R	.75	1.50
23 Kjeldoran Royal Guard R	.15	.30
24 Knight Errant C	.07	.15
25 Knighthood U	.20	.40
26 Longbow Archer U	.12	.25
27 Master Healer R	.15	.30
28 Northern Paladin R	.50	1.00
29 Pacifism C	.07	.15
30 Pariah R	1.00	2.00
31 Purify R	.15	.30
32 Razorfoot Griffin C	.07	.15
33 Reprisal U	.12	.25
34 Reverse Damage R	.15	.30
35 Rolling Stones R	.75	1.50
36 Sacred Ground R	.15	.30
37 Sacred Nectar C	.07	.15
38 Samite Healer C	.07	.15
39 Sanctimony U	.12	.25
40 Seasoned Marshal U	.12	.25
41 Serra Advocate U	.12	.25
42 Serra Angel R	.30	.60
43 Serra's Embrace U	.12	.25
44 Shield Wall C	.07	.15
45 Skyshroud Falcon C	.12	.25
46 Southern Paladin R	.15	.30
47 Spirit Link U	.25	.50
48 Standing Troops C	.07	.15
49 Starlight U	.12	.25
50 Staunch Defenders U	.12	.25
51 Sunweb R	.15	.30
52 Sustainer of the Realm U	.12	.25
53 Venerable Monk C	.07	.15
54 Vengeance U	.12	.25
55 Wall of Swords U	.12	.25
56 Worship R	1.25	2.50
57 Wrath of God R	6.00	12.00
58 Air Elemental U	.12	.25
59 Ancestral Memories R	.15	.30
60 Arcane Laboratory U	1.25	2.50
61 Archivist R	.20	.40
62 Baleful Stare U	.12	.25
63 Benthic Behemoth R	.50	1.00
64 Boomerang C	.07	.15
65 Confiscate U	.20	.40
66 Coral Merfolk C	.07	.15
67 Counterspell C	1.25	2.50
68 Daring Apprentice R	.15	.30
69 Deflection R	.15	.30
70 Delusions of Mediocrity R	.30	.75
71 Equilibrium R	6.00	12.00
72 Evacuation R	3.00	6.00
73 Fighting Drake U	.12	.25
74 Fleeting Image R	.15	.30
75 Flight C	.07	.15
76 Force Spike C	.15	.30
77 Giant Octopus C	.07	.15
78 Glacial Wall U	.12	.25
79 Hibernation U	.12	.25
80 Horned Turtle C	.07	.15
81 Inspiration C	.07	.15
82 Levitation U	.12	.25
83 Lord of Atlantis R	3.00	6.00
84 Mahamoti Djinn R	.15	.30
85 Mana Breach U	2.00	4.00
86 Mana Short R	.75	1.50
87 Mawcor R	.15	.30
88 Memory Lapse C	.07	.15
89 Merfolk Looter U	.12	.25
90 Merfolk of the Pearl Trident C	.07	.15
91 Opportunity U	.12	.25
92 Opposition R	7.50	15.00
93 Phantom Warrior U	.12	.25
94 Prodigal Sorcerer C	.07	.15
95 Remove Soul C	.07	.15
96 Sage Owl C	.07	.15
97 Sea Monster C	.07	.15
98 Sleight of Hand C	.50	1.00
99 Steal Artifact U	.12	.25
100 Storm Crow C	.07	.15
101 Telepathic Spies C	.07	.15
102 Telepathy U	.25	.50
103 Temporal Adept R	.15	.30
104 Thieving Magpie U	.12	.25
105 Tolarian Winds C	.75	1.50
106 Treasure Trove U	.12	.25
107 Twiddle C	.15	.30
108 Unsummon C	.07	.15
109 Vigilant Drake C	.07	.15
110 Vizzerdrix R	.15	.30
111 Wall of Air U	.12	.25
112 Wall of Wonder R	.15	.30
113 Wind Dancer U	.12	.25
114 Wind Drake C	.07	.15
115 Abyssal Horror R	.15	.30
116 Abyssal Specter U	.12	.25
117 Agonizing Memories U	.12	.25
118 Befoul U	.12	.25
119 Bellowing Fiend R	.15	.30
120 Bereavement U	.12	.25
121 Blood Pet C	.15	.30
122 Bog Imp C	.07	.15
123 Bog Wraith U	.12	.25
124 Corrupt C	.07	.15
125 Crypt Rats U	.20	.40
126 Dakmor Lancer U	.12	.25
127 Dark Banishing C	.07	.15
128 Darkest Hour R	3.00	6.00
129 Dregs of Sorrow R	.15	.30
130 Drudge Skeletons C	.07	.15
131 Duress C	.30	.60
132 Eastern Paladin R	.20	.40
133 Engineered Plague U	.20	.40
134 Fallen Angel R	.20	.40
135 Fear C	.07	.15
136 Foul Imp U	.12	.25
137 Fugue U	.12	.25
138 Giant Cockroach C	.07	.15
139 Gravedigger C	.07	.15
140 Greed R	2.50	5.00
141 Hollow Dogs C	.07	.15
142 Howl from Beyond C	.07	.15
143 Infernal Contract R	.25	.50
144 Leshrac's Rite U	.12	.25
145 Looming Shade C	.07	.15
146 Megrim U	.20	.40
147 Mind Rot C	.07	.15
148 Nausea C	.07	.15
149 Necrologia U	1.00	2.00
150 Nightmare R	.15	.30
151 Nocturnal Raid U	.12	.25
152 Oppression R	25.00	50.00
153 Ostracize C	.07	.15
154 Persecute R	.50	1.00
155 Plague Beetle C	.07	.15
156 Rag Man R	.15	.30
157 Raise Dead C	.07	.15
158 Razortooth Rats C	.07	.15
159 Reprocess R	.60	1.25
160 Revenant R	.15	.30
161 Scathe Zombies C	.07	.15
162 Serpent Warrior C	.07	.15
163 Soul Feast U	.12	.25
164 Spineless Thug C	.07	.15
165 Strands of Night U	.50	1.00
166 Stronghold Assassin R	.60	1.25
167 Tainted Aether R	7.50	15.00
168 Unholy Strength C	.07	.15
169 Wall of Bone U	.12	.25
170 Western Paladin R	.20	.40
171 Yawgmoth's Edict U	.12	.25
172 Aether Flash U	.30	.75
173 Balduvian Barbarians C	.07	.15
174 Bedlam R	3.00	6.00
175 Blaze U	.12	.25
176 Bloodshot Cyclops R	.15	.30
177 Boil U	3.00	6.00
178 Crimson Hellkite R	.30	.60
179 Disorder U	.12	.25
180 Earthquake R	.50	1.00
181 Fervor R	2.50	5.00
182 Final Fortune R	20.00	40.00
183 Fire Elemental U	.12	.25
184 Ghitu Fire-Eater U	.12	.25
185 Goblin Chariot C	.07	.15
186 Goblin Digging Team C	.07	.15
187 Goblin Elite Infantry C	.07	.15
188 Goblin Gardener C	.07	.15
189 Goblin Glider U	.12	.25
190 Goblin King R	2.00	4.00
191 Goblin Matron U	.30	.60
192 Goblin Raider C	.07	.15
193 Goblin Spelunkers C	.07	.15
194 Goblin War Drums U	.25	.50
195 Granite Grip C	.07	.15
196 Hill Giant C	.07	.15
197 Impatience R	.15	.30
198 Inferno R	.20	.40
199 Lava Axe C	.07	.15
200 Lightning Blast C	.07	.15
201 Lightning Elemental C	.07	.15
202 Mana Clash R	.15	.30
203 Ogre Taskmaster U	.12	.25
204 Okk R	.15	.30
205 Orcish Artillery U	.12	.25
206 Orcish Oriflamme U	.12	.25
207 Pillage U	.12	.25
208 Pygmy Pyrosaur C	.07	.15
209 Pyroclasm U	.12	.25
210 Pyrotechnics U	.12	.25
211 Raging Goblin C	.07	.15
212 Reckless Embermage R	.15	.30
213 Reflexes C	.07	.15
214 Relentless Assault R	1.25	2.50
215 Sabretooth Tiger C	.07	.15
216 Seismic Assault R	.75	1.50
217 Shatter C	.07	.15
218 Shivan Dragon R	.30	.60
219 Shock C	.07	.15
220 Spitting Earth C	.07	.15
221 Stone Rain C	.07	.15
222 Storm Shaman U	.12	.25
223 Sudden Impact U	.12	.25
224 Trained Orgg R	.15	.30
225 Tremor C	.07	.15
226 Volcanic Hammer C	.07	.15
227 Wall of Fire U	.12	.25
228 Wildfire R	.50	1.00
229 Anaconda U	.12	.25
230 Ancient Silverback R	.15	.30
231 Birds of Paradise R	10.00	20.00
232 Blanchwood Armor U	.12	.25
233 Bull Hippo U	.12	.25
234 Canopy Spider C	.07	.15
235 Compost U	2.00	4.00
236 Creeping Mold U	.12	.25
237 Early Harvest R	1.25	2.50
238 Elder Druid R	.25	.50
239 Elvish Archers R	.20	.40
240 Elvish Champion R	10.00	20.00
241 Elvish Lyrist U	.12	.25
242 Elvish Piper R	4.00	8.00
243 Familiar Ground U	.12	.25
244 Femeref Archers U	.12	.25
245 Fog C	.07	.15
246 Fyndhorn Elder U	.12	.25
247 Gang of Elk U	.12	.25
248 Giant Growth C	.07	.15
249 Giant Spider C	.07	.15
250 Gorilla Chieftain C	.07	.15
251 Grizzly Bears C	.07	.15
252 Hurricane R	.20	.40
253 Llanowar Elves C	.20	.40
254 Lone Wolf C	.07	.15
255 Lure U	.12	.25
256 Maro R	.15	.30
257 Might of Oaks R	.15	.30
258 Monstrous Growth C	.07	.15
259 Nature's Resurgence R	.15	.30
260 Nature's Revolt R	1.25	2.50
261 Pride of Lions U	.12	.25
262 Rampant Growth C	.50	1.00
263 Reclaim C	.07	.15
264 Redwood Treefolk C	.07	.15
265 Regeneration C	.07	.15
266 Rowen R	.15	.30
267 Scavenger Folk U	.12	.25
268 Seeker of Skybreak C	1.00	2.00
269 Shanodin Dryads C	.07	.15
270 Spined Wurm C	.07	.15
271 Squall C	.07	.15
272 Stream of Life C	.07	.15
273 Thorn Elemental R	.15	.30
274 Thoughtleech U	.12	.25
275 Trained Armodon C	.07	.15
276 Tranquility C	.07	.15
277 Treefolk Seedlings U	.20	.40
278 Uktabi Wildcats R	.15	.30
279 Untamed Wilds U	.12	.25
280 Verduran Enchantress R	2.00	4.00
281 Vernal Bloom R	3.00	6.00
282 Wild Growth C	.20	.40
283 Wing Snare U	.12	.25
284 Wood Elves C	.50	1.00
285 Yavimaya Enchantress U	.12	.25
286 Aladdin's Ring R	.15	.30
287 Beast of Burden R	.15	.30
288 Caltrops U	.30	.75
289 Charcoal Diamond U	1.00	2.00
290 Coat of Arms R	12.50	25.00
291 Crystal Rod U	.12	.25
292 Dingus Egg R	.25	.50
293 Disrupting Scepter R	.15	.30
294 Ensnaring Bridge R	15.00	30.00
295 Feroz's Ban R	.20	.40
296 Fire Diamond U	1.50	3.00
297 Flying Carpet R	.15	.30
298 Grafted Skullcap R	.25	.50
299 Grapeshot Catapult U	.12	.25
300 Howling Mine R	4.00	8.00
301 Iron Star U	.12	.25
302 Ivory Cup U	.12	.25
303 Jalum Tome R	.15	.30
304 Jandor's Saddlebags R	.25	.50
305 Jayemdae Tome R	.15	.30
306 Marble Diamond U	.75	1.50
307 Meekstone R	4.00	8.00
308 Millstone R	.15	.30
309 Moss Diamond U	.12	.25
310 Patagia Golem U	.12	.25
311 Phyrexian Colossus R	.15	.30
312 Phyrexian Hulk U	.12	.25
313 Pit Trap U	.12	.25
314 Rod of Ruin U	.12	.25
315 Sisay's Ring U	.75	1.50
316 Sky Diamond U	1.50	3.00
317 Soul Net U	.12	.25
318 Spellbook U	1.50	3.00
319 Static Orb R	17.50	35.00
320 Storm Cauldron R	3.00	6.00
321 Teferi's Puzzle Box R	5.00	10.00
322 Throne of Bone U	.12	.25
323 Wall of Spears U	.12	.25
324 Wooden Sphere U	.12	.25
325 Adarkar Wastes R	6.00	12.00
326 Brushland R	4.00	8.00
327 City of Brass R	12.50	25.00
328 Forest L	.07	.15
329 Forest L	.07	.15
330 Forest L	.07	.15
331 Forest L	.07	.15
332 Island L	.07	.15
333 Island L	.07	.15
334 Island L	.07	.15
335 Island L	.07	.15
336 Karplusan Forest R	3.00	6.00
337 Mountain L	.07	.15
338 Mountain L	.07	.15
339 Mountain L	.07	.15
340 Mountain L	.07	.15
341 Plains L	.07	.15
342 Plains L	.07	.15
343 Plains L	.07	.15

344 Plains L	.07	.15
345 Sulfurous Springs R	6.00	12.00
346 Swamp L	.07	.15
347 Swamp L	.07	.15
348 Swamp L	.07	.15
349 Swamp L	.07	.15
350 Underground River R	7.50	15.00

2002 Magic The Gathering Judge Gift Rewards

1 Hammer of Bogardan C	7.50	15.00
2 Tradewind Rider C	6.00	12.00

2002 Magic The Gathering Judgment

1 Ancestor's Chosen U	.12	.25
2 Aven Warcraft U	.12	.25
3 Battle Screech U	.30	.75
4 Battlewise Aven C	.07	.15
5 Benevolent Bodyguard C	.15	.30
6 Border Patrol C	.07	.15
7 Cagemail C	.07	.15
8 Chastise U	.12	.25
9 Commander Eesha R	2.00	4.00
10 Funeral Pyre C	.07	.15
11 Glory R	2.00	4.00
12 Golden Wish R	.30	.60
13 Guided Strike C	.07	.15
14 Lead Astray C	.07	.15
15 Nomad Mythmaker R	1.50	3.00
16 Phantom Flock U	.12	.25
17 Phantom Nomad C	.07	.15
18 Prismatic Strands C	.25	.50
19 Pulsemage Advocate R	.60	1.25
20 Ray of Revelation C	.07	.15
21 Selfless Exorcist R	.20	.40
22 Shieldmage Advocate C	.07	.15
23 Silver Seraph R	.30	.75
24 Solitary Confinement R	7.50	15.00
25 Soulcatchers' Aerie U	.75	1.50
26 Spirit Cairn U	.12	.25
27 Spurnmage Advocate U	.12	.25
28 Suntail Hawk C	.07	.15
29 Test of Endurance R	12.50	25.00
30 Trained Pronghorn C	.07	.15
31 Unquestioned Authority U	.30	.60
32 Valor U	.12	.25
33 Vigilant Sentry C	.07	.15
34 Aven Fogbringer C	.07	.15
35 Cephalid Constable R	4.00	8.00
36 Cephalid Inkshrouder U	.12	.25
37 Cunning Wish R	6.00	12.00
38 Defy Gravity C	.07	.15
39 Envelop C	.07	.15
40 Flash of Insight U	.12	.25
41 Grip of Amnesia C	.07	.15
42 Hapless Researcher C	.07	.15
43 Keep Watch C	.50	1.00
44 Laquatus's Disdain U	.12	.25
45 Lost in Thought C	.07	.15
46 Mental Note C	.20	.40
47 Mirror Wall C	.07	.15
48 Mist of Stagnation R	.25	.50
49 Quiet Speculation U	.12	.25
50 Scalpelexis R	.20	.40
51 Spelljack R	2.00	4.00
52 Telekinetic Bonds R	.20	.40
53 Web of Inertia U	.50	1.00
54 Wonder U	.50	1.00
55 Wormfang Behemoth R	.20	.40
56 Wormfang Crab U	.12	.25
57 Wormfang Drake C	.07	.15
58 Wormfang Manta R	.20	.40
59 Wormfang Newt C	.07	.15
60 Wormfang Turtle U	.12	.25
61 Balthor the Defiled R	7.50	15.00
62 Cabal Therapy U	2.00	4.00
63 Cabal Trainee C	.07	.15
64 Death Wish R	.30	.60
65 Earsplitting Rats C	.12	.25
66 Filth U	2.00	4.00
67 Grave Consequences U	.12	.25
68 Guiltfeeder R	1.00	2.00
69 Masked Gorgon R	.20	.40
70 Morality Shift R	1.25	2.50
71 Rats' Feast C	.07	.15
72 Stitch Together U	.75	1.50
73 Sutured Ghoul R	.20	.40
74 Toxic Stench C	.07	.15
75 Treacherous Vampire U	.12	.25
76 Treacherous Werewolf C	.07	.15
77 Anger U	2.00	4.00
78 Arcane Teachings C	.07	.15
79 Barbarian Bully C	.07	.15
80 Book Burning C	.07	.15
81 Breaking Point R	.30	.75
82 Browbeat U	.30	.60
83 Burning Wish R	1.50	3.00
84 Dwarven Bloodboiler R	12.50	25.00
85 Dwarven Driller U	2.00	4.00
86 Dwarven Scorcher C	.07	.15
87 Ember Shot C	.07	.15
88 Firecat Blitz U	.30	.60
89 Flaring Pain C	.50	1.00
90 Fledgling Dragon R	.60	1.25
91 Goretusk Firebeast C	.07	.15
92 Infectious Rage U	.12	.25
93 Jeska, Warrior Adept R	3.00	6.00
94 Lava Dart C	.30	.60
95 Liberated Dwarf C	.07	.15
96 Lightning Surge R	.20	.40
97 Planar Chaos U	1.25	2.50
98 Shaman's Trance R	.25	.50
99 Soulgorger Orgg U	.12	.25
100 Spellgorger Barbarian C	.07	.15
101 Swelter U	.12	.25
102 Swirling Sandstorm C	.30	.75
103 Worldgorger Dragon R	7.50	15.00
104 Anurid Barkripper C	.07	.15
105 Anurid Swarmsnapper U	.12	.25
106 Battlefield Scrounger C	.07	.15
107 Brawn U	.25	.50
108 Canopy Claws C	.07	.15
109 Centaur Rootcaster C	.07	.15
110 Crush of Wurms R	.75	1.50
111 Elephant Guide U	.12	.25
112 Epic Struggle R	3.00	6.00
113 Erhnam Djinn R	.20	.40
114 Exoskeletal Armor U	.12	.25
115 Folk Medicine C	.07	.15
116 Forcemage Advocate U	.12	.25
117 Genesis R	2.00	4.00
118 Giant Warthog C	.07	.15
119 Grizzly Fate U	.75	1.50
120 Harvester Druid C	.15	.30
121 Ironshell Beetle C	.07	.15
122 Krosan Reclamation U	.12	.25
123 Krosan Wayfarer C	.25	.50
124 Living Wish R	2.50	5.00
125 Nantuko Tracer C	.07	.15
126 Nullmage Advocate C	.07	.15
127 Phantom Centaur U	.12	.25
128 Phantom Nantuko R	.20	.40
129 Phantom Tiger C	.07	.15
130 Seedtime R	6.00	12.00
131 Serene Sunset U	.12	.25
132 Sudden Strength C	.07	.15
133 Sylvan Safekeeper R	10.00	20.00
134 Thriss, Nantuko Primus R	.20	.40
135 Tunneler Wurm U	.12	.25
136 Venomous Vines C	.07	.15
137 Anurid Brushhopper R	.20	.40
138 Hunting Grounds R	7.50	15.00
139 Mirari's Wake R	15.00	30.00
140 Phantom Nishoba R	1.25	2.50
141 Krosan Verge U	.50	1.00
142 Nantuko Monastery U	.12	.25
143 Riftstone Portal U	1.00	2.00

2002 Magic The Gathering Onslaught

1 Akroma's Blessing U	.20	.40
2 Akroma's Vengeance R	1.00	2.00
3 Ancestor's Prophet R	.50	1.00
4 Astral Slide U	1.50	3.00
5 Aura Extraction U	.12	.25
6 Aurification R	2.00	4.00
7 Aven Brigadier R	.75	1.50
8 Aven Soulgazer U	.12	.25
9 Battlefield Medic C	.07	.15
10 Catapult Master R	.30	.60
11 Catapult Squad U	.12	.25
12 Chain of Silence U	.25	.50
13 Circle of Solace R	.15	.30
14 Convalescent Care R	.15	.30
15 Crowd Favorites U	.12	.25
16 Crown of Awe C	.07	.15
17 Crude Rampart U	.12	.25
18 Daru Cavalier C	.07	.15
19 Daru Healer C	.07	.15
20 Daru Lancer C	.07	.15
21 Daunting Defender C	.07	.15
22 Dawning Purist U	.12	.25
23 Defensive Maneuvers C	.07	.15
24 Demystify C	.07	.15
25 Disciple of Grace C	.07	.15
26 Dive Bomber C	.07	.15
27 Doubtless One U	.12	.25
28 Exalted Angel R	2.50	5.00
29 Foothill Guide C	.07	.15
30 Glarecaster R	.25	.50
31 Glory Seeker C	.07	.15
32 Grassland Crusader C	.07	.15
33 Gravel Slinger C	.07	.15
34 Gustcloak Harrier C	.07	.15
35 Gustcloak Runner C	.07	.15
36 Gustcloak Savior R	.15	.30
37 Gustcloak Sentinel U	.12	.25
38 Gustcloak Skirmisher U	.12	.25
39 Harsh Mercy R	1.50	3.00
40 Improvised Armor U	.12	.25
41 Inspirit U	.12	.25
42 Ironfist Crusher U	.12	.25
43 Jareth, Leonine Titan R	.50	1.00
44 Mobilization R	.30	.75
45 Nova Cleric U	.12	.25
46 Oblation R	1.00	2.00
47 Pacifism C	.07	.15
48 Pearlspear Courier U	.12	.25
49 Piety Charm C	.07	.15
50 Renewed Faith C	.07	.15
51 Righteous Cause U	.20	.40
52 Sandskin C	.07	.15
53 Shared Triumph R	2.00	4.00
54 Shieldmage Elder U	.12	.25
55 Sigil of the New Dawn R	.25	.50
56 Sunfire Balm U	.12	.25
57 True Believer R	.75	1.50
58 Unified Strike C	.07	.15
59 Weathered Wayfarer R	.15	.30
60 Whipcorder U	.12	.25
61 Words of Worship R	.15	.30
62 Airborne Aid C	.07	.15
63 Annex U	.20	.40
64 Aphetto Alchemist U	2.00	4.00
65 Aphetto Grifter U	.12	.25
66 Arcanis the Omnipotent R	1.25	2.50
67 Artificial Evolution R	2.00	4.00
68 Ascending Aven C	.07	.15
69 Aven Fateshaper U	.12	.25
70 Backslide C	.10	.20
71 Blatant Thievery R	2.00	4.00
72 Callous Oppressor R	.60	1.25
73 Chain of Vapor U	6.00	12.00
74 Choking Tethers C	.07	.15
75 Clone R	.30	.75
76 Complicate U	2.00	4.00
77 Crafty Pathmage C	.07	.15
78 Crown of Ascension C	.07	.15
79 Discombobulate U	.12	.25
80 Dispersing Orb U	.12	.25
81 Disruptive Pitmage C	.10	.20
82 Essence Fracture U	.12	.25
83 Fleeting Aven U	.12	.25
84 Future Sight R	.60	1.25
85 Ghosthelm Courier U	.12	.25
86 Graxiplon U	.12	.25
87 Imagecrafter C	.07	.15
88 Information Dealer C	.07	.15
89 Ixidor, Reality Sculptor R	2.50	5.00
90 Ixidor's Will C	.07	.15
91 Mage's Guile C	.07	.15
92 Meddle U	.12	.25
93 Mistform Dreamer C	.07	.15
94 Mistform Mask C	.07	.15
95 Mistform Mutant U	.12	.25
96 Mistform Shrieker U	.12	.25
97 Mistform Skyreaver R	.15	.30
98 Mistform Stalker U	.12	.25
99 Mistform Wall C	.07	.15
100 Nameless One U	.12	.25
101 Peer Pressure R	.30	.75
102 Psychic Trance R	.15	.30
103 Quicksilver Dragon R	.50	1.00
104 Read the Runes R	.60	1.25
105 Reminisce U	.12	.25
106 Riptide Biologist C	.07	.15
107 Riptide Chronologist U	.12	.25
108 Riptide Entrancer R	2.00	4.00
109 Riptide Shapeshifter U	.12	.25
110 Rummaging Wizard U	.12	.25
111 Sage Aven C	.07	.15
112 Screaming Seahawk C	.07	.15
113 Sea's Claim C	.07	.15
114 Slipstream Eel C	.07	.15
115 Spy Network C	.07	.15
116 Standardize R	.50	1.00
117 Supreme Inquisitor R	.75	1.50
118 Trade Secrets R	.25	.50
119 Trickery Charm C	.07	.15
120 Voidmage Prodigy R	2.00	4.00
121 Wheel and Deal R	.15	.30
122 Words of Wind R	.15	.30
123 Accursed Centaur C	.07	.15
124 Anurid Murkdiver C	.07	.15
125 Aphetto Dredging C	.20	.40
126 Aphetto Vulture U	.12	.25
127 Blackmail U	.60	1.25
128 Boneknitter U	.25	.50
129 Cabal Archon U	.12	.25
130 Cabal Executioner U	.12	.25
131 Cabal Slaver U	.12	.25
132 Chain of Smog U	7.50	15.00
133 Cover of Darkness R	25.00	50.00
134 Crown of Suspicion C	.07	.15
135 Cruel Revival C	.07	.15
136 Death Match R	.25	.50
137 Death Pulse U	.12	.25
138 Dirge of Dread C	.07	.15
139 Disciple of Malice C	.07	.15
140 Doomed Necromancer R	.75	1.50
141 Ebonblade Reaper R	.30	.60
142 Endemic Plague R	.15	.30
143 Entrails Feaster R	.25	.50
144 Fade from Memory U	.12	.25
145 Fallen Cleric C	.07	.15
146 False Cure R	1.00	2.00
147 Feeding Frenzy U	.12	.25
148 Festering Goblin C	.07	.15
149 Frightshroud Courier U	.12	.25
150 Gangrenous Goliath R	.15	.30
151 Gluttonous Zombie U	.12	.25
152 Gravespawn Sovereign R	2.50	5.00
153 Grinning Demon R	.30	.75
154 Haunted Cadaver C	.07	.15
155 Head Games R	2.00	4.00
156 Headhunter U	.12	.25
157 Infest U	.12	.25
158 Misery Charm C	.07	.15
159 Nantuko Husk C	.07	.15
160 Oversold Cemetery R	12.50	25.00
161 Patriarch's Bidding R	25.00	50.00
162 Profane Prayers C	.07	.15
163 Prowling Pangolin U	.12	.25
164 Rotlung Reanimator R	6.00	12.00
165 Screeching Buzzard C	.07	.15
166 Severed Legion C	.07	.15
167 Shade's Breath U	.12	.25
168 Shepherd of Rot C	.50	1.00
169 Silent Specter R	.50	1.00
170 Smother U	.12	.25
171 Soulless One U	.75	1.50
172 Spined Basher C	.07	.15
173 Strongarm Tactics R	.25	.50
174 Swat C	.07	.15
175 Syphon Mind C	1.25	2.50
176 Syphon Soul C	.07	.15
177 Thrashing Mudspawn U	.12	.25
178 Undead Gladiator R	.30	.60
179 Visara the Dreadful R	1.25	2.50
180 Walking Desecration U	.12	.25
181 Withering Hex U	.12	.25
182 Words of Waste R	.15	.30
183 Wretched Anurid C	.07	.15
184 Aether Charge U	.12	.25
185 Aggravated Assault R	12.50	25.00
186 Airdrop Condor U	.12	.25
187 Avarax U	.12	.25
188 Battering Craghorn C	.07	.15
189 Blistering Firecat R	2.50	5.00
190 Break Open C	.07	.15
191 Brightstone Ritual C	.75	1.50
192 Butcher Orgg R	.15	.30
193 Chain of Plasma U	.25	.50
194 Charging Slateback C	.07	.15
195 Commando Raid U	.12	.25
196 Crown of Fury C	.07	.15
197 Custody Battle U	.30	.60
198 Dragon Roost R	.50	1.00
199 Dwarven Blastminer U	1.50	3.00
200 Embermage Goblin U	.12	.25
201 Erratic Explosion C	.07	.15
202 Fever Charm C	.07	.15
203 Flamestick Courier U	.12	.25
204 Goblin Machinist U	.12	.25
205 Goblin Piledriver R	4.00	8.00
206 Goblin Pyromancer R	.25	.50
207 Goblin Sharpshooter R	7.50	15.00
208 Goblin Sky Raider C	.07	.15
209 Goblin Sledder C	.20	.40
210 Goblin Taskmaster C	.07	.15
211 Grand Melee R	1.00	2.00
212 Gratuitous Violence R	3.00	6.00
213 Insurrection R	7.50	15.00
214 Kaboom! R	.20	.40
215 Lavamancer's Skill C	.07	.15
216 Lay Waste C	.07	.15
217 Lightning Rift U	.20	.40
218 Mana Echoes R	10.00	20.00
219 Menacing Ogre R	.15	.30
220 Nosy Goblin C	.07	.15
221 Pinpoint Avalanche C	.07	.15
222 Reckless One U	.50	1.00
223 Risky Move R	1.25	2.50
224 Rorix Bladewing R	.30	.60
225 Searing Flesh U	.12	.25
226 Shaleskin Bruiser U	.12	.25
227 Shock C	.07	.15
228 Skirk Commando C	.07	.15
229 Skirk Fire Marshal R	2.00	4.00
230 Skirk Prospector C	.20	.40
231 Skittish Valesk U	.12	.25
232 Slice and Dice U	.12	.25
233 Snapping Thragg U	.12	.25
234 Solar Blast C	.07	.15
235 Sparksmith C	.07	.15
236 Spitfire Handler U	.12	.25
237 Spurred Wolverine C	.07	.15
238 Starstorm R	.75	1.50
239 Tephraderm R	.15	.30
240 Thoughtbound Primoc U	.12	.25
241 Threaten U	.12	.25
242 Thunder of Hooves U	.12	.25
243 Wave of Indifference C	.07	.15
244 Words of War R	.15	.30
245 Animal Magnetism R	.15	.30
246 Barkhide Mauler C	.07	.15
247 Biorhythm R	1.25	2.50
248 Birchlore Rangers C	.30	.60
249 Bloodline Shaman U	.20	.40
250 Broodhatch Nantuko U	.20	.40
251 Centaur Glade U	.12	.25
252 Chain of Acid U	3.00	6.00
253 Crown of Vigor C	.07	.15
254 Elven Riders U	.12	.25
255 Elvish Guidance C	2.00	4.00
256 Elvish Pathcutter C	.07	.15
257 Elvish Pioneer C	.20	.40
258 Elvish Scrapper U	.12	.25
259 Elvish Vanguard R	1.00	2.00
260 Elvish Warrior C	.07	.15
261 Enchantress's Presence R	5.00	10.00
262 Everglove Courier U	.12	.25
263 Explosive Vegetation U	1.25	2.50
264 Gigapede R	.30	.60
265 Heedless One U	.60	1.25
266 Hystrodon R	1.00	2.00
267 Invigorating Boon U	.12	.25
268 Kamahl, Fist of Krosa R	4.00	8.00
269 Kamahl's Summons U	.50	1.00
270 Krosan Colossus R	.20	.40
271 Krosan Groundshaker U	.12	.25
272 Krosan Tusker C	.07	.15
273 Leery Fogbeast C	.07	.15
274 Mythic Proportions R	.30	.60
275 Naturalize C	.12	.25
276 Overwhelming Instinct U	.25	.50
277 Primal Boost U	.12	.25
278 Ravenous Baloth R	.50	1.00
279 Run Wild U	.12	.25
280 Serpentine Basilisk U	.12	.25
281 Silklash Spider R	.25	.50
282 Silvos, Rogue Elemental R	.75	1.50
283 Snarling Undorak C	.07	.15
284 Spitting Gourna C	.07	.15
285 Stag Beetle R	.30	.75
286 Steely Resolve R	10.00	20.00
287 Symbiotic Beast U	.12	.25
288 Symbiotic Elf C	.07	.15
289 Symbiotic Wurm R	.30	.60
290 Taunting Elf C	.12	.25
291 Tempting Wurm R	.75	1.50
292 Towering Baloth U	.12	.25
293 Treespring Lorian C	.07	.15
294 Tribal Unity U	.30	.60
295 Venomspout Brackus U	.12	.25
296 Vitality Charm C	.07	.15
297 Voice of the Woods R	.15	.30
298 Wall of Mulch U	.20	.40
299 Weird Harvest R	.15	.30
300 Wellwisher C	.75	1.50
301 Wirewood Elf C	.07	.15
302 Wirewood Herald C	.20	.40
303 Wirewood Pride C	.07	.15
304 Wirewood Savage C	.07	.15
305 Words of Wilding R	.15	.30
306 Cryptic Gateway R	5.00	10.00
307 Doom Cannon R	.20	.40
308 Dream Chisel R	1.00	2.00
309 Riptide Replicator R	2.00	4.00
310 Slate of Ancestry R	3.00	6.00
311 Tribal Golem R	.15	.30
312 Barren Moor C	.15	.30
313 Bloodstained Mire R	30.00	75.00
314 Contested Cliffs R	.30	.75
315 Daru Encampment U	.12	.25
316 Flooded Strand R	50.00	100.00
317 Forgotten Cave C	.15	.30
318 Goblin Burrows U	.12	.25
319 Grand Coliseum R	2.00	4.00
320 Lonely Sandbar C	.15	.30
321 Polluted Delta R	50.00	100.00
322 Riptide Laboratory R	5.00	10.00
323 Seaside Haven U	.12	.25
324 Secluded Steppe C	.07	.15
325 Starlit Sanctum U	.30	.75
326 Tranquil Thicket C	.12	.25
327 Unholy Grotto R	12.50	25.00
328 Windswept Heath R	.15	.30
329 Wirewood Lodge U	6.00	12.00
330 Wooded Foothills R	.15	.30
331 Plains L	.07	.15

332 Plains L	.07	.15
333 Plains L	.07	.15
334 Plains L	.07	.15
335 Island L	.07	.15
336 Island L	.07	.15
337 Island L	.07	.15
338 Island L	.07	.15
339 Swamp L	.07	.15
340 Swamp L	.07	.15
341 Swamp L	.07	.15
342 Swamp L	.07	.15
343 Mountain L	.07	.15
344 Mountain L	.07	.15
345 Mountain L	.07	.15
346 Mountain L	.07	.15
347 Forest L	.07	.15
348 Forest L	.07	.15
349 Forest L	.07	.15
350 Forest L	.07	.15

2002 Magic The Gathering Torment

1 Angel of Retribution R	.20	.40
2 Aven Trooper C	.07	.15
3 Cleansing Meditation U	.75	1.50
4 Equal Treatment U	.12	.25
5 Floating Shield C	.07	.15
6 Frantic Purification C	.07	.15
7 Hypochondria U	.12	.25
8 Major Teroh R	.30	.75
9 Militant Monk C	.07	.15
10 Morningtide R	.20	.40
11 Mystic Familiar C	.07	.15
12 Pay No Heed C	.07	.15
13 Possessed Nomad R	.20	.40
14 Reborn Hero R	.20	.40
15 Spirit Flare C	.07	.15
16 Stern Judge U	.12	.25
17 Strength of Isolation U	.12	.25
18 Teroh's Faithful C	.07	.15
19 Teroh's Vanguard U	.12	.25
20 Transcendence R	.75	1.50
21 Vengeful Dreams R	.30	.60
22 Alter Reality R	.50	1.00
23 Ambassador Laquatus R	.50	1.00
24 Aquamoeba C	.07	.15
25 Balshan Collaborator U	.12	.25
26 Breakthrough U	.20	.40
27 Cephalid Aristocrat C	.07	.15
28 Cephalid Illusionist U	.60	1.25
29 Cephalid Sage U	.12	.25
30 Cephalid Snitch C	.07	.15
31 Cephalid Vandal R	.20	.40
32 Churning Eddy C	.07	.15
33 Circular Logic U	.30	.75
34 Compulsion U	.12	.25
35 Coral Net C	.12	.25
36 Deep Analysis C	.15	.30
37 False Memories R	.20	.40
38 Ghostly Wings C	.07	.15
39 Hydromorph Guardian C	.07	.15
40 Hydromorph Gull U	.12	.25
41 Liquify C	.07	.15
42 Llawan, Cephalid Empress R	1.00	2.00
43 Obsessive Search C	.15	.30
44 Plagiarize R	.20	.40
45 Possessed Aven R	.20	.40
46 Retraced Image R	.75	1.50
47 Skywing Aven C	.07	.15
48 Stupefying Touch U	.12	.25
49 Turbulent Dreams R	.75	1.50
50 Boneshard Slasher U	.12	.25
51 Cabal Ritual C	3.00	6.00
52 Cabal Surgeon C	.07	.15
53 Cabal Torturer C	.07	.15
54 Carrion Rats C	.12	.25
55 Carrion Wurm U	.12	.25
56 Chainer, Dementia Master R	5.00	10.00
57 Chainer's Edict U	1.50	3.00
58 Crippling Fatigue C	.07	.15
59 Dawn of the Dead R	2.50	5.00
60 Faceless Butcher C	.07	.15
61 Gloomdrifter U	.12	.25
62 Gravegouger C	.07	.15
63 Grotesque Hybrid U	.12	.25
64 Hypnox R	.30	.75
65 Ichorid R	.75	1.50
66 Insidious Dreams R	7.50	15.00
67 Laquatus's Champion R	.30	.75
68 Last Laugh R	.30	.60
69 Mesmeric Fiend C	.20	.40
70 Mind Sludge U	.12	.25
71 Mortal Combat R	2.00	4.00
72 Mortiphobia U	.12	.25
73 Mutilate R	1.50	3.00
74 Nantuko Shade R	.60	1.25
75 Organ Grinder C	.07	.15
76 Psychotic Haze C	.15	.30
77 Putrid Imp C	.30	.60
78 Rancid Earth C	.20	.40
79 Restless Dreams C	.20	.40
80 Sengir Vampire R	.20	.40
81 Shade's Form C	.20	.40
82 Shambling Swarm R	.30	.60
83 Sickening Dreams U	.20	.40
84 Slithery Stalker U	.12	.25
85 Soul Scourge C	.07	.15
86 Strength of Lunacy U	.50	1.00
87 Unhinge C	.07	.15
88 Waste Away C	.07	.15
89 Zombie Trailblazer U	.60	1.25
90 Accelerate C	.30	.75
91 Balthor the Stout R	.30	.60
92 Barbarian Outcast C	.07	.15
93 Crackling Club C	.07	.15
94 Crazed Firecat U	.20	.40
95 Devastating Dreams R	.30	.75
96 Enslaved Dwarf C	.12	.25
97 Fiery Temper C	.12	.25
98 Flaming Gambit U	.12	.25
99 Flash of Defiance C	.07	.15
100 Grim Lavamancer R	4.00	8.00
101 Hell-Bent Raider R	.20	.40
102 Kamahl's Sledge C	.07	.15
103 Longhorn Firebeast C	.07	.15
104 Overmaster R	7.50	15.00
105 Pardic Arsonist U	.12	.25
106 Pardic Collaborator U	.12	.25
107 Pardic Lancer C	.07	.15
108 Petradon R	.20	.40
109 Petravark C	.07	.15
110 Pitchstone Wall U	.12	.25
111 Possessed Barbarian R	.20	.40
112 Pyromania U	.12	.25
113 Radiate R	2.00	4.00
114 Skullscorch R	.30	.60
115 Sonic Seizure C	.07	.15
116 Temporary Insanity U	.12	.25
117 Violent Eruption U	.12	.25
118 Acorn Harvest C	.15	.30
119 Anurid Scavenger U	.12	.25
120 Arrogant Wurm U	.50	1.00
121 Basking Rootwalla C	.12	.25
122 Centaur Chieftain U	.12	.25
123 Centaur Veteran C	.07	.15
124 Dwell on the Past U	.12	.25
125 Far Wanderings C	.15	.30
126 Gurzigost R	.25	.50
127 Insist R	.75	1.50
128 Invigorating Falls C	.07	.15
129 Krosan Constrictor C	.07	.15
130 Krosan Restorer C	.30	.60
131 Nantuko Blightcutter R	.20	.40
132 Nantuko Calmer C	.07	.15
133 Nantuko Cultivator R	.20	.40
134 Narcissism U	.12	.25
135 Nostalgic Dreams R	2.50	5.00
136 Parallel Evolution R	3.00	6.00
137 Possessed Centaur R	.20	.40
138 Seton's Scout U	.12	.25
139 Cabal Coffers U	75.00	150.00
140 Tainted Field U	.50	1.00
141 Tainted Isle U	3.00	6.00
142 Tainted Peak U	3.00	6.00
143 Tainted Wood U	2.00	4.00

2003 Magic The Gathering Eighth Edition

1 Angel of Mercy U	.12	.25
2 Angelic Page C	.07	.15
3 Ardent Militia U	.12	.25
4 Avatar of Hope R	.20	.40
5 Aven Cloudchaser C	.07	.15
6 Aven Flock C	.07	.15
7 Blessed Reversal R	.20	.40
8 Blinding Angel R	2.00	4.00
9 Chastise U	.12	.25
10 Circle of Protection Black U	.12	.25
11 Circle of Protection Blue U	.12	.25
12 Circle of Protection Green U	.12	.25
13 Circle of Protection Red U	.12	.25
14 Circle of Protection White U	.12	.25
15 Crossbow Infantry C	.07	.15
16 Demystify C	.07	.15
17 Diving Griffin C	.07	.15
18 Elite Archers R	.20	.40
19 Elite Javelineer U	.12	.25
20 Glorious Anthem R	.30	.75
21 Glory Seeker C	.07	.15
22 Healing Salve C	.07	.15
23 Holy Day C	.15	.30
24 Holy Strength C	.15	.30
25 Honor Guard C	.07	.15
26 Intrepid Hero R	.50	1.00
27 Ivory Mask R	.30	.60
28 Karma U	.12	.25
29 Master Decoy C	.07	.15
30 Master Healer R	.20	.40
31 Noble Purpose R	.30	.60
32 Oracle's Attendants R	.20	.40
33 Pacifism C	.07	.15
34 Peach Garden Oath U	.12	.25
35 Rain of Blades U	.12	.25
36 Razorfoot Griffin C	.07	.15
37 Redeem C	.07	.15
38 Rolling Stones R	1.00	2.00
39 Sacred Ground R	.20	.40
40 Sacred Nectar C	.07	.15
41 Samite Healer C	.07	.15
42 Sanctimony U	.12	.25
43 Savannah Lions R	.30	.75
44 Seasoned Marshal U	.12	.25
45 Serra Angel R	.30	.60
46 Solidarity C	.07	.15
47 Spirit Link U	.25	.50
48 Standing Troops C	.07	.15
49 Staunch Defenders U	.12	.25
50 Story Circle R	.30	.60
51 Suntail Hawk C	.07	.15
52 Sunweb R	.20	.40
53 Sword Dancer U	.12	.25
54 Tundra Wolves C	.07	.15
55 Venerable Monk C	.07	.15
56 Wall of Swords U	.12	.25
57 Worship R	.50	1.00
58 Wrath of God R	5.00	10.00
59 Air Elemental U	.12	.25
60 Archivist R	.20	.40
61 Aven Fisher C	.07	.15
62 Balance of Power R	.20	.40
63 Boomerang C	.07	.15
64 Bribery R	15.00	30.00
65 Catalog C	.07	.15
66 Coastal Hornclaw C	.07	.15
67 Coastal Piracy R	4.00	8.00
68 Concentrate U	.12	.25
69 Confiscate U	.12	.25
70 Coral Eel C	.07	.15
71 Cowardice R	.30	.60
72 Curiosity U	.60	1.25
73 Daring Apprentice R	.20	.40
74 Deflection R	.20	.40
75 Dehydration C	.07	.15
76 Evacuation R	3.00	6.00
77 Fighting Drake U	.12	.25
78 Flash Counter C	.07	.15
79 Fleeting Image R	.20	.40
80 Flight C	.07	.15
81 Fugitive Wizard C	.07	.15
82 Hibernation U	.12	.25
83 Horned Turtle C	.07	.15
84 Index C	.07	.15
85 Inspiration C	.07	.15
86 Intruder Alarm R	5.00	10.00
87 Invisibility U	.12	.25
88 Mahamoti Djinn R	.20	.40
89 Mana Leak C	.20	.40
90 Merchant of Secrets C	.07	.15
91 Merchant Scroll U	4.00	8.00
92 Mind Bend R	.20	.40
93 Phantom Warrior U	.12	.25
94 Puppeteer U	.12	.25
95 Remove Soul C	.07	.15
96 Rewind U	.25	.50
97 Sage of Lat-Nam R	.20	.40
98 Sage Owl C	.07	.15
99 Sea Monster C	.07	.15
100 Shifting Sky R	.20	.40
101 Sneaky Homunculus C	.07	.15
102 Spiketail Hatchling U	.12	.25
103 Steal Artifact U	.12	.25
104 Storm Crow C	.07	.15
105 Telepathy U	.25	.50
106 Temporal Adept R	.30	.60
107 Thieving Magpie U	.12	.25
108 Tidal Kraken R	.75	1.50
109 Trade Routes R	4.00	8.00
110 Treasure Trove U	.12	.25
111 Twiddle C	.20	.40
112 Unsummon C	.07	.15
113 Wall of Air U	.12	.25
114 Wind Drake C	.07	.15
115 Wrath of Marit Lage U	.12	.25
116 Zur's Weirding R	.30	.75
117 Abyssal Specter U	.12	.25
118 Ambition's Cost U	.30	.75
119 Bog Imp C	.07	.15
120 Bog Wraith U	.12	.25
121 Carrion Wall U	.25	.50
122 Coercion C	.07	.15
123 Dark Banishing C	.07	.15
124 Death Pit Offering R	.20	.40
125 Death Pits of Rath R	.20	.40
126 Deathgazer U	.12	.25
127 Deepwood Ghoul C	.07	.15
128 Diabolic Tutor U	1.00	2.00
129 Drudge Skeletons C	.07	.15
130 Dusk Imp C	.07	.15
131 Eastern Paladin R	.20	.40
132 Execute U	.12	.25
133 Fallen Angel R	.20	.40
134 Fear C	.07	.15
135 Giant Cockroach C	.07	.15
136 Gluttonous Zombie U	.12	.25
137 Grave Pact R	25.00	50.00
138 Gravedigger C	.07	.15
139 Larceny R	.20	.40
140 Looming Shade C	.07	.15
141 Lord of the Undead R	10.00	20.00
142 Maggot Carrier C	.07	.15
143 Megrim U	.30	.60
144 Mind Rot C	.07	.15
145 Mind Slash U	.60	1.25
146 Mind Sludge U	.12	.25
147 Murderous Betrayal R	.20	.40
148 Nausea C	.07	.15
149 Nekrataal U	.12	.25
150 Nightmare R	.20	.40
151 Persecute R	.20	.40
152 Phyrexian Arena R	10.00	20.00
153 Phyrexian Plaguelord R	.20	.40
154 Plague Beetle C	.07	.15
155 Plague Wind R	1.25	2.50
156 Primeval Shambler U	.12	.25
157 Raise Dead C	.07	.15
158 Ravenous Rats C	.07	.15
159 Royal Assassin R	.60	1.25
160 Scathe Zombies C	.07	.15
161 Serpent Warrior C	.07	.15
162 Sever Soul U	.12	.25
163 Severed Legion C	.07	.15
164 Slay U	.12	.25
165 Soul Feast U	.12	.25
166 Spineless Thug C	.07	.15
167 Swarm of Rats U	1.00	2.00
168 Underworld Dreams R	2.00	4.00
169 Unholy Strength C	.07	.15
170 Vampiric Spirit R	.20	.40
171 Vicious Hunger C	.07	.15
172 Warped Devotion R	.20	.40
173 Western Paladin R	.20	.40
174 Zombify U	.20	.40
175 Anaba Shaman C	.07	.15
176 Balduvian Barbarians C	.07	.15
177 Blaze U	.12	.25
178 Blood Moon R	6.00	12.00
179 Bloodshot Cyclops R	.20	.40
180 Boil U	2.50	5.00
181 Canyon Wildcat C	.07	.15
182 Cinder Wall C	.07	.15
183 Demolish U	.12	.25
184 Dwarven Demolition Team U	.12	.25
185 Enrage U	.12	.25
186 Flashfires U	.12	.25
187 Furnace of Rath R	4.00	8.00
188 Goblin Chariot C	.07	.15
189 Goblin Glider U	.12	.25
190 Goblin King R	1.50	3.00
191 Goblin Raider C	.07	.15
192 Guerrilla Tactics U	.12	.25
193 Hammer of Bogardan R	.20	.40
194 Hill Giant C	.07	.15
195 Hulking Cyclops U	.12	.25
196 Inferno R	.30	.60
197 Lava Axe C	.07	.15
198 Lava Hounds R	.20	.40
199 Lesser Gargadon U	.12	.25
200 Lightning Blast U	.12	.25
201 Lightning Elemental C	.07	.15
202 Mana Clash R	.20	.40
203 Mogg Sentry R	.20	.40
204 Obliterate R	2.50	5.00
205 Ogre Taskmaster U	.12	.25
206 Okk R	.20	.40
207 Orcish Artillery U	.12	.25
208 Orcish Spy C	.07	.15
209 Panic Attack C	.07	.15
210 Pyroclasm U	.12	.25
211 Pyrotechnics U	.12	.25
212 Raging Goblin C	.07	.15
213 Reflexes C	.07	.15
214 Relentless Assault R	.75	1.50
215 Ridgeline Rager C	.07	.15
216 Rukh Egg R	.30	.60
217 Sabretooth Tiger C	.07	.15
218 Searing Wind R	.20	.40
219 Seismic Assault R	.60	1.25
220 Shatter C	.07	.15
221 Shivan Dragon R	.20	.40
222 Shock C	.07	.15
223 Shock Troops C	.07	.15
224 Sizzle C	.12	.25
225 Stone Rain C	.07	.15
226 Sudden Impact U	.12	.25
227 Thieves' Auction R	2.00	4.00
228 Tremor C	.07	.15
229 Two-Headed Dragon R	.60	1.25
230 Viashino Sandstalker U	.12	.25
231 Volcanic Hammer C	.07	.15
232 Wall of Stone U	.12	.25
233 Birds of Paradise R	7.50	15.00
234 Blanchwood Armor U	.12	.25
235 Call of the Wild R	.30	.60
236 Canopy Spider C	.07	.15
237 Choke U	2.50	5.00
238 Collective Unconscious R	2.00	4.00
239 Craw Wurm C	.07	.15
240 Creeping Mold U	.12	.25
241 Elvish Champion R	15.00	30.00
242 Elvish Lyrist U	.12	.25
243 Elvish Pioneer C	.15	.30
244 Elvish Piper R	4.00	8.00
245 Elvish Scrapper U	.12	.25
246 Emperor Crocodile R	.20	.40
247 Fecundity U	.12	.25
248 Fertile Ground C	.07	.15
249 Foratog U	.12	.25
250 Fungusaur R	.20	.40
251 Fyndhorn Elder U	.12	.25
252 Gaea's Herald R	2.00	4.00
253 Giant Badger C	.07	.15
254 Giant Growth C	.07	.15
255 Giant Spider C	.07	.15
256 Grizzly Bears C	.07	.15
257 Horned Troll C	.07	.15
258 Hunted Wumpus U	.25	.50
259 Lhurgoyf R	.30	.60
260 Living Terrain U	.12	.25
261 Llanowar Behemoth U	.12	.25
262 Lone Wolf C	.07	.15
263 Lure U	.12	.25
264 Maro R	.20	.40
265 Might of Oaks R	.20	.40
266 Monstrous Growth C	.07	.15
267 Moss Monster C	.07	.15
268 Nantuko Disciple C	.07	.15
269 Natural Affinity R	.50	1.00
270 Naturalize C	.07	.15
271 Norwood Ranger C	.07	.15
272 Plow Under R	1.25	2.50
273 Primeval Force R	.20	.40
274 Rampant Growth C	.60	1.25
275 Regeneration C	.07	.15
276 Revive U	.12	.25
277 Rhox R	.20	.40
278 Rushwood Dryad C	.07	.15
279 Spined Wurm C	.07	.15
280 Spitting Spider U	.12	.25
281 Spreading Algae U	.20	.40
282 Stream of Life U	.12	.25
283 Thorn Elemental R	.20	.40
284 Trained Armodon C	.07	.15
285 Verduran Enchantress R	2.00	4.00
286 Vernal Bloom R	4.00	8.00
287 Vine Trellis C	.20	.40
288 Wing Snare U	.12	.25
289 Wood Elves C	.30	.75
290 Yavimaya Enchantress U	.12	.25
291 Aladdin's Ring R	.20	.40
292 Beast of Burden R	.20	.40
293 Brass Herald R	.20	.40
294 Coat of Arms R	7.50	15.00
295 Crystal Rod U	.12	.25
296 Defense Grid R	7.50	15.00
297 Dingus Egg R	.20	.40
298 Disrupting Scepter R	.20	.40
299 Distorting Lens R	.20	.40
300 Ensnaring Bridge R	10.00	20.00
301 Flying Carpet R	.20	.40
302 Fodder Cannon U	.12	.25
303 Howling Mine R	3.00	6.00
304 Iron Star U	.12	.25
305 Ivory Cup U	.12	.25
306 Jayemdae Tome R	.20	.40
307 Millstone R	.20	.40
308 Patagia Golem U	.12	.25
309 Phyrexian Colossus R	.20	.40
310 Phyrexian Hulk U	.12	.25
311 Planar Portal R	2.00	4.00
312 Rod of Ruin U	.12	.25
313 Skull of Orm R	.75	1.50
314 Spellbook U	2.00	4.00
315 Star Compass U	1.00	2.00
316 Teferi's Puzzle Box R	4.00	8.00
317 Throne of Bone U	.12	.25
318 Urza's Armor R	.20	.40
319 Vexing Arcanix R	.30	.75
320 Wall of Spears U	.12	.25
321 Wooden Sphere U	.12	.25
322 City of Brass R	12.50	25.00
323 Coastal Tower U	.30	.60
324 Elfhame Palace U	.12	.25
325 Salt Marsh U	.50	1.00
326 Shivan Oasis U	.12	.25
327 Urborg Volcano U	.25	.50

328 Urza's Mine U	1.50	3.00
329 Urza's Power Plant U	2.00	4.00
330 Urza's Tower U	1.50	3.00
331 Plains L	.20	.40
332 Plains L	.15	.30
333 Plains L	.25	.50
334 Plains L	.30	.60
335 Island L	.25	.50
336 Island L	.20	.40
337 Island L	.30	.75
338 Island L	.12	.25
339 Swamp L	.50	1.00
340 Swamp L	.50	1.00
341 Swamp L	.30	.60
342 Swamp L	.20	.40
343 Mountain L	.30	.60
344 Mountain L	.20	.40
345 Mountain L	.50	1.00
346 Mountain L	.15	.30
347 Forest L	.50	1.00
348 Forest L	.75	1.50
349 Forest L	.20	.40
350 Forest L	.30	.75
S1 Eager Cadet C	.07	.15
S2 Vengence U	.12	.25
S3 Giant Octopus C	.07	.15
S5 Vizzerdrix R	.20	.40
S6 Enormous Baloth U	.12	.25
S7 Silverback Ape U	.30	.60

2003 Magic The Gathering Legions

1 Akroma, Angel of Wrath R	4.00	8.00
2 Akroma's Devoted U	.12	.25
3 Aven Redeemer C	.07	.15
4 Aven Warhawk U	.12	.25
5 Beacon of Destiny R	.20	.40
6 Celestial Gatekeeper R	1.00	2.00
7 Cloudreach Cavalry U	.12	.25
8 Daru Mender U	.12	.25
9 Daru Sanctifier C	.07	.15
10 Daru Stinger C	.07	.15
11 Defender of the Order R	.20	.40
12 Deftblade Elite C	.20	.40
13 Essence Sliver R	7.50	15.00
14 Gempalm Avenger C	.30	.60
15 Glowrider R	3.00	6.00
16 Liege of the Axe U	.12	.25
17 Lowland Tracker C	.07	.15
18 Planar Guide R	.30	.60
19 Plated Sliver C	.30	.75
20 Starlight Invoker C	.07	.15
21 Stoic Champion U	.12	.25
22 Sunstrike Legionnaire R	.20	.40
23 Swooping Talon U	.12	.25
24 Wall of Hope C	.20	.40
25 Ward Sliver U	1.50	3.00
26 Whipgrass Entangler C	.07	.15
27 White Knight U	.12	.25
28 Windborn Muse R	4.00	8.00
29 Wingbeat Warrior C	.07	.15
30 Aven Envoy C	.07	.15
31 Cephalid Pathmage C	.07	.15
32 Chromeshell Crab R	.20	.40
33 Covert Operative C	.07	.15
34 Crookclaw Elder U	.12	.25
35 Dermoplasm R	.20	.40
36 Dreamborn Muse R	2.00	4.00
37 Echo Tracer C	.15	.30
38 Fugitive Wizard C	.07	.15
39 Gempalm Sorcerer U	.12	.25
40 Glintwing Invoker C	.07	.15
41 Keeneye Aven C	.07	.15
42 Keeper of the Nine Gales R	.75	1.50
43 Master of the Veil U	.75	1.50
44 Merchant of Secrets C	.07	.15
45 Mistform Seaswift C	.07	.15
46 Mistform Sliver C	.07	.15
47 Mistform Ultimus R	.20	.40
48 Mistform Wakecaster U	.12	.25
49 Primoc Escapee U	.15	.30
50 Riptide Director R	2.00	4.00
51 Riptide Mangler R	.20	.40
52 Shifting Sliver U	4.00	8.00
53 Synapse Sliver R	30.00	60.00
54 Voidmage Apprentice C	.25	.50
55 Wall of Deceit U	.12	.25
56 Warped Researcher U	.12	.25
57 Weaver of Lies R	.75	1.50
58 Willbender U	.12	.25
59 Aphetto Exterminator U	.12	.25
60 Bane of the Living R	.20	.40
61 Blood Celebrant C	.30	.75
62 Corpse Harvester U	.75	1.50
63 Crypt Sliver C	.75	1.50
64 Dark Supplicant U	.12	.25
65 Deathmark Prelate U	.12	.25
66 Drinker of Sorrow R	.20	.40
67 Dripping Dead C	.07	.15
68 Earthblighter U	.12	.25
69 Embalmed Brawler C	.07	.15
70 Gempalm Polluter C	.07	.15
71 Ghastly Remains R	.20	.40
72 Goblin Turncoat C	.07	.15
73 Graveborn Muse R	4.00	8.00
74 Havoc Demon R	.20	.40
75 Hollow Specter R	.20	.40
76 Infernal Caretaker C	.07	.15
77 Noxious Ghoul U	1.50	3.00
78 Phage the Untouchable R	4.00	8.00
79 Scion of Darkness R	2.50	5.00
80 Skinthinner C	.07	.15
81 Smokespew Invoker C	.07	.15
82 Sootfeather Flock C	.07	.15
83 Spectral Sliver U	.12	.25
84 Toxin Sliver R	3.00	6.00
85 Vile Deacon C	.07	.15
86 Withered Wretch U	.12	.25
87 Zombie Brute U	.12	.25
88 Blade Sliver U	.75	1.50
89 Bloodstoke Howler C	.07	.15
90 Clickslither R	.20	.40
91 Crested Craghorn C	.07	.15
92 Flamewave Invoker C	.07	.15
93 Frenetic Raptor U	.12	.25
94 Gempalm Incinerator U	.60	1.25
95 Goblin Assassin U	.60	1.25
96 Goblin Clearcutter U	.12	.25
97 Goblin Dynamo U	.12	.25
98 Goblin Firebug C	.07	.15
99 Goblin Goon R	.25	.50
100 Goblin Grappler C	.07	.15
101 Goblin Lookout C	.30	.60
102 Hunter Sliver C	.30	.75
103 Imperial Hellkite R	.20	.40
104 Kilnmouth Dragon R	.75	1.50
105 Lavaborn Muse R	.20	.40
106 Macetail Hystrodon C	.07	.15
107 Magma Sliver R	15.00	30.00
108 Ridgetop Raptor U	.12	.25
109 Rockshard Elemental R	.20	.40
110 Shaleskin Plower C	.07	.15
111 Skirk Alarmist R	.20	.40
112 Skirk Drill Sergeant U	.12	.25
113 Skirk Marauder C	.07	.15
114 Skirk Outrider C	.07	.15
115 Unstable Hulk R	.20	.40
116 Warbreak Trumpeter U	.12	.25
117 Berserk Murlodont C	.07	.15
118 Branchsnap Lorian U	.12	.25
119 Brontotherium U	.12	.25
120 Brood Sliver R	15.00	30.00
121 Caller of the Claw R	1.25	2.50
122 Canopy Crawler U	.12	.25
123 Defiant Elf C	.07	.15
124 Elvish Soultiller R	.30	.60
125 Enormous Baloth U	.12	.25
126 Feral Throwback R	.20	.40
127 Gempalm Strider U	.12	.25
128 Glowering Rogon C	.07	.15
129 Hundroog C	.07	.15
130 Krosan Cloudscraper R	.30	.60
131 Krosan Vorine C	.07	.15
132 Nantuko Vigilante C	.07	.15
133 Needleshot Gourna C	.07	.15
134 Patron of the Wild C	.07	.15
135 Primal Whisperer R	1.00	2.00
136 Quick Sliver C	.30	.75
137 Root Sliver U	7.50	15.00
138 Seedborn Muse R	10.00	20.00
139 Stonewood Invoker C	.07	.15
140 Timberwatch Elf C	.30	.60
141 Totem Speaker U	.12	.25
142 Tribal Forcemage R	.25	.50
143 Vexing Beetle R	.20	.40
144 Wirewood Channeler U	1.00	2.00
145 Wirewood Hivemaster U	.12	.25

2003 Magic The Gathering Mirrodin

1 Altar's Light U	.12	.25
2 Arrest C	.07	.15
3 Auriok Bladewarden U	.12	.25
4 Auriok Steelshaper R	1.00	2.00
5 Auriok Transfixer C	.07	.15
6 Awe Strike C	.07	.15
7 Blinding Beam C	.07	.15
8 Leonin Abunas R	1.00	2.00
9 Leonin Den-Guard C	.07	.15
10 Leonin Elder C	.07	.15
11 Leonin Skyhunter U	.12	.25
12 Loxodon Mender C	.07	.15
13 Loxodon Peacekeeper R	.20	.40
14 Loxodon Punisher R	.20	.40
15 Luminous Angel R	.30	.60
16 Raise the Alarm C	.07	.15
17 Razor Barrier C	.07	.15
18 Roar of the Kha U	.12	.25
19 Rule of Law R	.50	1.00
20 Second Sunrise R	4.00	8.00
21 Skyhunter Cub C	.07	.15
22 Skyhunter Patrol C	.07	.15
23 Slith Ascendant U	.12	.25
24 Solar Tide R	.60	1.25
25 Soul Nova U	.12	.25
26 Sphere of Purity C	.07	.15
27 Taj-Nar Swordsmith U	.12	.25
28 Tempest of Light U	.12	.25
29 Annul C	.07	.15
30 Assert Authority U	.12	.25
31 Broodstar R	.40	.80
32 Disarm C	.07	.15
33 Domineer U	.12	.25
34 Dream's Grip C	.30	.75
35 Fabricate U	4.00	8.00
36 Fatespinner R	2.50	5.00
37 Inertia Bubble C	.07	.15
38 Looming Hoverguard U	.12	.25
39 Lumengrid Augur R	.20	.40
40 Lumengrid Sentinel U	.12	.25
41 Lumengrid Warden C	.07	.15
42 March of the Machines R	.30	.75
43 Neurok Familiar C	.07	.15
44 Neurok Spy C	.07	.15
45 Override C	.07	.15
46 Psychic Membrane U	.12	.25
47 Quicksilver Elemental R	.60	1.25
48 Regress C	.07	.15
49 Shared Fate R	.60	1.25
50 Slith Strider U	.12	.25
51 Somber Hoverguard C	.07	.15
52 Temporal Cascade R	.20	.40
53 Thirst for Knowledge U	.12	.25
54 Thoughtcast C	.25	.50
55 Vedalken Archmage R	3.00	6.00
56 Wanderguard Sentry C	.07	.15
57 Barter in Blood U	.12	.25
58 Betrayal of Flesh U	.12	.25
59 Chimney Imp C	.07	.15
60 Consume Spirit C	.07	.15
61 Contaminated Bond C	.07	.15
62 Disciple of the Vault C	.07	.15
63 Dross Harvester R	.30	.75
64 Dross Prowler C	.07	.15
65 Flayed Nim U	.12	.25
66 Grim Reminder R	.20	.40
67 Irradiate C	.07	.15
68 Moriok Scavenger C	.07	.15
69 Necrogen Mists R	15.00	30.00
70 Nim Devourer R	.20	.40
71 Nim Lasher C	.07	.15
72 Nim Shambler U	.12	.25
73 Nim Shrieker C	.07	.15
74 Promise of Power R	.30	.60
75 Reiver Demon R	1.25	2.50
76 Relic Bane U	.12	.25
77 Slith Bloodletter U	.12	.25
78 Spoils of the Vault R	.50	1.00
79 Terror C	.07	.15
80 Vermiculos R	.20	.40
81 Wail of the Nim C	.07	.15
82 Wall of Blood U	.60	1.25
83 Woebearer U	.12	.25
84 Wrench Mind C	.07	.15
85 Arc-Slogger R	.20	.40
86 Atog U	.12	.25
87 Confusion in the Ranks R	2.00	4.00
88 Detonate U	.12	.25
89 Electrostatic Bolt C	.07	.15
90 Fiery Gambit R	1.25	2.50
91 Fists of the Anvil C	.07	.15
92 Forge Armor U	.12	.25
93 Fractured Loyalty U	.12	.25
94 Goblin Striker C	.07	.15
95 Grab the Reins U	.12	.25
96 Incite War C	.07	.15
97 Krark-Clan Grunt C	.07	.15
98 Krark-Clan Shaman C	.07	.15
99 Mass Hysteria R	6.00	12.00
100 Megatog R	.20	.40
101 Molten Rain C	.30	.75
102 Ogre Leadfoot C	.07	.15
103 Rustmouth Ogre U	.12	.25
104 Seething Song C	1.00	2.00
105 Shatter C	.07	.15
106 Shrapnel Blast U	.12	.25
107 Slith Firewalker U	.12	.25
108 Spikeshot Goblin C	.07	.15
109 Trash for Treasure R	.60	1.25
110 Vulshok Battlemaster R	.20	.40
111 Vulshok Berserker C	.07	.15
112 War Elemental R	.75	1.50
113 Battlegrowth C	.07	.15
114 Bloodscent U	.12	.25
115 Brown Ouphe U	.12	.25
116 Copperhoof Vorrac R	.20	.40
117 Creeping Mold U	.12	.25
118 Deconstruct C	.07	.15
119 Fangren Hunter C	.07	.15
120 Glissa Sunseeker R	.75	1.50
121 Groffskithur C	.07	.15
122 Hum of the Radix R	.30	.60
123 Journey of Discovery C	.07	.15
124 Living Hive R	.30	.60
125 Molder Slug R	.30	.60
126 One Dozen Eyes U	.12	.25
127 Plated Slagwurm R	.20	.40
128 Predator's Strike C	.07	.15
129 Slith Predator U	.12	.25
130 Sylvan Scrying U	1.00	2.00
131 Tel-Jilad Archers C	.07	.15
132 Tel-Jilad Chosen C	.07	.15
133 Tel-Jilad Exile C	.07	.15
134 Tooth and Nail R	20.00	40.00
135 Troll Ascetic R	.50	1.00
136 Trolls of Tel-Jilad U	.12	.25
137 Turn to Dust C	.07	.15
138 Viridian Joiner C	.17	.35
139 Viridian Shaman U	.12	.25
140 Wurmskin Forger C	.07	.15
141 Aether Spellbomb C	.15	.30
142 Alpha Myr C	.07	.15
143 Altar of Shadows R	.20	.40
144 Banshee's Blade U	.12	.25
145 Blinkmoth Urn R	1.00	2.00
146 Bonesplitter C	.20	.40
147 Bosh, Iron Golem R	.20	.40
148 Bottle Gnomes U	.12	.25
149 Cathodion U	.12	.25
150 Chalice of the Void R	25.00	50.00
151 Chromatic Sphere C	.60	1.25
152 Chrome Mox R	40.00	80.00
153 Clockwork Beetle C	.07	.15
154 Clockwork Condor C	.07	.15
155 Clockwork Dragon R	.50	1.00
156 Clockwork Vorrac U	.12	.25
157 Cobalt Golem C	.07	.15
158 Copper Myr C	.07	.15
159 Crystal Shard U	1.50	3.00
160 Culling Scales R	.20	.40
161 Damping Matrix R	.30	.60
162 Dead-Iron Sledge U	.12	.25
163 Dragon Blood U	.12	.25
164 Dross Scorpion C	.07	.15
165 Duplicant R	1.25	2.50
166 Duskworker U	.12	.25
167 Elf Replica C	.07	.15
168 Empyrial Plate R	.30	.60
169 Extraplanar Lens R	40.00	80.00
170 Farsight Mask U	.12	.25
171 Fireshrieker U	.50	1.00
172 Frogmite C	.07	.15
173 Galvanic Key C	.07	.15
174 Gate to the Aether R	1.25	2.50
175 Gilded Lotus R	4.00	8.00
176 Goblin Charbelcher R	2.00	4.00
177 Goblin Dirigible U	.12	.25
178 Goblin Replica C	.07	.15
179 Goblin War Wagon C	.07	.15
180 Gold Myr C	.07	.15
181 Golem-Skin Gauntlets U	.30	.60
182 Granite Shard U	.12	.25
183 Grid Monitor R	3.00	6.00
184 Heartwood Shard U	.12	.25
185 Hematite Golem C	.07	.15
186 Icy Manipulator U	.12	.25
187 Iron Myr C	.20	.40
188 Isochron Scepter U	7.50	15.00
189 Jinxed Choker R	.30	.60
190 Krark's Thumb R	12.50	25.00
191 Leaden Myr C	.07	.15
192 Leonin Bladetrap U	.12	.25
193 Leonin Scimitar C	.07	.15
194 Leonin Sun Standard R	.20	.40
195 Leveler R	1.50	3.00
196 Liar's Pendulum R	.20	.40
197 Lifespark Spellbomb C	.07	.15
198 Lightning Coils R	.50	1.00
199 Lightning Greaves U	4.00	8.00
200 Lodestone Myr R	.20	.40
201 Loxodon Warhammer U	.60	1.25
202 Malachite Golem C	.07	.15
203 Mask of Memory U	.75	1.50
204 Mesmeric Orb R	6.00	12.00
205 Mind's Eye R	5.00	10.00
206 Mindslaver R	3.00	6.00
207 Mindstorm Crown U	.12	.25
208 Mirror Golem U	.12	.25
209 Mourner's Shield U	.12	.25
210 Myr Adapter C	.07	.15
211 Myr Enforcer C	.07	.15
212 Myr Incubator R	.30	.60
213 Myr Mindservant U	.12	.25
214 Myr Prototype U	.12	.25
215 Myr Retriever U	.50	1.00
216 Necrogen Spellbomb C	.07	.15
217 Needlebug U	.12	.25
218 Neurok Hoversail C	.07	.15
219 Nightmare Lash R	2.00	4.00
220 Nim Replica C	.07	.15
221 Nuisance Engine U	.12	.25
222 Oblivion Stone R	3.00	6.00
223 Omega Myr C	.07	.15
224 Ornithopter U	.12	.25
225 Pearl Shard U	.12	.25
226 Pentavus R	.20	.40
227 Pewter Golem C	.07	.15
228 Platinum Angel R	7.50	15.00
229 Power Conduit U	.50	1.00
230 Proteus Staff R	7.50	15.00
231 Psychogenic Probe R	.20	.40
232 Pyrite Spellbomb C	.07	.15
233 Quicksilver Fountain R	2.00	4.00
234 Rust Elemental U	.12	.25
235 Rustspore Ram U	.12	.25
236 Scale of Chiss-Goria C	.07	.15
237 Scrabbling Claws U	.12	.25
238 Sculpting Steel R	3.00	6.00
239 Scythe of the Wretched R	3.00	6.00
240 Serum Tank U	.12	.25
241 Silver Myr C	.20	.40
242 Skeleton Shard U	.12	.25
243 Slagwurm Armor C	.07	.15
244 Soldier Replica C	.07	.15
245 Solemn Simulacrum R	3.00	6.00
246 Soul Foundry R	.50	1.00
247 Spellweaver Helix R	4.00	8.00
248 Steel Wall C	.20	.40
249 Sun Droplet U	.50	1.00
250 Sunbeam Spellbomb C	.07	.15
251 Sword of Kaldra R	10.00	20.00
252 Synod Sanctum U	.30	.75
253 Talisman of Dominance U	5.00	10.00
254 Talisman of Impulse U	.75	1.50
255 Talisman of Indulgence U	4.00	8.00
256 Talisman of Progress U	7.50	15.00
257 Talisman of Unity U	1.50	3.00
258 Tanglebloom C	.07	.15
259 Tangleroot R	.30	.75
260 Tel-Jilad Stylus U	.12	.25
261 Thought Prison U	.12	.25
262 Timesifter R	1.50	3.00
263 Titanium Golem C	.07	.15
264 Tooth of Chiss-Goria C	.07	.15
265 Tower of Champions R	.20	.40
266 Tower of Eons R	.20	.40
267 Tower of Fortunes R	.30	.75
268 Tower of Murmurs R	.20	.40
269 Triskelion R	1.25	2.50
270 Viridian Longbow C	.60	1.25
271 Vorrac Battlehorns C	.60	1.25
272 Vulshok Battlegear U	.12	.25
273 Vulshok Gauntlets C	.07	.15
274 Welding Jar C	.30	.60
275 Wizard Replica C	.07	.15
276 Worldslayer R	2.50	5.00
277 Yotian Soldier C	.07	.15
278 Ancient Den C	2.00	4.00
279 Blinkmoth Well U	.12	.25
280 Cloudpost C	.60	1.25
281 Glimmervoid R	3.00	6.00
282 Great Furnace C	.50	1.00
283 Seat of the Synod C	.75	1.50
284 Stalking Stones U	.12	.25
285 Tree of Tales C	.60	1.25
286 Vault of Whispers C	.75	1.50
287 Plains L	.07	.15
288 Plains L	.07	.15
289 Plains L	.07	.15
290 Plains L	.25	.50
291 Island L	.30	.60
292 Island L	.12	.25
293 Island L	.07	.15
294 Island L	.07	.15
295 Swamp L	.12	.25
296 Swamp L	.12	.25
297 Swamp L	.12	.25
298 Swamp L	.12	.25
299 Mountain L	.15	.30
300 Mountain L	.07	.15
301 Mountain L	.07	.15
302 Mountain L	.07	.15
303 Forest L	.20	.40
304 Forest L	.07	.15
305 Forest L	.07	.15
306 Forest L	.07	.15

2003 Magic The Gathering Scourge

1 Ageless Sentinels R	.20	.40
2 Astral Steel C	.07	.15
3 Aven Farseer C	.07	.15
4 Aven Liberator C	.07	.15

5 Daru Spiritualist C	.07	.15
6 Daru Warchief U	.75	1.50
7 Dawn Elemental R	.30	.75
8 Decree of Justice R	.75	1.50
9 Dimensional Breach R	.20	.40
10 Dragon Scales C	.07	.15
11 Dragonstalker U	.12	.25
12 Eternal Dragon R	.75	1.50
13 Exiled Doomsayer R	.20	.40
14 Force Bubble R	.20	.40
15 Frontline Strategist C	.07	.15
16 Gilded Light U	.12	.25
17 Guilty Conscience C	.20	.40
18 Karona's Zealot U	.12	.25
19 Noble Templar C	.07	.15
20 Rain of Blades U	.12	.25
21 Recuperate C	.07	.15
22 Reward the Faithful U	.12	.25
23 Silver Knight U	.12	.25
24 Trap Digger R	.20	.40
25 Wing Shards U	.12	.25
26 Wipe Clean C	.07	.15
27 Zealous Inquisitor C	.07	.15
28 Aphetto Runecaster U	.75	1.50
29 Brain Freeze U	5.00	10.00
30 Coast Watcher C	.07	.15
31 Day of the Dragons R	.25	.50
32 Decree of Silence R	10.00	20.00
33 Dispersal Shield C	.07	.15
34 Dragon Wings C	.07	.15
35 Faces of the Past R	.60	1.25
36 Frozen Solid C	.07	.15
37 Hindering Touch C	.07	.15
38 Long-Term Plans U	3.00	6.00
39 Mercurial Kite C	.07	.15
40 Metamorphose U	.12	.25
41 Mind's Desire R	.75	1.50
42 Mischievous Quanar R	.20	.40
43 Mistform Warchief U	.12	.25
44 Parallel Thoughts R	.30	.75
45 Pemmin's Aura U	7.50	15.00
46 Raven Guild Initiate C	.07	.15
47 Raven Guild Master R	1.25	2.50
48 Riptide Survivor U	.12	.25
49 Rush of Knowledge C	.15	.30
50 Scornful Egotist C	.07	.15
51 Shoreline Ranger C	.07	.15
52 Stifle R	17.50	35.00
53 Temporal Fissure C	.07	.15
54 Thundercloud Elemental U	.12	.25
55 Bladewing's Thrall U	.12	.25
56 Cabal Conditioning R	.30	.75
57 Cabal Interrogator U	.12	.25
58 Call to the Grave R	.75	1.50
59 Carrion Feeder C	.30	.75
60 Chill Haunting U	.12	.25
61 Clutch of Undeath C	.07	.15
62 Consumptive Goo R	.30	.60
63 Death's-Head Buzzard C	.07	.15
64 Decree of Pain R	2.50	5.00
65 Dragon Shadow C	.07	.15
66 Fatal Mutation U	.12	.25
67 Final Punishment R	.20	.40
68 Lethal Vapors R	3.00	6.00
69 Lingering Death C	.07	.15
70 Nefashu R	.20	.40
71 Putrid Raptor U	.12	.25
72 Reaping the Graves C	.60	1.25
73 Skulltap C	.07	.15
74 Soul Collector R	.50	1.00
75 Tendrils of Agony U	3.00	6.00
76 Twisted Abomination C	.07	.15
77 Unburden C	.07	.15
78 Undead Warchief U	3.00	6.00
79 Unspeakable Symbol U	3.00	6.00
80 Vengeful Dead C	.50	1.00
81 Zombie Cutthroat C	.07	.15
82 Bonethorn Valesk C	.07	.15
83 Carbonize U	.12	.25
84 Chartooth Cougar C	.07	.15
85 Decree of Annihilation R	3.00	6.00
86 Dragon Breath C	.07	.15
87 Dragon Mage R	.75	1.50
88 Dragon Tyrant R	1.25	2.50
89 Dragonspeaker Shaman U	2.50	5.00
90 Dragonstorm R	1.00	2.00
91 Enrage U	.12	.25
92 Extra Arms U	.12	.25
93 Form of the Dragon R	.30	.75
94 Goblin Brigand C	.07	.15
95 Goblin Psychopath U	.12	.25
96 Goblin War Strike C	.50	1.00
97 Goblin Warchief U	.75	1.50
98 Grip of Chaos R	1.25	2.50
99 Misguided Rage C	.07	.15
100 Pyrostatic Pillar U	.30	.60
101 Rock Jockey C	.07	.15
102 Scattershot C	.07	.15
103 Siege-Gang Commander R	1.00	2.00
104 Skirk Volcanist U	.12	.25
105 Spark Spray C	.07	.15
106 Sulfuric Vortex R	2.00	4.00
107 Torrent of Fire C	.07	.15
108 Uncontrolled Infestation C	.07	.15
109 Accelerated Mutation C	.07	.15
110 Alpha Status U	1.50	3.00
111 Ambush Commander R	.75	1.50
112 Ancient Ooze R	.75	1.50
113 Break Asunder C	.07	.15
114 Claws of Wirewood U	.12	.25
115 Decree of Savagery R	.60	1.25
116 Divergent Growth C	.07	.15
117 Dragon Fangs C	.07	.15
118 Elvish Aberration U	.12	.25
119 Fierce Empath C	.20	.40
120 Forgotten Ancient R	2.50	5.00
121 Hunting Pack U	.12	.25
122 Krosan Drover C	.07	.15
123 Krosan Warchief U	.12	.25
124 Kurgadon U	.12	.25
125 One with Nature U	2.50	5.00
126 Primitive Etchings R	.30	.60
127 Root Elemental R	.20	.40
128 Sprouting Vines C	.07	.15
129 Titanic Bulvox C	.07	.15
130 Treetop Scout C	.07	.15
131 Upwelling R	.60	1.25
132 Wirewood Guardian C	.07	.15
133 Wirewood Symbiote U	4.00	8.00
134 Woodcloaker C	.07	.15
135 Xantid Swarm R	.75	1.50
136 Bladewing the Risen R	.50	1.00
137 Edgewalker U	2.00	4.00
138 Karona, False God R	2.50	5.00
139 Sliver Overlord R	30.00	60.00
140 Ark of Blight U	.12	.25
141 Proteus Machine U	.12	.25
142 Stabilizer R	.20	.40
143 Temple of the False God U	.60	1.25

2004 Magic The Gathering Champions of Kamigawa

1 Blessed Breath C	.07	.15
2 Bushi Tenderfoot/Kenzo the Hardhearted U	.20	.40
3 Cage of Hands C	.07	.15
4 Call to Glory C	.07	.15
5 Candles' Glow U	.12	.25
6 Cleanfall U	.12	.25
7 Devoted Retainer C	.07	.15
8 Eight-and-a-Half-Tails R	1.50	3.00
9 Ethereal Haze C	.25	.50
10 Ghostly Prison U	2.50	5.00
11 Harsh Deceiver C	.07	.15
12 Hikari, Twilight Guardian R	.25	.50
13 Hold the Line R	.25	.50
14 Honden of Cleansing Fire U	1.50	3.00
15 Horizon Seed U	.12	.25
16 Hundred-Talon Kami C	.07	.15
17 Indomitable Will C	.07	.15
18 Innocence Kami U	.12	.25
19 Isamaru, Hound of Konda R	2.00	4.00
20 Kabuto Moth C	.07	.15
21 Kami of Ancient Law C	.07	.15
22 Kami of Old Stone U	.12	.25
23 Kami of the Painted Road C	.07	.15
24 Kami of the Palace Fields U	.12	.25
25 Kitsune Blademaster C	.07	.15
26 Kitsune Diviner C	.07	.15
27 Kitsune Healer C	.07	.15
28 Kitsune Mystic/Autumn-Tail, Kitsune Sage R	.30	.75
29 Kitsune Riftwalker C	.07	.15
30 Konda, Lord of Eiganjo R	2.00	4.00
31 Konda's Hatamoto U	.12	.25
32 Lantern Kami C	.07	.15
33 Masako the Humorless R	2.50	5.00
34 Mothrider Samurai C	.07	.15
35 Myojin of Cleansing Fire R	2.50	5.00
36 Nagao, Bound by Honor U	.12	.25
37 Otherworldly Journey U	.12	.25
38 Pious Kitsune C	.07	.15
39 Quiet Purity C	.07	.15
40 Reciprocate U	.12	.25
41 Reverse the Sands R	.25	.50
42 Samurai Enforcers U	.12	.25
43 Samurai of the Pale Curtain U	4.00	8.00
44 Sensei Golden-Tail R	1.25	2.50
45 Silent-Chant Zubera C	.07	.15
46 Takeno, Samurai General R	.50	1.00
47 Terashi's Cry C	.07	.15
48 Vassal's Duty R	.25	.50
49 Vigilance C	.07	.15
50 Yosei, the Morning Star R	1.50	3.00
51 Aura of Dominion U	.12	.25
52 Azami, Lady of Scrolls R	1.00	2.00
53 Callous Deceiver C	.07	.15
54 Consuming Vortex C	.07	.15
55 Counsel of the Soratami C	.07	.15
56 Cut the Tethers U	.12	.25
57 Dampen Thought U	.12	.25
58 Eerie Procession U	.12	.25
59 Eye of Nowhere C	.20	.40
60 Field of Reality C	.07	.15
61 Floating-Dream Zubera C	.20	.40
62 Gifts Ungiven R	2.50	5.00
63 Graceful Adept U	.60	1.25
64 Guardian of Solitude U	.12	.25
65 Hinder U	.30	.60
66 Hisoka, Minamo Sensei R	.25	.50
67 Hisoka's Defiance C	.07	.15
68 Hisoka's Guard C	.07	.15
69 Honden of Seeing Winds U	1.25	2.50
70 Jushi Apprentice/Tomoya the Revealer R	.50	1.00
71 Kami of Twisted Reflection C	.07	.15
72 Keiga, the Tide Star R	2.50	5.00
73 Lifted by Clouds C	.07	.15
74 Meloku the Clouded Mirror R	3.00	6.00
75 Myojin of Seeing Winds R	3.00	6.00
76 Mystic Restraints C	.07	.15
77 Part the Veil R	.25	.50
78 Peer Through Depths C	.07	.15
79 Petals of Insight U	.12	.25
80 Psychic Puppetry C	.20	.40
81 Reach Through Mists C	.07	.15
82 Reweave R	.30	.75
83 River Kaijin C	.07	.15
84 Sift Through Sands C	.07	.15
85 Sire of the Storm U	.12	.25
86 Soratami Cloudskater C	.07	.15
87 Soratami Mirror-Guard C	.07	.15
88 Soratami Mirror-Mage U	.12	.25
89 Soratami Rainshaper C	.07	.15
90 Soratami Savant U	.30	.60
91 Soratami Seer U	.12	.25
92 Squelch U	.20	.40
93 Student of Elements/Tobita, Master of Winds U	.12	.25
94 Swirl the Mists R	.25	.50
95 Teller of Tales C	.07	.15
96 Thoughtbind C	.07	.15
97 Time Stop R	2.50	5.00
98 The Unspeakable R	.25	.50
99 Uyo, Silent Prophet R	.30	.75
100 Wandering Ones C	.07	.15
101 Ashen-Skin Zubera C	.07	.15
102 Befoul C	.07	.15
103 Blood Speaker U	1.25	2.50
104 Bloodthirsty Ogre U	.12	.25
105 Cranial Extraction R	.75	1.50
106 Cruel Deceiver C	.07	.15
107 Cursed Ronin C	.07	.15
108 Dance of Shadows U	.12	.25
109 Deathcurse Ogre C	.07	.15
110 Devouring Greed C	.07	.15
111 Distress C	.07	.15
112 Gibbering Kami C	.07	.15
113 Gutwrencher Oni U	.12	.25
114 He Who Hungers R	.30	.75
115 Hideous Laughter U	.12	.25
116 Honden of Night's Reach U	.75	1.50
117 Horobi, Death's Wail R	2.00	4.00
118 Iname, Death Aspect R	.30	.60
119 Kami of Lunacy U	.12	.25
120 Kami of the Waning Moon C	.07	.15
121 Kiku, Night's Flower R	2.00	4.00
122 Kokusho, the Evening Star R	12.50	25.00
123 Kuro, Pitlord R	.25	.50
124 Marrow-Gnawer R	6.00	12.00
125 Midnight Covenant C	.07	.15
126 Myojin of Night's Reach R	6.00	12.00
127 Nezumi Bone-Reader U	.60	1.25
128 Nezumi Cutthroat C	.07	.15
129 Nezumi Graverobber Nighteyes the Desecrator U	.50	1.00
130 Nezumi Ronin C	.07	.15
131 Nezumi Shortfang/Stabwhisker the Odious R	2.50	5.00
132 Night Dealings R	1.00	2.00
133 Night of Souls' Betrayal R	.50	1.00
134 Numai Outcast U	.12	.25
135 Oni Possession U	.12	.25
136 Painwracker Oni U	.12	.25
137 Pull Under C	.07	.15
138 Rag Dealer C	.07	.15
139 Ragged Veins C	.07	.15
140 Rend Flesh C	.20	.40
141 Rend Spirit C	.07	.15
142 Scuttling Death C	.07	.15
143 Seizan, Perverter of Truth R	6.00	12.00
144 Soulless Revival C	.07	.15
145 Struggle for Sanity U	.12	.25
146 Swallowing Plague U	.12	.25
147 Thief of Hope U	.12	.25
148 Villainous Ogre C	.07	.15
149 Waking Nightmare C	.07	.15
150 Wicked Akuba C	.07	.15
151 Akki Avalanchers C	.07	.15
152 Akki Coalflinger U	.12	.25
153 Akki Lavarunner/Tok-Tok, Volcano Born R	.30	.60
154 Akki Rockspeaker C	.07	.15
155 Akki Underminer U	.12	.25
156 Battle-Mad Ronin C	.07	.15
157 Ben-Ben, Akki Hermit R	.30	.75
158 Blind with Anger U	.12	.25
159 Blood Rites U	.12	.25
160a Brothers Yamazaki U	.12	.25
160b Brothers Yamazaki U	.12	.25
161 Brutal Deceiver C	.07	.15
162 Crushing Pain C	.07	.15
163 Desperate Ritual C	.75	1.50
164 Devouring Rage C	.07	.15
165 Earthshaker U	.12	.25
166 Ember-Fist Zubera C	.07	.15
167 Frostwielder C	.07	.15
168 Glacial Ray C	.07	.15
169 Godo, Bandit Warlord R	3.00	6.00
170 Hanabi Blast U	.12	.25
171 Hearth Kami C	.07	.15
172 Honden of Infinite Rage U	1.00	2.00
173 Initiate of Blood/Goka the Unjust U	.12	.25
174 Kami of Fire's Roar C	.07	.15
175 Kiki-Jiki, Mirror Breaker R	20.00	40.00
176 Kumano, Master Yamabushi R	.25	.50
177 Kumano's Pupils U	.12	.25
178 Lava Spike C	2.00	4.00
179 Mana Seism U	.12	.25
180 Mindblaze R	.25	.50
181 Myojin of Infinite Rage R	1.50	3.00
182 Ore Gorger U	.12	.25
183 Pain Kami U	.12	.25
184 Ronin Houndmaster C	.07	.15
185 Ryusei, the Falling Star R	.75	1.50
186 Shimatsu the Bloodcloaked R	.25	.50
187 Sideswipe U	.12	.25
188 Sokenzan Bruiser C	.07	.15
189 Soul of Magma C	.07	.15
190 Soulblast R	.25	.50
191 Stone Rain C	.07	.15
192 Strange Inversion U	.12	.25
193 Through the Breach R	2.50	5.00
194 Tide of War R	1.00	2.00
195 Uncontrollable Anger C	.07	.15
196 Unearthly Blizzard C	.07	.15
197 Unnatural Speed C	.07	.15
198 Yamabushi's Flame C	.07	.15
199 Yamabushi's Storm C	.07	.15
200 Zo-Zu the Punisher R	5.00	10.00
201 Azusa, Lost but Seeking R	7.50	15.00
202 Budoka Gardener/Dokai, Weaver of Life R	2.00	4.00
203 Burr Grafter C	.07	.15
204 Commune with Nature C	.07	.15
205 Dosan the Falling Leaf R	7.50	15.00
206 Dripping-Tongue Zubera C	.07	.15
207 Feast of Worms U	.12	.25
208 Feral Deceiver C	.07	.15
209 Gale Force U	.12	.25
210 Glimpse of Nature R	15.00	30.00
211 Hana Kami U	.12	.25
212 Heartbeat of Spring R	2.50	5.00
213 Honden of Life's Web U	1.00	2.00
214 Humble Budoka C	.07	.15
215 Iname, Life Aspect R	.30	.75
216 Joyous Respite C	.07	.15
217 Jugan, the Rising Star R	.75	1.50
218 Jukai Messenger C	.07	.15
219 Kami of the Hunt C	.07	.15
220 Kashi-Tribe Reaver U	.12	.25
221 Kashi-Tribe Warriors C	.07	.15
222 Kodama of the North Tree R	.50	1.00
223 Kodama of the South Tree R	.50	1.00
224 Kodama's Might C	.07	.15
225 Kodama's Reach C	1.25	2.50
226 Lure U	.12	.25
227 Matsu-Tribe Decoy C	.07	.15
228 Moss Kami C	.07	.15
229 Myojin of Life's Web R	3.00	6.00
230 Nature's Will R	17.50	35.00
231 Orbweaver Kumo U	.12	.25
232 Order of the Sacred Bell C	.07	.15
233 Orochi Eggwatcher/Shidako, Broodmistress U	.20	.40
234 Orochi Leafcaller C	.07	.15
235 Orochi Ranger C	.07	.15
236 Orochi Sustainer C	.07	.15
237 Rootrunner U	.12	.25
238 Sachi, Daughter of Seshiro U	.12	.25
239 Sakura-Tribe Elder C	.75	1.50
240 Serpent Skin C	.07	.15
241 Seshiro the Anointed R	12.50	25.00
242 Shisato, Whispering Hunter R	.25	.50
243 Soilshaper U	.12	.25
244 Sosuke, Son of Seshiro U	.12	.25
245 Strength of Cedars U	.12	.25
246 Thousand-legged Kami U	.12	.25
247 Time of Need U	1.50	3.00
248 Venerable Kumo C	.07	.15
249 Vine Kami C	.07	.15
250 Wear Away C	.07	.15
251 General's Kabuto R	3.00	6.00
252 Hair-Strung Koto R	.25	.50
253 Hankyu U	.12	.25
254 Honor-Worn Shaku U	2.50	5.00
255 Imi Statue R	.25	.50
256 Jade Idol U	.12	.25
257 Journeyer's Kite R	.60	1.25
258 Junkyo Bell R	.25	.50
259 Konda's Banner R	7.50	15.00
260 Kusari-Gama R	1.50	3.00
261 Long-Forgotten Gohei R	.25	.50
262 Moonring Mirror R	.25	.50
263 Nine-Ringed Bo U	.12	.25
264 No-Dachi U	.12	.25
265 Oathkeeper, Takeno's Daisho R	1.25	2.50
266 Orochi Hatchery R	.50	1.00
267 Reito Lantern U	.12	.25
268 Sensei's Divining Top U	50.00	100.00
269 Shell of the Last Kappa R	.25	.50
270 Tatsumasa, the Dragon's Fang R	1.50	3.00
271 Tenza, Godo's Maul U	1.25	2.50
272 Uba Mask R	3.00	6.00
273 Boseiju, Who Shelters All R	20.00	40.00
274 Cloudcrest Lake U	.12	.25
275 Eiganjo Castle R	10.00	20.00
276 Forbidden Orchard R	12.50	25.00
277 Hall of the Bandit Lord R	25.00	50.00
278 Lantern-Lit Graveyard U	.12	.25
279 Minamo, School at Water's Edge R	10.00	20.00
280 Okina, Temple to the Grandfathers R	4.00	8.00
281 Pinecrest Ridge U	.12	.25
282 Shinka, the Bloodsoaked Keep R	6.00	12.00
283 Shizo, Death's Storehouse R	12.50	25.00
284 Tranquil Garden U	.12	.25
285 Untaidake, the Cloud Keeper R	2.00	4.00
286 Waterveil Cavern U	.12	.25
287 Plains L	.15	.30
288 Plains L	.30	.60
289 Plains L	.20	.40
290 Plains L	.20	.40
291 Island L	.30	.60
292 Island L	.30	.60
293 Island L	.60	1.25
294 Island L	.30	.75
295 Swamp L	.30	.60
296 Swamp L	.20	.40
297 Swamp L	.20	.40
298 Swamp L	.30	.75
299 Mountain L	.50	1.00
300 Mountain L	.30	.60
301 Mountain L	.60	1.25
302 Mountain L	.30	.75
303 Forest L	.20	.40
304 Forest L	.50	1.00
305 Forest L	.20	.40
306 Forest L	.20	.40

2004 Magic The Gathering Darksteel

1 Auriok Glaivemaster C	.07	.15
2 Echoing Calm C	.07	.15
3 Emissary of Hope U	.10	.20
5 Leonin Battlemage U	.10	.20
6 Leonin Shikari R	4.00	8.00
7 Loxodon Mystic C	.07	.15
8 Metal Fatigue C	.07	.15
9 Pristine Angel R	.75	1.50
10 Pteron Ghost C	.07	.15
11 Pulse of the Fields R	.25	.50
12 Purge U	.10	.20
13 Ritual of Restoration C	.07	.15
14 Soulscour R	.30	.60
15 Steelshaper Apprentice R	.50	1.00
16 Stir the Pride U	.10	.20
17 Test of Faith U	.10	.20
18 Turn the Tables R	.25	.50
19 Carry Away U	.10	.20
20 Chromescale Drake R	.25	.50
21 Echoing Truth C	.15	.30
22 Hoverguard Observer U	.10	.20
23 Last Word R	.75	1.50
24 Machinate C	.07	.15
25 Magnetic Flux C	.07	.15
26 Neurok Prodigy C	.07	.15
27 Neurok Transmuter U	.10	.20
28 Psychic Overload U	.10	.20
29 Pulse of the Grid R	.50	1.00
30 Quicksilver Behemoth C	.07	.15
31 Reshape R	1.25	2.50
32 Retract R	4.00	8.00
33 Second Sight U	.10	.20
34 Synod Artificer R	.25	.50
35 Vedalken Engineer C	.07	.15
36 Vex C	.07	.15
37 Aether Snap R	.50	1.00
38 Burden of Greed C	.07	.15
39 Chittering Rats C	.30	.75
40 Death Cloud R	12.50	25.00
41 Echoing Decay C	.15	.30
42 Emissary of Despair U	.10	.20
43 Essence Drain C	.07	.15

44 Greater Harvester R	.25	.50
45 Grimclaw Bats C	.07	.15
46 Hunger of the Nim C	.07	.15
47 Mephitic Ooze R	.25	.50
48 Murderous Spoils U	.10	.20
49 Nim Abomination U	.10	.20
50 Pulse of the Dross R	.25	.50
51 Scavenging Scarab C	.07	.15
52 Screams from Within U	.15	.30
53 Scrounge U	.10	.20
54 Shriveling Rot R	.30	.60
55 Barbed Lightning C	.07	.15
56 Crazed Goblin C	.07	.15
57 Dismantle U	.10	.20
58 Drooling Ogre C	.07	.15
59 Echoing Ruin C	.07	.15
60 Fireball U	.10	.20
61 Flamebreak R	1.00	2.00
62 Furnace Dragon R	.25	.50
63 Goblin Archaeologist U	.30	.60
63 Goblin Archaeologist U	.30	.60
64 Inflame C	.07	.15
65 Krark-Clan Stoker C	.07	.15
66 Pulse of the Forge R	.30	.75
67 Savage Beating R	10.00	20.00
68 Shunt R	.30	.60
69 Slobad, Goblin Tinkerer R	.75	1.50
70 Tears of Rage U	.10	.20
71 Unforge C	.07	.15
72 Vulshok War Boar U	.10	.20
73 Ageless Entity R	.50	1.00
74 Echoing Courage C	.07	.15
75 Fangren Firstborn R	.60	1.25
76 Infested Roothold U	.10	.20
77 Karstoderm U	.10	.20
78 Nourish C	.07	.15
79 Oxidize U	.20	.40
80 Pulse of the Tangle R	.25	.50
81 Reap and Sow C	.15	.30
82 Rebuking Ceremony R	.25	.50
83 Roaring Slagwurm R	.25	.50
84 Stand Together U	.10	.20
85 Tangle Spider C	.07	.15
86 Tanglewalker U	.10	.20
87 Tel-Jilad Outrider C	.07	.15
88 Tel-Jilad Wolf C	.07	.15
89 Viridian Acolyte C	.07	.15
90 Viridian Zealot R	.30	.75
91 Aether Vial U	30.00	60.00
92 Angel's Feather U	.10	.20
93 Arcane Spyglass C	.07	.15
94 Arcbound Bruiser C	.07	.15
95 Arcbound Crusher U	.30	.75
96 Arcbound Fiend U	.10	.20
97 Arcbound Hybrid C	.07	.15
98 Arcbound Lancer U	.10	.20
99 Arcbound Overseer R	1.00	2.00
100 Arcbound Ravager R	7.50	15.00
101 Arcbound Reclaimer R	.75	1.50
102 Arcbound Slith U	.30	.60
103 Arcbound Stinger C	.07	.15
104 Arcbound Worker C	.15	.30
105 Auriok Siege Sled U	.10	.20
106 Chimeric Egg U	.10	.20
107 Coretapper U	.60	1.25
108 Darksteel Brute U	.10	.20
109 Darksteel Colossus R	6.00	12.00
110 Darksteel Forge R	10.00	20.00
111 Darksteel Gargoyle U	.20	.40
112 Darksteel Ingot C	.30	.75
113 Darksteel Pendant C	.07	.15
114 Darksteel Reactor R	4.00	8.00
115 Death-Mask Duplicant U	.10	.20
116 Demon's Horn U	.10	.20
117 Dragon's Claw U	.30	.60
118 Drill-Skimmer C	.07	.15
119 Dross Golem C	.07	.15
120 Eater of Days R	1.00	2.00
121 Gemini Engine R	.25	.50
122 Genesis Chamber U	.75	1.50
123 Geth's Grimoire U	4.00	8.00
124 Heartseeker R	2.50	5.00
125 Juggernaut U	.10	.20
126 Kraken's Eye U	.10	.20
127 Leonin Bola C	.07	.15
128 Lich's Tomb R	.25	.50
129 Memnarch R	7.50	15.00
130 Mycosynth Lattice R	25.00	50.00
131 Myr Landshaper C	.15	.30
132 Myr Matrix R	3.00	6.00
133 Myr Moonvessel C	.15	.30
134 Nemesis Mask U	1.00	2.00
135 Oxidda Golem C	.07	.15
136 Panoptic Mirror R	2.50	5.00
137 Razor Golem C	.07	.15
138 Serum Powder R	.50	1.00
139 Shield of Kaldra R	7.50	15.00
140 Skullclamp U	5.00	10.00
141 Spawning Pit U	2.50	5.00
142 Specter's Shroud U	.10	.20
143 Spellbinder R	.75	1.50
144 Spincrusher U	.10	.20
145 Spire Golem C	.20	.40
146 Sundering Titan R	.75	1.50
147 Surestrike Trident U	.75	1.50
148 Sword of Fire and Ice R	30.00	60.00
149 Sword of Light and Shadow R	17.50	35.00
150 Talon of Pain U	.10	.20
151 Tangle Golem C	.07	.15
152 Thought Dissector R	.25	.50
153 Thunderstaff U	.10	.20
154 Trinisphere R	12.50	25.00
155 Ur-Golem's Eye C	.30	.60
156 Voltaic Construct U	.50	1.00
157 Vulshok Morningstar C	.07	.15
158 Wand of the Elements R	.25	.50
159 Well of Lost Dreams R	6.00	12.00
160 Whispersilk Cloak C	.07	.15
161 Wirefly Hive U	.15	.30
162 Wurm's Tooth U	.15	.30
163 Blinkmoth Nexus R	2.00	4.00
164 Darksteel Citadel C	.30	.75
165 Mirrodin's Core U	.20	.40

2004 Magic The Gathering Fifth Dawn

1 Abuna's Chant C	.07	.15
2 Armed Response C	.07	.15
3 Auriok Champion R	30.00	60.00
4 Auriok Salvagers U	.20	.40
5 Auriok Windwalker R	.30	.60
6 Beacon of Immortality R	1.50	3.00
7 Bringer of the White Dawn R	1.25	2.50
8 Circle of Protection Artifacts U	.10	.20
9 Leonin Squire C	.07	.15
10 Loxodon Anchorite C	.07	.15
11 Loxodon Stalwart U	.10	.20
12 Raksha Golden Cub R	.30	.75
13 Retaliate R	.20	.40
14 Roar of Reclamation R	.30	.60
15 Skyhunter Prowler C	.07	.15
16 Skyhunter Skirmisher U	.10	.20
17 Stand Firm C	.07	.15
18 Stasis Cocoon C	.07	.15
19 Steelshaper's Gift U	20.00	40.00
20 Vanquish U	.10	.20
21 Acquire R	2.50	5.00
22 Advanced Hoverguard C	.07	.15
23 Artificer's Intuition R	1.50	3.00
24 Beacon of Tomorrows R	3.00	6.00
25 Blinkmoth Infusion R	1.00	2.00
26 Bringer of the Blue Dawn R	3.00	6.00
27 Condescend C	.20	.40
28 Disruption Aura U	.10	.20
30 Eyes of the Watcher U	.20	.40
31 Fold into Aether U	.10	.20
32 Hoverguard Sweepers R	.20	.40
33 Into Thin Air C	.07	.15
34 Plasma Elemental U	.10	.20
35 Qumulox U	.10	.20
36 Serum Visions C	1.25	2.50
37 Spectral Shift R	.30	.60
38 Thought Courier C	.07	.15
39 Trinket Mage C	.20	.40
40 Vedalken Mastermind U	.10	.20
41 Beacon of Unrest R	.60	1.25
42 Blind Creeper C	.07	.15
43 Bringer of the Black Dawn R	1.50	3.00
44 Cackling Imp C	.07	.15
45 Desecration Elemental R	.20	.40
46 Devour in Shadow U	.10	.20
47 Dross Crocodile C	.07	.15
48 Ebon Drake U	.10	.20
48 Ebon Drake U	.10	.20
49 Endless Whispers R	2.50	5.00
50 Fill with Fright C	.07	.15
51 Fleshgrafter C	.07	.15
52 Lose Hope C	.07	.15
53 Mephidross Vampire R	3.00	6.00
54 Moriok Rigger R	.20	.40
55 Night's Whisper U	4.00	8.00
56 Nim Grotesque U	.10	.20
57 Plunge into Darkness R	6.00	12.00
58 Relentless Rats U	1.25	2.50
59 Shattered Dreams U	.10	.20
60 Vicious Betrayal C	.07	.15
61 Beacon of Destruction R	.20	.40
62 Bringer of the Red Dawn R	1.25	2.50
63 Cosmic Larva R	.20	.40
64 Feedback Bolt U	.15	.30
65 Furnace Whelp U	.10	.20
66 Goblin Brawler C	.07	.15
67 Granulate R	.20	.40
68 Ion Storm R	.20	.40
69 Iron-Barb Hellion U	.10	.20
70 Krark-Clan Engineers U	.10	.20
71 Krark-Clan Ogre C	.07	.15
72 Magma Giant R	.20	.40
73 Magma Jet U	.17	.35
74 Magnetic Theft U	4.00	8.00
75 Mana Geyser C	1.25	2.50
76 Rain of Rust C	.07	.15
77 Reversal of Fortune R	.60	1.25
78 Screaming Fury C	.07	.15
79 Spark Elemental C	.20	.40
80 Vulshok Sorcerer C	.15	.30
81 All Suns' Dawn R	.30	.60
82 Beacon of Creation R	6.00	12.00
83 Bringer of the Green Dawn R	1.00	2.00
84 Channel the Suns U	.30	.60
85 Dawn's Reflection C	.07	.15
86 Eternal Witness U	.10	.20
87 Fangren Pathcutter U	.10	.20
88 Ferocious Charge C	.07	.15
89 Joiner Adept R	2.00	4.00
90 Ouphe Vandals U	.10	.20
91 Rite of Passage R	1.25	2.50
92 Rude Awakening R	.60	1.25
93 Sylvok Explorer C	.07	.15
94 Tangle Asp C	.07	.15
95 Tel-Jilad Justice U	.10	.20
96 Tel-Jilad Lifebreather C	.07	.15
97 Tornado Elemental R	.20	.40
98 Tyrranax C	.07	.15
99 Viridian Lorebearers U	.10	.20
100 Viridian Scout C	.07	.15
101 Anodet Lurker C	.07	.15
102 Arachnoid U	.10	.20
103 Arcbound Wanderer U	.10	.20
104 Avarice Totem U	.20	.40
105 Baton of Courage C	.07	.15
106 Battered Golem C	.20	.40
107 Blasting Station U	4.00	8.00
108 Chimeric Coils U	.10	.20
109 Clearwater Goblet R	.50	1.00
110 Clock of Omens U	.50	1.00
111 Composite Golem U	.30	.60
112 Conjurer's Bauble C	.30	.75
113 Cranial Plating C	.07	.15
114 Crucible of Worlds R	30.00	60.00
115 Door to Nothingness R	1.00	2.00
116 Doubling Cube R	20.00	40.00
117 Energy Chamber U	.30	.75
118 Engineered Explosives R	6.00	12.00
119 Ensouled Scimitar U	.10	.20
120 Eon Hub R	.75	1.50
121 Etched Oracle U	.10	.20
122 Ferropede U	.20	.40
123 Fist of Suns R	5.00	10.00
124 Gemstone Array U	1.25	2.50
125 Goblin Cannon U	.20	.40
126 Grafted Wargear U	1.00	2.00
127 Grinding Station U	10.00	20.00
128 Guardian Idol U	.75	1.50
129 Healer's Headdress C	.07	.15
130 Heliophial C	.07	.15
131 Helm of Kaldra R	4.00	8.00
132 Horned Helm C	.07	.15
133 Infused Arrows U	.10	.20
134 Krark-Clan Ironworks U	20.00	40.00
135 Lantern of Insight U	.75	1.50
136 Lunar Avenger U	.10	.20
137 Mycosynth Golem R	17.50	35.00
138 Myr Quadropod C	.07	.15
139 Myr Servitor C	.07	.15
140 Neurok Stealthsuit C	.60	1.25
141 Opaline Bracers C	.07	.15
142 Paradise Mantle U	6.00	12.00
143 Pentad Prism C	.20	.40
144 Possessed Portal R	2.00	4.00
145 Razorgrass Screen C	.07	.15
146 Razormane Masticore R	.20	.40
147 Relic Barrier U	.10	.20
148 Salvaging Station R	.75	1.50
149 Sawtooth Thresher C	.07	.15
150 Silent Arbiter R	2.00	4.00
151 Skullcage U	.10	.20
152 Skyreach Manta C	.07	.15
153 Solarion R	.30	.75
154 Sparring Collar C	.07	.15
155 Spinal Parasite U	.10	.20
156 Staff of Domination R	12.50	25.00
157 Summoner's Egg R	2.00	4.00
158 Summoning Station R	1.25	2.50
159 Suncrusher R	.20	.40
1.60E+02 Suntouched Myr C	.07	.15
1.61E+02 Synod Centurion U	.10	.20
1.62E+02 Thermal Navigator C	.07	.15
1.63E+02 Vedalken Orrery R	30.00	60.00
1.64E+02 Vedalken Shackles R	5.00	10.00
1.65E+02 Wayfarer's Bauble C	3.00	6.00

2004 Magic The Gathering Unhinged

1.00E+00 Atinlay Igpay U	.20	.40
2 AWOL C	.30	.60
3 Bosom Buddy U	.20	.40
4 Cardpecker C	.10	.20
5 Cheap Ass C	.10	.20
6 Circle of Protection Art C	.10	.20
7 Collector Protector R	.30	.60
8 Drawn Together R	.30	.60
9 Emcee U	.30	.60
10 Erase C	.10	.20
11 Fascist Art Director C	.10	.20
12 First Come, First Served U	.20	.40
13 Frankie Peanuts R	1.25	2.50
14 Head to Head U	.20	.40
15 Ladies' Knight U	.20	.40
16 Little Girl C	.20	.40
17 Look at Me, I'm R&D R	.60	1.25
18 Man of Measure C	.10	.20
19 Save Life U	.20	.40
20 Standing Army C	.10	.20
21 Staying Power R	1.25	2.50
22 Wordmail C	.10	.20
23 ___ U	.50	1.00
24 Ambiguity R	.75	1.50
25 Artful Looter C	.10	.20
26 Avatar of Me R	1.00	2.00
27 Brushstroke Paintermage C	.10	.20
28 Bursting Beebles C	.10	.20
29 Carnivorous Death-Parrot C	.20	.40
30 Cheatyface U	1.00	2.00
31 Double Header C	.10	.20
32 Flaccify C	.10	.20
33 Framed! C	.10	.20
34 Greater Morphling R	2.00	4.00
35 Johnny, Combo Player R	2.50	5.00
36 Loose Lips C	.10	.20
37 Magical Hacker U	.30	.60
38 Mise U	.20	.40
39 Moniker Mage C	.10	.20
40 Mouth to Mouth U	.20	.40
41 Now I Know My ABC's R	2.00	4.00
42 Number Crunch C	.10	.20
43 Question Elemental? U	.20	.40
44 Richard Garfield, Ph.D. R	2.50	5.00
45 Smart Ass C	.10	.20
46 Spell Counter U	.75	1.50
47 Topsy Turvy R	.75	1.50
48 Aesthetic Consultation R	.30	.60
49 Bad Ass C	.10	.20
50 Bloodletter C	.10	.20
51 Booster Tutor U	.50	1.00
52 Duh C	.15	.30
53 Enter the Dungeon R	1.50	3.00
54 Eye to Eye U	.25	.50
55 The Fallen Apart C	.10	.20
56 Farewell to Arms C	.20	.40
57 Infernal Spawn of Infernal Spawn of Evil R	1.00	2.00
58 Kill! Destroy! U	1.00	2.00
59 Mother of Goons C	.10	.20
60 Necro-Impotence R	.30	.60
61 Persecute Artist U	.20	.40
62 Phyrexian Librarian U	.20	.40
63 Stop That C	.10	.20
64 Tainted Monkey C	.10	.20
65 Vile Bile C	.10	.20
66 Wet Willie of the Damned C	.10	.20
67 When Fluffy Bunnies Attack C	.10	.20
68 Working Stiff U	.20	.40
69 Zombie Fanboy U	.20	.40
70 Zzzyxas's Abyss R	1.00	2.00
71 Assquatch R	2.00	4.00
72 Blast from the Past R	2.00	4.00
73 Curse of the Fire Penguin R	1.00	2.00
74 Deal Damage U	.20	.40
75 Dumb Ass C	.15	.30
76 Face to Face U	.25	.50
77 Frazzled Editor C	.30	.60
78 Goblin Mime C	.10	.20
79 Goblin Secret Agent C	.10	.20
80 Goblin S.W.A.T. Team C	.10	.20
81 Mana Flair C	.10	.20
82 Mons's Goblin Waiters C	.10	.20
83 Orcish Paratroopers C	.10	.20
84 Punctuate C	.10	.20
85 Pygmy Giant U	.20	.40
86 Red-Hot Hottie C	.10	.20
87 Rocket-Powered Turbo Slug U	.30	.75
88 Saute C	.30	.75
89 Six-y Beast U	.20	.40
90 Touch and Go C	.10	.20
91 Yet Another Aether Vortex R	1.00	2.00
92 B-I-N-G-O R	.75	1.50
93 Creature Guy U	.20	.40
94 Elvish House Party U	.20	.40
95 Fat Ass C	.15	.30
96 Form of the Squirrel R	4.00	8.00
97 Fraction Jackson R	.30	.60
98 Gluetius Maximus U	.20	.40
99 Granny's Payback U	.25	.50
100 Graphic Violence C	.10	.20
101 Keeper of the Sacred Word C	.10	.20
102 Land Aid '04 C	.10	.20
103 Laughing Hyena C	.10	.20
104 Monkey Monkey Monkey C	.10	.20
105 Name Dropping U	.20	.40
106 Old Fogey R	1.00	2.00
107 Our Market Research Shows That Players Like/Really Long Card Names So We Mad This Card to Have the/Absolute Longest Card Name Ever Elemental C	.10	.20
108 Remodel C	.10	.20
109 Shoe Tree C	.10	.20
110 Side to Side U	.20	.40
111 S.N.O.T. C	.10	.20
112 Stone-Cold Basilisk U	.20	.40
113 Supersize C	.10	.20
114 Symbol Status U	.20	.40
115 Uktabi Kong R	.60	1.25
116 Ach! Hans, Run! R	3.00	6.00
117 Ass Whuppin' R	.60	1.25
118 Meddling Kids R	.75	1.50
119 Rare-B-Gone R	1.00	2.00
120 Who/What/When/Where/Why R	2.00	4.00
121 Gleemax R	2.50	5.00
122 Letter Bomb R	2.50	5.00
123 Mana Screw U	.75	1.50
124 Mox Lotus R	12.50	25.00
125 My First Tome U	.20	.40
126 Pointy Finger of Doom R	1.25	2.50
127 Rod of Spanking U	.50	1.00
128 Time Machine R	.75	1.50
129 Togglodyte U	.20	.40
130 Toy Boat U	.20	.40
131 Urza's Hot Tub U	.20	.40
132 Water Gun Balloon Game R	1.00	2.00
133 World-Bottling Kit R	.30	.75
134 City of Ass R	12.50	25.00
135 R&D's Secret Lair R	2.50	5.00
136 Plains L	2.50	5.00
137 Island L	2.50	5.00
138 Swamp L	2.50	5.00
139 Mountain L	2.50	5.00
140 Forest L	2.50	5.00
141 Super Secret Tech R	.30	.60

2005 Magic The Gathering Betrayers of Kamigawa

1 Day of Destiny R	4.00	8.00
2 Empty-Shrine Kannushi U	.10	.20
3 Faithful Squire/Kaiso, Memory of Loyalty U	.10	.20
4 Final Judgment R	2.00	4.00
5 Genju of the Fields U	.10	.20
6 Heart of Light C	.07	.15
7 Hokori, Dust Drinker R	5.00	10.00
8 Hundred-Talon Strike C	.07	.15
9 Indebted Samurai U	.30	.75
10 Kami of False Hope C	.75	1.50
11 Kami of Tattered Shoji C	.07	.15
12 Kami of the Honored Dead U	.10	.20
13 Kentaro, the Smiling Cat R	1.25	2.50
14 Kitsune Palliator U	.10	.20
15 Mending Hands C	.07	.15
16 Moonlit Strider C	.07	.15
17 Opal-Eye, Konda's Yojimbo R	3.00	6.00
18 Oyobi, Who Split the Heavens R	.75	1.50
19 Patron of the Kitsune R	1.00	2.00
20 Scour U	.10	.20
21 Shining Shoal R	.75	1.50
22 Silverstorm Samurai C	.07	.15
23 Split-Tail Miko C	.07	.15
24 Takeno's Cavalry C	.07	.15
25 Tallowisp U	.30	.60
26 Terashi's Grasp C	.07	.15
27 Terashi's Verdict U	.10	.20
28 Ward of Piety U	.10	.20
29 Waxmane Baku C	.07	.15
30 Yomiji, Who Bars the Way R	2.00	4.00
31 Callow Jushi/Jaraku the Interloper U	.10	.20
32 Chisei, Heart of Oceans R	.60	1.25
33 Disrupting Shoal R	.75	1.50
34 Floodbringer C	.07	.15
35 Genju of the Falls U	.10	.20
36 Heed the Mists U	.10	.20
37 Higure, the Still Wind R	5.00	10.00
38 Jetting Glasskite U	.10	.20
39 Kaijin of the Vanishing Touch U	.20	.40
40 Kira, Great Glass-Spinner R	7.50	15.00
41 Minamo Sightbender U	.10	.20
42 Minamo's Meddling C	.07	.15
43 Mistblade Shinobi C	.60	1.25
44 Ninja of the Deep Hours C	.60	1.25
45 Patron of the Moon R	2.00	4.00
46 Phantom Wings C	.07	.15
47 Quash U	.10	.20
48 Quillmane Baku C	.07	.15
49 Reduce to Dreams R	.25	.50
50 Ribbons of the Reikai C	.07	.15
51 Shimmering Glasskite C	.07	.15
52 Soratami Mindsweeper U	.10	.20
53 Stream of Consciousness U	.10	.20

54 Sway of the Stars R	.30	.75
55 Teardrop Kami C	.07	.15
56 Threads of Disloyalty R	.30	.75
57 Toils of Night and Day C	.07	.15
58 Tomorrow, Azami's Familiar R	.75	1.50
59 Veil of Secrecy C	.07	.15
60 Walker of Secret Ways U	2.50	5.00
61 Bile Urchin C	.07	.15
61 Bile Urchin C	.07	.15
62 Blessing of Leeches C	.30	.75
63 Call for Blood C	.07	.15
64 Crawling Filth C	.07	.15
65 Eradicate U	.10	.20
66 Genju of the Fens U	.10	.20
67 Goryo's Vengeance R	3.00	6.00
68 Hero's Demise R	1.00	2.00
69 Hired Muscle/Scarmaker U	.10	.20
70 Horobi's Whisper C	.07	.15
71 Ink-Eyes, Servant of Oni R	10.00	20.00
72 Kyoki, Sanity's Eclipse R	.75	1.50
73 Mark of the Oni U	.25	.50
74 Nezumi Shadow-Watcher U	.20	.40
75 Ogre Marauder U	.17	.35
76 Okiba-Gang Shinobi C	.60	1.25
77 Patron of the Nezumi R	.25	.50
78 Psychic Spear C	.07	.15
79 Pus Kami U	.10	.20
80 Scourge of Numai U	.10	.20
81 Shirei, Shizo's Caretaker R	.75	1.50
82 Sickening Shoal R	2.00	4.00
83 Skullmane Baku C	.07	.15
84 Skullsnatcher C	.30	.60
85 Stir the Grave C	.07	.15
86 Takenuma Bleeder C	.07	.15
87 Three Tragedies U	.10	.20
88 Throat Slitter U	5.00	10.00
89 Toshiro Umezawa R	10.00	20.00
90 Yukora, the Prisoner R	.25	.50
91 Akki Blizzard-Herder C	.07	.15
92 Akki Raider U	.10	.20
93 Ashen Monstrosity U	.10	.20
94 Aura Barbs U	.10	.20
95 Blademane Baku C	.07	.15
96 Blazing Shoal R	1.25	2.50
97 Clash of Realities R	.25	.50
98 Crack the Earth C	.15	.30
99 Cunning Bandit/Azamuki, Treachery Incarnate U	.10	.20
100 First Volley C	.07	.15
101 Flames of the Blood Hand U	.25	.50
102 Frost Ogre C	.07	.15
103 Frostling C	.07	.15
104 Fumiko the Lowblood R	.75	1.50
105 Genju of the Spires U	.10	.20
106 Goblin Cohort C	.17	.35
107 Heartless Hidetsugu R	2.50	5.00
108 In the Web of War R	1.50	3.00
109 Ire of Kaminari C	.07	.15
110 Ishi-Ishi, Akki Crackshot R	.25	.50
111 Kumano's Blessing C	.07	.15
112 Mannichi, the Fevered Dream R	.25	.50
113 Ogre Recluse U	.10	.20
114 Overblaze U	.25	.50
115 Patron of the Akki R	.25	.50
116 Ronin Cliffrider U	.20	.40
117 Shinka Gatekeeper C	.07	.15
118 Sowing Salt U	.10	.20
119 Torrent of Stone C	.07	.15
120 Twist Allegiance R	.25	.50
121 Body of Jukai U	.10	.20
122 Budoka Pupil/Ichiga, Who Topples Oaks U	.10	.20
123 Child of Thorns C	.07	.15
124 Enshrined Memories R	.30	.75
125 Forked-Branch Garami U	.10	.20
126 Genju of the Cedars U	.17	.35
127 Gnarled Mass C	.07	.15
128 Harbinger of Spring C	.07	.15
129 Isao, Enlightened Bushi R	.50	1.00
131 Kodama of the Center Tree R	.25	.50
132 Lifegift R	12.50	25.00
133 Lifespinner U	.30	.60
134 Loam Dweller U	.20	.40
135 Mark of Sakiko U	.25	.50
136 Matsu-Tribe Sniper C	.07	.15
137 Nourishing Shoal R	.75	1.50
138 Patron of the Orochi R	5.00	10.00
139 Petalmane Baku C	.07	.15
140 Roar of Jukai C	.07	.15
141 Sakiko, Mother of Summer R	2.50	5.00
142 Sakura-Tribe Springcaller C	.07	.15
143 Scaled Hulk C	.07	.15
144 Shizuko, Caller of Autumn R	3.00	6.00
145 Sosuke's Summons U	.30	.75
146 Splinter U	.20	.40
147 Traproot Kami C	.20	.40
148 Unchecked Growth U	.10	.20
149 Uproot C	.07	.15
150 Vital Surge C	.07	.15
151 Genju of the Realm R	3.00	6.00
152 Baku Altar R	.25	.50
153 Blinding Powder U	.20	.40
154 Mirror Gallery R	20.00	40.00
155 Neko-Te R	3.00	6.00
156 Orb of Dreams R	3.00	6.00
157 Ornate Kanzashi R	.25	.50
158 Ronin Warclub U	.25	.50
159 Shuko U	3.00	6.00
160 Shuriken U	.20	.40
161 Slumbering Tora R	.25	.50
162 That Which Was Taken R	6.00	12.00
163 Umezawa's Jitte R	17.50	35.00
164 Gods' Eye, Gate to the Reikai U	.20	.40
165 Tendo Ice Bridge R	3.00	6.00

2005 Magic The Gathering European Junior Series

1.00E+05 Slith Firewalker R	.50	1.00
1.00E+06 Sakura-Tribe Elder R	15.00	30.00
1.00E+07 Soltari Priest R	2.00	4.00
1.00E+08 Glorious Anthem R	25.00	50.00
2.00E+05 Royal Assassin R	40.00	80.00
2.00E+06 Shard Phoenix R	7.50	15.00
2.00E+07 Whirling Dervish R	.50	1.00
2.00E+08 Elvish Champion R	125.00	250.00

2005 Magic The Gathering Judge Gift Rewards

1 Gemstone Mine R	30.00	75.00
2 Regrowth R	20.00	40.00
3 Sol Ring R	250.00	500.00
4 Mishra's Factory R	20.00	40.00

2005 Magic The Gathering Magic Premiere Shop

287 Plains L	20.00	40.00
288 Plains L	4.00	8.00
289 Plains L	12.50	25.00
290 Plains L	12.50	25.00
291 Island L	12.50	25.00
292 Island L	20.00	40.00
293 Island L	15.00	30.00
294 Island L	17.50	35.00
295 Swamp L	15.00	30.00
296 Swamp L	15.00	30.00
297 Swamp L	12.50	25.00
298 Swamp L	12.50	25.00
299 Mountain L	12.50	25.00
300 Mountain L	10.00	20.00
301 Mountain L	10.00	20.00
302 Mountain L	12.50	25.00
303 Forest L	30.00	75.00
304 Forest L	12.50	25.00
305 Forest L	12.50	25.00
306 Forest L	15.00	30.00

2005 Magic The Gathering Ninth Edition

1 Angel of Mercy U	.10	.20
2 Angelic Blessing C	.07	.15
3 Aven Cloudchaser C	.07	.15
4 Aven Flock C	.07	.15
5 Ballista Squad U	.10	.20
6 Blessed Orator U	.10	.20
7 Blinding Angel R	1.50	3.00
8 Blinking Spirit R	.20	.40
9 Chastise U	.10	.20
10 Circle of Protection Black U	.10	.20
11 Circle of Protection Red U	.30	.60
12 Crossbow Infantry C	.07	.15
13 Demystify C	.07	.15
14 Foot Soldiers C	.07	.15
15 Gift of Estates U	2.00	4.00
16 Glorious Anthem R	.60	1.25
17 Glory Seeker C	.07	.15
18 Holy Day C	.07	.15
19 Holy Strength C	.07	.15
20 Honor Guard C	.07	.15
21 Infantry Veteran C	.07	.15
22 Inspirit U	.10	.20
23 Ivory Mask R	.60	1.25
24 Kami of Old Stone U	.10	.20
25 Leonin Skyhunter U	.10	.20
26 Marble Titan R	1.50	3.00
27 Master Decoy C	.07	.15
28 Master Healer R	.20	.40
29 Mending Hands C	.07	.15
30 Oracle's Attendants R	.20	.40
31 Pacifism C	.07	.15
32 Paladin en-Vec R	.50	1.00
33 Peace of Mind U	.10	.20
34 Pegasus Charger C	.07	.15
35 Reverse Damage R	.20	.40
36 Righteousness R	.20	.40
37 Sacred Ground R	.20	.40
38 Sacred Nectar C	.07	.15
39 Samite Healer C	.07	.15
40 Sanctum Guardian U	.10	.20
41 Savannah Lions R	.50	1.00
42 Seasoned Marshal U	.10	.20
43 Serra Angel R	.20	.40
44 Serra's Blessing U	.50	1.00
45 Skyhunter Prowler C	.07	.15
46 Soul Warden U	.50	1.00
47 Spirit Link U	.50	1.00
48 Story Circle R	.60	1.25
49 Suntail Hawk C	.07	.15
50 Tempest of Light U	.10	.20
51 Venerable Monk C	.07	.15
52 Veteran Cavalier C	.07	.15
53 Warrior's Honor C	.07	.15
54 Weathered Wayfarer R	6.00	12.00
55 Worship R	1.25	2.50
56 Wrath of God R	5.00	10.00
57 Zealous Inquisitor U	.10	.20
58 Air Elemental U	.10	.20
59 Annex U	.20	.40
60 Archivist R	.20	.40
61 Aven Fisher C	.07	.15
62 Aven Windreader C	.07	.15
63 Azure Drake U	.10	.20
64 Baleful Stare U	.10	.20
65 Battle of Wits R	.20	.40
66 Boomerang C	.07	.15
67 Clone R	.30	.60
68 Confiscate U	.10	.20
69 Counsel of the Soratami C	.07	.15
70 Cowardice R	.30	.60
71 Crafty Pathmage C	.07	.15
72 Daring Apprentice R	.25	.50
73 Dehydration C	.07	.15
74 Dream Prowler U	.10	.20
75 Evacuation R	5.00	10.00
76 Exhaustion U	.30	.75
77 Fishliver Oil C	.07	.15
78 Fleeting Image R	.20	.40
79 Flight C	.07	.15
80 Fugitive Wizard C	.07	.15
81 Horned Turtle C	.07	.15
82 Imaginary Pet R	.20	.40
83 Levitation U	.10	.20
84 Lumengrid Warden C	.07	.15
85 Mahamoti Djinn R	.20	.40
86 Mana Leak C	.15	.30
87 Mind Bend R	.20	.40
88 Phantom Warrior U	.10	.20
89 Plagiarize R	.20	.40
90 Polymorph R	1.00	2.00
91 Puppeteer U	.10	.20
92 Reminisce U	.10	.20
93 Remove Soul C	.07	.15
94 Rewind U	.30	.60
95 Sage Aven C	.07	.15
96 Sea Monster C	.07	.15
97 Sea's Claim C	.15	.30
98 Sift C	.07	.15
99 Sleight of Hand C	.60	1.25
100 Storm Crow C	.07	.15
101 Telepathy U	.25	.50
102 Temporal Adept R	.30	.75
103 Thieving Magpie U	.10	.20
104 Thought Courier U	.10	.20
105 Tidal Kraken R	.75	1.50
106 Tidings U	.10	.20
107 Time Ebb C	.07	.15
108 Trade Routes R	3.00	6.00
109 Traumatize R	2.50	5.00
110 Treasure Trove U	.10	.20
111 Wanderguard Sentry C	.07	.15
112 Wind Drake C	.07	.15
113 Withering Gaze U	.10	.20
114 Zur's Weirding R	.75	1.50
115 Blackmail U	.50	1.00
116 Bog Imp C	.07	.15
117 Bog Wraith U	.10	.20
118 Coercion C	.07	.15
119 Consume Spirit U	.10	.20
120 Contaminated Bond C	.07	.15
121 Cruel Edict U	.10	.20
122 Dark Banishing C	.07	.15
123 Death Pits of Rath R	.50	1.00
124 Deathgazer U	.10	.20
125 Diabolic Tutor U	.75	1.50
126 Drudge Skeletons U	.10	.20
127 Enfeeblement C	.07	.15
128 Execute U	.10	.20
129 Fear C	.07	.15
130 Festering Goblin C	.07	.15
131 Final Punishment R	.20	.40
132 Foul Imp C	.07	.15
133 Giant Cockroach C	.07	.15
134 Gluttonous Zombie U	.10	.20
135 Grave Pact R	17.50	35.00
136 Gravedigger C	.07	.15
137 Hell's Caretaker R	1.50	3.00
138 Highway Robber C	.07	.15
139 Hollow Dogs C	.07	.15
140 Horror of Horrors U	.10	.20
141 Hypnotic Specter R	1.25	2.50
142 Looming Shade C	.07	.15
143 Lord of the Undead R	10.00	20.00
144 Megrim U	.25	.50
145 Mind Rot C	.07	.15
146 Mindslicer R	12.50	25.00
147 Mortivore R	1.50	3.00
148 Nantuko Husk U	.15	.30
149 Nekrataal U	.10	.20
150 Nightmare R	.20	.40
151 Persecute R	.20	.40
152 Phyrexian Arena R	10.00	20.00
153 Phyrexian Gargantua U	.10	.20
154 Plague Beetle C	.07	.15
155 Plague Wind R	1.25	2.50
156 Raise Dead C	.07	.15
157 Ravenous Rats C	.07	.15
158 Razortooth Rats C	.07	.15
159 Royal Assassin R	.60	1.25
160 Scathe Zombies C	.07	.15
161 Sengir Vampire R	.30	.75
162 Serpent Warrior C	.07	.15
163 Slay U	.10	.20
164 Soul Feast U	.10	.20
165 Spineless Thug C	.07	.15
166 Swarm of Rats U	.75	1.50
167 Underworld Dreams R	1.25	2.50
168 Unholy Strength C	.07	.15
169 Will-o'-the-Wisp R	.60	1.25
170 Yawgmoth Demon R	.20	.40
171 Zombify U	.20	.40
172 Anaba Shaman C	.07	.15
173 Anarchist U	.10	.20
174 Balduvian Barbarians C	.07	.15
175 Blaze U	.10	.20
176 Blood Moon R	7.50	15.00
177 Bloodfire Colossus R	.20	.40
178 Boiling Seas U	.50	1.00
179 Demolish U	.10	.20
180 Enrage U	.10	.20
181 Firebreathing C	.07	.15
182 Flame Wave U	.10	.20
183 Flashfires U	.10	.20
184 Flowstone Crusher U	.10	.20
185 Flowstone Shambler C	.07	.15
186 Flowstone Slide R	.20	.40
187 Form of the Dragon R	.30	.75
188 Furnace of Rath R	4.00	8.00
189 Goblin Balloon Brigade U	.10	.20
190 Goblin Brigand C	.07	.15
191 Goblin Chariot C	.07	.15
192 Goblin King R	2.00	4.00
193 Goblin Mountaineer C	.07	.15
194 Goblin Piker C	.07	.15
195 Goblin Sky Raider C	.07	.15
196 Guerrilla Tactics U	.10	.20
197 Hill Giant C	.07	.15
198 Karplusan Yeti R	.20	.40
199 Kird Ape U	.20	.40
200 Lava Axe C	.07	.15
201 Lightning Elemental C	.07	.15
202 Magnivore R	.20	.40
203 Mana Clash R	.50	1.00
204 Mogg Sentry R	.30	.60
205 Ogre Taskmaster U	.25	.50
206 Orcish Artillery U	.10	.20
207 Panic Attack C	.07	.15
208 Pyroclasm U	.10	.20
209 Raging Goblin C	.07	.15
210 Rathi Dragon R	.20	.40
211 Reflexes C	.07	.15
212 Relentless Assault R	1.00	2.00
213 Rogue Kavu C	.07	.15
214 Rukh Egg R	.20	.40
215 Sandstone Warrior C	.07	.15
216 Seething Song C	1.25	2.50
217 Shard Phoenix R	.20	.40
218 Shatter C	.07	.15
219 Shivan Dragon R	.20	.40
220 Shock C	.07	.15
221 Stone Rain C	.20	.40
222 Sudden Impact U	.10	.20
223 Threaten U	.10	.20
224 Thundermare R	.30	.60
225 Viashino Sandstalker U	.10	.20
226 Volcanic Hammer C	.07	.15
227 Whip Sergeant U	.10	.20
228 Wildfire R	.20	.40
229 Anaconda U	.10	.20
230 Ancient Silverback R	.20	.40
231 Biorhythm R	.60	1.25
232 Blanchwood Armor U	.10	.20
233 Craw Wurm C	.07	.15
234 Creeping Mold U	.10	.20
235 Early Harvest R	1.50	3.00
236 Elvish Bard U	.10	.20
237 Elvish Berserker C	.07	.15
238 Elvish Champion R	7.50	15.00
239 Elvish Piper R	4.00	8.00
240 Elvish Warrior C	.07	.15
241 Emperor Crocodile R	.20	.40
242 Force of Nature R	.20	.40
243 Giant Growth C	.07	.15
244 Giant Spider C	.07	.15
245 Greater Good R	6.00	12.00
246 Grizzly Bears C	.07	.15
247 Groundskeeper U	.10	.20
248 Hunted Wumpus U	.10	.20
249 Kavu Climber C	.07	.15
250 King Cheetah U	.10	.20
251 Ley Druid U	.10	.20
252 Llanowar Behemoth U	.10	.20
253 Llanowar Elves C	.07	.15
254 Maro R	.20	.40
255 Might of Oaks R	.20	.40
256 Natural Affinity R	.50	1.00
257 Natural Spring C	.07	.15
258 Naturalize C	.07	.15
259 Needle Storm U	.10	.20
260 Norwood Ranger C	.07	.15
261 Order of the Sacred Bell C	.07	.15
262 Overgrowth C	.20	.40
263 Rampant Growth C	.60	1.25
264 Reclaim C	.07	.15
265 Regeneration U	.10	.20
266 River Bear U	2.50	5.00
267 Rootbreaker Wurm U	.10	.20
268 Rootwalla C	.07	.15
269 Scaled Wurm C	.07	.15
270 Seedborn Muse R	7.50	15.00
271 Silklash Spider R	.30	.75
272 Stream of Life U	.10	.20
273 Summer Bloom U	2.00	4.00
274 Trained Armodon C	.07	.15
275 Tree Monkey C	.07	.15
276 Treetop Bracers C	.07	.15
277 Utopia Tree R	1.50	3.00
278 Verdant Force R	.20	.40
279 Verduran Enchantress R	2.50	5.00
280 Viridian Shaman U	.10	.20
281 Web U	.10	.20
282 Weird Harvest R	1.25	2.50
283 Wood Elves C	.30	.75
284 Yavimaya Enchantress U	.10	.20
285 Zodiac Monkey C	.07	.15
286 Aladdin's Ring R	.20	.40
287 Angel's Feather U	.10	.20
288 Beast of Burden R	.25	.50
289 Booby Trap R	.20	.40
290 Bottle Gnomes U	.10	.20
291 Coat of Arms R	7.50	15.00
292 Dancing Scimitar U	.10	.20
293 Defense Grid R	7.50	15.00
294 Demon's Horn U	.10	.20
295 Disrupting Scepter R	.20	.40
296 Dragon's Claw U	.25	.50
297 Fellwar Stone U	4.00	8.00
298 Howling Mine R	3.00	6.00
299 Icy Manipulator U	.20	.40
300 Jade Statue R	.20	.40
301 Jester's Cap R	2.00	4.00
302 Kraken's Eye U	.10	.20
303 Loxodon Warhammer R	.20	.40
304 Millstone R	.20	.40
305 Ornithopter U	.20	.40
306 Phyrexian Hulk U	.10	.20
307 Rod of Ruin U	.10	.20
308 Slate of Ancestry R	4.00	8.00
309 Spellbook U	1.50	3.00
310 Storage Matrix R	2.50	5.00
311 Tanglebloom U	.10	.20
312 Teferi's Puzzle Box R	4.00	8.00
313 Thran Golem R	.20	.40
314 Ur-Golem's Eye U	.50	1.00
315 Vulshok Morningstar U	.10	.20
316 Wurm's Tooth U	.10	.20
317 Adarkar Wastes R	7.50	15.00
318 Battlefield Forge R	1.50	3.00
319 Brushland R	4.00	8.00
320 Caves of Koilos R	1.25	2.50
321 Karplusan Forest R	3.00	6.00
322 Llanowar Wastes R	1.25	2.50
323 Quicksand U	.10	.20
324 Shivan Reef R	3.00	6.00
325 Sulfurous Springs R	7.50	15.00
326 Underground River R	6.00	12.00
327 Urza's Mine U	1.50	3.00
328 Urza's Power Plant U	1.50	3.00
329 Urza's Tower U	2.00	4.00
330 Yavimaya Coast R	1.50	3.00
331 Plains L	.20	.40
332 Plains L	.12	.25
333 Plains L	.15	.30
334 Plains L	.20	.40
335 Island L	.25	.50
336 Island L	.17	.35
337 Island L	.25	.50
338 Island L	.10	.20
339 Swamp L	.60	1.25

340 Swamp L .30 .60
341 Swamp L .25 .50
342 Swamp L .25 .50
343 Mountain L .30 .60
344 Mountain L .17 .35
345 Mountain L .50 1.00
346 Mountain L .25 .50
347 Forest L .50 1.00
348 Forest L .30 .60
349 Forest L .17 .35
350 Forest L .17 .35
S1 Eager Cadet C .15 .30
S2 Vengeance U .10 .20
S3 Coral Eel C .15 .30
S4 Giant Octopus C .07 .15
S5 Index C .07 .15
S7 Vizzerdrix R .20 .40
S8 Goblin Raider C .07 .15
S9 Enormous Baloth U .20 .40
S10 Spined Wurm C .07 .15

2005 Magic The Gathering Ravnica City of Guilds

1 Auratouched Mage U .15 .30
2 Bathe in Light U .17 .35
3 Benevolent Ancestor C .07 .15
4 Blazing Archon R 1.50 3.00
5 Boros Fury-Shield C .07 .15
6 Caregiver C .07 .15
7 Chant of Vitu-Ghazi U .10 .20
8 Concerted Effort R 6.00 12.00
9 Conclave Equenaut C .07 .15
10 Conclave Phalanx U .10 .20
11 Conclave's Blessing C .07 .15
12 Courier Hawk C .07 .15
13 Devouring Light U .10 .20
14 Divebomber Griffin U .10 .20
15 Dromad Purebred C .07 .15
16 Faith's Fetters C .07 .15
17 Festival of the Guildpact U .10 .20
18 Flickerform R .75 1.50
19 Gate Hound C .07 .15
20 Ghosts of the Innocent R .20 .40
21 Hour of Reckoning R .50 1.00
22 Hunted Lammasu R .30 .60
23 Leave No Trace C .30 .75
24 Light of Sanction R .20 .40
25 Loxodon Gatekeeper R 2.50 5.00
26 Nightguard Patrol C .07 .15
27 Oathsworn Giant U .60 1.25
28 Sandsower U .10 .20
29 Screeching Griffin C .07 .15
30 Seed Spark U .20 .40
31 Suppression Field U 1.00 2.00
32 Three Dreams R 1.25 2.50
33 Twilight Drover R 2.00 4.00
34 Veteran Armorer C .07 .15
35 Votary of the Conclave C .07 .15
36 Wojek Apothecary U .10 .20
37 Wojek Siren C .07 .15
38 Belltower Sphinx U .10 .20
39 Cerulean Sphinx R .20 .40
40 Compulsive Research C .07 .15
41 Convolute C .07 .15
42 Copy Enchantment R 7.50 15.00
43 Dizzy Spell C .20 .40
44 Drake Familiar C .07 .15
45 Dream Leash R .25 .50
46 Drift of Phantasms C .50 1.00
47 Ethereal Usher U .20 .40
48 Eye of the Storm R 1.50 3.00
49 Flight of Fancy C .07 .15
50 Flow of Ideas U .15 .30
51 Followed Footsteps R 2.00 4.00
52 Grayscaled Gharial C .07 .15
53 Grozoth R 2.50 5.00
54 Halcyon Glaze U .10 .20
55 Hunted Phantasm R .30 .60
56 Induce Paranoia C .12 .25
57 Lore Broker U .20 .40
58 Mark of Eviction U .10 .20
59 Mnemonic Nexus U .10 .20
60 Muddle the Mixture C 4.00 8.00
61 Peel from Reality C .07 .15
62 Quickchange C .07 .15
63 Remand U 4.00 8.00
64 Snapping Drake C .07 .15
65 Spawnbroker R .20 .40
66 Stasis Cell C .10 .20
67 Surveilling Sprite C .07 .15
68 Tattered Drake C .07 .15
69 Telling Time U .10 .20
70 Terraformer C .07 .15
71 Tidewater Minion C .07 .15
72 Tunnel Vision R 2.50 5.00
73 Vedalken Dismisser C .07 .15
74 Vedalken Entrancer C .07 .15
75 Wizened Snitches U .17 .35
76 Zephyr Spirit C .07 .15
77 Blood Funnel R .75 1.50
78 Brainspoil C .20 .40
79 Carrion Howler U .10 .20
80 Clinging Darkness C .07 .15
81 Dark Confidant R 25.00 50.00
82 Darkblast U .30 .75
83 Dimir House Guard C .60 1.25
84 Dimir Machinations U 1.00 2.00
85 Disembowel C .07 .15
86 Empty the Catacombs R .20 .40
87 Golgari Thug U 1.00 2.00
88 Helldozer R .75 1.50
89 Hex R .30 .60
90 Hunted Horror R 3.00 6.00
91 Infectious Host C .07 .15
92 Keening Banshee U .10 .20
93 Last Gasp C .07 .15
94 Mausoleum Turnkey U .10 .20
95 Moonlight Bargain R .30 .75
96 Mortipede C .07 .15
97 Necromantic Thirst C .07 .15
98 Necroplasm R .20 .40
99 Netherborn Phalanx U .25 .50
100 Nightmare Void U .10 .20
101 Ribbons of Night U .10 .20
102 Roofstalker Wight C .07 .15
103 Sadistic Augermage C .07 .15
104 Sewerdreg C .07 .15
105 Shred Memory C .30 .60
106 Sins of the Past R .20 .40
107 Stinkweed Imp C .75 1.50
108 Strands of Undeath C .07 .15
109 Thoughtpicker Witch C .15 .30
110 Undercity Shade U .10 .20
111 Vigor Mortis U .20 .40
112 Vindictive Mob U .10 .20
113 Woebringer Demon R .20 .40
114 Barbarian Riftcutter C .07 .15
115 Blockbuster U .10 .20
116 Breath of Fury R 1.50 3.00
117 Char R .20 .40
118 Cleansing Beam U .10 .20
119 Coalhauler Swine C .07 .15
120 Dogpile C .07 .15
121 Excruciator R .20 .40
122 Fiery Conclusion C .07 .15
123 Flame Fusillade R .20 .40
124 Flash Conscription U .10 .20
125 Frenzied Goblin U .10 .20
126 Galvanic Arc C .07 .15
127 Goblin Fire Fiend C .07 .15
128 Goblin Spelunkers C .07 .15
129 Greater Forgeling U .10 .20
130 Hammerfist Giant R .20 .40
131 Hunted Dragon R .50 1.00
132 Incite Hysteria C .07 .15
133 Indentured Oaf U .10 .20
134 Instill Furor U .10 .20
135 Mindmoil R 2.50 5.00
136 Molten Sentry R .20 .40
137 Ordruun Commando C .07 .15
138 Rain of Embers C .07 .15
139 Reroute U .10 .20
140 Sabertooth Alley Cat C .07 .15
141 Seismic Spike C .07 .15
142 Sell-Sword Brute C .07 .15
143 Smash C .07 .15
144 Sparkmage Apprentice C .07 .15
145 Stoneshaker Shaman U .75 1.50
146 Surge of Zeal C .07 .15
147 Torpid Moloch C .07 .15
148 Viashino Fangtail C .07 .15
149 Viashino Slasher C .07 .15
150 Warp World R .60 1.25
151 War-Torch Goblin C .07 .15
152 Wojek Embermage U .10 .20
153 Birds of Paradise R 7.50 15.00
154 Bramble Elemental C .07 .15
155 Carven Caryatid U .25 .50
156 Chord of Calling R 4.00 8.00
157 Civic Wayfinder C .07 .15
158 Doubling Season R 50.00 100.00
159 Dowsing Shaman U .10 .20
160 Dryad's Caress C .07 .15
161 Elves of Deep Shadow C 1.50 3.00
162 Elvish Skysweeper C .07 .15
163 Farseek C 1.25 2.50
164 Fists of Ironwood C .07 .15
165 Gather Courage C .07 .15
166 Golgari Brownscale C .07 .15
167 Golgari Grave-Troll R 2.50 5.00
168 Goliath Spider U .10 .20
169 Greater Mossdog C .07 .15
170 Hunted Troll R 1.25 2.50
171 Ivy Dancer U .10 .20
172 Life from the Loam R 10.00 20.00
173 Moldervine Cloak U .10 .20
174 Nullmage Shepherd U .60 1.25
175 Overwhelm U .10 .20
176 Perilous Forays U 3.00 6.00
177 Primordial Sage R 1.25 2.50
178 Recollect U .10 .20
179 Rolling Spoil U .10 .20
180 Root-Kin Ally U .10 .20
181 Scatter the Seeds C .07 .15
182 Scion of the Wild R .20 .40
183 Siege Wurm C .07 .15
184 Stone-Seeder Hierophant C .20 .40
185 Sundering Vitae C .07 .15
186 Transluminant C .07 .15
187 Trophy Hunter U .10 .20
188 Ursapine R .20 .40
189 Vinelasher Kudzu R .25 .50
190 Agrus Kos, Wojek Veteran R .30 .60
191 Autochthon Wurm R 1.50 3.00
192 Bloodbond March R .50 1.00
193 Boros Swiftblade U .10 .20
194 Brightflame R .30 .75
195 Chorus of the Conclave R .20 .40
196 Circu, Dimir Lobotomist R .75 1.50
197 Clutch of the Undercity U .25 .50
198 Congregation at Dawn U 4.00 8.00
199 Consult the Necrosages C .07 .15
200 Dark Heart of the Wood U .10 .20
201 Dimir Cutpurse R .50 1.00
202 Dimir Doppelganger R .60 1.25
203 Dimir Infiltrator C .30 .75
204 Drooling Groodion U .10 .20
205 Firemane Angel R .30 .60
206 Flame-Kin Zealot U .10 .20
207 Glare of Subdual R .30 .75
208 Glimpse the Unthinkable R 7.50 15.00
209 Golgari Germination U .25 .50
210 Golgari Rotwurm C .07 .15
211 Grave-Shell Scarab R .20 .40
212 Guardian of Vitu-Ghazi C .07 .15
213 Lightning Helix U .75 1.50
214 Loxodon Hierarch R .50 1.00
215 Mindleech Mass R .75 1.50
216 Moroii U .10 .20
217 Perplex C 1.25 2.50
218 Phytohydra R 2.00 4.00
219 Pollenbright Wings U .10 .20
220 Psychic Drain U .50 1.00
221 Putrefy U .10 .20
222 Rally the Righteous C .07 .15
223 Razia, Boros Archangel R .60 1.25
224 Razia's Purification R .50 1.00
225 Savra, Queen of the Golgari R 4.00 8.00
226 Searing Meditation R .20 .40
227 Seeds of Strength C .07 .15
228 Selesnya Evangel C .07 .15
229 Selesnya Sagittars U .10 .20
230 Shambling Shell C .20 .40
231 Sisters of Stone Death R .75 1.50
232 Skyknight Legionnaire C .07 .15
233 Sunhome Enforcer U .10 .20
234 Szadek, Lord of Secrets R .30 .75
235 Thundersong Trumpeter C .07 .15
236 Tolsimir Wolfblood R 2.00 4.00
237 Twisted Justice U .10 .20
238 Vulturous Zombie R .20 .40
239 Watchwolf U .17 .35
240 Woodwraith Corrupter R .20 .40
241 Woodwraith Strangler C .07 .15
242 Boros Guildmage U .10 .20
243 Boros Recruit C .07 .15
244 Centaur Safeguard C .07 .15
245 Dimir Guildmage U .10 .20
246 Gaze of the Gorgon C .07 .15
247 Gleancrawler R .30 .60
248 Golgari Guildmage U .10 .20
249 Lurking Informant C .07 .15
250 Master Warcraft R .50 1.00
251 Privileged Position R 10.00 20.00
252 Selesnya Guildmage U .10 .20
253 Shadow of Doubt R 3.00 6.00
254 Bloodletter Quill R .20 .40
255 Boros Signet C .50 1.00
256 Bottled Cloister R .50 1.00
257 Cloudstone Curio R 40.00 80.00
258 Crown of Convergence R .20 .40
259 Cyclopean Snare U .10 .20
260 Dimir Signet C 1.50 3.00
261 Glass Golem U .10 .20
262 Golgari Signet C .75 1.50
263 Grifter's Blade U .10 .20
264 Junktroller U .10 .20
265 Leashling U .10 .20
266 Nullstone Gargoyle R 1.00 2.00
267 Pariah's Shield R 12.50 25.00
268 Peregrine Mask U .10 .20
269 Plague Boiler R .25 .50
270 Selesnya Signet C .75 1.50
271 Spectral Searchlight U .10 .20
272 Sunforger R 2.00 4.00
273 Terrarion C .07 .15
274 Voyager Staff U .30 .75
275 Boros Garrison C .20 .40
276 Dimir Aqueduct C .20 .40
277 Duskmantle, House of Shadow U .10 .20
278 Golgari Rot Farm C .20 .40
279 Overgrown Tomb R 12.50 25.00
280 Sacred Foundry R 12.50 25.00
281 Selesnya Sanctuary C .20 .40
282 Sunhome, Fortress of the Legion U .75 1.50
283 Svogthos, the Restless Tomb U .20 .40
284 Temple Garden R 12.50 25.00
285 Vitu-Ghazi, the City-Tree U .10 .20
286 Watery Grave R 12.50 25.00
287 Plains L .12 .25
288 Plains L .12 .25
289 Plains L .12 .25
290 Plains L .12 .25
291 Island L .12 .25
292 Island L .12 .25
293 Island L .12 .25
294 Island L .12 .25
295 Swamp L .15 .30
296 Swamp L .15 .30
297 Swamp L .15 .30
298 Swamp L .15 .30
299 Mountain L .12 .25
300 Mountain L .12 .25
301 Mountain L .12 .25
302 Mountain L .12 .25
303 Forest L .12 .25
304 Forest L .12 .25
305 Forest L .12 .25
306 Forest L .12 .25

2005 Magic The Gathering Saviors of Kamigawa

1 Aether Shockwave U .15 .30
2 Araba Mothrider C .20 .40
3 Celestial Kirin R .75 1.50
4 Charge Across the Araba U .10 .20
5 Cowed by Wisdom C .07 .15
6 Curtain of Light C .07 .15
7 Descendant of Kiyomaro U .10 .20
8 Eiganjo Free-Riders U .15 .30
9 Enduring Ideal R 4.00 8.00
10 Ghost-Lit Redeemer U .10 .20
11 Hail of Arrows U .10 .20
12 Hand of Honor U .60 1.25
13 Inner-Chamber Guard U .25 .50
14 Kataki, War's Wage R 2.00 4.00
15 Kitsune Bonesetter C .07 .15
16 Kitsune Dawnblade C .07 .15
17 Kitsune Loreweaver C .07 .15
18 Kiyomaro, First to Stand R .20 .40
19 Michiko Konda, Truth Seeker R 17.50 35.00
20 Moonwing Moth C .07 .15
21 Nikko-Onna U .10 .20
22 Plow Through Reito C .07 .15
23 Presence of the Wise U .10 .20
24 Promise of Bunrei R .60 1.25
25 Pure Intentions R .20 .40
26 Reverence R 3.00 6.00
27 Rune-Tail, Kitsune Ascendant
Rune-Tail's Essence R 2.50 5.00
28 Shinen of Stars' Light C .07 .15
29 Spiritual Visit C .07 .15
30 Torii Watchward C .07 .15
31 Cloudhoof Kirin R .30 .60
32 Cut the Earthly Bond C .07 .15
33 Descendant of Soramaro C .07 .15
34 Dreamcatcher C .07 .15
35 Erayo, Soratami Ascendant/Erayo's Essence R 7.50 15.00
36 Eternal Dominion R 2.50 5.00
37 Evermind U .15 .30
38 Freed from the Real C 2.00 4.00
39 Ghost-Lit Warder U .10 .20
40 Ideas Unbound C .75 1.50
41 Kaho, Minamo Historian R 1.50 3.00
42 Kami of the Crescent Moon R 4.00 8.00
43 Kiri-Onna U .20 .40
44 Meishin, the Mind Cage R 2.50 5.00
45 Minamo Scrollkeeper C .07 .15
46 Moonbow Illusionist C .07 .15
47 Murmurs from Beyond C .07 .15
48 Oboro Breezecaller C .07 .15
49 Oboro Envoy U .10 .20
50 Oppressive Will C .07 .15
51 Overwhelming Intellect U .20 .40
52 Rushing-Tide Zubera U .10 .20
53 Sakashima the Impostor R 15.00 30.00
54 Secretkeeper U .10 .20
55 Shape Stealer U .20 .40
56 Shifting Borders U 1.00 2.00
57 Shinen of Flight's Wings C .07 .15
58 Soramaro, First to Dream R .20 .40
59 Trusted Advisor U .20 .40
60 Twincast R 7.50 15.00
61 Akuta, Born of Ash R .20 .40
62 Choice of Damnations R 7.50 15.00
63 Death Denied C .07 .15
64 Death of a Thousand Stings C .07 .15
65 Deathknell Kami C .07 .15
66 Deathmask Nezumi C .07 .15
67 Exile into Darkness U .10 .20
68 Footsteps of the Goryo U 2.50 5.00
69 Ghost-Lit Stalker U .10 .20
70 Gnat Miser C .30 .60
71 Hand of Cruelty U .20 .40
72 Infernal Kirin R 1.50 3.00
73 Kagemaro, First to Suffer R 1.50 3.00
74 Kagemaro's Clutch C .07 .15
75 Kami of Empty Graves C .07 .15
76 Kemuri-Onna U .10 .20
77 Kiku's Shadow U .10 .20
78 Kuon, Ogre Ascendant/Kuon's Essence R .20 .40
79 Kuro's Taken C .07 .15
80 Locust Miser U 1.25 2.50
81 Maga, Traitor to Mortals R 2.50 5.00
82 Measure of Wickedness U .10 .20
83 Neverending Torment R .30 .60
84 One with Nothing R 1.25 2.50
85 Pain's Reward R 2.00 4.00
86 Raving Oni-Slave C .07 .15
87 Razorjaw Oni U .10 .20
88 Shinen of Fear's Chill C .07 .15
89 Sink into Takenuma C .07 .15
90 Skull Collector U .10 .20
91 Adamaro, First to Desire R .50 1.00
92 Akki Drillmaster C .07 .15
93 Akki Underling C .07 .15
94 Barrel Down Sokenzan C .07 .15
95 Burning-Eye Zubera U .10 .20
96 Captive Flame U .10 .20
97 Feral Lightning U .10 .20
98 Gaze of Adamaro U .10 .20
99 Ghost-Lit Raider U .10 .20
100 Glitterfang C .07 .15
101 Godo's Irregulars U .10 .20
102 Hidetsugu's Second Rite R .60 1.25
103 Homura, Human Ascendant
Homura's Essence R 2.00 4.00
104 Iizuka the Ruthless R .60 1.25
105 Inner Fire C .25 .50
106 Into the Fray C .07 .15
107 Jiwari, the Earth Aflame R .20 .40
108 Oni of Wild Places U .10 .20
109 Path of Anger's Flame C .07 .15
110 Rally the Horde R .20 .40
111 Ronin Cavekeeper C .07 .15
112 Shinen of Fury's Fire C .07 .15
113 Skyfire Kirin R .30 .75
114 Sokenzan Renegade U .10 .20
115 Sokenzan Spellblade C .07 .15
116 Spiraling Embers C .07 .15
117 Sunder from Within U .20 .40
118 Thoughts of Ruin R .20 .40
119 Undying Flames R .20 .40
120 Yuki-Onna U .20 .40
121 Arashi, the Sky Asunder R .50 1.00
122 Ayumi, the Last Visitor R .50 1.00
123 Bounteous Kirin R .30 .75
124 Briarknit Kami U .10 .20
125 Dense Canopy U .10 .20
126 Descendant of Masumaro U .10 .20
127 Dosan's Oldest Chant C .07 .15
128 Elder Pine of Jukai C .07 .15
129 Endless Swarm R .30 .75
130 Fiddlehead Kami C .07 .15
131 Ghost-Lit Nourisher U .20 .40
132 Haru-Onna U .20 .40
133 Inner Calm, Outer Strength C .07 .15
134 Kami of the Tended Garden U .10 .20
135 Kashi-Tribe Elite U .30 .75
136 Masumaro, First to Live R .50 1.00
137 Matsu-Tribe Birdstalker C .07 .15
138 Molting Skin U .10 .20
139 Nightsoil Kami C .07 .15
140 Okina Nightwatch C .07 .15
141 Promised Kannushi C .07 .15
142 Reki, the History of Kamigawa R 4.00 8.00
143 Rending Vines C .07 .15
144 Sakura-Tribe Scout C 2.50 5.00
145 Sasaya, Orochi Ascendant/Sasaya's Essence R 2.00 4.00
146 Seed the Land R 2.00 4.00
147 Seek the Horizon U .10 .20
148 Sekki, Seasons' Guide R 2.00 4.00
149 Shinen of Life's Roar C .07 .15
150 Stampeding Serow U .20 .40
151 Iname as One R .75 1.50
152 Ashes of the Fallen R .75 1.50
153 Blood Clock R 2.00 4.00
154 Ebony Owl Netsuke U .30 .75
155 Ivory Crane Netsuke U .10 .20
156 Manriki-Gusari U .25 .50
157 O-Naginata U .75 1.50
158 Pithing Needle R 4.00 8.00

159 Scroll of Origins R	.20	.40
160 Soratami Cloud Chariot U	.10	.20
161 Wine of Blood and Iron R	.20	.40
162 Mikokoro, Center of the Sea R	6.00	12.00
163 Miren, the Moaning Well R	7.50	15.00
164 Oboro, Palace in the Clouds R	50.00	100.00
165 Tomb of Urami R	.30	.75

2006 Magic The Gathering Coldsnap

1 Adarkar Valkyrie R	1.00	2.00
2 Boreal Griffin C	.07	.15
3 Cover of Winter R	.30	.60
4 Darien, King of Kjeldor R	4.00	8.00
5 Field Marshal R	2.00	4.00
6 Gelid Shackles C	.07	.15
7 Glacial Plating U	.12	.25
8 Jotun Grunt U	.12	.25
9 Jotun Owl Keeper U	.12	.25
10 Kjeldoran Gargoyle U	.12	.25
11 Kjeldoran Javelineer C	.07	.15
12 Kjeldoran Outrider C	.07	.15
13 Kjeldoran War Cry C	.07	.15
14 Luminesce U	.12	.25
15 Martyr of Sands C	.17	.35
16 Ronom Unicorn C	.07	.15
17 Squall Drifter C	.07	.15
18 Sun's Bounty C	.07	.15
19 Sunscour R	.75	1.50
20 Surging Sentinels C	.07	.15
21 Swift Maneuver C	.07	.15
22 Ursine Fylgja U	.12	.25
23 Wall of Shards U	1.25	2.50
24 White Shield Crusader U	.12	.25
25 Woolly Razorback R	.30	.75
26 Adarkar Windform U	.12	.25
27 Arcum Dagsson R	3.00	6.00
28 Balduvian Frostwaker U	.12	.25
29 Commandeer R	12.50	25.00
30 Controvert U	.12	.25
31 Counterbalance U	10.00	20.00
32 Drelnoch C	.07	.15
33 Flashfreeze U	.12	.25
34 Frost Raptor C	.07	.15
35 Frozen Solid C	.07	.15
36 Heidar, Rimewind Master R	.50	1.00
37 Jokulmorder R	.30	.60
38 Krovikan Mist C	.07	.15
39 Krovikan Whispers U	.12	.25
40 Martyr of Frost C	.07	.15
41 Perilous Research U	.25	.50
42 Rimefeather Owl R	4.00	8.00
43 Rimewind Cryomancer U	.25	.50
44 Rimewind Taskmage C	.07	.15
45 Ronom Serpent C	.07	.15
46 Rune Snag C	.07	.15
47 Surging Aether C	.07	.15
48 Survivor of the Unseen C	.07	.15
49 Thermal Flux C	.30	.75
50 Vexing Sphinx R	.50	1.00
51 Balduvian Fallen U	.12	.25
52 Chill to the Bone C	.07	.15
53 Chilling Shade C	.07	.15
54 Deathmark U	.12	.25
55 Disciple of Tevesh Szat C	.07	.15
56 Feast of Flesh C	.07	.15
57 Garza's Assassin R	.30	.75
58 Grim Harvest C	.15	.30
59 Gristle Grinner U	.12	.25
60 Gutless Ghoul C	.07	.15
61 Haakon, Stromgald Scourge R	2.00	4.00
62 Herald of Leshrac R	1.50	3.00
63 Krovikan Rot U	.12	.25
64 Krovikan Scoundrel C	.07	.15
65 Martyr of Bones C	.07	.15
66 Phobian Phantasm U	.12	.25
67 Phyrexian Etchings R	.30	.60
68 Rime Transfusion U	1.50	3.00
69 Rimebound Dead C	.20	.40
70 Soul Spike R	.60	1.25
71 Stromgald Crusader U	.75	1.50
72 Surging Dementia C	.07	.15
73 Tresserhorn Skyknight U	.12	.25
74 Void Maw R	.30	.60
75 Zombie Musher C	.07	.15
76 Balduvian Rage U	.30	.75
77 Balduvian Warlord U	.20	.40
78 Braid of Fire R	10.00	20.00
79 Cryoclasm U	.12	.25
80 Earthen Goo U	.12	.25
81 Fury of the Horde R	2.00	4.00
82 Goblin Furrier C	.07	.15
83 Goblin Rimerunner C	.07	.15
84 Greater Stone Spirit U	.12	.25
85 Icefall C	.07	.15
86 Karplusan Minotaur R	4.00	8.00
87 Karplusan Wolverine C	.07	.15
88 Lightning Serpent R	1.00	2.00
89 Lightning Storm U	.30	.75
90 Lovisa Coldeyes R	4.00	8.00
91 Magmatic Core U	.12	.25
92 Martyr of Ashes C	.20	.40
93 Ohran Yeti C	.07	.15
94 Orcish Bloodpainter C	.07	.15
95 Rimescale Dragon R	3.00	6.00
96 Rite of Flame C	1.00	2.00
97 Skred C	.75	1.50
98 Stalking Yeti U	.12	.25
99 Surging Flame C	.07	.15
100 Thermopod C	.75	1.50
101 Allosaurus Rider R	1.50	3.00
102 Arctic Nishoba U	.12	.25
103 Aurochs Herd C	.07	.15
104 Boreal Centaur C	.07	.15
105 Boreal Druid C	3.00	6.00
106 Brooding Saurian R	.30	.60
107 Bull Aurochs C	.07	.15
108 Freyalise's Radiance U	.15	.30
109 Frostweb Spider C	.15	.30
110 Hibernation's End R	1.50	3.00
111 Into the North C	2.50	5.00
112 Karplusan Strider U	.12	.25
113 Martyr of Spores C	.07	.15
114 Mystic Melting U	.12	.25
115 Ohran Viper R	1.25	2.50
116 Panglacial Wurm R	1.50	3.00
117 Resize U	.12	.25
118 Rimehorn Aurochs U	.12	.25
119 Ronom Hulk C	.07	.15
120 Shape of the Wiitigo R	.30	.60
121 Sheltering Ancient U	.50	1.00
122 Simian Brawler C	.07	.15
123 Sound the Call C	.07	.15
124 Steam Spitter U	.12	.25
125 Surging Might C	.07	.15
126 Blizzard Specter U	.20	.40
127 Deepfire Elemental U	.12	.25
128 Diamond Faerie R	.30	.60
129 Garza Zol, Plague Queen R	.50	1.00
130 Juniper Order Ranger U	.30	.60
131 Sek'Kuar, Deathkeeper R	.30	.60
132 Tamanoa R	.75	1.50
133 Vanish into Memory U	.20	.40
134 Wilderness Elemental U	.20	.40
135 Zur the Enchanter R	5.00	10.00
136 Coldsteel Heart U	4.00	8.00
137 Jester's Scepter R	.30	.60
138 Mishra's Bauble U	6.00	12.00
139 Phyrexian Ironfoot U	.12	.25
140 Phyrexian Snowcrusher U	.12	.25
141 Phyrexian Soulgorger R	1.50	3.00
142 Thrumming Stone R	30.00	75.00
143 Arctic Flats U	1.50	3.00
144 Boreal Shelf U	.75	1.50
145 Dark Depths R	20.00	40.00
146 Frost Marsh U	3.00	6.00
147 Highland Weald U	.30	.75
148 Mouth of Ronom U	4.00	8.00
149 Scrying Sheets R	20.00	40.00
150 Tresserhorn Sinks U	.75	1.50
151 Snow-Covered Plains C	.60	1.25
152 Snow-Covered Island C	1.25	2.50
153 Snow-Covered Swamp C	.75	1.50
154 Snow-Covered Mountain C	1.00	2.00
155 Snow-Covered Forest C	1.00	2.00

2006 Magic The Gathering Coldsnap Token

1 Marit Lage	6.00	12.00

2006 Magic The Gathering Dissension

1 Aurora Eidolon C	.07	.15
2 Azorius Herald U	.12	.25
3 Beacon Hawk C	.07	.15
4 Blessing of the Nephilim U	.30	.60
5 Brace for Impact U	.12	.25
6 Carom C	.07	.15
7 Celestial Ancient R	.30	.75
8 Condemn U	.25	.50
9 Freewind Equenaut C	.07	.15
10 Guardian of the Guildpact C	.60	1.25
11 Haazda Exonerator C	.07	.15
12 Haazda Shield Mate R	.20	.40
13 Mistral Charger U	.12	.25
14 Paladin of Prahv U	.12	.25
15 Proclamation of Rebirth R	1.00	2.00
16 Proper Burial R	.75	1.50
17 Soulsworn Jury C	.07	.15
18 Steeling Stance C	.07	.15
19 Stoic Ephemera U	.12	.25
20 Valor Made Real C	.07	.15
21 Wakestone Gargoyle R	.20	.40
22 Court Hussar U	.12	.25
23 Cytoplast Manipulator R	3.00	6.00
24 Enigma Eidolon C	.07	.15
25 Govern the Guildless R	.20	.40
26 Helium Squirter C	.07	.15
27 Novijen Sages R	.20	.40
28 Ocular Halo C	.07	.15
29 Plaxmanta U	.12	.25
30 Psychic Possession R	2.00	4.00
31 Silkwing Scout C	.07	.15
32 Skyscribing U	.12	.25
33 Spell Snare U	.75	1.50
34 Tidespout Tyrant R	4.00	8.00
35 Vigean Graftmage U	.12	.25
36 Vision Skeins C	.12	.25
37 Writ of Passage C	.07	.15
38 Bond of Agony U	.75	1.50
39 Brain Pry U	.12	.25
40 Crypt Champion U	.12	.25
41 Delirium Skeins C	.15	.30
42 Demon's Jester C	.07	.15
43 Drekavac U	.12	.25
44 Enemy of the Guildpact C	.07	.15
45 Entropic Eidolon C	.07	.15
46 Infernal Tutor R	6.00	12.00
47 Macabre Waltz C	.07	.15
48 Nettling Curse C	.07	.15
49 Nightcreep U	.12	.25
50 Nihilistic Glee R	.20	.40
51 Ragamuffyn U	.12	.25
52 Ratcatcher R	.75	1.50
53 Seal of Doom C	.07	.15
54 Slaughterhouse Bouncer C	.07	.15
55 Slithering Shade U	.12	.25
56 Unliving Psychopath R	.20	.40
57 Vesper Ghoul C	.07	.15
58 Wit's End R	.20	.40
59 Cackling Flames C	.07	.15
60 Demonfire R	.20	.40
61 Flame-Kin War Scout U	.12	.25
62 Flaring Flame-Kin U	.12	.25
63 Gnat Alley Creeper U	.12	.25
64 Ignorant Bliss U	.12	.25
65 Kill-Suit Cultist C	.07	.15
66 Kindle the Carnage U	.12	.25
67 Ogre Gatecrasher C	.07	.15
68 Psychotic Fury C	.30	.75
69 Rakdos Pit Dragon R	.30	.60
70 Sandstorm Eidolon C	.07	.15
71 Seal of Fire C	.25	.50
72 Squealing Devil U	.12	.25
73 Stalking Vengeance R	.75	1.50
74 Stormscale Anarch R	.20	.40
75 Taste for Mayhem C	.07	.15
76 Utvara Scalper C	.07	.15
77 War's Toll R	4.00	8.00
78 Weight of Spires U	4.00	8.00
79 Whiptail Moloch C	.07	.15
80 Aquastrand Spider C	.07	.15
81 Cytoplast Root-Kin R	.30	.60
82 Cytospawn Shambler C	.07	.15
83 Elemental Resonance R	2.00	4.00
84 Fertile Imagination U	.15	.30
85 Flash Foliage U	.12	.25
86 Indrik Stomphowler U	.12	.25
87 Loaming Shaman R	.30	.75
88 Might of the Nephilim U	.12	.25
89 Patagia Viper U	.12	.25
90 Protean Hulk R	6.00	12.00
91 Simic Basilisk U	.12	.25
92 Simic Initiate C	.07	.15
93 Simic Ragworm C	.07	.15
94 Sporeback Troll C	.07	.15
95 Sprouting Phytohydra R	2.50	5.00
96 Stomp and Howl U	.12	.25
97 Street Savvy C	.07	.15
98 Thrive C	.07	.15
99 Utopia Sprawl C	7.50	15.00
100 Verdant Eidolon C	.07	.15
101 Aethermage's Touch R	.20	.40
102 Anthem of Rakdos R	.30	.75
103 Assault Zeppelid C	.07	.15
104 Azorius Aethermage U	.12	.25
105 Azorius First-Wing C	.07	.15
106 Azorius Ploy U	.12	.25
107 Coiling Oracle C	.15	.30
108 Cytoshape R	.20	.40
109 Dread Slag R	.20	.40
110 Experiment Kraj R	2.50	5.00
111 Gobhobbler Rats C	.07	.15
112 Grand Arbiter Augustin IV R	25.00	50.00
113 Hellhole Rats U	.15	.30
114 Isperia the Inscrutable R	.20	.40
115 Jagged Poppet U	.12	.25
116 Leafdrake Roost U	.12	.25
117 Lyzolda, the Blood Witch R	.30	.75
118 Momir Vig, Simic Visionary R	.20	.40
119 Omnibian R	.20	.40
120 Overrule C	.07	.15
121 Pain Magnification U	3.00	6.00
122 Palliation Accord U	.12	.25
123 Plaxcaster Frogling U	.30	.75
124 Plumes of Peace C	.07	.15
125 Pride of the Clouds R	3.00	6.00
126 Rain of Gore R	7.50	15.00
127 Rakdos Augermage R	.30	.60
128 Rakdos Ickspitter C	.07	.15
129 Rakdos the Defiler R	1.25	2.50
130 Simic Sky Swallower R	.20	.40
131 Sky Hussar U	.20	.40
132 Swift Silence R	.20	.40
133 Trygon Predator U	.20	.40
134 Twinstrike U	.12	.25
135 Vigean Hydropon C	.07	.15
136 Vigean Intuition U	.12	.25
137 Voidslime R	6.00	12.00
138 Windreaver R	.20	.40
139 Wrecking Ball C	.07	.15
140 Avatar of Discord R	.50	1.00
141 Azorius Guildmage U	.12	.25
142 Biomantic Mastery R	.20	.40
143 Dovescape R	1.50	3.00
144 Minister of Impediments C	.07	.15
145 Rakdos Guildmage U	.12	.25
146 Riot Spikes C	.07	.15
147 Shielding Plax C	.07	.15
148 Simic Guildmage U	.30	.60
149 Bound/Determined R	.30	.60
150 Crime/Punishment R	.50	1.00
151 Hide/Seek R	2.50	5.00
152 Hit/Run U	.12	.25
153 Odds/Ends R	.50	1.00
154 Pure/Simple U	.12	.25
155 Research/Development R	.50	1.00
156 Rise/Fall U	.12	.25
157 Supply/Demand U	.25	.50
158 Trial/Error U	.12	.25
159 Azorius Signet C	.30	.75
160 Bronze Bombshell R	2.00	4.00
161 Evolution Vat R	.50	1.00
162 Magewrights Stone U	6.00	12.00
163 Muse Vessel R	.20	.40
164 Rakdos Riteknife R	.20	.40
165 Rakdos Signet C	.75	1.50
166 Simic Signet C	.30	.60
167 Skullmead Cauldron U	.12	.25
168 Transguild Courier U	.12	.25
169 Walking Archive R	2.50	5.00
170 Azorius Chancery C	.07	.15
171 Blood Crypt R	25.00	50.00
172 Breeding Pool R	20.00	40.00
173 Ghost Quarter U	2.00	4.00
174 Hallowed Fountain R	17.50	35.00
175 Novijen, Heart of Progress U	.60	1.25
176 Pillar of the Paruns R	10.00	20.00
177 Prahv, Spires of Order U	.20	.40
178 Rakdos Carnarium C	.20	.40
179 Rix Maadi, Dungeon Palace U	.20	.40
180 Simic Growth Chamber C	.30	.60

2006 Magic The Gathering Guildpact

1 Absolver Thrull C	.07	.15
2 Belfry Spirit U	.20	.40
3 Benediction of Moons C	.07	.15
4 Droning Bureaucrats U	.12	.25
5 Ghost Warden C	.07	.15
6 Ghostway R	12.50	25.00
7 Graven Dominator R	.20	.40
8 Guardian's Magemark C	.07	.15
9 Harrier Griffin U	.12	.25
10 Leyline of the Meek R	1.50	3.00
11 Lionheart Maverick C	.07	.15
12 Martyred Rusalka U	.12	.25
13 Order of the Stars U	.12	.25
14 Shadow Lance U	.12	.25
15 Shrieking Grotesque C	.07	.15
16 Sinstriker's Will U	.12	.25
17 Skyrider Trainee C	.07	.15
18 Spelltithe Enforcer R	1.25	2.50
19 Storm Herd R	.75	1.50
20 To Arms! U	.75	1.50
21 Withstand C	.07	.15
22 Aetherplasm U	.20	.40
23 Crystal Seer C	.07	.15
24 Drowned Rusalka U	.12	.25
25 Frazzle U	.12	.25
26 Gigadrowse C	.20	.40
27 Hatching Plans R	.30	.75
28 Infiltrator's Magemark C	.07	.15
29 Leyline of Singularity R	1.00	2.00
30 Mimeofacture R	.20	.40
31 Quicken R	.50	1.00
32 Repeal C	.07	.15
33 Runeboggle C	.07	.15
34 Sky Swallower R	.20	.40
35 Steamcore Weird C	.07	.15
36 Stratozeppelid U	.12	.25
37 Thunderheads U	.12	.25
38 Torch Drake C	.07	.15
39 Train of Thought C	.07	.15
40 Vacuumelt U	.12	.25
41 Vedalken Plotter U	.30	.75
42 Vertigo Spawn U	.12	.25
43 Abyssal Nocturnus R	.75	1.50
44 Caustic Rain U	.12	.25
45 Cremate C	.07	.15
46 Cry of Contrition C	.15	.30
47 Cryptwailing U	.12	.25
48 Daggerclaw Imp U	.12	.25
49 Douse in Gloom C	.07	.15
50 Exhumer Thrull U	.12	.25
51 Hissing Miasma U	.75	1.50
52 Leyline of the Void R	7.50	15.00
53 Necromancer's Magemark C	.07	.15
54 Orzhov Euthanist C	.07	.15
55 Ostiary Thrull C	.07	.15
56 Plagued Rusalka U	.12	.25
57 Poisonbelly Ogre C	.07	.15
58 Restless Bones C	.07	.15
59 Revenant Patriarch U	.12	.25
60 Sanguine Praetor R	.20	.40
61 Seize the Soul R	.20	.40
62 Skeletal Vampire R	.20	.40
63 Smogsteed Rider U	.12	.25
64 Bloodscale Prowler C	.07	.15
65 Fencer's Magemark C	.07	.15
66 Ghor-Clan Bloodscale U	.12	.25
67 Hypervolt Grasp U	.12	.25
68 Leyline of Lightning R	.20	.40
69 Living Inferno R	.20	.40
70 Ogre Savant C	.07	.15
71 Parallectric Feedback R	.20	.40
72 Pyromatics C	.07	.15
73 Rabble-Rouser U	.12	.25
74 Scorched Rusalka U	.12	.25
75 Shattering Spree U	2.00	4.00
76 Siege of Towers R	.20	.40
77 Skarrgan Firebird R	.20	.40
78 Tin Street Hooligan C	.07	.15
79 Battering Wurm U	.12	.25
80 Beastmaster's Magemark C	.07	.15
81 Bioplasm R	.20	.40
82 Crash Landing U	.12	.25
83 Dryad Sophisticate U	.12	.25
84 Earth Surge R	.30	.75
85 Gatherer of Graces U	.12	.25
86 Ghor-Clan Savage C	.07	.15
87 Gristleback U	.12	.25
88 Gruul Nodorog C	.07	.15
89 Gruul Scrapper C	.07	.15
90 Leyline of Lifeforce R	2.50	5.00
91 Petrified Wood-Kin R	.20	.40
92 Predatory Focus U	.12	.25
93 Primeval Light U	.12	.25
94 Silhana Ledgewalker C	.50	1.00
95 Silhana Starfletcher C	.07	.15
96 Skarrgan Pit-Skulk C	.07	.15
97 Starved Rusalka U	.12	.25
98 Wildsize C	.07	.15
99 Wurmweaver Coil R	.20	.40
100 Agent of Masks U	.12	.25
101 Angel of Despair R	1.00	2.00
102 Blind Hunter C	.07	.15
103 Borborygmos R	.20	.40
104 Burning-Tree Bloodscale C	.07	.15
105 Burning-Tree Shaman R	.30	.75
106 Castigate C	.15	.30
107 Cerebral Vortex R	.30	.60
108 Conjurer's Ban U	.12	.25
109 Culling Sun R	.20	.40
110 Dune-Brood Nephilim R	.60	1.25
111 Electrolyze U	.12	.25
112 Feral Animist U	.12	.25
113 Gelectrode U	.25	.50
114 Ghost Council of Orzhova R	.30	.60
115 Glint-Eye Nephilim R	.20	.40
116 Goblin Flectomancer U	.12	.25
117 Ink-Treader Nephilim R	.75	1.50
118 Invoke the Firemind R	.30	.60
119 Izzet Chronarch C	.07	.15
120 Killer Instinct R	.20	.40
121 Leap of Flame C	.07	.15
122 Mortify U	.20	.40
123 Niv-Mizzet, the Firemind R	1.25	2.50
124 Orzhov Pontiff R	.20	.40
125 Pillory of the Sleepless C	.07	.15
126 Rumbling Slum R	.20	.40
127 Savage Twister U	.12	.25
128 Scab-Clan Mauler C	.07	.15
129 Schismotivate U	.12	.25
130 Skarrgan Skybreaker U	.12	.25
131 Souls of the Faultless U	.30	.75
132 Stitch in Time R	6.00	12.00
133 Streetbreaker Wurm C	.07	.15
134 Teysa, Orzhov Scion R	4.00	8.00
135 Tibor and Lumia R	.20	.40
136 Ulasht, the Hate Seed R	1.00	2.00
137 Wee Dragonauts C	.07	.15
138 Witch-Maw Nephilim R	.75	1.50
139 Wreak Havoc U	.12	.25
140 Yore-Tiller Nephilim R	.50	1.00
141 Debtors' Knell R	2.00	4.00
142 Djinn Illuminatus R	.20	.40

143 Giant Solifuge R .20 .40
144 Gruul Guildmage U .12 .25
145 Izzet Guildmage U .12 .25
146 Mourning Thrull C .07 .15
147 Orzhov Guildmage U .12 .25
148 Petrahydrox C .07 .15
149 Wild Cantor C .15 .30
150 Gruul Signet C .50 1.00
151 Gruul War Plow R .25 .50
152 Izzet Signet C .75 1.50
153 Mizzium Transreliquat R .30 .75
154 Moratorium Stone R .20 .40
155 Orzhov Signet C .50 1.00
156 Sword of the Paruns R 6.00 12.00
157 Godless Shrine R 12.50 25.00
158 Gruul Turf C .20 .40
159 Izzet Boilerworks C .07 .15
160 Nivix, Aerie of the Firemind U .12 .25
161 Orzhov Basilica C .20 .40
162 Orzhova, the Church of Deals U .12 .25
163 Skarrg, the Rage Pits U .30 .60
164 Steam Vents R 12.50 25.00
165 Stomping Ground R 12.50 25.00

2006 Magic The Gathering Judge Gift Rewards

1 Exalted Angel R 30.00 75.00
2 Grim Lavamancer R 7.50 15.00
3 Meddling Mage R 15.00 30.00
4 Pernicious Deed R 40.00 80.00

2006 Magic The Gathering Magic Premiere Shop

1 Plains R L 7.50 15.00
2 Island R L 20.00 40.00
3 Swamp R L 7.50 15.00
4 Mountain R L 10.00 20.00
5 Forest R L 20.00 40.00

2006 Magic The Gathering Time Spiral

1 Amrou Scout C .07 .15
2 Amrou Seekers C .07 .15
3 Angel's Grace R 10.00 20.00
4 Benalish Cavalry C .07 .15
5 Castle Raptors C .07 .15
6 Cavalry Master U .12 .25
7 Celestial Crusader U .12 .25
8 Children of Korlis C .75 1.50
9 Chronosavant R .25 .50
10 Cloudchaser Kestrel C .07 .15
11 D'Avenant Healer C .07 .15
12 Detainment Spell C .07 .15
13 Divine Congregation C .07 .15
14 Duskrider Peregrine U .12 .25
15 Errant Doomsayers C .07 .15
16 Evangelize R .25 .50
17 Flickering Spirit C .07 .15
18 Foriysian Interceptor C .07 .15
19 Fortify C .07 .15
20 Gaze of Justice C .07 .15
21 Griffin Guide U .12 .25
22 Gustcloak Cavalier U .12 .25
23 Icatian Crier C .07 .15
24 Ivory Giant C .07 .15
25 Jedit's Dragoons C .07 .15
26 Knight of the Holy Nimbus U .12 .25
27 Magus of the Disk R .60 1.25
28 Mangara of Corondor R .30 .75
29 Momentary Blink C .15 .30
30 Opal Guardian R .25 .50
31 Outrider en-Kor U .12 .25
32 Pentarch Paladin R .75 1.50
33 Pentarch Ward C .07 .15
34 Plated Pegasus U .12 .25
35 Pull from Eternity U .75 1.50
36 Pulmonic Sliver R 6.00 12.00
37 Quilled Sliver U .25 .50
38 Restore Balance R 2.50 5.00
39 Return to Dust U .75 1.50
40 Serra Avenger R 1.25 2.50
41 Sidewinder Sliver C .50 1.00
42 Spirit Loop U .12 .25
43 Temporal Isolation C .20 .40
44 Tivadar of Thorn R .25 .50
45 Watcher Sliver C .07 .15
46 Weathered Bodyguards R .25 .50
47 Zealot il-Vec C .07 .15
48 Ancestral Vision R 5.00 10.00
49 Bewilder C .07 .15
50 Brine Elemental U .12 .25
51 Cancel C .07 .15
52 Careful Consideration U .12 .25
53 Clockspinning C .75 1.50
54 Coral Trickster C .07 .15
55 Crookclaw Transmuter C .07 .15
56 Deep-Sea Kraken R .75 1.50
57 Draining Whelk R 2.50 5.00
58 Dream Stalker C .30 .60
59 Drifter il-Dal C .07 .15
60 Errant Ephemeron C .07 .15
61 Eternity Snare C .07 .15
62 Fathom Seer C .07 .15
63 Fledgling Mawcor U .12 .25
64 Fool's Demise U .12 .25
65 Ixidron R .30 .75
66 Looter il-Kor C 1.00 2.00
67 Magus of the Jar R 1.50 3.00
68 Moonlace R .25 .50
69 Mystical Teachings C .20 .40
70 Ophidian Eye C 1.50 3.00
71 Paradox Haze U 6.00 12.00
72 Psionic Sliver R 2.50 5.00
73 Riftwing Cloudskate U .12 .25
74 Sage of Epityr C .25 .50
75 Screeching Sliver C .20 .40
76 Shadow Sliver C 1.00 2.00
77 Slipstream Serpent C .07 .15
78 Snapback C .07 .15
79 Spell Burst U .50 1.00
80 Spiketail Drakeling C .07 .15
81 Sprite Noble R .50 1.00
82 Stormcloud Djinn U .12 .25
83 Teferi, Mage of Zhalfir R 4.00 8.00
84 Telekinetic Sliver U 1.50 3.00
85 Temporal Eddy C .07 .15
86 Think Twice C .07 .15
87 Tolarian Sentinel C .07 .15
88 Trickbind R 5.00 10.00
89 Truth or Tale U .12 .25
90 Vesuvan Shapeshifter R .30 .75
91 Viscerid Deepwalker C .07 .15
92 Voidmage Husher U .50 1.00
93 Walk the Aeons R 6.00 12.00
94 Wipe Away U .30 .60
95 Assassinate C .07 .15
96 Basal Sliver C .60 1.25
97 Call to the Netherworld C .20 .40
98 Corpulent Corpse C .07 .15
99 Curse of the Cabal R 6.00 12.00
100 Cyclopean Giant C .07 .15
101 Dark Withering C .15 .30
102 Deathspore Thallid C .25 .50
103 Demonic Collusion R 2.50 5.00
104 Dread Return U .50 1.00
105 Drudge Reavers C .07 .15
106 Endrek Sahr, Master Breeder R 2.50 5.00
107 Evil Eye of Urborg U .12 .25
108 Faceless Devourer U .12 .25
109 Fallen Ideal U .20 .40
110 Feebleness C .07 .15
111 Gorgon Recluse C .15 .30
112 Haunting Hymn U .12 .25
113 Liege of the Pit R .25 .50
114 Lim-Dul the Necromancer R 1.25 2.50
115 Living End R 4.00 8.00
116 Magus of the Mirror R .25 .50
117 Mana Skimmer C .07 .15
118 Mindlash Sliver C .20 .40
119 Mindstab C .07 .15
120 Nether Traitor R 10.00 20.00
121 Nightshade Assassin U .12 .25
122 Phthisis U .12 .25
123 Pit Keeper C .07 .15
124 Plague Sliver R .60 1.25
125 Premature Burial U .12 .25
126 Psychotic Episode C .07 .15
127 Sangrophage C .07 .15
128 Sengir Nosferatu R .25 .50
129 Skittering Monstrosity U .12 .25
130 Skulking Knight C .07 .15
131 Smallpox U .50 1.00
132 Strangling Soot C .07 .15
133 Stronghold Overseer R .60 1.25
134 Sudden Death U .12 .25
135 Sudden Spoiling R 3.00 6.00
136 Tendrils of Corruption C .07 .15
137 Traitor's Clutch C .07 .15
138 Trespasser il-Vec C .07 .15
139 Urborg Syphon-Mage C .07 .15
140 Vampiric Sliver U .75 1.50
141 Viscid Lemures C .07 .15
142 Aetherflame Wall C .07 .15
143 Ancient Grudge C .15 .30
144 Barbed Shocker U .12 .25
145 Basalt Gargoyle U .12 .25
146 Blazing Blade Askari C .07 .15
147 Bogardan Hellkite R .50 1.00
148 Bogardan Rager C .07 .15
149 Bonesplitter Sliver C .30 .60
150 Coal Stoker C .07 .15
151 Conflagrate U .20 .40
152 Empty the Warrens C .30 .75
153 Firemaw Kavu U .12 .25
154 Flamecore Elemental C .07 .15
155 Flowstone Channeler C .07 .15
156 Fortune Thief R .25 .50
157 Fury Sliver U .75 1.50
158 Ghitu Firebreathing C .07 .15
159 Goblin Skycutter C .07 .15
160 Grapeshot C .50 1.00
161 Greater Gargadon R 1.25 2.50
162 Ground Rift C .60 1.25
163 Ib Halfheart, Goblin Tactician R 1.25 2.50
164 Ignite Memories U 1.25 2.50
165 Ironclaw Buzzardiers C .07 .15
166 Jaya Ballard, Task Mage R .60 1.25
167 Keldon Halberdier C .07 .15
168 Lightning Axe C .25 .50
169 Magus of the Scroll R .25 .50
170 Mogg War Marshal C .30 .75
171 Norin the Wary R 1.25 2.50
172 Orcish Cannonade C .07 .15
173 Pardic Dragon R .25 .50
174 Plunder C .07 .15
175 Reiterate R 10.00 20.00
176 Rift Bolt C .50 1.00
177 Sedge Sliver R 5.00 10.00
178 Subterranean Shambler C .07 .15
179 Sudden Shock U .12 .25
180 Sulfurous Blast U .12 .25
181 Tectonic Fiend U .12 .25
182 Thick-Skinned Goblin U .12 .25
183 Two-Headed Sliver C .50 1.00
184 Undying Rage U .12 .25
185 Viashino Bladescout C .07 .15
186 Volcanic Awakening U .12 .25
187 Wheel of Fate R 2.50 5.00
188 Word of Seizing R .25 .50
189 Aether Web C .07 .15
190 Ashcoat Bear C .30 .75
191 Aspect of Mongoose U .60 1.25
192 Chameleon Blur C .07 .15
193 Durkwood Baloth C .07 .15
194 Durkwood Tracker U .12 .25
195 Fungus Sliver R 1.25 2.50
196 Gemhide Sliver C 1.25 2.50
197 Glass Asp C .07 .15
198 Greenseeker C .07 .15
199 Havenwood Wurm C .07 .15
200 Herd Gnarr C .07 .15
201 Hypergenesis R 1.25 2.50
202 Krosan Grip U 2.00 4.00
203 Magus of the Candelabra R 1.00 2.00
204 Might of Old Krosa U 1.00 2.00
205 Might Sliver U 1.00 2.00
206 Molder C .07 .15
207 Mwonvuli Acid-Moss C .75 1.50
208 Nantuko Shaman C .07 .15
209 Pendelhaven Elder U .12 .25
210 Penumbra Spider C .07 .15
211 Phantom Wurm U .12 .25
212 Primal Forcemage U .12 .25
213 Savage Thallid C .25 .50
214 Scarwood Treefolk C .07 .15
215 Scryb Ranger U .75 1.50
216 Search for Tomorrow C .07 .15
217 Spectral Force R .25 .50
218 Spike Tiller R .25 .50
219 Spinneret Sliver C .50 1.00
220 Sporesower Thallid U .30 .75
221 Sprout C .07 .15
222 Squall Line R 1.25 2.50
223 Stonewood Invocation R .75 1.50
224 Strength in Numbers C .07 .15
225 Thallid Germinator C .07 .15
226 Thallid Shell-Dweller C .15 .30
227 Thelon of Havenwood R .75 1.50
228 Thelonite Hermit R .30 .60
229 Thrill of the Hunt C .07 .15
230 Tromp the Domains U .12 .25
231 Unyaro Bees R .25 .50
232 Verdant Embrace R 2.00 4.00
233 Wormwood Dryad C .07 .15
234 Wurmcalling R .75 1.50
235 Yavimaya Dryad U .25 .50
236 Dementia Sliver U .20 .40
237 Dralnu, Lich Lord R .75 1.50
238 Firewake Sliver U .25 .50
239 Ghostflame Sliver U .30 .75
240 Harmonic Sliver U 2.00 4.00
241 Ith, High Arcanist R .30 .60
242 Kaervek the Merciless R 7.50 15.00
243 Mishra, Artificer Prodigy R .25 .50
244 Opaline Sliver U 3.00 6.00
245 Saffi Eriksdotter R 6.00 12.00
246 Scion of the Ur-Dragon R 3.00 6.00
247 Stonebrow, Krosan Hero R .50 1.00
248 Assembly-Worker U .12 .25
249 Brass Gnat C .07 .15
250 Candles of Leng R .25 .50
251 Chromatic Star C .50 1.00
252 Chronatog Totem U .12 .25
253 Clockwork Hydra U .12 .25
254 Foriysian Totem U .12 .25
255 Gauntlet of Power R 12.50 25.00
256 Hivestone R 1.50 3.00
257 Jhoira's Timebug C .07 .15
258 Locket of Yesterdays U 2.00 4.00
259 Lotus Bloom R 4.00 8.00
260 Paradise Plume U .12 .25
261 Phyrexian Totem U .12 .25
262 Prismatic Lens C .30 .60
263 Sarpadian Empires, Vol. VII R .25 .50
264 Stuffy Doll R 5.00 10.00
265 Thunder Totem U .12 .25
266 Triskelavus R .25 .50
267 Venser's Sliver C .15 .30
268 Weatherseed Totem U .12 .25
269 Academy Ruins R 6.00 12.00
270 Calciform Pools U .50 1.00
271 Dreadship Reef U .20 .40
272 Flagstones of Trokair R 7.50 15.00
273 Fungal Reaches U .12 .25
274 Gemstone Caverns R 30.00 60.00
275 Kher Keep R 2.50 5.00
276 Molten Slagheap U .12 .25
277 Saltcrusted Steppe U .12 .25
278 Swarmyard R 6.00 12.00
279 Terramorphic Expanse C .20 .40
280 Urza's Factory U .20 .40
281 Vesuva R 20.00 40.00
282 Plains L .07 .15
283 Plains L .07 .15
284 Plains L .07 .15
285 Plains L .07 .15
286 Island L .07 .15
287 Island L .07 .15
288 Island L .07 .15
289 Island L .30 .60
290 Swamp L .12 .25
291 Swamp L .12 .25
292 Swamp L .12 .25
293 Swamp L .12 .25
294 Mountain L .12 .25
295 Mountain L .12 .25
296 Mountain L .12 .25
297 Mountain L .12 .25
298 Forest L .10 .20
299 Forest L .10 .20
300 Forest L .10 .20
301 Forest L .10 .20

2006 Magic The Gathering Time Spiral Timeshifted

1 Akroma, Angel of Wrath TR 2.50 5.00
2 Auratog TR .30 .75
3 Celestial Dawn TR 2.00 4.00
4 Consecrate Land TR .60 1.25
5 Defiant Vanguard TR .12 .25
6 Disenchant TR .75 1.50
7 Enduring Renewal TR 1.50 3.00
8 Essence Sliver TR 7.50 15.00
9 Honorable Passage TR .12 .25
10 Icatian Javelineers TR .12 .25
11 Moorish Cavalry TR .12 .25
12 Resurrection TR .20 .40
13 Sacred Mesa TR .20 .40
14 Soltari Priest TR .20 .40
15 Squire TR .12 .25
16 Valor TR .15 .30
17 Witch Hunter TR .15 .30
18 Zhalfirin Commander TR .12 .25
19 Dandan TR 1.00 2.00
20 Flying Men TR 1.50 3.00
21 Ghost Ship TR .12 .25
22 Giant Oyster TR .12 .25
23 Leviathan TR .20 .40
24 Lord of Atlantis TR 20.00 40.00
25 Merfolk Assassin TR .15 .30
26 Mistform Ultimus TR .20 .40
27 Ovinomancer TR .12 .25
28 Pirate Ship TR .20 .40
29 Prodigal Sorcerer TR .20 .40
30 Psionic Blast TR 4.00 8.00
31 Sindbad TR .12 .25
32 Stormscape Familiar TR .25 .50
33 Unstable Mutation TR .15 .30
34 Voidmage Prodigy TR 1.50 3.00
35 Whispers of the Muse TR .25 .50
36 Willbender TR .12 .25
37 Avatar of Woe TR 1.50 3.00
38 Bad Moon TR 2.00 4.00
39 Conspiracy TR 7.50 15.00
40 Darkness TR 15.00 30.00
41 Dauthi Slayer TR 1.00 2.00
42 Evil Eye of Orms-by-Gore TR .20 .40
43 Faceless Butcher TR .20 .40
44 Funeral Charm TR .75 1.50
45 Sengir Autocrat TR .30 .60
46 Shadow Guildmage TR .12 .25
47 Soul Collector TR .30 .75
48 Stupor TR .25 .50
49 Swamp Mosquito TR .30 .60
50 Twisted Abomination TR .15 .30
51 Uncle Istvan TR .15 .30
52 Undead Warchief TR 4.00 8.00
53 Undertaker TR .12 .25
54 Withered Wretch TR .25 .50
55 Avalanche Riders TR .50 1.00
56 Browbeat TR .30 .75
57 Desolation Giant TR .20 .40
58 Disintegrate TR .25 .50
59 Dragon Whelp TR .20 .40
60 Dragonstorm TR 2.00 4.00
61 Eron the Relentless TR .12 .25
62 Fiery Temper TR .25 .50
63 Fire Whip TR .15 .30
64 Goblin Snowman TR .20 .40
65 Kobold Taskmaster TR .20 .40
66 Orcish Librarian TR .20 .40
67 Orgg TR .12 .25
68 Pandemonium TR 2.00 4.00
69 Suq'Ata Lancer TR .12 .25
70 Tribal Flames TR .15 .30
71 Uthden Troll TR .12 .25
72 Wildfire Emissary TR .12 .25
73 Avoid Fate TR 4.00 8.00
74 Call of the Herd TR .20 .40
75 Cockatrice TR .60 1.25
76 Craw Giant TR .30 .75
77 Gaea's Blessing TR .30 .75
78 Gaea's Liege TR .20 .40
79 Hail Storm TR .12 .25
80 Hunting Moa TR .12 .25
81 Jolrael, Empress of Beasts TR 1.00 2.00
82 Krosan Cloudscraper TR .25 .50
83 Scragnoth TR .12 .25
84 Spike Feeder TR 1.50 3.00
85 Spitting Slug TR .12 .25
86 Thallid TR .30 .60
87 Thornscape Battlemage TR .12 .25
88 Verdeloth the Ancient TR 1.50 3.00
89 Wall of Roots TR .50 1.00
90 Whirling Dervish TR .15 .30
91 Coalition Victory TR 7.50 15.00
92 Fiery Justice TR .20 .40
93 Jasmine Boreal TR .25 .50
94 Lightning Angel TR .30 .60
95 Merieke Ri Berit TR 4.00 8.00
96 Mystic Enforcer TR .15 .30
97 Mystic Snake TR 1.00 2.00
98 Nicol Bolas TR 2.50 5.00
99 Shadowmage Infiltrator TR .25 .50
100 Sol'kanar the Swamp King TR .20 .40
101 Spined Sliver TR .30 .60
102 Stormbind TR .12 .25
103 Teferi's Moat TR .60 1.25
104 Vhati il-Dal TR 1.50 3.00
105 Void TR .30 .60
106 Assault/Battery TR .12 .25
107 Claws of Gix TR 7.50 15.00
108 Dodecapod TR .12 .25
109 Feldon's Cane TR .50 1.00
110 Grinning Totem TR .20 .40
111 Mindless Automaton TR .20 .40
112 Mirari TR .50 1.00
113 The Rack TR 3.00 6.00
114 Serrated Arrows TR .50 1.00
115 Tormod's Crypt TR 3.00 6.00
116 War Barge TR .12 .25
117 Arena TR 3.00 6.00
118 Desert TR 1.50 3.00
119 Gemstone Mine TR 6.00 12.00
120 Pendelhaven TR 3.00 6.00
121 Safe Haven TR .30 .60

2007 Magic The Gathering Duel Decks Elves vs. Goblins

1 Ambush Commander R 2.00 4.00
2 Allosaurus Rider R .50 1.00
3 Elvish Eulogist C .12 .25
4 Elvish Harbinger U 1.50 3.00
5 Elvish Warrior C .12 .25
6 Gempalm Strider U .25 .50
7 Heedless One U 2.00 4.00
8 Imperious Perfect U 3.00 6.00
9 Llanowar Elves C .25 .50
10 Lys Alana Huntmaster C .30 .75
11 Stonewood Invoker C .12 .25
12 Sylvan Messenger U 1.00 2.00
13 Timberwatch Elf C .75 1.50
14 Voice of the Woods R .75 1.50
15 Wellwisher C 1.00 2.00
16 Wirewood Herald C .30 .75
17 Wirewood Symbiote U 1.50 3.00
18 Wood Elves C .12 .25
19 Wren's Run Vanquisher U 1.00 2.00
20 Elvish Promenade U 2.00 4.00
21 Giant Growth C .12 .25
22 Harmonize U 1.00 2.00
23 Wildsize C .12 .25
24 Moonglove Extract C .12 .25

25 Slate of Ancestry R	.50	1.00
26 Wirewood Lodge U	1.50	3.00
27 Tranquil Thicket C	.12	.25
28 Forest L	.20	.40
29 Forest L	.20	.40
30 Forest L	.20	.40
31 Forest L	.20	.40
32 Siege-Gang Commander R	1.50	3.00
33 Akki Coalflinger U	.25	.50
34 Clickslither R	.30	.75
35 Emberwilde Augur C	.12	.25
36 Flamewave Invoker U	.25	.50
37 Gempalm Incinerator U	.75	1.50
38 Goblin Cohort C	.12	.25
39 Goblin Matron U	1.00	2.00
40 Goblin Ringleader U	1.50	3.00
41 Goblin Sledder C	.12	.25
42 Goblin Warchief U	2.00	4.00
43 Ib Halfheart, Goblin Tactician R	.30	.75
44 Mogg Fanatic U	.75	1.50
45 Mogg War Marshal C	.50	1.00
46 Mudbutton Torchrunner C	.12	.25
47 Raging Goblin C	.12	.25
48 Reckless One U	.30	.75
49 Skirk Drill Sergeant U	.25	.50
50 Skirk Fire Marshal R	.50	1.00
51 Skirk Prospector C	.25	.50
52 Skirk Shaman C	.12	.25
53 Tar Pitcher U	.25	.50
54 Boggart Shenanigans U	.25	.50
55 Spitting Earth C	.12	.25
56 Tarfire C	.12	.25
57 Forgotten Cave C	.12	.25
58 Goblin Burrows U	.25	.50
59 Mountain L	.20	.40
60 Mountain L	.20	.40
61 Mountain L	.20	.40
62 Mountain L	.20	.40

2007 Magic The Gathering Duel Decks Elves vs. Goblins Tokens

T1 Elemental	.30	.75
T2 Elf Warrior	.50	1.00
T3 Goblin	.50	1.00

2007 Magic The Gathering Future Sight

1 Angel of Salvation R	.25	.50
2 Augur il-Vec C	.12	.25
3 Barren Glory R	.60	1.25
4 Chronomantic Escape U	2.50	5.00
5 Dust of Moments U	.10	.20
6 Even the Odds U	.10	.20
7 Gift of Granite C	.07	.15
8 Intervention Pact R	2.00	4.00
9 Judge Unworthy C	.07	.15
10 Knight of Sursi C	.07	.15
11 Lost Auramancers U	.50	1.00
12 Magus of the Moat R	4.00	8.00
13 Marshaling Cry C	.07	.15
14 Saltskitter C	.07	.15
15 Samite Censer-Bearer C	.07	.15
16 Scout's Warning R	3.00	6.00
17 Spirit en-Dal U	.25	.50
18 Aven Mindcensor U	3.00	6.00
19 Blade of the Sixth Pride C	.07	.15
20 Bound in Silence U	.10	.20
21 Daybreak Coronet R	3.00	6.00
22 Goldmeadow Lookout U	.10	.20
23 Imperial Mask R	.25	.50
24 Lucent Liminid C	.07	.15
25 Lumithread Field C	.07	.15
26 Lymph Sliver C	.20	.40
27 Mistmeadow Skulk U	.10	.20
28 Oriss, Samite Guardian R	.60	1.25
29 Patrician's Scorn C	.07	.15
30 Ramosian Revivalist U	.10	.20
31 Seht's Tiger R	.50	1.00
32 Aven Augur C	.07	.15
33 Cloudseeder U	.20	.40
34 Cryptic Annelid U	.20	.40
35 Delay U	4.00	8.00
36 Foresee C	.07	.15
37 Infiltrator il-Kor C	.07	.15
38 Leaden Fists C	.07	.15
39 Maelstrom Djinn R	.25	.50
40 Magus of the Future R	1.00	2.00
41 Mystic Speculation U	2.50	5.00
42 Pact of Negation R	30.00	60.00
43 Reality Strobe U	.50	1.00
44 Take Possession R	.25	.50
45 Unblinking Bleb C	.25	.50
46 Venser, Shaper Savant R	7.50	15.00
47 Venser's Diffusion C	.07	.15
48 Arcanum Wings U	.60	1.25
49 Blind Phantasm C	.07	.15
50 Bonded Fetch U	.10	.20
51 Linessa, Zephyr Mage R	.30	.75
52 Logic Knot C	.25	.50
53 Mesmeric Sliver C	.20	.40
54 Narcomoeba U	1.25	2.50
55 Nix R	2.50	5.00
56 Sarcomite Myr C	.07	.15
57 Second Wind U	.10	.20
58 Shapeshifter's Marrow R	.25	.50
59 Spellweaver Volute R	2.00	4.00
60 Spin into Myth U	.10	.20
61 Vedalken Aethermage C	.75	1.50
62 Whip-Spine Drake C	.07	.15
63 Augur of Skulls C	.20	.40
64 Cutthroat il-Dal C	.07	.15
65 Festering March U	.10	.20
66 Gibbering Descent R	6.00	12.00
67 Grave Peril C	.07	.15
68 Ichor Slick C	.12	.25
69 Lost Hours C	.07	.15
70 Magus of the Abyss R	.30	.60
71 Minions' Murmurs U	.50	1.00
72 Nihilith R	.25	.50
73 Oblivion Crown C	.15	.30
74 Pooling Venom U	.20	.40
75 Putrid Cyclops C	.07	.15
76 Shimian Specter R	.25	.50
77 Skirk Ridge Exhumer U	.20	.40
78 Slaughter Pact R	4.00	8.00
79 Stronghold Rats U	2.50	5.00
80 Bitter Ordeal R	10.00	20.00
81 Bridge from Below R	3.00	6.00
82 Death Rattle C	.07	.15
83 Deepcavern Imp C	.07	.15
84 Fleshwrither U	.75	1.50
85 Frenzy Sliver C	.20	.40
86 Grave Scrabbler C	.12	.25
87 Korlash, Heir to Blackblade R	3.00	6.00
88 Mass of Ghouls C	.07	.15
89 Snake Cult Initiation U	.25	.50
90 Street Wraith U	3.00	6.00
91 Tombstalker R	1.25	2.50
92 Witch's Mist U	.10	.20
93 Yixlid Jailer U	.50	1.00
94 Arc Blade U	.20	.40
95 Bogardan Lancer C	.07	.15
96 Char-Rumbler U	.10	.20
97 Emberwilde Augur C	.07	.15
98 Fatal Attraction C	.07	.15
99 Gathan Raiders C	.07	.15
100 Haze of Rage U	.50	1.00
101 Magus of the Moon R	12.50	25.00
102 Molten Disaster R	.30	.60
103 Pact of the Titan R	1.25	2.50
104 Pyromancer's Swath R	.50	1.00
105 Riddle of Lightning C	.07	.15
106 Rift Elemental C	.07	.15
107 Scourge of Kher Ridges R	2.00	4.00
108 Shivan Sand-Mage U	.25	.50
109 Sparkspitter U	.10	.20
110 Bloodshot Trainee U	.10	.20
111 Boldwyr Intimidator U	.10	.20
112 Emblem of the Warmind U	.15	.30
113 Flowstone Embrace C	.07	.15
114 Fomori Nomad C	.07	.15
115 Ghostfire C	.07	.15
116 Grinning Ignus C	.15	.30
117 Henchfiend of Ukor C	.07	.15
118 Homing Sliver C	.30	.60
119 Shah of Naar Isle R	.25	.50
120 Skizzik Surger U	.10	.20
121 Steamflogger Boss R	.25	.50
122 Storm Entity U	.20	.40
123 Tarox Bladewing R	.25	.50
124 Thunderblade Charge R	.25	.50
125 Cyclical Evolution U	.10	.20
126 Force of Savagery R	1.00	2.00
127 Heartwood Storyteller R	6.00	12.00
128 Kavu Primarch C	.07	.15
129 Llanowar Augur C	.15	.30
130 Llanowar Empath C	.07	.15
131 Llanowar Mentor U	.60	1.25
132 Magus of the Vineyard R	3.00	6.00
133 Petrified Plating C	.07	.15
134 Quiet Disrepair C	.07	.15
135 Ravaging Riftwurm U	.10	.20
136 Riftsweeper U	1.00	2.00
137 Rites of Flourishing R	2.00	4.00
138 Sprout Swarm C	.30	.75
139 Summoner's Pact R	10.00	20.00
140 Utopia Mycon U	3.00	6.00
141 Wrap in Vigor C	.75	1.50
142 Baru, Fist of Krosa R	.75	1.50
143 Centaur Omenreader U	.20	.40
144 Edge of Autumn C	.75	1.50
145 Imperiosaur U	.10	.20
146 Muraganda Petroglyphs R	2.50	5.00
147 Nacatl War-Pride U	3.00	6.00
148 Nessian Courser C	.07	.15
149 Phosphorescent Feast U	.10	.20
150 Quagnoth R	.25	.50
151 Spellwild Ouphe U	.10	.20
152 Sporoloth Ancient C	.15	.30
153 Tarmogoyf R	30.00	75.00
154 Thornweald Archer C	.07	.15
155 Virulent Sliver C	.60	1.25
156 Glittering Wish R	1.25	2.50
157 Jhoira of the Ghitu R	1.25	2.50
158 Sliver Legion R	75.00	150.00
159 Akroma's Memorial R	20.00	40.00
160 Cloud Key R	20.00	40.00
161 Coalition Relic R	4.00	8.00
162 Epochrasite R	.25	.50
163 Sliversmith U	.25	.50
164 Soultether Golem U	.10	.20
165 Sword of the Meek U	2.00	4.00
166 Veilstone Amulet R	6.00	12.00
167 Darksteel Garrison R	.50	1.00
168 Whetwheel R	.25	.50
169 Dakmor Salvage U	.75	1.50
170 Keldon Megaliths U	.10	.20
171 Llanowar Reborn U	.75	1.50
172 New Benalia U	.10	.20
173 Tolaria West U	4.00	8.00
174 Dryad Arbor U	7.50	15.00
175 Graven Cairns R	4.00	8.00
176 Grove of the Burnwillows R	7.50	15.00
177 Horizon Canopy R	20.00	40.00
178 Nimbus Maze R	3.00	6.00
179 River of Tears R	3.00	6.00
180 Zoetic Cavern U	.20	.40

2007 Magic The Gathering Happy Holidays Promos

6 Fruitcake Elemental R	300.00	600.00
7 Gifts Given R	375.00	750.00
8 Evil Presents R	125.00	250.00
9 Season's Beatings R	75.00	150.00
10 Snow Mercy R	125.00	250.00
11 Yule Ooze R	75.00	150.00
12 Naughty/Nice R	25.00	50.00
13 Stocking Tiger R	50.00	100.00
14 Mishra's Toy Workshop M	50.00	100.00
15 Goblin Sleigh Ride M	25.00	50.00
16 Thopter Pie Network M	25.00	50.00
17 Some Disassembly Required M	15.00	30.00
18 Bog Humbugs M	25.00	50.00
19 Decorated Knight/Present Arms M	17.50	35.00
20 Topdeck the Halls M	30.00	75.00
21 Last-Minute Chopping M	30.00	75.00
22 Chaos Wrap M	30.00	60.00

2007 Magic The Gathering Judge Gift Rewards

1 Ravenous Baloth R	15.00	30.00
2 Cunning Wish R	25.00	50.00
3 Yawgmoth's Will R	400.00	800.00
4 Vindicate R	25.00	50.00
5 Decree of Justice R	12.50	25.00

2007 Magic The Gathering Lorwyn

1 Ajani Goldmane R	4.00	8.00
2 Arbiter of Knollridge R	.25	.50
3 Austere Command R	3.00	6.00
4 Avian Changeling C	.15	.30
5 Battle Mastery U	.12	.25
6 Brigid, Hero of Kinsbaile R	.60	1.25
7 Burrenton Forge-Tender U	.30	.75
8 Cenn's Heir C	.07	.15
9 Changeling Hero U	.25	.50
10 Cloudgoat Ranger U	.10	.20
11 Crib Swap U	.10	.20
12 Dawnfluke C	.07	.15
13 Entangling Trap U	.10	.20
14 Favor of the Mighty R	.30	.75
15 Galepowder Mage R	.25	.50
16 Goldmeadow Dodger C	.07	.15
17 Goldmeadow Harrier C	.07	.15
18 Goldmeadow Stalwart U	.10	.20
19 Harpoon Sniper U	.10	.20
20 Hillcomber Giant C	.07	.15
21 Hoofprints of the Stag R	.25	.50
22 Judge of Currents C	.07	.15
23 Kinsbaile Balloonist C	.07	.15
24 Kinsbaile Skirmisher C	.07	.15
25 Kithkin Greatheart C	.07	.15
26 Kithkin Harbinger U	.20	.40
27 Kithkin Healer C	.07	.15
28 Knight of Meadowgrain U	.75	1.50
29 Lairwatch Giant C	.07	.15
30 Militia's Pride R	1.00	2.00
31 Mirror Entity R	2.50	5.00
32 Neck Snap C	.07	.15
33 Oaken Brawler C	.07	.15
34 Oblivion Ring C	.25	.50
35 Plover Knights C	.07	.15
36 Pollen Lullaby U	.10	.20
37 Purity R	1.25	2.50
38 Sentry Oak U	.10	.20
39 Shields of Velis Vel C	.30	.75
40 Soaring Hope C	.07	.15
41 Springjack Knight C	.07	.15
42 Summon the School U	.15	.30
43 Surge of Thoughtweft C	.07	.15
44 Thoughtweft Trio R	.30	.75
45 Triclopean Sight C	.17	.35
46 Veteran of the Depths U	.10	.20
47 Wellgabber Apothecary C	.07	.15
48 Wispmare C	.20	.40
49 Wizened Cenn U	.10	.20
50 Aethersnipe C	.07	.15
51 Amoeboid Changeling C	.75	1.50
52 Aquitect's Will C	.20	.40
53 Benthicore U	.10	.20
54 Broken Ambitions C	.07	.15
55 Captivating Glance U	.10	.20
56 Cryptic Command R	15.00	30.00
57 Deeptread Merrow C	.07	.15
58 Drowner of Secrets U	.10	.20
59 Ego Erasure U	.10	.20
60 Ethereal Whiskergill U	.10	.20
61 Faerie Harbinger U	.75	1.50
62 Faerie Trickery C	.25	.50
63 Fallowsage U	.30	.75
64 Familiar's Ruse U	.50	1.00
65 Fathom Trawl R	.25	.50
66 Forced Fruition R	10.00	20.00
67 Glen Elendra Pranksters U	.10	.20
68 Glimmerdust Nap C	.07	.15
69 Guile R	.60	1.25
70 Inkfathom Divers C	.07	.15
71 Jace Beleren R	2.50	5.00
72 Merrow Commerce U	3.00	6.00
73 Merrow Harbinger U	1.25	2.50
74 Merrow Reejerey U	2.00	4.00
75 Mistbind Clique R	6.00	12.00
76 Mulldrifter C	.50	1.00
77 Paperfin Rascal C	.07	.15
78 Pestermite C	.30	.60
79 Ponder C	3.00	6.00
80 Protective Bubble C	.07	.15
81 Ringskipper C	.07	.15
82 Scattering Stroke U	.10	.20
83 Scion of Oona R	7.50	15.00
84 Sentinels of Glen Elendra C	.07	.15
85 Shapesharer R	10.00	20.00
86 Silvergill Adept U	.30	.60
87 Silvergill Douser C	.07	.15
88 Sower of Temptation R	3.00	6.00
89 Spellstutter Sprite C	1.50	3.00
90 Stonybrook Angler C	.07	.15
91 Streambed Aquitects C	.07	.15
92 Surgespanner R	2.50	5.00
93 Tideshaper Mystic C	.07	.15
94 Turtleshell Changeling U	.10	.20
95 Wanderwine Prophets R	3.00	6.00
96 Whirlpool Whelm C	.07	.15
97 Wings of Velis Vel C	.07	.15
98 Zephyr Net C	.07	.15
99 Black Poplar Shaman C	.07	.15
100 Bog Hoodlums C	.07	.15
101 Boggart Birth Rite C	.07	.15
102 Boggart Harbinger U	1.50	3.00
103 Boggart Loggers C	.07	.15
104 Boggart Mob R	.60	1.25
105 Cairn Wanderer R	.60	1.25
106 Colfenor's Plans R	.25	.50
107 Dread R	6.00	12.00
108 Dreamspoiler Witches C	.07	.15
109 Exiled Boggart C	.07	.15
110 Eyeblight's Ending C	.07	.15
111 Facevaulter C	.07	.15
112 Faerie Tauntings U	.20	.40
113 Final Revels U	.10	.20
114 Fodder Launch U	.17	.35
115 Footbottom Feast U	.20	.40
116 Ghostly Changeling U	.10	.20
117 Hoarder's Greed U	.10	.20
118 Hornet Harasser C	.07	.15
119 Hunter of Eyeblights C	.07	.15
120 Knucklebone Witch R	1.25	2.50
121 Liliana Vess R	7.50	15.00
122 Lys Alana Scarblade R	.25	.50
123 Mad Auntie R	.75	1.50
124 Makeshift Mannequin U	.10	.20
125 Marsh Flitter R	.25	.50
126 Moonglove Winnower U	.10	.20
127 Mournwhelk C	.07	.15
128 Nameless Inversion C	.07	.15
129 Nath's Buffoon C	.07	.15
130 Nectar Faerie R	.25	.50
131 Nettlevine Blight C	.50	1.00
132 Nightshade Stinger U	.10	.20
133 Oona's Prowler R	2.00	4.00
134 Peppersmoke C	.07	.15
135 Profane Command R	.50	1.00
136 Prowess of the Fair U	.30	.75
137 Quill-Slinger Boggart R	.25	.50
138 Scarred Vinebreeder U	.10	.20
139 Shriekmaw U	.60	1.25
140 Skeletal Changeling C	.30	.75
141 Spiderwig Boggart U	.10	.20
142 Squeaking Pie Sneak U	.15	.30
143 Thieving Sprite C	.07	.15
144 Thorntooth Witch U	.10	.20
145 Thoughtseize R	20.00	40.00
146 Warren Pilferers C	.07	.15
147 Weed Strangle C	.07	.15
148 Adder-Staff Boggart C	.07	.15
149 Ashling the Pilgrim R	2.00	4.00
150 Ashling's Prerogative R	.50	1.00
151 Axegrinder Giant C	.07	.15
152 Blades of Velis Vel C	.07	.15
153 Blind-Spot Giant C	.07	.15
154 Boggart Forager C	.07	.15
155 Boggart Shenanigans U	1.50	3.00
156 Boggart Sprite-Chaser C	.07	.15
157 Caterwauling Boggart C	.15	.30
158 Ceaseless Searblades U	.10	.20
159 Chandra Nalaar R	1.50	3.00
160 Changeling Berserker U	1.25	2.50
161 Consuming Bonfire C	.07	.15
162 Crush Underfoot U	.10	.20
163 Faultgrinder C	.07	.15
164 Fire-Belly Changeling C	.30	.60
165 Flamekin Bladewhirl U	.10	.20
166 Flamekin Brawler C	.07	.15
167 Flamekin Harbinger U	1.50	3.00
168 Flamekin Spitfire U	.10	.20
169 Giant Harbinger U	.30	.60
170 Giant's Ire C	.07	.15
171 Glarewielder U	.10	.20
172 Goatnapper U	.10	.20
173 Hamletback Goliath R	.25	.50
174 Hearthcage Giant U	.10	.20
175 Heat Shimmer R	2.00	4.00
176 Hostility R	.25	.50
177 Hurly-Burly C	.07	.15
178 Incandescent Soulstoke R	1.25	2.50
179 Incendiary Command R	1.25	2.50
180 Ingot Chewer C	.07	.15
181 Inner-Flame Acolyte C	.07	.15
182 Inner-Flame Igniter U	.10	.20
183 Lash Out C	.07	.15
184 Lowland Oaf C	.07	.15
185 Mudbutton Torchrunner C	.07	.15
186 Needle Drop C	.75	1.50
187 Nova Chaser R	2.50	5.00
188 Rebellion of the Flamekin U	.10	.20
189 Smokebraider C	.20	.40
190 Soulbright Flamekin C	.07	.15
191 Stinkdrinker Daredevil C	.07	.15
192 Sunrise Sovereign R	.25	.50
193 Tar Pitcher U	.10	.20
194 Tarfire C	.20	.40
195 Thundercloud Shaman U	.10	.20
196 Wild Ricochet R	.50	1.00
197 Battlewand Oak C	.07	.15
198 Bog-Strider Ash C	.07	.15
199 Briarhorn U	.10	.20
200 Changeling Titan U	1.50	3.00
201 Cloudcrown Oak C	.07	.15
202 Cloudthresher R	.30	.75
203 Dauntless Dourbark R	2.00	4.00
204 Elvish Branchbender C	.07	.15
205 Elvish Eulogist C	.07	.15
206 Elvish Handservant C	.07	.15
207 Elvish Harbinger U	7.50	15.00
208 Elvish Promenade U	3.00	6.00
209 Epic Proportions R	.25	.50
210 Eyes of the Wisent R	.30	.60
211 Fertile Ground C	.15	.30
212 Fistful of Force C	.07	.15
213 Garruk Wildspeaker R	4.00	8.00
214 Gilt-Leaf Ambush C	.15	.30
215 Gilt-Leaf Seer C	.07	.15
216 Guardian of Cloverdell U	.10	.20
217 Heal the Scars C	.07	.15
218 Hunt Down C	.07	.15
219 Immaculate Magistrate R	1.50	3.00
220 Imperious Perfect U	.75	1.50
221 Incremental Growth U	.10	.20
222 Jagged-Scar Archers U	.25	.50
223 Kithkin Daggerdare C	.07	.15
224 Kithkin Mourncaller U	.10	.20
225 Lace with Moonglove C	.07	.15
226 Lammastide Weave U	.10	.20
227 Leaf Gilder C	.07	.15
228 Lignify C	.50	1.00
229 Lys Alana Huntmaster C	.30	.75
230 Masked Admirers R	.25	.50
231 Nath's Elite C	.07	.15
232 Oakgnarl Warrior C	.07	.15
233 Primal Command R	1.50	3.00
234 Rootgrapple C	.07	.15
235 Seedguide Ash U	.75	1.50
236 Spring Cleaning C	.07	.15
237 Sylvan Echoes U	.10	.20
238 Timber Protector R	10.00	20.00

239 Treefolk Harbinger U 1.50 3.00
240 Vigor R 7.50 15.00
241 Warren-Scourge Elf C .07 .15
242 Woodland Changeling C .75 1.50
243 Woodland Guidance U .10 .20
244 Wren's Run Packmaster R .50 1.00
245 Wren's Run Vanquisher U .30 .60
246 Brion Stoutarm R .60 1.25
247 Doran, the Siege Tower R 3.00 6.00
248 Gaddock Teeg R 4.00 8.00
249 Horde of Notions R .60 1.25
250 Nath of the Gilt-Leaf R 3.00 6.00
251 Sygg, River Guide R .75 1.50
252 Wort, Boggart Auntie R 6.00 12.00
253 Wydwen, the Biting Gale R .50 1.00
254 Colfenor's Urn R 2.00 4.00
255 Deathrender R 2.50 5.00
256 Dolmen Gate R 5.00 10.00
257 Herbal Poultice C .20 .40
258 Moonglove Extract C .07 .15
259 Rings of Brighthearth R 7.50 15.00
260 Runed Stalactite C .07 .15
261 Springleaf Drum C .50 1.00
262 Thorn of Amethyst R 20.00 40.00
263 Thousand-Year Elixir R 17.50 35.00
264 Twinning Glass R .25 .50
265 Wanderer's Twig C .30 .75
266 Ancient Amphitheater R .50 1.00
267 Auntie's Hovel R 12.50 25.00
268 Gilt-Leaf Palace R 12.50 25.00
269 Howltooth Hollow R .25 .50
270 Mosswort Bridge R .75 1.50
271 Secluded Glen R 3.00 6.00
272 Shelldock Isle R 6.00 12.00
273 Shimmering Grotto C .07 .15
274 Spinerock Knoll R 1.50 3.00
275 Vivid Crag U .60 1.25
276 Vivid Creek U .50 1.00
277 Vivid Grove U .30 .75
278 Vivid Marsh U 1.00 2.00
279 Vivid Meadow U 1.00 2.00
280 Wanderwine Hub R 3.00 6.00
281 Windbrisk Heights R 1.00 2.00
282 Plains L .25 .50
283 Plains L .25 .50
284 Plains L .25 .50
285 Plains L .25 .50
286 Island L .25 .50
287 Island L 1.00 2.00
288 Island L .25 .50
289 Island L .25 .50
290 Swamp L .30 .60
291 Swamp L 1.00 2.00
292 Swamp L .30 .60
293 Swamp L .50 1.00
294 Mountain L .25 .50
295 Mountain L .25 .50
296 Mountain L .25 .50
297 Mountain L .25 .50
298 Forest L .25 .50
299 Forest L .25 .50
300 Forest L .25 .50
301 Forest L .25 .50

2007 Magic The Gathering Lorwyn Tokens

1 Avatar .50 1.00
2 Elemental .12 .25
3 Kithkin Soldier .07 .15
4 Merfolk Wizard .12 .25
5 Goblin Rogue .07 .15
6 Elemental Shaman .07 .15
7 Beast .10 .20
8 Elemental .07 .15
9 Elf Warrior .07 .15
10 Wolf .12 .25
11 Shapeshifter .10 .20

2007 Magic The Gathering Planar Chaos

1 Aven Riftwatcher C .07 .15
2 Benalish Commander R .50 1.00
3 Crovax, Ascendant Hero R 2.00 4.00
4 Dawn Charm C .25 .50
5 Dust Elemental R .30 .75
6 Ghost Tactician C .07 .15
7 Heroes Remembered R .60 1.25
8 Magus of the Tabernacle R .75 1.50
9 Mantle of Leadership U .10 .20
10 Pallid Mycoderm C .07 .15
11 Poultice Sliver C .15 .30
12 Rebuff the Wicked U 3.00 6.00
13 Retether R 3.00 6.00
14 Riftmarked Knight U .20 .40
15 Saltblast U .10 .20
16 Saltfield Recluse C .07 .15
17 Serra's Boon U .10 .20
18 Shade of Trokair C .07 .15
19 Stonecloaker U .20 .40
20 Stormfront Riders U .15 .30
21 Voidstone Gargoyle R .20 .40
22 Whitemane Lion C .07 .15
23 Calciderm U .10 .20
24 Malach of the Dawn U .15 .30
25 Mana Tithe C .75 1.50
26 Mesa Enchantress R 1.00 2.00
27 Mycologist U .10 .20
28 Porphyry Nodes R 1.25 2.50
29 Revered Dead C .07 .15
30 Sinew Sliver C 1.00 2.00
31 Sunlance C .07 .15
32 Aeon Chronicler R .20 .40
33 Aquamorph Entity C .07 .15
34 Auramancer's Guise U .75 1.50
35 Body Double R 1.25 2.50
36 Braids, Conjurer Adept R 1.25 2.50
37 Chronozoa R 1.00 2.00
38 Dichotomancy R .20 .40
39 Dismal Failure U .10 .20
40 Dreamscape Artist C .20 .40
41 Erratic Mutation C .07 .15
42 Jodah's Avenger U .10 .20
43 Magus of the Bazaar R .30 .75
44 Pongify U 2.00 4.00
45 Reality Acid C .20 .40
46 Shaper Parasite C .07 .15
47 Spellshift R .20 .40
48 Synchronous Sliver C .20 .40
49 Tidewalker U .10 .20
50 Timebender U .20 .40
51 Veiling Oddity C .07 .15
52 Venarian Glimmer U .10 .20
53 Wistful Thinking C .07 .15
54 Frozen Aether U .75 1.50
55 Gossamer Phantasm C .07 .15
56 Merfolk Thaumaturgist C .07 .15
57 Ovinize U .10 .20
58 Piracy Charm C .15 .30
59 Primal Plasma C .07 .15
60 Riptide Pilferer U .10 .20
61 Serendib Sorcerer R .20 .40
62 Serra Sphinx R .20 .40
63 Big Game Hunter U .30 .60
64 Blightspeaker C .07 .15
65 Brain Gorgers C .07 .15
66 Circle of Affliction U .15 .30
67 Cradle to Grave C .07 .15
68 Dash Hopes C .50 1.00
69 Deadly Grub C .07 .15
70 Enslave U .10 .20
71 Extirpate R 2.50 5.00
72 Imp's Mischief R 17.50 35.00
73 Magus of the Coffers R 6.00 12.00
74 Midnight Charm C .07 .15
75 Mirri the Cursed R 1.25 2.50
76 Muck Drubb U .75 1.50
77 Phantasmagorian U .30 .60
78 Ridged Kusite C .07 .15
79 Roiling Horror R .20 .40
80 Spitting Sliver C .15 .30
81 Temporal Extortion R 7.50 15.00
82 Treacherous Urge U .20 .40
83 Waning Wurm U .10 .20
84 Bog Serpent C .07 .15
85 Damnation R 25.00 50.00
86 Dunerider Outlaw U .10 .20
87 Kor Dirge U .10 .20
88 Melancholy C .07 .15
89 Null Profusion R .30 .75
90 Rathi Trapper C .07 .15
91 Shrouded Lore U .15 .30
92 Vampiric Link C .25 .50
93 Aether Membrane U .50 1.00
94 Akroma, Angel of Fury R 1.00 2.00
95 Battering Sliver C .25 .50
96 Detritivore R .50 1.00
97 Dust Corona C .07 .15
98 Fatal Frenzy R .30 .60
99 Firefright Mage C .07 .15
100 Fury Charm C .07 .15
101 Hammerheim Deadeye U .10 .20
102 Keldon Marauders C .07 .15
103 Lavacore Elemental U .10 .20
104 Magus of the Arena R .20 .40
105 Needlepeak Spider C .07 .15
106 Shivan Meteor U .17 .35
107 Stingscourger C .07 .15
108 Sulfur Elemental U .20 .40
109 Timecrafting U .30 .60
110 Torchling R .20 .40
111 Volcano Hellion R .50 1.00
112 Boom/Bust R 3.00 6.00
113 Dead/Gone C .07 .15
114 Rough/Tumble U .10 .20
115 Blood Knight U .20 .40
116 Brute Force C .15 .30
117 Molten Firebird R .20 .40
118 Prodigal Pyromancer C .07 .15
119 Pyrohemia U 4.00 8.00
120 Reckless Wurm U .15 .30
121 Shivan Wumpus R .30 .75
122 Simian Spirit Guide C 2.00 4.00
123 Skirk Shaman C .07 .15
124 Ana Battlemage U .12 .25
125 Citanul Woodreaders C .07 .15
126 Deadwood Treefolk U .15 .30
127 Evolution Charm C .15 .30
128 Fungal Behemoth R .75 1.50
129 Giant Dustwasp C .07 .15
130 Hunting Wilds U .30 .60
131 Jedit Ojanen of Efrava R .60 1.25
132 Kavu Predator U .10 .20
133 Life and Limb R 1.50 3.00
134 Magus of the Library R .30 .75
135 Mire Boa C .12 .25
136 Pouncing Wurm U .10 .20
137 Psychotrope Thallid U 3.00 6.00
138 Reflex Sliver C .15 .30
139 Sophic Centaur U .10 .20
140 Timbermare R .30 .60
141 Uktabi Drake C .07 .15
142 Utopia Vow C .07 .15
143 Vitaspore Thallid C .20 .40
144 Wild Pair R 1.25 2.50
145 Essence Warden C 4.00 8.00
146 Fa'adiyah Seer C .07 .15
147 Gaea's Anthem R .60 1.25
148 Groundbreaker R 1.25 2.50
149 Harmonize U .60 1.25
150 Healing Leaves C .07 .15
151 Hedge Troll U .10 .20
152 Keen Sense U 3.00 6.00
153 Seal of Primordium C .20 .40
154 Cautery Sliver U .25 .50
155 Darkheart Sliver U 1.00 2.00
156 Dormant Sliver U 1.25 2.50
157 Frenetic Sliver U 1.25 2.50
158 Intet, the Dreamer R .75 1.50
159 Necrotic Sliver U 3.00 6.00
160 Numot, the Devastator R 1.50 3.00
161 Oros, the Avenger R .30 .75
162 Radha, Heir to Keld R .75 1.50
163 Teneb, the Harvester R 1.50 3.00
164 Vorosh, the Hunter R .75 1.50
165 Urborg, Tomb of Yawgmoth R 20.00 40.00

2007 Magic The Gathering Tenth Edition

1 Ancestor's Chosen U .10 .20
2 Angel of Mercy U .10 .20
3 Angelic Blessing C .07 .15
4 Angelic Chorus R 1.25 2.50
5 Angelic Wall C .07 .15
6 Aura of Silence U 3.00 6.00
7 Aven Cloudchaser C .07 .15
8 Ballista Squad U .10 .20
9 Bandage C .20 .40
10 Beacon of Immortality R 1.25 2.50
11 Benalish Knight C .07 .15
12 Cho-Manno, Revolutionary R .20 .40
13 Condemn U .10 .20
14 Demystify C .07 .15
15 Field Marshal R 2.50 5.00
16 Ghost Warden C .07 .15
17 Glorious Anthem R 1.00 2.00
18 Hail of Arrows U .10 .20
19 Heart of Light C .07 .15
20 High Ground U .10 .20
21 Holy Day C .30 .60
22 Holy Strength C .07 .15
23 Honor Guard C .07 .15
24 Icatian Priest U .10 .20
25 Kjeldoran Royal Guard R .20 .40
26 Loxodon Mystic C .07 .15
27 Loyal Sentry R .20 .40
28 Luminesce U .10 .20
29 Mobilization R .50 1.00
30 Nomad Mythmaker R 2.50 5.00
31 Pacifism C .07 .15
32 Paladin en-Vec R .75 1.50
33 Pariah R 1.25 2.50
34 Reviving Dose C .07 .15
35 Reya Dawnbringer R 1.25 2.50
36 Righteousness R .20 .40
37 Rule of Law U .50 1.00
38 Samite Healer C .07 .15
39 Serra Angel R .30 .60
40 Serra's Embrace U .10 .20
41 Skyhunter Patrol C .07 .15
42 Skyhunter Prowler C .07 .15
43 Skyhunter Skirmisher U .10 .20
44 Soul Warden U .75 1.50
45 Spirit Link U .75 1.50
46 Spirit Weaver U .10 .20
47 Starlight Invoker U .10 .20
48 Steadfast Guard C .07 .15
49 Story Circle R 1.00 2.00
50 Suntail Hawk C .07 .15
51 Tempest of Light U .10 .20
52 Treasure Hunter U .10 .20
53 True Believer R .75 1.50
54 Tundra Wolves C .07 .15
55 Venerable Monk C .07 .15
56 Voice of All R .25 .50
57 Wall of Swords U .10 .20
58 Warrior's Honor C .07 .15
59 Wild Griffin C .07 .15
60 Windborn Muse R 4.00 8.00
61 Wrath of God R 5.00 10.00
62 Youthful Knight C .07 .15
63 Academy Researchers U .10 .20
64 Air Elemental U .10 .20
65 Ambassador Laquatus R 1.00 2.00
66 Arcanis the Omnipotent R 1.00 2.00
67 Aura Graft U .10 .20
68 Aven Fisher C .07 .15
69 Aven Windreader C .07 .15
70 Boomerang C .15 .30
71 Cancel C .07 .15
72 Cephalid Constable R 5.00 10.00
73 Clone R .60 1.25
74 Cloud Elemental C .07 .15
75 Cloud Sprite C .07 .15
76 Counsel of the Soratami C .07 .15
77 Crafty Pathmage C .07 .15
78 Dehydration C .07 .15
79 Deluge U .10 .20
80 Denizen of the Deep R .20 .40
81 Discombobulate U .10 .20
82 Dreamborn Muse R 2.00 4.00
83 Evacuation R 3.00 6.00
84 Flashfreeze U .10 .20
85 Fog Elemental U .10 .20
86 Fugitive Wizard C .07 .15
87 Horseshoe Crab C .07 .15
88 Hurkyl's Recall R 2.00 4.00
89 Lumengrid Warden C .07 .15
90 Mahamoti Djinn R .20 .40
91 March of the Machines R .30 .75
92 Merfolk Looter C .07 .15
93 Mind Bend R .20 .40
94 Peek C .25 .50
95 Persuasion U .20 .40
96 Phantom Warrior U .10 .20
97 Plagiarize R .20 .40
98 Puppeteer U .10 .20
99 Reminisce U .10 .20
100 Remove Soul C .07 .15
101 Robe of Mirrors C .07 .15
102 Rootwater Commando C .07 .15
103 Rootwater Matriarch R .30 .75
104 Sage Owl C .07 .15
105 Scalpelexis R .20 .40
106 Sea Monster C .07 .15
107 Shimmering Wings C .07 .15
108 Sift C .07 .15
109 Sky Weaver U .10 .20
110 Snapping Drake C .07 .15
111 Spiketail Hatchling U .10 .20
112 Sunken Hope R .20 .40
113 Telepathy U .30 .75
114 Telling Time U .10 .20
115 Thieving Magpie U .10 .20
116 Tidings U .10 .20
117 Time Stop R 3.00 6.00
118 Time Stretch R 15.00 30.00
119 Traumatize R 2.50 5.00
120 Twincast R 6.00 12.00
121 Twitch C .07 .15
122 Unsummon C .07 .15
123 Vedalken Mastermind U .25 .50
124 Wall of Air U .17 .35
125 Afflict C .07 .15
126 Agonizing Memories U .10 .20
127 Ascendant Evincar R .60 1.25
128 Assassinate C .07 .15
129 Beacon of Unrest R 1.00 2.00
130 Bog Wraith U .10 .20
131 Consume Spirit U .10 .20
132 Contaminated Bond C .07 .15
133 Cruel Edict U .10 .20
134 Deathmark U .10 .20
135 Diabolic Tutor U .75 1.50
136 Distress C .07 .15
137 Doomed Necromancer R 1.00 2.00
138 Dross Crocodile C .07 .15
139 Drudge Skeletons U .10 .20
140 Dusk Imp C .07 .15
141 Essence Drain C .07 .15
142 Fear C .07 .15
143 Festering Goblin C .07 .15
144 Grave Pact R 20.00 40.00
145 Graveborn Muse R 3.00 6.00
146 Gravedigger C .07 .15
147 Hate Weaver U .10 .20
148 Head Games R 2.50 5.00
149 Hidden Horror U .10 .20
150 Highway Robber C .07 .15
151 Hypnotic Specter R .75 1.50
152 Knight of Dusk U .30 .75
153 Looming Shade C .07 .15
154 Lord of the Pit R .20 .40
155 Lord of the Undead R 10.00 20.00
156 Mass of Ghouls C .07 .15
157 Megrim U .30 .60
158 Midnight Ritual R .20 .40
159 Mind Rot C .07 .15
160 Mortal Combat R 2.50 5.00
161 Mortivore R 1.25 2.50
162 Nantuko Husk U .10 .20
163 Nekrataal U .10 .20
164 Nightmare R .20 .40
165 No Rest for the Wicked U 1.00 2.00
166 Phage the Untouchable R 4.00 8.00
167 Phyrexian Rager C .07 .15
168 Plague Beetle C .07 .15
169 Plague Wind R 1.50 3.00
170 Rain of Tears U .50 1.00
171 Ravenous Rats C .07 .15
172 Recover C .07 .15
173 Relentless Rats U 1.25 2.50
174 Royal Assassin R .75 1.50
175 Scathe Zombies C .07 .15
176 Sengir Vampire R .20 .40
177 Severed Legion C .07 .15
178 Sleeper Agent R .60 1.25
179 Soul Feast U .10 .20
180 Spineless Thug C .07 .15
181 Stronghold Discipline U .10 .20
182 Terror C .07 .15
183 Thrull Surgeon U .10 .20
184 Underworld Dreams R 1.25 2.50
185 Unholy Strength C .07 .15
186 Vampire Bats C .07 .15
187 Anaba Bodyguard C .07 .15
188 Arcane Teachings U .10 .20
189 Beacon of Destruction R .20 .40
190 Blaze U .10 .20
191 Bloodfire Colossus R .20 .40
192 Bloodrock Cyclops C .07 .15
193 Bogardan Firefiend C .07 .15
194 Cone of Flame U .10 .20
195 Cryoclasm U .10 .20
196 Demolish C .07 .15
197 Dragon Roost R .75 1.50
198 Duct Crawler C .07 .15
199 Earth Elemental U .10 .20
200 Firebreathing C .07 .15
201 Fists of the Anvil C .12 .25
202 Flamewave Invoker U .10 .20
203 Flowstone Slide R .20 .40
204 Furnace of Rath R 4.00 8.00
205 Furnace Whelp U .10 .20
206 Goblin Elite Infantry C .07 .15
207 Goblin King R 7.50 15.00
208 Goblin Lore U 1.25 2.50
209 Goblin Piker C .07 .15
210 Goblin Sky Raider C .07 .15
211 Guerrilla Tactics U .10 .20
212 Hill Giant C .07 .15
213 Incinerate C .07 .15
214 Kamahl, Pit Fighter R .20 .40
215 Lava Axe C .07 .15
216 Lavaborn Muse R .20 .40
217 Lightning Elemental C .07 .15
218 Manabarbs R .75 1.50
219 Mogg Fanatic U .20 .40
220 Orcish Artillery U .10 .20
221 Prodigal Pyromancer C .07 .15
222 Pyroclasm U .10 .20
223 Rage Weaver U .10 .20
224 Raging Goblin C .07 .15
225 Relentless Assault R 1.25 2.50
226 Rock Badger C .07 .15
227 Scoria Wurm R .20 .40
228 Seismic Assault R 1.00 2.00
229 Shatterstorm U .30 .75
230 Shivan Dragon R .20 .40
231 Shivan Hellkite R .20 .40
232 Shock C .07 .15
233 Shunt R .20 .40
234 Siege-Gang Commander R .75 1.50
235 Smash C .07 .15
236 Soulblast R .20 .40
237 Spark Elemental U .50 1.00
238 Spitting Earth C .07 .15
239 Squee, Goblin Nabob R .75 1.50
240 Stun C .07 .15
241 Sudden Impact U .10 .20
242 Threaten U .20 .40
243 Thundering Giant U .10 .20
244 Uncontrollable Anger C .07 .15
245 Viashino Runner C .07 .15
246 Viashino Sandscout C .07 .15

247 Wall of Fire U	.10	.20
248 Warp World R	.75	1.50
249 Abundance R	1.25	2.50
250 Aggressive Urge C	.07	.15
251 Avatar of Might R	.60	1.25
252 Birds of Paradise R	6.00	12.00
253 Blanchwood Armor U	.15	.30
254 Canopy Spider C	.07	.15
255 Civic Wayfinder C	.07	.15
256 Commune with Nature C	.07	.15
257 Craw Wurm C	.07	.15
258 Creeping Mold U	.10	.20
259 Elven Riders U	.10	.20
260 Elvish Berserker C	.07	.15
261 Elvish Champion R	12.50	25.00
262 Elvish Piper R	4.00	8.00
263 Enormous Baloth U	.10	.20
264 Femeref Archers U	.10	.20
265 Gaea's Herald R	2.50	5.00
266 Giant Growth C	.07	.15
267 Giant Spider C	.07	.15
268 Grizzly Bears C	.07	.15
269 Hunted Wumpus U	.10	.20
270 Hurricane R	.50	1.00
271 Joiner Adept R	2.00	4.00
272 Karplusan Strider U	.10	.20
273 Kavu Climber C	.07	.15
274 Llanowar Elves C	.20	.40
275 Llanowar Sentinel C	.07	.15
276 Lure U	.10	.20
277 Might of Oaks R	.20	.40
278 Might Weaver U	.10	.20
279 Mirri, Cat Warrior R	3.00	6.00
280 Molimo, Maro-Sorcerer R	.30	.75
281 Natural Spring C	.07	.15
282 Naturalize C	.07	.15
283 Overgrowth C	.30	.60
284 Overrun U	.10	.20
285 Pincher Beetles C	.07	.15
286 Primal Rage U	2.00	4.00
287 Quirion Dryad R	.20	.40
288 Rampant Growth C	.60	1.25
289 Recollect U	.10	.20
290 Regeneration U	.10	.20
291 Rhox R	.20	.40
292 Root Maze R	5.00	10.00
293 Rootwalla C	.07	.15
294 Rushwood Dryad C	.07	.15
295 Scion of the Wild R	.20	.40
296 Seedborn Muse R	7.50	15.00
297 Skyshroud Ranger C	1.00	2.00
298 Spined Wurm C	.07	.15
299 Stalking Tiger C	.07	.15
300 Stampeding Wildebeests U	.10	.20
301 Sylvan Basilisk U	.17	.35
302 Sylvan Scrying U	.75	1.50
303 Tangle Spider U	.20	.40
304 Treetop Bracers C	.07	.15
305 Troll Ascetic R	.60	1.25
306 Upwelling R	2.00	4.00
307 Verdant Force R	.25	.50
308 Viridian Shaman U	.10	.20
309 Wall of Wood C	.07	.15
310 Yavimaya Enchantress U	.10	.20
311 Angel's Feather U	.10	.20
312 Bottle Gnomes U	.10	.20
313 Chimeric Staff R	.20	.40
314 Chromatic Star U	.75	1.50
315 Citanul Flute R	2.00	4.00
316 Coat of Arms R	10.00	20.00
317 Colossus of Sardia R	.20	.40
318 Composite Golem U	.30	.60
319 Crucible of Worlds R	30.00	60.00
320 Demon's Horn U	.10	.20
321 Doubling Cube R	20.00	40.00
322 Dragon's Claw U	.10	.20
323 Fountain of Youth U	.20	.40
324 The Hive R	.20	.40
325 Howling Mine R	3.00	6.00
326 Icy Manipulator U	.20	.40
327 Jayemdae Tome R	.20	.40
328 Juggernaut U	.10	.20
329 Kraken's Eye U	.10	.20
330 Legacy Weapon R	3.00	6.00
331 Leonin Scimitar U	.10	.20
332 Loxodon Warhammer R	.75	1.50
333 Mantis Engine U	.10	.20
334 Millstone R	.20	.40
335 Mind Stone U	1.25	2.50
336 Ornithopter U	.25	.50
337 Phyrexian Vault U	.10	.20
338 Pithing Needle R	3.00	6.00
339 Platinum Angel R	7.50	15.00
340 Razormane Masticore R	.20	.40
341 Rod of Ruin U	.10	.20
342 Sculpting Steel R	2.50	5.00
343 Spellbook U	2.00	4.00
344 Steel Golem U	.75	1.50
345 Whispersilk Cloak U	2.00	4.00
346 Wurm's Tooth U	.10	.20
347 Adarkar Wastes R	10.00	20.00
348 Battlefield Forge R	2.00	4.00
349 Brushland R	7.50	15.00
350 Caves of Koilos R	1.25	2.50
351 Faerie Conclave U	.75	1.50
352 Forbidding Watchtower U	.60	1.25
353 Ghitu Encampment U	.10	.20
354 Karplusan Forest R	3.00	6.00
355 Llanowar Wastes R	1.50	3.00
356 Quicksand U	.10	.20
357 Shivan Reef R	3.00	6.00
358 Spawning Pool U	.30	.60
359 Sulfurous Springs R	12.50	25.00
360 Terramorphic Expanse C	.20	.40
361 Treetop Village U	.30	.75
362 Underground River R	7.50	15.00
363 Yavimaya Coast R	2.50	5.00
364 Plains L	.15	.30
365 Plains L	.15	.30
366 Plains L	.15	.30
367 Plains L	.15	.30
368 Island L	.50	1.00
369 Island L	.15	.30
370 Island L	.15	.30
371 Island L	.15	.30
372 Swamp L	2.00	4.00
373 Swamp L	.15	.30
374 Swamp L	.15	.30
375 Swamp L	.15	.30
376 Mountain L	.25	.50
377 Mountain L	.15	.30
378 Mountain L	.15	.30
379 Mountain L	.15	.30
380 Forest L	.15	.30
381 Forest L	.25	.50
382 Forest L	.15	.30
383 Forest L	.15	.30

2007 Magic The Gathering Tenth Edition Tokens

1 Soldier	.12	.25
2 Zombie	.50	1.00
3 Dragon	.50	1.00
4 Goblin	.15	.30
5 Saproling	.12	.25
6 Wasp	.12	.25

2008 Magic The Gathering 15th Anniversary Promos

1 Char R	1.50	3.00
2 Kamahl, Pit Fighter R	.50	1.00

2008 Magic The Gathering Duel Decks Jace vs. Chandra

1 Jace Beleren M	7.50	15.00
2 Martyr of Frost C	.12	.25
3 Fathom Seer C	.12	.25
4 Voidmage Apprentice C	.12	.25
5 Wall of Deceit U	.25	.50
6 Willbender U	.30	.60
7 Bottle Gnomes U	.25	.50
8 Man-o'-War C	.30	.75
9 Ophidian C	.12	.25
10 Fledgling Mawcor U	.25	.50
11 Waterspout Djinn U	.25	.50
12 Mulldrifter C	.50	1.00
13 Air Elemental U	.25	.50
14 Guile R	.60	1.25
15 Riftwing Cloudskate U	.25	.50
16 Spire Golem C	.12	.25
17 Aethersnipe C	.12	.25
18 Brine Elemental U	.25	.50
19 Quicksilver Dragon R	.60	1.25
20 Errant Ephemeron C	.25	.50
21 Ancestral Vision R	2.50	5.00
22 Mind Stone U	.60	1.25
23 Daze C	2.00	4.00
24 Counterspell C	5.00	10.00
25 Repulse C	.12	.25
26 Fact or Fiction U	2.00	4.00
27 Gush C	.50	1.00
28 Condescend C	.25	.50
29 Terrain Generator U	.75	1.50
30 Island L	.12	.25
31 Island L	.12	.25
32 Island L	.12	.25
33 Island L	.12	.25
34 Chandra Nalaar M	4.00	8.00
35 Flamekin Brawler C	.12	.25
36 Fireslinger C	.12	.25
37 Soulbright Flamekin C	.25	.50
38 Pyre Charger U	.25	.50
39 Slith Firewalker U	.25	.50
40 Flamewave Invoker U	.25	.50
41 Inner-Flame Acolyte C	.12	.25
42 Flametongue Kavu U	.75	1.50
43 Furnace Whelp U	.25	.50
44 Rakdos Pit Dragon R	1.00	2.00
45 Ingot Chewer C	.25	.50
46 Oxidda Golem C	.12	.25
47 Chartooth Cougar C	.12	.25
48 Hostility R	.50	1.00
49 Firebolt C	.12	.25
50 Seal of Fire C	.25	.50
51 Incinerate C	.75	1.50
52 Magma Jet U	2.50	5.00
53 Flame Javelin U	.75	1.50
54 Cone of Flame U	.25	.50
55 Fireblast C	1.00	2.00
56 Fireball U	.25	.50
57 Demonfire R	.60	1.25
58 Keldon Megaliths U	.30	.60
60 Mountain L	.12	.25
61 Mountain L	.12	.25
62 Mountain L	.12	.25
63 Mountain L	.12	.25

2008 Magic The Gathering Duel Decks Jace vs. Chandra Token

1 Elemental Shaman	.10	.20

2008 Magic The Gathering Eventide

1 Archon of Justice R	.30	.75
2 Ballynock Trapper C	.07	.15
3 Cenn's Enlistment C	.07	.15
4 Endless Horizons R	7.50	15.00
5 Endure U	.10	.20
6 Flickerwisp U	.75	1.50
7 Hallowed Burial R	1.25	2.50
8 Kithkin Spellduster C	.07	.15
9 Kithkin Zealot C	.07	.15
10 Light from Within R	1.00	2.00
11 Loyal Gyrfalcon U	.10	.20
12 Patrol Signaler U	.10	.20
13 Recumbent Bliss C	.07	.15
14 Spirit of the Hearth R	.50	1.00
15 Springjack Shepherd U	.30	.75
16 Suture Spirit U	.10	.20
17 Banishing Knack C	.20	.40
18 Cache Raiders U	.10	.20
19 Dream Fracture U	.25	.50
20 Dream Thief C	.07	.15
21 Glamerdye R	3.00	6.00
22 Glen Elendra Archmage R	7.50	15.00
23 Idle Thoughts U	.10	.20
24 Indigo Faerie U	.10	.20
25 Inundate R	3.00	6.00
26 Merrow Levitator C	.07	.15
27 Oona's Grace C	.07	.15
28 Razorfin Abolisher U	.15	.30
29 Sanity Grinding R	3.00	6.00
30 Talonrend U	.10	.20
31 Wake Thrasher R	.50	1.00
32 Wilderness Hypnotist C	.07	.15
33 Ashling, the Extinguisher R	2.50	5.00
34 Creakwood Ghoul U	.10	.20
35 Crumbling Ashes U	5.00	10.00
36 Lingering Tormentor U	.20	.40
37 Merrow Bonegnawer C	.07	.15
38 Necroskitter R	6.00	12.00
39 Needle Specter R	4.00	8.00
40 Nightmare Incursion R	.50	1.00
41 Raven's Crime C	.75	1.50
42 Smoldering Butcher C	.07	.15
43 Soot Imp U	.15	.30
44 Soul Reap C	.07	.15
45 Soul Snuffers U	1.50	3.00
46 Syphon Life U	.15	.30
47 Talara's Bane C	.07	.15
48 Umbra Stalker R	.25	.50
49 Chaotic Backlash U	.10	.20
50 Cinder Pyromancer C	.15	.30
51 Duergar Cave-Guard U	.10	.20
52 Fiery Bombardment R	.25	.50
53 Flame Jab C	.07	.15
54 Hatchet Bully U	.10	.20
55 Hateflayer R	1.25	2.50
56 Heartlash Cinder C	.07	.15
57 Hotheaded Giant C	.07	.15
58 Impelled Giant U	.10	.20
59 Outrage Shaman U	.10	.20
60 Puncture Blast C	.07	.15
61 Rekindled Flame R	.25	.50
62 Stigma Lasher R	2.50	5.00
63 Thunderblust R	.25	.50
64 Unwilling Recruit U	.10	.20
65 Aerie Ouphes C	.12	.25
66 Bloom Tender R	25.00	50.00
67 Duskdale Wurm U	.10	.20
68 Helix Pinnacle R	6.00	12.00
69 Marshdrinker Giant U	.10	.20
70 Monstrify C	.07	.15
71 Nettle Sentinel C	.25	.50
72 Phosphorescent Feast U	.10	.20
73 Primalcrux R	4.00	8.00
74 Regal Force R	1.50	3.00
75 Savage Conception U	.10	.20
76 Swirling Spriggan U	.10	.20
77 Talara's Battalion R	.50	1.00
78 Tilling Treefolk C	.15	.30
79 Twinblade Slasher U	.15	.30
80 Wickerbough Elder C	.07	.15
81 Batwing Brume U	.75	1.50
82 Beckon Apparition C	.07	.15
83 Bloodied Ghost U	.10	.20
84 Cauldron Haze U	1.00	2.00
85 Deathbringer Liege R	7.50	15.00
86 Divinity of Pride R	2.50	5.00
87 Edge of the Divinity C	.50	1.00
88 Evershrike R	.50	1.00
89 Gwyllion Hedge-Mage U	.15	.30
90 Harvest Gwyllion C	.07	.15
91 Nightsky Mimic C	.10	.20
92 Nip Gwyllion C	.07	.15
93 Pyrrhic Revival R	.30	.75
94 Restless Apparition U	.15	.30
95 Stillmoon Cavalier R	3.00	6.00
96 Unmake C	.60	1.25
97 Voracious Hatchling U	.15	.30
98 Call the Skybreaker R	.25	.50
99 Clout of the Dominus C	.30	.75
100 Crackleburr R	.75	1.50
101 Crag Puca U	.10	.20
102 Dominus of Fealty R	1.25	2.50
103 Inside Out C	.12	.25
104 Mindwrack Liege R	2.50	5.00
105 Mirror Sheen R	1.00	2.00
106 Noggle Bandit C	.07	.15
107 Noggle Bridgebreaker C	.12	.25
108 Noggle Hedge-Mage U	.10	.20
109 Noggle Ransacker U	.10	.20
110 Nucklavee U	.10	.20
111 Riverfall Mimic C	.07	.15
112 Shrewd Hatchling U	.15	.30
113 Stream Hopper C	.07	.15
114 Unnerving Assault U	.10	.20
115 Canker Abomination U	.10	.20
116 Cankerous Thirst U	.10	.20
117 Creakwood Liege R	7.50	15.00
118 Deity of Scars R	1.50	3.00
119 Desecrator Hag C	.07	.15
120 Doomgape R	.30	.60
121 Drain the Well C	.07	.15
122 Gift of the Deity C	.07	.15
123 Hag Hedge-Mage U	.10	.20
124 Noxious Hatchling U	.30	.60
125 Odious Trow C	.07	.15
126 Quillspike U	1.00	2.00
127 Rendclaw Trow C	.15	.30
128 Sapling of Colfenor R	4.00	8.00
129 Stalker Hag U	.10	.20
130 Woodlurker Mimic C	.07	.15
131 Worm Harvest R	.50	1.00
132 Balefire Liege R	2.00	4.00
133 Battlegate Mimic C	.07	.15
134 Belligerent Hatchling U	.10	.20
135 Double Cleave C	.12	.25
136 Duergar Assailant C	.07	.15
137 Duergar Hedge-Mage U	.10	.20
138 Duergar Mine-Captain U	1.25	2.50
139 Figure of Destiny R	1.00	2.00
140 Fire at Will C	.07	.15
141 Hearthfire Hobgoblin U	.10	.20
142 Hobgoblin Dragoon C	.07	.15
143 Moonhold U	.10	.20
144 Nobilis of War R	.25	.50
145 Rise of the Hobgoblins R	2.00	4.00
146 Scourge of the Nobilis C	.07	.15
147 Spitemare U	1.00	2.00
148 Waves of Aggression R	7.50	15.00
149 Cold-Eyed Selkie R	.30	.75
150 Fable of Wolf and Owl R	7.50	15.00
151 Favor of the Overbeing C	.15	.30
152 Gilder Bairn U	1.00	2.00
153 Grazing Kelpie C	.07	.15
154 Groundling Pouncer U	.10	.20
155 Invert the Skies U	.10	.20
156 Murkfiend Liege R	2.50	5.00
157 Overbeing of Myth R	2.50	5.00
158 Selkie Hedge-Mage U	.10	.20
159 Shorecrasher Mimic C	.07	.15
160 Slippery Bogle C	1.00	2.00
161 Snakeform C	.17	.35
162 Spitting Image R	.30	.75
163 Sturdy Hatchling U	.10	.20
164 Trapjaw Kelpie C	.07	.15
165 Wistful Selkie U	.20	.40
166 Altar Golem R	.25	.50
167 Antler Skulkin C	.12	.25
168 Fang Skulkin C	.15	.30
169 Hoof Skulkin C	.07	.15
170 Jawbone Skulkin C	.25	.50
171 Leering Emblem R	.60	1.25
172 Scarecrone R	4.00	8.00
173 Shell Skulkin C	.15	.30
174 Ward of Bones R	7.50	15.00
175 Cascade Bluffs R	6.00	12.00
176 Fetid Heath R	5.00	10.00
177 Flooded Grove R	5.00	10.00
178 Rugged Prairie R	4.00	8.00
179 Springjack Pasture R	1.00	2.00
180 Twilight Mire R	6.00	12.00

2008 Magic The Gathering Eventide Tokens

1 Goat	.17	.35
2 Bird	.15	.30
3 Beast	.12	.25
4 Spirit	.15	.30
5 Elemental	.15	.30
6 Worm	.20	.40
7 Goblin Soldier	.12	.25

2008 Magic The Gathering From the Vault Dragons

1 Bladewing the Risen R	4.00	8.00
2 Bogarden Hellkite R	3.00	6.00
3 Draco R	2.50	5.00
4 Dragon Whelp R	1.00	2.00
5 Dragonstorm R	6.00	12.00
6 Ebon Dragon R	4.00	8.00
7 Form of the Dragon R	4.00	8.00
8 Hellkite Overlord R	4.00	8.00
9 Kokusho, the Evening Star R	10.00	20.00
10 Nicol Bolas R	25.00	50.00
11 Niv-Mizzet, the Firemind R	10.00	20.00
12 Rith, the Awakener R	4.00	8.00
13 Shivan Dragon R	2.00	4.00
14 Thunder Dragon R	5.00	10.00
15 Two-Headed Dragon R	2.50	5.00

2008 Magic The Gathering Judge Gift Rewards

1 Orim's Chant R	75.00	150.00
2 Mind's Desire R	10.00	20.00
3 Demonic Tutor R	175.00	350.00
4 Goblin Piledriver R	17.50	35.00
5 Living Wish R	15.00	30.00

2008 Magic The Gathering Magic Premiere Shop

1 Plains L	4.00	8.00
2 Island L	5.00	10.00
3 Swamp L	4.00	8.00
4 Mountain L	4.00	8.00
5 Forest L	3.00	6.00
A12007 Jaya Ballard, Task Mage R	.50	1.00

2008 Magic The Gathering Morningtide

1 Ballyrush Banneret C	.20	.40
2 Battletide Alchemist R	3.00	6.00
3 Burrenton Bombardier C	.07	.15
4 Burrenton Shield-Bearers C	.07	.15
5 Cenn's Tactician U	.10	.20
6 Changeling Sentinel C	.07	.15
7 Coordinated Barrage C	.07	.15
8 Daily Regimen U	.10	.20
9 Feudkiller's Verdict R	.25	.50
10 Forfend C	.07	.15
11 Graceful Reprieve U	.10	.20
12 Idyllic Tutor R	5.00	10.00
13 Indomitable Ancients R	3.00	6.00
14 Kinsbaile Borderguard R	1.00	2.00
15 Kinsbaile Cavalier R	4.00	8.00
16 Kithkin Zephyrnaut C	.07	.15
17 Meadowboon U	.10	.20
18 Mosquito Guard C	.07	.15
19 Order of the Golden Cricket C	.07	.15
20 Preeminent Captain R	.50	1.00
21 Redeem the Lost U	.10	.20
22 Reveillark R	1.00	2.00
23 Shinewend C	.07	.15
24 Stonehewer Giant R	3.00	6.00
25 Stonybrook Schoolmaster C	.15	.30
26 Swell of Courage U	.10	.20
27 Wandering Graybeard U	.10	.20
28 Weight of Conscience C	.07	.15
29 Declaration of Naught R	1.50	3.00
30 Dewdrop Spy C	.07	.15
31 Disperse C	.07	.15
32 Distant Melody C	.75	1.50
33 Fencer Clique C	.07	.15
34 Floodchaser C	.07	.15
35 Grimoire Thief R	1.25	2.50
36 Ink Dissolver C	.12	.25
37 Inspired Sprite U	.10	.20
38 Knowledge Exploitation R	15.00	30.00
39 Latchkey Faerie C	.07	.15
40 Merrow Witsniper C	.07	.15
41 Mind Spring R	.25	.50
42 Mothdust Changeling C	.75	1.50
43 Negate C	.07	.15
44 Nevermaker U	.60	1.25
45 Notorious Throng R	2.50	5.00
46 Research the Deep U	.15	.30
47 Sage of Fables U	1.50	3.00
48 Sage's Dousing U	.20	.40

49 Sigil Tracer R	6.00	12.00
50 Slithermuse R	.75	1.50
51 Stonybrook Banneret C	.75	1.50
52 Stream of Unconsciousness C	.15	.30
53 Supreme Exemplar R	.30	.75
54 Thieves' Fortune U	.20	.40
55 Vendilion Clique R	7.50	15.00
56 Waterspout Weavers U	.10	.20
57 Auntie's Snitch R	.25	.50
58 Bitterblossom R	30.00	75.00
59 Blightsoil Druid C	.07	.15
60 Earwig Squad R	1.50	3.00
61 Fendeep Summoner R	.25	.50
62 Festercreep C	.07	.15
63 Final-Sting Faerie C	.07	.15
64 Frogtosser Banneret C	.20	.40
65 Maralen of the Mornsong R	17.50	35.00
66 Mind Shatter R	.25	.50
67 Moonglove Changeling C	.15	.30
68 Morsel Theft C	.12	.25
69 Nightshade Schemers U	.15	.30
70 Noggin Whack U	.15	.30
71 Offalsnout U	.10	.20
72 Oona's Blackguard U	.75	1.50
73 Pack's Disdain C	.07	.15
74 Prickly Boggart C	.07	.15
75 Pulling Teeth C	.07	.15
76 Revive the Fallen U	.10	.20
77 Scarblade Elite R	.30	.60
78 Squeaking Pie Grubfellows C	.07	.15
79 Stenchskipper R	.25	.50
80 Stinkdrinker Bandit U	.25	.50
81 Violet Pall C	.07	.15
82 Warren Weirding U	.10	.20
83 Weed-Pruner Poplar C	.07	.15
84 Weirding Shaman R	.30	.75
85 Boldwyr Heavyweights R	.50	1.00
86 Boldwyr Intimidator U	.10	.20
87 Borderland Behemoth R	.25	.50
88 Brighthearth Banneret C	.30	.75
89 Countryside Crusher R	.60	1.25
90 Fire Juggler C	.07	.15
91 Hostile Realm C	.07	.15
92 Kindled Fury C	.07	.15
93 Lightning Crafter R	4.00	8.00
94 Lunk Errant C	.07	.15
95 Mudbutton Clanger C	.07	.15
96 Pyroclast Consul U	.10	.20
97 Rage Forger U	.25	.50
98 Release the Ants U	.10	.20
99 Rivals' Duel U	.10	.20
100 Roar of the Crowd C	.07	.15
101 Seething Pathblazer C	.07	.15
102 Sensation Gorger R	3.00	6.00
103 Shard Volley C	.30	.60
104 Shared Animosity R	3.00	6.00
105 Spitebellows U	.10	.20
106 Stingmoggie C	.07	.15
107 Stomping Slabs U	.10	.20
108 Sunflare Shaman C	.07	.15
109 Taurean Mauler R	1.50	3.00
110 Titan's Revenge R	.25	.50
111 Vengeful Firebrand R	.25	.50
112 War-Spike Changeling C	.07	.15
113 Ambassador Oak C	.07	.15
114 Bosk Banneret C	.15	.30
115 Bramblewood Paragon U	1.50	3.00
116 Chameleon Colossus R	2.50	5.00
117 Cream of the Crop R	5.00	10.00
118 Deglamer C	.30	.60
119 Earthbrawn C	.07	.15
120 Elvish Warrior C	.07	.15
121 Everbark Shaman C	.07	.15
122 Fertilid C	.15	.30
123 Game-Trail Changeling C	.20	.40
124 Gilt-Leaf Archdruid R	7.50	15.00
125 Greatbow Doyen R	.60	1.25
126 Heritage Druid U	7.50	15.00
127 Hunting Triad U	.10	.20
128 Leaf-Crowned Elder R	2.00	4.00
129 Luminescent Rain C	.15	.30
130 Lys Alana Bowmaster C	.07	.15
131 Orchard Warden U	.20	.40
132 Reach of Branches R	.25	.50
133 Recross the Paths U	.60	1.25
134 Reins of the Vinesteed C	.07	.15
135 Rhys the Exiled R	7.50	15.00
136 Scapeshift R	12.50	25.00
137 Unstoppable Ash R	1.25	2.50
138 Walker of the Grove U	.10	.20
139 Winnower Patrol C	.07	.15
140 Wolf-Skull Shaman U	.20	.40
141 Cloak and Dagger U	2.50	5.00
142 Diviner's Wand U	.30	.60
143 Door of Destinies R	12.50	25.00
144 Obsidian Battle-Axe U	.20	.40
145 Thornbite Staff U	7.50	15.00
146 Veteran's Armaments U	.20	.40
147 Murmuring Bosk R	1.25	2.50
148 Mutavault R	7.50	15.00
149 Primal Beyond R	6.00	12.00
150 Rustic Clachan R	.25	.50

2008 Magic The Gathering Morningtide Tokens

1 Giant Warrior	.12	.25
2 Faerie Rogue	1.00	2.00
3 Treefolk Shaman	.17	.35

2008 Magic The Gathering Shadowmoor

1 Apothecary Initiate C	.07	.15
2 Armored Ascension U	.20	.40
3 Ballynock Cohort C	.10	.20
4 Barrenton Medic C	.07	.15
5 Boon Reflection R	2.50	5.00
6 Goldenglow Moth C	.07	.15
7 Greater Auramancy R	30.00	75.00
8 Inquisitor's Snare C	.07	.15
9 Kithkin Rabble U	.10	.20
10 Kithkin Shielddare C	.07	.15
11 Last Breath C	.07	.15
12 Mass Calcify R	1.25	2.50
13 Mine Excavation C	.07	.15
14 Mistmeadow Skulk U	.10	.20
15 Niveous Wisps C	.30	.75
16 Order of Whiteclay R	1.50	3.00
17 Pale Wayfarer U	.10	.20
18 Prison Term U	.75	1.50
19 Resplendent Mentor U	.30	.60
20 Rune-Cervin Rider C	.07	.15
21 Runed Halo R	.75	1.50
22 Safehold Sentry C	.07	.15
23 Spectral Procession U	.60	1.25
24 Strip Bare C	.07	.15
25 Twilight Shepherd R	.50	1.00
26 Windbrisk Raptor R	1.00	2.00
27 Woeleecher C	.07	.15
28 Advice from the Fae U	.10	.20
29 Biting Tether U	.10	.20
30 Briarberry Cohort C	.07	.15
31 Cerulean Wisps C	.50	1.00
32 Consign to Dream C	.12	.25
33 Counterbore R	.25	.50
34 Cursecatcher U	.60	1.25
35 Deepchannel Mentor U	3.00	6.00
36 Drowner Initiate C	.15	.30
37 Faerie Swarm U	.75	1.50
38 Flow of Ideas U	.10	.20
39 Ghastly Discovery C	.07	.15
40 Isleback Spawn R	1.25	2.50
41 Kinscaer Harpoonist C	.07	.15
42 Knacksaw Clique R	2.50	5.00
43 Leech Bonder U	.20	.40
44 Merrow Wavebreakers C	.07	.15
45 Parapet Watchers C	.07	.15
46 Prismwake Merrow C	.07	.15
47 Puca's Mischief R	1.00	2.00
48 Put Away C	.07	.15
49 River Kelpie R	.50	1.00
50 Savor the Moment R	7.50	15.00
51 Sinking Feeling C	.07	.15
52 Spell Syphon C	.20	.40
53 Thought Reflection R	1.00	2.00
54 Whimwader C	.07	.15
55 Aphotic Wisps C	.25	.50
56 Ashenmoor Cohort C	.07	.15
57 Beseech the Queen U	3.00	6.00
58 Blowfly Infestation U	2.50	5.00
59 Cinderbones C	.07	.15
60 Cinderhaze Wretch C	.12	.25
61 Corrosive Mentor U	2.50	5.00
62 Corrupt U	.10	.20
63 Crowd of Cinders U	.10	.20
64 Disturbing Plot C	.07	.15
65 Dusk Urchins R	3.00	6.00
66 Faerie Macabre C	.50	1.00
67 Gloomlance C	.07	.15
68 Hollowborn Barghest R	.30	.60
69 Hollowsage U	.10	.20
70 Incremental Blight U	.75	1.50
71 Loch Korrigan C	.07	.15
72 Midnight Banshee R	1.50	3.00
73 Plague of Vermin R	4.00	8.00
74 Polluted Bonds R	30.00	60.00
75 Puppeteer Clique R	4.00	8.00
76 Rite of Consumption C	.60	1.25
77 Sickle Ripper C	.07	.15
78 Smolder Initiate C	.07	.15
79 Splitting Headache C	.07	.15
80 Torture C	.07	.15
81 Wound Reflection R	7.50	15.00
82 Blistering Dieflyn C	.07	.15
83 Bloodmark Mentor U	1.50	3.00
84 Bloodshed Fever C	.07	.15
85 Boggart Arsonists C	.07	.15
86 Burn Trail C	.07	.15
87 Cragganwick Cremator R	.30	.75
88 Crimson Wisps C	2.00	4.00
89 Deep-Slumber Titan R	.25	.50
90 Elemental Mastery R	3.00	6.00
91 Ember Gale C	.07	.15
92 Flame Javelin U	.10	.20
93 Furystoke Giant R	2.50	5.00
94 Horde of Boggarts U	.30	.75
95 Inescapable Brute C	.07	.15
96 Intimidator Initiate C	.07	.15
97 Jaws of Stone U	.10	.20
98 Knollspine Dragon R	12.50	25.00
99 Knollspine Invocation R	.25	.50
100 Mudbrawler Cohort C	.20	.40
101 Power of Fire C	.07	.15
102 Puncture Bolt C	.12	.25
103 Pyre Charger U	.10	.20
104 Rage Reflection R	.75	1.50
105 Rustrazor Butcher C	.07	.15
106 Slinking Giant U	.10	.20
107 Smash to Smithereens C	.20	.40
108 Wild Swing U	.10	.20
109 Crabapple Cohort C	.07	.15
110 Devoted Druid C	2.00	4.00
111 Dramatic Entrance R	1.00	2.00
112 Drove of Elves U	.75	1.50
113 Farhaven Elf C	.50	1.00
114 Flourishing Defenses U	.75	1.50
115 Foxfire Oak C	.07	.15
116 Gleeful Sabotage C	.75	1.50
117 Gloomwidow U	.10	.20
118 Gloomwidow's Feast C	.07	.15
119 Howl of the Night Pack U	.15	.30
120 Hungry Spriggan C	.07	.15
121 Juvenile Gloomwidow C	.20	.40
122 Mana Reflection R	7.50	15.00
123 Mossbridge Troll R	1.50	3.00
124 Nurturer Initiate C	.07	.15
125 Presence of Gond C	.20	.40
126 Prismatic Omen R	15.00	30.00
127 Raking Canopy U	.50	1.00
128 Roughshod Mentor U	.10	.20
129 Spawnwrithe R	.30	.75
130 Toil to Renown C	.07	.15
131 Tower Above U	.15	.30
132 Viridescent Wisps C	.07	.15
133 Wildslayer Elves C	.15	.30
134 Witherscale Wurm R	.25	.50
135 Woodfall Primus R	2.50	5.00
136 Aethertow C	.07	.15
137 Augury Adept R	.30	.75
138 Barrenton Cragtreads C	.07	.15
139 Curse of Chains C	.25	.50
140 Enchanted Evening R	2.50	5.00
141 Glamer Spinners U	.10	.20
142 Godhead of Awe R	3.00	6.00
143 Mirrorweave R	.50	1.00
144 Mistmeadow Witch U	.15	.30
145 Plumeveil U	.10	.20
146 Puresight Merrow U	.20	.40
147 Repel Intruders U	.10	.20
148 Silkbind Faerie C	.07	.15
149 Somnomancer C	.07	.15
150 Steel of the Godhead C	2.00	4.00
151 Swans of Bryn Argoll R	1.00	2.00
152 Thistledown Duo C	.12	.25
153 Thistledown Liege R	1.00	2.00
154 Thoughtweft Gambit U	.10	.20
155 Turn to Mist C	.15	.30
156 Worldpurge R	.50	1.00
157 Zealous Guardian C	.07	.15
158 Cemetery Puca R	2.00	4.00
159 Dire Undercurrents R	7.50	15.00
160 Dream Salvage U	.60	1.25
161 Fate Transfer C	.15	.30
162 Ghastlord of Fugue R	4.00	8.00
163 Glen Elendra Liege R	3.00	6.00
164 Gravelgill Axeshark C	.07	.15
165 Gravelgill Duo C	.07	.15
166 Helm of the Ghastlord C	.15	.30
167 Inkfathom Infiltrator U	4.00	8.00
168 Inkfathom Witch U	.30	.75
169 Memory Plunder R	2.00	4.00
170 Memory Sluice C	.50	1.00
171 Merrow Grimeblotter U	.10	.20
172 Oona, Queen of the Fae R	3.00	6.00
173 Oona's Gatewarden C	.15	.30
174 River's Grasp U	.10	.20
175 Scarscale Ritual C	.12	.25
176 Sygg, River Cutthroat R	4.00	8.00
177 Torpor Dust C	.07	.15
178 Wanderbrine Rootcutters C	.07	.15
179 Wasp Lancer U	.15	.30
180 Ashenmoor Gouger U	.10	.20
181 Ashenmoor Liege R	3.00	6.00
182 Cultbrand Cinder C	.07	.15
183 Demigod of Revenge R	1.50	3.00
184 Din of the Fireherd R	.30	.75
185 Emberstrike Duo C	.07	.15
186 Everlasting Torment R	2.00	4.00
187 Fists of the Demigod C	.20	.40
188 Fulminator Mage R	2.50	5.00
189 Grief Tyrant U	.10	.20
190 Kulrath Knight U	1.00	2.00
191 Manaforge Cinder C	.15	.30
192 Murderous Redcap U	.30	.75
193 Poison the Well C	.07	.15
194 Scar C	.07	.15
195 Sootstoke Kindler C	.07	.15
196 Sootwalkers C	.07	.15
197 Spiteflame Witch U	.10	.20
198 Spiteful Visions R	1.50	3.00
199 Torrent of Souls U	.10	.20
200 Traitor's Roar C	.07	.15
201 Tyrannize R	.25	.50
202 Boartusk Liege R	5.00	10.00
203 Boggart Ram-Gang U	.25	.50
204 Deus of Calamity R	.75	1.50
205 Firespout U	.60	1.25
206 Fossil Find U	.10	.20
207 Giantbaiting C	.07	.15
208 Guttural Response U	.75	1.50
209 Impromptu Raid R	.30	.60
210 Loamdragger Giant C	.07	.15
211 Manamorphose C	3.00	6.00
212 Morselhoarder C	.07	.15
213 Mudbrawler Raiders C	.07	.15
214 Rosheen Meanderer R	.30	.75
215 Runes of the Deus C	.20	.40
216 Scuzzback Marauders C	.07	.15
217 Scuzzback Scrapper C	.07	.15
218 Tattermunge Duo C	.07	.15
219 Tattermunge Maniac U	.25	.50
220 Tattermunge Witch U	.10	.20
221 Valleymaker R	.25	.50
222 Vexing Shusher R	6.00	12.00
223 Wort, the Raidmother R	.60	1.25
224 Barkshell Blessing C	.07	.15
225 Dawnglow Infusion U	.20	.40
226 Elvish Hexhunter C	.07	.15
227 Fracturing Gust R	1.50	3.00
228 Heartmender R	.50	1.00
229 Kitchen Finks U	.75	1.50
230 Medicine Runner C	.07	.15
231 Mercy Killing U	.75	1.50
232 Old Ghastbark C	.07	.15
233 Oracle of Nectars R	1.00	2.00
234 Oversoul of Dusk R	1.00	2.00
235 Raven's Run Dragoon C	.07	.15
236 Reknit U	.10	.20
237 Rhys the Redeemed R	4.00	8.00
238 Safehold Duo C	.07	.15
239 Safehold Elite C	.20	.40
240 Safewright Quest C	.20	.40
241 Seedcradle Witch U	.10	.20
242 Shield of the Oversoul C	2.50	5.00
243 Wheel of Sun and Moon R	15.00	30.00
244 Wilt-Leaf Cavaliers U	.20	.40
245 Wilt-Leaf Liege R	2.00	4.00
246 Blazethorn Scarecrow C	.15	.30
247 Blight Sickle C	.20	.40
248 Cauldron of Souls R	2.00	4.00
249 Chainbreaker C	.20	.40
250 Elsewhere Flask C	.20	.40
251 Gnarled Effigy U	.10	.20
252 Grim Poppet R	2.00	4.00
253 Heap Doll U	.25	.50
254 Illuminated Folio U	.10	.20
255 Lockjaw Snapper U	.75	1.50
256 Lurebound Scarecrow U	.30	.75
257 Painter's Servant R	30.00	75.00
258 Pili-Pala C	1.25	2.50
259 Rattleblaze Scarecrow C	.20	.40
260 Reaper King R	2.50	5.00
261 Revelsong Horn U	.20	.40
262 Scrapbasket C	.12	.25
263 Scuttlemutt C	.07	.15
264 Tatterkite U	.60	1.25
265 Thornwatch Scarecrow C	.20	.40
266 Trip Noose U	.10	.20
267 Umbral Mantle U	7.50	15.00
268 Watchwing Scarecrow C	.20	.40
269 Wicker Warcrawler U	.20	.40
270 Wingrattle Scarecrow C	.25	.50
271 Fire-Lit Thicket R	4.00	8.00
272 Graven Cairns R	4.00	8.00
273 Leechridden Swamp U	.60	1.25
274 Madblind Mountain U	.25	.50
275 Mistveil Plains U	1.00	2.00
276 Moonring Island U	.10	.20
277 Mystic Gate R	7.50	15.00
278 Reflecting Pool R	17.50	35.00
279 Sapseep Forest U	.20	.40
280 Sunken Ruins R	10.00	20.00
281 Wooded Bastion R	6.00	12.00
282 Plains L	.15	.30
283 Plains L	.15	.30
284 Plains L	.15	.30
285 Plains L	.15	.30
286 Island L	.15	.30
287 Island L	.15	.30
288 Island L	.15	.30
289 Island L	.15	.30
290 Swamp L	.15	.30
291 Swamp L	.15	.30
292 Swamp L	.15	.30
293 Swamp L	.15	.30
294 Mountain L	.15	.30
295 Mountain L	.15	.30
296 Mountain L	.15	.30
297 Mountain L	.15	.30
298 Forest L	.15	.30
299 Forest L	.15	.30
300 Forest L	.15	.30
301 Forest L	.15	.30

2008 Magic The Gathering Shadowmoor Tokens

1 Kithkin Soldier	.07	.15
2 Spirit	.20	.40
3 Rat	1.00	2.00
4 Elemental	.60	1.25
5 Elf Warrior	.25	.50
6 Spider	.15	.30
7 Wolf	.07	.15
8 Faerie Rogue	1.00	2.00
9 Elemental	.50	1.00
10 Giant Warrior	.07	.15
11 Goblin Warrior	.30	.55
12 Elf Warrior	.75	1.50

2008 Magic The Gathering Shards of Alara

1 Akrasan Squire C	.15	.30
2 Angel's Herald U	.10	.20
3 Angelic Benediction U	.10	.20
4 Angelsong C	.20	.40
5 Bant Battlemage U	.10	.20
6 Battlegrace Angel R	.50	1.00
7 Cradle of Vitality R	.75	1.50
8 Dispeller's Capsule C	.07	.15
9 Elspeth, Knight-Errant M	7.50	15.00
10 Ethersworn Canonist R	2.50	5.00
11 Excommunicate C	.07	.15
12 Guardians of Akrasa C	.07	.15
13 Gustrider Exuberant C	.07	.15
14 Invincible Hymn R	.30	.60
15 Knight of the Skyward Eye C	.07	.15
16 Knight of the White Orchid R	2.00	4.00
17 Knight-Captain of Eos R	3.00	6.00
18 Marble Chalice C	.07	.15
19 Metallurgeon U	.10	.20
20 Oblivion Ring C	.20	.40
21 Ranger of Eos R	2.00	4.00
22 Resounding Silence C	.07	.15
22 Resounding Silence C	.07	.15
23 Rockcaster Platoon U	.10	.20
24 Sanctum Gargoyle C	.07	.15
25 Scourglass R	4.00	8.00
26 Sighted-Caste Sorcerer C	.07	.15
27 Sigiled Paladin U	.20	.40
28 Soul's Grace C	.07	.15
29 Sunseed Nurturer U	.10	.20
30 Welkin Guide C	.07	.15
31 Yoked Plowbeast C	.07	.15
32 Call to Heel C	.07	.15
33 Cancel C	.07	.15
34 Cathartic Adept C	.15	.30
35 Cloudheath Drake C	.07	.15
36 Coma Veil C	.07	.15
37 Courier's Capsule C	.07	.15
38 Covenant of Minds R	.25	.50
39 Dawnray Archer U	.10	.20
40 Esper Battlemage U	.10	.20
41 Etherium Astrolabe U	.10	.20
42 Etherium Sculptor C	.25	.50
43 Fatestitcher U	2.00	4.00
44 Filigree Sages U	.50	1.00
45 Gather Specimens R	.60	1.25
46 Jhessian Lookout C	.07	.15
47 Kathari Screecher C	.07	.15
48 Kederekt Leviathan R	3.00	6.00
49 Master of Etherium R	.75	1.50
50 Memory Erosion R	1.50	3.00
51 Mindlock Orb R	.30	.75
52 Outrider of Jhess C	.07	.15
53 Protomatter Powder U	.10	.20
54 Resounding Wave C	.07	.15
55 Sharding Sphinx R	.25	.50
56 Skill Borrower R	.25	.50
57 Spell Snip C	.07	.15
58 Sphinx's Herald U	.10	.20
59 Steelclad Serpent C	.07	.15
60 Tezzeret the Seeker M	12.50	25.00
61 Tortoise Formation C	.07	.15
62 Vectis Silencers C	.07	.15
63 Ad Nauseam R	6.00	12.00

64 Archdemon of Unx R	.25	.50
65 Banewasp Affliction C	.12	.25
66 Blister Beetle C	.07	.15
67 Bone Splinters C	.07	.15
68 Corpse Connoisseur U	.60	1.25
69 Cunning Lethemancer R	6.00	12.00
70 Death Baron R	3.00	6.00
71 Deathgreeter C	1.25	2.50
72 Demon's Herald U	.10	.20
73 Dreg Reaver C	.07	.15
74 Dregscape Zombie C	.07	.15
75 Executioner's Capsule C	.20	.40
76 Fleshbag Marauder U	.20	.40
77 Glaze Fiend C	.07	.15
78 Grixis Battlemage U	.10	.20
79 Immortal Coil R	.25	.50
80 Infest U	.10	.20
81 Onyx Goblet C	.07	.15
82 Puppet Conjurer U	.10	.20
83 Resounding Scream C	.07	.15
84 Salvage Titan R	.30	.60
85 Scavenger Drake U	.10	.20
86 Shadowfeed C	.07	.15
87 Shore Snapper C	.07	.15
88 Skeletal Kathari C	.07	.15
89 Tar Fiend R	.25	.50
90 Undead Leotau C	.07	.15
91 Vein Drinker R	.25	.50
92 Viscera Dragger C	.15	.30
93 Bloodpyre Elemental C	.07	.15
94 Bloodthorn Taunter C	.07	.15
95 Caldera Hellion R	.25	.50
96 Crucible of Fire R	.75	1.50
97 Dragon Fodder C	.07	.15
98 Dragon's Herald U	.10	.20
99 Exuberant Firestoker U	.10	.20
100 Flameblast Dragon R	.25	.50
101 Goblin Assault R	.60	1.25
102 Goblin Mountaineer C	.07	.15
103 Hell's Thunder R	.25	.50
104 Hissing Iguanar C	.07	.15
105 Incurable Ogre C	.07	.15
106 Jund Battlemage U	.10	.20
107 Lightning Talons C	.07	.15
108 Magma Spray C	.07	.15
109 Predator Dragon R	.50	1.00
110 Resounding Thunder C	.07	.15
111 Ridge Rannet C	.07	.15
112 Rockslide Elemental U	.10	.20
113 Scourge Devil U	.10	.20
114 Skeletonize U	.10	.20
115 Soul's Fire C	.20	.40
116 Thorn-Thrash Viashino C	.07	.15
117 Thunder-Thrash Elder U	.10	.20
118 Viashino Skeleton C	.07	.15
119 Vicious Shadows R	.25	.50
120 Vithian Stinger C	.07	.15
121 Volcanic Submersion C	.07	.15
122 Where Ancients Tread R	.25	.50
123 Algae Gharial U	.10	.20
124 Behemoth's Herald U	.10	.20
125 Cavern Thoctar C	.07	.15
126 Court Archers C	.07	.15
127 Cylian Elf C	.07	.15
128 Druid of the Anima C	.20	.40
129 Drumhunter U	.30	.75
130 Elvish Visionary C	.15	.30
131 Feral Hydra R	.50	1.00
132 Gift of the Gargantuan C	.07	.15
133 Godtoucher C	.07	.15
134 Jungle Weaver C	.15	.30
135 Keeper of Progenitus R	2.00	4.00
136 Lush Growth C	.07	.15
137 Mighty Emergence U	.10	.20
138 Manaplasm R	.25	.50
139 Mosstodon C	.07	.15
140 Mycoloth R	2.50	5.00
141 Naturalize C	.07	.15
142 Naya Battlemage U	.10	.20
143 Ooze Garden R	.25	.50
144 Resounding Roar C	.07	.15
145 Rhox Charger U	.10	.20
146 Sacellum Godspeaker R	.25	.50
147 Savage Hunger C	.07	.15
148 Skullmulcher R	.25	.50
149 Soul's Might C	.15	.30
150 Spearbreaker Behemoth R	2.50	5.00
151 Topan Ascetic U	.10	.20
152 Wild Nacatl C	.25	.50
153 Agony Warp C	.12	.25
154 Ajani Vengeant M	4.00	8.00
155 Bant Charm U	.30	.75
156 Blightning C	.20	.40
157 Blood Cultist U	.15	.30
158 Branching Bolt C	.07	.15
159 Brilliant Ultimatum R	1.25	2.50
160 Broodmate Dragon R	.25	.50
161 Bull Cerodon U	.10	.20
162 Carrion Thrash C	.20	.40
163 Clarion Ultimatum R	.25	.50
164 Cruel Ultimatum R	.30	.75
165 Deft Duelist C	.07	.15
166 Empyrial Archangel M	2.00	4.00
167 Esper Charm U	.75	1.50
168 Fire-Field Ogre U	.10	.20
169 Goblin Deathraiders C	.07	.15
170 Godsire M	6.00	12.00
171 Grixis Charm U	.10	.20
172 Hellkite Overlord M	3.00	6.00
173 Hindering Light C	.50	1.00
174 Jhessian Infiltrator U	.20	.40
175 Jund Charm U	.20	.40
176 Kederekt Creeper C	.07	.15
177 Kiss of the Amesha U	.10	.20
178 Kresh the Bloodbraided M	3.00	6.00
179 Mayael the Anima M	1.25	2.50
180 Naya Charm U	.20	.40
181 Necrogenesis U	.20	.40
182 Prince of Thralls M	2.50	5.00
183 Punish Ignorance R	.25	.50
184 Qasali Ambusher U	.60	1.25
185 Rafiq of the Many M	6.00	12.00
186 Rakeclaw Gargantuan C	.07	.15
187 Realm Razer R	.25	.50
188 Rhox War Monk U	.10	.20
189 Rip-Clan Crasher C	.07	.15
190 Sangrite Surge U	.10	.20
191 Sarkhan Vol M	4.00	8.00
192 Sedraxis Specter R	.25	.50
193 Sedris, the Traitor King M	15.00	30.00
194 Sharuum the Hegemon M	.60	1.25
195 Sigil Blessing C	.07	.15
196 Sphinx Sovereign M	1.50	3.00
197 Sprouting Thrinax U	.10	.20
198 Steward of Valeron C	.15	.30
199 Stoic Angel R	.60	1.25
200 Swerve U	.20	.40
201 Thoughtcutter Agent U	.10	.20
202 Tidehollow Sculler U	.50	1.00
203 Tidehollow Strix C	.07	.15
204 Titanic Ultimatum R	1.50	3.00
205 Tower Gargoyle U	.10	.20
206 Violent Ultimatum R	.25	.50
207 Waveskimmer Aven C	.07	.15
208 Windwright Mage C	.07	.15
209 Woolly Thoctar U	.10	.20
210 Lich's Mirror M	2.50	5.00
211 Minion Reflector R	1.25	2.50
212 Obelisk of Bant C	.15	.30
213 Obelisk of Esper C	.15	.30
214 Obelisk of Grixis C	.12	.25
215 Obelisk of Jund C	.07	.15
216 Obelisk of Naya C	.07	.15
217 Quietus Spike R	3.00	6.00
218 Relic of Progenitus C	3.00	6.00
219 Sigil of Distinction R	.75	1.50
220 Arcane Sanctum U	1.00	2.00
221 Bant Panorama C	.75	1.50
223 Esper Panorama C	.75	1.50
224 Grixis Panorama C	.75	1.50
225 Jund Panorama C	1.00	2.00
226 Jungle Shrine U	.25	.50
227 Naya Panorama C	.20	.40
228 Savage Lands U	1.00	2.00
229 Seaside Citadel U	1.50	3.00
230 Plains L	.15	.30
231 Plains L	.15	.30
232 Plains L	.15	.30
233 Plains L	.50	1.00
234 Island L	.15	.30
235 Island L	.15	.30
236 Island L	.50	1.00
237 Island L	.12	.25
238 Swamp L	.50	1.00
239 Swamp L	.20	.40
240 Swamp L	.20	.40
241 Swamp L	.20	.40
242 Mountain L	.30	.60
243 Mountain L	.15	.30
244 Mountain L	.20	.40
245 Mountain L	.20	.40
246 Forest L	.50	1.00
247 Forest L	.15	.30
248 Forest L	.25	.50
249 Forest L	.20	.40

2008 Magic The Gathering Shards of Alara Tokens

1 Soldier	.12	.25
2 Homunculus	.07	.15
3 Thopter	.30	.75
4 Skeleton	.07	.15
5 Zombie	.12	.25
6 Dragon	.30	.60
7 Goblin	.12	.25
8 Ooze	.07	.15
9 Saproling	.12	.25
10 Beast	2.50	5.00

2009 Magic The Gathering Alara Reborn

1 Ardent Plea U	1.50	3.00
2 Aven Mimeomancer R	.50	1.00
3 Ethercaste Knight C	.10	.20
4 Ethersworn Shieldmage C	.10	.20
5 Fieldmist Borderpost C	.20	.40
6 Filigree Angel R	.25	.50
7 Glassdust Hulk C	.10	.20
8 Meddling Mage R	1.50	3.00
9 Offering to Asha C	.10	.20
10 Sanctum Plowbeast C	.10	.20
11 Shield of the Righteous U	.12	.25
12 Sovereigns of Lost Alara R	.60	1.25
13 Stormcaller's Boon C	.10	.20
14 Talon Trooper C	.10	.20
15 Unbender Tine U	.20	.40
16 Wall of Denial U	1.00	2.00
17 Architects of Will C	.20	.40
18 Brainbite C	.10	.20
19 Deny Reality C	.10	.20
20 Etherium Abomination C	.10	.20
21 Illusory Demon U	.12	.25
22 Jhessian Zombies C	.10	.20
23 Kathari Remnant U	.12	.25
24 Lich Lord of Unx R	7.50	15.00
25 Mask of Riddles U	.30	.60
26 Mind Funeral U	1.25	2.50
27 Mistvein Borderpost C	.20	.40
28 Nemesis of Reason R	2.50	5.00
29 Soul Manipulation C	.20	.40
30 Soulquake R	.25	.50
31 Time Sieve R	2.00	4.00
32 Vedalken Ghoul C	.10	.20
33 Anathemancer U	.25	.50
34 Bituminous Blast U	.12	.25
35 Breath of Malfegor C	.10	.20
36 Deathbringer Thoctar R	.75	1.50
37 Defiler of Souls M	1.25	2.50
38 Demonic Dread C	.17	.35
39 Demonspine Whip U	.12	.25
40 Igneous Pouncer C	.10	.20
41 Kathari Bomber C	.10	.20
42 Lightning Reaver R	.60	1.25
43 Monstrous Carabid C	.20	.40
44 Sanity Gnawers U	.12	.25
45 Singe-Mind Ogre C	.10	.20
46 Terminate C	.60	1.25
47 Thought Hemorrhage R	.25	.50
48 Veinfire Borderpost C	.17	.35
49 Blitz Hellion R	.25	.50
50 Bloodbraid Elf U	1.25	2.50
51 Colossal Might C	.15	.30
52 Deadshot Minotaur C	.10	.20
53 Dragon Broodmother M	7.50	15.00
54 Firewild Borderpost C	.20	.40
55 Godtracker of Jund C	.10	.20
56 Gorger Wurm C	.10	.20
57 Mage Slayer U	2.50	5.00
58 Predatory Advantage R	.25	.50
59 Rhox Brute C	.10	.20
60 Spellbreaker Behemoth R	.75	1.50
61 Valley Rannet C	.10	.20
62 Vengeful Rebirth U	.12	.25
63 Violent Outburst C	.75	1.50
64 Vithian Renegades U	.20	.40
65 Behemoth Sledge U	.20	.40
66 Captured Sunlight C	.10	.20
67 Dauntless Escort R	2.00	4.00
68 Enlisted Wurm U	.15	.30
69 Grizzled Leotau C	.15	.30
70 Knight of New Alara R	.75	1.50
71 Knotvine Paladin R	.25	.50
72 Leonin Armorguard C	.10	.20
73 Mycoid Shepherd R	.25	.50
74 Pale Recluse C	.10	.20
75 Qasali Pridemage C	.60	1.25
76 Reborn Hope U	.20	.40
77 Sigil Captain U	.20	.40
78 Sigil of the Nayan Gods C	.15	.30
79 Sigiled Behemoth C	.10	.20
80 Wildfield Borderpost C	.15	.30
81 Identity Crisis R	.30	.75
82 Necromancer's Covenant R	1.00	2.00
83 Tainted Sigil U	.75	1.50
84 Vectis Dominator C	.10	.20
85 Zealous Persecution U	.20	.40
86 Cloven Casting R	.25	.50
87 Double Negative U	.15	.30
88 Magefire Wings C	.10	.20
89 Skyclaw Thrash U	.15	.30
90 Spellbound Dragon R	.30	.60
91 Lord of Extinction M	7.50	15.00
92 Maelstrom Pulse R	1.50	3.00
93 Marrow Chomper U	.20	.40
94 Morbid Bloom U	.20	.40
95 Putrid Leech C	.10	.20
96 Cerodon Yearling C	.10	.20
97 Fight to the Death R	.30	.75
98 Glory of Warfare R	.60	1.25
99 Intimidation Bolt U	.30	.75
100 Stun Sniper U	.12	.25
101 Lorescale Coatl U	.12	.25
102 Nulltread Gargantuan U	.12	.25
103 Sages of the Anima R	.25	.50
104 Vedalken Heretic R	.25	.50
105 Winged Coatl C	.20	.40
106 Enigma Sphinx R	.30	.60
107 Esper Sojourners C	.10	.20
108 Etherwrought Page U	.15	.30
109 Sen Triplets M	7.50	15.00
110 Sphinx of the Steel Wind M	1.00	2.00
111 Drastic Revelation U	.12	.25
112 Grixis Sojourners C	.10	.20
113 Thraximundar M	1.00	2.00
114 Unscythe, Killer of Kings R	1.00	2.00
115 Dragon Appeasement U	.12	.25
116 Jund Sojourners C	.10	.20
117 Karrthus, Tyrant of Jund M	4.00	8.00
118 Lavalanche R	.25	.50
119 Madrush Cyclops R	.25	.50
120 Gloryscale Viashino U	.12	.25
121 Mayael's Aria R	6.00	12.00
122 Naya Sojourners C	.10	.20
123 Retaliator Griffin R	.25	.50
124 Uril, the Miststalker M	10.00	20.00
125 Bant Sojourners C	.10	.20
126 Finest Hour R	.50	1.00
127 Flurry of Wings U	.30	.60
128 Jenara, Asura of War M	2.00	4.00
129 Wargate R	2.00	4.00
130 Maelstrom Nexus M/K:	2.00	4.00
131 Arsenal Thresher C	.10	.20
132 Esper Stormblade C	.10	.20
133 Thopter Foundry U	.25	.50
134 Grixis Grimblade C	.15	.30
135 Sewn-Eye Drake C	.10	.20
136 Slave of Bolas U	.30	.60
137 Giant Ambush Beetle U	.12	.25
138 Jund Hackblade C	.17	.35
139 Sangrite Backlash C	.10	.20
140 Marisi's Twinclaws U	.15	.30
141 Naya Hushblade C	.15	.30
142 Trace of Abundance C	.30	.60
143 Bant Sureblade C	.10	.20
144 Crystallization C	.15	.30
145 Messenger Falcons U	.12	.25

2009 Magic The Gathering Alara Reborn Tokens

1 Bird Soldier	.07	.15
2 Lizard	.07	.15
3 Dragon	1.00	2.00
4 Zombie Wizard	.50	1.00

2009 Magic The Gathering Conflux

1 Aerie Mystics U	.10	.20
2 Asha's Favor C	.07	.15
3 Aven Squire C	.07	.15
4 Aven Trailblazer C	.07	.15
5 Celestial Purge U	.15	.30
6 Court Homunculus C	.07	.15
7 Darklit Gargoyle C	.07	.15
8 Gleam of Resistance C	.07	.15
9 Lapse of Certainty C	.75	1.50
10 Mark of Asylum R	1.25	2.50
11 Martial Coup R	.60	1.25
12 Mirror-Sigil Sergeant M	1.50	3.00
13 Nacatl Hunt-Pride U	.10	.20
14 Paragon of the Amesha U	.10	.20
15 Path to Exile U	3.00	6.00
16 Rhox Meditant C	.07	.15
17 Scepter of Dominance R	.25	.50
18 Sigil of the Empty Throne R	.60	1.25
19 Valiant Guard C	.07	.15
20 Wall of Reverence R	1.00	2.00
21 Brackwater Elemental C	.07	.15
22 Constricting Tendrils C	.07	.15
23 Controlled Instincts U	.10	.20
24 Cumber Stone U	.15	.30
25 Esperzoa U	.10	.20
26 Ethersworn Adjudicator M	2.50	5.00
27 Faerie Mechanist C	.07	.15
28 Frontline Sage C	.07	.15
29 Grixis Illusionist C	.07	.15
30 Inkwell Leviathan R	.50	1.00
31 Master Transmuter R	2.50	5.00
32 Parasitic Strix C	.07	.15
33 Scepter of Insight R	.25	.50
34 Scornful Aether-Lich U	.10	.20
35 Telemin Performance R	1.00	2.00
36 Traumatic Visions C	.07	.15
37 Unsummon C	.07	.15
38 View from Above U	.10	.20
39 Worldly Counsel C	.07	.15
40 Absorb Vis C	.07	.15
41 Corrupted Roots U	.10	.20
42 Drag Down C	.07	.15
43 Dreadwing U	.10	.20
44 Extractor Demon R	.25	.50
45 Fleshformer U	.10	.20
46 Grixis Slavedriver U	.10	.20
47 Infectious Horror C	.07	.15
48 Kederekt Parasite R	7.50	15.00
49 Nyxathid R	.30	.75
50 Pestilent Kathari C	.07	.15
51 Rotting Rats C	.07	.15
52 Salvage Slasher C	.07	.15
53 Scepter of Fugue R	.30	.75
54 Sedraxis Alchemist C	.12	.25
55 Voices from the Void U	.10	.20
56 Wretched Banquet C	.07	.15
57 Yoke of the Damned C	.07	.15
58 Banefire R	.60	1.25
59 Bloodhall Ooze R	.30	.75
60 Canyon Minotaur C	.07	.15
61 Dark Temper C	.07	.15
62 Dragonsoul Knight U	.10	.20
63 Fiery Fall C	.07	.15
64 Goblin Razerunners R	.25	.50
65 Hellspark Elemental U	.50	1.00
66 Ignite Disorder U	.10	.20
67 Kranioceros C	.07	.15
68 Maniacal Rage C	.07	.15
69 Molten Frame C	.07	.15
70 Quenchable Fire C	.07	.15
71 Rakka Mar R	.75	1.50
72 Toxic Iguanar C	.07	.15
73 Viashino Slaughtermaster U	.10	.20
74 Volcanic Fallout U	.20	.40
75 Voracious Dragon R	.75	1.50
76 Wandering Goblins C	.07	.15
77 Worldheart Phoenix R	.25	.50
78 Beacon Behemoth C	.12	.25
79 Cliffrunner Behemoth R	.25	.50
80 Cylian Sunsinger R	.25	.50
81 Ember Weaver C	.07	.15
82 Filigree Fracture U	.10	.20
83 Gluttonous Slime U	.10	.20
84 Matca Rioters C	.07	.15
85 Might of Alara C	.07	.15
86 Nacatl Savage C	.07	.15
87 Noble Hierarch R	12.50	25.00
88 Paleoloth R	.30	.75
89 Sacellum Archers U	.10	.20
90 Scattershot Archer C	.30	.60
91 Shard Convergence U	.30	.60
92 Soul's Majesty R	2.00	4.00
93 Spore Burst U	.10	.20
94 Sylvan Bounty C	.07	.15
95 Thornling M	2.00	4.00
96 Tukatongue Thallid C	.07	.15
97 Wild Leotau C	.07	.15
98 Apocalypse Hydra M	.75	1.50
99 Blood Tyrant R	.25	.50
100 Charnelhoard Wurm R	.25	.50
101 Child of Alara M	5.00	10.00
102 Conflux M	2.00	4.00
103 Countersquall U	.60	1.25
104 Elder Mastery U	.10	.20
105 Esper Cormorants C	.07	.15
106 Exploding Borders C	.07	.15
107 Fusion Elemental U	.15	.30
108 Giltspire Avenger R	.75	1.50
109 Goblin Outlander C	.07	.15
110 Gwafa Hazid, Profiteer R	.30	.60
111 Hellkite Hatchling U	.10	.20
112 Jhessian Balmgiver U	.10	.20
113 Knight of the Reliquary R	2.50	5.00
114 Knotvine Mystic U	.30	.75
115 Maelstrom Archangel M	2.00	4.00
116 Magister Sphinx R	2.50	5.00
117 Malfegor M	.60	1.25
118 Meglonoth R	.50	1.00
119 Nacatl Outlander C	.07	.15
120 Nicol Bolas, Planeswalker M	10.00	20.00
121 Progenitus M	7.50	15.00
122 Rhox Bodyguard C	.07	.15
123 Scarland Thrinax U	.10	.20
124 Shambling Remains U	.10	.20
125 Skyward Eye Prophets U	.10	.20
126 Sludge Strider U	.10	.20
127 Sphinx Summoner R	.30	.60
128 Suicidal Charge C	.07	.15
129 Vagrant Plowbeasts U	.10	.20
130 Valeron Outlander C	.07	.15
131 Vectis Agents C	.07	.15
132 Vedalken Outlander C	.07	.15
133 Zombie Outlander C	.07	.15
134 Armillary Sphere C	.07	.15
135 Bone Saw C	.07	.15
136 Font of Mythos R	3.00	6.00
137 Kaleidostone C	.07	.15
138 Mana Cylix C	.07	.15
139 Manaforce Mace U	.10	.20
140 Obelisk of Alara R	.30	.60

141 Ancient Ziggurat U	4.00	8.00
142 Exotic Orchard R	1.50	3.00
143 Reliquary Tower U	1.25	2.50
144 Rupture Spire C	.07	.15
145 Unstable Frontier U	.10	.20

2009 Magic The Gathering Conflux Tokens

1 Angel	.25	.50
2 Elemental	.12	.25

2009 Magic The Gathering Duel Decks Divine vs. Demonic

1 Akroma, Angel of Wrath M	15.00	30.00
2 Icatian Priest U	.25	.50
3 Angelic Page C	.25	.50
4 Charging Paladin C	.12	.25
5 Venerable Monk C	.12	.25
6 Angelic Protector U	.25	.50
7 Serra Advocate U	.25	.50
8 Sustainer of the Realm U	.25	.50
9 Angel of Mercy U	.25	.50
10 Serra Angel R	.30	.75
11 Twilight Shepherd R	1.50	3.00
12 Luminous Angel R	4.00	8.00
13 Reya Dawnbringer R	4.00	8.00
14 Healing Salve C	.12	.25
15 Angelsong C	.12	.25
16 Otherworldly Journey U	.25	.50
17 Pacifism C	.12	.25
18 Serra's Boon U	.25	.50
19 Angelic Benediction U	.25	.50
20 Faith's Fetters C	.30	.75
21 Serra's Embrace U	.30	.75
22 Righteous Cause U	.25	.50
23 Angel's Feather U	.25	.50
24 Marble Diamond U	.25	.50
25 Secluded Steppe C	.12	.25
26 Plains L	.25	.50
27 Plains L	.25	.50
28 Plains L	.25	.50
29 Plains L	.25	.50
30 Lord of the Pit M	2.00	4.00
31 Abyssal Gatekeeper C	.12	.25
32 Foul Imp C	.12	.25
33 Daggerclaw Imp U	.25	.50
34 Dusk Imp C	.12	.25
35 Overeager Apprentice C	.12	.25
36 Stinkweed Imp C	2.50	5.00
37 Soot Imp U	.25	.50
38 Demon's Jester C	.12	.25
39 Souldrinker U	.25	.50
40 Abyssal Specter U	.25	.50
41 Cackling Imp C	.12	.25
42 Fallen Angel R	.30	.75
43 Reiver Demon R	1.00	2.00
44 Kuro, Pitlord R	.30	.75
45 Dark Ritual C	1.50	3.00
46 Duress C	.50	1.00
47 Unholy Strength C	.12	.25
48 Cruel Edict U	.50	1.00
49 Demonic Tutor U	15.00	30.00
50 Dark Banishing C	.12	.25
51 Oni Possession U	.25	.50
52 Barter in Blood U	.50	1.00
53 Breeding Pit U	.30	.75
54 Promise of Power R	.50	1.00
55 Corrupt U	.25	.50
56 Consume Spirit U	.25	.50
57 Demon's Horn U	.25	.50
58 Barren Moor C	.25	.50
59 Swamp L	.25	.50
60 Swamp L	.25	.50
61 Swamp L	.25	.50
62 Swamp L	.25	.50

2009 Magic The Gathering Duel Decks Divine vs. Demonic Tokens

1 Spirit	.60	1.25
2 Demon	.25	.45
3 Thrull	.50	1.00

2009 Magic The Gathering Duel Decks Garruk vs. Liliana

1 Garruk Wildspeaker M	7.50	15.00
2 Basking Rootwalla C	.30	.75
3 Albino Troll U	.30	.75
4 Vine Trellis C	.12	.25
5 Wild Mongrel C	.12	.25
6 Wirewood Savage C	.12	.25
7 Blastoderm C	.12	.25
8 Ravenous Baloth R	2.00	4.00
9 Stampeding Wildebeests U	.25	.50
10 Indrik Stomphowler U	.25	.50
11 Krosan Tusker C	.12	.25
12 Plated Slagwurm R	1.50	3.00
13 Genju of the Cedars U	.25	.50
14 Giant Growth C	.12	.25
15 Rancor C	.12	.25
16 Lignify C	.12	.25
17 Nature's Lore C	.12	.25
18 Elephant Guide U	.25	.50
19 Invigorate C	.12	.25
20 Serrated Arrows C	.12	.25
21 Harmonize U	.25	.50
22 Rude Awakening R	.75	1.50
23 Beast Attack U	.25	.50
24 Overrun U	.25	.50
25 Windstorm U	.25	.50
26 Slippery Karst C	.12	.25
27 Treetop Village U	.25	.50
28 Forest L	.12	.25
29 Forest L	.12	.25
30 Forest L	.12	.25
31 Forest L	.12	.25
32 Liliana Vess M	7.50	15.00
33 Deathgreeter C	.12	.25
34 Ghost-Lit Stalker U	.25	.50
35 Vampire Bats C	.12	.25
36 Drudge Skeletons C	.12	.25
37 Ravenous Rats C	.12	.25
38 Fleshbag Marauder U	.25	.50
39 Phyrexian Rager C	.12	.25
40 Urborg Syphon-Mage C	.12	.25
41 Wall of Bone U	.25	.50
42 Faerie Macabre C	.12	.25
43 Howling Banshee U	.25	.50
44 Keening Banshee U	.25	.50
45 Twisted Abomination C	.12	.25
46 Skeletal Vampire R	1.50	3.00
47 Genju of the Fens U	.25	.50
48 Bad Moon R	3.00	6.00
49 Sign in Blood C	.12	.25
50 Vicious Hunger C	.12	.25
51 Ichor Slick C	.12	.25
52 Hideous End C	.12	.25
53 Snuff Out C	.12	.25
54 Tendrils of Corruption C	.12	.25
55 Mutilate R	3.00	6.00
56 Rise from the Grave U	.25	.50
57 Corrupt U	.25	.50
58 Enslave U	.25	.50
59 Polluted Mire C	.12	.25
60 Swamp L	.12	.25
61 Swamp L	.12	.25
62 Swamp L	.12	.25
63 Swamp L	.12	.25

2009 Magic The Gathering Duel Decks Garruk vs. Liliana Tokens

1 Beast	.50	1.00
2 Beast	.15	.30
3 Elephant	.30	.75

2009 Magic The Gathering From the Vault Exiled

1 Balance R	2.50	5.00
2 Berserk R	12.50	25.00
3 Channel R	1.50	3.00
4 Gifts Ungiven R	1.50	3.00
5 Goblin Lackey R	10.00	20.00
6 Kird Ape R	.60	1.25
7 Lotus Petal R	20.00	40.00
8 Mystical Tutor R	10.00	20.00
9 Necropotence R	15.00	30.00
10 Sensei's Divining Top R	30.00	60.00
11 Serendib Efreet R	.60	1.25
12 Skullclamp R	10.00	20.00
13 Strip Mine R	25.00	50.00
14 Tinker R	5.00	10.00
15 Trinisphere R	30.00	60.00

2009 Magic The Gathering Judge Gift Rewards

1 Dark Ritual R	30.00	60.00
2 Maze of Ith R	50.00	100.00
3 Stifle R	12.50	25.00
4 Survival of the Fittest R	300.00	600.00
5 Burning Wish R	12.50	25.00
6 Bloodstained Mire R	125.00	250.00
7 Flooded Strand R	100.00	200.00
8 Polluted Delta R	125.00	250.00
9 Windswept Heath R	50.00	100.00
10 Wooded Foothills R	75.00	150.00

2009 Magic The Gathering Magic 2010

1 Ajani Goldmane M	3.00	6.00
2 Angel's Mercy C	.07	.15
3 Armored Ascension U	.10	.20
4 Baneslayer Angel M	2.50	5.00
5 Blinding Mage C	.07	.15
6 Captain of the Watch R	.50	1.00
7 Celestial Purge U	.10	.20
8 Divine Verdict C	.07	.15
9 Elite Vanguard U	.10	.20
10 Excommunicate C	.07	.15
11 Glorious Charge C	.07	.15
12 Griffin Sentinel C	.07	.15
13 Guardian Seraph R	.30	.75
14 Harm's Way U	.10	.20
15 Holy Strength C	.07	.15
16 Honor of the Pure R	1.25	2.50
17 Indestructibility R	.75	1.50
18 Lifelink C	.07	.15
19 Lightwielder Paladin R	.25	.50
20 Mesa Enchantress R	1.25	2.50
21 Open the Vaults R	1.50	3.00
22 Pacifism C	.07	.15
23 Palace Guard C	.07	.15
24 Planar Cleansing R	.25	.50
25 Razorfoot Griffin C	.07	.15
26 Rhox Pikemaster U	.10	.20
27 Righteousness U	.10	.20
28 Safe Passage C	.07	.15
29 Serra Angel U	.10	.20
30 Siege Mastodon C	.07	.15
31 Silence R	6.00	12.00
32 Silvercoat Lion C	.07	.15
33 Solemn Offering C	.07	.15
34 Soul Warden C	.50	1.00
35 Stormfront Pegasus C	.07	.15
36 Tempest of Light U	.10	.20
37 Undead Slayer U	.10	.20
38 Veteran Armorsmith C	.07	.15
39 Veteran Swordsmith C	.15	.30
40 Wall of Faith C	.07	.15
41 White Knight U	.10	.20
42 Air Elemental U	.10	.20
43 Alluring Siren U	.10	.20
44 Cancel C	.07	.15
45 Clone R	.25	.50
46 Convincing Mirage C	.07	.15
47 Coral Merfolk C	.07	.15
48 Disorient C	.07	.15
49 Divination C	.07	.15
50 Djinn of Wishes R	.25	.50
51 Essence Scatter C	.07	.15
52 Fabricate U	4.00	8.00
53 Flashfreeze U	.10	.20
54 Hive Mind R	4.00	8.00
55 Horned Turtle C	.07	.15
56 Ice Cage C	.07	.15
57 Illusionary Servant C	.07	.15
58 Jace Beleren M	3.00	6.00
59 Jump C	.07	.15
60 Levitation U	.10	.20
61 Merfolk Looter C	.07	.15
62 Merfolk Sovereign R	.30	.60
63 Mind Control U	.10	.20
64 Mind Spring R	.30	.75
65 Negate C	.07	.15
66 Phantom Warrior U	.10	.20
67 Polymorph R	1.25	2.50
68 Ponder C	2.00	4.00
69 Sage Owl C	.07	.15
70 Serpent of the Endless Sea C	.07	.15
71 Sleep U	.10	.20
72 Snapping Drake C	.07	.15
73 Sphinx Ambassador M	4.00	8.00
74 Telepathy U	.25	.50
75 Time Warp M	10.00	20.00
76 Tome Scour C	.20	.40
77 Traumatize R	2.00	4.00
78 Twincast R	.25	.50
79 Unsummon C	.07	.15
80 Wall of Frost U	.20	.40
81 Wind Drake C	.07	.15
82 Zephyr Sprite C	.15	.30
83 Acolyte of Xathrid C	.07	.15
84 Assassinate C	.07	.15
85 Black Knight U	.10	.20
86 Bog Wraith U	.10	.20
87 Cemetery Reaper R	3.00	6.00
88 Child of Night C	.07	.15
89 Consume Spirit U	.10	.20
90 Deathmark U	.10	.20
91 Diabolic Tutor U	.50	1.00
92 Disentomb C	.07	.15
93 Doom Blade C	.07	.15
94 Dread Warlock C	.07	.15
95 Drudge Skeletons C	.07	.15
96 Duress C	.07	.15
97 Gravedigger C	.07	.15
98 Haunting Echoes R	.25	.50
99 Howling Banshee U	.10	.20
100 Hypnotic Specter R	1.25	2.50
101 Kelinore Bat C	.07	.15
102 Liliana Vess M	7.50	15.00
103 Looming Shade C	.07	.15
104 Megrim U	.25	.50
105 Mind Rot C	.07	.15
106 Mind Shatter R	.25	.50
107 Nightmare R	.25	.50
108 Relentless Rats U	1.50	3.00
109 Rise from the Grave U	.10	.20
110 Royal Assassin R	.75	1.50
111 Sanguine Bond R	2.50	5.00
112 Sign in Blood C	.20	.40
113 Soul Bleed C	.07	.15
114 Tendrils of Corruption C	.20	.40
115 Underworld Dreams R	.25	.50
116 Unholy Strength C	.07	.15
117 Vampire Aristocrat C	.07	.15
118 Vampire Nocturnus M	6.00	12.00
119 Wall of Bone U	.10	.20
120 Warpath Ghoul C	.07	.15
121 Weakness C	.07	.15
122 Xathrid Demon M	.30	.75
123 Zombie Goliath C	.07	.15
124 Act of Treason U	.10	.20
125 Ball Lightning R	1.00	2.00
126 Berserkers of Blood Ridge C	.07	.15
127 Bogardan Hellkite M	.50	1.00
128 Burning Inquiry C	1.50	3.00
129 Burst of Speed C	.07	.15
130 Canyon Minotaur C	.07	.15
131 Capricious Efreet R	.25	.50
132 Chandra Nalaar M	1.25	2.50
133 Dragon Whelp U	.10	.20
134 Earthquake R	.60	1.25
135 Fiery Hellhound C	.07	.15
136 Fireball U	.10	.20
137 Firebreathing C	.07	.15
138 Goblin Artillery U	.10	.20
139 Goblin Chieftain R	2.50	5.00
140 Goblin Piker C	.07	.15
141 Ignite Disorder U	.10	.20
142 Inferno Elemental U	.10	.20
143 Jackal Familiar C	.07	.15
144 Kindled Fury C	.07	.15
145 Lava Axe C	.07	.15
146 Lightning Bolt C	2.00	4.00
147 Lightning Elemental C	.07	.15
148 Magma Phoenix R	.25	.50
149 Manabarbs R	.30	.75
150 Panic Attack C	.07	.15
151 Prodigal Pyromancer U	.10	.20
152 Pyroclasm U	.10	.20
153 Raging Goblin C	.07	.15
154 Seismic Strike C	.07	.15
155 Shatter C	.07	.15
156 Shivan Dragon R	.25	.50
157 Siege-Gang Commander R	.75	1.50
158 Sparkmage Apprentice C	.07	.15
159 Stone Giant U	.10	.20
160 Trumpet Blast C	.07	.15
161 Viashino Spearhunter C	.07	.15
162 Wall of Fire U	.10	.20
163 Warp World R	.25	.50
164 Yawning Fissure C	.07	.15
165 Acidic Slime U	.20	.40
166 Ant Queen R	.50	1.00
167 Awakener Druid U	.10	.20
168 Birds of Paradise R	7.50	15.00
169 Borderland Ranger C	.07	.15
170 Bountiful Harvest C	.07	.15
171 Bramble Creeper C	.07	.15
172 Centaur Courser C	.07	.15
173 Craw Wurm C	.07	.15
174 Cudgel Troll U	.10	.20
175 Deadly Recluse C	.07	.15
176 Elvish Archdruid R	1.50	3.00
177 Elvish Piper R	4.00	8.00
178 Elvish Visionary C	.07	.15
179 Emerald Oryx C	.07	.15
180 Enormous Baloth U	.10	.20
181 Entangling Vines C	.07	.15
182 Fog C	.07	.15
183 Garruk Wildspeaker M	3.00	6.00
184 Giant Growth C	.07	.15
185 Giant Spider C	.07	.15
186 Great Sable Stag R	.30	.75
187 Howl of the Night Pack U	.10	.20
188 Kalonian Behemoth R	.25	.50
189 Llanowar Elves C	.17	.35
190 Lurking Predators R	4.00	8.00
191 Master of the Wild Hunt M	5.00	10.00
192 Might of Oaks R	.30	.60
193 Mist Leopard C	.07	.15
194 Mold Adder U	.20	.40
195 Naturalize C	.07	.15
196 Nature's Spiral U	.10	.20
197 Oakenform C	.07	.15
198 Overrun U	.20	.40
199 Prized Unicorn U	.10	.20
200 Protean Hydra M	4.00	8.00
201 Rampant Growth C	.60	1.25
202 Regenerate C	.07	.15
203 Runeclaw Bear C	.07	.15
204 Stampeding Rhino C	.07	.15
205 Windstorm U	.10	.20
206 Angel's Feather U	.10	.20
207 Coat of Arms R	12.50	25.00
208 Darksteel Colossus M	7.50	15.00
209 Demon's Horn U	.10	.20
210 Dragon's Claw U	.20	.40
211 Gorgon Flail U	1.50	3.00
212 Howling Mine R	4.00	8.00
213 Kraken's Eye U	.10	.20
214 Magebane Armor R	3.00	6.00
215 Mirror of Fate R	.50	1.00
216 Ornithopter U	.20	.40
217 Pithing Needle R	2.50	5.00
218 Platinum Angel M	7.50	15.00
219 Rod of Ruin U	.10	.20
220 Spellbook U	1.50	3.00
221 Whispersilk Cloak U	1.50	3.00
222 Wurms Tooth U	.10	.20
223 Dragonskull Summit R	3.00	6.00
224 Drowned Catacomb R	4.00	8.00
225 Gargoyle Castle R	.25	.50
226 Glacial Fortress R	4.00	8.00
227 Rootbound Crag R	2.50	5.00
228 Sunpetal Grove R	2.50	5.00
229 Terramorphic Expanse C	.07	.15
230 Plains L	.12	.25
231 Plains L	.12	.25
232 Plains L	.10	.20
233 Plains L	.20	.40
234 Island L	.12	.25
235 Island L	.10	.20
236 Island L	.10	.20
237 Island L	.20	.40
238 Swamp L	1.00	2.00
239 Swamp L	.12	.25
240 Swamp L	.07	.15
241 Swamp L	.07	.15
242 Mountain L	.12	.25
243 Mountain L	.12	.25
244 Mountain L	.12	.25
245 Mountain L	.12	.25
246 Forest L	.07	.15
247 Forest L	.12	.25
248 Forest L	.12	.25
249 Forest L	.12	.25

2009 Magic The Gathering Magic 2010 Tokens

1 Avatar	.50	1.00
2 Soldier	.10	.20
3 Zombie	.10	.20
4 Goblin	.12	.25
5 Beast	.15	.30
6 Insect	.17	.35
7 Wolf	.10	.20
8 Gargoyle	.10	.20

2009 Magic The Gathering Magic Premiere Shop

1 Plains L	3.00	6.00
2 Island L	2.50	5.00
3 Swamp L	1.00	2.00
4 Mountain L	1.25	2.50
5 Forest L	2.00	4.00

2009 Magic The Gathering Planechase

1 Akroma's Vengeance R	.50	1.00
2 Congregate C	.12	.25
3 Kor Sanctifiers C	.12	.25
4 Oblivion Ring C	.12	.25
5 Orim's Thunder C	.12	.25
6 Prison Term U	.25	.50
7 Soul Warden C	.12	.25
8 Broodstar R	.50	1.00
9 Fabricate U	1.00	2.00
10 Keep Watch C	.12	.25
11 Master of Etherium R	3.00	6.00
12 Qumulox U	.25	.50
13 Sarcomite Myr C	.12	.25
14 Thirst for Knowledge U	.25	.50
15 Vedalken Engineer C	.12	.25
16 Whiplash Trap C	.12	.25
17 Ascendant Evincar R	.50	1.00
18 Beacon of Unrest R	2.50	5.00
19 Beseech the Queen U	2.00	4.00
19 Festering Goblin C	.12	.25
20 Cadaverous Knight C	.12	.25
21 Consume Spirit U	.25	.50
22 Corpse Harvester U	.25	.50
23 Cruel Revival C	.12	.25
24 Dark Ritual C	1.00	2.00
25 Death Baron R	7.50	15.00
26 Dregscape Zombie C	.12	.25
28 Grave Pact R	5.00	10.00
29 Gravedigger C	.12	.25
30 Helldozer R	.50	1.00
31 Hideous End C	.12	.25
32 Incremental Blight U	.25	.50
33 Innocent Blood C	.12	.25
34 Nefashu R	.50	1.00
35 Noxious Ghoul U	.25	.50
36 Phyrexian Arena R	5.00	10.00
37 Phyrexian Ghoul C	.12	.25
38 Profane Command R	.50	1.00
39 Rotting Rats C	.12	.25
40 Shepherd of Rot C	.12	.25

41 Soulless One U	.25	.50
42 Syphon Mind C	.12	.25
43 Syphon Soul C	.12	.25
44 Undead Warchief U	2.50	5.00
45 Withered Wretch U	.25	.50
46 Arc Lightning C	.12	.25
47 Blaze U	.25	.50
48 Bogardan Firefiend C	.12	.25
49 Bogardan Rager C	.12	.25
50 Browbeat U	.60	1.25
51 Cinder Elemental U	.25	.50
52 Cone of Flame U	.25	.50
53 Flamekin Harbinger U	.50	1.00
54 Flametongue Kavu U	.25	.50
55 Furnace of Rath R	.50	1.00
56 Goblin Offensive U	.50	1.00
57 Insurrection R	2.00	4.00
58 Keldon Champion U	.25	.50
59 Menacing Ogre R	.50	1.00
60 Pyrotechnics U	.25	.50
61 Reckless Charge C	.12	.25
62 Relentless Assault R	.50	1.00
63 Rockslide Elemental U	.25	.50
64 Rolling Thunder C	.12	.25
65 Rorix Bladewing R	.50	1.00
66 Smokebraider C	.12	.25
67 Taurean Mauler R	.50	1.00
68 Beast Hunt C	.12	.25
69 Briarhorn U	.25	.50
70 Explosive Vegetation U	1.00	2.00
71 Fertile Ground C	.12	.25
72 Fertilid C	.12	.25
73 Forgotten Ancient R	1.50	3.00
74 Ivy Elemental R	.50	1.00
75 Living Hive R	.50	1.00
76 Rampant Growth C	.12	.25
77 Search for Tomorrow C	.12	.25
78 Silverglade Elemental C	.12	.25
79 Tornado Elemental R	.50	1.00
80 Tribal Unity U	.25	.50
81 Verdant Force R	.50	1.00
82 Boros Swiftblade U	.25	.50
83 Branching Bolt C	.12	.25
84 Bull Cerodon U	.25	.50
85 Captain's Maneuver U	.25	.50
86 Cerodon Yearling C	.12	.25
87 Fires of Yavimaya U	.25	.50
88 Glory of Warfare R	.50	1.00
89 Hull Breach C	1.00	2.00
90 Lightning Helix U	1.50	3.00
91 Mage Slayer U	.25	.50
92 Razia, Boros Archangel R	1.00	2.00
93 Rumbling Slum R	.50	1.00
94 Savage Twister U	.25	.50
95 Sludge Strider U	.25	.50
96 Arsenal Thresher C	.12	.25
97 Balefire Liege R	4.00	8.00
98 Battlegate Mimic C	.12	.25
99 Boros Guildmage U	.25	.50
100 Double Cleave C	.12	.25
101 Duergar Hedge-Mage U	.25	.50
102 Hearthfire Hobgoblin U	.25	.50
103 Assault/Battery U	.25	.50
104 Order/Chaos U	.25	.50
105 Arcbound Crusher U	.50	1.00
106 Arcbound Slith U	.25	.50
107 Boros Signet C	.12	.25
108 Bosh, Iron Golem R	.50	1.00
109 Copper Myr C	.12	.25
110 Cranial Plating C	1.50	3.00
111 Darksteel Forge R	2.00	4.00
112 Door to Nothingness R	.50	1.00
113 Etched Oracle U	.25	.50
114 Gold Myr C	.12	.25
115 Iron Myr C	.12	.25
116 Leaden Myr C	.12	.25
117 Lodestone Myr R	.50	1.00
118 Loxodon Warhammer R	.75	1.50
119 Mask of Memory U	.25	.50
120 Myr Enforcer C	.12	.25
121 Nuisance Engine U	.25	.50
122 Pentad Prism C	.12	.25
123 Pentavus R	.50	1.00
124 Relic of Progenitus C	.50	1.00
125 Serum Tank U	.25	.50
126 Silver Myr C	.12	.25
127 Skeleton Shard U	.25	.50
128 Suntouched Myr C	.12	.25
129 Wizard Replica C	.12	.25
130 Ancient Den C	1.00	2.00
131 Boros Garrison C	.30	.75
132 Cabal Coffers U	6.00	12.00
133 Great Furnace C	.50	1.00
134 Gruul Turf C	.12	.25
135 Leechridden Swamp U	.60	1.25
136 Seat of the Synod C	.12	.25
137 Shivan Oasis U	.25	.50
138 Sunhome, Fortress of the Legion U	.25	.50
139 Terramorphic Expanse C	.12	.25
140 Tree of Tales C	.12	.25
141 Vault of Whispers C	.12	.25
142 Plains L	.12	.25
143 Plains L	.12	.25
144 Plains L	.12	.25
145 Plains L	.12	.25
146 Plains L	.12	.25
147 Island L	.12	.25
148 Island L	.12	.25
149 Island L	.12	.25
150 Island L	.12	.25
151 Swamp L	.12	.25
152 Swamp L	.12	.25
153 Swamp L	.12	.25
154 Swamp L	.12	.25
155 Swamp L	.12	.25
156 Mountain L	.12	.25
157 Mountain L	.12	.25
158 Mountain L	.12	.25
159 Mountain L	.12	.25
160 Mountain L	.12	.25
161 Mountain L	.12	.25
162 Mountain L	.12	.25
163 Mountain L	.12	.25
164 Mountain L	.12	.25
165 Forest L	.12	.25
166 Forest L	.12	.25
167 Forest L	.12	.25
168 Forest L	.12	.25
169 Forest L	.12	.25

2009 Magic The Gathering Premium Deck Series Slivers

1 Metallic Sliver C	.30	.75
2 Virulent Sliver C	.30	.75
3 Amoeboid Changeline C	.25	.50
4 Winged Sliver C	1.50	3.00
5 Clot Sliver C	.25	.50
6 Frenzy Sliver C	.25	.50
7 Heart Sliver C	1.00	2.00
8 Gemhide Sliver C	1.00	2.00
9 Muscle Sliver C	1.00	2.00
10 Quick Sliver C	.25	.50
11 Crystalline Sliver U	2.50	5.00
12 Hibernation Sliver U	.30	.75
13 Acidic Sliver U	.50	1.00
14 Spined Sliver U	.30	.75
15 Victual Sliver U	.30	.75
16 Armor Sliver U	.30	.75
17 Spectral Sliver U	.30	.75
18 Barbed Sliver U	.30	.75
19 Homing Sliver C	.30	.75
20 Necrotic Sliver U	1.50	3.00
21 Fungus Sliver R	1.00	2.00
22 Brood Sliver R	2.00	4.00
23 Might Sliver U	.75	1.50
24 Sliver Overlord M	2.50	5.00
25 Fury Sliver U	.50	1.00
26 Heartstone U	.75	1.50
27 Distant Melody C	.25	.50
28 Aphetto Dredging C	.25	.50
29 Coat of Arms R	2.50	5.00
30 Wild Pair R	1.25	2.50
31 Ancient Ziggurat U	1.50	3.00
32 Rootbound Crag R	2.50	5.00
33 Rupture Spire C	.30	.75
34 Terramorphic Expanse C	.30	.75
35 Vivid Creek U	.75	1.50
36 Vivid Grove U	.75	1.50
37 Plains L	.30	.75
38 Island L	.30	.75
39 Swamp L	.30	.75
40 Mountain L	.30	.75
41 Forest L	.25	.50

2009 Magic The Gathering Zendikar

1 Armament Master R	.25	.50
2 Arrow Volley Trap U	.10	.20
3 Bold Defense C	.07	.15
4 Brave the Elements U	.25	.50
5 Caravan Hurda C	.07	.15
6 Celestial Mantle R	1.50	3.00
7 Cliff Threader C	.07	.15
8 Conqueror's Pledge R	.25	.50
9 Day of Judgment R	2.00	4.00
10 Devout Lightcaster R	.25	.50
11 Emeria Angel R	.75	1.50
12 Felidar Sovereign M	1.50	3.00
13 Iona, Shield of Emeria M	4.00	8.00
14 Journey to Nowhere C	.50	1.00
15 Kabira Evangel R	.30	.75
16 Kazandu Blademaster U	.25	.50
17 Kor Aeronaut U	.10	.20
18 Kor Cartographer C	.15	.30
19 Kor Duelist U	.10	.20
20 Kor Hookmaster C	.07	.15
21 Kor Outfitter C	.15	.30
22 Kor Sanctifiers C	.07	.15
23 Kor Skyfisher C	.07	.15
24 Landbind Ritual U	.10	.20
25 Luminarch Ascension R	7.50	15.00
26 Makindi Shieldmate C	.07	.15
27 Narrow Escape C	.07	.15
28 Nimbus Wings C	.07	.15
29 Noble Vestige C	.07	.15
30 Ondu Cleric C	.07	.15
31 Pillarfield Ox C	.07	.15
32 Pitfall Trap U	.10	.20
33 Quest for the Holy Relic U	.15	.30
34 Shepherd of the Lost U	.10	.20
35 Shieldmate's Blessing C	.07	.15
36 Steppe Lynx C	.07	.15
37 Sunspring Expedition C	.07	.15
38 Windborne Charge U	.10	.20
39 World Queller R	.25	.50
40 Aether Figment U	.10	.20
41 Archive Trap R	12.50	25.00
42 Archmage Ascension R	1.25	2.50
43 Caller of Gales C	.07	.15
44 Cancel C	.07	.15
45 Cosi's Trickster R	.30	.60
46 Gomazoa U	.10	.20
47 Hedron Crab U	4.00	8.00
48 Into the Roil C	.07	.15
49 Ior Ruin Expedition C	.07	.15
50 Kraken Hatchling C	.07	.15
51 Lethargy Trap C	.07	.15
52 Living Tsunami U	.10	.20
53 Lorthos, the Tidemaker M	2.50	5.00
54 Lullmage Mentor R	1.25	2.50
55 Merfolk Seastalkers U	.10	.20
56 Merfolk Wayfinder U	.10	.20
57 Mindbreak Trap M	12.50	25.00
58 Paralyzing Grasp C	.07	.15
59 Quest for Ancient Secrets U	.10	.20
60 Reckless Scholar C	.07	.15
61 Rite of Replication R	6.00	12.00
62 Roil Elemental R	7.50	15.00
63 Sea Gate Loremaster R	.30	.60
64 Seascape Aerialist U	.10	.20
65 Shoal Serpent C	.07	.15
66 Sky Ruin Drake C	.07	.15
67 Spell Pierce C	.30	.60
68 Sphinx of Jwar Isle R	.25	.50
69 Sphinx of Lost Truths R	.25	.50
70 Spreading Seas C	.50	1.00
71 Summoner's Bane U	.10	.20
72 Tempest Owl C	.07	.15
73 Trapfinder's Trick C	.07	.15
74 Trapmaker's Snare U	.10	.20
75 Umara Raptor C	.07	.15
76 Welkin Tern C	.07	.15
77 Whiplash Trap C	.07	.15
78 Windrider Eel C	.07	.15
79 Bala Ged Thief R	.25	.50
80 Blood Seeker C	.07	.15
81 Blood Tribute R	1.25	2.50
82 Bloodchief Ascension R	20.00	40.00
83 Bloodghast R	7.50	15.00
84 Bog Tatters C	.07	.15
85 Crypt Ripper C	.07	.15
86 Desecrated Earth C	.07	.15
87 Disfigure C	.07	.15
88 Feast of Blood U	.30	.75
89 Gatekeeper of Malakir U	.50	1.00
90 Giant Scorpion C	.07	.15
91 Grim Discovery C	.07	.15
92 Guul Draz Specter R	.25	.50
93 Guul Draz Vampire C	.15	.30
94 Hagra Crocodile C	.07	.15
95 Hagra Diabolist U	.15	.30
96 Halo Hunter R	.25	.50
97 Heartstabber Mosquito C	.07	.15
98 Hideous End C	.07	.15
99 Kalitas, Bloodchief of Ghet M	5.00	10.00
100 Malakir Bloodwitch R	.75	1.50
101 Marsh Casualties U	.10	.20
102 Mind Sludge U	.10	.20
103 Mindless Null C	.07	.15
104 Mire Blight C	.12	.25
105 Needlebite Trap U	.10	.20
106 Nimana Sell-Sword C	.07	.15
107 Ob Nixilis, the Fallen M	10.00	20.00
108 Quest for the Gravelord U	.10	.20
109 Ravenous Trap U	.20	.40
110 Sadistic Sacrament R	1.25	2.50
111 Sorin Markov M	7.50	15.00
112 Soul Stair Expedition C	.07	.15
113 Surrakar Marauder C	.07	.15
114 Vampire Hexmage U	.30	.60
115 Vampire Lacerator C	.07	.15
116 Vampire Nighthawk U	.30	.60
117 Vampire's Bite C	.07	.15
118 Bladetusk Boar C	.07	.15
119 Burst Lightning C	.15	.30
120 Chandra Ablaze M	3.00	6.00
121 Demolish C	.07	.15
122 Electropotence R	.25	.50
123 Elemental Appeal R	.25	.50
124 Geyser Glider U	.10	.20
125 Goblin Bushwhacker C	.30	.75
126 Goblin Guide R	4.00	8.00
127 Goblin Ruinblaster U	.10	.20
128 Goblin Shortcutter C	.07	.15
129 Goblin War Paint C	.07	.15
130 Hellfire Mongrel U	.10	.20
131 Hellkite Charger R	1.25	2.50
132 Highland Berserker C	.07	.15
133 Inferno Trap U	.10	.20
134 Kazuul Warlord R	.25	.50
135 Lavaball Trap R	.25	.50
136 Magma Rift C	.07	.15
137 Mark of Mutiny U	.10	.20
138 Molten Ravager C	.07	.15
139 Murasa Pyromancer U	.10	.20
140 Obsidian Fireheart M	.60	1.25
141 Plated Geopede C	.07	.15
142 Punishing Fire U	.20	.40
143 Pyromancer Ascension R	.30	.75
144 Quest for Pure Flame U	.20	.40
145 Ruinous Minotaur C	.07	.15
146 Runeflare Trap U	.10	.20
147 Seismic Shudder C	.07	.15
148 Shatterskull Giant C	.07	.15
149 Slaughter Cry C	.07	.15
150 Spire Barrage C	.07	.15
151 Torch Slinger C	.07	.15
152 Tuktuk Grunts C	.07	.15
153 Unstable Footing U	.10	.20
154 Warren Instigator M	5.00	10.00
155 Zektar Shrine Expedition C	.07	.15
156 Baloth Cage Trap U	.10	.20
157 Baloth Woodcrasher U	.10	.20
158 Beast Hunt C	.07	.15
159 Beastmaster Ascension R	6.00	12.00
160 Cobra Trap U	.10	.20
161 Frontier Guide U	.10	.20
162 Gigantiform R	.25	.50
163 Grazing Gladehart C	.07	.15
164 Greenweaver Druid U	.17	.35
165 Harrow C	.30	.60
166 Joraga Bard C	.07	.15
167 Khalni Heart Expedition C	.20	.40
168 Lotus Cobra M	3.00	6.00
169 Mold Shambler C	.12	.25
170 Nissa Revane M	7.50	15.00
171 Nissa's Chosen C	.07	.15
172 Oracle of Mul Daya R	20.00	40.00
173 Oran-Rief Recluse C	.07	.15
174 Oran-Rief Survivalist C	.07	.15
175 Predatory Urge R	.25	.50
176 Primal Bellow U	.20	.40
177 Quest for the Gemblades U	.10	.20
178 Rampaging Baloths M	1.00	2.00
179 Relic Crush C	.07	.15
180 River Boa U	.10	.20
181 Savage Silhouette C	.07	.15
182 Scute Mob R	.60	1.25
183 Scythe Tiger C	.07	.15
184 Summoning Trap R	.25	.50
185 Tajuru Archer U	.10	.20
186 Tanglesap C	.07	.15
187 Terra Stomper R	.25	.50
188 Territorial Baloth C	.07	.15
189 Timbermaw Larva C	.07	.15
190 Turntimber Basilisk U	.10	.20
191 Turntimber Ranger R	.75	1.50
192 Vastwood Gorger C	.07	.15
193 Vines of Vastwood C	.75	1.50
194 Zendikar Farguide C	.07	.15
195 Adventuring Gear C	.12	.25
196 Blade of the Bloodchief R	2.50	5.00
197 Blazing Torch U	.10	.20
198 Carnage Altar U	.15	.30
199 Eldrazi Monument M	7.50	15.00
200 Eternity Vessel M	6.00	12.00
201 Expedition Map C	1.00	2.00
202 Explorers Scope C	.07	.15
203 Grappling Hook R	.50	1.00
204 Hedron Scrabbler C	.07	.15
205 Khalni Gem U	.20	.40
206 Spidersilk Net C	.07	.15
207 Stonework Puma C	.07	.15
208 Trailblazers Boots U	1.50	3.00
209 Trusty Machete U	.10	.20
210 Akoum Refuge U	.10	.20
211 Arid Mesa R	25.00	50.00
212 Crypt of Agadeem R	3.00	6.00
213 Emeria, the Sky Ruin R	7.50	15.00
214 Graypelt Refuge U	.17	.35
215 Jwar Isle Refuge U	.20	.40
216 Kabira Crossroads C	.20	.40
217 Kazandu Refuge U	.20	.40
218 Magosi, the Waterveil R	.30	.75
219 Marsh Flats R	25.00	50.00
220 Misty Rainforest R	50.00	100.00
221 Oran-Rief, the Vastwood R	.75	1.50
222 Piranha Marsh C	.07	.15
223 Scalding Tarn R	50.00	90.00
224 Sejiri Refuge U	.20	.40
225 Soaring Seacliff C	.07	.15
226 Teetering Peaks C	.07	.15
227 Turntimber Grove C	.07	.15
228 Valakut, the Molten Pinnacle R	15.00	30.00
229 Verdant Catacombs R	30.00	75.00
230 Plains L FULL ART	.07	.15
230 Plains L	.07	.15
231 Plains L	.07	.15
231 Plains L FULL ART	.07	.15
232 Plains L FULL ART	.07	.15
232 Plains L	.07	.15
233 Plains L	.07	.15
233 Plains L FULL ART	.07	.15
234 Plains L FULL ART	.07	.15
234 Island L	.07	.15
235 Island L FULL ART	.07	.15
235 Island L	.07	.15
236 Island L	.07	.15
236 Island L FULL ART	.07	.15
237 Island L FULL ART	.07	.15
237 Island L	.07	.15
238 Swamp L	.07	.15
238 Swamp L FULL ART	.07	.15
239 Swamp L FULL ART	.07	.15
239 Swamp L	.07	.15
240 Swamp L	.07	.15
240 Swamp L FULL ART	.07	.15
241 Swamp L FULL ART	.07	.15
241 Swamp L	.07	.15
242 Mountain L	.07	.15
242 Mountain L	.07	.15
243 Mountain L	.07	.15
243 Mountain L FULL ART·	.07	.15
244 Mountain L	.07	.15
244 Mountain L FULL ART	.07	.15
245 Mountain L	.07	.15
245 Mountain L FULL ART	.07	.15
246 Forest L	.07	.15
246 Forest L	.07	.15
247 Forest L	.07	.15
247 Forest L FULL ART	.07	.15
248 Forest L	.07	.15
248 Forest L FULL ART	.07	.15
249 Forest L	.07	.15
249 Forest L FULL ART	.07	.15

2009 Magic The Gathering Zendikar Tokens

1 Angel	.30	.60
2 Bird	.12	.25
3 Kor Soldier	.12	.25
4 Illusion	.07	.15
5 Merfolk	.25	.50
6 Vampire	.75	1.50
7 Zombie Giant	.07	.15
8 Elemental	.07	.15
9 Beast	.15	.30
10 Snake	.10	.20
11 Wolf	.12	.25

2010 Magic The Gathering Archenemy

1 Leonin Abunas R	1.00	2.00
2 Metallurgeon U	.12	.25
3 Oblivion Ring C	.30	.75
4 Path to Exile U	6.00	12.00
5 Sanctum Gargoyle C	.12	.25
6 March of the Machines R	.25	.50
7 Master Transmuter R	17.50	35.00
8 Spin into Myth U	.30	.75
9 Avatar of Woe R	1.25	2.50
10 Beacon of Unrest R	2.00	4.00
11 Bog Witch C	.12	.25
12 Cemetery Reaper R	1.25	2.50
13 Corpse Connoisseur U	.15	.30
14 Dregscape Zombie C	.12	.25
15 Extractor Demon R	.25	.50
16 Festering Goblin C	.12	.25
17 Incremental Blight U	.12	.25
18 Infectious Horror C	.12	.25
19 Infest U	.12	.25
20 Makeshift Mannequin U	.17	.35
21 Reanimate U	6.00	11.00
22 Reassembling Skeleton U	.25	.50
23 Scion of Darkness R	1.00	1.75
24 Shriekmaw U	.60	1.25
25 Sign in Blood C	.12	.25
26 Twisted Abomination C	.12	.25
27 Urborg Syphon-Mage C	.12	.25
28 Zombie Infestation U	.50	1.00
29 Zombify U	.30	.75
30 Battering Craghorn C	.12	.25
31 Breath of Darigaaz U	.12	.25
32 Chandra's Outrage C	.12	.25
33 Dragon Breath C	.12	.25
34 Dragon Fodder C	.25	.50
35 Dragon Whelp U	.12	.25

36 Dragonspeaker Shaman U 2.50 4.50
37 Fireball U .15 .30
38 Flameblast Dragon R .30 .75
39 Furnace Whelp U .12 .25
40 Gathan Raiders C .12 .25
41 Hellkite Charger R .60 1.25
42 Imperial Hellkite R .30 .60
43 Inferno Trap U .12 .25
44 Kilnmouth Dragon R .75 1.50
45 Ryusei, the Falling Star R .75 1.50
46 Seething Song C .60 1.25
47 Skirk Commando C .12 .25
48 Skirk Marauder C .12 .25
49 Taurean Mauler R 1.00 2.00
50 Two-Headed Dragon R .75 1.50
51 Volcanic Fallout U .50 1.00
52 Chameleon Colossus R 1.00 2.00
53 Feral Hydra R 1.00 2.00
54 Fertilid C .12 .25
55 Fierce Empath C 1.50 3.00
56 Fog C .12 .25
57 Forgotten Ancient R 1.50 3.00
58 Gleeful Sabotage C .12 .25
59 Harmonize U .75 1.50
60 Hunting Moa U .25 .50
61 Kamahl, Fist of Krosa R 3.00 6.00
62 Krosan Tusker C .12 .25
63 Leaf Gilder C .12 .25
64 Molimo, Maro-Sorcerer R .25 .50
65 Plummet C .12 .25
66 Primal Command R 2.50 4.25
67 Rancor C 1.50 3.00
68 Sakura-Tribe Elder C .30 .75
69 Shinen of Life's Roar C .12 .25
70 Spider Umbra C .60 1.25
71 Thelonite Hermit R .30 .75
72 Verdeloth the Ancient R .30 .75
73 Wall of Roots C 1.50 3.00
74 Wickerbough Elder C .12 .25
75 Yavimaya Dryad U .12 .25
76 Agony Warp C .12 .25
77 Architects of Will C .20 .40
78 Armadillo Cloak C .60 1.25
79 Avatar of Discord R .60 1.25
80 Batwing Brume U 1.00 1.75
81 Bituminous Blast U .25 .50
82 Branching Bolt C .12 .25
83 Colossal Might C .12 .25
84 Ethersworn Shieldmage C .12 .25
85 Fieldmist Borderpost C .12 .25
86 Fires of Yavimaya U .30 .60
87 Heroes' Reunion U .25 .50
88 Kaervek the Merciless R 1.25 2.15
89 Magister Sphinx R .75 1.50
90 Mistvein Borderpost C .12 .25
91 Pale Recluse C .12 .25
92 Rakdos Guildmage U .25 .50
93 Savage Twister U .12 .25
94 Selesnya Guildmage U .12 .25
95 Terminate C 1.50 3.00
96 Torrent of Souls U .15 .30
97 Unbender Tine U .12 .25
98 Unmake C .60 1.25
99 Vampiric Dragon R 1.25 2.50
100 Watchwolf U .30 .75
101 Wax/Wane U .12 .25
102 AEther Spellbomb C .12 .25
103 Azorius Signet C .12 .25
104 Dimir Signet C 1.50 3.00
105 Dreamstone Hedron U .15 .30
106 Duplicant R 4.00 7.00
107 Everflowing Chalice U .30 .75
108 Gruul Signet C .12 .25
109 Juggernaut U .12 .25
110 Lightning Greaves U 2.50 5.00
111 Lodestone Golem R .50 1.00
112 Memnarch R 4.00 7.00
113 Obelisk of Esper C .12 .25
114 Rakdos Signet C .17 .35
115 Skullcage U .12 .25
116 Sorcerer's Strongbox U .12 .25
117 Sun Droplet U .75 1.50
118 Sundering Titan R 3.00 6.00
119 Synod Centurion U .12 .25
120 Synod Sanctum U .12 .25
121 Thran Dynamo U 5.00 8.50
122 Thunderstaff U .12 .25
123 Artisan of Kozilek U .60 1.25
124 Barren Moor C .12 .25
125 Graypelt Refuge U .25 .50
126 Kazandu Refuge U .15 .30
127 Khalni Garden C .15 .30
128 Krosan Verge U 2.00 3.25
129 Llanowar Reborn U .25 .50
130 Mosswort Bridge R 1.00 1.75
131 Nantuko Monastery U .25 .50
132 Rakdos Carnarium C .20 .40
133 Secluded Steppe C .12 .25
134 Terramorphic Expanse C .12 .25
135 Tranquil Thicket C .12 .25
136 Vitu-Ghazi, the City-Tree U .15 .30
137 Plains L .10 .20
138 Plains L .12 .25
139 Island L .12 .25
140 Island L .12 .25
141 Island L .12 .25
142 Swamp L .12 .25
143 Swamp L .12 .25
144 Swamp L .12 .25
145 Mountain L .12 .25
146 Mountain L .12 .25
147 Mountain L .12 .25
148 Forest L .12 .25
149 Forest L .12 .25
150 Forest L .12 .25

2010 Magic The Gathering Archenemy Oversized Schemes

1 All in Good Time 4.00 8.00
2 All Shall Smolder in My Wake .25 .50
3 Approach My Molten Realm .75 1.50
4 Behold the Power of Destruction 4.00 8.00
5 Choose Your Champion .25 .50
6 Dance, Pathetic Marionette 3.00 6.00
7 The Dead Shall Serve .25 .50
8 A Display of My Dark Power .75 1.50
9 Embrace My Diabolical Vision 1.50 3.00
10 Every Hope Shall Vanish .25 .50
11 Every Last Vestige Shall Rot .25 .50
12 Evil Comes to Fruition .75 1.50
13 The Fate of the Flammable .75 1.50
14 Feed the Machine .25 .50
15 I Bask in Your Silent Awe .25 .50
16 I Call on the Ancient Magics 1.50 3.00
17 I Delight in Your Convulsions .25 .50
18 I Know All, I See All .25 .50
19 Ignite the Cloneforge! .25 .50
20 Into the Earthen Maw 1.50 3.00
21 Introductions Are in Order .25 .50
22 The Iron Guardian Stirs .25 .50
23 Know Naught but Fire 1.50 3.00
24 Look Skyward and Despair .25 .50
25 May Civilization Collapse 1.25 2.50
26 Mortal Flesh Is Weak 2.50 5.00
27 My Crushing Masterstroke 4.00 8.00
28 My Genius Knows No Bounds 1.25 2.50
29 My Undead Horde Awakens 3.00 6.00
30 My Wish Is Your Command .25 .50
31 Nature Demands an Offering .25 .50
32 Nature Shields Its Own .25 .50
33 Nothing Can Stop Me Now .75 1.50
34 Only Blood Ends Your Nightmares .25 .50
35 The Pieces Are Coming Together .25 .50
36 Realms Befitting My Majesty .25 .50
37 Roots of All Evil .25 .50
38 Rotted Ones, Lay Siege .25 .50
39 Surrender Your Thoughts 1.50 3.00
40 Tooth, Claw, and Tail 4.00 8.00
41 The Very Soil Shall Shake 1.50 3.00
42 Which of You Burns Brightest .25 .50
43 Your Fate Is Thrice Sealed .25 .50
44 Your Puny Minds Cannot Fathom .25 .50
45 Your Will Is Not Your Own .25 .50

2010 Magic The Gathering Duel Decks Elspeth vs. Tezzeret

1 Elspeth, Knight-Errant M 6.00 12.00
2 Elite Vanguard U .12 .25
3 Goldmeadow Harrier C .10 .20
4 Infantry Veteran C .10 .20
5 Loyal Sentry R .20 .40
6 Mosquito Guard C .10 .20
7 Glory Seeker C .10 .20
8 Kor Skyfisher C .10 .20
9 Temple Acolyte C .10 .20
10 Kor Aeronaut U .12 .25
11 Burrenton Bombardier C .10 .20
12 Kor Hookmaster C .10 .20
13 Kemba's Skyguard C .10 .20
14 Celestial Crusader U .12 .25
15 Seasoned Marshal U .12 .25
16 Conclave Phalanx U .12 .25
17 Stormfront Riders U .12 .25
18 Catapult Master R .20 .40
19 Conclave Equenaut C .10 .20
20 Angel of Salvation R .20 .40
21 Sunlance C .10 .20
22 Swords to Plowshares U 1.25 2.50
23 Journey to Nowhere C 1.00 2.00
24 Mighty Leap C .10 .20
25 Raise the Alarm C .10 .20
26 Razor Barrier C .10 .20
27 Crusade R .30 .75
28 Blinding Beam C .10 .20
29 Abolish U .12 .25
30 Saltblast U .12 .25
31 Swell of Courage U .12 .25
32 Daru Encampment U .12 .25
33 Kabira Crossroads C .15 .30
34 Rustic Clachan R .20 .40
35 Plains L .10 .20
36 Plains L .10 .20
37 Plains L .10 .20
38 Plains L .10 .20
39 Tezzeret the Seeker M 4.00 8.00
40 Arcbound Worker C .10 .20
41 Steel Wall C .10 .20
42 Runed Servitor U .12 .25
43 Silver Myr C .10 .20
44 Steel Overseer R 6.00 12.00
45 Assembly-Worker U .12 .25
46 Serrated Biskelion U .12 .25
47 Esperzoa U .12 .25
48 Master of Etherium R 4.00 8.00
49 Trinket Mage C .15 .30
50 Clockwork Condor C .10 .20
51 Frogmite C .15 .30
52 Juggernaut U .12 .25
53 Synod Centurion U .12 .25
54 Faerie Mechanist C .10 .20
55 Clockwork Hydra U .12 .25
56 Razormane Masticore R .20 .40
57 Triskelion R .20 .40
58 Pentavus R .20 .40
59 Qumulox U .12 .25
60 Everflowing Chalice U .30 .60
61 Aether Spellbomb C .10 .20
62 Elixir of Immortality U .30 .60
63 Contagion Clasp U .20 .40
64 Energy Chamber U .50 1.00
65 Trip Noose U .12 .25
66 Echoing Truth C .25 .50
67 Moonglove Extract C .10 .20
68 Thirst for Knowledge U 1.00 2.00
69 Argivian Restoration U .12 .25
70 Foil U .25 .50
71 Thoughtcast C .50 1.00
72 Darksteel Citadel C .50 1.00
73 Mishra's Factory U 1.25 2.50
74 Seat of the Synod C 1.00 1.75
75 Stalking Stones U .12 .25
76 Island L .10 .20
77 Island L .10 .20
78 Island L .10 .20
79 Island L .10 .20

2010 Magic The Gathering Duel Decks Elspeth vs. Tezzeret Token

1 Soldier .07 .15

2010 Magic The Gathering Duel Decks Phyrexia vs. The Coalition

1 Phyrexian Negator M 1.50 3.00
2 Carrion Feeder C .25 .50
3 Phyrexian Battleflies C .12 .25
4 Phyrexian Denouncer C .12 .25
5 Bone Shredder U .25 .50
6 Phyrexian Ghoul C .12 .25
7 Priest of Gix U .25 .50
8 Phyrexian Broodlings C .12 .25
9 Sanguine Guard U .25 .50
10 Phyrexian Debaser C .12 .25
11 Order of Yawgmoth U .25 .50
12 Phyrexian Defiler U .25 .50
13 Phyrexian Plaguelord R .30 .75
14 Phyrexian Hulk U .25 .50
15 Phyrexian Gargantua U .25 .50
16 Phyrexian Colossus R .30 .75
17 Voltaic Key U .50 1.00
18 Dark Ritual C 1.00 2.00
19 Lightning Greaves U 1.25 2.50
20 Phyrexian Totem U .25 .50
21 Phyrexian Vault U .25 .50
22 Puppet Strings U .25 .50
23 Whispersilk Cloak U .30 .75
24 Worn Powerstone U .50 1.00
25 Slay U .25 .50
26 Hideous End C .12 .25
27 Phyrexian Arena R 1.50 3.00
28 Hornet Cannon U .25 .50
29 Phyrexian Processor R 1.00 2.00
30 Tendrils of Corruption C .12 .25
31 Living Death R 1.25 2.50
32 Swamp L .12 .25
33 Swamp L .12 .25
34 Swamp L .12 .25
35 Swamp L .12 .25
36 Urza's Rage M .75 1.50
37 Thornscape Apprentice C .12 .25
38 Nomadic Elf C .12 .25
39 Quirion Elves C .12 .25
40 Sunscape Battlemage U .25 .50
41 Thunderscape Battlemage U .25 .50
42 Thornscape Battlemage U .25 .50
43 Verduran Emissary U .25 .50
44 Yavimaya Elder C .50 1.00
45 Charging Troll U .25 .50
46 Gerrard Capashen R .30 .75
47 Darigaaz, the Igniter R .75 1.50
48 Rith, the Awakener R 1.00 2.00
49 Treva, the Renewer R 1.00 2.00
50 Evasive Action U .25 .50
51 Tribal Flames C .25 .50
52 Fertile Ground C .12 .25
53 Gerrard's Command C .12 .25
54 Coalition Relic R 2.00 4.00
55 Narrow Escape C .12 .25
56 Exotic Curse C .12 .25
57 Harrow C .25 .50
58 Armadillo Cloak C .50 1.00
59 Darigaaz's Charm U .25 .50
60 Rith's Charm U .25 .50
61 Treva's Charm U .25 .50
62 Power Armor U .25 .50
63 Allied Strategies U .25 .50
64 Elfhame Palace U .25 .50
65 Shivan Oasis U .25 .50
66 Terramorphic Expanse C .25 .50
67 Plains L .12 .25
68 Island L .12 .25
69 Mountain L .12 .25
70 Forest L .12 .25
70 Forest L .12 .25

2010 Magic The Gathering Duel Decks Phyrexia vs. The Coalition Tokens

1 Hornet 1.25 2.25
2 Minion 3.00 6.00
3 Saproling .12 .25

2010 Magic The Gathering From the Vault Relics

1 Aether Vial M 12.50 25.00
2 Black Vise M 1.50 3.00
3 Isochron Scepter M 5.00 10.00
4 Ivory Tower M 2.00 4.00
5 Jester's Cap M 1.50 3.00
6 Karn, Silver Golem M 3.00 6.00
7 Masticore M 1.50 3.00
8 Memory Jar M 2.50 5.00
9 Mirari M 2.00 4.00
10 Mox Diamond M 15.00 30.00
11 Nevinyrral's Disk M 7.50 15.00
12 Sol Ring M 15.00 30.00
13 Sundering Titan M 2.00 4.00
14 Sword of Body and Mind M 6.00 12.00
15 Zuran Orb M 1.50 3.00

2010 Magic The Gathering Judge Gift Rewards

1 Sinkhole R 20.00 40.00
2 Natural Order R 75.00 150.00
3 Phyrexian Dreadnought R 175.00 350.00
4 Thawing Glaciers R 100.00 200.00
5 Land Tax R 60.00 125.00
6 Morphling R 30.00 75.00
7 Wheel of Fortune R 1,250.00 2,500.00
8 Wasteland R 75.00 150.00

2010 Magic The Gathering Magic 2011

1 Ajani Goldmane M 3.00 6.00
2 Ajani's Mantra C .20 .40
3 Ajani's Pridemate U .17 .35
4 Angelic Arbiter R 1.50 3.00
5 Armored Ascension U .15 .30
6 Assault Griffin C .07 .15
7 Baneslayer Angel M 2.00 4.00
8 Blinding Mage C .07 .15
9 Celestial Purge U .10 .20
10 Cloud Crusader C .07 .15
11 Condemn U .10 .20
12 Day of Judgment R 2.00 4.00
13 Elite Vanguard U .10 .20
14 Excommunicate C .07 .15
15 Goldenglow Moth C .07 .15
16 Holy Strength C .07 .15
17 Honor of the Pure R 1.25 2.50
18 Infantry Veteran C .07 .15
19 Inspired Charge C .07 .15
20 Knight Exemplar R 7.50 15.00
21 Leyline of Sanctity R 2.00 4.00
22 Mighty Leap C .07 .15
23 Pacifism C .07 .15
24 Palace Guard C .07 .15
25 Roc Egg U .10 .20
26 Safe Passage C .07 .15
27 Serra Angel U .10 .20
28 Serra Ascendant R 15.00 30.00
29 Siege Mastodon C .07 .15
30 Silence R 3.00 6.00
31 Silvercoat Lion C .07 .15
32 Solemn Offering C .07 .15
33 Squadron Hawk C .15 .30
34 Stormfront Pegasus C .07 .15
35 Sun Titan M 1.25 2.50
36 Tireless Missionaries C .07 .15
37 Vengeful Archon R .15 .30
38 War Priest of Thune U .10 .20
39 White Knight U .10 .20
40 Wild Griffin C .07 .15
41 Aether Adept C .07 .15
42 Air Servant U .10 .20
43 Alluring Siren U .10 .20
44 Armored Cancrix C .07 .15
45 Augury Owl C .17 .35
46 Azure Drake U .10 .20
47 Call to Mind U .15 .30
48 Cancel C .07 .15
49 Clone R .25 .50
50 Cloud Elemental C .07 .15
51 Conundrum Sphinx R .15 .30
52 Diminish C .07 .15
53 Flashfreeze U .10 .20
54 Foresee C .07 .15
55 Frost Titan M .50 1.00
56 Harbor Serpent C .07 .15
57 Ice Cage C .07 .15
58 Jace Beleren M 2.50 5.00
59 Jace's Erasure C .15 .30
60 Jace's Ingenuity U .10 .20
61 Leyline of Anticipation R 5.00 10.00
62 Mana Leak C .17 .35
63 Maritime Guard C .07 .15
64 Mass Polymorph R .30 .75
65 Merfolk Sovereign R .15 .30
66 Merfolk Spy C .07 .15
67 Mind Control U .10 .20
68 Negate C .07 .15
69 Phantom Beast C .07 .15
70 Preordain C .60 1.25
71 Redirect R .15 .30
72 Scroll Thief C .07 .15
73 Sleep U .10 .20
74 Stormtide Leviathan R .60 1.25
75 Time Reversal M 4.00 8.00
76 Tome Scour C .15 .30
77 Traumatize R 2.00 4.00
78 Unsummon C .07 .15
79 Wall of Frost U .20 .40
80 Water Servant U .10 .20
81 Assassinate C .07 .15
82 Barony Vampire C .07 .15
83 Black Knight U .10 .20
84 Blood Tithe C .20 .40
85 Bloodthrone Vampire C .12 .25
86 Bog Raiders C .07 .15
87 Captivating Vampire R 4.00 8.00
88 Child of Night C .07 .15
89 Corrupt U .10 .20
90 Dark Tutelage R .50 1.00
91 Deathmark U .10 .20
92 Demon of Death's Gate M 6.00 12.00
93 Diabolic Tutor U .60 1.25
94 Disentomb C .07 .15
95 Doom Blade C .17 .35
96 Duress C .07 .15
97 Grave Titan M 7.50 15.00
98 Gravedigger C .07 .15
99 Haunting Echoes R .30 .75
100 Howling Banshee U .10 .20
101 Leyline of the Void R 4.00 8.00
102 Liliana Vess M 7.50 15.00
103 Liliana's Caress U 5.00 10.00
104 Liliana's Specter C .20 .40
105 Mind Rot C .07 .15
106 Nantuko Shade R .15 .30
107 Necrotic Plague C .07 .15
108 Nether Horror C .07 .15
109 Nightwing Shade C .07 .15
110 Phylactery Lich R .15 .30
111 Quag Sickness C .07 .15
112 Reassembling Skeleton U .25 .50
113 Relentless Rats U 1.50 3.00
114 Rise from the Grave U .10 .20
115 Rotting Legion C .07 .15
116 Royal Assassin R .50 1.00
117 Sign in Blood C .17 .35
118 Stabbing Pain C .07 .15
119 Unholy Strength C .07 .15
120 Viscera Seer C .20 .40
121 Act of Treason U .10 .20
122 Ancient Hellkite R .25 .50
123 Arc Runner C .07 .15
124 Berserkers of Blood Ridge C .07 .15
125 Bloodcrazed Goblin C .07 .15
126 Canyon Minotaur C .07 .15
127 Chandra Nalaar M 2.00 4.00
128 Chandra's Outrage C .07 .15
129 Chandra's Spitfire U .17 .35
130 Combust U .10 .20
131 Cyclops Gladiator R .15 .30
132 Demolish C .07 .15
133 Destructive Force R .15 .30

134 Earth Servant U .10 .20
135 Ember Hauler U .10 .20
136 Fiery Hellhound C .07 .15
137 Fire Servant U .30 .75
138 Fireball U .10 .20
139 Fling C .07 .15
140 Goblin Balloon Brigade C .07 .15
141 Goblin Chieftain R 2.50 5.00
142 Goblin Piker C .07 .15
143 Goblin Tunneler C .07 .15
144 Hoarding Dragon R .15 .30
145 Incite C .07 .15
146 Inferno Titan M 1.00 2.00
147 Lava Axe R .15 .30
148 Leyline of Punishment R 2.00 4.00
149 Lightning Bolt C 2.00 4.00
150 Magma Phoenix R .15 .30
151 Manic Vandal C .07 .15
152 Prodigal Pyromancer U .10 .20
153 Pyretic Ritual C 3.00 6.00
154 Pyroclasm U .10 .20
155 Reverberate R 4.00 8.00
156 Shiv's Embrace U .10 .20
157 Thunder Strike C .07 .15
158 Volcanic Strength C .07 .15
159 Vulshok Berserker C .07 .15
160 Wild Evocation R .30 .75
161 Acidic Slime U .17 .35
162 Autumn's Veil U .30 .60
163 Awakener Druid U .10 .20
164 Back to Nature U .10 .35
165 Birds of Paradise R 7.50 15.00
166 Brindle Boar C .07 .15
167 Cudgel Troll U .10 .20
168 Cultivate C .50 1.00
169 Dryad's Favor C .07 .15
170 Duskdale Wurm U .10 .20
171 Elvish Archdruid R 1.25 2.50
172 Fauna Shaman R 7.50 15.00
173 Fog C .07 .15
174 Gaea's Revenge M .50 1.00
175 Garruk Wildspeaker M 4.00 8.00
176 Garruk's Companion C .07 .15
177 Garruk's Packleader U .10 .20
178 Giant Growth C .07 .15
179 Giant Spider C .07 .15
180 Greater Basilisk C .07 .15
181 Hornet Sting C .07 .15
182 Hunters' Feast C .07 .15
183 Leyline of Vitality R 2.50 5.00
184 Llanowar Elves C .20 .40
185 Mitotic Slime R .75 1.50
186 Naturalize C .07 .15
187 Nature's Spiral U .10 .20
188 Obstinate Baloth U .50 1.00
189 Overwhelming Stampede R 2.50 5.00
190 Plummet C .07 .15
191 Primal Cocoon C .07 .15
192 Primeval Titan M 7.50 15.00
193 Prized Unicorn U .10 .20
194 Protean Hydra R 4.00 8.00
195 Runeclaw Bear C .07 .15
196 Sacred Wolf C .07 .15
197 Spined Wurm C .07 .15
198 Sylvan Ranger C .07 .15
199 Wall of Vines C .07 .15
200 Yavimaya Wurm C .07 .15
201 Angel's Feather U .10 .20
202 Brittle Effigy R .25 .50
203 Crystal Ball U .30 .60
204 Demon's Horn U .10 .20
205 Dragon's Claw U .20 .40
206 Elixir of Immortality U .60 1.25
207 Gargoyle Sentinel U .10 .20
208 Jinxed Idol R .15 .30
209 Juggernaut U .10 .20
210 Kraken's Eye U .10 .20
211 Ornithopter U .20 .40
212 Platinum Angel M 7.50 15.00
213 Sorcerer's Strongbox U .10 .20
214 Steel Overseer R 1.50 3.00
215 Stone Golem U .10 .20
216 Sword of Vengeance R 1.00 2.00
217 Temple Bell R 1.50 3.00
218 Triskelion R 1.25 2.50
219 Voltaic Key U .75 1.50
220 Warlord's Axe U .10 .20
221 Whispersilk Cloak U 2.00 4.00
222 Wurm's Tooth U .10 .20
223 Dragonskull Summit R 2.50 5.00
224 Drowned Catacomb R 4.00 8.00
225 Glacial Fortress R 4.00 8.00
226 Mystifying Maze R .50 1.00
227 Rootbound Crag R 2.50 5.00
228 Sunpetal Grove R 3.00 6.00
229 Terramorphic Expanse C .20 .40
230 Plains L .10 .20
231 Plains L .20 .40
232 Plains L .10 .20
233 Plains L .10 .20
234 Island L .12 .25
235 Island L .20 .40
236 Island L .17 .35
237 Island L .10 .20
238 Swamp L .17 .35
239 Swamp L .12 .25
240 Swamp L .12 .25
241 Swamp L .07 .15
242 Mountain L .20 .40
243 Mountain L .10 .20
244 Mountain L .15 .30
245 Mountain L .12 .25
246 Forest L .10 .20
247 Forest L .10 .20
248 Forest L .10 .20
249 Forest L .10 .20

2010 Magic The Gathering Magic 2011 Tokens

1 Avatar .30 .60
2 Bird .07 .15
3 Zombie .07 .15
4 Beast .07 .15
5 Ooze .07 .15
6 Ooze .20 .40

2010 Magic The Gathering Magic Premiere Shop

1 Plains L 1.25 2.50
2 Island L 1.25 2.50
3 Swamp L 1.50 3.00
4 Mountain L 1.50 3.00
5 Forest L .75 1.50

2010 Magic The Gathering Premium Deck Series Fire and Lightning

1 Grim Lavamancer R 3.00 6.00
2 Jackal Pup U .25 .50
3 Mogg Fanatic U .25 .50
4 Spark Elemental U .25 .50
5 Figure of Destiny R 1.00 2.00
6 Hellspark Elemental U 1.00 2.00
7 Keldon Marauders C .25 .50
8 Mogg Flunkies C .12 .25
9 Cinder Pyromancer C .12 .25
10 Jaya Ballard, Task Mage R .25 .50
11 Vulshok Sorcerer C .25 .50
12 Ball Lightning R 2.00 4.00
13 Boggart Ram-Gang U .30 .75
14 Keldon Champion U .25 .50
15 Fire Servant U .25 .50
16 Chain Lightning C 7.50 15.00
17 Lightning Bolt C 1.50 3.00
18 Price of Progress U 4.00 8.00
19 Thunderbolt C .12 .25
20 Reverberate R .50 1.00
21 Browbeat U .75 1.50
22 Flames of the Blood Hand U 2.00 4.00
23 Hammer of Bogardan R .50 1.00
24 Pillage U .30 .75
25 Sudden Impact U .25 .50
26 Fireblast C 1.25 2.50
27 Fireball U .25 .50
28 Barbarian Ring U .25 .50
29 Ghitu Encampment U .25 .50
30 Teetering Peaks C .12 .25
31 Mountain L .12 .25
32 Mountain L .12 .25
33 Mountain L .12 .25
34 Mountain L .12 .25

2010 Magic The Gathering Rise of the Eldrazi

1 All Is Dust M 5.00 10.00
2 Artisan of Kozilek U .10 .20
3 Eldrazi Conscription R .20 .40
4 Emrakul, the Aeons Torn M 12.50 25.00
5 Hand of Emrakul C .07 .15
6 Kozilek, Butcher of Truth M 20.00 40.00
7 It That Betrays R .20 .40
8 Not of This World U .10 .20
9 Pathrazer of Ulamog U .10 .20
10 Skittering Invasion U .10 .20
11 Spawnsire of Ulamog R .20 .40
12 Ulamog, the Infinite Gyre M 20.00 40.00
13 Ulamog's Crusher C .07 .15
14 Affa Guard Hound U .10 .20
15 Caravan Escort C .07 .15
16 Dawnglare Invoker C .07 .15
17 Deathless Angel R .20 .40
18 Demystify C .07 .15
19 Eland Umbra C .07 .15
20 Emerge Unscathed U .10 .20
21 Gideon Jura M 1.25 2.50
22 Glory Seeker C .07 .15
23 Guard Duty C .07 .15
24 Harmless Assault C .07 .15
25 Hedron-Field Purists R .20 .40
26 Hyena Umbra C .07 .15
27 Ikiral Outrider C .07 .15
28 Kabira Vindicator U .10 .20
29 Knight of Cliffhaven C .07 .15
30 Kor Line-Slinger C .07 .15
31 Kor Spiritdancer R .20 .40
32 Lightmine Field R .20 .40
33 Linvala, Keeper of Silence M 12.50 25.00
34 Lone Missionary C .07 .15
35 Luminous Wake U .10 .20
36 Makindi Griffin C .07 .15
37 Mammoth Umbra U .10 .20
38 Near-Death Experience R .20 .40
39 Nomads' Assembly R .20 .40
40 Oust U .10 .20
41 Puncturing Light C .07 .15
42 Repel the Darkness C .07 .15
43 Smite C .07 .15
44 Soul's Attendant C .07 .15
45 Soulbound Guardians U .10 .20
46 Stalwart Shield-Bearers C .07 .15
47 Student of Warfare R .20 .40
48 Survival Cache U .10 .20
49 Time of Heroes U .10 .20
50 Totem-Guide Hartebeest C .07 .15
51 Transcendent Master M 2.00 4.00
52 Umbra Mystic R .20 .40
53 Wall of Omens U .10 .20
54 Aura Finesse C .07 .15
55 Cast Through Time M 1.00 2.00
56 Champion's Drake C .07 .15
57 Coralhelm Commander R .20 .40
58 Crab Umbra U .10 .20
59 Deprive C .07 .15
60 Distortion Strike C .07 .15
61 Domestication U .10 .20
62 Dormant Gomazoa R .20 .40
63 Drake Umbra U .10 .20
64 Echo Mage R .20 .40
65 Eel Umbra C .07 .15
66 Enclave Cryptologist U .10 .20
67 Fleeting Distraction C .07 .15
68 Frostwind Invoker C .07 .15
69 Gravitational Shift R .20 .40
70 Guard Gomazoa U .10 .20
71 Hada Spy Patrol U .10 .20
72 Halimar Wavewatch C .07 .15
73 Jwari Scuttler C .07 .15
74 Lay Bare C .07 .15
75 Lighthouse Chronologist M 6.00 12.00
76 Merfolk Observer C .07 .15
77 Merfolk Skyscout U .10 .20
78 Mnemonic Wall C .07 .15
79 Narcolepsy C .07 .15
80 Phantasmal Abomination U .10 .20
81 Reality Spasm U .10 .20
82 Recurring Insight R .20 .40
83 Regress C .07 .15
84 Renegade Doppelganger R .20 .40
85 Sea Gate Oracle C .07 .15
86 See Beyond C .07 .15
87 Shared Discovery C .07 .15
88 Skywatcher Adept C .07 .15
89 Sphinx of Magosi R .20 .40
90 Surrakar Spellblade R .20 .40
91 Training Grounds R .20 .40
92 Unified Will U .10 .20
93 Venerated Teacher C .07 .15
94 Arrogant Bloodlord U .10 .20
95 Bala Ged Scorpion C .07 .15
96 Baneful Omen R .20 .40
97 Bloodrite Invoker C .07 .15
98 Bloodthrone Vampire C .07 .15
99 Cadaver Imp C .07 .15
100 Consume the Meek R .20 .40
101 Consuming Vapors R .20 .40
102 Contaminated Ground C .07 .15
103 Corpsehatch U .10 .20
104 Curse of Wizardry U .10 .20
105 Death Cultist C .07 .15
106 Demonic Appetite C .07 .15
107 Drana, Kalastria Bloodchief R .20 .40
108 Dread Drone C .07 .15
109 Escaped Null U .10 .20
110 Essence Feed C .07 .15
111 Gloomhunter C .07 .15
112 Guul Draz Assassin R .20 .40
113 Hellcarver Demon M .50 1.00
114 Induce Despair C .07 .15
115 Inquisition of Kozilek U .10 .20
116 Last Kiss C .07 .15
117 Mortician Beetle R .20 .40
118 Nighthaze C .07 .15
119 Nirkana Cutthroat U .10 .20
120 Nirkana Revenant M 6.00 12.00
121 Null Champion C .07 .15
122 Pawn of Ulamog U .10 .20
123 Perish the Thought C .07 .15
124 Pestilence Demon R .20 .40
125 Repay in Kind R .20 .40
126 Shrivel C .07 .15
127 Skeletal Wurm U .10 .20
128 Suffer the Past U .10 .20
129 Thought Gorger R .20 .40
130 Vendetta C .07 .15
131 Virulent Swipe U .10 .20
132 Zof Shade C .07 .15
133 Zulaport Enforcer C .07 .15
134 Akoum Boulderfoot U .10 .20
135 Battle Rampart C .07 .15
136 Battle-Rattle Shaman C .07 .15
137 Brimstone Mage U .10 .20
138 Brood Birthing C .07 .15
139 Conquering Manticore R .20 .40
140 Devastating Summons R .20 .40
141 Disaster Radius R .20 .40
142 Emrakul's Hatcher C .07 .15
143 Explosive Revelation U .10 .20
144 Fissure Vent C .07 .15
145 Flame Slash C .07 .15
146 Forked Bolt U .10 .20
147 Goblin Arsonist C .07 .15
148 Goblin Tunneler C .07 .15
149 Grotag Siege-Runner C .07 .15
150 Heat Ray C .07 .15
151 Hellion Eruption R .20 .40
152 Kargan Dragonlord M 1.50 3.00
153 Kiln Fiend C .07 .15
154 Lagac Lizard C .07 .15
155 Lavafume Invoker C .07 .15
156 Lord of Shatterskull Pass R .20 .40
157 Lust for War U .10 .20
158 Magmaw R .20 .40
159 Ogre Sentry C .07 .15
160 Rage Nimbus R .20 .40
161 Raid Bombardment C .07 .15
162 Rapacious One U .10 .20
163 Soulsurge Elemental U .10 .20
164 Spawning Breath C .07 .15
165 Splinter Twin R .20 .40
166 Staggershock C .07 .15
167 Surreal Memoir U .10 .20
168 Traitorous Instinct U .10 .20
169 Tuktuk the Explorer R .20 .40
170 Valakut Fireboar U .10 .20
171 Vent Sentinel C .07 .15
172 World at War R .20 .40
173 Wrap in Flames C .07 .15
174 Ancient Stirrings C .07 .15
175 Aura Gnarlid C .07 .15
176 Awakening Zone R .20 .40
177 Bear Umbra R .20 .40
178 Beastbreaker of Bala Ged U .10 .20
179 Boar Umbra U .10 .20
180 Bramblesnap U .10 .20
181 Broodwarden U .10 .20
182 Daggerback Basilisk C .07 .15
183 Gelatinous Genesis R .20 .40
184 Gigantomancer R .20 .40
185 Gravity Well U .10 .20
186 Growth Spasm C .07 .15
187 Haze Frog C .07 .15
188 Irresistible Prey U .10 .20
189 Jaddi Lifestrider U .10 .20
190 Joraga Treespeaker U .10 .20
191 Kazandu Tuskcaller R .20 .40
192 Khalni Hydra M 7.50 15.00
193 Kozilek's Predator C .07 .15
194 Leaf Arrow C .07 .15
195 Living Destiny C .07 .15
196 Might of the Masses C .07 .15
197 Momentous Fall R .20 .40
198 Mul Daya Channelers R .20 .40
199 Naturalize C .07 .15
200 Nema Siltlurker C .07 .15
201 Nest Invader C .07 .15
202 Ondu Giant C .07 .15
203 Overgrown Battlement C .07 .15
204 Pelakka Wurm U .10 .20
205 Prey's Vengeance U .10 .20
206 Realms Uncharted R .20 .40
207 Snake Umbra C .07 .15
208 Spider Umbra C .07 .15
209 Sporecap Spider C .07 .15
210 Stomper Cub C .07 .15
211 Tajuru Preserver R .20 .40
212 Vengevine M 7.50 15.00
213 Wildheart Invoker C .07 .15
214 Sarkhan the Mad M 3.00 6.00
215 Angelheart Vial R .20 .40
216 Dreamstone Hedron U .10 .20
217 Enatu Golem U .10 .20
218 Hedron Matrix R .20 .40
219 Keening Stone R .20 .40
220 Ogres Cleaver U .10 .20
221 Pennon Blade U .10 .20
222 Prophetic Prism C .07 .15
223 Reinforced Bulwark C .07 .15
224 Runed Servitor U .10 .20
225 Sphinx-Bone Wand R .20 .40
226 Warmonger's Chariot U .10 .20
227 Eldrazi Temple R .20 .40
228 Evolving Wilds C .07 .15
229 Plains L .07 .15
230 Plains L .07 .15
231 Plains L .07 .15
232 Plains L .07 .15
233 Island L .07 .15
234 Island L .07 .15
235 Island L .07 .15
236 Island L .07 .15
237 Swamp L .07 .15
238 Swamp L .07 .15
239 Swamp L .07 .15
240 Swamp L .07 .15
241 Mountain L .07 .15
242 Mountain L .07 .15
243 Mountain L .07 .15
244 Mountain L .07 .15
245 Forest L .07 .15
246 Forest L .07 .15
247 Forest L .07 .15
248 Forest L .07 .15

2010 Magic The Gathering Rise of the Eldrazi Tokens

1a Eldrazi Spawn .12 .25
1b Eldrazi Spawn .10 .20
1c Eldrazi Spawn .10 .20
2 Elemental .12 .25
3 Hellion .07 .15
4 Ooze .07 .15
5 Tuktuk the Returned .50 1.00

2010 Magic The Gathering Scars of Mirrodin

1 Abuna Acolyte U .10 .20
2 Arrest C .07 .15
3 Auriok Edgewright U .10 .20
4 Auriok Sunchaser C .07 .15
5 Dispense Justice U .10 .20
6 Elspeth Tirel M 7.50 15.00
7 Fulgent Distraction C .07 .15
8 Ghalma's Warden C .07 .15
9 Glimmerpoint Stag U .10 .20
10 Glint Hawk C .20 .40
11 Indomitable Archangel M 1.25 2.50
12 Kemba, Kha Regent R .20 .40
13 Kemba's Skyguard C .07 .15
14 Leonin Arbiter R 3.00 6.00
15 Loxodon Wayfarer C .07 .15
16 Myrsmith U .10 .20
17 Razor Hippogriff U .10 .20
18 Revoke Existence C .07 .15
19 Salvage Scout C .07 .15
20 Seize the Initiative C .07 .15
21 Soul Parry C .07 .15
22 Sunblast Angel R .30 .60
23 Sunspear Shikari C .07 .15
24 Tempered Steel R .50 1.00
25 True Conviction R 2.00 4.00
26 Vigil for the Lost U .10 .20
27 Whitesun's Passage C .07 .15
28 Argent Sphinx R .20 .40
29 Bonds of Quicksilver C .07 .15
30 Darkslick Drake U .10 .20
31 Disperse C .07 .15
32 Dissipation Field R 1.25 2.50
33 Grand Architect R .60 1.25
34 Halt Order U .10 .20
35 Inexorable Tide R 4.00 8.00
36 Lumengrid Drake C .07 .15
37 Neurok Invisimancer C .07 .15
38 Plated Seastrider C .07 .15
39 Quicksilver Gargantuan M .60 1.25
40 Riddlesmith U .10 .20
41 Scrapdiver Serpent C .07 .15
42 Screeching Silcaw C .07 .15
43 Shape Anew R .20 .40
44 Sky-Eel School C .07 .15
45 Steady Progress C .07 .15
46 Stoic Rebuttal C .07 .15
47 Thrummingbird U .20 .40
48 Trinket Mage U .20 .40
49 Turn Aside C .15 .30
50 Twisted Image U .10 .20
51 Vault Skyward C .07 .15
52 Vedalken Certarch C .07 .15
53 Volition Reins U .10 .20
54 Blackcleave Goblin C .07 .15
55 Bleak Coven Vampires C .07 .15
56 Blistergrub C .07 .15
57 Carnifex Demon R .75 1.50
58 Contagious Nim C .15 .30
59 Corrupted Harvester U .10 .20
60 Dross Hopper C .07 .15
61 Exsanguinate U 7.50 15.00
62 Flesh Allergy U .10 .20

63 Fume Spitter C .07 .15
64 Geth, Lord of the Vault M 1.50 3.00
65 Grasp of Darkness C .15 .30
66 Hand of the Praetors R 3.00 6.00
67 Ichor Rats U .75 1.50
68 Instill Infection C .07 .15
69 Memoricide R .20 .40
70 Moriok Reaver C .07 .15
71 Necrogen Scudder U .10 .20
72 Necrotic Ooze R 2.50 5.00
73 Painful Quandary R 17.50 35.00
74 Painsmith U .10 .20
75 Plague Stinger C .30 .75
76 Psychic Miasma C .07 .15
77 Relic Putrescence C .07 .15
78 Skinrender U .17 .35
79 Skithiryx, the Blight Dragon M 10.00 20.00
80 Tainted Strike C .75 1.50
81 Arc Trail U .10 .20
82 Assault Strobe C .30 .75
83 Barrage Ogre U .10 .20
84 Blade-Tribe Berserkers C .07 .15
85 Bloodshot Trainee U .10 .20
86 Cerebral Eruption R .20 .40
87 Embersmith U .10 .20
88 Ferrovore C .07 .15
89 Flameborn Hellion C .07 .15
90 Furnace Celebration U .10 .20
91 Galvanic Blast C .07 .15
92 Goblin Gaveleer C .07 .15
93 Hoard-Smelter Dragon R .20 .40
94 Koth of the Hammer M 4.00 8.00
95 Kuldotha Phoenix R .20 .40
96 Kuldotha Rebirth C .20 .40
97 Melt Terrain C .07 .15
98 Molten Psyche R 2.00 4.00
99 Ogre Geargrabber U .10 .20
R1 Rules Tip: Infect .07 .15
R2 Rules Tip: Metalcraft .07 .15
R3 Rules Tip: Proliferate .07 .15
R4 Rules Tip: Imprint .07 .15
R5 Rules Tip: Poison and Emblems .07 .15
100 Oxidda Daredevil C .07 .15
101 Oxidda Scrapmelter U .10 .20
102 Scoria Elemental C .07 .15
103 Shatter C .07 .15
104 Spikeshot Elder R .20 .40
105 Tunnel Ignus R .20 .40
106 Turn to Slag C .07 .15
107 Vulshok Heartstoker C .07 .15
108 Acid Web Spider U .10 .20
109 Alpha Tyrranax C .07 .15
110 Asceticism R 12.50 25.00
111 Bellowing Tanglewurm U .75 1.50
112 Blight Mamba C .75 1.50
113 Blunt the Assault C .07 .15
114 Carapace Forger C .07 .15
115 Carrion Call U .10 .20
116 Copperhorn Scout C .15 .30
117 Cystbearer C .07 .15
118 Engulfing Slagwurm R .60 1.25
119 Ezuri, Renegade Leader R 7.50 15.00
120 Ezuri's Archers C .07 .15
121 Ezuri's Brigade R .20 .40
122 Genesis Wave R 6.00 12.00
123 Liege of the Tangle M 2.00 4.00
124 Lifesmith U .10 .20
125 Molder Beast C .07 .15
126 Putrefax R .30 .75
127 Slice in Twain U .10 .20
128 Tangle Angler U .17 .35
129 Tel-Jilad Defiance C .07 .15
130 Tel-Jilad Fallen C .07 .15
131 Untamed Might C .07 .15
132 Viridian Revel U .10 .20
133 Wing Puncture C .07 .15
134 Withstand Death C .20 .40
135 Venser, the Sojourner M 12.50 25.00
136 Accorder's Shield C .07 .15
137 Argentum Armor R 2.50 5.00
138 Auriok Replica C .07 .15
139 Barbed Battlegear U .10 .20
140 Bladed Pinions C .12 .25
141 Chimeric Mass R .20 .40
142 Chrome Steed C .07 .15
143 Clone Shell U .10 .20
144 Contagion Clasp U .50 1.00
145 Contagion Engine R 12.50 25.00
146 Copper Myr C .07 .15
147 Corpse Cur C .07 .15
148 Culling Dais U .10 .20
149 Darksteel Axe U .10 .20
150 Darksteel Juggernaut R .75 1.50
151 Darksteel Myr U .30 .60
152 Darksteel Sentinel U .20 .40
153 Echo Circlet C .07 .15
154 Etched Champion R 1.25 2.50
155 Flight Spellbomb C .07 .15
156 Glint Hawk Idol C .07 .15
157 Gold Myr C .20 .40
158 Golden Urn C .07 .15
159 Golem Artisan U .10 .20
160 Golem Foundry C .25 .50
161 Golem's Heart U .10 .20
162 Grafted Exoskeleton U 3.00 6.00
163 Grindclock R .20 .40
164 Heavy Arbalest U .10 .20
165 Horizon Spellbomb C .07 .15
166 Ichorclaw Myr C .75 1.50
167 Infiltration Lens U .75 1.50
168 Iron Myr C .25 .50
169 Kuldotha Forgemaster R 4.00 8.00
170 Leaden Myr C .20 .40
171 Liquimetal Coating U .60 1.25
172 Livewire Lash R .30 .60
173 Lux Cannon M 1.25 2.50
174 Memnite U 1.50 3.00
175 Mimic Vat R .60 1.25
176 Mindslaver M 3.00 6.00
177 Molten-Tail Masticore M .30 .75
178 Moriok Replica C .07 .15
179 Mox Opal M 30.00 60.00
180 Myr Battlesphere R .30 .75
181 Myr Galvanizer U .30 .75
182 Myr Propagator R .30 .60
183 Myr Reservoir R .75 1.50
184 Necrogen Censer C .07 .15
185 Necropede U .30 .75
186 Neurok Replica C .07 .15
187 Nihil Spellbomb C .30 .60
188 Nim Deathmantle R 7.50 15.00
189 Origin Spellbomb C .07 .15
190 Palladium Myr U .30 .60
191 Panic Spellbomb C .07 .15
192 Perilous Myr C .07 .15
193 Platinum Emperion M 12.50 25.00
194 Precursor Golem R .20 .40
195 Prototype Portal R .30 .75
196 Ratchet Bomb R .50 1.00
197 Razorfield Thresher C .07 .15
198 Rust Tick U .10 .20
199 Rusted Relic U .10 .20
200 Saberclaw Golem C .07 .15
201 Semblance Anvil R 6.00 12.00
202 Silver Myr C .25 .50
203 Snapsail Glider C .07 .15
204 Soliton C .07 .15
205 Steel Hellkite R 1.00 2.00
206 Strata Scythe R .30 .60
207 Strider Harness C .07 .15
208 Sword of Body and Mind M 7.50 15.00
209 Sylvok Lifestaff C .07 .15
210 Sylvok Replica C .07 .15
211 Throne of Geth U .10 .20
212 Tower of Calamities R .20 .40
213 Trigon of Corruption U .10 .20
214 Trigon of Infestation U .17 .35
215 Trigon of Mending U .10 .20
216 Trigon of Rage U .10 .20
217 Trigon of Thought U .10 .20
218 Tumble Magnet C .07 .15
219 Vector Asp C .07 .15
220 Venser's Journal R 6.00 12.00
221 Vulshok Replica C .07 .15
222 Wall of Tanglecord C .20 .40
223 Wurmcoil Engine M 17.50 35.00
224 Blackcleave Cliffs R 12.50 25.00
225 Copperline Gorge R 3.00 6.00
226 Darkslick Shores R 7.50 15.00
227 Glimmerpost C .20 .40
228 Razorverge Thicket R 4.00 8.00
229 Seachrome Coast R 5.00 10.00
230 Plains L .10 .20
231 Plains L .12 .25
232 Plains L .07 .15
233 Plains L .07 .15
234 Island L .07 .15
235 Island L .07 .15
236 Island L .07 .15
237 Island L .07 .15
238 Swamp L .07 .15
239 Swamp L .07 .15
240 Swamp L .07 .15
241 Swamp L .12 .25
242 Mountain L .07 .15
243 Mountain L .07 .15
244 Mountain L .15 .30
245 Mountain L .07 .15
246 Forest L .12 .25
247 Forest L .07 .15
248 Forest L .15 .30
249 Forest L .07 .15

2010 Magic The Gathering Scars of Mirrodin Tokens

1 Cat .25 .50
2 Soldier .20 .40
3 Goblin .25 .50
4 Insect .12 .25
5 Wolf .50 1.00
6 Golem .10 .20
7 Myr .10 .20
8 Wurm 4.00 7.00
9 Wurm 2.50 5.00
10 Poison Counter .07 .15

2010 Magic The Gathering Worldwake

1 Admonition Angel M 4.00 8.00
2 Apex Hawks C .07 .15
3 Archon of Redemption R .20 .40
4 Battle Hurda C .07 .15
5 Fledgling Griffin C .07 .15
6 Guardian Zendikon C .07 .15
7 Hada Freeblade U .25 .50
8 Iona's Judgment C .07 .15
9 Join the Ranks C .07 .15
10 Kitesail Apprentice C .07 .15
11 Kor Firewalker U .30 .75
12 Lightkeeper of Emeria U .17 .35
13 Loam Lion U .25 .50
14 Marsh Threader C .07 .15
15 Marshal's Anthem R .30 .60
16 Perimeter Captain U .75 1.50
17 Refraction Trap U .10 .20
18 Rest for the Weary C .07 .15
19 Ruin Ghost U .30 .75
20 Stoneforge Mystic R 25.00 50.00
21 Talus Paladin R .50 1.00
22 Terra Eternal R 1.50 3.00
23 Veteran's Reflexes C .07 .15
24 Aether Tradewinds C .07 .15
25 Calcite Snapper C .07 .15
26 Dispel C .20 .40
27 Enclave Elite C .07 .15
28 Goliath Sphinx R .20 .40
29 Halimar Excavator C .07 .15
30 Horizon Drake U .10 .20
31 Jace, the Mind Sculptor M 40.00 80.00
32 Jwari Shapeshifter R .75 1.50
33 Mysteries of the Deep C .07 .15
34 Permafrost Trap U .10 .20
35 Quest for Ula's Temple R 3.00 6.00
36 Sejiri Merfolk U .10 .20
37 Selective Memory R 2.00 4.00
38 Spell Contortion U .10 .20
39 Surrakar Banisher C .07 .15
40 Thada Adel, Acquisitor R .20 .40
41 Tideforce Elemental U .20 .40
42 Treasure Hunt C .07 .15
43 Twitch C .07 .15
44 Vapor Snare U .10 .20
45 Voyager Drake U .10 .20
46 Wind Zendikon C .07 .15
47 Abyssal Persecutor M .75 1.50
48 Agadeem Occultist R .30 .75
49 Anowon, the Ruin Sage R 1.50 3.00
50 Bloodhusk Ritualist U .20 .40
51 Bojuka Brigand C .07 .15
52 Brink of Disaster C .07 .15
53 Butcher of Malakir R 1.50 3.00
54 Caustic Crawler U .10 .20
55 Corrupted Zendikon C .07 .15
56 Dead Reckoning C .07 .15
57 Death's Shadow R 5.00 10.00
58 Jagwasp Swarm C .07 .15
59 Kalastria Highborn R 4.00 8.00
60 Mire's Toll C .07 .15
61 Nemesis Trap U .10 .20
62 Pulse Tracker C .20 .40
63 Quag Vampires C .07 .15
64 Quest for the Nihil Stone R 4.00 8.00
65 Ruthless Cullblade C .07 .15
66 Scrib Nibblers U .20 .40
67 Shoreline Salvager U .10 .20
68 Smother U .10 .20
69 Tomb Hex C .07 .15
70 Urge to Feed U .15 .30
71 Akoum Battlesinger C .07 .15
72 Bazaar Trader R 2.50 5.00
73 Bull Rush C .07 .15
74 Chain Reaction R 1.25 2.50
75 Claws of Valakut C .07 .15
76 Comet Storm M .75 1.50
77 Cosi's Ravager C .07 .15
78 Crusher Zendikon C .07 .15
79 Cunning Sparkmage U .10 .20
80 Deathforge Shaman U .10 .20
81 Dragonmaster Outcast M 2.00 4.00
82 Goblin Roughrider C .07 .15
83 Grotag Thrasher C .07 .15
84 Kazuul, Tyrant of the Cliffs R 3.00 6.00
85 Mordant Dragon R .30 .75
86 Quest for the Goblin Lord U .75 1.50
87 Ricochet Trap U .30 .60
88 Roiling Terrain C .20 .40
89 Rumbling Aftershocks U .10 .20
90 Searing Blaze C .75 1.50
91 Skitter of Lizards C .07 .15
92 Slavering Nulls U .10 .20
93 Stone Idol Trap R .20 .40
94 Tuktuk Scrapper U .10 .20
95 Arbor Elf C .50 1.00
96 Avenger of Zendikar M 6.00 12.00
97 Bestial Menace U .10 .20
98 Canopy Cover U .75 1.50
99 Explore C .25 .50
100 Feral Contest C .07 .15
101 Gnarlid Pack C .07 .15
102 Grappler Spider C .07 .15
103 Graypelt Hunter C .07 .15
104 Groundswell C .50 1.00
105 Harabaz Druid R 1.50 3.00
106 Joraga Warcaller R 10.00 20.00
107 Leatherback Baloth U .20 .40
108 Nature's Claim C .60 1.25
109 Omnath, Locus of Mana M 12.50 25.00
110 Quest for Renewal U 4.00 8.00
111 Slingbow Trap U .10 .20
112 Snapping Creeper C .07 .15
113 Strength of the Tajuru R .50 1.00
114 Summit Apes U .10 .20
115 Terastodon R .60 1.25
116 Vastwood Animist U .10 .20
117 Vastwood Zendikon C .07 .15
118 Wolfbriar Elemental R .20 .40
119 Novablast Wurm M 1.50 3.00
120 Wrexial, the Risen Deep M 3.00 6.00
121 Amulet of Vigor R 12.50 25.00
122 Basilisk Collar R 4.00 8.00
123 Everflowing Chalice U .75 1.50
124 Hammer of Ruin U .10 .20
125 Hedron Rover C .07 .15
126 Kitesail C .07 .15
127 Lodestone Golem R .75 1.50
128 Pilgrim's Eye C .07 .15
129 Razor Boomerang U .10 .20
130 Seer's Sundial R .20 .40
131 Walking Atlas C 1.00 2.00
132 Bojuka Bog C 1.00 2.00
133 Celestial Colonnade R 3.00 6.00
134 Creeping Tar Pit R 2.00 4.00
135 Dread Statuary U .10 .20
136 Eye of Ugin M 10.00 20.00
137 Halimar Depths C .30 .60
138 Khalni Garden C .20 .40
139 Lavaclaw Reaches R 1.25 2.50
140 Quicksand C .07 .15
141 Raging Ravine R 2.00 4.00
142 Sejiri Steppe C .07 .15
143 Smoldering Spires C .07 .15
144 Stirring Wildwood R .30 .75
145 Tectonic Edge U .75 1.50
R1 Rules Tip: Allies and Quests .07 .15
R2 Rules Tip: Landfall .07 .15
R3 Rules Tip: Lands Alive .07 .15
R4 Rules Tip: Multikicker .07 .15
R5 Rules Tip: Traps .07 .15

2010 Magic The Gathering Worldwake Tokens

1 Soldier Ally .12 .25
2 Dragon .20 .40
3 Ogre .75 1.50
4 Elephant .12 .25
5 Plant .25 .50
6 Construct .12 .25

2011 Magic The Gathering Commander

1 Artisan of Kozilek U .60 1.25
2 Afterlife U .12 .25
3 Akroma's Vengeance R .25 .50
4 Alliance of Arms R 3.00 6.00
5 Angelic Arbiter R 1.25 2.50
6 Arbiter of Knollridge R .15 .30
7 Archangel of Strife R .60 1.25
8 Austere Command R 2.00 4.00
9 Bathe in Light U .12 .25
10 Celestial Force R .75 1.50
11 Congregate C .10 .20
12 Crescendo of War R 3.00 6.00
13 False Prophet R .75 1.50
14 Ghostly Prison U 2.50 5.00
15 Hour of Reckoning R .30 .75
16 Jotun Grunt U .12 .25
17 Journey to Nowhere C .60 1.25
18 Lightkeeper of Emeria U .12 .25
19 Martyr's Bond R .75 1.50
20 Monk Realist C .10 .20
21 Mother of Runes U 4.00 8.00
22 Oblation R 1.25 2.50
23 Oblivion Ring C .10 .20
24 Orim's Thunder C .10 .20
25 Path to Exile U 3.00 6.00
26 Pollen Lullaby U .12 .25
27 Prison Term U .75 1.50
28 Return to Dust U .75 1.50
29 Righteous Cause U .12 .25
30 Serra Angel U .12 .25
31 Shattered Angel U 1.00 2.00
32 Soul Snare U .12 .25
33 Spurnmage Advocate U .12 .25
34 Storm Herd R .15 .30
35 Voice of All U .12 .25
36 Vow of Duty U .12 .25
37 Wall of Omens U 1.00 2.00
38 Windborn Muse R 4.00 8.00
39 Aethersnipe C .10 .20
40 Brainstorm C 1.00 2.00
41 Chromeshell Crab R .15 .30
42 Conundrum Sphinx R .15 .30
43 Court Hussar U .12 .25
44 Dreamborn Muse R 1.50 3.00
45 Fact or Fiction U .25 .50
46 Flusterstorm R 15.00 30.00
47 Fog Bank U .25 .50
48 Gomazoa U .12 .25
49 Guard Gomazoa U .25 .50
50 Memory Erosion R 2.00 4.00
51 Minds Aglow R 2.50 5.00
52 Mulldrifter C .75 1.50
53 Murmurs from Beyond C .10 .20
54 Perilous Research U .12 .25
55 Propaganda U 4.00 8.00
56 Ray of Command C .10 .20
57 Reins of Power R 1.00 2.00
58 Repulse C .10 .20
59 Riddlekeeper R 3.00 6.00
60 Scattering Stroke U .12 .25
61 Skyscribing U .12 .25
62 Slipstream Eel C .10 .20
63 Spell Crumple U .30 .60
64 Trade Secrets R .20 .40
65 Trench Gorger R 2.50 5.00
66 Vedalken Plotter U .30 .75
67 Vision Skeins C .10 .20
68 Vow of Flight U .12 .25
69 Whirlpool Whelm C .10 .20
70 Windfall U 2.50 5.00
71 Wonder U .50 1.00
72 Attrition R 10.00 20.00
73 Avatar of Woe R 1.50 3.00
74 Buried Alive U 3.00 6.00
75 Butcher of Malakir R 1.50 3.00
76 Dark Hatchling R .15 .30
77 Diabolic Tutor U .75 1.50
78 Doom Blade C .10 .20
79 Dread Cacodemon R 2.50 5.00
80 Evincar's Justice C .30 .60
81 Extractor Demon R .15 .30
82 Fallen Angel R .15 .30
83 Fleshbag Marauder U .30 .75
84 Footbottom Feast C .10 .20
85 Grave Pact R 20.00 40.00
86 Gravedigger C .10 .20
87 Hex R .15 .30
88 Living Death R 5.00 10.00
89 Mortivore R 1.50 3.00
90 Nantuko Husk C .10 .20
91 Nemesis Trap U .12 .25
92 Nezumi Graverobber U .60 1.25
93 Patron of the Nezumi R .15 .30
94 Razorjaw Oni U .12 .25
95 Reiver Demon R 1.00 2.00
96 Rise from the Grave U .12 .25
97 Scythe Specter R 2.00 4.00
98 Sewer Nemesis R 1.25 2.50
99 Shared Trauma R .15 .30
100 Shriekmaw U .30 .60
101 Sign in Blood C .10 .20
102 Stitch Together U 1.25 2.50
103 Syphon Flesh U 1.00 2.00
104 Syphon Mind C 1.25 2.50
105 Unnerve C .10 .20
106 Vampire Nighthawk U .12 .25
107 Vow of Malice U .12 .25
108 Akroma, Angel of Fury R .15 .30
109 Anger U 2.50 5.00
110 Avatar of Fury R .15 .30
111 Avatar of Slaughter R 1.50 3.00
112 Breath of Darigaaz U .12 .25
113 Chain Reaction R .75 1.50
114 Chaos Warp R 2.50 5.00
115 Chartooth Cougar C .10 .20
116 Cleansing Beam U .12 .25
117 Comet Storm M .50 1.00
118 Death by Dragons U .12 .25
119 Disaster Radius R .15 .30
120 Dragon Whelp U .12 .25
121 Earthquake R .75 1.50
122 Faultgrinder C .10 .20
123 Flametongue Kavu U .12 .25
124 Furnace Whelp U .12 .25
125 Goblin Cadets U .12 .25

126 Insurrection R 12.50 25.00
127 Lash Out C .10 .20
128 Magmatic Force R .50 1.00
129 Mana-Charged Dragon R .75 1.50
130 Oni of Wild Places U .12 .25
131 Punishing Fire U .12 .25
132 Pyrohemia U 6.00 12.00
133 Rapacious One U .12 .25
134 Ruination R 5.00 10.00
135 Spitebellows U .12 .25
136 Stranglehold R 20.00 40.00
137 Sulfurous Blast U .12 .25
138 Vow of Lightning U .12 .25
139 Wild Ricochet R .25 .50
140 Acidic Slime U .12 .25
141 Aquastrand Spider C .10 .20
142 Awakening Zone R 3.00 6.00
143 Baloth Woodcrasher U .12 .25
144 Bestial Menace U .12 .25
145 Brawn U .30 .60
146 Cobra Trap U .12 .25
147 Collective Voyage R 4.00 8.00
148 Cultivate C .75 1.50
149 Deadly Recluse C .10 .20
150 Deadwood Treefolk U .12 .25
151 Elvish Aberration U .12 .25
152 Eternal Witness U 3.00 6.00
153 Explosive Vegetation U 1.00 2.00
154 Fertilid C .10 .20
155 Fierce Empath C .30 .60
156 Fists of Ironwood C .10 .20
157 Garruk Wildspeaker M 4.00 8.00
158 Harmonize U .12 .25
159 Hornet Queen R .75 1.50
160 Hunting Pack U .12 .25
161 Hydra Omnivore R 3.00 6.00
162 Invigorate C .15 .30
163 Kodama's Reach C 1.50 3.00
164 Krosan Tusker C .10 .20
165 Lhurgoyf R .25 .50
166 Magus of the Vineyard R 3.00 6.00
167 Penumbra Spider C .10 .20
168 Relic Crush C .10 .20
169 Sakura-Tribe Elder C .75 1.50
170 Scavenging Ooze R 1.50 3.00
171 Spawnwrithe R .30 .60
172 Spike Feeder U 3.00 6.00
173 Squallmonger U .12 .25
174 Symbiotic Wurm R .30 .60
175 Tribute to the Wild U .12 .25
176 Troll Ascetic R .15 .30
177 Veteran Explorer U .12 .25
178 Vow of Wildness U .12 .25
179 Yavimaya Elder C .20 .40
180 Angel of Despair R 1.00 2.00
181 Animar, Soul of Elements M 7.50 15.00
182 Aura Shards U 7.50 15.00
183 Azorius Guildmage U .12 .25
184 Basandra, Battle Seraph R 1.50 3.00
185 Bladewing the Risen R .75 1.50
186 Boros Guildmage U .12 .25
187 Brion Stoutarm R .30 .75
188 Call the Skybreaker R .15 .30
189 Chorus of the Conclave R .15 .30
190 Colossal Might C .25 .50
191 Damia, Sage of Stone M 6.00 12.00
192 Death Mutation U .12 .25
193 Desecrator Hag C .10 .20
194 Dominus of Fealty R 1.00 2.00
195 Duergar Hedge-Mage U 1.50 3.00
196 Edric, Spymaster of Trest R 2.50 5.00
197 Electrolyze U .12 .25
198 Fire/Ice U .30 .60
199 Firespout U .50 1.00
200 Ghave, Guru of Spores M 4.00 8.00
201 Golgari Guildmage U .12 .25
202 Gwyllion Hedge-Mage U .12 .25
203 Hull Breach C 2.00 4.00
204 Intet, the Dreamer R .75 1.50
205 Izzet Chronarch C .10 .20
206 Kaalia of the Vast M 12.50 25.00
207 Karador, Ghost Chieftain M 6.00 12.00
208 Malfegor M .50 1.00
209 Master Warcraft R .15 .30
210 The Mimeoplasm M 3.00 6.00
211 Mortify U .12 .25
212 Necrogenesis U .12 .25
213 Nin, the Pain Artist R .60 1.25
214 Nucklavee U .12 .25
215 Numot, the Devastator R 2.50 5.00
216 Oros, the Avenger R .30 .75
217 Orzhov Guildmage U .20 .40
218 Plumeveil U .12 .25
219 Prophetic Bolt R .15 .30
220 Riku of Two Reflections M 7.50 15.00
221 Ruhan of the Fomori M 7.50 15.00
222 Savage Twister U .12 .25
223 Selesnya Evangel C .10 .20
224 Selesnya Guildmage U .12 .25
225 Sigil Captain U .30 .75
226 Simic Sky Swallower R .15 .30
227 Skullbriar, the Walking Grave R 4.00 8.00
228 Szadek, Lord of Secrets R .25 .50
229 Tariel, Reckoner of Souls M 5.00 10.00
230 Teneb, the Harvester R 2.00 4.00
231 Terminate C .75 1.50
232 Valley Rannet C .10 .20
233 Vengeful Rebirth U .12 .25
234 Vish Kal, Blood Arbiter R 1.25 2.50
235 Vorosh, the Hunter R .75 1.50
236 Vulturous Zombie R .15 .30
237 Wall of Denial U 1.00 2.00
238 Wrecking Ball C .10 .20
239 Wrexial, the Risen Deep M 4.00 8.00
240 Zedruu the Greathearted M 2.00 4.00
241 Acorn Catapult R 7.50 15.00
242 Armillary Sphere C .10 .20
243 Boros Signet C .75 1.50
244 Champion's Helm R 20.00 40.00
245 Darksteel Ingot C .30 .75
246 Dimir Signet C 2.50 5.00
247 Dreamstone Hedron U .12 .25
248 Fellwar Stone U 4.00 8.00
249 Golgari Signet C 1.00 2.00
250 Gruul Signet C .50 1.00
251 Howling Mine R 5.00 10.00
252 Izzet Signet C 1.00 2.00
253 Lightning Greaves U 4.00 8.00
254 Oblivion Stone R 2.00 4.00
255 Orzhov Signet C .50 1.00
256 Prophetic Prism C .10 .20
257 Rakdos Signet C 1.00 2.00
258 Selesnya Signet C .75 1.50
259 Simic Signet C .10 .20
260 Skullclamp U 7.50 15.00
261 Solemn Simulacrum R 1.25 2.50
262 Sol Ring U 2.00 4.00
263 Triskelavus R .15 .30
264 Akoum Refuge U .20 .40
265 Azorius Chancery C .25 .50
266 Barren Moor C .10 .20
267 Bojuka Bog C 1.25 2.50
268 Boros Garrison C .10 .20
269 Command Tower C .50 1.00
270 Dimir Aqueduct C .10 .20
271 Dreadship Reef U .12 .25
272 Evolving Wilds C .10 .20
273 Forgotten Cave C .10 .20
274 Fungal Reaches U .12 .25
275 Golgari Rot Farm C .10 .20
276 Gruul Turf C .25 .50
277 Homeward Path R 10.00 20.00
278 Izzet Boilerworks C .10 .20
279 Jwar Isle Refuge U .30 .75
280 Kazandu Refuge U .12 .25
281 Lonely Sandbar C .10 .20
282 Molten Slagheap U .30 .75
283 Orzhov Basilica C .20 .40
284 Rakdos Carnarium C .20 .40
285 Rupture Spire C .10 .20
286 Secluded Steppe C .10 .20
287 Selesnya Sanctuary C .10 .20
288 Simic Growth Chamber C .10 .20
289 Svogthos, the Restless Tomb U .12 .25
290 Temple of the False God U .12 .25
291 Terramorphic Expanse C .10 .20
292 Tranquil Thicket C .10 .20
293 Vivid Crag U .30 .75
294 Vivid Creek U .30 .75
295 Vivid Grove U .12 .25
296 Vivid Marsh U 1.25 2.50
297 Vivid Meadow U .75 1.50
298 Zoetic Cavern U .12 .25
299 Plains L .10 .20
300 Plains L .10 .20
301 Plains L .10 .20
302 Plains L .10 .20
303 Island L .10 .20
304 Island L .10 .20
305 Island L .10 .20
306 Island L .10 .20
307 Swamp L .10 .20
308 Swamp L .10 .20
309 Swamp L .10 .20
310 Swamp L .10 .20
311 Mountain L .10 .20
312 Mountain L .10 .20
313 Mountain L .10 .20
314 Mountain L .10 .20
315 Forest L .10 .20
316 Forest L .10 .20
317 Forest L .10 .20
318 Forest L .10 .20

2011 Magic The Gathering Commander Launch Party

184 Basandra, Battle Seraph R 7.50 15.00
196 Edric, Spymaster of Trest R 3.00 6.00
213 Nin, the Pain Artist R 2.50 5.00
227 Skullbriar, the Walking Grave R 20.00 40.00
234 Vish Kal, Blood Arbiter R 6.00 12.00

2011 Magic The Gathering Commander Oversized

174 Intet, the Dreamer R 1.00 2.00
181 Animar, Soul of Elements M 4.00 8.00
191 Damia, Sage of Stone M 2.50 5.00
200 Ghave, Guru of Spores M 1.50 3.00
206 Kaalia of the Vast M 6.00 12.00
207 Karador, Ghost Chieftain M 2.00 4.00
210 The Mimeoplasm M 1.00 2.00
215 Numot, the Devastator R .75 1.50
216 Oros, the Avenger R 1.00 2.00
220 Riku of Two Reflections M 2.00 4.00
221 Ruhan of the Fomori M 1.00 2.00
229 Tariel, Reckoner of Souls M 1.00 2.00
230 Teneb, the Harvester R 1.25 2.50
235 Vorosh, the Hunter R .60 1.25
240 Zedruu the Greathearted M 1.25 2.50

2011 Magic The Gathering Duel Decks Ajani vs. Nicol Bolas

1 Ajani Vengeant M 3.00 6.00
2 Kird Ape U .60 1.25
3 Essence Warden C .25 .50
4 Wild Nacatl C .25 .50
5 Loam Lion U .25 .50
6 Canyon Wildcat C .12 .25
7 Jade Mage U .25 .50
8 Sylvan Ranger C .12 .25
9 Ajani's Pridemate U .50 1.00
10 Qasali Pridemage C .50 1.00
11 Grazing Gladehart C .12 .25
12 Fleetfoot Panther U .25 .50
13 Woolly Thoctar U .30 .75
14 Briarhorn U .25 .50
15 Loxodon Hierarch R .75 1.50
16 Spitemare U .25 .50
17 Marisi's Twinclaws U .25 .50
18 Ageless Entity R .60 1.25
19 Pride of Lions U .25 .50
20 Nacatl Hunt-Pride U .25 .50
21 Firemane Angel R 1.00 2.00
22 Ajani's Mantra C .12 .25
23 Lightning Helix U 2.00 4.00
24 Lead the Stampede U .25 .50
25 Griffin Guide U .25 .50
26 Recumbent Bliss C .12 .25
27 Searing Meditation R .50 1.00
28 Behemoth Sledge U .75 1.50
29 Naya Charm U .25 .50
30 Sylvan Bounty C .12 .25
31 Titanic Ultimatum R .50 1.00
32 Evolving Wilds C .30 .75
33 Graypelt Refuge U .30 .75
34 Jungle Shrine U 1.00 2.00
35 Kazandu Refuge U .30 .75
36 Sapseep Forest U .25 .50
37 Vitu-Ghazi, the City-Tree U .25 .50
38 Forest L .12 .25
39 Forest L .12 .25
40 Plains L .12 .25
41 Mountain L .12 .25
42 Nicol Bolas, Planeswalker M 6.00 12.00
43 Surveilling Sprite C .12 .25
44 Nightscape Familiar C .25 .50
45 Slavering Nulls U .25 .50
46 Brackwater Elemental C .12 .25
47 Morgue Toad C .12 .25
48 Hellfire Mongrel U .25 .50
49 Dimir Cutpurse R .75 1.50
50 Steamcore Weird C .12 .25
51 Moroii U .25 .50
52 Blazing Specter R .75 1.50
53 Fire-Field Ogre U .25 .50
54 Shriekmaw U .75 1.50
55 Ogre Savant C .12 .25
56 Jhessian Zombies C .12 .25
57 Igneous Pouncer C .12 .25
58 Vapor Snag C .60 1.25
59 Countersquall U .75 1.50
60 Obelisk of Grixis C .12 .25
61 Recoil C .25 .50
62 Undermine R 1.50 3.00
63 Grixis Charm U .25 .50
64 Icy Manipulator U .25 .50
65 Deep Analysis U .60 1.25
66 Agonizing Demise C .12 .25
67 Slave of Bolas U .25 .50
68 Elder Mastery U .25 .50
69 Cruel Ultimatum R 1.00 2.00
70 Profane Command R 1.00 2.00
71 Spite/Malice U .25 .50
72 Pain/Suffering U .25 .50
73 Rise/Fall U .25 .50
74 Crumbling Necropolis U 1.00 2.00
75 Rupture Spire C .25 .50
76 Terramorphic Expanse C .25 .50
77 Swamp L .12 .25
78 Swamp L .12 .25
79 Island L .12 .25
80 Mountain L .12 .25

2011 Magic The Gathering Duel Decks Ajani vs. Nicol Bolas Tokens

1 Griffin .12 .25
2 Saproling .12 .25

2011 Magic The Gathering Duel Decks Knights vs. Dragons

1 Knight of the Reliquary M 5.00 10.00
2 Caravan Escort C .12 .25
3 Lionheart Maverick C .12 .25
4 Knight of Cliffhaven C .12 .25
5 Knight of Meadowgrain U 1.50 3.00
6 Knight of the White Orchid R 1.50 3.00
7 Leonin Skyhunter U .25 .50
8 Silver Knight U 1.00 2.00
9 White Knight U .30 .75
10 Knotvine Paladin R .50 1.00
11 Steward of Valeron C .12 .25
12 Benalish Lancer C .12 .25
13 Zhalfirin Commander U .25 .50
14 Knight Exemplar R 2.00 4.00
15 Wilt-Leaf Cavaliers U 1.00 2.00
16 Kabira Vindicator U .25 .50
17 Kinsbaile Cavalier R 2.00 4.00
18 Alaborn Cavalier U .25 .50
19 Skyhunter Patrol C .12 .25
20 Plover Knights C .25 .50
21 Juniper Order Ranger U 1.00 2.00
22 Paladin of Prahv U .25 .50
23 Harm's Way U .25 .50
24 Reciprocate U .30 .75
25 Edge of Autumn C .12 .25
26 Mighty Leap C .12 .25
27 Reprisal U .25 .50
28 Test of Faith U .25 .50
29 Heroes' Reunion U .30 .75
30 Sigil Blessing C .12 .25
31 Loxodon Warhammer R 1.25 2.50
32 Spidersilk Armor C .25 .50
33 Griffin Guide U .25 .50
34 Oblivion Ring C 1.50 3.00
35 Grasslands U .25 .50
36 Sejiri Steppe C .12 .25
37 Selesnya Sanctuary C .25 .50
38 Treetop Village U 1.50 3.00
39 Plains L .12 .25
40 Plains L .12 .25
41 Plains L .12 .25
42 Plains L .12 .25
43 Forest L .12 .25
44 Forest L .12 .25
45 Forest L .12 .25
46 Forest L .12 .25
47 Bogardan Hellkite M 2.50 5.00
48 Cinder Wall C .12 .25
49 Skirk Prospector C .25 .50
50 Bloodmark Mentor U .50 1.00
51 Fire-Belly Changeling C .12 .25
52 Mudbutton Torchrunner C .25 .50
53 Dragonspeaker Shaman U 1.50 3.00
54 Dragon Whelp U .25 .50
55 Henge Guardian U .25 .50
56 Voracious Dragon R .50 1.00
57 Bogardan Rager C .12 .25
58 Mordant Dragon R .50 1.00
59 Kilnmouth Dragon R 1.50 3.00
60 Shivan Hellkite R .50 1.00
61 Thunder Dragon R 1.00 2.00
62 Armillary Sphere C .12 .25
63 Dragon's Claw U .25 .50
64 Breath of Darigaaz U .25 .50
65 Dragon Fodder C .25 .50
66 Punishing Fire U .50 1.00
67 Spitting Earth C .12 .25
68 Captive Flame U .25 .50
69 Ghostfire C .12 .25
70 Seething Song C 1.50 3.00
71 Seismic Strike C .25 .50
72 Claws of Valakut C .12 .25
73 Temporary Insanity U .25 .50
74 Shiv's Embrace U .50 1.00
75 Cone of Flame U .25 .50
76 Fiery Fall C .12 .25
77 Jaws of Stone U .25 .50
78 Mountain L .12 .25
79 Mountain L .12 .25
80 Mountain L .12 .25
81 Mountain L .12 .25

2011 Magic The Gathering Duel Decks Knights vs. Dragons Token

1 Goblin .20 .40

2011 Magic The Gathering From the Vault Legends

1 Cao Cao, Lord of Wei M 1.50 3.00
2 Captain Sisay M 2.00 4.00
3 Doran, the Siege Tower M 3.00 6.00
4 Kiki-Jiki, Mirror Breaker M 12.50 25.00
5 Kresh the Bloodbraided M 2.00 4.00
6 Mikaeus, the Lunarch M 1.50 3.00
7 Omnath, Locus of Mana M 4.00 8.00
8 Oona, Queen of the Fae M 2.50 5.00
9 Progenitus M 7.50 15.00
10 Rafiq of the Many M 5.00 10.00
11 Sharuum the Hegemon M 2.50 5.00
12 Sun Quan, Lord of Wu M 2.00 4.00
13 Teferi, Mage of Zhalfir M 5.00 10.00
14 Ulamog, the Infinite Gyre M 20.00 40.00
15 Visara the Dreadful M 4.00 8.00

2011 Magic The Gathering Innistrad

1 Abbey Griffin C .07 .15
2 Angel of Flight Alabaster R .15 .30
3 Angelic Overseer M 1.25 2.50
4 Avacynian Priest C .07 .15
5 Bonds of Faith C .07 .15
6 Champion of the Parish R 1.25 2.50
7 Chapel Geist C .07 .15
8 Cloistered Youth/Unholy Fiend U .10 .20
9 Dearly Departed R .15 .30
10 Divine Reckoning R .15 .30
11 Doomed Traveler C .07 .15
12 Elder Cathar C .07 .15
13 Elite Inquisitor R .15 .30
14 Feeling of Dread C .07 .15
15 Fiend Hunter U .10 .20
16 Gallows Warden U .10 .20
17 Geist-Honored Monk R .15 .30
18 Ghostly Possession C .07 .15
19 Intangible Virtue U .10 .20
20 Mausoleum Guard U .10 .20
21 Mentor of the Meek R .75 1.50
22 Midnight Haunting U .10 .20
23 Mikaeus, the Lunarch M 2.50 5.00
24 Moment of Heroism C .07 .15
25 Nevermore R .60 1.25
26 Paraselene U .10 .20
27 Purify the Grave U .10 .20
28 Rally the Peasants U .10 .20
29 Rebuke C .07 .15
30 Selfless Cathar C .07 .15
31 Silverchase Fox C .07 .15
32 Slayer of the Wicked U .10 .20
33 Smite the Monstrous C .07 .15
34 Spare from Evil C .07 .15
35 Spectral Rider U .10 .20
36 Stony Silence R 3.00 6.00
37 Thraben Purebloods C .07 .15
38 Thraben Sentry/Thraben Militia C .07 .15
39 Unruly Mob C .07 .15
40 Urgent Exorcism C .07 .15
41 Village Bell-Ringer C .07 .15
42 Voiceless Spirit C .07 .15
43 Armored Skaab C .07 .15
44 Back from the Brink R .15 .30
45 Battleground Geist U .10 .20
46 Cackling Counterpart R .75 1.50
47 Civilized Scholar/Homicidal Brute U .10 .20
48 Claustrophobia C .07 .15
49 Curiosity U .10 .20
50 Curse of the Bloody Tome C .07 .15
51 Delver of Secrets/Insectile Aberration C .75 1.50
52 Deranged Assistant C .07 .15
53 Dissipate U .10 .20
54 Dream Twist C .07 .15
55 Forbidden Alchemy C .07 .15
56 Fortress Crab C .07 .15
57 Frightful Delusion C .07 .15
58 Grasp of Phantoms U .10 .20
59 Hysterical Blindness C .07 .15
60 Invisible Stalker U .10 .20
61 Laboratory Maniac R 3.00 6.00
62 Lantern Spirit U .10 .20
63 Lost in the Mist C .07 .15
64 Ludevic's Test Subject
Ludevic's Abomination R .15 .30
65 Makeshift Mauler C .07 .15
66 Memory's Journey U .10 .20
67 Mindshrieker R .30 .75
68 Mirror-Mad Phantasm M .50 1.00
69 Moon Heron C .07 .15
70 Murder of Crows U .10 .20
71 Rooftop Storm R 7.50 15.00
72 Runic Repetition U .10 .20
73 Selhoff Occultist C .07 .15
74 Sensory Deprivation C .07 .15

75 Silent Departure C	.07	.15
76 Skaab Goliath U	.10	.20
77 Skaab Ruinator M	.75	1.50
78 Snapcaster Mage R	30.00	75.00
79 Spectral Flight C	.07	.15
80 Stitched Drake C	.07	.15
81 Stitcher's Apprentice C	.07	.15
82 Sturmgeist R	.15	.30
83 Think Twice C	.07	.15
84 Undead Alchemist R	1.00	2.00
85 Abattoir Ghoul U	.10	.20
86 Altar's Reap C	.07	.15
87 Army of the Damned M	1.50	3.00
88 Bitterheart Witch U	.10	.20
89 Bloodgift Demon R	.75	1.50
90 Bloodline Keeper/Lord of Lineage R	10.00	20.00
91 Brain Weevil C	.07	.15
92 Bump in the Night C	.07	.15
93 Corpse Lunge C	.07	.15
94 Curse of Death's Hold R	.15	.30
95 Curse of Oblivion C	.07	.15
96 Dead Weight C	.07	.15
97 Diregraf Ghoul U	.10	.20
98 Disciple of Griselbrand U	.10	.20
99 Endless Ranks of the Dead R	7.50	15.00
100 Falkenrath Noble U	.30	.60
101 Ghoulcaller's Chant C	.07	.15
102 Ghoulraiser C	.07	.15
103 Gruesome Deformity C	.07	.15
104 Heartless Summoning R	2.00	4.00
105 Liliana of the Veil M	60.00	120.00
106 Manor Skeleton C	.07	.15
107 Markov Patrician C	.07	.15
108 Maw of the Mire C	.07	.15
109 Moan of the Unhallowed U	.10	.20
110 Morkrut Banshee U	.10	.20
111 Night Terrors C	.07	.15
112 Reaper from the Abyss M	1.50	3.00
113 Rotting Fensnake C	.07	.15
114 Screeching Bat/Stalking Vampire U	.10	.20
115 Sever the Bloodline R	.15	.30
116 Skeletal Grimace C	.07	.15
117 Skirsdag High Priest R	.15	.30
118 Stromkirk Patrol C	.07	.15
119 Tribute to Hunger U	.10	.20
120 Typhoid Rats C	.07	.15
121 Unbreathing Horde R	.60	1.25
122 Unburial Rites U	.10	.20
123 Vampire Interloper C	.07	.15
124 Victim of Night C	.07	.15
125 Village Cannibals U	.10	.20
126 Walking Corpse C	.07	.15
127 Ancient Grudge C	.07	.15
128 Ashmouth Hound C	.07	.15
129 Balefire Dragon M	20.00	40.00
130 Blasphemous Act R	2.00	4.00
131 Bloodcrazed Neonate C	.07	.15
132 Brimstone Volley C	.07	.15
133 Burning Vengeance U	.10	.20
134 Charmbreaker Devils R	.15	.30
135 Crossway Vampire C	.07	.15
136 Curse of Stalked Prey R	.15	.30
137 Curse of the Nightly Hunt U	.10	.20
138 Curse of the Pierced Heart C	.07	.15
139 Desperate Ravings U	.10	.20
140 Devil's Play R	.15	.30
141 Falkenrath Marauders R	.15	.30
142 Feral Ridgewolf C	.07	.15
143 Furor of the Bitten C	.07	.15
144 Geistflame C	.07	.15
145 Hanweir Watchkeep/Bane of Hanweir U	.10	.20
146 Harvest Pyre C	.07	.15
147 Heretic's Punishment R	.15	.30
148 Infernal Plunge C	.07	.15
149 Instigator Gang/Wildblood Pack R	.50	1.00
150 Into the Maw of Hell U	.10	.20
151 Kessig Wolf C	.07	.15
152 Kruin Outlaw/Terror of Kruin Pass R	.50	1.00
153 Night Revelers C	.07	.15
154 Nightbird's Clutches C	.07	.15
155 Past in Flames M	2.00	4.00
156 Pitchburn Devils C	.07	.15
157 Rage Thrower U	.10	.20
158 Rakish Heir U	.10	.20
159 Reckless Waif/Merciless Predator U	.10	.20
160 Riot Devils C	.07	.15
161 Rolling Temblor U	.10	.20
162 Scourge of Geier Reach U	.10	.20
163 Skirsdag Cultist U	.10	.20
164 Stromkirk Noble R	.15	.30
165 Tormented Pariah/Rampaging Werewolf C	.07	.15
166 Traitorous Blood C	.07	.15
167 Vampiric Fury C	.07	.15
168 Village Ironsmith/Ironfang C	.07	.15
169 Ambush Viper C	.07	.15
170 Avacyn's Pilgrim C	.07	.15
171 Boneyard Wurm U	.10	.20
172 Bramblecrush U	.10	.20
173 Caravan Vigil C	.07	.15
174 Creeping Renaissance R	.50	1.00
175 Darkthicket Wolf C	.07	.15
176 Daybreak Ranger/Nightfall Predator R	2.00	4.00
177 Elder of Laurels R	.15	.30
178 Essence of the Wild M	.50	1.00
179 Festerhide Boar C	.07	.15
180 Full Moon's Rise U	.25	.50
181 Garruk Relentless/Garruk, the Veil-Cursed M	3.00	6.00
182 Gatstaf Shepherd/Gatstaf Howler U	.10	.20
183 Gnaw to the Bone C	.07	.15
184 Grave Bramble C	.07	.15
185 Grizzled Outcasts/Krallenhorde Wantons C	.07	.15
186 Gutter Grime R	.15	.30
187 Hamlet Captain U	.10	.20
188 Hollowhenge Scavenger U	.10	.20
189 Kessig Cagebreakers R	.15	.30
190 Kindercatch C	.07	.15
191 Lumberknot U	.10	.20
192 Make a Wish U	.10	.20
193 Mayor of Avabruck/Howlpack Alpha R	7.50	15.00
194 Moldgraf Monstrosity R	.15	.30
195 Moonmist C	.07	.15
196 Mulch C	.07	.15
197 Naturalize C	.07	.15
198 Orchard Spirit C	.07	.15
199 Parallel Lives R	30.00	60.00
200 Prey Upon C	.07	.15
201 Ranger's Guile C	.07	.15
202 Somberwald Spider C	.07	.15
203 Spider Spawning U	.10	.20
204 Spidery Grasp C	.07	.15
205 Splinterfright R	.15	.30
206 Travel Preparations C	.07	.15
207 Tree of Redemption M	3.00	6.00
208 Ulvenwald Mystics/Ulvenwald Primordials U	.10	.20
209 Villagers of Estwald/Howlpack of Estwald C	.07	.15
210 Woodland Sleuth C	.07	.15
211 Wreath of Geists U	.10	.20
212 Evil Twin R	.15	.30
213 Geist of Saint Traft M	2.50	5.00
214 Grimgrin, Corpse-Born M	5.00	10.00
215 Olivia Voldaren M	7.50	15.00
216 Blazing Torch C	.07	.15
217 Butcher's Cleaver U	.10	.20
218 Cellar Door U	.10	.20
219 Cobbled Wings C	.07	.15
220 Creepy Doll R	.30	.75
221 Demonmail Hauberk U	.10	.20
222 Galvanic Juggernaut U	.10	.20
223 Geistcatcher's Rig U	.10	.20
224 Ghoulcaller's Bell C	.07	.15
225 Graveyard Shovel U	.10	.20
226 Grimoire of the Dead M	.75	1.50
227 Inquisitor's Flail U	.30	.75
228 Manor Gargoyle R	.15	.30
229 Mask of Avacyn U	.10	.20
230 One-Eyed Scarecrow C	.07	.15
231 Runechanter's Pike R	.25	.50
232 Sharpened Pitchfork U	.10	.20
233 Silver-Inlaid Dagger U	.10	.20
234 Traveler's Amulet C	.07	.15
235 Trepanation Blade U	.10	.20
236 Witchbane Orb R	.30	.75
237 Wooden Stake C	.07	.15
238 Clifftop Retreat R	5.00	10.00
239 Gavony Township R	1.25	2.50
240 Ghost Quarter U	.75	1.50
241 Hinterland Harbor R	5.00	10.00
242 Isolated Chapel R	4.00	8.00
243 Kessig Wolf Run R	1.50	3.00
244 Moorland Haunt R	.25	.50
245 Nephalia Drownyard R	.30	.75
246 Shimmering Grotto C	.07	.15
247 Stensia Bloodhall R	.15	.30
248 Sulfur Falls R	4.00	8.00
249 Woodland Cemetery R	4.00	8.00
250 Plains L	.20	.40
251 Plains L	.20	.40
252 Plains L	.20	.40
253 Island L	.15	.30
254 Island L	.30	.75
255 Island L	.15	.30
256 Swamp L	.30	.60
257 Swamp L	.30	.60
258 Swamp L	.30	.60
259 Mountain L	.20	.40
260 Mountain L	.20	.40
261 Mountain L	.20	.40
262 Forest L	.20	.40
263 Forest L	.20	.40
264 Forest L	.20	.40

2011 Magic The Gathering Innistrad Tokens

1 Angel	.60	1.25
2 Spirit	.07	.15
3 Homunculus	.07	.15
4 Demon	.12	.25
5 Vampire	1.00	1.75
6 Wolf	1.00	2.00
7 Zombie	.07	.15
8 Zombie	.12	.25
9 Zombie	.12	.25
10 Ooze	.07	.15
11 Spider	.20	.40
12 Wolf	.12	.25
13 Innistrad CL	.07	.15

2011 Magic The Gathering Judge Gift Rewards

1 Bitterblossom R	75.00	150.00
2 Sword of Fire and Ice R	125.00	250.00
3 Vendilion Clique R	30.00	60.00
4 Entomb R	25.00	50.00
5 Mana Crypt R	200.00	400.00
6 Dark Confidant R	75.00	150.00
7 Doubling Season R	75.00	150.00
8 Goblin Welder R	30.00	75.00

2011 Magic The Gathering Magic 2012

1 Aegis Angel R	.30	.75
2 Alabaster Mage U	.10	.20
3 Angelic Destiny M	3.00	6.00
4 Angel's Mercy C	.07	.15
5 Arbalest Elite U	.10	.20
6 Archon of Justice R	.30	.60
7 Armored Warhorse C	.07	.15
8 Assault Griffin C	.07	.15
9 Auramancer C	.07	.15
10 Benalish Veteran C	.07	.15
11 Celestial Purge U	.10	.20
12 Day of Judgment R	1.50	3.00
13 Demystify C	.07	.15
14 Divine Favor C	.07	.15
15 Elite Vanguard U	.10	.20
16 Gideon Jura M	.75	1.50
17 Gideon's Avenger R	.30	.60
18 Gideon's Lawkeeper C	.07	.15
19 Grand Abolisher R	15.00	30.00
20 Griffin Rider C	.07	.15
21 Griffin Sentinel C	.07	.15
22 Guardians' Pledge C	.07	.15
23 Honor of the Pure R	1.00	2.00
24 Lifelink C	.07	.15
25 Mesa Enchantress R	2.00	4.00
26 Mighty Leap C	.07	.15
27 Oblivion Ring U	.10	.20
28 Pacifism C	.07	.15
29 Peregrine Griffin C	.07	.15
30 Personal Sanctuary R	.15	.30
31 Pride Guardian C	.07	.15
32 Roc Egg U	.10	.20
33 Serra Angel U	.10	.20
34 Siege Mastodon C	.07	.15
35 Spirit Mantle U	.40	.80
36 Stave Off C	.07	.15
37 Stonehorn Dignitary C	.30	.75
38 Stormfront Pegasus C	.07	.15
39 Sun Titan M	1.00	2.00
40 Timely Reinforcements U	.75	1.50
41 Aether Adept C	.07	.15
42 Alluring Siren U	.10	.20
43 Amphin Cutthroat C	.07	.15
44 Aven Fleetwing C	.07	.15
45 Azure Mage U	.10	.20
46 Belltower Sphinx U	.10	.20
47 Cancel C	.07	.15
48 Chasm Drake C	.07	.15
49 Coral Merfolk C	.07	.15
50 Divination C	.07	.15
51 Djinn of Wishes R	.15	.30
52 Flashfreeze U	.10	.20
53 Flight C	.07	.15
54 Frost Breath C	.07	.15
55 Frost Titan M	.60	1.25
56 Harbor Serpent C	.07	.15
57 Ice Cage C	.07	.15
58 Jace, Memory Adept M	6.00	12.00
59 Jace's Archivist R	3.00	6.00
60 Jace's Erasure C	.07	.15
61 Levitation U	.10	.20
62 Lord of the Unreal R	1.25	2.50
63 Mana Leak C	.07	.15
64 Master Thief U	.10	.20
65 Merfolk Looter C	.07	.15
66 Merfolk Mesmerist C	.07	.15
67 Mind Control U	.10	.20
68 Mind Unbound R	.30	.75
69 Negate C	.07	.15
70 Phantasmal Bear C	.07	.15
71 Phantasmal Dragon U	.10	.20
72 Phantasmal Image R	10.00	20.00
73 Ponder C	2.00	4.00
74 Redirect R	.25	.50
75 Skywinder Drake C	.07	.15
76 Sphinx of Uthuun R	.15	.30
77 Time Reversal M	2.00	4.00
78 Turn to Frog U	.10	.20
79 Unsummon C	.07	.15
80 Visions of Beyond R	7.50	15.00
81 Blood Seeker C	.07	.15
82 Bloodlord of Vaasgoth M	1.00	2.00
83 Bloodrage Vampire C	.07	.15
84 Brink of Disaster C	.07	.15
85 Call to the Grave R	.75	1.50
86 Cemetery Reaper R	4.00	8.00
87 Child of Night C	.07	.15
88 Consume Spirit U	.10	.20
89 Dark Favor C	.07	.15
90 Deathmark U	.10	.20
91 Devouring Swarm C	.07	.15
92 Diabolic Tutor U	.75	1.50
93 Disentomb C	.07	.15
94 Distress C	.07	.15
95 Doom Blade C	.07	.15
96 Drifting Shade C	.07	.15
97 Duskhunter Bat C	.07	.15
98 Grave Titan M	7.50	15.00
99 Gravedigger C	.07	.15
100 Hideous Visage C	.07	.15
101 Mind Rot C	.07	.15
102 Monomania R	.15	.30
103 Onyx Mage U	.10	.20
104 Reassembling Skeleton U	.10	.20
105 Royal Assassin R	.60	1.25
106 Rune-Scarred Demon R	.15	.30
107 Sengir Vampire U	.10	.20
108 Smallpox U	.10	.20
109 Sorin Markov M	7.50	15.00
110 Sorin's Thirst C	.07	.15
111 Sorin's Vengeance R	.50	1.00
112 Sutured Ghoul R	.15	.30
113 Taste of Blood C	.07	.15
114 Tormented Soul C	.07	.15
115 Vampire Outcasts U	.10	.20
116 Vengeful Pharaoh R	1.25	2.50
117 Warpath Ghoul C	.07	.15
118 Wring Flesh C	.07	.15
119 Zombie Goliath C	.07	.15
120 Zombie Infestation U	.10	.20
121 Act of Treason C	.07	.15
122 Blood Ogre C	.07	.15
123 Bonebreaker Giant C	.07	.15
124 Chandra, the Firebrand M	1.00	2.00
125 Chandra's Outrage C	.07	.15
126 Chandra's Phoenix R	.15	.30
127 Circle of Flame U	.10	.20
128 Combust U	.10	.20
129 Crimson Mage U	.10	.20
130 Fiery Hellhound C	.07	.15
131 Fireball U	.10	.20
132 Firebreathing C	.07	.15
133 Flameblast Dragon R	.25	.50
134 Fling C	.07	.15
135 Furyborn Hellkite M	1.50	3.00
136 Goblin Arsonist C	.07	.15
137 Goblin Bangchuckers U	.10	.20
138 Goblin Chieftain R	2.00	4.00
139 Goblin Fireslinger C	.07	.15
140 Goblin Grenade U	.60	1.25
141 Goblin Piker C	.07	.15
142 Goblin Tunneler C	.07	.15
143 Goblin War Paint C	.07	.15
144 Gorehorn Minotaurs C	.07	.15
145 Grim Lavamancer R	.60	1.25
146 Incinerate C	.07	.15
147 Inferno Titan M	1.25	2.50
148 Lava Axe C	.07	.15
149 Lightning Elemental C	.07	.15
150 Manabarbs R	.30	.75
151 Manic Vandal C	.07	.15
152 Reverberate R	3.00	6.00
153 Scrambleverse R	.15	.30
154 Shock C	.07	.15
155 Slaughter Cry C	.07	.15
156 Stormblood Berserker U	.10	.20
157 Tectonic Rift U	.10	.20
158 Volcanic Dragon U	.10	.20
159 Wall of Torches C	.07	.15
160 Warstorm Surge R	.75	1.50
161 Acidic Slime U	.10	.20
162 Arachnus Spinner R	.15	.30
163 Arachnus Web C	.07	.15
164 Autumn's Veil U	.30	.75
165 Birds of Paradise R	7.50	15.00
166 Bountiful Harvest C	.07	.15
167 Brindle Boar C	.07	.15
168 Carnage Wurm U	.10	.20
169 Cudgel Troll U	.10	.20
170 Doubling Chant R	.15	.30
171 Dungrove Elder R	.75	1.50
172 Elvish Archdruid R	.75	1.50
173 Fog C	.07	.15
174 Garruk, Primal Hunter M	1.50	3.00
175 Garruk's Companion C	.07	.15
176 Garruk's Horde R	.15	.30
177 Giant Spider C	.07	.15
178 Gladecover Scout C	.07	.15
179 Greater Basilisk C	.07	.15
180 Hunter's Insight U	.10	.20
181 Jade Mage U	.10	.20
182 Llanowar Elves C	.07	.15
183 Lure U	.10	.20
184 Lurking Crocodile C	.07	.15
185 Naturalize C	.07	.15
186 Overrun U	.10	.20
187 Plummet C	.07	.15
188 Primeval Titan M	6.00	12.00
189 Primordial Hydra M	12.50	25.00
190 Rampant Growth C	.30	.75
191 Reclaim C	.07	.15
192 Rites of Flourishing R	.30	.75
193 Runeclaw Bear C	.07	.15
194 Sacred Wolf C	.07	.15
195 Skinshifter R	.30	.60
196 Stampeding Rhino C	.07	.15
197 Stingerfling Spider U	.10	.20
198 Titanic Growth C	.07	.15
199 Trollhide C	.07	.15
200 Vastwood Gorger C	.07	.15
201 Adaptive Automaton R	2.00	4.00
202 Angel's Feather U	.10	.20
203 Crown of Empires U	.10	.20
204 Crumbling Colossus U	.10	.20
205 Demon's Horn U	.10	.20
206 Dragon's Claw U	.10	.20
207 Druidic Satchel R	.30	.60
208 Elixir of Immortality U	.10	.20
209 Greatsword U	.10	.20
210 Kite Shield U	.10	.20
211 Kraken's Eye U	.10	.20
212 Manalith C	.07	.15
213 Pentavus R	.15	.30
214 Quicksilver Amulet R	5.00	10.00
215 Rusted Sentinel U	.10	.20
216 Scepter of Empires U	.10	.20
217 Solemn Simulacrum R	1.00	2.00
218 Sundial of the Infinite R	3.00	6.00
219 Swiftfoot Boots U	1.25	2.50
220 Thran Golem U	.10	.20
221 Throne of Empires R	.25	.50
222 Worldslayer R	1.50	3.00
223 Wurm's Tooth U	.10	.20
224 Buried Ruin U	.50	1.00
225 Dragonskull Summit R	3.00	6.00
226 Drowned Catacomb R	5.00	10.00
227 Glacial Fortress R	4.00	8.00
228 Rootbound Crag R	2.50	5.00
229 Sunpetal Grove R	3.00	6.00
230 Plains L	.12	.25
231 Plains L	.12	.25
232 Plains L	.12	.25
233 Plains L	.12	.25
234 Island L	.12	.25
235 Island L	.12	.25
236 Island L	.12	.25
237 Island L	.12	.25
238 Swamp L	.12	.25
239 Swamp L	.12	.25
240 Swamp L	.12	.25
241 Swamp L	.12	.25
242 Mountain L	.12	.25
243 Mountain L	.12	.25
244 Mountain L	.12	.25
245 Mountain L	.12	.25
246 Forest L	.12	.25
247 Forest L	.12	.25
248 Forest L	.12	.25
249 Forest L	.12	.25

2011 Magic The Gathering Magic 2012 Tokens

1 Bird	.07	.15
2 Soldier	.07	.15
3 Zombie	.10	.20
4 Beast	.07	.15
5 Saproling	.07	.15
6 Wurm	.75	1.50
7 Pentavite	.07	.15

2011 Magic The Gathering Magic Premiere Shop

1 Plains L	1.75	3.50
2 Island L	4.00	8.00
3 Swamp L	2.00	4.00
4 Mountain L	2.50	5.00
5 Forest L	2.00	4.00

2011 Magic The Gathering Mirrodin Besieged

1 Accorder Paladin U	.10	.20
2 Ardent Recruit C	.07	.15
3 Banishment Decree C	.07	.15
4 Choking Fumes U	.10	.20
5 Divine Offering C	.07	.15

6 Frantic Salvage C .07 .15
7 Gore Vassal U .10 .20
8 Hero of Bladehold M 4.00 8.00
9 Kemba's Legion U .10 .20
10 Leonin Relic-Warder U .10 .20
11 Leonin Skyhunter C .07 .15
12 Loxodon Partisan C .07 .15
13 Master's Call C .07 .15
14 Mirran Crusader R .75 1.50
15 Phyrexian Rebirth R .20 .40
16 Priests of Norn C .07 .15
17 Tine Shrike C .07 .15
18 Victory's Herald R .20 .40
19 White Sun's Zenith R .20 .40
20 Blue Sun's Zenith R 2.00 4.00
21 Consecrated Sphinx M 25.00 50.00
22 Corrupted Conscience U .60 1.25
23 Cryptoplasm R 1.00 2.00
24 Distant Memories R .20 .40
25 Fuel for the Cause C .07 .15
26 Mirran Spy C .07 .15
27 Mitotic Manipulation R .20 .40
28 Neurok Commando U .10 .20
29 Oculus C .07 .15
30 Quicksilver Geyser C .07 .15
31 Serum Raker C .07 .15
32 Spire Serpent C .07 .15
33 Steel Sabotage C .07 .15
34 Treasure Mage U .10 .20
35 Turn the Tide C .07 .15
36 Vedalken Anatomist U .10 .20
37 Vedalken Infuser U .10 .20
38 Vivisection C .07 .15
39 Black Sun's Zenith R 6.00 12.00
40 Caustic Hound C .07 .15
41 Flensermite C .07 .15
42 Flesh-Eater Imp U .25 .50
43 Go for the Throat U 1.50 3.00
44 Gruesome Encore U .10 .20
45 Horrifying Revelation C .07 .15
46 Massacre Wurm M 3.00 6.00
47 Morbid Plunder C .07 .15
48 Nested Ghoul U .10 .20
49 Phyresis C .30 .60
50 Phyrexian Crusader R 7.50 15.00
51 Phyrexian Rager C .07 .15
52 Phyrexian Vatmother R .20 .40
53 Sangromancer R 1.00 2.00
54 Scourge Servant C .07 .15
55 Septic Rats U .50 1.00
56 Spread the Sickness C .07 .15
57 Virulent Wound C .07 .15
58 Blisterstick Shaman C .07 .15
59 Burn the Impure C .07 .15
60 Concussive Bolt C .07 .15
61 Crush C .07 .15
62 Galvanoth R .20 .40
63 Gnathosaur C .07 .15
64 Goblin Wardriver U .10 .20
65 Hellkite Igniter R .20 .40
66 Hero of Oxid Ridge M .50 1.00
67 Into the Core U .10 .20
68 Koth's Courier C .07 .15
69 Kuldotha Flamefiend U .10 .20
70 Kuldotha Ringleader C .07 .15
71 Metallic Mastery U .10 .20
72 Ogre Resister C .07 .15
73 Rally the Forces C .07 .15
74 Red Sun's Zenith R .50 1.00
75 Slagstorm R .30 .60
76 Spiraling Duelist U .10 .20
77 Blightwidow C .07 .15
78 Creeping Corrosion R .30 .60
79 Fangren Marauder C .07 .15
80 Glissa's Courier C .07 .15
81 Green Sun's Zenith R 17.50 35.00
82 Lead the Stampede U .10 .20
83 Melira's Keepers U .10 .20
84 Mirran Mettle C .07 .15
85 Phyrexian Hydra R 1.50 3.00
86 Pistus Strike C .07 .15
87 Plaguemaw Beast U .30 .60
88 Praetor's Counsel M 3.00 6.00
89 Quilled Slagwurm U .10 .20
90 Rot Wolf C .07 .15
91 Tangle Mantis C .07 .15
92 Thrun, the Last Troll M 3.00 6.00
93 Unnatural Predation C .07 .15
94 Viridian Corrupter U .30 .60
95 Viridian Emissary C .07 .15
96 Glissa, the Traitor M 3.00 6.00
97 Tezzeret, Agent of Bolas M 10.00 20.00
98 Bladed Sentinel C .07 .15
99 Blightsteel Colossus M 25.00 50.00
100 Bonehoard R .20 .40
101 Brass Squire U .10 .20
102 Copper Carapace C .07 .15
103 Core Prowler U .50 1.00
104 Darksteel Plate R 10.00 20.00
105 Decimator Web R .20 .40
106 Dross Ripper C .07 .15
107 Flayer Husk C .07 .15
108 Gust-Skimmer C .07 .15
109 Hexplate Golem C .07 .15
110 Ichor Wellspring C .07 .15
111 Knowledge Pool R .50 1.00
112 Lumengrid Gargoyle U .10 .20
113 Magnetic Mine R .20 .40
114 Mirrorworks R .75 1.50
115 Mortarpod U .10 .20
116 Myr Sire C .07 .15
117 Myr Turbine R 2.00 4.00
118 Myr Welder R .25 .50
119 Peace Strider U .10 .20
120 Phyrexian Digester C .07 .15
121 Phyrexian Juggernaut U .10 .20
122 Phyrexian Revoker R .75 1.50
123 Pierce Strider U .10 .20
124 Piston Sledge U .10 .20
125 Plague Myr U 1.00 2.00
126 Psychosis Crawler R .30 .75
127 Razorfield Rhino C .07 .15
128 Rusted Slasher C .07 .15
129 Shimmer Myr R .75 1.50
130 Shriekhorn C .07 .15
131 Signal Pest U .30 .75
132 Silverskin Armor U .10 .20
133 Skinwing U .10 .20
134 Sphere of the Suns U .20 .40
135 Spin Engine C .07 .15
136 Spine of Ish Sah R .75 1.50
137 Strandwalker U .10 .20
138 Sword of Feast and Famine M 50.00 100.00
139 Tangle Hulk C .07 .15
140 Thopter Assembly R .30 .60
141 Titan Forge R .40 .80
142 Training Drone C .07 .15
143 Viridian Claw U .10 .20
144 Contested War Zone R .20 .40
145 Inkmoth Nexus R 25.00 50.00
146 Plains L .12 .25
147 Plains L .12 .25
148 Island L .12 .25
149 Island L .12 .25
150 Swamp L .12 .25
151 Swamp L .12 .25
152 Mountain L .12 .25
153 Mountain L .12 .25
154 Forest L .12 .25
155 Forest L .12 .25

2011 Magic The Gathering Mirrodin Besieged Tokens

1 Germ .07 .15
2 Zombie .20 .40
3 Golem .20 .40
4 Horror 1.00 2.00
5 Thopter .30 .75
6 Poison Counter .07 .15

2011 Magic The Gathering New Phyrexia

1 Karn Liberated M 20.00 40.00
2 Apostle's Blessing C .20 .40
3 Auriok Survivors U .10 .20
4 Blade Splicer R .30 .75
5 Cathedral Membrane U .10 .20
6 Chancellor of the Annex R 2.00 4.00
7 Dispatch U 1.25 2.50
8 Due Respect U .10 .20
9 Elesh Norn, Grand Cenobite M 20.00 40.00
10 Exclusion Ritual U .10 .20
11 Forced Worship C .07 .15
12 Inquisitor Exarch U .10 .20
13 Lost Leonin C .07 .15
14 Loxodon Convert C .07 .15
15 Marrow Shards U .10 .20
16 Master Splicer U .10 .20
17 Norn's Annex R 4.00 8.00
18 Phyrexian Unlife R 4.00 8.00
19 Porcelain Legionnaire C .07 .15
20 Puresteel Paladin R 7.50 15.00
21 Remember the Fallen C .07 .15
22 Sensor Splicer C .07 .15
23 Shattered Angel U .75 1.50
24 Shriek Raptor C .07 .15
25 Suture Priest C .75 1.50
26 War Report C .07 .15
27 Argent Mutation U .10 .20
28 Arm with Aether U .10 .20
29 Blighted Agent C .60 1.25
30 Chained Throatseeker C .07 .15
31 Chancellor of the Spires R .75 1.50
32 Corrupted Resolve U .10 .20
33 Deceiver Exarch U .10 .20
34 Defensive Stance C .07 .15
35 Gitaxian Probe C 1.25 2.50
36 Impaler Shrike C .07 .15
37 Jin-Gitaxias, Core Augur M 12.50 25.00
38 Mental Misstep U 3.00 6.00
39 Mindculling U .10 .20
40 Numbing Dose C .07 .15
41 Phyrexian Ingester R .25 .50
42 Phyrexian Metamorph R 4.00 8.00
43 Psychic Barrier C .07 .15
44 Psychic Surgery R .25 .50
45 Spined Thopter C .07 .15
46 Spire Monitor C .07 .15
47 Tezzeret's Gambit U .20 .40
48 Vapor Snag C .25 .50
49 Viral Drake U 1.00 2.00
50 Wing Splicer U .10 .20
51 Xenograft R 1.00 2.00
52 Blind Zealot C .07 .15
53 Caress of Phyrexia U .10 .20
54 Chancellor of the Dross R .50 1.00
55 Dementia Bat C .07 .15
56 Despise U .10 .20
57 Dismember U 2.00 4.00
58 Enslave U .10 .20
59 Entomber Exarch U .10 .20
60 Evil Presence C .07 .15
61 Geth's Verdict C .25 .50
62 Glistening Oil R 1.25 2.50
63 Grim Affliction C .07 .15
64 Ichor Explosion U .10 .20
65 Life's Finale R 2.00 4.00
66 Mortis Dogs C .07 .15
67 Parasitic Implant C .07 .15
68 Phyrexian Obliterator M 20.00 40.00
69 Pith Driller C .07 .15
70 Postmortem Lunge U .30 .75
71 Praetor's Grasp R 10.00 20.00
72 Reaper of Sheoldred U .60 1.25
73 Sheoldred, Whispering One M 12.50 25.00
74 Surgical Extraction R 20.00 40.00
75 Toxic Nim C .07 .15
76 Vault Skirge C .25 .50
77 Whispering Specter U 1.00 2.00
78 Act of Aggression U .20 .40
79 Artillerize C .07 .15
80 Bludgeon Brawl R .20 .40
81 Chancellor of the Forge R 1.50 3.00
82 Fallen Ferromancer U .10 .20
83 Flameborn Viron C .07 .15
84 Furnace Scamp C .07 .15
85 Geosurge U .25 .50
86 Gut Shot U .75 1.50
87 Invader Parasite R .25 .50
88 Moltensteel Dragon R .75 1.50
89 Ogre Menial C .07 .15
90 Priest of Urabrask U .20 .40
91 Rage Extractor U .10 .20
92 Razor Swine C .07 .15
93 Ruthless Invasion C .07 .15
94 Scrapyard Salvo C .07 .15
95 Slag Fiend R .75 1.50
96 Slash Panther C .07 .15
97 Tormentor Exarch U .10 .20
98 Urabrask the Hidden M 6.00 12.00
99 Victorious Destruction C .07 .15
R1 Rules Tip: Phyrexian Mana .07 .15
R2 Rules Tip: Living Weapon .07 .15
R3 Rules Tip: Infect .07 .15
R4 Rules Tip: Proliferate .07 .15
100 Volt Charge C .07 .15
101 Vulshok Refugee U .10 .20
102 Whipflare U .10 .20
103 Beast Within U 1.25 2.50
104 Birthing Pod R 10.00 20.00
105 Brutalizer Exarch U .20 .40
106 Chancellor of the Tangle R .25 .50
107 Corrosive Gale U .10 .20
108 Death-Hood Cobra C .07 .15
109 Fresh Meat R .25 .50
110 Glissa's Scorn C .07 .15
111 Glistener Elf C .75 1.50
112 Greenhilt Trainee U .10 .20
113 Leeching Bite C .07 .15
114 Maul Splicer C .07 .15
115 Melira, Sylvok Outcast R 3.00 6.00
116 Mutagenic Growth C 1.50 3.00
117 Mycosynth Fiend U .10 .20
118 Noxious Revival U 7.50 15.00
119 Phyrexian Swarmlord R 4.00 8.00
120 Rotted Hystrix C .07 .15
121 Spinebiter U .30 .60
122 Thundering Tanadon C .07 .15
123 Triumph of the Hordes U 10.00 20.00
124 Viridian Betrayers C .07 .15
125 Viridian Harvest C .07 .15
126 Vital Splicer C .10 .20
127 Vorinclex, Voice of Hunger M 25.00 50.00
128 Jor Kadeen, the Prevailer R .25 .50
129 Alloy Myr U .20 .40
130 Batterskull M 7.50 15.00
131 Blinding Souleater C .07 .15
132 Caged Sun R 5.00 10.00
133 Conversion Chamber U .10 .20
134 Darksteel Relic U .30 .75
135 Etched Monstrosity M .30 .75
136 Gremlin Mine C .07 .15
137 Hex Parasite R 2.50 5.00
138 Hovermyr C .07 .15
139 Immolating Souleater C .07 .15
140 Insatiable Souleater C .07 .15
141 Isolation Cell U .10 .20
142 Kiln Walker U .10 .20
143 Lashwrithe R .50 1.00
144 Mindcrank U 3.00 6.00
145 Mycosynth Wellspring C .07 .15
146 Myr Superion R 1.25 2.50
147 Necropouncer U .10 .20
148 Omen Machine R .75 1.50
149 Pestilent Souleater C .07 .15
150 Phyrexian Hulk C .07 .15
151 Pristine Talisman C .20 .40
152 Shrine of Boundless Growth U .10 .20
153 Shrine of Burning Rage U .50 1.00
154 Shrine of Limitless Power U .10 .20
155 Shrine of Loyal Legions U .10 .20
156 Shrine of Piercing Vision U .10 .20
157 Sickleslicer U .10 .20
158 Soul Conduit R .30 .60
159 Spellskite R 3.00 6.00
160 Surge Node U .10 .20
161 Sword of War and Peace M 10.00 20.00
162 Torpor Orb R 12.50 25.00
163 Trespassing Souleater C .07 .15
164 Unwinding Clock R 7.50 15.00
165 Phyrexia's Core U .10 .20
166 Plains L .20 .40
167 Plains L .20 .40
168 Island L .30 .60
169 Island L .30 .60
170 Swamp L .75 1.50
171 Swamp L .75 1.50
172 Mountain L .75 1.50
173 Mountain L .25 .50
174 Forest L .50 1.00
175 Forest L .25 .50

2011 Magic The Gathering New Phyrexia Tokens

1 Beast .25 .50
2 Goblin 2.50 5.00
3 Golem .07 .15
4 Myr .17 .35
5 Poison Counter .07 .15

2011 Magic The Gathering Premium Deck Series Graveborn

1 Putrid Imp C .30 .75
2 Hidden Horror U .25 .50
3 Faceless Butcher C .25 .50
4 Twisted Abomination C .25 .50
5 Crosis, the Purger R 2.50 5.00
6 Avatar of Woe R .50 1.00
7 Terastodon R .75 1.50
8 Verdant Force R .50 1.00
9 Sphinx of the Steel Wind M .50 1.00
10 Inkwell Leviathan R 2.50 5.00
11 Blazing Archon R 2.00 4.00
12 Cabal Therapy U 6.00 12.00
13 Duress C .25 .50
14 Entomb R 12.50 25.00
15 Reanimate U 4.00 8.00
16 Animate Dead U 1.50 3.00
17 Exhume C .30 .75
18 Sickening Dreams U .25 .50
19 Zombie Infestation U .25 .50
20 Buried Alive U 1.25 2.50
21 Last Rites C .25 .50
22 Diabolic Servitude U .25 .50
23 Dread Return U 1.25 2.50
24 Crystal Vein U .25 .50
25 Ebon Stronghold U .25 .50
26 Polluted Mire C .25 .50
27 Swamp L .12 .25
28 Swamp L .12 .25
29 Swamp L .12 .25
30 Swamp L .12 .25

2012 Magic The Gathering Avacyn Restored

1 Angel of Glory's Rise R .30 .75
2 Angel of Jubilation R 4.00 8.00
3 Angel's Mercy C .07 .15
4 Angelic Wall C .07 .15
5 Archangel U .10 .20
6 Avacyn, Angel of Hope M 25.00 50.00
7 Banishing Stroke U .10 .20
8 Builder's Blessing U .10 .20
9 Call to Serve C .07 .15
10 Cathars' Crusade R 3.00 6.00
11 Cathedral Sanctifier C .07 .15
12 Cloudshift C .20 .40
13 Commander's Authority U .10 .20
14 Cursebreak C .07 .15
15 Defang C .07 .15
16 Defy Death U .20 .40
17 Devout Chaplain U .10 .20
18 Divine Deflection R .15 .30
19 Emancipation Angel U .10 .20
20 Entreat the Angels M 1.50 3.00
21 Farbog Explorer C .07 .15
22 Goldnight Commander U .10 .20
23 Goldnight Redeemer U .10 .20
24 Herald of War R 2.00 4.00
25 Holy Justiciar U .10 .20
26 Leap of Faith C .07 .15
27 Midnight Duelist C .07 .15
28 Midvast Protector C .07 .15
29 Moonlight Geist C .07 .15
30 Moorland Inquisitor C .07 .15
31 Nearheath Pilgrim U .10 .20
32 Restoration Angel R 1.00 2.00
33 Riders of Gavony R .15 .30
34 Righteous Blow C .07 .15
35 Seraph of Dawn C .07 .15
36 Silverblade Paladin R .30 .75
37 Spectral Gateguards C .07 .15
38 Terminus R 1.50 3.00
39 Thraben Valiant C .07 .15
40 Voice of the Provinces C .07 .15
41 Zealous Strike C .07 .15
42 Alchemist's Apprentice C .07 .15
43 Amass the Components C .07 .15
44 Arcane Melee R .15 .30
45 Captain of the Mists R .15 .30
46 Crippling Chill C .07 .15
47 Deadeye Navigator R 7.50 15.00
48 Devastation Tide R 1.25 2.50
49 Dreadwaters C .07 .15
50 Elgaud Shieldmate C .07 .15
51 Favorable Winds U .25 .50
52 Fettergeist U .10 .20
53 Fleeting Distraction C .07 .15
54 Galvanic Alchemist C .07 .15
55 Geist Snatch C .07 .15
56 Ghostform C .07 .15
57 Ghostly Flicker C .30 .75
58 Ghostly Touch U .10 .20
59 Gryff Vanguard C .07 .15
60 Havengul Skaab C .07 .15
61 Infinite Reflection R .15 .30
62 Into the Void U .10 .20
63 Latch Seeker U .10 .20
63 Latch Seeker U/(Full Art Promo) .10 .20
64 Lone Revenant R .15 .30
65 Lunar Mystic R .15 .30
66 Mass Appeal U .10 .20
67 Mist Raven C .07 .15
68 Misthollow Griffin M .75 1.50
69 Nephalia Smuggler U .10 .20
70 Outwit C .07 .15
71 Peel from Reality C .07 .15
72 Rotcrown Ghoul C .07 .15
73 Scrapskin Drake C .07 .15
74 Second Guess U .10 .20
75 Spectral Prison C .07 .15
76 Spirit Away R .15 .30
77 Stern Mentor U .10 .20
78 Stolen Goods R .15 .30
79 Tamiyo, the Moon Sage M 10.00 20.00
80 Tandem Lookout U .10 .20
81 Temporal Mastery M 6.00 12.00
82 Vanishment U .10 .20
83 Wingcrafter C .07 .15
84 Appetite for Brains U .10 .20
85 Barter in Blood U .10 .20
86 Blood Artist U 3.00 6.00
87 Bloodflow Connoisseur C .07 .15
88 Bone Splinters C .07 .15
89 Butcher Ghoul C .15 .30
90 Corpse Traders U .10 .20
91 Crypt Creeper C .07 .15
92 Dark Impostor R .30 .75
93 Death Wind C .07 .15
94 Demonic Rising R .15 .30
95 Demonic Taskmaster U .10 .20
96 Demonlord of Ashmouth R .15 .30
97 Descent into Madness M .30 .75
98 Dread Slaver R .15 .30
99 Driver of the Dead C .07 .15
100 Essence Harvest C .20 .40
101 Evernight Shade U .10 .20
102 Exquisite Blood R 25.00 50.00
103 Ghoulflesh C .07 .15
104 Gloom Surgeon R .15 .30
105 Grave Exchange C .07 .15
106 Griselbrand M 7.50 15.00
107 Harvester of Souls R .75 1.50
108 Homicidal Seclusion U .10 .20
109 Human Frailty U .10 .20
110 Hunted Ghoul C .07 .15

111 Killing Wave R	2.00	4.00
111 Killing Wave R/(Full Art Promo)	.15	.30
112 Maalfeld Twins U	.10	.20
113 Marrow Bats U	.10	.20
114 Mental Agony C	.07	.15
115 Necrobite C	.07	.15
116 Polluted Dead C	.07	.15
117 Predator's Gambit C	.07	.15
118 Renegade Demon C	.07	.15
119 Searchlight Geist C	.07	.15
120 Soulcage Fiend C	.07	.15
121 Treacherous Pit-Dweller R	.15	.30
122 Triumph of Cruelty U	.10	.20
123 Undead Executioner C	.07	.15
124 Unhallowed Pact C	.07	.15
125 Aggravate U	.10	.20
126 Archwing Dragon R	.15	.30
127 Banners Raised C	.07	.15
128 Battle Hymn C	.50	1.00
129 Bonfire of the Damned M	1.25	2.50
130 Burn at the Stake R	.60	1.25
131 Dangerous Wager C	.07	.15
132 Demolish C	.07	.15
133 Dual Casting R	.50	1.00
134 Falkenrath Exterminator U	.10	.20
135 Fervent Cathar C	.07	.15
136 Gang of Devils U	.10	.20
137 Guise of Fire C	.07	.15
138 Hanweir Lancer C	.07	.15
139 Havengul Vampire U	.10	.20
140 Heirs of Stromkirk C	.07	.15
141 Hound of Griselbrand R	.20	.40
142 Kessig Malcontents U	.10	.20
143 Kruin Striker C	.07	.15
144 Lightning Mauler U	.10	.20
145 Lightning Prowess U	.10	.20
146 Mad Prophet C	.07	.15
147 Malicious Intent C	.07	.15
148 Malignus M	4.00	8.00
149 Pillar of Flame C	.07	.15
150 Raging Poltergeist C	.07	.15
151 Reforge the Soul R	7.50	15.00
152 Riot Ringleader C	.07	.15
153 Rite of Ruin R	.15	.30
154 Rush of Blood U	.10	.20
155 Scalding Devil C	.07	.15
156 Somberwald Vigilante C	.07	.15
157 Stonewright U	.10	.20
158 Thatcher Revolt C	.07	.15
159 Thunderbolt C	.07	.15
160 Thunderous Wrath U	.10	.20
161 Tibalt, the Fiend-Blooded M	1.25	2.50
162 Tyrant of Discord R	.25	.50
163 Uncanny Speed C	.07	.15
164 Vexing Devil R	4.00	8.00
165 Vigilante Justice U	.10	.20
166 Zealous Conscripts R	1.25	2.50
167 Abundant Growth C	.30	.60
168 Blessings of Nature U	.10	.20
169 Borderland Ranger C	.07	.15
170 Bower Passage U	.10	.20
171 Champion of Lambholt R	1.25	2.50
172 Craterhoof Behemoth M	30.00	60.00
173 Descendants' Path R	6.00	12.00
174 Diregraf Escort C	.07	.15
175 Druid's Familiar U	.10	.20
176 Druids' Repository R	1.50	3.00
177 Eaten by Spiders U	.10	.20
178 Flowering Lumberknot C	.07	.15
179 Geist Trappers C	.07	.15
180 Gloomwidow U	.10	.20
181 Grounded C	.07	.15
182 Howlgeist U	.10	.20
183 Joint Assault C	.07	.15
184 Lair Delve C	.07	.15
185 Natural End C	.07	.15
186 Nettle Swine C	.07	.15
187 Nightshade Peddler C	.07	.15
188 Pathbreaker Wurm C	.07	.15
189 Primal Surge M	3.00	6.00
190 Rain of Thorns U	.10	.20
191 Revenge of the Hunted R	.15	.30
192 Sheltering Word C	.07	.15
193 Snare the Skies C	.07	.15
194 Somberwald Sage R	3.00	6.00
195 Soul of the Harvest R	.75	1.50
196 Terrifying Presence C	.07	.15
197 Timberland Guide C	.07	.15
198 Triumph of Ferocity U	.10	.20
199 Trusted Forcemage C	.07	.15
200 Ulvenwald Tracker R	1.50	3.00
201 Vorstclaw U	.10	.20
202 Wandering Wolf C	.07	.15
203 Wild Defiance R	.30	.60
204 Wildwood Geist C	.07	.15
205 Wolfir Avenger U	.15	.30
206 Wolfir Silverheart R	.50	1.00
207 Yew Spirit U	.10	.20
208 Bruna, Light of Alabaster M	.50	1.00
209 Gisela, Blade of Goldnight M	7.50	15.00
210 Sigarda, Host of Herons M	7.50	15.00
211 Angel's Tomb U	.10	.20
212 Angelic Armaments U	.10	.20
213 Bladed Bracers C	.07	.15
214 Conjurer's Closet R	3.00	6.00
215 Gallows at Willow Hill R	.15	.30
216 Haunted Guardian U	.10	.20
217 Moonsilver Spear R	.50	1.00
218 Narstad Scrapper C	.07	.15
219 Otherworld Atlas R	.75	1.50
220 Scroll of Avacyn C	.07	.15
221 Scroll of Griselbrand C	.07	.15
222 Tormentor's Trident U	.10	.20
223 Vanguard's Shield C	.07	.15
224 Vessel of Endless Rest U	.10	.20
225 Alchemist's Refuge R	4.00	8.00
226 Cavern of Souls R	60.00	120.00
227 Desolate Lighthouse R	.25	.50
228 Seraph Sanctuary C	.50	1.00
229 Slayers' Stronghold R	.30	.75
230 Plains L	.10	.20
231 Plains L	.10	.20
232 Plains L	.10	.20
233 Island L	.10	.20
234 Island L	.15	.30
235 Island L	.10	.20
236 Swamp L	.10	.20
237 Swamp L	.10	.20
238 Swamp L	.10	.20
239 Mountain L	.10	.20
240 Mountain L	.10	.20
241 Mountain L	.10	.20
242 Forest L	.10	.20
243 Forest L	.30	.60
244 Forest L	.20	.40

2012 Magic The Gathering Avacyn Restored Tokens

1 Angel	.12	.25
2 Human	.12	.25
3 Spirit	.12	.25
4 Spirit	.07	.15
5 Demon	.12	.25
6 Zombie	.07	.15
7 Human	.07	.15
8 Tamiyo, the Moon Sage Emblem	1.25	2.50

2012 Magic The Gathering Commander's Arsenal

1 Loyal Retainers U	15.00	30.00
2 Desertion R	5.00	10.00
3 Rhystic Study C	6.00	12.00
4 Decree of Pain R	6.00	12.00
5 Chaos Warp R	10.00	20.00
6 Diaochan, Artful Beauty R	2.50	5.00
7 Sylvan Library R	25.00	50.00
8 Dragonlair Spider R	4.00	8.00
9 Edric, Spymaster of Trest R	3.00	6.00
10 Kaalia of the Vast M	20.00	40.00
11 Maelstrom Wanderer M	12.50	25.00
12 Mirari's Wake R	10.00	20.00
13 The Mimeoplasm M	6.00	12.00
14 Vela the Night-Clad M	3.00	6.00
15 Command Tower C	7.50	15.00
16 Duplicant R	7.50	15.00
17 Mind's Eye R	5.00	10.00
18 Scroll Rack R	15.00	30.00

2012 Magic The Gathering Commander's Arsenal Oversized

1 Azusa, Lost but Seeking R	7.50	15.00
2 Brion Stoutarm R	2.50	5.00
3 Glissa, the Traitor M	4.00	8.00
4 Godo, Bandit Warlord R	2.50	5.00
5 Grimgrin, Corpse-Born M	15.00	20.00
6 Karn, Silver Golem R	15.00	20.00
7 Karrthus, Tyrant of Jund M	4.00	8.00
8 Mayael the Anima M	2.00	4.00
9 Sliver Queen R	75.00	150.00
10 Zur the Enchanter R	4.00	8.00

2012 Magic The Gathering Dark Ascension

1 Archangel's Light M	.50	1.00
2 Bar the Door C	.07	.15
3 Break of Day C	.07	.15
4 Burden of Guilt C	.07	.15
5 Curse of Exhaustion U	.30	.60
6 Elgaud Inquisitor C	.07	.15
7 Faith's Shield U	.10	.20
8 Gather the Townsfolk C	.07	.15
9 Gavony Ironwright U	.10	.20
10 Hollowhenge Spirit U	.10	.20
11 Increasing Devotion R	.15	.30
12 Lingering Souls U	.10	.20
13 Loyal Cathar/Unhallowed Cathar C	.07	.15
14 Midnight Guard C	.07	.15
15 Niblis of the Mist C	.07	.15
16 Niblis of the Urn U	.10	.20
17 Ray of Revelation C	.07	.15
18 Requiem Angel R	.50	1.00
19 Sanctuary Cat C	.07	.15
20 Seance R	.15	.30
21 Silverclaw Griffin C	.07	.15
22 Skillful Lunge C	.07	.15
23 Sudden Disappearance R	.15	.30
24 Thalia, Guardian of Thraben R	7.50	15.00
25 Thraben Doomsayer R	.15	.30
26 Thraben Heretic U	.10	.20
27 Artful Dodge C	.07	.15
28 Beguiler of Wills M	2.00	4.00
29 Bone to Ash C	.07	.15
30 Call to the Kindred R	.30	.60
31 Chant of the Skifsang C	.07	.15
32 Chill of Foreboding U	.10	.20
33 Counterlash R	.15	.30
34 Curse of Echoes R	.15	.30
35 Divination C	.07	.15
36 Dungeon Geists R	.15	.30
37 Geralf's Mindcrusher R	.15	.30
38 Griptide C	.07	.15
39 Havengul Runebinder R	.15	.30
40 Headless Skaab C	.07	.15
41 Increasing Confusion R	1.00	2.00
42 Mystic Retrieval U	.10	.20
43 Nephalia Seakite C	.07	.15
44 Niblis of the Breath U	.10	.20
45 Relentless Skaabs U	.10	.20
46 Saving Grasp C	.07	.15
47 Screeching Skaab C	.07	.15
48 Secrets of the Dead U	.10	.20
49 Shriekgeist C	.07	.15
50 Soul Seizer/Ghastly Haunting U	.10	.20
51 Stormbound Geist C	.07	.15
52 Thought Scour C	.30	.75
53 Tower Geist U	.10	.20
54 Black Cat C	.07	.15
55 Chosen of Markov/Markov's Servant C	.07	.15
56 Curse of Misfortunes R	.15	.30
57 Curse of Thirst U	.10	.20
58 Deadly Allure U	.10	.20
59 Death's Caress C	.07	.15
60 Falkenrath Torturer C	.07	.15
61 Farbog Boneflinger U	.10	.20
62 Fiend of the Shadows R	.15	.30
63 Geralf's Messenger R	10.00	20.00
64 Gravecrawler R	6.00	12.00
65 Gravepurge C	.07	.15
66 Gruesome Discovery C	.07	.15
67 Harrowing Journey U	.10	.20
68 Highborn Ghoul C	.07	.15
69 Increasing Ambition R	.75	1.50
70 Mikaeus, the Unhallowed M	25.00	50.00
71 Ravenous Demon/Archdemon of Greed R	.15	.30
72 Reap the Seagraf C	.07	.15
73 Sightless Ghoul C	.07	.15
74 Skirsdag Flayer U	.10	.20
75 Spiteful Shadows C	.07	.15
76 Tragic Slip C	.20	.40
77 Undying Evil C	.50	1.00
78 Vengeful Vampire U	.10	.20
79 Wakedancer U	.10	.20
80 Zombie Apocalypse R	3.00	6.00
81 Afflicted Deserter/Werewolf Ransacker U	.20	.40
82 Alpha Brawl R	.15	.30
83 Blood Feud U	.10	.20
84 Burning Oil U	.10	.20
85 Curse of Bloodletting R	1.00	2.00
86 Erdwal Ripper C	.07	.15
87 Faithless Looting C	.30	.60
88 Fires of Undeath C	.07	.15
89 Flayer of the Hatebound R	.15	.30
90 Fling C	.07	.15
91 Forge Devil C	.07	.15
92 Heckling Fiends U	.10	.20
93 Hellrider R	.25	.50
94 Hinterland Hermit/Hinterland Scourge C	.07	.15
95 Increasing Vengeance R	.40	.80
96 Markov Blademaster R	.30	.75
97 Markov Warlord U	.10	.20
98 Mondronen Shaman/Tovolar's Magehunter R	.60	1.25
99 Moonveil Dragon M	3.00	6.00
100 Nearheath Stalker C	.07	.15
101 Pyreheart Wolf U	.10	.20
102 Russet Wolves C	.07	.15
103 Scorch the Fields C	.07	.15
104 Shattered Perception U	.10	.20
105 Talons of Falkenrath C	.07	.15
106 Torch Fiend C	.07	.15
107 Wrack with Madness C	.07	.15
108 Briarpack Alpha U	.10	.20
109 Clinging Mists C	.07	.15
110 Crushing Vines C	.07	.15
111 Dawntreader Elk C	.07	.15
112 Deranged Outcast R	.15	.30
113 Favor of the Woods C	.07	.15
114 Feed the Pack R	.30	.60
115 Ghoultree R	.30	.75
116 Gravetiller Wurm U	.10	.20
117 Grim Flowering U	.10	.20
118 Hollowhenge Beast C	.07	.15
119 Hunger of the Howlpack C	.07	.15
120 Increasing Savagery R	.40	.80
121 Kessig Recluse C	.07	.15
122 Lambholt Elder/Silverpelt Werewolf U	.10	.20
123 Lost in the Woods R	.15	.30
124 Predator Ooze R	.50	1.00
125 Scorned Villager/Moonscarred Werewolf C	.07	.15
126 Somberwald Dryad C	.07	.15
127 Strangleroot Geist U	.30	.60
128 Tracker's Instincts U	.10	.20
129 Ulvenwald Bear C	.07	.15
130 Village Survivors U	.10	.20
131 Vorapede M	.60	1.25
132 Wild Hunger C	.07	.15
133 Wolfbitten Captive/Krallenhorde Killer R	.75	1.50
134 Young Wolf C	.30	.60
135 Diregraf Captain U	.25	.50
136 Drogskol Captain U	.30	.60
137 Drogskol Reaver M	4.00	8.00
138 Falkenrath Aristocrat M	.50	1.00
139 Havengul Lich M	2.50	5.00
140 Huntmaster of the Fells/Ravager of the Fells M	15.00	30.00
141 Immerwolf U	1.50	3.00
142 Sorin, Lord of Innistrad M	4.00	8.00
143 Stromkirk Captain U	.30	.75
144 Altar of the Lost U	.10	.20
145 Avacyn's Collar U	.10	.20
146 Chalice of Life/Chalice of Death U	.30	.75
147 Elbrus, the Binding Blade Withengar Unbound M	3.00	6.00
148 Executioner's Hood C	.07	.15
149 Grafdigger's Cage R	2.00	4.00
150 Heavy Mattock C	.07	.15
151 Helvault M	.30	.75
152 Jar of Eyeballs R	.15	.30
153 Warden of the Wall U	.10	.20
154 Wolfhunter's Quiver U	.10	.20
155 Evolving Wilds C	.07	.15
156 Grim Backwoods R	.15	.30
157 Haunted Fengraf C	.07	.15
158 Vault of the Archangel R	4.00	8.00

2012 Magic The Gathering Dark Ascension Tokens

1 Human	.07	.15
2 Vampire	2.00	4.00
3 Sorin, Lord of Innistrad Emblem	2.50	5.00
4 Dark Ascension CL	.07	.15

2012 Magic The Gathering Duel Decks Izzet vs. Golgari

1 Niv-Mizzet, the Firemind M	2.00	4.00
2 Kiln Fiend C	.50	1.00
3 Goblin Electromancer C	.25	.50
4 Izzet Guildmage U	.25	.50
5 Gelectrode U	.30	.75
6 Wee Dragonauts C	.12	.25
7 Steamcore Weird C	.12	.25
8 Shrewd Hatchling U	.25	.50
9 Ogre Savant C	.12	.25
10 Galvanoth R	.30	.75
11 Izzet Chronarch C	.12	.25
12 Djinn Illuminatus R	.30	.75
13 Brainstorm C	2.50	5.00
14 Force Spike C	.25	.50
15 Magma Spray C	.12	.25
16 Isochron Scepter U	3.00	6.00
17 Izzet Signet C	.12	.25
18 Call to Heel C	.12	.25
19 Train of Thought C	.12	.25
20 Pyromatics C	.12	.25
21 Izzet Charm U	.30	.75
22 Reminisce U	.25	.50
23 Thunderheads U	.25	.50
24 Vacuumelt U	.25	.50
25 Dissipate U	.30	.75
26 Quicksilver Dagger C	.12	.25
27 Prophetic Bolt R	.30	.75
28 Overwhelming Intellect U	.25	.50
29 Sphinx-Bone Wand R	.30	.75
30 Street Spasm U	.25	.50
31 Invoke the Firemind R	.30	.75
32 Fire/Ice U	.25	.50
33 Forgotten Cave C	.12	.25
34 Izzet Boilerworks C	.12	.25
35 Lonely Sandbar C	.12	.25
36 Nivix, Aerie of the Firemind U	.25	.50
37 Island L	.12	.25
38 Island L	.12	.25
39 Island L	.12	.25
40 Island L	.12	.25
41 Mountain L	.12	.25
42 Mountain L	.12	.25
43 Mountain L	.12	.25
44 Mountain L	.12	.25
45 Jarad, Golgari Lich Lord M	1.00	2.00
46 Plagued Rusalka U	.25	.50
47 Elves of Deep Shadow C	.12	.25
48 Golgari Thug U	.50	1.00
49 Ravenous Rats C	.12	.25
50 Reassembling Skeleton U	.25	.50
51 Boneyard Wurm U	.25	.50
52 Korozda Guildmage U	.25	.50
53 Putrid Leech C	.12	.25
54 Stinkweed Imp C	.12	.25
55 Eternal Witness U	1.50	3.00
56 Dreg Mangler U	.25	.50
57 Shambling Shell C	.12	.25
58 Brain Weevil C	.12	.25
59 Greater Mossdog C	.12	.25
60 Golgari Grave-Troll R	1.00	2.00
61 Stingerfling Spider U	.25	.50
62 Sadistic Hypnotist U	.25	.50
63 Golgari Rotwurm C	.12	.25
64 Gleancrawler R	.30	.75
65 Doomgape R	.30	.75
66 Golgari Signet C	.12	.25
67 Ghoul's Feast U	.25	.50
68 Yoke of the Damned C	.12	.25
69 Life from the Loam R	1.50	3.00
70 Golgari Germination U	.25	.50
71 Putrefy U	.30	.75
72 Feast or Famine C	.12	.25
73 Nightmare Void U	.25	.50
74 Vigor Mortis U	.25	.50
75 Grim Flowering U	.25	.50
76 Twilight's Call R	.30	.75
77 Life/Death U	.25	.50
78 Barren Moor C	.12	.25
79 Dakmor Salvage U	.25	.50
80 Golgari Rot Farm C	.30	.75
81 Svogthos, the Restless Tomb U	.25	.50
82 Tranquil Thicket C	.12	.25
83 Swamp L	.12	.25
84 Swamp L	.12	.25
85 Swamp L	.12	.25
86 Swamp L	.12	.25
87 Forest L	.12	.25
88 Forest L	.12	.25
89 Forest L	.12	.25
90 Forest L	.12	.25

2012 Magic The Gathering Duel Decks Izzet vs. Golgari Tokens

1 Saproling	.10	.20

2012 Magic The Gathering Duel Decks Venser vs. Koth

1 Venser, the Sojourner M	5.00	10.00
2 Whitemane Lion C	.25	.50
3 Augury Owl C	.12	.25
4 Coral Fighters U	.25	.50
5 Minamo Sightbender U	.25	.50
6 Mistmeadow Witch U	.25	.50
7 Scroll Thief C	.12	.25
8 Neurok Invisimancer C	.12	.25
9 Slith Strider U	.25	.50
10 Sky Spirit U	.25	.50
11 Wall of Denial U	.75	1.50
12 Galepowder Mage R	.50	1.00
13 Kor Cartographer C	.12	.25
14 Clone R	.50	1.00
15 Cryptic Annelid U	.25	.50
16 Primal Plasma C	.12	.25
17 Sawtooth Loon U	.25	.50
18 Cache Raiders U	.25	.50
19 Windreaver R	.50	1.00
20 Jedit's Dragoons C	.12	.25
21 Sunblast Angel R	.50	1.00
22 Sphinx of Uthuun R	.50	1.00
23 Path to Exile U	4.00	8.00
24 Preordain C	.75	1.50
25 Sigil of Sleep C	.25	.50
26 Revoke Existence C	.12	.25
27 Angelic Shield U	.25	.50
28 Oblivion Ring U	.75	1.50
29 Safe Passage C	.12	.25
30 Steel of the Godhead C	.30	.75
31 Vanish into Memory U	.25	.50
32 Overrule C	.25	.50
33 Azorius Chancery C	.25	.50
34 Flood Plain U	.30	.75
35 New Benalia U	.25	.50
36 Sejiri Refuge U	.30	.75
37 Soaring Seacliff C	.12	.25
38 Plains L	.12	.25
39 Plains L	.12	.25
40 Plains L	.12	.25
41 Island L	.12	.25
42 Island L	.12	.25
43 Island L	.12	.25
44 Koth of the Hammer M	5.00	10.00
45 Plated Geopede C	.30	.75
46 Pygmy Pyrosaur C	.12	.25
47 Pilgrim's Eye C	.25	.50

48 Aether Membrane U .25 .50
49 Fiery Hellhound C .12 .25
50 Vulshok Sorcerer C .12 .25
51 Anger U .75 1.50
52 Cosi's Ravager C .12 .25
53 Vulshok Berserker C .12 .25
54 Bloodfire Kavu U .25 .50
55 Stone Giant U .25 .50
56 Geyser Glider U .25 .50
57 Lithophage R .50 1.00
58 Torchling R .50 1.00
59 Chartooth Cougar C .30 .75
60 Earth Servant U .25 .50
61 Greater Stone Spirit U .25 .50
62 Bloodfire Colossus R .50 1.00
63 Wayfarer's Bauble C .25 .50
64 Armillary Sphere C .12 .25
65 Journeyer's Kite R 1.00 2.00
66 Vulshok Morningstar U .25 .50
67 Searing Blaze C .12 .25
68 Vulshok Battlegear U .25 .50
69 Downhill Charge C .12 .25
70 Seismic Strike C .12 .25
71 Spire Barrage C .12 .25
72 Jaws of Stone U .25 .50
73 Volley of Boulders R .50 1.00
74 Mountain L .12 .25
75 Mountain L .12 .25
76 Mountain L .12 .25
77 Mountain L .12 .25

2012 Magic The Gathering Duel Decks Venser vs. Koth Tokens

1 Venser, the Sojourner Emblem 3.00 6.00
2 Koth of the Hammer Emblem 1.00 2.00

2012 Magic The Gathering From the Vault Realms

1 Ancient Tomb M 20.00 40.00
2 Boseiju, Who Shelters All M 10.00 20.00
3 Cephalid Coliseum M 5.00 10.00
4 Desert M 1.50 3.00
5 Dryad Arbor M 12.50 25.00
6 Forbidden Orchard M 10.00 20.00
7 Glacial Chasm M 5.00 10.00
8 Grove of the Burnwillows M 4.00 8.00
9 High Market M 3.00 6.00
10 Maze of Ith M 12.50 25.00
11 Murmuring Bosk M 1.00 2.00
12 Shivan Gorge M 1.50 3.00
13 Urborg, Tomb of Yawgmoth M 15.00 30.00
14 Vesuva M 15.00 30.00
15 Windbrisk Heights M 1.50 3.00

2012 Magic The Gathering Judge Gift Rewards

1 Xiahou Dun, the One-Eyed R 30.00 75.00
2 Flusterstorm R 50.00 100.00
3 Noble Hierarch R 75.00 150.00
4 Karmic Guide R 12.50 25.00
5 Sneak Attack R 20.00 40.00
6 Karakas R 20.00 40.00
7 Sword of Light and Shadow R 30.00 60.00
8 Command Tower R 50.00 100.00
9 Centaur R 1.00 2.00

2012 Magic The Gathering League Tokens

1 Goblin 2.00 4.00
2 Knight 1.50 3.00

2012 Magic The Gathering Magic 2013

1 Ajani, Caller of the Pride M 2.50 5.00
2 Ajani's Sunstriker C .07 .15
3 Angel's Mercy C .07 .15
4 Angelic Benediction U .10 .20
5 Attended Knight C .07 .15
6 Aven Squire C .07 .15
7 Battleflight Eagle C .07 .15
8 Captain of the Watch R .30 .60
9 Captain's Call C .07 .15
10 Crusader of Odric U .10 .20
11 Divine Favor C .07 .15
12 Divine Verdict C .07 .15
13 Erase C .07 .15
14 Faith's Reward R 1.00 2.00
15 Glorious Charge C .07 .15
16 Griffin Protector C .07 .15
17 Guardian Lions C .07 .15
18 Guardians of Akrasa C .07 .15
19 Healer of the Pride U .10 .20
20 Intrepid Hero R .50 1.00
21 Knight of Glory U .10 .20
22 Oblivion Ring U .20 .40
23 Odric, Master Tactician R .15 .30
24 Pacifism C .07 .15
25 Pillarfield Ox C .07 .15
26 Planar Cleansing R .15 .30
27 Prized Elephant U .10 .20
28 Rain of Blades U .10 .20
29 Rhox Faithmender R 4.00 8.00
30 Safe Passage C .07 .15
31 Serra Angel U .10 .20
32 Serra Avatar M .50 1.00
33 Serra Avenger R .60 1.25
34 Show of Valor C .07 .15
35 Silvercoat Lion C .07 .15
36 Sublime Archangel M 1.50 3.00
37 Touch of the Eternal R .15 .30
38 War Falcon C .07 .15
39 War Priest of Thune U .10 .20
40 Warclamp Mastiff C .07 .15
41 Archaeomancer C .07 .15
42 Arctic Aven U .10 .20
43 Augur of Bolas U .10 .20
44 Battle of Wits R .15 .30
45 Clone R .15 .30
46 Courtly Provocateur U .10 .20
47 Divination C .07 .15
48 Downpour C .07 .15
49 Encrust C .07 .15
50 Essence Scatter C .07 .15
51 Faerie Invaders C .07 .15
52 Fog Bank U .20 .40
53 Harbor Serpent C .07 .15
54 Hydrosurge C .07 .15
55 Index C .07 .15
56 Jace, Memory Adept M 4.00 8.00
57 Jace's Phantasm U .20 .40
58 Kraken Hatchling C .07 .15
59 Master of the Pearl Trident R 3.00 6.00
60 Merfolk of the Pearl Trident C .07 .15
61 Mind Sculpt C .07 .15
62 Negate C .07 .15
63 Omniscience M 12.50 25.00
64 Redirect R .15 .30
65 Rewind U .10 .20
66 Scroll Thief C .07 .15
67 Sleep U .10 .20
68 Spelltwine R .20 .40
69 Sphinx of Uthuun R .15 .30
70 Stormtide Leviathan R .25 .50
71 Switcheroo U .10 .20
72 Talrand, Sky Summoner R .15 .30
73 Talrand's Invocation U .10 .20
74 Tricks of the Trade C .07 .15
75 Unsummon C .07 .15
76 Vedalken Entrancer C .07 .15
77 Void Stalker R .15 .30
78 Watercourser C .07 .15
79 Welkin Tern C .07 .15
80 Wind Drake C .07 .15
81 Blood Reckoning U .10 .20
82 Bloodhunter Bat C .07 .15
83 Bloodthrone Vampire C .07 .15
84 Cower in Fear U .10 .20
85 Crippling Blight C .07 .15
86 Dark Favor C .07 .15
87 Diabolic Revelation R 1.00 2.00
88 Disciple of Bolas R .25 .50
89 Disentomb C .07 .15
90 Duress C .07 .15
91 Duskmantle Prowler U .10 .20
92 Duty-Bound Dead C .07 .15
93 Essence Drain C .07 .15
94 Giant Scorpion C .07 .15
95 Harbor Bandit U .10 .20
96 Knight of Infamy U .10 .20
97 Liliana of the Dark Realms M 12.50 25.00
98 Liliana's Shade C .07 .15
99 Mark of the Vampire C .07 .15
100 Mind Rot C .07 .15
101 Murder C .07 .15
102 Mutilate R 1.25 2.50
103 Nefarox, Overlord of Grixis R .30 .75
104 Phylactery Lich R .15 .30
105 Public Execution U .10 .20
106 Ravenous Rats C .07 .15
107 Rise from the Grave U .10 .20
108 Servant of Nefarox C .07 .15
109 Shimian Specter R .15 .30
110 Sign in Blood C .07 .15
111 Tormented Soul C .07 .15
112 Vampire Nighthawk U .20 .40
113 Vampire Nocturnus M 4.00 8.00
114 Veilborn Ghoul U .10 .20
115 Vile Rebirth C .07 .15
116 Walking Corpse C .07 .15
117 Wit's End R .15 .30
118 Xathrid Gorgon R .15 .30
119 Zombie Goliath C .07 .15
120 Arms Dealer U .10 .20
121 Bladetusk Boar C .07 .15
122 Canyon Minotaur C .07 .15
123 Chandra, the Firebrand M 1.50 3.00
124 Chandra's Fury C .07 .15
125 Cleaver Riot U .10 .20
126 Craterize C .07 .15
127 Crimson Muckwader U .10 .20
128 Dragon Hatchling C .07 .15
129 Fervor R 2.00 4.00
130 Fire Elemental C .07 .15
131 Firewing Phoenix R .15 .30
132 Flames of the Firebrand U .10 .20
133 Furnace Whelp U .10 .20
134 Goblin Arsonist C .07 .15
135 Goblin Battle Jester C .07 .15
136 Hamletback Goliath R .15 .30
137 Kindled Fury C .07 .15
138 Krenko, Mob Boss R 4.00 8.00
139 Krenko's Command C .07 .15
140 Magmaquake R .15 .30
141 Mark of Mutiny U .10 .20
142 Mindclaw Shaman U .10 .20
143 Mogg Flunkies C .07 .15
144 Reckless Brute C .07 .15
145 Reverberate R 3.00 6.00
146 Rummaging Goblin C .07 .15
147 Searing Spear C .07 .15
148 Slumbering Dragon R 2.00 4.00
149 Smelt C .07 .15
150 Thundermaw Hellkite M 2.50 5.00
151 Torch Fiend U .10 .20
152 Trumpet Blast C .07 .15
153 Turn to Slag C .07 .15
154 Volcanic Geyser U .10 .20
155 Volcanic Strength C .07 .15
156 Wall of Fire C .07 .15
157 Wild Guess C .07 .15
158 Worldfire M 1.00 2.00
159 Acidic Slime U .10 .20
160 Arbor Elf C .30 .75
161 Bond Beetle C .07 .15
162 Boundless Realms R 2.50 5.00
163 Bountiful Harvest C .07 .15
164 Centaur Courser C .07 .15
165 Deadly Recluse C .07 .15
166 Duskdale Wurm C .10 .20
167 Elderscale Wurm M 2.00 4.00
168 Elvish Archdruid R .75 1.50
169 Elvish Visionary C .07 .15
170 Farseek C 1.50 3.00
171 Flinthoof Boar U .10 .20
172 Fog C .07 .15
173 Fungal Sprouting U .50 1.00
174 Garruk, Primal Hunter M 1.25 2.50
175 Garruk's Packleader U .10 .20
176 Ground Seal R .15 .30
177 Mwonvuli Beast Tracker U .10 .20
178 Naturalize C .07 .15
179 Plummet C .07 .15
180 Predatory Rampage R .15 .30
181 Prey Upon C .07 .15
182 Primal Huntbeast C .07 .15
183 Primordial Hydra M 12.50 25.00
184 Quirion Dryad R .15 .30
185 Rancor U .75 1.50
186 Ranger's Path C .07 .15
187 Revive U .10 .20
188 Roaring Primadox U .10 .20
189 Sentinel Spider C .07 .15
190 Serpent's Gift C .07 .15
191 Silklash Spider R .15 .30
192 Spiked Baloth C .07 .15
193 Thragtusk R .25 .50
194 Timberpack Wolf C .07 .15
195 Titanic Growth C .07 .15
196 Vastwood Gorger C .07 .15
197 Yeva, Nature's Herald R 1.50 3.00
198 Yeva's Forcemage C .07 .15
199 Nicol Bolas, Planeswalker M 4.00 8.00
200 Akroma's Memorial M 7.50 15.00
201 Chronomaton U .10 .20
202 Clock of Omens U .60 1.25
203 Door to Nothingness R 1.00 2.00
204 Elixir of Immortality U .30 .75
205 Gem of Becoming U .10 .20
206 Gilded Lotus R 3.00 6.00
207 Jayemdae Tome U .10 .20
208 Kitesail U .10 .20
209 Phyrexian Hulk U .10 .20
210 Primal Clay U .10 .20
211 Ring of Evos Isle U .10 .20
212 Ring of Kalonia U .50 1.00
213 Ring of Thune U .10 .20
214 Ring of Valkas U .10 .20
215 Ring of Xathrid U .30 .75
216 Sands of Delirium R .50 1.00
217 Staff of Nin R 1.25 2.50
218 Stuffy Doll R 1.50 3.00
219 Tormod's Crypt U .30 .60
220 Trading Post R .30 .75
221 Cathedral of War R .75 1.50
222 Dragonskull Summit R 3.00 6.00
223 Drowned Catacomb R 5.00 10.00
224 Evolving Wilds C .07 .15
225 Glacial Fortress R 4.00 8.00
226 Hellion Crucible R .15 .30
227 Reliquary Tower U 1.50 3.00
228 Rootbound Crag R 2.50 5.00
229 Sunpetal Grove R 2.50 5.00
230 Plains L .10 .20
231 Plains L .10 .20
232 Plains L .10 .20
233 Plains L .10 .20
234 Island L .10 .20
235 Island L .10 .20
236 Island L .10 .20
237 Island L .10 .20
238 Swamp L .10 .20
239 Swamp L .10 .20
240 Swamp L .10 .20
241 Swamp L .10 .20
242 Mountain L .10 .20
243 Mountain L .10 .20
244 Mountain L .10 .20
245 Mountain L .10 .20
246 Forest L .10 .20
247 Forest L .10 .20
248 Forest L .10 .20
249 Forest L .10 .20

2012 Magic The Gathering Magic 2013 Tokens

1 Cat .25 .50
2 Goat .12 .25
3 Soldier .07 .15
4 Drake .25 .50
5 Zombie .07 .15
6 Goblin .10 .20
7 Hellion .07 .15
8 Beast .07 .15
9 Saproling .07 .15
10 Wurm .20 .40
11 Liliana of the Dark Realms Emblem .20 .40

2012 Magic The Gathering Planechase

1 Armored Griffin U .12 .25
2 Auramancer C .10 .20
3 Auratouched Mage U .12 .25
4 Cage of Hands C .10 .20
5 Celestial Ancient R .25 .50
6 Felidar Umbra U 1.25 2.50
7 Ghostly Prison U .12 .25
8 Hyena Umbra C .30 .75
9 Kor Spiritdancer R 2.00 4.00
10 Mammoth Umbra U .12 .25
11 Sigil of the Empty Throne R .60 1.25
12 Spirit Mantle U 1.00 2.00
13 Three Dreams R 1.50 3.00
14 Augury Owl C .10 .20
15 Cancel C .10 .20
16 Concentrate U .12 .25
17 Guard Gomazoa U .25 .50
18 Higure, the Still Wind R 7.50 15.00
19 Illusory Angel U .12 .25
20 Mistblade Shinobi C .75 1.50
21 Ninja of the Deep Hours C .50 1.00
22 Peregrine Drake U 4.00 8.00
23 Primal Plasma C .10 .20
24 Sakashima's Student R 30.00 75.00
25 See Beyond C .10 .20
26 Sunken Hope R .15 .30
27 Walker of Secret Ways U 2.00 4.00
28 Wall of Frost U .12 .25
29 Whirlpool Warrior R 2.00 4.00
30 Assassinate C .25 .50
31 Cadaver Imp C .15 .30
32 Dark Hatchling R .25 .50
33 Ink-Eyes, Servant of Oni R 10.00 20.00
34 Liliana's Specter C .25 .50
35 Okiba-Gang Shinobi C .75 1.50
36 Skullsnatcher C .30 .75
37 Throat Slitter U 7.50 15.00
38 Tormented Soul C .10 .20
39 Arc Trail U .12 .25
40 Beetleback Chief U .12 .25
41 Erratic Explosion C .10 .20
42 Fiery Conclusion C .10 .20
43 Fiery Fall C .10 .20
44 Fling C .10 .20
45 Hellion Eruption R .15 .30
46 Hissing Iguanar C .10 .20
47 Mark of Mutiny U .12 .25
48 Mass Mutiny R .30 .75
49 Mudbutton Torchrunner C .10 .20
50 Preyseizer Dragon R .30 .75
51 Rivals' Duel U .12 .25
52 Thorn-Thrash Viashino C .10 .20
53 Thunder-Thrash Elder U .12 .25
54 Warstorm Surge R .75 1.50
55 Aura Gnarlid C .10 .20
56 Awakening Zone R 2.50 5.00
57 Beast Within U 1.50 3.00
58 Boar Umbra U .12 .25
59 Bramble Elemental C .10 .20
60 Brindle Shoat U .30 .75
61 Brutalizer Exarch U .25 .50
62 Cultivate C .50 1.00
63 Dowsing Shaman U .12 .25
64 Dreampod Druid U .25 .50
65 Gluttonous Slime U .12 .25
66 Lumberknot U .12 .25
67 Mitotic Slime R 1.50 3.00
68 Mycoloth R 2.50 5.00
69 Nest Invader C .15 .30
70 Nullmage Advocate C .10 .20
71 Ondu Giant C .10 .20
72 Overrun U .25 .50
73 Penumbra Spider C .10 .20
74 Predatory Urge R .15 .30
75 Quiet Disrepair C .10 .20
76 Rancor C 1.50 3.00
77 Silhana Ledgewalker C .75 1.50
78 Snake Umbra C .20 .40
79 Tukatongue Thallid C .10 .20
80 Viridian Emissary C .10 .20
81 Wall of Blossoms U .25 .50
82 Baleful Strix U 2.50 5.00
83 Bituminous Blast U .12 .25
84 Bloodbraid Elf U 2.00 4.00
85 Deny Reality C .10 .20
86 Dimir Infiltrator C .25 .50
87 Dragonlair Spider R 1.50 3.00
88 Elderwood Scion R .20 .40
89 Enigma Sphinx R .30 .60
90 Enlisted Wurm U .12 .25
91 Etherium-Horn Sorcerer R .30 .60
92 Fires of Yavimaya U .30 .60
93 Fusion Elemental U .20 .40
94 Glen Elendra Liege R 4.00 8.00
95 Hellkite Hatchling U .12 .25
96 Indrik Umbra R .50 1.00
97 Inkfathom Witch U .25 .50
98 Kathari Remnant U .12 .25
99 Krond the Dawn-Clad M .75 1.50
100 Last Stand R .15 .30
101 Maelstrom Wanderer M 7.50 15.00
102 Noggle Ransacker U .12 .25
103 Pollenbright Wings U .20 .40
104 Shardless Agent U 5.00 10.00
105 Silent-Blade Oni R 4.00 8.00
106 Thromok the Insatiable M 1.00 2.00
107 Vela the Night-Clad M 1.00 2.00
108 Armillary Sphere C .10 .20
109 Farsight Mask U .12 .25
110 Flayer Husk C .10 .20
111 Fractured Powerstone C .75 1.50
112 Quietus Spike R 4.00 8.00
113 Sai of the Shinobi U .12 .25
114 Thran Golem U .12 .25
115 Whispersilk Cloak U 2.00 4.00
116 Dimir Aqueduct C .25 .50
117 Exotic Orchard R .50 1.00
118 Graypelt Refuge U .12 .25
119 Gruul Turf C .20 .40
120 Jwar Isle Refuge U .12 .25
121 Kazandu Refuge U .12 .25
122 Khalni Garden C .10 .20
123 Krosan Verge U .30 .60
124 Rupture Spire C .10 .20
125 Selesnya Sanctuary C .10 .20
126 Shimmering Grotto C .10 .20
127 Skarg, the Rage Pits U .30 .60
128 Tainted Isle U 3.00 6.00
129 Terramorphic Expanse C .10 .20
130 Vitu-Ghazi, the City-Tree U .12 .25
131 Vivid Creek U .30 .60
132 Plains L .10 .20
133 Plains L .10 .20
134 Plains L .10 .20
135 Plains L .10 .20
136 Plains L .10 .20
137 Island L .12 .25
138 Island L .12 .25
139 Island L .12 .25
140 Island L .12 .25
141 Island L .12 .25
142 Swamp L .12 .25
143 Swamp L .12 .25
144 Swamp L .12 .25
145 Swamp L .12 .25
146 Swamp L .12 .25
147 Mountain L .12 .25
148 Mountain L .12 .25
149 Mountain L .12 .25
150 Mountain L .12 .25
151 Forest L .10 .20
152 Forest L .10 .20
153 Forest L .10 .20
154 Forest L .10 .20
155 Forest L .10 .20
156 Forest L .10 .20

2012 Magic The Gathering Return to Ravnica

1 Angel of Serenity M	.75	1.50
2 Armory Guard C	.07	.15
3 Arrest U	.10	.20
4 Avenging Arrow C	.07	.15
5 Azorius Arrester C	.07	.15
6 Azorius Justiciar U	.10	.20
7 Bazaar Krovod U	.10	.20
8 Concordia Pegasus C	.07	.15
9 Ethereal Armor C	.30	.75
10 Eyes in the Skies C	.07	.15
11 Fencing Ace U	.10	.20
12 Keening Apparition C	.07	.15
13 Knightly Valor C	.07	.15
14 Martial Law R	.15	.30
15 Palisade Giant R	.15	.30
16 Phantom General U	.10	.20
17 Precinct Captain R	.15	.30
18 Rest in Peace R	4.00	8.00
19 Rootborn Defenses C	.07	.15
20 Security Blockade U	.10	.20
21 Selesnya Sentry C	.07	.15
22 Seller of Songbirds C	.07	.15
23 Soul Tithe U	.10	.20
24 Sphere of Safety U	3.00	6.00
25 Sunspire Griffin C	.07	.15
26 Swift Justice C	.07	.15
27 Trained Caracal C	.07	.15
28 Trostani's Judgment C	.07	.15
29 Aqus Steed U	.10	.20
30 Blustersquall U	.10	.20
31 Cancel C	.07	.15
32 Chronic Flooding C	.07	.15
33 Conjured Currency R	.15	.30
34 Crosstown Courier C	.07	.15
35 Cyclonic Rift R	17.50	35.00
36 Dispel C	.07	.15
37 Doorkeeper C	.07	.15
38 Downsize C	.07	.15
39 Faerie Impostor U	.10	.20
40 Hover Barrier U	.30	.60
41 Inaction Injunction C	.07	.15
42 Inspiration C	.07	.15
43 Isperia's Skywatch C	.07	.15
44 Jace, Architect of Thought M	.60	1.25
45 Mizzium Skin C	.07	.15
46 Paralyzing Grasp C	.07	.15
47 Psychic Spiral U	.10	.20
48 Runewing C	.07	.15
49 Search the City R	.15	.30
50 Skyline Predator U	.10	.20
51 Soulsworn Spirit U	.10	.20
52 Sphinx of the Chimes R	.15	.30
53 Stealer of Secrets C	.07	.15
54 Syncopate U	.10	.20
55 Tower Drake C	.07	.15
56 Voidwielder C	.07	.15
57 Assassin's Strike U	.10	.20
58 Catacomb Slug C	.07	.15
59 Cremate C	.07	.15
60 Daggerdrome Imp C	.07	.15
61 Dark Revenant U	.10	.20
62 Dead Reveler C	.07	.15
63 Desecration Demon R	.50	1.00
64 Destroy the Evidence C	.07	.15
65 Deviant Glee C	.07	.15
66 Drainpipe Vermin C	.07	.15
67 Grave Betrayal R	1.25	2.50
68 Grim Roustabout C	.07	.15
69 Launch Party C	.07	.15
70 Mind Rot C	.07	.15
71 Necropolis Regent M	.50	1.00
72 Ogre Jailbreaker C	.07	.15
73 Pack Rat R	2.00	4.00
74 Perilous Shadow C	.07	.15
75 Sewer Shambler C	.07	.15
76 Shrieking Affliction U	.60	1.25
77 Slum Reaper U	.10	.20
78 Stab Wound C	.07	.15
79 Tavern Swindler U	.10	.20
80 Terrus Wurm C	.07	.15
81 Thrill-Kill Assassin U	.10	.20
82 Ultimate Price U	.10	.20
83 Underworld Connections R	.30	.60
84 Zanikev Locust U	.10	.20
85 Annihilating Fire C	.07	.15
86 Ash Zealot R	.15	.30
87 Batterhorn C	.07	.15
88 Bellows Lizard C	.07	.15
89 Bloodfray Giant U	.10	.20
90 Chaos Imps R	.15	.30
91 Cobblebrute C	.07	.15
92 Dynacharge C	.07	.15
93 Electrickery C	.07	.15
94 Explosive Impact C	.07	.15
95 Goblin Rally U	.10	.20
96 Gore-House Chainwalker C	.07	.15
97 Guild Feud R	.15	.30
98 Guttersnipe U	.10	.20
99 Lobber Crew C	.07	.15
100 Minotaur Aggressor U	.10	.20
101 Mizzium Mortars R	.30	.60
102 Pursuit of Flight C	.07	.15
103 Pyroconvergence U	.10	.20
104 Racecourse Fury U	.10	.20
105 Splatter Thug C	.07	.15
106 Street Spasm U	.10	.20
107 Survey the Wreckage C	.07	.15
108 Tenement Crasher C	.07	.15
109 Traitorous Instinct C	.07	.15
110 Utvara Hellkite M	7.50	15.00
111 Vandalblast U	2.00	4.00
112 Viashino Racketeer C	.07	.15
113 Aerial Predation C	.07	.15
114 Archweaver U	.10	.20
115 Axebane Guardian C	.07	.15
116 Axebane Stag C	.07	.15
117 Brushstrider U	.10	.20
118 Centaur's Herald C	.07	.15
119 Chorus of Might C	.07	.15
120 Deadbridge Goliath R	.15	.30
121 Death's Presence R	.30	.75
122 Drudge Beetle C	.07	.15
123 Druid's Deliverance C	.07	.15
124 Gatecreeper Vine C	.07	.15
125 Giant Growth C	.07	.15
126 Gobbling Ooze U	.10	.20
127 Golgari Decoy U	.10	.20
128 Horncaller's Chant C	.07	.15
129 Korozda Monitor C	.07	.15
130 Mana Bloom R	.30	.60
131 Oak Street Innkeeper U	.10	.20
132 Rubbleback Rhino C	.07	.15
133 Savage Surge U	.10	.20
134 Seek the Horizon U	.10	.20
135 Slime Molding U	.10	.20
136 Stonefare Crocodile C	.07	.15
137 Towering Indrik C	.07	.15
138 Urban Burgeoning C	.07	.15
139 Wild Beastmaster R	.15	.30
140 Worldspine Wurm M	6.00	12.00
141 Abrupt Decay R	3.00	6.00
142 Archon of the Triumvirate R	.15	.30
143 Armada Wurm M	.75	1.50
144 Auger Spree C	.07	.15
145 Azorius Charm U	.10	.20
146 Call of the Conclave U	.10	.20
147 Carnival Hellsteed R	.15	.30
148 Centaur Healer C	.07	.15
149 Chemister's Trick C	.07	.15
150 Collective Blessing R	.30	.75
151 Common Bond C	.07	.15
152 Corpsejack Menace R	.75	1.50
153 Counterflux R	.75	1.50
154 Coursers' Accord C	.07	.15
155 Detention Sphere R	.75	1.50
156 Dramatic Rescue C	.07	.15
157 Dreadbore R	2.00	4.00
158 Dreg Mangler U	.10	.20
158b Dreg Mangler FOIL ALT ART (issued in 2012 Holiday Gift Box)	.10	.20
159 Epic Experiment M	.30	.75
160 Essence Backlash C	.07	.15
161 Fall of the Gavel U	.10	.20
162 Firemind's Foresight R	.15	.30
163 Goblin Electromancer C	.07	.15
164 Golgari Charm U	.75	1.50
165 Grisly Salvage C	.07	.15
166 Havoc Festival R	.15	.30
167 Hellhole Flailer U	.10	.20
168 Heroes' Reunion U	.10	.20
169 Hussar Patrol C	.07	.15
170 Hypersonic Dragon R	.15	.30
171 Isperia, Supreme Judge M	.30	.75
172 Izzet Charm U	.25	.50
173 Izzet Staticaster U	.10	.20
174 Jarad, Golgari Lich Lord M	2.50	5.00
175 Jarad's Orders R	.75	1.50
176 Korozda Guildmage U	.10	.20
177 Lotleth Troll R	.30	.75
178 Loxodon Smiter R	.15	.30
179 Lyev Skyknight U	.10	.20
180 Mercurial Chemister R	.15	.30
181 New Prahv Guildmage U	.10	.20
182 Nivix Guildmage U	.10	.20
183 Niv-Mizzet, Dracogenius M	.50	1.00
184 Rakdos Charm U	.50	1.00
185 Rakdos Ragemutt U	.10	.20
186 Rakdos Ringleader U	.10	.20
187 Rakdos, Lord of Riots M	2.00	4.00
188 Rakdos's Return M	.60	1.25
189 Righteous Authority R	.15	.30
190 Risen Sanctuary U	.10	.20
191 Rites of Reaping U	.10	.20
192 Rix Maadi Guildmage U	.10	.20
193 Search Warrant C	.07	.15
194 Selesnya Charm U	.10	.20
195 Skull Rend C	.07	.15
196 Skymark Roc U	.10	.20
197 Slaughter Games R	.15	.30
198 Sluiceway Scorpion C	.07	.15
199 Spawn of Rix Maadi C	.07	.15
200 Sphinx's Revelation M	2.00	4.00
201 Supreme Verdict R	5.00	10.00
202 Teleportal U	.10	.20
203 Thoughtflare U	.10	.20
204 Treasured Find U	.10	.20
205 Trestle Troll C	.07	.15
206 Trostani, Selesnya's Voice M	.75	1.50
207 Vitu-Ghazi Guildmage U	.10	.20
208 Vraska the Unseen M	.75	1.50
209 Wayfaring Temple R	.15	.30
210 Azor's Elocutors R	.15	.30
211 Blistercoil Weird U	.10	.20
212 Cryptborn Horror R	.15	.30
213 Deathrite Shaman R	.15	.30
214 Dryad Militant U	.10	.20
215 Frostburn Weird C	.07	.15
216 Golgari Longlegs C	.07	.15
217 Growing Ranks R	.15	.30
218 Judge's Familiar U	.10	.20
219 Nivmagus Elemental R	.30	.60
220 Rakdos Cackler U	.10	.20
221 Rakdos Shred-Freak C	.07	.15
222 Slitherhead U	.10	.20
223 Sundering Growth C	.07	.15
224 Vassal Soul C	.07	.15
225 Azorius Keyrune U	.10	.20
226 Chromatic Lantern R	7.50	15.00
227 Civic Saber U	.10	.20
228 Codex Shredder U	.10	.20
229 Golgari Keyrune U	.10	.20
230 Izzet Keyrune U	.10	.20
231 Pithing Needle R	4.00	8.00
232 Rakdos Keyrune U	.10	.20
233 Selesnya Keyrune U	.10	.20
234 Street Sweeper U	.10	.20
235 Tablet of the Guilds U	.10	.20
236 Volatile Rig R	.15	.30
237 Azorius Guildgate C	.07	.15
238 Blood Crypt R	12.50	25.00
239 Golgari Guildgate C	.07	.15
240 Grove of the Guardian R	.15	.30
241 Hallowed Fountain R	6.00	12.00
242 Izzet Guildgate C	.07	.15
243 Overgrown Tomb R	10.00	20.00
244 Rakdos Guildgate C	.07	.15
245 Rogue's Passage U	.25	.50
246 Selesnya Guildgate C	.07	.15
247 Steam Vents R	12.50	25.00
248 Temple Garden R	7.50	15.00
249 Transguild Promenade C	.07	.15
250 Plains L	.10	.20
251 Plains L	.10	.20
252 Plains L	.10	.20
253 Plains L	.10	.20
254 Plains L	.10	.20
255 Island L	.10	.20
256 Island L	.10	.20
257 Island L	.10	.20
258 Island L	.10	.20
259 Island L	.10	.20
260 Swamp L	.10	.20
261 Swamp L	.10	.20
262 Swamp L	.10	.20
263 Swamp L	.10	.20
264 Swamp L	.10	.20
265 Mountain L	.10	.20
266 Mountain L	.10	.20
267 Mountain L	.10	.20
268 Mountain L	.10	.20
269 Mountain L	.10	.20
270 Forest L	.10	.20
271 Forest L	.10	.20
272 Forest L	.10	.20
273 Forest L	.10	.20
274 Forest L	.10	.20

2012 Magic The Gathering Return to Ravnica Tokens

1 Bird	.07	.15
2 Knight	.07	.15
3 Soldier	.07	.15
4 Assassin	.50	1.00
5 Dragon	1.50	3.00
6 Goblin	.12	.25
7 Centaur	.07	.15
8 Ooze	.07	.15
9 Rhino	.07	.15
10 Saproling	.12	.25
11 Wurm	.50	1.00
12 Elemental	.12	.25

2013 Magic The Gathering Commander 2013

1 Act of Authority R	1.50	3.00
2 Aerie Mystics U	.10	.20
3 Ajani's Pridemate U	.17	.35
4 Angel of Finality R	.50	1.00
5 Archangel U	.10	.20
6 Azorius Herald U	.10	.20
7 Cradle of Vitality R	.75	1.50
8 Curse of the Forsaken U	.10	.20
9 Darksteel Mutation U	1.25	2.50
10 Eternal Dragon R	.15	.30
11 Fiend Hunter U	.10	.20
12 Flickerform R	.75	1.50
13 Flickerwisp U	.25	.50
14 Karmic Guide R	6.00	12.00
15 Kirtar's Wrath R	.20	.40
16 Kongming, "Sleeping Dragon" R	.20	.40
17 Mirror Entity R	1.25	2.50
18 Mystic Barrier R	.75	1.50
19 Razor Hippogriff U	.10	.20
20 Serene Master R	.25	.50
21 Serra Avatar M	.30	.75
22 Stonecloaker U	.10	.20
23 Survival Cache U	.10	.20
24 Tempt with Glory R	.15	.30
25 Unexpectedly Absent R	.20	.40
26 Wall of Reverence R	1.00	2.00
27 Wrath of God R	4.00	8.00
28 Arcane Denial C	1.00	2.00
29 Arcane Melee R	.15	.30
30 Augur of Bolas U	.10	.20
31 Azami, Lady of Scrolls R	.75	1.50
32 Blue Sun's Zenith R	1.50	3.00
33 Borrowing 100,000 Arrows U	.10	.20
34 Brilliant Plan U	.10	.20
35 Control Magic U	.60	1.25
36 Curse of Inertia U	.10	.20
37 Deceiver Exarch U	.20	.40
38 Deep Analysis C	.20	.40
39 Dismiss U	.10	.20
40 Diviner Spirit U	.10	.20
41 Djinn of Infinite Deceits R	.25	.50
42 Dungeon Geists R	.15	.30
43 Echo Mage R	.25	.50
44 Fog Bank U	.20	.40
45 Guard Gomazoa U	.25	.50
46 Hada Spy Patrol U	.10	.20
47 Illusionist's Gambit R	1.25	2.50
48 Jace's Archivist R	3.00	6.00
49 Lu Xun, Scholar General R	.20	.40
50 Mnemonic Wall C	.15	.30
51 Opportunity U	.10	.20
52 Order of Succession R	.20	.40
53 Propaganda U	2.50	5.00
54 Prosperity U	1.25	2.50
55 Raven Familiar U	.10	.20
56 Sharding Sphinx R	.30	.60
57 Skyscribing U	.17	.35
58 Stormscape Battlemage U	.10	.20
59 Strategic Planning U	.10	.20
60 Tempt with Reflections R	2.00	4.00
61 Thornwind Faeries C	.07	.15
62 Tidal Force R	.15	.30
63 True-Name Nemesis R	4.00	8.00
64 Uyo, Silent Prophet R	.25	.50
65 Vision Skeins C	.17	.35
66 Wash Out U	.75	1.50
67 Wonder U	.75	1.50
68 Annihilate U	.10	.20
69 Army of the Damned M	2.00	4.00
70 Baleful Force R	.15	.30
71 Curse of Shallow Graves U	.30	.75
72 Decree of Pain R	3.00	6.00
73 Dirge of Dread C	.07	.15
74 Disciple of Griselbrand U	.20	.40
75 Endless Cockroaches R	1.50	3.00
76 Endrek Sahr, Master Breeder R	2.00	4.00
77 Famine U	.10	.20
78 Fell Shepherd R	.15	.30
79 Greed R	2.50	5.00
80 Hooded Horror U	.10	.20
81 Infest U	.10	.20
82 Marrow Bats U	.17	.35
83 Nightscape Familiar C	.50	1.00
84 Ophiomancer R	12.50	25.00
85 Phthisis U	.10	.20
86 Phyrexian Delver R	1.25	2.50
87 Phyrexian Gargantua U	.10	.20
88 Phyrexian Reclamation U	2.50	5.00
89 Price of Knowledge R	.50	1.00
90 Quagmire Druid C	.07	.15
91 Reckless Spite U	.10	.20
92 Sanguine Bond R	2.00	4.00
93 Stronghold Assassin R	.30	.75
94 Sudden Spoiling R	.75	1.50
95 Tempt with Immortality R	.50	1.00
96 Toxic Deluge R	12.50	25.00
97 Vampire Nighthawk U	.30	.75
98 Vile Requiem U	.10	.20
99 Viscera Seer C	.75	1.50
100 Wight of Precinct Six U	.10	.20
101 Blood Rites U	.10	.20
102 Capricious Efreet R	.15	.30
103 Charmbreaker Devils R	.15	.30
104 Crater Hellion R	.15	.30
105 Curse of Chaos U	.10	.20
106 Fireball U	.10	.20
107 Fissure Vent C	.07	.15
108 From the Ashes R	.75	1.50
109 Furnace Celebration U	.10	.20
110 Goblin Bombardment U	5.00	10.00
111 Goblin Sharpshooter R	7.50	15.00
112 Guttersnipe U	.10	.20
113 Incendiary Command R	1.00	2.00
114 Inferno Titan M	1.25	2.50
115 Magus of the Arena R	.15	.30
116 Mass Mutiny R	.20	.40
117 Molten Disaster R	.25	.50
118 Rough/Tumble U	.10	.20
119 Slice and Dice U	.10	.20
120 Spitebellows U	.10	.20
121 Stalking Vengeance R	.50	1.00
122 Starstorm R	.15	.30
123 Street Spasm U	.10	.20
124 Sudden Demise R	.25	.50
125 Tempt with Vengeance R	6.00	12.00
126 Terra Ravager U	.10	.20
127 Tooth and Claw R	.15	.30
128 War Cadence U	.25	.50
129 Warstorm Surge R	.75	1.50
130 Where Ancients Tread R	.30	.75
131 Widespread Panic R	.15	.30
132 Wild Ricochet R	.25	.50
133 Witch Hunt R	.30	.75
134 Acidic Slime U	.10	.20
135 Avenger of Zendikar M	4.00	8.00
136 Baloth Woodcrasher U	.10	.20
137 Bane of Progress R	3.00	6.00
138 Brooding Saurian R	.15	.30
139 Cultivate C	.60	1.25
140 Curse of Predation U	.20	.40
141 Deadwood Treefolk U	.10	.20
142 Drumhunter U	.30	.60
143 Elvish Skysweeper C	.07	.15
144 Farhaven Elf C	.75	1.50
145 Fecundity U	.30	.75
146 Foster R	.15	.30
147 Grazing Gladehart C	.07	.15
148 Harmonize U	.30	.75
149 Hua Tuo, Honored Physician R	.30	.75
150 Hunted Troll R	.60	1.25
151 Jade Mage U	.10	.20
152 Kazandu Tuskcaller R	.30	.60
153 Krosan Grip U	1.50	3.00
154 Krosan Tusker C	.07	.15
155 Krosan Warchief U	.10	.20
156 Mold Shambler C	.07	.15
157 Naya Soulbeast R	.15	.30
158 Night Soil C	2.00	4.00
159 One Dozen Eyes U	.10	.20
160 Phantom Nantuko R	.15	.30
161 Presence of Gond C	.20	.40
162 Primal Vigor R	20.00	40.00
163 Rain of Thorns U	.10	.20
164 Rampaging Baloths M	.30	.75
165 Ravenous Baloth R	.15	.30
166 Reincarnation U	.10	.20
167 Restore U	.10	.20
168 Sakura-Tribe Elder C	1.00	2.00
169 Silklash Spider R	.15	.30
170 Slice in Twain U	.10	.20
171 Spawning Grounds R	.15	.30
172 Spoils of Victory U	1.50	3.00
173 Sprouting Vines C	.07	.15
174 Tempt with Discovery R	1.00	2.00
175 Walker of the Grove U	.10	.20
176 Aethermage's Touch R	.15	.30
177 Baleful Strix U	2.50	5.00
178 Behemoth Sledge U	.10	.20
179 Boros Charm U	1.25	2.50
180 Charnelhoard Wurm R	.15	.30
181 Crosis's Charm U	.60	1.25
182 Cruel Ultimatum R	.30	.60
183 Death Grasp R	.15	.30
184 Deathbringer Thoctar R	.50	1.00
185 Deepfire Elemental U	.10	.20
186 Derevi, Empyrial Tactician M	2.50	5.00
187 Dromar's Charm U	.25	.50
188 Fiery Justice R	.15	.30
189 Filigree Angel R	.15	.30
190 Fires of Yavimaya U	.30	.60
191 Gahiji, Honored One M	2.50	5.00
192 Grixis Charm U	.10	.20
193 Hull Breach C	1.00	2.00
194 Jeleva, Nephalia's Scourge M	.75	1.50

195 Jund Charm U .10 .20
196 Leafdrake Roost U .10 .20
197 Lim-Dul's Vault U 7.50 15.00
198 Marath, Will of the Wild M .60 1.25
199 Mayael the Anima M 1.00 2.00
200 Naya Charm U .20 .40
201 Nekusar, the Mindrazer M 2.50 5.00
202 Nivix Guildmage U .10 .20
203 Oloro, Ageless Ascetic M 7.50 15.00
204 Prossh, Skyraider of Kher M 2.00 4.00
205 Rakeclaw Gargantuan C .07 .15
206 Roon of the Hidden Realm M 1.50 3.00
207 Rubinia Soulsinger R .15 .30
208 Savage Twister U .10 .20
209 Scarland Thrinax U .10 .20
210 Sek'Kuar, Deathkeeper R .20 .40
211 Selesnya Charm U .10 .20
212 Sharuum the Hegemon M .30 .60
213 Shattergang Brothers M 1.00 2.00
214 Skyward Eye Prophets U .10 .20
215 Soul Manipulation C .07 .15
216 Spellbreaker Behemoth R .75 1.50
217 Sphinx of the Steel Wind M .75 1.50
218 Spinal Embrace R .15 .30
219 Sprouting Thrinax U .10 .20
220 Sydri, Galvanic Genius M .75 1.50
221 Thraximundar M .60 1.25
222 Tidehollow Strix C .07 .15
223 Tower Gargoyle U .10 .20
224 Valley Rannet C .07 .15
225 Vizkopa Guildmage U .20 .40
226 Winged Coatl C .20 .40
227 Augury Adept R .15 .30
228 Divinity of Pride R 2.50 5.00
229 Golgari Guildmage U .10 .20
230 Mistmeadow Witch U .15 .30
231 Murkfiend Liege R .75 1.50
232 Selesnya Guildmage U .10 .20
233 Spiteful Visions R 2.00 4.00
234 Thopter Foundry U .20 .40
235 Armillary Sphere C .07 .15
236 Azorius Keyrune U .10 .20
237 Basalt Monolith U 1.25 2.50
238 Carnage Altar U .10 .20
239 Conjurer's Closet R 3.00 6.00
240 Crawlspace R 7.50 15.00
241 Darksteel Ingot U .50 1.00
242 Druidic Satchel R .25 .50
243 Eye of Doom R .15 .30
244 Jar of Eyeballs R .15 .30
245 Leonin Bladetrap U .10 .20
246 Mirari R .50 1.00
247 Myr Battlesphere R .30 .60
248 Nevinyrral's Disk R .75 1.50
249 Nihil Spellbomb C .30 .60
250 Obelisk of Esper C .15 .30
251 Obelisk of Grixis C .07 .15
252 Obelisk of Jund C .07 .15
253 Pilgrim's Eye C .07 .15
254 Plague Boiler R .20 .40
255 Pristine Talisman C .15 .30
256 Seer's Sundial R .15 .30
257 Selesnya Signet C .75 1.50
258 Simic Signet C .25 .50
259 Sol Ring U 1.25 2.50
260 Spine of Ish Sah R .75 1.50
261 Sun Droplet U .30 .75
262 Surveyor's Scope R .30 .75
263 Swiftfoot Boots U 1.25 2.50
264 Sword of the Paruns R 4.00 8.00
265 Temple Bell R 1.50 3.00
266 Thousand-Year Elixir R 4.00 8.00
267 Thunderstaff U .10 .20
268 Tower of Fortunes R .25 .50
269 Viseling U .17 .35
270 Wayfarer's Bauble C 2.00 4.00
271 Well of Lost Dreams R 3.00 6.00
272 Akoum Refuge U .10 .20
273 Arcane Sanctum U 1.25 2.50
274 Azorius Chancery C .07 .15
275 Azorius Guildgate C .07 .15
276 Bant Panorama C .75 1.50
277 Barren Moor C .07 .15
278 Bojuka Bog C 1.00 2.00
279 Boros Garrison C .07 .15
280 Boros Guildgate C .07 .15
281 Command Tower C .25 .50
282 Contested Cliffs R .25 .50
283 Crumbling Necropolis U .20 .40
284 Dimir Guildgate C .07 .15
285 Drifting Meadow C .07 .15
286 Esper Panorama C 1.00 2.00
287 Evolving Wilds C .07 .15
288 Faerie Conclave U .50 1.00
289 Forgotten Cave C .07 .15
290 Golgari Guildgate C .07 .15
291 Golgari Rot Farm C .07 .15
292 Grim Backwoods R .15 .30
293 Grixis Panorama C .75 1.50
294 Gruul Guildgate C .07 .15
295 Homeward Path R 7.50 15.00
296 Izzet Boilerworks C .20 .40
297 Izzet Guildgate C .07 .15
298 Jund Panorama C 1.00 2.00
299 Jungle Shrine U .20 .40
300 Jwar Isle Refuge U .20 .40
301 Kazandu Refuge U .10 .20
302 Khalni Garden C .17 .35
303 Kher Keep R .75 1.50
304 Llanowar Reborn U .30 .75
305 Lonely Sandbar C .07 .15
306 Molten Slagheap U .10 .20
307 Mosswort Bridge R .25 .50
308 Naya Panorama C .20 .40
309 New Benalia U .10 .20
310 Opal Palace C .07 .15
311 Orzhov Basilica C .17 .35
312 Orzhov Guildgate C .07 .15
313 Rakdos Carnarium C .17 .35
314 Rakdos Guildgate C .07 .15
315 Rupture Spire C .07 .15
316 Saltcrusted Steppe U .20 .40
317 Savage Lands U 1.00 2.00
318 Seaside Citadel U 1.50 3.00
319 Secluded Steppe C .07 .15
320 Sejiri Refuge U .20 .40
321 Selesnya Guildgate C .07 .15
322 Selesnya Sanctuary C .07 .15
323 Simic Guildgate C .07 .15
324 Slippery Karst C .15 .30
325 Smoldering Crater C .15 .30
326 Springjack Pasture R .15 .30
327 Temple of the False God U .10 .20
328 Terramorphic Expanse C .07 .15
329 Tranquil Thicket C .07 .15
330 Transguild Promenade C .07 .15
331 Urza's Factory U .10 .20
332 Vitu-Ghazi, the City-Tree U .10 .20
333 Vivid Crag U .50 1.00
334 Vivid Creek U .20 .40
335 Vivid Grove U .25 .50
336 Vivid Marsh U .75 1.50
337 Plains L .12 .25
338 Plains L .12 .25
339 Plains L .12 .25
340 Plains L .12 .25
341 Island L .10 .20
342 Island L .10 .20
343 Island L .10 .20
344 Island L .10 .20
345 Swamp L .10 .20
346 Swamp L .10 .20
347 Swamp L .10 .20
348 Swamp L .10 .20
349 Mountain L .10 .20
350 Mountain L .10 .20
351 Mountain L .10 .20
352 Mountain L .10 .20
353 Forest L .10 .20
354 Forest L .10 .20
355 Forest L .20 .40
356 Forest L .10 .20

2013 Magic The Gathering Commander 2013 Oversized

186 Derevi, Empyrial Tactician M .60 1.25
191 Gahiji, Honored One M .50 1.00
194 Jeleva, Nephalia's Scourge M .50 1.00
198 Marath, Will of the Wild M .60 1.25
199 Mayael the Anima M 1.25 2.50
201 Nekusar, the Mindrazer M .60 1.25
203 Oloro, Ageless Ascetic M 1.50 3.00
204 Prossh, Skyraider of Kher .75 1.50
206 Roon of the Hidden Realm M .50 1.00
207 Rubinia Soulsinger R .30 .75
210 Sek'Kuar, Deathkeeper R .30 .60
212 Sharuum the Hegemon M .30 .75
213 Shattergang Brothers M .30 .75
220 Sydri, Galvanic Genius M .60 1.25
221 Thraximundar M .30 .75

2013 Magic The Gathering Dragon's Maze

1 Boros Mastiff C .07 .15
2 Haazda Snare Squad C .07 .15
3 Lyev Decree C .07 .15
4 Maze Sentinel C .07 .15
5 Renounce the Guilds R .15 .30
6 Riot Control C .07 .15
7 Scion of Vitu-Ghazi R .15 .30
8 Steeple Roc C .07 .15
9 Sunspire Gatekeepers C .07 .15
10 Wake the Reflections C .07 .15
11 Aetherling R .20 .40
12 Hidden Strings C .07 .15
13 Maze Glider C .07 .15
14 Mindstatic C .07 .15
15 Murmuring Phantasm C .07 .15
16 Opal Lake Gatekeepers C .07 .15
17 Runner's Bane C .07 .15
18 Trait Doctoring R .15 .30
19 Uncovered Clues C .07 .15
20 Wind Drake C .07 .15
21 Bane Alley Blackguard C .07 .15
22 Blood Scrivener R .15 .30
23 Crypt Incursion C .20 .40
24 Fatal Fumes C .07 .15
25 Hired Torturer C .07 .15
26 Maze Abomination C .07 .15
27 Pontiff of Blight R .20 .40
28 Rakdos Drake C .07 .15
29 Sinister Possession C .07 .15
30 Ubul Sar Gatekeepers C .07 .15
31 Awe for the Guilds C .07 .15
32 Clear a Path C .07 .15
33 Maze Rusher C .07 .15
34 Possibility Storm R .50 1.00
35 Punish the Enemy C .07 .15
36 Pyrewild Shaman R .15 .30
37 Riot Piker C .07 .15
38 Rubblebelt Maaka C .07 .15
39 Smelt-Ward Gatekeepers C .07 .15
40 Weapon Surge C .07 .15
41 Battering Krasis C .07 .15
42 Kraul Warrior C .07 .15
43 Maze Behemoth C .07 .15
44 Mending Touch C .07 .15
45 Mutant's Prey C .07 .15
46 Phytoburst C .07 .15
47 Renegade Krasis R .15 .30
48 Saruli Gatekeepers C .07 .15
49 Skylasher R .15 .30
50 Thrashing Mossdog C .07 .15
51 Advent of the Wurm R .20 .40
52 Armored Wolf-Rider C .07 .15
53 Ascended Lawmage U .10 .20
54 Beetleform Mage C .07 .15
55 Blast of Genius U .10 .20
56 Blaze Commando U .10 .20
57 Blood Baron of Vizkopa M .30 .75
58 Boros Battleshaper R .15 .30
59 Bred for the Hunt U .10 .20
60 Bronzebeak Moa U .10 .20
61 Carnage Gladiator U .10 .20
62 Council of the Absolute M .25 .50
63 Deadbridge Chant M .50 1.00
64 Debt to the Deathless U .75 1.50
65 Deputy of Acquittals C .07 .15
66 Dragonshift R .15 .30
67 Drown in Filth C .07 .15
68 Emmara Tandris R .15 .30
69 Exava, Rakdos Blood Witch R .15 .30
70 Feral Animist U .10 .20
71 Fluxcharger U .10 .20
72 Gaze of Granite R .15 .30
73 Gleam of Battle U .10 .20
74 Goblin Test Pilot U .10 .20
75 Gruul War Chant U .10 .20
76 Haunter of Nightveil U .10 .20
77 Jelenn Sphinx U .10 .20
78 Korozda Gorgon U .10 .20
79 Krasis Incubation U .10 .20
80 Lavinia of the Tenth R .20 .40
81 Legion's Initiative M 2.00 4.00
82 Master of Cruelties M 7.50 15.00
83 Maw of the Obzedat U .10 .20
84 Melek, Izzet Paragon R .25 .50
85 Mirko Vosk, Mind Drinker R .75 1.50
86 Morgue Burst C .07 .15
87 Nivix Cyclops C .07 .15
88 Notion Thief R 2.50 5.00
89 Obzedat's Aid R .15 .30
90 Pilfered Plans C .07 .15
91 Plasm Capture R .50 1.00
92 Progenitor Mimic M 2.00 4.00
93 Putrefy U .10 .20
94 Ral Zarek M 1.00 2.00
95 Reap Intellect M .30 .60
96 Render Silent R 1.25 2.50
97 Restore the Peace U .10 .20
98 Rot Farm Skeleton U .10 .20
99 Ruric Thar, the Unbowed R .30 .60
100 Savageborn Hydra M .30 .75
101 Scab-Clan Giant U .10 .20
102 Showstopper U .10 .20
103 Sin Collector U .10 .20
104 Sire of Insanity R .75 1.50
105 Species Gorger U .10 .20
106 Spike Jester U .10 .20
107 Tajic, Blade of the Legion R .30 .75
108 Teysa, Envoy of Ghosts R .50 1.00
109 Tithe Drinker C .07 .15
110 Trostani's Summoner U .10 .20
111 Unflinching Courage U .10 .20
112 Varolz, the Scar-Striped R .30 .75
113 Viashino Firstblade C .07 .15
114 Voice of Resurgence M 3.00 6.00
115 Vorel of the Hull Clade R .75 1.50
116 Warleader's Helix U .10 .20
117 Warped Physique U .10 .20
118 Woodlot Crawler U .10 .20
119 Zhur-Taa Ancient R .25 .50
120 Zhur-Taa Druid C .07 .15
121 Alive/Well U .10 .20
122 Armed/Dangerous U .10 .20
123 Beck/Call R .15 .30
124 Breaking/Entering R .20 .40
125 Catch/Release R .15 .30
126 Down/Dirty U .10 .20
127 Far/Away U .10 .20
128 Flesh/Blood R .15 .30
129 Give/Take U .10 .20
130 Profit/Loss U .10 .20
131 Protect/Serve U .10 .20
132 Ready/Willing R .15 .30
133 Toil/Trouble U .10 .20
134 Turn/Burn U .10 .20
135 Wear/Tear U 2.00 4.00
136 Azorius Cluestone C .07 .15
137 Boros Cluestone C .07 .15
138 Dimir Cluestone C .07 .15
139 Golgari Cluestone C .07 .15
140 Gruul Cluestone C .07 .15
141 Izzet Cluestone C .07 .15
142 Orzhov Cluestone C .07 .15
143 Rakdos Cluestone C .07 .15
144 Selesnya Cluestone C .07 .15
145 Simic Cluestone C .07 .15
146 Azorius Guildgate C .07 .15
147 Boros Guildgate C .07 .15
148 Dimir Guildgate C .07 .15
149 Golgari Guildgate C .07 .15
150 Gruul Guildgate C .07 .15
151 Izzet Guildgate C .07 .15
152 Maze's End M 2.00 4.00
153 Orzhov Guildgate C .07 .15
154 Rakdos Guildgate C .07 .15
155 Selesnya Guildgate C .07 .15
156 Simic Guildgate C .07 .15

2013 Magic The Gathering Dragon's Maze Token

1 Elemental .75 1.50

2013 Magic The Gathering Duel Decks Heroes vs. Monsters

1 Sun Titan M 1.25 2.50
2 Somberwald Vigilante C .12 .25
3 Figure of Destiny R .75 1.50
4 Cavalry Pegasus C .12 .25
5 Fencing Ace U .12 .25
6 Thraben Valiant C .12 .25
7 Stun Sniper U .12 .25
8 Truefire Paladin U .12 .25
9 Auramancer C .12 .25
10 Freewind Equenaut C .12 .25
11 Anax and Cymede R .20 .40
12 Armory Guard C .12 .25
13 Gustcloak Sentinel U .12 .25
14 Dawnstrike Paladin C .12 .25
15 Nobilis of War R .20 .40
16 Kamahl, Pit Fighter R .12 .25
17 Condemn U .12 .25
18 Daily Regimen U .12 .25
19 Pay No Heed C .12 .25
20 Righteousness U .12 .25
21 Stand Firm C .12 .25
22 Magma Jet U .30 .75
23 Ordeal of Purphoros U .12 .25
24 Bonds of Faith C .12 .25
25 Moment of Heroism C .12 .25
26 Undying Rage U .12 .25
27 Battle Mastery U .12 .25
28 Griffin Guide U .12 .25
29 Smite the Monstrous C .12 .25
30 Miraculous Recovery U .12 .25
31 Winds of Rath R .50 1.00
32 Pyrokinesis U .20 .40
33 Boros Guildgate C .12 .25
34 New Benalia U .12 .25
35 Mountain L .12 .25
36 Mountain L .12 .25
37 Mountain L .12 .25
38 Mountain L .12 .25
39 Plains L .12 .25
40 Plains L .12 .25
41 Plains L .12 .25
42 Plains L .12 .25
43 Polukranos, World Eater M .75 1.50
44 Orcish Lumberjack C .12 .25
45 Deadly Recluse C .12 .25
46 Kavu Predator U .25 .50
47 Satyr Hedonist C .12 .25
48 Zhur-Taa Druid C .12 .25
49 Blood Ogre C .12 .25
50 Troll Ascetic R .30 .60
51 Crowned Ceratok U .12 .25
52 Gorehorn Minotaurs C .12 .25
53 Ghor Clan Savage C .12 .25
54 Deus of Calamity R .60 1.25
55 Conquering Manticore R .12 .25
56 Crater Hellion R .12 .25
57 Skarrgan Firebird R .12 .25
58 Valley Rannet C .12 .25
59 Krosan Tusker C .12 .25
60 Skarrgan Skybreaker U .12 .25
61 Shower of Sparks C .12 .25
62 Prey Upon C .12 .25
63 Pyroclasm U .30 .60
64 Regrowth U 1.50 3.00
65 Terrifying Presence C .12 .25
66 Destructive Revelry U .25 .50
67 Dragon Blood U .12 .25
68 Volt Charge C .12 .25
69 Beast Within U 2.00 4.00
70 Fires of Yavimaya U .12 .25
71 Kazandu Refuge U .12 .25
72 Llanowar Reborn U .25 .50
73 Skarrg, the Rage Pits U .12 .25
74 Mountain L .12 .25
75 Mountain L .12 .25
76 Mountain L .12 .25
77 Mountain L .12 .25
78 Forest L .12 .25
79 Forest L .12 .25
80 Forest L .12 .25
81 Forest L .12 .25

2013 Magic The Gathering Duel Decks Heroes vs. Monsters Tokens

1 Griffin .10 .20
2 Beast .12 .25

2013 Magic The Gathering Duel Decks Sorin vs. Tibalt

1 Sorin, Lord of Innistrad M 4.00 8.00
2 Doomed Traveler C .10 .20
3 Vampire Lacerator C .10 .20
4 Wall of Omens U 2.00 3.50
5 Child of Night C .10 .20
6 Duskhunter Bat C .10 .20
7 Mesmeric Fiend C .10 .20
8 Gatekeeper of Malakir U 1.00 1.75
9 Twilight Drover R .50 1.00
10 Bloodrage Vampire C .10 .20
11 Fiend Hunter U .10 .20
12 Vampire Nighthawk U .50 1.00
13 Mausoleum Guard U .10 .20
14 Phantom General U .10 .20
15 Vampire Outcasts U .10 .20
16 Revenant Patriarch U .10 .20
17 Sengir Vampire U .10 .20
18 Butcher of Malakir R .20 .40
19 Vampire's Bite C .10 .20
20 Decompose U .10 .20
21 Sorin's Thirst C .10 .20
22 Urge to Feed U .10 .20
23 Zealous Persecution U .25 .50
24 Lingering Souls U .50 1.00
25 Mortify U .30 .75
26 Spectral Procession U .20 .40
27 Unmake C .50 1.00
28 Ancient Craving R .20 .40
29 Mark of the Vampire C .10 .20
30 Field of Souls R .10 .20
31 Absorb Vis C .10 .20
32 Death Grasp R .10 .20
33 Evolving Wilds C .10 .20
34 Tainted Field U .25 .50
35 Swamp L .10 .20
36 Swamp L .10 .20
37 Swamp L .10 .20
38 Plains L .10 .20
39 Plains L .10 .20
40 Plains L .10 .20
41 Tibalt, the Fiend-Blooded M 2.00 4.00
42 Goblin Arsonist C .10 .20
43 Scorched Rusalka U .10 .20
44 Reassembling Skeleton U .10 .20
45 Ashmouth Hound C .10 .20
46 Hellspark Elemental U .60 1.25
47 Vithian Stinger C .10 .20
48 Shambling Remains U .10 .20
49 Coal Stoker C .10 .20
50 Lavaborn Muse R .10 .20
51 Mad Prophet C .10 .20
52 Hellrider R .30 .60
53 Skirsdag Cultist U .10 .20
54 Corpse Connoisseur U .10 .20
55 Scourge Devil U .10 .20
56 Gang of Devils U .10 .20
57 Bump in the Night C .10 .20
58 Blazing Salvo C .10 .20
59 Faithless Looting C .25 .50
60 Flame Slash C .25 .50
61 Geistflame C .10 .20
62 Pyroclasm U .25 .50

63 Recoup U	.10	.20
64 Terminate C	1.50	2.75
65 Strangling Soot C	.10	.20
66 Browbeat U	.60	1.25
67 Breaking Point R	.30	.60
68 Sulfuric Vortex R	.30	.75
69 Blightning C	.30	.75
70 Flame Javelin U	.10	.20
71 Torrent of Souls U	.10	.20
72 Devil's Play R	.10	.20
73 Akoum Refuge U	.10	.20
74 Rakdos Carnarium C	.10	.20
75 Mountain L	.10	.20
76 Mountain L	.10	.20
77 Mountain L	.10	.20
78 Swamp L	.10	.20
79 Swamp L	.10	.20
80 Swamp L	.10	.20

2013 Magic The Gathering Duel Decks Sorin vs. Tibalt Token

1 Spirit	.07	.15

2013 Magic The Gathering From the Vault Twenty

1 Dark Ritual M	1.50	3.00
2 Swords to Plowshares M	2.00	4.00
3 Hymn to Tourach M	1.00	2.00
4 Fyndhorn Elves M	12.50	25.00
5 Impulse M	1.00	2.00
6 Wall of Blossoms M	.60	1.25
7 Thran Dynamo M	3.00	6.00
8 Tangle Wire M	3.00	6.00
9 Fact or Fiction M	1.00	2.00
10 Chainer's Edict M	1.00	2.00
11 Akroma's Vengeance M	.50	1.00
12 Gilded Lotus M	5.00	10.00
13 Ink-Eyes, Servant of Oni M	7.50	15.00
14 Char M	.25	.50
15 Venser, Shaper Savant M	5.00	10.00
16 Chameleon Colossus M	1.50	3.00
17 Cruel Ultimatum M	.50	1.00
18 Jace, the Mind Sculptor M	50.00	100.00
19 Green Sun's Zenith M	7.50	15.00
20 Kessig Wolf Run M	2.00	4.00

2013 Magic The Gathering Gatecrash

1 Aerial Maneuver C	.07	.15
2 Angelic Edict C	.07	.15
3 Angelic Skirmisher R	.75	1.50
4 Assault Griffin C	.07	.15
5 Basilica Guards C	.07	.15
6 Blind Obedience R	4.00	8.00
7 Boros Elite U	.10	.20
8 Court Street Denizen C	.07	.15
9 Daring Skyjek C	.07	.15
10 Debtor's Pulpit U	.10	.20
11 Dutiful Thrull C	.07	.15
12 Frontline Medic R	.15	.30
13 Gideon, Champion of Justice M	1.00	2.00
14 Guardian of the Gateless U	.20	.40
15 Guildscorn Ward C	.07	.15
16 Hold the Gates U	.10	.20
17 Holy Mantle U	.10	.20
18 Knight of Obligation U	.10	.20
19 Knight Watch C	.07	.15
20 Luminate Primordial R	.15	.30
21 Murder Investigation U	.10	.20
22 Nav Squad Commandos C	.07	.15
23 Righteous Charge U	.10	.20
24 Shielded Passage C	.07	.15
25 Smite C	.07	.15
26 Syndic of Tithes C	.07	.15
27 Urbis Protector U	.10	.20
28 Zarichi Tiger C	.07	.15
29 Aetherize U	.50	1.00
30 Agoraphobia U	.10	.20
31 Clinging Anemones C	.07	.15
32 Cloudfin Raptor C	.07	.15
33 Diluvian Primordial R	.30	.75
34 Enter the Infinite M	3.00	6.00
35 Frilled Oculus C	.07	.15
36 Gridlock U	.10	.20
37 Hands of Binding C	.07	.15
38 Incursion Specialist U	.10	.20
39 Keymaster Rogue C	.07	.15
40 Last Thoughts C	.07	.15
41 Leyline Phantom C	.07	.15
42 Metropolis Sprite C	.07	.15
43 Mindeye Drake U	.10	.20
44 Rapid Hybridization U	1.25	2.50
45 Realmwright R	.20	.40
46 Sage's Row Denizen C	.07	.15
47 Sapphire Drake U	.10	.20
48 Scatter Arc C	.07	.15
49 Simic Fluxmage U	.10	.20
50 Simic Manipulator R	.15	.30
51 Skygames C	.07	.15
52 Spell Rupture C	.07	.15
53 Stolen Identity R	.25	.50
54 Totally Lost C	.07	.15
55 Voidwalk U	.20	.40
56 Way of the Thief C	.07	.15
57 Balustrade Spy C	.07	.15
58 Basilica Screecher C	.07	.15
59 Contaminated Ground C	.07	.15
60 Corpse Blockade C	.07	.15
61 Crypt Ghast R	6.00	12.00
62 Death's Approach C	.07	.15
63 Devour Flesh C	.07	.15
64 Dying Wish U	.10	.20
65 Gateway Shade U	.10	.20
66 Grisly Spectacle C	.07	.15
67 Gutter Skulk C	.07	.15
68 Horror of the Dim C	.07	.15
69 Illness in the Ranks U	.10	.20
70 Killing Glare U	.10	.20
71 Lord of the Void M	7.50	15.00
72 Mental Vapors U	.10	.20
73 Midnight Recovery C	.07	.15
74 Ogre Slumlord R	.30	.75
75 Sepulchral Primordial R	.50	1.00
76 Shadow Alley Denizen C	.07	.15
77 Shadow Slice C	.07	.15
78 Slate Street Ruffian C	.07	.15
79 Smog Elemental U	.10	.20
80 Syndicate Enforcer C	.07	.15
81 Thrull Parasite U	.30	.60
82 Undercity Informer U	.25	.50
83 Undercity Plague R	.15	.30
84 Wight of Precinct Six U	.10	.20
85 Act of Treason C	.07	.15
86 Bomber Corps C	.07	.15
87 Cinder Elemental U	.10	.20
88 Crackling Perimeter U	.10	.20
89 Ember Beast C	.07	.15
90 Firefist Striker U	.10	.20
91 Five-Alarm Fire R	.15	.30
92 Foundry Street Denizen C	.07	.15
93 Furious Resistance C	.07	.15
94 Hellkite Tyrant M	5.00	10.00
95 Hellraiser Goblin U	.10	.20
96 Homing Lightning U	.10	.20
97 Legion Loyalist R	6.00	12.00
98 Madcap Skills C	.07	.15
99 Mark for Death U	.10	.20
100 Massive Raid C	.07	.15
101 Molten Primordial R	.30	.75
102 Mugging C	.07	.15
103 Ripscale Predator U	.10	.20
104 Scorchwalker C	.07	.15
105 Skinbrand Goblin C	.07	.15
106 Skullcrack U	2.00	4.00
107 Structural Collapse C	.07	.15
108 Tin Street Market C	.07	.15
109 Towering Thunderfist C	.07	.15
110 Viashino Shanktail U	.10	.20
111 Warmind Infantry C	.07	.15
112 Wrecking Ogre R	.15	.30
113 Adaptive Snapjaw C	.07	.15
114 Alpha Authority U	.75	1.50
115 Burst of Strength C	.07	.15
116 Crocanura C	.07	.15
117 Crowned Ceratok U	.10	.20
118 Disciple of the Old Ways C	.07	.15
119 Experiment One U	.30	.60
120 Forced Adaptation C	.07	.15
121 Giant Adephage M	.75	1.50
122 Greenside Watcher C	.07	.15
123 Gyre Sage R	3.00	6.00
124 Hindervines U	.10	.20
125 Ivy Lane Denizen C	.07	.15
126 Miming Slime U	.10	.20
127 Naturalize C	.07	.15
128 Ooze Flux R	.15	.30
129 Predator's Rapport C	.07	.15
130 Rust Scarab U	.10	.20
131 Scab-Clan Charger C	.07	.15
132 Serene Remembrance U	.10	.20
133 Skarrg Goliath R	.15	.30
134 Slaughterhorn C	.07	.15
135 Spire Tracer C	.07	.15
136 Sylvan Primordial R	.15	.30
137 Tower Defense U	.15	.30
138 Verdant Haven C	.07	.15
139 Wasteland Viper U	.20	.40
140 Wildwood Rebirth C	.07	.15
141 Alms Beast R	.15	.30
142 Assemble the Legion R	2.00	4.00
143 Aurelia, the Warleader M	12.50	25.00
144 Aurelia's Fury M	.75	1.50
145 Bane Alley Broker U	.10	.20
146 Biovisionary R	.60	1.25
147 Borborygmos Enraged M	.75	1.50
148 Boros Charm U	1.25	2.50
149 Call of the Nightwing U	.10	.20
150 Cartel Aristocrat U	.10	.20
151 Clan Defiance R	.15	.30
152 Consuming Aberration R	.30	.75
153 Deathpact Angel M	.60	1.25
154 Dimir Charm U	.10	.20
155 Dinrova Horror U	.10	.20
156 Domri Rade M	1.50	3.00
157 Drakewing Krasis C	.07	.15
158 Duskmantle Guildmage U	.60	1.25
159 Duskmantle Seer M	.30	.60
160 Elusive Krasis U	.10	.20
161 Executioner's Swing C	.07	.15
162 Fathom Mage R	.20	.40
163 Firemane Avenger R	.15	.30
164 Fortress Cyclops U	.10	.20
165 Foundry Champion R	.15	.30
166 Frenzied Tilling U	.10	.20
167 Ghor-Clan Rampager U	.10	.20
168 Ground Assault U	.10	.20
169 Gruul Charm U	.10	.20
170 Gruul Ragebeast R	.20	.40
171 High Priest of Penance R	.15	.30
172 Hydroform C	.07	.15
173 Kingpin's Pet C	.07	.15
174 Lazav, Dimir Mastermind M	.60	1.25
175 Martial Glory C	.07	.15
176 Master Biomancer M	2.50	5.00
177 Merciless Eviction R	2.00	4.00
178 Mind Grind R	2.50	5.00
179 Mortus Strider C	.07	.15
180 Mystic Genesis R	.15	.30
181 Nimbus Swimmer U	.10	.20
182 Obzedat, Ghost Council M	1.00	2.00
183 One Thousand Lashes U	.10	.20
184 Ordruun Veteran U	.10	.20
185 Orzhov Charm U	.10	.20
186 Paranoid Delusions C	.07	.15
187 Primal Visitation C	.07	.15
188 Prime Speaker Zegana M	4.00	8.00
189 Psychic Strike C	.07	.15
190 Purge the Profane C	.07	.15
191 Rubblehulk R	.15	.30
192 Ruination Wurm C	.07	.15
193 Shambleshark C	.07	.15
194 Signal the Clans R	.25	.50
195 Simic Charm U	.10	.20
196 Skarrg Guildmage U	.10	.20
197 Skyknight Legionnaire C	.07	.15
198 Soul Ransom R	.15	.30
199 Spark Trooper R	.15	.30
200 Sunhome Guildmage U	.10	.20
201 Treasury Thrull R	.15	.30
202 Truefire Paladin U	.10	.20
203 Unexpected Results R	.30	.60
204 Urban Evolution U	.10	.20
205 Vizkopa Confessor U	.10	.20
206 Vizkopa Guildmage U	.20	.40
207 Whispering Madness R	.30	.75
208 Wojek Halberdiers C	.07	.15
209 Zameck Guildmage U	.10	.20
210 Zhur-Taa Swine C	.07	.15
211 Arrows of Justice U	.10	.20
212 Beckon Apparition C	.07	.15
213 Biomass Mutation R	.15	.30
214 Bioshift C	.07	.15
215 Boros Reckoner R	.50	1.00
216 Burning-Tree Emissary U	.25	.50
217 Coerced Confession U	.10	.20
218 Deathcult Rogue C	.07	.15
219 Gift of Orzhova U	.10	.20
220 Immortal Servitude R	.25	.50
221 Merfolk of the Depths U	.10	.20
222 Nightveil Specter R	.50	1.00
223 Pit Fight C	.07	.15
224 Rubblebelt Raiders R	.15	.30
225 Shattering Blow C	.07	.15
226 Armored Transport C	.07	.15
227 Boros Keyrune U	.10	.20
228 Dimir Keyrune U	.10	.20
229 Glaring Spotlight R	.50	1.00
230 Gruul Keyrune U	.10	.20
231 Illusionist's Bracers R	6.00	12.00
232 Millennial Gargoyle C	.07	.15
233 Orzhov Keyrune U	.10	.20
234 Prophetic Prism C	.07	.15
235 Razortip Whip C	.07	.15
236 Riot Gear C	.07	.15
237 Simic Keyrune U	.10	.20
238 Skyblinder Staff C	.07	.15
239 Boros Guildgate C	.07	.15
240 Breeding Pool R	17.50	35.00
241 Dimir Guildgate C	.07	.15
242 Godless Shrine R	7.50	15.00
243 Gruul Guildgate C	.07	.15
244 Orzhov Guildgate C	.07	.15
245 Sacred Foundry R	12.50	25.00
246 Simic Guildgate C	.07	.15
247 Stomping Ground R	7.50	15.00
248 Thespian's Stage R	.15	.30
249 Watery Grave R	7.50	15.00

2013 Magic The Gathering Gatecrash Tokens

1 Angel	.15	.30
2 Rat	.75	1.50
3 Frog Lizard	.10	.20
4 Cleric	.15	.30
5 Horror	.07	.15
6 Soldier	.07	.15
7 Spirit	.07	.15
8 Domri Rade Emblem	.25	.50

2013 Magic The Gathering Judge Gift Rewards

1 Swords to Plowshares R	25.00	50.00
2 Bribery R	20.00	40.00
3 Imperial Recruiter R	30.00	60.00
4 Crucible of Worlds R	30.00	75.00
5 Genesis R	3.00	6.00
6 Overwhelming Forces R	12.50	25.00
7 Vindicate R	7.50	15.00
8 Show and Tell R	15.00	30.00
9 Golem C	1.00	2.00

2013 Magic The Gathering League Tokens

1 Soldier	1.25	2.50
2 Bird	.60	1.25
3 Sliver	3.00	6.00
4 Soldier	4.00	8.00

2013 Magic The Gathering Magic 2014

1 Ajani, Caller of the Pride M	3.00	6.00
2 Ajani's Chosen R	.25	.50
3 Angelic Accord U	.10	.20
4 Angelic Wall C	.07	.15
5 Archangel of Thune M	12.50	25.00
6 Auramancer C	.07	.15
7 Banisher Priest U	.10	.20
8 Blessing U	.10	.20
9 Bonescythe Sliver R	5.00	10.00
10 Brave the Elements U	.15	.30
11 Capashen Knight C	.07	.15
12 Celestial Flare C	.07	.15
13 Charging Griffin C	.07	.15
14 Congregate U	.10	.20
15 Dawnstrike Paladin C	.07	.15
16 Devout Invocation M	1.25	2.50
17 Divine Favor C	.07	.15
18 Fiendslayer Paladin R	1.00	2.00
19 Fortify C	.07	.15
20 Griffin Sentinel C	.07	.15
21 Hive Stirrings C	.07	.15
22 Imposing Sovereign R	.15	.30
23 Indestructibility R	.75	1.50
24 Master of Diversion C	.07	.15
25 Pacifism C	.07	.15
26 Path of Bravery R	.15	.30
27 Pay No Heed C	.07	.15
28 Pillarfield Ox C	.07	.15
29 Planar Cleansing R	.15	.30
30 Sentinel Sliver C	.75	1.50
31 Seraph of the Sword R	.50	1.00
32 Serra Angel U	.10	.20
33 Show of Valor C	.07	.15
34 Siege Mastodon C	.07	.15
35 Silence R	2.50	5.00
36 Solemn Offering C	.07	.15
37 Soulmender C	.07	.15
38 Steelform Sliver U	.10	.20
39 Stonehorn Chanter U	.10	.20
40 Suntail Hawk C	.07	.15
41 Wall of Swords U	.10	.20
42 Air Servant U	.10	.20
43 Archaeomancer C	.07	.15
44 Armored Cancrix C	.07	.15
45 Cancel C	.07	.15
46 Claustrophobia C	.07	.15
47 Clone R	.25	.50
48 Colossal Whale R	.15	.30
49 Coral Merfolk C	.07	.15
50 Dismiss into Dream R	.50	1.00
51 Disperse C	.07	.15
52 Divination C	.07	.15
53 Domestication R	.15	.30
54 Elite Arcanist R	.25	.50
55 Essence Scatter C	.07	.15
56 Frost Breath C	.07	.15
57 Galerider Sliver R	6.00	12.00
58 Glimpse the Future U	.10	.20
59 Illusionary Armor U	.10	.20
60 Jace, Memory Adept M	5.00	10.00
61 Jace's Mindseeker R	.20	.40
62 Merfolk Spy C	.07	.15
63 Messenger Drake C	.07	.15
64 Negate C	.07	.15
65 Nephalia Seakite C	.07	.15
66 Opportunity U	.10	.20
67 Phantom Warrior U	.10	.20
68 Quicken R	.30	.75
69 Scroll Thief C	.07	.15
70 Seacoast Drake C	.07	.15
71 Sensory Deprivation C	.07	.15
72 Spell Blast U	.10	.20
73 Tidebinder Mage R	.25	.50
74 Time Ebb C	.07	.15
75 Tome Scour C	.07	.15
76 Trained Condor C	.07	.15
77 Traumatize R	2.00	4.00
78 Wall of Frost U	.10	.20
79 Warden of Evos Isle U	.10	.20
80 Water Servant U	.10	.20
81 Windreader Sphinx M	.30	.60
82 Zephyr Charge C	.07	.15
83 Accursed Spirit C	.07	.15
84 Altar's Reap C	.07	.15
85 Artificer's Hex U	.10	.20
86 Blightcaster U	.10	.20
87 Blood Bairn C	.07	.15
88 Bogbrew Witch R	.15	.30
89 Child of Night C	.07	.15
90 Corpse Hauler C	.07	.15
91 Corrupt U	.10	.20
92 Dark Favor C	.07	.15
93 Dark Prophecy R	2.00	4.00
94 Deathgaze Cockatrice C	.07	.15
95 Diabolic Tutor U	.75	1.50
96 Doom Blade U	.10	.20
97 Duress C	.07	.15
98 Festering Newt C	.07	.15
99 Gnawing Zombie U	.10	.20
100 Grim Return R	.30	.60
101 Lifebane Zombie R	.20	.40
102 Liliana of the Dark Realms M	12.50	25.00
103 Liliana's Reaver R	.75	1.50
104 Liturgy of Blood C	.07	.15
105 Mark of the Vampire C	.07	.15
106 Mind Rot C	.07	.15
107 Minotaur Abomination C	.07	.15
108 Nightmare R	.15	.30
109 Nightwing Shade C	.07	.15
110 Quag Sickness C	.07	.15
111 Rise of the Dark Realms M	10.00	20.00
112 Sanguine Bond R	1.00	2.00
113 Sengir Vampire U	.10	.20
114 Shadowborn Apostle C	.07	.15
115 Shadowborn Demon M	.60	1.25
116 Shrivel C	.07	.15
117 Syphon Sliver R	6.00	12.00
118 Tenacious Dead U	.10	.20
119 Undead Minotaur C	.07	.15
120 Vampire Warlord U	.10	.20
121 Vile Rebirth C	.07	.15
122 Wring Flesh C	.07	.15
123 Xathrid Necromancer R	.15	.30
124 Academy Raider C	.07	.15
125 Act of Treason C	.07	.15
126 Awaken the Ancient R	.15	.30
127 Barrage of Expendables U	.10	.20
128 Battle Sliver U	.50	1.00
129 Blur Sliver C	.12	.25
130 Burning Earth R	.30	.75
131 Canyon Minotaur C	.07	.15
132 Chandra, Pyromaster M	.75	1.50
133 Chandra's Outrage C	.07	.15
134 Chandra's Phoenix R	.15	.30
135 Cyclops Tyrant C	.07	.15
136 Demolish C	.07	.15
137 Dragon Egg U	.10	.20
138 Dragon Hatchling C	.07	.15
139 Flames of the Firebrand U	.10	.20
140 Fleshpulper Giant U	.10	.20
141 Goblin Diplomats R	.15	.30
142 Goblin Shortcutter C	.07	.15
143 Lava Axe C	.07	.15
144 Lightning Talons C	.07	.15
145 Marauding Maulhorn C	.07	.15
146 Mindsparker R	.15	.30
147 Molten Birth U	.10	.20
148 Ogre Battledriver R	.30	.75
149 Pitchburn Devils C	.07	.15
150 Regathan Firecat C	.07	.15
151 Scourge of Valkas M	2.50	5.00
152 Seismic Stomp C	.07	.15
153 Shiv's Embrace U	.10	.20
154 Shivan Dragon R	.15	.30
155 Shock C	.07	.15
156 Smelt C	.07	.15
157 Striking Sliver C	.30	.60
158 Thorncaster Sliver R	1.50	3.00
159 Thunder Strike C	.07	.15
160 Volcanic Geyser U	.10	.20
161 Wild Guess C	.07	.15
162 Wild Ricochet R	.25	.50

163 Young Pyromancer U .30 .75
164 Advocate of the Beast C .07 .15
165 Bramblecrush U .10 .20
166 Briarpack Alpha U .10 .20
167 Brindle Boar C .07 .15
168 Deadly Recluse C .07 .15
169 Elvish Mystic C .30 .75
170 Enlarge U .10 .20
171 Fog C .07 .15
172 Garruk, Caller of Beasts M 7.50 15.00
173 Garruk's Horde R .15 .30
174 Giant Growth C .07 .15
175 Giant Spider C .07 .15
176 Gladecover Scout C .07 .15
177 Groundshaker Sliver C .07 .15
178 Howl of the Night Pack U .10 .20
179 Hunt the Weak C .07 .15
180 Into the Wilds R .50 1.00
181 Kalonian Hydra M 10.00 20.00
182 Kalonian Tusker U .10 .20
183 Lay of the Land C .07 .15
184 Manaweft Sliver U 1.50 3.00
185 Megantic Sliver R .75 1.50
186 Naturalize C .07 .15
187 Oath of the Ancient Wood R .15 .30
188 Plummet C .07 .15
189 Predatory Sliver C .30 .75
190 Primeval Bounty M 4.00 8.00
191 Ranger's Guile C .07 .15
192 Rootwalla C .07 .15
193 Rumbling Baloth C .07 .15
194 Savage Summoning R .50 1.00
195 Scavenging Ooze R .75 1.50
196 Sporemound C .07 .15
197 Trollhide C .07 .15
198 Vastwood Hydra R .30 .60
199 Verdant Haven C .07 .15
200 Voracious Wurm U .10 .20
201 Windstorm U .10 .20
202 Witchstalker R .25 .50
203 Woodborn Behemoth U .10 .20
204 Accorder's Shield U .10 .20
205 Bubbling Cauldron U .10 .20
206 Darksteel Forge M 10.00 20.00
207 Darksteel Ingot U .30 .75
208 Door of Destinies R 10.00 20.00
209 Elixir of Immortality U .50 1.00
210 Fireshrieker U .10 .20
211 Guardian of the Ages R .15 .30
212 Haunted Plate Mail R .15 .30
213 Millstone U .10 .20
214 Pyromancer's Gauntlet R .20 .40
215 Ratchet Bomb R .30 .60
216 Ring of Three Wishes M 2.50 5.00
217 Rod of Ruin U .10 .20
218 Sliver Construct C .07 .15
219 Staff of the Death Magus U .17 .35
220 Staff of the Flame Magus U .10 .20
221 Staff of the Mind Magus U .10 .20
222 Staff of the Sun Magus U .10 .20
223 Staff of the Wild Magus U .10 .20
224 Strionic Resonator R 3.00 6.00
225 Trading Post R .30 .75
226 Vial of Poison U .10 .20
227 Encroaching Wastes U .10 .20
228 Mutavault R 7.50 15.00
229 Shimmering Grotto U .10 .20
230 Plains L .10 .20
231 Plains L .10 .20
232 Plains L .10 .20
233 Plains L .10 .20
234 Island L .10 .20
235 Island L .10 .20
236 Island L .10 .20
237 Island L .10 .20
238 Swamp L .10 .20
239 Swamp L .10 .20
240 Swamp L .10 .20
241 Swamp L .10 .20
242 Mountain L .10 .20
243 Mountain L .10 .20
244 Mountain L .10 .20
245 Mountain L .10 .20
246 Forest L .10 .20
247 Forest L .10 .20
248 Forest L .10 .20
249 Forest L .10 .20

2013 Magic The Gathering Magic 2014 Tokens

1 Sliver .30 .75
2 Angel .20 .40
3 Cat .20 .40
4 Goat .12 .25
5 Zombie .07 .15
6 Dragon .10 .20
7 Elemental .30 .60
8 Elemental .50 1.00
9 Beast .10 .20
10 Saproling .07 .15
11 Wolf .10 .20
12 Liliana of the Dark Realms Emblem .25 .50
13 Garruk, Caller of Beasts Emblem .12 .25

2013 Magic The Gathering Magic 2014 SDCC Black Variant

1 Ajani, Caller of the Pride M 50.00 100.00
60 Jace, Memory Adept M 50.00 100.00
102 Liliana of the Dark Realms M 100.00 200.00
132 Chandra, Pyromaster M 60.00 125.00
172 Garruk, Caller of Beasts M 60.00 125.00

2013 Magic The Gathering Modern Masters

1 Adarkar Valkyrie R .30 .60
2 Amrou Scout C .07 .15
3 Amrou Seekers C .07 .15
4 Angel's Grace R .30 .60
5 Auriok Salvagers R .30 .60
6 Avian Changeling C .07 .15
7 Blinding Beam C .07 .15
8 Bound in Silence C .07 .15
9 Cenn's Enlistment C .07 .15
10 Cloudgoat Ranger U .15 .30
11 Court Homunculus C .07 .15
12 Dispeller's Capsule C .07 .15
13 Elspeth, Knight-Errant M 7.50 15.00
14 Ethersworn Canonist R .30 .60
15 Feudkiller's Verdict U .15 .30
16 Flickerwisp U .15 .30
17 Gleam of Resistance C .07 .15
18 Hillcomber Giant C .07 .15
19 Ivory Giant C .07 .15
20 Kataki, War's Wage R .30 .60
21 Kithkin Greatheart C .07 .15
22 Meadowboon U .15 .30
23 Otherworldly Journey C .07 .15
24 Pallid Mycoderm C .07 .15
25 Path to Exile U .15 .30
26 Reveillark R .30 .60
27 Saltfield Recluse C .07 .15
28 Sanctum Gargoyle C .07 .15
29 Sandsower U .15 .30
30 Stir the Pride U .15 .30
31 Stonehewer Giant R .30 .60
32 Terashi's Grasp U .15 .30
33 Test of Faith C .07 .15
34 Veteran Armorer C .07 .15
35 Yosei, the Morning Star M 2.50 5.00
36 Aethersnipe C .07 .15
37 Careful Consideration U .15 .30
38 Cryptic Command R .30 .60
39 Dampen Thought C .07 .15
40 Echoing Truth C .07 .15
41 Errant Ephemeron C .07 .15
42 Erratic Mutation C .07 .15
43 Esperzoa U .15 .30
44 Etherium Sculptor C .07 .15
45 Faerie Mechanist C .07 .15
46 Gifts Ungiven R .30 .60
47 Glen Elendra Archmage R .30 .60
48 Keiga, the Tide Star M 3.00 6.00
49 Kira, Great Glass-Spinner R .30 .60
50 Latchkey Faerie C .07 .15
51 Logic Knot C .07 .15
52 Meloku the Clouded Mirror R .30 .60
53 Mothdust Changeling C .07 .15
54 Mulldrifter U .15 .30
55 Narcomoeba U .15 .30
56 Pact of Negation R .30 .60
57 Peer Through Depths C .07 .15
58 Perilous Research C .07 .15
59 Pestermite C .07 .15
60 Petals of Insight C .07 .15
61 Reach Through Mists C .07 .15
62 Riftwing Cloudskate U .15 .30
63 Scion of Oona R .30 .60
64 Spell Snare U .15 .30
65 Spellstutter Sprite C .07 .15
66 Take Possession U .15 .30
67 Thirst for Knowledge U .15 .30
68 Traumatic Visions C .07 .15
69 Vedalken Dismisser C .07 .15
70 Vendilion Clique M 7.50 15.00
71 Absorb Vis C .07 .15
72 Auntie's Snitch U .15 .30
73 Blightspeaker C .07 .15
74 Bridge from Below R .30 .60
75 Dark Confidant M 20.00 40.00
76 Death Cloud R .30 .60
77 Death Denied C .07 .15
78 Death Rattle U .15 .30
79 Deepcavern Imp C .07 .15
80 Drag Down C .07 .15
81 Dreamspoiler Witches C .07 .15
82 Earwig Squad R .30 .60
83 Executioner's Capsule U .15 .30
84 Extirpate R .30 .60
85 Facevaulter C .07 .15
86 Faerie Macabre C .07 .15
87 Festering Goblin C .07 .15
88 Horobi's Whisper U .15 .30
89 Kokusho, the Evening Star M 12.50 25.00
90 Mad Auntie U .15 .30
91 Marsh Flitter U .15 .30
92 Peppersmoke C .07 .15
93 Phthisis U .15 .30
94 Rathi Trapper C .07 .15
95 Raven's Crime C .07 .15
96 Skeletal Vampire R .30 .60
97 Slaughter Pact R .30 .60
98 Stinkweed Imp C .07 .15
99 Street Wraith C .07 .15
100 Syphon Life C .07 .15
101 Thieving Sprite C .07 .15
102 Tombstalker R .30 .60
103 Warren Pilferers C .07 .15
104 Warren Weirding C .07 .15
105 Blind-Spot Giant C .07 .15
106 Blood Moon R .30 .60
107 Brute Force C .07 .15
108 Countryside Crusher R .30 .60
109 Crush Underfoot C .07 .15
110 Desperate Ritual U .15 .30
111 Dragonstorm R .30 .60
112 Empty the Warrens C .07 .15
113 Fiery Fall C .07 .15
114 Fury Charm C .07 .15
115 Glacial Ray C .07 .15
116 Grapeshot C .07 .15
117 Greater Gargadon R .30 .60
118 Grinning Ignus U .15 .30
119 Hammerheim Deadeye C .07 .15
120 Kiki-Jiki, Mirror Breaker M 10.00 20.00
121 Lava Spike C .07 .15
122 Mogg War Marshal C .07 .15
123 Molten Disaster R .30 .60
124 Pardic Dragon U .15 .30
125 Pyromancer's Swath R .30 .60
126 Rift Bolt C .07 .15
127 Rift Elemental C .07 .15
128 Ryusei, the Falling Star M .75 1.50
129 Shrapnel Blast U .15 .30
130 Squee, Goblin Nabob R .30 .60
131 Stingscourger C .07 .15
132 Stinkdrinker Daredevil C .07 .15
133 Sudden Shock U .15 .30
134 Tar Pitcher U .15 .30
135 Thundercloud Shaman U .15 .30
136 Thundering Giant C .07 .15
137 Torrent of Stone C .07 .15
138 Tribal Flames U .15 .30
139 War-Spike Changeling C .07 .15
140 Citanul Woodreaders C .07 .15
141 Doubling Season R .30 .60
142 Durkwood Baloth C .07 .15
143 Echoing Courage C .07 .15
144 Eternal Witness U .15 .30
145 Giant Dustwasp C .07 .15
146 Greater Mossdog C .07 .15
147 Hana Kami C .07 .15
148 Imperiosaur C .07 .15
149 Incremental Growth U .15 .30
150 Jugan, the Rising Star M .60 1.25
151 Kodama's Reach C .07 .15
152 Krosan Grip U .15 .30
153 Life from the Loam R .30 .60
154 Masked Admirers U .15 .30
155 Moldervine Cloak C .07 .15
156 Nantuko Shaman C .07 .15
157 Penumbra Spider C .07 .15
158 Reach of Branches U .15 .30
159 Riftsweeper U .15 .30
160 Rude Awakening R .30 .60
161 Search for Tomorrow C .07 .15
162 Sporesower Thallid U .15 .30
163 Sporoloth Ancient C .07 .15
164 Summoner's Pact R .30 .60
165 Sylvan Bounty C .07 .15
166 Tarmogoyf M 25.00 50.00
167 Thallid C .07 .15
168 Thallid Germinator C .07 .15
169 Thallid Shell-Dweller C .07 .15
170 Tooth and Nail R .30 .60
171 Tromp the Domains U .15 .30
172 Verdeloth the Ancient R .30 .60
173 Walker of the Grove C .07 .15
174 Woodfall Primus R .30 .60
175 Electrolyze U .15 .30
176 Grand Arbiter Augustin IV R .30 .60
177 Jhoira of the Ghitu R .30 .60
178 Knight of the Reliquary R .30 .60
179 Lightning Helix U .15 .30
180 Maelstrom Pulse R .30 .60
181 Mind Funeral U .15 .30
182 Progenitus M 7.50 15.00
183 Sarkhan Vol M 5.00 10.00
184 Tidehollow Sculler U .15 .30
185 Trygon Predator U .15 .30
186 Cold-Eyed Selkie R .30 .60
187 Demigod of Revenge R .30 .60
188 Divinity of Pride R .30 .60
189 Figure of Destiny R .30 .60
190 Kitchen Finks U .15 .30
191 Manamorphose U .15 .30
192 Murderous Redcap U .15 .30
193 Oona, Queen of the Fae R .30 .60
194 Plumeveil U .15 .30
195 Worm Harvest U .15 .30
196 Aether Spellbomb C .07 .15
197 Aether Vial R .30 .60
198 Arcbound Ravager R .30 .60
199 Arcbound Stinger C .07 .15
200 Arcbound Wanderer C .07 .15
201 Arcbound Worker C .07 .15
202 Bonesplitter C .07 .15
203 Chalice of the Void R .30 .60
204 Engineered Explosives R .30 .60
205 Epochrasite U .15 .30
206 Etched Oracle U .15 .30
207 Frogmite C .07 .15
208 Lotus Bloom R .30 .60
209 Myr Enforcer C .07 .15
210 Myr Retriever U .15 .30
211 Paradise Mantle U .15 .30
212 Pyrite Spellbomb C .07 .15
213 Relic of Progenitus U .15 .30
214 Runed Stalactite C .07 .15
215 Skyreach Manta C .07 .15
216 Sword of Fire and Ice M 30.00 60.00
217 Sword of Light and Shadow M 15.00 30.00
218 Vedalken Shackles M 6.00 12.00
219 Academy Ruins R .30 .60
220 Blinkmoth Nexus R .30 .60
221 City of Brass R .30 .60
222 Dakmor Salvage U .15 .30
223 Glimmervoid R .30 .60
224 Terramorphic Expanse C .07 .15
225 Vivid Crag U .15 .30
226 Vivid Creek U .15 .30
227 Vivid Grove U .15 .30
228 Vivid Marsh U .15 .30
229 Vivid Meadow U .15 .30

2013 Magic The Gathering Modern Masters Tokens

1 Giant Warrior .10 .20
2 Kithkin Soldier .07 .15
3 Soldier .50 1.00
4 Illusion 1.00 2.00
5 Bat .20 .40
6 Goblin Rogue .07 .15
7 Spider .15 .30
8 Zombie .30 .75
9 Dragon .50 1.00
10 Goblin .10 .20
11 Elemental .10 .20
12 Saproling .07 .15
13 Treefolk Shaman .25 .50
14 Faerie Rogue .75 1.50
15 Worm .25 .50
16 Elspeth, Knight-Errant Emblem 4.00 8.00

2013 Magic The Gathering Theros

1 Battlewise Valor C .07 .15
2 Cavalry Pegasus C .07 .15
3 Celestial Archon R .15 .30
4 Chained to the Rocks R .30 .60
5 Chosen by Heliod C .07 .15
6 Dauntless Onslaught U .10 .20
7 Decorated Griffin U .10 .20
8 Divine Verdict C .07 .15
9 Elspeth, Sun's Champion M 7.50 15.00
10 Ephara's Warden C .07 .15
11 Evangel of Heliod U .10 .20
12 Fabled Hero R .20 .40
13 Favored Hoplite U .10 .20
14 Gift of Immortality R 2.00 4.00
15 Glare of Heresy U .10 .20
16 Gods Willing C .07 .15
17 Heliod, God of the Sun M 5.00 10.00
18 Heliod's Emissary U .10 .20
19 Hopeful Eidolon C .07 .15
20 Hundred-Handed One R .15 .30
21 Lagonna-Band Elder C .07 .15
22 Last Breath C .07 .15
23 Leonin Snarecaster C .07 .15
24 Observant Alseid C .07 .15
25 Ordeal of Heliod U .10 .20
26 Phalanx Leader U .10 .20
27 Ray of Dissolution C .07 .15
28 Scholar of Athreos C .07 .15
29 Setessan Battle Priest C .07 .15
30 Setessan Griffin C .07 .15
31 Silent Artisan C .07 .15
32 Soldier of the Pantheon R .15 .30
33 Spear of Heliod R .60 1.25
34 Traveling Philosopher C .07 .15
35 Vanquish the Foul U .10 .20
36 Wingsteed Rider C .07 .15
37 Yoked Ox C .07 .15
38 Annul C .07 .15
39 Aqueous Form C .12 .25
40 Artisan of Forms R .15 .30
41 Benthic Giant C .07 .15
42 Bident of Thassa R 1.50 3.00
43 Breaching Hippocamp C .07 .15
44 Coastline Chimera C .07 .15
45 Crackling Triton C .07 .15
46 Curse of the Swine R .20 .40
47 Dissolve U .10 .20
48 Fate Foretold C .07 .15
49 Gainsay U .10 .20
50 Griptide C .07 .15
51 Horizon Scholar U .10 .20
52 Lost in a Labyrinth C .07 .15
53 Master of Waves M 3.00 6.00
54 Meletis Charlatan R .15 .30
55 Mnemonic Wall C .07 .15
56 Nimbus Naiad C .07 .15
57 Omenspeaker C .07 .15
58 Ordeal of Thassa U .10 .20
59 Prescient Chimera C .07 .15
60 Prognostic Sphinx R .15 .30
61 Sea God's Revenge U .10 .20
62 Sealock Monster U .10 .20
63 Shipbreaker Kraken R .15 .30
64 Stymied Hopes C .07 .15
65 Swan Song R 7.50 15.00
66 Thassa, God of the Sea M 7.50 15.00
67 Thassa's Bounty C .07 .15
68 Thassa's Emissary U .10 .20
69 Triton Fortune Hunter U .10 .20
70 Triton Shorethief C .07 .15
71 Triton Tactics U .10 .20
72 Vaporkin C .07 .15
73 Voyage's End C .07 .15
74 Wavecrash Triton C .07 .15
75 Abhorrent Overlord R .25 .50
76 Agent of the Fates R .15 .30
77 Asphodel Wanderer C .07 .15
78 Baleful Eidolon C .07 .15
79 Blood-Toll Harpy C .07 .15
80 Boon of Erebos C .07 .15
81 Cavern Lampad C .07 .15
82 Cutthroat Maneuver U .10 .20
83 Dark Betrayal U .10 .20
84 Disciple of Phenax C .07 .15
85 Erebos, God of the Dead M 7.50 15.00
86 Erebos's Emissary U .10 .20
87 Felhide Minotaur C .07 .15
88 Fleshmad Steed C .07 .15
89 Gray Merchant of Asphodel C .30 .60
90 Hero's Downfall R 1.50 3.00
91 Hythonia the Cruel M .50 1.00
92 Insatiable Harpy U .10 .20
93 Keepsake Gorgon U .10 .20
94 Lash of the Whip C .07 .15
95 Loathsome Catoblepas C .07 .15
96 March of the Returned C .07 .15
97 Mogis's Marauder U .10 .20
98 Nighthowler R .15 .30
99 Ordeal of Erebos U .10 .20
100 Pharika's Cure C .07 .15
101 Read the Bones C .07 .15
102 Rescue from the Underworld U .10 .20
103 Returned Centaur C .07 .15
104 Returned Phalanx C .07 .15
105 Scourgemark C .07 .15
106 Sip of Hemlock C .07 .15
107 Thoughtseize R 10.00 20.00
108 Tormented Hero U .10 .20
109 Viper's Kiss C .07 .15
110 Whip of Erebos R 4.00 8.00
111 Akroan Crusader C .07 .15
112 Anger of the Gods R .75 1.50
113 Arena Athlete U .10 .20
114 Borderland Minotaur C .07 .15
115 Boulderfall C .07 .15
116 Coordinated Assault U .10 .20
117 Deathbellow Raider C .07 .15
118 Demolish C .07 .15
119 Dragon Mantle C .07 .15
120 Ember Swallower R .15 .30
121 Fanatic of Mogis U .10 .20
122 Firedrinker Satyr R .15 .30
123 Flamespeaker Adept U .10 .20
124 Hammer of Purphoros R .75 1.50
125 Ill-Tempered Cyclops C .07 .15
126 Labyrinth Champion R .15 .30
127 Lightning Strike C .07 .15
128 Magma Jet U .10 .20
129 Messenger's Speed C .07 .15

130 Minotaur Skullcleaver C	.07	.15
131 Ordeal of Purphoros U	.10	.20
132 Peak Eruption U	.10	.20
133 Portent of Betrayal C	.07	.15
134 Priest of Iroas C	.07	.15
135 Purphoros, God of the Forge M	12.50	25.00
136 Purphoros's Emissary U	.10	.20
137 Rage of Purphoros C	.07	.15
138 Rageblood Shaman R	.15	.30
139 Satyr Rambler C	.07	.15
140 Spark Jolt C	.07	.15
141 Spearpoint Oread C	.07	.15
142 Stoneshock Giant U	.10	.20
143 Stormbreath Dragon M	2.00	4.00
144 Titan of Eternal Fire R	.15	.30
145 Titan's Strength C	.07	.15
146 Two-Headed Cerberus C	.07	.15
147 Wild Celebrants C	.07	.15
148 Agent of Horizons C	.07	.15
149 Anthousa, Setessan Hero R	.15	.30
150 Arbor Colossus R	.15	.30
151 Artisan's Sorrow U	.10	.20
152 Boon Satyr R	.15	.30
153 Bow of Nylea R	2.50	5.00
154 Centaur Battlemaster U	.10	.20
155 Commune with the Gods C	.15	.30
156 Defend the Hearth C	.07	.15
157 Fade into Antiquity C	.07	.15
158 Feral Invocation C	.07	.15
159 Hunt the Hunter U	.10	.20
160a Karametra's Acolyte U	.25	.50
161 Leafcrown Dryad C	.07	.15
162 Mistcutter Hydra R	.75	1.50
163 Nemesis of Mortals U	.10	.20
164 Nessian Asp C	.07	.15
165 Nessian Courser C	.07	.15
166 Nylea, God of the Hunt M	5.00	10.00
167 Nylea's Disciple C	.07	.15
168 Nylea's Emissary U	.10	.20
169 Nylea's Presence C	.07	.15
170 Ordeal of Nylea U	.10	.20
171 Pheres-Band Centaurs C	.07	.15
172 Polukranos, World Eater M	1.25	2.50
173 Reverent Hunter R	.15	.30
174 Satyr Hedonist C	.07	.15
175 Satyr Piper U	.10	.20
176 Savage Surge C	.07	.15
177 Sedge Scorpion C	.07	.15
178 Shredding Winds C	.07	.15
179 Staunch-Hearted Warrior C	.07	.15
180 Sylvan Caryatid R	3.00	6.00
181 Time to Feed C	.07	.15
182 Voyaging Satyr C	.07	.15
183 Vulpine Goliath C	.07	.15
184 Warriors' Lesson U	.10	.20
185 Akroan Hoplite U	.10	.20
186 Anax and Cymede R	.15	.30
187 Ashen Rider M	1.50	3.00
188 Ashiok, Nightmare Weaver M	3.00	6.00
189 Battlewise Hoplite U	.10	.20
190 Chronicler of Heroes U	.10	.20
191 Daxos of Meletis R	.15	.30
192 Destructive Revelry U	.10	.20
193 Fleecemane Lion R	.50	1.00
194 Horizon Chimera U	.10	.20
195 Kragma Warcaller U	.10	.20
196 Medomai the Ageless M	1.25	2.50
197 Pharika's Mender U	.10	.20
198 Polis Crusher R	.15	.30
199 Prophet of Kruphix R	.15	.30
200 Psychic Intrusion R	.15	.30
201 Reaper of the Wilds R	.15	.30
202 Sentry of the Underworld U	.10	.20
203 Shipwreck Singer U	.10	.20
204 Spellheart Chimera U	.10	.20
205 Steam Augury R	.15	.30
206 Triad of Fates R	.15	.30
207 Tymaret, the Murder King R	.15	.30
208 Underworld Cerberus M	.30	.75
209 Xenagos, the Reveler M	3.00	6.00
210 Akroan Horse R	.15	.30
211 Anvilwrought Raptor U	.10	.20
212 Bronze Sable C	.07	.15
213 Burnished Hart U	.20	.40
214 Colossus of Akros R	.75	1.50
215 Flamecast Wheel U	.10	.20
216 Fleetfeather Sandals C	.07	.15
217 Guardians of Meletis C	.07	.15
218 Opaline Unicorn C	.07	.15
219 Prowler's Helm U	.75	1.50
220 Pyxis of Pandemonium R	.20	.40
221 Traveler's Amulet C	.07	.15
222 Witches' Eye U	.10	.20
223 Nykthos, Shrine to Nyx R	17.50	35.00
224 Temple of Abandon R	.75	1.50
225 Temple of Deceit R	.75	1.50
226 Temple of Mystery R	.25	.50
227 Temple of Silence R	.50	1.00
228 Temple of Triumph R	.25	.50
229 Unknown Shores C	.07	.15
230 Plains L	.10	.20
231 Plains L	.10	.20
232 Plains L	.10	.20
233 Plains L	.10	.20
234 Island L	.10	.20
235 Island L	.10	.20
236 Island L	.10	.20
237 Island L	.10	.20
238 Swamp L	.10	.20
239 Swamp L	.10	.20
240 Swamp L	.10	.20
241 Swamp L	.10	.20
242 Mountain L	.10	.20
243 Mountain L	.10	.20
244 Mountain L	.10	.20
245 Mountain L	.10	.20
246 Forest L	.10	.20
247 Forest L	.10	.20
248 Forest L	.10	.20
249 Forest L	.10	.20

2013 Magic The Gathering Theros Tokens

1 Cleric	1.50	3.00
2 Soldier	.07	.15
3 Soldier	.07	.15
4 Bird	.20	.40
5 Elemental	.25	.50
6 Harpy	.07	.15
7 Soldier	.07	.15
8 Boar	.20	.40
9 Satyr	.12	.25
10 Golem	.07	.15
11 Elspeth, Sun's Champion Emblem	1.50	3.00

2014 Magic The Gathering Born of the Gods

1 Acolyte's Reward U	.10	.20
2 Akroan Phalanx U	.10	.20
3 Akroan Skyguard C	.07	.15
4 Archetype of Courage U	.75	1.50
5 Brimaz, King of Oreskos M	7.50	15.00
6 Dawn to Dusk U	.10	.20
7 Eidolon of Countless Battles R	.75	1.50
8 Elite Skirmisher C	.07	.15
9 Ephara's Radiance C	.07	.15
10 Excoriate C	.07	.15
11 Fated Retribution R	.15	.30
12 Ghostblade Eidolon U	.10	.20
13 Glimpse the Sun God U	.10	.20
14 God-Favored General U	.10	.20
15 Great Hart C	.07	.15
16 Griffin Dreamfinder C	.07	.15
17 Hero of Iroas R	.20	.40
18 Hold at Bay C	.07	.15
19 Loyal Pegasus C	.07	.15
20 Mortal's Ardor C	.07	.15
21 Nyxborn Shieldmate C	.07	.15
22 Oreskos Sun Guide C	.07	.15
23 Ornitharch U	.10	.20
24 Plea for Guidance R	.30	.75
25 Revoke Existence C	.07	.15
26 Silent Sentinel R	.15	.30
27 Spirit of the Labyrinth R	1.50	3.00
28 Sunbond U	.40	.80
29 Vanguard of Brimaz U	.10	.20
30 Aerie Worshippers U	.10	.20
31 Arbiter of the Ideal R	.15	.30
32 Archetype of Imagination U	.75	1.50
33 Chorus of the Tides C	.07	.15
34 Crypsis C	.07	.15
35 Deepwater Hypnotist C	.07	.15
36 Divination C	.07	.15
37 Eternity Snare U	.10	.20
38 Evanescent Intellect C	.07	.15
39 Fated Infatuation R	.25	.50
40 Flitterstep Eidolon U	.10	.20
41 Floodtide Serpent C	.07	.15
42 Kraken of the Straits U	.10	.20
43 Meletis Astronomer U	.10	.20
44 Mindreaver R	.15	.30
45 Nullify C	.07	.15
46 Nyxborn Triton C	.07	.15
47 Oracle's Insight U	.10	.20
48 Perplexing Chimera R	.75	1.50
49 Retraction Helix C	.07	.15
50 Siren of the Fanged Coast U	.10	.20
51 Sphinx's Disciple C	.07	.15
52 Stratus Walk C	.07	.15
53 Sudden Storm C	.07	.15
54 Thassa's Rebuff U	.10	.20
55 Tromokratis R	.15	.30
56 Vortex Elemental U	.10	.20
57 Whelming Wave R	.25	.50
58 Archetype of Finality U	.75	1.50
59 Ashiok's Adept U	.10	.20
60 Asphyxiate C	.07	.15
61 Bile Blight U	.25	.50
62 Black Oak of Odunos U	.10	.20
63 Champion of Stray Souls M	.30	.60
64 Claim of Erebos C	.07	.15
65 Drown in Sorrow U	.10	.20
66 Eater of Hope R	.15	.30
67 Eye Gouge C	.07	.15
68 Fate Unraveler R	.30	.75
69 Fated Return R	.15	.30
70 Felhide Brawler C	.07	.15
71 Forlorn Pseudamma U	.10	.20
72 Forsaken Drifters C	.07	.15
73 Gild R	.15	.30
74 Grisly Transformation C	.07	.15
75 Herald of Torment R	.15	.30
76 Marshmist Titan C	.07	.15
77 Necrobite C	.07	.15
78 Nyxborn Eidolon C	.07	.15
79 Odunos River Trawler U	.10	.20
80 Pain Seer R	.15	.30
81 Sanguimancy U	.10	.20
82 Servant of Tymaret C	.07	.15
83 Shrike Harpy U	.10	.20
84 Spiteful Returned U	.10	.20
85 Warchanter of Mogis C	.07	.15
86 Weight of the Underworld C	.07	.15
87 Akroan Conscriptor U	.10	.20
88 Archetype of Aggression U	.50	1.00
89 Bolt of Keranos C	.07	.15
90 Cyclops of One-Eyed Pass C	.07	.15
91 Epiphany Storm C	.07	.15
92 Everflame Eidolon U	.10	.20
93 Fall of the Hammer C	.07	.15
94 Fated Conflagration R	.15	.30
95 Fearsome Temper C	.07	.15
96 Felhide Spiritbinder R	.15	.30
97 Flame-Wreathed Phoenix M	.30	.60
98 Forgestoker Dragon R	.15	.30
99 Impetuous Sunchaser C	.07	.15
100 Kragma Butcher C	.07	.15
101 Lightning Volley U	.10	.20
102 Nyxborn Rollicker C	.07	.15
103 Oracle of Bones R	.15	.30
104 Pharagax Giant C	.07	.15
105 Pinnacle of Rage U	.10	.20
106 Reckless Reveler C	.07	.15
107 Rise to the Challenge C	.07	.15
108 Satyr Firedancer R	.25	.50
109 Satyr Nyx-Smith U	.10	.20
110 Scouring Sands C	.07	.15
111 Searing Blood U	.15	.30
112 Stormcaller of Keranos U	.10	.20
113 Thunder Brute U	.10	.20
114 Thunderous Might U	.10	.20
115 Whims of the Fates R	.15	.30
116 Archetype of Endurance U	1.00	2.00
117 Aspect of Hydra C	.07	.15
118 Charging Badger C	.07	.15
119 Courser of Kruphix R	2.50	5.00
120 Culling Mark C	.07	.15
121 Fated Intervention R	.15	.30
122 Graverobber Spider U	.10	.20
123 Hero of Leina Tower R	.15	.30
124 Hunter's Prowess R	.15	.30
125 Karametra's Favor C	.07	.15
126 Mischief and Mayhem U	.10	.20
127 Mortal's Resolve C	.07	.15
128 Nessian Demolok U	.10	.20
129 Nessian Wilds Ravager R	.15	.30
130 Noble Quarry U	.10	.20
131 Nyxborn Wolf C	.07	.15
132 Peregrination U	.10	.20
133 Pheres-Band Raiders U	.10	.20
134 Pheres-Band Tromper C	.07	.15
135 Raised by Wolves U	.20	.40
136 Satyr Wayfinder C	.07	.15
137 Scourge of Skola Vale R	.20	.40
138 Setessan Oathsworn C	.07	.15
139 Setessan Starbreaker C	.07	.15
140 Skyreaping U	.10	.20
141 Snake of the Golden Grove C	.07	.15
142 Swordwise Centaur C	.07	.15
143 Unravel the Aether U	.60	1.25
144 Chromanticore M	1.00	2.00
145 Ephara, God of the Polis M	4.00	8.00
146 Ephara's Enlightenment U	.10	.20
147 Fanatic of Xenagos U	.10	.20
148 Karametra, God of Harvests M	2.00	4.00
149 Kiora, the Crashing Wave M	1.50	3.00
150 Kiora's Follower U	.10	.20
151 Mogis, God of Slaughter M	7.50	15.00
152 Phenax, God of Deception M	6.00	12.00
153 Ragemonger U	.10	.20
154 Reap What Is Sown U	.10	.20
155 Siren of the Silent Song U	.17	.35
156 Xenagos, God of Revels M	7.50	15.00
157 Astral Cornucopia R	1.00	2.00
158 Gorgon's Head U	.50	1.00
159 Heroes' Podium R	.20	.40
160 Pillar of War U	.10	.20
161 Siren Song Lyre U	.10	.20
162 Springleaf Drum U	1.50	3.00
163 Temple of Enlightenment R	.50	1.00
164 Temple of Malice R	1.00	2.00
165 Temple of Plenty R	.75	1.50

2014 Magic The Gathering Born of the Gods Tokens

1 Bird	.07	.15
2 Cat Soldier	.75	1.50
3 Soldier	.07	.15
4 Bird	.07	.15
5 Kraken	.75	1.50
6 Zombie	.10	.20
7 Elemental	.07	.15
8 Centaur	.07	.15
9 Wolf	.10	.20
10 Gold	.15	.30
11 Kiora, the Crashing Wave Emblem	4.00	8.00

2014 Magic The Gathering Commander 2014

1 Angel of the Dire Hour R	.75	1.50
2 Angelic Field Marshal R	4.00	8.00
3 Benevolent Offering R	2.00	4.00
4 Comeuppance R	7.50	15.00
5 Containment Priest R	.30	.60
6 Deploy to the Front R	.75	1.50
7 Fell the Mighty R	2.50	5.00
8 Hallowed Spiritkeeper R	3.00	6.00
9 Jazal Goldmane M	2.00	4.00
10A Nahiri, the Lithomancer M	7.50	15.00
11 Aether Gale R	.30	.60
12 Breaching Leviathan R	4.00	8.00
13 Domineering Will R	1.00	2.00
14 Dulcet Sirens R	.60	1.25
15 Intellectual Offering R	1.50	3.00
16 Reef Worm R	1.50	3.00
17 Stitcher Geralf M	1.25	2.50
18 Stormsurge Kraken R	5.00	10.00
19A Teferi, Temporal Archmage M	2.50	5.00
20 Well of Ideas R	.75	1.50
21 Demon of Wailing Agonies R	1.50	3.00
22 Flesh Carver R	.75	1.50
23 Ghoulcaller Gisa M	5.00	10.00
24 Infernal Offering R	.25	.50
25 Malicious Affliction R	1.50	3.00
26 Necromantic Selection R	.20	.40
27A Ob Nixilis of the Black Oath M	5.00	10.00
28 Overseer of the Damned R	.50	1.00
29 Raving Dead R	1.25	2.50
30 Spoils of Blood R	.25	.50
31 Wake the Dead R	4.00	8.00
32 Bitter Feud R	.30	.75
33A Daretti, Scrap Savant M	1.25	2.50
34 Dualcaster Mage R	.20	.40
35 Feldon of the Third Path M	.60	1.25
36 Impact Resonance R	.60	1.25
37 Incite Rebellion R	.15	.30
38 Scrap Mastery R	3.00	6.00
39 Tyrant's Familiar R	1.25	2.50
40 Volcanic Offering R	1.50	3.00
41 Warmonger Hellkite R	.50	1.00
42 Creeperhulk R	.15	.30
43A Freyalise, Llanowar's Fury M	4.00	8.00
44 Grave Sifter R	.25	.50
45 Lifeblood Hydra C	7.50	15.00
46 Siege Behemoth R	1.25	2.50
47 Song of the Dryads R	7.50	15.00
48 Sylvan Offering R	2.50	5.00
49 Thunderfoot Baloth R	3.00	6.00
50 Titania, Protector of Argoth M	5.00	10.00
51 Wave of Vitriol R	.60	1.25
52 Wolfcaller's Howl C	.60	1.25
53 Assault Suit U	.30	.75
54 Commander's Sphere C	.10	.20
55 Crown of Doom R	2.50	5.00
56 Loreseeker's Stone U	.12	.25
57 Masterwork of Ingenuity R	2.00	4.00
58 Unstable Obelisk U	.12	.25
59 Arcane Lighthouse U	3.00	6.00
60 Flamekin Village R	2.00	4.00
61 Myriad Landscape U	.20	.40
62 Artisan of Kozilek U	.50	1.00
63 Adarkar Valkyrie R	.50	1.00
64 Afterlife U	.12	.25
65 Armistice R	.15	.30
66 Brave the Elements U	.20	.40
67 Cathars' Crusade R	3.00	6.00
68 Celestial Crusader U	.12	.25
69 Condemn U	.12	.25
70 Decree of Justice R	.15	.30
71 Flickerwisp U	.12	.25
72 Geist-Honored Monk R	.15	.30
73 Gift of Estates U	1.00	2.00
74 Grand Abolisher R	15.00	30.00
75 Kemba, Kha Regent R	.15	.30
76 Kor Sanctifiers C	.10	.20
77 Marshal's Anthem R	.15	.30
78 Martial Coup R	.50	1.00
79 Mentor of the Meek R	.75	1.50
80 Midnight Haunting U	.12	.25
81 Mobilization R	.30	.60
82 Nomads' Assembly R	.25	.50
83 Oblation R	.25	.50
84 Requiem Angel R	.50	1.00
85 Return to Dust U	.12	.25
86 Sacred Mesa R	.20	.40
87 Serra Avatar M	.50	1.00
88 Silverblade Paladin R	.50	1.00
89 Skyhunter Skirmisher U	.12	.25
90 Spectral Procession U	.25	.50
91 Sun Titan M	.50	1.00
92 Sunblast Angel R	.25	.50
93 True Conviction R	2.50	5.00
94 Twilight Shepherd R	.30	.75
95 White Sun's Zenith R	.25	.50
96 Whitemane Lion C	.10	.20
97 Wing Shards U	.12	.25
98 Azure Mage U	.12	.25
99 Brine Elemental U	.12	.25
100 Cackling Counterpart R	.75	1.50
101 Call to Mind U	.12	.25
102 Compulsive Research C	.10	.20
103 Concentrate U	.12	.25
104 Cyclonic Rift R	17.50	35.00
105 Deep-Sea Kraken R	.60	1.25
106 Dismiss U	.12	.25
107 Distorting Wake R	.25	.50
108 Exclude C	.10	.20
109 Fathom Seer C	.10	.20
110 Fog Bank U	.20	.40
111 Fool's Demise U	.20	.40
112 Frost Titan M	.50	1.00
113 Hoverguard Sweepers R	.15	.30
114 Infinite Reflection R	.15	.30
115 Into the Roil C	.10	.20
116 Ixidron R	.15	.30
117 Lorthos, the Tidemaker M	2.50	5.00
118 Mulldrifter C	.30	.60
119 Phyrexian Ingester R	.15	.30
120 Pongify U	2.00	4.00
121 Riptide Survivor U	.12	.25
122 Rite of Replication R	2.50	5.00
123 Rush of Knowledge C	.10	.20
124 Sea Gate Oracle C	.10	.20
125 Shaper Parasite C	.10	.20
126 Sphinx of Jwar Isle R	.15	.30
127 Sphinx of Magosi R	.15	.30
128 Sphinx of Uthuun R	.15	.30
129 Stroke of Genius R	3.00	6.00
130 Turn to Frog U	.12	.25
131 Willbender U	.12	.25
132 Abyssal Persecutor M	.60	1.25
133 AEther Snap R	.30	.75
134 Annihilate U	.12	.25
135 Bad Moon R	1.00	2.00
136 Black Sun's Zenith R	6.00	12.00
137 Bloodgift Demon R	1.25	2.50
138 Butcher of Malakir R	1.25	2.50
139 Crypt Ghast R	7.50	15.00
140 Disciple of Bolas R	.20	.40
141 Drana, Kalastria Bloodchief R	.30	.75
142 Dread Return U	.50	1.00
143 Dregs of Sorrow R	.15	.30
144 Evernight Shade U	.12	.25
145 Grave Titan M	7.50	15.00
146 Gray Merchant of Asphodel C	.30	.60
147 Liliana's Reaver R	.50	1.00
148 Magus of the Coffers R	4.00	8.00
149 Morkrut Banshee U	.12	.25
150 Mutilate R	1.25	2.50
151 Nantuko Shade R	.15	.30
152 Nekrataal U	.12	.25
153 Pestilence Demon R	.40	.80
154 Phyrexian Gargantua U	.12	.25
155 Pontiff of Blight R	.50	1.00
156 Profane Command R	.25	.50
157 Promise of Power R	.30	.75
158 Read the Bones C	.30	.60
159 Reaper from the Abyss M	2.00	4.00
160 Shriekmaw U	.25	.50
161 Sign in Blood C	.20	.40
162 Skeletal Scrying U	.20	.40
163 Skirsdag High Priest R	.25	.50
164 Sudden Spoiling R	2.00	4.00
165 Syphon Mind C	1.25	2.50
166 Tendrils of Corruption C	.10	.20
167 Tragic Slip C	.25	.50
168 Vampire Hexmage U	.20	.40
169 Victimize U	.75	1.50
170 Xathrid Demon M	.30	.75
171 Beetleback Chief U	.20	.40
172 Blasphemous Act R	1.50	3.00
173 Bogardan Hellkite M	.30	.60
174 Chaos Warp R	1.25	2.50
175 Faithless Looting C	.30	.60
176 Flametongue Kavu U	.12	.25

177 Goblin Welder R	6.00	12.00
178 Hoard-Smelter Dragon R	.15	.30
179 Ingot Chewer C	.10	.20
180 Magmaquake R	.15	.30
181 Spitebellows U	.12	.25
182 Starstorm R	.20	.40
183 Tuktuk the Explorer R	.15	.30
184 Whipflare U	.12	.25
185 Word of Seizing R	.15	.30
186 Beastmaster Ascension R	7.50	15.00
187 Collective Unconscious R	1.25	2.50
188 Desert Twister U	.12	.25
189 Drove of Elves U	.60	1.25
190 Elvish Archdruid R	1.00	2.00
191 Elvish Mystic C	.30	.75
192 Elvish Skysweeper C	.10	.20
193 Elvish Visionary C	.10	.20
194 Essence Warden C	4.00	8.00
195 Ezuri, Renegade Leader R	7.50	15.00
196 Farhaven Elf C	.20	.40
197 Fresh Meat R	.15	.30
198 Grim Flowering U	.12	.25
199 Harrow C	.25	.50
200 Hunting Triad U	.12	.25
201 Immaculate Magistrate R	.60	1.25
202 Imperious Perfect U	.30	.75
203 Joraga Warcaller R	7.50	15.00
204 Llanowar Elves C	.20	.40
205 Lys Alana Huntmaster C	.25	.50
206 Masked Admirers R	.15	.30
207 Overrun U	.20	.40
208 Overwhelming Stampede R	2.50	5.00
209 Praetor's Counsel M	2.50	5.00
210 Priest of Titania C	6.00	12.00
211 Primordial Sage R	.75	1.50
212 Rampaging Baloths M	.30	.75
213 Reclamation Sage U	.12	.25
214 Silklash Spider R	.20	.40
215 Soul of the Harvest R	.75	1.50
216 Sylvan Ranger C	.10	.20
217 Sylvan Safekeeper R	7.50	15.00
218 Terastodon R	.20	.40
219 Thornweald Archer C	.10	.20
220 Timberwatch Elf C	.20	.40
221 Titania's Chosen U	.12	.25
222 Tornado Elemental R	.20	.40
223 Wellwisher C	2.00	4.00
224 Whirlwind R	.20	.40
225 Wolfbriar Elemental R	.20	.40
226 Wood Elves C	.75	1.50
227 Wren's Run Packmaster R	.30	.75
228 Argentum Armor R	2.00	4.00
229 Bonehoard R	.15	.30
230 Bosh, Iron Golem R	.15	.30
231 Bottle Gnomes U	.12	.25
232 Burnished Hart U	.30	.60
233 Caged Sun R	6.00	12.00
234 Cathodion U	.12	.25
235 Charcoal Diamond U	.30	.75
236 Dreamstone Hedron U	.12	.25
237 Emerald Medallion R	7.50	15.00
238 Epochrasite R	.15	.30
239 Everflowing Chalice U	.60	1.25
240 Fire Diamond U	.60	1.25
241 Ichor Wellspring C	.10	.20
242 Jalum Tome R	.15	.30
243 Jet Medallion R	25.00	50.00
244 Junk Diver R	3.00	6.00
245 Lashwrithe R	.50	1.00
246 Liquimetal Coating U	.75	1.50
247 Loxodon Warhammer R	.50	1.00
248 Marble Diamond U	.12	.25
249 Mask of Memory U	.30	.60
250 Mind Stone U	.50	1.00
251 Moonsilver Spear R	.60	1.25
252 Moss Diamond U	.12	.25
253 Mycosynth Wellspring C	.10	.20
254 Myr Battlesphere R	.25	.50
255 Myr Retriever U	.25	.50
256 Myr Sire C	.10	.20
257 Nevinyrral's Disk R	1.00	2.00
258 Palladium Myr U	.30	.75
259 Panic Spellbomb C	.10	.20
260 Pearl Medallion R	10.00	20.00
261 Pentavus R	.15	.30
262 Pilgrim's Eye C	.10	.20
263 Predator, Flagship R	.20	.40
264 Pristine Talisman C	.20	.40
265 Ruby Medallion R	17.50	35.00
266 Sapphire Medallion R	20.00	40.00
267 Seer's Sundial R	.15	.30
268 Skullclamp U	6.00	12.00
269 Sky Diamond U	.30	.75
270 Sol Ring U	1.25	2.50
271 Solemn Simulacrum R	.75	1.50
272 Spine of Ish Sah R	.75	1.50
273 Steel Hellkite R	.60	1.25
274 Strata Scythe R	.30	.75
275 Swiftfoot Boots U	1.25	2.50
276 Sword of Vengeance R	.30	.75
277 Thran Dynamo U	3.00	6.00
278 Tormod's Crypt U	.25	.50
279 Trading Post R	.50	1.00
280 Ur-Golem's Eye C	.25	.50
281 Wayfarer's Bauble C	2.50	5.00
282 Worn Powerstone U	1.00	2.00
283 Wurmcoil Engine M	15.00	30.00
284 Barren Moor C	.10	.20
285 Bojuka Bog C	.75	1.50
286 Buried Ruin U	.50	1.00
287 Coral Atoll U	.25	.50
288 Crypt of Agadeem R	4.00	8.00
289 Crystal Vein U	1.25	2.50
290 Darksteel Citadel U	.30	.60
291 Dormant Volcano U	.20	.40
292 Drifting Meadow C	.10	.20
293 Emeria, the Sky Ruin R	7.50	15.00
294 Everglades U	.30	.75
295 Evolving Wilds C	.10	.20
296 Forgotten Cave C	.10	.20
297 Gargoyle Castle R	.15	.30
298 Ghost Quarter U	.75	1.50
299 Great Furnace C	.50	1.00
300 Haunted Fengraf C	.10	.20
301 Havenwood Battleground U	.12	.25
302 Jungle Basin U	.12	.25
303 Karoo U	.50	1.00
304 Lonely Sandbar C	.10	.20
305 Oran-Rief, the Vastwood R	.50	1.00
306 Phyrexia's Core U	.12	.25
307 Polluted Mire C	.15	.30
308 Reliquary Tower U	1.50	3.00
309 Remote Isle C	.15	.30
310 Secluded Steppe C	.10	.20
311 Slippery Karst C	.10	.20
312 Smoldering Crater C	.10	.20
313 Tectonic Edge U	.75	1.50
314 Temple of the False God U	.12	.25
315 Terramorphic Expanse C	.20	.40
316 Tranquil Thicket C	.10	.20
317 Zoetic Cavern U	.15	.30
318 Plains L	.10	.20
319 Plains L	.10	.20
320 Plains L	.10	.20
321 Plains L	.10	.20
322 Island L	.10	.20
323 Island L	.10	.20
324 Island L	.10	.20
325 Island L	.10	.20
326 Swamp L	.10	.20
327 Swamp L	.10	.20
328 Swamp L	.10	.20
329 Swamp L	.10	.20
330 Mountain L	.10	.20
331 Mountain L	.10	.20
332 Mountain L	.10	.20
333 Mountain L	.10	.20
334 Forest L	.10	.20
335 Forest L	.10	.20
336 Forest L	.10	.20
337 Forest L	.10	.20

2014 Magic The Gathering Commander 2014 Oversized

10 Nahiri, the Lithomancer M	.60	1.25
19 Teferi, Temporal Archmage M	.50	1.00
27 Ob Nixilis of the Black Oath M	.75	1.50
33 Daretti, Scrap Savant M	.60	1.25
43 Freyalise, Llanowar's Fury M	1.25	2.50

2014 Magic The Gathering Commander 2014 Tokens

1 Angel	.10	.20
2 Cat	.10	.20
3 Goat	.10	.20
4 Kor Soldier	.10	.20
5 Pegasus	.10	.20
6 Soldier	.10	.20
7 Spirit	.10	.20
8 Fish	.10	.20
9 Kraken	.10	.20
10 Whale	.10	.20
11 Zombie	.10	.20
12 Demon	.10	.20
13 Demon	.10	.20
14 Germ	.10	.20
15 Horror	.10	.20
16 Zombie	.10	.20
17 Goblin	.10	.20
18 Ape	.10	.20
19 Beast	.10	.20
20 Beast	.10	.20
21 Elemental	1.00	2.00
22 Elephant	.10	.20
23 Elf Druid	.75	1.50
24 Elf Warrior	.10	.20
25 Treefolk	.10	.20
26 Wolf	.10	.20
27 Gargoyle	.10	.20
28 Myr	.10	.20
29 Pentavite	.10	.20
30 Stoneforged Blade	.50	1.00
31 Tuktuk the Returned	.10	.20
32 Wurm	1.00	2.00
33 Wurm	1.00	2.00
34 Teferi, Temporal Archmage Emblem	.25	.50
35 Ob Nixilis of the Black Oath Emblem	.10	.20
36 Daretti, Scrap Savant Emblem	.10	.20

2014 Magic The Gathering Conspiracy

1 Advantageous Proclamation U	.10	.20
2 Backup Plan R	.20	.40
3 Brago's Favor C	.07	.15
4 Double Stroke U	.15	.30
5 Immediate Action C	.07	.15
6 Iterative Analysis U	.10	.20
7 Muzzio's Preparations C	.07	.15
8 Power Play U	.10	.20
9 Secret Summoning U	.10	.20
10 Secrets of Paradise C	.07	.15
11 Sentinel Dispatch C	.07	.15
12 Unexpected Potential U	.10	.20
13 Worldknit R	.15	.30
14 Brago's Representative C	.07	.15
15 Council Guardian U	.10	.20
16 Council's Judgment R	2.00	4.00
17 Custodi Soulbinders R	.17	.35
18 Custodi Squire C	.07	.15
19 Rousing of Souls C	.07	.15
20 Academy Elite R	.15	.30
21 Marchesa's Emissary C	.15	.30
22 Marchesa's Infiltrator U	.10	.20
23 Muzzio, Visionary Architect M	2.50	5.00
24 Plea for Power R	2.00	4.00
25 Split Decision U	.50	1.00
26 Bite of the Black Rose U	.10	.20
27 Drakestown Forgotten R	.20	.40
28 Grudge Keeper C	.07	.15
29 Reign of the Pit R	.20	.40
30 Tyrant's Choice C	.20	.40
31 Enraged Revolutionary C	.07	.15
32 Grenzo's Cutthroat C	.07	.15
33 Grenzo's Rebuttal R	.15	.30
34 Ignition Team R	.15	.30
35 Scourge of the Throne M	7.50	15.00
36 Treasonous Ogre U	3.00	6.00
37 Predator's Howl U	.25	.50
38 Realm Seekers R	.25	.50
39 Selvala's Charge U	.10	.20
40 Selvala's Enforcer C	.07	.15
41 Brago, King Eternal R	.75	1.50
42 Dack Fayden M	12.50	25.00
43 Dack's Duplicate R	2.50	5.00
44 Deathreap Ritual U	.30	.75
45 Extract from Darkness U	.12	.25
46 Flamewright U	.10	.20
47 Grenzo, Dungeon Warden R	.30	.60
48 Magister of Worth R	.30	.60
49 Marchesa, the Black Rose M	4.00	8.00
50 Marchesa's Smuggler U	.10	.20
51 Selvala, Explorer Returned R	3.00	6.00
52 Woodvine Elemental U	.10	.20
53 Aether Searcher R	.15	.30
54 Agent of Acquisitions U	.10	.20
55 Canal Dredger R	.20	.40
56 Coercive Portal M	7.50	15.00
57 Cogwork Grinder R	.15	.30
58 Cogwork Librarian C	.17	.35
59 Cogwork Spy C	.07	.15
60 Cogwork Tracker U	.10	.20
61 Deal Broker R	.30	.60
62 Lore Seeker R	.20	.40
63 Lurking Automaton C	.07	.15
64 Whispergear Sneak C	.07	.15
65 Paliano, the High City R	.15	.30
66 Ajani's Sunstriker C	.07	.15
67 Apex Hawks C	.07	.15
68 Courier Hawk C	.07	.15
69 Doomed Traveler C	.07	.15
70 Glimmerpoint Stag U	.10	.20
71 Guardian Zendikon C	.07	.15
72 Intangible Virtue U	.10	.20
73 Kor Chant C	.07	.15
74 Moment of Heroism C	.07	.15
75 Noble Templar C	.07	.15
76 Pillarfield Ox C	.07	.15
77 Pride Guardian C	.07	.15
78 Pristine Angel M	.30	.75
79 Reya Dawnbringer R	1.00	2.00
80 Rout R	.60	1.25
81 Silverchase Fox C	.07	.15
82 Soulcatcher U	.10	.20
83 Stave Off C	.07	.15
84 Swords to Plowshares U	2.00	4.00
85 Unquestioned Authority U	.10	.20
86 Valor Made Real C	.07	.15
87 Vow of Duty U	.10	.20
88 Wakestone Gargoyle U	.10	.20
89 Aether Tradewinds C	.07	.15
90 Air Servant U	.10	.20
91 Brainstorm C	.50	1.00
92 Breakthrough U	.15	.30
93 Compulsive Research C	.07	.15
94 Crookclaw Transmuter C	.07	.15
95 Dream Fracture C	.17	.35
96 Enclave Elite C	.07	.15
97 Fact or Fiction U	.12	.25
98 Favorable Winds U	.25	.50
99 Grixis Illusionist C	.07	.15
100 Jetting Glasskite U	.10	.20
101 Minamo Scrollkeeper C	.07	.15
102 Misdirection R	2.50	5.00
103 Plated Seastrider C	.07	.15
104 Reckless Scholar C	.07	.15
105 Screaming Seahawk C	.07	.15
106 Shoreline Ranger C	.07	.15
107 Stasis Cell C	.07	.15
108 Stifle R	6.00	12.00
109 Traveler's Cloak C	.07	.15
110 Turn the Tide C	.07	.15
111 Wind Dancer U	.10	.20
112 Altar's Reap C	.07	.15
113 Assassinate C	.07	.15
114 Ill-Gotten Gains R	.25	.50
115 Infectious Horror C	.07	.15
116 Liliana's Specter C	.20	.40
117 Magus of the Mirror R	.25	.50
118 Morkrut Banshee U	.10	.20
119 Necromantic Thirst C	.07	.15
120 Phage the Untouchable M	4.00	8.00
121 Plagued Rusalka U	.10	.20
122 Quag Vampires C	.07	.15
123 Reckless Spite U	.10	.20
124 Skeletal Scrying U	.10	.20
125 Smallpox U	.20	.40
126 Stronghold Discipline C	.07	.15
127 Syphon Soul C	.07	.15
128 Tragic Slip C	.20	.40
129 Twisted Abomination C	.07	.15
130 Typhoid Rats C	.07	.15
131 Unhallowed Pact C	.07	.15
132 Vampire Hexmage U	.20	.40
133 Victimize U	.50	1.00
134 Wakedancer C	.07	.15
135 Zombie Goliath C	.07	.15
136 Barbed Shocker U	.10	.20
137 Boldwyr Intimidator U	.10	.20
138 Brimstone Volley C	.07	.15
139 Chartooth Cougar C	.07	.15
140 Cinder Wall C	.07	.15
141 Deathforge Shaman U	.10	.20
142 Flaring Flame-Kin U	.10	.20
143 Flowstone Blade C	.07	.15
144 Heartless Hidetsugu R	2.50	5.00
145 Heckling Fiends U	.10	.20
146 Lizard Warrior C	.07	.15
147 Mana Geyser C	.75	1.50
148 Orcish Cannonade C	.07	.15
149 Pitchburn Devils C	.07	.15
150 Power of Fire C	.07	.15
151 Skitter of Lizards C	.07	.15
152 Sulfuric Vortex R	.75	1.50
153 Torch Fiend C	.07	.15
154 Trumpet Blast C	.07	.15
155 Uncontrollable Anger U	.10	.20
156 Vent Sentinel C	.07	.15
157 Volcanic Fallout U	.10	.20
158 Wrap in Flames C	.07	.15
159 Charging Rhino C	.07	.15
160 Copperhorn Scout C	.17	.35
161 Echoing Courage C	.07	.15
162 Elephant Guide U	.17	.35
163 Elvish Aberration C	.07	.15
164 Exploration R	12.50	25.00
165 Gamekeeper U	.10	.20
166 Gnarlid Pack C	.07	.15
167 Howling Wolf C	.07	.15
168 Hunger of the Howlpack C	.07	.15
169 Hydra Omnivore M	2.50	5.00
170 Lead the Stampede U	.10	.20
171 Nature's Claim C	.75	1.50
172 Pelakka Wurm U	.10	.20
173 Plummet C	.07	.15
174 Provoke C	.07	.15
175 Relic Crush U	.10	.20
176 Respite C	.07	.15
177 Sakura-Tribe Elder C	.75	1.50
178 Scaled Wurm C	.07	.15
179 Sporecap Spider C	.07	.15
180 Squirrel Nest U	.30	.60
181 Terastodon R	.17	.35
182 Wolfbriar Elemental R	.25	.50
183 Wrap in Vigor C	1.00	2.00
184 Basandra, Battle Seraph R	2.00	4.00
185 Decimate R	2.00	4.00
186 Dimir Doppelganger R	.60	1.25
187 Edric, Spymaster of Trest R	2.50	5.00
188 Fires of Yavimaya U	.30	.75
189 Mirari's Wake M	12.50	25.00
190 Mortify U	.20	.40
191 Pernicious Deed M	5.00	10.00
192 Sky Spirit U	.10	.20
193 Spiritmonger R	.15	.30
194 Spontaneous Combustion U	.10	.20
195 Wood Sage U	.10	.20
196 Altar of Dementia R	4.00	8.00
197 Deathrender R	3.00	6.00
198 Explorer's Scope U	.12	.25
199 Fireshrieker U	.20	.40
200 Galvanic Juggernaut U	.10	.20
201 Peace Strider U	.10	.20
202 Reito Lantern U	.10	.20
203 Runed Servitor U	.10	.20
204 Silent Arbiter R	1.00	2.00
205 Spectral Searchlight U	.10	.20
206 Vedalken Orrery R	25.00	50.00
207 Warmonger's Chariot U	.10	.20
208 Mirrodin's Core U	.20	.40
209 Quicksand U	.15	.30
210 Reflecting Pool R	20.00	40.00

2014 Magic The Gathering Conspiracy Tokens

1 Spirit	.07	.15
2 Demon	.12	.25
3 Zombie	.07	.15
4 Ogre	.20	.40
5 Elephant	.12	.25
6 Squirrel	.50	1.00
7 Wolf	.12	.25
8 Construct	.07	.15
9 Dack Fayden Emblem	1.00	2.00

2014 Magic The Gathering Duel Decks Jace vs. Vraska

1 Jace, Architect of Thought M	2.00	3.50
2 Chronomaton U	.10	.20
3 Jace's Phantasm U	.75	1.50
4 Phantasmal Bear C	.10	.20
5 Aether Figment U	.10	.20
6 Crosstown Courier C	.10	.20
7 Dream Stalker C	.10	.20
8 Krovikan Mist C	.10	.20
9 Merfolk Wayfinder U	.10	.20
10 Sea Gate Oracle C	.10	.20
11 Stealer of Secrets C	.10	.20
12 Aether Adept C	.10	.20
13 Archaeomancer C	.10	.20
14 Phantasmal Dragon U	.10	.20
15 Body Double R	.30	.75
16 Leyline Phantom C	.10	.20
17 Aeon Chronicler R	.17	.35
18 Riftwing Cloudskate U	.10	.20
19 Jace's Mindseeker R	.15	.30
20 Errant Ephemeron C	.10	.20
21 Thought Scour C	.50	1.00
22 Agoraphobia U	.10	.20
23 Into the Roil C	.10	.20
24 Memory Lapse C	.10	.20
25 Prohibit C	.10	.20
26 Remand U	2.50	5.00
27 Claustrophobia C	.10	.20
28 Griptide C	.10	.20
29 Ray of Command C	.10	.20
30 Control Magic U	.30	.60
31 Summoner's Bane U	.10	.20
32 Jace's Ingenuity U	.10	.20
33 Future Sight R	.30	.60
34 Spelltwine R	.17	.35
35 Dread Statuary U	.10	.20
36 Halimar Depths C	.30	.75
37 Island L	.10	.20
37 Island L	.10	.20
38 Island L	.10	.20
38 Island L	.10	.20
39 Island L	.10	.20
42 Vraska the Unseen M	2.50	5.00
43 Pulse Tracker C	.10	.20
44 Shadow Alley Denizen C	.10	.20
45 Tavern Swindler U	.10	.20
46 Wight of Precinct Six U	.20	.40
47 Death-Hood Cobra C	.10	.20
48 Gatecreeper Vine C	.10	.20
49 River Boa U	.10	.20
50 Vinelasher Kudzu R	.17	.35
51 Putrid Leech C	.10	.20
52 Sadistic Augermage C	.10	.20
53 Slate Street Ruffian C	.10	.20
54 Oran-Rief Recluse C	.10	.20
55 Spawnwrithe R	.17	.35
56 Stonefare Crocodile C	.10	.20
57 Ohran Viper R	.17	.35
58 Corpse Traders U	.10	.20
59 Festerhide Boar C	.10	.20
60 Mold Shambler C	.10	.20
61 Highway Robber C	.10	.20
62 Nekrataal U	.10	.20

63 Reaper of the Wilds R .17 .35
64 Acidic Slime U .10 .20
65 Drooling Groodion U .10 .20
66 Tragic Slip C .10 .20
67 Hypnotic Cloud C .10 .20
68 Night's Whisper U 1.00 1.75
69 Marsh Casualties U .10 .20
70 Treasured Find U .10 .20
71 Last Kiss C .10 .20
72 Stab Wound C .10 .20
73 Underworld Connections R .20 .40
74 Consume Strength C .10 .20
75 Grisly Spectacle C .10 .20
76 Golgari Guildgate C .10 .20
77 Rogue's Passage U .10 .20
78 Tainted Wood U .17 .35
79 Swamp L .10 .20
79 Swamp L .10 .20
80 Swamp L .10 .20
80 Swamp L .10 .20
81 Swamp L .10 .20
84 Forest L .10 .20
84 Forest L .10 .20
85 Forest L .10 .20
85 Forest L .10 .20
86 Forest L .10 .20

2014 Magic The Gathering Duel Decks Jace vs. Vraska Tokens

1 Assassin .30 .75

2014 Magic The Gathering Duel Decks Speed vs. Cunning

1 Zurgo Helmsmasher M 3.00 6.00
2 Frenzied Goblin U .25 .50
3 Infantry Veteran C .12 .25
4 Leonin Snarecaster C .12 .25
5 Dregscape Zombie C .12 .25
6 Goblin Deathraiders C .12 .25
7 Hellraiser Goblin U .25 .50
8 Fleshbag Marauder U .25 .50
9 Goblin Warchief U 1.00 2.00
10 Hell's Thunder R .50 1.00
11 Kathari Bomber C .12 .25
12 Shambling Remains U .25 .50
13 Mardu Heart-Piercer U .25 .50
14 Beetleback Chief U .25 .50
15 Krenko, Mob Boss R 2.00 4.00
16 Ogre Battledriver R .50 1.00
17 Flame-Kin Zealot U .25 .50
18 Scourge Devil U .25 .50
19 Oni of Wild Places U .25 .50
20 Reckless Abandon C .12 .25
21 Shock C .12 .25
22 Bone Splinters C .12 .25
23 Arc Trail U .25 .50
24 Goblin Bombardment U .25 .50
25 Krenko's Command C .12 .25
26 Act of Treason C .12 .25
27 Dauntless Onslaught U .25 .50
28 Orcish Cannonade C .12 .25
29 Fiery Fall C .12 .25
30 Fury of the Horde R .75 1.50
31 Banefire R .50 1.00
32 Evolving Wilds C .12 .25
33 Ghitu Encampment U .25 .50
34 Nomad Outpost U .30 .60
35 Mountain L .12 .25
35 Mountain L .12 .25
36 Mountain L .12 .25
36 Mountain L .12 .25
38 Plains L .12 .25
38 Plains L .12 .25
39 Swamp L .12 .25
39 Swamp L .12 .25
40 Swamp L .12 .25
42 Arcanis the Omnipotent M 3.00 6.00
43 Faerie Impostor U .25 .50
44 Coral Trickster C .12 .25
45 Fathom Seer C .12 .25
46 Jeskai Elder U .25 .50
47 Willbender U .25 .50
48 Sparkmage Apprentice C .12 .25
49 Lone Missionary C .12 .25
50 Master Decoy C .12 .25
51 Echo Tracer C .12 .25
52 Kor Hookmaster C .12 .25
53 Stonecloaker U .25 .50
54 Aquamorph Entity C .12 .25
55 Hussar Patrol C .12 .25
56 Lightning Angel R .50 1.00
57 Faerie Invaders C .12 .25
58 Thousand Winds R .50 1.00
59 Sphinx of Uthuun R .50 1.00
60 Fleeting Distraction C .12 .25
61 Stave Off C .12 .25
62 Swift Justice C .12 .25
63 Impulse C .12 .25
64 Mana Leak C .25 .50
65 Lightning Helix U 1.50 3.00
66 Hold the Line R .50 1.00
67 Inferno Trap U .25 .50
68 Steam Augury R .50 1.00
69 Traumatic Visions C .12 .25
70 Whiplash Trap C .12 .25
71 Arrow Volley Trap U .25 .50
72 Repeal C .12 .25
73 Mystic Monastery U .30 .75
74 Terramorphic Expanse C .12 .25
75 Island L .12 .25
75 Island L .12 .25
76 Island L .12 .25
79 Plains L .12 .25
79 Plains L .12 .25

2014 Magic The Gathering From the Vault Annihilation

1 Armageddon M 2.50 5.00
2 Burning of Xinye M .75 1.50
3 Cataclysm M 3.00 6.00
4 Child of Alara M 12.50 25.00
5 Decree of Annihilation M 7.50 15.00
6 Firespout M .75 1.50
7 Fracturing Gust M 1.00 2.00
8 Living Death M 4.00 8.00
9 Martial Coup M 1.00 2.00
10 Rolling Earthquake M 7.50 15.00
11 Smokestack M 3.00 6.00
12 Terminus M 1.50 3.00
13 Upheaval M .75 1.50
14 Virtue's Ruin M .50 1.00
15 Wrath of God M 4.00 8.00

2014 Magic The Gathering Journey into Nyx

1 Aegis of the Gods R 1.25 2.50
2 Ajani's Presence C .07 .15
3 Akroan Mastiff C .07 .15
4 Armament of Nyx C .07 .15
5 Banishing Light U .10 .20
6 Dawnbringer Charioteers R .15 .30
7 Deicide R .15 .30
8 Dictate of Heliod R .30 .60
9 Eagle of the Watch C .07 .15
10 Eidolon of Rhetoric U .60 1.25
11 Font of Vigor C .07 .15
12 Godsend M 10.00 20.00
13 Harvestguard Alseids C .07 .15
14 Lagonna-Band Trailblazer C .07 .15
15 Launch the Fleet R .15 .30
16 Leonin Iconoclast U .10 .20
17 Mortal Obstinacy C .07 .15
18 Nyx-Fleece Ram U .30 .60
19 Oppressive Rays C .07 .15
20 Oreskos Swiftclaw C .07 .15
21 Phalanx Formation U .10 .20
22 Quarry Colossus U .10 .20
23 Reprisal U .10 .20
24 Sightless Brawler U .10 .20
25 Skybind R .20 .40
26 Skyspear Cavalry U .10 .20
27 Stonewise Fortifier C .07 .15
28 Supply-Line Cranes C .07 .15
29 Tethmos High Priest U .10 .20
30 Aerial Formation C .07 .15
31 Battlefield Thaumaturge R .15 .30
32 Cloaked Siren C .07 .15
33 Countermand C .07 .15
34 Crystalline Nautilus U .10 .20
35 Dakra Mystic U .10 .20
36 Daring Thief R .15 .30
37 Dictate of Kruphix R 1.00 2.00
38 Font of Fortunes C .07 .15
39 Godhunter Octopus C .07 .15
40 Hour of Need U .10 .20
41 Hubris C .07 .15
42 Hypnotic Siren R .20 .40
43 Interpret the Signs U .10 .20
44 Kiora's Dismissal U .10 .20
45 Pin to the Earth C .07 .15
46 Polymorphous Rush R .15 .30
47 Pull from the Deep U .10 .20
48 Riptide Chimera U .10 .20
49 Rise of Eagles U .10 .20
50 Sage of Hours M 2.50 5.00
51 Scourge of Fleets R .15 .30
52 Sigiled Starfish C .07 .15
53 Thassa's Devourer C .07 .15
54 Thassa's Ire U .10 .20
55 Triton Cavalry U .10 .20
56 Triton Shorestalker C .07 .15
57 War-Wing Siren C .07 .15
58 Whitewater Naiads U .10 .20
59 Agent of Erebos U .20 .40
60 Aspect of Gorgon C .07 .15
61 Bloodcrazed Hoplite C .07 .15
62 Brain Maggot U .10 .20
63 Cast into Darkness C .07 .15
64 Cruel Feeding C .07 .15
65 Dictate of Erebos R 7.50 15.00
66 Doomwake Giant R .15 .30
67 Dreadbringer Lampads C .07 .15
68 Extinguish All Hope R .15 .30
69 Feast of Dreams C .07 .15
70 Felhide Petrifier U .10 .20
71 Font of Return C .07 .15
72 Gnarled Scarhide U .10 .20
73 Grim Guardian C .07 .15
74 King Macar, the Gold-Cursed R .25 .50
75 Master of the Feast R .50 1.00
76 Nightmarish End U .10 .20
77 Nyx Infusion C .07 .15
78 Pharika's Chosen C .07 .15
79 Returned Reveler C .07 .15
80 Ritual of the Returned U .10 .20
81 Rotted Hulk U .10 .20
82 Silence the Believers R .15 .30
83 Spiteful Blow U .10 .20
84 Squelching Leeches U .10 .20
85 Thoughtrender Lamia U .10 .20
86 Tormented Thoughts U .10 .20
87 Worst Fears M 1.25 2.50
88 Akroan Line Breaker U .10 .20
89 Bearer of the Heavens R .25 .50
90 Bladetusk Boar C .07 .15
91 Blinding Flare U .10 .20
92 Cyclops of Eternal Fury U .10 .20
93 Dictate of the Twin Gods R 1.25 2.50
94 Eidolon of the Great Revel R 7.50 15.00
95 Flamespeaker's Will C .07 .15
96 Flurry of Horns C .07 .15
97 Font of Ire C .07 .15
98 Forgeborn Oreads U .10 .20
99 Gluttonous Cyclops C .07 .15
100 Harness by Force R .15 .30
101 Knowledge and Power U .10 .20
102 Lightning Diadem C .07 .15
103 Magma Spray C .07 .15
104 Mogis's Warhound U .10 .20
105 Pensive Minotaur C .07 .15
106 Prophetic Flamespeaker M .50 1.00
107 Riddle of Lightning U .10 .20
108 Rollick of Abandon U .10 .20
109 Rouse the Mob C .07 .15
110 Satyr Hoplite C .07 .15
111 Sigiled Skink C .07 .15
112 Spawn of Thraxes R .15 .30
113 Spite of Mogis U .10 .20
114 Starfall C .07 .15
115 Twinflame R 1.50 3.00
116 Wildfire Cerberus U .10 .20
117 Bassara Tower Archer U .15 .30
118 Colossal Heroics U .10 .20
119 Consign to Dust U .10 .20
120 Desecration Plague C .07 .15
121 Dictate of Karametra R .75 1.50
122 Eidolon of Blossoms R .75 1.50
123 Font of Fertility C .30 .60
124 Golden Hind C .07 .15
125 Goldenhide Ox U .10 .20
126 Heroes' Bane R .15 .30
127 Humbler of Mortals C .07 .15
128 Hydra Broodmaster R .75 1.50
129 Kruphix's Insight C .07 .15
130 Market Festival C .07 .15
131 Nature's Panoply C .07 .15
132 Nessian Game Warden U .10 .20
133 Oakheart Dryads C .07 .15
134 Pheres-Band Thunderhoof C .07 .15
135 Pheres-Band Warchief R .15 .30
136 Ravenous Leucrocota C .07 .15
137 Renowned Weaver C .07 .15
138 Reviving Melody U .10 .20
139 Satyr Grovedancer C .07 .15
140 Setessan Tactics R .25 .50
141 Solidarity of Heroes U .75 1.50
142 Spirespine U .10 .20
143 Strength from the Fallen U .10 .20
144 Swarmborn Giant U .10 .20
145 Ajani, Mentor of Heroes M 7.50 15.00
146 Athreos, God of Passage M 7.50 15.00
147 Desperate Stand U .10 .20
148 Disciple of Deceit U .10 .20
149 Fleetfeather Cockatrice U .10 .20
150 Iroas, God of Victory M 7.50 15.00
151 Keranos, God of Storms M 4.00 8.00
152 Kruphix, God of Horizons M 4.00 8.00
153 Nyx Weaver U .10 .20
154 Pharika, God of Affliction M 1.25 2.50
155 Revel of the Fallen God R .15 .30
156 Stormchaser Chimera U .10 .20
157 Underworld Coinsmith U .10 .20
158 Armory of Iroas U .10 .20
159 Chariot of Victory U .30 .75
160 Deserter's Quarters U .10 .20
161 Gold-Forged Sentinel U .10 .20
162 Hall of Triumph R .25 .50
163 Mana Confluence R 12.50 25.00
164 Temple of Epiphany R .50 1.00
165 Temple of Malady R .50 1.00

2014 Magic The Gathering Journey into Nyx Tokens

1 Sphinx .07 .15
2 Zombie .12 .25
3 Minotaur .07 .15
4 Hydra .75 1.50
5 Spider .07 .15
6 Snake .30 .75

2014 Magic The Gathering Judge Gift Rewards

1 Karador, Ghost Chieftain R 15.00 30.00
2 Greater Good R 12.50 25.00
3 Riku of Two Reflections M 25.00 50.00
4 Force of Will R 200.00 400.00
5 Hanna, Ship's Navigator R 10.00 20.00
6 Sword of Feast and Famine R 60.00 125.00
7 Nekusar, the Mindrazer R 15.00 30.00
8 Elesh Norn, Grand Cenobite R 100.00 200.00
9 Oloro, Ageless Ascetic R 20.00 40.00

2014 Magic The Gathering Judge Gift Rewards Lands

1 Plains R 30.00 75.00
2 Island R 75.00 150.00
3 Swamp R 30.00 60.00
4 Mountain R 30.00 60.00
5 Forest R 50.00 100.00

2014 Magic The Gathering Khans of Tarkir

1 Abzan Battle Priest U .10 .20
2 Abzan Falconer U .10 .20
3 Ainok Bond-Kin C .07 .15
4 Alabaster Kirin C .07 .15
5 Brave the Sands U .75 1.50
6 Dazzling Ramparts U .10 .20
7 Defiant Strike C .07 .15
8 End Hostilities R .15 .30
9 Erase C .07 .15
10 Feat of Resistance C .07 .15
11 Firehoof Cavalry C .07 .15
12 Herald of Anafenza R .15 .30
13 High Sentinels of Arashin R .15 .30
14 Jeskai Student C .07 .15
15 Kill Shot C .07 .15
16 Mardu Hateblade C .07 .15
17 Mardu Hordechief C .07 .15
18 Master of Pearls R .15 .30
19 Rush of Battle C .07 .15
20 Sage-Eye Harrier C .07 .15
21 Salt Road Patrol C .07 .15
22 Seeker of the Way U .10 .20
23 Siegecraft C .07 .15
24 Smite the Monstrous C .07 .15
25 Suspension Field U .10 .20
26 Take Up Arms U .10 .20
27 Timely Hordemate U .10 .20
28 Venerable Lammasu U .10 .20
29 War Behemoth U .10 .20
30 Watcher of the Roost U .10 .20
31 Wingmate Roc M .30 .75
32 Blinding Spray U .10 .20
33 Cancel C .07 .15
34 Clever Impersonator M 1.50 3.00
35 Crippling Chill C .07 .15
36 Dig Through Time R .75 1.50
37 Disdainful Stroke C .07 .15
38 Dragon's Eye Savants U .10 .20
39 Embodiment of Spring C .07 .15
40 Force Away C .07 .15
41 Glacial Stalker C .07 .15
42 Icy Blast R .15 .30
43 Jeskai Elder U .10 .20
44 Jeskai Windscout C .07 .15
45 Kheru Spellsnatcher R .15 .30
46 Mistfire Weaver U .10 .20
47 Monastery Flock C .07 .15
48 Mystic of the Hidden Way C .07 .15
49 Pearl Lake Ancient M .30 .60
50 Quiet Contemplation U .10 .20
51 Riverwheel Aerialists U .10 .20
52 Scaldkin C .07 .15
53 Scion of Glaciers U .10 .20
54 Set Adrift U .10 .20
55 Singing Bell Strike C .07 .15
56 Stubborn Denial U .75 1.50
57 Taigam's Scheming C .07 .15
58 Thousand Winds R .15 .30
59 Treasure Cruise C .07 .15
60 Waterwhirl U .10 .20
61 Weave Fate C .07 .15
62 Wetland Sambar C .07 .15
63 Whirlwind Adept C .07 .15
64 Bellowing Saddlebrute U .10 .20
65 Bitter Revelation C .07 .15
66 Bloodsoaked Champion R .75 1.50
67 Dead Drop U .10 .20
68 Debilitating Injury C .07 .15
69 Despise U .10 .20
70 Disowned Ancestor C .07 .15
71 Dutiful Return C .07 .15
72 Empty the Pits M .30 .75
73 Grim Haruspex R .50 1.00
74 Gurmag Swiftwing U .10 .20
75 Kheru Bloodsucker U .10 .20
75 Kheru Bloodsucker U .10 .20
76 Kheru Dreadmaw C .07 .15
77 Krumar Bond-Kin C .07 .15
78 Mardu Skullhunter C .07 .15
79 Mer-Ek Nightblade U .10 .20
80 Molting Snakeskin C .07 .15
81 Murderous Cut U .10 .20
82 Necropolis Fiend R .15 .30
83 Raiders' Spoils U .10 .20
84 Rakshasa's Secret C .07 .15
85 Retribution of the Ancients R .15 .30
86 Rite of the Serpent C .07 .15
87 Rotting Mastodon C .07 .15
88 Ruthless Ripper U .10 .20
90 Sidisi's Pet C .07 .15
91 Sultai Scavenger C .07 .15
92 Swarm of Bloodflies U .10 .20
93 Throttle C .07 .15
94 Unyielding Krumar C .07 .15
95 Act of Treason C .07 .15
96 Ainok Tracker C .07 .15
97 Arc Lightning U .10 .20
98 Arrow Storm C .07 .15
99 Ashcloud Phoenix M .25 .50
100 Barrage of Boulders C .07 .15
101 Bloodfire Expert C .07 .15
102 Bloodfire Mentor C .07 .15
103 Bring Low C .07 .15
104 Burn Away U .10 .20
105 Canyon Lurkers C .07 .15
106 Crater's Claws R .15 .30
107 Dragon Grip U .10 .20
108 Dragon-Style Twins R .15 .30
109 Goblinslide U .10 .20
110 Horde Ambusher U .10 .20
111 Hordeling Outburst U .20 .40
112 Howl of the Horde R .20 .40
113 Jeering Instigator R .15 .30
114 Leaping Master C .07 .15
115 Mardu Blazebringer U .10 .20
116 Mardu Heart-Piercer U .10 .20
117 Mardu Warshrieker C .07 .15
118 Monastery Swiftspear U 1.50 3.00
119 Sarkhan, the Dragonspeaker M .75 1.50
120 Shatter C .07 .15
121 Summit Prowler C .07 .15
122 Swift Kick C .07 .15
123 Tormenting Voice C .07 .15
124 Trumpet Blast C .07 .15
125 Valley Dasher C .07 .15
126 War-Name Aspirant U .10 .20
127 Alpine Grizzly C .07 .15
128 Archers' Parapet C .07 .15
129 Awaken the Bear C .07 .15
130 Become Immense U .10 .20
131 Dragonscale Boon C .07 .15
132 Feed the Clan C .07 .15
133 Hardened Scales R 5.00 10.00
134 Heir of the Wilds U .10 .20
135 Highland Game C .07 .15
136 Hooded Hydra M .75 1.50
137 Hooting Mandrills C .07 .15
138 Incremental Growth U .10 .20
139 Kin-Tree Warden C .07 .15
140 Longshot Squad C .07 .15
141 Meandering Towershell R .15 .30
142 Naturalize C .07 .15
143 Pine Walker U .10 .20
144 Rattleclaw Mystic R .15 .30
145 Roar of Challenge U .10 .20
146 Sagu Archer C .07 .15
147 Savage Punch C .07 .15
148 Scout the Borders C .07 .15
149 See the Unwritten M .60 1.25
150 Seek the Horizon U .10 .20
151 Smoke Teller C .07 .15
152 Sultai Flayer U .10 .20
153 Temur Charger U .10 .20
154 Trail of Mystery R .15 .30
155 Tusked Colossodon C .07 .15
156 Tuskguard Captain U .10 .20
157 Windstorm U .10 .20
158 Woolly Loxodon C .07 .15
159 Abomination of Gudul C .07 .15
160 Abzan Ascendancy R .15 .30
161 Abzan Charm U .10 .20
162 Abzan Guide C .07 .15
163 Anafenza, the Foremost M 1.00 2.00

164 Ankle Shanker R	.15	.30
165 Armament Corps U	.10	.20
166 Avalanche Tusker R	.15	.30
167 Bear's Companion U	.10	.20
168 Butcher of the Horde R	.15	.30
169 Chief of the Edge U	.10	.20
170 Chief of the Scale U	.10	.20
171 Crackling Doom R	.15	.30
172 Death Frenzy U	.10	.20
173 Deflecting Palm R	.50	1.00
174 Duneblast R	.15	.30
175 Efreet Weaponmaster C	.07	.15
176 Flying Crane Technique R	.15	.30
177 Highspire Mantis U	.10	.20
178 Icefeather Aven U	.10	.20
179 Ivorytusk Fortress R	.15	.30
180 Jeskai Ascendancy R	.75	1.50
181 Jeskai Charm U	.10	.20
182 Kheru Lich Lord R	.15	.30
183 Kin-Tree Invocation U	.10	.20
184 Mantis Rider R	.75	1.50
185 Mardu Ascendancy R	.15	.30
186 Mardu Charm U	.10	.20
187 Mardu Roughrider U	.10	.20
188 Master the Way U	.10	.20
189 Mindswipe R	.15	.30
190 Narset, Enlightened Master M	.75	1.50
191 Ponyback Brigade C	.07	.15
192 Rakshasa Deathdealer R	.15	.30
193 Rakshasa Vizier R	.15	.30
194 Ride Down U	.10	.20
195 Sage of the Inward Eye R	.15	.30
196 Sagu Mauler R	.15	.30
197 Savage Knuckleblade R	.15	.30
198 Secret Plans U	.10	.20
199 Sidisi, Brood Tyrant M	1.00	2.00
200 Siege Rhino R	.50	1.00
201 Snowhorn Rider C	.07	.15
202 Sorin, Solemn Visitor M	2.50	5.00
203 Sultai Ascendancy R	.15	.30
204 Sultai Charm U	.10	.20
205 Sultai Soothsayer U	.10	.20
206 Surrak Dragonclaw M	2.00	4.00
207 Temur Ascendancy R	.75	1.50
208 Temur Charm U	.10	.20
209 Trap Essence R	.15	.30
210 Utter End R	.60	1.25
211 Villainous Wealth R	.30	.60
212 Warden of the Eye U	.10	.20
213 Winterflame U	.10	.20
214 Zurgo Helmsmasher M	.30	.60
215 Abzan Banner C	.07	.15
216 Altar of the Brood R	4.00	8.00
217 Briber's Purse U	.10	.20
218 Cranial Archive U	.10	.20
219 Dragon Throne of Tarkir R	.25	.50
220 Ghostfire Blade R	.25	.50
221 Heart-Piercer Bow U	.10	.20
222 Jeskai Banner C	.07	.15
223 Lens of Clarity C	.07	.15
224 Mardu Banner C	.07	.15
225 Sultai Banner C	.07	.15
226 Temur Banner C	.07	.15
227 Ugin's Nexus M	1.50	3.00
228 Witness of the Ages U	.10	.20
229 Bloodfell Caves C	.07	.15
230 Bloodstained Mire R	25.00	50.00
231 Blossoming Sands C	.07	.15
232 Dismal Backwater C	.07	.15
233 Flooded Strand R	20.00	40.00
234 Frontier Bivouac U	.25	.50
235 Jungle Hollow C	.07	.15
236 Mystic Monastery U	.10	.20
237 Nomad Outpost U	.30	.75
238 Opulent Palace U	.20	.40
239 Polluted Delta R	30.00	60.00
240 Rugged Highlands C	.07	.15
241 Sandsteppe Citadel U	.30	.60
242 Scoured Barrens C	.07	.15
243 Swiftwater Cliffs C	.07	.15
244 Thornwood Falls C	.07	.15
245 Tomb of the Spirit Dragon U	.30	.75
246 Tranquil Cove C	.07	.15
247 Wind-Scarred Crag C	.07	.15
248 Windswept Heath R	17.50	35.00
249 Wooded Foothills R	25.00	50.00
250 Plains L	.10	.20
251 Plains L	.10	.20
252 Plains L	.10	.20
253 Plains L	.10	.20
254 Island L	.12	.25
255 Island L	.12	.25
256 Island L	.12	.25
257 Island L	.12	.25
258 Swamp L	.10	.20
259 Swamp L	.10	.20
260 Swamp L	.10	.20
261 Swamp L	.10	.20
262 Mountain L	.10	.20
263 Mountain L	.10	.20
264 Mountain L	.10	.20
265 Mountain L	.10	.20
266 Forest L	.10	.20
267 Forest L	.10	.20
268 Forest L	.10	.20
269 Forest L	.10	.20

2014 Magic The Gathering Khans of Tarkir Tokens

1 Bird	.30	.75
2 Spirit	.07	.15
3 Warrior	.07	.15
4 Warrior	.07	.15
5 Vampire	1.00	2.00
6 Zombie	.30	.60
7 Goblin	.07	.15
8 Bear	.10	.20
9 Snake	.12	.25
10 Spirit Warrior	.07	.15
11 Morph	.07	.15
12 Sarkhan, the Dragonspeaker Emblem	.12	.25
13 Sorin, Solemn Visitor Emblem	.25	.50

2014 Magic The Gathering League Tokens

1 Soldier	4.00	8.00
2 Minotaur	1.00	2.00
3 Squid	7.50	15.00
4 Warrior	12.50	25.00

2014 Magic The Gathering Magic 2015

1 Ajani Steadfast M	4.00	8.00
2 Ajani's Pridemate U	.10	.20
3 Avacyn, Guardian Angel R	.30	.75
4 Battle Mastery U	.10	.20
5 Boonweaver Giant U	.10	.20
6 Congregate U	.10	.20
7 Constricting Sliver U	.75	1.50
8 Dauntless River Marshal U	.10	.20
9 Devouring Light U	.10	.20
10 Divine Favor C	.07	.15
11 Ephemeral Shields C	.07	.15
12 First Response U	.10	.20
13 Geist of the Moors U	.10	.20
14 Heliod's Pilgrim C	.07	.15
15 Hushwing Gryff R	.20	.40
16 Kinsbaile Skirmisher C	.07	.15
17 Marked by Honor C	.07	.15
18 Mass Calcify R	.30	.75
19 Meditation Puzzle C	.07	.15
20 Midnight Guard C	.07	.15
21 Oppressive Rays C	.07	.15
22 Oreskos Swiftclaw C	.07	.15
23 Paragon of New Dawns U	.10	.20
24 Pillar of Light C	.07	.15
25 Preeminent Captain R	.25	.50
26 Raise the Alarm C	.07	.15
27 Razorfoot Griffin C	.07	.15
28 Resolute Archangel R	.75	1.50
29 Return to the Ranks R	.75	1.50
30 Sanctified Charge C	.07	.15
31 Selfless Cathar C	.07	.15
32 Seraph of the Masses U	.10	.20
33 Solemn Offering C	.07	.15
34 Soul of Theros M	.30	.60
35 Soulmender C	.07	.15
36 Spectra Ward R	.75	1.50
37 Spirit Bonds R	.30	.60
38 Sungrace Pegasus C	.07	.15
39 Tireless Missionaries C	.07	.15
40 Triplicate Spirits C	.07	.15
41 Wall of Essence U	.20	.40
42 Warden of the Beyond U	.10	.20
43 Aeronaut Tinkerer C	.07	.15
44 Aetherspouts R	.50	1.00
45 Amphin Pathmage C	.07	.15
46 Chasm Skulker R	3.00	6.00
47 Chief Engineer R	.50	1.00
48 Chronostutter C	.07	.15
49 Coral Barrier C	.07	.15
50 Diffusion Sliver U	1.25	2.50
51 Dissipate U	.10	.20
52 Divination C	.07	.15
53 Encrust C	.07	.15
54 Ensoul Artifact U	.30	.60
55 Frost Lynx C	.07	.15
56 Fugitive Wizard C	.07	.15
57 Glacial Crasher C	.07	.15
58 Hydrosurge C	.07	.15
59 Illusory Angel U	.10	.20
60 Into the Void U	.10	.20
61 Invisibility C	.07	.15
62 Jace, the Living Guildpact M	.75	1.50
63 Jace's Ingenuity U	.10	.20
64 Jalira, Master Polymorphist R	.15	.30
65 Jorubai Murk Lurker U	.10	.20
66 Kapsho Kitefins U	.10	.20
67 Master of Predicaments R	.15	.30
68 Mercurial Pretender R	.15	.30
69 Military Intelligence U	.10	.20
70 Mind Sculpt C	.07	.15
71 Negate C	.07	.15
72 Nimbus of the Isles C	.07	.15
73 Paragon of Gathering Mists U	.10	.20
74 Peel from Reality C	.07	.15
75 Polymorphist's Jest R	.75	1.50
76 Quickling U	.20	.40
77 Research Assistant C	.07	.15
78 Soul of Ravnica M	.25	.50
79 Statute of Denial C	.07	.15
80 Stormtide Leviathan R	.20	.40
81 Turn to Frog U	.10	.20
82 Void Snare C	.15	.30
83 Wall of Frost U	.10	.20
84 Welkin Tern C	.07	.15
85 Accursed Spirit C	.07	.15
86 Black Cat C	.07	.15
87 Blood Host U	.10	.20
88 Carrion Crow C	.07	.15
89 Caustic Tar U	.10	.20
90 Child of Night C	.50	1.00
91 Covenant of Blood C	.07	.15
92 Crippling Blight C	.07	.15
93 Cruel Sadist R	.15	.30
94 Endless Obedience U	.10	.20
95 Eternal Thirst C	.07	.15
96 Feast on the Fallen U	.15	.30
97 Festergloom C	.07	.15
98 Flesh to Dust C	.07	.15
99 Gravedigger C	.07	.15
100 In Garruk's Wake R	.60	1.25
101 Indulgent Tormentor R	.30	.75
102 Leeching Sliver U	1.25	2.50
103 Liliana Vess M	7.50	15.00
104 Mind Rot C	.07	.15
105 Necrobite C	.07	.15
106 Necrogen Scudder U	.10	.20
107 Necromancer's Assistant C	.07	.15
108 Necromancer's Stockpile R	.25	.50
109 Nightfire Giant U	.10	.20
110 Ob Nixilis, Unshackled R	4.00	8.00
111 Paragon of Open Graves U	.15	.30
112 Rotfeaster Maggot C	.07	.15
113 Shadowcloak Vampire C	.07	.15
114 Sign in Blood C	.15	.30
115 Soul of Innistrad M	.25	.50
116 Stab Wound C	.07	.15
117 Stain the Mind R	.17	.35
118 Typhoid Rats C	.07	.15
119 Ulcerate U	.10	.20
120 Unmake the Graves C	.07	.15
121 Wall of Limbs U	.10	.20
122 Waste Not R	10.00	20.00
123 Witch's Familiar C	.07	.15
124 Xathrid Slyblade U	.10	.20
125 Zof Shade C	.12	.25
126 Act on Impulse U	.10	.20
127 Aggressive Mining R	.15	.30
128 Altac Bloodseeker U	.10	.20
129 Belligerent Sliver U	.30	.60
130 Blastfire Bolt C	.07	.15
131 Borderland Marauder C	.07	.15
132 Brood Keeper U	.10	.20
133 Burning Anger R	.15	.30
134 Chandra, Pyromaster M	.75	1.50
135 Circle of Flame U	.10	.20
136 Clear a Path C	.07	.15
137 Cone of Flame U	.10	.20
138 Crowd's Favor C	.07	.15
139 Crucible of Fire R	.75	1.50
140 Forge Devil C	.07	.15
141 Foundry Street Denizen C	.07	.15
142 Frenzied Goblin U	.10	.20
143 Generator Servant C	.07	.15
144 Goblin Kaboomist R	.20	.40
145 Goblin Rabblemaster R	2.00	4.00
146 Goblin Roughrider C	.07	.15
147 Hammerhand C	.07	.15
148 Heat Ray C	.07	.15
149 Hoarding Dragon R	.15	.30
150 Inferno Fist C	.07	.15
151 Kird Chieftain U	.10	.20
152 Krenko's Enforcer C	.07	.15
153 Kurkesh, Onakke Ancient R	.20	.40
154 Lava Axe C	.07	.15
155 Lightning Strike C	.07	.15
156 Might Makes Right U	.10	.20
157 Miner's Bane C	.07	.15
158 Paragon of Fierce Defiance U	.10	.20
159 Rummaging Goblin C	.07	.15
160 Scrapyard Mongrel C	.07	.15
161 Shrapnel Blast U	.10	.20
162 Siege Dragon R	.15	.30
163 Soul of Shandalar M	.30	.75
164 Stoke the Flames U	.15	.30
165 Thundering Giant C	.07	.15
166 Torch Fiend C	.07	.15
167 Wall of Fire C	.07	.15
168 Ancient Silverback U	.10	.20
169 Back to Nature U	.10	.20
170 Carnivorous Moss-Beast C	.07	.15
171 Charging Rhino C	.07	.15
172 Chord of Calling R	4.00	8.00
173 Elvish Mystic C	.30	.60
174 Feral Incarnation U	.10	.20
175 Gather Courage U	.10	.20
176 Genesis Hydra R	.30	.60
177 Hornet Nest R	.75	1.50
178 Hornet Queen R	.50	1.00
179 Hunt the Weak C	.07	.15
180 Hunter's Ambush C	.07	.15
181 Invasive Species C	.07	.15
182 Kalonian Twingrove R	.30	.60
183 Life's Legacy R	1.25	2.50
184 Living Totem U	.10	.20
185 Naturalize C	.07	.15
186 Netcaster Spider C	.07	.15
187 Nissa, Worldwaker M	3.00	6.00
188 Nissa's Expedition U	.10	.20
189 Overwhelm U	.10	.20
190 Paragon of Eternal Wilds U	.10	.20
191 Phytotitan R	.15	.30
192 Plummet C	.07	.15
193 Ranger's Guile C	.07	.15
194 Reclamation Sage U	.10	.20
195 Restock R	.15	.30
196 Roaring Primadox U	.10	.20
197 Runeclaw Bear C	.07	.15
198 Satyr Wayfinder C	.07	.15
199 Shaman of Spring C	.07	.15
200 Siege Wurm C	.07	.15
201 Soul of Zendikar M	.30	.60
202 Sunblade Elf U	.10	.20
203 Titanic Growth C	.07	.15
204 Undergrowth Scavenger C	.07	.15
205 Venom Sliver U	2.00	4.00
206 Verdant Haven C	.07	.15
207 Vineweft C	.07	.15
208 Wall of Mulch U	.15	.30
209 Yisan, the Wanderer Bard R	.75	1.50
210 Garruk, Apex Predator M	10.00	20.00
211 Sliver Hivelord M	12.50	25.00
212 Avarice Amulet R	.15	.30
213 Brawler's Plate U	.10	.20
214 Bronze Sable C	.07	.15
215 The Chain Veil M	10.00	20.00
216 Gargoyle Sentinel U	.10	.20
217 Grindclock R	.20	.40
218 Haunted Plate Mail R	.15	.30
219 Hot Soup U	.25	.50
220 Juggernaut U	.10	.20
221 Meteorite U	.10	.20
222 Obelisk of Urd R	1.50	3.00
223 Ornithopter U	.20	.40
224 Perilous Vault M	2.50	5.00
225 Phyrexian Revoker R	.75	1.50
226 Profane Memento U	2.50	5.00
227 Rogue's Gloves U	.15	.30
228 Sacred Armory U	.10	.20
229 Scuttling Doom Engine R	.15	.30
230 Shield of the Avatar R	.15	.30
231 Soul of New Phyrexia M	1.50	3.00
232 Staff of the Death Magus U	.15	.30
233 Staff of the Flame Magus U	.10	.20
234 Staff of the Mind Magus U	.10	.20
235 Staff of the Sun Magus U	.10	.20
236 Staff of the Wild Magus U	.10	.20
237 Tormod's Crypt U	.30	.60
238 Tyrant's Machine C	.07	.15
239 Will-Forged Golem C	.07	.15
240 Battlefield Forge R	.60	1.25
241 Caves of Koilos R	.50	1.00
242 Darksteel Citadel U	.30	.60
243 Evolving Wilds C	.07	.15
244 Llanowar Wastes R	.50	1.00
245 Radiant Fountain C	.15	.30
246 Shivan Reef R	.75	1.50
247 Sliver Hive R	10.00	20.00
248 Urborg, Tomb of Yawgmoth R	17.50	35.00
249 Yavimaya Coast R	.50	1.00
250 Plains L	.10	.20
251 Plains L	.10	.20
252 Plains L	.10	.20
253 Plains L	.10	.20
254 Island L	.10	.20
255 Island L	.10	.20
256 Island L	.10	.20
257 Island L	.10	.20
258 Swamp L	.10	.20
259 Swamp L	.10	.20
260 Swamp L	.10	.20
261 Swamp L	.10	.20
262 Mountain L	.10	.20
263 Mountain L	.10	.20
264 Mountain L	.10	.20
265 Mountain L	.10	.20
266 Forest L	.10	.20
267 Forest L	.10	.20
268 Forest L	.10	.20
269 Forest L	.10	.20
270 Aegis Angel R	.15	.30
271 Divine Verdict C	.07	.15
272 Inspired Charge C	.07	.15
273 Serra Angel U	.10	.20
274 Cancel C	.07	.15
275 Mahamoti Djinn R	.15	.30
276 Nightmare R	.15	.30
277 Sengir Vampire U	.10	.20
278 Walking Corpse C	.07	.15
279 Furnace Whelp U	.10	.20
280 Seismic Strike C	.07	.15
281 Shivan Dragon R	.15	.30
282 Centaur Courser C	.07	.15
283 Garruk's Packleader U	.10	.20
284 Terra Stomper R	.15	.30

2014 Magic The Gathering Magic 2015 Tokens

1 Sliver	.30	.60
2 Soldier	.07	.15
3 Spirit	.07	.15
4 Squid	.30	.60
5 Beast	.50	1.00
6 Zombie	.07	.15
7 Dragon	.12	.25
8 Goblin	.15	.30
9 Beast	.07	.15
10 Insect	2.50	5.00
11 Treefolk Warrior	.07	.15
12 Land Mine	.07	.15
13 Ajani Steadfast Emblem	.75	1.50
14 Garruk, Apex Predator Emblem	.50	1.00

2014 Magic The Gathering Magic 2015 SDCC Black Variant

1 Ajani Steadfast M	25.00	50.00
62 Jace, The Living Guildpact M	15.00	30.00
103 Liliana Vess M	30.00	60.00
134 Chandra Pyromaster M	15.00	30.00
187 Nissa, Worldwaker M	25.00	50.00
210 Garruk, Apex Predator M	25.00	50.00
NNO Garruk's Axe NERF prop	20.00	40.00

2014 Magic The Gathering Modern Event Deck 2014

1 Soul Warden C	.30	.75
2 Tidehollow Sculler U	.60	1.25
3 Path to Exile U	2.50	5.00
4 Inquisition of Kozilek U	2.50	5.00
5 Shrine of Loyal Legions U	.10	.20
6 Honor of the Pure R	.75	1.50
7 Intangible Virtue U	.15	.30
8 Raise the Alarm C	.10	.20
9 Zealous Persecution U	.12	.25
10 Sword of Feast and Famine M	30.00	75.00
11 Lingering Souls U	.30	.75
12 Spectral Procession U	.25	.50
13 Elspeth, Knight-Errant M	7.50	15.00
14 Caves of Koilos R	.50	1.00
15 City of Brass R	7.50	15.00
16 Isolated Chapel R	2.50	5.00
17 Vault of the Archangel R	2.00	4.00
18 Windbrisk Heights R	.50	1.00
19 Plains L	.15	.30
20 Swamp L	.30	.60
21 Relic of Progenitus U	.60	1.25
22 Burrenton Forge-Tender U	.15	.30
23 Duress C	.07	.15
24 Kataki, War's Wage R	.50	1.00
25 Dismember U	1.25	2.50
26 Ghost Quarter U	.60	1.25

2014 Magic The Gathering Modern Event Deck 2014 Tokens

1 Soldier	.07	.15
2 Spirit	.07	.15
3 Myr	.07	.15
4 Elspeth, Knight-Errant Emblem	3.00	6.00

2015 Magic The Gathering Battle for Zendikar

1 Bane of Bala Ged U	.60	1.25
2 Blight Herder R	.15	.30
3 Breaker of Armies U	.20	.40
4 Conduit of Ruin R	1.25	2.50
5 Deathless Behemoth U	.10	.20
6 Desolation Twin R	.15	.30
7 Eldrazi Devastator C	.07	.15
8 Endless One R	.75	1.50
9 Gruesome Slaughter R	.15	.30
10 Kozilek's Channeler C	.07	.15
11 Oblivion Sower M	2.00	4.00
12 Ruin Processor C	.07	.15
13 Scour from Existence C	.07	.15
14 Titan's Presence U	.10	.20
15 Ulamog, the Ceaseless Hunger M	30.00	60.00

16 Ulamog's Despoiler U	.10	.20
17 Void Winnower M	6.00	12.00
18 Angel of Renewal U	.10	.20
19 Angelic Gift C	.07	.15
20 Cliffside Lookout C	.07	.15
21 Courier Griffin C	.07	.15
22 Emeria Shepherd R	.30	.60
23 Encircling Fissure U	.10	.20
24 Expedition Envoy U	.10	.20
25 Felidar Cub C	.07	.15
26 Felidar Sovereign R	1.25	2.50
27 Fortified Rampart C	.07	.15
28 Ghostly Sentinel C	.07	.15
29 Gideon, Ally of Zendikar M	3.00	6.00
30 Gideon's Reproach C	.07	.15
31 Hero of Goma Fada R	.15	.30
32 Inspired Charge C	.07	.15
33 Kitesail Scout C	.07	.15
34 Kor Bladewhirl U	.10	.20
35 Kor Castigator C	.07	.15
36 Kor Entanglers U	.10	.20
37 Lantern Scout R	.15	.30
38 Lithomancer's Focus C	.07	.15
39 Makindi Patrol C	.07	.15
40 Ondu Greathorn C	.07	.15
41 Ondu Rising U	.10	.20
42 Planar Outburst R	.15	.30
43 Quarantine Field M	.30	.75
44 Retreat to Emeria U	.10	.20
45 Roil's Retribution U	.10	.20
46 Serene Steward U	.10	.20
47 Shadow Glider C	.07	.15
48 Sheer Drop C	.07	.15
49 Smite the Monstrous C	.07	.15
50 Stasis Snare U	.10	.20
51 Stone Haven Medic C	.07	.15
52 Tandem Tactics C	.07	.15
53 Unified Front U	.10	.20
54 Adverse Conditions U	.10	.20
55 Benthic Infiltrator C	.07	.15
56 Cryptic Cruiser U	.10	.20
57 Drowner of Hope R	.15	.30
58 Eldrazi Skyspawner C	.07	.15
59 Horribly Awry U	.10	.20
60 Incubator Drone C	.07	.15
61 Mist Intruder C	.07	.15
62 Murk Strider C	.07	.15
63 Oracle of Dust C	.07	.15
64 Ruination Guide U	.10	.20
65 Salvage Drone C	.07	.15
66 Spell Shrivel C	.07	.15
67 Tide Drifter U	.10	.20
68 Ulamog's Reclaimer U	.10	.20
69 Anticipate C	.07	.15
70 Brilliant Spectrum C	.07	.15
71 Cloud Manta C	.07	.15
72 Clutch of Currents C	.07	.15
73 Coastal Discovery U	.10	.20
74 Coralhelm Guide C	.07	.15
75 Dampening Pulse U	.10	.20
76 Dispel C	.07	.15
77 Exert Influence R	.15	.30
78 Guardian of Tazeem R	.15	.30
79 Halimar Tidecaller U	.10	.20
80 Part the Waterveil M	1.25	2.50
81 Prism Array R	.15	.30
82 Retreat to Coralhelm U	.10	.20
83 Roilmage's Trick C	.07	.15
84 Rush of Ice C	.07	.15
85 Scatter to the Winds R	.15	.30
86 Tightening Coils C	.07	.15
87 Ugin's Insight R	.15	.30
88 Wave-Wing Elemental C	.07	.15
89 Windrider Patrol U	.10	.20
90 Complete Disregard C	.07	.15
91 Culling Drone C	.07	.15
92 Dominator Drone C	.07	.15
93 Grave Birthing C	.07	.15
94 Grip of Desolation U	.10	.20
95 Mind Raker C	.07	.15
96 Silent Skimmer C	.07	.15
97 Skitterskin U	.10	.20
98 Sludge Crawler C	.07	.15
99 Smothering Abomination R	.30	.75
100 Swarm Surge C	.07	.15
101 Transgress the Mind U	.10	.20
102 Wasteland Strangler R	.15	.30
103 Altar's Reap C	.07	.15
104 Bloodbond Vampire U	.10	.20
105 Bone Splinters C	.07	.15
106 Carrier Thrall U	.10	.20
107 Defiant Bloodlord R	.15	.30
108 Demon's Grasp C	.07	.15
109 Drana, Liberator of Malakir M	2.50	5.00
110 Dutiful Return C	.07	.15
111 Geyserfield Stalker C	.07	.15
112 Guul Draz Overseer R	.15	.30
113 Hagra Sharpshooter U	.10	.20
114 Kalastria Healer C	.07	.15
115 Kalastria Nightwatch C	.07	.15
116 Malakir Familiar U	.10	.20
117 Mire's Malice C	.07	.15
118 Nirkana Assassin C	.07	.15
119 Ob Nixilis Reignited M	.60	1.25
120 Painful Truths R	.15	.30
121 Retreat to Hagra U	.10	.20
122 Rising Miasma U	.10	.20
123 Ruinous Path R	.15	.30
124 Vampiric Rites U	.50	1.00
125 Voracious Null C	.07	.15
126 Zulaport Cutthroat U	.60	1.25
127 Barrage Tyrant R	.15	.30
128 Crumble to Dust U	.10	.20
129 Kozilek's Sentinel C	.07	.15
130 Molten Nursery U	.10	.20
131 Nettle Drone C	.07	.15
132 Processor Assault U	.10	.20
133 Serpentine Spike R	.15	.30
134 Touch of the Void C	.07	.15
135 Turn Against U	.10	.20
136 Vestige of Emrakul C	.07	.15
137 Vile Aggregate U	.10	.20
138 Akoum Firebird M	.25	.50
139 Akoum Hellkite R	.15	.30
140 Akoum Stonewaker U	.10	.20
141 Belligerent Whiptail C	.07	.15
142 Boiling Earth C	.07	.15
143 Chasm Guide U	.10	.20
144 Dragonmaster Outcast M	1.25	2.50
145 Firemantle Mage U	.10	.20
146 Goblin War Paint C	.07	.15
147 Lavastep Raider C	.07	.15
148 Makindi Sliderunner C	.07	.15
149 Ondu Champion C	.07	.15
150 Outnumber C	.07	.15
151 Radiant Flames R	.15	.30
152 Reckless Cohort C	.07	.15
153 Retreat to Valakut U	.10	.20
154 Rolling Thunder U	.10	.20
155 Shatterskull Recruit C	.07	.15
156 Stonefury C	.07	.15
157 Sure Strike C	.07	.15
158 Tunneling Geopede U	.10	.20
159 Valakut Invoker C	.07	.15
160 Valakut Predator C	.07	.15
161 Volcanic Upheaval C	.07	.15
162 Zada, Hedron Grinder R	.25	.50
163 Blisterpod C	.07	.15
164 Brood Monitor U	.10	.20
165 Call the Scions C	.07	.15
166 Eyeless Watcher C	.07	.15
167 From Beyond R	.50	1.00
168 Unnatural Aggression C	.07	.15
169 Void Attendant U	.10	.20
170 Beastcaller Savant R	.30	.60
171 Broodhunter Wurm C	.07	.15
172 Earthen Arms C	.07	.15
173 Giant Mantis C	.07	.15
174 Greenwarden of Murasa M	.75	1.50
175 Infuse with the Elements U	.10	.20
176 Jaddi Offshoot U	.10	.20
177 Lifespring Druid C	.07	.15
178 Murasa Ranger U	.10	.20
179 Natural Connection C	.07	.15
180 Nissa's Renewal R	.15	.30
181 Oran-Rief Hydra R	.15	.30
182 Oran-Rief Invoker C	.07	.15
183 Plated Crusher U	.10	.20
184 Plummet C	.07	.15
185 Reclaiming Vines C	.07	.15
186 Retreat to Kazandu U	.10	.20
187 Rot Shambler U	.10	.20
188 Scythe Leopard U	.10	.20
189 Seek the Wilds C	.07	.15
190 Snapping Gnarlid C	.07	.15
191 Swell of Growth C	.07	.15
192 Sylvan Scrying U	.50	1.00
193 Tajuru Beastmaster C	.07	.15
194 Tajuru Stalwart C	.07	.15
195 Tajuru Warcaller U	.10	.20
196 Territorial Baloth C	.07	.15
197 Undergrowth Champion M	1.50	3.00
198 Woodland Wanderer R	.15	.30
199 Brood Butcher R	.15	.30
200 Brutal Expulsion R	.15	.30
201 Catacomb Sifter U	.10	.20
202 Dust Stalker R	.15	.30
203 Fathom Feeder R	.15	.30
204 Forerunner of Slaughter U	.10	.20
205 Herald of Kozilek U	.10	.20
206 Sire of Stagnation M	2.50	5.00
207 Ulamog's Nullifier U	.10	.20
208 Angelic Captain R	.15	.30
209 Bring to Light R	1.00	2.00
210 Drana's Emissary U	.30	.75
211 Grove Rumbler U	.10	.20
212 Grovetender Druids U	.10	.20
213 Kiora, Master of the Depths M	2.50	5.00
214 March from the Tomb R	.15	.30
215 Munda, Ambush Leader R	.15	.30
216 Noyan Dar, Roil Shaper R	.15	.30
217 Omnath, Locus of Rage M	1.25	2.50
218 Resolute Blademaster U	.10	.20
219 Roil Spout U	.10	.20
220 Skyrider Elf U	.10	.20
221 Veteran Warleader R	.15	.30
222 Aligned Hedron Network R	.15	.30
223 Hedron Archive U	.10	.20
224 Hedron Blade C	.07	.15
225 Pathway Arrows U	.10	.20
226 Pilgrim's Eye U	.10	.20
227 Slab Hammer U	.10	.20
228 Ally Encampment R	.15	.30
229 Blighted Cataract U	.10	.20
230 Blighted Fen U	.10	.20
231 Blighted Gorge U	.10	.20
232 Blighted Steppe U	.10	.20
233 Blighted Woodland U	.10	.20
234 Canopy Vista R	1.00	2.00
235 Cinder Glade R	.75	1.50
236 Evolving Wilds C	.07	.15
237 Fertile Thicket C	.07	.15
238 Looming Spires C	.07	.15
239 Lumbering Falls R	.15	.30
240 Mortuary Mire C	.07	.15
241 Prairie Stream R	.50	1.00
242 Sanctum of Ugin R	.75	1.50
243 Sandstone Bridge C	.07	.15
244 Shambling Vent R	.75	1.50
245 Shrine of the Forsaken Gods R	.15	.30
246 Skyline Cascade C	.07	.15
247 Smoldering Marsh R	.15	.30
248 Spawning Bed U	.10	.20
249 Sunken Hollow R	.75	1.50
250 Plains L	.10	.20
250 Plains L FULL ART	.10	.20
251 Plains L	.10	.20
251 Plains L FULL ART	.10	.20
252 Plains L	.10	.20
252 Plains L FULL ART	.10	.20
253 Plains L	.10	.20
253 Plains L FULL ART	.10	.20
254 Plains L	.10	.20
254 Plains L FULL ART	.10	.20
255 Island L	.10	.20
255 Island L FULL ART	.20	.40
256 Island L	.10	.20
256 Island L FULL ART	.20	.40
257 Island L	.10	.20
257 Island L FULL ART	.20	.40
258 Island L	.10	.20
258 Island L FULL ART	.20	.40
259 Island L	.10	.20
259 Island L FULL ART	.20	.40
260 Swamp L	.10	.20
260 Swamp L FULL ART	.10	.20
261 Swamp L	.10	.20
261 Swamp L FULL ART	.10	.20
262 Swamp L	.10	.20
262 Swamp L FULL ART	.10	.20
263 Swamp L	.10	.20
263 Swamp L FULL ART	.10	.20
264 Swamp L	.10	.20
264 Swamp L FULL ART	.10	.20
265 Mountain L	.10	.20
265 Mountain L FULL ART	.17	.35
266 Mountain L	.10	.20
266 Mountain L FULL ART	.17	.35
267 Mountain L	.10	.20
267 Mountain L FULL ART	.17	.35
268 Mountain L	.10	.20
268 Mountain L FULL ART	.17	.35
269 Mountain L	.10	.20
269 Mountain L FULL ART	.17	.35
270 Forest L	.10	.20
270 Forest L FULL ART	.20	.40
271 Forest L	.10	.20
271 Forest L FULL ART	.20	.40
272 Forest L	.10	.20
272 Forest L FULL ART	.20	.40
273 Forest L	.10	.20
273 Forest L FULL ART	.20	.40
274 Forest L	.10	.20
274 Forest L FULL ART	.20	.40

2015 Magic The Gathering Battle for Zendikar Tokens

1 Eldrazi	.30	.75
2 Eldrazi Scion	.07	.15
3 Eldrazi Scion	.07	.15
4 Eldrazi Scion	.07	.15
5 Knight Ally	.07	.15
6 Kor Ally	.07	.15
7 Octopus	.07	.15
8 Dragon	.15	.30
9 Elemental	.07	.15
10 Plant	.07	.15
11 Elemental	.60	1.25
12 Gideon, Ally of Zendikar Emblem	.17	.35
13 Ob Nixilis Reignited Emblem	.10	.20
14 Kiora, Master of the Depths Emblem	.07	.15

2015 Magic The Gathering Battle for Zendikar Standard Series

234 Canopy Vista R	3.00	6.00
235 Cinder Glade R	3.00	6.00
241 Prairie Stream R	2.50	5.00
247 Smoldering Marsh R	2.00	4.00
249 Sunken Hollow R	2.50	5.00

2015 Magic The Gathering Commander 2015

1 Bastion Protector R	3.00	6.00
2 Dawnbreak Reclaimer R	.20	.40
3 Grasp of Fate R	2.00	4.00
4 Herald of the Host U	.12	.25
5 Kalemne's Captain R	.20	.40
6 Oreskos Explorer U	.20	.40
7 Righteous Confluence R	.50	1.00
8 Shielded by Faith R	1.25	2.50
9 Aethersnatch R	.30	.75
10 Broodbirth Viper U	.12	.25
11 Gigantoplasm R	.20	.40
12 Illusory Ambusher U	.15	.30
13 Mirror Match U	.12	.25
14 Mystic Confluence R	5.00	10.00
15 Synthetic Destiny R	.20	.40
16 Banshee of the Dread Choir U	.12	.25
17 Corpse Augur U	.15	.30
18 Daxos's Torment R	.20	.40
19 Deadly Tempest R	.30	.75
20 Dread Summons R	.50	1.00
21 Scourge of Nel Toth R	1.00	2.00
22 Elephant/Saproling	.12	.25
23 Elemental Shaman/Shapeshifter	.12	.25
24 Seal of Doom C	.10	.20
25 Breath of Darigaaz U	.12	.25
26 Curse of the Nightly Hunt U	.12	.25
27 Fiery Confluence R	5.00	9.00
28 Fumiko the Lowblood R	.20	.40
29 Hammerfist Giant R	.20	.40
30 Hostility R	.20	.40
31 Mizzix's Mastery R	2.00	4.00
32 Sunrise Sovereign R	.20	.40
33 Vandalblast U	.30	.75
34 Warstorm Surge R	.20	.40
35 Word of Seizing R	.20	.40
36 Caller of the Pack U	.12	.25
37 Chameleon Colossus R	.20	.40
38 Krosan Grip U	.50	1.00
39 Ohran Viper R	.20	.40
40 Rampant Growth C	.10	.20
41 Thelonite Hermit R	.20	.40
42 Tribute to the Wild U	.12	.25
43 Wall of Blossoms U	.50	1.00
44 Biomantic Mastery R	.20	.40
45 Epic Experiment M	.30	.75
46 Etherium-Horn Sorcerer R	.20	.40
47 Ezuri, Claw of Progress M	2.50	5.00
48 Golgari Charm U	.20	.40
49 Jarad, Golgari Lich Lord M	.50	1.00
50 Kalemne, Disciple of Iroas M	.50	1.00
51 Snakeform C	.10	.20
52 Golgari Signet C	.10	.20
53 Izzet Signet C	.10	.20
54 Lightning Greaves U	2.00	4.00
55 Seer's Sundial R	.20	.40
56 Thought Vessel C	2.00	3.50
57 Ajani's Chosen R	.20	.40
58 Angel of Serenity M	.60	1.25
59 Arbiter of Knollridge R	.20	.40
60 Aura of Silence U	.60	1.25
61 Banishing Light U	.12	.25
62 Cage of Hands C	.10	.20
63 Celestial Ancient R	.20	.40
64 Celestial Archon R	.20	.40
65 Crib Swap U	.12	.25
66 Dawn to Dusk U	.12	.25
67 Dawnglare Invoker C	.10	.20
68 Dictate of Heliod R	.20	.40
69 Faith's Fetters C	.10	.20
70 Ghostblade Eidolon U	.12	.25
71 Jareth, Leonine Titan R	.20	.40
72 Karmic Justice R	.75	1.50
73 Kor Sanctifiers C	.10	.20
74 Marshal's Anthem R	.20	.40
75 Mesa Enchantress R	.20	.40
76 Monk Idealist U	.12	.25
77 Open the Vaults R	.50	1.00
78 Orim's Thunder C	.10	.20
79 Seal of Cleansing C	.10	.20
80 Sigil of the Empty Throne R	.20	.40
81 Silent Sentinel R	.20	.40
82 Sun Titan M	2.00	3.25
83 Victory's Herald R	.20	.40
84 Vow of Duty U	.12	.25
85 Aetherize U	.12	.25
86 Bident of Thassa R	.20	.40
87 Blatant Thievery R	.60	1.25
88 Blue Sun's Zenith R	.50	1.00
89 Blustersquall U	.12	.25
90 Brainstorm C	.60	1.25
91 Day of the Dragons R	.20	.40
92 Dominate U	.12	.25
93 Echoing Truth C	.10	.20
94 Fact or Fiction U	.25	.50
95 Jace's Archivist R	.20	.40
96 Lone Revenant R	.20	.40
97 Mulldrifter U	.30	.60
98 Mystic Retrieval U	.12	.25
99 Ninja of the Deep Hours C	.60	1.25
100 Plaxmanta U	.12	.25
101 Preordain C	1.00	2.00
102 Rapid Hybridization U	.25	.50
103 Reins of Power R	.20	.40
104 Repeal C	.10	.20
105 Rite of Replication R	1.00	2.00
106 Sleep U	.12	.25
107 Stolen Goods R	.20	.40
108 Stroke of Genius R	.20	.40
109 Talrand, Sky Summoner R	.50	1.00
110 Thought Reflection R	.20	.40
111 Windfall U	1.00	2.00
112 Altar's Reap C	.10	.20
113 Ambition's Cost U	.12	.25
114 Ancient Craving R	.20	.40
115 Barter in Blood U	.12	.25
116 Black Market R	3.00	6.00
117 Blood Bairn C	.10	.20
118 Butcher of Malakir R	.20	.40
119 Champion of Stray Souls M	.30	.75
120 Diabolic Servitude U	.12	.25
121 Doomwake Giant R	.20	.40
122 Dreadbringer Lampads C	.10	.20
123 Eater of Hope R	.20	.40
124 Extractor Demon R	.20	.40
125 Fallen Ideal U	.12	.25
126 Fate Unraveler R	.20	.40
127 Gild R	.20	.40
128 Grave Peril C	.10	.20
129 Nighthowler R	.20	.40
130 Phyrexian Arena R	2.50	5.00
131 Phyrexian Plaguelord R	.20	.40
132 Phyrexian Rager C	.10	.20
133 Phyrexian Reclamation U	.25	.50
134 Rise from the Grave U	.12	.25
135 Angel/Knight	.12	.25
136 Bear/Spider	.12	.25
137 Beast/Snake	.12	.25
138 Cat/Zombie	.12	.25
139 Dragon/Dragon	.12	.25
140 Drake/Elemental	.12	.25
141 Experience	.12	.25
142 Sever the Bloodline R	.20	.40
143 Shriekmaw U	.50	1.00
144 Underworld Connections R	.20	.40
145 Victimize U	.12	.25
146 Vow of Malice U	.12	.25
147 Wretched Confluence R	.50	1.00
148 Thief of Blood U	.12	.25
149 Act of Aggression U	.12	.25
150 Awaken the Sky Tyrant R	.20	.40
151 Borderland Behemoth R	.20	.40
152 Chain Reaction R	.20	.40
153 Charmbreaker Devils R	.20	.40
154 Comet Storm M	.50	1.00
155 Desolation Giant R	.20	.40
156 Desperate Ravings U	.12	.25
157 Disaster Radius R	.20	.40
158 Dragon Mage R	.30	.75
159 Dream Pillager R	.20	.40
160 Earthquake R	.20	.40
161 Faithless Looting C	.30	.60
162 Fall of the Hammer C	.10	.20
163 Hamletback Goliath R	.20	.40
164 Hunted Dragon R	.20	.40
165 Inferno Titan M	.60	1.25
166 Magma Giant R	.20	.40
167 Magmaquake R	.20	.40
168 Magus of the Wheel R	2.00	4.00
169 Meteor Blast U	.12	.25
170 Mizzium Mortars R	.20	.40
171 Rite of the Raging Storm U	.12	.25
172 Stinkdrinker Daredevil C	.10	.20
173 Stoneshock Giant U	.12	.25
174 Taurean Mauler R	.30	.75
175 Thundercloud Shaman U	.12	.25
176 Urza's Rage R	.20	.40
177 Warchief Giant U	.12	.25
178 Acidic Slime U	.12	.25
179 Arachnogenesis R	3.00	6.00
180 Arbor Colossus R	.20	.40
181 Bane of Progress R	1.00	2.00
182 Beastmaster Ascension R	.75	1.50

183 Bloodspore Thrinax R	3.00	6.00
184 Caller of the Claw R	.20	.40
185 Centaur Vinecrasher R	.30	.75
186 Cloudthresher R	.20	.40
187 Cobra Trap U	.12	.25
188 Desert Twister U	.12	.25
189 Elvish Visionary C	.10	.20
190 Eternal Witness U	2.50	5.00
191 Experiment One U	1.00	1.75
192 Ezuri's Predation R	.20	.40
193 Forgotten Ancient R	.50	1.00
194 Great Oak Guardian U	.12	.25
195 Indrik Stomphowler U	.12	.25
196 Kessig Cagebreakers R	.20	.40
197 Kodama's Reach C	1.00	1.75
198 Loaming Shaman R	.20	.40
199 Mulch C	.10	.20
200 Mycoloth R	1.00	2.00
201 Noble Quarry U	.12	.25
202 Overrun U	.12	.25
203 Overwhelming Stampede R	.20	.40
204 Patagia Viper U	.12	.25
205 Pathbreaker Ibex R	3.00	6.00
206 Primal Growth C	.10	.20
207 Sakura-Tribe Elder C	.25	.50
208 Satyr Wayfinder C	.10	.20
209 Skullwinder U	.20	.40
210 Spider Spawning U	.12	.25
211 Stingerfling Spider U	.12	.25
212 Terastodon R	.20	.40
213 Viridian Emissary C	.10	.20
214 Viridian Zealot R	.20	.40
215 Wood Elves C	.10	.20
216 Anya, Merciless Angel M	1.00	2.00
217 Arjun, the Shifting Flame M	.50	1.00
218 Call the Skybreaker R	.20	.40
219 Coiling Oracle C	.20	.40
220 Cold-Eyed Selkie R	.20	.40
221 Counterflux R	.60	1.25
222 Daxos the Returned M	.50	1.00
223 Death Grasp R	.20	.40
224 Firemind's Foresight R	.20	.40
225 Gisela, Blade of Goldnight M	3.00	6.00
226 Goblin Electromancer C	.10	.20
227 Grisly Salvage C	.10	.20
228 Karlov of the Ghost Council M	2.50	5.00
229 Kaseto, Orochi Archmage M	.50	1.00
230 Korozda Guildmage U	.12	.25
231 Lorescale Coatl U	.12	.25
232 Lotleth Troll R	.30	.75
233 Melek, Izzet Paragon R	.20	.40
234 Meren of Clan Nel Toth M	4.00	8.00
235 Mizzix of the Izmagnus M	.60	1.25
236 Mystic Snake R	.30	.60
237 Necromancer's Covenant R	.20	.40
238 Prime Speaker Zegana M	.50	1.00
239 Verdant Confluence R	1.00	2.00
240 Verdant Force R	.20	.40
241 Viridian Shaman U	.12	.25
242 Mazirek, Kraul Death Priest M	1.50	2.75
243 Prophetic Bolt R	.20	.40
244 Putrefy U	.15	.30
245 Steam Augury R	.20	.40
246 Teysa, Envoy of Ghosts R	.20	.40
247 Treasury Thrull R	.20	.40
248 Trygon Predator U	.20	.40
249 Underworld Coinsmith U	.12	.25
250 Vulturous Zombie R	.20	.40
251 Wistful Selkie U	.12	.25
252 Basalt Monolith U	.60	1.25
253 Blade of Selves R	4.00	7.00
254 Bonehoard R	.20	.40
255 Boros Cluestone C	.10	.20
256 Boros Signet C	.10	.20
257 Burnished Hart U	.25	.50
258 Coldsteel Heart U	.60	1.25
259 Crystal Chimes U	.12	.25
260 Darksteel Ingot U	.20	.40
261 Dreamstone Hedron U	.12	.25
262 Eldrazi Monument M	2.50	4.50
263 Fellwar Stone U	.30	.75
264 Loxodon Warhammer R	.30	.75
265 Mind Stone U	.12	.25
266 Orochi Hatchery R	.20	.40
267 Orzhov Cluestone C	.10	.20
268 Orzhov Signet C	.10	.20
269 Psychosis Crawler R	.30	.75
270 Sandstone Oracle U	.12	.25
271 Scytheclaw R	.20	.40
272 Seal of the Guildpact R	.50	1.00
273 Simic Keyrune U	.12	.25
274 Simic Signet C	.10	.20
275 Skullclamp U	1.25	2.15
276 Sol Ring U	2.00	3.25
277 Solemn Simulacrum R	2.50	5.00
278 Staff of Nin R	.60	1.25
279 Swiftfoot Boots U	.50	1.00
280 Sword of Vengeance R	.20	.40
281 Urza's Incubator R	3.00	6.00
282 Wayfarer's Bauble C	.10	.20
283 Worn Powerstone U	.30	.60
284 Boros Guildgate C	.10	.20
285 Command Beacon R	4.00	8.00
286 Command Tower C	.75	1.50
287 Drifting Meadow C	.10	.20
288 Evolving Wilds C	.10	.20
289 Forest L	.10	.20
290 Ghost Quarter U	.75	1.50
291 Golgari Guildgate C	.10	.20
292 Golgari Rot Farm C	.15	.30
293 Grim Backwoods R	.20	.40
294 High Market R	.50	1.00
295 Izzet Boilerworks C	.10	.20
296 Izzet Guildgate C	.10	.20
297 Jungle Hollow C	.10	.20
298 Llanowar Reborn U	.12	.25
299 Mosswort Bridge R	.50	1.00
300 New Benalia U	.12	.25
301 Novijen, Heart of Progress U	.12	.25
302 Oran-Rief, the Vastwood R	.60	1.25
303 Orzhov Basilica C	.15	.30
304 Orzhov Guildgate C	.10	.20
305 Plains L	.10	.20
306 Plains L	.10	.20
307 Plains L	.10	.20
308 Plains L	.10	.20
309 Polluted Mire C	.10	.20
310 Simic Growth Chamber C	.30	.75
311 Simic Guildgate C	.10	.20
312 Slippery Karst C	.10	.20
313 Smoldering Crater C	.10	.20
314 Spinerock Knoll R	.20	.40
315 Swamp L	.10	.20
316 Swamp L	.10	.20
317 Swamp L	.10	.20
318 Swamp L	.10	.20
319 Swiftwater Cliffs C	.10	.20
320 Tainted Field U	.25	.50
321 Tainted Wood U	.12	.25
322 Temple of the False God U	.25	.50
323 Mountain L	.10	.20
324 Mountain L	.10	.20
325 Mountain L	.10	.20
326 Mountain L	.10	.20
327 Forest L	.10	.20
328 Forest L	.10	.20
329 Forest L	.10	.20
330 Forgotten Cave C	.10	.20
331 Reliquary Tower U	1.50	3.00
332 Rogue's Passage U	.12	.25
333 Scoured Barrens C	.10	.20
334 Terramorphic Expanse C	.10	.20
334 Secluded Steppe C	.10	.20
335 Thornwood Falls C	.10	.20
335 Island L	.10	.20
336 Vivid Crag U	.12	.25
336 Island L	.10	.20
337 Vivid Creek U	.12	.25
337 Island L	.10	.20
338 Vivid Grove U	.12	.25
338 Island L	.10	.20
339 Vivid Marsh U	.12	.25
339 Ancient Amphitheater R	.20	.40
340 Barren Moor C	.10	.20
340 Vivid Meadow U	.12	.25
341 Wind-Scarred Crag C	.10	.20
341 Blasted Landscape U	.12	.25
342 Boros Garrison C	.10	.20
342 Zoetic Cavern U	.12	.25

2015 Magic The Gathering Commander 2015 Oversized

43 Daxos the Returned M	.50	1.00
44 Ezuri, Claw of Progress M	.60	1.25
45 Kalemne, Disciple of Iroas M	.50	1.00
49 Meren of Clan Nel Toth M	1.25	2.50
50 Mizzix of the Izmagnus M	.75	1.50

2015 Magic The Gathering Commander 2015 Tokens

0 Experience Counter	.07	.15
1 Shapeshifter	.07	.15
2 Angel	.07	.15
3 Cat	.07	.15
4 Knight	.07	.15
5 Knight	.17	.35
6 Drake	.07	.15
7 Germ	.07	.15
8 Zombie	.07	.15
9 Dragon	.07	.15
10 Elemental Shaman	.07	.15
11 Lightning Rager	.07	.15
12 Bear	.75	1.50
13 Beast	.07	.15
14 Elephant	.07	.15
15 Frog Lizard	.07	.15
16 Saproling	.07	.15
17 Snake	.07	.15
18 Spider	.07	.15
19 Wolf	.07	.15
20 Elemental	.07	.15
21 Snake	.07	.15
22 Spirit	.07	.15
23 Spirit	.30	.75
24 Gold	.07	.15

2015 Magic The Gathering Dragons of Tarkir

1 Scion of Ugin U	.10	.20
2 Anafenza, Kin-Tree Spirit R	.75	1.50
3 Arashin Foremost R	.15	.30
4 Artful Maneuver C	.07	.15
5 Aven Sunstriker U	.10	.20
6 Aven Tactician C	.07	.15
7 Battle Mastery U	.10	.20
8 Center Soul C	.07	.15
9 Champion of Arashin C	.07	.15
10 Dragon Hunter U	.10	.20
11 Dragon's Eye Sentry C	.07	.15
12 Dromoka Captain U	.10	.20
13 Dromoka Dunecaster C	.07	.15
14 Dromoka Warrior C	.07	.15
15 Echoes of the Kin Tree U	.10	.20
16 Enduring Victory C	.07	.15
17 Fate Forgotten C	.07	.15
18 Glaring Aegis C	.07	.15
19 Gleam of Authority R	.15	.30
20 Graceblade Artisan U	.10	.20
21 Great Teacher's Decree U	.10	.20
22 Herald of Dromoka C	.07	.15
23 Hidden Dragonslayer R	.15	.30
24 Lightwalker C	.07	.15
25 Misthoof Kirin C	.07	.15
26 Myth Realized R	.15	.30
27 Ojutai Exemplars M	.30	.75
28 Orator of Ojutai U	.10	.20
29 Pacifism C	.07	.15
30 Profound Journey R	.15	.30
31 Radiant Purge R	.15	.30
32 Resupply C	.07	.15
33 Sandcrafter Mage C	.07	.15
34 Sandstorm Charger C	.07	.15
35 Scale Blessing U	.10	.20
36 Secure the Wastes R	2.50	5.00
37 Shieldhide Dragon U	.10	.20
38 Silkwrap U	.10	.20
39 Strongarm Monk U	.10	.20
40 Student of Ojutai C	.07	.15
41 Sunscorch Regent R	.60	1.25
42 Surge of Righteousness U	.10	.20
43 Territorial Roc C	.07	.15
44 Ancient Carp C	.07	.15
45 Anticipate C	.07	.15
46 Belltoll Dragon R	.15	.30
47 Blessed Reincarnation R	.15	.30
48 Clone Legion M	2.50	5.00
49 Contradict C	.07	.15
50 Dance of the Skywise U	.10	.20
51 Dirgur Nemesis C	.07	.15
52 Dragonlord's Prerogative R	.15	.30
53 Elusive Spellfist C	.07	.15
54 Encase in Ice U	.10	.20
55 Glint C	.07	.15
56 Gudul Lurker U	.40	.80
57 Gurmag Drowner C	.07	.15
58 Icefall Regent R	.30	.60
59 Illusory Gains R	.15	.30
60 Learn from the Past U	.10	.20
61 Living Lore R	.15	.30
62 Mirror Mockery R	.25	.50
63 Monastery Loremaster C	.07	.15
64 Mystic Meditation C	.07	.15
65 Negate C	.07	.15
66 Ojutai Interceptor C	.07	.15
67 Ojutai's Breath C	.07	.15
68 Ojutai's Summons C	.07	.15
69 Palace Familiar C	.07	.15
70 Profaner of the Dead R	.15	.30
71 Qarsi Deceiver U	.10	.20
72 Reduce in Stature C	.07	.15
73 Shorecrasher Elemental M	.25	.50
74 Sidisi's Faithful C	.07	.15
75 Sight Beyond Sight U	.10	.20
76 Silumgar Sorcerer U	.10	.20
77 Silumgar Spell-Eater U	.10	.20
78 Silumgar's Scorn U	.10	.20
79 Skywise Teachings U	.10	.20
80 Stratus Dancer R	.15	.30
81 Taigam's Strike C	.07	.15
82 Updraft Elemental C	.07	.15
83 Void Squall U	.10	.20
84 Youthful Scholar U	.10	.20
85 Zephyr Scribe C	.07	.15
86 Acid-Spewer Dragon U	.10	.20
87 Ambuscade Shaman U	.10	.20
88 Blood-Chin Fanatic R	.15	.30
89 Blood-Chin Rager U	.10	.20
90 Butcher's Glee C	.07	.15
91 Coat with Venom C	.07	.15
92 Corpseweft R	.15	.30
93 Damnable Pact R	.15	.30
94 Deadly Wanderings U	.10	.20
95 Death Wind U	.10	.20
96 Deathbringer Regent R	.15	.30
97 Defeat C	.07	.15
98 Duress C	.07	.15
99 Dutiful Attendant C	.07	.15
100 Flatten C	.07	.15
101 Foul Renewal R	.15	.30
102 Foul-Tongue Invocation U	.10	.20
103 Foul-Tongue Shriek C	.07	.15
104 Gravepurge C	.07	.15
105 Hand of Silumgar C	.07	.15
106 Hedonist's Trove R	.15	.30
107 Kolaghan Skirmisher C	.07	.15
108 Marang River Skeleton U	.10	.20
109 Marsh Hulk C	.07	.15
110 Mind Rot C	.07	.15
111 Minister of Pain U	.10	.20
112 Pitiless Horde R	.15	.30
113 Qarsi Sadist C	.07	.15
114 Rakshasa Gravecaller U	.10	.20
115 Reckless Imp C	.07	.15
116 Risen Executioner M	2.00	4.00
117 Self-Inflicted Wound U	.10	.20
118 Shambling Goblin C	.07	.15
119 Sibsig Icebreakers C	.07	.15
120 Sidisi, Undead Vizier R	6.00	12.00
121 Silumgar Assassin R	.15	.30
122 Silumgar Butcher C	.07	.15
123 Ukud Cobra U	.10	.20
124 Ultimate Price U	.10	.20
125 Virulent Plague U	.10	.20
126 Vulturous Aven C	.07	.15
127 Wandering Tombshell C	.07	.15
128 Atarka Efreet C	.07	.15
129 Atarka Pummeler U	.10	.20
130 Berserkers' Onslaught R	.60	1.25
131 Commune with Lava R	.15	.30
132 Crater Elemental R	.15	.30
133 Descent of the Dragons M	3.00	6.00
134 Draconic Roar U	.10	.20
135 Dragon Fodder C	.07	.15
136 Dragon Tempest R	4.00	8.00
137 Dragon Whisperer M	.75	1.50
138 Dragonlord's Servant U	.30	.60
139 Hardened Berserker C	.07	.15
140 Impact Tremors C	2.00	4.00
141 Ire Shaman R	.15	.30
142 Kindled Fury C	.07	.15
143 Kolaghan Aspirant C	.07	.15
144 Kolaghan Forerunners U	.10	.20
145 Kolaghan Stormsinger C	.07	.15
146 Lightning Berserker U	.10	.20
147 Lose Calm C	.07	.15
148 Magmatic Chasm C	.07	.15
149 Qal Sisma Behemoth U	.10	.20
150 Rending Volley U	.10	.20
151 Roast U	.10	.20
152 Sabertooth Outrider C	.07	.15
153 Sarkhan's Rage C	.07	.15
154 Sarkhan's Triumph U	.75	1.50
155 Screamreach Brawler C	.07	.15
156 Seismic Rupture U	.10	.20
157 Sprinting Warbrute C	.07	.15
158 Stormcrag Elemental U	.10	.20
159 Stormwing Dragon U	.10	.20
160 Summit Prowler C	.07	.15
161 Tail Slash C	.07	.15
162 Thunderbreak Regent R	1.25	2.50
163 Tormenting Voice C	.07	.15
164 Twin Bolt C	.07	.15
165 Vandalize C	.07	.15
166 Volcanic Rush C	.07	.15
167 Volcanic Vision R	.15	.30
168 Warbringer U	.10	.20
169 Zurgo Bellstriker R	.30	.60
170 Aerie Bowmasters C	.07	.15
171 Ainok Artillerist C	.07	.15
172 Ainok Survivalist U	.10	.20
173 Assault Formation R	.60	1.25
174 Atarka Beastbreaker C	.07	.15
175 Avatar of the Resolute R	.15	.30
176 Circle of Elders U	.10	.20
177 Collected Company R	10.00	20.00
178 Colossodon Yearling C	.07	.15
179 Conifer Strider C	.07	.15
180 Deathmist Raptor M	.50	1.00
181 Den Protector R	.15	.30
182 Display of Dominance U	.10	.20
183 Dragon-Scarred Bear C	.07	.15
184 Dromoka's Gift U	.10	.20
185 Epic Confrontation C	.07	.15
186 Explosive Vegetation U	.75	1.50
187 Foe-Razer Regent R	.25	.50
188 Glade Watcher C	.07	.15
189 Guardian Shield-Bearer C	.07	.15
190 Herdchaser Dragon U	.10	.20
191 Inspiring Call U	.50	1.00
192 Lurking Arynx U	.10	.20
193 Naturalize C	.07	.15
194 Obscuring Aether R	.15	.30
195 Pinion Feast C	.07	.15
196 Press the Advantage U	.10	.20
197 Revealing Wind C	.07	.15
198 Salt Road Ambushers U	.10	.20
199 Salt Road Quartermasters U	.10	.20
200 Sandsteppe Scavenger C	.07	.15
201 Scaleguard Sentinels U	.10	.20
202 Segmented Krotiq C	.07	.15
203 Servant of the Scale C	.07	.15
204 Shaman of Forgotten Ways M	4.00	8.00
205 Shape the Sands C	.07	.15
206 Sheltered Aerie C	.07	.15
207 Sight of the Scalelords U	.20	.40
208 Stampeding Elk Herd C	.07	.15
209 Sunbringer's Touch R	.15	.30
210 Surrak, the Hunt Caller R	.15	.30
211 Tread Upon C	.07	.15
212 Arashin Sovereign R	.15	.30
213 Atarka's Command R	2.00	4.00
214 Boltwing Marauder R	.15	.30
215 Cunning Breezedancer U	.10	.20
216 Dragonlord Atarka M	5.00	10.00
217 Dragonlord Dromoka M	25.00	50.00
218 Dragonlord Kolaghan M	6.00	12.00
219 Dragonlord Ojutai M	3.00	6.00
220 Dragonlord Silumgar M	10.00	20.00
221 Dromoka's Command R	.75	1.50
222 Enduring Scalelord U	.10	.20
223 Harbinger of the Hunt R	.15	.30
224 Kolaghan's Command R	7.50	15.00
225 Narset Transcendent M	5.00	10.00
226 Necromaster Dragon R	.15	.30
227 Ojutai's Command R	.15	.30
228 Pristine Skywise R	.15	.30
229 Ruthless Deathfang U	.10	.20
230 Sarkhan Unbroken M	12.50	25.00
231 Savage Ventmaw U	.10	.20
232 Silumgar's Command R	.15	.30
233 Swift Warkite U	.10	.20
234 Ancestral Statue C	.07	.15
235 Atarka Monument U	.10	.20
236 Custodian of the Trove C	.07	.15
237 Dragonloft Idol U	.10	.20
238 Dromoka Monument U	.10	.20
239 Gate Smasher U	.10	.20
240 Keeper of the Lens C	.07	.15
241 Kolaghan Monument U	.10	.20
242 Ojutai Monument U	.15	.30
243 Silumgar Monument U	.10	.20
244 Spidersilk Net C	.07	.15
245 Stormrider Rig U	.10	.20
246 Tapestry of the Ages U	.10	.20
247 Vial of Dragonfire C	.07	.15
248 Evolving Wilds C	.07	.15
249 Haven of the Spirit Dragon R	2.00	4.00
250 Plains L	.15	.30
251 Plains L	.15	.30
252 Plains L	.15	.30
253 Island L	.15	.30
254 Island L	.15	.30
255 Island L	.15	.30
256 Swamp L	.15	.30
257 Swamp L	.15	.30
258 Swamp L	.15	.30
259 Mountain L	.15	.30
260 Mountain L	.15	.30
261 Mountain L	.15	.30
262 Forest L	.15	.30
263 Forest L	.15	.30
264 Forest L	.15	.30

2015 Magic The Gathering Dragons of Tarkir Tokens

1 Warrior	.30	.75
2 Djinn Monk	.07	.15
3 Zombie	.12	.25
4 Zombie Horror	.07	.15
5 Dragon	.20	.40
6 Goblin	.12	.25
7 Morph	.07	.15
8 Narset Transcendent Emblem	.50	1.00

2015 Magic The Gathering Duel Decks Elspeth vs. Kiora

1 Elspeth, Sun's Champion M	5.00	10.00
2 Banisher Priest U	.10	.20
3 Captain of the Watch R	.30	.75
4 Celestial Flare C	.10	.20
5 Court Street Denizen C	.10	.20
6 Dauntless Onslaught U	.10	.20
7 Decree of Justice R	.17	.35
8 Dictate of Heliod R	.17	.35
9 Gempalm Avenger C	.10	.20
10 Gustcloak Harrier C	.10	.20
11 Gustcloak Savior R	.17	.35
12 Gustcloak Sentinel U	.10	.20

13 Gustcloak Skirmisher U .10 .20
14 Icatian Javeliners C .10 .20
15 Kinsbaile Skirmisher C .10 .20
16 Kor Skyfisher C .10 .20
17 Loxodon Partisan C .10 .20
18 Mighty Leap C .10 .20
19 Mortal's Ardor C .10 .20
20 Mother of Runes U 1.25 2.25
21 Noble Templar C .10 .20
22 Precinct Captain R .25 .50
23 Raise the Alarm C .10 .20
24 Soul Parry C .10 .20
25 Standing Troops C .10 .20
26 Sunlance C .10 .20
27 Veteran Armorsmith C .10 .20
28 Veteran Swordsmith C .10 .20
29 Secluded Steppe C .10 .20
30 Plains L .10 .20
31 Plains L .10 .20
32 Plains L .10 .20
33 Plains L .10 .20
34 Kiora, the Crashing Wave M 2.00 4.00
35 Accumulated Knowledge C .10 .20
36 Aetherize U .10 .20
37 Inkwell Leviathan R .30 .60
38 Man-o'-War C .10 .20
39 Omenspeaker C .10 .20
40 Peel from Reality C .10 .20
41 Scourge of Fleets R .17 .35
42 Sealock Monster U .10 .20
43 Surrakar Banisher C .10 .20
44 Whelming Wave R .20 .40
45 Explore C .25 .50
46 Explosive Vegetation U .60 1.25
47 Grazing Gladehart C .10 .20
48 Nessian Asp C .10 .20
49 Netcaster Spider C .10 .20
50 Time to Feed C .10 .20
51 Coiling Oracle C .10 .20
52 Kiora's Follower U .10 .20
53 Lorescale Coatl U .10 .20
54 Nimbus Swimmer U .10 .20
55 Plasm Capture R .17 .35
56 Simic Sky Swallower R .17 .35
57 Urban Evolution U .10 .20
58 Evolving Wilds C .10 .20
59 Temple of the False God U .30 .75
60 Island L .10 .20
61 Island L .10 .20
62 Island L .10 .20
63 Forest L .10 .20
64 Forest L .10 .20
65 Forest L .10 .20
66 Soldier C .12 .25
67 Kraken C .75 1.50

2015 Magic The Gathering Duel Decks Zendikar vs. Eldrazi

1 Avenger of Zendikar M 3.00 6.00
2 Affa Guard Hound U .10 .20
3 Caravan Escort C .10 .20
4 Kabira Vindicator U .10 .20
5 Knight of Cliffhaven C .10 .20
6 Makindi Griffin C .10 .20
7 Oust U .10 .20
8 Repel the Darkness C .10 .20
9 Sheer Drop C .10 .20
10 Beastbreaker of Bala Ged U .10 .20
11 Daggerback Basilisk C .10 .20
12 Frontier Guide U .10 .20
13 Graypelt Hunter C .10 .20
14 Grazing Gladehart C .10 .20
15 Groundswell C .50 1.00
16 Harrow C .10 .20
17 Joraga Bard C .10 .20
18 Khalni Heart Expedition C .10 .20
19 Ondu Giant C .10 .20
20 Primal Command R .60 1.25
21 Retreat to Kazandu U .10 .20
22 Scute Mob R .30 .60
23 Tajuru Archer U .10 .20
24 Territorial Baloth C .10 .20
25 Turntimber Basilisk U .10 .20
26 Wildheart Invoker C .10 .20
27 Veteran Warleader R .25 .50
28 Explorer's Scope C .10 .20
29 Seer's Sundial R .17 .35
30 Stonework Puma C .10 .20
31 Evolving Wilds C .10 .20
32 Graypelt Refuge U .10 .20
33 Stirring Wildwood R .60 1.25
34 Turntimber Grove C .10 .20
35 Plains L .10 .20
36 Plains L .10 .20
37 Plains L .10 .20
38 Forest L .10 .20
39 Forest L .10 .20
40 Forest L .10 .20
41 Oblivion Sower M .75 1.50
42 Artisan of Kozilek U .20 .40
43 It That Betrays R 1.25 2.25
44 Ulamog's Crusher C .10 .20
45 Bloodrite Invoker C .10 .20
46 Bloodthrone Vampire C .10 .20
47 Butcher of Malakir R .20 .40
48 Cadaver Imp C .10 .20
49 Consume the Meek R .20 .40
50 Corpsehatch U .10 .20
51 Dominator Drone C .10 .20
52 Heartstabber Mosquito C .10 .20
53 Induce Despair C .10 .20
54 Marsh Casualties U .10 .20
55 Pawn of Ulamog U .10 .20
56 Read the Bones C .10 .20
57 Smother U .10 .20
58 Vampire Nighthawk U .50 1.00
59 Emrakul's Hatcher C .10 .20
60 Forked Bolt C .20 .40
61 Hellion Eruption R .20 .40
62 Magmaw R .20 .40
63 Torch Slinger C .10 .20
64 Forerunner of Slaughter U .10 .20
65 Mind Stone U .10 .20
66 Runed Servitor U .10 .20
67 Akoum Refuge U .10 .20
68 Eldrazi Temple U 4.00 7.00
69 Rocky Tar Pit U .10 .20
70 Swamp L .10 .20
71 Swamp L .10 .20
72 Swamp L .10 .20
73 Mountain L .10 .20
74 Mountain L .10 .20
75 Mountain L .10 .20
76 Eldrazi Spawn C .10 .20
77 Eldrazi Spawn C .10 .20
78 Eldrazi Spawn C .10 .20
79 Hellion C .10 .20
80 Plant C .10 .20

2015 Magic The Gathering Fate Reforged

1 Ugin, the Spirit Dragon M 15.00 30.00
2 Abzan Advantage C .07 .15
3 Abzan Runemark C .07 .15
4 Abzan Skycaptain C .07 .15
5 Arashin Cleric C .07 .15
6 Aven Skirmisher C .07 .15
7 Channel Harm U .10 .20
8 Citadel Siege R .15 .30
9 Daghatar the Adamant R .15 .30
10 Dragon Bell Monk C .07 .15
11 Dragonscale General R .15 .30
12 Elite Scaleguard U .10 .20
13 Great-Horn Krushok C .07 .15
14 Honor's Reward U .10 .20
15 Jeskai Barricade U .30 .60
16 Lightform U .10 .20
17 Lotus-Eye Mystics U .10 .20
18 Mardu Woe-Reaper U .20 .40
19 Mastery of the Unseen R .15 .30
20 Monastery Mentor M 7.50 15.00
21 Pressure Point C .07 .15
22 Rally the Ancestors R .30 .75
23 Sage's Reverie U .20 .40
24 Sandblast C .07 .15
25 Sandsteppe Outcast C .07 .15
26 Soul Summons C .07 .15
27 Soulfire Grand Master M 1.50 3.00
28 Valorous Stance U .10 .20
29 Wandering Champion U .10 .20
30 Wardscale Dragon U .10 .20
31 Aven Surveyor C .07 .15
32 Cloudform U .10 .20
33 Enhanced Awareness C .07 .15
34 Fascination U .15 .30
35 Frost Walker U .10 .20
36 Jeskai Infiltrator R .15 .30
37 Jeskai Runemark C .07 .15
38 Jeskai Sage C .07 .15
39 Lotus Path Djinn C .07 .15
40 Marang River Prowler U .10 .20
41 Mindscour Dragon U .10 .20
42 Mistfire Adept U .10 .20
43 Monastery Siege R .50 1.00
44 Neutralizing Blast U .10 .20
45 Rakshasa's Disdain C .07 .15
46 Reality Shift U .75 1.50
47 Refocus C .07 .15
48 Renowned Weaponsmith U .10 .20
49 Rite of Undoing U .10 .20
50 Sage-Eye Avengers R .15 .30
51 Shifting Loyalties U .10 .20
52 Shu Yun, the Silent Tempest R .20 .40
53 Sultai Skullkeeper C .07 .15
54 Supplant Form R .15 .30
55 Temporal Trespass M 5.00 10.00
56 Torrent Elemental M .50 1.00
57 Whisk Away C .07 .15
58 Will of the Naga C .07 .15
59 Write into Being C .07 .15
60 Alesha's Vanguard C .07 .15
61 Ancestral Vengeance C .07 .15
62 Archfiend of Depravity R 2.50 5.00
63 Battle Brawler U .10 .20
64 Brutal Hordechief M .50 1.00
65 Crux of Fate R 1.25 2.50
66 Dark Deal U 2.00 4.00
67 Diplomacy of the Wastes U .10 .20
68 Douse in Gloom C .07 .15
69 Fearsome Awakening U .15 .30
70 Ghastly Conscription M .30 .75
71 Grave Strength U .10 .20
72 Gurmag Angler C .07 .15
73 Hooded Assassin C .07 .15
74 Mardu Shadowspear U .10 .20
75 Mardu Strike Leader R .15 .30
76 Merciless Executioner U .10 .20
77 Noxious Dragon U .10 .20
78 Orc Sureshot U .10 .20
79 Palace Siege R .75 1.50
80 Qarsi High Priest U .10 .20
81 Reach of Shadows C .07 .15
82 Sibsig Host C .07 .15
83 Sibsig Muckdraggers U .10 .20
84 Soulflayer R .15 .30
85 Sultai Emissary C .07 .15
86 Sultai Runemark C .07 .15
87 Tasigur, the Golden Fang R .15 .30
88 Tasigur's Cruelty C .07 .15
89 Typhoid Rats C .07 .15
90 Alesha, Who Smiles at Death R .15 .30
91 Arcbond R .25 .50
92 Bathe in Dragonfire C .07 .15
93 Bloodfire Enforcers U .10 .20
94 Break Through the Line U .10 .20
95 Collateral Damage C .07 .15
96 Defiant Ogre C .07 .15
97 Dragonrage U .10 .20
98 Fierce Invocation C .07 .15
99 Flamerush Rider R .15 .30
100 Flamewake Phoenix R .30 .60
101 Friendly Fire U .10 .20
102 Goblin Heelcutter C .07 .15
103 Gore Swine C .07 .15
104 Humble Defector U .10 .20
105 Hungering Yeti U .10 .20
106 Lightning Shrieker C .07 .15
107 Mardu Runemark C .07 .15
108 Mardu Scout C .07 .15
109 Mob Rule R .60 1.25
110 Outpost Siege R .20 .40
111 Pyrotechnics U .10 .20
112 Rageform U .10 .20
113 Shaman of the Great Hunt M .30 .75
114 Shockmaw Dragon U .10 .20
115 Smoldering Efreet C .07 .15
116 Temur Battle Rage C .07 .15
117 Vaultbreaker U .10 .20
118 Wild Slash U .20 .40
119 Abzan Beastmaster U .10 .20
120 Abzan Kin-Guard U .10 .20
121 Ainok Guide C .07 .15
122 Ambush Krotiq C .07 .15
123 Arashin War Beast U .10 .20
124 Archers of Qarsi C .07 .15
125 Battlefront Krushok U .10 .20
126 Cached Defenses U .10 .20
127 Destructor Dragon U .10 .20
128 Feral Krushok C .07 .15
129 Formless Nurturing C .07 .15
130 Frontier Mastodon C .07 .15
131 Frontier Siege R .30 .75
132 Fruit of the First Tree U .10 .20
133 Hunt the Weak C .07 .15
134 Map the Wastes C .07 .15
135 Return to the Earth C .07 .15
136 Ruthless Instincts U .10 .20
137 Sandsteppe Mastodon R .15 .30
138 Shamanic Revelation R .30 .60
139 Sudden Reclamation U .10 .20
140 Temur Runemark C .07 .15
141 Temur Sabertooth U 2.00 4.00
142 Temur War Shaman R .15 .30
143 Warden of the First Tree M .30 .75
144 Whisperer of the Wilds C .07 .15
145 Whisperwood Elemental M .50 1.00
146 Wildcall R .15 .30
147 Winds of Qal Sisma U .10 .20
148 Yasova Dragonclaw R .15 .30
149 Atarka, World Render R .50 1.00
150 Cunning Strike C .07 .15
151 Dromoka, the Eternal R .20 .40
152 Ethereal Ambush C .07 .15
153 Grim Contest C .07 .15
154 Harsh Sustenance C .07 .15
155 Kolaghan, the Storm's Fury R .30 .60
156 Ojutai, Soul of Winter R .15 .30
157 Silumgar, the Drifting Death R .30 .60
158 War Flare C .07 .15
159 Goblin Boom Keg U .10 .20
160 Hero's Blade U .10 .20
161 Hewed Stone Retainers U .10 .20
162 Pilgrim of the Fires U .10 .20
163 Scroll of the Masters R .15 .30
164 Ugin's Construct U .10 .20
165 Bloodfell Caves C .07 .15
166 Blossoming Sands C .07 .15
167 Crucible of the Spirit Dragon R .25 .50
168 Dismal Backwater C .07 .15
169 Jungle Hollow C .07 .15
170 Rugged Highlands C .07 .15
171 Scoured Barrens C .07 .15
172 Swiftwater Cliffs C .07 .15
173 Thornwood Falls C .07 .15
174 Tranquil Cove C .07 .15
175 Wind-Scarred Crag C .07 .15
176 Plains L .15 .30
177 Plains L .15 .30
178 Plains L .15 .30
179 Island L .15 .30
180 Swamp L .15 .30
181 Swamp L .15 .30
182 Mountain L .15 .30
183 Mountain L .15 .30
184 Forest L .15 .30
185 Forest L .15 .30

2015 Magic The Gathering Fate Reforged Tokens

1 Monk .60 1.25
2 Spirit .07 .15
3 Warrior .07 .15
4 Manifest .07 .15

2015 Magic The Gathering From the Vault Angels

1 Akroma, Angel of Fury M 2.50 5.00
2 Akroma, Angel of Wrath M 3.00 6.00
3 Archangel of Strife M .50 1.00
4 Aurelia, the Warleader M 6.00 12.00
5 Avacyn, Angel of Hope M 30.00 60.00
6 Baneslayer Angel M 5.00 10.00
7 Entreat the Angels M 1.00 2.00
8 Exalted Angel M .75 1.50
9 Iona, Shield of Emeria M 3.00 6.00
10 Iridescent Angel M .60 1.25
11 Jenara, Asura of War M 1.25 2.50
12 Lightning Angel M .50 1.00
13 Platinum Angel M 4.00 8.00
14 Serra Angel M .75 1.50
15 Tariel, Reckoner of Souls M 1.50 3.00

2015 Magic The Gathering Judge Gift Rewards

1 Temporal Manipulation R 12.50 25.00
2 Shardless Agent R 5.00 10.00
3 Rishadan Port R 7.50 15.00
4 Ravages of War R 60.00 125.00
5 Damnation R 30.00 60.00
6 Dualcaster Mage R 6.00 12.00
7 Feldon of the Third Path R 6.00 12.00
8 Wasteland R 30.00 75.00

2015 Magic The Gathering League Token

1 Monk 20.00 40.00

2015 Magic The Gathering Modern Masters 2015

1 All Is Dust R 7.50 15.00
2 Artisan of Kozilek U .50 1.00
3 Emrakul, the Aeons Torn M 30.00 60.00
4 Karn Liberated M 20.00 40.00
5 Kozilek, Butcher of Truth M 50.00 100.00
6 Ulamog, the Infinite Gyre M 30.00 75.00
7 Ulamog's Crusher C .07 .15
8 Apostle's Blessing C .15 .30
9 Arrest C .07 .15
10 Battlegrace Angel R .30 .75
11 Celestial Purge U .15 .30
12 Conclave Phalanx C .12 .25
13 Court Homunculus C .07 .15
14 Daybreak Coronet R 3.00 6.00
15 Dispatch U 1.00 2.00
16 Elesh Norn, Grand Cenobite M 20.00 40.00
17 Fortify C .07 .15
18 Hikari, Twilight Guardian U .10 .20
19 Indomitable Archangel R .75 1.50
20 Iona, Shield of Emeria M 4.00 8.00
21 Kami of Ancient Law C .07 .15
22 Kor Duelist U .15 .30
23 Leyline of Sanctity R 4.00 8.00
24 Mighty Leap C .07 .15
25 Mirran Crusader R 1.00 2.00
26 Mirror Entity R 1.25 2.50
27 Moonlit Strider C .07 .15
28 Myrsmith U .10 .20
29 Oblivion Ring U .20 .40
30 Otherworldly Journey C .07 .15
31 Raise the Alarm C .07 .15
32 Skyhunter Skirmisher C .15 .30
33 Spectral Procession U .25 .50
34 Sunlance C .07 .15
35 Sunspear Shikari C .07 .15
36 Taj-Nar Swordsmith U .12 .25
37 Terashi's Grasp C .07 .15
38 Waxmane Baku C .07 .15
39 Aethersnipe C .07 .15
40 Air Servant U .10 .20
41 Argent Sphinx R .15 .30
42 Cloud Elemental C .07 .15
43 Cryptic Command R 17.50 35.00
44 Faerie Mechanist C .07 .15
45 Flashfreeze U .10 .20
46 Guile R .50 1.00
47 Helium Squirter C .07 .15
48 Hurkyl's Recall R 4.00 8.00
49 Inexorable Tide R 4.00 8.00
50 Mana Leak C .20 .40
51 Mulldrifter U .25 .50
52 Narcolepsy C .07 .15
53 Novijen Sages U .10 .20
54 Qumulox U .10 .20
55 Remand U 3.00 6.00
56 Repeal C .07 .15
57 Somber Hoverguard C .07 .15
58 Steady Progress C .12 .25
59 Stoic Rebuttal C .12 .25
60 Surrakar Spellblade R .15 .30
61 Telling Time C .07 .15
62 Tezzeret the Seeker M 12.50 25.00
63 Tezzeret's Gambit U .20 .40
64 Thoughtcast C .60 1.25
65 Thrummingbird C .20 .40
66 Vapor Snag C .25 .50
67 Vendilion Clique M 6.00 12.00
68 Vigean Graftmage C .12 .25
69 Water Servant U .10 .20
70 Wings of Velis Vel C .07 .15
71 Bitterblossom M 30.00 60.00
72 Bloodthrone Vampire C .07 .15
73 Bone Splinters C .07 .15
74 Daggerclaw Imp U .10 .20
75 Dark Confidant M 20.00 40.00
76 Death Denied C .07 .15
77 Deathmark U .10 .20
78 Devouring Greed U .10 .20
79 Dismember U 2.50 5.00
80 Dread Drone C .07 .15
81 Duskhunter Bat C .07 .15
82 Endrek Sahr, Master Breeder R 2.50 5.00
83 Ghostly Changeling C .07 .15
84 Grim Affliction C .15 .30
85 Instill Infection C .07 .15
86 Midnight Banshee R 1.00 2.00
87 Nameless Inversion C .07 .15
88 Necroskitter R 5.00 10.00
89 Plagued Rusalka C .07 .15
90 Profane Command R .20 .40
91 Puppeteer Clique R 3.00 6.00
92 Reassembling Skeleton U .20 .40
93 Scavenger Drake U .10 .20
94 Scuttling Death C .07 .15
95 Shrivel C .07 .15
96 Sickle Ripper C .07 .15
97 Sign in Blood C .20 .40
98 Spread the Sickness U .15 .30
99 Surgical Extraction R 20.00 40.00
100 Thief of Hope C .07 .15
101 Vampire Lacerator C .07 .15
102 Vampire Outcasts U .10 .20
103 Waking Nightmare C .07 .15
104 Banefire R .50 1.00
105 Blades of Velis Vel C .07 .15
106 Blood Ogre C .07 .15
107 Bloodshot Trainee U .10 .20
108 Brute Force C .15 .30
109 Burst Lightning C .20 .40
110 Combust U .10 .20
111 Comet Storm M .75 1.50
112 Dragonsoul Knight C .07 .15
113 Fiery Fall C .07 .15
114 Goblin Fireslinger C .07 .15
115 Goblin War Paint C .07 .15
116 Gorehorn Minotaurs C .07 .15
117 Gut Shot C .75 1.50
118 Hellkite Charger R 2.00 4.00
119 Incandescent Soulstoke U 1.00 2.00
120 Inner-Flame Igniter C .07 .15
121 Kiki-Jiki, Mirror Breaker M 7.50 15.00
122 Lightning Bolt U 2.00 4.00
123 Skarrgan Firebird U .10 .20
124 Smash to Smithereens C .15 .30

125 Smokebraider C	.07	.15
126 Soulbright Flamekin C	.07	.15
127 Spikeshot Elder R	.15	.30
128 Spitebellows U	.10	.20
129 Splinter Twin R	7.50	15.00
130 Stormblood Berserker U	.10	.20
131 Thunderblust R	.25	.50
132 Tribal Flames C	.07	.15
133 Viashino Slaughtermaster C	.07	.15
134 Wildfire R	.30	.75
135 Worldheart Phoenix U	.12	.25
136 Wrap in Flames C	.07	.15
137 Algae Gharial U	.10	.20
138 All Suns' Dawn R	.25	.50
139 Ant Queen R	.75	1.50
140 Aquastrand Spider C	.07	.15
141 Bestial Menace U	.10	.20
142 Commune with Nature C	.07	.15
143 Cytoplast Root-Kin U	.10	.20
144 Gnarlid Pack C	.07	.15
145 Karplusan Strider U	.10	.20
146 Kavu Primarch C	.07	.15
147 Kozilek's Predator C	.07	.15
148 Matca Rioters C	.07	.15
149 Mutagenic Growth U	2.50	5.00
150 Nest Invader C	.15	.30
151 Noble Hierarch R	12.50	25.00
152 Overwhelm U	.10	.20
153 Overwhelming Stampede R	2.00	4.00
154 Pelakka Wurm U	.10	.20
155 Plummet C	.07	.15
156 Primeval Titan M	5.00	10.00
157 Rampant Growth C	.50	1.00
158 Root-Kin Ally U	.10	.20
159 Scatter the Seeds C	.07	.15
160 Scion of the Wild C	.07	.15
161 Scute Mob R	.75	1.50
162 Simic Initiate C	.07	.15
163 Sundering Vitae C	.07	.15
164 Sylvan Bounty C	.07	.15
165 Tarmogoyf M	25.00	50.00
166 Thrive C	.07	.15
167 Tukatongue Thallid C	.07	.15
168 Vines of Vastwood C	.75	1.50
169 Wolfbriar Elemental R	.25	.50
170 Agony Warp U	.10	.20
171 Apocalypse Hydra R	.30	.75
172 Boros Swiftblade U	.10	.20
173 Drooling Groodion U	.10	.20
174 Electrolyze U	.10	.20
175 Ethercaste Knight U	.10	.20
176 Ghost Council of Orzhova R	.20	.40
177 Glassdust Hulk U	.10	.20
178 Horde of Notions R	.50	1.00
179 Lorescale Coatl U	.10	.20
180 Mystic Snake R	.75	1.50
181 Necrogenesis U	.15	.30
182 Niv-Mizzet, the Firemind R	.30	.60
183 Pillory of the Sleepless U	.10	.20
184 Plaxcaster Frogling U	.25	.50
185 Savage Twister U	.10	.20
186 Shadowmage Infiltrator R	.20	.40
187 Sigil Blessing U	.10	.20
188 Vengeful Rebirth U	.10	.20
189 Wrecking Ball U	.10	.20
190 Ashenmoor Gouger U	.10	.20
191 Creakwood Liege R	7.50	15.00
192 Dimir Guildmage U	.10	.20
193 Fulminator Mage R	1.00	2.00
194 Hearthfire Hobgoblin U	.10	.20
195 Nobilis of War R	.15	.30
196 Restless Apparition U	.10	.20
197 Selesnya Guildmage U	.10	.20
198 Shrewd Hatchling U	.10	.20
199 Swans of Bryn Argoll R	.60	1.25
200 Wilt-Leaf Liege R	1.50	3.00
201 Alloy Myr C	.15	.30
202 Blinding Souleater C	.07	.15
203 Cathodion C	.07	.15
204 Chimeric Mass R	.20	.40
205 Copper Carapace C	.07	.15
206 Cranial Plating U	.30	.60
207 Culling Dais U	.10	.20
208 Darksteel Axe U	.10	.20
209 Etched Champion R	4.00	8.00
210 Etched Monstrosity R	.25	.50
211 Etched Oracle U	.10	.20
212 Everflowing Chalice U	.75	1.50
213 Expedition Map U	1.50	3.00
214 Flayer Husk C	.07	.15
215 Frogmite C	.15	.30
216 Glint Hawk Idol C	.07	.15
217 Gust-Skimmer C	.07	.15
218 Kitesail C	.07	.15
219 Lodestone Golem R	.75	1.50
220 Lodestone Myr R	.20	.40
221 Long-Forgotten Gohei R	.20	.40
222 Mortarpod U	.10	.20
223 Mox Opal M	30.00	60.00
224 Myr Enforcer C	.25	.50
225 Precursor Golem R	.20	.40
226 Runed Servitor C	.07	.15
227 Rusted Relic C	.07	.15
228 Sickleslicer C	.07	.15
229 Skyreach Manta C	.07	.15
230 Spellskite R	2.50	5.00
231 Sphere of the Suns C	.20	.40
232 Sunforger R	.75	1.50
233 Tumble Magnet U	.10	.20
234 Wayfarer's Bauble C	1.25	2.50
235 Azorius Chancery U	.15	.30
236 Blinkmoth Nexus R	1.50	3.00
237 Boros Garrison U	.15	.30
238 Darksteel Citadel C	.30	.60
239 Dimir Aqueduct U	.20	.40
240 Eldrazi Temple U	5.00	10.00
241 Evolving Wilds C	.07	.15
242 Eye of Ugin R	7.50	15.00
243 Golgari Rot Farm U	.15	.30
244 Gruul Turf U	.15	.30
245 Izzet Boilerworks U	.15	.30
246 Orzhov Basilica U	.20	.40
247 Rakdos Carnarium U	.15	.30
248 Selesnya Sanctuary U	.15	.30
249 Simic Growth Chamber U	.30	.60

2015 Magic The Gathering Modern Masters 2015 Tokens

1 Eldrazi Spawn	.10	.20
2 Eldrazi Spawn	.10	.20
3 Eldrazi Spawn	.10	.20
4 Soldier	.07	.15
5 Spirit	.07	.15
6 Faerie Rogue	.60	1.25
7 Germ	.07	.15
8 Thrull	.30	.75
9 Elephant	.07	.15
10 Insect	.12	.25
11 Saproling	.10	.20
12 Snake	.10	.20
13 Wolf	.12	.25
14 Worm	.17	.35
15 Golem	.17	.35
16 Myr	.15	.30

2015 Magic The Gathering Origins

1 Akroan Jailer C	.07	.15
2 Ampryn Tactician C	.07	.15
3 Anointer of Champions U	.10	.20
4 Archangel of Tithes M	7.50	15.00
5 Auramancer C	.07	.15
6 Aven Battle Priest C	.07	.15
7 Blessed Spirits U	.10	.20
8 Celestial Flare C	.07	.15
9 Charging Griffin C	.07	.15
10 Cleric of the Forward Order C	.07	.15
11 Consul's Lieutenant U	.10	.20
12 Enlightened Ascetic C	.07	.15
13 Enshrouding Mist C	.07	.15
14 Gideon's Phalanx R	.15	.30
15 Grasp of the Hieromancer C	.07	.15
16 Hallowed Moonlight R	.15	.30
17 Healing Hands C	.07	.15
18 Heavy Infantry C	.07	.15
19 Hixus, Prison Warden R	.15	.30
20 Knight of the Pilgrim's Road C	.07	.15
21 Knight of the White Orchid R	.60	1.25
22 Knightly Valor U	.10	.20
23 Kytheon, Hero of Akros Gideon, Battle-Forged M	2.50	5.00
25 Kytheon's Tactics C	.07	.15
25 Kytheon's Tactics C	.07	.15
26 Mighty Leap C	.07	.15
27 Murder Investigation U	.10	.20
28 Patron of the Valiant U	.10	.20
29 Relic Seeker R	.15	.30
30 Sentinel of the Eternal Watch U	.10	.20
31 Sigil of the Empty Throne R	.75	1.50
32 Stalwart Aven C	.07	.15
33 Starfield of Nyx M	7.50	15.00
34 Suppression Bonds C	.07	.15
35 Swift Reckoning U	.10	.20
36 Topan Freeblade C	.07	.15
37 Totem-Guide Hartebeest U	.10	.20
38 Tragic Arrogance R	.50	1.00
39 Valor in Akros U	.10	.20
40 Vryn Wingmare R	.15	.30
41 War Oracle U	.10	.20
42 Yoked Ox C	.07	.15
43 Alhammarret, High Arbiter M	4.00	8.00
44 Anchor to the Aether U	.10	.20
45 Artificer's Epiphany C	.07	.15
46 Aspiring Aeronaut C	.07	.15
47 Bone to Ash C	.07	.15
48 Calculated Dismissal C	.07	.15
49 Clash of Wills U	.10	.20
50 Claustrophobia C	.07	.15
51 Day's Undoing M	3.00	6.00
52 Deep-Sea Terror C	.07	.15
53 Disciple of the Ring M	.30	.75
54 Disperse C	.07	.15
55 Displacement Wave R	.50	1.00
56 Dreadwaters C	.07	.15
57 Faerie Miscreant C	.07	.15
58 Harbinger of the Tides R	.30	.75
59 Hydrolash U	.10	.20
60 Jace, Vryn's Prodigy/Jace, Telepath Unbound M	7.50	15.00
61 Jace's Sanctum R	.50	1.00
62 Jhessian Thief U	.10	.20
63 Maritime Guard C	.07	.15
64 Mizzium Meddler R	.15	.30
65 Negate C	.07	.15
66 Nivix Barrier C	.07	.15
67 Psychic Rebuttal U	.10	.20
68 Ringwarden Owl C	.07	.15
69 Scrapskin Drake C	.07	.15
70 Screeching Skaab C	.07	.15
71 Send to Sleep C	.07	.15
72 Separatist Voidmage C	.07	.15
73 Sigiled Starfish U	.10	.20
74 Skaab Goliath U	.10	.20
75 Soulblade Djinn R	.15	.30
76 Sphinx's Tutelage U	1.25	2.50
77 Stratus Walk C	.07	.15
78 Talent of the Telepath R	.40	.80
79 Thopter Spy Network R	.75	1.50
80 Tower Geist U	.10	.20
81 Turn to Frog U	.10	.20
82 Watercourser C	.07	.15
83 Whirler Rogue U	.10	.20
84 Willbreaker R	.75	1.50
85 Blightcaster U	.10	.20
86 Catacomb Slug C	.07	.15
87 Consecrated by Blood U	.10	.20
88 Cruel Revival U	.10	.20
89 Dark Dabbling C	.07	.15
90 Dark Petition R	2.50	5.00
91 Deadbridge Shaman C	.07	.15
92 Demonic Pact M	1.50	3.00
93 Despoiler of Souls R	.15	.30
94 Erebos's Titan M	.30	.75
95 Eyeblight Assassin C	.07	.15
96 Eyeblight Massacre U	.10	.20
97 Fetid Imp C	.07	.15
98 Fleshbag Marauder U	.10	.20
99 Gilt-Leaf Winnower R	.15	.30
100 Gnarlroot Trapper U	.20	.40
101 Graveblade Marauder R	.15	.30
102 Infernal Scarring C	.07	.15
103 Infinite Obliteration R	.15	.30
104 Kothophed, Soul Hoarder R	.15	.30
105 Languish R	.40	.80
106 Liliana Heretical Healer/Defiant Necromancer M :K:	12.50	25.00
107 Macabre Waltz C	.07	.15
108 Malakir Cullblade U	.10	.20
109 Nantuko Husk C	.07	.15
110 Necromantic Summons U	.10	.20
111 Nightsnare C	.07	.15
112 Priest of the Blood Rite R	.15	.30
113 Rabid Bloodsucker C	.07	.15
114 Read the Bones C	.20	.40
115 Reave Soul C	.07	.15
116 Returned Centaur C	.07	.15
117 Revenant U	.10	.20
118 Shadows of the Past U	.20	.40
119 Shambling Ghoul C	.07	.15
120 Tainted Remedy R	2.50	5.00
121 Thornbow Archer C	.07	.15
122 Tormented Thoughts U	.10	.20
123 Touch of Moonglove C	.07	.15
124 Undead Servant C	.07	.15
125 Unholy Hunger C	.07	.15
126 Weight of the Underworld C	.07	.15
127 Abbot of Keral Keep R	.60	1.25
128 Acolyte of the Inferno U	.10	.20
129 Act of Treason C	.07	.15
130 Akroan Sergeant C	.07	.15
131 Avaricious Dragon M	.75	1.50
132 Bellows Lizard C	.07	.15
133 Boggart Brute C	.07	.15
134 Call of the Full Moon U	.10	.20
135 Chandra Fire of Kaladesh Roaring Flame M :R:	2.00	4.00
136 Chandra's Fury C	.07	.15
137 Chandra's Ignition R	4.00	8.00
138 Cobblebrute C	.07	.15
139 Demolish C	.07	.15
140 Dragon Fodder C	.07	.15
141 Embermaw Hellion R	.20	.40
142 Enthralling Victor U	.10	.20
143 Exquisite Firecraft R	.15	.30
144 Fiery Conclusion U	.10	.20
145 Fiery Impulse C	.07	.15
146 Firefiend Elemental C	.07	.15
147 Flameshadow Conjuring R	2.00	4.00
148 Ghirapur Aether Grid U	.25	.50
149 Ghirapur Gearcrafter C	.07	.15
150 Goblin Glory Chaser U	.10	.20
151 Goblin Piledriver R	1.00	2.00
152 Infectious Bloodlust C	.07	.15
153 Lightning Javelin C	.07	.15
154 Mage-Ring Bully C	.07	.15
155 Magmatic Insight U	.20	.40
156 Molten Vortex R	.15	.30
157 Pia and Kiran Nalaar R	.20	.40
158 Prickleboar C	.07	.15
159 Ravaging Blaze U	.10	.20
160 Scab-Clan Berserker R	.25	.50
161 Seismic Elemental U	.10	.20
162 Skyraker Giant U	.10	.20
163 Smash to Smithereens C	.07	.15
164 Subterranean Scout C	.07	.15
165 Thopter Engineer U	.10	.20
166 Titan's Strength C	.07	.15
167 Volcanic Rambler C	.07	.15
168 Aerial Volley C	.07	.15
169 Animist's Awakening R	.60	1.25
170 Caustic Caterpillar C	.30	.75
171 Conclave Naturalists U	.10	.20
172 Dwynen, Gilt-Leaf Daen R	.30	.60
173 Dwynen's Elite U	.20	.40
174 Elemental Bond U	2.00	4.00
175 Elvish Visionary C	.07	.15
176 Evolutionary Leap R	.50	1.00
177 Gaea's Revenge R	.15	.30
178 Gather the Pack U	.10	.20
179 The Great Aurora M	.60	1.25
180 Herald of the Pantheon R	.75	1.50
181 Hitchclaw Recluse C	.07	.15
182 Honored Hierarch R	.15	.30
183 Joraga Invocation U	.10	.20
184 Leaf Gilder C	.07	.15
185 Llanowar Empath C	.07	.15
186 Managorger Hydra R	1.00	2.00
187 Mantle of Webs C	.07	.15
188 Might of the Masses C	.07	.15
190 Nissa's Pilgrimage C	.07	.15
190 Nissa's Pilgrimage C	.07	.15
191 Nissa's Revelation R	.15	.30
191 Nissa's Revelation R	.15	.30
192 Orchard Spirit C	.07	.15
193 Outland Colossus R	.15	.30
194 Pharika's Disciple C	.07	.15
195 Reclaim C	.07	.15
196 Rhox Maulers C	.07	.15
197 Skysnare Spider U	.10	.20
198 Somberwald Alpha U	.10	.20
199 Sylvan Messenger U	.10	.20
200 Timberpack Wolf C	.07	.15
201 Titanic Growth C	.07	.15
202 Undercity Troll U	.10	.20
203 Valeron Wardens U	.10	.20
204 Vastwood Gorger C	.07	.15
205 Vine Snare C	.07	.15
206 Wild Instincts C	.07	.15
207 Woodland Bellower M	3.00	6.00
208 Yeva's Forcemage C	.07	.15
209 Zendikar's Roil U	.30	.75
210 Blazing Hellhound U	.10	.20
211 Blood-Cursed Knight U	.10	.20
212 Bounding Krasis U	.10	.20
213 Citadel Castellan U	.10	.20
214 Iroas's Champion U	.10	.20
215 Possessed Skaab U	.10	.20
216 Reclusive Artificer U	.10	.20
217 Shaman of the Pack U	.20	.40
218 Thunderclap Wyvern U	.10	.20
219 Zendikar Incarnate U	.10	.20
220 Alchemist's Vial C	.07	.15
221 Alhammarret's Archive M	4.00	8.00
222 Angel's Tomb U	.10	.20
223 Bonded Construct C	.07	.15
224 Brawler's Plate U	.10	.20
225 Chief of the Foundry U	.10	.20
226 Gold-Forged Sentinel U	.10	.20
227 Guardian Automaton C	.07	.15
228 Guardians of Meletis C	.07	.15
229 Hangarback Walker R	4.00	8.00
230 Helm of the Gods R	.75	1.50
231 Jayemdae Tome U	.10	.20
232 Mage-Ring Responder R	.15	.30
233 Meteorite U	.10	.20
234 Orbs of Warding R	.50	1.00
235 Prism Ring U	.20	.40
236 Pyromancer's Goggles M	3.00	6.00
237 Ramroller U	.10	.20
238 Runed Servitor U	.10	.20
239 Sigil of Valor U	.10	.20
240 Sword of the Animist R	4.00	8.00
241 Throwing Knife U	.10	.20
242 Veteran's Sidearm C	.07	.15
243 War Horn U	.10	.20
244 Battlefield Forge R	.50	1.00
245 Caves of Koilos R	.50	1.00
246 Evolving Wilds C	.07	.15
247 Foundry of the Consuls U	.10	.20
248 Llanowar Wastes R	.50	1.00
249 Mage-Ring Network U	.10	.20
250 Rogue's Passage U	.10	.20
251 Shivan Reef R	.75	1.50
252 Yavimaya Coast R	.50	1.00
253 Plains L	.10	.20
254 Plains L	.10	.20
255 Plains L	.10	.20
256 Plains L	.10	.20
257 Island L	.10	.20
258 Island L	.10	.20
259 Island L	.10	.20
260 Island L	.10	.20
261 Swamp L	.10	.20
262 Swamp L	.10	.20
263 Swamp L	.10	.20
264 Swamp L	.10	.20
265 Mountain L	.10	.20
266 Mountain L	.10	.20
267 Mountain L	.10	.20
268 Mountain L	.10	.20
269 Forest L	.10	.20
270 Forest L	.10	.20
271 Forest L	.10	.20
272 Forest L	.10	.20
273 Aegis Angel R	.25	.50
274 Divine Verdict C	.07	.15
275 Eagle of the Watch C	.07	.15
276 Serra Angel U	.20	.40
277 Into the Void U	.15	.30
278 Mahamoti Djinn R	.15	.30
279 Weave Fate C	.07	.15
280 Flesh to Dust C	.07	.15
281 Mind Rot C	.25	.50
282 Nightmare R	.15	.30
283 Sengir Vampire U	.10	.20
284 Fiery Hellhound C	.20	.40
285 Shivan Dragon R	.15	.30
286 Plummet C	.20	.40
287 Prized Unicorn U	.20	.40
288 Terra Stomper R	.15	.30

2015 Magic The Gathering Origins Tokens

0 Magic Origins CL	.15	.30
1 Angel	.17	.35
2 Knight	.07	.15
3 Soldier	.07	.15
4 Demon	.10	.20
5 Zombie	.07	.15
6 Goblin	.12	.25
7 Ashaya, the Awoken World	.12	.25
8 Elemental	.12	.25
9 Elf Warrior	.20	.40
10 Thopter	.07	.15
11 Thopter	.07	.15
12 Jace, Telepath Unbound Emblem	.20	.40
13 Liliana, Defiant Necromancer Emblem	.30	.75
14 Chandra, Roaring Flame Emblem	.25	.50

2015 Magic The Gathering Ugin's Fate

1 Ugin, the Spirit Dragon M	60.00	125.00
19 Mastery of the Unseen R	5.00	10.00
24 Smite the Monstrous C	1.50	3.00
26 Soul Summons C	2.50	5.00
30 Watcher of the Roost U	1.50	3.00
36 Jeskai Infiltrator R	5.00	10.00
46 Reality Shift U	6.00	12.00
48 Mystic of the Hidden Way C	1.50	3.00
59 Write into Being C	2.00	4.00
68 Debilitating Injury C	1.50	3.00
73 Grim Haruspex R	4.00	8.00
85 Sultai Emissary C	2.00	4.00
88 Ruthless Ripper U	3.00	6.00
96 Ainok Tracker (AA)	1.50	3.00
97 Arc Lightning U	2.50	5.00
98 Fierce Invocation C	1.50	3.00
113 Jeering Instigator R	4.00	8.00
123 Arashin War Beast U	1.50	3.00
129 Formless Nurturing C	2.00	4.00
131 Dragonscale Boon C	2.00	4.00
146 Wildcall R	7.50	15.00
161 Hewed Stone Retainers U	1.50	3.00
164 Ugins Construct U	2.50	5.00
216 Altar of the Brood R	5.00	10.00
217 Bribers Purse U	1.50	3.00
220 Ghostfire Blade (AA)	4.00	8.00

2015-16 Magic The Gathering Zendikar Expeditions

24 Arid Mesa M	60.00	125.00
8 Blood Crypt M	50.00	100.00
18 Bloodstained Mire M	60.00	125.00
15 Breeding Pool M	40.00	80.00
5 Canopy Vista M	20.00	40.00
4 Cinder Glade M	20.00	40.00
16 Flooded Strand M	100.00	180.00
11 Godless Shrine M	50.00	100.00

6 Hallowed Fountain M 40.00 80.00
21 Marsh Flats M 60.00 125.00
25 Misty Rainforest M 125.00 250.00
13 Overgrown Tomb M 40.00 80.00
17 Polluted Delta M 125.00 250.00
1 Prairie Stream M 25.00 50.00
14 Sacred Foundry M 40.00 80.00
22 Scalding Tarn M 125.00 250.00
3 Smoldering Marsh M 20.00 40.00
12 Steam Vents M 60.00 125.00
9 Stomping Ground M 50.00 100.00
2 Sunken Hollow M 25.00 50.00
10 Temple Garden M 40.00 80.00
23 Verdant Catacombs M 100.00 180.00
7 Watery Grave M 40.00 80.00
20 Windswept Heath M 60.00 125.00
19 Wooded Foothills M 75.00 150.00
26 Mystic Gate M 25.00 50.00
27 Sunken Ruins M 25.00 50.00
28 Graven Cairns M 25.00 50.00
29 Fire-Lit Thicket M 25.00 50.00
30 Wooded Bastion M 25.00 50.00
31 Fetid Heath M 25.00 50.00
32 Cascade Bluffs M 30.00 60.00
33 Twilight Mire M 30.00 70.00
34 Rugged Prairie M 25.00 50.00
35 Flooded Grove M 30.00 60.00
36 Ancient Tomb M 40.00 80.00
37 Dust Bowl M 20.00 50.00
38 Eye of Ugin M 40.00 80.00
40 Horizon Canopy M 60.00 125.00
41 Kor Haven M 20.00 40.00
42 Mana Confluence M 25.00 50.00
43 Strip Mine M 30.00 70.00
44 Tectonic Edge M 20.00 50.00
45 Wasteland M 75.00 150.00

2016 Magic The Gathering Commander 2016

1 Duelist's Heritage R 1.25 2.50
2 Entrapment Maneuver R 1.25 2.50
3 Orzhov Advokist U .20 .40
4 Selfless Squire R 2.00 4.00
5 Sublime Exhalation R .75 1.50
6 Coastal Breach R 4.00 8.00
7 Deepglow Skate R 1.50 3.00
8 Faerie Artisans R 10.00 20.00
9 Grip of Phyresis U .15 .30
10 Manifold Insights R .50 1.00
11 Cruel Entertainment R 2.50 5.00
12 Curse of Vengeance R 3.00 6.00
13 Curtains' Call R 5.00 10.00
14 Magus of the Will R .30 .60
15 Parting Thoughts U .12 .25
16 Charging Cinderhorn R .30 .60
17 Divergent Transformations R 3.00 6.00
18 Frenzied Fugue U .30 .75
19 Gobline Spymaster R .20 .40
20 Runehorn Hellkite R 3.00 6.00
21 Benefactor's Draught R 7.50 15.00
22 Evolutionary Escalation U .30 .60
23 Primeval Protector R 2.50 5.00
24 Seeds of Renewal R .50 1.00
25 Stonehoof Chieftain R 10.00 20.00
26 Akiri, Line-Slinger R .20 .40
27 Ancient Excavation U 1.25 2.50
28 Atraxa, Praetors' Voice M 15.00 30.00
29 Breya, Etherium Shaper M 4.00 8.00
30 Bruse Tarl, Boorish Herder M 2.50 5.00
31 Grave Upheaval U .60 1.25
32 Ikra Shidiqi, the Usurper M 2.50 5.00
33 Ishai, Ojutai Dragonspeaker M 2.00 4.00
34 Kraum, Ludevic's Opus R .20 .40
35 Kydele, Chosen of Kruphix M 2.50 5.00
36 Kynaios and Tiro of Meletis M 7.50 15.00
37 Ludevic, Necro-Alchemist M 2.00 4.00
38 Migratory Route U .12 .25
39 Ravos, Soultender M 5.00 10.00
40 Reyhan, Last of the Abzan R .20 .40
41 Saskia the Unyielding M 2.50 5.00
42 Sidar Kondo of Jamuraa M 2.50 5.00
43 Silas Renn, Seeker Adept M 3.00 6.00
44 Sylvan Reclamation U .15 .30
45 Tana, the Bloodsower M 3.00 6.00
46 Thrasios, Triton Hero R .20 .40
47 Treacherous Terrain U .12 .25
48 Tymna the Weaver R .20 .40
49 Vial Smasher the Fierce M 7.50 15.00
50 Yidris, Maelstrom Wielder M 7.50 15.00
51 Armory Automation R 3.00 6.00
52 Boompile R 1.25 2.50
53 Conqueror's Flail R 17.50 35.00
54 Crystalline Crawler R 6.00 12.00
55 Prismatic Geoscope R .75 1.50
56 Ash Barrens C .30 .75
57 Abzan Falconer U .12 .25
58 Blazing Archon R 1.50 3.00
59 Blind Obedience R 4.00 8.00
60 Brave the Sands U 1.25 2.50
61 Cathars' Crusade R 3.00 6.00
62 Citadel Siege R .20 .40
63 Custodi Soulbinders R .20 .40
64 Dispeller's Capsule C .10 .20
65 Elite Scaleguard U .12 .25
66 Ghostly Prison U 1.50 3.00
67 Hoofprints of the Stag R .20 .40
68 Hushwing Gryff R .25 .50
69 Mentor of the Meek R .75 1.50
70 Mirror Entity R 1.50 3.00
71 Oblation R 1.00 2.00
72 Open the Vaults R 2.00 4.00
73 Phyrexian Rebirth R .25 .50
74 Reveillark R .30 .75
75 Reverse the Sands R .20 .40
76 Sanctum Gargoyle C .10 .20
77 Sphere of Safety U 3.00 6.00
78 Swords to Plowshares U 2.00 4.00
79 Wave of Reckoning R 2.50 5.00
80 Windborn Muse R 1.50 3.00
81 Academy Elite R .20 .40
82 Aeon Chronicler R .20 .40
83 Arcane Denial C 1.00 2.00
84 Chain of Vapor U 6.00 12.00
85 Chasm Skulker R 4.00 8.00
86 Chief Engineer R .50 1.00
87 Devastation Tide R 1.25 2.50
88 Disdainful Stroke C .10 .20
89 Etherium Sculptor C .30 .75
90 Elersworn Adjudicator M 2.00 4.00
91 Evacuation R 3.00 6.00
92 Master of Etherium R .75 1.50
93 Minds Aglow R 2.50 5.00
94 Propaganda U 2.00 4.00
95 Read the Runes R .60 1.25
96 Reins of Power R 1.25 2.50
97 Spelltwine R .20 .40
98 Swan Song R 7.50 15.00
99 Tezzeret's Gambit U .20 .40
100 Thrummingbird U .25 .50
101 Treasure Cruise C .15 .30
102 Trinket Mage C .25 .50
103 Vedalken Engineer C .20 .40
104 Windfall U 2.00 4.00
105 Army of the Damned M 2.00 4.00
106 Bane of the Living R .20 .40
107 Beacon of Unrest R .20 .40
108 Brutal Hordechief M .50 1.00
109 Executioner's Capsule U .12 .25
110 Festercreep C .10 .20
111 Ghastly Conscription M .50 1.00
112 Guiltfeeder R 1.00 2.00
113 In Garruk's Wake R .60 1.25
114 Languish R .50 1.00
115 Necroplasm R .30 .60
116 Sangromancer R 1.25 2.50
117 Waste Not R 10.00 20.00
118 Wight of Precinct Six U .12 .25
119 Alesha, Who Smiles at Death R .20 .40
120 Blasphemous Act R 1.50 3.00
121 Breath of Fury R 1.25 2.50
122 Chaos Warp R 1.50 3.00
123 Daretti, Scrap Savant M 1.50 3.00
124 Dragon Mage R .25 .50
125 Godo, Bandit Warlord R .20 .40
126 Grab the Reins U .20 .40
127 Hellkite Igniter R .20 .40
128 Hellkite Tyrant M 4.00 8.00
129 Humble Defector U .12 .25
130 Kazuul, Tyrant of the Cliffs R 3.00 6.00
131 Past in Flames M 1.25 2.50
132 Reforge the Soul R 7.50 15.00
133 Slobad, Goblin Tinkerer R 1.25 2.50
134 Stalking Vengeance R .50 1.00
135 Taurean Mauler R 1.50 3.00
136 Trash for Treasure R .30 .75
137 Volcanic Vision R .20 .40
138 Wheel of Fate R 2.00 4.00
139 Whims of the Fates R .20 .40
140 Whipflare U .12 .25
141 Beast Within U 1.00 2.00
142 Beastmaster Ascension R 7.50 15.00
143 Burgeoning R 15.00 30.00
144 Champion of Lambholt R 1.50 3.00
145 Collective Voyage R 4.00 8.00
146 Cultivate C .60 1.25
147 Den Protector R .20 .40
148 Far Wanderings C .25 .50
149 Farseek C 1.50 3.00
150 Forgotten Ancient R 1.00 2.00
151 Gamekeeper U .12 .25
152 Hardened Scales R 6.00 12.00
153 Inspiring Call U .30 .75
154 Kalonian Hydra M 10.00 20.00
155 Kodama's Reach C 1.00 2.00
156 Lurking Predators R 5.00 10.00
157 Managorger Hydra R 1.50 3.00
158 Mycoloth R 3.00 6.00
159 Oath of Druids R 2.50 5.00
160 Quirion Explorer C .10 .20
161 Rampant Growth C .75 1.50
162 Realm Seekers R .25 .50
163 Rites of Flourishing R .60 1.25
164 Sakura-Tribe Elder C .75 1.50
165 Satyr Wayfinder C .10 .20
166 Scavenging Ooze R .60 1.25
167 Shamanic Revelation R .75 1.50
168 Solidarity of Heroes U .75 1.50
169 Sylvok Explorer C .10 .20
170 Tempt with Discovery R .75 1.50
171 Thelonite Hermit R .20 .40
172 Thunderfoot Baloth R 3.00 6.00
173 Tuskguard Captain U .12 .25
174 Veteran Explorer U .12 .25
175 Wall of Blossoms U .12 .25
176 Wild Beastmaster R .20 .40
177 Abzan Charm U .12 .25
178 Ankle Shanker R .20 .40
179 Artifact Mutation R .30 .60
180 Aura Mutation R 1.50 3.00
181 Baleful Strix U 2.00 4.00
182 Bituminous Blast U .12 .25
183 Blood Tyrant R .20 .40
184 Bloodbraid Elf U 1.25 2.50
185 Boros Charm U 1.00 2.00
186 Bred for the Hunt U .12 .25
187 Clan Defiance R .20 .40
188 Coiling Oracle C .10 .20
189 Consuming Aberration R .50 1.00
190 Corpsejack Menace R .75 1.50
191 Crackling Doom R .20 .40
192 Dauntless Escort R 2.00 4.00
193 Decimate R 2.00 4.00
194 Duneblast R .20 .40
195 Edric, Spymaster of Trest R 2.50 5.00
196 Enduring Scalelord U .12 .25
197 Etherium-Horn Sorcerer R .20 .40
198 Fathom Mage R .25 .50
199 Filigree Angel R .20 .40
200 Ghave, Guru of Spores M 3.00 6.00
201 Glint-Eye Nephilim R .20 .40
202 Gwafa Hazid, Profiteer R .30 .60
203 Hanna, Ship's Navigator R 1.25 2.50
204 Horizon Chimera U .12 .25
205 Iroas, God of Victory M 7.50 15.00
206 Jor Kadeen, the Prevailer R .20 .40
207 Juniper Order Ranger U .20 .40
208 Korozda Guildmage U .12 .25
209 Lavalanche R .20 .40
210 Master Biomancer M 1.50 3.00
211 Merciless Eviction R 1.50 3.00
212 Mortify U .20 .40
213 Nath of the Gilt-Leaf R 3.00 6.00
214 Naya Charm U .15 .30
215 Necrogenesis U .15 .30
216 Progenitor Mimic M 2.00 4.00
217 Putrefy U .12 .25
218 Rakdos Charm U .75 1.50
219 Rubblehulk R .20 .40
220 Selvala, Explorer Returned R 2.00 4.00
221 Sharuum the Hegemon M .50 1.00
222 Spellheart Chimera U .12 .25
223 Sphinx Summoner R .20 .40
224 Sydri, Galvanic Genius M .75 1.50
225 Terminate C .50 1.00
226 Utter End R 1.50 3.00
227 Vorel of the Hull Clade R 1.25 2.50
228 Vulturous Zombie R .20 .40
229 Whispering Madness R .60 1.25
230 Wilderness Elemental U .12 .25
231 Zedruu the Greathearted M .75 1.50
232 Zhur-Taa Druid C .10 .20
233 Everlasting Torment R 1.50 3.00
234 Mirrorweave R .30 .60
235 Selesnya Guildmage U .12 .25
236 Spitting Image R .20 .40
237 Thopter Foundry U .25 .50
238 Worm Harvest R .20 .40
239 Trial/Error U .12 .25
240 Order/Chaos U .12 .25
241 Akroan Horse R .20 .40
242 Assault Suit U .25 .50
243 Astral Cornucopia R 1.25 2.50
244 Blinkmoth Urn R 1.00 2.00
245 Bonehoard R .20 .40
246 Cauldron of Souls R 2.50 5.00
247 Chromatic Lantern R 7.50 15.00
248 Commander's Sphere C .20 .40
249 Cranial Plating U .30 .60
250 Darksteel Ingot U .30 .75
251 Empyrial Plate R .30 .75
252 Etched Oracle U .12 .25
253 Everflowing Chalice U .60 1.25
254 Fellwar Stone U 1.50 3.00
255 Golgari Signet C 1.00 2.00
256 Gruul Signet C .50 1.00
257 Howling Mine R 5.00 10.00
258 Ichor Wellspring C .10 .20
259 Keening Stone R 2.00 4.00
260 Lightning Greaves U 4.00 8.00
261 Loxodon Warhammer U .30 .60
262 Mycosynth Wellspring C .10 .20
263 Myr Battlesphere R .25 .50
264 Myr Retriever U .30 .75
265 Nevinyrral's Disk R .75 1.50
266 Orzhov Signet C .50 1.00
267 Psychosis Crawler R .30 .75
268 Rakdos Signet C .75 1.50
269 Shimmer Myr R .75 1.50
270 Simic Signet C .30 .60
271 Skullclamp U 7.50 15.00
272 Sol Ring U 1.00 2.00
273 Solemn Simulacrum R 1.25 2.50
274 Soul of New Phyrexia M 1.50 3.00
275 Sunforger R .50 1.00
276 Swiftfoot Boots U 1.50 3.00
277 Temple Bell R 1.50 3.00
278 Trading Post R .50 1.00
279 Venser's Journal R 4.00 8.00
280 Whispersilk Cloak U 2.50 5.00
281 Arcane Sanctum U 1.00 2.00
282 Azorius Chancery U .15 .30
283 Boros Garrison U .12 .25
284 Buried Ruin U .75 1.50
285 Caves of Koilos R .60 1.25
286 Command Tower C .20 .40
287 Crumbling Necropolis U .20 .40
288 Darksteel Citadel U .30 .60
289 Darkwater Catacombs R .25 .50
290 Dimir Aqueduct U .30 .75
291 Dismal Backwater C .10 .20
292 Dragonskull Summit R 3.00 6.00
293 Dreadship Reef U .20 .40
294 Evolving Wilds C .10 .20
295 Exotic Orchard R .40 .80
296 Forbidden Orchard R 12.50 25.00
297 Frontier Bivouac U .25 .50
298 Golgari Rot Farm C .10 .20
299 Grand Coliseum R 2.50 5.00
300 Gruul Turf U .12 .25
301 Homeward Path R 10.00 20.00
302 Izzet Boilerworks C .15 .30
303 Jungle Hollow C .12 .25
304 Jungle Shrine U .17 .35
305 Karplusan Forest R 3.00 6.00
306 Krosan Verge U .12 .25
307 Mosswort Bridge R .25 .50
308 Murmuring Bosk R 1.50 3.00
309 Myriad Landscape U .25 .50
310 Mystic Monastery U .25 .50
311 Nomad Outpost U .50 1.00
312 Opal Palace C .10 .20
313 Opulent Palace U .25 .50
314 Orzhov Basilica U .17 .35
315 Rakdos Carnarium U .12 .25
316 Reliquary Tower U 1.50 3.00
317 Rootbound Crag R 2.50 5.00
318 Rugged Highlands C .10 .20
319 Rupture Spire C .10 .20
320 Sandsteppe Citadel U .30 .60
321 Savage Lands U 1.00 2.00
322 Seaside Citadel U 1.50 3.00
323 Seat of the Synod C 1.25 2.50
324 Selesnya Sanctuary U .12 .25
325 Shadowblood Ridge R .30 .75
326 Simic Growth Chamber U .12 .25
327 Spinerock Knoll R .25 .50
328 Sungrass Prairie R .20 .40
329 Sunpetal Grove R 3.00 6.00
330 Swiftwater Cliffs C .10 .20
331 Temple of the False God U .12 .25
332 Terramorphic Expanse C .15 .30
333 Thornwood Falls C .10 .20
334 Transguild Promenade C .10 .20
335 Underground River R 7.50 15.00
336 Windbrisk Heights R .20 .40
337 Plains L .30 .75
338 Plains L .10 .20
339 Plains L .10 .20
340 Island L .10 .20
341 Island L .10 .20
342 Island L .10 .20
343 Swamp L .30 .75
344 Swamp L .15 .30
345 Swamp L .10 .20
346 Mountain L .25 .50
347 Mountain L .10 .20
348 Mountain L .10 .20
349 Forest L .20 .40
350 Forest L .10 .20
351 Forest L .10 .20

2016 Magic The Gathering Commander 2016 Oversized

28 Atraxa, Praetors' Voice M 7.50 15.00
29 Breya, Etherium Shaper M 1.50 3.00
36 Kynaios and Tiro of Meletis M .50 1.00
41 Saskia the Unyielding M .30 .75
50 Yidris, Maelstrom Wielder M .60 1.25

2016 Magic The Gathering Commander 2016 Tokens

1 Spirit .07 .15
2 Bird .07 .15
3 Elemental .07 .15
4 Goat .12 .25
5 Soldier .07 .15
6 Spirit .07 .15
7 Bird .07 .15
8 Squid .07 .15
9 Thopter .17 .35
10 Germ .07 .15
11 Zombie .07 .15
12 Goblin .17 .35
13 Ogre .17 .35
14 Beast .15 .30
15 Elf Warrior .17 .35
16 Saproling .07 .15
17 Saproling .07 .15
18 Worm .07 .15
19 Horror .07 .15
20 Myr .07 .15
21 Daretti, Scrap Savant Emblem .10 .20

2016 Magic The Gathering Conspiracy Take the Crown

1 Adriana's Valor C .07 .15
2 Assemble the Rank and Vile C .07 .15
3 Echoing Boon U .10 .20
4 Emissary's Ploy R .15 .30
5 Hired Heist C .07 .15
6 Hold the Perimeter R .15 .30
7 Hymn of the Wilds M .50 1.00
8 Incendiary Dissent C .07 .15
9 Natuarl Unity C .07 .15
10 Sovereign's Realm M .50 1.00
11 Summoner's Bond U .10 .20
12 Weight Advantage R .15 .30
13 Ballot Broker C .07 .15
14 Custodi Peacekeeper C .07 .15
15 Custodi Soulcaller U .10 .20
16 Lieutenants of the Guard C .07 .15
17 Noble Banneret U .10 .20
18 Palace Jailer U 1.00 2.00
19 Palace Sentinels C .07 .15
20 Paliano Vanguard R .15 .30
21 Protector of the Crown R 2.00 4.00
22 Recruiter of the Guard R 20.00 40.00
23 Sanctum Prelate M 15.00 30.00
24 Spectral Grasp U .20 .40
25 Throne Warden C .07 .15
26 Wings of the Guard C .07 .15
27 Arcane Savant R .15 .30
28 Canal Courier C .07 .15
29 Coveted Peacock U .10 .20
30 Expropriate M 15.00 30.00
31 Illusion of Choice U .10 .20
32 Illusionary Informant C .07 .15
33 Jeering Homunculus C .07 .15
34 Keeper of Keys R 3.00 6.00
35 Messenger Jays C .07 .15
36 Skittering Crustacean C .07 .15
37 Spire Phantasm U .10 .20
38 Stunt Double R 3.00 6.00
39 Archdemon of Paliano R .15 .30
40 Capital Punishment R 2.00 4.00
41 Custodi Lich R 2.50 5.00
42 Deadly Designs U .10 .20
43 Garrulous Sycophant C .07 .15
44 Marchesa's Decree U 2.50 5.00
45 Regicide C .07 .15
46 Sinuous Vermin C .15 .30
47 Smuggler Captain U .10 .20
48 Thorn of the Black Rose C .20 .40
49 Besmirch U .75 1.50
50 Crown-Hunter Hireling C .07 .15
51 Deputized Protester C .07 .15
52 Garbage Fire C .07 .15
53 Goblin Racketeer C .07 .15
54 Grenzo, Havoc Raiser R 20.00 40.00
55 Grenzo's Ruffians U .10 .20
56 Pyretic Hunter U .10 .20
57 Skyline Despot R 7.50 15.00
58 Subterranean Tremors M 4.00 8.00
59 Volatile Chimera R .15 .30
60 Animus of Predation U .10 .20
61 Borderland Explorer C .07 .15
62 Caller of the Untamed R .15 .30
63 Domesticated Hydra U .20 .40
64 Entourage of Trest C .07 .15
65 Fang of the Pack U .10 .20
66 Leovold's Operative C .07 .15

67 Menagerie Liberator C	.07	.15
68 Orchard Elemental C	.07	.15
69 Regal Behemoth R	12.50	25.00
70 Selvala, Heart of the Wilds M	10.00	20.00
71 Selvala's Stampede R	6.00	12.00
72 Splitting Slime R	.30	.60
73 Adriana, Captain of the Guard R	.30	.75
74 Daretti, Ingenious Iconoclast M	12.50	25.00
75 Kaya, Ghost Assassin M	4.00	8.00
76 Knights of the Black Rose U	.30	.60
77 Leovold, Emissary of Trest M	4.00	8.00
78 Queen Marchesa M	4.00	8.00
79 Spy Kit U	.15	.30
80 Throne of the High City R	3.00	6.00
81 Affa Guard Hound U	.10	.20
82 Disenchant C	.07	.15
83 Doomed Traveler C	.07	.15
84 Faith's Reward R	1.25	2.50
85 Ghostly Possession C	.07	.15
86 Ghostly Prison U	1.50	3.00
87 Gleam of Resistance C	.07	.15
88 Gods Willing C	.07	.15
89 Guardian of the Gateless U	.15	.30
90 Hall of Arrows U	.10	.20
91 Hallowed Burial R	.60	1.25
92 Hollowhenge Spirit U	.10	.20
93 Hundred-Handed One R	.17	.35
94 Kill Shot C	.07	.15
95 Pariah R	1.25	2.50
96 Raise the Alarm C	.07	.15
97 Reviving Dose C	.07	.15
98 Spirit of the Hearth R	.15	.30
99 Wild Griffin C	.07	.15
100 Windborne Charge U	.10	.20
101 Zealous Strike C	.07	.15
102 Bonds of Quicksilver C	.07	.15
103 Caller of Gales C	.07	.15
104 Cloaked Siren C	.07	.15
105 Covenant of Minds R	.15	.30
106 Deceiver Exarch U	.15	.30
107 Desertion R	3.00	6.00
108 Dismiss U	.10	.20
109 Divination C	.07	.15
110 Fleeting Distraction C	.07	.15
111 Followed Footsteps R	1.50	3.00
112 Into the Void U	.10	.20
113 Kami of the Crescent Moon R	3.00	6.00
114 Merfolk Looter U	.10	.20
115 Merfolk Skyscout U	.10	.20
116 Mnemonic Wall C	.07	.15
117 Negate C	.07	.15
118 Omenspeaker C	.07	.15
119 Repulse C	.07	.15
120 Serum Visions U	1.50	3.00
121 Show and Tell M	10.00	20.00
122 Sphinx of Magosi R	.15	.30
123 Traumatic Visions C	.07	.15
124 Vaporkin C	.07	.15
125 Vertigo Spawn U	.10	.20
126 Absorb Vis C	.07	.15
127 Altar's Reap C	.07	.15
128 Avatar of Woe M	2.00	4.00
129 Blood-Toll Harpy C	.07	.15
130 Child of Night C	.07	.15
131 Death Wind C	.07	.15
132 Diabolic Tutor U	.60	1.25
133 Festergloom C	.07	.15
134 Driver of the Dead C	.07	.15
135 Farbog Boneflinger U	.10	.20
136 Fleshbag Marauder U	.10	.20
137 Guul Draz Specter R	.15	.30
138 Harvester of Souls R	.75	1.50
139 Infest U	.10	.20
140 Inquisition of Kozilek R	3.00	6.00
141 Keepsake Gorgon U	.10	.20
142 Mausoleum Turnkey U	.10	.20
143 Murder C	.07	.15
144 Phyrexian Arena R	10.00	20.00
145 Public Execution U	.10	.20
146 Raise Dead C	.07	.15
147 Sangromancer R	1.00	2.00
148 Shambling Goblin C	.07	.15
149 Stormkirk Patrol C	.07	.15
150 Unnerve C	.07	.15
151 Burn Away U	.10	.20
152 Burning Wish R	.30	.75
153 Charmbreaker Devils R	.15	.30
154 Coordinated Assault U	.10	.20
155 Ember Beast C	.07	.15
156 Fiery Fall C	.07	.15
157 Flame Slash C	.20	.40
158 Gang of Devils U	.10	.20
159 Goblin Balloon Brigade C	.07	.15
160 Goblin Tunneler C	.07	.15
161 Gratuitous Violence R	3.00	6.00
162 Guttersnipe U	.10	.20
163 Hamletback Goliath R	.15	.30
164 Havengul Vampire U	.10	.20
165 Hurly-Burly C	.07	.15
166 Ill-Tempered Cyclops C	.07	.15
167 Kilin Fiend C	.07	.15
168 Ogre Sentry C	.07	.15
169 Stoneshock Giant U	.10	.20
170 Sulfurous Blast U	.10	.20
171 Tormenting Voice C	.07	.15
172 Trumpet Blast C	.07	.15
173 Twing Bolt C	.07	.15
174 Beast Within U	.75	1.50
175 Berserk M	20.00	40.00
176 Birds of Paradise R	7.50	15.00
177 Bushstrider U	.10	.20
178 Burgeoning R	17.50	35.00
179 Copperhorn Scout C	.15	.30
180 Explosive Vegetation U	1.00	2.00
181 Fade into Antiquity C	.07	.15
182 Forgotten Ancient R	.75	1.50
183 Irresistible Prey U	.10	.20
184 Lace with Moonglove C	.07	.15
185 Lay of the Land C	.07	.15
186 Manaplasm U	.10	.20
187 Nessian Asp U	.10	.20
188 Netcaster Spider C	.07	.15
189 Overrun U	.10	.20
190 Plummet C	.07	.15
191 Prey Upon C	.07	.15
192 Ravenous Leucrocota C	.07	.15
193 Stength in Numbers C	.07	.15
194 Sylvan Bounty C	.07	.15
195 Voyaging Satyr C	.07	.15
196 Wild Pair R	1.50	3.00
197 Akroan Hoplite U	.10	.20
198 Ascended Lawmage U	.10	.20
199 Carnage Gladiator U	.10	.20
200 Coiling Oracle U	.10	.20
201 Dragonlair Spider R	1.25	2.50
202 Duskmantle Seer R	.15	.30
203 Gruul War Chant U	.10	.20
204 Juniper Order Ranger U	.17	.35
205 Pharika's Mender U	.10	.20
206 Shipwreck Singer U	.10	.20
207 Stormchaser Chimera U	.10	.20
208 Bronze Sable C	.07	.15
209 Hedron Matrix R	.25	.50
210 Hexplate Golem C	.07	.15
211 Horn of Greed R	6.00	12.00
212 Kitesail C	.07	.15
213 Opaline Unicorn C	.07	.15
214 Platinum Angel M	7.50	15.00
215 Psychosis Crawler R	.60	1.25
216 Runed Servitor U	.10	.20
217 Dread Statuary U	.10	.20
218 Evolving Wilds C	.07	.15
219 Exotic Orchard R	.60	1.25
220 Rogue's Passage U	.25	.50
221 Shimmering Grotto U	.10	.20
222 Kaya Ghost Assassin M ALT ART	75.00	150.00

2016 Magic The Gathering Conspiracy Take the Crown Tokens

1 The Monarch	.07	.15
2 Soldier	.07	.15
3 Soldier	.07	.15
4 Spirit	.07	.15
5 Assassin	.30	.75
6 Zombie	.07	.15
7 Dragon	.12	.25
8 Goblin	.07	.15
9 Lizard	.07	.15
10 Beast	.07	.15
11 Insect	.07	.15
12 Construct	.07	.15

2016 Magic The Gathering Duel Decks Blessed vs. Cursed

1 Geist of Saint Traft M	3.00	6.00
2 Bonds of Faith C	.10	.20
3 Cathedral Sanctifier C	.10	.20
4 Champion of the Parish R	1.25	2.50
5 Chapel Geist C	.10	.20
6 Dearly Departed R	.10	.20
7 Doomed Traveler C	.10	.20
8 Eerie Interlude R	.30	.60
9 Elder Cathar C	.10	.20
10 Emancipation Angel U	.10	.20
11 Fiend Hunter U	.10	.20
12 Gather the Townsfolk C	.10	.20
13 Goldnight Redeemer U	.10	.20
14 Increasing Devotion R	.20	.40
15 Momentary Blink C	.20	.40
16 Moorland Inquisitor C	.10	.20
17 Rebuke C	.10	.20
18 Slayer of the Wicked U	.10	.20
19 Spectral Gateguards C	.10	.20
20 Thraben Heretic U	.10	.20
21 Topplegeist U	.10	.20
22 Village Bell-Ringer C	.10	.20
23 Voice of the Provinces C	.10	.20
24 Captain of the Mists R	.10	.20
25 Gryff Vanguard C	.10	.20
26 Mist Raven C	.10	.20
27 Nephalia Smuggler U	.10	.20
28 Pore Over the Pages U	.10	.20
29 Tandem Lookout U	.10	.20
30 Tower Geist U	.10	.20
31 Butcher's Cleaver U	.10	.20
32 Sharpened Pitchfork U	.10	.20
33 Seraph Sanctuary C	.10	.20
34 Tranquil Cove C	.10	.20
35 Island L	.10	.20
36 Island L	.10	.20
37 Island L	.10	.20
38 Plains L	.10	.20
39 Plains L	.10	.20
40 Plains L	.10	.20
41 Mindwrack Demon M	1.50	3.00
42 Compelling Deterrence U	.10	.20
43 Forbidden Alchemy C	.10	.20
44 Havengul Runebinder R	.10	.20
45 Makeshift Mauler C	.10	.20
46 Relentless Skaabs U	.10	.20
47 Scrapskin Drake C	.10	.20
48 Screeching Skaab C	.10	.20
49 Stitched Drake C	.10	.20
50 Abattoir Ghoul U	.10	.20
51 Appetite for Brains U	.10	.20
52 Barter in Blood U	.10	.20
53 Butcher Ghoul C	.10	.20
54 Diregraf Ghoul U	.10	.20
55 Dread Return U	.50	1.00
56 Driver of the Dead C	.10	.20
57 Falkenrath Noble U	.10	.20
58 Ghoulraiser C	.10	.20
59 Gravecrawler R	2.50	4.50
60 Harvester of Souls R	.17	.35
61 Human Frailty U	.10	.20
62 Moan of the Unhallowed U	.10	.20
63 Sever the Bloodline R	.10	.20
64 Tooth Collector U	.10	.20
65 Tribute to Hunger U	.10	.20
66 Unbreathing Horde R	.50	1.00
67 Victim of Night C	.10	.20
68 Diregraf Captain U	.30	.75
69 Cobbled Wings C	.10	.20
70 Dismal Backwater C	.10	.20
71 Island L	.10	.20
72 Island L	.10	.20
73 Island L	.10	.20
74 Swamp L	.10	.20
75 Swamp L	.10	.20
76 Swamp L	.10	.20
77 Angel C	.07	.15
78 Human C	.07	.15
79 Spirit C	.07	.15
80 Zombie C	.07	.15

2016 Magic The Gathering Duel Decks Nissa vs. Ob Nixilis

1 Nissa, Voice of Zendikar M	6.00	12.00
2 Abundance R	.50	1.00
3 Briarhorn U	.10	.20
4 Citanul Woodreaders C	.10	.20
5 Civic Wayfinder C	.10	.20
6 Cloudthresher R	.10	.20
7 Crop Rotation C	.75	1.50
8 Elvish Visionary C	.10	.20
9 Fertilid C	.15	.30
10 Gaea's Blessing U	.10	.20
11 Gilt-Leaf Seer C	.10	.20
12 Jaddi Lifestrider U	.10	.20
13 Natural Connection C	.10	.20
14 Nissa's Chosen C	.10	.20
15 Oakgnarl Warrior C	.10	.20
16 Oran-Rief Hydra R	.10	.20
17 Oran-Rief Invoker C	.10	.20
18 Saddleback Lagac C	.10	.20
19 Scythe Leopard U	.10	.20
20 Seek the Horizon U	.10	.20
21 Thicket Elemental R	.10	.20
22 Thornweald Archer C	.10	.20
23 Vines of the Recluse C	.10	.20
24 Walker of the Grove U	.10	.20
25 Wood Elves C	.10	.20
26 Woodborn Behemoth U	.10	.20
27 Fertile Thicket C	.10	.20
28 Khalni Garden C	.10	.20
29 Mosswort Bridge R	.25	.50
30 Treetop Village U	.60	1.25
31 Forest L	.10	.20
32 Forest L	.10	.20
33 Forest L	.10	.20
34 Forest L	.10	.20
35 Forest L	.10	.20
36 Ob Nixilis Reignited M	2.50	4.50
37 Altar's Reap C	.10	.20
38 Ambition's Cost U	.10	.20
39 Bala Ged Scorpion C	.10	.20
40 Blistergrub C	.10	.20
41 Cadaver Imp C	.10	.20
42 Carrier Thrall U	.10	.20
43 Demon's Grasp C	.10	.20
44 Desecration Demon R	.30	.75
45 Despoiler of Souls R	.10	.20
46 Disfigure C	.20	.40
47 Doom Blade U	.20	.40
48 Fetid Imp C	.10	.20
49 Foul Imp C	.10	.20
50 Giant Scorpion C	.10	.20
51 Grim Discovery C	.10	.20
52 Hideous End C	.10	.20
53 Indulgent Tormentor R	.20	.40
54 Innocent Blood C	.10	.20
55 Mire's Toll C	.10	.20
56 Pestilence Demon R	.15	.30
57 Priest of the Blood Rite R	.15	.30
58 Quest for the Gravelord U	.10	.20
59 Renegade Demon C	.10	.20
60 Shadows of the Past U	.10	.20
61 Smallpox U	.10	.20
62 Squelching Leeches U	.10	.20
63 Tendrils of Corruption C	.10	.20
64 Unhallowed Pact C	.10	.20
65 Leechridden Swamp U	.10	.20
66 Swamp L	.10	.20
67 Swamp L	.10	.20
68 Swamp L	.10	.20
69 Swamp L	.10	.20
70 Swamp L	.10	.20
71 Eldrazi Scion C	.10	.20
72 Demon C	.10	.20
73 Zombie Giant C	.10	.20
74 Elemental C	.10	.20
75 Plant C	.10	.20

2016 Magic The Gathering Eldritch Moon

1 Abundant Maw U	.10	.20
2 Decimator of the Provinces M	1.00	2.00
3 Distended Mindbender R	.15	.30
4 Drownyard Behemoth U	.10	.20
5 Elder Deep-Fiend R	.15	.30
6 Emrakul, the Promised End M	20.00	40.00
7 Eternal Scourge R	.50	1.00
8 It of the Horrid Swarm C	.07	.15
9 Lashweed Lurker U	.10	.20
10 Mockery of Nature U	.10	.20
11 Vexing Scuttler U	.10	.20
12 Wretched Gryff C	.07	.15
13 Blessed Alliance U	.17	.35
14 Borrowed Grace C	.07	.15
15 Bruna, The Fading Light R	1.50	3.00
16 Choking Restraints C	.07	.15
17 Collective Effort R	.30	.60
18 Courageous Outrider U	.10	.20
19 Dawn Gryff C	.07	.15
20 Deploy the Gatewatch M	.60	1.25
21 Desperate Sentry C	.07	.15
22 Drogskol Shieldmate U	.10	.20
23 Extricator of Sin/Extricator of Flesh U	.10	.20
24 Faith Unbroken U	.10	.20
25 Faith Bearer Paladin C	.07	.15
26 Fiend Binder C	.07	.15
27 Geist of the Lonely Vigil U	.10	.20
28 Gisela, the Broken Blade M	12.50	25.00
29 Give No Ground U	.10	.20
30 Guardian of Pilgrims C	.07	.15
31 Ironclad Slayer C	.07	.15
32 Ironwright's Cleansing C	.07	.15
33 Lone Rider/It That Rides as One U	.30	.60
34 Long Road Home U	.10	.20
35 Lunarch Mantle C	.07	.15
36 Peace of Mind U	.10	.20
37 Providence R	.15	.30
38 Repel the Abominable U	.10	.20
39 Sanctifier of Souls R	.15	.30
40 Selfless Spirit R	5.00	10.00
41 Sigarda's Aid R	7.50	15.00
42 Sigardian Priest C	.07	.15
43 Spectral Reserves C	.07	.15
44 Steadfast Cathar C	.07	.15
45 Subjugator Angel U	.10	.20
46 Thalia, Heretic Cathar R	2.50	5.00
47 Thalia's Lancers R	.25	.50
48 Thraben Standard Bearer C	.07	.15
49 Advanced Stitchwing U	.10	.20
50 Chilling Grasp U	.10	.20
51 Coax from the Blind Eternities R	.15	.30
52 Contingency Plan C	.07	.15
53 Convolute C	.07	.15
54 Curious Homunculus/Voracious Reader U	.10	.20
55 Displace C	.30	.60
56 Docent of Perfection/Final Iteration R	2.50	5.00
57 Drag Under C	.07	.15
58 Enlightened Maniac C	.07	.15
59 Exultant Cultist C	.07	.15
60 Fogwalker C	.07	.15
61 Fortune's Favor U	.10	.20
62 Geist of the Archives U	.10	.20
63 Grizzled Angler/Grisly Anglerfish U	.10	.20
64 Identity Thief R	.15	.30
65 Imprisoned in the Moon R	1.50	3.00
66 Ingenious Skaab C	.07	.15
67 Laboratory Brute C	.07	.15
68 Lunar Force U	.10	.20
69 Mausoleum Wanderer R	1.50	3.00
70 Mind's Dilation M	6.00	12.00
71 Nebelgast Herald U	.10	.20
72 Niblis of Frost R	.15	.30
73 Scour the Laboratory U	.10	.20
74 Spontaneous Mutation C	.07	.15
75 Summary Dismissal R	.25	.50
76 Take Inventory C	.07	.15
77 Tattered Haunter C	.07	.15
78 Turn Aside C	.07	.15
79 Unsubstantiate U	.10	.20
80 Wharf Infiltrator R	.15	.30
81 Boon of Emrakul C	.07	.15
82 Borrowed Malevolence C	.07	.15
83 Cemetery Recruitment C	.07	.15
84 Certain Death C	.07	.15
85 Collective Brutality R	4.00	8.00
86 Cryptbreaker R	4.00	8.00
87 Dark Salvation R	.75	1.50
88 Dusk Feaster U	.10	.20
89 Gavony Unhallowed C	.07	.15
90 Graf Harvest U	.20	.40
91 Graf Rats C	.07	.15
92 Haunted Dead U	.10	.20
93 Liliana, the Last Hope M	12.50	25.00
94 Liliana's Elite U	.10	.20
95 Markov Crusader U	.10	.20
96 Midnight Scavengers C	.07	.15
97 Murder U	.10	.20
98 Noosegraf Mob R	.25	.50
99 Oath of Liliana R	.25	.50
100 Olivia's Dragoon C	.07	.15
101 Prying Questions C	.07	.15
102 Rise from the Grave U	.10	.20
103 Ruthless Disposal U	.10	.20
104 Skirsdag Supplicant C	.07	.15
105 Strange Augmentation C	.07	.15
106 Stromkirk Condemned R	.15	.30
107 Succumb to Temptation C	.07	.15
108 Thraben Foulbloods C	.07	.15
109 Tree of Perdition M	7.50	15.00
110 Vampire Cutthroat U	.60	1.25
111 Voldaren Pariah/Abolisher of Bloodlines R	1.00	2.00
112 Wailing Ghoul C	.07	.15
113 Weirded Vampire C	.07	.15
114 Whispers of Emrakul U	.10	.20
115 Abandon Reason U	.10	.20
116 Alchemist's Greeting C	.07	.15
117 Assembled Alphas R	.15	.30
118 Bedlam Reveler R	1.00	2.00
119 Blood Mist U	.17	.35
120 Bold Impaler C	.07	.15
121 Borrowed Hostility C	.07	.15
122 Brazen Wolves C	.07	.15
123 Collective Defiance R	.50	1.00
124 Conduit of Storms/Conduit of Emrakul U	.10	.20
125 Deranged Whelp U	.10	.20
126 Distemper of the Blood C	.07	.15
127 Falkenrath Reaver C	.07	.15
128 Furyblade Vampire U	.10	.20
129 Galvanic Bombardment C	.07	.15
130 Hanweir Garrison R	1.50	3.00
131 Harmless Offering R	.30	.60
132 Impetuous Devils R	.15	.30
133 Incendiary Flow U	.10	.20
134 Insatiable Gorgers U	.10	.20
135 Make Mischief C	.07	.15
136 Mirrorwing Dragon M	2.50	5.00
137 Nahiri's Wrath M	.50	1.00
138 Otherworldly Outburst C	.07	.15
139 Prophetic Ravings C	.07	.15
140 Savage Alliance U	.10	.20
141 Shreds of Sanity U	.10	.20
142 Smoldering Werewolf/Erupting Dreadwolf U	.10	.20
143 Spreading Flames U	.10	.20
144 Stensia Banquet C	.07	.15
145 Stensia Innkeeper C	.07	.15
146 Stromkirk Occulist R	.15	.30
147 Thermo-Alchemist C	.07	.15
148 Vildin-Pack Outcast/Dronepack Kindred C	.07	.15
149 Weaver of Lightning U	.10	.20
150 Backwoods Survivalists C	.07	.15
151 Bloodbriar C	.07	.15
152 Clear Shot U	.10	.20
153 Crop Sigil U	.10	.20
154 Crossroads Consecrator C	.07	.15
155 Eldritch Evolution R	4.00	8.00
156 Emrakul's Evangel R	.15	.30
157 Emrakul's Influence U	.10	.20
158 Foul Emissary U	.10	.20
159 Gnarlwood Dryad U	.20	.40
160 Grapple with the Past C	.07	.15
161 Hamlet Captain U	.10	.20

162 Ishkanah, Grafwidow M .75 1.50
163 Kessig Prowler/Sinuous Predator U .10 .20
164 Noose Constrictor U .10 .20
165 Permeating Mass R .15 .30
166 Prey Upon C .07 .15
167 Primal Druid C .07 .15
168 Shrill Howler, Howling Chorus U .10 .20
169 Somberwald Stag U .10 .20
170 Spirit of the Hunt R .30 .75
171 Splendid Reclamation R 3.00 6.00
172 Springsage Ritual C .07 .15
173 Swift Spinner C .07 .15
174 Tangleclaw Werewolf/Fibrous Entangler U .10 .20
175 Ulvenwald Captive/Ulvenwald Abomination C .07 .15
176 Ulvenwald Observer R .15 .30
177 Waxing Moon C .07 .15
178 Wolfkin Bond C .07 .15
179 Woodcutter's Grit C .07 .15
180 Woodland Patrol C .07 .15
181 Bloodhall Priest R .15 .30
182 Campaign of Vengeance U .10 .20
183 Gisa and Geralf M 4.00 8.00
184 Grim Flayer M 3.00 6.00
185 Heron's Grace Champion R .15 .30
186 Mercurial Geists U .10 .20
187 Mournwillow U .10 .20
188 Ride Down U .10 .20
189 Spell Queller R 2.50 5.00
190 Tamiyo, Field Researcher M 5.00 10.00
191 Ulrich of Krallenhorde
Uncontested Alpha M :R/:G: 5.00 10.00
192 Cathar's Shield U .10 .20
193 Cryptolith Fragment/Aurora of Emrakul U .30 .60
194 Cultist's Staff C .07 .15
195 Field Creeper C .07 .15
196 Geist-Fueled Scarecrow U .10 .20
197 Lupine Prototype R .15 .30
198 Slayer's Cleaver U .10 .20
199 Soul Separator R .15 .30
200 Stitcher's Graft R .15 .30
201 Terrarion C .07 .15
202 Thirsting Axe U .10 .20
203 Geier Reach Sanitarium R .60 1.25
204 Hanweir Battlements R 2.50 5.00
205 Nephalia Academy U .10 .20

2016 Magic The Gathering Eldritch Moon Tokens

1 Eldrazi Horror .07 .15
2 Human Wizard .60 1.25
3 Zombie .07 .15
4 Zombie .17 .35
5 Zombie .07 .15
6 Zombie .07 .15
7 Human Wizard .07 .15
8 Spider .15 .30
9 Liliana, the Last Hope Emblem .20 .40
10 Tamiyo, Field Researcher Emblem .07 .15
CH1 Eldritch Moon CL .07 .15

2016 Magic The Gathering Eternal Masters

1 Aven Riftwatcher C .07 .15
2 Balance M 2.50 5.00
3 Ballynock Cohort C .07 .15
4 Benevolent Bodyguard C .07 .15
5 Calciderm U .10 .20
6 Coalition Honor Guard C .07 .15
7 Eight-and-a-Half-Tails R 2.00 4.00
8 Elite Vanguard C .07 .15
9 Enlightened Tutor R 25.00 50.00
10 Faith's Fetters U .10 .20
11 Field of Souls U .25 .50
12 Glimmerpoint Stag U .10 .20
13 Honden of Cleansing Fire U 1.50 3.00
14 Humble C .07 .15
15 Intangible Virtue U .10 .20
16 Jareth, Leonine Titan R .20 .40
17 Karmic Guide R 6.00 12.00
18 Kor Hookmaster C .07 .15
19 Mesa Enchantress U 1.25 2.50
20 Mistral Charger C .07 .15
21 Monk Idealist C .12 .25
22 Mother of Runes R 4.00 8.00
23 Pacifism C .07 .15
24 Raise the Alarm C .07 .15
25 Rally the Peasants C .07 .15
26 Seal of Cleansing C .07 .15
27 Second Thoughts C .07 .15
28 Serra Angel U .10 .20
29 Shelter C .07 .15
30 Soulcatcher U .10 .20
31 Squadron Hawk C .15 .30
32 Swords to Plowshares U 2.00 4.00
33 Unexpectedly Absent R .20 .40
34 Wall of Omens U 1.00 2.00
35 War Priest of Thune U .15 .30
36 Welkin Guide C .07 .15
37 Whitemane Lion C .07 .15
38 Wrath of God R 3.00 6.00
39 Arcanis the Omnipotent R 1.00 2.00
40 Brainstorm U .50 1.00
41 Cephalid Sage C .07 .15
42 Control Magic R .75 1.50
43 Counterspell C 1.00 2.00
44 Daze U .75 1.50
45 Deep Analysis C .07 .15
46 Diminishing Returns R .25 .50
47 Dream Twist C .07 .15
48 Fact or Fiction U .15 .30
49 Force of Will M 75.00 150.00
50 Future Sight R .15 .30
51 Gaseous Form C .07 .15
52 Giant Tortoise C .07 .15
53 Glacial Wall C .15 .30
54 Honden of Seeing Winds U 1.25 2.50
55 Hydroblast U .30 .75
56 Inkwell Leviathan R .30 .60
57 Jace, the Mind Sculptor M 40.00 80.00
58 Jetting Glasskite U .10 .20
59 Man-o'-War C .07 .15
60 Memory Lapse C .15 .30
61 Merfolk Looter U .10 .20
62 Mystical Tutor R 15.00 30.00
63 Oona's Grace C .07 .15
64 Peregrine Drake C 2.00 4.00
65 Phantom Master C .07 .15
66 Phyrexian Ingester U .20 .40
67 Prodigal Sorcerer U .10 .20
68 Quiet Speculation U .15 .30
69 Screeching Skaab C .07 .15
70 Serendib Efreet R .15 .30
71 Shoreline Ranger C .07 .15
72 Silent Departure C .07 .15
73 Sprite Noble U .30 .75
74 Stupefying Touch C .07 .15
75 Tidal Wave C .07 .15
76 Warden of Evos Isle C .07 .15
77 Wonder U .75 1.50
78 Animate Dead U 2.50 5.00
79 Annihilate U .10 .20
80 Blightsoil Druid C .07 .15
81 Blood Artist U 4.00 8.00
82 Braids, Cabal Minion R .25 .50
83 Cabal Therapy U .75 1.50
84 Carrion Feeder C .30 .75
85 Deadbridge Shaman C .07 .15
86 Duress C .07 .15
87 Entomb R 15.00 30.00
88 Eyeblight's Ending C .07 .15
89 Gravedigger C .07 .15
90 Havoc Demon U .15 .30
91 Honden of Night's Reach U .75 1.50
92 Hymn to Tourach U .75 1.50
93 Ichorid R .30 .75
94 Innocent Blood C .07 .15
95 Lys Alana Scarblade U .12 .25
96 Malicious Affliction R 1.50 3.00
97 Nausea C .07 .15
98 Necropotence M 30.00 60.00
99 Nekrataal U .10 .20
100 Night's Whisper C 3.00 6.00
101 Phyrexian Gargantua U .10 .20
102 Phyrexian Rager C .07 .15
103 Plague Witch C .07 .15
104 Prowling Pangolin C .07 .15
105 Sengir Autocrat U .30 .75
106 Sinkhole R 4.00 8.00
107 Skulking Ghost C .07 .15
108 Toxic Deluge R 15.00 30.00
109 Tragic Slip C .25 .50
110 Twisted Abomination C .07 .15
111 Urborg Uprising C .07 .15
112 Vampiric Tutor M 30.00 60.00
113 Victimize U .30 .75
114 Visara the Dreadful R .75 1.50
115 Wake of Vultures C .07 .15
116 Wakedancer C .07 .15
117 Avarax C .07 .15
118 Battle Squadron U .20 .40
119 Beetleback Chief U .20 .40
120 Borderland Marauder C .07 .15
121 Burning Vengeance U .10 .20
122 Carbonize C .07 .15
123 Chain Lightning U 1.50 3.00
124 Crater Hellion R .15 .30
125 Desperate Ravings C .07 .15
126 Dragon Egg C .07 .15
127 Dualcaster Mage R .30 .60
128 Faithless Looting C .30 .60
129 Fervent Cathar C .07 .15
130 Firebolt C .07 .15
131 Flame Jab U .10 .20
132 Gamble R 12.50 25.00
133 Ghitu Slinger U .10 .20
134 Honden of Infinite Rage U .75 1.50
135 Keldon Champion U .10 .20
136 Keldon Marauders C .07 .15
137 Kird Ape C .07 .15
138 Mogg Fanatic C .07 .15
139 Mogg War Marshal C .17 .35
140 Orcish Oriflamme C .07 .15
141 Price of Progress U 1.50 3.00
142 Pyroblast U 2.50 5.00
143 Pyrokinesis R .25 .50
144 Reckless Charge C .07 .15
145 Rorix Bladewing R .20 .40
146 Seismic Stomp C .07 .15
147 Siege-Gang Commander R .75 1.50
148 Sneak Attack M 10.00 20.00
149 Stingscourger C .07 .15
150 Sulfuric Vortex R .75 1.50
151 Tooth and Claw U .12 .25
152 Undying Rage C .07 .15
153 Wildfire Emissary C .07 .15
154 Worldgorger Dragon M 12.50 25.00
155 Young Pyromancer U .50 1.00
156 Abundant Growth C .50 1.00
157 Ancestral Mask U .10 .20
158 Argothian Enchantress M 30.00 60.00
159 Brawn U .30 .60
160 Centaur Chieftain U .10 .20
161 Civic Wayfinder C .07 .15
162 Commune with the Gods C .07 .15
163 Elephant Guide C .07 .15
164 Elvish Vanguard C .20 .40
165 Emperor Crocodile C .07 .15
166 Flinthoof Boar U .10 .20
167 Fog C .15 .30
168 Gaea's Blessing U .20 .40
169 Green Sun's Zenith R 20.00 40.00
170 Harmonize U .15 .30
171 Heritage Druid R 7.50 15.00
172 Honden of Life's Web U .75 1.50
173 Imperious Perfect R .30 .60
174 Invigorate U .10 .20
175 Llanowar Elves C .20 .40
176 Lys Alana Huntmaster C .20 .40
177 Natural Order M 12.50 25.00
178 Nature's Claim C .60 1.25
179 Nimble Mongoose C .07 .15
180 Rancor U .75 1.50
181 Regal Force R 1.50 3.00
182 Roar of the Wurm U .10 .20
183 Roots C .07 .15
184 Seal of Strenght C .07 .15
185 Sentinel Spider C .07 .15
186 Silvos, Rogue Elemental R .25 .50
187 Sylvan Library R 30.00 60.00
188 Sylvan Might C .07 .15
189 Thornweald Archer C .07 .15
190 Timberwatch Elf U .20 .40
191 Werebear C .15 .30
192 Wirewood Symbiote U 2.50 5.00
193 Xantid Swarm R .40 .80
194 Yavimaya Enchantress C .07 .15
195 Armadillo Cloak U .30 .75
196 Baleful Strix R 2.50 5.00
197 Bloodbraid Elf U 1.50 3.00
198 Brago, King Eternal R 1.00 2.00
199 Dack Fayden M 15.00 30.00
200 Extract from Darkness U .10 .20
201 Flame-Kin Zealot U .10 .20
202 Glare of Subdual R .25 .50
203 Goblin Trenches R .15 .30
204 Maelstrom Wanderer M 7.50 15.00
205 Shaman of the Pack U .50 1.00
206 Shardless Agent R .15 .30
207 Sphinx of the Steel Wind M .75 1.50
208 Thunderclap Wyvern U .15 .30
209 Trygon Predator U .15 .30
210 Vindicate R 4.00 8.00
211 Void R .20 .40
212 Wee Dragonauts U .10 .20
213 Zealous Persecution U .10 .20
214 Call the Skybreaker R .15 .30
215 Deathrite Shaman R 5.00 10.00
216 Giant Solifuge R .15 .30
217 Torrent of Souls U .12 .25
218 Ashnod's Altar U 7.50 15.00
219 Chrome Mox M 30.00 75.00
220 Duplicant R .75 1.50
221 Emmessi Tome U .10 .20
222 Goblin Charbelcher R .75 1.50
223 Isochron Scepter R 7.50 15.00
224 Juggernaut U .10 .20
225 Mana Crypt M 100.00 200.00
226 Millikin U .75 1.50
227 Mindless Automaton U .12 .25
228 Nevinyrral's Disk R 1.00 2.00
229 Pilgrim's Eye C .07 .15
230 Prismatic Lens U .20 .40
231 Relic of Progenitus U 3.00 6.00
232 Sensei's Divining Top R 30.00 75.00
233 Ticking Gnomes U .10 .20
234 Winter Orb R 10.00 20.00
235 Worn Powerstone U 1.00 2.00
236 Bloodfell Caves C .07 .15
237 Blossoming Sands C .07 .15
238 Dismal Backwater C .07 .15
239 Jungle Hollow C .07 .15
240 Karakas M 20.00 40.00
241 Maze of Ith R 7.50 15.00
242 Mishra's Factory U .20 .40
243 Rugged Highlands C .07 .15
244 Scoured Barrens C .07 .15
245 Swiftwater Cliffs C .07 .15
246 Thornwood Falls C .07 .15
247 Tranquil Cove C .07 .15
248 Wasteland R 20.00 40.00
249 Wind-Scarred Crag C .07 .15

2016 Magic The Gathering Eternal Masters Tokens

1 Spirit .30 .75
2 Soldier .07 .15
3 Spirit .07 .15
4 Wall .07 .15
5 Serf .15 .30
6 Zombie .07 .15
7 Carnivore .07 .15
8 Dragon .07 .15
9 Elemental .30 .60
10 Goblin .07 .15
11 Elephant .07 .15
12 Elf Warrior .17 .35
13 Wurm .25 .50
14 Elemental .07 .15
15 Goblin Soldier .07 .15
16 Dack Fayden Emblem .75 1.50

2016 Magic The Gathering From the Vault Lore

1 Beseech the Queen M 1.25 2.50
2 Cabal Ritual M 2.00 3.75
3 Conflux M .60 1.25
4 Dark Depths M 15.00 30.00
5 Glissa the Traitor M .75 1.50
6 Helvault M .50 1.00
7 Memnarch M 2.50 4.75
8 Minds Desire M 1.00 1.75
9 Momir Vig Simic Visionary M 2.00 3.50
10 Near-Death Experience M .50 1.00
11 Obliterate M .60 1.25
12 Phyrexian Processor M .60 1.25
13 Tolaria West M 2.50 4.25
14 Umezawas Jitte M 10.00 18.00
15 Unmask M 1.50 2.75
16 Marit Lage Token M 2.50 4.50

2016 Magic The Gathering Judge Gift Rewards

1 Stoneforge Mystic R 30.00 60.00
2 Mana Drain R 75.00 150.00
3 Azusa, Lost but Seeking R 17.50 35.00
4 Command Beacon R 12.50 25.00
5 Mystic Confluence R 6.00 12.00
6 Imperial Seal R 200.00 400.00
7 Defense of the Heart R 50.00 100.00
8 Zur the Enchanter R 12.50 25.00

2016 Magic The Gathering Kaladesh

1 Acrobatic Maneuver C .07 .15
2 Aerial Responder U .10 .20
3 Aetherstorm Roc R .15 .30
4 Angel of Invention M 2.00 4.00
5 Authority of the Consuls R 4.00 8.00
6 Aviary Mechanic C .07 .15
7 Built to Last C .07 .15
8 Captured by the Consulate R .15 .30
9 Cataclysmic Gearhulk M .50 1.00
10 Consulate Surveillance U .10 .20
11 Consul's Shieldguard U .10 .20
12 Eddytrail Hawk C .07 .15
13 Fairgrounds Warden U .10 .20
14 Fragmentize C .07 .15
15 Fumigate R 1.25 2.50
16 Gearshift Ace U .10 .20
17 Glint-Sleeve Artisan C .07 .15
18 Herald of the Fair C .07 .15
19 Impeccable Timing C .07 .15
20 Inspired Charge C .07 .15
21 Master Trinketeer R .15 .30
22 Ninth Bridge Patrol C .07 .15
23 Pressure Point C .07 .15
24 Propeller Pioneer C .07 .15
25 Refurbish U .10 .20
26 Revoke Privileges C .07 .15
27 Servo Exhibition U .10 .20
28 Skyswirl Harrier C .07 .15
29 Skywhaler's Shot U .10 .20
30 Tasseled Dromedary C .07 .15
31 Thriving Ibex C .07 .15
32 Toolcraft Exemplar R .15 .30
33 Trusty Companion U .10 .20
34 Visionary Augmenter U .10 .20
35 Wispweaver Angel U .10 .20
36 Aether Meltdown U .10 .20
37 Aether Theorist C .07 .15
38 Aether Tradewinds C .07 .15
39 Aethersquall Ancient R .15 .30
40 Ceremonious Rejection U .10 .20
41 Confiscation Coup R .15 .30
42 Curio Vendor C .07 .15
43 Disappearing Trick U .10 .20
44 Dramatic Reversal C .50 1.00
45 Era of Innovation U .10 .20
46 Experimental Aviator U .10 .20
47 Failed Inspection C .07 .15
48 Gearseeker Serpent C .07 .15
49 Glimmer of Genius U .10 .20
50 Glint-Nest Crane U .10 .20
51 Hightide Hermit C .07 .15
52 Insidious Will R .50 1.00
53 Janjeet Sentry U .10 .20
54 Long-Finned Skywhale U .10 .20
55 Malfunction C .07 .15
56 Metallurgic Summonings M .75 1.50
57 Minister of Inquiries U .10 .20
58 Nimble Innovator C .07 .15
59 Padeem, Consul of Innovation R .75 1.50
60 Paradoxical Outcome R .30 .75
61 Revolutionary Rebuff C .07 .15
62 Saheeli's Artistry R .15 .30
63 Select for Inspection C .07 .15
64 Shrewd Negotiation U .10 .20
65 Tezzeret's Ambition C .07 .15
66 Thriving Turtle C .07 .15
67 Torrential Gearhulk M 4.00 8.00
68 Vedalken Blademaster C .07 .15
69 Weldfast Wingsmith C .07 .15
70 Wind Drake C .07 .15
71 Aetherborn Marauder U .10 .20
72 Ambitious Aetherborn C .07 .15
73 Demon of Dark Schemes M .75 1.50
74 Dhund Operative C .07 .15
75 Diabolic Tutor U .60 1.25
76 Die Young C .07 .15
77 Dukhara Scavenger C .07 .15
78 Eliminate the Competition R .15 .30
79 Embraal Bruiser U .10 .20
80 Essence Extraction U .10 .20
81 Fortuitous Find C .07 .15
82 Foundry Screecher C .07 .15
83 Fretwork Colony U .10 .20
84 Gonti, Lord of Luxury R .20 .40
85 Harsh Scrutiny U .10 .20
86 Lawless Broker C .07 .15
87 Live Fast C .07 .15
88 Lost Legacy R .15 .30
89 Make Obsolete U .10 .20
90 Marionette Master R .30 .60
91 Maulfist Squad C .07 .15
92 Midnight Oil R .15 .30
93 Mind Rot C .07 .15
94 Morbid Curiosity U .10 .20
95 Night Market Lookout C .07 .15
96 Noxious Gearhulk M 1.25 2.50
97 Ovalchase Daredevil U .75 1.50
98 Prakhata Club Security C .07 .15
99 Rush of Vitality C .07 .15
100 Subtle Strike C .07 .15
101 Syndicate Trafficker R .15 .30
102 Thriving Rats C .07 .15
103 Tidy Conclusion C .07 .15
104 Underhanded Designs U .10 .20
105 Weaponcraft Enthusiast U .10 .20
106 Aethertorch Renegade U .10 .20
107 Brazen Scourge U .10 .20
108 Built to Smash C .07 .15
109 Cathartic Reunion C .07 .15
110 Chandra, Torch of Defiance M 6.00 12.00
111 Chandra's Pyrohelix C .07 .15
112 Combustible Gearhulk M .75 1.50
113 Demolish C .07 .15
114 Fateful Showdown R .15 .30
115 Furious Reprisal U .10 .20
116 Giant Spectacle C .07 .15
117 Harnessed Lightning U .10 .20
118 Hijack C .07 .15
119 Incendiary Sabotage U .10 .20
120 Inventor's Apprentice U .10 .20
121 Lathnu Hellion R .15 .30
122 Madcap Experiment R .15 .30
123 Maulfist Doorbuster U .10 .20
124 Pia Nalaar R .15 .30
125 Quicksmith Genius U .10 .20
126 Reckless Fireweaver C .07 .15
127 Renegade Tactics C .07 .15
128 Ruinous Gremlin C .07 .15
129 Salivating Gremlins C .07 .15
130 Skyship Stalker R .15 .30
131 Spark of Creativity U .10 .20

132 Speedway Fanatic U	.10	.20
133 Spireside Infiltrator C	.07	.15
134 Spontaneous Artist C	.07	.15
135 Start Your Engines U	.10	.20
136 Territorial Gorger R	.15	.30
137 Terror of the Fairgrounds C	.07	.15
138 Thriving Grubs C	.07	.15
139 Wayward Giant C	.07	.15
140 Welding Sparks C	.07	.15
141 Appetite for the Unnatural C	.07	.15
142 Arborback Stomper U	.10	.20
143 Architect of the Untamed R	.15	.30
144 Armorcraft Judge U	.10	.20
145 Attune with Aether C	.07	.15
146 Blossoming Defense U	.30	.60
147 Bristling Hydra R	.15	.30
148 Commencement of Festivities C	.07	.15
149 Cowl Prowler C	.07	.15
150 Creeping Mold U	.10	.20
151 Cultivator of Blades R	.15	.30
152 Dubious Challenge R	.15	.30
153 Durable Handicraft U	.10	.20
154 Elegant Edgecrafters U	.10	.20
155 Fairgrounds Trumpeter U	.10	.20
156 Ghirapur Guide U	.10	.20
157 Highspire Artisan C	.07	.15
158 Hunt the Weak C	.07	.15
159 Kurjar Seedsculptor C	.07	.15
160 Larger Than Life C	.07	.15
161 Longtusk Cub U	.10	.20
162 Nature's Way U	.10	.20
163 Nissa, Vital Force M	4.00	8.00
164 Ornamental Courage C	.07	.15
165 Oviya Pashiri, Sage Lifecrafter R	.15	.30
166 Peema Outrider C	.07	.15
167 Riparian Tiger C	.07	.15
168 Sage of Shaila's Claim C	.07	.15
169 Servant of the Conduit U	.10	.20
170 Take Down C	.07	.15
171 Thriving Rhino C	.07	.15
172 Verdurous Gearhulk M	.50	1.00
173 Wild Wanderer C	.07	.15
174 Wildest Dreams R	.20	.40
175 Wily Bandar C	.07	.15
176 Cloudblazer U	.10	.20
177 Contraband Kingpin U	.10	.20
178 Depala, Pilot Exemplar R	.15	.30
179 Dovin Baan M	.75	1.50
180 Empyreal Voyager U	.10	.20
181 Engineered Might U	.10	.20
182 Hazardous Conditions U	.10	.20
183 Kambal, Consul of Allocation R	2.00	4.00
184 Rashmi, Eternities Crafter M	.50	1.00
185 Restoration Gearsmith U	.10	.20
186 Saheeli Rai M	3.00	6.00
187 Unlicensed Disintegration U	.10	.20
188 Veteran Motorist U	.10	.20
189 Voltaic Brawler U	.10	.20
190 Whirler Virtuoso U	.10	.20
191 Accomplished Automaton C	.07	.15
192 Aetherflux Reservoir R	7.50	15.00
193 Aetherworks Marvel M	1.00	2.00
194 Animation Module R	.60	1.25
195 Aradara Express C	.07	.15
196 Ballista Charger U	.10	.20
197 Bastion Mastodon C	.07	.15
198 Bomat Bazaar Barge U	.30	.60
199 Bomat Courier R	.20	.40
200 Chief of the Foundry U	.10	.20
201 Cogworker's Puzzleknot C	.07	.15
202 Consulate Skygate C	.07	.15
203 Cultivator's Caravan R	.15	.30
204 Deadlock Trap R	.15	.30
205 Decoction Module U	.10	.20
206 Demolition Stomper U	.10	.20
207 Dukhara Peafowl C	.07	.15
208 Dynavolt Tower R	.15	.30
209 Eager Construct C	.07	.15
210 Electrostatic Pummeler R	.15	.30
211 Fabrication Module U	.10	.20
212 Filigree Familiar U	.10	.20
213 Fireforger's Puzzleknot C	.07	.15
214 Fleetwheel Cruiser R	.15	.30
215 Foundry Inspector U	.15	.30
216 Ghirapur Orrery R	.50	1.00
217 Glassblower's Puzzleknot C	.07	.15
218 Inventor's Goggles C	.07	.15
219 Iron League Steed U	.10	.20
220 Key to the City R	.15	.30
221 Metalspinner's Puzzleknot C	.07	.15
222 Metalwork Colossus R	.75	1.50
223 Multiform Wonder R	.15	.30
224 Narnam Cobra C	.07	.15
225 Ovalchase Dragster U	.10	.20
226 Panharmonicon R	5.00	10.00
227 Perpetual Timepiece U	.30	.75
228 Prakhata Pillar-Bug C	.07	.15
229 Prophetic Prism C	.07	.15
230 Renegade Freighter C	.07	.15
231 Scrapheap Scrounger R	.15	.30
232 Self-Assembler C	.07	.15
233 Sky Skiff C	.07	.15
234 Skysovereign, Consul Flagship M	1.50	3.00
235 Smuggler's Copter R	2.00	4.00
236 Snare Thopter U	.10	.20
237 Torch Gauntlet C	.07	.15
238 Weldfast Monitor C	.07	.15
239 Whirlermaker U	.10	.20
240 Woodweaver's Puzzleknot C	.07	.15
241 Workshop Assistant C	.07	.15
242 Aether Hub U	.10	.20
243 Blooming Marsh R	6.00	12.00
244 Botanical Sanctum R	4.00	8.00
245 Concealed Courtyard R	3.00	6.00
246 Inspiring Vantage R	4.00	8.00
247 Inventors' Fair R	5.00	10.00
248 Sequestered Stash U	.10	.20
249 Spirebluff Canal R	10.00	20.00
250 Plains L	.07	.15
251 Plains L	.07	.15
252 Plains L	.07	.15
253 Island L	.07	.15
254 Island L	.07	.15
255 Island L	.07	.15
256 Swamp L	.07	.15
257 Swamp L	.07	.15
258 Swamp L	.07	.15
259 Mountain L	.07	.15
260 Mountain L	.07	.15
261 Mountain L	.07	.15
262 Forest L	.07	.15
263 Forest L	.07	.15
264 Forest L	.07	.15
265 Chandra, Pyrogenius M	1.00	2.00
266 Flame Lash C	.07	.15
267 Liberating Combustion R	.15	.30
268 Renegade Firebrand U	.10	.20
269 Stone Quarry C	.07	.15
270 Nissa, Nature's Artisan M	2.00	4.00
271 Guardian of the Great Conduit U	.10	.20
272 Terrain Elemental C	.07	.15
273 Verdant Crescendo R	.15	.30
274 Woodland Stream C	.07	.15

2016 Magic The Gathering Kaladesh Inventions

1 Cataclysmic Gearhulk M	12.50	25.00
2 Torrential Gearhulk M	25.00	50.00
3 Noxious Gearhulk M	25.00	50.00
4 Combustible Gearhulk M	20.00	40.00
5 Verdurous Gearhulk M	15.00	30.00
6 Aether Vial M	60.00	125.00
7 Champions Helm M	20.00	40.00
8 Chromatic Lantern M	50.00	100.00
9 Chrome Mox M	100.00	200.00
10 Cloudstone Curio M	50.00	100.00
11 Crucible of Worlds M	60.00	125.00
12 Gauntlet of Power M	30.00	60.00
13 Hangarback Walker M	30.00	75.00
14 Lightning Greaves M	50.00	100.00
15 Lotus Petal M	75.00	150.00
16 Mana Crypt M	300.00	750.00
17 Mana Vault M	100.00	200.00
18 Minds Eye M	15.00	30.00
19 Mox Opal M	100.00	200.00
20 Painters Servant M	60.00	125.00
21 Rings of Brighthearth M	60.00	125.00
22 Scroll Rack M	100.00	200.00
23 Sculpting Steel M	25.00	50.00
24 Sol Ring M	300.00	600.00
25 Solemn Simulacrum M	50.00	100.00
26 Static Orb M	30.00	75.00
27 Steel Overseer M	20.00	40.00
28 Sword of Feast and Famine M	100.00	200.00
29 Sword of Fire and Ice M	75.00	150.00
30 Sword of Light and Shadow M	60.00	125.00
31 Arcbound Ravager M	25.00	50.00
32 Black Vise M	15.00	30.00
33 Chalice of the Void M	75.00	150.00
34 Defense Grid M	25.00	50.00
35 Duplicant M	20.00	40.00
36 Engineered Explosives M	30.00	75.00
37 Ensnaring Bridge M	60.00	125.00
38 Extraplanar Lens M	50.00	100.00
39 Grindstone M	50.00	100.00
40 Meekstone M	25.00	50.00
41 Oblivion Stone M	25.00	50.00
42 Ornithopter M	25.00	50.00
43 Paradox Engine M	25.00	50.00
44 Pithing Needle M	30.00	75.00
45 Planar Bridge M	25.00	50.00
46 Platinum Angel M	50.00	100.00
47 Sphere of Resistance M	25.00	50.00
48 Staff of Domination M	60.00	125.00
49 Sundering Titan M	15.00	30.00
50 Sword of Body and Mind M	30.00	75.00
51 Sword of War and Peace M	30.00	75.00
52 Trinisphere M	60.00	125.00
53 Vedalken Shackles M	20.00	40.00
54 Wurmcoil Engine M	60.00	125.00

2016 Magic The Gathering Kaladesh Tokens

1 Beast	.07	.15
2 Construct	.07	.15
3 Construct	.10	.20
4 Servo	.07	.15
5 Servo	.07	.15
6 Servo	.07	.15
7 Thopter	.07	.15
8 Thopter	.07	.15
9 Thopter	.07	.15
10 Chandra, Torch of Defiance Emblem	.17	.35
11 Nissa, Vital Force Emblem	.12	.25
12 Dovin Baan Emblem	.07	.15
13 Energy Reserve	.07	.15

2016 Magic The Gathering League Token

1 Servo//Thopter C	7.50	15.00

2016 Magic The Gathering Oath of the Gatewatch

1 Deceiver of Form R	.15	.30
2 Eldrazi Mimic R	.50	1.00
3 Endbringer R	.50	1.00
4 Kozilek, the Great Distortion M	10.00	20.00
5 Kozilek's Pathfinder C	.07	.15
6 Matter Reshaper R	2.00	4.00
7 Reality Smasher R	2.00	4.00
8 Spatial Contortion U	.10	.20
9 Thought-Knot Seer R	2.50	5.00
10 Walker of the Wastes U	.10	.20
11 Warden of Geometries C	.07	.15
12 Warping Wail U	.50	1.00
13 Eldrazi Displacer R	2.50	5.00
14 Affa Protector C	.07	.15
15 Allied Reinforcements U	.10	.20
16 Call the Gatewatch R	.15	.30
17 Dazzling Reflection C	.07	.15
18 Expedition Raptor C	.07	.15
19 General Tazri M	.30	.75
20 Immolating Glare U	.10	.20
21 Iona's Blessing U	.10	.20
22 Isolation Zone C	.07	.15
23 Kor Scythemaster C	.07	.15
24 Kor Sky Climber C	.07	.15
25 Linvala, the Preserver M	.50	1.00
26 Make a Stand U	.10	.20
27 Makindi Aeronaut C	.07	.15
28 Mighty Leap C	.07	.15
29 Munda's Vanguard R	.15	.30
30 Oath of Gideon R	.20	.40
31 Ondu War Cleric C	.07	.15
32 Relief Captain U	.10	.20
33 Searing Light C	.07	.15
34 Shoulder to Shoulder C	.07	.15
35 Spawnbinder Mage C	.07	.15
36 Steppe Glider U	.10	.20
37 Stone Haven Outfitter R	.25	.50
38 Stoneforge Acolyte U	.10	.20
39 Wall of Resurgence U	.10	.20
40 Abstruse Interference C	.07	.15
41 Blinding Drone C	.07	.15
42 Cultivator Drone C	.07	.15
43 Deepfathom Skulker R	.15	.30
44 Dimensional Infiltrator R	.15	.30
45 Gravity Negator C	.07	.15
46 Prophet of Distortion U	.10	.20
47 Slip Through Space C	.07	.15
48 Thought Harvester U	.10	.20
49 Void Shatter U	.10	.20
50 Ancient Crab C	.07	.15
51 Comparative Analysis C	.07	.15
52 Containment Membrane C	.07	.15
53 Crush of Tentacles M	1.25	2.50
54 Cyclone Sire U	.10	.20
55 Gift of Tusks U	.10	.20
56 Grip of the Roil U	.10	.20
57 Hedron Alignment R	.15	.30
58 Jwar Isle Avenger C	.07	.15
59 Negate C	.07	.15
60 Oath of Jace R	.20	.40
61 Overwhelming Denial R	.15	.30
62 Roiling Waters U	.10	.20
63 Sphinx of the Final Word M	.75	1.50
64 Sweep Away C	.07	.15
65 Umara Entangler C	.07	.15
66 Unity of Purpose U	.10	.20
67 Bearer of Silence R	.15	.30
68 Dread Defiler R	.15	.30
69 Essence Depleter U	.10	.20
70 Flaying Tendrils U	.10	.20
71 Havoc Sower U	.10	.20
72 Inverter of Truth M	.75	1.50
73 Kozilek's Shrieker C	.07	.15
74 Kozilek's Translator C	.07	.15
75 Oblivion Strike C	.07	.15
76 Reaver Drone U	.10	.20
77 Sifter of Skulls R	.75	1.50
78 Sky Scourer C	.07	.15
79 Slaughter Drone C	.07	.15
80 Unnatural Endurance C	.07	.15
81 Visions of Brutality U	.10	.20
82 Witness the End C	.07	.15
83 Corpse Churn C	.07	.15
84 Drana's Chosen R	.15	.30
85 Grasp of Darkness U	.10	.20
86 Kalitas, Traitor of Ghet M	7.50	15.00
87 Malakir Soothsayer U	.10	.20
88 Null Caller U	.10	.20
89 Remorseless Punishment R	.15	.30
90 Tar Snare C	.07	.15
91 Untamed Hunger C	.07	.15
92 Vampire Envoy C	.07	.15
93 Zulaport Chainmage C	.07	.15
94 Consuming Sinkhole C	.07	.15
95 Eldrazi Aggressor C	.07	.15
96 Eldrazi Obligator R	.15	.30
97 Immobilizer Eldrazi U	.10	.20
98 Kozilek's Return M	7.50	15.00
99 Maw of Kozilek C	.07	.15
100 Reality Hemorrhage C	.07	.15
101 Akoum Flameseeker C	.07	.15
102 Boulder Salvo C	.07	.15
103 Brute Strength C	.07	.15
104 Chandra, Flamecaller M	.50	1.00
105 Cinder Hellion C	.07	.15
106 Devour in Flames U	.10	.20
107 Embodiment of Fury U	.10	.20
108 Expedite C	.07	.15
109 Fall of the Titans R	.15	.30
110 Goblin Dark-Dwellers R	.20	.40
111 Goblin Freerunner C	.07	.15
112 Kazuul's Toll Collector U	.10	.20
113 Oath of Chandra R	.20	.40
114 Press into Service U	.10	.20
115 Pyromancer's Assault U	.10	.20
116 Reckless Bushwhacker U	.20	.40
117 Sparkmage's Gambit C	.07	.15
118 Tears of Valakut U	.10	.20
119 Tyrant of Valakut R	.15	.30
120 Zada's Commando C	.07	.15
121 Birthing Hulk U	.10	.20
122 Ruin in Their Wake U	.10	.20
123 Scion Summoner C	.07	.15
124 Stalking Drone C	.07	.15
125 Vile Redeemer R	.15	.30
126 World Breaker M	2.00	4.00
127 Baloth Pup U	.10	.20
128 Bonds of Mortality U	.10	.20
129 Canopy Gorger C	.07	.15
130 Elemental Uprising C	.07	.15
131 Embodiment of Insight U	.10	.20
132 Gladehart Cavalry R	.15	.30
133 Harvester Troll U	.10	.20
134 Lead by Example C	.07	.15
135 Loam Larva C	.07	.15
136 Natural State C	.07	.15
137 Netcaster Spider C	.07	.15
138 Nissa, Voice of Zendikar M	2.50	5.00
139 Nissa's Judgment U	.10	.20
140 Oath of Nissa R	2.00	4.00
141 Pulse of Murasa C	.07	.15
142 Saddleback Lagac C	.07	.15
143 Seed Guardian U	.10	.20
144 Sylvan Advocate R	.15	.30
145 Tajuru Pathwarden C	.07	.15
146 Vines of the Recluse C	.07	.15
147 Zendikar Resurgent R	4.00	8.00
148 Flayer Drone U	.10	.20
149 Mindmelter U	.10	.20
150 Void Grafter U	.10	.20
151 Ayli, Eternal Pilgrim R	.75	1.50
152 Baloth Null U	.10	.20
153 Cliffhaven Vampire U	.50	1.00
154 Joraga Auxiliary U	.10	.20
155 Jori En, Ruin Diver R	.20	.40
156 Mina and Denn, Wildborn R	.50	1.00
157 Reflector Mage U	.50	1.00
158 Relentless Hunter U	.10	.20
159 Stormchaser Mage U	.10	.20
160 Weapons Trainer U	.10	.20
161 Bone Saw C	.07	.15
162 Captain's Claws R	.15	.30
163 Chitinous Cloak U	.10	.20
164 Hedron Crawler C	.07	.15
165 Seer's Lantern C	.07	.15
166 Stoneforge Masterwork R	1.50	3.00
167 Strider Harness U	.10	.20
168 Cinder Barrens U	.10	.20
169 Corrupted Crossroads R	.15	.30
170 Crumbling Vestige C	.07	.15
171 Hissing Quagmire R	.75	1.50
172 Holdout Settlement C	.07	.15
173 Meandering River U	.10	.20
174 Mirrorpool M	1.50	3.00
175 Needle Spires R	.15	.30
176 Ruins of Oran-Rief R	.15	.30
177 Sea Gate Wreckage R	.15	.30
178 Submerged Boneyard U	.10	.20
179 Timber Gorge U	.10	.20
180 Tranquil Expanse U	.10	.20
181 Unknown Shores C	.07	.15
182 Wandering Fumarole R	.50	1.00
183a Wastes C	1.50	3.00
183b Wastes C FULL ART	.40	.80
184a Wastes C	1.25	2.50
184b Wastes C FULL ART	.40	.80

2016 Magic The Gathering Oath of the Gatewatch Tokens

1 Eldrazi Scion	.07	.15
2 Eldrazi Scion	.07	.15
3 Eldrazi Scion	.07	.15
4 Eldrazi Scion	.07	.15
5 Eldrazi Scion	.07	.15
6 Eldrazi Scion	.07	.15
7 Angel	.07	.15
8 Zombie	.07	.15
9 Elemental	.07	.15
10 Elemental	.07	.15
11 Plant	.17	.35

2016 Magic The Gathering Planechase Anthology

1 Armored Griffin U	.20	.40
2 Auramancer C	.10	.20
3 Auratouched Mage U	.20	.40
4 Cage of Hands C	.10	.20
5 Celestial Ancient R	.12	.25
6 Felidar Umbra U	.20	.40
7 Ghostly Prison U	.20	.40
8 Hyena Umbra C	.10	.20
9 Kor Spiritdancer R	.12	.25
10 Mammoth Umbra U	.20	.40
11 Sigil of the Empty Throne R	.12	.25
12 Spirit Mantle U	.20	.40
13 Three Dreams R	.12	.25
14 Augury Owl C	.10	.20
15 Cancel C	.10	.20
16 Concentrate U	.20	.40
17 Guard Gomazoa U	.20	.40
18 Higure the Still Wind R	.12	.25
19 Illusory Angel U	.20	.40
20 Mistblade Shinobi C	.10	.20
21 Ninja of the Deep Hours C	.10	.20
22 Peregrine Drake U	.20	.40
23 Primal Plasma C	.10	.20
24 Sakashimas Student R	.12	.25
25 See Beyond C	.10	.20
26 Sunken Hope R	.12	.25
27 Walker of Secret Ways U	.20	.40
28 Wall of Frost U	.20	.40
29 Whirlpool Warrior R	.12	.25
30 Assassinate C	.10	.20
31 Cadaver Imp C	.10	.20
32 Dark Hatchling R	.12	.25
33 InkEyes Servant of Oni R	.12	.25
34 Lilianas Specter C	.10	.20
35 OkibaGang Shinobi C	.10	.20
36 Skullsnatcher C	.10	.20
37 Throat Slitter U	.20	.40
38 Tormented Soul C	.10	.20
39 Arc Trail U	.20	.40
40 Beetleback Chief U	.10	.20
41 Erratic Explosion C	.10	.20
42 Fiery Conclusion C	.10	.20
43 Fiery Fall C	.10	.20
44 Fling C	.10	.20
45 Hellion Eruption R	.12	.25
46 Hissing Iguanar C	.10	.20
47 Mark of Mutiny U	.20	.40
48 Mass Mutiny R	.12	.25
49 Mudbutton Torchrunner C	.10	.20
50 Preyseizer Dragon R	.12	.25
51 Rivals Duel U	.20	.40
52 ThornThrash Viashino C	.10	.20
53 ThunderThrash Elder U	.20	.40
54 Warstorm Surge R	.12	.25
55 Aura Gnarlid C	.10	.20
56 Awakening Zone R	.12	.25
57 Beast Within U	.20	.40
58 Boar Umbra U	.20	.40
59 Bramble Elemental C	.10	.20
60 Brindle Shoat U	.20	.40
61 Brutalizer Exarch U	.20	.40
62 Cultivate C	.10	.20
63 Dowsing Shaman U	.20	.40
64 Dreampod Druid U	.20	.40
65 Gluttonous Slime U	.20	.40
66 Lumberknot U	.20	.40
67 Mitotic Slime R	.12	.25
68 Mycoloth R	.12	.25
69 Nest Invader C	.10	.20
70 Nullmage Advocate C	.10	.20
71 Ondu Giant C	.10	.20

72 Overrun U	.20	.40
73 Penumbra Spider C	.10	.20
74 Predatory Urge R	.12	.25
75 Quiet Disrepair C	.10	.20
76 Rancor C	.10	.20
77 Silhana Ledgewalker C	.10	.20
78 Snake Umbra C	.10	.20
79 Tukatongue Thallid C	.10	.20
80 Viridian Emissary C	.10	.20
81 Wall of Blossoms U	.20	.40
82 Baleful Strix U	.20	.40
83 Bituminous Blast U	.20	.40
84 Bloodbraid Elf U	.20	.40
85 Deny Reality C	.10	.20
86 Dimir Infiltrator C	.10	.20
87 Dragonlair Spider R	.12	.25
88 Elderwood Scion R	.12	.25
89 Enigma Sphinx R	.12	.25
90 Enlisted Wurm U	.20	.40
91 EtheriumHorn Sorcerer R	.12	.25
92 Fires of Yavimaya U	.20	.40
93 Fusion Elemental U	.20	.40
94 Glen Elendra Liege R	.12	.25
95 Hellkite Hatchling U	.20	.40
96 Indrik Umbra R	.12	.25
97 Inkfathom Witch U	.20	.40
98 Kathari Remnant U	.20	.40
99 Krond the DawnClad MR	1.25	2.50
100 Last Stand R	.12	.25
101 Maelstrom Wanderer MR	5.00	10.00
102 Noggle Ransacker U	.20	.40
103 Pollenbright Wings U	.20	.40
104 Shardless Agent U	.20	.40
105 SilentBlade Oni R	.12	.25
106 Thromok the Insatiable MR	2.00	4.00
107 Vela the NightClad MR	1.50	3.00
108 Armillary Sphere C	.10	.20
109 Farsight Mask U	.20	.40
110 Flayer Husk C	.10	.20
111 Fractured Powerstone C	.10	.20
112 Quietus Spike R	.12	.25
113 Sai of the Shinobi U	.20	.40
114 Thran Golem U	.20	.40
115 Whispersilk Cloak U	.20	.40
116 Dimir Aqueduct C	.10	.20
117 Exotic Orchard R	.12	.25
118 Graypelt Refuge U	.20	.40
119 Gruul Turf C	.10	.20
120 Jwar Isle Refuge U	.20	.40
121 Kazandu Refuge U	.20	.40
122 Khalni Garden C	.10	.20
123 Krosan Verge U	.20	.40
124 Rupture Spire C	.10	.20
125 Selesnya Sanctuary C	.10	.20
126 Shimmering Grotto C	.10	.20
127 Skarrg the Rage Pits U	.20	.40
128 Tainted Isle U	.20	.40
129 Terramorphic Expanse C	.10	.20
130 VituGhazi the CityTree U	.20	.40
131 Vivid Creek U	.20	.40
132 Plains L	.10	.20
133 Plains L	.10	.20
134 Plains L	.10	.20
135 Plains L	.10	.20
136 Plains L	.10	.20
137 IsL L	.10	.20
138 IsL L	.10	.20
139 IsL L	.10	.20
140 IsL L	.10	.20
141 IsL L	.10	.20
142 Swamp L	.10	.20
143 Swamp L	.10	.20
144 Swamp L	.10	.20
145 Swamp L	.10	.20
146 Swamp L	.10	.20
147 Mountain L	.10	.20
148 Mountain L	.10	.20
149 Mountain L	.10	.20
150 Mountain L	.10	.20
151 Forest L	.10	.20
152 Forest L	.10	.20
153 Forest L	.10	.20
154 Forest L	.10	.20
155 Forest L	.10	.20
156 Forest L	.10	.20

2016 Magic The Gathering Planechase Anthology Planes

1 Chaotic Aether	.50	1.00
2 Interplanar Tunnel	.50	1.00
3 Morphic Tide	.50	1.00
4 Mutual Epiphany	.50	1.00
5 Planewide Disaster	.50	1.00
6 Reality Shaping	.50	1.00
7 Spatial Merging	.50	1.00
8 Time Distortion	.50	1.00
9 Academy at Tolaria West	.50	1.00
10 The Aether Flues	.75	1.50
11 Agyrem	.50	1.00
12 Akoum	.50	1.00
13 Aretopolis	.30	.75
14 Astral Arena	.50	1.00
15 Bant	.50	1.00
16 Bloodhill Bastion	.50	1.00
17 Celestine Reef	.50	1.00
18 Cliffside Market	.50	1.00
19 The Dark Barony	.60	1.25
20 Edge of Malacol	.30	.75
21 Eloren Wilds	.60	1.25
22 The Eon Fog	.60	1.25
23 Feeding Grounds	.50	1.00
24 Fields of Summer	.75	1.50
25 The Fourth Sphere	.60	1.25
26 Furnace Layer	.30	.75
27 Gavony	.50	1.00
28 Glen Elendra	.50	1.00
29 Glimmervoid Basin	.50	1.00
30 Goldmeadow	.60	1.25
31 Grand Ossuary	.50	1.00
32 The Great Forest	.60	1.25
33 Grixis	.75	1.50
34 Grove of the Dreampods	.50	1.00
35 Hedron Fields of Agadeem	.50	1.00
36 The Hippodrome	.60	1.25
37 Horizon Boughs	.75	1.50
38 Immersturm	.60	1.25
39 Isle of Vesuva	.75	1.50
40 Izzet Steam Maze	.60	1.25
41 Jund	.30	.75
42 Kessig	.50	1.00
43 Kharasha Foothills	.30	.75
44 Kilnspire District	.30	.75
45 Krosa	.60	1.25
46 Lair of the Ashen Idol	.30	.75
47 Lethe Lake	.50	1.00
48 Llanowar	.60	1.25
49 The Maelstrom	.75	1.50
50 Minamo	.60	1.25
51 Mirrored Depths	.50	1.00
52 Mount Keralia	.30	.75
53 Murasa	.50	1.00
54 Naar Isle	.50	1.00
55 Naya	.50	1.00
56 Nephalia	.30	.75
57 Norn's Dominion	.30	.75
58 Onakke Catacomb	.30	.75
59 Orochi Colony	.30	.75
60 Orzhova	.30	.75
61 Otaria	.60	1.25
62 Panopticon	.60	1.25
63 Pools of Becoming	1.00	2.00
64 Prahv	.50	1.00
65 Quicksilver Sea	.50	1.00
66 Raven's Run	.50	1.00
67 Sanctum of Serra	.60	1.25
68 Sea of Sand	.60	1.25
69 Selesnya Loft Gardens	.50	1.00
70 Shiv	.30	.75
71 Skybreen	.60	1.25
72 Sokenzan	.60	1.25
73 Stairs to Infinity	1.25	2.50
74 Stensia	.30	.75
75 Stronghold Furnace	.60	1.25
76 Takenuma	.30	.75
77 Talon Gates	.30	.75
78 Tazeem	2.50	5.00
79 Tember City	1.00	2.00
80 Trail of the Mage-Rings	.30	.75
81 Truga Jungle	.30	.75
82 Turri Island	.60	1.25
83 Undercity Reaches	.75	1.50
84 Velis Vel	.60	1.25
85 Windriddle Palaces	.30	.75
86 The Zephyr Maze	.30	.75

2016 Magic The Gathering Planechase Anthology Tokens

1 Eldrazi	.07	.15
2 Eldrazi Spawn	.07	.15
3 Eldrazi Spawn	.07	.15
4 Eldrazi Spawn	.07	.15
5 Angel	.07	.15
6 Goat	.07	.15
7 Germ	.07	.15
8 Spider	.07	.15
9 Zombie	.07	.15
10 Dragon	.07	.15
11 Goblin	.07	.15
12 Hellion	.07	.15
13 Beast	.07	.15
14 Boar	.07	.15
15 Insect	.07	.15
16 Ooze	.07	.15
17 Ooze	.07	.15
18 Plant	.07	.15
19 Saproling	.07	.15

2016 Magic The Gathering Shadows over Innistrad

1 Always Watching R	.75	1.50
2 Angel of Deliverance R	.15	.30
3 Angelic Purge C	.07	.15
4 Apothecary Geist C	.07	.15
5 Archangel Avacyn/Avacyn the Purifier M	4.00	8.00
6 Avacynian Missionaries/Lunarch Inquisitors U	.10	.20
7 Bound by Moonsilver U	.10	.20
8 Bygone Bishop R	.30	.60
9 Cathar's Companion C	.07	.15
10 Chaplain's Blessing C	.07	.15
11 Dauntless Cathar C	.07	.15
12 Declaration in Stone R	.30	.60
13 Descend upon the Sinful M	.30	.75
14 Devilthorn Fox C	.07	.15
15 Drogskol Cavalry R	.15	.30
16 Eerie Interlude R	1.00	2.00
17 Emissary of the Sleepless C	.07	.15
18 Ethereal Guidance C	.07	.15
19 Expose Evil C	.07	.15
20 Gryff's Boon U	.10	.20
21 Hanweir Militia Captain/Westvale Cult Leader R	.50	1.00
22 Hope Against Hope U	.10	.20
23 Humble the Brute U	.10	.20
24 Inquisitor's Ox C	.07	.15
25 Inspiring Captain C	.07	.15
26 Militant Inquisitor C	.07	.15
27 Moorland Drifter C	.07	.15
28 Nahiri's Machinations U	.10	.20
29 Nearheath Chaplain U	.10	.20
30 Not Forgotten U	.10	.20
31 Odric, Lunarch Marshal R	.15	.30
32 Open the Armory U	.50	1.00
33 Paranoid Parish-Blade U	.10	.20
34 Pious Evangel/Wayward Disciple U	.20	.40
35 Puncturing Light C	.07	.15
36 Reaper of Flight Moonsilver U	.10	.20
37 Silverstrike U	.10	.20
38 Spectral Shepherd U	.10	.20
39 Stern Constable C	.07	.15
40 Strength of Arms C	.07	.15
41 Survive the Night C	.07	.15
42 Tenacity U	.10	.20
43 Thalia's Lieutenant R	.50	1.00
44 Thraben Inspector C	.07	.15
45 Topplegeist U	.10	.20
46 Town Gossipmonger/Incited Rabble U	.10	.20
47 Unruly Mob C	.07	.15
48 Vessel of Ephemera C	.07	.15
49 Aberrant Researcher/Perfected Form U	.10	.20
50 Broken Concentration U	.10	.20
51 Catalog C	.07	.15
52 Compelling Deterrence U	.10	.20
53 Confirm Suspicions R	.15	.30
54 Daring Sleuth/Bearer of Overwhelming Truths U	.10	.20
55 Deny Existence C	.07	.15
56 Drownyard Explorers C	.07	.15
57 Drunau Corpse Trawler U	.10	.20
58 Engulf the Shore R	.30	.75
59 Epiphany at the Drownyard R	.15	.30
60 Erdwal Illuminator U	.10	.20
61 Essence Flux U	.75	1.50
62 Fleeting Memories U	.10	.20
63 Forgotten Creation R	.30	.75
64 Furtive Homunculus C	.07	.15
65 Geralf's Masterpiece M	.30	.60
66 Ghostly Wings C	.07	.15
67 Gone Missing C	.07	.15
68 Invasive Surgery U	.10	.20
69 Jace, Unraveler of Secrets M	3.00	6.00
70 Jace's Scrutiny C	.07	.15
71 Just the Wind C	.07	.15
72 Lamplighter of Selhoff C	.07	.15
73 Manic Scribe U	.20	.40
74 Nagging Thoughts C	.07	.15
75 Nephalia Moondrakes R	.15	.30
76 Niblis of Dusk C	.07	.15
77 Ongoing Investigation U	.10	.20
78 Pieces of the Puzzle C	.07	.15
79 Pore Over the Pages U	.10	.20
80 Press for Answers C	.07	.15
81 Rattlechains R	.30	.60
82 Reckless Scholar U	.10	.20
83 Rise from the Tides U	.10	.20
84 Seagraf Skaab C	.07	.15
85 Silburlind Snapper C	.07	.15
86 Silent Observer C	.07	.15
87 Sleep Paralysis C	.07	.15
88 Startled Awake/Persistent Nightmare M	1.50	3.00
89 Stitched Mangler C	.07	.15
90 Stitchwing Skaab U	.10	.20
91 Stormrider Spirit C	.07	.15
92 Thing in the Ice/Awoken Horror R	.15	.30
93 Trail of Evidence U	.10	.20
94 Uninvited Geist/Unimpeded Trespasser U	.10	.20
95 Vessel of Paramnesia C	.07	.15
96 Welcome to the Fold R	.15	.30
97 Accursed Witch/Infectious Curse U	.20	.40
98 Alms of the Vein C	.07	.15
99 Asylum Visitor R	.15	.30
100 Behind the Scenes U	.10	.20
101 Behold the Beyond M	.50	1.00
102 Biting Rain U	.10	.20
103 Call the Bloodline U	.10	.20
104 Creeping Dread U	.10	.20
105 Crow of Dark Tidings C	.07	.15
106 Dead Weight C	.07	.15
107 Diregraf Colossus R	4.00	8.00
108 Elusive Tormentor/Insidious Mist R	.15	.30
109 Ever After R	.15	.30
110 Farbog Revenant C	.07	.15
111 From Under the Floorboards R	.15	.30
112 Ghoulcaller's Accomplice C	.07	.15
113 Ghoulsteed U	.10	.20
114 Gisa's Bidding U	.10	.20
115 Grotesque Mutation C	.07	.15
116 Heir of Falkenrath/Heir to the Night U	.10	.20
117 Hound of the Farbogs C	.07	.15
118 Indulgent Aristocrat U	.30	.75
119 Kindly Stranger/Demon-Possessed Witch U	.10	.20
120 Liliana's Indignation U	.10	.20
121 Macabre Waltz C	.07	.15
122 Markov Dreadknight R	.15	.30
123 Merciless Resolve C	.07	.15
124 Mindwrack Demon M	.30	.60
125 Morkrut Necropod U	.10	.20
126 Murderous Compulsion C	.07	.15
127 Olivia's Bloodsworn U	.10	.20
128 Pale Rider of Trostad U	.10	.20
129 Pick the Brain U	.10	.20
130 Rancid Rats C	.07	.15
131 Relentless Dead M	10.00	20.00
132 Rottenheart Ghoul C	.07	.15
133 Sanitarium Skeleton C	.07	.15
134 Shamble Back C	.07	.15
135 Sinister Concoction U	.10	.20
136 Stallion of Ashmouth C	.07	.15
137 Stromkirk Mentor C	.07	.15
138 Throttle C	.07	.15
139 To the Slaughter R	.15	.30
140 Tooth Collector U	.10	.20
141 Triskaidekaphobia R	.15	.30
142 Twins of Maurer Estate C	.07	.15
143 Vampire Noble C	.07	.15
144 Vessel of Malignity C	.07	.15
145 Avacyn's Judgment R	.15	.30
146 Bloodmad Vampire C	.07	.15
147 Breakneck Rider/Neck Breaker U	.25	.50
148 Burn from Within R	.15	.30
149 Convicted Killer/Branded Howler C	.07	.15
150 Dance with Devils U	.10	.20
151 Devils' Playground R	.15	.30
152 Dissension in the Ranks U	.10	.20
153 Dual Shot C	.07	.15
154 Ember-Eye Wolf C	.07	.15
155 Falkenrath Gorger R	.15	.30
156 Fiery Temper C	.07	.15
157 Flameblade Angel R	.15	.30
158 Gatstaf Arsonists/Gatstaf Ravagers C	.07	.15
159 Geier Reach Bandit/Vildin-Pack Alpha R	1.25	2.50
160 Geistblast U	.10	.20
161 Gibbering Fiend U	.10	.20
162 Goldnight Castigator M	.30	.75
163 Harness the Storm R	.15	.30
164 Howlpack Wolf C	.07	.15
165 Hulking Devil C	.07	.15
166 Incorrigible Youths U	.10	.20
167 Inner Struggle U	.10	.20
168 Insolent Neonate C	.20	.40
169 Kessig Forgemaster/Flameheart Werewolf U	.25	.50
170 Lightning Axe U	.10	.20
171 Mad Prophet U	.10	.20
172 Magmatic Chasm C	.07	.15
173 Malevolent Whispers U	.10	.20
174 Pyre Hound C	.07	.15
175 Ravenous Bloodseeker U	.10	.20
176 Reduce to Ashes C	.07	.15
177 Rush of Adrenaline C	.07	.15
178 Sanguinary Mage C	.07	.15
179 Scourge Wolf R	.15	.30
180 Senseless Rage C	.07	.15
181 Sin Prodder R	.15	.30
182 Skin Invasion/Skin Shedder U	.10	.20
183 Spiteful Motives U	.10	.20
184 Stensia Masquerade U	.50	1.00
185 Structural Distortion C	.07	.15
186 Tormenting Voice C	.07	.15
187 Ulrich's Kindred U	.10	.20
188 Uncaged Fury C	.07	.15
189 Vessel of Volatility C	.07	.15
190 Village Messenger/Moonrise Intruder U	.30	.60
191 Voldaren Duelist C	.07	.15
192 Wolf of Devil's Breach M	.30	.75
193 Aim High C	.07	.15
194 Autumnal Gloom/Ancient of the Equinox U	.10	.20
195 Briarbridge Patrol U	.10	.20
196 Byway Courier C	.07	.15
197 Clip Wings C	.07	.15
198 Confront the Unknown C	.07	.15
199 Crawling Sensation U	.10	.20
200 Cryptolith Rite R	7.50	15.00
201 Cult of the Waxing Moon U	.20	.40
202 Deathcap Cultivator R	.20	.40
203 Duskwatch Recruiter/Krallenhorde Howler U	.75	1.50
204 Equestrian Skill C	.07	.15
205 Fork in the Road C	.07	.15
206 Gloomwidow U	.10	.20
207 Graf Mole U	.10	.20
208 Groundskeeper U	.10	.20
209 Hermit/Lone Wolf of Natterknolls U :G:	.30	.60
210 Hinterland Logger/Timber Shredder C	.07	.15
211 Howlpack Resurgence U	1.25	2.50
212 Inexorable Blob R	.15	.30
213 Intrepid Provisioner C	.07	.15
214 Kessig Dire Swine C	.07	.15
215 Lambholt Pacifist/Lambholt Butcher U	.20	.40
216 Loam Dryad C	.07	.15
217 Might Beyond Reason C	.07	.15
218 Moldgraf Scavenger C	.07	.15
219 Moonlight Hunt U	.75	1.50
220 Obsessive Skinner U	.10	.20
221 Pack Guardian U	.10	.20
222 Quilled Wolf C	.07	.15
223 Rabid Bite C	.07	.15
224 Root Out C	.07	.15
225 Sage of Ancient Lore Werewolf of Ancient Hunger R	.30	.60
226 Seasons Past M	2.50	5.00
227 Second Harvest R	3.00	6.00
228 Silverfur Partisan R	.50	1.00
229 Solitary Hunter/One of the Pack C	.07	.15
230 Soul Swallower R	.15	.30
231 Stoic Builder C	.07	.15
232 Thornhide Wolves C	.07	.15
233 Tireless Tracker R	4.00	8.00
234 Traverse the Ulvenwald R	1.00	2.00
235 Ulvenwald Hydra M	2.00	4.00
236 Ulvenwald Mysteries U	.10	.20
237 Vessel of Nascency C	.07	.15
238 Veteran Cathar U	.10	.20
239 Watcher in the Web C	.07	.15
240 Weirding Wood U	.20	.40
241 Altered Ego R	.60	1.25
242 Anguished Unmaking R	6.00	12.00
243 Arlinn Kord/Arlinn, Embraced by the Moon M	6.00	12.00
244 Fevered Visions R	.50	1.00
245 The Gitrog Monster M	3.00	6.00
246 Invocation of Saint Traft R	.15	.30
247 Nahiri, the Harbinger M	2.00	4.00
248 Olivia, Mobilized for War M	1.25	2.50
249 Prized Amalgam R	.75	1.50
250 Sigarda, Heron's Grace M	.60	1.25
251 Sorin, Grim Nemesis M	3.00	6.00
252 Brain in a Jar R	.15	.30
253 Corrupted Grafstone R	.15	.30
254 Epitaph Golem U	.10	.20
255 Explosive Apparatus C	.07	.15
256 Harvest Hand/Scrounged Scythe U	.10	.20
257 Haunted Cloak U	.30	.60
258 Magnifying Glass U	.10	.20
259 Murderer's Axe U	.10	.20
260 Neglected Heirloom/Ashmouth Blade U	.20	.40
261 Runaway Carriage U	.10	.20
262 Shard of Broken Glass C	.07	.15
263 Skeleton Key U	.10	.20
264 Slayer's Plate R	.15	.30
265 Tamiyo's Journal R	1.25	2.50
266 Thraben Gargoyle/Stonewing Antagonizer U	.10	.20
267 True-Faith Censer C	.07	.15
268 Wicker Witch C	.07	.15
269 Wild-Field Scarecrow U	.10	.20
270 Choked Estuary R	1.50	3.00
271 Drownyard Temple R	.15	.30
272 Foreboding Ruins R	1.50	3.00
273 Forsaken Sanctuary U	.10	.20
274 Fortified Village R	1.00	2.00
275 Foul Orchard U	.10	.20
276 Game Trail R	.75	1.50
277 Highland Lake U	.10	.20
278 Port Town R	.60	1.25
279 Stone Quarry U	.10	.20
280 Warped Landscape C	.25	.50
281 Westvale Abbey/Ormendahl Profane Prince R	4.00	8.00
282 Woodland Stream U	.10	.20
283 Plains L	.07	.15
284 Plains L	.07	.15
285 Plains L	.07	.15
286 Island L	.07	.15
287 Island L	.07	.15
288 Island L	.07	.15
289 Swamp L	.07	.15
290 Swamp L	.07	.15
291 Swamp L	.07	.15

292 Mountain L	.07	.15
293 Mountain L	.07	.15
294 Mountain L	.07	.15
295 Forest L	.07	.15
296 Forest L	.07	.15
297 Forest L	.07	.15

2016 Magic The Gathering Shadows over Innistrad Tokens

1 Angel	.30	.60
2 Human Soldier	.07	.15
3 Spirit	.07	.15
4 Vampire Knight	.50	1.00
5 Zombie	.07	.15
6 Devil	.20	.40
7 Insect	.12	.25
8 Ooze	.07	.15
9 Wolf	.17	.35
10 Human Cleric	2.00	4.00
11 Clue	.07	.15
12 Clue	.07	.15
13 Clue	.07	.15
14 Clue	.07	.15
15 Clue	.07	.15
16 Clue	.07	.15
17 Jace, Unraveler of Secrets Emblem	1.50	3.00
18 Arlinn Kord Emblem	.30	.60
CH1 Shadows over Innistrad CL 1	.07	.15
CH2 Shadows over Innistrad CL 2	.12	.25

2016 Magic The Gathering Welcome Deck 2016

1 Aegis Angel R	.15	.30
2 Marked by Honor C	.07	.10
3 Serra Angel U	.07	.15
4 Air Servant U	.07	.10
5 Disperse C	.07	.10
6 Sphinx of Magosi R	.12	.25
7 Mind Rot C	.07	.10
8 Nightmare R	.12	.25
9 Sengir Vampire U	.07	.10
10 Walking Corpse C	.07	.15
11 Borderland Marauder C	.07	.15
12 Cone of Flame U	.07	.10
13 Shiyan Dragon R	.07	.15
14 Incremental Growth U	.07	.10
15 Oakenform C	.07	.15
16 Soul of the Harvest R	.60	1.25

2017 Magic The Gathering Aether Revolt

1 Aerial Modification U	.10	.20
2 Aeronaut Admiral U	.10	.20
3 Aether Inspector C	.07	.15
4 Aethergeode Miner R	.15	.30
5 Airdrop Aeronauts U	.10	.20
6 Alley Evasion C	.07	.15
7 Audacious Infiltrator C	.07	.15
8 Bastion Enforcer C	.07	.15
9 Call for Unity R	.15	.30
10 Caught in the Brights C	.07	.15
11 Consulate Crackdown R	.15	.30
12 Conviction C	.07	.15
13 Countless Gears Renegade C	.07	.15
14 Dawnfeather Eagle C	.07	.15
15 Deadeye Harpooner U	.10	.20
16 Decommission C	.07	.15
17 Deft Dismissal U	.10	.20
18 Exquisite Archangel M	2.00	4.00
19 Felidar Guardian U	.75	1.50
20 Ghirapur Osprey C	.07	.15
21 Restoration Specialist U	.10	.20
22 Solemn Recruit R	.15	.30
23 Sram, Senior Edificer R	.40	.80
24 Sram's Expertise R	.25	.50
25 Thopter Arrest U	.10	.20
26 Aether Swooper C	.07	.15
27 Aethertide Whale R	.15	.30
28 Baral, Chief of Compliance R	3.00	6.00
29 Baral's Expertise R	.30	.60
30 Bastion Inventor C	.07	.15
31 Disallow R	3.00	6.00
32 Dispersal Technician C	.07	.15
33 Efficient Construction U	.50	1.00
34 Hinterland Drake C	.07	.15
35 Ice Over C	.07	.15
36 Illusionist's Stratagem U	.30	.60
37 Leave in the Dust C	.07	.15
38 Mechanized Production M	7.50	15.00
39 Metallic Rebuke C	.07	.15
40 Negate C	.07	.15
41 Quicksmith Spy R	.15	.30
42 Reverse Engineer U	.10	.20
43 Salvage Scuttler U	.10	.20
44 Shielded Aether Thief U	.10	.20
45 Shipwreck Moray C	.07	.15
46 Skyship Plunderer U	.10	.20
47 Take Into Custody C	.07	.15
48 Trophy Mage U	.25	.50
49 Whir of Invention R	2.50	5.00
50 Wind-Kin Raiders U	.10	.20
51 Aether Poisoner C	.07	.15
52 Alley Strangler C	.07	.15
53 Battle at the Bridge R	.15	.30
54 Cruel Finality C	.07	.15
55 Daring Demolition C	.07	.15
56 Defiant Salvager C	.07	.15
57 Fatal Push U	2.00	4.00
58 Fen Hauler C	.07	.15
59 Foundry Hornet U	.10	.20
60 Fourth Bridge Prowler C	.07	.15
61 Gifted Aetherborn U	.60	1.25
62 Glint-Sleeve Siphoner R	.15	.30
63 Gonti's Machinations U	.10	.20
64 Herald of Anguish M	.75	1.50
65 Ironclad Revolutionary U	.10	.20
66 Midnight Entourage R	.15	.30
67 Night Market Aeronaut C	.07	.15
68 Perilous Predicament U	.10	.20
69 Renegade's Getaway C	.07	.15
70 Resourceful Return C	.07	.15
71 Secret Salvage R	.15	.30
72 Sly Requisitioner U	.10	.20
73 Vengeful Rebel U	.10	.20
74 Yahenni, Undying Partisan R	4.00	8.00
75 Yahenni's Expertise R	.15	.30
76 Aether Chaser C	.07	.15
77 Chandra's Revolution C	.07	.15
78 Destructive Tampering C	.07	.15
79 Embraal Gear Smasher C	.07	.15
80 Enraged Giant U	.10	.20
81 Freejam Regent R	.15	.30
82 Frontline Rebel C	.07	.15
83 Gremlin Infestation U	.10	.20
84 Hungry Flames U	.10	.20
85 Indomitable Creativity M	4.00	8.00
86 Invigorated Rampage U	.10	.20
87 Kari Zev, Skyship Raider R	.15	.30
88 Kari Zev's Expertise R	.25	.50
89 Lathnu Sailback C	.07	.15
90 Lightning Runner M	.30	.75
91 Pia's Revolution R	.20	.40
92 Precise Strike C	.07	.15
93 Quicksmith Rebel R	.15	.30
94 Ravenous Intruder U	.10	.20
95 Reckless Racer U	.10	.20
96 Release the Gremlins R	.15	.30
97 Scrapper Champion U	.10	.20
98 Shock C	.07	.15
99 Siege Modification U	.10	.20
100 Sweatworks Brawler C	.07	.15
101 Wrangle C	.07	.15
102 Aether Herder C	.07	.15
103 Aetherstream Leopard C	.07	.15
104 Aetherwind Basker M	.30	.60
105 Aid from the Cowl R	.15	.30
106 Druid of the Cowl C	.07	.15
107 Greenbelt Rampager R	.15	.30
108 Greenwheel Liberator R	.15	.30
109 Heroic Intervention R	6.00	12.00
110 Hidden Herbalists U	.10	.20
111 Highspire Infusion C	.07	.15
112 Lifecraft Awakening U	.10	.20
113 Lifecraft Cavalry C	.07	.15
114 Lifecrafter's Gift U	.10	.20
115 Maulfist Revolutionary U	.10	.20
116 Monstrous Onslaught U	.10	.20
117 Narnam Renegade U	.17	.35
118 Natural Obsolescence C	.07	.15
119 Peema Aether-Seer U	.10	.20
120 Prey Upon C	.07	.15
121 Ridgescale Tusker U	.10	.20
122 Rishkar, Peema Renegade R	.15	.30
123 Rishkar's Expertise R	2.00	4.00
124 Scrounging Bandar C	.07	.15
125 Silkweaver Elite C	.07	.15
126 Unbridled Growth C	.07	.15
127 Ajani Unyielding M	.60	1.25
128 Dark Intimations R	.15	.30
129 Hidden Stockpile U	.10	.20
130 Maverick Thopterist U	.10	.20
131 Oath of Ajani R	.30	.75
132 Outland Boar U	.10	.20
133 Renegade Rallier U	.10	.20
134 Renegade Wheelsmith U	.10	.20
135 Rogue Refiner U	.10	.20
136 Spire Patrol U	.10	.20
137 Tezzeret the Schemer M	.75	1.50
138 Tezzeret's Touch U	.10	.20
139 Weldfast Engineer U	.10	.20
140 Winding Constrictor U	.25	.50
141 Aegis Automaton C	.07	.15
142 Aethersphere Harvester R	.15	.30
143 Augmenting Automaton C	.07	.15
144 Barricade Breaker U	.10	.20
145 Cogwork Assembler U	.10	.20
146 Consulate Dreadnought U	.20	.40
147 Consulate Turret C	.07	.15
148 Crackdown Construct U	.10	.20
149 Daredevil Dragster U	.10	.20
150 Filligree Crawler C	.07	.15
151 Foundry Assembler C	.07	.15
152 Gonti's Aether Heart M	.50	1.00
153 Heart of Kiran M	.50	1.00
154 Hope of Ghirapur R	1.25	2.50
155 Implement of Combustion C	.07	.15
156 Implement of Examination C	.07	.15
157 Implement of Ferocity C	.07	.15
158 Implement of Improvement C	.07	.15
159 Implement of Malice C	.07	.15
160 Inspiring Statuary R	3.00	6.00
161 Irontread Crusher C	.07	.15
162 Lifecrafter's Bestiary R	1.00	2.00
163 Merchant's Dockhand R	.15	.30
164 Metallic Mimic R	6.00	12.00
165 Mobile Garrison C	.07	.15
166 Night Market Guard C	.07	.15
167 Ornithopter U	.20	.40
168 Pacification Array U	.10	.20
169 Paradox Engine M	3.00	6.00
170 Peacewalker Colossus R	.15	.30
171 Planar Bridge M	5.00	10.00
172 Prizefighter Construct C	.07	.15
173 Renegade Map C	.07	.15
174 Reservoir Walker C	.07	.15
175 Scrap Trawler R	.30	.60
176 Servo Schematic U	.10	.20
177 Treasure Keeper U	.10	.20
178 Universal Solvent C	.07	.15
179 Untethered Express U	.20	.40
180 Verdant Automation C	.07	.15
181 Walking Ballista R	10.00	20.00
182 Watchful Automaton C	.07	.15
183 Welder Automaton C	.07	.15
184 Spire of Industry R	2.50	5.00
185 Ajani, Valiant Protector M	3.00	6.00
186 Inspiring Roar C	.07	.15
187 Ajani's Comrade U	.10	.20
188 Ajani's Aid R	.15	.30
189 Tranquil Expanse C	.07	.15
190 Tezzeret, Master of Metal M	1.00	2.00
191 Tezzeret's Betrayal R	.15	.30
192 Pendulum of Patterns C	.07	.15
193 Tezzeret's Simulacrum U	.10	.20
194 Submerged Boneyard C	.07	.15

2017 Magic The Gathering Aether Revolt Masterpiece Series

31 Arcbound Ravager M	60.00	120.00
32 Black Vise M	20.00	40.00
33 Chalice of the Void M	100.00	200.00
34 Defense Grid M	25.00	45.00
35 Duplicant M	20.00	40.00
36 Engineered Explosives M	60.00	120.00
37 Ensnaring Bridge M	75.00	150.00
38 Extraplanar Lens M	25.00	45.00
39 Grindstone M	40.00	80.00
40 Meekstone M	20.00	40.00
41 Oblivion Stone M	50.00	100.00
42 Ornithopter M	30.00	54.00
43 Paradox Engine M	30.00	75.00
44 Pithing Needle M	30.00	65.00
45 Planar Bridge M	30.00	75.00
46 Platinum Angel M	30.00	60.00
47 Sphere of Resistance M	25.00	50.00
48 Staff od Domination M	50.00	100.00
49 Sundering Titan M	30.00	55.00
50 Sword of Body and Mind M	30.00	65.00
51 Sword of War and Peace M	50.00	100.00
52 Trinisphere M	30.00	60.00
53 Vedalken Shackles M	30.00	60.00
54 Wurmcoil Engine M	50.00	100.00

2017 Magic The Gathering Aether Revolt Tokens

1 Gremlin	.07	.10
2 Ragavan	.17	.35
3 Etherium Cell	.07	.15
4 Tezzeret the Schemer Emblem	.07	.15

2017 Magic The Gathering Amonkhet

1 Angel of Sanctions M	.50	1.00
2 Anointed Procession R	20.00	40.00
3 Anointer Priest C	.07	.15
4 Approach of the Second Sun R	.75	1.50
5 Aven Mindcensor R	.75	1.50
6 Binding Mummy C	.07	.15
7 Cartouche of Solidarity C	.07	.15
8 Cast Out U	.10	.20
9 Compulsory Rest C	.07	.15
10 Devoted Crop Mate U	.10	.20
11 Djeru's Resolve C	.07	.15
12 Fan Bearer C	.07	.15
13 Forsake the Worldly C	.07	.15
14 Gideon of the Trials M	3.00	6.00
15 Gideon's Intervention R	.15	.30
16 Glory-Bound Initiate R	.15	.30
17 Gust Walker C	.07	.15
18 Impeccable Timing C	.07	.15
19 In Oketra's Name C	.07	.15
20 Mighty Leap U	.10	.20
21 Oketra the True M	2.50	5.00
22 Oketra's Attendant U	.10	.20
23 Protection of the Hekma U	.10	.20
24 Regal Caracal R	.50	1.00
25 Renewed Faith U	.10	.20
26 Rhet-Crop Spearmaster C	.07	.15
27 Sacred Cat C	.07	.15
28 Seraph of the Suns U	.10	.20
29 Sparring Mummy C	.07	.15
30 Supply Caravan C	.07	.15
31 Tah-Crop Elite C	.07	.15
32 Those Who Serve C	.07	.15
33 Time to Reflect U	.10	.20
34 Trial of Solidarity U	.10	.20
35 Trueheart Duelist U	.10	.20
36 Unwavering Initiate C	.07	.15
37 Vizier of Deferment U	.10	.20
38 Vizier of Remedies U	.15	.30
39 Winged Shepherd U	.10	.20
40 Ancient Crab C	.07	.15
41 Angler Drake U	.10	.20
42 As Foretold M	7.50	15.00
43 Aven Initiate C	.07	.15
44 Cancel C	.07	.15
45 Cartouche of Knowledge C	.07	.15
46 Censor U	.10	.20
47 Compelling Argument C	.07	.15
48 Cryptic Serpent U	.10	.20
49 Curator of Mysteries R	.30	.60
50 Decision Paralysis C	.07	.15
51 Drake Haven R	.15	.30
52 Essence Scatter C	.07	.15
53 Floodwaters C	.07	.15
54 Galestrike U	.10	.20
55 Glyph Keeper R	.15	.30
56 Hekma Sentinels C	.07	.15
57 Hieroglyphic Illumination C	.07	.15
58 Illusory Wrappings C	.07	.15
59 Kefnet the Mindful M	.50	1.00
60 Labyrinth Guardian U	.10	.20
61 Lay Claim U	.10	.20
62 Naga Oracle C	.07	.15
63 New Perspectives R	.15	.30
64 Open into Wonder U	.10	.20
65 Pull from Tomorrow R	2.50	5.00
66 River Serpent C	.07	.15
67 Sacred Excavation U	.10	.20
68 Scribe of the Mindful C	.07	.15
69 Seeker of Insight C	.07	.15
70 Shimmerscale Drake C	.07	.15
71 Slither Blade C	.17	.35
72 Tah-Crop Skirmisher C	.07	.15
73 Trial of Knowledge U	.10	.20
74 Vizier of Many Faces R	.50	1.00
75 Vizier of Tumbling Sands U	.10	.20
76 Winds of Rebuke C	.15	.30
77 Zenith Seeker U	.10	.20
78 Archfiend of Ifnir R	1.25	2.50
79 Baleful Ammit U	.10	.20
80 Blighted Bat C	.07	.15
81 Bone Picker U	.10	.20
82 Bontu the Glorified M	1.50	3.00
83 Cartouche of Ambition C	.07	.15
84 Cruel Reality M	1.25	2.50
85 Cursed Minotaur C	.07	.15
86 Dispossess R	.15	.30
87 Doomed Dissenter C	.07	.15
88 Dread Wanderer R	.75	1.50
89 Dune Beetle C	.07	.15
90 Faith of the Devoted U	.10	.20
91 Festering Mummy C	.07	.15
92 Final Reward C	.07	.15
93 Gravedigger U	.10	.20
94 Grim Strider U	.10	.20
95 Horror of the Broken Lands C	.07	.15
96 Lay Bare the Heart U	.10	.20
97 Liliana Death's Majesty M	5.00	10.00
98 Liliana's Mastery R	.75	1.50
99 Lord of the Accursed U	.75	1.50
100 Miasmic Mummy C	.07	.15
101 Nest of Scarabs U	.30	.60
102 Painful Lesson C	.07	.15
103 Pitiless Vizier C	.07	.15
104 Plague Belcher R	.75	1.50
105 Ruthless Sniper U	.10	.20
106 Scarab Feast C	.07	.15
107 Shadow of the Grave R	.30	.60
108 Soulstinger C	.07	.15
109 Splendid Agony C	.07	.15
110 Stir the Sands U	.10	.20
111 Supernatural Stamina C	.07	.15
112 Trespasser's Curse C	.20	.40
113 Trial of Ambition U	.10	.20
114 Unburden C	.07	.15
115 Wander in Death C	.07	.15
116 Wasteland Scorpion C	.07	.15
117 Ahn-Crop Crasher U	.10	.20
118 Battlefield Scavenger U	.10	.20
119 Blazing Volley C	.07	.15
120 Bloodlust Inciter C	.07	.15
121 Bloodrage Brawler U	.10	.20
122 Brute Strength C	.07	.15
123 By Force U	.75	1.50
124 Cartouche of Zeal C	.07	.15
125 Combat Celebrant M	7.50	15.00
126 Consuming Fervor U	.10	.20
127 Deem Worthy U	.10	.20
128 Desert Cerodon C	.07	.15
129 Electrify C	.07	.15
130 Emberhorn Minotaur C	.07	.15
131 Flameblade Adept U	.10	.20
132 Fling C	.07	.15
133 Glorious End M	.75	1.50
134 Glorybringer R	.75	1.50
135 Harsh Mentor R	.20	.40
136 Hazoret the Fervent M	1.25	2.50
137 Hazoret's Favor R	.15	.30
138 Heart-Piercer Manticore R	.15	.30
139 Hyena Pack C	.07	.15
140 Limits of Solidarity U	.10	.20
141 Magma Spray C	.07	.15
142 Manticore of the Gauntlet C	.07	.15
143 Minotaur Sureshot C	.07	.15
144 Nef-Crop Entangler C	.07	.15
145 Nimble-Blade Khenra C	.07	.15
146 Pathmaker Initiate C	.07	.15
147 Pursue Glory C	.07	.15
148 Soul-Scar Mage R	3.00	6.00
149 Sweltering Suns R	.50	1.00
150 Thresher Lizard C	.07	.15
151 Tormenting Voice C	.07	.15
152 Trail of Zeal U	.10	.20
153 Trueheart Twins U	.10	.20
154 Violent Impact C	.07	.15
155 Warfire Javelineer U	.10	.20
156 Benefaction of Rhonas C	.07	.15
157 Bitterblade Warrior C	.07	.15
158 Cartouche of Strength C	.07	.15
159 Champion of Rhonas R	.15	.30
160 Channeler Initiate R	.15	.30
161 Colossapede C	.07	.15
162 Crocodile of the Crossing U	.10	.20
163 Defiant Greatmaw U	.10	.20
164 Dissenter's Deliverance C	.07	.15
165 Exemplar of Strength U	.10	.20
166 Giant Spider C	.07	.15
167 Gift of Paradise C	.07	.15
168 Greater Sandwurm C	.07	.15
169 Hapatra's Mark U	.10	.20
170 Harvest Season R	1.50	3.00
171 Haze of Pollen C	.07	.15
172 Honored Hydra R	.15	.30
173 Hooded Brawler C	.07	.15
174 Initiate's Companion C	.07	.15
175 Manglehorn U	.25	.50
176 Naga Vitalist C	.07	.15
177 Oashra Cultivator C	.07	.15
178 Ornery Kudu C	.07	.15
179 Pouncing Cheetah C	.07	.15
180 Prowling Serpopard R	2.50	5.00
181 Quarry Hauler C	.07	.15
182 Rhonas the Indomitable M	6.00	12.00
183 Sandwurm Convergence R	1.25	2.50
184 Scaled Behemoth U	.10	.20
185 Shed Weakness C	.07	.15
186 Shefet Monitor U	.10	.20
187 Sixth Sense U	.10	.20
188 Spidery Grasp C	.07	.15
189 Stinging Shot C	.07	.15
190 Synchronized Strike U	.10	.20
191 Trial of Strength U	.10	.20
192 Vizier of the Menagerie M	5.00	10.00
193 Watchful Naga U	.10	.20
194 Ahn-Crop Champion U	.10	.20
195 Aven Wind Guide U	.10	.20
196 Bounty of the Luxa R	.15	.30
197 Decimator Beetle U	.10	.20
198 Enigma Drake U	.10	.20
199 Hapatra, Vizier of Poisons R	.60	1.25
200 Honored Crop-Captain U	.10	.20
201 Khenra Charioteer U	.10	.20
202 Merciless Javelineer U	.10	.20
203 Neheb, the Worthy R	.15	.30
204 Nissa, Steward of Elements M	.75	1.50
205 Samut, Voice of Dissent M	2.50	5.00
206 Shadowstorm Vizier U	.10	.20
207 Temmet, Vizier of Naktamun R	.15	.30
208 Wayward Servant U	.17	.35
209 Weaver of Currents U	.10	.20
210 Dusk/Dawn R	.30	.60
211 Commit/Memory R	1.50	3.00
212 Never/Return R	.30	.75
213 Insult/Injury R	.30	.75
214 Mouth/Feed R	.15	.30

215 Start/Finish U .10 .20
216 Reduce/Rubble U .10 .20
217 Destined/Lead U .10 .20
218 Onward/Victory U .10 .20
219 Spring/Mind U .10 .20
220 Prepare/Fight R .15 .30
221 Failure/Comply R .15 .30
222 Rags/Riches R .15 .30
223 Cut/Ribbons R .20 .40
224 Heaven/Earth R .15 .30
225 Bontu's Monument U 2.50 5.00
226 Edifice of Authority U .10 .20
227 Embalmer's Tools U .10 .20
228 Gate to the Afterlife U .10 .20
229 Hazoret's Monument U .75 1.50
230 Honed Khopesh C .07 .15
231 Kefnet's Monument U .17 .35
232 Luxa River Shrine C .07 .15
233 Oketra's Monument U 1.00 2.00
234 Oracle's Vault R .15 .30
235 Pyramid of the Pantheon R .15 .30
236 Rhonas's Monument R .75 1.50
237 Throne of the God-Pharaoh R 2.50 5.00
238 Watchers of the Dead U .10 .20
239 Canyon Slough R 2.50 5.00
240 Cascading Cataracts R 3.00 6.00
241 Cradle of the Accursed C .07 .15
242 Evolving Wilds C .07 .15
243 Fetid Pools R 2.50 5.00
244 Grasping Dunes U .15 .30
245 Irrigated Farmland R .20 .40
246 Painted Bluffs C .07 .15
247 Scattered Groves R 2.00 4.00
248 Sheltered Thicket R 1.50 3.00
249 Sunscorched Desert C .07 .15
250 Plains Full Art L .17 .35
251 Island Full Art L .20 .40
252 Swamp Full Art L .30 .60
253 Mountain Full Art L .20 .40
254 Forest Full Art L .07 .15
255 Plains L .07 .15
256 Plains L .07 .15
257 Plains L .07 .15
258 Island L .07 .15
259 Island L .07 .15
260 Island L .07 .15
261 Swamp L .07 .15
262 Swamp L .07 .15
263 Swamp L .07 .15
264 Mountain L .07 .15
265 Mountain L .07 .15
266 Mountain L .07 .15
267 Forest L .07 .15
268 Forest L .07 .15
269 Forest L .07 .15
270 Gideon, Martial Paragon M 1.00 2.00
271 Companion of the Trials U .10 .20
272 Gideon's Resolve R .15 .30
273 Graceful Cat C .07 .15
274 Stone Quarry C .07 .15
275 Liliana, Death Wielder M 3.00 6.00
276 Desiccated Naga U .10 .20
277 Liliana's Influence R .20 .40
278 Tattered Mummy C .12 .25

2017 Magic The Gathering Amonkhet Invocations

1 Austere Command M 25.00 50.00
2 Aven Mindcensor M 30.00 75.00
3 Containment Priest M 20.00 40.00
4 Loyal Retainers M 30.00 60.00
5 Oketra the True M 30.00 75.00
6 Worship M 20.00 40.00
7 Wrath of God M 50.00 100.00
8 Consecrated Sphinx M 75.00 150.00
9 Counterbalance M 40.00 80.00
10 Counterspell M 100.00 200.00
11 Cryptic Command M 60.00 120.00
12 Daze M 75.00 150.00
13 Divert M 20.00 40.00
14 Force of Will M 150.00 300.00
15 Kefnet the Mindful M 30.00 60.00
16 Pact of Negation M 75.00 150.00
17 Spell Pierce M 30.00 75.00
18 Stifle M 30.00 75.00
19 Attrition M 25.00 50.00
20 Bontu the Glorified M 30.00 75.00
21 Dark Ritual M 50.00 100.00
22 Diabolic Intent M 60.00 120.00
23 Entomb M 60.00 120.00
24 Mind Twist M 40.00 80.00
25 Aggravated Assault M 30.00 60.00
26 Chain Lightning M 20.00 40.00
27 Hazoret the Fervent M 50.00 100.00
28 Rhonas the Indomitable M 50.00 90.00
29 Maelstrom Pulse M 20.00 40.00
30 Vindicate M 25.00 50.00
31 Armageddon M 30.00 60.00
32 Capsize M 30.00 75.00
33 Forbid M 30.00 60.00
34 Omniscience M 125.00 250.00
35 Opposition M 30.00 60.00
36 Sunder M 25.00 50.00
37 Threads of Disloyalty M 20.00 40.00
38 Avatar of Woe M 25.00 50.00
39 Damnation M 125.00 250.00
40 Desolation Angel M 20.00 40.00
41 Diabolic Edict M 20.00 40.00
42 Doomsday M 60.00 120.00
43 No Mercy M 60.00 120.00
44 Slaughter Pact M 25.00 50.00
45 Thoughtseize M 75.00 150.00
46 Blood Moon M 50.00 100.00
47 Boil M 30.00 75.00
48 Shatterstorm M 20.00 40.00
49 Through the Breach M 20.00 40.00
50 Choke M 30.00 60.00
51 The Locust God M 75.00 150.00
52 Lord of Extinction M 25.00 50.00
53 The Scarab God M 125.00 250.00
54 The Scorpion God M 30.00 75.00

2017 Magic The Gathering Amonkhet Tokens

1 Angel of Sanctions .50 1.00
2 Anointer Priest .07 .10
3 Aven Initiate .07 .10
4 Aven Wind Guide .07 .10
5 Glyph Keeper .15 .30
6 Heart-Piercer Manticore .07 .10
7 Honored Hydra .12 .25
8 Labyrinth Guardian .07 .10
9 Oketra's Attendant .07 .10
10 Sacred Cat .12 .25
11 Tah-Crop Skirmisher .07 .10
12 Temmet, Vizier of Naktamun .10 .20
13 Trueheart Duelist .07 .10
14 Unwavering Initiate .07 .10
15 Vizier of Many Faces .25 .50
16 Cat .17 .35
17 Warrior .07 .10
18 Drake .07 .10
19 Insect .50 1.00
20 Zombie .07 .10
21 Beast .07 .10
22 Hippo .20 .40
23 Snake .50 1.00
24 Wurm .75 1.50
25 Gideon of the Trials Emblem 1.00 2.00
26 Punchcard .07 .10
27 Punchcard .07 .10

2017 Magic The Gathering Archenemy Nicol Bolas

1 Aegis Angel R .10 .20
2 Aerial Responder U .10 .20
3 Anointer of Champions U .10 .20
4 Doomed Traveler C .10 .20
5 Excoriate C .10 .20
6 Expedition Raptor C .10 .20
7 Fencing Ace U .10 .20
8 Fiendslayer Paladin R 1.00 2.00
9 Flickerwisp U .50 1.00
10 Gideon Jura M 4.00 8.00
11 Gideons Lawkeeper C .10 .20
12 Grand Abolisher R 3.00 6.00
13 Grasp of the Hieromancer C .10 .20
14 Lightwielder Paladin R .10 .20
15 Mentor of the Meek R .40 .80
16 Moment of Heroism C .10 .20
17 Odric Master Tactician R .60 1.25
18 Precinct Captain R .10 .20
19 Relief Captain U .10 .20
20 Shoulder to Shoulder C .10 .20
21 Sun Titan M 2.50 5.00
22 Youthful Knight C .10 .20
23 Compulsive Research C .10 .20
24 Icefall Regent R .10 .20
25 Ior Ruin Expedition C .10 .20
26 Prognostic Sphinx R .10 .20
27 Reckless Scholar U .10 .20
28 Sphinx of Jwar Isle R .10 .20
29 Vision Skeins C .10 .20
30 Windrider Eel C .10 .20
31 Archfiend of Depravity R .10 .20
32 Deathbringer Regent R .17 .35
33 Doom Blade U .10 .20
34 Harvester of Souls R .10 .20
35 Nightscape Familiar C .10 .20
36 Overseer of the Damned R 1.25 2.50
37 Reckless Spite U .10 .20
38 Vampire Nighthawk U .30 .60
39 Avatar of Fury R .25 .50
40 Battle-Rattle Shaman C .10 .20
41 Blood Ogre C .10 .20
42 Chandra Pyromaster M 1.25 2.50
43 Chandras Outrage C .10 .20
44 Chandras Phoenix R .20 .40
45 Coordinated Assault U .10 .20
46 Dualcaster Mage R .25 .50
47 Fiery Fall C .10 .20
48 Flametongue Kavu U .10 .20
49 Gorehorn Minotaurs C .10 .20
50 Grim Lavamancer R 2.50 5.00
51 Guttersnipe U .10 .20
52 Hammerhand C .10 .20
53 Inferno Titan M .60 1.25
54 Lightning Bolt U 1.00 2.00
55 Obsidian Fireheart M .50 1.00
56 Searing Spear C .10 .20
57 Skarrgan Firebird U .10 .20
58 Stormblood Berserker U .10 .20
59 Sudden Demise R .40 .80
60 Torchling R .10 .20
61 Volcanic Geyser U .10 .20
62 Cultivate C .75 1.50
63 Explore C .10 .20
64 Fertilid C .10 .20
65 Forgotten Ancient R .10 .20
66 Hunters Prowess R .10 .20
67 Khalni Heart Expedition C .10 .20
68 Nissa Worldwaker M 4.00 8.00
69 Oran-Rief Hydra R .10 .20
70 Press the Advantage U .10 .20
71 Rampaging Baloths M .60 1.25
72 Retreat to Kazandu U .10 .20
73 Scute Mob R .25 .50
74 Sylvan Bounty C .10 .20
75 Thragtusk R .75 1.50
76 Turntimber Basilisk U .10 .20
77 Vastwood Zendikon C .10 .20
78 Vines of the Recluse C .10 .20
79 Woodborn Behemoth U .10 .20
80 Baleful Strix U 1.25 2.50
81 Blood Tyrant R .10 .20
82 Cruel Ultimatum R .10 .20
83 Dreadbore R 1.25 2.50
84 Extract from Darkness U .10 .20
85 Nicol Bolas Planeswalker M 4.00 8.00
86 Slave of Bolas U .10 .20
87 Soul Ransom U .10 .20
88 Obelisk of Grixis C .10 .20
89 Sword of the Animist R 2.00 3.50
90 Talisman of Dominance U .75 1.50
91 Talisman of Indulgence U .25 .50
92 Crumbling Necropolis U .10 .20
93 Dragonskull Summit R 1.25 2.50
94 Drowned Catacomb R 2.00 3.50
95 Grixis Panorama C .10 .20
96 Smoldering Spires C .10 .20
97 Plains L .10 .20
98 Island L .10 .20
99 Swamp L .10 .20
100 Mountain L .10 .20
101 Forest L .10 .20
102 Plains L .10 .20
103 Island L .10 .20
104 Swamp L .10 .20
105 Mountain L .10 .20
106 Forest L .10 .20

2017 Magic The Gathering Archenemy Nicol Bolas Schemes

1 Because I Have Willed It .75 1.50
2 Behold My Grandeur .75 1.50
3 Bow to My Command .75 1.50
4 Choose Your Demise .75 1.50
5 Delight in the Hunt .75 1.50
6 Every Dream a Nightmare .75 1.50
7 For Each of You, a Gift .50 1.00
8 Know Evil .60 1.25
9 Make Yourself Useful .60 1.25
10 The Mighty Will Fall .60 1.25
11 My Forces Are Innumerable 1.25 2.50
12 My Laughter Echoes .60 1.25
13 No One Will Hear Your Cries .60 1.25
14 Pay Tribute to Me .75 1.50
15 Power Without Equal .75 1.50
16 A Reckoning Approaches 1.00 2.00
17 There Is No Refuge .75 1.50
18 This World Belongs to Me .60 1.25
19 What's Yours Is Now Mine .60 1.25
20 When Will You Learn? .60 1.25

2017 Magic The Gathering Archenemy Nicol Bolas Tokens

1 Soldier .07 .15
2 Spirit .07 .15
3 Horror .07 .10
4 Beast .07 .10
5 Beast .12 .25

2017 Magic The Gathering Commander 2017

1 Alms Collector R 7.50 15.00
2 Balan, Wandering Knight R 7.50 15.00
3 Curse of Vitality U .25 .50
4 Fortunate Few R .25 .50
5 Kindred Boon R 3.00 6.00
6 Scalelord Reckoner R 10.00 20.00
7 Stalking Leonin R .75 1.50
8 Teferi's Protection R 12.50 25.00
9 Curse of Verbosity U 1.00 2.00
10 Galecaster Colossus R 2.50 5.00
11 Kindred Discovery R 12.50 25.00
12 Magus of the Mind R .15 .30
13 Portal Mage R .15 .30
14 Bloodline Necromancer U 2.50 5.00
15 Boneyard Scourge R 4.00 8.00
16 Curse of Disturbance U .75 1.50
17 Kheru Mind-Eater R .50 1.00
18 Kindred Dominance R 15.00 30.00
19 New Blood R 4.00 8.00
20 Patron of the Vein R 7.50 15.00
21 Vindictive Lich R 6.00 12.00
22 Bloodsworn Steward R 2.00 4.00
23 Crimson Honor Guard R .30 .60
24 Curse of Opulence U 7.50 15.00
25 Disrupt Decorum R 7.50 15.00
26 Izzet Chemister R .15 .30
27 Kindred Charge R 4.00 8.00
28 Shifting Shadow R .20 .40
29 Territorial Hellkite R .15 .30
30 Curse of Bounty U 1.50 3.00
31 Hungry Lynx R 3.00 6.00
32 Kindred Summons R 7.50 15.00
33 Qasali Slingers R 3.00 6.00
34 Traverse the Outlands R 7.50 15.00
37 Fractured Identity R 7.50 15.00
39 Kess, Dissident Mage M 2.00 4.00
40 Licia, Sanguine Tribune M 1.00 2.00
41 Mairsil, the Pretender M .50 1.00
42 Mathas, Fiend Seeker M 3.00 6.00
43 Mirri, Weatherlight Duelist M 12.50 25.00
44 Nazahn, Revered Bladesmith M 1.00 2.00
45 O-Kagachi, Vengeful Kami M 7.50 15.00
46 Taigam, Ojutai Master R 7.50 15.00
47 Taigam, Sidisi's Hand R .75 1.50
48 The Ur-Dragon M 30.00 75.00
49 Wasitora, Nekoru Queen R 5.00 10.00
50 Bloodforged Battle-Axe R 10.00 20.00
51 Hammer of Nazahn R 7.50 15.00
52 Heirloom Blade U .20 .40
53 Herald's Horn U 5.00 10.00
54 Mirror of the Forebears U 1.00 2.00
55 Ramos, Dragon Engine M 7.50 15.00
56 Path of Ancestry C .30 .60
57 Blind Obedience R 4.00 8.00
58 Condemn U .10 .20
59 Divine Reckoning R .25 .50
60 Fell the Mighty R 4.00 8.00
61 Jareth, Leonine Titan R .25 .50
62 Jazal Goldmane M 2.00 4.00
63 Kemba, Kha Regent R .20 .40
64 Leonin Arbiter R 2.50 5.00
65 Leonin Relic-Warder U .20 .40
66 Leonin Shikari R 4.00 8.00
67 Orator of Ojutai U .20 .40
68 Oreskos Explorer U .17 .35
69 Raksha Golden Cub R .30 .60
70 Return to Dust U .15 .30
71 Rout R .15 .30
72 Seht's Tiger R .30 .60
73 Spirit of the Hearth R .17 .35
74 Sunscorch Regent R 1.25 2.50
75 Sunspear Shikari C .07 .15
76 Swords to Plowshares U 2.00 4.00
77 Taj-Nar Swordsmith U .15 .30
78 White Sun's Zenith R .17 .35
79 Wing Shards U .10 .20
80 Arcanis the Omnipotent R 1.00 2.00
81 Archaeomancer C .20 .40
82 Azami, Lady of Scrolls R .75 1.50
83 Body Double R .75 1.50
84 Clone Legion M 3.00 6.00
85 Harbinger of the Tides R .30 .75
86 Into the Roil C .07 .15
87 Merchant of Secrets C .07 .15
88 Monastery Siege R .50 1.00
89 Opportunity U .10 .20
90 Polymorphist's Jest R .75 1.50
91 Reality Shift U .75 1.50
92 Sea Gate Oracle C .12 .25
93 Serendib Sorcerer R .15 .30
94 Spelltwine R .25 .50
95 Ambition's Cost U .15 .30
96 Anowon, the Ruin Sage R 2.50 5.00
97 Apprentice Necromancer R 1.00 2.00
98 Black Market R 3.00 6.00
99 Blood Artist U 4.00 8.00
100 Blood Tribute R 1.50 3.00
101 Bloodhusk Ritualist U .17 .35
102 Bloodlord of Vaasgoth M .75 1.50
103 Butcher of Malakir R 1.00 2.00
104 Captivating Vampire R 7.50 15.00
105 Consuming Vapors R .25 .50
106 Corpse Augur U .30 .60
107 Crux of Fate R 1.50 3.00
108 Damnable Pact R .15 .30
109 Dark Imposter R .30 .60
110 Deathbringer Regent R .20 .40
111 Decree of Pain R 2.50 5.00
112 Drana, Kalastria Bloodchief R .25 .50
113 Falkenrath Noble C .30 .75
114 Go for the Throat U 2.00 4.00
115 Magus of the Abyss R .20 .40
116 Malakir Bloodwitch R .75 1.50
117 Necromantic Selection R .30 .75
118 Painful Truths R .25 .50
119 Palace Siege R .75 1.50
120 Pawn of Ulamog U 2.00 4.00
121 Puppeteer Clique R 3.00 6.00
122 Read the Bones C 1.25 2.50
123 Sangromancer R .60 1.25
124 Sanguine Bond R .75 1.50
125 Skeletal Scrying U .15 .30
126 Skeletal Vampire R .15 .30
127 Syphon Mind C 1.25 2.50
128 Underworld Connections R .40 .80
129 Vampire Nighthawk U .30 .60
130 Vein Drinker R .15 .30
131 Chaos Warp R 1.00 2.00
132 Comet Storm M .30 .75
133 Crucible of Fire R 1.00 2.00
134 Dragon Tempest R 4.00 8.00
135 Dragonlord's Servant U .50 1.00
136 Dragonspeaker Shaman U 2.50 5.00
137 Earthquake R .50 1.00
138 Hellkite Charger R 2.50 5.00
139 Outpost Siege R .25 .50
140 Rakish Heir U .17 .35
141 Ryusei, the Falling Star M 1.25 2.50
142 Scourge of Valkas M 1.50 3.00
143 Tyrant's Familiar R 1.00 2.00
144 Utvara Hellkite M 10.00 20.00
145 Abundance R .50 1.00
146 Crushing Vines C .12 .25
147 Cultivate C .30 .60
148 Elemental Bond U 2.00 4.00
149 Farseek C 1.50 3.00
150 Frontier Siege R .30 .75
151 Harmonize U .17 .35
152 Hunter's Prowess R .17 .35
153 Jedit Ojanen of Efrava R .75 1.50
154 Kodama's Reach C 1.00 2.00
155 Nissa's Pilgrimage C .25 .50
156 Rain of Thorns U .10 .20
157 Relic Crush U .10 .20
158 Soul's Majesty R 2.50 5.00
159 Temur Sabertooth U 2.50 5.00
160 Zendikar Resurgent R 4.00 8.00
161 Atarka, World Render R .50 1.00
162 Behemoth Sledge U .17 .35
163 Bladewing the Risen R .60 1.25
164 Blood Baron of Vizkopa M .50 1.00
165 Broodmate Dragon R .30 .60
166 Cauldron Dance U .25 .50
167 Crackling Doom R .15 .30
168 Crosis, the Purger R 1.50 3.00
169 Crosis's Charm U .60 1.25
170 Dromoka, the Eternal R .20 .40
171 Etherium-Horn Sorcerer R .15 .30
172 Fleecemane Lion R .75 1.50
173 Havengul Lich M 3.00 6.00
174 Intet, the Dreamer R .75 1.50
175 Izzet Chronarch C .15 .30
176 Kolaghan, the Storm's Fury R .30 .75
177 Marchesa, the Black Rose M 4.00 8.00
178 Memory Plunder R 3.00 6.00
179 Merciless Eviction R 2.00 4.00
180 Mercurial Chemister R .15 .30
181 Mirari's Wake M 4.00 8.00
182 Mortify U .20 .40
183 Nin, the Pain Artist R .25 .50
184 Niv-Mizzet, Dracogenius R .40 .80
185 Niv-Mizzet, the Firemind R .30 .75
186 Nivix Guildmage U .10 .20
187 Ojutai, Soul of Winter R .30 .60
188 Phantom Nishoba R .50 1.00
189 Qasali Pridemage C .50 1.00
190 Rakdos Charm U .75 1.50
191 Savage Ventmaw U .30 .60
192 Scion of the Ur-Dragon R 7.50 15.00
193 Shadowmage Infiltrator R .20 .40
194 Silumgar, the Drifting Death R .30 .75
195 Silumgar's Command R .15 .30
196 Spellbound Dragon R .25 .50
197 Stromkirk Captain U .50 1.00
198 Teneb, the Harvester R 2.00 4.00
199 Terminate U .50 1.00
200 Tithe Drinker C .15 .30
201 Vela the Night-Clad M 1.00 2.00
202 Argentum Armor R 2.00 4.00
203 Armillary Sphere C .12 .25
204 Blade of the Bloodchief R 3.00 6.00
205 Boros Signet U .30 .60

206 Commander's Sphere C .12 .25
207 Darksteel Ingot U .30 .75
208 Door of Destinies R 10.00 20.00
209 Dreamstone Hedron U .10 .20
210 Fellwar Stone U 3.00 6.00
211 Fist of Suns R 7.50 15.00
212 Grappling Hook R .50 1.00
213 Hedron Archive U .30 .75
214 Hero's Blade U .15 .30
215 Lightning Greaves U 4.00 8.00
216 Loxodon Warhammer U .50 1.00
217 Nevinyrral's Disk R .75 1.50
218 Nihil Spellbomb C .30 .60
219 Orzhov Signet U .50 1.00
220 Quietus Spike R 3.00 6.00
221 Rakdos Signet U 1.00 2.00
222 Skullclamp U 6.00 12.00
223 Sol Ring U 1.25 2.50
224 Staff of Nin R 1.00 2.00
225 Steel Hellkite R .75 1.50
226 Swiftfoot Boots U 1.25 2.50
227 Sword of the Animist R 4.00 8.00
228 Sword of Vengeance R .50 1.00
229 Unstable Obelisk U .30 .60
230 Wayfarer's Bauble C 2.00 4.00
231 Well of Lost Dreams R 1.50 3.00
232 Worn Powerstone U .75 1.50
233 Akoum Refuge U .15 .30
234 Arcane Sanctum U 1.25 2.50
235 Blighted Woodland U .10 .20
236 Bloodfell Caves C .07 .15
237 Blossoming Sands C .07 .15
238 Bojuka Bog C 1.25 2.50
239 Boros Garrison C .07 .15
240 Boros Guildgate C .07 .15
241 Cinder Barrens U .10 .20
242 Command Tower C .20 .40
243 Crucible of the Spirit Dragon R .30 .60
244 Crumbling Necropolis U .25 .50
245 Dimir Aqueduct U .20 .40
246 Dismal Backwater C .15 .30
247 Elfhame Palace U .15 .30
248 Evolving Wilds C .07 .15
249 Exotic Orchard R .75 1.50
250 Forsaken Sanctuary U .10 .20
251 Frontier Bivouac U .50 1.00
252 Grasslands U 1.25 2.50
253 Graypelt Refuge U .20 .40
254 Grixis Panorama C .75 1.50
255 Haven of the Spirit Dragon R 2.00 4.00
256 Izzet Boilerworks U .12 .25
257 Jungle Shrine U .20 .40
258 Jwar Isel Refuge U .10 .20
259 Kabira Crossroads C .20 .40
260 Krosan Verge U .20 .40
261 Mosswort Bridge R .30 .75
262 Myriad Landscape U .17 .35
263 Mystic Monastery U .20 .40
264 Mystifying Maze R .50 1.00
265 Nomad Outpost U .50 1.00
266 Opal Palace C .15 .30
267 Opulent Palace U .50 1.00
268 Orzhov Basilica C .20 .40
269 Orzhov Guildgate C .12 .25
270 Rakdos Carnarium C .15 .30
271 Rakdos Guildgate C .07 .15
272 Rogue's Passage U .25 .50
273 Saltcrusted Steppe U .10 .20
274 Sandsteppe Citadel U .30 .75
275 Savage Lands U 1.00 2.00
276 Scoured Barrens C .07 .15
277 Seaside Citadel U 1.25 2.50
278 Secluded Steppe C .07 .15
279 Selesnya Guildgate C .07 .15
280 Selesnya Sanctuary C .15 .30
281 Stirring Wildwood R .25 .50
282 Stone Quarry U .10 .20
283 Swiftwater Cliffs C .07 .15
284 Temple of the False God U .12 .25
285 Terramorphic Expanse C .15 .30
286 Tranquil Expanse U .10 .20
287 Tranquil Thicket C .07 .15
288 Urborg Volcano U .30 .60
289 Vivid Crag U .50 1.00
290 Vivid Creek U .25 .50
291 Vivid Grove U .25 .50
292 Vivid Marsh U .75 1.50
293 Vivid Meadow U .75 1.50
294 Wind-Scarred Crag C .07 .15
295 Plains L .30 .75
296 Plains L .07 .15
297 Plains L .07 .15
298 Island L .15 .30
299 Island L .07 .15
300 Island L .07 .15
301 Swamp L .30 .75
302 Swamp L .12 .25
303 Swamp L .07 .15
304 Mountain L .17 .35
305 Mountain L .07 .15
306 Mountain L .07 .15
307 Forest L .30 .60
308 Forest L .07 .15
309 Forest L .07 .15

2017 Magic The Gathering Commander 2017 Oversized

35 Arahbo, Roar of the World M 2.00 4.00
36 Edgar Markov M 10.00 20.00
38 Inalla, Archmage Ritualist M 1.50 3.00
48 The Ur-Dragon M 12.50 25.00

2017 Magic The Gathering Commander 2017 Tokens

1 Cat .07 .10
2 Bat .12 .25
3 Rat .07 .15
4 Vampire .25 .50
5 Zombie .07 .10
6 Dragon .07 .15
7 Dragon .12 .25
8 Cat Warrior .07 .15
9 Cat Dragon .17 .35
10 Gold .07 .15
11 Eldrazi Spawn .17 .35

2017 Magic The Gathering Commander Anthology

1 Aerie Mystics U .10 .20
2 Akroma's Vengeance R .15 .30
3 Angel of Finality R .15 .30
4 Angelic Arbiter R .15 .30
5 Archangel of Strife R .15 .30
6 Bathe in Light U .10 .20
7 Congregate C .07 .15
8 Curse of the Forsaken U .10 .20
9 Darksteel Mutation U .10 .20
10 Fiend Hunter U .10 .20
11 Flickerform R .15 .30
12 Flickerwisp U .10 .20
13 Karmic Guide R .15 .30
14 Kirtar's Wrath R .15 .30
15 Lightkeeper of Emeria U .10 .20
16 Mirror Entity R .15 .30
17 Mother of Runes U .10 .20
18 Orim's Thunder C .07 .15
19 Path to Exile U .10 .20
20 Return to Dust U .10 .20
21 Righteous Cause U .10 .20
22 Serra Angel U .10 .20
23 Shattered Angel U .10 .20
24 Soul Snare U .10 .20
25 Stonecloaker U .10 .20
26 Tempt with Glory R .15 .30
27 Unexpectedly Absent R .15 .30
28 Voice of All R .15 .30
29 Vow of Duty U .10 .20
30 Arcane Denial C .07 .15
31 Azami, Lady of Scrolls R .15 .30
32 Blue Sun's Zenith R .15 .30
33 Borrowing 100,000 Arrows U .10 .20
34 Control Magic U .10 .20
35 Curse of Inertia U .10 .20
36 Deceiver Exarch U .10 .20
37 Diviner Spirit U .10 .20
38 Djinn of Infinite Deceits R .15 .30
39 Dungeon Geists R .15 .30
40 Hada Spy Patrol U .10 .20
41 Lu Xun, Scholar General R .15 .30
42 Thornwind Faeries C .07 .15
43 Wash Out U .10 .20
44 Wonder U .10 .20
45 Altar's Reap C .07 .15
46 Ambition's Cost U .10 .20
47 Banshee of the Dread Choir U .10 .20
48 Barter in Blood U .10 .20
49 Blood Bairn C .07 .15
50 Butcher of Malakir R .15 .30
51 Champion of Stray Souls M .20 .40
52 Corpse Augur U .10 .20
53 Diabolic Servitude U .10 .20
54 Diabolic Tutor U .10 .20
55 Dread Cacodemon R .15 .30
56 Dread Summons R .15 .30
57 Eater of Hope R .15 .30
58 Evincar's Justice C .07 .15
59 Extractor Demon R .15 .30
60 Fallen Angel R .15 .30
61 Phyrexian Plaguelord R .15 .30
62 Phyrexian Rager C .07 .15
63 Razorjaw Oni U .10 .20
64 Reiver Demon R .15 .30
65 Rise from the Grave U .10 .20
66 Scourge of Nel Toth R .15 .30
67 Sever the Bloodline R .15 .30
68 Shriekmaw U .10 .20
69 Syphon Flesh U .10 .20
70 Syphon Mind C .07 .15
71 Thief of Blood U .10 .20
72 Victimize U .10 .20
73 Vow of Malice U .10 .20
74 Wretched Confluence R .15 .30
75 Akroma, Angel of Fury R .15 .30
76 Anger U .10 .20
77 Avatar of Slaughter R .15 .30
78 Cleansing Beam U .10 .20
79 Comet Storm M .60 1.25
80 Death by Dragons U .10 .20
81 Dragon Whelp U .10 .20
82 Earthquake R .15 .30
83 Furnace Whelp U .10 .20
84 Mana-Charged Dragon R .15 .30
85 Oni of Wild Places U .10 .20
86 Pyrohemia U .10 .20
87 Stranglehold R .15 .30
88 Sulfurous Blast U .10 .20
89 Vow of Lightning U .10 .20
90 Acidic Slime U .10 .20
91 Bane of Progress R .15 .30
92 Beastmaster Ascension R .15 .30
93 Bloodspore Thrinax R .15 .30
94 Caller of the Pack U .10 .20
95 Centaur Vinecrasher R .15 .30
96 Cloudthresher R .15 .30
97 Collective Unconscious R .15 .30
98 Creeperhulk R .15 .30
99 Curse of Predation U .10 .20
100 Desert Twister U .10 .20
101 Drove of Elves U .10 .20
102 Elvish Archdruid R .15 .30
103 Elvish Mystic C .07 .15
104 Elvish Skysweeper C .07 .15
105 Elvish Visionary C .07 .15
106 Essence Warden C .07 .15
107 Eternal Witness U .10 .20
108 Ezuri, Renegade Leader R .15 .30
109 Farhaven Elf C .07 .15
110 Fresh Meat R .15 .30
111 Freyalise, Llanowar's Fury M 4.00 8.00
112 Grave Sifter R .15 .30
113 Great Oak Guardian U .10 .20
114 Grim Flowering U .10 .20
115 Harrow C .07 .15
116 Hunting Triad U .10 .20
117 Immaculate Magistrate R .15 .30
118 Imperious Perfect U .10 .20
119 Indrik Stomphowler U .10 .20
120 Joraga Warcaller R .15 .30
121 Kazandu Tuskcaller R .15 .30
122 Kessig Cagebreakers R .15 .30
123 Krosan Grip U .10 .20
124 Lifeblood Hydra R .15 .30
125 Llanowar Elves C .07 .15
126 Lys Alana Huntmaster C .07 .15
127 Masked Admirers R .15 .30
128 Mulch C .07 .15
129 Mycoloth R .15 .30
130 Overrun U .10 .20
131 Overwhelming Stampede R .15 .30
132 Pathbreaker Ibex R .15 .30
133 Phantom Nantuko R .15 .30
134 Praetor's Counsel M 1.25 2.50
135 Presence of Gond C .07 .15
136 Priest of Titania C .07 .15
137 Primal Growth C .07 .15
138 Primordial Sage R .15 .30
139 Rampaging Baloths M .30 .60
140 Reclamation Sage U .10 .20
141 Restore U .10 .20
142 Sakura-Tribe Elder C .07 .15
143 Satyr Wayfinder C .07 .15
144 Siege Behemoth R .15 .30
145 Silklash Spider R .15 .30
146 Skullwinder U .10 .20
147 Song of the Dryads R .15 .30
148 Soul of the Harvest R .15 .30
149 Spider Spawning U .10 .20
150 Sylvan Offering R .15 .30
151 Sylvan Ranger C .07 .15
152 Sylvan Safekeeper R .15 .30
153 Terastodon R .15 .30
154 Thornweald Archer C .07 .15
155 Thunderfoot Baloth R .15 .30
156 Timberwatch Elf C .07 .15
157 Titania, Protector of Argoth M .75 1.50
158 Titania's Chosen U .10 .20
159 Tornado Elemental R .15 .30
160 Tribute to the Wild U .10 .20
161 Verdant Force R .07 .15
162 Viridian Emissary C .07 .15
163 Viridian Zealot R .15 .30
164 Wall of Blossoms U .10 .20
165 Wave of Vitriol R .15 .30
166 Wellwisher C .07 .15
167 Whirlwind R .15 .30
168 Wolfbriar Elemental R .15 .30
169 Wolfcaller's Howl R .15 .30
170 Wood Elves C .07 .15
171 Wren's Run Packmaster R .15 .30
172 Aethermage's Touch R .15 .30
173 Angel of Despair R .15 .30
174 Basandra, Battle Seraph R .15 .30
175 Bladewing the Risen R .15 .30
176 Derevi, Empyrial Tactician M 2.00 4.00
177 Golgari Charm U .10 .20
178 Grisly Salvage C .07 .15
179 Jarad, Golgari Lich Lord M 1.25 2.50
180 Kaalia of the Vast M 7.50 15.00
181 Korozda Guildmage U .10 .20
182 Leafdrake Roost U .10 .20
183 Lotleth Troll R .15 .30
184 Malfegor M .30 .75
185 Mazirek, Kraul Death Priest M 6.00 12.00
186 Meren of Clan Nel Toth M 5.00 10.00
187 Mortify U .10 .20
188 Oros, the Avenger R .15 .30
189 Putrefy U .10 .20
190 Roon of the Hidden Realm M .20 .40
191 Rubinia Soulsinger R .15 .30
192 Selesnya Charm U .10 .20
193 Skyward Eye Prophets U .10 .20
194 Tariel, Reckoner of Souls M .75 1.50
195 Terminate C .07 .15
196 Vulturous Zombie R .15 .30
197 Winged Coatl C .07 .15
198 Wrecking Ball C .07 .15
199 Boros Guildmage U .10 .20
200 Duergar Hedge-Mage U .10 .20
201 Gwyllion Hedge-Mage U .10 .20
202 Master Warcraft R .15 .30
203 Mistmeadow Witch U .10 .20
204 Murkfiend Liege R .15 .30
205 Orzhov Guildmage U .10 .20
206 Selesnya Guildmage U .10 .20
207 Armillary Sphere C .07 .15
208 Assault Suit U .10 .20
209 Azorius Keyrune U .10 .20
210 Basalt Monolith U .10 .20
211 Bonehoard R .15 .30
212 Boros Signet C .07 .15
213 Commander's Sphere C .07 .15
214 Conjurer's Closet R .15 .30
215 Darksteel Ingot U .10 .20
216 Eldrazi Monument M 7.50 15.00
217 Emerald Medallion R .15 .30
218 Golgari Signet C .07 .15
219 Leonin Bladetrap U .10 .20
220 Lightning Greaves U .10 .20
221 Loreseeker's Stone U .10 .20
222 Moss Diamond U .10 .20
223 Orzhov Signet C .07 .15
224 Pilgrim's Eye C .07 .15
225 Predator, Flagship R .15 .30
226 Rakdos Signet C .07 .15
227 Seer's Sundial R .15 .30
228 Selesnya Signet C .07 .15
229 Simic Signet C .07 .15
230 Skullclamp U .10 .20
231 Sol Ring U .10 .20
232 Surveyor's Scope R .15 .30
233 Swiftfoot Boots U .10 .20
234 Sword of the Paruns R .15 .30
235 Thought Vessel C .07 .15
236 Thousand-Year Elixir R .15 .30
237 Thunderstaff U .10 .20
238 Akoum Refuge U .10 .20
239 Azorius Chancery C .07 .15
240 Azorius Guildgate C .07 .15
241 Bant Panorama C .07 .15
242 Barren Moor C .07 .15
243 Bojuka Bog C .07 .15
244 Boros Garrison C .07 .15
245 Command Tower C .07 .15
246 Crystal Vein U .10 .20
247 Evolving Wilds C .07 .15
248 Faerie Conclave U .10 .20
249 Forgotten Cave C .07 .15
250 Gargoyle Castle R .15 .30
251 Ghost Quarter U .10 .20
252 Golgari Guildgate C .07 .15
253 Golgari Rot Farm C .07 .15
254 Grim Backwoods R .15 .30
255 Haunted Fengraf C .07 .15
256 Havenwood Battleground U .10 .20
257 High Market R .15 .30
258 Jungle Basin U .10 .20
259 Jungle Hollow C .07 .15
260 Molten Slagheap U .10 .20
261 Myriad Landscape U .10 .20
262 Opal Palace C .07 .15
263 Oran-Rief, the Vastwood R .15 .30
264 Orzhov Basilica C .07 .15
265 Polluted Mire C .07 .15
266 Rakdos Carnarium C .07 .15
267 Rupture Spire C .07 .15
268 Saltcrusted Steppe U .10 .20
269 Seaside Citadel U .10 .20
270 Secluded Steppe C .07 .15
271 Sejiri Refuge U .10 .20
272 Selesnya Guildgate C .07 .15
273 Selesnya Sanctuary C .07 .15
274 Simic Guildgate C .07 .15
275 Slippery Karst C .07 .15
276 Tainted Wood U .10 .20
277 Temple of the False God U .10 .20
278 Terramorphic Expanse C .07 .15
279 Tranquil Thicket C .07 .15
280 Transguild Promenade C .07 .15
281 Vivid Grove U .10 .20
282 Vivid Marsh U .10 .20
283 Vivid Meadow U .10 .20
284 Zoetic Cavern U .10 .20
285 Plains L .07 .15
286 Plains L .07 .15
287 Plains L .07 .15
288 Plains L .07 .15
289 Plains L .07 .15
290 Plains L .07 .15
291 Plains L .07 .15
292 Plains L .07 .15
293 Island L .07 .15
294 Island L .07 .15
295 Island L .07 .15
296 Island L .07 .15
297 Swamp L .07 .15
298 Swamp L .07 .15
299 Swamp L .07 .15
300 Swamp L .07 .15
301 Swamp L .07 .15
302 Swamp L .07 .15
303 Swamp L .07 .15
304 Swamp L .07 .15
305 Mountain L .07 .15
306 Mountain L .07 .15
307 Mountain L .07 .15
308 Mountain L .07 .15
309 Forest L .07 .15
310 Forest L .07 .15
311 Forest L .07 .15
312 Forest L .07 .15
313 Forest L .07 .15
314 Forest L .07 .15
315 Forest L .07 .15
316 Forest L .07 .15
317 Forest L .07 .15
318 Forest L .07 .15
319 Forest L .07 .15
320 Forest L .07 .15

2017 Magic The Gathering Commander Anthology Tokens

0 Experience Counter 1.50 3.00
1 Kithkin Soldier .10 .20
2 Knight .10 .20
3 Spirit .15 .30
4 Germ .10 .20
5 Zombie .10 .20
6 Dragon .15 .30
7 Beast .10 .20
8 Beast .10 .20
9 Elemental .60 1.25
10 Elephant .15 .30
11 Elf Druid 2.50 5.00
12 Elf Warrior .10 .20
13 Saproling .10 .20
14 Spider .12 .25
15 Treefolk 1.50 3.00
16 Wolf .12 .25
17 Wolf .12 .25
18 Drake .20 .40
19 Gargoyle .10 .20

2017 Magic The Gathering Duel Decks Merfolk vs. Goblins Tokens

1 Elemental .12 .25
2 Wall .07 .15
3 Goblin .12 .25

2017 Magic The Gathering Duel Decks Mind vs. Might

1 Jhoira of the Ghitu M .75 1.50
2 Beacon of Tomorrows R 1.00 2.00
3 Deep Sea Kraken R .17 .35
4 Minds Desire R .17 .35
5 Peer Through Depths C .17 .35
6 Quicken R .17 .35
7 Reach Through Mists C .17 .35
8 Sage Eye Avengers R .17 .35
9 Sift Through Sands C .17 .35
10 Snap C .40 .80
11 Talrand Sky Summoner R .40 .80
12 Temporal Fissure C .17 .35
13 The Unspeakable R .17 .35
14 Desperate Ritual U 1.00 2.00
15 Empty the Warrens C .17 .35
16 Grapeshot C .17 .35
17 Rift Bolt C 1.00 2.00
18 Shivan Meteor U .17 .35
19 Volcanic Vision R .17 .35

20 Young Pyromancer U .50 1.00
21 Fireminds Foresight R .17 .35
22 Goblin Electromancer C .17 .35
23 Jori En Ruin Diver R .17 .35
24 Nivix Cyclops C .17 .35
25 Spellheart Chimera U .17 .35
26 Nucklavee U .17 .35
27 Swiftwater Cliffs C .17 .35
28 Island L .17 .35
29 Island L .17 .35
30 Island L .17 .35
31 Mountain L .17 .35
32 Mountain L .17 .35
33 Mountain L .17 .35
34 Lovisa Coldeyes M .60 1.25
35 Beacon of Destruction R .17 .35
36 Boldwyr Intimidator U .17 .35
37 Firebolt C .17 .35
38 Gorehorn Minotaurs C .17 .35
39 Kamahl Pit Fighter R .17 .35
40 Kruin Striker C .17 .35
41 Zo Zu the Punisher R .17 .35
42 Ambassador Oak C .17 .35
43 Beast Attack U .17 .35
44 Call of the Herd R .17 .35
45 Cloudcrown Oak C .17 .35
46 Harmonize U .30 .60
47 Increasing Savagery R .17 .35
48 Rampant Growth C .17 .35
49 Roar of the Wurm U .17 .35
50 Skarrgan Pit Skulk C .17 .35
51 Sylvan Might C .17 .35
52 Talaras Battalion R .40 .80
53 Radha Heir to Keld R .17 .35
54 Relentless Hunter U .17 .35
55 Burning Tree Emissary U .17 .35
56 Guttural Response U .50 1.00
57 Rubblebelt Raiders R .17 .35
58 Coat of Arms R 4.00 8.00
59 Rugged Highlands C .17 .35
60 Mountain L .17 .35
61 Mountain L .17 .35
62 Mountain L .17 .35
63 Forest L .17 .35
64 Forest L .17 .35
65 Forest L .17 .35

2017 Magic The Gathering Duel Decks Mind vs. Might Tokens

1 Drake .20 .40
2 Elemental .30 .75
3 Goblin .10 .20
4 Beast .07 .15
5 Elephant .07 .15
6 Elf Warrior .20 .40
7 Wurm .25 .50

2017 Magic The Gathering Explorers of Ixalan

1 Beacon of Immortality R 1.00 2.00
2 Day of Judgment R 1.50 3.00
3 Path to Exile U 6.00 12.00
4 Shielded by Faith R .75 1.50
5 Veteran's Reflexes C .07 .15
6 Vow of Duty U .10 .20
7 Aether Gale R .30 .60
8 Blatant Thievery R 1.50 3.00
9 Concentrate U .10 .20
10 Merfolk Sovereign R .25 .50
11 Threads of Disloyalty R .15 .30
12 Time Warp M 6.00 12.00
13 Unsummon C .07 .15
14 Vow of Flight U .10 .20
15 Bloodbond Vampire U .10 .20
16 Child of Night C .07 .15
17 Coat with Venom C .07 .15
18 Doom Blade U .10 .20
19 Innocent Blood C .07 .15
20 Necropolis Regent M .50 1.00
21 Urge to Feed U .10 .20
22 Vampire Interloper C .07 .15
23 Vampire Nighthawk U .30 .60
24 Vampire Noble C .07 .15
25 Aggravated Assault R 3.00 6.00
26 Disaster Radius R .12 .25
27 Mass Mutiny R .12 .25
28 Rush of Adrenaline C .07 .15
29 Shared Animosity R 3.00 6.00
30 Vow of Lightning U .10 .20
31 Borderland Ranger C .07 .15
32 Giant Growth C .07 .15
33 Hunter's Prowess R .12 .25
34 Prey Upon C .07 .15
35 Rancor U .75 1.50
36 Soul of the Harvest R 1.50 3.00
37 Vow of Wildness U .10 .20
38 Jungle Barrier U .10 .20
39 Lightning Helix U .75 1.50
40 Mortify U .20 .40
41 Zealous Persecution U .10 .20
42 Adaptive Automaton R 4.00 8.00
43 Prismatic Lens U .10 .20
44 Quicksilver Amulet R 3.00 6.00
45 Crumbling Necropolis U .10 .20
46 Jungle Shrine U .20 .40
47 Tainted Field U .10 .20

2017 Magic The Gathering Explorers of Ixalan Token

1 Saproling .12 .25

2017 Magic The Gathering From the Vault Transform

1 Archangel Avacyn/Avacyn, the Purifer M 5.00 10.00
2 Arguel's Blood Fast/Temple of Aclazotz M .75 1.50
3 Arlinn Kord/Arlinn Embraced...Moon M :R:/:G:3.00 6.00
4 Bloodline Keeper/Lord of Lineage M 12.50 25.00
5a Bruna, the Fading Light M 6.00 12.00
5b Brisela, Voice of Nightmares M 15.00 30.00
6 Chandra Fire of Kaladesh/Roaring Flame M :R:2.00 4.00
7 Delver of Secrets/Insectile Aberration M 2.50 5.00
8 Elbrus, the Binding Blade/Withengar Unbound M4.00 8.00
9 Garruk Relentless/Garruk, the Veil-Cursed M2.00 4.00
10 Gisela, the Broken Blade M 20.00 40.00
11 Huntmaster & Ravager of the Fells M :R:/:G:6.00 12.00
12 Jace Vryn's Prodigy/Telepath Unbound M :B:12.50 25.00
13 Kytheon/Gideon M :W: 5.00 10.00
14 Liliana Heretical Healer
Defiant Necromancer M :K: 4.00 8.00
15 Nissa, Vastwood Seer/Nissa, Sage Animist M6.00 12.00

2017 Magic The Gathering HasCon 2017 Promos

1 Grimlock, Dinobot Leader
Ferocious King M :R:/:G:/:W: 200.00 400.00
2 Nerf War M 12.50 25.00
3 Sword of Dungeons & Dragons M 17.50 35.00
4 Dragon M 7.50 15.00

2017 Magic The Gathering Hour of Devastation

1 Act of Heroism C .07 .15
2 Adorned Pouncer R .75 1.50
3 Angel of Condemnation R .30 .60
4 Angel of the God-Pharaoh U .10 .20
5 Aven of Enduring Hope C .07 .15
6 Crested Sunmare M 3.00 6.00
7 Dauntless Aven C .07 .15
8 Desert's Hold U .10 .20
9 Disposal Mummy C .07 .15
10 Djeru, With Eyes Open R .15 .30
11 Djeru's Renunciation C .07 .15
12 Dutiful Servants C .07 .15
13 Gideon's Defeat U .10 .20
14 God-Pharaoh's Faithful C .30 .75
15 Hour of Revelation R .30 .60
16 Mummy Paramount C .07 .15
17 Oketra's Avenger C .07 .15
18 Oketra's Last Mercy R .15 .30
19 Overwhelming Splendor M 3.00 6.00
20 Sandblast C .07 .15
21 Saving Grace U .10 .20
22 Solemnity R 2.00 4.00
23 Solitary Camel C .07 .15
24 Steadfast Sentinel C .07 .15
25 Steward of Solidarity U .10 .20
26 Sunscourge Champion U .10 .20
27 Unconventional Tactics U .10 .20
28 Vizier of the True U .10 .20
29 Aerial Guide C .07 .15
30 Aven Reedstalker C .07 .15
31 Champion of Wits R .25 .50
32 Countervailing Winds C .17 .35
33 Cunning Survivor C .07 .15
34 Eternal of Harsh Truths U .10 .20
35 Fraying Sanity R 4.00 8.00
36 Hour of Eternity R .40 .80
37 Imaginary Threats U .10 .20
38 Jace's Defeat U .10 .20
39 Kefnet's Last Word R .15 .30
40 Nimble Obstructionist R .15 .30
41 Ominous Sphinx U .10 .20
42 Proven Combatant C .07 .15
43 Riddleform U .10 .20
44 Seer of the Last Tomorrow C .07 .15
45 Sinuous Striker U .10 .20
46 Spellweaver Eternal C .07 .15
47 Strategic Planning C .07 .15
48 Striped Riverwinder C .25 .50
49 Supreme Will U .10 .20
50 Swarm Intelligence R .15 .30
51 Tragic Lesson C .07 .15
52 Unesh, Criosphinx Sovereign M .75 1.50
53 Unquenchable Thirst C .07 .15
54 Unsummon C .07 .15
55 Vizier of the Anointed U .10 .20
56 Accursed Horde U .10 .20
57 Ammit Eternal R .15 .30
58 Apocalypse Demon R .15 .30
59 Bleinwing Punisher U .20 .40
60 Bontu's Last Reckoning R 1.00 2.00
61 Carrion Screecher C .07 .15
62 Doomfall U .10 .20
63 Dreamstealer R .15 .30
64 Grisly Survivor C .07 .15
65 Hour of Glory R .15 .30
66 Khenra Eternal C .07 .15
67 Lethal Sting C .07 .15
68 Liliana's Defeat U .10 .20
69 Lurching Rotbeast C .07 .15
70 Marauding Boneslasher C .07 .15
71 Merciless Eternal U .10 .20
72 Moaning Wall C .07 .15
73 Razaketh, the Foulblooded M 15.00 30.00
74 Razaketh's Rite U .30 .60
75 Ruin Rat C .07 .15
76 Scrounger of Souls C .07 .15
77 Torment of Hailfire R 12.50 25.00
78 Torment of Scarabs U .30 .75
79 Torment of Venom C .07 .15
80 Vile Manifestation U .10 .20
81 Without Weakness C .07 .15
82 Wretched Camel C .07 .15
83 Abrade U .30 .75
84 Blur of Blades C .07 .15
85 Burning-Fist Minotaur U .10 .20
86 Chandra's Defeat U .10 .20
87 Chaos Maw R .15 .30
88 Crash Through C .07 .15
89 Defiant Khenra C .07 .15
90 Earthshaker Khenra R .15 .30
91 Fervent Paincaster U .10 .20
92 Firebrand Archer C .20 .40
93 Frontline Devastator C .07 .15
94 Gilded Cerodon C .07 .15
95 Granitic Titan C .07 .15
96 Hazoret's Undying Fury R .15 .30
97 Hour of Devastation R .40 .80
98 Imminent Doom R .15 .30
99 Inferno Jet U .10 .20
100 Khenra Scrapper C .07 .15
101 Kindled Fury C .07 .15
102 Magmaroth U .10 .20
103 Manticore Eternal U .10 .20
104 Neheb, the Eternal M 10.00 20.00
105 Open Fire C .07 .15
106 Puncturing Blow C .07 .15
107 Sand Strangler U .10 .20
108 Thorned Moloch C .07 .15
109 Wildfire Eternal R .15 .30
110 Ambuscade C .07 .15
111 Beneath the Sands C .07 .15
112 Bitterbow Sharpshooters C .07 .15
113 Devotee of Strength U .10 .20
114 Dune Diviner U .10 .20
115 Feral Prowler C .07 .15
116 Frilled Sandwalla C .07 .15
117 Gift of Strength C .07 .15
118 Harrier Naga C .07 .15
119 Hope Tender U .10 .20
120 Hour of Promise R .75 1.50
121 Life Goes On C .07 .15
122 Majestic Myriarch M .50 1.00
123 Nissa's Defeat U .10 .20
124 Oasis Ritualist C .07 .15
125 Overcome U .10 .20
126 Pride Sovereign R 1.50 3.00
127 Quarry Beetle U .10 .20
128 Rampaging Hippo C .07 .15
129 Ramunap Excavator R 2.00 4.00
130 Ramunap Hydra R .15 .30
131 Resilient Khenra R .15 .30
132 Rhonas's Last Stand R .15 .30
133 Rhonas's Stalwart C .07 .15
134 Sidewinder Naga C .07 .15
135 Sifter Wurm U .10 .20
136 Tenacious Hunter U .10 .20
137 Uncage the Menagerie M .75 1.50
138 Bloodwater Entity U .15 .30
139 The Locust God M 2.50 5.00
140 Nicol Bolas, God-Pharaoh M 7.50 15.00
141 Obelisk Spider U .25 .50
142 Resolute Survivors U .10 .20
143 River Hoopoe U .10 .20
144 Samut, the Tested M .75 1.50
145 The Scarab God M 10.00 20.00
146 The Scorpion God M 2.50 5.00
147 Unraveling Mummy U .10 .20
148 Farm/Market U .10 .20
149 Consign/Oblivion U .17 .35
150 Claim/Fame U .17 .35
151 Struggle/Survive U .10 .20
152 Appeal/Authority U .10 .20
153 Leave/Chance R .25 .50
154 Reason/Believe R .15 .30
155 Grind/Dust R .15 .30
156 Refuse/Cooperate R .15 .30
157 Driven/Despair R .30 .60
158 Abandoned Sarcophagus R .15 .30
159 Crook of Condemnation U .10 .20
160 Dagger of the Worthy U .10 .20
161 God-Pharaoh's Gift R .15 .30
162 Graven Abomination C .07 .15
163 Hollow One R .75 1.50
164 Manalith C .07 .15
165 Mirage Mirror R 4.00 8.00
166 Sunset Pyramid U .10 .20
167 Traveler's Amulet C .07 .15
168 Wall of Forgotten Pharaohs C .07 .15
169 Crypt of the Eternals U .10 .20
170 Desert of the Fervent C .07 .15
171 Desert of the Glorified C .07 .15
172 Desert of the Indomitable C .07 .15
173 Desert of the Mindful C .07 .15
174 Desert of the True C .07 .15
175 Dunes of the Dead U .10 .20
176 Endless Sands R .15 .30
177 Hashep Oasis U .10 .20
178 Hostile Desert R .15 .30
179 Ifnir Deadlands U .10 .20
180 Ipnu Rivulet U .10 .20
181 Ramunap Ruins U .25 .50
182 Scavenger Grounds R .75 1.50
183 Shefet Dunes U .17 .35
184 Survivors' Encampment C .20 .40
185 Plains Full Art L .20 .40
186 Island Full Art L .25 .50
187 Swamp Full Art L .50 1.00
188 Mountain Full Art L .20 .40
189 Forest Full Art L .25 .50
190 Plains L .10 .20
191 Plains L .07 .15
192 Island L .07 .15
193 Island L .07 .15
194 Swamp L .07 .15
195 Swamp L .07 .15
196 Mountain L .07 .15
197 Mountain L .07 .15
198 Forest L .07 .15
199 Forest L .07 .15
201 Avid Reclaimer U .10 .20
202 Bramblewelt Behemoth C .07 .15
203 Nissa's Encouragement R .15 .30
204 Woodland Stream C .07 .15
206 Wasp of the Bitter End U .10 .20
207 Zealot of the God-Pharaoh C .07 .15
208 Visage of Bolas R .15 .30
209 Cinder Barrens C .07 .15

2017 Magic The Gathering Hour of Devastation Tokens

1 Adorned Pouncer .20 .40
2 Champion of Wits .07 .15
3 Dreamstealer .07 .10
4 Earthshaker Khenra .07 .15
5 Proven Combatant .07 .10
6 Resilient Khenra .07 .15
7 Sinuous Striker .07 .10
8 Steadfast Sentinel .07 .10
9 Sunscourge Champion .07 .10
10 Horse .30 .75
11 Snake .10 .20
12 Insect 1.00 1.75
13 Punchcard .07 .10
14 Punchcard .07 .10

2017 Magic The Gathering Iconic Masters

1 Scion of Ugin C .07 .15
2 Abzan Battle Priest U .25 .50
3 Abzan Falconer U .10 .20
4 Ainok Bond Kin C .07 .15
5 Ajanis Pridemate U .10 .20
6 Angel of Mercy C .07 .15
7 Angelic Accord U .75 1.50
8 Archangel of Thune M 12.50 25.00
9 Auriok Champion R 17.50 35.00
10 Austere Command R 1.50 3.00
11 Avacyn, Angel of Hope M 25.00 50.00
12 Benevolent Ancestor C .07 .15
13 Blinding Mage C .07 .15
14 Burrenton Forge-Tender U .17 .35
15 Disenchant C .07 .15
16 Doomed Traveler C .07 .15
17 Dragon Bell Monk C .07 .15
18 Elesh Norn, Grand Cenobite M 12.50 25.00
19 Emerge Unscathed C .20 .40
20 Emeria Angel R .50 1.00
21 Great Teacher's Decree U .10 .20
22 Guard Duty C .07 .15
23 Guided Strike C .07 .15
24 Infantry Veteran C .07 .15
25 Iona's Judgment C .07 .15
26 Path of Bravery R .15 .30
27 Pentarch Ward C .07 .15
28 Restoratoin Angel R .75 1.50
29 Seeker of the Way C .07 .15
30 Serra Angel U .10 .20
31 Serra Ascendant R 12.50 25.00
32 Stalwart Aven C .07 .15
33 Student of Ojutai C .07 .15
34 Survival Cache C .07 .15
35 Sustainer of the Realm C .07 .15
36 Swords to Plowshares U 2.00 4.00
37 Topan Freeblade U .10 .20
38 Wing Shards U .10 .20
39 Yosei, the Morning Star R 2.00 4.00
40 Aetherize U .50 1.00
41 Amass the Components C .07 .15
42 Ancestral Vision R 3.00 6.00
43 Bewilder C .07 .15
44 Cephalid Broker U .10 .20
45 Claustrophobia C .07 .15
46 Condescend U .20 .40
47 Consecrated Sphinx M 25.00 50.00
48 Cryptic Command R 12.50 25.00
49 Day of the Dragons R .15 .30
50 Diminish C .07 .15
51 Dissolve C .20 .40
52 Distortion Strike U .30 .75
53 Doorkeeper C .07 .15
54 Elusive Spellfist C .07 .15
55 Flusterstorm R 15.00 30.00
56 Fog Bank U .20 .40
57 Frost Lynx C .07 .15
58 Illusory Ambusher U .10 .20
59 Illusory Angel U .10 .20
60 Jace's Phantasm C .25 .50
61 Jhessian Thief C .07 .15
62 Jin-Gitaxias, Core Augur M 12.50 25.00
63 Keiga, the Tide Star R 3.00 6.00
64 Mahamoti Djinn U .10 .20
65 Mana Drain M 30.00 75.00
66 Mana Leak C .15 .30
67 Mnemonic Wall C .07 .15
68 Ojutai's Breath C .07 .15
69 Phantom Monster C .07 .15
70 Repeal C .07 .15
71 Riverwheel Aerialists C .07 .15
72 Shriekgeist C .07 .15
73 Skywise Teachings U .10 .20
74 Sphinx of Uthuun R .15 .30
75 Teferi, Mage of Zhalfir R 2.00 4.00
76 Thought Scour C .30 .60
77 Windfall U 2.00 4.00
78 Abyssal Persecutor R .40 .80
79 Bala Ged Scorpion C .07 .15
80 Balustrade Spy C .07 .15
81 Bladewing's Thrall U .10 .20
82 Bloodghast R 7.50 15.00
83 Bogbrew Witch U .10 .20
84 Butcher's Glee C .07 .15
85 Child of Night C .07 .15
86 Dead Reveler C .07 .15
87 Doom Blade U .15 .30
88 Duress C .07 .15
89 Eternal Thirst C .07 .15
90 Festering Newt C .07 .15
91 Foul-Tongue Invocation C .07 .15
92 Grisly Spectacle C .07 .15
93 Haunting Hymn U .10 .20
94 Indulgent Tormentor U .30 .75
95 Kokusho, the Evening Star R 12.50 25.00
96 Lord of the Pit R .15 .30
97 Mer-Ek Nightblade U .10 .20
98 Necropotence M 30.00 60.00
99 Night of Souls' Betrayal R .20 .40
100 Noxious Dragon U .10 .20
101 Ob Nixilis, the Fallen M 7.50 15.00
102 Phyrexian Rager C .07 .15
103 Rakdos Drake C .07 .15
104 Reave Soul C .07 .15
105 Rotfeaster Maggot C .07 .15
106 Rune-Scarred Demon R 4.00 8.00
107 Sanguine Bond U .75 1.50
108 Sheoldred, Whispering One M 10.00 20.00
109 Tavern Swindler U .10 .20
110 Thoughtseize R 10.00 20.00
111 Thrill-Kill Assassin C .07 .15
112 Ulcerate U .10 .20
113 Virulent Swipe C .07 .15
114 Wight of Precinct Six C .15 .30
115 Wrench Mind C .07 .15
116 Anger of the Gods R .75 1.50
117 Battle-Rattle Shaman C .07 .15
118 Bogardan Hellkite R .25 .50
119 Borderland Marauder C .07 .15
120 Charmbreaker Devils R .15 .30
121 Coordinated Assault U .10 .20
122 Crucible of Fire R 1.00 2.00
123 Draconic Roar C .07 .15
124 Dragon Egg C .07 .15
125 Dragon Tempest U 4.00 8.00
126 Dragonlord's Servant C .25 .50
127 Earth Elemental C .07 .15

128 Fireball U .10 .20
129 Furnace Whelp C .07 .15
130 Fury Charm C .07 .15
131 Guttersnipe U .10 .20
132 Hammerhand C .07 .15
133 Heat Ray C .07 .15
134 Hoarding Dragon U .17 .35
135 Keldon Halberdier C .07 .15
136 Kiki Jiki, Mirror Breaker M 7.50 15.00
137 Kiln Fiend C .07 .15
138 Magus of the Moon R 3.00 6.00
139 Mark of Mutiny C .07 .15
140 Monastery Swiftspear U 2.00 4.00
141 Pillar of Flame C .07 .15
142 Prodigal Pyromancer U .10 .20
143 Rift Bolt U .30 .75
144 Ryusei, the Falling Star R 1.00 2.00
145 Scourge of Valkas R .75 1.50
146 Splatter Thug C .07 .15
147 Staggershock U .10 .20
148 Surreal Memoir U .10 .20
149 Thundermaw Hellkite M 2.50 5.00
150 Tormenting Voice C .07 .15
151 Trumpet Blast C .07 .15
152 Urabrask the Hidden M 7.50 15.00
153 Vent Sentinel C .07 .15
154 Aerial Predation C .07 .15
155 Assault Formation U .60 1.25
156 Carven Caryatid U .25 .50
157 Channel M .50 1.00
158 Crowned Ceratok C .07 .15
159 Curse of Predation R .25 .50
160 Durkwood Baloth C .07 .15
161 Duskdale Wurm C .07 .15
162 Enlarge U .10 .20
163 Genesis Hydra R .25 .50
164 Genesis Wave R 7.50 15.00
165 Greater Basilisk C .07 .15
166 Heroes' Bane U .20 .40
167 Hunt the Weak C .07 .15
168 Hunting Pack U .10 .20
169 Inspiring Call U .30 .75
170 Ivy Elemental C .07 .15
171 Jaddi Offshoot C .07 .15
172 Jugan, the Rising Star R .60 1.25
173 Lead the Stampede C .07 .15
174 Lotus Cobra R 2.50 5.00
175 Lure U .10 .20
176 Nantuko Shaman C .07 .15
177 Nature's Claim C .07 .15
178 Netcaster Spider C .07 .15
179 Obstinate Baloth R .30 .75
180 Overgrown Battlement U .25 .50
181 Phantom Tiger C .07 .15
182 Prey's Vengeance C .07 .15
183 Primeval Titan M 5.00 10.00
184 Rampaging Baloths R .25 .50
185 Search for Tomorrow C .20 .40
186 Sultai Flayer U .10 .20
187 Timberland Guide C .07 .15
188 Undercity Troll U .10 .20
189 Vorinclex, Voice of Hunger M 15.00 30.00
190 Wall of Roots C .17 .35
191 Wildsize C .07 .15
192 Azorius Charm U .15 .30
193 Bladewing the Risen U .75 1.50
194 Blizzard Specter U .15 .30
195 Blood Baron of Vizkopa R .25 .50
196 Chronicler of Heroes U .10 .20
197 Corpsejack Menace U .75 1.50
198 Electrolyze U .10 .20
199 Firemane Angel R .15 .30
200 Glimpse the Unthinkable R 7.50 15.00
201 Hypersonic Dragon R .15 .30
202 Jungle Barrier U .10 .20
203 Knight of the Reliquary R 1.25 2.50
204 Lightning Helix U .60 1.25
205 Maelegor R .30 .60
206 Rosheen Meanderer U .10 .20
207 Savageborn Hydra R .15 .30
208 Simic Sky Swallower R .15 .30
209 Spiritmonger R .15 .30
210 Supreme Verdict R 4.00 8.00
211 Vizkopa Guildmage U .20 .40
212 Aether Vial R 25.00 50.00
213 Bubbling Cauldron U .10 .20
214 Darksteel Axe C .07 .15
215 Dragonloft Idol U .10 .20
216 Guardian Idol C .50 1.00
217 Kolaghan Monument U .10 .20
218 Manakin C .25 .50
219 Mind Stone C .50 1.00
220 Mindcrank U 3.00 6.00
221 Mishra's Bauble U 7.50 15.00
222 Moonglove Extract C .07 .15
223 Oblivion Stone R 2.00 4.00
224 Palladium Myr U .30 .75
225 Pristine Talisman U .20 .40
226 Runed Servitor C .07 .15
227 Sandstone Oracle U .10 .20
228 Serum Powder R .50 1.00
229 Star Compass C .75 1.50
230 Thran Dynamo U 3.00 6.00
231 Trepanation Blade U .10 .20
232 Azorius Chancery U .15 .30
233 Boros Garrison U .17 .35
234 Dimir Aqueduct U .15 .30
235 Evolving Wilds C .07 .15
236 Golgari Rot Farm U .15 .30
237 Graven Cairns R 4.00 8.00
238 Grove of the Burnwillows R 3.00 6.00
239 Gruul Turf U .17 .35
240 Horizon Canopy R 20.00 40.00
241 Izzet Boilerworks U .10 .20
242 Nimbus Maze R 2.00 4.00
243 Orzhov Basilica U .20 .40
244 Radiant Fountain C .07 .15
245 Rakdos Carnarium U .10 .20
246 River of Tears R 2.50 5.00
247 Selesnya Sanctuary U .15 .30
248 Shimmering Grotto C .07 .15
249 Simic Growth Chamber U .25 .50

2017 Magic The Gathering Iconic Masters Tokens

1 Angel .10 .20
2 Bird .07 .10
3 Spirit .07 .10
4 Djinn Monk .07 .10
5 Dragon .07 .15
6 Dragon .07 .15
7 Beast .07 .15

2017 Magic The Gathering Ixalan

1 Adanto Vanguard U .10 .20
2 Ashes of the Abhorrent R .30 .60
3 Axis of Mortality M .60 1.25
4 Bellowing Aegisaur U .15 .30
5 Bishop of Rebirth R .15 .30
6 Bishops Soldier C .07 .15
7 Bright Reprisal U .10 .20
8 Demystify C .07 .15
9 Duskborne Skymarcher U .10 .20
10 Emissary of Sunrise U .10 .20
11 Encampment Keeper C .07 .15
12 Glorifier of Dusk U .10 .20
13 Goring Ceratops R .25 .50
14 Imperial Aerosaur U .10 .20
15 Imperial Lancer U .10 .20
16 Inspiring Cleric U .10 .20
17 Ixalan's Binding U .20 .40
18 Kinjalli's Caller C .07 .15
19 Kinjalli's Sunwing R 1.50 3.00
20 Legion Conquistador C .07 .15
21 Legion's Judgment C .07 .15
22 Legion's Landing/Adanto, the First Fort R 2.00 4.00
23 Looming Altisaur C .07 .15
24 Mavren Fein Dusk Apostle R .75 1.50
25 Paladin of the Bloodstained C .07 .15
26 Pious Interdiction C .07 .15
27 Priest of the Wakening Sun R .20 .40
28 Pterodon Knight C .07 .15
29 Queens Commission C .07 .15
30 Rallying Roar U .10 .20
31 Raptor Companion C .07 .15
32 Ritual of Rejuvenation C .07 .15
33 Sanguine Sacrament R .15 .30
34 Settle the Wreckage R 2.00 4.00
35 Sheltering Light U .10 .20
36 Shining Aerosaur C .07 .15
37 Skyblade of the Legion C .07 .15
38 Slash of Talons C .07 .15
39 Steadfast Armasaur U .10 .20
40 Sunrise Seeker C .07 .15
41 Territorial Hammerskull C .07 .15
42 Vampires Zeal C .07 .15
43 Tocatli Honor Guard R .15 .30
44 Wakening Sun's Avatar M 4.00 8.00
45 Air Elemental U .10 .20
46 Arcane Adaptation R 2.00 4.00
47 Cancel C .07 .15
48 Chart a Course U .25 .50
49 Daring Saboteur R .15 .30
50 Deadeye Quartermaster U .20 .40
51 Deeproot Waters U .25 .50
52 Depths of Desire C .07 .15
53 Dive Down C .07 .15
54 Dreamcaller Siren R .15 .30
55 Entrancing Melody R .15 .30
56 Favorable Winds U .25 .50
57 Fleet Swallower R .75 1.50
58 Headwater Sentries C .07 .15
59 Herald of Secret Streams R 2.00 4.00
60 Jace Cunning Castaway M 1.00 2.00
61 Kopala Warden of Waves R .50 1.00
62 Lookout's Dispersal U .20 .40
63 Navigator's Ruin U .10 .20
64 One With the Wind C .07 .15
65 Overflowing Insight M .50 1.00
66 Opt C .07 .15
67 Perilous Voyage U .10 .20
68 Pirates Prize C .07 .15
69 Prosperous Pirates C .07 .15
70 River Sneak U .10 .20
71 River's Rebuke R 1.00 2.00
72 Run Aground C .07 .15
73 Sailor of Means C .07 .15
74 Search for Azcanta/Azcanta, the Sunken Ruin R 4.00 8.00
75 Shaper Apprentice C .07 .15
76 Shipwreck Looter C .07 .15
77 Shore Keeper C .07 .15
78 Siren Lookout C .07 .15
79 Siren Stormtamer U .25 .50
80 Siren's Ruse C .07 .15
81 Spell Pierce C .07 .15
82 Spell Swindle R 2.50 5.00
83 Storm Fleet Aerialist U .10 .20
84 Storm Fleet Spy U .10 .20
85 Storm Sculptor C .07 .15
86 Tempest Caller U .10 .20
87 Watertrap Weaver C .07 .15
88 Wind Strider C .07 .15
89 Anointed Deacon C .07 .15
90 Arguel's Blood Fast/Temple of Aclazotz R .25 .50
91 Bishop of the Bloodstained U .10 .20
92 Blight Keeper C .07 .15
93 Bloodcrazed Paladin R .15 .30
94 Boneyard Parley M .50 1.00
95 Contract Killing C .07 .15
96 Costly Plunder C .12 .25
97 Dark Nourishment U .10 .20
98 Deadeye Tormentor C .07 .15
99 Deadeye Tracker R .25 .50
100 Deathless Ancient U .10 .20
101 Desperate Castaways C .07 .15
102 Dire Fleet Hoarder C .07 .15
103 Dire Fleet Interloper C .07 .15
104 Dire Fleet Ravager M 2.00 4.00
105 Duress C .07 .15
106 Fathom Fleet Captain R .15 .30
107 Fathom Fleet Cutthroat C .07 .15
108 Grim Captains Call U .10 .20
109 Heartless Pillage U .10 .20
110 Kitesail Freebooter U .20 .40
111 Lurking Chupacabra U .10 .20
112 March of the Drowned C .07 .15
113 Mark of the Vampire C .07 .15
114 Queens Agent C .07 .15
115 Queens Bay Soldier C .07 .15
116 Raiders' Wake U .30 .75
117 Revel in Riches R 7.50 15.00
118 Ruin Raider R .15 .30
119 Ruthless Knave U .17 .35
120 Sanctum Seeker R 2.00 4.00
121 Seekers Squire U .10 .20
122 Skittering Heartstopper C .07 .15
123 Skulduggery C .07 .15
124 Skymarch Bloodletter C .07 .15
125 Spreading Rot C .07 .15
126 Sword Point Diplomacy R .15 .30
127 Vanquish the Weak C .07 .15
128 Vicious Conquistador U .25 .50
129 Vraska's Contempt R 1.00 2.00
130 Walk the Plank U .10 .20
131 Wanted Scoundrels U .10 .20
132 Angrath's Marauders R .30 .75
133 Bonded Horncrest U .10 .20
134 Brazen Buccaneers C .07 .15
135 Burning Suns Avatar R .15 .30
136 Captain Lannery Storm R 2.50 5.00
137 Captivating Crew R .25 .50
138 Charging Monstrosaur U .10 .20
139 Demolish C .07 .15
140 Dinosaur Stampede U .10 .20
141 Dual Shot C .07 .15
142 Fathom Fleet Firebrand C .07 .15
143 Fiery Cannonade U .10 .20
144 Fire Shrine Keeper C .07 .15
145 Firecannon Blast C .07 .15
146 Frenzied Raptor C .07 .15
147 Headstrong Brute C .07 .15
148 Hijack C .07 .15
149 Lightning Strike U .10 .20
150 Lightning-Rig Crew U .10 .20
151 Makeshift Munitions U .10 .20
152 Nest Robber C .07 .15
153 Otepec Huntmaster U .60 1.25
154 Rampaging Ferocidon R 2.50 5.00
155 Raptor Hatchling U .15 .30
156 Repeating Barrage R .15 .30
157 Rigging Runner U .10 .20
158 Rile C .07 .15
159 Rowdy Crew M .30 .75
160 Rummaging Goblin C .07 .15
161 Star of Extinction M 2.50 5.00
162 Storm Fleet Arsonist U .10 .20
163 Storm Fleet Pyromancer C .07 .15
164 Sun-Crowned Hunters C .07 .15
165 Sunbird's Invocation R .50 1.00
166 Sure Strike C .07 .15
167 Swashbuckling C .07 .15
168 Thrash of Raptors C .07 .15
169 Tilonalli's Knight C .07 .15
170 Tilonalli's Skinshifter R .15 .30
171 Trove of Temptation U .10 .20
172 Unfriendly Fire C .07 .15
173 Vance's Blasting Cannons Spitfire Bastion R .30 .60
174 Wily Goblin U .30 .75
175 Ancient Brontodon C .07 .15
176 Atzocan Archer U .10 .20
177 Blinding Fog C .07 .15
178 Blossom Dryad C .07 .15
179 Carnage Tyrant M 7.50 15.00
180 Colossal Dreadmaw C .07 .15
181 Commune with Dinosaurs C .07 .15
182 Crash the Ramparts C .07 .15
183 Crushing Canopy C .07 .15
184 Deathgorge Scavenger R .25 .50
185 Deeproot Champion R .15 .30
186 Deeproot Warrior C .07 .15
187 Drover of the Mighty U .10 .20
188 Emergent Growth U .10 .20
189 Emperors Vanguard R .15 .30
190 Gazing Whiptail C .07 .15
191 Growing Rites of Itlimoc/Cradle of Sun R :G:12.50 25.00
192 Ixalli's Diviner C .07 .15
193 Ixalli's Keeper C .07 .15
194 Jade Guardian C .07 .15
195 Jungle Delver C .07 .15
196 Kumena's Speaker U .10 .20
197 Merfolk Branchwalker U .15 .30
198 New Horizons C .07 .15
199 Old-Growth Dryads R .15 .30
200 Pounce C .15 .30
201 Ranging Raptors U .50 1.00
202 Ravenous Daggertooth C .07 .15
203 Ripjaw Raptor R 1.50 3.00
204 River Heralds' Boon C .07 .15
205 Savage Stomp U .10 .20
206 Shapers' Sanctuary R .75 1.50
207 Slice in Twain U .10 .20
208 Snapping Sailback U .20 .40
209 Spike-Tailed Ceratops C .07 .15
210 Thundering Spineback U .10 .20
211 Tishana's Wayfinder C .07 .15
212 Verdant Rebirth U .10 .20
213 Verdant Sun's Avatar R .15 .30
214 Vineshaper Mystic U .10 .20
215 Waker of the Wilds R .15 .30
216 Wildgrowth Walker U .10 .20
217 Admiral Beckett Brass M 2.50 5.00
218 Belligerent Brontodon U .10 .20
219 Call to the Feast U .15 .30
220 Deadeye Plunderers U .12 .25
221 Dire Fleet Captain U .10 .20
222 Gishath, Sun's Avatar M 12.50 25.00
223 Hostage Taker R 1.50 3.00
224 Huatli, Warrior Poet M 2.50 5.00
225 Marauding Looter U .10 .20
226 Raging Swordtooth U .20 .40
227 Regisaur Alpha R .75 1.50
228 Shapers of Nature U .10 .20
229 Sky Terror U .10 .20
230 Tishana, Voice of Thunder M 3.00 6.00
231 Vona, Butcher of Magan M 4.00 8.00
232 Vraska, Relic Seeker M 2.50 5.00
233 Cobbled Wings C .07 .15
234 Conqueror's Galleon/Conqueror's Foothold R .50 1.00
235 Dowsing Dagger/Lost Vale R 3.00 6.00
236 Dusk Legion Dreadnought U .10 .20
237 Elaborate Firecannon U .10 .20
238 Fell Flagship R .30 .60
239 Gilded Sentinel C .07 .15
240 Hierophant's Chalice C .07 .15
241 Pillar of Origins U .50 1.00
242 Pirate's Cutlass C .07 .15
243 Primal Amulet/Primal Wellspring R 6.00 12.00
244 Prying Blade C .20 .40
245 Sentinel Totem U .10 .20
246 Shadowed Caravel R .15 .30
247 Sleek Schooner U .10 .20
248 Sorcerous Spyglass R .15 .30
249 Thaumatic Compass/Spires of Orazca R 2.50 5.00
250 Treasure Map/Treasure Cove R 5.00 10.00
251 Vanquisher's Banner R 7.50 15.00
252 Dragonskull Summit R 3.00 6.00
253 Drowned Catacomb R 5.00 10.00
254 Field of Ruin U .30 .75
255 Glacial Fortress R 4.00 8.00
256 Rootbound Crag R 3.00 6.00
257 Sunpetal Grove R 3.00 6.00
258 Unclaimed Territory U 1.25 2.50
259 Unknown Shores C .07 .15
260 Plains L .07 .15
261 Plains L .07 .15
262 Plains L .07 .15
263 Plains L .07 .15
264 Island L .07 .15
265 Island L .07 .15
266 Island L .07 .15
267 Island L .07 .15
268 Swamp L .07 .15
269 Swamp L .07 .15
270 Swamp L .07 .15
271 Swamp L .07 .15
272 Mountain L .07 .15
273 Mountain L .07 .15
274 Mountain L .07 .15
275 Mountain L .07 .15
276 Forest L .07 .15
277 Forest L .07 .15
278 Forest L .07 .15
279 Forest L .07 .15
281 Castaway's Despair C .07 .15
282 Grasping Current R .15 .30
283 Jace's Sentinel U .10 .20
284 Woodland Stream C .07 .15
286 Huatli's Snubhorn C .15 .30
287 Huatli's Spurring U .10 .20
288 Sun-Blessed Mount R .20 .40
289 Stone Quarry C .07 .15

2017 Magic The Gathering Ixalan Tokens

1 Vampire .15 .30
2 Illusion .07 .15
3 Merfolk .07 .10
4 Pirate .07 .15
5 Dinosaur .07 .10
6 Plant .07 .10
7 Treasure .07 .10
8 Treasure .07 .10
9 Treasure .07 .10
10 Treasure .07 .10
CH1 Ixalan CL .07 .10

2017 Magic The Gathering Judge Gift Rewards

1 Avacyn, Angel of Hope M 75.00 150.00
2 Capture of Jingzhou R 60.00 120.00
3 Gaddock Teeg R 10.00 20.00
4 Homeward Path R 15.00 30.00
5 Doran, the Siege Tower M 7.50 15.00
6 Prismatic Geoscope R 2.50 5.00
7 Spellskite R 12.50 25.00
8 Pendelhaven R 3.00 6.00
9 Rules Lawyer R 2.50 5.00

2017 Magic The Gathering League Token

1 Gremlin/Energy Reserve C 2.00 4.00

2017 Magic The Gathering Modern Masters 2017

1 Attended Knight C .07 .15
2 Banishing Stroke U .10 .20
3 Blade Splicer R .30 .60
4 Entreat the Angels M 1.25 2.50
5 Eyes in the Skies C .07 .15
6 Flickerwisp U .20 .40
7 Gideon's Lawkeeper C .07 .15
8 Graceful Reprieve C .07 .15
9 Intangible Virtue U .15 .30
10 Kor Hookmaster C .07 .15
11 Kor Skyfisher C .07 .15
12 Lingering Souls U .20 .40
13 Linvala, Keeper of Silence M 12.50 25.00
14 Lone Missionary C .07 .15
15 Master Splicer U .10 .20
16 Momentary Blink C .07 .15
17 Path to Exile U 2.50 5.00
18 Pitfall Trap C .07 .15
19 Ranger of Eos R 1.50 3.00
20 Restoration Angel R .75 1.50
21 Rootborn Defenses C .15 .30
22 Seance R .17 .35
23 Sensor Splicer C .07 .15
24 Soul Warden C .50 1.00
25 Stony Silence R 4.00 8.00
26 Terminus R .15 .30
27 Urbis Protector U .10 .20
28 Wake the Reflections C .07 .15
29 Youthful Knight C .07 .15
30 Augur of Bolas C .20 .40
31 Azure Mage U .10 .20
32 Cackling Counterpart R .30 .75
33 Compulsive Research U .10 .20
34 Crippling Chill C .07 .15
35 Cyclonic Rift R 20.00 40.00
36 Deadeye Navigator R 7.50 15.00
37 Familiar's Ruse U .40 .80
38 Forbidden Alchemy C .07 .15
39 Ghostly Flicker C .30 .75
40 Gifts Ungiven R 1.00 2.00
41 Grasp of Phantoms C .07 .15

42 Kraken Hatchling C .07 .15
43 Mist Raven C .07 .15
44 Mystical Teachings C .07 .15
45 Opportunity U .10 .20
46 Phantasmal Image R 4.00 8.00
47 Rewind C .20 .40
48 Sea Gate Oracle C .07 .15
49 Serum Visions U 2.00 4.00
50 Snapcaster Mage M 50.00 100.00
51 Spell Pierce C .20 .40
52 Spire Monitor C .07 .15
53 Tandem Lookout C .07 .15
54 Temporal Mastery M 7.50 15.00
55 Vendilion Clique, Shaper Savant R 1.25 2.50
56 Wall of Frost U .15 .30
57 Wing Splicer U .10 .20
58 Wingcrafter C .07 .15
59 Abyssal Specter U .10 .20
60 Bone Splinters C .07 .15
61 Corpse Connoisseur U .30 .60
62 Cower in Fear C .07 .15
63 Damnation R 15.00 30.00
64 Death's Shadow R 4.00 8.00
65 Delirium Skeins C .12 .25
66 Desecration Demon R .30 .75
67 Dregscape Zombie C .07 .15
68 Entomber Exarch U .10 .20
69 Extractor Demon R .15 .30
70 Falkenrath Noble C .30 .60
71 Gnawing Zombie C .07 .15
72 Griselbrand M 7.50 15.00
73 Grisly Spectacle C .07 .15
74 Grixis Slavedriver C .07 .15
75 Inquisition of Kozilek U 2.50 5.00
76 Liliana of the Veil M 60.00 120.00
77 Mind Shatter R .15 .30
78 Mortician Beetle C .17 .35
79 Night Terrors C .07 .15
80 Ogre Jailbreaker C .07 .15
81 Pit Keeper C .07 .15
82 Recover U .15 .30
83 Seal of Doom U .10 .20
84 Sever the Bloodline R .15 .30
85 Unburial Rites U .10 .20
86 Vampire Aristocrat C .07 .15
87 Vampire Nighthawk U .25 .50
88 Ancient Grudge U .15 .30
89 Battle-Rattle Shaman C .07 .15
90 Blood Moon R 12.50 25.00
91 Bonfire of the Damned M 1.25 2.50
92 Chandra's Outrage C .07 .15
93 Dragon Fodder C .07 .15
94 Dynacharge C .07 .15
95 Goblin Assault U .40 .80
96 Goblin Guide R 4.00 8.00
97 Hanweir Lancer C .07 .15
98 Hellrider R .25 .50
99 Madcap Skills C .07 .15
100 Magma Jet C .07 .15
101 Mizzium Mortars R .30 .60
102 Mogg Flunkies C .07 .15
103 Molten Rain U .10 .20
104 Mudbutton Torchrunner C .07 .15
105 Past in Flames M 2.00 4.00
106 Pyrewild Shaman U .10 .20
107 Pyroclasm U .10 .20
108 Pyromancer Ascension R .25 .50
109 Rubblebelt Maaka C .07 .15
110 Scorched Rusalka C .07 .15
111 Scourge Devil C .07 .15
112 Skirsdag Cultist U .10 .20
113 Thunderous Wrath C .07 .15
114 Traitorous Instinct C .07 .15
115 Vithian Stinger U .10 .20
116 Zealous Conscripts R 1.25 2.50
117 Arachnus Spinner U .15 .30
118 Archnus Web C .07 .15
119 Avacyn's Pilgrim C .20 .40
120 Baloth Cage Trap U .10 .20
121 Call of the Herd R .15 .30
122 Craterhoof Behemoth M 30.00 60.00
123 Death-Hood Cobra C .07 .15
124 Druid's Deliverance C .07 .15
125 Explore C .07 .15
126 Fists of Ironwood C .07 .15
127 Gaea's Anthem U .25 .50
128 Harmonize U .25 .50
129 Hungry Spriggan C .07 .15
130 Might of Old Krosa U .40 .80
131 Penumbra Spider C .07 .15
132 Primal Command R .75 1.50
133 Revive C .07 .15
134 Scavenging Ooze R .60 1.25
135 Seal of Primordium C .07 .15
136 Slaughterhorn C .07 .15
137 Slime Molding C .07 .15
138 Strength in Numbers C .07 .15
139 Summoning Trap R .20 .40
140 Sylvan Ranger C .15 .30
141 Tarmogoyf M 20.00 40.00
142 Thornscape Battlemage U .10 .20
143 Thragtusk R .25 .50
144 Ulvenwald Tracker R 1.50 3.00
145 Vital Splicer U .10 .20
146 Abrupt Decay R 3.00 6.00
147 Advent of the Wurm R .20 .40
148 Aethermage's Touch R .15 .30
149 Agent of Masks U .17 .35
150 Agony Warp C .07 .15
151 Auger Spree C .07 .15
152 Bronzebeak Moa U .10 .20
153 Broodmate Dragon R .25 .50
154 Call of the Conclave C .07 .15
155 Carnage Gladiator U .10 .20
156 Centaur Healer C .07 .15
157 Coiling Oracle C .07 .15
158 Cruel Ultimatum R .30 .60
159 Deputy of Acquittals C .07 .15
160 Dinrova Horror C .07 .15
161 Domri Rade M 2.00 4.00
162 Evil Twin R .25 .50
163 Falkenrath Aristocrat R .30 .60
164 Fiery Justice R .15 .30
165 Ghor-Clan Rampager U .10 .20
166 Goblin Electromancer C .07 .15
167 Golgari Germination U .30 .75
168 Golgari Rotwurm C .07 .15
169 Ground Assault C .07 .15
170 Gruul War Chant U .10 .20
171 Izzet Charm U .25 .50
172 Kathari Bomber C .07 .15
173 Moroii U .10 .20
174 Mystic Genesis U .10 .20
175 Niv-Mizzet, Dracogenius R .60 1.25
176 Obzedat, Ghost Council R .75 1.50
177 Olivia Voldaren M 6.00 12.00
178 Pilfered Plans C .07 .15
179 Putrefy U .15 .30
180 Rhox War Monk U .10 .20
181 Sedraxis Specter U .10 .20
182 Simic Sky Swallower R .15 .30
183 Sin Collector U .10 .20
184 Skyknight Legionnaire C .07 .15
185 Soul Manipulation U .15 .30
186 Soul Ransom U .10 .20
187 Sphinx's Revelation M 2.50 5.00
188 Spike Jester C .07 .15
189 Sprouting Thrinax U .10 .20
190 Stoic Angel R .30 .75
191 Sunhome Guildmage U .10 .20
192 Talon Trooper C .07 .15
193 Teleportal U .15 .30
194 Terminate U .50 1.00
195 Thundersong Trumpeter U .10 .20
196 Tower Gargoyle U .10 .20
197 Unflinching Courage U .10 .20
198 Urban Evolution U .10 .20
199 Vanish into Memory U .10 .20
200 Voice of Resurgence M 2.50 5.00
201 Wall of Denial U 1.25 2.50
202 Wayfaring Temple U .15 .30
203 Woolly Thoctar U .10 .20
204 Zur the Enchanter R 2.00 4.00
205 Aethertow U .10 .20
206 Boros Reckoner R .30 .75
207 Burning-Tree Emissary C .20 .40
208 Giantbaiting C .07 .15
209 Gift of Orzhova C .07 .15
210 Mistmeadow Witch U .10 .20
211 Sundering Growth C .07 .15
212 Tattermunge Witch U .10 .20
213 Torrent of Souls U .10 .20
214 Wort, the Raidmother R .20 .40
215 Azorius Signet U .60 1.25
216 Basilisk Collar R 2.50 5.00
217 Boros Signet U .30 .60
218 Damping Matrix R .25 .50
219 Dimir Signet U 2.00 4.00
220 Golgari Signet U .10 .20
221 Grafdigger's Cage R 1.50 3.00
222 Gruul Signet U .30 .60
223 Izzet Signet U .50 1.00
224 Orzhov Signet U .30 .75
225 Rakdos Signet U .75 1.50
226 Selesnya Signet U .75 1.50
227 Simic Signet U .25 .50
228 Arcane Sanctum U 1.00 2.00
229 Arid Mesa R 12.50 25.00
230 Azorius Guildgate C .07 .15
231 Boros Guildgate C .07 .15
232 Cavern of Souls M 60.00 120.00
233 Crumbling Necropolis U .20 .40
234 Dimir Guildgate C .07 .15
235 Golgari Guildgate C .07 .15
236 Gruul Guildgate C .15 .30
237 Izzet Guildgate C .07 .15
238 Jungle Shrine U .20 .40
239 Marsh Flats R 15.00 30.00
240 Misty Rainforest R 20.00 40.00
241 Orzhov Guildgate C .07 .15
242 Rakdos Guildgate C .07 .15
243 Savage Lands U 1.00 2.00
244 Scalding Tarn R 25.00 50.00
245 Seaside Citadel U 1.00 2.00
246 Selesnya Guildgate C .07 .15
247 Shimmering Grotto C .07 .15
248 Simic Guildgate C .07 .15
249 Verdant Catacombs R 25.00 50.00

2017 Magic The Gathering Modern Masters 2017 Tokens

1 Angel .17 .35
2 Bird .07 .15
3 Soldier .15 .30
4 Spirit .07 .15
5 Spider .10 .20
6 Zombie .07 .15
7 Dragon .12 .25
8 Goblin .12 .25
9 Beast .12 .25
10 Beast .15 .30
11 Centaur .07 .15
12 Elephant .10 .20
13 Ooze .07 .15
14 Saproling .07 .15
15 Wurm .25 .50
16 Elemental .17 .35
17 Giant Warrior .07 .15
18 Goblin Warrior .07 .15
19 Soldier .07 .15
20 Golem .07 .15
21 Domri Rade Emblem .30 .75

2017 Magic The Gathering Unstable

1 Adorable Kitten C .07 .15
2 Aerial Toastmaster U .10 .20
3 Amateur Auteur U :W:/Innistrad .10 .20
3 Amateur Auteur U :W:/Theros .10 .20
3 Amateur Auteur U :W:/Zendikar .10 .20
3 Amateur Auteur U :W:/Ravnica .10 .20
4 By Gnome Means R .15 .30
5 Chivalrous Chevalier C .07 .15
6 Do-It-Yourself Seraph M .60 1.25
7 Gimme Five U .10 .20
8 GO TO JAIL C .07 .15
9 Half-Kitten, Half- U .10 .20
10 Humming- C .07 .15
11 Jackknight R .15 .30
12 Knight of Kitch.Sink U :W:/Two-Word Names .10 .20
12 Knight of Kitch.Sink U :W:/Odd Numbers .10 .20
12 Knight of Kitch.Sink U :W:/Loose Lips .10 .20
12 Knight of Kitch.Sink U :W:/Even Numbers .10 .20
12 Knight of Kitch.Sink U :W:/Black Borders .10 .20
12 Knight of Kitch.Sink U :W:/Watermarks .10 .20
13 Knight of the Widget U .10 .20
14 Midlife Upgrade U .10 .20
15 Oddly Uneven R .15 .30
16 Old Guard C .07 .15
17 Ordinary Pony C .07 .15
18 Rhino- U .10 .20
19 Riveting Rigger C .07 .15
20 Rules Lawyer R .15 .30
21 Sacrifice Play C .07 .15
22 Shaggy Camel C .07 .15
23 Side Quest U .10 .20
24 Success! C .07 .15
25 Teacher's Pet U .10 .20
26 Animate Library R .15 .30
27 Blurry Beeble C .07 .15
28 Chipper Chopper C .07 .15
29 Clocknapper R .15 .30
30 Crafty Octopus C .07 .15
31 Crow Storm U .10 .20
32 Defective Detective C .07 .15
33 Five-Finger Discount R .15 .30
34 Graveyard Busybody R .15 .30
35 Half-Shark, Half U .10 .20
36 Incite Insight R .15 .30
37 Kindly Cognician U .10 .20
38 Magic Word C .07 .15
39 Mer Man C .07 .15
40 More or Less U .10 .20
41 Novellamental C :B:/Heart .07 .15
41 Novellamental C :B:/Chain .07 .15
41 Novellamental C :B:/Pendant .07 .15
41 Novellamental C :B:/Grandmother .07 .15
42 Numbing Jellyfish C .07 .15
43 S.N.E.A.K. Dispatcher U .10 .20
44 Socketed Sprocketer U .10 .20
45 Spell Suck C .07 .15
46 Spye Eye U .10 .20
47 Suspicious Nanny U .10 .20
48 Time Out C .07 .15
49 Very Crypt.Command R :B:/Scry 3 .15 .30
49 Very Crypt.Command R :B:
Counter Black Border .15 .30
49 Very Crypt.Command R :B:/Return Target .15 .30
49 Very Crypt.Command R :B:/Draw Card .15 .30
49 Very Crypt.Command R :B:/Untap Two Target .15 .30
49 Very Crypt.Command R :B: ALT ART .15 .30
50 Wall of Fortune C .07 .15
51 Big Boa Constrictor C .07 .15
52 capital offense C .07 .15
53 Dirty Rat C .07 .15
54 Extremely Slow Zombie C :K:/Spring .07 .15
54 Extremely Slow Zombie C :K:/Summer .07 .15
54 Extremely Slow Zombie C :K:/Winter .07 .15
54 Extremely Slow Zombie C :K:/Fall .07 .15
55 Finders, Keepers C .07 .15
56 Hangman R .15 .30
57 Hazmat Suit (Used) C .07 .15
58 Hoisted Hireling C .07 .15
59 Inhumaniac U .10 .20
60 Masterful Ninja R .15 .30
61 Ninja U .10 .20
62 Old-Fashioned Vampire U .10 .20
63 Over My Daed Bodies R .15 .30
64 Overt Operative U .10 .20
65 Rumors of My Death... U .10 .20
66 Skull Saucer U .10 .20
67 Sly Spy U :K:/Subpar... .10 .20
67 Sly Spy U :K:/Spies... .10 .20
67 Sly Spy U :K:/Skilled... .10 .20
67 Sly Spy U :K:/Serious... .10 .20
67 Sly Spy U :K:/Sinister... .10 .20
67 Sly Spy U :K:/Silent... .10 .20
68 Snickering Squirrel C .07 .15
69 Spike, Tournament Grinder R .15 .30
70 Squirrel-Powered Scheme U .10 .20
71 Steady-Handed Mook C .07 .15
72 Stinging Scorpion C .07 .15
73 Subcontract C .07 .15
74 Summon the Pack M .60 1.25
75 Zombified U .10 .20
76 The Big Idea R .15 .30
77 Box of Free-Range Goblins C .07 .15
78 Bumbling Pangolin C .07 .15
79 Common Iguana C .07 .15
80 The Countdown Is at One R .15 .30
81 Feisty Stegosaurus C .07 .15
82 Garbage Elemental U :R:/Last Strike .10 .20
82 Garbage Elemental U :R:/Unleash .10 .20
82 Garbage Elemental U :R:/Cascade .10 .20
82 Garbage Elemental U :R:/Battle Cry .10 .20
82 Garbage Elemental U :R:/Undying .10 .20
82 Garbage Elemental U :R:/Frenzy 2 .10 .20
83 Goblin Haberdasher U .10 .20
84 Half-Orc, Half- U .10 .20
85 Hammer Helper C .07 .15
86 Hammer Jammer U .10 .20
87 Hammerfest Boomtacular U .10 .20
88 Infinity Elemental M .60 1.25
89 It That Gets Left Hanging C .07 .15
90 Just Desserts C .07 .15
91 Painiac C .07 .15
92 Party Crasher U .10 .20
93 Steamflogger Boss R .15 .30
94 Steamflogger of the Month R .15 .30
95 Steamflogger Temp U .10 .20
96 Steamfloggery U .10 .20
97 Super-Duper Death Ray U .10 .20
98 Target Minotaur C :R:/Vines .07 .15
98 Target Minotaur C :R:/Fireballs .07 .15
98 Target Minotaur C :R:/Blood Rain .07 .15
98 Target Minotaur C :R:/Frozen .07 .15
99 Three-Headed Goblin R .15 .30
100 Work a Double C .07 .15
101 Wrench-Rigger C .07 .15
102 As Luck Would Have It R .15 .30
103 Beast in Show C :G:/Ox .07 .15
103 Beast in Show C :G:/Dragon .07 .15
103 Beast in Show C :G:/Goat .07 .15
103 Beast in Show C :G:/Dinosaur .07 .15
104 Chittering Doom U .10 .20
105 Clever Combo U .10 .20
106 Druid of the Sacred Beaker U .10 .20
107 Eager Beaver C .07 .15
108 Earl of the Squirrel R .15 .30
109 First Pick U .10 .20
110 Ground Pounder C .07 .15
111 Half-Squirrel, Half- U .10 .20
112 Hydradoodle R .15 .30
113 Ineffable Blessing R :G:/Number .15 .30
113 Ineffable Blessing R :G:/Odd or Even .15 .30
113 Ineffable Blessing R :G:/Rarity .15 .30
113 Ineffable Blessing R :G:/White or Silver Border .15 .30
113 Ineffable Blessing R :G:/Artist .15 .30
113 Ineffable Blessing R :G:/Flavorful or Bland .15 .30
114 Joyride Rigger C .07 .15
115 Monkey- U .10 .20
116 Mother Kangaroo C .07 .15
117 Multi-Headed C .07 .15
118 Really Epic Punch C .07 .15
119 Selfie Preservation C .07 .15
120 Serpentine R .15 .30
121 Shellephant U .10 .20
122 Slaying Mantis U .10 .20
123 Squirrel Dealer C .07 .15
124 Steamflogger Service Rep U .10 .20
125 Wild Crocodile C .07 .15
126 Willing Test Subject C .07 .15
127 Baron Von Count M .60 1.25
128 Better Than One R .15 .30
129 Cramped Bunker R .15 .30
130 Dr. Julius Jumblemorph M .60 1.25
131 The Grand Calcutron M .60 1.25
132 Grusilda, Monster Masher R .15 .30
133 Hot Fix R .15 .30
134 Ol' Buzzbark M .60 1.25
135 Phoebe, Head of S.N.E.A.K. M 1.25 2.50
136 Urza, Academy Headmaster M 4.00 8.00
137 X R .15 .30
138 Mary O'Kill R .15 .30
139 Angelic Rocket R .15 .30
140 Border Guardian U .10 .20
141 Buzzing Whack-a-Doodle U .10 .20
142 Clock of DOOOOOOOOOOOOM! U .10 .20
143 Cogmentor U .10 .20
144 Contraption Cannon U .10 .20
145 Curious Killbot C .07 .15
145 Enraged Killbot C .07 .15
145 Despondent Killbot C .07 .15
145 Delighted Killbot C .07 .15
146 Entirely Normal Armchair U .10 .20
147 Everythingamajig R/Scry 2 .15 .30
147 Everythingamajig R/Sacrifice Land .15 .30
147 Everythingamajig R/Add One Mana .15 .30
147 Everythingamajig R/Flip Coin .15 .30
147 Everythingamajig R/Draw Card .15 .30
147 Everythingamajig R/Move Counter .15 .30
148 Gnome-Made Engine C .07 .15
149 Handy Dandy Clone Machine R .15 .30
150 Kindslaver R .15 .30
151 Krark's Other Thumb U .10 .20
152 Labro Bot U .10 .20
153 Lobe Lobber U .10 .20
154 Mad Science Fair Project C .07 .15
155 Modular Monstrosity R .15 .30
156 Proper Laboratory Attire U .10 .20
157 Robo- U .10 .20
158 Split Screen R .15 .30
159 Staff of the Letter Magus U .10 .20
160 Stamp of Approval U .10 .20
161 Steam-Powered U .10 .20
162 Steel Squirrel U .10 .20
163 Sword of Dungeons & Dragons M 2.50 5.00
164 Voracious Vacuum C .07 .15
165 Secret Base C/Agents of SNEAK .07 .15
165 Secret Base C/League of Dastardly Doom .07 .15
165 Secret Base C/Goblin Explosioneers .07 .15
165 Secret Base C/Crossbreed Labs .07 .15
165 Secret Base C/Order of Widget .07 .15
166 Watermarket R .15 .30
167 Accessories to Murder U .10 .20
168 Applied Aeronautics C .07 .15
169 Arms Depot U .10 .20
170 Auto-Key C .07 .15
171 Bee-Bee Gun M .60 1.25
172 Boomflinger C .07 .15
173 Buzz Buggy C .07 .15
174 Deadly Poison Sampler R .15 .30
175 Dictation Quillograph C .07 .15
176 Dispatch Dispensary U .10 .20
177 Division Table C .07 .15
178 Dogsnail Engine U .10 .20
179 Dual Doomsuits R .15 .30
180 Duplication Device R .15 .30
181 Faerie Aerie M .60 1.25
182 Genetic Recombinator U .10 .20
183 Gift Horse R .15 .30
184 Gnomeball Machine U .10 .20
185 Goblin Slingshot R .15 .30
186 Guest List R .15 .30
187 Hard Hat Area M .60 1.25
188 Head Banger C .07 .15
189 Hypnotic Swirly Disc R .15 .30
190 Inflation Station C .07 .15
191 Insufferable Syphon U .10 .20
192 Jamming Device U .10 .20
193 Lackey Recycler C .07 .15
194 Mandatory Friendship Shackles C .07 .15
195 Neural Network U .10 .20
196 Oaken Power Suit R .15 .30
197 Optical Optimizer U .10 .20
198 Pet Project M .60 1.25
199 Quick-Stick Lick Trick C .07 .15
200 Rapid Prototyper M .60 1.25
201 Record Store R .15 .30
202 Refibrillator R .15 .30
203 Sap Sucker C .07 .15
204 Sundering Fork U .10 .20

205 Targeting Rocket U .10 .20
206 Thud-for-Duds U .10 .20
207 Top-Secret Tunnel C .07 .15
208 Tread Mill C .07 .15
209 Turbo-Thwacking Auto-Hammer U .10 .20
210 Twiddlestick Charger C .07 .15
211 Widget Contraption U .10 .20
212 Plains L .07 .15
213 Island L .07 .15
214 Swamp L .07 .15
215 Mountain L .07 .15
216 Forest L .07 .15

2017 Magic The Gathering Unstable Tokens

1 Angel/Angel .75 1.50
2 Goat .15 .30
3 Spirit/Spirit .50 1.00
4 Faerie Spy .07 .15
5 Storm Crow .10 .20
6 Thopter/Thopter .50 1.00
7 Rogue .07 .15
8 Vampire/Vampire .50 1.00
9 Zombie/Zombie .30 .75
10 Brainiac .07 .15
11 Elemental/Elemental .50 1.00
12 Goblin .50 1.00
13 Beast/Beast .12 .25
14 Saproling/Saproling .25 .50
15 Squirrel .30 .75
16 Dragon .17 .35
17 Elemental/Elemental .15 .30
18 Clue/Clue .25 .50
19 Construct .15 .30
20 Gnome .07 .15

2017 Magic The Gathering Welcome Deck 2017

1 Divine Verdict C .07 .15
2 Glory Seeker C .07 .15
3 Serra Angel U .10 .20
4 Standing Troops C .07 .15
5 Stormfront Pegasus U .15 .30
6 Victory's Herald R .12 .25
7 Air Elemental U .07 .15
8 Coral Merfolk C .07 .15
9 Drag Under C .20 .40
10 Inspiration C .10 .20
11 Sleep Paralysis C .07 .15
12 Sphinx of Magosi R .12 .25
13 Stealer of Secrets C .07 .15
14 Tricks of the Trade C .07 .15
15 Bloodhunter Bat C .12 .25
16 Certain Death C .07 .15
17 Nightmare R .07 .15
18 Raise Dead C .07 .15
19 Sengir Vampire U .10 .20
20 Untamed Hunger C .07 .15
21 Falkenrath Reaver C .07 .15
22 Shivan Dragon R .07 .15
23 Thundering Giant C .07 .15
24 Garruk's Horde R .12 .25
25 Oakenform C .07 .15
26 Rabid Bite C .07 .15
27 Rootwalla C .07 .15
28 Stalking Tiger C .07 .15
29 Stampeding Rhino C .07 .15
30 Wing Snare U .07 .15

2018 Magic The Gathering Battlebond

1 Will Kenrith M 4.00 8.00
2 Rowan Kenrith M 2.00 4.00
3 Regna, the Redeemer R 1.00 2.00
4 Krav, the Unredeemed R 3.00 6.00
5 Zndrsplt, Eye of Wisdom R .50 1.00
6 Okaun, Eye of Chaos R .50 1.00
7 Virtus the Veiled R .75 1.50
8 Gorm the Great R .30 .60
9 Khorvath Brightflame R .30 .75
10 Sylvia Brightspear R 1.25 2.50
11 Pir, Imaginative Rascal R .15 .30
12 Toothy, Imaginary Friend R 7.50 15.00
13 Blaring Recruiter U .10 .20
14 Blaring Captain U .10 .20
15 Chakram Retriever U .30 .60
16 Chakram Slinger U .10 .20
17 Soulblade Corrupter U .10 .20
18 Soulblade Renewer U .10 .20
19 Impetuous Protege U .10 .20
20 Proud Mentor U .10 .20
21 Ley Weaver U .30 .60
22 Lore Weaver U .10 .20
23 Arena Rector M 7.50 15.00
24 Aurora Champion C .07 .15
25 Brightling M .75 1.50
26 Bring Down U .10 .20
27 Dwarven Lightsmith C .07 .15
28 Jubilant Mascot U .10 .20
29 Play of the Game R .20 .40
30 Regna's Sanction R .20 .40
31 Skystreamer C .07 .15
32 Together Forever R .15 .30
33 Arcane Artisan M .75 1.50
34 Fumble U .17 .35
35 Game Plan R .75 1.50
36 Huddle Up C .07 .15
37 Nimbus Champion U .10 .20
38 Out of Bounds U .10 .20
39 Saltwater Stalwart C .07 .15
40 Soaring Show-Off C .07 .15
41 Spellseeker R 20.00 40.00
42 Spellweaver Duo C .07 .15
43 Zndrsplt's Judgment R .30 .60
44 Archfiend of Despair M 20.00 40.00
45 Bloodborn Scoundrels C .07 .15
46 Fan Favorite C .07 .15
47 Gang Up U .07 .15
48 Inner Demon U .15 .30
49 Mindblade Render R .15 .30
50 Sickle Dancer C .07 .15
51 Stunning Reversal M 1.25 2.50
52 Thrasher Brute U .10 .20
53 Thrilling Encore R 4.00 8.00
54 Virtus's Maneuver R .50 1.00
55 Azra Bladeseeker C .07 .15
56 Bonus Round R 4.00 8.00
57 Bull-Rush Bruiser C .07 .15
58 Cheering Fanatic U .10 .20
59 Khorvath's Fury R 2.00 4.00
60 Lava-Field Overlord U .10 .20
61 Magma Hellion C .07 .15
62 Najeela, the Blade-Blossom M 5.00 10.00
63 Stadium Vendors C .07 .15
64 Stolen Strategy R 12.50 25.00
65 Bramble Sovereign M 12.50 25.00
66 Charging Binox C .07 .15
67 Combo Attack C .07 .15
68 The Crowd Goes Wild U .10 .20
69 Decorated Champion U .20 .40
70 Generous Patron R 2.00 4.00
71 Grothama, All-Devouring M 3.00 6.00
72 Jungle Wayfinder C .07 .15
73 Pir's Whim R 2.00 4.00
74 Archon of Valor's Reach R .25 .50
75 Azra Oddsmaker U 1.00 2.00
76 Last One Standing R 2.50 5.00
77 Rushblade Commander U .15 .30
78 Vampire Charmseeker U .10 .20
79 Sentinel Tower R 1.25 2.50
80 Victory Chimes R .15 .30
81 Bountiful Promenade R 10.00 20.00
82 Luxury Suite R 20.00 40.00
83 Morphic Pool R 15.00 30.00
84 Sea of Clouds R 10.00 20.00
85 Spire Garden R 10.00 20.00
86 Angel of Retribution U .10 .20
87 Angelic Chorus R 1.25 2.50
88 Angelic Gift C .12 .25
89 Battle Mastery U .17 .35
90 Champion of Arashin C .07 .15
91 Doomed Traveler C .07 .15
92 Expedition Raptor C .07 .15
93 Kor Spiritdancer R 2.00 4.00
94 Land Tax M 20.00 40.00
95 Lightwalker C .07 .15
96 Long Road Home U .10 .20
97 Loyal Pegasus U .10 .20
98 Mangara of Corondor R .25 .50
99 Midnight Guard C .07 .15
100 Oreskos Explorer U .15 .30
101 Pacifism C .07 .15
102 Raptor Companion C .07 .15
103 Rebuke C .07 .15
104 Royal Trooper C .07 .15
105 Shoulder to Shoulder C .07 .15
106 Silverchase Fox C .07 .15
107 Solemn Offering U .10 .20
108 Sparring Mummy C .07 .15
109 Steppe Glider U .10 .20
110 Swords to Plowshares U 1.50 3.00
111 Take Up Arms U .10 .20
112 Tandem Tactics C .07 .15
113 Benthic Giant C .07 .15
114 Call to Heel C .07 .15
115 Claustrophobia C .07 .15
116 Coralhelm Guide C .07 .15
117 Fog Bank U .25 .50
118 Frost Lynx C .07 .15
119 Impulse C .30 .60
120 Kitesail Corsair C .07 .15
121 Kraken Hatchling C .07 .15
122 Mystic Confluence R 2.00 4.00
123 Negate C .07 .15
124 Nimbus of the Isles C .07 .15
125 Omenspeaker C .07 .15
126 Opportunity U .10 .20
127 Oracle's Insight U .10 .20
128 Peregrine Drake U 1.50 3.00
129 Phantom Warrior U .10 .20
130 Reckless Scholar U .10 .20
131 Sower of Temptation R 2.00 4.00
132 Spell Snare U .30 .75
133 Switcheroo U .10 .20
134 Tidespout Tyrant R 3.00 6.00
135 Totally Lost C .07 .15
136 True-Name Nemesis M 3.00 6.00
137 Watercourser C .07 .15
138 Assassin's Strike U .10 .20
139 Assassinate C .07 .15
140 Daggerdrome Imp C .07 .15
141 Diabolic Intent R 20.00 40.00
142 Doomed Dissenter C .07 .15
143 Eyeblight Assassin C .07 .15
144 Fill with Fright C .07 .15
145 Grotesque Mutation C .07 .15
146 Hand of Silumgar C .07 .15
147 Last Gasp C .07 .15
148 Liturgy of Blood C .07 .15
149 Morbid Curiosity U .10 .20
150 Nirkana Revenant M 10.00 20.00
151 Noosegraf Mob R .25 .50
152 Noxious Dragon U .10 .20
153 Nyxathid R .20 .40
154 Painful Lesson C .07 .15
155 Prakhata Club Security C .07 .15
156 Quest for the Gravelord U .10 .20
157 Rotfeaster Maggot C .07 .15
158 Screeching Buzzard C .07 .15
159 Shambling Ghoul C .07 .15
160 Slum Reaper U .10 .20
161 Swarm of Bloodflies U .10 .20
162 Tavern Swindler U .10 .20
163 Tenacious Dead U .10 .20
164 Bathe in Dragonfire C .07 .15
165 Battle Rampart C .07 .15
166 Battle-Rattle Shaman U .10 .20
167 Blaze U .10 .20
168 Blood Feud U .10 .20
169 Boldwyr Intimidator U .10 .20
170 Borderland Marauder C .07 .15
171 Chain Lightning U 1.00 2.00
172 Dragon Breath U .12 .25
173 Dragon Hatchling C .07 .15
174 Earth Elemental C .07 .15
175 Ember Beast C .07 .15
176 Enthralling Victor U .10 .20
177 Expedite C .07 .15
178 Flamewave Invoker U .10 .20
179 Goblin Razerunners R .15 .30
180 Lightning Talons C .07 .15
181 Magmatic Force R .30 .60
182 Pathmaker Initiate C .07 .15
183 Reckless Reveler C .07 .15
184 Shock C .07 .15
185 Thunder Strike C .07 .15
186 Trumpet Blast U .10 .20
187 War's Toll R 2.50 5.00
188 Wrap in Flames C .07 .15
189 Aim High U .10 .20
190 Beast Within U .75 1.50
191 Canopy Spider C .07 .15
192 Charging Rhino C .07 .15
193 Cowl Prowler C .07 .15
194 Daggerback Basilisk C .07 .15
195 Doubling Season M 50.00 100.00
196 Elvish Visionary C .07 .15
197 Feral Hydra U .30 .60
198 Fertile Ground C .17 .35
199 Fertilid U .17 .35
200 Giant Growth C .07 .15
201 Greater Good R 2.50 5.00
202 Hunted Wumpus U .10 .20
203 Karametra's Favor U .10 .20
204 Kraul Warrior C .07 .15
205 Lead by Example C .07 .15
206 Magus of the Candelabra R .60 1.25
207 Plated Crusher U .10 .20
208 Primal Huntbeast C .07 .15
209 Pulse of Murasa U .10 .20
210 Return to the Earth C .07 .15
211 Saddleback Lagac C .07 .15
212 Seedborn Muse R 7.50 15.00
213 Skyshroud Claim C 2.00 4.00
214 Veteran Explorer U .15 .30
215 Vigor R 7.50 15.00
216 Wandering Wolf C .07 .15
217 Apocalypse Hydra R .25 .50
218 Auger Spree C .07 .15
219 Centaur Healer C .07 .15
220 Dinrova Horror U .10 .20
221 Enduring Scalelord U .10 .20
222 Evil Twin R .30 .60
223 Gwafa Hazid, Profiteer R .25 .50
224 Jelenn Sphinx U .10 .20
225 Kiss of the Amesha U .10 .20
226 Relentless Hunter U .10 .20
227 Rhox Brute C .07 .15
228 Riptide Crab C .07 .15
229 Savage Ventmaw U .30 .75
230 Unflinching Courage U .10 .20
231 Urborg Drake C .07 .15
232 Consulate Skygate C .07 .15
233 Culling Dais U .10 .20
234 Eager Construct C .07 .15
235 Genesis Chamber U .60 1.25
236 Gold-Forged Sentinel U .10 .20
237 Hexplate Golem C .07 .15
238 Juggernaut U .10 .20
239 Millennial Gargoyle C .07 .15
240 Mind's Eye R 7.50 15.00
241 Mycosynth Lattice M 25.00 50.00
242 Night Market Guard C .07 .15
243 Peace Strider C .07 .15
244 Pierce Strider C .07 .15
245 Seer's Lantern C .07 .15
246 Spectral Searchlight U .10 .20
247 Stone Golem C .07 .15
248 Tyrant's Machine C .07 .15
249 Yotian Soldier C .07 .15
250 Plains L .12 .25
251 Island L .25 .50
252 Swamp L .20 .40
253 Mountain L .25 .50
254 Forest L .30 .75

2018 Magic The Gathering Battlebond Tokens

1 Spirit .07 .15
2 Warrior .12 .25
3 Zombie .07 .15
4 Zombie Giant .07 .15
5 Beast .07 .15
6 Myr .07 .15
7 Will Kenrith Emblem .07 .15
8 Rowan Kenrith Emblem .10 .20

2018 Magic The Gathering Commander 2018

1 Boreas Charger R .15 .30
2 Empyrial Storm R .15 .30
3 Heavenly Blademaster R .15 .30
4 Loyal Unicorn U .10 .20
5 Magus of the Balance R .15 .30
6 Aminatou's Augury R .15 .30
7 Echo Storm R .15 .30
8 Estrid's Invocation R .15 .30
9 Ever-Watching Threshold R .15 .30
10 Loyal Drake U .10 .20
11 Octopus Umbra R .15 .30
12 Primordial Mist R .15 .30
13 Vedalken Humiliator R .15 .30
14 Bloodtracker R .15 .30
15 Entreat the Dead R .15 .30
16 Loyal Subordinate U .10 .20
17 Night Incarnate R .15 .30
18 Skull Storm R .15 .30
19 Sower of Discord R .15 .30
20 Emissary of Grudges R .15 .30
21 Enchanter's Bane R .15 .30
22 Fury Storm R .15 .30
23 Loyal Apprentice U .10 .20
24 Nesting Dragon R .15 .30
25 Reality Scramble R .15 .30
26 Saheeli's Directive R .15 .30
27 Treasure Nabber R .15 .30
28 Varchild, Betrayer of Kjeldor R .15 .30
29 Crash of Rhino Beetles R .15 .30
30 Genesis Storm R .15 .30
31 Loyal Guardian U .10 .20
32 Myth Unbound R .15 .30
33 Nylea's Colossus R .15 .30
34 Ravenous Slime R .15 .30
35 Turntimber Sower R .15 .30
36 Whiptongue Hydra R .15 .30
37 Aminatou, the Fateshifter M 5.00 10.00
38 Arixmethes, Slumbering Isle R .15 .30
39 Brudiclad, Telchor Engineer M 1.50 3.00
40 Estrid, the Masked M 3.00 6.00
41 Gyrus, Waker of Corpses M 1.25 2.50
42 Kestia, the Cultivator M 1.50 3.00
43 Lord Windgrace M 4.00 8.00
44 Saheeli, the Gifted M 4.00 7.50
45 Tawnos, Urza's Apprentice M 1.50 3.00
46 Thantis, the Warweaver M .75 1.50
47 Tuvasa the Sunlit M 2.50 5.00
48 Varina, Lich Queen M 1.50 3.00
49 Windgrace's Judgment R .15 .30
50 Xantcha, Sleeper Agent R .15 .30
51 Yennett, Cryptic Sovereign M 1.50 3.00
52 Yuriko, the Tiger's Shadow R .15 .30
53 Ancient Stone Idol R .15 .30
54 Coveted Jewel R .15 .30
55 Endless Atlas R .15 .30
56 Geode Golem U .10 .20
57 Retrofitter Foundry R .15 .30
58 Forge of Heroes C .10 .20
59 Isolated Watchtower R .15 .30
60 Adarkar Valkyrie R .15 .30
61 Ajani's Chosen R .15 .30
62 Akroma's Vengeance R .15 .30
63 Banishing Stroke U .10 .20
64 Celestial Archon R .15 .30
65 Crib Swap U .10 .20
66 Dismantling Blow C .07 .15
67 Entreat the Angels M 1.25 2.50
68 Lightform U .10 .20
69 Martial Coup R .15 .30
70 Phyrexian Rebirth R .15 .30
71 Return to Dust U .10 .20
72 Sage's Reverie U .10 .20
73 Serra Avatar M .12 .25
74 Sigil of the Empty Throne R .15 .30
75 Silent Sentinel R .15 .30
76 Soul Snare U .10 .20
77 Terminus R .15 .30
78 Unquestioned Authority U .10 .20
79 Winds of Rath R .15 .30
80 Aether Gale R .15 .30
81 Archetype of Imagination U .10 .20
82 Brainstorm U .10 .20
83 Cloudform U .10 .20
84 Conundrum Sphinx R .15 .30
85 Devastation Tide R .15 .30
86 Dictate of Kruphix R .15 .30
87 Djinn of Wishes R .15 .30
88 Dream Cache C .07 .15
89 Eel Umbra C .07 .15
90 Etherium Sculptor C .07 .15
91 Inkwell Leviathan R .15 .30
92 Into the Roil C .07 .15
93 Jeskai Infiltrator R .15 .30
94 Mulldrifter U .10 .20
95 Ninja of the Deep Hours C .07 .15
96 Ponder C .07 .15
97 Portent C .07 .15
98 Predict U .10 .20
99 Reverse Engineer U .10 .20
100 Saheeli's Artistry R .15 .30
101 Sharding Sphinx R .15 .30
102 Sigiled Starfish U .10 .20
103 Sphinx of Jwar Isle R .15 .30
104 Sphinx of Uthuun R .15 .30
105 Telling Time C .07 .15
106 Thirst for Knowledge U .10 .20
107 Thopter Spy Network R .15 .30
108 Tidings U .10 .20
109 Treasure Hunt C .07 .15
110 Vow of Flight U .10 .20
111 Whirler Rogue U .10 .20
112 Whitewater Naiads U .10 .20
113 Army of the Damned M .12 .25
114 Moonlight Bargain R .15 .30
115 Phyrexian Delver R .15 .30
116 Retreat to Hagra U .10 .20
117 Ruinous Path R .15 .30
118 Soul of Innistrad M .12 .25
119 Stitch Together U .10 .20
120 Blasphemous Act R .15 .30
121 Chain Reaction R .15 .30
122 Chaos Warp R .15 .30
123 Flameblast Dragon R .15 .30
124 Hellkite Igniter R .15 .30
125 Magmaquake R .15 .30
126 Thopter Engineer U .10 .20
127 Acidic Slime U .10 .20
128 Aura Gnarlid C .07 .15
129 Avenger of Zendikar M 2.00 3.50
130 Baloth Woodcrasher U .10 .20
131 Bear Umbra R .15 .30
132 Boon Satyr R .15 .30
133 Borderland Explorer C .07 .15
134 Budoka Gardener/Dokai, Weaver of Life R .15 .30
135 Centaur Vinecrasher R .15 .30
136 Consign to Dust U .10 .20
137 Creeping Renaissance R .15 .30
138 Cultivate C .07 .15
139 Dawn's Reflection C .07 .15
140 Eidolon of Blossoms R .15 .30
141 Enchantress's Presence R .15 .30
142 Epic Proportions R .15 .30
143 Explore C .07 .15
144 Explosive Vegetation U .10 .20
145 Far Wanderings C .07 .15
146 Farhaven Elf C .07 .15
147 Fertile Ground C .07 .15
148 Grapple with the Past C .07 .15
149 Ground Seal R .15 .30
150 Harrow C .07 .15
151 Herald of the Pantheon R .15 .30
152 Hunting Wilds U .10 .20
153 Hydra Omnivore M .60 1.25
154 Khalni Heart Expedition C .07 .15
155 Kruphix's Insight C .07 .15

156 Moldgraf Monstrosity R	.15	[illegible]
157 Overgrowth C	.07	.15
158 Rampaging Baloths R	.15	.30
159 Reclamation Sage U	.10	.20
160 Sakura-Tribe Elder C	.07	.15
161 Scute Mob R	.15	.30
162 Snake Umbra C	.07	.15
163 Spawning Grounds R	.15	.30
164 Vow of Wildness U	.10	.20
165 Wild Growth C	.07	.15
166 Yavimaya Elder C	.07	.15
167 Yavimaya Enchantress C	.07	.15
168 Aethermage's Touch R	.15	.30
169 Bant Charm U	.10	.20
170 Bruna, Light of Alabaster M	.12	.25
171 Charnelhoard Wurm R	.15	.30
172 Cold-Eyed Selkie R	.15	.30
173 Daxos of Meletis R	.15	.30
174 Deathreap Ritual U	.10	.20
175 Decimate R	.15	.30
176 Duskmantle Seer R	.15	.30
177 Elderwood Scion R	.15	.30
178 Enigma Sphinx R	.15	.30
179 Esper Charm U	.10	.20
180 Finest Hour R	.15	.30
181 Gaze of Granite R	.15	.30
182 Grisly Salvage C	.07	.15
183 High Priest of Penance R	.15	.30
184 Lavalanche R	.15	.30
185 Maverick Thopterist U	.10	.20
186 Mortify U	.10	.20
187 Putrefy U	.10	.20
188 Righteous Authority R	.15	.30
189 Rubblehulk R	.15	.30
190 Savage Twister U	.10	.20
191 Silent-Blade Oni R	.15	.30
192 Unflinching Courage U	.10	.20
193 Utter End R	.15	.30
194 Worm Harvest R	.15	.30
195 Zendikar Incarnate U	.10	.20
196 Azorius Signet U	.10	.20
197 Blinkmoth Urn R	.15	.30
198 Bosh, Iron Golem R	.15	.30
199 Chief of the Foundry U	.10	.20
200 Commander's Sphere C	.07	.15
201 Crystal Ball U	.10	.20
202 Darksteel Juggernaut R	.15	.30
203 Dimir Signet U	.10	.20
204 Dreamstone Hedron U	.10	.20
205 Duplicant R	.15	.30
206 Hedron Archive U	.10	.20
207 Izzet Signet U	.10	.20
208 Magnifying Glass U	.10	.20
209 Mimic Vat R	.15	.30
210 Mind Stone C	.07	.15
211 Mirrorworks R	.15	.30
212 Myr Battlesphere R	.15	.30
213 Orzhov Signet C	.07	.15
214 Pilgrim's Eye C	.07	.15
215 Prismatic Lens U	.10	.20
216 Prototype Portal R	.15	.30
217 Psychosis Crawler R	.15	.30
218 Scrabbling Claws U	.10	.20
219 Scuttling Doom Engine R	.15	.30
220 Seer's Lantern C	.07	.15
221 Seer's Sundial R	.15	.30
222 Sol Ring U	.10	.20
223 Soul of New Phyrexia M	.07	.15
224 Steel Hellkite R	.15	.30
225 Swiftfoot Boots U	.10	.20
226 Thopter Assembly R	.15	.30
227 Unstable Obelisk U	.10	.20
228 Unwinding Clock R	.15	.30
229 Vessel of Endless Rest U	.10	.20
230 Worn Powerstone U	.10	.20
231 Akoum Refuge U	.10	.20
232 Arcane Sanctum U	.10	.20
233 Azorius Chancery U	.10	.20
234 Azorius Guildgate C	.07	.15
235 Barren Moor C	.07	.15
236 Blighted Woodland U	.10	.20
237 Blossoming Sands C	.07	.15
238 Bojuka Bog C	.07	.15
239 Buried Ruin U	.10	.20
240 Command Tower C	.07	.15
241 Darksteel Citadel U	.10	.20
242 Dimir Aqueduct U	.10	.20
243 Dimir Guildgate C	.07	.15
244 Dismal Backwater C	.07	.15
245 Evolving Wilds C	.07	.15
246 Forgotten Cave C	.07	.15
247 Forsaken Sanctuary U	.10	.20
248 Foundry of the Consuls U	.10	.20
249 Golgari Rot Farm U	.10	.20
250 Great Furnace C	.07	.15
251 Grim Backwoods R	.15	.30
252 Gruul Turf U	.10	.20
253 Halimar Depths C	.07	.15
254 Haunted Fengraf C	.07	.15
255 Highland Lake U	.10	.20
256 Izzet Boilerworks U	.10	.20
257 Izzet Guildgate C	.07	.15
258 Jund Panorama C	.07	.15
259 Jungle Hollow C	.07	.15
260 Jwar Isle Refuge U	.10	.20
261 Kazandu Refuge U	.10	.20
262 Khalni Garden C	.07	.15
263 Krosan Verge U	.10	.20
264 Lonely Sandbar C	.07	.15
265 Meandering River U	.10	.20
266 Mortuary Mire C	.07	.15
267 Mosswort Bridge R	.15	.30
268 Mountain Valley U	.10	.20
269 Myriad Landscape U	.10	.20
270 New Benalia U	.10	.20
271 Orzhov Basilica U	.10	.20
272 Orzhov Guildgate C	.07	.15
273 Rakdos Carnarium C	.07	.15
274 Rocky Tar Pit U	.10	.20
275 Savage Lands U	.10	.20
276 Scoured Barrens C	.07	.15
277 Seaside Citadel U	.10	.20
278 Seat of the Synod C	.07	.15
279 Secluded Steppe C	.07	.15
280 Sejiri Refuge U	.10	.20
281 Selesnya Sanctuary C	.07	.15
282 Simic Growth Chamber U	.10	.20
283 Submerged Boneyard U	.10	.20
284 Swiftwater Cliffs C	.07	.15
285 Temple of the False God U	.10	.20
286 Terramorphic Expanse C	.07	.15
287 Thornwood Falls C	.07	.15
288 Tranquil Cove C	.07	.15
289 Tranquil Expanse U	.10	.20
290 Tranquil Thicket C	.07	.15
291 Warped Landscape C	.07	.15
292 Woodland Stream C	.07	.15
293 Plains L	.07	.15
294 Plains L	.07	.15
295 Plains L	.07	.15
296 Island L	.07	.15
297 Island L	.07	.15
298 Island L	.07	.15
299 Swamp L	.07	.15
300 Swamp L	.07	.15
301 Swamp L	.07	.15
302 Mountain L	.07	.15
303 Mountain L	.07	.15
304 Mountain L	.07	.15
305 Forest L	.07	.15
306 Forest L	.07	.15
307 Forest L	.07	.15

2018 Magic The Gathering Commander 2018 Oversized

37 Aminatou, the Fateshifter M	1.25	2.50
40 Estrid, the Masked M	.75	1.50
43 Lord Windgrace M	2.00	4.00
44 Saheeli, the Gifted M	.75	1.50

2018 Magic The Gathering Commander 2018 Tokens

1 Manifest	.07	.10
2 Shapeshifter	.07	.10
3 Angel	.07	.15
4 Mask	.07	.15
5 Cat	.07	.10
6 Soldier	.07	.10
7 Myr	.07	.15
8 Thopter	.07	.10
9 Zombie	.07	.10
10 Dragon Egg	.60	1.25
11 Dragon	.07	.10
12 Survivor	.15	.30
13 Beast	.07	.10
14 Beast	.07	.10
15 Cat Warrior	.07	.10
16 Elemental	.07	.10
17 Plant	.07	.10
18 Worm	.07	.10
19 Clue	.07	.10
20 Construct	.07	.10
21 Construct	.07	.10
22 Horror	.07	.10
23 Myr	.15	.30
24 Servo	.07	.10
25 Thopter	.07	.10
26 Thopter	.07	.10

2018 Magic The Gathering Commander Anthology Volume II

1 The Mimeoplasm M	.50	1.00
2 Damia, Sage of Stone M	4.00	8.00
3 Vorosh, the Hunter R	.15	.30
4 Daretti, Scrap Savant M	7.50	15.00
5 Bosh, Iron Golem R	.15	.30
6 Feldon of the Third Path M	1.25	2.50
7 Kalemne, Disciple of Iroas M	.75	1.50
8 Anya, Merciless Angel M	[illegible]	[illegible]
9 Gisela, Blade of Goldnight M	10.00	20.00
10 Atraxa, Praetors' Voice M	30.00	60.00
11 Ikra Shidiqi, the Usurper M	2.50	5.00
12 Ishai, Ojutai Dragonspeaker M	4.00	8.00
13 Reyhan, Last of the Abzan R	.15	.30
14 Artisan of Kozilek U	.10	.20
15 Abzan Falconer U	.10	.20
16 Angel of Serenity M	.30	.75
17 Arbiter of Knollridge R	.15	.30
18 Banishing Light U	.10	.20
19 Brave the Sands U	.10	.20
20 Cathars' Crusade R	.15	.30
21 Citadel Siege R	.15	.30
22 Crib Swap U	.10	.20
23 Custodi Soulbinders R	.15	.30
24 Dawnbreak Reclaimer R	.15	.30
25 Dawnglare Invoker C	.07	.15
26 Duelist's Heritage R	.15	.30
27 Elite Scaleguard U	.10	.20
28 Faith's Fetters C	.07	.15
29 Herald of the Host U	.10	.20
30 Jareth, Leonine Titan R	.15	.30
31 Kalemne's Captain R	.15	.30
32 Oreskos Explorer U	.10	.20
33 Orim's Thunder C	.07	.15
34 Orzhov Advokist U	.10	.20
35 Reveillark R	.15	.30
36 Sublime Exhalation R	.15	.30
37 Sun Titan M	1.00	2.00
38 Victory's Herald R	.15	.30
39 Deepglow Skate R	.15	.30
40 Disdainful Stroke C	.07	.15
41 Dreamborn Muse R	.15	.30
42 Fact or Fiction U	.10	.20
43 Grip of Phyresis U	.10	.20
44 Manifold Insights R	.15	.30
45 Memory Erosion R	.15	.30
46 Minds Aglow R	.15	.30
47 Mulldrifter C	.07	.15
48 Riddlekeeper R	.15	.30
49 Slipstream Eel C	.07	.15
50 Spell Crumple U	.10	.20
51 Tezzeret's Gambit U	.10	.20
52 Thrummingbird U	.10	.20
53 Treasure Cruise C	.07	.15
54 Vow of Flight U	.10	.20
55 Windfall U	.10	.20
56 Wonder U	.10	.20
57 Avatar of Woe R	.15	.30
58 Bane of the Living R	.15	.30
59 Buried Alive U	.10	.20
60 Butcher of Malakir R	.15	.30
61 Dark Hatchling R	.15	.30
62 Extractor Demon R	.15	.30
63 Festercreep C	.07	.15
64 Fleshbag Marauder U	.10	.20
65 Grave Pact R	.15	.30
66 Gravedigger C	.07	.15
67 Languish R	.15	.30
68 Living Death R	.15	.30
69 Mortivore R	.15	.30
70 Necroplasm R	.15	.30
71 Nezumi Graverobber Nighteyes the Desecrator U	.10	.20
72 Patron of the Nezumi R	.15	.30
73 Rise from the Grave U	.10	.20
74 Scythe Specter R	.15	.30
75 Sewer Nemesis R	.15	.30
76 Shared Trauma R	.15	.30
77 Sign in Blood C	.07	.15
78 Stitch Together U	.10	.20
79 Syphon Flesh U	.10	.20
80 Syphon Mind C	.07	.15
81 Unnerve C	.07	.15
82 Vow of Malice U	.10	.20
83 Beetleback Chief U	.10	.20
84 Bitter Feud R	.15	.30
85 Blasphemous Act R	.15	.30
86 Bogardan Hellkite M	.25	.50
87 Borderland Behemoth R	.15	.30
88 Breath of Darigaaz U	.10	.20
89 Chaos Warp R	.15	.30
90 Curse of the Nightly Hunt U	.10	.20
91 Desolation Giant R	.15	.30
92 Disaster Radius R	.15	.30
93 Dream Pillager R	.15	.30
94 Dualcaster Mage R	.15	.30
95 Earthquake R	.15	.30
96 Faithless Looting C	.07	.15
97 Fall of the Hammer C	.07	.15
98 Fiery Confluence R	.15	.30
99 Flametongue Kavu U	.10	.20
100 Fumiko the Lowblood R	.15	.30
101 Goblin Welder R	.15	.30
102 Hamletback Goliath R	.15	.30
103 Hammerfist Giant R	.15	.30
104 Hoard-Smelter Dragon R	.15	.30
105 Hostility R	[illegible]	[illegible]
106 Hunted Dragon R	.15	.30
107 Impact Resonance R	.15	.30
108 Incite Rebellion R	.15	.30
109 Inferno Titan M	.50	1.00
110 Ingot Chewer C	.07	.15
111 Magma Giant R	.15	.30
112 Magmaquake R	.15	.30
113 Magus of the Wheel R	.15	.30
114 Meteor Blast U	.10	.20
115 Rite of the Raging Storm U	.10	.20
116 Scrap Mastery R	.15	.30
117 Spitebellows U	.10	.20
118 Starstorm R	.15	.30
119 Stinkdrinker Daredevil C	.07	.15
120 Stoneshock Giant U	.10	.20
121 Sunrise Sovereign R	.15	.30
122 Taurean Mauler R	.15	.30
123 Thundercloud Shaman U	.10	.20
124 Tuktuk the Explorer R	.15	.30
125 Tyrant's Familiar R	.15	.30
126 Volcanic Offering R	.15	.30
127 Warchief Giant U	.10	.20
128 Warmonger Hellkite R	.15	.30
129 Warstorm Surge R	.15	.30
130 Whipflare U	.10	.20
131 Word of Seizing R	.15	.30
132 Acidic Slime U	.10	.20
133 Brawn U	.10	.20
134 Champion of Lambholt R	.15	.30
135 Cultivate C	.07	.15
136 Eternal Witness U	.10	.20
137 Forgotten Ancient R	.15	.30
138 Hardened Scales R	.15	.30
139 Inspiring Call U	.10	.20
140 Kalonian Hydra M	7.50	15.00
141 Lhurgoyf R	.15	.30
142 Relic Crush C	.07	.15
143 Scavenging Ooze R	.15	.30
144 Solidarity of Heroes U	.10	.20
145 Tribute to the Wild U	.10	.20
146 Troll Ascetic R	.15	.30
147 Tuskguard Captain U	.10	.20
148 Vow of Wildness U	.10	.20
149 Yavimaya Elder C	.07	.15
150 Ancient Excavation U	.10	.20
151 Bred for the Hunt U	.10	.20
152 Corpsejack Menace R	.15	.30
153 Desecrator Hag C	.07	.15
154 Duneblast R	.15	.30
155 Enduring Scalelord U	.10	.20
156 Fathom Mage R	.15	.30
157 Ghave, Guru of Spores M	.75	1.50
158 Juniper Order Ranger U	.10	.20
159 Master Biomancer M	.30	.75
160 Merciless Eviction R	.15	.30
161 Migratory Route U	.10	.20
162 Mirrorweave R	.15	.30
163 Mortify U	.10	.20
164 Putrefy U	.10	.20
165 Skullbriar, the Walking Grave R	.15	.30
166 Spitting Image R	.15	.30
167 Sylvan Reclamation U	.10	.20
168 Szadek, Lord of Secrets R	.15	.30
169 Vorel of the Hull Clade R	.15	.30
170 Vulturous Zombie R	.15	.30
171 Wrexial, the Risen Deep M	1.25	2.50
172 Astral Cornucopia R	.15	.30
173 Basalt Monolith U	.10	.20
174 Blade of Selves R	.15	.30
175 Boros Cluestone C	.07	.15
176 Boros Signet C	.07	.15
177 Bottle Gnomes U	.10	.20
178 Caged Sun R	.15	.30
179 Cathodion U	.10	.20
180 Cauldron of Souls R	.15	.30
181 Coldsteel Heart U	.10	.20
182 Commander's Sphere C	.07	.15
183 Crystalline Crawler R	.15	.30
184 Darksteel Ingot U	.10	.20
185 Dimir Signet C	.07	.15
186 Dreamstone Hedron U	.10	.20
187 Epochrasite R	.15	.30
188 Everflowing Chalice U	.10	.20
189 Fellwar Stone U	.10	.20
190 Fire Diamond U	.10	.20
191 Golgari Signet C	.07	.15
192 Golgari Signet C	.07	.15
193 Ichor Wellspring C	.07	.15
194 Jalum Tome R	.15	.30
195 Junk Diver R	.15	.30
196 Lightning Greaves U	.10	.20
197 Liquimetal Coating U	.10	.20
198 Loreseeker's Stone U	.10	.20
199 Loxodon Warhammer R	.15	.30
200 Mind Stone M	.30	.75
201 Mycosynth Wellspring C	.07	.15
202 Myr Battlesphere R	.15	.30
203 Myr Retriever U	.10	.20
204 Myr Sire C	.07	.15
205 Oblivion Stone R	.15	.30
206 Orzhov Signet C	.07	.15
207 Palladium Myr U	.10	.20
208 Panic Spellbomb C	.07	.15
209 Pentavus R	.15	.30
210 Pilgrim's Eye C	.07	.15
211 Pristine Talisman C	.07	.15
212 Ruby Medallion R	.15	.30
213 Sandstone Oracle U	.10	.20
214 Seer's Sundial R	.15	.30
215 Simic Signet C	.07	.15
216 Simic Signet C	.07	.15
217 Sol Ring U	.10	.20
218 Solemn Simulacrum R	.15	.30
219 Solemn Simulacrum R	.15	.30
220 Spine of Ish Sah R	.15	.30
221 Staff of Nin R	.15	.30
222 Steel Hellkite R	.15	.30
223 Swiftfoot Boots U	.10	.20
224 Thought Vessel C	.07	.15
225 Trading Post R	.15	.30
226 Triskelavus R	.15	.30
227 Unstable Obelisk U	.10	.20
228 Urza's Incubator R	.15	.30
229 Wayfarer's Bauble C	.07	.15
230 Worn Powerstone U	.10	.20
231 Wurmcoil Engine M	7.50	15.00
232 Ancient Amphitheater R	.15	.30
233 Arcane Lighthouse U	.10	.20
234 Arcane Sanctum U	.10	.20
235 Ash Barrens C	.07	.15
236 Azorius Chancery U	.10	.20
237 Barren Moor C	.07	.15
238 Blasted Landscape U	.10	.20
239 Boros Garrison C	.07	.15
240 Boros Guildgate C	.07	.15
241 Buried Ruin U	.10	.20
242 Command Tower C	.07	.15
243 Darksteel Citadel U	.10	.20
244 Darkwater Catacombs R	.15	.30
245 Dimir Aqueduct C	.07	.15
246 Dormant Volcano U	.10	.20
247 Dreadship Reef U	.10	.20
248 Drifting Meadow C	.07	.15
249 Evolving Wilds C	.07	.15
250 Exotic Orchard R	.15	.30
251 Flamekin Village R	.15	.30
252 Forgotten Cave C	.07	.15
253 Ghost Quarter U	.10	.20
254 Golgari Rot Farm U	.10	.20
255 Great Furnace C	.07	.15
256 Jwar Isle Refuge U	.10	.20
257 Lonely Sandbar C	.07	.15
258 Murmuring Bosk R	.15	.30
259 Opal Palace C	.07	.15
260 Opulent Palace U	.10	.20
261 Phyrexia's Core U	.10	.20
262 Reliquary Tower U	.10	.20
263 Rupture Spire C	.07	.15
264 Sandsteppe Citadel U	.10	.20
265 Seaside Citadel U	.10	.20
266 Secluded Steppe C	.07	.15
267 Simic Growth Chamber C	.07	.15
268 Smoldering Crater C	.07	.15
269 Sungrass Prairie R	.15	.30
270 Svogthos, the Restless Tomb U	.10	.20
271 Temple of the False God U	.10	.20
272 Temple of the False God U	.10	.20
273 Terramorphic Expanse C	.07	.15
274 Tranquil Thicket C	.07	.15
275 Underground River R	.15	.30
276 Vivid Crag U	.10	.20
277 Vivid Meadow U	.10	.20
278 Wind-Scarred Crag C	.07	.15
279 Plains L	.07	.15
280 Plains L	.07	.15
281 Plains L	.07	.15
282 Plains L	.07	.15
283 Plains L	.07	.15
284 Plains L	.07	.15
285 Plains L	.07	.15
286 Island L	.07	.15
287 Island L	.07	.15
288 Island L	.07	.15
289 Island L	.07	.15
290 Island L	.07	.15
291 Island L	.07	.15
292 Island L	.07	.15
293 Swamp L	.07	.15
294 Swamp L	.07	.15
295 Swamp L	.07	.15
296 Swamp L	.07	.15
297 Swamp L	.07	.15
298 Swamp L	.07	.15
299 Swamp L	.07	.15
300 Mountain L	.07	.15

301 Mountain L .07 .15
302 Mountain L .07 .15
303 Mountain L .07 .15
304 Mountain L .07 .15
305 Mountain L .07 .15
306 Forest L .07 .15
307 Forest L .07 .15
308 Forest L .07 .15
309 Forest L .07 .15
310 Forest L .07 .15
311 Forest L .07 .15
312 Forest L .07 .15

2018 Magic The Gathering Commander Anthology Volume II Tokens

1 Shapeshifter .12 .25
2 Bird .12 .25
3 Goat .12 .25
4 Knight .12 .25
5 Spirit .12 .25
6 Germ .12 .25
7 Zombie .12 .25
8 Elemental Shaman .12 .25
9 Goblin .12 .25
10 Lightning Rager .12 .25
11 Saproling .12 .25
12 Myr .12 .25
13 Pentavite .12 .25
14 Triskelavite .12 .25
15 Tuktuk the Returned .12 .25
16 Wurm (Deathtouch) 2.00 3.50
17 Wurm (Lifelink) 2.00 3.50
18 Daretti, Scrap Savant .12 .25
19 Experience Counter .12 .25

2018 Magic The Gathering Core Set 2019

1 Aegis of the Heavens U .10 .20
2 Aethershield Artificer U .10 .20
3 Ajani, Adversary of Tyrants M 7.50 13.00
4 Ajani's Last Stand R .15 .30
5 Ajani's Pridemate U .10 .20
6 Ajani's Welcome U .10 .20
7 Angel of the Dawn C .07 .15
8 Cavalry Drillmaster C .07 .15
9 Cleansing Nova R .15 .30
10 Daybreak Chaplain C .07 .15
11 Dwarven Priest C .07 .15
12 Ilant Cavalry C .07 .15
13 Herald of Faith U .10 .20
14 Hieromancer's Cage U .10 .20
15 Inspired Charge C .07 .15
16 Invoke the Divine C .07 .15
17 Isolate R .15 .30
18 Knight of the Tusk C .07 .15
19 Knight's Pledge C .07 .15
20 Knightly Valor U .10 .20
21 Lena, Selfless Champion R .15 .30
22 Leonin Vanguard U .10 .20
23 Leonin Warleader R .15 .30
24 Loxodon Line Breaker C .07 .15
25 Luminous Bonds C .07 .15
26 Make a Stand U .10 .20
27 Mentor of the Meek R .15 .30
28 Mighty Leap C .07 .15
29 Militia Bugler U .10 .20
30 Novice Knight U .10 .20
31 Oreskos Swiftclaw C .07 .15
32 Pegasus Courser C .07 .15
33 Remorseful Cleric R .15 .30
34 Resplendent Angel M 10.00 17.00
35 Revitalize C .07 .15
36 Rustwing Falcon C .07 .15
37 Shield Mare U .10 .20
38 Star-Crowned Stag C .07 .15
39 Suncleanser R .15 .30
40 Take Vengeance C .07 .15
41 Trusty Packbeast C .07 .15
42 Valiant Knight R .15 .30
43 Aether Tunnel U .10 .20
44 Anticipate C .07 .15
45 Aven Wind Mage C .07 .15
46 Aviation Pioneer C .07 .15
47 Bone to Ash U .10 .20
48 Cancel C .07 .15
49 Departed Deckhand U .10 .20
50 Disperse C .07 .15
51 Divination C .07 .15
52 Djinn of Wishes R .15 .30
53 Dwindle C .07 .15
54 Essence Scatter C .07 .15
55 Exclusion Mage U .10 .20
56 Frilled Sea Serpent C .07 .15
57 Gearsmith Prodigy C .07 .15
58 Ghostform C .07 .15
59 Horizon Scholar U .10 .20
60 Metamorphic Alteration R .15 .30
61 Mirror Image U .10 .20
62 Mistcaller R .15 .30
63 Mystic Archaeologist R .15 .30
64 Omenspeaker C .07 .15
65 Omniscience M 4.00 7.00
66 One with the Machine R .15 .30
67 Patient Rebuilding R .15 .30
68 Psychic Corrosion U .10 .20
69 Sai, Master Thopterist R .15 .30
70 Salvager of Secrets C .07 .15
71 Scholar of Stars C .07 .15
72 Sift U .10 .20
73 Skilled Animator U .10 .20
74 Sleep U .10 .20
75 Snapping Drake C .07 .15
76 Supreme Phantom R .15 .30
77 Surge Mare U .10 .20
78 Switcheroo U .10 .20
79 Tezzeret, Artifice Master M 10.00 20.00
80 Tolarian Scholar C .07 .15
81 Totally Lost C .07 .15
82 Uncomfortable Chill C .07 .15
83 Wall of Mist C .07 .15
84 Windreader Sphinx R .15 .30
85 Abnormal Endurance C .07 .15
86 Blood Divination U .10 .20
87 Bogstomper C .07 .15
88 Bone Dragon M .75 1.50
89 Child of Night C .07 .15
90 Death Baron R .15 .30
91 Demon of Catastrophes R .15 .30
92 Diregraf Ghoul U .10 .20
93 Doomed Dissenter C .07 .15
94 Duress C .07 .15
95 Epicure of Blood C .07 .15
96 Fell Specter U .10 .20
97 Fraying Omnipotence R .15 .30
98 Gravedigger U .10 .20
99 Graveyard Marshal R .15 .30
100 Hired Blade C .07 .15
101 Infectious Horror C .07 .15
102 Infernal Reckoning R .15 .30
103 Infernal Scarring C .07 .15
104 Isareth the Awakener R .15 .30
105 Lich's Caress C .07 .15
106 Liliana, Untouched by Death M 5.00 10.00
107 Liliana's Contract R .15 .30
108 Macabre Waltz C .07 .15
109 Mind Rot C .07 .15
110 Murder U .10 .20
111 Nightmare's Thirst U .10 .20
112 Open the Graves R .15 .30
113 Phylactery Lich R .15 .30
114 Plague Mare U .10 .20
115 Ravenous Harpy U .10 .20
116 Reassembling Skeleton U .10 .20
117 Rise from the Grave U .10 .20
118 Skeleton Archer C .07 .15
119 Skymarch Bloodletter C .07 .15
120 Sovereign's Bite C .07 .15
121 Stitcher's Supplier U .10 .20
122 Strangling Spores C .07 .15
123 Two-Headed Zombie C .07 .15
124 Vampire Neonate C .07 .15
125 Vampire Sovereign U .10 .20
126 Walking Corpse C .07 .15
127 Act of Treason C .07 .15
128 Alpine Moon R .15 .30
129 Apex of Power M .50 1.00
130 Banefire R .15 .30
131 Boggart Brute C .07 .15
132 Catalyst Elemental C .07 .15
133 Crash Through C .07 .15
134 Dark-Dweller Oracle R .15 .30
135 Demanding Dragon R .15 .30
136 Dismissive Pyromancer R .15 .30
137 Doublecast U .10 .20
138 Dragon Egg U .10 .20
139 Electrify C .07 .15
140 Fiery Finish U .10 .20
141 Fire Elemental C .07 .15
142 Goblin Instigator C .07 .15
143 Goblin Motivator C .07 .15
144 Goblin Trashmaster R .15 .30
145 Guttersnipe U .10 .20
146 Havoc Devils C .07 .15
147 Hostile Minotaur C .07 .15
148 Inferno Hellion U .10 .20
149 Lathliss, Dragon Queen R .15 .30
150 Lava Axe C .07 .15
151 Lightning Mare U .10 .20
152 Lightning Strike U .10 .20
153 Onakke Ogre C .07 .15
154 Sarkhan, Fireblood M 6.00 11.00
155 Sarkhan's Unsealing R .15 .30
156 Shock C .07 .15
157 Siegebreaker Giant U .10 .20
158 Smelt C .07 .15
159 Sparktongue Dragon C .07 .15
160 Spit Flame R .15 .30
161 Sure Strike C .07 .15
162 Tectonic Rift U .10 .20
163 Thud U .10 .20
164 Tormenting Voice C .07 .15
165 Trumpet Blast C .07 .15
166 Viashino Pyromancer C .07 .15
167 Volcanic Dragon U .10 .20
168 Volley Veteran U .10 .20
169 Blanchwood Armor U .10 .20
170 Bristling Boar C .07 .15
171 Centaur Courser C .07 .15
172 Colossal Dreadmaw C .07 .15
173 Colossal Majesty U .10 .20
174 Daggerback Basilisk C .07 .15
175 Declare Dominance U .10 .20
176 Druid of Horns U .10 .20
177 Druid of the Cowl C .07 .15
178 Dryad Greenseeker U .10 .20
179 Elvish Clancaller R .15 .30
180 Elvish Rejuvenator C .07 .15
181 Ghastbark Twins U .10 .20
182 Ghirapur Guide U .10 .20
183 Giant Spider C .07 .15
184 Gift of Paradise U .10 .20
185 Gigantosaurus R .15 .30
186 Goreclaw, Terror of Qal Sisma R .15 .30
187 Greenwood Sentinel C .07 .15
188 Highland Game C .07 .15
189 Hungering Hydra R .15 .30
190 Naturalize C .07 .15
191 Oakenform C .07 .15
192 Pelakka Wurm R .15 .30
193 Plummet C .07 .15
194 Prodigious Growth R .15 .30
195 Rabid Bite C .07 .15
196 Reclamation Sage U .10 .20
197 Recollect U .10 .20
198 Rhox Oracle C .07 .15
199 Root Snare C .07 .15
200 Runic Armasaur R .15 .30
201 Scapeshift M .50 1.00
202 Talons of Wildwood C .07 .15
203 Thorn Lieutenant R .25 .50
204 Thornhide Wolves C .07 .15
205 Titanic Growth C .07 .15
206 Vigilant Baloth U .10 .20
207 Vine Mare U .10 .20
208 Vivien Reid M 4.00 8.00
209 Vivien's Invocation R .15 .30
210 Wall of Vines C .07 .15
211 Aerial Engineer U .10 .20
212 Arcades, the Strategist M 3.00 6.00
213 Brawl-Bash Ogre U .10 .20
214 Chromium, the Mutable M 4.00 8.00
215 Draconic Disciple U .10 .20
216 Enigma Drake U .10 .20
217 Heroic Reinforcements U .10 .20
218 Nicol Bolas Ravager/Arisen M :B/:K/:R:15.00 30.00
219 Palladia-Mors, the Ruiner M 1.50 3.00
220 Poison-Tip Archer U .10 .20
221 Psychic Symbiont U .10 .20
222 Regal Bloodlord U .10 .20
223 Satyr Enchanter U .10 .20
224 Skyrider Patrol U .10 .20
225 Vaevictis Asmadi, the Dire M 1.00 2.00
226 Amulet of Safekeeping R .15 .30
227 Arcane Encyclopedia U .10 .20
228 Chaos Wand R .15 .30
229 Crucible of Worlds M 10.00 20.00
230 Desecrated Tomb R .15 .30
231 Diamond Mare U .10 .20
232 Dragon's Hoard R .15 .30
233 Explosive Apparatus C .07 .15
234 Field Creeper C .07 .15
235 Fountain of Renewal U .10 .20
236 Gargoyle Sentinel U .10 .20
237 Gearsmith Guardian C .07 .15
238 Magistrate's Scepter R .15 .30
239 Manalith C .07 .15
240 Marauder's Axe C .07 .15
241 Meteor Golem U .10 .20
242 Millstone U .10 .20
243 Rogue's Gloves U .10 .20
244 Sigiled Sword of Valeron R .15 .30
245 Skyscanner C .07 .15
246 Suspicious Bookcase U .10 .20
247 Transmogrifying Wand R .15 .30
248 Cinder Barrens C .07 .15
249 Detection Tower R .15 .30
250 Forsaken Sanctuary C .07 .15
251 Foul Orchard C .07 .15
252 Highland Lake C .07 .15
253 Meandering River C .07 .15
254 Reliquary Tower U .10 .20
255 Rupture Spire U .10 .20
256 Stone Quarry C .07 .15
257 Submerged Boneyard C .07 .15
258 Timber Gorge C .07 .15
259 Tranquil Expanse C .07 .15
260 Woodland Stream C .07 .15
261 Plains L .07 .15
262 Plains L .07 .15
263 Plains L .07 .15
264 Plains L .07 .15
265 Island L .07 .15
266 Island L .07 .15
267 Island L .07 .15
268 Island L .07 .15
269 Swamp L .07 .15
270 Swamp L .07 .15
271 Swamp L .07 .15
272 Swamp L .07 .15
273 Mountain L .07 .15
274 Mountain L .07 .15
275 Mountain L .07 .15
276 Mountain L .07 .15
277 Forest L .07 .15
278 Forest L .07 .15
279 Forest L .07 .15
280 Forest L .07 .15

2018 Magic The Gathering Core Set 2019 Gift Pack

GP1 Angelic Guardian R .75 1.50
GP2 Angler Turtle R .20 .40
GP3 Vengeant Vampire R .30 .75
GP4 Immortal Phoenix R .20 .40
GP5 Rampaging Brontodon R 1.00 2.00

2018 Magic The Gathering Core Set 2019 Standard Showdown

1 Plains L .50 1.00
2 Island L .50 1.00
3 Swamp L .30 .75
4 Mountain L .40 .80
5 Forest L .30 .60

2018 Magic The Gathering Core Set 2019 Tokens

1 Angel .20 .40
2 Avatar .07 .10
3 Cat .25 .50
4 Knight .10 .20
5 Ox .07 .10
6 Soldier .12 .25
7 Bat .10 .20
8 Zombie .07 .15
9 Dragon .07 .10
10 Dragon .12 .25
11 Goblin .07 .15
12 Beast .10 .20
13 Elf Warrior .17 .35
14 Thopter .10 .20
15 Ajani, Adversary of Tyrants Emblem .10 .20
16 Tezzeret, Artifice Master Emblem .15 .30
17 Vivien Reid Emblem .12 .25
CH1 Core Set 2019 CL .07 .15

2018 Magic The Gathering Dominaria

1 Karn, Scion of Urza M 17.50 35.00
2 Adamant Will C .07 .15
3 Aven Sentry C .07 .15
4 Baird, Steward of Argive U .10 .20
5 Benalish Honor Guard C .07 .15
6 Benalish Marshal R .15 .30
7 Blessed Light C .07 .15
8 Board the Weatherlight U .10 .20
9 Call the Cavalry C .07 .15
10 Charge C .07 .15
11 D'Avenant Trapper C .07 .15
12 Danitha Capashen, Paragon U .10 .20
13 Daring Archaeologist R .15 .30
14 Dauntless Bodyguard U .10 .20
15 Dub C .07 .15
16 Evra, Halcyon Witness R .15 .30
17 Evxcavation Elephant C .07 .15
18 Fall of the Thran R .15 .30
19 Gideon's Reproach C .07 .15
20 Healing Grace C .07 .15
21 History of Benalia M 6.00 12.00
22 Invoke the Divine C .07 .15
23 Knight of Grace U .10 .20
24 Knight of New Benalia C .07 .15
25 Kwende, Pride of Femeref U .10 .20
26 Lyra Dawnbringer M 7.50 15.00
27 Mesa Unicorn C .07 .15
28 On Serra's Wings U .10 .20
29 Pegasus Courser C .07 .15
30 Sanctum Spirit U .10 .20
31 Seal Away U .10 .20
32 Sergeant-at-Arms C .07 .15
33 Serra Angel U .10 .20
34 Serra Disciple C .07 .15
35 Shalai, Voice of Plenty R .15 .30
36 Teshar, Ancestor's Apostle R .15 .30
37 Tragic Poet C .07 .15
38 Triumph of Gerrard U .10 .20
39 Urza's Ruinous Blast R .15 .30
40 Academy Drake C .07 .15
41 Academy Journeymage C .07 .15
42 The Antiquities War R .15 .30
43 Arcane Flight C .07 .15
44 Artificer's Assistant C .07 .15
45 Befuddle C .07 .15
46 Blink of an Eye C .07 .15
47 Cloudreader Sphinx C .07 .15
48 Cold-Water Snapper C .07 .15
49 Curator's Ward U .10 .20
50 Deep Freeze C .07 .15
51 Diligent Excavator U .10 .20
52 Divination C .07 .15
53 Homarid Explorer C .07 .15
54 In Bolas's Clutches U .10 .20
55 Karn's Temporal Sundering R .15 .30
56 Merfolk Trickster U .10 .20
57 The Mirari Conjecture R .15 .30
58 Naban, Dean of Iteration R .15 .30
59 Naru Meha, Master Wizard M .75 1.50
60 Opt C .07 .15
61 Precognition Field R .15 .30
62 Relic Runner C .07 .15
63 Rescue C .07 .15
64 Sage of Lat-Nam U .10 .20
65 Sentinel of the Pearl Trident U .10 .20
66 Slinn Voda, the Rising Deep U .10 .20
67 Syncopate C .07 .15
68 Tempest Djinn R .15 .30
69 Tetsuko Umezawa, Fugitive U .10 .20
70 Time of Ice U .10 .20
71 Tolarian Scholar C .07 .15
72 Unwind C .07 .15
73 Vodalian Arcanist C .07 .15
74 Weight of Memory U .10 .20
75 Wizard's Retort U .10 .20
76 Zahid, Djinn of the Lamp R .15 .30
77 Blessing of Belzenlok C .07 .15
78 Cabal Evangel C .07 .15
79 Cabal Paladin C .07 .15
80 Caligo Skin-Witch C .07 .15
81 Cast Down U .10 .20
82 Chainer's Torment U .10 .20
83 Dark Bargain C .07 .15
84 Deathbloom Thallid C .07 .15
85 Demonic Vigor C .07 .15
86 Demonlord Belzenlok M .75 1.50
87 Divest C .07 .15
88 Dread Shade R .15 .30
89 Drudge Sentinel C .07 .15
90 The Eldest Reborn U .10 .20
91 Eviscerate C .07 .15
92 Feral Abomination C .07 .15
93 Final Parting U .10 .20
94 Fungal Infection C .07 .15
95 Josu Vess, Lich Knight R .15 .30
96 Kazarov, Sengir Pureblod R .15 .30
97 Knight of Malice U .10 .20
98 Lich's Mastery R .15 .30
99 Lingering Phantom U .10 .20
100 Phyrexian Scriptures M 1.00 2.00
101 Rat Colony C .07 .15
102 Rite of Belzenlok R .15 .30
103 Settle the Score U .10 .20
104 Soul Salvage C .07 .15
105 Stronghold Confessor C .07 .15
106 Thallid Omnivore C .07 .15
107 Thallid Soothsayer U .10 .20
108 Torgaar, Famine Incarnate R .15 .30
109 Urgoros, the Empty One U .10 .20
110 Vicious Offering C .07 .15
111 Whisper, Blood Liturgist U .10 .20
112 Windgrace Acolyte C .07 .15
113 Yargle, Glutton of Urborg U .10 .20
114 Yawgmoth's Vile Offering R .15 .30
115 Bloodstone Goblin C .07 .15
116 Champion of the Flame U .10 .20
117 Fervent Strike C .07 .15
118 Fiery Intervention C .07 .15
119 Fight with Fire U .10 .20
120 Fire Elemental C .07 .15
121 Firefist Adept U .10 .20
122 The First Eruption R .15 .30
123 The Flame of Keld U .10 .20
124 Frenzied Rage C .07 .15
125 Ghitu Chronicler C .07 .15
126 Ghitu Journeymage C .07 .15
127 Ghitu Lavarunner C .07 .15
128 Goblin Barrage U .10 .20
129 Goblin Chainwhirler R .15 .30
130 Goblin Warchief U .10 .20
131 Haphazard Bombardment R .15 .30
132 Jaya Ballard M 2.50 5.00
133 Jaya's Immolating Inferno R .15 .30
134 Keldon Overseer C .07 .15
135 Keldon Raider C .07 .15
136 Keldon Warcaller C .07 .15
137 Orcish Vandal U .10 .20
138 Radiating Lightning C .07 .15
139 Rampaging Cyclops C .07 .15
140 Run Amok C .07 .15
141 Seismic Shift C .07 .15
142 Shivan Fire C .07 .15

143 Siege-Gang Commander R	.15	.30
144 Skirk Prospector C	.07	.15
145 Skizzik U	.10	.20
146 Squee, the Immortal R	.15	.30
147 Two-Headed Giant R	.15	.30
148 Valduk, Keeper of the Flame U	.10	.20
149 Verix Bladewing M	1.50	3.00
150 Warcry Phoenix U	.10	.20
151 Warlord's Fury C	.07	.15
152 Wizard's Lightning U	.10	.20
153 Adventurous Impulse C	.07	.15
154 Ancient Animus C	.07	.15
155 Arbor Armament C	.07	.15
156 Baloth Gorger C	.07	.15
157 Broken Bond C	.07	.15
158 Corrosive Ooze C	.07	.15
159 Elfhame Druid U	.10	.20
160 Fungal Plots U	.10	.20
161 Gaea's Blessing U	.10	.20
162 Gaea's Protector C	.07	.15
163 Gift of Growth C	.07	.15
164 Grow from the Ashes C	.07	.15
165 Grunn, the Lonely King U	.10	.20
166 Kamahl's Druidic Vow R	.15	.30
167 Krosan Druid C	.07	.15
168 Llanowar Elves C	.07	.15
169 Llanowar Envoy C	.07	.15
170 Llanowar Scout C	.07	.15
171 Mammoth Spider U	.10	.20
172 Marwyn, the Nurturer R	.15	.30
173 The Mending of Dominaria R	.15	.30
174 Multani, Yavimaya's Avatar M	1.00	2.00
175 Nature's Spiral U	.10	.20
176 Pierce the Sky C	.07	.15
177 Primordial Wurm C	.07	.15
178 Saproling Migration C	.07	.15
179 Song of Freyalise U	.10	.20
180 Spore Swarm U	.10	.20
181 Sporecrown Thallid U	.10	.20
182 Steel Leaf Champion R	.15	.30
183 Sylvan Awakening R	.15	.30
184 Territorial Allosaurus R	.15	.30
185 Thorn Elemental U	.10	.20
186 Untamed Kavu U	.10	.20
187 Verdant Force R	.15	.30
188 Wild Onslaught U	.10	.20
189 Yavimaya Sapherd C	.07	.15
190 Adeliz, the Cinder Wind U	.10	.20
191 Arvad the Cursed U	.10	.20
192 Aryel, Knight of Windgrace R	.15	.30
193 Darigaaz Reincarnated M	.75	1.50
194 Garna, the Bloodflame U	.10	.20
195 Grand Warlord Radha R	.15	.30
196 Hallar, the Firefletcher U	.10	.20
197 Jhoira, Weatherlight Captain M	1.00	2.00
198 Jodah, Archmage Eternal R	.15	.30
199 Muldrotha, the Gravetide M	2.00	4.00
200 Oath of Teferi R	.15	.30
201 Primevals' Glorious Rebirth R	.15	.30
202 Raff Capashen, Ship's Mage U	.10	.20
203 Rona, Disciple of Gix U	.10	.20
204 Shanna, Sisay's Legacy U	.10	.20
205 Slimefoot, the Stowaway U	.10	.20
206 Tatyova, Benthic Druid U	.10	.20
207 Teferi, Hero of Dominaria M	17.50	35.00
208 Tiana, Ship's Caretaker U	.10	.20
209 Aesthir Glider C	.07	.15
210 Amaranthine Wall U	.10	.20
211 Blackblade Reforged R	.15	.30
212 Bloodtallow Candle C	.07	.15
213 Damping Sphere U	.10	.20
214 Forebear's Blade R	.15	.30
215 Gilded Lotus R	.15	.30
216 Guardians of Koilos C	.07	.15
217 Helm of the Host R	.15	.30
218 Howling Golem U	.10	.20
219 Icy Manipulator U	.10	.20
220 Jhoira's Familiar U	.10	.20
221 Jousting Lance C	.07	.15
222 Juggernaut U	.10	.20
223 Mishra's Self-Replicator R	.15	.30
224 Mox Amber M	6.00	12.00
225 Navigator's Compass C	.07	.15
226 Pardic Wanderer C	.07	.15
227 Powerstone Shard C	.07	.15
228 Shield of the Realm U	.10	.20
229 Short Sword C	.07	.15
230 Skittering Surveyor C	.07	.15
231 Sorcerer's Wand U	.10	.20
232 Sparring Construct C	.07	.15
233 Thran Temporal Gateway R	.15	.30
234 Traxos, Scourge of Kroog R	.15	.30
235 Urza's Tome U	.10	.20
236 Voltaic Servant C	.07	.15
237 Weatherlight M	.50	1.00
238 Cabal Stronghold R	.15	.30
239 Clifftop Retreat R	.15	.30
240 Hinterland Harbor R	.15	.30
241 Isolated Chapel R	.15	.30
242 Memorial to Folly U	.10	.20
243 Memorial to Genius U	.10	.20
244 Memorial to Glory U	.10	.20
245 Memorial to Unity U	.10	.20
246 Memorial to War U	.10	.20
247 Sulfur Falls R	.15	.30
248 Woodland Cemetery R	.15	.30
249 Zhalfirin Void U	.10	.20
250 Plains L	.07	.15
251 Plains L	.07	.15
252 Plains L	.07	.15
253 Plains L	.07	.15
254 Island L	.07	.15
255 Island L	.07	.15
256 Island L	.07	.15
257 Island L	.07	.15
258 Swamp L	.07	.15
259 Swamp L	.07	.15
260 Swamp L	.07	.15
261 Swamp L	.07	.15
262 Mountain L	.07	.15
263 Mountain L	.07	.15
264 Mountain L	.07	.15
265 Mountain L	.07	.15
266 Forest L	.07	.15
267 Forest L	.07	.15
268 Forest L	.07	.15
269 Forest L	.07	.15
270 Teferi, Timebender M	2.50	5.00
271 Temporal Machinations C	.07	.15
272 Niambi, Faithful Healer R	.15	.30
273 Teferi's Sentinel U	.10	.20
274 Meandering River C	.07	.15
275 Chandra, Bold Pyromancer M	2.50	5.00
276 Chandra's Outburst R	.15	.30
277 Karplusan Hound U	.10	.20
278 Pyromantic Pilgrim C	.07	.15
279 Timber Gorge C	.07	.15

2018 Magic The Gathering Dominaria Tokens

1 Knight	.07	.10
2 Knight	.60	1.25
3 Soldier	.07	.15
4 Cleric	.07	.15
5 Zombie Knight	.60	1.25
6 Nightmare Horror	.07	.10
7 Demon	.15	.30
8 Elemental	.07	.15
9 Goblin	.10	.20
10 Karox Bladewing	.30	.60
11 Saproling	.07	.10
12 Saproling	.07	.10
13 Saproling	.07	.10
14 Construct	2.00	3.50
15 Jaya Ballard Emblem	.20	.40
16 Teferi, Hero of Dominaria Emblem	.50	1.00

2018 Magic The Gathering Duel Decks Elves vs. Inventors

1 Ezuri, Renegade Leader M	3.00	6.00
2 Dwynen, Gilt-Leaf Daen R	.30	.60
3 Dwynen's Elite U	.12	.25
4 Elvish Aberration C	.06	.12
5 Elvish Archdruid R	.75	1.50
6 Elvish Branchbender C	.05	.10
7 Elvish Mystic C	.30	.75
8 Elvish Vanguard C	.25	.50
9 Ezuri's Archers C	.05	.10
10 Fierce Empath C	.12	.25
11 Gladehart Cavalry R	.12	.25
12 Ivy Lane Denizen C	.10	.20
13 Jagged-Scar Archers U	.12	.25
14 Krosan Tusker C	.06	.12
15 Kujar Seedsculptor C	.05	.10
16 Lead the Stampede C	.12	.25
17 Leaf Gilder C	.05	.10
18 Llanowar Empath C	.07	.15
19 Naturalize C	.07	.15
20 Nature's Way U	.12	.25
21 Nissa's Judgment U	.07	.15
22 Regal Force R	2.00	4.00
23 Sylvan Advocate R	.12	.25
24 Talara's Battalion R	.15	.30
25 Viridian Shaman U	.05	.10
26 Wildheart Invoker C	.05	.10
27 Yeva, Nature's Herald R	2.00	4.00
28 Oran-Rief, the Vastwood R	.30	.75
29 Tranquil Thicket C	.10	.20
30 Treetop Village U	.15	.30
31 Forest L	.12	.25
32 Forest L	.07	.15
33 Forest L	.07	.15
34 Forest L	.12	.25
35 Goblin Welder M	7.50	15.00
36 Artificer's Epiphany C	.07	.15
37 Etherium Sculptor C	.30	.60
38 Faerie Mechanist C	.05	.10
39 Riddlesmith U	.05	.10
40 Treasure Mage U	.10	.20
41 Trinket Mage C	.17	.35
42 Trophy Mage U	.30	.60
43 Whirler Rogue U	.07	.15
44 Barrage Ogre U	.15	.30
45 Galvanic Blast C	.75	1.50
46 Ghirapur Gearcrafter C	.07	.15
47 Pia and Kiran Nalaar R	.12	.25
48 Shrapnel Blast U	.15	.30
49 Welding Sparks C	.30	.60
50 Maverick Thopterist U	.05	.10
51 Reclusive Artificer U	.07	.15
52 Darksteel Plate R	5.00	10.00
53 Filigree Familiar U	.07	.15
54 Ichor Wellspring C	.12	.25
55 Inventor's Goggles C	.07	.15
56 Mycosynth Wellspring C	.10	.20
57 Myr Battlesphere R	.30	.60
58 Myr Sire C	.12	.25
59 Neurok Replica C	.05	.10
60 Pyrite Spellbomb C	.12	.25
61 Scuttling Doom Engine R	.12	.25
62 Solemn Simulacrum R	.40	.80
63 Thopter Assembly R	.30	.60
64 Voyager Staff U	1.00	2.00
65 Darksteel Citadel U	.30	.75
66 Foundry of the Consuls U	.12	.25
67 Great Furnace C	1.25	2.50
68 Phyrexia's Core U	.07	.15
69 Seat of the Synod C	.75	1.50
70 Shivan Reef R	.50	1.00
71 Swiftwater Cliffs C	.06	.12
72 Temple of Epiphany R	.20	.40
73 Island L	.07	.15
74 Island L	.06	.12
75 Mountain L	.06	.12
76 Mountain L	.07	.15

2018 Magic The Gathering Duel Decks Elves vs. Inventors Tokens

1 Elf Warrior	.15	.30
2 Myr	.75	1.50
3 Thopter	.12	.25
4 Thopter	.10	.20

2018 Magic The Gathering Guilds of Ravnica

1 Blade Instructor C	.07	.15
2 Bounty Agent R	.15	.30
3 Candlelight Vigil C	.07	.15
4 Citywide Bust R	.15	.30
5 Collar the Culprit C	.07	.15
6 Conclave Tribunal U	.10	.20
7 Crush Contraband U	.10	.20
8 Dawn of Hope R	.15	.30
9 Demotion U	.10	.20
10 Divine Visitation M	3.00	6.00
11 Flight of Equenauts U	.10	.20
12 Gird for Battle U	.10	.20
13 Haazda Marshal U	.10	.20
14 Healer's Hawk C	.07	.15
15 Hunted Witness C	.07	.15
16 Inspiring Unicorn U	.10	.20
17 Intrusive Packbeast C	.07	.15
18 Ledev Guardian C	.07	.15
19 Light of the Legion R	.15	.30
20 Loxodon Restorer C	.07	.15
21 Luminous Bonds C	.07	.15
22 Parhelion Patrol C	.07	.15
23 Righteous Blow C	.07	.15
24 Roc Charger U	.10	.20
25 Skyline Scout C	.07	.15
26 Sunhome Stalwart U	.10	.20
27 Sworn Companions C	.07	.15
28 Take Heart C	.07	.15
29 Tenth District Guard C	.07	.15
30 Venerated Loxodon R	.15	.30
31 Capture Sphere C	.07	.15
32 Chemister's Insight U	.10	.20
33 Citywatch Sphinx U	.10	.20
34 Dazzling Lights C	.07	.15
35 Devious Cover-up C	.07	.15
36 Dimir Informant C	.07	.15
37 Disdainful Stroke C	.07	.15
38 Dream Eater M	4.00	8.00
39 Drowned Secrets R	.15	.30
40 Enhanced Surveillance U	.10	.20
41 Guild Summit U	.10	.20
42 Leapfrog C	.07	.15
43 Maximize Altitude C	.07	.15
44 Mission Briefing R	.15	.30
45 Murmuring Mystic U	.10	.20
46 Muse Drake C	.07	.15
47 Narcomoeba R	.15	.30
48 Nightveil Sprite U	.10	.20
49 Omnispell Adept R	.15	.30
50 Passwall Adept C	.07	.15
51 Quasiduplicate R	.15	.30
52 Radical Idea C	.07	.15
53 Selective Snare U	.10	.20
54 Sinister Sabotage U	.10	.20
55 Thoughtbound Phantasm U	.10	.20
56 Unexplained Disappearance C	.07	.15
57 Vedalken Mesmerist C	.07	.15
58 Wall of Mist C	.07	.15
59 Watcher in the Mist C	.07	.15
60 Wishcoin Crab C	.07	.15
61 Barrier of Bones C	.07	.15
62 Bartizan Bats C	.07	.15
63 Blood Operative R	.15	.30
64 Burglar Rat C	.07	.15
65 Child of Night C	.07	.15
66 Creeping Chill U	.10	.20
67 Dead Weight C	.07	.15
68 Deadly Visit C	.07	.15
69 Doom Whisperer M	12.50	25.00
70 Douser of Lights C	.07	.15
71 Gruesome Menagerie R	.15	.30
72 Hired Poisoner C	.07	.15
73 Kraul Swarm U	.10	.20
74 Lotleth Giant U	.10	.20
75 Mausoleum Secrets R	.15	.30
76 Mephitic Vapors C	.07	.15
77 Midnight Reaper R	.15	.30
78 Moodmark Painter C	.07	.15
79 Necrotic Wound U	.10	.20
80 Never Happened C	.07	.15
81 Pilfering Imp U	.10	.20
82 Plaguecrafter U	.10	.20
83 Price of Fame U	.10	.20
84 Ritual of Soot R	.15	.30
85 Severed Strands C	.07	.15
86 Spinal Centipede C	.07	.15
87 Undercity Necrolisk U	.10	.20
88 Veiled Shade C	.07	.15
89 Vicious Rumors C	.07	.15
90 Whispering Snitch U	.10	.20
91 Arclight Phoenix M	2.00	4.00
92 Barging Sergeant C	.07	.15
93 Book Devourer U	.10	.20
94 Command the Storm C	.07	.15
95 Cosmotronic Wave C	.07	.15
96 Direct Current C	.07	.15
97 Electrostatic Field U	.10	.20
98 Erratic Cyclops R	.15	.30
99 Experimental Frenzy R	.15	.30
100 Fearless Halberdier C	.07	.15
101 Fire Urchin C	.07	.15
102 Goblin Banneret U	.10	.20
103 Goblin Cratermaker U	.10	.20
104 Goblin Locksmith C	.07	.15
105 Gravitic Punch C	.07	.15
106 Hellkite Whelp U	.10	.20
107 Inescapable Blaze U	.10	.20
108 Lava Coil U	.10	.20
109 Legion Warboss R	.15	.30
110 Maniacal Rage C	.07	.15
111 Maximize Velocity C	.07	.15
112 Ornery Goblin C	.07	.15
113 Risk Factor R	.15	.30
114 Rubblebelt Boar C	.07	.15
115 Runaway Steam-Kin R	.15	.30
116 Smelt-Ward Minotaur U	.10	.20
117 Street Riot U	.10	.20
118 Sure Strike C	.07	.15
119 Torch Courier C	.07	.15
120 Wojek Bodyguard C	.07	.15
121 Affectionate Indrik U	.10	.20
122 Arboretum Elemental U	.10	.20
123 Beast Whisperer R	.15	.30
124 Bounty of Might R	.15	.30
125 Circuitous Route U	.10	.20
126 Crushing Canopy C	.07	.15
127 Devkarin Dissident C	.07	.15
128 District Guide U	.10	.20
129 Generous Stray C	.07	.15
130 Golgari Raiders U	.10	.20
131 Grappling Sundew U	.10	.20
132 Hatchery Spider R	.15	.30
133 Hitchclaw Recluse C	.07	.15
134 Ironshell Beetle C	.07	.15
135 Kraul Foragers C	.07	.15
136 Kraul Harpooner U	.10	.20
137 Might of the Masses U	.10	.20
138 Nullhide Ferox M	4.00	8.00
139 Pack's Favor C	.07	.15
140 Pause for Reflection C	.07	.15
141 Pelt Collector R	.15	.30
142 Portcullis Vine C	.07	.15
143 Prey Upon C	.07	.15
144 Siege Wurm C	.07	.15
145 Sprouting Renewal U	.10	.20
146 Urban Utopia C	.07	.15
147 Vigorspore Wurm C	.07	.15
148 Vivid Revival R	.15	.30
149 Wary Okapi C	.07	.15
150 Wild Ceratok C	.07	.15
151 Artful Takedown C	.07	.15
152 Assassin's Trophy R	.15	.30
153 Aurelia, Exemplar of Justice M	7.50	15.00
154 Beacon Bolt U	.10	.20
155 Beamsplitter Mage U	.10	.20
156 Boros Challenger U	.10	.20
157 Camaraderie R	.15	.30
158 Centaur Peacemaker C	.07	.15
159 Chance for Glory M	1.25	2.50
160 Charnel Troll R	.15	.30
161 Conclave Cavalier U	.10	.20
162 Conclave Guildmage U	.10	.20
163 Crackling Drake U	.10	.20
164 Darkblade Agent C	.07	.15
165 Deafening Clarion R	.15	.30
166 Dimir Spybug U	.10	.20
167 Disinformation Campaign U	.10	.20
168 Emmara, Soul of the Accord R	.15	.30
169 Erstwhile Trooper C	.07	.15
170 Etrata, the Silencer R	.15	.30
171 Firemind's Research R	.15	.30
172 Garrison Sergeant C	.07	.15
173 Glowspore Shaman U	.10	.20
174 Goblin Electromancer C	.07	.15
175 Golgari Findbroker U	.10	.20
176 Hammer Dropper C	.07	.15
177 House Guildmage U	.10	.20
178 Hypothesizzle C	.07	.15
179 Ionize R	.15	.30
180 Izoni, Thousand-Eyed R	.15	.30
181 Join Shields U	.10	.20
182 Justice Strike U	.10	.20
183 Knight of Autumn R	.15	.30
184 Lazav, the Multifarious M	2.50	5.00
185 League Guildmage U	.10	.20
186 Ledev Champion U	.10	.20
187 Legion Guildmage U	.10	.20
188 March of the Multitudes M	7.50	15.00
189 Mnemonic Betrayal M	1.25	2.50
190 Molderhulk U	.10	.20
191 Nightveil Predator U	.10	.20
192 Niv-Mizzet, Parun R	.15	.30
193 Notion Rain C	.07	.15
194 Ochran Assassin U	.10	.20
195 Ral, Izzet Viceroy M	5.00	10.00
196 Rhizome Lurcher C	.07	.15
197 Rosemane Centaur C	.07	.15
198 Skyknight Legionnaire C	.07	.15
199 Sonic Assault C	.07	.15
200 Sumala Woodshaper C	.07	.15
201 Swarm Guildmage U	.10	.20
202 Swathcutter Giant U	.10	.20
203 Swiftblade Vindicator R	.15	.30
204 Tajic, Legion's Edge R	.15	.30
205 Thief of Sanity R	.15	.30
206 Thought Erasure U	.10	.20
207 Thousand-Year Storm M	1.50	3.00
208 Trostani Discordant M	2.00	4.00
209 Truefire Captain U	.10	.20
210 Undercity Uprising C	.07	.15
211 Underrealm Lich M	2.50	5.00
212 Unmoored Ego R	.15	.30
213 Vraska, Golgari Queen M	6.00	12.00
214 Wee Dragonauts U	.10	.20
215 Worldsoul Colossus U	.10	.20
216 Fresh-Faced Recruit C	.07	.15
217 Piston-Fist Cyclops C	.07	.15
218 Pitiless Gorgon C	.07	.15
219 Vernadi Shieldmate C	.07	.15
220 Whisper Agent C	.07	.15
221 Assure/Assemble R	.15	.30
222 Connive/Concoct R	.15	.30
223 Discovery/Dispersal U	.10	.20
224 Expansion/Explosion R	.15	.30
225 Find/Finality R	.15	.30
226 Flower/Flourish U	.10	.20
227 Integrity/Intervention U	.10	.20
228 Invert/Invent U	.10	.20
229 Response/Resurgence R	.15	.30
230 Status/Statue U	.10	.20
231 Boros Locket C	.07	.15
232 Chamber Sentry R	.15	.30
233 Chromatic Lantern R	.15	.30
234 Dimir Locket C	.07	.15
235 Gatekeeper Gargoyle U	.10	.20
236 Glaive of the Guildpact U	.10	.20
237 Golgari Locket C	.07	.15
238 Izzet Locket C	.07	.15
239 Rampaging Monument U	.10	.20
240 Selesnya Locket C	.07	.15
241 Silent Dart U	.10	.20
242 Wand of Vertebrae U	.10	.20
243 Boros Guildgate C	.07	.15
244 Boros Guildgate C	.07	.15
245 Dimir Guildgate C	.07	.15
246 Dimir Guildgate C	.07	.15
247 Gateway Plaza C	.07	.15
248 Golgari Guildgate C	.07	.15
249 Golgari Guildgate C	.07	.15

250 Guildmages' Forum R .15 .30
251 Izzet Guildgate C .07 .15
252 Izzet Guildgate C .07 .15
253 Overgrown Tomb R .15 .30
254 Sacred Foundry R .15 .30
255 Selesnya Guildgate C .07 .15
256 Selesnya Guildgate C .07 .15
257 Steam Vents R .15 .30
258 Temple Garden R .15 .30
259 Watery Grave R .15 .30
260 Plains L .07 .15
261 Island L .07 .15
262 Swamp L .07 .15
263 Mountain L .07 .15
264 Forest L .07 .15
265 Ral, Caller of Storms M 3.00 6.00
266 Ral's Dispersal R .15 .30
267 Precision Bolt C .07 .15
268 Ral's Staticaster U .10 .20
269 Vraska, Regal Gorgon M 3.00 6.00
270 Kraul Raider C .07 .15
271 Attendant of Vraska U .10 .20
272 Vraska's Stoneglare R .15 .30
273 Impervious Greatwurm M 2.50 5.00

2018 Magic The Gathering Guilds of Ravnica Ravnica Weekend

A01 Island L 2.00 4.00
A02 Swamp L 1.50 3.00
A03 Island L 3.00 6.00
A04 Mountain L 2.00 4.00
A05 Swamp L 1.25 2.50
A06 Forest L 1.50 3.00
A07 Mountain L 1.25 2.50
A08 Plains L 1.50 3.00
A09 Forest L 1.50 3.00
A10 Plains L 1.25 2.50

2018 Magic The Gathering Guilds of Ravnica Tokens

1 Angel .25 .50
2 Soldier .07 .15
3 Bird Illusion .07 .15
4 Goblin .07 .15
5 Insect .07 .15
6 Elf Knight .07 .15
7 Ral, Izzet Viceroy Emblem .07 .15
8 Vraska, Golgari Queen Emblem .07 .15

2018 Magic The Gathering Judge Gift Rewards

1 Merchant Scroll R 20.00 40.00
2 Vampiric Tutor R 75.00 150.00
3 Nin, the Pain Artist R 3.00 6.00
4 Commander's Sphere R 6.00 12.00
5 Teferi's Protection R 25.00 50.00
6 Lord of Atlantis R 25.00 50.00
7 Rhystic Study R 150.00 300.00
8 Food Chain R 40.00 80.00

2018 Magic The Gathering Lunar New Year 2018

1 Treasure R 25.00 50.00

2018 Magic The Gathering Masters 25

1 Act of Heroism U .10 .20
2 Akroma, Angel of Wrath M 2.50 5.00
3 Akroma's Vengeance R .15 .30
4 Angelic Page U .10 .20
5 Armageddon M 2.50 5.00
6 Auramancer U .10 .20
7 Cloudshift C .07 .15
8 Congregate U .10 .20
9 Darien, King of Kjeldor R .15 .30
10 Dauntless Cathar C .07 .15
11 Decree of Justice R .15 .30
12 Disenchant C .07 .15
13 Fencing Ace C .07 .15
14 Fiend Hunter U .10 .20
15 Geist of the Moors C .07 .15
16 Gods Willing C .07 .15
17 Griffin Protector C .07 .15
18 Karona's Zealot U .10 .20
19 Knight of the Skyward Eye C .07 .15
20 Kongming, ""Sleeping Dragon"" U .10 .20
21 Kor Firewalker U .10 .20
22 Loyal Sentry C .07 .15
23 Luminarch Ascension R .15 .30
24 Lunarch Mantle C .07 .15
25 Noble Templar C .07 .15
26 Nyx-Fleece Ram U .10 .20
27 Ordeal of Heliod U .10 .20
28 Pacifism C .07 .15
29 Path of Peace C .07 .15
30 Promise of Bunrei U .10 .20
31 Renewed Faith C .07 .15
32 Rest in Peace R .15 .30
33 Savannah Lions C .07 .15
34 Squadron Hawk C .07 .15
35 Swords to Plowshares U .10 .20
36 Thalia, Guardian of Thraben R .15 .30
37 Urbis Protector U .10 .20
38 Valor in Akros U .10 .20
39 Whitemane Lion C .07 .15
40 Accumulated Knowledge C .07 .15
41 Arcane Denial C .07 .15
42 Bident of Thassa R .15 .30
43 Blue Elemental Blast U .10 .20
44 Blue Sun's Zenith R .15 .30
45 Borrowing 100,000 Arrows C .07 .15
46 Brainstorm C .07 .15
47 Brine Elemental U .10 .20
48 Choking Tethers C .07 .15
49 Coralhelm Guide C .07 .15
50 Counterspell C .07 .15
51 Court Hussar C .07 .15
52 Curiosity U .10 .20
53 Cursecatcher U .10 .20
54 Dragon's Eye Savants C .07 .15
55 Exclude U .10 .20
56 Fathom Seer C .07 .15
57 Flash R .15 .30
58 Freed from the Real U .10 .20
59 Genju of the Falls U .10 .20
60 Ghost Ship C .07 .15
61 Horseshoe Crab C .07 .15
62 Jace, the Mind Sculptor M 60.00 120.00
63 Jalira, Master Polymorphist U .10 .20
64 Man-o'-War C .07 .15
65 Merfolk Looter U .10 .20
66 Murder of Crows U .10 .20
67 Mystic of the Hidden Way C .07 .15
68 Pact of Negation R .15 .30
69 Phantasmal Bear C .07 .15
70 Reef Worm R .15 .30
71 Retraction Helix C .07 .15
72 Shoreline Ranger C .07 .15
73 Sift C .07 .15
74 Totally Lost C .07 .15
75 Twisted Image U .10 .20
76 Vendilion Clique M 12.50 25.00
77 Vesuvan Shapeshifter R .15 .30
78 Willbender U .10 .20
79 Ancient Craving U .10 .20
80 Bloodhunter Bat C .07 .15
81 Caustic Tar U .10 .20
82 Dark Ritual C .07 .15
83 Deadly Designs U .10 .20
84 Death's-Head Buzzard C .07 .15
85 Diabolic Edict C .07 .15
86 Dirge of Dread C .07 .15
87 Disfigure C .07 .15
88 Doomsday M 2.50 5.00
89 Dusk Legion Zealot C .07 .15
90 Erg Raiders C .07 .15
91 Fallen Angel U .10 .20
92 Hell's Caretaker R .15 .30
93 Horror of the Broken Lands U .10 .20
94 Ihsan's Shade U .10 .20
95 Laquatus's Champion R .15 .30
96 Living Death R .15 .30
97 Mesmeric Fiend U .10 .20
98 Murder C .07 .15
99 Nezumi Cutthroat C .07 .15
100 Phyrexian Ghoul C .07 .15
101 Phyrexian Obliterator M 10.00 18.00
102 Plague Wind R .15 .30
103 Ratcatcher R .15 .30
104 Ravenous Chupacabra U .10 .20
105 Relentless Rats C .07 .15
106 Returned Phalanx C .07 .15
107 Ruthless Ripper C .07 .15
108 Street Wraith U .10 .20
109 Supernatural Stamina C .07 .15
110 Triskaidekaphobia R .15 .30
111 Twisted Abomination C .07 .15
112 Undead Gladiator U .10 .20
113 Unearth C .07 .15
114 Vampire Lacerator C .07 .15
115 Will-o'-the-Wisp U .10 .20
116 Zombify U .10 .20
117 Zulaport Cutthroat U .10 .20
118 Act of Treason C .07 .15
119 Akroma, Angel of Fury M 2.50 5.00
120 Balduvian Horde C .07 .15
121 Ball Lghtning R .15 .30
122 Blood Moon R .15 .30
123 Browbeat U .10 .20
124 Chandra's Outrage C .07 .15
125 Chartooth Cougar C .07 .15
126 Cinder Storm C .07 .15
127 Crimson Mage C .07 .15
128 Eidolon of the Great Revel R .15 .30
129 Enthralling Victor U .10 .20
130 Fortune Thief R .15 .30
131 Frenzied Goblin C .07 .15
132 Genju of the Spires U .10 .20
133 Goblin Hawk Drums U .10 .20
134 Hordeling Outburst C .07 .15
135 Humble Defector U .10 .20
136 Imperial Recruiter M 30.00 75.00
137 Ire Shaman U .10 .20
138 Izzet Chemister R .15 .30
139 Jackal Pup C .07 .15
140 Kindle C .07 .15
141 Lightning Bolt U .10 .20
142 Magus of the Wheel R .15 .30
143 Mogg Flunkies C .07 .15
144 Pillage C .07 .15
145 Pyre Hound C .07 .15
146 Pyroclasm U .10 .20
147 Red Elemental Blast U .10 .20
148 Simian Spirit Guide U .10 .20
149 Skeletonize C .07 .15
150 Skirk Commando C .07 .15
151 Soulbright Flamekin C .07 .15
152 Spikeshot Goblin U .10 .20
153 Thresher Lizard C .07 .15
154 Trumpet Blast C .07 .15
155 Uncaged Fury C .07 .15
156 Zada, Hedron Grinder U .10 .20
157 Ainok Survivalist C .07 .15
158 Ambassador Oak C .07 .15
159 Ancient Stirrings U .10 .20
160 Arbor Elf C .07 .15
161 Azusa, Lost but Seeking R .15 .30
162 Broodhatch Nantuko U .10 .20
163 Colossal Dreadmaw C .07 .15
164 Courser of Kruphix R .15 .30
165 Cultivate C .07 .15
166 Echoing Courage C .07 .15
167 Elvish Aberration C .07 .15
168 Elvish Piper R .15 .30
169 Ember Weaver C .07 .15
170 Epic Confrontation C .07 .15
171 Fierce Empath U .10 .20
172 Giant Growth C .07 .15
173 Invigorate U .10 .20
174 Iwamori of the Open Fist U .10 .20
175 Kavu Climber C .07 .15
176 Kavu Predator U .10 .20
177 Krosan Colossus U .10 .20
178 Krosan Tusker U .10 .20
179 Living Wish R .15 .30
180 Lull C .07 .15
181 Master of the Wild Hunt M 2.50 5.00
182 Nettle Sentinel C .07 .15
183 Plummet C .07 .15
184 Presence of Gond C .07 .15
185 Protean Hulk R .15 .30
186 Rancor U .10 .20
187 Regrowth U .10 .20
188 Stampede Driver U .10 .20
189 Summoner's Pact R .15 .30
190 Timberpack Wolf C .07 .15
191 Tree of Redemption M 2.50 5.00
192 Utopia Sprawl U .10 .20
193 Vessel of Nascency C .07 .15
194 Wildheart Invoker C .07 .15
195 Woolly Loxodon C .07 .15
196 Animar, Soul of Elements M 7.50 16.00
197 Baloth Null U .10 .20
198 Blightning U .10 .20
199 Boros Charm U .10 .20
200 Brion Stoutarm R .15 .30
201 Cloudblazer U .10 .20
202 Conflux R .15 .30
203 Eladamri's Call R .15 .30
204 Gisela, Blade of Goldnight M 2.50 5.00
205 Grenzo, Dungeon Warden R .15 .30
206 Hanna, Ship's Navigator R .15 .30
207 Lorescale Coatl U .10 .20
208 Mystic Snake R .15 .30
209 Nicol Bolas R .15 .30
210 Niv-Mizzet, the Firemind R .15 .30
211 Notion Thief R .15 .30
212 Pernicious Deed R .15 .30
213 Pillory of the Sleepless U .10 .20
214 Prossh, Skyraider of Kher M .17 .35
215 Quicksilver Dagger U .10 .20
216 Ruric Thar, the Unbowed R .15 .30
217 Shadowmage Infiltrator U .10 .20
218 Stangg U .10 .20
219 Vindicate R .15 .30
220 Watchwolf U .10 .20
221 Assembly-Worker C .07 .15
222 Chalice of the Void M 30.00 55.00
223 Coalition Relic R .15 .30
224 Ensnaring Bridge M 17.50 35.00
225 Heavy Arbalest U .10 .20
226 Nihil Spellbomb U .10 .20
227 Perilous Myr U .10 .20
228 Primal Clay C .07 .15
229 Prophetic Prism C .07 .15
230 Sai of the Shinobi U .10 .20
231 Self-Assembler C .07 .15
232 Strionic Resonator R .15 .30
233 Sundering Titan R .15 .30
234 Swiftfoot Boots U .10 .20
235 Treasure Keeper U .10 .20
236 Ash Barrens U .10 .20
237 Cascade Bluffs R .15 .30
238 Fetid Heath R .15 .30
239 Flooded Grove R .15 .30
240 Haunted Fengraf R .15 .30
241 Mikokoro, Center of the Sea R .15 .30
242 Mishra's Factory U .10 .20
243 Myriad Landscape U .10 .20
244 Pendelhaven R .15 .30
245 Quicksand U .10 .20
246 Rishadan Port R .15 .30
247 Rugged Prairie R .15 .30
248 Twilight Mire R .15 .30
249 Zoetic Cavern U .10 .20

2018 Magic The Gathering Masters 25 Tokens

1 Spirit .12 .25
2 Angel .07 .10
3 Soldier .07 .10
4 Spirit .07 .10
5 Fish .15 .30
6 Kraken .75 1.50
7 Whale .15 .30
8 Skeleton .07 .10
9 Goblin .10 .20
10 Kobolds of Kher Keep 1.00 1.75
11 Elf Warrior .10 .20
12 Insect .07 .15
13 Wolf .07 .15
14 Stangg Twin .07 .10
15 Morph .07 .10

2018 Magic The Gathering Rivals of Ixalan

1 Baffling End U .10 .20
2 Bishop of Binding R .15 .30
3 Blazing Hope U .10 .20
4 Cleansing Ray C .07 .15
5 Divine Verdict C .07 .15
6 Everdawn Champion U .10 .20
7 Exultant Skymarcher C .07 .15
8 Famished Paladin U .10 .20
9 Forerunner of the Legion U .25 .50
10 Imperial Ceratops U .10 .20
11 Legion Conquistador C .07 .15
12 Luminous Bonds C .07 .15
13 Majestic Heliopterus U .10 .20
14 Martyr of Dusk C .07 .15
15 Moment of Triumph C .07 .15
16 Paladin of Atonement R .15 .30
17 Pride of Conquerors U .10 .20
18 Radiant Destiny R .75 1.50
19 Raptor Companion C .07 .15
20 Sanguine Glorifier C .07 .15
21 Skymarcher Aspirant U .10 .20
22 Slaughter the Strong R .20 .40
23 Snubhorn Sentry C .07 .15
24 Sphinx's Decree R .15 .30
25 Squire's Devotion C .07 .15
26 Sun Sentinel C .07 .15
27 Sun-Crested Pterodon C .07 .15
28 Temple Altisaur R .75 1.50
29 Trapjaw Tyrant M 4.00 8.00
30 Zetalpa, Primal Dawn R .30 .60
31 Admiral's Order R .25 .50
32 Aquatic Incursion U .10 .20
33 Crafty Cutpurse R .20 .40
34 Crashing Tide C .07 .15
35 Curious Obsession U .50 1.00
36 Deadeye Rig-Hauler C .07 .15
37 Expel from Orazca U .10 .20
38 Flood of Recollection U .10 .20
39 Hornswoggle U .10 .20
40 Induced Amnesia R .15 .30
41 Kitesail Corsair C .07 .15
42 Kumena's Awakening R .30 .75
43 Mist-Cloaked Herald C .20 .40
44 Negate C .07 .15
45 Nezahal, Primal Tide R .75 1.50
46 Release to the Wind R .25 .50
47 River Darter C .07 .15
48 Riverwise Augur U .10 .20
49 Sailor of Means C .07 .15
50 Sea Legs C .07 .15
51 Seafloor Oracle R .50 1.00
52 Secrets of the Golden City C .07 .15
53 Silvergill Adept U .15 .30
54 Siren Reaver U .10 .20
55 Slippery Scoundrel U .10 .20
56 Soul of the Rapids C .07 .15
57 Spire Winder C .07 .15
58 Sworn Guardian C .07 .15
59 Timestream Navigator M 3.00 6.00
60 Warkite Marauder R 1.25 2.50
61 Waterknot C .07 .15
62 Arterial Flow U .30 .60
63 Canal Monitor C .07 .15
64 Champion of Dusk R .75 1.50
65 Dark Inquiry C .07 .15
66 Dead Man's Chest R .20 .40
67 Dinosaur Hunter C .07 .15
68 Dire Fleet Poisoner R .50 1.00
69 Dusk Charger C .07 .15
70 Dusk Legion Zealot C .20 .40
71 Fathom Fleet Boarder C .07 .15
72 Forerunner of the Coalition U .20 .40
73 Golden Demise U .10 .20
74 Grasping Scoundrel C .07 .15
75 Gruesome Fate C .07 .15
76 Impale C .07 .15
77 Mastermind's Acquisition R 1.00 2.00
78 Mausoleum Harpy U .10 .20
79 Moment of Craving C .07 .15
80 Oathsworn Vampire U .15 .30
81 Pitiless Plunderer U 7.50 15.00
82 Ravenous Chupacabra U .75 1.50
83 Reaver Ambush U .10 .20
84 Recover C .07 .15
85 Sadistic Skymarcher U .10 .20
86 Tetzimoc, Primal Death R .30 .60
87 Tomb Robber R .15 .30
88 Twilight Prophet M 20.00 40.00
89 Vampire Revenant C .07 .15
90 Vona's Hunger R 2.50 5.00
91 Voracious Vampire C .07 .15
92 Blood Sun R .30 .75
93 Bombard C .07 .15
94 Brass's Bounty R 1.25 2.50
95 Brazen Freebooter C .07 .15
96 Buccaneer's Bravado C .07 .15
97 Charging Tuskodon U .15 .30
98 Daring Buccaneer U .10 .20
99 Dire Fleet Daredevil R 1.00 2.00
100 Etali, Primal Storm R .60 1.25
101 Fanatical Firebrand C .07 .15
102 Forerunner of the Empire U .50 1.00
103 Form of the Dinosaur R .15 .30
104 Frilled Deathspitter C .07 .15
105 Goblin Trailblazer C .07 .15
106 Mutiny C .07 .15
107 Needletooth Raptor U .10 .20
108 Orazca Raptor C .07 .15
109 Pirate's Pillage U .75 1.50
110 Reckless Rage U .20 .40
111 Rekindling Phoenix M 1.25 2.50
112 See Red U .10 .20
113 Shake the Foundations U .10 .20
114 Shatter C .07 .15
115 Silverclad Ferocidons R 1.50 3.00
116 Stampeding Horncrest C .07 .15
117 Storm Fleet Swashbuckler U .10 .20
118 Sun-Collared Raptor C .07 .15
119 Swaggering Corsair C .07 .15
120 Tilonalli's Crown C .07 .15
121 Tilonalli's Summoner R .30 .60
122 Aggressive Urge C .07 .15
123 Cacophodon U .10 .20
124 Cherished Hatchling U .10 .20
125 Colossal Dreadmaw C .07 .15
126 Crested Herdcaller U .10 .20
127 Deeproot Elite R .75 1.50
128 Enter the Unknown U .15 .30
129 Forerunner of the Heralds U .10 .20
130 Ghalta, Primal Hunger R 2.00 4.00
131 Giltgrove Stalker C .07 .15
132 Hardy Veteran C .07 .15
133 Hunt the Weak C .07 .15
134 Jade Bearer C .07 .15
135 Jadecraft Artisan C .07 .15
136 Jadelight Ranger R .30 .60
137 Jungleborn Pioneer C .07 .15
138 Knight of the Stampede C .20 .40
139 Naturalize C .07 .15
140 Orazca Frillback C .07 .15
141 Overgrown Armasaur C .07 .15
142 Path of Discovery R 1.50 3.00
143 Plummet C .07 .15
144 Polyraptor M 10.00 20.00
145 Strength of the Pack U .10 .20
146 Swift Warden U .10 .20
147 Tendershoot Dryad R 7.50 15.00
148 Thrashing Brontodon U .10 .20
149 Thunderherd Migration U .15 .30
150 Wayward Swordtooth R 7.50 15.00
151 World Shaper R 3.00 6.00
152 Angrath, the Flame-Chained M 5.00 10.00
153 Atzocan Seer U .20 .40
154 Azor, the Lawbringer M 2.00 4.00
155 Deadeye Brawler U .10 .20
156 Dire Fleet Neckbreaker U .15 .30
157 Elenda, the Dusk Rose M 12.50 25.00
158 Hadana's Climb/Winged Temple of Orazca R2.50 5.00

159 Huatli, Radiant Champion M 5.00 10.00
160 Journey to Eternity/Atzal, Cave of Eternity R3.00 6.00
161 Jungle Creeper U .10 .20
162 Kumena, Tyrant of Orazca M 4.00 8.00
163 Legion Lieutenant U .75 1.50
164 Merfolk Mistbinder U .25 .50
165 Path of Mettle/Metzali, Tower of Triumph R .20 .40
166 Profane Procession/Tomb of the Dusk Rose R.50 1.00
167 Protean Raider R .30 .75
168 Raging Regisaur U .17 .35
169 Relentless Raptor U .10 .20
170 Resplendent Griffin U .10 .20
171 Siegehorn Ceratops R .50 1.00
172 Storm Fleet Sprinter U .15 .30
173 Storm the Vault/Vault of Catlacan R 4.00 8.00
174 Zacama, Primal Calamity M 20.00 40.00
175 Awakened Amalgam R .15 .30
176 Azor's Gateway/Sanctum of the Sun M 3.00 6.00
177 Captain's Hook R .15 .30
178 Gleaming Barrier C .07 .15
179 Golden Guardian/Gold-Forge Garrison R 1.00 2.00
180 The Immortal Sun M 17.50 35.00
181 Orazca Relic C .07 .15
182 Silent Gravestone R .15 .30
183 Strider Harness C .07 .15
184 Traverl's Amulet C .07 .15
185 Arch of Orazca R .60 1.25
186 Evolving Wilds C .07 .15
187 Forsaken Sanctuary U .10 .20
188 Foul Orchard U .10 .20
189 Highland Lake U .10 .20
190 Stone Quarry U .10 .20
191 Woodland Stream U .10 .20
192 Plains L .15 .30
193 Island L .30 .60
194 Swamp L .20 .40
195 Mountain L .25 .50
196 Forest L .30 .60

2018 Magic The Gathering Rivals of Ixalan Tokens

1 Elemental .10 .20
2 Elemental .10 .20
3 Saproling .07 .15
4 Golem .07 .15
5 Huatli, Radiant Champion Emblem .07 .15
6 City's Blessing .07 .15
CH1 Rivals of Ixalan CL .07 .15

2018 Magic The Gathering Signature Spellbook Jace

1 Jace Beleren M 1.50 3.00
2 Blue Elemental Blast R .30 .60
3 Brainstorm R 1.00 2.00
4 Counterspell R 1.25 2.50
5 Gifts Ungiven R .25 .50
6 Mystical Tutor R 4.00 8.00
7 Negate R .20 .40
8 Threads of Disloyalty R .20 .40

2018 Magic The Gathering Ultimate Masters

1 All Is Dust R 7.50 15.00
2 Artisan of Kozilek U .50 1.00
3 Eldrazi Conscription R 7.50 15.00
4 Emrakul, the Aeons Torn M 30.00 60.00
5 Karn Liberated M 20.00 40.00
6 Kozilek, Butcher of Truth M 30.00 75.00
7 Ulamog, the Infinite Gyre M 30.00 75.00
8 Ulamog's Crusher C .07 .15
9 Ancestor's Chosen U .10 .20
10 Angelic Renewal C .15 .30
11 Containment Priest R .17 .35
12 Conviction C .07 .15
13 Dawn Charm U .20 .40
14 Daybreak Coronet R 3.00 6.00
15 Emancipation Angel U .15 .30
16 Faith's Fetters C .07 .15
17 Fiend Hunter U .15 .30
18 Gods Willing C .07 .15
19 Heliod's Pilgrim C .07 .15
20 Hero of Iroas U .20 .40
21 Hyena Umbra C .25 .50
22 Icatian Crier C .07 .15
23 Lotus-Eye Mystics C .07 .15
24 Mammoth Umbra C .07 .15
25 Martyr of Sands C .07 .15
26 Miraculous Recovery U .10 .20
27 Phalanx Leader U .15 .30
28 Rally the Peasants U .10 .20
29 Repel the Darkness C .07 .15
30 Resurrection C .07 .15
31 Reveillark R .30 .75
32 Reya Dawnbringer R 1.00 2.00
33 Ronom Unicorn C .07 .15
34 Runed Halo R .20 .40
35 Sigil of the New Dawn U .15 .30
36 Skyspear Cavalry C .07 .15
37 Spirit Cairn U .10 .20
38 Sublime Archangel R 1.25 2.50
39 Swift Reckoning U .10 .20
40 Tethmos High Priest C .07 .15
41 Wall of Reverence R 1.00 2.00
42 Wandering Champion C .07 .15
43 Wingsteed Rider C .07 .15
44 Aethersnipe C .07 .15
45 Archaeomancer C .15 .30
46 Back to Basics R 7.50 15.00
47 Circular Logic U .20 .40
48 Defy Gravity C .07 .15
49 Deranged Assistant C .07 .15
50 Dig Through Time R 1.00 2.00
51 Disrupting Shoal R .30 .75
52 Dreamscape Artist U .12 .25
53 Eel Umbra C .07 .15
54 Flight of Fancy C .07 .15
55 Foil C .25 .50
56 Forbidden Alchemy U .12 .25
57 Frantic Search C .75 1.50
58 Glen Elendra Archmage R 6.00 12.00
59 Iridescent Drake U .10 .20
60 Just the Wind C .07 .15
61 Laboratory Maniac U 2.50 5.00
62 Living Lore U .10 .20
63 Magus of the Bazaar R .30 .60
64 Mahamoti Djinn U .10 .20
65 Marang River Prowler U .10 .20
66 Mystic Retrieval U .10 .20
67 Rise from the Tides U .15 .30
68 Rune Snag C .07 .15
69 Skywing Aven C .07 .15
70 Sleight of Hand U .75 1.50
71 Snapcaster Mage M 40.00 80.00
72 Stitched Drake C .07 .15
73 Stitcher's Apprentice C .07 .15
74 Stream of Consciousness U .10 .20
75 Sultai Skullkeeper C .07 .15
76 Talrand, Sky Summoner R .15 .30
77 Temporal Manipulation M 12.50 25.00
78 Think Twice C .07 .15
79 Treasure Cruise C .07 .15
80 Unstable Mutation U .10 .20
81 Visions of Beyond R 7.50 15.00
82 Whirlwind Adept C .07 .15
83 Appetite for Brains U .10 .20
84 Apprentice Necromancer U .75 1.50
85 Bitterblossom M 30.00 60.00
86 Bloodflow Connoisseur C .12 .25
87 Bridge from Below R .75 1.50
88 Buried Alive U 3.00 6.00
89 Chainer's Edict U 2.50 5.00
90 Crow of Dark Tidings C .07 .15
91 Dark Dabbling C .07 .15
92 Death Denied C .15 .30
93 Demonic Tutor R 20.00 40.00
94 Entomb R 15.00 30.00
95 Fume Spitter C .12 .25
96 Ghoulcaller's Accomplice C .07 .15
97 Ghoulsteed U .10 .20
98 Golgari Thug U .60 1.25
99 Goryo's Vengeance R 2.00 4.00
100 Grave Scrabbler C .07 .15
101 Grave Strength U .10 .20
102 Gurmag Angler C .15 .30
103 Last Gasp C .07 .15
104 Liliana of the Veil M 60.00 120.00
105 Mark of the Vampire C .07 .15
106 Mikaeus, the Unhallowed M 30.00 60.00
107 Moan of the Unhallowed C .07 .15
108 Offalsnout C .07 .15
109 Olivia's Dragoon C .07 .15
110 Reanimate R 7.50 15.00
111 Sanitarium Skeleton C .07 .15
112 Shirei, Shizo's Caretaker U .25 .50
113 Shriekmaw U .25 .50
114 Slum Reaper C .07 .15
115 Songs of the Damned U .30 .75
116 Spoils of the Vault R .30 .75
117 Tasigur, the Golden Fang R .20 .40
118 Twins of Maurer Estate C .07 .15
119 Unburial Rites U .15 .30
120 Unholy Hunger C .07 .15
121 Akroan Crusader C .07 .15
122 Anger U 1.50 3.00
123 Arena Athlete C .07 .15
124 Balefire Dragon M 20.00 40.00
125 Brazen Scourge U .10 .20
126 Conflagrate U .17 .35
127 Desperate Ritual U .75 1.50
128 Faithless Looting C .30 .75
129 Fiery Temper C .07 .15
130 Firewing Phoenix U .10 .20
131 Furnace Celebration U .10 .20
132 Gamble R 10.00 20.00
133 Generator Servant C .07 .15
134 Hissing Iguanar C .07 .15
135 Ingot Chewer C .07 .15
136 Lava Spike U 1.50 3.00
137 Mad Prophet C .07 .15
138 Magmaw U .10 .20
139 Malevolent Whispers U .10 .20
140 Molten Birth C .07 .15
141 Nightbird's Clutches C .07 .15
142 Raid Bombardment C .10 .20
143 Reckless Charge C .07 .15
144 Reckless Wurm C .07 .15
145 Rolling Temblor U .10 .20
146 Seismic Assault R .25 .50
147 Seize the Day R 5.00 10.00
148 Soul's Fire C .07 .15
149 Sparkspitter C .07 .15
150 Squee, Goblin Nabob R .20 .40
151 Thermo-Alchemist C .07 .15
152 Through the Breach R 2.50 5.00
153 Undying Rage C .07 .15
154 Vexing Devil R 3.00 6.00
155 Young Pyromancer U .50 1.00
156 Basking Rootwalla C .10 .20
157 Become Immense U .12 .25
158 Boar Umbra U .15 .30
159 Boneyard Wurm U .15 .30
160 Brawn U .30 .60
161 Crushing Canopy C .07 .15
162 Devoted Druid U 1.25 2.50
163 Eternal Witness U 3.00 6.00
164 Fauna Shaman R 7.50 15.00
165 Fecundity U .50 1.00
166 Golgari Brownscale C .07 .15
167 Golgari Grave-Troll R 2.50 5.00
168 Groundskeeper C .07 .15
169 Hero of Leina Tower U .10 .20
170 Hooting Mandrills C .07 .15
171 Kodama's Reach C 1.00 2.00
172 Life from the Loam R 10.00 20.00
173 Miming Slime C .07 .15
174 Noble Hierarch R 10.00 20.00
175 Nourishing Shoal R .15 .30
176 Pattern of Rebirth R 3.00 6.00
177 Penumbra Wurm U .10 .20
178 Prey Upon C .07 .15
179 Pulse of Murasa C .07 .15
180 Satyr Wayfinder C .07 .15
181 Shed Weakness C .07 .15
182 Snake Umbra U .30 .60
183 Spider Spawning U .20 .40
184 Spider Umbra C .07 .15
185 Staunch-Hearted Warrior C .07 .15
186 Stingerfling Spider U .10 .20
187 Tarmogoyf M 20.00 40.00
188 Travel Preparations U .10 .20
189 Vengevine M 10.00 20.00
190 Verdant Eidolon C .07 .15
191 Walker of the Grove C .07 .15
192 Wickerbough Elder C .07 .15
193 Wild Hunger U .10 .20
194 Wild Mongrel C .12 .25
195 Woodfall Primus R 2.00 4.00
196 Angel of Despair U .25 .50
197 Blast of Genius U .10 .20
198 Countersquall U .60 1.25
199 Gaddock Teeg R 4.00 8.00
200 Garna, the Bloodflame U .10 .20
201 Golgari Charm U .75 1.50
202 Leovold, Emissary of Trest M 4.00 8.00
203 Lord of Extinction M 6.00 12.00
204 Maelstrom Pulse R 1.00 2.00
205 Reviving Vapors U .10 .20
206 Sigarda, Host of Herons M 7.50 15.00
207 Sovereigns of Lost Alara R 1.00 2.00
208 Urban Evolution U .15 .30
209 Vengeful Rebirth U .10 .20
210 Warleader's Helix U .10 .20
211 Beckon Apparition C .07 .15
212 Canker Abomination C .07 .15
213 Dimir Guildmage C .07 .15
214 Double Cleave C .12 .25
215 Fulminator Mage R 1.25 2.50
216 Kitchen Finks U .50 1.00
217 Murderous Redcap U .17 .35
218 Plumeveil U .10 .20
219 Rakdos Shred-Freak C .07 .15
220 Safehold Elite C .10 .20
221 Scuzzback Marauders C .07 .15
222 Shielding Plax C .07 .15
223 Slippery Bogle U 1.00 2.00
224 Turn to Mist C .15 .30
225 Fire/Ice C .07 .15
226 Cathodion C .07 .15
227 Engineered Explosives R 12.50 25.00
228 Heap Doll U .20 .40
229 Mana Vault M 60.00 120.00
230 Myr Servitor C .07 .15
231 Patchwork Gnomes C .07 .15
232 Phyrexian Altar R 40.00 80.00
233 Platinum Emperion M 12.50 25.00
234 Prismatic Lens U .30 .60
235 Vessel of Endless Rest C .15 .30
236 Ancient Tomb R 30.00 60.00
237 Cavern of Souls M 60.00 120.00
238 Celestial Colonnade R 2.50 5.00
239 Creeping Tar Pit R 2.50 5.00
240 Dakmor Salvage U .50 1.00
241 Dark Depths M 12.50 25.00
242 Desolate Lighthouse R .15 .30
243 Flagstones of Trokair R 2.50 5.00
244 Karakas M 20.00 40.00
245 Lavaclaw Reachers R .50 1.00
246 Mage-Ring Network U .15 .30
247 Mistveil Plains U 1.25 2.50
248 Phyrexian Tower R 10.00 20.00
249 Raging Ravine R 1.25 2.50
250 Rogue's Passage U .25 .50
251 Stirring Wildwood R .30 .60
252 Terramorphic Expanse C .10 .20
253 Thespian's Stage R 1.00 2.00
254 Urborg, Tomb of Yawgmoth R 20.00 40.00

2018 Magic The Gathering Ultimate Masters Box-Toppers

U1 Emrakul, the Aeons Torn M 30.00 60.00
U2 Karn Liberated M 60.00 120.00
U3 Kozilek, Butcher of Truth M 30.00 75.00
U4 Ulamog, the Infinite Gyre M 30.00 60.00
U5 Snapcaster Mage M 75.00 150.00
U6 Temporal Manipulation M 20.00 40.00
U7 Bitterblossom M 30.00 75.00
U8 Demonic Tutor M 50.00 100.00
U9 Goryo's Vengeance M 10.00 20.00
U10 Liliana of the Veil M 150.00 300.00
U11 Mikaeus, the Unhallowed M 30.00 60.00
U12 Reanimate M 20.00 40.00
U13 Tasigur, the Golden Fang M 12.50 25.00
U14 Balefire Dragon M 20.00 40.00
U15 Through the Breach M 15.00 30.00
U16 Eternal Witness M 30.00 60.00
U17 Life from the Loam M 30.00 60.00
U18 Noble Hierarch M 30.00 75.00
U19 Tarmogoyf M 60.00 120.00
U20 Vengevine M 20.00 40.00
U21 Gaddock Teeg M 15.00 30.00
U22 Leovold, Emissary of Trest M 15.00 30.00
U23 Lord of Extinction M 10.00 20.00
U24 Maelstrom Pulse M 15.00 30.00
U25 Sigarda, Hose of Herons M 20.00 40.00
U26 Fulminator Mage M 20.00 40.00
U27 Kitchen Finks M 12.50 25.00
U28 Engineered Explosives M 25.00 50.00
U29 Mana Vault M 60.00 120.00
U30 Platinum Emperion M 12.50 25.00
U31 Ancient Tomb M 50.00 100.00
U32 Cavern of Souls M 100.00 200.00
U33 Celestial Colonnade M 25.00 50.00
U34 Creeping Tar Pit M 15.00 30.00
U35 Dark Depths M 50.00 100.00
U36 Karakas M 25.00 50.00
U37 Lavaclaw Reaches M 10.00 20.00
U38 Raging Ravine M 20.00 40.00
U39 Stirring Wildwood M 10.00 20.00
U40 Urborg, Tomb of Yawgmoth M 60.00 120.00

2018 Magic The Gathering Ultimate Masters Tokens

1 Citizen .07 .15
2 Spirit .07 .10
3 Drake .30 .60
4 Homunculus .07 .10
5 Faerie Rogue .60 1.25
6 Marit Lage .50 1.00
7 Wurm .07 .15
8 Zombie .10 .20
9 Elemental .12 .25
10 Elemental .15 .30
11 Soldier .07 .15
12 Spark Elemental .07 .10
13 Elemental .07 .10
14 Ooze .07 .10
15 Spider .10 .20
16 Spirit .07 .10

2019 Magic The Gathering Commander 2019

1 Cliffside Rescuer U .10 .20
2 Commander's Insignia R .15 .30
3 Doomed Artisan R .15 .30
4 Mandate of Peace R .15 .30
5 Sevinne's Reclamation R .15 .30
6 Song of the Worldsoul R .15 .30
7 Thalia's Geistcaller R .15 .30
8 Kadena's Silencer R .15 .30
9 Leadership Vacuum U .10 .20
10 Mass Diminish R .15 .30
11 Sudden Substitution R .15 .30
12 Thought Sponge R .15 .30
13 Wall of Stolen Identity R .15 .30
14 Archfiend of Spite R .15 .30
15 Bone Miser R .15 .30
16 Curse of Fool's Wisdom R .15 .30
17 Gift of Doom R .15 .30
18 K'rrik, Son of Yawgmoth R .15 .30
19 Mire in Misery U .10 .20
20 Nightmare Unmaking R .15 .30
21 Thieving Amalgam R .15 .30
22 Anje's Ravager R .15 .30
23 Backdraft Hellkite R .15 .30
24 Dockside Extortionist R .15 .30
25 Ghired's Belligerence R .15 .30
26 Hate Mirage U .10 .20
27 Ignite the Future R .15 .30
28 Skyfire Phoenix R .15 .30
29 Tectonic Hellion R .15 .30
30 Wildfire Devils R .15 .30
31 Apex Altisaur R .15 .30
32 Full Flowering R .15 .30
33 Ohran Frostfang R .15 .30
34 Road of Return R .15 .30
35 Selesnya Eulogist R .15 .30
36 Voice of Many U .10 .20
37 Anje Falkenrath M 2.50 5.00
38 Atla Palani, Nest Tender M 4.00 8.00
39 Chainer, Nightmare Adept M 2.50 5.00
40 Elsha of the Infinite M 3.00 6.00
41 Gerrard, Weatherlight Hero R .15 .30
42 Ghired, Conclave Exile M 2.50 5.00
43 Greven, Predator Captain M 1.25 2.50
44 Grismold, the Dreadsower R .15 .30
45 Kadena, Slinking Sorcerer M 2.00 4.00
46 Marisi, Breaker of the Coil M 2.00 4.00
47 Pramikon, Sky Rampant M 1.50 3.00
48 Rayami, First of the Fallen M 1.00 2.00
49 Sevinne, the Chronoclasm M 1.25 2.50
50 Tahngarth, First Mate R .15 .30
51 Volrath, the Shapestealer M 2.00 4.00
52 Aeon Engine R .15 .30
53 Bloodthirsty Blade U .10 .20
54 Empowered Autogenerator R .15 .30
55 Idol of Oblivion R .15 .30
56 Pendant of Prosperity R .15 .30
57 Scareteller C .07 .15
58 Scroll of Fate R .15 .30
59 Sanctum of Eternity R .15 .30
60 Desolation Twin R .15 .30
61 Angel of Sanctions M .25 .50
62 Divine Reckoning R .15 .30
63 Dusk/Dawn R .15 .30
64 Ghostly Prison U .10 .20
65 Hour of Reckoning R .15 .30
66 Increasing Devotion R .15 .30
67 Intangible Virtue U .10 .20
68 Phyrexian Rebirth R .15 .30
69 Prismatic Strands C .07 .15
70 Pristine Angel M .25 .50
71 Purify the Grave U .10 .20
72 Ray of Distortion C .07 .15
73 Roc Egg U .10 .20
74 Rootborn Defenses C .07 .15
75 Storm Herd R .15 .30
76 Sun Titan M 1.25 2.50
77 Trostani's Judgment C .07 .15
78 Wingmate Roc M .25 .50
79 Zetalpa, Primal Dawn R .15 .30
80 Chemister's Insight U .10 .20
81 Chromeshell Crab R .15 .30
82 Clever Impersonator M 1.50 3.00
83 Deep Analysis C .07 .15
84 Echoing Truth C .07 .15
85 Fact or Fiction U .10 .20
86 Fervent Denial U .10 .20
87 Ixidron R .15 .30
88 Jace's Sanctum R .15 .30
89 Kheru Spellsnatcher R .15 .30
90 Mystic Retrieval U .10 .20
91 Oona's Grace C .07 .15
92 Reality Shift U .10 .20
93 River Kelpie R .15 .30
94 Runic Repetition U .10 .20
95 Secrets of the Dead U .10 .20
96 Stratus Dancer R .15 .30
97 Talrand, Sky Summoner R .15 .30
98 Tezzeret's Gambit U .10 .20
99 Think Twice C .07 .15
100 Thousand Winds R .15 .30
101 Vesuvan Shapeshifter R .15 .30
102 Willbender U .10 .20
103 Asylum Visitor R .15 .30
104 Bane of the Living R .15 .30
105 Beacon of Unrest R .15 .30
106 Big Game Hunter U .10 .20
107 Boneyard Parley M .25 .50
108 Call to the Netherworld C .07 .15
109 Champion of Stray Souls M .25 .50
110 Dark Withering C .07 .15
111 Doomed Necromancer R .15 .30
112 Faith of the Devoted U .10 .20
113 From Under the Floorboards R .15 .30
114 Geth, Lord of the Vault M 2.00 4.00

115 Ghastly Conscription M	.25	.50
116 Gorgon Recluse C	.07	.16
117 Grave Scrabbler C	.07	.15
118 Grim Haruspex R	.15	.30
119 Hedonist's Trove R	.15	.30
120 Hex R	.15	.30
121 In Garruk's Wake R	.15	.30
122 Murderous Compulsion C	.07	.15
123 Nightshade Assassin U	.10	.20
124 Ob Nixilis Reignited M	.60	1.25
125 Overseer of the Damned R	.15	.30
126 Plaguecrafter U	.10	.20
127 Sanitarium Skeleton C	.07	.15
128 Silumgar Assassin R	.15	.30
129 Skinthinner C	.07	.15
130 Soul of Innistrad M	.25	.50
131 The Eldest Reborn U	.10	.20
132 Zombie Infestation U	.10	.20
133 Alchemist's Greeting C	.07	.15
134 Avacyn's Judgment R	.15	.30
135 Burning Vengeance U	.10	.20
136 Chaos Warp R	.15	.30
137 Desperate Ravings U	.10	.20
138 Devil's Play R	.15	.30
139 Dragonmaster Outcast M	.60	1.25
140 Faithless Looting C	.07	.15
141 Feldon of the Third Path M	.30	.75
142 Fiery Temper C	.07	.15
143 Flamerush Rider R	.15	.30
144 Flayer of the Hatebound R	.15	.30
145 Guttersnipe U	.10	.20
146 Heart-Piercer Manticore R	.15	.30
147 Increasing Vengeance R	.15	.30
148 Magmaquake R	.15	.30
149 Magus of the Wheel R	.15	.30
150 Malevolent Whispers U	.10	.20
151 Rolling Temblor U	.10	.20
152 Squee, Goblin Nabob R	.15	.30
153 Stromkirk Occultist R	.15	.30
154 Violent Eruption U	.10	.20
155 Warstorm Surge R	.15	.30
156 Ainok Survivalist C	.07	.15
157 Beast Within U	.10	.20
158 Colossal Majesty U	.10	.20
159 Cultivate C	.07	.15
160 Deathmist Raptor M	.30	.60
161 Den Protector R	.15	.30
162 Druid's Deliverance C	.07	.15
163 Elemental Bond U	.10	.20
164 Explore C	.07	.15
165 Farseek C	.07	.15
166 Fresh Meat R	.15	.30
167 Garruk, Primal Hunter M	1.50	3.00
168 Garruk's Packleader U	.10	.20
169 Giant Adephage M	.30	.60
170 Great Oak Guardian U	.10	.20
171 Harmonize U	.10	.20
172 Hooded Hydra M	.30	.75
173 Momentous Fall R	.15	.30
174 Nanfuko Vigilante C	.07	.15
175 Overwhelming Stampede R	.15	.30
176 Rampaging Baloths R	.15	.30
177 Sakura-Tribe Elder C	.07	.15
178 Second Harvest R	.15	.30
179 Seedborn Muse R	.15	.30
180 Shamanic Revelation R	.15	.30
181 Slice in Twain U	.10	.20
182 Soul of Zendikar M	.25	.50
183 Tempt with Discovery R	.15	.30
184 Thelonite Hermit R	.15	.30
185 Thragtusk R	.15	.30
186 Trail of Mystery R	.15	.30
187 Biomass Mutation R	.15	.30
188 Bloodhall Priest R	.15	.30
189 Bounty of the Luxa R	.15	.30
190 Crackling Drake U	.10	.20
191 Emmara Tandris R	.15	.30
192 Farm/Market U	.10	.20
193 Growing Ranks R	.15	.30
194 Icefeather Aven U	.10	.20
195 Naya Charm U	.10	.20
196 Pristine Skywise R	.15	.30
197 Putrefy U	.10	.20
198 Ral Zarek M	1.00	2.00
199 Refuse/Cooperate R	.15	.30
200 Sagu Mauler R	.15	.30
201 Secret Plans U	.10	.20
202 Sultai Charm U	.10	.20
203 Sundering Growth C	.07	.15
204 Trostani, Selesnya's Voice M	.30	.60
205 Urban Evolution U	.10	.20
206 Vitu-Ghazi Guildmage U	.10	.20
207 Vraska the Unseen M	.75	1.50
208 Wayfaring Temple R	.15	.30
209 Armillary Sphere C	.07	.15
210 Azorius Locket C	.07	.15
211 Burnished Hart U	.10	.20
212 Commander's Sphere C	.07	.15
213 Grimoire of the Dead M	.50	1.00
214 Hedron Archive U	.10	.20
215 Izzet Locket C	.07	.15
216 Key to the City R	.15	.30
217 Lightning Greaves U	.10	.20
218 Meteor Golem U	.10	.20
219 Mimic Vat R	.15	.30
220 Rakdos Locket C	.07	.15
221 Sol Ring U	.10	.20
222 Solemn Simulacrum R	.15	.30
223 Soul Foundry R	.15	.30
224 Strionic Resonator R	.15	.30
225 Thran Dynamo U	.10	.20
226 Akoum Refuge U	.10	.20
227 Ash Barrens C	.07	.15
228 Azorius Chancery U	.10	.20
229 Barren Moor U	.10	.20
230 Bloodfell Caves C	.07	.15
231 Blossoming Sands C	.07	.15
232 Bojuka Bog C	.07	.15
233 Boros Garrison C	.07	.15
234 Boros Guildgate C	.07	.15
235 Cinder Barrens R	.15	.30
236 Cinder Glade R	.15	.30
237 Command Tower C	.07	.15
238 Darkwater Catacombs R	.15	.30
239 Dimir Aqueduct U	.10	.20
240 Drownyard Temple R	.15	.30
241 Evolving Wilds C	.07	.15
242 Exotic Orchard R	.15	.30
243 Forgotten Cave C	.07	.15
244 Foul Orchard U	.10	.20
245 Gargoyle Castle R	.15	.30
246 Geier Reach Sanitarium R	.15	.30
247 Golgari Guildgate C	.07	.15
248 Golgari Rot Farm U	.10	.20
249 Graypelt Refuge U	.10	.20
250 Gruul Turf U	.10	.20
251 Highland Lake U	.10	.20
252 Izzet Boilerworks U	.10	.20
253 Izzet Guildgate C	.07	.15
254 Jungle Hollow C	.07	.15
255 Jungle Shrine U	.10	.20
256 Kazandu Refuge U	.10	.20
257 Krosan Verge U	.10	.20
258 Llanowar Wastes R	.15	.30
259 Memorial to Folly U	.10	.20
260 Mortuary Mire C	.07	.15
261 Myriad Landscape U	.10	.20
262 Mystic Monastery U	.10	.20
263 Naya Panorama C	.07	.15
264 Opulent Palace U	.10	.20
265 Prairie Stream R	.15	.30
266 Rakdos Carnarium C	.07	.15
267 Rakdos Guildgate C	.07	.15
268 Reliquary Tower U	.10	.20
269 Rix Maadi, Dungeon Palace U	.10	.20
270 Rogue's Passage U	.10	.20
271 Rugged Highlands C	.07	.15
272 Selesnya Sanctuary C	.07	.15
273 Shrine of the Forsaken Gods R	.15	.30
274 Simic Growth Chamber U	.10	.20
275 Simic Guildgate C	.07	.15
276 Stone Quarry U	.10	.20
277 Sungrass Prairie R	.15	.30
278 Sunken Hollow R	.15	.30
279 Swiftwater Cliffs C	.07	.15
280 Temple of the False God U	.10	.20
281 Terramorphic Expanse C	.07	.15
282 Thespian's Stage R	.15	.30
283 Thornwood Falls C	.07	.15
284 Tranquil Cove C	.07	.15
285 Wind-Scarred Crag C	.07	.15
286 Woodland Stream C	.07	.15
287 Yavimaya Coast R	.15	.30
288 Plains L	.07	.15
289 Plains L	.07	.15
290 Plains L	.07	.15
291 Island L	.07	.15
292 Island L	.07	.15
293 Island L	.07	.15
294 Swamp L	.07	.15
295 Swamp L	.07	.15
296 Swamp L	.07	.15
297 Mountain L	.07	.15
298 Mountain L	.07	.15
299 Mountain L	.07	.15
300 Forest L	.07	.15
301 Forest L	.07	.15
302 Forest L	.07	.15

2019 Magic The Gathering Commander 2019 Tokens

1 Bird	.20	.40
2 Bird	.20	.40
3 Human	.20	.40
4 Pegasus	.20	.40
5 Spirit	.20	.40
6 Angel of Sanctions	.20	.40
7 Heart-Piercer Manticore	.20	.40
8 Drake	.20	.40
9 Assassin	.20	.40
10 Zombie	.20	.40
11 Zombie	.20	.40
12 Dragon	.20	.40
13 Beast	.20	.40
14 Beast	.20	.40
15 Centaur	.20	.40
16 Egg	.20	.40
17 Plant	.20	.40
18 Rhino	.20	.40
19 Saproling	.20	.40
20 Snake	.20	.40
21 Wurm	.20	.40
22 Gargoyle	.20	.40
23 Horror	.20	.40
24 Sculpture	.20	.40
25 Treasure	.20	.40
26 Eldrazi	.20	.40
27 Morph	.20	.40
28 Manifest	.20	.40
29 Ob Nixilis Reignited Emblem	.20	.40

2019 Magic The Gathering Core Set 2020

1 Aerial Assault C	.07	.15
2 Ajani, Strength of the Pride M	3.00	6.00
3 Ancestral Blade U	.10	.20
4 Angel of Vitality U	.10	.20
5 Angelic Gift C	.07	.15
6 Apostle of Purifying Light U	.10	.20
7 Battalion Foot Soldier C	.07	.15
8 Bishop of Wings R	.15	.30
9 Brought Back R	.15	.30
10 Cavalier of Dawn M	2.00	3.50
11 Dawning Angel C	.07	.15
12 Daybreak Chaplain C	.07	.15
13 Devout Decree U	.10	.20
14 Disenchant C	.07	.15
15 Eternal Isolation U	.10	.20
16 Fencing Ace U	.10	.20
17 Gauntlets of Light U	.10	.20
18 Glaring Aegis C	.07	.15
19 Gods Willing U	.10	.20
20 Griffin Protector C	.07	.15
21 Griffin Sentinel C	.07	.15
22 Hanged Executioner R	.15	.30
23 Herald of the Sun U	.10	.20
24 Inspired Charge C	.07	.15
25 Inspiring Captain C	.07	.15
26 Leyline of Sanctity R	.15	.30
27 Loxodon Lifechanter R	.15	.30
28 Loyal Pegasus U	.10	.20
29 Master Splicer U	.10	.20
30 Moment of Heroism C	.07	.15
31 Moorland Inquisitor C	.07	.15
32 Pacifism C	.07	.15
33 Planar Cleansing R	.15	.30
34 Raise the Alarm C	.07	.15
35 Rule of Law U	.10	.20
36 Sephara, Sky's Blade R	.15	.30
37 Soulmender C	.07	.15
38 Squad Captain C	.07	.15
39 Starfield Mystic R	.15	.30
40 Steadfast Sentry C	.07	.15
41 Yoked Ox C	.07	.15
42 Aether Gust U	.10	.20
43 Agent of Treachery R	.15	.30
44 Air Elemental U	.10	.20
45 Anticipate C	.07	.15
46 Atemsis, All-Seeing R	.15	.30
47 Befuddle C	.07	.15
48 Bone to Ash C	.07	.15
49 Boreal Elemental C	.07	.15
50 Brineborn Cutthroat U	.10	.20
51 Captivating Gyre U	.10	.20
52 Cavalier of Gales M	2.00	4.00
53 Cerulean Drake U	.10	.20
54 Cloudkin Seer C	.07	.15
55 Convolute C	.07	.15
56 Drawn from Dreams R	.15	.30
57 Dungeon Geists R	.15	.30
58 Faerie Miscreant C	.07	.15
59 Flood of Tears R	.15	.30
60 Fortress Crab C	.07	.15
61 Frilled Sea Serpent C	.07	.15
62 Frost Lynx C	.07	.15
63 Hard Cover U	.10	.20
64 Leyline of Anticipation R	.15	.30
65 Masterful Replication R	.15	.30
66 Metropolis Sprite C	.07	.15
67 Moat Piranhas C	.07	.15
68 Mu Yanling, Sky Dancer M	6.00	12.00
69 Negate C	.07	.15
70 Octoprophet C	.07	.15
71 Portal of Sanctuary U	.10	.20
72 Renowned Weaponsmith U	.10	.20
73 Sage's Row Denizen C	.07	.15
74 Scholar of the Ages U	.10	.20
75 Sleep Paralysis C	.07	.15
76 Spectral Sailor U	.10	.20
77 Tale's End R	.15	.30
78 Unsummon C	.07	.15
79 Warden of Evos Isle U	.10	.20
80 Winged Words C	.07	.15
81 Yarok's Wavecrasher U	.10	.20
82 Zephyr Charge C	.07	.15
83 Agonizing Syphon C	.07	.15
84 Audacious Thief C	.07	.15
85 Barony Vampire C	.07	.15
86 Bladebrand C	.07	.15
87 Blightbeetle U	.10	.20
88 Blood Burglar C	.07	.15
89 Blood for Bones U	.10	.20
90 Bloodsoaked Altar U	.10	.20
91 Bloodthirsty Aerialist U	.10	.20
92 Bone Splinters C	.07	.15
93 Boneclad Necromancer C	.07	.15
94 Cavalier of Night M	2.00	4.00
95 Disfigure U	.10	.20
96 Dread Presence R	.15	.30
97 Duress C	.07	.15
98 Embodiment of Agonies R	.15	.30
99 Epicure of Blood C	.07	.15
100 Fathom Fleet Cutthroat C	.07	.15
101 Feral Abomination C	.07	.15
102 Gorging Vulture C	.07	.15
103 Gravedigger U	.10	.20
104 Gruesome Scourger U	.10	.20
105 Knight of the Ebon Legion R	.15	.30
106 Legion's End R	.15	.30
107 Leyline of the Void R	.15	.30
108 Mind Rot C	.07	.15
109 Murder C	.07	.15
110 Noxious Grasp U	.10	.20
111 Rotting Regisaur R	.15	.30
112 Sanitarium Skeleton C	.07	.15
113 Scheming Symmetry R	.15	.30
114 Sorcerer of the Fang C	.07	.15
115 Sorin, Imperious Bloodlord M	10.00	20.00
116 Soul Salvage C	.07	.15
117 Thought Distortion U	.10	.20
118 Undead Servant C	.07	.15
119 Unholy Indenture C	.07	.15
120 Vampire of the Dire Moon U	.10	.20
121 Vengeful Warchief U	.10	.20
122 Vilis, Broker of Blood R	.15	.30
123 Yarok's Fenlurker U	.10	.20
124 Act of Treason C	.07	.15
125 Cavalier of Flame M	2.00	3.50
126 Chandra, Acolyte of Flame R	.15	.30
127 Chandra, Awakened Inferno M	12.50	25.00
128 Chandra, Novice Pyromancer U	.10	.20
129 Chandra's Embercat C	.07	.15
130 Chandra's Outrage C	.07	.15
131 Chandra's Regulator R	.15	.30
132 Chandra's Spitfire U	.10	.20
133 Daggersail Aeronaut C	.07	.15
134 Destructive Digger C	.07	.15
135 Dragon Mage U	.10	.20
136 Drakuseth, Maw of Flames R	.15	.30
137 Ember Hauler U	.10	.20
138 Fire Elemental C	.07	.15
139 Flame Sweep U	.10	.20
140 Fry U	.10	.20
141 Glint-Horn Buccaneer R	.15	.30
142 Goblin Bird-Grabber C	.07	.15
143 Goblin Ringleader U	.10	.20
144 Goblin Smuggler C	.07	.15
145 Infuriate C	.07	.15
146 Keldon Raider C	.07	.15
147 Lavakin Brawler C	.07	.15
148 Leyline of Combustion R	.15	.30
149 Maniacal Rage C	.07	.15
150 Marauding Raptor R	.15	.30
151 Mask of Immolation U	.10	.20
152 Pack Mastiff C	.07	.15
153 Rapacious Dragon U	.10	.20
154 Reckless Air Strike C	.07	.15
155 Reduce to Ashes C	.07	.15
156 Repeated Reverberation R	.15	.30
157 Ripscale Predator C	.07	.15
158 Scampering Scorcher U	.10	.20
159 Scorch Spitter C	.07	.15
160 Shock C	.07	.15
161 Tectonic Rift C	.07	.15
162 Thunderkin Awakener R	.15	.30
163 Uncaged Fury U	.10	.20
164 Unchained Berserker U	.10	.20
165 Barkhide Troll U	.10	.20
166 Brightwood Tracker C	.07	.15
167 Cavalier of Thorns M	6.00	12.00
168 Centaur Courser C	.07	.15
169 Elvish Reclaimer R	.15	.30
170 Feral Invocation C	.07	.15
171 Ferocious Pup C	.07	.15
172 Gargos, Vicious Watcher R	.15	.30
173 Gift of Paradise C	.07	.15
174 Greenwood Sentinel C	.07	.15
175 Growth Cycle C	.07	.15
176 Healer of the Glade C	.07	.15
177 Howling Giant U	.10	.20
178 Leafkin Druid C	.07	.15
179 Leyline of Abundance R	.15	.30
180 Loaming Shaman U	.10	.20
181 Mammoth Spider C	.07	.15
182 Might of the Masses U	.10	.20
183 Natural End C	.07	.15
184 Netcaster Spider C	.07	.15
185 Nightpack Ambusher R	.15	.30
186 Overcome U	.10	.20
187 Overgrowth Elemental U	.10	.20
188 Plummet C	.07	.15
189 Pulse of Murasa U	.10	.20
190 Rabid Bite C	.07	.15
191 Season of Growth U	.10	.20
192 Sedge Scorpion C	.07	.15
193 Shared Summons R	.15	.30
194 Shifting Ceratops R	.15	.30
195 Silverback Shaman C	.07	.15
196 Thicket Crasher C	.07	.15
197 Thrashing Brontodon U	.10	.20
198 Veil of Summer U	.10	.20
199 Vivien, Arkbow Ranger M	2.50	5.00
200 Voracious Hydra R	.15	.30
201 Vorstclaw C	.07	.15
202 Wakeroot Elemental R	.15	.30
203 Wolfkin Bond C	.07	.15
204 Wolfrider's Saddle U	.10	.20
205 Woodland Champion U	.10	.20
206 Corpse Knight U	.10	.20
207 Creeping Trailblazer U	.10	.20
208 Empyrean Eagle U	.10	.20
209 Ironroot Warlord U	.10	.20
210 Kaalia, Zenith Seeker M	2.00	4.00
211 Kethis, the Hidden Hand M	2.00	3.50
212 Kykar, Wind's Fury M	2.00	4.00
213 Lightning Stormkin U	.10	.20
214 Moldervine Reclamation U	.10	.20
215 Ogre Siegebreaker U	.10	.20
216 Omnath, Locus of the Roil M	10.00	20.00
217 Risen Reef U	.10	.20
218 Skyknight Vanguard U	.10	.20
219 Tomebound Lich U	.10	.20
220 Yarok, the Desecrated M	7.50	15.00
221 Anvilwrought Raptor C	.07	.15
222 Bag of Holding R	.15	.30
223 Colossus Hammer U	.10	.20
224 Diamond Knight U	.10	.20
225 Diviner's Lockbox U	.10	.20
226 Golos, Tireless Pilgrim R	.15	.30
227 Grafdigger's Cage R	.15	.30
228 Heart-Piercer Bow C	.07	.15
229 Icon of Ancestry R	.15	.30
230 Manifold Key U	.10	.20
231 Marauder's Axe C	.07	.15
232 Meteor Golem U	.10	.20
233 Mystic Forge R	.15	.30
234 Pattern Matcher U	.10	.20
235 Prismite C	.07	.15
236 Retributive Wand U	.10	.20
237 Salvager of Ruin U	.10	.20
238 Scuttlemutt U	.10	.20
239 Steel Overseer R	.15	.30
240 Stone Golem C	.07	.15
241 Vial of Dragonfire C	.07	.15
242 Bloodfell Caves C	.07	.15
243 Blossoming Sands C	.07	.15
244 Cryptic Caves U	.10	.20
245 Dismal Backwater C	.07	.15
246 Evolving Winds C	.07	.15
247 Field of the Dead R	.15	.30
248 Jungle Hollow C	.07	.15
249 Lotus Field R	.15	.30
250 Rugged Highlands C	.07	.15
251 Scoured Barrens C	.07	.15
252 Swiftwater Cliffs C	.07	.15
253 Temple of Epiphany R	.15	.30
254 Temple of Malady R	.15	.30
255 Temple of Mystery R	.15	.30
256 Temple of Silence R	.15	.30
257 Temple of Triumph R	.15	.30
258 Thornwood Falls C	.07	.15
259 Tranquil Cove C	.07	.15
260 Wind-Scarred Crag C	.07	.15
261 Plains L	.07	.15
262 Plains L	.07	.15
263 Plains L	.07	.15
264 Plains L	.07	.15
265 Island L	.07	.15
266 Island L	.07	.15
267 Island L	.07	.15
268 Island L	.07	.15
269 Swamp L	.07	.15
270 Swamp L	.07	.15
271 Swamp L	.07	.15
272 Swamp L	.07	.15
273 Mountain L	.07	.15

274 Mountain L	.07	.15
275 Mountain L	.07	.15
276 Mountain L	.07	.15
277 Forest L	.07	.15
278 Forest L	.07	.15
279 Forest L	.07	.15
280 Forest L	.07	.15
281 Rienne, Angel of Rebirth M (Buy-A-Box Exclusive)	2.50	5.00
282 Ajani, Inspiring Leader M	3.00	6.00
283 Goldmane Griffin R	.15	.30
284 Savannah Sage C	.07	.15
285 Twinblade Paladin U	.10	.20
286 Mu Yanling, Celestial Wind M	3.00	6.00
287 Celestial Messenger C	.07	.15
288 Waterkin Shaman U	.10	.20
289 Yanling's Harbinger R	.15	.30
290 Sorin, Vampire Lord M	3.00	6.00
291 Savage Gorger C	.07	.15
292 Sorin's Guide R	.15	.30
293 Thirsting Bloodlord U	.10	.20
294 Chandra, Flame's Fury M	2.50	5.00
295 Chandra's Flame Wave R	.15	.30
296 Pyroclastic Elemental U	.10	.20
297 Wildfire Elemental C	.07	.15
298 Vivien, Nature's Avenger M	4.00	8.00
299 Ethereal Elk R	.15	.30
300 Gnarlback Rhino U	.10	.20
301 Vivien's Crocodile C	.07	.15
302 Angelic Guardian R	.15	.30
303 Bastion Enforcer C	.07	.15
304 Concordia Pegasus C	.07	.15
305 Haazda Officer C	.07	.15
306 Impassioned Orator C	.07	.15
307 Imperial Outrider C	.07	.15
308 Ironclad Krovod C	.07	.15
309 Prowling Caracal C	.07	.15
310 Serra's Guardian R	.15	.30
311 Show of Valor C	.07	.15
312 Siege Mastodon C	.07	.15
313 Take Vengeance C	.07	.15
314 Trusted Pegasus C	.07	.15
315 Coral Merfolk C	.07	.15
316 Phantom Warrior U	.10	.20
317 Riddlemaster Sphinx R	.15	.30
318 Snapping Drake C	.07	.15
319 Bartizan Bats C	.07	.15
320 Bogstomper C	.07	.15
321 Dark Remedy C	.07	.15
322 Disentomb C	.07	.15
323 Gravewalker R	.15	.30
324 Skeleton Archer C	.07	.15
325 Sorin's Thrust C	.07	.15
326 Vampire Opportunist C	.07	.15
327 Walking Corpse C	.07	.15
328 Engulfing Eruption C	.07	.15
329 Fearless Halberdier C	.07	.15
330 Goblin Assailant C	.07	.15
331 Hostile Minotaur C	.07	.15
332 Immortal Phoenix R	.15	.30
333 Nimble Birdsticker C	.07	.15
334 Rubblebelt Recluse C	.07	.15
335 Shivan Dragon R	.15	.30
336 Volcanic Dragon U	.10	.20
337 Aggressive Mammoth R	.15	.30
338 Bristling Boar C	.07	.15
339 Canopy Spider C	.07	.15
340 Frilled Sandwalla C	.07	.15
341 Oakenform C	.07	.15
342 Prized Unicorn U	.10	.20
343 Titanic Growth C	.07	.15
344 Woodland Mystic C	.07	.15

2019 Magic The Gathering Core Set 2020 Tokens

1 Ajani's Pridemate	.12	.25
2 Soldier	.12	.25
3 Spirit	.12	.25
4 Elemental Bird	.12	.25
5 Demon	.12	.25
6 Zombie	.12	.25
7 Elemental	.12	.25
8 Wolf	.12	.25
9 Golem	.12	.25
10 Treasure	.12	.25
11 Chandra, Awakened Inferno Emblem	.12	.25
12 Mu Yanling, Sky Dancer Emblem	.12	.25

2019 Magic The Gathering Judge Gift Rewards

1 Mirri's Guile M	20.00	40.00
2 Sliver Legion M	60.00	120.00
3 Mox Opal M	50.00	100.00
4 Isolated Watchtower M	2.50	5.00
5 Monastery Mentor M	15.00	30.00
6 Yuriko, the Tiger's Shadow M	12.50	25.00
7 Chalice of the Void M	50.00	100.00
8 Reflecting Pool M	25.00	50.00

2019 Magic The Gathering MagicFest

1 Lightning Bolt R	6.00	12.00
2 Plains L	1.50	3.00
3 Island L	.60	1.25
4 Swamp L	.60	1.25
5 Mountain L	.50	1.00
6 Forest L	.60	1.25
7 Sol Ring R	6.00	12.00

2019 Magic The Gathering Modern Horizons

1 Morophon, the Boundless M	5.00	10.00
2 Answered Prayers C	.07	.15
3 Astral Drift R	.15	.30
4 Battle Screech U	.10	.20
5 Dismantling Blow U	.10	.20
6 Enduring Sliver C	.07	.15
7 Ephemerate C	.07	.15
8 Face of Divinity U	.10	.20
9 First Silver's Chosen U	.10	.20
10 Force of Virtue R	.15	.30
11 Generous Gift U	.10	.20
12 Gilded Light C	.07	.15
13 Giver of Runes R	.15	.30
14 Imposter of the Sixth Pride C	.07	.15
15 Irregular Cohort C	.07	.15
16 King of the Pride U	.10	.20
17 Knight of Old Benalia C	.07	.15
18 Lancer Silver C	.07	.15
19 Martyr's Soul C	.07	.15
20 On Thin Ice R	.15	.30
21 Ranger-Captain of Eos M	10.00	20.00
22 Recruit the Worthy C	.07	.15
23 Reprobation C	.07	.15
24 Rhox Veteran C	.07	.15
25 Segovian Angel C	.07	.15
26 Serra the Benevolent M	7.50	15.00
27 Settle Beyond Reality C	.07	.15
28 Shelter C	.07	.15
29 Sisay, Weatherlight Captain R	.15	.30
30 Soul-Strike Technique C	.07	.15
31 Splicer's Skill U	.10	.20
32 Stirring Address C	.07	.15
33 Trustworthy Scout C	.07	.15
34 Valiant Changeling U	.10	.20
35 Vesperlark U	.10	.20
36 Wall of One Thousand Cuts C	.07	.15
37 Winds of Abandon R	.15	.30
38 Wing Shards U	.10	.20
39 Zhalfirin Decoy U	.10	.20
40 Archmage's Charm R	.15	.30
41 Bazaar Trademage R	.15	.30
42 Blizzard Strix U	.10	.20
43 Chillerpillar C	.07	.15
44 Choking Tethers C	.07	.15
45 Cunning Evasion U	.10	.20
46 Echo of Eons M	6.00	12.00
47 Everdream U	.10	.20
48 Exclude U	.10	.20
49 Eyekite C	.07	.15
50 Fact or Fiction U	.10	.20
51 Faerie Seer C	.07	.15
52 Force of Negation R	.15	.30
53 Future Sight R	.15	.30
54 Iceberg Cancrix C	.07	.15
55 Man-o-War C	.07	.15
56 Marit Lage's Slumber R	.15	.30
57 Mirrodin Besieged R	.15	.30
58 Mist-Syndicate Naga R	.15	.30
59 Moonblade Shinobi C	.07	.15
60 Oneirophage U	.10	.20
61 Phantasmal Form C	.07	.15
62 Phantom Ninja C	.07	.15
63 Pondering Mage C	.07	.15
64 Prohibit C	.07	.15
65 Rain of Revelation C	.07	.15
66 Rebuild U	.10	.20
67 Scour All Possibilities C	.07	.15
68 Scuttling Sliver U	.10	.20
69 Smoke Shroud C	.07	.15
70 Spell Snuff C	.07	.15
71 Stream of Thought C	.07	.15
72 String of Disappearances C	.07	.15
73 Tribute Mage U	.10	.20
74 Twisted Reflection U	.10	.20
75 Urza, Lord High Artificer M	25.00	45.00
76 Watcher for Tomorrow U	.10	.20
77 Windcaller Aven C	.07	.15
78 Winter's Rest C	.07	.15
79 Azra Smokeshaper C	.07	.15
80 Cabal Therapist R	.15	.30
81 Carrion Feeder U	.10	.20
82 Changeling Outcast C	.07	.15
83 Cordial Vampire R	.15	.30
84 Crypt Rats U	.10	.20
85 Dead of Winter R	.15	.30
86 Defile C	.07	.15
87 Diabolic Edict C	.07	.15
88 Dregscape Sliver U	.10	.20
89 Endling R	.15	.30
90 Feaster of Fools U	.10	.20
91 First-Sphere Gargantua C	.07	.15
92 Force of Despair R	.15	.30
93 Gluttonous Slug C	.07	.15
94 Graveshifter U	.10	.20
95 Headless Specter C	.07	.15
96 Mind Rake C	.07	.15
97 Mob C	.07	.15
98 Nether Spirit R	.15	.30
99 Ninja of the New Moon C	.07	.15
100 Plague Engineer R	.15	.30
101 Putrid Goblin C	.07	.15
102 Rank Officer C	.07	.15
103 Ransack the Lab C	.07	.15
104 Return from Extinction C	.07	.15
105 Sadistic Obsession U	.10	.20
106 Shatter Assumptions U	.10	.20
107 Silumgar Scavenger C	.07	.15
108 Sling-Gang Lieutenant U	.10	.20
109 Smiting Helix U	.10	.20
110 Throatseeker U	.10	.20
111 Umezawa's Charm C	.07	.15
112 Undead Augur U	.10	.20
113 Unearth C	.07	.15
114 Venomous Changeling C	.07	.15
115 Warteye Witch C	.07	.15
116 Yawgmoth, Thran Physician M	10.00	20.00
117 Alpine Guide U	.10	.20
118 Aria of Flame R	.15	.30
119 Bladeback Sliver C	.07	.15
120 Bogardan Dragonheart C	.07	.15
121 Cleaving Sliver C	.07	.15
122 Firebolt U	.10	.20
123 Fists of Flame C	.07	.15
124 Force of Rage R	.15	.30
125 Geomancer's Gambit C	.07	.15
126 Goatnap C	.07	.15
127 Goblin Champion C	.07	.15
128 Goblin Engineer R	.15	.30
129 Goblin Matron U	.10	.20
130 Goblin Oriflamme U	.10	.20
131 Goblin War Party C	.07	.15
132 Hollowhead Sliver U	.10	.20
133 Igneous Elemental C	.07	.15
134 Lava Dart C	.07	.15
135 Magmatic Sinkhole C	.07	.15
136 Orcish Hellraiser C	.07	.15
137 Ore-Scale Guardian U	.10	.20
138 Pashalik Mons R	.15	.30
139 Pillage U	.10	.20
140 Planebound Accomplice R	.15	.30
141 Pyrophobia C	.07	.15
142 Quakefoot Cyclops C	.07	.15
143 Ravenous Giant U	.10	.20
144 Reckless Charge C	.07	.15
145 Seasoned Pyromancer M	15.00	30.00
146 Shenanigans C	.07	.15
147 Spinehorn Minotaur C	.07	.15
148 Spiteful Sliver R	.15	.30
149 Tectonic Reformation R	.15	.30
150 Throes of Chaos U	.10	.20
151 Urza's Rage U	.10	.20
152 Vengeful Devil U	.10	.20
153 Viashino Sandsprinter C	.07	.15
154 Volatile Claws C	.07	.15
155 Ayula, Queen Among Bears R	.15	.30
156 Ayula's Influence R	.15	.30
157 Bellowing Elk C	.07	.15
158 Collector Ouphe R	.15	.30
159 Conifer Wurm U	.10	.20
160 Crashing Footfalls R	.15	.30
161 Deep Forest Hermit R	.15	.30
162 Elvish Fury C	.07	.15
163 Excavating Anurid C	.07	.15
164 Force of Vigor R	.15	.30
165 Frostwalla C	.07	.15
166 Genesis R	.15	.30
167 Glacial Revelation U	.10	.20
168 Hexdrinker M	12.50	25.00
169 Krosan Tusker C	.07	.15
170 Llanowar Tribe U	.10	.20
171 Mother Bear C	.07	.15
172 Murasa Behemoth C	.07	.15
173 Nantuko Cultivator U	.10	.20
174 Nimble Mongoose C	.07	.15
175 Regrowth U	.10	.20
176 Rime Tender C	.07	.15
177 Saddled Rimestag U	.10	.20
178 Savage Swipe C	.07	.15
179 Scale Up U	.10	.20
180 Spore Frog C	.07	.15
181 Springbloom Druid C	.07	.15
182 Squirrel Nest U	.10	.20
183 Tempered Sliver U	.10	.20
184 Thornado C	.07	.15
185 Treefolk Umbra C	.07	.15
186 Treetop Ambusher C	.07	.15
187 Trumpeting Herd C	.07	.15
188 Twin-Silk Spider C	.07	.15
189 Unbound Flourishing M	6.00	12.00
190 Wall of Blossoms U	.10	.20
191 Weather the Storm C	.07	.15
192 Webweaver Changeling U	.10	.20
193 Winding Way C	.07	.15
194 Abominable Treefolk U	.10	.20
195 Cloudshredder Sliver R	.15	.30
196 Collected Conjuring R	.15	.30
197 Eladamri's Call R	.15	.30
198 Etchings of the Chosen U	.10	.20
199 Fallen Shinobi R	.15	.30
200 The First Sliver M	10.00	20.00
201 Good-Fortune Unicorn U	.10	.20
202 Hogaak, Arisen Necropolis R	.15	.30
203 Ice-Fang Coatl R	.15	.30
204 Ingenious Infiltrator U	.10	.20
205 Kaya's Guile R	.15	.30
206 Kess, Dissident Mage M	1.50	3.00
207 Lavabelly Sliver U	.10	.20
208 Lightning Skelemental R	.15	.30
209 Munitions Expert U	.10	.20
210 Nature's Chant C	.07	.15
211 Reap the Past R	.15	.30
212 Rotwidow Pack U	.10	.20
213 Ruination Rioter U	.10	.20
214 Soulherder U	.10	.20
215 Thundering Djinn U	.10	.20
216 Unsettled Mariner R	.15	.30
217 Wrenn and Six M	50.00	90.00
218 Altar of Dementia R	.15	.30
219 Amorphous Axe C	.07	.15
220 Arcum's Astrolabe C	.07	.15
221 Birthing Boughs U	.10	.20
222 Farmstead Gleaner U	.10	.20
223 Fountain of Ichor C	.07	.15
224 Icehide Golem U	.10	.20
225 Lesser Masticore U	.10	.20
226 Mox Tantalite M	4.00	8.00
227 Scrapyard Recombiner R	.15	.30
228 Sword of Sinew and Steel M	6.00	12.00
229 Sword of Truth and Justice M	7.50	15.00
230 Talisman of Conviction U	.10	.20
231 Talisman of Creativity U	.10	.20
232 Talisman of Curiosity U	.10	.20
233 Talisman of Hierarchy U	.10	.20
234 Talisman of Resilience U	.10	.20
235 Universal Automaton C	.07	.15
236 Barren Moor U	.10	.20
237 Cave of Temptation C	.07	.15
238 Fiery Islet R	.15	.30
239 Forgotten Cave U	.10	.20
240 Frostwalk Bastion U	.10	.20
241 Hall of Heliod's Generosity R	.15	.30
242 Lonely Sandbar U	.10	.20
243 Nurturing Peatland R	.15	.30
244 Prismatic Vista R	.15	.30
245 Secluded Steppe U	.10	.20
246 Silent Clearing R	.15	.30
247 Sunbaked Canyon R	.15	.30
248 Tranquil Thicket U	.10	.20
249 Waterlogged Grove R	.15	.30
250 Snow-Covered Plains L	.07	.15
251 Snow-Covered Island L	.07	.15
252 Snow-Covered Swamp L	.07	.15
253 Snow-Covered Mountain L	.07	.15
254 Snow-Covered Forest L	.07	.15
255 Flusterstorm R	.15	.30

2019 Magic The Gathering Modern Horizons Tokens

1 Shapeshifter	.12	.25
2 Angel	.12	.25
3 Bird	.12	.25
4 Soldier	.12	.25
5 Illusion	.12	.25
6 Marit Lage	.12	.25
7 Zombie	.12	.25
8 Elemental	.12	.25
9 Elemental	.12	.25
10 Goblin	.12	.25
11 Bear	.12	.25
12 Elephant	.12	.25
13 Rhino	.12	.25
14 Spider	.12	.25
15 Squirrel	.12	.25
16 Spirit	.12	.25
17 Construct	.12	.25
18 Golem	.12	.25
19 Myr	.12	.25
20 Serra the Benevolent Emblem	.12	.25
21 Wrenn and Six Emblem	.12	.25

2019 Magic The Gathering Mystery Booster

1 All Is Dust R	6.00	12.00
2 Artisan of Kozilek U	.30	.75
3 Breaker of Armies U	.25	.50
4 Desolation Twin R	.20	.40
5 Eldrazi Devastator C	.17	.35
6 Pathrazer of Ulamog U	2.50	5.00
7 Abzan Falconer U	.12	.25
8 Abzan Runemark C	.15	.30
9 Acrobatic Maneuver C	.17	.35
10 Adanto Vanguard U	.17	.35
11 Adorned Pouncer R	.30	.75
12 Affa Protector C	.07	.15
13 Ainok Bond-Kin C	.07	.15
14 Ajani's Pridemate U	.12	.25
15 Alley Evasion C	.07	.15
16 Angelic Destiny M	2.50	5.00
17 Angelic Gift C	.05	.10
18 Angelic Purge C	.07	.15
19 Angel of Mercy C	.07	.15
20 Angel of Renewal U	.12	.25
21 Angel of the Dire Hour R	.60	1.25
22 Angelsong C	.12	.25
23 Apostle's Blessing C	.17	.35
24 Approach of the Second Sun R	1.50	3.00
25 Archangel U	.07	.15
26 Arrest C	.07	.15
27 Arrester's Zeal C	.12	.25
28 Artful Maneuver C	.10	.20
29 Aura of Silence U	2.50	5.00
30 Aven Battle Priest C	.07	.15
31 Aven Sentry C	.05	.10
32 Ballynock Cohort C	.12	.25
33 Bartered Cow C	.05	.10
34 Battle Mastery U	.17	.35
35 Beacon of Immortality R	3.00	6.00
36 Benevolent Ancestor C	.12	.25
37 Blade Instructor C	.05	.10
38 Blessed Spirits U	.07	.15
39 Bonds of Faith C	.05	.10
40 Borrowed Grace C	.05	.10
41 Built to Last C	.05	.10
42 Bulwark Giant C	.07	.15
43 Candlelight Vigil C	.07	.15
44 Caravan Escort C	.07	.15
45 Cartouche of Solidarity C	.17	.35
46 Cast Out U	.12	.25
47 Cathar's Companion C	.05	.10
48 Caught in the Brights C	.07	.15
49 Celestial Crusader U	.07	.15
50 Celestial Flare C	.15	.30
51 Center Soul C	.07	.15
52 Champion of Arashin C	.05	.10
53 Champion of the Parish R	3.00	6.00
54 Chancellor of the Annex R	2.00	4.00
55 Charge C	.07	.15
56 Cliffside Lookout C	.07	.15
57 Cloudshift C	.25	.50
58 Coalition Honor Guard C	.07	.15
59 Collar the Culprit C	.05	.10
60 Congregate U	.15	.30
61 Conviction C	.07	.15
62 Countless Gears Renegade C	.07	.15
63 Court Homunculus C	.05	.10
64 Court Street Denizen C	.10	.20
65 Crib Swap U	.12	.25
66 Danitha Capashen, Paragon U	.30	.75
67 Daring Skyjek C	.10	.20
68 Darksteel Mutation U	1.25	2.50
69 Dauntless Cathar C	.07	.15
70 Dawnglare Invoker C	.10	.20
71 Decommission C	.05	.10
72 Decree of Justice R	.12	.25
73 Defiant Strike C	.05	.10
74 Desperate Sentry C	.07	.15
75 Devilthorn Fox C	.07	.15
76 Dictate of Heliod R	.25	.50
77 Disenchant C	.10	.20
78 Dismantling Blow U	.07	.15
79 Disposal Mummy C	.05	.10
80 Divine Favor C	.05	.10
81 Djeru's Renunciation C	.05	.10
82 Djeru's Resolve C	.07	.15
83 Doomed Traveler C	.07	.15
84 Dragon Bell Monk C	.07	.15
85 Dragon's Eye Sentry C	.05	.10
86 Dragon's Presence C	.07	.15
87 Eddytrail Hawk C	.05	.10
88 Elesh Norn, Grand Cenobite M	7.50	15.00
89 Emerge Unscathed C	.20	.40
90 Empyrial Armor C	.07	.15
91 Encampment Keeper C	.07	.15
92 Encircling Fissure U	.07	.15
93 Enduring Victory C	.07	.15
94 Enlightened Ascetic C	.12	.25
95 Ephemeral Shields C	.07	.15
96 Ephemerate C	1.25	2.50

97 Evra, Halcyon Witness R	.10	.20
98 Excavation Elephant C	.07	.15
99 Excoriate C	.07	.15
100 Expedition Raptor C	.07	.15
101 Expose Evil C	.07	.15
102 Exultant Skymarcher C	.05	.10
103 Eyes in the Skies C	.05	.10
104 Faithbearer Paladin C	.10	.20
105 Faith's Fetters C	.05	.10
106 Feat of Resistance C	.05	.10
107 Felidar Guardian U	1.00	2.00
108 Felidar Sovereign R	1.25	2.50
109 Felidar Umbra U	1.50	3.00
110 Fencing Ace C	.17	.35
111 Fiend Hunter U	.12	.25
112 Firehoof Cavalry C	.07	.15
113 Forsake the Worldly C	.15	.30
114 Fortify C	.05	.10
115 Fragmentize C	.07	.15
116 Geist of the Moors C	.05	.10
117 Ghostblade Eidolon U	.07	.15
118 Gideon Jura M	.25	.50
119 Gideon's Lawkeeper C	.07	.15
120 Gift of Estates U	.75	1.50
121 Glaring Aegis C	.07	.15
122 Gleam of Resistance C	.12	.25
123 Glint-Sleeve Artisan C	.05	.10
124 God-Pharaoh's Faithful C	.10	.20
125 Gods Willing C	.12	.25
126 Grasp of Fate R	4.00	8.00
127 Grasp of the Hieromancer C	.07	.15
128 Great-Horn Krushok C	.05	.10
129 Guided Strike C	.12	.25
130 Gustcloak Skirmisher U	.05	.10
131 Gust Walker C	.05	.10
132 Healer's Hawk C	.12	.25
133 Healing Grace C	.05	.10
134 Healing Hands C	.07	.15
135 Heavy Infantry C	.07	.15
136 Humble C	.07	.15
137 Hyena Umbra C	.17	.35
138 Infantry Veteran C	.07	.15
139 Inquisitor's Ox C	.05	.10
140 Inspired Charge C	.05	.10
141 Intrusive Packbeast C	.05	.10
142 Iona's Judgment C	.10	.20
143 Isolation Zone C	.05	.10
144 Jubilant Mascot U	.05	.10
145 Knight of Cliffhaven C	.07	.15
146 Knight of Dawn U	.10	.20
147 Knight of Old Benalia C	.07	.15
148 Knight of Sorrows C	.10	.20
149 Knight of the Skyward Eye C	.05	.10
150 Knight of the Tusk C	.10	.20
151 Kor Bladewhirl U	.07	.15
152 Kor Chant C	.05	.10
153 Kor Firewalker U	.12	.25
154 Kor Hookmaster C	.07	.15
155 Kor Sky Climber C	.07	.15
156 Kor Skyfisher C	.15	.30
157 Lashknife Barrier U	.10	.20
158 Leonin Relic-Warder U	.15	.30
159 Lieutenants of the Guard C	.12	.25
160 Lightform U	.05	.10
161 Lightwalker C	.10	.20
162 Lingering Souls U	.15	.30
163 Lone Missionary C	.15	.30
164 Lonesome Unicorn // Rider in Need C	.07	.15
165 Looming Altisaur C	.12	.25
166 Lotus-Eye Mystics C	.07	.15
167 Loxodon Partisan C	.05	.10
168 Loyal Sentry C	.07	.15
169 Lunarch Mantle C	.05	.10
170 Magus of the Moat R	1.50	3.00
171 Mana Tithe C	.20	.40
172 Mardu Hordechief C	.05	.10
173 Marked by Honor C	.05	.10
174 Martyr's Bond R	.25	.50
175 Martyr's Cause U	.75	1.50
176 Meditation Puzzle C	.07	.15
177 Midnight Guard C	.12	.25
178 Mirran Crusader R	.30	.60
179 Mirror Entity R	.50	1.00
180 Momentary Blink C	.07	.15
181 Moonlit Strider C	.05	.10
182 Mortal's Ardor C	.07	.15
183 Mother of Runes U	2.00	4.00
184 Ninth Bridge Patrol C	.05	.10
185 Nyx-Fleece Ram U	.25	.50
186 Odric, Lunarch Marshal R	.20	.40
187 Ondu Greathorn C	.07	.15
188 Ondu War Cleric C	.07	.15
189 Oreskos Swiftclaw C	.05	.10
190 Oust U	.12	.25
191 Pacifism C	.12	.25
192 Palace Jailer U	.75	1.50
193 Palace Sentinels C	.10	.20
194 Paladin of the Bloodstained C	.07	.15
195 Path of Peace C	.05	.10
196 Path to Exile U	1.25	2.50
197 Peace of Mind U	.07	.15
198 Pegasus Courser C	.05	.10
199 Pentarch Ward C	.10	.20
200 Pitfall Trap C	.07	.15
201 Pressure Point C	.05	.10
202 Promise of Bunrei U	.12	.25
203 Prowling Caracal C	.07	.15
204 Rally the Peasants C	.07	.15
205 Raptor Companion C	.12	.25
206 Recruiter of the Guard R	15.00	30.00
207 Refurbish U	.10	.20
208 Renewed Faith C	.17	.35
209 Resurrection C	.07	.15
210 Retreat to Emeria U	.12	.25
211 Reviving Dose C	.05	.10
212 Rhet-Crop Spearmaster C	.12	.25
213 Righteous Cause U	.25	.50
214 Rootborn Defenses C	.17	.35
215 Sacred Cat C	.30	.75
216 Sanctum Gargoyle C	.05	.10
217 Sandstorm Charger C	.05	.10
218 Savannah Lions C	.15	.30
219 Seal of Cleansing C	.12	.25
220 Searing Light C	.07	.15
221 Seeker of the Way U	.07	.15
222 Sensor Splicer C	.07	.15
223 Seraph of the Suns U	.07	.15
224 Serra Disciple C	.07	.15
225 Serra's Embrace U	.10	.20
226 Sheer Drop C	.07	.15
227 Shining Aerosaur C	.07	.15
228 Shining Armor C	.05	.10
229 Shoulder to Shoulder C	.10	.20
230 Siegecraft C	.07	.15
231 Silverchase Fox C	.05	.10
232 Skyhunter Skirmisher C	.12	.25
233 Skymarcher Aspirant U	.07	.15
234 Skyspear Cavalry C	.10	.20
235 Slash of Talons C	.05	.10
236 Snubhorn Sentry C	.07	.15
237 Soulmender C	.10	.20
238 Soul Parry C	.05	.10
239 Soul-Strike Technique C	.05	.10
240 Soul Summons C	.05	.10
241 Soul Warden C	1.00	2.00
242 Sparring Mummy C	.05	.10
243 Spectral Gateguards C	.05	.10
244 Stalwart Aven C	.10	.20
245 Star-Crowned Stag C	.05	.10
246 Stave Off C	.07	.15
247 Steadfast Sentinel C	.05	.10
248 Stone Haven Medic C	.07	.15
249 Sunlance C	.07	.15
250 Sunrise Seeker C	.05	.10
251 Suppression Bonds C	.05	.10
252 Survive the Night C	.07	.15
253 Swords to Plowshares U	.75	1.50
254 Take Vengeance C	.05	.10
255 Tandem Tactics C	.07	.15
256 Teferi's Protection R	15.00	30.00
257 Terashi's Grasp C	.07	.15
258 Territorial Hammerskull C	.07	.15
259 Thalia's Lancers R	.30	.75
260 Thraben Inspector C	.20	.40
261 Thraben Standard Bearer C	.05	.10
262 Timely Reinforcements U	.12	.25
263 Topan Freeblade C	.07	.15
264 Unwavering Initiate C	.05	.10
265 Veteran Swordsmith C	.10	.20
266 Village Bell-Ringer C	.17	.35
267 Voice of the Provinces C	.07	.15
268 Volunteer Reserves U	.05	.10
269 Wake the Reflections C	.07	.15
270 Wall of Omens U	.40	.80
271 Wall of One Thousand Cuts C	.07	.15
272 Wandering Champion C	.07	.15
273 War Behemoth C	.05	.10
274 Weathered Wayfarer R	1.25	2.50
275 Wild Griffin C	.07	.15
276 Windborne Charge U	.05	.10
277 Winged Shepherd C	.05	.10
278 Wing Shards U	.05	.10
279 Youthful Knight C	.07	.15
280 Zealous Strike C	.07	.15
281 Academy Journeymage C	.07	.15
282 Aethersnipe C	.07	.15
283 Aether Tradewinds C	.05	.10
284 Amass the Components C	.07	.15
285 Aminatou's Augury R	1.25	2.50
286 Amphin Pathmage C	.07	.15
287 Anticipate C	.07	.15
288 Arcane Denial C	3.00	6.00
289 Archaeomancer C	.20	.40
290 Archetype of Imagination U	6.00	12.00
291 Artificer's Assistant C	.15	.30
292 Augur of Bolas C	.12	.25
293 Augury Owl C	.12	.25
294 Bastion Inventor C	.07	.15
295 Befuddle C	.07	.15
296 Benthic Giant C	.07	.15
297 Benthic Infiltrator C	.07	.15
298 Bewilder C	.05	.10
299 Blue Elemental Blast U	.25	.50
300 Borrowing 100,000 Arrows C	.15	.30
301 Brainstorm C	.75	1.50
302 Brilliant Spectrum C	.05	.10
303 Brine Elemental U	.07	.15
304 Calculated Dismissal C	.05	.10
305 Caller of Gales C	.07	.15
306 Call to Heel C	.05	.10
307 Cancel C	.12	.25
308 Capture Sphere C	.05	.10
309 Cartouche of Knowledge C	.12	.25
310 Castaway's Despair C	.07	.15
311 Catalog C	.07	.15
312 Chart a Course U	.20	.40
313 Chasm Skulker R	1.25	2.50
314 Chillbringer C	.05	.10
315 Choking Tethers C	.07	.15
316 Chronostutter C	.07	.15
317 Circular Logic U	.10	.20
318 Citywatch Sphinx U	.05	.10
319 Claustrophobia C	.05	.10
320 Clear the Mind C	.15	.30
321 Cloak of Mists C	.12	.25
322 Cloud Elemental C	.07	.15
323 Cloudkin Seer C	.15	.30
324 Cloudreader Sphinx C	.05	.10
325 Clutch of Currents C	.07	.15
326 Compelling Argument C	.12	.25
327 Concentrate U	.07	.15
328 Condescend U	.17	.35
329 Containment Membrane C	.07	.15
330 Contingency Plan C	.10	.20
331 Contradict C	.05	.10
332 Convolute C	.05	.10
333 Coralhelm Guide C	.05	.10
334 Coral Trickster C	.05	.10
335 Corrupted Conscience U	.75	1.50
336 Counterspell C	.75	1.50
337 Court Hussar C	.05	.10
338 Crashing Tide C	.10	.20
339 Crush Dissent C	.07	.15
340 Curiosity U	.30	.75
341 Curio Vendor C	.05	.10
342 Daze C	.75	1.50
343 Dazzling Lights C	.10	.20
344 Decision Paralysis C	.05	.10
345 Deep Analysis C	.10	.20
346 Deep Freeze C	.10	.20
347 Deepglow Skate R	2.00	4.00
348 Diminish C	.05	.10
349 Dirgur Nemesis C	.05	.10
350 Dispel C	.40	.80
351 Displace C	.30	.75
352 Distortion Strike U	.20	.40
353 Divination C	.07	.15
354 Djinn of Wishes R	.07	.15
355 Doorkeeper C	.15	.30
356 Dragon's Eye Savants U	.07	.15
357 Drag Under C	.07	.15
358 Dreadwaters C	.07	.15
359 Dream Cache C	.12	.25
360 Dream Twist C	.07	.15
361 Eel Umbra C	.07	.15
362 Embodiment of Spring C	.10	.20
363 Energy Field R	.25	.50
364 Enlightened Maniac C	.07	.15
365 Ensoul Artifact U	.15	.30
366 Errant Ephemeron C	.05	.10
367 Essence Scatter C	.12	.25
368 Everdream U	.05	.10
369 Exclude U	.07	.15
370 Expropriate M	10.00	20.00
371 Fact or Fiction U	.12	.25
372 Faerie Invaders C	.05	.10
373 Faerie Mechanist C	.05	.10
374 Failed Inspection C	.10	.20
375 Fascination U	.17	.35
376 Fathom Seer C	.05	.10
377 Fblthp, the Lost R	.15	.30
378 Flashfreeze U	.07	.15
379 Fledgling Mawcor U	.07	.15
380 Fleeting Distraction C	.07	.15
381 Floodgate U	.07	.15
382 Fog Bank U	.15	.30
383 Fogwalker C	.07	.15
384 Foil C	.25	.50
385 Forbidden Alchemy C	.05	.10
386 Frantic Search C	.15	.30
387 Frilled Sea Serpent C	.07	.15
388 Frost Lynx C	.07	.15
389 Gaseous Form C	.07	.15
390 Ghost Ship C	.07	.15
391 Glacial Crasher C	.05	.10
392 Glint C	.07	.15
393 Gone Missing C	.10	.20
394 Grasp of Phantoms C	.07	.15
395 Guard Gomazoa U	.15	.30
396 Gurmag Drowner C	.10	.20
397 Gush C	.40	.80
398 Hedron Crab U	3.00	6.00
399 Hieroglyphic Illumination C	.07	.15
400 Hightide Hermit C	.07	.15
401 Hinterland Drake C	.10	.20
402 Horseshoe Crab C	.12	.25
403 Humongulus C	.05	.10
404 Impulse C	.15	.30
405 Inkfathom Divers C	.05	.10
406 Invisibility C	.05	.10
407 Ior Ruin Expedition C	.05	.10
408 Jace's Phantasm C	.15	.30
409 Jeering Homunculus C	.07	.15
410 Jeskai Sage C	.12	.25
411 Jushi Apprentice // Tomoya the Revealer R	.12	.25
412 Jwar Isle Avenger C	.05	.10
413 Kiora's Dambreaker C	.07	.15
414 Laboratory Brute C	.07	.15
415 Laboratory Maniac U	1.50	3.00
416 Labyrinth Guardian U	.05	.10
417 Lay Claim U	.10	.20
418 Leapfrog C	.07	.15
419 Mahamoti Djinn U	.05	.10
420 Mana Leak C	.12	.25
421 Man-o'-War C	.05	.10
422 Master Transmuter R	.30	.75
423 Maximize Altitude C	.05	.10
424 Memory Erosion R	2.00	4.00
425 Memory Lapse C	.17	.35
426 Merfolk Looter U	.07	.15
427 Messenger Jays C	.07	.15
428 Metallic Rebuke C	.17	.35
429 Mind Sculpt C	.15	.30
430 Mind Spring R	.15	.30
431 The Mirari Conjecture R	.30	.75
432 Misdirection R	1.50	3.00
433 Mistform Shrieker U	.05	.10
434 Mist Raven C	.05	.10
435 Mnemonic Wall C	.15	.30
436 Monastery Loremaster C	.07	.15
437 Mulldrifter C	.25	.50
438 Murder of Crows U	.05	.10
439 Mystical Teachings C	.10	.20
440 Mystic Confluence R	.75	1.50
441 Mystic of the Hidden Way C	.05	.10
442 Nagging Thoughts C	.07	.15
443 Negate C	.25	.50
444 Niblis of Dusk C	.12	.25
445 Nine-Tail White Fox C	.12	.25
446 Ninja of the Deep Hours C	.75	1.50
447 Ojutai Interceptor C	.07	.15
448 Ojutai's Breath C	.05	.10
449 Omenspeaker C	.05	.10
450 Opportunity U	.07	.15
451 Opt C	.12	.25
452 Peel from Reality C	.05	.10
453 Phantasmal Bear C	.05	.10
454 Phantasmal Dragon U	.12	.25
455 Phyrexian Ingester U	.12	.25
456 Phyrexian Metamorph R	5.00	10.00
457 Pondering Mage C	.10	.20
458 Portent C	.20	.40
459 Predict U	.75	1.50
460 Preordain C	.30	.75
461 Prodigal Sorcerer U	.12	.25
462 Propaganda U	2.50	5.00
463 Prosperous Pirates C	.05	.10
464 Purple-Crystal Crab C	.12	.25
465 Refocus C	.12	.25
466 Repulse C	.07	.15
467 Retraction Helix C	.12	.25
468 Rhystic Study C	25.00	50.00
469 Riftwing Cloudskate U	.07	.15
470 Ringwarden Owl C	.05	.10
471 Rishadan Footpad U	.15	.30
472 River Darter C	.30	.75
473 River Serpent C	.12	.25
474 Riverwheel Aerialists C	.05	.10
475 Sage of Lat-Nam U	.07	.15
476 Sailor of Means C	.05	.10
477 Sakashima the Impostor R	2.00	4.00
478 Sapphire Charm C	.10	.20
479 Scroll Thief C	.05	.10
480 Sea Gate Oracle C	.07	.15
481 Sealock Monster U	.07	.15
482 Secrets of the Golden City C	.12	.25
483 Send to Sleep C	.05	.10
484 Serendib Efreet R	.07	.15
485 Shaper Parasite C	.05	.10
486 Shimmerscale Drake C	.10	.20
487 Shipwreck Looter C	.05	.10
488 Sigiled Starfish U	.07	.15
489 Silent Observer C	.07	.15
490 Silvergill Adept U	.15	.30
491 Singing Bell Strike C	.07	.15
492 Skaab Goliath U	.07	.15
493 Skitter Eel C	.10	.20
494 Skittering Crustacean C	.10	.20
495 Sleep U	.12	.25
496 Slipstream Eel C	.05	.10
497 Slither Blade C	.17	.35
498 Snap C	.75	1.50
499 Snapping Drake C	.05	.10
500 Somber Hoverguard C	.07	.15
501 Soothsaying U	1.25	2.50
502 Sphinx's Tutelage U	1.00	2.00
503 Spire Monitor C	.07	.15
504 Steady Progress C	.17	.35
505 Stitched Drake C	.05	.10
506 Storm Sculptor C	.05	.10
507 Strategic Planning C	.05	.10
508 Stream of Thought C	.12	.25
509 Stunt Double R	2.00	4.00
510 Surrakar Banisher C	.05	.10
511 Syncopate C	.07	.15
512 Syr Elenora, the Discerning U	.10	.20
513 Talrand, Sky Summoner R	.15	.30
514 Tandem Lookout C	.17	.35
515 Teferi, Temporal Archmage M	2.50	5.00
516 Temporal Fissure C	.15	.30
517 Temporal Mastery M	3.00	6.00
518 Thieving Magpie U	.05	.10
519 Thornwind Faeries C	.15	.30
520 Thoughtcast C	.50	1.00
521 Thought Collapse C	.12	.25
522 Thought Scour C	.15	.30
523 Thrummingbird U	.12	.25
524 Thunder Drake C	.05	.10
525 Tidal Warrior C	.12	.25
526 Tidal Wave C	.05	.10
527 Tinker U	.75	1.50
528 Totally Lost C	.05	.10
529 Trail of Evidence U	.17	.35
530 Treasure Cruise C	.15	.30
531 Treasure Hunt C	.10	.20
532 Treasure Mage U	.10	.20
533 Trinket Mage C	.17	.35
534 Triton Tactics U	.07	.15
535 Turn Aside C	.12	.25
536 Uncomfortable Chill C	.05	.10
537 Vapor Snag C	.15	.30
538 Vigean Graftmage C	.12	.25
539 Wall of Frost U	.12	.25
540 Warden of Evos Isle C	.07	.15
541 Watercourser C	.05	.10
542 Wave-Wing Elemental C	.10	.20
543 Weldfast Wingsmith C	.05	.10
544 Welkin Tern C	.07	.15
545 Whelming Wave R	.25	.50
546 Whiplash Trap C	.05	.10
547 Whir of Invention R	.75	1.50
548 Windcaller Aven C	.07	.15
549 Wind Drake C	.05	.10
550 Wind-Kin Raiders U	.05	.10
551 Windrider Eel C	.07	.15
552 Wind Strider C	.05	.10
553 Wishcoin Crab C	.05	.10
554 Wishful Merfolk C	.07	.15
555 Wretched Gryff C	.12	.25
556 Write into Being C	.07	.15
557 Youthful Scholar U	.07	.15
558 Absorb Vis C	.05	.10
559 Accursed Spirit C	.07	.15
560 Aid the Fallen C	.15	.30
561 Alesha's Vanguard C	.07	.15
562 Alley Strangler C	.05	.10
563 Altar's Reap C	.12	.25
564 Ambitious Aetherborn C	.05	.10
565 Ancestral Vengeance C	.05	.10
566 Animate Dead U	4.00	8.00
567 Annihilate U	.05	.10
568 Bala Ged Scorpion C	.07	.15
569 Baleful Ammit U	.07	.15
570 Balustrade Spy C	.07	.15
571 Bartizan Bats C	.05	.10
572 Bitter Revelation C	.07	.15
573 Black Cat C	.07	.15
574 Black Knight U	.07	.15
575 Black Market R	1.50	3.00
576 Bladebrand C	.05	.10
577 Blessing of Belzenlok C	.05	.10
578 Blighted Bat C	.07	.15
579 Blightsoil Druid C	.05	.10
580 Blistergrub C	.07	.15
581 Blood Artist U	1.25	2.50
582 Bloodrite Invoker C	.07	.15
583 Bone Splinters C	.07	.15
584 Boon of Emrakul C	.07	.15
585 Breeding Pit U	.12	.25
586 Butcher's Glee C	.07	.15
587 Cabal Therapy U	.25	.50
588 Cackling Imp C	.05	.10
589 Cadaver Imp C	.10	.20
590 Cairn Wanderer R	.12	.25
591 Caligo Skin-Witch C	.05	.10

592 Carrion Feeder U	1.00	2.00
593 Carrion Imp C	.05	.10
594 Catacomb Crocodile C	.05	.10
595 Catacomb Slug C	.05	.10
596 Caustic Tar U	.07	.15
597 Certain Death C	.07	.15
598 Child of Night C	.05	.10
599 Coat with Venom C	.07	.15
600 Collective Brutality R	1.25	2.50
601 Corpsehatch U	.07	.15
602 Costly Plunder C	.15	.30
603 Covenant of Blood C	.05	.10
604 Cower in Fear C	.07	.15
605 Crippling Blight C	.05	.10
606 Crow of Dark Tidings C	.07	.15
607 Cursed Minotaur C	.05	.10
608 Daring Demolition C	.07	.15
609 Darkblast U	.20	.40
610 Dark Dabbling C	.10	.20
611 Dark Ritual C	.60	1.25
612 Dark Withering C	.05	.10
613 Dauthi Mindripper U	.07	.15
614 Deadbridge Shaman C	.07	.15
615 Deadeye Tormentor C	.05	.10
616 Deadly Tempest R	.25	.50
617 Dead Reveler C	.05	.10
618 Death Denied C	.05	.10
619 Defeat C	.05	.10
620 Demonic Tutor U	20.00	40.00
621 Demonic Vigor C	.15	.30
622 Demon's Grasp C	.05	.10
623 Desperate Castaways C	.05	.10
624 Diabolic Edict C	.07	.15
625 Dictate of Erebos R	7.50	15.00
626 Die Young C	.05	.10
627 Dinosaur Hunter C	.07	.15
628 Dirge of Dread C	.07	.15
629 Dismember U	1.50	3.00
630 Disowned Ancestor C	.07	.15
631 Doomed Dissenter C	.05	.10
632 Douse in Gloom C	.05	.10
633 Drana, Kalastria Bloodchief R	.20	.40
634 Dreadbringer Lampads C	.12	.25
635 Dread Drone C	.07	.15
636 Dread Return U	.15	.30
637 Dregscape Zombie C	.05	.10
638 Driver of the Dead C	.05	.10
639 Drudge Sentinel C	.07	.15
640 Dukhara Scavenger C	.07	.15
641 Dune Beetle C	.05	.10
642 Duress C	.05	.10
643 Dusk Charger C	.05	.10
644 Dusk Legion Zealot C	.12	.25
645 The Eldest Reborn U	.40	.80
646 Epicure of Blood C	.10	.20
647 Erg Raiders C	.05	.10
648 Eternal Thirst C	.10	.20
649 Evincar's Justice C	.12	.25
650 Executioner's Capsule C	.07	.15
651 Exsanguinate U	4.00	8.00
652 Eyeblight's Ending C	.05	.10
653 Fallen Angel U	.07	.15
654 Farbog Revenant C	.07	.15
655 Fatal Push U	1.25	2.50
656 Fen Hauler C	.05	.10
657 Feral Abomination C	.05	.10
658 Festercreep C	.07	.15
659 Festering Newt C	.10	.20
660 Fetid Imp C	.12	.25
661 Fill with Fright C	.05	.10
662 First-Sphere Gargantua C	.07	.15
663 Flesh to Dust C	.07	.15
664 Fretwork Colony U	.05	.10
665 Fungal Infection C	.07	.15
666 Genju of the Fens U	.07	.15
667 Ghostly Changeling C	.07	.15
668 Ghoulcaller's Accomplice C	.05	.10
669 Gifted Aetherborn U	.30	.75
670 Go for the Throat U	.40	.80
671 Gonti, Lord of Luxury R	.30	.60
672 Grasping Scoundrel C	.07	.15
673 Gravecrawler R	2.00	4.00
674 Gravedigger C	.05	.10
675 Gravepurge C	.25	.50
676 Grave Titan M	3.00	6.00
677 Gray Merchant of Asphodel C	.30	.75
678 Grim Affliction C	.15	.30
679 Grim Discovery C	.12	.25
680 Grixis Slavedriver C	.10	.20
681 Grotesque Mutation C	.05	.10
682 Gruesome Fate C	.12	.25
683 Gurmag Angler C	.12	.25
684 Haakon, Stromgald Scourge R	.60	1.25
685 Hideous End C	.07	.15
686 Hired Blade C	.05	.10
687 Hound of the Farbogs C	.05	.10
688 Hunter of Eyeblights U	.10	.20
689 Hypnotic Specter R	.60	1.25
690 Induce Despair C	.05	.10
691 Infernal Scarring C	.07	.15
692 Infest U	.05	.10
693 Innocent Blood C	.10	.20
694 Inquisition of Kozilek U	.25	.50
695 Instill Infection C	.07	.15
696 Kalastria Nightwatch C	.05	.10
697 Krumar Bond-Kin C	.05	.10
698 Lawless Broker C	.05	.10
699 Lazotep Behemoth C	.05	.10
700 Lethal Sting C	.07	.15
701 Liliana, Death's Majesty M	.75	1.50
702 Living Death R	1.25	2.50
703 Lord of the Accursed U	.17	.35
704 Macabre Waltz C	.07	.15
705 Marauding Boneslasher C	.07	.15
706 March of the Drowned C	.12	.25
707 Mark of the Vampire C	.07	.15
708 Marsh Hulk C	.12	.25
709 Mephitic Vapors C	.07	.15
710 Merciless Resolve C	.07	.15
711 Miasmic Mummy C	.07	.15
712 Mind Rake C	.12	.25
713 Mind Rot C	.05	.10
714 Mind Shatter R	.12	.25
715 Mire's Malice C	.05	.10
716 Moment of Craving C	.05	.10
717 Murder C	.07	.15
718 Murderous Compulsion C	.10	.20
719 Nameless Inversion C	.12	.25
720 Nantuko Husk C	.10	.20
721 Never Happened C	.05	.10
722 Nighthowler R	.12	.25
723 Night's Whisper C	.75	1.50
724 Nirkana Assassin C	.07	.15
725 Noxious Dragon U	.05	.10
726 Okiba-Gang Shinobi C	.50	1.00
727 Painful Lesson C	.07	.15
728 Perish U	.12	.25
729 Pestilence C	.15	.30
730 Phyrexian Arena R	2.00	4.00
731 Phyrexian Plaguelord R	.10	.20
732 Phyrexian Rager C	.05	.10
733 Phyrexian Reclamation U	3.00	6.00
734 Pit Keeper C	.07	.15
735 Plaguecrafter U	.30	.60
736 Plagued Rusalka C	.07	.15
737 Plague Wight C	.05	.10
738 Prakhata Club Security C	.05	.10
739 Prowling Pangolin C	.07	.15
740 Queen's Agent C	.05	.10
741 Quest for the Gravelord U	.07	.15
742 Rabid Bloodsucker C	.05	.10
743 Rakdos Drake C	.05	.10
744 Rakshasa's Secret C	.05	.10
745 Ravenous Chupacabra U	.25	.50
746 Read the Bones C	.15	.30
747 Reaper of Night // Harvest Fear C	.07	.15
748 Reassembling Skeleton U	.15	.30
749 Reckless Imp C	.10	.20
750 Reckless Spite U	.07	.15
751 Recover C	.10	.20
752 Renegade Demon C	.05	.10
753 Renegade's Getaway C	.07	.15
754 Returned Centaur C	.10	.20
755 Revel in Riches R	6.00	12.00
756 Revenant U	.05	.10
757 Rite of the Serpent C	.05	.10
758 Rotfeaster Maggot C	.07	.15
759 Ruin Rat C	.15	.30
760 Rune-Scarred Demon R	3.00	6.00
761 Sadistic Hypnotist U	.30	.75
762 Scarab Feast C	.07	.15
763 Scrounger of Souls C	.05	.10
764 Scuttling Death C	.05	.10
765 Seal of Doom C	.10	.20
766 Sengir Vampire U	.05	.10
767 Sewer Nemesis R	.15	.30
768 Shadowcloak Vampire C	.05	.10
769 Shambling Attendants C	.05	.10
770 Shambling Goblin C	.07	.15
771 Shriekmaw U	.17	.35
772 Shrouded Lore U	.10	.20
773 Silumgar Butcher C	.05	.10
774 Skeletal Scrying U	.12	.25
775 Skeleton Archer C	.05	.10
776 Skulking Ghost C	.05	.10
777 Smiting Helix U	.05	.10
778 Sorin Markov M	2.50	5.00
779 Spreading Rot C	.05	.10
780 Stab Wound U	.05	.10
781 Stallion of Ashmouth C	.05	.10
782 Stinkweed Imp C	.30	.60
783 Street Wraith U	.12	.25
784 Stromkirk Patrol C	.12	.25
785 Subtle Strike C	.05	.10
786 Sultai Runemark C	.07	.15
787 Tar Snare C	.05	.10
788 Tavern Swindler U	.07	.15
789 Tendrils of Corruption C	.10	.20
790 Thallid Omnivore C	.07	.15
791 Thornbow Archer C	.10	.20
792 Thorn of the Black Rose C	.17	.35
793 Thraben Foulbloods C	.05	.10
794 Tidy Conclusion C	.07	.15
795 Torment of Hailfire R	10.00	20.00
796 Torment of Venom C	.07	.15
797 Touch of Moonglove C	.07	.15
798 Toxin Sliver R	1.00	2.00
799 Tragic Slip C	.17	.35
800 Trespasser's Curse C	.25	.50
801 Trial of Ambition U	.07	.15
802 Twins of Maurer Estate C	.07	.15
803 Typhoid Rats C	.15	.30
804 Unburden C	.05	.10
805 Undercity's Embrace C	.07	.15
806 Untamed Hunger C	.05	.10
807 Unyielding Krumar C	.05	.10
808 Urborg Uprising C	.07	.15
809 Vampire Champion C	.12	.25
810 Vampire Envoy C	.10	.20
811 Vampire Hexmage U	.20	.40
812 Vampire Lacerator C	.07	.15
813 Vampire Nighthawk U	.12	.25
814 Vessel of Malignity C	.05	.10
815 Virulent Swipe C	.07	.15
816 Voracious Null C	.07	.15
817 Vraska's Finisher C	.05	.10
818 Wake of Vultures C	.07	.15
819 Walking Corpse C	.05	.10
820 Walk the Plank U	.10	.20
821 Wander in Death C	.07	.15
822 Warteye Witch C	.10	.20
823 Weight of the Underworld C	.05	.10
824 Weirded Vampire C	.12	.25
825 Wight of Precinct Six U	.10	.20
826 Will-o'-the-Wisp U	.12	.25
827 Windgrace Acolyte C	.05	.10
828 Wrench Mind C	.10	.20
829 Yargle, Glutton of Urborg U	.12	.25
830 Zulaport Chainmage C	.07	.15
831 Act of Treason C	.05	.10
832 Act on Impulse U	.10	.20
833 Ahn-Crop Crasher U	.10	.20
834 Ainok Tracker C	.05	.10
835 Akroan Sergeant C	.05	.10
836 Alchemist's Greeting C	.05	.10
837 Alesha, Who Smiles at Death R	.15	.30
838 Ancient Grudge U	.10	.20
839 Anger U	3.00	6.00
840 Anger of the Gods R	.25	.50
841 Arc Trail U	.07	.15
842 Arrow Storm C	.07	.15
843 Atarka Efreet C	.05	.10
844 Avalanche Riders U	.12	.25
845 Avarax C	.10	.20
846 Azra Bladeseeker C	.07	.15
847 Balduvian Horde C	.05	.10
848 Barging Sergeant C	.07	.15
849 Barrage of Boulders C	.10	.20
850 Battle Rampart C	.05	.10
851 Battle-Rattle Shaman C	.05	.10
852 Beetleback Chief U	.30	.60
853 Bellows Lizard C	.05	.10
854 Blades of Velis Vel C	.12	.25
855 Blastfire Bolt C	.05	.10
856 Blazing Volley C	.12	.25
857 Blindblast C	.05	.10
858 Bloodfire Expert C	.07	.15
859 Bloodlust Inciter C	.07	.15
860 Bloodmad Vampire C	.12	.25
861 Blood Ogre C	.07	.15
862 Bloodstone Goblin C	.15	.30
863 Blow Your House Down C	.07	.15
864 Blur of Blades C	.05	.10
865 Boggart Brute C	.05	.10
866 Boiling Earth C	.07	.15
867 Bombard C	.07	.15
868 Bomber Corps C	.05	.10
869 Borrowed Hostility C	.07	.15
870 Boulder Salvo C	.07	.15
871 Brazen Buccaneers C	.05	.10
872 Brazen Wolves C	.07	.15
873 Brimstone Dragon R	.12	.25
874 Brimstone Mage U	.10	.20
875 Bring Low C	.05	.10
876 Browbeat U	.15	.30
877 Brute Strength C	.05	.10
878 Built to Smash C	.12	.25
879 Burst Lightning C	.10	.20
880 Canyon Lurkers C	.05	.10
881 Cartouche of Zeal C	.10	.20
882 Cathartic Reunion C	.10	.20
883 Chandra's Pyrohelix C	.07	.15
884 Chandra's Revolution C	.07	.15
885 Chaos Warp R	.75	1.50
886 Charging Monstrosaur U	.12	.25
887 Chartooth Cougar C	.05	.10
888 Cinder Hellion C	.05	.10
889 Cleansing Screech C	.07	.15
890 Cobblebrute C	.07	.15
891 Cosmotronic Wave C	.10	.20
892 Cragganwick Cremator R	.10	.20
893 Crash Through C	.12	.25
894 Crowd's Favor C	.07	.15
895 Crown-Hunter Hireling C	.05	.10
896 Curse of Opulence U	.75	1.50
897 Curse of the Nightly Hunt U	.12	.25
898 Daretti, Scrap Savant M	.40	.80
899 Death by Dragons U	.12	.25
900 Defiant Ogre C	.07	.15
901 Demolish C	.07	.15
902 Desert Cerodon C	.05	.10
903 Desperate Ravings U	.05	.10
904 Destructive Tampering C	.07	.15
905 Direct Current C	.05	.10
906 Distemper of the Blood C	.07	.15
907 Dragon Breath U	.12	.25
908 Dragon Egg C	.05	.10
909 Dragon Fodder C	.12	.25
910 Dragonsoul Knight C	.10	.20
911 Dragon Whelp U	.05	.10
912 Dual Shot C	.07	.15
913 Dynacharge C	.07	.15
914 Earth Elemental C	.05	.10
915 Emrakul's Hatcher C	.12	.25
916 Enthralling Victor U	.07	.15
917 Erratic Explosion C	.05	.10
918 Expedite C	.15	.30
919 Faithless Looting C	.30	.75
920 Falkenrath Reaver C	.05	.10
921 Fall of the Hammer C	.12	.25
922 Fervent Strike C	.05	.10
923 Fierce Invocation C	.07	.15
924 Fiery Hellhound C	.07	.15
925 Fiery Temper C	.07	.15
926 Fireball U	.07	.15
927 Firebolt C	.05	.10
928 Firebrand Archer C	.75	1.50
929 Fire Elemental C	.07	.15
930 Flame Jab U	.07	.15
931 Flameshot U	.07	.15
932 Flametongue Kavu U	.07	.15
933 Flamewave Invoker U	.07	.15
934 Fling C	.12	.25
935 Forge Devil C	.10	.20
936 Foundry Street Denizen C	.12	.25
937 Frenzied Raptor C	.07	.15
938 Frilled Deathspitter C	.12	.25
939 Frontline Devastator C	.05	.10
940 Frontline Rebel C	.07	.15
941 Furnace Whelp C	.12	.25
942 Fury Charm C	.07	.15
943 Galvanic Blast C	1.00	2.00
944 Generator Servant C	.10	.20
945 Genju of the Spires U	.07	.15
946 Geomancer's Gambit C	.05	.10
947 Ghitu Lavarunner C	.07	.15
948 Ghitu War Cry U	.07	.15
949 Giant Spectacle C	.07	.15
950 Goblin Assault U	.60	1.25
951 Goblin Balloon Brigade C	.07	.15
952 Goblin Bombardment U	1.25	2.50
953 Goblin Fireslinger C	.10	.20
954 Goblin Game R	.25	.50
955 Goblin Locksmith C	.07	.15
956 Goblin Matron U	.20	.40
957 Goblin Motivator C	.12	.25
958 Goblin Oriflamme U	.12	.25
959 Goblin Piledriver R	.60	1.25
960 Goblin Roughrider C	.07	.15
961 Goblin Warchief U	.30	.60
962 Goblin War Paint C	.07	.15
963 Gorehorn Minotaurs C	.05	.10
964 Gore Swine C	.05	.10
965 Granitic Titan C	.15	.30
966 Grapeshot C	.12	.25
967 Gravitic Punch C	.07	.15
968 Greater Gargadon R	.07	.15
969 Gut Shot C	.75	1.50
970 Guttersnipe U	.15	.30
971 Hammerhand C	.07	.15
972 Hanweir Lancer C	.05	.10
973 Hardened Berserker C	.05	.10
974 Hijack C	.07	.15
975 Hulking Devil C	.05	.10
976 Hyena Pack C	.07	.15
977 Ill-Tempered Cyclops C	.05	.10
978 Impact Tremors C	2.00	4.00
979 Impending Disaster R	.25	.50
980 Incorrigible Youths U	.07	.15
981 Inferno Fist C	.05	.10
982 Inferno Jet U	.10	.20
983 Ingot Chewer C	.10	.20
984 Insolent Neonate C	.17	.35
985 Jackal Pup C	.07	.15
986 Kaervek's Torch C	.10	.20
987 Kargan Dragonlord M	.25	.50
988 Keldon Halberdier C	.07	.15
989 Keldon Overseer C	.07	.15
990 Khenra Scrapper C	.05	.10
991 Kiki-Jiki, Mirror Breaker M	3.00	6.00
992 Kiln Fiend C	.07	.15
993 Kird Ape C	.15	.30
994 Knollspine Dragon R	.40	.80
995 Kolaghan Stormsinger C	.10	.20
996 Krenko, Mob Boss R	3.00	6.00
997 Krenko's Command C	.20	.40
998 Krenko's Enforcer C	.07	.15
999 Leaping Master C	.05	.10
1000 Leopard-Spotted Jiao C	.05	.10
1001 Lightning Bolt U	.40	.80
1002 Lightning Javelin C	.07	.15
1003 Lightning Shrieker C	.07	.15
1004 Lightning Talons C	.12	.25
1005 Madcap Skills C	.07	.15
1006 Magma Spray C	.05	.10
1007 Makindi Sliderunner C	.07	.15
1008 Mardu Warshrieker C	.05	.10
1009 Mark of Mutiny U	.10	.20
1010 Maximize Velocity C	.07	.15
1011 Miner's Bane C	.05	.10
1012 Mizzix's Mastery R	4.00	8.00
1013 Mogg Fanatic U	.07	.15
1014 Mogg Flunkies C	.05	.10
1015 Mogg War Marshal C	.07	.15
1016 Molten Rain U	.15	.30
1017 Monastery Swiftspear U	.30	.75
1018 Mutiny C	.15	.30
1019 Nimble-Blade Khenra C	.05	.10
1020 Ondu Champion C	.07	.15
1021 Orcish Cannonade C	.05	.10
1022 Orcish Oriflamme C	.05	.10
1023 Outnumber C	.07	.15
1024 Pillage C	.07	.15
1025 Preyseizer Dragon R	.15	.30
1026 Price of Progress U	2.00	4.00
1027 Prickleboar C	.05	.10
1028 Prophetic Ravings C	.07	.15
1029 Purphoros, God of the Forge M	10.00	20.00
1030 Pyrotechnics U	.05	.10
1031 Quakefoot Cyclops C	.07	.15
1032 Rage Reflection R	.30	.75
1033 Rampaging Cyclops C	.05	.10
1034 Reality Scramble R	.25	.50
1035 Reckless Fireweaver C	.60	1.25
1036 Reckless Wurm C	.07	.15
1037 Recoup U	.15	.30
1038 Release the Ants U	.05	.10
1039 Release the Gremlins R	.15	.30
1040 Renegade Tactics C	.10	.20
1041 Rivals' Duel U	.05	.10
1042 Roast U	.17	.35
1043 Rolling Thunder U	.12	.25
1044 Rubblebelt Maaka C	.10	.20
1045 Ruinous Gremlin C	.07	.15
1046 Rummaging Goblin C	.05	.10
1047 Run Amok C	.05	.10
1048 Rush of Adrenaline C	.05	.10
1049 Salivating Gremlins C	.05	.10
1050 Samut's Sprint C	.10	.20
1051 Sarkhan's Rage C	.05	.10
1052 Screamreach Brawler C	.07	.15
1053 Seismic Shift C	.07	.15
1054 Seismic Stomp C	.05	.10
1055 Shatter C	.05	.10
1056 Shattering Spree U	3.00	6.00
1057 Shenanigans C	.10	.20
1058 Shock C	.05	.10
1059 Skirk Commando C	.05	.10
1060 Skirk Prospector C	.17	.35
1061 Smash to Smithereens C	.17	.35
1062 Smelt C	.07	.15
1063 Sparkmage Apprentice C	.05	.10
1064 Sparkspitter C	.05	.10
1065 Sparktongue Dragon C	.05	.10
1066 Spikeshot Goblin U	.07	.15
1067 Staggershock U	.07	.15
1068 Star of Extinction M	1.25	2.50
1069 Steamflogger Boss R	.07	.15
1070 Stormblood Berserker U	.07	.15
1071 Sudden Demise R	.12	.25
1072 Sulfurous Blast U	.10	.20
1073 Summit Prowler C	.05	.10
1074 Sun-Crowned Hunters C	.12	.25
1075 Swashbuckling C	.05	.10
1076 Sweatworks Brawler C	.05	.10
1077 Swift Kick C	.05	.10
1078 Tarfire C	.12	.25
1079 Taurean Mauler R	.50	1.00
1080 Tectonic Rift U	.07	.15
1081 Temur Battle Rage C	.15	.30

1082 Thresher Lizard C .05 .10
1083 Thrill of Possibility C .10 .20
1084 Tibalt's Rager U .07 .15
1085 Torch Courier C .15 .30
1086 Two-Headed Giant R .07 .15
1087 Uncaged Fury C .05 .10
1088 Undying Rage C .05 .10
1089 Urza's Rage R .05 .10
1090 Valakut Invoker C .07 .15
1091 Valakut Predator C .07 .15
1092 Valley Dasher C .07 .15
1093 Vandalize C .07 .15
1094 Vent Sentinel C .07 .15
1095 Vessel of Volatility C .12 .25
1096 Viashino Sandstalker U .05 .10
1097 Volcanic Dragon U .05 .10
1098 Volcanic Rush C .05 .10
1099 Voldaren Duelist C .07 .15
1100 Wall of Fire C .05 .10
1101 Wayward Giant C .07 .15
1102 Wheel of Fate R 1.50 3.00
1103 Wildfire Emissary C .05 .10
1104 Wojek Bodyguard C .05 .10
1105 Young Pyromancer U .15 .30
1106 Zada's Commando C .05 .10
1107 Zealot of the God-Pharaoh C .07 .15
1108 Abundant Growth C .25 .50
1109 Acidic Slime U .12 .25
1110 Adventurous Impulse C .05 .10
1111 Aerie Bowmasters C .10 .20
1112 Affectionate Indrik U .15 .30
1113 Aggressive Instinct C .12 .25
1114 Aggressive Urge C .10 .20
1115 Ainok Survivalist U .07 .15
1116 Alpine Grizzly C .12 .25
1117 Ambassador Oak C .07 .15
1118 Ana Sanctuary U .10 .20
1119 Ancestral Mask U 3.00 6.00
1120 Ancient Brontodon C .12 .25
1121 Ancient Stirrings U .17 .35
1122 Arachnus Web C .07 .15
1123 Arbor Armament C .07 .15
1124 Arbor Elf C .25 .50
1125 Asceticism R 5.00 10.00
1126 Aura Gnarlid C .15 .30
1127 Avacyn's Pilgrim C .17 .35
1128 Backwoods Survivalists C .15 .30
1129 Baloth Gorger C .05 .10
1130 Basking Rootwalla C .07 .15
1131 Bear Cub C .75 1.50
1132 Beastbreaker of Bala Ged U .05 .10
1133 Beastmaster Ascension R 2.50 5.00
1134 Beast Within U 1.00 2.00
1135 Become Immense U .12 .25
1136 Beneath the Sands C .12 .25
1137 Bestial Menace U .05 .10
1138 Birds of Paradise R 4.00 8.00
1139 Bitterblade Warrior C .05 .10
1140 Bitterbow Sharpshooters C .07 .15
1141 Blanchwood Armor U .10 .20
1142 Blastoderm C .07 .15
1143 Bloom Tender R 7.50 15.00
1144 Blossom Dryad C .10 .20
1145 Borderland Explorer C .07 .15
1146 Borderland Ranger C .05 .10
1147 Bow of Nylea R 2.00 4.00
1148 Briarhorn U .07 .15
1149 Bristling Boar C .05 .10
1150 Broken Bond C .17 .35
1151 Broodhunter Wurm C .07 .15
1152 Byway Courier C .07 .15
1153 Call the Scions C .07 .15
1154 Canopy Spider C .05 .10
1155 Carnivorous Moss-Beast C .05 .10
1156 Carpet of Flowers U 7.50 15.00
1157 Caustic Caterpillar C .30 .60
1158 Centaur Courser C .05 .10
1159 Centaur Glade U .07 .15
1160 Charging Rhino C .07 .15
1161 Chatter of the Squirrel C .15 .30
1162 Citanul Woodreaders C .05 .10
1163 Clip Wings C .07 .15
1164 Colossal Dreadmaw C .05 .10
1165 Combo Attack C .05 .10
1166 Commune with Nature C .07 .15
1167 Commune with the Gods C .12 .25
1168 Conifer Strider C .07 .15
1169 Courser of Kruphix R 1.25 2.50
1170 Creeping Mold U .05 .10
1171 Crop Rotation C .75 1.50
1172 Crossroads Consecrator C .07 .15
1173 The Crowd Goes Wild U .12 .25
1174 Crowned Ceratok C .10 .20
1175 Crushing Canopy C .05 .10
1176 Cultivate C .30 .75
1177 Daggerback Basilisk C .10 .20
1178 Dawn's Reflection C .15 .30
1179 Death-Hood Cobra C .07 .15
1180 Defense of the Heart R 7.50 15.00
1181 Desert Twister U .07 .15
1182 Destructor Dragon U .15 .30
1183 Dissenter's Deliverance C .07 .15
1184 Domesticated Hydra U .12 .25
1185 Dragonscale Boon C .10 .20
1186 Dragon-Scarred Bear C .17 .35
1187 Dungrove Elder R .50 1.00
1188 Durkwood Baloth C .07 .15
1189 Earthen Arms C .07 .15
1190 Eldritch Evolution R 4.00 8.00
1191 Elemental Uprising C .15 .30
1192 Elephant Guide C .12 .25
1193 Elves of Deep Shadow C 1.00 2.00
1194 Elvish Fury C .05 .10
1195 Elvish Visionary C .12 .25
1196 Elvish Warrior C .07 .15
1197 Ember Weaver C .05 .10
1198 Epic Confrontation C .05 .10
1199 Essence Warden C 2.50 5.00
1200 Eternal Witness U 1.00 2.00
1201 Experiment One U .12 .25
1202 Explore C .17 .35
1203 Explosive Vegetation U .25 .50
1204 Ezuri's Archers C .10 .20
1205 Fade into Antiquity C .07 .15
1206 Farseek C 1.25 2.50
1207 Feed the Clan C .12 .25
1208 Feral Krushok C .05 .10
1209 Feral Prowler C .07 .15
1210 Ferocious Zheng C .10 .20
1211 Fertile Ground C .25 .50
1212 Fierce Empath C .12 .25
1213 Fog C .12 .25
1214 Formless Nurturing C .05 .10
1215 Frontier Mastodon C .05 .10
1216 Gaea's Blessing U .15 .30
1217 Gaea's Protector C .07 .15
1218 Giant Growth C .07 .15
1219 Giant Spider C .12 .25
1220 Gift of Growth C .05 .10
1221 Gift of Paradise C .12 .25
1222 Glade Watcher C .05 .10
1223 Gnarlid Pack C .05 .10
1224 Grapple with the Past C .15 .30
1225 Grazing Gladehart C .12 .25
1226 Greater Basilisk C .15 .30
1227 Greater Sandwurm C .10 .20
1228 Greenbelt Rampager R .07 .15
1229 Greenwood Sentinel C .07 .15
1230 Groundswell C .12 .25
1231 Guardian Shield-Bearer C .07 .15
1232 Hamlet Captain U .05 .10
1233 Hardy Veteran C .05 .10
1234 Harmonize U .17 .35
1235 Harrow C .60 1.25
1236 Hooded Brawler C .07 .15
1237 Hooting Mandrills C .10 .20
1238 Hornet Nest R .60 1.25
1239 Hunter's Ambush C .07 .15
1240 Hunt the Weak C .05 .10
1241 Hurricane R .15 .30
1242 Imperious Perfect U .10 .20
1243 Invigorate U .12 .25
1244 Ivy Lane Denizen C .12 .25
1245 Jungle Delver C .25 .50
1246 Jungle Wayfinder C .05 .10
1247 Kavu Climber C .05 .10
1248 Kavu Primarch C .05 .10
1249 Khalni Heart Expedition C .15 .30
1250 Kin-Tree Warden C .07 .15
1251 Kozilek's Predator C .05 .10
1252 Kraul Foragers C .07 .15
1253 Kraul Warrior C .05 .10
1254 Krosan Druid C .05 .10
1255 Krosan Tusker C .05 .10
1256 Larger Than Life C .07 .15
1257 Lay of the Land C .07 .15
1258 Lead by Example C .07 .15
1259 Lead the Stampede C .15 .30
1260 Lifespring Druid C .05 .10
1261 Lignify C 1.00 2.00
1262 Llanowar Elves C .25 .50
1263 Llanowar Empath C .05 .10
1264 Longshot Squad C .10 .20
1265 Lure U .10 .20
1266 Manglehorn U .30 .75
1267 Mantle of Webs C .05 .10
1268 Map the Wastes C .15 .30
1269 Meandering Towershell R .07 .15
1270 Might of the Masses C .07 .15
1271 Mulch C .05 .10
1272 Mycoloth R 2.00 4.00
1273 Natural Connection C .07 .15
1274 Naturalize C .12 .25
1275 Nature's Claim C .75 1.50
1276 Nature's Lore C 1.25 2.50
1277 Nest Invader C .15 .30
1278 Nettle Sentinel C .15 .30
1279 New Horizons C .07 .15
1280 Nimble Mongoose C .05 .10
1281 Nissa, Voice of Zendikar M 1.25 2.50
1282 Oakgnarl Warrior C .07 .15
1283 Ondu Giant C .07 .15
1284 Oran-Rief Invoker C .05 .10
1285 Overgrown Armasaur C .15 .30
1286 Overgrown Battlement U .15 .30
1287 Overrun U .17 .35
1288 Pack's Favor C .05 .10
1289 Peema Outrider C .07 .15
1290 Pelakka Wurm U .07 .15
1291 Penumbra Spider C .10 .20
1292 Phantom Centaur U .10 .20
1293 Pierce the Sky C .12 .25
1294 Pinion Feast C .07 .15
1295 Plummet C .05 .10
1296 Pouncing Cheetah C .07 .15
1297 Prey's Vengeance C .05 .10
1298 Prey Upon C .05 .10
1299 Priest of Titania C 2.50 5.00
1300 Pulse of Murasa C .12 .25
1301 Quiet Disrepair C .12 .25
1302 Rain of Thorns U .07 .15
1303 Rampant Growth C .25 .50
1304 Rancor U .75 1.50
1305 Ranger's Guile C .12 .25
1306 Ravenous Leucrocota C .05 .10
1307 Reclaim C .12 .25
1308 Reclaiming Vines C .07 .15
1309 Regrowth U .25 .50
1310 Relic Crush C .07 .15
1311 Return to the Earth C .05 .10
1312 Revive C .07 .15
1313 Rhox Maulers C .05 .10
1314 Riparian Tiger C .07 .15
1315 River Boa U .07 .15
1316 Roar of the Wurm U .07 .15
1317 Root Out C .10 .20
1318 Roots C .05 .10
1319 Rosethorn Halberd C .12 .25
1320 Runeclaw Bear C .07 .15
1321 Sagu Archer C .05 .10
1322 Sakura-Tribe Elder C 1.00 2.00
1323 Saproling Migration C .15 .30
1324 Savage Punch C .15 .30
1325 Scatter the Seeds C .12 .25
1326 Seal of Strength C .07 .15
1327 Search for Tomorrow C .25 .50
1328 Seek the Horizon U .07 .15
1329 Seek the Wilds C .05 .10
1330 Selvala, Heart of the Wilds M 7.50 15.00
1331 Shamanic Revelation R .30 .75
1332 Shape the Sands C .05 .10
1333 Siege Wurm C .07 .15
1334 Silhana Ledgewalker C .25 .50
1335 Silkweaver Elite C .07 .15
1336 Snake Umbra C .30 .75
1337 Snapping Sailback U .12 .25
1338 Spawning Grounds R .10 .20
1339 Spider Spawning U .10 .20
1340 Squirrel Wrangler R .60 1.25
1341 Stalking Tiger C .05 .10
1342 Stoic Builder C .07 .15
1343 Strength in Numbers C .05 .10
1344 Sylvan Bounty C .05 .10
1345 Sylvan Scrying U .25 .50
1346 Tajuru Pathwarden C .12 .25
1347 Tajuru Warcaller U .10 .20
1348 Take Down C .05 .10
1349 Talons of Wildwood C .12 .25
1350 Tempt with Discovery R 2.50 5.00
1351 Terrain Elemental C .10 .20
1352 Territorial Baloth C .07 .15
1353 Thornhide Wolves C .07 .15
1354 Thornscape Battlemage U .05 .10
1355 Thornweald Archer C .07 .15
1356 Thrashing Brontodon U .07 .15
1357 Thrive C .07 .15
1358 Thrun, the Last Troll M 1.25 2.50
1359 Timberwatch Elf U .17 .35
1360 Time to Feed C .05 .10
1361 Tireless Tracker R 1.25 2.50
1362 Titanic Growth C .07 .15
1363 Triumph of the Hordes U 7.50 15.00
1364 Tukatongue Thallid C .10 .20
1365 Turntimber Basilisk U .12 .25
1366 Vastwood Gorger C .05 .10
1367 Venom Sliver U 1.00 2.00
1368 Vigor R 7.50 15.00
1369 Watcher in the Web C .10 .20
1370 Wellwisher C .75 1.50
1371 Wild Growth C .17 .35
1372 Wild Mongrel C .10 .20
1373 Wild Nacatl C .20 .40
1374 Wildsize C .05 .10
1375 Wolfkin Bond C .07 .15
1376 Woodborn Behemoth U .05 .10
1377 Woolly Loxodon C .07 .15
1378 Wren's Run Vanquisher U .12 .25
1379 Yavimaya Elder C .15 .30
1380 Yavimaya Sapherd C .07 .15
1381 Yeva's Forcemage C .05 .10
1382 Zendikar's Roil U .50 1.00
1383 Abzan Charm U .12 .25
1384 Abzan Guide C .07 .15
1385 Agony Warp C .12 .25
1386 Akroan Hoplite U .07 .15
1387 Animar, Soul of Elements M 5.00 10.00
1388 Armadillo Cloak U .50 1.00
1389 Armament Corps U .07 .15
1390 Assemble the Legion R .12 .25
1391 Athreos, God of Passage M 7.50 15.00
1392 Aura Shards U 3.00 6.00
1393 Azorius Charm U .15 .30
1394 Azra Oddsmaker U .75 1.50
1395 Baleful Strix U 1.25 2.50
1396 Baloth Null U .07 .15
1397 Bear's Companion U .05 .10
1398 Belligerent Brontodon U .07 .15
1399 Bituminous Blast U .07 .15
1400 Bladewing the Risen U 1.00 2.00
1401 Blightning U .12 .25
1402 Bloodbraid Elf U .12 .25
1403 Boros Challenger U .05 .10
1404 Bounding Krasis U .07 .15
1405 Call of the Nightwing U .07 .15
1406 Campaign of Vengeance U .20 .40
1407 Cauldron Dance U .15 .30
1408 Citadel Castellan U .05 .10
1409 Coiling Oracle C .07 .15
1410 Contraband Kingpin U .12 .25
1411 Corpsejack Menace U .75 1.50
1412 Crosis's Charm U .25 .50
1413 Cunning Breezedancer U .10 .20
1414 Deathreap Ritual U .20 .40
1415 Deny Reality C .05 .10
1416 Draconic Disciple U .10 .20
1417 Dragon Broodmother M 3.00 6.00
1418 Dragonlord Ojutai M .25 .50
1419 Drana's Emissary U .30 .60
1420 Engineered Might U .05 .10
1421 Esper Charm U .30 .75
1422 Ethercaste Knight U .07 .15
1423 Ethereal Ambush C .05 .10
1424 Extract from Darkness U .10 .20
1425 Fires of Yavimaya U .60 1.25
1426 Flame-Kin Zealot U .05 .10
1427 Fusion Elemental U .10 .20
1428 Gelectrode U .40 .80
1429 Ghor-Clan Rampager U .05 .10
1430 The Gitrog Monster M 3.00 6.00
1431 Goblin Deathraiders C .07 .15
1432 Grim Contest C .07 .15
1433 Guided Passage R .17 .35
1434 Hammer Dropper C .07 .15
1435 Hidden Stockpile U .12 .25
1436 Highspire Mantis U .05 .10
1437 Hypothesizzle C .05 .10
1438 Iroas's Champion U .07 .15
1439 Join Shields U .12 .25
1440 Jungle Barrier U .10 .20
1441 Kathari Remnant U .07 .15
1442 Kin-Tree Invocation U .07 .15
1443 Kiora's Follower U .17 .35
1444 Kiss of the Amesha U .05 .10
1445 Kolaghan's Command R 1.00 2.00
1446 Kruphix, God of Horizons M 2.00 4.00
1447 Lawmage's Binding C .07 .15
1448 Lightning Helix U .25 .50
1449 Maelstrom Archangel M .30 .75
1450 Mardu Roughrider U .05 .10
1451 Martial Glory C .07 .15
1452 Maverick Thopterist U .07 .15
1453 Meddling Mage R .40 .80
1454 Mercurial Geists U .05 .10
1455 Meren of Clan Nel Toth M 4.00 8.00
1456 Migratory Route U .12 .25
1457 Mortify U .15 .30
1458 Naya Charm U .15 .30
1459 Nemesis of Reason R .75 1.50
1460 Nin, the Pain Artist R .25 .50
1461 Obelisk Spider U .17 .35
1462 Ochran Assassin U .10 .20
1463 Pillory of the Sleepless U .10 .20
1464 Plaxcaster Frogling U .15 .30
1465 Pollenbright Wings U .15 .30
1466 Putrefy U .15 .30
1467 Qasali Pridemage C .12 .25
1468 Queen Marchesa M 2.00 4.00
1469 Questing Phelddagrif R .12 .25
1470 Raff Capashen, Ship's Mage U .12 .25
1471 Raging Swordtooth U .15 .30
1472 Reclusive Artificer U .07 .15
1473 Reflector Mage U .17 .35
1474 Rhox War Monk U .05 .10
1475 Riptide Crab C .07 .15
1476 Rith, the Awakener R .15 .30
1477 River Hoopoe U .07 .15
1478 Rosemane Centaur C .05 .10
1479 Satyr Enchanter U .75 1.50
1480 Savage Knuckleblade R .07 .15
1481 Savage Twister U .12 .25
1482 Sedraxis Specter U .05 .10
1483 Shambling Remains U .07 .15
1484 Shardless Agent U .30 .75
1485 Shipwreck Singer U .10 .20
1486 Skyward Eye Prophets U .07 .15
1487 Sliver Hivelord M 7.50 15.00
1488 Soul Manipulation U .12 .25
1489 Sprouting Thrinax U .07 .15
1490 Stormchaser Chimera U .05 .10
1491 Sultai Charm U .10 .20
1492 Sultai Soothsayer U .05 .10
1493 Supreme Verdict R 2.50 5.00
1494 Tatyova, Benthic Druid U .30 .75
1495 Terminate C .25 .50
1496 Thought Erasure U .12 .25
1497 Time Sieve R 4.00 8.00
1498 Tithe Drinker C .17 .35
1499 Tower Gargoyle U .07 .15
1500 Treacherous Terrain U .12 .25
1501 Underworld Coinsmith U .15 .30
1502 Unflinching Courage U .10 .20
1503 Unlicensed Disintegration U .07 .15
1504 Urban Evolution U .10 .20
1505 Vengeful Rebirth U .07 .15
1506 Violent Ultimatum R .15 .30
1507 Warden of the Eye U .10 .20
1508 Wargate R 2.00 4.00
1509 Wayfaring Temple U .10 .20
1510 Weapons Trainer U .07 .15
1511 Wee Dragonauts U .05 .10
1512 Winding Constrictor U .30 .60
1513 Woolly Thoctar U .05 .10
1514 Yavimaya's Embrace R .05 .10
1515 Yuriko, the Tiger's Shadow R 3.00 6.00
1516 Zealous Persecution U .07 .15
1517 Zhur-Taa Druid C .12 .25
1518 Boros Reckoner R .25 .50
1519 Debtors' Knell R .30 .75
1520 Dominus of Fealty R .30 .75
1521 Doomgape R .12 .25
1522 Enchanted Evening R 1.25 2.50
1523 Giantbaiting C .07 .15
1524 Gift of Orzhova C .05 .10
1525 Gwyllion Hedge-Mage U .07 .15
1526 Manamorphose C 1.50 3.00
1527 Mistmeadow Witch U .07 .15
1528 Nucklavee U .07 .15
1529 Oracle of Nectars R .15 .30
1530 Rhys the Redeemed R 2.00 4.00
1531 Rosheen Meanderer U .12 .25
1532 Selesnya Guildmage U .05 .10
1533 Shrewd Hatchling U .05 .10
1534 Slave of Bolas U .17 .35
1535 Thopter Foundry U .15 .30
1536 Claim // Fame U .12 .25
1537 Commit // Memory R .17 .35
1538 Fire // Ice C .12 .25
1539 Aetherflux Reservoir R 5.00 10.00
1540 Aether Spellbomb C .17 .35
1541 Akroan Horse R .17 .35
1542 Alchemist's Vial C .12 .25
1543 Alhammarret's Archive M 7.50 15.00
1544 Alloy Myr C .20 .40
1545 Armillary Sphere C .10 .20
1546 Ashnod's Altar U 4.00 8.00
1547 Basilisk Collar R 1.25 2.50
1548 Belbe's Portal R 1.00 2.00
1549 Blinding Souleater C .05 .10
1550 Bomat Bazaar Barge U .10 .20
1551 Bone Saw C .12 .25
1552 Bonesplitter C .07 .15
1553 Boompile R .60 1.25
1554 Bottle Gnomes U .07 .15
1555 Burnished Hart U .15 .30
1556 Caged Sun R 1.25 2.50
1557 Cathodion U .05 .10
1558 Cauldron of Souls R 2.50 5.00
1559 Chromatic Lantern R 2.00 4.00
1560 Chromatic Star C .15 .30
1561 Coat of Arms R 10.00 20.00
1562 Coldsteel Heart U .75 1.50
1563 Consulate Dreadnought U .15 .30
1564 Contagion Clasp U .30 .60
1565 Copper Carapace C .05 .10
1566 Coveted Jewel R .40 .80
1567 Crenellated Wall U .07 .15
1568 Crystal Ball U .25 .50
1569 Crystal Chimes U 1.25 2.50
1570 Crystal Shard U .40 .80
1571 Darksteel Garrison R .12 .25
1572 Diamond Mare U .15 .30
1573 Dolmen Gate R 7.50 15.00
1574 Draco R .60 1.25
1575 Dragon Mask U .07 .15
1576 Eater of Days R .40 .80

1577 Eldrazi Monument M	7.50	15.00
1578 Elixir of Immortality U	.30	.75
1579 Emmessi Tome U	.07	.15
1580 Etched Oracle U	.10	.20
1581 Farmstead Gleaner U	.12	.25
1582 Filigree Familiar U	.10	.20
1583 Flayer Husk C	.05	.10
1584 Font of Mythos R	7.50	15.00
1585 Foundry Inspector U	.20	.40
1586 Fountain of Renewal U	.50	1.00
1587 Frogmite C	.25	.50
1588 Goblin Charbelcher R	.15	.30
1589 Gruul Signet C	.50	1.00
1590 Guardians of Meletis C	.05	.10
1591 Heavy Arbalest U	.05	.10
1592 Helm of Awakening U	.75	1.50
1593 Herald's Horn U	2.50	5.00
1594 Hexplate Golem C	.05	.10
1595 Hot Soup U	.17	.35
1596 Icy Manipulator U	.07	.15
1597 Implement of Malice C	.07	.15
1598 Irontread Crusher C	.07	.15
1599 Juggernaut U	.05	.10
1600 Lightning Greaves U	4.00	8.00
1601 Lotus Petal C	15.00	30.00
1602 Loxodon Warhammer U	.15	.30
1603 Mana Crypt M	100.00	200.00
1604 Mask of Memory U	.15	.30
1605 Meteorite U	.05	.10
1606 Millikin U	.17	.35
1607 Millstone U	.10	.20
1608 Mimic Vat R	.25	.50
1609 Mind Stone C	.15	.30
1610 Mishra's Bauble U	.75	1.50
1611 Moonglove Extract C	.10	.20
1612 Mortarpod U	.10	.20
1613 Myr Retriever U	.75	1.50
1614 Myr Sire C	.15	.30
1615 Ornithopter C	.10	.20
1616 Palladium Myr U	.60	1.25
1617 Peace Strider C	.05	.10
1618 Perilous Myr U	.07	.15
1619 Phyrexian Soulgorger R	.75	1.50
1620 Pilgrim's Eye U	.07	.15
1621 Precursor Golem R	.07	.15
1622 Prophetic Prism C	.05	.10
1623 Renegade Map C	.07	.15
1624 Rhonas's Monument U	.75	1.50
1625 Sandstone Oracle U	.07	.15
1626 Serrated Arrows C	.15	.30
1627 Short Sword C	.07	.15
1628 Sigil of Valor U	.12	.25
1629 Simic Locket C	.07	.15
1630 Skullclamp U	2.00	4.00
1631 Skyscanner C	.10	.20
1632 Solemn Simulacrum R	.50	1.00
1633 Sol Ring U	1.25	2.50
1634 Sorcerer's Broom U	.12	.25
1635 Spy Kit U	.10	.20
1636 Sunset Pyramid U	.05	.10
1637 Suspicious Bookcase U	.12	.25
1638 Sword of the Animist R	6.00	12.00
1639 Thought Vessel C	1.50	3.00
1640 Thran Dynamo U	2.00	4.00
1641 Thran Golem U	.10	.20
1642 Tormod's Crypt U	.17	.35
1643 Tower of Eons R	.10	.20
1644 Trading Post R	.25	.50
1645 Trepanation Blade U	.15	.30
1646 Umbral Mantle U	4.00	8.00
1647 Universal Automaton C	.17	.35
1648 Universal Solvent C	.05	.10
1649 Whispersilk Cloak U	2.00	4.00
1650 Aether Hub U	.10	.20
1651 Akoum Refuge U	.12	.25
1652 Ancient Den C	.75	1.50
1653 Ancient Ziggurat U	1.50	3.00
1654 Arcane Sanctum U	.15	.30
1655 Arch of Orazca R	.40	.80
1656 Ash Barrens C	.15	.30
1657 Blasted Landscape U	1.25	2.50
1658 Blighted Fen U	.07	.15
1659 Blossoming Sands C	.07	.15
1660 Bojuka Bog C	.75	1.50
1661 Crumbling Necropolis U	.20	.40
1662 Darksteel Citadel C	.50	1.00
1663 Dismal Backwater C	.10	.20
1664 Dreadship Reef U	.12	.25
1665 Evolving Wilds C	.20	.40
1666 Faerie Conclave U	.75	1.50
1667 Field of Ruin U	.40	.80
1668 Forgotten Cave C	.10	.20
1669 Frontier Bivouac U	.20	.40
1670 Gateway Plaza C	.15	.30
1671 Ghost Quarter U	.50	1.00
1672 Gilt-Leaf Palace R	2.50	5.00
1673 Goblin Burrows U	.10	.20
1674 Graypelt Refuge U	.15	.30
1675 Great Furnace C	1.00	2.00
1676 Jungle Hollow C	.07	.15
1677 Jungle Shrine U	.30	.60
1678 Kazandu Refuge U	.10	.20
1679 Krosan Verge U	.15	.30
1680 Mishra's Factory U	.07	.15
1681 New Benalia U	.10	.20
1682 Orzhov Basilica C	.12	.25
1683 Reliquary Tower U	2.00	4.00
1684 Rogue's Passage U	.60	1.25
1685 Sandsteppe Citadel U	.25	.50
1686 Scoured Barrens C	.07	.15
1687 Sejiri Refuge U	.12	.25
1688 Skarrg, the Rage Pits U	.60	1.25
1689 Swiftwater Cliffs C	.10	.20
1690 Tectonic Edge U	.40	.80
1691 Temple of the False God U	.15	.30
1692 Thornwood Falls C	.07	.15
1693 Unclaimed Territory U	.40	.80
1694 Wirewood Lodge U	2.50	5.00
1695 Goblin Trenches R	.17	.35
1696 Prophetic Bolt R	.10	.20

2019 Magic The Gathering Mystery Booster Convention Exclusives

1 Ral's Vanguard	3.00	6.00
2 Banding Sliver	10.00	20.00
3 Baneslayer Aspirant	3.00	6.00
4 Enroll in the Coalition	3.00	6.00
5 Five Kids in a Trenchcoat	3.00	6.00
6 Frontier Explorer	4.00	8.00
7 Imaginary Friends	2.50	5.00
8 Metagamer	3.00	6.00
9 Priority Avenger	5.00	10.00
10 Ruff, Underdog Champ	3.00	6.00
11 Sarah's Wings	4.00	8.00
12 Scaled Destruction	3.00	6.00
13 Stack of Paperwork	6.00	12.00
14 Wizened Arbiter	3.00	6.00
15 You're In Command	6.00	12.00
16 Animate Spell	4.00	8.00
17 Biting Remark	3.00	6.00
18 Command the Chaff	5.00	10.00
19 Control Win Condition	4.00	8.00
20 Do-Over	2.00	4.00
21 Enchantmentize	3.00	6.00
22 Form of the Mulldrifter	6.00	12.00
23 Innocuous Insect	3.00	6.00
24 Khod, Etlan Shiis Envoy	6.00	12.00
25 Learned Learner	2.50	5.00
26 Loopy Lobster	3.00	6.00
27 Memory Bank	5.00	10.00
28 Recycla-bird	5.00	10.00
29 Squidnapper	6.00	12.00
30 The Grand Tour	3.00	6.00
31 Time Sidewalk	15.00	30.00
32 Truth or Dare	6.00	12.00
33 Visitor from Planet Q	4.00	8.00
34 Blood Poet	4.00	8.00
35 Bone Rattler	5.00	10.00
36 Buried Ogre	3.00	6.00
37 Celestine Cave Witch	6.00	12.00
38 Chimney Goyf	3.00	6.00
39 Corrupted Key	2.00	4.00
40 Cyclopean Titan	3.00	6.00
41 Everlasting Lich	4.00	8.00
42 Frogkin Kidnapper	6.00	12.00
43 Gunk Slug	4.00	8.00
44 Largepox	4.00	8.00
45 One With Death	6.00	12.00
46 Spellmorph Raise Dead	3.00	6.00
47 Sunimret	3.00	6.00
48 Swarm of Locus	3.00	6.00
49 Underdark Beholder	5.00	10.00
50 Witty Demon	3.00	6.00
51 Xyru Specter	3.00	6.00
52 Yawgmoth's Testament	4.00	8.00
53 Bombardment	4.00	8.00
54 Geometric Weird	3.00	6.00
55 High Troller	3.00	6.00
56 Impatient Iguana	6.00	12.00
57 Lazier Goblin	4.00	8.00
58 Lightning Colt	2.00	4.00
59 Mana Abundance	5.00	10.00
60 Planequake	2.00	4.00
61 Problematic Volcano	5.00	10.00
62 Queue of Beetles	3.00	6.00
63 Red Herring	3.00	6.00
64 Seasoned Weaponsmith	4.00	8.00
65 Siege Elemental	3.00	6.00
66 Throat Wolf	4.00	8.00
67 Tibalt the Chaotic	15.00	30.00
68 Transcantation	5.00	10.00
69 Trial and Error	3.00	6.00
70 Whammy Burn	4.00	8.00
71 Bear with Set's Mechanic	6.00	12.00
72 Domesticated Mammoth	2.00	4.00
73 Experiment Five	2.00	4.00
74 Frenemy of the Guildpact	3.00	6.00
75 Generated Horizons	3.00	6.00
76 Gorilla Tactics	2.00	4.00
77 Growth Charm	4.00	8.00
78 Inspirational Antelope	2.00	4.00
79 Interplanar Brushwagg	3.00	6.00
80 Krosan Adaptation	2.00	4.00
81 Maro's Gone Nuts	7.50	15.00
82 Patient Turtle	2.00	4.00
83 Plane-Merge Elf	2.50	5.00
84 Soulmates	12.50	25.00
85 Vazal, the Compleat	12.50	25.00
86 A Good Thing	2.50	5.00
87 Abian, Luvion Usurper	7.50	15.00
88 Bind // Liberate	2.50	5.00
89 Bucket List	5.00	10.00
90 Evil Boros Charm	4.00	8.00
91 Golgari Death Swarm	2.50	5.00
92 Graveyard Dig	3.00	6.00
93 How to Keep an Izzet Mage Busy	5.00	10.00
94 Kaya, Ghost Haunter	6.00	12.00
95 Louvaq, the Aberrant	5.00	10.00
96 Personal Decoy	7.50	15.00
97 Pick Your Poison	3.00	6.00
98 Seek Bolas's Counsel	10.00	20.00
99 Sliv-Mizzet, Hivemind	30.00	75.00
100 Smelt // Herd // Saw	2.50	5.00
101 Start // Fire	2.50	5.00
102 Slivdrazi Monstrosity	50.00	100.00
103 Wrath of Sod	5.00	10.00
104 Zyym, Mesmeric Lord	5.00	10.00
105 Chronobot	2.50	5.00
106 Lantern of Undersight	5.00	10.00
107 Mirrored Lotus	25.00	50.00
108 Pithing Spyglass	2.50	5.00
109 Puresteel Angel	12.50	25.00
110 Unicycle	2.50	5.00
111 Weaponized Scrap	2.00	4.00
112 Aggressive Crag	4.00	8.00
113 Barry's Land	3.00	6.00
114 Domesticated Watercourse	4.00	8.00
115 Enchanted Prairie	4.00	8.00
116 Gold Mine	3.00	6.00
117 Jasconian Isle	3.00	6.00
118 Noxious Bayou	4.00	8.00
119 Rift	5.00	10.00
120 Taiga Stadium	6.00	12.00
121 Waste Land	5.00	10.00

2019 Magic The Gathering Ravnica Allegiance

1 Angel of Grace M	4.00	8.00
2 Angelic Exaltation U	.10	.20
3 Archway Angel U	.10	.20
4 Arrester's Zeal C	.07	.15
5 Bring to Trial C	.07	.15
6 Civic Stalwart C	.07	.15
7 Concordia Pegasus C	.07	.15
8 Expose to Daylight C	.07	.15
9 Forbidding Spirit U	.10	.20
10 Haazda Officer C	.07	.15
11 Hero of Precinct One R	.15	.30
12 Impassioned Orator C	.07	.15
13 Justiciar's Portal C	.07	.15
14 Knight of Sorrows C	.07	.15
15 Lumbering Battlement R	.15	.30
16 Ministrant of Obligation U	.10	.20
17 Prowling Caracal C	.07	.15
18 Rally to Battle U	.10	.20
19 Resolute Watchdog U	.10	.20
20 Sentinel's Mark U	.10	.20
21 Sky Tether U	.10	.20
22 Smothering Tithe R	.15	.30
23 Spirit of the Spires U	.10	.20
24 Summary Judgment C	.07	.15
25 Syndicate Messenger C	.07	.15
26 Tenth District Veteran C	.07	.15
27 Tithe Taker R	.15	.30
28 Twilight Panther C	.07	.15
29 Unbreakable Formation R	.15	.30
30 Watchful Giant C	.07	.15
31 Arrester's Admonition C	.07	.15
32 Benthic Biomancer R	.15	.30
33 Chillbringer C	.07	.15
34 Clear the Mind C	.07	.15
35 Code of Constraint U	.10	.20
36 Coral Commando C	.07	.15
37 Essence Capture U	.10	.20
38 Eyes Everywhere U	.10	.20
39 Faerie Duelist C	.07	.15
40 Gateway Sneak U	.10	.20
41 Humongulus C	.07	.15
42 Mass Manipulation R	.15	.30
43 Mesmerizing Benthid M	1.50	3.00
44 Persistent Petitioners C	.07	.15
45 Precognitive Perception R	.15	.30
46 Prying Eyes C	.07	.15
47 Pteramander U	.10	.20
48 Quench C	.07	.15
49 Sage's Row Savant C	.07	.15
50 Senate Courier C	.07	.15
51 Shimmer of Possibility C	.07	.15
52 Skatewing Spy U	.10	.20
53 Skitter Eel C	.07	.15
54 Slimebind C	.07	.15
55 Sphinx of Foresight R	.15	.30
56 Swirling Torrent U	.10	.20
57 Thought Collapse C	.07	.15
58 Verity Circle R	.15	.30
59 Wall of Lost Thoughts U	.10	.20
60 Windstorm Drake U	.10	.20
61 Awaken the Erstwhile R	.15	.30
62 Bankrupt in Blood U	.10	.20
63 Blade Juggler C	.07	.15
64 Bladebrand C	.07	.15
65 Bloodmist Infiltrator U	.10	.20
66 Carrion Imp C	.07	.15
67 Catacomb Crocodile C	.07	.15
68 Clear the Stage U	.10	.20
69 Consign to the Pit C	.07	.15
70 Cry of the Carnarium U	.10	.20
71 Dead Revels C	.07	.15
72 Debtors' Transport C	.07	.15
73 Drill Bit U	.10	.20
74 Font of Agonies R	.15	.30
75 Grotesque Demise C	.07	.15
76 Gutterbones R	.15	.30
77 Ill-Gotten Inheritance C	.07	.15
78 Noxious Groodion C	.07	.15
79 Orzhov Enforcer U	.10	.20
80 Orzhov Racketeers U	.10	.20
81 Pestilent Spirit R	.15	.30
82 Plague Wight C	.07	.15
83 Priest of Forgotten Gods R	.15	.30
84 Rakdos Trumpeter C	.07	.15
85 Spawn of Mayhem M	6.00	12.00
86 Spire Mangler U	.10	.20
87 Thirsting Shade C	.07	.15
88 Undercity Scavenger C	.07	.15
89 Undercity's Embrace C	.07	.15
90 Vindictive Vampire U	.10	.20
91 Act of Treason C	.07	.15
92 Amplifire R	.15	.30
93 Burn Bright C	.07	.15
94 Burning-Tree Vandal C	.07	.15
95 Cavalcade of Calamity U	.10	.20
96 Clamor Shaman U	.10	.20
97 Dagger Caster U	.10	.20
98 Deface C	.07	.15
99 Electrodominance R	.15	.30
100 Feral Maaka C	.07	.15
101 Flames of the Raze-Boar U	.10	.20
102 Gates Ablaze U	.10	.20
103 Ghor-Clan Wrecker C	.07	.15
104 Goblin Gathering C	.07	.15
105 Gravel-Hide Goblin C	.07	.15
106 Immolation Shaman R	.15	.30
107 Light Up the Stage U	.10	.20
108 Mirror March R	.15	.30
109 Rix Maadi Reveler R	.15	.30
110 Rubble Reading C	.07	.15
111 Rubblebelt Recluse C	.07	.15
112 Rumbling Ruin U	.10	.20
113 Scorchmark C	.07	.15
114 Skarrgan Hellkite M	5.00	10.00
115 Skewer the Critics C	.07	.15
116 Smelt-Ward Ignus U	.10	.20
117 Spear Spewer C	.07	.15
118 Spikewheel Acrobat C	.07	.15
119 Storm Strike C	.07	.15
120 Tin Street Dodger U	.10	.20
121 Axebane Beast C	.07	.15
122 Biogenic Ooze M	6.00	12.00
123 Biogenic Upgrade U	.10	.20
124 End-Raze Forerunners R	.15	.30
125 Enraged Ceratok U	.10	.20
126 Gatebreaker Ram U	.10	.20
127 Gift of Strength C	.07	.15
128 Growth-Chamber Guardian R	.15	.30
129 Gruul Beastmaster U	.10	.20
130 Guardian Project R	.15	.30
131 Incubation Druid R	.15	.30
132 Mammoth Spider C	.07	.15
133 Open the Gates C	.07	.15
134 Rampage of the Clans R	.15	.30
135 Rampaging Rendhorn C	.07	.15
136 Regenesis U	.10	.20
137 Root Snare C	.07	.15
138 Sagittars' Volley C	.07	.15
139 Saruli Caretaker C	.07	.15
140 Sauroform Hybrid C	.07	.15
141 Silhana Wayfinder U	.10	.20
142 Steeple Creeper C	.07	.15
143 Stony Strength C	.07	.15
144 Sylvan Brushstrider C	.07	.15
145 Territorial Boar C	.07	.15
146 Titanic Brawl C	.07	.15
147 Tower Defense U	.10	.20
148 Trollbred Guardian U	.10	.20
149 Wilderness Reclamation U	.10	.20
150 Wrecking Beast C	.07	.15
151 Absorb R	.15	.30
152 Aeromunculus C	.07	.15
153 Applied Biomancy C	.07	.15
154 Azorius Knight-Arbiter C	.07	.15
155 Azorius Skyguard U	.10	.20
156 Basilica Bell-Haunt U	.10	.20
157 Bedevil R	.15	.30
158 Biomancer's Familiar R	.15	.30
159 Bolrac-Clan Crusher U	.10	.20
160 Captive Audience M	1.50	3.00
161 Cindervines R	.15	.30
162 Clan Guildmage U	.10	.20
163 Combine Guildmage U	.10	.20
164 Cult Guildmage U	.10	.20
165 Deputy of Detention R	.15	.30
166 Domri, Chaos Bringer M	5.00	10.00
167 Dovin, Grand Arbiter M	4.00	8.00
168 Dovin's Acuity U	.10	.20
169 Emergency Powers M	1.50	3.00
170 Ethereal Absolution R	.15	.30
171 Final Payment C	.07	.15
172 Fireblade Artist U	.10	.20
173 Frenzied Arynx C	.07	.15
174 Frilled Mystic U	.10	.20
175 Galloping Lizrog U	.10	.20
176 Get the Point C	.07	.15
177 Grasping Thrull C	.07	.15
178 Growth Spiral C	.07	.15
179 Gruul Spellbreaker R	.15	.30
180 Gyre Engineer U	.10	.20
181 Hackrobat U	.10	.20
182 High Alert U	.10	.20
183 Hydroid Krasis M	25.00	45.00
184 Imperious Oligarch C	.07	.15
185 Judith, the Scourge Diva R	.15	.30
186 Kaya, Orzhov Usurper M	4.00	8.00
187 Kaya's Wrath R	.15	.30
188 Knight of the Last Breath U	.10	.20
189 Lavinia, Azorius Renegade R	.15	.30
190 Lawmage's Binding C	.07	.15
191 Macabre Mockery U	.10	.20
192 Mortify U	.10	.20
193 Nikya of the Old Ways R	.15	.30
194 Pitiless Pontiff U	.10	.20
195 Prime Speaker Vannifar M	7.50	15.00
196 Rafter Demon C	.07	.15
197 Rakdos Firewheeler U	.10	.20
198 Rakdos Roustabout C	.07	.15
199 Rakdos, the Showstopper M	1.50	3.00
200 Ravager Wurm M	2.00	4.00
201 Rhythm of the Wild U	.10	.20
202 Rubblebelt Runner C	.07	.15
203 Savage Smash C	.07	.15
204 Senate Guildmage U	.10	.20
205 Seraph of the Scales M	7.50	15.00
206 Sharktocrab U	.10	.20
207 Simic Ascendancy R	.15	.30
208 Sphinx of New Prahv U	.10	.20
209 Sphinx's Insight C	.07	.15
210 Sunder Shaman U	.10	.20
211 Syndicate Guildmage U	.10	.20
212 Teysa Karlov R	.15	.30
213 Theater of Horrors R	.15	.30
214 Zegana, Utopian Speaker R	.15	.30
215 Zhur-Taa Goblin U	.10	.20
216 Footlight Fiend C	.07	.15
217 Rubble Slinger C	.07	.15
218 Scuttlegator C	.07	.15
219 Senate Griffin C	.07	.15
220 Vizkopa Vampire C	.07	.15
221 Bedeck/Bedazzle R	.15	.30
222 Carnival/Carnage U	.10	.20
223 Collision/Colossus U	.10	.20
224 Consecrate/Consume U	.10	.20
225 Depose/Deploy U	.10	.20
226 Incubation/Incongruity U	.10	.20
227 Repudiate/Replicate R	.15	.30
228 Revival/Revenge R	.15	.30
229 Thrash/Threat R	.15	.30
230 Warrant/Warden R	.15	.30
231 Azorius Locket C	.07	.15
232 Gate Colossus U	.10	.20
233 Glass of the Guildpact R	.15	.30
234 Gruul Locket C	.07	.15
235 Junktroller U	.10	.20
236 Orzhov Locket C	.07	.15
237 Rakdos Locket C	.07	.15
238 Scrabbling Claws U	.10	.20
239 Screaming Shield U	.10	.20
240 Simic Locket C	.07	.15
241 Sphinx of the Guildpact U	.10	.20

242 Tome of the Guildpact R .15 .30
243 Azorius Guildgate C .07 .15
244 Azorius Guildgate C .07 .15
245 Blood Crypt R .15 .30
246 Breeding Pool R .15 .30
247 Gateway Plaza C .07 .15
248 Godless Shrine R .15 .30
249 Gruul Guildgate C .07 .15
250 Gruul Guildgate C .07 .15
251 Hallowed Fountain R .15 .30
252 Orzhov Guildgate C .07 .15
253 Orzhov Guildgate C .07 .15
254 Plaza of Harmony R .15 .30
255 Rakdos Guildgate C .07 .15
256 Rakdos Guildgate C .07 .15
257 Simic Guildgate C .07 .15
258 Simic Guildgate C .07 .15
259 Stomping Ground R .15 .30
260 Plains L .07 .15
261 Island L .07 .15
262 Swamp L .07 .15
263 Mountain L .07 .15
264 Forest L .07 .15
265 Dovin, Architect of Law M 4.00 8.00
266 Elite Arrester C .07 .15
267 Dovin's Dismissal R .15 .30
268 Dovin's Automaton U .10 .20
269 Domri, City Smasher M 5.00 10.00
270 Ragefire C .07 .15
271 Charging War Boar U .10 .20
272 Domri's Nodorog R .15 .30
273 The Haunt of Hightower M 4.00 8.00

2019 Magic The Gathering Ravnica Allegiance Mythic Edition

RA1 Karn, Scion of Urza 30.00 70.00
RA2 Tamiyo, the Moon Sage 40.00 80.00
RA3 Sorin Markov 25.00 50.00
RA4 Jaya Ballard 10.00 20.00
RA5 Ajani, Mentor of Heroes 17.50 35.00
RA6 Dack Fayden 25.00 50.00
RA7 Domri, Chaos Bringer 20.00 40.00
RA8 Kaya, Orzhov Usurper 17.50 35.00

2019 Magic The Gathering Ravnica Allegiance Ravnica Weekend

B1 Plains L 1.50 3.00
B2 Island L 1.25 2.50
B3 Plains L 2.50 5.00
B4 Swamp L 4.00 8.00
B5 Swamp L 2.50 5.00
B6 Mountain L 2.00 4.00
B7 Mountain L 1.00 2.00
B8 Forest L 1.00 2.00
B9 Forest L 1.75 3.50
B10 Island L 1.50 3.00

2019 Magic The Gathering Ravnica Allegiance Tokens

1 Human .07 .10
2 Illusion .07 .10
3 Zombie .07 .10
4 Goblin .07 .15
5 Centaur .07 .10
6 Frog Lizard .07 .10
7 Ooze .07 .10
8 Beast .07 .10
9 Sphinx .07 .10
10 Spirit .07 .10
11 Thopter .07 .15
12 Treasure .12 .25
13 Domri, Chaos Bringer Emblem .07 .10

2019 Magic The Gathering Secret Lair Drop Series Bitterblossom Dreams

12 Bitterblossom M 12.00 30.00
13 Faerie Rogue T 3.00 8.00
14 Faerie Rogue T 2.50 6.00
15 Faerie Rogue T 1.50 4.00
16 Faerie Rogue T 4.00 10.00

2019 Magic The Gathering Secret Lair Drop Series Eldraine Wonderland

1 Snow-Covered Plains FOIL R 4.00 10.00
2 Snow-Covered Island FOIL R 6.00 15.00
3 Snow-Covered Swamp FOIL R 2.50 6.00
4 Snow-Covered Mountain FOIL R 2.00 5.00
5 Snow-Covered Forest FOIL R 3.00 8.00

2019 Magic The Gathering Secret Lair Drop Series Explosion Sounds

17 Goblin Bushwhacker R 4.00 10.00
18 Goblin Sharpshooter R 15.00 40.00
19 Goblin King R 10.00 25.00
20 Goblin Lackey R 8.00 20.00
21 Goblin Piledriver R 2.00 5.00

2019 Magic The Gathering Secret Lair Drop Series Kaleidoscope Killers

9 Reaper King FOIL M 2.50 6.00
10 Sliver Overlord FOIL M 40.00 100.00
11 The Ur-Dragon FOIL M 25.00 60.00

2019 Magic The Gathering Secret Lair Drop Series OMG Kitties

22 Leonin Warleader FOIL R 15.00 40.00
23 Regal Caracal FOIL R 10.00 25.00
24 Qasali Slingers FOIL R 10.00 25.00
25 Arahbo, Roar of the World FOIL M 25.00 60.00
26 Mirri, Weatherlight Duelist FOIL M 20.00 50.00
27 Cat FOIL T 3.00 8.00

2019 Magic The Gathering Secret Lair Drop Series Restless in Peace

6 Bloodghast R 8.00 20.00
7 Golgari Thug R 1.50 4.00
8 Life from the Loam R 8.00 20.00

2019 Magic The Gathering Secret Lair Drop Series Seeing Visions

29 Serum Visions FOIL R 2.00 5.00
30 Serum Visions FOIL R 1.25 3.00
31 Serum Visions FOIL R 1.25 3.00
32 Serum Visions FOIL R 1.25 3.00

2019 Magic The Gathering Signature Spellbook Gideon

1 Gideon Jura M .60 1.25
2 Martyr's Bond R .30 .75
3 Path to Exile R 4.00 8.00
4 Rest in Peace R 3.00 6.00
5 Shielded by Faith R 1.50 3.00
6 True Conviction R 1.25 2.50
7 Worship R .50 1.00
8 Blackblade Reforged R .75 1.50

2019 Magic The Gathering Throne of Eldraine

1 Acclaimed Contender R .15 .30
2 All That Glitters U .10 .20
3 Archon of Absolution U .10 .20
4 Ardenvale Paladin C .07 .15
5 Ardenvale Tactician/Dizzying Swoop C .07 .15
6 Bartered Cow C .07 .15
7 Beloved Princess C .07 .15
8 Charming Prince R .15 .30
9 The Circle of Loyalty M 1.00 2.00
10 Deafening Silence U .10 .20
11 Faerie Guidemother/Gift of the Fae C .07 .15
12 Flutterfox C .07 .15
13 Fortifying Provisions C .07 .15
14 Giant Killer/Chop Down R .15 .30
15 Glass Casket U .10 .20
16 Happily Ever After R .15 .30
17 Harmonious Archon M .30 .75
18 Hushbringer R .15 .30
19 Knight of the Keep C .07 .15
20 Linden, the Steadfast Queen R .15 .30
21 Lonesome Unicorn/Rider in Need C .07 .15
22 Mysterious Pathlighter U .10 .20
23 Outflank C .07 .15
24 Prized Griffin C .07 .15
25 Rally for the Throne U .10 .20
26 Realm-Cloaked Giant/Cast Off M .75 1.50
27 Righteousness U .10 .20
28 Shepherd of the Flock/Usher to Safety U .10 .20
29 Shining Armor C .07 .15
30 Silverflame Ritual C .07 .15
31 Silverflame Squire/On Alert C .07 .15
32 Syr Alin, the Lion's Claw U .10 .20
33 Trapped in the Tower C .07 .15
34 True Love's Kiss C .07 .15
35 Venerable Knight U .10 .20
36 Worthy Knight R .15 .30
37 Youthful Knight C .07 .15
38 Animating Faerie/Bring to Life U .10 .20
39 Brazen Borrower/Petty Theft M 10.00 20.00
40 Charmed Sleep C .07 .15
41 Corridor Monitor C .07 .15
42 Didn't Say Please C .07 .15
43 Emry, Lurker of the Loch R .15 .30
44 Fae of Wishes/Granted R .15 .30
45 Faerie Vandal U .10 .20
46 Folio of Fancies R .15 .30
47 Frogify U .10 .20
48 Gadwick, the Wizened R .15 .30
49 Hypnotic Sprite/Mesmeric Glare U .10 .20
50 Into the Story U .10 .20
51 The Magic Mirror M 1.50 3.00
52 Mantle of Tides C .07 .15
53 Merfolk Secretkeeper/Venture Deeper C .07 .15
54 Midnight Clock R .15 .30
55 Mirrormade R .15 .30
56 Mistford River Turtle C .07 .15
57 Moonlit Scavengers C .07 .15
58 Mystical Dispute U .10 .20
59 Opt C .07 .15
60 Overwhelmed Apprentice U .10 .20
61 Queen of Ice/Rage of Winter C .07 .15
62 Run Away Together C .07 .15
63 Sage of the Falls U .10 .20
64 So Tiny C .07 .15
65 Steelgaze Griffin C .07 .15
66 Stolen by the Fae R .15 .30
67 Syr Elenora, the Discerning U .10 .20
68 Tome Raider C .07 .15
69 Turn into a Pumpkin U .10 .20
70 Unexplained Vision C .07 .15
71 Vantress Gargoyle R .15 .30
72 Vantress Paladin C .07 .15
73 Wishful Merfolk C .07 .15
74 Witching Well C .07 .15
75 Ayara, First of Locthwain R .15 .30
76 Bake into a Pie C .07 .15
77 Barrow Witches C .07 .15
78 Belle of the Brawl U .10 .20
79 Blacklance Paragon R .15 .30
80 Bog Naughty U .10 .20
81 Cauldron Familiar U .10 .20
82 The Cauldron of Eternity M 1.00 2.00
83 Cauldron's Gift U .10 .20
84 Clackbridge Troll R .15 .30
85 Epic Downfall U .10 .20
86 Eye Collector C .07 .15
87 Festive Funeral C .07 .15
88 Foreboding Fruit C .07 .15
89 Forever Young C .07 .15
90 Foulmire Knight/Profane Insight U .10 .20
91 Giant Skewer C .07 .15
92 Lash of Thorns C .07 .15
93 Locthwain Paladin C .07 .15
94 Lost Legion C .07 .15
95 Malevolent Noble C .07 .15
96 Memory Theft C .07 .15
97 Murderous Rider/Swift End R .15 .30
98 Oathsworn Knight R .15 .30
99 Order of Midnight/Alter Fate U .10 .20
100 Piper of the Swarm R .15 .30
101 Rankle, Master of Pranks M 5.00 10.00
102 Reaper of Night/Harvest Fear C .07 .15
103 Reave Soul C .07 .15
104 Revenge of Ravens U .10 .20
105 Smitten Swordmaster/Curry Favor C .07 .15
106 Specter's Shriek U .10 .20
107 Syr Konrad, the Grim U .10 .20
108 Tempting Witch C .07 .15
109 Wicked Guardian C .07 .15
110 Wishclaw Talisman R .15 .30
111 Witch's Vengeance R .15 .30
112 Barge In C .07 .15
113 Bloodhaze Wolverine C .07 .15
114 Blow Your House Down C .07 .15
115 Bonecrusher Giant/Stomp R .15 .30
116 Brimstone Trebuchet C .07 .15
117 Burning-Yard Trainer U .10 .20
118 Claim the Firstborn U .10 .20
119 Crystal Slipper C .07 .15
120 Embercleave M 10.00 20.00
121 Embereth Paladin C .07 .15
122 Embereth Shieldbreaker/Battle Display U .10 .20
123 Ferocity of the Wilds U .10 .20
124 Fervent Champion R .15 .30
125 Fires of Invention R .15 .30
126 Fling C .07 .15
127 Irencrag Feat R .15 .30
128 Irencrag Pyromancer R .15 .30
129 Joust U .10 .20
130 Mad Ratter U .10 .20
131 Merchant of the Vale/Haggle C .07 .15
132 Ogre Errant C .07 .15
133 Opportunistic Dragon R .15 .30
134 Raging Redcap C .07 .15
135 Redcap Melee U .10 .20
136 Redcap Raiders C .07 .15
137 Rimrock Knight/Boulder Rush C .07 .15
138 Robber of the Rich M 4.00 8.00
139 Scorching Dragonfire C .07 .15
140 Searing Barrage C .07 .15
141 Seven Dwarves C .07 .15
142 Skullknocker Ogre U .10 .20
143 Slaying Fire U .10 .20
144 Sundering Stroke R .15 .30
145 Syr Carah, the Bold U .10 .20
146 Thrill of Possibility C .07 .15
147 Torbran, Thane of Red Fell R .15 .30
148 Weaselback Redcap C .07 .15
149 Beanstalk Giant/Fertile Footsteps U .10 .20
150 Curious Pair/Treats to Share C .07 .15
151 Edgewall Innkeeper U .10 .20
152 Feasting Troll King R .15 .30
153 Fell the Pheasant C .07 .15
154 Fierce Witchstalker C .07 .15
155 Flaxen Intruder/Welcome Home U .10 .20
156 Garenbrig Carver/Shield's Might C .07 .15
157 Garenbrig Paladin C .07 .15
158 Garenbrig Squire C .07 .15
159 Giant Opportunity U .10 .20
160 Gilded Goose R .15 .30
161 The Great Henge M 10.00 20.00
162 Insatiable Appetite C .07 .15
163 Keeper of Fables U .10 .20
164 Kenrith's Transformation U .10 .20
165 Lovestruck Beast/Heart Desire R .15 .30
166 Maraleaf Rider C .07 .15
167 Oakhame Adversary U .10 .20
168 Once and Future U .10 .20
169 Once Upon a Time R .15 .30
170 Outmuscle C .07 .15
171 Questing Beast M 7.50 15.00
172 Return of the Wildspeaker R .15 .30
173 Return to Nature C .07 .15
174 Rosethorn Acolyte/Seasonal Ritual C .07 .15
175 Rosethorn Halberd C .07 .15
176 Sporecap Spider C .07 .15
177 Syr Faren, the Hengehammer U .10 .20
178 Tall as a Beanstalk C .07 .15
179 Trail of Crumbs U .10 .20
180 Tuinvale Treefolk/Oaken Boon C .07 .15
181 Wicked Wolf R .15 .30
182 Wildborn Preserver R .15 .30
183 Wildwood Tracker C .07 .15
184 Wolf's Quarry C .07 .15
185 Yorvo, Lord of Garenbrig R .15 .30
186 Dance of the Manse R .15 .30
187 Doom Foretold R .15 .30
188 Drown in the Loch U .10 .20
189 Escape to the Wilds R .15 .30
190 Faeburrow Elder R .15 .30
191 Garruk, Cursed Huntsman M 2.50 5.00
192 Grumgully, the Generous U .10 .20
193 Improbable Alliance U .10 .20
194 Inspiring Veteran U .10 .20
195 Lochmere Serpent R .15 .30
196 Maraleaf Pixie U .10 .20
197 Oko, Thief of Crowns M 7.50 15.00
198 Outlaws' Merriment M .60 1.25
199 The Royal Scions M 4.00 8.00
200 Savvy Hunter U .10 .20
201 Shinechaser U .10 .20
202 Steelclaw Lance U .10 .20
203 Stormfist Crusader R .15 .30
204 Wandermare U .10 .20
205 Wintermoor Commander U .10 .20
206 Arcanist's Owl U .10 .20
207 Covetous Urge U .10 .20
208 Deathless Knight U .10 .20
209 Elite Headhunter U .10 .20
210 Fireborn Knight U .10 .20
211 Loch Dragon U .10 .20
212 Oakhame Ranger/Bring Back U .10 .20
213 Rampart Smasher U .10 .20
214 Resolute Rider U .10 .20
215 Thunderous Snapper U .10 .20
216 Clockwork Servant U .10 .20
217 Crashing Drawbridge C .07 .15
218 Enchanted Carriage U .10 .20
219 Gingerbrute C .07 .15
220 Golden Egg C .07 .15
221 Henge Walker C .07 .15
222 Heraldic Banner U .10 .20
223 Inquisitive Puppet U .10 .20
224 Jousting Dummy C .07 .15
225 Locthwain Gargoyle C .07 .15
226 Lucky Clover U .10 .20
227 Prophet of the Peak C .07 .15
228 Roving Keep C .07 .15
229 Scalding Cauldron C .07 .15
230 Shambling Suit U .10 .20
231 Signpost Scarecrow C .07 .15
232 Sorcerer's Broom U .10 .20
233 Sorcerous Spyglass R .15 .30
234 Spinning Wheel U .10 .20
235 Stonecoil Serpent R .15 .30
236 Weapon Rack C .07 .15
237 Witch's Oven U .10 .20
238 Castle Ardenvale R .15 .30
239 Castle Embereth R .15 .30
240 Castle Garenbrig R .15 .30
241 Castle Locthwain R .15 .30
242 Castle Vantress R .15 .30
243 Dwarven Mine C .07 .15
244 Fabled Passage R .15 .30
245 Gingerbread Cabin C .07 .15
246 Idyllic Grange C .07 .15
247 Mystic Sanctuary C .07 .15
248 Tournament Grounds U .10 .20
249 Witch's Cottage C .07 .15
250 Plains L .07 .15
251 Plains L .07 .15
252 Plains L .07 .15
253 Plains L .07 .15
254 Island L .07 .15
255 Island L .07 .15
256 Island L .07 .15
257 Island L .07 .15
258 Swamp L .07 .15
259 Swamp L .07 .15
260 Swamp L .07 .15
261 Swamp L .07 .15
262 Mountain L .07 .15
263 Mountain L .07 .15
264 Mountain L .07 .15
265 Mountain L .07 .15
266 Forest L .07 .15
267 Forest L .07 .15
268 Forest L .07 .15
269 Forest L .07 .15
270 Garruk, Cursed Huntsman M 6.00 12.00
271 Oko, Thief of Crowns M 12.50 25.00
272 The Royal Scions M 7.50 15.00
273 Ardenvale Tactician/Dizzying Swoop C .07 .15
274 Faerie Guidemother/Gift of the Fae C .07 .15
275 Giant Killer/Chop Down R .15 .30
276 Lonesome Unicorn/Rider in Need C .07 .15
277 Realm-Cloaked Giant/Cast Off M 3.00 6.00
278 Shepherd of the Flock/Usher to Safety U .10 .20
279 Silverflame Squire/On Alert C .07 .15
280 Animating Faerie/Bring to Life U .10 .20
281 Brazen Borrower/Petty Theft M 20.00 40.00
282 Fae of Wishes/Granted R .15 .30
283 Hypnotic Sprite/Mesmeric Glare U .10 .20
284 Merfolk Secretkeeper/Venture Deeper C .07 .15
285 Queen of Ice/Rage of Winter C .07 .15
286 Foulmire Knight/Profane Insight U .10 .20
287 Murderous Rider/Swift End R .15 .30
288 Order of Midnight/Alter Fate U .10 .20
289 Reaper of Night/Harvest Fear C .07 .15
290 Smitten Swordmaster/Curry Favor C .07 .15
291 Bonecrusher Giant/Stomp R .15 .30
292 Embereth Shieldbreaker/Battle Display U .10 .20
293 Merchant of the Vale/Haggle C .07 .15
294 Rimrock Knight/Boulder Rush C .07 .15
295 Beanstalk Giant/Fertile Footsteps U .10 .20
296 Curious Pair/Treats to Share C .07 .15
297 Flaxen Intruder/Welcome Home U .10 .20
298 Garenbrig Carver/Shield's Might C .07 .15
299 Lovestruck Beast/Heart Desire R .15 .30
300 Rosethorn Acolyte/Seasonal Ritual C .07 .15
301 Tuinvale Treefolk/Oaken Boon C .07 .15
302 Oakhame Ranger/Bring Back U .10 .20
303 Kenrith, the Returned King M
(Buy-a-Box Exclusive) 4.00 8.00
304 Rowan, Fearless Sparkmage M 1.00 2.00
305 Garrison Griffin C .07 .15
306 Rowan's Battleguard U .10 .20
307 Rowan's Stalwarts R .15 .30
308 Wind-Scarred Crag C .07 .15
309 Oko, the Trickster M 1.50 3.00
310 Oko's Accomplices C .07 .15
311 Bramblefort Fink U .10 .20
312 Oko's Hospitality R .15 .30
313 Thornwood Falls C .07 .15
314 Mace of the Valiant R .15 .30
315 Silverwing Squadron R .15 .30
316 Faerie Formation R .15 .30
317 Shimmer Dragon R .15 .30
318 Workshop Elders R .15 .30
319 Chittering Witch R .15 .30
320 Taste of Death R .15 .30
321 Embereth Skyblazer R .15 .30
322 Steelbane Hydra R .15 .30
323 Thorn Mammoth R .15 .30
324 Alela, Artful Provocateur M 3.00 6.00
325 Banish into Fable R .20 .40
326 Chulane, Teller of Tales M 2.50 5.00
327 Gluttonous Troll R .20 .40
328 Knights' Charge R .50 1.00
329 Korvold, Fae-Cursed King M 7.50 15.00
330 Syr Gwyn, Hero of Ashvale M 1.00 2.00
331 Arcane Signet C .07 .15
332 Tome of Legends R .15 .30
333 Command Tower C .07 .15
334 Acclaimed Contender R FULL ART .15 .30
335 Charming Prince R FULL ART .15 .30
336 The Circle of Loyalty M FULL ART 3.00 6.00
337 Happily Ever After R FULL ART .15 .30
338 Harmonious Archon M FULL ART 1.50 3.00
339 Hushbringer R FULL ART .15 .30
340 Linden, the Steadfast Queen R FULL ART .15 .30
341 Worthy Knight R FULL ART .15 .30
342 Emry, Lurker of the Loch R FULL ART .15 .30
343 Folio of Fancies R FULL ART .15 .30
344 Gadwick, the Wizened R FULL ART .15 .30
345 The Magic Mirror M FULL ART 3.00 6.00
346 Midnight Clock R FULL ART .15 .30
347 Mirrormade R FULL ART .15 .30
348 Stolen by the Fae R FULL ART .15 .30
349 Vantress Gargoyle R FULL ART .15 .30
350 Ayara, First of Locthwain R FULL ART .15 .30

351 Blacklance Paragon R FULL ART .15 .30
352 The Cauldron of Eternity M FULL ART 3.00 6.00
353 Clackbridge Troll R FULL ART .15 .30
354 Oathsworn Knight R FULL ART .15 .30
355 Piper of the Swarm R FULL ART .15 .30
356 Rankle, Master of Pranks M FULL ART 7.50 15.00
357 Wishclaw Talisman R FULL ART .15 .30
358 Witch's Vengeance R FULL ART .15 .30
359 Embercleave M FULL ART 15.00 30.00
360 Fervent Champion R FULL ART .15 .30
361 Fires of Invention R FULL ART .15 .30
362 Irencrag Feat R FULL ART .15 .30
363 Irencrag Pyromancer R FULL ART .15 .30
364 Opportunistic Dragon R FULL ART .15 .30
365 Robber of the Rich M FULL ART 7.50 15.00
366 Sundering Stroke R FULL ART .15 .30
367 Torbran, Thane of Red Fell R FULL ART .15 .30
368 Feasting Troll King R FULL ART .15 .30
369 Gilded Goose R FULL ART .15 .30
370 The Great Henge M FULL ART 17.50 35.00
371 Once Upon a Time R FULL ART .15 .30
372 Questing Beast M FULL ART 12.50 25.00
373 Return of the Wildspeaker R FULL ART .15 .30
374 Wicked Wolf R FULL ART .15 .30
375 Wildborn Preserver R FULL ART .15 .30
376 Yorvo, Lord of Garenbrig R FULL ART .15 .30
377 Dance of the Manse R FULL ART .15 .30
378 Doom Foretold R FULL ART .15 .30
379 Escape to the Wilds R FULL ART .15 .30
380 Faeburrow Elder R FULL ART .15 .30
381 Lochmere Serpent R FULL ART .15 .30
382 Outlaws' Merriment M FULL ART 1.50 3.00
383 Stormfist Crusader R FULL ART .15 .30
384 Sorcerous Spyglass R FULL ART .15 .30
385 Stonecoil Serpent R FULL ART .15 .30
386 Castle Ardenvale R FULL ART .15 .30
387 Castle Embereth R FULL ART .15 .30
388 Castle Garenbrig R FULL ART .15 .30
389 Castle Locthwain R FULL ART .15 .30
390 Castle Vantress R FULL ART .15 .30
391 Fabled Passage R FULL ART .15 .30

2019 Magic The Gathering Throne of Eldraine Tokens

1 Goat .20 .40
2 Human .15 .30
3 Knight .07 .15
4 Mouse .07 .15
5 Faerie 1.00 2.00
6 Rat .75 1.50
7 Dwarf .15 .30
8 Bear .15 .30
9 Boar .07 .15
10 Giant .07 .15
11 Human Cleric .50 1.00
12 Human Rogue .30 .75
13 Human Warrior .30 .75
14 Wolf 1.25 2.50
15 Food .15 .30
16 Food .12 .25
17 Food .12 .25
18 Food .15 .30
19 Garruk, Cursed Huntsman Emblem .07 .15
20 On an Adventure .07 .15

2019 Magic The Gathering War of the Spark

1 Karn, the Great Creator R 12.00 30.00
2 Ugin, the Ineffable R 4.00 10.00
3 Ugin's Conjurant U .60 1.50
4 Ajani's Pridemate U 1.00 2.50
5 Battlefield Promotion C .15 .40
6 Bond of Discipline U 5.00 12.00
7 Bulwark Giant C .08 .20
8 Charmed Stray C .75 2.00
9 Defiant Strike C .12 .30
10 Divine Arrow C .12 .30
11 Enforcer Griffin C .08 .20
12 Finale of Glory M 3.00 8.00
13 Gideon Blackblade M 2.00 5.00
14 Gideon's Sacrifice C .30 .75
15 Gideon's Triumph U .30 .75
16 God-Eternal Oketra M 6.00 15.00
17 Grateful Apparition U 2.00 5.00
18 Ignite the Beacon R .40 1.00
19 Ironclad Krovod C .08 .20
20 Law-Rune Enforcer C .25 .60
21 Loxodon Sergeant C .08 .20
22 Makeshift Battalion C .08 .20
23 Martyr for the Cause C .20 .50
24 Parhelion II R 2.50 6.00
25 Pouncing Lynx C .08 .20
26 Prison Realm U .50 1.25
27 Rally of Wings U .30 .75
28 Ravnica at War R .40 1.00
29 Rising Populace C .08 .20
30 Single Combat R 1.00 2.50
31 Sunblade Angel U .30 .75
32 Teyo, the Shieldmage U .50 1.25
33 Teyo's Lightshield C .20 .50
34 Tomik, Distinguished Advokist R .50 1.25
35 Topple the Statue C .08 .20
36 Trusted Pegasus C .12 .30
37 The Wanderer U 1.25 3.00
38 Wanderer's Strike C .20 .50
39 War Screecher C .08 .20
40 Ashiok's Skulker C .08 .20
41 Augur of Bolas U .25 .60
42 Aven Eternal C .40 1.00
43 Bond of Insight U .40 1.00
44 Callous Dismissal C .20 .50
45 Commence the Endgame R .40 1.00
46 Contentious Plan C 4.00 10.00
47 Crush Dissent C .12 .30
48 Erratic Visionary C .08 .20
49 Eternal Skylord U 4.00 10.00
50 Fblthp, the Lost R .50 1.25
51 Finale of Revelation M 5.00 12.00
52 Flux Channeler U 8.00 20.00
53 God-Eternal Kefnet M 4.00 10.00
54 Jace, Wielder of Mysteries R 4.00 10.00
55 Jace's Triumph U .15 .40
56 Kasmina, Enigmatic Mentor U .60 1.50
57 Kasmina's Transmutation C .25 .60
58 Kiora's Dambreaker C .20 .50
59 Lazotep Plating U 4.00 10.00
60 Naga Eternal C .08 .20
61 Narset, Parter of Veils U 6.00 15.00
62 Narset's Reversal R 6.00 15.00
63 No Escape C .15 .40
64 Relentless Advance C .12 .30
65 Rescuer Sphinx U .20 .50
66 Silent Submersible R .50 1.25
67 Sky Theater Strix C .08 .20
68 Spark Double R 5.00 12.00
69 Spellkeeper Weird C .08 .20
70 Stealth Mission C .25 .60
71 Tamiyo's Epiphany C 3.00 8.00
72 Teferi's Time Twist C 1.50 4.00
73 Thunder Drake C .12 .30
74 Totally Lost C .08 .20
75 Wall of Runes C .30 .75
76 Aid the Fallen C .20 .50
77 Banehound C 2.00 5.00
78 Bleeding Edge U .12 .30
79 Bolas's Citadel R 5.00 12.00
80 Bond of Revival U .60 1.50
81 Charity Extractor C .12 .30
82 Command the Dreadhorde R 1.50 4.00
83 Davriel, Rogue Shadowmage U .60 1.50
84 Davriel's Shadowfugue C .08 .20
85 Deliver Unto Evil R .40 1.00
86 Dreadhorde Invasion R 4.00 10.00
87 Dreadmalkin U .50 1.25
88 Duskmantle Operative C .08 .20
89 The Elderspell R 2.00 5.00
90 Eternal Taskmaster U .25 .60
91 Finale of Eternity M 1.25 3.00
92 God-Eternal Bontu M 4.00 10.00
93 Herald of the Dreadhorde C .25 .60
94 Kaya's Ghostform C 10.00 25.00
95 Lazotep Behemoth C .08 .20
96 Lazotep Reaver C 1.25 3.00
97 Liliana, Dreadhorde General M 12.00 30.00
98 Liliana's Triumph U 1.00 2.50
99 Massacre Girl R 2.00 5.00
100 Ob Nixilis, the Hate-Twisted U .75 2.00
101 Ob Nixilis's Cruelty C .25 .60
102 Price of Betrayal U 1.50 4.00
103 Shriekdiver C .20 .50
104 Sorin's Thirst C .12 .30
105 Spark Harvest C .75 2.00
106 Spark Reaper C .12 .30
107 Tithebearer Giant C .12 .30
108 Toll of the Invasion C .08 .20
109 Unlikely Aid C .20 .50
110 Vampire Opportunist C .08 .20
111 Vizier of the Scorpion U 2.00 5.00
112 Vraska's Finisher C .15 .40
113 Ahn-Crop Invader C .08 .20
114 Blindblast C .08 .20
115 Bolt Bend U 8.00 20.00
116 Bond of Passion U .12 .30
117 Burning Prophet C 1.00 2.50
118 Chainwhip Cyclops C .12 .30
119 Chandra, Fire Artisan R 1.00 2.50
120 Chandra's Pyrohelix C .08 .20
121 Chandra's Triumph U .50 1.25
122 Cyclops Electromancer U .08 .20
123 Demolish C .08 .20
124 Devouring Hellion U .12 .30
125 Dreadhorde Arcanist R 3.00 8.00
126 Dreadhorde Twins U 2.00 5.00
127 Finale of Promise M 4.00 10.00
128 Goblin Assailant C .08 .20
129 Goblin Assault Team C .12 .30
130 Grim Initiate C .25 .60
131 Heartfire C .15 .40
132 Honor the God-Pharaoh C .25 .60
133 Ilharg, the Raze-Boar M 4.00 10.00
134 Invading Manticore C .12 .30
135 Jaya, Venerated Firemage U .25 .60
136 Jaya's Greeting C .15 .40
137 Krenko, Tin Street Kingpin R 2.00 5.00
138 Mizzium Tank R .20 .50
139 Nahiri's Stoneblades C .20 .50
140 Neheb, Dreadhorde Champion R 1.00 2.50
141 Raging Kronch C .08 .20
142 Samut's Sprint C .25 .60
143 Sarkhan the Masterless R 1.00 2.50
144 Sarkhan's Catharsis C .12 .30
145 Spellgorger Weird C .12 .30
146 Tibalt, Rakish Instigator U .60 1.50
147 Tibalt's Rager U .12 .30
148 Turret Ogre C .08 .20
149 Arboreal Grazer C 10.00 25.00
150 Arlinn, Voice of the Pack U .30 .75
151 Arlinn's Wolf C .08 .20
152 Awakening of Vitu-Ghazi R .20 .50
153 Band Together C .08 .20
154 Bloom Hulk C .50 1.25
155 Bond of Flourishing U .15 .40
156 Centaur Nurturer C .08 .20
157 Challenger Troll U .15 .40
158 Courage in Crisis C .30 .75
159 Evolution Sage U 6.00 15.00
160 Finale of Devastation M 20.00 50.00
161 Forced Landing C .12 .30
162 Giant Growth C .12 .30
163 God-Eternal Rhonas M 4.00 10.00
164 Jiang Yanggu, Wildcrafter U .60 1.50
165 Kraul Stinger C .20 .50
166 Kronch Wrangler C .08 .20
167 Mowu, Loyal Companion U 1.25 3.00
168 New Horizons C .15 .40
169 Nissa, Who Shakes the World R 3.00 8.00
170 Nissa's Triumph U .25 .60
171 Paradise Druid U .60 1.50
172 Planewide Celebration R 1.25 3.00
173 Pollenbright Druid C 2.50 6.00
174 Primordial Wurm C .12 .30
175 Return of Nature C .30 .75
176 Snarespinner C .08 .20
177 Steady Aim C .08 .20
178 Storm the Citadel U .12 .30
179 Thundering Ceratok C .08 .20
180 Vivien, Champion of the Wilds R .60 1.50
181 Vivien's Arkbow R .25 .60
182 Vivien's Grizzly C .30 .75
183 Wardscale Crocodile C .08 .20
184 Ajani, the Greathearted R 1.25 3.00
185 Angrath's Rampage U .75 2.00
186 Bioessence Hydra R .25 .60
187 Casualties of War R 1.50 4.00
188 Cruel Celebrant U 6.00 15.00
189 Deathsprout U 2.00 5.00
190 Despark U 1.25 3.00
191 Domri, Anarch of Bolas R 1.25 3.00
192 Domri's Ambush U .60 1.50
193 Dovin's Veto U 3.00 8.00
194 Dreadhorde Butcher R .75 2.00
195 Elite Guardmage U 1.25 3.00
196 Enter the God-Eternals R .50 1.25
197 Feather, the Redeemed R 2.00 5.00
198 Gleaming Overseer U 6.00 15.00
199 Heartwarming Redemption U .50 1.25
200 Huatli's Raptor U 1.00 2.50
201 Invade the City U .50 1.25
202 Leyline Prowler U 1.50 4.00
203 Living Twister R .20 .50
204 Mayhem Devil U 12.00 30.00
205 Merfolk Skydiver U 1.00 2.50
206 Neoform U 8.00 20.00
207 Nicol Bolas, Dragon-God M 10.00 25.00
208 Niv-Mizzet Reborn M 4.00 10.00
209 Oath of Kaya R .50 1.25
210 Pledge of Unity U 1.00 2.50
211 Ral, Storm Conduit R 1.25 3.00
212 Ral's Outburst U .20 .50
213 Roalesk, Apex Hybrid M 1.50 4.00
214 Role Reversal R .30 .75
215 Rubblebelt Rioters U .30 .75
216 Solar Blaze R .25 .60
217 Sorin, Vengeful Bloodlord R 2.00 5.00
218 Soul Diviner R .30 .75
219 Storrev, Devkarin Lich R .30 .75
220 Tamiyo, Collector of Tales R .75 2.00
221 Teferi, Time Raveler R 12.00 30.00
222 Tenth District Legionnaire U .30 .75
223 Time Wipe R 1.50 4.00
224 Tolsimir, Friend to Wolves R 1.00 2.50
225 Tyrant's Scorn U .50 1.25
226 Widespread Brutality R 1.50 4.00
227 Angrath, Captain of Chaos U .40 1.00
228 Ashiok, Dream Render U 2.50 6.00
229 Dovin, Hand of Control U .40 1.00
230 Huatli, the Sun's Heart U .40 1.00
231 Kaya, Bane of the Dead U .20 .50
232 Kiora, Behemoth Beckoner U 2.50 6.00
233 Nahiri, Storm of Stone U .20 .50
234 Saheeli, Sublime Artificer U .75 2.00
235 Samut, Tyrant Smasher U .15 .40
236 Vraska, Swarm's Eminence U .30 .75
237 Firemind Vessel U .60 1.50
238 God-Pharaoh's Statue U 5.00 12.00
239 Guild Globe C .25 .60
240 Iron Bully C .15 .40
241 Mana Geode C .40 1.00
242 Prismite C .15 .40
243 Saheeli's Silverwing C .08 .20
244 Blast Zone R .75 2.00
245 Emergence Zone U 10.00 25.00
246 Gateway Plaza C 2.50 6.00
247 Interplanar Beacon U 2.00 5.00
248 Karn's Bastion R 2.00 5.00
249 Mobilized District R .20 .50
250 Plains L .30 .75
251 Plains L .25 .60
252 Plains L .40 1.00
253 Island L .30 .75
254 Island L .50 1.25
255 Island L .50 1.25
256 Swamp L .40 1.00
257 Swamp L .30 .75
258 Swamp L .50 1.25
259 Mountain L .30 .75
260 Mountain L .20 .50
261 Mountain L .40 1.00
262 Forest L .25 .60
263 Forest L .20 .50
264 Forest L .20 .50
265 Gideon, the Oathsworn M .50 1.25
266 Desperate Lunge C .20 .50
267 Gideon's Battle Cry R .25 .60
268 Gideon's Company U .15 .40
269 Orzhov Guildgate C .60 1.50
270 Jace, Arcane Strategist M 1.00 2.50
271 Guildpact Informant C .25 .60
272 Jace's Projection U .20 .50
273 Jace's Ruse R .15 .40
274 Simic Guildgate C 12.00 30.00
275 Tezzeret, Master of the Bridge M 6.00 12.00

2019 Magic The Gathering War of the Spark Foil

1 Karn, the Great Creator R .30 .75
2 Ugin, the Ineffable R .30 .75
3 Ugin's Conjurant U .20 .40
4 Ajani's Pridemate U .20 .40
5 Battlefield Promotion C .12 .25
6 Bond of Discipline U .20 .40
7 Bulwark Giant C .12 .25
8 Charmed Stray C .12 .25
9 Defiant Strike C .12 .25
10 Divine Arrow C .12 .25
11 Enforcer Griffin C .12 .25
12 Finale of Glory M 3.00 6.00
13 Gideon Blackblade M 3.00 6.00
14 Gideon's Sacrifice C .12 .25
15 Gideon's Triumph U .20 .40
16 God-Eternal Oketra M 3.00 6.00
17 Grateful Apparition U .20 .40
18 Ignite the Beacon R .30 .75
19 Ironclad Krovod C .12 .25
20 Law-Rune Enforcer C .12 .25
21 Loxodon Sergeant C .12 .25
22 Makeshift Battalion C .12 .25
23 Martyr for the Cause C .12 .25
24 Parhelion II R .30 .75
25 Pouncing Lynx C .12 .25
26 Prison Realm U .20 .40
27 Rally of Wings U .20 .40
28 Ravnica at War R .30 .75
29 Rising Populace C .12 .25
30 Single Combat R .30 .75
31 Sunblade Angel U .20 .40
32 Teyo, the Shieldmage U .20 .40
33 Teyo's Lightshield C .12 .25
34 Tomik, Distinguished Advokist R .30 .75
35 Topple the Statue C .12 .25
36 Trusted Pegasus C .12 .25
37 The Wanderer U .20 .40
38 Wanderer's Strike C .12 .25
39 War Screecher C .12 .25
40 Ashiok's Skulker C .12 .25
41 Augur of Bolas U .20 .40
42 Aven Eternal C .12 .25
43 Bond of Insight U .20 .40
44 Callous Dismissal C .12 .25
45 Commence the Endgame R .30 .75
46 Contentious Plan C .12 .25
47 Crush Dissent C .12 .25
48 Erratic Visionary C .12 .25
49 Eternal Skylord U .20 .40
50 Fblthp, the Lost R .30 .75
51 Finale of Revelation M 7.50 15.00
52 Flux Channeler U .20 .40
53 God-Eternal Kefnet M 5.00 10.00
54 Jace, Wielder of Mysteries R .30 .75
55 Jace's Triumph U .20 .40
56 Kasmina, Enigmatic Mentor U .20 .40
57 Kasmina's Transmutation C .12 .25
58 Kiora's Dambreaker C .12 .25
59 Lazotep Plating U .20 .40
60 Naga Eternal C .12 .25
61 Narset, Parter of Veils U .20 .40
62 Narset's Reversal R .30 .75
63 No Escape C .12 .25
64 Relentless Advance C .12 .25
65 Rescuer Sphinx U .20 .40
66 Silent Submersible R .30 .75
67 Sky Theater Strix C .12 .25
68 Spark Double R .30 .75
69 Spellkeeper Weird C .12 .25
70 Stealth Mission C .12 .25
71 Tamiyo's Epiphany C .12 .25
72 Teferi's Time Twist C .12 .25
73 Thunder Drake C .12 .25
74 Totally Lost C .12 .25
75 Wall of Runes C .12 .25
76 Aid the Fallen C .12 .25
77 Banehound C .12 .25
78 Bleeding Edge U .20 .40
79 Bolas's Citadel R .30 .75
80 Bond of Revival U .20 .40
81 Charity Extractor C .12 .25
82 Command the Dreadhorde R .30 .75
83 Davriel, Rogue Shadowmage U .20 .40
84 Davriel's Shadowfugue C .12 .25
85 Deliver Unto Evil R .30 .75
86 Dreadhorde Invasion R .30 .75
87 Dreadmalkin U .20 .40
88 Duskmantle Operative C .12 .25
89 The Elderspell R .30 .75
90 Eternal Taskmaster U .20 .40
91 Finale of Eternity M 4.00 8.00
92 God-Eternal Bontu M 3.00 6.00
93 Herald of the Dreadhorde C .12 .25
94 Kaya's Ghostform C .12 .25
95 Lazotep Behemoth C .12 .25
96 Lazotep Reaver C .12 .25
97 Liliana, Dreadhorde General M 30.00 60.00
98 Liliana's Triumph U .20 .40
99 Massacre Girl R .30 .75
100 Ob Nixilis, the Hate-Twisted U .20 .40
101 Ob Nixilis's Cruelty C .12 .25
102 Price of Betrayal U .20 .40
103 Shriekdiver C .12 .25
104 Sorin's Thirst C .12 .25
105 Spark Harvest C .12 .25
106 Spark Reaper C .12 .25
107 Tithebearer Giant C .12 .25
108 Toll of the Invasion C .12 .25
109 Unlikely Aid C .12 .25
110 Vampire Opportunist C .12 .25
111 Vizier of the Scorpion U .20 .40
112 Vraska's Finisher C .12 .25
113 Ahn-Crop Invader C .12 .25
114 Blindblast C .12 .25
115 Bolt Bend U .20 .40
116 Bond of Passion U .20 .40
117 Burning Prophet C .12 .25
118 Chainwhip Cyclops C .12 .25
119 Chandra, Fire Artisan R .30 .75
120 Chandra's Pyrohelix C .12 .25
121 Chandra's Triumph U .20 .40
122 Cyclops Electromancer U .20 .40
123 Demolish C .12 .25
124 Devouring Hellion U .20 .40
125 Dreadhorde Arcanist R .30 .75
126 Dreadhorde Twins U .20 .40
127 Finale of Promise M 6.00 12.00
128 Goblin Assailant C .12 .25
129 Goblin Assault Team C .12 .25
130 Grim Initiate C .12 .25
131 Heartfire C .12 .25
132 Honor the God-Pharaoh C .12 .25
133 Ilharg, the Raze-Boar M 12.50 25.00
134 Invading Manticore C .12 .25
135 Jaya, Venerated Firemage U .20 .40
136 Jaya's Greeting C .12 .25
137 Krenko, Tin Street Kingpin R .30 .75
138 Mizzium Tank R .30 .75
139 Nahiri's Stoneblades C .12 .25
140 Neheb, Dreadhorde Champion R .30 .75
141 Raging Kronch C .12 .25
142 Samut's Sprint C .12 .25
143 Sarkhan the Masterless R .30 .75
144 Sarkhan's Catharsis C .12 .25
145 Spellgorger Weird C .12 .25
146 Tibalt, Rakish Instigator U .20 .40
147 Tibalt's Rager U .20 .40
148 Turret Ogre C .12 .25
149 Arboreal Grazer C .12 .25

150 Arlinn, Voice of the Pack U	.20	.40
151 Arlinn's Wolf C	.12	.25
152 Awakening of Vitu-Ghazi R	.30	.75
153 Band Together C	.12	.25
154 Bloom Hulk C	.12	.25
155 Bond of Flourishing U	.20	.40
156 Centaur Nurturer C	.12	.25
157 Challenger Troll U	.20	.40
158 Courage in Crisis C	.12	.25
159 Evolution Sage U	.20	.40
160 Finale of Devastation M	40.00	80.00
161 Forced Landing C	.12	.25
162 Giant Growth C	.12	.25
163 God-Eternal Rhonas M	2.50	5.00
164 Jiang Yanggu, Wildcrafter U	.20	.40
165 Kraul Stinger C	.12	.25
166 Kronch Wrangler C	.12	.25
167 Mowu, Loyal Companion U	.20	.40
168 New Horizons C	.12	.25
169 Nissa, Who Shakes the World R	.30	.75
170 Nissa's Triumph U	.20	.40
171 Paradise Druid U	.20	.40
172 Planewide Celebration R	.30	.75
173 Pollenbright Druid C	.12	.25
174 Primordial Wurm C	.12	.25
175 Return of Nature C	.12	.25
176 Snarespinner C	.12	.25
177 Steady Aim C	.12	.25
178 Storm the Citadel U	.20	.40
179 Thundering Ceratok C	.12	.25
180 Vivien, Champion of the Wilds R	.30	.75
181 Vivien's Arkbow R	.30	.75
182 Vivien's Grizzly C	.12	.25
183 Wardscale Crocodile C	.12	.25
184 Ajani, the Greathearted R	.30	.75
185 Angrath's Rampage U	.20	.40
186 Bioessence Hydra R	.30	.75
187 Casualties of War R	.30	.75
188 Cruel Celebrant U	.20	.40
189 Deathsprout U	.20	.40
190 Despark U	.20	.40
191 Domri, Anarch of Bolas R	.30	.75
192 Domri's Ambush U	.20	.40
193 Dovin's Veto U	.20	.40
194 Dreadhorde Butcher R	.30	.75
195 Elite Guardmage U	.20	.40
196 Enter the God-Eternals R	.30	.75
197 Feather, the Redeemed R	.30	.75
198 Gleaming Overseer U	.20	.40
199 Heartwarming Redemption U	.20	.40
200 Huatli's Raptor U	.20	.40
201 Invade the City U	.20	.40
202 Leyline Prowler U	.20	.40
203 Living Twister R	.30	.75
204 Mayhem Devil U	.20	.40
205 Merfolk Skydiver U	.20	.40
206 Neoform U	.20	.40
207 Nicol Bolas, Dragon-God M	12.50	25.00
208 Niv-Mizzet Reborn M	20.00	40.00
209 Oath of Kaya R	.30	.75
210 Pledge of Unity U	.20	.40
211 Ral, Storm Conduit R	.30	.75
212 Ral's Outburst U	.20	.40
213 Roalesk, Apex Hybrid M	3.00	6.00
214 Role Reversal R	.30	.75
215 Rubblebelt Rioters U	.20	.40
216 Solar Blaze R	.30	.75
217 Sorin, Vengeful Bloodlord R	.30	.75
218 Soul Diviner R	.30	.75
219 Storrev, Devkarin Lich R	.30	.75
220 Tamiyo, Collector of Tales R	.30	.75
221 Teferi, Time Raveler R	.30	.75
222 Tenth District Legionnaire U	.20	.40
223 Time Wipe R	.30	.75
224 Tolsimir, Friend to Wolves R	.30	.75
225 Tyrant's Scorn U	.20	.40
226 Widespread Brutality R	.30	.75
227 Angrath, Captain of Chaos U	.20	.40
228 Ashiok, Dream Render U	.20	.40
229 Dovin, Hand of Control U	.20	.40
230 Huatli, the Sun's Heart U	.20	.40
231 Kaya, Bane of the Dead U	.20	.40
232 Kiora, Behemoth Beckoner U	.20	.40
233 Nahiri, Storm of Stone U	.20	.40
234 Saheeli, Sublime Artificer U	.20	.40
235 Samut, Tyrant Smasher U	.20	.40
236 Vraska, Swarm's Eminence U	.20	.40
237 Firemind Vessel U	.20	.40
238 God-Pharaoh's Statue U	.20	.40
239 Guild Globe C	.12	.25
240 Iron Bully C	.12	.25
241 Mana Geode C	.12	.25
242 Prismite C	.12	.25
243 Saheeli's Silverwing C	.12	.25
244 Blast Zone R	.30	.75
245 Emergence Zone U	.20	.40
246 Gateway Plaza C	.12	.25
247 Interplanar Beacon U	.20	.40
248 Karn's Bastion R	.30	.75
249 Mobilized District R	.30	.75
250 Plains L	.12	.25
251 Plains L	.12	.25
252 Plains L	.12	.25
253 Island L	.12	.25
254 Island L	.12	.25
255 Island L	.12	.25
256 Swamp L	.12	.25
257 Swamp L	.12	.25
258 Swamp L	.12	.25
259 Mountain L	.12	.25
260 Mountain L	.12	.25
261 Mountain L	.12	.25
262 Forest L	.12	.25
263 Forest L	.12	.25
264 Forest L	.12	.25
266 Desperate Lunge C	.12	.25
267 Gideon's Battle Cry R	.30	.75
268 Gideon's Company U	.20	.40
269 Orzhov Guildgate C	.12	.25
270 Jane, Arcane Strategist M	3.00	6.00
271 Guildpact Informant C	.12	.25
272 Jace's Projection U	.20	.40
273 Jace's Ruse R	.30	.75
274 Simic Guildgate C	.12	.25

2019 Magic The Gathering War of the Spark Mythic Edition

WS1 Ugin, the Spirit Dragon	150.00	300.00
WS2 Gideon Blackblade	30.00	60.00
WS3 Jace, the Mind Sculptor	150.00	300.00
WS4 Tezzeret the Seeker	30.00	75.00
WS5 Garruk, Apex Predator	25.00	50.00
WS6 Nicol Bolas, Dragon-God	60.00	120.00
WS7 Nahiri, the Harbinger	25.00	50.00
WS8 Sarkhan Unbroken	15.00	30.00

2019 Magic The Gathering War of the Spark Tokens

1 Spirit	.07	.15
2 Angel	.12	.25
3 Soldier	.07	.15
4 Wall	.07	.10
5 Wizard	.07	.10
6 Assassin	.07	.10
7 Zombie	.12	.25
8 Zombie Army	.07	.10
9 Zombie Army	.07	.10
10 Zombie Army	.07	.10
11 Zombie Warrior	.50	1.00
12 Devil	.07	.10
13 Dragon	.07	.15
14 Goblin	.07	.15
15 Wolf	.07	.10
16 Citizen	.07	.10
17 Voja, Friend to Elves	.07	.15
18 Servo	.07	.15
19 Nissa, Who Shakes the World Emblem	.12	.25

2020 Magic The Gathering Commander 2020

1 Trynn, Champion of Freedom M :W:	.75	1.50
2 Haldan, Avid Arcanist M :B:	.60	1.25
3 Nikara, Lair Scavenger M :K:	1.25	2.50
4 Brallin, Skyshark Rider M :R:	1.25	2.50
5 Cazur, Ruthless Stalker M :G:	1.50	3.00
6 Akim, the Soaring Wind M :B:/:R:/:W:	.50	1.00
7 Gavi, Nest Warden M :B:/:R:/:W:	1.00	2.00
8 Jirina Kudro M :R:/:W:/:K:	.30	.75
9 Kalamax, the Stormsire M :G:/:B:/:R:	2.50	5.00
10 Kathril, Aspect Warper M :W:/:K:/:G:	1.25	2.50
11 Kelsien, the Plague M :R:/:W:/:K:	1.00	2.00
12 Otrimi, the Ever-Playful M :K:/:G:/:B:	1.50	3.00
13 Pako, Arcane Retriever M :R:/:G:	1.00	2.00
14 Shabraz, the Skyshark M :W:/:B:	.75	1.50
15 Silvar, Devourer of the Free M :K:/:R:	1.00	2.00
16 Tayam, Luminous Enigma M :W:/:K:/:G:	2.00	4.00
17 Ukkima, Stalking Shadow M :B:/:K:	2.00	4.00
18 Xyris, the Writhing Storm M :G:/:B:/:R:	4.00	8.00
19 Yannik, Scavenging Sentinel M :G:/:W:	1.25	2.50
20 Zaxara, the Exemplary M :K:/:G:/:B:	7.50	15.00
21 Cryptic Trilobite R	.15	.30
22 Avenging Huntbonder R :W:	.15	.30
23 Call the Coppercoats R :W:	.15	.30
24 Cartographer's Hawk R :W:	.15	.30
25 Dismantling Wave R :W:	.15	.30
26 Flawless Maneuver R :W:	.15	.30
27 Herald of the Forgotten R :W:	.15	.30
28 Martial Impetus U :W:	.10	.20
29 Verge Rangers R :W:	.15	.30
30 Vitality Hunter R :W:	.15	.30
31 Crystalline Resonance R :B:	.15	.30
32 Decoy Gambit R :B:	.15	.30
33 Eon Frolicker R :B:	.15	.30
34 Ethereal Forager R :B:	.15	.30
35 Fierce Guardianship R :B:	.15	.30
36 Nascent Metamorph R :B:	.15	.30
37 Psychic Impetus U :B:	.10	.20
38 Souvenir Snatcher R :B:	.15	.30
39 Tidal Barracuda R :B:	.15	.30
40 Boneyard Mycodrax R :K:	.15	.30
41 Daring Fiendbonder R :K:	.15	.30
42 Deadly Rollick R :K:	.15	.30
43 Dredge the Mire R :K:	.15	.30
44 Mindleecher R :K:	.15	.30
45 Netherborn Altar R :K:	.15	.30
46 Parasitic Impetus U :K:	.10	.20
47 Species Specialist R :K:	.15	.30
48 Titan Hunter R :K:	.15	.30
49 Agitator Ant R :R:	.15	.30
50 Deflecting Swat R :R:	.15	.30
51 Fireflux Squad R :R:	.15	.30
52 Frontier Warmonger R :R:	.15	.30
53 Lavabrink Floodgates R :R:	.15	.30
54 Molten Echoes R :R:	.15	.30
55 Shiny Impetus U :R:	.10	.20
56 Spellpyre Phoenix R :R:	.15	.30
57 Surly Badgersaur R :R:	.15	.30
58 Capricopian R :G:	.15	.30
59 Curious Herd R :G:	.15	.30
60 Glademuse R :G:	.15	.30
61 Obscuring Haze R :G:	.15	.30
62 Predatory Impetus U :G:	.10	.20
63 Ravenous Gigantotherium R :G:	.15	.30
64 Sawtusk Demolisher R :G:	.15	.30
65 Selective Adaptation R :G:	.15	.30
66 Slippery Bogbonder R :G:	.15	.30
67 Bonder's Ornament C	.07	.15
68 Manascape Refractor R	.15	.30
69 Sanctuary Blade R	.15	.30
70 Twinning Staff R	.15	.30
71 Nesting Grounds R	.15	.30
72 Aerial Responder U :W:	.10	.20
73 Akroma, Angel of Wrath M :W:	.60	1.25
74 Akroma's Vengeance R :W:	.15	.30
75 Angel of Finality R :W:	.15	.30
76 Astral Drift R :W:	.15	.30
77 Banisher Priest U :W:	.10	.20
78 Bounty Agent R :W:	.15	.30
79 Cast Out U :W:	.10	.20
80 Cataclysmic Gearhulk M :W:	.30	.75
81 Cavalry Pegasus C :W:	.07	.15
82 Citywide Bust R :W:	.15	.30
83 Cleansing Nova R :W:	.15	.30
84 Dearly Departed R :W:	.15	.30
85 Decree of Justice R :W:	.15	.30
86 Descend upon the Sinful M :W:	.30	.60
87 Devout Chaplain U :W:	.10	.20
88 Eternal Dragon R :W:	.15	.30
89 Frontline Medic R :W:	.15	.30
90 Hoofprints of the Stag R :W:	.15	.30
91 Increasing Devotion R :W:	.15	.30
92 Kalemne's Captain R :W:	.15	.30
93 Knight of the White Orchid R :W:	.15	.30
94 Magus of the Disk R :W:	.15	.30
95 Odric, Lunarch Marshal R :W:	.15	.30
96 Odric, Master Tactician R :W:	.15	.30
97 Reveillark R :W:	.15	.30
98 Riders of Gavony R :W:	.15	.30
99 Solemn Recruit R :W:	.15	.30
100 Spirit Cairn U :W:	.10	.20
101 Sun Titan M :W:	.60	1.25
102 Sunblast Angel R :W:	.15	.30
103 Thalia's Lieutenant R :W:	.15	.30
104 Thraben Doomsayer R :W:	.15	.30
105 Together Forever R :W:	.15	.30
106 Unexpectedly Absent R :W:	.15	.30
107 Zetalpa, Primal Dawn R :W:	.15	.30
108 Chemister's Insight U :B:	.10	.20
109 Curator of Mysteries R :B:	.15	.30
110 Drake Haven R :B:	.15	.30
111 Frantic Search C :B:	.07	.15
112 Hieroglyphic Illumination C :B:	.07	.15
113 Illusory Ambusher U :B:	.10	.20
114 Jace, Architect of Thought M :B:	.60	1.25
115 Lunar Mystic R :B:	.15	.30
116 Mind Spring R :B:	.15	.30
117 Mulldrifter U :B:	.10	.20
118 Murmuring Mystic U :B:	.10	.20
119 New Perspectives R :B:	.15	.30
120 Niblis of Frost R :B:	.15	.30
121 Nimble Obstructionist R :B:	.15	.30
122 Portal Mage R :B:	.15	.30
123 Propaganda U :B:	.10	.20
124 Swarm Intelligence R :B:	.15	.30
125 Talrand, Sky Summoner R :B:	.15	.30
126 Vizier of Tumbling Sands U :B:	.10	.20
127 Whiplash Trap C :B:	.07	.15
128 Windfall U :B:	.10	.20
129 Ambition's Cost U :K:	.10	.20
130 Cairn Wanderer R :K:	.15	.30
131 Deadly Tempest R :K:	.15	.30
132 Disciple of Bolas R :K:	.15	.30
133 Ever After R :K:	.15	.30
134 Painful Truths R :K:	.15	.30
135 Profane Command R :K:	.15	.30
136 Shriekmaw U :K:	.10	.20
137 Soul of Innistrad M :K:	.30	.60
138 Soulflayer R :K:	.15	.30
139 Unburial Rites U :K:	.10	.20
140 Vampire Nighthawk U :K:	.10	.20
141 Xathrid Necromancer R :K:	.15	.30
142 Zulaport Cutthroat U :K:	.10	.20
143 Alesha, Who Smiles at Death R :R:	.15	.30
144 Captivating Crew R :R:	.15	.30
145 Chandra, Flamecaller M :R:	.60	1.25
146 Chaos Warp R :R:	.15	.30
147 Charmbreaker Devils R :R:	.15	.30
148 Comet Storm M :R:	.30	.75
149 Commune with Lava R :R:	.15	.30
150 Dualcaster Mage R :R:	.15	.30
151 Etali, Primal Storm R :R:	.15	.30
152 Fumiko the Lowblood R :R:	.15	.30
153 Goblin Dark-Dwellers R :R:	.15	.30
154 Humble Defector U :R:	.10	.20
155 Lightning Rift U :R:	.10	.20
156 Magus of the Wheel R :R:	.15	.30
157 Outpost Siege R :R:	.15	.30
158 Shared Animosity R :R:	.15	.30
159 Slice and Dice U :R:	.10	.20
160 Starstorm R :R:	.15	.30
161 Surreal Memoir U :R:	.10	.20
162 Tectonic Reformation R :R:	.15	.30
163 Titan of Eternal Fire R :R:	.15	.30
164 Vigilante Justice U :R:	.10	.20
165 Acidic Slime U :G:	.10	.20
166 Animist's Awakening R :G:	.15	.30
167 Beast Whisperer R :G:	.15	.30
168 Beast Within U :G:	.10	.20
169 Crop Rotation C :G:	.07	.15
170 Cultivate C :G:	.07	.15
171 Evolution Charm C :G:	.07	.15
172 Genesis Hydra R :G:	.15	.30
173 Harmonize U :G:	.10	.20
174 Harrow C :G:	.07	.15
175 Heroes' Bane U :G:	.10	.20
176 Hornet Queen R :G:	.15	.30
177 Hungering Hydra R :G:	.15	.30
178 Hunter's Insight U :G:	.10	.20
179 Hunting Pack U :G:	.10	.20
180 Kodama's Reach C :G:	.07	.15
181 Krosan Grip U :G:	.10	.20
182 Majestic Myriarch M :G:	.30	.75
183 Masked Admirers R :G:	.15	.30
184 Natural Connection C :G:	.07	.15
185 Predator Ooze R :G:	.15	.30
186 Reclamation Sage U :G:	.10	.20
187 Sakura-Tribe Elder C :G:	.07	.15
188 Satyr Wayfinder C :G:	.07	.15
189 Skullwinder U :G:	.10	.20
190 Slice in Twain U :G:	.10	.20
191 Splinterfright R :G:	.15	.30
192 Strength of the Tajuru R :G:	.15	.30
193 Tribute to the Wild U :G:	.10	.20
194 Vastwood Hydra R :G:	.15	.30
195 Vorapede M :G:	.30	.60
196 Wilderness Reclamation U :G:	.10	.20
197 Yavimaya Dryad U :G:	.10	.20
198 Abzan Ascendancy R :W:/:K:/:G:	.15	.30
199 Abzan Charm U :W:/:K:/:G:	.10	.20
200 Adriana, Captain of the Guard R :R:/:W:	.15	.30
201 Ajani Unyielding M :G:/:W:	.50	1.00
202 Archon of Valor's Reach R :G:/:W:	.15	.30
203 Artifact Mutation R :G:	.15	.30
204 Cold-Eyed Selkie R :G:/:B:	.15	.30
205 Crackling Doom R :R:/:W:/:K:	.15	.30
206 Crackling Drake U :B:/:R:	.10	.20
207 Deadbridge Chant M :K:/:G:	.50	1.00
208 Deathsprout U :K:/:G:	.10	.20
209 Despark U :W:/:K:	.10	.20
210 Djinn Illuminatus R :B:/:R:	.15	.30
211 Duneblast R :W:/:K:/:G:	.15	.30
212 Find // Finality R :K:/:G:	.15	.30
213 Gama, the Bloodflame U :K:/:R:	.10	.20
214 Gaze of Granite R :K:/:G:	.15	.30
215 Grisly Salvage C :K:/:G:	.07	.15
216 Growth Spiral C :G:/:B:	.07	.15
217 Isperia, Supreme Judge M :W:/:B:	.30	.60
218 Karametra, God of Harvests M :G:/:W:	3.00	6.00
219 The Locust God M :B:/:R:	4.00	8.00
220 Melek, Izzet Paragon R :B:/:R:	.15	.30
221 Mercurial Chemister R :B:/:R:	.15	.30
222 Migratory Route U :W:/:B:	.10	.20
223 Nahiri, the Harbinger M :R:/:W:	2.00	4.00
224 Nissa, Steward of Elements M :G:/:B:	1.25	2.50
225 Niv-Mizzet, the Firemind R :B:/:R:	.15	.30
226 Nyx Weaver U :K:/:G:	.10	.20
227 Prophetic Bolt R :B:/:R:	.15	.30
228 Putrefy U :K:/:G:	.10	.20
229 Rashmi, Eternities Crafter R :G:/:B:	.15	.30
230 Temur Charm U :G:/:B:/:R:	.10	.20
231 Terminate U :K:/:R:	.10	.20
232 Trygon Predator U :G:/:B:	.10	.20
233 Villainous Wealth R :K:/:G:/:B:	.15	.30
234 Wort, the Raidmother R :R:/:G:	.15	.30
235 Wydwen, the Biting Gale R :B:/:K:	.15	.30
236 Abandoned Sarcophagus R	.15	.30
237 Arcane Signet C	.07	.15
238 Azorius Signet U	.10	.20
239 Boros Signet U	.10	.20
240 Commander's Sphere C	.07	.15
241 Fluctuator R	.15	.30
242 Heirloom Blade U	.10	.20
243 Izzet Signet U	.10	.20
244 Lifecrafter's Bestiary R	.15	.30
245 Lightning Greaves U	.10	.20
246 Mimic Vat R	.15	.30
247 Orzhov Signet U	.10	.20
248 Psychosis Crawler R	.15	.30
249 Rakdos Signet U	.10	.20
250 Silent Arbiter R	.15	.30
251 Skullclamp U	.10	.20
252 Sol Ring U	.10	.20
253 Solemn Simulacrum R	.15	.30
254 Swiftfoot Boots U	.10	.20
255 Ash Barrens C	.07	.15
256 Azorius Chancery U	.10	.20
257 Battlefield Forge R	.15	.30
258 Blighted Woodland U	.10	.20
259 Bojuka Bog C	.07	.15
260 Boros Garrison C	.07	.15
261 Canopy Vista R	.15	.30
262 Caves of Koilos R	.15	.30
263 Cinder Glade R	.15	.30
264 Command Tower C	.07	.15
265 Darkwater Catacombs R	.15	.30
266 Desert of the Fervent C	.07	.15
267 Desert of the Mindful C	.07	.15
268 Desert of the True C	.07	.15
269 Desolate Lighthouse R	.15	.30
270 Dimir Aqueduct U	.10	.20
271 Drifting Meadow C	.07	.15
272 Endless Sands R	.15	.30
273 Exotic Orchard R	.15	.30
274 Forgotten Cave U	.10	.20
275 Frontier Bivouac U	.10	.20
276 Gavony Township R	.15	.30
277 Golgari Rot Farm U	.10	.20
278 Grim Backwoods R	.15	.30
279 Gruul Turf U	.10	.20
280 Halimar Depths C	.07	.15
281 Hostile Desert R	.15	.30
282 Irrigated Farmland R	.15	.30
283 Izzet Boilerworks U	.10	.20
284 Kessig Wolf Run R	.15	.30
285 Krosan Verge U	.10	.20
286 Llanowar Wastes R	.15	.30
287 Lonely Sandbar U	.10	.20
288 Memorial to Folly U	.10	.20
289 Mortuary Mire C	.07	.15
290 Mossfire Valley R	.15	.30
291 Mosswort Bridge R	.15	.30
292 Myriad Landscape U	.10	.20
293 Mystic Monastery U	.10	.20
294 Nomad Outpost U	.10	.20
295 Opulent Palace U	.10	.20
296 Oran-Rief, the Vastwood R	.15	.30
297 Orzhov Basilica C	.07	.15
298 Path of Ancestry C	.07	.15
299 Prairie Stream R	.15	.30
300 Rakdos Carnarium C	.07	.15
301 Reliquary Tower U	.10	.20
302 Remote Isle C	.07	.15
303 Rogue's Passage U	.10	.20
304 Rupture Spire C	.07	.15
305 Sandsteppe Citadel U	.10	.20
306 Scavenger Grounds R	.15	.30
307 Secluded Steppe U	.10	.20
308 Selesnya Sanctuary C	.07	.15
309 Shadowblood Ridge R	.15	.30
310 Shivan Reef R	.15	.30
311 Simic Growth Chamber U	.10	.20
312 Skycloud Expanse R	.15	.30
313 Smoldering Crater C	.07	.15
314 Smoldering Marsh R	.15	.30
315 Soaring Seacliff C	.07	.15
316 Spinerock Knoll R	.15	.30
317 Sungrass Prairie R	.15	.30
318 Sunken Hollow R	.15	.30
319 Temple of the False God U	.10	.20
320 Unclaimed Territory U	.10	.20
321 Windbrisk Heights R	.15	.30
322 Yavimaya Coast R	.15	.30

2020 Magic The Gathering Commander 2020 Oversized

7 Gavi, Nest Warden M :B:/:R:/:W:	.10	.20
8 Jirina Kudro M :R:/:W:/:K:	.20	.40
9 Kalamax, the Stormsire M :G:/:B:/:R:	.25	.50
10 Kathril, Aspect Warper M :W:/:K:/:G:	.30	.75
12 Otrimi, the Ever-Playful M :K:/:G:/:B:	.30	.60

2020 Magic The Gathering Commander 2020 Tokens

1 Angel	.25	.50
2 Bird	.25	.50
3 Elemental	.30	.60
4 Human	.30	.60
5 Soldier	.30	.60
6 Spirit	.30	.60

7 Bird Illusion .30 .60
8 Drake .25 .50
9 Zombie .30 .60
10 Elemental .25 .50
11 Beast .25 .50
12 Hydra .60 1.25
13 Insect .75 1.50
14 Saproling .25 .50
15 Snake .30 .60
16 Dinosaur Cat .60 1.25
17 Goblin Warrior .30 .60
18 Insect .30 .60
19 Treasure .25 .50

2020 Magic The Gathering Commander Legends

1 The Prismatic Piper C .10 .20
2 Akroma, Vision of Ixidor M :W: 2.00 4.00
3 Akroma's Will R :W: 6.00 12.00
4 Alharu, Solemn Ritualist U :W: .07 .15
5 Ancestral Blade C :W: .07 .15
6 Angel of the Dawn C :W: .07 .15
7 Angelic Gift C :W: .07 .15
8 Anointer of Valor C :W: .07 .15
9 Archon of Coronation M :W: .20 .40
10 Ardenn, Intrepid Archaeologist U :W: .15 .30
11 Armored Skyhunter R :W: .50 1.00
12 Austere Command R :W: .30 .75
13 Benevolent Blessing C :W: .10 .20
14 Cage of Hands C :W: .07 .15
15 Captain's Call C :W: .07 .15
16 Court of Grace R :W: 1.50 3.00
17 Court Street Denizen C :W: .07 .15
18 Dispeller's Capsule C :W: .07 .15
19 Doomed Traveler C :W: .07 .15
20 Faith's Fetters U :W: .07 .15
21 Fencing Ace U :W: .07 .15
22 First Response U :W: .07 .15
23 Inspiring Roar C :W: .07 .15
24 Intangible Virtue U :W: .10 .20
25 Iona's Judgment C :W: .07 .15
26 Kangee's Lieutenant U :W: .10 .20
27 Keeper of the Accord R :W: 1.50 3.00
28 Keleth, Sunmane Familiar U :W: .07 .15
29 Kinsbaile Courier C :W: .07 .15
30 Kor Cartographer C :W: .07 .15
31 Livio, Oathsworn Sentinel R :W: .10 .20
32 Make a Stand U :W: .10 .20
33 Ninth Bridge Patrol C :W: .07 .15
34 Open the Armory U :W: .25 .50
35 Orzhov Advokist U :W: .07 .15
36 Palace Sentinels C :W: .07 .15
37 Patron of the Valiant U :W: .07 .15
38 Prava of the Steel Legion U :W: .12 .25
39 Promise of Tomorrow R :W: .12 .25
40 Radiant, Serra Archangel U :W: .10 .20
41 Raise the Alarm C :W: .07 .15
42 Rebbec, Architect of Ascension U :W: .12 .25
43 Return to Dust U :W: .10 .20
44 Seraph of Dawn C :W: .07 .15
45 Seraphic Greatsword M :W: .20 .40
46 Skywhaler's Shot C :W: .07 .15
47 Slash the Ranks R :W: .15 .30
48 Slaughter the Strong U :W: .12 .25
49 Slith Ascendant C :W: .07 .15
50 Soul of Eternity R :W: .12 .25
51 Squad Captain C :W: .07 .15
52 Triumphant Reckoning M :W: .25 .50
53 Trusty Packbeast C :W: .07 .15
54 Vow of Duty U :W: .07 .15
55 Amphin Mutineer R :B: .15 .30
56 Aqueous Form C :B: .12 .25
57 Aven Surveyor C :B: .07 .15
58 Azure Fleet Admiral C :B: .07 .15
59 Body of Knowledge R :B: .15 .30
60 Brinelin, the Moon Kraken U :B: .10 .20
61 Flood of Recollection C :B: .07 .15
62 Confiscate U :B: .07 .15
63 Court of Cunning R :B: 1.50 3.00
64 Daring Saboteur U :B: .07 .15
65 Deranged Assistant C :B: .07 .15
66 Eligeth, Crossroads Augur R :B: .12 .25
67 Esior, Wardwing Familiar U :B: .07 .15
68 Fall from Favor C :B: .07 .15
69 Forceful Denial C :B: .07 .15
70 Galestrike C :B: .07 .15
71 Ghost of Ramirez DePietro U :B: .10 .20
72 Glacian, Powerstone Engineer U :B: .07 .15
73 Horizon Scholar U :B: .07 .15
74 Hullbreacher R :B: .75 1.50
75 Interpret the Signs U :B: .07 .15
76 Kitesail Corsair C :B: .07 .15
77 Kitesail Skirmisher C :B: .07 .15
78 Laboratory Drudge R :B: .07 .15
79 Malcolm, Keen-Eyed Navigator U :B: .07 .15
80 Mana Drain M :B: 30.00 60.00
81 Merchant Raiders U :B: .10 .20
82 Mnemonic Deluge M :B: 2.00 4.00
83 Omenspeaker C :B: .07 .15
84 Preordain C :B: .15 .30
85 Prosperous Pirates C :B: .07 .15
86 Prying Eyes C :B: .07 .15
87 Run Away Together C :B: .07 .15
88 Sailor of Means C :B: .07 .15
89 Sakashima of a Thousand Faces M :B: 12.50 25.00
90 Sakashima's Protege R :B: .15 .30
91 Sakashima's Will R :B: .15 .30
92 Scholar of Stars C :B: .07 .15
93 Scholar of the Ages U :B: .07 .15
94 Scrapdiver Serpent C :B: .07 .15
95 Siani, Eye of the Storm U :B: .10 .20
96 Siren Stormtamer U :B: .15 .30
97 Skaab Goliath C :B: .07 .15
98 Skilled Animator U :B: .07 .15
99 Sphinx of the Second Sun M :B: 2.00 4.00
100 Spontaneous Mutation C :B: .07 .15
101 Strategic Planning C :B: .07 .15
102 Supreme Will U :B: .07 .15
103 Thirst for Knowledge U :B: .07 .15
104 Trove Tracker C :B: .07 .15
105 Vow of Flight U :B: .07 .15
106 Warden of Evos Isle U :B: .07 .15
107 Wrong Turn R :B: .12 .25
108 Armix, Filigree Thrasher U :K: .07 .15
109 Bitter Revelation C :K: .07 .15
110 Bladebrand C :K: .07 .15
111 Briarblade Adept C :K: .07 .15
112 Cast Down U :K: .10 .20
113 Corpse Churn C :K: .07 .15
114 Court of Ambition R :K: .75 1.50
115 Crow of Dark Tidings C :K: .07 .15
116 Cuombajj Witches U :K: .10 .20
117 Defiant Salvager C :K: .07 .15
118 Demonic Lore U :K: .07 .15
119 Dhund Operative C :K: .07 .15
120 Elvish Doomsayer C :K: .07 .15
121 Elvish Dreadlord R :K: .15 .30
122 Exquisite Huntmaster C :K: .07 .15
123 Eyeblight Assassin C :K: .07 .15
124 Eyeblight Cullers C :K: .07 .15
125 Eyeblight Massacre C :K: .07 .15
126 Falthis, Shadowcat Familiar U :K: .10 .20
127 Feast of Succession U :K: .07 .15
128 Fleshbag Marauder C :K: .10 .20
129 Ghastly Demise C :K: .07 .15
130 Gilt-Leaf Winnower U :K: .07 .15
131 Keskit, the Flesh Sculptor U :K: .07 .15
132 Maalfeld Twins C :K: .07 .15
133 Miara, Thorn of the Glade U :K: .10 .20
134 Murder C :K: .07 .15
135 Nadier, Agent of the Duskenel U :K: .10 .20
136 Nadier's Nightblade U :K: 1.00 2.00
137 Necrotic Hex R :K: .20 .40
138 Nightshade Harvester R :K: .12 .25
139 Noxious Dragon U :K: .07 .15
140 Null Caller U :K: .07 .15
141 Opposition Agent R :K: 7.50 15.00
142 Phyrexian Rager C :K: .07 .15
143 Plague Reaver R :K: .12 .25
144 Pride of the Perfect U :K: .07 .15
145 Profane Transfusion M :K: .25 .50
146 Rakshasa Debaser R :K: .25 .50
147 Revenant U :K: .07 .15
148 Sanitarium Skeleton C :K: .07 .15
149 Sengir, the Dark Baron R :K: .10 .20
150 Spark Harvest C :K: .07 .15
151 Supernatural Stamina C :K: .07 .15
152 Szat's Will R :K: .15 .30
153 Tevesh Szat, Doom of Fools M :K: 4.00 8.00
154 Thorn of the Black Rose C :K: .07 .15
155 Tormod, the Desecrator U :K: .12 .25
156 Vampiric Tutor M :K: 25.00 50.00
157 Victimize U :K: .15 .30
158 Viscera Seer C :K: .12 .25
159 Vow of Torment U :K: .07 .15
160 Alena, Kessig Trapper U :R: .10 .20
161 Aurora Phoenix R :R: .10 .20
162 Blasphemous Act R :R: 1.50 3.00
163 Boarding Party C :R: .10 .20
164 Brazen Freebooter C :R: .07 .15
165 Breeches, Brazen Plunderer U :R: .10 .20
166 Burning Anger U :R: .07 .15
167 Champion of the Flame C :R: .07 .15
168 Coastline Marauders U :R: .15 .30
169 Coercive Recruiter R :R: .15 .30
170 Court of Ire R :R: .15 .30
171 Crimson Fleet Commodore C :R: .07 .15
172 Dargo, the Shipwrecker U :R: .10 .20
173 Dragon Egg C :R: .07 .15
174 Dragon Mantle C :R: .07 .15
175 Emberwilde Captain R :R: .30 .75
176 Explosion of Riches U :R: .07 .15
177 Fathom Fleet Swordjack U :R: .10 .20
178 Fiery Cannonade C :R: .10 .20
179 Flamekin Herald R :R: .10 .20
180 Frenzied Saddlebrute U :R: .10 .20
181 Furnace Celebration U :R: .07 .15
182 Goblin Trailblazer C :R: .07 .15
183 Hellkite Courser M :R: 2.00 4.00
184 Humble Defector U :R: .10 .20
185 Impulsive Pilferer C :R: .12 .25
186 Jeska, Thrice Reborn M :R: 1.50 3.00
187 Jeska's Will R :R: 7.50 15.00
188 Kediss, Emberclaw Familiar U :R: .15 .30
189 Krark, the Thumbless R :R: .15 .30
190 Lightning-Rig Crew U :R: .07 .15
191 Makeshift Munitions C :R: .10 .20
192 Meteoric Mace U :R: .10 .20
193 Port Razer M :R: 2.00 4.00
194 Portent of Betrayal C :R: .07 .15
195 Renegade Tactics C :R: .07 .15
196 Ripscale Predator C :R: .07 .15
197 Rograkh, Son of Rohgahh U :R: .12 .25
198 Rummaging Goblin C :R: .07 .15
199 Skyraker Giant C :R: .07 .15
200 Soul's Fire C :R: .10 .20
201 Soulfire Eruption M :R: .50 1.00
202 Sparktongue Dragon C :R: .07 .15
203 Stonefury C :R: .07 .15
204 Toggo, Goblin Weaponsmith U :R: .12 .25
205 Undying Rage C :R: .07 .15
206 Valakut Invoker C :R: .07 .15
207 Volcanic Dragon U :R: .07 .15
208 Volcanic Torrent U :R: .07 .15
209 Vow of Lightning U :R: .07 .15
210 Welding Sparks C :R: .07 .15
211 Wheel of Misfortune R :R: 1.00 2.00
212 Wild Celebrants C :R: .07 .15
213 Ambush Viper C :G: .07 .15
214 Anara, Wolvid Familiar U :G: .10 .20
215 Ancient Animus C :G: .07 .15
216 Annoyed Altisaur C :G: .10 .20
217 Apex Devastator M :G: 7.50 15.00
218 Armorcraft Judge U :G: .10 .20
219 Biowaste Blob R :G: .12 .25
220 Court of Bounty R :G: .30 .75
221 Crushing Vines C :G: .07 .15
222 Dawnglade Regent R :G: .15 .30
223 Elvish Visionary C :G: .07 .15
224 Entourage of Trest C :G: .07 .15
225 Farhaven Elf C :G: .10 .20
226 Fertilid C :G: .07 .15
227 Fin-Clade Fugitives C :G: .07 .15
228 Fyndhorn Elves C :G: .20 .40
229 Gift of Paradise C :G: .07 .15
230 Gilanra, Caller of Wirewood U :G: .10 .20
231 Halana, Kessig Ranger U :G: .10 .20
232 Hunter's Insight U :G: .10 .20
233 Ich-Tekik, Salvage Splicer U :G: .07 .15
234 Immaculate Magistrate R :G: .15 .30
235 Imperious Perfect U :G: .10 .20
236 Ivy Lane Denizen C :G: .10 .20
237 Kamahl, Heart of Krosa M :G: 1.50 3.00
238 Kamahl's Will R :G: .12 .25
239 Kodama of the East Tree R :G: 1.50 3.00
240 Lifecrafter's Gift C :G: .07 .15
241 Lys Alana Bowmaster C :G: .07 .15
242 Magus of the Order R :G: .10 .20
243 Molder Beast C :G: .07 .15
244 Monstrous Onslaught U :G: .07 .15
245 Natural Reclamation C :G: .07 .15
246 Numa, Joraga Chieftain U :G: .07 .15
247 Ordeal of Nylea U :G: .07 .15
248 Reclamation Sage U :G: .07 .15
249 Reshape the Earth M :G: 2.50 5.00
250 Rootweaver Druid R :G: .12 .25
251 Scaled Behemoth U :G: .07 .15
252 Scrounging Bandar C :G: .07 .15
253 Sentinel Spider C :G: .07 .15
254 Sifter Wurm U :G: .07 .15
255 Silverback Shaman C :G: .07 .15
256 Slurrk, All-Ingesting U :G: .07 .15
257 Soul's Might C :G: .07 .15
258 Stingerfling Spider U :G: .07 .15
259 Strength of the Pack U :G: .07 .15
260 Sweet-Gum Recluse R :G: .12 .25
261 Three Visits U :G: 3.00 6.00
262 Vow of Wildness U :G: .07 .15
263 Wildheart Invoker C :G: .07 .15
264 Wildsize C :G: .07 .15
265 Abomination of Llanowar U :K:/:G: .07 .15
266 Amareth, the Lustrous R :G:/:W:/:B: .12 .25
267 Araumi of the Dead Tide U :B:/:K: .10 .20
268 Archelos, Lagoon Mystic R :K:/:G:/:B: .12 .25
269 Averna, the Chaos Bloom R :G:/:B:/:R: .12 .25
270 Belbe, Corrupted Observer R :K:/:G: .12 .25
271 Bell Borca, Spectral Sergeant R :R:/:W: .10 .20
272 Blim, Comedic Genius R :K:/:R: .10 .20
273 Captain Vargus Wrath U :B:/:R: .07 .15
274 Colfenor, the Last Yew R :W:/:K:/:G: .12 .25
275 Ghen, Arcanum Weaver R :R:/:W:/:K: .10 .20
276 Gnostro, Voice of the Crags R :B:/:R:/:W: .10 .20
277 Gor Muldrak, Amphinologist R :G:/:B: .10 .20
278 Hamza, Guardian of Arashin U :G:/:W: .12 .25
279 Hans Eriksson R :R:/:G: .10 .20
280 Imoti, Celebrant of Bounty U :G:/:B: .10 .20
281 Jared Carthalion, True Heir R :R:/:G:/:W: .10 .20
282 Juri, Master of the Revue U :K:/:R: .15 .30
283 Kangee, Sky Warden U :W:/:B: .10 .20
284 Kwain, Itinerant Meddler R :W:/:B: .15 .30
285 Lathiel, the Bounteous Dawn R :G:/:W: .15 .30
286 Liesa, Shroud of Dusk R :W:/:K: .15 .30
287 Nevinyrral, Urborg Tyrant R :W:/:B:/:K: .12 .25
288 Nymris, Oona's Trickster R :B:/:K: .10 .20
289 Obeka, Brute Chronologist R :B:/:K:/:R: .12 .25
290 Reyav, Master Smith U :R:/:W: .10 .20
291 Thalisse, Reverent Medium U :W:/:K: .12 .25
292 Tuya Bearclaw U :R:/:G: .10 .20
293 Yurlok of Scorch Thrash R :K:/:R:/:G: .12 .25
294 Zara, Renegade Recruiter R :B:/:R: .12 .25
295 Amorphous Axe C .07 .15
296 Angelic Armaments U .07 .15
297 Arcane Signet U .50 1.00
298 Armillary Sphere C .07 .15
299 Armory of Iroas C .07 .15
300 Bladegriff Prototype R .12 .25
301 Brass Herald U .07 .15
302 Burnished Hart U .12 .25
303 Charcoal Diamond C .10 .20
304 Codex Shredder U .10 .20
305 Commander's Plate M 10.00 20.00
306 Commander's Sphere C .10 .20
307 Dreamstone Hedron U .12 .25
308 Filigree Familiar C .07 .15
309 Fire Diamond C .10 .20
310 Foundry Inspector C .12 .25
311 Golem Artisan U .07 .15
312 Grafted Wargear U .07 .15
313 Haunted Cloak C .07 .15
314 Hero's Blade U .07 .15
315 Horizon Stone R .25 .50
316 Howling Golem C .07 .15
317 Ingenuity Engine U .10 .20
318 Jalum Tome C .07 .15
319 Jeweled Lotus M 60.00 125.00
320 Loreseeker's Stone U .07 .15
321 Lumengrid Gargoyle C .07 .15
322 Maelstrom Colossus C .10 .20
323 Marble Diamond C .07 .15
324 Mask of Memory U .15 .30
325 Meteor Golem U .07 .15
326 Mindless Automaton U .07 .15
327 Moss Diamond C .07 .15
328 Nevinyrral's Disk R .15 .30
329 Pennon Blade U .07 .15
330 Perilous Myr C .07 .15
331 Phyrexian Triniform M 1.25 2.50
332 Pilgrim's Eye C .07 .15
333 Pirate's Cutlass C .07 .15
334 Prophetic Prism C .07 .15
335 Rings of Brighthearth R 1.50 3.00
336 Sandstone Oracle U .10 .20
337 Scroll Rack M 10.00 20.00
338 Seer's Lantern C .07 .15
339 Shimmer Myr U .10 .20
340 Sisay's Ring C .07 .15
341 Sky Diamond C .07 .15
342 Spectral Searchlight C .07 .15
343 Staff of Domination R 2.00 4.00
344 Staunch Throneguard C .07 .15
345 Sunset Pyramid U .07 .15
346 Thought Vessel U 2.50 5.00
347 Universal Solvent C .07 .15
348 Workshop Assistant C .07 .15
349 Command Beacon R 3.00 6.00
350 Command Tower C .12 .25
351 Guildless Commons U .15 .30
352 Opal Palace C .10 .20
353 Path of Ancestry C .12 .25
354 Rejuvenating Springs R 6.00 12.00
355 Rupture Spire C .07 .15
356 Spectator Seating R 4.00 8.00
357 Terramorphic Expanse C .10 .20
358 Training Center R 5.00 10.00
359 Undergrowth Stadium R 5.00 10.00
360 Vault of Champions R 6.00 12.00
361 War Room R 1.50 3.00
362 Wyleth, Soul of Steel M :R:/:W: .15 .30
363 Timely Ward R :W: 3.00 6.00
364 Blazing Sunsteel R :R: .12 .25
365 Aesi, Tyrant of Gyre Strait M :G:/:B: 5.00 10.00
366 Trench Behemoth R :B: .12 .25
367 Stumpsquall Hydra R :G: .10 .20
368 Elder Deep-Fiend R .12 .25
369 Condemn U :W: .10 .20
370 Danitha Capashen, Paragon U :W: .15 .30
371 Dawn Charm U :W: .15 .30
372 Disenchant C :W: .07 .15
373 Faith Unbroken U :W: .07 .15
374 Flickerwisp U :W: .10 .20
375 Generous Gift U :W: 1.50 3.00
376 Ironclad Slayer C :W: .07 .15
377 Kor Cartographer C :W: .07 .15
378 Martial Coup R :W: .15 .30
379 Odric, Lunarch Marshal R :W: .12 .25
380 On Serra's Wings U :W: .10 .20
381 Oreskos Explorer U :W: .10 .20
382 Relic Seeker R :W: .12 .25
383 Return to Dust U :W: .07 .15
384 Sigarda's Aid R :W: 3.00 6.00
385 Spirit Mantle U :W: .30 .60
386 Sram, Senior Edificer R :W: .12 .25
387 Swords to Plowshares U :W: 1.25 2.50
388 Unbreakable Formation R :W: .15 .30
389 Unquestioned Authority U :W: .20 .40
390 Valorous Stance U :W: .12 .25
391 White Sun's Zenith R :W: .15 .30
392 Winds of Rath R :W: .12 .25
393 Arcane Denial C :B: 1.25 2.50
394 Compulsive Research C :B: .10 .20
395 Counterspell C :B: 1.25 2.50
396 Fact or Fiction U :B: .10 .20
397 Into the Roil C :B: .10 .20
398 Ior Ruin Expedition C :B: .07 .15
399 Meloku the Clouded Mirror R :B: .12 .25
400 Mulldrifter U :B: .15 .30
401 Nezahal, Primal Tide R :B: 1.00 2.00
402 Peel from Reality C :B: .07 .15
403 Scourge of Fleets R :B: .15 .30
404 Shipbreaker Kraken R :B: .12 .25
405 Slinn Voda, the Rising Deep U :B: .12 .25
406 Sphinx of Uthuun R :B: .10 .20
407 Stormtide Leviathan R :B: .12 .25
408 Tromokratis R :B: .12 .25
409 Whelming Wave R :B: .12 .25
410 Abrade U :R: .10 .20
411 Comet Storm M :R: .30 .60
412 Dualcaster Mage R :R: .12 .25
413 Expedite C :R: .12 .25
414 Fists of Flame C :R: .10 .20
415 Jaya's Immolating Inferno R :R: .10 .20
416 Relentless Assault R :R: 1.25 2.50
417 Temur Battle Rage C :R: .10 .20
418 Volcanic Fallout U :R: .07 .15
419 Wild Ricochet R :R: .10 .20
420 Word of Seizing R :R: .12 .25
421 Acidic Slime U :G: .10 .20
422 Avenger of Zendikar M :G: 2.00 4.00
423 Beast Within U :G: .50 1.00
424 Cultivate C :G: .25 .50
425 Eternal Witness U :G: 2.00 4.00
426 Explore C :G: .12 .25
427 Harmonize U :G: .15 .30
428 Khalni Heart Expedition C :G: .10 .20
429 Kodama's Reach C :G: .75 1.50
430 Molimo, Maro-Sorcerer R :G: .10 .20
431 Rampaging Baloths R :G: .12 .25
432 Rampant Growth C :G: .15 .30
433 Ramunap Excavator R :G: 1.50 3.00
434 Reclamation Sage U :G: .10 .20
435 Retreat to Kazandu U :G: .10 .20
436 Search for Tomorrow C :G: .15 .30
437 Sporemound C :G: .10 .20
438 Terastodon R :G: .12 .25
439 Verdant Sun's Avatar R :G: .12 .25
440 Wickerbough Elder C :G: .07 .15
441 Yavimaya Elder C :G: .07 .15
442 Boros Charm U :R:/:W: .75 1.50
443 Coiling Oracle C :G:/:B: .10 .20
444 Deflecting Palm R :R:/:W: 1.00 2.00
445 Fathom Mage R :G:/:B: .12 .25
446 Growth Spiral C :G:/:B: .15 .30
447 Master Warcraft R :R:/:W: .12 .25
448 Murkfiend Liege R :G:/:B: .30 .75
449 Response // Resurgence R :R:/:W: .12 .25
450 Sharktocrab U :G:/:B: .07 .15
451 Simic Charm U :G:/:B: .12 .25
452 Simic Sky Swallower R :G:/:B: .10 .20
453 Spitting Image R :G:/:B: .10 .20
454 Tiana, Ship's Caretaker U :R:/:W: .07 .15
455 Urban Evolution U :G:/:B: .10 .20
456 Wear // Tear U :R:/:W: .60 1.25
457 Blackblade Reforged R .60 1.25
458 Bonesplitter C .10 .20
459 Boros Signet C .25 .50
460 Brass Squire U .10 .20
461 Explorer's Scope C .10 .20
462 Fireshrieker U .12 .25
463 Haunted Cloak C .07 .15
464 Hero's Blade U .10 .20
465 Loxodon Warhammer R .15 .30
466 Mask of Avacyn U .20 .40
467 Meteor Golem U .10 .20
468 Ring of Thune U .07 .15
469 Ring of Valkas U .10 .20
470 Seer's Sundial R .12 .25
471 Simic Signet C .15 .30
472 Sol Ring U .75 1.50
473 Sunforger R .12 .25
474 Swiftfoot Boots U .60 1.25
475 Sword of Vengeance R .12 .25

476 Blighted Woodland U .10 .20
477 Boros Garrison U .12 .25
478 Boros Guildgate C .10 .20
479 Command Tower C .12 .25
480 Coral Atoll U .10 .20
481 Encroaching Wastes U .10 .20
482 Evolving Wilds C .10 .20
483 Forgotten Cave C .10 .20
484 Jungle Basin U .12 .25
485 Memorial to Genius U .07 .15
486 Memorial to War U .07 .15
487 Myriad Landscape U .10 .20
488 Reliquary Tower U 2.50 5.00
489 Rogue's Passage U .20 .40
490 Rupture Spire C .07 .15
491 Secluded Steppe U .10 .20
492 Simic Growth Chamber U .12 .25
493 Simic Guildgate C .10 .20
494 Slayers' Stronghold R .12 .25
495 Stone Quarry U .07 .15
496 Sunhome, Fortress of the Legion U .12 .25
497 Terramorphic Expanse C .10 .20
498 Thornwood Falls C .10 .20
499 Transguild Promenade C .10 .20
500 Vivid Creek U .15 .30
501 Vivid Grove U .15 .30
502 Wind-Scarred Crag C .10 .20
503 Woodland Stream C .07 .15
504 Plains L .07 .15
505 Plains L .10 .20
506 Island L .10 .20
507 Island L .10 .20
508 Mountain L .10 .20
509 Mountain L .10 .20
510 Forest L .10 .20
511 Forest L .10 .20
512 Tevesh Szat, Doom of Fools M :K: 4.00 8.00
513 Jeska, Thrice Reborn M :R: 1.50 3.00
514 Najeela, the Blade-Blossom M :R: 6.00 12.00
515 Akiri, Line-Slinger M :R:/:W: 1.50 3.00
516 Brago, King Eternal M :W:/:B: 2.50 5.00
517 Bruse Tarl, Boorish Herder M :R:/:W: 3.00 6.00
518 Derevi, Empyrial Tactician M :G:/:W:/:B: 2.50 5.00
519 Ikra Shidiqi, the Usurper M :K:/:G: 2.50 5.00
520 Ishai, Ojutai Dragonspeaker M :W:/:B: 3.00 6.00
521 Karador, Ghost Chieftain M :W:/:K:/:G: 1.50 3.00
522 Karametra, God of Harvests M :G:/:W: 2.00 4.00
523 Kraum, Ludevic's Opus M :B:/:R: 2.50 5.00
524 Kydele, Chosen of Kruphix M :G:/:B: 1.25 2.50
525 Ludevic, Necro-Alchemist M :B:/:R: .75 1.50
526 Maelstrom Wanderer M :G:/:B:/:R: 5.00 10.00
527 Marath, Will of the Wild M :R:/:G:/:W: .30 .75
528 Muldrotha, the Gravetide M :K:/:G:/:B: 4.00 8.00
529 Nekusar, the Mindrazer M :B:/:K:/:R: 4.00 8.00
530 Prossh, Skyraider of Kher M :K:/:R:/:G: 2.00 4.00
531 Queen Marchesa M :R:/:W:/:K: 4.00 8.00
532 Rakdos, Lord of Riots M :K:/:R: 3.00 6.00
533 Ravos, Soultender M :W:/:K: 4.00 8.00
534 Reyhan, Last of the Abzan M :K:/:G: 4.00 8.00
535 Sidar Kondo of Jamuraa M :G:/:W: 1.50 3.00
536 Silas Renn, Seeker Adept M :B:/:K: 4.00 8.00
537 Tana, the Bloodsower M :R:/:G: 3.00 6.00
538 Thrasios, Triton Hero M :G:/:B: 12.50 25.00
539 Tymna the Weaver M :W:/:K: 15.00 30.00
540 Vial Smasher the Fierce M :K:/:R: 7.50 15.00
541 Xenagos, God of Revels M :R:/:G: 7.50 15.00
542 Yuriko, the Tiger's Shadow M :B:/:K: 12.50 25.00
543 Zedruu the Greathearted M :B:/:R:/:W: .75 1.50
544 Zur the Enchanter M :W:/:B:/:K: 3.00 6.00
545 Ramos, Dragon Engine M 10.00 20.00
546 The Prismatic Piper C .30 .60
547 Akroma, Vision of Ixidor M :W: 5.00 10.00
548 Alharu, Solemn Ritualist U :W: .15 .30
549 Ardenn, Intrepid Archaeologist U :W: 3.00 6.00
550 Keleth, Sunmane Familiar U :W: .30 .75
551 Livio, Oathsworn Sentinel R :W: .15 .30
552 Prava of the Steel Legion U :W: 1.25 2.50
553 Radiant, Serra Archangel U :W: .30 .75
554 Rebbec, Architect of Ascension U :W: 1.25 2.50
555 Brinelin, the Moon Kraken U :B: 1.25 2.50
556 Eligeth, Crossroads Augur R :B: .50 1.00
557 Esior, Wardwing Familiar U :B: .75 1.50
558 Ghost of Ramirez DePietro U :B: .25 .50
559 Glacian, Powerstone Engineer U :B: .15 .30
560 Malcolm, Keen-Eyed Navigator U :B: 3.00 6.00
561 Sakashima of a Thousand Faces M :B: 20.00 40.00
562 Siani, Eye of the Storm U :B: .30 .60
563 Armix, Filigree Thrasher U :K: 1.25 2.50
564 Falthis, Shadowcat Familiar U :K: 1.25 2.50
565 Keskit, the Flesh Sculptor U :K: .25 .50
566 Miara, Thorn of the Glade U :K: .30 .75
567 Nadier, Agent of the Duskenel U :K: .75 1.50
568 Sengir, the Dark Baron R :K: .30 .60
569 Tormod, the Desecrator U :K: 1.50 3.00
570 Alena, Kessig Trapper U :R: .30 .75
571 Breeches, Brazen Plunderer U :R: .75 1.50
572 Dargo, the Shipwrecker U :R: .30 .75
573 Kediss, Emberclaw Familiar U :R: 3.00 6.00
574 Krark, the Thumbless R :R: 1.50 3.00
575 Rograkh, Son of Rohgahh U 3.00 6.00
576 Toggo, Goblin Weaponsmith U :R: 1.00 2.00
577 Anara, Wolvid Familiar U :G: 1.00 2.00
578 Gilanra, Caller of Wirewood U :G: .30 .75
579 Halana, Kessig Ranger U :G: .50 1.00
580 Ich-Tekik, Salvage Splicer U :G: .20 .40
581 Kamahl, Heart of Krosa M :G: 3.00 6.00
582 Kodama of the East Tree R :G: 3.00 6.00
583 Numa, Joraga Chieftain U :G: .20 .40
584 Slurrk, All-Ingesting U :G: .50 1.00
585 Abomination of Llanowar U :K:/:G: .60 1.25
586 Amareth, the Lustrous R :G:/:W:/:B: .30 .75
587 Araumi of the Dead Tide U :B:/:K: .60 1.25
588 Archelos, Lagoon Mystic R :K:/:G:/:B: .75 1.50
589 Averna, the Chaos Bloom R :G:/:B:/:R: .30 .60
590 Belbe, Corrupted Observer R :K:/:G: .25 .50
591 Bell Borca, Spectral Sergeant R :R:/:W: .15 .30
592 Blim, Comedic Genius R :K:/:R: .15 .30
593 Captain Vargus Wrath U :B:/:R: .15 .30
594 Colfenor, the Last Yew R :W:/:K:/:G: .25 .50
595 Ghen, Arcanum Weaver R :R:/:W:/:K: .20 .40
596 Gnostro, Voice of the Crags R :B:/:R:/:W: .12 .25
597 Gor Muldrak, Amphinologist R :G:/:B: .15 .30
598 Hamza, Guardian of Arashin U :G:/:W: 1.25 2.50
599 Hans Eriksson R :R:/:G: .15 .30
600 Imoti, Celebrant of Bounty U :G:/:B: 1.50 3.00
601 Jared Carthalion, True Heir R :R:/:G:/:W: .15 .30
602 Juri, Master of the Revue U :K:/:R: 2.50 5.00
603 Kangee, Sky Warden U :W:/:B: .30 .75
604 Kwain, Itinerant Meddler R :W:/:B: 1.00 2.00
605 Lathiel, the Bounteous Dawn R :G:/:W: .60 1.25
606 Liesa, Shroud of Dusk R :W:/:K: 2.00 4.00
607 Nevinyrral, Urborg Tyrant R :W:/:B:/:K: .30 .60
608 Nymris, Oona's Trickster R :B:/:K: .20 .40
609 Obeka, Brute Chronologist R :B:/:K:/:R: .60 1.25
610 Reyav, Master Smith U :R:/:W: .75 1.50
611 Thalisse, Reverent Medium U :W:/:K: 1.25 2.50
612 Tuya Bearclaw U :R:/:G: .25 .50
613 Yurlok of Scorch Thrash R :K:/:R:/:G: .30 .75
614 Zara, Renegade Recruiter R :B:/:R: .30 .60
615 Akroma's Will R :W: 7.50 15.00
616 Archon of Coronation M :W: 1.50 3.00
617 Armored Skyhunter R :W: 2.00 4.00
618 Austere Command R :W: 2.50 5.00
619 Court of Grace R :W: 3.00 6.00
620 Generous Gift U :W: 2.50 5.00
621 Keeper of the Accord R :W: 2.50 5.00
622 Promise of Tomorrow R :W: .30 .60
623 Return to Dust U :W: .20 .40
624 Seraphic Greatsword M :W: 1.25 2.50
625 Slash the Ranks R :W: .75 1.50
626 Soul of Eternity R :W: .25 .50
627 Swords to Plowshares U :W: 1.50 3.00
628 Triumphant Reckoning M :W: 1.50 3.00
629 Amphin Mutineer R :B: 1.50 3.00
630 Arcane Denial C :B: 2.00 4.00
631 Body of Knowledge R :B: .75 1.50
632 Counterspell C :B: 2.00 4.00
633 Court of Cunning R :B: 4.00 8.00
634 Fact or Fiction U :B: .50 1.00
635 Hullbreacher R :B: 3.00 6.00
636 Laboratory Drudge R :B: .12 .25
637 Mana Drain M :B: 40.00 80.00
638 Mnemonic Deluge M :B: 3.00 6.00
639 Muldrifter U :B: .60 1.25
640 Preordain C :B: 2.00 4.00
641 Sakashima's Protege R :B: .30 .75
642 Sakashima's Will R :B: .30 .75
643 Sphinx of the Second Sun M :B: 5.00 10.00
644 Wrong Turn R :B: .50 1.00
645 Court of Ambition R :K: 2.00 4.00
646 Cuombajj Witches U :K: .50 1.00
647 Elvish Dreadlord R :K: .60 1.25
648 Fleshbag Marauder C :K: .50 1.00
649 Necrotic Hex R :K: .75 1.50
650 Nightshade Harvester R :K: .20 .40
651 Opposition Agent R :K: 10.00 20.00
652 Plague Reaver R :K: .25 .50
653 Profane Transfusion M :K: 1.50 3.00
654 Rakshasa Debaser R :K: 1.25 2.50
655 Szat's Will R :K: .60 1.25
656 Vampiric Tutor M :K: 30.00 75.00
657 Victimize U :K: 1.00 2.00
658 Viscera Seer C :K: 2.00 4.00
659 Abrade U :R: 1.50 3.00
660 Aurora Phoenix R :R: .50 1.00
661 Blasphemous Act R :R: 5.00 10.00
662 Coercive Recruiter R :R: .60 1.25
663 Court of Ire R :R: .75 1.50
664 Emberwilde Captain R :R: 1.00 2.00
665 Flamekin Herald R :R: .30 .60
666 Hellkite Courser M :R: 7.50 15.00
667 Humble Defector U :R: .20 .40
668 Jeska's Will R :R: 15.00 30.00
669 Port Razer M :R: 3.00 6.00
670 Soulfire Eruption M :R: 2.00 4.00
671 Temur Battle Rage C :R: 1.00 2.00
672 Wheel of Misfortune R :R: 3.00 6.00
673 Acidic Slime U :G: .30 .60
674 Apex Devastator M :G: 12.50 25.00
675 Biowaste Blob R :G: .75 1.50
676 Court of Bounty R :G: 1.50 3.00
677 Dawnglade Regent R :G: .60 1.25
678 Fyndhorn Elves C :G: 1.50 3.00
679 Immaculate Magistrate R :G: 1.00 2.00
680 Kamahl's Will R :G: .30 .60
681 Kodama's Reach C :G: 2.00 4.00
682 Magus of the Order R :G: .25 .50
683 Reshape the Earth M :G: 7.50 15.00
684 Rootweaver Druid R :G: .25 .50
685 Sweet-Gum Recluse R :G: .30 .75
686 Three Visits U :G: 7.50 15.00
687 Boros Charm U :R:/:W: 2.50 5.00
688 Coiling Oracle C :G:/:B: .30 .75
689 Arcane Signet U 5.00 10.00
690 Bladegriff Prototype R .25 .50
691 Burnished Hart U .75 1.50
692 Commander's Plate M 12.50 25.00
693 Commander's Sphere C 1.25 2.50
694 Horizon Stone R 1.00 2.00
695 Jeweled Lotus M 125.00 250.00
696 Nevinyrral's Disk R .75 1.50
697 Phyrexian Triniform M 4.00 8.00
698 Rings of Brighthearth R 4.00 8.00
699 Scroll Rack M 15.00 30.00
700 Sol Ring U 7.50 15.00
701 Staff of Domination R 3.00 6.00
702 Swiftfoot Boots U 3.00 6.00
703 Thought Vessel U 4.00 8.00
704 Command Beacon R 7.50 15.00
705 Command Tower C 7.50 15.00
706 Myriad Landscape U 2.00 4.00
707 Opal Palace C 1.25 2.50
708 Path of Ancestry C 1.50 3.00
709 Rejuvenating Springs R 12.50 25.00
710 Reliquary Tower U 4.00 8.00
711 Spectator Seating R 7.50 15.00
712 Terramorphic Expanse C .75 1.50
713 Training Center R 7.50 15.00
714 Undergrowth Stadium R 10.00 20.00
715 Vault of Champions R 10.00 20.00
716 War Room R 4.00 8.00

2020 Magic The Gathering Commander Legends Tokens

1 Angel .50 1.00
2 Soldier .07 .15
3 Spirit .10 .20
4 Salamander Warrior .15 .30
5 Thrull .50 1.00
6 Zombie .07 .15
7 Dragon .15 .30
8 Elf Warrior .12 .25
9 Golem .07 .15
10 Horror .07 .15
11 Rock .30 .60
12 Treasure .07 .15
13 Copy .15 .30
14 The Monarch .07 .15
15 Cat .07 .15
16 Soldier .07 .15
17 Illusion .07 .15
18 Beast .07 .15
19 Beast .07 .15
20 Elephant .07 .15
21 Plant .07 .15
22 Saproling .07 .15
23 Copy .07 .15

2020 Magic The Gathering Core Set 2021

1 Ugin, the Spirit Dragon M 15.00 30.00
2 Alpine Watchdog C :W: .07 .15
3 Angelic Ascension U :W: .10 .20
4 Anointed Chorister C :W: .07 .15
5 Aven Gagglemaster U :W: .10 .20
6 Baneslayer Angel M :W: 2.00 4.00
7 Basri Ket M :W: 2.00 4.00
8 Basri's Acolyte C :W: .07 .15
9 Basri's Lieutenant R :W: .15 .30
10 Basri's Solidarity U :W: .10 .20
11 Celestial Enforcer C :W: .07 .15
12 Concordia Pegasus C :W: .07 .15
13 Containment Priest R :W: .15 .30
14 Daybreak Charger C :W: .07 .15
15 Defiant Strike C :W: .07 .15
16 Dub C :W: .07 .15
17 Faith's Fetters U :W: .10 .20
18 Falconer Adept U :W: .10 .20
19 Feat of Resistance C :W: .07 .15
20 Gale Swooper C :W: .07 .15
21 Glorious Anthem R :W: .15 .30
22 Griffin Aerie U :W: .10 .20
23 Idol of Endurance R :W: .15 .30
24 Legion's Judgment C :W: .07 .15
25 Light of Promise U :W: .10 .20
26 Makeshift Battalion C :W: .07 .15
27 Mangara, the Diplomat M :W: 4.00 8.00
28 Nine Lives R :W: .15 .30
29 Pack Leader R :W: .15 .30
30 Rambunctious Mutt C :W: .07 .15
31 Revitalize C :W: .07 .15
32 Runed Halo R :W: .15 .30
33 Sanctum of Tranquil Light U :W: .10 .20
34 Seasoned Hallowblade U :W: .10 .20
35 Secure the Scene C :W: .07 .15
36 Selfless Savior U :W: .10 .20
37 Siege Striker U :W: .10 .20
38 Speaker of the Heavens R :W: .15 .30
39 Staunch Shieldmate C :W: .07 .15
40 Swift Response C :W: .07 .15
41 Tempered Veteran U :W: .10 .20
42 Valorous Steed C :W: .07 .15
43 Vryn Wingmare U :W: .10 .20
44 Warded Battlements C :W: .07 .15
45 Barrin, Tolarian Archmage R :B: .15 .30
46 Cancel C :B: .07 .15
47 Capture Sphere C :B: .07 .15
48 Discontinuity M :B: 1.25 2.50
49 Enthralling Hold U :B: .10 .20
50 Frantic Inventory C :B: .07 .15
51 Frost Breath C :B: .07 .15
52 Ghostly Pilferer R :B: .15 .30
53 Jeskai Elder U :B: .10 .20
54 Keen Glidemaster C :B: .07 .15
55 Library Larcenist C :B: .07 .15
56 Lofty Denial C :B: .07 .15
57 Miscast U :B: .75 1.50
58 Mistral Singer C :B: .07 .15
59 Opt C :B: .07 .15
60 Pursued Whale R :B: .15 .30
61 Rain of Revelation U :B: .10 .20
62 Read the Tides C :B: .07 .15
63 Rewind U :B: .10 .20
64 Riddleform U :B: .10 .20
65 Roaming Ghostlight C :B: .07 .15
66 Rookie Mistake C :B: .07 .15
67 Rousing Read C :B: .07 .15
68 Sanctum of Calm Waters U :B: .10 .20
69 See the Truth R :B: .15 .30
70 Shacklegeist R :B: .15 .30
71 Shipwreck Dowser U :B: .10 .20
72 Spined Megalodon C :B: .07 .15
73 Stormwing Entity R :B: .15 .30
74 Sublime Epiphany R :B: .15 .30
75 Teferi, Master of Time M :B: 12.50 25.00
76 Teferi's Ageless Insight R :B: .15 .30
77 Teferi's Protege C :B: .07 .15
78 Teferi's Tutelage U :B: .10 .20
79 Tide Skimmer U :B: .10 .20
80 Tolarian Kraken U :B: .10 .20
81 Tome Anima C :B: .07 .15
82 Unsubstantiate U :B: .10 .20
83 Vodalian Arcanist C :B: .07 .15
84 Waker of Waves U :B: .10 .20
85 Wall of Runes C :B: .07 .15
86 Wishcoin Crab C :B: .07 .15
87 Alchemist's Gift C :K: .07 .15
88 Archfiend's Vessel U :K: .10 .20
89 Bad Deal U :K: .10 .20
90 Blood Glutton C :K: .07 .15
91 Caged Zombie C :K: .07 .15
92 Carrion Grub U :K: .10 .20
93 Crypt Lurker C :K: .07 .15
94 Deathbloom Thallid C :K: .07 .15
95 Demonic Embrace R :K: .15 .30
96 Duress C :K: .07 .15
97 Eliminate U :K: .10 .20
98 Fetid Imp C :K: .07 .15
99 Finishing Blow C :K: .07 .15
100 Gloom Sower C :K: .07 .15
101 Goremand U :K: .10 .20
102 Grasp of Darkness C :K: .07 .15
103 Grim Tutor M :K: 7.50 15.00
104 Hooded Blightfang R :K: .15 .30
105 Infernal Scarring C :K: .07 .15
106 Kaervek, the Spiteful R :K: .15 .30
107 Kitesail Freebooter U :K: .10 .20
108 Liliana, Waker of the Dead M :K: 3.00 6.00
109 Liliana's Devotee U :K: .10 .20
110 Liliana's Standard Bearer R :K: .15 .30
111 Liliana's Steward C :K: .07 .15
112 Malefic Scythe U :K: .10 .20
113 Masked Blackguard C :K: .07 .15
114 Massacre Wurm M :K: 2.50 5.00
115 Mind Rot C :K: .07 .15
116 Necromentia R :K: .15 .30
117 Peer into the Abyss R :K: .15 .30
118 Pestilent Haze U :K: .10 .20
119 Rise Again C :K: .07 .15
120 Sanctum of Stone Fangs U :K: .10 .20
121 Sanguine Indulgence C :K: .07 .15
122 Silversmote Ghoul U :K: .10 .20
123 Skeleton Archer C :K: .07 .15
124 Tavern Swindler U :K: .10 .20
125 Thieves' Guild Enforcer R :K: .15 .30
126 Village Rites C :K: .07 .15
127 Vito, Thorn of the Dusk Rose R :K: .15 .30
128 Walking Corpse C :K: .07 .15
129 Witch's Cauldron U :K: .10 .20
130 Battle-Rattle Shaman U :R: .10 .20
131 Bolt Hound U :R: .10 .20
132 Bone Pit Brute C :R: .07 .15
133 Brash Taunter R :R: .15 .30
134 Burn Bright C :R: .07 .15
135 Chandra, Heart of Fire M :R: 1.00 2.00
136 Chandra's Incinerator R :R: .15 .30
137 Chandra's Magmutt C :R: .07 .15
138 Chandra's Pyreling U :R: .10 .20
139 Conspicuous Snoop R :R: .15 .30
140 Crash Through C :R: .07 .15
141 Destructive Tampering C :R: .07 .15
142 Double Vision R :R: .15 .30
143 Fiery Emancipation M :R: 6.00 12.00
144 Furious Rise U :R: .10 .20
145 Furor of the Bitten C :R: .07 .15
146 Gadrak, the Crown-Scourge R :R: .15 .30
147 Goblin Arsonist C :R: .07 .15
148 Goblin Wizardry C :R: .07 .15
149 Havoc Jester U :R: .10 .20
150 Heartfire Immolator U :R: .10 .20
151 Hellkite Punisher U :R: .10 .20
152 Hobblefiend C :R: .07 .15
153 Igneous Cur C :R: .07 .15
154 Kinetic Augur U :R: .10 .20
155 Onakke Ogre C :R: .07 .15
156 Pitchburn Devils C :R: .07 .15
157 Sanctum of Shattered Heights U :R: .10 .20
158 Scorching Dragonfire C :R: .07 .15
159 Shock C :R: .07 .15
160 Soul Sear U :R: .10 .20
161 Spellgorger Weird C :R: .07 .15
162 Subira, Tulzidi Caravanner R :R: .15 .30
163 Sure Strike C :R: .07 .15
164 Terror of the Peaks M :R: 7.50 15.00
165 Thrill of Possibility C :R: .07 .15
166 Traitorous Greed U :R: .10 .20
167 Transmogrify R :R: .15 .30
168 Turn to Slag C :R: .07 .15
169 Turret Ogre C :R: .07 .15
170 Unleash Fury U :R: .10 .20
171 Volcanic Geyser U :R: .10 .20
172 Volcanic Salvo R :R: .15 .30
173 Azusa, Lost but Seeking R :G: 5.00 10.00
174 Burlfist Oak U :G: .10 .20
175 Canopy Stalker U :G: .10 .20
176 Colossal Dreadmaw C :G: .07 .15
177 Cultivate U :G: .10 .20
178 Drowsing Tyrannodon C :G: .07 .15
179 Elder Gargaroth M :G: 5.00 10.00
180 Feline Sovereign R :G: .15 .30
181 Fierce Empath U :G: .10 .20
182 Fungal Rebirth U :G: .10 .20
183 Garruk, Unleashed M :G: 2.00 4.00
184 Garruk's Gorehorn C :G: .07 .15
185 Garruk's Harbinger R :G: .15 .30
186 Garruk's Uprising U :G: .10 .20
187 Gnarled Sage C :G: .07 .15
188 Heroic Intervention R :G: .15 .30
189 Hunter's Edge C :G: .07 .15
190 Invigorating Surge U :G: .10 .20
191 Jolrael, Mwonvuli Recluse R :G: .15 .30
192 Life Goes On C :G: .07 .15
193 Llanowar Visionary C :G: .07 .15
194 Ornery Dilophosaur C :G: .07 .15
195 Portcullis Vine C :G: .07 .15
196 Pridemalkin C :G: .07 .15
197 Primal Might R :G: .15 .30
198 Quirion Dryad U :G: .10 .20
199 Ranger's Guile C :G: .07 .15
200 Return to Nature C :G: .07 .15
201 Run Afoul C :G: .07 .15
202 Sabertooth Mauler C :G: .07 .15
203 Sanctum of Fruitful Harvest U :G: .10 .20
204 Scavenging Ooze R :G: .15 .30
205 Setessan Training C :G: .07 .15
206 Skyway Sniper U :G: .10 .20
207 Snarespinner C :G: .07 .15
208 Sporeweb Weaver R :G: .15 .30
209 Thrashing Brontodon U :G: .10 .20
210 Titanic Growth C :G: .07 .15
211 Track Down C :G: .07 .15
212 Trufflesnout C :G: .07 .15
213 Warden of the Woods U :G: .10 .20
214 Wildwood Scourge U :G: .10 .20
215 Alpine Houndmaster U :R:/:W: .10 .20
216 Conclave Mentor U :G:/:W: .10 .20
217 Dire Fleet Warmonger U :K:/:R: .10 .20
218 Experimental Overload U :B:/:R: .10 .20
219 Indulging Patrician U :W:/:K: .10 .20
220 Leafkin Avenger U :R:/:G: .10 .20
221 Lorescale Coatl U :G:/:B: .10 .20
222 Niambi, Esteemed Speaker R :W:/:B: .15 .30
223 Obsessive Stitcher U :B:/:K: .10 .20
224 Radha, Heart of Keld R :R:/:G: .15 .30
225 Sanctum of All R :W:/:B:/:K:/:R:/:G: .15 .30
226 Twinblade Assassin U :K:/:G: .10 .20

2020 Magic The Gathering Core Set 2021

227 Watcher of the Spheres U :W:/:B:	.10	.20
228 Chromatic Orrery M	6.00	12.00
229 Chrome Replicator U	.10	.20
230 Epitaph Golem U	.10	.20
231 Forgotten Sentinel C	.07	.15
232 Mazemind Tome R	.15	.30
233 Meteorite U	.10	.20
234 Palladium Myr U	.10	.20
235 Prismite C	.07	.15
236 Short Sword C	.07	.15
237 Silent Dart C	.07	.15
238 Skyscanner C	.07	.15
239 Solemn Simulacrum R	.15	.30
240 Sparkhunter Masticore R	.15	.30
241 Tormod's Crypt U	.10	.20
242 Animal Sanctuary R	.60	1.25
243 Bloodfell Caves C	.07	.15
244 Blossoming Sands C	.07	.15
245 Dismal Backwater C	.07	.15
246 Fabled Passage R	.15	.30
247 Jungle Hollow C	.07	.15
248 Radiant Fountain C	.07	.15
249 Rugged Highlands C	.07	.15
250 Scoured Barrens C	.07	.15
251 Swiftwater Cliffs C	.07	.15
252 Temple of Epiphany R	.15	.30
253 Temple of Malady R	.15	.30
254 Temple of Mystery R	.15	.30
255 Temple of Silence R	.15	.30
256 Temple of Triumph R	.15	.30
257 Thornwood Falls C	.07	.15
258 Tranquil Cove C	.07	.15
259 Wind-Scarred Crag C	.07	.15
260 Plains L	.07	.15
261 Plains L	.07	.15
262 Plains L	.07	.15
263 Island L	.07	.15
264 Island L	.07	.15
265 Island L	.07	.15
266 Swamp L	.07	.15
267 Swamp L	.07	.15
268 Swamp L	.07	.15
269 Mountain L	.07	.15
270 Mountain L	.07	.15
271 Mountain L	.07	.15
272 Forest L	.07	.15
273 Forest L	.07	.15
274 Forest L	.07	.15
275 Teferi, Master of Time M :B:	12.50	25.00
276 Teferi, Master of Time M :B:	12.50	25.00
277 Teferi, Master of Time M :B:	12.50	25.00
278 Rin and Seri, Inseparable M :R:/:G:/:W:/(Buy-a-Box Exclusive)	12.50	25.00
279 Ugin, the Spirit Dragon M	20.00	40.00
280 Basri Ket M :W:	2.50	5.00
281 Teferi, Master of Time M :B:	20.00	40.00
282 Liliana, Waker of the Dead M :K:	10.00	20.00
283 Chandra, Heart of Fire M :R:	2.00	4.00
284 Garruk, Unleashed M :G:	2.50	5.00
285 Ugin, the Spirit Dragon M	20.00	40.00
286 Basri Ket M :W:	1.50	3.00
287 Basri's Acolyte C :W:	.07	.15
288 Basri's Lieutenant R :W:	.15	.30
289 Basri's Solidarity U :W:	.10	.20
290 Teferi, Master of Time M :B:	15.00	30.00
291 Teferi, Master of Time M :B:	12.50	25.00
292 Teferi, Master of Time M :B:	12.50	25.00
293 Teferi, Master of Time M :B:	12.50	25.00
294 Teferi's Ageless Insight R :B:	.15	.30
295 Teferi's Protege C :B:	.07	.15
296 Teferi's Tutelage U :B:	.10	.20
297 Liliana, Waker of the Dead M :K:	3.00	6.00
298 Liliana's Devotee U :K:	.10	.20
299 Liliana's Standard Bearer R :K:	.15	.30
300 Liliana's Steward C :K:	.07	.15
301 Chandra, Heart of Fire M :R:	1.25	2.50
302 Chandra's Incinerator R :R:	.15	.30
303 Chandra's Magmutt C :R:	.07	.15
304 Chandra's Pyreling U :R:	.10	.20
305 Garruk, Unleashed M :G:	1.50	3.00
306 Garruk's Gorehorn C :G:	.07	.15
307 Garruk's Harbinger R :G:	.15	.30
308 Garruk's Uprising U :G:	.10	.20
309 Plains L	.07	.15
310 Island L	.07	.15
311 Swamp L	.07	.15
312 Mountain L	.07	.15
313 Forest L	.07	.15
314 Containment Priest R :W:	.15	.30
315 Grim Tutor M :K:	10.00	20.00
316 Massacre Wurm M :K:	3.00	6.00
317 Cultivate R :G:	.15	.30
318 Scavenging Ooze R :G:	.15	.30
319 Solemn Simulacrum R	.15	.30
320 Basri, Devoted Paladin M :W:	4.00	8.00
321 Adherent of Hope C :W:	.07	.15
322 Basri's Aegis R :W:	.15	.30
323 Sigiled Contender U :W:	.10	.20
324 Teferi, Timeless Voyager M :B:	3.00	6.00
325 Historian of Zhalfir U :B:	.10	.20
326 Mystic Skyfish C :B:	.07	.15
327 Teferi's Wavecaster R :B:	.15	.30
328 Liliana, Death Mage M :K:	6.00	12.00
329 Liliana's Scorn R :K:	.15	.30
330 Liliana's Scrounger U :K:	.10	.20
331 Spirit of Malevolence C :K:	.07	.15
332 Chandra, Flame's Catalyst M :R:	6.00	12.00
333 Chandra's Firemaw R :R:	.15	.30
334 Keral Keep Disciples U :R:	.10	.20
335 Storm Caller C :R:	.07	.15
336 Garruk, Savage Herald M :G:	3.00	6.00
337 Garruk's Warsteed R :G:	.15	.30
338 Predatory Wurm U :G:	.10	.20
339 Wildwood Patrol C :G:	.07	.15
340 Baneslayer Angel M :W:	4.00	8.00
341 Glorious Anthem R :W:	.15	.30
342 Idol of Endurance R :W:	.15	.30
343 Mangara, the Diplomat M :W:	6.00	12.00
344 Nine Lives R :W:	.15	.30
345 Pack Leader R :W:	.15	.30
346 Runed Halo R :W:	.15	.30
347 Speaker of the Heavens R :W:	.15	.30
348 Barrin, Tolarian Archmage R :B:	.15	.30
349 Discontinuity M :B:	2.50	5.00
350 Ghostly Pilferer R :B:	.15	.30
351 Pursued Whale R :B:	.15	.30
352 See the Truth R :B:	.15	.30
353 Shacklegeist R :B:	.15	.30
354 Stormwing Entity R :B:	.15	.30
355 Sublime Epiphany R :B:	.15	.30
356 Demonic Embrace R :K:	.15	.30
357 Hooded Blightfang R :K:	.15	.30
358 Kaervek, the Spiteful R :K:	.15	.30
359 Necromentia R :K:	.15	.30
360 Peer into the Abyss R :K:	.15	.30
361 Thieves' Guild Enforcer R :K:	.15	.30
362 Vito, Thorn of the Dusk Rose R :K:	.15	.30
363 Brash Taunter R :R:	.15	.30
364 Conspicuous Snoop R :R:	.15	.30
365 Double Vision R :R:	.15	.30
366 Fiery Emancipation M :R:	7.50	15.00
367 Gadrak, the Crown-Scourge R :R:	.15	.30
368 Subira, Tulzidi Caravanner R :R:	.15	.30
369 Terror of the Peaks M :R:	12.50	25.00
370 Transmogrify R :R:	.15	.30
371 Volcanic Salvo R :R:	.15	.30
372 Azusa, Lost but Seeking R :G:	7.50	15.00
373 Elder Gargaroth M :G:	7.50	15.00
374 Feline Sovereign R :G:	.15	.30
375 Heroic Intervention R :G:	.15	.30
376 Jolrael, Mwonvuli Recluse R :G:	.15	.30
377 Primal Might R :G:	.15	.30
378 Sporeweb Weaver R :G:	.15	.30
379 Niambi, Esteemed Speaker R :W:/:B:	.15	.30
380 Radha, Heart of Keld R :R:/:G:	.15	.30
381 Sanctum of All R :W:/:B:/:K:/:R:/:G:	.15	.30
382 Chromatic Orrery M	10.00	20.00
383 Mazemind Tome R	.15	.30
384 Sparkhunter Masticore R	.15	.30
385 Animal Sanctuary R	2.50	5.00
386 Fabled Passage R	.15	.30
387 Temple of Epiphany R	.15	.30
388 Temple of Malady R	.15	.30
389 Temple of Mystery R	.15	.30
390 Temple of Silence R	.15	.30
391 Temple of Triumph R	.15	.30
392 Pack Leader R :W:/(Bundle Exclusive)	.15	.30
393 Selfless Savior U :W:	.10	.20
394 Frantic Inventory C :B:	.07	.15
395 Eliminate U :K:	.10	.20
396 Heartfire Immolator U :R:	.10	.20
397 Llanowar Visionary C :G:	.07	.15

2020 Magic The Gathering Core Set 2021 Tokens

1 Angel	.12	.25
2 Bird	.10	.20
3 Griffin	.10	.20
4 Knight	.10	.20
5 Soldier	.10	.20
6 Demon	.12	.25
7 Zombie	.10	.20
8 Goblin Wizard	.10	.20
9 Pirate	.12	.25
10 Beast	.10	.20
11 Cat	.12	.25
12 Saproling	.10	.20
13 Weird	.20	.40
14 Construct	.12	.25
15 Treasure	.15	.30
16 Basri Ket Emblem	.30	.60
17 Garruk, Unleashed Emblem	.30	.60
18 Liliana, Waker of the Dead Emblem	.30	.75

2020 Magic The Gathering Double Masters

1 Karn Liberated M	20.00	40.00
2 Alabaster Mage C :W:	.07	.15
3 Ancestral Blade C :W:	.07	.15
4 Angel of the Dawn C :W:	.07	.15
5 Archangel of Thune M :W:	7.50	15.00
6 Auriok Salvagers U :W:	.10	.20
7 Austere Command R :W:	.15	.30
8 Avacyn, Angel of Hope M :W:	20.00	40.00
9 Blade Splicer R :W:	.15	.30
10 Boon Reflection R :W:	.15	.30
11 Council's Judgment R :W:	.15	.30
12 Crib Swap C :W:	.07	.15
13 Crusader of Odric C :W:	.07	.15
14 Ethersworn Canonist R :W:	.15	.30
15 Fencing Ace U :W:	.10	.20
16 Flickerwisp U :W:	.10	.20
17 Fortify C :W:	.07	.15
18 Glint-Sleeve Artisan C :W:	.07	.15
19 Kemba, Kha Regent R :W:	.15	.30
20 Land Tax M :W:	20.00	40.00
21 Leonin Abunas R :W:	.15	.30
22 Master Splicer U :W:	.10	.20
23 Myrsmith U :W:	.10	.20
24 Open the Vaults R :W:	.15	.30
25 Path to Exile U :W:	.10	.20
26 Puresteel Paladin R :W:	.15	.30
27 Remember the Fallen C :W:	.07	.15
28 Revoke Existence C :W:	.07	.15
29 Sanctum Gargoyle C :W:	.07	.15
30 Sanctum Spirit C :W:	.07	.15
31 Stoneforge Mystic R :W:	.15	.30
32 Stonehewer Giant R :W:	.15	.30
33 Strength of Arms C :W:	.07	.15
34 Tempered Steel R :W:	.15	.30
35 Thraben Inspector C :W:	.07	.15
36 Topple the Statue U :W:	.10	.20
37 Valor in Akros U :W:	.10	.20
38 Valorous Stance U :W:	.10	.20
39 Wrath of God R :W:	.15	.30
40 Apprentice Wizard C :B:	.07	.15
41 Arcum Dagsson M :B:	4.00	8.00
42 Argivian Restoration C :B:	.07	.15
43 Braids, Conjurer Adept R :B:	.15	.30
44 Brainstorm C :B:	.07	.15
45 Cloudreader Sphinx C :B:	.07	.15
46 Corridor Monitor C :B:	.07	.15
47 Cyclonic Rift R :B:	.15	.30
48 Deepglow Skate R :B:	.15	.30
49 Esperzoa U :B:	.10	.20
50 Faerie Mechanist C :B:	.07	.15
51 Force of Will M :B:	60.00	125.00
52 Frogify C :B:	.07	.15
53 Grand Architect R :B:	.15	.30
54 Hinder U :B:	.10	.20
55 Inkwell Leviathan R :B:	.15	.30
56 Jace, the Mind Sculptor M :B:	30.00	75.00
57 Master of Etherium R :B:	.15	.30
58 Master Transmuter R :B:	.15	.30
59 Metallic Rebuke C :B:	.07	.15
60 Parasitic Strix C :B:	.07	.15
61 Phyrexian Metamorph R :B:	.15	.30
62 Pongify U :B:	.10	.20
63 Relic Runner C :B:	.07	.15
64 Reshape R :B:	.15	.30
65 Riddlesmith U :B:	.10	.20
66 Rush of Knowledge U :B:	.10	.20
67 Sentinel of the Pearl Trident U :B:	.10	.20
68 Serra Sphinx U :B:	.10	.20
69 Sift C :B:	.07	.15
70 Steel Sabotage C :B:	.07	.15
71 Thirst for Knowledge U :B:	.10	.20
72 Thought Reflection R :B:	.15	.30
73 Treasure Mage U :B:	.10	.20
74 Vedalken Infuser C :B:	.07	.15
75 Well of Ideas R :B:	.15	.30
76 Ad Nauseam R :K:	.15	.30
77 Beacon of Unrest R :K:	.15	.30
78 Bone Picker C :K:	.07	.15
79 Cast Down C :K:	.07	.15
80 Costly Plunder C :K:	.07	.15
81 Dark Confidant M :K:	20.00	40.00
82 Death's Shadow R :K:	.15	.30
83 Defiant Salvager C :K:	.07	.15
84 Dire Fleet Hoarder C :K:	.07	.15
85 Disciple of Bolas R :K:	.15	.30
86 Disciple of the Vault U :K:	.10	.20
87 Divest C :K:	.07	.15
88 Doomed Necromancer R :K:	.15	.30
89 Dread Return U :K:	.10	.20
90 Driver of the Dead C :K:	.07	.15
91 Drown in Sorrow U :K:	.10	.20
92 Executioner's Capsule C :K:	.07	.15
93 Fatal Push U :K:	.10	.20
94 Geth, Lord of the Vault M :K:	.60	1.25
95 Glaze Fiend C :K:	.07	.15
96 Heartless Pillage C :K:	.07	.15
97 Magus of the Abyss R :K:	.15	.30
98 Magus of the Will R :K:	.15	.30
99 Morkrut Banshee U :K:	.10	.20
100 Oubliette U :K:	.10	.20
101 Ovalchase Daredevil U :K:	.10	.20
102 Painsmith U :K:	.10	.20
103 Ravenous Trap R :K:	.15	.30
104 Salvage Titan R :K:	.15	.30
105 Silumgar Scavenger C :K:	.07	.15
106 Skirsdag High Priest R :K:	.15	.30
107 Skithiryx, the Blight Dragon M :K:	12.50	25.00
108 Supernatural Stamina C :K:	.07	.15
109 Thoughtseize R :K:	.15	.30
110 Toxic Deluge R :K:	.15	.30
111 Twisted Abomination C :K:	.07	.15
112 Vampire Hexmage U :K:	.10	.20
113 Wound Reflection R :K:	.15	.30
114 Abrade C :R:	.07	.15
115 Balduvian Rage C :R:	.07	.15
116 Battle-Rattle Shaman C :R:	.07	.15
117 Blasphemous Act R :R:	.15	.30
118 Blood Moon R :R:	.15	.30
119 Bloodshot Trainee U :R:	.10	.20
120 Brimstone Volley U :R:	.10	.20
121 Cathartic Reunion C :R:	.07	.15
122 Cragganwick Cremator R :R:	.15	.30
123 Dismantle U :R:	.10	.20
124 Dualcaster Mage R :R:	.15	.30
125 Galvanic Blast U :R:	.10	.20
126 Goblin Gaveleer C :R:	.07	.15
127 Goblin Guide R :R:	.15	.30
128 Godo, Bandit Warlord R :R:	.15	.30
129 Grim Lavamancer R :R:	.15	.30
130 Heat Shimmer R :R:	.15	.30
131 Imperial Recruiter M :R:	15.00	30.00
132 Ion Storm R :R:	.15	.30
133 Kazuul's Toll Collector C :R:	.07	.15
134 Kuldotha Flamefiend U :R:	.10	.20
135 Lightning Axe C :R:	.07	.15
136 Mana Echoes M :R:	15.00	30.00
137 Orcish Vandal C :R:	.07	.15
138 Pyrewild Shaman U :R:	.10	.20
139 Rage Reflection R :R:	.15	.30
140 Rapacious Dragon C :R:	.07	.15
141 Ravenous Intruder U :R:	.10	.20
142 Rolling Earthquake R :R:	.15	.30
143 Salivating Gremlins C :R:	.07	.15
144 Skinbrand Goblin C :R:	.07	.15
145 Sneak Attack M :R:	7.50	15.00
146 Temur Battle Rage C :R:	.07	.15
147 Thopter Engineer U :R:	.10	.20
148 Trash for Treasure U :R:	.10	.20
149 Tuktuk the Explorer R :R:	.15	.30
150 Weapon Surge C :R:	.07	.15
151 Ancient Stirrings C :G:	.07	.15
152 Avenger of Zendikar M :G:	4.00	8.00
153 Awakening Zone R :G:	.15	.30
154 Bloodbriar C :G:	.07	.15
155 Bloodspore Thrinax R :G:	.15	.30
156 Champion of Lambholt R :G:	.15	.30
157 Chatter of the Squirrel C :G:	.07	.15
158 Chord of Calling R :G:	.15	.30
159 Clear Shot C :G:	.07	.15
160 Conclave Naturalists C :G:	.07	.15
161 Crop Rotation U :G:	.10	.20
162 Crushing Vines C :G:	.07	.15
163 Death-Hood Cobra C :G:	.07	.15
164 Doubling Season M :G:	25.00	50.00
165 Elvish Aberration C :G:	.07	.15
166 Enlarge U :G:	.10	.20
167 Exploration R :G:	.15	.30
168 Fierce Empath C :G:	.07	.15
169 Gelatinous Genesis U :G:	.10	.20
170 Greater Good R :G:	.15	.30
171 Heartbeat of Spring R :G:	.15	.30
172 Invigorate U :G:	.10	.20
173 Kozilek's Predator C :G:	.07	.15
174 Liege of the Tangle R :G:	.15	.30
175 Mana Reflection R :G:	.15	.30
176 Might of the Masses C :G:	.07	.15
177 Noble Hierarch R :G:	.15	.30
178 Reclamation Sage U :G:	.10	.20
179 Shamanic Revelation R :G:	.15	.30
180 Skullmulcher U :G:	.10	.20
181 Sylvan Might C :G:	.07	.15
182 Terastodon R :G:	.15	.30
183 Thragtusk R :G:	.15	.30
184 Ulvenwald Mysteries U :G:	.10	.20
185 Vengevine M :G:	4.00	8.00
186 Veteran Explorer U :G:	.10	.20
187 Whisperer of the Wilds C :G:	.07	.15
188 Woodland Champion U :G:	.10	.20
189 Arixmethes, Slumbering Isle R :G:/:B:	.15	.30
190 Atraxa, Praetors' Voice M :G:/:W:/:B:/:K:	12.50	25.00
191 Baleful Strix R :B:/:K:	.15	.30
192 Breya, Etherium Shaper M :W:/:B:/:K:/:R:	4.00	8.00
193 Brudiclad, Telchor Engineer R :B:/:R:	.15	.30
194 Deathreap Ritual U :K:/:G:	.10	.20
195 Falkenrath Aristocrat R :K:/:R:	.15	.30
196 Fulminator Mage R :K:/:R:	.15	.30
197 Geist of Saint Traft M :W:/:B:	1.25	2.50
198 Ghor-Clan Rampager U :R:/:G:	.10	.20
199 Glassdust Hulk U :W:/:B:	.10	.20
200 Hanna, Ship's Navigator R :W:/:B:	.15	.30
201 Hidden Stockpile U :W:/:K:	.10	.20
202 Izzet Charm U :B:/:R:	.10	.20
203 Jhoira, Weatherlight Captain R :B:/:R:	.15	.30
204 Kaalia of the Vast M :R:/:W:/:K:	12.50	25.00
205 Karrthus, Tyrant of Jund M :K:/:R:/:G:	1.25	2.50
206 Maelstrom Nexus M :W:/:B:/:K:/:R:/:G:	1.25	2.50
207 Maelstrom Pulse R :K:/:G:	.15	.30
208 Manamorphose U :R:/:G:	.10	.20
209 Mazirek, Kraul Death Priest R :K:/:G:	.15	.30
210 Meddling Mage R :W:/:B:	.15	.30
211 Merciless Eviction R :W:/:K:	.15	.30
212 Progenitor Mimic R :G:/:B:	.15	.30
213 Rhys the Redeemed R :G:/:W:	.15	.30
214 Riku of Two Reflections M :G:/:B:/:R:	6.00	12.00
215 Savageborn Hydra R :R:/:G:	.15	.30
216 The Scarab God M :B:/:K:	10.00	20.00
217 Selesnya Guildmage U :G:/:W:	.10	.20
218 Sen Triplets M :W:/:B:/:K:	4.00	8.00
219 Sharuum the Hegemon R :W:/:B:/:K:	.15	.30
220 Sphinx Summoner U :B:/:K:	.10	.20
221 Switblade Vindicator R :R:/:W:	.15	.30
222 Thopter Foundry U :W:/:K:/:B:	.10	.20
223 Time Sieve R :B:/:K:	.15	.30
224 Unlicensed Disintegration U :K:/:R:	.10	.20
225 Vexing Shusher R :R:/:G:	.15	.30
226 Vish Kal, Blood Arbiter R :W:/:K:	.15	.30
227 Voice of Resurgence R :G:/:W:	.15	.30
228 Weapons Trainer U :R:/:W:	.10	.20
229 Yavimaya's Embrace U :G:/:B:	.10	.20
230 Accomplished Automaton C	.07	.15
231 Adaptive Automaton R	.15	.30
232 Basalt Monolith U	.10	.20
233 Basilisk Collar R	.15	.30
234 Batterskull M	6.00	12.00
235 Blightsteel Colossus M	25.00	50.00
236 Bosh, Iron Golem R	.15	.30
237 Cathodion C	.07	.15
238 Chief of the Foundry U	.10	.20
239 Chromatic Star C	.07	.15
240 Chrome Mox M	30.00	60.00
241 Clone Shell U	.10	.20
242 Cogwork Assembler U	.10	.20
243 Conjurer's Closet R	.15	.30
244 Coretapper U	.10	.20
245 Cranial Plating U	.10	.20
246 Culling Dais U	.10	.20
247 Darksteel Axe C	.07	.15
248 Darksteel Forge M	7.50	15.00
249 Duplicant R	.15	.30
250 Eager Construct C	.07	.15
251 Endless Atlas R	.15	.30
252 Engineered Explosives R	.15	.30
253 Ensnaring Bridge M	12.50	25.00
254 Everflowing Chalice C	.07	.15
255 Expedition Map C	.07	.15
256 Flayer Husk C	.07	.15
257 Gleaming Barrier C	.07	.15
258 Golem Artisan U	.10	.20
259 Golem-Skin Gauntlets C	.07	.15
260 Hammer of Nazahn R	.15	.30
261 Ichor Wellspring C	.07	.15
262 Iron Bully C	.07	.15
263 Iron League Steed C	.07	.15
264 Isochron Scepter R	.15	.30
265 Jhoira's Familiar U	.10	.20
266 Kuldotha Forgemaster R	.15	.30
267 Lightning Greaves U	.10	.20
268 Lux Cannon R	.15	.30
269 Magnifying Glass C	.07	.15
270 Mana Crypt M	75.00	150.00
271 Masterwork of Ingenuity R	.15	.30
272 Mesmeric Orb R	.15	.30
273 Metalspinner's Puzzleknot C	.07	.15
274 Mishra's Bauble U	.10	.20
275 Mox Opal M	25.00	50.00
276 Myr Battlesphere R	.15	.30
277 Myr Retriever C	.07	.15
278 O-Naginata U	.10	.20
279 Oblivion Stone R	.15	.30
280 Peace Strider C	.07	.15
281 Pentad Prism U	.10	.20
282 Phyrexian Revoker R	.15	.30
283 Pyrite Spellbomb C	.07	.15
284 Ratchet Bomb R	.15	.30
285 Sandstone Oracle U	.10	.20
286 Sculpting Steel R	.15	.30
287 Sicklesl icer C	.07	.15
288 Skinwing C	.07	.15

289 Spellskite R	.15	.30
290 Sphinx of the Guildpact U	.10	.20
291 Springleaf Drum U	.10	.20
292 Sundering Titan R	.15	.30
293 Sunforger R	.15	.30
294 Surge Node C	.07	.15
295 Sword of Body and Mind M	7.50	15.00
296 Sword of Feast and Famine M	30.00	60.00
297 Sword of Fire and Ice M	30.00	60.00
298 Sword of Light and Shadow M	15.00	30.00
299 Sword of the Meek R	.15	.30
300 Sword of War and Peace M	7.50	15.00
301 Throne of Geth U	.10	.20
302 Treasure Keeper U	.10	.20
303 Trinisphere M	12.50	25.00
304 Tumble Magnet C	.07	.15
305 Vulshok Gauntlets C	.07	.15
306 Walking Ballista R	.15	.30
307 Welding Jar U	.10	.20
308 Wurmcoil Engine M	12.50	25.00
309 Academy Ruins R	.15	.30
310 Ash Barrens U	.10	.20
311 Blinkmoth Nexus R	.15	.30
312 Buried Ruin U	.10	.20
313 Cascade Bluffs R	.15	.30
314 Dark Depths M	7.50	15.00
315 Darksteel Citadel U	.10	.20
316 Fetid Heath R	.15	.30
317 Fire-Lit Thicket R	.15	.30
318 Flooded Grove R	.15	.30
319 Glimmervoid R	.15	.30
320 Graven Cairns R	.15	.30
321 High Market R	.15	.30
322 Maze of Ith R	.15	.30
323 Mishra's Factory U	.10	.20
324 Mystic Gate R	.15	.30
325 Rugged Prairie R	.15	.30
326 Sunken Ruins R	.15	.30
327 Thespian's Stage R	.15	.30
328 Twilight Mire R	.15	.30
329 Urza's Mine C	.07	.15
330 Urza's Power Plant C	.07	.15
331 Urza's Tower C	.07	.15
332 Wooded Bastion R	.15	.30
333 Karn Liberated M	50.00	100.00
334 Jace, the Mind Sculptor M :B:	60.00	125.00
335 Avacyn, Angel of Hope M :W:	50.00	100.00
336 Council's Judgment R :W:	.15	.30
337 Stoneforge Mystic R :W:	.15	.30
338 Brainstorm R :B:	.15	.30
339 Cyclonic Rift R :B:	.15	.30
340 Force of Will M :B:	300.00	600.00
341 Phyrexian Metamorph R :B:	.15	.30
342 Dark Confidant M :B:	20.00	40.00
343 Fatal Push R :B:	.15	.30
344 Thoughtseize R :B:	.15	.30
345 Toxic Deluge R :B:	.15	.30
346 Blood Moon R :K:	.15	.30
347 Goblin Guide R :K:	.15	.30
348 Sneak Attack M :K:	7.50	15.00
349 Crop Rotation R :G:	.15	.30
350 Doubling Season M :G:	50.00	100.00
351 Exploration R :G:	.15	.30
352 Noble Hierarch R :G:	.15	.30
353 Atraxa, Praetors' Voice M :G:/:W:/:B:/:K:	30.00	60.00
354 Kaalia of the Vast M :R:/:W:/:K:	30.00	75.00
355 Meddling Mage R :W:/:B:	.15	.30
356 Batterskull M :R:/:W:/:K:	6.00	12.00
357 Blightsteel Colossus M	30.00	75.00
358 Chrome Mox M	50.00	100.00
359 Expedition Map R	.15	.30
360 Lightning Greaves R	.15	.30
361 Mana Crypt M	150.00	300.00
362 Mox Opal M	30.00	75.00
363 Sword of Body and Mind M	20.00	40.00
364 Sword of Feast and Famine M	75.00	150.00
365 Sword of Fire and Ice M	60.00	125.00
366 Sword of Light and Shadow M	30.00	60.00
367 Sword of War and Peace M	25.00	50.00
368 Wurmcoil Engine M	25.00	50.00
369 Academy Ruins R	.15	.30
370 Urza's Mine R	.15	.30
371 Urza's Power Plant R	.15	.30
372 Urza's Tower R	.15	.30
373 Plains L	.07	.15
374 Plains L	.07	.15
375 Island L	.07	.15
376 Island L	.07	.15
377 Swamp L	.07	.15
378 Swamp L	.07	.15
379 Mountain L	.07	.15
380 Mountain L	.07	.15
381 Forest L	.07	.15
382 Forest L	.07	.15
383 Wrath of God R :W:	.15	.30
384 Chord of Calling R :G:	.15	.30

2020 Magic The Gathering Double Masters Tokens

1 Eldrazi Spawn	.75	1.50
2 Shapeshifter	.15	.30
3 Angel	.30	.60
4 Cat	.25	.50
5 Human Soldier	.15	.30
6 Soldier	.07	.15
7 Myr	.30	.60
8 Thopter	.30	.60
9 Demon	.07	.15
10 Germ	.10	.20
11 Marit Lage	.30	.75
12 Ape	.50	1.00
13 Beast	.15	.30
14 Elephant	.30	.60
15 Ooze	.15	.30
16 Plant	.20	.40
17 Saproling	.10	.20
18 Squirrel	.10	.20
19 Wolf	.07	.15
20 Elemental	.12	.25
21 Elf Warrior	.50	1.00
22 Clue	.07	.15
23 Golem	.07	.15
24 Myr	.10	.20
25 Servo	.15	.30
26 Thopter	.07	.15
27 Treasure	.15	.30
28 Tuktuk the Returned	.20	.40
29 Wurm	1.50	3.00
30 Wurm	3.00	6.00
31 Copy	.25	.50

2020 Magic The Gathering Ikoria Lair of Behemoths

1 Adaptive Shimmerer C	.07	.15
2 Farfinder C	.07	.15
3 Mysterious Egg C	.07	.15
4 Blade Banish C	.07	.15
5 Checkpoint Officer C	.07	.15
6 Coordinated Charge C	.07	.15
7 Cubwarden R	.15	.30
8 Daysquad Marshal C	.07	.15
9 Divine Arrow C	.07	.15
10 Drannith Healer C	.07	.15
11 Drannith Magistrate R	.15	.30
12 Fight as One U	.10	.20
13 Flourishing Fox U	.10	.20
14 Garrison Cat C	.07	.15
15 Helica Glider C	.07	.15
16 Huntmaster Liger U	.10	.20
17 Imposing Vantasaur C	.07	.15
18 Keensight Mentor U	.10	.20
19 Lavabrink Venturer R	.15	.30
20 Light of Hope C	.07	.15
21 Luminous Broodmoth M	7.50	15.00
22 Majestic Auricorn U	.10	.20
23 Maned Serval C	.07	.15
24 Mythos of Snapdax R	.15	.30
25 Pacifism C	.07	.15
26 Patagia Tiger C	.07	.15
27 Perimeter Sergeant C	.07	.15
28 Sanctuary Lockdown U	.10	.20
29 Savai Sabertooth C	.07	.15
30 Snare Tactician C	.07	.15
31 Solid Footing C	.07	.15
32 Splendor Mare U	.10	.20
33 Spontaneous Flight C	.07	.15
34 Stormwild Capridor U	.10	.20
35 Swallow Whole U	.10	.20
36 Valiant Rescuer U	.10	.20
37 Vulpikeet C	.07	.15
38 Will of the All-Hunter U	.10	.20
39 Aegis Turtle C	.07	.15
40 Anticipate C	.07	.15
41 Archipelagore U	.10	.20
42 Avian Oddity U	.10	.20
43 Boon of the Wish-Giver U	.10	.20
44 Capture Sphere C	.07	.15
45 Convolute C	.07	.15
46 Crystacean C	.07	.15
47 Dreamtail Heron C	.07	.15
48 Escape Protocol U	.10	.20
49 Essence Scatter C	.07	.15
50 Facet Reader C	.07	.15
51 Frost Lynx C	.07	.15
52 Frostveil Ambush C	.07	.15
53 Glimmerbell C	.07	.15
54 Gust of Wind C	.07	.15
55 Hampering Snare C	.07	.15
56 Keep Safe C	.07	.15
57 Mystic Subdual U	.10	.20
58 Mythos of Illuna R	.15	.30
59 Neutralize U	.10	.20
60 Of One Mind C	.07	.15
61 Ominous Seas U	.25	.50
62 Phase Dolphin C	.07	.15
63 Pollywog Symbiote U	.10	.20
64 Pouncing Shoreshark U	.10	.20
65 Reconnaissance Mission U	.10	.20
66 Sea-Dasher Octopus R	.75	1.50
67 Shark Typhoon R	6.00	12.00
68 Startling Development C	.07	.15
69 Thieving Otter C	.07	.15
70 Voracious Greatshark R	.15	.30
71 Wingfold Pteron C	.07	.15
72 Wingspan Mentor U	.10	.20
73 Bastion of Remembrance U	2.00	4.00
74 Blitz Leech C	.07	.15
75 Blood Curdle C	.07	.15
76 Boot Nipper C	.07	.15
77 Bushmeat Poacher C	.07	.15
78 Call of the Death-Dweller U	.30	.75
79 Cavern Whisperer C	.07	.15
80 Chittering Harvester U	.10	.20
81 Corpse Churn C	.07	.15
82 Dark Bargain C	.07	.15
83 Dead Weight C	.07	.15
84 Dirge Bat R	.30	.60
85 Durable Coilbug C	.07	.15
86 Duskfang Mentor U	.10	.20
87 Easy Prey U	.10	.20
88 Extinction Event R	.50	1.00
89 Gloom Pangolin C	.07	.15
90 Grimdancer U	.10	.20
91 Heartless Act U	.75	1.50
92 Hunted Nightmare R	.15	.30
93 Insatiable Hemophage U	.10	.20
94 Lurking Deadeye C	.07	.15
95 Memory Leak C	.07	.15
96 Mutual Destruction C	.07	.15
97 Mythos of Nethroi R	.25	.50
98 Nightsquad Commando C	.07	.15
99 Serrated Scorpion C	.07	.15
100 Suffocating Fumes C	.07	.15
101 Unbreakable Bond U	.10	.20
102 Unexpected Fangs C	.07	.15
103 Unlikely Aid C	.07	.15
104 Void Beckoner U	.10	.20
105 Whisper Squad C	.07	.15
106 Zagoth Mamba U	.10	.20
107 Blazing Volley C	.07	.15
108 Blisterspit Gremlin C	.07	.15
109 Blitz of the Thunder-Raptor U	.10	.20
110 Cathartic Reunion C	.07	.15
111 Clash of Titans U	.10	.20
112 Cloudpiercer C	.07	.15
113 Drannith Stinger C	.07	.15
114 Everquill Phoenix R	.15	.30
115 Ferocious Tigorilla C	.07	.15
116 Fire Prophecy C	.07	.15
117 Flame Spill U	.10	.20
118 Footfall Crater U	.10	.20
119 Forbidden Friendship C	.07	.15
120 Frenzied Raptor C	.07	.15
121 Frillscare Mentor U	.10	.20
122 Go for Blood C	.07	.15
123 Heightened Reflexes C	.07	.15
124 Lava Serpent C	.07	.15
125 Lukka, Coppercoat Outcast M	1.25	2.50
126 Momentum Rumbler U	.10	.20
127 Mythos of Vadrok R	.15	.30
128 Porcuparrot U	.10	.20
129 Prickly Marmoset C	.07	.15
130 Pyroceratops C	.07	.15
131 Raking Claws C	.07	.15
132 Reptilian Reflection U	.10	.20
133 Rooting Moloch U	.10	.20
134 Rumbling Rockslide C	.07	.15
135 Sanctuary Smasher U	.10	.20
136 Shredded Sails C	.07	.15
137 Spelleater Wolverine C	.07	.15
138 Tentative Connection C	.07	.15
139 Unpredictable Cyclone R	.15	.30
140 Weaponize the Monsters U	.10	.20
141 Yidaro, Wandering Monster R	.15	.30
142 Adventurous Impulse C	.07	.15
143 Almighty Brushwagg C	.07	.15
144 Auspicious Starrix U	.10	.20
145 Barrier Breach U	.10	.20
146 Bristling Boar C	.07	.15
147 Charge of the Forever-Beast U	.10	.20
148 Colossification R	.20	.40
149 Essence Symbiote C	.07	.15
150 Excavation Mole C	.07	.15
151 Exuberant Wolfbear U	.10	.20
152 Fertilid C	.07	.15
153 Flycatcher Giraffid C	.07	.15
154 Fully Grown C	.07	.15
155 Gemrazer R	.30	.75
156 Glowstone Recluse U	.10	.20
157 Greater Sandwurm C	.07	.15
158 Honey Mammoth C	.07	.15
159 Hornbash Mentor U	.10	.20
160 Humble Naturalist C	.07	.15
161 Ivy Elemental U	.10	.20
162 Kogla, the Titan Ape R	.75	1.50
163 Lead the Stampede U	.10	.20
164 Migration Path U	.75	1.50
165 Migratory Greathorn C	.07	.15
166 Monstrous Step U	.10	.20
167 Mosscoat Goriak C	.07	.15
168 Mythos of Brokkos R	.15	.30
169 Plummet C	.07	.15
170 Ram Through C	.07	.15
171 Sudden Spinnerets C	.07	.15
172 Survivors' Bond C	.07	.15
173 Thwart the Enemy C	.07	.15
174 Titanoth Rex U	.10	.20
175 Vivien, Monsters' Advocate M	4.00	8.00
176 Wilt C	.07	.15
177 Back for More U	.10	.20
178 Boneyard Lurker U	.10	.20
179 Brokkos, Apex of Forever M	1.00	2.00
180 Channeled Force U	.10	.20
181 Chevill, Bane of Monsters M	1.00	2.00
182 Death's Oasis R	.15	.30
183 Dire Tactics U	.10	.20
184 Eerie Ultimatum R	2.00	4.00
185 Emergent Ultimatum R	.50	1.00
186 Frondland Felidar R	.15	.30
187 General Kudro of Drannith M	1.25	2.50
188 General's Enforcer U	.10	.20
189 Genesis Ultimatum R	.75	1.50
190 Illuna, Apex of Wishes M	2.00	1.50
191 Inspired Ultimatum R	.15	.30
192 Kinnan, Bonder Prodigy M	4.00	8.00
193 Labyrinth Raptor R	.15	.30
194 Lore Drakkis U	.10	.20
195 Narset of the Ancient Way M	3.00	1.50
196 Necropanther U	.10	.20
197 Nethroi, Apex of Death M	2.00	4.00
198 Offspring's Revenge R	.15	.30
199 Parcelbeast U	.10	.20
200 Primal Empathy U	.10	.20
201 Quartzwood Crasher R	.75	1.50
202 Regal Leosaur U	.10	.20
203 Rielle, the Everwise M	1.25	2.50
204 Ruinous Ultimatum R	2.50	5.00
205 Savai Thundermane U	.10	.20
206 Skull Prophet U	.10	.20
207 Skycat Sovereign R	.15	.30
208 Slitherwisp R	.15	.30
209 Snapdax, Apex of the Hunt M	.50	1.00
210 Song of Creation R	.15	.30
211 Sprite Dragon U	1.00	2.00
212 Titans' Nest R	.15	.30
213 Trumpeting Gnarr U	.10	.20
214 Vadrok, Apex of Thunder M	.50	1.00
215 Whirlwind of Thought R	.50	1.00
216 Winota, Joiner of Forces M	3.00	6.00
217 Zenith Flare U	.10	.20
218 Alert Heedbonder U	.10	.20
219 Cunning Nightbonder U	.10	.20
220 Fiend Artisan M	4.00	8.00
221 Gyruda, Doom of Depths R	.15	.30
222 Jegantha, the Wellspring R	.60	1.25
223 Jubilant Skybonder U	.10	.20
224 Kaheera, the Orphanguard R	.50	1.00
225 Keruga, the Macrosage R	.15	.30
226 Lurrus of the Dream-Den R	7.50	15.00
227 Lutri, the Spellchaser R	.15	.30
228 Obosh, the Preypiercer R	.30	.60
229 Proud Wildbonder U	.10	.20
230 Sonorous Howlbonder U	.10	.20
231 Umori, the Collector R	.15	.30
232 Yorion, Sky Nomad R	1.50	3.00
233 Zirda, the Dawnwaker R	.75	1.50
234 Crystalline Giant R	.30	.75
235 Indatha Crystal U	.10	.20
236 Ketria Crystal U	.10	.20
237 The Ozolith R	10.00	20.00
238 Raugrin Crystal U	.10	.20
239 Savai Crystal U	.10	.20
240 Sleeper Dart C	.07	.15
241 Springjaw Trap C	.07	.15
242 Zagoth Crystal U	.10	.20
243 Bloodfell Caves C	.07	.15
244 Blossoming Sands C	.07	.15
245 Bonder's Enclave R	1.25	2.50
246 Dismal Backwater C	.07	.15
247 Evolving Wilds C	.07	.15
248 Indatha Triome R	5.00	10.00
249 Jungle Hollow C	.07	.15
250 Ketria Triome R	7.50	15.00
251 Raugrin Triome R	7.50	15.00
252 Rugged Highlands C	.07	.15
253 Savai Triome R	6.00	12.00
254 Scoured Barrens C	.07	.15
255 Swiftwater Cliffs C	.07	.15
256 Thornwood Falls C	.07	.15
257 Tranquil Cove C	.07	.15
258 Wind-Scarred Crag C	.07	.15
259 Zagoth Triome R	7.50	15.00
260 Plains L	.07	.15
261 Plains L	.07	.15
262 Plains L	.07	.15
263 Island L	.07	.15
264 Island L	.07	.15
265 Island L	.07	.15
266 Swamp L	.07	.15
267 Swamp L	.07	.15
268 Swamp L	.07	.15
269 Mountain L	.07	.15
270 Mountain L	.07	.15
271 Mountain L	.07	.15
272 Forest L	.50	1.00
273 Forest L	.07	.15
274 Forest L	.07	.15
275 Zilortha, Strength Incarnate M	4.00	8.00
276 Lukka, Coppercoat Outcast M	1.50	3.00
277 Vivien, Monsters' Advocate M	5.00	10.00
278 Narset of the Ancient Way M	1.25	2.50
279 Cubwarden R	.30	.75
280 Huntmaster Liger U	.10	.20
281 Majestic Auricorn U	.10	.20
282 Vulpikeet C	.07	.15
283 Archipelagore U	.10	.20
284 Dreamtail Heron C	.07	.15
285 Pouncing Shoreshark U	.10	.20
286 Sea-Dasher Octopus R	.60	1.25
287 Cavern Whisperer C	.07	.15
288 Chittering Harvester U	.10	.20
289 Dirge Bat R	.30	.75
290 Insatiable Hemophage U	.10	.20
291 Cloudpiercer C	.07	.15
292 Everquill Phoenix R	.15	.30
293 Porcuparrot U	.10	.20
294 Auspicious Starrix U	.30	.60
295 Gemrazer R	1.00	2.00
296 Glowstone Recluse U	.10	.20
297 Migratory Greathorn C	.07	.15
298 Boneyard Lurker U	.10	.20
299 Brokkos, Apex of Forever M	2.00	4.00
300 Illuna, Apex of Wishes M	1.00	2.00
301 Lore Drakkis U	.10	.20
302 Necropanther U	.10	.20
303 Nethroi, Apex of Death M	2.00	4.00
304 Parcelbeast U :G:/:B:	.10	.20
305 Regal Leosaur U	.10	.20
306 Snapdax, Apex of the Hunt M	.75	1.50
307 Trumpeting Gnarr U	.10	.20
308 Vadrok, Apex of Thunder M	1.00	2.00
309 Indatha Triome R	6.00	12.00
310 Ketria Triome R	10.00	20.00
311 Raugrin Triome R	10.00	20.00
312 Savai Triome R	6.00	12.00
313 Zagoth Triome R	10.00	20.00
314 Drannith Magistrate R	6.00	12.00
315 Lavabrink Venturer R	.15	.30
316 Luminous Broodmoth M	10.00	20.00
317 Mythos of Snapdax R	1.50	3.00
318 Mythos of Illuna R	.75	1.50
319 Shark Typhoon R	10.00	20.00
320 Voracious Greatshark R	.75	1.50
321 Extinction Event R	2.00	4.00
322 Hunted Nightmare R	.20	.40
323 Mythos of Nethroi R	1.25	2.50
324 Mythos of Vadrok R	.20	.40
325 Unpredictable Cyclone R	.20	.40
326 Yidaro, Wandering Monster R	.75	1.50
327 Colossification R	1.00	2.00
328 Kogla, the Titan Ape R	3.00	6.00
329 Mythos of Brokkos R	.50	1.00
330 Chevill, Bane of Monsters M	3.00	6.00
331 Death's Oasis R	.25	.50
332 Eerie Ultimatum R	5.00	10.00
333 Emergent Ultimatum R	2.50	5.00
334 Frondland Felidar R	.25	.50
335 General Kudro of Drannith M	3.00	6.00
336 Genesis Ultimatum R	2.50	5.00
337 Inspired Ultimatum R	.50	1.00
338 Kinnan, Bonder Prodigy M	7.50	15.00
339 Labyrinth Raptor R	.30	.75
340 Offspring's Revenge R	.15	.30
341 Quartzwood Crasher R	2.00	4.00
342 Rielle, the Everwise M	4.00	8.00
343 Ruinous Ultimatum R	6.00	12.00
344 Skycat Sovereign R	.75	1.50
345 Slitherwisp R	.60	1.25
346 Song of Creation R	.75	1.50
347 Titans' Nest R	.30	.75
348 Whirlwind of Thought R	1.50	3.00
349 Winota, Joiner of Forces M	7.50	15.00
350 Fiend Artisan M	7.50	15.00
351 Gyruda, Doom of Depths R	.75	1.50
352 Jegantha, the Wellspring R	3.00	6.00
353 Kaheera, the Orphanguard R	2.50	5.00
354 Keruga, the Macrosage R	.60	1.25
355 Lurrus of the Dream-Den R	12.50	25.00
356 Lutri, the Spellchaser R	1.00	2.00
357 Obosh, the Preypiercer R	2.00	4.00
358 Umori, the Collector R	.75	1.50
359 Yorion, Sky Nomad R	6.00	12.00
360 Zirda, the Dawnwaker R	4.00	8.00

361 Crystalline Giant R 1.25 2.50
362 The Ozolith R 12.50 25.00
363 Bonder's Enclave R 2.50 5.00
364 Colossification R .50 1.00
365 Flourishing Fox U .25 .50
366 Heartless Act U 1.50 3.00
367 Forbidden Friendship C .20 .40
368 Migration Path U 1.00 2.00
369 Sprite Dragon U 2.00 4.00
370 King Caesar, Ancient Guardian U .20 .40
371 Mothra, Supersonic Queen M 25.00 50.00
372 Babygodzilla, Ruin Reborn U 1.00 2.00
373 Spacegodzilla, Death Corona U 3.00 6.00
374 Destoroyah, Perfect Lifeform R 2.50 5.00
375 Godzilla, Doom Inevitable R 7.50 15.00
376 Anguirus, Armored Killer R 3.00 6.00
377 Godzilla, Primeval Champion U 2.00 4.00
378 Bio-Quartz Spacegodzilla M 10.00 20.00
379 Ghidorah, King of the Cosmos M 30.00 60.00
380 Biollante, Plant Beast Form M 17.50 35.00
381 King Caesar, Awoken Titan M 6.00 12.00
382 Dorat, the Perfect Pet U 1.50 3.00
383 Rodan, Titan of Winged Fury M 10.00 20.00
384 Gigan, Cyberclaw Terror R 3.00 6.00
385 Mothra's Giant Cocoon C .20 .40
386 Battra, Terror of the City R 3.00 6.00
387 Mechagodzilla R 4.00 8.00

2020 Magic The Gathering Ikoria Lair of Behemoths Tokens

1 Cat .12 .25
2 Cat Bird .30 .60
3 Human Soldier .25 .50
4 Human Soldier .12 .25
5 Human Soldier .30 .60
6 Kraken .60 1.25
7 Shark .25 .50
8 Dinosaur .12 .25
9 Feather .30 .60
10 Beast .15 .30
11 Dinosaur Beast .20 .40
12 Narset of the Ancient Way Emblem 1.00 2.00
13 Companion .30 .60

2020 Magic The Gathering Judge Gift Rewards

1 Arena Rector R :W: 25.00 50.00
2 Enlightened Tutor R :W: 50.00 100.00
3 Spellseeker R :B: 50.00 100.00
4 Demonic Tutor :K: 100.00 200.00
5 Infernal Tutor R :K: 30.00 60.00
6 Gamble R :R: 20.00 40.00
7 Birthing Pod R :G: 25.00 50.00
8 Sylvan Tutor R :G: 50.00 100.00
9 Sterling Grove R :G:/:W: 15.00 30.00
10 Eye of Ugin R 15.00 30.00

2020 Magic The Gathering Jumpstart

1 Blessed Sanctuary R :W: .15 .30
2 Brightmare U :W: .10 .20
3 Emiel the Blessed M :W: 25.00 50.00
4 Release the Dogs U :W: .10 .20
5 Steel-Plume Marshal R :W: .15 .30
6 Stone Haven Pilgrim U :W: .10 .20
7 Supply Runners U :W: .10 .20
8 Trusty Retriever C :W: .07 .15
9 Archaeomender C :B: .07 .15
10 Bruvac the Grandiloquent M :B: 25.00 50.00
11 Corsair Captain R :B: .15 .30
12 Inniaz, the Gale Force R :B: .15 .30
13 Ormos, Archive Keeper R :B: .15 .30
14 Scholar of the Lost Trove R :B: .15 .30
15 Kels, Fight Fixer R :K: .15 .30
16 Nocturnal Feeder C :K: .07 .15
17 Tinybones, Trinket Thief M :K: 30.00 60.00
18 Witch of the Moors R :K: .15 .30
19 Chained Brute U :R: .10 .20
20 Immolating Gyre M :R: 4.00 8.00
21 Lightning Phoenix R :R: .15 .30
22 Lightning Visionary C :R: .07 .15
23 Living Lightning U :R: .10 .20
24 Muxus, Goblin Grandee R :R: .15 .30
25 Sethron, Hurloon General R :R: .15 .30
26 Spiteful Prankster U :R: .10 .20
27 Zurzoth, Chaos Rider R :R: .15 .30
28 Allosaurus Shepherd M :G: 60.00 125.00
29 Branching Evolution R :G: .15 .30
30 Neyith of the Dire Hunt R :G: .15 .30
31 Towering Titan M :G: 4.00 8.00
32 Lightning-Core Excavator C :G: .07 .15
33 Thriving Bluff C .07 .15
34 Thriving Grove C .07 .15
35 Thriving Heath C .07 .15
36 Thriving Isle C .07 .15
37 Thriving Moor C .07 .15
38 Plains L .07 .15
39 Plains L .07 .15
40 Plains L .07 .15
41 Plains L .07 .15
42 Plains L .07 .15
43 Plains L .07 .15
44 Plains L .07 .15
45 Plains L .07 .15
46 Island L .07 .15
47 Island L .07 .15
48 Island L .07 .15
49 Island L .07 .15
50 Island L .07 .15
51 Island L .07 .15
52 Island L .07 .15
53 Island L .07 .15
54 Swamp L .07 .15
55 Swamp L .07 .15
56 Swamp L .07 .15
57 Swamp L .07 .15
58 Swamp L .07 .15
59 Swamp L .07 .15
60 Swamp L .07 .15
61 Swamp L .07 .15
62 Mountain L .07 .15
63 Mountain L .07 .15
64 Mountain L .07 .15
65 Mountain L .07 .15
66 Mountain L .07 .15
67 Mountain L .07 .15
68 Mountain L .07 .15
69 Mountain L .07 .15
70 Forest L .07 .15
71 Forest L .07 .15
72 Forest L .07 .15
73 Forest L .07 .15
74 Forest L .07 .15
75 Forest L .07 .15
76 Forest L .07 .15
77 Forest L .07 .15
78 Terramorphic Expanse C .07 .15
79 Aegis of the Heavens U :W: .10 .20
80 Aerial Assault C :W: .07 .15
81 Affa Guard Hound U :W: .10 .20
82 Ajani's Chosen R :W: .15 .30
83 Alabaster Mage U :W: .10 .20
84 Angel of Mercy C :W: .07 .15
85 Angel of the Dire Hour R :W: .15 .30
86 Angelic Arbiter R :W: .15 .30
87 Angelic Edict C :W: .07 .15
88 Angelic Page C :W: .07 .15
89 Archon of Justice R :W: .15 .30
90 Archon of Redemption R :W: .15 .30
91 Battlefield Promotion C :W: .07 .15
92 Blessed Spirits U :W: .10 .20
93 Bulwark Giant C :W: .07 .15
94 Cathar's Companion C :W: .07 .15
95 Cathars' Crusade R :W: .15 .30
96 Celestial Mantle R :W: .15 .30
97 Cloudshift C :W: .07 .15
98 Cradle of Vitality R :W: .15 .30
99 Dauntless Onslaught U :W: .10 .20
100 Divine Arrow C :W: .07 .15
101 Duelist's Heritage R :W: .15 .30
102 Emancipation Angel U :W: .10 .20
103 Face of Divinity U :W: .10 .20
104 Forced Worship C :W: .07 .15
105 Fortify C :W: .07 .15
106 Gird for Battle U :W: .10 .20
107 Healer's Hawk C :W: .07 .15
108 High Sentinels of Arashin R :W: .15 .30
109 Indomitable Will C :W: .07 .15
110 Inspired Charge C :W: .07 .15
111 Inspiring Captain C :W: .07 .15
112 Inspiring Unicorn U :W: .10 .20
113 Isamaru, Hound of Konda R :W: .15 .30
114 Knight of the Tusk C :W: .07 .15
115 Knightly Valor C :W: .07 .15
116 Kor Spiritdancer R :W: .15 .30
117 Lena, Selfless Champion R :W: .15 .30
118 Lightwalker C :W: .07 .15
119 Linvala, Keeper of Silence M :W: 12.50 25.00
120 Long Road Home U :W: .10 .20
121 Mentor of the Meek R :W: .15 .30
122 Mesa Unicorn C :W: .07 .15
123 Mikaeus, the Lunarch M :W: 2.50 5.00
124 Moment of Heroism C :W: .07 .15
125 Pacifism C :W: .07 .15
126 Path of Bravery R :W: .15 .30
127 Path to Exile U :W: .10 .20
128 Patron of the Valiant U :W: .10 .20
129 Raise the Alarm C :W: .07 .15
130 Rhox Faithmender R :W: .15 .30
131 Ronom Unicorn C :W: .07 .15
132 Serra Angel U :W: .10 .20
133 Sky Tether U :W: .10 .20
134 Take Heart C :W: .07 .15
135 Tandem Tactics C :W: .07 .15
136 Valorous Stance U :W: .10 .20
137 Voice of the Provinces C :W: .07 .15
138 Aegis Turtle C :B: .07 .15
139 Battleground Geist U :B: .10 .20
140 Befuddle C :B: .07 .15
141 Belltower Sphinx U :B: .10 .20
142 Chart a Course U :B: .10 .20
143 Cloudreader Sphinx C :B: .07 .15
144 Coastal Piracy U :B: .10 .20
145 Crookclaw Transmuter C :B: .07 .15
146 Cryptic Serpent U :B: .10 .20
147 Curiosity U :B: .10 .20
148 Curious Obsession U :B: .10 .20
149 Departed Deckhand U :B: .10 .20
150 Erratic Visionary C :B: .07 .15
151 Essence Flux U :B: .10 .20
152 Exclude U :B: .10 .20
153 Exclusion Mage U :B: .10 .20
154 Kira, Great Glass-Spinner R :B: .15 .30
155 Kitesail Corsair C :B: .07 .15
156 Leave in the Dust C :B: .07 .15
157 Murmuring Phantasm C :B: .07 .15
158 Mystic Archaeologist R :B: .15 .30
159 Narcolepsy C :B: .07 .15
160 Nebelgast Herald U :B: .10 .20
161 Octoprophet C :B: .07 .15
162 Oneirophage U :B: .10 .20
163 Peel from Reality C :B: .07 .15
164 Prescient Chimera C :B: .07 .15
165 Prosperous Pirates C :B: .07 .15
166 Rattlechains R :B: .15 .30
167 Read the Runes R :B: .15 .30
168 Reckless Scholar U :B: .10 .20
169 Rhystic Study R :B: .15 .30
170 Rishadan Airship C :B: .07 .15
171 Sage's Row Savant C :B: .07 .15
172 Sailor of Means C :B: .07 .15
173 Sea Gate Oracle C :B: .07 .15
174 Selhoff Occultist C :B: .07 .15
175 Serendib Efreet R :B: .15 .30
176 Sharding Sphinx R :B: .15 .30
177 Sigiled Starfish U :B: .10 .20
178 Spectral Sailor U :B: .10 .20
179 Storm Sculptor C :B: .07 .15
180 Sweep Away C :B: .07 .15
181 Talrand, Sky Summoner R :B: .15 .30
182 Talrand's Invocation U :B: .10 .20
183 Thirst for Knowledge U :B: .10 .20
184 Thought Collapse C :B: .07 .15
185 Thought Scour C :B: .07 .15
186 Towering-Wave Mystic C :B: .07 .15
187 Vedalken Archmage R :B: .15 .30
188 Vedalken Entrancer C :B: .07 .15
189 Voyage's End C :B: .07 .15
190 Wall of Lost Thoughts U :B: .10 .20
191 Warden of Evos Isle U :B: .10 .20
192 Waterknot C :B: .07 .15
193 Whelming Wave R :B: .15 .30
194 Windreader Sphinx R :B: .15 .30
195 Windstorm Drake U :B: .10 .20
196 Winged Words C :B: .07 .15
197 Wishful Merfolk C :B: .07 .15
198 Wizard's Retort U :B: .10 .20
199 Agonizing Syphon C :K: .07 .15
200 Assassin's Strike U :K: .10 .20
201 Bake into a Pie C :K: .07 .15
202 Barter in Blood U :K: .10 .20
203 Black Cat C :K: .07 .15
204 Black Market R :K: .15 .30
205 Blighted Bat C :K: .07 .15
206 Blood Artist U :K: .10 .20
207 Blood Divination U :K: .10 .20
208 Blood Host U :K: .10 .20
209 Bloodbond Vampire U :K: .10 .20
210 Bloodhunter Bat C :K: .07 .15
211 Bogbrew Witch R :K: .15 .30
212 Bone Picker U :K: .10 .20
213 Bone Splinters C :K: .07 .15
214 Burglar Rat C :K: .07 .15
215 Cadaver Imp C :K: .07 .15
216 Cauldron Familiar C :K: .07 .15
217 Cemetery Recruitment C :K: .07 .15
218 Child of Night C :K: .07 .15
219 Corpse Hauler C :K: .07 .15
220 Corpse Traders U :K: .10 .20
221 Crow of Dark Tidings C :K: .07 .15
222 Death's Approach C :K: .07 .15
223 Douse in Gloom C :K: .07 .15
224 Drainpipe Vermin C :K: .07 .15
225 Drana, Liberator of Malakir M :K: 2.50 5.00
226 Dutiful Attendant C :K: .07 .15
227 Entomber Exarch U :K: .10 .20
228 Eternal Taskmaster U :K: .10 .20
229 Eternal Thirst C :K: .07 .15
230 Exhume U :K: .10 .20
231 Exquisite Blood R :K: .15 .30
232 Falkenrath Noble U :K: .10 .20
233 Fell Specter U :K: .10 .20
234 Festering Newt C :K: .07 .15
235 Funeral Rites C :K: .07 .15
236 Ghoulcaller Gisa M :K: 7.50 15.00
237 Ghoulcaller's Accomplice C :K: .07 .15
238 Ghoulraiser C :K: .07 .15
239 Gifted Aetherborn U :K: .10 .20
240 Gonti, Lord of Luxury R :K: .15 .30
241 Gravewaker R :K: .15 .30
242 Gristle Grinner U :K: .10 .20
243 Harvester of Souls R :K: .15 .30
244 Innocent Blood C :K: .07 .15
245 Kalastria Nightwatch C :K: .07 .15
246 Languish R :K: .15 .30
247 Last Gasp C :K: .07 .15
248 Launch Party C :K: .07 .15
249 Lawless Broker C :K: .07 .15
250 Liliana's Elite U :K: .10 .20
251 Liliana's Reaver R :K: .15 .30
252 Macabre Waltz C :K: .07 .15
253 Malakir Familiar U :K: .10 .20
254 Mark of the Vampire C :K: .07 .15
255 Mausoleum Turnkey U :K: .10 .20
256 Miasmic Mummy C :K: .07 .15
257 Mire Triton U :K: .10 .20
258 Nightshade Stinger C :K: .07 .15
259 Nyxathid R :K: .15 .30
260 Ogre Slumlord R :K: .15 .30
261 Oona's Blackguard U :K: .10 .20
262 Parasitic Implant C :K: .07 .15
263 Phyrexian Broodlings C :K: .07 .15
264 Phyrexian Debaser C :K: .07 .15
265 Phyrexian Gargantua U :K: .10 .20
266 Phyrexian Rager C :K: .07 .15
267 Phyrexian Reclamation U :K: .10 .20
268 Plagued Rusalka C :K: .07 .15
269 Ravenous Chupacabra U :K: .10 .20
270 Reanimate R :K: .15 .30
271 Rise of the Dark Realms M :K: 10.00 20.00
272 Sangromancer R :K: .15 .30
273 Sanitarium Skeleton C :K: .07 .15
274 Scourge of Nel Toth R :K: .15 .30
275 Sengir Vampire U :K: .10 .20
276 Settle the Score U :K: .10 .20
277 Shambling Goblin C :K: .07 .15
278 Sheoldred, Whispering One M :K: 12.50 25.00
279 Slate Street Ruffian C :K: .07 .15
280 Soul Salvage C :K: .07 .15
281 Stab Wound U :K: .10 .20
282 Swarm of Bloodflies U :K: .10 .20
283 Tempting Witch U :K: .10 .20
284 Tithebearer Giant C :K: .07 .15
285 Vampire Neonate C :K: .07 .15
286 Wailing Ghoul C :K: .07 .15
287 Wight of Precinct Six C :K: .07 .15
288 Zombie Infestation U :K: .10 .20
289 Act of Treason C :R: .07 .15
290 Ashmouth Hound C :R: .07 .15
291 Ball Lightning R :R: .15 .30
292 Barrage of Expendables U :R: .10 .20
293 Bathe in Dragonfire C :R: .07 .15
294 Beetleback Chief U :R: .10 .20
295 Blindblast C :R: .07 .15
296 Bloodrage Brawler U :R: .10 .20
297 Bloodrock Cyclops C :R: .07 .15
298 Bloodshot Trainee U :R: .10 .20
299 Boggart Brute C :R: .07 .15
300 Borderland Marauder C :R: .07 .15
301 Borderland Minotaur C :R: .07 .15
302 Chain Lightning U :R: .10 .20
303 Charmbreaker Devils R :R: .15 .30
304 Cinder Elemental U :R: .10 .20
305 Collateral Damage C :R: .07 .15
306 Dance with Devils U :R: .10 .20
307 Doublecast U :R: .10 .20
308 Draconic Roar U :R: .10 .20
309 Dragon Fodder C :R: .07 .15
310 Dragon Hatchling C :R: .07 .15
311 Dragonlord's Servant U :R: .10 .20
312 Dragonspeaker Shaman U :R: .10 .20
313 Dualcaster Mage R :R: .15 .30
314 Etali, Primal Storm R :R: .15 .30
315 Fanatical Firebrand C :R: .07 .15
316 Flame Lash C :R: .07 .15
317 Flames of the Firebrand U :R: .10 .20
318 Flames of the Raze-Boar U :R: .10 .20
319 Flametongue Kavu U :R: .10 .20
320 Fling C :R: .07 .15
321 Flurry of Horns C :R: .07 .15
322 Forge Devil C :R: .07 .15
323 Furnace Whelp U :R: .10 .20
324 Goblin Chieftain R :R: .15 .30
325 Goblin Commando U :R: .10 .20
326 Goblin Goon R :R: .15 .30
327 Goblin Instigator C :R: .07 .15
328 Goblin Lore U :R: .10 .20
329 Goblin Rally U :R: .10 .20
330 Goblin Shortcutter C :R: .07 .15
331 Grim Lavamancer R :R: .15 .30
332 Hamletback Goliath R :R: .15 .30
333 Heartfire C :R: .07 .15
334 Hellrider R :R: .15 .30
335 Homing Lightning U :R: .10 .20
336 Hungry Flames C :R: .07 .15
337 Inferno Hellion U :R: .10 .20
338 Kiln Fiend C :R: .07 .15
339 Krenko, Mob Boss R :R: .15 .30
340 Lathliss, Dragon Queen R :R: .15 .30
341 Lightning Axe U :R: .10 .20
342 Lightning Bolt U :R: .10 .20
343 Lightning Diadem C :R: .07 .15
344 Lightning Elemental C :R: .07 .15
345 Lightning Shrieker C :R: .07 .15
346 Magma Jet U :R: .10 .20
347 Magmaquake R :R: .15 .30
348 Makeshift Munitions U :R: .10 .20
349 Minotaur Skullcleaver C :R: .07 .15
350 Minotaur Sureshot C :R: .07 .15
351 Molten Ravager C :R: .07 .15
352 Mugging C :R: .07 .15
353 Ornery Goblin C :R: .07 .15
354 Outnumber C :R: .07 .15
355 Pillar of Flame C :R: .07 .15
356 Pyroclastic Elemental U :R: .10 .20
357 Rageblood Shaman R :R: .15 .30
358 Rapacious Dragon U :R: .10 .20
359 Riddle of Lightning U :R: .10 .20
360 Sarkhan's Rage C :R: .07 .15
361 Sarkhan's Unsealing R :R: .15 .30
362 Seismic Elemental U :R: .10 .20
363 Sin Prodder R :R: .15 .30
364 Spitting Earth C :R: .07 .15
365 Thermo-Alchemist C :R: .07 .15
366 Tibalt's Rager U :R: .10 .20
367 Torch Fiend C :R: .07 .15
368 Volcanic Fallout U :R: .10 .20
369 Volley Veteran U :R: .10 .20
370 Warfire Javelineer U :R: .10 .20
371 Weaver of Lightning U :R: .10 .20
372 Young Pyromancer U :R: .10 .20
373 Affectionate Indrik U :G: .10 .20
374 Aggressive Urge C :G: .07 .15
375 Ambassador Oak C :G: .07 .15
376 Arbor Armament C :G: .07 .15
377 Armorcraft Judge U :G: .10 .20
378 Assault Formation R :G: .15 .30
379 Awakener Druid U :G: .10 .20
380 Brindle Shoat U :G: .10 .20
381 Brushstrider U :G: .10 .20
382 Carven Caryatid U :G: .10 .20
383 Champion of Lambholt R :G: .15 .30
384 Commune with Dinosaurs C :G: .07 .15
385 Craterhoof Behemoth M :G: 25.00 50.00
386 Crushing Canopy C :G: .07 .15
387 Dawntreader Elk C :G: .07 .15
388 Drover of the Mighty U :G: .10 .20
389 Dwynen's Elite U :G: .10 .20
390 Elemental Uprising C :G: .07 .15
391 Elvish Archdruid R :G: .15 .30
392 Enlarge U :G: .10 .20
393 Explore C :G: .07 .15
394 Fa'adiyah Seer C :G: .07 .15
395 Feral Hydra U :G: .10 .20
396 Feral Invocation C :G: .07 .15
397 Feral Prowler C :G: .07 .15
398 Fertilid C :G: .07 .15
399 Ghalta, Primal Hunger R :G: .15 .30
400 Ghirapur Guide U :G: .10 .20
401 Grave Bramble C :G: .07 .15
402 Hunter's Insight U :G: .10 .20
403 Initiate's Companion C :G: .07 .15
404 Inspiring Call U :G: .10 .20
405 Ironshell Beetle C :G: .07 .15
406 Irresistible Prey U :G: .10 .20
407 Keeper of Fables U :G: .10 .20
408 Leaf Gilder C :G: .07 .15
409 Lifecrafter's Gift U :G: .10 .20
410 Lurking Predators R :G: .15 .30
411 Momentous Fall R :G: .15 .30
412 Nature's Way U :G: .10 .20
413 Nessian Hornbeetle U :G: .10 .20
414 New Horizons C :G: .07 .15
415 Oracle of Mul Daya R :G: .15 .30
416 Orazca Frillback C :G: .07 .15
417 Overgrown Battlement U :G: .10 .20
418 Penumbra Bobcat C :G: .07 .15
419 Pouncing Cheetah C :G: .07 .15
420 Presence of Gond C :G: .07 .15
421 Primeval Bounty M :G: 3.00 6.00
422 Primordial Sage R :G: .15 .30
423 Rampaging Brontodon R :G: .15 .30
424 Ravenous Baloth R :G: .15 .30
425 Rishkar, Peema Renegade R :G: .15 .30
426 Rumbling Baloth C :G: .07 .15
427 Savage Stomp U :G: .10 .20
428 Scrounging Bandar C :G: .07 .15
429 Selvala, Heart of the Wilds M :G: 12.50 25.00
430 Silhana Wayfinder U :G: .10 .20

431 Somberwald Stag U :G:	.10	.20
432 Soul of the Harvest R :G:	.15	.30
433 Sporemound C :G:	.07	.15
434 Sylvan Brushstrider C :G:	.07	.15
435 Sylvan Ranger C :G:	.07	.15
436 Thragtusk R :G:	.15	.30
437 Thundering Spineback U :G:	.10	.20
438 Time to Feed C :G:	.07	.15
439 Ulvenwald Hydra M :G:	3.00	6.00
440 Vastwood Zendikon C :G:	.07	.15
441 Verdant Embrace R :G:	.15	.30
442 Wall of Blossoms U :G:	.10	.20
443 Wall of Vines C :G:	.07	.15
444 Wildheart Invoker C :G:	.07	.15
445 Wildsize C :G:	.07	.15
446 Woodborn Behemoth U :G:	.10	.20
447 Wren's Run Vanquisher U :G:	.10	.20
448 Zendikar's Roil U :G:	.10	.20
449 Auger Spree C :K/:R:	.07	.15
450 Dinrova Horror U :B/:K:	.10	.20
451 Fusion Elemental U :W/:B/:K/:R/:G:	.10	.20
452 Ironroot Warlord U :G/:W:	.10	.20
453 Lawmage's Binding C :W/:B:	.07	.15
454 Maelstrom Archangel M :W/:B/:K/:R/:G:	2.00	4.00
455 Raging Regisaur U :R/:G:	.10	.20
456 Aether Spellbomb C	.07	.15
457 Alloy Myr C	.07	.15
458 Ancestral Statue C	.07	.15
459 Arcane Encyclopedia U	.10	.20
460 Bubbling Cauldron U	.10	.20
461 Chamber Sentry R	.15	.30
462 Chromatic Sphere C	.07	.15
463 Dragonloft Idol U	.10	.20
464 Dreamstone Hedron U	.10	.20
465 Gargoyle Sentinel U	.10	.20
466 Gingerbrute C	.07	.15
467 Guardian Idol U	.10	.20
468 Hedron Archive U	.10	.20
469 Herald's Horn U	.10	.20
470 Jousting Dummy C	.07	.15
471 Juggernaut U	.10	.20
472 Mana Geode C	.07	.15
473 Marauder's Axe C	.07	.15
474 Meteor Golem U	.10	.20
475 Myr Sire C	.07	.15
476 Perilous Myr U	.10	.20
477 Pirate's Cutlass C	.07	.15
478 Prophetic Prism C	.07	.15
479 Rogue's Gloves U	.10	.20
480 Roving Keep C	.07	.15
481 Runed Servitor C	.07	.15
482 Scarecrone R	.15	.30
483 Scroll of Avacyn C	.07	.15
484 Scuttlemutt U	.10	.20
485 Signpost Scarecrow C	.07	.15
486 Skittering Surveyor C	.07	.15
487 Suspicious Bookcase U	.10	.20
488 Terrarion C	.07	.15
489 Unstable Obelisk U	.10	.20
490 Warmonger's Chariot U	.10	.20
491 Buried Ruin U	.10	.20
492 Mirrodin's Core U	.10	.20
493 Phyrexian Tower R	.15	.30
494 Riptide Laboratory R	.15	.30
495 Rupture Spire C	.07	.15

2020 Magic The Gathering MagicFest

1 Path to Exile R	5.00	10.00
2 Plains R	1.25	2.50
3 Island R	2.00	4.00
4 Swamp R	2.50	5.00
5 Mountain R	1.25	2.50
6 Forest R	2.00	4.00

2020 Magic The Gathering Secret Lair Drop Series A Box of Rocks

201 Arcane Signet R	5.00	12.00
202 Chromatic Lantern R	4.00	10.00
203 Commander's Sphere R	2.50	6.00
204 Darksteel Ingot R	.60	1.50
205 Gilded Lotus R	1.50	4.00

2020 Magic The Gathering Secret Lair Drop Series A Box of Rocks Foil

201 Arcane Signet R	5.00	12.00
202 Chromatic Lantern R	4.00	10.00
203 Commander's Sphere R	2.50	6.00
204 Darksteel Ingot R	.60	1.50
205 Gilded Lotus R	1.50	4.00

2020 Magic The Gathering Secret Lair Drop Series April Fools

60 Storm Crow FOIL R	5.00	12.00
61 Goblin Snowman FOIL R	6.00	15.00
62 Mudhole FOIL R	2.00	5.00
537 Tibalt, the Fiend-Blooded FOIL M	10.00	25.00

2020 Magic The Gathering Secret Lair Drop Series Artist Series Seb McKinnon

119 Swamp R	2.50	6.00
120 Sower of Temptation R	2.00	5.00
121 Damnation R	12.00	30.00
122 Enchanted Evening R	1.25	3.00
539 Swamp R	2.50	6.00

2020 Magic The Gathering Secret Lair Drop Series Artist Series Seb McKinnon Foil

119 Swamp R	2.50	6.00
120 Sower of Temptation R	2.00	5.00
121 Damnation R	12.00	30.00
122 Enchanted Evening R	1.25	3.00
539 Swamp R	2.50	6.00

2020 Magic The Gathering Secret Lair Drop Series Can You Feel With A Heart Of Steel?

56 Arcbound Ravager FOIL R	6.00	15.00
57 Darksteel Colossus FOIL M	5.00	12.00
58 Walking Ballista FOIL R	15.00	40.00

2020 Magic The Gathering Secret Lair Drop Series Every Dog Has Its Day

96 Rest in Peace R	10.00	25.00
97 Dig Through Time R	4.00	10.00
98 Ancient Grudge R	5.00	12.00
99 Lightning Greaves R	20.00	50.00

2020 Magic The Gathering Secret Lair Drop Series Every Dog Has Its Day Foil

96 Rest in Peace R	10.00	25.00
97 Dig Through Time R	4.00	10.00
98 Ancient Grudge R	5.00	12.00
99 Lightning Greaves R	20.00	50.00

2020 Magic The Gathering Secret Lair Drop Series Extra Life 2020

164 Teferi's Protection FOIL R	20.00	50.00
165 Consecrated Sphinx FOIL R	15.00	40.00
166 Collected Company FOIL R	5.00	12.00
167 Amulet of Vigor FOIL R	20.00	50.00

2020 Magic The Gathering Secret Lair Drop Series Full Sleeves The Tattoo Pack

41 Spell Pierce R	3.00	8.00
42 Blood Artist R	3.00	8.00
43 Eternal Witness R	2.50	6.00
44 Pithing Needle R	2.00	5.00
45 Inkmoth Nexus R	12.00	30.00

2020 Magic The Gathering Secret Lair Drop Series Happy Little Gathering

100 Plains R	1.50	4.00
101 Plains R	1.00	2.50
102 Island R	2.00	5.00
103 Island R	1.00	2.50
104 Swamp R	2.00	5.00
105 Swamp R	2.50	6.00
106 Mountain R	2.00	5.00
107 Mountain R	2.00	5.00
108 Forest R	1.50	4.00
109 Forest R	2.00	5.00
538 Evolving Wilds R	2.50	6.00

2020 Magic The Gathering Secret Lair Drop Series Happy Little Gathering Foil

100 Plains R	1.50	4.00
101 Plains R	1.00	2.50
102 Island R	2.00	5.00
103 Island R	1.00	2.50
104 Swamp R	2.00	5.00
105 Swamp R	2.50	6.00
106 Mountain R	2.00	5.00
107 Mountain R	2.00	5.00
108 Forest R	1.50	4.00
109 Forest R	2.00	5.00
538 Evolving Wilds R	2.50	6.00

2020 Magic The Gathering Secret Lair Drop Series Happy Yargle Day!

110 Swords to Plowshares R	6.00	15.00
111 Opt R	2.50	6.00
112 Fatal Push R	12.00	30.00
113 Anger of the Gods R	1.25	3.00
114 Explore R	6.00	15.00

2020 Magic The Gathering Secret Lair Drop Series Happy Yargle Day! Foil

110 Swords to Plowshares R	6.00	15.00
111 Opt R	2.50	6.00
112 Fatal Push R	12.00	30.00
113 Anger of the Gods R	1.25	3.00
114 Explore R	6.00	15.00

2020 Magic The Gathering Secret Lair Drop Series Hope You Like Squirrels

195 Chatter of the Squirrel FOIL R	2.50	6.00
196 Krosan Beast FOIL R	4.00	10.00
197 Squirrel Mob FOIL R	4.00	10.00
198 Squirrel Wrangler FOIL R	2.00	5.00
199 Swarmyard FOIL R	20.00	50.00
200 Squirrel FOIL T	6.00	15.00

2020 Magic The Gathering Secret Lair Drop Series International Women's Day

51 Captain Sisay FOIL M	20.00	50.00
52 Meren of Clan Nel Toth FOIL M	15.00	40.00
53 Narset, Enlightened Master FOIL M	8.00	20.00
54 Oona, Queen of the Fae FOIL M	5.00	12.00
55 Saskia the Unyielding FOIL M	6.00	15.00

2020 Magic The Gathering Secret Lair Drop Series Mountains Go

83 Lightning Bolt FOIL R	3.00	8.00
84 Lightning Bolt FOIL R	3.00	8.00
85 Lightning Bolt FOIL R	2.50	6.00
86 Lightning Bolt FOIL R	3.00	8.00

2020 Magic The Gathering Secret Lair Drop Series Ornithological Studies

91 Swan Song R	10.00	25.00
92 Birds of Paradise R	5.00	12.00
93 Gilded Goose R	2.00	5.00
94 Baleful Strix R	4.00	10.00
95 Dovescape R	1.25	3.00

2020 Magic The Gathering Secret Lair Drop Series Party Hard Shred Harder

138 Anguished Unmaking R	5.00	12.00
139 Assassin's Trophy R	10.00	25.00
140 Decimate R	2.00	5.00
141 Dreadbore R	1.50	4.00
142 Thraximundar R	5.00	12.00

2020 Magic The Gathering Secret Lair Drop Series Prime Slime

133 Necrotic Ooze R	4.00	10.00
134 Acidic Slime R	3.00	8.00
135 Scavenging Ooze R	4.00	10.00
136 The Mimeoplasm M	3.00	8.00
137 Voidslime R	2.50	6.00

2020 Magic The Gathering Secret Lair Drop Series Showcase Zendikar Revisited

154 Admonition Angel M	15.00	40.00
155 Roil Elemental R	10.00	25.00
156 Zulaport Cutthroat R	12.00	30.00
157 Warren Instigator M	10.00	25.00
158 Avenger of Zendikar M	20.00	50.00

2020 Magic The Gathering Secret Lair Drop Series Showcase Zendikar Revisited Foil

154 Admonition Angel M	15.00	40.00
155 Roil Elemental R	10.00	25.00
156 Zulaport Cutthroat R	12.00	30.00
157 Warren Instigator M	10.00	25.00
158 Avenger of Zendikar M	20.00	50.00

2020 Magic The Gathering Secret Lair Drop Series Thalia Beyond the Helvault

37 Thalia, Guardian of Thraben FOIL R	3.00	8.00
38 Thalia, Guardian of Thraben FOIL R	2.50	6.00
39 Thalia, Guardian of Thraben FOIL R	2.00	5.00
40 Thalia, Guardian of Thraben FOIL R	4.00	10.00

2020 Magic The Gathering Secret Lair Drop Series The Godzilla Lands

63 Plains FOIL L	8.00	20.00
64 Island FOIL L	8.00	20.00
65 Swamp FOIL L	8.00	20.00
66 Mountain FOIL L	10.00	25.00
67 Forest FOIL L	10.00	25.00

2020 Magic The Gathering Secret Lair Drop Series The Path Not Traveled

87 Ajani Steadfast FOIL M	2.00	5.00
88 Domri Rade FOIL M	.60	1.50
89 Tamiyo, Field Researcher FOIL M	4.00	10.00
90 Vraska, Golgari Queen FOIL M	3.00	8.00

2020 Magic The Gathering Secret Lair Drop Series The Walking Dead

143 Rick, Steadfast Leader FOIL M	25.00	60.00
144 Daryl, Hunter of Walkers FOIL M	2.00	5.00
145 Glenn, the Voice of Calm FOIL M	2.00	5.00
146 Michonne, Ruthless Survivor FOIL M	1.00	2.50
147 Negan, the Cold-Blooded FOIL M	5.00	12.00
148 Walker (Bicycle Girl) FOIL T	.75	2.00
149 Walker (Well Walker) FOIL T	.60	1.50
150 Walker (Blade Walker) FOIL T	.60	1.50
151 Walker (Winslow) FOIL T	.75	2.00
152 Walker (Metal Head) FOIL T	.60	1.50
153 Treasure FOIL T	.75	2.00
581 Lucille FOIL M	6.00	15.00

2020 Magic The Gathering Secret Lair Drop Series Theros Stargazing Volume I

68 Heliod, God of the Sun M	3.00	8.00
69 Karametra, God of Harvests M	10.00	25.00
70 Iroas, God of Victory M	20.00	50.00

2020 Magic The Gathering Secret Lair Drop Series Theros Stargazing Volume II

71 Thassa, God of the Sea FOIL M	10.00	25.00
72 Ephara, God of the Polis FOIL M	4.00	10.00
73 Kruphix, God of Horizons FOIL M	10.00	25.00

2020 Magic The Gathering Secret Lair Drop Series Theros Stargazing Volume III

74 Erebos, God of the Dead FOIL M	12.00	30.00
75 Phenax, God of Deception FOIL M	15.00	40.00
76 Athreos, God of Passage FOIL M	20.00	50.00

2020 Magic The Gathering Secret Lair Drop Series Theros Stargazing Volume IV

77 Purphoros, God of the Forge FOIL M	20.00	50.00
78 Mogis, God of Slaughter FOIL M	2.50	6.00
79 Keranos, God of Storms FOIL M	4.00	10.00

2020 Magic The Gathering Secret Lair Drop Series Theros Stargazing Volume V

80 Nylea, God of the Hunt FOIL M	10.00	25.00
81 Xenagos, God of Revels FOIL M	12.00	30.00
82 Pharika, God of Affliction FOIL M	2.00	5.00

2020 Magic The Gathering Secret Lair Drop Series Year of the Rat

33 Ink-Eyes, Servant of Oni FOIL R	10.00	25.00
34 Marrow-Gnawer FOIL R	25.00	60.00
35 Pack Rat FOIL R	8.00	20.00
36 Rat Colony FOIL R	5.00	12.00

2020 Magic The Gathering Secret Lair Ultimate Edition

1 Marsh Flats R	20.00	40.00
2 Scalding Tarn R	30.00	75.00
3 Verdant Catacombs R	30.00	75.00
4 Arid Mesa R	20.00	40.00
5 Misty Rainforest R	30.00	75.00
11 Barkchannel Pathway // Tidechannel Pathway R	5.00	12.00
12 Blightstep Pathway // Searstep Pathway R	5.00	10.00
13 Branchloft Pathway // Boulderloft Pathway R	3.00	6.00
14 Brightclimb Pathway // Grimclimb Pathway R	5.00	10.00
15 Clearwater Pathway // Murkwater Pathway R	5.00	10.00
16 Cragcrown Pathway // Timbercrown Pathway R	3.00	6.00
17 Darkbore Pathway // Slitherbore Pathway R	6.00	12.00
18 Hengegate Pathway // Mistgate Pathway R	4.00	8.00
19 Needleverge Pathway // Pillarverge Pathway R	4.00	8.00
20 Riverglide Pathway // Lavaglide Pathway R	6.00	12.00
504 Blast Zone R	5.00	10.00

2020 Magic The Gathering Signature Spellbook Chandra

1 Chandra, Torch of Defiance M :R:	4.00	8.00
2 Past in Flames R :R:	.20	.40
3 Fiery Confluence R :R:	.75	1.50
4 Past in Flames M :R:	1.25	2.50
5 Pyroblast R :R:	1.25	2.50
6 Pyromancer Ascension R :R:	.20	.40
7 Rite of Flame R :R:	.30	.60
8 Young Pyromancer R :R:	.30	.75

2020 Magic The Gathering Theros Beyond Death

1 Alseid of Life's Bounty U :W:	.10	.20
2 Archon of Falling Stars U :W:	.10	.20
3 Archon of Sun's Grace R :W:	.15	.30
4 Banishing Light U :W:	.10	.20
5 The Birth of Meletis U :W:	.10	.20
6 Captivating Unicorn C :W:	.07	.15
7 Commanding Presence U :W:	.10	.20
8 Dawn Evangel U :W:	.10	.20
9 Daxos, Blessed by the Sun U :W:	.10	.20
10 Daybreak Chimera C :W:	.07	.15
11 Dreadful Apathy C :W:	.07	.15
12 Eidolon of Obstruction R :W:	.15	.30
13 Elspeth Conquers Death R :W:	.15	.30
14 Elspeth, Sun's Nemesis M :W:	2.50	5.00
15 Favored of Iroas U :W:	.10	.20
16 Flicker of Fate C :W:	.07	.15
17 Glory Bearers C :W:	.07	.15
18 Heliod, Sun-Crowned M :W:	7.50	15.00
19 Heliod's Intervention R :W:	.15	.30
20 Heliod's Pilgrim C :W:	.07	.15
21 Heliod's Punishment U :W:	.10	.20
22 Hero of the Pride C :W:	.07	.15
23 Hero of the Winds U :W:	.10	.20
24 Idyllic Tutor R :W:	.15	.30
25 Indomitable Will C :W:	.07	.15
26 Karametra's Blessing C :W:	.07	.15
27 Lagonna-Band Storyteller U :W:	.10	.20
28 Leonin of the Lost Pride C :W:	.07	.15
29 Nyxborn Courser C :W:	.07	.15
30 Omen of the Sun C :W:	.07	.15
31 Phalanx Tactics U :W:	.10	.20
32 Pious Wayfarer C :W:	.07	.15
33 Reverent Hoplite U :W:	.10	.20
34 Revoke Existence C :W:	.07	.15
35 Rumbling Sentry C :W:	.07	.15
36 Sentinel's Eyes C :W:	.07	.15
37 Shatter the Sky R :W:	.15	.30
38 Sunmane Pegasus C :W:	.07	.15
39 Taranika, Akroan Veteran R :W:	.15	.30
40 Transcendent Envoy C :W:	.07	.15
41 Triumphant Surge C :W:	.07	.15
42 Alirios, Enraptured U :B:	.10	.20
43 Ashiok's Erasure R :B:	.15	.30
44 Brine Giant C :B:	.07	.15
45 Callaphe, Beloved of the Sea U :B:	.10	.20
46 Chain to Memory C :B:	.07	.15
47 Deny the Divine C :B:	.07	.15
48 Eidolon of Philosophy C :B:	.07	.15
49 Elite Instructor C :B:	.07	.15
50 Glimpse of Freedom U :B:	.10	.20
51 Ichthyomorphosis C :B:	.07	.15
52 Kiora Bests the Sea God M :B:	1.50	3.00
53 Medomai's Prophecy U :B:	.10	.20
54 Memory Drain C :B:	.07	.15
55 Nadir Kraken R :B:	.15	.30
56 Naiad of Hidden Coves C :B:	.07	.15
57 Nyxborn Seaguard C :B:	.07	.15
58 Omen of the Sea C :B:	.07	.15
59 One with the Stars U :B:	.10	.20
60 Protean Thaumaturge R :B:	.15	.30
61 Riptide Turtle C :B:	.07	.15
62 Sage of Mysteries U :B:	.10	.20
63 Sea God's Scorn U :B:	.10	.20
64 Shimmerwing Chimera U :B:	.10	.20
65 Shoal Kraken U :B:	.10	.20
66 Sleep of the Dead C :B:	.07	.15
67 Starlit Mantle C :B:	.07	.15
68 Stern Dismissal C :B:	.07	.15
69 Stinging Lionfish U :B:	.10	.20
70 Sweet Oblivion U :B:	.10	.20
71 Thassa, Deep-Dwelling M :B:	6.00	12.00
72 Thassa's Intervention R :B:	.15	.30
73 Thassa's Oracle R :B:	.15	.30
74 Thirst for Meaning C :B:	.07	.15
75 Threnody Singer U :B:	.10	.20
76 Thryx, the Sudden Storm R :B:	.15	.30
77 Towering-Wave Mystic C :B:	.07	.15
78 Triton Waverider C :B:	.07	.15
79 Vexing Gull C :B:	.07	.15
80 Wavebreak Hippocamp R :B:	.15	.30
81 Whirlwind Denial U :B:	.10	.20
82 Witness of Tomorrows C :B:	.07	.15
83 Agonizing Remorse U :K:	.10	.20
84 Aphemia, the Cacophony R :K:	.15	.30
85 Aspect of Lamprey C :K:	.07	.15
86 Blight-Breath Catoblepas C :K:	.07	.15
87 Cling to Dust U :K:	.10	.20
88 Discordant Piper C :K:	.07	.15
89 Drag to the Underworld U :K:	.10	.20
90 Eat to Extinction R :K:	.15	.30
91 Elspeth's Nightmare U :K:	.10	.20
92 Enemy of Enlightenment U :K:	.10	.20
93 Erebos, Bleak-Hearted M :K:	2.00	4.00
94 Erebos's Intervention R :K:	.15	.30
95 Final Death C :K:	.07	.15
96 Fruit of Tizerus C :K:	.07	.15
97 Funeral Rites C :K:	.07	.15
98 Gravebreaker Lamia R :K:	.15	.30
99 Gray Merchant of Asphodel U :K:	.10	.20
100 Grim Physician C :K:	.07	.15
101 Hateful Eidolon U :K:	.10	.20
102 Inevitable End U :K:	.10	.20
103 Lampad of Death's Vigil C :K:	.07	.15
104 Minion's Return U :K:	.10	.20
105 Mire Triton U :K:	.10	.20
106 Mire's Grasp C :K:	.07	.15
107 Mogis's Favor C :K:	.07	.15
108 Nightmare Shepherd R :K:	.15	.30
109 Nyxborn Marauder C :K:	.07	.15
110 Omen of the Dead C :K:	.07	.15
111 Pharika's Libation C :K:	.07	.15
112 Pharika's Spawn U :K:	.10	.20

113 Rage-Scarred Berserker C :K: .07 .15
114 Scavenging Harpy C :K: .07 .15
115 Soulreaper of Mogis C :K: .07 .15
116 Temple Thief C :K: .07 .15
117 Treacherous Blessing R :K: .15 .30
118 Tymaret Calls the Dead R :K: .15 .30
119 Tymaret, Chosen from Death U :K: .10 .20
120 Underworld Charger C :K: .07 .15
121 Underworld Dreams U :K: .10 .20
122 Venomous Hierophant C :K: .07 .15
123 Woe Strider R :K: .15 .30
124 The Akroan War R :R: .15 .30
125 Anax, Hardened in the Forge U :R: .10 .20
126 Arena Trickster C :R: .07 .15
127 Aspect of Manticore C :R: .07 .15
128 Blood Aspirant U :R: .10 .20
129 Careless Celebrant U :R: .10 .20
130 Dreamshaper Shaman U :R: .10 .20
131 Dreamstalker Manticore U :R: .10 .20
132 Escape Velocity U :R: .10 .20
133 Fateful End U :R: .10 .20
134 Final Flare C :R: .07 .15
135 Flummoxed Cyclops C :R: .07 .15
136 Furious Rise U :R: .10 .20
137 Hero of the Games C :R: .07 .15
138 Heroes of the Revel U :R: .10 .20
139 Impending Doom U :R: .10 .20
140 Incendiary Oracle C :R: .07 .15
141 Infuriate C :R: .07 .15
142 Iroas's Blessing C :R: .07 .15
143 Irreverent Revelers C :R: .07 .15
144 Nyxborn Brute C :R: .07 .15
145 Omen of the Forge C :R: .07 .15
146 Oread of Mountain's Blaze C :R: .07 .15
147 Ox of Agonas M :R: 2.00 4.00
148 Phoenix of Ash R :R: .15 .30
149 Portent of Betrayal C :R: .07 .15
150 Purphoros, Bronze-Blooded M :R: 2.00 4.00
151 Purphoros's Intervention R :R: .15 .30
152 Satyr's Cunning C :R: .07 .15
153 Skophos Maze-Warden U :R: .10 .20
154 Skophos Warleader C :R: .07 .15
155 Stampede Rider C :R: .07 .15
156 Storm Herald R :R: .15 .30
157 Storm's Wrath R :R: .15 .30
158 Tectonic Giant R :R: .15 .30
159 Thrill of Possibility C :R: .07 .15
160 The Triumph of Anax U :R: .10 .20
161 Underworld Breach R :R: .15 .30
162 Underworld Fires U :R: .10 .20
163 Underworld Rage-Hound C :R: .07 .15
164 Wrap in Flames C :R: .07 .15
165 Arasta of the Endless Web R :G: .15 .30
166 The Binding of the Titans U :G: .10 .20
167 Chainweb Aracnir U :G: .10 .20
168 Destiny Spinner U :G: .10 .20
169 Dryad of the Ilysian Grove R :G: .15 .30
170 The First Iroan Games R :G: .15 .30
171 Gift of Strength C :G: .07 .15
172 Hydra's Growth U :G: .10 .20
173 Hyrax Tower Scout C :G: .07 .15
174 Ilysian Caryatid C :G: .07 .15
175 Inspire Awe C :G: .07 .15
176 Klothys's Design U :G: .10 .20
177 Loathsome Chimera C :G: .07 .15
178 Mantle of the Wolf R :G: .15 .30
179 Moss Viper C :G: .07 .15
180 Mystic Repeal U :G: .10 .20
181 Nessian Boar R :G: .15 .30
182 Nessian Hornbeetle U :G: .10 .20
183 Nessian Wanderer U :G: .10 .20
184 Nexus Wardens C :G: .07 .15
185 Nylea, Keen-Eyed M :G: 2.50 5.00
186 Nylea's Forerunner C :G: .07 .15
187 Nylea's Huntmaster C :G: .07 .15
188 Nylea's Intervention R :G: .15 .30
189 Nyx Herald U :G: .10 .20
190 Nyxbloom Ancient M :G: 7.50 15.00
191 Nyxborn Colossus C :G: .07 .15
192 Omen of the Hunt C :G: .07 .15
193 Pheres-Band Brawler U :G: .10 .20
194 Plummet C :G: .07 .15
195 Relentless Pursuit C :G: .07 .15
196 Renata, Called to the Hunt U :G: .10 .20
197 Return to Nature C :G: .07 .15
198 Setessan Champion R :G: .15 .30
199 Setessan Petitioner U :G: .10 .20
200 Setessan Skirmisher C :G: .07 .15
201 Setessan Training C :G: .07 .15
202 Skola Grovedancer C :G: .07 .15
203 Voracious Typhon C :G: .07 .15
204 Warbriar Blessing C :G: .07 .15
205 Wolfwillow Haven U :G: .10 .20
206 Acolyte of Affliction U :K/:G: .10 .20
207 Allure of the Unknown R :K/:R: .15 .30
208 Ashiok, Nightmare Muse M :B/:K: 4.00 8.00
209 Atris, Oracle of Half-Truths R :B/:K: .15 .30
210 Bronzehide Lion R :G/:W: .15 .30
211 Calix, Destiny's Hand M :G/:W: 2.00 4.00
212 Dalakos, Crafter of Wonders R :B/:R: .15 .30
213 Devourer of Memory U :B/:K: .10 .20
214 Dream Trawler R :W/:B: .15 .30
215 Enigmatic Incarnation R :G/:B: .15 .30
216 Eutropia the Twice-Favored U :G/:B: .10 .20
217 Gallia of the Endless Dance R :R/:G: .15 .30
218 Haktos the Unscarred R :R/:W: .15 .30
219 Hero of the Nyxborn U :R/:W: .10 .20
220 Klothys, God of Destiny M :R/:G: 3.00 6.00
221 Kroxa, Titan of Death's Hunger M :K/:R: 10.00 20.00
222 Kunoros, Hound of Athreos R :W/:K: .15 .30
223 Mischievous Chimera U :B/:R: .10 .20
224 Polukranos, Unchained M :K/:G: 2.00 4.00
225 Rise to Glory U :W/:K: .10 .20
226 Siona, Captain of the Pyleas U :G/:W: .10 .20
227 Slaughter-Priest of Mogis U :K/:R: .10 .20
228 Staggering Insight U :W/:B: .10 .20
229 Uro, Titan of Nature's Wrath M :G/:B: 20.00 40.00
230 Warden of the Chained U :R/:G: .10 .20
231 Altar of the Pantheon C .07 .15
232 Bronze Sword C .07 .15
233 Entrancing Lyre U .10 .20
234 Mirror Shield U .10 .20
235 Nyx Lotus R .15 .30
236 Shadowspear R .15 .30
237 Soul-Guide Lantern U .10 .20
238 Thaumaturge's Familiar C .07 .15
239 Thundering Chariot U .10 .20
240 Traveler's Amulet C .07 .15
241 Wings of Hubris C .07 .15
242 Field of Ruin U .10 .20
243 Labyrinth of Skophos R .15 .30
244 Temple of Abandon R .15 .30
245 Temple of Deceit R .15 .30
246 Temple of Enlightenment R .15 .30
247 Temple of Malice R .15 .30
248 Temple of Plenty R .15 .30
249 Unknown Shores C .07 .15
250 Plains L .07 .15
251 Island L .07 .15
252 Swamp L .07 .15
253 Mountain L .07 .15
254 Forest L .07 .15
255 Elspeth, Sun's Nemesis M :W: 2.50 5.00
256 Ashiok, Nightmare Muse M :B/:K: 4.00 8.00
257 Calix, Destiny's Hand M :G/:W: 2.00 4.00
258 Daxos, Blessed by the Sun U :W: .10 .20
259 Heliod, Sun-Crowned M :W: 7.50 15.00
260 Callaphe, Beloved of the Sea U :B: .10 .20
261 Thassa, Deep-Dwelling M :B: 7.50 15.00
262 Erebos, Bleak-Hearted M :K: 2.00 4.00
263 Tymaret, Chosen from Death U :K: .10 .20
264 Anax, Hardened in the Forge U :R: .10 .20
265 Purphoros, Bronze-Blooded M :R: 2.00 4.00
266 Nylea, Keen-Eyed M :G: 2.50 5.00
267 Renata, Called to the Hunt U :G: .10 .20
268 Klothys, God of Destiny M :R/:G: 2.50 5.00
269 Athreos, Shroud-Veiled M :W/:K: 3.00 6.00
270 Elspeth, Undaunted Hero M :W: .75 1.50
271 Eidolon of Inspiration U :W: .10 .20
272 Elspeth's Devotee R :W: .15 .30
273 Sunlit Hoplite C :W: .07 .15
274 Ashiok, Sculptor of Fears M :B/:K: .75 1.50
275 Swimmer in Nightmares U :B: .10 .20
276 Mindwrack Harpy C :K: .07 .15
277 Ashiok's Forerunner R :B/:K: .15 .30
278 Plains L .07 .15
279 Plains L .07 .15
280 Island L .07 .15
281 Island L .07 .15
282 Swamp L .07 .15
283 Swamp L .07 .15
284 Mountain L .07 .15
285 Mountain L .07 .15
286 Forest L .07 .15
287 Forest L .07 .15
288 Grasping Giant R :W: .15 .30
289 Victory's Envoy R :W: .15 .30
290 Sphinx Mindbreaker R :B: .15 .30
291 Serpent of Yawning Depths R :B: .15 .30
292 Demon of Loathing R :K: .15 .30
293 Underworld Sentinel R :K: .15 .30
294 Deathbellow War Cry R :R: .15 .30
295 Terror of Mount Velus R :R: .15 .30
296 Ironscale Hydra R :G: .15 .30
297 Treeshaker Chimera R :G: .15 .30
298 Archon of Sun's Grace R :W: .15 .30
299 Eidolon of Obstruction R :W: .15 .30
300 Heliod's Intervention R :W: .15 .30
301 Idyllic Tutor R :W: .15 .30
302 Shatter the Sky R :W: .15 .30
303 Taranika, Akroan Veteran R :W: .15 .30
304 Ashiok's Erasure R :B: .15 .30
305 Nadir Kraken R :B: .15 .30
306 Protean Thaumaturge R :B: .15 .30
307 Thassa's Intervention R :B: .15 .30
308 Thassa's Oracle R :B: .15 .30
309 Thryx, the Sudden Storm R :B: .15 .30
310 Wavebreak Hippocamp R :B: .15 .30
311 Aphemia, the Cacophony R :K: .15 .30
312 Eat to Extinction R :K: .15 .30
313 Erebos's Intervention R :K: .15 .30
314 Gravebreaker Lamia R :K: .15 .30
315 Nightmare Shepherd R :K: .15 .30
316 Treacherous Blessing R :K: .15 .30
317 Woe Strider R :K: .15 .30
318 Ox of Agonas M :R: 5.00 10.00
319 Phoenix of Ash R :R: .15 .30
320 Purphoros's Intervention R :R: .15 .30
321 Storm Herald R :R: .15 .30
322 Storm's Wrath R :R: .15 .30
323 Tectonic Giant R :R: .15 .30
324 Underworld Breach R :R: .15 .30
325 Arasta of the Endless Web R :G: .15 .30
326 Dryad of the Ilysian Grove R :G: .15 .30
327 Mantle of the Wolf R :G: .15 .30
328 Nessian Boar R :G: .15 .30
329 Nylea's Intervention R :G: .15 .30
330 Nyxbloom Ancient M :G: 12.50 25.00
331 Setessan Champion R :G: .15 .30
332 Allure of the Unknown R :K/:R: .15 .30
333 Atris, Oracle of Half-Truths R :B/:K: .15 .30
334 Bronzehide Lion R :G/:W: .15 .30
335 Dalakos, Crafter of Wonders R :B/:R: .15 .30
336 Dream Trawler R :W/:B: .15 .30
337 Enigmatic Incarnation R :G/:B: .15 .30
338 Gallia of the Endless Dance R :R/:G: .15 .30
339 Haktos the Unscarred R :R/:W: .15 .30
340 Kroxa, Titan of Death's Hunger M :K/:R: 15.00 30.00
341 Kunoros, Hound of Athreos R :W/:K: .15 .30
342 Polukranos, Unchained M :K/:G: 3.00 6.00
343 Uro, Titan of Nature's Wrath M :G/:B: 30.00 60.00
344 Nyx Lotus R .15 .30
345 Shadowspear R .15 .30
346 Labyrinth of Skophos R .15 .30
347 Temple of Abandon R .15 .30
348 Temple of Deceit R .15 .30
349 Temple of Enlightenment R .15 .30
350 Temple of Malice R .15 .30
351 Temple of Plenty R .15 .30
352 Arasta of the Endless Web R :G: .15 .30
353 Alseid of Life's Bounty U :W: .10 .20
354 Thirst for Meaning C :B: .07 .15
355 Gray Merchant of Asphodel U :K: .10 .20
356 Thrill of Possibility C :R: .07 .15
357 Wolfwillow Haven U :G: .10 .20

2020 Magic The Gathering Theros Beyond Death Tokens

1 Goat .10 .20
2 Human Soldier .10 .20
3 Pegasus .15 .30
4 Kraken .12 .25
5 Reflection .12 .25
6 Tentacle .20 .40
7 Zombie .12 .25
8 Elemental .12 .25
9 Satyr .10 .20
10 Spider .12 .25
11 Wolf .10 .20
12 Nightmare .20 .40
13 Gold .10 .20
14 Wall .10 .20

2020 Magic The Gathering Unsanctioned

1 Adorable Kitten C .07 .15
2 AWOL C .07 .15
3 Emcee U .10 .20
4 Flavor Judge R .15 .30
5 Frankie Peanuts R .15 .30
6 GO TO JAIL C .07 .15
7 Humming C .07 .15
8 Knight of the Hokey Pokey C .07 .15
9 Look at Me, I'm R&D R .15 .30
10 Look at Me, I'm the DCI R .15 .30
11 Old Guard C .07 .15
12 Ordinary Pony C .07 .15
13 Staying Power R .15 .30
14 Strutting Turkey U .10 .20
15 Syr Cadian, Knight Owl R .15 .30
16 Alexander Clamilton R .15 .30
17 Avatar of Me R .15 .30
18 B.O.B. (Bevy of Beebles) M 1.00 2.00
19 Carnivorous Death-Parrot C .07 .15
20 Cheatyface U .10 .20
21 Chicken à la King R .15 .30
22 Common Courtesy U .10 .20
23 Johnny, Combo Player R .15 .30
24 Magic Word C .07 .15
25 Mer Man C .07 .15
26 Richard Garfield, Ph.D. R .15 .30
27 Rings a Bell U .10 .20
28 Time Out C .07 .15
29 Topsy Turvy U .10 .20
30 Wall of Fortune C .07 .15
31 Acornelia, Fashionable Filcher R .15 .30
32 Bat- U .10 .20
33 Booster Tutor U .10 .20
34 Dirty Rat C .07 .15
35 Duh C .07 .15
36 Enter the Dungeon R .15 .30
37 Hoisted Hireling C .07 .15
38 Infernal Spawn of Evil R .15 .30
39 Infernal Spawn of Infernal Spawn of Evil R .15 .30
40 Infernius Spawnington III, Esq. R .15 .30
41 Inhumaniac U .10 .20
42 Jumbo Imp U .10 .20
43 Poultrygeist C .07 .15
44 Skull Saucer U .10 .20
45 Snickering Squirrel C .07 .15
46 Stinging Scorpion C .07 .15
47 Abstract Iguanart U .10 .20
48 Blast from the Past R .15 .30
49 Boomstacker R .15 .30
50 Common Iguana C .07 .15
51 Goblin Haberdasher U .10 .20
52 Goblin S.W.A.T. Team C .07 .15
53 Goblin Tutor U .10 .20
54 Infinity Elemental M 1.00 2.00
55 Painiac C .07 .15
56 Six-y Beast U .10 .20
57 Stet, Draconic Proofreader R .15 .30
58 Strategy, Schmategy R .15 .30
59 Super-Duper Death Ray U .10 .20
60 Yet Another Aether Vortex R .15 .30
61 B-I-N-G-O R .15 .30
62 Elvish Impersonators C .07 .15
63 Free-Range Chicken C .07 .15
64 Growth Spurt C .07 .15
65 Half-Squirrel, Half U .10 .20
66 Mother Kangaroo C .07 .15
67 Old Fogey R .15 .30
68 Pippa, Duchess of Dice R .15 .30
69 Slaying Mantis U .10 .20
70 Spirit of the Season U .10 .20
71 Squirrel Farm R .15 .30
72 Surgeon General Commander M 1.00 2.00
73 Timmy, Power Gamer R .15 .30
74 Wild Crocodile C .07 .15
75 Who // What // When // Where // Why R .15 .30
76 Bronze Calendar U .10 .20
77 Entirely Normal Armchair U .10 .20
78 Jack-in-the-Mox R .15 .30
79 Krark's Other Thumb U .10 .20
80 Paper Tiger C .07 .15
81 Pointy Finger of Doom R .15 .30
82 Rock Lobster C .07 .15
83 Scissors Lizard C .07 .15
84 Sword of Dungeons & Dragons M 1.00 2.00
85 Water Gun Balloon Game R .15 .30
86 Underdome C .07 .15
87 Plains L .07 .15
88 Plains L FULL ART .07 .15
89 Island L .07 .15
90 Island L FULL ART .07 .15
91 Swamp L .07 .15
92 Swamp L FULL ART .07 .15
93 Mountain L .07 .15
94 Mountain L FULL ART .07 .15
95 Forest L .07 .15
96 Forest L FULL ART .07 .15

2020 Magic The Gathering Unsanctioned Tokens

1 Beeble .12 .25
2 Goblin .12 .25
3 Squirrel .12 .25
4 Dragon .12 .25
5 Giant Teddy Bear .12 .25
6 Acorn Stash .12 .25

2020 Magic The Gathering Zendikar Rising

1 Allied Assault U :W: .10 .20
2 Angel of Destiny M :W: 3.00 6.00
3 Angelheart Protector C :W: .07 .15
4 Archon of Emeria R :W: .15 .30
5 Archpriest of Iona R :W: .15 .30
6 Attended Healer U :W: .10 .20
7 Canyon Jerboa U :W: .10 .20
8 Cliffhaven Sell-Sword C :W: .07 .15
9 Dauntless Unity C :W: .07 .15
10 Disenchant C :W: .07 .15
11 Emeria Captain U :W: .10 .20
12 Emeria's Call/Emeria, Shattered Skyclave M :W: 4.00 8.00
13 Expedition Healer C :W: .07 .15
14 Farsight Adept C :W: .07 .15
15 Fearless Fledgling U :W: .10 .20
16 Felidar Retreat R :W: .15 .30
17 Journey to Oblivion U :W: .10 .20
18 Kabira Outrider C :W: .07 .15
19 Kabira Takedown/Kabira Plateau U :W: .10 .20
20 Kitesail Cleric U :W: .10 .20
21 Kor Blademaster U :W: .10 .20
22 Kor Celebrant C :W: .07 .15
23 Legion Angel R :W: .15 .30
24 Luminarch Aspirant R :W: .15 .30
25 Makindi Ox C :W: .07 .15
26 Makindi Stampede/Makindi Mesas U :W: .10 .20
27 Maul of the Skyclaves R :W: .15 .30
28 Mesa Lynx C :W: .07 .15
29 Nahiri's Binding C :W: .07 .15
30 Ondu Inversion/Ondu Skyruins R :W: .15 .30
31 Paired Tactician U :W: .10 .20
32 Practiced Tactics C :W: .07 .15
33 Pressure Point C :W: .07 .15
34 Prowling Felidar C :W: .07 .15
35 Resolute Strike C :W: .07 .15
36 Sea Gate Banneret C :W: .07 .15
37 Sejiri Shelter/Sejiri Glacier U :W: .10 .20
38 Shepherd of Heroes C :W: .07 .15
39 Skyclave Apparition R :W: .15 .30
40 Skyclave Cleric/Skyclave Basilica U :W: .10 .20
41 Squad Commander R :W: .15 .30
42 Smite the Monstrous C :W: .07 .15
43 Tazeem Raptor C :W: .07 .15
44 Tazri, Beacon of Unity M :W: .20 .40
45 Anticognition C :B: .07 .15
46 Beyeen Veil/Beyeen Coast U :B: .10 .20
47 Bubble Snare C :B: .07 .15
48 Cascade Seer C :B: .07 .15
49 Charix, the Raging Isle R :B: .15 .30
50 Chilling Trap C :B: .07 .15
51 Cleric of Chill Depths C :B: .07 .15
52 Concerted Defense U :B: .10 .20
53 Confounding Conundrum R :B: .15 .30
54 Coralhelm Chronicler R :B: .15 .30
55 Cunning Geysermage C :B: .07 .15
56 Deliberate C :B: .07 .15
57 Expedition Diviner C :B: .07 .15
58 Field Research C :B: .07 .15
59 Glacial Grasp C :B: .07 .15
60 Glasspool Mimic/Glasspool Shore R :B: .15 .30
61 Inscription of Insight R :B: .15 .30
62 Into the Roil C :B: .07 .15
63 Jace, Mirror Mage M :B: .30 .75
64 Jwari Disruption/Jwari Ruins U :B: .10 .20
65 Living Tempest C :B: .07 .15
66 Lullmage's Domination U :B: .10 .20
67 Maddening Cacophony R :B: .15 .30
68 Master of Winds R :B: .15 .30
69 Merfolk Falconer U :B: .10 .20
70 Merfolk Windrobber U :B: .10 .20
71 Negate C :B: .07 .15
72 Nimble Trapfinder R :B: .15 .30
73 Risen Riptide C :B: .07 .15
74 Roost of Drakes U :B: .10 .20
75 Ruin Crab U :B: .10 .20
76 Sea Gate Restoration/Sea Gate, Reborn M :B: 10.00 20.00
77 Sea Gate Stormcaller M :B: .20 .40
78 Seafloor Stalker C :B: .07 .15
79 Shell Shield C :B: .07 .15
80 Silundi Vision/Silundi Isle U :B: .10 .20
81 Skyclave Plunder U :B: .10 .20
82 Skyclave Squid C :B: .07 .15
83 Sure-Footed Infiltrator U :B: .10 .20
84 Tazeem Roilmage C :B: .07 .15
85 Thieving Skydiver R :B: .15 .30
86 Umara Wizard/Umara Skyfalls U :B: .10 .20
87 Windrider Wizard U :B: .10 .20
88 Zulaport Duelist C :B: .07 .15
89 Acquisitions Expert U :K: .10 .20
90 Agadeem's Awakening Agadeem, the Undercrypt M :K: 10.00 20.00
91 Blackbloom Rogue/Blackbloom Bog U :K: .10 .20
92 Blood Beckoning C :K: .07 .15
93 Blood Price C :K: .07 .15
94 Bloodchief's Thirst U :K: .10 .20
95 Coveted Prize R :K: .15 .30
96 Deadly Alliance C :K: .07 .15
97 Demon's Disciple U :K: .10 .20
98 Drana, the Last Bloodchief M :K: 1.00 2.00
99 Drana's Silencer C :K: .07 .15
100 Dreadwurm C :K: .07 .15
101 Expedition Skulker C :K: .07 .15
102 Feed the Swarm C :K: .07 .15
103 Ghastly Gloomhunter C :K: .07 .15
104 Guul Draz Mucklord C :K: .07 .15
105 Hagra Constrictor C :K: .07 .15
106 Hagra Mauling/Hagra Broodpit R :K: .15 .30
107 Highborn Vampire C :K: .07 .15
108 Inscription of Ruin R :K: .15 .30
109 Lithoform Blight U :K: .10 .20
110 Malakir Blood-Priest C :K: .07 .15
111 Malakir Rebirth/Malakir Mire U :K: .10 .20
112 Marauding Blight-Priest C :K: .07 .15
113 Mind Carver U :K: .10 .20
114 Mind Drain C :K: .07 .15
115 Nighthawk Scavenger R :K: .15 .30
116 Nimana Skitter-Sneak C :K: .07 .15
117 Nimana Skydancer C :K: .07 .15
118 Nullpriest of Oblivion R :K: .15 .30
119 Oblivion's Hunger C :K: .07 .15

120 Pelakka Predation/Pelakka Caverns U :K: .10 .20
121 Scion of the Swarm U :K: .10 .20
122 Scourge of the Skyclaves M :K: .30 .60
123 Shadow Stinger U :K: .10 .20
124 Shadows' Verdict R :K: .15 .30
125 Skyclave Shade R :K: .15 .30
126 Skyclave Shadowcat U :K: .10 .20
127 Soul Shatter R :K: .15 .30
128 Subtle Strike C :K: .07 .15
129 Taborax, Hope's Demise R :K: .15 .30
130 Thwart the Grave U :K: .10 .20
131 Vanquish the Weak C :K: .07 .15
132 Zof Consumption/Zof Bloodbog U :K: .10 .20
133 Akoum Hellhound C :R: .07 .15
134 Akoum Warrior/Akoum Teeth U :R: .10 .20
135 Ardent Electromancer C :R: .07 .15
136 Cinderclasm U :R: .10 .20
137 Cleansing Wildfire C :R: .07 .15
138 Expedition Champion C :R: .07 .15
139 Fireblade Charger U :R: .10 .20
140 Fissure Wizard C :R: .07 .15
141 Goma Fada Vanguard U :R: .10 .20
142 Grotag Bug-Catcher C :R: .07 .15
143 Grotag Night-Runner U :R: .10 .20
144 Inordinate Rage C :R: .07 .15
145 Kargan Intimidator R :R: .15 .30
146 Kazuul's Fury/Kazuul's Cliffs U :R: .10 .20
147 Leyline Tyrant M :R: 1.50 3.00
148 Magmatic Channeler R :R: .15 .30
149 Molten Blast C :R: .07 .15
150 Moraug, Fury of Akoum M :R: 4.00 8.00
151 Nahiri's Lithoforming R :R: .15 .30
152 Pyroclastic Hellion C :R: .07 .15
153 Relic Robber R :R: .15 .30
154 Rockslide Sorcerer U :R: .10 .20
155 Roil Eruption C :R: .07 .15
156 Roiling Vortex R :R: .15 .30
157 Scavenged Blade C :R: .07 .15
158 Scorch Rider C :R: .07 .15
159 Shatterskull Charger R :R: .15 .30
160 Shatterskull Minotaur U :R: .10 .20
161 Shatterskull Smashing
Shatterskull, the Hammer Pass M :R: 3.00 6.00
162 Sizzling Barrage C :R: .07 .15
163 Skyclave Geopede U :R: .10 .20
164 Sneaking Guide C :R: .07 .15
165 Song-Mad Treachery/Song-Mad Ruins U :R: .10 .20
166 Spikefield Hazard/Spikefield Cave U :R: .10 .20
167 Spitfire Lagac C :R: .07 .15
168 Synchronized Spellcraft C :R: .07 .15
169 Teeterpeak Ambusher C :R: .07 .15
170 Thundering Rebuke U :R: .10 .20
171 Thundering Sparkmage U :R: .10 .20
172 Tormenting Voice C :R: .07 .15
173 Tuktuk Rubblefort C :R: .07 .15
174 Valakut Awakening/Valakut Stoneforge R :R: .15 .30
175 Valakut Exploration R :R: .15 .30
176 Wayward Guide-Beast R :R: .15 .30
177 Adventure Awaits C :G: .07 .15
178 Ancient Greenwarden M :G: 7.50 15.00
179 Ashaya, Soul of the Wild M :G: 7.50 15.00
180 Bala Ged Recovery/Bala Ged Sanctuary U :G: .10 .20
181 Broken Wings C :G: .07 .15
182 Canopy Baloth C :G: .07 .15
183 Cragplate Baloth R :G: .15 .30
184 Dauntless Survivor C :G: .07 .15
185 Gnarlid Colony C :G: .07 .15
186 Inscription of Abundance R :G: .15 .30
187 Iridescent Hornbeetle U :G: .10 .20
188 Joraga Visionary C :G: .07 .15
189 Kazandu Mammoth/Kazandu Valley R :G: .15 .30
190 Kazandu Nectarpot C :G: .07 .15
191 Kazandu Stomper C :G: .07 .15
192 Khalni Ambush/Khalni Territory U :G: .10 .20
193 Lotus Cobra R :G: .15 .30
194 Might of Murasa C :G: .07 .15
195 Murasa Brute C :G: .07 .15
196 Murasa Sproutling U :G: .10 .20
197 Nissa's Zendikon C :G: .07 .15
198 Oran-Rief Ooze R :G: .15 .30
199 Rabid Bite C :G: .07 .15
200 Reclaim the Wastes C :G: .07 .15
201 Roiling Regrowth U :G: .10 .20
202 Scale the Heights C :G: .07 .15
203 Scute Swarm R :G: .15 .30
204 Skyclave Pick-Axe U :G: .10 .20
205 Springmantle Cleric U :G: .10 .20
206 Strength of Solidarity C :G: .07 .15
207 Swarm Shambler R :G: .15 .30
208 Tajuru Blightblade C :G: .07 .15
209 Tajuru Paragon R :G: .15 .30
210 Tajuru Snarecaster C :G: .07 .15
211 Tangled Florahedron/Tangled Vale U :G: .10 .20
212 Taunting Arbormage U :G: .10 .20
213 Territorial Scythecat C :G: .07 .15
214 Turntimber Ascetic C :G: .07 .15
215 Turntimber Symbiosis/Turntimber,
Serpentine Wood M :G: 2.00 4.00
216 Vastwood Fortification/Vastwood Thicket U :G: .10 .20
217 Vastwood Surge U :G: .10 .20
218 Veteran Adventurer U :G: .10 .20
219 Vine Gecko U :G: .10 .20
220 Akiri, Fearless Voyager R :R:/:W: .15 .30
221 Brushfire Elemental U :R:/:G: .10 .20
222 Cleric of Life's Bond U :W:/:K: .10 .20
223 Grakmaw, Skyclave Ravager R :K:/:G: .15 .30
224 Kargan Warleader U :R:/:W: .10 .20
225 Kaza, Roil Chaser R :B:/:R: .15 .30
226 Linvala, Shield of Sea Gate R :W:/:B: .15 .30
227 Lullmage's Familiar U :G:/:B: .10 .20
228 Moss-Pit Skeleton U :K:/:G: .10 .20
229 Murasa Rootgrazer U :G:/:W: .10 .20
230 Nahiri, Heir of the Ancients M :R:/:W: .75 1.50
231 Nissa of Shadowed Boughs M :K:/:G: 1.00 2.00
232 Omnath, Locus of Creation M :R:/:G:/:W:/:B: 10.00 20.00
233 Orah, Skyclave Hierophant R :W:/:K: .15 .30
234 Phylath, World Sculptor R :R:/:G: .15 .30
235 Ravager's Mace U :K:/:R: .10 .20
236 Soaring Thought-Thief U :B:/:K: .10 .20
237 Spoils of Adventure U :W:/:B: .10 .20
238 Umara Mystic U :B:/:R: .10 .20
239 Verazol, the Split Current R :G:/:B: .15 .30
240 Yasharn, Implacable Earth R :G:/:W: .15 .30
241 Zagras, Thief of Heartbeats R :K:/:R: .15 .30
242 Zareth San, the Trickster R :B:/:K: .15 .30
243 Cliffhaven Kitesail C .07 .15
244 Forsaken Monument M 4.00 8.00
245 Lithoform Engine M 2.00 4.00
246 Myriad Construct R .15 .30
247 Relic Amulet U .10 .20
248 Relic Axe U .10 .20
249 Relic Golem U .10 .20
250 Relic Vial U .10 .20
251 Sea Gate Colossus C .07 .15
252 Skyclave Relic R .15 .30
253 Skyclave Sentinel C .07 .15
254 Spare Supplies C .07 .15
255 Stonework Packbeast C .07 .15
256 Utility Knife C .07 .15
257 Base Camp U .10 .20
258 Branchloft Pathway/Boulderloft Pathway R .15 .30
259 Brightclimb Pathway/Grimclimb Pathway R .15 .30
260 Clearwater Pathway/Murkwater Pathway R .15 .30
261 Cragcrown Pathway/Timbercrown Pathway R .15 .30
262 Crawling Barrens R .15 .30
263 Needleverge Pathway/Pillarverge Pathway R .15 .30
264 Riverglide Pathway/Lavaglide Pathway R .15 .30
265 Throne of Makindi R .15 .30
266 Plains C .07 .15
267 Plains C .07 .15
268 Plains C .07 .15
269 Island C .07 .15
270 Island C .07 .15
271 Island C .07 .15
272 Swamp C .07 .15
273 Swamp C .07 .15
274 Swamp C .07 .15
275 Mountain C .07 .15
276 Mountain C .07 .15
277 Mountain C .07 .15
278 Forest C .07 .15
279 Forest C .07 .15
280 Forest C .07 .15
281 Jace, Mirror Mage M :B: .30 .75
282 Nahiri, Heir of the Ancients M :R:/:W: .50 1.00
283 Nissa of Shadowed Boughs M :K:/:G: .75 1.50
284 Branchloft Pathway/Boulderloft Pathway R .15 .30
285 Brightclimb Pathway/Grimclimb Pathway R .15 .30
286 Clearwater Pathway/Murkwater Pathway R .15 .30
287 Cragcrown Pathway/Timbercrown Pathway R .15 .30
288a Needleverge Pathway/Pillarverge Pathway R .15 .30
288b Needleverge Pathway/Pillarverge Pathway R .15 .30
289 Riverglide Pathway/Lavaglide Pathway R .15 .30
290 Canyon Jerboa U :W: .10 .20
291 Fearless Fledgling U :W: .10 .20
292 Felidar Retreat R :W: .15 .30
293 Makindi Ox C :W: .07 .15
294 Prowling Felidar C :W: .07 .15
295 Ruin Crab U :B: .10 .20
296 Skyclave Squid C :B: .07 .15
297 Dreadwurm C :K: .07 .15
298 Skyclave Shade R :K: .15 .30
299 Akoum Hellhound C :R: .07 .15
300 Moraug, Fury of Akoum M :R: 4.00 8.00
301 Skyclave Geopede U :R: .10 .20
302 Spitfire Lagac C :R: .07 .15
303 Valakut Exploration R :R: .15 .30
304 Canopy Baloth C :G: .07 .15
305 Kazandu Mammoth/Kazandu Valley R :G: .15 .30
306 Kazandu Nectarpot C :G: .07 .15
307 Lotus Cobra R :G: .15 .30
308 Scute Swarm R :G: .15 .30
309 Skyclave Pick-Axe U :G: .10 .20
310 Territorial Scythecat C :G: .07 .15
311 Brushfire Elemental U :R:/:G: .10 .20
312 Omnath, Locus of Creation M :R:/:G:/:W:/:B: 7.50 15.00
313 Phylath, World Sculptor R :R:/:G: .15 .30
314 Angel of Destiny M :W: 4.00 8.00
315 Archon of Emeria R :W: .15 .30
316 Archpriest of Iona R :W: .15 .30
317 Emeria's Call/Emeria,
Shattered Skyclave M :W: 10.00 20.00
318 Legion Angel R :W: .15 .30
319 Luminarch Aspirant R :W: .15 .30
320 Maul of the Skyclaves R :W: .15 .30
321 Ondu Inversion/Ondu Skyruins R :W: .15 .30
322 Skyclave Apparition R :W: .15 .30
323 Squad Commander R :W: .15 .30
324 Tazri, Beacon of Unity M :W: .50 1.00
325 Charix, the Raging Isle R :B: .15 .30
326 Confounding Conundrum R :B: .15 .30
327 Coralhelm Chronicler R :B: .15 .30
328 Glasspool Mimic/Glasspool Shore R :B: .15 .30
329 Inscription of Insight R :B: .15 .30
330 Maddening Cacophony R :B: .15 .30
331 Master of Winds R :B: .15 .30
332 Nimble Trapfinder R :B: .15 .30
333 Sea Gate Restoration/Sea Gate, Reborn M :B: 15.00 30.00
334 Sea Gate Stormcaller M :B: .30 .75
335 Thieving Skydiver R :B: .15 .30
336 Agadeem's Awakening/Agadeem,
the Undercrypt M :K: 15.00 30.00
337 Coveted Prize R :K: .15 .30
338 Drana, the Last Bloodchief M :K: 2.50 5.00
339 Hagra Mauling/Hagra Broodpit R :K: .15 .30
340 Inscription of Ruin R :K: .15 .30
341 Nighthawk Scavenger R :K: .15 .30
342 Nullpriest of Oblivion R :K: .15 .30
343 Scourge of the Skyclaves M :K: .75 1.50
344 Shadows' Verdict R :K: .15 .30
345 Soul Shatter R :K: .15 .30
346 Taborax, Hope's Demise R :K: .15 .30
347 Kargan Intimidator R :R: .15 .30
348 Leyline Tyrant M :R: 2.50 5.00
349 Magmatic Channeler R :R: .15 .30
350 Nahiri's Lithoforming R :R: .15 .30
351 Relic Robber R :R: .15 .30
352 Roiling Vortex R :R: .15 .30
353 Shatterskull Charger R :R: .15 .30
354 Shatterskull Smashing/Shatterskull,
the Hammer Pass M :R: 7.50 15.00
355 Valakut Awakening/Valakut Stoneforge R :R: .15 .30
356 Wayward Guide-Beast R :R: .15 .30
357 Ancient Greenwarden M :G: 10.00 20.00
358 Ashaya, Soul of the Wild M :G: 7.50 15.00
359 Cragplate Baloth R :G: .15 .30
360 Inscription of Abundance R :G: .15 .30
361 Oran-Rief Ooze R :G: .15 .30
362 Swarm Shambler R :G: .15 .30
363 Tajuru Paragon R :G: .15 .30
364 Turntimber Symbiosis
Turntimber, Serpentine Wood M :G: 4.00 8.00
365 Akiri, Fearless Voyager R :R:/:W: .15 .30
366 Grakmaw, Skyclave Ravager R :K:/:G: .15 .30
367 Kaza, Roil Chaser R :B:/:R: .15 .30
368 Linvala, Shield of Sea Gate R :W:/:B: .15 .30
369 Orah, Skyclave Hierophant R :W:/:K: .15 .30
370 Verazol, the Split Current R :G:/:B: .15 .30
371 Yasharn, Implacable Earth R :G:/:W: .15 .30
372 Zagras, Thief of Heartbeats R :K:/:R: .15 .30
373 Zareth San, the Trickster R :B:/:K: .15 .30
374 Forsaken Monument M 7.50 15.00
375 Lithoform Engine M 3.00 6.00
376 Myriad Construct R .15 .30
377 Skyclave Relic R .15 .30
378 Crawling Barrens R .15 .30
379 Throne of Makindi R .15 .30
380 Plains C .07 .15
381 Island C .07 .15
382 Swamp C .07 .15
383 Mountain C .07 .15
384 Forest C .07 .15
385 Orah, Skyclave Hierophant R :W:/:K: .15 .30
386 Charix, the Raging Isle R :B: .15 .30
387 Into the Roil C :B: .07 .15
388 Bloodchief's Thirst U :K: .10 .20
389 Roil Eruption C :R: .07 .15
390 Roiling Regrowth U :G: .10 .20
391 Kargan Warleader U :R:/:W: .10 .20

2020 Magic The Gathering Zendikar Rising Expeditions

1 Flooded Strand M 25.00 50.00
2 Polluted Delta M 30.00 75.00
3 Bloodstained Mire M 30.00 75.00
4 Wooded Foothills M 30.00 75.00
5 Windswept Heath M 25.00 50.00
6 Marsh Flats M 12.50 25.00
7 Scalding Tarn M 20.00 40.00
8 Verdant Catacombs M 20.00 40.00
9 Arid Mesa M 12.50 25.00
10 Misty Rainforest M 15.00 40.00
11 Seachrome Coast M 4.00 8.00
12 Darkslick Shores M 4.00 8.00
13 Blackcleave Cliffs M 4.00 8.00
14 Copperline Gorge M 3.00 6.00
15 Razorverge Thicket M 4.00 8.00
16 Sea of Clouds M 5.00 10.00
17 Morphic Pool M 7.50 15.00
18 Luxury Suite M 7.50 15.00
19 Spire Garden M 5.00 10.00
20 Bountiful Promenade M 4.00 8.00
21 Ancient Tomb M 40.00 80.00
22 Cavern of Souls M 30.00 75.00
23 Celestial Colonnade M 1.50 3.00
24 Creeping Tar Pit M 1.50 3.00
25 Grove of the Burnwillows M 4.00 8.00
26 Horizon Canopy M 7.50 15.00
27 Prismatic Vista M 20.00 40.00
28 Strip Mine M 12.50 25.00
29 Valakut, the Molten Pinnacle M 15.00 30.00
30 Wasteland M 15.00 30.00

2020 Magic The Gathering Zendikar Rising Tokens

1 Angel Warrior .15 .30
2 Cat .12 .25
3 Cat Beast .30 .60
4 Kor Warrior .07 .15
5 Drake .12 .25
6 Illusion .15 .30
7 Insect .12 .25
8 Plant .07 .15
9 Hydra .30 .60
10 Construct .07 .15
11 Goblin Construct .07 .15
12 Copy .20 .40

2021 Magic The Gathering Commander 2021

1 Breena, the Demagogue M :W:/:K: 2.50 5.00
2 Felisa, Fang of Silverquill M :W:/:K: .30 .75
3 Veyran, Voice of Duality M :B:/:R: 3.00 6.00
4 Zaffai, Thunder Conductor M :B:/:R: .50 1.00
5 Gyome, Master Chef M :K:/:G: .30 .75
6 Willowdusk, Essence Seer M :K:/:G: .25 .50
7 Alibou, Ancient Witness M :R:/:W: .25 .50
8 Osgir, the Reconstructor M :R:/:W: .25 .50
9 Adrix and Nev, Twincasters M :G:/:B: 4.00 8.00
10 Esix, Fractal Bloom M :G:/:B: .50 1.00
11 Angel of the Ruins R :W: .60 1.25
12 Archaeomancer's Map R :W: 7.50 15.00
13 Bronze Guardian R :W: .50 1.00
14 Combat Calligrapher R :W: .25 .50
15 Digsite Engineer R :W: .25 .50
16 Excavation Technique R :W: .20 .40
17 Guardian Archon R :W: .20 .40
18 Losheel, Clockwork Scholar R :W: .60 1.25
19 Monologue Tax R :W: 2.00 4.00
20 Nils, Discipline Enforcer R :W: .50 1.00
21 Promise of Loyalty R :W: 2.50 5.00
22 Scholarship Sponsor R :W: .20 .40
23 Commander's Insight R :B: .20 .40
24 Curiosity Crafter R :B: 1.25 2.50
25 Dazzling Sphinx R :B: .20 .40
26 Deekah, Fractal Theorist R :B: 3.00 6.00
27 Inspiring Refrain R :B: .20 .40
28 Muse Vortex R :B: .20 .40
29 Octavia, Living Thesis R :B: .30 .75
30 Perplexing Test R :B: 1.25 2.50
31 Replication Technique R :B: .20 .40
32 Sly Instigator R :B: .20 .40
33 Spawning Kraken R :B: 2.50 5.00
34 Theoretical Duplication R :B: .20 .40
35 Author of Shadows R :K: .30 .75
36 Blight Mound R :K: .30 .75
37 Bold Plagiarist R :K: .20 .40
38 Cunning Rhetoric R :K: 7.50 15.00
39 Essence Pulse R :K: .20 .40
40 Fain, the Broker R :K: .50 1.00
41 Incarnation Technique R :K: 2.00 4.00
42 Keen Duelist R :K: 1.50 3.00
43 Marshland Bloodcaster R :K: .20 .40
44 Stinging Study R :K: 3.00 6.00
45 Tivash, Gloom Summoner R :K: .20 .40
46 Veinwitch Coven R :K: 1.00 2.00
47 Audacious Reshapers R :R: .20 .40
48 Battlemage's Bracers R :R: .50 1.00
49 Creative Technique R :R: .20 .40
50 Cursed Mirror R :R: 4.00 8.00
51 Fiery Encore R :R: .20 .40
52 Inferno Project R :R: .20 .40
53 Laelia, the Blade Reforged R :R: 1.00 2.00
54 Radiant Performer R :R: .20 .40
55 Rionya, Fire Dancer R :R: .30 .75
56 Rousing Refrain R :R: .30 .75
57 Ruin Grinder R :R: .20 .40
58 Surge to Victory R :R: .25 .50
59 Blossoming Bogbeast R :G: .50 1.00
60 Ezzaroot Channeler R :G: .20 .40
61 Fractal Harness R :G: .20 .40
62 Guardian Augmenter R :G: 1.00 2.00
63 Healing Technique R :G: .20 .40
64 Paradox Zone R :G: .50 1.00
65 Pest Infestation R :G: 4.00 8.00
66 Ruxa, Patient Professor R :G: .20 .40
67 Sequence Engine R :G: .30 .40
68 Sproutback Trudge R :G: .30 .60
69 Trudge Garden R :G: .20 .40
70 Yedora, Grave Gardener R :G: .50 1.00
71 Inkshield R :W:/:K: 7.50 15.00
72 Oversimplify R :G:/:B: .20 .40
73 Reinterpret R :B:/:R: .20 .40
74 Revival Experiment R :K:/:G: .20 .40
75 Wake the Past R :R:/:W: .20 .40
76 Elementalist's Palette R .30 .75
77 Geometric Nexus R .20 .40
78 Tempting Contract R 1.50 3.00
79 Triplicate Titan R .30 .75
80 Study Hall C .07 .15
81 Witch's Clinic R 2.00 4.00
82 Desolation Twin R .20 .40
83 Angel of Serenity M :W: .50 1.00
84 Boreas Charger R :W: .20 .40
85 Citadel Siege R :W: .20 .40
86 Cleansing Nova R :W: .30 .75
87 Darksteel Mutation U :W: 1.25 2.50
88 Dispatch U :W: .20 .40
89 Dispeller's Capsule C :W: .07 .15
90 Duelist's Heritage R :W: .50 1.00
91 Elite Scaleguard U :W: .12 .25
92 Ghostly Prison U :W: 1.50 3.00
93 Gideon, Champion of Justice M :W: .25 .50
94 Hunted Lammasu R :W: .20 .40
95 Knight of the White Orchid R :W: .25 .50
96 Martial Impetus U :W: .12 .25
97 Oblation R :W: .50 1.00
98 Oreskos Explorer U :W: .12 .25
99 Orzhov Advokist U :W: .12 .25
100 Return to Dust U :W: .12 .25
101 Rout R :W: .20 .40
102 Sanctum Gargoyle C :W: .07 .15
103 Selfless Squire R :W: .30 .60
104 Soul Snare U :W: .12 .25
105 Stalking Leonin R :W: .30 .60
106 Sun Titan M :W: .50 1.00
107 Sunscorch Regent R :W: .60 1.25
108 Together Forever R :W: .20 .40
109 Tragic Arrogance R :W: 1.00 2.00
110 Vow of Duty U :W: .12 .25
111 Windborn Muse R :W: .50 1.00
112 Zetalpa, Primal Dawn R :W: .20 .40
113 Aether Gale R :B: .50 1.00
114 Aetherspouts R :B: .20 .40
115 Brainstorm C :B: .07 .15
116 Champion of Wits R :B: .20 .40
117 Crafty Cutpurse R :B: .20 .40
118 Curse of the Swine R :B: .20 .40
119 Dig Through Time R :B: .30 .75
120 Diluvian Primordial R :B: .50 1.00
121 Living Lore U :B: .12 .25
122 Metallurgic Summonings M :B: 1.00 2.00
123 Mind's Desire R :B: .20 .40
124 Naru Meha, Master Wizard M :B: .30 .60
125 Ponder C :B: 1.25 2.50
126 Rapid Hybridization U :B: 2.00 4.00
127 Reef Worm R :B: .20 .40
128 Rite of Replication R :B: 2.50 5.00
129 Serum Visions U :B: .30 .75
130 Swarm Intelligence R :B: .20 .40
131 Talrand, Sky Summoner R :B: .20 .40
132 Traumatic Visions C :B: .07 .15
133 Treasure Cruise C :B: .20 .40
134 Ambition's Cost U :K: .12 .25
135 Ancient Craving U :K: .12 .25
136 Bloodthirsty Aerialist U :K: .12 .25
137 Bloodtracker R :K: .20 .40
138 Curse of Disturbance U :K: .60 1.25
139 Damnable Pact R :K: .20 .40
140 Deadly Tempest R :K: .25 .50
141 Deathbringer Regent R :K: .20 .40
142 Defiant Bloodlord R :K: .20 .40
143 Epicure of Blood C :K: .07 .15
144 Feed the Swarm C :K: .30 .60
145 Greed R :K: .20 .40
146 Internal Offering R :K: .30 .60
147 Necropolis Regent M :K: .30 .60
148 Noxious Gearhulk M :K: .50 1.00
149 Ob Nixilis Reignited M :K: .50 1.00
150 Parasitic Impetus U :K: .12 .25
151 Reckless Spite U :K: .12 .25
152 Sangromancer R :K: .30 .60
153 Sanguine Bond R :K: 1.50 3.00
154 Silversmote Ghoul U :K: .12 .25
155 Suffer the Past U :K: .12 .25
156 Taste of Death R :K: .30 .60
157 Vampire Nighthawk U :K: .12 .25
158 Apex of Power M :R: .20 .40
159 Blasphemous Act R :R: 1.50 3.00
160 Brass's Bounty R :R: 1.25 2.50
161 Chain Reaction R :R: .30 .60
162 Charmbreaker Devils R :R: .30 .60
163 Combustible Gearhulk M :R: .50 1.00
164 Daretti, Scrap Savant M :R: .50 1.00
165 Dualcaster Mage R :R: .20 .40
166 Erratic Cyclops R :R: .30 .60
167 Etali, Primal Storm R :R: .25 .50

168 Faithless Looting C :R:	.30	.75
169 Feldon of the Third Path M :R:	.50	1.00
170 Fiery Fall C :R:	.07	.15
171 Hellkite Igniter R :R:	.20	.40
172 Hellkite Tyrant M :R:	6.00	12.00
173 Hoard-Smelter Dragon R :R:	.20	.40
174 Humble Defector U :R:	.12	.25
175 Jaya Ballard M :R:	.50	1.00
176 Mana Geyser C :R:	.75	1.50
177 Pia Nalaar R :R:	.20	.40
178 Quicksmith Genius U :R:	.12	.25
179 Seething Song C :R:	.50	1.00
180 Sunbird's Invocation R :R:	.50	1.00
181 Thopter Engineer U :R:	.12	.25
182 Volcanic Vision R :R:	.30	.60
183 Wildfire Devils R :R:	.30	.60
184 Ageless Entity R :G:	.30	.60
185 Arashi, the Sky Asunder R :G:	.20	.40
186 Beast Within U :G:	.75	1.50
187 Cultivate U :G:	.30	.75
188 Ezuri's Predation R :G:	.75	1.50
189 Forgotten Ancient R :G:	.25	.50
190 Garruk, Primal Hunter M :G:	.75	1.50
191 Gift of Paradise C :G:	.07	.15
192 Hornet Nest R :G:	.50	1.00
193 Hornet Queen R :G:	.30	.75
194 Hydra Broodmaster R :G:	.20	.40
195 Incubation Druid R :G:	.30	.75
196 Kazandu Tuskcaller R :G:	.20	.40
197 Kodama's Reach C :G:	1.00	2.00
198 Krosan Grip U :G:	.30	.75
199 Managorger Hydra R :G:	.75	1.50
200 Nissa's Expedition U :G:	.12	.25
201 Nissa's Renewal R :G:	.30	.60
202 Pulse of Murasa U :G:	.12	.25
203 Rampaging Baloths R :G:	.30	.60
204 Rampant Growth C :G:	.07	.15
205 Return of the Wildspeaker R :G:	.75	1.50
206 Shamanic Revelation R :G:	.30	.60
207 Terastodon R :G:	.30	.60
208 Verdant Sun's Avatar R :G:	.30	.60
209 Biomass Mutation R :G:/:B:	.20	.40
210 Boros Charm U :R:/:W:	.75	1.50
211 Call the Skybreaker R :B:/:R:	.20	.40
212 Coiling Oracle C :G:/:B:	.07	.15
213 Crackling Drake U :B:/:R:	.12	.25
214 Deathbringer Liege R :W:/:K:	.50	1.00
215 Debtors' Knell R :W:/:K:	.30	.60
216 Epic Experiment M :B:/:R:	.30	.75
217 Gaze of Granite R :K:/:G:	.20	.40
218 Gluttonous Troll R :K:/:G:	.20	.40
219 Incubation // Incongruity U :G:/:B:	.12	.25
220 Jor Kadeen, the Prevailer R :R:/:W:	.20	.40
221 Kaseto, Orochi Archmage M :G:/:B:	.30	.75
222 Leyline Prowler U :K:/:G:	.12	.25
223 Magister of Worth R :W:/:K:	.30	.60
224 Master Biomancer M :G:/:B:	.50	1.00
225 Moldervine Reclamation U :K:/:G:	.25	.50
226 Plaxcaster Frogling U :G:/:B:	.12	.25
227 Primal Empathy U :G:/:B:	.12	.25
228 Sapling of Colfenor R :K:/:G:	.20	.40
229 Spitting Image R :G:/:B:	.20	.40
230 Teysa, Envoy of Ghosts R :W:/:K:	.20	.40
231 Trygon Predator U :G:/:B:	.12	.25
232 Utter End R :W:/:K:	.30	.60
233 Alhammarret's Archive M	4.00	8.00
234 Arcane Signet C	.60	1.25
235 Bloodthirsty Blade U	.12	.25
236 Boros Locket C	.07	.15
237 Bosh, Iron Golem R	.20	.40
238 Burnished Hart U	.12	.25
239 Commander's Sphere C	.07	.15
240 Coveted Jewel R	.30	.60
241 Druidic Satchel R	.20	.40
242 Duplicant R	.20	.40
243 Elixir of Immortality U	.30	.75
244 Hedron Archive U	.20	.40
245 Ichor Wellspring C	.07	.15
246 Idol of Oblivion R	.60	1.25
247 Izzet Signet C	.30	.60
248 Key to the City R	.20	.40
249 Loxodon Warhammer R	.25	.50
250 Meteor Golem U	.12	.25
251 Mind Stone U	.50	1.00
252 Mycosynth Wellspring C	.07	.15
253 Myr Battlesphere R	.30	.60
254 Orzhov Signet U	.20	.40
255 Paradise Plume U	.12	.25
256 Pendant of Prosperity R	.30	.60
257 Pilgrim's Eye C	.07	.15
258 Pristine Talisman C	.07	.15
259 Pyromancer's Goggles M	.75	1.50
260 Scrap Trawler R	.30	.60
261 Sculpting Steel R	.50	1.00
262 Simic Signet C	.20	.40
263 Sol Ring U	.75	1.50
264 Solemn Simulacrum R	.50	1.00
265 Spectral Searchlight U	.12	.25
266 Steel Hellkite R	.30	.60
267 Steel Overseer R	.50	1.00
268 Sun Droplet U	.12	.25
269 Talisman of Creativity U	.75	1.50
270 Talisman of Resilience U	.25	.50
271 Thousand-Year Elixir R	3.00	6.00
272 Unstable Obelisk U	.12	.25
273 Venser's Journal R	2.00	4.00
274 Victory Chimes R	.30	.60
275 Well of Lost Dreams R	1.25	2.50
276 Ancient Den C	.30	.75
277 Barren Moor U	.12	.25
278 Battlefield Forge R	1.00	2.00
279 Blighted Cataract U	.12	.25
280 Blighted Woodland U	.12	.25
281 Bojuka Bog C	.75	1.50
282 Boros Garrison U	.12	.25
283 Caves of Koilos R	.50	1.00
284 Command Tower C	.20	.40
285 Darksteel Citadel U	.25	.50
286 Desert of the Fervent C	.07	.15
287 Desert of the Mindful C	.07	.15
288 Exotic Orchard R	.30	.60
289 Forgotten Cave C	.07	.15
290 Gingerbread Cabin C	.07	.15
291 Golgari Rot Farm U	.12	.25
292 Great Furnace C	.50	1.00
293 High Market R	1.00	2.00
294 Izzet Boilerworks U	.17	.35
295 Jungle Hollow C	.07	.15
296 Llanowar Reborn U	.12	.25
297 Llanowar Wastes R	.75	1.50
298 Lonely Sandbar C	.07	.15
299 Lumbering Falls R	.30	.60
300 Mage-Ring Network U	.12	.25
301 Memorial to Genius U	.12	.25
302 Mikokoro, Center of the Sea R	2.00	4.00
303 Mosswort Bridge R	.30	.60
304 Myriad Landscape U	.12	.25
305 Novijen, Heart of Progress U	.12	.25
306 Opal Palace C	.07	.15
307 Oran-Rief, the Vastwood R	.30	.60
308 Orzhov Basilica U	.12	.25
309 Phyrexia's Core U	.12	.25
310 Radiant Fountain C	.07	.15
311 Reliquary Tower U	2.50	5.00
312 Rogue's Passage U	.30	.75
313 Sapseep Forest U	.12	.25
314 Scavenger Grounds R	1.00	2.00
315 Secluded Steppe C	.07	.15
316 Shivan Reef R	2.00	4.00
317 Simic Growth Chamber U	.12	.25
318 Slayers' Stronghold R	.30	.60
319 Sunhome, Fortress of the Legion U	.12	.25
320 Tainted Field U	.12	.25
321 Tainted Wood U	.60	1.25
322 Temple of Epiphany R	.20	.40
323 Temple of Malady R	.20	.40
324 Temple of Mystery R	.20	.40
325 Temple of Silence R	.20	.40
326 Temple of the False God U	.12	.25
327 Temple of Triumph R	.30	.60
328 Breena, the Demagogue M :W:/:K:	7.50	15.00
329 Felisa, Fang of Silverquill M :W:/:K:	4.00	8.00
330 Veyran, Voice of Duality M :B:/:R:	7.50	15.00
331 Zaffai, Thunder Conductor M :B:/:R:	2.50	5.00
332 Gyome, Master Chef M :K:/:G:	3.00	6.00
333 Willowdusk, Essence Seer M :K:/:G:	.60	1.25
334 Alibou, Ancient Witness M :R:/:W:	3.00	6.00
335 Osgir, the Reconstructor M :R:/:W:	4.00	8.00
336 Adrix and Nev, Twincasters M :G:/:B:	10.00	20.00
337 Esix, Fractal Bloom M :G:/:B:	2.50	5.00
338 Angel of the Ruins R :W:	2.00	4.00
339 Archaeomancer's Map R :W:	7.50	15.00
340 Bronze Guardian R :W:	2.00	4.00
341 Combat Calligrapher R :W:	.50	1.00
342 Digsite Engineer R :W:	.75	1.50
343 Excavation Technique R :W:	.30	.60
344 Guardian Archon R :W:	.30	.60
345 Losheel, Clockwork Scholar R :W:	2.00	4.00
346 Monologue Tax R :W:	3.00	6.00
347 Nils, Discipline Enforcer R :W:	.50	1.00
348 Promise of Loyalty R :W:	2.50	5.00
349 Scholarship Sponsor R :W:	.50	1.00
350 Commander's Insight R :B:	.30	.75
351 Curiosity Crafter R :B:	2.00	4.00
352 Dazzling Sphinx R :B:	.75	1.50
353 Deekah, Fractal Theorist R :B:	4.00	8.00
354 Inspiring Refrain R :B:	.30	.75
355 Muse Vortex R :B:	.20	.40
356 Octavia, Living Thesis R :B:	1.50	3.00
357 Perplexing Test R :B:	1.50	3.00
358 Replication Technique R :B:	.30	.60
359 Sly Instigator R :B:	.30	.60
360 Spawning Kraken R :B:	3.00	6.00
361 Theoretical Duplication R :B:	.50	1.00
362 Author of Shadows R :K:	.75	1.50
363 Blight Mound R :K:	1.00	2.00
364 Bold Plagiarist R :K:	.30	.60
365 Cunning Rhetoric R :K:	6.00	12.00
366 Essence Pulse R :K:	.30	.60
367 Fain, the Broker R :K:	1.50	3.00
368 Incarnation Technique R :K:	2.50	5.00
369 Keen Duelist R :K:	3.00	6.00
370 Marshland Bloodcaster R :K:	.50	1.00
371 Stinging Study R :K:	3.00	6.00
372 Tivash, Gloom Summoner R :K:	.50	1.00
373 Veinwitch Coven R :K:	1.25	2.50
374 Audacious Reshapers R :R:	.30	.60
375 Battlemage's Bracers R :R:	2.00	4.00
376 Creative Technique R :R:	.50	1.00
377 Cursed Mirror R :R:	5.00	10.00
378 Fiery Encore R :R:	.30	.60
379 Inferno Project R :R:	.30	.60
380 Laelia, the Blade Reforged R :R:	7.50	15.00
381 Radiant Performer R :R:	.30	.60
382 Rionya, Fire Dancer R :R:	1.50	3.00
383 Rousing Refrain R :R:	1.50	3.00
384 Ruin Grinder R :R:	.75	1.50
385 Surge to Victory R :R:	.50	1.00
386 Blossoming Bogbeast R :G:	1.00	2.00
387 Ezzaroot Channeler R :G:	.50	1.00
388 Fractal Harness R :G:	.75	1.50
389 Guardian Augmenter R :G:	1.50	3.00
390 Healing Technique R :G:	.30	.60
391 Paradox Zone R :G:	.75	1.50
392 Pest Infestation R :G:	5.00	10.00
393 Ruxa, Patient Professor R :G:	1.00	2.00
394 Sequence Engine R :G:	.30	.60
395 Sproutback Trudge R :G:	.30	.60
396 Trudge Garden R :G:	.75	1.50
397 Yedora, Grave Gardener R :G:	1.50	3.00
398 Inkshield R :W:/:K:	7.50	15.00
399 Oversimplify R :G:/:B:	.50	1.00
400 Reinterpret R :B:/:R:	.60	1.25
401 Revival Experiment R :K:/:G:	.20	.40
402 Wake the Past R :R:/:W:	.30	.60
403 Elementalist's Palette R	.75	1.50
404 Geometric Nexus R	.30	.60
405 Tempting Contract R	1.50	3.00
406 Triplicate Titan R	1.25	2.50
407 Witch's Clinic R	3.00	6.00
408 Tranquil Thicket C	.07	.15
409 Yavimaya Coast R	.50	1.00

2021 Magic The Gathering Commander 2021 Tokens

1 Eldrazi	.07	.15
2 Drake	.07	.15
3 Fish	.07	.15
4 Kraken	.07	.15
5 Whale	.07	.15
6 Champion of Wits	.07	.15
7 Demon	.07	.15
8 Horror	.07	.15
9 Zombie	.07	.15
10 Beast	.07	.15
11 Beast	.07	.15
12 Boar	.07	.15
13 Elephant	.07	.15
14 Frog Lizard	.07	.15
15 Fungus Beast	.07	.15
16 Hydra	.07	.15
17 Insect	.07	.15
18 Saproling	.07	.15
19 Wurm	.07	.15
20 Elemental	.07	.15
21 Spirit	.07	.15
22 Construct	.07	.15
23 Construct	.07	.15
24 Food	.07	.15
25 Golem	.07	.15
26 Golem	.07	.15
27 Golem	.07	.15
28 Myr	.07	.15
29 Thopter	.07	.15
30 Copy	.07	.15

2021 Magic The Gathering Dungeons and Dragons Adventures in the Forgotten Realms

1 +2 Mace C :W:	.07	.15
2 Arborea Pegasus C :W:	.07	.15
3 Blink Dog U :W:	.12	.25
4 The Book of Exalted Deeds M :W:	5.00	10.00
5 Celestial Unicorn C :W:	.07	.15
6 Cleric Class U :W:	.12	.25
7 Cloister Gargoyle U :W:	.12	.25
8 Dancing Sword R :W:	.30	.60
9 Dawnbringer Cleric C :W:	.07	.15
10 Delver's Torch C :W:	.07	.15
11 Devoted Paladin C :W:	.07	.15
12 Divine Smite U :W:	.12	.25
13 Dragon's Disciple U :W:	.12	.25
14 Dwarfhold Champion C :W:	.07	.15
15 Flumph R :W:	.30	.60
16 Gloom Stalker C :W:	.07	.15
17 Grand Master of Flowers M :W:	2.00	4.00
18 Guardian of Faith R :W:	.30	.60
19 Half-Elf Monk C :W:	.07	.15
20 Icingdeath, Frost Tyrant M :W:	2.50	5.00
21 Ingenious Smith U :W:	.12	.25
22 Keen-Eared Sentry U :W:	.12	.25
23 Loyal Warhound R :W:	.30	.60
24 Minimus Containment C :W:	.07	.15
25 Monk of the Open Hand U :W:	.12	.25
26 Moon-Blessed Cleric U :W:	.12	.25
27 Nadaar, Selfless Paladin R :W:	.30	.60
28 Oswald Fiddlebender R :W:	.30	.60
29 Paladin Class R :W:	.30	.60
30 Paladin's Shield C :W:	.07	.15
31 Planar Ally C :W:	.07	.15
32 Plate Armor U :W:	.12	.25
33 Portable Hole U :W:	.12	.25
34 Potion of Healing C :W:	.07	.15
35 Priest of Ancient Lore C :W:	.07	.15
36 Rally Maneuver U :W:	.12	.25
37 Ranger's Hawk C :W:	.07	.15
38 Steadfast Paladin C :W:	.07	.15
39 Teleportation Circle R :W:	.30	.60
40 Veteran Dungeoneer C :W:	.07	.15
41 White Dragon U :W:	.12	.25
42 You Hear Something on Watch C :W:	.07	.15
43 You're Ambushed on the Road C :W:	.07	.15
44 Aberrant Mind Sorcerer U :B:	.12	.25
45 Air-Cult Elemental C :B:	.07	.15
46 Arcane Investigator C :B:	.07	.15
47 Bar the Gate C :B:	.07	.15
48 The Blackstaff of Waterdeep R :B:	.30	.60
49 Blue Dragon U :B:	.12	.25
50 Charmed Sleep C :B:	.07	.15
51 Clever Conjurer C :B:	.07	.15
52 Contact Other Plane C :B:	.07	.15
53 Demilich M :B:	5.00	10.00
54 Displacer Beast U :B:	.12	.25
55 Djinni Windseer C :B:	.07	.15
56 Dragon Turtle R :B:	.30	.60
57 Eccentric Apprentice U :B:	.12	.25
58 Feywild Trickster U :B:	.12	.25
59 Fly U :B:	.12	.25
60 Grazilaxx, Illithid Scholar R :B:	.30	.60
61 Guild Thief U :B:	.12	.25
62 Iymrith, Desert Doom M :B:	5.00	10.00
63 Mind Flayer R :B:	.30	.60
64 Mordenkainen M :B:	2.50	5.00
6.50E+01 Mordenkainen's Polymorph C :B:	.07	.15
6.60E+01 Pixie Guide C :B:	.07	.15
6.70E+01 Power of Persuasion U :B:	.12	.25
6.80E+01 Ray of Frost U :B:	.12	.25
6.90E+01 Rimeshield Frost Giant C :B:	.07	.15
7.00E+01 Scion of Stygia C :B:	.07	.15
7.10E+01 Secret Door C :B:	.07	.15
7.20E+01 Shocking Grasp C :B:	.07	.15
73 Shortcut Seeker C :B:	.07	.15
74 Silver Raven C :B:	.07	.15
75 Soulknife Spy C :B:	.07	.15
76 Split the Party U :B:	.12	.25
77 Sudden Insight U :B:	.12	.25
78 Tasha's Hideous Laughter R :B:	.30	.60
79 Trickster's Talisman U :B:	.12	.25
80 True Polymorph R :B:	.30	.60
81 Wizard Class U :B:	.12	.25
82 Wizard's Spellbook R :B:	.30	.60
83 You Come to a River C :B:	.07	.15
84 You Find the Villains' Lair C :B:	.07	.15
85 You See a Guard Approach C :B:	.07	.15
86 Yuan-Ti Malison R :B:	.30	.60
87 Acererak the Archlich M :K:	5.00	10.00
88 Asmodeus the Archfiend R :K:	.30	.60
89 Baleful Beholder C :K:	.07	.15
90 Black Dragon U :K:	.12	.25
91 The Book of Vile Darkness M :K:	2.00	4.00
92 Check for Traps U :K:	.12	.25
93 Clattering Skeletons C :K:	.07	.15
94 Deadly Dispute C :K:	.07	.15
95 Death-Priest of Myrkul U :K:	.12	.25
96 Demogorgon's Clutches U :K:	.12	.25
97 Devour Intellect C :K:	.07	.15
98 Drider U :K:	.12	.25
99 Dungeon Crawler U :K:	.12	.25
100 Ebondeath, Dracolich M :K:	6.00	12.00
101 Eyes of the Beholder C :K:	.07	.15
102 Fates' Reversal C :K:	.07	.15
103 Feign Death C :K:	.07	.15
104 Forsworn Paladin R :K:	.30	.60
105 Gelatinous Cube R :K:	.30	.60
106 Grim Bounty C :K:	.07	.15
107 Grim Wanderer U :K:	.12	.25
108 Herald of Hadar C :K:	.07	.15
109 Hired Hexblade C :K:	.07	.15
110 Hoard Robber C :K:	.07	.15
111 Lightfoot Rogue U :K:	.12	.25
112 Lolth, Spider Queen M :K:	7.50	15.00
113 Manticore C :K:	.07	.15
114 Power Word Kill U :K:	.12	.25
115 Precipitous Drop C :K:	.07	.15
116 Ray of Enfeeblement U :K:	.12	.25
117 Reaper's Talisman U :K:	.12	.25
118 Sepulcher Ghoul C :K:	.07	.15
119 Shambling Ghast C :K:	.07	.15
120 Skullport Merchant U :K:	.12	.25
121 Sphere of Annihilation R :K:	.30	.60
122 Thieves' Tools C :K:	.07	.15
123 Vampire Spawn C :K:	.07	.15
124 Vorpal Sword R :K:	.30	.60
125 Warlock Class U :K:	.12	.25
126 Westgate Regent R :K:	.30	.60
127 Wight R :K:	.30	.60
128 Yuan-Ti Fang-Blade C :K:	.07	.15
129 Zombie Ogre C :K:	.07	.15
130 Armory Veteran C :R:	.07	.15
131 Barbarian Class U :R:	.12	.25
132 Battle Cry Goblin U :R:	.12	.25
133 Boots of Speed C :R:	.07	.15
134 Brazen Dwarf C :R:	.07	.15
135 Burning Hands U :R:	.12	.25
136 Chaos Channeler U :R:	.12	.25
137 Critical Hit U :R:	.12	.25
138 Delina, Wild Mage R :R:	.30	.60
139 Dragon's Fire C :R:	.07	.15
140 Dueling Rapier C :R:	.07	.15
141 Earth-Cult Elemental C :R:	.07	.15
142 Farideh's Fireball C :R:	.07	.15
143 Flameskull M :R:	.75	1.50
144 Goblin Javelineer C :R:	.07	.15
145 Goblin Morningstar U :R:	.12	.25
146 Hoarding Ogre C :R:	.07	.15
147 Hobgoblin Bandit Lord R :R:	.30	.60
148 Hobgoblin Captain C :R:	.07	.15
149 Hulking Bugbear U :R:	.12	.25
150 Improvised Weaponry C :R:	.07	.15
151 Inferno of the Star Mounts M :R:	6.00	12.00
152 Jaded Sell-Sword C :R:	.07	.15
153 Kick in the Door C :R:	.07	.15
154 Magic Missile U :R:	.12	.25
155 Meteor Swarm R :R:	.30	.60
156 Minion of the Mighty R :R:	.30	.60
157 Orb of Dragonkind R :R:	.30	.60
158 Plundering Barbarian C :R:	.07	.15
159 Price of Loyalty C :R:	.07	.15
160 Red Dragon U :R:	.12	.25
161 Rust Monster U :R:	.12	.25
162 Swarming Goblins C :R:	.07	.15
163 Tiger-Tribe Hunter U :R:	.12	.25
164 Unexpected Windfall C :R:	.07	.15
165 Valor Singer C :R:	.07	.15
166 Wish R :R:	.30	.60
167 Xorn R :R:	.30	.60
168 You Come to the Gnoll Camp C :R:	.07	.15
169 You Find Some Prisoners U :R:	.12	.25
170 You See a Pair of Goblins U :R:	.12	.25
171 Zalto, Fire Giant Duke R :R:	.30	.60
172 Zariel, Archduke of Avernus M :R:	2.50	5.00
173 Bulette C :G:	.07	.15
174 Bull's Strength C :G:	.07	.15
175 Choose Your Weapon U :G:	.12	.25
176 Circle of Dreams Druid R :G:	.30	.60
177 Circle of the Moon Druid C :G:	.07	.15
178 Compelled Duel C :G:	.07	.15
179 Dire Wolf Prowler C :G:	.07	.15
180 Druid Class U :G:	.12	.25
181 Ellywick Tumblestrum M :G:	2.00	4.00
182 Elturgard Ranger C :G:	.07	.15
183 Find the Path C :G:	.07	.15
184 Froghemoth R :G:	.30	.60
185 Gnoll Hunter C :G:	.07	.15
186 Green Dragon U :G:	.12	.25
187 Hill Giant Herdgorger C :G:	.07	.15
188 Hunter's Mark U :G:	.12	.25
189 Inspiring Bard C :G:	.07	.15
190 Instrument of the Bards R :G:	.30	.60
191 Intrepid Outlander U :G:	.12	.25
192 Loathsome Troll U :G:	.12	.25
193 Long Rest R :G:	.30	.60
194 Lurking Roper U :G:	.12	.25
195 Neverwinter Dryad C :G:	.07	.15
196 Ochre Jelly R :G:	.30	.60
197 Old Gnawbone M :G:	20.00	40.00
198 Owlbear C :G:	.07	.15
199 Plummet C :G:	.07	.15
200 Prosperous Innkeeper U :G:	.12	.25
201 Purple Worm U :G:	.12	.25
202 Ranger Class R :G:	.30	.60
203 Ranger's Longbow C :G:	.07	.15
204 Scaled Herbalist C :G:	.07	.15
205 Spoils of the Hunt C :G:	.07	.15
206 Sylvan Shepherd C :G:	.07	.15
207 The Tarrasque M :G:	2.50	5.00
208 Underdark Basilisk C :G:	.07	.15
209 Varis, Silverymoon Ranger R :G:	.30	.60
210 Wandering Troubadour U :G:	.12	.25
211 Werewolf Pack Leader R :G:	.30	.60
212 Wild Shape U :G:	.12	.25

213 You Find a Cursed Idol C :G: .07 .15
214 You Happen On a Glade U :G: .12 .25
215 You Meet in a Tavern U :G: .12 .25
216 Adult Gold Dragon R :R:/:W: .30 .60
217 Bard Class R :R:/:G: .30 .60
218 Barrowin of Clan Undurr U :W:/:K: .12 .25
219 Bruenor Battlehammer U :R:/:W: .12 .25
220 Drizzt Do'Urden R :G:/:W: .30 .60
221 Farideh, Devil's Chosen U :B:/:R: .12 .25
222 Fighter Class R :R:/:W: .30 .60
223 Gretchen Titchwillow U :G:/:B: .12 .25
224 Hama Pashar, Ruin Seeker U :W:/:B: .12 .25
225 Kalain, Reclusive Painter U :K:/:R: .12 .25
226 Krydle of Baldur's Gate U :B:/:K: .12 .25
227 Minsc, Beloved Ranger M :R:/:G:/:W: 2.00 4.00
228 Monk Class R :W:/:B: .30 .60
229 Orcus, Prince of Undeath R :K:/:R: .30 .60
230 Rogue Class R :B:/:K: .30 .60
231 Shessra, Death's Whisper U :K:/:G: .12 .25
232 Skeletal Swarming R :K:/:G: .30 .60
233 Sorcerer Class R :B:/:R: .30 .60
234 Targ Nar, Demon-Fang Gnoll U :R:/:G: .12 .25
235 Tiamat M :W:/:B:/:K:/:R:/:G: 10.00 20.00
236 Trelasarra, Moon Dancer U :G:/:W: .12 .25
237 Triumphant Adventurer R :W:/:K: .30 .60
238 Volo, Guide to Monsters R :G:/:B: .30 .60
239 Xanathar, Guild Kingpin M :B:/:K: 5.00 10.00
240 Bag of Holding U .12 .25
241 The Deck of Many Things M 2.00 4.00
242 Dungeon Map U .12 .25
243 Eye of Vecna R .30 .60
244 Fifty Feet of Rope U .12 .25
245 Greataxe C .07 .15
246 Hand of Vecna R .30 .60
247 Iron Golem U .12 .25
248 Leather Armor C .07 .15
249 Mimic C .07 .15
250 Spare Dagger C .07 .15
251 Spiked Pit Trap C .07 .15
252 Treasure Chest R .30 .60
253 Cave of the Frost Dragon R .30 .60
254 Den of the Bugbear R .30 .60
255 Dungeon Descent R .30 .60
256 Evolving Wilds C .07 .15
257 Hall of Storm Giants R .30 .60
258 Hive of the Eye Tyrant R .30 .60
259 Lair of the Hydra R .30 .60
260 Temple of the Dragon Queen U .12 .25
261 Treasure Vault R .30 .60
262 Plains L .07 .15
263 Plains L .07 .15
264 Plains L .07 .15
265 Plains L .07 .15
266 Island L .07 .15
267 Island L .07 .15
268 Island L .07 .15
269 Island L .07 .15
270 Swamp L .07 .15
271 Swamp L .07 .15
272 Swamp L .07 .15
273 Swamp L .07 .15
274 Mountain L .07 .15
275 Mountain L .07 .15
276 Mountain L .07 .15
277 Mountain L .07 .15
278 Forest L .07 .15
279 Forest L .07 .15
280 Forest L .07 .15
281 Forest L .07 .15
282 Grand Master of Flowers M :W: 3.00 6.00
283 Mordenkainen M :B: 4.00 8.00
284 Lolth, Spider Queen M :K: 10.00 20.00
285 Zariel, Archduke of Avernus M :R: 6.00 12.00
286 Ellywick Tumblestrum M :G: 3.00 6.00
287 Icingdeath, Frost Tyrant M :W: 6.00 12.00
288 White Dragon U :W: .12 .25
289 Blue Dragon U :B: .12 .25
290 Iymrith, Desert Doom M :B: 7.50 15.00
291 Black Dragon U :K: .12 .25
292 Ebondeath, Dracolich M :K: 7.50 15.00
293 Inferno of the Star Mounts M :R: 10.00 20.00
294 Red Dragon U :R: .12 .25
295 Green Dragon U :G: .12 .25
296 Old Gnawbone M :G: 25.00 50.00
297 Adult Gold Dragon R :R:/:W: .30 .60
298 Tiamat M :W:/:B:/:K:/:R:/:G: 17.50 35.00
299 Arborea Pegasus C :W: .07 .15
300 Blink Dog U :W: .12 .25
301 Celestial Unicorn C :W: .07 .15
302 Cloister Gargoyle U :W: .12 .25
303 Nadaar, Selfless Paladin R :W: .30 .60
304 Oswald Fiddlebender R :W: .30 .60
305 Displacer Beast U :B: .12 .25
306 Djinni Windseer C :B: .07 .15
307 Dragon Turtle R :B: .30 .60
308 Mind Flayer R :B: .30 .60
309 Pixie Guide C :B: .07 .15
310 Rimeshield Frost Giant C :B: .07 .15
311 Baleful Beholder C :K: .07 .15
312 Clattering Skeletons C :K: .07 .15
313 Gelatinous Cube R :K: .30 .60
314 Manticore C :K: .07 .15
315 Westgate Regent R :K: .30 .60
316 Wight R :K: .30 .60
317 Delina, Wild Mage R :R: .30 .60
318 Goblin Javelineer C :R: .07 .15
319 Hulking Bugbear U :R: .12 .25
320 Minion of the Mighty R :R: .30 .60
321 Rust Monster U :R: .12 .25
322 Xorn R :R: .30 .60
323 Zalto, Fire Giant Duke R :R: .30 .60
324 Bulette C :G: .07 .15
325 Dire Wolf Prowler C :G: .07 .15
326 Gnoll Hunter C :G: .07 .15
327 Loathsome Troll U :G: .12 .25
328 Lurking Roper U :G: .12 .25
329 Neverwinter Dryad C :G: .07 .15
330 Ochre Jelly R :G: .30 .60
331 Owlbear C :G: .07 .15
332 Purple Worm U :G: .12 .25
333 The Tarrasque M :G: 2.50 5.00
334 Underdark Basilisk C :G: .07 .15
335 Varis, Silverymoon Ranger R :G: .30 .60
336 Barrowin of Clan Undurr U :W:/:K: .12 .25
337 Bruenor Battlehammer U :R:/:W: .12 .25
338 Drizzt Do'Urden R :G:/:W: .30 .60
339 Farideh, Devil's Chosen U :B:/:R: .12 .25
340 Gretchen Titchwillow U :G:/:B: .12 .25
341 Hama Pashar, Ruin Seeker U :W:/:B: .12 .25
342 Kalain, Reclusive Painter U :K:/:R: .12 .25
343 Krydle of Baldur's Gate U :B:/:K: .12 .25
344 Minsc, Beloved Ranger M :R:/:G:/:W: 2.50 5.00
345 Shessra, Death's Whisper U :K:/:G: .12 .25
346 Trelasarra, Moon Dancer U :G:/:W: .12 .25
347 Volo, Guide to Monsters R :G:/:B: .30 .60
348 Iron Golem U .12 .25
349 Mimic C .07 .15
350 Cave of the Frost Dragon R .30 .60
351 Den of the Bugbear R .30 .60
352 Dungeon Descent R .30 .60
353 Evolving Wilds C .07 .15
354 Hall of Storm Giants R .30 .60
355 Hive of the Eye Tyrant R .30 .60
356 Lair of the Hydra R .30 .60
357 Temple of the Dragon Queen U .12 .25
358 Treasure Vault R .30 .60
359 The Book of Exalted Deeds M :W: 7.50 15.00
360 Dancing Sword R :W: .30 .60
361 Flumph R :W: .30 .60
362 Guardian of Faith R :W: .30 .60
363 Loyal Warhound R :W: .30 .60
364 Teleportation Circle R :W: .30 .60
365 The Blackstaff of Waterdeep R :B: .30 .60
366 Demilich M :B: 7.50 15.00
367 Grazilaxx, Illithid Scholar R :B: .30 .60
368 Tasha's Hideous Laughter R :B: .30 .60
369 True Polymorph R :B: .30 .60
370 Wizard's Spellbook R :B: .30 .60
371 Yuan-Ti Malison R :B: .30 .60
372 Acererak the Archlich M :K: 7.50 15.00
373 Asmodeus the Archfiend R :K: .30 .60
374 The Book of Vile Darkness M :K: 3.00 6.00
375 Forsworn Paladin R :K: .30 .60
376 Sphere of Annihilation R :K: .30 .60
377 Vorpal Sword R :K: .30 .60
378 Flameskull M :R: 1.50 3.00
379 Hobgoblin Bandit Lord R :R: .30 .60
380 Meteor Swarm R :R: .30 .60
381 Orb of Dragonkind R :R: .30 .60
382 Wish R :R: .30 .60
383 Circle of Dreams Druid R :G: .30 .60
384 Froghemoth R :G: .30 .60
385 Instrument of the Bards R :G: .30 .60
386 Long Rest R :G: .30 .60
387 Werewolf Pack Leader R :G: .30 .60
388 Orcus, Prince of Undeath R :K:/:R: .30 .60
389 Skeletal Swarming R :K:/:G: .30 .60
390 Triumphant Adventurer R :W:/:K: .30 .60
391 Xanathar, Guild Kingpin M :B:/:K: 7.50 15.00
392 The Deck of Many Things M 3.00 6.00
393 Eye of Vecna R .30 .60
394 Hand of Vecna R .30 .60
395 Treasure Chest R .30 .60
396 Vorpal Sword R :K: .30 .60
397 Treasure Chest R .30 .60
398 Portable Hole U :W: .12 .25
399 You Find the Villains' Lair C :B: .07 .15
400 Power Word Kill U :K: .12 .25
401 Magic Missile U :R: .12 .25
402 Prosperous Innkeeper U :G: .12 .25

2021 Magic The Gathering Dungeons and Dragons Adventures in the Forgotten Realms Foil

1 +2 Mace C :W: .20 .40
2 Arborea Pegasus C :W: .20 .40
3 Blink Dog U :W: .25 .50
5 Celestial Unicorn C :W: .20 .40
6 Cleric Class U :W: .25 .50
7 Cloister Gargoyle U :W: .25 .50
8 Dancing Sword R :W: .30 .60
9 Dawnbringer Cleric C :W: .20 .40
10 Delver's Torch C :W: .20 .40
11 Devoted Paladin C :W: .20 .40
12 Divine Smite U :W: .25 .50
13 Dragon's Disciple U :W: .25 .50
14 Dwarfhold Champion C :W: .20 .40
15 Flumph R :W: .30 .60
16 Gloom Stalker C :W: .20 .40
18 Guardian of Faith R :W: .30 .60
19 Half-Elf Monk C :W: .20 .40
21 Ingenious Smith U :W: .25 .50
22 Keen-Eared Sentry U :W: .25 .50
23 Loyal Warhound R :W: .30 .60
24 Minimus Containment C :W: .20 .40
25 Monk of the Open Hand U :W: .25 .50
26 Moon-Blessed Cleric U :W: .25 .50
27 Nadaar, Selfless Paladin R :W: .30 .60
28 Oswald Fiddlebender R :W: .30 .60
29 Paladin Class R :W: .30 .60
30 Paladin's Shield C :W: .20 .40
31 Planar Ally C :W: .20 .40
32 Plate Armor U :W: .25 .50
33 Portable Hole U :W: .25 .50
34 Potion of Healing C :W: .20 .40
35 Priest of Ancient Lore C :W: .20 .40
36 Rally Maneuver U :W: .25 .50
37 Ranger's Hawk C :W: .20 .40
38 Steadfast Paladin C :W: .20 .40
39 Teleportation Circle R :W: .30 .60
40 Veteran Dungeoneer C :W: .20 .40
41 White Dragon U :W: .25 .50
42 You Hear Something on Watch C :W: .20 .40
43 You're Ambushed on the Road C :W: .20 .40
44 Aberrant Mind Sorcerer U :B: .25 .50
45 Air-Cult Elemental C :B: .20 .40
46 Arcane Investigator C :B: .20 .40
47 Bar the Gate C :B: .20 .40
48 The Blackstaff of Waterdeep R :B: .30 .60
49 Blue Dragon U :B: .25 .50
50 Charmed Sleep C :B: .20 .40
51 Clever Conjurer C :B: .20 .40
52 Contact Other Plane C :B: .20 .40
54 Displacer Beast U :B: .25 .50
55 Djinni Windseer C :B: .20 .40
56 Dragon Turtle R :B: .30 .60
57 Eccentric Apprentice U :B: .25 .50
58 Feywild Trickster U :B: .25 .50
59 Fly U :B: .25 .50
60 Grazilaxx, Illithid Scholar R :B: .30 .60
61 Guild Thief U :B: .25 .50
63 Mind Flayer R :B: .30 .60
65 Mordenkainen's Polymorph C :B: .20 .40
66 Pixie Guide C :B: .20 .40
67 Power of Persuasion U :B: .25 .50
68 Ray of Frost U :B: .25 .50
69 Rimeshield Frost Giant C :B: .20 .40
70 Scion of Stygia C :B: .20 .40
71 Secret Door C :B: .20 .40
72 Shocking Grasp C :B: .20 .40
73 Shortcut Seeker C :B: .20 .40
74 Silver Raven C :B: .20 .40
75 Soulknife Spy C :B: .20 .40
76 Split the Party U :B: .25 .50
77 Sudden Insight U :B: .25 .50
78 Tasha's Hideous Laughter R :B: .30 .60
79 Trickster's Talisman U :B: .25 .50
80 True Polymorph R :B: .30 .60
81 Wizard Class U :B: .25 .50
82 Wizard's Spellbook R :B: .30 .60
83 You Come to a River C :B: .20 .40
84 You Find the Villains' Lair C :B: .20 .40
85 You See a Guard Approach C :B: .20 .40
86 Yuan-Ti Malison R :B: .30 .60
88 Asmodeus the Archfiend R :K: .30 .60
89 Baleful Beholder C :K: .20 .40
90 Black Dragon U :K: .25 .50
92 Check for Traps U :K: .25 .50
93 Clattering Skeletons C :K: .20 .40
94 Deadly Dispute C :K: .20 .40
95 Death-Priest of Myrkul U :K: .25 .50
96 Demogorgon's Clutches U :K: .25 .50
97 Devour Intellect C :K: .20 .40
98 Drider U :K: .25 .50
99 Dungeon Crawler U :K: .25 .50
101 Eyes of the Beholder C :K: .20 .40
102 Fates' Reversal C :K: .20 .40
103 Feign Death C :K: .20 .40
104 Forsworn Paladin R :K: .30 .60
105 Gelatinous Cube R :K: .30 .60
106 Grim Bounty C :K: .20 .40
107 Grim Wanderer U :K: .25 .50
108 Herald of Hadar C :K: .20 .40
109 Hired Hexblade C :K: .20 .40
110 Hoard Robber C :K: .20 .40
111 Lightfoot Rogue U :K: .25 .50
113 Manticore C :K: .20 .40
114 Power Word Kill U :K: .25 .50
115 Precipitous Drop C :K: .20 .40
116 Ray of Enfeeblement U :K: .25 .50
117 Reaper's Talisman U :K: .25 .50
118 Sepulcher Ghoul C :K: .20 .40
119 Shambling Ghast C :K: .20 .40
120 Skullport Merchant U :K: .25 .50
121 Sphere of Annihilation R :K: .30 .60
122 Thieves' Tools C :K: .20 .40
123 Vampire Spawn C :K: .20 .40
124 Vorpal Sword R :K: .30 .60
125 Warlock Class U :K: .25 .50
126 Westgate Regent R :K: .30 .60
127 Wight R :K: .30 .60
128 Yuan-Ti Fang-Blade C :K: .20 .40
129 Zombie Ogre C :K: .20 .40
130 Armory Veteran C :R: .20 .40
131 Barbarian Class U :R: .25 .50
132 Battle Cry Goblin U :R: .25 .50
133 Boots of Speed C :R: .20 .40
134 Brazen Dwarf C :R: .20 .40
135 Burning Hands U :R: .25 .50
136 Chaos Channeler U :R: .25 .50
137 Critical Hit U :R: .25 .50
138 Delina, Wild Mage R :R: .30 .60
139 Dragon's Fire C :R: .20 .40
140 Dueling Rapier C :R: .20 .40
141 Earth-Cult Elemental C :R: .20 .40
142 Farideh's Fireball C :R: .20 .40
144 Goblin Javelineer C :R: .20 .40
145 Goblin Morningstar U :R: .25 .50
146 Hoarding Ogre C :R: .20 .40
147 Hobgoblin Bandit Lord R :R: .30 .60
148 Hobgoblin Captain C :R: .20 .40
149 Hulking Bugbear U :R: .25 .50
150 Improvised Weaponry C :R: .20 .40
152 Jaded Sell-Sword C :R: .20 .40
153 Kick in the Door C :R: .20 .40
154 Magic Missile U :R: .25 .50
155 Meteor Swarm R :R: .30 .60
156 Minion of the Mighty R :R: .30 .60
157 Orb of Dragonkind R :R: .30 .60
158 Plundering Barbarian C :R: .20 .40
159 Price of Loyalty C :R: .20 .40
160 Red Dragon U :R: .25 .50
161 Rust Monster U :R: .25 .50
162 Swarming Goblins C :R: .20 .40
163 Tiger-Tribe Hunter U :R: .25 .50
164 Unexpected Windfall C :R: .20 .40
165 Valor Singer C :R: .20 .40
166 Wish R :R: .30 .60
167 Xorn R :R: .30 .60
168 You Come to the Gnoll Camp C :R: .20 .40
169 You Find Some Prisoners U :R: .25 .50
170 You See a Pair of Goblins U :R: .25 .50
171 Zalto, Fire Giant Duke R :R: .30 .60
173 Bulette C :G: .20 .40
174 Bull's Strength C :G: .20 .40
175 Choose Your Weapon U :G: .25 .50
176 Circle of Dreams Druid R :G: .30 .60
177 Circle of the Moon Druid C :G: .20 .40
178 Compelled Duel C :G: .20 .40
179 Dire Wolf Prowler C :G: .20 .40
180 Druid Class U :G: .25 .50
182 Elturgard Ranger C :G: .20 .40
183 Find the Path C :G: .20 .40
184 Froghemoth R :G: .30 .60
185 Gnoll Hunter C :G: .20 .40
186 Green Dragon U :G: .25 .50
187 Hill Giant Herdgorger C :G: .20 .40
188 Hunter's Mark U :G: .25 .50
189 Inspiring Bard C :G: .20 .40
190 Instrument of the Bards R :G: .30 .60
191 Intrepid Outlander U :G: .25 .50
192 Loathsome Troll U :G: .25 .50
193 Long Rest R :G: .30 .60
194 Lurking Roper U :G: .25 .50
195 Neverwinter Dryad C :G: .20 .40
196 Ochre Jelly R :G: .30 .60
198 Owlbear C :G: .20 .40
199 Plummet C :G: .20 .40
200 Prosperous Innkeeper U :G: .25 .50
201 Purple Worm U :G: .25 .50
202 Ranger Class R :G: .30 .60
203 Ranger's Longbow C :G: .20 .40
204 Scaled Herbalist C :G: .20 .40
205 Spoils of the Hunt C :G: .20 .40
206 Sylvan Shepherd C :G: .20 .40
208 Underdark Basilisk C :G: .20 .40
209 Varis, Silverymoon Ranger R :G: .30 .60
210 Wandering Troubadour U :G: .25 .50
211 Werewolf Pack Leader R :G: .30 .60
212 Wild Shape U :G: .25 .50
213 You Find a Cursed Idol C :G: .20 .40
214 You Happen On a Glade U :G: .25 .50
215 You Meet in a Tavern U :G: .25 .50
216 Adult Gold Dragon R :R:/:W: .30 .60
217 Bard Class R :R:/:G: .30 .60
218 Barrowin of Clan Undurr U :W:/:K: .25 .50
219 Bruenor Battlehammer U :R:/:W: .25 .50
220 Drizzt Do'Urden R :G:/:W: .30 .60
221 Farideh, Devil's Chosen U :B:/:R: .25 .50
222 Fighter Class R :R:/:W: .30 .60
223 Gretchen Titchwillow U :G:/:B: .25 .50
224 Hama Pashar, Ruin Seeker U :W:/:B: .25 .50
225 Kalain, Reclusive Painter U :K:/:R: .25 .50
226 Krydle of Baldur's Gate U :B:/:K: .25 .50
228 Monk Class R :W:/:B: .30 .60
229 Orcus, Prince of Undeath R :K:/:R: .30 .60
230 Rogue Class R :B:/:K: .30 .60
231 Shessra, Death's Whisper U :K:/:G: .25 .50
232 Skeletal Swarming R :K:/:G: .30 .60
233 Sorcerer Class R :B:/:R: .30 .60
234 Targ Nar, Demon-Fang Gnoll U :R:/:G: .25 .50
236 Trelasarra, Moon Dancer U :G:/:W: .25 .50
237 Triumphant Adventurer R :W:/:K: .30 .60
238 Volo, Guide to Monsters R :G:/:B: .30 .60
240 Bag of Holding U .25 .50
242 Dungeon Map U .25 .50
243 Eye of Vecna R .30 .60
244 Fifty Feet of Rope U .25 .50
245 Greataxe C .20 .40
246 Hand of Vecna R .30 .60
247 Iron Golem U .25 .50
248 Leather Armor C .20 .40
249 Mimic C .20 .40
250 Spare Dagger C .20 .40
251 Spiked Pit Trap C .20 .40
252 Treasure Chest R .30 .60
253 Cave of the Frost Dragon R .30 .60
254 Den of the Bugbear R .30 .60
255 Dungeon Descent R .30 .60
256 Evolving Wilds C .20 .40
257 Hall of Storm Giants R .30 .60
258 Hive of the Eye Tyrant R .30 .60
259 Lair of the Hydra R .30 .60
260 Temple of the Dragon Queen U .25 .50
261 Treasure Vault R .30 .60
262 Plains L .20 .40
263 Plains L .20 .40
264 Plains L .20 .40
265 Plains L .20 .40
266 Island L .20 .40
267 Island L .20 .40
268 Island L .20 .40
269 Island L .20 .40
270 Swamp L .20 .40
271 Swamp L .20 .40
272 Swamp L .20 .40
273 Swamp L .20 .40
274 Mountain L .20 .40
275 Mountain L .20 .40
276 Mountain L .20 .40
277 Mountain L .20 .40
278 Forest L .20 .40
279 Forest L .20 .40
280 Forest L .20 .40
281 Forest L .20 .40
288 White Dragon U :W: .25 .50
289 Blue Dragon U :B: .25 .50
291 Black Dragon U :K: .25 .50
294 Red Dragon U :R: .25 .50
295 Green Dragon U :G: .25 .50
297 Adult Gold Dragon R :R:/:W: .30 .60
299 Arborea Pegasus C :W: .20 .40
300 Blink Dog U :W: .25 .50
301 Celestial Unicorn C :W: .20 .40
302 Cloister Gargoyle U :W: .25 .50
303 Nadaar, Selfless Paladin R :W: .30 .60
304 Oswald Fiddlebender R :W: .30 .60
305 Displacer Beast U :B: .25 .50
306 Djinni Windseer C :B: .20 .40
307 Dragon Turtle R :B: .30 .60
308 Mind Flayer R :B: .30 .60
309 Pixie Guide C :B: .20 .40
310 Rimeshield Frost Giant C :B: .20 .40
311 Baleful Beholder C :K: .20 .40
312 Clattering Skeletons C :K: .20 .40
313 Gelatinous Cube R :K: .30 .60
314 Manticore C :K: .20 .40
315 Westgate Regent R :K: .30 .60
316 Wight R :K: .30 .60
317 Delina, Wild Mage R :R: .30 .60
318 Goblin Javelineer C :R: .20 .40
319 Hulking Bugbear U :R: .25 .50
320 Minion of the Mighty R :R: .30 .60
321 Rust Monster U :R: .25 .50
322 Xorn R :R: .30 .60
323 Zalto, Fire Giant Duke R :R: .30 .60
324 Bulette C :G: .20 .40
325 Dire Wolf Prowler C :G: .20 .40
326 Gnoll Hunter C :G: .20 .40
327 Loathsome Troll U :G: .25 .50
328 Lurking Roper U :G: .25 .50
329 Neverwinter Dryad C :G: .20 .40
330 Ochre Jelly R :G: .30 .60
331 Owlbear C :G: .20 .40
332 Purple Worm U :G: .25 .50
334 Underdark Basilisk C :G: .20 .40

335 Varis, Silverymoon Ranger R :G: .30 .60
336 Barrowin of Clan Undurr U :W:/:K: .25 .50
337 Bruenor Battlehammer U :R:/:W: .25 .50
338 Drizzt Do'Urden R :G:/:W: .30 .60
339 Farideh, Devil's Chosen U :B:/:R: .25 .50
340 Gretchen Titchwillow U :G:/:B: .25 .50
341 Hama Pashar, Ruin Seeker U :W:/:B: .25 .50
342 Kalain, Reclusive Painter U :K:/:R: .25 .50
343 Krydle of Baldur's Gate U :B:/:K: .25 .50
345 Shessra, Death's Whisper U :K:/:G: .25 .50
346 Trelasarra, Moon Dancer U :G:/:W: .25 .50
347 Volo, Guide to Monsters R :G:/:B: .30 .60
348 Iron Golem U .25 .50
349 Mimic C .20 .40
350 Cave of the Frost Dragon R .30 .60
351 Den of the Bugbear R .30 .60
352 Dungeon Descent R .30 .60
353 Evolving Wilds C .20 .40
354 Hall of Storm Giants R .30 .60
355 Hive of the Eye Tyrant R .30 .60
356 Lair of the Hydra R .30 .60
357 Temple of the Dragon Queen U .25 .50
358 Treasure Vault R .30 .60
360 Dancing Sword R :W: .30 .60
361 Flumph R :W: .30 .60
362 Guardian of Faith R :W: .30 .60
363 Loyal Warhound R :W: .30 .60
364 Teleportation Circle R :W: .30 .60
365 The Blackstaff of Waterdeep R :B: .30 .60
367 Grazilaxx, Illithid Scholar R :B: .30 .60
368 Tasha's Hideous Laughter R :B: .30 .60
369 True Polymorph R :B: .30 .60
370 Wizard's Spellbook R :B: .30 .60
371 Yuan-Ti Malison R :B: .30 .60
373 Asmodeus the Archfiend R :K: .30 .60
375 Forsworn Paladin R :K: .30 .60
376 Sphere of Annihilation R :K: .30 .60
377 Vorpal Sword R :K: .30 .60
379 Hobgoblin Bandit Lord R :R: .30 .60
380 Meteor Swarm R :R: .30 .60
381 Orb of Dragonkind R :R: .30 .60
382 Wish R :R: .30 .60
383 Circle of Dreams Druid R :G: .30 .60
384 Froghemoth R :G: .30 .60
385 Instrument of the Bards R :G: .30 .60
386 Long Rest R :G: .30 .60
387 Werewolf Pack Leader R :G: .30 .60
388 Orcus, Prince of Undeath R :K:/:R: .30 .60
389 Skeletal Swarming R :K:/:G: .30 .60
390 Triumphant Adventurer R :W:/:K: .30 .60
393 Eye of Vecna R .30 .60
394 Hand of Vecna R .30 .60
395 Treasure Chest R .30 .60
396 Vorpal Sword R :K: .30 .60
397 Treasure Chest R .30 .60
398 Portable Hole U :W: .25 .50
399 You Find the Villains' Lair C :B: .20 .40
400 Power Word Kill U :K: .25 .50
401 Magic Missile U :R: .25 .50
402 Prosperous Innkeeper U :G: .25 .50

2021 Magic The Gathering Dungeons and Dragons Adventures in the Forgotten Realms Tokens

1 Angel .50 1.00
2 Icingdeath, Frost Tongue 1.25 2.50
3 Dog Illusion .20 .40
4 Faerie Dragon .15 .30
7 Spider .20 .40
8 Vecna 1.50 3.00
9 Zombie .10 .20
10 Boo .75 1.50
11 Devil .07 .15
13 Guenhwyvar .25 .50
14 Wolf .07 .15
15 Treasure .10 .20
16 Ellywick Tumblestrum Emblem .17 .35
17 Lolth, Spider Queen Emblem .30 .75
18 Mordenkainen Emblem .15 .30
19 Zariel, Archduke of Avernus Emblem .20 .40
21 Lost Mine of Phandelver .25 .50

2021 Magic The Gathering Dungeons and Dragons Forgotten Realms Commander

1 Galea, Kindler of Hope M :G:/:B:/:W: .50 1.00
2 Prosper, Tome-Bound M :K:/:R: .50 1.00
3 Sefris of the Hidden Ways M :W:/:B:/:K: .50 1.00
4 Vrondiss, Rage of Ancients M :R:/:G: .50 1.00
5 Fey Steed R :W: .30 .60
6 Holy Avenger R :W: .30 .60
7 Immovable Rod R :W: .30 .60
8 Mantle of the Ancients R :W: .30 .60
9 Radiant Solar R :W: .30 .60
10 Revivify R :W: .30 .60
11 Robe of Stars R :W: .30 .60
12 Thorough Investigation R :W: .30 .60
13 Valiant Endeavor R :W: .30 .60
14 Arcane Endeavor R :B: .30 .60
15 Diviner's Portent R :B: .30 .60
16 Minn, Wily Illusionist R :B: .30 .60
17 Netherese Puzzle-Ward R :B: .30 .60
18 Phantom Steed R :B: .30 .60
19 Rod of Absorption R :B: .30 .60
20 Winged Boots R :B: .30 .60
21 Bag of Devouring R :K: .30 .60
22 Danse Macabre R :K: .30 .60
23 Death Tyrant R :K: .30 .60
24 Grave Endeavor R :K: .30 .60
25 Grim Hireling R :K: .30 .60
26 Hellish Rebuke R :K: .30 .60
27 Lorcan, Warlock Collector R :K: .30 .60
28 Wand of Orcus R :K: .30 .60
29 Berserker's Frenzy R :R: .30 .60
30 Chaos Dragon R :R: .30 .60
31 Fiendlash R :R: .30 .60
32 Maddening Hex R :R: .30 .60
33 Reckless Endeavor R :R: .30 .60
34 Share the Spoils R :R: .30 .60
35 Vengeful Ancestor R :R: .30 .60
36 Wild-Magic Sorcerer R :R: .30 .60
37 Bag of Tricks R :G: .30 .60
38 Belt of Giant Strength R :G: .30 .60
39 Druid of Purification R :G: .30 .60
40 Indomitable Might R :G: .30 .60
41 Neverwinter Hydra R :G: .30 .60
42 Song of Inspiration R :G: .30 .60
43 Wild Endeavor R :G: .30 .60
44 Catti-brie of Mithral Hall R :G:/:W: .30 .60
45 Dragonborn Champion R :R:/:G: .30 .60
46 Extract Brain R :B:/:K: .30 .60
47 Fevered Suspicion R :K:/:R: .30 .60
48 Hurl Through Hell R :K:/:R: .30 .60
49 Karazikar, the Eye Tyrant M :K:/:R: .50 1.00
50 Klauth, Unrivaled Ancient M :R:/:G: .50 1.00
51 Klauth's Will R :R:/:G: .30 .60
52 Midnight Pathlighter R :W:/:B: .30 .60
53 Nihiloor M :W:/:B:/:K: .50 1.00
54 Ride the Avalanche R :G:/:B: .30 .60
55 Storvald, Frost Giant Jarl M :G:/:W:/:B: .50 1.00
56 Wulfgar of Icewind Dale R :R:/:G: .30 .60
57 Bucknard's Everfull Purse U .12 .25
58 Clay Golem U .12 .25
59 Component Pouch U .12 .25
60 Ebony Fly U .12 .25
61 Sword of Hours U .12 .25
62 Underdark Rift U .12 .25
63 Angel of Finality R :W: .30 .60
64 Angelic Gift C :W: .07 .15
65 Cataclysmic Gearhulk M :W: .50 1.00
66 Eternal Dragon R :W: .30 .60
67 Gryff's Boon U :W: .12 .25
68 Karmic Guide R :W: .30 .60
69 Puresteel Paladin R :W: .30 .60
70 Realm-Cloaked Giant // Cast Off M :W: .50 1.00
71 Ronom Unicorn C :W: .07 .15
72 Sram, Senior Edificer R :W: .30 .60
73 Sun Titan M :W: .50 1.00
74 Sunblast Angel R :W: .30 .60
75 Swords to Plowshares U :W: .12 .25
76 Valorous Stance U :W: .12 .25
77 Wall of Omens U :W: .12 .25
78 Winds of Rath R :W: .30 .60
79 Brainstorm C :B: .07 .15
80 Champion of Wits R :B: .30 .60
81 Curator of Mysteries R :B: .30 .60
82 Curse of Verbosity U :B: .12 .25
83 Eel Umbra C :B: .07 .15
84 Forbidden Alchemy U :B: .12 .25
85 Imprisoned in the Moon R :B: .30 .60
86 Merfolk Looter U :B: .12 .25
87 Mulldrifter U :B: .12 .25
88 Murder of Crows U :B: .12 .25
89 Phantasmal Image R :B: .30 .60
90 Prognostic Sphinx R :B: .30 .60
91 Propaganda U :B: .12 .25
92 Psychic Impetus U :B: .12 .25
93 Riverwise Augur U :B: .12 .25
94 Serum Visions U :B: .12 .25
95 Chittering Witch R :K: .30 .60
96 Consuming Vapors R :K: .30 .60
97 Dead Man's Chest R :K: .30 .60
98 Doomed Necromancer R :K: .30 .60
99 Fiend of the Shadows R :K: .30 .60
100 Gonti, Lord of Luxury R :K: .30 .60
101 Hex R :K: .30 .60
102 Marionette Master R :K: .30 .60
103 Necromantic Selection R :K: .30 .60
104 Ogre Slumlord R :K: .30 .60
105 Phthisis U :K: .12 .25
106 Piper of the Swarm R :K: .30 .60
107 Plaguecrafter U :K: .12 .25
108 Pontiff of Blight R :K: .30 .60
109 Reassembling Skeleton U :K: .12 .25
110 Shriekmaw U :K: .12 .25
111 Unburial Rites U :K: .12 .25
112 Victimize U :K: .12 .25
113 Anger U :R: .12 .25
114 Apex of Power M :R: .50 1.00
115 Bogardan Hellkite M :R: .50 1.00
116 Chain Reaction R :R: .30 .60
117 Chaos Warp R :R: .30 .60
118 Commune with Lava R :R: .30 .60
119 Dark-Dweller Oracle R :R: .30 .60
120 Demanding Dragon R :R: .30 .60
121 Dire Fleet Daredevil R :R: .30 .60
122 Disrupt Decorum R :R: .30 .60
123 Dragonlord's Servant U :R: .12 .25
124 Dragonmaster Outcast M :R: .50 1.00
125 Dream Pillager R :R: .30 .60
126 Etali, Primal Storm R :R: .30 .60
127 Gratuitous Violence R :R: .30 .60
128 Hoard-Smelter Dragon R :R: .30 .60
129 Ignite the Future R :R: .30 .60
130 Izzet Chemister R :R: .30 .60
131 Light Up the Stage U :R: .12 .25
132 Loyal Apprentice U :R: .12 .25
133 Magmaquake R :R: .30 .60
134 Opportunistic Dragon R :R: .30 .60
135 Outpost Siege R :R: .30 .60
136 Rile C :R: .07 .15
137 Scourge of Valkas R :R: .30 .60
138 Shiny Impetus U :R: .12 .25
139 Shivan Hellkite R :R: .30 .60
140 Skyline Despot R :R: .30 .60
141 Skyship Stalker R :R: .30 .60
142 Spit Flame R :R: .30 .60
143 Taurean Mauler R :R: .30 .60
144 Tectonic Giant R :R: .30 .60
145 Terror of Mount Velus R :R: .30 .60
146 Throes of Chaos U :R: .12 .25
147 Thunderbreak Regent R :R: .30 .60
148 Vandalblast U :R: .12 .25
149 Warstorm Surge R :R: .30 .60
150 Abundant Growth C :G: .07 .15
151 Acidic Slime U :G: .12 .25
152 Beast Within U :G: .12 .25
153 Chameleon Colossus R :G: .30 .60
154 Colossal Majesty U :G: .12 .25
155 Cultivate U :G: .12 .25
156 Decree of Savagery R :G: .30 .60
157 Explore C :G: .07 .15
158 Fertile Ground C :G: .07 .15
159 Garruk's Uprising U :G: .12 .25
160 Greater Good R :G: .30 .60
161 Heroic Intervention R :G: .30 .60
162 Kenrith's Transformation U :G: .12 .25
163 Kindred Summons R :G: .30 .60
164 Nature's Lore C :G: .07 .15
165 Paradise Druid U :G: .12 .25
166 Rampant Growth C :G: .07 .15
167 Rancor U :G: .12 .25
168 Return of the Wildspeaker R :G: .30 .60
169 Return to Nature C :G: .07 .15
170 Rishkar's Expertise R :G: .30 .60
171 Shamanic Revelation R :G: .30 .60
172 Utopia Sprawl C :G: .07 .15
173 Verdant Embrace R :G: .30 .60
174 Wild Growth C :G: .07 .15
175 Ashen Rider M :W:/:K: .50 1.00
176 Atarka, World Render R :R:/:G: .30 .60
177 Baleful Strix R :B:/:K: .30 .60
178 Bant Charm U :G:/:W:/:B: .12 .25
179 Bedevil R :K:/:R: .30 .60
180 Behemoth Sledge U :G:/:W: .12 .25
181 Bituminous Blast U :K:/:R: .12 .25
182 Cloudblazer U :W:/:B: .12 .25
183 Cold-Eyed Selkie R :G:/:B: .30 .60
184 Despark U :W:/:K: .12 .25
185 Fleecemane Lion R :G:/:W: .30 .60
186 Hostage Taker R :B:/:K: .30 .60
187 Knight of Autumn R :G:/:W: .30 .60
188 Necrotic Sliver U :W:/:K: .12 .25
189 Obsessive Stitcher U :B:/:K: .12 .25
190 Rakdos Charm U :K:/:R: .12 .25
191 Savage Ventmaw U :R:/:G: .12 .25
192 Shielding Plax C :G:/:B: .07 .15
193 Terminate U :K:/:R: .12 .25
194 Theater of Horrors R :K:/:R: .30 .60
195 Utter End R :W:/:K: .30 .60
196 Vanish into Memory U :W:/:B: .12 .25
197 Arcane Signet C .07 .15
198 Argentum Armor R .30 .60
199 Basilisk Collar R .30 .60
200 Burnished Hart U .12 .25
201 Chaos Wand R .30 .60
202 Colossus Hammer U .12 .25
203 Commander's Sphere C .07 .15
204 Dragon's Hoard R .30 .60
205 Explorer's Scope C .07 .15
206 Fellwar Stone U .12 .25
207 Gruul Signet C .07 .15
208 Heirloom Blade U .12 .25
209 Masterwork of Ingenuity R .30 .60
210 Meteor Golem U .12 .25
211 Mind Stone U .12 .25
212 Moonsilver Spear R .30 .60
213 Orazca Relic C .07 .15
214 Rakdos Signet U .12 .25
215 Sol Ring U .12 .25
216 Solemn Simulacrum R .30 .60
217 Swiftfoot Boots U .12 .25
218 Sword of the Animist R .30 .60
219 Talisman of Indulgence U .12 .25
220 Unstable Obelisk U .12 .25
221 Viridian Longbow C .07 .15
222 Wayfarer's Bauble C .07 .15
223 Arcane Sanctum U .12 .25
224 Azorius Chancery U .12 .25
225 Bant Panorama C .07 .15
226 Bojuka Bog C .07 .15
227 Canopy Vista R .30 .60
228 Choked Estuary R .30 .60
229 Cinder Glade R .30 .60
230 Command Tower C .07 .15
231 Crucible of the Spirit Dragon R .30 .60
232 Darkwater Catacombs R .30 .60
233 Desert U .12 .25
234 Dimir Aqueduct U .12 .25
235 Esper Panorama C .07 .15
236 Exotic Orchard R .30 .60
237 Flood Plain U .12 .25
238 Foreboding Ruins R .30 .60
239 Fortified Village R .30 .60
240 Game Trail R .30 .60
241 Geier Reach Sanitarium R .30 .60
242 Grasslands U .12 .25
243 Gruul Turf U .12 .25
244 Halimar Depths C .07 .15
245 Haven of the Spirit Dragon R .30 .60
246 High Market R .30 .60
247 Lumbering Falls R .30 .60
248 Mishra's Factory U .12 .25
249 Mortuary Mire C .07 .15
250 Mossfire Valley R .30 .60
251 Mosswort Bridge R .30 .60
252 Nimbus Maze R .30 .60
253 Orzhov Basilica U .12 .25
254 Path of Ancestry C .07 .15
255 Port Town R .30 .60
256 Prairie Stream R .30 .60
257 Rakdos Carnarium U .12 .25
258 Seaside Citadel U .12 .25
259 Shadowblood Ridge R .30 .60
260 Simic Growth Chamber U .12 .25
261 Skycloud Expanse R .30 .60
262 Smoldering Marsh R .30 .60
263 Spinerock Knoll R .30 .60
264 Sungrass Prairie R .30 .60
265 Sunken Hollow R .30 .60
266 Tainted Peak U .12 .25
267 Terramorphic Expanse C .07 .15
268 Thriving Grove C .07 .15
269 Thriving Heath C .07 .15
270 Thriving Isle C .07 .15
271 Thriving Moor C .07 .15
272 Vitu-Ghazi, the City-Tree U .12 .25
273 Zhalfirin Void U .12 .25
274 Fey Steed R :W: .30 .60
275 Holy Avenger R :W: .30 .60
276 Immovable Rod R :W: .30 .60
277 Mantle of the Ancients R :W: .30 .60
278 Radiant Solar R :W: .30 .60
279 Revivify R :W: .30 .60
280 Robe of Stars R :W: .30 .60
281 Thorough Investigation R :W: .30 .60
282 Valiant Endeavor R :W: .30 .60
283 Arcane Endeavor R :B: .30 .60
284 Diviner's Portent R :B: .30 .60
285 Minn, Wily Illusionist R :B: .30 .60
286 Netherese Puzzle-Ward R :B: .30 .60
287 Phantom Steed R :B: .30 .60
288 Rod of Absorption R :B: .30 .60
289 Winged Boots R :B: .30 .60
290 Bag of Devouring R :K: .30 .60
291 Danse Macabre R :K: .30 .60
292 Death Tyrant R :K: .30 .60
293 Grave Endeavor R :K: .30 .60
294 Grim Hireling R :K: .30 .60
295 Hellish Rebuke R :K: .30 .60
296 Lorcan, Warlock Collector R :K: .30 .60
297 Wand of Orcus R :K: .30 .60
298 Berserker's Frenzy R :R: .30 .60
299 Chaos Dragon R :R: .30 .60
300 Fiendlash R :R: .30 .60
301 Maddening Hex R :R: .30 .60
302 Reckless Endeavor R :R: .30 .60
303 Share the Spoils R :R: .30 .60
304 Vengeful Ancestor R :R: .30 .60
305 Wild-Magic Sorcerer R :R: .30 .60
306 Bag of Tricks R :G: .30 .60
307 Belt of Giant Strength R :G: .30 .60
308 Druid of Purification R :G: .30 .60
309 Indomitable Might R :G: .30 .60
310 Neverwinter Hydra R :G: .30 .60
311 Song of Inspiration R :G: .30 .60
312 Wild Endeavor R :G: .30 .60
313 Catti-brie of Mithral Hall R :G:/:W: .30 .60
314 Dragonborn Champion R :R:/:G: .30 .60
315 Extract Brain R :B:/:K: .30 .60
316 Fevered Suspicion R :K:/:R: .30 .60
317 Galea, Kindler of Hope M :G:/:B:/:W: .50 1.00
318 Hurl Through Hell R :K:/:R: .30 .60
319 Karazikar, the Eye Tyrant M :K:/:R: .50 1.00
320 Klauth, Unrivaled Ancient M :R:/:G: .50 1.00
321 Klauth's Will R :R:/:G: .30 .60
322 Midnight Pathlighter R :W:/:B: .30 .60
323 Nihiloor M :W:/:B:/:K: .50 1.00
324 Prosper, Tome-Bound M :K:/:R: .50 1.00
325 Ride the Avalanche R :G:/:B: .30 .60
326 Sefris of the Hidden Ways M :W:/:B:/:K: .50 1.00
327 Storvald, Frost Giant Jarl M :G:/:W:/:B: .50 1.00
328 Vrondiss, Rage of Ancients M :R:/:G: .50 1.00
329 Wulfgar of Icewind Dale R :R:/:G: .30 .60
330 Dragonspeaker Shaman U :R: .12 .25
331 Lightning Greaves U .12 .25

2021 Magic The Gathering Innistrad Crimson Vow

1 Adamant Will C :W: .07 .15
2 Angelic Quartermaster U :W: .12 .25
3 Arm the Cathars U :W: .12 .25
4 Bride's Gown U :W: .12 .25
5 By Invitation Only R :W: .50 1.00
6 Cemetery Protector M :W: .75 1.50
7 Circle of Confinement U :W: .12 .25
8 Dawnhart Geist U :W: .12 .25
9 Distracting Geist/Clever Distraction U :W: .12 .25
10 Drogskol Infantry/Drogskol Armaments C :W: .07 .15
11 Estwald Shieldbasher C :W: .07 .15
12 Faithbound Judge/Sinner's Judgment M :W: .75 1.50
13 Fierce Retribution C :W: .07 .15
14 Fleeting Spirit U :W: .12 .25
15 Gryff Rider C :W: .07 .15
16 Gryffwing Cavalry U :W: .12 .25
17 Hallowed Haunting M :W: 5.00 10.00
18 Heron of Hope C :W: .07 .15
19 Heron-Blessed Geist C :W: .07 .15
20 Hopeful Initiate R :W: 1.50 3.00
21 Katilda, Dawnhart Martyr
Katilda's Rising Dawn R :W: .30 .60
22 Kindly Ancestor/Ancestor's Embrace C :W: .07 .15
23 Lantern Flare R :W: .30 .60
24 Militia Rallier C :W: .07 .15
25 Nebelgast Beguiler C :W: .07 .15
26 Nurturing Presence C :W: .07 .15
27 Ollenbock Escort U :W: .12 .25
28 Panicked Bystander/Cackling Culprit U :W: .12 .25
29 Parish-Blade Trainee C :W: .07 .15
30 Piercing Light C :W: .07 .15
31 Radiant Grace/Radiant Restraints U :W: .12 .25
32 Resistance Squad U :W: .12 .25
33 Sanctify C :W: .07 .15
34 Savior of Ollenbock M :W: .50 1.00
35 Sigarda's Imprisonment C :W: .07 .15
36 Sigarda's Summons R :W: .30 .60
37 Supernatural Rescue C :W: .07 .15
38 Thalia, Guardian of Thraben R :W: 1.25 2.50
39 Traveling Minister C :W: .07 .15
40 Twinblade Geist/Twinblade Invocation U :W: .12 .25
41 Unholy Officiant C :W: .07 .15
42 Valorous Stance U :W: .12 .25
43 Vampire Slayer C :W: .07 .15
44 Voice of the Blessed R :W: 1.50 3.00
45 Wedding Announcement
Wedding Festivity R :W: .75 1.50
46 Welcoming Vampire R :W: 3.00 6.00
47 Alchemist's Retrieval C :B: .07 .15
48 Binding Geist/Spectral Binding C :B: .07 .15
49 Biolume Egg/Biolume Serpent U :B: .12 .25
50 Cemetery Illuminator M :B: 1.25 2.50
51 Chill of the Grave C :B: .07 .15
52 Cobbled Lancer U :B: .12 .25
53 Consuming Tide R :B: .30 .60
54 Cradle of Safety C :B: .07 .15
55 Cruel Witness C :B: .07 .15
56 Diver Skaab U :B: .12 .25
57 Dreadlight Monstrosity C :B: .07 .15
58 Dreamshackle Geist R :B: .30 .60
59 Fear of Death C :B: .07 .15
60 Geistlight Snare U :B: .30 .60
61 Geralf, Visionary Stitcher R :B: .30 .60
62 Gutter Skulker/Gutter Shortcut U :B: .12 .25
63 Hullbreaker Horror R :B: 1.50 3.00
64 Inspired Idea R :B: .30 .60
65 Jacob Hauken, Inspector
Hauken's Insight M :B: .30 .75
66 Lantern Bearer/Lanterns' Lift C :B: .07 .15
67 Lunar Rejection U :B: .12 .25
68 Mirrorhall Mimic/Ghastly Mimicry R :B: .75 1.50
69 Mischievous Catgeist/Catlike Curiosity U :B: .12 .25
70 Necroduality M :B: 7.50 15.00
71 Overcharged Amalgam R :B: .30 .60

72 Patchwork Crawler R :B: .30 .60
73 Repository Skaab C :B: .07 .15
74 Scattered Thoughts C :B: .07 .15
75 Screaming Swarm U :B: .12 .25
76 Selhoff Entomber C :B: .07 .15
77 Serpentine Ambush C :B: .07 .15
78 Skywarp Skaab C :B: .07 .15
79 Soulcipher Board/Cipherbound Spirit U :B: .12 .25
80 Steelclad Spirit C :B: .07 .15
81 Stitched Assistant C :B: .07 .15
82 Stormchaser Drake U :B: .12 .25
83 Syncopate C :B: .07 .15
84 Syphon Essence C :B: .07 .15
85 Thirst for Discovery U :B: .12 .25
86 Wanderlight Spirit C :B: .07 .15
87 Wash Away U :B: .30 .75
88 Whispering Wizard U :B: .12 .25
89 Winged Portent R :B: .30 .60
90 Witness the Future U :B: .12 .25
91 Wretched Throng C :B: .07 .15
92 Aim for the Head C :K: .07 .15
93 Archghoul of Thraben U :K: .12 .25
94 Bleed Dry C :K: .07 .15
95 Blood Fountain C :K: .07 .15
96 Bloodcrazed Socialite C :K: .07 .15
97 Bloodsworn Squire/Bloodsworn Knight U :K: .12 .25
98 Bloodvial Purveyor R :K: .30 .60
99 Catapult Fodder/Catapult Captain U :K: .12 .25
100 Cemetery Desecrator M :K: .50 1.00
101 Concealing Curtains/Revealing Eye R :K: .30 .60
102 Courier Bat C :K: .07 .15
103 Demonic Bargain R :K: .30 .60
104 Desperate Farmer/Depraved Harvester C :K: .07 .15
105 Diregraf Scavenger C :K: .07 .15
106 Doomed Dissenter C :K: .07 .15
107 Dread Fugue U :K: .12 .25
108 Dreadfeast Demon R :K: .30 .60
109 Dying to Serve R :K: .30 .60
110 Edgar's Awakening U :K: .12 .25
111 Falkenrath Forebear R :K: .30 .60
112 Fell Stinger U :K: .12 .25
113 Gift of Fangs C :K: .07 .15
114 Gluttonous Guest C :K: .07 .15
115 Graf Reaver R :K: .30 .60
116 Grisly Ritual C :K: .07 .15
117 Groom's Finery U :K: .12 .25
118 Headless Rider R :K: 1.00 2.00
119 Henrika Domnathi/Henrika, Infernal Seer M :K: .75 1.50
120 Hero's Downfall U :K: .12 .25
121 Innocent Traveler/Malicious Invader U :K: .12 .25
122 Mindleech Ghoul C :K: .07 .15
123 Parasitic Grasp U :K: .12 .25
124 Path of Peril R :K: .30 .60
125 Persistent Specimen C :K: .07 .15
126 Pointed Discussion C :K: .07 .15
127 Ragged Recluse/Odious Witch C :K: .07 .15
128 Restless Bloodseeker
Bloodsoaked Reveler U :K: .12 .25
129 Rot-Tide Gargantua C :K: .07 .15
130 Skulking Killer U :K: .12 .25
131 Sorin the Mirthless M :K: 6.00 12.00
132 Toxrill, the Corrosive M :K: 10.00 20.00
133 Undead Butler U :K: .12 .25
134 Undying Malice C :K: .07 .15
135 Unhallowed Phalanx C :K: .07 .15
136 Vampire's Kiss C :K: .07 .15
137 Voldaren Bloodcaster
Bloodbat Summoner R :K: .30 .60
138 Wedding Security U :K: .12 .25
139 Abrade C :R: .07 .15
140 Alchemist's Gambit R :R: .30 .60
141 Alluring Suitor/Deadly Dancer U :R: .12 .25
142 Ancestral Anger C :R: .07 .15
143 Ballista Watcher/Ballista Wielder U :R: .12 .25
144 Belligerent Guest C :R: .07 .15
145 Blood Hypnotist U :R: .12 .25
146 Blood Petal Celebrant C :R: .07 .15
147 Bloody Betrayal C :R: .07 .15
148 Cemetery Gatekeeper M :R: 2.00 4.00
149 Chandra, Dressed to Kill M :R: 12.50 25.00
150 Change of Fortune R :R: .30 .60
151 Creepy Puppeteer R :R: .30 .60
152 Curse of Hospitality R :R: .30 .60
153 Daybreak Combatants C :R: .07 .15
154 Dominating Vampire R :R: .30 .60
155 End the Festivities C :R: .07 .15
156 Falkenrath Celebrants C :R: .07 .15
157 Fearful Villager/Fearsome Werewolf C :R: .07 .15
158 Flame-Blessed Bolt C :R: .07 .15
159 Frenzied Devils U :R: .12 .25
160 Honeymoon Hearse U :R: .12 .25
161 Hungry Ridgewolf C :R: .07 .15
162 Ill-Tempered Loner/Howlpack Avenger R :R: .30 .60
163 Into the Night U :R: .12 .25
164 Kessig Flamebreather C :R: .07 .15
165 Kessig Wolfrider R :R: .30 .60
166 Lacerate Flesh C :R: .07 .15
167 Lambholt Raconteur/Lambholt Ravager U :R: .12 .25
168 Lightning Wolf C :R: .07 .15
169 Magma Pummeler U :R: .12 .25
170 Manaform Hellkite M :R: 2.50 5.00
171 Markov Retribution U :R: .12 .25
172 Olivia's Attendants R :R: .30 .60
173 Pyre Spawn C :R: .07 .15
174 Reckless Impulse C :R: .07 .15
175 Rending Flame U :R: .12 .25
176 Runebound Wolf U :R: .12 .25
177 Sanguine Statuette U :R: .12 .25
178 Stensia Uprising R :R: .30 .60
179 Sure Strike C :R: .07 .15
180 Vampires' Vengeance U :R: .12 .25
181 Volatile Arsonist/Dire-Strain Anarchist M :R: .75 1.50
182 Voldaren Epicure C :R: .07 .15
183 Voltaic Visionary/Volt
Charged Berserker U :R: .12 .25
184 Weary Prisoner/Wrathful Jailbreaker C :R: .07 .15
185 Apprentice Sharpshooter C :G: .07 .15
186 Ascendant Packleader R :G: .30 .75
187 Avabruck Caretaker/Hollowhenge
Huntmaster M :G: 4.00 8.00
188 Bramble Armor C :G: .07 .15
189 Bramble Wurm U :G: .12 .25
190 Cartographer's Survey U :G: .12 .25
191 Cemetery Prowler M :G: 1.50 3.00
192 Cloaked Cadet U :G: .12 .25
193 Crawling Infestation U :G: .12 .25
194 Crushing Canopy C :G: .07 .15
195 Cultivator Colossus M :G: 12.50 25.00
196 Dawnhart Disciple C :G: .07 .15
197 Dig Up R :G: .75 1.50
198 Dormant Grove/Gnarled Grovestrider U :G: .12 .25
199 Flourishing Hunter C :G: .07 .15
200 Glorious Sunrise R :G: .60 1.25
201 Hamlet Vanguard R :G: .30 .60
202 Hiveheart Shaman R :G: .30 .60
203 Hookhand Mariner/Riphook Raider C :G: .07 .15
204 Howling Moon R :G: .30 .60
205 Howlpack Piper/Wildsong Howler R :G: .60 1.25
206 Infestation Expert/Infested Werewolf U :G: .12 .25
207 Laid to Rest U :G: .12 .25
208 Massive Might C :G: .07 .15
209 Moldgraf Millipede C :G: .07 .15
210 Mulch C :G: .07 .15
211 Nature's Embrace C :G: .07 .15
212 Oakshade Stalker/Moonlit Ambusher U :G: .12 .25
213 Packsong Pup U :G: .12 .25
214 Reclusive Taxidermist U :G: .12 .25
215 Retrieve U :G: .12 .25
216 Rural Recruit C :G: .07 .15
217 Sawblade Slinger U :G: .12 .25
218 Sheltering Boughs C :G: .07 .15
219 Snarling Wolf C :G: .07 .15
220 Spiked Ripsaw U :G: .12 .25
221 Splendid Reclamation R :G: .60 1.25
222 Spore Crawler C :G: .07 .15
223 Sporeback Wolf C :G: .07 .15
224 Toxic Scorpion C :G: .07 .15
225 Ulvenwald Oddity/Ulvenwald Behemoth R :G: .30 .60
226 Weaver of Blossoms
Blossom-Clad Werewolf C :G: .07 .15
227 Witch's Web C :G: .07 .15
228 Wolf Strike C :G: .07 .15
229 Wolfkin Outcast/Wedding Crasher U :G: .12 .25
230 Ancient Lumberknot U :K/:G: .12 .25
231 Anje, Maid of Dishonor R :K/:R: .30 .60
232 Bloodtithe Harvester U :K/:R: .12 .25
233 Brine Comber/Brinebound Gift U :W/:B: .12 .25
234 Child of the Pack/Savage Packmate U :R/:G: .12 .25
235 Dorothea Vengeful
Victim/Retribution R :W/:B: .30 .60
236 Edgar Charmed Groom/Coffin R :W/:K: .30 .75
237 Eruth, Tormented Prophet R :B/:R: .30 .60
238 Grolnok, the Omnivore R :G/:B: .30 .60
239 Halana and Alena, Partners R :R/:G: .30 .60
240 Kaya, Geist Hunter M :W/:K: 1.50 3.00
241 Markov Purifier U :W/:K: .12 .25
242 Markov Waltzer U :R/:W: .12 .25
243 Odric, Blood-Cursed R :R/:W: .30 .60
244 Old Rutstein R :K/:G: .30 .60
245 Olivia, Crimson Bride M :K/:R: 4.00 8.00
246 Runo Stromkirk/Krothuss,
Lord of the Deep R :B/:K: .30 .60
247 Sigardian Paladin U :G/:W: .12 .25
248 Skull Skaab U :B/:K: .12 .25
249 Torens, Fist of the Angels R :G/:W: .50 1.00
250 Vilespawn Spider U :G/:B: .12 .25
251 Wandering Mind U :B/:R: .12 .25
252 Blood Servitor C .07 .15
253 Boarded Window U .12 .25
254 Ceremonial Knife C .07 .15
255 Dollhouse of Horrors R .30 .60
256 Foreboding Statue/Forsaken Thresher U .12 .25
257 Honored Heirloom C .07 .15
258 Investigator's Journal R .30 .60
259 Lantern of the Lost U .12 .25
260 Wedding Invitation C .07 .15
261 Deathcap Glade R 4.00 8.00
262 Dreamroot Cascade R 3.00 6.00
263 Evolving Wilds C .07 .15
264 Shattered Sanctum R 4.00 8.00
265 Stormcarved Coast R 7.50 15.00
266 Sundown Pass R 4.00 8.00
267 Voldaren Estate R .30 .60
268 Plains C .15 .30
269 Plains C .15 .30
270 Island C .30 .60
271 Island C .30 .60
272 Swamp C .30 .75
273 Swamp C .30 .75
274 Mountain C .20 .40
275 Mountain C .20 .40
276 Forest C .20 .40
277 Forest C .20 .40
278 Sorin the Mirthless M :K: 7.50 15.00
279 Chandra, Dressed to Kill M :R: 15.00 30.00
280 Kaya, Geist Hunter M :W/:K: 2.50 5.00
281 Deathcap Glade R 4.00 8.00
282 Dreamroot Cascade R 4.00 8.00
283 Shattered Sanctum R 4.00 8.00
284 Stormcarved Coast R 7.50 15.00
285 Sundown Pass R 5.00 10.00
286 Unholy Officiant C :W: .20 .40
287 Welcoming Vampire R :W: 3.00 6.00
288 Bloodcrazed Socialite C :K: .07 .15
289 Bloodsworn Squire/Bloodsworn Knight U :K: .12 .25
290 Bloodvial Purveyor R :K: .30 .60
291 Falkenrath Forebear R :K: .30 .60
292 Gluttonous Guest C :K: .07 .15
293 Henrika Domnathi/Henrika, Infernal Seer M :K: .75 1.50
294 Innocent Traveler/Malicious Invader U :K: .12 .25
295 Restless Bloodseeker
Bloodsoaked Reveler U :K: .12 .25
296 Skulking Killer U :K: .12 .25
297 Sorin the Mirthless M :K: 12.50 25.00
298 Voldaren Bloodcaster
Bloodbat Summoner R :K: .30 .60
299 Wedding Security U :K: .12 .25
300 Alluring Suitor/Deadly Dancer U :R: .12 .25
301 Belligerent Guest C :R: .07 .15
302 Blood Hypnotist U :R: .12 .25
303 Blood Petal Celebrant C :R: .07 .15
304 Cemetery Gatekeeper M :R: 2.00 4.00
305 Dominating Vampire R :R: .30 .60
306 Falkenrath Celebrants C :R: .07 .15
307 Olivia's Attendants R :R: .30 .60
308 Voldaren Epicure C :R: .07 .15
309 Anje, Maid of Dishonor R :K/:R: .50 1.00
310 Bloodtithe Harvester U :K/:R: .25 .50
311 Edgar Charmed Groom/Coffin R :W/:K: .50 1.00
312 Markov Purifier U :W/:K: .12 .25
313 Markov Waltzer U :R/:W: .12 .25
314 Odric, Blood-Cursed R :R/:W: .30 .60
315 Olivia, Crimson Bride M :K/:R: 7.50 15.00
316 Runo Stromkirk/Krothuss,
Lord of the Deep R :B/:K: .75 1.50
317 Katilda Dawnhart Martyr/Rising Dawn R :W: .30 .60
318 Thalia, Guardian of Thraben R :W: .30 .60
319 Geralf, Visionary Stitcher R :B: .30 .60
320 Jacob Hauken, Inspector
Hauken's Insight M :B: .50 1.00
321 Toxrill, the Corrosive M :K: 7.50 15.00
322 Dorothea Vengeful Victim
Retribution R :W/:B: .20 .40
323 Eruth, Tormented Prophet R :B/:R: .20 .40
324 Grolnok, the Omnivore R :G/:B: .20 .40
325 Halana and Alena, Partners R :R/:G: .60 1.25
326 Old Rutstein R :K/:G: .20 .40
327 Runo Stromkirk/Krothuss,
Lord of the Deep R :B/:K: .50 1.00
328 Torens, Fist of the Angels R :G/:W: .25 .50
329 Circle of Confinement U :W: .12 .25
330 Savior of Ollenbock M :W: .75 1.50
331 Thalia, Guardian of Thraben R :W: 2.00 4.00
332 Jacob Hauken, Inspector
Hauken's Insight M :B: .75 1.50
333 Thirst for Discovery U :B: .12 .25
334 Falkenrath Forebear R :K: .75 1.50
335 Henrika Domnathi/Henrika, Infernal Seer M :K: 2.00 4.00
336 Innocent Traveler/Malicious Invader U :K: .12 .25
337 Sorin the Mirthless M :K: 7.50 15.00
338 Voldaren Bloodcaster
Bloodbat Summoner R :K: 1.50 3.00
339 Vampires' Vengeance U :R: .12 .25
340 Reclusive Taxidermist U :G: .12 .25
341 Edgar Charmed Groom/Coffin R :W/:K: 1.00 2.00
342 Eruth, Tormented Prophet R :B/:R: .30 .60
343 Olivia, Crimson Bride M :K/:R: 4.00 8.00
344 Torens, Fist of the Angels R :G/:W: .30 .60
345 Investigator's Journal R .20 .40
346 By Invitation Only R :W: .75 1.50
347 Cemetery Protector M :W: 1.00 2.00
348 Faithbound Judge/Sinner's Judgment M :W: 1.50 3.00
349 Hallowed Haunting M :W: 7.50 15.00
350 Hopeful Initiate R :W: 2.50 5.00
351 Lantern Flare R :W: .20 .40
352 Savior of Ollenbock M :W: .50 1.00
353 Sigarda's Summons R :W: .30 .60
354 Voice of the Blessed R :W: 2.00 4.00
355 Wedding Announcement
Wedding Festivity R :W: 1.50 3.00
356 Cemetery Illuminator M :B: 2.00 4.00
357 Consuming Tide R :B: .30 .60
358 Dreamshackle Geist R :B: .20 .40
359 Hullbreaker Horror R :B: 7.50 15.00
360 Inspired Idea R :B: .30 .60
361 Mirrorhall Mimic/Ghastly Mimicry R :B: 1.25 2.50
362 Necroduality M :B: 7.50 15.00
363 Overcharged Amalgam R :B: 1.25 2.50
364 Patchwork Crawler R :B: .20 .40
365 Winged Portent R :B: .20 .40
366 Cemetery Desecrator M :K: .50 1.00
367 Concealing Curtains/Revealing Eye R :K: .25 .50
368 Demonic Bargain R :K: .25 .50
369 Dreadfeast Demon R :K: .25 .50
370 Dying to Serve R :K: .30 .60
371 Graf Reaver R :K: .30 .60
372 Headless Rider R :K: 1.50 3.00
373 Path of Peril R :K: .50 1.00
374 Alchemist's Gambit R :R: .30 .60
375 Change of Fortune R :R: .30 .60
376 Creepy Puppeteer R :R: .20 .40
377 Curse of Hospitality R :R: .50 1.00
378 Ill-Tempered Loner/Howlpack Avenger R :R: .75 1.50
379 Kessig Wolfrider R :R: .20 .40
380 Manaform Hellkite M :R: 4.00 8.00
381 Stensia Uprising R :R: .20 .40
382 Volatile Arsonist/Dire-Strain Anarchist M :R: 1.25 2.50
383 Ascendant Packleader R :G: .75 1.50
384 Avabruck Caretaker
Hollowhenge Huntmaster M :G: 7.50 15.00
385 Cemetery Prowler M :G: 3.00 6.00
386 Cultivator Colossus M :G: 20.00 40.00
387 Dig Up R :G: 1.25 2.50
388 Glorious Sunrise R :G: .75 1.50
389 Hamlet Vanguard R :G: .20 .40
390 Hiveheart Shaman R :G: .20 .40
391 Howling Moon R :G: .75 1.50
392 Howlpack Piper/Wildsong Howler R :G: 1.00 2.00
393 Splendid Reclamation R :G: 1.50 3.00
394 Ulvenwald Oddity/Ulvenwald Behemoth R :G: 1.00 2.00
395 Dollhouse of Horrors R .30 .75
396 Investigator's Journal R .20 .40
397 Voldaren Estate R .60 1.25
398 Plains C .07 .15
399 Island C .07 .15
400 Swamp C .07 .15
401 Mountain C .07 .15
402 Forest C .07 .15
403 Voldaren Estate R .30 .60
404 Sigarda's Summons R :W: .30 .60
405 Geistlight Snare U :B: .50 1.00
406 Fell Stinger U :K: .75 1.50
407 Dominating Vampire R :R: 2.00 4.00

2021 Magic The Gathering Innistrad Crimson Vow Tokens

1 Human .07 .15
2 Spirit .07 .15
3 Spirit .07 .15
4 Spirit Cleric 1.50 3.00
5 Zombie .07 .15
6 Slug 3.00 6.00
7 Vampire 4.00 8.00
8 Zombie .12 .25
9 Dragon Illusion .75 1.50
10 Human .07 .15
11 Wolf .07 .15
12 Boar .07 .15
13 Insect .15 .30
14 Wolf .07 .15
15 Human Soldier .75 1.50
16 Vampire .30 .75
17 Blood .12 .25
18 Treasure .12 .25
19 Copy .30 .75
20 Chandra, Dressed to Kill .25 .50
21 Day/Night .07 .15

2021 Magic The Gathering Innistrad Crimson Vow Commander

1 Millicent, Restless Revenant M :W/:B: .20 .40
2 Strefan, Maurer Progenitor M :K/:R: .30 .60
3 Donal, Herald of Wings M :B: .25 .50
4 Timothar, Baron of Bats M :K: .17 .35
5 Drogskol Reinforcements R :W: .10 .20
6 Haunted Library R :W: .12 .25
7 Priest of the Blessed Graf R :W: .07 .15
8 Rhoda, Geist Avenger R :W: .07 .15
9 Storm of Souls R :W: .25 .50
10 Sudden Salvation R :W: .07 .15
11 Breath of the Sleepless R :B: .07 .15
12 Ethereal Investigator R :B: .75 1.50
13 Haunting Imitation R :B: .10 .20
14 Occult Epiphany R :B: .17 .35
15 Spectral Arcanist R :B: .07 .15
16 Timin, Youthful Geist R :B: .07 .15
17 Crossway Troublemakers R :K: .40 .80
18 Glass-Cast Heart R :K: .30 .60
19 Kamber, the Plunderer R :K: .10 .20
20 Olivia's Wrath R :K: 1.00 2.00
21 Predators' Hour R :K: .20 .40
22 Shadowgrange Archfiend R :K: 1.00 2.00
23 Arterial Alchemy R :R: .10 .20
24 Imposing Grandeur R :R: .60 1.25
25 Laurine, the Diversion R :R: .12 .25
26 Markov Enforcer R :R: .10 .20
27 Midnight Arsonist R :R: .07 .15
28 Scion of Opulence R :R: .12 .25
29 Disorder in the Court R :W/:B: .30 .60
30 Sinister Waltz R :K/:R: .07 .15
31 Breathkeeper Seraph R :W: .75 1.50
32 Wedding Ring M :W: 10.00 20.00
33 Imperious Mindbreaker R :B: .17 .35
34 Doom Weaver R :K: 1.25 2.50
35 Mirage Phalanx R :R: .60 1.25
36 Hollowhenge Overlord R :G: 1.50 3.00
37 Thundering Mightmare R :G: .40 .80
38 Umbris, Fear Manifest M :B/:K: 4.00 8.00
39 Millicent, Restless Revenant M :W/:B: 1.25 2.50
40 Strefan, Maurer Progenitor M :K/:R: 1.25 2.50
41 Donal, Herald of Wings M :B: 1.00 2.00
42 Timothar, Baron of Bats M :K: .75 1.50
43 Drogskol Reinforcements R :W: .12 .25
44 Haunted Library R :W: .75 1.50
45 Priest of the Blessed Graf R :W: .15 .30
46 Rhoda, Geist Avenger R :W: .15 .30
47 Storm of Souls R :W: .75 1.50
48 Sudden Salvation R :W: .12 .25
49 Breath of the Sleepless R :B: .15 .30
50 Ethereal Investigator R :B: .75 1.50
51 Haunting Imitation R :B: .12 .25
52 Occult Epiphany R :B: .20 .40
53 Spectral Arcanist R :B: .12 .25
54 Timin, Youthful Geist R :B: .12 .25
55 Crossway Troublemakers R :K: 1.50 3.00
56 Glass-Cast Heart R :K: .75 1.50
57 Kamber, the Plunderer R :K: .40 .80
58 Olivia's Wrath R :K: 1.25 2.50
59 Predators' Hour R :K: .40 .80
60 Shadowgrange Archfiend R :K: 1.50 3.00
61 Arterial Alchemy R :R: .20 .40
62 Imposing Grandeur R :R: .40 .80
63 Laurine, the Diversion R :R: .20 .40
64 Markov Enforcer R :R: .17 .35
65 Midnight Arsonist R :R: .12 .25
66 Scion of Opulence R :R: .20 .40
67 Disorder in the Court R :W/:B: .75 1.50
68 Sinister Waltz R :K/:R: .20 .40
69 Breathkeeper Seraph R :W: 1.00 2.00
70 Wedding Ring M :W: 12.50 25.00
71 Imperious Mindbreaker R :B: .25 .50
72 Doom Weaver R :K: 3.00 6.00
73 Mirage Phalanx R :R: 1.25 2.50
74 Hollowhenge Overlord R :G: 1.50 3.00
75 Thundering Mightmare R :G: .40 .80
76 Umbris, Fear Manifest M :B/:K: 4.00 8.00
77 Angel of Flight Alabaster R :W: .07 .15
78 Benevolent Offering R :W: .17 .35
79 Boreas Charger R :W: .07 .15
80 Bygone Bishop R :W: .07 .15
81 Crush Contraband U :W: .12 .25
82 Custodi Soulbinders R :W: .07 .15
83 Custodi Squire C :W: .07 .15
84 Darksteel Mutation U :W: 1.25 2.50
85 Fell the Mighty R :W: .07 .15
86 Field of Souls U :W: .07 .15
87 Ghostly Prison U :W: 1.50 3.00
88 Hallowed Spiritkeeper R :W: .12 .25
89 Hanged Executioner R :W: .07 .15
90 Karmic Guide R :W: .17 .35
91 Kirtar's Wrath R :W: .07 .15
92 Knight of the White Orchid R :W: .30 .60
93 Mentor of the Meek R :W: .12 .25
94 Mirror Entity R :W: 1.00 2.00
95 Oyobi, Who Split the Heavens R :W: .07 .15
96 Promise of Bunrei R :W: .07 .15
97 Remorseful Cleric R :W: .10 .20
98 Spectral Shepherd U :W: .07 .10
99 Swords to Plowshares U :W: .60 1.25
100 Twilight Drover R :W: .10 .20
101 Windborn Muse R :W: .15 .30
102 Arcane Denial C :B: 2.50 5.00
103 Distant Melody C :B: .30 .60
104 Flood of Tears R :B: .20 .40
105 Ghostly Pilferer R :B: .07 .15
106 Imprisoned in the Moon R :B: .30 .75
107 Kami of the Crescent Moon R :B: .75 1.50
108 Midnight Clock R :B: .25 .50
109 Nebelgast Herald U :B: .07 .10
110 Rattlechains R :B: .10 .20
111 Reconnaissance Mission U :B: .30 .75
112 Shacklegeist R :B: .12 .25
113 Sire of the Storm U :B: .07 .10
114 Spectral Sailor U :B: .12 .25
115 Supreme Phantom R :B: .25 .50

116 Verity Circle R :B: .10 .20
117 Ancient Craving U :K: .12 .25
118 Anowon, the Ruin Sage R :K: .25 .50
119 Blood Artist U :K: .75 1.50
120 Bloodline Necromancer U :K: .30 .60
121 Bloodlord of Vaasgoth M :K: .17 .35
122 Bloodtracker R :K: .10 .20
123 Butcher of Malakir R :K: .12 .25
124 Champion of Dusk R :K: .12 .25
125 Cordial Vampire R :K: 1.25 2.50
126 Damnable Pact R :K: .10 .20
127 Dark Impostor R :K: .07 .15
128 Falkenrath Noble U :K: .20 .40
129 Feed the Swarm C :K: .40 .80
130 Indulgent Aristocrat U :K: .20 .40
131 Malakir Bloodwitch R :K: .25 .50
132 Necropolis Regent M :K: .30 .60
133 Night's Whisper C :K: .75 1.50
134 Nirkana Revenant M :K: 2.00 4.00
135 Patron of the Vein R :K: .40 .80
136 Sanctum Seeker R :K: .40 .80
137 Stromkirk Condemned R :K: .07 .10
138 Underworld Connections R :K: .15 .30
139 Urge to Feed U :K: .07 .15
140 Vampire Nighthawk U :K: .12 .25
141 Anje's Ravager R :R: .12 .25
142 Avacyn's Judgment R :R: .07 .10
143 Blasphemous Act R :R: 1.25 2.50
144 Bloodsworn Steward R :R: .07 .15
145 Crimson Honor Guard R :R: .07 .10
146 Falkenrath Gorger R :R: .07 .15
147 Mob Rule R :R: .30 .60
148 Molten Echoes R :R: 1.25 2.50
149 Rakish Heir U :R: .07 .15
150 Stensia Masquerade U :R: .12 .25
151 Stromkirk Occultist R :R: .07 .10
152 Vandalblast U :R: 3.00 6.00
153 Dovin, Grand Arbiter M :W:/:B: .25 .50
154 Drogskol Captain U :W:/:B: .10 .20
155 Geist of Saint Traft M :W:/:B: .50 .40
156 Rakdos Charm U :K:/:R: .25 .50
157 Stromkirk Captain U :K:/:R: .30 .75
158 Vampiric Dragon R :K:/:R: .07 .15
159 Arcane Signet C .40 .80
160 Azorius Locket C .07 .15
161 Azorius Signet U .30 .60
162 Charcoal Diamond C .10 .20
163 Commander's Sphere C .07 .15
164 Fire Diamond C .60 1.25
165 Marble Diamond C .07 .15
166 Rakdos Signet U .75 1.50
167 Sky Diamond C .07 .15
168 Sol Ring U 1.00 2.00
169 Swiftfoot Boots U .75 1.50
170 Unstable Obelisk U .07 .10
171 Azorius Chancery U .10 .20
172 Command Tower C .15 .30
173 Exotic Orchard R .12 .25
174 Foreboding Ruins R .12 .25
175 Moorland Haunt R .07 .10
176 Myriad Landscape U .12 .25
177 Path of Ancestry C .10 .20
178 Port Town R .07 .15
179 Prairie Stream R .12 .25
180 Rakdos Carnarium C .17 .35
181 Shadowblood Ridge R .12 .25
182 Skycloud Expanse R .07 .15
183 Smoldering Marsh R .30 .60
184 Tainted Peak U .60 1.25
185 Temple of Enlightenment R .07 .15
186 Temple of Malice R .17 .35
187 Temple of the False God U .07 .15
188 Unclaimed Territory U .30 .75

2021 Magic The Gathering Innistrad Crimson Vow Commander Tokens

1 Spirit .12 .25
2 Angel .12 .25
3 Spirit .12 .25
4 Bat .12 .25
5 Clue .12 .25
6 Thopter .12 .25

2021 Magic The Gathering Innistrad Midnight Hunt

1 Adeline, Resplendent Cathar R :W: 4.00 8.00
2 Ambitious Farmhand/Seasoned Cathar U :W: .12 .25
3 Beloved Beggar/Generous Soul U :W: .12 .25
4 Bereaved Survivor/Dauntless Avenger U :W: .12 .25
5 Blessed Defiance C :W: .07 .15
6 Borrowed Time U :W: .12 .25
7 Brutal Cathar/Moonrage Brute R :W: 1.25 2.50
8 Candlegrove Witch C :W: .07 .15
9 Candletrap C :W: .07 .15
10 Cathar Commando C :W: .07 .15
11 Cathar's Call U :W: .12 .25
12 Celestus Sanctifier C :W: .07 .15
13 Chaplain of Alms/Chapel Shieldgeist U :W: .12 .25
14 Clarion Cathars C :W: .07 .15
15 Curse of Silence R :W: .30 .60
16 Duelcraft Trainer U :W: .12 .25
17 Enduring Angel/Angelic Enforcer M :W: 1.00 2.00
18 Fateful Absence R :W: 1.00 2.00
19 Flare of Faith C :W: .07 .15
20 Gavony Dawnguard U :W: .12 .25
21 Gavony Silversmith C :W: .07 .15
22 Gavony Trapper C :W: .07 .15
23 Hedgewitch's Mask C :W: .07 .15
24 Homestead Courage C :W: .07 .15
25 Intrepid Adversary M :W: 1.25 2.50
26 Loyal Gryff U :W: .12 .25
27 Lunarch Veteran/Luminous Phantom C :W: .07 .15
28 Mourning Patrol/Morning Apparition C :W: .07 .15
29 Odric's Outrider U :W: .12 .25
30 Ritual Guardian C :W: .07 .15
31 Ritual of Hope U :W: .12 .25
32 Search Party Captain C :W: .07 .15
33 Sigarda's Splendor R :W: .30 .60
34 Sigardian Savior M :W: .50 1.00
35 Soul-Guide Gryff C :W: .07 .15
36 Sungold Barrage C :W: .07 .15
37 Sungold Sentinel R :W: .30 .60
38 Sunset Revelry U :W: .12 .25
39 Thraben Exorcism C :W: .07 .15
40 Unruly Mob C :W: .07 .15
41 Vanquish the Horde R :W: 3.00 6.00
42 Baithook Angler/Hook-Haunt Drifter C :B: .07 .15
43 Component Collector C :B: .07 .15
44 Consider C :B: 1.00 2.00
45 Covetous Castaway/Ghostly Castigator U :B: .12 .25
46 Curse of Surveillance R :B: .30 .60
47 Delver of Secrets/Insectile Aberration U :B: .12 .25
48 Devious Cover-Up C :B: .07 .15
49 Dissipate U :B: .12 .25
50 Drownyard Amalgam C :B: .07 .15
51 Fading Hope U :B: .12 .25
52 Falcon Abomination C :B: .07 .15
53 Firmament Sage U :B: .12 .25
54 Flip the Switch C :B: .07 .15
55 Galedrifter/Waildrifter C :B: .07 .15
56 Geistwave C :B: .07 .15
57 Grafted Identity R :B: .30 .60
58 Larder Zombie C :B: .07 .15
59 Lier, Disciple of the Drowned M :B: 6.00 12.00
60 Locked in the Cemetery C :B: .07 .15
61 Malevolent Hermit/Benevolent Geist R :B: 1.25 2.50
62 Memory Deluge R :B: .40 .80
63 Mysterious Tome/Chilling Chronicle U :B: .12 .25
64 Nebelgast Intruder U :B: .12 .25
65 Ominous Roost U :B: .12 .25
66 Organ Hoarder C :B: .07 .15
67 Otherworldly Gaze C :B: .07 .15
68 Overwhelmed Archivist/Archive Haunt U :B: .12 .25
69 Patrician Geist R :B: .30 .60
70 Phantom Carriage U :B: .12 .25
71 Poppet Stitcher/Poppet Factory M :B: 4.00 8.00
72 Revenge of the Drowned C :B: .07 .15
73 Secrets of the Key C :B: .07 .15
74 Shipwreck Sifters C :B: .07 .15
75 Skaab Wrangler U :B: .12 .25
76 Sludge Monster R :B: .30 .60
77 Spectral Adversary M :B: 1.25 2.50
78 Startle C :B: .07 .15
79 Stormrider Spirit C :B: .07 .15
80 Suspicious Stowaway/Seafaring Werewolf R :B: .30 .60
81 Triskaidekaphile R :B: .75 1.50
82 Unblinking Observer C :B: .07 .15
83 Vivisection U :B: .12 .25
84 Arrogant Outlaw C :K: .07 .15
85 Baneblade Scoundrel/Baneclaw Marauder U :K: .12 .25
86 Bat Whisperer C :K: .07 .15
87 Bladebrand C :K: .07 .15
88 Blood Pact C :K: .07 .15
89 Bloodline Culling R :K: .30 .60
90 Bloodtithe Collector U :K: .12 .25
91 Champion of the Perished R :K: 1.00 2.00
92 Covert Cutpurse/Covetous Geist U :K: .12 .25
93 Crawl from the Cellar C :K: .07 .15
94 Curse of Leeches/Leeching Lurker R :K: .30 .60
95 Defenestrate C :K: .07 .15
96 Diregraf Horde C :K: .07 .15
97 Dreadhound U :K: .12 .25
98 Duress C :K: .07 .15
99 Eaten Alive C :K: .07 .15
100 Ecstatic Awakener/Awoken Demon C :K: .07 .15
101 Foul Play U :K: .12 .25
102 Ghoulish Procession U :K: .12 .25
103 Gisa, Glorious Resurrector R :K: .75 1.50
104 Graveyard Trespasser/Graveyard Glutton R :K: 1.00 2.00
105 Heirloom Mirror/Inherited Fiend U :K: .12 .25
106 Hobbling Zombie C :K: .07 .15
107 Infernal Grasp U :K: .30 .75
108 Jadar, Ghoulcaller of Nephalia R :K: 1.25 2.50
109 Jerren /Ormendahl M :K: .50 1.00
110 Lord of the Forsaken M :K: .60 1.25
111 Mask of Griselbrand R :K: .30 .60
112 The Meathook Massacre M :K: 30.00 75.00
113 Morbid Opportunist U :K: .75 1.50
114 Morkrut Behemoth C :K: .07 .15
115 Necrosynthesis U :K: .12 .25
116 No Way Out C :K: .07 .15
117 Novice Occultist C :K: .07 .15
118 Olivia's Midnight Ambush C :K: .07 .15
119 Rotten Reunion C :K: .07 .15
120 Shady Traveler/Stalking Predator C :K: .07 .15
121 Siege Zombie C :K: .07 .15
122 Slaughter Specialist R :K: .30 .60
123 Stromkirk Bloodthief U :K: .12 .25
124 Tainted Adversary M :K: 2.00 4.00
125 Vampire Interloper C :K: .07 .15
126 Vengeful Strangler/Strangling Grasp U :K: .12 .25
127 Abandon the Post C :R: .07 .15
128 Ardent Elementalist C :R: .07 .15
129 Bloodthirsty Adversary M :R: 2.50 5.00
130 Brimstone Vandal C :R: .07 .15
131 Burn Down the House R :R: .30 .75
132 Burn the Accursed C :R: .07 .15
133 Cathartic Pyre U :R: .12 .25
134 Curse of Shaken Faith R :R: .30 .60
135 Electric Revelation C :R: .07 .15
136 Falkenrath Perforator C :R: .07 .15
137 Falkenrath Pit Fighter R :R: .30 .60
138 Famished Foragers C :R: .07 .15
139 Fangblade Brigand
Fangblade Eviscerator U :R: .12 .25
140 Festival Crasher C :R: .07 .15
141 Flame Channeler/Embodiment of Flame U :R: .12 .25
142 Geistflame Reservoir R :R: .30 .60
143 Harvesttide Infiltrator
Harvesttide Assailant C :R: .07 .15
144 Immolation C :R: .07 .15
145 Lambholt Harrier C :R: .07 .15
146 Light Up the Night R :R: .30 .60
147 Lunar Frenzy U :R: .12 .25
148 Moonrager's Slash C :R: .07 .15
149 Moonveil Regent M :R: .60 1.25
150 Mounted Dreadknight C :R: .07 .15
151 Neonate's Rush C :R: .07 .15
152 Obsessive Astronomer U :R: .12 .25
153 Pack's Betrayal C :R: .07 .15
154 Play with Fire U :R: 1.25 2.50
155 Purifying Dragon U :R: .12 .25
156 Raze the Effigy C :R: .07 .15
157 Reckless Stormseeker
Storm-Charged Slasher R :R: .75 1.50
158 Seize the Storm U :R: .12 .25
159 Smoldering Egg/Ashmouth Dragon R :R: .50 1.00
160 Spellrune Painter/Spellrune Howler U :R: .12 .25
161 Stolen Vitality C :R: .07 .15
162 Sunstreak Phoenix M :R: .50 1.00
163 Tavern Ruffian/Tavern Smasher C :R: .07 .15
164 Thermo-Alchemist U :R: .12 .25
165 Village Watch/Village Reavers U :R: .12 .25
166 Voldaren Ambusher U :R: .12 .25
167 Voldaren Stinger C :R: .07 .15
168 Augur of Autumn R :G: 3.00 6.00
169 Bird Admirer/Wing Shredder C :G: .07 .15
170 Bounding Wolf C :G: .07 .15
171 Bramble Armor C :G: .07 .15
172 Briarbridge Tracker R :G: .30 .60
173 Brood Weaver U :G: .12 .25
174 Burly Breaker/Dire-Strain Demolisher U :G: .12 .25
175 Candlelit Cavalry C :G: .07 .15
176 Clear Shot U :G: .12 .25
177 Consuming Blob M :G: .30 .75
178 Contortionist Troupe U :G: .12 .25
179 Dawnhart Mentor U :G: .12 .25
180 Dawnhart Rejuvenator C :G: .07 .15
181 Deathbonnet Sprout/Deathbonnet Hulk U :G: .12 .25
182 Defend the Celestus U :G: .12 .25
183 Dryad's Revival U :G: .12 .25
184 Duel for Dominance C :G: .07 .15
185 Eccentric Farmer C :G: .07 .15
186 Harvesttide Sentry C :G: .07 .15
187 Hound Tamer/Untamed Pup U :G: .12 .25
188 Howl of the Hunt C :G: .07 .15
189 Might of the Old Ways C :G: .07 .15
190 Outland Liberator/Frenzied Trapbreaker U :G: .50 1.00
191 Path to the Festival C :G: .07 .15
192 Pestilent Wolf C :G: .07 .15
193 Plummet C :G: .07 .15
194 Primal Adversary M :G: .60 1.25
195 Return to Nature C :G: .07 .15
196 Rise of the Ants U :G: .12 .25
197 Saryth, the Viper's Fang R :G: 1.00 2.00
198 Shadowbeast Sighting C :G: .07 .15
199 Snarling Wolf C :G: .07 .15
200 Storm the Festival R :G: .50 1.00
201 Tapping at the Window C :G: .07 .15
202 Timberland Guide C :G: .07 .15
203 Tireless Hauler/Dire-Strain Brawler C :G: .07 .15
204 Tovolar's Huntmaster
Tovolar's Packleader R :G: .30 .60
205 Turn the Earth U :G: .12 .25
206 Unnatural Growth R :G: 4.00 8.00
207 Willow Geist R :G: .30 .60
208 Wrenn and Seven M :G: 6.00 12.00
209 Angelfire Ignition R :R:/:W: .30 .60
210 Arcane Infusion U :B:/:R: .12 .25
211 Arlinn, the Pack's Hope
Moon's Fury M :R:/:G: 3.00 6.00
212 Bladestitched Skaab U :B:/:K: .12 .25
213 Can't Stay Away R :W:/:K: .30 .60
214 Corpse Cobble U :B:/:K: .12 .25
215 Croaking Counterpart R :G:/:B: .30 .60
216 Dawnhart Wardens U :G:/:W: .12 .25
217 Dennick, Pious Apprentice
Apparition R :W:/:B: .30 .60
218 Devoted Grafkeeper
Departed Soulkeeper U :W:/:B: .12 .25
219 Dire-Strain Rampage R :R:/:G: .30 .60
220 Diregraf Rebirth U :K:/:G: .12 .25
221 Faithful Mending U :W:/:B: .50 1.00
222 Fleshtaker U :W:/:K: .12 .25
223 Florian, Voldaren Scion R :K:/:R: .30 .60
224 Galvanic Iteration R :B:/:R: 1.50 3.00
225 Ghoulcaller's Harvest R :K:/:G: .30 .60
226 Grizzly Ghoul U :K:/:G: .12 .25
227 Hallowed Respite R :W:/:B: .30 .60
228 Hungry for More U :K:/:R: .12 .25
229 Join the Dance U :G:/:W: .12 .25
230 Katilda, Dawnhart Prime R :G:/:W: .30 .60
231 Kessig Naturalist/Lord of
the Ulvenwald U :R:/:G: .12 .25
232 Liesa, Forgotten Archangel R :W:/:K: 1.25 2.50
233 Ludevic, Necrogenius/Olag,
Ludevic's Hubris R :B:/:K: .30 .60
234 Old Stickfingers R :K:/:G: .30 .60
235 Rem Karolus, Stalwart Slayer R :R:/:W: .30 .60
236 Rite of Harmony R :G:/:W: .60 1.25
237 Rite of Oblivion U :W:/:K: .12 .25
238 Rootcoil Creeper U :G:/:B: .12 .25
239 Sacred Fire U :R:/:W: .12 .25
240 Sigarda, Champion of Light M :G:/:W: .75 1.50
241 Siphon Insight R :B:/:K: .30 .60
242 Slogurk, the Overslime R :G:/:B: .30 .60
243 Storm Skreelix U :B:/:R: .12 .25
244 Sunrise Cavalier U :R:/:W: .12 .25
245 Teferi, Who Slows the Sunset M :W:/:B: 2.50 5.00
246 Tovolar, Dire Overlord
Midnight Scourge R :R:/:G: .30 .60
247 Unnatural Moonrise U :R:/:G: .12 .25
248 Vadrik, Astral Archmage R :B:/:R: .30 .60
249 Vampire Socialite U :K:/:R: .12 .25
250 Wake to Slaughter R :K:/:R: .30 .60
251 Winterthorn Blessing U :G:/:B: .12 .25
252 The Celestus R .75 1.50
253 Crossroads Candleguide C .07 .15
254 Jack-o'-Lantern C .07 .15
255 Moonsilver Key U .25 .50
256 Mystic Skull/Mystic Monstrosity U .12 .25
257 Pithing Needle R .50 1.00
258 Silver Bolt C .07 .15
259 Stuffed Bear C .07 .15
260 Deserted Beach R 5.00 10.00
261 Evolving Wilds C .07 .15
262 Field of Ruin U .20 .40
263 Haunted Ridge R 7.50 15.00
264 Hostile Hostel/Creeping Inn M .60 1.25
265 Overgrown Farmland R 3.00 6.00
266 Rockfall Vale R 1.25 2.50
267 Shipwreck Marsh R 2.00 4.00
268 Plains L .20 .40
269 Plains L .20 .40
270 Island L .20 .40
271 Island L .20 .40
272 Swamp L .20 .40
273 Swamp L .20 .40
274 Mountain L .20 .40
275 Mountain L .20 .40
276 Forest L .20 .40
277 Forest L .20 .40
278 Wrenn and Seven M :G: 7.50 15.00
279 Arlinn, the Pack's Hope
Moon's Fury M :R:/:G: 4.00 8.00
280 Teferi, Who Slows the Sunset M :W:/:B: 2.50 5.00
281 Deserted Beach R 6.00 12.00
282 Haunted Ridge R 7.50 15.00
283 Overgrown Farmland R 4.00 8.00
284 Rockfall Vale R .30 5.00
285 Shipwreck Marsh R 4.00 8.00
286 Brutal Cathar/Moonrage Brute R :W: 1.25 2.50
287 Candlegrove Witch C :W: .07 .15
288 Suspicious Stowaway
Seafaring Werewolf R :B: .30 .60
289 Baneblade Scoundrel
Baneclaw Marauder U :K: .12 .25
290 Graveyard Trespasser/Graveyard Glutton R :K: 2.50 5.00
291 Shady Traveler/Stalking Predator C :K: .07 .15
292 Fangblade Brigand
Fangblade Eviscerator U :R: .12 .25
293 Harvesttide Infiltrator
Harvesttide Assailant C :R: .07 .15
294 Reckless Stormseeker
Storm-Charged Slasher R :R: .75 1.50
295 Spellrune Painter/Spellrune Howler U :R: .12 .25
296 Tavern Ruffian/Tavern Smasher C :R: .07 .15
297 Village Watch/Village Reavers U :R: .12 .25
298 Bird Admirer/Wing Shredder C :G: .07 .15
299 Burly Breaker/Dire-Strain Demolisher U :G: .12 .25
300 Dawnhart Mentor U :G: .12 .25
301 Dawnhart Rejuvenator C :G: .07 .15
302 Hound Tamer/Untamed Pup U :G: .12 .25
303 Outland Liberator/Frenzied Trapbreaker U :G: .20 .40
304 Saryth, the Viper's Fang R :G: 1.00 2.00
305 Tireless Hauler/Dire-Strain Brawler C :G: .07 .15
306 Tovolar's Huntmaster
Tovolar's Packleader R :G: .30 .75
307 Arlinn, the Pack's Hope
Moon's Fury M :R:/:G: 7.50 15.00
308 Dawnhart Wardens U :G:/:W: .12 .25
309 Katilda, Dawnhart Prime R :G:/:W: .30 .60
310 Kessig Naturalist
Lord of the Ulvenwald U :R:/:G: .12 .25
311 Tovolar, Dire Overlord
Midnight Scourge R :R:/:G: .75 1.50
312 Adeline, Resplendent Cathar R :W: 3.00 6.00
313 Lier, Disciple of the Drowned M :B: 4.00 8.00
314 Gisa, Glorious Resurrector R :K: .75 1.50
315 Jadar, Ghoulcaller of Nephalia R :K: .75 1.50
316 Jerren/Ormendahl M :K: .50 1.00
317 Dennick, Pious Apprentice
Apparition R :W:/:B: .30 .60
318 Florian, Voldaren Scion R :K:/:R: .30 .60
319 Liesa, Forgotten Archangel R :W:/:K: .30 .60
320 Ludevic, Necrogenius
Olag, Ludevic's Hubris R :B:/:K: .30 .60
321 Old Stickfingers R :K:/:G: .30 .60
322 Rem Karolus, Stalwart Slayer R :R:/:W: .30 .60
323 Sigarda, Champion of Light M :G:/:W: .50 1.00
324 Slogurk, the Overslime R :G:/:B: .30 .60
325 Vadrik, Astral Archmage R :B:/:R: .30 .60
326 Curse of Silence R :W: .30 .60
327 Enduring Angel/Angelic Enforcer M :W: 2.50 5.00
328 Fateful Absence R :W: 2.00 4.00
329 Intrepid Adversary M :W: 4.00 8.00
330 Sigarda's Splendor R :W: .60 1.25
331 Sigardian Savior M :W: .75 1.50
332 Sungold Sentinel R :W: .30 .60
333 Vanquish the Horde R :W: 3.00 6.00
334 Curse of Surveillance R :B: .30 .60
335 Grafted Identity R :B: .30 .60
336 Malevolent Hermit/Benevolent Geist R :B: 2.50 5.00
337 Memory Deluge R :B: 3.00 6.00
338 Patrician Geist R :B: .50 1.00
339 Poppet Stitcher/Poppet Factory M :B: 6.00 12.00
340 Sludge Monster R :B: .75 1.50
341 Spectral Adversary M :B: 2.00 4.00
342 Triskaidekaphile R :B: .75 1.50
343 Bloodline Culling R :K: .30 .60
344 Champion of the Perished R :K: 1.00 2.00
345 Curse of Leeches/Leeching Lurker R :K: .30 .60
346 Lord of the Forsaken M :K: 1.50 3.00
347 Mask of Griselbrand R :K: .60 1.25
348 The Meathook Massacre M :K: 40.00 80.00
349 Slaughter Specialist R :K: .50 1.00
350 Tainted Adversary M :K: 3.00 6.00
351 Bloodthirsty Adversary M :R: 3.00 6.00
352 Burn Down the House R :R: .75 1.50
353 Curse of Shaken Faith R :R: .30 .60
354 Falkenrath Pit Fighter R :R: .30 .60
355 Geistflame Reservoir R :R: .30 .60
356 Light Up the Night R :R: .30 .60
357 Moonveil Regent M :R: 2.00 4.00
358 Smoldering Egg/Ashmouth Dragon R :R: .75 1.50
359 Sunstreak Phoenix M :R: .50 1.00
360 Augur of Autumn R :G: 3.00 6.00
361 Briarbridge Tracker R :G: .30 .60
362 Consuming Blob M :G: .75 1.50
363 Primal Adversary M :G: 1.00 2.00
364 Storm the Festival R :G: 2.00 4.00
365 Unnatural Growth R :G: 4.00 8.00
366 Willow Geist R :G: .30 .60
367 Angelfire Ignition R :R:/:W: .75 1.50
368 Can't Stay Away R :W:/:K: .75 1.50
369 Croaking Counterpart R :G:/:B: .30 .60
370 Dire-Strain Rampage R :R:/:G: .30 .60
371 Galvanic Iteration R :B:/:R: 1.50 3.00
372 Ghoulcaller's Harvest R :K:/:G: .30 .60
373 Hallowed Respite R :W:/:B: .30 .60
374 Rite of Harmony R :G:/:W: .75 1.50
375 Siphon Insight R :B:/:K: 1.50 3.00
376 Wake to Slaughter R :K:/:R: .30 .60
377 The Celestus R 1.25 2.50
378 Pithing Needle R 1.25 2.50
379 Hostile Hostel/Creeping Inn M 1.50 3.00
380 Plains L .07 .15
381 Island L .07 .15
382 Swamp L .07 .15
383 Mountain L .07 .15
384 Forest L .07 .15
385 Champion of the Perished R :K: .30 .60

386 Triskaidekaphile R :B: .30 .60
387 Gavony Dawnguard U :W: .12 .25
388 Consider C :B: 2.00 4.00
389 Infernal Grasp U :K: 1.25 2.50
390 Play with Fire U :R: 1.25 2.50
391 Join the Dance U :G:/:W: .12 .25

2021 Magic The Gathering Innistrad Midnight Hunt Tokens

1 Human .10 .20
2 Spirit .07 .15
3 Bird .07 .15
4 Bat .10 .20
5 Zombie .10 .20
6 Devil .15 .30
7 Elemental .07 .15
8 Beast .07 .15
9 Insect .15 .30
10 Ooze .07 .15
11 Spider .15 .30
12 Treefolk .25 .50
13 Wolf .15 .30
14 Vampire .12 .25
15 Zombie .07 .15
16 Clue .10 .20
17 Teferi, Who Slows the Sunset .50 1.00
18 Wrenn and Seven .30 .60
19 Day/Night .07 .15

2021 Magic The Gathering Innistrad Midnight Hunt Commander

1 Leinore, Autumn Sovereign M :G:/:W: .25 .50
2 Wilhelt, the Rotcleaver M :B:/:K: 1.25 2.50
3 Eloise, Nephalia Sleuth M :B:/:K: .17 .35
4 Kyler, Sigardian Emissary M :G:/:W: .30 .75
5 Celestial Judgment R :W: .07 .15
6 Curse of Conformity R :W: .07 .15
7 Moorland Rescuer R :W: .12 .25
8 Sigarda's Vanguard R :W: .17 .35
9 Stalwart Pathlighter R :W: .10 .20
10 Wall of Mourning R :W: .07 .15
11 Cleaver Skaab R :B: .75 1.50
12 Curse of Unbinding R :B: .50 1.00
13 Drown in Dreams R :B: 2.00 4.00
14 Empty the Laboratory R :B: .20 .40
15 Hordewing Skaab R :B: .60 1.25
16 Shadow Kin R :B: .30 .75
17 Crowded Crypt R :K: 1.00 2.00
18 Curse of the Restless Dead R :K: 1.25 2.50
19 Ghouls' Night Out R :K: .15 .30
20 Gorex, the Tombshell R :K: .17 .35
21 Prowling Geistcatcher R :K: .15 .30
22 Ravenous Rotbelly R :K: .15 .30
23 Tomb Tyrant R :K: .60 1.25
24 Celebrate the Harvest R :G: .07 .15
25 Curse of Clinging Webs R :G: 1.00 2.00
26 Heronblade Elite R :G: .60 1.25
27 Kurbis, Harvest Celebrant R :G: .15 .30
28 Ruinous Intrusion R :G: .20 .40
29 Sigardian Zealot R :G: .07 .15
30 Somberwald Beastmaster R :G: .12 .25
31 Avacyn's Memorial M :W: .50 12.00
32 Visions of Glory R :W: .20 .40
33 Visions of Duplicity R :B: .10 .20
34 Visions of Dread R :K: .10 .20
35 Curse of Obsession R :R: .17 .35
36 Visions of Ruin R :R: .25 .50
37 Visions of Dominance R :G: .25 .50
38 Lynde, Cheerful Tormentor M :B:/:K:/:R: .75 1.50
39 Leinore, Autumn Sovereign M :G:/:W: 2.00 4.00
40 Wilhelt, the Rotcleaver M :B:/:K: 5.00 10.00
41 Eloise, Nephalia Sleuth M :B:/:K: 1.00 2.00
42 Kyler, Sigardian Emissary M :G:/:W: 2.50 5.00
43 Celestial Judgment R :W: .07 .15
44 Curse of Conformity R :W: .15 .30
45 Moorland Rescuer R :W: .15 .30
46 Sigarda's Vanguard R :W: .30 .60
47 Stalwart Pathlighter R :W: .17 .35
48 Wall of Mourning R :W: .15 .30
49 Cleaver Skaab R :B: 1.25 2.50
50 Curse of Unbinding R :B: .75 1.50
51 Drown in Dreams R :B: 2.50 5.00
52 Empty the Laboratory R :B: .30 .75
53 Hordewing Skaab R :B: 1.00 2.00
54 Shadow Kin R :B: 1.00 2.00
55 Crowded Crypt R :K: 1.25 2.50
56 Curse of the Restless Dead R :K: 1.00 2.00
57 Ghouls' Night Out R :K: .25 .50
58 Gorex, the Tombshell M :K: 1.00 2.00
59 Prowling Geistcatcher R :K: .25 .50
60 Ravenous Rotbelly R :K: .25 .50
61 Tomb Tyrant R :K: .75 1.50
62 Celebrate the Harvest R :G: .12 .25
63 Curse of Clinging Webs R :G: 1.00 2.00
64 Heronblade Elite R :G: 1.50 3.00
65 Kurbis, Harvest Celebrant M :G: 1.00 2.00
66 Ruinous Intrusion R :G: .75 1.50
67 Sigardian Zealot R :G: .12 .25
68 Somberwald Beastmaster R :G: .17 .35
69 Avacyn's Memorial M :W: 4.00 8.00
70 Visions of Glory R :W: .25 .50
71 Visions of Duplicity R :B: .10 .20
72 Visions of Dread R :K: .12 .25
73 Curse of Obsession R :R: .17 .35
74 Visions of Ruin R :R: .75 1.50
75 Visions of Dominance R :G: .50 1.00
76 Lynde, Cheerful Tormentor M :B:/:K:/:R: 1.50 3.00
77 Abzan Falconer U :W: .07 .15
78 Ainok Bond-Kin C :W: .07 .15
79 Angel of Glory's Rise R :W: .12 .25
80 Bastion Protector R :W: .25 .50
81 Citadel Siege R :W: .10 .20
82 Cleansing Nova R :W: .25 .50
83 Custodi Soulbinders R :W: .07 .15
84 Dearly Departed R :W: .07 .15
85 Elite Scaleguard U :W: .07 .15
86 Herald of War R :W: 1.25 2.50
87 Hour of Reckoning R :W: .10 .20
88 Knight of the White Orchid R :W: .17 .35
89 Mikaeus, the Lunarch M :W: .15 .30
90 Odric, Master Tactician R :W: .17 .35
91 Orzhov Advokist U :W: .07 .15
92 Return to Dust U :W: .10 .20
93 Riders of Gavony R :W: .07 .15
94 Swords to Plowshares U :W: .60 1.25
95 Unbreakable Formation R :W: .15 .30
96 Victory's Envoy R :W: .12 .25
97 Aetherspouts R :B: .15 .30
98 Distant Melody C :B: .40 .80
99 Eternal Skylord U :B: .07 .15
100 Forgotten Creation R :B: .10 .20
101 Havengul Runebinder R :B: .07 .15
102 Hour of Eternity R :B: .07 .15
103 Rooftop Storm R :B: .75 1.50
104 Stitcher Geralf M :B: .15 .30
105 Undead Alchemist R :B: .17 .35
106 Army of the Damned M :K: .25 .50
107 Butcher of Malakir R :K: .12 .25
108 Cemetery Reaper R :K: .40 .80
109 Corpse Augur U :K: .07 .15
110 Dark Salvation R :K: .12 .25
111 Death Baron R :K: 1.25 2.50
112 Diregraf Colossus R :K: 1.00 2.00
113 Dread Summons R :K: .15 .30
114 Dreadhorde Invasion R :K: .75 1.50
115 Eater of Hope R :K: .07 .15
116 Endless Ranks of the Dead R :K: .50 1.00
117 Feed the Swarm C :K: .15 .30
118 Fleshbag Marauder U :K: .10 .20
119 Go for the Throat U :K: .17 .35
120 Gravespawn Sovereign R :K: .07 .15
121 Liliana, Death's Majesty M :K: .75 1.50
122 Liliana's Devotee U :K: .07 .15
123 Liliana's Mastery R :K: .15 .30
124 Lord of the Accursed U :K: .12 .25
125 Midnight Reaper R :K: .15 .30
126 Open the Graves R :K: .15 .30
127 Overseer of the Damned R :K: .12 .25
128 Spark Reaper C :K: .07 .15
129 Syphon Flesh U :K: .07 .15
130 Undead Augur U :K: .15 .30
131 Zombie Apocalypse R :K: .15 .30
132 Avacyn's Pilgrim C :G: .20 .40
133 Beast Within U :G: .75 1.50
134 Bestial Menace U :G: .07 .15
135 Biogenic Upgrade U :G: .07 .15
136 Champion of Lambholt R :G: .20 .40
137 Death's Presence R :G: .10 .20
138 Eternal Witness U :G: 1.00 2.00
139 Growth Spasm C :G: .07 .15
140 Gyre Sage R :G: .60 1.25
141 Inspiring Call U :G: .20 .40
142 Kessig Cagebreakers R :G: .07 .15
143 Shamanic Revelation R :G: .25 .50
144 Somberwald Sage R :G: .75 1.50
145 Verdurous Gearhulk M :G: .20 .40
146 Wild Beastmaster R :G: .07 .15
147 Yavimaya Elder C :G: .07 .15
148 Diregraf Captain U :B:/:K: .12 .25
149 Enduring Scalelord U :G:/:W: .07 .15
150 Gisa and Geralf M :B:/:K: .17 .35
151 Gleaming Overseer U :B:/:K: .12 .25
152 Heron's Grace Champion R :G:/:W: .07 .15
153 Juniper Order Ranger U :G:/:W: .07 .15
154 Ruthless Deathfang U :B:/:K: .07 .15
155 Sigarda, Heron's Grace M :G:/:W: .20 .40
156 Trostani's Summoner U :G:/:W: .07 .15
157 Arcane Signet C .40 .80
158 Charcoal Diamond C .12 .25
159 Commander's Sphere C .12 .25
160 Lifecrafter's Bestiary R .50 1.00
161 Sky Diamond C .10 .20
162 Sol Ring U 1.00 2.00
163 Swiftfoot Boots U .60 1.25
164 Talisman of Dominance U 1.25 2.50
165 Talisman of Unity U .30 .75
166 Blighted Woodland U .12 .25
167 Bojuka Bog C .75 1.50
168 Canopy Vista R .25 .50
169 Choked Estuary R .15 .30
170 Command Tower C .15 .30
171 Darkwater Catacombs R .12 .25
172 Dimir Aqueduct U .10 .20
173 Exotic Orchard R .07 .15
174 Fortified Village R .12 .25
175 Krosan Verge U .12 .25
176 Mortuary Mire C .07 .15
177 Myriad Landscape U .12 .25
178 Path of Ancestry C .10 .20
179 Rogue's Passage U .25 .50
180 Selesnya Sanctuary U .15 .30
181 Sungrass Prairie R .12 .25
182 Sunken Hollow R .15 .30
183 Tainted Isle U .75 1.50
184 Temple of Deceit R .12 .25
185 Temple of Plenty R .15 .30
186 Temple of the False God U .07 .15
187 Unclaimed Territory U .75 1.50

2021 Magic The Gathering Innistrad Midnight Hunt Commander Tokens

1 Eldrazi Spawn .12 .25
2 Human Soldier .12 .25
3 Knight .12 .25
4 Zombie .12 .25
5 Zombie .12 .25
6 Zombie Army .12 .25
7 Beast .12 .25
8 Centaur .12 .25
9 Elephant .12 .25
10 Rhino .12 .25
11 Snake .12 .25

2021 Magic The Gathering Kaldheim

1 Axgard Braggart C :W: .07 .15
2 Battershield Warrior U :W: .10 .20
3 Battlefield Raptor C :W: .07 .15
4 Beskir Shieldmate C :W: .07 .15
5 Bound in Gold C :W: .07 .15
6 Clarion Spirit U :W: .12 .25
7 Codespell Cleric C :W: .07 .15
8 Divine Gambit U :W: .10 .20
9 Doomskar R :W: .15 .30
10 Doomskar Oracle C :W: .07 .15
11 Giant Ox C :W: .07 .15
12 Glorious Protector R :W: .15 .30
13 Gods' Hall Guardian C :W: .07 .15
14 Goldmaw Champion C :W: .07 .15
15 Halvar, God of Battle/Sword of the Realms M :W: 5.00 10.00
16 Invoke the Divine C :W: .07 .15
17 Iron Verdict C :W: .07 .15
18 Kaya's Onslaught U :W: .10 .20
19 Master Skald C :W: .07 .15
20 Rally the Ranks R :W: .15 .30
21 Reidane/Valkmira R :W: .15 .30
22 Resplendent Marshal M :W: 1.00 2.00
23 Revitalize C :W: .07 .15
24 Righteous Valkyrie R :W: .15 .30
25 Rune of Sustenance U :W: .10 .20
26 Runeforge Champion R :W: .15 .30
27 Search for Glory R :W: .15 .30
28 Shepherd of the Cosmos U :W: .10 .20
29 Sigrid, God-Favored R :W: .15 .30
30 Spectral Steel U :W: .10 .20
31 Stalwart Valkyrie C :W: .07 .15
32 Starnheim Courser C :W: .07 .15
33 Starnheim Unleashed M :W: 3.00 6.00
34 Story Seeker C :W: .07 .15
35 Usher of the Fallen U :W: .10 .20
36 Valkyrie's Sword U :W: .10 .20
37 Valor of the Worthy C :W: .07 .15
38 Warhorn Blast C :W: .07 .15
39 Wings of the Cosmos C :W: .07 .15
40 Alrund/Hakka M :B: 1.25 2.50
41 Alrund's Epiphany M :B: 5.00 10.00
42 Annul C :B: .07 .15
43 Ascendant Spirit R :B: .15 .30
44 Augury Raven C :B: .07 .15
45 Avalanche Caller U :B: .10 .20
46 Behold the Multiverse C :B: .07 .15
47 Berg Strider C :B: .07 .15
48 Bind the Monster C :B: .07 .15
49 Brinebarrow Intruder C :B: .07 .15
50 Cosima, God of the Voyage The Omenkeel R :B: .15 .30
51 Cosmos Charger R :B: .15 .30
52 Cyclone Summoner R :B: .15 .30
53 Depart the Realm C :B: .07 .15
54 Disdainful Stroke C :B: .07 .15
55 Draugr Thought-Thief C :B: .07 .15
56 Frost Augur U :B: .10 .20
57 Frostpeak Yeti C :B: .07 .15
58 Frostpyre Arcanist U :B: .10 .20
59 Giant's Amulet U :B: .10 .20
60 Glimpse the Cosmos U :B: .10 .20
61 Graven Lore R :B: .15 .30
62 Icebind Pillar U :B: .10 .20
63 Icebreaker Kraken R :B: .15 .30
64 Inga Rune-Eyes U :B: .10 .20
65 Karfell Harbinger C :B: .07 .15
66 Littjara Kinseekers C :B: .07 .15
67 Mists of Littjara C :B: .07 .15
68 Mistwalker C :B: .07 .15
69 Mystic Reflection R :B: .15 .30
70 Orvar, the All-Form M :B: 4.00 8.00
71 Pilfering Hawk C :B: .07 .15
72 Ravenform C :B: .07 .15
73 Reflections of Littjara R :B: .15 .30
74 Run Ashore C :B: .07 .15
75 Rune of Flight U :B: .10 .20
76 Saw It Coming U :B: .10 .20
77 Strategic Planning C :B: .07 .15
78 Undersea Invader C :B: .07 .15
79 Blood on the Snow R :K: .15 .30
80 Bloodsky Berserker U :K: .10 .20
81 Burning-Rune Demon M :K: 2.00 4.00
82 Crippling Fear R :K: .15 .30
83 Deathknell Berserker C :K: .07 .15
84 Demonic Gifts C :K: .07 .15
85 Dogged Pursuit C :K: .07 .15
86 Draugr Necromancer R :K: .15 .30
87 Draugr Recruiter C :K: .07 .15
88 Draugr's Helm U :K: .10 .20
89 Dread Rider C :K: .07 .15
90 Dream Devourer R :K: .15 .30
91 Duskwielder C :K: .07 .15
92 Egon, God of Death/Throne of Death R :K: .15 .30
93 Elderfang Disciple C :K: .07 .15
94 Eradicator Valkyrie M :K: 3.00 6.00
95 Feed the Serpent C :K: .07 .15
96 Grim Draugr C :K: .07 .15
97 Hailstorm Valkyrie U :K: .10 .20
98 Haunting Voyage M :K: 2.50 5.00
99 Infernal Pet C :K: .07 .15
100 Jarl of the Forsaken C :K: .07 .15
101 Karfell Kennel-Master C :K: .07 .15
102 Koma's Faithful C :K: .07 .15
103 Poison the Cup U :K: .10 .20
104 Priest of the Haunted Edge C :K: .07 .15
105 Raise the Draugr C :K: .07 .15
106 Return Upon the Tide U :K: .10 .20
107 Rise of the Dread Marn R :K: .15 .30
108 Rune of Mortality U :K: .10 .20
109 Skemfar Avenger R :K: .15 .30
110 Skemfar Shadowsage U :K: .10 .20
111 Skull Raid C :K: .07 .15
112 Tergrid, God of Fright/Tergrid's Lantern R :K: .15
113 Tergrid's Shadow U :K: .10 .20
114 Valki, God of Lies/Tibalt, Cosmic Impostor M :K: 12.50 25.00
115 Varragoth, Bloodsky Sire R :K: .15 .30
116 Vengeful Reaper U :K: .10 .20
117 Village Rites C :K: .07 .15
118 Weigh Down C :K: .07 .15
119 Withercrown C :K: .07 .15
120 Arni Brokenbrow R :R: .15 .30
121 Axgard Cavalry C :R: .07 .15
122 Basalt Ravager U :R: .10 .20
123 Birgi/Harnfel R :R: .15 .30
124 Breakneck Berserker C :R: .07 .15
125 Calamity Bearer R :R: .15 .30
126 Cinderheart Giant C :R: .07 .15
127 Craven Hulk C :R: .07 .15
128 Crush the Weak U :R: .10 .20
129 Demon Bolt C :R: .07 .15
130 Doomskar Titan U :R: .10 .20
131 Dragonkin Berserker R :R: .15 .30
132 Dual Strike U :R: .10 .20
133 Dwarven Hammer U :R: .10 .20
134 Dwarven Reinforcements C :R: .07 .15
135 Fearless Liberator U :R: .10 .20
136 Fearless Pup C :R: .07 .15
137 Frenzied Raider U :R: .10 .20
138 Frost Bite C :R: .07 .15
139 Goldspan Dragon M :R: 12.50 25.00
140 Hagi Mob C :R: .07 .15
141 Immersturm Raider C :R: .07 .15
142 Magda, Brazen Outlaw R :R: .15 .30
143 Open the Omenpaths C :R: .07 .15
144 Provoke the Trolls U :R: .10 .20
145 Quakebringer M :R: 2.00 4.00
146 Reckless Crew R :R: .15 .30
147 Run Amok C :R: .07 .15
148 Rune of Speed U :R: .10 .20
149 Seize the Spoils C :R: .07 .15
150 Shackles of Treachery C :R: .07 .15
151 Smashing Success C :R: .07 .15
152 Squash C :R: .07 .15
153 Tibalt's Trickery R :R: .15 .30
154 Toralf, God of Fury/Toralf's Hammer M :R: 3.00 6.00
155 Tormentor's Helm C :R: .07 .15
156 Tundra Fumarole R :R: .15 .30
157 Tuskeri Firewalker C :R: .07 .15
158 Vault Robber C :R: .07 .15
159 Arachnoform C :G: .07 .15
160 Battle Mammoth M :G: 1.00 2.00
161 Blessing of Frost R :G: .15 .30
162 Blizzard Brawl U :G: .10 .20
163 Boreal Outrider U :G: .10 .20
164 Broken Wings C :G: .07 .15
165 Elderleaf Mentor C :G: .07 .15
166 Elven Bow U :G: .10 .20
167 Elvish Warmaster R :G: .15 .30
168 Esika, God of the Tree/The Prismatic Bridge M :G: 7.50 15.00
169 Esika's Chariot R :G: .15 .30
170 Fynn, the Fangbearer U :G: .10 .20
171 Glittering Frost C :G: .07 .15
172 Gnottvold Recluse C :G: .07 .15
173 Grizzled Outrider C :G: .07 .15
174 Guardian Gladewalker C :G: .07 .15
175 Horizon Seeker C :G: .07 .15
176 Icehide Troll C :G: .07 .15
177 In Search of Greatness R :G: .15 .30
178 Jaspera Sentinel C :G: .07 .15
179 Jorn, God of Winter/Kaldring, the Rimestaff R :G: .15 .30
180 King Harald's Revenge C :G: .07 .15
181 Kolvori, God of Kinship The Ringhart Crest R :G: .15 .30
182 Littjara Glade-Warden U :G: .10 .20
183 Mammoth Growth C :G: .07 .15
184 Masked Vandal C :G: .07 .15
185 Old-Growth Troll R :G: .15 .30
186 Path to the World Tree U :G: .10 .20
187 Ravenous Lindwurm C :G: .07 .15
188 Realmwalker R :G: .15 .30
189 Rootless Yew U :G: .10 .20
190 Roots of Wisdom C :G: .07 .15
191 Rune of Might U :G: .10 .20
192 Sarulf's Packmate C :G: .07 .15
193 Sculptor of Winter C :G: .07 .15
194 Snakeskin Veil C :G: .07 .15
195 Spirit of the Aldergard U :G: .10 .20
196 Struggle for Skemfar C :G: .07 .15
197 Toski, Bearer of Secrets R :G: .15 .30
198 Tyvar Kell M :G: 6.00 12.00
199 Vorinclex, Monstrous Raider M :G: 25.00 50.00
200 Aegar, the Freezing Flame U :B:/:R: .10 .20
201 Arni Slays the Troll U :R:/:G: .10 .20
202 Ascent of the Worthy U :W:/:K: .10 .20
203 Battle for Bretagard R :G:/:W: .15 .30
204 Battle of Frost and Fire R :B:/:R: .15 .30
205 The Bears of Littjara R :G:/:B: .15 .30
206 Binding the Old Gods U :K:/:G: .10 .20
207 The Bloodsky Massacre R :K:/:R: .15 .30
208 Fall of the Impostor U :G:/:W: .10 .20
209 Firja, Judge of Valor U :W:/:K: .10 .20
210 Firja's Retribution R :W:/:K: .15 .30
211 Forging the Tyrite Sword U :R:/:W: .10 .20
212 Harald, King of Skemfar U :K:/:G: .10 .20
213 Harald Unites the Elves R :K:/:G: .15 .30
214 Immersturm Predator R :K:/:R: .15 .30
215 Invasion of the Giants U :B:/:R: .10 .20
216 Kardur, Doomscourge U :K:/:R: .10 .20
217 Kardur's Vicious Return U :K:/:R: .10 .20
218 Kaya the Inexorable M :W:/:K: 2.50 5.00
219 King Narfi's Betrayal R :B:/:K: .15 .30
220 Koll, the Forgemaster U :R:/:W: .10 .20
221 Koma, Cosmos Serpent M :G:/:B: 10.00 20.00
222 Maja, Bretagard Protector U :G:/:W: .10 .20
223 Moritte of the Frost U :G:/:B: .10 .20
224 Narfi, Betrayer King U :B:/:K: .10 .20
225 Niko Aris M :W:/:B: 1.25 2.50
226 Niko Defies Destiny U :W:/:B: .10 .20
227 The Raven's Warning R :W:/:B: .15 .30
228 Sarulf, Realm Eater R :K:/:G: .15 .30
229 Showdown of the Skalds R :R:/:W: .15 .30
230 Svella, Ice Shaper U :R:/:G: .10 .20
231 The Three Seasons U :G:/:B: .10 .20
232 The Trickster-God's Heist U :B:/:K: .10 .20
233 Vega, the Watcher U :W:/:B: .10 .20
234 Waking the Trolls R :R:/:G: .15 .30
235 Bloodline Pretender U .10 .20
236 Colossal Plow U .10 .20
237 Cosmos Elixir R .15 .30
238 Funeral Longboat C .07 .15
239 Goldvein Pick C .07 .15
240 Maskwood Nexus R .15 .30
241 Pyre of Heroes R .15 .30
242 Raiders' Karve C .07 .15
243 Raven Wings C .07 .15
244 Replicating Ring U .10 .20
245 Runed Crown U .10 .20
246 Scorn Effigy C .07 .15
247 Weathered Runestone U .10 .20
248 Alpine Meadow C .07 .15
249 Arctic Treeline C .07 .15
250 Axgard Armory U .10 .20
251 Barkchannel Pathway/Tidechannel Pathway R .15 .30
252 Blightstep Pathway/Searstep Pathway R .15 .30
253 Bretagard Stronghold U .10 .20
254 Darkbore Pathway/Slitherbore Pathway R .15 .30
255 Faceless Haven R .15 .30

2021 Magic The Gathering Kaldheim

256 Gates of Istfell U .10 .20
257 Glacial Floodplain C .07 .15
258 Gnottvold Slumbermound U .10 .20
259 Great Hall of Starnheim U .10 .20
260 Hengegate Pathway/Mistgate Pathway R .15 .30
261 Highland Forest C .07 .15
262 Ice Tunnel C .07 .15
263 Immersturm Skullcairn U .10 .20
264 Littjara Mirrorlake U .10 .20
265 Port of Karfell U .10 .20
266 Rimewood Falls C .07 .15
267 Shimmerdrift Vale C .07 .15
268 Skemfar Elderhall U .10 .20
269 Snowfield Sinkhole C .07 .15
270 Sulfurous Mire C .07 .15
271 Surtland Frostpyre U .10 .20
272 Tyrite Sanctum R .15 .30
273 Volatile Fjord C .07 .15
274 Woodland Chasm C .07 .15
275 The World Tree R .15 .30
276 Snow-Covered Plains C .07 .15
277 Snow-Covered Plains C .07 .15
278 Snow-Covered Island C .07 .15
279 Snow-Covered Island C .07 .15
280 Snow-Covered Swamp C .07 .15
281 Snow-Covered Swamp C .07 .15
282 Snow-Covered Mountain C .07 .15
283 Snow-Covered Mountain C .07 .15
284 Snow-Covered Forest C .07 .15
285 Snow-Covered Forest C .07 .15
286 Valki, God of Lies/Tibalt, Cosmic Impostor M :K:/:R: 1.00 2.00
287 Tyvar Kell M :G: 1.00 2.00
288 Kaya the Inexorable M :W:/:K: 1.00 2.00
289 Niko Aris M :W:/:B: 1.00 2.00
290 Barkchannel Pathway/Tidechannel Pathway R .15 .30
291 Blightstep Pathway/Searstep Pathway R .15 .30
292 Darkbore Pathway/Slitherbore Pathway R .15 .30
293 Hengegate Pathway/Mistgate Pathway R .15 .30
294 Starnheim Unleashed M :W: 1.00 2.00
295 Alrund's Epiphany M :B: 1.00 2.00
296 Haunting Voyage M :K: 1.00 2.00
297 Quakebringer M :R: 1.00 2.00
298 Battle Mammoth M :G: 1.00 2.00
299 Halvar, God of Battle Sword of the Realms M :W: 1.00 2.00
300 Reidane/Valkmira R :W: .15 .30
301 Sigrid, God-Favored R :W: .15 .30
302 Alrund/Hakka M :B: 1.00 2.00
303 Cosima, God of the Voyage/The Omenkeel R :B: .15 .30
304 Inga Rune-Eyes U :B: .10 .20
305 Orvar, the All-Form M :B: 1.00 2.00
306 Egon, God of Death/Throne of Death R :K: .15 .30
307 Tergrid, God of Fright/Tergrid's Lantern R :K: .15 .30
308 Valki, God of Lies/Tibalt, Cosmic Impostor M :K:/:R: 1.00 2.00
309 Varragoth, Bloodsky Sire R :K: .15 .30
310 Arni Brokenbrow R :R: .15 .30
311 Birgi, God of Storytelling Harnfel, Horn of Bounty R :R: .15 .30
312 Magda, Brazen Outlaw R :R: .15 .30
313 Toralf, God of Fury/Toralf's Hammer M :R: 1.00 2.00
314 Esika/Prismatic Bridge M :W:/:B:/:K:/:R:/:G: 10.00 20.00
315 Esika's Chariot R :G: .15 .30
316 Fynn, the Fangbearer U :G: .10 .20
317 Jorn/Kaldring R :G:/:B:/:K: .15 .30
318 Kolvori, God of Kinship The Ringhart Crest R :G: .15 .30
319 Toski, Bearer of Secrets R :G: .15 .30
320 Vorinclex, Monstrous Raider M :G: 1.00 2.00
321 Aegar, the Freezing Flame U :B:/:R: .10 .20
322 Firja, Judge of Valor U :W:/:K: .10 .20
323 Harald, King of Skemfar U :K:/:G: .10 .20
324 Kardur, Doomscourge U :K:/:R: .10 .20
325 Koll, the Forgemaster U :R:/:W: .10 .20
326 Koma, Cosmos Serpent M :G:/:B: 1.00 2.00
327 Maja, Bretagard Protector U :G:/:W: .10 .20
328 Moritte of the Frost U :G:/:B: .10 .20
329 Narfi, Betrayer King U :B:/:K: .10 .20
330 Sarulf, Realm Eater R :K:/:G: .15 .30
331 Svella, Ice Shaper U :R:/:G: .10 .20
332 Vega, the Watcher U :W:/:B: .10 .20
333 Vorinclex, Monstrous Raider (Phyrexian) M :G: 1.00 2.00
334 Doomskar R :W: FULL ART .15 .30
335 Glorious Protector R :W: FULL ART .15 .30
336 Rally the Ranks R :W: FULL ART .15 .30
337 Resplendent Marshal M :W: FULL ART 1.00 2.00
338 Righteous Valkyrie R :W: FULL ART .15 .30
339 Runeforge Champion R :W: FULL ART .15 .30
340 Search for Glory R :W: FULL ART .15 .30
341 Ascendant Spirit R :B: FULL ART .15 .30
342 Cosmos Charger R :B: FULL ART .15 .30
343 Cyclone Summoner R :B: FULL ART .15 .30
344 Graven Lore R :B: FULL ART .15 .30
345 Icebreaker Kraken R :B: FULL ART .15 .30
346 Mystic Reflection R :B: FULL ART .15 .30
347 Reflections of Littjara R :B: FULL ART .15 .30
348 Blood on the Snow R :K: FULL ART .15 .30
349 Burning-Rune Demon M :K: FULL ART 1.00 2.00
350 Crippling Fear R :K: FULL ART .15 .30
351 Draugr Necromancer R :K: FULL ART .15 .30
352 Dream Devourer R :K: FULL ART .15 .30
353 Eradicator Valkyrie M :K: FULL ART 1.00 2.00
354 Rise of the Dread Marn R :K: FULL ART .15 .30
355 Skemfar Avenger R :K: FULL ART .15 .30
356 Calamity Bearer R :R: FULL ART .15 .30
357 Dragonkin Berserker R :R: FULL ART .15 .30
358 Goldspan Dragon M :R: FULL ART 1.00 2.00
359 Reckless Crew R :R: FULL ART .15 .30
360 Tibalt's Trickery R :R: FULL ART .15 .30
361 Tundra Fumarole R :R: FULL ART .15 .30
362 Blessing of Frost R :G: FULL ART .15 .30
363 Elvish Warmaster R :G: FULL ART .15 .30
364 In Search of Greatness R :G: FULL ART .15 .30
365 Old-Growth Troll R :G: FULL ART .15 .30
366 Realmwalker R :G: FULL ART .15 .30
367 Immersturm Predator R :K:/:R: FULL ART .15 .30
368 Cosmos Elixir R FULL ART .15 .30
369 Maskwood Nexus R FULL ART .15 .30
370 Pyre of Heroes R FULL ART .15 .30
371 Faceless Haven R FULL ART .15 .30
372 Tyrite Sanctum R FULL ART .15 .30
373 The World Tree R FULL ART .15 .30
374 Valkyrie Harbinger R :W: .15 .30
375 Surtland Elementalist R :B: .15 .30
376 Cleaving Reaper R :K: .15 .30
377 Surtland Flinger R :R: .15 .30
378 Canopy Tactician R :G: .15 .30
379 Armed and Armored U :W: .10 .20
380 Starnheim Aspirant U :W: .10 .20
381 Warchanter Skald U :W: .10 .20
382 Youthful Valkyrie U :W: .10 .20
383 Absorb Identity U :B: .10 .20
384 Giant's Grasp U :B: .10 .20
385 Elderfang Ritualist U :K: .10 .20
386 Renegade Reaper U :K: .10 .20
387 Thornmantle Striker U :K: .10 .20
388 Bearded Axe U :R: .10 .20
389 Fire Giant's Fury U :R: .10 .20
390 Gilded Assault Cart U :R: .10 .20
391 Elven Ambush U :G: .10 .20
392 Gladewalker Ritualist U :G: .10 .20
393 Rampage of the Valkyries U :W:/:K: .10 .20
394 Plains C .07 .15
395 Island C .07 .15
396 Swamp C .07 .15
397 Mountain C .07 .15
398 Forest C .07 .15
399 Realmwalker R :G: .15 .30
400 Reflections of Littjara R :B: .15 .30
401 Usher of the Fallen U :W: .10 .20
402 Strategic Planning C :B: .07 .15
403 Poison the Cup U :K: .10 .20
404 Frost Bite C :R: .07 .15
405 Masked Vandal C :G: .07 .15

2021 Magic The Gathering Kaldheim Tokens

1 Shard .30 .60
2 Angel Warrior .15 .30
3 Human Warrior .07 .15
4 Spirit .07 .15
5 Bird .07 .15
6 Giant Wizard .07 .15
7 Koma's Coil 3.00 6.00
8 Shapeshifter .30 .60
9 Zombie Berserker .07 .15
10 Demon Berserker .07 .15
11 Dragon .30 .60
12 Dwarf Berserker .07 .15
13 Bear .15 .30
14 Cat .75 1.50
15 Elf Warrior .15 .30
16 Troll Warrior .07 .15
17 Icy Manalith .07 .15
18 Replicated Ring .20 .40
19 Treasure .07 .15
20 Kaya the Inexorable Emblem .30 .60
21 Tibalt, Cosmic Impostor Emblem .30 .60
22 Tyvar Kell Emblem .20 .40
23 Foretell .07 .15

2021 Magic The Gathering Kaldheim Commander

1 Lathril, Blade of the Elves M :K:/:G: 2.50 5.00
2 Ranar the Ever-Watchful M :W:/:B: .15 .30
3 Cosmic Intervention R :W: 2.00 4.00
4 Hero of Bretagard R :W: .10 .20
5 Stoic Farmer R :W: .15 .25
6 Sage of the Beyond R :B: .17 .35
7 Spectral Deluge R :B: .75 1.50
8 Tales of the Ancestors R :B: .15 .25
9 Pact of the Serpent R :K: 3.00 6.00
10 Ruthless Winnower R :K: .20 .40
11 Serpent's Soul-Jar R :K: .15 .30
12 Bounty of Skemfar R :G: .15 .30
13 Crown of Skemfar R :G: .20 .40
14 Wolverine Riders R :G: 1.25 2.50
15 Elderfang Venom R :K:/:G: .40 .80
16 Ethereal Valkyrie R :W:/:B: .17 .35
17 Angel of Finality R :W: .15 .30
18 Angel of Serenity M :W: .25 .50
19 Banishing Light U :W: .07 .15
20 Cleansing Nova R :W: .25 .50
21 Cloudgoat Ranger U :W: .07 .15
22 Eerie Interlude R :W: 2.50 5.00
23 Evangel of Heliod U :W: .10 .20
24 Flickerwisp U :W: .07 .15
25 Geist-Honored Monk R :W: .15 .30
26 Ghostly Prison U :W: 1.50 3.00
27 Goldnight Commander U :W: .07 .15
28 Kor Cartographer C :W: .07 .15
29 Marshal's Anthem R :W: .15 .25
30 Momentary Blink C :W: .07 .15
31 Restoration Angel R :W: .17 .35
32 Return to Dust U :W: .07 .15
33 Storm Herd R :W: .20 .40
34 Sun Titan M :W: .30 .75
35 Wall of Omens U :W: .15 .25
36 Arcane Artisan M :B: .17 .35
37 Curse of the Swine R :B: .20 .40
38 Day of the Dragons R :B: .07 .15
39 Ghostly Flicker C :B: .75 1.50
40 Inspired Sphinx M :B: .15 .25
41 Mist Raven C :B: .07 .15
42 Mulldrifter U :B: .17 .35
43 Sea Gate Oracle C :B: .10 .20
44 Synthetic Destiny R :B: .07 .15
45 Whirler Rogue U :B: .07 .15
46 Windfall U :B: 4.00 8.00
47 Ambition's Cost U :K: .07 .15
48 Eyeblight Cullers C :K: .07 .15
49 Eyeblight Massacre U :K: .07 .15
50 Lys Alana Scarblade U :K: .07 .15
51 Miara, Thorn of the Glade U :K: .10 .20
52 Pride of the Perfect U :K: .07 .15
53 Prowess of the Fair U :K: .17 .35
54 Beast Whisperer R :G: 2.50 5.00
55 Cultivator of Blades R :G: .15 .25
56 Dwynen, Gilt-Leaf Daen R :G: .30 .75
57 Elvish Archdruid R :G: .40 .80
58 Elvish Mystic C :G: .75 1.50
59 Elvish Promenade U :G: 2.00 4.00
60 Elvish Rejuvenator C :G: .07 .15
61 End-Raze Forerunners R :G: .15 .30
62 Farhaven Elf C :G: .10 .20
63 Harvest Season R :G: .75 1.50
64 Imperious Perfect R :G: .20 .40
65 Jagged-Scar Archers U :G: .15 .25
66 Llanowar Tribe U :G: .25 .50
67 Lys Alana Huntmaster C :G: .15 .30
68 Marwyn, the Nurturer R :G: 1.25 2.50
69 Masked Admirers R :G: .07 .15
70 Nullmage Shepherd U :G: .15 .25
71 Numa, Joraga Chieftain U :G: .07 .15
72 Reclamation Sage U :G: .17 .35
73 Rhys the Exiled R :G: .17 .35
74 Springbloom Druid C :G: .75 1.50
75 Sylvan Messenger U :G: .07 .15
76 Timberwatch Elf C :G: .20 .40
77 Voice of Many U :G: .07 .15
78 Voice of the Woods R :G: .15 .25
79 Wirewood Channeler U :G: 1.25 2.50
80 Wood Elves C :G: .20 .40
81 Abomination of Llanowar U :K:/:G: .15 .25
82 Brago, King Eternal R :W:/:B: 1.00 2.00
83 Casualties of War R :K:/:G: .75 1.50
84 Cloudblazer U :W:/:B: .07 .15
85 Empyrean Eagle U :W:/:B: .20 .40
86 Golgari Findbroker U :K:/:G: .07 .15
87 Migratory Route U :W:/:B: .07 .15
88 Mistmeadow Witch U :W:/:B: .07 .15
89 Moldervine Reclamation U :K:/:G: .20 .40
90 Poison-Tip Archer U :K:/:G: 1.00 2.00
91 Putrefy U :K:/:G: .17 .35
92 Shaman of the Pack U :K:/:G: .20 .40
93 Soulherder U :W:/:B: .30 .75
94 Thunderclap Wyvern U :W:/:B: .15 .30
95 Twinblade Assassins U :K:/:G: .07 .15
96 Arcane Signet C .50 1.00
97 Azorius Signet U .25 .50
98 Burnished Hart U .10 .20
99 Commander's Sphere C .10 .20
100 Marble Diamond C .07 .15
101 Meteor Golem U .07 .15
102 Mind Stone C .15 .30
103 Sky Diamond C .15 .25
104 Sol Ring U 1.00 2.00
105 Swiftfoot Boots U .75 1.50
106 Azorius Chancery U .07 .15
107 Azorius Guildgate C .75 1.50
108 Command Tower C .15 .30
109 Cryptic Caves U .07 .15
110 Foul Orchard U .07 .15
111 Golgari Guildgate C .15 .25
112 Golgari Rot Farm U .20 .40
113 Jungle Hollow C .07 .15
114 Meandering River C .07 .15
115 Myriad Landscape U .15 .25
116 Opal Palace C .07 .15
117 Path of Ancestry C .15 .25
118 Sejiri Refuge U .15 .25
119 Tranquil Cove C .07 .15

2021 Magic The Gathering Modern Horizons 2

1 Abiding Grace U :W: .12 .25
2 Arcbound Javelineer U :W: .12 .25
3 Arcbound Mouser C :W: .07 .15
4 Arcbound Prototype C :W: .07 .15
5 Barbed Spike U :W: .12 .25
6 Blacksmith's Skill C :W: .07 .15
7 Blossoming Calm U :W: .12 .25
8 Break Ties C :W: .07 .15
9 Caprichrome U :W: .12 .25
10 Constable of the Realm U :W: .12 .25
11 Disciple of the Sun C :W: .07 .15
12 Esper Sentinel R :W: 12.50 25.00
13 Fairgrounds Patrol C :W: .07 .15
14 Glorious Enforcer U :W: .12 .25
15 Guardian Kirin C :W: .07 .15
16 Healer's Flock U :W: .12 .25
17 Knighted Myr C :W: .07 .15
18 Landscaper Colos C :W: .07 .15
19 Late to Dinner C :W: .07 .15
20 Lens Flare C :W: .07 .15
21 Marble Gargoyle C :W: .07 .15
22 Nykthos Paragon R :W: .20 .40
23 Out of Time R :W: .20 .40
24 Piercing Rays C :W: .07 .15
25 Prismatic Ending U :W: .60 1.25
26 Resurgent Belief R .20 .40
27 Sanctifier en-Vec R :W: .75 1.50
28 Scour the Desert U :W: .12 .25
29 Search the Premises R :W: .20 .40
30 Serra's Emissary M :W: 2.00 4.00
31 Skyblade's Boon U :W: .12 .25
32 Solitude M :W: 25.00 50.00
33 Soul of Migration C :W: .07 .15
34 Thraben Watcher U :W: .12 .25
35 Timeless Dragon R :W: .20 .40
36 Unbounded Potential C :W: .07 .15
37 Aeromoeba C :B: .07 .15
38 Burdened Aerialist C :B: .07 .15
39 Dress Down R :B: 1.25 2.50
40 Etherium Spinner C :B: .07 .15
41 Filigree Attendant U :B: .12 .25
42 Floodhound C :B: .07 .15
43 Foul Watcher C :B: .07 .15
44 Fractured Sanity R :B: .30 .75
45 Ghost-Lit Drifter U :B: .12 .25
46 Hard Evidence C :B: .07 .15
47 Inevitable Betrayal R .20 .40
48 Junk Winder U :B: .12 .25
49 Lose Focus C :B: .07 .15
50 Lucid Dreams U :B: .12 .25
51 Mental Journey C :B: .07 .15
52 Murktide Regent M :B: 10.00 20.00
53 Mystic Redaction U :B: .12 .25
54 Parcel Myr C :B: .07 .15
55 Phantasmal Dreadmaw C :B: .07 .15
56 Raving Visionary U :B: .12 .25
57 Recalibrate C :B: .07 .15
58 Rise and Shine R :B: .20 .40
59 Rishadan Dockhand R :B: .20 .40
60 Said // Done U :B: .12 .25
61 Scuttletide U :B: .12 .25
62 Shattered Ego C :B: .07 .15
63 So Shiny C :B: .07 .15
64 Specimen Collector U :B: .12 .25
65 Steelfin Whale C :B: .07 .15
66 Step Through C :B: .07 .15
67 Subtlety M :B: 7.50 15.00
68 Suspend R :B: .20 .40
69 Svyelun of Sea and Sky M :B: .75 1.50
70 Sweep the Skies U :B: .12 .25
71 Thought Monitor R :B: 1.00 2.00
72 Tide Shaper U :B: .12 .25
73 Vedalken Infiltrator U :B: .12 .25
74 Archfiend of Sorrows U :K: .12 .25
75 Archon of Cruelty M :K: 7.50 15.00
76 Bone Shards C :K: .07 .15
77 Break the Ice U :K: .12 .25
78 Cabal Initiate C :K: .07 .15
79 Clattering Augur U :K: .12 .25
80 Damn R :K: 2.00 4.00
81 Dauthi Voidwalker R :K: 5.00 10.00
82 Discerning Taste C :K: .07 .15
83 Echoing Return C :K: .07 .15
84 Feast of Sanity U :K: .12 .25
85 Flay Essence U :K: .12 .25
86 Gilt-Blade Prowler C :K: .07 .15
87 Grief M :K: 7.50 15.00
88 Hell Mongrel C :K: .07 .15
89 Kitchen Imp C :K: .07 .15
90 Legion Vanguard U :K: .12 .25
91 Loathsome Curator C :K: .07 .15
92 Magus of the Bridge R :K: .20 .40
93 Necrogoyf R :K: .20 .40
94 Necromancer's Familiar U :K: .12 .25
95 Nested Shambler C :K: .07 .15
96 Persist R :K: .75 1.50
97 Profane Tutor R 1.25 2.50
98 Radiant Epicure U :K: .12 .25
99 Sinister Starfish C :K: .07 .15
100 Sudden Edict U :K: .12 .25
101 Tizerus Charger C :K: .07 .15
102 Tourach, Dread Cantor M :K: 2.00 4.00
103 Tourach's Canticle C :K: .07 .15
104 Tragic Fall C :K: .07 .15
105 Underworld Hermit U :K: .12 .25
106 Unmarked Grave R :K: 1.00 2.00
107 Vermin Gorger C :K: .07 .15
108 Vile Entomber U :K: .12 .25
109 World-Weary C :K: .07 .15
110 Young Necromancer U :K: .12 .25
111 Arcbound Slasher C :R: .07 .15
112 Arcbound Tracker C :R: .07 .15
113 Arcbound Whelp U :R: .12 .25
114 Battle Plan C :R: .07 .15
115 Blazing Rootwalla U :R: .12 .25
116 Bloodbraid Marauder R :R: .20 .40
117 Breya's Apprentice R :R: .20 .40
118 Calibrated Blast R :R: .20 .40
119 Captain Ripley Vance U :R: .12 .25
120 Chef's Kiss R :R: .20 .40
121 Dragon's Rage Channeler U :R: .75 1.50
122 Faithless Salvaging C :R: .07 .15
123 Fast // Furious U :R: .12 .25
124 Flame Blitz U :R: .12 .25
125 Flametongue Yearling U :R: .12 .25
126 Fury M :R: 15.00 30.00
127 Galvanic Relay C :R: .07 .15
128 Gargadon C :R: .07 .15
129 Glimpse of Tomorrow R .20 .40
130 Goblin Traprunner U :R: .12 .25
131 Gouged Zealot C :R: .07 .15
132 Harmonic Prodigy R :R: .75 1.50
133 Kaleidoscorch U :R: .12 .25
134 Lightning Spear C :R: .07 .15
135 Mine Collapse C :R: .07 .15
136 Mount Velus Manticore C :R: .07 .15
137 Obsidian Charmaw R :R: .20 .40
138 Ragavan, Nimble Pilferer M :R: 45.00 90.00
139 Revolutionist C :R: .07 .15
140 Skophos Reaver C :R: .07 .15
141 Slag Strider U :R: .12 .25
142 Spreading Insurrection U :R: .12 .25
143 Strike It Rich U :R: .12 .25
144 Tavern Scoundrel C :R: .07 .15
145 Unholy Heat C :R: .07 .15
146 Viashino Lashclaw C :R: .07 .15
147 Abundant Harvest C :G: .07 .15
148 Aeve, Progenitor Ooze R :G: .20 .40
149 Bannerhide Krushok C :G: .07 .15
150 Blessed Respite U :G: .12 .25
151 Chatterfang, Squirrel General M :G: 2.50 5.00
152 Chatterstorm C :G: .07 .15
153 Chitterspitter R :G: .20 .40
154 Crack Open C :G: .07 .15
155 Deepwood Denizen C :G: .07 .15
156 Duskshell Crawler C :G: .07 .15
157 Endurance M :G: 30.00 60.00
158 Fae Offering U :G: .12 .25
159 Flourishing Strike C :G: .07 .15
160 Foundation Breaker U :G: .12 .25
161 Funnel-Web Recluse C :G: .07 .15
162 Gaea's Will R .20 .40
163 Glimmer Bairn C :G: .07 .15
164 Glinting Creeper U :G: .12 .25
165 Herd Baloth U :G: .12 .25
166 Ignoble Hierarch R :G: 2.00 4.00
167 Jade Avenger C :G: .07 .15
168 Jewel-Eyed Cobra C :G: .07 .15
169 Orchard Strider C :G: .07 .15
170 Rift Sower C :G: .07 .15
171 Sanctum Weaver R :G: 2.00 4.00
172 Scurry Oak U :G: .25 .50
173 Smell Fear C :G: .07 .15
174 Squirrel Sanctuary U :G: .12 .25
175 Squirrel Sovereign U :G: .12 .25
176 Sylvan Anthem R :G: .50 1.00
177 Terramorph U :G: .12 .25
178 Thrasta, Tempest's Roar M :G: .75 1.50
179 Timeless Witness U :G: .12 .25
180 Tireless Provisioner U :G: .75 1.50
181 Urban Daggertooth C :G: .07 .15
182 Verdant Command R :G: .20 .40
183 Wren's Run Hydra U :G: .12 .25
184 Arcbound Shikari U :R:/:W: .12 .25
185 Arcus Acolyte U :G:/:W: .12 .25
186 Asmoranomardicadaistinaculdacar R .20 .40

187 Breathless Knight C :W:/:K: .07 .15
188 Captured by Lagacs C :G:/:W: .07 .15
189 Carth the Lion R :K:/:G: .20 .40
190 Chrome Courier C :W:/:B: .07 .15
191 Combine Chrysalis U :G:/:B: .12 .25
192 Dakkon, Shadow Slayer M :W:/:B:/:K: .75 1.50
193 Dihada's Ploy C :B:/:K: .07 .15
194 Drey Keeper C :K:/:G: .07 .15
195 Ethersworn Sphinx U :W:/:B: .12 .25
196 Foundry Helix C :R:/:W: .07 .15
197 Garth One-Eye M :W:/:B:/:K:/:R:/:G: .30 .60
198 General Ferrous Rokiric R :R:/:W: .20 .40
199 Geyadrone Dihada M :B:/:K:/:R: .50 1.00
200 Goblin Anarchomancer C :R:/:G: .07 .15
201 Graceful Restoration U :W:/:K: .12 .25
202 Grist, the Hunger Tide M :K:/:G: 4.00 8.00
203 Lazotep Chancellor U :B:/:K: .12 .25
204 Lonis, Cryptozoologist R :G:/:B: .20 .40
205 Master of Death R :B:/:K: .20 .40
206 Moderation R :W:/:B: .20 .40
207 Piru, the Volatile R :R:/:W:/:K: .20 .40
208 Priest of Fell Rites R :W:/:K: .20 .40
209 Prophetic Titan U :B:/:R: .12 .25
210 Rakdos Headliner U :K:/:R: .12 .25
211 Ravenous Squirrel U :K:/:G: .12 .25
212 Road // Ruin U :G:/:R: .12 .25
213 Storm God's Oracle C :B:/:R: .07 .15
214 Sythis, Harvest's Hand R :G:/:W: 1.00 2.00
215 Terminal Agony C :K:/:R: .07 .15
216 Territorial Kavu R :R:/:G: .20 .40
217 Wavesifter C :G:/:B: .07 .15
218 Yusri, Fortune's Flame R :B:/:R: .20 .40
219 Academy Manufactor R .20 .40
220 Altar of the Goyf U 3.00 6.00
221 Batterbone U .12 .25
222 Bottle Golems C .07 .15
223 Brainstone U .12 .25
224 Dermotaxi R .20 .40
225 Diamond Lion R .20 .40
226 Fodder Tosser C .07 .15
227 Kaldra Compleat M 2.50 5.00
228 Liquimetal Torque U .60 1.25
229 Monoskelion U .12 .25
230 Myr Scrapling C .07 .15
231 Nettlecyst R 1.00 2.00
232 Ornithopter of Paradise C .07 .15
233 Sanctuary Raptor U .12 .25
234 Scion of Draco M 1.25 2.50
235 Sojourner's Companion C .07 .15
236 Sol Talisman R .20 .40
237 Steel Dromedary U .12 .25
238 Sword of Hearth and Home M 6.00 12.00
239 Tormod's Cryptkeeper C .07 .15
240 The Underworld Cookbook U .12 .25
241 Vectis Gloves U .12 .25
242 Void Mirror R .20 .40
243 Zabaz, the Glimmerwasp R .20 .40
244 Arid Mesa R 10.00 20.00
245 Darkmoss Bridge C .07 .15
246 Drossforge Bridge C .07 .15
247 Goldmire Bridge C .07 .15
248 Marsh Flats R 7.50 15.00
249 Mistvault Bridge C .07 .15
250 Misty Rainforest R .20 .40
251 Power Depot U 12.50 25.00
252 Razortide Bridge C .07 .15
253 Rustvale Bridge C .07 .15
254 Scalding Tarn R 17.50 35.00
255 Silverbluff Bridge C .07 .15
256 Slagwoods Bridge C .07 .15
257 Tanglepool Bridge C .07 .15
258 Thornglint Bridge C .07 .15
259 Urza's Saga R 20.00 40.00
260 Verdant Catacombs R 10.00 20.00
261 Yavimaya, Cradle of Growth R 5.00 10.00
262 Angelic Curator U :W: .12 .25
263 Karmic Guide R :W: .20 .40
264 Seal of Cleansing U :W: .12 .25
265 Solitary Confinement R :W: .20 .40
266 Soul Snare U :W: .12 .25
267 Counterspell U :B: .75 1.50
268 Sea Drake U :B: .12 .25
269 Seal of Removal U :B: .12 .25
270 Upheaval R :B: .20 .40
271 Wonder R :B: .20 .40
272 Bone Shredder U :K: .12 .25
273 Braids, Cabal Minion R :K: .20 .40
274 Greed U :K: .12 .25
275 Patriarch's Bidding R :K: 1.00 2.00
276 Skirge Familiar U :K: .12 .25
277 Chance Encounter R :R: .20 .40
278 Flame Rift U :R: .12 .25
279 Goblin Bombardment R :R: .75 1.50
280 Gorilla Shaman U :R: .12 .25
281 Imperial Recruiter M :R: 4.00 8.00
282 Mogg Salvage U :R: .12 .25
283 Enchantress's Presence R :G: .50 1.00
284 Hunting Pack U :G: .12 .25
285 Quirion Ranger U :G: .12 .25
286 Squirrel Mob R :G: .20 .40
287 Titania, Protector of Argoth M :G: .50 1.00
288 Yavimaya Elder U :G: .12 .25
289 Chainer, Nightmare Adept R :K:/:R: .20 .40
290 Fire // Ice R :R:/:B: .20 .40
291 Mirari's Wake M :G:/:W: 3.00 6.00
292 Shardless Agent R :G:/:B: .20 .40
293 Sterling Grove R :G:/:W: 2.00 4.00
294 Vindicate R :W:/:K: .30 .75
295 Cursed Totem R .20 .40
296 Extruder U .12 .25
297 Millikin U .12 .25
298 Nevinyrral's Disk R .20 .40
299 Patchwork Gnomes U .12 .25
300 Zuran Orb U .12 .25
301 Cabal Coffers M 10.00 20.00
302 Mishra's Factory U .12 .25
303 Riptide Laboratory R .20 .40
304 Dakkon, Shadow Slayer M :W:/:B:/:K: 1.50 3.00
305 Geyadrone Dihada M :B:/:K:/:R: 1.50 3.00
306 Grist, the Hunger Tide M :K:/:G: 7.50 15.00
307 Solitude M :W: 30.00 75.00
308 Counterspell R :B: 4.00 8.00
309 Subtlety M :B: 12.50 25.00
310 Svyelun of Sea and Sky M :B: 1.50 3.00
311 Grief M :K: 12.50 25.00
312 Tourach, Dread Cantor M :K: 3.00 6.00
313 Fury M :R: 17.50 35.00
314 Imperial Recruiter M :R: 7.50 15.00
315 Ragavan, Nimble Pilferer M :R: 50.00 100.00
316 Chatterfang, Squirrel General M :G: 6.00 12.00
317 Endurance M :G: 40.00 80.00
318 Thrasta, Tempest's Roar M :G: 2.00 4.00
319 Titania, Protector of Argoth M :G: 2.00 4.00
320 Mirari's Wake M :G:/:W: 6.00 12.00
321 Shardless Agent R :G:/:B: 1.25 2.50
322 Vindicate R :W:/:K: 1.50 3.00
323 Scion of Draco M 4.00 8.00
324 Sword of Hearth and Home M 7.50 15.00
325 Cabal Coffers M 20.00 40.00
326 Mishra's Factory R .75 1.50
327 Blossoming Calm U :W: .12 .25
328 Esper Sentinel R :W: 12.50 25.00
329 Late to Dinner C :W: .07 .15
330 Lens Flare C :W: .07 .15
331 Nykthos Paragon R :W: .20 .40
332 Search the Premises R :W: .20 .40
333 Serra's Emissary M :W: 2.50 5.00
334 Dress Down R :B: 1.25 2.50
335 Floodhound C :B: .07 .15
336 Fractured Sanity R :B: .30 .75
337 Murktide Regent M :B: 10.00 20.00
338 Mystic Redaction U :B: .12 .25
339 Phantasmal Dreadmaw C :B: .07 .15
340 Rise and Shine R :B: .20 .40
341 Thought Monitor R :B: 1.25 2.50
342 Archon of Cruelty M :K: 7.50 15.00
343 Kitchen Imp C :K: .07 .15
344 Magus of the Bridge R :K: .20 .40
345 Persist R :K: .50 1.00
346 Sudden Edict U :K: .12 .25
347 Underworld Hermit U :K: .12 .25
348 World-Weary C :K: .07 .15
349 Faithless Salvaging C :R: .07 .15
350 Flametongue Yearling U :R: .12 .25
351 Gargadon C :R: .07 .15
352 Harmonic Prodigy R :R: .75 1.50
353 Obsidian Charmaw R :R: .20 .40
354 Abundant Harvest C :G: .07 .15
355 Ignoble Hierarch R :G: 2.50 5.00
356 Jade Avenger C :G: .07 .15
357 Sylvan Anthem R :G: .30 .75
358 Timeless Witness U :G: .12 .25
359 Verdant Command R :G: .20 .40
360 Arcbound Shikari U :R:/:W: .12 .25
361 Arcus Acolyte U :G:/:W: .12 .25
362 Combine Chrysalis U :G:/:B: .12 .25
363 Dakkon, Shadow Slayer M :W:/:B:/:K: .50 1.00
364 Ethersworn Sphinx U :W:/:B: .12 .25
365 Garth One-Eye M :W:/:B:/:K:/:R:/:G: .30 .75
366 General Ferrous Rokiric R :R:/:W: .20 .40
367 Geyadrone Dihada M :B:/:K:/:R: .50 1.00
368 Grist, the Hunger Tide M :K:/:G: 4.00 8.00
369 Lazotep Chancellor U :B:/:K: .12 .25
370 Lonis, Cryptozoologist R :G:/:B: .20 .40
371 Moderation R :W:/:B: .20 .40
372 Priest of Fell Rites R :W:/:K: .20 .40
373 Prophetic Titan U :B:/:R: .12 .25
374 Rakdos Headliner U :K:/:R: .12 .25
375 Ravenous Squirrel U :K:/:G: .12 .25
376 Road // Ruin U :G:/:R: .12 .25
377 Sythis, Harvest's Hand R :G:/:W: .20 .40
378 Dermotaxi R .20 .40
379 Kaldra Compleat M 2.50 5.00
380 Urza's Saga R .20 .40
381 Blacksmith's Skill C :W: .07 .15
382 Marble Gargoyle C :W: .07 .15
383 Out of Time R :W: .50 1.00
384 Prismatic Ending U :W: 1.00 2.00
385 Resurgent Belief R .20 .40
386 Sanctifier en-Vec R :W: 1.50 3.00
387 Soul Snare U :W: .12 .25
388 Timeless Dragon R :W: 1.25 2.50
389 Aeromoeba C :B: .07 .15
390 Inevitable Betrayal R .25 .50
391 Rishadan Dockhand R :B: .20 .40
392 Step Through C :B: .07 .15
393 Svyelun of Sea and Sky M :B: 2.00 4.00
394 Tide Shaper U :B: .12 .25
395 Bone Shards C :K: .07 .15
396 Damn R :K: 2.50 5.00
397 Dauthi Voidwalker R :K: 7.50 15.00
398 Necrogoyf R :K: .20 .40
399 Nested Shambler C :K: .07 .15
400 Persist R :K: 1.25 2.50
401 Profane Tutor R 2.50 5.00
402 Tourach, Dread Cantor M :K: 7.50 15.00
403 Vile Entomber U :K: .12 .25
404 Blazing Rootwalla U :R: .12 .25
405 Calibrated Blast R :R: .20 .40
406 Galvanic Relay C :R: .07 .15
407 Glimpse of Tomorrow R .20 .40
408 Mine Collapse C :R: .07 .15
409 Aeve, Progenitor Ooze R :G: .20 .40
410 Chatterfang, Squirrel General M :G: 4.00 8.00
411 Chatterstorm C :G: .07 .15
412 Gaea's Will R .20 .40
413 Glimmer Bairn C :G: .07 .15
414 Ignoble Hierarch R :G: 4.00 8.00
415 Squirrel Sovereign U :G: .12 .25
416 Titania, Protector of Argoth M :G: 2.00 4.00
417 Asmoranomardicadaistinaculdacar R .20 .40
418 Carth the Lion R :K:/:G: .20 .40
419 Chainer, Nightmare Adept R :K:/:R: .20 .40
420 Garth One-Eye M :W:/:B:/:K:/:R:/:G: .75 1.50
421 Goblin Anarchomancer C :R:/:G: .07 .15
422 Piru, the Volatile R :R:/:W:/:K: .20 .40
423 Shardless Agent R :G:/:B: .75 1.50
424 Terminal Agony C :K:/:R: .07 .15
425 Territorial Kavu R :R:/:G: .20 .40
426 Brainstone U .12 .25
427 Diamond Lion R .20 .40
428 Liquimetal Torque U .50 1.00
429 Monoskelion U .12 .25
430 Ornithopter of Paradise C .07 .15
431 Scion of Draco M 2.50 5.00
432 Sol Talisman R .20 .40
433 Sword of Hearth and Home M 7.50 15.00
434 The Underworld Cookbook U .12 .25
435 Void Mirror R .60 1.25
436 Arid Mesa R 15.00 30.00
437 Marsh Flats R 12.50 25.00
438 Misty Rainforest R 25.00 50.00
439 Scalding Tarn R 30.00 60.00
440 Verdant Catacombs R 20.00 40.00
441 Yavimaya, Cradle of Growth R 7.50 15.00
442 Out of Time R :W: .20 .40
443 Resurgent Belief R .50 1.00
444 Sanctifier en-Vec R :W: 1.00 2.00
445 Timeless Dragon R :W: .25 .50
446 Inevitable Betrayal R .25 .50
447 Rishadan Dockhand R :B: .20 .40
448 Suspend R :B: .30 .75
449 Damn R :K: 3.00 6.00
450 Dauthi Voidwalker R :K: 7.50 15.00
451 Necrogoyf R :K: .20 .40
452 Profane Tutor R 2.00 4.00
453 Unmarked Grave R :K: 2.00 4.00
454 Bloodbraid Marauder R :R: .20 .40
455 Breya's Apprentice R :R: .25 .50
456 Calibrated Blast R :R: .20 .40
457 Chef's Kiss R :R: .20 .40
458 Glimpse of Tomorrow R .20 .40
459 Aeve, Progenitor Ooze R :G: .20 .40
460 Chitterspitter R :G: .30 .75
461 Gaea's Will R .20 .40
462 Sanctum Weaver R :G: 2.00 4.00
463 Asmoranomardicadaistinaculdacar R .60 1.25
464 Carth the Lion R :K:/:G: .20 .40
465 Master of Death R :B:/:K: .30 .60
466 Piru, the Volatile R :R:/:W:/:K: .20 .40
467 Territorial Kavu R :R:/:G: .20 .40
468 Yusri, Fortune's Flame R :B:/:R: .20 .40
469 Academy Manufactor R 5.00 10.00
470 Diamond Lion R .20 .40
471 Nettlecyst R 1.25 2.50
472 Sol Talisman R .30 .75
473 Void Mirror R .30 .60
474 Zabaz, the Glimmerwasp R .25 .50
475 Arid Mesa R 10.00 20.00
476 Marsh Flats R 7.50 15.00
477 Misty Rainforest R 15.00 30.00
478 Scalding Tarn R 20.00 40.00
479 Verdant Catacombs R 12.50 25.00
480 Yavimaya, Cradle of Growth R 7.50 15.00
481 Plains C .07 .15
482 Plains C .07 .15
483 Island C .07 .15
484 Island C .07 .15
485 Swamp C .07 .15
486 Swamp C .07 .15
487 Mountain C .07 .15
488 Mountain C .07 .15
489 Forest C .07 .15
490 Forest C .07 .15
491 Sanctum Prelate M :W: 3.00 6.00
492 Yusri, Fortune's Flame R :B:/:R: 1.25 2.50

2021 Magic The Gathering Modern Horizons 2 Tokens

1 Bird .07 .15
2 Crab .07 .15
3 Phyrexian Germ .07 .15
4 Timeless Dragon .30 .60
5 Timeless Witness .07 .15
6 Zombie .10 .20
7 Zombie Army .07 .15
8 Goblin .20 .40
9 Beast .07 .15
10 Elemental .75 1.50
11 Squirrel .15 .30
12 Golem .60 1.25
13 Insect .50 1.00
14 Clue .07 .15
15 Clue .07 .15
16 Construct 1.50 3.00
17 Food .07 .15
18 Food .07 .15
19 Thopter .07 .15
20 Treasure .07 .15
21 Treasure .07 .15

2021 Magic The Gathering Secret Lair Drop Series Arcane

477 Path to Exile R 1.25 3.00
478 Unstable Harmonics R/(Rhystic Study R 25.00 60.00
479 Duress R 2.00 5.00
480 Round Two R/(Seize the Day R 5.00 12.00
481 Denting Blows R/(Krosan Grip R .60 1.50
482 Counterflux R 2.50 6.00
483 The Hexcore R/(Thran Dynamo R 2.50 6.00
696 Gromp R/(Spore Frog R 2.00 5.00

2021 Magic The Gathering Secret Lair Drop Series Arcane Foil

477 Path to Exile R 1.25 3.00
478 Unstable Harmonics R/(Rhystic Study R 25.00 60.00
479 Duress R 2.00 5.00
480 Round Two R/(Seize the Day R 5.00 12.00
481 Denting Blows R/(Krosan Grip R .60 1.50
482 Counterflux R 2.50 6.00
483 The Hexcore R/(Thran Dynamo R 2.50 6.00
696 Gromp R/(Spore Frog R 2.00 5.00

2021 Magic The Gathering Secret Lair Drop Series Arcane Lands

484 Plains R .60 1.50
485 Island R 1.25 3.00
486 Swamp R 1.25 3.00
487 Mountain R .60 1.50
488 Forest R 1.25 3.00
697 Summoner's Rift R/(Command Tower R 3.00 8.00

2021 Magic The Gathering Secret Lair Drop Series Arcane Lands Foil

484 Plains R .60 1.50
485 Island R 1.25 3.00
486 Swamp R 1.25 3.00
487 Mountain R .60 1.50
488 Forest R 1.25 3.00
697 Summoner's Rift R/(Command Tower R 3.00 8.00

2021 Magic The Gathering Secret Lair Drop Series Artist Series Johannes Voss

278 Sanctum Prelate M 1.50 4.00
279 Carpet of Flowers R 12.00 30.00
280 Sphere of Safety R 6.00 15.00
281 Karmic Guide R 4.00 10.00
588 Sphere of Safety R 3.00 8.00

2021 Magic The Gathering Secret Lair Drop Series Artist Series Johannes Voss Foil

278 Sanctum Prelate M 1.50 4.00
279 Carpet of Flowers R 12.00 30.00
280 Sphere of Safety R 6.00 15.00
281 Karmic Guide R 4.00 10.00
588 Sphere of Safety R 3.00 8.00

2021 Magic The Gathering Secret Lair Drop Series Artist Series Mark Poole

173 Balance M 1.25 3.00
174 Brainstorm R 1.25 3.00
175 Counterspell R 1.25 3.00
176 Birds of Paradise R 3.00 8.00
177 Howling Mine R 2.00 5.00
178 Wasteland R 12.00 30.00
582 Brainstorm R 1.00 2.50

2021 Magic The Gathering Secret Lair Drop Series Artist Series Mark Poole Foil

173 Balance M 1.25 3.00
174 Brainstorm R 1.25 3.00
175 Counterspell R 1.25 3.00
176 Birds of Paradise R 3.00 8.00
177 Howling Mine R 2.00 5.00
178 Wasteland R 12.00 30.00
582 Brainstorm R 1.00 2.50

2021 Magic The Gathering Secret Lair Drop Series Artist Series Thomas Baxa

274 Ob Nixilis Reignited M 1.00 2.50
275 Sire of Insanity R 3.00 8.00
276 Sliver Hivelord M 5.00 12.00
277 Spellskite R 5.00 12.00
587 Spellskite R 5.00 12.00

2021 Magic The Gathering Secret Lair Drop Series Artist Series Thomas Baxa Foil

274 Ob Nixilis Reignited M 1.00 2.50
275 Sire of Insanity R 3.00 8.00
276 Sliver Hivelord M 5.00 12.00
277 Spellskite R 5.00 12.00
587 Spellskite R 5.00 12.00

2021 Magic The Gathering Secret Lair Drop Series Black is Magic

244 Shalai, Voice of Plenty R 6.00 15.00
245 Ponder R 5.00 12.00
246 Cultivate R 3.00 8.00
247 Kaya, Ghost Assassin R 1.25 3.00
248 Teferi, Hero of Dominaria M 12.00 30.00
249 Sol Ring R 6.00 15.00
250 Path of Ancestry R 4.00 10.00

2021 Magic The Gathering Secret Lair Drop Series Black is Magic Foil

244 Shalai, Voice of Plenty R 6.00 15.00
245 Ponder R 5.00 12.00
246 Cultivate R 3.00 8.00
247 Kaya, Ghost Assassin R 1.25 3.00
248 Teferi, Hero of Dominaria M 12.00 30.00
249 Sol Ring R 6.00 15.00
250 Path of Ancestry R 4.00 10.00

2021 Magic The Gathering Secret Lair Drop Series Crocodile Jackson's Monstrous Menagerie

305 Ravenous Chupacabra R 8.00 20.00
306 Managorger Hydra R 8.00 20.00
307 Pathbreaker Ibex R 10.00 25.00
308 Temur Sabertooth R 8.00 20.00
309 Winding Constrictor R 2.00 5.00
590 Lurking Crocodile R .50 1.25

2021 Magic The Gathering Secret Lair Drop Series Crocodile Jackson's Monstrous Menagerie Foil

305 Ravenous Chupacabra R 8.00 20.00
306 Managorger Hydra R 8.00 20.00
307 Pathbreaker Ibex R 10.00 25.00
308 Temur Sabertooth R 8.00 20.00
309 Winding Constrictor R 2.00 5.00
590 Lurking Crocodile R .50 1.25

2021 Magic The Gathering Secret Lair Drop Series Culture Shocks

123 Hallowed Fountain R 5.00 12.00
124 Watery Grave R 8.00 20.00
125 Blood Crypt R 10.00 25.00
126 Stomping Ground R 8.00 20.00
127 Temple Garden R 6.00 15.00
128 Godless Shrine R 8.00 20.00
129 Steam Vents R 10.00 25.00
130 Overgrown Tomb R 8.00 20.00
131 Sacred Foundry R 10.00 25.00
132 Breeding Pool R 10.00 25.00

2021 Magic The Gathering Secret Lair Drop Series Dan Frazier is Back The Allied Signets

286 Azorius Signet R 5.00 12.00
287 Dimir Signet R 8.00 20.00
288 Gruul Signet R 4.00 10.00
289 Rakdos Signet R 6.00 15.00
290 Selesnya Signet R 2.50 6.00
589 Arcane Signet R 10.00 25.00

2021 Magic The Gathering Secret Lair Drop Series Dan Frazier is Back The Allied Signets Etched Foil

286 Azorius Signet R 5.00 12.00
287 Dimir Signet R 8.00 20.00
288 Gruul Signet R 4.00 10.00
289 Rakdos Signet R 6.00 15.00

290 Selesnya Signet R 2.50 6.00
589 Arcane Signet R 10.00 25.00

2021 Magic The Gathering Secret Lair Drop Series Dan Frazier is Back The Enemy Signets

291 Boros Signet R 6.00 15.00
292 Golgari Signet R 4.00 10.00
293 Izzet Signet R 8.00 20.00
294 Orzhov Signet R 8.00 20.00
295 Simic Signet R 8.00 20.00

2021 Magic The Gathering Secret Lair Drop Series Dan Frazier is Back The Enemy Signets Etched Foil

291 Boros Signet R 6.00 15.00
292 Golgari Signet R 4.00 10.00
293 Izzet Signet R 8.00 20.00
294 Orzhov Signet R 8.00 20.00
295 Simic Signet R 8.00 20.00

2021 Magic The Gathering Secret Lair Drop Series Extra Life 2021

373 Mulldrifter R 1.00 2.50
374 Mulldrifter R .75 2.00
375 Craterhoof Behemoth M 15.00 40.00
376 Craterhoof Behemoth M 15.00 40.00
377 Metalwork Colossus R .60 1.50
378 Metalwork Colossus R .40 1.00
671 Questing Phelddagrif R .20 .50
672 Questing Phelddagrif R .25 .60

2021 Magic The Gathering Secret Lair Drop Series Extra Life 2021 Foil

373 Mulldrifter R 1.00 2.50
374 Mulldrifter R .75 2.00
375 Craterhoof Behemoth M 15.00 40.00
376 Craterhoof Behemoth M 15.00 40.00
377 Metalwork Colossus R .60 1.50
378 Metalwork Colossus R .40 1.00
671 Questing Phelddagrif R .20 .50
672 Questing Phelddagrif R .25 .60

2021 Magic The Gathering Secret Lair Drop Series Faerie Faerie Faerie Rad

115 Glen Elendra Archmage FOIL R 20.00 50.00
116 Mistbind Clique FOIL R 12.00 30.00
117 Spellstutter Sprite FOIL R 10.00 25.00
118 Vendilion Clique FOIL R 10.00 25.00

2021 Magic The Gathering Secret Lair Drop Series Far Out Man

330 Aether Gust R 2.50 6.00
331 Counterspell R 8.00 20.00
332 Fabricate R 5.00 12.00
333 Fact or Fiction R 2.50 6.00
334 Mystical Tutor R 10.00 25.00

2021 Magic The Gathering Secret Lair Drop Series Far Out Man Foil

330 Aether Gust R 2.50 6.00
331 Counterspell R 8.00 20.00
332 Fabricate R 5.00 12.00
333 Fact or Fiction R 2.50 6.00
334 Mystical Tutor R 10.00 25.00

2021 Magic The Gathering Secret Lair Drop Series Fblthp Completely Utterly Totally Lost

226 Path to Exile R 4.00 10.00
227 Well of Lost Dreams R 2.00 5.00
228 Frantic Search R 3.00 8.00
229 Intruder Alarm R 4.00 10.00
230 Shelldock Isle R 1.25 3.00
583 Fblthp, the Lost R 2.50 6.00

2021 Magic The Gathering Secret Lair Drop Series Fblthp Completely Utterly Totally Lost Foil

226 Path to Exile R 4.00 10.00
227 Well of Lost Dreams R 2.00 5.00
228 Frantic Search R 3.00 8.00
229 Intruder Alarm R 4.00 10.00
230 Shelldock Isle R 1.25 3.00
583 Fblthp, the Lost R 2.50 6.00

2021 Magic The Gathering Secret Lair Drop Series Kamigawa Ink

259 Michiko Konda, Truth Seeker R 6.00 15.00
260 Kami of the Crescent Moon R 10.00 25.00
261 Toshiro Umezawa R 4.00 10.00
262 Heartless Hidetsugu R 4.00 10.00
263 Reki, the History of Kamigawa R 5.00 12.00

2021 Magic The Gathering Secret Lair Drop Series Kamigawa Ink Foil

259 Michiko Konda, Truth Seeker R 6.00 15.00
260 Kami of the Crescent Moon R 10.00 25.00
261 Toshiro Umezawa R 4.00 10.00
262 Heartless Hidetsugu R 4.00 10.00
263 Reki, the History of Kamigawa R 5.00 12.00

2021 Magic The Gathering Secret Lair Drop Series Math is for Blockers

234 Brazen Borrower // Petty Theft M 10.00 25.00
235 Vindictive Lich R 1.25 3.00
236 Meandering Towershell R .25 .60
237 Ohran Frostfang R 3.00 8.00
238 Thragtusk R .75 2.00
584 Wrexial, the Risen Deep M 5.00 12.00

2021 Magic The Gathering Secret Lair Drop Series Math is for Blockers Foil

234 Brazen Borrower // Petty Theft M 10.00 25.00
235 Vindictive Lich R 1.25 3.00
236 Meandering Towershell R .25 .60
237 Ohran Frostfang R 3.00 8.00
238 Thragtusk R .75 2.00
584 Wrexial, the Risen Deep M 5.00 12.00

2021 Magic The Gathering Secret Lair Drop Series Mirrodinsanity

300 Ancient Den R 6.00 15.00
301 Seat of the Synod R 8.00 20.00
302 Vault of Whispers R 5.00 12.00
303 Great Furnace R 10.00 25.00
304 Tree of Tales R 4.00 10.00
608 Darksteel Citadel R 8.00 20.00

2021 Magic The Gathering Secret Lair Drop Series Mirrodinsanity Foil

300 Ancient Den R 6.00 15.00
301 Seat of the Synod R 8.00 20.00
302 Vault of Whispers R 5.00 12.00
303 Great Furnace R 10.00 25.00
304 Tree of Tales R 4.00 10.00
608 Darksteel Citadel R 8.00 20.00

2021 Magic The Gathering Secret Lair Drop Series Monster Anatomy 101

316 Fleet Swallower R 3.00 8.00
317 Goblin Trashmaster R 6.00 15.00
318 Ilharg, the Raze-Boar M 3.00 8.00
319 Protean Hulk R 5.00 12.00
320 Gishath, Sun's Avatar M 15.00 40.00

2021 Magic The Gathering Secret Lair Drop Series Monster Anatomy 101 Etched Foil

316 Fleet Swallower R 3.00 8.00
317 Goblin Trashmaster R 6.00 15.00
318 Ilharg, the Raze-Boar M 3.00 8.00
319 Protean Hulk R 5.00 12.00
320 Gishath, Sun's Avatar M 15.00 40.00

2021 Magic The Gathering Secret Lair Drop Series Monster Movie Marathon

321 Dismember R 8.00 20.00
322 Blasphemous Act R 12.00 30.00
323 Beast Within R 10.00 25.00
324 Grafdigger's Cage R 6.00 15.00

2021 Magic The Gathering Secret Lair Drop Series Monster Movie Marathon Foil

321 Dismember R 8.00 20.00
322 Blasphemous Act R 12.00 30.00
323 Beast Within R 10.00 25.00
324 Grafdigger's Cage R 6.00 15.00

2021 Magic The Gathering Secret Lair Drop Series Mother's Day 2021

296 Mother of Runes R 4.00 10.00
297 Mother of Runes R 5.00 12.00
298 Mother of Runes R 5.00 12.00
299 Mother of Runes R 4.00 10.00

2021 Magic The Gathering Secret Lair Drop Series Mother's Day 2021 Foil

296 Mother of Runes R 4.00 10.00
297 Mother of Runes R 5.00 12.00
298 Mother of Runes R 5.00 12.00
299 Mother of Runes R 4.00 10.00

2021 Magic The Gathering Secret Lair Drop Series MSCHF

364 Swords to Plowshares FOIL ETCHED R 20.00 50.00
365 Grim Tutor FOIL R 12.00 30.00
366 Blood Moon FOIL ETCHED R 10.00 25.00
367 Cut // Ribbons FOIL ETCHED R 1.50 4.00
368 Teferi's Puzzle Box FOIL R 5.00 12.00
669 Battlefield Forge R 4.00 10.00
670 Plains R/(Peeled) 4.00 10.00

2021 Magic The Gathering Secret Lair Drop Series Our Show Is On Friday Can You Make It?

185 Wrath of God R 4.00 10.00
186 Preordain R 8.00 20.00
187 Decree of Pain R 2.50 6.00
188 Gamble R 8.00 20.00
189 Nature's Lore R 20.00 50.00

2021 Magic The Gathering Secret Lair Drop Series Phyrexian Praetors Compleat Edition

209 Elesh Norn, Grand Cenobite M 8.00 20.00
210 Jin-Gitaxias, Core Augur M 2.50 6.00
211 Sheoldred, Whispering One M 8.00 20.00
212 Urabrask the Hidden M 1.00 2.50
213 Vorinclex, Voice of Hunger M 2.50 6.00

2021 Magic The Gathering Secret Lair Drop Series Phyrexian Praetors Compleat Edition Foil

209 Elesh Norn, Grand Cenobite M 8.00 20.00
210 Jin-Gitaxias, Core Augur M 2.50 6.00
211 Sheoldred, Whispering One M 8.00 20.00
212 Urabrask the Hidden M 1.00 2.50
213 Vorinclex, Voice of Hunger M 2.50 6.00

2021 Magic The Gathering Secret Lair Drop Series PixelSnowLands.jpg

325 Snow-Covered Plains R 4.00 10.00
326 Snow-Covered Island R 10.00 25.00
327 Snow-Covered Swamp R 8.00 20.00
328 Snow-Covered Mountain R 3.00 8.00
329 Snow-Covered Forest R 5.00 12.00

2021 Magic The Gathering Secret Lair Drop Series PixelSnowLands.jpg Foil

325 Snow-Covered Plains R 4.00 10.00
326 Snow-Covered Island R 10.00 25.00
327 Snow-Covered Swamp R 8.00 20.00
328 Snow-Covered Mountain R 3.00 8.00
329 Snow-Covered Forest R 5.00 12.00

2021 Magic The Gathering Secret Lair Drop Series Purrfection

369 Generous Gift R 15.00 40.00
370 Chain Lightning R 10.00 25.00
371 Kodama's Reach R 40.00 100.00
372 Heirloom Blade R 15.00 40.00

2021 Magic The Gathering Secret Lair Drop Series Purrfection Foil

369 Generous Gift R 15.00 40.00
370 Chain Lightning R 10.00 25.00
371 Kodama's Reach R 40.00 100.00
372 Heirloom Blade R 15.00 40.00

2021 Magic The Gathering Secret Lair Drop Series Read The Fine Print

159 Demonlord Belzenlok M .75 2.00
160 Griselbrand M 5.00 12.00
161 Liliana's Contract R 4.00 10.00
162 Kothophed, Soul Hoarder R .25 .60
163 Razaketh, the Foulblooded M 8.00 20.00

2021 Magic The Gathering Secret Lair Drop Series Read The Fine Print Etched Foil

159 Demonlord Belzenlok M .75 2.00
160 Griselbrand M 5.00 12.00
161 Liliana's Contract R 4.00 10.00
162 Kothophed, Soul Hoarder R .25 .60
163 Razaketh, the Foulblooded M 8.00 20.00

2021 Magic The Gathering Secret Lair Drop Series Read The Fine Print Foil

159 Demonlord Belzenlok M .75 2.00
160 Griselbrand M 5.00 12.00
161 Liliana's Contract R 4.00 10.00
162 Kothophed, Soul Hoarder R .25 .60
163 Razaketh, the Foulblooded M 8.00 20.00

2021 Magic The Gathering Secret Lair Drop Series Saturday Morning D and D

310 Unbreakable Formation R 3.00 8.00
311 Whir of Invention R 4.00 10.00
312 Hero's Downfall R 4.00 10.00
313 Impact Tremors R 3.00 8.00
314 Primal Vigor R 8.00 20.00
315 Commander's Sphere R 2.00 5.00
591 Crash Through R 4.00 10.00

2021 Magic The Gathering Secret Lair Drop Series Saturday Morning D and D Foil

310 Unbreakable Formation R 3.00 8.00
311 Whir of Invention R 4.00 10.00
312 Hero's Downfall R 4.00 10.00
313 Impact Tremors R 3.00 8.00
314 Primal Vigor R 8.00 20.00
315 Commander's Sphere R 2.00 5.00
591 Crash Through R 4.00 10.00

2021 Magic The Gathering Secret Lair Drop Series Showcase Kaldheim Part 1

220 Frost Titan M 1.25 3.00
221 Primeval Titan M 5.00 12.00
222 Uro, Titan of Nature's Wrath M 15.00 40.00

2021 Magic The Gathering Secret Lair Drop Series Showcase Kaldheim Part 1 Foil

220 Frost Titan M 1.25 3.00
221 Primeval Titan M 5.00 12.00
222 Uro, Titan of Nature's Wrath M 15.00 40.00

2021 Magic The Gathering Secret Lair Drop Series Showcase Kaldheim Part 2

223 Grave Titan M 5.00 12.00
224 Inferno Titan M 2.00 5.00
225 Kroxa, Titan of Death's Hunger M 6.00 15.00

2021 Magic The Gathering Secret Lair Drop Series Showcase Kaldheim Part 2 Foil

223 Grave Titan M 5.00 12.00
224 Inferno Titan M 2.00 5.00
225 Kroxa, Titan of Death's Hunger M 6.00 15.00

2021 Magic The Gathering Secret Lair Drop Series Showcase Midnight Hunt

349 Moorland Haunt R .60 1.50
350 Vault of the Archangel R 8.00 20.00
351 Nephalia Drownyard R 3.00 8.00
352 Desolate Lighthouse R 1.00 2.50
353 Stensia Bloodhall R .50 1.25
354 Grim Backwoods R 2.00 5.00
355 Kessig Wolf Run R 6.00 15.00
356 Slayers' Stronghold R 3.00 8.00
357 Gavony Township R 4.00 10.00
358 Alchemist's Refuge R 3.00 8.00

2021 Magic The Gathering Secret Lair Drop Series Showcase Midnight Hunt Foil

349 Moorland Haunt R .60 1.50
350 Vault of the Archangel R 8.00 20.00
351 Nephalia Drownyard R 3.00 8.00
352 Desolate Lighthouse R 1.00 2.50
353 Stensia Bloodhall R .50 1.25
354 Grim Backwoods R 2.00 5.00
355 Kessig Wolf Run R 6.00 15.00
356 Slayers' Stronghold R 3.00 8.00
357 Gavony Township R 4.00 10.00
358 Alchemist's Refuge R 3.00 8.00

2021 Magic The Gathering Secret Lair Drop Series Showcase Strixhaven

268 All Is Dust R 10.00 25.00
269 Artifact Mutation R 4.00 10.00
270 Drown in the Loch R 6.00 15.00
271 Fire Covenant R 15.00 40.00
272 Fractured Identity R 1.50 4.00
273 Fracturing Gust R 1.50 4.00

2021 Magic The Gathering Secret Lair Drop Series Showcase Strixhaven Foil

268 All Is Dust R 10.00 25.00
269 Artifact Mutation R 4.00 10.00
270 Drown in the Loch R 6.00 15.00
271 Fire Covenant R 15.00 40.00
272 Fractured Identity R 1.50 4.00
273 Fracturing Gust R 1.50 4.00

2021 Magic The Gathering Secret Lair Drop Series Special Guest Fiona Staples

190 Soul-Scar Mage R 6.00 15.00
191 Dryad of the Ilysian Grove R 20.00 50.00
192 Sakura-Tribe Elder R 8.00 20.00
193 Spell Queller R 2.50 6.00
194 Metallic Mimic R 6.00 15.00

2021 Magic The Gathering Secret Lair Drop Series Special Guest Fiona Staples Foil

190 Soul-Scar Mage R 6.00 15.00
191 Dryad of the Ilysian Grove R 20.00 50.00
192 Sakura-Tribe Elder R 8.00 20.00
193 Spell Queller R 2.50 6.00
194 Metallic Mimic R 6.00 15.00

2021 Magic The Gathering Secret Lair Drop Series Special Guest Jen Bartel

282 Mesa Enchantress R 4.00 10.00
283 Archaeomancer R 12.00 30.00
284 Bloom Tender R 20.00 50.00
285 Meteor Golem R 2.50 6.00

2021 Magic The Gathering Secret Lair Drop Series Special Guest Jen Bartel Foil

282 Mesa Enchantress R 4.00 10.00
283 Archaeomancer R 12.00 30.00
284 Bloom Tender R 20.00 50.00
285 Meteor Golem R 2.50 6.00

2021 Magic The Gathering Secret Lair Drop Series Stranger Things

340 Mind Flayer, the Shadow M 8.00 20.00
341 Chief Jim Hopper R 2.00 5.00
342 Dustin, Gadget Genius R 1.25 3.00
343 Eleven, the Mage R 4.00 10.00
344 Lucas, the Sharpshooter R 1.50 4.00
345 Max, the Daredevil R 1.50 4.00
346 Mike, the Dungeon Master R 1.50 4.00
347 Will the Wise R 2.50 6.00
348 Clue T 4.00 10.00
609 Hawkins National Laboratory // The Upside Down R 2.00 5.00

2021 Magic The Gathering Secret Lair Drop Series Stranger Things Foil

340 Mind Flayer, the Shadow M 8.00 20.00
341 Chief Jim Hopper R 2.00 5.00
342 Dustin, Gadget Genius R 1.25 3.00
343 Eleven, the Mage R 4.00 10.00
344 Lucas, the Sharpshooter R 1.50 4.00
345 Max, the Daredevil R 1.50 4.00
346 Mike, the Dungeon Master R 1.50 4.00
347 Will the Wise R 2.50 6.00
348 Clue C 4.00 10.00
609 Hawkins National Laboratory // The Upside Down R 2.00 5.00

2021 Magic The Gathering Secret Lair Drop Series Teferi's Time Trouble

251 Dack Fayden M 4.00 10.00
252 Teferi, Time Raveler R 8.00 20.00
253 Karn, the Great Creator R 12.00 30.00

2021 Magic The Gathering Secret Lair Drop Series The Dracula Lands

359 Plains R 4.00 10.00
360 Island R 2.00 5.00
361 Swamp R 12.00 30.00
362 Mountain R 2.50 6.00
363 Forest R 2.00 5.00

2021 Magic The Gathering Secret Lair Drop Series The Dracula Lands Foil

359 Plains R 4.00 10.00
360 Island R 2.00 5.00
361 Swamp R 12.00 30.00
362 Mountain R 2.50 6.00
363 Forest R 2.00 5.00

2021 Magic The Gathering Secret Lair Drop Series The Full-Text Lands

254 Plains R 3.00 8.00
255 Island R 4.00 10.00
256 Swamp R 4.00 10.00
257 Mountain R 3.00 8.00
258 Forest R 3.00 8.00
585 Terramorphic Expanse R 1.25 3.00

2021 Magic The Gathering Secret Lair Drop Series The Full-Text Lands Foil

254 Plains R 3.00 8.00
255 Island R 4.00 10.00
256 Swamp R 4.00 10.00
257 Mountain R 3.00 8.00
258 Forest R 3.00 8.00
585 Terramorphic Expanse R 1.25 3.00

2021 Magic The Gathering Secret Lair Drop Series The Unfathomable Crushing Brutality of Basic Lands

239 Plains R 2.50 6.00
240 Island R 4.00 10.00
241 Swamp R 10.00 25.00
242 Mountain R 4.00 10.00
243 Forest R 3.00 8.00

2021 Magic The Gathering Secret Lair Drop Series The Unfathomable Crushing Brutality of Basic Lands Foil

239 Plains R 2.50 6.00
240 Island R 4.00 10.00
241 Swamp R 10.00 25.00
242 Mountain R 4.00 10.00
243 Forest R 3.00 8.00

2021 Magic The Gathering Secret Lair Drop Series Thrilling Tales of the Undead

231 Gravecrawler R 12.00 30.00
232 Liliana, Death's Majesty M 6.00 15.00
233 Rise of the Dark Realms M 15.00 40.00

2021 Magic The Gathering Secret Lair Drop Series Thrilling Tales of the Undead Foil

231 Gravecrawler R 12.00 30.00
232 Liliana, Death's Majesty M 6.00 15.00
233 Rise of the Dark Realms M 15.00 40.00

2021 Magic The Gathering Secret Lair Drop Series Valentines Day 2021

214 Heliod, Sun-Crowned M 10.00 25.00
215 Goblin Rabblemaster R 4.00 10.00
216 Monastery Swiftspear R 8.00 20.00
217 Boros Charm R 10.00 25.00

218 Gisela, Blade of Goldnight M 2.50 6.00
219 Goblin T 1.00 2.50

2021 Magic The Gathering Secret Lair Drop Series Valentines Day 2021 Foil

214 Heliod, Sun-Crowned M 10.00 25.00
215 Goblin Rabblemaster R 4.00 10.00
216 Monastery Swiftspear R 8.00 20.00
217 Boros Charm R 10.00 25.00
218 Gisela, Blade of Goldnight M 2.50 6.00
219 Goblin T 1.00 2.50

2021 Magic The Gathering Secret Lair Drop Series Welcome to Castle Dracula

206 Hunger of the Ancient One R
(Exquisite Blood R 15.00 40.00
207 Nightfeeder's Visitation R/(Night's Whisper R3.00 8.00
208 Dracula's Tomb R/(Phyrexian Tower R 25.00 60.00

2021 Magic The Gathering Secret Lair Drop Series Welcome to Castle Dracula Foil

206 Hunger of the Ancient One R
(Exquisite Blood R 15.00 40.00
207 Nightfeeder's Visitation R/(Night's Whisper R3.00 8.00
208 Dracula's Tomb R/(Phyrexian Tower R 25.00 60.00

2021 Magic The Gathering Strixhaven School of Mages

1 Environmental Sciences C .10 .20
2 Expanded Anatomy C .10 .20
3 Introduction to Annihilation C .10 .20
4 Introduction to Prophecy C .10 .20
5 Mascot Exhibition M .75 1.50
6 Wandering Archaic/Explore the Vastlands R 5.00 10.00
7 Academic Probation R :W: .20 .40
8 Ageless Guardian C :W: .10 .20
9 Beaming Defiance C :W: .10 .20
10 Clever Lumimancer U :W: .25 .50
11 Combat Professor C :W: .10 .20
12 Defend the Campus C :W: .10 .20
13 Detention Vortex U :W: .12 .25
14 Devastating Mastery R :W: .20 .40
15 Dueling Coach U :W: .12 .25
16 Eager First-Year C :W: .10 .20
17 Elite Spellbinder R :W: 1.25 2.50
18 Expel C :W: .10 .20
19 Guiding Voice C :W: .10 .20
20 Leonin Lightscribe R :W: .25 .50
21 Mavinda, Students' Advocate M :W: .75 1.50
22 Pilgrim of the Ages C :W: .10 .20
23 Pillardrop Rescuer C :W: .10 .20
24 Professor of Symbology U :W: .12 .25
25 Reduce to Memory U :W: .12 .25
26 Secret Rendezvous U :W: .12 .25
27 Semester's End R :W: .20 .40
28 Show of Confidence U :W: .12 .25
29 Sparring Regimen R :W: .20 .40
30 Star Pupil C :W: .10 .20
31 Stonebinder's Familiar U :W: .12 .25
32 Stonerise Spirit C :W: .10 .20
33 Strict Proctor R :W: .20 .40
34 Study Break C :W: .10 .20
35 Thunderous Orator U :W: .12 .25
36 Arcane Subtraction C :B: .10 .20
37 Archmage Emeritus R :B: 1.25 2.50
38 Burrog Befuddler C :B: .10 .20
39 Bury in Books C :B: .10 .20
40 Curate C :B: .10 .20
41 Divide by Zero U :B: .12 .25
42 Dream Strix R :B: .20 .40
43 Frost Trickster C :B: .10 .20
44 Ingenious Mastery R :B: .20 .40
45 Kelpie Guide U :B: .12 .25
46 Mentor's Guidance U :B: .12 .25
47 Mercurial Transformation U :B: .12 .25
48 Multiple Choice R :B: .20 .40
49 Pop Quiz C :B: .10 .20
50 Reject C :B: .10 .20
51 Resculpt C :B: .10 .20
52 Serpentine Curve C :B: .10 .20
53 Snow Day U :B: .12 .25
54 Solve the Equation U :B: 1.50 3.00
55 Soothsayer Adept C :B: .10 .20
56 Symmetry Sage U :B: .12 .25
57 Teachings of the Archaics R :B: .20 .40
58 Tempted by the Oriq R :B: .20 .40
59 Test of Talents U :B: .30 .75
60 Vortex Runner C :B: .10 .20
61 Waterfall Aerialist C :B: .10 .20
62 Wormhole Serpent U :B: .12 .25
63 Arrogant Poet C :K: .10 .20
64 Baleful Mastery R :K: 1.25 2.50
65 Brackish Trudge U :K: .12 .25
66 Callous Bloodmage R :K: .20 .40
67 Confront the Past R :K: .20 .40
68 Crushing Disappointment C :K: .10 .20
69 Essence Infusion C :K: .10 .20
70 Eyetwitch U :K: .20 .40
71 Flunk U :K: .12 .25
72 Go Blank U :K: .12 .25
73 Hunt for Specimens C :K: .10 .20
74 Lash of Malice C :K: .10 .20
75 Leech Fanatic C :K: .10 .20
76 Mage Hunter U :K: .12 .25
77 Mage Hunters' Onslaught C :K: .10 .20
78 Necrotic Fumes U :K: .12 .25
79 Novice Dissector C :K: .10 .20
80 Oriq Loremage R :K: .20 .40
81 Plumb the Forbidden U :K: 1.25 2.50
82 Poet's Quill R :K: .20 .40
83 Professor Onyx M :K: 7.50 15.00
84 Professor's Warning C :K: .10 .20
85 Promising Duskmage C :K: .10 .20
86 Sedgemoor Witch R :K: 2.50 5.00
87 Specter of the Fens C :K: .10 .20
88 Tenured Inkcaster U :K: .12 .25
89 Umbral Juke U :K: .12 .25
90 Unwilling Ingredient C :K: .10 .20
91 Academic Dispute U :R: .12 .25
92 Ardent Dustspeaker U :R: .12 .25
93 Blood Age General C :R: .10 .20
94 Conspiracy Theorist R :R: .30 .60
95 Crackle with Power M :R: 2.00 4.00
96 Draconic Intervention R :R: .20 .40
97 Dragon's Approach C :R: 1.00 2.00
98 Efreet Flamepainter R :R: .20 .40
99 Enthusiastic Study C :R: .10 .20
100 Explosive Welcome U :R: .12 .25
101 Fervent Mastery R :R: .20 .40
102 First Day of Class C :R: .10 .20
103 Fuming Effigy C :R: .10 .20
104 Grinning Ignus U :R: .12 .25
105 Hall Monitor U :R: .12 .25
106 Heated Debate C :R: .10 .20
107 Igneous Inspiration U :R: .12 .25
108 Illuminate History R :R: .20 .40
109 Illustrious Historian C :R: .10 .20
110 Mascot Interception U :R: .12 .25
111 Pigment Storm C :R: .10 .20
112 Pillardrop Warden C :R: .10 .20
113 Retriever Phoenix R :R: .20 .40
114 Start from Scratch U :R: .12 .25
115 Storm-Kiln Artist U :R: 1.00 2.00
116 Sudden Breakthrough C :R: .10 .20
117 Tome Shredder C :R: .10 .20
118 Twinscroll Shaman C :R: .10 .20
119 Accomplished Alchemist R :G: .25 .50
120 Basic Conjuration R :G: .20 .40
121 Bayou Groff C :G: .10 .20
122 Big Play C :G: .10 .20
123 Bookwurm U :G: .12 .25
124 Charge Through C :G: .10 .20
125 Containment Breach U :G: .12 .25
126 Devouring Tendrils U :G: .12 .25
127 Dragonsguard Elite R :G: .20 .40
128 Ecological Appreciation M :G: .75 1.50
129 Emergent Sequence U :G: .12 .25
130 Exponential Growth R :G: .20 .40
131 Field Trip C :G: .10 .20
132 Fortifying Draught U :G: .12 .25
133 Gnarled Professor R :G: .20 .40
134 Honor Troll U :G: .12 .25
135 Karok Wrangler U :G: .12 .25
136 Leyline Invocation C :G: .10 .20
137 Mage Duel C :G: .10 .20
138 Master Symmetrist U :G: .12 .25
139 Overgrown Arch U :G: .12 .25
140 Professor of Zoomancy C :G: .10 .20
141 Reckless Amplimancer C :G: .10 .20
142 Scurrid Colony C :G: .10 .20
143 Spined Karok C :G: .10 .20
144 Springmane Cervin C :G: .10 .20
145 Tangletrap C :G: .10 .20
146 Verdant Mastery R :G: .20 .40
147 Augmenter Pugilist
Echoing Equation R :G:/:B: .20 .40
148 Blex, Vexing Pest/Search for Blex M :G:/:K:1.00 2.00
149 Extus/Awaken the Blood Avatar M :W:/:K:/:R:1.00 2.00
150 Flamescroll Celebrant/Revel Silence R :R:/:W:.20 .40
151 Jadzi/Journey to the Oracle M :B:/:G: 1.00 2.00
152 Kianne/Imbraham R :G:/:B: .20 .40
153 Mila/Lukka M :W:/:R: 1.00 2.00
154 Pestilent Cauldron/Restorative Burst R :K:/:G:.20 .40
155 Plargg/Augusta R :R:/:W: .20 .40
156 Rowan/Will M :R:/:B: 2.50 5.00
157 Selfless Glyphweaver/Deadly Vanity R :W:/:K:.20 .40
158 Shaile/Embrose R :W:/:K: .20 .40
159 Torrent Sculptor
Flamethrower Sonata R :B:/:R: .20 .40
160 Uvilda/Nassari R :B:/:R: .20 .40
161 Valentin/Lisette R :K:/:G: .75 1.50
162 Aether Helix U :G:/:B: .12 .25
163 Beledros Witherbloom M :K:/:G: 10.00 20.00
164 Biomathematician C :G:/:B: .10 .20
165 Blade Historian R :R:/:W: .20 .40
166 Blood Researcher C :K:/:G: .10 .20
167 Blot Out the Sky M :W:/:K: .75 1.50
168 Body of Research M :G:/:B: 1.00 2.00
169 Closing Statement U :W:/:K: .12 .25
170 Cram Session C :K:/:G: .10 .20
171 Creative Outburst U :B:/:R: .12 .25
172 Culling Ritual R :K:/:G: 2.50 5.00
173 Culmination of Studies R :B:/:R: .20 .40
174 Daemogoth Titan R :K:/:G: .30 .75
175 Daemogoth Woe-Eater U :K:/:G: .12 .25
176 Deadly Brew U :K:/:G: .12 .25
177 Decisive Denial U :G:/:B: .12 .25
178 Dina, Soul Steeper U :K:/:G: .12 .25
179 Double Major R :G:/:B: 1.00 2.00
180 Dramatic Finale R :W:/:K: .20 .40
181 Elemental Expressionist R :B:/:R: .20 .40
182 Elemental Masterpiece C :B:/:R: .10 .20
183 Elemental Summoning C :B:/:R: .10 .20
184 Eureka Moment C :G:/:B: .10 .20
185 Exhilarating Elocution C :W:/:K: .12 .25
186 Expressive Iteration U :B:/:R: 4.00 8.00
187 Fractal Summoning C :G:/:B: .10 .20
188 Fracture U :W:/:K: .30 .60
189 Galazeth Prismari M :B:/:R: 4.00 8.00
190 Golden Ratio U :G:/:B: .12 .25
191 Harness Infinity M :K:/:G: .75 1.50
192 Hofri Ghostforge M :R:/:W: 1.00 2.00
193 Humiliate U :W:/:K: .12 .25
194 Infuse with Vitality C :K:/:G: .10 .20
195 Inkling Summoning C :W:/:K: .10 .20
196 Kasmina, Enigma Sage M :G:/:B: 1.50 3.00
197 Killian, Ink Duelist U :W:/:K: .12 .25
198 Lorehold Apprentice U :R:/:W: .12 .25
199 Lorehold Command R :R:/:W: .20 .40
200 Lorehold Excavation U :R:/:W: .12 .25
201 Lorehold Pledgemage C :R:/:W: .10 .20
202 Maelstrom Muse U :B:/:R: .12 .25
203 Magma Opus M :B:/:R: 1.25 2.50
204 Make Your Mark C :R:/:W: .10 .20
205 Manifestation Sage R :G:/:B: .20 .40
206 Moldering Karok C :K:/:G: .10 .20
207 Mortality Spear U :K:/:G: .12 .25
208 Needlethorn Drake C :G:/:B: .10 .20
209 Oggyar Battle-Seer C :B:/:R: .10 .20
210 Owlin Shieldmage C :W:/:K: .10 .20
211 Pest Summoning C :K:/:G: .10 .20
212 Practical Research U :B:/:R: .12 .25
213 Prismari Apprentice U :B:/:R: .12 .25
214 Prismari Command R :B:/:R: 5.00 10.00
215 Prismari Pledgemage C :B:/:R: .10 .20
216 Quandrix Apprentice U :G:/:B: .12 .25
217 Quandrix Command R :G:/:B: .30 .75
218 Quandrix Cultivator U :G:/:B: .12 .25
219 Quandrix Pledgemage C :G:/:B: .10 .20
220 Quintorius, Field Historian U :R:/:W: .12 .25
221 Radiant Scrollwielder R :R:/:W: .20 .40
222 Reconstruct History U :R:/:W: .12 .25
223 Relic Sloth C :R:/:W: .10 .20
224 Returned Pastcaller U :R:/:W: .12 .25
225 Rip Apart U :R:/:W: .30 .60
226 Rise of Extus C :W:/:K: .10 .20
227 Rootha, Mercurial Artist U :B:/:R: .12 .25
228 Rushed Rebirth R :K:/:G: .30 .60
229 Shadewing Laureate U :W:/:K: .12 .25
230 Shadrix Silverquill M :W:/:K: 4.00 8.00
231 Silverquill Apprentice U :W:/:K: .12 .25
232 Silverquill Command R :W:/:K: .20 .40
233 Silverquill Pledgemage C :W:/:K: .10 .20
234 Silverquill Silencer R :W:/:K: .20 .40
235 Spectacle Mage C :B:/:R: .10 .20
236 Spirit Summoning C :R:/:W: .10 .20
237 Spiteful Squad C :W:/:K: .10 .20
238 Square Up C :G:/:B: .10 .20
239 Stonebound Mentor C :R:/:W: .10 .20
240 Tanazir Quandrix M :G:/:B: 1.50 3.00
241 Teach by Example C :B:/:R: .10 .20
242 Tend the Pests U :K:/:G: .12 .25
243 Thrilling Discovery C :R:/:W: .10 .20
244 Vanishing Verse R :W:/:K: 1.50 3.00
245 Velomachus Lorehold M :R:/:W: 2.50 5.00
246 Venerable Warsinger R :R:/:W: .20 .40
247 Witherbloom Apprentice U :K:/:G: .12 .25
248 Witherbloom Command R :K:/:G: .30 .75
249 Witherbloom Pledgemage C :K:/:G: .10 .20
250 Zimone, Quandrix Prodigy U :G:/:B: .12 .25
251 Biblioplex Assistant C .10 .20
252 Campus Guide C .10 .20
253 Codie, Vociferous Codex R .30 .60
254 Cogwork Archivist C .10 .20
255 Excavated Wall C .10 .20
256 Letter of Acceptance C .10 .20
257 Reflective Golem U .12 .25
258 Spell Satchel U .12 .25
259 Strixhaven Stadium R .50 1.00
260 Team Pennant U .12 .25
261 Zephyr Boots U .12 .25
262 Access Tunnel U .12 .25
263 Archway Commons C .10 .20
264 The Biblioplex R .20 .40
265 Frostboil Snarl R .20 .40
266 Furycalm Snarl R 1.50 3.00
267 Hall of Oracles R .20 .40
268 Lorehold Campus C .10 .20
269 Necroblossom Snarl R 2.00 4.00
270 Prismari Campus C .10 .20
271 Quandrix Campus C .10 .20
272 Shineshadow Snarl R 1.50 3.00
273 Silverquill Campus C .10 .20
274 Vineglimmer Snarl R 1.25 2.50
275 Witherbloom Campus C .10 .20
276 Professor Onyx M :K: 7.50 15.00
277 Mila/Lukka M :W:/:R: 2.50 5.00
278 Rowan/Will M :R:/:B: 4.00 8.00
279 Kasmina, Enigma Sage M :G:/:B: 2.50 5.00
280 Shadrix Silverquill M :W:/:K: 6.00 12.00
281 Galazeth Prismari M :B:/:R: 5.00 10.00
282 Beledros Witherbloom M :K:/:G: 12.50 25.00
283 Velomachus Lorehold M :R:/:W: 4.00 8.00
284 Tanazir Quandrix M :G:/:B: 2.50 5.00
285 Mascot Exhibition M 2.00 4.00
286 Wandering Archaic/Explore the Vastlands R7.50 15.00
287 Academic Probation R :W: .20 .40
288 Devastating Mastery R :W: .30 .60
289 Elite Spellbinder R :W: 2.50 5.00
290 Leonin Lightscribe R :W: .75 1.50
291 Mavinda, Students' Advocate M :W: 2.00 4.00
292 Semester's End R :W: 1.00 2.00
293 Sparring Regimen R :W: .40 .80
294 Strict Proctor R :W: 1.00 2.00
295 Archmage Emeritus R :B: 2.50 5.00
296 Dream Strix R :B: .20 .40
297 Ingenious Mastery R :B: .20 .40
298 Multiple Choice R :B: .30 .75
299 Teachings of the Archaics R :B: .20 .40
300 Tempted by the Oriq R :B: .30 .75
301 Baleful Mastery R :K: 2.00 4.00
302 Callous Bloodmage R :K: 1.00 2.00
303 Confront the Past R :K: .30 .60
304 Oriq Loremage R :K: .75 1.50
305 Poet's Quill R :K: .30 .60
306 Sedgemoor Witch R :K: 4.00 8.00
307 Conspiracy Theorist R :R: .75 1.50
308 Crackle with Power M :R: 4.00 8.00
309 Draconic Intervention R :R: .30 .75
310 Efreet Flamepainter R :R: .30 .75
311 Fervent Mastery R :R: .25 .50
312 Illuminate History R :R: .20 .40
313 Retriever Phoenix R :R: .20 .40
314 Accomplished Alchemist R :G: .60 1.25
315 Basic Conjuration R :G: .20 .40
316 Dragonsguard Elite R :G: .30 .75
317 Ecological Appreciation M :G: 1.50 3.00
318 Exponential Growth R :G: .30 .75
319 Gnarled Professor R :G: .30 .60
320 Verdant Mastery R :G: .20 .40
321 Augmenter Pugilist
Echoing Equation R :G:/:B: .50 1.00
322 Blex, Vexing Pest/Search for Blex M :G:/:K:2.50 5.00
323 Extus/Awaken the Blood Avatar M :W:/:K:/:R:4.00 8.00
324 Flamescroll Celebrant
Revel in Silence R :R:/:W: .30 .75
325 Jadzi/Journey to the Oracle M :B:/:G: 2.50 5.00
326 Kianne/Imbraham R :G:/:B: .20 .40
327 Pestilent Cauldron/Restorative Burst R :K:/:G:.30 .60
328 Plargg/Augusta R :R:/:W: .60 1.25
329 Selfless Glyphweaver/Deadly Vanity R :W:/:K:.50 1.00
330 Shaile/Embrose R :W:/:K: .75 1.50
331 Torrent Sculptor
Flamethrower Sonata R :B:/:R: .20 .40
332 Uvilda/Nassari R :B:/:R: .30 .75
333 Valentin/Lisette R :K:/:G: 1.50 3.00
334 Blade Historian R :R:/:W: 1.00 2.00
335 Blot Out the Sky M :W:/:K: 2.00 4.00
336 Body of Research M :G:/:B: 2.50 5.00
337 Culling Ritual R :K:/:G: 4.00 8.00
338 Culmination of Studies R :B:/:R: .25 .50
339 Daemogoth Titan R :K:/:G: .75 1.50
340 Double Major R :G:/:B: 2.50 5.00
341 Dramatic Finale R :W:/:K: .40 .80
342 Elemental Expressionist R :B:/:R: .20 .40
343 Harness Infinity M :K:/:G: 2.00 4.00
344 Hofri Ghostforge M :R:/:W: 2.00 4.00
345 Lorehold Command R :R:/:W: .30 .75
346 Magma Opus M :B:/:R: 3.00 6.00
347 Manifestation Sage R :G:/:B: .20 .40
348 Prismari Command R :B:/:R: 7.50 15.00
349 Quandrix Command R :G:/:B: .75 1.50
350 Radiant Scrollwielder R :R:/:W: .30 .60
351 Rushed Rebirth R :K:/:G: .75 1.50
352 Silverquill Command R :W:/:K: .50 1.00
353 Silverquill Silencer R :W:/:K: .30 .75
354 Vanishing Verse R :W:/:K: 2.50 5.00
355 Venerable Warsinger R :R:/:W: .30 .75
356 Witherbloom Command R :K:/:G: 1.25 2.50
357 Codie, Vociferous Codex R 1.00 2.00
358 Strixhaven Stadium R 2.00 4.00
359 The Biblioplex R .75 1.50
360 Frostboil Snarl R .20 .40
361 Furycalm Snarl R 2.00 4.00
362 Hall of Oracles R .50 1.00
363 Necroblossom Snarl R 2.50 5.00
364 Shineshadow Snarl R 1.50 3.00
365 Vineglimmer Snarl R 2.50 5.00
366 Plains L .10 .20
367 Plains L .10 .20
368 Island L .10 .20
369 Island L .10 .20
370 Swamp L .10 .20
371 Swamp L .10 .20
372 Mountain L .10 .20
373 Mountain L .10 .20
374 Forest L .10 .20
375 Forest L .10 .20
376 Dragonsguard Elite R :G: .30 .60
377 Archmage Emeritus R :B: 1.00 2.00
378 Fracture U :W:/:K: .75 1.50
379 Expressive Iteration U :B:/:R: 6.00 12.00
380 Mortality Spear U :K:/:G: .30 .75
381 Rip Apart U :R:/:W: .75 1.50
382 Decisive Denial U :G:/:B: .30 .60

2021 Magic The Gathering Strixhaven School of Mages Mystical Archive

1 Approach of the Second Sun M :W: 1.50 3.00
2 Day of Judgment M :W: 1.25 2.50
3 Defiant Strike U :W: .07 .10
4 Divine Gambit U :W: .07 .10
5 Ephemerate R :W: 1.50 3.00
6 Gift of Estates R :W: .60 1.25
7 Gods Willing R :W: .20 .40
8 Mana Tithe R :W: .30 .60
9 Revitalize U :W: .07 .10
10 Swords to Plowshares R :W: 1.25 2.50
11 Teferi's Protection M :W: 15.00 30.00
12 Blue Sun's Zenith M :B: 2.00 4.00
13 Brainstorm R :B: 1.50 3.00
14 Compulsive Research R :B: .12 .25
15 Counterspell R :B: 1.50 3.00
16 Memory Lapse R :B: .25 .50
17 Mind's Desire M :B: .75 1.50
18 Negate U :B: .60 1.25
19 Opt U :B: .12 .25
20 Strategic Planning U :B: .07 .10
21 Tezzeret's Gambit R :B: .20 .40
22 Time Warp M :B: 7.50 15.00
23 Whirlwind Denial U :B: .07 .10
24 Agonizing Remorse U :K: .07 .10
25 Crux of Fate M :K: 2.50 5.00
26 Dark Ritual R :K: 4.00 8.00
27 Demonic Tutor M :K: 30.00 60.00
28 Doom Blade R :K: .15 .30
29 Duress U :K: .07 .15
30 Eliminate U :K: .07 .10
31 Inquisition of Kozilek R :K: .25 .50
32 Sign in Blood R :K: 2.00 4.00
33 Tainted Pact M :K: 7.50 15.00
34 Tendrils of Agony R :K: .20 .40
35 Village Rites U :K: .20 .40
36 Chaos Warp M :R: 2.50 5.00
37 Claim the Firstborn U :R: .10 .20
38 Faithless Looting R :R: .75 1.50
39 Grapeshot R :R: .25 .50
40 Increasing Vengeance M :R: .75 1.50
41 Infuriate U :R: .07 .10
42 Lightning Bolt R :R: 1.25 2.50
43 Mizzix's Mastery M :R: 4.00 8.00
44 Shock U :R: .07 .15
45 Stone Rain R :R: .10 .20
46 Thrill of Possibility U :R: .07 .15
47 Urza's Rage R :R: .07 .15
48 Abundant Harvest R :G: .12 .25
49 Adventurous Impulse U :G: .07 .10
50 Channel M :G: .20 .40
51 Cultivate U :G: .50 1.00
52 Harmonize R :G: .20 .40
53 Krosan Grip R :G: 1.00 2.00
54 Natural Order M :G: 7.50 15.00
55 Primal Command M :G: .75 1.50
56 Regrowth R :G: .40 .80
57 Snakeskin Veil U :G: .12 .25
58 Weather the Storm R :G: .25 .50
59 Despark R :W:/:K: .75 1.50
60 Electrolyze R :B:/:R: .10 .20
61 Growth Spiral R :G:/:B: 1.00 2.00
62 Lightning Helix R :R:/:W: .25 .50
63 Putrefy R :K:/:G: .30 .60
65 Day of Judgment M :W: 3.00 6.00
66 Defiant Strike U :W: .20 .40
67 Divine Gambit U :W: .25 .50

2021 Magic The Gathering Strixhaven School of Mages Tokens

1 Avatar .30 .75
2 Elemental .07 .15
3 Fractal .10 .20
4 Inkling .12 .25
5 Pest .30 .60
6 Spirit .07 .15

2021 Magic The Gathering Time Spiral Remastered

1 Amrou Scout C :W:	.07	.15
2 Amrou Seekers C :W:	.07	.15
3 Angel of Salvation R :W:	.15	.30
4 Angel's Grace R :W:	2.50	5.00
5 Aven Mindcensor U :W:	.75	1.50
6 Aven Riftwatcher C :W:	.07	.15
7 Benalish Cavalry C :W:	.07	.15
8 Benalish Commander R :W:	.15	.30
9 Blade of the Sixth Pride C :W:	.07	.15
10 Bound in Silence C :W:	.07	.15
11 Calciderm U :W:	.10	.20
12 Castle Raptors C :W:	.07	.15
13 Celestial Crusader U :W:	.10	.20
14 Children of Korlis C :W:	.07	.15
15 Crovax, Ascendant Hero M :W:	.50	1.00
16 Duskrider Peregrine U :W:	.10	.20
17 Errant Doomsayers C :W:	.07	.15
18 Fortify C :W:	.07	.15
19 Griffin Guide U :W:	.10	.20
20 Ivory Giant C :W:	.07	.15
21 Judge Unworthy C :W:	.07	.15
22 Knight of Sursi C :W:	.07	.15
23 Knight of the Holy Nimbus U :W:	.10	.20
24 Lost Auramancers U :W:	.10	.20
25 Lymph Sliver C :W:	.07	.15
26 Mana Tithe C :W:	.25	.50
27 Mangara of Corondor R :W:	.15	.30
28 Momentary Blink C :W:	.07	.15
29 Mycologist U :W:	.10	.20
30 Outrider en-Kor U :W:	.10	.20
31 Pallid Mycoderm C :W:	.07	.15
32 Porphyry Nodes R :W:	.30	.60
33 Poultice Sliver U :W:	.10	.20
34 Pulmonic Sliver R :W:	.50	1.00
35 Rebuff the Wicked U :W:	.30	.60
36 Restore Balance M	1.00	2.00
37 Return to Dust U :W:	.12	.25
38 Riftmarked Knight U :W:	.10	.20
39 Saltblast U :W:	.10	.20
40 Saltfield Recluse U :W:	.10	.20
41 Serra Avenger R :W:	.20	.40
42 Shade of Trokair C :W:	.07	.15
43 Sidewinder Sliver C :W:	.12	.25
44 Sinew Sliver C :W:	.20	.40
45 Stonecloaker U :W:	.10	.20
46 Stormfront Riders U :W:	.10	.20
47 Sunlance C :W:	.07	.15
48 Temporal Isolation C :W:	.07	.15
49 Watcher Sliver C :W:	.07	.15
50 Whitemane Lion C :W:	.07	.15
51 Aeon Chronicler R :B:	.15	.30
52 Ancestral Vision M	3.00	6.00
53 Bewilder C :B:	.07	.15
54 Bonded Fetch U :B:	.10	.20
55 Brine Elemental U :B:	.10	.20
56 Careful Consideration U :B:	.10	.20
57 Cloudseeder U :B:	.10	.20
58 Coral Trickster C :B:	.07	.15
59 Crookclaw Transmuter C :B:	.07	.15
60 Cryptic Annelid U :B:	.10	.20
61 Delay U :B:	1.00	2.00
62 Draining Whelk R :B:	.20	.40
63 Dream Stalker C :B:	.07	.15
64 Dreamscape Artist C :B:	.07	.15
65 Drifter il-Dal C :B:	.07	.15
66 Errant Ephemeron C :B:	.07	.15
67 Erratic Mutation C :B:	.07	.15
68 Fathom Seer C :B:	.07	.15
69 Foresee C :B:	.07	.15
70 Gossamer Phantasm C :B:	.07	.15
71 Infiltrator il-Kor C :B:	.07	.15
72 Jodah's Avenger U :B:	.10	.20
73 Logic Knot C :B:	.07	.15
74 Looter il-Kor C :B:	.07	.15
75 Magus of the Future R :B:	.15	.30
76 Mystical Teachings U :B:	.10	.20
77 Pact of Negation R	12.50	25.00
78 Piracy Charm C :B:	.07	.15
79 Pongify U :B:	.50	1.00
80 Primal Plasma C :B:	.07	.15
81 Reality Acid C :B:	.07	.15
82 Riftwing Cloudskate U :B:	.10	.20
83 Riptide Pilferer U :B:	.10	.20
84 Sarcomite Myr C :B:	.07	.15
85 Shaper Parasite U :B:	.10	.20
86 Slipstream Serpent C :B:	.07	.15
87 Snapback C :B:	.07	.15
88 Spell Burst U :B:	.10	.20
89 Spiketail Drakeling C :B:	.07	.15
90 Stormcloud Djinn U :B:	.10	.20
91 Teferi, Mage of Zhalfir M :B:	2.50	5.00
92 Think Twice C :B:	.07	.15
93 Timebender U :B:	.10	.20
94 Tolarian Sentinel C :B:	.07	.15
95 Veiling Oddity C :B:	.07	.15
96 Venser, Shaper Savant R :B:	2.00	4.00
97 Vesuvan Shapeshifter R :B:	.15	.30
98 Walk the Aeons R :B:	1.25	2.50
99 Whip-Spine Drake U :B:	.10	.20
100 Wipe Away U :B:	.10	.20
101 Assassinate C :K:	.07	.15
102 Big Game Hunter U :K:	.10	.20
103 Blightspeaker C :K:	.07	.15
104 Corpulent Corpse C :K:	.07	.15
105 Cutthroat il-Dal C :K:	.07	.15
106 Damnation M :K:	20.00	40.00
107 Dark Withering C :K:	.07	.15
108 Deadly Grub C :K:	.07	.15
109 Deathspore Thallid C :K:	.07	.15
110 Deepcavern Imp C :K:	.07	.15
111 Dread Return U :K:	.10	.20
112 Dunerider Outlaw U :K:	.10	.20
113 Enslave U :K:	.10	.20
114 Extirpate R :K:	.50	1.00
115 Faceless Devourer U :K:	.10	.20
116 Feebleness C :K:	.07	.15
117 Gorgon Recluse C :K:	.07	.15
118 Grave Scrabbler C :K:	.07	.15
119 Ichor Slick C :K:	.07	.15
120 Kor Dirge U :K:	.10	.20
121 Living End M	2.50	5.00
122 Mass of Ghouls C :K:	.07	.15
123 Mindstab C :K:	.07	.15
124 Minions' Murmurs U :K:	.10	.20
125 Mirri the Cursed R :K:	.20	.40
126 Muck Drubb U :K:	.10	.20
127 Nether Traitor R :K:	1.00	2.00
128 Nightshade Assassin U :K:	.10	.20
129 Phthisis U :K:	.10	.20
130 Pit Keeper C :K:	.07	.15
131 Premature Burial U :K:	.10	.20
132 Psychotic Episode C :K:	.07	.15
133 Rathi Trapper C :K:	.07	.15
134 Ridged Kusite C :K:	.07	.15
135 Sangrophage C :K:	.07	.15
136 Sengir Nosferatu R :K:	.15	.30
137 Skittering Monstrosity U :K:	.10	.20
138 Slaughter Pact R	1.25	2.50
139 Smallpox U :K:	.12	.25
140 Strangling Soot C :K:	.07	.15
141 Street Wraith U :K:	.30	.60
142 Stronghold Rats U :K:	.10	.20
143 Sudden Death U :K:	.10	.20
144 Sudden Spoiling R :K:	.75	1.50
145 Tendrils of Corruption C :K:	.07	.15
146 Tombstalker R :K:	.15	.30
147 Trespasser il-Vec C :K:	.07	.15
148 Urborg Syphon-Mage C :K:	.07	.15
149 Yixlid Jailer U :K:	.10	.20
150 Akroma, Angel of Fury M :R:	.50	1.00
151 Ancient Grudge C :R:	.07	.15
152 Arc Blade U :R:	.10	.20
153 Basalt Gargoyle U :R:	.10	.20
154 Battering Sliver C :R:	.07	.15
155 Bonesplitter Sliver C :R:	.07	.15
156 Boom // Bust R :R:	.20	.40
157 Brute Force C :R:	.07	.15
158 Char-Rumbler U :R:	.10	.20
159 Coal Stoker C :R:	.07	.15
160 Conflagrate U :R:	.10	.20
161 Dead // Gone C :R:	.07	.15
162 Empty the Warrens C :R:	.07	.15
163 Firemaw Kavu U :R:	.10	.20
164 Fury Sliver U :R:	.20	.40
165 Gathan Raiders C :R:	.07	.15
166 Grapeshot C :R:	.07	.15
167 Greater Gargadon R :R:	.20	.40
168 Grinning Ignus C :R:	.07	.15
169 Haze of Rage U :R:	.10	.20
170 Henchfiend of Ukor U :R:	.10	.20
171 Homing Sliver C :R:	.07	.15
172 Jaya Ballard, Task Mage R :R:	.15	.30
173 Keldon Halberdier C :R:	.07	.15
174 Lightning Axe U :R:	.10	.20
175 Magus of the Moon R :R:	3.00	6.00
176 Mogg War Marshal C :R:	.07	.15
177 Needlepeak Spider C :R:	.07	.15
178 Orcish Cannonade C :R:	.07	.15
179 Pact of the Titan R	.15	.30
180 Prodigal Pyromancer U :R:	.10	.20
181 Reckless Wurm C :R:	.07	.15
182 Reiterate R :R:	1.25	2.50
183 Riddle of Lightning C :R:	.07	.15
184 Rift Bolt C :R:	.12	.25
185 Rift Elemental C :R:	.07	.15
186 Rough // Tumble U :R:	.10	.20
187 Sedge Sliver R :R:	.60	1.25
188 Shivan Meteor U :R:	.10	.20
189 Shivan Sand-Mage U :R:	.10	.20
190 Simian Spirit Guide C :R:	.30	.60
191 Skirk Shaman C :R:	.07	.15
192 Stingscourger C :R:	.07	.15
193 Storm Entity U :R:	.10	.20
194 Sudden Shock U :R:	.10	.20
195 Sulfur Elemental U :R:	.10	.20
196 Thick-Skinned Goblin U :R:	.10	.20
197 Two-Headed Sliver C :R:	.07	.15
198 Wheel of Fate M	1.50	3.00
199 Citanul Woodreaders C :G:	.07	.15
200 Durkwood Baloth C :G:	.07	.15
201 Edge of Autumn C :G:	.12	.25
202 Evolution Charm C :G:	.07	.15
203 Fungus Sliver R :G:	.20	.40
204 Gaea's Anthem U :G:	.10	.20
205 Gemhide Sliver C :G:	.20	.40
206 Giant Dustwasp C :G:	.07	.15
207 Greenseeker C :G:	.07	.15
208 Harmonize U :G:	.10	.20
209 Heartwood Storyteller R :G:	.50	1.00
210 Hypergenesis M	.50	1.00
211 Imperiosaur U :G:	.10	.20
212 Kavu Primarch C :G:	.07	.15
213 Keen Sense U :G:	.25	.50
214 Krosan Grip U :G:	.25	.50
215 Life and Limb R :G:	.20	.40
216 Llanowar Mentor U :G:	.10	.20
217 Might of Old Krosa U :G:	.10	.20
218 Might Sliver U :G:	.20	.40
219 Mire Boa U :G:	.10	.20
220 Muraganda Petroglyphs R :G:	.25	.50
221 Nantuko Shaman C :G:	.07	.15
222 Pendelhaven Elder U :G:	.10	.20
223 Penumbra Spider C :G:	.07	.15
224 Phantom Wurm U :G:	.10	.20
225 Primal Forcemage U :G:	.10	.20
226 Reflex Sliver C :G:	.07	.15
227 Scryb Ranger U :G:	.20	.40
228 Seal of Primordium C :G:	.07	.15
229 Search for Tomorrow C :G:	.12	.25
230 Spinneret Sliver C :G:	.07	.15
231 Sporesower Thallid U :G:	.10	.20
232 Sporoloth Ancient C :G:	.07	.15
233 Strength in Numbers C :G:	.07	.15
234 Summoner's Pact R	2.50	5.00
235 Tarmogoyf M :G:	20.00	40.00
236 Thallid Germinator C :G:	.07	.15
237 Thallid Shell-Dweller C :G:	.07	.15
238 Thelon of Havenwood R :G:	.15	.30
239 Thelonite Hermit R :G:	.15	.30
240 Thornweald Archer C :G:	.07	.15
241 Thrill of the Hunt C :G:	.07	.15
242 Tromp the Domains U :G:	.10	.20
243 Uktabi Drake C :G:	.07	.15
244 Utopia Mycon U :G:	.10	.20
245 Utopia Vow C :G:	.07	.15
246 Virulent Sliver C :G:	.15	.30
247 Yavimaya Dryad U :G:	.10	.20
248 Cautery Sliver U :R:/:W:	.10	.20
249 Darkheart Sliver U :K:/:G:	.15	.30
250 Dormant Sliver U :G:/:B:	.20	.40
251 Dralnu, Lich Lord R :B:/:K:	.15	.30
252 Firewake Sliver U :R:/:G:	.12	.25
253 Glittering Wish R :G:/:W:	.15	.30
254 Harmonic Sliver U :G:/:W:	.25	.50
255 Ith, High Arcanist R :W:/:B:	.15	.30
256 Jhoira of the Ghitu R :B:/:R:	.15	.30
257 Kaervek the Merciless R :K:/:R:	1.00	2.00
258 Necrotic Sliver U :W:/:K:	.25	.50
259 Radha, Heir to Keld R :R:/:G:	.15	.30
260 Saffi Eriksdotter R :G:/:W:	.60	1.25
261 Sliver Legion M :W:/:B:/:K:/:R:/:G:	30.00	60.00
262 Akroma's Memorial M	12.50	25.00
263 Chromatic Star C	.15	.30
264 Clockwork Hydra U	.10	.20
265 Cloud Key R	4.00	8.00
266 Coalition Relic R	1.25	2.50
267 Gauntlet of Power M	7.50	15.00
268 Hivestone R	.30	.75
269 Jhoira's Timebug C	.07	.15
270 Lotus Bloom R	2.00	4.00
271 Paradise Plume U	.10	.20
272 Prismatic Lens U	.12	.25
273 Sliversmith U	.10	.20
274 Stuffy Doll R	1.00	2.00
275 Calciform Pools U	.10	.20
276 Dreadship Reef U	.10	.20
277 Dryad Arbor R	4.00	8.00
278 Flagstones of Trokair R	2.50	5.00
279 Fungal Reaches U	.10	.20
280 Gemstone Caverns M	20.00	40.00
281 Kher Keep R	.30	.60
282 Molten Slagheap U	.10	.20
283 Saltcrusted Steppe U	.10	.20
284 Swarmyard R	2.00	4.00
285 Terramorphic Expanse C	.15	.30
286 Tolaria West R	1.50	3.00
287 Urborg, Tomb of Yawgmoth R	10.00	20.00
288 Urza's Factory U	.10	.20
289 Vesuva M	12.50	25.00
290 Ajani's Pridemate S :W:	.25	.50
291 Banishing Light S :W:	.30	.60
292 Containment Priest S :W:	1.25	2.50
293 Ethereal Armor S :W:	.75	1.50
294 Flickerwisp S :W:	2.00	4.00
295 Intangible Virtue S :W:	.30	.75
296 Lingering Souls S :W:	1.00	2.00
297 Mirror Entity S :W:	1.25	2.50
298 Palace Jailer S :W:	1.25	2.50
299 Path to Exile S :W:	5.00	10.00
300 Restoration Angel S :W:	1.50	3.00
301 Sigil of the Empty Throne S :W:	.50	1.00
302 Silence S :W:	2.50	5.00
303 Sram, Senior Edificer S :W:	1.25	2.50
304 Stonehorn Dignitary S :W:	.60	1.25
305 Thraben Inspector S :W:	1.50	3.00
306 Baral, Chief of Compliance S :B:	4.00	8.00
307 Disdainful Stroke S :B:	.60	1.25
308 Fblthp, the Lost S :B:	.60	1.25
309 Laboratory Maniac S :B:	2.50	5.00
310 Master of the Pearl Trident S :B:	2.00	4.00
311 Mulldrifter R :B:	1.50	3.00
312 Mystic Confluence S :B:	2.50	5.00
313 Ninja of the Deep Hours S :B:	1.00	2.00
314 Paradoxical Outcome S :B:	1.00	2.00
315 Ponder S :B:	10.00	20.00
316 Remand S :B:	4.00	8.00
317 Repeal S :B:	.60	1.25
318 Talrand, Sky Summoner S :B:	.50	1.00
319 Treasure Cruise S :B:	1.25	2.50
320 Trinket Mage S :B:	.75	1.50
321 True-Name Nemesis S :B:	6.00	12.00
322 Dismember S :K:	5.00	10.00
323 Gray Merchant of Asphodel S :K:	1.50	3.00
324 Gurmag Angler S :K:	2.00	4.00
325 Harvester of Souls S :K:	.75	1.50
326 Leyline of the Void S :K:	6.00	12.00
327 Liliana's Triumph S :K:	.50	1.00
328 Read the Bones S :K:	.75	1.50
329 Relentless Rats S :K:	2.00	4.00
330 Sanguine Bond S :K:	2.00	4.00
331 Shriekmaw S :K:	.60	1.25
332 Stinkweed Imp S :K:	1.50	3.00
333 Tasigur, the Golden Fang S :K:	1.50	3.00
334 Thoughtseize S :K:	25.00	50.00
335 Vampire Hexmage S :K:	1.00	2.00
336 Yawgmoth, Thran Physician S :K:	12.50	25.00
337 Zulaport Cutthroat S :K:	1.00	2.00
338 Alesha, Who Smiles at Death S :R:	.60	1.25
339 Anger of the Gods S :R:	1.50	3.00
340 Bedlam Reveler S :R:	1.25	2.50
341 Dreadhorde Arcanist S :R:	2.50	5.00
342 Etali, Primal Storm S :R:	1.50	3.00
343 Exquisite Firecraft S :R:	.75	1.50
344 Feldon of the Third Path S :R:	.75	1.50
345 Goblin Engineer S :R:	1.25	2.50
346 Kiki-Jiki, Mirror Breaker S :R:	7.50	15.00
347 Lava Spike S :R:	3.00	6.00
348 Molten Rain S :R:	.60	1.25
349 Monastery Swiftspear S :R:	6.00	12.00
350 Past in Flames S :R:	2.00	4.00
351 Temur Battle Rage S :R:	1.25	2.50
352 Vandalblast S :R:	3.00	6.00
353 Young Pyromancer S :R:	3.00	6.00
354 Zealous Conscripts S :R:	.75	1.50
355 Ancient Stirrings S :G:	1.50	3.00
356 Beast Whisperer S :G:	2.00	4.00
357 Beast Within S :G:	2.00	4.00
358 Become Immense S :G:	.30	.60
359 Courser of Kruphix S :G:	2.50	5.00
360 Elvish Mystic S :G:	2.50	5.00
361 Eternal Witness S :G:	3.00	6.00
362 Evolutionary Leap S :G:	.75	1.50
363 Farseek S :G:	1.50	3.00
364 Nature's Claim S :G:	2.50	5.00
365 Primeval Titan S :G:	6.00	12.00
366 Reclamation Sage S :G:	1.50	3.00
367 Sylvan Scrying S :G:	1.25	2.50
368 Thragtusk S :G:	1.00	2.00
369 Time of Need S :G:	1.25	2.50
370 Abrupt Decay S :K:/:G:	7.50	15.00
371 Arcades, the Strategist S :G:/:W:/:B:	2.50	5.00
372 Bloodbraid Elf S :R:/:G:	2.00	4.00
373 Cloudshredder Sliver S :R:/:W:	1.50	3.00
374 Consuming Aberration S :B:/:K:	.60	1.25
375 Dovin's Veto S :W:/:B:	2.00	4.00
376 Epic Experiment S :B:/:R:	.50	1.00
377 Feather, the Redeemed S :R:/:W:	1.00	2.00
378 Grenzo, Dungeon Warden S :K:/:R:	.60	1.25
379 Knight of the Reliquary S :G:/:W:	2.50	5.00
380 Lavinia, Azorius Renegade S :W:/:B:	.75	1.50
381 Mortify S :W:/:K:	.60	1.25
382 Prized Amalgam S :B:/:K:	2.00	4.00
383 Qasali Pridemage S :G:/:W:	.75	1.50
384 Rakdos Charm S :K:/:R:	.75	1.50
385 Secret Plans S :G:/:B:	.25	.50
386 Slimefoot, the Stowaway S :K:/:G:	.25	.50
387 Temur Ascendancy S :G:/:B:/:R:	.60	1.25
388 Tidehollow Sculler S :W:/:K:	.75	1.50
389 Trygon Predator S :G:/:B:	.50	1.00
390 Chalice of the Void S	25.00	50.00
391 Contagion Clasp S	.60	1.25
392 Cranial Plating S	.75	1.50
393 Crystal Shard S	1.00	2.00
394 Everflowing Chalice S	1.25	2.50
395 Hedron Archive S	.75	1.50
396 Hollow One S	.75	1.50
397 Leveler S	.50	1.00
398 Manifold Key S	1.00	2.00
399 Panharmonicon S	6.00	12.00
400 Solemn Simulacrum S	2.50	5.00
401 Sorcerous Spyglass S	.75	1.50
402 Vanquisher's Banner S	6.00	12.00
403 Ancient Den S	1.25	2.50
404 Arch of Orazca S	1.00	2.00
405 Blighted Woodland S	.60	1.25
406 Bojuka Bog S	3.00	6.00
407 Field of Ruin S	3.00	6.00
408 Mystic Sanctuary S	3.00	6.00
409 Ramunap Ruins S	.60	1.25
410 Wastes S	4.00	8.00
411 Lotus Bloom R	.15	.30

2021 Magic The Gathering Time Spiral Remastered Tokens

1 Griffin	.07	.15
2 Soldier	.12	.25
3 Cloud Sprite	.07	.15
4 Bat	.07	.15
5 Knight	.07	.15
6 Spider	.07	.15
7 Giant	.12	.25
8 Goblin	.15	.30
9 Kobolds of Kher Keep	.25	.50
10 Ape	.25	.50
11 Insect	.07	.15
12 Llanowar Elves	.07	.15
13 Saproling	.10	.20
14 Assembly-Worker	.07	.15
15 Metallic Sliver	.15	.30

2022 Magic The Gathering 30th Anniversary

1 Animate Wall R :W:	30.00	60.00
2 Armageddon R :W:	75.00	150.00
3 Balance R :W:	30.00	60.00
4 Benalish Hero C :W:	2.50	5.00
5 Black Ward U :W:	2.50	5.00
6 Blaze of Glory R :W:	30.00	75.00
7 Blessing R :W:	20.00	40.00
8 Blue Ward U :W:	5.00	10.00
9 Castle U :W:	6.00	12.00
10 Circle of Protection: Black C :W:	2.00	4.00
11 Circle of Protection: Blue C :W:	2.00	4.00
12 Circle of Protection: Green C :W:	2.00	4.00
13 Circle of Protection: Red C :W:	2.50	5.00
14 Circle of Protection: White C :W:	2.00	4.00
15 Consecrate Land U :W:	3.00	8.00
16 Conversion U :W:	4.00	8.00
17 Death Ward C :W:	2.00	4.00
18 Disenchant C :W:	4.00	8.00
19 Farmstead R :W:	30.00	75.00
20 Green Ward U :W:	6.00	12.00
21 Guardian Angel C :W:	3.00	6.00
22 Healing Salve C :W:	1.50	3.00
23 Holy Armor C :W:	2.00	4.00
24 Holy Strength C :W:	2.00	4.00
25 Island Sanctuary R :W:	20.00	40.00
26 Karma U :W:	5.00	10.00
27 Lance U :W:	4.00	8.00
28 Mesa Pegasus C :W:	3.00	6.00
29 Northern Paladin R :W:	50.00	100.00
30 Pearled Unicorn C :W:	2.00	4.00
31 Personal Incarnation R :W:	30.00	75.00
32 Purelace R :W:	20.00	40.00
33 Red Ward U :W:	4.00	8.00
34 Resurrection U :W:	6.00	12.00
35 Reverse Damage R :W:	50.00	100.00
36 Righteousness R :W:	12.50	25.00
37 Samite Healer C :W:	2.50	5.00
38 Savannah Lions R :W:	30.00	60.00
39 Serra Angel U :W:	30.00	75.00
40 Swords to Plowshares U :W:	20.00	40.00
41 Veteran Bodyguard R :W:	30.00	75.00
42 Wall of Swords U :W:	7.50	15.00
43 White Knight U :W:	6.00	12.00
44 White Ward U :W:	4.00	8.00
45 Wrath of God R :W:	100.00	200.00
46 Air Elemental U :B:	7.50	15.00
47 Ancestral Recall R :B:	500.00	1,000.00
48 Animate Artifact U :B:	5.00	10.00
49 Blue Elemental Blast C :B:	4.00	8.00
50 Braingeyser R :B:	60.00	125.00
51 Clone U :B:	7.50	15.00
52 Control Magic U :B:	15.00	30.00
53 Copy Artifact R :B:	60.00	125.00
54 Counterspell U :B:	10.00	20.00
55 Creature Bond C :B:	2.00	4.00
56 Drain Power R :B:	2.50	5.00
57 Feedback U :B:	5.00	10.00
58 Flight C :B:	1.50	3.00

59 Invisibility C :B:	1.50	3.00
60 Jump C :B:	1.50	3.00
61 Lifetap U :B:	5.00	10.00
62 Lord of Atlantis R :B:	75.00	150.00
63 Magical Hack R :B:	60.00	125.00
64 Mahamoti Djinn R :B:	50.00	100.00
65 Mana Short R :B:	50.00	100.00
66 Merfolk of the Pearl Trident C :B:	2.50	5.00
67 Phantasmal Forces U :B:	6.00	12.00
68 Phantasmal Terrain C :B:	2.50	5.00
69 Phantom Monster U :B:	6.00	12.00
70 Pirate Ship R :B:	25.00	50.00
71 Power Leak C :B:	4.00	8.00
72 Power Sink C :B:	4.00	8.00
73 Prodigal Sorcerer C :B:	3.00	6.00
74 Psionic Blast U :B:	12.50	25.00
75 Psychic Venom C :B:	4.00	8.00
76 Sea Serpent C :B:	2.50	5.00
77 Siren's Call U :B:	6.00	12.00
78 Sleight of Mind R :B:	30.00	75.00
79 Spell Blast C :B:	2.50	5.00
80 Stasis R :B:	75.00	150.00
81 Steal Artifact U :B:	4.00	8.00
82 Thoughtlace R :B:	30.00	75.00
83 Time Walk R :B:	1,000.00	2,000.00
84 Timetwister R :B:	1,250.00	2,500.00
85 Twiddle C :B:	3.00	6.00
86 Unsummon C :B:	2.50	5.00
87 Vesuvan Doppelganger R :B:	150.00	300.00
88 Volcanic Eruption R :B:	60.00	125.00
89 Wall of Air U :B:	6.00	12.00
90 Wall of Water U :B:	4.00	8.00
91 Water Elemental U :B:	4.00	8.00
92 Animate Dead U :K:	10.00	20.00
93 Bad Moon R :K:	75.00	150.00
94 Black Knight U :K:	5.00	12.00
95 Bog Wraith U :K:	5.00	10.00
96 Cursed Land U :K:	5.00	10.00
97 Dark Ritual C :K:	7.50	15.00
98 Deathgrip U :K:	7.50	15.00
99 Deathlace R :K:	20.00	40.00
100 Demonic Hordes R :K:	30.00	60.00
101 Demonic Tutor U :K:	50.00	100.00
102 Drain Life C :K:	2.00	4.00
103 Drudge Skeletons C :K:	3.00	6.00
104 Evil Presence U :K:	5.00	10.00
105 Fear C :K:	2.00	4.00
106 Frozen Shade C :K:	3.00	6.00
107 Gloom U :K:	4.00	8.00
108 Howl from Beyond C :K:	3.00	6.00
109 Hypnotic Specter U :K:	20.00	40.00
110 Lich R :K:	100.00	200.00
112 Mind Twist R :K:	75.00	150.00
113 Nether Shadow R :K:	60.00	125.00
114 Nettling Imp U :K:	12.50	25.00
115 Nightmare R :K:	25.00	50.00
116 Paralyze C :K:	4.00	8.00
117 Pestilence C :K:	2.50	5.00
118 Plague Rats C :K:	3.00	6.00
119 Raise Dead C :K:	3.00	6.00
120 Royal Assassin R :K:	60.00	125.00
121 Sacrifice U :K:	6.00	12.00
122 Scathe Zombies C :K:	3.00	6.00
123 Scavenging Ghoul U :K:	5.00	10.00
124 Sengir Vampire U :K:	10.00	20.00
125 Simulacrum U :K:	7.50	15.00
126 Sinkhole C :K:	5.00	10.00
127 Terror C :K:	2.00	4.00
128 Unholy Strength C :K:	4.00	8.00
129 Wall of Bone U :K:	7.50	15.00
130 Warp Artifact R :K:	30.00	75.00
131 Sol Ring C	10.00	20.00
132 Will-o'-the-Wisp R :K:	30.00	75.00
133 Word of Command R :K:	75.00	150.00
134 Zombie Master R :K:	100.00	200.00
135 Burrowing U :R:	10.00	20.00
136 Chaoslace R :R:	20.00	40.00
137 Disintegrate C :R:	2.00	4.00
138 Dragon Whelp U :R:	5.00	10.00
139 Dwarven Demolition Team U :R:	7.50	15.00
140 Dwarven Warriors C :R:	2.50	5.00
141 Earth Elemental U :R:	7.50	15.00
142 Earthquake R :R:	30.00	75.00
143 False Orders C :R:	3.00	6.00
144 Fire Elemental U :R:	7.50	15.00
145 Fireball C :R:	4.00	8.00
146 Firebreathing C :R:	2.00	4.00
147 Flashfires U :R:	4.00	8.00
148 Fork R :R:	100.00	200.00
149 Goblin Balloon Brigade U :R:	12.50	25.00
150 Goblin King R :R:	60.00	125.00
151 Granite Gargoyle R :R:	15.00	30.00
152 Gray Ogre C :R:	2.00	4.00
153 Hill Giant C :R:	2.00	4.00
154 Hurloon Minotaur C :R:	3.00	6.00
155 Ironclaw Orcs C :R:	1.50	3.00
156 Keldon Warlord U :R:	5.00	10.00
157 Lightning Bolt C :R:	10.00	20.00
158 Mana Flare R :R:	30.00	75.00
159 Manabarbs R :R:	200.00	400.00
160 Mons's Goblin Raiders C :R:	3.00	6.00
161 Orcish Artillery U :R:	4.00	8.00
162 Orcish Oriflamme U :R:	7.50	15.00
163 Power Surge R :R:	40.00	80.00
164 Raging River R :R:	75.00	150.00
165 Red Elemental Blast C :R:	4.00	8.00
166 Roc of Kher Ridges R :R:	12.50	25.00
167 Rock Hydra R :R:	50.00	100.00
168 Sedge Troll R :R:	60.00	125.00
169 Shatter C :R:	4.00	8.00
170 Shivan Dragon R :R:	150.00	300.00
171 Smoke R :R:	15.00	30.00
172 Stone Giant U :R:	4.00	8.00
173 Stone Rain C :R:	2.50	5.00
174 Tunnel U :R:	3.00	6.00
175 Two-Headed Giant of Foriys R :R:	60.00	125.00
176 Uthden Troll U :R:	4.00	8.00
177 Wall of Fire U :R:	6.00	12.00
178 Wall of Stone U :R:	5.00	10.00
179 Wheel of Fortune R :R:	200.00	400.00
180 Aspect of Wolf R :G:	25.00	50.00
181 Berserk U :G:	25.00	50.00
182 Birds of Paradise R :G:	150.00	300.00
183 Camouflage U :G:	10.00	20.00
184 Channel U :G:	5.00	10.00
185 Cockatrice R :G:	60.00	125.00
186 Craw Wurm C :G:	5.00	10.00
187 Elvish Archers R :G:	60.00	125.00
188 Fastbond R :G:	50.00	100.00
189 Fog C :G:	4.00	8.00
190 Force of Nature R :G:	60.00	125.00
191 Fungusaur R :G:	100.00	200.00
192 Gaea's Liege R :G:	60.00	125.00
193 Giant Growth C :G:	6.00	12.00
194 Giant Spider C :G:	2.00	4.00
195 Grizzly Bears C :G:	3.00	6.00
196 Hurricane U :G:	7.50	15.00
197 Ice Storm U :G:	12.50	25.00
198 Instill Energy U :G:	7.50	15.00
199 Ironroot Treefolk C :G:	2.00	4.00
200 Kudzu R :G:	30.00	75.00
201 Ley Druid U :G:	7.50	15.00
202 Lifeforce U :G:	10.00	20.00
203 Lifelace R :G:	50.00	100.00
204 Living Artifact R :G:	15.00	30.00
205 Living Lands R :G:	50.00	100.00
206 Llanowar Elves C	6.00	12.00
207 Lure U :G:	7.50	15.00
208 Natural Selection R :G:	60.00	125.00
209 Regeneration C :G:	3.00	6.00
210 Regrowth U :G:	10.00	20.00
211 Scryb Sprites C :G:	3.00	6.00
212 Shanodin Dryads C :G:	4.00	8.00
213 Stream of Life C :G:	2.50	5.00
214 Thicket Basilisk U :G:	6.00	12.00
215 Timber Wolves R :G:	30.00	60.00
216 Tranquility C :G:	3.00	6.00
217 Tsunami U :G:	6.00	12.00
218 Verduran Enchantress R :G:	25.00	50.00
219 Wall of Brambles U :G:	4.00	8.00
220 Wall of Ice U :G:	4.00	8.00
221 Wall of Wood C :G:	2.50	5.00
222 Wanderlust U :G:	5.00	10.00
223 War Mammoth C :G:	2.00	4.00
224 Web R :G:	7.50	15.00
225 Wild Growth C :G:	4.00	8.00
226 Ankh of Mishra R	75.00	150.00
227 Basalt Monolith U	6.00	12.00
228 Black Lotus R	5,000.00	10,000.00
229 Black Vise U	10.00	20.00
230 Celestial Prism U	5.00	10.00
231 Chaos Orb R	400.00	800.00
232 Clockwork Beast R	40.00	80.00
233 Conservator U	3.00	6.00
234 Copper Tablet U	15.00	30.00
235 Crystal Rod U	7.50	15.00
236 Cyclopean Tomb R	150.00	300.00
237 Dingus Egg R	50.00	100.00
238 Disrupting Scepter R	60.00	125.00
239 Forcefield R	100.00	200.00
240 Gauntlet of Might R	250.00	500.00
241 Glasses of Urza U	6.00	12.00
242 Helm of Chatzuk R	30.00	60.00
243 The Hive R	30.00	60.00
244 Howling Mine R	100.00	200.00
245 Icy Manipulator U	15.00	30.00
246 Illusionary Mask R	100.00	200.00
247 Iron Star U	5.00	10.00
248 Ivory Cup U	6.00	12.00
249 Jade Monolith R	25.00	50.00
250 Jade Statue U	6.00	12.00
251 Jayemdae Tome R	50.00	100.00
252 Juggernaut U	7.50	15.00
253 Kormus Bell R	30.00	60.00
254 Library of Leng U	12.50	25.00
255 Living Wall U	6.00	12.00
256 Mana Vault R	100.00	200.00
257 Meekstone R	50.00	100.00
258 Mox Emerald R	1,250.00	2,500.00
259 Mox Jet R	1,000.00	2,000.00
260 Mox Pearl R	750.00	1,500.00
261 Mox Ruby R	750.00	1,500.00
262 Mox Sapphire R	1,000.00	2,000.00
263 Nevinyrral's Disk R	50.00	100.00
264 Obsianus Golem U	4.00	8.00
265 Rod of Ruin U	6.00	12.00
266 Sol Ring C	20.00	40.00
267 Soul Net U	6.00	12.00
268 Sunglasses of Urza R	20.00	40.00
269 Throne of Bone U	3.00	6.00
270 Time Vault R	250.00	500.00
271 Winter Orb R	150.00	300.00
272 Wooden Sphere U	3.00	6.00
273 Badlands R	175.00	350.00
274 Bayou R	200.00	400.00
275 Plateau R	150.00	300.00
276 Savannah R	175.00	350.00
277 Scrubland R	200.00	400.00
278 Taiga R	250.00	500.00
279 Tropical Island R	300.00	600.00
280 Tundra R	175.00	350.00
281 Underground Sea R	300.00	600.00
282 Volcanic Island R	300.00	600.00
283 Plains C	2.50	5.00
284 Plains C	2.50	5.00
285 Plains C	2.50	5.00
286 Island C	2.50	5.00
287 Island C	2.50	5.00
288 Island C	2.50	5.00
289 Swamp C	2.50	5.00
290 Swamp C	2.50	5.00
291 Swamp C	2.50	5.00
292 Mountain C	2.50	5.00
293 Mountain C	2.50	5.00
294 Mountain C	2.50	5.00
295 Forest C	2.50	5.00
296 Forest C	2.50	5.00
297 Forest C	2.50	5.00
298 Animate Wall R :W:	250.00	500.00
299 Armageddon R :W:	100.00	200.00
300 Balance R :W:	150.00	300.00
301 Benalish Hero C :W:	30.00	75.00
302 Black Ward U :W:	20.00	40.00
303 Blaze of Glory R :W:	150.00	300.00
304 Blessing R :W:	150.00	300.00
305 Blue Ward U :W:	60.00	125.00
306 Castle U :W:	60.00	125.00
307 Circle of Protection: Black C :W:	30.00	75.00
308 Circle of Protection: Blue C :W:	25.00	50.00
309 Circle of Protection: Green C :W:	50.00	100.00
310 Circle of Protection: Red C :W:	300.00	600.00
311 Circle of Protection: White C :W:	60.00	125.00
313 Conversion U :W:	200.00	400.00
314 Death Ward C :W:	25.00	50.00
315 Disenchant C :W:	30.00	75.00
316 Farmstead R :W:	60.00	125.00
317 Green Ward U :W:	60.00	125.00
318 Guardian Angel C :W:	50.00	100.00
319 Healing Salve C :W:	30.00	60.00
320 Holy Armor C :W:	60.00	125.00
321 Holy Strength C :W:	100.00	200.00
322 Island Sanctuary R :W:	75.00	150.00
323 Karma U :W:	150.00	300.00
324 Lance U :W:	60.00	125.00
325 Mesa Pegasus C :W:	60.00	125.00
327 Pearled Unicorn C :W:	30.00	60.00
328 Personal Incarnation R :W:	600.00	1,200.00
329 Purelace R :W:	30.00	75.00
330 Red Ward U :W:	50.00	100.00
331 Resurrection U :W:	30.00	60.00
332 Reverse Damage R :W:	125.00	250.00
333 Righteousness R :W:	150.00	300.00
334 Samite Healer C :W:	40.00	80.00
335 Savannah Lions R :W:	400.00	800.00
336 Serra Angel U :W:	300.00	600.00
337 Swords to Plowshares U :W:	200.00	400.00
338 Veteran Bodyguard R :W:	150.00	300.00
340 White Knight U :W:	60.00	125.00
341 White Ward U :W:	125.00	250.00
343 Air Elemental U :B:	50.00	100.00
344 Ancestral Recall R :B:	750.00	1,500.00
345 Animate Artifact U :B:	75.00	150.00
346 Blue Elemental Blast C :B:	30.00	75.00
347 Braingeyser R :B:	1,250.00	2,500.00
348 Clone U :B:	50.00	100.00
349 Control Magic U :B:	75.00	150.00
350 Copy Artifact R :B:	300.00	600.00
351 Counterspell U :B:	150.00	300.00
352 Creature Bond C :B:	75.00	150.00
353 Drain Power R :B:	250.00	500.00
354 Feedback U :B:	40.00	80.00
355 Flight C :B:	25.00	50.00
356 Invisibility C :B:	50.00	100.00
357 Jump C :B:	20.00	40.00
358 Lifetap U :B:	30.00	75.00
359 Lord of Atlantis R :B:	300.00	600.00
360 Magical Hack R :B:	100.00	200.00
361 Mahamoti Djinn R :B:	100.00	200.00
363 Merfolk of the Pearl Trident C :B:	50.00	100.00
364 Phantasmal Forces U :B:	125.00	250.00
365 Phantasmal Terrain C :B:	30.00	60.00
366 Phantom Monster U :B:	100.00	200.00
367 Pirate Ship R :B:	60.00	125.00
368 Power Leak C :B:	12.50	25.00
369 Power Sink C :B:	60.00	125.00
370 Prodigal Sorcerer C :B:	25.00	50.00
371 Psionic Blast U :B:	100.00	200.00
372 Psychic Venom C :B:	40.00	80.00
373 Sea Serpent C :B:	30.00	75.00
374 Siren's Call U :B:	100.00	200.00
375 Sleight of Mind R :B:	125.00	250.00
376 Spell Blast C :B:	60.00	125.00
377 Stasis R :B:	600.00	1,200.00
378 Steal Artifact U :B:	75.00	150.00
379 Thoughtlace R :B:	125.00	250.00
380 Time Walk R :B:	1,500.00	3,000.00
381 Timetwister R :B:	5,000.00	10,000.00
382 Twiddle C :B:	25.00	50.00
383 Unsummon C :B:	50.00	100.00
384 Vesuvan Doppelganger R :B:	300.00	600.00
385 Volcanic Eruption R :B:	150.00	300.00
386 Wall of Air U :B:	50.00	100.00
387 Wall of Water U :B:	30.00	75.00
388 Water Elemental U :B:	60.00	125.00
389 Animate Dead U :K:	100.00	200.00
390 Bad Moon R :K:	300.00	600.00
391 Black Knight U :K:	60.00	125.00
392 Bog Wraith U :K:	75.00	150.00
394 Dark Ritual C :K:	200.00	400.00
395 Deathgrip U :K:	100.00	200.00
397 Demonic Hordes R :K:	300.00	600.00
398 Demonic Tutor U :K:	1,000.00	2,000.00
399 Drain Life C :K:	30.00	75.00
400 Drudge Skeletons C :K:	20.00	40.00
401 Evil Presence U :K:	30.00	60.00
402 Fear C :K:	60.00	125.00
403 Frozen Shade C :K:	60.00	125.00
404 Gloom U :K:	50.00	100.00
405 Howl from Beyond C :K:	60.00	125.00
406 Hypnotic Specter U :K:	125.00	250.00
407 Lich R :K:	400.00	800.00
409 Mind Twist R :K:	400.00	800.00
410 Nether Shadow R :K:	100.00	200.00
411 Nettling Imp U :K:	100.00	200.00
412 Nightmare R :K:	250.00	500.00
413 Paralyze C :K:	30.00	60.00
414 Pestilence C :K:	75.00	150.00
415 Plague Rats C :K:	75.00	150.00
417 Royal Assassin R :K:	250.00	500.00
418 Sacrifice U :K:	12.50	25.00
419 Scathe Zombies C :K:	25.00	50.00
420 Scavenging Ghoul U :K:	250.00	500.00
421 Sengir Vampire U :K:	600.00	1,200.00
422 Simulacrum U :K:	75.00	150.00
423 Sinkhole C :K:	125.00	250.00
424 Terror C :K:	100.00	200.00
425 Unholy Strength C :K:	60.00	125.00
426 Wall of Bone U :K:	20.00	40.00
427 Warp Artifact R :K:	150.00	300.00
428 Sol Ring U	125.00	250.00
429 Will-o'-the-Wisp R :K:	250.00	500.00
431 Zombie Master R :K:	300.00	750.00
432 Burrowing U :R:	20.00	40.00
433 Chaoslace R :R:	250.00	500.00
434 Disintegrate C :R:	25.00	50.00
435 Dragon Whelp U :R:	100.00	200.00
436 Dwarven Demolition Team U :R:	60.00	125.00
437 Dwarven Warriors C :R:	30.00	75.00
438 Earth Elemental U :R:	30.00	60.00
439 Earthquake R :R:	175.00	350.00
440 False Orders C :R:	60.00	125.00
441 Fire Elemental U :R:	50.00	100.00
442 Fireball C :R:	75.00	150.00
443 Firebreathing C :R:	50.00	100.00
444 Flashfires U :R:	30.00	60.00
445 Fork R :R:	250.00	500.00
446 Goblin Balloon Brigade U :R:	50.00	100.00
447 Goblin King R :R:	125.00	250.00
448 Granite Gargoyle R :R:	50.00	100.00
449 Gray Ogre C :R:	30.00	75.00
450 Hill Giant C :R:	30.00	60.00
452 Ironclaw Orcs C :R:	30.00	60.00
453 Keldon Warlord U :R:	100.00	200.00
454 Lightning Bolt C :R:	125.00	250.00
455 Mana Flare R :R:	150.00	300.00
456 Manabarbs R :R:	500.00	1,000.00
457 Mons's Goblin Raiders C :R:	125.00	250.00
458 Orcish Artillery U :R:	25.00	50.00
459 Orcish Oriflamme U :R:	400.00	800.00
460 Power Surge R :R:	60.00	125.00
461 Raging River R :R:	150.00	300.00
462 Red Elemental Blast C :R:	25.00	50.00
463 Roc of Kher Ridges R :R:	100.00	200.00
464 Rock Hydra R :R:	300.00	600.00
465 Sedge Troll R :R:	100.00	200.00
466 Shatter C :R:	75.00	150.00
468 Smoke R :R:	100.00	200.00
469 Stone Giant U :R:	25.00	50.00
470 Stone Rain C :R:	50.00	100.00
471 Tunnel U :R:	40.00	80.00
472 Two-Headed Giant of Foriys R :R:	150.00	300.00
473 Uthden Troll U :R:	30.00	75.00
474 Wall of Fire U :R:	60.00	125.00
475 Wall of Stone U :R:	60.00	125.00
476 Wheel of Fortune R :R:	600.00	1,200.00
477 Aspect of Wolf R :G:	60.00	125.00
478 Berserk U :G:	125.00	250.00
479 Birds of Paradise R :G:	1,000.00	2,000.00
480 Camouflage U :G:	60.00	125.00
481 Channel U :G:	125.00	250.00
483 Craw Wurm C :G:	100.00	200.00
484 Elvish Archers R :G:	75.00	150.00
485 Fastbond R :G:	150.00	300.00
486 Fog C :G:	75.00	150.00
487 Force of Nature R :G:	300.00	600.00
488 Fungusaur R :G:	75.00	150.00
490 Giant Growth C :G:	100.00	200.00
491 Giant Spider C :G:	25.00	50.00
492 Grizzly Bears C :G:	200.00	400.00
493 Hurricane U :G:	50.00	100.00
494 Ice Storm U :G:	150.00	300.00
495 Instill Energy U :G:	125.00	250.00
496 Ironroot Treefolk C :G:	20.00	40.00
498 Ley Druid U :G:	150.00	300.00
499 Lifeforce U :G:	100.00	200.00
500 Lifelace R :G:	75.00	150.00
501 Living Artifact R :G:	75.00	150.00
502 Living Lands R :G:	250.00	500.00
503 Llanowar Elves C :G:	150.00	300.00
504 Lure U :G:	100.00	200.00
506 Regeneration C :G:	25.00	50.00
507 Regrowth U :G:	30.00	60.00
508 Scryb Sprites C :G:	15.00	30.00
509 Shanodin Dryads C :G:	30.00	75.00
510 Stream of Life C :G:	30.00	60.00
511 Thicket Basilisk U :G:	25.00	50.00
512 Timber Wolves R :G:	150.00	300.00
513 Tranquility C :G:	125.00	250.00
514 Tsunami U :G:	60.00	125.00
515 Verduran Enchantress R :G:	100.00	200.00
517 Wall of Ice U :G:	60.00	125.00
518 Wall of Wood C :G:	30.00	60.00
519 Wanderlust U :G:	125.00	250.00
520 War Mammoth C :G:	60.00	125.00
521 Web R :G:	20.00	40.00
522 Wild Growth C :G:	125.00	250.00
523 Ankh of Mishra R	200.00	400.00
524 Basalt Monolith U	200.00	400.00
525 Black Lotus R	12,500.00	25,000.00
526 Black Vise U	125.00	250.00
527 Celestial Prism U	20.00	40.00
528 Chaos Orb R	1,500.00	3,000.00
529 Clockwork Beast R	75.00	150.00
530 Conservator U	40.00	80.00
531 Copper Tablet U	125.00	250.00
532 Crystal Rod U	30.00	75.00
533 Cyclopean Tomb R	500.00	1,000.00
534 Dingus Egg R	100.00	200.00
535 Disrupting Scepter R	75.00	150.00
536 Forcefield R	500.00	1,000.00
537 Gauntlet of Might R	500.00	1,000.00
538 Glasses of Urza U	125.00	250.00
539 Helm of Chatzuk R	100.00	200.00
540 The Hive R	75.00	150.00
541 Howling Mine R	600.00	1,200.00
542 Icy Manipulator U	100.00	200.00
543 Illusionary Mask R	250.00	500.00
544 Iron Star U	250.00	500.00
545 Ivory Cup U	40.00	80.00
546 Jade Monolith R	75.00	150.00
547 Jade Statue U	75.00	150.00
548 Jayemdae Tome R	100.00	200.00
549 Juggernaut U	125.00	250.00
550 Kormus Bell R	300.00	600.00
551 Library of Leng U	150.00	300.00
553 Mana Vault R	250.00	500.00
554 Meekstone R	175.00	350.00
556 Mox Jet R	1,250.00	2,500.00
560 Nevinyrral's Disk R	250.00	500.00
561 Obsianus Golem U	75.00	150.00
562 Rod of Ruin U	20.00	40.00
563 Sol Ring U	300.00	600.00
564 Soul Net U	30.00	60.00
565 Sunglasses of Urza R	150.00	300.00
566 Throne of Bone U	250.00	500.00
567 Time Vault R	600.00	1,200.00
568 Winter Orb R	500.00	1,000.00
569 Wooden Sphere U	50.00	100.00
570 Badlands R	500.00	1,000.00
571 Bayou R	500.00	1,000.00
572 Plateau R	400.00	800.00
573 Savannah R	300.00	600.00
574 Scrubland R	750.00	1,500.00
575 Taiga R	600.00	1,200.00
576 Tropical Island R	450.00	900.00

577 Tundra R 750.00 1,500.00
578 Underground Sea R 1,000.00 2,000.00
579 Volcanic Island R 1,000.00 2,000.00
580 Plains C 7.50 15.00
581 Plains C 7.50 15.00
582 Plains C 7.50 15.00
583 Island C 10.00 20.00
584 Island C 10.00 20.00
585 Island C 10.00 20.00
586 Swamp C 7.50 15.00
587 Swamp C 7.50 15.00
588 Swamp C 7.50 15.00
589 Mountain C 5.00 10.00
590 Mountain C 5.00 10.00
591 Mountain C 5.00 10.00
592 Forest C 7.50 15.00
593 Forest C 7.50 15.00
594 Forest C 7.50 15.00

2022 Magic The Gathering Commander Collection Black

1 Liliana, Heretical Healer
Liliana, Defiant Necromancer M :K: 2.00 4.00
2 Ghoulcaller Gisa M :K: 2.00 4.00
3 Ophiomancer R :K: 4.00 8.00
4 Phyrexian Arena R :K: 2.00 4.00
5 Reanimate R :K: 7.50 15.00
6 Toxic Deluge R :K: 7.50 15.00
7 Sol Ring R 3.00 6.00
8 Command Tower R 1.50 3.00
9 Snake/Zombie C .75 1.50

2022 Magic The Gathering Commander Legends Dungeons and Dragons Battle for Baldur's Gate

1 Faceless One S .07 .10
2 Abdel Adrian, Gorion's Ward U :W: .07 .15
3 Ancient Gold Dragon M :W: 7.50 15.00
4 Archivist of Oghma R :W: 4.00 8.00
5 Ascend from Avernus R :W: .30 .75
6 Astral Confrontation C :W: .07 .10
7 Bane's Invoker C :W: .07 .10
8 Banishment U :W: .07 .10
9 Battle Angels of Tyr M :W: 10.00 20.00
10 Beckoning Will-o'-Wisp U :W: .07 .10
11 Blessed Hippogriff/Tyr's Blessing C :W: .07 .10
12 Contraband Livestock U :W: .07 .15
13 Crystal Dragon/Rob the Hoard U :W: .07 .15
14 Cut a Deal U :W: .10 .20
15 Dawnbringer Cleric C :W: .07 .15
16 Ellyn Harbreeze, Busybody U :W: .07 .10
17 Far Traveler U :W: .07 .15
18 Flaming Fist C :W: .07 .10
19 Flaming Fist Officer C :W: .07 .10
20 Githzerai Monk U :W: .07 .10
21 Goliath Paladin C :W: .12 .25
22 Greatsword of Tyr C :W: .07 .15
23 Guardian Naga/Banishing Coils C :W: .07 .10
24 Guiding Bolt C :W: .07 .10
25 Hammers of Moradin U :W: .07 .15
26 Horn of Valhalla/Ysgard's Call R :W: .25 .50
27 Icewind Stalwart C :W: .07 .10
28 Inspiring Leader U :W: .12 .25
29 Lae'zel, Vlaakith's Champion R :W: .75 1.50
30 Lae'zel's Acrobatics R :W: .40 .80
31 Legion Loyalty M :W: 2.50 5.00
32 Lulu, Loyal Hollyphant U :W: .07 .10
33 Martial Impetus C :W: .07 .10
34 Minimus Containment C :W: .07 .10
35 Noble Heritage R :W: .07 .15
36 Pegasus Guardian/Rescue the Foal C :W: .07 .15
37 Rasaad yn Bashir U :W: .07 .10
38 Recruitment Drive C :W: .07 .10
39 Rescuer Chwinga U :W: .07 .10
40 Roving Harper C :W: .07 .10
41 Scouting Hawk C :W: .07 .10
42 Sculpted Sunburst R :W: .07 .15
43 Slaughter the Strong U :W: .12 .25
44 Steadfast Unicorn C :W: .07 .10
45 Stoneskin U :W: .12 .25
46 Tabaxi Toucaneers C :W: .07 .10
47 Undercellar Sweep U :W: .07 .15
48 Veteran Soldier U :W: .07 .10
49 White Plume Adventurer R :W: .75 1.50
50 Windshaper Planetar R :W: .07 .15
51 Wyrm's Crossing Patrol C :W: .07 .15
52 Your Temple Is Under Attack C :W: .17 .35
53 You're Confronted by Robbers C :W: .07 .10
54 Aarakocra Sneak C :B: .07 .10
55 Alora, Merry Thief U :B: .07 .10
56 Ancient Silver Dragon M :B: 12.50 25.00
57 Bane's Contingency U :B: .07 .15
58 Blur C :B: .12 .25
59 Candlekeep Inspiration U :B: .07 .15
60 Candlekeep Sage C :B: .07 .10
61 Cone of Cold U :B: .07 .15
62 Contact Other Plane C :B: .07 .10
63 Displacer Kitten R :B: 7.50 15.00
64 Draconic Lore C :B: .07 .10
65 Dragonborn Looter C :B: .07 .10
66 Dream Fracture C :B: .07 .10
67 Dungeon Delver U :B: .07 .10
68 Elminster's Simulacrum M :B: .75 1.50
69 Feywild Caretaker U :B: .07 .15
70 Feywild Visitor U :B: .07 .10
71 Font of Magic M :B: .20 .40
72 Gale, Waterdeep Prodigy R :B: .12 .25
73 Gale's Redirection R :B: .12 .25
74 Goggles of Night C :B: .07 .10
75 Gray Harbor Merfolk C :B: .07 .10
76 Illithid Harvester/Plant Tadpoles R :B: .12 .25
77 Imoen, Mystic Trickster U :B: .07 .15
78 Irenicus's Vile Duplication U :B: 1.75 3.50
79 Juvenile Mist Dragon U :B: .07 .15
80 Kenku Artificer C :B: .12 .25
81 Kindred Discovery R :B: 7.50 15.00
82 Lapis Orb of Dragonkind C :B: .07 .15
83 Modify Memory U :B: .07 .15
84 Moonshae Pixie/Pixie Dust U :B: .07 .10
85 Mystery Key U :B: .07 .10
86 Nimbleclaw Adept C :B: .07 .15
87 Oceanus Dragon C :B: .07 .10
88 Pseudodragon Familiar C :B: .07 .10
89 Psychic Impetus C :B: .07 .10
90 Renari, Merchant of Marvels U :B: .07 .15
91 Robe of the Archmagi R :B: .17 .35
92 Run Away Together C :B: .07 .10
93 Sailors' Bane U :B: .07 .15
94 Sapphire Dragon/Psionic Pulse U :B: .07 .10
95 Sea Hag/Aquatic Ingress C :B: .07 .10
96 Shameless Charlatan R :B: .07 .10
97 Stunning Strike C :B: .07 .10
98 Sword Coast Sailor U :B: .07 .10
99 Sword Coast Serpent/Capsizing Wave C :B: .12 .25
100 Tomb of Horrors Adventurer R :B: .15 .30
101 Tymora's Invoker C :B: .07 .10
102 Vhal, Candlekeep Researcher U :B: .07 .10
103 Volo, Itinerant Scholar M :B: .20 .40
104 Winter Eladrin C :B: .07 .10
105 Wizards of Thay R :B: .75 1.50
106 Young Blue Dragon/Sand Augury C :B: .07 .15
107 Agent of the Iron Throne U :K: .17 .35
108 Agent of the Shadow Thieves U :K: .07 .15
109 Altar of Bhaal/Bone Offering R :K: .12 .25
110 Ambition's Cost U :K: .07 .15
111 Ancient Brass Dragon M :K: 7.50 15.00
112 Armor of Shadows C :K: .07 .15
113 Arms of Hadar C :K: .07 .15
114 Astarion's Thirst R :K: .17 .35
115 Atrocious Experiment C :K: .07 .15
116 Blood Money M :K: 3.00 6.00
117 Bonecaller Cleric U :K: .07 .15
118 Call to the Void R :K: .07 .10
119 Cast Down U :K: .12 .25
120 Chain Devil C :K: .07 .10
121 Cloudkill U :K: .07 .10
122 Criminal Past U :K: .07 .10
123 Cultist of the Absolute R :K: .07 .15
124 Deadly Dispute C :K: 1.00 2.00
125 Elder Brain R :K: .30 .75
126 Eldritch Pact R :K: .12 .25
127 Ghastly Death Tyrant C :K: .07 .10
128 Ghost Lantern/Bind Spirit U :K: .12 .25
129 Gray Slaad/Entropic Decay C :K: .07 .10
130 Guildsworn Prowler C :K: .07 .10
131 Hezrou/Demonic Stench C :K: .07 .10
132 Intellect Devourer R :K: .12 .25
133 Mold Folk C :K: .07 .10
134 Murder C :K: .07 .10
135 Myrkul's Edict C :K: .07 .10
136 Myrkul's Invoker C :K: .07 .10
137 Nefarious Imp C :K: .07 .10
138 Nothic U :K: .07 .10
139 Pact Weapon M :K: .40 .80
140 Parasitic Impetus C :K: .07 .10
141 Passageway Seer U :K: .07 .15
142 Ravenloft Adventurer R :K: .15 .30
143 Safana, Calimport Cutthroat U :K: .07 .15
144 Sarevok, Deathbringer U :K: .07 .15
145 Scion of Halaster C :K: .07 .10
146 Shadowheart, Dark Justiciar R :K: .12 .25
147 Sigil of Myrkul U :K: .07 .10
148 Sivriss, Nightmare Speaker U :K: .07 .15
149 Skullport Merchant U :K: .07 .15
150 Stirge C :K: .07 .10
151 Summon Undead C :K: .07 .10
152 Thieves' Tools C :K: .07 .10
153 Topaz Dragon/Entropic Cloud U :K: .07 .15
154 Underdark Explorer C :K: .07 .10
155 Vicious Battlerager C :K: .07 .10
156 Viconia, Drow Apostate U :K: .07 .10
157 Vrock U :K: .07 .15
158 Zhentarim Bandit C :K: .07 .10
159 Amber Gristle O'Maul U :R: .07 .10
160 Amethyst Dragon/Explosive Crystal U :R: .07 .15
161 Ancient Copper Dragon M :R: 30.00 75.00
162 Balor M :R: 2.50 5.00
163 Bhaal's Invoker C :R: .07 .10
164 Bloodboil Sorcerer U :R: .07 .15
165 Breath Weapon C :R: .12 .25
166 Carnelian Orb of Dragonkind C :R: .12 .25
167 Caves of Chaos Adventurer R :R: .60 1.25
168 Coronation of Chaos C :R: .07 .15
169 Descent into Avernus R :R: 1.00 2.00
170 Dragon Cultist U :R: .07 .10
171 Earth Tremor C :R: .07 .10
172 Elturel Survivors R :R: .15 .30
173 Fang Dragon/Forktail Sweep C :R: .07 .15
174 Firbolg Flutist R :R: .12 .25
175 Fireball U :R: .07 .10
176 Ganax, Astral Hunter U :R: .12 .25
177 Genasi Enforcers C :R: .07 .10
178 Gnoll War Band U :R: .07 .10
179 Guild Artisan U :R: .07 .15
180 Gut, True Soul Zealot U :R: .07 .15
181 Hoarding Ogre C :R: .07 .10
182 Ingenious Artillerist C :R: .12 .25
183 Inspired Tinkering U :R: .17 .35
184 Insufferable Balladeer C :R: .07 .10
185 Javelin of Lightning C :R: .07 .10
186 Karlach, Fury of Avernus M :R: 3.00 6.00
187 Lightning Bolt C :R: .30 .75
188 Livaan, Cultist of Tiamat U :R: .07 .15
189 Nemesis Phoenix U :R: .07 .10
190 Pack Attack C :R: .07 .10
191 Patron of the Arts C :R: .12 .25
192 Popular Entertainer R :R: .07 .15
193 Reckless Barbarian C :R: .07 .15
194 Shiny Impetus C :R: .07 .10
195 Stirring Bard C :R: .07 .15
196 Storm King's Thunder M :R: 1.00 2.00
197 Street Urchin U :R: .07 .10
198 Swashbuckler Extraordinaire U :R: .12 .25
199 Taunting Kobold U :R: .12 .25
200 Tavern Brawler C :R: .07 .10
201 Thunderwave U :R: .07 .10
202 Tiamat's Fanatics C :R: .07 .10
203 Two-Handed Axe/Sweeping Cleave U :R: .25 .50
204 Wand of Wonder R :R: .30 .75
205 Warehouse Thief C :R: .07 .10
206 Wild Magic Surge U :R: 1.00 2.00
207 Wrathful Red Dragon R :R: 1.25 2.50
208 Wyll, Blade of Frontiers R :R: .12 .25
209 Wyll's Reversal R :R: .17 .35
210 Young Red Dragon/Bathe in Gold C :R: .07 .15
211 You've Been Caught Stealing C :R: .07 .10
212 Acolyte of Bahamut U :G: .07 .15
213 Ambitious Dragonborn C :G: .07 .10
214 Ancient Bronze Dragon M :G: 6.00 12.00
215 Avenging Hunter C :G: .20 .40
216 Band Together C :G: .07 .10
217 Barroom Brawl R :G: .07 .15
218 Bramble Sovereign M :G: 1.25 2.50
219 Carefree Swinemaster C :G: .07 .10
220 Circle of the Land Druid C :G: .07 .10
221 Cloakwood Hermit U :G: .07 .15
222 Cloakwood Swarmkeeper C :G: .07 .10
223 Colossal Badger/Dig Deep C :G: .07 .10
224 Draconic Muralists U :G: .12 .25
225 Dread Linnorm/Scale Deflection C :G: .07 .15
226 Druid of the Emerald Grove C :G: .07 .10
227 Druidic Ritual C :G: .07 .15
228 Earthquake Dragon R :G: 1.00 2.00
229 Emerald Dragon/Dissonant Wave U :G: .07 .15
230 Erinis, Gloom Stalker U :G: .12 .25
231 Ettercap/Web Shot C :G: .07 .10
232 Explore the Underdark U :G: .12 .25
233 Giant Ankheg U :G: .12 .25
234 Halsin, Emerald Archdruid U :G: .07 .10
235 Hardy Outlander U :G: .07 .10
236 Jade Orb of Dragonkind C :G: .07 .15
237 Jaheira, Friend of the Forest R :G: 4.00 8.00
238 Jaheira's Respite R :G: .25 .50
239 Lurking Green Dragon C :G: .07 .10
240 Majestic Genesis M :G: 1.25 2.50
241 Master Chef C :G: .07 .15
242 Monster Manual/Zoological Study R :G: 1.50 3.00
243 Myconid Spore Tender C :G: .07 .10
244 Nature's Lore C :G: 1.00 2.00
245 Overwhelming Encounter U :G: .07 .15
246 Owlbear Cub R :G: .12 .25
247 Owlbear Shepherd U :G: .07 .10
248 Poison the Blade C :G: .07 .10
249 Predatory Impetus C :G: .07 .10
250 Raised by Giants R :G: .07 .15
251 Saddle of the Cavalier U :G: .07 .10
252 Scaled Nurturer C :G: .10 .20
253 Sharpshooter Elf U :G: .07 .10
254 Silvanus's Invoker C :G: .07 .10
255 Skanos Dragonheart U :G: .07 .15
256 Skullwinder U :G: .07 .15
257 Split the Spoils U :G: .07 .10
258 Traverse the Outlands R :G: 1.25 2.50
259 Undercellar Myconid C :G: .07 .15
260 Undermountain Adventurer R :G: .20 .40
261 Wilson, Refined Grizzly U :G: .07 .10
262 You Look Upon the Tarrasque U :G: .12 .25
263 You Meet in a Tavern C :G: .07 .10
264 Alaundo the Seer R :G:/:B: .07 .10
265 Astarion, the Decadent R :W:/:K: .07 .15
266 Baba Lysaga, Night Witch R :K:/:G: .07 .15
267 Bane, Lord of Darkness R :W:/:B:/:K: .07 .15
268 Bhaal, Lord of Murder R :K:/:R:/:G: .07 .10
269 Cadira, Caller of the Small U :G:/:W: .07 .15
270 Commander Liara Portyr U :R:/:W: .07 .15
271 The Council of Four R :W:/:B: .25 .50
272 Duke Ulder Ravengard R :R:/:W: .12 .25
273 Dynaheir, Invoker Adept R :B:/:R:/:W: .07 .15
274 Elminster M :W:/:B: .50 1.00
275 Gluntch, the Bestower R :G:/:W: .12 .25
276 Gorion, Wise Mentor R :G:/:W:/:B: .07 .15
277 Jan Jansen, Chaos Crafter R :R:/:W:/:K: .07 .15
278 Jon Irenicus, Shattered One R :B:/:K: .12 .25
279 Kagha, Shadow Archdruid U :K:/:G: .12 .25
280 Korlessa, Scale Singer U :G:/:B: .12 .25
281 Lozhan, Dragons' Legacy U :B:/:R: .07 .15
282 Mahadi, Emporium Master U :K:/:R: .10 .20
283 Mazzy, Truesword Paladin R :R:/:G:/:W: .07 .10
284 Miirym, Sentinel Wyrm R :G:/:B:/:R: 1.00 2.00
285 Minsc & Boo, Timeless Heroes M :R:/:G: 7.50 15.00
286 Minthara, Merciless Soul U :W:/:K: .07 .15
287 Myrkul, Lord of Bones R :W:/:K:/:G: .12 .25
288 Neera, Wild Mage R :B:/:R: .07 .15
289 Nine-Fingers Keene R :K:/:G:/:B: .07 .15
290 Oji, the Exquisite Blade U :W:/:B: .07 .15
291 Raggadragga, Goreguts Boss R :R:/:G: .07 .15
292 Raphael, Fiendish Savior R :K:/:R: .12 .25
293 Rilsa Rael, Kingpin U :B:/:K: .07 .10
294 Tasha, the Witch Queen M :B:/:K: 1.25 2.50
295 Thrakkus the Butcher U :R:/:G: .12 .25
296 Zevlor, Elturel Exile R :B:/:K:/:R: .07 .15
297 Arcane Encyclopedia U .07 .15
298 Arcane Signet U .50 1.00
299 Bag of Holding U .07 .10
300 Basilisk Collar R 1.25 2.50
301 Blade of Selves R 2.00 4.00
302 Bronze Walrus C .07 .10
303 Burnished Hart U .07 .15
304 Campfire U .12 .25
305 Charcoal Diamond C .12 .25
306 Chardalyn Dragon C .07 .10
307 Cloak of the Bat C .07 .15
308 Clockwork Fox C .07 .10
309 Decanter of Endless Water C 1.25 2.50
310 Dire Mimic C .07 .10
311 Drillworks Mole U .07 .15
312 Dungeoneer's Pack U .07 .10
313 Fire Diamond C .07 .15
314 Fraying Line R .07 .15
315 Gate Colossus U .07 .10
316 Geode Golem U .12 .25
317 Iron Mastiff U .07 .10
318 Lantern of Revealing C .07 .10
319 Manifold Key U .15 .30
320 Marble Diamond C .07 .15
321 Marching Duodrone C .07 .10
322 Marut C .07 .10
323 Meteor Golem U .07 .15
324 Mighty Servant of Leuk-o R .12 .25
325 Mind Stone U .15 .30
326 Mirror of Life Trapping R .12 .25
327 Moss Diamond C .07 .15
328 Nautiloid Ship M 1.50 3.00
329 Navigation Orb C .07 .15
330 Nimblewright Schematic C .07 .10
331 Noble's Purse U .07 .15
332 Patriar's Seal U 1.00 2.00
333 Pilgrim's Eye C .07 .10
334 Prized Statue C .12 .25
335 Prophetic Prism C .07 .10
336 Rug of Smothering U .12 .25
337 Sky Diamond C .07 .15
338 Stonespeaker Crystal U .17 .35
339 Swiftfoot Boots U .75 1.50
340 Trailblazer's Torch C .07 .10
341 Treasure Keeper U .07 .10
342 Universal Solvent C .07 .10
343 Vexing Puzzlebox M 1.25 2.50
344 Wayfarer's Bauble C .17 .35
345 Baldur's Gate R .75 1.50
346 Basilisk Gate C .20 .40
347 Black Dragon Gate C .20 .40
348 Bountiful Promenade R 4.00 8.00
349 Citadel Gate C .30 .60
350 Cliffgate C .12 .25
351 Command Tower C .12 .25
352 Evolving Wilds C .07 .15
353 Gond Gate U .12 .25
354 Heap Gate C .12 .25
355 Luxury Suite R 4.00 8.00
356 Manor Gate C .15 .30
357 Morphic Pool R 7.50 15.00
358 Reflecting Pool R 3.00 6.00
359 Sea Gate C .20 .40
360 Sea of Clouds R 3.00 6.00
361 Spire Garden R 3.00 6.00
362 Elminster M :W:/:B: .75 1.50
363 Minsc & Boo, Timeless Heroes M :R:/:G: 7.50 15.00
364 Tasha, the Witch Queen M :B:/:K: 1.50 3.00
365 Ancient Gold Dragon M :W: 7.50 15.00
366 Ancient Silver Dragon M :B: 17.50 35.00
367 Ancient Brass Dragon M :K: 12.50 25.00
368 Ancient Copper Dragon M :R: 40.00 80.00
369 Ancient Bronze Dragon M :G: 7.50 15.00
370 Battle Angels of Tyr M :W: 7.50 15.00
371 Legion Loyalty M :W: 1.50 3.00
372 Bramble Sovereign M :G: 1.25 2.50
373 Nautiloid Ship M 1.50 3.00
374 Vexing Puzzlebox M 1.25 2.50
375 Abdel Adrian, Gorion's Ward U :W: .07 .10
376 Ancient Gold Dragon M :W: 6.00 12.00
377 Ellyn Harbreeze, Busybody U :W: .07 .10
378 Lae'zel, Vlaakith's Champion R :W: .20 .40
379 Lulu, Loyal Hollyphant U :W: .07 .10
380 Rasaad yn Bashir U :W: .07 .15
381 Alora, Merry Thief U :B: .07 .15
382 Ancient Silver Dragon M :B: 10.00 20.00
383 Gale, Waterdeep Prodigy R :B: .07 .15
384 Goggles of Night C :B: .07 .10
385 Imoen, Mystic Trickster U :B: .07 .10
386 Renari, Merchant of Marvels U :B: .07 .15
387 Vhal, Candlekeep Researcher U :B: .07 .10
388 Volo, Itinerant Scholar M :B: .12 .25
389 Ancient Brass Dragon M :K: 7.50 15.00
390 Safana, Calimport Cutthroat U :K: .07 .10
391 Sarevok, Deathbringer U :K: .07 .10
392 Shadowheart, Dark Justiciar R :K: .12 .25
393 Sivriss, Nightmare Speaker U :K: .07 .15
394 Viconia, Drow Apostate U :K: .07 .10
395 Amber Gristle O'Maul U :R: .07 .10
396 Ancient Copper Dragon M :R: 30.00 60.00
397 Fireball U :R: .07 .10
398 Ganax, Astral Hunter U :R: .07 .15
399 Gut, True Soul Zealot U :R: .07 .10
400 Karlach, Fury of Avernus M :R: 1.75 3.50
401 Lightning Bolt C :R: .17 .35
402 Livaan, Cultist of Tiamat U :R: .07 .10
403 Nemesis Phoenix U :R: .07 .10
404 Taunting Kobold U :R: .07 .10
405 Wyll, Blade of Frontiers R :R: .07 .15
406 Ancient Bronze Dragon M :G: 4.00 8.00
407 Erinis, Gloom Stalker U :G: .07 .10
408 Halsin, Emerald Archdruid U :G: .07 .15
409 Jaheira, Friend of the Forest R :G: 1.25 2.50
410 Skanos Dragonheart U :G: .07 .15
411 Wilson, Refined Grizzly U :G: .07 .15
412 Alaundo the Seer R :G:/:B: .07 .10
413 Astarion, the Decadent R :W:/:K: .07 .15
414 Baba Lysaga, Night Witch R :K:/:G: .07 .15
415 Bane, Lord of Darkness R :W:/:B:/:K: .07 .15
416 Bhaal, Lord of Murder R :K:/:R:/:G: .12 .25
417 Cadira, Caller of the Small U :G:/:W: .07 .15
418 Commander Liara Portyr U :R:/:W: .07 .10
419 The Council of Four R :W:/:B: .12 .25
420 Duke Ulder Ravengard R :R:/:W: .07 .15
421 Dynaheir, Invoker Adept R :B:/:R:/:W: .07 .15
422 Gluntch, the Bestower R :G:/:W: .07 .15
423 Gorion, Wise Mentor R :G:/:W:/:B: .07 .10
424 Jan Jansen, Chaos Crafter R :R:/:W:/:K: .07 .15
425 Jon Irenicus, Shattered One R :B:/:K: .07 .10
426 Kagha, Shadow Archdruid U :K:/:G: .07 .10
427 Korlessa, Scale Singer U :G:/:B: .07 .15
428 Lozhan, Dragons' Legacy U :B:/:R: .07 .10
429 Mahadi, Emporium Master U :K:/:R: .07 .15
430 Mazzy, Truesword Paladin R :R:/:G:/:W: .07 .10
431 Miirym, Sentinel Wyrm R :G:/:B:/:R: .20 .40
432 Minthara, Merciless Soul U :W:/:K: .07 .10
433 Myrkul, Lord of Bones R :W:/:K:/:G: .12 .25
434 Neera, Wild Mage R :B:/:R: .07 .10
435 Nine-Fingers Keene R :K:/:G:/:B: .07 .15
436 Oji, the Exquisite Blade U :W:/:B: .07 .15
437 Raggadragga, Goreguts Boss R :R:/:G: .07 .10
438 Raphael, Fiendish Savior R :K:/:R: .07 .15
439 Rilsa Rael, Kingpin U :B:/:K: .07 .15
440 Thrakkus the Butcher U :R:/:G: .07 .15
441 Zevlor, Elturel Exile R :B:/:K:/:R: .07 .15
442 Charcoal Diamond C .07 .10
443 Cloak of the Bat C .07 .10
444 Decanter of Endless Water C .15 .30
445 Fire Diamond C .07 .10
446 Marble Diamond C .07 .10
447 Marching Duodrone C .07 .10
448 Moss Diamond C .07 .10
449 Sky Diamond C .07 .10
450 Stonespeaker Crystal U .07 .10
451 Plains C .07 .10
452 Plains C .07 .10
453 Plains C .07 .10
454 Plains C .07 .10
455 Island C .07 .10

456 Island C	.07	.10
457 Island C	.07	.10
458 Island C	.07	.10
459 Swamp C	.07	.10
460 Swamp C	.07	.10
461 Swamp C	.07	.10
462 Swamp C	.07	.10
463 Mountain C	.07	.10
464 Mountain C	.07	.10
465 Mountain C	.07	.10
466 Mountain C	.07	.10
467 Forest C	.07	.10
468 Forest C	.07	.10
469 Forest C	.07	.10
470 Forest C	.07	.10
471 Abdel Adrian, Gorion's Ward U :W:	.17	.35
472 Ellyn Harbreeze, Busybody U :W:	.07	.15
473 Far Traveler U :W:	.12	.25
474 Flaming Fist C :W:	.07	.10
475 Inspiring Leader U :W:	1.00	2.00
476 Lae'zel, Vlaakith's Champion R :W:	.25	.50
477 Lulu, Loyal Hollyphant U :W:	.07	.15
478 Noble Heritage R :W:	.12	.25
479 Rasaad yn Bashir U :W:	.07	.15
480 Veteran Soldier U :W:	.07	.15
481 Alora, Merry Thief U :B:	.10	.20
482 Candlekeep Sage C :B:	.07	.15
483 Dungeon Delver U :B:	.12	.25
484 Feywild Visitor U :B:	.07	.15
485 Gale, Waterdeep Prodigy R :B:	.12	.25
486 Imoen, Mystic Trickster U :B:	.07	.15
487 Renari, Merchant of Marvels U :B:	.10	.20
488 Shameless Charlatan R :B:	.07	.15
489 Sword Coast Sailor U :B:	.12	.25
490 Vhal, Candlekeep Researcher U :B:	.07	.15
491 Volo, Itinerant Scholar M :B:	.17	.35
492 Agent of the Iron Throne U :K:	1.25	2.50
493 Agent of the Shadow Thieves U :K:	.12	.25
494 Criminal Past U :K:	.12	.25
495 Cultist of the Absolute R :K:	.12	.25
496 Safana, Calimport Cutthroat U :K:	.07	.15
497 Sarevok, Deathbringer U :K:	.07	.10
498 Scion of Halaster C :K:	.07	.10
499 Shadowheart, Dark Justiciar R :K:	.12	.25
500 Sivriss, Nightmare Speaker U :K:	.07	.15
501 Viconia, Drow Apostate U :K:	.07	.15
502 Amber Gristle O'Maul U :R:	.07	.10
503 Dragon Cultist U :R:	.12	.25
504 Ganax, Astral Hunter U :R:	.25	.50
505 Guild Artisan U :R:	.15	.30
506 Gut, True Soul Zealot U :R:	.12	.25
507 Karlach, Fury of Avernus M :R:	1.75	3.50
508 Livaan, Cultist of Tiamat U :R:	.12	.25
509 Popular Entertainer R :R:	.07	.15
510 Street Urchin U :R:	.10	.20
511 Tavern Brawler C :R:	.07	.15
512 Wyll, Blade of Frontiers R :R:	.07	.15
513 Acolyte of Bahamut U :G:	.10	.20
514 Cloakwood Hermit U :G:	.12	.25
515 Erinis, Gloom Stalker U :G:	.15	.30
516 Halsin, Emerald Archdruid U :G:	.07	.15
517 Hardy Outlander U :G:	.12	.25
518 Jaheira, Friend of the Forest R :G:	1.25	2.50
519 Master Chef C :G:	.07	.15
520 Raised by Giants R :G:	.12	.25
521 Skanos Dragonheart U :G:	.07	.15
522 Wilson, Refined Grizzly U :G:	.15	.30
523 Alaundo the Seer R :G:/:B:	.07	.10
524 Astarion, the Decadent R :W:/:K:	.12	.25
525 Baba Lysaga, Night Witch R :K:/:G:	.07	.15
526 Bane, Lord of Darkness R :W:/:B:/:K:	.07	.15
527 Bhaal, Lord of Murder R :K:/:R:/:G:	.07	.15
528 Cadira, Caller of the Small U :G:/:W:	.12	.25
529 Commander Liara Portyr U :R:/:W:	.12	.25
530 The Council of Four R :W:/:B:	.15	.30
531 Duke Ulder Ravengard R :R:/:W:	.07	.15
532 Dynaheir, Invoker Adept R :B:/:R:/:W:	.07	.15
533 Gluntch, the Bestower R :G:/:W:	.12	.25
534 Gorion, Wise Mentor R :G:/:W:/:B:	.07	.15
535 Jan Jansen, Chaos Crafter R :R:/:W:/:K:	.12	.25
536 Jon Irenicus, Shattered One R :B:/:K:	.10	.20
537 Kagha, Shadow Archdruid U :K:/:G:	.10	.20
538 Korlessa, Scale Singer U :G:/:B:	.12	.25
539 Lozhan, Dragons' Legacy U :B:/:R:	.12	.25
540 Mahadi, Emporium Master U :K:/:R:	.60	1.25
541 Mazzy, Truesword Paladin R :R:/:G:/:W:	.07	.15
542 Miirym, Sentinel Wyrm R :G:/:B:/:R:	.75	1.50
543 Minthara, Merciless Soul U :W:/:K:	.12	.25
544 Myrkul, Lord of Bones R :W:/:K:/:G:	.12	.25
545 Neera, Wild Mage R :B:/:R:	.12	.25
546 Nine-Fingers Keene R :K:/:G:/:B:	.07	.15
547 Oji, the Exquisite Blade U :W:/:B:	.12	.25
548 Raggadragga, Goreguts Boss R :R:/:G:	.12	.25
549 Raphael, Fiendish Savior R :K:/:R:	.12	.25
550 Rilsa Rael, Kingpin U :B:/:K:	.12	.25
551 Thrakkus the Butcher U :R:/:G:	.12	.25
552 Zevlor, Elturel Exile R :B:/:K:/:R:	.07	.10
553 Archivist of Oghma R :W:	4.00	8.00
554 Ascend from Avernus R :W:	.75	1.50
555 Horn of Valhalla/Ysgard's Call R :W:	.40	.80
556 Lae'zel's Acrobatics R :W:	.30	.75
557 Sculpted Sunburst R :W:	.07	.15
558 White Plume Adventurer R :W:	.75	1.50
559 Windshaper Planetar R :W:	.12	.25
560 Displacer Kitten R :B:	7.50	15.00
561 Elminster's Simulacrum M :B:	1.00	2.00
562 Font of Magic M :B:	.60	1.25
563 Gale's Redirection R :B:	.12	.25
564 Illithid Harvester/Plant Tadpoles R :B:	.12	.25
565 Kindred Discovery R :B:	7.50	15.00
566 Robe of the Archmagi R :B:	.30	.60
567 Tomb of Horrors Adventurer R :B:	.12	.25
568 Wizards of Thay R :B:	.40	.80
569 Altar of Bhaal/Bone Offering R :K:	.12	.25
570 Astarion's Thirst R :K:	.15	.30
571 Blood Money M :K:	2.00	4.00
572 Call to the Void R :K:	.07	.15
573 Elder Brain R :K:	.20	.40
574 Eldritch Pact R :K:	.12	.25
575 Intellect Devourer R :K:	.12	.25
576 Pact Weapon M :K:	.75	1.50
577 Ravenloft Adventurer R :K:	.30	.60
578 Balor M :R:	3.00	6.00
579 Caves of Chaos Adventurer R :R:	.60	1.25
580 Descent into Avernus R :R:	1.25	2.50
581 Elturel Survivors R :R:	.15	.30
582 Firbolg Flutist R :R:	.12	.25
583 Storm King's Thunder M :R:	1.00	2.00
584 Wand of Wonder R :R:	.40	.80
585 Wrathful Red Dragon R :R:	1.00	2.00
586 Wyll's Reversal R :R:	.40	.80
587 Barroom Brawl R :G:	.07	.15
588 Earthquake Dragon R :G:	1.00	2.00
589 Jaheira's Respite R :G:	.30	.75
590 Majestic Genesis M :G:	1.25	2.50
591 Monster Manual/Zoological Study R :G:	1.25	2.50
592 Owlbear Cub R :G:	.12	.25
593 Traverse the Outlands R :G:	1.00	2.00
594 Undermountain Adventurer R :G:	.25	.50
595 Basilisk Collar R	1.25	2.50
596 Blade of Selves R	2.00	4.00
597 Fraying Line R	.07	.15
598 Mighty Servant of Leuk-o R	.17	.35
599 Mirror of Life Trapping R	.12	.25
600 Baldur's Gate R	.30	.75
601 Bountiful Promenade R	4.00	8.00
602 Luxury Suite R	4.00	8.00
603 Morphic Pool R	6.00	12.00
604 Reflecting Pool R	4.00	8.00
605 Sea of Clouds R	4.00	8.00
606 Spire Garden R	3.00	6.00
607 Deep Gnome Terramancer R :W:	1.50	3.00
608 Folk Hero M :W:	2.50	5.00
609 Harper Recruiter R :W:	.15	.30
610 Seasoned Dungeoneer R :W:	1.50	3.00
611 Stick Together R :W:	.12	.25
612 Aboleth Spawn R :B:	.75	1.50
613 Astral Dragon R :B:	2.50	5.00
614 Clan Crafter M :B:	.30	.75
615 Endless Evil R :B:	.50	1.00
616 Grell Philosopher R :B:	.12	.25
617 Mocking Doppelganger R :B:	.25	.50
618 Psionic Ritual R :B:	.07	.15
619 Zellix, Sanity Flayer M :B:	1.75	3.50
620 Black Market Connections R :K:	12.50	25.00
621 Brainstealer Dragon R :K:	1.50	3.00
622 Burakos, Party Leader M :K:	.50	1.00
623 From the Catacombs R :K:	.15	.30
624 Haunted One M :K:	3.00	6.00
625 Solemn Doomguide R :K:	.10	.20
626 Uchuulon R :K:	.17	.35
627 Baeloth Barrityl, Entertainer M :R:	1.50	3.00
628 Bothersome Quasit R :R:	.75	1.50
629 Death Kiss R :R:	.17	.35
630 Delayed Blast Fireball R :R:	4.00	8.00
631 Loot Dispute R :R:	.12	.25
632 Nalfeshnee R :R:	1.25	2.50
633 Passionate Archaeologist M :R:	7.50	15.00
634 Spectacular Showdown R :R:	.25	.50
635 Durnan of the Yawning Portal M :G:	.30	.75
636 Green Slime R :G:	.30	.60
637 Journey to the Lost City R :G:	.07	.15
638 Tlincalli Hunter/Retrieve Prey R :G:	.15	.30
639 Venture Forth R :G:	.15	.30
640 Captain N'ghathrod M :B:/:K:	1.00	2.00
641 Faldorn, Dread Wolf Herald M :R:/:G:	1.00	2.00
642 Firkraag, Cunning Instigator M :B:/:R:	1.25	2.50
643 Nalia de'Arnise M :W:/:K:	.30	.60
644 Multiclass Baldric R	.12	.25
645 Sarevok's Tome R	.30	.75
646 Captain N'ghathrod M :B:/:K:	.17	.35
647 Faldorn, Dread Wolf Herald M :R:/:G:	.20	.40
648 Firkraag, Cunning Instigator M :B:/:R:	.20	.40
649 Nalia de'Arnise M :W:/:K:	.10	.20
650 Folk Hero M :W:	.25	.50
651 Clan Crafter M :B:	.12	.25
652 Zellix, Sanity Flayer M :B:	.30	.75
653 Burakos, Party Leader M :K:	.15	.30
654 Haunted One M :K:	1.50	3.00
655 Baeloth Barrityl, Entertainer M :R:	.20	.40
656 Passionate Archaeologist M :R:	2.50	5.00
657 Durnan of the Yawning Portal M :G:	.15	.30
658 Deep Gnome Terramancer R :W:	1.25	2.50
659 Harper Recruiter R :W:	.07	.15
660 Seasoned Dungeoneer R :W:	.75	1.50
661 Stick Together R :W:	.07	.10
662 Aboleth Spawn R :B:	.30	.60
663 Artificer Class R :B:	1.50	3.00
664 Astral Dragon R :B:	1.75	3.50
665 Endless Evil R :B:	.12	.25
666 Grell Philosopher R :B:	.12	.25
667 Mocking Doppelganger R :B:	.12	.25
668 Psionic Ritual R :B:	.07	.15
669 Black Market Connections R :K:	12.50	25.00
670 Brainstealer Dragon R :K:	1.50	3.00
671 From the Catacombs R :K:	.15	.30
672 Solemn Doomguide R :K:	.07	.10
673 Uchuulon R :K:	.15	.30
674 Bothersome Quasit R :R:	.40	.80
675 Death Kiss R :R:	.12	.25
676 Delayed Blast Fireball R :R:	2.50	5.00
677 Loot Dispute R :R:	.12	.25
678 Nalfeshnee R :R:	.75	1.50
679 Spectacular Showdown R :R:	.17	.35
680 Green Slime R :G:	.12	.25
681 Journey to the Lost City R :G:	.07	.10
682 Tlincalli Hunter/Retrieve Prey R :G:	.12	.25
683 Venture Forth R :G:	.12	.25
684 Multiclass Baldric R	.07	.15
685 Sarevok's Tome R	.12	.25
686 Archpriest of Iona R :W:	.07	.10
687 Austere Command R :W:	.50	1.00
688 Aven Mindcensor U :W:	.12	.25
689 Bygone Bishop R :W:	.07	.15
690 Crib Swap C :W:	.12	.25
691 Dusk/Dawn R :W:	.07	.15
692 Eight-and-a-Half-Tails R :W:	.07	.15
693 Frontline Medic R :W:	.07	.15
694 Galepowder Mage R :W:	.07	.10
695 Glorious Protector R :W:	.07	.15
696 Irregular Cohort C :W:	.07	.15
697 Jazal Goldmane M :W:	.12	.25
698 Mage's Attendant U :W:	.07	.10
699 Magus of the Balance R :W:	.07	.10
700 Mikaeus, the Lunarch M :W:	.17	.35
701 Mirror Entity R :W:	.15	.30
702 Mother of Runes U :W:	1.25	2.50
703 Order of Whiteclay R :W:	.07	.10
704 Priest of Ancient Lore C :W:	.07	.10
705 Rumor Gatherer U :W:	.12	.25
706 Selfless Spirit R :W:	.60	1.25
707 Sevinne's Reclamation R :W:	.25	.50
708 Solemn Recruit R :W:	.07	.10
709 Squad Commander R :W:	.07	.10
710 Unbreakable Formation R :W:	.12	.25
711 Valiant Changeling U :W:	.07	.10
712 Aether Gale R :B:	.17	.35
713 Angler Turtle R :B:	.07	.15
714 Chasm Skulker R :B:	.25	.50
715 Compulsive Research C :B:	.07	.15
716 Curse of the Swine R :B:	.17	.35
717 Curse of Verbosity U :B:	.17	.35
718 Dissipation Field R :B:	.15	.30
719 Domineering Will R :B:	.12	.25
720 Fact or Fiction U :B:	.12	.25
721 Forgotten Creation R :B:	.12	.25
722 Fractured Sanity R :B:	.20	.40
723 Grazilaxx, Illithid Scholar R :B:	.12	.25
724 Hullbreaker Horror R :B:	2.00	4.00
725 Keiga, the Tide Star R :B:	.12	.25
726 Leyline of Anticipation R :B:	1.50	3.00
727 Midnight Clock R :B:	.17	.35
728 Mind Flayer R :B:	.10	.20
729 Overcharged Amalgam R :B:	.12	.25
730 Propaganda U :B:	2.50	5.00
731 Pull from Tomorrow R :B:	.12	.25
732 Pursued Whale R :B:	.07	.10
733 Reflections of Littjara R :B:	1.00	2.00
734 Reins of Power R :B:	.12	.25
735 Sludge Monster R :B:	.10	.20
736 Sly Instigator R :B:	.07	.15
737 Wharf Infiltrator R :B:	.07	.15
738 Will Kenrith M :B:	.20	.40
739 Black Market R :K:	1.50	3.00
740 Bloodsoaked Champion R :K:	.07	.15
741 Butcher of Malakir R :K:	.12	.25
742 Calculating Lich M :K:	.15	.30
743 Changeling Outcast C :K:	.15	.30
744 Corpse Augur U :K:	.07	.15
745 Crippling Fear R :K:	.12	.25
746 Curtains' Call R :K:	.17	.35
747 Dark Hatchling R :K:	.07	.10
748 Dauthi Horror C :K:	.07	.15
749 Dire Fleet Ravager M :K:	.20	.40
750 Dross Harvester R :K:	.07	.15
751 Dusk Mangler U :K:	.07	.15
752 Feed the Swarm C :K:	.17	.35
753 Gonti, Lord of Luxury R :K:	.07	.15
754 Grim Haruspex R :K:	.20	.40
755 Grim Hireling R :K:	1.25	2.50
756 Guiltfeeder R :K:	.12	.25
757 Hex R :K:	.07	.15
758 Hunted Horror R :K:	.17	.35
759 In Garruk's Wake R :K:	.40	.80
760 Malakir Blood-Priest C :K:	.07	.15
761 Mardu Strike Leader R :K:	.07	.10
762 Mindblade Render R :K:	.07	.15
763 Nighthawk Scavenger R :K:	.20	.40
764 Nighthowler R :K:	.07	.15
765 Nihilith R :K:	.07	.15
766 Phyrexian Rager C :K:	.07	.10
767 Plague Spitter U :K:	.12	.25
768 Pontiff of Blight R :K:	.07	.15
769 Puppeteer Clique R :K:	.07	.15
770 Ravenous Chupacabra U :K:	.20	.40
771 Sewer Nemesis R :K:	.12	.25
772 Syphon Mind C :K:	.15	.30
773 Thwart the Grave U :K:	.07	.10
774 Woe Strider R :K:	.15	.30
775 Zulaport Cutthroat U :K:	.60	1.25
776 Agitator Ant R :R:	.12	.25
777 The Akroan War R :R:	.17	.35
778 Aurora Phoenix R :R:	.12	.25
779 Avatar of Slaughter R :R:	.12	.25
780 Blasphemous Act R :R:	1.25	2.50
781 Bonecrusher Giant/Stomp R :R:	.25	.50
782 Brash Taunter R :R:	.50	1.00
783 Chain Reaction R :R:	.12	.25
784 Chaos Dragon R :R:	.15	.30
785 Chaos Warp R :R:	.75	1.50
786 Curse of Opulence U :R:	1.00	2.00
787 Demon Bolt C :R:	.07	.15
788 Dire Fleet Daredevil R :R:	.12	.25
789 Disrupt Decorum R :R:	.40	.80
790 Drakuseth, Maw of Flames R :R:	.50	1.00
791 Dream Pillager R :R:	.12	.25
792 Embereth Shieldbreaker/Battle Display U :R:	.07	.10
793 Etali, Primal Storm R :R:	.15	.30
794 Geode Rager R :R:	.12	.25
795 Goblin Spymaster R :R:	.12	.25
796 Greater Gargadon R :R:	.07	.10
797 Ignite the Future R :R:	.12	.25
798 Izzet Chemister R :R:	.07	.15
799 Jeska's Will R :R:	7.50	15.00
800 Kazuul, Tyrant of the Cliffs R :R:	.12	.25
801 Laelia, the Blade Reforged R :R:	1.00	2.00
802 Light Up the Stage U :R:	.15	.30
803 Mizzium Mortars R :R:	.10	.20
804 Outpost Siege R :R:	.12	.25
805 Rowan Kenrith M :R:	.20	.40
806 Ryusei, the Falling Star R :R:	.20	.40
807 Stolen Strategy R :R:	.12	.25
808 Tectonic Giant R :R:	.12	.25
809 Territorial Hellkite R :R:	.12	.25
810 Thunder Dragon R :R:	.12	.25
811 Urabrask the Hidden M :R:	.30	.60
812 Vengeful Ancestor R :R:	.12	.25
813 Volcanic Torrent U :R:	.07	.10
814 Warmonger Hellkite R :R:	.10	.20
815 Warstorm Surge R :R:	.17	.35
816 Wild-Magic Sorcerer R :R:	.25	.50
817 Arasta of the Endless Web R :G:	.17	.35
818 Battle Mammoth M :G:	.15	.30
819 Beanstalk Giant/Fertile Footsteps U :G:	.07	.15
820 Beast Within U :G:	.75	1.50
821 Cultivate U :G:	.30	.75
822 End-Raze Forerunners R :G:	.15	.30
823 Explore C :G:	.12	.25
824 Ezuri's Predation R :G:	.30	.60
825 Hornet Queen R :G:	.12	.25
826 Kodama's Reach C :G:	1.00	2.00
827 Lovestruck Beast/Heart's Desire R :G:	.07	.15
828 Managorger Hydra R :G:	.12	.25
829 Natural Reclamation C :G:	.07	.10
830 Primeval Bounty M :G:	.30	.60
831 Return of the Wildspeaker R :G:	1.25	2.50
832 Sakura-Tribe Elder C :G:	.75	1.50
833 Sandwurm Convergence R :G:	.12	.25
834 Search for Tomorrow C :G:	.12	.25
835 Sweet-Gum Recluse R :G:	.12	.25
836 Terramorph U :G:	.07	.10
837 Three Visits U :G:	3.00	6.00
838 Vivien, Champion of the Wilds R :G:	.17	.35
839 Bloodbraid Elf U :R:/:G:	.07	.10
840 Consuming Aberration R :B:/:K:	.12	.25
841 Despark U :W:/:K:	.12	.25
842 Drown in the Loch U :B:/:K:	.30	.75
843 Escape to the Wilds R :R:/:G:	.15	.30
844 Extract from Darkness U :B:/:K:	.07	.10
845 Felisa, Fang of Silverquill M :W:/:K:	.17	.35
846 Firja's Retribution R :W:/:K:	.12	.25
847 Grumgully, the Generous U :R:/:G:	.07	.15
848 High Priest of Penance R :W:/:K:	.07	.15
849 Memory Plunder R :B:/:K:	.15	.30
850 Nemesis of Reason R :B:/:K:	.12	.25
851 Niv-Mizzet, Parun R :B:/:R:	1.00	2.00
852 Sprite Dragon U :B:/:R:	.15	.30
853 Xenagos, the Reveler M :R:/:G:	.20	.40
854 Bloodthirsty Blade U	.12	.25
855 Chaos Wand R	.12	.25
856 Dimir Keyrune U	.12	.25
857 Dimir Signet C	.40	.80
858 Dragon's Hoard R	.25	.50
859 Everflowing Chalice U	.25	.50
860 Fellwar Stone U	.30	.60
861 Hedron Archive U	.12	.25
862 Herald's Horn U	2.50	5.00
863 Izzet Signet C	.30	.75
864 Lightning Greaves U	5.00	10.00
865 Maskwood Nexus R	1.25	2.50
866 Mindcrank U	1.25	2.50
867 Orzhov Signet C	.17	.35
868 Phyrexian Revoker R	.12	.25
869 Psychosis Crawler R	.15	.30
870 Skullclamp U	2.50	5.00
871 Sol Ring U	1.00	2.00
872 Solemn Simulacrum R	.30	.75
873 Spellskite R	1.25	2.50
874 Steel Hellkite R	.12	.25
875 Stuffy Doll R	.30	.75
876 Talisman of Creativity U	.75	1.50
877 Talisman of Dominance U	.12	2.00
878 Talisman of Hierarchy U	.20	.40
879 Thought Vessel U	1.25	2.50
880 Ash Barrens U	.12	.25
881 Blighted Woodland U	.10	.20
882 Bojuka Bog C	.75	1.50
883 Castle Embereth R	.12	.25
884 Castle Locthwain R	1.25	2.50
885 Castle Vantress R	.25	.50
886 Choked Estuary R	.12	.25
887 Cinder Glade R	.15	.30
888 Creeping Tar Pit R	.15	.30
889 Darkwater Catacombs R	.12	.25
890 Desolate Lighthouse R	.07	.15
891 Dimir Aqueduct U	.12	.25
892 Drownyard Temple R	.12	.25
893 Exotic Orchard R	.12	.25
894 Game Trail R	.07	.15
895 Gruul Turf U	.12	.25
896 Highland Forest C	.10	.20
897 Izzet Boilerworks U	.12	.25
898 Kessig Wolf Run R	.15	.30
899 Kher Keep R	.12	.25
900 Mortuary Mire C	.12	.25
901 Mossfire Valley R	.07	.15
902 Mosswort Bridge R	.15	.30
903 Mutavault R	4.00	8.00
904 Myriad Landscape U	.12	.25
905 Nephalia Drownyard R	.12	.25
906 Orzhov Basilica U	.07	.15
907 Path of Ancestry C	.12	.25
908 Port of Karfell U	.07	.15
909 Prismari Campus C	.07	.10
910 Raging Ravine R	.07	.15
911 Reliquary Tower U	2.50	5.00
912 River of Tears R	.12	.25
913 Rogue's Passage U	.30	.60
914 Shambling Vent R	.12	.25
915 Snowfield Sinkhole C	.07	.15
916 Spinerock Knoll R	.12	.25
917 Starlit Sanctum U	.07	.10
918 Sunken Hollow R	.15	.30
919 Tainted Field U	.07	.15
920 Tainted Isle U	.30	.60
921 Temple of Abandon R	.10	.20
922 Temple of Deceit R	.12	.25
923 Temple of Epiphany R	.12	.25
924 Temple of Silence R	.12	.25
925 Temple of the False God U	.07	.15
926 Terrain Generator U	.30	.75
927 Vault of the Archangel R	.17	.35
928 Wandering Fumarole R	.12	.25
929 War Room R	2.50	5.00
930 Windbrisk Heights R	.07	.15
931 Captain N'ghathrod M :B:/:K:	.12	.25
932 Faldorn, Dread Wolf Herald M :R:/:G:	.07	.15
933 Firkraag, Cunning Instigator M :B:/:R:	.12	.25
934 Nalia de'Arnise M :W:/:K:	.12	.25
935 Wand of Wonder R :R:	.17	.35
936 Elder Brain R :K:	.30	.75

2022 Magic The Gathering Dominaria United

1 Karn, Living Legacy M	.75	1.50
2 Anointed Peacekeeper R :W:	.30	.60
3 Archangel of Wrath R :W:	.07	.15
4 Argivian Cavalier C :W:	.05	.10
5 Argivian Phalanx C :W:	.05	.10
6 Artillery Blast C :W:	.05	.10
7 Benalish Faithbonder C :W:	.05	.10
8 Benalish Sleeper C :W:	.05	.10
9 Captain's Call C :W:	.05	.10
10 Charismatic Vanguard C :W:	.05	.10
11 Citizen's Arrest C :W:	.05	.10

2022 Magic The Gathering Double Masters 2022

12 Cleaving Skyrider U :W: .05 .10
13 Clockwork Drawbridge C :W: .05 .10
14 Coalition Skyknight U :W: .05 .10
15 Danitha, Benalia's Hope R :W: .25 .50
16 Defiler of Faith R :W: .25 .50
17 Destroy Evil C :W: .30 .60
18 Griffin Protector C :W: .05 .10
19 Guardian of New Benalia R :W: .12 .25
20 Heroic Charge C :W: .05 .10
21 Join Forces U :W: .05 .10
22 Juniper Order Rootweaver C :W: .05 .10
23 Knight of Dawn's Light U :W: .05 .10
24 Leyline Binding R :W: 5.00 10.00
25 Love Song of Night and Day U :W: .05 .10
26 Mesa Cavalier C :W: .05 .10
27 Phyrexian Missionary U :W: .05 .10
28 Prayer of Binding U :W: .05 .10
29 Resolute Reinforcements U :W: .15 .30
30 Runic Shot U :W: .05 .10
31 Samite Herbalist C :W: .05 .10
32 Serra Paragon M :W: 4.00 8.00
33 Shalai's Acolyte U :W: .05 .10
34 Stall for Time C :W: .05 .10
35 Take Up the Shield C :W: .05 .10
36 Temporary Lockdown R :W: 1.25 2.50
37 Urza Assembles the Titans R :W: .12 .25
38 Valiant Veteran R :W: .20 .40
39 Wingmantle Chaplain U :W: .05 .10
40 Academy Loremaster R :B: .07 .15
41 Academy Wall C :B: .05 .10
42 Aether Channeler R :B: .60 1.25
43 Battlewing Mystic U :B: .05 .10
44 Combat Research U :B: .12 .25
45 Coral Colony U :B: .05 .10
46 Defiler of Dreams R :B: .25 .50
47 Djinn of the Fountain U :B: .05 .10
48 Ertai's Scorn U :B: .05 .10
49 Essence Scatter C :B: .05 .10
50 Founding the Third Path U :B: .15 .30
51 Frostfist Strider U :B: .05 .10
52 Haughty Djinn R :B: .75 1.50
53 Haunting Figment C :B: .05 .10
54 Impede Momentum C :B: .05 .10
55 Impulse C :B: .05 .10
56 Joint Exploration U :B: .15 .30
57 Micromancer U :B: .05 .10
58 Negate C :B: .06 .12
59 The Phasing of Zhalfir R :B: .25 .50
60 Phyrexian Espionage C :B: .05 .10
61 Pixie Illusionist C :B: .05 .10
62 Protect the Negotiators U :B: .05 .10
63 Rona's Vortex U :B: .05 .10
64 Shore Up C :B: .07 .15
65 Silver Scrutiny R :B: .12 .25
66 Soaring Drake C :B: .05 .10
67 Sphinx of Clear Skies M :B: .15 .30
68 Talas Lookout C :B: .05 .10
69 Tidepool Turtle C :B: .05 .10
70 Timely Interference C :B: .05 .10
71 Tolarian Geyser C :B: .05 .10
72 Tolarian Terror C :B: .40 .80
73 Vesuvan Duplimancy M :B: 1.50 3.00
74 Voda Sea Scavenger C :B: .05 .10
75 Vodalian Hexcatcher R :B: .75 1.50
76 Vodalian Mindsinger R :B: .05 .10
77 Volshe Tideturner C :B: .05 .10
78 Aggressive Sabotage C :K: .05 .10
79 Balduvian Atrocity U :K: .05 .10
80 Battle-Rage Blessing C :K: .05 .10
81 Battlefly Swarm C :K: .05 .10
82 Blight Pile U :K: .05 .10
83 Bone Splinters C :K: .05 .10
84 Braids, Arisen Nightmare R :K: 2.50 5.00
85 Braids's Frightful Return U :K: .05 .10
86 Choking Miasma U :K: .05 .10
87 The Cruelty of Gix R :K: 2.50 5.00
88 Cult Conscript U :K: .07 .15
89 Cut Down U :K: .25 .50
90 Defiler of Flesh R :K: .15 .30
91 Drag to the Bottom R :K: .05 .10
92 Eerie Soultender C :K: .05 .10
93 Evolved Sleeper R :K: .15 .30
94 Extinguish the Light C :K: .05 .10
95 Gibbering Barricade C :K: .05 .10
96 Knight of Dusk's Shadow U :K: .07 .15
97 Liliana of the Veil M :K: 7.50 15.00
98 Monstrous War-Leech U :K: .05 .10
99 Phyrexian Rager C :K: .05 .10
100 Phyrexian Vivisector C :K: .05 .10
101 Phyrexian Warhorse C :K: .05 .10
102 Pilfer U :K: .05 .10
103 The Raven Man R :K: .15 .30
104 Sengir Connoisseur U :K: .05 .10
105 Shadow Prophecy C :K: .05 .10
106 Shadow-Rite Priest R :K: .12 .25
107 Sheoldred, the Apocalypse M :K: 40.00 80.00
108 Sheoldred's Restoration U :K: .05 .10
109 Splatter Goblin C :K: .05 .10
110 Stronghold Arena R :K: .05 .10
111 Tattered Apparition C :K: .05 .10
112 Toxic Abomination C :K: .05 .10
113 Tribute to Urborg C :K: .05 .10
114 Urborg Repossession C :K: .05 .10
115 Writhing Necromass C :K: .05 .10
116 Balduvian Berserker U :R: .05 .10
117 Chaotic Transformation R :R: .07 .15
118 Coalition Warbrute C :R: .05 .10
119 Defiler of Instinct R :R: .15 .30
120 Dragon Whelp U :R: .05 .10
121 The Elder Dragon War R :R: .30 .60
122 Electrostatic Infantry U :R: .10 .20
123 Fires of Victory U :R: .05 .10
124 Flowstone Infusion C :R: .05 .10
125 Flowstone Kavu C :R: .05 .10
126 Furious Bellow C :R: .05 .10
127 Ghitu Amplifier C :R: .05 .10
128 Goblin Picker C :R: .05 .10
129 Hammerhand C :R: .05 .10
130 Hurler Cyclops U :R: .05 .10
131 Hurloon Battle Hymn U :R: .05 .10
132 In Thrall to the Pit C :R: .05 .10
133 Jaya, Fiery Negotiator M :R: .50 1.00
134 Jaya's Firenado C :R: .05 .10
135 Keldon Flamesage R :R: .05 .10
136 Keldon Strike Team C :R: .05 .10
137 Lightning Strike C :R: .06 .12
138 Meria's Outrider C :R: .05 .10
139 Molten Monstrosity C :R: .05 .10
140 Phoenix Chick U :R: .25 .50
141 Radha's Firebrand R :R: .05 .10
142 Rundvelt Hordemaster R :R: .75 1.50
143 Shivan Devastator M :R: 2.50 5.00
144 Smash to Dust C :R: .07 .15
145 Sprouting Goblin U :R: .05 .10
146 Squee, Dubious Monarch R :R: .25 .50
147 Temporal Firestorm R :R: .05 .10
148 Thrill of Possibility C :R: .05 .10
149 Twinferno U :R: .12 .25
150 Viashino Branchrider C :R: .05 .10
151 Warhost's Frenzy U :R: .05 .10
152 Yavimaya Steelcrusher C :R: .05 .10
153 Yotia Declares War U :R: .05 .10
154 Barkweave Crusher C :G: .05 .10
155 Bite Down C :G: .06 .12
156 Bog Badger C :G: .05 .10
157 Broken Wings C :G: .05 .10
158 Colossal Growth C :G: .05 .10
159 Deathbloom Gardener C :G: .05 .10
160 Defiler of Vigor R :G: 1.50 3.00
161 Elfhame Wurm C :G: .05 .10
162 Elvish Hydromancer U :G: .05 .10
163 Floriferous Vinewall C :G: .05 .10
164 Gaea's Might C :G: .05 .10
165 Herd Migration R :G: .07 .15
166 Hexbane Tortoise C :G: .05 .10
167 Leaf-Crowned Visionary R :G: 2.50 5.00
168 Linebreaker Baloth U :G: .05 .10
169 Llanowar Greenwidow R :G: .12 .25
170 Llanowar Loamspeaker R :G: .15 .30
171 Llanowar Stalker C :G: .05 .10
172 Magnigoth Sentry C :G: .05 .10
173 Mossbeard Ancient U :G: .05 .10
174 Nishoba Brawler U :G: .05 .10
175 Quirion Beastcaller R :G: .25 .50
176 Scout the Wilderness C :G: .05 .10
177 Silverback Elder M :G: 3.00 6.00
178 Slimefoot's Survey U :G: .05 .10
179 Snarespinner C :G: .05 .10
180 Strength of the Coalition U :G: .05 .10
181 Sunbathing Rootwalla C :G: .05 .10
182 Tail Swipe U :G: .12 .25
183 Tear Asunder U :G: 1.25 2.50
184 Territorial Maro U :G: .05 .10
185 Threats Undetected R :G: .15 .30
186 Urborg Lhurgoyf R :G: .12 .25
187 Vineshaper Prodigy C :G: .05 .10
188 The Weatherseed Treaty U :G: .07 .15
189 The World Spell M :G: 1.00 2.00
190 Yavimaya Iconoclast U :G: .05 .10
191 Yavimaya Sojourner C :G: .05 .10
192 Ajani, Sleeper Agent M :G:/W: 2.00 4.00
193 Aron, Benalia's Ruin U :W:/K: .05 .10
194 Astor, Bearer of Blades R :R:/W: .25 .50
195 Baird, Argivian Recruiter U :R:/W: .05 .10
196 Balmor, Battlemage Captain U :B:/R: .12 .25
197 Bortuk Bonerattle U :K:/G: .05 .10
198 Elas il-Kor, Sadistic Pilgrim U :W:/K: .75 1.50
199 Ertai Resurrected R :B:/K: .40 .80
200 Garna, Bloodfist of Keld U :K:/R: .05 .10
201 Ivy, Gleeful Spellthief R :G:/B: .25 .50
202 Jhoira, Ageless Innovator R :B:/R: .10 .20
203 Jodah, the Unifier M :W:/B:/K:/R:/G: 2.00 4.00
204 King Darien XLVIII R :G:/W: .25 .50
205 Lagomos, Hand of Hatred U :K:/R: .06 .12
206 Meria, Scholar of Antiquity R :R:/G: .12 .25
207 Nael, Avizoa Aeronaut U :G:/B: .05 .10
208 Najal, the Storm Runner U :B:/R: .05 .10
209 Nemata, Primeval Warden R :K:/G: .25 .50
210 Queen Allenal of Ruadach U :G:/W: .07 .15
211 Radha, Coalition Warlord U :R:/G: .05 .10
212 Raff, Weatherlight Stalwart U :W:/B: .05 .10
213 Ratadrabik of Urborg R :W:/K: .75 1.50
214 Rith, Liberated Primeval M :R:/G:/W: 1.00 2.00
215 Rivaz of the Claw R :K:/R: .40 .80
216 Rona, Sheoldred's Faithful U :B:/K: .05 .10
217 Rulik Mons, Warren Chief U :R:/G: .05 .10
218 Shanna, Purifying Blade M :G:/W:/B: .20 .40
219 Sol'Kanar the Tainted M :B:/K:/R: .15 .30
220 Soul of Windgrace M :K:/R:/G: .40 .80
221 Stenn, Paranoid Partisan R :W:/B: .12 .25
222 Tatyova, Steward of Tides U :G:/B: .05 .10
223 Tori D'Avenant, Fury Rider U :R:/W: .07 .15
224 Tura Kennerüd, Skyknight U :W:/B: .05 .10
225 Uurg, Spawn of Turg U :K:/G: .05 .10
226 Vohar, Vodalian Desecrator U :B:/K: .05 .10
227 Zar Ojanen, Scion of Efrava U :G:/W: .05 .10
228 Zur, Eternal Schemer M :W:/B:/K: .75 1.50
229 Automatic Librarian C .05 .10
230 Golden Argosy R .25 .50
231 Hero's Heirloom U .07 .15
232 Inscribed Tablet U .05 .10
233 Jodah's Codex U .05 .10
234 Karn's Sylex M .75 1.50
235 Meteorite C .05 .10
236 Relic of Legends U 1.00 2.00
237 Salvaged Manaworker C .05 .10
238 Shield-Wall Sentinel C .06 .12
239 Timeless Lotus M 7.50 15.00
240 Vanquisher's Axe C .05 .10
241 Walking Bulwark U .05 .10
242 Weatherlight Compleated M .75 1.50
243 Adarkar Wastes R 2.50 5.00
244 Caves of Koilos R .20 .40
245 Contaminated Aquifer C .25 .50
246 Crystal Grotto C .10 .20
247 Geothermal Bog C .12 .25
248 Haunted Mire C .15 .30
249 Idyllic Beachfront C .10 .20
250 Karplusan Forest R .75 1.50
251 Molten Tributary C .12 .25
252 Plaza of Heroes R 5.00 10.00
253 Radiant Grove C .10 .20
254 Sacred Peaks C .10 .20
255 Shivan Reef R .40 .80
256 Sulfurous Springs R 2.00 4.00
257 Sunlit Marsh C .12 .25
258 Tangled Islet C .12 .25
259 Thran Portal R .20 .40
260 Wooded Ridgeline C .10 .20
261 Yavimaya Coast R .75 1.50
262 Plains C .05 .10
263 Plains C .06 .12
264 Plains C .05 .10
265 Island C .05 .10
266 Island C .05 .10
267 Island C .05 .10
268 Swamp C .05 .10
269 Swamp C .05 .10
270 Swamp C .05 .10
271 Mountain C .06 .12
272 Mountain C .05 .10
273 Mountain C .06 .12
274 Forest C .06 .12
275 Forest C .05 .10
276 Forest C .07 .15
277 Plains C 1.00 2.00
278 Island C .75 1.50
279 Swamp C .75 1.50
280 Mountain C .75 1.50
281 Forest C .75 1.50
282 Serra Redeemer R :W: .12 .25
283 Cosmic Epiphany R :B: .05 .10
284 Tyrannical Pitlord R :K: .06 .12
285 Ragefire Hellkite R :R: .06 .12
286 Briar Hydra R :G: .05 .10
287 Danitha, Benalia's Hope R :W: .10 .20
288 Braids, Arisen Nightmare R :K: 1.25 2.50
289 The Raven Man R :K: .10 .20
290 Sheoldred, the Apocalypse M :K: 30.00 75.00
291 Squee, Dubious Monarch R :R: .12 .25
292 Aron, Benalia's Ruin U :W:/K: .05 .10
293 Astor, Bearer of Blades R :R:/W: .15 .30
294 Baird, Argivian Recruiter U :R:/W: .05 .10
295 Balmor, Battlemage Captain U :B:/R: .05 .10
296 Bortuk Bonerattle U :K:/G: .05 .10
297 Elas il-Kor, Sadistic Pilgrim U :W:/K: .06 .12
298 Ertai Resurrected R :B:/K: .15 .30
299 Garna, Bloodfist of Keld U :K:/R: .05 .10
300 Ivy, Gleeful Spellthief R :G:/B: .15 .30
301 Jhoira, Ageless Innovator R :B:/R: .06 .12
302 Jodah, the Unifier M :W:/B:/K:/R:/G: 1.25 2.50
303 King Darien XLVIII R :G:/W: .12 .25
304 Lagomos, Hand of Hatred U :K:/R: .05 .10
305 Meria, Scholar of Antiquity R :R:/G: .07 .15
306 Nael, Avizoa Aeronaut U :G:/B: .05 .10
307 Najal, the Storm Runner U :B:/R: .05 .10
308 Nemata, Primeval Warden R :K:/G: .10 .20
309 Queen Allenal of Ruadach U :G:/W: .05 .10
310 Radha, Coalition Warlord U :R:/G: .05 .10
311 Raff, Weatherlight Stalwart U :W:/B: .05 .10
312 Ratadrabik of Urborg R :W:/K: .25 .50
313 Rith, Liberated Primeval M :R:/G:/W: .25 .50
314 Rivaz of the Claw R :K:/R: .12 .25
315 Rona, Sheoldred's Faithful U :B:/K: .05 .10
316 Rulik Mons, Warren Chief U :R:/G: .05 .10
317 Shanna, Purifying Blade M :G:/W:/B: .15 .30
318 Sol'Kanar the Tainted M :B:/K:/R: .15 .30
319 Soul of Windgrace M :K:/R:/G: .25 .50
320 Stenn, Paranoid Partisan R :W:/B: .07 .15
321 Tatyova, Steward of Tides U :G:/B: .05 .10
322 Tori D'Avenant, Fury Rider U :R:/W: .05 .10
323 Tura Kennerüd, Skyknight U :W:/B: .05 .10
324 Uurg, Spawn of Turg U :K:/G: .05 .10
325 Vohar, Vodalian Desecrator U :B:/K: .05 .10
326 Zar Ojanen, Scion of Efrava U :G:/W: .05 .10
327 Zur, Eternal Schemer M :W:/B:/K: .25 .50
328 Danitha, Benalia's Hope R :W: .30 .60
329 Braids, Arisen Nightmare R :K: 2.00 4.00
330 The Raven Man R :K: .20 .40
331 Sheoldred, the Apocalypse M :K: 40.00 80.00
332 Squee, Dubious Monarch R :R: .50 1.00
333 Aron, Benalia's Ruin U :W:/K: .12 .25
334 Astor, Bearer of Blades R :R:/W: .20 .40
335 Baird, Argivian Recruiter U :R:/W: .12 .25
336 Balmor, Battlemage Captain U :B:/R: .40 .80
337 Bortuk Bonerattle U :K:/G: .12 .25
338 Elas il-Kor, Sadistic Pilgrim U :W:/K: 1.00 2.00
339 Ertai Resurrected R :B:/K: .30 .60
340 Garna, Bloodfist of Keld U :K:/R: .15 .30
341 Ivy, Gleeful Spellthief R :G:/B: .75 1.50
342 Jhoira, Ageless Innovator R :B:/R: .15 .30
343 Jodah, the Unifier M :W:/B:/K:/R:/G: 6.00 12.00
344 King Darien XLVIII R :G:/W: .25 .50
345 Lagomos, Hand of Hatred U :K:/R: .15 .30
346 Meria, Scholar of Antiquity R :R:/G: .25 .50
347 Nael, Avizoa Aeronaut U :G:/B: .10 .20
348 Najal, the Storm Runner U :B:/R: .12 .25
349 Nemata, Primeval Warden R :K:/G: .30 .60
350 Queen Allenal of Ruadach U :G:/W: .20 .40
351 Radha, Coalition Warlord U :R:/G: .12 .25
352 Raff, Weatherlight Stalwart U :W:/B: .15 .30
353 Ratadrabik of Urborg R :W:/K: 1.50 3.00
354 Rith, Liberated Primeval M :R:/G:/W: 1.25 2.50
355 Rivaz of the Claw R :K:/R: .75 1.50
356 Rona, Sheoldred's Faithful U :B:/K: .15 .30
357 Rulik Mons, Warren Chief U :R:/G: .12 .25
358 Shanna, Purifying Blade M :G:/W:/B: 1.00 2.00
359 Sol'Kanar the Tainted M :B:/K:/R: .30 .60
360 Soul of Windgrace M :K:/R:/G: 3.00 6.00
361 Stenn, Paranoid Partisan R :W:/B: .12 .25
362 Tatyova, Steward of Tides U :G:/B: .12 .25
363 Tori D'Avenant, Fury Rider U :R:/W: .15 .30
364 Tura Kennerüd, Skyknight U :W:/B: .12 .25
365 Uurg, Spawn of Turg U :K:/G: .12 .25
366 Vohar, Vodalian Desecrator U :B:/K: .25 .50
367 Zar Ojanen, Scion of Efrava U :G:/W: .10 .20
368 Zur, Eternal Schemer M :W:/B:/K: 1.25 2.50
369 |gOcdrd,nETemk. M :K: 30.00 75.00
370 |DFaUnEED lugtkenvr. M :G:/W: 1.50 3.00
371 Ajani, Sleeper Agent M :G:/W: 2.00 4.00
372 Karn, Living Legacy M .75 1.50
373 Liliana of the Veil M :K: 7.50 15.00
374 Jaya, Fiery Negotiator M :R: .30 .60
375 Ajani, Sleeper Agent M :G:/W: 3.00 6.00
376 Ajani, Sleeper Agent M :G:/W: 5.00 10.00
377 Adarkar Wastes R 2.00 4.00
378 Caves of Koilos R .75 1.50
379 Karplusan Forest R 1.25 2.50
380 Shivan Reef R 1.00 2.00
381 Sulfurous Springs R 1.25 2.50
382 Yavimaya Coast R .75 1.50
383 Anointed Peacekeeper R :W: .75 1.50
384 Archangel of Wrath R :W: .30 .60
385 Defiler of Faith R :W: .50 1.00
386 Guardian of New Benalia R :W: .12 .25
387 Leyline Binding R :W: 7.50 15.00
388 Serra Paragon M :W: 7.50 15.00
389 Temporary Lockdown R :W: 1.50 3.00
390 Valiant Veteran R :W: .50 1.00
391 Academy Loremaster R :B: .12 .25
392 Aether Channeler R :B: .75 1.50
393 Defiler of Dreams R :B: .30 .60
394 Haughty Djinn R :B: 1.25 2.50
395 Silver Scrutiny R :B: .20 .40
396 Sphinx of Clear Skies M :B: .25 .50
397 Vesuvan Duplimancy M :B: 2.50 5.00
398 Vodalian Hexcatcher R :B: 1.25 2.50
399 Vodalian Mindsinger R :B: .10 .20
400 Defiler of Flesh R :K: .30 .60
401 Drag to the Bottom R :K: .12 .25
402 Evolved Sleeper R :K: .25 .50
403 Shadow-Rite Priest R :K: .15 .30
404 Stronghold Arena R :K: .10 .20
405 Chaotic Transformation R :R: .12 .25
406 Defiler of Instinct R :R: .30 .60
407 Keldon Flamesage R :R: .10 .20
408 Radha's Firebrand R :R: .10 .20
409 Rundvelt Hordemaster R :R: .75 1.50
410 Shivan Devastator M :R: 4.00 8.00
411 Temporal Firestorm R :R: .07 .15
412 Defiler of Vigor R :G: 1.50 3.00
413 Herd Migration R :G: .15 .30
414 Leaf-Crowned Visionary R :G: 2.00 4.00
415 Llanowar Greenwidow R :G: .12 .25
416 Llanowar Loamspeaker R :G: .15 .30
417 Quirion Beastcaller R :G: .30 .60
418 Silverback Elder M :G: 6.00 12.00
419 Threats Undetected R :G: .30 .60
420 Urborg Lhurgoyf R :G: .15 .30
421 Plaza of Heroes R 6.00 12.00
422 Thran Portal R .20 .40
423 Serra Redeemer R :W: .75 1.50
424 Cosmic Epiphany R :B: .12 .25
425 Tyrannical Pitlord R :K: .12 .25
426 Ragefire Hellkite R :R: .15 .30
427 Briar Hydra R :G: .12 .25
428 Llanowar Loamspeaker R :G: .20 .40
429 Herd Migration R :G: .07 .15
430 Resolute Reinforcements U :W: .60 1.25
431 Micromancer U :B: .20 .40
432 Cut Down U :K: 1.25 2.50
433 Lightning Strike C :R: .25 .50
434 Nishoba Brawler U :G: .75 1.50
435 Sheoldred, the Apocalypse M :K: 50.00 100.00
436 Sheoldred, the Apocalypse M :K: 75.00 150.00

2022 Magic The Gathering Dominaria United Commander

1 Dihada, Binder of Wills M :R:/W:/K: 1.25 2.50
2 Jared Carthalion M :W:/B:/K:/R:/G: .60 1.25
3 Jenson Carthalion, Druid Exile M :G:/W: .75 1.50
4 Shanid, Sleepers' Scourge M :R:/W:/K: .75 1.50
5 Zeriam, Golden Wind R :W: .10 .20
6 Moira, Urborg Haunt R :K: .10 .20
7 Mana Cannons R :R: .25 .50
8 The Reaver Cleaver R :R: 7.50 15.00
9 Bladewing, Deathless Tyrant R :K:/R: .20 .40
10 Cadric, Soul Kindler R :R:/W: .30 .75
11 Fallaji Wayfarer R :G: 2.00 4.00
12 Iridian Maelstrom R :W:/B:/K:/R:/G: .20 .40
13 Primeval Spawn R :W:/B:/K:/R:/G: .15 .30
14 Two-Headed Hellkite R :W:/B:/K:/R:/G: 2.50 5.00
15 Unite the Coalition R :W:/B:/K:/R:/G: .20 .40
16 Verrak, Warped Sengir R :W:/K: .07 .15
17 Gerrard's Hourglass Pendant R .50 1.00
18 Obsidian Obelisk R .25 .50
19 The Peregrine Dynamo R .15 .30
20 Tiller Engine R 2.00 4.00
21 Historian's Boon R :W: 2.50 5.00
22 Robaran Mercenaries R :W: .12 .25
23 Emperor Mihail II R :B: .75 1.50
24 Activated Sleeper R :K: .60 1.25
25 Rosnakht, Heir of Rohgahh R :R: .20 .40
26 Baru, Wurmspeaker R :G: .12 .25
27 Greensleeves, Maro-Sorcerer M :G: 20.00 40.00
28 The Mana Rig M .75 1.50
29 Ayesha Tanaka, Armorer R :W:/B: .07 .15
30 The Ever-Changing 'Dane R :W:/B:/K: .12 .25
31 General Marhault Elsdragon U :R:/G: .07 .15
32 Hazezon, Shaper of Sand R :R:/G:/W: .10 .20
33 Jasmine Boreal of the Seven U :G:/W: .05 .10
34 Jedit Ojanen, Mercenary M :W:/B: .20 .40
35 The Lady of Otaria M :R:/G: .20 .40
36 Ohabi Caleria R :G:/W: .10 .20
37 Orca, Siege Demon R :K:/R: .15 .30
38 Ramirez DePietro, Pillager U :B:/K: .12 .25
39 Ramses, Assassin Lord R :B:/K: .15 .30
40 Rasputin, the Oneiromancer R :W:/B: .10 .20
41 Rohgahh, Kher Keep Overlord R :K:/R: .12 .25
42 Stangg, Echo Warrior R :R:/G: .15 .30
43 Sivitri, Dragon Master M :B:/K: 3.00 6.00
44 Tetsuo, Imperial Champion M :B:/K:/R: .30 .75
45 Tobias, Doomed Conqueror U :W:/B: .05 .10
46 Tor Wauki the Younger U :K:/R: .12 .25
47 Torsten, Founder of Benalia M :G:/W: .30 .60
48 Xira, the Golden Sting R :K:/R:/G: .10 .20
49 Dihada, Binder of Wills M :R:/W:/K: .20 .40
50 Jared Carthalion M :W:/B:/K:/R:/G: .20 .40
51 Ayesha Tanaka, Armorer R :W:/B: .10 .20
52 The Ever-Changing 'Dane R :W:/B:/K: .10 .20
53 General Marhault Elsdragon U :R:/G: .07 .15
54 Hazezon, Shaper of Sand R :R:/G:/W: .12 .25
55 Jasmine Boreal of the Seven U :G:/W: .06 .12
56 Jedit Ojanen, Mercenary M :W:/B: .15 .30
57 The Lady of Otaria M :R:/G: .15 .30
58 Ohabi Caleria R :G:/W: .12 .25
59 Orca, Siege Demon R :K:/R: .12 .25
60 Ramirez DePietro, Pillager U :B:/K: .07 .15
61 Ramses, Assassin Lord R :B:/K: .20 .40
62 Rasputin, the Oneiromancer R :W:/B: .10 .20
63 Rohgahh, Kher Keep Overlord R :K:/R: .12 .25
64 Stangg, Echo Warrior R :R:/G: .15 .30

65 Sivitri, Dragon Master M :D:/:K: 1.00 2.00
66 Tetsuo, Imperial Champion M :B:/:K:/:R: .40 .80
67 Tobias, Doomed Conqueror U :W:/:B: .05 .10
68 Tor Wauki the Younger U :K:/:R: .10 .20
69 Torsten, Founder of Benalia M :G:/:W: .25 .50
70 Xira, the Golden Sting R :K:/:R:/:G: .12 .25
71 Historian's Boon R :W: 2.00 4.00
72 Robaran Mercenaries R :W: .12 .25
73 Emperor Mihail II R :B: .75 1.50
74 Activated Sleeper R :K: .50 1.00
75 Rosnakht, Heir of Rohgahh R :R: .15 .30
76 Baru, Wurmspeaker R :G: .15 .30
77 Greensleeves, Maro-Sorcerer M :G: 20.00 40.00
78 Jenson Carthalion, Druid Exile M :G:/:W: .75 1.50
79 Shanid, Sleepers' Scourge M :R:/:W:/:K: 1.50 3.00
80 The Mana Rig M .75 1.50
81 Zeriam, Golden Wind R :W: .20 .40
82 Moira, Urborg Haunt R :K: .25 .50
83 Mana Cannons R :R: .75 1.50
84 The Reaver Cleaver R :R: 7.50 15.00
85 Bladewing, Deathless Tyrant R :K:/:R: 1.25 2.50
86 Cadric, Soul Kindler R :R:/:W: 1.25 2.50
87 Fallaji Wayfarer R :G: 1.25 2.50
88 Iridian Maelstrom R :W:/:B:/:K:/:R:/:G: .50 1.00
89 Primeval Spawn R :W:/:B:/:K:/:R:/:G: .75 1.50
90 Two-Headed Hellkite R :W:/:B:/:K:/:R:/:G: 4.00 8.00
91 Unite the Coalition R :W:/:B:/:K:/:R:/:G: .50 1.00
92 Verrak, Warped Sengir R :W:/:K: .40 .80
93 Gerrard's Hourglass Pendant R 1.00 2.00
94 Obsidian Obelisk R .30 .60
95 The Peregrine Dynamo R 1.00 2.00
96 Tiller Engine R 2.50 5.00
97 Anafenza, Kin-Tree Spirit R :W: .07 .15
98 The Circle of Loyalty M :W: .30 .75
99 Day of Destiny R :W: .12 .25
100 Generous Gift U :W: .75 1.50
101 Hero of Precinct One R :W: .10 .20
102 Jazal Goldmane M :W: .12 .25
103 Odric, Lunarch Marshal R :W: .15 .30
104 Path to Exile U :W: 1.25 2.50
105 Teshar, Ancestor's Apostle R :W: .10 .20
106 Unbreakable Formation R :W: .12 .25
107 Urza's Ruinous Blast R :W: .20 .40
108 Zetalpa, Primal Dawn R :W: .15 .30
109 Echoing Truth C :B: .12 .25
110 Ambition's Cost U :K: .10 .20
111 Drana, Liberator of Malakir M :K: .25 .50
112 Hero's Downfall U :K: .10 .20
113 Josu Vess, Lich Knight R :K: .07 .15
114 Kothophed, Soul Hoarder R :K: .06 .12
115 Night's Whisper C :K: .75 1.50
116 Painful Truths R :K: .12 .25
117 Read the Bones C :K: .15 .30
118 Alesha, Who Smiles at Death R :R: .05 .10
119 Ashling the Pilgrim R :R: .10 .20
120 Captain Lannery Storm R :R: .10 .20
121 Etali, Primal Storm R :R: .30 .60
122 Faithless Looting C :R: .30 .60
123 Kari Zev, Skyship Raider R :R: .10 .20
124 Krenko, Tin Street Kingpin R :R: .30 .75
125 Neheb, Dreadhorde Champion R :R: .15 .30
126 Radiant Flames R :R: .06 .12
127 Thrill of Possibility C :R: .05 .10
128 Abundant Growth C :G: .25 .50
129 Beast Within U :G: .75 1.50
130 Cultivate C :G: .30 .75
131 Explore C :G: .12 .25
132 Explosive Vegetation U :G: .30 .60
133 Farseek C :G: 1.25 2.50
134 Kodama's Reach C :G: 1.00 2.00
135 Migration Path U :G: .20 .40
136 Path to the World Tree U :G: .07 .15
137 Search for Tomorrow C :G: .12 .25
138 Abzan Charm U :W:/:K:/:G: .10 .20
139 Adriana, Captain of the Guard R :R:/:W: .10 .20
140 Archelos, Lagoon Mystic R :K:/:G:/:B: .10 .20
141 Arvad the Cursed U :W:/:K: .10 .20
142 Atla Palani, Nest Tender R :R:/:G:/:W: .20 .40
143 Baleful Strix R :B:/:K: 1.50 3.00
144 Bedevil R :K:/:R: .30 .60
145 Bell Borca, Spectral Sergeant R :R:/:W: .05 .10
146 Chromanticore M :W:/:B:/:K:/:R:/:G: .20 .40
147 Coiling Oracle C :G: .07 .15
148 Duneblast R :W:/:K:/:G: .12 .25
149 Faeburrow Elder R :G:/:W: 2.00 4.00
150 Fusion Elemental U :W:/:B:/:K:/:R:/:G: .06 .12
151 Garna, the Bloodflame U :K:/:R: .05 .10
152 Glint-Eye Nephilim R :B:/:K:/:R:/:G: .07 .15
153 Growth Spiral C :G: .25 .50
154 Illuna, Apex of Wishes M :G:/:B:/:R: .15 .30
155 Kaya's Wrath R :W:/:K: .12 .25
156 Knight of New Alara R :G:/:W: .15 .30
157 Lavalanche R :K:/:R:/:G: .07 .15
158 Maelstrom Archangel M :W:/:B:/:K:/:R:/:G: .30 .60
159 Maelstrom Nexus M :W:/:B:/:K:/:R:/:G: .40 .80
160 Merciless Eviction R :W:/:K: .15 .30
161 Mortify U :W:/:K: .10 .20
162 Naya Charm U :R:/:G:/:W: .12 .25
163 Nethroi, Apex of Death M :W:/:K:/:G: .20 .40
164 O-Kagachi, Vengeful Kami M :W:/:R:/:K:/:R:/:G: .40 .80
165 Primevals' Glorious Rebirth R :W:/:K: .40 .80
166 Rienne, Angel of Rebirth M :R:/:G:/:W: .30 .60
167 Selvala, Explorer Returned R :G:/:W: .12 .25
168 Sultai Charm U :K:/:G:/:B: .10 .20
169 Surrak Dragonclaw M :G:/:B:/:R: .60 1.25
170 Sylvan Reclamation U :G:/:W: .10 .20
171 Tajic, Blade of the Legion R :R:/:W: .07 .15
172 Terminate C :K:/:R: .25 .50
173 Time Wipe R :W:/:B: .12 .25
174 Wear // Tear U :R:/:W: .40 .80
175 Xyris, the Writhing Storm M :G:/:B:/:R: .20 .40
176 Zaxara, the Exemplary M :K:/:G:/:B: .25 .50
177 Arcane Signet C .50 1.00
178 Blackblade Reforged R .20 .40
179 Bontu's Monument U 1.50 3.00
180 Coalition Relic R .25 .50
181 Commander's Sphere C .07 .15
182 Fellwar Stone U .30 .60
183 Hazoret's Monument U .20 .40
184 Hedron Archive U .07 .15
185 Heroes' Podium R .20 .40
186 Hero's Blade U .10 .20
187 Honor-Worn Shaku U .10 .20
188 Oketra's Monument U 1.25 2.50
189 Prophetic Prism C .07 .15
190 Sol Ring U .75 1.50
191 Solemn Simulacrum R .30 .75
192 Sword of the Chosen R .07 .15
193 Tenza, Godo's Maul U .10 .20
194 Transguild Courier U .05 .10
195 Traxos, Scourge of Kroog R .06 .12
196 Arcane Sanctum U .12 .25
197 Bad River U .30 .75
198 Battlefield Forge R .30 .75
199 Bojuka Bog C .60 1.25
200 Boros Garrison U .07 .15
201 Canopy Vista R .30 .60
202 Cascading Cataracts R 1.50 3.00
203 Cinder Glade R .20 .40
204 Command Tower C .15 .30
205 Crumbling Necropolis U .15 .30
206 Crystal Quarry R .40 .80
207 Dragonskull Summit R 1.50 3.00
208 Evolving Wilds C .06 .12
209 Exotic Orchard R .12 .25
210 Flood Plain U .12 .25
211 Foreboding Ruins R .12 .25
212 Frontier Bivouac U .15 .30
213 Geier Reach Sanitarium R 1.25 2.50
214 Grasslands U .12 .25
215 Jungle Shrine U .20 .40
216 Krosan Verge U .12 .25
217 Mikokoro, Center of the Sea R .75 1.50
218 Mobilized District R .06 .12
219 Mountain Valley U .25 .50
220 Murmuring Bosk R .25 .50
221 Mystic Monastery U .20 .40
222 Nomad Outpost U .30 .60
223 Opulent Palace U .30 .60
224 Orzhov Basilica U .10 .20
225 Prairie Stream R .12 .25
226 Rakdos Carnarium U .12 .25
227 Reliquary Tower U 2.50 5.00
228 Rocky Tar Pit U .20 .40
229 Sandsteppe Citadel U .25 .50
230 Savage Lands U .40 .80
231 Seaside Citadel U .30 .60
232 Shivan Gorge R .15 .30
233 Shizo, Death's Storehouse R 4.00 8.00
234 Smoldering Marsh R .20 .40
235 Sunken Hollow R .15 .30
236 Temple of Malice R .15 .30
237 Temple of Silence R .07 .15
238 Temple of Triumph R .10 .20
239 Terramorphic Expanse C .10 .20
240 Tyrite Sanctum R .25 .50

2022 Magic The Gathering Dominaria United Commander Tokens

1 Angel .75 1.50
3 Knight .07 .15
5 Merfolk .20 .40
7 Insect .12 .25
9 Zombie .07 .15
13 Kobolds of Kher Keep .20 .40
15 Badger 1.50 3.00
17 Cat Warrior .10 .20
19 Wurm .20 .40
20 Sand Warrior .50 1.00
21 Stangg Twin .10 .20
24 Treasure .15 .30

2022 Magic The Gathering Double Masters 2022

1 Emrakul, the Aeons Torn M 12.50 25.00
2 Kozilek, Butcher of Truth M 25.00 50.00
3 Ulamog, the Infinite Gyre M 25.00 50.00
4 Abzan Falconer U :W: .12 .25
5 Alnok Bond-Kin C :W: .07 .15
6 Anointer of Valor C :W: .07 .16
7 Battlefield Promotion C :W: .07 .15
8 Divine Visitation M :W: 5.00 10.00
9 Doomed Traveler C :W: .07 .15
10 Emiel the Blessed M :W: 3.00 6.00
11 Flickerwisp U :W: .12 .25
12 Gods Willing C :W: .07 .15
13 Hyena Umbra C :W: .07 .15
14 Knightly Valor C :W: .07 .15
15 Last Breath C :W: .07 .15
16 Leonin Arbiter R :W: .75 1.50
17 Mentor of the Meek U :W: .12 .25
18 Mikaeus, the Lunarch R :W: .20 .40
19 Militia Bugler C :W: .07 .15
20 Momentary Blink C :W: .07 .15
21 Monastery Mentor M :W: 7.50 15.00
22 Myth Realized U :W: .12 .25
23 Path to Exile U :W: 1.50 3.00
24 Relief Captain C :W: .07 .15
25 Restoration Angel R :W: .30 .75
26 Reveillark R :W: .25 .50
27 Scale Blessing U :W: .12 .25
28 Seeker of the Way C :W: .07 .15
29 Sensor Splicer C :W: .07 .15
30 Settle Beyond Reality C :W: .07 .15
31 Smothering Tithe R :W: 20.00 40.00
32 Teferi's Protection R :W: 15.00 30.00
33 Wall of Omens U :W: .12 .25
34 Weathered Wayfarer R :W: 2.00 4.00
35 Wingsteed Rider C :W: .07 .15
36 Advanced Stitchwing C :B: .07 .15
37 Aethersnipe C :B: .07 .15
38 As Foretold M :B: 3.00 6.00
39 Aven Initiate C :B: .07 .15
40 Body Double U :B: .20 .40
41 Breakthrough U :B: .12 .25
42 Capture Sphere C :B: .07 .15
43 Consecrated Sphinx M :B: 17.50 35.00
44 Deep Analysis C :B: .07 .15
45 Deranged Assistant C :B: .07 .15
46 Disciple of the Ring R :B: .20 .40
47 Domestication U :B: .12 .25
48 Eel Umbra C :B: .07 .15
49 Forbidden Alchemy C :B: .07 .15
50 Force of Negation R :B: 25.00 50.00
51 Gifts Ungiven R :B: .30 .75
52 Ingenious Skaab C :B: .07 .15
53 Jeskai Elder C :B: .07 .15
54 Kasmina's Transmutation C :B: .07 .15
55 Kederekt Leviathan R :B: .20 .40
56 Makeshift Mauler C :B: .07 .15
57 Mana Drain M :B: 30.00 60.00
58 Mana Leak C :B: .07 .15
59 Mistfire Adept U :B: .12 .25
60 Mulldrifter U :B: .12 .25
61 Nephalia Smuggler U :B: .12 .25
62 Pull from Tomorrow R :B: .50 1.00
63 Spell Pierce C :B: .07 .15
64 Talrand, Sky Summoner R :B: .20 .40
65 Thought Scour C :B: .07 .15
66 Venser, Shaper Savant R :B: .75 1.50
67 Wash Out U :B: .12 .25
68 Balustrade Spy C :K: .07 .15
69 Bitterblossom M :K: 15.00 30.00
70 Blood Artist U :K: 1.50 3.00
71 Bloodflow Connoisseur C :K: .07 .15
72 Carrier Thrall C :K: .07 .15
73 Damnation R :K: 10.00 20.00
74 Disfigure C :K: .07 .15
75 Eyeblight's Ending C :K: .07 .15
76 Go for the Throat U :K: .20 .40
77 Graveblade Marauder U :K: .12 .25
78 Gravecrawler R :K: 3.00 6.00
79 Imperial Seal M :K: 75.00 150.00
80 Inquisition of Kozilek U :K: .30 .75
81 Liliana, the Last Hope M :K: 7.50 15.00
82 Liliana's Elite C :K: .07 .15
83 Necrotic Ooze R :K: 1.00 2.00
84 Ob Nixilis, Unshackled R :K: 1.00 2.00
85 Oona's Prowler R :K: .20 .40
86 Scion of Darkness U :K: .12 .25
87 Seekers' Squire C :K: .07 .15
88 Severed Strands C :K: .07 .15
89 Shadowborn Apostle C :K: 1.50 3.00
90 Skeleton Archer C :K: .07 .15
91 Skinrender U :K: .12 .25
92 Strands of Undeath C :K: .07 .15
93 Supernatural Stamina C :K: .07 .15
94 Surgical Extraction R :K: 4.00 8.00
95 Unburial Rites U :K: .12 .25
96 Unearth C :K: .07 .15
97 Vampire Sovereign C :K: .07 .15
98 Vampiric Rites U :K: .12 .25
99 Yahenni, Undying Partisan R :K: 1.50 3.00
100 Abbot of Keral Keep R :R: .20 .40
101 Alesha, Who Smiles at Death R :R: .20 .40
102 Anger of the Gods R :R: .50 1.00
103 Backdraft Hellkite R :R: .30 .60
104 Bedlam Reveler R :R: .20 .40
106 Chaos Warp R :R: 1.00 2.00
106 Dark-Dweller Oracle C :R: .07 .15
107 Dockside Extortionist M :R: 40.00 80.00
108 Dreamshaper Shaman U :R: .12 .25
109 Fiery Fall C :R: .07 .15
110 Goblin Banneret U :R: .12 .25
111 Greater Gargadon R :R: .20 .40
112 Hero of the Games C :R: .07 .15
113 Hissing Iguanar C :R: .07 .15
114 Kruin Striker C :R: .07 .15
115 Labyrinth Champion U :R: .12 .25
116 Lava Coil C :R: .07 .15
117 Lightning Bolt U :R: .75 1.50
118 Living Lightning C :R: .07 .15
119 Monastery Swiftspear C :R: .30 .75
120 Pirate's Pillage C :R: .07 .15
121 Purphoros's Emissary C :R: .07 .15
122 Rift Bolt C :R: .07 .15
123 Seasoned Pyromancer M :R: 12.50 25.00
124 Sparkmage's Gambit C :R: .07 .15
125 Staggershock U :R: .12 .25
126 Storm Fleet Pyromancer C :R: .07 .15
127 Surreal Memoir U :R: .12 .25
128 Titan's Strength C :R: .07 .15
129 Twinflame R :R: 1.25 2.50
130 Warrior's Oath M :R: 10.00 20.00
131 Young Pyromancer U :R: .12 .25
132 Allosaurus Shepherd M :G: 25.00 50.00
133 Ambuscade C :G: .07 .15
134 Annoyed Altisaur C :G: .07 .15
135 Arachnus Spinner U :G: .12 .25
136 Arachnus Web C :G: .07 .15
137 Biogenic Upgrade U :G: .12 .25
138 Bloom Tender R :G: 7.50 15.00
139 Brindle Shoat C :G: .07 .15
140 Centaur Battlemaster U :G: .12 .25
141 Concordant Crossroads M :G: 15.00 30.00
142 Deadly Recluse C :G: .07 .15
143 Devoted Druid U :G: .75 1.50
144 Elvish Rejuvenator C :G: .07 .15
145 Eternal Witness U :G: 1.00 2.00
146 Experiment One C :G: .07 .15
147 Food Chain M :G: 25.00 50.00
148 Gnarlback Rhino C :G: .07 .15
149 Grapple with the Past C :G: .07 .15
150 Green Sun's Zenith R :G: 7.50 15.00
151 Hardened Scales R :G: 3.00 6.00
152 Impervious Greatwurm R :G: 1.25 2.50
153 Might of Old Krosa C :G: .07 .15
154 Oracle of Mul Daya R :G: 5.00 10.00
155 Rampant Growth C :G: .15 .30
156 Rancor U :G: .25 .50
157 Rishkar, Peema Renegade R :G: .20 .40
158 Spider Spawning U :G: .12 .25
159 Splinterfright R :G: .20 .40
160 Summer Bloom U :G: .30 .75
161 Thrive C :G: .07 .15
162 Travel Preparations U :G: .12 .25
163 Tuskguard Captain C :G: .07 .15
164 Webweaver Changeling C :G: .07 .15
165 Abzan Ascendancy R :W:/:K:/:G: .20 .40
166 Abzan Charm U :W:/:K:/:G: .12 .25
167 Aethermage's Touch U :W:/:B: .12 .25
168 Agony Warp C :B:/:K: .07 .15
169 Aminatou, the Fateshifter M :W:/:B:/:K: 2.00 4.00
170 Anguished Unmaking R :W:/:K: 2.50 5.00
171 Animar, Soul of Elements M :G:/:B:/:R: 4.00 8.00
172 Arjun, the Shifting Flame R :B:/:R: .25 .50
173 Ashen Rider R :W:/:K: .20 .40
174 Ashenmoor Liege R :K:/:R: .50 1.00
175 Assassin's Trophy R :K:/:G: 4.00 8.00
176 Atarka's Command R :R:/:G: .30 .75
177 Atla Palani, Nest Tender R :R:/:G:/:W: .25 .50
178 Auger Spree C :K:/:R: .07 .15
179 Aurelia, the Warleader M :R:/:W: 7.50 15.00
180 Balefire Liege R :R:/:W: .50 1.00
181 Bant Charm U :G:/:W:/:B: .12 .25
182 Bear's Companion U :G:/:B:/:R: .12 .25
183 Blazing Hellhound U :K:/:R: .12 .25
184 Bloodbraid Elf U :R:/:G: .12 .25
185 Bloodwater Entity C :B:/:R: .07 .15
186 Boartusk Liege R :R:/:G: .30 .75
187 Bounty of the Luxa U :G:/:B: .12 .25
188 Bring to Light R :G:/:B: .20 .40
189 Burning-Tree Emissary C :R:/:G: .07 .15
190 Call to the Feast C :W:/:K: .07 .15
191 Cartel Aristocrat C :W:/:K: .07 .15
192 Child of Alara R :W:/:B:/:K:/:R:/:G: .75 1.50
193 Chronicler of Heroes C :G:/:W: .07 .15
194 Coiling Oracle C :G:/:B: .07 .15
195 Conclave Mentor U :G:/:W: .12 .25
196 Crackling Doom U :R:/:W:/:K: .12 .25
197 Creakwood Liege R :K:/:G: 1.00 2.00
198 Dack's Duplicate R :B:/:R: .30 .75
199 Dauntless Escort R :G:/:W: .25 .50
200 Deathbringer Liege R :W:/:K: .50 1.00
201 Doran, the Siege Tower R :W:/:K:/:G: .50 1.00
202 Dragonlord Dromoka M :G:/:W: 7.50 15.00
203 Dragonlord Silumgar M :B:/:K: 2.00 4.00
204 Dreg Mangler C :K:/:G: .07 .15
205 Drogskol Reaver R :W:/:B: 1.25 2.50
206 Dromoka's Command R :G:/:W: .30 .60
207 Elenda, the Dusk Rose M :W:/:K: 7.50 15.00
208 Elsha of the Infinite R :B:/:R:/:W: .25 .50
209 Empyrial Archangel R :G:/:W:/:B: .20 .40
210 Extract from Darkness U :B:/:K: .12 .25
211 Ezuri, Claw of Progress M :G:/:B: 2.00 4.00
212 Fiery Justice R :R:/:G:/:W: .20 .40
213 Figure of Destiny R :R:/:W: .20 .40
214 Fireblade Artist C :K:/:R: .07 .15
215 Firesong and Sunspeaker R :R:/:W: .25 .50
216 Ghave, Guru of Spores M :W:/:K:/:G: 1.25 2.50
217 Glen Elendra Liege R :B:/:K: .30 .75
218 Glimpse the Unthinkable R :B:/:K: 1.50 3.00
219 Gloryscale Viashino U :R:/:G:/:W: .12 .25
220 Glowspore Shaman C :K:/:G: .07 .15
221 Grand Arbiter Augustin IV R :W:/:B: 2.00 4.00
222 Grim Flayer R :K:/:G: .50 1.00
223 Ground Assault C :R:/:G: .07 .15
224 Guided Passage R :G:/:B:/:R: .20 .40
225 Hellkite Overlord M :K:/:R:/:G: .75 1.50
226 Heroic Reinforcements U :R:/:W: .12 .25
227 Hostage Taker R :B:/:K: .30 .60
228 Hydroid Krasis R :G:/:B: 2.50 5.00
229 Intet, the Dreamer R :G:/:B:/:R: .25 .50
230 Izzet Charm C :B:/:R: .07 .15
231 Jeskai Ascendancy R :B:/:R:/:W: .25 .50
232 Jeskai Charm U :B:/:R:/:W: .12 .25
233 Jodah, Archmage Eternal R :B:/:R:/:W: .20 .40
234 Judith, the Scourge Diva R :K:/:R: .20 .40
235 Kaalia of the Vast M :R:/:W:/:K: 7.50 15.00
236 Kaervek the Merciless R :K:/:R: .20 .40
237 Kambal, Consul of Allocation R :W:/:K: .60 1.25
238 Karador, Ghost Chieftain M :W:/:K:/:G: .75 1.50
239 Kolaghan's Command R :K:/:R: 2.00 4.00
240 Lavalanche R :K:/:R:/:G: .20 .40
241 League Guildmage U :B:/:R: .12 .25
242 Legion's Initiative R :R:/:W: .20 .40
243 Lightning Helix U :R:/:W: .12 .25
244 Lord of Extinction M :K:/:G: 3.00 6.00
245 Lotleth Troll U :K:/:G: .12 .25
246 Lyev Skyknight C :W:/:B: .07 .15
247 Magister Sphinx R :W:/:B:/:K: .50 1.00
248 Marchesa, the Black Rose R :B:/:K:/:R: .75 1.50
249 Martial Glory C :R:/:W: .07 .15
250 Master Biomancer R :G:/:B: .30 .60
251 Master of Cruelties M :K:/:R: 2.50 5.00
252 Mathas, Fiend Seeker R :R:/:W:/:K: .25 .50
253 Mayael's Aria R :R:/:G:/:W: .75 1.50
254 The Mimeoplasm R :K:/:G:/:B: .30 .75
255 Mindwrack Liege R :B:/:R: .25 .50
256 Mistmeadow Witch U :W:/:B: .12 .25
257 Mizzix of the Izmagnus M :B:/:R: 2.00 4.00
258 Muldrotha, the Gravetide M :K:/:G:/:B: 2.50 5.00
259 Murkfiend Liege R :G:/:B: .30 .75
260 Nicol Bolas, God-Pharaoh M :B:/:K:/:R: 2.50 5.00
261 Orzhov Pontiff U :W:/:K: .12 .25
262 Phyrexian Tyranny R :B:/:K:/:R: .60 1.25
263 Privileged Position R :G:/:W: 2.50 5.00
264 Prized Amalgam R :B:/:K: .20 .40
265 Prophetic Bolt U :B:/:R: .12 .25
266 Psychic Symbiont U :B:/:K: .12 .25
267 Qasali Pridemage C :G:/:W: .07 .15
268 Rafiq of the Many R :G:/:W:/:B: .50 1.00
269 River Hoopoe U :G:/:B: .12 .25
270 Roon of the Hidden Realm R :G:/:W:/:B: .20 .40
271 Ruric Thar, the Unbowed R :R:/:G: .20 .40
272 Scab-Clan Giant U :R:/:G: .12 .25
273 Sedraxis Specter U :B:/:K:/:R: .12 .25
274 Sedris, the Traitor King M :B:/:K:/:R: 1.25 2.50
275 Shattergang Brothers R :K:/:R:/:G: .20 .40
276 Sidisi, Brood Tyrant R :K:/:G:/:B: .20 .40
277 Skullbriar, the Walking Grave R :K:/:G: .75 1.50
278 Sprouting Thrinax U :K:/:R:/:G: .12 .25
279 Sultai Soothsayer U :K:/:G:/:B: .12 .25
280 Supreme Verdict R :W:/:B: 4.00 8.00
281 Tariel, Reckoner of Souls R :R:/:W:/:K: .75 1.50
282 Teneb, the Harvester R :W:/:K:/:G: .25 .50
283 Tenth District Legionnaire C :R:/:W: .07 .15
284 Terminate U :K:/:R: .25 .50
285 Thistledown Liege R :W:/:B: .30 .75
286 Thousand-Year Storm R :B:/:R: 1.50 3.00
287 Thraximundar R :B:/:K:/:R: .20 .40
288 Tower Gargoyle U :W:/:B:/:K: .12 .25
289 Ulasht, the Hate Seed R :R:/:G: .20 .40
290 Uril, the Miststalker M :R:/:G:/:W: 2.00 4.00
291 Varina, Lich Queen R :W:/:B:/:K: .25 .50
292 Villainous Wealth R :K:/:G:/:B: .20 .40
293 Wasitora, Nekoru Queen R :K:/:R:/:G: .25 .50
294 Wilt-Leaf Liege R :G:/:W: .30 .75
295 Winged Coatl C :G:/:B: .07 .15
296 Wrenn and Six M :R:/:G: 40.00 80.00
297 Zur the Enchanter R :W:/:B:/:K: .75 1.50
298 Aether Vial R 7.50 15.00
299 Bloodforged Battle-Axe R 2.50 5.00
300 Civic Saber U .12 .25
301 Coldsteel Heart U .30 .75

302 Conqueror's Flail R	3.00	6.00
303 Crucible of Worlds M	15.00	30.00
304 Darksteel Plate R	4.00	8.00
305 Dragon Arch U	.50	1.00
306 Firemind Vessel U	.12	.25
307 Livewire Lash U	.12	.25
308 Mana Vault M	30.00	75.00
309 Nim Deathmantle R	2.00	4.00
310 Panharmonicon R	4.00	8.00
311 Phyrexian Altar R	25.00	50.00
312 Pithing Needle R	.30	.75
313 Planar Bridge R	.75	1.50
314 Sensei's Divining Top R	20.00	40.00
315 Thrumming Stone R	4.00	8.00
316 Traveler's Amulet C	.07	.15
317 Vedalken Orrery R	7.50	15.00
318 Azorius Chancery U	.12	.25
319 Boros Garrison U	.12	.25
320 Cavern of Souls M	40.00	80.00
321 City of Brass R	7.50	15.00
322 Dimir Aqueduct U	.15	.30
323 Forbidden Orchard R	4.00	8.00
324 Golgari Rot Farm U	.12	.25
325 Gruul Turf U	.12	.25
326 Izzet Boilerworks U	.12	.25
327 Orzhov Basilica U	.12	.25
328 Pillar of the Paruns R	1.25	2.50
329 Rakdos Carnarium U	.15	.30
330 Selesnya Sanctuary U	.12	.25
331 Simic Growth Chamber U	.12	.25
332 Cryptic Spires C	.07	.15
333 Liliana, the Last Hope M :K:	10.00	20.00
334 Wrenn and Six M :R:/:G:	50.00	100.00
335 Emrakul, the Aeons Torn M	17.50	35.00
336 Kozilek, Butcher of Truth M	30.00	75.00
337 Ulamog, the Infinite Gyre M	30.00	75.00
338 Emiel the Blessed M :W:	4.00	8.00
339 Flickerwisp U :W:	.50	1.00
340 Mentor of the Meek U :W:	.30	.60
341 Seeker of the Way C :W:	.07	.15
342 Smothering Tithe R :W:	30.00	60.00
343 Teferi's Protection R :W:	12.50	25.00
344 Wall of Omens U :W:	.50	1.00
345 Consecrated Sphinx M :B:	20.00	40.00
346 Force of Negation R :B:	30.00	75.00
347 Gifts Ungiven R :B:	.75	1.50
348 Mana Drain M :B:	30.00	75.00
349 Mulldrifter U :B:	1.50	3.00
350 Spell Pierce C :B:	.50	1.00
351 Thought Scour C :B:	.30	.75
352 Blood Artist U :K:	1.50	3.00
353 Damnation R :K:	12.50	25.00
354 Imperial Seal M :K:	100.00	200.00
355 Inquisition of Kozilek U :K:	1.25	2.50
356 Surgical Extraction R :K:	5.00	10.00
357 Unearth C :K:	.50	1.00
358 Anger of the Gods R :R:	1.25	2.50
359 Chaos Warp R :R:	4.00	8.00
360 Dockside Extortionist M :R:	40.00	80.00
361 Lightning Bolt U :R:	1.50	3.00
362 Monastery Swiftspear C :R:	1.00	2.00
363 Seasoned Pyromancer M :R:	25.00	50.00
364 Young Pyromancer U :R:	.75	1.50
365 Allosaurus Shepherd M :G:	30.00	60.00
366 Bloom Tender R :G:	7.50	15.00
367 Concordant Crossroads M :G:	20.00	40.00
368 Eternal Witness U :G:	1.25	2.50
369 Hardened Scales R :G:	3.00	6.00
370 Oracle of Mul Daya R :G:	7.50	15.00
371 Rampant Growth C :G:	.60	1.25
372 Assassin's Trophy R :K:/:G:	6.00	12.00
373 Bloodbraid Elf U :R:/:G:	.50	1.00
374 Burning-Tree Emissary C :R:/:G:	.30	.75
375 Coiling Oracle C :G:/:B:	.12	.25
376 Dragonlord Dromoka M :G:/:W:	7.50	15.00
377 Elenda, the Dusk Rose M :W:/:K:	7.50	15.00
378 Glimpse the Unthinkable R :B:/:K:	1.50	3.00
379 Grand Arbiter Augustin IV R :W:/:B:	2.50	5.00
380 Grim Flayer R :K:/:G:	1.50	3.00
381 Kolaghan's Command R :K:/:R:	3.00	6.00
382 Marchesa, the Black Rose R :B:/:K:/:R:	1.50	3.00
383 The Mimeoplasm R :K:/:G:/:B:	1.00	2.00
384 Muldrotha, the Gravetide M :K:/:G:/:B:	7.50	15.00
385 Privileged Position R :G:/:W:	3.00	6.00
386 Qasali Pridemage C :G:/:W:	.07	.15
387 Sedris, the Traitor King M :B:/:K:/:R:	2.50	5.00
388 Supreme Verdict R :W:/:B:	4.00	8.00
389 Terminate U :K:/:R:	1.25	2.50
390 Thousand-Year Storm R :B:/:R:	2.50	5.00
391 Aether Vial R	12.50	25.00
392 Bloodforged Battle-Axe R	3.00	6.00
393 Crucible of Worlds M	25.00	50.00
394 Mana Vault M	50.00	100.00
395 Panharmonicon R	4.00	8.00
396 Phyrexian Altar R	30.00	60.00
397 Pithing Needle R	1.50	3.00
398 Sensei's Divining Top R	25.00	50.00
399 Vedalken Orrery R	10.00	20.00
400 Azorius Chancery U	.60	1.25
401 Boros Garrison U	.75	1.50
402 Cavern of Souls M	50.00	100.00
403 City of Brass R	10.00	20.00
404 Dimir Aqueduct U	.75	1.50
405 Forbidden Orchard R	6.00	12.00
406 Golgari Rot Farm U	.75	1.50
407 Gruul Turf U	1.00	2.00
408 Izzet Boilerworks U	.50	1.00
409 Orzhov Basilica U	.75	1.50
410 Rakdos Carnarium U	.75	1.50
411 Selesnya Sanctuary U	1.25	2.50
412 Simic Growth Chamber U	1.25	2.50
413 Emrakul, the Aeons Torn M	40.00	80.00
414 Kozilek, Butcher of Truth M	30.00	75.00
415 Ulamog, the Infinite Gyre M	30.00	75.00
416 Divine Visitation M :W:	10.00	20.00
417 Emiel the Blessed M :W:	12.50	25.00
418 Leonin Arbiter R :W:	3.00	6.00
419 Mikaeus, the Lunarch R :W:	1.50	3.00
420 Monastery Mentor M :W:	12.50	25.00
421 Restoration Angel R :W:	2.50	5.00
422 Reveillark R :W:	2.50	5.00
423 Smothering Tithe R :W:	30.00	60.00
424 Teferi's Protection R :W:	20.00	40.00
425 Weathered Wayfarer R :W:	4.00	8.00
426 As Foretold M :B:	10.00	20.00
427 Consecrated Sphinx M :B:	25.00	50.00
428 Disciple of the Ring R :B:	.75	1.50
429 Force of Negation R :B:	50.00	100.00
430 Gifts Ungiven R :B:	1.50	3.00
431 Kederekt Leviathan R :B:	1.25	2.50
432 Mana Drain M :B:	60.00	125.00
433 Pull from Tomorrow R :B:	2.50	5.00
434 Talrand, Sky Summoner R :B:	2.00	4.00
435 Venser, Shaper Savant R :B:	3.00	6.00
436 Bitterblossom M :K:	30.00	75.00
437 Damnation R :K:	25.00	50.00
438 Gravecrawler R :K:	6.00	12.00
439 Imperial Seal M :K:	200.00	400.00
440 Liliana, the Last Hope M :K:	30.00	60.00
441 Necrotic Ooze R :K:	3.00	6.00
442 Ob Nixilis, Unshackled R :K:	3.00	6.00
443 Oona's Prowler R :K:	1.00	2.00
444 Surgical Extraction R :K:	7.50	15.00
445 Yahenni, Undying Partisan R :K:	4.00	8.00
446 Abbot of Keral Keep R :R:	.75	1.50
447 Alesha, Who Smiles at Death R :R:	1.25	2.50
448 Anger of the Gods R :R:	2.00	4.00
449 Backdraft Hellkite R :R:	2.00	4.00
450 Bedlam Reveler R :R:	1.50	3.00
451 Chaos Warp R :R:	4.00	8.00
452 Dockside Extortionist M :R:	100.00	200.00
453 Greater Gargadon R :R:	.50	1.00
454 Seasoned Pyromancer M :R:	25.00	50.00
455 Twinflame R :R:	2.50	5.00
456 Warrior's Oath M :R:	30.00	60.00
457 Allosaurus Shepherd M :G:	40.00	80.00
458 Bloom Tender R :G:	10.00	20.00
459 Concordant Crossroads M :G:	25.00	50.00
460 Food Chain M :G:	45.00	90.00
461 Green Sun's Zenith R :G:	20.00	40.00
462 Hardened Scales R :G:	4.00	8.00
463 Impervious Greatwurm R :G:	3.00	6.00
464 Oracle of Mul Daya R :G:	10.00	20.00
465 Rishkar, Peema Renegade R :G:	1.50	3.00
466 Splinterfright R :G:	.75	1.50
467 Abzan Ascendancy R :W:/:K:/:G:	.75	1.50
468 Aminatou, the Fateshifter M :W:/:B:/:K:	20.00	40.00
469 Anguished Unmaking R :W:/:K:	5.00	10.00
470 Animar, Soul of Elements M :G:/:B:/:R:	25.00	50.00
471 Arjun, the Shifting Flame R :B:/:R:	1.50	3.00
472 Ashen Rider R :W:/:K:	2.00	4.00
473 Ashenmoor Liege R :K:/:R:	1.50	3.00
474 Assassin's Trophy R :K:/:G:	10.00	20.00
475 Atarka's Command R :R:/:G:	2.00	4.00
476 Atla Palani, Nest Tender R :R:/:G:/:W:	3.00	6.00
477 Aurelia, the Warleader M :R:/:W:	20.00	40.00
478 Balefire Liege R :R:/:W:	2.00	4.00
479 Boartusk Liege R :R:/:G:	2.00	4.00
480 Bring to Light R :G:/:B:	3.00	6.00
481 Child of Alara R :W:/:B:/:K:/:R:/:G:	3.00	6.00
482 Creakwood Liege R :K:/:G:	3.00	6.00
483 Dack's Duplicate R :B:/:R:	1.50	3.00
484 Dauntless Escort R :G:/:W:	1.00	2.00
485 Deathbringer Liege R :W:/:K:	3.00	6.00
486 Doran, the Siege Tower R :W:/:K:/:G:	3.00	6.00
487 Dragonlord Dromoka M :G:/:W:	15.00	30.00
488 Dragonlord Silumgar M :B:/:K:	7.50	15.00
489 Drogskol Reaver R :W:/:B:	3.00	6.00
490 Dromoka's Command R :G:/:W:	.75	1.50
491 Elenda, the Dusk Rose M :W:/:K:	12.50	25.00
492 Elsha of the Infinite R :B:/:R:/:W:	2.50	5.00
493 Empyrial Archangel R :G:/:W:/:B:	1.25	2.50
494 Ezuri, Claw of Progress M :G:/:B:	7.50	15.00
495 Fiery Justice R :R:/:G:/:W:	.60	1.25
496 Figure of Destiny R :R:/:W:	1.50	3.00
497 Firesong and Sunspeaker R :R:/:W:	1.50	3.00
498 Ghave, Guru of Spores M :W:/:K:/:G:	17.50	35.00
499 Glen Elendra Liege R :B:/:K:	1.50	3.00
500 Glimpse the Unthinkable R :B:/:K:	4.00	8.00
501 Grand Arbiter Augustin IV R :W:/:B:	6.00	12.00
502 Grim Flayer R :K:/:G:	1.50	3.00
503 Guided Passage R :G:/:B:/:R:	.75	1.50
504 Hellkite Overlord M :K:/:R:/:G:	4.00	8.00
505 Hostage Taker R :B:/:K:	3.00	6.00
506 Hydroid Krasis R :G:/:B:	5.00	10.00
507 Intet, the Dreamer R :G:/:B:/:R:	2.00	4.00
508 Jeskai Ascendancy R :B:/:R:/:W:	2.00	4.00
509 Jodah, Archmage Eternal R :B:/:R:/:W:	4.00	8.00
510 Judith, the Scourge Diva R :K:/:R:	1.50	3.00
511 Kaalia of the Vast M :R:/:W:/:K:	17.50	35.00
512 Kaervek the Merciless R :K:/:R:	1.50	3.00
513 Kambal, Consul of Allocation R :W:/:K:	5.00	10.00
514 Karador, Ghost Chieftain M :W:/:K:/:G:	3.00	6.00
515 Kolaghan's Command R :K:/:R:	4.00	8.00
516 Lavalanche R :K:/:R:/:G:	.75	1.50
517 Legion's Initiative R :R:/:W:	1.50	3.00
518 Lord of Extinction M :K:/:G:	6.00	12.00
519 Magister Sphinx R :W:/:B:/:K:	1.50	3.00
520 Marchesa, the Black Rose R :B:/:K:/:R:	3.00	6.00
521 Master Biomancer R :G:/:B:	1.50	3.00
522 Master of Cruelties M :K:/:R:	12.50	25.00
523 Mathas, Fiend Seeker R :R:/:W:/:K:	1.25	2.50
524 Mayael's Aria R :R:/:G:/:W:	2.00	4.00
525 The Mimeoplasm R :K:/:G:/:B:	1.50	3.00
526 Mindwrack Liege R :B:/:R:	1.50	3.00
527 Mizzix of the Izmagnus M :B:/:R:	5.00	10.00
528 Muldrotha, the Gravetide M :K:/:G:/:B:	4.00	8.00
529 Murkfiend Liege R :G:/:B:	2.50	5.00
530 Nicol Bolas, God-Pharaoh M :B:/:K:/:R:	12.50	25.00
5.31E+02 Phyrexian Tyranny R :B:/:K:/:R:	1.50	3.00
5.32E+02 Privileged Position R :G:/:W:	4.00	8.00
5.33E+02 Prized Amalgam R :B:/:K:	1.25	2.50
5.34E+02 Rafiq of the Many R :G:/:W:/:B:	2.50	5.00
5.35E+02 Roon of the Hidden Realm R :G:/:W:/:B:	3.00	6.00
5.36E+02 Ruric Thar, the Unbowed R :R:/:G:	2.50	5.00
5.37E+02 Sedris, the Traitor King M :B:/:K:/:R:	6.00	12.00
538 Shattergang Brothers R :K:/:R:/:G:	1.50	3.00
539 Sidisi, Brood Tyrant R :K:/:G:/:B:	1.50	3.00
540 Skullbriar, the Walking Grave R :K:/:G:	7.50	15.00
541 Supreme Verdict R :W:/:B:	7.50	15.00
542 Tariel, Reckoner of Souls R :R:/:W:/:K:	1.50	3.00
543 Teneb, the Harvester R :W:/:K:/:G:	1.50	3.00
544 Thistledown Liege R :W:/:B:	.75	1.50
545 Thousand-Year Storm R :B:/:R:	2.50	5.00
546 Thraximundar R :B:/:K:/:R:	1.00	2.00
547 Ulasht, the Hate Seed R :R:/:G:	1.25	2.50
548 Uril, the Miststalker M :R:/:G:/:W:	10.00	20.00
549 Varina, Lich Queen R :W:/:B:/:K:	4.00	8.00
550 Villainous Wealth R :K:/:G:/:B:	2.50	5.00
551 Wasitora, Nekoru Queen R :K:/:R:/:G:	3.00	6.00
552 Wilt-Leaf Liege R :G:/:W:	1.50	3.00
553 Wrenn and Six M :R:/:G:	75.00	150.00
554 Zur the Enchanter R :W:/:B:/:K:	3.00	6.00
555 Aether Vial R	12.50	25.00
556 Bloodforged Battle-Axe R	4.00	8.00
557 Conqueror's Flail R	7.50	15.00
558 Crucible of Worlds M	30.00	60.00
559 Darksteel Plate R	7.50	15.00
560 Mana Vault M	75.00	150.00
561 Nim Deathmantle R	4.00	8.00
562 Panharmonicon R	7.50	15.00
563 Phyrexian Altar R	40.00	80.00
564 Pithing Needle R	2.00	4.00
565 Planar Bridge R	4.00	8.00
566 Sensei's Divining Top R	30.00	60.00
567 Thrumming Stone R	10.00	20.00
568 Vedalken Orrery R	12.50	25.00
569 Cavern of Souls M	75.00	150.00
570 City of Brass R	20.00	40.00
571 Forbidden Orchard R	7.50	15.00
572 Pillar of the Paruns R	3.00	6.00
573 Liliana, the Last Hope M :K:	100.00	200.00
574 Wrenn and Six M :R:/:G:	200.00	400.00
575 Emrakul, the Aeons Torn M	100.00	200.00
576 Kozilek, Butcher of Truth M	150.00	300.00
577 Ulamog, the Infinite Gyre M	125.00	250.00
578 Weathered Wayfarer R :W:	.20	.40
579 Bring to Light R :G:/:B:	.20	.40

2022 Magic The Gathering Double Masters 2022 Tokens

1 Eldrazi Scion	3.00	6.00
2 Spirit	4.00	8.00
3 Angel	3.00	6.00
4 Aven Initiate	3.00	6.00
5 Knight	2.00	4.00
6 Monk	4.00	8.00
7 Soldier	.50	1.00
8 Spirit	3.00	6.00
9 Vampire	1.50	3.00
10 Drake	1.50	3.00
11 Faerie Rogue	1.25	2.50
12 Zombie	.50	1.00
13 Elemental	1.25	2.50
14 Bear	1.50	3.00
15 Boar	1.00	2.00
16 Egg	2.50	5.00
17 Saproling	1.50	3.00
18 Spider	1.25	2.50
19 Cat Dragon	2.00	4.00
20 Worm	2.50	5.00
21 Phyrexian Golem	3.00	6.00
22 Treasure	3.00	6.00
23 Liliana, the Last Hope Emblem	4.00	8.00
24 Wrenn and Six Emblem	2.00	4.00

2022 Magic The Gathering Game Night Free-for-All

1 Zamriel, Seraph of Steel M :W:	2.50	5.00
2 Maeve, Insidious Singer M :B:	1.25	2.50
3 Vogar, Necropolis Tyrant M :K:	4.00	8.00
4 Nogi, Draco-Zealot M :R:	7.50	15.00
5 Imaryll, Elfhame Elite M :G:	6.00	12.00
6 Ancestral Blade C :W:	.07	.15
7 Banisher Priest U :W:	.12	.25
8 Captain of the Watch R :W:	.20	.40
9 Danitha Capashen, Paragon U :W:	.12	.25
10 Forbidding Spirit U :W:	.12	.25
11 Heavenly Blademaster R :W:	.20	.40
12 Kitesail Apprentice C :W:	.07	.15
13 Kor Duelist U :W:	.12	.25
14 Kor Outfitter C :W:	.07	.15
15 Path to Exile U :W:	.12	.25
16 Pilgrim of the Ages C :W:	.07	.15
17 Serra Angel U :W:	.12	.25
18 Strength of Arms C :W:	.07	.15
19 Swords to Plowshares U :W:	.12	.25
20 Valorous Stance U :W:	.12	.25
21 Vow of Duty U :W:	.12	.25
22 Angler Drake U :B:	.12	.25
23 Angler Turtle R :B:	.20	.40
24 Brineborn Cutthroat U :B:	.12	.25
25 Counterspell U :B:	.12	.25
26 Diluvian Primordial R :B:	.20	.40
27 Fact or Fiction U :B:	.12	.25
28 Fog Bank U :B:	.12	.25
29 Illusory Ambusher U :B:	.12	.25
30 Impulse C :B:	.07	.15
31 Jeering Homunculus C :B:	.07	.15
32 Murmuring Mystic U :B:	.12	.25
33 Plea for Power R :B:	.20	.40
34 Precognitive Perception R :B:	.20	.40
35 Pull from Tomorrow R :B:	.20	.40
36 Repulse C :B:	.07	.15
37 Run Away Together C :B:	.07	.15
38 Sea Gate Oracle C :B:	.07	.15
39 Split Decision U :B:	.12	.25
40 Supreme Will U :B:	.12	.25
41 Talrand's Invocation U :B:	.12	.25
42 Vow of Flight U :B:	.12	.25
43 Bloodsoaked Altar U :K:	.12	.25
44 Bushmeat Poacher C :K:	.07	.15
45 Demon of Loathing R :K:	.20	.40
46 Demonic Embrace R :K:	.20	.40
47 Doom Blade C :K:	.07	.15
48 Doomed Dissenter C :K:	.07	.15
49 Dusk Legion Zealot C :K:	.07	.15
50 Fleshbag Marauder C :K:	.07	.15
51 Gavony Unhallowed C :K:	.07	.15
52 Gifted Aetherborn U :K:	.12	.25
53 Gravewaker R :K:	.20	.40
54 Liliana's Mastery R :K:	.20	.40
55 Lord of the Accursed U :K:	.12	.25
56 Maalfeld Twins C :K:	.07	.15
57 Moan of the Unhallowed U :K:	.12	.25
58 Priest of the Blood Rite R :K:	.20	.40
59 Ravenous Chupacabra U :K:	.12	.25
60 Reassembling Skeleton U :K:	.12	.25
61 Sign in Blood C :K:	.07	.15
62 Supernatural Stamina C :K:	.07	.15
63 Vilis, Broker of Blood R :K:	.20	.40
64 Village Rites C :K:	.07	.15
65 Vow of Torment U :K:	.12	.25
67 Abrade C :R:	.07	.15
68 Ancient Hellkite R :R:	.20	.40
69 Blaze U :R:	.12	.25
70 Crucible of Fire R :R:	.20	.40
71 Dragon Egg C :R:	.07	.15
72 Dragon Hatchling C :R:	.07	.15
73 Dragon Mage U :R:	.12	.25
74 Dragon Tempest U :R:	.12	.25
75 Dragonspeaker Shaman U :R:	.12	.25
76 Drakuseth, Maw of Flames R :R:	.20	.40
77 Flameblast Dragon R :R:	.20	.40
78 Flametongue Kavu U :R:	.12	.25
79 Furnace Whelp U :R:	.12	.25
80 Goblin Motivator C :R:	.07	.15
81 Kargan Dragonrider C :R:	.07	.15
82 Knollspine Dragon R :R:	.20	.40
83 Lightning Bolt U :R:	.12	.25
84 Mana Geyser C :R:	.07	.15
85 Rapacious Dragon C :R:	.07	.15
86 Seize the Spoils C :R:	.07	.15
87 Shivan Dragon R :R:	.20	.40
88 Vow of Lightning U :R:	.12	.25
89 Beast Whisperer R :G:	.20	.40
90 Broken Wings C :G:	.07	.15
91 Dwynen's Elite U :G:	.12	.25
92 Elven Ambush U :G:	.12	.25
93 Elvish Archdruid R :G:	.20	.40
94 Elvish Rejuvenator C :G:	.07	.15
95 Elvish Skysweeper C :G:	.07	.15
96 Elvish Visionary C :G:	.07	.15
97 End-Raze Forerunners R :G:	.20	.40
98 Immaculate Magistrate R :G:	.20	.40
99 Invigorate U :G:	.12	.25
100 Joraga Visionary C :G:	.07	.15
101 Llanowar Elves C :G:	.07	.15
102 Llanowar Tribe U :G:	.12	.25
103 Overrun U :G:	.12	.25
104 Rabid Bite C :G:	.07	.15
105 Ram Through C :G:	.07	.15
106 Regrowth U :G:	.12	.25
107 Sylvan Messenger U :G:	.12	.25
108 Taunting Elf C :G:	.07	.15
109 Thorn Lieutenant R :G:	.20	.40
110 Thornweald Archer C :G:	.07	.15
111 Vow of Wildness U :G:	.12	.25
112 Wirewood Pride C :G:	.07	.15
113 Argentum Armor R	.20	.40
114 Bloodthirsty Blade U	.12	.25
115 Colossus Hammer U	.12	.25
116 Greatsword U	.12	.25
117 Howling Golem C	.07	.15
118 Moonsilver Spear R	.20	.40
119 Ring of Thune U	.12	.25
120 Sword of Vengeance R	.20	.40
121 Trusty Machete U	.12	.25
122 Plains C	.07	.15
123 Plains C	.07	.15
124 Plains C	.07	.15
125 Island C	.07	.15
126 Island C	.07	.15
127 Island C	.07	.15
128 Swamp C	.07	.15
129 Swamp C	.07	.15
130 Swamp C	.07	.15
131 Mountain C	.07	.15
132 Mountain C	.07	.15
133 Mountain C	.07	.15
134 Forest C	.07	.15
135 Forest C	.07	.15
136 Forest C	.07	.15

2022 Magic The Gathering Game Night Free-for-All Tokens

1 Angel	.12	.25
2 Human Soldier	.12	.25
3 Soldier	.12	.25
4 Bird Illusion	.12	.25
5 Drake	.12	.25
6 Demon	.12	.25
7 Zombie	.12	.25
8 Dragon	.12	.25
9 Elf Warrior	.12	.25
10 Treasure	.12	.25

2022 Magic The Gathering Judge Gift Rewards

1 Greater Auramancy R :W:	25.00	50.00
2 Omniscience R :B:	25.00	50.00
3 Parallel Lives R :G:	30.00	60.00
4 Stranglehold R :R:	7.50	15.00
5 Smothering Tithe R :W:	30.00	75.00
6 Training Grounds R :B:	20.00	40.00
7 Animate Dead R :K:	40.00	80.00
8 Purphoros, God of the Forge R :R:	20.00	40.00
9 No Mercy R :B:	20.00	40.00
10 Growing Rites of Itlimoc/Itlimoc, Cradle of the Sun R :G:	30.00	75.00

2022 Magic The Gathering Jumpstart

1 Agrus Kos, Eternal Soldier R :W:	.75	1.50
2 Angelic Cub U :W:	.15	.30
3 Chains of Custody C :W:	.10	.20
4 Distinguished Conjurer U :W:	.50	1.00
5 Ingenious Leonin U :W:	.07	.15
6 Lita, Mechanical Engineer M :W:	10.00	20.00
7 Magnanimous Magistrate U :W:	.07	.15
8 Preston, the Vanisher R :W:	7.50	15.00
9 Alandra, Sky Dreamer R :B:	7.50	15.00
10 Biblioplex Kraken U :B:	.15	.30
11 Hold for Questioning U :B:	.10	.20
12 Isu the Abominable M :B:	1.25	2.50
13 Kenessos, Priest of Thassa R :B:	2.50	5.00
14 Launch Mishap U :B:	.10	.20
15 Merfolk Pupil C :B:	.05	.10
16 Pirated Copy M :B:	7.50	15.00
17 Soul Read C :B:	.06	.12
18 Synchronized Eviction U :B:	.06	.12
19 Ashcoat of the Shadow Swarm M :K:	20.00	40.00
20 Conductor of Cacophony U :K:	.10	.20
21 Creeping Bloodsucker C :K:	1.25	2.50
22 Deadly Plot U :K:	.15	.30

23 Disciple of Perdition U :K:	.10	.20
24 Ossuary Rats C :K:	.05	.10
25 Rodolf Duskbringer R :K:	6.00	12.00
26 Skullslither Worm U :K:	.07	.15
27 Suspicious Shambler C :K:	.06	.12
28 Termination Facilitator R :K:	.25	.50
29 Ardoz, Cobbler of War R :R:	2.50	5.00
30 Auntie Blyte, Bad Influence M :R:	4.00	8.00
31 Brazen Cannonade R :R:	3.00	6.00
32 Coalborn Entity U :R:	.05	.10
33 Daring Piracy U :R:	.15	.30
34 Goblin Researcher C :R:	.05	.10
35 Mizzix, Replica Rider R :R:	1.00	2.00
36 Ogre Battlecaster R :R:	.10	.20
37 Plundering Predator C :R:	.06	.12
38 Benevolent Hydra R :G:	7.50	15.00
39 Giant Ladybug C :G:	.06	.12
40 Kibo, Uktabi Prince M :G:	4.00	8.00
41 Mild-Mannered Librarian U :G:	.06	.12
42 Primeval Herald U :G:	1.50	3.00
43 Rampaging Growth U :G:	.07	.15
44 Runadi, Behemoth Caller R :G:	4.00	8.00
45 Spectral Hunt-Caller C :G:	.06	.12
46 Towering Gibbon U :G:	.12	.25
47 Zask, Skittering Swarmlord R :G:	1.50	3.00
48 Dutiful Replicator C	.07	.15
49 Infernal Idol C	.10	.20
50 Instruments of War U	.12	.25
51 Planar Atlas U	1.00	2.00
52 Arrest U :W:	.05	.10
53 Balan, Wandering Knight R :W:	12.50	25.00
54 Eidolon of Rhetoric U :W:	1.00	2.00
55 Emancipation Angel U :W:	.20	.40
56 Flicker of Fate C :W:	.12	.25
57 King of the Pride U :W:	.12	.25
58 Sage's Reverie U :W:	.40	.80
59 Valorous Stance U :W:	.12	.25
60 Kasmina, Enigmatic Mentor U :B:	.25	.50
61 Merrow Reejerey U :B:	.15	.30
62 Mirror Image U :B:	2.00	4.00
63 Preordain C :B:	1.00	2.00
64 Spectral Sailor U :B:	1.25	2.50
65 Spellstutter Sprite C :B:	2.00	4.00
66 Whirler Rogue U :B:	.07	.15
67 Diabolic Edict C :K:	.12	.25
68 Feast on the Fallen U :K:	.07	.15
69 Lord of the Accursed U :K:	.20	.40
70 Oathsworn Vampire U :K:	.15	.30
71 Ogre Slumlord R :K:	.30	.60
72 Plaguecrafter U :K:	.15	.30
73 Stitcher's Supplier U :K:	1.25	2.50
74 Tragic Slip C :K:	1.00	2.00
75 Tree of Perdition M :K:	3.00	6.00
76 Dragon Fodder C :R:	.06	.12
77 Dragon Mage U :R:	.25	.50
78 Drannith Stinger C :R:	.15	.30
79 Kiki-Jiki, Mirror Breaker M :R:	7.50	15.00
8.00E+01 Rapacious Dragon U :R:	.12	.25
8.10E+01 Rigging Runner U :R:	.05	.10
8.20E+01 Spear Spewer C :R:	.30	.60
8.30E+01 Thermo-Alchemist C :R:	.12	.25
8.40E+01 Thrill of Possibility C :R:	.15	.30
8.50E+01 Arlinn, Voice of the Pack U :G:	.12	.25
8.60E+01 Caustic Caterpillar C :G:	.12	.25
8.70E+01 Colossal Majesty U :G:	.75	1.50
88 Elvish Rejuvenator C :G:	.07	.15
89 Hydra's Growth U :G:	.75	1.50
90 Khalni Heart Expedition C :G:	.12	.25
91 Ram Through C :G:	4.00	8.00
92 Thrashing Brontodon U :G:	.10	.20
93 World Breaker M :G:	.75	1.50
94 Coldsteel Heart U	2.50	5.00
95 Magnifying Glass U	.10	.20
96 Peacewalker Colossus R	.15	.30
97 Karn Liberated M	7.50	15.00
98 Plains C	.05	.10
99 Plains C	.05	.10
100 Plains C	.05	.10
101 Island C	.05	.10
102 Island C	.05	.10
103 Island C	.06	.12
104 Swamp C	.05	.10
105 Swamp C	.05	.10
106 Swamp C	.05	.10
107 Mountain C	.05	.10
108 Mountain C	.05	.10
109 Mountain C	.06	.12
110 Forest C	.05	.10
111 Forest C	.05	.10
112 Forest C	.05	.10
113 Task Force C :W:	.05	.10
114 Rhystic Study R :B:	25.00	50.00
115 Tragic Lesson C :B:	.07	.15
116 Wizard Mentor C :B:	.07	.15
117 Blood Artist U :K:	1.50	3.00
118 Feast of Blood U :K:	.12	.25
119 Festering Evil U :K:	.07	.15
120 Ghoul's Feast C :K:	.12	.25
121 Morkrut Banshee U :K:	.05	.10
122 Nezumi Bone-Reader U :K:	.20	.40
123 Phyrexian Plaguelord R :K:	.12	.25
124 Phyrexian Reclamation U :K:	4.00	8.00
125 Reassembling Skeleton U :K:	.60	1.25
126 Renegade Demon C :K:	.10	.20
127 Swarm of Bloodflies U :K:	.10	.20
128 Wakedancer C :K:	.10	.20
129 Aftershock C :R:	.07	.15
130 Fireslinger C :R:	.10	.20
131 Flameblade Adept U :R:	.12	.25
132 Ruin in Their Wake U :G:	.12	.25
133 Uktabi Orangutan U :G:	.75	1.50
134 Wicked Wolf R :G:	.15	.30
135 Clockwork Hydra U	.07	.15
136 Spawning Pit U	1.25	2.50
137 Leechridden Swamp U	.75	1.50
138 Acrobatic Maneuver C :W:	.12	.25
139 Aerial Modification U :W:	.12	.25
140 Aethershield Artificer U :W:	.12	.25
141 Ajani, Strength of the Pride M :W:	1.50	3.00
142 Ajani's Pridemate U :W:	.12	.25
143 Alseid of Life's Bounty U :W:	.15	.30
144 Angel of Flight Alabaster R :W:	.10	.20
145 Angelic Edict C :W:	.06	.12
146 Angelic Page C :W:	.10	.20
147 Angelic Protector U :W:	.05	.10
148 Anointer of Valor C :W:	.05	.10
149 Apothecary Geist C :W:	.05	.10
150 Archon of Justice R :W:	.10	.20
151 Archon of Sun's Grace R :W:	.50	1.00
152 Attended Healer U :W:	.10	.20
153 Auramancer C :W:	.10	.20
154 Basri's Acolyte C :W:	.05	.10
155 Benalish Honor Guard C :W:	.10	.20
156 Blessed Defiance C :W:	.06	.12
157 Blessed Sanctuary R :W:	.75	1.50
158 Blessed Spirits U :W:	.05	.10
159 Brightmare U :W:	.05	.10
160 Bring to Trial C :W:	.05	.10
161 Built to Last C :W:	.07	.15
162 Cage of Hands C :W:	.07	.15
163 Captivating Unicorn C :W:	.05	.10
164 Caught in the Brights C :W:	.12	.25
165 Cavalry Drillmaster C :W:	.05	.10
166 The Circle of Loyalty M :W:	.40	.80
167 Combat Professor C :W:	.05	.10
168 Danitha Capashen, Paragon U :W:	.20	.40
169 Dawn of Hope R :W:	.75	1.50
170 Dawning Angel C :W:	.05	.10
171 Daybreak Chaplain C :W:	.06	.12
172 Daybreak Charger C :W:	.07	.15
173 Decree of Justice R :W:	.12	.25
174 Defy Death U :W:	.12	.25
175 Devouring Light U :W:	.06	.12
176 Divine Arrow C :W:	.05	.10
177 Divine Verdict C :W:	.05	.10
178 Doomed Traveler C :W:	.05	.10
179 Dreadful Apathy C :W:	.10	.20
180 Emiel the Blessed M :W:	1.50	3.00
181 Faith's Fetters U :W:	.05	.10
182 Favored of Iroas U :W:	.05	.10
183 Felidar Cub C :W:	.10	.20
184 Felidar Retreat R :W:	.50	1.00
185 Forced Worship C :W:	.07	.15
186 Gallant Cavalry C :W:	.07	.15
187 Gallows Warden U :W:	.05	.10
188 Giant Ox C :W:	.10	.20
189 Gideon, Champion of Justice M :W:	.25	.50
190 Gideon's Lawkeeper C :W:	.06	.12
191 Glory Bearers C :W:	.05	.10
192 Goldnight Commander U :W:	.12	.25
193 Hotshot Mechanic U :W:	.10	.20
194 Hour of Reckoning R :W:	.15	.30
195 Impeccable Timing C :W:	.05	.10
196 Imperial Aerosaur U :W:	.07	.15
197 Imperial Recovery Unit U :W:	.07	.15
198 Infantry Veteran C :W:	.05	.10
199 Inspiring Cleric U :W:	.05	.10
200 Inspiring Overseer C :W:	.15	.30
201 Isamaru, Hound of Konda R :W:	.25	.50
202 Justiciar's Portal C :W:	.10	.20
203 Kami of Ancient Law C :W:	.05	.10
204 Kitsune Ace C :W:	.10	.20
205 Kwende, Pride of Femeref U :W:	.10	.20
206 Law-Rune Enforcer C :W:	.07	.15
207 Leonin Snarecaster C :W:	.05	.10
208 Leonin Warleader R :W:	2.50	5.00
209 Light of Hope C :W:	.07	.15
210 Lyra Dawnbringer M :W:	2.00	4.00
211 Make a Stand U :W:	.10	.20
212 Martyr's Soul C :W:	.07	.15
213 Mausoleum Guard U :W:	.05	.10
214 Mesa Lynx C :W:	.07	.15
215 Michiko Konda, Truth Seeker R :W:	1.00	2.00
216 Midnight Guard C :W:	.05	.10
217 Miraculous Recovery U :W:	.12	.25
218 Moment of Triumph C :W:	.10	.20
219 Murder Investigation U :W:	.07	.15
220 Nightguard Patrol C :W:	.05	.10
221 Ninth Bridge Patrol C :W:	.05	.10
222 Not Forgotten U :W:	.07	.15
223 Order of the Golden Cricket C :W:	.10	.20
224 Phalanx Tactics U :W:	.06	.12
225 Pilgrim of the Ages C :W:	.05	.10
226 Pillardrop Rescuer C :W:	.07	.15
227 Pious Wayfarer C :W:	.07	.15
228 Pouncing Lynx C :W:	.06	.12
229 Prowling Felidar C :W:	.10	.20
230 Radiant's Judgment C :W:	.07	.15
231 Rambunctious Mutt C :W:	.07	.15
232 Regal Caracal R :W:	1.25	2.50
233 Restoration Angel R :W:	.15	.30
234 Righteous Valkyrie R :W:	2.00	4.00
235 Righteousness U :W:	.07	.15
236 Sanctum Gargoyle C :W:	.10	.20
237 Savannah Lions U :W:	.05	.10
238 Savannah Sage C :W:	.07	.15
239 Selfless Spirit R :W:	.60	1.25
240 Seller of Songbirds C :W:	.05	.10
241 Serene Steward U :W:	.10	.20
242 Settle Beyond Reality C :W:	.05	.10
243 Shining Armor C :W:	.10	.20
244 Sigil of the Empty Throne R :W:	1.00	2.00
245 Skyhunter Patrol C :W:	.05	.10
246 Skyhunter Prowler C :W:	.07	.15
247 Spectral Steel U :W:	.05	.10
248 Spirited Companion C :W:	.15	.30
249 Stalwart Valkyrie C :W:	.05	.10
250 Starnheim Aspirant U :W:	1.00	2.00
251 Steppe Lynx C :W:	.10	.20
252 Syr Alin, the Lion's Claw U :W:	.07	.15
253 Taranika, Akroan Veteran R :W:	.07	.15
254 Tempered Veteran U :W:	.07	.15
255 Thraben Inspector C :W:	.15	.30
256 Trained Caracal C :W:	.10	.20
257 Transcendent Envoy C :W:	.12	.25
258 Triplicate Spirits C :W:	.15	.30
259 Trove Warden R :W:	.20	.40
260 Unquestioned Authority U :W:	.12	.25
261 Valkyrie Harbinger R :W:	.75	1.50
262 Valor in Akros U :W:	.07	.15
263 Valorous Stance U :W:	.10	.20
264 Valorous Steed C :W:	.07	.15
265 Weight of Conscience C :W:	.05	.10
266 Wispweaver Angel U :W:	.07	.15
267 Academy Journeymage C :B:	.05	.10
268 Aeronaut Tinkerer C :B:	.06	.12
269 Amoeboid Changeling C :B:	.20	.40
270 Anchor to the Aether U :B:	.06	.12
271 Aquatic Incursion U :B:	.05	.10
272 Artificer's Epiphany C :B:	.05	.10
273 Augury Owl C :B:	.12	.25
274 Avalanche Caller U :B:	.05	.10
275 Aviation Pioneer C :B:	.05	.10
276 Barrin, Tolarian Archmage R :B:	.10	.20
277 Berg Strider C :B:	.07	.15
278 Brineborn Cutthroat U :B:	.12	.25
279 Bury in Books C :B:	.05	.10
280 Chillerpillar C :B:	.07	.15
281 Chilling Trap C :B:	.06	.12
282 Condescend U :B:	.15	.30
283 Crashing Tide C :B:	.05	.10
284 Crippling Chill C :B:	.06	.12
285 Cryptic Serpent U :B:	.06	.12
286 Dismiss U :B:	.07	.15
287 Djinn of Wishes R :B:	.06	.12
288 Drag Under C :B:	.07	.15
289 Drownyard Explorers C :B:	.05	.10
290 Elite Instructor C :B:	.05	.10
291 Erdwal Illuminator U :B:	.12	.25
292 Eternity Snare U :B:	.06	.12
293 Eyekite C :B:	.10	.20
294 Faerie Formation R :B:	.15	.30
295 Faerie Seer C :B:	.25	.50
296 Faerie Vandal U :B:	.05	.10
297 Fallowsage U :B:	.15	.30
298 Filigree Attendant U :B:	.07	.15
299 Fleeting Distraction C :B:	.07	.15
300 Floodhound C :B:	.05	.10
301 Frostpeak Yeti C :B:	.07	.15
302 Gearseeker Serpent C :B:	.05	.10
303 Gearsmith Prodigy C :B:	.06	.12
304 Gigantoplasm R :B:	.12	.25
305 Glen Elendra Pranksters U :B:	.07	.15
306 Harbinger of the Tides R :B:	.20	.40
307 Hieroglyphic Illumination C :B:	.07	.15
308 Icebind Pillar U :B:	.07	.15
309 Interpret the Signs U :B:	.10	.20
310 Jace, Arcane Strategist M :B:	.30	.60
311 Jace's Scrutiny C :B:	.05	.10
312 Lay Claim U :B:	.06	.12
313 Leave in the Dust C :B:	.07	.15
314 Library Larcenist C :B:	.06	.12
315 Littjara Kinseekers C :B:	.07	.15
316 Lookout's Dispersal U :B:	.07	.15
317 Lumengrid Sentinel U :B:	.07	.15
318 Mantle of Tides C :B:	.07	.15
319 Marit Lage's Slumber R :B:	.20	.40
320 Mechanized Production M :B:	2.50	5.00
321 Morfolk Sovereign R :B:	.20	.40
322 Military Intelligence U :B:	.12	.25
323 Mistwalker C :B:	.07	.15
324 Moonfolk Puzzlemaker C :B:	.07	.15
325 Multiple Choice R :B:	.07	.15
326 Mystic Skyfish C :B:	.05	.10
327 Neutralize U :B:	.10	.20
328 No Escape C :B:	.07	.15
329 Octoprophet C :B:	.10	.20
330 One With the Wind C :B:	.05	.10
331 Oneirophage U :B:	.07	.15
332 Opt C :B:	.12	.25
333 Overwhelmed Apprentice U :B:	.07	.15
334 Perilous Voyage U :B:	.07	.15
335 Pestermite C :B:	.12	.25
336 Pilfering Hawk C :B:	.06	.12
337 Press for Answers C :B:	.05	.10
338 Renowned Weaponsmith U :B:	.07	.15
339 River Sneak U :B:	.05	.10
340 Sage of the Falls U :B:	.07	.15
341 Sage's Row Savant C :B:	.07	.15
342 Saltwater Stalwart C :B:	.05	.10
343 Seafloor Oracle R :B:	.15	.30
344 Sentinels of Glen Elendra C :B:	.06	.12
345 Serum Visions U :B:	.75	1.50
346 Shaper Apprentice C :B:	.05	.10
347 Shimmer Dragon R :B:	.20	.40
348 Skilled Animator U :B:	.06	.12
349 So Tiny C :B:	.07	.15
350 Startling Development C :B:	.06	.12
351 Steelgaze Griffin C :B:	.05	.10
352 Stinging Lionfish U :B:	.10	.20
353 Stolen by the Fae R :B:	.12	.25
354 Stonybrook Angler C :B:	.06	.12
355 Storm Sculptor C :B:	.05	.10
356 Svyelun of Sea and Sky M :B:	.75	1.50
357 Syr Elenora, the Discerning U :B:	.06	.12
358 Tamiyo, the Moon Sage M :B:	2.00	4.00
359 Teferi's Protege C :B:	.05	.10
360 Tezzeret, Artifice Master M :B:	1.25	2.50
361 Thopter Spy Network R :B:	.20	.40
362 Tolarian Kraken U :B:	.07	.15
363 Tolarian Sentinel C :B:	.05	.10
364 Tome Anima C :B:	.05	.10
365 Triton Shorestalker C :B:	.12	.25
366 Undersea Invader C :B:	.06	.12
367 Vedalken Engineer C :B:	.05	.10
368 Vendilion Clique M :B:	1.25	2.50
369 Wake Thrasher R :B:	.15	.30
370 Watertrap Weaver C :B:	.05	.10
371 Wavebreak Hippocamp R :B:	.15	.30
372 Weldfast Wingsmith C :B:	.07	.15
373 Windrider Patrol U :B:	.06	.12
374 Winter's Rest C :B:	.12	.25
375 Alley Strangler C :K:	.05	.10
376 Ancient Craving U :K:	.12	.25
377 Black Cat C :K:	.07	.15
378 Blight Keeper C :K:	.05	.10
379 Blood Price C :K:	.06	.12
380 Bloodbond Vampire U :K:	.06	.12
381 Bloodthirsty Aerialist U :K:	.12	.25
382 Bloodtracker R :K:	.12	.25
383 Bone Picker U :K:	.06	.12
384 Burglar Rat C :K:	.12	.25
385 Cemetery Recruitment C :K:	.05	.10
386 Certain Death C :K:	.05	.10
387 Chittering Rats C :K:	.25	.50
388 Consign to the Pit C :K:	.07	.15
389 Corpse Churn C :K:	.06	.12
390 Crow of Dark Tidings C :K:	.05	.10
391 Cruel Sadist R :K:	.06	.12
392 Crypt Rats U :K:	.15	.30
393 Dead Weight C :K:	.05	.10
394 Death Wind U :K:	.07	.15
395 Deathbloom Thallid C :K:	.05	.10
396 Deathbringer Regent R :K:	.10	.20
397 Demon of Catastrophes R :K:	.12	.25
398 Demonic Gifts C :K:	.10	.20
399 Demon's Disciple U :K:	.12	.25
400 Demon's Grasp C :K:	.05	.10
401 Devouring Swarm C :K:	.06	.12
402 Doomed Dissenter C :K:	.05	.10
403 Dread Presence R :K:	1.00	2.00
404 Dread Rider C :K:	.07	.15
405 Dread Slaver R :K:	.10	.20
406 Dreadhound U :K:	.10	.20
407 Dune Beetle C :K:	.10	.20
408 Durable Coilbug C :K:	.05	.10
409 Eaten Alive C :K:	.07	.15
410 Endless Ranks of the Dead R :K:	1.00	2.00
411 Epicure of Blood C :K:	.07	.15
412 Eviscerate C :K:	.05	.10
413 Exsanguinate U :K:	4.00	8.00
414 Falkenrath Noble U :K:	.12	.25
415 Fetid Imp C :K:	.07	.15
416 Fungal Infection C :K:	.07	.15
417 Gavony Unhallowed C :K:	.05	.10
418 Ghoulraiser C :K:	.07	.15
419 Gnawing Zombie C :K:	.05	.10
420 Gorging Vulture C :K:	.07	.15
421 Graf Harvest U :K:	.12	.25
422 Graveblade Marauder R :K:	.05	.10
423 Gravecrawler R :K:	2.00	4.00
424 Gravedigger U :K:	.05	.10
425 Grotesque Mutation C :K:	.05	.10
426 Hooded Assassin C :K:	.05	.10
427 Ill-Gotten Inheritance C :K:	.05	.10
428 Inner Demon U :K:	.10	.20
429 Kalastria Nightwatch C :K:	.07	.15
430 Karfell Kennel-Master C :K:	.06	.12
431 Kothophed, Soul Hoarder R :K:	.12	.25
432 Kraul Swarm U :K:	.07	.15
433 Liliana, Death's Majesty M :K:	.75	1.50
434 Liliana's Elite U :K:	.12	.25
435 Liliana's Mastery R :K:	.12	.25
436 Liliana's Steward C :K:	.07	.15
437 Lurking Deadeye C :K:	.06	.12
438 Maalfeld Twins C :K:	.05	.10
439 Marauding Blight-Priest C :K:	.15	.30
440 Marauding Boneslasher C :K:	.07	.15
441 Massacre Wurm M :K:	1.50	3.00
442 Mire Blight C :K:	.05	.10
443 Mire Triton U :K:	.07	.15
444 Moment of Craving C :K:	.05	.10
445 Moodmark Painter C :K:	.06	.12
446 Necromancer's Stockpile R :K:	.12	.25
447 Necrotic Wound U :K:	.06	.12
448 Nested Ghoul U :K:	.05	.10
449 Nirkana Assassin C :K:	.07	.15
450 Ob Nixilis, the Hate-Twisted U :K:	.20	.40
451 Ob Nixilis's Cruelty C :K:	.10	.20
452 Ophiomancer R :K:	3.00	6.00
453 Oversold Cemetery R :K:	.40	.80
454 Phyrexian Debaser C :K:	.06	.12
455 Pit Keeper C :K:	.07	.15
456 Plague Spitter U :K:	.10	.20
457 Priest of the Blood Rite R :K:	.15	.30
458 Reaper from the Abyss M :K:	.75	1.50
459 Reave Soul C :K:	.05	.10
460 Returned Reveler C :K:	.07	.15
461 Revenant U :K:	.07	.15
462 Ruthless Disposal U :K:	.07	.15
463 Seizan, Perverter of Truth R :K:	.75	1.50
464 Shadowborn Demon M :K:	.20	.40
465 Shambling Ghoul C :K:	.07	.15
466 Sinuous Vermin C :K:	.15	.30
467 Skirsdag High Priest R :K:	.12	.25
468 Skirsdag Supplicant C :K:	.07	.15
469 Sling-Gang Lieutenant U :K:	.20	.40
470 Soulcage Fiend C :K:	.06	.12
471 Spark Reaper C :K:	.07	.15
472 Stitcher's Supplier U :K:	1.25	2.50
473 Strangling Spores C :K:	.07	.15
474 Syr Konrad, the Grim U :K:	1.00	2.00
475 Takenuma Bleeder C :K:	.06	.12
476 Tivash, Gloom Summoner R :K:	.12	.25
477 Tormented Soul C :K:	.15	.30
478 Tragic Slip C :K:	.15	.30
479 Triskaidekaphobia R :K:	.10	.20
480 Typhoid Rats C :K:	.12	.25
481 Ulcerate U :K:	.07	.15
482 Undead Augur U :K:	.12	.25
483 Vampire Envoy C :K:	.05	.10
484 Vampiric Rites U :K:	.12	.25
485 Vermin Gorger C :K:	.10	.20
486 Village Rites C :K:	.15	.30
487 Vito, Thorn of the Dusk Rose R :K:	3.00	6.00
488 Wailing Ghoul C :K:	.06	.12
489 Wicked Guardian C :K:	.07	.15
490 Witch's Cauldron U :K:	.10	.20
491 Yargle, Glutton of Urborg U :K:	.10	.20
492 Act on Impulse U :R:	.07	.15
493 Arms Dealer U :R:	.10	.20
494 Axgard Cavalry C :R:	.07	.15
495 Banefire R :R:	.30	.60
496 Barrage Ogre U :R:	.07	.15
497 Battle Squadron U :R:	.15	.30
498 Big Score C :R:	1.00	2.00
499 Blaze U :R:	.07	.15
500 Blisterspit Gremlin C :R:	.10	.20
501 Blood Aspirant U :R:	.05	.10
502 Bloodhaze Wolverine C :R:	.06	.12
503 Bogardan Dragonheart C :R:	.07	.15
504 Bolt Hound U :R:	.20	.40
505 Borderland Marauder C :R:	.05	.10
506 Brazen Freebooter C :R:	.05	.10
507 Brazen Wolves C :R:	.05	.10
508 Burn Bright C :R:	.07	.15
509 Captain Lannery Storm R :R:	.12	.25
510 Catalyst Elemental C :R:	.06	.12
511 Chandra, Flame's Fury M :R:	.50	1.00
512 Chandra's Magmutt C :R:	.10	.20
513 Chandra's Pyreling U :R:	.05	.10
514 Chandra's Pyrohelix C :R:	.06	.12
515 Chandra's Spitfire U :R:	.05	.10
516 Coalhauler Swine C :R:	.10	.20
517 Cone of Flame U :R:	.06	.12

518 Cyclops Electromancer U :R: .07 .15
519 Dance with Devils U :R: .07 .15
520 Deem Worthy U :R: .05 .10
521 Destructive Tampering C :R: .05 .10
522 Dragon Egg U :R: .07 .15
523 Dragon Fodder C :R: .10 .20
524 Dragonlord's Servant U :R: .25 .50
525 Dragonspeaker Shaman U :R: .75 1.50
526 Electric Revelation C :R: .05 .10
527 Electrify C :R: .05 .10
528 Fanatical Firebrand C :R: .07 .15
529 Fervent Strike C :R: .07 .15
530 Fiery Conclusion U :R: .07 .15
531 Fiery Intervention C :R: .05 .10
532 Firebolt C :R: .06 .12
533 Firecannon Blast C :R: .05 .10
534 Flame Lash C :R: .05 .10
535 Flames of the Firebrand U :R: .07 .15
536 Frenzied Goblin C :R: .07 .15
537 Furnace Whelp U :R: .07 .15
538 Gadrak, the Crown-Scourge R :R: .25 .50
539 Glint-Horn Buccaneer R :R: .60 1.25
540 Go for Blood C :R: .06 .12
541 Goblin Artillery U :R: .07 .15
542 Goblin Grenade U :R: .15 .30
543 Goblin Oriflamme U :R: .07 .15
544 Goblin Psychopath U :R: .05 .10
545 Goblin Rabblemaster R :R: 1.25 2.50
546 Goblin Rally U :R: .12 .25
547 Goblin Trailblazer C :R: .05 .10
548 Goblin Warchief U :R: .30 .60
549 Goldhound C :R: .07 .15
550 Goldspan Dragon M :R: 7.50 15.00
551 Grotag Night-Runner U :R: .06 .12
552 Hordeling Outburst U :R: .10 .20
553 Hungry Flames C :R: .06 .12
554 Ib Halfheart, Goblin Tactician R :R: .20 .40
555 Ignite the Future R :R: .12 .25
556 Immersturm Raider C :R: .10 .20
557 Impending Doom U :R: .07 .15
558 Improvised Weaponry C :R: .05 .10
559 Irencrag Pyromancer R :R: .15 .30
560 Irreverent Revelers C :R: .07 .15
561 Kargan Dragonrider C :R: .07 .15
562 Kari Zev, Skyship Raider R :R: .15 .30
563 Keldon Raider C :R: .05 .10
564 Krenko, Mob Boss R :R: 3.00 6.00
565 Kuldotha Flamefiend U :R: .05 .10
566 Lathliss, Dragon Queen R :R: 1.50 3.00
567 Lava Serpent C :R: .06 .12
568 Lavastep Raider C :R: .06 .12
569 Lightning Axe U :R: .07 .15
570 Mad Ratter U :R: .10 .20
571 Magmatic Channeler R :R: .10 .20
572 Mardu Heart-Piercer U :R: .07 .15
573 Markov Warlord U :R: .07 .15
574 Mudbutton Torchrunner C :R: .10 .20
575 Muxus, Goblin Grandee R :R: 3.00 6.00
576 Nest Robber C :R: .10 .20
577 Ordeal of Purphoros U :R: .07 .15
578 Outnumber C :R: .10 .20
579 Pillar of Flame C :R: .05 .10
580 Prickly Marmoset C :R: .05 .10
581 Professional Face-Breaker R :R: 4.00 8.00
582 Pyre-Sledge Arsonist U :R: .07 .15
583 Quakefoot Cyclops C :R: .07 .15
584 Raking Claws C :R: .07 .15
585 Ravenous Giant U :R: .07 .15
586 Raze the Effigy C :R: .10 .20
587 Reckless Fireweaver C :R: .25 .50
588 Reptilian Reflection U :R: .05 .10
589 Ripscale Predator C :R: .05 .10
590 Rooting Moloch U :R: .05 .10
591 Rummaging Goblin C :R: .05 .10
592 Rush of Adrenaline C :R: .07 .15
593 Sarkhan, the Dragonspeaker M :R: .15 .30
594 Sarkhan's Rage C :R: .07 .15
595 Sarkhan's Whelp U :R: .07 .15
596 Scorching Dragonfire C :R: .07 .15
597 Searing Spear C :R: .10 .20
598 Seize the Storm U :R: .05 .10
599 Shredded Sails C :R: .07 .15
600 Smoldering Efreet C :R: .06 .12
601 Sokenzan Smelter U :R: .05 .10
602 Spark of Creativity U :R: .07 .15
603 Sparkmage Apprentice C :R: .07 .15
604 Sparktongue Dragon C :R: .07 .15
605 Spellgorger Weird C :R: .07 .15
606 Spiteful Prankster U :R: .15 .30
607 Starstorm R :R: .12 .25
608 Storm Fleet Pyromancer C :R: .05 .10
609 Subterranean Scout C :R: .07 .15
610 Sudden Breakthrough C :R: .10 .20
611 Swaggering Corsair C :R: .05 .10
612 Swift Kick C :R: .10 .20
613 Thermo-Alchemist C :R: .12 .25
614 Torch Courier C :R: .10 .20
615 Tormenting Voice C :R: .05 .10
616 Trove of Temptation U :R: .06 .12
617 Vault Robber C :R: .05 .10
618 Viashino Pyromancer C :R: .07 .15
619 Volley Veteran U :R: .07 .15
620 War-Name Aspirant U :R: .05 .10
621 Warcry Phoenix U :R: .07 .15
622 Weaselback Redcap C :R: .07 .15
623 Welding Sparks C :R: .05 .10
624 Wildfire Elemental C :R: .05 .10
625 Yidaro, Wandering Monster R :R: .20 .40
626 Young Pyromancer U :R: .15 .30
627 Adventurous Impulse C :G: .07 .15
628 Ancient Stirrings C :G: .12 .25
629 Avenger of Zendikar M :G: 2.50 5.00
630 Baloth Woodcrasher U :G: .07 .15
631 Band Together C :G: .05 .10
632 Blisterpod C :G: .10 .20
633 Bounding Wolf C :G: .05 .10
634 Briarpack Alpha U :G: .06 .12
635 Bristling Boar C :G: .07 .15
636 Broken Bond C :G: .15 .30
637 Brood Monitor U :G: .10 .20
638 Canopy Baloth C :G: .05 .10
639 Challenger Troll U :G: .05 .10
640 Colossal Dreadmaw C :G: .06 .12
641 Courser of Kruphix R :G: 1.25 2.50
642 Crawling Sensation U :G: .07 .15
643 Creeperhulk R :G: .10 .20
644 Cultivate C :G: .50 1.00
645 Deadbridge Goliath R :G: .07 .15
646 Declare Dominance U :G: .07 .15
647 Domesticated Hydra U :G: .07 .15
648 Drowsing Tyrannodon C :G: .05 .10
649 Drudge Beetle C :G: .07 .15
650 Duskshell Crawler C :G: .12 .25
651 Dwynen's Elite U :G: .07 .15
652 Elderleaf Mentor C :G: .05 .10
653 Elven Bow U :G: .05 .10
654 Elvish Warmaster R :G: 1.00 2.00
655 Engulfing Slagwurm R :G: .20 .40
656 Enlarge U :G: .07 .15
657 Feed the Pack R :G: .12 .25
658 Feral Hydra U :G: .12 .25
659 Ferocious Pup C :G: .05 .10
660 Fertilid C :G: .06 .12
661 Fierce Witchstalker C :G: .07 .15
662 Flourishing Hunter C :G: .10 .20
663 Frontier Mastodon C :G: .05 .10
664 Gaea's Protector C :G: .10 .20
665 Ghirapur Guide U :G: .06 .12
666 Giant Caterpillar C :G: .07 .15
667 Gift of the Gargantuan C :G: .06 .12
668 Goreclaw, Terror of Qal Sisma R :G: .75 1.50
669 Groundswell C :G: .12 .25
670 Havenwood Wurm C :G: .07 .15
671 Hooting Mandrills C :G: .12 .25
672 Howl of the Hunt C :G: .06 .12
673 Howlgeist U :G: .07 .15
674 Hunger of the Howlpack C :G: .07 .15
675 Hunter's Edge C :G: .05 .10
676 Ilysian Caryatid C :G: .07 .15
677 Imperious Perfect R :G: .12 .25
678 Iridescent Hornbeetle U :G: .07 .15
679 Ironshell Beetle C :G: .05 .10
680 Ivy Lane Denizen C :G: .10 .20
681 Kessig Cagebreakers R :G: .10 .20
682 Kraul Foragers C :G: .06 .12
683 Kraul Harpooner U :G: .07 .15
684 Kraul Warrior C :G: .07 .15
685 Kujar Seedsculptor C :G: .07 .15
686 Lys Alana Huntmaster C :G: .12 .25
687 Mammoth Spider C :G: .10 .20
688 Master of the Wild Hunt M :G: .60 1.25
689 Master's Rebuke C :G: .07 .15
690 Might of the Masses C :G: .05 .10
691 Moldgraf Millipede C :G: .05 .10
692 Moonlight Hunt U :G: .12 .25
693 Naga Vitalist C :G: .07 .15
694 Nantuko Cultivator U :G: .05 .10
695 Nessian Hornbeetle U :G: .05 .10
696 Nightpack Ambusher R :G: .15 .30
697 Oashra Cultivator C :G: .05 .10
698 Ondu Giant C :G: .07 .15
699 Ordeal of Nylea U :G: .07 .15
700 Ornery Dilophosaur C :G: .05 .10
701 Overcome U :G: .06 .12
702 Overgrowth C :G: .12 .25
703 Packsong Pup U :G: .12 .25
704 Paradise Druid U :G: .15 .30
705 Pestilent Wolf C :G: .05 .10
706 Phantom Nantuko R :G: .12 .25
707 Pounce C :G: .10 .20
708 Predator's Howl U :G: .10 .20
709 Presence of Gond C :G: .07 .15
710 Prey Upon C :G: .05 .10
711 Pridemalkin C :G: .10 .20
712 Primordial Hydra M :G: 5.00 10.00
713 Prowling Serpopard R :G: 1.25 2.50
714 Quarry Beetle U :G: .07 .15
715 Rampaging Baloths R :G: .20 .40
716 Reckless Amplimancer C :G: .05 .10
717 Reclamation Sage U :G: .20 .40
718 Relentless Pursuit C :G: .05 .10
719 Rhonas the Indomitable M :G: 2.00 4.00
720 Roar of Challenge U :G: .10 .20
721 Roots of Wisdom C :G: .05 .10
722 Rosethorn Halberd C :G: .07 .15
723 Savage Punch C :G: .05 .10
724 Scale the Heights C :G: .07 .15
725 Scion Summoner C :G: .12 .25
726 Scrounging Bandar C :G: .10 .20
727 Servant of the Scale C :G: .07 .15
728 Silverback Shaman C :G: .10 .20
729 Simian Brawler C :G: .10 .20
730 Snapping Gnarlid C :G: .05 .10
731 Soul's Might C :G: .07 .15
732 Sporeback Wolf C :G: .06 .12
733 Stalking Drone C :G: .10 .20
734 Swarm Shambler R :G: .07 .15
735 Titanic Brawl C :G: .07 .15
736 Turntimber Basilisk U :G: .07 .15
737 Unnatural Aggression C :G: .10 .20
738 Wildborn Preserver R :G: .07 .15
739 Wily Bandar C :G: .12 .25
740 Wolf's Quarry C :G: .10 .20
741 Wolfkin Bond C :G: .12 .25
742 Wolfwillow Haven U :G: .20 .40
743 Wolverine Riders R :G: 1.25 2.50
744 Woodborn Behemoth U :G: .07 .15
745 Woodland Champion U :G: .07 .15
746 Young Wolf C :G: .30 .60
747 Zendikar's Roil U :G: .50 1.00
748 Endbringer R .30 .60
749 Titan's Presence U .15 .30
750 Warden of Geometries C .12 .25
751 Adventuring Gear C .12 .25
752 Aether Spellbomb C .12 .25
753 Alchemist's Vial C .12 .25
754 Aradara Express C .10 .20
755 Assembly-Worker C .06 .12
756 Bag of Holding R .07 .15
757 Bloodline Pretender U .25 .50
758 Campus Guide C .07 .15
759 Cellar Door U .07 .15
760 Circuit Mender U .12 .25
761 Cogwork Assembler U .07 .15
762 Dragon Blood U .07 .15
763 Dragon's Hoard R .75 1.50
764 Edifice of Authority U .06 .12
765 Expedition Map C 1.50 3.00
766 Explorer's Scope C .12 .25
767 Gearsmith Guardian C .10 .20
768 Gleaming Barrier C .07 .15
769 Goldvein Pick C .10 .20
770 Golem Artisan U .07 .15
771 Hammer of Ruin U .05 .10
772 Hangarback Walker R 3.00 6.00
773 Heart-Piercer Bow C .07 .15
774 Hedron Archive U .10 .20
775 Heirloom Blade U .15 .30
776 Hero's Blade U .10 .20
777 Infiltration Lens U .50 1.00
778 Iron Bully C .05 .10
779 Jousting Lance C .07 .15
780 Juggernaut U .06 .12
781 Kitesail C .06 .12
782 Leonin Scimitar C .05 .10
783 Lothwain Gargoyle C .07 .15
784 Loxodon Warhammer R .15 .30
785 Manakin C .15 .30
786 Meteor Golem U .07 .15
787 Monkey Cage R .75 1.50
788 Panharmonicon R 3.00 6.00
789 Phyrexian Ironfoot U .07 .15
790 Pierce Strider U .06 .12
791 Pilgrim's Eye C .06 .12
792 Psychosis Crawler R .12 .25
793 Raiders' Karve C .10 .20
794 Runed Servitor C .10 .20
795 Self-Assembler C .12 .25
796 Shambling Suit U .06 .12
797 Solemn Simulacrum R .50 1.00
798 Steel Overseer R .75 1.50
799 Talon of Pain U .05 .10
800 Tamiyo's Journal R 2.50 5.00
801 Teferi's Puzzle Box R 3.00 6.00
802 Thaumaturge's Familiar C .06 .12
803 Universal Automaton C .12 .25
804 Universal Solvent C .06 .12
805 Vial of Dragonfire C .05 .10
806 Walking Ballista R 7.50 15.00
807 Weapon Rack C .05 .10
808 Whirlermaker U .07 .15
809 Ash Barrens C .12 .25
810 Blighted Fen U .06 .12
811 Bonders' Enclave R 1.25 2.50
812 Desert of the Mindful C .06 .12
813 Evolving Wilds C .06 .12
814 Forgotten Cave C .07 .15
815 Memorial to Genius U .05 .10
816 Mishra's Factory U .07 .15
817 Mortuary Mire C .10 .20
818 Piranha Marsh C .12 .25
819 Sandstone Bridge C .05 .10
820 Seat of the Synod C .75 1.50
821 Shimmerdrift Vale C .06 .12
822 Thriving Bluff C .06 .12
823 Thriving Grove C .06 .12
824 Thriving Heath C .06 .12
825 Thriving Isle C .05 .10
826 Thriving Moor C .05 .10
827 Treetop Village U .15 .30
828 Urza's Factory U .12 .25
829 Urza's Mine C .75 1.50
830 Urza's Power Plant C .75 1.50
831 Urza's Tower C .60 1.25
832 Warped Landscape C .10 .20
833 Snow-Covered Island C 1.00 2.00
834 Wastes C 1.50 3.00
835 Kibo, Uktabi Prince M :G: 1.00 2.00

2022 Magic The Gathering Kamigawa Neon Dynasty

1 Ancestral Katana C :W: .07 .15
2 Ao, the Dawn Sky M :W: 1.00 2.00
3 Banishing Slash U :W: .12 .25
4 Befriending the Moths/Imperial Moth C :W: .07 .15
5 Blade-Blizzard Kitsune U :W: .12 .25
6 Born to Drive U :W: .12 .25
7 Brilliant Restoration R :W: .20 .40
8 Cloudsteel Kirin R :W: .20 .40
9 Dragonfly Suit C :W: .07 .15
10 Eiganjo Exemplar C :W: .07 .15
11 Era of Enlightenment
Hand of Enlightenment C :W: .07 .15
12 The Fall of Lord Konda
Fragment of Konda U :W: .12 .25
13 Farewell R :W: 4.00 8.00
14 Go-Shintai of Shared Purpose U :W: .12 .25
15 Golden-Tail Disciple C :W: .07 .15
16 Hotshot Mechanic U :W: .12 .25
17 Imperial Oath C :W: .07 .15
18 Imperial Recovery Unit U :W: .12 .25
19 Imperial Subduer C :W: .07 .15
20 Intercessor's Arrest C :W: .07 .15
21 Invoke Justice R :W: .20 .40
22 Kitsune Ace C :W: .07 .15
23 Kyodai, Soul of Kamigawa R :W: .20 .40
24 Light the Way C :W: .07 .15
25 Light-Paws, Emperor's Voice R :W: .20 .40
26 Lion Sash R :W: 1.25 2.50
27 Lucky Offering C :W: .07 .15
28 March of Otherworldly Light R :W: 2.50 5.00
29 Michiko's Reign of Truth
Portrait of Michiko U :W: .12 .25
30 Mothrider Patrol C :W: .07 .15
31 Norika Yamazaki, the Poet U :W: .12 .25
32 Regent's Authority C :W: .07 .15
33 Repel the Vile C :W: .07 .15
34 Restoration/Architect of Restoration R :W: .25 .50
35 Selfless Samurai U :W: .12 .25
36 Seven-Tail Mentor C :W: .07 .15
37 Sky-Blessed Samurai U :W: .12 .25
38 Spirited Companion C :W: .12 .25
39 Sunblade Samurai C :W: .07 .15
40 Touch the Spirit Realm U :W: .12 .25
41 Wanderer's Intervention C :W: .07 .15
42 The Wandering Emperor M :W: 20.00 40.00
43 When We Were Young U :W: .12 .25
44 Acquisition Octopus U :B: .12 .25
45 Anchor to Reality U :B: .12 .25
46 Armguard Familiar C :B: .07 .15
47 Awakened Awareness U :B: .12 .25
48 Behold Unspeakable
Vision of Unspeakable U :B: .12 .25
49 Covert Technician U :B: .12 .25
50 Discover the Impossible U :B: .12 .25
51 Disruption Protocol C :B: .07 .15
52 Essence Capture U :B: .12 .25
53 Futurist Operative U :B: .12 .25
54 Futurist Sentinel C :B: .07 .15
55 Go-Shintai of Lost Wisdom U :B: .12 .25
56 Guardians of Oboro C :B: .07 .15
57 Inventive Iteration/Living Breakthrough R :B: .20 .40
58 Invoke the Winds R :B: .20 .40
59 Jin-Gitaxias, Progress Tyrant M :B: 7.50 15.00
60 Kairi, the Swirling Sky M :B: .75 1.50
61 March of Swirling Mist R :B: .75 1.50
62 Mindlink Mech R :B: .20 .40
63 Mirrorshell Crab C :B: .07 .15
64 Mnemonic Sphere C :B: .07 .15
65 Mobilizer Mech U :B: .12 .25
66 The Modern Age/Vector Glider C :B: .07 .15
67 Moon-Circuit Hacker C :B: .07 .15
68 Moonfolk Puzzlemaker C :B: .07 .15
69 Moonsnare Prototype C :B: .07 .15
70 Moonsnare Specialist C :B: .07 .15
71 Network Disruptor C :B: .07 .15
72 Planar Incision C :B: .07 .15
73 Prosperous Thief U :B: .12 .25
74 The Reality Chip R :B: 1.25 2.50
75 Reality Heist U :B: .12 .25
76 Replication Specialist U :B: .12 .25
77 Saiba Trespassers C :B: .07 .15
78 Short Circuit C :B: .07 .15
79 Skyswimmer Koi C :B: .07 .15
80 Spell Pierce C :B: .07 .15
81 Suit Up C :B: .07 .15
82 Tameshi, Reality Architect R :B: .20 .40
83 Tamiyo's Compleation C :B: .07 .15
84 Tezzeret, Betrayer of Flesh M :B: 1.50 3.00
85 Thirst for Knowledge U :B: .12 .25
86 Thousand-Faced Shadow R :B: .30 .60
87 Assassin's Ink U :K: .12 .25
88 Biting-Palm Ninja R :K: .20 .40
89 Blade of the Oni M :K: .50 1.00
90 Chainflail Centipede C :K: .07 .15
91 Clawing Torment C :K: .07 .15
92 Debt to the Kami C :K: .07 .15
93 Dockside Chef U :K: .12 .25
94 Dokuchi Shadow-Walker C :K: .07 .15
95 Dokuchi Silencer U :K: .12 .25
96 Enormous Energy Blade U :K: .12 .25
97 Go-Shintai of Hidden Cruelty U :K: .12 .25
98 Gravelighter U :K: .12 .25
99 Hidetsugu, Devouring Chaos R :K: .20 .40
100 Inkrise Infiltrator C :K: .07 .15
101 Invoke Despair R :K: .20 .40
102 Junji, the Midnight Sky M :K: 4.00 8.00
103 Kaito's Pursuit C :K: .07 .15
104 Kami of Restless Shadows C :K: .07 .15
105 Kami of Terrible Secrets C :K: .07 .15
106 Leech Gauntlet U :K: .12 .25
107 Lethal Exploit C :K: .07 .15
108 Toshiro Umezawa/Memory of Toshiro U :K: .12 .25
109 Long Reach of Night/Animus
of Night's Reach U :K: .12 .25
110 Malicious Malfunction U :K: .12 .25
111 March of Wretched Sorrow R :K: .20 .40
112 Mukotai Ambusher C :K: .07 .15
113 Mukotai Soulripper R :K: .20 .40
114 Nashi, Moon Sage's Scion M :K: 2.00 4.00
115 Nezumi Bladeblesser C :K: .07 .15
116 Nezumi Prowler U :K: .12 .25
117 Okiba Reckoner Raid/Nezumi
Road Captain C :K: .07 .15
118 Okiba Salvage U :K: .12 .25
119 Reckoner Shakedown C :K: .07 .15
120 Reckoner's Bargain C :K: .07 .15
121 Return to Action C :K: .07 .15
122 Soul Transfer R :K: .20 .40
123 Tatsunari, Toad Rider R :K: .20 .40
124 Tribute to Horobi/Echo of Death's Wail R :K: .20 .40
125 Twisted Embrace C :K: .07 .15
126 Undercity Scrounger C :K: .07 .15
127 Unforgiving One U :K: .12 .25
128 Virus Beetle C :K: .07 .15
129 You Are Already Dead C :K: .07 .15
130 Akki Ember-Keeper C :R: .07 .15
131 Akki Ronin C :R: .07 .15
132 Akki War Paint C :R: .07 .15
133 Ambitious Assault C :R: .07 .15
134 Atsushi, the Blazing Sky M :R: 4.00 8.00
135 Bronzeplate Boar U :R: .12 .25
136 Crackling Emergence C :R: .07 .15
137 Dragonspark Reactor U :R: .12 .25
138 Experimental Synthesizer C :R: .20 .40
139 Explosive Entry C :R: .07 .15
140 Explosive Singularity M :R: .15 .30
141 Fable of Mirror-Breaker
Reflection of Kiki-Jiki R :R: 7.50 15.00
142 Flame Discharge U :R: .12 .25
143 Gift of Wrath C :R: .07 .15
144 Go-Shintai of Ancient Wars U :R: .12 .25
145 Goro-Goro, Disciple of Ryusei R :R: .20 .40
146 Heiko Yamazaki, the General U :R: .12 .25
147 Invoke Calamity R :R: .20 .40
148 Ironhoof Boar C :R: .07 .15
149 Kami of Industry C :R: .07 .15
150 Kami's Flare C :R: .07 .15
151 Kindled Fury C :R: .07 .15
152 Kumano Faces Kakkazan
Etching of Kumano U :R: .12 .25
153 Lizard Blades R :R: .30 .60
154 March of Reckless Joy R :R: .20 .40
155 Ogre-Head Helm R :R: .20 .40
156 Peerless Samurai C :R: .07 .15
157 Rabbit Battery U :R: .12 .25
158 Reinforced Ronin U :R: .12 .25
159 Scrap Welder R :R: .20 .40
160 Scrapyard Steelbreaker C :R: .07 .15
161 Seismic Wave U :R: .12 .25
162 The Shattered States Era

Nameless Conqueror C :R: .07 .15
163 Simian Sling C :R: .07 .15
164 Sokenzan Smelter U :R: .12 .25
165 Tempered in Solitude U :R: .12 .25
166 Thundering Raiju R :R: .20 .40
167 Towashi Songshaper C :R: .07 .15
168 Twinshot Sniper U :R: .12 .25
169 Unstoppable Ogre C :R: .07 .15
170 Upriser Renegade U :R: .12 .25
171 Voltage Surge C :R: .07 .15
172 Azusa's Many Journeys
Likeness of the Seeker U :G: .12 .25
173 Bamboo Grove Archer C :G: .07 .15
174 Bearer of Memory C :G: .07 .15
175 Blossom Prancer U :G: .12 .25
176 Boon of Boseiju U :G: .12 .25
177 Boseiju Reaches Skyward
Branch of Boseiju U :G: .12 .25
178 Careful Cultivation C :G: .07 .15
179 Coiling Stalker C :G: .07 .15
180 Commune with Spirits C :G: .07 .15
181 The Dragon-Kami Reborn
Dragon-Kami's Egg R :G: .20 .40
182 Fade into Antiquity C :G: .07 .15
183 Fang of Shigeki C :G: .07 .15
184 Favor of Jukai C :G: .07 .15
185 Generous Visitor U :G: .12 .25
186 Geothermal Kami C :G: .07 .15
187 Go-Shintai of Boundless Vigor U :G: .12 .25
188 Grafted Growth C :G: .07 .15
189 Greater Tanuki C :G: .07 .15
190 Harmonious Emergence C :G: .07 .15
191 Heir of the Ancient Fang C :G: .07 .15
192 Historian's Wisdom U :G: .12 .25
193 Invoke the Ancients R :G: .20 .40
194 Jugan Defends Temple
Remnant of Rising Star M :G: .75 1.50
195 Jukai Preserver C :G: .07 .15
196 Jukai Trainee C :G: .07 .15
197 Kami of Transience R :G: .20 .40
198 Kappa Tech-Wrecker U :G: .12 .25
199 Kodama of the West Tree M :G: 3.00 6.00
200 Kura, the Boundless Sky M :G: 2.50 5.00
201 March of Burgeoning Life R :G: .20 .40
202 Master's Rebuke C :G: .07 .15
203 Orochi Merge-Keeper U :G: .12 .25
204 Roaring Earth U :G: .12 .25
205 Season of Renewal C :G: .07 .15
206 Shigeki, Jukai Visionary R :G: .20 .40
207 Spinning Wheel Kick U :G: .12 .25
208 Spring-Leaf Avenger R :G: .20 .40
209 Storyweave U :G: .12 .25
210 Master Seshiro/Seshiro's Living Legacy C :G:.07 .15
211 Tamiyo's Safekeeping C :G: .07 .15
212 Teachings of the Kirin
Kirin-Touched Orochi R :G: .20 .40
213 Weaver of Harmony R :G: .75 1.50
214 Webspinner Cuff U :G: .12 .25
215 Asari Captain U :R:/:W: .12 .25
216 Colossal Skyturtle U :G:/:B: .12 .25
217 Eiganjo Uprising R :R:/:W: .20 .40
218 Enthusiastic Mechanaut U :B:/:R: .12 .25
219 Gloomshrieker U :K:/:G: .12 .25
220 Greasefang, Okiba Boss R :W:/:K: .20 .40
221 Hidetsugu Consumes All
Vessel of All-Consuming M :K:/:R: 1.25 2.50
222 Hinata, Dawn-Crowned R :B:/:R:/:W: .20 .40
223 Invigorating Hot Spring U :R:/:G: .12 .25
224 Isshin, Two Heavens as One R :R:/:W:/:K: .20 .40
225 Jukai Naturalist U :G:/:W: .12 .25
226 Kaito Shizuki M :B:/:K: 4.00 8.00
227 Kami War/O-Kagachi Made
Manifest M :W:/:B:/:K:/:R:/:G: .30 .75
228 Kotose, the Silent Spider R :B:/:K: .20 .40
229 Naomi, Pillar of Order U :W:/:K: .12 .25
230 Oni-Cult Anvil U :K:/:R: .12 .25
231 Prodigy's Prototype U :W:/:B: .12 .25
232 Raiyuu, Storm's Edge R :R:/:W: .20 .40
233 Risona, Asari Commander R :R:/:W: .20 .40
234 Satoru Umezawa R :B:/:K: .20 .40
235 Satsuki, the Living Lore R :G:/:W: .20 .40
236 Silver-Fur Master U :B:/:K: .12 .25
237 Spirit-Sister's Call M :W:/:K: .20 .40
238 Tamiyo, Compleated Sage M :G:/:B: 1.00 2.00
239 Automated Artificer C .07 .15
240 Bronze Cudgels U .12 .25
241 Brute Suit C .07 .15
242 Circuit Mender U .12 .25
243 Containment Construct U .30 .60
244 Dramatist's Puppet C .07 .15
245 Eater of Virtue R .20 .40
246 Ecologist's Terrarium C .07 .15
247 High-Speed Hoverbike U .12 .25
248 Iron Apprentice C .07 .15
249 Mechtitan Core R .20 .40
250 Mirror Box R 1.25 2.50
251 Network Terminal C .07 .15
252 Ninja's Kunai C .07 .15
253 Papercraft Decoy C .07 .15
254 Patchwork Automaton U .12 .25
255 Reckoner Bankbuster R .20 .40
256 Reito Sentinel U .12 .25
257 Runaway Trash-Bot U .12 .25
258 Searchlight Companion C .07 .15
259 Shrine Steward C .07 .15
260 Surgehacker Mech R .20 .40
261 Thundersteel Colossus C .07 .15
262 Towashi Guide-Bot U .12 .25
263 Walking Skyscraper U .12 .25
264 Bloodfell Caves C .07 .15
265 Blossoming Sands C .07 .15
266 Boseiju, Who Endures R 15.00 30.00
267 Dismal Backwater C .07 .15
268 Eiganjo, Seat of the Empire R 2.50 5.00
269 Jungle Hollow C .07 .15
270 Mech Hangar U .12 .25
271 Otawara, Soaring City R 7.50 15.00
272 Roadside Reliquary U .12 .25
273 Rugged Highlands C .07 .15
274 Scoured Barrens C .07 .15
275 Secluded Courtyard U 2.00 4.00
276 Sokenzan, Crucible of Defiance R 2.00 4.00
277 Swiftwater Cliffs C .07 .15
278 Takenuma, Abandoned Mire R 3.00 6.00
279 Thornwood Falls C .07 .15
280 Tranquil Cove C .07 .15
281 Uncharted Haven C .07 .15
282 Wind-Scarred Crag C .07 .15
283 Plains C .07 .15
284 Plains C .07 .15
285 Island C .07 .15
286 Island C .07 .15
287 Swamp C .15 .30
288 Swamp C .15 .30
289 Mountain C .07 .15
290 Mountain C .07 .15
291 Forest C .07 .15
292 Forest C .07 .15
293 Plains C 1.00 2.00
294 Plains C 1.00 2.00
295 Island C 1.00 2.00
296 Island C 1.00 2.00
297 Swamp C 1.00 2.00
298 Swamp C 1.00 2.00
299 Mountain C 1.00 2.00
300 Mountain C 1.00 2.00
301 Forest C 1.00 2.00
302 Forest C 1.00 2.00
303 The Wandering Emperor M :W: 20.00 40.00
304 Tezzeret, Betrayer of Flesh M :B: 3.00 6.00
305 Kaito Shizuki M :B:/:K: 7.50 15.00
306 Tamiyo, Compleated Sage M :G:/:B: 4.00 8.00
307 Jin-Gitaxias, Progress Tyrant M :B: 15.00 30.00
308 Tamiyo, Completed Sage M :G:/:B: 6.00 12.00
309 Eiganjo Exemplar C :W: .07 .15
310 Imperial Subduer C :W: .07 .15
311 Norika Yamazaki, the Poet U :W: .12 .25
312 Selfless Samurai U :W: .12 .25
313 Seven-Tail Mentor C :W: .07 .15
314 Sky-Blessed Samurai U :W: .12 .25
315 Sunblade Samurai C :W: .07 .15
316 The Wandering Emperor M :W: 50.00 100.00
317 Guardians of Oboro C :B: .07 .15
318 Nezumi Bladeblesser C :K: .07 .15
319 Akki Ronin C :R: .07 .15
320 Goro-Goro, Disciple of Ryusei R :R: 1.25 2.50
321 Heiko Yamazaki, the General U :R: .12 .25
322 Peerless Samurai C :R: .07 .15
323 Reinforced Ronin U :R: .12 .25
324 Upriser Renegade U :R: .12 .25
325 Heir of the Ancient Fang C :G: .07 .15
326 Jukai Trainee C :G: .07 .15
327 Asari Captain U :R:/:W: .12 .25
328 Isshin, Two Heavens as One R :R:/:W:/:K: 3.00 6.00
329 Raiyuu, Storm's Edge R :R:/:W: 1.50 3.00
330 Risona, Asari Commander R :R:/:W: .75 1.50
331 Blade-Blizzard Kitsune U :W: .12 .25
332 Covert Technician U :B: .12 .25
333 Futurist Operative U :B: .12 .25
334 Moon-Circuit Hacker C :B: .07 .15
335 Moonsnare Specialist C :B: .07 .15
336 Prosperous Thief U :B: .12 .25
337 Thousand-Faced Shadow R :B: 1.25 2.50
338 Biting-Palm Ninja R :K: .75 1.50
339 Dokuchi Shadow-Walker C :K: .07 .15
340 Dokuchi Silencer U :K: .12 .25
341 Inkrise Infiltrator C :K: .07 .15
342 Mukotai Ambusher C :K: .07 .15
343 Nashi, Moon Sage's Scion M :K: 3.00 6.00
344 Nezumi Prowler U :K: .12 .25
345 Tatsunari, Toad Rider R :K: .75 1.50
346 Coiling Stalker C :G: .07 .15
347 Fang of Shigeki C :G: .07 .15
348 Kappa Tech-Wrecker U :G: .12 .25
349 Spring-Leaf Avenger R :G: .20 .40
350 Kaito Shizuki M :B:/:K: 10.00 20.00
351 Kotose, the Silent Spider R :B:/:K: .50 1.00
352 Satoru Umezawa R :B:/:K: .30 .75
353 Silver-Fur Master U :B:/:K: .12 .25
354 Restoration of Eiganjo
Architect of Restoration R :W: .75 1.50
355 Inventive Iteration/Living Breakthrough R :B:.20 .40
356 Tribute to Horobi/Echo of Death's Wail R :K:.20 .40
357 Fable of Mirror-Breaker
Reflection of Kiki-Jiki R :R: 12.50 25.00
358 The Dragon-Kami Reborn
Dragon-Kami's Egg R :G: .20 .40
359 Jugan Defends Temple
Remnant of Rising Star M :G: 1.25 2.50
360 Teachings of the Kirin
Kirin-Touched Orochi R :G: .20 .40
361 Hidetsugu Consumes All
Vessel of All-Consuming M :K:/:R: 2.50 5.00
362 Kami War/O-Kagachi Made
Manifest M :W:/:B:/:K:/:R:/:G: 1.25 2.50
363 Brilliant Restoration R :W: 1.00 2.00
364 Cloudsteel Kirin R :W: .30 .75
365 Farewell R :W: 6.00 12.00
366 Invoke Justice R :W: .25 .50
367 Light-Paws, Emperor's Voice R :W: 1.25 2.50
368 Lion Sash R :W: 2.50 5.00
369 March of Otherworldly Light R :W: 4.00 8.00
370 Invoke the Winds R :B: .20 .40
371 Jin-Gitaxias, Progress Tyrant M :B: 12.50 25.00
372 March of Swirling Mist R :B: 1.50 3.00
373 Mindlink Mech R :B: .50 1.00
374 The Reality Chip R :B: 3.00 6.00
375 Tameshi, Reality Architect R :B: .50 1.00
376 Tezzeret, Betrayer of Flesh M :B: 3.00 6.00
377 Blade of the Oni M :K: 1.25 2.50
378 Hidetsugu, Devouring Chaos R :K: .30 .60
379 Invoke Despair R :K: .75 1.50
380 March of Wretched Sorrow R :K: .30 .75
381 Mukotai Soulripper R :K: .20 .40
382 Soul Transfer R :K: .20 .40
383 Explosive Singularity M :R: .50 1.00
384 Invoke Calamity R :R: .50 1.00
385 Lizard Blades R :R: 1.00 2.00
386 March of Reckless Joy R :R: .30 .60
387 Ogre-Head Helm R :R: .20 .40
388 Scrap Welder R :R: .20 .40
389 Thundering Raiju R :R: .40 .80
390 Invoke the Ancients R :G: .20 .40
391 Kami of Transience R :G: .50 1.00
392 Kodama of the West Tree M :G: 4.00 8.00
393 March of Burgeoning Life R :G: .20 .40
394 Shigeki, Jukai Visionary R :G: .50 1.00
395 Weaver of Harmony R :G: .60 1.25
396 Eiganjo Uprising R :R:/:W: .20 .40
397 Greasefang, Okiba Boss R :W:/:K: 2.00 4.00
398 Hinata, Dawn-Crowned R :B:/:R:/:W: 1.00 2.00
399 Satsuki, the Living Lore R :G:/:W: .30 .60
400 Spirit-Sister's Call M :W:/:K: .30 .60
401 Eater of Virtue R .75 1.50
402 Mechtitan Core R 1.25 2.50
403 Mirror Box R 1.25 2.50
404 Reckoner Bankbuster R 1.00 2.00
405 Surgehacker Mech R .30 .75
406 Ao, the Dawn Sky M :W: 3.00 6.00
407 Kyodai, Soul of Kamigawa R :W: .25 .50
408 Kairi, the Swirling Sky M :B: 2.50 5.00
409 Junji, the Midnight Sky M :K: 7.50 15.00
410 Atsushi, the Blazing Sky M :R: 7.50 15.00
411 Kura, the Boundless Sky M :G: 4.00 8.00
412 Boseiju, Who Endures R 20.00 40.00
413 Eiganjo, Seat of the Empire R 4.00 8.00
414 Otawara, Soaring City R 12.50 25.00
415 Sokenzan, Crucible of Defiance R 4.00 8.00
416 Takenuma, Abandoned Mire R 7.50 15.00
417 Farewell R :W: 10.00 20.00
418 The Wandering Emperor M :W: 125.00 250.00
419 Tezzeret, Betrayer of Flesh M :B: 10.00 20.00
420 Blade of the Oni M :K: 4.00 8.00
421 Nashi, Moon Sage's Scion M :K: 10.00 20.00
422 Explosive Singularity M :R: 3.00 6.00
423 Kodama of the West Tree M :G: 7.50 15.00
424 Kaito Shizuki M :B:/:K: 20.00 40.00
425 Risona, Asari Commander R :R:/:W: 4.00 8.00
426 Satoru Umezawa R :B:/:K: 4.00 8.00
427 Jin-Gitaxias, Progress Tyrant M :B: 60.00 125.00
428 Tamiyu, Completed Sage M :G:/:B: 25.00 50.00
429 Hidetsugu, Devouring Chaos R :K: 750.00 1,500.00
430 Hidetsugu, Devouring Chaos R :K: 150.00 300.00
431 Hidetsugu, Devouring Chaos R :K: 60.00 125.00
432 Hidetsugu, Devouring Chaos R :K: 100.00 200.00
433 Ao, the Dawn Sky M :W: 1.25 2.50
434 Brilliant Restoration R :W: .30 .60
435 Cloudsteel Kirin R :W: .20 .40
436 Farewell R :W: 6.00 12.00
437 Invoke Justice R :W: .20 .40
438 Kyodai, Soul of Kamigawa R :W: .20 .40
439 Light-Paws, Emperor's Voice R :W: .75 1.50
440 Lion Sash R :W: 1.50 3.00
441 March of Otherworldly Light R :W: 2.50 5.00
442 Restoration of Eiganjo
Architect of Restoration R :W: .50 1.00
443 Inventive Iteration/Living Breakthrough R :B:.20 .40
444 Invoke the Winds R :B: .20 .40
445 Jin-Gitaxias, Progress Tyrant M :B: 7.50 15.00
446 Kairi, the Swirling Sky M :B: 1.25 2.50
447 March of Swirling Mist R :B: 1.00 2.00
448 Mindlink Mech R :B: .20 .40
449 The Reality Chip R :B: 1.50 3.00
450 Tameshi, Reality Architect R :B: .50 1.00
451 Thousand-Faced Shadow R :B: .50 1.00
452 Biting-Palm Ninja R :K: .25 .50
453 Blade of the Oni M :K: .75 1.50
454 Hidetsugu, Devouring Chaos R :K: .20 .40
455 Invoke Despair R :K: .50 1.00
456 Junji, the Midnight Sky M :K: 4.00 8.00
457 March of Wretched Sorrow R :K: .30 .75
458 Mukotai Soulripper R :K: .20 .40
459 Nashi, Moon Sage's Scion M :K: 2.50 5.00
460 Soul Transfer R :K: .20 .40
461 Tatsunari, Toad Rider R :K: .20 .40
462 Tribute to Horobi/Echo of Death's Wail R :K:.20 .40
463 Atsushi, the Blazing Sky M :R: 6.00 12.00
464 Explosive Singularity M :R: .25 .50
465 Fable of Mirror-Breaker
Reflection of Kiki-Jiki R :R: 7.50 15.00
466 Goro-Goro, Disciple of Ryusei R :R: .50 1.00
467 Invoke Calamity R :R: .20 .40
468 Lizard Blades R :R: .75 1.50
469 March of Reckless Joy R :R: .20 .40
470 Ogre-Head Helm R :R: .20 .40
471 Scrap Welder R :R: .20 .40
472 Thundering Raiju R :R: .30 .60
473 The Dragon-Kami Reborn
Dragon-Kami's Egg R :G: .20 .40
474 Invoke the Ancients R :G: .20 .40
475 Jugan Defends Temple
Remnant of Rising Star M :G: 1.00 2.00
476 Kami of Transience R :G: .25 .50
477 Kodama of the West Tree M :G: 4.00 8.00
478 Kura, the Boundless Sky M :G: 2.50 5.00
479 March of Burgeoning Life R :G: .20 .40
480 Shigeki, Jukai Visionary R :G: .30 .75
481 Spring-Leaf Avenger R :G: .20 .40
482 Teachings of the Kirin
Kirin-Touched Orochi R :G: .20 .40
483 Weaver of Harmony R :G: .75 1.50
484 Eiganjo Uprising R :R:/:W: .20 .40
485 Greasefang, Okiba Boss R :W:/:K: .75 1.50
486 Hidetsugu Consumes All
Vessel of All-Consuming M :K:/:R: 2.00 4.00
487 Hinata, Dawn-Crowned R :B:/:R:/:W: .30 .75
488 Isshin, Two Heavens as One R :R:/:W:/:K: .75 1.50
489 Kami War/O-Kagachi Made
Manifest M :W:/:B:/:K:/:R:/:G: .75 1.50
490 Kotose, the Silent Spider R :B:/:K: .20 .40
491 Raiyuu, Storm's Edge R :R:/:W: .20 .40
492 Risona, Asari Commander R :R:/:W: .20 .40
493 Satoru Umezawa R :B:/:K: .30 .75
494 Satsuki, the Living Lore R :G:/:W: .20 .40
495 Spirit-Sister's Call M :W:/:K: .50 1.00
496 Eater of Virtue R .30 .60
497 Mechtitan Core R .20 .40
498 Mirror Box R 1.50 3.00
499 Reckoner Bankbuster R .50 1.00
500 Surgehacker Mech R .20 .40
501 Boseiju, Who Endures R 17.50 35.00
502 Eiganjo, Seat of the Empire R 3.00 6.00
503 Otawara, Soaring City R 10.00 20.00
504 Sokenzan, Crucible of Defiance R 2.50 5.00
505 Takenuma, Abandoned Mire R 4.00 8.00

2022 Magic The Gathering Kamigawa Neon Dynasty Tokens

1 Pilot .10 .20
2 Spirit .07 .15
3 Samurai .07 .15
4 Ninja 2.00 4.00
5 Rat Rogue .10 .20
6 Construct .07 .15
7 Dragon Spirit .30 .75
8 Goblin Shaman 6.00 12.00
9 Spirit .07 .15
10 Human Monk .07 .15
11 Spirit .15 .30
12 Spirit .15 .30
13 Keimi .60 1.25
14 Mechtitan 1.50 3.00
15 Construct .07 .15
16 Tamiyo's Notebook .30 .75
17 Treasure .07 .15
18 Kaito Shizuki Emblem .20 .40
19 Tezzeret, Betrayer of Flesh Emblem .25 .50

2022 Magic The Gathering Kamigawa Neon Dynasty Commander

1 Chishiro, the Shattered Blade M :R:/:G: .15 .30
2 Kotori, Pilot Prodigy M :W:/:B: .17 .35
3 Kaima, the Fractured Calm M :R:/:G: .12 .25
4 Shorikai, Genesis Engine M :W:/:B: .75 1.50
5 Aerial Surveyor R :W: .15 .30
6 Drumbellower R :W: 2.00 4.00
7 Ironsoul Enforcer R :W: .15 .30
8 Organic Extinction R :W: 2.50 5.00
9 Release to Memory R :W: .12 .25
10 Swift Reconfiguration R :W: .75 1.50
11 Access Denied R :B: .30 .75
12 Cyberdrive Awakener R :B: 1.25 2.50
13 Imposter Mech R :B: .50 1.00
14 Kappa Cannoneer R :B: 1.50 3.00
15 Katsumasa, the Animator R :B: .12 .25
16 Research Thief R :B: .12 .25
17 Universal Surveillance R :B: .12 .25
18 Akki Battle Squad R :R: .30 .75
19 Collision of Realms R :R: .07 .15
20 Kami of Celebration R :R: .12 .25
21 Komainu Battle Armor R :R: 1.00 2.00
22 Smoke Spirits' Aid R :R: .12 .25
23 Unquenchable Fury R :R: .15 .30
24 Ascendant Acolyte R :G: .12 .25
25 Concord with the Kami R :G: .07 .15
26 Kosei, Penitent Warlord R :G: .07 .15
27 One with the Kami R :G: .12 .25
28 Rampant Rejuvenator R :G: 1.00 2.00
29 Silkguard R :G: 1.25 2.50
30 Tanuki Transplanter R :G: .40 .80
31 Myojin of Blooming Dawn R :W: .12 .25
32 Yoshimaru, Ever Faithful M :W: 3.00 6.00
33 Myojin of Cryptic Dreams R :B: .17 .35
34 Myojin of Grim Betrayal R :K: .07 .15
35 Ruthless Technomancer R :K: 2.00 4.00
36 Myojin of Roaring Blades R :R: .07 .15
37 Go-Shintai of Life's Origin M :G: 2.50 5.00
38 Myojin of Towering Might R :G: .07 .15
39 Aerial Surveyor R :W: .25 .50
40 Drumbellower R :W: 1.50 3.00
41 Ironsoul Enforcer R :W: .40 .80
42 Myojin of Blooming Dawn R :W: .25 .50
43 Organic Extinction R :W: 1.50 3.00
44 Release to Memory R :W: .15 .30
45 Swift Reconfiguration R :W: .75 1.50
46 Yoshimaru, Ever Faithful M :W: 4.00 8.00
47 Access Denied R :B: .30 .60
48 Cyberdrive Awakener R :B: 1.25 2.50
49 Imposter Mech R :B: 1.00 2.00
50 Kappa Cannoneer R :B: 1.50 3.00
51 Katsumasa, the Animator R :B: .12 .25
52 Myojin of Cryptic Dreams R :B: .20 .40
53 Research Thief R :B: .17 .35
54 Universal Surveillance R :B: .15 .30
55 Myojin of Grim Betrayal R :K: .15 .30
56 Ruthless Technomancer R :K: 1.25 2.50
57 Akki Battle Squad R :R: .40 .80
58 Collision of Realms R :R: .07 .15
59 Kami of Celebration R :R: .20 .40
60 Komainu Battle Armor R :R: .75 1.50
61 Myojin of Roaring Blades R :R: .12 .25
62 Smoke Spirits' Aid R :R: .17 .35
63 Unquenchable Fury R :R: .17 .35
64 Ascendant Acolyte R :G: .12 .25
65 Concord with the Kami R :G: .10 .20
66 Go-Shintai of Life's Origin M :G: 3.00 6.00
67 Kosei, Penitent Warlord R :G: .12 .25
68 Myojin of Towering Might R :G: .15 .30
69 One with the Kami R :G: .12 .25
70 Rampant Rejuvenator R :G: 1.25 2.50
71 Silkguard R :G: 1.25 2.50
72 Tanuki Transplanter R :G: .30 .75
73 Chishiro, the Shattered Blade M :R:/:G: .30 .75
74 Kaima, the Fractured Calm M :R:/:G: .17 .35
75 Kotori, Pilot Prodigy M :W:/:B: .60 1.25
76 Shorikai, Genesis Engine M :W:/:B: 2.50 5.00
77 Chishiro, the Shattered Blade M :R:/:G: .10 .20
78 Kotori, Pilot Prodigy M :W:/:B: .12 .25
79 Aeronaut Admiral U :W: .07 .15
80 Armed and Armored U :W: .10 .20
81 Cataclysmic Gearhulk M :W: .17 .35
82 Crush Contraband U :W: .10 .20
83 Dispatch U :W: 1.50 3.00
84 Generous Gift U :W: .75 1.50
85 Indomitable Archangel M :W: .20 .40
86 Myrsmith U :W: .07 .15
87 Parhelion II R :W: .75 1.50
88 Sram, Senior Edificer R :W: .20 .40
89 Swords to Plowshares U :W: .75 1.50
90 Teshar, Ancestor's Apostle R :W: .12 .25
91 Emry, Lurker of the Loch R :B: .25 .50
92 Etherium Sculptor C :B: .30 .60
93 Jace, Architect of Thought M :B: .15 .30
94 Master of Etherium R :B: .12 .25
95 Reality Shift U :B: .60 1.25
96 Riddlesmith U :B: .07 .15
97 Sai, Master Thopterist R :B: .75 1.50
98 Thopter Spy Network R :B: .10 .20
99 Thoughtcast C :B: .50 1.00
100 Vedalken Engineer C :B: .10 .20
101 Whirler Rogue U :B: .07 .15

102 Agitator Ant R :R: .12 .25
103 Chain Reaction R :R: .12 .25
104 Chaos Warp R :R: .60 1.25
105 Elemental Mastery R :R: .12 .25
106 Goblin Razerunners R :R: .07 .15
107 Krenko, Tin Street Kingpin R :R: .30 .75
108 Ox of Agonas M :R: .20 .40
109 Shifting Shadow R :R: .07 .15
110 Starstorm R :R: .12 .25
111 Taurean Mauler R :R: .50 1.00
112 Acidic Slime U :G: .07 .15
113 Bear Umbra R :G: 4.00 8.00
114 Beast Within U :G: 1.00 2.00
115 Champion of Lambholt R :G: .20 .40
116 Fertilid C :G: .07 .15
117 Forgotten Ancient R :G: .12 .25
118 Genesis Hydra R :G: .12 .25
119 Hunter's Insight U :G: .12 .25
120 Kodama's Reach C :G: 1.25 2.50
121 Loyal Guardian U :G: .25 .50
123 Ordeal of Nylea U :G: .07 .15
124 Primeval Protector R :G: .20 .40
125 Rampant Growth C :G: .17 .35
126 Rishkar, Peema Renegade R :G: .12 .25
127 Rishkar's Expertise R :G: 2.00 4.00
128 Sakura-Tribe Elder C :G: .75 1.50
129 Shamanic Revelation R :G: .30 .60
130 Snake Umbra U :G: .25 .50
131 Soul's Majesty R :G: .60 1.25
132 Spearbreaker Behemoth R :G: .12 .25
133 Vastwood Surge U :G: .10 .20
134 Whiptongue Hydra R :G: .17 .35
135 Arcanist's Owl U :W:/:B: .07 .15
136 Dance of the Manse R :W:/:B: .30 .75
137 Decimate R :R:/:G: .20 .40
138 Grumgully, the Generous U :R:/:G: .07 .15
139 Hanna, Ship's Navigator R :W:/:B: .15 .30
140 Mage Slayer U :R:/:G: .15 .30
141 Raff Capashen, Ship's Mage U :W:/:B: .07 .15
142 Rhythm of the Wild U :R:/:G: 3.00 6.00
143 Ulasht, the Hate Seed R :R:/:G: .07 .15
144 Arcane Signet C .50 1.00
145 Azorius Signet U .25 .50
146 Blackblade Reforged R .15 .30
147 Bonehoard R .10 .20
148 Colossal Plow U .10 .20
149 Cultivator's Caravan R .12 .25
150 Fellwar Stone U .75 1.50
151 Fireshrieker U .15 .30
152 Foundry Inspector C .12 .25
153 Gold Myr C .12 .25
154 Mirage Mirror R 1.00 2.00
155 Peacewalker Colossus R .12 .25
156 Raiders' Karve C .07 .15
157 Shimmer Myr U .12 .25
158 Silver Myr C .12 .25
159 Skysovereign, Consul Flagship M 2.00 4.00
160 Smuggler's Copter R .25 .50
161 Sol Ring U 1.00 2.00
162 Solemn Simulacrum R .40 .80
163 Swiftfoot Boots U 1.00 2.00
164 Sword of Vengeance R .17 .35
165 Weatherlight M .17 .35
166 Cinder Glade R .15 .30
167 Command Tower C .15 .30
168 Exotic Orchard R .10 .20
169 Game Trail R .12 .25
170 Gruul Turf U .10 .20
171 Mossfire Valley R .07 .15
172 Opal Palace C .10 .20
173 Oran-Rief, the Vastwood R .30 .75
174 Port Town R .10 .20
175 Prairie Stream R .12 .25
176 Raging Ravine R .10 .20
177 Skycloud Expanse R .10 .20
178 Spire of Industry R .30 .75
179 Temple of Abandon R .12 .25
180 Temple of Enlightenment R .15 .30

2022 Magic The Gathering Kamigawa Neon Dynasty Commander Tokens

1 Shrine 3.00 6.00
2 Angel .12 .25
3 Phyrexian Germ .07 .15
4 Elemental .10 .20
5 Goblin .07 .15
6 Smoke Blessing .07 .15
7 Beast .07 .15
8 Elephant .12 .25
9 Plant .12 .30
10 Saproling .07 .15
11 Myr .12 .25
12 Thopter .07 .15

2022 Magic The Gathering Regional Championship Qualifiers

1 Gideon, Ally of Zendikar M :W: 20.00 40.00
2 Selfless Spirit R :W: 3.00 6.00
3 Thraben Inspector R :W: .75 1.50

2022 Magic The Gathering Secret Lair Drop Series Artist Series Aleksi Briclot

720 Thought-Knot Seer R 5.00 12.00
1151 Thought-Knot Seer R 8.00 20.00
1152 Inquisition of Kozilek R 4.00 10.00
1153 Reality Smasher R 15.00 40.00
1154 Eldrazi Temple R 40.00 100.00

2022 Magic The Gathering Secret Lair Drop Series Artist Series Aleksi Briclot Foil

720 Thought-Knot Seer R 5.00 12.00
1151 Thought-Knot Seer R 8.00 20.00
1152 Inquisition of Kozilek R 4.00 10.00
1153 Reality Smasher R 15.00 40.00
1154 Eldrazi Temple R 40.00 100.00

2022 Magic The Gathering Secret Lair Drop Series Artist Series Chris Rahn

493 Kozilek, the Great Distortion M 10.00 25.00
494 Primeval Titan M 3.00 8.00
495 Huntmaster of the Fells // Ravager of the Fells M 2.50 6.00
496 Platinum Angel R 5.00 12.00
700 Huntmaster of the Fells // Ravager of the Fells M .75 2.00

2022 Magic The Gathering Secret Lair Drop Series Artist Series Chris Rahn Foil

493 Kozilek, the Great Distortion M 10.00 25.00
494 Primeval Titan M 3.00 8.00
495 Huntmaster of the Fells // Ravager of the Fells M 2.50 6.00
496 Platinum Angel R 5.00 12.00
700 Huntmaster of the Fells // Ravager of the Fells M .75 2.00

2022 Magic The Gathering Secret Lair Drop Series Artist Series Livia Prima

489 Akroma, Angel of Wrath M 5.00 12.00
490 Mikaeus, the Unhallowed M 6.00 15.00
491 Glissa Sunseeker R 1.25 3.00
492 Olivia, Mobilized for War M 8.00 20.00
699 Olivia, Mobilized for War M .75 2.00

2022 Magic The Gathering Secret Lair Drop Series Artist Series Livia Prima Foil

489 Akroma, Angel of Wrath M 5.00 12.00
490 Mikaeus, the Unhallowed M 6.00 15.00
491 Glissa Sunseeker R 1.25 3.00
492 Olivia, Mobilized for War M 8.00 20.00
699 Olivia, Mobilized for War M .75 2.00

2022 Magic The Gathering Secret Lair Drop Series Artist Series Magali Villeneuve

473 Mother of Runes R 5.00 12.00
474 Death's Shadow R 6.00 15.00
475 Elvish Mystic R 6.00 15.00
476 Forest R 6.00 15.00
690 Forest R 3.00 8.00

2022 Magic The Gathering Secret Lair Drop Series Artist Series Magali Villeneuve Foil

473 Mother of Runes R 5.00 12.00
474 Death's Shadow R 6.00 15.00
475 Elvish Mystic R 6.00 15.00
476 Forest R 6.00 15.00
690 Forest R 3.00 8.00

2022 Magic The Gathering Secret Lair Drop Series Artist Series Nils Hamm

711 Tireless Tracker R 2.00 5.00
1093 Deepglow Skate R 2.00 5.00
1094 Tireless Tracker R 2.00 5.00
1095 Contagion Engine R 6.00 15.00
1096 Sword of Truth and Justice M 20.00 50.00

2022 Magic The Gathering Secret Lair Drop Series Artist Series Nils Hamm Foil

711 Tireless Tracker R 2.00 5.00
1093 Deepglow Skate R 2.00 5.00
1094 Tireless Tracker R 2.00 5.00
1095 Contagion Engine R 6.00 15.00
1096 Sword of Truth and Justice M 20.00 50.00

2022 Magic The Gathering Secret Lair Drop Series Artist Series Sidharth Chaturvedi

465 Nomad Outpost R 2.50 6.00
466 Island R 1.50 4.00
467 Concordant Crossroads R 10.00 25.00
468 Ghost Quarter R 1.50 4.00
679 Ghost Quarter R 1.00 2.50

2022 Magic The Gathering Secret Lair Drop Series Artist Series Sidharth Chaturvedi Foil

465 Nomad Outpost R 2.50 6.00
466 Island R 1.50 4.00
467 Concordant Crossroads R 10.00 25.00
468 Ghost Quarter R 1.50 4.00
679 Ghost Quarter R 1.00 2.50

2022 Magic The Gathering Secret Lair Drop Series Artist Series Victor Adame Minguez

707 Knight Exemplar R 1.25 3.00
1044 Knight Exemplar R 2.50 6.00
1045 Knight of the White Orchid R 6.00 15.00
1046 Lord of the Undead R 10.00 25.00
1047 Compost R 1.50 4.00

2022 Magic The Gathering Secret Lair Drop Series Artist Series Victor Adame Minguez Foil

707 Knight Exemplar R 1.25 3.00
1044 Knight Exemplar R 2.50 6.00
1045 Knight of the White Orchid R 6.00 15.00
1046 Lord of the Undead R 10.00 25.00
1047 Compost R 1.50 4.00

2022 Magic The Gathering Secret Lair Drop Series Artist Series Volkan Baga

701 Elspeth, Knight-Errant M 3.00 8.00
1001 Elspeth, Knight-Errant M 4.00 10.00
1002 Patron Wizard R 2.50 6.00
1003 Berserk M 10.00 25.00
1004 Verduran Enchantress R 2.00 5.00

2022 Magic The Gathering Secret Lair Drop Series Artist Series Volkan Baga Foil

701 Elspeth, Knight-Errant M 3.00 8.00
1001 Elspeth, Knight-Errant M 4.00 10.00
1002 Patron Wizard R 2.50 6.00
1003 Berserk M 10.00 25.00
1004 Verduran Enchantress R 2.00 5.00

2022 Magic The Gathering Secret Lair Drop Series Artist Series Wayne Reynolds

461 Sram, Senior Edificer R 4.00 10.00
462 Balthor the Defiled R 8.00 20.00
463 Torbran, Thane of Red Fell R 3.00 8.00
464 Depala, Pilot Exemplar R .40 1.00
678 Torbran, Thane of Red Fell R 1.50 4.00

2022 Magic The Gathering Secret Lair Drop Series Artist Series Wayne Reynolds Foil

461 Sram, Senior Edificer R 4.00 10.00
462 Balthor the Defiled R 8.00 20.00
463 Torbran, Thane of Red Fell R 3.00 8.00
464 Depala, Pilot Exemplar R .40 1.00
678 Torbran, Thane of Red Fell R 1.50 4.00

2022 Magic The Gathering Secret Lair Drop Series Beadle and Grimms Here Be Dragons

709 Dragon's Hoard FOIL R 20.00 50.00
1012 Icingdeath, Frost Tyrant FOIL M 3.00 8.00
1013 Iymrith, Desert Doom FOIL M 4.00 10.00
1014 Ebondeath, Dracolich FOIL M 6.00 15.00
1015 Inferno of the Star Mounts FOIL M 4.00 10.00
1016 Old Gnawbone FOIL M 40.00 100.00
1017 Tiamat FOIL M 25.00 60.00
1018 Icingdeath, Frost Tongue FOIL T 4.00 10.00

2022 Magic The Gathering Secret Lair Drop Series Blood Bowl

706 Wastes R 3.00 8.00
1035 Touchdown! R/(Approach of the Second Sun R 3.00 8.00
1036 Re-Roll R/(Rewind R 2.50 6.00
1037 Both Down R/(Bone Splinters R .60 1.50
1038 Throw Team-Mate R/(Fling R 2.50 6.00
1039 Perfect Defense R/(Defense of the Heart R6.00 15.00
1040 The Ball R/(Fellwar Stone R 8.00 20.00

2022 Magic The Gathering Secret Lair Drop Series Blood Bowl Foil

706 Wastes R 3.00 8.00
1035 Touchdown! R/(Approach of the Second Sun R 3.00 8.00
1036 Re-Roll R/(Rewind R 2.50 6.00
1037 Both Down R/(Bone Splinters R .60 1.50
1038 Throw Team-Mate R/(Fling R 2.50 6.00
1039 Perfect Defense R/(Defense of the Heart R6.00 15.00
1040 The Ball R/(Fellwar Stone R 8.00 20.00

2022 Magic The Gathering Secret Lair Drop Series Dan Frazier Is Back Again The Allied Talismans

1052 Talisman of Progress R 6.00 15.00
1053 Talisman of Dominance R 10.00 25.00
1054 Talisman of Indulgence R 10.00 25.00
1055 Talisman of Impulse R 2.50 6.00
1056 Talisman of Unity R 2.00 5.00

2022 Magic The Gathering Secret Lair Drop Series Dan Frazier Is Back Again The Allied Talismans Foil

1052 Talisman of Progress R 6.00 15.00
1053 Talisman of Dominance R 10.00 25.00
1054 Talisman of Indulgence R 10.00 25.00
1055 Talisman of Impulse R 2.50 6.00
1056 Talisman of Unity R 2.00 5.00

2022 Magic The Gathering Secret Lair Drop Series Dan Frazier is Back Again The Enemy Talismans

708 Fellwar Stone R 2.50 6.00
1057 Talisman of Hierarchy R 5.00 12.00
1058 Talisman of Creativity R 8.00 20.00
1059 Talisman of Resilience R 4.00 10.00
1060 Talisman of Conviction R 2.50 6.00
1061 Talisman of Curiosity R 2.50 6.00

2022 Magic The Gathering Secret Lair Drop Series Dan Frazier is Back Again The Enemy Talismans Foil

708 Fellwar Stone R 2.50 6.00
1057 Talisman of Hierarchy R 5.00 12.00
1058 Talisman of Creativity R 8.00 20.00
1059 Talisman of Resilience R 4.00 10.00
1060 Talisman of Conviction R 2.50 6.00
1061 Talisman of Curiosity R 2.50 6.00

2022 Magic The Gathering Secret Lair Drop Series Extra Life 2022

718 Maro R .25 .60
719 Maro R .25 .60
1145 Lathliss, Dragon Queen R 2.50 6.00
1146 Lathliss, Dragon Queen R 3.00 8.00
1147 Birds of Paradise R 4.00 10.00
1148 Birds of Paradise R 6.00 15.00
1149 Sliver Legion M 25.00 60.00
1150 Sliver Legion M 20.00 50.00

2022 Magic The Gathering Secret Lair Drop Series Extra Life 2022 Foil

718 Maro R .25 .60
719 Maro R .25 .60
1145 Lathliss, Dragon Queen R 2.50 6.00
1146 Lathliss, Dragon Queen R 3.00 8.00
1147 Birds of Paradise R 4.00 10.00
1148 Birds of Paradise R 6.00 15.00
1149 Sliver Legion M 25.00 60.00
1150 Sliver Legion M 20.00 50.00

2022 Magic The Gathering Secret Lair Drop Series Finally! Left-Handed Magic Cards

698 Dakkon Blackblade R 1.00 2.50
9995 Garruk, Caller of Beasts M 2.00 5.00
9996 Rograkh, Son of Rohgahh R 10.00 25.00
9997 Geralf's Messenger R 6.00 15.00
9998 Empress Galina R 10.00 25.00
9999 Sisay, Weatherlight Captain R 3.00 8.00

2022 Magic The Gathering Secret Lair Drop Series Finally! Left-Handed Magic Cards Foil

698 Dakkon Blackblade R 1.00 2.50
9995 Garruk, Caller of Beasts M 2.00 5.00
9996 Rograkh, Son of Rohgahh R 10.00 25.00
9997 Geralf's Messenger R 6.00 15.00
9998 Empress Galina R 10.00 25.00
9999 Sisay, Weatherlight Captain R 3.00 8.00

2022 Magic The Gathering Secret Lair Drop Series Fortnight Landmarks and Locations

448 Plains R 4.00 10.00
449 Island R 5.00 12.00
450 Swamp R 3.00 8.00
451 Mountain R 4.00 10.00
452 Forest R 5.00 12.00
677 The Spire R/(Command Tower R 8.00 20.00

2022 Magic The Gathering Secret Lair Drop Series Fortnight Landmarks and Locations Foil

448 Plains R 4.00 10.00
449 Island R 5.00 12.00
450 Swamp R 3.00 8.00
451 Mountain R 4.00 10.00
452 Forest R 5.00 12.00
677 The Spire R/(Command Tower R 8.00 20.00

2022 Magic The Gathering Secret Lair Drop Series Fortnite

441 Shrinking Storm R/(Wrath of God R 3.00 8.00
442 Dance Battle R/(Dance of Many R 1.25 3.00
443 Supply Llama R/(Etherium Sculptor R 4.00 10.00
444 Crack the Vault M/(Grim Tutor M 10.00 25.00
445 Battle Royale R/(Triumph of the Hordes R10.00 25.00
446 Battle Bus R/(Smuggler's Copter R 12.00 30.00
447 The Cube M/(Planar Bridge M 3.00 8.00
676 Boogie Bomb R/(Pyrite Spellbomb R 2.50 6.00

2022 Magic The Gathering Secret Lair Drop Series Fortnite Foil

441 Shrinking Storm R/(Wrath of God R 3.00 8.00
442 Dance Battle R/(Dance of Many R 1.25 3.00
443 Supply Llama R/(Etherium Sculptor R 4.00 10.00
444 Crack the Vault M/(Grim Tutor M 10.00 25.00
445 Battle Royale R/(Triumph of the Hordes R10.00 25.00
446 Battle Bus R/(Smuggler's Copter R 12.00 30.00
447 The Cube M/(Planar Bridge M 3.00 8.00
676 Boogie Bomb R/(Pyrite Spellbomb R 2.50 6.00

2022 Magic The Gathering Secret Lair Drop Series If Looks Could Kill

1106 Azami, Lady of Scrolls R 6.00 15.00
1107 Liliana of the Dark Realms M 20.00 50.00
1108 Reflector Mage R 3.00 8.00
1109 Adaptive Automaton R 3.00 8.00

2022 Magic The Gathering Secret Lair Drop Series If Looks Could Kill Foil

1106 Azami, Lady of Scrolls R 6.00 15.00
1107 Liliana of the Dark Realms M 20.00 50.00
1108 Reflector Mage R 3.00 8.00
1109 Adaptive Automaton R 3.00 8.00

2022 Magic The Gathering Secret Lair Drop Series Imaginary Friends

1048 Matter Reshaper R 4.00 10.00
1049 Toothy, Imaginary Friend R 8.00 20.00
1050 Pir, Imaginative Rascal R 5.00 12.00
1051 The Gitrog Monster M 15.00 40.00

2022 Magic The Gathering Secret Lair Drop Series Imaginary Friends Foil

1048 Matter Reshaper R 4.00 10.00
1049 Toothy, Imaginary Friend R 8.00 20.00
1050 Pir, Imaginative Rascal R 5.00 12.00
1051 The Gitrog Monster M 15.00 40.00

2022 Magic The Gathering Secret Lair Drop Series In Memoriam Jaya Ballard

1062 Jaya Ballard M 1.50 4.00
1063 Jaya's Immolating Inferno R 3.00 8.00
1064 Pyretic Ritual R 20.00 50.00
1065 Repercussion R 4.00 10.00
1066 Pyromancer's Goggles M 5.00 12.00

2022 Magic The Gathering Secret Lair Drop Series In Memoriam Jaya Ballard Foil

1062 Jaya Ballard M 1.50 4.00
1063 Jaya's Immolating Inferno R 3.00 8.00
1064 Pyretic Ritual R 20.00 50.00
1065 Repercussion R 4.00 10.00
1066 Pyromancer's Goggles M 5.00 12.00

2022 Magic The Gathering Secret Lair Drop Series Introducing Kaito Shizuki

410 Brain Freeze R 10.00 25.00
411 Bribery R 4.00 10.00
412 Snap R 5.00 12.00
413 Unmask R 1.50 4.00
414 Shadow of Doubt R 2.00 5.00

2022 Magic The Gathering Secret Lair Drop Series Introducing Kaito Shizuki Foil

410 Brain Freeze R 10.00 25.00
411 Bribery R 4.00 10.00
412 Snap R 5.00 12.00
413 Unmask R 1.50 4.00
414 Shadow of Doubt R 2.00 5.00

2022 Magic The Gathering Secret Lair Drop Series Just Add Milk!

1122 Ulamog, the Ceaseless Hunger // Ulamog, the Ceaseless Hunger M 20.00 50.00
1123 Etali, Primal Storm // Etali, Primal Storm R5.00 12.00
1124 Ghalta, Primal Hunger // Ghalta, Primal Hunger R 5.00 12.00

2022 Magic The Gathering Secret Lair Drop Series Just Add Milk! Foil

1122 Ulamog, the Ceaseless Hunger // Ulamog, the Ceaseless Hunger M 20.00 50.00
1123 Etali, Primal Storm // Etali, Primal Storm R5.00 12.00
1124 Ghalta, Primal Hunger // Ghalta, Primal Hunger R 5.00 12.00

2022 Magic The Gathering Secret Lair Drop Series Just Some Totally Normal Guys

1075 Void Winnower M 25.00 60.00
1076 Goblin Settler R 1.00 2.50
1077 Collector Ouphe R 5.00 12.00
1078 Vengevine M 5.00 12.00

2022 Magic The Gathering Secret Lair Drop Series Just Some Totally Normal Guys Foil

1075 Void Winnower M 25.00 60.00
1076 Goblin Settler R 1.00 2.50
1077 Collector Ouphe R 5.00 12.00
1078 Vengevine M 5.00 12.00

2022 Magic The Gathering Secret Lair Drop Series Kamigawa The Manga The Cards

1020 Idyllic Tutor R 5.00 12.00
1021 Swords to Plowshares R 8.00 20.00
1022 Solve the Equation R 2.50 6.00
1023 Praetor's Grasp R 10.00 25.00
1024 Veil of Summer R 8.00 20.00

2022 Magic The Gathering Secret Lair Drop Series Kamigawa The Manga The Cards Foil

1020 Idyllic Tutor R 5.00 12.00
1021 Swords to Plowshares R 8.00 20.00
1022 Solve the Equation R 2.50 6.00
1023 Praetor's Grasp R 10.00 25.00
1024 Veil of Summer R 8.00 20.00

2022 Magic The Gathering Secret Lair Drop Series Lil Walkers

396 Tamiyo, the Moon Sage M 5.00 12.00
397 Ajani, Mentor of Heroes M 4.00 10.00
398 Angrath, the Flame-Chained M 1.50 4.00
399 Ashiok, Dream Render R 12.00 30.00
400 Sorin, Grim Nemesis M 4.00 10.00

2022 Magic The Gathering Secret Lair Drop Series Lil Walkers Foil

396 Tamiyo, the Moon Sage M 5.00 12.00
397 Ajani, Mentor of Heroes M 4.00 10.00
398 Angrath, the Flame-Chained M 1.50 4.00
399 Ashiok, Dream Render R 12.00 30.00
400 Sorin, Grim Nemesis M 4.00 10.00

2022 Magic The Gathering Secret Lair Drop Series Liler Walkers

1140 Elspeth, Sun's Champion M 10.00 25.00
1141 Narset, Parter of Veils R 15.00 40.00
1142 Garruk Wildspeaker R 4.00 10.00
1143 Saheeli, Sublime Artificer R 4.00 10.00
1144 Sarkhan Vol M 2.00 5.00

2022 Magic The Gathering Secret Lair Drop Series Liler Walkers Foil

1140 Elspeth, Sun's Champion M 10.00 25.00
1141 Narset, Parter of Veils R 15.00 40.00
1142 Garruk Wildspeaker R 4.00 10.00
1143 Saheeli, Sublime Artificer R 4.00 10.00
1144 Sarkhan Vol M 2.00 5.00

2022 Magic The Gathering Secret Lair Drop Series Look at the Kitties

1182 Felidar Sovereign FOIL R 25.00 60.00
1183 Descendants' Path FOIL R 20.00 50.00
1184 Lord Windgrace FOIL M 40.00 100.00
1185 Violent Outburst FOIL R 10.00 25.00

2022 Magic The Gathering Secret Lair Drop Series Pictures of the Floating World

436 Windbrisk Heights R 3.00 8.00
437 Shelldock Isle R 1.25 3.00
438 Howltooth Hollow R .50 1.25
439 Spinerock Knoll R 2.50 6.00
440 Mosswort Bridge R 8.00 20.00

2022 Magic The Gathering Secret Lair Drop Series Pictures of the Floating World Foil

436 Windbrisk Heights R 3.00 8.00
437 Shelldock Isle R 1.25 3.00
438 Howltooth Hollow R .50 1.25
439 Spinerock Knoll R 2.50 6.00
440 Mosswort Bridge R 8.00 20.00

2022 Magic The Gathering Secret Lair Drop Series Post Malone Backstage Pass

726 Post the Enchanter R/(Zur the Enchanter R12.00 30.00
1186 Post, Son of Rich R/(K'rrik, Son of Yawgmoth R 15.00 40.00
1187 Post's Citadel R/(Bolas's Citadel R 10.00 25.00
1188 Post's Sigil R/(Leshrac's Sigil R 1.00 2.50
1189 Jet Medallion R 10.00 25.00

2022 Magic The Gathering Secret Lair Drop Series Post Malone Backstage Pass Foil

726 Post the Enchanter R/(Zur the Enchanter R12.00 30.00
1186 Post, Son of Rich R/(K'rrik, Son of Yawgmoth R 15.00 40.00
1187 Post's Citadel R/(Bolas's Citadel R 10.00 25.00
1188 Post's Sigil R/(Leshrac's Sigil R 1.00 2.50
1189 Jet Medallion R 10.00 25.00

2022 Magic The Gathering Secret Lair Drop Series Post Malone The Lands

727 Fabled Passage R 8.00 20.00
1190 Plains R 4.00 10.00
1191 Island R 5.00 12.00
1192 Swamp R 8.00 20.00
1193 Mountain R 4.00 10.00
1194 Forest R 4.00 10.00

2022 Magic The Gathering Secret Lair Drop Series Post Malone The Lands Foil

727 Fabled Passage R 8.00 20.00
1190 Plains R 4.00 10.00
1191 Island R 5.00 12.00
1192 Swamp R 8.00 20.00
1193 Mountain R 4.00 10.00
1194 Forest R 4.00 10.00

2022 Magic The Gathering Secret Lair Drop Series Pride Across the Multiverse

1005 Triumphant Reckoning M .60 1.50
1006 Savor the Moment R 2.00 5.00
1007 Alesha, Who Smiles at Death R .50 1.25
1008 Bearscape R 5.00 12.00
1009 Collective Voyage R 4.00 10.00
1010 Heartbeat of Spring R 2.00 5.00
1011 Sol Ring R 10.00 25.00
1012 Mana Confluence R 30.00 80.00

2022 Magic The Gathering Secret Lair Drop Series Pride Across the Multiverse Foil

1005 Triumphant Reckoning M .60 1.50
1006 Savor the Moment R 2.00 5.00
1007 Alesha, Who Smiles at Death R .50 1.25
1008 Bearscape R 5.00 12.00
1009 Collective Voyage R 4.00 10.00
1010 Heartbeat of Spring R 2.00 5.00
1011 Sol Ring R 10.00 25.00
1012 Mana Confluence R 30.00 80.00

2022 Magic The Gathering Secret Lair Drop Series Promos

721 Diabolic Tutor R/(Brain Dead Studios Collab Promo) 25.00 60.00
900 The Scarab God M/(Secretversary 2022 Shop Exclusive) 10.00 25.00

2022 Magic The Gathering Secret Lair Drop Series Rule the Room

497 Brimaz, King of Oreskos M 12.00 30.00
498 Arcanis the Omnipotent R 2.00 5.00
499 Queen Marchesa M 2.50 6.00
500 Savra, Queen of the Golgari R 2.00 5.00

2022 Magic The Gathering Secret Lair Drop Series Rule the Room Foil

497 Brimaz, King of Oreskos M 12.00 30.00
498 Arcanis the Omnipotent R 2.00 5.00
499 Queen Marchesa M 2.50 6.00
500 Savra, Queen of the Golgari R 2.00 5.00

2022 Magic The Gathering Secret Lair Drop Series Shades Not Included

415 Plains R 4.00 10.00
416 Island R 5.00 12.00
417 Swamp R 6.00 15.00
418 Mountain R 5.00 12.00
419 Forest R 4.00 10.00

2022 Magic The Gathering Secret Lair Drop Series Shades Not Included Foil

415 Plains R 4.00 10.00
416 Island R 5.00 12.00
417 Swamp R 6.00 15.00
418 Mountain R 5.00 12.00
419 Forest R 4.00 10.00

2022 Magic The Gathering Secret Lair Drop Series Showcase Dominaria United

1067 Arcades Sabboth TEXTURED FOIL R 1.25 3.00
1068 Chromium TEXTURED FOIL R 2.00 5.00
1069 Nicol Bolas TEXTURED FOIL R 10.00 25.00
1070 Vaevictis Asmadi TEXTURED FOIL R 3.00 8.00
1071 Palladia-Mors TEXTURED FOIL R 2.00 5.00

2022 Magic The Gathering Secret Lair Drop Series Showcase Neon Destiny

424 Ghostly Prison NEON INK FOIL R 8.00 20.00
425 Freed from the Real NEON INK FOIL R 5.00 12.00
426 Boseiju, Who Shelters All NEON INK FOIL R8.00 20.00
427 Hall of the Bandit Lord NEON INK FOIL R10.00 25.00

2022 Magic The Gathering Secret Lair Drop Series Showcase Streets of New Capenna Gilded Foil Edition

453 Atraxa, Praetors' Voice M 20.00 50.00
454 Breya, Etherium Shaper M 6.00 15.00
455 Yidris, Maelstrom Wielder M 2.50 6.00

2022 Magic The Gathering Secret Lair Drop Series Special Guest Junji Ito Foil

1114 Carrion Feeder R 12.00 30.00
1115 Doomsday R 8.00 20.00
1116 Plaguecrafter R 6.00 15.00
1117 Thoughtseize R 20.00 50.00

2022 Magic The Gathering Secret Lair Drop Series Special Guest Kelogsloops

406 Mystic Remora R 20.00 50.00
407 Retreat to Coralhelm R 3.00 8.00
408 Burgeoning R 20.00 50.00
409 Utopia Sprawl R 4.00 10.00

2022 Magic The Gathering Secret Lair Drop Series Special Guest Kelogsloops Foil

406 Mystic Remora R 20.00 50.00
407 Retreat to Coralhelm R 3.00 8.00
408 Burgeoning R 20.00 50.00
409 Utopia Sprawl R 4.00 10.00

2022 Magic The Gathering Secret Lair Drop Series Special Guest Kozyndan Another Story

1125 Serra Ascendant R 12.00 30.00
1126 Rapid Hybridization R 8.00 20.00
1127 Demonic Consultation R 20.00 50.00
1128 Winds of Change R 10.00 25.00
1129 Llanowar Elves R 6.00 15.00

2022 Magic The Gathering Secret Lair Drop Series Special Guest Kozyndan Another Story Foil

1125 Serra Ascendant R 12.00 30.00
1126 Rapid Hybridization R 8.00 20.00
1127 Demonic Consultation R 20.00 50.00
1128 Winds of Change R 10.00 25.00
1129 Llanowar Elves R 6.00 15.00

2022 Magic The Gathering Secret Lair Drop Series Special Guest Kozyndan The Lands

1130 Plains R 15.00 40.00
1131 Island R 12.00 30.00
1132 Swamp R 8.00 20.00
1133 Mountain R 6.00 15.00
1134 Forest R 10.00 25.00

2022 Magic The Gathering Secret Lair Drop Series Special Guest Kozyndan The Lands Foil

1130 Plains R 15.00 40.00
1131 Island R 12.00 30.00
1132 Swamp R 8.00 20.00
1133 Mountain R 6.00 15.00
1134 Forest R 10.00 25.00

2022 Magic The Gathering Secret Lair Drop Series Special Guest Matt Jukes

456 Glacial Fortress R 5.00 12.00
457 Drowned Catacomb R 8.00 20.00
458 Dragonskull Summit R 6.00 15.00
459 Rootbound Crag R 5.00 12.00
460 Sunpetal Grove R 5.00 12.00

2022 Magic The Gathering Secret Lair Drop Series Special Guest Matt Jukes Foil

456 Glacial Fortress R 5.00 12.00
457 Drowned Catacomb R 8.00 20.00
458 Dragonskull Summit R 6.00 15.00
459 Rootbound Crag R 5.00 12.00
460 Sunpetal Grove R 5.00 12.00

2022 Magic The Gathering Secret Lair Drop Series Special Guest Yoji Shinkawa

1110 Phyrexian Metamorph R 20.00 50.00
1111 Tezzeret the Seeker M 20.00 50.00
1112 Skullclamp R 25.00 60.00
1113 Solemn Simulacrum R 8.00 20.00

2022 Magic The Gathering Secret Lair Drop Series Special Guest Yoji Shinkawa Foil

1110 Phyrexian Metamorph R 20.00 50.00
1111 Tezzeret the Seeker M 20.00 50.00
1112 Skullclamp R 25.00 60.00
1113 Solemn Simulacrum R 8.00 20.00

2022 Magic The Gathering Secret Lair Drop Series Special Guest Yuko Shimizu

420 Hokori, Dust Drinker R 1.25 3.00
421 Kira, Great Glass-Spinner R 4.00 10.00
422 Eidolon of the Great Revel R 3.00 8.00
423 Elvish Spirit Guide R 5.00 12.00

2022 Magic The Gathering Secret Lair Drop Series Special Guest Yuko Shimizu Foil

420 Hokori, Dust Drinker R 1.25 3.00
421 Kira, Great Glass-Spinner R 4.00 10.00
422 Eidolon of the Great Revel R 3.00 8.00
423 Elvish Spirit Guide R 5.00 12.00

2022 Magic The Gathering Secret Lair Drop Series Street Fighter

428 E. Honda, Sumo Champion R 2.00 5.00
429 Ryu, World Warrior R 2.50 6.00
430 Ken, Burning Brawler R 1.50 4.00
431 Blanka, Ferocious Friend R 3.00 8.00
432 Chun-Li, Countless Kicks R 10.00 25.00
433 Dhalsim, Pliable Pacifist R 1.50 4.00
434 Guile, Sonic Soldier R 1.25 3.00
435 Zangief, the Red Cyclone R 2.50 6.00
675 Hadoken R/(Lightning Bolt R 5.00 12.00

2022 Magic The Gathering Secret Lair Drop Series Street Fighter Foil

428 E. Honda, Sumo Champion R 2.00 5.00
429 Ryu, World Warrior R 2.50 6.00
430 Ken, Burning Brawler R 1.50 4.00
431 Blanka, Ferocious Friend R 3.00 8.00
432 Chun-Li, Countless Kicks R 10.00 25.00
433 Dhalsim, Pliable Pacifist R 1.50 4.00
434 Guile, Sonic Soldier R 1.25 3.00
435 Zangief, the Red Cyclone R 2.50 6.00
675 Hadoken R/(Lightning Bolt R 5.00 12.00

2022 Magic The Gathering Secret Lair Drop Series The Art of Frank Franzetta

724 Lightning Strike R 5.00 12.00
1168 Field Marshal R 5.00 12.00
1169 Temporal Manipulation M 12.00 30.00
1170 Dark Ritual R 40.00 100.00
1171 Midnight Reaper R 8.00 20.00
1172 Seize the Day R 10.00 25.00

2022 Magic The Gathering Secret Lair Drop Series The Art of Frank Franzetta Foil

724 Lightning Strike R 5.00 12.00
1168 Field Marshal R 5.00 12.00
1169 Temporal Manipulation M 12.00 30.00
1170 Dark Ritual R 40.00 100.00
1171 Midnight Reaper R 8.00 20.00
1172 Seize the Day R 10.00 25.00

2022 Magic The Gathering Secret Lair Drop Series The Astrology Lands

384 Swamp R 3.00 8.00
385 Island R 2.00 5.00
386 Island R 3.00 8.00
387 Mountain R 4.00 10.00
388 Forest R 2.00 5.00
389 Mountain R 3.00 8.00
390 Plains R 3.00 8.00
391 Plains R 2.50 6.00
392 Island R 3.00 8.00
393 Plains R 5.00 12.00
394 Swamp R 10.00 25.00
395 Forest R 25.00 60.00

2022 Magic The Gathering Secret Lair Drop Series The Astrology Lands Foil

384 Swamp R 3.00 8.00
385 Island R 2.00 5.00
386 Island R 3.00 8.00
387 Mountain R 4.00 10.00
388 Forest R 2.00 5.00
389 Mountain R 3.00 8.00
390 Plains R 3.00 8.00
391 Plains R 2.50 6.00
392 Island R 3.00 8.00
393 Plains R 5.00 12.00
394 Swamp R 10.00 25.00
395 Forest R 25.00 60.00

2022 Magic The Gathering Secret Lair Drop Series The Meaning of Life, Maybe

1177 Forced Fruition R 4.00 10.00
1178 Future Sight R 2.00 5.00
1179 Mental Misstep R 40.00 100.00
1180 Mind's Dilation M 6.00 15.00
1181 Well of Lost Dreams R 2.50 6.00

2022 Magic The Gathering Secret Lair Drop Series The Meaning of Life, Maybe Foil

1177 Forced Fruition R 4.00 10.00
1178 Future Sight R 2.00 5.00
1179 Mental Misstep R 40.00 100.00
1180 Mind's Dilation M 6.00 15.00
1181 Well of Lost Dreams R 2.50 6.00

2022 Magic The Gathering Secret Lair Drop Series The Space Beyond the Stars

1102 Imprisoned in the Moon R 4.00 10.00
1103 Stasis R 8.00 20.00
1104 Prismatic Omen R 2.50 6.00
1105 Wheel of Sun and Moon R 2.00 5.00

2022 Magic The Gathering Secret Lair Drop Series The Space Beyond the Stars Foil

1102 Imprisoned in the Moon R 4.00 10.00
1103 Stasis R 8.00 20.00
1104 Prismatic Omen R 2.50 6.00
1105 Wheel of Sun and Moon R 2.00 5.00

2022 Magic The Gathering Secret Lair Drop Series The Tokyo Lands

46 Plains R 6.00 15.00
47 Island R 6.00 15.00
48 Swamp R 8.00 20.00
49 Mountain R 4.00 10.00
50 Forest R 8.00 20.00

2022 Magic The Gathering Secret Lair Drop Series The Tokyo Lands Foil

46 Plains R 6.00 15.00
47 Island R 6.00 15.00
48 Swamp R 8.00 20.00
49 Mountain R 4.00 10.00
50 Forest R 8.00 20.00

2022 Magic The Gathering Secret Lair Drop Series The Weirdest Pets in the Multiverse

1097 Laboratory Maniac R 8.00 20.00
1098 Stitcher's Supplier R 6.00 15.00
1099 Beast Whisperer R 8.00 20.00
1100 Vizier of the Menagerie M 3.00 8.00
1101 Wood Elves R 4.00 10.00

2022 Magic The Gathering Secret Lair Drop Series The Weirdest Pets in the Multiverse Foil

1097 Laboratory Maniac R 8.00 20.00
1098 Stitcher's Supplier R 6.00 15.00
1099 Beast Whisperer R 8.00 20.00
1100 Vizier of the Menagerie M 3.00 8.00
1101 Wood Elves R 4.00 10.00

2022 Magic The Gathering Secret Lair Drop Series Time Trouble Two

1041 Narset, Parter of Veils R 20.00 50.00
1042 Nissa, Who Shakes the World R 4.00 10.00
1043 Tezzeret, Agent of Bolas M 2.00 5.00

2022 Magic The Gathering Secret Lair Drop Series Time Trouble Two Foil

1041 Narset, Parter of Veils R 20.00 50.00
1042 Nissa, Who Shakes the World R 4.00 10.00
1043 Tezzeret, Agent of Bolas M 2.00 5.00

2022 Magic The Gathering Secret Lair Drop Series Totally Spaced Out

469 Ash Barrens FOIL R 4.00 10.00
470 Command Beacon FOIL R 15.00 40.00
471 Fabled Passage FOIL R 15.00 40.00
472 Strip Mine FOIL R 25.00 60.00

2022 Magic The Gathering Secret Lair Drop Series Transformers One Shall Stand One Shall Fall

1088 Plains R 6.00 15.00
1089 Island R 5.00 12.00
1090 Swamp R 5.00 12.00
1091 Mountain R 8.00 20.00
1092 Forest R 2.50 6.00

2022 Magic The Gathering Secret Lair Drop Series Transformers One Shall Stand One Shall Fall Foil

1088 Plains R 6.00 15.00
1089 Island R 5.00 12.00
1090 Swamp R 5.00 12.00
1091 Mountain R 8.00 20.00
1092 Forest R 2.50 6.00

2022 Magic The Gathering Secret Lair Drop Series Transformers Optimus Prime vs. Megatron

710 Cybertron R/(Command Tower R 1.25 3.00
1079 Megatron // Megatron M/(Blightsteel Colossus // Blightsteel Colossus M 25.00 60.00
1080 The AllSpark // The AllSpark R/(Doubling Cube // Doubling Cube R 10.00 25.00
1081 Optimus Prime // Optimus Prime M/(Darksteel Colossus // Darksteel Colossus M 5.00 12.00

2022 Magic The Gathering Secret Lair Drop Series Transformers Optimus Prime vs. Megatron Foil

710 Cybertron R/(Command Tower R 1.25 3.00
1079 Megatron // Megatron M/(Blightsteel Colossus // Blightsteel Colossus M 25.00 60.00
1080 The AllSpark // The AllSpark R/(Doubling Cube // Doubling Cube R 10.00 25.00
1081 Optimus Prime // Optimus Prime M/(Darksteel Colossus // Darksteel Colossus M 5.00 12.00

2022 Magic The Gathering Secret Lair Drop Series Transformers Roll Out or Rise Up

1082 True Conviction R 8.00 20.00
1083 Dramatic Reversal R 15.00 40.00
1084 Fabricate R 8.00 20.00
1085 Collective Brutality R 4.00 10.00
1086 By Force R 1.50 4.00
1087 Greater Good R 10.00 25.00

2022 Magic The Gathering Secret Lair Drop Series Transformers Roll Out or Rise Up Foil

1082 True Conviction R 8.00 20.00
1083 Dramatic Reversal R 15.00 40.00
1084 Fabricate R 8.00 20.00
1085 Collective Brutality R 4.00 10.00
1086 By Force R 1.50 4.00
1087 Greater Good R 10.00 25.00

2022 Magic The Gathering Secret Lair Drop Series Warhammer 40,000 Orks

704 Wastes R 4.00 10.00
1025 Ork Kommando R/(Merciless Executioner R2.00 5.00
1026 Aggravated Assault R 8.00 20.00
1027 Makari the Lucky Grot R/(Krenko, Tin Street Kingpin R 10.00 25.00
1028 Ghazghkull, Prophet of the Waaagh! M/(Zurgo Helmsmasher M 10.00 25.00
1029 Da Vulcha M/(Skysovereign, Consul Flagship M 4.00 10.00

2022 Magic The Gathering Secret Lair Drop Series Warhammer 40,000 Orks Foil

704 Wastes R 4.00 10.00
1025 Ork Kommando R/(Merciless Executioner R2.00 5.00
1026 Aggravated Assault R 8.00 20.00
1027 Makari the Lucky Grot R (Krenko, Tin Street Kingpin R 10.00 25.00
1028 Ghazghkull, Prophet of the Waaagh! M (Zurgo Helmsmasher M 10.00 25.00
1029 Da Vulcha M/(Skysovereign, Consul Flagship M 4.00 10.00

2022 Magic The Gathering Secret Lair Drop Series Warhammer Age of Sigmar

705 Wastes R 3.00 8.00
1030 Blind Obedience R 10.00 25.00
1031 Neave Blacktalon R/(Danitha Capashen, Paragon R 5.00 12.00
1032 Archaeon the Everchosen M (Najeela, the Blade-Blossom M 20.00 50.00
1033 Stardrake M/(Scourge of the Throne M 10.00 25.00
1034 Ghal Maraz, the Great Shatterer R/(Loxodon Warhammer R 4.00 10.00

2022 Magic The Gathering Secret Lair Drop Series Warhammer Age of Sigmar Foil

705 Wastes R 3.00 8.00
1030 Blind Obedience R 10.00 25.00
1031 Neave Blacktalon R/(Danitha Capashen, Paragon R 5.00 12.00
1032 Archaeon the Everchosen M (Najeela, the Blade-Blossom M 20.00 50.00
1033 Stardrake M/(Scourge of the Throne M 10.00 25.00
1034 Ghal Maraz, the Great Shatterer R (Loxodon Warhammer R 4.00 10.00

2022 Magic The Gathering Secret Lair Drop Series Welcome to the Fungal

1135 Abundant Growth R 6.00 15.00
1136 Mycoloth R 8.00 20.00
1137 Ghave, Guru of Spores M 12.00 30.00
1138 Slimefoot, the Stowaway R 4.00 10.00
1139 Saproling T 6.00 15.00

2022 Magic The Gathering Secret Lair Drop Series Welcome to the Fungal Foil

1135 Abundant Growth R 6.00 15.00
1136 Mycoloth R 8.00 20.00
1137 Ghave, Guru of Spores M 12.00 30.00
1138 Slimefoot, the Stowaway R 4.00 10.00
1139 Saproling T 6.00 15.00

2022 Magic The Gathering Secret Lair Drop Series Wizards of the Street

1164 Baral, Chief of Compliance R 4.00 10.00
1165 Spellseeker R 10.00 25.00
1166 Magus of the Wheel R 5.00 12.00
1167 Kess, Dissident Mage M 4.00 10.00

2022 Magic The Gathering Secret Lair Drop Series Wizards of the Street Foil

1164 Baral, Chief of Compliance R 4.00 10.00
1165 Spellseeker R 10.00 25.00
1166 Magus of the Wheel R 5.00 12.00
1167 Kess, Dissident Mage M 4.00 10.00

2022 Magic The Gathering Starter Commander Decks

1 Atarka, World Render M :R:/:G: 1.00 2.00
2 Emmara, Soul of the Accord M :G:/:W: .30 .75
3 Gisa and Geralf M :B:/:K: .75 1.50
4 Isperia, Supreme Judge M :W:/:B: .17 .35
5 Kardur, Doomscourge M :K:/:R: .40 .80
6 Ajani, Caller of the Pride M :W: 1.00 2.00
7 Archon of Redemption R :W: .07 .15
8 Aven Gagglemaster U :W: .05 .10
9 Banishing Light U :W: .07 .15
10 Cartographer's Hawk R :W: .12 .25
11 Citywide Bust R :W: .07 .15
12 Cleansing Nova R :W: .30 .60
13 Commander's Insignia R :W: .12 .25
14 Conclave Tribunal U :W: .07 .15
15 Condemn U :W: .07 .15
16 Crush Contraband U :W: .10 .20
17 Dawn of Hope R :W: .75 1.50
18 Devouring Light U :W: .05 .10
19 Dictate of Heliod R :W: .25 .50
20 Disenchant C :W: .05 .10
21 Emeria Angel R :W: .12 .25
22 Felidar Retreat R :W: .50 1.00
23 Generous Gift U :W: .75 1.50
24 Gideon Jura M :W: .20 .40
25 Hanged Executioner R :W: .07 .15
26 Hour of Reckoning R :W: .12 .25
27 Kangee's Lieutenant U :W: .05 .10
28 Mentor of the Meek R :W: .12 .25
29 Path to Exile U :W: 1.25 2.50
30 Rally of Wings U :W: .07 .15
31 Remorseful Cleric R :W: .12 .25
32 Rootborn Defenses C :W: .15 .30
33 Sephara, Sky's Blade R :W: 2.50 5.00
34 Soul Snare U :W: .05 .10
35 Steel-Plume Marshal R :W: .10 .20
36 Storm Herd R :W: .12 .25
37 Swords to Plowshares U :W: .75 1.50
38 True Conviction R :W: 2.50 5.00
39 Valor in Akros U :W: .07 .15
40 Vow of Duty U :W: .05 .10
41 White Sun's Zenith R :W: .10 .20
42 Aetherize U :B: .30 .60
43 Angler Turtle R :B: .07 .15
44 Bident of Thassa R :B: 1.25 2.50
45 Counterspell C :B: .75 1.50
46 Deep Analysis C :B: .07 .15
47 Diluvian Primordial R :B: .12 .25
48 Distant Melody C :B: .30 .60
49 Eternal Skylord U :B: .07 .15
50 Ever-Watching Threshold R :B: .17 .35
51 Faerie Formation R :B: .12 .25
52 Favorable Winds U :B: .15 .30
53 Geralf's Mindcrusher R :B: .10 .20
54 Gravitational Shift R :B: .60 1.25
55 Inspired Sphinx M :B: .15 .30
56 Laboratory Drudge R :B: .07 .15
57 Lazotep Plating U :B: .30 .75
58 Negate C :B: .07 .15
59 Sharding Sphinx R :B: .10 .20
60 Sinister Sabotage U :B: .05 .10
61 Sphinx of Enlightenment M :B: .25 .50
62 Tide Skimmer U :B: .05 .10
63 Warden of Evos Isle U :B: .05 .10
64 Windreader Sphinx R :B: .10 .20
65 Winged Words C :B: .07 .15
66 Ambition's Cost U :K: .07 .15
67 Archfiend of Depravity R :K: 2.00 4.00
68 Army of the Damned M :K: .30 .60
69 Bloodgift Demon R :K: 1.00 2.00
70 Cemetery Reaper R :K: .40 .80
71 Champion of the Perished R :K: .75 1.50
72 Crippling Fear R :K: .15 .30
73 Cruel Revival U :K: .05 .10
74 Curse of Disturbance U :K: .30 .60
75 Deadly Tempest R :K: .25 .50
76 Dredge the Mire R :K: .10 .20
77 Feed the Swarm C :K: .30 .60
78 Fleshbag Marauder C :K: .07 .15
79 Gravespawn Sovereign R :K: .10 .20
80 Gray Merchant of Asphodel U :K: .75 1.50
81 Indulgent Tormentor U :K: .20 .40
82 Josu Vess, Lich Knight R :K: .12 .25
83 Lazotep Reaver C :K: .07 .15
84 Liliana, Untouched by Death M :K: 1.25 2.50
85 Liliana's Devotee U :K: .05 .10
86 Liliana's Mastery R :K: .12 .25
87 Liliana's Standard Bearer R :K: .12 .25
88 Lord of the Accursed U :K: .12 .25
89 Lotleth Giant U :K: .05 .10
90 Loyal Subordinate U :K: .50 1.00
91 Midnight Reaper R :K: .25 .50
92 Mire Triton U :K: .07 .15
93 Murder C :K: .05 .10
94 Necromantic Selection R :K: .15 .30
95 Necrotic Hex R :K: .15 .30
96 Ob Nixilis Reignited M :K: .25 .50
97 Open the Graves R :K: .15 .30
98 Overseer of the Damned R :K: .15 .30
99 Profane Command R :K: .10 .20
100 Rakshasa Debaser R :K: .17 .35
101 Read the Bones C :K: .12 .25
102 Reign of the Pit R :K: .07 .15
103 Sangromancer R :K: .30 .60
104 Scourge of Nel Toth R :K: .15 .30
105 Scythe Specter R :K: .12 .25
106 Sepulchral Primordial R :K: .60 1.25
107 Sign in Blood C :K: .17 .35
108 Soul Shatter R :K: .75 1.50
109 Spark Reaper C :K: .05 .10
110 Syphon Flesh U :K: .07 .15
111 Syphon Mind C :K: .30 .75
112 Titan Hunter R :K: .07 .15
113 Unbreathing Horde R :K: .15 .30
114 Undead Augur U :K: .12 .25
115 Vampire Nighthawk U :K: .10 .20
116 Vampiric Rites U :K: .12 .25
117 Vengeful Dead C :K: .30 .75
118 Victimize U :K: .30 .60
119 Vizier of the Scorpion U :K: .12 .25
120 Withered Wretch U :K: .05 .10
121 Zombie Apocalypse R :K: .15 .30
122 Abrade U :R: .10 .20
123 Akoum Hellkite R :R: .12 .25
124 Blasphemous Act R :R: 1.50 3.00
125 Brash Taunter R :R: .75 1.50
126 Chain Reaction R :R: .12 .25
127 Chaos Warp R :R: .60 1.25
128 Combustible Gearhulk M :R: 1.00 2.00
129 Crucible of Fire R :R: .50 1.00
130 Demanding Dragon R :R: .12 .25
131 Dictate of the Twin Gods R :R: .75 1.50
132 Dragon Mage U :R: .12 .25
133 Dragon Tempest U :R: 2.50 5.00
134 Dragonkin Berserker R :R: .10 .20
135 Dragonlord's Servant U :R: .25 .50
136 Dragonmaster Outcast M :R: .30 .60
137 Dragonspeaker Shaman U :R: .75 1.50
138 Drakuseth, Maw of Flames R :R: .75 1.50
139 Dream Pillager R :R: .07 .15
140 Explosion of Riches U :R: .05 .10
141 Fiery Confluence R :R: .50 1.00
142 Flameblast Dragon R :R: .12 .25
143 Furnace Whelp U :R: .05 .10
144 Geode Rager R :R: .12 .25
145 Guttersnipe U :R: .15 .30
146 Hate Mirage U :R: .07 .15
147 Hoard-Smelter Dragon R :R: .07 .15
148 Kazuul, Tyrant of the Cliffs R :R: .12 .25
149 Magmaquake R :R: .10 .20
150 Magmatic Force R :R: .12 .25
151 Mana Geyser C :R: 1.25 2.50
152 Mordant Dragon R :R: .12 .25
153 Provoke the Trolls U :R: .05 .10
154 Rapacious Dragon C :R: .07 .15
155 Runehorn Hellkite R :R: .30 .75
156 Sarkhan, the Dragonspeaker M :R: .17 .35
157 Scourge of Valkas M :R: 1.00 2.00
158 Spit Flame R :R: .12 .25
159 Sunbird's Invocation R :R: .25 .50
160 Sweltering Suns R :R: .17 .35
161 Tectonic Giant R :R: .15 .30
162 Thermo-Alchemist C :R: .10 .20
163 Thunderbreak Regent R :R: .75 1.50
164 Thundermaw Hellkite M :R: 1.00 2.00
165 Tyrant's Familiar R :R: .30 .60
166 Unleash Fury U :R: .17 .35
167 Vandalblast U :R: 4.00 8.00
168 Verix Bladewing M :R: .20 .40
169 Wild Ricochet R :R: .12 .25
170 Wildfire Devils R :R: .12 .25
171 Avacyn's Pilgrim C :G: .20 .40
172 Beast Within U :G: 1.00 2.00
173 Blossoming Defense U :G: .17 .35
174 Champion of Lambholt R :G: .30 .75
175 Citanul Hierophants R :G: .40 .80
176 Collective Unconscious R :G: .20 .40
177 Cultivate U :G: .40 .80
178 Curse of Bounty U :G: .25 .50
179 Drumhunter U :G: .10 .20
180 Elemental Bond U :G: 3.00 6.00
181 Eternal Witness U :G: 1.25 2.50
182 Farhaven Elf C :G: .10 .20
183 Foe-Razer Regent R :G: .12 .25
184 Frontier Siege R :G: .30 .75
185 Garruk's Uprising U :G: 2.00 4.00
186 Great Oak Guardian U :G: .07 .15
187 Harmonize U :G: .17 .35
188 Harvest Season R :G: .75 1.50
189 Hornet Nest R :G: .50 1.00
190 Hornet Queen R :G: .15 .30
191 Hunter's Insight U :G: .15 .30
192 Hunter's Prowess R :G: .12 .25
193 Jade Mage U :G: .10 .20
194 Jaspera Sentinel C :G: .07 .15
195 Karametra's Favor U :G: .07 .15
196 Leafkin Druid C :G: .07 .15
197 Loaming Shaman U :G: .07 .15
198 Loyal Guardian U :G: .25 .50
199 Nissa's Expedition U :G: .07 .15
200 Nullmage Shepherd U :G: .10 .20
201 Overrun U :G: .17 .35
202 Overwhelming Instinct U :G: .10 .20
203 Presence of Gond C :G: .07 .15
204 Primal Might R :G: .12 .25
205 Reclamation Sage U :G: .15 .30
206 Return to Nature C :G: .07 .15
207 Rishkar, Peema Renegade R :G: .12 .25
208 Sakura-Tribe Elder C :G: .75 1.50
209 Scatter the Seeds C :G: .10 .20
210 Scavenging Ooze R :G: .12 .25
211 Shamanic Revelation R :G: .30 .60
212 Sporemound C :G: .12 .25
213 Thunderfoot Baloth R :G: .25 .50
214 Verdant Force R :G: .15 .30
215 Voice of Many U :G: .07 .15
216 Absorb R :W:/:B: .15 .30
217 Aura Mutation R :G:/:W: .17 .35
218 Breath of Malfegor C :K:/:R: .10 .20
219 Camaraderie R :G:/:W: .15 .30
220 Clan Defiance R :R:/:G: .10 .20
221 Cloudblazer U :W:/:B: .07 .15
222 Collective Blessing R :G:/:W: .25 .50
223 Dauntless Escort R :G:/:W: .12 .25
224 Diregraf Captain U :B:/:K: .10 .20
225 Draconic Disciple U :R:/:G: .07 .15
226 Empyrean Eagle U :W:/:B: .12 .25
227 Enter the God-Eternals R :B:/:K: .12 .25
228 Fires of Yavimaya U :R:/:G: .40 .80
229 Gleaming Overseer U :B:/:K: .10 .20
230 Harbinger of the Hunt R :R:/:G: .12 .25
231 Havengul Lich M :B:/:K: 1.00 2.00
232 Jubilant Skybonder U :W:/:B: .07 .15
233 Kaervek the Merciless R :K:/:R: .12 .25
234 Kangee, Sky Warden U :W:/:B: .05 .10
235 Maja, Bretagard Protector U :G:/:W: .15 .30
236 March of the Multitudes M :G:/:W: .30 .75
237 Migratory Route U :W:/:B: .07 .15
238 Pilfered Plans C :B:/:K: .05 .10
239 Rakdos Charm U :K:/:R: .25 .50
240 Savage Ventmaw U :R:/:G: .30 .75
241 Selesnya Evangel C :G:/:W: .07 .15
242 Selesnya Guildmage U :G:/:W: .05 .10
243 Skycat Sovereign R :W:/:B: .12 .25
244 Sphinx's Revelation M :W:/:B: .30 .60
245 Spiteful Visions R :K:/:R: .60 1.25
246 Staggering Insight U :W:/:B: .10 .20
247 Stormfist Crusader R :K:/:R: .30 .60
248 Sylvan Reclamation U :G:/:W: .07 .15
249 Terminate U :K:/:R: .25 .50
250 Theater of Horrors R :K:/:R: .12 .25
251 Thunderclap Wyvern U :W:/:B: .07 .15
252 Time Wipe R :W:/:B: .12 .25
253 Trostani Discordant M :G:/:W: .25 .50
254 Undermine R :B:/:K: .12 .25
255 Unlicensed Disintegration U :K:/:R: .05 .10
256 Vela the Night-Clad M :B:/:K: .30 .60
257 Arcane Signet C .30 .75
258 Atarka Monument U .07 .15
259 Azorius Signet U .25 .50
260 Burnished Hart U .07 .15
261 Commander's Sphere C .07 .15
262 Coveted Jewel R .40 .80
263 Dimir Signet U .50 1.00
264 Dragon's Hoard R .40 .80
265 Grimoire of the Dead M .25 .50
266 Hedron Archive U .10 .20
267 Heraldic Banner U .75 1.50
268 Idol of Oblivion R .40 .80
269 Lightning Greaves U 7.50 15.00
270 Nihil Spellbomb C .30 .60
271 Pilgrim's Eye C .05 .10
272 Rakdos Signet U .75 1.50
273 Sky Diamond C .07 .15
274 Skyscanner C .05 .10
275 Slate of Ancestry R .75 1.50
276 Sol Ring U 1.00 2.00
277 Solemn Simulacrum R .40 .80
278 Steel Hellkite R .12 .25
279 Swiftfoot Boots U .75 1.50
280 Talisman of Dominance U 1.25 2.50
281 Talisman of Impulse U 2.00 4.00
282 Talisman of Indulgence U 2.50 5.00
283 Talisman of Progress U 4.00 8.00
284 Talisman of Unity U .75 1.50
285 Thought Vessel U 2.50 5.00
286 Unstable Obelisk U .07 .15
287 Wayfarer's Bauble C .20 .40
288 Worn Powerstone U .50 1.00
289 Akoum Refuge U .10 .20
290 Bloodfell Caves C .07 .15
291 Blossoming Sands C .07 .15
292 Canopy Vista R .30 .60
293 Choked Estuary R .12 .25
294 Cinder Barrens U .07 .15
295 Cinder Glade R .15 .30
296 Coastal Tower U .07 .15
297 Command Tower C .10 .20
298 Dismal Backwater C .07 .15
299 Elfhame Palace U .07 .15
300 Foreboding Ruins R .12 .25
301 Fortified Village R .10 .20
302 Game Trail R .12 .25
303 Graypelt Refuge U .10 .20
304 Haven of the Spirit Dragon R 1.00 2.00
305 Holdout Settlement C .10 .20
306 Jwar Isle Refuge U .12 .25
307 Kazandu Refuge U .07 .15
308 Meandering River U .05 .10
309 Molten Slagheap U .05 .10
310 Moorland Haunt R .10 .20
311 Myriad Landscape U .12 .25
312 Path of Ancestry C .10 .20
313 Port Town R .12 .25
314 Prairie Stream R .12 .25
315 Rugged Highlands C .05 .10
316 Salt Marsh U .07 .15
317 Sejiri Refuge U .07 .15
318 Shivan Oasis U .07 .15
319 Smoldering Marsh R .17 .35
320 Stensia Bloodhall R .07 .15
321 Submerged Boneyard U .07 .15
322 Sunken Hollow R .17 .35
323 Temple of Abandon R .12 .25
324 Temple of Deceit R .12 .25
325 Temple of Enlightenment R .12 .25
326 Temple of Malice R .25 .50
327 Temple of Plenty R .15 .30
328 Timber Gorge U .05 .10
329 Tranquil Cove C .07 .15
330 Tranquil Expanse U .05 .10
331 Urborg Volcano U .07 .15
332 Vitu-Ghazi, the City-Tree U .07 .15
333 Plains C .07 .15
334 Plains C .10 .20
335 Plains C .07 .15
336 Plains C .07 .15
337 Island C .07 .15
338 Island C .10 .20
339 Island C .10 .20
340 Island C .12 .25
341 Swamp C .10 .20
342 Swamp C .07 .15
343 Swamp C .07 .15
344 Swamp C .07 .15
345 Mountain C .05 .10
346 Mountain C .10 .20
347 Mountain C .10 .20
348 Mountain C .12 .25
349 Forest C .07 .15
350 Forest C .12 .25
351 Forest C .10 .20
352 Forest C .12 .25

2022 Magic The Gathering Starter Commander Decks Tokens

1 Eldrazi .12 .25
2 Bird .07 .15
3 Cat .15 .30
4 Cat Beast .25 .50
5 Cat Bird .25 .50
6 Human Warrior .12 .25
7 Pegasus .10 .20
8 Soldier .07 .15
9 Spirit .07 .15
10 Faerie .10 .20
11 Thopter .07 .15
12 Demon .10 .20
13 Zombie .07 .15
14 Zombie Army .07 .15
15 Zombie Knight .07 .15
16 Dragon .10 .20
17 Karox Bladewing .15 .30
18 Ogre .07 .15
19 Beast .15 .30
20 Elephant .12 .25
21 Elf Warrior .12 .25
22 Insect .12 .25
23 Saproling .10 .20
24 Thopter .07 .15
25 Treasure .07 .15
26 Ob Nixilis Reignited Emblem .15 .30
27 Sarkhan, the Dragonspeaker Emblem .12 .25

2022 Magic The Gathering Store Championships

1 Flame Slash R :R: .20 .40
2 Archmage's Charm R :B: 4.00 8.00
3 Dark Confidant R :K: 75.00 150.00
4 Spell Pierce R :B: .75 1.50
5 Gilded Goose R :G: 2.00 4.00
6 Omnath, Locus of Creation M :R:/:G:/:W:/:B:100.00 200.00
7 Annex Sentry R :W: .20 .40

8 Memory Deluge R :B:	1.50	3.00
9 Koth, Fire of Resistance R :R:	7.50	15.00
10 Strangle R :R:	.30	.60
11 Aether Channeler R :B:	.60	1.25
12 Thalia and the Gitrog Monster M :W:/:K:/:G:	75.00	150.00

2022 Magic The Gathering Streets of New Capenna

1 Angelic Observer U :W:	.12	.25
2 Backup Agent C :W:	.07	.15
3 Ballroom Brawlers U :W:	.12	.25
4 Boon of Safety C :W:	.07	.15
5 Brokers Initiate C :W:	.07	.15
6 Buy Your Silence C :W:	.07	.15
7 Celebrity Fencer C :W:	.07	.15
8 Citizen's Crowbar U :W:	.12	.25
9 Dapper Shieldmate C :W:	.07	.15
10 Depopulate R :W:	.20	.40
11 Elspeth Resplendent M :W:	2.50	5.00
12 Extraction Specialist R :W:	.75	1.50
13 Gathering Throng C :W:	.07	.15
14 Giada, Font of Hope R :W:	1.50	3.00
15 Halo Fountain M :W:	3.00	6.00
16 Hold for Ransom C :W:	.07	.15
17 Illuminator Virtuoso U :W:	.20	.40
18 Inspiring Overseer C :W:	.12	.25
19 Kill Shot C :W:	.07	.15
20 Knockout Blow U :W:	.12	.25
21 Mage's Attendant U :W:	.12	.25
22 Mysterious Limousine R :W:	.20	.40
23 Patch Up U :W:	.12	.25
24 Rabble Rousing R :W:	.75	1.50
25 Raffine's Guidance C :W:	.07	.15
26 Raffine's Informant C :W:	.07	.15
27 Refuse to Yield U :W:	.12	.25
28 Revelation of Power C :W:	.07	.15
29 Rumor Gatherer U :W:	.15	.30
30 Sanctuary Warden M :W:	1.00	2.00
31 Sky Crier C :W:	.07	.15
32 Speakeasy Server C :W:	.07	.15
33 Swooping Protector U :W:	.12	.25
34 All-Seeing Arbiter M :B:	.25	.50
35 Backstreet Bruiser C :B:	.07	.15
36 Brokers Veteran C :B:	.07	.15
37 Case the Joint C :B:	.07	.15
38 Cut Your Losses R :B:	.30	.60
39 Disdainful Stroke C :B:	.07	.15
40 Echo Inspector C :B:	.07	.15
41 Errant, Street Artist R :B:	.20	.40
42 Even the Score M :B:	.30	.75
43 Expendable Lackey C :B:	.07	.15
44 Faerie Vandal U :B:	.12	.25
45 Hypnotic Grifter U :B:	.12	.25
46 Ledger Shredder R :B:	15.00	30.00
47 A Little Chat U :B:	.12	.25
48 Majestic Metamorphosis C :B:	.07	.15
49 Make Disappear C :B:	.07	.15
50 Obscura Initiate C :B:	.07	.15
51 An Offer You Can't Refuse U :B:	1.25	2.50
52 Out of the Way U :B:	.12	.25
53 Psionic Snoop C :B:	.07	.15
54 Psychic Pickpocket U :B:	.12	.25
55 Public Enemy U :B:	.12	.25
56 Reservoir Kraken R :B:	.20	.40
57 Rooftop Nuisance C :B:	.07	.15
58 Run Out of Town C :B:	.07	.15
59 Security Bypass C :B:	.07	.15
60 Sewer Crocodile C :B:	.07	.15
61 Sleep with the Fishes U :B:	.12	.25
62 Slip Out the Back U :B:	1.25	2.50
63 Undercover Operative R :B:	.25	.50
64 Wingshield Agent U :B:	.12	.25
65 Wiretapping R :B:	.20	.40
66 Witness Protection C :B:	.20	.40
67 Angel of Suffering M :K:	1.00	2.00
68 Body Launderer M :K:	1.25	2.50
69 Cemetery Tampering R :K:	.20	.40
70 Corrupt Court Official C :K:	.07	.15
71 Crooked Custodian C :K:	.07	.15
72 Cut of the Profits R :K:	.20	.40
73 Cutthroat Contender C :K:	.07	.15
74 Deal Gone Bad C :K:	.07	.15
75 Demon's Due C :K:	.07	.15
76 Dig Up the Body C :K:	.07	.15
77 Dusk Mangler U :K:	.12	.25
78 Extract the Truth C :K:	.07	.15
79 Fake Your Own Death C :K:	.07	.15
80 Girder Goons C :K:	.07	.15
81 Graveyard Shift U :K:	.12	.25
82 Grisly Sigil U :K:	.12	.25
83 Illicit Shipment U :K:	.12	.25
84 Incriminate C :K:	.07	.15
85 Join the Maestros C :K:	.07	.15
86 Maestros Initiate C :K:	.07	.15
87 Midnight Assassin C :K:	.07	.15
88 Murder C :K:	.07	.15
89 Night Clubber U :K:	.12	.25
90 Raffine's Silencer U :K:	.12	.25
91 Revel Ruiner C :K:	.07	.15
92 Rogues' Gallery U :K:	.12	.25
93 Sanguine Spy R :K:	.20	.40
94 Shadow of Mortality R :K:	.20	.40
95 Shakedown Heavy R :K:	.30	.60
96 Tavern Swindler U :K:	.12	.25
97 Tenacious Underdog R :K:	.75	1.50
98 Vampire Scrivener U :K:	.12	.25
99 Whack U :K:	.12	.25
100 Antagonize C :R:	.07	.15
101 Arcane Bombardment M :R:	3.00	6.00
102 Big Score C :R:	.30	.75
103 Call In a Professional U :R:	.12	.25
104 Daring Escape C :R:	.07	.15
105 Devilish Valet R :R:	.50	1.00
106 Exhibition Magician C :R:	.07	.15
107 Glittering Stockpile U :R:	.12	.25
108 Goldhound C :R:	.07	.15
109 Hoard Hauler R :R:	.20	.40
110 Involuntary Employment U :R:	.12	.25
111 Jackhammer C :R:	.07	.15
112 Jaxis, the Troublemaker R :R:	.30	.75
113 Light 'Em Up C :R:	.07	.15
114 Mayhem Patrol C :R:	.07	.15
115 Plasma Jockey C :R:	.07	.15
116 Professional Face-Breaker R :R:	3.00	6.00
117 Pugnacious Pugilist U :R:	.12	.25
118 Pyre-Sledge Arsonist U :R:	.12	.25
119 Ready to Rumble C :R:	.07	.15
120 Riveteers Initiate C :R:	.07	.15
121 Riveteers Requisitioner U :R:	.12	.25
122 Rob the Archives U :R:	.12	.25
123 Sizzling Soloist U :R:	.12	.25
124 Sticky Fingers C :R:	.15	.30
125 Strangle C :R:	.15	.30
126 Structural Assault R :R:	.20	.40
127 Torch Breath U :R:	.12	.25
128 Unlucky Witness U :R:	.12	.25
129 Urabrask, Heretic Praetor M :R:	3.00	6.00
130 Widespread Thieving R :R:	.20	.40
131 Witty Roastmaster C :R:	.12	.25
132 Wrecking Crew C :R:	.07	.15
133 Attended Socialite C :G:	.07	.15
134 Bootleggers' Stash M :G:	7.50	15.00
135 Bouncer's Beatdown U :G:	.12	.25
136 Broken Wings C :G:	.07	.15
137 Cabaretti Initiate C :G:	.07	.15
138 Caldaia Strongarm C :G:	.07	.15
139 Capenna Express C :G:	.07	.15
140 Civic Gardener C :G:	.07	.15
141 Cleanup Crew U :G:	.12	.25
142 Courier's Briefcase U :G:	.12	.25
143 Elegant Entourage U :G:	.12	.25
144 Evolving Door R :G:	.20	.40
145 Fight Rigging R :G:	1.00	2.00
146 For the Family C :G:	.07	.15
147 Freelance Muscle U :G:	.12	.25
148 Gala Greeters R :G:	.50	1.00
149 Glittermonger C :G:	.07	.15
150 High-Rise Sawjack C :G:	.07	.15
151 Jewel Thief C :G:	.07	.15
152 Luxurious Libation U :G:	.12	.25
153 Most Wanted C :G:	.07	.15
154 Prizefight C :G:	.07	.15
155 Rhox Pummeler C :G:	.07	.15
156 Riveteers Decoy U :G:	.12	.25
157 Social Climber C :G:	.07	.15
158 Take to the Streets U :G:	.12	.25
159 Titan of Industry M :G:	2.50	5.00
160 Topiary Stomper R :G:	1.00	2.00
161 Venom Connoisseur U :G:	.12	.25
162 Vivien on the Hunt M :G:	2.00	4.00
163 Voice of the Vermin U :G:	.12	.25
164 Warm Welcome C :G:	.07	.15
165 Workshop Warchief R :G:	.20	.40
166 Aven Heartstabber R :B:/:K:	.20	.40
167 Black Market Tycoon R :R:/:G:	.20	.40
168 Body Dropper C :K:/:R:	.07	.15
169 Brazen Upstart U :R:/:G:/:W:	.12	.25
170 Brokers Ascendancy R :G:/:W:/:B:	.75	1.50
171 Brokers Charm U :G:/:W:/:B:	.12	.25
172 Cabaretti Ascendancy R :R:/:G:/:W:	.20	.40
173 Cabaretti Charm U :R:/:G:/:W:	.12	.25
174 Celestial Regulator C :W:/:B:	.07	.15
175 Ceremonial Groundbreaker U :G:/:W:	.12	.25
176 Civil Servant C :G:/:W:	.07	.15
177 Cormela, Glamour Thief U :B:/:K:/:R:	.12	.25
178 Corpse Appraiser U :B:/:K:/:R:	.12	.25
179 Corpse Explosion R :K:/:R:	.20	.40
180 Crew Captain U :K:/:R:/:G:	.12	.25
181 Darling of the Masses U :G:/:W:	.12	.25
182 Disciplined Duelist U :G:/:W:/:B:	.12	.25
183 Endless Detour R :G:/:W:/:B:	.20	.40
184 Evelyn, the Covetous R :B:/:K:/:R:	.20	.40
185 Exotic Pets U :W:/:B:	.12	.25
186 Falco Spara, Pactweaver M :G:/:W:/:B:	.60	1.25
187 Fatal Grudge U :K:/:R:	.12	.25
188 Fleetfoot Dancer R :R:/:G:/:W:	.20	.40
189 Forge Boss U :K:/:R:	.12	.25
190 Glamorous Outlaw C :B:/:K:/:R:	.07	.15
191 Hostile Takeover R :B:/:K:/:R:	.20	.40
192 Incandescent Aria R :R:/:G:/:W:	.20	.40
193 Jetmir, Nexus of Revels M :R:/:G:/:W:	3.00	6.00
194 Jetmir's Fixer C :R:/:G:	.07	.15
195 Jinnie Fay, Jetmir's Second R :R:/:G:/:W:	.30	.60
196 Lagrella, the Magpie U :G:/:W:/:B:	.12	.25
197 Lord Xander, the Collector M :B:/:K:/:R:	1.50	3.00
198 Maestros Ascendancy R :B:/:K:/:R:	.20	.40
199 Maestros Charm U :B:/:K:/:R:	.12	.25
200 Maestros Diabolist R :B:/:K:/:R:	.20	.40
201 Masked Bandits C :K:/:R:/:G:	.07	.15
202 Meeting of the Five M :W:/:B:/:K:/:R:/:G:	.25	.50
203 Metropolis Angel U :W:/:B:	.12	.25
204 Mr. Orfeo, the Boulder U :K:/:R:/:G:	.12	.25
205 Nimble Larcenist U :W:/:B:/:K:	.12	.25
206 Ob Nixilis, the Adversary M :K:/:R:	7.50	15.00
207 Obscura Ascendancy R :W:/:B:/:K:	.20	.40
208 Obscura Charm U :W:/:B:/:K:	.12	.25
209 Obscura Interceptor R :W:/:B:/:K:	.20	.40
210 Ognis, the Dragon's Lash R :K:/:R:/:G:	.20	.40
211 Park Heights Pegasus R :G:/:W:	.20	.40
212 Queza, Augur of Agonies U :W:/:B:/:K:	.12	.25
213 Raffine, Scheming Seer M :W:/:B:/:K:	2.00	4.00
214 Rakish Revelers C :R:/:G:/:W:	.07	.15
215 Rigo, Streetwise Mentor R :G:/:W:/:B:	.20	.40
216 Riveteers Ascendancy R :K:/:R:/:G:	.20	.40
217 Riveteers Charm U :K:/:R:/:G:	.12	.25
218 Rocco, Cabaretti Caterer U :R:/:G:/:W:	.12	.25
219 Scheming Fence R :W:/:B:	.20	.40
220 Security Rhox U :R:/:G:	.12	.25
221 Shattered Seraph C :W:/:B:/:K:	.07	.15
222 Snooping Newsie C :B:/:K:	.07	.15
223 Soul of Emancipation R :G:/:W:/:B:	.20	.40
224 Spara's Adjudicators C :G:/:W:/:B:	.07	.15
225 Stimulus Package U :R:/:G:	.12	.25
226 Syndicate Infiltrator U :B:/:K:	.12	.25
227 Tainted Indulgence U :B:/:K:	.75	1.50
228 Toluz, Clever Conductor R :W:/:B:/:K:	.20	.40
229 Unleash the Inferno R :K:/:R:/:G:	.20	.40
230 Void Rend R :W:/:B:/:K:	1.25	2.50
231 Ziatora, the Incinerator M :K:/:R:/:G:	2.50	5.00
232 Ziatora's Envoy R :K:/:R:/:G:	.20	.40
233 Arc Spitter U	.12	.25
234 Brass Knuckles U	.12	.25
235 Cement Shoes U	.12	.25
236 Chrome Cat C	.07	.15
237 Getaway Car R	.20	.40
238 Gilded Pinions C	.07	.15
239 Halo Scarab C	.07	.15
240 Luxior, Giada's Gift M	4.00	8.00
241 Ominous Parcel C	.07	.15
242 Paragon of Modernity C	.07	.15
243 Quick-Draw Dagger C	.07	.15
244 Scuttling Butler U	.12	.25
245 Suspicious Bookcase U	.12	.25
246 Unlicensed Hearse R	10.00	20.00
247 Botanical Plaza C	.07	.15
248 Brokers Hideout C	.15	.30
249 Cabaretti Courtyard C	.15	.30
250 Jetmir's Garden R	5.00	10.00
251 Maestros Theater C	.20	.40
252 Obscura Storefront C	.20	.40
253 Racers' Ring C	.07	.15
254 Raffine's Tower R	7.50	15.00
255 Riveteers Overlook C	.15	.30
256 Skybridge Towers C	.07	.15
257 Spara's Headquarters R	5.00	10.00
258 Tramway Station C	.07	.15
259 Waterfront District C	.07	.15
260 Xander's Lounge R	4.00	8.00
261 Ziatora's Proving Ground R	5.00	10.00
262 Plains C	.07	.15
263 Plains C	.07	.15
264 Island C	.07	.15
265 Island C	.07	.15
266 Swamp C	.07	.15
267 Swamp C	.07	.15
268 Mountain C	.07	.15
269 Mountain C	.07	.15
270 Forest C	.07	.15
271 Forest C	.07	.15
272 Plains C	.50	1.00
273 Plains C	.30	.75
274 Island C	.25	.50
275 Island C	.25	.50
276 Swamp C	.50	1.00
277 Swamp C	.25	.50
278 Mountain C	.25	.50
279 Mountain C	.60	1.25
280 Forest C	.30	.60
281 Forest C	.30	.60
282 Elspeth Resplendent M :W:	4.00	8.00
283 Vivien on the Hunt M :G:	6.00	12.00
284 Ob Nixilis, the Adversary M :K:/:R:	7.50	15.00
285 Halo Fountain M :W:	3.00	6.00
286 All-Seeing Arbiter M :B:	.30	.75
287 Shadow of Mortality R :K:	.30	.75
288 Bootleggers' Stash M :G:	10.00	20.00
289 Titan of Industry M :G:	4.00	8.00
290 Topiary Stomper R :G:	1.25	2.50
291 Jetmir's Garden R	12.50	25.00
292 Raffine's Tower R	15.00	30.00
293 Spara's Headquarters R	12.50	25.00
294 Xander's Lounge R	10.00	20.00
295 Ziatora's Proving Ground R	12.50	25.00
296 Brazen Upstart U :R:/:G:/:W:	.12	.25
297 Brokers Ascendancy R :G:/:W:/:B:	.50	1.00
298 Brokers Charm U :G:/:W:/:B:	.12	.25
299 Cabaretti Ascendancy R :R:/:G:/:W:	.20	.40
300 Cabaretti Charm U :R:/:G:/:W:	.12	.25
301 Cormela, Glamour Thief U :B:/:K:/:R:	.12	.25
302 Corpse Appraiser U :B:/:K:/:R:	.12	.25
303 Crew Captain U :K:/:R:/:G:	.12	.25
304 Disciplined Duelist U :G:/:W:/:B:	.12	.25
305 Endless Detour R :G:/:W:/:B:	.20	.40
306 Evelyn, the Covetous R :B:/:K:/:R:	.20	.40
307 Falco Spara, Pactweaver M :G:/:W:/:B:	1.00	2.00
308 Fleetfoot Dancer R :R:/:G:/:W:	.20	.40
309 Glamorous Outlaw C :B:/:K:/:R:	.07	.15
310 Hostile Takeover R :B:/:K:/:R:	.20	.40
311 Incandescent Aria R :R:/:G:/:W:	.20	.40
312 Jetmir, Nexus of Revels M :R:/:G:/:W:	3.00	6.00
313 Jinnie Fay, Jetmir's Second R :R:/:G:/:W:	.50	1.00
314 Lagrella, the Magpie U :G:/:W:/:B:	.12	.25
315 Lord Xander, the Collector M :B:/:K:/:R:	1.25	2.50
316 Maestros Ascendancy R :B:/:K:/:R:	.20	.40
317 Maestros Charm U :B:/:K:/:R:	.12	.25
318 Maestros Diabolist R :B:/:K:/:R:	.20	.40
319 Masked Bandits C :K:/:R:/:G:	.07	.15
320 Mr. Orfeo, the Boulder U :K:/:R:/:G:	.12	.25
321 Nimble Larcenist U :W:/:B:/:K:	.12	.25
322 Obscura Ascendancy R :W:/:B:/:K:	.20	.40
323 Obscura Charm U :W:/:B:/:K:	.12	.25
324 Obscura Interceptor R :W:/:B:/:K:	.20	.40
325 Ognis, the Dragon's Lash R :K:/:R:/:G:	.20	.40
326 Queza, Augur of Agonies U :W:/:B:/:K:	.12	.25
327 Raffine, Scheming Seer M :W:/:B:/:K:	3.00	6.00
328 Rakish Revelers C :R:/:G:/:W:	.07	.15
329 Rigo, Streetwise Mentor R :G:/:W:/:B:	.20	.40
330 Riveteers Ascendancy R :K:/:R:/:G:	.20	.40
331 Riveteers Charm U :K:/:R:/:G:	.12	.25
332 Rocco, Cabaretti Caterer U :R:/:G:/:W:	.12	.25
333 Shattered Seraph C :W:/:B:/:K:	.07	.15
334 Soul of Emancipation R :G:/:W:/:B:	.20	.40
335 Spara's Adjudicators C :G:/:W:/:B:	.07	.15
336 Toluz, Clever Conductor R :W:/:B:/:K:	.20	.40
337 Unleash the Inferno R :K:/:R:/:G:	.20	.40
338 Void Rend R :W:/:B:/:K:	1.25	2.50
339 Ziatora, the Incinerator M :K:/:R:/:G:	3.00	6.00
340 Ziatora's Envoy R :K:/:R:/:G:	.20	.40
341 Elspeth Resplendent M :W:	3.00	6.00
342 Giada, Font of Hope R :W:	1.50	3.00
343 Sanctuary Warden M :W:	.75	1.50
344 Errant, Street Artist R :B:	.20	.40
345 Tenacious Underdog R :K:	1.00	2.00
346 Urabrask, Heretic Praetor M :R:	4.00	8.00
347 Vivien on the Hunt M :G:	2.50	5.00
348 Ob Nixilis, the Adversary M :K:/:R:	10.00	20.00
349 Scheming Fence R :W:/:B:	.20	.40
350 Botanical Plaza C	.07	.15
351 Jetmir's Garden R	5.00	10.00
352 Racers' Ring C	.07	.15
353 Raffine's Tower R	7.50	15.00
354 Skybridge Towers C	.07	.15
355 Spara's Headquarters R	6.00	12.00
356 Tramway Station C	.07	.15
357 Waterfront District C	.07	.15
358 Xander's Lounge R	5.00	10.00
359 Ziatora's Proving Ground R	5.00	10.00
360 Urabrask, Heretic Praetor M :R:	7.50	15.00
361 Brazen Upstart U :R:/:G:/:W:	.15	.30
362 Brokers Ascendancy R :G:/:W:/:B:	6.00	12.00
363 Brokers Charm U :G:/:W:/:B:	.60	1.25
364 Cabaretti Ascendancy R :R:/:G:/:W:	1.50	3.00
365 Cabaretti Charm U :R:/:G:/:W:	.50	1.00
366 Cormela, Glamour Thief U :B:/:K:/:R:	.75	1.50
367 Corpse Appraiser U :B:/:K:/:R:	.40	.80
368 Crew Captain U :K:/:R:/:G:	.25	.50
369 Disciplined Duelist U :G:/:W:/:B:	.50	1.00
370 Endless Detour R :G:/:W:/:B:	1.50	3.00
371 Evelyn, the Covetous R :B:/:K:/:R:	4.00	8.00
372 Falco Spara, Pactweaver M :G:/:W:/:B:	17.50	35.00
373 Fleetfoot Dancer R :R:/:G:/:W:	1.25	2.50
374 Glamorous Outlaw C :B:/:K:/:R:	.20	.40
375 Hostile Takeover R :B:/:K:/:R:	1.00	2.00
376 Incandescent Aria R :R:/:G:/:W:	.75	1.50
377 Jetmir, Nexus of Revels M :R:/:G:/:W:	25.00	50.00
378 Jinnie Fay, Jetmir's Second R :R:/:G:/:W:	7.50	15.00
379 Lagrella, the Magpie U :G:/:W:/:B:	.50	1.00
380 Lord Xander, the Collector M :B:/:K:/:R:	25.00	50.00
381 Maestros Ascendancy R :B:/:K:/:R:	2.00	4.00
382 Maestros Charm U :B:/:K:/:R:	.75	1.50
383 Maestros Diabolist R :B:/:K:/:R:	.75	1.50
384 Masked Bandits C :K:/:R:/:G:	.20	.40
385 Mr. Orfeo, the Boulder U :K:/:R:/:G:	.50	1.00
386 Nimble Larcenist U :W:/:B:/:K:	.25	.50
387 Obscura Ascendancy R :W:/:B:/:K:	.75	1.50
388 Obscura Charm U :W:/:B:/:K:	1.25	2.50
389 Obscura Interceptor R :W:/:B:/:K:	2.50	5.00
390 Ognis, the Dragon's Lash R :K:/:R:/:G:	2.50	5.00
391 Queza, Augur of Agonies U :W:/:B:/:K:	1.25	2.50
392 Raffine, Scheming Seer M :W:/:B:/:K:	30.00	60.00
393 Rakish Revelers C :R:/:G:/:W:	.12	.25
394 Rigo, Streetwise Mentor R :G:/:W:/:B:	2.00	4.00
395 Riveteers Ascendancy R :K:/:R:/:G:	2.50	5.00
396 Riveteers Charm U :K:/:R:/:G:	2.50	5.00
397 Rocco, Cabaretti Caterer U :R:/:G:/:W:	2.50	5.00
398 Shattered Seraph C :W:/:B:/:K:	.20	.40
399 Soul of Emancipation R :G:/:W:/:B:	1.00	2.00
400 Spara's Adjudicators C :G:/:W:/:B:	.20	.40
401 Toluz, Clever Conductor R :W:/:B:/:K:	2.00	4.00
402 Unleash the Inferno R :K:/:R:/:G:	.75	1.50
403 Void Rend R :W:/:B:/:K:	7.50	15.00
404 Ziatora, the Incinerator M :K:/:R:/:G:	30.00	60.00
405 Ziatora's Envoy R :K:/:R:/:G:	2.50	5.00
406 Depopulate R :W:	.20	.40
407 Extraction Specialist R :W:	1.25	2.50
408 Mysterious Limousine R :W:	.20	.40
409 Rabble Rousing R :W:	.75	1.50
410 Cut Your Losses R :B:	.25	.50
411 Even the Score M :B:	.50	1.00
412 Ledger Shredder R :B:	20.00	40.00
413 Reservoir Kraken R :B:	.20	.40
414 Undercover Operative R :B:	.25	.50
415 Wiretapping R :B:	.20	.40
416 Angel of Suffering M :K:	1.50	3.00
417 Body Launderer M :K:	1.50	3.00
418 Cemetery Tampering R :K:	.20	.40
419 Cut of the Profits R :K:	.20	.40
420 Sanguine Spy R :K:	.20	.40
421 Shakedown Heavy R :K:	.30	.60
422 Arcane Bombardment M :R:	3.00	6.00
423 Devilish Valet R :R:	.60	1.25
424 Hoard Hauler R :R:	.20	.40
425 Jaxis, the Troublemaker R :R:	.30	.75
426 Professional Face-Breaker R :R:	4.00	8.00
427 Structural Assault R :R:	.20	.40
428 Widespread Thieving R :R:	.20	.40
429 Evolving Door R :G:	.20	.40
430 Fight Rigging R :G:	1.00	2.00
431 Gala Greeters R :G:	.20	.40
432 Workshop Warchief R :G:	.20	.40
433 Aven Heartstabber R :B:/:K:	.20	.40
434 Black Market Tycoon R :R:/:G:	.20	.40
435 Corpse Explosion R :K:/:R:	.20	.40
436 Meeting of the Five M :W:/:B:/:K:/:R:/:G:	.25	.50
437 Park Heights Pegasus R :G:/:W:	.20	.40
438 Getaway Car R	.20	.40
439 Luxior, Giada's Gift M	4.00	8.00
440 Unlicensed Hearse R	12.50	25.00
441 Elspeth Resplendent M :W:	25.00	50.00
442 Giada, Font of Hope R :W:	15.00	30.00
443 Sanctuary Warden M :W:	7.50	15.00
444 Errant, Street Artist R :B:	1.25	2.50
445 Tenacious Underdog R :K:	3.00	6.00
446 Urabrask, Heretic Praetor M :R:	17.50	35.00
447 Vivien on the Hunt M :G:	20.00	40.00
448 Ob Nixilis, the Adversary M :K:/:R:	50.00	100.00
449 Scheming Fence R :W:/:B:	2.00	4.00
450 Gala Greeters R :G:	.20	.40
451 Gala Greeters R :G:	12.50	25.00
452 Gala Greeters R :G:	75.00	150.00
453 Gala-Begrüßer R :G:	15.00	30.00
454 Presonnel d'accueil du gala R :G:	5.00	10.00
455 Comitato di Benvenuto al Galà R :G:	12.50	25.00
456 Gala Greeters R :G:	2.00	4.00
457 Gala Greeters R :G:	75.00	150.00
460 Saludadores de la gala R :G:	15.00	30.00
461 Jaxis, the Troublemaker R :R:	.30	.60
462 Mysterious Limousine R :W:	.12	.25
463 Rumor Gatherer U :W:	.25	.50
464 An Offer You Can't Refuse U :B:	2.50	5.00
465 Incriminate C :K:	.07	.15
466 Light 'Em Up C :R:	.07	.15
467 Courier's Briefcase U :G:	.12	.25
468 Urabrask, Heretic Praetor M :R:	4.00	8.00
469 Urabrask, Heretic Praetor M :R:	7.50	15.00

2022 Magic The Gathering Streets of New Capenna Tokens

1 Copy	.40	.80
2 Angel	.50	1.00
3 Spirit	.07	.15
4 Fish	.07	.15
5 Wizard	.07	.15
6 Ogre Warrior	.07	.15
7 Rogue	.07	.15

8 Devil	.07	.15
9 Cat	.25	.50
10 Dog	.50	1.00
11 Rhino Warrior	.12	.25
12 Citizen	.10	.20
13 Treasure	.07	.15
14 Treasure	.07	.15
15 Treasure	.07	.15
16 Treasure	.07	.15
17 Treasure	.07	.15

2022 Magic The Gathering Streets of New Capenna Commander

1 Anhelo, the Painter M :B/:K/:R:	.25	.50
2 Henzie "Toolbox" Torre M :K/:R/:G:	.20	.40
3 Kamiz, Obscura Oculus M :W/:B/:K:	.17	.35
4 Kitt Kanto, Mayhem Diva M :R/:G/:W:	.20	.40
5 Perrie, the Pulverizer M :G/:B/:W:	.15	.30
6 The Beamtown Bullies M :K/:R/:G:	.20	.40
7 Kros, Defense Contractor M :G/:W/:B:	.15	.30
8 Parnesse, the Subtle Brush M :B/:K/:R:	.20	.40
9 Phabine, Boss's Confidant M :R/:G/:W:	.20	.40
10 Tivit, Seller of Secrets M :W/:B/:K:	.20	.40
11 Aerial Extortionist R :W:	.20	.40
12 Angelic Sleuth R :W:	.20	.40
13 Boss's Chauffeur R :W:	.20	.40
14 Contractual Safeguard R :W:	.20	.40
15 Damning Verdict R :W:	.20	.40
16 Grand Crescendo R :W:	.20	.40
17 Jailbreak R :W:	.20	.40
18 Master of Ceremonies R :W:	.20	.40
19 Resourceful Defense R :W:	.20	.40
20 Skyboon Evangelist R :W:	.20	.40
21 Smuggler's Share R :W:	.20	.40
22 Aven Courier R :B:	.20	.40
23 Cephalid Facetaker R :B:	.20	.40
24 Change of Plans R :B:	.20	.40
25 Extravagant Replication R :B:	.20	.40
26 Flawless Forgery R :B:	.20	.40
27 In Too Deep R :B:	.20	.40
28 Mask of the Schemer R :B:	.20	.40
29 Shield Broker R :B:	.20	.40
30 Sinister Concierge R :B:	.20	.40
31 Skyway Robber R :B:	.20	.40
32 Storm of Forms R :B:	.20	.40
33 Bellowing Mauler R :K:	.20	.40
34 Body Count R :K:	.20	.40
35 Dogged Detective R :K:	.20	.40
36 Lethal Scheme R :K:	.20	.40
37 Make an Example R :K:	.20	.40
38 Misfortune Teller R :K:	.20	.40
39 Protection Racket R :K:	.20	.40
40 Waste Management R :K:	.20	.40
41 Wave of Rats R :K:	.20	.40
42 Writ of Return R :K:	.20	.40
43 Xander's Pact R :K:	.20	.40
44 Audacious Swap R :R:	.20	.40
45 Determined Iteration R :R:	.20	.40
46 Indulge // Excess R :R:	.20	.40
47 Industrial Advancement R :R:	.20	.40
48 Life of the Party R :R:	.20	.40
49 Mezzio Mugger R :R:	.20	.40
50 Rain of Riches R :R:	.20	.40
51 Rose Room Treasurer R :R:	.20	.40
52 Seize the Spotlight R :R:	.20	.40
53 Spellbinding Soprano R :R:	.20	.40
54 Turf War R :R:	.20	.40
55 Bribe Taker R :G:	.20	.40
56 Caldaia Guardian R :G:	.20	.40
57 Crash the Party R :G:	.20	.40
58 Dodgy Jalopy R :G:	.20	.40
59 Family's Favor R :G:	.20	.40
60 First Responder R :G:	.20	.40
61 Killer Service R :G:	.20	.40
62 Next of Kin R :G:	.20	.40
63 Park Heights Maverick R :G:	.20	.40
64 Scepter of Celebration R :G:	.20	.40
65 Vivien's Stampede R :G:	.20	.40
66 Agent's Toolkit R :G/:B:	.20	.40
67 Bess, Soul Nourisher R :G/:W:	.20	.40
68 Brokers Confluence R :G/:W/:B:	.20	.40
69 Cabaretti Confluence R :R/:G/:W:	.20	.40
70 Cryptic Pursuit R :B/:R:	.20	.40
71 Denry Klin, Editor in Chief R :W/:B:	.20	.40
72 Grime Gorger R :K/:G:	.20	.40
73 Jolene, the Plunder Queen R :R/:G:	.20	.40
74 Life Insurance R :W/:K:	.20	.40
75 Maestros Confluence R :B/:K/:R:	.20	.40
76 Obscura Confluence R :W/:B/:K:	.20	.40
77 Oskar, Rubbish Reclaimer R :B/:K:	.20	.40
78 Prosperous Partnership R :R/:W:	.20	.40
79 Riveteers Confluence R :K/:R/:G:	.20	.40
80 Syrix, Carrier of the Flame R :K/:R:	.20	.40
81 Currency Converter R	.20	.40
82 False Floor R	.20	.40
83 Gavel of the Righteous R	.20	.40
84 Smuggler's Buggy R	.20	.40
85 Weathered Sentinels R	.20	.40
87 Tenuous Truce R :W:	.20	.40
88 Swindler's Scheme R :B:	.20	.40
89 Mari, the Killing Quill R :K:	.20	.40
90 Spiteful Repossession R :R:	.20	.40
91 Boxing Ring R :G:	.20	.40
92 Vazi, Keen Negotiator R :K/:R/:G:	.20	.40
95 Tenuous Truce R :W:	.20	.40
96 Swindler's Scheme R :B:	.20	.40
97 Mari, the Killing Quill R :K:	.20	.40
98 Spiteful Repossession R :R:	.20	.40
99 Boxing Ring R :G:	.20	.40
110 Vazi, Keen Negotiator R :K/:R/:G:	.20	.40
112 Aerial Extortionist R :W:	.20	.40
113 Angelic Sleuth R :W:	.20	.40
114 Boss's Chauffeur R :W:	.20	.40
115 Contractual Safeguard R :W:	.20	.40
116 Damning Verdict R :W:	.20	.40
117 Grand Crescendo R :W:	.20	.40
118 Jailbreak R :W:	.20	.40
119 Master of Ceremonies R :W:	.20	.40
120 Resourceful Defense R :W:	.20	.40
121 Skyboon Evangelist R :W:	.20	.40
122 Smuggler's Share R :W:	.20	.40
123 Aven Courier R :B:	.20	.40
124 Cephalid Facetaker R :B:	.20	.40
125 Change of Plans R :B:	.20	.40
126 Extravagant Replication R :B:	.20	.40
127 Flawless Forgery R :B:	.20	.40
128 In Too Deep R :B:	.20	.40
129 Mask of the Schemer R :B:	.20	.40
130 Shield Broker R :B:	.20	.40
131 Sinister Concierge R :B:	.20	.40
132 Skyway Robber R :B:	.20	.40
133 Storm of Forms R :B:	.20	.40
134 Bellowing Mauler R :K:	.20	.40
135 Body Count R :K:	.20	.40
136 Dogged Detective R :K:	.20	.40
137 Lethal Scheme R :K:	.20	.40
138 Make an Example R :K:	.20	.40
139 Misfortune Teller R :K:	.20	.40
140 Protection Racket R :K:	.20	.40
141 Waste Management R :K:	.20	.40
142 Wave of Rats R :K:	.20	.40
143 Writ of Return R :K:	.20	.40
144 Xander's Pact R :K:	.20	.40
145 Audacious Swap R :R:	.20	.40
146 Determined Iteration R :R:	.20	.40
147 Industrial Advancement R :R:	.20	.40
148 Life of the Party R :R:	.20	.40
149 Mezzio Mugger R :R:	.20	.40
150 Rain of Riches R :R:	.20	.40
151 Rose Room Treasurer R :R:	.20	.40
152 Seize the Spotlight R :R:	.20	.40
153 Spellbinding Soprano R :R:	.20	.40
154 Turf War R :R:	.20	.40
155 Bribe Taker R :G:	.20	.40
156 Caldaia Guardian R :G:	.20	.40
157 Crash the Party R :G:	.20	.40
158 Dodgy Jalopy R :G:	.20	.40
159 Family's Favor R :G:	.20	.40
160 First Responder R :G:	.20	.40
161 Killer Service R :G:	.20	.40
162 Next of Kin R :G:	.20	.40
163 Park Heights Maverick R :G:	.20	.40
164 Scepter of Celebration R :G:	.20	.40
165 Vivien's Stampede R :G:	.20	.40
166 Agent's Toolkit R :G/:B:	.20	.40
167 Bess, Soul Nourisher R :G/:W:	.20	.40
168 Brokers Confluence R :G/:W/:B:	.20	.40
169 Cabaretti Confluence R :R/:G/:W:	.20	.40
170 Cryptic Pursuit R :B/:R:	.20	.40
171 Denry Klin, Editor in Chief R :W/:B:	.20	.40
172 Grime Gorger R :K/:G:	.20	.40
173 Jolene, the Plunder Queen R :R/:G:	.20	.40
174 Life Insurance R :W/:K:	.20	.40
175 Maestros Confluence R :B/:K/:R:	.20	.40
176 Obscura Confluence R :W/:B/:K:	.20	.40
177 Oskar, Rubbish Reclaimer R :B/:K:	.20	.40
178 Prosperous Partnership R :R/:W:	.20	.40
179 Riveteers Confluence R :K/:R/:G:	.20	.40
180 Syrix, Carrier of the Flame R :K/:R:	.20	.40
181 Currency Converter R	.20	.40
182 False Floor R	.20	.40
183 Gavel of the Righteous R	.20	.40
184 Smuggler's Buggy R	.20	.40
185 Weathered Sentinels R	.20	.40
191 Artisan of Kozilek U	.12	.25
193 Austere Command R :W:	.20	.40
194 Avenging Huntbonder R :W:	.20	.40
195 Call the Coppercoats R :W:	.20	.40
196 Declaration in Stone R :W:	.20	.40
197 Duelist's Heritage R :W:	.20	.40
198 Dusk // Dawn R :W:	.20	.40
199 Felidar Retreat R :W:	.20	.40
200 Fell the Mighty R :W:	.20	.40
201 Generous Gift U :W:	.12	.25
202 Grateful Apparition U :W:	.12	.25
203 Hoofprints of the Stag R :W:	.20	.40
204 Intangible Virtue U :W:	.12	.25
205 Luminarch Aspirant R :W:	.20	.40
206 Martial Coup R :W:	.20	.40
207 Orzhov Advokist U :W:	.12	.25
208 Path to Exile U :W:	.12	.25
209 Planar Outburst R :W:	.20	.40
211 Swords to Plowshares U :W:	.12	.25
212 Together Forever R :W:	.20	.40
213 Champion of Wits R :B:	.20	.40
214 Chasm Skulker R :B:	.20	.40
216 Commit // Memory R :B:	.20	.40
217 Daring Saboteur U :B:	.12	.25
218 Deep Analysis C :B:	.07	.15
219 Dig Through Time R :B:	.20	.40
220 Drawn from Dreams R :B:	.20	.40
221 Fact or Fiction U :B:	.12	.25
222 Frantic Search C :B:	.07	.15
223 Ghostly Pilferer R :B:	.20	.40
224 Identity Thief R :B:	.20	.40
225 Looter il-Kor C :B:	.07	.15
226 Midnight Clock R :B:	.20	.40
227 Mystic Confluence R :B:	.20	.40
228 Nadir Kraken R :B:	.20	.40
229 Ponder C :B:	.07	.15
230 Preordain C :B:	.07	.15
231 River's Rebuke R :B:	.20	.40
232 Skyship Plunderer U :B:	.12	.25
233 Stolen Identity R :B:	.20	.40
234 Talrand's Invocation U :B:	.12	.25
235 Tezzeret's Gambit R :B/:R:	.20	.40
236 Thrummingbird U :B:	.12	.25
237 Treasure Cruise C :B:	.07	.15
238 Whirler Rogue U :B:	.12	.25
239 Wingspan Mentor U :B:	.12	.25
240 Zndrsplt's Judgment R :B:	.20	.40
241 Aether Snap R :K:	.20	.40
243 Bloodsoaked Champion R :K:	.20	.40
244 Custodi Lich R :K:	.20	.40
245 Damnable Pact R :K:	.20	.40
246 Deathbringer Regent R :K:	.20	.40
247 Disciple of Bolas R :K:	.20	.40
249 Dread Summons R :K:	.20	.40
250 Feed the Swarm C :K:	.07	.15
251 Graveblade Marauder R :K:	.20	.40
252 Hex R :K:	.20	.40
253 Nightmare Unmaking R :K:	.20	.40
255 Painful Truths R :K:	.20	.40
256 Profane Command R :K:	.20	.40
257 Puppeteer Clique R :K:	.20	.40
258 Reign of the Pit R :K:	.20	.40
259 Sever the Bloodline R :K:	.20	.40
260 Skyclave Shade R :K:	.20	.40
261 Victimize U :K:	.12	.25
262 Woe Strider R :K:	.20	.40
263 Agitator Ant R :R:	.20	.40
264 Blasphemous Act R :R:	.20	.40
265 Chain Reaction R :R:	.20	.40
266 Chaos Warp R :R:	.20	.40
267 Double Vision R :R:	.20	.40
268 Etali, Primal Storm R :R:	.20	.40
270 Kazuul, Tyrant of the Cliffs R :R:	.20	.40
271 Magus of the Wheel R :R:	.20	.40
272 Outpost Siege R :R:	.20	.40
274 Rite of the Raging Storm U :R:	.12	.25
275 Squee, the Immortal R :R:	.20	.40
276 Stalking Vengeance R :R:	.20	.40
277 Warstorm Surge R :R:	.20	.40
278 Zurzoth, Chaos Rider R :R:	.20	.40
279 Arasta of the Endless Web R :G:	.20	.40
281 Awakening Zone R :G:	.20	.40
282 Beast Within U :G:	.12	.25
283 Beastmaster Ascension R :G:	.20	.40
284 Champion of Lambholt R :G:	.20	.40
285 Cultivate U :G:	.12	.25
286 Devoted Druid U :G:	.12	.25
287 Evolution Sage U :G:	.12	.25
288 Evolutionary Leap R :G:	.20	.40
289 Explore C :G:	.07	.15
290 Farseek C :G:	.07	.15
291 Forgotten Ancient R :G:	.20	.40
292 Garruk's Uprising U :G:	.12	.25
295 Harmonize U :G:	.12	.25
296 Incubation Druid R :G:	.20	.40
297 Indrik Stomphowler U :G:	.12	.25
298 Kodama's Reach C :G:	.07	.15
299 Leafkin Druid C :G:	.07	.15
300 Life's Legacy R :G:	.20	.40
301 Migration Path U :G:	.12	.25
302 Mitotic Slime R :G:	.20	.40
303 Overgrown Battlement U :G:	.12	.25
304 Rampant Growth C :G:	.07	.15
305 Rishkar, Peema Renegade R :G:	.20	.40
306 Rishkar's Expertise R :G:	.20	.40
307 Sakura-Tribe Elder C :G:	.07	.15
308 Sandwurm Convergence R :G:	.20	.40
309 Scavenging Ooze R :G:	.20	.40
310 Scute Swarm R :G:	.20	.40
311 Shamanic Revelation R :G:	.20	.40
312 Slippery Bogbonder R :G:	.20	.40
313 Steelbane Hydra R :G:	.20	.40
314 Sylvan Offering R :G:	.20	.40
315 Temur Sabertooth U :G:	.12	.25
316 Thragtusk R :G:	.20	.40
317 Thunderfoot Baloth R :G:	.20	.40
318 Treeshaker Chimera R :G:	.20	.40
319 Wall of Roots C :G:	.07	.15
320 Wickerbough Elder C :G:	.07	.15
321 Wood Elves C :G:	.07	.15
322 Woodfall Primus R :G:	.20	.40
323 World Shaper R :G:	.20	.40
326 Artifact Mutation R :R/:G:	.20	.40
327 Assemble the Legion R :R/:W:	.20	.40
328 Aura Mutation R :G/:W:	.20	.40
329 Aven Mimeomancer R :W/:B:	.20	.40
330 Bant Charm U :G/:W/:B:	.12	.25
331 Bedevil R :K/:R:	.20	.40
332 Boros Charm U :R/:W:	.12	.25
333 Call the Skybreaker R :B/:R:	.20	.40
334 Camaraderie R :G/:W:	.20	.40
335 Daxos of Meletis R :W/:B:	.20	.40
336 Deathreap Ritual U :K/:G:	.12	.25
338 Fallen Shinobi R :B/:K:	.20	.40
339 Fathom Mage R :G/:B:	.20	.40
341 Goblin Electromancer C :B/:R:	.07	.15
342 Inkfathom Witch U :B/:K:	.12	.25
347 Mask of Riddles U :B/:K:	.12	.25
348 Primal Empathy U :G/:B:	.12	.25
350 Selvala, Explorer Returned R :G/:W:	.20	.40
351 Shadowmage Infiltrator R :B/:K:	.20	.40
352 Silent-Blade Oni R :B/:K:	.20	.40
353 Terminate U :K/:R:	.12	.25
354 Thief of Sanity R :B/:K:	.20	.40
355 Urban Evolution U :G/:B:	.12	.25
356 Utter End R :W/:K:	.20	.40
357 Vorel of the Hull Clade R :G/:B:	.20	.40
358 Windgrace's Judgment R :K/:G:	.20	.40
360 Arcane Signet C	.07	.15
361 Azorius Signet U	.12	.25
362 Bloodthirsty Blade U	.12	.25
363 Commander's Sphere C	.07	.15
364 Crystalline Giant R	.20	.40
365 Dimir Signet C	.07	.15
366 Everflowing Chalice C	.07	.15
367 Fellwar Stone U	.12	.25
368 Idol of Oblivion R	.20	.40
369 Izzet Signet U	.12	.25
370 Lifecrafter's Bestiary R	.20	.40
371 Lightning Greaves U	.12	.25
372 Mimic Vat R	.20	.40
373 Oblivion Stone R	.20	.40
374 Oracle's Vault R	.20	.40
375 Orzhov Signet U	.12	.25
376 Power Conduit U	.12	.25
377 Quietus Spike R	.20	.40
378 Rakdos Signet U	.12	.25
379 Sol Ring U	.12	.25
380 Solemn Simulacrum R	.20	.40
381 Strionic Resonator R	.20	.40
382 Swiftfoot Boots U	.12	.25
383 Twinning Staff R	.20	.40
384 Wayfarer's Bauble C	.07	.15
385 Arcane Sanctum U	.12	.25
386 Ash Barrens U	.12	.25
387 Bant Panorama C	.07	.15
388 Blighted Woodland U	.12	.25
389 Canopy Vista R	.20	.40
390 Cascade Bluffs R	.20	.40
391 Castle Ardenvale R	.20	.40
392 Castle Embereth R	.20	.40
393 Choked Estuary R	.20	.40
394 Cinder Glade R	.20	.40
395 Command Tower C	.07	.15
396 Creeping Tar Pit R	.20	.40
397 Crumbling Necropolis U	.12	.25
398 Darkwater Catacombs R	.20	.40
399 Esper Panorama C	.07	.15
400 Exotic Orchard R	.20	.40
401 Fetid Heath R	.20	.40
402 Flooded Grove R	.20	.40
403 Foreboding Ruins R	.20	.40
404 Fortified Village R	.20	.40
405 Game Trail R	.20	.40
406 Gavony Township R	.20	.40
407 Grixis Panorama C	.07	.15
408 Jund Panorama C	.07	.15
409 Jungle Shrine U	.12	.25
410 Karn's Bastion R	.20	.40
411 Kessig Wolf Run R	.20	.40
412 Littjara Mirrorlake U	.12	.25
413 Llanowar Reborn U	.12	.25
414 Mossfire Valley R	.20	.40
415 Mosswort Bridge R	.20	.40
416 Myriad Landscape U	.12	.25
417 Naya Panorama C	.07	.15
418 Nesting Grounds R	.20	.40
419 Path of Ancestry C	.07	.15
420 Port Town R	.20	.40
421 Prairie Stream R	.20	.40
422 Rogue's Passage U	.12	.25
423 Rugged Prairie R	.20	.40
424 Savage Lands U	.12	.25
425 Seaside Citadel U	.12	.25
426 Shadowblood Ridge R	.20	.40
427 Skycloud Expanse R	.20	.40
428 Smoldering Marsh R	.20	.40
429 Spinerock Knoll R	.20	.40
430 Sungrass Prairie R	.20	.40
431 Sunken Hollow R	.20	.40
432 Temple of Epiphany R	.20	.40
433 Temple of Malady R	.20	.40
434 Temple of Mystery R	.20	.40
435 Temple of Silence R	.20	.40
436 Temple of the False God U	.12	.25
437 Temple of Triumph R	.20	.40
438 Thriving Bluff C	.07	.15
439 Thriving Grove C	.07	.15
440 Thriving Heath C	.07	.15
441 Thriving Isle C	.07	.15
442 Thriving Moor C	.07	.15
443 Twilight Mire R	.20	.40
444 Vivid Creek U	.12	.25
445 Vivid Grove U	.12	.25
446 Vivid Meadow U	.12	.25
447 Windbrisk Heights R	.20	.40

2022 Magic The Gathering Streets of New Capenna Commander Tokens

1 Eldrazi	.20	.40
2 Eldrazi Spawn	.20	.40
3 Manifest	.20	.40
4 Cat Beast	.20	.40
5 Elemental	.20	.40
6 Goat	.20	.40
7 Human	.20	.40
8 Human Soldier	.20	.40
9 Soldier	.20	.40
10 Drake	.20	.40
11 Faerie	.20	.40
12 Squid	.20	.40
13 Tentacle	.20	.40
14 Champion of Wits	.20	.40
15 Demon	.20	.40
16 Zombie	.20	.40
17 Devil	.20	.40
18 Elemental	.20	.40
19 Lightning Rager	.20	.40
20 Ogre	.20	.40
21 Beast	.20	.40
22 Elephant	.20	.40
23 Elf Warrior	.20	.40
24 Insect	.20	.40
25 Ooze	.20	.40
26 Ooze	.20	.40
27 Plant	.20	.40
28 Saproling	.20	.40
29 Spider	.20	.40
30 Treefolk	.20	.40
31 Wurm	.20	.40
32 Elemental	.20	.40
33 Soldier	.20	.40
34 Clue	.20	.40
35 Food	.20	.40
36 Thopter	.20	.40

2022 Magic The Gathering The Brothers' War

1 Aeronaut Cavalry C :W:	.05	.10
2 Airlift Chaplain C :W:	.05	.10
3 Ambush Paratrooper C :W:	.05	.10
4 Calamity's Wake U :W:	.10	.20
5 Deadly Riposte C :W:	.05	.10
6 Disenchant C :W:	.05	.10
7 Great Desert Prospector U :W:	.05	.10
8 In the Trenches M :W:	.40	.80
9 Kayla's Command R :W:	.12	.25
10 Kayla's Reconstruction R :W:	.15	.30
11 Lay Down Arms U :W:	.12	.25
12 Loran of the Third Path R :W:	5.00	10.00
13 Loran, Disciple of History U :W:	.05	.10
14 Loran's Escape C :W:	.12	.25
15 Mass Production U :W:	.05	.10
16 Meticulous Excavation U :W:	.05	.10
17 Military Discipline C :W:	.05	.10
18 Myrel, Shield of Argive M :W:	10.00	20.00
19 Phalanx Vanguard C :W:	.05	.10
20 Powerstone Engineer C :W:	.05	.10
21 Prison Sentence C :W:	.05	.10
22 Recommission C :W:	.10	.20
23 Recruitment Officer U :W:	.20	.40
24 Repair and Recharge U :W:	.05	.10

25 Siege Veteran R :W: .30 .60
26 Soul Partition R :W: .75 1.50
27 Static Net U :W: .05 .10
28 Survivor of Korlis C :W: .05 .10
29 Thopter Architect U :W: .05 .10
30 Tocasia's Welcome R :W: 1.50 3.00
31 Union of the Third Path C :W: .05 .10
32 Warlord's Elite C :W: .05 .10
33 Yotian Medic C :W: .05 .10
34 Autonomous Assembler R .05 .10
35 Combat Thresher U .05 .10
36 Platoon Dispenser M .75 1.50
37 Scrapwork Cohort C .05 .10
38 Steel Seraph R .60 1.25
39 Tocasia's Onulet C .05 .10
40 Urza's Sylex M .25 .50
41 Veteran's Powerblade C .05 .10
42 Yotian Frontliner U .05 .10
43 Air Marshal C :B: .05 .10
44 Curate C :B: .05 .10
45 Defabricate U :B: .07 .15
46 Desynchronize C :B: .05 .10
47 Drafna, Founder of Lat-Nam R :B: .20 .40
48 Fallaji Archaeologist C :B: .06 .12
49 Flow of Knowledge U :B: .10 .20
50 Forging the Anchor U :B: .05 .10
51 Hurkyl, Master Wizard R :B: .12 .25
52 Hurkyl's Final Meditation R :B: .07 .15
53 Involuntary Cooldown U :B: .05 .10
54 Keeper of the Cadence U :B: .05 .10
55 Koilos Roc C :B: .05 .10
56 Lat-Nam Adept C :B: .05 .10
57 Machine Over Matter C :B: .05 .10
58 Mightstone's Animation C :B: .05 .10
59 One with the Multiverse M :B: 2.50 5.00
60 Retrieval Agent C :B: .05 .10
61 Scatter Ray C :B: .05 .10
62 Skystrike Officer R :B: .20 .40
63 Splitting the Powerstone U :B: .05 .10
64 Stern Lesson C :B: .05 .10
65 Take Flight U :B: .05 .10
66 Teferi, Temporal Pilgrim M :B: 3.00 6.00
67 Third Path Savant C :B: .05 .10
68 Thopter Mechanic U :B: .05 .10
69 Urza, Powerstone Prodigy U :B: .05 .10
70 Urza's Command R :B: .12 .25
71 Urza's Rebuff C :B: .05 .10
72 Weakstone's Subjugation C :B: .05 .10
73 Wing Commando C :B: .05 .10
74 Zephyr Sentinel U :B: .05 .10
75 Arcane Proxy M .60 1.25
76 Coastal Bulwark C .05 .10
77 Combat Courier C .05 .10
78 Depth Charge Colossus C .05 .10
79 Hulking Metamorph U .06 .12
80 Spotter Thopter U .05 .10
81 Surge Engine M .40 .80
82 The Temporal Anchor R :B: .15 .30
83 Terisian Mindbreaker R .25 .50
84 Ashnod, Flesh Mechanist R :K: .10 .20
85 Ashnod's Intervention C :K: .05 .10
86 Battlefield Butcher U :K: .05 .10
87 Carrion Locust C :K: .05 .10
88 Corrupt U :K: .05 .10
89 Diabolic Intent R :K: 3.00 6.00
90 Disciples of Gix U :K: .05 .10
91 Disfigure C :K: .05 .10
92 Dreams of Steel and Oil U :K: .05 .10
93 Emergency Weld C :K: .07 .15
94 Fateful Handoff R :K: .12 .25
95 Gix, Yawgmoth Praetor M :K: 4.00 8.00
96 Gix's Caress C :K: .05 .10
97 Gix's Command R :K: .25 .50
98 Gixian Infiltrator C :K: .05 .10
99 Gixian Puppeteer R :K: .75 1.50
100 Gixian Skullflayer C :K: .05 .10
101 Gnawing Vermin U :K: .06 .12
102 Go for the Throat U :K: .30 .60
103 Gruesome Realization U :K: .05 .10
104 Gurgling Anointer U :K: .05 .10
105 Hostile Negotiations R :K: .25 .50
106 Kill-Zone Acrobat C :K: .05 .10
107 Misery's Shadow R :K: .30 .60
108 Moment of Defiance C :K: .05 .10
109 No One Left Behind U :K: .05 .10
110 Overwhelming Remorse C :K: .07 .15
111 Painful Quandary R :K: .75 1.50
112 Powerstone Fracture C :K: .05 .10
113 Ravenous Gigamole C :K: .05 .10
114 Thran Vigil U :K: .05 .10
115 Thraxodemon C :K: .05 .10
116 Trench Stalker C :K: .05 .10
117 Ashnod's Harvester U .05 .10
118 Clay Revenant C .05 .10
119 Dredging Claw C .05 .10
120 Goring Warplow C .05 .10
121 Phyrexian Fleshgorger M 2.00 4.00
122 Razorlash Transmogrant R .20 .40
123 Scrapwork Rager C .05 .10
124 Transmogrant Altar U .06 .12
125 Transmogrant's Crown R .15 .30
126 Arms Race U :R: .05 .10
127 Bitter Reunion C :R: .25 .50
128 Brotherhood's End R :R: 2.00 4.00
129 Conscripted Infantry C :R: .05 .10
130 Draconic Destiny M :R: .25 .50
131 Dwarven Forge-Chanter C :R: .05 .10
132 Excavation Explosion C :R: .05 .10
133 The Fall of Kroog U :R: .05 .10
134 Fallaji Chaindancer C :R: .05 .10
135 Feldon, Ronom Excavator R :R: .20 .40
136 Giant Cindermaw U :R: .06 .12
137 Goblin Blast-Runner C :R: .06 .12
138 Horned Stoneseeker U :R: .05 .10
139 Mechanized Warfare R :R: .75 1.50
140 Mishra, Excavation Prodigy U :R: .05 .10
141 Mishra's Command R :R: .15 .30
142 Mishra's Domination C :R: .05 .10
143 Mishra's Onslaught C :R: .05 .10
144 Monastery Swiftspear U :R: .12 .25
145 Obliterating Bolt U :R: .12 .25
146 Over the Top R :R: .10 .20
147 Penregon Strongbull C :R: .05 .10
148 Pyrrhic Blast U :R: .05 .10
149 Raze to the Ground C :R: .05 .10
150 Roc Hunter C :R: .05 .10
151 Sardian Cliffstomper U :R: .05 .10
152 Sibling Rivalry C :R: .05 .10
153 Tomakul Scrapsmith C :R: .05 .10
154 Tyrant of Kher Ridges R :R: .12 .25
155 Unleash Shell C :R: .05 .10
156 Visions of Phyrexia R :R: .15 .30
157 Whirling Strike C :R: .05 .10
158 Blitz Automaton C .05 .10
159 Fallaji Dragon Engine U .05 .10
160 Heavyweight Demolisher U .05 .10
161 Mishra's Juggernaut C .05 .10
162 Mishra's Research Desk U .07 .15
163a Phyrexian Dragon Engine R .75 1.50
164 Scrapwork Mutt C .10 .20
165 Skitterbeam Battalion M .30 .60
166 Alloy Animist U :G: .05 .10
167 Argothian Opportunist C :G: .05 .10
168 Argothian Sprite C :G: .05 .10
169 Audacity U :G: .20 .40
170 Awaken the Woods M :G: 7.50 15.00
171 Blanchwood Armor U :G: .05 .10
172 Blanchwood Prowler C :G: .05 .10
173 Burrowing Razormaw C :G: .05 .10
174 Bushwhack U :G: .25 .50
175 Citanul Stalwart C :G: .05 .10
176 Epic Confrontation C :G: .05 .10
177 Fade from History R :G: .25 .50
178 Fallaji Excavation U :G: .05 .10
179 Fauna Shaman R :G: 1.00 2.00
180 Fog of War C :G: .05 .10
181 Gaea's Courser U :G: .05 .10
182 Gaea's Gift C :G: .25 .50
183 Giant Growth C :G: .05 .10
184 Gnarlroot Pallbearer C :G: .05 .10
185 Gwenna, Eyes of Gaea R :G: 1.50 3.00
186 Hoarding Recluse C :G: .05 .10
187 Obstinate Baloth U :G: .05 .10
188 Perimeter Patrol C :G: .05 .10
189 Sarinth Steelseeker U :G: .15 .30
190 Shoot Down C :G: .05 .10
191 Tawnos's Tinkering C :G: .05 .10
192 Teething Wurmlet R :G: .15 .30
193 Titania, Voice of Gaea M :G: 5.00 10.00
194 Titania's Command R :G: .40 .80
195 Tomakul Honor Guard C :G: .05 .10
196 Wasteful Harvest C :G: .05 .10
197 Boulderbranch Golem C .05 .10
198 Cradle Clearcutter U .05 .10
199 Haywire Mite U 1.50 3.00
200 Iron-Craw Crusher U .05 .10
201 Mask of the Jadecrafter U .05 .10
202 Perennial Behemoth R .40 .80
203 Rootwire Amalgam M .25 .50
204 Rust Goliath C .05 .10
205 Simian Simulacrum R .15 .30
206 Arbalest Engineers U :R:/:G: .05 .10
207 Battery Bearer U :G:/:B: .05 .10
208 Deathbloom Ritualist R :K:/:G: .12 .25
209 Evangel of Synthesis U :B:/:K: .05 .10
210 Fallaji Vanguard U :R:/:W: .05 .10
211 Hajar, Loyal Bodyguard R :R:/:G: .25 .50
212 Harbin, Vanguard Aviator R :W:/:B: .15 .30
213 Hero of the Dunes U :W:/:K: .05 .10
214 Junkyard Genius U :K:/:R: .05 .10
215 Legions to Ashes R :W:/:K: .15 .30
216 Mishra, Claimed by Gix M :K:/:R: 2.50 5.00
217 Mishra, Tamer of Mak Fawa R :K:/:R: .12 .25
218 Queen Kayla bin-Kroog R :R:/:W: .07 .15
219 Saheeli, Filigree Master M :B:/:R: .75 1.50
220 Sarinth Greatwurm M :R:/:G: .25 .50
221 Skyfisher Spider U :K:/:G: .10 .20
222 Tawnos, the Toymaker R :G:/:B: .10 .20
223 Third Path Iconoclast U :B:/:R: 1.00 2.00
224 Tocasia, Dig Site Mentor R :G:/:W:/:B: .07 .15
225 Urza, Lord Protector M :W:/:B: 7.50 15.00
226 Urza, Prince of Kroog R :W:/:B: .25 .50
227 Yotian Dissident U :G:/:W: .05 .10
228 Yotian Tactician U :W:/:B: .05 .10
229 Bladecoil Serpent M .20 .40
230 Clay Champion M .20 .40
231 Aeronaut's Wings C .05 .10
232 Argivian Avenger U .05 .10
233 Cityscape Leveler M 10.00 20.00
234 Energy Refractor C .10 .20
235 Goblin Firebomb C .05 .10
236 Levitating Statue U .05 .10
237 Liberator, Urza's Battlethopter R 1.25 2.50
238a The Mightstone and Weakstone R 1.50 3.00
239 Mine Worker C .05 .10
240 Portal to Phyrexia M 12.50 25.00
241 Power Plant Worker C .05 .10
242 Reconstructed Thopter U .05 .10
243 Slagstone Refinery U .05 .10
244 Spectrum Sentinel U .06 .12
245 The Stasis Coffin R .10 .20
246 Steel Exemplar U .05 .10
247 The Stone Brain R 1.50 3.00
248 Stone Retrieval Unit C .05 .10
249 Su-Chi Cave Guard U .05 .10
250 Supply Drop C .05 .10
251 Swiftgear Drake C .05 .10
252 Symmetry Matrix U .10 .20
253 Thran Power Suit U .10 .20
254 Thran Spider R .10 .20
255 Tower Worker C .05 .10
256a Argoth, Sanctum of Nature R 1.00 2.00
257 Battlefield Forge R 1.00 2.00
258 Blast Zone R .30 .75
259 Brushland R 1.50 3.00
260 Demolition Field U 1.25 2.50
261 Evolving Wilds C .06 .12
262 Fortified Beachhead R .20 .40
263 Hall of Tagsin R .12 .25
264 Llanowar Wastes R 1.00 2.00
265 Mishra's Foundry R .30 .60
266 Tocasia's Dig Site C .05 .10
267 Underground River R 2.00 4.00
268 Plains C .05 .10
269 Plains C .05 .10
270 Island C .07 .15
271 Island C .06 .12
272 Swamp C .12 .25
273 Swamp C .05 .10
274 Mountain C .07 .15
275 Mountain C .05 .10
276 Forest C .07 .15
277 Forest C .05 .10
278 Plains C .25 .50
279 Plains C .15 .30
280 Island C .30 .60
281 Island C .30 .60
282 Swamp C .30 .75
283 Swamp C .10 .20
284 Mountain C .25 .50
285 Mountain C .25 .50
286 Forest C .20 .40
287 Forest C .25 .50
288 Rescue Retriever R :W: .30 .60
289 Geology Enthusiast R :B: .12 .25
290 Terror Ballista R .12 .25
291 Artificer's Dragon R .12 .25
292 Woodcaller Automaton R .15 .30
293 Teferi, Temporal Pilgrim M :B: 2.50 5.00
294 Saheeli, Filigree Master M :B:/:R: .75 1.50
295 Mishra, Tamer of Mak Fawa R :K:/:R: .12 .25
296 Urza, Prince of Kroog R :W:/:B: .25 .50
297 Battlefield Forge R 1.25 2.50
298 Brushland R 1.50 3.00
299 Llanowar Wastes R 1.25 2.50
300 Underground River R 2.00 4.00
301 In the Trenches M :W: .75 1.50
302 Kayla's Command R :W: .12 .25
303 Kayla's Reconstruction R :W: .25 .50
304 Loran of the Third Path R :W: 5.00 10.00
305 Myrel, Shield of Argive M :W: 12.50 25.00
306 Siege Veteran R :W: .40 .80
307 Soul Partition R :W: 1.25 2.50
308 Tocasia's Welcome R :W: 2.00 4.00
309 Autonomous Assembler R .12 .25
310 Platoon Dispenser M 1.25 2.50
311 Steel Seraph R 1.00 2.00
312 Urza's Sylex M .50 1.00
313 Drafna, Founder of Lat-Nam R :B: .50 1.00
314 Hurkyl, Master Wizard R :B: .40 .80
315 Hurkyl's Final Meditation R :B: .12 .25
316 One with the Multiverse M :B: 4.00 8.00
317 Skystrike Officer R :B: .60 1.25
318 Urza's Command R :B: .15 .30
319 Arcane Proxy M 1.50 3.00
320 Surge Engine M .75 1.50
321 The Temporal Anchor R :B: .20 .40
322 Terisian Mindbreaker R .50 1.00
323 Ashnod, Flesh Mechanist R :K: .20 .40
324 Diabolic Intent R :K: 4.00 8.00
325 Fateful Handoff R :K: .12 .25
326 Gix, Yawgmoth Praetor M :K: 7.50 15.00
327 Gix's Command R :K: .75 1.50
328 Gixian Puppeteer R :K: .60 1.25
329 Hostile Negotiations R :K: .40 .80
330 Misery's Shadow R :K: 1.00 2.00
331 Painful Quandary R :K: .75 1.50
332 Phyrexian Fleshgorger M 3.00 6.00
333 Razorlash Transmogrant R .60 1.25
334 Transmogrant's Crown R .25 .50
335 Brotherhood's End R :R: 2.50 5.00
336 Draconic Destiny M :R: .50 1.00
337 Feldon, Ronom Excavator R :R: .15 .30
338 Mechanized Warfare R :R: .50 1.00
339 Mishra's Command R :R: .12 .25
340 Over the Top R :R: .15 .30
341 Tyrant of Kher Ridges R :R: .20 .40
342 Visions of Phyrexia R :R: .25 .50
343 Skitterbeam Battalion M .75 1.50
344 Awaken the Woods M :G: 10.00 20.00
345 Fade from History R :G: .40 .80
346 Fauna Shaman R :G: 1.25 2.50
347 Gwenna, Eyes of Gaea R :G: 2.00 4.00
348 Teething Wurmlet R :G: .25 .50
349 Titania's Command R :G: .40 .80
350 Perennial Behemoth R .60 1.25
351 Rootwire Amalgam M .50 1.00
352 Simian Simulacrum R .15 .30
353 Deathbloom Ritualist R :K:/:G: .20 .40
354 Hajar, Loyal Bodyguard R :R:/:G: .75 1.50
355 Harbin, Vanguard Aviator R :W:/:B: .15 .30
356 Legions to Ashes R :W:/:K: .20 .40
357 Queen Kayla bin-Kroog R :R:/:W: .12 .25
358 Sarinth Greatwurm M :R:/:G: .75 1.50
359 Tawnos, the Toymaker R :G:/:B: .12 .25
360 Tocasia, Dig Site Mentor R :G:/:W:/:B: .12 .25
361 Bladecoil Serpent M .50 1.00
362 Clay Champion M .60 1.25
363 Cityscape Leveler M 12.50 25.00
364 Liberator, Urza's Battlethopter R 1.25 2.50
365 Portal to Phyrexia M 15.00 30.00
366 The Stasis Coffin R .15 .30
367 The Stone Brain R 1.50 3.00
368 Thran Spider R .20 .40
369 Blast Zone R .75 1.50
370 Fortified Beachhead R .30 .60
371 Hall of Tagsin R .15 .30
372 Mishra's Foundry R .75 1.50
373 Rescue Retriever R :W: .15 .30
374 Geology Enthusiast R :B: .10 .20
375 Terror Ballista R .10 .20
376 Artificer's Dragon R .15 .30
377 Woodcaller Automaton R .12 .25
378 Mishra's Foundry R .30 .60
379 Queen Kayla bin-Kroog R :R:/:W: .07 .15
380 Lay Down Arms U :W: .40 .80
381 Flow of Knowledge U :B: .25 .50
382 Corrupt U :K: .12 .25
383 Sardian Cliffstomper U :R: .12 .25
384 Blanchwood Armor U :G: .15 .30

2022 Magic The Gathering The Brothers' War Tokens

1 Spirit .75 1.50
2 Bear .20 .40
3 Forest Dryad 3.00 6.00
4 Construct .12 .25
5 Construct 1.00 2.00
6 Golem .12 .25
7 Powerstone .20 .40
8 Soldier .15 .30
9 Soldier .20 .40
10 Thopter .15 .30
11 Zombie .15 .30
12 Saheeli, Filigree Master Emblem .12 .25

2022 Magic The Gathering The Brothers' War Commander

1 Mishra, Eminent One M :B:/:K:/:R: .20 .40
2 Urza, Chief Artificer M :W:/:B:/:K: .30 .75
3 Tawnos, Solemn Survivor M :B: .15 .30
4 Ashnod the Uncaring M :B:/:K:/:R: .20 .40
5 Sanwell, Avenger Ace R :W: .07 .15
6 Scholar of New Horizons R :W: 1.25 2.50
7 Glint Raker R :B: .05 .10
8 March of Progress R :B: .15 .30
9 Terisiare's Devastation R :K: .07 .15
10 Wire Surgeons R :K: .07 .15
11 Wreck Hunter R :K: .05 .10
12 Blast-Furnace Hellkite R :R: 1.25 2.50
13 Farid, Enterprising Salvager R :R: .07 .15
14 Hexavus R .07 .15
15 Kayla's Music Box R .05 .10
16 Machine God's Effigy R .75 1.50
17 Scavenged Brawler R .25 .50
18 Smelting Vat R .07 .15
19 Thopter Shop R .12 .25
20 Wondrous Crucible R .40 .80
21 Disciple of Caelus Nin R :W: .20 .40
22 The Brothers' War R :R: 1.00 2.00
23 Sardian Avenger R :R: 1.50 3.00
24 Rootpath Purifier M :G: 7.50 15.00
25 Titania, Nature's Force M :G: 7.50 15.00
26 The Archimandrite R :B:/:R:/:W: .15 .30
27 Staff of Titania R 2.50 5.00
28 Urza's Workshop R 2.50 5.00
29 Plains C .07 .15
30 Plains C .07 .15
31 Island C .05 .10
32 Island C .07 .15
33 Swamp C .05 .10
34 Swamp C .07 .15
35 Mountain C .07 .15
36 Mountain C .05 .10
39 Mishra, Eminent One M :B:/:K:/:R: .20 .40
40 Urza, Chief Artificer M :W:/:B:/:K: .20 .40
41 Disciple of Caelus Nin R :W: .10 .20
42 Tawnos, Solemn Survivor M :B: .15 .30
43 Sardian Avenger R :R: .30 .60
44 Rootpath Purifier M :G: 3.00 6.00
45 Titania, Nature's Force M :G: 3.00 6.00
46 The Archimandrite R :B:/:R:/:W: .10 .20
47 Ashnod the Uncaring M :B:/:K:/:R: .25 .50
48 Mishra, Eminent One M :B:/:K:/:R: .20 .40
49 Urza, Chief Artificer M :W:/:B:/:K: .75 1.50
50 Staff of Titania R .75 1.50
51 Urza's Workshop R .75 1.50
52 Sanwell, Avenger Ace R :W: .15 .30
53 Scholar of New Horizons R :W: .75 1.50
54 Glint Raker R :B: .07 .15
55 March of Progress R :B: .15 .30
56 Terisiare's Devastation R :K: .15 .30
57 Wire Surgeons R :K: .07 .15
58 Wreck Hunter R :K: .07 .15
59 Blast-Furnace Hellkite R :R: .75 1.50
60 Farid, Enterprising Salvager R :R: .10 .20
61 Hexavus R .10 .20
62 Kayla's Music Box R .10 .20
63 Machine God's Effigy R .75 1.50
64 Scavenged Brawler R .30 .75
65 Smelting Vat R .12 .25
66 Thopter Shop R .15 .30
67 Wondrous Crucible R .20 .40
68 Angel of the Ruins R :W: .15 .30
69 Austere Command R :W: .50 1.00
70 Bronze Guardian R :W: .30 .60
71 Digsite Engineer R :W: .07 .15
72 Indomitable Archangel M :W: .15 .30
73 Losheel, Clockwork Scholar R :W: 1.25 2.50
74 Phyrexian Rebirth R :W: .10 .20
75 Swords to Plowshares U :W: .75 1.50
76 Tempered Steel R :W: .25 .50
77 Teshar, Ancestor's Apostle R :W: .12 .25
78 Unbreakable Formation R :W: .12 .25
79 Urza's Ruinous Blast R :W: .15 .30
80 Bident of Thassa R :B: 1.00 2.00
81 Emry, Lurker of the Loch R :B: .40 .80
82 Etherium Sculptor C :B: .30 .60
83 Ethersworn Adjudicator M :B: .20 .40
84 Fact or Fiction U :B: .10 .20
85 Filigree Attendant U :B: .05 .10
86 Master of Etherium R :B: .10 .20
87 Master Transmuter R :B: .30 .60
88 Mnemonic Sphere C :B: .05 .10
89 Muzzio, Visionary Architect M :B: .20 .40
90 One with the Machine R :B: .07 .15
91 Padeem, Consul of Innovation R :B: .75 1.50
92 Preordain C :B: .75 1.50
93 Sai, Master Thopterist R :B: .75 1.50
94 Sharding Sphinx R :B: .07 .15
95 Shimmer Dragon R :B: .30 .60
96 Thirst for Knowledge U :B: .05 .10
97 Thopter Spy Network R :B: .12 .25
98 Thought Monitor R :B: .75 1.50
99 Thoughtcast C :B: .75 1.50
100 Vedalken Humiliator R :B: .07 .15
101 Whirler Rogue U :B: .05 .10
102 Workshop Elders R :B: .05 .10
103 Armix, Filigree Thrasher U :K: .07 .15
104 Executioner's Capsule C :K: .05 .10
105 Fain, the Broker R :K: .12 .25
106 Feed the Swarm C :K: .40 .80
107 Geth, Lord of the Vault M :K: .15 .30
108 Herald of Anguish M :K: .20 .40
109 Marionette Master R :K: .40 .80
110 Noxious Gearhulk M :K: .30 .60
111 Abrade U :R: .50 1.00
112 Audacious Reshapers R :R: .07 .15
113 Blasphemous Act R :R: 1.25 2.50

114 Chaos Warp R :R: .75 1.50
115 Cursed Mirror R :R: 1.50 3.00
116 Faithless Looting C :R: .60 1.25
117 Hellkite Igniter R :R: .07 .15
118 Slobad, Goblin Tinkerer R :R: .07 .15
119 Alela, Artful Provocateur M :W:/:B:/:K: .15 .30
120 Baleful Strix R :B:/:K: 1.50 3.00
121 Bedevil R :K:/:R: .30 .60
122 Brudiclad, Telchor Engineer R :B:/:R: .15 .30
123 Chrome Courier C :W:/:B: .05 .10
124 Despark U :W:/:K: .20 .40
125 Expressive Iteration U :B:/:R: 1.25 2.50
126 Jhoira, Weatherlight Captain M :B:/:R: 1.25 2.50
127 Oni-Cult Anvil U :K:/:R: .10 .20
128 Sharuum the Hegemon R :W:/:B:/:K: .07 .15
129 Silas Renn, Seeker Adept M :B:/:K: .15 .30
130 Sphinx's Revelation M :W:/:B: .20 .40
131 Vindicate R :W:/:K: .25 .50
132 Arcane Signet C .75 1.50
133 Azorius Signet U .25 .50
134 Chief of the Foundry U .10 .20
135 Commander's Sphere C .10 .20
136 Cranial Plating U .15 .30
137 Darksteel Juggernaut R .12 .25
138 Dimir Signet C .30 .60
139 Dreamstone Hedron U .10 .20
140 Etched Champion R .15 .30
141 Fellwar Stone U .30 .75
142 Hedron Archive U .10 .20
143 Ichor Wellspring U .10 .20
144 Idol of Oblivion R .50 1.00
145 Liquimetal Torque U .30 .60
146 Lithoform Engine M 1.50 3.00
147 Metalwork Colossus R .25 .50
148 Mind Stone C .15 .30
149 Mirrorworks R .25 .50
150 Mycosynth Wellspring C .10 .20
151 Myr Battlesphere R .12 .25
152 Nihil Spellbomb C .40 .80
153 Oblivion Stone R .15 .30
154 Orzhov Signet C .25 .50
155 Prophetic Prism C .05 .10
156 Rakdos Signet U .75 1.50
157 Relic of Progenitus U 3.00 6.00
158 Servo Schematic U .07 .15
159 Skullclamp U 2.00 4.00
160 Sol Ring U 1.25 2.50
161 Solemn Simulacrum R .50 1.00
162 Spine of Ish Sah R .10 .20
163 Steel Hellkite R .15 .30
164 Steel Overseer R .75 1.25
165 Strionic Resonator R 1.25 2.50
166 Swiftfoot Boots U .75 1.50
167 Thought Vessel U 2.00 4.00
168 Thran Dynamo U 2.00 4.00
169 Trading Post R .20 .40
170 Traxos, Scourge of Kroog R .07 .15
171 Wayfarer's Bauble C .25 .50
172 Ancient Den C .75 1.50
173 Arcane Sanctum U .12 .25
174 Ash Barrens C .10 .20
175 Azorius Chancery U .10 .20
176 Bojuka Bog C .75 1.50
177 Buried Ruin U .30 .60
178 Command Tower C .50 1.00
179 Crumbling Necropolis U .15 .30
180 Darksteel Citadel U .75 1.50
181 Darkwater Catacombs R .12 .25
182 Dimir Aqueduct U .10 .20
183 Drossforge Bridge C .25 .50
184 Evolving Wilds C .10 .20
185 Exotic Orchard R .15 .30
186 Goldmire Bridge C .10 .20
187 Great Furnace C 1.50 3.00
188 Izzet Boilerworks U .12 .25
189 Mistvault Bridge C .12 .25
190 Myriad Landscape U .12 .25
191 Orzhov Basilica U .10 .20
192 Path of Ancestry C .10 .20
193 Prairie Stream R .12 .25
194 Rakdos Carnarium U .12 .25
195 Razortide Bridge C .15 .30
196 Reliquary Tower U 2.50 5.00
197 River of Tears R .07 .15
198 Seat of the Synod C .75 1.50
199 Shadowblood Ridge R .12 .25
200 Silverbluff Bridge C .25 .50
201 Skycloud Expanse R .10 .20
202 Smoldering Marsh R .20 .40
203 Spire of Industry R .40 .80
204 Sunken Hollow R .20 .40
205 Temple of Deceit R .12 .25
206 Temple of Enlightenment R .12 .25
207 Temple of Epiphany R .12 .25
208 Temple of Malice R .20 .40
209 Temple of Silence R .12 .25
210 Terramorphic Expanse C .15 .30
211 Vault of Whispers C .50 1.00

2022 Magic The Gathering The Brothers' War Commander Tokens

1 Copy .15 .30
2 Eldrazi .15 .30
3 Goat .15 .30
4 Faerie .15 .30
5 Phyrexian Myr .15 .30
6 Thopter .15 .30
7 Inkling .15 .30
8 Construct .15 .30
9 Mishra's Warform .15 .30
10 Myr .15 .30
11 Phyrexian Horror .15 .30
12 Scrap .15 .30
13 Servo .15 .30
14 Elemental .15 .30

2022 Magic The Gathering Transformers PulseCon Exclusives

1 Prowl, Stoic Strategist/Prowl, Pursuit Vehicle M :W: .75 1.50
2 Ratchet M :W: .60 1.25
3 Jetfire M :B: .30 .60
4 Blitzwing M :K: .60 1.25
5 Starscream M :K: .75 1.50
6 Slicer M :R: .75 1.50
7 Arcee M :R:/:W: .60 1.25
8 Blaster M :R:/:G: .30 .60
9 Cyclonus M :B:/:K: .25 .50
10 Flamewar M :K:/:R: .30 .60
11 Goldbug M :W:/:B: .50 1.00
12 Megatron M :R:/:W:/:K: .60 1.25
13 Optimus Prime M :B:/:R:/:W: 1.00 2.00
14 Soundwave M :W:/:B:/:K: .75 1.50
15 Ultra Magnus M :R:/:G:/:W: .30 .60
16 Prowl M :W: 3.00 6.00
17 Ratchet M :W: 3.00 6.00
18 Jetfire M :B: 2.50 5.00
19 Blitzwing M :K: 4.00 8.00
20 Starscream M :K: 6.00 12.00
21 Slicer M :R: 7.50 15.00
22 Blaster M :R:/:G: 2.50 5.00
23 Cyclonus M :B:/:K: 2.00 4.00
24 Flamewar M :K:/:R: 4.00 8.00
25 Goldbug M :W:/:B: 3.00 6.00
26 Megatron M :R:/:W:/:K: 7.50 15.00
27 Optimus Prime M :B:/:R:/:W: 7.50 15.00
28 Soundwave M :W:/:B:/:K: 3.00 6.00
29 Ultra Magnus M :R:/:G:/:W: 3.00 6.00

2022 Magic The Gathering Transformers PulseCon Exclusives Tokens

1 Laserbeak 2.00 4.00
2 Ravage 2.00 4.00

2022 Magic The Gathering Unfinity

1 Standard Procedure M .12 .25
2 Aerialephant C :W: .05 .10
3 Assembled Ensemble U :W: .05 .10
4 Bar Entry C :W: .05 .10
5 _____ Bird Gets the Worm C :W: .05 .10
6 Clowning Around C :W: .05 .10
7 Complaints Clerk U :W: .05 .10
8 Far Out M :W: .07 .15
9 Form of the Approach of the Second Sun R :W: .05 .10
10 Get Your Head in the Game U :W: .05 .10
11 Gobsmacked C :W: .05 .10
12 A Good Day to Pie C :W: .05 .10
13 Hat Trick C :W: .05 .10
14 Impounding Lot-Bot C :W: .05 .10
15 Jetpack Janitor C :W: .05 .10
16 Katerina of Myra's Marvels R :W: .05 .10
17 Knight in _____ Armor U :W: .05 .10
18 Leading Performance C :W: .05 .10
19 Main Event Horizon R :W: .05 .10
20 Now You See Me . . . C :W: .05 .10
21 Park Bleater U :W: .05 .10
22 Park Re-Entry U :W: .05 .10
23 Pin Collection U :W: .05 .10
24 Ride Guide C :W: .05 .10
25 Robo-Piñata C :W: .05 .10
26 Sanguine Sipper C :W: .05 .10
27 Solaflora, Intergalactic Icon R :W: .05 .10
28 Starlight Spectacular R :W: .40 .80
29 Surprise Party R :W: .05 .10
30 Sword-Swallowing Seraph U :W: .05 .10
31 T.A.P.P.E.R. C :W: .05 .10
32 Trapeze Artist U :W: .05 .10
33 Animate Object U :B: .05 .10
34 Astroquarium U :B: .05 .10
35 Baaallerina U :B: .05 .10
36 Bag Check C :B: .05 .10
37 Bamboozling Beeble C :B: .05 .10
38 Bioluminary U :B: .05 .10
39 Blufferfish C :B: .05 .10
40 Boing! C :B: .05 .10
41 Busted! U :B: .05 .10
42 Command Performance C :B: .05 .10
43 Croakid Amphibonaut C :B: .05 .10
44 Decisions, Decisions C :B: .05 .10
45 Exchange of Words R :B: .50 1.00
46 Fluros of Myra's Marvels R :B: .05 .10
47 Focused Funambulist C :B: .05 .10
48 Glitterflitter C :B: .05 .10
49 How Is This a Par Three?! R :B: .05 .10
50 Make a _____ Splash U :B: .05 .10
51 Mobile Clone R :B: .05 .10
52 Monitor Monitor U :B: .05 .10
53 Motion Sickness C :B: .05 .10
54 Octo Opus U :B: .05 .10
55 Phone a Friend M :B: .10 .20
56 Plate Spinning M :B: .07 .15
57 Prize Wall C :B: .05 .10
58 Seasoned Buttoneer C :B: .05 .10
59 Super-Duper Lost C :B: .05 .10
60 Treacherous Trapezist R :B: .05 .10
61 _____ _____ Trespasser U :B: .05 .10
62 Unlawful Entry C :B: .05 .10
63 Vedalken Squirrel-Whacker R :B: .10 .20
64 Wizards of the _____ C :B: .05 .10
65 Animate Graveyard R :K: .05 .10
66 Attempted Murder U :K: .05 .10
67 Black Hole R :K: .07 .15
68 Carnival Carnivore C :K: .05 .10
69 Deadbeat Attendant C :K: .05 .10
70 Discourtesy Clerk U :K: .05 .10
71 Disemvowel C :K: .05 .10
72 Dissatisfied Customer C :K: .05 .10
73 Down for Repairs C :K: .05 .10
74 Exit Through the Grift Shop M :K: .07 .15
75 Gray Merchant of Alphabet U :K: .05 .10
76 Haberthrasher U :K: .05 .10
77 Knife and Death R :K: .05 .10
78 Last Voyage of the _____ U :K: .05 .10
79 Lifetime** Pass Holder R :K: .10 .20
80 Line Cutter C :K: .05 .10
81 Night Shift of the Living Dead U :K: .05 .10
82 Nocturno of Myra's Marvels R :K: .05 .10
83 Photo Op M :K: .07 .15
84 Questionable Cuisine C :K: .05 .10
85 Quick Fixer U :K: .05 .10
86 Rat in the Hat C :K: .05 .10
87 A Real Handful U :K: .05 .10
88 Saw in Half R :K: 3.00 6.00
89 Scampire U :K: .05 .10
90 Scared Stiff C :K: .05 .10
91 Scooch C :K: .05 .10
92 Six-Sided Die C :K: .05 .10
93 Soul Swindler C :K: .05 .10
94 Step Right Up C :K: .05 .10
95 Wolf in _____ Clothing C :K: .05 .10
96 Xenosquirrels C :K: .05 .10
97 Aardwolf's Advantage C :R: .05 .10
98 Amped Up C :R: .05 .10
99 Art Appreciation C :R: .05 .10
100 _____ Balls of Fire U :R: .05 .10
101 Big Winner C :R: .05 .10
102 Carnival Barker R :R: .05 .10
103 Circuits Act C :R: .05 .10
104 Devil K. Nevil R :R: .05 .10
105 Don't Try This at Home R :R: .05 .10
106 Eelectrocute C :R: .05 .10
107 _____ Goblin C :R: .05 .10
108 Goblin Airbrusher U :R: .05 .10
109 Goblin Blastronauts U :R: .05 .10
110 Goblin Cruciverbalist R :R: .05 .10
111 Goblin Girder Gang U :R: .05 .10
112 Ignacio of Myra's Marvels R :R: .05 .10
113 Juggletron U :R: .05 .10
114 Minotaur de Force C :R: .05 .10
115 Non-Human Cannonball C :R: .05 .10
116 Omniclown Colossus/Pie-roclasm R :R: .05 .10
117 One-Clown Band C :R: .05 .10
118 Opening Ceremony M :R: .12 .25
119 Priority Boarding U :R: .05 .10
120 Proficient Pyrodancer U :R: .05 .10
121 Rad Rascal C :R: .05 .10
122 Rock Star C :R: .05 .10
123 Slight Malfunction C :R: .05 .10
124 Ticking Mime Bomb U :R: .05 .10
125 Trigger Happy U :R: .05 .10
126 Vorthos, Steward of Myth M :R: .12 .25
127 Wee Champion C :R: .05 .10
128 Well Done C :R: .05 .10
129 Alpha Guard C :G: .05 .10
130 Atomwheel Acrobats C :G: .05 .10
131 Blorbian Buddy C :G: .05 .10
132 Centaur of Attention R :G: .07 .15
133 Chicken Troupe C :G: .05 .10
134 Clandestine Chameleon U :G: .05 .10
135 Coming Attraction C :G: .05 .10
136 Done for the Day U :G: .05 .10
137 Embiggen C :G: .05 .10
138 Fight the _____ Fight U :G: .05 .10
139 Finishing Move C :G: .05 .10
140 Grabby Tabby C :G: .05 .10
141 Hardy of Myra's Marvels R :G: .05 .10
142 Icing Manipulator U :G: .05 .10
143 An Incident Has Occurred C :G: .05 .10
144 Jermane, Pride of the Circus R :G: .05 .10
145 Killer Cosplay M :G: .10 .20
146 Lineprancers U :G: .05 .10
147 Mistakes Were Made C :G: .05 .10
148 _____-o-saurus C :G: .05 .10
149 Pair o' Dice Lost U :G: .10 .20
150 Petting Zookeeper C :G: .05 .10
151 Pie-Eating Contest U :G: .05 .10
152 Plot Armor C :G: .05 .10
153 Resolute Veggiesaur U :G: .05 .10
154 Sole Performer R :G: .05 .10
155 Spelling Bee R :G: .05 .10
156 Squirrel Squatters U :G: .05 .10
157 Stiltstrider C :G: .05 .10
158 Tchotchke Elemental R :G: .05 .10
159 Tug of War M :G: .07 .15
160 Vegetation Abomination C :G: .05 .10
161 Ambassador Blorpityblorpboop U :G:/:B: .05 .10
162 Angelic Harold U :W:/:B: .05 .10
163 Brims** Barone, Midway Mobster U :W:/:K: .05 .10
164 Captain Rex Nebula R :R:/:W: .05 .10
165 Claire D'Loon, Joy Sculptor R :W:/:B: .05 .10
166 Comet, Stellar Pup M :R:/:W: 2.50 5.00
167 Dee Kay, Finder of the Lost U :B:/:K: .05 .10
168 Grand Marshal Macie M :W:/:K: .12 .25
169 It Came from Planet Glurg M :G:/:B: .12 .25
170 Lila, Hospitality Hostess M :G:/:W: .07 .15
171 Magar of the Magic Strings M :K:/:R: .12 .25
172 Meet and Greet "Sisay" R :R:/:G: .05 .10
173 Monoxa, Midway Manager U :K:/:R: .05 .10
174 The Most Dangerous Gamer R :K:/:G: .07 .15
175 Myra the Magnificent M :B:/:R: .12 .25
176 Pietra, Crafter of Clowns U :R:/:W: .05 .10
177 Roxi, Publicist to the Stars U :B:/:R: .05 .10
178 Space Beleren M :W:/:B: .25 .50
179 The Space Family Goblinson U :R:/:G: .05 .10
180 Spinnerette, Arachnobat U :K:/:G: .05 .10
181 Truss, Chief Engineer R :B:/:K: .05 .10
182 Tusk and Whiskers U :G:/:W: .05 .10
183 Autograph Book U .05 .10
184 Blue Ribbon R .05 .10
185 Celebr-8000 R .12 .25
186 Clown Car R .30 .60
187 D00-DL, Caricaturist R .05 .10
188 Draconian Gate-Bot C .05 .10
189 Greatest Show in the Multiverse M .12 .25
190 Park Map C .05 .10
191 _____ _____ Rocketship U .05 .10
192 Souvenir T-Shirt R .05 .10
193 Strength-Testing Hammer U .10 .20
194 Ticket Turbotubes C .05 .10
195 Ticketomaton C .05 .10
196 Wicker Picker U .05 .10
197 The Big Top U .05 .10
198 Nearby Planet C .05 .10
199 Urza's Fun House R .05 .10
200a Balloon Stand U .05 .10
200b Balloon Stand U .05 .10
200c Balloon Stand U .10 .20
200d Balloon Stand U .12 .25
201a Bounce Chamber U .05 .10
201b Bounce Chamber U .10 .20
201c Bounce Chamber U .05 .10
201d Bounce Chamber U .25 .50
202a Bumper Cars U .07 .15
202b Bumper Cars U .07 .15
202c Bumper Cars U .07 .15
202d Bumper Cars U .07 .15
202e Bumper Cars U .07 .15
202f Bumper Cars U .12 .25
203a Centrifuge R .07 .15
203b Centrifuge R .10 .20
204a Clown Extruder C .05 .10
204b Clown Extruder C .05 .10
204c Clown Extruder C .05 .10
204d Clown Extruder C .07 .15
205a Concession Stand U .10 .20
205b Concession Stand U .05 .10
205c Concession Stand U .07 .15
205d Concession Stand U .07 .15
206a Costume Shop C .07 .15
206b Costume Shop C .05 .10
206c Costume Shop C .05 .10
206d Costume Shop C .07 .15
206e Costume Shop C .05 .10
206f Costume Shop C .05 .10
207a Cover the Spot C .05 .10
207b Cover the Spot C .05 .10
207c Cover the Spot C .05 .10
207d Cover the Spot C .05 .10
208a Dart Throw C .05 .10
208b Dart Throw C .05 .10
208c Dart Throw C .05 .10
208d Dart Throw C .05 .10
209a Drop Tower C .10 .20
209b Drop Tower C .05 .10
209c Drop Tower C .05 .10
209d Drop Tower C .05 .10
209e Drop Tower C .05 .10
209f Drop Tower C .50 1.00
210 Ferris Wheel R .17 .35
211a Foam Weapons Kiosk C .05 .10
211b Foam Weapons Kiosk C .05 .10
211c Foam Weapons Kiosk C .05 .10
211d Foam Weapons Kiosk C .07 .15
212a Fortune Teller C .05 .10
212b Fortune Teller C .07 .15
212c Fortune Teller C .05 .10
212d Fortune Teller C .05 .10
212e Fortune Teller C .10 .20
212f Fortune Teller C .07 .15
213a Gallery of Legends R .07 .15
213b Gallery of Legends R .05 .10
214a Gift Shop R .12 .25
214b Gift Shop R .07 .15
215a Guess Your Fate U .05 .10
215b Guess Your Fate U .05 .10
215c Guess Your Fate U .05 .10
215d Guess Your Fate U .05 .10
216a Hall of Mirrors R .12 .25
216b Hall of Mirrors R .12 .25
217a Haunted House R .12 .25
217b Haunted House R .25 .50
218a Information Booth U .07 .15
218b Information Booth U .07 .15
218c Information Booth U .12 .25
218d Information Booth U .25 .50
219a Kiddie Coaster C .05 .10
219b Kiddie Coaster C .05 .10
219c Kiddie Coaster C .07 .15
219d Kiddie Coaster C .05 .10
219e Kiddie Coaster C .05 .10
219f Kiddie Coaster C .15 .30
220a Log Flume R .07 .15
220b Log Flume R .07 .15
221a Memory Test R .07 .15
221b Memory Test R .05 .10
222a Merry-Go-Round R .07 .15
222b Merry-Go-Round R .15 .30
223a Pick-a-Beeble C .05 .10
223b Pick-a-Beeble C .05 .10
223c Pick-a-Beeble C .07 .15
223d Pick-a-Beeble C .17 .35
223e Pick-a-Beeble C .05 .10
223f Pick-a-Beeble C .10 .20
224a Push Your Luck R .07 .15
224b Push Your Luck R .10 .20
225a Roller Coaster U .07 .15
225b Roller Coaster U .07 .15
225c Roller Coaster U .07 .15
225d Roller Coaster U .07 .15
226a Scavenger Hunt U .07 .15
226b Scavenger Hunt U .07 .15
226c Scavenger Hunt U .07 .15
226d Scavenger Hunt U .05 .10
226e Scavenger Hunt U .05 .10
226f Scavenger Hunt U .07 .15
227a Spinny Ride C .05 .10
227b Spinny Ride C .07 .15
227c Spinny Ride C .05 .10
227d Spinny Ride C .05 .10
227e Spinny Ride C .07 .15
227f Spinny Ride C .10 .20
228a Squirrel Stack U .07 .15
228b Squirrel Stack U .07 .15
228c Squirrel Stack U .07 .15
228d Squirrel Stack U .05 .10
228e Squirrel Stack U .07 .15
228f Squirrel Stack U .10 .20
229a Storybook Ride R .25 .50
229b Storybook Ride R .17 .35
230a The Superlatorium U .05 .10
230b The Superlatorium U .05 .10
230c The Superlatorium U .05 .10
230d The Superlatorium U .05 .10
230e The Superlatorium U .07 .15
230f The Superlatorium U .07 .15
231a Swinging Ship R .10 .20
231b Swinging Ship R .15 .30
232a Trash Bin U .07 .15
232b Trash Bin U .07 .15
232c Trash Bin U .05 .10
232d Trash Bin U .25 .50
233a Trivia Contest U .05 .10
233b Trivia Contest U .07 .15
233c Trivia Contest U .05 .10
233d Trivia Contest U .05 .10
233e Trivia Contest U .05 .10
233f Trivia Contest U .07 .15
234a Tunnel of Love R .12 .25
234b Tunnel of Love R .17 .35
235 Plains C .25 .50
236 Island C .30 .75

237 Swamp C .60 1.25
238 Mountain C .60 1.25
239 Forest C .40 .80
240 Plains C .75 1.50
241 Island C .75 1.50
242 Swamp C 1.25 2.50
243 Mountain C 1.25 2.50
244 Forest C 1.25 2.50
245 Katerina of Myra's Marvels R :W: .12 .25
246 Solaflora, Intergalactic Icon R :W: .10 .20
247 Fluros of Myra's Marvels R :B: .10 .20
248 Nocturno of Myra's Marvels R :K: .07 .15
249 Devil K. Nevil R :R: .07 .15
250 Ignacio of Myra's Marvels R :R: .07 .15
251 Vorthos, Steward of Myth M :R: .12 .25
252 Hardy of Myra's Marvels R :G: .07 .15
253 Jermane, Pride of the Circus R :G: .07 .15
254 Ambassador Blorpityblorpboop U :G:/B: .07 .15
255 Angelic Harold U :W:/B: .05 .10
256 Brims" Barone, Midway Mobster U :W:/:K: .05 .10
257 Captain Rex Nebula R :R:/:W: .12 .25
258 Claire D'Loon, Joy Sculptor R :W:/:B: .07 .15
259 Dee Kay, Finder of the Lost U :B:/:K: .07 .15
260 Grand Marshal Macie M :W:/:K: .17 .35
261 It Came from Planet Glurg M :G:/:B: .15 .30
262 Lila, Hospitality Hostess M :G:/:W: .12 .25
263 Magar of the Magic Strings M :K:/:R: .30 .60
264 Meet and Greet "Sisay" R :R:/:G: .07 .15
265 Monoxa, Midway Manager U :K:/:R: .05 .10
266 The Most Dangerous Gamer R :K:/:G: .10 .20
267 Myra the Magnificent M :B:/:R: .15 .30
268 Pietra, Crafter of Clowns U :R:/:W: .05 .10
269 Roxi, Publicist to the Stars U :B:/:R: .05 .10
270 The Space Family Goblinson U :R:/:G: .07 .15
271 Spinnerette, Arachnobat U :K:/:G: .05 .10
272 Truss, Chief Engineer R :B:/:K: .07 .15
273 Tusk and Whiskers U :G:/:W: .05 .10
274 D00-DL, Caricaturist R .10 .20
275 Comet, Stellar Pup M :R:/:W: 2.00 4.00
276 Space Beleren M :W:/:B: .30 .60
277 Hallowed Fountain R 17.50 35.00
278 Watery Grave R 20.00 40.00
279 Blood Crypt R 20.00 40.00
280 Stomping Ground R 12.50 25.00
281 Temple Garden R 12.50 25.00
282 Godless Shrine R 12.50 25.00
283 Steam Vents R 20.00 40.00
284 Overgrown Tomb R 12.50 25.00
285 Sacred Foundry R 15.00 30.00
286 Breeding Pool R 17.50 35.00
287 Standard Procedure M .20 .40
288 Aerialephant C :W: .15 .30
289 Assembled Ensemble U :W: .17 .35
290 Bar Entry C :W: .15 .30
291 ____ Bird Gets the Worm C :W: .12 .25
292 Clowning Around C :W: 1.50 3.00
293 Complaints Clerk U :W: 1.25 2.50
294 Far Out M :W: .20 .40
295 Form of the Approach
of the Second Sun R :W: .12 .25
296 Get Your Head in the Game U :W: .20 .40
297 Gobsmacked C :W: .15 .30
298 A Good Day to Pie C :W: .12 .25
299 Hat Trick C :W: .12 .25
300 Impounding Lot-Bot C :W: .17 .35
301 Jetpack Janitor C :W: .12 .25
302 Katerina of Myra's Marvels R :W: .12 .25
303 Knight in ____ Armor U :W: .20 .40
304 Leading Performance C :W: .15 .30
305 Main Event Horizon R :W: .07 .15
306 Now You See Me . . . C :W: .17 .35
307 Park Bleater U :W: .75 1.50
308 Park Re-Entry U :W: .15 .30
309 Pin Collection U :W: .75 1.50
310 Ride Guide C :W: .17 .35
311 Robo-Piñata C :W: .15 .30
312 Sanguine Sipper C :W: .15 .30
313 Solaflora, Intergalactic Icon R :W: .10 .20
314 Starlight Spectacular R :W: 2.50 5.00
315 Surprise Party R :W: .07 .15
316 Sword-Swallowing Seraph U :W: .60 1.25
317 T.A.P.P.E.R. C :W: .17 .35
318 Trapeze Artist U :W: .25 .50
319 Animate Object U :B: .25 .50
320 Astroquarium U :B: .25 .50
321 Baaallerina U :B: .30 .60
322 Bag Check C :B: .15 .30
323 Bamboozling Beeble C :B: 1.25 2.50
324 Bioluminary U :B: .60 1.25
325 Blufferfish C :B: .12 .25
326 Boing! C :B: .75 1.50
327 Busted! U :B: .30 .75
328 Command Performance C :B: 4.00 8.00
329 Croakid Amphibonaut C :B: .12 .25
330 Decisions, Decisions C :B: .12 .25
331 Exchange of Words R :B: 1.00 2.00
332 Fluros of Myra's Marvels R :B: .10 .20
333 Focused Funambulist C :B: .10 .20
334 Glitterflitter C :B: .25 .50
335 How Is This a Par Three?! R :B: .12 .25
336 Make a ____ Splash U :B: .17 .35
337 Mobile Clone R :B: .40 .80
338 Monitor Monitor U :B: 4.00 8.00
339 Motion Sickness C :B: .17 .35
340 Octo Opus U :B: .20 .40
341 Phone a Friend M :B: .15 .30
342 Plate Spinning M :B: .12 .25
343 Prize Wall C :B: .17 .35
344 Seasoned Buttoneer C :B: .75 1.50
345 Carnival Carnivore C :K: .15 .30
346 Treacherous Trapezist R :B: .07 .15
347 ____ Trespasser U :B: .25 .50
348 Unlawful Entry C :B: .10 .20
349 Vedalken Squirrel-Whacker R :B: .17 .35
350 Wizards of the ____ C :B: .17 .35
351 Animate Graveyard R :K: .10 .20
352 Attempted Murder U :K: 3.00 6.00
353 Black Hole R :K: .12 .25
354 Carnival Carnivore C :K: .15 .30
355 Deadbeat Attendant C :K: 7.50 15.00
356 Discourtesy Clerk U :K: 5.00 10.00
357 Disemvowel C :K: .12 .25
358 Dissatisfied Customer C :K: .15 .30
359 Down for Repairs C :K: .15 .30
360 Exit Through the Grift Shop M :K: .15 .30
361 Gray Merchant of Alphabet U :K: 1.50 3.00
362 Haberthrasher U :K: .20 .40
363 Knife and Death R :K: .07 .15
364 Last Voyage of the ____ U :K: .60 1.25
365 Lifetime" Pass Holder R :K: .60 1.25
366 Line Cutter C :K: 1.00 2.00
367 Night Shift of the Living Dead U :K: 2.00 4.00
368 Nocturno of Myra's Marvels R :K: .07 .15
369 Photo Op M :K: .17 .35
370 Questionable Cuisine C :K: .12 .25
371 Quick Fixer U :K: 5.00 10.00
372 Rat in the Hat C :K: .15 .30
373 A Real Handful U :K: .25 .50
374 Saw in Half R :K: 7.50 15.00
375 Scampire U :K: .40 .80
376 Scared Stiff C :K: .12 .25
377 Scooch C :K: .12 .25
378 Six-Sided Die C :K: .75 1.50
379 Soul Swindler C :K: .50 1.00
380 Step Right Up C :K: .75 1.50
381 Wolf in ____ Clothing C :K: .07 .15
382 Xenosquirrels C :K: 1.00 2.00
383 Aardwolf's Advantage C :R: .12 .25
384 Amped Up C :R: .10 .20
385 Art Appreciation C :R: .10 .20
386 ____ Balls of Fire U :R: .25 .50
387 Big Winner C :R: .12 .25
388 Carnival Barker R :R: .12 .25
389 Circuits Act C :R: .75 1.50
390 Devil K. Nevil R :R: .07 .15
391 Don't Try This at Home R :R: .07 .15
392 Electrocute C :R: .20 .40
393 ____ Goblin C :R: 2.50 5.00
394 Goblin Airbrusher U :R: .40 .80
395 Goblin Blastronauts U :R: .60 1.25
396 Goblin Cruciverbalist R :R: .07 .15
397 Goblin Girder Gang U :R: .40 .80
398 Ignacio of Myra's Marvels R :R: .10 .20
399 Juggletron U :R: .30 .75
400 Minotaur de Force C :R: .12 .25
401 Non-Human Cannonball C :R: .15 .30
402 Omniclown Colossus/Pie-roclasm R :R: .12 .25
403 One-Clown Band C :R: .15 .30
404 Opening Ceremony M :R: .30 .60
405 Priority Boarding U :R: 2.50 5.00
406 Proficient Pyrodancer U :R: .20 .40
407 Rad Rascal C :R: .30 .60
408 Rock Star C :R: .15 .30
409 Slight Malfunction C :R: 1.00 2.00
410 Ticking Mime Bomb U :R: .25 .50
411 Trigger Happy U :R: 1.00 2.00
412 Vorthos, Steward of Myth M :R: .60 1.25
413 Wee Champion C :R: .15 .30
414 Well Done C :R: .15 .30
415 Alpha Guard C :G: .12 .25
416 Atomwheel Acrobats C :G: .30 .75
417 Blorbian Buddy C :G: .20 .40
418 Centaur of Attention R :G: .15 .30
419 Chicken Troupe C :G: .15 .30
420 Clandestine Chameleon U :G: 1.25 2.50
421 Coming Attraction C :G: 1.00 2.00
422 Done for the Day U :G: .75 1.50
423 Embiggen C :G: 3.00 6.00
424 Fight the ____ Fight U :G: .30 .60
425 Finishing Move C :G: .17 .35
426 Grabby Tabby C :G: .15 .30
427 Hardy of Myra's Marvels R :G: .07 .15
428 Icing Manipulator U :G: .40 .80
429 An Incident Has Occurred C :G: .12 .25
430 Jermane, Pride of the Circus R :G: .10 .20
431 Killer Cosplay M :G: .20 .40
432 Lineprancers U :G: .50 1.00
433 Mistakes Were Made C :G: .15 .30
434 ____-o-saurus C :G: .17 .35
435 Pair o' Dice Lost U :G: 7.50 15.00
436 Petting Zookeeper C :G: 1.00 2.00
437 Pie-Eating Contest U :G: .25 .50
438 Plot Armor C :G: .12 .25
439 Resolute Veggiesaur U :G: 2.00 4.00
440 Sole Performer R :G: .12 .25
441 Spelling Bee R :G: .07 .15
442 Squirrel Squatters U :G: 2.50 5.00
443 Stiltstrider C :G: .12 .25
444 Tchotchke Elemental R :G: .07 .15
445 Tug of War M :G: .12 .25
446 Vegetation Abomination C :G: .17 .35
447 Ambassador Blorpityblorpboop U :G:/B: .75 1.50
448 Angelic Harold U :W:/:B: .25 .50
449 Brims" Barone, Midway Mobster U :W:/:K: .20 .40
450 Captain Rex Nebula R :R:/:W: .12 .25
451 Claire D'Loon, Joy Sculptor R :W:/:B: .15 .30
452 Comet, Stellar Pup M :R:/:W: 4.00 8.00
453 Dee Kay, Finder of the Lost U :B:/:K: 1.00 2.00
454 Grand Marshal Macie M :W:/:K: .15 .30
455 It Came from Planet Glurg M :G:/:B: .25 .50
456 Lila, Hospitality Hostess M :G:/:W: .17 .35
457 Magar of the Magic Strings M :K:/:R: 1.25 2.50
458 Meet and Greet "Sisay" R :R:/:G: .07 .15
459 Monoxa, Midway Manager U :K:/:R: 1.25 2.50
460 The Most Dangerous Gamer R :K:/:G: .30 .75
461 Myra the Magnificent M :B:/:R: .75 1.50
462 Pietra, Crafter of Clowns U :R:/:W: .30 .75
463 Roxi, Publicist to the Stars U :B:/:R: .25 .50
464 Space Beleren M :W:/:B: 1.00 2.00
465 The Space Family Goblinson U :R:/:G: .75 1.50
466 Spinnerette, Arachnobat U :K:/:G: .75 1.50
467 Truss, Chief Engineer R :B:/:K: .07 .15
468 Tusk and Whiskers U :G:/:W: .40 .80
469 Autograph Book U 3.00 6.00
470 Blue Ribbon R .10 .20
471 Celebr-8000 R .25 .50
472 Clown Car R 1.25 2.50
473 D00-DL, Caricaturist R .07 .15
474 Draconian Gate-Bot C .75 1.50
475 Greatest Show in the Multiverse M .20 .40
476 Park Map C .30 .75
477 ____ Rocketship U .30 .75
478 Souvenir T-Shirt R .07 .15
479 Strength-Testing Hammer U 6.00 12.00
480 Ticket Turbotubes C .25 .50
481 Ticketomaton C .15 .30
482 Wicker Picker U 2.50 5.00
483 The Big Top U 1.00 2.00
484 Nearby Planet C 1.25 2.50
485 Urza's Fun House R .25 .50
486 Plains C .75 1.50
487 Island C 1.25 2.50
488 Swamp C 1.00 2.00
489 Mountain C 1.25 2.50
490 Forest C .75 1.50
491 Plains C 4.00 8.00
492 Island C 4.00 8.00
493 Swamp C 4.00 8.00
494 Mountain C 5.00 10.00
495 Forest C 4.00 8.00
496 Katerina of Myra's Marvels R :W: .12 .25
497 Solaflora, Intergalactic Icon R :W: .10 .20
498 Fluros of Myra's Marvels R :B: .07 .15
499 Nocturno of Myra's Marvels R :K: .10 .20
500 Devil K. Nevil R :R: .12 .25
501 Ignacio of Myra's Marvels R :R: .12 .25
502 Vorthos, Steward of Myth M :R: .30 .75
503 Hardy of Myra's Marvels R :G: .10 .20
504 Jermane, Pride of the Circus R :G: .10 .20
505 Ambassador Blorpityblorpboop U :G:/B: .07 .15
506 Angelic Harold U :W:/:B: .07 .15
507 Brims" Barone, Midway Mobster U :W:/:K: .07 .15
508 Captain Rex Nebula R :R:/:W: .12 .25
509 Claire D'Loon, Joy Sculptor R :W:/:B: .15 .30
510 Dee Kay, Finder of the Lost U :B:/:K: .12 .25
511 Grand Marshal Macie M :W:/:K: .25 .50
512 It Came from Planet Glurg M :G:/:B: .15 .30
513 Lila, Hospitality Hostess M :G:/:W: .12 .25
514 Magar of the Magic Strings M :K:/:R: 1.25 2.50
515 Meet and Greet "Sisay" R :R:/:G: .10 .20
516 Monoxa, Midway Manager U :K:/:R: .10 .20
517 The Most Dangerous Gamer R :K:/:G: .50 1.00
518 Myra the Magnificent M :B:/:R: 1.50 3.00
519 Pietra, Crafter of Clowns U :R:/:W: .07 .15
520 Roxi, Publicist to the Stars U :B:/:R: .07 .15
521 The Space Family Goblinson U :R:/:G: .12 .25
522 Spinnerette, Arachnobat U :K:/:G: .10 .20
523 Truss, Chief Engineer R :B:/:K: .07 .15
524 Tusk and Whiskers U :G:/:W: .07 .15
525 D00-DL, Caricaturist R .10 .20
526 Comet, Stellar Pup M :R:/:W: 5.00 10.00
527 Space Beleren M :W:/:B: 1.25 2.50
528 Hallowed Fountain R 75.00 150.00
529 Watery Grave R 75.00 150.00
530 Blood Crypt R 75.00 150.00
531 Stomping Ground R 60.00 125.00
532 Temple Garden R 50.00 100.00
533 Godless Shrine R 75.00 150.00
534 Steam Vents R 100.00 200.00
535 Overgrown Tomb R 60.00 125.00
536 Sacred Foundry R 75.00 150.00
537 Breeding Pool R 75.00 150.00
538 Water Gun Balloon Game R .07 .15

2022 Magic The Gathering Unfinity Sticker Sheets

1 Eldrazi Guacamole Tightrope .25 .50
2 Trendy Circus Pirate .12 .25
3 Night Brushwagg Ringmaster .12 .25
4 Urza's Dark Cannonball .12 .25
5 Misunderstood Trapeze Elf .25 .50
6 Zombie Cheese Magician .10 .20
7 Carnival Elephant Meteor .12 .25
8 Happy Dead Squirrel .12 .25
9 Slimy Burrito Illusion .12 .25
10 Spooky Clown Mox .10 .20
11 Mystic Doom Sandwich .10 .20
12 Narrow-Minded Baloney Fireworks .20 .40
13 Unsanctioned Ancient Juggler .25 .50
14 Deep-Fried Plague Myr .12 .25
15 Contortionist Otter Storm .12 .25
16 Sticky Kavu Daredevil .12 .25
17 Goblin Coward Parade .10 .20
18 Phyrexian Midway Bamboozle .30 .60
19 Eternal Acrobat Toast .12 .25
20 Jetpack Death Seltzer .10 .20
21 Demonic Tourist Laser .12 .25
22 Cursed Firebreathing Yogurt .10 .20
23 Ancestral Hot Dog Minotaur .25 .50
24 Familiar Beeble Mascot .12 .25
25 Giant Mana Cake .10 .20
26 Snazzy Aether Homunculus .12 .25
27 Squid Fire Knight .10 .20
28 Cool Fluffy Loxodon .12 .25
29 Space Fungus Snickerdoodle .12 .25
30 Playable Delusionary Hydra .30 .60
31 Wrinkly Monkey Shenanigans .10 .20
32 Geek Lotus Warrior .10 .20
33 Primal Elder Kitty .10 .20
34 Sassy Gremlin Blood .12 .25
35 Yawgmoth Merfolk Soul .12 .25
36 Unassuming Gelatinous Serpent .25 .50
37 Squishy Sphinx Ninja .10 .20
38 Unique Charmed Pants .10 .20
39 Unhinged Beast Hunt .10 .20
40 Wild Ogre Bupkis .10 .20
41 Notorious Sliver War .12 .25
42 Weird Angel Flame .12 .25
43 Vampire Champion Fury .12 .25
44 Trained Blessed Mind .25 .50
45 Unglued Pea-Brained Dinosaur .25 .50
46 Elemental Time Flamingo .12 .25
47 Unstable Robot Dragon .10 .20
48 Werewolf Lightning Mage .10 .20

2022 Magic The Gathering Unfinity Tokens

1 Cat .40 .80
2 Clown Robot .07 .15
3 Clown Robot .07 .15
4 Contortionist/Contortionist .07 .15
5 Storm Crow .07 .15
6 Zombie Employee .10 .20
7 Balloon .10 .20
8 Squirrel .20 .40
9 Teddy Bear .07 .15
10 Food .10 .20
11 Food .10 .20
12 Treasure .07 .15
13 Treasure .07 .15
14 Ticket Bucket-Bot .07 .15

2022 Magic The Gathering Warhammer 40,000

1 Szarekh, the Silent King M :K: .40 .80
2 Abaddon the Despoiler M :B:/:K:/:R: 1.00 2.00
3 Inquisitor Greyfax M :W:/:B:/:K: .50 1.00
4 The Swarmlord M :G:/:B:/:R: .25 .50
5 Imotekh the Stormlord M :K: 2.00 4.00
6 Be'lakor, the Dark Master M :B:/:K:/:R: 4.00 8.00
7 Magus Lucea Kane M :G:/:B:/:R: 1.50 3.00
8 Marneus Calgar M :W:/:B:/:K: 4.00 8.00
9 And They Shall Know No Fear U :W: 4.00 8.00
10 Celestine, the Living Saint R :W: 3.00 6.00
11 Defenders of Humanity R :W: .10 .20
12 For the Emperor! R :W: .10 .20
13 Grey Knight Paragon U :W: .10 .20
14 Space Marine Devastator R :W: .15 .30
15 Space Marine Scout U :W: .07 .15
16 Thunderwolf Cavalry U :W: .05 .10
17 Triumph of Saint Katherine R :W: 1.50 3.00
18 Ultramarines Honour Guard R :W: .15 .30
19 Vexilus Praetor R :W: 1.50 3.00
20 Zephyrim R :W: .07 .15
21 Genestealer Locus U :B: .05 .10
22 Genestealer Patriarch R :B: .07 .15
23 Heralds of Tzeentch U :B: .10 .20
24 Lord of Change R :B: .25 .50
25 Sicarian Infiltrator U :B: .75 1.50
26 Sister of Silence R :B: .15 .30
27 Vanguard Suppressor R :B: .12 .25
28 Anrakyr the Traveller R :K: .15 .30
29 Arco-Flagellant R :K: .05 .10
30 Biotransference R :K: 1.50 3.00
31 Blight Grenade R :K: .07 .15
32 Chronomancer R :K: .12 .25
33 Cryptek R :K: .07 .15
34 Flayed One U :K: .05 .10
35 Great Unclean One R :K: .40 .80
36 Hexmark Destroyer U :K: .07 .15
37 Illuminor Szeras R :K: .30 .60
38 Lokhust Heavy Destroyer R :K: .07 .15
39 Lychguard R :K: .07 .15
40 Mandate of Abaddon R :K: .25 .50
41 Mortarion, Daemon Primarch R :K: .10 .20
42 Necron Deathmark R :K: .40 .80
43 Necron Overlord R :K: .07 .15
44 Nurgle's Conscription R :K: .10 .20
45 Nurgle's Rot U :K: .07 .15
46 Out of the Tombs R :K: .75 1.50
47 Plague Drone R :K: .15 .30
48 Plasmancer U :K: .07 .15
49 Poxwalkers R :K: .50 1.00
50 Primaris Eliminator R :K: .10 .20
51 Psychomancer U :K: .10 .20
52 Royal Warden R :K: .10 .20
53 Sanguinary Priest U :K: .25 .50
54 Sautekh Immortal U :K: .05 .10
55 Shard of the Nightbringer R :K: .15 .30
56 Shard of the Void Dragon R :K: .10 .20
57 Skorpekh Destroyer U :K: .05 .10
58 Skorpekh Lord R :K: .25 .50
59 Sloppity Bilepiper R :K: .10 .20
60 Tallyman of Nurgle R :K: .10 .20
61 Technomancer R :K: .07 .15
62 Their Name Is Death R :K: 1.00 2.00
63 Their Number Is Legion R :K: .07 .15
64 Tomb Blade R :K: .07 .15
65 Trazyn the Infinite R :K: .15 .30
66 Triarch Praetorian U :K: .15 .30
67 Triarch Stalker R :K: .07 .15
68 Venomcrawler R :K: .10 .20
69 The War in Heaven R :K: .12 .25
70 Acolyte Hybrid U :R: .05 .10
71 Aspiring Champion R :R: .10 .20
72 Bloodcrusher of Khorne U :R: .10 .20
73 Bloodthirster R :R: 4.00 8.00
74 Chaos Terminator Lord U :R: .07 .15
75 Dark Apostle R :R: .07 .15
76 Exocrine R :R: .15 .30
77 Herald of Slaanesh U :R: .50 1.00
78 Keeper of Secrets R :R: 2.00 4.00
79 Khârn the Betrayer R :R: .15 .30
80 Knight Rampager R :R: .07 .15
81 Let the Galaxy Burn R :R: .15 .30
82 Noise Marine U :R: .10 .20
83 The Red Terror R :R: 2.50 5.00
84 Screamer-Killer R :R: .07 .15
85 Seeker of Slaanesh U :R: .07 .15
86 Aberrant U :G: .10 .20
87 Biophagus R :G: 3.00 6.00
88 Bone Sabres R :G: .75 1.50
89 Broodlord R :G: .07 .15
90 Clamavus R :G: .15 .30
91 Haruspex R :G: .07 .15
92 Hierophant Bio-Titan R :G: .10 .20
93 Hormagaunt Horde R :G: .10 .20
94 Lictor R :G: .05 .10
95 Nexos R :G: .20 .40
96 Old One Eye R :G: .75 1.50
97 Purestrain Genestealer U :G: .05 .10
98 Sporocyst R :G: .30 .60
99 Termagant Swarm R :G: .15 .30
100 Tervigon R :G: .15 .30
101 Toxicrene R :G: .10 .20
102 Tyranid Invasion U :G: .05 .10
103 Tyrant Guard R :G: .12 .25
104 Assault Intercessor R :W:/:K: .15 .30
105 Atalan Jackal R :R:/:G: .25 .50
106 Belisarius Cawl R :W:/:B: .07 .15
107 Birth of the Imperium R :W:/:B:/:K: 4.00 8.00
108 Blood for the Blood God! R :K:/:R: 2.00 4.00
109 Callidus Assassin R :B:/:K: .12 .25
110 Chaos Defiler R :K:/:R: 2.00 4.00
111 Chaos Mutation R :B:/:R: .07 .15
112 Commissar Severina Raine R :W:/:K: 1.25 2.50
113 Company Commander R :W:/:K: .12 .25
114 Cybernetica Datasmith R :B:/:K: .07 .15
115 Deathleaper, Terror Weapon R :R:/:G: .12 .25
116 Deny the Witch U :W:/:B:/:K: .10 .20
117 Drach'Nyen R :K:/:R: .10 .20
118 Epistolary Librarian R :W:/:B: .10 .20
119 Exalted Flamer of Tzeentch R :B:/:R: 4.00 8.00
120 Exterminatus R :W:/:K: .10 .20
121 The First Tyrannic War R :G:/:B:/:R: .25 .50
122 The Flesh Is Weak R :W:/:B:/:K: .10 .20
123 Gargoyle Flock R :G:/:B: .07 .15
124 Ghyrson Starn, Kelermorph R :B:/:R: 2.50 5.00

125 Helbrute R :K:/:R: .07 .15
126 The Horus Heresy R :B:/:K:/:R: 3.00 6.00
127 Inquisitor Eisenhorn R :B:/:K: .07 .15
128 Kill! Maim! Burn! R :K:/:R: .10 .20
129 The Lost and the Damned U :B:/:R: .12 .25
130 Lucius the Eternal R :K:/:R: .07 .15
131 Magnus the Red R :B:/:R: .75 1.50
132 Malanthrope R :G:/:B: .12 .25
133 Mawloc R :R:/:G: 1.50 3.00
134 Mutalith Vortex Beast R :B:/:R: .10 .20
135 Neyam Shai Murad R :W:/:K: .07 .15
136 Pink Horror R :B:/:R: .25 .50
137 Primaris Chaplain U :W:/:K: .07 .15
138 Ravener R :G:/:B: .07 .15
139 The Ruinous Powers R :K:/:R: .25 .50
140 Shadow in the Warp R :R:/:G: 6.00 12.00
141 Sister Hospitaller R :W:/:K: .12 .25
142 Sister Repentia R :W:/:K: .07 .15
143 Trygon Prime U :G:/:B: .07 .15
144 Tyranid Harridan R :G:/:B: .07 .15
145 Tyranid Prime R :G:/:B: .15 .30
146 Tzaangor Shaman R :B:/:R: .07 .15
147 Venomthrope U :G:/:B: .10 .20
148 Winged Hive Tyrant R :B:/:R: .10 .20
149 Zoanthrope R :B:/:R: .10 .20
150 Canoptek Scarab Swarm R 1.25 2.50
151 Canoptek Spyder R 1.00 2.00
152 Canoptek Tomb Sentinel R .25 .50
153 Canoptek Wraith R 4.00 8.00
154 Convergence of Dominion R .15 .30
155 Cryptothrall R 1.25 2.50
156 Ghost Ark R .10 .20
157 The Golden Throne R 1.25 2.50
158 Goliath Truck U .07 .15
159 Inquisitorial Rosette R .15 .30
160 Knight Paladin R .40 .80
161 Necron Monolith R .10 .20
162 Night Scythe U .07 .15
163 Reaver Titan R 1.25 2.50
164 Redemptor Dreadnought R .07 .15
165 Resurrection Orb R 1.50 3.00
166 Sceptre of Eternal Glory R 4.00 8.00
167 Thunderhawk Gunship R .75 1.50
168 Tomb Fortress R .60 1.25
169 Imotekh the Stormlord M :K: .30 .60
170 Szarekh, the Silent King M :K: .12 .25
171 Abaddon the Despoiler M :B:/:K:/:R: .20 .40
172 Be'lakor, the Dark Master M :B:/:K:/:R: .20 .40
173 Inquisitor Greyfax M :W:/:B:/:K: .15 .30
174 Magus Lucea Kane M :G:/:B:/:R: .25 .50
175 Marneus Calgar M :W:/:B:/:K: .30 .60
176 The Swarmlord M :G:/:B:/:R: .15 .30
177 Szarekh, the Silent King M :K: .30 .60
178 Abaddon the Despoiler M :B:/:K:/:R: .60 1.25
179 Inquisitor Greyfax M :W:/:B:/:K: 1.00 2.00
180 The Swarmlord M :G:/:B:/:R: .25 .50
181 Fabricate R :B: 2.50 5.00
182 Bastion Protector R :W: .30 .60
183 Collective Effort R :W: .12 .25
184 Deploy to the Front R :W: .12 .25
185 Entrapment Maneuver R :W: .12 .25
186 Fell the Mighty R :W: .07 .15
187 Hour of Reckoning R :W: .10 .20
188 Launch the Fleet R :W: .12 .25
189 Martial Coup R :W: .12 .25
190 Swords to Plowshares U :W: .75 1.50
191 Aetherize U :B: .30 .60
192 Brainstorm C :B: 1.00 2.00
193 Reconnaissance Mission U :B: .25 .50
194 Beacon of Unrest R :K: .12 .25
195 Bile Blight U :K: .07 .15
196 Dark Ritual C :K: 1.00 2.00
197 Darkness C :K: 1.25 2.50
198 Decree of Pain R :K: .25 .50
199 Defile U :K: .25 .50
200 Dread Return U :K: .15 .30
201 Go for the Throat C :K: .30 .75
202 Living Death R :K: 1.25 2.50
203 Mutilate R :K: .30 .75
204 Blasphemous Act R :R: 1.25 2.50
205 Chaos Warp R :R: .75 1.50
206 Past in Flames M :R: .30 .75
207 Reverberate R :R: .60 1.25
208 Starstorm R :R: .10 .20
209 Warstorm Surge R :R: .30 .75
210 Abundance R :G: .15 .30
211 Cultivate C :G: .75 1.50
212 Death's Presence R :G: .10 .20
213 Explore C :G: .12 .25
214 Farseek C :G: 1.25 2.50
215 Hardened Scales R :G: 2.50 5.00
216 Harrow C :G: .30 .60
217 Inspiring Call U :G: .25 .50
218 New Horizons C :G: .05 .10
219 Overgrowth C :G: .10 .20
220 Rampant Growth C :G: .15 .30
221 Bituminous Blast U :K:/:R: .05 .10
222 Bred for the Hunt U :G:/:B: .10 .20
223 Deny Reality C :B:/:K: .07 .15
224 Hull Breach U :R:/:G: .30 .60
225 Mortify U :W:/:K: .10 .20
226 Utter End R :W:/:K: .10 .20
227 Arcane Signet C .75 1.50
228 Arcane Signet C .30 .60
229 Arcane Signet C .75 1.50
230 Assault Suit U .12 .25
231 Caged Sun R 1.25 2.50
232 Chromatic Lantern R 2.50 5.00
233 Commander's Sphere C .10 .20
234 Commander's Sphere C .07 .15
235 Commander's Sphere C .10 .20
236 Cranial Plating U .15 .30
237 Endless Atlas R .60 1.25
238 Everflowing Chalice R .30 .60
239 Gilded Lotus R .75 1.50
240 Hedron Archive U .10 .20
241 Herald's Horn U 2.50 5.00
242 Icon of Ancestry R .75 1.50
243 Mask of Memory U .10 .20
244 Mind Stone U .12 .25
245 Mind Stone U .10 .20
246 Mystic Forge R 1.25 2.50
247 Sculpting Steel R .15 .30
248 Skullclamp U 2.50 5.00
249 Sol Ring U 1.00 2.00
250 Sol Ring U 1.00 2.00
251 Sol Ring U 1.00 2.00
252 Sol Ring U 1.25 2.50
253 Talisman of Creativity U .60 1.25
254 Talisman of Dominance U .40 .80
255 Talisman of Dominance U .60 1.25
256 Talisman of Hierarchy U .30 .60
257 Talisman of Indulgence U 2.00 4.00
258 Talisman of Progress U 2.00 4.00
259 Thought Vessel C 2.00 4.00
260 Unstable Obelisk C .07 .15
261 Wayfarer's Bauble C .15 .30
262 Wayfarer's Bauble C .12 .25
263 Worn Powerstone U .40 .80
264 Arcane Sanctum U .12 .25
265 Ash Barrens U .10 .20
266 Barren Moor U .10 .20
267 Cave of Temptation C .05 .10
268 Choked Estuary R .12 .25
269 Cinder Glade R .15 .30
270 Command Tower C .12 .25
271 Command Tower C .20 .40
272 Command Tower C .12 .25
273 Crumbling Necropolis U .15 .30
274 Darkwater Catacombs R .12 .25
275 Desert of the Glorified C .07 .15
276 Dismal Backwater C .07 .15
277 Evolving Wilds C .10 .20
278 Exotic Orchard R .12 .25
279 Foreboding Ruins R .12 .25
280 Forgotten Cave C .07 .15
281 Frontier Bivouac U .15 .30
282 Game Trail R .12 .25
283 Memorial to Glory U .05 .10
284 Molten Slagheap U .05 .10
285 Myriad Landscape U .12 .25
286 Opal Palace C .12 .25
287 Path of Ancestry C .10 .20
288 Polluted Mire C .05 .10
289 Port Town R .10 .20
290 Prairie Stream R .12 .25
291 Reliquary Tower U 2.50 5.00
292 Rugged Highlands C .07 .15
293 Scoured Barrens C .07 .15
294 Skycloud Expanse R .10 .20
295 Sunken Hollow R .15 .30
296 Swiftwater Cliffs C .07 .15
297 Temple of Abandon R .12 .25
298 Temple of Epiphany R .12 .25
299 Temple of Mystery R .15 .30
300 Temple of the False God U .10 .20
301 Terramorphic Expanse C .12 .25
302 Thornwood Falls C .05 .10
303 Tranquil Cove C .05 .10
304 Unclaimed Territory U .60 1.25
305 Vault of Whispers C .40 .80
306 Plains C .05 .10
307 Island C .05 .10
308 Island C .05 .10
309 Island C .05 .10
310 Swamp C .05 .10
311 Swamp C .05 .10
312 Swamp C .05 .10
313 Swamp C .05 .10
314 Swamp C .05 .10
315 Mountain C .05 .10
316 Mountain C .07 .15
317 Forest C .05 .10
318 Szarekh, the Silent King M :K: .15 .30
319 Abaddon the Despoiler M :B:/:K:/:R: .20 .40
320 Inquisitor Greyfax M :W:/:B:/:K: .07 .15
321 The Swarmlord M :G:/:B:/:R: .12 .25

2022 Magic The Gathering Warhammer 40,000 Tokens

1 Astartes Warrior FOIL .50 1.00
1 Astartes Warrior .12 .25
2 Soldier FOIL .50 1.00
2 Soldier .12 .25
3 Soldier FOIL .50 1.00
3 Soldier .12 .25
4 Soldier FOIL .50 1.00
4 Soldier .12 .25
5 Space Marine Devastator .12 .25
6 Ultramarines Honour Guard .12 .25
7 Zephyrim .12 .25
8 Sicarian Infiltrator .12 .25
9 Tyranid Gargoyle .12 .25
10 Vanguard Suppressor .12 .25
11 Arco-Flagellant .12 .25
12 Astartes Warrior .12 .25
13 Cherubael .12 .25
14 Necron Warrior FOIL .30 .60
14 Necron Warrior .12 .25
15 Plaguebearer of Nurgle FOIL .15 .30
15 Plaguebearer of Nurgle .12 .25
16 Spawn FOIL .15 .30
16 Spawn .12 .25
17 Tyranid FOIL 1.00 2.00
17 Tyranid .12 .25
18 Tyranid .12 .25
19 Tyranid Warrior .12 .25
20 Blue Horror .12 .25
21 Clue .12 .25
22 Insect .12 .25
23 Robot .12 .25

2022 Magic The Gathering Year of the Tiger Promos

1 Temur Sabertooth R :G: 17.50 35.00
2 Jedit Ojanen R :W:/:B: 6.00 12.00
3 Snapdax, Apex of the Hunt R :R:/:W:/:K: 20.00 40.00
4 Yuriko, the Tiger's Shadow R :B:/:K: 50.00 100.00
5 Herald's Horn R 30.00 60.00

2023 Magic The Gathering Commander Masters

1 The Prismatic Piper S .04 .10
2 Kozilek, the Great Distortion M 2.50 6.00
3 Morophon, the Boundless M 5.00 12.00
4 Pathrazer of Ulamog U 1.00 2.50
5 Ulamog, the Ceaseless Hunger M 25.00 60.00
6 Ulamog's Crusher C .10 .25
7 Ainok Bond-Kin C .03 .08
8 Alharu, Solemn Ritualist U .03 .08
9 All That Glitters C .40 1.00
10 Alms Collector R .25 .60
11 Anafenza, Kin-Tree Spirit U .08 .20
12 Ancestral Blade C .03 .08
13 Angelic Field Marshal R .40 1.00
14 Avacyn, Angel of Hope M 20.00 50.00
15 Baird, Steward of Argive U .12 .30
16 Balan, Wandering Knight R .30 .75
17 Battle Screech C .03 .08
18 Cartographer's Hawk U .04 .10
19 Custodi Squire C .03 .08
20 Danitha Capashen, Paragon U .15 .40
21 Darksteel Mutation U 1.00 2.50
22 Elite Scaleguard U .03 .08
23 Fencing Ace U .03 .08
24 Flawless Maneuver R 5.00 12.00
25 Gavony Silversmith C .03 .08
26 Generous Gift C .25 .60
27 Grand Abolisher R 3.00 8.00
28 Heavenly Blademaster R .10 .25
29 Heliod, Sun-Crowned M 8.00 20.00
30 Herald of the Host U .10 .25
31 Intangible Virtue U .05 .12
32 Jazal Goldmane R .12 .30
33 Keleth, Sunmane Familiar U .05 .12
34 Kemba, Kha Regent U .05 .12
35 Kirtar's Wrath U .04 .10
36 Knighted Myr C .03 .08
37 Land Tax M 8.00 20.00
38 Losheel, Clockwork Scholar U 1.00 2.50
39 Loyal Retainers M 1.25 3.00
40 Loyal Unicorn U .12 .30
41 Mace of the Valiant U .04 .10
42 Mangara, the Diplomat R 1.00 2.50
43 Ministrant of Obligation C .04 .10
44 Myrsmith C .04 .10
45 Nahiri, the Lithomancer R .25 .60
46 Odric, Master Tactician R .20 .50
47 Palace Jailer U .08 .20
48 Palace Sentinels C .03 .08
49 Path to Exile U .50 1.25
50 Pianna, Nomad Captain U .03 .08
51 Puresteel Paladin R .75 2.00
52 Return to Dust U .10 .25
53 Righteous Confluence R .08 .20
54 Sephara, Sky's Blade R 1.00 2.50
55 Sevinne's Reclamation R .20 .50
56 Shelter C .04 .10
57 Smothering Tithe M 15.00 40.00
58 Spectral Grasp C .03 .08
59 Steelshaper's Gift R 1.50 4.00
60 Sublime Exhalation R .10 .25
61 Sunblade Angel C .04 .10
62 Sunspear Shikari C .03 .08
63 Supply Runners C .04 .10
64 Swift Response C .03 .08
65 Teshar, Ancestor's Apostle U .10 .25
66 Thraben Inspector C .10 .25
67 Unbounded Potential C .03 .08
68 Wakening Sun's Avatar R .25 .60
69 Wanderer's Strike C .03 .08
70 Wrath of God R 1.25 3.00
72 Aether Gale U .12 .30
73 Aminatou's Augury R .20 .50
74 Azami, Lady of Scrolls R .15 .40
75 Body Double U .05 .12
76 Braids, Conjurer Adept R .25 .60
77 Bribery M 3.00 8.00
78 Brinelin, the Moon Kraken U .10 .25
79 Capture of Jingzhou M 5.00 12.00
80 Commandeer R .30 .75
81 Counterspell C 1.00 2.50
82 Coveted Peacock U .03 .08
83 Cryptic Serpent C .10 .25
84 Cyclonic Rift R 20.00 50.00
85 Day's Undoing R 1.00 2.50
86 Deep Analysis C .04 .10
87 Deranged Assistant C .03 .08
88 Efficient Construction U .15 .40
89 Evacuation R .15 .40
90 Exclude C .04 .10
91 Fact or Fiction U .10 .25
92 Faerie Artisans R .40 1.00
93 Fall from Favor C .03 .08
94 Fierce Guardianship R 20.00 50.00
95 Filigree Attendant C .03 .08
96 Frantic Search C .12 .30
97 Ghost of Ramirez DePietro U .03 .08
98 Ghostly Flicker C .30 .75
99 Goliath Sphinx C .03 .08
100 Inga Rune-Eyes U .03 .08
101 Kaho, Minamo Historian U .03 .08
102 Looter il-Kor C .04 .10
103 Lorthos, the Tidemaker R .12 .30
104 Loyal Drake U .10 .25
105 Minds Aglow R .30 .75
106 Murder of Crows U .03 .08
107 Murmuring Mystic C .10 .25
108 Mystic Confluence R .20 .50
109 Padeem, Consul of Innovation U .60 1.50
110 Personal Tutor R 2.50 6.00
111 Phyrexian Ingester U .04 .10
112 Portal Mage U .04 .10
113 Reality Shift U .20 .50
114 Renowned Weaponsmith C .03 .08
115 Resculpt C .12 .30
116 Reverse Engineer C .03 .08
117 Rise from the Tides U .04 .10
118 Sai, Master Thopterist R .60 1.50
119 Shipwreck Dowser C .03 .08
120 Spellseeker M 6.00 15.00
121 Stitcher Geralf R .10 .25
122 Stormsurge Kraken R .20 .50
123 Sun Quan, Lord of Wu M 2.50 6.00
124 Talrand, Sky Summoner R .10 .25
125 Teferi, Temporal Archmage R .50 1.25
126 Tetsuko Umezawa, Fugitive U .10 .25
127 Thryx, the Sudden Storm U .12 .30
128 Torrential Gearhulk R .30 .75
129 Tromokratis U .10 .25
130 Urza, Lord High Artificer M 5.00 12.00
131 Vizier of Tumbling Sands C .08 .20
132 Whirler Rogue U .03 .08
133 Windcaller Aven C .03 .08
134 Windrider Wizard C .03 .08
135 Witching Well C .03 .08
137 Archfiend of Despair M 6.00 15.00
138 Bastion of Remembrance U .50 1.25
139 Bloodchief Ascension R 5.00 12.00
140 Cabal Patriarch U .03 .08
141 Cadaver Imp C .05 .12
142 Carrier Thrall C .03 .08
143 Carrion Grub C .03 .08
144 Chainer, Dementia Master R .10 .25
145 Corpse Augur U .05 .12
146 Curtains' Call R .12 .30
147 Deadly Rollick R 10.00 25.00
148 Decree of Pain R .15 .40
149 Demon's Disciple C .08 .20
150 Demonic Tutor M 25.00 60.00
151 Demonlord Belzenlok R .15 .40
152 Dread Drone C .04 .10
153 Dread Return C .12 .30
154 Drown in Sorrow C .10 .25
155 Endrek Sahr, Master Breeder R .25 .60
156 Exsanguinate U 1.25 3.00
157 Extinguish All Hope U .10 .25
158 Feast of Succession U .04 .10
159 Feed the Swarm C .10 .25
160 Final Parting U .20 .50
161 Ghoulcaller Gisa R 1.00 2.50
162 Gonti, Lord of Luxury U .10 .25
163 Goremand U .03 .08
164 Gorex, the Tombshell U .08 .20
165 Grave Pact M 5.00 12.00
166 Heartless Act U .10 .25
167 Imp's Mischief R 1.25 3.00
168 Isareth the Awakener U .04 .10
169 Kindred Dominance R 3.00 8.00
170 Legion Vanguard C .03 .08
171 Lotleth Giant C .04 .10
172 Loyal Subordinate U .10 .25
173 Mikaeus, the Unhallowed M 4.00 10.00
174 Mire Triton C .08 .20
175 Nadier's Nightblade C .15 .40
176 Ob Nixilis of the Black Oath R .40 1.00
177 Ogre Slumlord R .15 .40
178 Phyrexian Gargantua C .03 .08
179 Priest of the Blood Rite U .04 .10
180 Rankle, Master of Pranks R .40 1.00
181 Razaketh, the Foulblooded M 4.00 10.00
182 Read the Bones C .12 .30
183 Reassembling Skeleton U .15 .40
184 Rune-Scarred Demon R 1.50 4.00
185 Serrated Scorpion C .05 .12
186 Shirei, Shizo's Caretaker U .05 .12
187 Sower of Discord R 1.00 2.50
188 Supernatural Stamina C .08 .20
189 Taborax, Hope's Demise U .10 .25
190 Thorn of the Black Rose C .10 .25
191 Toxic Deluge R 2.50 6.00
192 Tragic Slip C .10 .25
193 Twilight Prophet M 1.25 3.00
194 Twisted Abomination C .03 .08
195 Victimize U .50 1.25
196 Vindictive Lich R .12 .30
197 Wake the Dead R .10 .25
198 Whisper, Blood Liturgist U .10 .25
199 Witch's Cauldron C .03 .08
200 Wretched Confluence R .10 .25
201 Yahenni, Undying Partisan U .15 .40
202 Yargle, Glutton of Urborg U .05 .12
203 Abrade C .10 .25
204 Anax, Hardened in the Forge U .05 .12
205 Ashling the Pilgrim R .10 .25
206 Avatar of Slaughter R .10 .25
207 Balefire Dragon M 6.00 15.00
208 Blood Aspirant C .03 .08
209 Captain Ripley Vance U .03 .08
210 Champion of the Flame C .03 .08
211 Crimson Fleet Commodore C .03 .08
212 Cyclops Electromancer C .03 .08
213 Daretti, Scrap Savant R 1.00 2.50
214 Deflecting Swat R 20.00 50.00
215 Disrupt Decorum R .12 .30
216 Divergent Transformations R .10 .25
217 Dragon Fodder C .04 .10
218 Drakuseth, Maw of Flames R .50 1.25
219 Dwarven Hammer C .03 .08
220 Faithless Looting C .10 .25
221 Fiendlash U .10 .25
222 Fiery Confluence R .25 .60
223 Fists of Flame C .05 .12
224 Frontier Warmonger U .08 .20
225 Furious Rise U .03 .08
226 Gargadon C .03 .08
227 Godo, Bandit Warlord R .50 1.25
228 Grenzo, Havoc Raiser R .30 .75
229 Guttersnipe C .10 .25
230 Havoc Jester U .04 .10
231 Heartless Hidetsugu R .60 1.50
232 Hellkite Charger R .75 2.00
233 Hoarding Dragon U .05 .12
234 Impulsive Pilferer C .10 .25
235 Inferno Titan R .12 .30
236 Insurrection M 3.00 8.00
237 Kazuul, Tyrant of the Cliffs U .08 .20
238 Krenko, Mob Boss R .75 2.00
239 Living Lightning C .03 .08
240 Loyal Apprentice U .20 .50
241 Magus of the Wheel R .25 .60
242 Makeshift Munitions C .08 .20
243 Meteoric Mace U .03 .08
244 Neheb, the Eternal M 1.25 3.00
245 Nesting Dragon R .40 1.00
246 Purphoros, God of the Forge M 10.00 25.00
247 Rakka Mar U .03 .08
248 Rapacious Dragon C .05 .12
249 Rapacious One C .05 .12
250 Ravaging Blaze U .04 .10

251 Rorix Bladewing U .04 .10
252 Savage Beating M 3.00 8.00
253 Scourge of the Throne R .20 .50
254 Skyline Despot U .50 1.25
255 Slice and Dice U .03 .08
256 Spikeshot Goblin C .03 .08
257 Spitebellows C .04 .10
258 Squee, Goblin Nabob U .10 .25
259 Star of Extinction R .50 1.25
260 Storm-Kiln Artist U .60 1.50
261 Subira, Tulzidi Caravanner U .04 .10
262 Sulfurous Blast C .03 .08
263 Tempt with Vengeance R .60 1.50
264 Temur Battle Rage C .10 .25
265 Treasure Nabber R .30 .75
266 Valduk, Keeper of the Flame U .03 .08
267 Vandalblast U 1.25 3.00
269 Abundant Harvest C .03 .08
270 Acidic Slime U .08 .20
271 Animal Magnetism U .03 .08
272 Arachnogenesis R 1.25 3.00
273 Armorcraft Judge U .08 .20
274 Azusa, Lost but Seeking R 3.00 8.00
275 Beanstalk Giant // Fertile Footsteps U .10 .25
276 Bloodspore Thrinax R .10 .25
277 Broken Wings C .05 .12
278 Courage in Crisis C .03 .08
279 Crash of Rhino Beetles C .05 .12
280 Craterhoof Behemoth M 15.00 40.00
281 Crawling Infestation C .05 .12
282 Deadly Recluse C .05 .12
283 Doubling Season M 25.00 60.00
284 Elvish Mystic C .25 .60
285 Entourage of Trest C .03 .08
286 Eternal Witness U 1.00 2.50
287 Ezuri's Predation R 1.25 3.00
288 Fierce Empath C .05 .12
289 Finale of Devastation M 15.00 40.00
290 Freyalise, Llanowar's Fury R 1.00 2.50
291 Fungal Plots U .08 .20
292 Ghalta, Primal Hunger R 2.00 5.00
293 Goreclaw, Terror of Qal Sisma U .30 .75
294 The Great Henge M 30.00 80.00
295 Heroic Intervention R 5.00 12.00
296 Hunter's Insight U .15 .40
297 Ilysian Caryatid C .10 .25
298 Jade Mage U .04 .10
299 Jolrael, Mwonvuli Recluse R .05 .12
300 Kodama's Reach C .60 1.50
301 Kozilek's Predator C .04 .10
302 Krosan Tusker C .03 .08
303 Lifeblood Hydra R 1.00 2.50
304 Loyal Guardian U .12 .30
305 Molimo, Maro-Sorcerer U .04 .10
306 Mowu, Loyal Companion U .08 .20
307 Nemata, Grove Guardian U .10 .25
308 Obscuring Haze R 1.25 3.00
309 Ohran Frostfang R 1.00 2.50
310 Omnath, Locus of Mana M 1.25 3.00
311 Oviya Pashiri, Sage Lifecrafter U .04 .10
312 Pollenbright Druid C .04 .10
313 Predatory Rampage U .04 .10
314 Ram Through C .12 .30
315 Rampaging Brontodon U .15 .40
316 Regal Behemoth R .20 .50
317 Rishkar, Peema Renegade U .12 .30
318 Rot Shambler C .04 .10
319 Sakiko, Mother of Summer R .15 .40
320 Selvala, Heart of the Wilds M 5.00 12.00
321 Skyshroud Claim C 1.00 2.50
322 Skysnare Spider C .05 .12
323 Snakeskin Veil C .08 .20
324 Song of the Dryads R 2.00 5.00
325 Stonehoof Chieftain R 1.00 2.50
326 Surrak, the Hunt Caller U .08 .20
327 Tooth and Nail R 1.00 2.50
328 Tuskguard Captain C .04 .10
329 Verdant Confluence R .12 .30
330 Verdeloth the Ancient U .10 .25
331 Wayward Swordtooth R 2.00 5.00
332 Wildwood Scourge U .10 .25
333 Yedora, Grave Gardener U .08 .20
334 Yisan, the Wanderer Bard R .10 .25
335 Akiri, Fearless Voyager U .12 .30
336 Aryel, Knight of Windgrace U .08 .20
337 Experiment Kraj R .12 .30
338 Gisela, Blade of Goldnight R 1.00 2.50
339 Hamza, Guardian of Arashin U .10 .25
340 Hanna, Ship's Navigator R .10 .25
341 Judith, the Scourge Diva U .10 .25
342 Karador, Ghost Chieftain R .10 .25
343 Kykar, Wind's Fury R .12 .30
344 Maelstrom Wanderer R .50 1.25
345 Melek, Izzet Paragon U .10 .25
346 Meren of Clan Nel Toth R 1.50 4.00
347 Mirri, Weatherlight Duelist R 1.25 3.00
348 Mizzix of the Izmagnus R .20 .50
349 Nekusar, the Mindrazer R .50 1.25
350 Queen Marchesa R .12 .30
351 Raff Capashen, Ship's Mage U .05 .12
352 Rafiq of the Many R .10 .25
353 The Scarab God M 6.00 15.00
354 Sek'Kuar, Deathkeeper R .08 .20
355 Sidisi, Brood Tyrant R .15 .40
356 Slimefoot, the Stowaway U .10 .25
357 Taigam, Sidisi's Hand U .04 .10
358 Tatyova, Benthic Druid U .10 .25
359 Teysa Karlov R .50 1.25
360 Tuya Bearclaw U .04 .10
361 The Ur-Dragon M 10.00 25.00
362 Xantcha, Sleeper Agent R .25 .60
363 Yennett, Cryptic Sovereign R .10 .25
367 Arcane Signet U .25 .60
368 Ashnod's Altar U 4.00 10.00
369 Assault Suit U .08 .20
370 Bonder's Ornament C .04 .10
371 Boompile R .12 .30
372 Brass Knuckles C .05 .12
373 Burnished Hart U .05 .12
374 Campfire C .10 .25
375 Champion's Helm R .75 2.00
376 Chromatic Lantern R 1.25 3.00
377 Commander's Sphere C .10 .25
378 Darksteel Ingot C .10 .25
379 Emerald Medallion R 1.50 4.00
380 Explorer's Scope C .05 .12
381 Extraplanar Lens M 4.00 10.00
382 Fellwar Stone U .50 1.25
383 Firemind Vessel C .10 .25
384 Forebear's Blade U .08 .20
385 Foundry Inspector C .10 .25
386 Geode Golem U .10 .25
387 Gilded Lotus R 1.00 2.50
388 Hammer of Nazahn R 5.00 12.00
389 Haunted Cloak C .10 .25
390 Heart-Piercer Bow C .03 .08
391 Hero's Blade U .10 .25
392 Idol of Oblivion R .60 1.50
393 The Immortal Sun M 6.00 15.00
394 Inspiring Statuary R .12 .30
395 Jet Medallion R 2.50 6.00
396 Jeweled Lotus M 50.00 120.00
397 Letter of Acceptance C .03 .08
398 Lightning Greaves U 3.00 8.00
399 Meteor Golem U .10 .25
400 Myr Sire C .04 .10
401 Pearl Medallion R 1.50 4.00
402 Pilgrim's Eye C .03 .08
403 Prismatic Lens C .08 .20
404 Prophetic Prism C .03 .08
405 Ruby Medallion R 4.00 10.00
406 Sandstone Oracle U .05 .12
407 Sapphire Medallion R 2.00 5.00
408 Scytheclaw R .10 .25
409 Shimmer Myr U .10 .25
410 Sol Ring U .60 1.50
411 Spectral Searchlight U .04 .10
412 Staunch Throneguard C .03 .08
413 Sword of the Animist R 4.00 10.00
414 Thought Vessel U .75 2.00
415 Thran Dynamo U 1.25 3.00
416 Unstable Obelisk C .05 .12
417 Vial of Dragonfire C .03 .08
418 Vulshok Battlegear C .03 .08
419 Ash Barrens C .08 .20
420 Command Tower C .10 .25
421 Myriad Landscape U .08 .20
422 Opal Palace C .10 .25
423 Path of Ancestry C .08 .20
424 Rejuvenating Springs R 2.50 6.00
425 Reliquary Tower U 1.00 2.50
426 Rogue's Passage U .25 .60
427 Spectator Seating R 5.00 12.00
428 Terramorphic Expanse C .10 .25
429 Thriving Bluff C .04 .10
430 Thriving Grove C .05 .12
431 Thriving Heath C .04 .10
432 Thriving Isle C .10 .25
433 Thriving Moor C .05 .12
434 Training Center R 5.00 12.00
435 Undergrowth Stadium R 4.00 10.00
436 Vault of Champions R 4.00 10.00
437 Plains RETRO FRAME C .20 .50
438 Plains RETRO FRAME C .60 1.50
439 Plains RETRO FRAME C .10 .25
440 Island RETRO FRAME C .30 .75
441 Island RETRO FRAME C .20 .50
442 Island RETRO FRAME C .12 .30
443 Swamp RETRO FRAME C .15 .40
444 Swamp RETRO FRAME C 1.00 2.50
445 Swamp RETRO FRAME C .20 .50
446 Mountain RETRO FRAME C .15 .40
447 Mountain RETRO FRAME C .75 2.00
448 Mountain RETRO FRAME C .10 .25
449 Forest RETRO FRAME C .20 .50
450 Forest RETRO FRAME C .75 2.00
451 Forest RETRO FRAME C .15 .40
452 Kozilek, the Great Distortion FOIL ETCHED M4.00 10.00
453 Morophon, the Boundless FOIL ETCHED M6.00 15.00
454 Ulamog, the Ceaseless
Hunger FOIL ETCHED M 25.00 60.00
455 Alms Collector FOIL ETCHED R 1.00 2.50
456 Angelic Field Marshal FOIL ETCHED R 2.00 5.00
457 Avacyn, Angel of Hope FOIL ETCHED M 25.00 60.00
458 Balan, Wandering Knight FOIL ETCHED R 1.00 2.50
459 Flawless Maneuver FOIL ETCHED R 6.00 15.00
460 Grand Abolisher FOIL ETCHED R 8.00 20.00
461 Heavenly Blademaster FOIL ETCHED R .60 1.50
462 Heliod, Sun-Crowned FOIL ETCHED M 8.00 20.00
463 Jazal Goldmane FOIL ETCHED R 1.50 4.00
464 Land Tax FOIL ETCHED M 10.00 25.00
465 Loyal Retainers FOIL ETCHED M 2.00 5.00
466 Mangara, the Diplomat FOIL ETCHED R 1.50 4.00
467 Nahiri, the Lithomancer FOIL ETCHED R 2.00 5.00
468 Odric, Master Tactician FOIL ETCHED R 5.00 12.00
469 Puresteel Paladin FOIL ETCHED R .60 1.50
470 Righteous Confluence FOIL ETCHED R .15 .40
471 Sephara, Sky's Blade FOIL ETCHED R 5.00 12.00
472 Sevinne's Reclamation FOIL ETCHED R 5.00 12.00
473 Smothering Tithe FOIL ETCHED M 15.00 40.00
474 Steelshaper's Gift FOIL ETCHED R 2.50 6.00
475 Sublime Exhalation FOIL ETCHED R .25 .60
476 Wakening Sun's Avatar FOIL ETCHED R 1.50 4.00
477 Wrath of God FOIL ETCHED R 1.00 2.50
479 Aminatou's Augury FOIL ETCHED R 1.50 4.00
480 Azami, Lady of Scrolls FOIL ETCHED R .60 1.50
481 Braids, Conjurer Adept FOIL ETCHED R 2.00 5.00
482 Bribery FOIL ETCHED M 4.00 10.00
483 Capture of Jingzhou FOIL ETCHED M 8.00 20.00
484 Commandeer FOIL ETCHED R 10.00 25.00
485 Cyclonic Rift FOIL ETCHED R 25.00 60.00
486 Day's Undoing FOIL ETCHED R 3.00 8.00
487 Evacuation FOIL ETCHED R 1.50 4.00
488 Faerie Artisans FOIL ETCHED R 2.00 5.00
489 Fierce Guardianship FOIL ETCHED R 40.00 100.00
490 Lorthos, the Tidemaker FOIL ETCHED R .60 1.50
491 Minds Aglow FOIL ETCHED R 1.50 4.00
492 Mystic Confluence FOIL ETCHED R 2.00 5.00
493 Personal Tutor FOIL ETCHED R 4.00 10.00
494 Sai, Master Thopterist FOIL ETCHED R 4.00 10.00
495 Spellseeker FOIL ETCHED M 8.00 20.00
496 Stitcher Geralf FOIL ETCHED R .20 .50
497 Stormsurge Kraken FOIL ETCHED R 1.25 3.00
498 Sun Quan, Lord of Wu FOIL ETCHED M 4.00 10.00
499 Talrand, Sky Summoner FOIL ETCHED R 1.00 2.50
500 Teferi, Temporal Archmage FOIL ETCHED R3.00 8.00
501 Torrential Gearhulk FOIL ETCHED R 1.25 3.00
502 Urza, Lord High Artificer FOIL ETCHED M6.00 15.00
503 Archfiend of Despair FOIL ETCHED M 10.00 25.00
504 Bloodchief Ascension FOIL ETCHED R 5.00 12.00
505 Chainer, Dementia Master FOIL ETCHED R .25 .60
506 Curtains' Call FOIL ETCHED R 1.00 2.50
507 Deadly Rollick FOIL ETCHED R 20.00 50.00
508 Decree of Pain FOIL ETCHED R .50 1.25
509 Demonic Tutor FOIL ETCHED M 25.00 60.00
510 Demonlord Belzenlok FOIL ETCHED R .50 1.25
511 Endrek Sahr, Master Breeder FOIL ETCHED R2.00 5.00
512 Ghoulcaller Gisa FOIL ETCHED R 4.00 10.00
513 Grave Pact FOIL ETCHED M 6.00 15.00
514 Imp's Mischief FOIL ETCHED R 10.00 25.00
515 Kindred Dominance FOIL ETCHED R 4.00 10.00
516 Mikaeus, the Unhallowed FOIL ETCHED M4.00 10.00
517 Ob Nixilis of the Black Oath FOIL ETCHED R1.00 2.50
518 Ogre Slumlord FOIL ETCHED R .60 1.50
519 Rankle, Master of Pranks FOIL ETCHED R2.50 6.00
520 Razaketh, the Foulblooded FOIL ETCHED M6.00 15.00
521 Rune-Scarred Demon FOIL ETCHED R 4.00 10.00
522 Sower of Discord FOIL ETCHED R 3.00 8.00
523 Toxic Deluge FOIL ETCHED R 15.00 40.00
524 Twilight Prophet FOIL ETCHED M 4.00 10.00
525 Vindictive Lich FOIL ETCHED R 1.00 2.50
526 Wake the Dead FOIL ETCHED R .30 .75
527 Wretched Confluence FOIL ETCHED R .30 .75
528 Ashling the Pilgrim FOIL ETCHED R 1.00 2.50
529 Avatar of Slaughter FOIL ETCHED R .15 .40
530 Balefire Dragon FOIL ETCHED M 6.00 15.00
531 Daretti, Scrap Savant FOIL ETCHED R 5.00 12.00
532 Deflecting Swat FOIL ETCHED R 30.00 80.00
533 Disrupt Decorum FOIL ETCHED R 2.00 5.00
534 Divergent Transformations FOIL ETCHED R .50 1.25
535 Drakuseth, Maw of Flames FOIL ETCHED R5.00 12.00
536 Fiery Confluence FOIL ETCHED R 2.00 5.00
537 Godo, Bandit Warlord FOIL ETCHED R 2.00 5.00
538 Grenzo, Havoc Raiser FOIL ETCHED R 2.00 5.00
539 Heartless Hidetsugu FOIL ETCHED R 1.00 2.50
540 Hellkite Charger FOIL ETCHED R 4.00 10.00
541 Inferno Titan FOIL ETCHED R .12 .30
542 Insurrection FOIL ETCHED M 2.50 6.00
543 Krenko, Mob Boss FOIL ETCHED R 6.00 15.00
544 Magus of the Wheel FOIL ETCHED R .50 1.25
545 Neheb, the Eternal FOIL ETCHED M 2.50 6.00
546 Nesting Dragon FOIL ETCHED R 2.50 6.00
547 Purphoros, God of the Forge FOIL ETCHED M10.00 25.00
548 Savage Beating FOIL ETCHED M 4.00 10.00
549 Scourge of the Throne FOIL ETCHED R 2.00 5.00
550 Star of Extinction FOIL ETCHED R 4.00 10.00
551 Tempt with Vengeance FOIL ETCHED R 1.25 3.00
552 Treasure Nabber FOIL ETCHED R 1.50 4.00
553 Arachnogenesis FOIL ETCHED R 2.00 5.00
554 Azusa, Lost but Seeking FOIL ETCHED R 5.00 12.00
555 Bloodspore Thrinax FOIL ETCHED R .40 1.00
556 Craterhoof Behemoth FOIL ETCHED M 20.00 50.00
557 Doubling Season FOIL ETCHED M 25.00 60.00
558 Ezuri's Predation FOIL ETCHED R 1.25 3.00
559 Finale of Devastation FOIL ETCHED M 20.00 50.00
560 Freyalise, Llanowar's Fury FOIL ETCHED R2.50 6.00
561 Ghalta, Primal Hunger FOIL ETCHED R 3.00 8.00
562 The Great Henge FOIL ETCHED M 40.00 100.00
563 Heroic Intervention FOIL ETCHED R 10.00 25.00
564 Jolrael, Mwonvuli Recluse FOIL ETCHED R .25 .60
565 Lifeblood Hydra FOIL ETCHED R 2.50 6.00
566 Obscuring Haze FOIL ETCHED R 2.00 5.00
567 Ohran Frostfang FOIL ETCHED R 4.00 10.00
568 Omnath, Locus of Mana FOIL ETCHED M 1.50 4.00
569 Regal Behemoth FOIL ETCHED R 1.00 2.50
570 Sakiko, Mother of Summer FOIL ETCHED R.60 1.50
571 Selvala, Heart of the Wilds FOIL ETCHED M10.00 25.00
572 Song of the Dryads FOIL ETCHED R 2.50 6.00
573 Stonehoof Chieftain FOIL ETCHED R 2.00 5.00
574 Tooth and Nail FOIL ETCHED R 2.50 6.00
575 Verdant Confluence FOIL ETCHED R .15 .40
576 Wayward Swordtooth FOIL ETCHED R 4.00 10.00
577 Yisan, the Wanderer Bard FOIL ETCHED R1.00 2.50
578 Experiment Kraj FOIL ETCHED R .50 1.25
579 Gisela, Blade of Goldnight FOIL ETCHED R3.00 8.00
580 Hanna, Ship's Navigator FOIL ETCHED R .50 1.25
581 Karador, Ghost Chieftain FOIL ETCHED R .25 .60
582 Kykar, Wind's Fury FOIL ETCHED R 1.25 3.00
583 Maelstrom Wanderer FOIL ETCHED R .60 1.50
584 Meren of Clan Nel Toth FOIL ETCHED R 5.00 12.00
585 Mirri, Weatherlight Duelist FOIL ETCHED R1.50 4.00
586 Mizzix of the Izmagnus FOIL ETCHED R .75 2.00
587 Nekusar, the Mindrazer FOIL ETCHED R 1.50 4.00
588 Queen Marchesa FOIL ETCHED R 2.00 5.00
589 Rafiq of the Many FOIL ETCHED R .30 .75
590 The Scarab God FOIL ETCHED M 10.00 25.00
591 Sek'Kuar, Deathkeeper FOIL ETCHED R .20 .50
592 Sidisi, Brood Tyrant FOIL ETCHED R .50 1.25
593 Teysa Karlov FOIL ETCHED R .60 1.50
594 The Ur-Dragon FOIL ETCHED M 15.00 40.00
595 Xantcha, Sleeper Agent FOIL ETCHED R 1.25 3.00
596 Yennett, Cryptic Sovereign FOIL ETCHED R.50 1.25
600 Boompile FOIL ETCHED R .60 1.50
601 Champion's Helm FOIL ETCHED R 1.25 3.00
602 Chromatic Lantern FOIL ETCHED R 4.00 10.00
603 Emerald Medallion FOIL ETCHED R 8.00 20.00
604 Extraplanar Lens FOIL ETCHED M 4.00 10.00
605 Gilded Lotus FOIL ETCHED R 5.00 12.00
606 Hammer of Nazahn FOIL ETCHED R 6.00 15.00
607 Idol of Oblivion FOIL ETCHED R 6.00 15.00
608 The Immortal Sun FOIL ETCHED M 8.00 20.00
609 Inspiring Statuary FOIL ETCHED R 2.00 5.00
610 Jet Medallion FOIL ETCHED R 15.00 40.00
611 Jeweled Lotus FOIL ETCHED M 100.00 250.00
612 Pearl Medallion FOIL ETCHED R 10.00 25.00
613 Ruby Medallion FOIL ETCHED R 12.00 30.00
614 Sapphire Medallion FOIL ETCHED R 4.00 10.00
615 Scytheclaw FOIL ETCHED R .15 .40
616 Sword of the Animist FOIL ETCHED R 4.00 10.00
617 Rejuvenating Springs FOIL ETCHED R 4.00 10.00
618 Spectator Seating FOIL ETCHED R 6.00 15.00
619 Training Center FOIL ETCHED R 5.00 12.00
620 Undergrowth Stadium FOIL ETCHED R 6.00 15.00
621 Vault of Champions FOIL ETCHED R 4.00 10.00
622 All That Glitters BORDERLESS C .15 .40
623 Darksteel Mutation BORDERLESS U 1.00 2.50
624 Generous Gift BORDERLESS C .25 .60
625 Grand Abolisher BORDERLESS R 4.00 10.00
626 Path to Exile BORDERLESS U 1.00 2.50
627 Puresteel Paladin BORDERLESS R .75 2.00
628 Return to Dust BORDERLESS U .20 .50
629 Steelshaper's Gift BORDERLESS R 1.25 3.00
630 Counterspell BORDERLESS C .75 2.00
631 Fact or Fiction BORDERLESS U .10 .25
632 Frantic Search BORDERLESS C .10 .25
633 Personal Tutor BORDERLESS R 2.00 5.00
634 Reality Shift BORDERLESS U .40 1.00
635 Spellseeker BORDERLESS M 6.00 15.00
636 Bloodchief Ascension BORDERLESS R 5.00 12.00
637 Dread Return BORDERLESS C .15 .40
638 Exsanguinate BORDERLESS U 1.50 4.00
639 Grave Pact BORDERLESS M 6.00 15.00
640 Kindred Dominance BORDERLESS R 3.00 8.00
641 Nadier's Nightblade BORDERLESS C .10 .25
642 Faithless Looting BORDERLESS C .12 .30
643 Magus of the Wheel BORDERLESS R .25 .60
644 Storm-Kiln Artist BORDERLESS U .75 2.00
645 Treasure Nabber BORDERLESS R .40 1.00
646 Vandalblast BORDERLESS U 1.50 4.00
647 Arachnogenesis BORDERLESS R 1.50 4.00
648 Elvish Mystic BORDERLESS C .20 .50
649 Kodama's Reach BORDERLESS C .60 1.50
650 Ohran Frostfang BORDERLESS R 2.00 5.00
651 Regal Behemoth BORDERLESS R .60 1.50
652 Tooth and Nail BORDERLESS R 1.00 2.50
653 Arcane Signet BORDERLESS U 1.50 4.00
654 Champion's Helm BORDERLESS R .60 1.50
655 Commander's Sphere BORDERLESS C .20 .50
656 Extraplanar Lens BORDERLESS M 3.00 8.00
657 Fellwar Stone BORDERLESS U 1.25 3.00
658 Thran Dynamo BORDERLESS U 2.00 5.00
659 Command Tower BORDERLESS C 1.00 2.50
660 Myriad Landscape BORDERLESS U .50 1.25
661 Path of Ancestry BORDERLESS C .20 .50
662 Rejuvenating Springs BORDERLESS R 3.00 8.00
663 Reliquary Tower BORDERLESS U 1.50 4.00
664 Spectator Seating BORDERLESS R 5.00 12.00
665 Training Center BORDERLESS R 4.00 10.00
666 Undergrowth Stadium BORDERLESS R 4.00 10.00
667 Vault of Champions BORDERLESS R 4.00 10.00
668 Kozilek, the Great Distortion
BORDERLESS PROFILE M 3.00 8.00
669 Morophon, the Boundless
BORDERLESS PROFILE M 5.00 12.00
670 Ulamog, the Ceaseless Hunger
BORDERLESS PROFILE M 25.00 60.00
671 Kemba, Kha Regent BORDERLESS PROFILE U.08 .20
672 Azami, Lady of Scrolls
BORDERLESS PROFILE R .20 .50
673 Talrand, Sky Summoner
BORDERLESS PROFILE R .40 1.00
674 Urza, Lord High Artificer
BORDERLESS PROFILE M 5.00 12.00
675 Mikaeus, the Unhallowed
BORDERLESS PROFILE M 5.00 12.00
676 Shirei, Shizo's Caretaker
BORDERLESS PROFILE U .10 .25
677 Grenzo, Havoc Raiser
BORDERLESS PROFILE R .50 1.25
678 Neheb, the Eternal BORDERLESS PROFILE M1.50 4.00
679 Azusa, Lost but Seeking
BORDERLESS PROFILE R 4.00 10.00
680 Omnath, Locus of Mana
BORDERLESS PROFILE M 1.50 4.00
681 Selvala, Heart of the Wilds
BORDERLESS PROFILE M 6.00 15.00
682 Gisela, Blade of Goldnight
BORDERLESS PROFILE R .75 2.00
683 Kykar, Wind's Fury BORDERLESS PROFILE R.25 .60
684 Maelstrom Wanderer
BORDERLESS PROFILE R .60 1.50
685 Meren of Clan Nel Toth
BORDERLESS PROFILE R 1.00 2.50
686 Slimefoot, the Stowaway
BORDERLESS PROFILE U .12 .30
687 Tatyova, Benthic Druid
BORDERLESS PROFILE U .40 1.00
688 Teysa Karlov BORDERLESS PROFILE R .40 1.00
689 The Ur-Dragon BORDERLESS PROFILE M10.00 25.00
692 Flawless Maneuver FRAME BREAK R 6.00 15.00
693 Smothering Tithe FRAME BREAK M 15.00 40.00
694 Fierce Guardianship FRAME BREAK R 25.00 60.00
695 Deadly Rollick FRAME BREAK R 12.00 30.00
696 Demonic Tutor FRAME BREAK M 30.00 80.00
697 Balefire Dragon FRAME BREAK M 8.00 20.00
698 Deflecting Swat FRAME BREAK R 25.00 60.00
699 Insurrection FRAME BREAK M 3.00 8.00
700 Finale of Devastation FRAME BREAK M 20.00 50.00
701 Obscuring Haze FRAME BREAK R 1.50 4.00
702 Jeweled Lotus FRAME BREAK M 75.00 200.00
703 Sol Ring FRAME BREAK U 5.00 12.00
712 Abstruse Archaic R 1.50 4.00
713 Calamity of the Titans R 2.00 5.00
714 Desecrate Reality R 2.00 5.00
715 Flayer of Loyalties R 15.00 40.00
716 Rise of the Eldrazi R 4.00 10.00
717 Skittering Cicada R 5.00 12.00
718 Ugin's Mastery R .25 .60
719 Battle at the Helvault R .50 1.25
720 Boon of the Spirit Realm R .50 1.25
721 Gatewatch Beacon R .10 .25
722 Onakke Oathkeeper R .10 .25
723 Ondu Spiritdancer R 5.00 12.00
724 Regal Sliver R .25 .60
725 Teyo, Geometric Tactician R 1.25 3.00
726 Sparkshaper Visionary R .08 .20
727 Taunting Sliver R .20 .50
728 Titan of Littjara R 2.50 6.00
729 Vronos, Masked Inquisitor R 1.00 2.50
730 Cacophony Unleashed R .10 .25
731 Demon of Fate's Design R .30 .75
732 Ghoulish Impetus R 2.00 5.00
733 Lazotep Sliver R 1.00 2.50
734 Capricious Sliver R .15 .40
735 Chandra, Legacy of Fire R .25 .60
736 Descendants' Fury R .75 2.00
737 Guff Rewrites History R .25 .60
738 Jaya's Phoenix R .20 .50
739 Composer of Spring R 2.00 5.00
740 For the Ancestors R 1.25 3.00
741 Hatchery Sliver R 1.00 2.50
742 Nyxborn Behemoth R .20 .50
743 Darksteel Monolith R 10.00 25.00
744 Abstruse Archaic EXT ART R 1.00 2.50
745 Calamity of the Titans EXT ART R 5.00 12.00

746 Desecrate Reality EXT ART R 1.50 4.00
747 Flayer of Loyalties EXT ART R 12.00 30.00
748 Omarthis, Ghostfire Initiate EXT ART M .75 2.00
749 Rise of the Eldrazi EXT ART R 5.00 12.00
750 Skittering Cicada EXT ART R 6.00 15.00
751 Ugin's Mastery EXT ART R .40 1.00
753 Boon of the Spirit Realm EXT ART R .50 1.25
754 Gatewatch Beacon EXT ART R .10 .25
755 Onakke Oathkeeper EXT ART R .12 .30
756 Ondu Spiritdancer EXT ART R 4.00 10.00
757 Regal Sliver EXT ART R .10 .25
758 Sparkshaper Visionary EXT ART R .05 .12
759 Taunting Sliver EXT ART R .25 .60
760 Titan of Littjara EXT ART R 3.00 8.00
761 Cacophony Unleashed EXT ART R .10 .25
762 Demon of Fate's Design EXT ART R .40 1.00
763 Ghoulish Impetus EXT ART R 1.50 4.00
764 Lazotep Sliver EXT ART R .50 1.25
765 Capricious Sliver EXT ART R .12 .30
766 Descendants' Fury EXT ART R .75 2.00
767 Guff Rewrites History EXT ART R 1.00 2.50
768 Jaya's Phoenix EXT ART R .15 .40
769 Composer of Spring EXT ART R 2.00 5.00
770 For the Ancestors EXT ART R 1.25 3.00
771 Hatchery Sliver EXT ART R .75 2.00
772 Nyxborn Behemoth EXT ART R .20 .50
773 Anikthea, Hand of Erebos EXT ART M 1.50 4.00
774 Leori, Sparktouched Hunter EXT ART M .25 .60
775 Narci, Fable Singer EXT ART M 1.50 4.00
776 Rukarumel, Biologist EXT ART M 1.50 4.00
777 Sliver Gravemother EXT ART M 5.00 12.00
778 Darksteel Monolith EXT ART R 10.00 25.00
780 Anikthea, Hand of Erebos FOIL ETCHED M .20 .50
781 Commodore Guff FOIL ETCHED M .12 .30
782 Sliver Gravemother FOIL ETCHED M .30 .75
783 Plains C .05 .12
784 Plains C .05 .12
785 Plains C .04 .10
786 Plains C .08 .20
787 Plains C .04 .10
788 Island C .04 .10
789 Island C .10 .25
790 Island C .08 .20
791 Swamp C .05 .12
792 Swamp C .05 .12
793 Swamp C .08 .20
794 Mountain C .08 .20
795 Mountain C .04 .10
796 Mountain C .10 .25
797 Forest C .05 .12
798 Forest C .05 .12
799 Forest C .10 .25
800 All Is Dust M 4.00 10.00
801 Artisan of Kozilek U .15 .40
802 Bane of Bala Ged U .30 .75
803 Endbringer R .12 .30
804 Endless One R .20 .50
805 It That Betrays R 6.00 15.00
806 Matter Reshaper R .50 1.25
807 Not of This World U 2.00 5.00
808 Oblivion Sower M .40 1.00
809 Spatial Contortion U .10 .25
810 Titan's Presence U .10 .25
811 Ugin, the Ineffable R 1.00 2.50
812 Warping Wail U .20 .50
813 Ajani Steadfast M .40 1.00
814 Archon of Sun's Grace R .30 .75
815 Bonescythe Sliver R .60 1.50
816 Cast Out U .04 .10
817 Cleansing Nova R .30 .75
818 Constricting Sliver U .20 .50
819 Deploy the Gatewatch M .12 .30
820 Elspeth, Sun's Champion M .60 1.50
821 Felidar Retreat R .50 1.25
822 Gideon Jura M .10 .25
823 Grasp of Fate R .10 .25
824 Grateful Apparition U .10 .25
825 Harsh Mercy R .12 .30
826 Heliod, God of the Sun M .25 .60
827 Love Song of Night and Day U .03 .08
828 Mesa Enchantress R .15 .40
829 Norn's Annex R .40 1.00
830 Oath of Gideon R .10 .25
831 Omen of the Sun C .04 .10
832 Oreskos Explorer U .05 .12
833 Promise of Loyalty R .10 .25
834 Semester's End R .10 .25
835 Sentinel Sliver C .30 .75
836 Sigil of the Empty Throne R .60 1.50
837 Sinew Sliver C .12 .30
838 Spirited Companion C .10 .25
839 Starfield Mystic R .25 .60
840 Starfield of Nyx M 1.25 3.00
841 Swords to Plowshares U .75 2.00
842 Urza's Ruinous Blast R .10 .25
843 The Wanderer U .10 .25
844 Deepglow Skate R .50 1.25
845 Diffusion Sliver U .30 .75
846 Distant Melody C .15 .40
847 Flux Channeler U .60 1.50
848 Fog Bank U .10 .25
849 Galerider Sliver R 1.50 4.00
850 Jace Beleren M .60 1.50
851 Jace, Architect of Thought M .10 .25
852 Jace, Mirror Mage M .15 .40
853 Narset, Parter of Veils U 1.00 2.50
854 Oath of Jace R .08 .20
855 Shifting Sliver U .30 .75
856 Spark Double R 2.00 5.00
857 Synapse Sliver R 1.00 2.50
858 Thrummingbird U .10 .25
859 Windfall U 1.50 4.00
860 Winged Sliver C .20 .50
861 Clot Sliver C .10 .25
862 Crippling Fear R .30 .75
863 Crypt Sliver C .20 .50
864 Cunning Rhetoric R .50 1.25
865 Doomwake Giant R .25 .60
866 Dreadhorde Invasion R .40 1.00
867 The Eldest Reborn U .12 .30
868 Erebos, Bleak-Hearted M .30 .75
869 Mindwrack Harpy C .10 .25
870 Syphon Sliver R 1.00 2.50
871 Blade Sliver U .10 .25
872 Blasphemous Act R 1.25 3.00
873 Blur Sliver C .10 .25
874 Bonesplitter Sliver C .10 .25
875 Chandra, Awakened Inferno M 1.00 2.50
876 Chandra, Torch of Defiance M 1.25 3.00
877 Cleaving Sliver C .10 .25
878 Hollowhead Sliver U .10 .25
879 Repeated Reverberation R .10 .25
880 Sarkhan the Masterless R .15 .40
881 Spiteful Sliver R .30 .75
882 Striking Sliver C .20 .50
883 Two-Headed Sliver C .10 .25
884 Abundance R .10 .25
885 Arasta of the Endless Web R .15 .40
886 The Binding of the Titans U .08 .20
887 Brood Sliver R .60 1.50
888 Courser of Kruphix R .60 1.50
889 Cultivate C .40 1.00
890 Destiny Spinner U .15 .40
891 Dryad of the Ilysian Grove R 5.00 12.00
892 Eidolon of Blossoms R .25 .60
893 Enchantress's Presence R .12 .30
894 Farseek C .60 1.50
895 Font of Fertility C .10 .25
896 Gemhide Sliver C .25 .60
897 Greater Tanuki C .04 .10
898 Herald of the Pantheon R .60 1.50
899 Khalni Heart Expedition C .10 .25
900 Manaweft Sliver U 2.00 5.00
901 Megantic Sliver R .30 .75
902 The Mending of Dominaria R .12 .30
903 Might Sliver U .10 .25
904 Nature's Lore C 1.00 2.50
905 Nessian Wanderer U .04 .10
906 Omen of the Hunt C .04 .10
907 Quick Sliver C .20 .50
908 Rampant Growth C .25 .60
909 Realmwalker R 2.00 5.00
910 Sanctum Weaver R .60 1.50
911 Sandwurm Convergence R .12 .30
912 Setessan Champion R .50 1.25
913 Three Visits U 2.50 6.00
914 Venom Sliver U .50 1.25
915 Verduran Enchantress R 1.00 2.50
916 Battle for Bretagard R .10 .25
917 Binding the Old Gods U .25 .60
918 Calix, Destiny's Hand M .40 1.00
919 Cloudshredder Sliver R .50 1.25
920 Crystalline Sliver U .75 2.00
921 Culling Ritual R .50 1.25
922 Decimate R .15 .40
923 Firewake Sliver U .12 .30
924 Harmonic Sliver U .20 .50
925 Hibernation Sliver U .25 .60
926 Jukai Naturalist U .10 .25
927 Lavabelly Sliver U .10 .25
928 Mirari's Wake M 3.00 8.00
929 Nahiri, the Harbinger M .20 .50
930 Narset of the Ancient Way M .20 .50
931 Narset, Enlightened Master M .15 .40
932 Necrotic Sliver U .10 .25
933 Nyx Weaver U .10 .25
934 Oath of Teferi R .12 .30
935 Saheeli, Sublime Artificer U .15 .40
936 Satyr Enchanter U .25 .60
937 Sliver Hivelord M 1.50 4.00
938 Sythis, Harvest's Hand R .75 2.00
939 Wall of Denial U .20 .50
940 Ancient Stone Idol R .12 .30
941 Azorius Signet U .15 .40
942 Boros Signet U .50 1.25
943 The Chain Veil M 1.50 4.00
944 Crashing Drawbridge C .75 2.00
945 Dreamstone Hedron U .10 .25
946 Duplicant R .10 .25
947 Endless Atlas R .40 1.00
948 Everflowing Chalice U .20 .50
949 Fireshrieker U .20 .50
950 Forsaken Monument M 2.50 6.00
951 Hangarback Walker R .75 2.00
952 Hedron Archive U .25 .60
953 Herald's Horn U 2.50 6.00
954 Honor-Worn Shaku U .10 .25
955 Icon of Ancestry R .20 .50
956 Investigator's Journal R .10 .25
957 Izzet Signet U .20 .50
958 Kaldra Compleat M 1.25 3.00
959 Mazemind Tome R .10 .25
960 Metalwork Colossus R .20 .50
961 Mind Stone C .12 .30
962 Mirage Mirror R .60 1.50
963 Myriad Construct R .05 .12
964 Mystic Forge R .40 1.00
965 Nevinyrral's Disk R .12 .30
966 Ornithopter of Paradise C 1.00 2.50
967 Palladium Myr U .40 1.00
968 Perilous Vault M .15 .40
969 Phyrexian Triniform M .25 .60
970 Pillar of Origins U .20 .50
971 Scaretiller C .08 .20
972 Silent Arbiter R 4.00 10.00
973 Solemn Simulacrum R .30 .75
974 Soul of New Phyrexia M .20 .50
975 Steel Hellkite R .12 .30
976 Stonecoil Serpent R .50 1.25
977 Suspicious Bookcase U .08 .20
978 Talisman of Conviction U .15 .40
979 Talisman of Creativity U .60 1.50
980 Talisman of Progress U .25 .60
981 Transmogrifying Wand R .10 .25
982 Vanquisher's Banner R 2.00 5.00
983 Wayfarer's Bauble C .10 .25
984 Worn Powerstone U .40 1.00
985 Arcane Lighthouse U 2.50 6.00
986 Arch of Orazca R .10 .25
987 Blast Zone R .15 .40
988 Bonders' Enclave R .50 1.25
989 Canopy Vista R .12 .30
990 Cascade Bluffs R 1.25 3.00
991 Cinder Glade R .15 .40
992 Eldrazi Temple U 4.00 10.00
993 Exotic Orchard R .10 .25
994 Flood Plain U .10 .25
995 Forge of Heroes C .10 .25
996 Fortified Village R .10 .25
997 Frontier Bivouac U .25 .60
998 Frostboil Snarl R .10 .25
999 Furycalm Snarl R .10 .25
1000 Geier Reach Sanitarium R 1.00 2.50
1001 Golgari Rot Farm C .20 .50
1002 Grasslands U .10 .25
1003 Guildless Commons U .50 1.25
1004 Interplanar Beacon U .08 .20
1005 Irrigated Farmland R .10 .25
1006 Jungle Shrine U .12 .30
1007 Karn's Bastion R .75 2.00
1008 Krosan Verge U .10 .25
1009 Mage-Ring Network U .10 .25
1010 Mirrorpool M .75 2.00
1011 Mobilized District R .05 .12
1012 Mountain Valley U .12 .30
1013 Mystic Gate R 2.50 6.00
1014 Mystic Monastery U .10 .25
1015 Necroblossom Snarl R .50 1.25
1016 Nomad Outpost U .75 2.00
1017 Opulent Palace U .20 .50
1018 Orzhov Basilica U .10 .25
1019 Port Town R .10 .25
1020 Prairie Stream R .10 .25
1021 Rocky Tar Pit U .12 .30
1022 Rugged Prairie R 1.00 2.50
1023 Ruins of Oran-Rief R .10 .25
1024 Sandsteppe Citadel U .15 .40
1025 Savage Lands U .50 1.25
1026 Scattered Groves R .12 .30
1027 Scavenger Grounds R .40 1.00
1028 Sea Gate Wreckage R .12 .30
1029 Seaside Citadel U .25 .60
1030 Secluded Courtyard U .30 .75
1031 Selesnya Sanctuary C .10 .25
1032 Sheltered Thicket R .10 .25
1033 Shineshadow Snarl R .12 .30
1034 Shrine of the Forsaken Gods R .10 .25
1035 Skycloud Expanse R .08 .20
1036 Smoldering Marsh R .40 1.00
1037 Sungrass Prairie R .10 .25
1038 Sunken Hollow R .10 .25
1039 Tainted Field U .10 .25
1040 Tainted Wood U .40 1.00
1041 Temple of Enlightenment R .08 .20
1042 Temple of Epiphany R .08 .20
1043 Temple of Malady R .15 .40
1044 Temple of Plenty R .10 .25
1045 Temple of Silence R .08 .20
1046 Temple of the False God U .10 .25
1047 Temple of Triumph R .05 .12
1048 Tomb of the Spirit Dragon U .15 .40
1049 Tyrite Sanctum R .50 1.25
1050 Unclaimed Territory U .25 .60
1051 Urza's Mine C .60 1.50
1052 Urza's Power Plant C .60 1.50
1053 Urza's Tower C .60 1.50
1054 War Room R 1.00 2.50
1055 Wastes C .40 1.00
1056 Wastes C .30 .75
1057 Kozilek, the Great Distortion
TEX FOIL BORDERLESS M 15.00 40.00
1058 Morophon, the Boundless
TEX FOIL BORDERLESS M 12.00 30.00
1059 Ulamog, the Ceaseless Hunger
TEX FOIL BORDERLESS M 30.00 80.00
1060 Urza, Lord High Artificer
TEX FOIL BORDERLESS M 20.00 50.00
1061 Mikaeus, the Unhallowed
TEX FOIL BORDERLESS M 12.00 30.00
1062 Neheb, the Eternal
TEX FOIL BORDERLESS M 10.00 25.00
1063 Omnath, Locus of Mana
TEX FOIL BORDERLESS M 10.00 25.00
1064 Selvala, Heart of the Wilds
TEX FOIL BORDERLESS M 20.00 50.00
1065 The Ur-Dragon TEX FOIL BORDERLESS M40.00 100.00
1066 Jeweled Lotus TEX FOIL BORDERLESS M300.00 800.00

2023 Magic The Gathering Commander Masters Foil

2 Kozilek, the Great Distortion M 4.00 10.00
3 Morophon, the Boundless M 6.00 15.00
4 Pathrazer of Ulamog U 1.00 2.50
5 Ulamog, the Ceaseless Hunger M 25.00 60.00
6 Ulamog's Crusher C .60 1.50
7 Ainok Bond-Kin C .05 .12
8 Alharu, Solemn Ritualist U .04 .10
9 All That Glitters C .40 1.00
10 Alms Collector R .40 1.00
11 Anafenza, Kin-Tree Spirit U .10 .25
12 Ancestral Blade C .04 .10
13 Angelic Field Marshal R .30 .75
14 Avacyn, Angel of Hope M 25.00 60.00
15 Baird, Steward of Argive U .15 .40
16 Balan, Wandering Knight R .25 .60
17 Battle Screech C .08 .20
18 Cartographer's Hawk U .10 .25
19 Custodi Squire C .05 .12
20 Danitha Capashen, Paragon U 1.25 3.00
21 Darksteel Mutation U 1.00 2.50
22 Elite Scaleguard U .05 .12
23 Fencing Ace U .04 .10
24 Flawless Maneuver R 5.00 12.00
25 Gavony Silversmith C .03 .08
26 Generous Gift C 1.25 3.00
27 Grand Abolisher R 3.00 8.00
28 Heavenly Blademaster R .20 .50
29 Heliod, Sun-Crowned M 8.00 20.00
30 Herald of the Host U .15 .40
31 Intangible Virtue U .12 .30
32 Jazal Goldmane R .20 .50
33 Keleth, Sunmane Familiar U .10 .25
34 Kemba, Kha Regent U .10 .25
35 Kirtar's Wrath U .05 .12
36 Knighted Myr C .08 .20
37 Land Tax M 10.00 25.00
38 Losheel, Clockwork Scholar U 1.25 3.00
39 Loyal Retainers M 1.50 4.00
40 Loyal Unicorn U .15 .40
41 Mace of the Valiant U .10 .25
42 Mangara, the Diplomat R 1.25 3.00
43 Ministrant of Obligation C .04 .10
44 Myrsmith C .08 .20
45 Nahiri, the Lithomancer R .30 .75
46 Odric, Master Tactician R .40 1.00
47 Palace Jailer U .15 .40
48 Palace Sentinels C .04 .10
49 Path to Exile U .50 1.25
50 Pianna, Nomad Captain U .10 .25
51 Puresteel Paladin R 1.00 2.50
52 Return to Dust U .10 .25
53 Righteous Confluence R .15 .40
54 Sephara, Sky's Blade R 1.00 2.50
55 Sevinne's Reclamation R .50 1.25
56 Shelter C .10 .25
57 Smothering Tithe M 15.00 40.00
58 Spectral Grasp C .04 .10
59 Steelshaper's Gift R 2.00 5.00
60 Sublime Exhalation R .10 .25
61 Sunblade Angel C .08 .20
62 Sunspear Shikari C .03 .08
63 Supply Runners C .05 .12
64 Swift Response C .04 .10
65 Teshar, Ancestor's Apostle U .12 .30
66 Thraben Inspector C .15 .40
67 Unbounded Potential C .05 .12
68 Wakening Sun's Avatar R .50 1.25
69 Wanderer's Strike C .03 .08
70 Wrath of God R 1.25 3.00
72 Aether Gale U .20 .50
73 Aminatou's Augury R .25 .60
74 Azami, Lady of Scrolls R .20 .50
75 Body Double U .10 .25
76 Braids, Conjurer Adept R .25 .60
77 Bribery M 4.00 10.00
78 Brinelin, the Moon Kraken U .10 .25
79 Capture of Jingzhou M 10.00 25.00
80 Commandeer R 1.50 4.00
81 Counterspell C 1.25 3.00
82 Coveted Peacock U .03 .08
83 Cryptic Serpent C .12 .30
84 Cyclonic Rift R 20.00 50.00
85 Day's Undoing R 1.25 3.00
86 Deep Analysis C .05 .12
87 Deranged Assistant C .04 .10
88 Efficient Construction U .20 .50
89 Evacuation R .50 1.25
90 Exclude C .05 .12
91 Fact or Fiction U .10 .25
92 Faerie Artisans R .50 1.25
93 Fall from Favor C .08 .20
94 Fierce Guardianship R 25.00 60.00
95 Filigree Attendant C .04 .10
96 Frantic Search C .12 .30
97 Ghost of Ramirez DePietro U .08 .20
98 Ghostly Flicker C 1.25 3.00
99 Goliath Sphinx C .03 .08
100 Inga Rune-Eyes U .03 .08
101 Kaho, Minamo Historian U .08 .20
102 Looter il-Kor C .10 .25
103 Lorthos, the Tidemaker R .20 .50
104 Loyal Drake U .15 .40
105 Minds Aglow R .40 1.00
106 Murder of Crows U .05 .12
107 Murmuring Mystic C .30 .75
108 Mystic Confluence R .40 1.00
109 Padeem, Consul of Innovation U .75 2.00
110 Personal Tutor R 3.00 8.00
111 Phyrexian Ingester U .08 .20
112 Portal Mage U .10 .25
113 Reality Shift U .25 .60
114 Renowned Weaponsmith C .03 .08
115 Resculpt C 1.50 4.00
116 Reverse Engineer C .05 .12
117 Rise from the Tides U .10 .25
118 Sai, Master Thopterist R .60 1.50
119 Shipwreck Dowser C .04 .10
120 Spellseeker M 8.00 20.00
121 Stitcher Geralf R .10 .25
122 Stormsurge Kraken R .30 .75
123 Sun Quan, Lord of Wu M 3.00 8.00
124 Talrand, Sky Summoner R .20 .50
125 Teferi, Temporal Archmage R .60 1.50
126 Tetsuko Umezawa, Fugitive U .12 .30
127 Thryx, the Sudden Storm U .15 .40
128 Torrential Gearhulk R .30 .75
129 Tromokratis U .12 .30
130 Urza, Lord High Artificer M 6.00 15.00
131 Vizier of Tumbling Sands C .12 .30
132 Whirler Rogue U .10 .25
133 Windcaller Aven C .04 .10
134 Windrider Wizard C .08 .20
135 Witching Well C .03 .08
137 Archfiend of Despair M 8.00 20.00
138 Bastion of Remembrance U .50 1.25
139 Bloodchief Ascension R 6.00 15.00
140 Cabal Patriarch U .10 .25
141 Cadaver Imp C .05 .12
142 Carrier Thrall C .04 .10
143 Carrion Grub C .04 .10
144 Chainer, Dementia Master R .10 .25
145 Corpse Augur U .10 .25
146 Curtains' Call R .25 .60
147 Deadly Rollick R 12.00 30.00
148 Decree of Pain R .20 .50
149 Demon's Disciple C .15 .40
150 Demonic Tutor M 25.00 60.00
151 Demonlord Belzenlok R .20 .50
152 Dread Drone C .04 .10
153 Dread Return C .15 .40
154 Drown in Sorrow C .10 .25
155 Endrek Sahr, Master Breeder R .25 .60
156 Exsanguinate U 1.50 4.00
157 Extinguish All Hope U .10 .25
158 Feast of Succession U .04 .10
159 Feed the Swarm C 1.50 4.00
160 Final Parting U .25 .60
161 Ghoulcaller Gisa R 1.00 2.50
162 Gonti, Lord of Luxury U .15 .40
163 Goremand U .04 .10
164 Gorex, the Tombshell U .10 .25
165 Grave Pact M 6.00 15.00

166 Heartless Act U .15 .40
167 Imp's Mischief R 3.00 8.00
168 Isareth the Awakener U .08 .20
169 Kindred Dominance R 4.00 10.00
170 Legion Vanguard C .04 .10
171 Lotleth Giant C .08 .20
172 Loyal Subordinate U .20 .50
173 Mikaeus, the Unhallowed M 5.00 12.00
174 Mire Triton C .10 .25
175 Nadier's Nightblade C .30 .75
176 Ob Nixilis of the Black Oath R .40 1.00
177 Ogre Slumlord R .25 .60
178 Phyrexian Gargantua C .03 .08
179 Priest of the Blood Rite U .10 .25
180 Rankle, Master of Pranks R .60 1.50
181 Razaketh, the Foulblooded M 6.00 15.00
182 Read the Bones C 1.25 3.00
183 Reassembling Skeleton U 2.00 5.00
184 Rune-Scarred Demon R 1.50 4.00
185 Serrated Scorpion C .10 .25
186 Shirei, Shizo's Caretaker U .10 .25
187 Sower of Discord R 2.00 5.00
188 Supernatural Stamina C .08 .20
189 Taborax, Hope's Demise U .10 .25
190 Thorn of the Black Rose C .20 .50
191 Toxic Deluge R 5.00 12.00
192 Tragic Slip C .25 .60
193 Twilight Prophet M 2.00 5.00
194 Twisted Abomination C .03 .08
195 Victimize U .60 1.50
196 Vindictive Lich R .20 .50
197 Wake the Dead R .15 .40
198 Whisper, Blood Liturgist U .12 .30
199 Witch's Cauldron C .05 .12
200 Wretched Confluence R .15 .40
201 Yahenni, Undying Partisan U .30 .75
202 Yargle, Glutton of Urborg U .10 .25
203 Abrade C .12 .30
204 Anax, Hardened in the Forge U .08 .20
205 Ashling the Pilgrim R .12 .30
206 Avatar of Slaughter R .10 .25
207 Balefire Dragon M 6.00 15.00
208 Blood Aspirant C .03 .08
209 Captain Ripley Vance U .04 .10
210 Champion of the Flame C .04 .10
211 Crimson Fleet Commodore C .04 .10
212 Cyclops Electromancer C .03 .08
213 Daretti, Scrap Savant R .75 2.00
214 Deflecting Swat R 25.00 60.00
215 Disrupt Decorum R .30 .75
216 Divergent Transformations R .12 .30
217 Dragon Fodder C .25 .60
218 Drakuseth, Maw of Flames R .60 1.50
219 Dwarven Hammer C .03 .08
220 Faithless Looting C 1.50 4.00
221 Fiendlash U .10 .25
222 Fiery Confluence R .75 2.00
223 Fists of Flame C 1.00 2.50
224 Frontier Warmonger U .10 .25
225 Furious Rise U .05 .12
226 Gargadon C .03 .08
227 Godo, Bandit Warlord R .50 1.25
228 Grenzo, Havoc Raiser R .75 2.00
229 Guttersnipe C .12 .30
230 Havoc Jester U .03 .08
231 Heartless Hidetsugu R .75 2.00
232 Hellkite Charger R 1.00 2.50
233 Hoarding Dragon U .10 .25
234 Impulsive Pilferer C .20 .50
235 Inferno Titan R .15 .40
236 Insurrection M 3.00 8.00
237 Kazuul, Tyrant of the Cliffs U .10 .25
238 Krenko, Mob Boss R 1.00 2.50
239 Living Lightning C .04 .10
240 Loyal Apprentice U 1.25 3.00
241 Magus of the Wheel R .40 1.00
242 Makeshift Munitions C .10 .25
243 Meteoric Mace U .05 .12
244 Neheb, the Eternal M 2.50 6.00
245 Nesting Dragon R .75 2.00
246 Purphoros, God of the Forge M 10.00 25.00
247 Rakka Mar U .05 .12
248 Rapacious Dragon C .10 .25
249 Rapacious One C .12 .30
250 Ravaging Blaze U .08 .20
251 Rorix Bladewing U .12 .30
252 Savage Beating M 4.00 10.00
253 Scourge of the Throne R .50 1.25
254 Skyline Despot U 3.00 8.00
255 Slice and Dice U .04 .10
256 Spikeshot Goblin C .08 .20
257 Spitebellows C .03 .08
258 Squee, Goblin Nabob U .12 .30
259 Star of Extinction R .50 1.25
260 Storm-Kiln Artist U .75 2.00
261 Subira, Tulzidi Caravanner U .08 .20
262 Sulfurous Blast C .04 .10
263 Tempt with Vengeance R .60 1.50
264 Temur Battle Rage C .12 .30
265 Treasure Nabber R .75 2.00
266 Valduk, Keeper of the Flame U .08 .20
267 Vandalblast U 1.50 4.00
269 Abundant Harvest C .04 .10
270 Acidic Slime U .10 .25
271 Animal Magnetism U .03 .08
272 Arachnogenesis R 2.00 5.00
273 Armorcraft Judge U .10 .25
274 Azusa, Lost but Seeking R 4.00 10.00
275 Beanstalk Giant U .15 .40
276 Bloodspore Thrinax R .15 .40
277 Broken Wings C .03 .08
278 Courage in Crisis C .04 .10
279 Crash of Rhino Beetles C .10 .25
280 Craterhoof Behemoth M 20.00 50.00
281 Crawling Infestation C .10 .25
282 Deadly Recluse C .10 .25
283 Doubling Season M 25.00 60.00
284 Elvish Mystic C 2.50 6.00
285 Entourage of Trest C .04 .10
286 Eternal Witness U 1.00 2.50
287 Ezuri's Predation R 1.25 3.00
288 Fierce Empath C .20 .50
289 Finale of Devastation M 15.00 40.00
290 Freyalise, Llanowar's Fury R 1.00 2.50
291 Fungal Plots U .10 .25
292 Ghalta, Primal Hunger R 2.00 5.00
293 Goreclaw, Terror of Qal Sisma U .50 1.25
294 The Great Henge M 30.00 80.00
295 Heroic Intervention R 5.00 12.00
296 Hunter's Insight U .15 .40
297 Ilysian Caryatid C .12 .30
298 Jade Mage U .10 .25
299 Jolrael, Mwonvuli Recluse R .12 .30
300 Kodama's Reach C .75 2.00
301 Kozilek's Predator C .10 .25
302 Krosan Tusker C .04 .10
303 Lifeblood Hydra R 1.00 2.50
304 Loyal Guardian U .20 .50
305 Molimo, Maro-Sorcerer U .05 .12
306 Mowu, Loyal Companion U .10 .25
307 Nemata, Grove Guardian U .10 .25
308 Obscuring Haze R 1.25 3.00
309 Ohran Frostfang R 1.00 2.50
310 Omnath, Locus of Mana M 1.50 4.00
311 Oviya Pashiri, Sage Lifecrafter U .05 .12
312 Pollenbright Druid C .12 .30
313 Predatory Rampage U .05 .12
314 Ram Through C .75 2.00
315 Rampaging Brontodon U .12 .30
316 Regal Behemoth R .40 1.00
317 Rishkar, Peema Renegade U .25 .60
318 Rot Shambler C .05 .12
319 Sakiko, Mother of Summer R .20 .50
320 Selvala, Heart of the Wilds M 10.00 25.00
321 Skyshroud Claim C 4.00 10.00
322 Skysnare Spider C .08 .20
323 Snakeskin Veil C .12 .30
324 Song of the Dryads R 2.00 5.00
325 Stonehoof Chieftain R 1.00 2.50
326 Surrak, the Hunt Caller U .10 .25
327 Tooth and Nail R 1.25 3.00
328 Tuskguard Captain C .04 .10
329 Verdant Confluence R .12 .30
330 Verdeloth the Ancient U .12 .30
331 Wayward Swordtooth R 2.50 6.00
332 Wildwood Scourge U .20 .50
333 Yedora, Grave Gardener U .10 .25
334 Yisan, the Wanderer Bard R .20 .50
335 Akiri, Fearless Voyager U .20 .50
336 Aryel, Knight of Windgrace U .08 .20
337 Experiment Kraj R .15 .40
338 Gisela, Blade of Goldnight R 1.50 4.00
339 Hamza, Guardian of Arashin U .10 .25
340 Hanna, Ship's Navigator R .20 .50
341 Judith, the Scourge Diva U .40 1.00
342 Karador, Ghost Chieftain R .15 .40
343 Kykar, Wind's Fury R .25 .60
344 Maelstrom Wanderer R 1.00 2.50
345 Melek, Izzet Paragon U .10 .25
346 Meren of Clan Nel Toth R 1.50 4.00
347 Mirri, Weatherlight Duelist R 1.50 4.00
348 Mizzix of the Izmagnus R .20 .50
349 Nekusar, the Mindrazer R .50 1.25
350 Queen Marchesa R 1.25 3.00
351 Raff Capashen, Ship's Mage U .12 .30
352 Rafiq of the Many R .15 .40
353 The Scarab God M 6.00 15.00
354 Sek'Kuar, Deathkeeper R .10 .25
355 Sidisi, Brood Tyrant R .20 .50
356 Slimefoot, the Stowaway U .12 .30
357 Taigam, Sidisi's Hand U .10 .25
358 Tatyova, Benthic Druid U .15 .40
359 Teysa Karlov R .60 1.50
360 Tuya Bearclaw U .08 .20
361 The Ur-Dragon M 12.00 30.00
362 Xantcha, Sleeper Agent R .30 .75
363 Yennett, Cryptic Sovereign R .10 .25
364 Yuriko, the Tiger's Shadow R .50 1.25
367 Arcane Signet U .60 1.50
368 Ashnod's Altar U 4.00 10.00
369 Assault Suit U .10 .25
370 Bonder's Ornament C .10 .25
371 Boompile R .20 .50
372 Brass Knuckles C .10 .25
373 Burnished Hart U .10 .25
374 Campfire C .15 .40
375 Champion's Helm R 1.00 2.50
376 Chromatic Lantern R 2.00 5.00
377 Commander's Sphere C 2.50 6.00
378 Darksteel Ingot C .15 .40
379 Emerald Medallion R 3.00 8.00
380 Explorer's Scope C .12 .30
381 Extraplanar Lens M 4.00 10.00
382 Fellwar Stone U 1.25 3.00
383 Firemind Vessel C .10 .25
384 Forebear's Blade U .10 .25
385 Foundry Inspector C .75 2.00
386 Geode Golem U .30 .75
387 Gilded Lotus R 1.00 2.50
388 Hammer of Nazahn R 5.00 12.00
389 Haunted Cloak C .50 1.25
390 Heart-Piercer Bow C .04 .10
391 Hero's Blade U .12 .30
392 Idol of Oblivion R 1.00 2.50
393 The Immortal Sun M 6.00 15.00
394 Inspiring Statuary R .25 .60
395 Jet Medallion R 8.00 20.00
396 Jeweled Lotus M 60.00 150.00
397 Letter of Acceptance C .05 .12
398 Lightning Greaves U 3.00 8.00
399 Meteor Golem U .15 .40
400 Myr Sire C .10 .25
401 Pearl Medallion R 3.00 8.00
402 Pilgrim's Eye C .03 .08
403 Prismatic Lens C .15 .40
404 Prophetic Prism C .04 .10
405 Ruby Medallion R 8.00 20.00
406 Sandstone Oracle U .10 .25
407 Sapphire Medallion R 6.00 15.00
408 Scytheclaw R .12 .30
409 Shimmer Myr U .20 .50
410 Sol Ring U 1.50 4.00
411 Spectral Searchlight U .05 .12
412 Staunch Throneguard C .10 .25
413 Sword of the Animist R 4.00 10.00
414 Thought Vessel U .75 2.00
415 Thran Dynamo U 1.50 4.00
416 Unstable Obelisk C .10 .25
417 Vial of Dragonfire C .03 .08
418 Vulshok Battlegear C .05 .12
419 Ash Barrens C .10 .25
420 Command Tower C 1.00 2.50
421 Myriad Landscape U .30 .75
422 Opal Palace C .25 .60
423 Path of Ancestry C .20 .50
424 Rejuvenating Springs R 3.00 8.00
425 Reliquary Tower U 1.00 2.50
426 Rogue's Passage U 2.00 5.00
427 Spectator Seating R 5.00 12.00
428 Terramorphic Expanse C .40 1.00
429 Thriving Bluff C .10 .25
430 Thriving Grove C .10 .25
431 Thriving Heath C .10 .25
432 Thriving Isle C .10 .25
433 Thriving Moor C .05 .12
434 Training Center R 5.00 12.00
435 Undergrowth Stadium R 4.00 10.00
436 Vault of Champions R 5.00 12.00
437 Plains RETRO FRAME L .20 .50
438 Plains RETRO FRAME L .50 1.25
439 Plains RETRO FRAME L .15 .40
440 Island RETRO FRAME L .60 1.50
441 Island RETRO FRAME L .50 1.25
442 Island RETRO FRAME L .20 .50
443 Swamp RETRO FRAME L .25 .60
444 Swamp RETRO FRAME L 1.25 3.00
445 Swamp RETRO FRAME L .40 1.00
446 Mountain RETRO FRAME L .25 .60
447 Mountain RETRO FRAME L .50 1.25
448 Mountain RETRO FRAME L .25 .60
449 Forest RETRO FRAME L .25 .60
450 Forest RETRO FRAME L 1.00 2.50
451 Forest RETRO FRAME L .25 .60
622 All That Glitters BORDERLESS C .20 .50
623 Darksteel Mutation BORDERLESS U 1.25 3.00
624 Generous Gift BORDERLESS C .40 1.00
625 Grand Abolisher BORDERLESS R 4.00 10.00
626 Path to Exile BORDERLESS U 1.50 4.00
627 Puresteel Paladin BORDERLESS R .75 2.00
628 Return to Dust BORDERLESS U .15 .40
629 Steelshaper's Gift BORDERLESS R 1.25 3.00
630 Counterspell BORDERLESS C .75 2.00
631 Fact or Fiction BORDERLESS U .20 .50
632 Frantic Search BORDERLESS C .12 .30
633 Personal Tutor BORDERLESS R 2.00 5.00
634 Reality Shift BORDERLESS U .60 1.50
635 Spellseeker BORDERLESS M 8.00 20.00
636 Bloodchief Ascension BORDERLESS R 5.00 12.00
637 Dread Return BORDERLESS C .30 .75
638 Exsanguinate BORDERLESS U 2.00 5.00
639 Grave Pact BORDERLESS M 8.00 20.00
640 Kindred Dominance BORDERLESS R 4.00 10.00
641 Nadier's Nightblade BORDERLESS C .20 .50
642 Faithless Looting BORDERLESS C .15 .40
643 Magus of the Wheel BORDERLESS R .30 .75
644 Storm-Kiln Artist BORDERLESS U 2.00 5.00
645 Treasure Nabber BORDERLESS R .50 1.25
646 Vandalblast BORDERLESS U 2.00 5.00
647 Arachnogenesis BORDERLESS R 1.50 4.00
648 Elvish Mystic BORDERLESS C .75 2.00
649 Kodama's Reach BORDERLESS C 1.00 2.50
650 Ohran Frostfang BORDERLESS R 2.00 5.00
651 Regal Behemoth BORDERLESS R .60 1.50
652 Tooth and Nail BORDERLESS R 1.00 2.50
653 Arcane Signet BORDERLESS U 2.50 6.00
654 Champion's Helm BORDERLESS R .75 2.00
655 Commander's Sphere BORDERLESS C .30 .75
656 Extraplanar Lens BORDERLESS M 3.00 8.00
657 Fellwar Stone BORDERLESS U 2.50 6.00
658 Thran Dynamo BORDERLESS U 2.50 6.00
659 Command Tower BORDERLESS C 1.50 4.00
660 Myriad Landscape BORDERLESS U 1.00 2.50
661 Path of Ancestry BORDERLESS C .40 1.00
662 Rejuvenating Springs BORDERLESS R 3.00 8.00
663 Reliquary Tower BORDERLESS U 3.00 8.00
664 Spectator Seating BORDERLESS R 5.00 12.00
665 Training Center BORDERLESS R 5.00 12.00
666 Undergrowth Stadium BORDERLESS R 4.00 10.00
667 Vault of Champions BORDERLESS R 4.00 10.00
668 Kozilek, the Great Distortion BORDERLESS M4.00 10.00
669 Morophon, the Boundless BORDERLESS M6.00 15.00
670 Ulamog, the Ceaseless Hunger BORDERLESS M 25.00 60.00
671 Kemba, Kha Regent BORDERLESS U .10 .25
672 Azami, Lady of Scrolls BORDERLESS R .20 .50
673 Talrand, Sky Summoner BORDERLESS R .50 1.25
674 Urza, Lord High Artificer BORDERLESS M6.00 15.00
675 Mikaeus, the Unhallowed BORDERLESS M5.00 12.00
676 Shirei, Shizo's Caretaker BORDERLESS U .10 .25
677 Grenzo, Havoc Raiser BORDERLESS R .75 2.00
678 Neheb, the Eternal BORDERLESS M 2.00 5.00
679 Azusa, Lost but Seeking BORDERLESS R 4.00 10.00
680 Omnath, Locus of Mana BORDERLESS M 2.00 5.00
681 Selvala, Heart of the Wilds BORDERLESS M8.00 20.00
682 Gisela, Blade of Goldnight BORDERLESS R1.00 2.50
683 Kykar, Wind's Fury BORDERLESS R .30 .75
684 Maelstrom Wanderer BORDERLESS R 1.25 3.00
685 Meren of Clan Nel Toth BORDERLESS R 1.00 2.50
686 Slimefoot, the Stowaway BORDERLESS U .25 .60
687 Tatyova, Benthic Druid BORDERLESS U 2.00 5.00
688 Teysa Karlov BORDERLESS R .50 1.25
689 The Ur-Dragon BORDERLESS M 12.00 30.00
692 Flawless Maneuver FRAME BREAK R 8.00 20.00
693 Smothering Tithe FRAME BREAK M 15.00 40.00
694 Fierce Guardianship FRAME BREAK R 40.00 100.00
695 Deadly Rollick FRAME BREAK R 15.00 40.00
696 Demonic Tutor FRAME BREAK M 40.00 100.00
697 Balefire Dragon FRAME BREAK M 8.00 20.00
698 Deflecting Swat FRAME BREAK R 30.00 80.00
699 Insurrection FRAME BREAK M 3.00 8.00
700 Finale of Devastation FRAME BREAK M 20.00 50.00
701 Obscuring Haze FRAME BREAK R 2.00 5.00
702 Jeweled Lotus FRAME BREAK M 100.00 250.00
703 Sol Ring FRAME BREAK U 10.00 25.00
705 Anikthea, Hand of Erebos M .30 .75
706 Commodore Guff M .25 .60
707 Sliver Gravemother M 4.00 10.00
708 Omarthis, Ghostfire Initiate M .30 .75
709 Leori, Sparktouched Hunter M .12 .30
710 Narci, Fable Singer M .50 1.25
711 Rukarumel, Biologist M .40 1.00
733 Lazotep Sliver R 2.00 5.00
744 Abstruse Archaic EXT ART R 2.00 5.00
745 Calamity of the Titans EXT ART R 10.00 25.00
746 Desecrate Reality EXT ART R 5.00 12.00
747 Flayer of Loyalties EXT ART R 20.00 50.00
748 Omarthis, Ghostfire Initiate EXT ART M 2.00 5.00
749 Rise of the Eldrazi EXT ART R 12.00 30.00
750 Skittering Cicada EXT ART R 10.00 25.00
751 Ugin's Mastery EXT ART R 1.25 3.00
753 Boon of the Spirit Realm EXT ART R .50 1.25
754 Gatewatch Beacon EXT ART R .40 1.00
755 Onakke Oathkeeper EXT ART R .40 1.00
756 Ondu Spiritdancer EXT ART R 5.00 12.00
757 Regal Sliver EXT ART R .75 2.00
758 Sparkshaper Visionary EXT ART R .12 .30
759 Taunting Sliver EXT ART R 1.00 2.50
760 Titan of Littjara EXT ART R 6.00 15.00
761 Cacophony Unleashed EXT ART R .20 .50
762 Demon of Fate's Design EXT ART R .75 2.00
763 Ghoulish Impetus EXT ART R 2.50 6.00
764 Lazotep Sliver EXT ART R 1.25 3.00
765 Capricious Sliver EXT ART R .40 1.00
766 Descendants' Fury EXT ART R 1.50 4.00
767 Guff Rewrites History EXT ART R 2.00 5.00
768 Jaya's Phoenix EXT ART R .75 2.00
769 Composer of Spring EXT ART R 2.50 6.00
770 For the Ancestors EXT ART R 1.25 3.00
771 Hatchery Sliver EXT ART R 2.50 6.00
772 Nyxborn Behemoth EXT ART R .60 1.50
773 Anikthea, Hand of Erebos EXT ART M 10.00 25.00
774 Leori, Sparktouched Hunter EXT ART M 1.00 2.50
775 Narci, Fable Singer EXT ART M 4.00 10.00
776 Rukarumel, Biologist EXT ART M 2.50 6.00
777 Sliver Gravemother EXT ART M 20.00 50.00
778 Darksteel Monolith EXT ART R 30.00 80.00

2023 Magic The Gathering Dominaria Remastered

1 Auramancer C .08 .20
2 Battle Screech U .08 .20
3 Cleric of the Forward Order C .08 .20
4 Congregate U .08 .20
5 Divine Sacrament R .08 .20
6 Enlightened Tutor R 10.00 25.00
7 Glory R .08 .20
8 Griffin Guide U .08 .20
9 Icatian Javelineers C .08 .20
10 Improvised Armor U .08 .20
11 Kjeldoran Gargoyle C .08 .20
12 Lieutenant Kirtar R .08 .20
13 Lyra Dawnbringer M 2.00 5.00
14 Mesa Enchantress U .20 .50
15 Momentary Blink C .08 .20
16 Mystic Zealot C .08 .20
17 Nomad Decoy C .08 .20
18 Orim's Thunder C .08 .20
19 Pacifism C .08 .20
20 Phantom Flock C .08 .20
21 Radiant's Judgment C .08 .20
22 Remedy C .08 .20
23 Renewed Faith C .08 .20
24 Savannah Lions C .08 .20
25 Serra Angel U .08 .20
26 Serra Avatar M .20 .50
27 Sevinne's Reclamation R .40 1.00
28 Spectral Lynx U .08 .20
29 Spirit Link C .08 .20
30 Sun Clasp C .08 .20
31 Swords to Plowshares U .50 1.25
32 Test of Endurance M 2.00 5.00
33 Vigilant Sentry C .08 .20
34 Voice of All U .08 .20
35 Whitemane Lion C .08 .20
36 Windborn Muse R .15 .40
37 Wrath of God R 1.00 2.50
38 Aquamoeba C .08 .20
39 Arcanis the Omnipotent R .20 .50
40 Aven Fateshaper U .08 .20
41 Aven Fisher C .08 .20
42 Circular Logic U .08 .20
43 Cloud of Faeries C .08 .20
44 Confiscate U .08 .20
45 Counterspell C .75 2.00
46 Deep Analysis C .08 .20
47 Denizen of the Deep R .08 .20
48 Fact or Fiction U .08 .20
49 Floodgate U .08 .20
50 Force of Will M 25.00 60.00
51 Frantic Search C .12 .30
52 Glintwing Invoker C .08 .20
53 Hermetic Study C .08 .20
54 High Tide U .20 .50
55 Horseshoe Crab C .08 .20
56 Impulse C .08 .20
57 Leaden Fists C .08 .20
58 Man-o'-War C .08 .20
59 Mystic Remora R 3.00 8.00
60 Mystical Tutor R 4.00 10.00
61 Obsessive Search C .08 .20
62 Opposition R 1.00 2.50
63 Ovinize C .08 .20
64 Ovinomancer U .08 .20
65 Peregrine Drake C .08 .20
66 Snap C .40 1.00
67 Stroke of Genius R .08 .20
68 Thieving Magpie U .08 .20
69 Time Stretch M 2.00 5.00
70 Turnabout U .08 .20
71 Urza, Lord High Artificer M 5.00 12.00
72 Veiled Serpent C .08 .20
73 Vexing Sphinx R .08 .20
74 Wormfang Drake C .08 .20
75 Body Snatcher R .08 .20
76 Cackling Fiend C .08 .20
77 Chainer, Dementia Master R .08 .20
78 Chainer's Edict U .30 .75
79 Dark Withering U .08 .20
80 Dread Return U .08 .20
81 Duress C .08 .20
82 Entomb R 4.00 10.00
83 Evil Eye of Orms-by-Gore C :K: .08 .20
84 Faceless Butcher U .08 .20
85 Festering Goblin C .08 .20
86 Flesh Reaver U .08 .20

87 Goblin Turncoat C	.08	.20
88 Howl from Beyond C	.08	.20
89 Hyalopterous Lemure C	.08	.20
90 Ichor Slick C	.08	.20
91 Mindslicer R	.15	.40
92 Nantuko Shade R	.08	.20
93 Necrosavant U	.08	.20
94 Nightscape Familiar C	.12	.30
95 No Mercy M	5.00	12.00
96 Oversold Cemetery R	.30	.75
97 Phyrexian Debaser C	.08	.20
98 Phyrexian Ghoul C	.08	.20
99 Phyrexian Rager C	.08	.20
100 Phyrexian Scuta U	.08	.20
101 Royal Assassin R	.40	1.00
102 Street Wraith C	.08	.20
103 Terror C	.08	.20
104 Twisted Experiment C	.08	.20
105 Undead Gladiator U	.08	.20
106 Urborg Syphon-Mage C	.08	.20
107 Urborg Uprising C	.08	.20
108 Vampiric Tutor M	15.00	40.00
109 Wretched Anurid C	.08	.20
110 Yawgmoth, Thran Physician M	8.00	20.00
111 Zombie Infestation U	.08	.20
112 Avarax C	.08	.20
113 Chain Lightning C	.12	.30
114 Coal Stoker C	.08	.20
115 Deadapult U	.08	.20
116 Dragon Whelp U	.08	.20
117 Ember Beast C	.08	.20
118 Empty the Warrens C	.08	.20
119 Fireblast U	.12	.30
120 Flametongue Kavu U	.08	.20
121 Gamble R	2.50	6.00
122 Gempalm Incinerator U	.08	.20
123 Goblin Matron C	.08	.20
124 Goblin Medics C	.08	.20
125 Grapeshot C	.08	.20
126 Grim Lavamancer R	.08	.20
127 Last Chance M	.60	1.50
128 Lightning Reflexes C	.08	.20
129 Lightning Rift U	.08	.20
130 Macetail Hystrodon C	.08	.20
131 Mogg War Marshal C	.08	.20
132 Overmaster R	.30	.75
133 Pashalik Mons R	.50	1.25
134 Ridgetop Raptor C	.08	.20
135 Shivan Dragon R	.08	.20
136 Siege-Gang Commander R	.08	.20
137 Skirk Prospector C	.08	.20
138 Slice and Dice U	.08	.20
139 Sneak Attack M	3.00	8.00
140 Solar Blast C	.08	.20
141 Spark Spray C	.08	.20
142 Storm Entity U	.08	.20
143 Subterranean Scout C	.08	.20
144 Sulfuric Vortex R	.20	.50
145 Suq'Ata Lancer C	.08	.20
146 Undying Rage C	.08	.20
147 Valduk, Keeper of the Flame U	.08	.20
148 Worldgorger Dragon M	.50	1.25
149 Arboria R	.08	.20
150 Battlefield Scrounger C	.08	.20
151 Birds of Paradise R	3.00	8.00
152 Break Asunder C	.08	.20
153 Call of the Herd U	.08	.20
154 Crop Rotation U	.50	1.25
155 Deadwood Treefolk U	.08	.20
156 Elvish Aberration C	.08	.20
157 Elvish Spirit Guide U	.50	1.25
158 Emerald Charm C	.08	.20
159 Exploration R	8.00	20.00
160 Fa'adiyah Seer C	.08	.20
161 Forgotten Ancient R	.30	.75
162 Gamekeeper U	.08	.20
163 Giant Spider C	.08	.20
164 Invigorating Boon U	.08	.20
165 Jolrael, Mwonvuli Recluse R	.08	.20
166 Kamahl, Fist of Krosa M	.40	1.00
167 Kavu Primarch C	.08	.20
168 Krosan Restorer C	.08	.20
169 Lull C	.08	.20
170 Nature's Lore U	1.00	2.50
171 Nut Collector M	.50	1.25
172 Penumbra Bobcat C	.08	.20
173 Primal Boost C	.08	.20
174 Sandstorm C	.08	.20
175 Saproling Symbiosis R	.20	.50
176 Seton's Desire C	.08	.20
177 Squirrel Nest U	.08	.20
178 Stonewood Invoker C	.08	.20
179 Sylvan Library M	10.00	25.00
180 Symbiotic Beast C	.08	.20
181 Terravore U	.08	.20
182 Werebear C	.08	.20
183 Wild Dogs C	.08	.20
184 Wild Growth C	.15	.40
185 Worldly Tutor R	6.00	15.00
186 Absorb R	.20	.50
187 Arcades Sabboth R	.08	.20
188 Decimate R	.20	.50
189 Dralnu's Crusade U	.08	.20
190 Gerrard's Verdict U	.08	.20
191 Hunting Grounds M	.60	1.50
192 Mystic Enforcer U	.08	.20
193 Phantom Nishoba R	.08	.20
194 Pyre Zombie R	.08	.20
195 Quicksilver Dagger U	.08	.20
196 Radha, Heir to Keld U	.08	.20
197 Recoil U	.08	.20
198 Rith, the Awakener R	.08	.20
199 Sawtooth Loon U	.08	.20
200 Sol'kanar the Swamp King R	.08	.20
201 Spinal Embrace R	.08	.20
202 Spiritmonger U	.08	.20
203 Tatyova, Benthic Druid U	.12	.30
204 Tiana, Ship's Caretaker U	.08	.20
205 Xira Arien R	.08	.20
206 Zur the Enchanter R	.25	.60
207 Stand // Deliver U	.08	.20
208 Spite // Malice U	.08	.20
209 Pain // Suffering U	.08	.20
210 Assault // Battery U	.08	.20
211 Wax // Wane U	.08	.20
212 Order // Chaos U	.08	.20
213 Illusion // Reality U	.08	.20
214 Night // Day U	.08	.20
215 Fire // Ice U	.12	.30
216 Life // Death U	.08	.20
217 Crawlspace R	1.50	4.00
218 Cryptic Gateway R	2.00	5.00
219 Damping Sphere U	.20	.50
220 Dodecapod U	.08	.20
221 Dragon Blood U	.08	.20
222 Dragon Engine C	.08	.20
223 Gauntlet of Power M	1.25	3.00
224 Helm of Awakening R	.60	1.50
225 Icy Manipulator U	.08	.20
226 Jalum Tome C	.08	.20
227 Jester's Cap R	.08	.20
228 Juggernaut C	.08	.20
229 Legacy Weapon M	.20	.50
230 Lotus Blossom R	.12	.30
231 Millikin U	.08	.20
232 Mind Stone C	.08	.20
233 Ornithopter C	.08	.20
234 Thran Golem U	.08	.20
235 Tormod's Crypt U	.20	.50
236 Triskelion R	.08	.20
237 Umbilicus R	.08	.20
238 Urza's Blueprints R	.08	.20
239 Urza's Incubator M	15.00	40.00
240 Wall of Junk U	.08	.20
241 Clifftop Retreat R	1.25	3.00
242 Crosis's Catacombs U	.08	.20
243 Darigaaz's Caldera U	.08	.20
244 Dark Depths M	3.00	8.00
245 Drifting Meadow C	.08	.20
246 Dromar's Cavern U	.08	.20
247 Gemstone Mine R	.50	1.25
248 Hinterland Harbor R	1.25	3.00
249 Isolated Chapel R	1.50	4.00
250 Maze of Ith R	2.00	5.00
251 Mishra's Factory U	.08	.20
252 Nantuko Monastery U	.08	.20
253 Polluted Mire C	.08	.20
254 Remote Isle C	.08	.20
255 Rith's Grove U	.08	.20
256 Slippery Karst C	.08	.20
257 Smoldering Crater C	.08	.20
258 Sulfur Falls R	.75	2.00
259 Terminal Moraine C	.08	.20
260 Treva's Ruins U	.08	.20
261 Woodland Cemetery R	1.50	4.00
262 Divine Sacrament R	.08	.20
263 Enlightened Tutor R	8.00	20.00
264 Glory R	.08	.20
265 Lieutenant Kirtar R	.08	.20
266 Lyra Dawnbringer M	1.50	4.00
267 Mesa Enchantress U	.15	.40
268 Momentary Blink C	.08	.20
269 Renewed Faith C	.08	.20
270 Savannah Lions C	.08	.20
271 Serra Angel U	.08	.20
272 Serra Avatar M	.15	.40
273 Sevinne's Reclamation R	.60	1.50
274 Spirit Link C	.08	.20
275 Swords to Plowshares U	.75	2.00
276 Test of Endurance M	.50	1.25
277 Whitemane Lion C	.08	.20
278 Windborn Muse R	.12	.30
279 Wrath of God R	1.00	2.50
280 Arcanis the Omnipotent R	.12	.30
281 Counterspell C	.40	1.00
282 Denizen of the Deep R	.08	.20
283 Fact or Fiction U	.08	.20
284 Force of Will M	25.00	60.00
285 Frantic Search C	.08	.20
286 High Tide U	.20	.50
287 Impulse C	.08	.20
288 Mystic Remora R	2.50	6.00
289 Mystical Tutor R	3.00	8.00
290 Opposition R	.50	1.25
291 Ovinize C	.08	.20
292 Peregrine Drake C	.08	.20
293 Stroke of Genius R	.12	.30
294 Time Stretch M	1.50	4.00
295 Turnabout U	.08	.20
296 Urza, Lord High Artificer M	5.00	12.00
297 Vexing Sphinx R	.08	.20
298 Body Snatcher R	.08	.20
299 Chainer, Dementia Master R	.08	.20
300 Chainer's Edict U	.30	.75
301 Dark Withering U	.08	.20
302 Dread Return U	.25	.60
303 Duress C	.08	.20
304 Entomb R	3.00	8.00
305 Mindslicer R	.15	.40
306 Nantuko Shade R	.08	.20
307 Necrosavant U	.08	.20
308 No Mercy M	3.00	8.00
309 Oversold Cemetery R	.20	.50
310 Royal Assassin R	.25	.60
311 Street Wraith C	.08	.20
312 Terror C	.08	.20
313 Undead Gladiator U	.08	.20
314 Vampiric Tutor M	15.00	40.00
315 Yawgmoth, Thran Physician M	8.00	20.00
316 Chain Lightning C	.12	.30
317 Dragon Whelp U	.08	.20
318 Empty the Warrens C	.08	.20
319 Fireblast U	.12	.30
320 Flametongue Kavu U	.08	.20
321 Gamble R	2.00	5.00
322 Gempalm Incinerator U	.08	.20
323 Goblin Matron C	.08	.20
324 Grim Lavamancer R	.08	.20
325 Last Chance M	.60	1.50
326 Mogg War Marshal C	.08	.20
327 Overmaster R	.25	.60
328 Pashalik Mons R	.30	.75
329 Shivan Dragon R	.08	.20
330 Siege-Gang Commander R	.08	.20
331 Sneak Attack M	2.50	6.00
332 Sulfuric Vortex R	.12	.30
333 Valduk, Keeper of the Flame U	.08	.20
334 Worldgorger Dragon M	.40	1.00
335 Arboria R	.08	.20
336 Birds of Paradise R	2.50	6.00
337 Deadwood Treefolk U	.08	.20
338 Elvish Spirit Guide U	.50	1.25
339 Exploration R	5.00	12.00
340 Fa'adiyah Seer C	.08	.20
341 Forgotten Ancient R	.25	.60
342 Invigorating Boon U	.08	.20
343 Jolrael, Mwonvuli Recluse R	.08	.20
344 Kamahl, Fist of Krosa M	.25	.60
345 Lull C	.08	.20
346 Nature's Lore U	1.25	3.00
347 Nut Collector M	.40	1.00
348 Saproling Symbiosis R	.12	.30
349 Squirrel Nest U	.08	.20
350 Sylvan Library M	10.00	25.00
351 Wild Dogs C	.08	.20
352 Wild Growth C	.12	.30
353 Worldly Tutor R	5.00	12.00
354 Absorb R	.12	.30
355 Arcades Sabboth R	.08	.20
356 Decimate R	.15	.40
357 Dralnu's Crusade U	.08	.20
358 Gerrard's Verdict U	.08	.20
359 Hunting Grounds M	.30	.75
360 Mystic Enforcer U	.08	.20
361 Phantom Nishoba R	.08	.20
362 Pyre Zombie R	.08	.20
363 Quicksilver Dagger U	.08	.20
364 Radha, Heir to Keld U	.08	.20
365 Recoil U	.08	.20
366 Rith, the Awakener R	.08	.20
367 Sawtooth Loon U	.08	.20
368 Sol'kanar the Swamp King R	.08	.20
369 Spinal Embrace R	.08	.20
370 Spiritmonger U	.08	.20
371 Tatyova, Benthic Druid U	.08	.20
372 Tiana, Ship's Caretaker U	.08	.20
373 Xira Arien R	.08	.20
374 Zur the Enchanter R	.12	.30
375 Crawlspace R	1.25	3.00
376 Cryptic Gateway R	.20	.50
377 Damping Sphere U	.60	1.50
378 Gauntlet of Power M	1.00	2.50
379 Helm of Awakening R	.25	.60
380 Icy Manipulator U	.08	.20
381 Jester's Cap R	.08	.20
382 Juggernaut C	.08	.20
383 Legacy Weapon M	.15	.40
384 Lotus Blossom R	.08	.20
385 Mind Stone C	.08	.20
386 Ornithopter C	.08	.20
387 Thran Golem U	.08	.20
388 Tormod's Crypt U	.50	1.25
389 Triskelion R	.08	.20
390 Umbilicus R	.08	.20
391 Urza's Blueprints R	.08	.20
392 Urza's Incubator M	12.00	30.00
393 Clifftop Retreat R	1.25	3.00
394 Dark Depths M	3.00	8.00
395 Gemstone Mine R	.50	1.25
396 Hinterland Harbor R	1.00	2.50
397 Isolated Chapel R	1.50	4.00
398 Maze of Ith R	2.00	5.00
399 Mishra's Factory U	.12	.30
400 Sulfur Falls R	1.00	2.50
401 Woodland Cemetery R	1.25	3.00
402 Plains C	.08	.20
403 Plains C	.08	.20
404 Island C	.25	.60
405 Island C	.08	.20
406 Swamp C	.08	.20
407 Swamp C	.12	.30
408 Mountain C	.08	.20
409 Mountain C	.25	.60
410 Forest C	.25	.60
411 Forest C	.08	.20
412 Enlightened Tutor R	8.00	20.00
413 Lyra Dawnbringer M	3.00	8.00
414 Test of Endurance M	.60	1.50
415 Windborn Muse R	.50	1.25
416 Wrath of God R	1.25	3.00
417 Denizen of the Deep R	.08	.20
418 Force of Will M	30.00	80.00
419 High Tide U	.60	1.50
420 Mystic Remora R	3.00	8.00
421 Mystical Tutor R	4.00	10.00
422 Time Stretch M	2.00	5.00
423 Urza, Lord High Artificer M	5.00	12.00
424 Chainer, Dementia Master R	.12	.30
425 Chainer's Edict U	.40	1.00
426 Entomb R	4.00	10.00
427 No Mercy M	3.00	8.00
428 Oversold Cemetery R	.50	1.25
429 Street Wraith C	.15	.40
430 Vampiric Tutor M	20.00	50.00
431 Yawgmoth, Thran Physician M	6.00	15.00
432 Flametongue Kavu U	.08	.20
433 Gamble R	2.50	6.00
434 Grim Lavamancer R	.08	.20
435 Last Chance M	1.00	2.50
436 Siege-Gang Commander R	.12	.30
437 Worldgorger Dragon M	.50	1.25
438 Arboria R	.20	.50
439 Birds of Paradise R	4.00	10.00
440 Nut Collector M	.60	1.50
441 Sylvan Library M	12.00	30.00
442 Worldly Tutor R	5.00	12.00
443 Absorb R	.25	.60
444 Decimate R	.40	1.00
445 Hunting Grounds M	.60	1.50
446 Radha, Heir to Keld U	.08	.20
447 Gauntlet of Power M	1.25	3.00
448 Helm of Awakening R	.30	.75
449 Jester's Cap R	.12	.30
450 Legacy Weapon M	.25	.60
451 Lotus Blossom R	.20	.50
452 Triskelion R	.12	.30
453 Urza's Incubator M	15.00	40.00
454 Dark Depths M	3.00	8.00
455 Gemstone Mine R	.60	1.50
456 Maze of Ith R	2.50	6.00
457 Counterspell R	2.50	6.00

2023 Magic The Gathering Dominaria Remastered Tokens

1 Bird	.12	.25
2 Griffin	.12	.25
3 Cat	.12	.25
4 Marit Lage	1.50	3.00
5 Zombie	.12	.25
6 Elemental	.12	.25
7 Goblin	.12	.25
8 Cat	.12	.25
9 Elephant	.12	.25
10 Insect	.12	.25
11 Saproling	.12	.25
12 Sheep	.12	.25
13 Squirrel	.15	.30
14 Construct	1.50	3.00

2023 Magic The Gathering Judge Gift Rewards

1 Painter's Servant R	40.00	80.00
2 Grindstone R	30.00	75.00
3 Mycosynth Lattice R	25.00	50.00
4 Retrofitter Foundry R	60.00	125.00
5 Sword of War and Peace M	40.00	80.00

2023 Magic The Gathering Lord of the Rings Tales of Middle-Earth

1 Banish from Edoras C	.08	.20
2 The Battle of Bywater R	.40	1.00
3 Bill the Pony U	.08	.20
4 Boromir, Warden of the Tower R	1.50	4.00
5 Dawn of a New Age M	3.00	8.00
6 Dunedain Blade C	.08	.20
7 Eagles of the North C	.04	.10
8 Eastfarthing Farmer C	.04	.10
9 East-Mark Cavalier C	.04	.10
10 Eowyn, Lady of Rohan U	.04	.10
11 Errand-Rider of Gondor C	.04	.10
12 Escape from Orthanc C	.04	.10
13 Esquire of the King C	.04	.10
14 Faramir, Field Commander U	.04	.10
15 Flowering of the White Tree R	2.00	5.00
16 Fog on the Barrow-Downs C	.04	.10
17 Forge Anew R	1.25	3.00
18 Frodo, Sauron's Bane R	.12	.30
19 Gandalf the White M	6.00	15.00
20 Hobbit's Sting C	.04	.10
21 Landroval, Horizon Witness U	.04	.10
22 Lost to Legend U	.04	.10
23 Nimble Hobbit C	.04	.10
24 Now for Wrath, Now for Ruin! C	.04	.10
25 Protector of Gondor C	.04	.10
26 Reprieve U :W:	.75	2.00
27 Rosie Cotton of South Lane U	.06	.15
28 Samwise the Stouthearted U	.06	.15
29 Second Breakfast C	.04	.10
30 Shire Shirriff U	.04	.10
31 Slip On the Ring C	.04	.10
32 Soldier of the Grey Host C	.04	.10
33 Stalwarts of Osgiliath C	.04	.10
34 Tale of Tinuviel U	.06	.15
35 Took Reaper C	.04	.10
36 War of the Last Alliance R	.75	2.00
37 Westfold Rider C	.04	.10
38 You Cannot Pass! U	.04	.10
39 Arwen's Gift C	.04	.10
40 The Bath Song U	.08	.20
41 Bewitching Leechcraft C	.04	.10
42 Bill Ferny, Bree Swindler U	.04	.10
43 Birthday Escape C	.08	.20
44 Borne Upon a Wind R	.30	.75
45 Captain of Umbar C	.04	.10
46 Council's Deliberation U	.06	.15
47 Deceive the Messenger C	.04	.10
48 Dreadful as the Storm C	.04	.10
49 Elrond, Lord of Rivendell U	.04	.10
50 Gandalf, Friend of the Shire U	.04	.10
51 Glorious Gale C	.04	.10
52 Goldberry, River-Daughter R	.15	.40
53 Grey Havens Navigator C	.04	.10
54 Hithlain Knots C	.04	.10
55 Horses of the Bruinen U	.04	.10
56 Ioreth of the Healing House U	.06	.15
57 Isolation at Orthanc C	.04	.10
58 Ithilien Kingfisher C	.04	.10
59 Knights of Dol Amroth C	.04	.10
60 Lorien Revealed C	2.00	5.00
61 Lost Isle Calling R	.08	.20
62 Meneldor, Swift Savior U	.04	.10
63 Nimrodel Watcher C	.04	.10
64 Pelargir Survivor C	.04	.10
65 Press the Enemy R	.10	.25
66 Rangers of Ithilien R	.10	.25
67 Saruman the White U	.06	.15
68 Saruman's Trickery U	.04	.10
69 Scroll of Isildur R	.20	.50
70 Soothing of Smeagol C	.04	.10
71 Stern Scolding U	.30	.75
72 Storm of Saruman M	2.50	6.00
73 Surrounded by Orcs C	.04	.10
74 Treason of Isengard C	.04	.10
75 The Watcher in the Water M	1.25	3.00
76 Willow-Wind C	.04	.10
77 Bitter Downfall U	.04	.10
78 The Black Breath C	.04	.10
79 Call of the Ring R	2.50	6.00
80 Cirith Ungol Patrol C	.04	.10
81 Claim the Precious C	.04	.10
82 Dunland Crebain C	.04	.10
83 Easterling Vanguard C	.04	.10
84 Gollum, Patient Plotter U	.04	.10
85 Gollum's Bite U	.04	.10
86 Gorbag of Minas Morgul U	.06	.15
87 Gothmog, Morgul Lieutenant U	.04	.10
88 Grima Wormtongue U	.06	.15
89 Grond, the Gatebreaker U	.04	.10
90 Haunt of the Dead Marshes C	.04	.10
91 Isildur's Fateful Strike R	.10	.25
92 Lash of the Balrog C	.04	.10
93 Lobelia Sackville-Baggins R	.15	.40

94 March from the Black Gate U	.08	.20
95 Mirkwood Bats C	.15	.40
96 Mordor Muster C	.04	.10
97 Mordor Trebuchet C	.04	.10
98 Morgul-Knife Wound C	.04	.10
99 Nasty End C	.04	.10
100 Nazgul U	6.00	15.00
101 Oath of the Grey Host U	.04	.10
102 One Ring to Rule Them All R	1.25	3.00
103 Orcish Bowmasters R	25.00	60.00
104 Orcish Medicine C	.04	.10
105 Sam's Desperate Rescue C	.05	.12
106 Sauron, the Necromancer R	.15	.40
107 Shadow of the Enemy M	1.00	2.50
108 Shelob's Ambush C	.04	.10
109 Snarling Warg C	.04	.10
110 The Torment of Gollum C	.04	.10
111 Troll of Khazad-dum C	.75	2.00
112 Uruk-hai Berserker C	.04	.10
113 Voracious Fell Beast U	.04	.10
114 Witch-king of Angmar M	4.00	10.00
115 Battle-Scarred Goblin C	.04	.10
116 Book of Mazarbul U	.04	.10
117 Breaking of the Fellowship C	.04	.10
118 Cast into the Fire C	.50	1.25
119 Display of Power R	.20	.50
120 Eomer, Marshal of Rohan R	.15	.40
121 Eomer of the Riddermark U	.04	.10
122 Erebor Flamesmith C	.04	.10
123 Erkenbrand, Lord of Westfold U	.04	.10
124 Fall of Cair Andros R	.15	.40
125 Fear, Fire, Foes! U	.04	.10
126 Fiery Inscription U	.10	.25
127 Fire of Orthanc C	.04	.10
128 Foray of Orcs U	.04	.10
129 Gimli, Counter of Kills U	.05	.12
130 Gimli's Axe C	.04	.10
131 Gimli's Fury C	.04	.10
132 Gloin, Dwarf Emissary R	.25	.60
133 Goblin Fireleaper U	.04	.10
134 Grishnakh, Brash Instigator U	.04	.10
135 Haradrim Spearmaster C	.04	.10
136 Hew the Entwood M	.50	1.25
137 Improvised Club C	.04	.10
138 Moria Marauder R	.40	1.00
139 Oliphaunt C	.08	.20
140 Olog-hai Crusher C	.04	.10
141 Quarrel's End C	.04	.10
142 Rally at the Hornburg C	.04	.10
143 Ranger's Firebrand U	.04	.10
144 Relentless Firebrand U	.04	.10
145 Rising of the Day U	.12	.30
146 Rohirrim Lancer C	.04	.10
147 Rush the Room C	.04	.10
148 Smite the Deathless C	.04	.10
149 Spiteful Banditry M	5.00	12.00
150 Swarming of Moria C	.04	.10
151 There and Back Again R	2.00	5.00
152 Warbeast of Gorgoroth C	.04	.10
153 Bag End Porter C	.04	.10
154 Bombadil's Song C	.05	.12
155 Brandywine Farmer C	.04	.10
156 Celeborn the Wise U	.04	.10
157 Chance-Met Elves C	.04	.10
158 Delighted Halfling R	8.00	20.00
159 Dunedain Rangers U	.04	.10
160 Elven Chorus R	2.50	6.00
161 Elven Farsight C	.04	.10
162 Enraged Huorn C	.04	.10
163 Entish Restoration U	.50	1.25
164 Ent's Fury C	.04	.10
165 Fall of Gil-galad R	.15	.40
166 Fangorn, Tree Shepherd R	.12	.30
167 Galadhrim Bow C	.04	.10
168 Galadhrim Guide C	.04	.10
169 Generous Ent C	.20	.50
170 Gift of Strands U	.04	.10
171 Glorfindel, Dauntless Rescuer U	.04	.10
172 Last March of the Ents M	8.00	20.00
173 Legolas, Master Archer R	.15	.40
174 Long List of the Ents U	.04	.10
175 Lothlorien Lookout C	.04	.10
176 Many Partings C	.04	.10
177 Meriadoc Brandybuck U	.04	.10
178 Mirkwood Spider C	.04	.10
179 Mirrormere Guardian C	.04	.10
180 Mushroom Watchdogs C	.04	.10
181 Peregrin Took U	.08	.20
182 Pippin's Bravery C	.04	.10
183 Quickbeam, Upstart Ent U	.04	.10
184 Radagast the Brown M	.60	1.50
185 Revive the Shire C	.04	.10
186 The Ring Goes South R	.12	.30
187 Shortcut to Mushrooms U	.04	.10
188 Shower of Arrows C	.04	.10
189 Stew the Coneys U	.04	.10
190 Wose Pathfinder C	.04	.10
191 Aragorn, Company Leader R	.10	.25
192 Aragorn, the Uniter M	6.00	15.00
193 Arwen, Mortal Queen M	1.50	4.00
194 Arwen Undomiel U	.08	.20
195 The Balrog, Durin's Bane R	.20	.50
196 Bilbo, Retired Burglar U	.04	.10
197 Butterbur, Bree Innkeeper U	.04	.10
198 Denethor, Ruling Steward U	.04	.10
199 Doors of Durin R	.75	2.00
200 Elrond, Master of Healing R	.12	.30
201 Eowyn, Fearless Knight R	.20	.50
202 Faramir, Prince of Ithilien R	.12	.30
203 Flame of Anor R	2.00	5.00
204 Friendly Rivalry U	.04	.10
205 Frodo Baggins U	.04	.10
206 Galadriel of Lothlorien R	.15	.40
207 Gandalf the Grey R	.20	.50
208 Gandalf's Sanction U	.04	.10
209 Gimli, Mournful Avenger R	.08	.20
210 Gwaihir the Windlord U	.04	.10
211 King of the Oathbreakers R	.12	.30
212 Legolas, Counter of Kills U	.04	.10
213 Lotho, Corrupt Shirriff R	2.00	5.00
214 Mauhur, Uruk-hai Captain U	.04	.10
215 Merry, Esquire of Rohan R	.12	.30
216 The Mouth of Sauron U	.04	.10
217 Old Man Willow U	.04	.10
218 Pippin, Guard of the Citadel R	.25	.60
219 Prince Imrahil the Fair U	.04	.10
220 Ringsight U	.12	.30
221 Rise of the Witch-king U	.15	.40
222 Samwise Gamgee R	2.00	5.00
223 Saruman of Many Colors M	1.00	2.50
224 Sauron, the Dark Lord M	4.00	10.00
225 Sauron's Ransom R	2.00	5.00
226 Shadow Summoning U	.04	.10
227 Shadowfax, Lord of Horses U	.08	.20
228 Shagrat, Loot Bearer R	.08	.20
229 Sharkey, Tyrant of the Shire R	.08	.20
230 Shelob, Child of Ungoliant R	.75	2.00
231 Smeagol, Helpful Guide R	.20	.50
232 Strider, Ranger of the North U	.04	.10
233 Theoden, King of Rohan U	.04	.10
234 Tom Bombadil M	2.50	6.00
235 Ugluk of the White Hand U	.04	.10
236 Anduril, Flame of the West M	2.50	6.00
237 Barrow-Blade U	.04	.10
238 Ent-Draught Basin U	.04	.10
239 Glamdring M	2.00	5.00
240 Horn of Gondor R	1.00	2.50
241 Horn of the Mark R	.60	1.50
242 Inherited Envelope C	.04	.10
243 Lembas C	.15	.40
244 Mirror of Galadriel U	.04	.10
245 Mithril Coat R	5.00	12.00
246 The One Ring M	40.00	100.00
247 Palantir of Orthanc M	10.00	25.00
248 Phial of Galadriel R	.20	.50
249 Shire Scarecrow C	.04	.10
250 Sting, the Glinting Dagger R	1.00	2.50
251 Stone of Erech U	.15	.40
252 Wizard's Rockets C	.04	.10
253 Barad-dur R	.60	1.50
254 Great Hall of the Citadel C	.10	.25
255 The Grey Havens U	.08	.20
256 Minas Tirith R	1.50	4.00
257 Mines of Moria R	.40	1.00
258 Mount Doom M	3.00	8.00
259 Rivendell R	.60	1.50
260 The Shire R	.75	2.00
261 Shire Terrace C	.05	.10
262 Plains C	.05	.10
263 Plains C	.05	.10
264 Island C	.05	.10
265 Island C	.05	.10
266 Swamp C	.05	.10
267 Swamp C	.05	.10
268 Mountain C	.05	.10
269 Mountain C	.05	.10
270 Forest C	.05	.10
271 Forest C	.05	.10
272 Plains C	.20	.40
273 Plains C	.25	.50
274 Island C	.20	.40
275 Island C	.25	.50
276 Swamp C	.30	.60
277 Swamp C	.50	1.00
278 Mountain C	.15	.30
279 Mountain C	.25	.50
280 Forest C	.30	.60
281 Forest C	.25	.50
282 Saradoc, Master of Buckland R	.15	.40
283 Elvish Mariner R	.75	2.00
284 Ringwraiths R	.50	1.25
285 Assault on Osgiliath R	.30	.75
286 Elanor Gardner R	1.00	2.50
287 Aragorn and Arwen, Wed M	8.00	20.00
288 Sauron, the Lidless Eye M	2.50	6.00
289 Frodo, Determined Hero R	1.25	3.00
290 Gandalf, White Rider R	1.25	3.00
291 Knight of the Keep C	.12	.30
292 Gollum, Scheming Guide R	1.00	2.50
293 Witch-king, Bringer of Ruin R	5.00	12.00
294 Fires of Mount Doom R	.60	1.50
295 Goblin Assailant C	.12	.30
296 Galadriel, Gift-Giver R	2.50	6.00
297 The Balrog, Flame of Udun R	.25	.60
298 Bilbo's Ring R	6.00	15.00
302 Boromir, Warden of the Tower R	1.50	4.00
303 Faramir, Field Commander U	.04	.10
304 Frodo, Sauron's Bane R	.12	.30
305 Gandalf the White M	6.00	15.00
306 Samwise the Stouthearted U	.06	.15
307 Elrond, Lord of Rivendell U	.04	.10
308 Gandalf, Friend of the Shire U	.05	.10
309 Gollum, Patient Plotter U	.04	.10
310 Sauron, the Necromancer R	.20	.50
311 Witch-king of Angmar M	8.00	20.00
312 Gimli, Counter of Kills U	.04	.10
313 Legolas, Master Archer R	.25	.60
314 Meriadoc Brandybuck U	.06	.15
315 Peregrin Took U	.06	.15
316 Aragorn, Company Leader R	.40	1.00
317 Aragorn, the Uniter M	6.00	15.00
318 Elrond, Master of Healing R	.20	.50
319 Faramir, Prince of Ithilien R	.10	.25
320 Frodo Baggins U	.08	.20
321 Galadriel of Lothlorien R	.25	.60
322 Gandalf the Grey R	.15	.40
323 Gimli, Mournful Avenger R	.20	.50
324 Legolas, Counter of Kills U	.04	.10
325 Merry, Esquire of Rohan R	.30	.75
326 Pippin, Guard of the Citadel R	.75	2.00
327 Samwise Gamgee R	.75	2.00
328 Saruman of Many Colors M	1.25	3.00
329 Sauron, the Dark Lord M	3.00	10.00
330 Smeagol, Helpful Guide R	.20	.50
331 Tom Bombadil M	1.50	4.00
332 Nazgul U	6.00	15.00
333 Nazgul U	6.00	15.00
334 Nazgul U	6.00	15.00
335 Nazgul U	6.00	15.00
336 Nazgul U	6.00	15.00
337 Nazgul U	6.00	15.00
338 Nazgul U	6.00	15.00
339 Nazgul U	6.00	15.00
340 Barad-dur R	.75	2.00
341 Minas Tirith R	3.00	8.00
342 Mines of Moria R	.50	1.25
343 Mount Doom M	4.00	10.00
344 Rivendell R	.75	2.00
345 The Shire R	1.00	2.50
346 The Battle of Bywater R	.75	2.00
347 Dawn of a New Age M	3.00	8.00
348 Flowering of the White Tree R	3.00	8.00
349 Forge Anew R	2.00	5.00
350 Borne Upon a Wind R	6.00	1.50
351 Goldberry, River-Daughter R	.75	2.00
352 Press the Enemy R	.25	.60
353 Rangers of Ithilien R	.15	.40
354 The Watcher in the Water M	2.00	5.00
355 Call of the Ring R	3.00	8.00
356 Isildur's Fateful Strike R	.25	.60
357 Lobelia Sackville-Baggins R	.25	.60
358 Display of Power R	.30	.75
359 Fall of Cair Andros R	.40	1.00
360 Gloin, Dwarf Emissary R	.30	.75
361 Hew the Entwood M	.60	1.50
362 Moria Marauder R	.60	1.50
363 Delighted Halfling R	10.00	25.00
364 Elven Chorus R	3.00	8.00
365 Radagast the Brown M	1.25	3.00
366 The Ring Goes South R	.25	.60
367 Arwen, Mortal Queen M	2.00	5.00
368 Doors of Durin R	1.25	3.00
369 King of the Oathbreakers R	.15	.40
370 Lotho, Corrupt Shirriff R	1.50	4.00
371 Sauron's Ransom R	2.50	6.00
372 Shagrat, Loot Bearer R	.15	.40
373 Sharkey, Tyrant of the Shire R	.12	.30
374 Shelob, Child of Ungoliant R	.75	2.00
375 Anduril, Flame of the West M	2.50	5.00
376 Glamdring M	2.50	6.00
377 Horn of Gondor R	1.25	3.00
378 Horn of the Mark R	.75	2.00
379 Mithril Coat R	5.00	12.00
380 The One Ring M	40.00	100.00
381 Palantir of Orthanc M	8.00	20.00
382 Phial of Galadriel R	.50	1.25
383 Saradoc, Master of Buckland R	.50	1.25
384 Elvish Mariner R	2.50	6.00
385 Ringwraiths R	4.00	10.00
386 Assault on Osgiliath R	1.00	2.50
387 Elanor Gardner R	2.00	5.00
388 Frodo, Determined Hero R	3.00	8.00
389 Gandalf, White Rider R	3.00	8.00
390 Gollum, Scheming Guide R	2.50	6.00
391 Witch-king, Bringer of Ruin R	6.00	15.00
392 Fires of Mount Doom R	2.00	5.00
393 Galadriel, Gift-Giver R	4.00	10.00
394 Aragorn and Arwen, Wed M	12.00	30.00
395 The Balrog, Flame of Udun R	2.50	6.00
396 Sauron, the Lidless Eye M	10.00	25.00
397 Bilbo's Ring R	6.00	15.00
400 Wizard's Rockets C	.20	.50
401 Gandalf, Friend of the Shire U	.50	1.25
402 Delighted Halfling R	10.00	25.00
403 Bilbo, Retired Burglar U	.30	.75
404 Frodo Baggins U	.30	.75
405 The Balrog, Durin's Bane R	.50	1.25
406 Flame of Anor R	2.50	6.00
407 Boromir, Warden of the Tower R	3.00	8.00
408 Lash of the Balrog C	.04	.10
409 Sting, the Glinting Dagger R	1.00	2.50
410 Aragorn, Company Leader R	.75	2.00
411 Dunland Crebain C	.04	.10
412 Saruman of Many Colors M	6.00	15.00
413 Storm of Saruman M	3.00	8.00
414 Pippin's Bravery C	.04	.10
415 Fangorn, Tree Shepherd R	.25	.60
416 Nasty End C	.04	.10
417 Foray of Orcs U	.04	.10
418 Last March of the Ents M	8.00	20.00
419 Quickbeam, Upstart Ent U	.08	.20
420 Minas Tirith R	3.00	8.00
421 Mirkwood Bats C	.15	.40
422 Voracious Fell Beast U	.06	.15
423 Witch-king of Angmar M	15.00	40.00
424 Shadow of the Enemy M	2.00	5.00
425 Barad-dur R	1.50	4.00
426 Oliphaunt C	.06	.15
427 Rising of the Day U	.15	.40
428 Eomer, Marshal of Rohan R	.30	.75
429 Gothmog, Morgul Lieutenant U	.06	.15
430 Eowyn, Fearless Knight R	.50	1.25
431 Prince Imrahil the Fair U	.06	.15
432 Knights of Dol Amroth C	.04	.10
433 Orcish Bowmasters R	25.00	60.00
434 Aragorn, the Uniter M	12.00	30.00
435 Legolas, Master Archer R	1.50	4.00
436 Gimli, Mournful Avenger R	1.50	4.00
437 Merry, Esquire of Rohan R	1.00	2.50
438 Pippin, Guard of the Citadel R	1.25	3.00
439 Spiteful Banditry M	6.00	15.00
440 Rosie Cotton of South Lane U	.08	.20
441 Shire Shirriff U	.04	.10
442 Gandalf the White M	12.00	30.00
443 The Grey Havens U	.08	.20
444 Lost Isle Calling R	.20	.50
445 Many Partings C	.04	.10
446 Galadriel of Lothlorien R	2.00	5.00
447 Elrond, Master of Healing R	1.50	4.00
448 Frodo, Sauron's Bane R	.20	.50
449 Samwise the Stouthearted U	.12	.30
450 Gollum, Patient Plotter U	.15	.40
451 The One Ring M	30.00	80.00
649 Denethor, Ruling Steward U	.04	.10
753 Mines of Moria R	1.00	2.50
760 Forge Anew R	.50	1.25
763 Press the Enemy R	.20	.50
764 Rangers of Ithilien R	.20	.50
765 The Watcher in the Water M	2.00	5.00
767 Isildur's Fateful Strike R	.75	2.00
770 Fall of Cair Andros R	.15	.40
780 King of the Oathbreakers R	.40	1.00
785 Shelob, Child of Ungoliant R	.40	1.00
787 Glamdring M	2.00	5.00

2023 Magic The Gathering Lord of the Rings Tales of Middle-Earth Tokens

1 Human Soldier	.12	.25
2 Human Soldier	.12	.25
3 Spirit	.12	.25
4 Tentacle	.12	.25
5 Orc Army	.12	.25
6 Orc Army	.12	.25
7 Smaug	.12	.25
8 Ballistic Boulder	.12	.25
9 Food	.12	.25
10 Food	.12	.25
11 Food	.12	.25
12 Treasure	.12	.25
H13 The Ring // The Ring Tempts You	.12	.25

2023 Magic The Gathering Lord of the Rings Tales of Middle-Earth Commander

1 Eowyn, Shieldmaiden M :B:/:R:/:W:	.15	.30
2 Frodo, Adventurous Hobbit M :W:/:K:	.20	.40
3 Galadriel, Elven-Queen M :G:/:B:	.10	.20
4 Sauron, Lord of the Rings M :B:/:K:/:R:	.25	.50
5 Aragorn, King of Gondor M :B:/:R:/:W:	1.25	2.50
6 Gandalf, Westward Voyager M :G:/:B:	.12	.25
7 Sam, Loyal Attendant M :G:/:W:	.15	.30
8 Saruman, the White Hand M :B:/:K:/:R:	.40	.80
9 Beregond of the Guard R :W:	1.00	2.00
10 Champions of Minas Tirith R :W:	.15	.30
11 Field-Tested Frying Pan R :W:	.12	.25
12 The Gaffer R :W:	1.50	3.00
13 Gilraen, Dunedain Protector R :W:	.30	.60
14 Grey Host Reinforcements R :W:	.10	.20
15 Gwaihir, Greatest of the Eagles R :W:	.25	.50
16 Lossarnach Captain R :W:	.30	.75
17 Of Herbs and Stewed Rabbit R :W:	.75	1.50
18 Archivist of Gondor R :B:	.15	.30
19 Corsairs of Umbar R :B:	.20	.40
20 Denethor, Stone Seer R :B:	.15	.30
21 Fealty to the Realm R :B:	.20	.40
22 Monstrosity of the Lake R :B:	.20	.40
23 Raise the Palisade R :B:	7.50	15.00
24 Subjugate the Hobbits R :B:	.20	.40
25 Trap the Trespassers R :B:	.05	.10
26 Gollum, Obsessed Stalker R :K:	.75	1.50
27 Lobelia, Defender of Bag End R :K:	.12	.25
28 Rapacious Guest R :K:	.25	.50
29 Shelob, Dread Weaver R :K:	2.00	4.00
30 Call for Aid R :R:	.30	.75
31 Cavern-Hoard Dragon R :R:	15.00	30.00
32 Gimli of the Glittering Caves R :R:	1.25	2.50
33 Orcish Siegemaster R :R:	.25	.50
34 Rampaging War Mammoth R :R:	.10	.20
35 Arwen, Weaver of Hope R :G:	2.50	5.00
36 Assemble the Entmoot R :G:	.30	.60
37 Feasting Hobbit R :G:	.25	.50
38 Galadhrim Ambush R :G:	3.00	6.00
39 Haldir, Lorien Lieutenant R :G:	.30	.60
40 Legolas Greenleaf R :G:	.20	.40
41 Mirkwood Elk R :G:	.05	.10
42 Motivated Pony R :G:	.12	.25
43 Prize Pig R :G:	.25	.50
44 Travel Through Caradhras R :G:	.05	.10
45 Windswift Slice R :G:	.25	.50
46 The Balrog of Moria R :K:/:R:	.50	1.00
47 Banquet Guests R :G:/:W:	.20	.40
48 Bilbo, Birthday Celebrant R :W:/:K:/:G:	.30	.75
49 Boromir, Gondor's Hope R :W:/:B:	.30	.60
50 Cirdan the Shipwright R :G:/:B:	.07	.15
51 Elrond of the White Council R :G:/:B:	.10	.20
52 Eomer, King of Rohan R :R:/:W:	.30	.75
53 Erestor of the Council R :G:/:B:	.07	.15
54 Faramir, Steward of Gondor R :W:/:B:	.75	1.50
55 Farmer Cotton R :G:/:W:	1.00	2.00
56 Forth Eorlingas! R :R:/:W:	10.00	20.00
57 Grima, Saruman's Footman R :B:/:K:	.50	1.00
58 In the Darkness Bind Them R :B:/:K:/:R:	7.50	15.00
59 Lidless Gaze R :K:/:R:	.15	.30
60 Lord of the Nazgul R :B:/:K:	10.00	20.00
61 Merry, Warden of Isengard R :G:/:W:	.20	.40
62 Mirkwood Trapper R :G:/:B:	.05	.10
63 Moria Scavenger R :K:/:R:	.20	.40
64 Oath of Eorl R :R:/:W:	1.00	2.00
65 Pippin, Warden of Isengard R :K:/:G:	.30	.60
66 Radagast, Wizard of Wilds R :G:/:B:	.10	.20
67 Riders of Rohan R :R:/:W:	.25	.50
68 Sail into the West R :G:/:B:	.12	.25
69 Song of Earendil R :G:/:B:	.30	.60
70 Summons of Saruman R :B:/:R:	.12	.25
71 Taunt from the Rampart R :R:/:W:	.75	1.50
72 Too Greedily, Too Deep R :K:/:R:	.20	.40
73 Treebeard, Gracious Host R :G:/:W:	.60	1.25
74 Wake the Dragon R :K:/:R:	.10	.20
75 Crown of Gondor R	1.00	2.00
76 Hithlain Rope R	.12	.25
77 Lothlorien Blade R	.20	.40
78 Model of Unity R	.05	.10
79 Relic of Sauron R	1.50	3.00
80 The Black Gate R	7.50	15.00
81 Eowyn, Shieldmaiden M :B:/:R:/:W:	.20	.40
82 Frodo, Adventurous Hobbit M :W:/:K:	.20	.40
83 Galadriel, Elven-Queen M :G:/:B:	.20	.40
84 Sauron, Lord of the Rings M :B:/:K:/:R:	.30	.60
85 Aragorn, King of Gondor M :B:/:R:/:W:	1.50	3.00
86 Eowyn, Shieldmaiden M :B:/:R:/:W:	.75	1.50
87 Frodo, Adventurous Hobbit M :W:/:K:	.75	1.50
88 Galadriel, Elven-Queen M :G:/:B:	.30	.60
89 Gandalf, Westward Voyager M :G:/:B:	.30	.75
90 Sam, Loyal Attendant M :G:/:W:	.75	1.50
91 Saruman, the White Hand M :B:/:K:/:R:	1.50	3.00
92 Sauron, Lord of the Rings M :B:/:K:/:R:	1.25	2.50
93 Beregond of the Guard R :W:	.75	1.50
94 Champions of Minas Tirith R :W:	.75	1.50
95 Field-Tested Frying Pan R :W:	.40	.80
96 The Gaffer R :W:	2.50	5.00
97 Gilraen, Dunedain Protector R :W:	1.25	2.50
98 Grey Host Reinforcements R :W:	.25	.50
99 Gwaihir, Greatest of the Eagles R :W:	.75	1.50
100 Lossarnach Captain R :W:	1.00	2.00
101 Archivist of Gondor R :B:	.30	.75
102 Corsairs of Umbar R :B:	.30	.60
103 Denethor, Stone Seer R :B:	.25	.50
104 Fealty to the Realm R :B:	.30	.75
105 Monstrosity of the Lake R :B:	.50	1.00
106 Raise the Palisade R :B:	7.50	15.00
107 Subjugate the Hobbits R :B:	.30	.60
108 Trap the Trespassers R :B:	.20	.40
109 Gollum, Obsessed Stalker R :K:	2.00	4.00
110 Lobelia, Defender of Bag End R :K:	.60	1.25
111 Rapacious Guest R :K:	.60	1.25
112 Shelob, Dread Weaver R :K:	3.00	6.00

113 Call for Aid R :R: .75 1.50
114 Cavern-Hoard Dragon R :R: 15.00 30.00
115 Gimli of the Glittering Caves R :R: 3.00 6.00
116 Orcish Siegemaster R :R: .60 1.25
117 Rampaging War Mammoth R :R: .30 .75
118 Arwen, Weaver of Hope R :G: 3.00 6.00
119 Assemble the Entmoot R :G: 1.00 2.00
120 Feasting Hobbit R :G: .50 1.00
121 Galadhrim Ambush R :G: 3.00 6.00
122 Haldir, Lorien Lieutenant R :G: .75 1.50
123 Legolas Greenleaf R :G: 1.25 2.50
124 Mirkwood Elk R :G: .15 .30
125 Motivated Pony R :G: .25 .50
126 Prize Pig R :G: .50 1.00
127 Travel Through Caradhras R :G: .20 .40
128 Windswift Slice R :G: .75 1.50
129 The Balrog of Moria R :K:/:R: 1.50 3.00
130 Banquet Guests R :G:/:W: .75 1.50
131 Bilbo, Birthday Celebrant R :W:/:K:/:G: 1.25 2.50
132 Boromir, Gondor's Hope R :W:/:B: .60 1.25
133 Cirdan the Shipwright R :G:/:B: .30 .75
134 Elrond of the White Council R :G:/:B: .30 .75
135 Eomer, King of Rohan R :R:/:W: 1.50 3.00
136 Erestor of the Council R :G:/:B: .25 .50
137 Faramir, Steward of Gondor R :W:/:B: 1.00 2.00
138 Farmer Cotton R :G:/:W: 1.50 3.00
139 Forth Eorlingas! R :R:/:W: 10.00 20.00
140 Grima, Saruman's Footman R :B:/:K: 1.50 3.00
141 Lidless Gaze R :K:/:R: .25 .50
142 Lord of the Nazgûl R :B:/:K: 12.50 25.00
143 Merry, Warden of Isengard R :G:/:W: 1.25 2.50
144 Mirkwood Trapper R :G:/:B: .20 .40
145 Moria Scavenger R :K:/:R: .30 .60
146 Pippin, Warden of Isengard R :K:/:G: .75 1.50
147 Radagast, Wizard of Wilds R :G:/:B: .40 .80
148 Riders of Rohan R :R:/:W: .30 .60
149 Sail into the West R :G:/:B: .40 .80
150 Summons of Saruman R :B:/:R: .50 1.00
151 Taunt from the Rampart R :R:/:W: 1.25 2.50
152 Too Greedily, Too Deep R :K:/:R: .75 1.50
153 Treebeard, Gracious Host R :G:/:W: 3.00 6.00
154 Wake the Dragon R :K:/:R: .30 .75
155 Crown of Gondor R 1.25 2.50
156 Hithlain Rope R .50 1.00
157 Lothlorien Blade R .50 1.00
158 Model of Unity R .20 .40
159 Relic of Sauron R 2.50 5.00
160 The Black Gate R 7.50 15.00
161 Banishing Light U :W: .05 .10
162 Bastion Protector R :W: .15 .30
163 Call for Unity R :W: .05 .10
164 Dawn of Hope R :W: .10 .20
165 Dearly Departed R :W: .05 .10
166 Dusk // Dawn R :W: .10 .20
167 Fell the Mighty R :W: .07 .15
168 Fiend Hunter U :W: .05 .10
169 Frontline Medic R :W: .05 .10
170 Fumigate R :W: .15 .30
171 Increasing Devotion R :W: .07 .15
172 Marshal's Anthem R :W: .10 .20
173 Mentor of the Meek R :W: .10 .20
174 Palace Jailer U :W: .12 .25
175 Path to Exile U :W: .75 1.50
176 Selfless Squire R :W: .12 .25
177 Sunset Revelry U :W: .07 .15
178 Swords to Plowshares U :W: .75 1.50
179 Unbreakable Formation R :W: .12 .25
180 Verge Rangers R :W: .12 .25
181 Village Bell-Ringer C :W: .05 .10
182 Visions of Glory R :W: .10 .20
183 Weathered Wayfarer R :W: .50 1.00
184 Arcane Denial C :B: 3.00 6.00
185 Boon of the Wish-Giver U :B: .05 .10
186 Colossal Whale R :B: .05 .10
187 Consider C :B: .30 .75
188 Deep Analysis C :B: .07 .15
189 Devastation Tide R :B: .12 .25
190 Fact or Fiction U :B: .10 .20
191 Forbidden Alchemy C :B: .05 .10
192 Learn from the Past U :B: .05 .10
193 Mystic Confluence R :B: .20 .40
194 Opt C :B: .05 .10
195 Plea for Power R :B: .10 .20
196 Preordain C :B: .25 .50
197 Swan Song R :B: 6.00 12.00
198 Crypt Incursion C :K: .07 .15
199 Decree of Pain R :K: .12 .25
200 Feed the Swarm C :K: .15 .30
201 Go for the Throat U :K: .20 .40
202 Languish R :K: .12 .25
203 Living Death R :K: 1.25 2.50
204 Merciless Executioner U :K: .10 .20
205 Night's Whisper C :K: 1.00 2.00
206 Reanimate R :K: 7.50 15.00
207 Revenge of Ravens U :K: .12 .25
208 Sanguine Bond R :K: .75 1.50
209 Toxic Deluge R :K: 7.50 15.00
210 Anger U :R: 1.50 3.00
211 Blasphemous Act R :R: 1.50 3.00
212 Combat Celebrant M :R: 4.00 8.00
213 Court of Ire R :R: .10 .20
214 Earthquake R :R: .12 .25
215 Faithless Looting C :R: .20 .40
216 Flamerush Rider R :R: .05 .10
217 Frontier Warmonger R :R: .10 .20
218 Goblin Cratermaker U :R: .05 .10
219 Goblin Dark-Dwellers R :R: .05 .10
220 Guttersnipe U :R: .12 .25
221 Harsh Mentor R :R: .07 .15
222 Humble Defector U :R: .05 .10
223 Inferno Titan M :R: .15 .30
224 Knollspine Dragon R :R: .12 .25
225 Scourge of the Throne M :R: 2.50 5.00
226 Shared Animosity R :R: 2.00 4.00
227 Shiny Impetus U :R: .05 .10
228 Siege-Gang Commander R :R: .07 .15
229 Thrill of Possibility C :R: .05 .10
230 Treasure Nabber R :R: 2.50 5.00
231 Zealous Conscripts R :R: .12 .25
232 Arbor Elf C :G: .12 .25
233 Asceticism R :G: 2.50 5.00
234 Beast Within U :G: .75 1.50
235 Birds of Paradise R :G: 5.00 10.00
236 Cultivate C :G: .30 .60
237 Elvish Archdruid R :G: .20 .40
238 Elvish Mystic C :G: .30 .60
239 Elvish Piper R :G: 2.00 4.00
240 Elvish Visionary C :G: .07 .15
241 Elvish Warmaster R :G: .30 .60
242 Essence Warden C :G: 1.00 2.00
243 Farhaven Elf C :G: .12 .25
244 Farseek C :G: 1.50 3.00
245 Genesis Wave R :G: 1.00 2.00
246 Gilded Goose R :G: .75 1.50
247 Great Oak Guardian U :G: .07 .15
248 Harmonize U :G: .12 .25
249 Heroic Intervention R :G: 7.50 15.00
250 Hornet Queen R :G: .12 .25
251 Inscription of Abundance R :G: .10 .20
252 Lignify C :G: .12 .25
253 Orchard Strider C :G: .05 .10
254 Overwhelming Stampede R :G: .75 1.50
255 Paradise Druid U :G: .15 .30
256 Prosperous Innkeeper U :G: .20 .40
257 Rampant Growth C :G: .30 .60
258 Realm Seekers R :G: .05 .10
259 Reclamation Sage U :G: .10 .20
260 Seeds of Renewal R :G: .05 .10
261 Sylvan Offering R :G: .07 .15
262 Tireless Provisioner U :G: 1.25 2.50
263 Wood Elves C :G: .12 .25
264 Woodfall Primus R :G: .12 .25
265 Anguished Unmaking R :W:/:K: 2.50 5.00
266 Extract from Darkness U :B:/:K: .07 .15
267 Growth Spiral C :G:/:B: .12 .25
268 Hostage Taker R :B:/:K: .12 .25
269 Mortify U :W:/:K: .10 .20
270 Notion Thief R :B:/:K: .30 .75
271 Savvy Hunter U :K:/:G: .10 .20
272 Supreme Verdict R :W:/:B: 2.00 4.00
273 Arcane Signet C .50 1.00
274 Basalt Monolith U .75 1.50
275 Chromatic Lantern R 2.50 5.00
276 Commander's Sphere C .10 .20
277 Door of Destinies R 7.50 15.00
278 Everflowing Chalice U .15 .30
279 Heirloom Blade U .07 .15
280 Herald's Horn U 2.00 4.00
281 Lightning Greaves U 5.00 10.00
282 Mind Stone U .10 .20
283 Pristine Talisman C .07 .15
284 Sol Ring U 1.25 2.50
285 Talisman of Conviction U .25 .50
286 Talisman of Progress U 1.00 2.00
287 Thought Vessel C 1.50 3.00
288 Trading Post R .12 .25
289 Vanquisher's Banner R 4.00 8.00
290 Wayfarer's Bauble C .25 .50
291 Well of Lost Dreams R .15 .30
292 Whispersilk Cloak U 1.50 3.00
293 Worn Powerstone U .20 .40
294 Access Tunnel U .15 .30
295 Ash Barrens U .07 .15
296 Battlefield Forge R .25 .50
297 Brushland R .75 1.50
298 Canopy Vista R .25 .50
299 Choked Estuary R .12 .25
300 Clifftop Retreat R .75 1.50
301 Command Tower C .15 .30
302 Crumbling Necropolis U .12 .25
303 Desolate Lighthouse R .07 .15
304 Dragonskull Summit R 1.25 2.50
305 Drowned Catacomb R 2.00 4.00
306 Evolving Wilds C .05 .10
307 Exotic Orchard R .15 .30
308 Field of Ruin U .05 .10
309 Flooded Grove R .75 1.50
310 Foreboding Ruins R .12 .25
311 Fortified Village R .12 .25
312 Frostboil Snarl R .20 .40
313 Furycalm Snarl R .12 .25
314 Ghost Quarter U .20 .40
315 Glacial Fortress R 1.50 3.00
316 Graypelt Refuge U .05 .10
317 Hinterland Harbor R 1.25 2.50
318 Isolated Chapel R 1.25 2.50
319 Lonely Sandbar U .07 .15
320 Murmuring Bosk R .12 .25
321 Necroblossom Snarl R .25 .50
322 Path of Ancestry C .12 .25
323 Port Town R .12 .25
324 Prairie Stream R .20 .40
325 Rejuvenating Springs R 2.50 5.00
326 Rogue's Passage U .20 .40
327 Sandsteppe Citadel U .12 .25
328 Scattered Groves R .15 .30
329 Scoured Barrens C .07 .15
330 Secluded Courtyard U .40 .80
331 Shineshadow Snarl R .12 .25
332 Smoldering Marsh R .20 .40
333 Sulfur Falls R .50 1.00
334 Sulfurous Springs R .75 1.50
335 Sunken Hollow R .20 .40
336 Sunpetal Grove R 2.50 5.00
337 Terramorphic Expanse C .07 .15
338 Thornwood Falls C .05 .10
339 Throne of the High City R .20 .40
340 Tranquil Cove C .05 .10
341 Tranquil Thicket U .05 .10
342 Underground River R 2.00 4.00
343 Vineglimmer Snarl R .15 .30
344 Wind-Scarred Crag C .07 .15
345 Windbrisk Heights R .10 .20
346 Woodland Cemetery R 1.50 3.00
347 Woodland Stream C .05 .10
348 The Great Henge M :G: 30.00 60.00
349 Cloudstone Curio M 12.50 25.00
350 Ensnaring Bridge M 7.50 15.00
351 The Ozolith M 12.50 25.00
352 Rings of Brighthearth M 3.00 6.00
353 Shadowspear M 12.50 25.00
354 Sword of Hearth and Home M 7.50 15.00
355 Sword of the Animist M 7.50 15.00
356 Thorn of Amethyst M .75 1.50
357 Ancient Tomb M 40.00 80.00
358 Bojuka Bog M 7.50 15.00
359 Boseiju, Who Shelters All M 7.50 15.00
360 Cabal Coffers M 20.00 40.00
361 Castle Ardenvale M 4.00 8.00
362 Cavern of Souls M 30.00 60.00
363 Deserted Temple M 4.00 8.00
364 Gemstone Caverns M 25.00 50.00
365 Homeward Path M 7.50 15.00
366 Horizon Canopy M 7.50 15.00
367 Karakas M 7.50 15.00
368 Kor Haven M 5.00 10.00
369 Minamo, School at Water's Edge M 12.50 25.00
370 Mouth of Ronom M .30 .75
371 Oboro, Palace in the Clouds M 10.00 20.00
372 Pillar of the Paruns M 3.00 6.00
373 Reflecting Pool M 7.50 15.00
374 Shinka, the Bloodsoaked Keep M 7.50 15.00
375 Urborg, Tomb of Yawgmoth M 25.00 50.00
376 Wasteland M 12.50 25.00
377 Yavimaya, Cradle of Growth M 12.50 25.00
378 The Party Tree M SUR FOIL 150.00 300.00
379 Elessar, The Elfstone M SUR FOIL 75.00 150.00
380 Bridge of Khazad-dum M SUR FOIL 100.00 200.00
381 Argonath, Pillars of the Kings M SUR FOIL150.00 300.00
382 Three Rings for the Elven
Kings M SUR FOIL 100.00 200.00
383 Morgul-Knife M SUR FOIL 125.00 250.00
384 Herugrim, Sword of Rohan M SUR FOIL 75.00 150.00
385 Ring of Barahir M SUR FOIL 75.00 150.00
386 Shards of Narsil M SUR FOIL 75.00 150.00
387 Balin's Tomb M SUR FOIL 200.00 400.00
388 Barrow-Downs M SUR FOIL 100.00 200.00
389 Isengard, Saruman's Fortress M SUR FOIL100.00 200.00
390 Minas Morgul M SUR FOIL 150.00 300.00
391 Meduseld, Golden Hall of Edoras M SUR FOIL40.0080.00
392 Paths of the Dead M SUR FOIL 250.00 500.00
393 Weathertop M SUR FOIL 150.00 300.00
394 Glittering Caves of Aglarond M SUR FOIL200.00 400.00
395 Green Dragon Inn M SUR FOIL 75.00 150.00
396 Bag End M SUR FOIL 125.00 250.00
397 White Tower of Ecthelion M SUR FOIL 50.00 100.00
398 Osgiliath, Fallen Capital M SUR FOIL 60.00 125.00
399 Dol Amroth M SUR FOIL 100.00 200.00
400 Redhorn Pass M SUR FOIL 30.00 75.00
401 Buckelbury Ferry M SUR FOIL 125.00 250.00
402 Inn of the Prancing Pony M SUR FOIL 40.00 80.00
403 Henneth Annun M SUR FOIL 125.00 250.00
404 Helm's Deep M SUR FOIL 125.00 250.00
405 The Dead Marshes M SUR FOIL 125.00 250.00
406 Valley of Gorgoroth M SUR FOIL 125.00 250.00
407 Fangorn Forest M SUR FOIL 75.00 150.00
408 Sol Ring Elven M/3000* 400.00 800.00
408 Sol Ring Elven Foil M/300 6,000.00 12,000.00
409 Sol Ring Dwarven Foil M/700 2,500.00 5,000.00
409 Sol Ring Dwarven M/7000* 150.00 300.00
410 Sol Ring Human M/9000* 150.00 300.00
410 Sol Ring Human Foil M/900 1,500.00 3,000.00

2023 Magic The Gathering March of the Machine

1 Invasion of Ravnica/Guildpact Paragon M .60 1.25
2 Aerial Boost C :W: .05 .10
3 Alabaster Host Intercessor C :W: .05 .10
4 Alabaster Host Sanctifier C :W: .05 .10
5 Angelic Intervention C :W: .05 .10
6 Archangel Elspeth M :W: 2.00 4.00
7 Attentive Skywarden C :W: .05 .10
8 Bola Slinger C :W: .05 .10
9 Boon-Bringer Valkyrie R :W: .15 .30
10 Cut Short C :W: .05 .10
11 Dusk Legion Duelist R :W: .50 1.00
12 Elesh Norn/The Argent Etchings M :W: 7.50 15.00
13 Elspeth's Smite U :W: .05 .10
14 Enduring Bondwarden C :W: .05 .10
15 Golden-Scale Aeronaut C :W: .05 .10
16 Guardian of Ghirapur R :W: .15 .30
17 Heliod Radiant Dawn/Warped Eclipse R :W: .25 .50
18 Infected Defector C :W: .05 .10
19 Inspired Charge C :W: .05 .10
20 Invasion of Belenon
Belenon War Anthem U :W: .05 .10
21 Invasion of Dominaria/Serra Faithkeeper U :W:.05 .10
22 Invasion of Gobakhan/Lightshield Array R :W:3.00 6.00
23 Invasion of Theros
Ephara, Ever-Sheltering R :W: .30 .60
24 Kithkin Billyrider C :W: .05 .10
25 Knight of the New Coalition C :W: .05 .10
26 Knight-Errant of Eos R :W: .75 1.50
27 Kor Halberd C :W: .05 .10
28 Monastery Mentor M :W: 1.50 3.00
29 Norn's Inquisitor U :W: .05 .10
30 Phyrexian Awakening U :W: .05 .10
31 Phyrexian Censor U :W: .12 .25
32 Progenitor Exarch R :W: .15 .30
33 Realmbreaker's Grasp C :W: .05 .10
34 Scrollshift C :W: .05 .10
35 Seal from Existence U :W: .07 .15
36 Seraph of New Capenna
Seraph of New Phyrexia U :W: .05 .10
37 Sigiled Sentinel C :W: .05 .10
38 Sun-Bless.Guardian/Furnace
Bless.Conqueror U :W: .05 .10
39 Sunder the Gateway C :W: .05 .10
40 Sunfall R :W: 1.50 3.00
41 Surge of Salvation U :W: .75 1.50
42 Swordsworn Cavalier C :W: .05 .10
43 Tarkir Duneshaper
Burnished Dunestomper C :W: .05 .10
44 Tiller of Flesh U :W: .05 .10
45 Zhalfirin Lancer U :W: .05 .10
46 Artistic Refusal U :B: .05 .10
47 Assimilate Essence C :B: .05 .10
48 Astral Wingspan U :B: .05 .10
49 Captive Weird/Compleated Conjurer U :B: .05 .10
50 Change the Equation U :B: .15 .30
51 Chrome Host Seedshark R :B: 1.25 2.50
52 Complete the Circuit R :B: .12 .25
53 Corruption of Towashi U :B: .05 .10
54 Disturbing Conversion C :B: .05 .10
55 Ephara's Dispersal C :B: .05 .10
56 Expedition Lookout C :B: .05 .10
57 Eyes of Gitaxias C :B: .05 .10
58 Faerie Mastermind R :B: 4.00 8.00
59 Furtive Analyst C :B: .05 .10
60 Halo-Charged Skaab C :B: .05 .10
61 Invasion of Arcavios/Invocation
of the Founders R :B: .15 .30
62 Invasion of Kamigawa/Rooftop Saboteurs U :B:.05 .10
63 Invasion of Segovia/Caetus,
Sea Tyrant of Segovia R :B: .50 1.00
64 Invasion of Vryn/Overloaded Mage-Ring U :B:.05 .10
65 Jin-Gitaxias/The Great Synthesis M :B: 3.00 6.00
66 Meeting of Minds C :B: .07 .15
67 Moment of Truth C :B: .05 .10
68 Negate C :B: .12 .25
69 Oculus Whelp C :B: .05 .10
70 Omen Hawker U :B: .05 .10
71 Oracle of Tragedy U :B: .05 .10
72 Order of the Mirror/Order of
the Alabaster Host C :B: .05 .10
73 Preening Champion C :B: .05 .10
74 Protocol Knight C :B: .05 .10
75 Rona, Herald of Invasion/Rona,
Tolarian Obliterator R :B: .75 1.50
76 Saiba Cryptomancer C :B: .05 .10
77 See Double R :B: .75 1.50
78 Skyclave Aerialist/Skyclave Invader U :B: .05 .10
79 Stasis Field C :B: .05 .10
80 Temporal Cleansing C :B: .05 .10
81 Thunderhead Squadron C :B: .05 .10
82 Tidal Terror C :B: .05 .10
83 Transcendent Message R :B: .15 .30
84 Wicked Slumber U :B: .05 .10
85 Xerex Strobe-Knight U :B: .05 .10
86 Zephyr Singer R :B: .10 .20
87 Zhalfirin Shapecraft C :B: .05 .10
88 Aetherblade Agent/Gitaxian Mindstinger C :K:.05 .10
89 Archpriest of Shadows R :K: .20 .40
90 Ayara, Widow of the Realm/Ayara,
Furnace Queen R :K: .15 .30
91 Bladed Battle-Fan C :K: .05 .10
92 Blightreaper Thallid/Blightsower Thallid U :K:.05 .10
93 Bloated Processor R :K: .10 .20
94 Breach the Multiverse R :K: 2.00 4.00
95 Collective Nightmare U :K: .05 .10
96 Compleated Huntmaster U :K: .05 .10
97 Consuming Aetherborn C :K: .05 .10
98 Corrupted Conviction C :K: .30 .60
99 Deadly Derision C :K: .05 .10
100 Dreg Recycler C :K: .05 .10
101 Etched Familiar C :K: .05 .10
102 Etched Host Doombringer C :K: .05 .10
103 Failed Conversion C :K: .05 .10
104 Final Flourish C :K: .05 .10
105 Flitting Guerrilla C :K: .05 .10
106 Gift of Compleation U :K: .05 .10
107 Glistening Deluge U :K: .05 .10
108 Gloomfang Mauler C :K: .05 .10
109 Grafted Butcher R :K: .20 .40
110 Hoarding Broodlord R :K: .75 1.50
111 Ichor Drinker C :K: .05 .10
112 Ichor Shade C :K: .05 .10
113 Invasion of Eldraine/Prickle Faeries U :K: .05 .10
114 Invasion of Fiora/Marchesa,
Resolute Monarch R :K: .50 1.00
115 Invasion of Innistrad/Deluge of the Dead M :K:1.00 2.00
116 Invasion of Ulgrotha
Grandmother Ravi Sengir U :K: .05 .10
117 Merciless Repurposing U :K: .05 .10
118 Mirrodin Avenged C :K: .05 .10
119 Nezumi Freewheeler
Hideous Fleshwheeler U :K: .05 .10
120 Nezumi Informant C :K: .05 .10
121 Phyrexian Gargantua U :K: .05 .10
122 Pile On R :K: .30 .75
123 Render Inert U :K: .05 .10
124 Scorn-Blade Berserker U :K: .05 .10
125 Sheoldred/The True Scriptures M :K: 12.50 25.00
126 Tenured Oilcaster C :K: .05 .10
127 Traumatic Revelation C :K: .05 .10
128 Unseal the Necropolis C :K: .05 .10
129 Vanquish the Weak C :K: .05 .10
130 Akki Scrapchomper C :R: .05 .10
131 Beamtown Beatstick C :R: .07 .15
132 Bloodfeather Phoenix R :R: .20 .40
133 Burning Sun's Fury C :R: .05 .10
134 Chandra, Hope's Beacon M :R: 4.00 8.00
135 City on Fire R :R: 2.00 4.00
136 Coming In Hot C :R: .05 .10
137 Etali, Primal Conqueror
Etali, Primal Sickness R :R: 3.00 6.00
138 Fearless Skald U :R: .05 .10
139 Furnace Gremlin U :R: .05 .10
140 Furnace Host Charger C :R: .05 .10
141 Furnace Reins U :R: .05 .10
142 Hangar Scrounger C :R: .05 .10
143 Harried Artisan/Phyrexian Skyflayer U :R: .05 .10
144 Into the Fire R :R: .20 .40
145 Invasion of Kaldheim/Pyre
of the World Tree R :R: .30 .75
146 Invasion of Karsus/Refraction Elemental R :R:.20 .40
147 Invasion of Mercadia/Kyren Flamewright U :R:.05 .10
148 Invasion of Regatha
Disciples of the Inferno U :R: .07 .15
149 Invasion of Tarkir/Defiant Thundermaw M :R:4.00 8.00
150 Karsus Depthguard C :R: .05 .10
151 Khenra Spellspear/Gitaxian Spellstalker U :R:.05 .10
152 Lithomantic Barrage U :R: .07 .15
153 Marauding Dreadship C :R: .05 .10
154 Mirran Banesplitter C :R: .05 .10
155 Nahiri's Warcrafting R :R: .15 .30
156 Onakke Javelineer C :R: .05 .10
157 Pyretic Prankster
Glistening Goremonger C :R: .05 .10
158 Ral's Reinforcements C :R: .05 .10
159 Ramosian Greatsword U :R: .05 .10
160 Rampaging Raptor R :R: .12 .25
161 Redcap Heelslasher C :R: .05 .10
162 Scrappy Bruiser U :R: .05 .10
163 Searing Barb C :R: .05 .10
164 Shatter the Source C :R: .05 .10
165 Shivan Branch-Burner U :R: .05 .10
166 Stoke the Flames U :R: .05 .10
167 Thrashing Frontliner C :R: .05 .10
168 Trailblazing Historian C :R: .05 .10
169 Urabrask/The Great Work M :R: 7.50 15.00

170 Volcanic Spite C :R: .10 .20
171 Voldaren Thrillseeker R :R: .30 .60
172 War-Trained Slasher C :R: .05 .10
173 Wrenn's Resolve C :R: .75 1.50
174 Ancient Imperiosaur R :G: .30 .75
175 Arachnoid Adaptation C :G: .05 .10
176 Atraxa's Fall C :G: .05 .10
177 Blighted Burgeoning C :G: .05 .10
178 Bonded Herdbeast/Plated Kilnbeast C :G: .05 .10
179 Chomping Kavu C :G: .05 .10
180 Converter Beast C :G: .05 .10
181 Copper Host Crusher U :G: .05 .10
182 Cosmic Hunger C :G: .05 .10
183 Crystal Carapace C :G: .05 .10
184 Deeproot Wayfinder R :G: .15 .30
185 Doomskar Warrior R :G: .07 .15
186 Fertilid's Favor C :G: .05 .10
187 Glistening Dawn R :G: .07 .15
188 Gnottvold Hermit/Chrome Host Hulk U :G: .05 .10
189 Herbology Instructor/Malady Invoker U :G: .05 .10
190 Invasion of Ikoria/Zilortha, Apex of Ikoria R :G:5.00 10.00
191 Invasion of Ixalan/Belligerent Regisaur R :G:.60 1.25
192 Invasion of Muraganda
Primordial Plasm U :G: .05 .10
193 Invasion of Shandalar/Leyline Surge M :G:1.00 2.00
194 Invasion of Zendikar/Awakened Skyclave U :G:.12 .25
195 Iridescent Blademaster C :G: .05 .10
196 Kami of Whispered Hopes U :G: .25 .50
197 Overgrown Pest C :G: .05 .10
198 Ozolith, the Shattered Spire R :G: 3.00 6.00
199 Placid Rottentail C :G: .05 .10
200 Polukranos Reborn/Polukranos,
Engine of Ruin R :G: .60 1.25
201 Portent Tracker C :G: .05 .10
202 Ravenous Sailback U :G: .05 .10
203 Sandstalker Moloch U :G: .05 .10
204 Seed of Hope C :G: .05 .10
205 Serpent-Blade Assailant C :G: .05 .10
206 Storm the Seedcore U :G: .05 .10
207 Streetwise Negotiator U :G: .05 .10
208 Tandem Takedown U :G: .05 .10
209 Tangled Skyline U :G: .05 .10
210 Timberland Ancient C :G: .05 .10
211 Tribute to the World Tree R :G: 5.00 10.00
212 Vengeant Earth C :G: .05 .10
213 Vorinclex/The Grand Evolution M :G: 5.00 10.00
214 War Historian C :G: .05 .10
215 Wary Thespian C :G: .05 .10
216 Wildwood Escort C :G: .05 .10
217 Wrenn and Realmbreaker M :G: 5.00 10.00
218 Baral and Kari Zev R :B:/:R: .15 .30
219 Borborygmos and Fblthp M :G:/:B:/:R: .15 .30
220 Botanical Brawler U :G:/:W: .07 .15
221 Djeru and Hazoret R :R:/:W: .15 .30
222 Drana and Linvala R :W:/:K: 1.00 2.00
223 Elvish Vatkeeper U :K:/:G: .05 .10
224 Errant and Giada R :W:/:B: .20 .40
225 Ghalta and Mavren R :G:/:W: .75 1.50
226 Glissa, Herald of Predation R :K:/:G: .15 .30
227 Halo Forager U :B:/:K: .05 .10
228 Hidetsugu and Kairi R :B:/:K: .15 .30
229 Inga and Esika R :G:/:B: .30 .60
230 Awaken Maelstrom R :W:/:B:/:K:/:R:/:G: .20 .40
231 Lazotep Convert U :B:/:K: .10 .20
232 Ashen Reaper U :K:/:R: .05 .10
233 Truga Cliffcharger U :R:/:G: .05 .10
234 Aetherwing, Golden-Scale Flagship U :B:/:R:.05 .10
235 Valor's Reach Tag Team U :R:/:W: .05 .10
236 Winnowing Forces U :K:/:G: .05 .10
237 Bloomwielder Dryads U :G:/:W: .05 .10
238 Holy Frazzle-Cannon U :W:/:K: .05 .10
239 Teferi Akosa of Zhalfir M :W:/:B: 2.00 4.00
240 Gargantuan Slabhorn U :G:/:B: .05 .10
241 The Broken Sky R :W:/:K: .25 .50
242 Vertex Paladin U :W:/:K: .05 .10
243 Joyful Stormsculptor U :B:/:R: .05 .10
244 Kogla and Yidaro R :R:/:G: .30 .60
245 Kroxa and Kunoros M :R:/:W:/:K: .25 .50
246 Marshal of Zhalfir U :W:/:B: .05 .10
247 Mirror-Shield Hoplite U :R:/:W: .05 .10
248 Mutagen Connoisseur U :G:/:B: .05 .10
249 Omnath, Locus of All R :W:/:B:/:K:/:R:/:G: .20 .40
250 Quintorius, Loremaster R :R:/:W: .07 .15
251 Rampaging Geoderm U :R:/:G: .05 .10
252 Rankle and Torbran R :K:/:R: .10 .20
253 Sculpted Perfection U :W:/:K: .05 .10
254 Stormclaw Rager U :K:/:R: .05 .10
255 Thalia and The Gitrog Monster M :W:/:K:/:G:2.00 4.00
256 Yargle and Multani R :K:/:G: .30 .75
257 Zimone and Dina M :K:/:G:/:B: .50 1.00
258 Zurgo and Ojutai M :B:/:R:/:W: .75 1.50
259 Flywheel Racer C .05 .10
260 Halo Hopper C .05 .10
261 Kitesail C .05 .10
262 Phyrexian Archivist C .05 .10
263 Realmbreaker, the Invasion Tree R .75 1.50
264 Skittering Surveyor C .05 .10
265 Sword of Once and Future M 3.00 6.00
266 Urn of Godfire C .05 .10
267 Bloodfell Caves C .05 .10
268 Blossoming Sands C .05 .10
269 Dismal Backwater C .05 .10
270 Jungle Hollow C .05 .10
271 Rugged Highlands C .05 .10
272 Scoured Barrens C .05 .10
273 Swiftwater Cliffs C .05 .10
274 Thornwood Falls C .05 .10
275 Tranquil Cove C .05 .10
276 Wind-Scarred Crag C .05 .10
277 Plains C .05 .10
278 Island C .05 .10
279 Swamp C .05 .10
280 Mountain C .05 .10
281 Forest C .07 .15
282 Plains C .25 .50
283 Plains C .07 .15
284 Island C .10 .20
285 Island C .10 .20
286 Swamp C .20 .40
287 Swamp C .25 .50
288 Mountain C .12 .25
289 Mountain C .07 .15
290 Forest C .12 .25
291 Forest C .10 .20
292 Elesh Norn/The Argent Etchings M :W: 6.00 12.00
293 Heliod, the Radiant Dawn
Heliod, the Warped Eclipse R :W: .30 .60
294 Jin-Gitaxias/The Great Synthesis M :B: 4.00 8.00
295 Rona, Herald of Invasion
Rona, Tolarian Obliterator R :B: .75 1.50
296 Ayara, Widow of the Realm
Ayara, Furnace Queen R :K: .12 .25
297 Sheoldred/The True Scriptures M :K: 12.50 25.00
298 Etali, Primal Conqueror
Etali, Primal Sickness R :R: 2.00 4.00
299 Urabrask/The Great Work M :R: 6.00 12.00
300 Polukranos Reborn
Polukranos, Engine of Ruin R :G: .75 1.50
301 Vorinclex/The Grand Evolution M :G: 4.00 8.00
302 Baral and Kari Zev R :B:/:R: .20 .40
303 Borborygmos and Fblthp M :G:/:B:/:R: .15 .30
304 Djeru and Hazoret R :R:/:W: .20 .40
305 Drana and Linvala R :W:/:K: 1.25 2.50
306 Errant and Giada R :W:/:B: .15 .30
307 Ghalta and Mavren R :G:/:W: .20 .40
308 Glissa, Herald of Predation R :K:/:G: .12 .25
309 Hidetsugu and Kairi R :B:/:K: .25 .50
310 Inga and Esika R :G:/:B: .25 .50
311 Kogla and Yidaro R :R:/:G: .30 .75
312 Kroxa and Kunoros M :R:/:W:/:K: .75 1.50
313 Omnath, Locus of All R :W:/:B:/:K:/:R:/:G: .20 .40
314 Quintorius, Loremaster R :R:/:W: .10 .20
315 Rankle and Torbran R :K:/:R: .15 .30
316 Thalia and The Gitrog Monster M :W:/:K:/:G:2.00 4.00
317 Yargle and Multani R :K:/:G: .30 .60
318 Zimone and Dina M :K:/:G:/:B: .75 1.50
319 Zurgo and Ojutai M :B:/:R:/:W: .30 .75
320 Archangel Elspeth M :W: 2.50 5.00
321 Chandra, Hope's Beacon M :R: 5.00 10.00
322 Wrenn and Realmbreaker M :G: 6.00 12.00
323 Essence of Orthodoxy R :W: .25 .50
324 Phyrexian Pegasus C :W: .07 .15
325 Seedpod Caretaker U :W: .12 .25
326 Interdisciplinary Mascot R :B: .07 .15
327 Referee Squad U :B: .20 .40
328 Zephyr Winder C :B: .05 .10
329 Injector Crocodile C :K: .10 .20
330 Seer of Stolen Sight U :K: .25 .50
331 Terror of Towashi R :K: .15 .30
332 Axgard Artisan U :R: .75 1.50
333 Cragsmasher Yeti C :R: .07 .15
334 Orthion, Hero of Lavabrink R :R: 1.25 2.50
335 Fairgrounds Trumpeter C :G: .05 .10
336 Ruins Recluse U :G: 4.00 8.00
337 Surrak and Goreclaw R :G: 2.50 5.00
338 Elesh Norn/The Argent
Etchings SERIAL M 1,500.00 3,000.00
339 Jin-Gitaxias/The Great Synthesis SERIAL M300.00 750.00
340 Sheoldred/The True Scriptures SERIAL M750.00 1,500.00
341 Urabrask/The Great Work SERIAL M 750.00 1,500.00
342 Vorinclex/The Grand Evolution SERIAL M600.00 1,200.00
343 Boon-Bringer Valkyrie R :W: .30 .60
344 Dusk Legion Duelist R :W: .30 .60
345 Guardian of Ghirapur R :W: .20 .40
346 Knight-Errant of Eos R :W: 1.25 2.50
347 Monastery Mentor M :W: 1.50 3.00
348 Progenitor Exarch R :W: .20 .40
349 Sunfall R :W: 1.50 3.00
350 Chrome Host Seedshark R :B: 1.50 3.00
351 Complete the Circuit R :B: .10 .20
352 Faerie Mastermind R :B: 4.00 8.00
353 See Double R :B: 1.00 2.00
354 Transcendent Message R :B: .12 .25
355 Zephyr Singer R :B: .15 .30
356 Archpriest of Shadows R :K: .25 .50
357 Bloated Processor R :K: .12 .25
358 Breach the Multiverse R :K: 1.50 3.00
359 Grafted Butcher R :K: .20 .40
360 Hoarding Broodlord R :K: 1.25 2.50
361 Pile On R :K: .60 1.25
362 Bloodfeather Phoenix R :R: .25 .50
363 City on Fire R :R: 2.50 5.00
364 Into the Fire R :R: .20 .40
365 Nahiri's Warcrafting R :R: .12 .25
366 Rampaging Raptor R :R: .20 .40
367 Voldaren Thrillseeker R :R: .60 1.25
368 Ancient Imperiosaur R :G: .75 1.50
369 Deeproot Wayfinder R :G: .25 .50
370 Doomskar Warrior R :G: .12 .25
371 Glistening Dawn R :G: .12 .25
372 Ozolith, the Shattered Spire R :G: 4.00 8.00
373 Tribute to the World Tree R :G: 4.00 8.00
374 Realmbreaker, the Invasion Tree R .75 1.50
375 Sword of Once and Future M 3.00 6.00
376 Essence of Orthodoxy R :W: .30 .60
377 Interdisciplinary Mascot R :B: .07 .15
378 Terror of Towashi R :K: .20 .40
379 Orthion, Hero of Lavabrink R :R: 1.25 2.50
380 Surrak and Goreclaw R :G: 3.00 6.00
381 Norn's Inquisitor U :W: .10 .20
382 Scrappy Bruiser U :R: .10 .20
383 Kami of Whispered Hopes U :G: .75 1.50
384 Botanical Brawler U :G:/:W: .20 .40
385 Halo Forager U :B:/:K: .12 .25
386 Ghalta and Mavren R :G:/:W: .25 .50
387 Omnath, Locus of All R :W:/:B:/:K:/:R:/:G: .30 .60

2023 Magic The Gathering March of the Machine The Aftermath

1 Coppercoat Vanguard U :W: .75 1.50
2 Deification R :W: .25 .50
3 Harnessed Snubhorn U :W: .05 .10
4 Metropolis Reformer R :W: .75 1.50
5 Spark Rupture R :W: .12 .25
6 Tazri, Stalwart Survivor R :W: .06 .12
7 Filter Out U :B: .25 .50
8 Tolarian Contempt U :B: .05 .10
9 Training Grounds R :B: 2.50 5.00
10 Vesuvan Drifter R :B: .75 1.50
11 Ayara's Oathsworn R :K: .50 1.00
12 Blot Out U :K: .05 .10
13 Death-Rattle Oni U :K: .05 .10
14 Markov Baron U :K: .07 .15
15 Urborg Scavengers R :K: .50 1.00
16 Arni Metalbrow R :R: .12 .25
17 Kolaghan Warmonger U :R: .05 .10
18 Plargg and Nassari R :R: .30 .60
19 Reckless Handling U :R: .10 .20
20 Animist's Might U :G: .05 .10
21 Leyline Immersion R :G: .60 1.25
22 Nissa, Resurgent Animist M :G: 20.00 40.00
23 Open the Way R :G: .75 1.50
24 Tranquil Frillback R :G: .60 1.25
25 Undercity Upheaval U :G: .05 .10
26 Calix, Guided by Fate M :G:/:W: 7.50 15.00
27 Campus Renovation U :R:/:W: .06 .12
28 Cosmic Rebirth U :G:/:W: .12 .25
29 Danitha, New Benalia's Light R :G:/:W: .20 .40
30 Feast of the Victorious Dead U :W:/:K: .06 .12
31 Gold-Forged Thopteryx U :W:/:B: .07 .15
32 Jirina, Dauntless General R :W:/:K: .60 1.25
33 Jolrael, Voice of Zhalfir R :G:/:B: .10 .20
34 The Kenriths' Royal Funeral R :W:/:K: .15 .30
35 Kiora, Sovereign of the Deep M :G:/:B: 1.25 2.50
36 Nahiri, Forged in Fury M :R:/:W: 2.00 4.00
37 Nahiri's Resolve R :R:/:W: .40 .80
38 Narset, Enlightened Exile M :B:/:R:/:W: 4.00 8.00
39 Nashi, Moon's Legacy R :K:/:G:/:B: .10 .20
40 Niv-Mizzet, Supreme R :W:/:B:/:K:/:R:/:G: .15 .30
41 Ob Nixilis, Captive Kingpin M :K:/:R: 4.00 8.00
42 Pia Nalaar, Consul of Revival R :R:/:W: .75 1.50
43 Rebuild the City R :K:/:R:/:G: .10 .20
44 Rocco, Street Chef R :R:/:G:/:W: .07 .15
45 Samut, Vizier of Naktamun M :R:/:G: 2.00 4.00
46 Sarkhan, Soul Aflame M :B:/:R: 4.00 8.00
47 Sigarda, Font of Blessings R :G:/:W: 2.50 5.00
48 Tyvar the Bellicose M :K:/:G: 2.50 5.00
49 Karn, Legacy Reforged M 7.50 15.00
50 Drannith Ruins R .30 .75
51 Coppercoat Vanguard U :W: .75 1.50
52 Deification R :W: 1.00 2.00
53 Harnessed Snubhorn U :W: .05 .10
54 Metropolis Reformer R :W: .75 1.50
55 Spark Rupture R :W: 1.00 2.00
56 Tazri, Stalwart Survivor R :W: .30 .75
57 Filter Out U :B: .20 .40
58 Tolarian Contempt U :B: .05 .10
59 Training Grounds R :B: 4.00 8.00
60 Vesuvan Drifter R :B: 1.50 3.00
61 Ayara's Oathsworn R :K: 1.25 2.50
62 Blot Out U :K: .06 .12
63 Death-Rattle Oni U :K: .05 .10
64 Markov Baron U :K: .10 .20
65 Urborg Scavengers R :K: 1.50 3.00
66 Arni Metalbrow R :R: .60 1.25
67 Kolaghan Warmonger U :R: .05 .10
68 Plargg and Nassari R :R: 1.00 2.00
69 Reckless Handling U :R: .12 .25
70 Animist's Might U :G: .05 .10
71 Leyline Immersion R :G: .75 1.50
72 Nissa, Resurgent Animist M :G: 30.00 60.00
73 Open the Way R :G: 1.00 2.00
74 Tranquil Frillback R :G: .30 .75
75 Undercity Upheaval U :G: .05 .10
76 Calix, Guided by Fate M :G:/:W: 7.50 15.00
77 Campus Renovation U :R:/:W: .05 .10
78 Cosmic Rebirth U :G:/:W: .12 .25
79 Danitha, New Benalia's Light R :G:/:W: .25 .50
80 Feast of the Victorious Dead U :W:/:K: .06 .12
81 Gold-Forged Thopteryx U :W:/:B: .06 .12
82 Jirina, Dauntless General R :W:/:K: 1.50 3.00
83 Jolrael, Voice of Zhalfir R :G:/:B: .25 .50
84 The Kenriths' Royal Funeral R :W:/:K: .75 1.50
85 Kiora, Sovereign of the Deep M :G:/:B: 5.00 10.00
86 Nahiri, Forged in Fury M :R:/:W: 7.50 15.00
87 Nahiri's Resolve R :R:/:W: .75 1.50
88 Narset, Enlightened Exile M :B:/:R:/:W: 4.00 8.00
89 Nashi, Moon's Legacy R :K:/:G:/:B: 1.25 2.50
90 Niv-Mizzet, Supreme R :W:/:B:/:K:/:R:/:G: .75 1.50
91 Ob Nixilis, Captive Kingpin M :K:/:R: 10.00 20.00
92 Pia Nalaar, Consul of Revival R :R:/:W: 1.00 2.00
93 Rebuild the City R :K:/:R:/:G: .20 .40
94 Rocco, Street Chef R :R:/:G:/:W: .30 .60
95 Samut, Vizier of Naktamun M :R:/:G: 2.50 5.00
96 Sarkhan, Soul Aflame M :B:/:R: 6.00 12.00
97 Sigarda, Font of Blessings R :G:/:W: 4.00 8.00
98 Tyvar the Bellicose M :K:/:G: 7.50 15.00
99 Karn, Legacy Reforged M 15.00 30.00
100 Drannith Ruins R 1.00 2.00
101 Coppercoat Vanguard U :W: .40 .80
102 Deification R :W: .30 .60
103 Harnessed Snubhorn U :W: .12 .25
104 Metropolis Reformer R :W: .75 1.50
105 Spark Rupture R :W: .20 .40
106 Tazri, Stalwart Survivor R :W: .15 .30
107 Filter Out U :B: .75 1.50
108 Tolarian Contempt U :B: .07 .15
109 Training Grounds R :B: 3.00 6.00
110 Vesuvan Drifter R :B: .75 1.50
111 Ayara's Oathsworn R :K: .40 .80
112 Blot Out U :K: .12 .25
113 Death-Rattle Oni U :K: .07 .15
114 Markov Baron U :K: .25 .50
115 Urborg Scavengers R :K: .40 .80
116 Arni Metalbrow R :R: .30 .60
117 Kolaghan Warmonger U :R: .07 .15
118 Plargg and Nassari R :R: .50 1.00
119 Reckless Handling U :R: .25 .50
120 Animist's Might U :G: .10 .20
121 Leyline Immersion R :G: .75 1.50
122 Nissa, Resurgent Animist M :G: 20.00 40.00
123 Open the Way R :G: .75 1.50
124 Tranquil Frillback R :G: .50 1.00
125 Undercity Upheaval U :G: .06 .12
126 Calix, Guided by Fate M :G:/:W: 5.00 10.00
127 Campus Renovation U :R:/:W: .06 .12
128 Cosmic Rebirth U :G:/:W: .20 .40
129 Danitha, New Benalia's Light R :G:/:W: .30 .60
130 Feast of the Victorious Dead U :W:/:K: .12 .25
131 Gold-Forged Thopteryx U :W:/:B: .15 .30
132 Jirina, Dauntless General R :W:/:K: .60 1.25
133 Jolrael, Voice of Zhalfir R :G:/:B: .15 .30
134 The Kenriths' Royal Funeral R :W:/:K: .30 .60
135 Kiora, Sovereign of the Deep M :G:/:B: 1.25 2.50
136 Nahiri, Forged in Fury M :R:/:W: 2.50 5.00
137 Nahiri's Resolve R :R:/:W: .40 .80
138 Narset, Enlightened Exile M :B:/:R:/:W: 7.50 15.00
139 Nashi, Moon's Legacy R :K:/:G:/:B: .25 .50
140 Niv-Mizzet, Supreme R :W:/:B:/:K:/:R:/:G: .25 .50
141 Ob Nixilis, Captive Kingpin M :K:/:R: 5.00 10.00
142 Pia Nalaar, Consul of Revival R :R:/:W: .50 1.00
143 Rebuild the City R :K:/:R:/:G: .25 .50
144 Rocco, Street Chef R :R:/:G:/:W: .25 .50
145 Samut, Vizier of Naktamun M :R:/:G: 2.00 4.00
146 Sarkhan, Soul Aflame M :B:/:R: 4.00 8.00
147 Sigarda, Font of Blessings R :G:/:W: 2.50 5.00
148 Tyvar the Bellicose M :K:/:G: 2.50 5.00
149 Karn, Legacy Reforged M 7.50 15.00
150 Drannith Ruins R .30 .75
151 Deification R :W: .40 .80
152 Metropolis Reformer R :W: 1.25 2.50
153 Spark Rupture R :W: .20 .40
154 Tazri, Stalwart Survivor R :W: .15 .30
155 Training Grounds R :B: 3.00 6.00
156 Vesuvan Drifter R :B: .75 1.50
157 Ayara's Oathsworn R :K: .75 1.50
158 Urborg Scavengers R :K: .75 1.50
159 Arni Metalbrow R :R: .30 .60
160 Plargg and Nassari R :R: .75 1.50
161 Leyline Immersion R :G: .75 1.50
162 Nissa, Resurgent Animist M :G: 30.00 60.00
163 Open the Way R :G: .75 1.50
164 Tranquil Frillback R :G: .75 1.50
165 Calix, Guided by Fate M :G:/:W: 6.00 12.00
166 Danitha, New Benalia's Light R :G:/:W: .75 1.50
167 Jirina, Dauntless General R :W:/:K: .75 1.50
168 Jolrael, Voice of Zhalfir R :G:/:B: .30 .60
169 The Kenriths' Royal Funeral R :W:/:K: .30 .75
170 Kiora, Sovereign of the Deep M :G:/:B: 2.00 4.00
171 Nahiri, Forged in Fury M :R:/:W: 4.00 8.00
172 Nahiri's Resolve R :R:/:W: .40 .80
173 Narset, Enlightened Exile M :B:/:R:/:W: 7.50 15.00
174 Nashi, Moon's Legacy R :K:/:G:/:B: .25 .50
175 Niv-Mizzet, Supreme R :W:/:B:/:K:/:R:/:G: .40 .80
176 Ob Nixilis, Captive Kingpin M :K:/:R: 7.50 15.00
177 Pia Nalaar, Consul of Revival R :R:/:W: .40 .80
178 Rebuild the City R :K:/:R:/:G: .25 .50
179 Rocco, Street Chef R :R:/:G:/:W: .20 .40
180 Samut, Vizier of Naktamun M :R:/:G: 1.50 3.00
181 Sarkhan, Soul Aflame M :B:/:R: 5.00 10.00
182 Sigarda, Font of Blessings R :G:/:W: 3.00 6.00
183 Tyvar the Bellicose M :K:/:G: 3.00 6.00
184 Karn, Legacy Reforged M 7.50 15.00
185 Drannith Ruins R .50 1.00
186 Coppercoat Vanguard U :W: 4.00 8.00
187 Deification R :W: 6.00 12.00
188 Harnessed Snubhorn U :W: 1.00 2.00
189 Metropolis Reformer R :W: 4.00 8.00
190 Tazri, Stalwart Survivor R :W: 3.00 6.00
191 Filter Out U :B: 7.50 15.00
192 Tolarian Contempt U :B: .60 1.25
193 Training Grounds R :B: 25.00 50.00
194 Vesuvan Drifter R :B: 6.00 12.00
195 Ayara's Oathsworn R :K: 7.50 15.00
196 Blot Out U :K: 1.00 2.00
197 Death-Rattle Oni U :K: .75 1.50
198 Markov Baron U :K: 2.00 4.00
199 Urborg Scavengers R :K: 4.00 8.00
200 Arni Metalbrow R :R: 4.00 8.00
201 Kolaghan Warmonger U :R: .75 1.50
202 Plargg and Nassari R :R: 5.00 10.00
203 Reckless Handling U :R: 4.00 8.00
204 Tranquil Frillback R :G: 2.50 5.00
205 Undercity Upheaval U :G: .60 1.25
206 Calix, Guided by Fate M :G:/:W: 30.00 60.00
207 Campus Renovation U :R:/:W: .50 1.00
208 Cosmic Rebirth U :G:/:W: 2.50 5.00
209 Danitha, New Benalia's Light R :G:/:W: 2.00 4.00
210 Feast of the Victorious Dead U :W:/:K: 1.50 3.00
211 Gold-Forged Thopteryx U :W:/:B: 1.50 3.00
212 Jirina, Dauntless General R :W:/:K: 6.00 12.00
213 The Kenriths' Royal Funeral R :W:/:K: 4.00 8.00
214 Kiora, Sovereign of the Deep M :G:/:B: 20.00 40.00
215 Nahiri, Forged in Fury M :R:/:W: 30.00 60.00
216 Nahiri's Resolve R :R:/:W: 6.00 12.00
217 Narset, Enlightened Exile M :B:/:R:/:W: 30.00 60.00
218 Nashi, Moon's Legacy R :K:/:G:/:B: 7.50 15.00
219 Niv-Mizzet, Supreme R :W:/:B:/:K:/:R:/:G: 7.50 15.00
220 Ob Nixilis, Captive Kingpin M :K:/:R: 50.00 100.00
221 Pia Nalaar, Consul of Revival R :R:/:W: 5.00 10.00
222 Rebuild the City R :K:/:R:/:G: 2.00 4.00
223 Rocco, Street Chef R :R:/:G:/:W: 5.00 10.00
224 Samut, Vizier of Naktamun M :R:/:G: 12.50 25.00
225 Sarkhan, Soul Aflame M :B:/:R: 30.00 60.00
226 Sigarda, Font of Blessings R :G:/:W: 15.00 30.00
227 Tyvar the Bellicose M :K:/:G: 20.00 40.00
228 Drannith Ruins R 12.50 25.00
229 Spark Rupture R :W: .60 1.25
230 Jolrael, Voice of Zhalfir R :G:/:B: .15 .30

2023 Magic The Gathering March of the Machine Commander

1 Bright-Palm, Soul Awakener M :R:/:G:/:W: .25 .50
2 Brimaz, Blight of Oreskos M :W:/:K: .15 .30
3 Gimbal, Gremlin Prodigy M :G:/:B:/:R: .12 .25
4 Kasla, the Broken Halo M :B:/:R:/:W: .15 .30
5 Sidar Jabari of Zhalfir M :W:/:B:/:K: .20 .40
6 Elenda and Azor M :W:/:B:/:K: .15 .30
7 Moira and Teshar M :W:/:K: .12 .25
8 Rashmi and Ragavan M :G:/:B:/:R: .20 .40
9 Saint Traft and Rem Karolus M :B:/:R:/:W: .12 .25
10 Shalai and Hallar M :R:/:G:/:W: .30 .75
11 Chivalric Alliance R :W: 4.00 8.00
12 Conjurer's Mantle R :W: .25 .50
13 Darksteel Splicer R :W: .15 .30
14 Excise the Imperfect R :W: 1.25 2.50
15 Filigree Vector R :W: .30 .60
16 Guardian Scalelord R :W: 1.50 3.00
17 Nesting Dovehawk R :W: .75 1.50
18 Path of the Ghosthunter R :W: .15 .30
19 Vulpine Harvester R :W: .12 .25
20 Wand of the Worldsoul R :W: 1.25 2.50
21 Deluxe Dragster R :B: .20 .40
22 Herald of Hoofbeats R :B: .15 .30
23 Path of the Enigma R :B: .06 .12
24 Schema Thief R :B: .15 .30
25 Blight Titan R :K: .12 .25
26 Exsanguinator Cavalry R :K: .20 .40
27 Locthwain Lancer R :K: .07 .15
28 Path of the Schemer R :K: .07 .15
29 Dance with Calamity R :R: .75 1.50
30 Death-Greeter's Champion R :R: .12 .25
31 Hedron Detonator R :R: .75 1.50

32 Mirror-Style Master R :R:	.15	.30
33 Pain Distributor R :R:	.75	1.50
34 Path of the Pyromancer R :R:	.60	1.25
35 Uncivil Unrest R :R:	4.00	8.00
36 Conclave Sledge-Captain R :G:	.30	.60
37 Emergent Woodwurm R :G:	.25	.50
38 Path of the Animist R :G:	.07	.15
39 Sandsteppe War Riders R :G:	.05	.10
40 Cutthroat Negotiator R :B:/:R:	.12	.25
41 Flockchaser Phantom R :W:/:B:	.12	.25
42 Mistmeadow Vanisher R :W:/:B:	.07	.15
43 Vodalian Wave-Knight R :W:/:B:	.20	.40
44 Wildfire Awakener R :R:/:W:	.12	.25
45 Bitterthorn, Nissa's Animus R	7.50	15.00
46 Ichor Elixir R	.05	.10
47 The Caldaia C	1.00	2.00
48 Enigma Ridges C	1.25	2.50
49 Esper C	1.00	2.00
50 The Fertile Lands of Saulvinia C	1.50	3.00
51 Ghirapur C	1.50	3.00
52 The Golden City of Orazca C	1.50	3.00
53 The Great Aerie C	1.50	3.00
54 Inys Haen C	1.25	2.50
55 Ketria C	.75	1.50
56 Littjara C	1.25	2.50
57 Megaflora Jungle C	1.00	2.00
58 Naktamun C	1.00	2.00
59 New Argive C	1.50	3.00
60 Norn's Seedcore C	1.50	3.00
61 Nyx C	1.25	2.50
62 Paliano C	1.25	2.50
63 The Pit C	.75	1.50
64 Riptide Island C	1.50	3.00
65 Strixhaven C	1.25	2.50
66 Ten Wizards Mountain C	2.00	4.00
67 Towashi C	1.25	2.50
68 Unyaro C	1.25	2.50
69 Valor's Reach C	1.25	2.50
70 The Western Cloud C	1.50	3.00
71 The Wilds C	1.50	3.00
72 Elspeth's Talent R :W:	.15	.30
73 Firemane Commando R :W:	1.25	2.50
74 Teferi's Talent R :B:	.15	.30
75 Infernal Sovereign M :K:	.75	1.50
76 Liliana's Talent R :K:	.20	.40
77 Rowan's Talent R :R:	.12	.25
78 Vivien's Talent R :G:	.10	.20
79 Begin the Invasion M :W:/:B:/:K:/:R:/:G:	.15	.30
80 Elspeth's Talent R :W:	.15	.30
81 Firemane Commando R :W:	1.00	2.00
82 Teferi's Talent R :B:	.15	.30
83 Infernal Sovereign M :K:	.40	.80
84 Liliana's Talent R :K:	.15	.30
85 Rowan's Talent R :R:	.12	.25
86 Vivien's Talent R :G:	.12	.25
87 Begin the Invasion M :W:/:B:/:K:/:R:/:G:	.20	.40
88 Bright-Palm, Soul Awakener M :R:/:G:/:W:	.20	.40
89 Brimaz, Blight of Oreskos M :W:/:K:	.30	.75
90 Elenda and Azor M :W:/:B:/:K:	.25	.50
91 Gimbal, Gremlin Prodigy M :G:/:B:/:R:	.12	.25
92 Kasla, the Broken Halo M :B:/:R:/:W:	.20	.40
93 Moira and Teshar M :W:/:K:	.20	.40
94 Rashmi and Ragavan M :G:/:B:/:R:	.75	1.50
95 Saint Traft and Rem Karolus M :B:/:R:/:W:	.12	.25
96 Shalai and Hallar M :R:/:G:/:W:	1.00	2.00
97 Sidar Jabari of Zhalfir M :W:/:B:/:K:	.50	1.00
98 Chivalric Alliance R :W:	3.00	6.00
99 Conjurer's Mantle R :W:	.75	1.50
100 Darksteel Splicer R :W:	.20	.40
101 Excise the Imperfect R :W:	1.25	2.50
102 Filigree Vector R :W:	.30	.75
103 Guardian Scalelord R :W:	1.25	2.50
104 Nesting Dovehawk R :W:	.75	1.50
105 Path of the Ghosthunter R :W:	.07	.15
106 Vulpine Harvester R :W:	.12	.25
107 Wand of the Worldsoul R :W:	1.25	2.50
108 Deluxe Dragster R :B:	.20	.40
109 Herald of Hoofbeats R :B:	.25	.50
110 Path of the Enigma R :B:	.07	.15
111 Schema Thief R :B:	.20	.40
112 Blight Titan R :K:	.12	.25
113 Exsanguinator Cavalry R :K:	.30	.60
114 Locthwain Lancer R :K:	.12	.25
115 Path of the Schemer R :K:	.07	.15
116 Dance with Calamity R :R:	.50	1.00
117 Death-Greeter's Champion R :R:	.15	.30
118 Hedron Detonator R :R:	1.25	2.50
119 Mirror-Style Master R :R:	.15	.30
120 Pain Distributor R :R:	1.50	3.00
121 Path of the Pyromancer R :R:	.60	1.25
122 Uncivil Unrest R :R:	3.00	6.00
123 Conclave Sledge-Captain R :G:	.30	.75
124 Emergent Woodwurm R :G:	.25	.50
125 Path of the Animist R :G:	.07	.15
126 Sandsteppe War Riders R :G:	.06	.12
127 Cutthroat Negotiator R :B:/:R:	.15	.30
128 Flockchaser Phantom R :W:/:B:	.12	.25
129 Mistmeadow Vanisher R :W:/:B:	.10	.20

130 Vodalian Wave-Knight R :W:/:B:	.25	.50
131 Wildfire Awakener R :R:/:W:	.20	.40
132 Bitterthorn, Nissa's Animus R	7.50	15.00
133 Ichor Elixir R	.07	.15
134 Bright-Palm, Soul Awakener M :R:/:G:/:W:	.20	.40
135 Brimaz, Blight of Oreskos M :W:/:K:	.30	.60
136 Gimbal, Gremlin Prodigy M :G:/:B:/:R:	.30	.75
137 Kasla, the Broken Halo M :B:/:R:/:W:	.30	.60
138 Sidar Jabari of Zhalfir M :W:/:B:/:K:	.30	.75
139 The Aether Flues C	.40	.80
140 Bloodhill Bastion C	.75	1.50
141 Chaotic Aether C	.60	1.25
142 Gavony C	1.00	2.00
143 Glimmervoid Basin C	.75	1.50
144 The Great Forest C	.40	.80
145 Grove of the Dreampods C	.30	.75
146 Hedron Fields of Agadeem C	.75	1.50
147 Isle of Vesuva C	.75	1.50
148 Jund C	.50	1.00
149 Kharasha Foothills C	.75	1.50
150 Krosa C	1.25	2.50
151 Mutual Epiphany C	.75	1.50
152 Orochi Colony C	.75	1.50
153 Panopticon C	.75	1.50
154 Planewide Disaster C	1.25	2.50
155 Reality Shaping C	1.00	2.00
156 Selesnya Loft Gardens C	1.25	2.50
157 Sokenzan C	.75	1.50
158 Spatial Merging C	.75	1.50
159 Stensia C	1.00	2.00
160 Stronghold Furnace C	1.25	2.50
161 Truga Jungle C	.50	1.00
162 Turri Island C	.50	1.00
163 Undercity Reaches C	.60	1.25
164 Abzan Battle Priest U :W:	.07	.15
165 Abzan Falconer U :W:	.07	.15
166 Acclaimed Contender R :W:	.07	.15
167 Adeline, Resplendent Cathar R :W:	7.50	15.00
168 Alharu, Solemn Ritualist U :W:	.06	.12
169 Angel of Finality R :W:	.10	.20
170 Angel of Salvation R :W:	.05	.10
171 Angel of the Ruins R :W:	.12	.25
172 Austere Command R :W:	.50	1.00
173 Banisher Priest U :W:	.05	.10
174 Battle Screech U :W:	.05	.10
175 Blade Splicer R :W:	.12	.25
176 Cataclysmic Gearhulk M :W:	.15	.30
177 Chant of Vitu-Ghazi U :W:	.06	.12
178 Conclave Tribunal U :W:	.05	.10
179 Constable of the Realm U :W:	.05	.10
180 Devouring Light U :W:	.05	.10
181 Elite Scaleguard U :W:	.05	.10
182 Elspeth, Sun's Champion M :W:	2.50	5.00
183 Emeria Angel R :W:	.12	.25
184 Ephemeral Shields C :W:	.05	.10
185 Fell the Mighty R :W:	.07	.15
186 Flight of Equenauts U :W:	.05	.10
187 Generous Gift U :W:	.75	1.50
188 Hero of Bladehold M :W:	1.25	2.50
189 High Sentinels of Arashin R :W:	.06	.12
190 Hour of Reckoning R :W:	.10	.20
191 Keeper of the Accord R :W:	1.00	2.00
192 Knight Exemplar R :W:	.75	1.50
193 Knight of the White Orchid R :W:	.20	.40
194 Master Splicer U :W:	.07	.15
195 Maul of the Skyclaves R :W:	.07	.15
196 Mentor of the Meek U :W:	.12	.25
197 Mikaeus, the Lunarch M :W:	.20	.40
198 Path to Exile U :W:	1.00	2.00
199 Phyrexian Rebirth R :W:	.10	.20
200 Promise of Loyalty R :W:	.25	.50
201 Restoration Angel R :W:	.12	.25
202 Return to Dust U :W:	.07	.15
203 Secure the Wastes R :W:	.75	1.50
204 Semester's End R :W:	.20	.40
205 Seraph of the Masses U :W:	.05	.10
206 Shattered Angel U :W:	.07	.15
207 Silverwing Squadron R :W:	.07	.15
208 Spirited Companion C :W:	.15	.30
209 Sunscorch Regent R :W:	.25	.50
210 Suture Priest C :W:	.75	1.50
211 Swords to Plowshares U :W:	.50	1.00
212 Together Forever R :W:	.10	.20
213 Unbreakable Formation R :W:	.12	.25
214 Valiant Knight R :W:	.10	.20
215 Venerated Loxodon R :W:	1.25	2.50
216 Village Bell-Ringer C :W:	.07	.15
217 Worthy Knight R :W:	.07	.15
218 Chasm Skulker R :B:	.30	.60
219 Cloud of Faeries C :B:	.10	.20
220 Distant Melody C :B:	.20	.40
221 Echo Storm R :B:	.07	.15
222 Ethersworn Adjudicator M :B:	.15	.30
223 Fallowsage U :B:	.10	.20
224 Imprisoned in the Moon R :B:	.50	1.00
225 Junk Winder U :B:	.10	.20
226 Master of Etherium R :B:	.07	.15
227 Masterful Replication R :B:	.10	.20

228 Nadir Kraken R :B:	.30	.60
229 Perplexing Test R :B:	.60	1.25
230 Pull from Tomorrow R :B:	.15	.30
231 Reality Shift U :B:	.30	.75
232 Reverse Engineer U :B:	.05	.10
233 Rise and Shine R :B:	.10	.20
234 Saheeli's Artistry R :B:	.10	.20
235 Sharding Sphinx R :B:	.10	.20
236 Shimmer Dragon R :B:	.20	.40
237 Spell Swindle R :B:	.75	1.50
238 Stroke of Genius R :B:	.10	.20
239 Syr Elenora, the Discerning U :B:	.05	.10
240 Tetsuko Umezawa, Fugitive U :B:	.06	.12
241 Thopter Spy Network R :B:	.12	.25
242 Thoughtcast C :B:	.25	.50
243 Vedalken Humiliator R :B:	.07	.15
244 Whirler Rogue U :B:	.05	.10
245 Workshop Elders R :B:	.05	.10
246 Ambition's Cost U :K:	.06	.12
247 Bone Shredder U :K:	.05	.10
248 First-Sphere Gargantua C :K:	.05	.10
249 Foulmire Knight // Profane Insight U :K:	.06	.12
250 Go for the Throat U :K:	.20	.40
251 Graveshifter U :K:	.12	.25
252 Haakon, Stromgald Scourge R :K:	.10	.20
253 Josu Vess, Lich Knight R :K:	.06	.12
254 Keskit, the Flesh Sculptor U :K:	.05	.10
255 Liliana's Standard Bearer R :K:	.07	.15
256 Massacre Wurm M :K:	1.25	2.50
257 Midnight Reaper R :K:	.15	.30
258 Murderous Rider // Swift End R :K:	.30	.75
259 Night's Whisper C :K:	.75	1.50
260 Noxious Gearhulk M :K:	.20	.40
261 Order of Midnight // Alter Fate U :K:	.05	.10
262 Painful Truths R :K:	.10	.20
263 Phyrexian Delver R :K:	.12	.25
264 Phyrexian Ghoul C :K:	.05	.10
265 Phyrexian Rager C :K:	.05	.10
266 Phyrexian Scriptures M :K:	.40	.80
267 Read the Bones C :K:	.12	.25
268 Smitten Swordmaster // Curry Favor C :K:	.05	.10
269 Syr Konrad, the Grim U :K:	.75	1.50
270 Victimize U :K:	.20	.40
271 Yawgmoth's Vile Offering R :K:	.12	.25
272 Brass's Bounty R :R:	.20	.40
273 Chaos Warp R :R:	.75	1.50
274 Curse of Opulence U :R:	.75	1.50
275 Everquill Phoenix R :R:	.05	.10
276 Falkenrath Exterminator U :R:	.05	.10
277 Feldon of the Third Path M :R:	.20	.40
278 Fiery Confluence R :R:	.25	.50
279 Flamerush Rider R :R:	.07	.15
280 Flameshadow Conjuring R :R:	.60	1.25
281 Ghirapur Aether Grid U :R:	.10	.20
282 Goblin Instigator C :R:	.07	.15
283 Goblin Medics C :R:	.07	.15
284 Hellkite Igniter R :R:	.06	.12
285 Impact Tremors C :R:	2.00	4.00
286 Ion Storm R :R:	.06	.12
287 Krenko, Tin Street Kingpin R :R:	.40	.80
288 Pia and Kiran Nalaar R :R:	.10	.20
289 Vampires' Vengeance U :R:	.05	.10
290 Aid from the Cowl R :G:	.07	.15
291 Armorcraft Judge U :G:	.06	.12
292 Brawn U :G:	.12	.25
293 Champion of Lambholt R :G:	.25	.50
294 Crack Open C :G:	.07	.15
295 Cultivate C :G:	.30	.60
296 Fertilid C :G:	.05	.10
297 Forgotten Ancient R :G:	.15	.30
298 Genesis Hydra R :G:	.12	.25
299 Gilded Goose R :G:	.75	1.50
300 Gyre Sage R :G:	.75	1.50
301 Hindervines U :G:	.05	.10
302 Incubation Druid R :G:	.25	.50
303 Inscription of Abundance R :G:	.10	.20
304 Inspiring Call U :G:	.20	.40
305 Kalonian Hydra M :G:	3.00	6.00
306 Kodama's Reach C :G:	1.00	2.00
307 Managorger Hydra R :G:	.75	1.50
308 Pridemalkin C :G:	.07	.15
309 Return to Nature C :G:	.07	.15
310 Rishkar, Peema Renegade R :G:	.12	.25
311 Root Out C :G:	.05	.10
312 Slurrk, All-Ingesting U :G:	.05	.10
313 Tireless Provisioner U :G:	.75	1.50
314 Tireless Tracker R :G:	1.25	2.50
315 Weirding Wood U :G:	.07	.15
316 Wood Elves C :G:	.15	.30
317 Arvad the Cursed U :W:/:K:	.07	.15
318 Aryel, Knight of Windgrace R :W:/:K:	.07	.15
319 Combine Chrysalis U :G:/:B:	.05	.10
320 Conclave Mentor U :G:/:W:	.12	.25
321 Corpse Knight U :W:/:K:	.25	.50
322 Despark U :W:/:K:	.10	.20
323 Dromoka's Command R :G:/:W:	.10	.20
324 Duergar Hedge-Mage U :R:/:W:	.10	.20
325 Enduring Scalelord U :G:/:W:	.05	.10

326 Good-Fortune Unicorn U :G:/:W:	.10	.20
327 Hamza, Guardian of Arashin U :G:/:W:	.10	.20
328 Heaven // Earth R :G:/:R:	.06	.12
329 Improbable Alliance U :B:/:R:	.05	.10
330 Juniper Order Ranger U :G:/:W:	.06	.12
331 Knight of the Last Breath U :W:/:K:	.05	.10
332 Knights of the Black Rose U :W:/:K:	.05	.10
333 Knights' Charge R :W:/:K:	.10	.20
334 Kykar, Wind's Fury M :B:/:R:/:W:	.50	1.00
335 The Locust God M :B:/:R:	.75	1.50
336 Migratory Route U :W:/:B:	.05	.10
337 Mortify U :W:/:K:	.12	.25
338 Saheeli, Sublime Artificer U :B:/:R:	.15	.30
339 Struggle // Survive U :R:/:G:	.06	.12
340 Time Wipe R :W:/:B:	.12	.25
341 Utter End R :W:/:K:	.10	.20
342 Vona, Butcher of Magan M :W:/:K:	.25	.50
343 Wear // Tear U :R:/:W:	.30	.75
344 Whirlwind of Thought R :B:/:R:/:W:	.30	.60
345 Wintermoor Commander U :W:/:K:	.05	.10
346 Academy Manufactor R	7.50	15.00
347 Ancient Stone Idol R	.30	.75
348 Arcane Signet C	.40	.80
349 Bloodforged Battle-Axe R	1.25	2.50
350 Bloodline Pretender U	.20	.40
351 Burnished Hart U	.07	.15
352 Commander's Sphere C	.07	.15
353 Coveted Jewel R	.20	.40
354 Cultivator's Caravan R	.10	.20
355 Duplicant R	.12	.25
356 Fellwar Stone U	.30	.60
357 Fractured Powerstone C	.06	.12
358 Gruul Signet C	.30	.60
359 Hedron Archive U	.07	.15
360 Herald's Horn U	3.00	6.00
361 Inspiring Statuary R	.20	.40
362 Izzet Signet C	.30	.60
363 Meteor Golem U	.10	.20
364 Mind Stone U	.10	.20
365 Mindless Automaton U	.05	.10
366 Myr Battlesphere R	.12	.25
367 Nettlecyst R	1.25	2.50
368 Orzhov Locket C	.05	.10
369 Orzhov Signet C	.15	.30
370 Phyrexian Triniform M	.20	.40
371 Psychosis Crawler R	.12	.25
372 Replicating Ring U	.15	.30
373 Scrap Trawler R	.12	.25
374 Sculpting Steel R	.20	.40
375 Scytheclaw R	.10	.20
376 Shimmer Myr U	.10	.20
377 Sigiled Sword of Valeron R	.10	.20
378 Simic Signet C	.20	.40
379 Skullclamp U	2.00	4.00
380 Skyclave Relic R	.50	1.00
381 Sol Ring U	.75	1.50
382 Soul of New Phyrexia M	.20	.40
383 Spine of Ish Sah R	.10	.20
384 Strionic Resonator R	1.25	2.50
385 Talisman of Hierarchy U	.25	.50
386 Thopter Assembly R	.10	.20
387 Triskelion R	.10	.20
388 Vanquisher's Banner R	4.00	8.00
389 Wayfarer's Bauble C	.20	.40
390 Arcane Sanctum U	.12	.25
391 Bojuka Bog C	.50	1.00
392 Bretagard Stronghold U	.05	.10
393 Canopy Vista R	.25	.50
394 Choked Estuary R	.12	.25
395 Cinder Glade R	.15	.30
396 Command Tower C	.15	.30
397 Evolving Wilds C	.07	.15
398 Exotic Orchard R	.12	.25
399 Fetid Heath R	.75	1.50
400 Field of Ruin U	.10	.20
401 Fortified Village R	.12	.25
402 Frontier Bivouac U	.15	.30
403 Frostboil Snarl R	.30	.60
404 Furycalm Snarl R	.12	.25
405 Game Trail R	.12	.25
406 Gavony Township R	.75	1.50
407 Goldmire Bridge C	.07	.15
408 Jungle Shrine U	.20	.40
409 Karn's Bastion R	1.25	2.50
410 Kessig Wolf Run R	.15	.30
411 Kher Keep R	.10	.20
412 Krosan Verge U	.12	.25
413 Llanowar Reborn U	.07	.15
414 Mossfire Valley R	.12	.25
415 Mosswort Bridge R	.15	.30
416 Myriad Landscape U	.12	.25
417 Mystic Monastery U	.15	.30
418 Path of Ancestry C	.10	.20
419 Port Town R	.10	.20
420 Prairie Stream R	.12	.25
421 Rogue's Passage U	.25	.50
422 Shineshadow Snarl R	.12	.25
423 Silverquill Campus C	.05	.10

424 Simic Growth Chamber C	.10	.20
425 Skycloud Expanse R	.10	.20
426 Spire of Industry R	.30	.75
427 Sungrass Prairie R	.10	.20
428 Sunken Hollow R	.15	.30
429 Tainted Field U	.07	.15
430 Temple of Abandon R	.12	.25
431 Temple of Deceit R	.10	.20
432 Temple of Enlightenment R	.10	.20
433 Temple of Epiphany R	.10	.20
434 Temple of Mystery R	.15	.30
435 Temple of Plenty R	.15	.30
436 Temple of Silence R	.10	.20
437 Temple of the False God U	.07	.15
438 Temple of Triumph R	.10	.20
439 Terramorphic Expanse C	.07	.15
440 Thriving Heath C	.06	.12
441 Thriving Isle C	.06	.12
442 Thriving Moor C	.05	.10
443 Vault of the Archangel R	.40	.80
444 Vineglimmer Snarl R	.75	1.50
445 Goro-Goro and Satoru M :B:/:K:/:R:	.30	.60
446 Katilda and Lier M :G:/:W:/:B:	.20	.40
447 Slimefoot and Squee M :K:/:R:/:G:	1.25	2.50
448 Goro-Goro and Satoru M :B:/:K:/:R:	4.00	8.00
449 Katilda and Lier M :G:/:W:/:B:	1.25	2.50
450 Slimefoot and Squee M :K:/:R:/:G:	5.00	10.00

2023 Magic The Gathering March of the Machine Multiverse Legends

1 Anafenza, Kin-Tree Spirit R :W:	.10	.20
2 Daxos, Blessed by the Sun U :W:	.05	.10
3 Elesh Norn, Grand Cenobite M :W:	7.50	15.00
4 Kenrith, the Returned King M :W:	1.50	3.00
5 Kwende, Pride of Femeref U :W:	.05	.10
6 Sram, Senior Edificer R :W:	.30	.60
7 Thalia, Guardian of Thraben R :W:	.60	1.25
8 Baral, Chief of Compliance R :B:	.60	1.25
9 Emry, Lurker of the Loch R :B:	.40	.80
10 Inga Rune-Eyes U :B:	.05	.10
11 Jin-Gitaxias, Core Augur M :B:	2.00	4.00
12 Tetsuko Umezawa, Fugitive U :B:	.05	.10
13 Ayara, First of Locthwain R :K:	.75	1.50
14 Horobi, Death's Wail R :K:	.10	.20
15 Seizan, Perverter of Truth R :K:	.15	.30
16 Sheoldred, Whispering One M :K:	4.00	8.00
17 Skithiryx, the Blight Dragon M :K:	4.00	8.00
18 Tymaret, Chosen from Death U :K:	.05	.10
19 Yargle, Glutton of Urborg U :K:	.05	.10
20 Captain Lannery Storm R :R:	.10	.20
21 Ragavan, Nimble Pilferer M :R:	25.00	50.00
22 Squee, the Immortal R :R:	.12	.25
23 Urabrask the Hidden M :R:	.75	1.50
24 Valduk, Keeper of the Flame U :R:	.05	.10
25 Zada, Hedron Grinder U :R:	.05	.10
26 Fynn, the Fangbearer U :G:	.05	.10
27 Goreclaw, Terror of Qal Sisma R :G:	.75	1.50
28 Renata, Called to the Hunt U :G:	.05	.10
29 Vorinclex, Voice of Hunger M :G:	3.00	6.00
30 Yedora, Grave Gardener R :G:	.12	.25
31 Aegar, the Freezing Flame U :B:/:R:	.05	.10
32 Arixmethes, Slumbering Isle R :G:/:B:	.30	.60
33 Atraxa, Praetors' Voice M :G:/:W:/:B:/:K:	7.50	15.00
34 Atris, Oracle of Half-Truths R :B:/:K:	.05	.10
35 Aurelia, the Warleader M :R:/:W:	2.00	4.00
36 Brudiclad, Telchor Engineer R :B:/:R:	.15	.30
37 Dina, Soul Steeper U :K:/:G:	.05	.10
38 Ezuri, Claw of Progress M :G:/:B:	.25	.50
39 Firesong and Sunspeaker R :R:/:W:	.07	.15
40 Firja, Judge of Valor U :W:/:K:	.05	.10
41 Grimgrin, Corpse-Born M :B:/:K:	.75	1.50
42 Gyruda, Doom of Depths R :B:/:K:	.20	.40
43 Imoti, Celebrant of Bounty U :G:/:B:	.05	.10
44 Jegantha, the Wellspring R :R:/:G:	.60	1.25
45 Judith, the Scourge Diva R :K:/:R:	.10	.20
46 Juri, Master of the Revue U :K:/:R:	.05	.10
47 Kaheera, the Orphanguard R :G:/:W:	.20	.40
48 Keruga, the Macrosage R :G:/:B:	.12	.25
49 Kroxa, Titan of Death's Hunger M :K:/:R:	2.50	5.00
50 Lathiel, the Bounteous Dawn R :G:/:W:	.15	.30
51 Lurrus of the Dream-Den R :W:/:K:	.30	.75
52 Lutri, the Spellchaser R :B:/:R:	.10	.20
53 Niv-Mizzet Reborn M :W:/:B:/:K:/:R:/:G:	.75	1.50
54 Obosh, the Preypiercer R :K:/:R:	.15	.30
55 Radha, Coalition Warlord U :R:/:G:	.05	.10
56 Raff, Weatherlight Stalwart U :W:/:B:	.05	.10
57 Reyav, Master Smith U :R:/:W:	.05	.10
58 Rona, Sheoldred's Faithful U :B:/:K:	.05	.10
59 Shanna, Sisay's Legacy U :G:/:W:	.05	.10
60 Taigam, Ojutai Master R :W:/:B:	.10	.20
61 Teysa Karlov R :W:/:K:	.40	.80
62 Umori, the Collector R :K:/:G:	.12	.25
63 Yarok, the Desecrated M :K:/:G:/:B:	1.25	2.50
64 Yorion, Sky Nomad R :W:/:B:	.30	.60
65 Zirda, the Dawnwaker R :R:/:W:	.25	.50
66 Anafenza, Kin-Tree Spirit R :W:	.25	.50
67 Daxos, Blessed by the Sun U :W:	.05	.10
68 Elesh Norn, Grand Cenobite M :W:	15.00	30.00

69 Kenrith, the Returned King M :W: 2.50 5.00
70 Kwende, Pride of Femeref U :W: .05 .10
71 Sram, Senior Edificer R :W: .40 .80
72 Thalia, Guardian of Thraben R :W: 1.25 2.50
73 Baral, Chief of Compliance R :B: .75 1.50
74 Emry, Lurker of the Loch R :B: 1.50 3.00
75 Inga Rune-Eyes U :B: .05 .10
76 Jin-Gitaxias, Core Augur M :B: 6.00 12.00
77 Tetsuko Umezawa, Fugitive U :B: .06 .12
78 Ayara, First of Locthwain R :K: 1.00 2.00
79 Horobi, Death's Wail R :K: .30 .75
80 Seizan, Perverter of Truth R :K: .75 1.50
81 Sheoldred, Whispering One M :K: 7.50 15.00
82 Skithiryx, the Blight Dragon M :K: 12.50 25.00
83 Tymaret, Chosen from Death U :K: .05 .10
84 Yargle, Glutton of Urborg U :K: .06 .12
85 Captain Lannery Storm R :R: .30 .75
86 Ragavan, Nimble Pilferer M :R: 30.00 75.00
87 Squee, the Immortal R :R: .30 .60
88 Urabrask the Hidden M :R: 2.50 5.00
89 Valduk, Keeper of the Flame U :R: .05 .10
90 Zada, Hedron Grinder U :R: .05 .10
91 Fynn, the Fangbearer U :G: .10 .20
92 Goreclaw, Terror of Qal Sisma R :G: .75 1.50
93 Renata, Called to the Hunt U :G: .05 .10
94 Vorinclex, Voice of Hunger M :G: 7.50 15.00
95 Yedora, Grave Gardener R :G: .30 .75
96 Aegar, the Freezing Flame U :B/:R: .05 .10
97 Arixmethes, Slumbering Isle R :G/:B: .75 1.50
98 Atraxa, Praetors' Voice M :G/:W/:B/:K: 17.50 35.00
99 Atris, Oracle of Half-Truths R :B/:K: .15 .30
100 Aurelia, the Warleader M :R/:W: 5.00 10.00
101 Brudiclad, Telchor Engineer R :B/:R: .75 1.50
102 Dina, Soul Steeper U :K/:G: .07 .15
103 Ezuri, Claw of Progress M :G/:B: .75 1.50
104 Firesong and Sunspeaker R :R/:W: .20 .40
105 Firja, Judge of Valor U :W/:K: .05 .10
106 Grimgrin, Corpse-Born M :B/:K: 2.00 4.00
107 Gyruda, Doom of Depths R :B/:K: .30 .75
108 Imoti, Celebrant of Bounty U :G/:B: .07 .15
109 Jegantha, the Wellspring R :R/:G: .75 1.50
110 Judith, the Scourge Diva R :K/:R: .20 .40
111 Juri, Master of the Revue U :K/:R: .07 .15
112 Kaheera, the Orphanguard R :G/:W: .30 .60
113 Keruga, the Macrosage R :G/:B: .25 .50
114 Kroxa, Titan of Death's Hunger M :K/:R: 4.00 8.00
115 Lathiel, the Bounteous Dawn R :G/:W: .25 .50
116 Lurrus of the Dream-Den R :W/:K: .75 1.50
117 Lutri, the Spellchaser R :B/:R: .15 .30
118 Niv-Mizzet Reborn M :W/:B/:K/:R/:G: 2.50 5.00
119 Obosh, the Preypiercer R :K/:R: .30 .75
120 Radha, Coalition Warlord U :R/:G: .05 .10
121 Raff, Weatherlight Stalwart U :W/:B: .05 .10
122 Reyav, Master Smith U :R/:W: .05 .10
123 Rona, Sheoldred's Faithful U :B/:K: .05 .10
124 Shanna, Sisay's Legacy U :G/:W: .05 .10
125 Taigam, Ojutai Master R :W/:B: .30 .75
126 Teysa Karlov R :W/:K: 1.25 2.50
127 Umori, the Collector R :K/:G: .20 .40
128 Yarok, the Desecrated M :K/:G/:B: 2.50 5.00
129 Yorion, Sky Nomad R :W/:B: .75 1.50
130 Zirda, the Dawnwaker R :R/:W: .75 1.50
131 Anafenza, Kin-Tree Spirit R :W: 75.00 150.00
132 Daxos, Blessed by the Sun U :W: .20 .40
132 Daxos, Blessed by the Sun U :W:/500 75.00 150.00
133 Elesh Norn, Grand Cenobite M :W: 30.00 60.00
133 Elesh Norn, Grand Cenobite M :W:/500500.00 1,000.00
134 Kenrith, the Returned King M :W: 40.00 80.00
135 Kwende, Pride of Femeref U :W: .12 .25
135 Kwende, Pride of Femeref U :W:/500 75.00 150.00
136 Sram, Senior Edificer R :W: 7.50 15.00
136 Sram, Senior Edificer R :W:/500 100.00 200.00
137 Thalia, Guardian of Thraben R :W: 7.50 15.00
137 Thalia, Guardian of Thraben R :W:/500 150.00 300.00
138 Baral, Chief of Compliance R :B: 7.50 15.00
138 Baral, Chief of Compliance R :B:/500 175.00 350.00
139 Emry, Lurker of the Loch R :B: 7.50 15.00
140 Inga Rune-Eyes U :B: .12 .25
140 Inga Rune-Eyes U :B:/500 125.00 250.00
141 Jin-Gitaxias, Core Augur M :B: 12.50 25.00
141 Jin-Gitaxias, Core Augur M :B:/500 300.00 600.00
142 Tetsuko Umezawa, Fugitive U :B: .25 .50
142 Tetsuko Umezawa, Fugitive U :B:/500 125.00 250.00
143 Ayara, First of Locthwain R :K: 5.00 10.00
143 Ayara, First of Locthwain R :K:/500 200.00 400.00
144 Horobi, Death's Wail R :K: 2.00 4.00
144 Horobi, Death's Wail R :K:/500 75.00 150.00
145 Seizan, Perverter of Truth R :K: 2.50 5.00
145 Seizan, Perverter of Truth R :K:/500 300.00 750.00
146 Sheoldred, Whispering One M :K: 20.00 40.00
146 Sheoldred, Whispering One M :K:/500 400.00 800.00
147 Skithiryx, the Blight Dragon M :K: 30.00 75.00
147 Skithiryx, the Blight Dragon M :K:/500 250.00 500.00
148 Tymaret, Chosen from Death U :K: .12 .25
148 Tymaret, Chosen from Death U :K:/500 100.00 200.00
149 Yargle, Glutton of Urborg U :K: .12 .25
149 Yargle, Glutton of Urborg U :K:/500 75.00 150.00
150 Captain Lannery Storm R :R: 1.50 3.00
150 Captain Lannery Storm R :R:/500 40.00 80.00
151 Ragavan, Nimble Pilferer M :R: 100.00 200.00
151 Ragavan, Nimble Pilferer M :R:/500 750.00 1,500.00
152 Squee, the Immortal R :R: 2.00 4.00
152 Squee, the Immortal R :R:/500 75.00 150.00
153 Urabrask the Hidden M :R: 7.50 15.00
154 Valduk, Keeper of the Flame U :R: .12 .25
154 Valduk, Keeper of the Flame U :R:/500 75.00 150.00
155 Zada, Hedron Grinder U :R: 1.00 2.00
155 Zada, Hedron Grinder U :R:/500 100.00 200.00
156 Fynn, the Fangbearer U :G: 1.00 2.00
156 Fynn, the Fangbearer U :G:/500 75.00 150.00
157 Goreclaw, Terror of Qal Sisma R :G: 3.00 6.00
157 Goreclaw, Terror of Qal Sisma R :G:/500150.00 300.00
158 Renata, Called to the Hunt U :G: .25 .50
158 Renata, Called to the Hunt U :G:/500 75.00 150.00
159 Vorinclex, Voice of Hunger M :G: 12.50 25.00
160 Yedora, Grave Gardener R :G: 2.00 4.00
160 Yedora, Grave Gardener R :G:/500 75.00 150.00
161 Aegar, the Freezing Flame U :B/:R: .20 .40
161 Aegar, the Freezing Flame U :B/:R:/500 75.00 150.00
162 Arixmethes, Slumbering Isle R :G/:B: 5.00 10.00
163 Atraxa, Praetors' Voice M :G/:W/:B/:K: 30.00 75.00
163 Atraxa, Praetors' Voice
M :G/:W/:B/:K:/500 600.00 1,200.00
164 Atris, Oracle of Half-Truths R :B/:K: 1.25 2.50
164 Atris, Oracle of Half-Truths R :B/:K:/500125.00 250.00
165 Aurelia, the Warleader M :R/:W: 20.00 40.00
166 Brudiclad, Telchor Engineer R :B/:R: 3.00 6.00
166 Brudiclad, Telchor Engineer R :B/:R:/500125.00 250.00
167 Dina, Soul Steeper U :K/:G: .75 1.50
167 Dina, Soul Steeper U :K/:G:/500 100.00 200.00
168 Ezuri, Claw of Progress M :G/:B: 4.00 8.00
169 Firesong and Sunspeaker R :R/:W: 1.50 3.00
169 Firesong and Sunspeaker R :R/:W:/500 75.00 150.00
170 Firja, Judge of Valor U :W/:K: .12 .25
171 Grimgrin, Corpse-Born M :B/:K: 7.50 15.00
171 Grimgrin, Corpse-Born M :B/:K:/500 150.00 300.00
172 Gyruda, Doom of Depths R :B/:K: 2.50 5.00
172 Gyruda, Doom of Depths R :B/:K:/500 150.00 300.00
173 Imoti, Celebrant of Bounty U :G/:B: .30 .60
173 Imoti, Celebrant of Bounty U :G/:B:/500100.00 200.00
174 Jegantha, the Wellspring R :R/:G: 12.50 25.00
175 Judith, the Scourge Diva R :K/:R: 2.00 4.00
176 Juri, Master of the Revue U :K/:R: .30 .60
176 Juri, Master of the Revue U :K/:R:/500 100.00 200.00
177 Kaheera, the Orphanguard R :G/:W:/500175.00 350.00
177 Kaheera, the Orphanguard R :G/:W: 7.50 15.00
178 Keruga, the Macrosage R :G/:B: 4.00 8.00
178 Keruga, the Macrosage R :G/:B:/500 125.00 250.00
179 Kroxa, Titan of Death's Hunger M :K/:R: 15.00 30.00
179 Kroxa, Titan of Death's
Hunger M :K/:R:/500 250.00 500.00
180 Lathiel, the Bounteous Dawn R :G/:W: 5.00 10.00
180 Lathiel, the Bounteous Dawn R :G/:W:/50075.00 150.00
181 Lurrus of the Dream-Den R :W/:K: 12.50 25.00
182 Lutri, the Spellchaser R :B/:R: 1.25 2.50
182 Lutri, the Spellchaser R :B/:R:/500 150.00 300.00
183 Niv-Mizzet Reborn M :W/:B/:K/:R/:G: 15.00 30.00
183 Niv-Mizzet Reborn M :W/:B/:K/:R/:G:/500300.00750.00
184 Obosh, the Preypiercer R :K/:R: 4.00 8.00
184 Obosh, the Preypiercer R :K/:R:/500 175.00 350.00
185 Radha, Coalition Warlord U :R/:G: .12 .25
185 Radha, Coalition Warlord U :R/:G:/500 40.00 80.00
186 Raff, Weatherlight Stalwart U :W/:B: .12 .25
187 Reyav, Master Smith U :R/:W: .30 .60
187 Reyav, Master Smith U :R/:W:/500 75.00 150.00
188 Rona, Sheoldred's Faithful U :B/:K: .12 .25
188 Rona, Sheoldred's Faithful U :B/:K:/500 30.00 75.00
189 Shanna, Sisay's Legacy U :G/:W: .12 .25
189 Shanna, Sisay's Legacy U :G/:W:/500 75.00 150.00
190 Taigam, Ojutai Master R :W/:B: 1.50 3.00
190 Taigam, Ojutai Master R :W/:B:/500 125.00 250.00
191 Teysa Karlov R :W/:K: 7.50 15.00
192 Umori, the Collector R :K/:G: 2.00 4.00
193 Yarok, the Desecrated M :K/:G/:B: 15.00 30.00
193 Yarok, the Desecrated M :K/:G/:B:/500200.00 400.00
194 Yorion, Sky Nomad R :W/:B: 7.50 15.00
194 Yorion, Sky Nomad R :W/:B:/500 250.00 500.00
195 Zirda, the Dawnwaker R :R/:W: 7.50 15.00
195 Zirda, the Dawnwaker R :R/:W:/500 200.00 400.00

2023 Magic The Gathering Phyrexia All Will Be One

1 Against All Odds U :W: .05 .10
2 Annex Sentry U :W: .06 .12
3 Apostle of Invasion U :W: .05 .10
4 Basilica Shepherd C :W: .05 .10
5 Bladed Ambassador U :W: .05 .10
6 Charge of the Mites C :W: .05 .10
7 Compleat Devotion C :W: .05 .10
8 Crawling Chorus C :W: .06 .12
9 Duelist of Deep Faith C :W: .05 .10
10 Elesh Norn, Mother of Machines M :W: 15.00 30.00
11 The Eternal Wanderer R :W: .75 1.50
12 Flensing Raptor C :W: .05 .10
13 Goldwarden's Helm C :W: .05 .10
14 Hexgold Hoverwings U :W: .06 .12
15 Incisor Glider C :W: .05 .10
16 Indoctrination Attendant C :W: .05 .10
17 Infested Fleshcutter U :W: .05 .10
18 Jawbone Duelist U :W: .06 .12
19 Kemba, Kha Enduring R :W: .15 .30
20 Leonin Lightbringer C :W: .05 .10
21 Mandible Justiciar C :W: .05 .10
22 Mirran Bardiche C :W: .05 .10
23 Mondrak, Glory Dominus M :W: 15.00 30.00
24 Norn's Wellspring R :W: .12 .25
25 Orthodoxy Enforcer C :W: .05 .10
26 Ossification U :W: 1.00 2.00
27 Phyrexian Vindicator M :W: 2.00 4.00
28 Planar Disruption C :W: .05 .10
29 Plated Onslaught U :W: .05 .10
30 Porcelain Zealot U :W: .05 .10
31 Resistance Reunited U :W: .05 .10
32 Sinew Dancer C :W: .05 .10
33 Skrelv, Defector Mite R :W: 2.50 5.00
34 Skrelv's Hive R :W: 1.25 2.50
35 Swooping Lookout U :W: .05 .10
36 Vanish into Eternity C :W: .05 .10
37 Veil of Assimilation U :W: .05 .10
38 White Sun's Twilight R :W: 1.25 2.50
39 Zealot's Conviction C :W: .05 .10
40 Aspirant's Ascent C :B: .05 .10
41 Atmosphere Surgeon U :B: .05 .10
42 Blade of Shared Souls R :B: .12 .25
43 Blue Sun's Twilight R :B: .40 .80
44 Bring the Ending C :B: .06 .12
45 Chrome Prowler C :B: .05 .10
46 Distorted Curiosity U :B: .05 .10
47 Encroaching Mycosynth R :B: .15 .30
48 Escaped Experiment C :B: .05 .10
49 Experimental Augury C :B: .25 .50
50 Eye of Malcator C :B: .05 .10
51 Font of Progress U :B: .05 .10
52 Gitaxian Anatomist C :B: .05 .10
53 Gitaxian Raptor C :B: .05 .10
54 Glistener Seer C :B: .05 .10
55 Ichor Synthesizer C :B: .05 .10
56 Ichormoon Gauntlet M :B: 2.00 4.00
57 Jace, the Perfected Mind M :B: 2.00 4.00
58 Malcator's Watcher C :B: .05 .10
59 Meldweb Curator C :B: .05 .10
60 Meldweb Strider C :B: .05 .10
61 Mercurial Spelldancer R :B: .25 .50
62 Mesmerizing Dose C :B: .05 .10
63 Mindsplice Apparatus R :B: .25 .50
64 Minor Misstep U :B: .07 .15
65 Prologue to Phyresis C :B: .25 .50
66 Quicksilver Fisher C :B: .05 .10
67 Reject Imperfection U :B: .10 .20
68 Serum Snare U :B: .10 .20
69 Tamiyo's Immobilizer U :B: .05 .10
70 Tamiyo's Logbook U :B: .05 .10
71 Tekuthal, Inquiry Dominus M :B: 2.00 4.00
72 Thrummingbird U :B: .06 .12
73 Transplant Theorist U :B: .05 .10
74 Trawler Drake U :B: .05 .10
75 Unctus, Grand Metatect R :B: .12 .25
76 Unctus's Retrofitter U :B: .05 .10
77 Vivisurgeon's Insight C :B: .05 .10
78 Watchful Blisterzoa U :B: .05 .10
79 Ambulatory Edifice U :K: .05 .10
80 Annihilating Glare C :K: .05 .10
81 Anoint with Affliction C :K: .06 .12
82 Archfiend of the Dross R :K: .60 1.25
83 Bilious Skulldweller U :K: .06 .12
84 Black Sun's Twilight R :K: .25 .50
85 Blightbelly Rat C :K: .05 .10
86 Bonepicker Skirge C :K: .05 .10
87 Chittering Skitterling U :K: .05 .10
88 Cruel Grimnarch C :K: .05 .10
89 Cutthroat Centurion C :K: .05 .10
90 Drivnod, Carnage Dominus M :K: 2.50 5.00
91 Drown in Ichor U :K: .30 .60
92 Duress C :K: .05 .10
93 Feed the Infection U :K: .05 .10
94 Fleshless Gladiator C :K: .05 .10
95 Geth, Thane of Contracts R :K: .10 .20
96 Gulping Scraptrap C :K: .05 .10
97 Infectious Inquiry C :K: .10 .20
98 Karumonix, the Rat King R :K: .15 .30
99 Necrogen Communion U :K: .10 .20
100 Necrosquito U :K: .05 .10
101 Nimraiser Paladin U :K: .05 .10
102 Offer Immortality C :K: .05 .10
103 Pestilent Syphoner C :K: .05 .10
104 Phyrexian Arena R :K: 1.75 3.50
105 Phyrexian Obliterator M :K: 3.00 6.00
106 Ravenous Necrotitan U :K: .05 .10
107 Scheming Aspirant U :K: .05 .10
108 Sheoldred's Edict U :K: 1.25 2.50
109 Sheoldred's Headcleaver C :K: .05 .10
110 Stinghive Master C :K: .05 .10
111 Testament Bearer C :K: .05 .10
112 Vat Emergence U :K: .05 .10
113 Vat of Rebirth U :K: .20 .40
114 Vraan, Executioner Thane R :K: .30 .60
115 Vraska, Betrayal's Sting M :K: 4.00 8.00
116 Vraska's Fall C :K: .07 .15
117 Whisper of the Dross C :K: .06 .12
118 All Will Be One M :R: 7.50 15.00
119 Awaken the Sleeper U :R: .05 .10
120 Axiom Engraver C :R: .05 .10
121 Barbed Batterfist C :R: .05 .10
122 Bladegraft Aspirant C :R: .05 .10
123 Blazing Crescendo C :R: .05 .10
124 Cacophony Scamp U :R: .06 .12
125 Capricious Hellraiser M :R: .30 .60
126 Chimney Rabble C :R: .05 .10
127 Churning Reservoir U :R: .05 .10
128 Dragonwing Glider R :R: .07 .15
129 Exuberant Fuseling U :R: .05 .10
130 Forgehammer Centurion C :R: .05 .10
131 Free from Flesh C :R: .05 .10
132 Furnace Punisher U :R: .05 .10
133 Furnace Strider C :R: .05 .10
134 Gleeful Demolition U :R: .50 1.00
135 Hazardous Blast C :R: .05 .10
136 Hexgold Halberd U :R: .05 .10
137 Hexgold Slash C :R: .05 .10
138 Koth, Fire of Resistance R :R: .20 .40
139 Kuldotha Cackler C :R: .05 .10
140 Magmatic Sprinter U :R: .05 .10
141 Molten Rebuke C :R: .05 .10
142 Nahiri's Sacrifice U :R: .05 .10
143 Oxidda Finisher U :R: .05 .10
144 Rebel Salvo U :R: .06 .12
145 Red Sun's Twilight R :R: .12 .25
146 Resistance Skywarden U :R: .05 .10
147 Sawblade Scamp C :R: .05 .10
148 Shrapnel Slinger C :R: .05 .10
149 Slobad, Iron Goblin R :R: .07 .15
150 Solphim, Mayhem Dominus M :R: 4.00 8.00
151 Thrill of Possibility C :R: .05 .10
152 Urabrask's Anointer U :R: .05 .10
153 Urabrask's Forge R :R: .20 .40
154 Vindictive Flamestoker R :R: .07 .15
155 Volt Charge C :R: .05 .10
156 Vulshok Splitter C :R: .05 .10
157 Adaptive Sporesinger C :G: .05 .10
158 Armored Scrapgorger U :G: .12 .25
159 Bloated Contaminator R :G: .75 1.50
160 Branchblight Stalker C :G: .05 .10
161 Cankerbloom U :G: .15 .30
162 Carnivorous Canopy C :G: .05 .10
163 Conduit of Worlds R :G: 1.75 3.50
164 Contagious Vorrac C :G: .05 .10
165 Copper Longlegs C :G: .05 .10
166 Evolved Spinoderm R :G: .05 .10
167 Evolving Adaptive U :G: .05 .10
168 Expand the Sphere U :G: .05 .10
169 Green Sun's Twilight R :G: .25 .50
170 Ichorspit Basilisk C :G: .05 .10
171 Incubation Sac U :G: .05 .10
172 Infectious Bite U :G: .30 .60
173 Lattice-Blade Mantis C :G: .05 .10
174 Maze's Mantle C :G: .05 .10
175 Nissa, Ascended Animist M :G: 1.75 3.50
176 Noxious Assault U :G: .05 .10
177 Oil-Gorger Troll C :G: .05 .10
178 Paladin of Predation U :G: .05 .10
179 Plague Nurse C :G: .05 .10
180 Predation Steward C :G: .05 .10
181 Rustvine Cultivator C :G: .05 .10
182 Ruthless Predation C :G: .05 .10
183 Skyscythe Engulfer C :G: .05 .10
184 Sylvok Battle-Chair U :G: .05 .10
185 Thirsting Roots C :G: .15 .30
186 Thrun, Breaker of Silence R :G: .20 .40
187 Titanic Growth C :G: .05 .10
188 Tyrranax Atrocity C :G: .05 .10
189 Tyrranax Rex M :G: 2.50 5.00
190 Tyvar's Stand U :G: 1.00 2.00
191 Unnatural Restoration U :G: .25 .50
192 Venerated Rotpriest R :G: 1.25 2.50
193 Venomous Brutalizer U :G: .05 .10
194 Viral Spawning U :G: .05 .10
195 Zopandrel, Hunger Dominus M :G: 3.00 6.00
196 Atraxa, Grand Unifier M :G/:W/:B/:K: 10.00 20.00
197 Bladehold War-Whip U :R/:W: .05 .10
198 Cephalopod Sentry U :W/:B: .05 .10
199 Charforger U :K/:R: .05 .10
200 Cinderslash Ravager U :R/:G: .05 .10
201 Ezuri, Stalker of Spheres R :G/:B: .25 .50
202 Glissa Sunslayer R :K/:G: 1.25 2.50
203 Jor Kadeen, First Goldwarden R :R/:W: .10 .20
204 Kaito, Dancing Shadow R :B/:K: .20 .40
205 Kaya, Intangible Slayer R :W/:K: .20 .40
206 Kethek, Crucible Goliath R :K/:R: .07 .15
207 Lukka, Bound to Ruin M :R/:G: .30 .75
208 Malcator, Purity Overseer R :W/:B: .07 .15
209 Melira, the Living Cure R :G/:W: .10 .20
210 Migloz, Maze Crusher R :R/:G: .12 .25
211 Nahiri, the Unforgiving M :R/:W: .25 .50
212 Necrogen Rotpriest U :K/:G: .06 .12
213 Ovika, Enigma Goliath R :B/:R: .15 .30
214 Ria Ivor, Bane of Bladehold R :W/:K: .12 .25
215 Serum-Core Chimera U :B/:R: .05 .10
216 Slaughter Singer U :G/:W: .06 .12
217 Tainted Observer U :G/:B: .06 .12
218 Tyvar, Jubilant Brawler R :K/:G: .75 1.50
219 Venser, Corpse Puppet R :B/:K: .10 .20
220 Vivisection Evangelist U :W/:K: .05 .10
221 Voidwing Hybrid U :B/:K: .10 .20
222 Argentum Masticore R .07 .15
223 Atraxa's Skitterfang U .05 .10
224 Basilica Skullbomb C .05 .10
225 Dross Skullbomb C .05 .10
226 Dune Mover C .05 .10
227 The Filigree Sylex R .15 .30
228 Furnace Skullbomb C .05 .10
229 Graaz, Unstoppable Juggernaut R .10 .20
230 Ichorplate Golem U .05 .10
231 Maze Skullbomb C .05 .10
232 Mirran Safehouse R .07 .15
233 Monument to Perfection R .06 .12
234 Myr Convert U .07 .15
235 Myr Custodian C .05 .10
236 Myr Kinsmith C .05 .10
237 Phyrexian Atlas C .05 .10
238 Prophetic Prism C .05 .10
239 Prosthetic Injector U .05 .10
240 Ribskiff U .05 .10
241 Soulless Jailer R .50 1.00
242 Staff of Compleation M 2.50 5.00
243 Surgical Skullbomb C .05 .10
244 Sword of Forge and Frontier M 7.50 15.00
245 Tablet of Compleation R .07 .15
246 Zenith Chronicler R .15 .30
247 The Autonomous Furnace C .05 .10
248 Blackcleave Cliffs R 1.25 2.50
249 Copperline Gorge R 1.00 2.00
250 Darkslick Shores R 1.75 3.50
251 The Dross Pits C .05 .10
252 The Fair Basilica C .05 .10
253 The Hunter Maze C .05 .10
254 Mirrex R .75 1.50
255 The Monumental Facade R .07 .15
256 The Mycosynth Gardens R 1.50 3.00
257 Razorverge Thicket R 1.25 2.50
258 Seachrome Coast R 1.25 2.50
259 The Seedcore R .20 .40
260 The Surgical Bay C .05 .10
261 Terramorphic Expanse C .07 .15
262 Plains C .20 .40
263 Island C .12 .25
264 Swamp C .10 .20
265 Mountain C .10 .20
266 Forest C .10 .20
267 Plains C .40 .80
268 Island C .40 .80
269 Swamp C .75 1.50
270 Mountain C .30 .75
271 Forest C .30 .75
272 Plains C .05 .10
273 Island C .07 .15
274 Swamp C .06 .12
275 Mountain C .05 .10
276 Forest C .07 .15
277 Ossification U :W: 1.25 2.50
278 Experimental Augury C :B: .25 .50
279 Sheoldred's Edict U :K: 1.25 2.50
280 Bladehold War-Whip U :R/:W: .20 .40
281 Slaughter Singer U :G/:W: .20 .40
282 Karumonix, the Rat King R :K: .07 .15
283 Phyrexian Arena R :K: .75 1.50
284 Green Sun's Twilight R :G: .25 .50
285 Bladed Ambassador U :W: .05 .10
286 Sinew Dancer C :W: .05 .10
287 Quicksilver Fisher C :B: .05 .10
288 Thrummingbird U :B: .05 .10
289 Blightbelly Rat C :K: .05 .10
290 Bonepicker Skirge C :K: .05 .10
291 Furnace Punisher U :R: .05 .10
292 Sawblade Scamp C :R: .05 .10
293 Urabrask's Anointer U :R: .05 .10
294 Cankerbloom U :G: .05 .10
295 Rustvine Cultivator C :G: .05 .10
296 Necrogen Rotpriest U :K/:G: .05 .10
297 Myr Convert U .05 .10
298 Elesh Norn, Mother of Machines M :W: 17.50 35.00
299 Mondrak, Glory Dominus M :W: 15.00 30.00
300 Phyrexian Vindicator M :W: 1.75 3.50
301 Skrelv, Defector Mite R :W: 1.75 3.50
302 Tekuthal, Inquiry Dominus M :B: 1.50 3.00
303 Unctus, Grand Metatect R :B: .20 .40
304 Archfiend of the Dross R :K: .40 .80
305 Drivnod, Carnage Dominus M :K: 2.00 4.00
306 Geth, Thane of Contracts R :K: .06 .12
307 Karumonix, the Rat King R :K: .15 .30
308 Phyrexian Obliterator M :K: 2.50 5.00
309 Vraan, Executioner Thane R :K: .20 .40
310 Capricious Hellraiser M :R: .30 .60
311 Slobad, Iron Goblin R :R: .06 .12
312 Solphim, Mayhem Dominus M :R: 3.00 6.00
313 Evolved Spinoderm R :G: .07 .15

314 Tyrranax Rex M :G: 2.00 4.00
315 Zopandrel, Hunger Dominus M :G: 2.50 5.00
316 Atraxa, Grand Unifier M :G:/W:/B:/K: 10.00 20.00
317 Ezuri, Stalker of Spheres R :G:/B: .15 .30
318 Glissa Sunslayer R :K:/G: 1.25 2.50
319 Kethek, Crucible Goliath R :K:/R: .06 .12
320 Malcator, Purity Overseer R :W:/B: .07 .15
321 Migloz, Maze Crusher R :R:/G: .20 .40
322 Ovika, Enigma Goliath R :B:/R: .15 .30
323 Ria Ivor, Bane of Bladehold R :W:/K: .15 .30
324 Venser, Corpse Puppet R :B:/K: .10 .20
325 Jace, the Perfected Mind M :B: 1.50 3.00
326 Vraska, Betrayal's Sting M :K: 3.00 6.00
327 Nissa, Ascended Animist M :G: 1.25 2.50
328 Lukka, Bound to Ruin M :R:/G: .30 .75
329 Nahiri, the Unforgiving M :R:/W: .30 .75
330 Kemba, Kha Enduring R :W: .12 .25
331 Thrun, Breaker of Silence R :G: .20 .40
332 Jor Kadeen, First Goldwarden R :R:/W: .10 .20
333 Melira, the Living Cure R :G:/W: .20 .40
334 Graaz, Unstoppable Juggernaut R .15 .30
335 The Eternal Wanderer R :W: 1.00 2.00
336 Jace, the Perfected Mind M :B: 3.00 6.00
337 Vraska, Betrayal's Sting M :K: 7.50 15.00
338 Koth, Fire of Resistance R :R: .12 .25
339 Nissa, Ascended Animist M :G: 2.50 5.00
340 Kaito, Dancing Shadow R :B:/K: .25 .50
341 Kaya, Intangible Slayer R :W:/K: .20 .40
342 Lukka, Bound to Ruin M :R:/G: .30 .75
343 Nahiri, the Unforgiving M :R:/W: .75 1.50
344 Tyvar, Jubilant Brawler R :K:/G: .75 1.50
345 Elesh Norn, Mother of Machines M :W: 30.00 60.00
346 Mondrak, Glory Dominus M :W: 20.00 40.00
347 Phyrexian Vindicator M :W: 7.50 15.00
348 Ichormoon Gauntlet M :B: 10.00 20.00
349 Tekuthal, Inquiry Dominus M :B: 7.50 15.00
350 Drivnod, Carnage Dominus M :K: 7.50 15.00
351 Phyrexian Obliterator M :K: 10.00 20.00
352 All Will Be One M :R: 17.50 35.00
353 Capricious Hellraiser M :R: 2.50 5.00
354 Solphim, Mayhem Dominus M :R: 10.00 20.00
355 Tyrranax Rex M :G: 7.50 15.00
356 Zopandrel, Hunger Dominus M :G: 7.50 15.00
357 Atraxa, Grand Unifier M :G:/W:/B:/K: 30.00 75.00
358 Staff of Compleation M 10.00 20.00
359 Sword of Forge and Frontier M 17.50 35.00
360 Jace, the Perfected Mind M :B: 7.50 15.00
361 Vraska, Betrayal's Sting M :K: 10.00 20.00
362 Nissa, Ascended Animist M :G: 7.50 15.00
363 Lukka, Bound to Ruin M :R:/G: 2.50 5.00
364 Nahiri, the Unforgiving M :R:/W: 2.50 5.00
365 Plains C 2.00 4.00
366 Island C 2.00 4.00
367 Swamp C 5.00 10.00
368 Mountain C 1.75 3.50
369 Forest C 1.75 3.50
370 Blackcleave Cliffs R 1.75 3.50
371 Copperline Gorge R 1.00 2.00
372 Darkslick Shores R 1.50 3.00
373 Razorverge Thicket R 1.25 2.50
374 Seachrome Coast R 1.50 3.00
375 Norn's Wellspring R :W: .15 .30
376 Skrelv's Hive R :W: .75 1.50
377 White Sun's Twilight R :W: 1.25 2.50
378 Blade of Shared Souls R :B: .12 .25
379 Blue Sun's Twilight R :B: .25 .50
380 Encroaching Mycosynth R :B: .20 .40
381 Mercurial Spelldancer R :B: .30 .60
382 Mindsplice Apparatus R :B: .50 1.00
383 Black Sun's Twilight R :K: .30 .60
384 Phyrexian Arena R :K: 1.25 2.50
385 Dragonwing Glider R :R: .10 .20
386 Red Sun's Twilight R :R: .15 .30
387 Urabrask's Forge R :R: .25 .50
388 Vindictive Flamestoker R :R: .12 .25
389 Bloated Contaminator R :G: .75 1.50
390 Conduit of Worlds R :G: 1.75 3.50
391 Green Sun's Twilight R :G: .20 .40
392 Venerated Rotpriest R :G: 1.25 2.50
393 Argentum Masticore R .07 .15
394 The Filigree Sylex R .25 .50
395 Mirran Safehouse R .12 .25
396 Monument to Perfection R .07 .15
397 Soulless Jailer R 1.00 2.00
398 Tablet of Compleation R .07 .15
399 Zenith Chronicler R .12 .25
400 Mirrex R 1.00 2.00
401 The Monumental Facade R .07 .15
402 The Mycosynth Gardens R 1.50 3.00
403 The Seedcore R .30 .75
404 Mite Overseer R :W: 1.25 2.50
405 Serum Sovereign R :B: .12 .25
406 Kinzu of the Bleak Coven R :K: .15 .30
407 Rhuk, Hexgold Nabber R :R: .10 .20
408 Goliath Hatchery R :G: .10 .20
409 Mite Overseer R :W: .75 1.50
410 Serum Sovereign R :B: .20 .40
411 Kinzu of the Bleak Coven R :K: .12 .25
412 Rhuk, Hexgold Nabber R :R: .12 .25
413 Goliath Hatchery R :G: .12 .25
414 Elesh Norn, Mother of Machines M 17.50 35.00
415 Elesh Norn, Mother of Machines M :W: 30.00 75.00
416 Elesh Norn, Mother of Machines M :W: 25.00 50.00
417 Bladed Ambassador U :W: .07 .15
418 Elesh Norn Mother of Machines M :W: 25.00 50.00
419 Elesh Norn, Mother of Machines M :W: 75.00 150.00
420 Elesh Norn, Mother of Machines M :W: 20.00 40.00
421 Elesh Norn, Mother of Machines M :W: 25.00 50.00
422 The Eternal Wanderer R :W: 3.00 6.00
423 Kemba, Kha Enduring R :W: .75 1.50
424 Mondrak, Glory Dominus M :W: 17.50 35.00
425 Phyrexian Vindicator M :W: 4.00 8.00
426 Sinew Dancer C :W: .05 .10
427 Skrelv, Defector Mite R :W: 5.00 10.00
428 Jace, the Perfected Mind M :B: 7.50 15.00
429 Jace, the Perfected Mind M :B: 4.00 8.00
430 Quicksilver Fisher C :B: .05 .10
431 Tekuthal, Inquiry Dominus M :B: 6.00 12.00
432 Thrummingbird U :B: .30 .75
433 Unctus, Grand Metatect R :B: 1.25 2.50
434 Archfiend of the Dross R :K: 2.50 5.00
435 Blightbelly Rat C :K: .15 .30
436 Bonepicker Skirge C :K: .05 .10
437 Drivnod, Carnage Dominus M :K: 5.00 10.00
438 Geth, Thane of Contracts R :K: .30 .75
439 Karumonix, the Rat King R :K: 1.00 2.00
440 Phyrexian Obliterator M :K: 6.00 12.00
441 Vraan, Executioner Thane R :K: 1.25 2.50
442 Vraska, Betrayal's Sting M :K: 20.00 40.00
443 Vraska, Betrayal's Sting M :K: 3.00 6.00
444 Capricious Hellraiser M :R: 2.00 4.00
445 Furnace Punisher U :R: .15 .30
446 Koth, Fire of Resistance R :R: 1.00 2.00
447 Sawblade Scamp C :R: .06 .12
448 Slobad, Iron Goblin R :R: .60 1.25
449 Solphim, Mayhem Dominus M :R: 7.50 15.00
450 Urabrask's Anointer U :R: .07 .15
451 Cankerbloom U :G: .75 1.50
452 Evolved Spinoderm R :G: .30 .75
453 Nissa, Ascended Animist M :G: 4.00 8.00
454 Nissa, Ascended Animist M :G: 7.50 15.00
455 Rustvine Cultivator C :G: .06 .12
456 Thrun, Breaker of Silence R :G: 1.25 2.50
457 Tyrranax Rex M :G: 6.00 12.00
458 Zopandrel, Hunger Dominus M :G: 6.00 12.00
459 Atraxa, Grand Unifier M :G:/W:/B:/K: 30.00 75.00
460 Ezuri, Stalker of Spheres R :G:/B: 1.25 2.50
461 Glissa Sunslayer R :K:/G: 3.00 6.00
462 Jor Kadeen, First Goldwarden R :R:/W: .40 .80
463 Kaito, Dancing Shadow R :B:/K: 1.25 2.50
464 Kaya, Intangible Slayer R :W:/K: .75 1.50
465 Kethek, Crucible Goliath R :K:/R: .50 1.00
466 Lukka, Bound to Ruin M :R:/G: 2.00 4.00
467 Lukka, Bound to Ruin M :R:/G: 1.25 2.50
468 Malcator, Purity Overseer R :W:/B: .40 .80
469 Melira, the Living Cure R :G:/W: .75 1.50
470 Migloz, Maze Crusher R :R:/G: .75 1.50
471 Nahiri, the Unforgiving M :R:/W: 3.00 6.00
472 Nahiri, the Unforgiving M :R:/W: 1.50 3.00
473 Necrogen Rotpriest U :K:/G: .20 .40
474 Ovika, Enigma Goliath R :B:/R: 1.75 3.50
475 Ria Ivor, Bane of Bladehold R :W:/K: .75 1.50
476 Tyvar, Jubilant Brawler R :K:/G: 4.00 8.00
477 Venser, Corpse Puppet R :B:/K: .75 1.50
478 Graaz, Unstoppable Juggernaut R .75 1.50
479 Myr Convert U .15 .30

2023 Magic The Gathering Phyrexia All Will Be One Commander

1 Ixhel, Scion of Atraxa M :W:/K:/G: .25 .50
2 Neyali, Suns' Vanguard M :R:/W: .25 .50
3 Otharri, Suns' Glory M :R:/W: .17 .35
4 Vishgraz, the Doomhive M :W:/K:/G: .20 .40
5 Clever Concealment R :W: 5.00 10.00
6 Glimmer Lens R :W: .15 .30
7 Kemba's Banner R :W: .12 .25
8 Norn's Choirmaster R :W: 2.50 5.00
9 Norn's Decree R :W: 1.25 2.50
10 Staff of the Storyteller R :W: 4.00 8.00
11 Geth's Summons R :K: .10 .20
12 Phyresis Outbreak R :K: 2.00 4.00
13 Goldwardens' Gambit R :R: .10 .20
14 Hexplate Wallbreaker R :R: .40 .80
15 Roar of Resistance R :R: .25 .50
16 Vulshok Factory R :R: .05 .10
17 Contaminant Grafter R :G: 1.00 2.00
18 Glissa's Retriever R :G: .12 .25
19 Wurmquake R :G: .10 .20
20 Glistening Sphere R 1.25 2.50
21 Skyhunter Strike Force R :W: 1.50 3.00
22 Mirage Mockery R :B: .15 .30
23 Synthesis Pod R :B: .12 .25
24 Monumental Corruption R :K: .30 .60
25 Chiss-Goria, Forge Tyrant M :R: 2.00 4.00
26 Tangleweave Armor R :G: .12 .25
27 Lux Artillery R .25 .50
28 Urtet, Remnant of Memnarch M 1.25 2.50
29 Ixhel, Scion of Atraxa M :W:/K:/G: .15 .30
30 Neyali, Suns' Vanguard M :R:/W: .12 .25
31 Skyhunter Strike Force R :W: .75 1.50
32 Mirage Mockery R :B: .12 .25
33 Synthesis Pod R :B: .12 .25
34 Monumental Corruption R :K: .15 .30
35 Chiss-Goria, Forge Tyrant M :R: 1.50 3.00
36 Tangleweave Armor R :G: .07 .15
37 Ixhel, Scion of Atraxa M :W:/K:/G: .75 1.50
38 Neyali, Suns' Vanguard M :R:/W: .75 1.50
39 Otharri, Suns' Glory M :R:/W: .50 1.00
40 Vishgraz, the Doomhive M :W:/K:/G: .75 1.50
41 Lux Artillery R .12 .25
42 Urtet, Remnant of Memnarch M .75 1.50
43 Clever Concealment R :W: 5.00 10.00
44 Glimmer Lens R :W: .25 .50
45 Kemba's Banner R :W: .12 .25
46 Norn's Choirmaster R :W: 2.00 4.00
47 Norn's Decree R :W: .75 1.50
48 Staff of the Storyteller R :W: 4.00 8.00
49 Geth's Summons R :K: .12 .25
50 Phyresis Outbreak R :K: 1.00 2.00
51 Goldwardens' Gambit R :R: .15 .30
52 Hexplate Wallbreaker R :R: .75 1.50
53 Roar of Resistance R :R: .30 .60
54 Vulshok Factory R :R: .07 .15
55 Contaminant Grafter R :G: 1.25 2.50
56 Glissa's Retriever R :G: .15 .30
57 Wurmquake R :G: .12 .25
58 Glistening Sphere R 1.50 3.00
59 Battle Screech U :W: .05 .10
60 Call the Coppercoats R :W: .30 .60
61 Collective Effort R :W: .12 .25
62 Court of Grace R :W: .30 .60
63 Cut a Deal U :W: .12 .25
64 Elspeth Tirel M :W: .50 1.00
65 Emeria Angel R :W: .12 .25
66 Felidar Retreat R :W: .40 .80
67 Finale of Glory M :W: .25 .50
68 Flawless Maneuver R :W: 7.50 15.00
69 Fumigate R :W: .25 .50
70 Generous Gift U :W: .75 1.50
71 Ghostly Prison U :W: 1.50 3.00
72 Goldnight Commander U :W: .06 .12
73 Grateful Apparition U :W: .10 .20
74 Harmonious Archon M :W: .15 .30
75 Hour of Reckoning R :W: .10 .20
76 Increasing Devotion R :W: .07 .15
77 Intangible Virtue U :W: .10 .20
78 Mace of the Valiant R :W: .06 .12
79 Martial Coup R :W: .12 .25
80 Maul of the Skyclaves R :W: .07 .15
81 Mentor of the Meek R :W: .10 .20
82 Midnight Haunting U :W: .05 .10
83 Norn's Annex R :W: 1.00 2.00
84 Path to Exile U :W: 1.25 2.50
85 Phantom General U :W: .05 .10
86 Phyrexian Rebirth R :W: .12 .25
87 Prava of the Steel Legion U :W: .10 .20
88 Silverwing Squadron R :W: .06 .12
89 Swords to Plowshares U :W: .75 1.50
90 White Sun's Zenith R :W: .10 .20
91 Windborn Muse R :W: .12 .25
92 Caress of Phyrexia U :K: .10 .20
93 Ichor Rats U :K: .75 1.50
94 Night's Whisper C :K: .75 1.50
95 Painful Truths R :K: .12 .25
96 Plague Stinger C :K: .12 .25
97 Chain Reaction R :R: .12 .25
98 Dragonmaster Outcast M :R: .30 .60
99 Hate Mirage U :R: .05 .10
100 Hordeling Outburst U :R: .10 .20
101 Legion Warboss R :R: .20 .40
102 Loyal Apprentice U :R: .30 .60
103 Siege-Gang Commander R :R: .12 .25
104 Beast Within S :G: .75 1.50
105 Blight Mamba C :G: .12 .25
106 Carrion Call U :G: .05 .10
107 Cultivate C :G: .75 1.50
108 Evolution Sage U :G: 1.00 2.00
109 Mycosynth Fiend U :G: .05 .10
110 Noxious Revival U :G: 2.00 4.00
111 Phyrexian Swarmlord R :G: .75 1.50
112 Scavenging Ooze R :G: .15 .30
113 Viridian Corrupter U :G: .12 .25
114 Adriana, Captain of the Guard R :R:/W: .10 .20
115 Assemble the Legion R :R:/W: .12 .25
116 Boros Charm U :R:/W: 1.00 2.00
117 Culling Ritual R :K:/G: .75 1.50
118 Heroic Reinforcements U :R:/W: .05 .10
119 Jor Kadeen, the Prevailer R :R:/W: .05 .10
120 Merciless Eviction R :W:/K: .25 .50
121 Moldervine Reclamation U :K:/G: .20 .40
122 Mortify U :W:/K: .12 .25
123 Putrefy U :K:/G: .15 .30
124 Rip Apart U :R:/W: .10 .20
125 Arcane Signet C .40 .80
126 Boros Signet U .25 .50
127 Chromatic Lantern R 2.00 4.00
128 Commander's Sphere C .10 .20
129 Contagion Clasp U .30 .75
130 Fellwar Stone U .30 .75
131 Golgari Signet U .75 1.50
132 Grafted Exoskeleton U 1.00 2.00
133 Ichorclaw Myr C .30 .60
134 Idol of Oblivion R .30 .75
135 Loxodon Warhammer R .15 .30
136 Mask of Memory U .10 .20
137 Mind Stone U .12 .25
138 Myr Battlesphere R .12 .25
139 Plague Myr U .75 1.50
140 Sol Ring U .75 1.50
141 Solemn Simulacrum R .40 .80
142 Soul-Guide Lantern U .07 .15
143 Talisman of Conviction U .40 .80
144 Trailblazer's Boots U .75 1.50
145 Bojuka Bog C .75 1.50
146 Boros Garrison U .10 .20
147 Buried Ruin U .20 .40
148 Canopy Vista R .30 .60
149 Castle Ardenvale R .30 .75
150 Castle Embereth R .12 .25
151 Command Tower C .15 .30
152 Exotic Orchard R .12 .25
153 Forgotten Cave U .07 .15
154 Fortified Village R .12 .25
155 Furycalm Snarl R .12 .25
156 Karn's Bastion R 1.50 3.00
157 Kher Keep R .12 .25
158 Krosan Verge U .17 .35
159 Myriad Landscape U .12 .25
160 Necroblossom Snarl R .75 1.50
161 Path of Ancestry C .10 .20
162 Sandsteppe Citadel U .50 1.00
163 Secluded Steppe U .05 .10
164 Shineshadow Snarl R .12 .25
165 Slayers' Stronghold R .12 .25
166 Sungrass Prairie R .12 .25
167 Tainted Field U .10 .20
168 Tainted Wood U .75 1.50
169 Temple of Malady R .30 .60
170 Temple of Plenty R .17 .35
171 Temple of Silence R .12 .25
172 Temple of the False God U .07 .15
173 Temple of Triumph R .10 .20
174 Windbrisk Heights R .12 .25

2023 Magic The Gathering Regional Championship Qualifiers

1 Mystical Dispute R :B: 1.50 3.00
2 Snapcaster Mage M :B: 25.00 50.00
3 Thing in the Ice/Awoken Horror R :B: 4.00 8.00

2023 Magic The Gathering Secret Lair Drop Series Absolute Annihilation

1424 Oppression R 5.00 12.00
1425 Abrade R 8.00 20.00
1426 Mass Hysteria R 8.00 20.00
1427 Terminate R 6.00 15.00

2023 Magic The Gathering Secret Lair Drop Series Absolute Annihilation Foil

1424 Oppression R 5.00 12.00
1425 Abrade R 8.00 20.00
1426 Mass Hysteria R 8.00 20.00
1427 Terminate R 6.00 15.00

2023 Magic The Gathering Secret Lair Drop Series Angels They're Just Like Us but Cooler and with Wings

731 Sigarda's Aid R 15.00 40.00
1335 Gisela, the Broken Blade FOIL M 30.00 80.00
1336 Bruna, the Fading Light FOIL R 25.00 60.00
1337 Archangel of Thune FOIL M 30.00 80.00
1338 Court of Grace FOIL R 10.00 25.00
1339 Commander's Plate FOIL M 40.00 100.00
1342 Angel of Finality FOIL R .25 .60
1343 Angel of the Ruins FOIL R 1.50 4.00
1344 Arden Angel FOIL R 5.00 12.00
1345 Breathkeeper Seraph FOIL R .75 2.00
1346 Dawnbreak Reclaimer FOIL R .75 2.00
1347 Valkyrie Harbinger FOIL R 1.00 2.50
1348 Plains FOIL C .05 .12
1349 Plains FOIL C .10 .25
1350 Plains FOIL C .10 .25
1351 Plains FOIL C .08 .20
1387 Gisela, the Broken Blade FOIL M 10.00 25.00
1388 Bruna, the Fading Light FOIL R 5.00 12.00

2023 Magic The Gathering Secret Lair Drop Series Artist Series Alayna Danner

733 Seraph Sanctuary R 1.25 3.00
1289 Linvala, Keeper of Silence M 15.00 40.00
1290 Sunblast Angel R 2.00 5.00
1291 Emeria, the Sky Ruin R 12.00 30.00
1292 Seraph Sanctuary R 4.00 10.00

2023 Magic The Gathering Secret Lair Drop Series Artist Series Alayna Danner Foil

733 Seraph Sanctuary R 1.25 3.00
1289 Linvala, Keeper of Silence M 15.00 40.00
1290 Sunblast Angel R 2.00 5.00
1291 Emeria, the Sky Ruin R 12.00 30.00
1292 Seraph Sanctuary R 4.00 10.00

2023 Magic The Gathering Secret Lair Drop Series Artist Series John Avon

723 Brainstorm R 1.00 2.50
1160 Emrakul, the Promised End M 40.00 100.00
1161 Serra Angel R .25 .60
1162 Brainstorm R 1.25 3.00
1163 Progenitus M 2.50 6.00

2023 Magic The Gathering Secret Lair Drop Series Artist Series Kev Walker

725 Fleshbag Marauder R 2.00 5.00
1173 Faeburrow Elder R 8.00 20.00
1174 Carnage Tyrant M 6.00 15.00
1175 Fleshbag Marauder R 4.00 10.00
1176 It That Betrays R 12.00 30.00

2023 Magic The Gathering Secret Lair Drop Series Artist Series Kev Walker Foil

725 Fleshbag Marauder R 2.00 5.00
1173 Faeburrow Elder R 8.00 20.00
1174 Carnage Tyrant M 6.00 15.00
1175 Fleshbag Marauder R 4.00 10.00
1176 It That Betrays R 12.00 30.00

2023 Magic The Gathering Secret Lair Drop Series Artist Series Randy Vargas

732 Selfless Savior R 2.00 5.00
1285 Grand Abolisher R 10.00 25.00
1286 Selfless Savior R 6.00 15.00
1287 Akroma, Angel of Fury M 1.00 2.50
1288 Umezawa's Jitte R 5.00 12.00

2023 Magic The Gathering Secret Lair Drop Series Artist Series Randy Vargas Foil

732 Selfless Savior R 2.00 5.00
1285 Grand Abolisher R 10.00 25.00
1286 Selfless Savior R 6.00 15.00
1287 Akroma, Angel of Fury M 1.00 2.50
1288 Umezawa's Jitte R 5.00 12.00

2023 Magic The Gathering Secret Lair Drop Series Artist Series Rebecca Guay

730 Cleansing Nova R .50 1.25
1251 Cleansing Nova R .60 1.50
1252 Serra the Benevolent M 5.00 12.00
1253 Stoneforge Mystic R 15.00 40.00
1254 Muddle the Mixture R 2.50 6.00

2023 Magic The Gathering Secret Lair Drop Series Artist Series Rebecca Guay Foil

730 Cleansing Nova R .50 1.25
1251 Cleansing Nova R .60 1.50
1252 Serra the Benevolent M 5.00 12.00
1253 Stoneforge Mystic R 15.00 40.00
1254 Muddle the Mixture R 2.50 6.00

2023 Magic The Gathering Secret Lair Drop Series Artist Series Ryan Alexander Lee

735 Gaea's Blessing R .60 1.50
1302 Nemesis of Reason R 2.50 6.00
1303 Gaea's Blessing R 1.50 4.00
1304 Twilight Prophet R 4.00 10.00
1305 Worldspine Wurm M 10.00 25.00
1306 Wurm C 2.50 6.00

2023 Magic The Gathering Secret Lair Drop Series Artist Series Ryan Alexander Lee Foil

735 Gaea's Blessing R .60 1.50
1302 Nemesis of Reason R 2.50 6.00
1303 Gaea's Blessing R 1.50 4.00
1304 Twilight Prophet R 4.00 10.00
1305 Worldspine Wurm M 10.00 25.00
1306 Wurm C 2.50 6.00

2023 Magic The Gathering Secret Lair Drop Series Artist Series Sam Burley

729 Braid of Fire R 10.00 25.00
1247 Braid of Fire R 10.00 25.00
1248 Koth of the Hammer M 2.00 5.00
1249 Master of the Wild Hunt M 4.00 10.00
1250 Karrthus, Tyrant of Jund M 5.00 12.00

2023 Magic The Gathering Secret Lair Drop Series Artist Series Sam Burley Foil

729 Braid of Fire R 10.00 25.00
1247 Braid of Fire R 10.00 25.00
1248 Koth of the Hammer M 2.00 5.00

1249 Master of the Wild Hunt M 4.00 10.00
1250 Karthus, Tyrant of Jund M 5.00 12.00

2023 Magic The Gathering Secret Lair Drop Series Bad to the Bones

1404 Bottomless Pit R 10.00 25.00
1406 Reassembling Skeleton U 10.00 25.00
1407 Tinybones, Trinket Thief M 12.00 30.00
1408 Geier Reach Sanitarium R 15.00 40.00

2023 Magic The Gathering Secret Lair Drop Series Bad to the Bones Foil

1404 Bottomless Pit R 10.00 25.00
1405 Necrogen Mists R 6.00 15.00
1406 Reassembling Skeleton U 10.00 25.00
1407 Tinybones, Trinket Thief M 12.00 30.00
1408 Geier Reach Sanitarium R 15.00 40.00

2023 Magic The Gathering Secret Lair Drop Series Buggin' Out

1414 Eldritch Evolution R 6.00 15.00
1415 Giant Adephage M 2.00 5.00
1416 Noxious Revival R 8.00 20.00
1417 Grist, the Hunger Tide M 12.00 30.00
1418 Mazirek, Kraul Death Priest R 6.00 15.00

2023 Magic The Gathering Secret Lair Drop Series Buggin' Out Foil

1414 Eldritch Evolution R 6.00 15.00
1415 Giant Adephage M 2.00 5.00
1416 Noxious Revival R 8.00 20.00
1417 Grist, the Hunger Tide M 12.00 30.00
1418 Mazirek, Kraul Death Priest R 6.00 15.00

2023 Magic The Gathering Secret Lair Drop Series Calling All Hydra Heads

1329 Gargos, Vicious Watcher R 1.00 2.50
1330 Primordial Hydra M 6.00 15.00
1331 Unbound Flourishing M 10.00 25.00
1332 Hydroid Krasis R 2.50 6.00
1333 Zaxara, the Exemplary M 2.00 5.00
1334 Hydra C 2.50 6.00

2023 Magic The Gathering Secret Lair Drop Series Calling All Hydra Heads Foil

1329 Gargos, Vicious Watcher R 1.00 2.50
1330 Primordial Hydra M 6.00 15.00
1331 Unbound Flourishing M 10.00 25.00
1332 Hydroid Krasis R 2.50 6.00
1333 Zaxara, the Exemplary M 2.00 5.00
1334 Hydra C 2.50 6.00

2023 Magic The Gathering Secret Lair Drop Series City Styles

1232 Sakashima the Impostor R 10.00 25.00
1233 Massacre Girl R 20.00 50.00
1234 Azusa, Lost but Seeking R 25.00 60.00
1235 Teysa Karlov R 20.00 50.00
1236 Paradise Mantle R 8.00 20.00

2023 Magic The Gathering Secret Lair Drop Series City Styles Foil

1232 Sakashima the Impostor R 10.00 25.00
1233 Massacre Girl R 20.00 50.00
1234 Azusa, Lost but Seeking R 25.00 60.00
1235 Teysa Karlov R 20.00 50.00
1236 Paradise Mantle R 8.00 20.00

2023 Magic The Gathering Secret Lair Drop Series Cool Ocean Breeze

1277 Llawan, Cephalid Empress R 1.00 2.50
1278 Master of Waves M 1.00 2.50
1279 Thassa, Deep-Dwelling M 10.00 25.00
1280 Thassa's Oracle R 50.00 120.00

2023 Magic The Gathering Secret Lair Drop Series Cool Ocean Breeze Foil

1277 Llawan, Cephalid Empress R 1.00 2.50
1278 Master of Waves M 1.00 2.50
1279 Thassa, Deep-Dwelling M 10.00 25.00
1280 Thassa's Oracle R 50.00 120.00

2023 Magic The Gathering Secret Lair Drop Series Creepshow

1458 Death Baron // Death Baron R 5.00 12.00
1459 Noxious Ghoul // Noxious Ghoul R 4.00 10.00
1460 Zombie Master // Zombie Master R 8.00 20.00
1461 Grimgrin, Corpse-Born // Grimgrin, Corpse-Born M 4.00 10.00
1462 Unholy Grotto // Unholy Grotto R 6.00 15.00

2023 Magic The Gathering Secret Lair Drop Series Dan Fraziers Mox Box

1072 Mox Opal ETCHED FOIL M 60.00 150.00
1073 Mox Tantalite ETCHED FOIL M 5.00 12.00
1074 Sol Ring ETCHED FOIL R 15.00 40.00

2023 Magic The Gathering The Lost Caverns of Ixalan

1 Abuelo's Awakening R .08 .20
2 Acrobatic Leap C .08 .20
3 Adaptive Gemguard C .08 .20
4 Attentive Sunscribe C .08 .20
5 Bat Colony U .08 .20
6 Clay-Fired Bricks U/(Cosmium Kiln) .08 .20
7 Cosmium Blast C .08 .20
8 Dauntless Dismantler U .25 .60
9 Deconstruction Hammer C .08 .20
10 Dusk Rose Reliquary U .08 .20
11 Envoy of Okinec Ahau C .08 .20
12 Fabrication Foundry R .12 .30
13 Family Reunion C .08 .20
14 Get Lost R 2.50 6.00
15 Glorifier of Suffering C .08 .20
16 Guardian of the Great Door U .08 .20
17 Helping Hand U .12 .30
18 Ironpaw Aspirant C .08 .20
19 Kinjalli's Dawnrunner U .08 .20
20 Kutzil's Flanker R .12 .30
21 Malamet War Scribe U .08 .20
22 Market Gnome U .08 .20
23 Might of the Ancestors U .08 .20
24 Miner's Guidewing C .08 .20
25 Mischievous Pup U .08 .20
26 Ojer Taq, Deepest Foundation M/(Temple of Civilization) 12.00 30.00
27 Oltec Archaeologists C .08 .20
28 Oltec Cloud Guard C .08 .20
29 Oteclan Landmark C/(Oteclan Levitator) .08 .20
30 Petrify C .08 .20
31 Quicksand Whirlpool C .08 .20
32 Resplendent Angel M 2.50 6.00
33 Ruin-Lurker Bat U .08 .20
34 Sanguine Evangelist R .12 .30
35 Soaring Sandwing C .08 .20
36 Spring-Loaded Sawblades U (Bladewheel Chariot) .08 .20
37 Thousand Moons Crackshot C .08 .20
38 Thousand Moons Infantry C .08 .20
39 Thousand Moons Smithy R (Barracks of the Thousand) 1.00 2.50
40 Tinker's Tote C .08 .20
41 Unstable Glyphbridge R (Sandswirl Wanderglyph) .20 .50
42 Vanguard of the Rose U .08 .20
43 Warden of the Inner Sky R .75 2.00
44 Akal Pakal, First Among Equals R .08 .20
45 Ancestral Reminiscence C .08 .20
46 Brackish Blunder C .08 .20
47 Braided Net R/(Braided Quipu) .08 .20
48 Chart a Course U .08 .20
49 Cogwork Wrestler C .08 .20
50 Confounding Riddle U .08 .20
51 Council of Echoes U .08 .20
52 Deeproot Pilgrimage R 1.25 3.00
53 Didact Echo C .08 .20
54 Eaten by Piranhas U .08 .20
55 The Enigma Jewel M/(Locus of Enlightenment)1.25 3.00
56 The Everflowing Well R/(The Myriad Pools) .20 .50
57 Frilled Cave-Wurm C .08 .20
58 Hermitic Nautilus U .08 .20
59 Hurl into History U .08 .20
60 Inverted Iceberg C/(Iceberg Titan) .08 .20
61 Kitesail Larcenist R .75 2.00
62 Lodestone Needle U/(Guidestone Compass) .08 .20
63 Malcolm, Alluring Scoundrel R .60 1.50
64 Marauding Brinefang C .08 .20
65 Merfolk Cave-Diver U .08 .20
66 Oaken Siren C .08 .20
67 Ojer Pakpatiq, Deepest Epoch M (Temple of Cyclical Time) 1.25 3.00
68 Orazca Puzzle-Door C .08 .20
69 Out of Air C .08 .20
70 Pirate Hat C .08 .20
71 Relic's Roar C .08 .20
72 River Herald Scout C .08 .20
73 Sage of Days C .08 .20
74 Self-Reflection U .08 .20
75 Shipwreck Sentry C .08 .20
76 Sinuous Benthisaur U .08 .20
77 Song of Stupefaction C .08 .20
78 Spyglass Siren U .12 .30
79 Staunch Crewmate U .08 .20
80 Subterranean Schooner R 1.25 3.00
81 Tishana's Tidebinder R 10.00 25.00
82 Unlucky Drop C .08 .20
83 Waterlogged Hulk U/(Watertight Gondola) .08 .20
84 Waterwind Scout C .08 .20
85 Waylaying Pirates C .08 .20
86 Zoetic Glyph U .08 .20
87 Abyssal Gorestalker U .08 .20
88 Aclazotz, Deepest Betrayal M (Temple of the Dead) 2.50 6.00
89 Acolyte of Aclazotz C .08 .20
90 Another Chance C .08 .20
91 Bitter Triumph U .60 1.50
92 Bloodletter of Aclazotz M 8.00 20.00
93 Bloodthorn Flail U .08 .20
94 Bringer of the Last Gift R .15 .40
95 Broodrage Mycoid C .08 .20
96 Canonized in Blood U .08 .20
97 Chupacabra Echo U .08 .20
98 Corpses of the Lost R .08 .20
99 Dead Weight C .08 .20
100 Deathcap Marionette C .08 .20
101 Deep Goblin Skulltaker C .08 .20
102 Deep-Cavern Bat U .08 .20
103 Defossilize U .08 .20
104 Echo of Dusk C .08 .20
105 Fanatical Offering C .08 .20
106 Fungal Fortitude C .08 .20
107 Gargantuan Leech U .08 .20
108 Grasping Shadows U/(Shadows' Lair) .08 .20
109 Greedy Freebooter C .08 .20
110 Join the Dead C .08 .20
111 Malicious Eclipse U .08 .20
112 Mephitic Draught C .08 .20
113 Preacher of the Schism R .30 .75
114 Primordial Gnawer C .08 .20
115 Queen's Bay Paladin R .08 .20
116 Rampaging Spiketail C .08 .20
117 Ray of Ruin C .08 .20
118 Screaming Phantom C .08 .20
119 Skullcap Snail C .08 .20
120 Soulcoil Viper U .08 .20
121 Souls of the Lost R .75 2.00
122 Stalactite Stalker R .50 1.25
123 Starving Revenant R .15 .40
124 Stinging Cave Crawler U .08 .20
125 Synapse Necromage U .08 .20
126 Tarrian's Journal R/(The Tomb of Aclazotz) .50 1.25
127 Terror Tide R .20 .50
128 Tithing Blade C/(Consuming Sepulcher) .08 .20
129 Visage of Dread U/(Dread Osseosaur) .08 .20
130 Vito's Inquisitor C .08 .20
131 Abrade C .08 .20
132 Ancestors' Aid C .08 .20
133 Belligerent Yearling U .08 .20
134 Bonehoard Dracosaur M 10.00 25.00
135 Brass's Tunnel-Grinder R (Tecutlan, the Searing Rift) .60 1.50
136 Brazen Blademaster C .08 .20
137 Breeches, Eager Pillager R .40 1.00
138 Burning Sun Cavalry C .08 .20
139 Calamitous Cave-In U .08 .20
140 Child of the Volcano C .08 .20
141 Curator of Sun's Creation U .08 .20
142 Daring Discovery C .08 .20
143 Diamond Pick-Axe U .12 .30
144 Dinotomaton C .08 .20
145 Dire Flail R/(Dire Blunderbuss) .08 .20
146 Dowsing Device U/(Geode Grotto) .08 .20
147 Dreadmaw's Ire U .08 .20
148 Enterprising Scallywag U .08 .20
149 Etali's Favor C .08 .20
150 Geological Appraiser U .15 .40
151 Goblin Tomb Raider C .08 .20
152 Goldfury Strider U .08 .20
153 Hit the Mother Lode R .12 .30
154 Hotfoot Gnome C .08 .20
155 Idol of the Deep King C (Sovereign's Macuahuitl) .08 .20
156 Inti, Seneschal of the Sun R 1.00 2.50
157 Magmatic Galleon R .08 .20
158 Ojer Axonil, Deepest Might M (Temple of Power) 6.00 15.00
159 Panicked Altisaur C .08 .20
160 Plundering Pirate C .08 .20
161 Poetic Ingenuity R .20 .50
162 Rampaging Ceratops U .08 .20
163 Rumbling Rockslide C .08 .20
164 Saheeli's Lattice U/(Mastercraft Raptor) .08 .20
165 Scytheclaw Raptor U .08 .20
166 Seismic Monstrosaur C .08 .20
167 Sunfire Torch C .08 .20
168 Sunshot Militia C .08 .20
169 Tectonic Hazard C .08 .20
170 Triumphant Chomp U .08 .20
171 Trumpeting Carnosaur R 2.00 5.00
172 Volatile Wanderglyph C .08 .20
173 Zoyowa's Justice U .08 .20
174 Armored Kincaller C .08 .20
175 Basking Capybara C .08 .20
176 Bedrock Tortoise R .12 .30
177 Cavern Stomper C .08 .20
178 Cenote Scout U .12 .30
179 Coati Scavenger U .08 .20
180 Colossadactyl U .08 .20
181 Cosmium Confluence R .08 .20
182 Disturbed Slumber C .08 .20
183 Earthshaker Dreadmaw U .08 .20
184 Explorer's Cache U .08 .20
185 Ghalta, Stampede Tyrant M 10.00 25.00
186 Glimpse the Core U .08 .20
187 Glowcap Lantern U .08 .20
188 Growing Rites of Itlimoc R (Itlimoc, Cradle of the Sun) 2.50 6.00
189 Huatli, Poet of Unity M (Roar of the Fifth People) 1.25 3.00
190 Huatli's Final Strike C .08 .20
191 Hulking Raptor R .60 1.50
192 In the Presence of Ages C .08 .20
193 Intrepid Paleontologist R .25 .60
194 Ixalli's Lorekeeper U .08 .20
195 Jade Seedstones U/(Jadeheart Attendant) .08 .20
196 Jadelight Spelunker R .20 .50
197 Kaslem's Stonetree C/(Kaslem's Strider) .08 .20
198 Malamet Battle Glyph U .08 .20
199 Malamet Brawler C .08 .20
200 Malamet Scythe C .08 .20
201 Malamet Veteran C .08 .20
202 Mineshaft Spider C .08 .20
203 Nurturing Bristleback C .08 .20
204 Ojer Kaslem, Deepest Growth M (Temple of Cultivation) 4.00 10.00
205 Over the Edge C .08 .20
206 Pathfinding Axejaw C .08 .20
207 Poison Dart Frog C .15 .40
208 Pugnacious Hammerskull R .50 1.25
209 River Herald Guide C .08 .20
210 Seeker of Sunlight C .08 .20
211 Sentinel of the Nameless City R .30 .75
212 The Skullspore Nexus M 5.00 12.00
213 Spelunking U .60 1.50
214 Staggering Size C .08 .20
215 Tendril of the Mycotyrant U .08 .20
216 Thrashing Brontodon U .08 .20
217 Twists and Turns U/(Mycoid Maze) .08 .20
218 Walk with the Ancestors C .08 .20
219 Abuelo, Ancestral Echo R .08 .20
220 Akawalli, the Seething Tower U .08 .20
221 Amalia Benavides Aguirre R .60 1.50
222 The Ancient One M 1.25 3.00
223 Anim Pakal, Thousandth Moon R .25 .60
224 Bartolome del Presidio U .08 .20
225 The Belligerent R .12 .30
226 Caparocti Sunborn U .08 .20
227 Captain Storm, Cosmium Raider U .08 .20
228 Deepfathom Echo R .15 .40
229 Gishath, Sun's Avatar M 5.00 12.00
230 Itzquinth, Firstborn of Gishath U .08 .20
231 Kellan, Daring Traveler R/(Journey On) .12 .30
232 Kutzil, Malamet Exemplar U .20 .50
233 Master's Guide-Mural U (Master's Manufactory) .08 .20
234 Molten Collapse R 1.00 2.50
235 The Mycotyrant M 1.25 3.00
236 Nicanzil, Current Conductor U .08 .20
237 Palani's Hatcher R .30 .75
238 Quintorius Kand M 3.00 8.00
239 Saheeli, the Sun's Brilliance M .60 1.50
240 Sovereign Okinec Ahau M 2.00 5.00
241 Squirming Emergence R .30 .75
242 Uchbenbak, the Great Mistake U .08 .20
243 Vito, Fanatic of Aclazotz M .75 2.00
244 Wail of the Forgotten R .08 .20
245 Zoyowa Lava-Tongue U .08 .20
246 Buried Treasure C .08 .20
247 Careening Mine Cart U .08 .20
248 Cartographer's Companion C .08 .20
249 Chimil, the Inner Sun M 10.00 25.00
250 Compass Gnome C .08 .20
251 Contested Game Ball U .08 .20
252 Digsite Conservator U .08 .20
253 Disruptor Wanderglyph C .08 .20
254 Hoverstone Pilgrim U .08 .20
255 Hunter's Blowgun C .08 .20
256 Matzalantli, the Great Door R/(The Core) .60 1.50
257 The Millennium Calendar M 1.50 4.00
258 Roaming Throne R 10.00 25.00
259 Runaway Boulder C .08 .20
260 Scampering Surveyor U .08 .20
261 Sorcerous Spyglass U .08 .20
262 Sunbird Standard U/(Sunbird Effigy) .08 .20
263 Swashbuckler's Whip U .08 .20
264 Tarrian's Soulcleaver R 1.00 2.50
265 Threefold Thunderhulk R .15 .40
266 Throne of the Grim Captain R (The Grim Captain) .08 .20
267 Treasure Map R/(Treasure Cove) .20 .50
268 Captivating Cave C .08 .20
269 Cavern of Souls M 20.00 50.00
270 Cavernous Maw U .08 .20
271 Echoing Deeps R .60 1.50
272 Forgotten Monument U .08 .20
273 Hidden Cataract C .08 .20
274 Hidden Courtyard C .08 .20
275 Hidden Necropolis C .08 .20
276 Hidden Nursery C .08 .20
277 Hidden Volcano C .08 .20
278 Pit of Offerings U .12 .30
279 Promising Vein C .08 .20
280 Restless Anchorage R .60 1.50
281 Restless Prairie R .25 .60
282 Restless Reef R .30 .75
283 Restless Ridgeline R .30 .75
284 Restless Vents R .20 .50
285 Sunken Citadel R .30 .75
286 Volatile Fault U .08 .20
287 Plains C .30 .75
288 Island C .40 1.00
289 Swamp C .25 .60
290 Mountain C .40 1.00
291 Forest C .40 1.00
292 Akal Pakal, First Among Equals SHOWCASE R .08 .20
293 Malcolm, Alluring Scoundrel SHOWCASE R.25 .60
294 Breeches, Eager Pillager SHOWCASE R .25 .60
295 Inti, Seneschal of the Sun SHOWCASE R .60 1.50
296 Huatli, Poet of Unity SHOWCASE M (Roar of the Fifth People) 1.00 2.50
297 Abuelo, Ancestral Echo SHOWCASE R .08 .20
298 Akawalli, the Seething Tower SHOWCASE U.08 .20
299 Amalia Benavides Aguirre SHOWCASE R .50 1.25
300 Anim Pakal, Thousandth Moon SHOWCASE R.20 .50
301 Bartolome del Presidio SHOWCASE U .08 .20
302 Caparocti Sunborn SHOWCASE U .08 .20
303 Captain Storm, Cosmium Raider SHOWCASE U .08 .20
304 Kutzil, Malamet Exemplar SHOWCASE U .15 .40
305 The Mycotyrant SHOWCASE M 1.00 2.50
306 Nicanzil, Current Conductor SHOWCASE U.08 .20
307 Quintorius Kand BORDERLESS M 4.00 10.00
308 Saheeli, the Sun's Brilliance BORDERLESS M.40 1.00
309 Sovereign Okinec Ahau BORDERLESS M 1.25 3.00
310 Uchbenbak, the Great Mistake BORDERLESS U .08 .20
311 Vito, Fanatic of Aclazotz BORDERLESS M .50 1.25
312 Zoyowa Lava-Tongue BORDERLESS U .08 .20
313 Throne of the Grim Captain BORDERLESS R (The Grim Captain) .08 .20
314 Ojer Taq, Deepest Foundation BORDERLESS M (Temple of Civilization) 12.00 30.00
315 Ojer Pakpatiq, Deepest Epoch BORDERLESS M (Temple of Cyclical Time) 1.25 3.00
316 Aclazotz, Deepest Betrayal BORDERLESS M (Temple of the Dead) 1.25 3.00
317 Ojer Axonil, Deepest Might BORDERLESS M (Temple of Power) 5.00 12.00
318 Ojer Kaslem, Deepest Growth BORDERLESS M (Temple of Cultivation) 2.00 5.00
319 The Ancient One BORDERLESS M .75 2.00
320 Belligerent Yearling BORDERLESS U .08 .20
321 Bonehoard Dracosaur BORDERLESS M 8.00 20.00
322 Rampaging Ceratops BORDERLESS U .08 .20
323 Scytheclaw Raptor BORDERLESS U .08 .20
324 Trumpeting Carnosaur BORDERLESS R 2.00 5.00
325 Earthshaker Dreadmaw BORDERLESS U .08 .20
326 Ghalta, Stampede Tyrant BORDERLESS M10.00 25.00
327 Hulking Raptor BORDERLESS R .60 1.50
328 Pugnacious Hammerskull BORDERLESS R .50 1.25
329 Thrashing Brontodon BORDERLESS U .08 .20
330 Gishath, Sun's Avatar BORDERLESS M 4.00 10.00
331 Itzquinth, Firstborn of Gishath BORDERLESS U .08 .20
332 Palani's Hatcher BORDERLESS R .30 .75
333 Get Lost BORDERLESS R 2.50 6.00
334 Resplendent Angel BORDERLESS M 2.00 5.00
335 Tishana's Tidebinder BORDERLESS R 8.00 20.00
336 Bloodletter of Aclazotz BORDERLESS M 6.00 15.00
337 Bringer of the Last Gift BORDERLESS R .15 .40
338 Starving Revenant BORDERLESS R .12 .30
339 Huatli, Poet of Unity BORDERLESS M/(Roar of the Fifth People) 1.00 2.50
340 The Skullspore Nexus BORDERLESS M 5.00 12.00
341 Kellan, Daring Traveler BORDERLESS R/(Journey On) .08 .20
342 Molten Collapse BORDERLESS R .60 1.50
343 Wail of the Forgotten BORDERLESS R .08 .20
344 Roaming Throne BORDERLESS R 8.00 20.00
345 Cavern of Souls BORDERLESS M 20.00 50.00
346 Echoing Deeps BORDERLESS R .50 1.25
347 Restless Anchorage BORDERLESS R .75 2.00
348 Restless Prairie BORDERLESS R .40 1.00
349 Restless Reef BORDERLESS R .50 1.25
350 Restless Ridgeline BORDERLESS R .40 1.00
351 Restless Vents BORDERLESS R .40 1.00
352 Quintorius Kand BORDERLESS M 8.00 20.00
353 Abuelo's Awakening EXT ART R .08 .20
354 Fabrication Foundry EXT ART R .12 .30
355 Kutzil's Flanker EXT ART R .20 .50
356 Sanguine Evangelist EXT ART R .12 .30
357 Thousand Moons Smithy EXT ART R (Barracks of the Thousand) .60 1.50
358 Unstable Glyphbridge EXT ART R (Sandswirl Wanderglyph) .20 .50
359 Warden of the Inner Sky EXT ART R .50 1.25
360 Braided Net EXT ART R/(Braided Quipu) .08 .20
361 Deeproot Pilgrimage EXT ART R 1.00 2.50
362 The Enigma Jewel EXT ART M (Locus of Enlightenment) 1.25 3.00
363 The Everflowing Well EXT ART R

(The Myriad Pools)	.25	.60
364 Kitesail Larcenist EXT ART R	.60	1.50
365 Subterranean Schooner EXT ART R	1.50	4.00
366 Corpses of the Lost EXT ART R	.08	.20
367 Preacher of the Schism EXT ART R	.30	.75
368 Queen's Bay Paladin EXT ART R	.12	.30
369 Souls of the Lost EXT ART R	.50	1.25
370 Stalactite Stalker EXT ART R	.50	1.25
371 Tarrian's Journal EXT ART R (The Tomb of Aclazotz)	.30	.75
372 Terror Tide EXT ART R	.15	.40
373 Brass's Tunnel-Grinder EXT ART R/(Tecutlan, the Searing Rift)	.60	1.50
374 Dire Flail EXT ART R/(Dire Blunderbuss)	.08	.20
375 Hit the Mother Lode EXT ART R	.15	.40
376 Magmatic Galleon EXT ART R	.08	.20
377 Poetic Ingenuity EXT ART R	.12	.30
378 Bedrock Tortoise EXT ART R	.08	.20
379 Cosmium Confluence EXT ART R	.08	.20
380 Growing Rites of Itlimoc EXT ART R/(Itlimoc, Cradle of the Sun)	2.50	6.00
381 Intrepid Paleontologist EXT ART R	.25	.60
382 Jadelight Spelunker EXT ART R	.15	.40
383 Sentinel of the Nameless City EXT ART R	.30	.75
384 The Belligerent EXT ART R	.12	.30
385 Deepfathom Echo EXT ART R	.08	.20
386 Squirming Emergence EXT ART R	.30	.75
387 Matzalantli, the Great Door EXT ART R/(The Core)	.50	1.25
388 The Millennium Calendar EXT ART M	2.00	5.00
389 Tarrian's Soulcleaver EXT ART R	.75	2.00
390 Threefold Thunderhulk EXT ART R	.20	.50
391 Treasure Map EXT ART R/(Treasure Cove)	.15	.40
392 Sunken Citadel EXT ART R	.50	1.25
393 Plains C	.08	.20
394 Plains C	.08	.20
395 Island C	.08	.20
396 Island C	.08	.20
397 Swamp C	.08	.20
398 Swamp C	.08	.20
399 Mountain C	.08	.20
400 Mountain C	.08	.20
401 Forest C	.08	.20
402 Forest C	.08	.20
403 Jadelight Spelunker P	.30	.75
404 Hit the Mother Lode P	.12	.30
405 Spyglass Siren P	1.25	3.00
406 Deep-Cavern Bat P	.60	1.50
407 Geological Appraiser P	2.50	6.00
408 Cenote Scout P	.60	1.50
410c Cavern of Souls NEON INK BORDERLESS ALT ART M	100.00	250.00
410d Cavern of Souls NEON INK BORDERLESS ALT ART M	125.00	300.00
410e Cavern of Souls NEON INK BORDERLESS ALT ART M	200.00	500.00
410f Cavern of Souls NEON INK BORDERLESS ALT ART M	100.00	250.00

2023 Magic The Gathering The Lost Caverns of Ixalan Special Guests Foil

1 Lord of Atlantis BORDERLESS R	12.00	30.00
2 Malcolm, Keen-Eyed Navigator BORDERLESS U	3.00	8.00
3 Bridge from Below BORDERLESS R	.75	2.00
4 Mephidross Vampire BORDERLESS R	.75	2.00
5 Pitiless Plunderer BORDERLESS U	10.00	25.00
6 Breeches, Brazen Plunderer BORDERLESS U	1.50	4.00
7 Dargo, the Shipwrecker BORDERLESS U	1.50	4.00
8 Rampaging Ferocidon BORDERLESS R	2.50	6.00
9 Underworld Breach BORDERLESS R	20.00	50.00
10 Carnage Tyrant BORDERLESS M	5.00	12.00
11 Ghalta, Primal Hunger BORDERLESS R	8.00	20.00
12 Polyraptor BORDERLESS M	12.00	30.00
13 Kalamax, the Stormsire BORDERLESS M	3.00	8.00
14 Lord Windgrace BORDERLESS M	3.00	8.00
15 Mirri, Weatherlight Duelist BORDERLESS M	2.00	5.00
16 Thrasios, Triton Hero BORDERLESS R	10.00	25.00
17 Mana Crypt BORDERLESS M	100.00	250.00
18 Star Compass BORDERLESS U	1.00	2.50
17b Mana Crypt NEON INK BORDERLESS ALT ART M	125.00	300.00
17c Mana Crypt NEON INK BORDERLESS ALT ART M	250.00	600.00
17d Mana Crypt NEON INK BORDERLESS ALT ART M	400.00	1,000.00
17e Mana Crypt NEON INK BORDERLESS ALT ART M	600.00	1,500.00
17f Mana Crypt NEON INK BORDERLESS ALT ART M	200.00	500.00

2023 Magic The Gathering Universes Beyond Doctor Who

1 Davros, Dalek Creator M	.12	.30
2 The Fourth Doctor M	.08	.20
3 The Tenth Doctor M	.20	.50
4 The Thirteenth Doctor M	.15	.40
5 Rose Tyler R	.08	.20
6 Sarah Jane Smith R	.12	.30
7 Yasmin Khan R	.08	.20
8 Missy R	.12	.30
9 Clara Oswald R	.75	2.00
10 Adipose Offspring R	.08	.20
11 Astrid Peth R	.20	.50
12 Atraxi Warden U	.08	.20
13 Banish to Another Universe U	.08	.20
14 Barbara Wright R	.12	.30
15 The Caves of Androzani R	.08	.20
16 Crack in Time R	.08	.20
17 Crisis of Conscience R	.08	.20
18 Everybody Lives! R	10.00	25.00
19 Everything Comes to Dust R	1.00	2.50
20 Four Knocks R	.30	.75
21 The Girl in the Fireplace R	.08	.20
22 Ian Chesterton R	.08	.20
23 Jo Grant R	.08	.20
24 The Night of the Doctor R	.20	.50
25 The Pandorica R	.12	.30
26 Peri Brown R	.08	.20
27 Romana II R	.08	.20
28 Tegan Jovanka R	.08	.20
29 Trial of a Time Lord R	.08	.20
30 The War Games R	.08	.20
31 The Wedding of River Song R	.08	.20
32 Wilfred Mott R	.08	.20
33 Adric, Mathematical Genius R	.12	.30
34 All of History, All at Once R	.08	.20
35 An Unearthly Child R	.08	.20
36 Auton Soldier R	2.50	6.00
37 Become the Pilot R	.08	.20
38 Cyber Conversion R	3.00	8.00
39 Danny Pink R	.50	1.25
40 Don't Blink U	.08	.20
41 The Eleventh Hour R	.08	.20
42 Five Hundred Year Diary R	.12	.30
43 Flatline R	.40	1.00
44 Flesh Duplicate R	4.00	10.00
45 The Flood of Mars R	.20	.50
46 Hunted by The Family R	.08	.20
47 K-9, Mark I R	.40	1.00
48 Martha Jones R	.08	.20
49 Nanogene Conversion R	2.00	5.00
50 Nardole, Resourceful Cyborg R	.08	.20
51 Nyssa of Traken R	.08	.20
52 Quantum Misalignment R	2.00	5.00
53 Renegade Silent U	.08	.20
54 Reverse the Polarity R	.60	1.50
55 Star Whale U	.12	.30
56 Start the TARDIS U	.08	.20
57 Surge of Brilliance U	.08	.20
58 Time Beetle U	.12	.30
59 Time Lord Regeneration U	.08	.20
60 Traverse Eternity R	.08	.20
61 Twice Upon a Time R	.08	.20
62 Wibbly-wobbly, Timey-wimey C	.12	.30
63 Zygon Infiltrator U	.08	.20
64 Dalek Drone R	.30	.75
65 Dalek Squadron U	.15	.40
66 Death in Heaven R	.20	.50
67 Doomsday Confluence R	.12	.30
68 Exterminate! U	.12	.30
69 Genesis of the Daleks R	.25	.60
70 This Is How It Ends R	.12	.30
71 Time Reaper R	.08	.20
72 The Toymaker's Trap R	.08	.20
73 Vashta Nerada R	1.00	2.50
74 Vislor Turlough R	.08	.20
75 Amy Pond R	.08	.20
76 Bill Potts R	.08	.20
77 Coward // Killer R	.08	.20
78 Dan Lewis R	.08	.20
79 Day of the Moon R	.08	.20
80 Decaying Time Loop U	.20	.50
81 Delete R	.25	.60
82 Donna Noble R	.15	.40
83 Ecstatic Beauty R	.12	.30
84 Ensnared by the Mara R	.60	1.50
85 Flaming Tyrannosaurus R	6.00	15.00
86 The Flux R	.50	1.25
87 Impending Flux R	.08	.20
88 Into the Time Vortex R	.20	.50
89 Iraxxa, Empress of Mars U	.12	.30
90 Memory Worm U	.08	.20
91 The Parting of the Ways R	.12	.30
92 Return the Past R	.40	1.00
93 RMS Titanic R	.15	.40
94 Ryan Sinclair R	.08	.20
95 Sibylline Soothsayer U	.08	.20
96 Sontaran General U	.08	.20
97 The Sound of Drums R	.25	.60
98 Ace, Fearless Rebel R	.08	.20
99 City of Death R	4.00	10.00
100 Displaced Dinosaurs U	8.00	20.00
101 The Five Doctors R	.08	.20
102 The Foretold Soldier R	.08	.20
103 Fugitive of the Judoon R	.08	.20
104 Graham O'Brien R	.08	.20
105 Jamie McCrimmon R	.08	.20
106 Karvanista, Loyal Lupari R	.12	.30
107 Leela, Sevateem Warrior R	.08	.20
108 The Sea Devils R	.08	.20
109 Sisterhood of Karn R	.08	.20
110 Susan Foreman R	.08	.20
111 Thijarian Witness U	.08	.20
112 Alistair, the Brigadier R	.08	.20
113 Ashad, the Lone Cyberman R	.08	.20
114 The Beast, Deathless Prince R	.15	.40
115 Bigger on the Inside U	.50	1.25
116 Blink R	.15	.40
117 Cult of Skaro R	.12	.30
118 The Curse of Fenric R	.08	.20
119 The Cyber-Controller R	.25	.60
120 The Dalek Emperor R	.08	.20
121 The Day of the Doctor R	.08	.20
122 Dinosaurs on a Spaceship R	8.00	20.00
123 Duggan, Private Detective R	.08	.20
124 The Eighth Doctor R	.08	.20
125 The Eleventh Doctor R	.08	.20
126 The Face of Boe R	.08	.20
127 The Fifth Doctor R	.08	.20
128 The First Doctor R	.08	.20
129 Frost Fair Lure Fish R	.08	.20
130 The Fugitive Doctor R	.08	.20
131 Gallifrey Falls // No More R	.20	.50
132 Gallifrey Stands R	.08	.20
133 Great Intelligence's Plan U	.15	.40
134 Heaven Sent R	.25	.60
135 Idris, Soulu of the TARDIS R	.08	.20
136 Jenny Flint R	.08	.20
137 Jenny, Generated Anomaly R	.08	.20
138 Judoon Enforcers U	.08	.20
139 Kate Stewart R	.08	.20
140 Last Night Together R	.12	.30
141 Lunar Hatchling R	.08	.20
142 Madame Vastra R	.08	.20
143 The Master, Formed Anew R	.08	.20
144 The Master, Gallifrey's End R	.08	.20
145 The Master, Mesmerist R	.08	.20
146 The Master, Multiplied R	1.00	2.50
147 Me, the Immortal R	.08	.20
148 The Ninth Doctor R	.12	.30
149 The Rani R	.08	.20
150 Rassilon, the War President R	.08	.20
151 Regenerations Restored R	.08	.20
152 River Song R	.20	.50
153 Rory Williams R	.08	.20
154 Run for Your Life R	.08	.20
155 Sally Sparrow R	.08	.20
156 The Second Doctor R	.12	.30
157 Sergeant John Benton R	.08	.20
158 The Seventh Doctor R	.08	.20
159 The Sixth Doctor R	.08	.20
160 Strax, Sontaran Nurse R	.08	.20
161 Sycorax Commander R	.08	.20
162 The Third Doctor R	.08	.20
163 Truth or Consequences U	.08	.20
164 The Twelfth Doctor R	.08	.20
165 The Valeyard R	.08	.20
166 Vrestin, Menoptra Leader R	.15	.40
167 The War Doctor R	.30	.75
168 Weeping Angel R	.40	1.00
169 Wreck and Rebuild U	.08	.20
170 Ace's Baseball Bat R	.08	.20
171 Bessie, the Doctor's Roadster R	.08	.20
172 Clockwork Droid U	.08	.20
173 Confession Dial R	.08	.20
174 Cyberman Patrol U	1.50	4.00
175 Cybermat U	.08	.20
176 Cybermen Squadron R	4.00	10.00
177 Cybership R	.12	.30
178 Laser Screwdriver U	.20	.50
179 Midnight Crusader Shuttle U	.08	.20
180 The Moment R	.08	.20
181 Psychic Paper U	.08	.20
182 River Song's Diary R	1.25	3.00
183 Rotating Fireplace R	.12	.30
184 Sonic Screwdriver U	.50	1.25
185 Sonic Screwdriver U	.60	1.50
186 Sonic Screwdriver U	.40	1.00
187 TARDIS U	.08	.20
188 Gallifrey Council Chamber R	.08	.20
189 Ominous Cemetery R	.08	.20
190 Trenzalore Clocktower R	.08	.20
191 Osgood, Operation Double R	.08	.20
192 Davros, Dalek Creator - Thick Stock M	.08	.20
193 The Fourth Doctor - Thick Stock M	.20	.50
194 The Tenth Doctor - Thick Stock M	.12	.30
195 The Thirteenth Doctor - Thick Stock M	.20	.50
196 Plains L	.08	.20
197 Plains L	.08	.20
198 Island L	.08	.20
199 Island L	.08	.20
200 Swamp L	.12	.30
201 Swamp L	.15	.40
202 Mountain L	.08	.20
203 Mountain L	.08	.20
204 Forest L	.08	.20
205 Forest L	.08	.20
206 Day of Destiny R	.08	.20
207 Farewell R	4.00	10.00
208 Grasp of Fate R	.08	.20
209 Out of Time R	.08	.20
210 Path to Exile U	.50	1.25
211 Return to Dust U	.08	.20
212 Swords to Plowshares U	.50	1.25
213 Wedding Ring M	1.50	4.00
214 As Foretold R	.12	.30
215 Clockspinning C	.12	.30
216 Inspiring Refrain R	.08	.20
217 Ponder C	.75	2.00
218 Preordain C	.60	1.50
219 Propaganda U	2.00	5.00
220 Think Twice C	.08	.20
221 Feed the Swarm C	.12	.30
222 Snuff Out U	4.00	10.00
223 Wound Reflection R	.25	.60
224 Blasphemous Act R	1.00	2.50
225 Chaos Warp R	.50	1.25
226 Cursed Mirror R	.50	1.25
227 Throes of Chaos U	.08	.20
228 Beast Within U	.60	1.50
229 Carpet of Flowers R	2.50	6.00
230 Cultivate C	.30	.75
231 Explore C	.08	.20
232 Farseek C	.75	2.00
233 Heroic Intervention R	5.00	12.00
234 Search for Tomorrow C	.08	.20
235 Three Visits U	3.00	8.00
236 Fractured Identity R	.12	.30
237 Growth Spiral C	.12	.30
238 Time Wipe R	.08	.20
239 Arcane Signet C	.30	.75
240 Commander's Sphere C	.08	.20
241 Hero's Blade U	.08	.20
242 Heroes' Podium R	.12	.30
243 Lightning Greaves U	2.50	6.00
244 Mind Stone U	.08	.20
245 Sol Ring U	.75	2.00
246 Solemn Simulacrum R	.40	1.00
247 Talisman of Conviction U	.25	.60
248 Talisman of Creativity U	.60	1.50
249 Talisman of Curiosity U	.20	.50
250 Talisman of Dominance U	.50	1.25
251 Talisman of Impulse U	.40	1.00
252 Talisman of Indulgence U	1.25	3.00
253 Talisman of Progress U	.60	1.50
254 Talisman of Unity U	.20	.50
255 Thought Vessel U	.50	1.25
256 Wayfarer's Bauble C	.15	.40
257 Ash Barrens U	.08	.20
258 Canopy Vista R	.15	.40
259 Canyon Slough R	.15	.40
260 Celestial Colonnade R	.12	.30
261 Choked Estuary R	.08	.20
262 Cinder Glade R	.15	.40
263 Command Tower C	.08	.20
264 Command Tower C	.08	.20
265 Command Tower C	.08	.20
266 Command Tower C	.08	.20
267 Creeping Tar Pit R	.08	.20
268 Crumbling Necropolis U	.12	.30
269 Darkwater Catacombs R	.08	.20
270 Deserted Beach R	1.25	3.00
271 Desolate Lighthouse R	.08	.20
272 Dragonskull Summit R	.75	2.00
273 Dreamroot Cascade R	.75	2.00
274 Drowned Catacomb R	1.25	3.00
275 Evolving Wilds C	.08	.20
276 Exotic Orchard R	.08	.20
277 Fetid Pools R	.15	.40
278 Fiery Islet R	.50	1.25
279 Foreboding Ruins R	.08	.20
280 Fortified Village R	.08	.20
281 Frontier Bivouac U	.12	.30
282 Frostboil Snarl R	.08	.20
283 Furycalm Snarl R	.08	.20
284 Game Trail R	.08	.20
285 Glacial Fortress R	.50	1.25
286 Haunted Ridge R	2.50	6.00
287 Horizon Canopy R	1.25	3.00
288 Irrigated Farmland R	.08	.20
289 Lavaclaw Reaches R	.08	.20
290 Myriad Landscape U	.08	.20
291 Mystic Monastery U	.08	.20
292 Overgrown Farmland R	1.25	3.00
293 Path of Ancestry C	.08	.20
294 Port Town R	.08	.20
295 Prairie Stream R	.08	.20
296 Reliquary Tower U	1.00	2.50
297 River of Tears R	.08	.20
298 Rockfall Vale R	.50	1.25
299 Rogue's Passage U	.20	.50
300 Rootbound Crag R	1.00	2.50
301 Scattered Groves R	.08	.20
302 Seaside Citadel U	.15	.40
303 Shadowblood Ridge R	.08	.20
304 Sheltered Thicket R	.08	.20
305 Shipwreck Marsh R	1.50	4.00
306 Skycloud Expanse R	.08	.20
307 Smoldering Marsh R	.20	.50
308 Stormcarved Coast R	1.00	2.50
309 Sunbaked Canyon R	4.00	10.00
310 Sundown Pass R	2.00	5.00
311 Sungrass Prairie R	.08	.20
312 Sunken Hollow R	.15	.40
313 Temple of Abandon R	.08	.20
314 Temple of Deceit R	.08	.20
315 Temple of Enlightenment R	.08	.20
316 Temple of Epiphany R	.08	.20
317 Temple of Malice R	.15	.40
318 Temple of Mystery R	.08	.20
319 Temple of Plenty R	.08	.20
320 Temple of the False God U	.08	.20
321 Temple of Triumph R	.08	.20
322 Terramorphic Expanse C	.08	.20
323 Thespian's Stage R	.40	1.00
324 Thriving Bluff C	.08	.20
325 Thriving Grove C	.08	.20
326 Thriving Heath C	.08	.20
327 Thriving Isle C	.08	.20
328 Thriving Moor C	.08	.20
329 Vineglimmer Snarl R	.08	.20
330 War Room R	1.00	2.50
331 Waterlogged Grove R	.50	1.25
332 Clara Oswald EXT ART R	2.50	6.00
333 Adipose Offspring EXT ART R	.25	.60
334 Astrid Peth EXT ART R	.60	1.50
335 Barbara Wright EXT ART R	.25	.60
336 Crack in Time EXT ART R	.40	1.00
337 Crisis of Conscience EXT ART R	.25	.60
338 Everybody Lives! EXT ART R	12.00	30.00
339 Everything Comes to Dust EXT ART R	1.50	4.00
340 Four Knocks EXT ART R	.75	2.00
341 Ian Chesterton EXT ART R	.30	.75
342 Jo Grant EXT ART R	.20	.50
343 The Pandorica EXT ART R	.50	1.25
344 Peri Brown EXT ART R	.40	1.00
345 Romana II EXT ART R	.60	1.50
346 Rose Tyler EXT ART R	.75	2.00
347 Sarah Jane Smith EXT ART R	.50	1.25
348 Tegan Jovanka EXT ART R	.40	1.00
349 The Wedding of River Song EXT ART R	.50	1.25
350 Wilfred Mott EXT ART R	.30	.75
351 Adric, Mathematical Genius EXT ART R	.40	1.00
352 All of History, All at Once EXT ART R	.20	.50
353 Auton Soldier EXT ART R	3.00	8.00
354 Become the Pilot EXT ART R	.15	.40
355 Cyber Conversion EXT ART R	4.00	10.00
356 Danny Pink EXT ART R	.75	2.00
357 Five Hundred Year Diary EXT ART R	.40	1.00
358 Flatline EXT ART R	1.50	4.00
359 Flesh Duplicate EXT ART R	5.00	12.00
360 The Flood of Mars EXT ART R	.40	1.00
361 Hunted by The Family EXT ART R	.30	.75
362 K-9, Mark I EXT ART R	.60	1.50
363 Martha Jones EXT ART R	.25	.60
364 Nanogene Conversion EXT ART R	2.50	6.00
365 Nardole, Resourceful Cyborg EXT ART R	.50	1.25
366 Nyssa of Traken EXT ART R	.30	.75
367 Osgood, Operation Double EXT ART R	.40	1.00
368 Quantum Misalignment EXT ART R	2.00	5.00
369 Reverse the Polarity EXT ART R	2.00	5.00
370 Traverse Eternity EXT ART R	.40	1.00
371 Dalek Drone EXT ART R	.50	1.25
372 Doomsday Confluence EXT ART R	.60	1.50
373 This Is How It Ends EXT ART R	.50	1.25
374 Time Reaper EXT ART R	.30	.75
375 The Toymaker's Trap EXT ART R	.20	.50
376 Vashta Nerada EXT ART R	2.00	5.00
377 Vislor Turlough EXT ART R	.30	.75
378 Amy Pond EXT ART R	.50	1.25
379 Bill Potts EXT ART R	.25	.60
380 Dan Lewis EXT ART R	.30	.75
381 Delete EXT ART R	.60	1.50
382 Donna Noble EXT ART R	.50	1.25
383 Ecstatic Beauty EXT ART R	.75	2.00
384 Ensnared by the Mara EXT ART R	.75	2.00
385 Flaming Tyrannosaurus EXT ART R	4.00	10.00
386 Impending Flux EXT ART R	.40	1.00
387 Into the Time Vortex EXT ART R	.75	2.00
388 Return the Past EXT ART R	1.50	4.00
389 RMS Titanic EXT ART R	.60	1.50
390 Ryan Sinclair EXT ART R	.50	1.25
391 The Sound of Drums EXT ART R	.60	1.50
392 Yasmin Khan EXT ART R	.25	.60
393 Ace, Fearless Rebel EXT ART R	.25	.60
394 The Five Doctors EXT ART R	.60	1.50
395 The Foretold Soldier EXT ART R	.25	.60
396 Graham O'Brien EXT ART R	.40	1.00
397 Jamie McCrimmon EXT ART R	.30	.75
398 Leela, Sevateem Warrior EXT ART R	.08	.20
399 Sisterhood of Karn EXT ART R	.25	.60
400 Susan Foreman EXT ART R	.25	.60

401 Alistair, the Brigadier EXT ART R .25 .60
402 Ashad, the Lone Cyberman EXT ART R .20 .50
403 The Beast, Deathless Prince EXT ART R .30 .75
404 Cult of Skaro EXT ART R .30 .75
405 The Cyber-Controller EXT ART R 1.50 4.00
406 The Dalek Emperor EXT ART R 1.00 2.50
407 Davros, Dalek Creator EXT ART M .60 1.50
408 Dinosaurs on a Spaceship EXT ART R 10.00 25.00
409 Duggan, Private Detective EXT ART R .50 1.25
410 The Eighth Doctor EXT ART R .25 .60
411 The Eleventh Doctor EXT ART R 1.50 4.00
412 The Face of Boe EXT ART R .40 1.00
413 The Fifth Doctor EXT ART R .50 1.25
414 The First Doctor EXT ART R .30 .75
415 The Fourth Doctor EXT ART M .75 2.00
416 Frost Fair Lure Fish EXT ART R .12 .30
417 The Fugitive Doctor EXT ART R .20 .50
418 Gallifrey Stands EXT ART R .60 1.50
419 Idris, Soulu of the TARDIS EXT ART R .30 .75
420 Jenny Flint EXT ART R .20 .50
421 Jenny, Generated Anomaly EXT ART R .25 .60
422 Kate Stewart EXT ART R .30 .75
423 Last Night Together EXT ART R .60 1.50
424 Lunar Hatchling EXT ART R .20 .50
425 Madame Vastra EXT ART R .50 1.25
426 The Master, Formed Anew EXT ART R .60 1.50
427 The Master, Gallifrey's End EXT ART R .20 .50
428 The Master, Mesmerist EXT ART R .12 .30
429 The Master, Multiplied EXT ART R 2.00 5.00
430 Me, the Immortal EXT ART R 1.00 2.50
431 Missy EXT ART R .60 1.50
432 The Ninth Doctor EXT ART R 1.00 2.50
433 The Rani EXT ART R .40 1.00
434 Rassilon, the War President EXT ART R .40 1.00
435 Regenerations Restored EXT ART R .25 .60
436 River Song EXT ART R 1.00 2.50
437 Rory Williams EXT ART R .60 1.50
438 Run for Your Life EXT ART R .40 1.00
439 Sally Sparrow EXT ART R .20 .50
440 The Second Doctor EXT ART R .50 1.25
441 Sergeant John Benton EXT ART R .25 .60
442 The Seventh Doctor EXT ART R .25 .60
443 The Sixth Doctor EXT ART R .50 1.25
444 Strax, Sontaran Nurse EXT ART R .30 .75
445 Sycorax Commander EXT ART R .20 .50
446 The Tenth Doctor EXT ART M 2.00 5.00
447 The Third Doctor EXT ART R .20 .50
448 The Thirteenth Doctor EXT ART M .50 1.25
449 The Twelfth Doctor EXT ART R .60 1.50
450 The Valeyard EXT ART R .50 1.25
451 Vrestin, Menoptra Leader EXT ART R .60 1.50
452 The War Doctor EXT ART R .75 2.00
453 Weeping Angel EXT ART R 1.00 2.50
454 Ace's Baseball Bat EXT ART R .25 .60
455 Bessie, the Doctor's Roadster EXT ART R .30 .75
456 Confession Dial EXT ART R .40 1.00
457 Cybermen Squadron EXT ART R 4.00 10.00
458 Cybership EXT ART R .40 1.00
459 The Moment EXT ART R .30 .75
460 River Song's Diary EXT ART R 2.00 5.00
461 Rotating Fireplace EXT ART R .15 .40
462 Gallifrey Council Chamber EXT ART R .20 .50
463 Trenzalore Clocktower EXT ART R .60 1.50
464 Day of Destiny EXT ART R .25 .60
465 Farewell EXT ART R 4.00 10.00
466 Grasp of Fate EXT ART R .12 .30
467 Out of Time EXT ART R .12 .30
468 Wedding Ring EXT ART M 1.50 4.00
469 As Foretold EXT ART R .12 .30
470 Inspiring Refrain EXT ART R .15 .40
471 Wound Reflection EXT ART R .50 1.25
472 Blasphemous Act EXT ART R 1.25 3.00
473 Chaos Warp EXT ART R .50 1.25
474 Cursed Mirror EXT ART R .60 1.50
475 Carpet of Flowers EXT ART R 2.50 6.00
476 Heroic Intervention EXT ART R 5.00 12.00
477 Fractured Identity EXT ART R .20 .50
478 Time Wipe EXT ART R .08 .20
479 Heroes' Podium EXT ART R .12 .30
480 Solemn Simulacrum EXT ART R .50 1.25
481 Canopy Vista EXT ART R .50 1.25
482 Canyon Slough EXT ART R .15 .40
483 Celestial Colonnade EXT ART R .15 .40
484 Choked Estuary EXT ART R .20 .50
485 Cinder Glade EXT ART R .50 1.25
486 Creeping Tar Pit EXT ART R .15 .40
487 Darkwater Catacombs EXT ART R .20 .50
488 Deserted Beach EXT ART R 2.00 5.00
489 Desolate Lighthouse EXT ART R .12 .30
490 Dragonskull Summit EXT ART R 1.25 3.00
491 Dreamroot Cascade EXT ART R 1.00 2.50
492 Drowned Catacomb EXT ART R 2.00 5.00
493 Exotic Orchard EXT ART R 1.50 4.00
494 Fetid Pools EXT ART R .30 .75
495 Fiery Islet EXT ART R 1.50 4.00
496 Foreboding Ruins EXT ART R .15 .40
497 Fortified Village EXT ART R .15 .40
498 Frostboil Snarl EXT ART R .20 .50
499 Furycalm Snarl EXT ART R .20 .50
500 Game Trail EXT ART R .20 .50
501 Glacial Fortress EXT ART R 1.00 2.50
502 Haunted Ridge EXT ART R 2.50 6.00
503 Horizon Canopy EXT ART R 1.25 3.00
504 Irrigated Farmland EXT ART R .20 .50
505 Lavaclaw Reaches EXT ART R .12 .30
506 Overgrown Farmland EXT ART R 2.00 5.00
507 Port Town EXT ART R .20 .50
508 Prairie Stream EXT ART R .40 1.00
509 River of Tears EXT ART R .15 .40
510 Rockfall Vale EXT ART R .60 1.50
511 Rootbound Crag EXT ART R .75 2.00
512 Scattered Groves EXT ART R .20 .50
513 Shadowblood Ridge EXT ART R .12 .30
514 Sheltered Thicket EXT ART R .15 .40
515 Shipwreck Marsh EXT ART R 2.00 5.00
516 Skycloud Expanse EXT ART R .20 .50
517 Smoldering Marsh EXT ART R .40 1.00
518 Stormcarved Coast EXT ART R 1.50 4.00
519 Sunbaked Canyon EXT ART R 4.00 10.00
520 Sundown Pass EXT ART R 2.00 5.00
521 Sungrass Prairie EXT ART R .15 .40
522 Sunken Hollow EXT ART R .40 1.00
523 Temple of Abandon EXT ART R .15 .40
524 Temple of Deceit EXT ART R .20 .50
525 Temple of Enlightenment EXT ART R .20 .50
526 Temple of Epiphany EXT ART R .20 .50
527 Temple of Malice EXT ART R .15 .40
528 Temple of Mystery EXT ART R .15 .40
529 Temple of Plenty EXT ART R .12 .30
530 Temple of Triumph EXT ART R .12 .30
531 Thespian's Stage EXT ART R 1.00 2.50
532 Vineglimmer Snarl EXT ART R .20 .50
533 War Room EXT ART R 1.25 3.00
534 Waterlogged Grove EXT ART R 1.00 2.50
535 Rose Tyler SHOWCASE R .30 .75
536 Sarah Jane Smith SHOWCASE R .15 .40
537 K-9, Mark I SHOWCASE R .60 1.50
538 Dalek Squadron SHOWCASE U .25 .60
539 Yasmin Khan SHOWCASE R .12 .30
540 Davros, Dalek Creator SHOWCASE M .15 .40
541 The Fugitive Doctor SHOWCASE R .15 .40
542 The Master, Formed Anew SHOWCASE R .12 .30
543 The Master, Gallifrey's End SHOWCASE R .15 .40
544 The Master, Mesmerist SHOWCASE R .12 .30
545 The Master, Multiplied SHOWCASE R 1.00 2.50
546 Missy SHOWCASE R .20 .50
547 River Song SHOWCASE R 1.00 2.50
548 The War Doctor SHOWCASE R .60 1.50
549 Weeping Angel SHOWCASE R .60 1.50
550 Cyberman Patrol SHOWCASE U 1.50 4.00
551 TARDIS SHOWCASE U 1.50 4.00
552 The First Doctor SERIAL R .25 .60
552 The First Doctor SHOWCASE R .08 .20
553 The Second Doctor SERIAL R .40 1.00
553 The Second Doctor SHOWCASE R .08 .20
554 The Third Doctor SERIAL R .30 .75
554 The Third Doctor SHOWCASE R .08 .20
555 The Fourth Doctor SERIAL M .75 2.00
555 The Fourth Doctor SHOWCASE M 100.00 250.00
556 The Fifth Doctor SERIAL R .50 1.25
556 The Fifth Doctor SHOWCASE R 100.00 250.00
557 The Sixth Doctor SERIAL R .30 .75
557 The Sixth Doctor SHOWCASE R 125.00 300.00
558 The Seventh Doctor SERIAL R .20 .50
558 The Seventh Doctor SHOWCASE R .08 .20
559 The Eighth Doctor SERIAL R .25 .60
559 The Eighth Doctor SHOWCASE R 150.00 400.00
560 The Ninth Doctor SERIAL R .75 2.00
560 The Ninth Doctor SHOWCASE R 150.00 400.00
561 The Tenth Doctor SHOWCASE M 400.00 1,000.00
561 The Tenth Doctor SERIAL M 2.50 6.00
562 The Eleventh Doctor SERIAL R .50 1.25
562 The Eleventh Doctor SHOWCASE R 250.00 600.00
563 The Twelfth Doctor SERIAL R .50 1.25
563 The Twelfth Doctor SHOWCASE R 125.00 300.00
564 The Thirteenth Doctor SERIAL M .75 2.00
564 The Thirteenth Doctor SHOWCASE M 200.00 500.00
606 Davros, Dalek Creator SURGE FOIL M 1.25 3.00
607 The Fourth Doctor SURGE FOIL M .50 1.25
608 The Tenth Doctor SURGE FOIL M .30 .75
609 The Thirteenth Doctor SURGE FOIL M .20 .50
610 Rose Tyler SURGE FOIL R 1.50 4.00
611 Sarah Jane Smith SURGE FOIL R 1.00 2.50
612 Yasmin Khan SURGE FOIL R .60 1.50
613 Missy SURGE FOIL R 2.00 5.00
614 Clara Oswald SURGE FOIL R 8.00 20.00
615 Adipose Offspring SURGE FOIL R 1.00 2.50
616 Astrid Peth SURGE FOIL R 1.25 3.00
617 Atraxi Warden SURGE FOIL U 1.00 2.50
618 Banish to Another Universe SURGE FOIL U2.00 5.00
619 Barbara Wright SURGE FOIL R 1.25 3.00
620 The Caves of Androzani SURGE FOIL R 1.50 4.00
621 Crack in Time SURGE FOIL R .50 1.25
622 Crisis of Conscience SURGE FOIL R 3.00 8.00
623 Everybody Lives! SURGE FOIL R 15.00 40.00
624 Everything Comes to Dust SURGE FOIL R2.50 6.00
625 Four Knocks SURGE FOIL R 1.00 2.50
626 The Girl in the Fireplace SURGE FOIL R 2.50 6.00
627 Ian Chesterton SURGE FOIL R .30 .75
628 Jo Grant SURGE FOIL R 6.00 15.00
629 The Night of the Doctor SURGE FOIL R 2.50 6.00
630 The Pandorica SURGE FOIL R 2.00 5.00
631 Peri Brown SURGE FOIL R 1.00 2.50
632 Romana II SURGE FOIL R 2.00 5.00
633 Tegan Jovanka SURGE FOIL R 1.25 3.00
634 Trial of a Time Lord SURGE FOIL R 4.00 10.00
635 The War Games SURGE FOIL R 2.50 6.00
636 The Wedding of River Song SURGE FOIL R1.25 3.00
637 Wilfred Mott SURGE FOIL R 1.50 4.00
638 Adric, Mathematical Genius SURGE FOIL R1.25 3.00
639 All of History, All at Once SURGE FOIL R 1.00 2.50
640 An Unearthly Child SURGE FOIL R 1.50 4.00
641 Auton Soldier SURGE FOIL R 3.00 8.00
642 Become the Pilot SURGE FOIL R .12 .30
643 Cyber Conversion SURGE FOIL R 8.00 20.00
644 Danny Pink SURGE FOIL R 2.50 6.00
645 Don't Blink SURGE FOIL U 4.00 10.00
646 The Eleventh Hour SURGE FOIL R .25 .60
647 Five Hundred Year Diary SURGE FOIL R 2.00 5.00
648 Flatline SURGE FOIL R 3.00 8.00
649 Flesh Duplicate SURGE FOIL R 8.00 20.00
650 The Flood of Mars SURGE FOIL R 1.00 2.50
651 Hunted by The Family SURGE FOIL R 1.25 3.00
652 K-9, Mark I SURGE FOIL R 3.00 8.00
653 Martha Jones SURGE FOIL R 1.00 2.50
654 Nanogene Conversion SURGE FOIL R 2.50 6.00
655 Nardole, Resourceful Cyborg SURGE FOIL R.50 1.25
656 Nyssa of Traken SURGE FOIL R .40 1.00
657 Quantum Misalignment SURGE FOIL R 2.50 6.00
658 Renegade Silent SURGE FOIL U 2.50 6.00
659 Reverse the Polarity SURGE FOIL R 2.00 5.00
660 Star Whale SURGE FOIL U 3.00 8.00
661 Start the TARDIS SURGE FOIL U 1.50 4.00
662 Surge of Brilliance SURGE FOIL U 1.50 4.00
663 Time Beetle SURGE FOIL U 4.00 10.00
664 Time Lord Regeneration SURGE FOIL U 2.50 6.00
665 Traverse Eternity SURGE FOIL R 1.25 3.00
666 Twice Upon a Time SURGE FOIL R 2.00 5.00
667 Wibbly-wobbly, Timey-wimey SURGE FOIL C3.00 8.00
668 Zygon Infiltrator SURGE FOIL U 2.00 5.00
669 Dalek Drone SURGE FOIL R 1.50 4.00
670 Dalek Squadron SURGE FOIL U 2.00 5.00
671 Death in Heaven SURGE FOIL R 4.00 10.00
672 Doomsday Confluence SURGE FOIL R 2.00 5.00
673 Exterminate! SURGE FOIL U 5.00 12.00
674 Genesis of the Daleks SURGE FOIL R 6.00 15.00
675 This Is How It Ends SURGE FOIL R 2.00 5.00
676 Time Reaper SURGE FOIL R .75 2.00
677 The Toymaker's Trap SURGE FOIL R .08 .20
678 Vashta Nerada SURGE FOIL R 2.50 6.00
679 Vislor Turlough SURGE FOIL R 1.25 3.00
680 Amy Pond SURGE FOIL R 1.25 3.00
681 Bill Potts SURGE FOIL R 1.00 2.50
682 Coward // Killer SURGE FOIL R 1.50 4.00
683 Dan Lewis SURGE FOIL R 1.50 4.00
684 Day of the Moon SURGE FOIL R 1.50 4.00
685 Decaying Time Loop SURGE FOIL U 2.50 6.00
686 Delete SURGE FOIL R 1.00 2.50
687 Donna Noble SURGE FOIL R 2.00 5.00
688 Ecstatic Beauty SURGE FOIL R 2.00 5.00
689 Ensnared by the Mara SURGE FOIL R 2.00 5.00
690 Flaming Tyrannosaurus SURGE FOIL R 5.00 12.00
691 The Flux SURGE FOIL R 8.00 20.00
692 Impending Flux SURGE FOIL R 2.50 6.00
693 Into the Time Vortex SURGE FOIL R 1.50 4.00
694 Iraxxa, Empress of Mars SURGE FOIL U 2.50 6.00
695 Memory Worm SURGE FOIL U 1.50 4.00
696 The Parting of the Ways SURGE FOIL R 5.00 12.00
697 Return the Past SURGE FOIL R 3.00 8.00
698 RMS Titanic SURGE FOIL R 1.50 4.00
699 Ryan Sinclair SURGE FOIL R 1.25 3.00
700 Sibylline Soothsayer SURGE FOIL U 1.25 3.00
701 Sontaran General SURGE FOIL U 2.00 5.00
702 The Sound of Drums SURGE FOIL R 1.50 4.00
703 Ace, Fearless Rebel SURGE FOIL R 1.00 2.50
704 City of Death SURGE FOIL R 6.00 15.00
705 Displaced Dinosaurs SURGE FOIL U 25.00 60.00
706 The Five Doctors SURGE FOIL R .75 2.00
707 The Foretold Soldier SURGE FOIL R 1.00 2.50
708 Fugitive of the Judoon SURGE FOIL R .20 .50
709 Graham O'Brien SURGE FOIL R 1.25 3.00
710 Jamie McCrimmon SURGE FOIL R .75 2.00
711 Karvanista, Loyal Lupari SURGE FOIL R 4.00 10.00
712 Leela, Sevateem Warrior SURGE FOIL R .60 1.50
713 The Sea Devils SURGE FOIL R 1.25 3.00
714 Sisterhood of Karn SURGE FOIL R 1.50 4.00
715 Susan Foreman SURGE FOIL R 1.00 2.50
716 Thijarian Witness SURGE FOIL U 2.00 5.00
717 Alistair, the Brigadier SURGE FOIL R 1.25 3.00
718 Ashad, the Lone Cyberman SURGE FOIL R2.00 5.00
719 The Beast, Deathless Prince SURGE FOIL R.60 1.50
720 Bigger on the Inside SURGE FOIL U 8.00 20.00
721 Blink SURGE FOIL R 2.50 6.00
722 Cult of Skaro SURGE FOIL R 2.00 5.00
723 The Curse of Fenric SURGE FOIL R 1.25 3.00
724 The Cyber-Controller SURGE FOIL R 5.00 12.00
725 The Dalek Emperor SURGE FOIL R 3.00 8.00
726 The Day of the Doctor SURGE FOIL R 2.50 6.00
727 Dinosaurs on a Spaceship SURGE FOIL R8.00 20.00
728 Duggan, Private Detective SURGE FOIL R .75 2.00
729 The Eighth Doctor SURGE FOIL R .20 .50
730 The Eleventh Doctor SURGE FOIL R .50 1.25
731 The Face of Boe SURGE FOIL R 1.25 3.00
732 The Fifth Doctor SURGE FOIL R .12 .30
733 The First Doctor SURGE FOIL R .15 .40
734 Frost Fair Lure Fish SURGE FOIL R .50 1.25
735 The Fugitive Doctor SURGE FOIL R 2.00 5.00
736 Gallifrey Falls // No More SURGE FOIL R 5.00 12.00
737 Gallifrey Stands SURGE FOIL R .75 2.00
738 Great Intelligence's Plan SURGE FOIL U 2.50 6.00
739 Heaven Sent SURGE FOIL R 2.50 6.00
740 Idris, Soulu of the TARDIS SURGE FOIL R .40 1.00
741 Jenny Flint SURGE FOIL R 1.25 3.00
742 Jenny, Generated Anomaly SURGE FOIL R1.00 2.50
743 Judoon Enforcers SURGE FOIL U 1.50 4.00
744 Kate Stewart SURGE FOIL R .75 2.00
745 Last Night Together SURGE FOIL R 2.00 5.00
746 Lunar Hatchling SURGE FOIL R .75 2.00
747 Madame Vastra SURGE FOIL R 1.25 3.00
748 The Master, Formed Anew SURGE FOIL R2.00 5.00
749 The Master, Gallifrey's End SURGE FOIL R1.50 4.00
750 The Master, Mesmerist SURGE FOIL R .75 2.00
751 The Master, Multiplied SURGE FOIL R 5.00 12.00
752 Me, the Immortal SURGE FOIL R 6.00 15.00
753 The Ninth Doctor SURGE FOIL R .30 .75
754 The Rani SURGE FOIL R 1.00 2.50
755 Rassilon, the War President SURGE FOIL R.50 1.25
756 Regenerations Restored SURGE FOIL R 1.00 2.50
757 River Song SURGE FOIL R 4.00 10.00
758 Rory Williams SURGE FOIL R 1.25 3.00
759 Run for Your Life SURGE FOIL R 1.00 2.50
760 Sally Sparrow SURGE FOIL R 1.00 2.50
761 The Second Doctor SURGE FOIL R .30 .75
762 Sergeant John Benton SURGE FOIL R 1.00 2.50
763 The Seventh Doctor SURGE FOIL R .20 .50
764 The Sixth Doctor SURGE FOIL R .25 .60
765 Strax, Sontaran Nurse SURGE FOIL R .75 2.00
766 Sycorax Commander SURGE FOIL R 1.00 2.50
767 The Third Doctor SURGE FOIL R .25 .60
768 Truth or Consequences SURGE FOIL U 2.00 5.00
769 The Twelfth Doctor SURGE FOIL R 2.50 6.00
770 The Valeyard SURGE FOIL R 1.25 3.00
771 Vrestin, Menoptra Leader SURGE FOIL R 2.00 5.00
772 The War Doctor SURGE FOIL R 2.00 5.00
773 Weeping Angel SURGE FOIL R 2.50 6.00
774 Wreck and Rebuild SURGE FOIL U 2.50 6.00
775 Ace's Baseball Bat SURGE FOIL R .40 1.00
776 Bessie, the Doctor's Roadster SURGE FOIL R1.00 2.50
777 Clockwork Droid SURGE FOIL U 3.00 8.00
778 Confession Dial SURGE FOIL R .75 2.00
779 Cyberman Patrol SURGE FOIL U 15.00 40.00
780 Cybermat SURGE FOIL U 2.00 5.00
781 Cybermen Squadron SURGE FOIL R 4.00 10.00
782 Cybership SURGE FOIL R 1.25 3.00
783 Laser Screwdriver SURGE FOIL U 5.00 12.00
784 Midnight Crusader Shuttle SURGE FOIL U2.50 6.00
785 The Moment SURGE FOIL R .50 1.25
786 Psychic Paper SURGE FOIL U 2.50 6.00
787 River Song's Diary SURGE FOIL R 5.00 12.00
788 Rotating Fireplace SURGE FOIL R 1.50 4.00
789 Sonic Screwdriver SURGE FOIL U 8.00 20.00
790 Sonic Screwdriver SURGE FOIL U 12.00 30.00
791 Sonic Screwdriver SURGE FOIL U 8.00 20.00
792 TARDIS SURGE FOIL U 2.00 5.00
793 Gallifrey Council Chamber SURGE FOIL R1.50 4.00
794 Ominous Cemetery SURGE FOIL R 2.50 6.00
795 Trenzalore Clocktower SURGE FOIL R 2.00 5.00
796 Osgood, Operation Double SURGE FOIL R2.00 5.00
797 Day of Destiny SURGE FOIL R .75 2.00
798 Farewell SURGE FOIL R 4.00 10.00
799 Grasp of Fate SURGE FOIL R .60 1.50
800 Out of Time SURGE FOIL R 1.00 2.50
801 Path to Exile SURGE FOIL U 2.50 6.00
802 Return to Dust SURGE FOIL R 2.50 6.00
803 Swords to Plowshares SURGE FOIL U 4.00 10.00
804 Wedding Ring SURGE FOIL M 4.00 10.00
805 As Foretold SURGE FOIL R .75 2.00
806 Clockspinning SURGE FOIL C 3.00 8.00
807 Inspiring Refrain SURGE FOIL R 1.00 2.50
808 Ponder SURGE FOIL C 5.00 12.00
809 Preordain SURGE FOIL C 5.00 12.00
810 Propaganda SURGE FOIL U 4.00 10.00
811 Think Twice SURGE FOIL C .75 2.00
812 Feed the Swarm SURGE FOIL C 2.50 6.00
813 Snuff Out SURGE FOIL U 10.00 25.00
814 Wound Reflection SURGE FOIL R .75 2.00
815 Blasphemous Act SURGE FOIL R 1.50 4.00
816 Chaos Warp SURGE FOIL R 2.00 5.00
817 Cursed Mirror SURGE FOIL R 2.00 5.00
818 Thrones of Chaos SURGE FOIL U 3.00 8.00
819 Beast Within SURGE FOIL U 4.00 10.00
820 Carpet of Flowers SURGE FOIL R 6.00 15.00
821 Cultivate SURGE FOIL C 2.00 5.00
822 Explore SURGE FOIL C 1.00 2.50
823 Farseek SURGE FOIL C 4.00 10.00
824 Heroic Intervention SURGE FOIL R 6.00 15.00
825 Search for Tomorrow SURGE FOIL C 1.00 2.50
826 Three Visits SURGE FOIL U 5.00 12.00
827 Fractured Identity SURGE FOIL R 1.00 2.50
828 Growth Spiral SURGE FOIL C 4.00 10.00
829 Time Wipe SURGE FOIL R .30 .75
830 Arcane Signet SURGE FOIL C 2.00 5.00
831 Commander's Sphere SURGE FOIL C 1.25 3.00
832 Hero's Blade SURGE FOIL U 1.25 3.00
833 Heroes' Podium SURGE FOIL R .20 .50
834 Lightning Greaves SURGE FOIL U 5.00 12.00
835 Mind Stone SURGE FOIL U 1.25 3.00
836 Sol Ring SURGE FOIL U 5.00 12.00
837 Solemn Simulacrum SURGE FOIL R 2.50 6.00
838 Talisman of Conviction SURGE FOIL U 2.50 6.00
839 Talisman of Creativity SURGE FOIL U 4.00 10.00
840 Talisman of Curiosity SURGE FOIL U 2.50 6.00
841 Talisman of Dominance SURGE FOIL U 4.00 10.00
842 Talisman of Impulse SURGE FOIL U 2.00 5.00
843 Talisman of Indulgence SURGE FOIL U 2.00 5.00
844 Talisman of Progress SURGE FOIL U 2.50 6.00
845 Talisman of Unity SURGE FOIL U 1.50 4.00
846 Thought Vessel SURGE FOIL U 2.50 6.00
847 Wayfarer's Bauble SURGE FOIL C 2.50 6.00
848 Ash Barrens SURGE FOIL U .40 1.00
849 Canopy Vista SURGE FOIL R 1.25 3.00
850 Canyon Slough SURGE FOIL R 1.25 3.00
851 Celestial Colonnade SURGE FOIL R 1.25 3.00
852 Choked Estuary SURGE FOIL R 1.00 2.50
853 Cinder Glade SURGE FOIL R 1.50 4.00
854 Command Tower SURGE FOIL C 3.00 8.00
855 Command Tower SURGE FOIL C 4.00 10.00
856 Command Tower SURGE FOIL C 2.50 6.00
857 Command Tower SURGE FOIL C 4.00 10.00
858 Creeping Tar Pit SURGE FOIL R .60 1.50
859 Crumbling Necropolis SURGE FOIL U 1.25 3.00
860 Darkwater Catacombs SURGE FOIL R 1.00 2.50
861 Deserted Beach SURGE FOIL R 2.00 5.00
862 Desolate Lighthouse SURGE FOIL R .60 1.50
863 Dragonskull Summit SURGE FOIL R 1.50 4.00
864 Dreamroot Cascade SURGE FOIL R 1.50 4.00
865 Drowned Catacomb SURGE FOIL R 2.50 6.00
866 Evolving Wilds SURGE FOIL C 4.00 10.00
867 Exotic Orchard SURGE FOIL R 1.25 3.00
868 Fetid Pools SURGE FOIL R 1.25 3.00
869 Fiery Islet SURGE FOIL R 1.50 4.00
870 Foreboding Ruins SURGE FOIL R .60 1.50
871 Fortified Village SURGE FOIL R .60 1.50
872 Frontier Bivouac SURGE FOIL U 2.00 5.00
873 Frostboil Snarl SURGE FOIL R 1.00 2.50
874 Furycalm Snarl SURGE FOIL R 1.00 2.50
875 Game Trail SURGE FOIL R .40 1.00
876 Glacial Fortress SURGE FOIL R 1.25 3.00
877 Haunted Ridge SURGE FOIL R 2.50 6.00
878 Horizon Canopy SURGE FOIL R 1.50 4.00
879 Irrigated Farmland SURGE FOIL R 1.00 2.50
880 Lavaclaw Reaches SURGE FOIL R .40 1.00
881 Myriad Landscape SURGE FOIL U 1.00 2.50
882 Mystic Monastery SURGE FOIL U 2.00 5.00
883 Overgrown Farmland SURGE FOIL R 1.25 3.00
884 Path of Ancestry SURGE FOIL C 2.00 5.00
885 Port Town SURGE FOIL R .30 .75
886 Prairie Stream SURGE FOIL R .75 2.00
887 Reliquary Tower SURGE FOIL U 2.50 6.00
888 River of Tears SURGE FOIL R 1.00 2.50
889 Rockfall Vale SURGE FOIL R 1.00 2.50
890 Rogue's Passage SURGE FOIL U 3.00 8.00
891 Rootbound Crag SURGE FOIL R 1.00 2.50
892 Scattered Groves SURGE FOIL R 1.00 2.50
893 Seaside Citadel SURGE FOIL U 1.00 2.50
894 Shadowblood Ridge SURGE FOIL R 1.00 2.50
895 Sheltered Thicket SURGE FOIL R .60 1.50
896 Shipwreck Marsh SURGE FOIL R 1.25 3.00
897 Skycloud Expanse SURGE FOIL R 1.00 2.50
898 Smoldering Marsh SURGE FOIL R .50 1.25
899 Stormcarved Coast SURGE FOIL R 1.50 4.00
900 Sunbaked Canyon SURGE FOIL R 4.00 10.00
901 Sundown Pass SURGE FOIL R 2.00 5.00
902 Sungrass Prairie SURGE FOIL R .30 .75
903 Sunken Hollow SURGE FOIL R 1.00 2.50
904 Temple of Abandon SURGE FOIL R .40 1.00
905 Temple of Deceit SURGE FOIL R .20 .50
906 Temple of Enlightenment SURGE FOIL R .50 1.25
907 Temple of Epiphany SURGE FOIL R .30 .75
908 Temple of Malice SURGE FOIL R .60 1.50
909 Temple of Mystery SURGE FOIL R .50 1.25
910 Temple of Plenty SURGE FOIL R 1.00 2.50
911 Temple of the False God SURGE FOIL U 1.25 3.00
912 Temple of Triumph SURGE FOIL R .60 1.50
913 Terramorphic Expanse SURGE FOIL C 1.00 2.50
914 Thespian's Stage SURGE FOIL R 3.00 8.00
915 Thriving Bluff SURGE FOIL C 1.00 2.50
916 Thriving Grove SURGE FOIL C 1.00 2.50
917 Thriving Heath SURGE FOIL C .75 2.00
918 Thriving Isle SURGE FOIL C .75 2.00
919 Thriving Moor SURGE FOIL C .60 1.50
920 Vineglimmer Snarl SURGE FOIL R 1.00 2.50
921 War Room SURGE FOIL R 4.00 10.00
922 Waterlogged Grove SURGE FOIL R 1.25 3.00
923 Clara Oswald EXT ART SURGE FOIL R 10.00 25.00

924 Adipose Offspring EXT ART SURGE FOIL R .50 1.25
925 Astrid Peth EXT ART SURGE FOIL R 1.00 2.50
926 Barbara Wright EXT ART SURGE FOIL R .40 1.00
927 Crack in Time EXT ART SURGE FOIL R .20 .50
928 Crisis of Conscience EXT ART SURGE FOIL R.25 .60
929 Everybody Lives! EXT ART SURGE FOIL R25.00 60.00
930 Everything Comes to Dust EXT ART SURGE FOIL R 2.50 6.00
931 Four Knocks EXT ART SURGE FOIL R 1.00 2.50
932 Ian Chesterton EXT ART SURGE FOIL R .40 1.00
933 Jo Grant EXT ART SURGE FOIL R .30 .75
934 The Pandorica EXT ART SURGE FOIL R .60 1.50
935 Peri Brown EXT ART SURGE FOIL R 1.00 2.50
936 Romana II EXT ART SURGE FOIL R 1.50 4.00
937 Rose Tyler EXT ART SURGE FOIL R 3.00 8.00
938 Sarah Jane Smith EXT ART SURGE FOIL R .40 1.00
939 Tegan Jovanka EXT ART SURGE FOIL R .40 1.00
940 The Wedding of River Song EXT ART SURGE FOIL R .40 1.00
941 Wilfred Mott EXT ART SURGE FOIL R .60 1.50
942 Adric, Mathematical Genius EXT ART SURGE FOIL R 1.25 3.00
943 All of History, All at Once EXT ART SURGE FOIL R .50 1.25
944 Auton Soldier EXT ART SURGE FOIL R 5.00 12.00
945 Become the Pilot EXT ART SURGE FOIL R .30 .75
946 Cyber Conversion EXT ART SURGE FOIL R8.00 20.00
947 Danny Pink EXT ART SURGE FOIL R 1.50 4.00
948 Five Hundred Year Diary EXT ART SURGE FOIL R 1.00 2.50
949 Flatline EXT ART SURGE FOIL R 2.00 5.00
950 Flesh Duplicate EXT ART SURGE FOIL R10.00 25.00
951 The Flood of Mars EXT ART SURGE FOIL R.75 2.00
952 Hunted by The Family EXT ART SURGE FOIL R .40 1.00
953 K-9, Mark I EXT ART SURGE FOIL R 1.50 4.00
954 Martha Jones EXT ART SURGE FOIL R .50 1.25
955 Nanogene Conversion EXT ART SURGE FOIL R 4.00 10.00
956 Nardole, Resourceful Cyborg EXT ART SURGE FOIL R .60 1.50
957 Nyssa of Traken EXT ART SURGE FOIL R .50 1.25
958 Osgood, Operation Double EXT ART SURGE FOIL R .30 .75
959 Quantum Misalignment EXT ART SURGE FOIL R 3.00 8.00
960 Reverse the Polarity EXT ART SURGE FOIL R2.50 6.00
961 Traverse Eternity EXT ART SURGE FOIL R .75 2.00
962 Dalek Drone EXT ART SURGE FOIL R 1.00 2.50
963 Doomsday Confluence EXT ART SURGE FOIL R .75 2.00
964 This Is How It Ends EXT ART SURGE FOIL R1.00 2.50
965 Time Reaper EXT ART SURGE FOIL R .25 .60
966 The Toymaker's Trap EXT ART SURGE FOIL R.30 .75
967 Vashta Nerada EXT ART SURGE FOIL R 2.50 6.00
968 Vislor Turlough EXT ART SURGE FOIL R 1.25 3.00
969 Amy Pond EXT ART SURGE FOIL R 2.00 5.00
970 Bill Potts EXT ART SURGE FOIL R .25 .60
971 Dan Lewis EXT ART SURGE FOIL R .60 1.50
972 Delete EXT ART SURGE FOIL R 2.50 6.00
973 Donna Noble EXT ART SURGE FOIL R .75 2.00
974 Ecstatic Beauty EXT ART SURGE FOIL R 2.50 6.00
975 Ensnared by the Mara EXT ART SURGE FOIL R 1.50 4.00
976 Flaming Tyrannosaurus EXT ART SURGE FOIL R 8.00 20.00
977 Impending Flux EXT ART SURGE FOIL R .75 2.00
978 Into the Time Vortex EXT ART SURGE FOIL R.75 2.00
979 Return the Past EXT ART SURGE FOIL R 1.00 2.50
980 RMS Titanic EXT ART SURGE FOIL R 1.25 3.00
981 Ryan Sinclair EXT ART SURGE FOIL R .75 2.00
982 The Sound of Drums EXT ART SURGE FOIL R.75 2.00
983 Yasmin Khan EXT ART SURGE FOIL R .30 .75
984 Ace, Fearless Rebel EXT ART SURGE FOIL R.25 .60
985 The Five Doctors EXT ART SURGE FOIL R .30 .75
986 The Foretold Soldier EXT ART SURGE FOIL R.30 .75
987 Graham O'Brien EXT ART SURGE FOIL R .40 1.00
988 Jamie McCrimmon EXT ART SURGE FOIL R.40 1.00
989 Leela, Sevateem Warrior EXT ART SURGE FOIL R .40 1.00
990 Sisterhood of Karn EXT ART SURGE FOIL R.50 1.25
991 Susan Foreman EXT ART SURGE FOIL R .60 1.50
992 Alistair, the Brigadier EXT ART SURGE FOIL R.60 1.50
993 Ashad, the Lone Cyberman EXT ART SURGE FOIL R 2.00 5.00
994 The Beast, Deathless Prince EXT ART SURGE FOIL R 1.00 2.50
995 Cult of Skaro EXT ART SURGE FOIL R 2.00 5.00
996 The Cyber-Controller EXT ART SURGE FOIL R4.00 10.00
997 The Dalek Emperor EXT ART SURGE FOIL R1.00 2.50
998 Davros, Dalek Creator EXT ART SURGE FOIL M 1.25 3.00
999 Dinosaurs on a Spaceship EXT ART SURGE FOIL R 15.00 40.00
1000 Duggan, Private Detective EXT ART SURGE FOIL R .30 .75
1001 The Eighth Doctor EXT ART SURGE FOIL R.40 1.00
1002 The Eleventh Doctor EXT ART SURGE FOIL R3.00 8.00
1003 The Face of Boe EXT ART SURGE FOIL R1.25 3.00
1004 The Fifth Doctor EXT ART SURGE FOIL R .50 1.25
1005 The First Doctor EXT ART SURGE FOIL R .60 1.50
1006 The Fourth Doctor EXT ART SURGE FOIL M1.00 2.50
1007 Frost Fair Lure Fish EXT ART SURGE FOIL R.30 .75
1008 The Fugitive Doctor EXT ART SURGE FOIL R.30 .75
1009 Gallifrey Stands EXT ART SURGE FOIL R1.00 2.50
1010 Idris, Soulu of the TARDIS EXT ART SURGE FOIL R .40 1.00
1011 Jenny Flint EXT ART SURGE FOIL R 1.00 2.50
1012 Jenny, Generated Anomaly EXT ART SURGE FOIL R .75 2.00
1013 Kate Stewart EXT ART SURGE FOIL R .30 .75
1014 Last Night Together EXT ART SURGE FOIL R1.25 3.00
1015 Lunar Hatchling EXT ART SURGE FOIL R .40 1.00
1016 Madame Vastra EXT ART SURGE FOIL R1.25 3.00
1017 The Master, Formed Anew EXT ART SURGE FOIL R .25 .60
1018 The Master, Gallifrey's End EXT ART SURGE FOIL R 1.00 2.50
1019 The Master, Mesmerist EXT ART SURGE FOIL R .20 .50
1020 The Master, Multiplied EXT ART SURGE FOIL R 4.00 10.00
1021 Me, the Immortal EXT ART SURGE FOIL R3.00 8.00
1022 Missy EXT ART SURGE FOIL R 1.25 3.00
1023 The Ninth Doctor EXT ART SURGE FOIL R2.00 5.00
1024 The Rani EXT ART SURGE FOIL R .75 2.00
1025 Rassilon, the War President EXT ART SURGE FOIL R .25 .60
1026 Regenerations Restored EXT ART SURGE FOIL R .50 1.25
1027 River Song EXT ART SURGE FOIL R 3.00 8.00
1028 Rory Williams EXT ART SURGE FOIL R 1.00 2.50
1029 Run for Your Life EXT ART SURGE FOIL R.75 2.00
1030 Sally Sparrow EXT ART SURGE FOIL R .50 1.25
1031 The Second Doctor EXT ART SURGE FOIL R.50 1.25
1032 Sergeant John Benton EXT ART SURGE FOIL R .50 1.25
1033 The Seventh Doctor EXT ART SURGE FOIL R.60 1.50
1034 The Sixth Doctor EXT ART SURGE FOIL R1.25 3.00
1035 Strax, Sontaran Nurse EXT ART SURGE FOIL R .60 1.50
1036 Sycorax Commander EXT ART SURGE FOIL R .50 1.25
1037 The Tenth Doctor EXT ART SURGE FOIL M6.00 15.00
1038 The Third Doctor EXT ART SURGE FOIL R.50 1.25
1039 The Thirteenth Doctor EXT ART SURGE FOIL M .50 1.25
1040 The Twelfth Doctor EXT ART SURGE FOIL R2.50 6.00
1041 The Valeyard EXT ART SURGE FOIL R .60 1.50
1042 Vrestin, Menoptra Leader EXT ART SURGE FOIL R 1.50 4.00
1043 The War Doctor EXT ART SURGE FOIL R3.00 8.00
1044 Weeping Angel EXT ART SURGE FOIL R 2.00 5.00
1045 Ace's Baseball Bat EXT ART SURGE FOIL R.30 .75
1046 Bessie, the Doctor's Roadster EXT ART SURGE FOIL R .50 1.25
1047 Confession Dial EXT ART SURGE FOIL R .60 1.50
1048 Cybermen Squadron EXT ART SURGE FOIL R 5.00 12.00
1049 Cybership EXT ART SURGE FOIL R .75 2.00
1050 The Moment EXT ART SURGE FOIL R 1.00 2.50
1051 River Song's Diary EXT ART SURGE FOIL R3.00 8.00
1052 Rotating Fireplace EXT ART SURGE FOIL R.40 1.00
1053 Gallifrey Council Chamber EXT ART SURGE FOIL R 2.00 5.00
1054 Trenzalore Clocktower EXT ART SURGE FOIL R 2.00 5.00
1055 Day of Destiny EXT ART SURGE FOIL R .15 .40
1056 Farewell EXT ART SURGE FOIL R 6.00 15.00
1057 Grasp of Fate EXT ART SURGE FOIL R .30 .75
1058 Out of Time EXT ART SURGE FOIL R .30 .75
1059 Wedding Ring EXT ART SURGE FOIL M 2.00 5.00
1060 As Foretold EXT ART SURGE FOIL R .20 .50
1061 Inspiring Refrain EXT ART SURGE FOIL R .20 .50
1062 Wound Reflection EXT ART SURGE FOIL R.75 2.00
1063 Blasphemous Act EXT ART SURGE FOIL R3.00 8.00
1064 Chaos Warp EXT ART SURGE FOIL R .75 2.00
1065 Cursed Mirror EXT ART SURGE FOIL R 1.50 4.00
1066 Carpet of Flowers EXT ART SURGE FOIL R4.00 10.00
1067 Heroic Intervention EXT ART SURGE FOIL R6.00 15.00
1068 Fractured Identity EXT ART SURGE FOIL R.30 .75
1069 Time Wipe EXT ART SURGE FOIL R .20 .50
1070 Heroes' Podium EXT ART SURGE FOIL R .25 .60
1071 Solemn Simulacrum EXT ART SURGE FOIL R 1.50 4.00
1072 Canopy Vista EXT ART SURGE FOIL R .60 1.50
1073 Canyon Slough EXT ART SURGE FOIL R .25 .60
1074 Celestial Colonnade EXT ART SURGE FOIL R.30 .75
1075 Choked Estuary EXT ART SURGE FOIL R .40 1.00
1076 Cinder Glade EXT ART SURGE FOIL R 1.00 2.50
1077 Creeping Tar Pit EXT ART SURGE FOIL R .25 .60
1078 Darkwater Catacombs (Extended Art SURGE FOIL R .40 1.00
1079 Deserted Beach EXT ART SURGE FOIL R2.00 5.00
1080 Desolate Lighthouse EXT ART SURGE FOIL R .20 .50
1081 Dragonskull Summit EXT ART SURGE FOIL R 1.00 2.50
1082 Dreamroot Cascade EXT ART SURGE FOIL R2.00 5.00
1083 Drowned Catacomb EXT ART SURGE FOIL R1.50 4.00
1084 Exotic Orchard EXT ART SURGE FOIL R 8.00 20.00
1085 Fetid Pools EXT ART SURGE FOIL R .50 1.25
1086 Fiery Islet EXT ART SURGE FOIL R 4.00 10.00
1087 Foreboding Ruins EXT ART SURGE FOIL R.25 .60
1088 Fortified Village EXT ART SURGE FOIL R .25 .60
1089 Frostboil Snarl EXT ART SURGE FOIL R .40 1.00
1090 Furycalm Snarl EXT ART SURGE FOIL R .25 .60
1091 Game Trail EXT ART SURGE FOIL R .25 .60
1092 Glacial Fortress EXT ART SURGE FOIL R1.00 2.50
1093 Haunted Ridge EXT ART SURGE FOIL R 2.00 5.00
1094 Horizon Canopy EXT ART SURGE FOIL R2.00 5.00
1095 Irrigated Farmland EXT ART SURGE FOIL R.50 1.25
1096 Lavaclaw Reaches EXT ART SURGE FOIL R.20 .50
1097 Overgrown Farmland EXT ART SURGE FOIL R 2.50 6.00
1098 Port Town EXT ART SURGE FOIL R .40 1.00
1099 Prairie Stream EXT ART SURGE FOIL R .60 1.50
1100 River of Tears EXT ART SURGE FOIL R .25 .60
1101 Rockfall Vale EXT ART SURGE FOIL R 1.25 3.00
1102 Rootbound Crag EXT ART SURGE FOIL R1.25 3.00
1103 Scattered Groves EXT ART SURGE FOIL R.40 1.00
1104 Shadowblood Ridge EXT ART SURGE FOIL R.40 1.00
1105 Sheltered Thicket EXT ART SURGE FOIL R.30 .75
1106 Shipwreck Marsh EXT ART SURGE FOIL R2.00 5.00
1107 Skycloud Expanse EXT ART SURGE FOIL R.50 1.25
1108 Smoldering Marsh EXT ART SURGE FOIL R.75 2.00
1109 Stormcarved Coast EXT ART SURGE FOIL R2.00 5.00
1110 Sunbaked Canyon EXT ART SURGE FOIL R5.00 12.00
1111 Sundown Pass EXT ART SURGE FOIL R 2.50 6.00
1112 Sungrass Prairie EXT ART SURGE FOIL R .50 1.25
1113 Sunken Hollow EXT ART SURGE FOIL R .60 1.50
1114 Temple of Abandon EXT ART SURGE FOIL R.15 .40
1115 Temple of Deceit EXT ART SURGE FOIL R .30 .75
1116 Temple of Enlightenment EXT ART SURGE FOIL R .25 .60
1117 Temple of Epiphany EXT ART SURGE FOIL R.30 .75
1118 Temple of Malice EXT ART SURGE FOIL R.30 .75
1119 Temple of Mystery EXT ART SURGE FOIL R.40 1.00
1120 Temple of Plenty EXT ART SURGE FOIL R .20 .50
1121 Temple of Triumph EXT ART SURGE FOIL R.20 .50
1122 Thespian's Stage EXT ART SURGE FOIL R3.00 8.00
1123 Vineglimmer Snarl EXT ART SURGE FOIL R.40 1.00
1124 War Room EXT ART SURGE FOIL R 1.50 4.00
1125 Waterlogged Grove EXT ART SURGE FOIL R2.50 6.00
1126 Rose Tyler SHOWCASE SURGE FOIL R 10.00 25.00
1127 Sarah Jane Smith S HOWCASE SURGE FOIL R 3.00 8.00
1128 K-9, Mark I SHOWCASE SURGE FOIL R 6.00 15.00
1129 Dalek Squadron SHOWCASE SURGE FOIL U8.00 20.00
1130 Yasmin Khan SHOWCASE SURGE FOIL R2.50 6.00
1131 Davros, Dalek Creator SHOWCASE SURGE FOIL M 12.00 30.00
1132 The Fugitive Doctor SHOWCASE SURGE FOIL R 2.50 6.00
1133 The Master, Formed Anew SHOWCASE SURGE FOIL R 3.00 8.00
1134 The Master, Gallifrey's End SHOWCASE SURGE FOIL R 3.00 8.00
1135 The Master, Mesmerist SHOWCASE SURGE FOIL R 2.00 5.00
1136 The Master, Multiplied SHOWCASE SURGE FOIL R 12.00 30.00
1137 Missy SHOWCASE SURGE FOIL R 8.00 20.00
1138 River Song SHOWCASE SURGE FOIL R12.00 30.00
1139 The War Doctor SHOWCASE SURGE FOIL R10.00 25.00
1140 Weeping Angel SHOWCASE SURGE FOIL R15.00 40.00
1141 Cyberman Patrol SHOWCASE SURGE FOIL U 6.00 15.00
1142 TARDIS SHOWCASE SURGE FOIL U 20.00 50.00
1143 The First Doctor SHOWCASE SURGE FOIL R8.00 20.00
1144 The Second Doctor SHOWCASE SURGE FOIL R 5.00 12.00
1145 The Third Doctor SHOWCASE SURGE FOIL R 3.00 8.00
1146 The Fourth Doctor SHOWCASE SURGE FOIL M 5.00 12.00
1147 The Fifth Doctor SHOWCASE SURGE FOIL R6.00 15.00
1148 The Sixth Doctor SHOWCASE SURGE FOIL R 12.00 30.00
1149 The Seventh Doctor SHOWCASE SURGE FOIL R 3.00 8.00
1150 The Eighth Doctor SHOWCASE SURGE FOIL R 5.00 12.00
1151 The Ninth Doctor SHOWCASE SURGE FOIL R 10.00 25.00
1152 The Tenth Doctor SHOWCASE SURGE FOIL M 30.00 80.00
1153 The Eleventh Doctor SHOWCASE SURGE FOIL R 12.00 30.00
1154 The Twelfth Doctor SHOWCASE SURGE FOIL R 12.00 30.00
1155 The Thirteenth Doctor SHOWCASE SURGE FOIL M 6.00 15.00
1156 Plains SURGE FOIL L .20 .50
1157 Plains SURGE FOIL L .50 1.25
1158 Island SURGE FOIL L .50 1.25
1159 Island SURGE FOIL L .60 1.50
1160 Swamp SURGE FOIL L .40 1.00
1161 Swamp SURGE FOIL L .50 1.25
1162 Mountain SURGE FOIL L .50 1.25
1163 Mountain SURGE FOIL L .50 1.25
1164 Forest SURGE FOIL L .30 .75
1165 Forest SURGE FOIL L .20 .50

2023 Magic The Gathering Universes Beyond Doctor Who Planechase

566 Amy's Home T 1.00 2.50
567 Antarctic Research Base T .50 1.25
568 Aplan Mortarium T .50 1.25
569 Bad Wolf Bay T .50 1.25
570 Besieged Viking Village T .75 2.00
571 Bowie Base One T .60 1.50
572 Caught in a Parallel Universe T .50 1.25
573 The Cave of Skulls T .50 1.25
574 The Cheetah Planet T .50 1.25
575 City of the Daleks T .50 1.25
576 Coal Hill School T .50 1.25
577 Dalek Intensive Care T .50 1.25
578 The Dining Car T .50 1.25
579 The Doctor's Childhood Barn T .60 1.50
580 The Doctor's Tomb T .60 1.50
581 The Drum, Mining Facility T .50 1.25
582 Fixed Point in Time T .60 1.50
583 Gardens of Tranquil Repose T .75 2.00
584 Hotel of Fears T .50 1.25
585 Human-Time Lord Meta-Crisis T .60 1.50
586 Kerblam! Warehouse T .50 1.25
587 Lake Silencio T .60 1.50
588 The Lux Foundation Library T .50 1.25
589 The Matrix of Time T .50 1.25
590 Mondassian Colony Ship T .50 1.25
591 The Moonbase T .50 1.25
592 New New York T .50 1.25
593 North Pole Research Base T .50 1.25
594 Ood Sphere T .60 1.50
595 Pompeii T .50 1.25
596 Prime Minister's Cabinet Room T .60 1.50
597 The Pyramid of Mars T .50 1.25
598 Singing Towers of Darillium T .60 1.50
599 Spectrox Mines T .60 1.50
600 Stormcage Containment Facility T .50 1.25
601 TARDIS Bay T .60 1.50
602 Temple of Atropos T .30 .75
603 Two Streams Facility T .60 1.50
604 UNIT Headquarters T .50 1.25
605 Unleash the Flux T .50 1.25

2023 Magic The Gathering Wilds of Eldraine

1 Archon of the Wild Rose R .12 .30
2 Archon's Glory C .08 .20
3 Armory Mice C .08 .20
4 Besotted Knight C .08 .20
5 Break the Spell C .08 .20
6 Charmed Clothier C .08 .20
7 Cheeky House-Mouse U .08 .20
8 Cooped Up C .08 .20
9 Cursed Courtier U .08 .20
10 Discerning Financier U .08 .20
11 Dutiful Griffin U .08 .20
12 Eerie Interference U .08 .20
13 Expel the Interlopers R .15 .40
14 Frostbridge Guard C .08 .20
15 Gallant Pie-Wielder U .08 .20
16 Glass Casket U .08 .20
17 Hopeful Vigil C .08 .20
18 Kellan's Lightblades C .08 .20
19 Knight of Doves U .08 .20
20 Moment of Valor C .08 .20
21 Moonshaker Cavalry M 8.00 20.00
22 Plunge into Winter C .08 .20
23 The Princess Takes Flight U .08 .20
24 Protective Parents C .08 .20
25 Regal Bunnicorn R .75 2.00
26 Return Triumphant C .08 .20
27 Rimefur Reindeer C .08 .20
28 Savior of the Sleeping C .08 .20
29 Slumbering Keepguard C .08 .20
30 Solitary Sanctuary U .08 .20
31 Spellbook Vendor R .15 .40
32 Stockpiling Celebrant C .08 .20
33 Stroke of Midnight U 1.00 2.50
34 A Tale for the Ages R .08 .20
35 Three Blind Mice R .20 .50
36 Tuinvale Guide C .08 .20
37 Unassuming Sage C .08 .20
38 Virtue of Loyalty M 8.00 20.00
39 Werefox Bodyguard R .50 1.25
40 Aquatic Alchemist C .08 .20
41 Archive Dragon U .08 .20
42 Asinine Antics M 1.00 2.50
43 Beluna's Gatekeeper C .08 .20
44 Bitter Chill U .08 .20
45 Chancellor of Tales U .08 .20
46 Diminisher Witch C .08 .20
47 Disdainful Stroke U .08 .20
48 Extraordinary Journey R .08 .20
49 Farsight Ritual R .08 .20
50 Freeze in Place C .08 .20
51 Gadwick's First Duel U .08 .20
52 Galvanic Giant U .08 .20
53 Horned Loch-Whale R .20 .50
54 Ice Out C .08 .20
55 Icewrought Sentry U .08 .20
56 Ingenious Prodigy R .25 .60
57 Into the Fae Court C .08 .20
58 Johann's Stopgap C .08 .20
59 Living Lectern C .08 .20
60 Merfolk Coralsmith C .08 .20
61 Misleading Motes C .08 .20
62 Mocking Sprite C .08 .20
63 Obyra's Attendants C .08 .20
64 Picklock Prankster U .08 .20
65 Quick Study C .08 .20
66 Sleep-Cursed Faerie R .40 1.00
67 Sleight of Hand C .08 .20
68 Snaremaster Sprite C .08 .20
69 Spell Stutter C .08 .20
70 Splashy Spellcaster U .08 .20
71 Stormkeld Prowler C .08 .20
72 Succumb to the Cold U .08 .20
73 Talion's Messenger R .12 .30
74 Tenacious Tomeseeker U .08 .20
75 Vantress Transmuter C .08 .20
76 Virtue of Knowledge M 3.00 8.00
77 Water Wings C .08 .20
78 Ashiok, Wicked Manipulator M .40 1.00
79 Ashiok's Reaper U .08 .20
80 Back for Seconds U .08 .20
81 Barrow Naughty C .08 .20
82 Beseech the Mirror M 12.00 30.00
83 Candy Grapple C .08 .20
84 Conceited Witch C .08 .20
85 Dream Spoilers U .08 .20
86 Ego Drain U .08 .20
87 The End R .25 .60
88 Eriette's Whisper C .08 .20
89 Faerie Dreamthief U .08 .20
90 Faerie Fencing U .08 .20
91 Feed the Cauldron C .08 .20
92 Fell Horseman C .08 .20
93 Gumdrop Poisoner R .12 .30
94 High Fae Negotiator U .08 .20
95 Hopeless Nightmare C .08 .20
96 Lich-Knights' Conquest R .75 2.00
97 Lord Skitter, Sewer King R 1.00 2.50
98 Lord Skitter's Blessing R .20 .50
99 Lord Skitter's Butcher U .08 .20
100 Mintstrosity C .08 .20
101 Not Dead After All C .30 .75
102 Rankle's Prank R .25 .60
103 Rat Out C .08 .20
104 Rowan's Grim Search C .08 .20
105 Scream Puff C .08 .20
106 Shatter the Oath C .08 .20
107 Specter of Mortality R .08 .20
108 Spiteful Hexmage R .08 .20
109 Stingblade Assassin C .08 .20
110 Sugar Rush C .08 .20
111 Sweettooth Witch C .08 .20
112 Taken by Nightmares U .08 .20
113 Tangled Colony R .20 .50
114 Twisted Sewer-Witch U .08 .20
115 Virtue of Persistence M 10.00 25.00
116 Voracious Vermin C .08 .20
117 Warehouse Tabby C .08 .20
118 Wicked Visitor C .08 .20
119 The Witch's Vanity U .08 .20
120 Belligerent of the Ball U .08 .20
121 Bellowing Bruiser C .08 .20
122 Bespoke Battlegarb C .08 .20
123 Boundary Lands Ranger U .08 .20
124 Charming Scoundrel R 1.00 2.50
125 Cut In C .08 .20
126 Edgewall Pack C .08 .20
127 Embereth Veteran U .08 .20
128 Flick a Coin C .08 .20
129 Food Fight R .08 .20
130 Frantic Firebolt C .08 .20
131 Gnawing Crescendo C .08 .20
132 Goddric, Cloaked Reveler R .20 .50
133 Grabby Giant C .08 .20
134 Grand Ball Guest C .08 .20
135 Harried Spearguard C .08 .20
136 Hearth Elemental U .08 .20
137 Imodane, the Pyrohammer R .15 .40
138 Kindled Heroism C .08 .20
139 Korvold and the Noble Thief U .08 .20
140 Merry Bards C .08 .20
141 Minecart Daredevil C .08 .20

142 Monstrous Rage U .15 .40
143 Raging Battle Mouse R .08 .20
144 Ratcatcher Trainee C .08 .20
145 Realm-Scorcher Hellkite M .50 1.25
146 Redcap Gutter-Dweller R .08 .20
147 Redcap Thief C .08 .20
148 Rotisserie Elemental R .08 .20
149 Skewer Slinger C .08 .20
150 Song of Totentanz R .60 1.50
151 Stonesplitter Bolt U .08 .20
152 Tattered Ratter U .08 .20
153 Torch the Tower C .08 .20
154 Twisted Fealty U .08 .20
155 Two-Headed Hunter U .08 .20
156 Unruly Catapult C .08 .20
157 Virtue of Courage R 1.50 4.00
158 Witch's Mark C .08 .20
159 Witchstalker Frenzy U .08 .20
160 Agatha's Champion U .08 .20
161 Beanstalk Wurm C .08 .20
162 Bestial Bloodline C .08 .20
163 Blossoming Tortoise M 4.00 10.00
164 Bramble Familiar R .25 .60
165 Brave the Wilds C .08 .20
166 Commune with Nature C .08 .20
167 Curse of the Werefox C .08 .20
168 Elvish Archivist R .20 .50
169 Feral Encounter R .08 .20
170 Ferocious Werefox C .08 .20
171 Graceful Takedown U .08 .20
172 Gruff Triplets R .50 1.25
173 Hamlet Glutton C .08 .20
174 Hollow Scavenger C .08 .20
175 Howling Galefang U .08 .20
176 The Huntsman's Redemption R .60 1.50
177 Leaping Ambush C .08 .20
178 Night of the Sweets' Revenge U .15 .40
179 Redtooth Genealogist C .08 .20
180 Redtooth Vanguard U .08 .20
181 Return from the Wilds C .08 .20
182 Rootrider Faun C .08 .20
183 Royal Treatment U .08 .20
184 Sentinel of Lost Lore R .08 .20
185 Skybeast Tracker C .08 .20
186 Spider Food C .08 .20
187 Stormkeld Vanguard U .08 .20
188 Tanglespan Lookout U .08 .20
189 Territorial Witchstalker C .08 .20
190 Thunderous Debut R .12 .30
191 Titanic Growth C .08 .20
192 Toadstool Admirer C .08 .20
193 Tough Cookie U .08 .20
194 Troublemaker Ouphe C .08 .20
195 Up the Beanstalk U 1.25 3.00
196 Verdant Outrider C .08 .20
197 Virtue of Strength M 3.00 8.00
198 Welcome to Sweettooth U .08 .20
199 Agatha of the Vile Cauldron M .60 1.50
200 The Apprentice's Folly R .08 .20
201 Ash, Party Crasher U .08 .20
202 Eriette of the Charmed Apple M 1.50 4.00
203 Faunsbane Troll R .08 .20
204 The Goose Mother R .50 1.25
205 Greta, Sweettooth Scourge U .08 .20
206 Hylda of the Icy Crown M 1.50 4.00
207 Johann, Apprentice Sorcerer U .08 .20
208 Likeness Looter R .75 2.00
209 Neva, Stalked by Nightmares U .08 .20
210 Obyra, Dreaming Duelist U .08 .20
211 Rowan, Scion of War M .50 1.25
212 Ruby, Daring Tracker U .08 .20
213 Sharae of Numbing Depths U .08 .20
214 Syr Armont, the Redeemer U .08 .20
215 Talion, the Kindly Lord M 2.50 6.00
216 Totentanz, Swarm Piper U .08 .20
217 Troyan, Gutsy Explorer U .08 .20
218 Will, Scion of Peace M .25 .60
219 Yenna, Redtooth Regent R .40 1.00
220 Beluna Grandsquall M .20 .50
221 Callous Sell-Sword U .08 .20
222 Cruel Somnophage R .20 .50
223 Decadent Dragon R 1.00 2.50
224 Devouring Sugarmaw R .08 .20
225 Elusive Otter R .20 .50
226 Frolicking Familiar U .08 .20
227 Gingerbread Hunter U .08 .20
228 Heartflame Duelist R .25 .60
229 Imodane's Recruiter U .08 .20
230 Kellan, the Fae-Blooded M 1.00 2.50
231 Mosswood Dreadknight R 1.00 2.50
232 Picnic Ruiner U .08 .20
233 Pollen-Shield Hare R .08 .20
234 Questing Druid R 2.50 6.00
235 Scalding Viper R .15 .40
236 Shrouded Shepherd U .08 .20
237 Spellscorn Coven U .08 .20
238 Tempest Hart U .08 .20
239 Threadbind Clique U .08 .20
240 Twining Twins R .08 .20
241 Woodland Acolyte U .08 .20
242 Agatha's Soul Cauldron M 25.00 60.00
243 Candy Trail C .08 .20
244 Collector's Vault U .25 .60
245 Eriette's Tempting Apple U .08 .20
246 Gingerbrute C .08 .20
247 Hylda's Crown of Winter R .20 .50
248 The Irencrag R .50 1.25
249 Prophetic Prism C .08 .20
250 Scarecrow Guide C .08 .20
251 Soul-Guide Lantern U .08 .20
252 Syr Ginger, the Meal Ender R 1.25 3.00
253 Three Bowls of Porridge U .08 .20
254 Crystal Grotto C .08 .20
255 Edgewall Inn U .08 .20
256 Evolving Wilds C .08 .20
257 Restless Bivouac R .30 .75
258 Restless Cottage R 1.25 3.00
259 Restless Fortress R .30 .75
260 Restless Spire R .40 1.00
261 Restless Vinestalk R .25 .60
262 Plains (0262) L .12 .30
263 Island (0263) L .25 .60
264 Swamp (0264) L .30 .75
265 Mountain (0265) L .20 .50
266 Forest (0266) L .25 .60
267 Plains (0267) L .08 .20
268 Plains (0268) L .08 .20
269 Island (0269) L .08 .20
270 Island (0270) L .08 .20
271 Swamp (0271) L .08 .20
272 Swamp (0272) L .08 .20
273 Mountain (0273) L .08 .20
274 Mountain (0274) L .08 .20
275 Forest (0275) L .08 .20
276 Forest (0276) L .08 .20
277 Virtue of Loyalty SHOWCASE M 8.00 20.00
278 Horned Loch-Whale SHOWCASE R .20 .50
279 Virtue of Knowledge SHOWCASE M 2.50 6.00
280 Gumdrop Poisoner SHOWCASE R .08 .20
281 Virtue of Persistence SHOWCASE M 8.00 20.00
282 Virtue of Courage SHOWCASE M 1.25 3.00
283 Bramble Familiar SHOWCASE R .25 .60
284 Virtue of Strength SHOWCASE M 2.00 5.00
285 Beluna Grandsquall SHOWCASE M .20 .50
286 Cruel Somnophage SHOWCASE R .20 .50
287 Decadent Dragon SHOWCASE R 1.00 2.50
288 Devouring Sugarmaw SHOWCASE R .08 .20
289 Elusive Otter SHOWCASE R .20 .50
290 Heartflame Duelist SHOWCASE R .08 .20
291 Kellan, the Fae-Blooded SHOWCASE M 1.25 3.00
292 Mosswood Dreadknight SHOWCASE R 1.00 2.50
293 Pollen-Shield Hare SHOWCASE R .08 .20
294 Questing Druid SHOWCASE R 2.00 5.00
295 Scalding Viper SHOWCASE R .15 .40
296 Twining Twins SHOWCASE R .15 .40
297 Ashiok, Wicked Manipulator BORDERLESS M .50 1.25
298 Kellan, the Fae-Blooded BORDERLESS M 1.50 4.00
299 Eriette of the Charmed Apple BORDERLESS M .60 1.50
300 Rowan, Scion of War BORDERLESS M .75 2.00
301 Talion, the Kindly Lord BORDERLESS M 3.00 8.00
302 Will, Scion of Peace BORDERLESS M .40 1.00
303 Restless Bivouac BORDERLESS R .50 1.25
304 Restless Cottage BORDERLESS R .75 2.00
305 Restless Fortress BORDERLESS R .40 1.00
306 Restless Spire BORDERLESS R .50 1.25
307 Restless Vinestalk BORDERLESS R .40 1.00
308 Food Coma U .08 .20
309 Lady of Laughter R .20 .50
310 Pests of Honor U .08 .20
311 Faerie Slumber Party R 1.00 2.50
312 Rowdy Research U .12 .30
313 Storyteller Pixie U .08 .20
314 Experimental Confectioner U .75 2.00
315 Malevolent Witchkite R .30 .75
316 Old Flitterfang U .25 .60
317 Become Brutes U .08 .20
318 Charging Hooligan U .08 .20
319 Ogre Chitterlord R .25 .60
320 Intrepid Trufflesnout U .08 .20
321 Provisions Merchant U .08 .20
322 Wildwood Mentor R .30 .75
323 Archon of the Wild Rose EXT ART R .12 .30
324 Expel the Interlopers EXT ART R .15 .40
325 Moonshaker Cavalry EXT ART M 10.00 25.00
326 Regal Bunnicorn EXT ART R 1.00 2.50
327 Spellbook Vendor EXT ART R .30 .75
328 A Tale for the Ages EXT ART R .15 .40
329 Werefox Bodyguard EXT ART R 1.00 2.50
330 Asinine Antics EXT ART M 1.50 4.00
331 Extraordinary Journey EXT ART R .20 .50
332 Farsight Ritual EXT ART R .15 .40
333 Ingenious Prodigy EXT ART R .40 1.00
334 Sleep-Cursed Faerie EXT ART R .60 1.50
335 Talion's Messenger EXT ART R .25 .60
336 Beseech the Mirror EXT ART M 20.00 50.00
337 The End EXT ART R .50 1.25
338 Lich-Knights' Conquest EXT ART R .75 2.00
339 Lord Skitter, Sewer King EXT ART R 2.00 5.00
340 Lord Skitter's Blessing EXT ART R .25 .60
341 Rankle's Prank EXT ART R .50 1.25
342 Specter of Mortality EXT ART R .08 .20
343 Spiteful Hexmage EXT ART R .12 .30
344 Tangled Colony EXT ART R .30 .75
345 Charming Scoundrel EXT ART R .60 1.50
346 Food Fight EXT ART R .08 .20
347 Goddric, Cloaked Reveler EXT ART R .25 .60
348 Imodane, the Pyrohammer EXT ART R .60 1.50
349 Raging Battle Mouse EXT ART R .12 .30
350 Realm-Scorcher Hellkite EXT ART M 1.00 2.50
351 Redcap Gutter-Dweller EXT ART R .12 .30
352 Rotisserie Elemental EXT ART R .08 .20
353 Song of Totentanz EXT ART R .75 2.00
354 Blossoming Tortoise EXT ART M 5.00 12.00
355 Elvish Archivist EXT ART R .30 .75
356 Feral Encounter EXT ART R .20 .50
357 Gruff Triplets EXT ART R 1.00 2.50
358 Sentinel of Lost Lore EXT ART R .12 .30
359 Thunderous Debut EXT ART R .12 .30
360 Agatha of the Vile Cauldron EXT ART M 2.00 5.00
361 Faunsbane Troll EXT ART R .08 .20
362 The Goose Mother EXT ART R 1.25 3.00
363 Hylda of the Icy Crown EXT ART M 4.00 10.00
364 Likeness Looter EXT ART R 1.25 3.00
365 Yenna, Redtooth Regent EXT ART R 1.50 4.00
366 Agatha's Soul Cauldron EXT ART M 30.00 80.00
367 Hylda's Crown of Winter EXT ART R .40 1.00
368 The Irencrag EXT ART R .75 2.00
369 Syr Ginger, the Meal Ender EXT ART R 2.00 5.00
370 Lady of Laughter EXT ART R .20 .50
371 Faerie Slumber Party EXT ART R 1.50 4.00
372 Malevolent Witchkite EXT ART R .25 .60
373 Ogre Chitterlord EXT ART R .20 .50
374 Wildwood Mentor EXT ART R .40 1.00
375 Stroke of Midnight EXT ART U 1.50 4.00
376 Sleight of Hand EXT ART C .40 1.00
377 Faerie Dreamthief EXT ART U .20 .50
378 Torch the Tower EXT ART C .25 .60
379 Tanglespan Lookout EXT ART C .20 .50
380 Lich-Knights' Conquest EXT ART R .25 .60
381 Expel the Interlopers EXT ART R .12 .30

2023 Magic the Gathering Wilds of Eldraine Enchanting Tales

1 Blind Obedience R 1.25 3.00
2 Dawn of Hope R .12 .30
3 Grasp of Fate U .08 .20
4 Greater Auramancy M 4.00 10.00
5 Griffin Aerie U .08 .20
6 Intangible Virtue U .08 .20
7 Karmic Justice R .50 1.25
8 Knightly Valor U .08 .20
9 Land Tax M 8.00 20.00
10 Leyline of Sanctity R .75 2.00
11 Phyrexian Unlife R .12 .30
12 Rest in Peace R .50 1.25
13 Smothering Tithe M 10.00 25.00
14 As Foretold R .40 1.00
15 Compulsion U .08 .20
16 Copy Enchantment R .30 .75
17 Curiosity U .08 .20
18 Forced Fruition R .25 .60
19 Fraying Sanity R .15 .40
20 Hatching Plans U .08 .20
21 Intruder Alarm R 1.25 3.00
22 Kindred Discovery M 4.00 10.00
23 Leyline of Anticipation R .60 1.50
24 Omniscience M 3.00 8.00
25 Rhystic Study M 20.00 50.00
26 Spreading Seas U .12 .30
27 Bitterblossom M 8.00 20.00
28 Dark Tutelage U .08 .20
29 Grave Pact M 5.00 12.00
30 Leyline of the Void R 1.25 3.00
31 Necropotence M 6.00 15.00
32 Oppression R .30 .75
33 Oversold Cemetery R .25 .60
34 Polluted Bonds R .50 1.25
35 Sanguine Bond R .75 2.00
36 Stab Wound U .08 .20
37 Vampiric Rites U .08 .20
38 Waste Not R 1.00 2.50
39 Aggravated Assault R 2.50 6.00
40 Blood Moon M 3.00 8.00
41 Dragon Mantle U .08 .20
42 Fiery Emancipation R 2.50 6.00
43 Goblin Bombardment R .50 1.25
44 Impact Tremors U .20 .50
45 Leyline of Lightning R .08 .20
46 Mana Flare R .25 .60
47 Raid Bombardment U .08 .20
48 Repercussion M 2.00 5.00
49 Shared Animosity R .40 1.00
50 Sneak Attack M 3.00 8.00
51 Defense of the Heart M 4.00 10.00
52 Doubling Season M 20.00 50.00
53 Garruk's Uprising U .30 .75
54 Ground Seal U .08 .20
55 Hardened Scales R 1.00 2.50
56 Leyline of Abundance R .20 .50
57 Nature's Will R .50 1.25
58 Parallel Lives M 12.00 30.00
59 Primal Vigor R 2.50 6.00
60 Prismatic Omen R .40 1.00
61 Season of Growth U .08 .20
62 Unnatural Growth R 1.25 3.00
63 Utopia Sprawl U .25 .60
64 Greater Auramancy ANIME ART M 8.00 20.00
65 Karmic Justice ANIME ART R .75 2.00
66 Land Tax ANIME ART M 8.00 20.00
67 Smothering Tithe ANIME ART M 30.00 80.00
68 As Foretold ANIME ART R 1.00 2.50
69 Kindred Discovery ANIME ART M 5.00 12.00
70 Omniscience ANIME ART M 12.00 30.00
71 Rhystic Study ANIME ART M 40.00 100.00
72 Bitterblossom ANIME ART M 8.00 20.00
73 Grave Pact ANIME ART M 5.00 12.00
74 Necropotence ANIME ART M 8.00 20.00
75 Polluted Bonds ANIME ART R 1.50 4.00
76 Aggravated Assault ANIME ART R 2.00 5.00
77 Blood Moon ANIME ART M 6.00 15.00
78 Repercussion ANIME ART M 1.50 4.00
79 Sneak Attack ANIME ART M 4.00 10.00
80 Defense of the Heart ANIME ART M 5.00 12.00
81 Doubling Season ANIME ART M 25.00 60.00
82 Nature's Will ANIME ART R .60 1.50
83 Parallel Lives ANIME ART M 15.00 40.00
84 Greater Auramancy ANIME ART CON FOIL M40.00 100.00
85 Karmic Justice ANIME ART CON FOIL R 8.00 20.00
86 Land Tax ANIME ART CON FOIL M 20.00 50.00
87 Smothering Tithe ANIME ART CON FOIL M125.00 300.00
88 As Foretold ANIME ART CON FOIL R 10.00 25.00
89 Kindred Discovery ANIME ART CON FOIL M25.00 60.00
90 Omniscience ANIME ART CON FOIL M 60.00 150.00
91 Rhystic Study ANIME ART CON FOIL M 200.00 500.00
92 Bitterblossom ANIME ART CON FOIL M 40.00 100.00
93 Grave Pact ANIME ART CON FOIL M 25.00 60.00
94 Necropotence ANIME ART CON FOIL M 40.00 100.00
95 Polluted Bonds ANIME ART CON FOIL R 15.00 40.00
96 Aggravated Assault ANIME ART CON FOIL R12.00 30.00
97 Blood Moon ANIME ART CON FOIL M 30.00 80.00
98 Repercussion ANIME ART CON FOIL M 8.00 20.00
99 Sneak Attack ANIME ART CON FOIL M 25.00 60.00
100 Defense of the Heart ANIME ART CON FOIL M25.00 60.00
101 Doubling Season ANIME ART CON FOIL M75.00 200.00
102 Nature's Will ANIME ART CON FOIL R 6.00 15.00
103 Parallel Lives ANIME ART CON FOIL M 50.00 120.00

2023 Magic The Gathering Wilds of Eldraine Enchanting Tales Foil

1 Blind Obedience R FOIL 2.50 6.00
2 Dawn of Hope R FOIL .25 .60
3 Grasp of Fate U FOIL .08 .20
4 Greater Auramancy M FOIL 6.00 15.00
5 Griffin Aerie U FOIL .08 .20
6 Intangible Virtue U FOIL .08 .20
7 Karmic Justice R FOIL .75 2.00
8 Knightly Valor U FOIL .08 .20
9 Land Tax M FOIL 10.00 25.00
10 Leyline of Sanctity R FOIL 2.50 6.00
11 Phyrexian Unlife R FOIL .50 1.25
12 Rest in Peace R FOIL 1.25 3.00
13 Smothering Tithe M FOIL 10.00 25.00
14 As Foretold R FOIL 1.00 2.50
15 Compulsion U FOIL .08 .20
16 Copy Enchantment R FOIL .60 1.50
17 Curiosity U FOIL .12 .30
18 Forced Fruition R FOIL .30 .75
19 Fraying Sanity R FOIL .30 .75
20 Hatching Plans U FOIL .08 .20
21 Intruder Alarm R FOIL 1.50 4.00
22 Kindred Discovery M FOIL 6.00 15.00
23 Leyline of Anticipation R FOIL 1.50 4.00
24 Omniscience M FOIL 6.00 15.00
25 Rhystic Study M FOIL 30.00 80.00
26 Spreading Seas U FOIL .08 .20
27 Bitterblossom M FOIL 10.00 25.00
28 Dark Tutelage U FOIL .08 .20
29 Grave Pact M FOIL 5.00 12.00
30 Leyline of the Void R FOIL 4.00 10.00
31 Necropotence M FOIL 10.00 25.00
32 Oppression R FOIL .50 1.25
33 Oversold Cemetery R FOIL .50 1.25
34 Polluted Bonds R FOIL 1.25 3.00
35 Sanguine Bond R FOIL 1.25 3.00
36 Stab Wound U FOIL .08 .20
37 Vampiric Rites U FOIL .08 .20
38 Waste Not R FOIL 2.00 5.00
39 Aggravated Assault R FOIL 3.00 8.00
40 Blood Moon M FOIL 6.00 15.00
41 Dragon Mantle U FOIL .08 .20
42 Fiery Emancipation R FOIL 3.00 8.00
43 Goblin Bombardment R FOIL 1.00 2.50
44 Impact Tremors U FOIL .20 .50
45 Leyline of Lightning R FOIL .15 .40
46 Mana Flare R FOIL .75 2.00
47 Raid Bombardment U FOIL .08 .20
48 Repercussion M FOIL 2.00 5.00
49 Shared Animosity R FOIL 1.00 2.50
50 Sneak Attack M FOIL 3.00 8.00
51 Defense of the Heart M FOIL 5.00 12.00
52 Doubling Season M FOIL 25.00 60.00
53 Garruk's Uprising U FOIL .30 .75
54 Ground Seal U FOIL .08 .20
55 Hardened Scales R FOIL 2.00 5.00
56 Leyline of Abundance R FOIL .40 1.00
57 Nature's Will R FOIL .75 2.00
58 Parallel Lives M FOIL 15.00 40.00
59 Primal Vigor R FOIL 4.00 10.00
60 Prismatic Omen R FOIL .75 2.00
61 Season of Growth U FOIL .08 .20
62 Unnatural Growth R FOIL 2.00 5.00
63 Utopia Sprawl U FOIL .50 1.25
64 Greater Auramancy ANIME ART FOIL M 25.00 60.00
65 Karmic Justice ANIME ART FOIL R 2.50 6.00
66 Land Tax ANIME ART FOIL M 8.00 20.00
67 Smothering Tithe ANIME ART FOIL M 60.00 150.00
68 As Foretold ANIME ART FOIL R 4.00 10.00
69 Kindred Discovery ANIME ART FOIL M 10.00 25.00
70 Omniscience ANIME ART FOIL M 25.00 60.00
71 Rhystic Study ANIME ART FOIL M 100.00 250.00
72 Bitterblossom ANIME ART FOIL M 15.00 40.00
73 Grave Pact ANIME ART FOIL M 8.00 20.00
74 Necropotence ANIME ART FOIL M 20.00 50.00
75 Polluted Bonds ANIME ART FOIL R 4.00 10.00
76 Aggravated Assault ANIME ART FOIL R 4.00 10.00
77 Blood Moon ANIME ART FOIL M 15.00 40.00
78 Repercussion ANIME ART FOIL M 4.00 10.00
79 Sneak Attack ANIME ART FOIL M 8.00 20.00
80 Defense of the Heart ANIME ART FOIL M 12.00 30.00
81 Doubling Season ANIME ART FOIL M 40.00 100.00
82 Nature's Will ANIME ART FOIL R 2.00 5.00
83 Parallel Lives ANIME ART FOIL M 25.00 60.00

2023 Magic The Gathering Year of the Rabbit

1 Rabbit Battery R :R: 2.00 5.00
3 Kwain, Itinerant Meddler R :W:/:B: 30.00 60.00
4 Swiftfoot Boots R 8.00 20.00
5 Ethereal Armor R :W: 25.00 60.00
6 Arcbound Ravager R 25.00 60.00

2024 Magic The Gathering Modern Horizons 3

1 Breaker of Creation U .10 .25
2 Devourer of Destiny R 2.00 5.00
4 Echoes of Eternity R 1.50 4.00
5 Eldrazi Ravager U .08 .20
6 Emrakul, the World Anew M 12.00 30.00
7 Glaring Fleshraker U .30 .75
8 Herigast, Erupting Nullkite M 1.25 3.00
9 It That Heralds the End U .20 .50
10 Kozilek, the Broken Reality M 8.00 20.00
11 Kozilek's Command R 6.00 15.00
12 Null Elemental Blast U .25 .60
13 Nulldrifter R 1.50 4.00
15 Ulamog, the Defiler M 25.00 60.00
17 Wastescape Battlemage U .10 .25
18 Aerie Auxiliary C .40 1.00
20 Argent Dais R .10 .25
21 Charitable Levy U .08 .20
23 Envoy of the Ancestors U .08 .20
26 Flare of Fortitude R 2.00 5.00
27 Glyph Elemental U .08 .20
29 Guide of Souls R 2.50 6.00
31 Indebted Spirit U .08 .20
35 Metastatic Evangel U .10 .25
36 Muster the Departed U .08 .20
38 Ocelot Pride M 10.00 25.00
39 Pearl-Ear, Imperial Advisor R .20 .50
40 Phelia, Exuberant Shepherd R 1.50 4.00
44 Static Prison U .40 1.00
45 Thraben Charm C .08 .20
47 White Orchid Phantom R 1.00 2.50
49 Wrath of the Skies R 4.00 10.00
51 Amphibian Downpour R .25 .60
53 Brainsurge U .12 .30
54 Consign to Memory U .40 1.00
55 Copycrook U .08 .20
59 Dreamtide Whale R .50 1.25
61 Emrakul's Messenger U .10 .25
62 Flare of Denial R 5.00 12.00
63 Harbinger of the Seas R 1.50 4.00
64 Hope-Ender Coatl U .08 .20
65 Kozilek's Unsealing U .50 1.25
70 Shadow of the Second Sun M .75 2.00
71 Strix Serenade R 1.25 3.00
75 Tune the Narrative C .08 .20
76 Ugin's Binding M 5.00 12.00
79 Volatile Stormdrake R 1.00 2.50
80 Accursed Marauder C .10 .25
83 Chthonian Nightmare R 1.50 4.00
84 Consuming Corruption U .08 .20
85 Crabomination R .12 .30
86 The Creation of Avacyn U .08 .20
90 Emperor of Bones R .12 .30

95 Flare of Malice R 2.00 5.00
100 Marionette Apprentice U .40 1.00
102 Necrodominance M 10.00 25.00
103 Nethergoyf M 10.00 25.00
104 Quest for the Necropolis U .08 .20
105 Refurbished Familiar C .08 .20
107 Ripples of Undeath R 1.00 2.50
108 Scurrilous Sentry C .08 .20
109 Shilgengar, Sire of Famine R .12 .30
110 Warren Soultrader R 2.50 6.00
112 Wurmcoil Larva U .08 .20
113 Aether Revolt R .20 .50
114 Amped Raptor U .40 1.00
115 Ashling, Flame Dancer M 1.00 2.50
116 Detective's Phoenix R .08 .20
117 Eldrazi Linebreaker R .50 1.25
119 Flare of Duplication R 1.00 2.50
120 Frogmyr Enforcer U .10 .25
122 Galvanic Discharge C .12 .30
123 Ghostfire Slice U .10 .25
124 Glimpse the Impossible C .10 .25
128 Molten Gatekeeper C .08 .20
129 Party Thrasher R .30 .75
131 Powerbalance R .40 1.00
137 Skittering Precursor U .08 .20
140 Spawn-Gang Commander U .08 .20
142 Unstable Amulet U .15 .40
144 Wheel of Potential R .15 .40
145 Basking Broodscale C .10 .25
146 Birthing Ritual M 2.50 6.00
147 Collective Resistance U .25 .60
149 Eladamri, Korvecdal M 4.00 10.00
151 Evolution Witness C .08 .20
152 Fanatic of Rhonas R 2.00 5.00
153 Fangs of Kalonia U .10 .25
154 Flare of Cultivation R 2.00 5.00
156 Gift of the Viper C .08 .20
160 Lion Umbra U .08 .20
161 Malevolent Rumble C .08 .20
162 Monstrous Vortex U .10 .25
163 Nightshade Dryad C .10 .25
164 Nyxborn Hydra C .08 .20
165 Path of Annihilation U .12 .30
166 Primal Prayers R .15 .40
167 Propagator Drone U .08 .20
169 Six R 2.00 5.00
170 Sowing Mycospawn R 1.00 2.50
171 Springheart Nantuko R 2.50 6.00
172 Temperamental Oozewagg C .08 .20
174 Thief of Existence R .25 .60
175 Trickster's Elk U .08 .20
176 Wumpus Aberration U .08 .20
177 Abstruse Appropriation R .20 .50
178 Arna Kennerüd, Skycaptain M .50 1.25
181 Cursed Wombat U .08 .20
186 Genku, Future Shaper R .10 .25
187 Golden-Tail Trainer U .10 .25
189 Imskir Iron-Eater R .12 .30
190 Invert Polarity R 1.50 4.00
192 Kudo, King Among Bears R .15 .40
193 Nadu, Winged Wisdom R 3.00 8.00
194 The Necrobloom R .25 .60
197 Phlage, Titan of Fire's Fury M 20.00 50.00
198 Planar Genesis U .15 .40
199 Psychic Frog R 4.00 10.00
200 Pyretic Rebirth U .08 .20
202 Rosheen, Roaring Prophet R .10 .25
205 Sneaky Snacker C .10 .25
207 Wight of the Reliquary R 1.25 3.00
208 Writhing Chrysalis C .08 .20
209 Disruptor Flute R 1.00 2.50
210 Idol of False Gods U .10 .25
211 Solar Transformer U .10 .25
212 Vexing Bauble U .75 2.00
213 Winter Moon R .40 1.00
214 Archway of Innovation R .40 1.00
215 Arena of Glory R 1.50 4.00
216 Bloodstained Mire R 6.00 15.00
217 Bountiful Landscape C .08 .20
218 Contaminated Landscape C .08 .20
219 Deceptive Landscape C .08 .20
220 Flooded Strand R 6.00 15.00
221 Foreboding Landscape C .08 .20
222 Monumental Henge R .30 .75
223 Perilous Landscape C .08 .20
224 Polluted Delta R 8.00 20.00
225 Seething Landscape C .08 .20
226 Shattered Landscape C .08 .20
227 Sheltering Landscape C .10 .25
228 Shifting Woodland R 2.50 6.00
229 Snow-Covered Wastes U .15 .40
230 Spymaster's Vault R .60 1.50
231 Tranquil Landscape C .08 .20
232 Twisted Landscape C .08 .20
233 Ugin's Labyrinth M 20.00 50.00
234 Urza's Cave U 1.00 2.50
235 Windswept Heath R 5.00 12.00
236 Wooded Foothills R 8.00 20.00
237 Ajani, Nacatl Pariah // Ajani, Nacatl Avenger M 12.00 30.00
238 Razorgrass Ambush // Razorgrass Field U .12 .30
239 Witch Enchanter // Witch-Blessed Meadow U1.00 2.50
240 Hydroelectric Specimen // Hydroelectric Laboratory U .20 .50
241 Sink into Stupor // Soporific Springs U 2.00 5.00
242 Tamiyo, Inquisitive Student // Tamiyo, Seasoned Scholar M 15.00 40.00
243 Boggart Trawler // Boggart Bog U .40 1.00
244 Fell the Profane // Fell Mire U 1.25 3.00
245 Sorin of House Markov // Sorin, Ravenous Neonate M 6.00 15.00
246 Pinnacle Monk // Mystic Peak U .25 .60
247 Ral, Monsoon Mage // Ral, Leyline Prodigy M6.00 15.00
248 Sundering Eruption // Volcanic Fissure U .40 1.00
249 Bridgeworks Battle // Tanglespan Bridgeworks U .30 .75
250 Disciple of Freyalise // Garden of Freyalise U.60 1.50
251 Grist, Voracious Larva // Grist, the Plague Swarm M 2.50 6.00
252 Bloodsoaked Insight // Sanguine Morass U.10 .25
253 Drowner of Truth // Drowned Jungle U .15 .40
254 Glasswing Grace // Age-Graced Chapel U .12 .30
255 Legion Leadership // Legion Stronghold U .30 .75
256 Revitalizing Repast // Old-Growth Grove U .50 1.25
257 Rush of Inspiration // Crackling Falls U .08 .20
258 Strength of the Harvest // Haven of the Harvest U .25 .60
259 Stump Stomp // Burnwillow Clearing U .25 .60
260 Suppression Ray // Orderly Plaza U .08 .20
261 Waterlogged Teachings // Inundated Archive U.20 .50
264 Distinguished Conjurer U .08 .20
265 Orim's Chant R .60 1.50
266 Recruiter of the Guard M 2.50 6.00
267 Sevinne's Reclamation R .10 .25
269 Estrid's Invocation R .25 .60
270 Kappa Cannoneer R .50 1.25
273 Buried Alive U .20 .50
274 K'rrik, Son of Yawgmoth R .15 .40
275 Nadier's Nightblade U .08 .20
276 Ophiomancer R .25 .60
277 Toxic Deluge R 2.00 5.00
278 Victimize U .10 .25
279 Cursed Mirror R .15 .40
281 Laelia, the Blade Reforged R .15 .40
282 Meltdown U .10 .25
285 Branching Evolution R 1.00 2.50
286 Priest of Titania U .15 .40
287 Sylvan Safekeeper R 1.25 3.00
288 Wirewood Symbiote U .08 .20
289 Breya, Etherium Shaper M .20 .50
290 Kaalia of the Vast M .60 1.50
291 Emerald Medallion R 1.00 2.50
292 Jet Medallion R 2.00 5.00
293 Junk Diver U .08 .20
294 Pearl Medallion R 1.00 2.50
295 Ruby Medallion R 4.00 10.00
296 Sapphire Medallion R 1.50 4.00
297 Urza's Incubator R 6.00 15.00
298 Worn Powerstone U .08 .20
299 Barbarian Ring U .08 .20
300 Cephalid Coliseum U .12 .30
301 Deserted Temple R .50 1.25
302 Nesting Grounds U .08 .20
303 Phyrexian Tower M 10.00 25.00
304 Plains FULL ART C .10 .25
305 Island FULL ART C .12 .30
306 Swamp FULL ART C .15 .40
307 Mountain FULL ART C .12 .30
308 Forest FULL ART C .12 .30
309 Snow-Covered Wastes FULL ART U 1.00 2.50
311 Plains C .08 .20
313 Island C .08 .20
320 Echoes of Eternity FRAME BREAK R 2.00 5.00
321 Flare of Fortitude FRAME BREAK R 5.00 12.00
322 Ocelot Pride FRAME BREAK M 20.00 50.00
323 Orim's Chant FRAME BREAK R 1.25 3.00
324 White Orchid Phantom FRAME BREAK R 2.00 5.00
325 Wrath of the Skies FRAME BREAK R 6.00 15.00
326 Flare of Denial FRAME BREAK R 10.00 25.00
327 Strix Serenade FRAME BREAK R 2.50 6.00
328 Ugin's Binding FRAME BREAK M 6.00 15.00
329 Volatile Stormdrake FRAME BREAK R 4.00 10.00
330 Chthonian Nightmare FRAME BREAK R 5.00 12.00
331 Flare of Malice FRAME BREAK R 2.50 6.00
332 Warren Soultrader FRAME BREAK R 4.00 10.00
333 Flare of Duplication FRAME BREAK R 2.50 6.00
334 Party Thrasher FRAME BREAK R 1.25 3.00
335 Powerbalance FRAME BREAK R .75 2.00
336 Wheel of Potential FRAME BREAK R .60 1.50
337 Birthing Ritual FRAME BREAK M 3.00 8.00
338 Flare of Cultivation FRAME BREAK R 5.00 12.00
339 Primal Prayers FRAME BREAK R .75 2.00
340 Sowing Mycospawn FRAME BREAK R 1.25 3.00
341 Springheart Nantuko FRAME BREAK R 4.00 10.00
342 Abstruse Appropriation FRAME BREAK R .60 1.50
343 Kaalia of the Vast FRAME BREAK M 12.00 30.00
344 Psychic Frog FRAME BREAK R 10.00 25.00
345 Emerald Medallion FRAME BREAK R 2.00 5.00
346 Jet Medallion FRAME BREAK R 5.00 12.00
347 Pearl Medallion FRAME BREAK R 3.00 8.00
348 Ruby Medallion FRAME BREAK R 5.00 12.00
349 Sapphire Medallion FRAME BREAK R 3.00 8.00
350 Archway of Innovation FRAME BREAK R .60 1.50
351 Arena of Glory FRAME BREAK R 2.50 6.00
352 Bloodstained Mire BORDERLESS R 10.00 25.00
353 Flooded Strand BORDERLESS R 10.00 25.00
354 Monumental Henge BORDERLESS R .60 1.50
355 Phyrexian Tower BORDERLESS M 12.00 30.00
356 Polluted Delta BORDERLESS R 10.00 25.00
357 Shifting Woodland BORDERLESS R 4.00 10.00
358 Spymaster's Vault BORDERLESS R 1.00 2.50
359 Ugin's Labyrinth BORDERLESS M 25.00 60.00
360 Windswept Heath BORDERLESS R 8.00 20.00
361 Wooded Foothills BORDERLESS R 8.00 20.00
362 Herigast, Erupting Nullkite BORDERLESS PROFILE M 1.50 4.00
363 Pearl-Ear, Imperial Advisor BORDERLESS PROFILE R .20 .50
364 Phelia, Exuberant Shepherd BORDERLESS PROFILE R 2.00 5.00
365 K'rrik, Son of Yawgmoth BORDERLESS PROFILE R .40 1.00
366 Shilgengar, Sire of Famine BORDERLESS PROFILE R .12 .30
367 Ashling, Flame Dancer BORDERLESS PROFILE M 2.50 6.00
368 Laelia, the Blade Reforged BORDERLESS PROFILE R .25 .60
369 Eladamri, Korvecdal BORDERLESS PROFILE M 5.00 12.00
370 Six BORDERLESS PROFILE R 6.00 15.00
371 Arna Kennerüd, Skycaptain BORDERLESS PROFILE M .50 1.25
372 Breya, Etherium Shaper BORDERLESS PROFILE M 1.00 2.50
373 Genku, Future Shaper BORDERLESS PROFILE R .20 .50
374 Imskir Iron-Eater BORDERLESS PROFILE R.50 1.25
375 Kaalia of the Vast BORDERLESS PROFILE M4.00 10.00
376 Kudo, King Among Bears BORDERLESS PROFILE R .30 .75
377 Nadu, Winged Wisdom BORDERLESS PROFILE R 4.00 10.00
378 The Necrobloom BORDERLESS PROFILE R.75 2.00
379 Phlage, Titan of Fire's Fury BORDERLESS PROFILE M 25.00 60.00
380 Rosheen, Roaring Prophet BORDERLESS PROFILE R .15 .40
381 Emrakul, the World Anew BORDERLESS CONCEPT M 25.00 60.00
382 Kozilek, the Broken Reality BORDERLESS CONCEPT M 20.00 50.00
383 Ulamog, the Defiler BORDERLESS CONCEPT M 40.00 100.00
384 Emrakul, the World Anew RETRO FRAME M15.00 40.00
385 It That Heralds the End RETRO FRAME U .20 .50
386 Kozilek, the Broken Reality RETRO FRAME M10.00 25.00
387 Null Elemental Blast RETRO FRAME U .50 1.25
388 Nulldrifter RETRO FRAME R 2.00 5.00
389 Ulamog, the Defiler RETRO FRAME M 25.00 60.00
390 Charitable Levy RETRO FRAME U .10 .25
391 Flare of Fortitude RETRO FRAME R 2.00 5.00
393 Metastatic Evangel RETRO FRAME U .10 .25
394 Ocelot Pride RETRO FRAME M 12.00 30.00
395 Recruiter of the Guard RETRO FRAME M 2.50 6.00
396 White Orchid Phantom RETRO FRAME R 2.00 5.00
397 Wrath of the Skies RETRO FRAME R 6.00 15.00
398 Aether Spike RETRO FRAME C .08 .20
399 Brainsurge RETRO FRAME U .20 .50
400 Flare of Denial RETRO FRAME R 8.00 20.00
401 Kappa Cannoneer RETRO FRAME R .50 1.25
402 Shadow of the Second Sun RETRO FRAME M.50 1.25
403 Tune the Narrative RETRO FRAME C .30 .75
404 Volatile Stormdrake RETRO FRAME R 2.00 5.00
405 Accursed Marauder RETRO FRAME C .15 .40
406 Chthonian Nightmare RETRO FRAME R 3.00 8.00
407 Consuming Corruption RETRO FRAME U .10 .25
408 Flare of Malice RETRO FRAME R 3.00 8.00
409 Grim Servant RETRO FRAME U .12 .30
410 Marionette Apprentice RETRO FRAME U .50 1.25
411 Necrodominance RETRO FRAME M 12.00 30.00
412 Toxic Deluge RETRO FRAME R 2.50 6.00
413 Victimize RETRO FRAME U .10 .25
414 Warren Soultrader RETRO FRAME R 4.00 10.00
415 Ashling, Flame Dancer RETRO FRAME M 1.25 3.00
416 Flare of Duplication RETRO FRAME R 1.25 3.00
417 Galvanic Discharge RETRO FRAME C .75 2.00
418 Meltdown RETRO FRAME U .12 .30
419 Party Thrasher RETRO FRAME R .50 1.25
421 Unstable Amulet RETRO FRAME U .50 1.25
422 Wheel of Potential RETRO FRAME R .20 .50
423 Eladamri, Korvecdal RETRO FRAME M 5.00 12.00
424 Evolution Witness RETRO FRAME C .12 .30
425 Flare of Cultivation RETRO FRAME R 2.50 6.00
426 Lion Umbra RETRO FRAME U .10 .25
427 Monstrous Vortex RETRO FRAME U .12 .30
428 Priest of Titania RETRO FRAME U .20 .50
429 Primal Prayers RETRO FRAME R .20 .50
430 Six RETRO FRAME R 3.00 8.00
431 Imskir Iron-Eater RETRO FRAME R .10 .25
432 Kudo, King Among Bears RETRO FRAME R.25 .60
433 Psychic Frog RETRO FRAME R 8.00 20.00
434 Rosheen, Roaring Prophet RETRO FRAME R.08 .20
435 Bloodstained Mire RETRO FRAME R 8.00 20.00
436 Flooded Strand RETRO FRAME R 8.00 20.00
437 Nesting Grounds RETRO FRAME U .08 .20
438 Polluted Delta RETRO FRAME R 10.00 25.00
439 Snow-Covered Wastes RETRO FRAME U .30 .75
440 Windswept Heath RETRO FRAME R 5.00 12.00
441 Wooded Foothills RETRO FRAME R 8.00 20.00
442 Ajani, Nacatl Pariah // Ajani, Nacatl Avenger BORDERLESS M 12.00 30.00
443 Tamiyo, Inquisitive Student // Tamiyo, Seasoned Scholar BORDERLESS M 20.00 50.00
444 Sorin of House Markov // Sorin, Ravenous Neonate BORDERLESS M 10.00 25.00
445 Ral, Monsoon Mage // Ral, Leyline Prodigy BORDERLESS M 10.00 25.00
446 Grist, Voracious Larva // Grist, the Plague Swarm BORDERLESS M 4.00 10.00
447 Argent Dais EXTENDED ART R .10 .25
448 Guide of Souls EXTENDED ART R 2.50 6.00
449 Amphibian Downpour EXTENDED ART R .40 1.00
450 Dreamtide Whale EXTENDED ART R .60 1.50
451 Harbinger of the Seas EXTENDED ART R 2.00 5.00
452 Crabomination EXTENDED ART R .15 .40
453 Emperor of Bones EXTENDED ART R .25 .60
454 Nethergoyf EXTENDED ART M 10.00 25.00
455 Ripples of Undeath EXTENDED ART R 1.00 2.50
456 Aether Revolt EXTENDED ART R .12 .30
457 Detective's Phoenix EXTENDED ART R .10 .25
458 Fanatic of Rhonas EXTENDED ART R 2.50 6.00
459 Invert Polarity EXTENDED ART R 1.50 4.00
460 Wight of the Reliquary EXTENDED ART R 1.25 3.00
461 Disruptor Flute EXTENDED ART R 1.25 3.00
462 Winter Moon EXTENDED ART R .75 2.00
463 Bloodstained Mire EXTENDED ART R 6.00 15.00
464 Flooded Strand EXTENDED ART R 6.00 15.00
465 Polluted Delta EXTENDED ART R 8.00 20.00
466 Windswept Heath EXTENDED ART R 5.00 12.00
467 Wooded Foothills EXTENDED ART R 6.00 15.00
468 Ajani, Nacatl Pariah // Ajani, Nacatl Avenger TEXTURED M 30.00 80.00
469 Tamiyo, Inquisitive Student // Tamiyo, Seasoned Scholar TEXTURED M 40.00 100.00
470 Sorin of House Markov // Sorin, Ravenous Neonate TEXTURED M 40.00 100.00
471 Ral, Monsoon Mage // Ral, Leyline Prodigy TEXTURED M 25.00 60.00
472 Grist, Voracious Larva // Grist, the Plague Swarm TEXTURED M 15.00 40.00
473 Emrakul, the World Anew FOIL ETCHED M15.00 40.00
474 Herigast, Erupting Nullkite FOIL ETCHED M3.00 8.00
475 Kozilek, the Broken Reality FOIL ETCHED M12.00 30.00
476 Ulamog, the Defiler FOIL ETCHED M 30.00 80.00
477 Pearl-Ear, Imperial Advisor FOIL ETCHED R.75 2.00
478 Phelia, Exuberant Shepherd FOIL ETCHED R3.00 8.00
479 K'rrik, Son of Yawgmoth FOIL ETCHED R 1.00 2.50
480 Shilgengar, Sire of Famine FOIL ETCHED R1.50 4.00
481 Ashling, Flame Dancer FOIL ETCHED M 2.00 5.00
482 Laelia, the Blade Reforged FOIL ETCHED R .40 1.00
483 Eladamri, Korvecdal FOIL ETCHED M 8.00 20.00
484 Six FOIL ETCHED R 3.00 8.00
485 Arna Kennerüd, Skycaptain FOIL ETCHED M2.00 5.00
486 Breya, Etherium Shaper FOIL ETCHED M 1.50 4.00
487 Genku, Future Shaper FOIL ETCHED R .20 .50
488 Imskir Iron-Eater FOIL ETCHED R .25 .60
489 Kaalia of the Vast FOIL ETCHED M 2.50 6.00
490 Kudo, King Among Bears FOIL ETCHED R .75 2.00
491 Nadu, Winged Wisdom FOIL ETCHED R 8.00 20.00
492 The Necrobloom FOIL ETCHED R 1.25 3.00
493 Phlage, Titan of Fire's Fury FOIL ETCHED M30.00 80.00
494 Rosheen, Roaring Prophet FOIL ETCHED R.12 .30
497 Plains C .20 .50
498 Plains C .20 .50
499 Island C .20 .50
500 Island C 1.25 3.00
501 Swamp C 1.00 2.50
502 Swamp C .60 1.50
503 Mountain C .30 .75
504 Mountain C .30 .75
505 Forest C .30 .75
506 Forest C .30 .75
514 Unstable Amulet U 12.00 30.00
516 Scurry of Gremlins U 2.50 6.00
507 Glaring Fleshraker RIPPLE FOIL U .30 .75
508 Wastescape Battlemage RIPPLE FOIL U 2.00 5.00
509 Jolted Awake RIPPLE FOIL C 2.00 5.00
510 Bespoke Battlewagon RIPPLE FOIL U 1.50 4.00
511 Roil Cartographer RIPPLE FOIL U 8.00 20.00
512 Accursed Marauder RIPPLE FOIL C 4.00 10.00
513 Amped Raptor RIPPLE FOIL U 1.50 4.00
515 Izzet Generatorium RIPPLE FOIL U .60 1.50
517 Snapping Voidcraw RIPPLE FOIL C 1.25 3.00
518 Titans' Vanguard RIPPLE FOIL U 1.50 4.00
519 Solar Transformer RIPPLE FOIL U 2.00 5.00
520 Tranquil Landscape RIPPLE FOIL C 8.00 20.00
521 Twisted Landscape RIPPLE FOIL C 2.50 6.00

2024 Magic The Gathering Modern Horizons 3 Commander

1 Disa the Restless M .12 .30
2 Omo, Queen of Vesuva M .15 .40
3 Satya, Aetherflux Genius M .20 .50
4 Ulalek, Fused Atrocity M 1.25 3.00
5 Azlask, the Swelling Scourge M .40 1.00
6 Cayth, Famed Mechanist M .20 .50
7 Coram, the Undertaker M .20 .50
8 Jyoti, Moag Ancient M .15 .40
9 Azlask, the Swelling Scourge M 1.00 2.50
10 Cayth, Famed Mechanist M .12 .30
11 Coram, the Undertaker M .30 .75
12 Disa the Restless M .20 .50
13 Jyoti, Moag Ancient M .25 .60
14 Omo, Queen of Vesuva M .60 1.50
15 Satya, Aetherflux Genius M .20 .50
16 Ulalek, Fused Atrocity M 2.00 5.00
25 Azlask, the Swelling Scourge M .50 1.25
26 Cayth, Famed Mechanist M .12 .30
27 Coram, the Undertaker M .40 1.00
28 Disa the Restless M .15 .40
29 Jyoti, Moag Ancient M .12 .30
30 Omo, Queen of Vesuva M .20 .50
31 Satya, Aetherflux Genius M .25 .60
32 Eldrazi Confluence R 2.00 5.00
33 Eldritch Immunity R 6.00 15.00
34 Inversion Behemoth R .12 .30
35 Selective Obliteration R .40 1.00
36 Spawnbed Protector R 5.00 12.00
37 Twins of Discord R .25 .60
38 Ulamog's Dreadsire R 1.00 2.50
39 Angelic Aberration R .30 .75
40 Hourglass of the Lost R .40 1.00
41 Localized Destruction R .12 .30
42 Razorfield Ripper R .10 .25
43 Salvation Colossus R .25 .60
44 Silverquill Lecturer R .25 .60
45 Aurora Shifter R .12 .30
46 Benthic Anomaly R .20 .50
47 Copy Land R 1.00 2.50
48 March from Velis Vel R .20 .50
49 Wonderscape Sage R .12 .30
50 Barrowgoyf R 2.50 6.00
51 Bismuth Mindrender R .12 .30
52 Final Act R 1.50 4.00
53 Mutated Cultist R 2.00 5.00
54 Aether Refinery R .25 .60
55 Blaster Hulk R .10 .25
56 Filigree Racer R .10 .25
57 Hideous Taskmaster R 1.00 2.50
58 Overclocked Electromancer R .10 .25
59 Pyrogoyf R .40 1.00
60 Sawhorn Nemesis R .75 2.00
61 Siege-Gang Lieutenant R 1.25 3.00
62 Tempt with Mayhem R .50 1.25
63 Chittering Dispatcher R .40 1.00
64 Desert Warfare R .50 1.25
65 Polygoyf R .20 .50
66 Rampant Frogantua R .50 1.25
67 Sage of the Maze R .25 .60
68 Tarmogoyf Nest R .40 1.00
69 Aggressive Biomancy R .25 .60
70 Bloodbraid Challenger R .25 .60
71 Broodmate Tyrant R .15 .40
72 Exterminator Magmarch R .20 .50
73 Gluttonous Hellkite R .25 .60
74 Infested Thrinax R .12 .30
75 Sphinx of the Revelation R .30 .75
76 Conversion Apparatus R .20 .50
77 Stone Idol Generator R .15 .40
78 Horizon of Progress R 3.00 8.00
79 Lazotep Quarry R 1.25 3.00
80 Planar Nexus R 8.00 20.00
81 Sunken Palace R .50 1.25
82 Talon Gates of Madara R 8.00 20.00
83 Trenchpost R .40 1.00
92 Hourglass of the Lost R .40 1.00
93 Localized Destruction R .10 .25
94 Razorfield Ripper R .10 .25
95 Salvation Colossus R .10 .25
96 Silverquill Lecturer R .20 .50
97 Aurora Shifter R .10 .25
99 Copy Land R .60 1.50
100 March from Velis Vel R .15 .40
101 Wonderscape Sage R .10 .25
102 Barrowgoyf R 4.00 10.00
104 Final Act R 1.25 3.00
106 Aether Refinery R .20 .50
107 Blaster Hulk R .10 .25
108 Filigree Racer R .08 .20
110 Overclocked Electromancer R .08 .20

111 Pyrogoyf R .20 .50
112 Sawhorn Nemesis R .60 1.50
113 Siege-Gang Lieutenant R 1.00 2.50
114 Tempt with Mayhem R .40 1.00
116 Desert Warfare R .20 .50
117 Polygoyf R .10 .25
118 Rampant Frogantua R .40 1.00
119 Sage of the Maze R .15 .40
120 Tarmogoyf Nest R .25 .60
121 Aggressive Biomancy R .15 .40
122 Bloodbraid Challenger R .10 .25
123 Broodmate Tyrant R .10 .25
124 Exterminator Magmarch R .08 .20
125 Gluttonous Hellkite R .10 .25
126 Infested Thrinax R .10 .25
127 Sphinx of the Revelation R .15 .40
128 Conversion Apparatus R .10 .25
129 Stone Idol Generator R .12 .30
130 Horizon of Progress R 3.00 8.00
131 Lazotep Quarry R 1.25 3.00
132 Planar Nexus R 10.00 25.00
133 Sunken Palace R .40 1.00
134 Talon Gates of Madara R 8.00 20.00
135 Trenchpost R .25 .60
152 All Is Dust M 4.00 10.00
153 Artisan of Kozilek U .15 .40
154 Elder Deep-Fiend R .10 .25
155 Eldrazi Conscription R 3.00 8.00
156 Endbringer R .10 .25
157 Morophon, the Boundless M 2.50 6.00
158 Oblivion Sower M .20 .50
159 Skittering Invasion U .30 .75
160 Ugin, the Ineffable R 1.00 2.50
161 Ulamog's Crusher C .10 .25
162 Warping Wail U .12 .30
163 Aethergeode Miner R .08 .20
164 Aetherstorm Roc R .08 .20
165 Akroma's Will R 5.00 12.00
166 Angel of Invention M .20 .50
167 Austere Command R .20 .50
168 Crib Swap U .10 .25
169 Eldrazi Displacer R .40 1.00
170 Farewell R 2.50 6.00
171 Legion Loyalty M .30 .75
172 Skyclave Apparition R .20 .50
173 Swords to Plowshares U .60 1.50
174 Aethersquall Ancient R .08 .20
175 Aethertide Whale R .08 .20
176 Arcane Denial C 1.00 2.50
177 Bident of Thassa R .25 .60
178 Confiscation Coup R .08 .20
179 Curse of the Swine R .10 .25
180 Deepfathom Skulker R .10 .25
181 Drown in Dreams R .20 .50
182 Drowner of Hope R .10 .25
183 Era of Innovation U .08 .20
184 Evacuation R .10 .25
185 Finale of Revelation M .12 .30
188 Imprisoned in the Moon R .20 .50
189 Midnight Clock R .10 .25
190 Pongify U .75 2.00
191 Propaganda U 1.00 2.50
192 Replication Technique R .08 .20
193 Summary Dismissal R .08 .20
194 Tezzeret's Gambit U .08 .20
195 Treasure Cruise C .10 .25
196 Ugin's Insight R .08 .20
197 Archon of Cruelty M 2.50 6.00
198 Graveshifter U .08 .20
199 Junji, the Midnight Sky M .40 1.00
200 Liliana, Death's Majesty M .20 .50
201 Mortivore R .10 .25
202 Necrogoyf R .08 .20
203 Sifter of Skulls R .25 .60
204 Stitcher's Supplier U .75 2.00
206 Syphon Mind C .10 .25
207 Syr Konrad, the Grim U .30 .75
208 Anger U .75 2.00
209 Chandra's Ignition R 1.25 3.00
210 Combustible Gearhulk M .20 .50
211 Faithless Looting C .12 .30
212 Goldspan Dragon M 6.00 15.00
213 Grenzo, Havoc Raiser R .10 .25
214 Kozilek's Return M .25 .60
215 Lightning Runner M .10 .25
216 Professional Face-Breaker R 1.50 4.00
217 The Reaver Cleaver R 4.00 10.00
219 Ancient Stirrings C .10 .25
220 Apex Devastator M 4.00 10.00
221 Avenger of Zendikar M .75 2.00
222 Awakening Zone R .30 .75
223 Beast Within U .60 1.50
224 Brawn U .10 .25
225 Dryad of the Ilysian Grove R 4.00 10.00
227 Eternal Witness U .50 1.25
228 Floriferous Vinewall C .08 .20
229 Garruk's Uprising U .50 1.25
231 Harmonize U .10 .25
232 Hour of Promise R .08 .20
233 Hydra Broodmaster R .10 .25
234 Ignoble Hierarch R .60 1.50
235 Lhurgoyf R .08 .20
236 Magus of the Candelabra R .10 .25
237 Mana Reflection R 2.00 5.00
238 Poison Dart Frog C .08 .20
239 Rampaging Baloths M .20 .50
240 Rampant Growth C .20 .50
241 Ramunap Excavator R .50 1.25
242 Return of the Wildspeaker R .50 1.25
243 Sakura-Tribe Elder C .60 1.50
245 Scute Swarm R 1.50 4.00
246 Selvala, Heart of the Wilds M 3.00 8.00
247 Skullwinder U .08 .20
248 Sylvan Scrying U .10 .25
249 Terastodon R .10 .25
250 Ulvenwald Hydra M .15 .40
251 Vile Redeemer R .10 .25
252 Vivien Reid M .25 .60
253 World Breaker M 2.50 6.00
257 Brudiclad, Telchor Engineer M .10 .25
258 Deadbridge Chant M .10 .25
259 Deathreap Ritual U .10 .25
260 Eureka Moment C .08 .20
262 Garruk, Apex Predator M .20 .50
263 Grisly Salvage C .08 .20
264 Grist, the Hunger Tide M .75 2.00
265 Growth Spiral C .12 .30
266 Hydroid Krasis R .12 .30
267 Izoni, Thousand-Eyed R .08 .20
268 Kolaghan's Command R .15 .40
269 Maelstrom Pulse R .12 .30
270 Nissa, Steward of Elements M .10 .25
272 Sire of Stagnation M .60 1.50
273 Tatyova, Benthic Druid U .08 .20
274 Terminate C .15 .40
275 Ulamog's Nullifier U .08 .20
276 Urban Evolution U .08 .20
277 Uro, Titan of Nature's Wrath M 1.50 4.00
278 Whirler Virtuoso U .08 .20
279 Ziatora, the Incinerator M .12 .30
280 Aethersphere Harvester R .08 .20
281 Aetherworks Marvel M .50 1.25
283 Arcane Signet C .20 .50
284 Burnished Hart U .08 .20
285 Chromatic Lantern R 1.00 2.50
286 Coalition Relic R .10 .25
287 Coveted Jewel R .12 .30
288 Decoction Module U .10 .25
289 Dreamstone Hedron U .10 .25
290 Eldrazi Monument M 4.00 10.00
291 Everflowing Chalice U .12 .30
292 Expedition Map C .60 1.50
293 Forsaken Monument M 2.50 6.00
294 Gonti's Aether Heart M 1.00 2.50
295 Hedron Archive U .10 .25
296 Herald's Horn U 2.50 6.00
297 Idol of Oblivion U .25 .60
298 Lightning Greaves U 2.50 6.00
299 Maskwood Nexus R 2.00 5.00
300 Mirage Mirror R .20 .50
301 Myr Battlesphere R .10 .25
302 Mystic Forge R .25 .60
303 Oblivion Stone R .10 .25
304 Seer's Sundial R .08 .20
305 Sol Ring U .60 1.50
306 Solemn Simulacrum R .25 .60
307 Talisman of Conviction U .12 .30
308 Talisman of Creativity U .40 1.00
309 Talisman of Curiosity U .12 .30
310 Talisman of Dominance U .40 1.00
311 Talisman of Impulse U .20 .50
312 Talisman of Indulgence U .75 2.00
313 Talisman of Progress U .20 .50
314 Talisman of Resilience U .12 .30
315 Wayfarer's Bauble C .12 .30
316 Adarkar Wastes R .60 1.50
317 Aether Hub U .15 .40
318 Ash Barrens C .08 .20
319 Azorius Chancery U .08 .20
320 Basilisk Gate C .10 .25
321 Battlefield Forge R .40 1.00
322 Blast Zone R .10 .25
323 Bonders' Enclave R .15 .40
324 Brushland R 1.25 3.00
325 Canyon Slough R .10 .25
326 Cascading Cataracts R .50 1.25
327 Castle Vantress R .12 .30
328 Caves of Koilos R .40 1.00
329 Cinder Glade R .10 .25
330 Cloudpost C .10 .25
331 Command Tower C .12 .30
332 Corrupted Crossroads R .10 .25
333 Dakmor Salvage U .12 .30
334 Dark Depths M 1.25 3.00
335 Demolition Field U .20 .50
336 Desert of the Indomitable C .08 .20
338 Dreamroot Cascade R .60 1.50
339 Eldrazi Temple R 4.00 10.00
340 Evolving Wilds C .10 .25
341 Exotic Orchard R .10 .25
342 Flooded Grove R .30 .75
344 Frostboil Snarl R .10 .25
345 Furycalm Snarl R .10 .25
346 Glimmerpost C .10 .25
349 Hidden Nursery C .08 .20
350 Izzet Boilerworks U .10 .25
351 Karplusan Forest R 1.50 4.00
352 Kessig Wolf Run R .10 .25
353 Lair of the Hydra R .12 .30
354 Llanowar Wastes R .75 2.00
355 Lumbering Falls R .08 .20
356 Lush Oasis C .08 .20
357 Mossfire Valley R .08 .20
358 Myriad Landscape U .10 .25
359 Mystic Gate R 1.00 2.50
360 Mystic Monastery U .10 .25
361 Opal Palace C .08 .20
362 Overflowing Basin R .12 .30
363 Path of Ancestry C .10 .25
364 Port Town R .10 .25
365 Prairie Stream R .10 .25
367 Raging Ravine R .08 .20
368 Reliquary Tower U 1.00 2.50
369 Riveteers Overlook C .10 .25
370 Ruins of Oran-Rief R .08 .20
371 Savage Lands U .20 .50
372 Secluded Courtyard U .20 .50
373 Shadowblood Ridge R .10 .25
374 Sheltered Thicket R .08 .20
375 Shivan Reef R .30 .75
376 Shrine of the Forsaken Gods R .10 .25
377 Simic Growth Chamber C .10 .25
379 Smoldering Marsh R .10 .25
380 Spawning Bed U .10 .25
381 Sulfurous Springs R 1.25 3.00
382 Tainted Peak U .10 .25
383 Tainted Wood U .12 .30
384 Tectonic Edge U .10 .25
385 Temple of Abandon R .08 .20
386 Temple of Enlightenment R .10 .25
387 Temple of Epiphany R .10 .25
388 Temple of Malady R .10 .25
389 Temple of Malice R .10 .25
390 Temple of Mystery R .08 .20
391 Temple of Silence R .10 .25
392 Temple of Triumph R .08 .20
393 Tendo Ice Bridge R .12 .30
394 Terramorphic Expanse C .10 .25
395 Thespian's Stage R .30 .75
397 Tomb of the Spirit Dragon U .10 .25
398 Tranquil Thicket C .08 .20
399 Unclaimed Territory U .12 .30
400 Underground River R 2.00 5.00
401 Urza's Mine C .40 1.00
402 Urza's Power Plant C .30 .75
403 Urza's Tower C .40 1.00
404 Vesuva R 4.00 10.00
405 Vineglimmer Snarl R .10 .25
406 Viridescent Bog R .15 .40
407 Volatile Fault U .08 .20
408 Wastes C .50 1.25
409 Yavimaya, Cradle of Growth R 4.00 10.00
410 Yavimaya Coast R .25 .60
411 Rishkar's Expertise R 1.25 3.00

2024 Magic The Gathering Modern Horizons 3 Special Guests

39 Thought-Knot Seer BORDERLESS R 5.00 12.00
40 Prismatic Ending BORDERLESS M 2.00 5.00
41 Dismember BORDERLESS M 3.00 8.00
42 Persist BORDERLESS M 1.00 2.50
43 Expressive Iteration BORDERLESS M 2.00 5.00
44 Solitude BORDERLESS M 10.00 25.00
45 Subtlety BORDERLESS M 8.00 20.00
46 Grief BORDERLESS M 10.00 25.00
47 Fury BORDERLESS M 2.00 5.00
48 Endurance BORDERLESS M 5.00 12.00

2024 Magic The Gathering Modern Horizons 3 Special Guests Foil

39 Thought-Knot Seer BORDERLESS R 5.00 12.00
40 Prismatic Ending BORDERLESS M 4.00 10.00
41 Dismember BORDERLESS M 5.00 12.00
42 Persist BORDERLESS M 2.50 6.00
43 Expressive Iteration BORDERLESS M 3.00 8.00
44 Solitude BORDERLESS M 12.00 30.00
45 Subtlety BORDERLESS M 10.00 25.00
46 Grief BORDERLESS M 10.00 25.00
47 Fury BORDERLESS M 3.00 8.00
48 Endurance BORDERLESS M 10.00 25.00
49 Solitude BORDERLESS TEXTURED M 20.00 50.00
50 Subtlety BORDERLESS TEXTURED M 15.00 40.00
51 Grief BORDERLESS TEXTURED M 20.00 50.00
52 Fury BORDERLESS TEXTURED M 8.00 20.00
53 Endurance BORDERLESS TEXTURED M 20.00 50.00

2024 Magic The Gathering Murders at Karlov Manor

1 Case of the Shattered Pact U .05 .12
3 Assemble the Players R .10 .25
4 Aurelia's Vindicator M .30 .75
6 Call a Surprise Witness U .05 .12
8 Case of the Gateway Express U .10 .25
10 Case of the Uneaten Feast R .15 .40
12 Delney, Streetwise Lookout M 6.00 15.00
13 Doorkeeper Thrull R .60 1.50
16 Forum Familiar U .05 .12
20 Karlov Watchdog U .05 .12
27 No Witnesses R .10 .25
29 Novice Inspector C .12 .30
34 Tenth District Hero R .05 .12
35 Unyielding Gatekeeper R .08 .20
36 Wojek Investigator R .12 .30
37 Wrench U .05 .12
43 Candlestick U .05 .12
44 Case of the Filched Falcon U .08 .20
45 Case of the Ransacked Lab R .50 1.25
47 Conspiracy Unraveler M .20 .50
48 Coveted Falcon R .10 .25
50 Cryptic Coat R .50 1.25
51 Curious Inquiry U .05 .12
52 Deduce C .08 .20
55 Exit Specialist U .05 .12
57 Forensic Gadgeteer R 1.50 4.00
58 Forensic Researcher U .05 .12
61 Intrude on the Mind M .12 .30
64 Lost in the Maze R .10 .25
65 Mistway Spy U .05 .12
67 Proft's Eidetic Memory R 1.25 3.00
70 Reenact the Crime R .15 .40
71 Steamcore Scholar R .10 .25
74 Unauthorized Exit C .05 .12
77 Barbed Servitor R .10 .25
80 Case of the Stashed Skeleton R .40 1.00
83 Deadly Cover-Up R .25 .60
84 Extract a Confession C .05 .12
86 Homicide Investigator R .05 .12
87 Hunted Bonebrute R .10 .25
88 Illicit Masquerade R .10 .25
92 Long Goodbye U .12 .30
93 Macabre Reconstruction C .05 .12
94 Massacre Girl, Known Killer M 4.00 10.00
96 Nightdrinker Moroii U .05 .12
97 Outrageous Robbery R .40 1.00
98 Persuasive Interrogators U .05 .12
103 Slice from the Shadows C .05 .12
105 Snarling Gorehound C .08 .20
106 Soul Enervation U .05 .12
108 Undercity Eliminator U .05 .12
109 Unscrupulous Agent C .05 .12
110 Vein Ripper M 12.00 30.00
111 Anzrag's Rampage R .12 .30
114 Case of the Crimson Pulse R .25 .60
115 Caught Red-Handed U .05 .12
118 Connecting the Dots R .12 .30
119 Convenient Target U .08 .20
121 Crime Novelist U .75 2.00
122 Demand Answers C .25 .60
123 Expedited Inheritance M .12 .30
124 Expose the Culprit U .05 .12
126 Frantic Scapegoat U .05 .12
127 Fugitive Codebreaker R .25 .60
128 Galvanize C .05 .12
132 Incinerator of the Guilty M .40 1.00
135 Krenko, Baron of Tin Street R .10 .25
136 Krenko's Buzzcrusher R .10 .25
137 Lamplight Phoenix R .05 .12
140 Pyrotechnic Performer R .10 .25
144 Shock C .05 .12
146 Torch the Witness U .05 .12
147 Vengeful Tracker U .05 .12
148 Aftermath Analyst U 1.50 4.00
149 Airtight Alibi C .05 .12
150 Analyze the Pollen R .10 .25
151 Archdruid's Charm R 5.00 12.00
152 Audience with Trostani R .10 .25
153 Axebane Ferox R .10 .25
155 Case of the Locked Hothouse R 2.00 5.00
156 Case of the Trampled Garden U .08 .20
157 Chalk Outline U .05 .12
160 Flourishing Bloom-Kin U .08 .20
161 Get a Leg Up U .05 .12
164 Hard-Hitting Question U .10 .25
166 Hide in Plain Sight R .05 .12
167 A Killer Among Us U .05 .12
168 Loxodon Eavesdropper C .05 .12
169 Nervous Gardener C .05 .12
170 Pick Your Poison C 1.25 3.00
172 The Pride of Hull Clade M 1.00 2.50
173 Rope U .05 .12
174 Rubblebelt Maverick C .05 .12
176 Sharp-Eyed Rookie R .08 .20
177 Slime Against Humanity C 1.00 2.50
178 They Went This Way C .05 .12
179 Topiary Panther C .05 .12
181 Undergrowth Recon M 2.00 5.00
184 Agrus Kos, Spirit of Justice M .10 .25
185 Alquist Proft, Master Sleuth M .15 .40
186 Anzrag, the Quake-Mole M 1.50 4.00
187 Assassin's Trophy R 2.00 5.00
188 Aurelia, the Law Above R .75 2.00
189 Blood Spatter Analysis R .05 .12
190 Break Out U .10 .25
191 Buried in the Garden U .05 .12
192 Coerced to Kill U .05 .12
196 Detective's Satchel U .05 .12
198 Doppelgang R .75 2.00
199 Drag the Canal R .05 .12
200 Etrata, Deadly Fugitive M .50 1.25
202 Ezrim, Agency Chief R .08 .20
203 Faerie Snoop C .05 .12
205 Gleaming Geardrake U .08 .20
206 Granite Witness C .05 .12
207 Ill-Timed Explosion R .10 .25
208 Insidious Roots U .75 2.00
209 Izoni, Center of the Web R .08 .20
210 Judith, Carnage Connoisseur R .15 .40
211 Kaya, Spirits' Justice M .20 .50
212 Kellan, Inquisitive Prodigy //
Tail the Suspect R .20 .50
214 Kylox, Visionary Inventor R .05 .12
215 Kylox's Voltstrider M .10 .25
216 Lazav, Wearer of Faces R .10 .25
217 Leyline of the Guildpact R 4.00 10.00
218 Lightning Helix U .10 .25
220 Niv-Mizzet, Guildpact R .10 .25
221 No More Lies U .50 1.25
222 Officious Interrogation R .10 .25
224 Rakdos, Patron of Chaos M 4.00 10.00
226 Relive the Past R .05 .12
227 Repulsive Mutation U .12 .30
228 Riftburst Hellion C .05 .12
232 Soul Search U .05 .12
234 Teysa, Opulent Oligarch R .10 .25
236 Tolsimir, Midnight's Light R .10 .25
237 Treacherous Greed R .10 .25
238 Trostani, Three Whispers M .30 .75
240 Urgent Necropsy M .10 .25
241 Vannifar, Evolved Enigma M .20 .50
242 Warleader's Call R 4.00 10.00
243 Wispdrinker Vampire U .10 .25
244 Worldsoul's Rage R .40 1.00
245 Yarus, Roar of the Old Gods R .08 .20
247 Flotsam // Jetsam U .05 .12
257 Thinking Cap C .05 .12
258 Branch of Vitu-Ghazi U .05 .12
259 Commercial District R 5.00 12.00
260 Elegant Parlor R 8.00 20.00
261 Escape Tunnel C .10 .25
262 Hedge Maze R 5.00 12.00
263 Lush Portico R 2.50 6.00
264 Meticulous Archive R 5.00 12.00
265 Public Thoroughfare C .05 .12
266 Raucous Theater R 4.00 10.00
267 Scene of the Crime U .10 .25
268 Shadowy Backstreet R 4.00 10.00
269 Thundering Falls R 5.00 12.00
270 Undercity Sewers R 8.00 20.00
271 Underground Mortuary R 8.00 20.00
272 Plains IMPOSSIBLE L .20 .50
273 Island IMPOSSIBLE L .20 .50
274 Swamp IMPOSSIBLE L .20 .50
275 Mountain IMPOSSIBLE L .12 .30
276 Forest IMPOSSIBLE L .10 .25
277 Plains L .05 .12
278 Plains L .05 .12
279 Island L .05 .12
280 Island L .05 .12
281 Swamp L .05 .12
282 Swamp L .05 .12
283 Mountain L .05 .12
284 Mountain L .05 .12
285 Forest L .05 .12
286 Forest L .05 .12
287 Assemble the Players
MAGNIFIED SHOWCASE R .12 .30
288 Auspicious Arrival MAGNIFIED SHOWCASE C .05 .12
289 Call a Surprise Witness
MAGNIFIED SHOWCASE U .08 .20
291 Not on My Watch MAGNIFIED SHOWCASE U .05 .12
293 Deduce MAGNIFIED SHOWCASE C .08 .20
295 Fae Flight MAGNIFIED SHOWCASE U .05 .12
296 Intrude on the Mind
MAGNIFIED SHOWCASE M .20 .50
297 Reenact the Crime MAGNIFIED SHOWCASE R .12 .30
298 Unauthorized Exit MAGNIFIED SHOWCASE C .05 .12
300 Murder MAGNIFIED SHOWCASE C .05 .12
301 Slice from the Shadows
MAGNIFIED SHOWCASE C .05 .12
302 Soul Enervation MAGNIFIED SHOWCASE U .08 .20
303 Anzrag's Rampage MAGNIFIED SHOWCASE R .10 .25
305 Convenient Target MAGNIFIED SHOWCASE U .05 .12
306 Demand Answers MAGNIFIED SHOWCASE C .12 .30

308 Analyze the Pollen MAGNIFIED SHOWCASE R .20 .50
309 Audience with Trostani MAGNIFIED SHOWCASE R .08 .20
310 Fanatical Strength MAGNIFIED SHOWCASE C .05 .12
311 Coerced to Kill MAGNIFIED SHOWCASE U .05 .12
313 Insidious Roots MAGNIFIED SHOWCASE U .60 1.50
314 Officious Interrogation MAGNIFIED SHOWCASE R .10 .25
315 Warleader's Call MAGNIFIED SHOWCASE R 4.00 10.00
316 Worldsoul's Rage MAGNIFIED SHOWCASE R 1.00 2.50
317 Aurelia, the Law Above RAVNICA SHOWCASE R 1.25 3.00
317 Aurelia, the Law Above SERIAL RAV SHOWCASE FOIL R 800.00 2,000.00
318 Lazav, Wearer of Faces RAVNICA SHOWCASE R .25 .60
319 Niv-Mizzet, Guildpact RAVNICA SHOWCASE R .20 .50
319 Niv-Mizzet, Guildpact SERIAL RAV SHOWCASE FOIL R 500.00 1,200.00
320 Rakdos, Patron of Chaos RAVNICA SHOWCASE M 4.00 10.00
320 Rakdos, Patron of Chaos SERIAL RAV SHOWCASE FOIL M 500.00 1,200.00
321 Teysa, Opulent Oligarch RAVNICA SHOWCASE R 1.00 2.50
321 Teysa, Opulent Oligarch SERIAL RAV SHOWCASE FOIL R 500.00 1,200.00
322 Trostani, Three Whispers RAVNICA SHOWCASE M 1.25 3.00
322 Trostani, Three Whispers SERIAL RAV SHOWCASE FOIL M 500.00 1,200.00
323 Vannifar, Evolved Enigma RAVNICA SHOWCASE M .75 2.00
323 Vannifar, Evolved Enigma SERIAL RAV SHOWCASE FOIL M 500.00 1,200.00
324 Commercial District BORDERLESS R 6.00 15.00
325 Elegant Parlor BORDERLESS R 12.00 30.00
326 Hedge Maze BORDERLESS R 8.00 20.00
327 Lush Portico BORDERLESS R 4.00 10.00
328 Meticulous Archive BORDERLESS R 8.00 20.00
329 Raucous Theater BORDERLESS R 6.00 15.00
330 Shadowy Backstreet BORDERLESS R 6.00 15.00
331 Thundering Falls BORDERLESS R 6.00 15.00
332 Undercity Sewers BORDERLESS R 10.00 25.00
333 Underground Mortuary BORDERLESS R 8.00 20.00
334 Kellan, Inquisitive Prodigy // Tail the Suspect BORDERLESS R .25 .60
335 Kaya, Spirits' Justice BORDERLESS M .40 1.00
336 Aurelia's Vindicator DOSSIER SHOWCASE M .25 .60
337 Delney, Streetwise Lookout DOSSIER SHOWCASE M 6.00 15.00
338 Doorkeeper Thrull DOSSIER SHOWCASE R .60 1.50
339 Neighborhood Guardian DOSSIER SHOWCASE U .05 .12
340 Wojek Investigator DOSSIER SHOWCASE R .15 .40
341 Conspiracy Unraveler DOSSIER SHOWCASE M .30 .75
342 Forensic Gadgeteer DOSSIER SHOWCASE R 1.00 2.50
343 Homicide Investigator DOSSIER SHOWCASE R .08 .20
344 Massacre Girl, Known Killer DOSSIER SHOWCASE M 3.00 8.00
346 Vein Ripper DOSSIER SHOWCASE M 10.00 25.00
348 Fugitive Codebreaker DOSSIER SHOWCASE R .25 .60
349 Incinerator of the Guilty DOSSIER SHOWCASE M .20 .50
350 Krenko, Baron of Tin Street DOSSIER SHOWCASE R .10 .25
352 The Pride of Hull Clade DOSSIER SHOWCASE M .75 2.00
353 Sharp-Eyed Rookie DOSSIER SHOWCASE R .10 .25
354 Agrus Kos, Spirit of Justice DOSSIER SHOWCASE M .10 .25
355 Alquist Proft, Master Sleuth DOSSIER SHOWCASE M .12 .30
356 Anzrag, the Quake-Mole DOSSIER SHOWCASE M 1.50 4.00
357 Aurelia, the Law Above DOSSIER SHOWCASE R .50 1.25
359 Etrata, Deadly Fugitive DOSSIER SHOWCASE M .30 .75
360 Ezrim, Agency Chief DOSSIER SHOWCASE R .10 .25
361 Gleaming Geardrake DOSSIER SHOWCASE U .05 .12
362 Izoni, Center of the Web DOSSIER SHOWCASE R .05 .12
363 Judith, Carnage Connoisseur DOSSIER SHOWCASE R .15 .40
364 Kraul Whipcracker DOSSIER SHOWCASE U .05 .12
365 Kylox, Visionary Inventor DOSSIER SHOWCASE R .08 .20
366 Lazav, Wearer of Faces DOSSIER SHOWCASE R .05 .12
367 Meddling Youths DOSSIER SHOWCASE U .05 .12
368 Niv-Mizzet, Guildpact DOSSIER SHOWCASE R .15 .40
369 Rakdos, Patron of Chaos DOSSIER SHOWCASE M 2.00 5.00
370 Teysa, Opulent Oligarch DOSSIER SHOWCASE R .12 .30
371 Tolsimir, Midnight's Light DOSSIER SHOWCASE R .10 .25
372 Trostani, Three Whispers DOSSIER SHOWCASE M .40 1.00
373 Vannifar, Evolved Enigma DOSSIER SHOWCASE M .20 .50
374 Wispdrinker Vampire DOSSIER SHOWCASE U .05 .12
375 Yarus, Roar of the Old Gods DOSSIER SHOWCASE R .10 .25
377 Aurelia's Vindicator INVIS INK SHOWCASE FOIL M 1.25 3.00
378 Delney, Streetwise Lookout INVIS INK SHOWCASE FOIL M 12.00 30.00
379 Conspiracy Unraveler INVIS INK SHOWCASE FOIL M .75 2.00
380 Massacre Girl, Known Killer INVIS INK SHOWCASE FOIL M 6.00 15.00
381 Incinerator of the Guilty INVIS INK SHOWCASE FOIL M 1.50 4.00
382 The Pride of Hull Clade INVIS INK SHOWCASE FOIL M 2.00 5.00
383 Agrus Kos, Spirit of Justice INVIS INK SHOWCASE FOIL M .50 1.25
384 Alquist Proft, Master Sleuth INVIS INK SHOWCASE FOIL M 1.25 3.00
385 Anzrag, the Quake-Mole INVIS INK SHOWCASE FOIL M 4.00 10.00
386 Etrata, Deadly Fugitive INVIS INK SHOWCASE FOIL M 3.00 8.00
387 Rakdos, Patron of Chaos INVIS INK SHOWCASE FOIL M 3.00 8.00
388 Trostani, Three Whispers INVIS INK SHOWCASE FOIL M 1.25 3.00
389 Vannifar, Evolved Enigma INVIS INK SHOWCASE FOIL M 1.25 3.00
390 No Witnesses EXT ART R .10 .25
391 Tenth District Hero EXT ART R .08 .20
392 Unyielding Gatekeeper EXT ART R .10 .25
393 Coveted Falcon EXT ART R .10 .25
394 Cryptic Coat EXT ART R 1.00 2.50
395 Lost in the Maze EXT ART R .12 .30
396 Proft's Eidetic Memory EXT ART R 1.50 4.00
397 Steamcore Scholar EXT ART R .10 .25
398 Barbed Servitor EXT ART R .10 .25
399 Deadly Cover-Up EXT ART R .50 1.25
400 Hunted Bonebrute EXT ART R .15 .40
401 Illicit Masquerade EXT ART R .08 .20
402 Outrageous Robbery EXT ART R .50 1.25
403 Connecting the Dots EXT ART R .10 .25
404 Expedited Inheritance EXT ART M .20 .50
405 Krenko's Buzzcrusher EXT ART R .20 .50
406 Lamplight Phoenix EXT ART R .08 .20
407 Pyrotechnic Performer EXT ART R .10 .25
408 Archdruid's Charm EXT ART R 5.00 12.00
409 Axebane Ferox EXT ART R .10 .25
410 Hide in Plain Sight EXT ART R .08 .20
411 Undergrowth Recon EXT ART M 2.50 6.00
412 Assassin's Trophy EXT ART R 1.25 3.00
413 Blood Spatter Analysis EXT ART R .05 .12
414 Doppelgang EXT ART R 1.25 3.00
415 Drag the Canal EXT ART R .08 .20
416 Ill-Timed Explosion EXT ART R .20 .50
417 Kylox's Voltstrider EXT ART M .12 .30
418 Leyline of the Guildpact EXT ART R 4.00 10.00
419 Relive the Past EXT ART R .05 .12
420 Treacherous Greed EXT ART R .10 .25
421 Urgent Necropsy EXT ART M .25 .60
422 Cryptex EXT ART R .05 .12
433 Vein Ripper INVIS INK SHOWCASE M 15.00 40.00

2024 Magic The Gathering Murders at Karlov Manor Commander

1 Kaust, Eyes of the Glade FOIL M .05 .12
2 Mirko, Obsessive Theorist FOIL M .08 .20
3 Morska, Undersea Sleuth FOIL M .10 .25
4 Nelly Borca, Impulsive Accuser FOIL M .10 .25
5 Duskana, the Rage Mother FOIL M .12 .30
6 Feather, Radiant Arbiter FOIL M .12 .30
7 Marvo, Deep Operative FOIL M .12 .30
8 Sophia, Dogged Detective FOIL M .10 .25
9 Armed with Proof R .08 .20
10 Immortal Obligation R .10 .25
11 Merchant of Truth R .12 .30
12 Otherworldly Escort R .05 .12
13 Redemption Arc R .20 .50
14 Serene Sleuth R .08 .20
15 Trouble in Pairs R 12.00 30.00
16 True Identity R .10 .25
17 Unexplained Absence R .25 .60
18 Veiled Ascension R .08 .20
19 Case of the Shifting Visage R .08 .20
20 Copy Catchers R .05 .12
21 Detective of the Month R .08 .20
22 Final-Word Phantom R .10 .25
23 Follow the Bodies R .05 .12
24 Tangletrove Kelp R .10 .25
25 Watcher of Hours R .08 .20
26 Charnel Serenade R .05 .12
27 Eye of Duskmantle R .05 .12
28 Foreboding Steamboat R .05 .12
29 Unshakable Tail R .10 .25
30 Boltbender R .08 .20
31 Havoc Eater R .08 .20
32 Hot Pursuit R .10 .25
33 Mob Verdict R .10 .25
34 Prisoner's Dilemma R .50 1.25
35 Showstopping Surprise R .05 .12
36 Tesak, Judith's Hellhound R .08 .20
37 Experiment Twelve R .08 .20
38 Innocuous Researcher R .08 .20
39 On the Trail R .30 .75
40 Printlifter Ooze R .08 .20
41 Counterpoint R .08 .20
42 Knowledge Is Power R .10 .25
43 Take the Bait R .50 1.25
44 Panoptic Projektor R .10 .25
45 Ransom Note R .05 .12
46 Ransom Note R .05 .12
47 Ransom Note R .05 .12
48 Ransom Note R .05 .12
49 Kaust, Eyes of the Glade THICK STOCK FOIL M .10 .25
50 Mirko, Obsessive Theorist THICK STOCK FOIL M .10 .25
51 Morska, Undersea Sleuth THICK STOCK FOIL M .10 .25
52 Nelly Borca, Impulsive Accuser THICK STOCK FOIL M .10 .25
53 Ugin's Mastery R .12 .30
54 Aerial Extortionist R .15 .40
55 Angel of the Ruins R .10 .25
56 Austere Command R .20 .50
57 Bennie Bracks, Zoologist M 4.00 10.00
58 Comeuppance R .30 .75
59 Darien, King of Kjeldor R .12 .30
60 Duelist's Heritage R .12 .30
61 Dusk // Dawn R .10 .25
62 Elspeth, Sun's Champion M .50 1.25
63 Exalted Angel R .10 .25
64 Farewell R 3.00 8.00
65 Fell the Mighty R .08 .20
66 Fumigate R .12 .30
67 Ghostly Prison U 2.00 5.00
68 Gideon's Sacrifice C .05 .12
69 Hidden Dragonslayer R .05 .12
70 Keeper of the Accord R .12 .30
71 Loran of the Third Path R 2.00 5.00
72 Martial Impetus U .05 .12
73 Master of Pearls R .05 .12
74 Mastery of the Unseen R .05 .12
75 Mirror Entity R .12 .30
76 Organic Extinction R .40 1.00
77 Orzhov Advokist U .05 .12
78 Path to Exile U .50 1.25
79 Promise of Loyalty R .10 .25
80 Seal of Cleansing U .05 .12
81 Search the Premises R .08 .20
82 Selfless Squire R .10 .25
83 Sevinne's Reclamation R .10 .25
84 Smuggler's Share R .75 2.00
85 Soul Snare U .05 .12
86 Stalking Leonin R .05 .12
87 Sun Titan M .15 .40
88 Swords to Plowshares U .60 1.50
89 Vow of Duty U .05 .12
90 Wall of Omens U .10 .25
91 Welcoming Vampire R .30 .75
92 Windborn Muse R .10 .25
93 Winds of Rath R .10 .25
94 Alandra, Sky Dreamer R .30 .75
95 Amphin Mutineer R .05 .12
96 Brainstorm C .75 2.00
97 Confirm Suspicions R .08 .20
98 Consider C .40 1.00
99 Curate C .05 .12
100 Deep Analysis C .05 .12
101 Dream Eater M .08 .20
102 Enhanced Surveillance U .05 .12
103 Ephara's Dispersal C .05 .12
104 Erdwal Illuminator U .08 .20
105 Ethereal Investigator R .10 .25
106 Finale of Revelation M .10 .25
107 Junk Winder U .10 .25
108 Kappa Cannoneer R 1.50 4.00
109 Mechanized Production M .30 .75
110 Mission Briefing R .08 .20
111 Mulldrifter U .10 .25
112 Nadir Kraken R .10 .25
113 Nightveil Sprite U .05 .12
114 Ongoing Investigation U .05 .12
115 Otherworldly Gaze C .10 .25
116 Phyrexian Metamorph R 3.00 8.00
117 Shimmer Dragon R .10 .25
118 Sphinx of the Second Sun M .40 1.00
119 Teferi's Ageless Insight R 1.00 2.50
120 Tezzeret, Betrayer of Flesh M .15 .40
121 Thought Monitor R .75 2.00
122 Thoughtbound Phantasm U .05 .12
123 Vizier of Many Faces R .10 .25
124 Whirler Rogue U .05 .12
125 Animate Dead U 2.50 6.00
126 Black Sun's Zenith R .20 .50
127 Dogged Detective R .08 .20
128 Doom Whisperer M .25 .60
129 Grave Titan M .75 2.00
130 Massacre Wurm M .60 1.50
131 Necromancy U 3.00 8.00
132 Overseer of the Damned R .10 .25
133 Phyrexian Arena R 2.00 5.00
134 Pile On R .10 .25
135 Price of Fame U .05 .12
136 Ravenous Chupacabra U .12 .30
137 Reanimate R 4.00 10.00
138 Rise of the Dark Realms M 5.00 12.00
139 Shriekmaw U .10 .25
140 Sinister Starfish C .05 .12
141 Syr Konrad, the Grim U .50 1.25
142 Toxic Deluge R 4.00 10.00
143 Twilight Prophet M 1.00 2.50
144 Whispering Snitch U .05 .12
145 Agitator Ant R .08 .20
146 Akroma, Angel of Fury M .12 .30
147 Ashcloud Phoenix M .08 .20
148 Brash Taunter R .50 1.25
149 Chaos Warp R .25 .60
150 Curse of Opulence U .40 1.00
151 Disrupt Decorum R .10 .25
152 Etali, Primal Storm R .20 .50
153 Fiendish Duo M .30 .75
154 Frontier Warmonger R .05 .12
155 Imperial Hellkite R .05 .12
156 Jeska's Will R 10.00 25.00
157 Kazuul, Tyrant of the Cliffs U .08 .20
158 Neheb, the Eternal M .75 2.00
159 Rite of the Raging Storm U .08 .20
160 Scourge of the Throne R .10 .25
161 Shiny Impetus U .05 .12
162 Spectacular Showdown R .10 .25
163 Vengeful Ancestor R .15 .40
164 Vow of Lightning U .05 .12
165 Ainok Survivalist U .05 .12
166 Beast Whisperer R 1.00 2.50
167 Broodhatch Nantuko U .05 .12
168 Deathmist Raptor M .08 .20
169 Den Protector R .08 .20
170 Graf Mole U .05 .12
171 Hooded Hydra M .15 .40
172 Hornet Queen R .10 .25
173 Jolrael, Mwonvuli Recluse R .08 .20
174 Killer Service R .10 .25
175 Krosan Cloudscraper R .05 .12
176 Krosan Colossus U .05 .12
177 Nantuko Vigilante C .05 .12
178 Nature's Lore U .75 2.00
179 Obscuring Aether R .05 .12
180 Ohran Frostfang R 1.00 2.50
181 Return of the Wildspeaker R .40 1.00
182 Root Elemental R .08 .20
183 Sakura-Tribe Elder C .50 1.25
184 Salt Road Ambushers U .05 .12
185 Saryth, the Viper's Fang R .25 .60
186 Seedborn Muse R 5.00 12.00
187 Temur War Shaman R .05 .12
188 Thelonite Hermit R .08 .20
189 Three Visits U 2.50 6.00
190 Tireless Tracker R .25 .60
191 Toski, Bearer of Secrets R 4.00 10.00
192 Trail of Mystery R .05 .12
193 Ulvenwald Mysteries U .05 .12
194 Whisperwood Elemental M .10 .25
195 Wild Growth C .15 .40
196 Wilderness Reclamation U .40 1.00
197 Yedora, Grave Gardener U .05 .12
198 Adrix and Nev, Twincasters M 2.50 6.00
199 Anya, Merciless Angel M .10 .25
200 Baleful Strix R .30 .75
201 Boros Reckoner R .08 .20
202 Chulane, Teller of Tales M .40 1.00
203 Connive // Concoct R .05 .12
204 Decimate R .08 .20
205 Deflecting Palm R .20 .50
206 Dimir Spybug U .05 .12
207 Discovery // Dispersal U .05 .12
208 Disinformation Campaign U .05 .12
209 Disorder in the Court R .08 .20
210 Esix, Fractal Bloom M .12 .30
211 Gisela, Blade of Goldnight M .50 1.25
212 Hydroid Krasis M .20 .50
213 Koma, Cosmos Serpent M 2.50 6.00
214 Lazav, the Multifarious R .10 .25
215 Lonis, Cryptozoologist R .08 .20
216 Master of Death R .05 .12
217 Notion Rain C .05 .12
218 Selvala, Explorer Returned R .08 .20
219 Sidar Kondo of Jamuraa M .15 .40
220 Wavesifter C .05 .12
221 Academy Manufactor R 2.00 5.00
222 Ancient Stone Idol R .10 .25
223 Arcane Signet C .12 .30
224 Azorius Signet U .12 .30
225 Bloodthirsty Blade U .10 .25
226 Dimir Signet U .15 .40
227 Everflowing Chalice U .12 .30
228 Fellwar Stone U .40 1.00
229 Idol of Oblivion R .25 .60
230 Inspiring Statuary R .12 .30
231 Lifecrafter's Bestiary R .10 .25
232 Mind Stone U .10 .25
233 Nettlecyst R .75 2.00
234 Psychosis Crawler R .12 .30
235 Scroll of Fate R .08 .20
236 Simic Signet U .10 .25
237 Sol Ring U .60 1.50
238 Solemn Simulacrum R .25 .60
239 Steel Hellkite R .12 .30
240 Talisman of Conviction U .10 .25
241 Talisman of Curiosity U .12 .30
242 Talisman of Dominance U .30 .75
243 Talisman of Progress U .20 .50
244 Talisman of Unity U .15 .40
245 Thought Vessel U .60 1.50
246 Tome of Legends R .15 .40
247 Access Tunnel U .12 .30
248 Ash Barrens U .05 .12
249 Azorius Chancery C .08 .20
250 Bojuka Bog C .60 1.50
251 Boros Garrison U .10 .25
252 Canopy Vista R .10 .25
253 Castle Ardenvale R .10 .25
254 Choked Estuary R .10 .25
255 Cinder Glade R .10 .25
256 Command Tower C .10 .25
257 Darkwater Catacombs R .10 .25
258 Dimir Aqueduct U .10 .25
259 Drownyard Temple R .08 .20
260 Exotic Orchard R .10 .25
261 Fetid Pools R .10 .25
262 Fortified Village R .08 .20
263 Furycalm Snarl R .10 .25
264 Game Trail R .10 .25
265 Gruul Turf U .10 .25
266 Hostile Desert R .08 .20
267 Irrigated Farmland R .08 .20
268 Jungle Shrine U .10 .25
269 Kessig Wolf Run R .10 .25
270 Kher Keep R .10 .25
271 Krosan Verge U .08 .20
272 Labyrinth of Skophos R .08 .20
273 Lonely Sandbar U .10 .25
274 Mossfire Valley R .08 .20
275 Mosswort Bridge R .12 .30
276 Myriad Landscape U .10 .25
277 Mystic Sanctuary C .60 1.50
278 Needle Spires R .08 .20
279 Path of Ancestry C .08 .20
280 Port of Karfell U .05 .12
281 Prairie Stream R .10 .25
282 Reliquary Tower U 1.00 2.50
283 River of Tears R .10 .25
284 Rogue's Passage U .10 .25
285 Sacred Peaks C .08 .20
286 Scattered Groves R .08 .20
287 Scavenger Grounds R .12 .30
288 Seaside Citadel U .15 .40
289 Secluded Steppe C .08 .20
290 Selesnya Sanctuary U .08 .20
291 Sheltered Thicket R .08 .20
292 Shrine of the Forsaken Gods R .10 .25
293 Simic Growth Chamber U .10 .25
294 Skycloud Expanse R .08 .20
295 Slayers' Stronghold R .10 .25
296 Spire of Industry R .10 .25
297 Sungrass Prairie R .08 .20
298 Sunhome, Fortress of the Legion U .08 .20
299 Sunken Hollow R .10 .25
300 Tainted Isle U .12 .30
301 Temple of Abandon R .08 .20
302 Temple of Enlightenment R .08 .20
303 Temple of Mystery R .08 .20
304 Temple of Plenty R .08 .20
305 Temple of the False God U .08 .20
306 Temple of Triumph R .08 .20
307 Throne of the High City R .08 .20
308 Tocasia's Dig Site C .05 .12
309 Tranquil Thicket C .08 .20
310 War Room R .75 2.00
311 Zoetic Cavern U .05 .12
312 Duskana, the Rage Mother EXT ART FOIL M 1.00 2.50
312 Duskana, the Rage Mother EXT ART M .75 2.00
313 Feather, Radiant Arbiter EXT ART FOIL M .30 .75
313 Feather, Radiant Arbiter EXT ART M .30 .75

314 Kaust, Eyes of the Glade EXT ART FOIL M .10 .25
314 Kaust, Eyes of the Glade EXT ART M .12 .30
315 Marvo, Deep Operative EXT ART FOIL M .50 1.25
315 Marvo, Deep Operative EXT ART M .40 1.00
316 Mirko, Obsessive Theorist EXT ART FOIL M.20 .50
316 Mirko, Obsessive Theorist EXT ART M .20 .50
317 Morska, Undersea Sleuth EXT ART FOIL M .20 .50
317 Morska, Undersea Sleuth EXT ART M .20 .50
318 Nelly Borca, Impulsive
Accuser EXT ART FOIL M .40 1.00
318 Nelly Borca, Impulsive Accuser EXT ART M.30 .75
319 Sophia, Dogged Detective EXT ART FOIL M.15 .40
319 Sophia, Dogged Detective EXT ART M .20 .50
320 Armed with Proof EXT ART R .10 .25
321 Immortal Obligation EXT ART R .15 .40
322 Merchant of Truth EXT ART R .60 1.50
323 Otherworldly Escort EXT ART R .08 .20
324 Redemption Arc EXT ART R .30 .75
325 Serene Sleuth EXT ART R .05 .12
326 Trouble in Pairs EXT ART R 12.00 30.00
327 True Identity EXT ART R .08 .20
328 Unexplained Absence EXT ART R .50 1.25
329 Veiled Ascension EXT ART R .10 .25
330 Copy Catchers EXT ART R .08 .20
331 Detective of the Month EXT ART R .15 .40
332 Final-Word Phantom EXT ART R .50 1.25
333 Follow the Bodies EXT ART R .10 .25
334 Tangletrove Kelp EXT ART R .25 .60
335 Watcher of Hours EXT ART R .10 .25
336 Charnel Serenade EXT ART R .12 .30
337 Eye of Duskmantle EXT ART R .08 .20
338 Foreboding Steamboat EXT ART R .10 .25
339 Unshakable Tail EXT ART R .15 .40
340 Boltbender EXT ART R .10 .25
341 Havoc Eater EXT ART R .10 .25
342 Hot Pursuit EXT ART R .15 .40
343 Mob Verdict EXT ART R .10 .25
344 Prisoner's Dilemma EXT ART R 1.25 3.00
345 Showstopping Surprise EXT ART R .10 .25
346 Tesak, Judith's Hellhound EXT ART R .20 .50
347 Experiment Twelve EXT ART R .10 .25
348 Innocuous Researcher EXT ART R .10 .25
349 On the Trail EXT ART R .50 1.25
350 Printlifter Ooze EXT ART R .15 .40
351 Counterpoint EXT ART R .15 .40
352 Knowledge Is Power EXT ART R .20 .50
353 Take the Bait EXT ART R 1.25 3.00
354 Panoptic Projektor EXT ART R .10 .25
355 Ransom Note EXT ART R .10 .25
356 Ransom Note EXT ART R .08 .20
357 Ransom Note EXT ART R .08 .20
358 Ransom Note EXT ART R .05 .12

2024 Magic The Gathering Murders at Karlov Manor Foil

1 Case of the Shattered Pact U .08 .20
3 Assemble the Players R .10 .25
4 Aurelia's Vindicator M .50 1.25
6 Call a Surprise Witness U .08 .20
7 Case File Auditor U .05 .12
8 Case of the Gateway Express U .10 .25
9 Case of the Pilfered Proof U .05 .12
10 Case of the Uneaten Feast R .30 .75
12 Delney, Streetwise Lookout M 6.00 15.00
13 Doorkeeper Thrull R 1.00 2.50
15 Essence of Antiquity U .08 .20
20 Karlov Watchdog U .05 .12
21 Krovod Haunch U .05 .12
22 Make Your Move C .05 .12
27 No Witnesses R .10 .25
28 Not on My Watch U .08 .20
29 Novice Inspector C .15 .40
32 Sanctuary Wall U .05 .12
34 Tenth District Hero R .10 .25
35 Unyielding Gatekeeper R .05 .12
36 Wojek Investigator R .10 .25
38 Agency Outfitter U .05 .12
43 Candlestick U .05 .12
44 Case of the Filched Falcon U .10 .25
45 Case of the Ransacked Lab R .50 1.25
47 Conspiracy Unraveler M .40 1.00
48 Coveted Falcon R .12 .30
50 Cryptic Coat R 1.00 2.50
51 Curious Inquiry U .05 .12
52 Deduce C .10 .25
55 Exit Specialist U .05 .12
56 Fae Flight U .08 .20
57 Forensic Gadgeteer R 1.50 4.00
58 Forensic Researcher U .10 .25
61 Intrude on the Mind M .50 1.25
64 Lost in the Maze R .15 .40
66 Out Cold C .05 .12
67 Proft's Eidetic Memory R 1.25 3.00
69 Reasonable Doubt C .05 .12
70 Reenact the Crime R .20 .50
71 Steamcore Scholar R .15 .40
77 Barbed Servitor R .15 .40
79 Case of the Gorgon's Kiss U .05 .12
80 Case of the Stashed Skeleton R .60 1.50
82 Clandestine Meddler U .05 .12
83 Deadly Cover-Up R .30 .75
84 Extract a Confession C .10 .25
86 Homicide Investigator R .10 .25
87 Hunted Bonebrute R .15 .40
88 Illicit Masquerade R .10 .25
89 It Doesn't Add Up R .05 .12
91 Leering Onlooker U .05 .12
92 Long Goodbye U .15 .40
94 Massacre Girl, Known Killer M 5.00 12.00
95 Murder C .08 .20
97 Outrageous Robbery R .50 1.25
98 Persuasive Interrogators U .05 .12
100 Presumed Dead U .05 .12
102 Rot Farm Mortipede C .05 .12
103 Slice from the Shadows C .05 .12
105 Snarling Gorehound C .10 .25
106 Soul Enervation U .08 .20
107 Toxin Analysis C .05 .12
108 Undercity Eliminator U .08 .20
110 Vein Ripper M 12.00 30.00
111 Anzrag's Rampage R .15 .40
114 Case of the Crimson Pulse R .60 1.50
117 Concealed Weapon U .05 .12
118 Connecting the Dots R .12 .30
121 Crime Novelist U 1.00 2.50
122 Demand Answers C .40 1.00
123 Expedited Inheritance M .20 .50
124 Expose the Culprit U .05 .12
126 Frantic Scapegoat U .08 .20
127 Fugitive Codebreaker R .60 1.50
129 Gearbane Orangutan C .05 .12
131 Harried Dronesmith U .05 .12
132 Incinerator of the Guilty M .50 1.25
134 Knife U .05 .12
135 Krenko, Baron of Tin Street R .12 .30
136 Krenko's Buzzcrusher R .10 .25
137 Lamplight Phoenix R .10 .25
140 Pyrotechnic Performer R .12 .30
142 Red Herring C .05 .12
144 Shock C .05 .12
146 Torch the Witness U .08 .20
147 Vengeful Tracker U .08 .20
148 Aftermath Analyst U 2.50 6.00
150 Analyze the Pollen R .12 .30
151 Archdruid's Charm R 5.00 12.00
152 Audience with Trostani R .10 .25
153 Axebane Ferox R .12 .30
155 Case of the Locked Hothouse R 2.50 6.00
156 Case of the Trampled Garden U .10 .25
157 Chalk Outline U .05 .12
159 Fanatical Strength C .05 .12
160 Flourishing Bloom-Kin U .08 .20
161 Get a Leg Up U .08 .20
162 Glint Weaver U .08 .20
163 Greenbelt Radical U .05 .12
164 Hard-Hitting Question U .10 .25
166 Hide in Plain Sight R .08 .20
167 A Killer Among Us U .08 .20
168 Loxodon Eavesdropper C .05 .12
169 Nervous Gardener C .05 .12
170 Pick Your Poison C 1.50 4.00
172 The Pride of Hull Clade M 1.00 2.50
173 Rope U .08 .20
174 Rubblebelt Maverick C .10 .25
176 Sharp-Eyed Rookie R .12 .30
177 Slime Against Humanity C 1.25 3.00
178 They Went This Way C .08 .20
179 Topiary Panther C .05 .12
181 Undergrowth Recon M 2.00 5.00
182 Vengeful Creeper C .05 .12
184 Agrus Kos, Spirit of Justice M .20 .50
185 Alquist Proft, Master Sleuth M .25 .60
186 Anzrag, the Quake-Mole M 2.00 5.00
187 Assassin's Trophy R 2.00 5.00
188 Aurelia, the Law Above R 1.00 2.50
189 Blood Spatter Analysis R .08 .20
190 Break Out U .20 .50
191 Buried in the Garden U .10 .25
192 Coerced to Kill U .05 .12
194 Curious Cadaver U .05 .12
195 Deadly Complication U .05 .12
196 Detective's Satchel U .05 .12
198 Doppelgang R .75 2.00
199 Drag the Canal R .10 .25
200 Etrata, Deadly Fugitive M 1.00 2.50
202 Ezrim, Agency Chief R .10 .25
205 Gleaming Geardrake U .10 .25
207 Ill-Timed Explosion R .15 .40
208 Insidious Roots U 2.00 5.00
209 Izoni, Center of the Web R .12 .30
210 Judith, Carnage Connoisseur R .25 .60
211 Kaya, Spirits' Justice M .25 .60
212 Kellan, Inquisitive Prodigy // T
ail the Suspect R .25 .60
213 Kraul Whipcracker U .05 .12
214 Kylox, Visionary Inventor R .10 .25
215 Kylox's Voltstrider M .12 .30
216 Lazav, Wearer of Faces R .12 .30
217 Leyline of the Guildpact R 4.00 10.00
218 Lightning Helix U .10 .25
219 Meddling Youths U .05 .12
220 Niv-Mizzet, Guildpact R .15 .40
221 No More Lies U .50 1.25
222 Officious Interrogation R .12 .30
223 Private Eye U .05 .12
224 Rakdos, Patron of Chaos M 4.00 10.00
225 Rakish Scoundrel C .05 .12
226 Relive the Past R .08 .20
227 Repulsive Mutation U .20 .50
232 Soul Search U .08 .20
234 Teysa, Opulent Oligarch R .20 .50
236 Tolsimir, Midnight's Light R .20 .50
237 Treacherous Greed R .10 .25
238 Trostani, Three Whispers M .50 1.25
240 Urgent Necropsy M .15 .40
241 Vannifar, Evolved Enigma M .30 .75
242 Warleader's Call R 4.00 10.00
243 Wispdrinker Vampire U .15 .40
244 Worldsoul's Rage R 1.00 2.50
245 Yarus, Roar of the Old Gods R .10 .25
246 Cease // Desist U .05 .12
247 Flotsam // Jetsam U .08 .20
250 Push // Pull U .08 .20
251 Cryptex R .08 .20
255 Magnifying Glass C .05 .12
258 Branch of Vitu-Ghazi U .08 .20
259 Commercial District R 5.00 12.00
260 Elegant Parlor R 5.00 12.00
261 Escape Tunnel C .12 .30
262 Hedge Maze R 5.00 12.00
263 Lush Portico R 2.50 6.00
264 Meticulous Archive R 5.00 12.00
265 Public Thoroughfare C .10 .25
266 Raucous Theater R 4.00 10.00
267 Scene of the Crime U .12 .30
268 Shadowy Backstreet R 4.00 10.00
269 Thundering Falls R 5.00 12.00
270 Undercity Sewers R 8.00 20.00
271 Underground Mortuary R 8.00 20.00
272 Plains IMPOSSIBLE L .25 .60
273 Island IMPOSSIBLE L .25 .60
274 Swamp IMPOSSIBLE L .40 1.00
275 Mountain IMPOSSIBLE L .20 .50
276 Forest IMPOSSIBLE L .15 .40
277 Plains L .05 .12
278 Plains L .05 .12
279 Island L .05 .12
280 Island L .05 .12
281 Swamp L .05 .12
282 Swamp L .05 .12
283 Mountain L .05 .12
284 Mountain L .05 .12
285 Forest L .08 .20
286 Forest L .08 .20
287 Assemble the Players
MAGNIFIED SHOWCASE R .25 .60
289 Call a Surprise Witness
MAGNIFIED SHOWCASE U .08 .20
290 Makeshift Binding MAGNIFIED SHOWCASE C.05 .12
291 Not on My Watch MAGNIFIED SHOWCASE U.05 .12
292 On the Job MAGNIFIED SHOWCASE C .05 .12
293 Deduce MAGNIFIED SHOWCASE C .10 .25
295 Fae Flight MAGNIFIED SHOWCASE U .05 .12
296 Intrude on the Mind
MAGNIFIED SHOWCASE M .50 1.25
297 Reenact the Crime MAGNIFIED SHOWCASE R.50 1.25
298 Unauthorized Exit MAGNIFIED SHOWCASE C.05 .12
299 It Doesn't Add Up MAGNIFIED SHOWCASE U.05 .12
300 Murder MAGNIFIED SHOWCASE C .05 .12
301 Slice from the Shadows
MAGNIFIED SHOWCASE C .05 .12
302 Soul Enervation MAGNIFIED SHOWCASE U.08 .20
303 Anzrag's Rampage MAGNIFIED SHOWCASE R.20 .50
304 The Chase Is On MAGNIFIED SHOWCASE C.05 .12
305 Convenient Target MAGNIFIED SHOWCASE U.08 .20
306 Demand Answers MAGNIFIED SHOWCASE C.20 .50
307 Expose the Culprit MAGNIFIED SHOWCASE U.05 .12
308 Analyze the Pollen MAGNIFIED SHOWCASE R.50 1.25
309 Audience with Trostani
MAGNIFIED SHOWCASE R .12 .30
310 Fanatical Strength MAGNIFIED SHOWCASE C.05 .12
311 Coerced to Kill MAGNIFIED SHOWCASE U .08 .20
312 Deadly Complication
MAGNIFIED SHOWCASE U .05 .12
313 Insidious Roots MAGNIFIED SHOWCASE U1.25 3.00
314 Officious Interrogation
MAGNIFIED SHOWCASE R .15 .40
315 Warleader's Call MAGNIFIED SHOWCASE R5.00 12.00
316 Worldsoul's Rage MAGNIFIED SHOWCASE R2.00 5.00
317 Aurelia, the Law Above
RAVNICA SHOWCASE R 4.00 10.00
318 Lazav, Wearer of Faces
RAVNICA SHOWCASE R .40 1.00
319 Niv-Mizzet, Guildpact
RAVNICA SHOWCASE R .60 1.50
320 Rakdos, Patron of Chaos
RAVNICA SHOWCASE M 5.00 12.00
321 Teysa, Opulent Oligarch
RAVNICA SHOWCASE R 2.00 5.00
322 Trostani, Three Whispers
RAVNICA SHOWCASE M 4.00 10.00
323 Vannifar, Evolved Enigma
RAVNICA SHOWCASE M 4.00 10.00
324 Commercial District BORDERLESS R 10.00 25.00
325 Elegant Parlor BORDERLESS R 12.00 30.00
326 Hedge Maze BORDERLESS R 12.00 30.00
327 Lush Portico BORDERLESS R 8.00 20.00
328 Meticulous Archive BORDERLESS R 12.00 30.00
329 Raucous Theater BORDERLESS R 12.00 30.00
330 Shadowy Backstreet BORDERLESS R 10.00 25.00
331 Thundering Falls BORDERLESS R 12.00 30.00
332 Undercity Sewers BORDERLESS R 20.00 50.00
333 Underground Mortuary BORDERLESS R 12.00 30.00
334 Kellan, Inquisitive Prodigy //
Tail the Suspect BORDERLESS R .25 .60
335 Kaya, Spirits' Justice BORDERLESS M 1.00 2.50
336 Aurelia's Vindicator DOSSIER SHOWCASE M.50 1.25
337 Delney, Streetwise Lookout
DOSSIER SHOWCASE M 8.00 20.00
338 Doorkeeper Thrull DOSSIER SHOWCASE R1.00 2.50
339 Neighborhood Guardian
DOSSIER SHOWCASE U .05 .12
340 Wojek Investigator DOSSIER SHOWCASE R.20 .50
341 Conspiracy Unraveler
DOSSIER SHOWCASE M .60 1.50
342 Forensic Gadgeteer DOSSIER SHOWCASE R1.25 3.00
343 Homicide Investigator
DOSSIER SHOWCASE R .08 .20
344 Massacre Girl, Known Killer
DOSSIER SHOWCASE M 3.00 8.00
345 Persuasive Interrogators
DOSSIER SHOWCASE U .05 .12
346 Vein Ripper DOSSIER SHOWCASE M 12.00 30.00
347 Frantic Scapegoat DOSSIER SHOWCASE U.05 .12
348 Fugitive Codebreaker DOSSIER SHOWCASE R.20 .50
349 Incinerator of the Guilty
DOSSIER SHOWCASE M .40 1.00
350 Krenko, Baron of Tin Street
DOSSIER SHOWCASE R .15 .40
352 The Pride of Hull Clade
DOSSIER SHOWCASE M 1.00 2.50
353 Sharp-Eyed Rookie DOSSIER SHOWCASE R.15 .40
354 Agrus Kos, Spirit of Justice
DOSSIER SHOWCASE M .25 .60
355 Alquist Proft, Master Sleuth
DOSSIER SHOWCASE M .20 .50
356 Anzrag, the Quake-Mole
DOSSIER SHOWCASE M 1.50 4.00
357 Aurelia, the Law Above
DOSSIER SHOWCASE R .75 2.00
358 Curious Cadaver DOSSIER SHOWCASE U .05 .12
359 Etrata, Deadly Fugitive
DOSSIER SHOWCASE M .30 .75
360 Ezrim, Agency Chief DOSSIER SHOWCASE R.10 .25
361 Gleaming Geardrake DOSSIER SHOWCASE U.08 .20
362 Izoni, Center of the Web
DOSSIER SHOWCASE R .10 .25
363 Judith, Carnage Connoisseur
DOSSIER SHOWCASE R .50 1.25
364 Kraul Whipcracker DOSSIER SHOWCASE U.08 .20
365 Kylox, Visionary Inventor
DOSSIER SHOWCASE R .10 .25
366 Lazav, Wearer of Faces
DOSSIER SHOWCASE R .25 .60
368 Niv-Mizzet, Guildpact
DOSSIER SHOWCASE R .30 .75
369 Rakdos, Patron of Chaos
DOSSIER SHOWCASE M 2.00 5.00
370 Teysa, Opulent Oligarch
DOSSIER SHOWCASE R .40 1.00
371 Tolsimir, Midnight's Light
DOSSIER SHOWCASE R .10 .25
372 Trostani, Three Whispers
DOSSIER SHOWCASE M 1.25 3.00
373 Vannifar, Evolved Enigma
DOSSIER SHOWCASE M .40 1.00
374 Wispdrinker Vampire DOSSIER SHOWCASE U.10 .25
375 Yarus, Roar of the Old Gods
DOSSIER SHOWCASE R .15 .40
376 Magnetic Snuffler DOSSIER SHOWCASE U.08 .20
390 No Witnesses EXT ART R .12 .30
391 Tenth District Hero EXT ART R .08 .20
392 Unyielding Gatekeeper EXT ART R .12 .30
393 Coveted Falcon EXT ART R .15 .40
394 Cryptic Coat EXT ART R 2.00 5.00
395 Lost in the Maze EXT ART R .20 .50
396 Proft's Eidetic Memory EXT ART R 2.00 5.00
397 Steamcore Scholar EXT ART R .20 .50
398 Barbed Servitor EXT ART R .25 .60
399 Deadly Cover-Up EXT ART R 1.25 3.00
400 Hunted Bonebrute EXT ART R .20 .50
401 Illicit Masquerade EXT ART R .25 .60
402 Outrageous Robbery EXT ART R 1.25 3.00
403 Connecting the Dots EXT ART R .25 .60
404 Expedited Inheritance EXT ART M .60 1.50
405 Krenko's Buzzcrusher EXT ART R .30 .75
406 Lamplight Phoenix EXT ART R .10 .25
407 Pyrotechnic Performer EXT ART R .20 .50
408 Archdruid's Charm EXT ART R 10.00 25.00
409 Axebane Ferox EXT ART R .12 .30
410 Hide in Plain Sight EXT ART R .12 .30
411 Undergrowth Recon EXT ART M 4.00 10.00
412 Assassin's Trophy EXT ART R 2.00 5.00
413 Blood Spatter Analysis EXT ART R .10 .25
414 Doppelgang EXT ART R 1.50 4.00
415 Drag the Canal EXT ART R .10 .25
416 Ill-Timed Explosion EXT ART R .50 1.25
417 Kylox's Voltstrider EXT ART M .40 1.00
418 Leyline of the Guildpact EXT ART R 8.00 20.00
419 Relive the Past EXT ART R .08 .20
420 Treacherous Greed EXT ART R .12 .30
421 Urgent Necropsy EXT ART M .30 .75
422 Cryptex EXT ART R .08 .20

2024 Magic The Gathering Murders at Karlov Manor Prism Alt

7 Case File Auditor FOIL U/(Black Ink) .08 .20
36 Wojek Investigator FOIL R/(Red Feather) .25 .60
36 Wojek Investigator R/(Red Feather) .15 .40
72 Sudden Setback FOIL U/(Dark Bottle) .05 .12
73 Surveillance Monitor FOIL U
(Black Picture Frame) .10 .25
79 Case of the Gorgon's Kiss
FOIL U/(Green Cloth) .05 .12
82 Clandestine Meddler FOIL U/(White Curtains).08 .20
82 Clandestine Meddler U/(White Curtains) .05 .12
146 Torch the Witness U/(Green Lampshade) .05 .12
146 Torch the Witness FOIL U/(Green Lampshade).05 .12
190 Break Out FOIL U/(White Beam of Light) .40 1.00
190 Break Out U/(White Beam of Light) .10 .25
213 Kraul Whipcracker U/(Black Whip) .05 .12
213 Kraul Whipcracker FOIL U/(Black Whip) .05 .12

2024 Magic The Gathering Outlaws of Thunder Junction

1 Another Round R .12 .30
2 Archangel of Tithes M 1.00 2.50
3 Armored Armadillo C .03 .08
4 Aven Interrupter R 1.25 3.00
5 Bounding Felidar U .04 .10
6 Bovine Intervention U .08 .20
7 Bridled Bighorn C .03 .08
8 Claim Jumper R .60 1.50
9 Dust Animus R .10 .25
10 Eriette's Lullaby C .03 .08
11 Final Showdown M 4.00 10.00
12 Fortune, Loyal Steed R .08 .20
13 Frontier Seeker U .03 .08
14 Getaway Glamer U .04 .10
15 High Noon R .30 .75
16 Holy Cow C .04 .10
17 Inventive Wingsmith C .03 .08
18 Lassoed by the Law U .03 .08
19 Mystical Tether C .03 .08
20 Nurturing Pixie U .04 .10
21 Omenport Vigilante U .03 .08
22 One Last Job R .10 .25
23 Outlaw Medic C .04 .10
24 Prairie Dog U .04 .10
25 Prosperity Tycoon U .03 .08
26 Requisition Raid U .25 .60
27 Rustler Rampage U .04 .10
28 Shepherd of the Clouds U .03 .08
29 Sheriff of Safe Passage U .04 .10
30 Stagecoach Security C .03 .08
31 Steer Clear C .03 .08
32 Sterling Keykeeper C .03 .08
33 Sterling Supplier C .03 .08
34 Take Up the Shield C .03 .08
35 Thunder Lasso U .04 .10
36 Trained Arynx C .03 .08
37 Vengeful Townsfolk C .03 .08
38 Wanted Griffin C .03 .08
39 Archmage's Newt R .04 .10
40 Canyon Crab U .03 .08
41 Daring Thunder-Thief C .03 .08
42 Deepmuck Desperado U .03 .08
43 Djinn of Fool's Fall C .03 .08
44 Double Down M 1.25 3.00
45 Duelist of the Mind R .12 .30
46 Emergent Haunting U .03 .08
47 Failed Fording C .03 .08
48 Fblthp, Lost on the Range R .10 .25
49 Fleeting Reflection U .08 .20
50 Geralf, the Fleshwright M 1.25 3.00
51 Geyser Drake C .05 .12
52 Harrier Strix C .03 .08
53 Jailbreak Scheme C .03 .08
54 The Key to the Vault R .20 .50
55 Loan Shark C .03 .08
56 Marauding Sphinx U .03 .08
57 Metamorphic Blast U .04 .10
58 Nimble Brigand U .03 .08
59 Outlaw Stitcher U .03 .08
60 Peerless Ropemaster C .03 .08

61 Phantom Interference C .03 .08
62 Plan the Heist U .03 .08
63 Razzle-Dazzler C .03 .08
64 Seize the Secrets C .03 .08
65 Shackle Slinger U .05 .12
66 Shifting Grift U .05 .12
67 Slickshot Lockpicker U .03 .08
68 Slickshot Vault-Buster C .03 .08
69 Spring Splasher C .03 .08
70 Step Between Worlds R .10 .25
71 Stoic Sphinx R .08 .20
72 Stop Cold C .03 .08
73 Take the Fall C .03 .08
74 This Town Ain't Big Enough U .03 .08
75 Three Steps Ahead R 2.50 6.00
76 Visage Bandit U .04 .10
77 Ambush Gigapede C .03 .08
78 Binding Negotiation U .03 .08
79 Blacksnag Buzzard C .03 .08
80 Blood Hustler U .04 .10
81 Boneyard Desecrator C .03 .08
82 Caustic Bronco R .75 2.00
83 Consuming Ashes C .03 .08
84 Corrupted Conviction C .04 .10
85 Desert's Due C .03 .08
86 Desperate Bloodseeker C .03 .08
87 Fake Your Own Death C .03 .08
88 Forsaken Miner U .15 .40
89 Gisa, the Hellraiser M 3.00 8.00
90 Hollow Marauder U .03 .08
91 Insatiable Avarice R 2.00 5.00
92 Kaervek, the Punisher R .20 .50
93 Lively Dirge U .25 .60
94 Mourner's Surprise C .03 .08
95 Neutralize the Guards U .03 .08
96 Nezumi Linkbreaker C .03 .08
97 Overzealous Muscle C .03 .08
98 Pitiless Carnage R .12 .30
99 Rakish Crew U .03 .08
100 Rattleback Apothecary U .03 .08
101 Raven of Fell Omens C .03 .08
102 Rictus Robber U .03 .08
103 Rooftop Assassin C .04 .10
104 Rush of Dread R .40 1.00
105 Servant of the Stinger U .04 .10
106 Shoot the Sheriff U .08 .20
107 Skulduggery C .03 .08
108 Tinybones Joins Up R .25 .60
109 Tinybones, the Pickpocket M 5.00 12.00
110 Treasure Dredger U .04 .10
111 Unfortunate Accident U .03 .08
112 Unscrupulous Contractor U .03 .08
113 Vadmir, New Blood R .10 .25
114 Vault Plunderer C .03 .08
115 Brimstone Roundup U .03 .08
116 Calamity, Galloping Inferno R .15 .40
117 Caught in the Crossfire U .03 .08
118 Cunning Coyote U .03 .08
119 Deadeye Duelist C .03 .08
120 Demonic Ruckus U .10 .25
121 Discerning Peddler C .04 .10
122 Explosive Derailment C .03 .08
123 Ferocification U .03 .08
124 Gila Courser U .03 .08
125 Great Train Heist R 1.25 3.00
126 Hell to Pay R .20 .50
127 Hellspur Brute U .03 .08
128 Hellspur Posse Boss R .10 .25
129 Highway Robbery C .08 .20
130 Irascible Wolverine C .03 .08
131 Iron-Fist Pulverizer C .03 .08
132 Longhorn Sharpshooter U .03 .08
133 Magda, the Hoardmaster R .50 1.25
134 Magebane Lizard U .20 .50
135 Mine Raider C .03 .08
136 Outlaws' Fury C .03 .08
137 Prickly Pair C .03 .08
138 Quick Draw C .03 .08
139 Quilled Charger C .03 .08
140 Reckless Lackey C .08 .20
141 Resilient Roadrunner U .03 .08
142 Return the Favor U .50 1.25
143 Rodeo Pyromancers C .04 .10
144 Scalestorm Summoner U .04 .10
145 Scorching Shot U .05 .12
146 Slickshot Show-Off R 5.00 12.00
147 Stingerback Terror R .10 .25
148 Take for a Ride U .03 .08
149 Terror of the Peaks M 10.00 25.00
150 Thunder Salvo C .03 .08
151 Trick Shot C .03 .08
152 Aloe Alchemist U .03 .08
153 Ankle Biter C .04 .10
154 Beastbond Outcaster U .03 .08
155 Betrayal at the Vault U .04 .10
156 Bristlepack Sentry C .03 .08
157 Bristly Bill, Spine Sower M 12.00 30.00
158 Cactarantula C .03 .08
159 Colossal Rattlewurm R .10 .25
160 Dance of the Tumbleweeds C .03 .08
161 Drover Grizzly C .03 .08
162 Freestrider Commando C .03 .08
163 Freestrider Lookout R .40 1.00
164 Full Steam Ahead U .03 .08
165 Giant Beaver C .03 .08
166 Gold Rush U .04 .10
167 Goldvein Hydra M 5.00 12.00
168 Hardbristle Bandit C .03 .08
169 Intrepid Stablemaster U .03 .08
170 Map the Frontier U .04 .10
171 Ornery Tumblewagg R .12 .30
172 Outcaster Greenblade U .04 .10
173 Outcaster Trailblazer R 2.00 5.00
174 Patient Naturalist C .03 .08
175 Railway Brawler M 4.00 10.00
176 Rambling Possum U .04 .10
177 Raucous Entertainer U .03 .08
178 Reach for the Sky C .04 .10
179 Rise of the Varmints U .04 .10
180 Smuggler's Surprise R 1.50 4.00
181 Snakeskin Veil C .04 .10
182 Spinewoods Armadillo U .05 .12
183 Spinewoods Paladin C .03 .08
184 Stubborn Burrowfiend U .03 .08
185 Throw from the Saddle C .03 .08
186 Trash the Town U .08 .20
187 Tumbleweed Rising C .03 .08
188 Voracious Varmint C .04 .10
189 Akul the Unrepentant R .10 .25
190 Annie Flash, the Veteran M .12 .30
191 Annie Joins Up R 1.00 2.50
192 Assimilation Aegis M .60 1.50
193 At Knifepoint U .04 .10
194 Badlands Revival U .03 .08
195 Baron Bertram Graywater U .10 .25
196 Bonny Pall, Clearcutter R .30 .75
197 Breeches, the Blastmaker R .10 .25
198 Bruse Tarl, Roving Rancher R .08 .20
199 Cactusfolk Sureshot U .04 .10
200 Congregation Gryff U .03 .08
201 Doc Aurlock, Grizzled Genius U .05 .12
202 Eriette, the Beguiler R .10 .25
203 Ertha Jo, Frontier Mentor U .04 .10
204 Form a Posse U .03 .08
205 Ghired, Mirror of the Wilds M .25 .60
206 The Gitrog, Ravenous Ride M 1.50 4.00
207 Honest Rutstein U .25 .60
208 Intimidation Campaign U .04 .10
209 Jem Lightfoote, Sky Explorer U .03 .08
210 Jolene, Plundering Pugilist U .04 .10
211 Kambal, Profiteering Mayor R .75 2.00
212 Kellan Joins Up R .10 .25
213 Kellan, the Kid M .60 1.50
214 Kraum, Violent Cacophony U .04 .10
215 Laughing Jasper Flint R .20 .50
216 Lazav, Familiar Stranger U .03 .08
217 Lilah, Undefeated Slickshot R .20 .50
218 Make Your Own Luck U .03 .08
219 Malcolm, the Eyes R .10 .25
220 Marchesa, Dealer of Death R .10 .25
221 Miriam, Herd Whisperer U .03 .08
222 Obeka, Splitter of Seconds R .20 .50
223 Oko, the Ringleader M .75 2.00
224 Pillage the Bog R .60 1.50
225 Rakdos Joins Up R .15 .40
226 Rakdos, the Muscle M 1.00 2.50
227 Riku of Many Paths R .08 .20
228 Roxanne, Starfall Savant R .30 .75
229 Ruthless Lawbringer U .10 .25
230 Satoru, the Infiltrator R 1.50 4.00
231 Selvala, Eager Trailblazer M .20 .50
232 Seraphic Steed R .10 .25
233 Slick Sequence U .10 .25
234 Taii Wakeen, Perfect Shot R .10 .25
235 Vial Smasher, Gleeful Grenadier U .04 .10
236 Vraska Joins Up R .25 .60
237 Vraska, the Silencer M 1.00 2.50
238 Wrangler of the Damned U .03 .08
239 Wylie Duke, Atiin Hero R .10 .25
240 Bandit's Haul U .03 .08
241 Boom Box U .04 .10
242 Gold Pan C .03 .08
243 Lavaspur Boots U 1.00 2.50
244 Luxurious Locomotive U .03 .08
245 Mobile Homestead U .03 .08
246 Oasis Gardener C .03 .08
247 Redrock Sentinel U .03 .08
248 Silver Deputy C .03 .08
249 Sterling Hound C .03 .08
250 Tomb Trawler U .03 .08
251 Abraded Bluffs C .10 .25
252 Arid Archway U .25 .60
253 Bristling Backwoods C .08 .20
254 Conduit Pylons C .05 .12
255 Creosote Heath C .04 .10
256 Eroded Canyon C .08 .20
257 Festering Gulch C .08 .20
258 Forlorn Flats C .08 .20
259 Jagged Barrens C .12 .30
260 Lonely Arroyo C .05 .12
261 Lush Oasis C .04 .10
262 Mirage Mesa C .05 .12
263 Sandstorm Verge U .04 .10
264 Soured Springs C .08 .20
265 Bucolic Ranch U .04 .10
266 Blooming Marsh R 1.00 2.50
267 Botanical Sanctum R .75 2.00
268 Concealed Courtyard R .50 1.25
269 Inspiring Vantage R .75 2.00
270 Spirebluff Canal R 1.50 4.00
271 Jace Reawakened M 1.25 3.00
272 Plains WESTERN FULL ART C .10 .25
273 Island WESTERN FULL ART C .20 .50
274 Swamp WESTERN FULL ART C .20 .50
275 Mountain WESTERN FULL ART C .20 .50
276 Forest WESTERN FULL ART C .20 .50
277 Plains C .04 .10
278 Plains C .04 .10
279 Island C .04 .10
280 Island C .04 .10
281 Swamp C .04 .10
282 Swamp C .04 .10
283 Mountain C .04 .10
284 Mountain C .04 .10
285 Forest C .04 .10
286 Forest C .04 .10
287 Geralf, the Fleshwright WANTED POSTER M1.25 3.00
288 Gisa, the Hellraiser WANTED POSTER M 4.00 10.00
289 Kaervek, the Punisher WANTED POSTER R .50 1.25
290 Tinybones, the Pickpocket WANTED POSTER M 8.00 20.00
291 Annie Flash, the Veteran WANTED POSTER M.25 .60
292 Breeches, the Blastmaker WANTED POSTER R.10 .25
293 Eriette, the Beguiler WANTED POSTER R .25 .60
294 Kellan, the Kid WANTED POSTER M 1.25 3.00
295 Malcolm, the Eyes WANTED POSTER R .15 .40
296 Oko, the Ringleader WANTED POSTER M 3.00 8.00
297 Rakdos, the Muscle WANTED POSTER M 2.00 5.00
298 Satoru, the Infiltrator WANTED POSTER R 1.50 4.00
299 Vraska, the Silencer WANTED POSTER M 1.50 4.00
300 Blooming Marsh BORDERLESS R 1.50 4.00
301 Botanical Sanctum BORDERLESS R 1.25 3.00
302 Concealed Courtyard BORDERLESS R 1.00 2.50
303 Inspiring Vantage BORDERLESS R 1.00 2.50
304 Spirebluff Canal BORDERLESS R 2.00 5.00
305 Oko, the Ringleader BORDERLESS M 4.00 10.00
306 Jace Reawakened BORDERLESS M 3.00 8.00
307 Another Round EXT ART R .25 .60
308 Archangel of Tithes EXT ART M 1.25 3.00
309 Aven Interrupter EXT ART R 2.50 6.00
310 Claim Jumper EXT ART R 1.00 2.50
311 Dust Animus EXT ART R .20 .50
312 Final Showdown EXT ART M 6.00 15.00
313 Fortune, Loyal Steed EXT ART R .12 .30
314 High Noon EXT ART R .75 2.00
315 One Last Job EXT ART R .15 .40
316 Archmage's Newt EXT ART R .10 .25
317 Double Down EXT ART M 2.50 6.00
318 Duelist of the Mind EXT ART R .40 1.00
319 Fblthp, Lost on the Range EXT ART R .30 .75
320 The Key to the Vault EXT ART R .50 1.25
321 Step Between Worlds EXT ART R .15 .40
322 Stoic Sphinx EXT ART R .15 .40
323 Three Steps Ahead EXT ART R 4.00 10.00
324 Caustic Bronco EXT ART R 1.50 4.00
325 Insatiable Avarice EXT ART R 3.00 8.00
326 Pitiless Carnage EXT ART R .40 1.00
327 Rush of Dread EXT ART R .60 1.50
328 Tinybones Joins Up EXT ART R .50 1.25
329 Vadmir, New Blood EXT ART R .25 .60
330 Calamity, Galloping Inferno EXT ART R .30 .75
331 Great Train Heist EXT ART R 2.00 5.00
332 Hell to Pay EXT ART R 1.25 3.00
333 Hellspur Posse Boss EXT ART R .12 .30
334 Magda, the Hoardmaster EXT ART R .75 2.00
335 Slickshot Show-Off EXT ART R 5.00 12.00
336 Stingerback Terror EXT ART R .15 .40
337 Terror of the Peaks EXT ART M 12.00 30.00
338 Bristly Bill, Spine Sower EXT ART M 20.00 50.00
339 Colossal Rattlewurm EXT ART R .30 .75
340 Freestrider Lookout EXT ART R 1.00 2.50
341 Goldvein Hydra EXT ART M 8.00 20.00
342 Ornery Tumblewagg EXT ART R .15 .40
343 Outcaster Trailblazer EXT ART R 2.50 6.00
344 Railway Brawler EXT ART M 6.00 15.00
345 Smuggler's Surprise EXT ART R 2.00 5.00
346 Akul the Unrepentant EXT ART R .25 .60
347 Annie Joins Up EXT ART R 2.50 6.00
348 Assimilation Aegis EXT ART M 1.25 3.00
349 Bonny Pall, Clearcutter EXT ART R 1.00 2.50
350 Bruse Tarl, Roving Rancher EXT ART R .08 .20
351 Ghired, Mirror of the Wilds EXT ART M 1.50 4.00
352 The Gitrog, Ravenous Ride EXT ART M 2.50 6.00
353 Kambal, Profiteering Mayor EXT ART R 2.00 5.00
354 Kellan Joins Up EXT ART R .15 .40
355 Laughing Jasper Flint EXT ART R .50 1.25
356 Lilah, Undefeated Slickshot EXT ART R .25 .60
357 Marchesa, Dealer of Death EXT ART R .25 .60
358 Obeka, Splitter of Seconds EXT ART R .50 1.25
359 Pillage the Bog EXT ART R 1.50 4.00
360 Rakdos Joins Up EXT ART R .50 1.25
361 Riku of Many Paths EXT ART R .12 .30
362 Roxanne, Starfall Savant EXT ART R 2.00 5.00
363 Selvala, Eager Trailblazer EXT ART M .40 1.00
364 Seraphic Steed EXT ART R .12 .30
365 Taii Wakeen, Perfect Shot EXT ART R .25 .60
366 Vraska Joins Up EXT ART R .50 1.25
367 Wylie Duke, Atiin Hero EXT ART R .12 .30

2024 Magic The Gathering Outlaws of Thunder Junction Breaking News

1 Fell the Mighty R .10 .25
2 Fierce Retribution U .03 .08
3 Journey to Nowhere U .04 .10
4 Leyline Binding M 1.25 3.00
5 Pariah R .12 .30
6 Path to Exile R .60 1.50
7 Archive Trap R .60 1.50
8 Archmage's Charm R .40 1.00
9 Commandeer R .25 .60
10 Essence Capture U .03 .08
11 Mana Drain M 15.00 40.00
12 Mindbreak Trap M 8.00 20.00
13 Repulse U .03 .08
14 Heartless Pillage U .04 .10
15 Imp's Mischief R .75 2.00
16 Murder U .05 .12
17 Overwhelming Forces M .50 1.25
18 Reanimate R 4.00 10.00
19 Surgical Extraction R .60 1.50
20 Thoughtseize M 4.00 10.00
21 Collective Defiance R .08 .20
22 Crackle with Power M 1.00 2.50
23 Electrodominance R .15 .40
24 Fling U .03 .08
25 Indomitable Creativity M .60 1.50
26 Skewer the Critics U .08 .20
27 Skullcrack R .10 .25
28 Clear Shot U .03 .08
29 Force of Vigor M 4.00 10.00
30 Pest Infestation R .40 1.00
31 Primal Command R .10 .25
32 Primal Might R .08 .20
33 Thornado U .03 .08
34 Abrupt Decay R .50 1.25
35 Anguished Unmaking M .60 1.50
36 Back for More U .03 .08
37 Bedevil R .20 .50
38 Buried in the Garden U .03 .08
39 Crime // Punishment M .10 .25
40 Cruel Ultimatum R .08 .20
41 Decimate R .10 .25
42 Decisive Denial U .03 .08
43 Detention Sphere R .04 .10
44 Endless Detour R .04 .10
45 Fractured Identity M .12 .30
46 Hindering Light U .03 .08
47 Humiliate U .03 .08
48 Hypothesizzle U .03 .08
49 Ionize R .05 .12
50 Oko, Thief of Crowns M 2.00 5.00
51 Outlaws' Merriment R .08 .20
52 Ride Down U .04 .10
53 Savage Smash U .04 .10
54 Siphon Insight R .05 .12
55 Terminal Agony U .04 .10
56 Tyrant's Scorn U .03 .08
57 Vanishing Verse R .12 .30
58 Villainous Wealth R .05 .12
59 Void Rend R .20 .50
60 Voidslime R .10 .25
61 Contagion Engine M 2.00 5.00
62 Grindstone M .75 2.00
63 Mindslaver M .50 1.25
64 Unlicensed Hearse R 1.00 2.50
65 Dust Bowl R .25 .60

2024 Magic The Gathering Outlaws of Thunder Junction Breaking News Foil

1 Fell the Mighty R .10 .25
2 Fierce Retribution U .04 .10
3 Journey to Nowhere U .10 .25
4 Leyline Binding M 2.50 6.00
5 Pariah R .25 .60
6 Path to Exile R .75 2.00
7 Archive Trap R 1.25 3.00
8 Archmage's Charm R .50 1.25
9 Commandeer R .60 1.50
10 Essence Capture U .05 .12
11 Mana Drain M 20.00 50.00
12 Mindbreak Trap M 15.00 40.00
13 Repulse U .04 .10
14 Heartless Pillage U .03 .08
15 Imp's Mischief R 1.00 2.50
16 Murder U .04 .10
17 Overwhelming Forces M .60 1.50
18 Reanimate R 5.00 12.00
19 Surgical Extraction R 1.25 3.00
20 Thoughtseize M 6.00 15.00
21 Collective Defiance R .10 .25
22 Crackle with Power M 2.00 5.00
23 Electrodominance R .25 .60
24 Fling U .03 .08
25 Indomitable Creativity M 1.25 3.00
26 Skewer the Critics U .10 .25
27 Skullcrack R .20 .50
28 Clear Shot U .03 .08
29 Force of Vigor M 6.00 15.00
30 Pest Infestation R .60 1.50
31 Primal Command R .10 .25
32 Primal Might R .10 .25
33 Thornado U .03 .08
34 Abrupt Decay R .75 2.00
35 Anguished Unmaking M 1.25 3.00
36 Back for More U .04 .10
37 Bedevil R .25 .60
38 Buried in the Garden U .05 .12
39 Crime // Punishment M .25 .60
40 Cruel Ultimatum R .10 .25
41 Decimate R .10 .25
42 Decisive Denial U .04 .10
43 Detention Sphere R .10 .25
44 Endless Detour R .10 .25
45 Fractured Identity M .50 1.25
46 Hindering Light U .10 .25
47 Humiliate U .03 .08
48 Hypothesizzle U .03 .08
49 Ionize R .10 .25
50 Oko, Thief of Crowns M 3.00 8.00
51 Outlaws' Merriment R .12 .30
52 Ride Down U .04 .10
53 Savage Smash U .03 .08
54 Siphon Insight R .10 .25
55 Terminal Agony U .03 .08
56 Tyrant's Scorn U .04 .10
57 Vanishing Verse R .20 .50
58 Villainous Wealth R .25 .60
59 Void Rend R .25 .60
60 Voidslime R .12 .30
61 Contagion Engine M 3.00 8.00
62 Grindstone M 2.00 5.00
63 Mindslaver M .75 2.00
64 Unlicensed Hearse R 1.00 2.50
65 Dust Bowl R .60 1.50
66 Leyline Binding TEXTURED M 20.00 50.00
67 Mana Drain TEXTURED M 100.00 250.00
68 Mindbreak Trap TEXTURED M 100.00 250.00
69 Overwhelming Forces TEXTURED M 12.00 30.00
70 Thoughtseize TEXTURED M 30.00 80.00
71 Crackle with Power TEXTURED M 12.00 30.00
72 Indomitable Creativity TEXTURED M 15.00 40.00
73 Force of Vigor TEXTURED M 50.00 120.00
74 Anguished Unmaking TEXTURED M 20.00 50.00
75 Crime // Punishment TEXTURED M 20.00 50.00
76 Fractured Identity TEXTURED M 12.00 30.00
77 Oko, Thief of Crowns TEXTURED M 50.00 120.00
78 Contagion Engine TEXTURED M 25.00 60.00
79 Grindstone TEXTURED M 20.00 50.00
80 Mindslaver TEXTURED M 15.00 40.00

2024 Magic The Gathering Outlaws of Thunder Junction Commander

1 Gonti, Canny Acquisitor M .25 .60
2 Olivia, Opulent Outlaw M 1.25 3.00
3 Stella Lee, Wild Card M 2.00 5.00
4 Yuma, Proud Protector M .15 .40
9 Angel of Indemnity R 2.50 6.00
10 Angelic Sell-Sword R .10 .25
11 Sand Scout R .10 .25
12 We Ride at Dawn R .12 .30
13 Arcane Heist R .20 .50
14 Forger's Foundry R .10 .25
15 Lock and Load R .12 .30
16 Smirking Spelljacker R .25 .60
17 Thunderclap Drake R 2.50 6.00
18 Back in Town R .20 .50
19 Charred Graverobber R .05 .12
20 Discreet Retreat R .08 .20
21 Heartless Conscription R .20 .50
22 Orochi Soul-Reaver R .75 2.00
23 Thieving Varmint R .10 .25
24 Cataclysmic Prospecting R .05 .12
25 Crackling Spellslinger R .25 .60
26 Dead Before Sunrise R .05 .12
27 Elemental Eruption R .60 1.50
28 Embrace the Unknown R .12 .30
29 Pyretic Charge R .05 .12
30 Smoldering Stagecoach R .10 .25
31 Dune Chanter R .20 .50
32 Rumbleweed R .20 .50
33 Savvy Trader R .40 1.00

34 Tower Winder R	1.50	4.00
35 Vengeful Regrowth R	.05	.12
36 Graywater's Fixer R	.08	.20
37 Bounty Board R	.15	.40
38 Dream-Thief's Bandana R	.12	.30
39 Leyline Dowser R	.60	1.50
40 Cactus Preserve R	.60	1.50
41 Eris, Roar of the Storm M	1.00	2.50
42 Felix Five-Boots M	.60	1.50
43 Kirri, Talented Sprout M	.15	.40
44 Vihaan, Goldwaker M	1.00	2.50
45 Angel of Indemnity R	2.00	5.00
46 Angelic Sell-Sword R	.12	.30
47 Sand Scout R	.15	.40
48 We Ride at Dawn R	.20	.50
49 Arcane Heist R	.20	.50
50 Forger's Foundry R	.10	.25
51 Lock and Load R	.15	.40
52 Smirking Spelljacker R	.20	.50
53 Thunderclap Drake R	1.50	4.00
54 Back in Town R	.20	.50
55 Charred Graverobber R	.08	.20
56 Discreet Retreat R	.12	.30
57 Heartless Conscription R	.20	.50
58 Orochi Soul-Reaver R	.30	.75
59 Thieving Varmint R	.10	.25
60 Cataclysmic Prospecting R	.05	.12
61 Crackling Spellslinger R	.30	.75
62 Dead Before Sunrise R	.05	.12
63 Elemental Eruption R	.20	.50
64 Embrace the Unknown R	.20	.50
65 Pyretic Charge R	.10	.25
66 Smoldering Stagecoach R	.10	.25
67 Dune Chanter R	.20	.50
68 Rumbleweed R	.15	.40
69 Savvy Trader R	.20	.50
70 Tower Winder R	1.25	3.00
71 Vengeful Regrowth R	.10	.25
72 Graywater's Fixer R	.10	.25
73 Bounty Board R	.12	.30
74 Dream-Thief's Bandana R	.15	.40
75 Leyline Dowser R	.30	.75
76 Cactus Preserve R	.30	.75
77 Oblivion Sower M	.20	.50
78 Angel of the Ruins U	.10	.25
79 Council's Judgment R	.10	.25
80 Descend upon the Sinful M	.10	.25
81 Heliod's Intervention R	.30	.75
82 Marshal's Anthem R	.05	.12
83 Mirror Entity R	.15	.40
84 Mistmeadow Skulk U	.03	.08
85 Path to Exile U	.50	1.25
86 Sevinne's Reclamation R	.10	.25
87 Sun Titan M	.15	.40
88 Valorous Stance U	.04	.10
89 Arcane Denial C	1.50	4.00
90 Archmage Emeritus R	1.00	2.50
91 Baral's Expertise R	.08	.20
92 Curse of the Swine R	.10	.25
93 Dazzling Sphinx R	.05	.12
94 Deep Analysis C	.04	.10
95 Dig Through Time R	.12	.30
96 Diluvian Primordial R	.10	.25
97 Finale of Revelation M	.10	.25
98 Ghostly Pilferer R	.05	.12
99 Haughty Djinn R	.20	.50
100 Midnight Clock R	.12	.30
101 Mind's Dilation M	.40	1.00
102 Murmuring Mystic U	.10	.25
103 Octavia, Living Thesis R	.10	.25
104 Opt C	.08	.20
105 Ponder C	1.00	2.50
106 Pongify U	1.50	4.00
107 Preordain C	.60	1.50
108 Propaganda U	2.50	6.00
109 Pteramander U	.04	.10
110 Radical Idea C	.05	.12
111 Sage of the Beyond R	.10	.25
112 Serum Visions U	.20	.50
113 Shark Typhoon R	2.00	5.00
114 Slither Blade C	.12	.30
115 Stolen Goods R	.05	.12
116 Talrand, Sky Summoner R	.10	.25
117 Tezzeret's Gambit R	.10	.25
118 Thieving Skydiver R	.10	.25
119 Think Twice C	.03	.08
120 Treasure Cruise C	.12	.30
121 Triton Shorestalker C	.10	.25
122 Whirler Rogue U	.03	.08
123 Windfall U	1.50	4.00
124 Winged Boots R	1.00	2.50
125 Aetherborn Marauder U	.04	.10
126 Baleful Mastery R	.25	.60
127 Brainstealer Dragon R	1.00	2.50
128 Changeling Outcast C	.50	1.25
129 Cunning Rhetoric R	.12	.30
130 Curtains' Call R	.10	.25
131 Deadly Dispute C	.50	1.25
132 Dire Fleet Ravager M	.08	.20
133 Fain, the Broker R	.10	.25
134 Feed the Swarm C	.10	.25
135 Gonti, Lord of Luxury R	.10	.25
136 Hex R	.05	.12
137 Kamber, the Plunderer R	.08	.20
138 Mari, the Killing Quill R	1.00	2.50
139 Marshland Bloodcaster R	.05	.12
140 Massacre Girl R	.12	.30
141 Misfortune Teller R	.05	.12
142 Morbid Opportunist U	.40	1.00
143 Nashi, Moon Sage's Scion M	.25	.60
144 Nighthawk Scavenger R	.10	.25
145 Ogre Slumlord R	.10	.25
146 Painful Truths R	.10	.25
147 Predators' Hour R	.05	.12
148 Rankle, Master of Pranks R	.20	.50
149 Tenured Inkcaster U	.04	.10
150 Thieving Amalgam R	.10	.25
151 Veinwitch Coven R	.10	.25
152 Witch of the Moors R	.30	.75
153 Angrath's Marauders R	.10	.25
154 Arcane Bombardment M	.50	1.25
155 Big Score C	.60	1.50
156 Bitter Reunion C	.10	.25
157 Bloodthirsty Adversary M	.30	.75
158 Captain Lannery Storm R	.08	.20
159 Captivating Crew R	.10	.25
160 Chaos Warp R	.25	.60
161 Cursed Mirror R	.25	.60
162 Dire Fleet Daredevil R	.10	.25
163 Electric Revelation C	.03	.08
164 Electrostatic Field U	.50	1.25
165 Faithless Looting C	.10	.25
166 Finale of Promise M	.12	.30
167 Glittering Stockpile U	.10	.25
168 Grenzo, Havoc Raiser R	.12	.30
169 Guttersnipe C	.10	.25
170 Humble Defector U	.04	.10
171 Impulsive Pilferer C	.10	.25
172 Laurine, the Diversion R	.05	.12
173 Magmatic Insight U	.04	.10
174 Mass Mutiny R	.08	.20
175 Mizzix's Mastery R	.30	.75
176 Nesting Dragon R	.12	.30
177 Rain of Riches R	1.00	2.50
178 Rousing Refrain R	.75	2.00
179 Seize the Spotlight R	.75	2.00
180 Shiny Impetus U	.03	.08
181 Storm-Kiln Artist U	.50	1.25
182 Unholy Heat C	.04	.10
183 Vandalblast U	1.25	3.00
184 Volcanic Torrent U	.03	.08
185 Young Pyromancer U	.10	.25
186 Ancient Greenwarden M	4.00	10.00
187 Avenger of Zendikar M	1.25	3.00
188 Cazur, Ruthless Stalker M	.12	.30
189 Crawling Sensation U	.10	.25
190 Eccentric Farmer C	.04	.10
191 Elvish Rejuvenator C	.04	.10
192 Explore C	.10	.25
193 Genesis Hydra R	.10	.25
194 Harrow C	.20	.50
195 Hour of Promise R	.10	.25
196 Kodama's Reach C	.60	1.50
197 The Mending of Dominaria R	.08	.20
198 Nantuko Cultivator U	.03	.08
199 Ohran Frostfang R	.75	2.00
200 Oracle of Mul Daya R	3.00	8.00
201 Rampant Growth C	.20	.50
202 Ramunap Excavator R	1.00	2.50
203 Return of the Wildspeaker R	.50	1.25
204 Satyr Wayfinder C	.04	.10
205 Scute Swarm R	2.00	5.00
206 Silhana Ledgewalker C	.04	.10
207 Skullwinder U	.04	.10
208 Springbloom Druid C	.10	.25
209 Three Visits U	2.50	6.00
210 Titania, Protector of Argoth M	.30	.75
211 Turntimber Sower R	.10	.25
212 Void Attendant U	.04	.10
213 Winding Way C	.10	.25
214 World Shaper R	.60	1.50
215 Baleful Strix R	.40	1.00
216 Boros Charm U	1.50	4.00
217 Breena, the Demagogue M	.60	1.50
218 Cold-Eyed Selkie R	.10	.25
219 Culling Ritual R	.30	.75
220 Decimate R	.08	.20
221 Edric, Spymaster of Trest R	.12	.30
222 Epic Experiment M	.10	.25
223 Escape to the Wilds R	.10	.25
224 Expressive Iteration U	.25	.60
225 Extract Brain R	.08	.20
226 Fallen Shinobi R	.50	1.25
227 Galvanic Iteration R	.15	.40
228 Goblin Electromancer C	.08	.20
229 Hazezon, Shaper of Sand R	.04	.10
230 Heaven // Earth R	.05	.12
231 Hostage Taker R	.10	.25
232 Kaza, Roil Chaser R	.08	.20
233 Life Insurance R	.10	.25
234 The Mimeoplasm R	.08	.20
235 Niv-Mizzet, Parun R	.40	1.00
236 Omnath, Locus of Rage M	.30	.75
237 Plasm Capture R	.05	.12
238 Putrefy U	.10	.25
239 Queen Marchesa R	.12	.30
240 Shadowmage Infiltrator R	.04	.10
241 Silent-Blade Oni R	.15	.40
242 Siphon Insight R	.04	.10
243 Thief of Sanity R	.10	.25
244 Third Path Iconoclast U	.25	.60
245 Thrilling Discovery C	.05	.12
246 Trygon Predator U	.08	.20
247 Ukkima, Stalking Shadow M	.12	.30
248 Veyran, Voice of Duality M	1.50	4.00
249 Villainous Wealth R	.08	.20
250 Wreck and Rebuild U	.05	.12
251 Academy Manufactor R	2.00	5.00
252 Arcane Signet C	.15	.40
253 Bladegriff Prototype R	.05	.12
254 Chaos Wand R	.08	.20
255 Chromatic Lantern R	1.25	3.00
256 Darksteel Ingot U	.10	.25
257 Fellwar Stone U	.50	1.25
258 Idol of Oblivion R	.30	.75
259 Izzet Signet C	.15	.40
260 Lightning Greaves U	3.00	8.00
261 Orzhov Signet C	.12	.30
262 Perennial Behemoth R	.10	.25
263 Perpetual Timepiece U	.10	.25
264 Prismatic Lens U	.10	.25
265 Rakdos Signet U	.25	.60
266 Scaretiller C	.04	.10
267 Sol Ring U	.60	1.50
268 Swiftfoot Boots U	1.00	2.50
269 Trailblazer's Boots U	.75	2.00
270 Access Tunnel U	.15	.40
271 Battlefield Forge R	.50	1.25
272 Blackcleave Cliffs R	1.00	2.50
273 Bojuka Bog C	.60	1.50
274 Bonders' Enclave R	.20	.50
275 Canyon Slough R	.10	.25
276 Cascade Bluffs R	1.25	3.00
277 Caves of Koilos R	.30	.75
278 Clifftop Retreat R	.25	.60
279 Command Beacon R	4.00	10.00
280 Command Tower C	.12	.30
281 Darkslick Shores R	1.00	2.50
282 Darkwater Catacombs R	.08	.20
283 Demolition Field U	.40	1.00
284 Desert of the Fervent C	.04	.10
285 Desert of the Indomitable C	.05	.12
286 Desert of the True C	.05	.12
287 Desolate Mire R	.50	1.25
288 Dimir Aqueduct C	.10	.25
289 Dragonskull Summit R	.60	1.50
290 Drowned Catacomb R	1.00	2.50
291 Dunes of the Dead U	.04	.10
292 Evolving Wilds C	.05	.12
293 Exotic Orchard R	.10	.25
294 Ferrous Lake R	.50	1.25
295 Fetid Heath R	1.25	3.00
296 Fetid Pools R	.10	.25
297 Flooded Grove R	.50	1.25
298 Frostboil Snarl R	.10	.25
299 Hashep Oasis U	.05	.12
300 Hinterland Harbor R	.50	1.25
301 Isolated Chapel R	.75	2.00
302 Izzet Boilerworks U	.10	.25
303 Jungle Shrine U	.10	.25
304 Krosan Verge U	.10	.25
305 Llanowar Wastes R	.60	1.50
306 Nomad Outpost U	.12	.30
307 Opulent Palace U	.12	.30
308 Overflowing Basin R	.25	.60
309 Painted Bluffs C	.04	.10
310 Path of Ancestry C	.08	.20
311 Ramunap Ruins U	.15	.40
312 Reliquary Tower U	1.00	2.50
313 Rogue's Passage U	.15	.40
314 Rugged Prairie R	1.00	2.50
315 Scattered Groves R	.10	.25
316 Scavenger Grounds R	.20	.50
317 Shadowblood Ridge R	.10	.25
318 Shefet Dunes U	.05	.12
319 Sheltered Thicket R	.08	.20
320 Shivan Reef R	.60	1.50
321 Smoldering Marsh R	.10	.25
322 Sulfur Falls R	.50	1.25
323 Sulfurous Springs R	1.25	3.00
324 Sunhome, Fortress of the Legion U	.08	.20
325 Sunken Hollow R	.10	.25
326 Sunscorched Divide R	.50	1.25
327 Tainted Peak U	.10	.25
328 Temple of Deceit R	.10	.25
329 Temple of Epiphany R	.10	.25
330 Temple of Malady R	.10	.25
331 Temple of Malice R	.10	.25
332 Temple of Mystery R	.08	.20
333 Temple of Silence R	.10	.25
334 Temple of the False God U	.10	.25
335 Temple of Triumph R	.08	.20
336 Terramorphic Expanse C	.08	.20
337 Twilight Mire R	1.50	4.00
338 Underground River R	1.50	4.00
339 Vault of the Archangel R	.20	.50
340 Viridescent Bog R	.30	.75
341 Woodland Cemetery R	.75	2.00
342 Yavimaya Coast R	.40	1.00

2024 Magic The Gathering Outlaws of Thunder Junction Foil

1 Another Round R	.20	.50
2 Archangel of Tithes M	1.25	3.00
3 Armored Armadillo C	.03	.08
4 Aven Interrupter R	1.50	4.00
5 Bounding Felidar U	.10	.25
6 Bovine Intervention U	.10	.25
7 Bridled Bighorn C	.03	.08
8 Claim Jumper R	.50	1.25
9 Dust Animus R	.20	.50
10 Eriette's Lullaby C	.04	.10
11 Final Showdown M	4.00	10.00
12 Fortune, Loyal Steed R	.10	.25
13 Frontier Seeker U	.04	.10
14 Getaway Glamer U	.10	.25
15 High Noon R	.25	.60
16 Holy Cow C	.10	.25
17 Inventive Wingsmith C	.03	.08
18 Lassoed by the Law U	.04	.10
19 Mystical Tether C	.03	.08
20 Nurturing Pixie U	.10	.25
21 Omenport Vigilante U	.03	.08
22 One Last Job R	.10	.25
23 Outlaw Medic C	.10	.25
24 Prairie Dog U	.04	.10
25 Prosperity Tycoon U	.03	.08
26 Requisition Raid U	.40	1.00
27 Rustler Rampage U	.10	.25
28 Shepherd of the Clouds U	.03	.08
29 Sheriff of Safe Passage U	.04	.10
30 Stagecoach Security C	.03	.08
31 Steer Clear C	.03	.08
32 Sterling Keykeeper C	.04	.10
33 Sterling Supplier C	.03	.08
34 Take Up the Shield C	.05	.12
35 Thunder Lasso U	.05	.12
36 Trained Arynx C	.05	.12
37 Vengeful Townsfolk C	.03	.08
38 Wanted Griffin C	.03	.08
39 Archmage's Newt R	.10	.25
40 Canyon Crab U	.04	.10
41 Daring Thunder-Thief C	.03	.08
42 Deepmuck Desperado U	.04	.10
43 Djinn of Fool's Fall C	.04	.10
44 Double Down M	1.25	3.00
45 Duelist of the Mind R	.25	.60
46 Emergent Haunting U	.04	.10
47 Failed Fording C	.03	.08
48 Fblthp, Lost on the Range R	.15	.40
49 Fleeting Reflection U	.10	.25
50 Geralf, the Fleshwright M	1.50	4.00
51 Geyser Drake C	.04	.10
52 Harrier Strix C	.04	.10
53 Jailbreak Scheme C	.03	.08
54 The Key to the Vault R	.25	.60
55 Loan Shark C	.03	.08
56 Marauding Sphinx U	.03	.08
57 Metamorphic Blast U	.10	.25
58 Nimble Brigand U	.03	.08
59 Outlaw Stitcher U	.03	.08
60 Peerless Ropemaster C	.03	.08
61 Phantom Interference C	.04	.10
62 Plan the Heist U	.03	.08
63 Razzle-Dazzler C	.03	.08
64 Seize the Secrets C	.04	.10
65 Shackle Slinger U	.03	.08
66 Shifting Grift U	.12	.30
67 Slickshot Lockpicker U	.05	.12
68 Slickshot Vault-Buster C	.03	.08
69 Spring Splasher C	.03	.08
70 Step Between Worlds R	.12	.30
71 Stoic Sphinx R	.10	.25
72 Stop Cold C	.03	.08
73 Take the Fall C	.03	.08
74 This Town Ain't Big Enough U	.03	.08
75 Three Steps Ahead R	2.50	6.00
76 Visage Bandit U	.10	.25
77 Ambush Gigapede C	.03	.08
78 Binding Negotiation U	.04	.10
79 Blacksnag Buzzard C	.03	.08
80 Blood Hustler U	.15	.40
81 Boneyard Desecrator C	.03	.08
82 Caustic Bronco R	1.00	2.50
83 Consuming Ashes C	.04	.10
84 Corrupted Conviction C	.10	.25
85 Desert's Due C	.03	.08
86 Desperate Bloodseeker C	.10	.25
87 Fake Your Own Death C	.04	.10
88 Forsaken Miner U	.20	.50
89 Gisa, the Hellraiser M	4.00	10.00
90 Hollow Marauder U	.04	.10
91 Insatiable Avarice R	2.50	6.00
92 Kaervek, the Punisher R	.50	1.25
93 Lively Dirge U	.40	1.00
94 Mourner's Surprise C	.03	.08
95 Neutralize the Guards U	.03	.08
96 Nezumi Linkbreaker C	.04	.10
97 Overzealous Muscle C	.03	.08
98 Pitiless Carnage R	.20	.50
99 Rakish Crew U	.10	.25
100 Rattleback Apothecary U	.04	.10
101 Raven of Fell Omens C	.04	.10
102 Rictus Robber U	.04	.10
103 Rooftop Assassin C	.04	.10
104 Rush of Dread R	.50	1.25
105 Servant of the Stinger U	.10	.25
106 Shoot the Sheriff U	.10	.25
107 Skulduggery C	.03	.08
108 Tinybones Joins Up R	.20	.50
109 Tinybones, the Pickpocket M	6.00	15.00
110 Treasure Dredger U	.10	.25
111 Unfortunate Accident U	.03	.08
112 Unscrupulous Contractor U	.08	.20
113 Vadmir, New Blood R	.10	.25
114 Vault Plunderer C	.04	.10
115 Brimstone Roundup U	.04	.10
116 Calamity, Galloping Inferno R	.20	.50
117 Caught in the Crossfire U	.04	.10
118 Cunning Coyote U	.04	.10
119 Deadeye Duelist C	.03	.08
120 Demonic Ruckus U	.12	.30
121 Discerning Peddler C	.03	.08
122 Explosive Derailment C	.03	.08
123 Ferocification U	.04	.10
124 Gila Courser U	.03	.08
125 Great Train Heist R	1.25	3.00
126 Hell to Pay R	.30	.75
127 Hellspur Brute U	.05	.12
128 Hellspur Posse Boss R	.12	.30
129 Highway Robbery C	.10	.25
130 Irascible Wolverine C	.04	.10
131 Iron-Fist Pulverizer C	.03	.08
132 Longhorn Sharpshooter U	.05	.12
133 Magda, the Hoardmaster R	.40	1.00
134 Magebane Lizard U	.25	.60
135 Mine Raider C	.04	.10
136 Outlaws' Fury C	.03	.08
137 Prickly Pair C	.03	.08
138 Quick Draw C	.04	.10
139 Quilled Charger C	.03	.08
140 Reckless Lackey C	.12	.30
141 Resilient Roadrunner U	.03	.08
142 Return the Favor U	2.00	5.00
143 Rodeo Pyromancers C	.05	.12
144 Scalestorm Summoner U	.03	.08
145 Scorching Shot U	.10	.25
146 Slickshot Show-Off R	5.00	12.00
147 Stingerback Terror R	.12	.30
148 Take for a Ride U	.04	.10
149 Terror of the Peaks M	10.00	25.00
150 Thunder Salvo C	.03	.08
151 Trick Shot C	.03	.08
152 Aloe Alchemist U	.05	.12
153 Ankle Biter C	.04	.10
154 Beastbond Outcaster U	.08	.20
155 Betrayal at the Vault U	.04	.10
156 Bristlepack Sentry C	.03	.08
157 Bristly Bill, Spine Sower M	15.00	40.00
158 Cactarantula C	.05	.12
159 Colossal Rattlewurm R	.15	.40
160 Dance of the Tumbleweeds C	.05	.12
161 Drover Grizzly C	.05	.12
162 Freestrider Commando C	.03	.08
163 Freestrider Lookout R	1.00	2.50
164 Full Steam Ahead U	.05	.12
165 Giant Beaver C	.04	.10
166 Gold Rush U	.05	.12
167 Goldvein Hydra M	5.00	12.00
168 Hardbristle Bandit C	.05	.12
169 Intrepid Stablemaster U	.04	.10
170 Map the Frontier U	.10	.25
171 Ornery Tumblewagg R	.15	.40
172 Outcaster Greenblade U	.04	.10
173 Outcaster Trailblazer R	2.00	5.00
174 Patient Naturalist C	.03	.08
175 Railway Brawler M	4.00	10.00
176 Rambling Possum U	.08	.20
177 Raucous Entertainer U	.04	.10
178 Reach for the Sky C	.04	.10
179 Rise of the Varmints U	.05	.12
180 Smuggler's Surprise R	1.25	3.00
181 Snakeskin Veil C	.10	.25
182 Spinewoods Armadillo U	.08	.20
183 Spinewoods Paladin C	.04	.10
184 Stubborn Burrowfiend U	.04	.10
185 Throw from the Saddle C	.03	.08
186 Trash the Town U	.12	.30
187 Tumbleweed Rising C	.05	.12

188 Voracious Varmint C .04 .10
189 Akul the Unrepentant R .20 .50
190 Annie Flash, the Veteran M .20 .50
191 Annie Joins Up R 3.00 8.00
192 Assimilation Aegis M .75 2.00
193 At Knifepoint U .05 .12
194 Badlands Revival U .04 .10
195 Baron Bertram Graywater U .12 .30
196 Bonny Pall, Clearcutter R .30 .75
197 Breeches, the Blastmaker R .12 .30
198 Bruse Tarl, Roving Rancher R .08 .20
199 Cactusfolk Sureshot U .10 .25
200 Congregation Gryff U .08 .20
201 Doc Aurlock, Grizzled Genius U .12 .30
202 Eriette, the Beguiler R .10 .25
203 Ertha Jo, Frontier Mentor U .10 .25
204 Form a Posse U .04 .10
205 Ghired, Mirror of the Wilds M .50 1.25
206 The Gitrog, Ravenous Ride M 2.00 5.00
207 Honest Rutstein U .50 1.25
208 Intimidation Campaign U .08 .20
209 Jem Lightfoote, Sky Explorer U .10 .25
210 Jolene, Plundering Pugilist U .10 .25
211 Kambal, Profiteering Mayor R 1.50 4.00
212 Kellan Joins Up R .12 .30
213 Kellan, the Kid M 1.00 2.50
214 Kraum, Violent Cacophony U .10 .25
215 Laughing Jasper Flint R .20 .50
216 Lazav, Familiar Stranger U .10 .25
217 Lilah, Undefeated Slickshot R .12 .30
218 Make Your Own Luck U .10 .25
219 Malcolm, the Eyes R .15 .40
220 Marchesa, Dealer of Death R .15 .40
221 Miriam, Herd Whisperer U .04 .10
222 Obeka, Splitter of Seconds R .25 .60
223 Oko, the Ringleader M 1.00 2.50
224 Pillage the Bog R 1.00 2.50
225 Rakdos Joins Up R .25 .60
226 Rakdos, the Muscle M 1.25 3.00
227 Riku of Many Paths R .12 .30
228 Roxanne, Starfall Savant R .40 1.00
229 Ruthless Lawbringer U .10 .25
230 Satoru, the Infiltrator R 2.00 5.00
231 Selvala, Eager Trailblazer M .30 .75
232 Seraphic Steed R .10 .25
233 Slick Sequence U .08 .20
234 Taii Wakeen, Perfect Shot R .15 .40
235 Vial Smasher, Gleeful Grenadier U .12 .30
236 Vraska Joins Up R .50 1.25
237 Vraska, the Silencer M 2.00 5.00
238 Wrangler of the Damned U .08 .20
239 Wylie Duke, Atiin Hero R .12 .30
240 Bandit's Haul U .05 .12
241 Boom Box U .05 .12
242 Gold Pan C .08 .20
243 Lavaspur Boots U 2.50 6.00
244 Luxurious Locomotive U .10 .25
245 Mobile Homestead U .04 .10
246 Oasis Gardener C .04 .10
247 Redrock Sentinel U .03 .08
248 Silver Deputy C .04 .10
249 Sterling Hound C .04 .10
250 Tomb Trawler U .04 .10
251 Abraded Bluffs C .10 .25
252 Arid Archway U .30 .75
253 Bristling Backwoods C .08 .20
254 Conduit Pylons C .10 .25
255 Creosote Heath C .10 .25
256 Eroded Canyon C .10 .25
257 Festering Gulch C .10 .25
258 Forlorn Flats C .10 .25
259 Jagged Barrens C .12 .30
260 Lonely Arroyo C .08 .20
261 Lush Oasis C .10 .25
262 Mirage Mesa C .05 .12
263 Sandstorm Verge U .10 .25
264 Soured Springs C .10 .25
265 Bucolic Ranch U .08 .20
266 Blooming Marsh R 1.00 2.50
267 Botanical Sanctum R 1.00 2.50
268 Concealed Courtyard R .50 1.25
269 Inspiring Vantage R 1.00 2.50
270 Spirebluff Canal R 1.50 4.00
271 Jace Reawakened M 2.00 5.00
272 Plains WESTERN FULL ART C .15 .40
273 Island WESTERN FULL ART C .20 .50
274 Swamp WESTERN FULL ART C .20 .50
275 Mountain WESTERN FULL ART C .25 .60
276 Forest WESTERN FULL ART C .25 .60
277 Plains C .05 .12
278 Plains C .04 .10
279 Island C .04 .10
280 Island C .04 .10
281 Swamp C .08 .20
282 Swamp C .05 .12
283 Mountain C .04 .10
284 Mountain C .04 .10
285 Forest C .04 .10
286 Forest C .04 .10
287 Geralf, the Fleshwright WANTED POSTER M2.00 5.00
288 Gisa, the Hellraiser WANTED POSTER M 5.00 12.00
289 Kaervek, the Punisher WANTED POSTER R1.00 2.50
290 Tinybones, the Pickpocket WANTED POSTER M 12.00 30.00
291 Annie Flash, the Veteran WANTED POSTER M.60 1.50
292 Breeches, the Blastmaker WANTED POSTER R.25 .60
293 Eriette, the Beguiler WANTED POSTER R .50 1.25
294 Kellan, the Kid WANTED POSTER M 3.00 8.00
295 Malcolm, the Eyes WANTED POSTER R .20 .50
296 Oko, the Ringleader WANTED POSTER M 6.00 15.00
297 Rakdos, the Muscle WANTED POSTER M 4.00 10.00
298 Satoru, the Infiltrator WANTED POSTER R 2.00 5.00
299 Vraska, the Silencer WANTED POSTER M 4.00 10.00
300 Blooming Marsh BORDERLESS R 2.00 5.00
301 Botanical Sanctum BORDERLESS R 1.50 4.00
302 Concealed Courtyard BORDERLESS R 1.50 4.00
303 Inspiring Vantage BORDERLESS R 1.25 3.00
304 Spirebluff Canal BORDERLESS R 2.50 6.00
305 Oko, the Ringleader BORDERLESS M 6.00 15.00
306 Jace Reawakened BORDERLESS M 8.00 20.00
307 Another Round EXT ART R .40 1.00
308 Archangel of Tithes EXT ART M 2.50 6.00
309 Aven Interrupter EXT ART R 4.00 10.00
310 Claim Jumper EXT ART R 1.25 3.00
311 Dust Animus EXT ART R .25 .60
312 Final Showdown EXT ART M 12.00 30.00
313 Fortune, Loyal Steed EXT ART R .12 .30
314 High Noon EXT ART R 1.25 3.00
315 One Last Job EXT ART R .20 .50
316 Archmage's Newt EXT ART R .25 .60
317 Double Down EXT ART M 2.50 6.00
318 Duelist of the Mind EXT ART R .60 1.50
319 Fblthp, Lost on the Range EXT ART R .60 1.50
320 The Key to the Vault EXT ART R .60 1.50
321 Step Between Worlds EXT ART R .20 .50
322 Stoic Sphinx EXT ART R .20 .50
323 Three Steps Ahead EXT ART R 4.00 10.00
324 Caustic Bronco EXT ART R 2.50 6.00
325 Insatiable Avarice EXT ART R 4.00 10.00
326 Pitiless Carnage EXT ART R .60 1.50
327 Rush of Dread EXT ART R 1.00 2.50
328 Tinybones Joins Up EXT ART R .60 1.50
329 Vadmir, New Blood EXT ART R .25 .60
330 Calamity, Galloping Inferno EXT ART R .60 1.50
331 Great Train Heist EXT ART R 2.50 6.00
332 Hell to Pay EXT ART R 1.25 3.00
333 Hellspur Posse Boss EXT ART R .20 .50
334 Magda, the Hoardmaster EXT ART R 1.25 3.00
335 Slickshot Show-Off EXT ART R 8.00 20.00
336 Stingerback Terror EXT ART R .20 .50
337 Terror of the Peaks EXT ART M 20.00 50.00
338 Bristly Bill, Spine Sower EXT ART M 20.00 50.00
339 Colossal Rattlewurm EXT ART R .30 .75
340 Freestrider Lookout EXT ART R 2.50 6.00
341 Goldvein Hydra EXT ART M 10.00 25.00
342 Ornery Tumblewagg EXT ART R .25 .60
343 Outcaster Trailblazer EXT ART R 3.00 8.00
344 Railway Brawler EXT ART M 10.00 25.00
345 Smuggler's Surprise EXT ART R 3.00 8.00
346 Akul the Unrepentant EXT ART R .40 1.00
347 Annie Joins Up EXT ART R 3.00 8.00
348 Assimilation Aegis EXT ART M 2.00 5.00
349 Bonny Pall, Clearcutter EXT ART R 1.00 2.50
350 Bruse Tarl, Roving Rancher EXT ART R .20 .50
351 Ghired, Mirror of the Wilds EXT ART M 2.50 6.00
352 The Gitrog, Ravenous Ride EXT ART M 6.00 15.00
353 Kambal, Profiteering Mayor EXT ART R 3.00 8.00
354 Kellan Joins Up EXT ART R .20 .50
355 Laughing Jasper Flint EXT ART R 1.00 2.50
356 Lilah, Undefeated Slickshot EXT ART R .50 1.25
357 Marchesa, Dealer of Death EXT ART R .60 1.50
358 Obeka, Splitter of Seconds EXT ART R 1.50 4.00
359 Pillage the Bog EXT ART R 3.00 8.00
360 Rakdos Joins Up EXT ART R .60 1.50
361 Riku of Many Paths EXT ART R .20 .50
362 Roxanne, Starfall Savant EXT ART R 4.00 10.00
363 Selvala, Eager Trailblazer EXT ART M .60 1.50
364 Seraphic Steed EXT ART R .15 .40
365 Taii Wakeen, Perfect Shot EXT ART R .25 .60
366 Vraska Joins Up EXT ART R .60 1.50
367 Wylie Duke, Atiin Hero EXT ART R .20 .50

2024 Magic The Gathering Outlaws of Thunder Junction Special Guests

29 Stoneforge Mystic M 12.00 30.00
30 Brazen Borrower // Petty Theft M 4.00 10.00
31 Desertion M 1.00 2.50
32 Morbid Opportunist M 5.00 12.00
33 Port Razer M 2.00 5.00
34 Scapeshift M 12.00 30.00
35 Mystic Snake M 2.00 5.00
36 Notion Thief M 3.00 8.00
37 Desert M 2.00 5.00
38 Prismatic Vista M 20.00 50.00

2024 Magic The Gathering Outlaws of Thunder Junction Special Guests Foil

29 Stoneforge Mystic M 20.00 50.00
30 Brazen Borrower // Petty Theft M 8.00 20.00
31 Desertion M 1.25 3.00
32 Morbid Opportunist M 10.00 25.00
33 Port Razer M 4.00 10.00
34 Scapeshift M 20.00 50.00
35 Mystic Snake M 2.50 6.00
36 Notion Thief M 8.00 20.00
37 Desert M 2.50 6.00
38 Prismatic Vista M 25.00 60.00

2024 Magic The Gathering Outlaws of Thunder Junction The Big Score

1 Collector's Cage M 1.50 4.00
2 Grand Abolisher M 3.00 8.00
3 Oltec Matterweaver M 1.50 4.00
4 Rest in Peace M .40 1.00
5 Esoteric Duplicator M .75 2.00
6 Simulacrum Synthesizer M 12.00 30.00
7 Worldwalker Helm M 3.00 8.00
8 Greed's Gambit M .15 .40
9 Harvester of Misery M 1.25 3.00
10 Hostile Investigator M 4.00 10.00
11 Generous Plunderer M 3.00 8.00
12 Legion Extruder M 1.25 3.00
13 Memory Vessel M .30 .75
14 Molten Duplication M 4.00 10.00
15 Territory Forge M .15 .40
16 Ancient Cornucopia M 2.50 6.00
17 Bristlebud Farmer M .75 2.00
18 Omenpath Journey M 2.50 6.00
19 Sandstorm Salvager M 1.25 3.00
20 Vaultborn Tyrant M 15.00 40.00
21 Loot, the Key to Everything M .60 1.50
22 Pest Control M 3.00 8.00
23 Lost Jitte M 2.50 6.00
24 Lotus Ring M 1.00 2.50
25 Nexus of Becoming M 1.25 3.00
26 Sword of Wealth and Power M 12.00 30.00
27 Torpor Orb M 1.25 3.00
28 Transmutation Font M 1.25 3.00
29 Fomori Vault M 6.00 15.00
30 Tarnation Vista M 1.25 3.00
31 Collector's Cage M 6.00 15.00
32 Grand Abolisher M 4.00 10.00
33 Oltec Matterweaver M 3.00 8.00
34 Rest in Peace M 1.50 4.00
35 Esoteric Duplicator M 4.00 10.00
36 Simulacrum Synthesizer M 40.00 100.00
37 Worldwalker Helm M 6.00 15.00
38 Greed's Gambit M .60 1.50
39 Harvester of Misery M 4.00 10.00
40 Hostile Investigator M 10.00 25.00
41 Generous Plunderer M 10.00 25.00
42 Legion Extruder M 3.00 8.00
43 Memory Vessel M 2.00 5.00
44 Molten Duplication M 8.00 20.00
45 Territory Forge M 1.00 2.50
46 Ancient Cornucopia M 8.00 20.00
47 Bristlebud Farmer M 2.00 5.00
48 Omenpath Journey M 5.00 12.00
49 Sandstorm Salvager M 2.50 6.00
50 Vaultborn Tyrant M 30.00 80.00
51 Loot, the Key to Everything M 10.00 25.00
52 Pest Control M 10.00 25.00
53 Lost Jitte M 10.00 25.00
54 Lotus Ring M 4.00 10.00
55 Nexus of Becoming M 4.00 10.00
56 Sword of Wealth and Power M 30.00 80.00
57 Torpor Orb M 4.00 10.00
58 Transmutation Font M 4.00 10.00
59 Fomori Vault M 15.00 40.00
60 Tarnation Vista M 4.00 10.00
66 Collector's Cage M 3.00 8.00
67 Grand Abolisher M 3.00 8.00
68 Oltec Matterweaver M 2.50 6.00
69 Rest in Peace M .75 2.00
70 Esoteric Duplicator M 2.00 5.00
71 Simulacrum Synthesizer M 20.00 50.00
72 Worldwalker Helm M 4.00 10.00
73 Greed's Gambit M .40 1.00
74 Harvester of Misery M 2.50 6.00
75 Hostile Investigator M 5.00 12.00
76 Generous Plunderer M 4.00 10.00
77 Legion Extruder M 2.00 5.00
78 Memory Vessel M 1.00 2.50
79 Molten Duplication M 6.00 15.00
80 Territory Forge M .50 1.25
81 Ancient Cornucopia M 4.00 10.00
82 Bristlebud Farmer M 1.00 2.50
83 Omenpath Journey M 3.00 8.00
84 Sandstorm Salvager M 2.00 5.00
85 Vaultborn Tyrant M 20.00 50.00
86 Loot, the Key to Everything M 3.00 8.00
87 Pest Control M 6.00 15.00
88 Lost Jitte M 5.00 12.00
89 Lotus Ring M 4.00 10.00
90 Nexus of Becoming M 1.25 3.00
91 Sword of Wealth and Power M 15.00 40.00
92 Torpor Orb M 2.00 5.00
93 Transmutation Font M 1.50 4.00
94 Fomori Vault M 10.00 25.00
95 Tarnation Vista M 2.00 5.00

2024 Magic The Gathering Ravnica Remastered

1 Karn, the Great Creator M 5.00 12.00
2 Angelic Exaltation U .05 .12
3 Armory Guard C .03 .08
4 Arrester's Zeal C .04 .10
5 Azorius Arrester C .03 .08
6 Azorius Justiciar U .03 .08
7 Basilica Guards C .03 .08
8 Blazing Archon R .25 .60
9 Blind Obedience R 1.00 2.50
10 Boros Elite C .03 .08
11 Bulwark Giant C .03 .08
12 Carom C .03 .08
13 Conclave Equenaut C .03 .08
14 Condemn U .05 .12
15 Devouring Light U .03 .08
16 Divine Visitation M 4.00 10.00
17 Eyes in the Skies C .03 .08
18 Faith's Fetters C .03 .08
19 Ghostway R 1.00 2.50
20 Gideon Blackblade M .50 1.25
21 Keening Apparition C .03 .08
22 Makeshift Battalion C .03 .08
23 Ministrant of Obligation U .03 .08
24 Mistral Charger U .03 .08
25 Rising Populace C .03 .08
26 Rootborn Defenses C .10 .25
27 Summary Judgment C .03 .08
28 Sunhome Stalwart U .03 .08
29 Syndicate Messenger C .03 .08
30 To Arms! U .10 .25
31 Tomik, Distinguished Advokist R .10 .25
32 Unbreakable Formation R 1.00 2.50
33 Urbis Protector U .03 .08
34 Aetherplasm U .04 .10
35 Bruvac the Grandiloquent M 10.00 25.00
36 Cerulean Sphinx U .03 .08
37 Cloudfin Raptor C .03 .08
38 Compulsive Research C .03 .08
39 Copy Enchantment R .20 .50
40 Cyclonic Rift M 20.00 50.00
41 Downsize C .03 .08
42 Drift of Phantasms C .10 .25
43 Eyes Everywhere U .04 .10
44 Fblthp, the Lost R .12 .30
45 Helium Squirter C .05 .12
46 Kasmina's Transmutation C .03 .08
47 Keymaster Rogue C .04 .10
48 Kiora's Dambreaker C .03 .08
49 Leapfrog C .03 .08
50 Muddle the Mixture U .75 2.00
51 Murmuring Mystic U .30 .75
52 Nightveil Sprite U .03 .08
53 Persistent Petitioners C .60 1.50
54 Pteramander U .03 .08
55 Quasiduplicate R .20 .50
56 Quench C .03 .08
57 Quicken U .10 .25
58 Radical Idea C .03 .08
59 Remand U .20 .50
60 Repeal C .03 .08
61 Sinister Sabotage C .03 .08
62 Spark Double R 3.00 8.00
63 Tidespout Tyrant R .60 1.50
64 Totally Lost C .03 .08
65 Vedalken Mesmerist C .04 .10
66 Balustrade Spy C .03 .08
67 Blade Juggler C .03 .08
68 Bladebrand C .03 .08
69 Burglar Rat C .08 .20
70 Crypt Ghast R 4.00 10.00
71 Dark Confidant M 4.00 10.00
72 Debtors' Transport C .03 .08
73 Dimir House Guard C .05 .12
74 Disembowel C .03 .08
75 Dreadmalkin U .03 .08
76 Golgari Thug U .12 .30
77 Ill-Gotten Inheritance C .04 .10
78 Infernal Tutor R .20 .50
79 Last Gasp C .04 .10
80 Liliana, Dreadhorde General M 8.00 20.00
81 Lord of the Void M 3.00 8.00
82 Macabre Waltz C .04 .10
83 Massacre Girl R .50 1.25
84 Mausoleum Turnkey U .03 .08
85 Mephitic Vapors C .03 .08
86 Midnight Reaper R .12 .30
87 Orzhov Enforcer U .05 .12
88 Orzhov Euthanist C .03 .08
89 Plaguecrafter U .20 .50
90 Priest of Forgotten Gods R .75 2.00
91 Sewer Shambler C .03 .08
92 Shadow Alley Denizen C .04 .10
93 Stab Wound C .04 .10
94 Thrill-Kill Assassin C .08 .20
95 Ultimate Price U .03 .08
96 Undercity's Embrace C .03 .08
97 Vindictive Vampire U .10 .25
98 Woebringer Demon U .03 .08
99 Act of Treason C .03 .08
100 Arclight Phoenix R 2.00 5.00
101 Bloodfray Giant U .03 .08
102 Bomber Corps C .03 .08
103 Burn Bright C .03 .08
104 Burning Prophet C .03 .08
105 Burning-Tree Vandal C .03 .08
106 Demolish C .03 .08
107 Demonfire U .03 .08
108 Dogpile C .03 .08
109 Greater Forgeling C .03 .08
110 Guttersnipe U .10 .25
111 Hellkite Tyrant R 2.00 5.00
112 Homing Lightning U .03 .08
113 Illharg, the Raze-Boar M 2.00 5.00
114 Krenko, Mob Boss R .75 2.00
115 Krenko's Command C .10 .25
116 Legion Warboss R .25 .60
117 Light Up the Stage U .12 .30
118 Mizzix's Mastery R 1.00 2.50
119 Mugging C .03 .08
120 Rakdos Pit Dragon U .03 .08
121 Rubblebelt Maaka C .03 .08
122 Scorched Rusalka C .03 .08
123 Siege of Towers U .03 .08
124 Skewer the Critics C .05 .12
125 Skullcrack U .10 .25
126 Stalking Vengeance U .08 .20
127 Taste for Mayhem C .03 .08
128 Tin Street Dodger C .03 .08
129 Utvara Hellkite M 5.00 12.00
130 Wojek Bodyguard C .03 .08
131 Arboreal Grazer C .10 .25
132 Band Together C .03 .08
133 Birds of Paradise R 4.00 10.00
134 Chord of Calling R 4.00 10.00
135 Crocanura C .03 .08
136 Drudge Beetle C .03 .08
137 Experiment One U .05 .12
138 Farseek U .60 1.50
139 Fists of Ironwood C .03 .08
140 Forced Adaptation C .04 .10
141 Forced Landing C .03 .08
142 Fungal Rebirth U .10 .25
143 Gather Courage C .03 .08
144 Golgari Grave-Troll R 1.25 3.00
145 Greater Mossdog C .03 .08
146 Guardian Project M 5.00 12.00
147 Horncaller's Chant C .03 .08
148 Life from the Loam R 5.00 12.00
149 Loaming Shaman U .03 .08
150 Moldervine Cloak U .03 .08
151 Open the Gates C .05 .12
152 Overwhelm U .03 .08
153 Protean Hulk M 2.50 6.00
154 Rampaging Rendhorn C .03 .08
155 Siege Wurm C .03 .08
156 Silhana Ledgewalker C .04 .10
157 Sprouting Renewal C .03 .08
158 Titanic Brawl C .03 .08
159 Utopia Sprawl U .20 .50
160 Wasteland Viper U .10 .25
161 Wurmweaver Coil U .03 .08
162 Yeva, Nature's Herald R .40 1.00
163 Assemble the Legion R .10 .25
164 Aurelia, Exemplar of Justice M 1.00 2.50
165 Azorius Guildmage U .04 .10
166 Blind Hunter C .03 .08
167 Borborygmos Enraged R .12 .30
168 Boros Guildmage U .04 .10
169 Call of the Conclave C .03 .08
170 Cartel Aristocrat U .04 .10
171 Cindervines R .12 .30
172 Coiling Oracle C .08 .20
173 Conclave Cavalier U .03 .08
174 Crackling Drake U .08 .20
175 Deathrite Shaman R 2.00 5.00
176 Debt to the Deathless U .15 .40
177 Deputy of Acquittals C .03 .08
178 Dimir Guildmage U .03 .08
179 Domri Rade M .50 1.25
180 Dreadbore R .20 .50
181 Footlight Fiend C .03 .08
182 Fresh-Faced Recruit C .03 .08
183 Frilled Mystic U .04 .10
184 Glowspore Shaman C .03 .08
185 Gobhobbler Rats C .03 .08
186 Goblin Electromancer C .10 .25
187 Golgari Findbroker U .08 .20
188 Golgari Guildmage U .03 .08
189 Gruul Guildmage U .03 .08

190 Izzet Charm U .12 .30
191 Izzet Guildmage U .03 .08
192 Judge's Familiar C .04 .10
193 Karlov of the Ghost Council M 2.50 6.00
194 Kaya, Orzhov Usurper R .10 .25
195 Lavinia, Azorius Renegade R .30 .75
196 Lazav, the Multifarious R .12 .30
197 Lightning Helix U .10 .25
198 Master of Cruelties M 1.50 4.00
199 Mayhem Devil U .50 1.25
200 Merfolk of the Depths C .03 .08
201 Mindleech Mass R .50 1.25
202 Moroii U .03 .08
203 Mortus Strider C .03 .08
204 Mourning Thrull C .03 .08
205 Nicol Bolas, Dragon-God M 1.50 4.00
206 Nightveil Predator U .05 .12
207 Niv-Mizzet, Parun R .75 2.00
208 Orzhov Guildmage U .03 .08
209 Petrahydrox C .04 .10
210 Phytohydra R .12 .30
211 Prime Speaker Zegana R .20 .50
212 Putrefy U .10 .25
213 Rakdos Firewheeler U .03 .08
214 Rakdos Guildmage U .03 .08
215 Rakdos, Lord of Riots R 1.00 2.50
216 Ral Zarek M .40 1.00
217 Rhythm of the Wild U 2.00 5.00
218 Savra, Queen of the Golgari R .60 1.50
219 Scab-Clan Mauler C .03 .08
220 Selesnya Evangel U .04 .10
221 Selesnya Guildmage U .03 .08
222 Sharktocrab U .03 .08
223 Simic Guildmage U .03 .08
224 Sky Hussar U .03 .08
225 Skyknight Legionnaire C .03 .08
226 Slitherhead C .04 .10
227 Sphinx of New Prahv U .03 .08
228 Sphinx's Revelation R .60 1.50
229 Stitch in Time R .50 1.25
230 Sunder Shaman U .05 .12
231 Tajic, Legion's Edge R .30 .75
232 Teferi, Time Raveler M 4.00 10.00
233 Teysa, Orzhov Scion R 1.00 2.50
234 Tolsimir Wolfblood R 1.25 3.00
235 Truefire Captain U .04 .10
236 Vernadi Shieldmate C .03 .08
237 Voidslime R .25 .60
238 Whisper Agent C .03 .08
239 Wild Cantor C .04 .10
240 Warrant // Warden R .04 .10
241 Revival // Revenge R .12 .30
242 Connive // Concoct R .08 .20
243 Expansion // Explosion R .15 .40
244 Bedeck // Bedazzle R .08 .20
245 Find // Finality R .10 .25
246 Thrash // Threat R .10 .25
247 Response // Resurgence R .15 .40
248 Assure // Assemble R .04 .10
249 Repudiate // Replicate R .12 .30
250 Azorius Signet U .12 .30
251 Boros Signet U .50 1.25
252 Bottled Cloister R .10 .25
253 Chromatic Lantern R 1.25 3.00
254 Civic Saber U .03 .08
255 Cloudstone Curio M 8.00 20.00
256 Dimir Signet U .60 1.50
257 Gate Colossus U .04 .10
258 Golgari Signet U .25 .60
259 Gruul Signet U .60 1.50
260 Illusionist's Bracers R 1.50 4.00
261 Izzet Signet U .20 .50
262 Junktroller U .03 .08
263 Orzhov Signet U .30 .75
264 Pariah's Shield R .50 1.25
265 Rakdos Signet U 1.25 3.00
266 Seal of the Guildpact R .15 .40
267 Selesnya Signet U .40 1.00
268 Silent Dart U .04 .10
269 Simic Signet U .20 .50
270 Sword of the Paruns R .50 1.25
271 Voyager Staff U .10 .25
272 Azorius Guildgate C .08 .20
273 Blood Crypt R 8.00 20.00
274 Boros Guildgate C .08 .20
275 Breeding Pool R 10.00 25.00
276 Dimir Guildgate C .08 .20
277 Godless Shrine R 6.00 15.00
278 Golgari Guildgate C .10 .25
279 Gruul Guildgate C .08 .20
280 Hallowed Fountain R 5.00 12.00
281 Izzet Guildgate C .10 .25
282 Orzhov Guildgate C .05 .12
283 Overgrown Tomb R 8.00 20.00
284 Rakdos Guildgate C .05 .12
285 Sacred Foundry R 12.00 30.00
286 Selesnya Guildgate C .08 .20
287 Simic Guildgate C .08 .20
288 Steam Vents R 10.00 25.00
289 Stomping Ground R 6.00 15.00
290 Temple Garden R 8.00 20.00
291 Watery Grave R 8.00 20.00
292 Blood Crypt BORDERLESS R 10.00 25.00
293 Breeding Pool BORDERLESS R 12.00 30.00
294 Godless Shrine BORDERLESS R 10.00 25.00
295 Hallowed Fountain BORDERLESS R 8.00 20.00
296 Overgrown Tomb BORDERLESS R 10.00 25.00
297 Sacred Foundry BORDERLESS R 12.00 30.00
298 Steam Vents BORDERLESS R 10.00 25.00
299 Stomping Ground BORDERLESS R 10.00 25.00
300 Temple Garden BORDERLESS R 10.00 25.00
301 Watery Grave BORDERLESS R 10.00 25.00
302 Blazing Archon RETRO SERIAL R 60.00 150.00
302 Blazing Archon RETRO R .10 .25
303 Blind Obedience RETRO R .75 2.00
303 Blind Obedience RETRO SERIAL R 75.00 200.00
304 Condemn RETRO U .04 .10
305 Devouring Light RETRO U .03 .08
306 Divine Visitation RETRO SERIAL M 60.00 150.00
306 Divine Visitation RETRO M 3.00 8.00
307 Faith's Fetters RETRO C .04 .10
308 Ghostway RETRO R .25 .60
309 Bruvac the Grandiloquent RETRO M 8.00 20.00
309 Bruvac the Grandiloquent RETRO SERIAL M100.00250.00
310 Cloudfin Raptor RETRO C .03 .08
311 Compulsive Research RETRO C .04 .10
312 Copy Enchantment RETRO SERIAL R 50.00 120.00
312 Copy Enchantment RETRO R .12 .30
313 Cyclonic Rift RETRO SERIAL M 400.00 1,000.00
313 Cyclonic Rift RETRO M 20.00 50.00
314 Drift of Phantasms RETRO C .08 .20
315 Muddle the Mixture RETRO U .75 2.00
316 Persistent Petitioners RETRO C .60 1.50
317 Pteramander RETRO U .04 .10
318 Quicken RETRO U .08 .20
319 Spark Double RETRO SERIAL R 75.00 200.00
319 Spark Double RETRO R 2.50 6.00
320 Tidespout Tyrant RETRO SERIAL R 75.00 200.00
320 Tidespout Tyrant RETRO R .20 .50
321 Totally Lost RETRO C .03 .08
322 Crypt Ghast RETRO SERIAL R 100.00 250.00
322 Crypt Ghast RETRO R 3.00 8.00
323 Dark Confidant RETRO SERIAL M 125.00 300.00
323 Dark Confidant RETRO M 3.00 8.00
324 Dimir House Guard RETRO C .08 .20
325 Golgari Thug RETRO U .20 .50
326 Infernal Tutor RETRO R .20 .50
326 Infernal Tutor RETRO SERIAL R 75.00 200.00
327 Lord of the Void RETRO M 2.00 5.00
327 Lord of the Void RETRO SERIAL M 75.00 200.00
328 Massacre Girl RETRO R .20 .50
329 Ultimate Price RETRO U .05 .12
330 Vindictive Vampire RETRO U .10 .25
331 Arclight Phoenix RETRO R 2.00 5.00
331 Arclight Phoenix RETRO SERIAL R 125.00 300.00
332 Guttersnipe RETRO U .10 .25
333 Hellkite Tyrant RETRO R 2.00 5.00
333 Hellkite Tyrant RETRO SERIAL R 125.00 300.00
334 Ilharg, the Raze-Boar RETRO M 1.00 2.50
334 Ilharg, the Raze-Boar RETRO SERIAL M 60.00 150.00
335 Krenko, Mob Boss RETRO R .75 2.00
335 Krenko, Mob Boss RETRO SERIAL R 200.00 500.00
336 Krenko's Command RETRO C .03 .08
337 Legion Warboss RETRO R .15 .40
337 Legion Warboss RETRO SERIAL R 60.00 150.00
338 Light Up the Stage RETRO U .20 .50
339 Mizzix's Mastery RETRO R .25 .60
339 Mizzix's Mastery RETRO SERIAL R 50.00 120.00
340 Skewer the Critics RETRO C .12 .30
341 Skullcrack RETRO U .15 .40
342 Utvara Hellkite RETRO M 3.00 8.00
342 Utvara Hellkite RETRO SERIAL M 100.00 250.00
343 Arboreal Grazer RETRO C .25 .60
344 Birds of Paradise RETRO R 2.50 6.00
344 Birds of Paradise RETRO SERIAL R 300.00 800.00
345 Chord of Calling RETRO R 4.00 10.00
345 Chord of Calling RETRO SERIAL R 100.00 250.00
346 Experiment One RETRO U .03 .08
347 Farseek RETRO U 1.00 2.50
348 Golgari Grave-Troll RETRO R .75 2.00
348 Golgari Grave-Troll RETRO SERIAL R 60.00 150.00
349 Guardian Project RETRO M 4.00 10.00
350 Life from the Loam RETRO R 4.00 10.00
350 Life from the Loam RETRO SERIAL R 125.00 300.00
351 Loaming Shaman RETRO U .04 .10
352 Moldervine Cloak RETRO U .04 .10
353 Protean Hulk RETRO M 2.00 5.00
353 Protean Hulk RETRO SERIAL M 60.00 150.00
354 Silhana Ledgewalker RETRO C .04 .10
355 Utopia Sprawl RETRO U .50 1.25
356 Aurelia, Exemplar of Justice RETRO M .40 1.00
356 Aurelia, Exemplar of Justice
RETRO SERIAL M 60.00 150.00
357 Borborygmos Enraged RETRO R .08 .20
358 Call of the Conclave RETRO C .03 .08
359 Cartel Aristocrat RETRO U .04 .10
360 Cindervines RETRO R .12 .30
360 Cindervines RETRO SERIAL R 40.00 100.00
361 Coiling Oracle RETRO C .08 .20
362 Crackling Drake RETRO U .25 .60
363 Deathrite Shaman RETRO SERIAL R 200.00 500.00
363 Deathrite Shaman RETRO R 2.00 5.00
364 Debt to the Deathless RETRO U .12 .30
365 Dreadbore RETRO R .12 .30
366 Frilled Mystic RETRO U .04 .10
367 Goblin Electromancer RETRO C .05 .12
368 Izzet Charm RETRO U .10 .25
369 Karlov of the Ghost Council
RETRO SERIAL M 125.00 300.00
369 Karlov of the Ghost Council RETRO M 2.00 5.00
370 Lavinia, Azorius Renegade RETRO R .12 .30
371 Lazav, the Multifarious RETRO SERIAL R60.00 150.00
371 Lazav, the Multifarious RETRO R .10 .25
372 Lightning Helix RETRO U .20 .50
373 Master of Cruelties RETRO SERIAL M 100.00 250.00
373 Master of Cruelties RETRO M 1.00 2.50
374 Mayhem Devil RETRO U .60 1.50
375 Mindleech Mass RETRO R .10 .25
375 Mindleech Mass RETRO SERIAL R 40.00 100.00
376 Niv-Mizzet, Parun RETRO R .30 .75
376 Niv-Mizzet, Parun RETRO SERIAL R 200.00 500.00
377 Prime Speaker Zegana RETRO R .12 .30
377 Prime Speaker Zegana RETRO SERIAL R 75.00 200.00
378 Putrefy RETRO U .08 .20
379 Rakdos, Lord of Riots RETRO SERIAL R100.00 250.00
379 Rakdos, Lord of Riots RETRO R .15 .40
380 Rhythm of the Wild RETRO U 2.00 5.00
381 Savra, Queen of the Golgari RETRO SERIAL R50.00120.00
381 Savra, Queen of the Golgari RETRO R .12 .30
382 Sky Hussar RETRO U .04 .10
383 Sphinx's Revelation RETRO SERIAL R 40.00 100.00
383 Sphinx's Revelation RETRO R .12 .30
384 Stitch in Time RETRO SERIAL R 50.00 120.00
384 Stitch in Time RETRO R .10 .25
385 Tajic, Legion's Edge RETRO R .10 .25
385 Tajic, Legion's Edge RETRO SERIAL R 50.00 120.00
386 Teysa, Orzhov Scion RETRO R .20 .50
386 Teysa, Orzhov Scion RETRO SERIAL R 75.00 200.00
387 Tolsimir Wolfblood RETRO SERIAL R 60.00 150.00
387 Tolsimir Wolfblood RETRO R .10 .25
388 Voidslime RETRO R .10 .25
389 Bottled Cloister RETRO SERIAL R 40.00 100.00
389 Bottled Cloister RETRO R .04 .10
390 Chromatic Lantern RETRO SERIAL R 100.00 250.00
390 Chromatic Lantern RETRO R 1.25 3.00
391 Cloudstone Curio RETRO SERIAL M 100.00 250.00
391 Cloudstone Curio RETRO M 5.00 12.00
392 Illusionist's Bracers RETRO R .75 2.00
393 Pariah's Shield RETRO SERIAL R 40.00 100.00
393 Pariah's Shield RETRO R .12 .30
394 Seal of the Guildpact RETRO SERIAL R 40.00 100.00
394 Seal of the Guildpact RETRO R .10 .25
395 Sword of the Paruns RETRO R .10 .25
395 Sword of the Paruns RETRO SERIAL R 50.00 120.00
396 Azorius Guildgate RETRO C .05 .12
397 Blood Crypt RETRO R 10.00 25.00
397 Blood Crypt RETRO SERIAL R 250.00 600.00
398 Boros Guildgate RETRO C .04 .10
3.99E+02 Breeding Pool RETRO R 10.00 25.00
3.99E+02 Breeding Pool RETRO SERIAL R 250.00 600.00
4.00E+02 Dimir Guildgate RETRO C .04 .10
4.01E+02 Godless Shrine RETRO R 8.00 20.00
4.01E+02 Godless Shrine RETRO SERIAL R 250.00 600.00
4.02E+02 Golgari Guildgate RETRO C .04 .10
4.03E+02 Gruul Guildgate RETRO C .04 .10
4.04E+02 Hallowed Fountain RETRO R 10.00 25.00
404 Hallowed Fountain RETRO SERIAL R 250.00 600.00
405 Izzet Guildgate RETRO C .04 .10
406 Orzhov Guildgate RETRO C .04 .10
407 Overgrown Tomb RETRO R 8.00 20.00
407 Overgrown Tomb RETRO SERIAL R 250.00 600.00
408 Rakdos Guildgate RETRO C .04 .10
409 Sacred Foundry RETRO R 12.00 30.00
409 Sacred Foundry RETRO SERIAL R 200.00 500.00
410 Selesnya Guildgate RETRO C .04 .10
411 Simic Guildgate RETRO C .05 .12
412 Steam Vents RETRO R 12.00 30.00
412 Steam Vents RETRO SERIAL R 500.00 1,200.00
413 Stomping Ground RETRO R 10.00 25.00
413 Stomping Ground RETRO SERIAL R 150.00 400.00
414 Temple Garden RETRO R 8.00 20.00
414 Temple Garden RETRO SERIAL R 200.00 500.00
415 Watery Grave RETRO R 10.00 25.00
415 Watery Grave RETRO SERIAL R 300.00 800.00
416 Divine Visitation BORDERLESS ANIME M8.00 20.00
417 Tomik, Distinguished Advokist
BORDERLESS ANIME R .15 .40
418 Bruvac the Grandiloquent
BORDERLESS ANIME M 8.00 20.00
419 Cyclonic Rift BORDERLESS ANIME M 30.00 80.00
420 Fblthp, the Lost BORDERLESS ANIME R .15 .40
421 Spark Double BORDERLESS ANIME R 4.00 10.00
422 Tidespout Tyrant BORDERLESS ANIME R .30 .75
423 Crypt Ghast BORDERLESS ANIME R 4.00 10.00
424 Lord of the Void BORDERLESS ANIME M 3.00 8.00
425 Massacre Girl BORDERLESS ANIME R 2.50 6.00
426 Pack Rat BORDERLESS ANIME R 1.00 2.50
427 Arclight Phoenix BORDERLESS ANIME R 2.00 5.00
428 Hellkite Tyrant BORDERLESS ANIME R 3.00 8.00
429 Ilharg, the Raze-Boar BORDERLESS ANIME M2.00 5.00
430 Krenko, Mob Boss BORDERLESS ANIME R2.00 5.00
431 Utvara Hellkite BORDERLESS ANIME M 8.00 20.00
432 Birds of Paradise BORDERLESS ANIME R5.00 12.00
433 Guardian Project BORDERLESS ANIME M6.00 15.00
434 Life from the Loam BORDERLESS ANIME R5.00 12.00
435 Protean Hulk BORDERLESS ANIME M 3.00 8.00
436 Aurelia, Exemplar of Justice
BORDERLESS ANIME M 5.00 12.00
437 Karlov of the Ghost Council
BORDERLESS ANIME M 2.00 5.00
438 Niv-Mizzet, Parun BORDERLESS ANIME R2.50 6.00
439 Prime Speaker Zegana
BORDERLESS ANIME R .60 1.50
440 Savra, Queen of the Golgari
BORDERLESS ANIME R 1.50 4.00
441 Teysa, Orzhov Scion BORDERLESS ANIME R2.00 5.00
442 Chromatic Lantern BORDERLESS ANIME R3.00 8.00
443 Cloudstone Curio BORDERLESS ANIME M6.00 15.00
444 Domri Rade BORDERLESS ANIME M .40 1.00
445 Ral Zarek BORDERLESS ANIME M .60 1.50
446 Rest in Peace RETRO R .40 1.00
447 Sphere of Safety RETRO U 2.00 5.00
448 Aetherize RETRO U .75 2.00
449 Enter the Infinite RETRO M 1.25 3.00
450 Gigantoplasm RETRO R .10 .25
451 Narcomoeba RETRO U .75 2.00
452 Turnabout RETRO U .12 .30
453 Creeping Chill RETRO U .50 1.25
454 Darkblast RETRO U .20 .50
455 Pack Rat RETRO R .40 1.00
456 Shattering Spree RETRO U .60 1.50
457 Perilous Forays RETRO U .40 1.00
458 Wilderness Reclamation RETRO U 1.00 2.50
459 Niv-Mizzet Reborn RETRO M .60 1.50
460 Shambling Shell C .08 .20
461 Supreme Verdict RETRO R 1.25 3.00
462 Magewright's Stone RETRO U 2.00 5.00
463 Pithing Needle RETRO R 1.25 3.00
464 Karn's Bastion RETRO R 1.00 2.50
465 Maze's End RETRO M 4.00 10.00
466 Thespian's Stage RETRO R 2.00 5.00
467 Niv-Mizzet, the Firemind RETRO R .25 .60

2024 Magic The Gathering Ravnica Remastered Foil

1 Karn, the Great Creator M 5.00 12.00
2 Angelic Exaltation U .10 .25
3 Armory Guard C .03 .08
4 Arrester's Zeal C .04 .10
5 Azorius Arrester C .04 .10
6 Azorius Justiciar U .04 .10
7 Basilica Guards C .03 .08
8 Blazing Archon R .30 .75
9 Blind Obedience R 1.50 4.00
10 Boros Elite C .04 .10
11 Bulwark Giant C .03 .08
12 Carom C .03 .08
13 Conclave Equenaut C .04 .10
14 Condemn U .10 .25
15 Devouring Light U .03 .08
16 Divine Visitation M 4.00 10.00
17 Eyes in the Skies C .03 .08
18 Faith's Fetters C .03 .08
19 Ghostway R 1.25 3.00
20 Gideon Blackblade M .50 1.25
21 Keening Apparition C .03 .08
22 Makeshift Battalion C .03 .08
23 Ministrant of Obligation U .04 .10
24 Mistral Charger U .03 .08
25 Rising Populace C .03 .08
26 Rootborn Defenses C .20 .50
27 Summary Judgment C .03 .08
28 Sunhome Stalwart U .03 .08
29 Syndicate Messenger C .04 .10
30 To Arms! U .12 .30
31 Tomik, Distinguished Advokist R .08 .20
32 Unbreakable Formation R 1.00 2.50
33 Urbis Protector U .03 .08
34 Aetherplasm U .04 .10
35 Bruvac the Grandiloquent M 10.00 25.00
36 Cerulean Sphinx U .03 .08
37 Cloudfin Raptor C .04 .10
38 Compulsive Research C .04 .10
39 Copy Enchantment R .25 .60
40 Cyclonic Rift M 25.00 60.00
41 Downsize C .03 .08
42 Drift of Phantasms C .20 .50
43 Eyes Everywhere U .05 .12
44 Fblthp, the Lost R .12 .30
45 Helium Squirter C .03 .08
46 Kasmina's Transmutation C .04 .10
47 Keymaster Rogue C .03 .08
48 Kiora's Dambreaker C .03 .08
49 Leapfrog C .04 .10
50 Muddle the Mixture U 1.00 2.50
51 Murmuring Mystic U 1.00 2.50
52 Nightveil Sprite U .03 .08
53 Persistent Petitioners C 1.00 2.50
54 Pteramander U .04 .10
55 Quasiduplicate R .25 .60
56 Quench C .04 .10
57 Quicken U .10 .25
58 Radical Idea C .03 .08
59 Remand U .25 .60
60 Repeal C .04 .10
61 Sinister Sabotage C .08 .20
62 Spark Double R 2.50 6.00
63 Tidespout Tyrant R .75 2.00
64 Totally Lost C .03 .08
65 Vedalken Mesmerist C .03 .08
66 Balustrade Spy C .05 .12
67 Blade Juggler C .03 .08
68 Bladebrand C .04 .10
69 Burglar Rat C .10 .25
70 Crypt Ghast R 4.00 10.00
71 Dark Confidant M 4.00 10.00
72 Debtors' Transport C .03 .08
73 Dimir House Guard C .10 .25
74 Disembowel C .04 .10
75 Dreadmalkin U .03 .08
76 Golgari Thug U .20 .50
77 Ill-Gotten Inheritance C .04 .10
78 Infernal Tutor R .20 .50
79 Last Gasp C .04 .10
80 Liliana, Dreadhorde General M 10.00 25.00
81 Lord of the Void M 4.00 10.00
82 Macabre Waltz C .04 .10
83 Massacre Girl R .40 1.00
84 Mausoleum Turnkey U .03 .08
85 Mephitic Vapors C .03 .08
86 Midnight Reaper R .20 .50
87 Orzhov Enforcer U .05 .12
88 Orzhov Euthanist C .05 .12
89 Plaguecrafter U .40 1.00
90 Priest of Forgotten Gods R 1.00 2.50
91 Sewer Shambler C .04 .10
92 Shadow Alley Denizen C .04 .10
93 Stab Wound U .04 .10
94 Thrill-Kill Assassin C .05 .12
95 Ultimate Price U .03 .08
96 Undercity's Embrace C .03 .08
97 Vindictive Vampire U .12 .30
98 Woebringer Demon U .04 .10
99 Act of Treason C .04 .10
100 Arclight Phoenix R 2.00 5.00
101 Bloodfray Giant U .03 .08
102 Bomber Corps C .03 .08
103 Burn Bright C .04 .10
104 Burning Prophet C .04 .10
105 Burning-Tree Vandal C .03 .08
106 Demolish C .04 .10
107 Demonfire U .05 .12
108 Dogpile C .05 .12
109 Greater Forgeling C .03 .08
110 Guttersnipe U .12 .30
111 Hellkite Tyrant R 3.00 8.00
112 Homing Lightning U .03 .08
113 Ilharg, the Raze-Boar M 2.00 5.00
114 Krenko, Mob Boss R .75 2.00
115 Krenko's Command C .12 .30
116 Legion Warboss R .25 .60
117 Light Up the Stage U .15 .40
118 Mizzix's Mastery R 1.00 2.50
119 Mugging C .03 .08
120 Rakdos Pit Dragon U .03 .08
121 Rubblebelt Maaka C .03 .08
122 Scorched Rusalka C .08 .20
123 Siege of Towers U .03 .08
124 Skewer the Critics C .12 .30
125 Skullcrack U .10 .25
126 Stalking Vengeance U .10 .25
127 Taste for Mayhem C .03 .08
128 Tin Street Dodger C .08 .20
129 Utvara Hellkite M 5.00 12.00
130 Wojek Bodyguard C .03 .08
131 Arboreal Grazer C .12 .30
132 Band Together C .03 .08
133 Birds of Paradise R 4.00 10.00
134 Chord of Calling R 3.00 8.00
135 Crocanura C .05 .12
136 Drudge Beetle C .03 .08
137 Experiment One U .10 .25
138 Farseek U .75 2.00
139 Fists of Ironwood C .04 .10
140 Forced Adaptation C .08 .20
141 Forced Landing C .03 .08
142 Fungal Rebirth U .10 .25
143 Gather Courage C .03 .08
144 Golgari Grave-Troll R 1.50 4.00
145 Greater Mossdog C .04 .10
146 Guardian Project M 4.00 10.00
147 Horncaller's Chant C .04 .10
148 Life from the Loam R 5.00 12.00
149 Loaming Shaman U .04 .10
150 Moldervine Cloak U .04 .10
151 Open the Gates C .10 .25

152 Overwhelm U .03 .08
153 Protean Hulk M 2.00 5.00
154 Rampaging Rendhorn C .03 .08
155 Siege Wurm C .04 .10
156 Silhana Ledgewalker C .08 .20
157 Sprouting Renewal C .05 .12
158 Titanic Brawl C .04 .10
159 Utopia Sprawl U .20 .50
160 Wasteland Viper U .10 .25
161 Wurmweaver Coil U .04 .10
162 Yeva, Nature's Herald R .50 1.25
163 Assemble the Legion R .12 .30
164 Aurelia, Exemplar of Justice M 1.00 2.50
165 Azorius Guildmage U .10 .25
166 Blind Hunter C .03 .08
167 Borborygmos Enraged R .12 .30
168 Boros Guildmage U .03 .08
169 Call of the Conclave C .04 .10
170 Cartel Aristocrat U .04 .10
171 Cindervines R .20 .50
172 Coiling Oracle C .08 .20
173 Conclave Cavalier U .03 .08
174 Crackling Drake U .10 .25
175 Deathrite Shaman R 2.50 6.00
176 Debt to the Deathless U .25 .60
177 Deputy of Acquittals C .04 .10
178 Dimir Guildmage U .03 .08
179 Domri Rade M .50 1.25
180 Dreadbore R .30 .75
181 Footlight Fiend C .04 .10
182 Fresh-Faced Recruit C .03 .08
183 Frilled Mystic U .04 .10
184 Glowspore Shaman C .04 .10
185 Gobhobbler Rats C .03 .08
186 Goblin Electromancer C .10 .25
187 Golgari Findbroker U .05 .12
188 Golgari Guildmage U .04 .10
189 Gruul Guildmage U .03 .08
190 Izzet Charm U .12 .30
191 Izzet Guildmage U .03 .08
192 Judge's Familiar C .05 .12
193 Karlov of the Ghost Council M 3.00 8.00
194 Kaya, Orzhov Usurper R .15 .40
195 Lavinia, Azorius Renegade R .30 .75
196 Lazav, the Multifarious R .15 .40
197 Lightning Helix U .12 .30
198 Master of Cruelties M 1.50 4.00
199 Mayhem Devil U .75 2.00
200 Merfolk of the Depths C .03 .08
201 Mindleech Mass R .50 1.25
202 Moroii U .04 .10
203 Mortus Strider C .03 .08
204 Mourning Thrull C .03 .08
205 Nicol Bolas, Dragon-God M 2.00 5.00
206 Nightveil Predator U .10 .25
207 Niv-Mizzet, Parun R 1.25 3.00
208 Orzhov Guildmage U .04 .10
209 Petrahydrox C .03 .08
210 Phytohydra R .12 .30
211 Prime Speaker Zegana R .20 .50
212 Putrefy U .12 .30
213 Rakdos Firewheeler U .03 .08
214 Rakdos Guildmage U .03 .08
215 Rakdos, Lord of Riots R 1.25 3.00
216 Ral Zarek M .30 .75
217 Rhythm of the Wild U 2.50 6.00
218 Savra, Queen of the Golgari R .60 1.50
219 Scab-Clan Mauler C .03 .08
220 Selesnya Evangel U .05 .12
221 Selesnya Guildmage U .03 .08
222 Sharktocrab U .04 .10
223 Simic Guildmage U .03 .08
224 Sky Hussar U .03 .08
225 Skyknight Legionnaire C .04 .10
226 Slitherhead C .04 .10
227 Sphinx of New Prahv U .03 .08
228 Sphinx's Revelation R .40 1.00
229 Stitch in Time R .50 1.25
230 Sunder Shaman U .08 .20
231 Tajic, Legion's Edge R .40 1.00
232 Teferi, Time Raveler M 5.00 12.00
233 Teysa, Orzhov Scion R 1.00 2.50
234 Tolsimir Wolfblood R 2.50 6.00
235 Truefire Captain U .04 .10
236 Vernadi Shieldmate C .03 .08
237 Voidslime R .25 .60
238 Whisper Agent C .03 .08
239 Wild Cantor C .04 .10
240 Warrant // Warden R .04 .10
241 Revival // Revenge R .25 .60
242 Connive // Concoct R .05 .12
243 Expansion // Explosion R .25 .60
244 Bedeck // Bedazzle R .10 .25
245 Find // Finality R .08 .20
246 Thrash // Threat R .10 .25
247 Response // Resurgence R .20 .50
248 Assure // Assemble R .08 .20
249 Repudiate // Replicate R .10 .25
250 Azorius Signet U .30 .75
251 Boros Signet U .75 2.00
252 Bottled Cloister R .10 .25
253 Chromatic Lantern R 1.50 4.00
254 Civic Saber U .03 .08
255 Cloudstone Curio M 6.00 15.00
256 Dimir Signet U .60 1.50
257 Gate Colossus U .04 .10
258 Golgari Signet U .40 1.00
259 Gruul Signet U 1.00 2.50
260 Illusionist's Bracers R 1.50 4.00
261 Izzet Signet U 1.00 2.50
262 Junktroller U .03 .08
263 Orzhov Signet U 2.00 5.00
264 Pariah's Shield R .60 1.50
265 Rakdos Signet U 1.50 4.00
266 Seal of the Guildpact R .15 .40
267 Selesnya Signet U .60 1.50
268 Silent Dart U .04 .10
269 Simic Signet U .20 .50
270 Sword of the Paruns R .50 1.25
271 Voyager Staff U .10 .25
272 Azorius Guildgate C .10 .25
273 Blood Crypt R 10.00 25.00
274 Boros Guildgate C .10 .25
275 Breeding Pool R 10.00 25.00
276 Dimir Guildgate C .08 .20
277 Godless Shrine R 6.00 15.00
278 Golgari Guildgate C .12 .30
279 Gruul Guildgate C .10 .25
280 Hallowed Fountain R 6.00 15.00
281 Izzet Guildgate C .10 .25
282 Orzhov Guildgate C .10 .25
283 Overgrown Tomb R 8.00 20.00
284 Rakdos Guildgate C .10 .25
285 Sacred Foundry R 12.00 30.00
286 Selesnya Guildgate C .05 .12
287 Simic Guildgate C .10 .25
288 Steam Vents R 10.00 25.00
289 Stomping Ground R 8.00 20.00
290 Temple Garden R 8.00 20.00
291 Watery Grave R 8.00 20.00
292 Blood Crypt BORDERLESS R 12.00 30.00
293 Breeding Pool BORDERLESS R 12.00 30.00
294 Godless Shrine BORDERLESS R 12.00 30.00
295 Hallowed Fountain BORDERLESS R 12.00 30.00
296 Overgrown Tomb BORDERLESS R 12.00 30.00
297 Sacred Foundry BORDERLESS R 12.00 30.00
298 Steam Vents BORDERLESS R 15.00 40.00
299 Stomping Ground BORDERLESS R 10.00 25.00
300 Temple Garden BORDERLESS R 15.00 40.00
301 Watery Grave BORDERLESS R 15.00 40.00
302 Blazing Archon RETRO R .15 .40
303 Blind Obedience RETRO R 1.25 3.00
304 Condemn RETRO U .12 .30
305 Devouring Light RETRO U .05 .12
306 Divine Visitation RETRO M 3.00 8.00
307 Faith's Fetters RETRO C .04 .10
308 Ghostway RETRO R .60 1.50
309 Bruvac the Grandiloquent RETRO M 8.00 20.00
310 Cloudfin Raptor RETRO C .08 .20
311 Compulsive Research RETRO C .04 .10
312 Copy Enchantment RETRO R .20 .50
313 Cyclonic Rift RETRO M 40.00 100.00
314 Drift of Phantasms RETRO C .15 .40
315 Muddle the Mixture RETRO U 2.00 5.00
316 Persistent Petitioners RETRO C 1.00 2.50
317 Pteramander RETRO U .10 .25
318 Quicken RETRO U .12 .30
319 Spark Double RETRO R 3.00 8.00
320 Tidespout Tyrant RETRO R 1.00 2.50
321 Totally Lost RETRO C .04 .10
322 Crypt Ghast RETRO R 4.00 10.00
323 Dark Confidant RETRO M 4.00 10.00
324 Dimir House Guard RETRO C .25 .60
325 Golgari Thug RETRO U .75 2.00
326 Infernal Tutor RETRO R .40 1.00
327 Lord of the Void RETRO M 2.50 6.00
328 Massacre Girl RETRO R .50 1.25
329 Ultimate Price RETRO U .08 .20
330 Vindictive Vampire RETRO U .15 .40
331 Arclight Phoenix RETRO R 4.00 10.00
332 Guttersnipe RETRO U .20 .50
333 Hellkite Tyrant RETRO R 2.00 5.00
334 Ilharg, the Raze-Boar RETRO M 1.25 3.00
335 Krenko, Mob Boss RETRO R 1.25 3.00
336 Krenko's Command RETRO C .10 .25
337 Legion Warboss RETRO R .25 .60
338 Light Up the Stage RETRO U .60 1.50
339 Mizzix's Mastery RETRO R .40 1.00
340 Skewer the Critics RETRO C .50 1.25
341 Skullcrack RETRO U 1.00 2.50
342 Utvara Hellkite RETRO M 4.00 10.00
343 Arboreal Grazer RETRO C 2.50 6.00
344 Birds of Paradise RETRO R 4.00 10.00
345 Chord of Calling RETRO R 5.00 12.00
346 Experiment One RETRO U .15 .40
347 Farseek RETRO U 2.00 5.00
348 Golgari Grave-Troll RETRO R 1.50 4.00
349 Guardian Project RETRO M 4.00 10.00
350 Life from the Loam RETRO R 5.00 12.00
351 Loaming Shaman RETRO U .10 .25
352 Moldervine Cloak RETRO U .05 .12
353 Protean Hulk RETRO M 2.50 6.00
354 Silhana Ledgewalker RETRO C .12 .30
355 Utopia Sprawl RETRO U 1.50 4.00
356 Aurelia, Exemplar of Justice RETRO M .50 1.25
357 Borborygmos Enraged RETRO R .10 .25
358 Call of the Conclave RETRO C .04 .10
359 Cartel Aristocrat RETRO U .10 .25
360 Cindervines RETRO R .10 .25
361 Coiling Oracle RETRO C .12 .30
362 Crackling Drake RETRO U .50 1.25
363 Deathrite Shaman RETRO R 4.00 10.00
364 Debt to the Deathless RETRO U .20 .50
365 Dreadbore RETRO R .15 .40
366 Frilled Mystic RETRO U .10 .25
367 Goblin Electromancer RETRO C .12 .30
368 Izzet Charm RETRO U .20 .50
369 Karlov of the Ghost Council RETRO M 2.00 5.00
370 Lavinia, Azorius Renegade RETRO R .25 .60
371 Lazav, the Multifarious RETRO R .15 .40
372 Lightning Helix RETRO U .75 2.00
373 Master of Cruelties RETRO M 1.00 2.50
374 Mayhem Devil RETRO U 2.00 5.00
375 Mindleech Mass RETRO R .20 .50
376 Niv-Mizzet, Parun RETRO R 1.00 2.50
377 Prime Speaker Zegana RETRO R .15 .40
378 Putrefy RETRO U .10 .25
379 Rakdos, Lord of Riots RETRO R .20 .50
380 Rhythm of the Wild RETRO U 2.50 6.00
381 Savra, Queen of the Golgari RETRO R .20 .50
382 Sky Hussar RETRO U .08 .20
383 Sphinx's Revelation RETRO R .15 .40
384 Stitch in Time RETRO R .15 .40
385 Tajic, Legion's Edge RETRO R .08 .20
386 Teysa, Orzhov Scion RETRO R .40 1.00
387 Tolsimir Wolfblood RETRO R .20 .50
388 Voidslime RETRO R .15 .40
389 Bottled Cloister RETRO R .15 .40
390 Chromatic Lantern RETRO R 1.50 4.00
391 Cloudstone Curio RETRO M 5.00 12.00
392 Illusionist's Bracers RETRO R 1.00 2.50
393 Pariah's Shield RETRO R .20 .50
394 Seal of the Guildpact RETRO R .10 .25
395 Sword of the Paruns RETRO R .15 .40
396 Azorius Guildgate RETRO C .15 .40
397 Blood Crypt RETRO R 20.00 50.00
398 Boros Guildgate RETRO C .12 .30
399 Breeding Pool RETRO R 20.00 50.00
400 Dimir Guildgate RETRO C .12 .30
401 Godless Shrine RETRO R 15.00 40.00
402 Golgari Guildgate RETRO C .15 .40
403 Gruul Guildgate RETRO C .10 .25
404 Hallowed Fountain RETRO R 25.00 60.00
405 Izzet Guildgate RETRO C .15 .40
406 Orzhov Guildgate RETRO C .12 .30
407 Overgrown Tomb RETRO R 25.00 60.00
408 Rakdos Guildgate RETRO C .12 .30
409 Sacred Foundry RETRO R 15.00 40.00
410 Selesnya Guildgate RETRO C .12 .30
411 Simic Guildgate RETRO C .15 .40
412 Steam Vents RETRO R 25.00 60.00
413 Stomping Ground RETRO R 15.00 40.00
414 Temple Garden RETRO R 15.00 40.00
415 Watery Grave RETRO R 25.00 60.00
416 Divine Visitation BORDERLESS ANIME M 15.00 40.00
417 Tomik, Distinguished Advokist
BORDERLESS ANIME R .20 .50
418 Bruvac the Grandiloquent
BORDERLESS ANIME M 10.00 25.00
419 Cyclonic Rift BORDERLESS ANIME M 60.00 150.00
420 Fblthp, the Lost BORDERLESS ANIME R .30 .75
421 Spark Double BORDERLESS ANIME R 8.00 20.00
422 Tidespout Tyrant BORDERLESS ANIME R 1.50 4.00
423 Crypt Ghast BORDERLESS ANIME R 6.00 15.00
424 Lord of the Void BORDERLESS ANIME M 6.00 15.00
425 Massacre Girl BORDERLESS ANIME R 5.00 12.00
426 Pack Rat BORDERLESS ANIME R 1.25 3.00
427 Arclight Phoenix BORDERLESS ANIME R 5.00 12.00
428 Hellkite Tyrant BORDERLESS ANIME R 8.00 20.00
429 Ilharg, the Raze-Boar BORDERLESS ANIME M 3.00 8.00
430 Krenko, Mob Boss BORDERLESS ANIME R 5.00 12.00
431 Utvara Hellkite BORDERLESS ANIME M 15.00 40.00
432 Birds of Paradise BORDERLESS ANIME R 12.00 30.00
433 Guardian Project BORDERLESS ANIME M 15.00 40.00
434 Life from the Loam BORDERLESS ANIME R 8.00 20.00
435 Protean Hulk BORDERLESS ANIME M 6.00 15.00
436 Aurelia, Exemplar of Justice
BORDERLESS ANIME M 15.00 40.00
437 Karlov of the Ghost Council
BORDERLESS ANIME M 4.00 10.00
438 Niv-Mizzet, Parun BORDERLESS ANIME R 10.00 25.00
439 Prime Speaker Zegana
BORDERLESS ANIME R 2.00 5.00
440 Savra, Queen of the Golgari
BORDERLESS ANIME R 4.00 10.00
441 Teysa, Orzhov Scion BORDERLESS ANIME R 6.00 15.00
442 Chromatic Lantern BORDERLESS ANIME R 8.00 20.00
443 Cloudstone Curio BORDERLESS ANIME M 8.00 20.00
444 Domri Rade BORDERLESS ANIME M .75 2.00
445 Ral Zarek BORDERLESS ANIME M 1.25 3.00
446 Rest in Peace RETRO R 1.00 2.50
447 Sphere of Safety RETRO U 2.00 5.00
448 Aetherize RETRO U 1.00 2.50
449 Enter the Infinite RETRO M 1.25 3.00
450 Gigantoplasm RETRO R .12 .30
451 Narcomoeba RETRO U 1.25 3.00
452 Turnabout RETRO U .12 .30
453 Creeping Chill RETRO U 1.25 3.00
454 Darkblast RETRO U .50 1.25
455 Pack Rat RETRO R .40 1.00
456 Shattering Spree RETRO U 1.00 2.50
457 Perilous Forays RETRO U 1.25 3.00
458 Wilderness Reclamation RETRO U 1.50 4.00
459 Niv-Mizzet Reborn RETRO M .75 2.00
460 Shambling Shell C .08 .20
461 Supreme Verdict RETRO R 1.50 4.00
462 Magewright's Stone RETRO U 2.00 5.00
463 Pithing Needle RETRO R 1.00 2.50
464 Karn's Bastion RETRO R 1.50 4.00
465 Maze's End RETRO M 3.00 8.00
466 Thespian's Stage RETRO R 2.50 6.00

2024 Magic The Gathering Universes Beyond Fallout

9 Aradesh, the Founder FOIL R .10 .25
10 Automated Assembly Line FOIL R .12 .30
11 Battle of Hoover Dam FOIL R .25 .60
12 Brotherhood Outcast FOIL U .60 1.50
13 Brotherhood Scribe FOIL R .20 .50
14 Codsworth, Handy Helper FOIL R 8.00 20.00
15 Commander Sofia Daguerre FOIL U .75 2.00
16 Gary Clone FOIL U .40 1.00
17 Idolized FOIL R 6.00 15.00
18 Overencumbered FOIL R .25 .60
19 Overseer of Vault 76 FOIL R .12 .30
20 Paladin Danse, Steel Maverick FOIL U 2.50 6.00
21 Pre-War Formalwear FOIL R 1.50 4.00
22 The Prydwen, Steel Flagship FOIL R .50 1.25
23 Securitron Squadron FOIL R .75 2.00
24 Sentry Bot FOIL R .20 .50
25 Sierra, Nuka's Biggest Fan FOIL R .15 .40
26 Vault 13: Dweller's Journey FOIL R .25 .60
27 Vault 75: Middle School FOIL R .40 1.00
28 Vault 101: Birthday Party FOIL R .20 .50
29 Yes Man, Personal Securitron FOIL R .25 .60
30 Curie, Emergent Intelligence FOIL R .20 .50
31 James, Wandering Dad // Follow Him FOIL R .30 .75
32 Jason Bright, Glowing Prophet FOIL R .40 1.00
33 Mirelurk Queen FOIL R .12 .30
34 Nerd Rage FOIL U 12.00 30.00
35 Nick Valentine, Private Eye FOIL R .30 .75
36 Piper Wright, Publick Reporter FOIL R .25 .60
37 Radstorm FOIL R 4.00 10.00
38 Robobrain War Mind FOIL U .20 .50
39 Struggle for Project Purity FOIL R 2.50 6.00
40 Synth Infiltrator FOIL R .25 .60
41 Vexing Radgull FOIL U .75 2.00
42 Bloatfly Swarm FOIL U 1.50 4.00
43 Butch DeLoria, Tunnel Snake FOIL U 1.00 2.50
44 Feral Ghoul FOIL R 1.00 2.50
45 Hancock, Ghoulish Mayor FOIL R .20 .50
46 Infesting Radroach FOIL U 1.00 2.50
47 Nuclear Fallout FOIL R 2.00 5.00
48 Ruthless Radrat FOIL U .50 1.25
49 Screeching Scorchbeast FOIL R .30 .75
50 V.A.T.S. FOIL R 2.00 5.00
51 Vault 12: The Necropolis FOIL R .30 .75
52 Wasteland Raider FOIL R .25 .60
53 Acquired Mutation FOIL U .40 1.00
54 Assaultron Dominator FOIL R .20 .50
55 Bottle-Cap Blast FOIL U 3.00 8.00
56 Crimson Caravaneer FOIL U .30 .75
57 Duchess, Wayward Tavernkeep FOIL R .10 .25
58 Grim Reaper's Sprint FOIL R 2.00 5.00
59 Ian the Reckless FOIL U .20 .50
60 Junk Jet FOIL R .15 .40
61 Megaton's Fate FOIL R .15 .40
62 The Motherlode, Excavator FOIL R .10 .25
63 Mysterious Stranger FOIL R .20 .50
64 Plasma Caster FOIL R .20 .50
65 Powder Ganger FOIL R .12 .30
66 Rose, Cutthroat Raider FOIL R 1.00 2.50
67 Synth Eradicator FOIL R .10 .25
68 Thrill-Kill Disciple FOIL R .12 .30
69 Vault 21: House Gambit FOIL R .20 .50
70 Veronica, Dissident Scribe FOIL R .25 .60
71 Wild Wasteland FOIL R 1.25 3.00
72 Animal Friend FOIL R .20 .50
73 Bighorner Rancher FOIL U 1.00 2.50
74 Break Down FOIL U .25 .60
75 Cathedral Acolyte FOIL U 1.00 2.50
76 Glowing One FOIL U .75 2.00
77 Gunner Conscript FOIL U .25 .60
78 Harold and Bob, First Numens FOIL R .20 .50
79 Lily Bowen, Raging Grandma FOIL R .30 .75
80 Lumbering Megasloth FOIL U 2.00 5.00
81 Power Fist FOIL R 8.00 20.00
82 Rampaging Yao Guai FOIL R 1.25 3.00
83 Strong Back FOIL R 2.00 5.00
84 Strong, the Brutish Thespian FOIL R .25 .60
85 Super Mutant Scavenger FOIL U .20 .50
86 Tato Farmer FOIL R .20 .50
87 Watchful Radstag FOIL R 2.00 5.00
88 Well Rested FOIL U 5.00 12.00
89 Agent Frank Horrigan FOIL R .50 1.25
90 Almost Perfect FOIL R .25 .60
91 Alpha Deathclaw FOIL R 1.25 3.00
92 Arcade Gannon FOIL R .10 .25
93 Armory Paladin FOIL R .40 1.00
94 Atomize FOIL R 2.00 5.00
95 Boomer Scrapper FOIL R .15 .40
96 Cait, Cage Brawler FOIL R .20 .50
97 Cass, Hand of Vengeance FOIL R .20 .50
98 Colonel Autumn FOIL R .25 .60
99 Contaminated Drink FOIL U .50 1.25
100 Craig Boone, Novac Guard FOIL U 1.25 3.00
101 Desdemona, Freedom's Edge FOIL R .10 .25
102 Elder Arthur Maxson FOIL R .25 .60
103 Elder Owyn Lyons FOIL U 1.00 2.50
104 Electrosiphon FOIL R .25 .60
105 Inventory Management FOIL R 3.00 8.00
106 Kellogg, Dangerous Mind FOIL R 8.00 20.00
107 Legate Lanius, Caesar's Ace FOIL U .60 1.50
108 MacCready, Lamplight Mayor FOIL R 1.50 4.00
109 Marcus, Mutant Mayor FOIL R .20 .50
110 Moira Brown, Guide Author FOIL R .12 .30
111 Mutational Advantage FOIL R 1.00 2.50
112 Nightkin Ambusher FOIL U .50 1.25
113 The Nipton Lottery FOIL R .25 .60
114 Paladin Elizabeth Taggerdy FOIL R .40 1.00
115 Raul, Trouble Shooter FOIL U 8.00 20.00
116 Red Death, Shipwrecker FOIL R .25 .60
117 Rex, Cyber-Hound FOIL R .12 .30
118 Sentinel Sarah Lyons FOIL R .20 .50
119 Shaun, Father of Synths FOIL R .25 .60
120 Three Dog, Galaxy News DJ FOIL R .12 .30
121 Vault 11: Voter's Dilemma FOIL R .20 .50
122 Vault 87: Forced Evolution FOIL R .20 .50
123 Vault 112: Sadistic Simulation FOIL R .20 .50
124 White Glove Gourmand FOIL U .30 .75
125 Young Deathclaws FOIL U .40 1.00
126 Agility Bobblehead FOIL U 3.00 8.00
127 Behemoth of Vault 0 FOIL U .30 .75
128 Brotherhood Vertibird FOIL R 2.00 5.00
129 C.A.M.P. FOIL U .20 .50
130 Charisma Bobblehead FOIL U 2.50 6.00
131 ED-E, Lonesome Eyebot FOIL R .15 .40
132 Endurance Bobblehead FOIL U 5.00 12.00
133 Expert-Level Safe FOIL U .30 .75
134 Intelligence Bobblehead FOIL U 3.00 8.00
135 Luck Bobblehead FOIL U 5.00 12.00
136 Mister Gutsy FOIL R .20 .50
137 Nuka-Cola Vending Machine FOIL U 10.00 25.00
138 Nuka-Nuke Launcher FOIL R .25 .60
139 Perception Bobblehead FOIL U 4.00 10.00
140 Pip-Boy 3000 FOIL R 3.00 8.00
141 Recon Craft Theta FOIL R .20 .50
142 Silver Shroud Costume FOIL U 20.00 50.00
143 Strength Bobblehead FOIL U 4.00 10.00
144 Survivor's Med Kit FOIL U .20 .50
145 T-45 Power Armor FOIL R .20 .50
146 Desolate Mire FOIL R 2.50 6.00
147 Diamond City FOIL R 2.00 5.00
148 Ferrous Lake FOIL R 1.00 2.50
149 HELIOS One FOIL R .30 .75
150 Junktown FOIL R .25 .60
151 Mariposa Military Base FOIL R .20 .50
152 Overflowing Basin FOIL R 1.25 3.00
153 Sunscorched Divide FOIL R .60 1.50
154 Viridescent Bog FOIL R 1.25 3.00
155 All That Glitters FOIL C 1.00 2.50
156 Austere Command FOIL R .75 2.00
157 Captain of the Watch FOIL R .12 .30
158 Crush Contraband FOIL U .25 .60
159 Dispatch FOIL U 2.00 5.00
160 Entrapment Maneuver FOIL R .10 .25
161 Hour of Reckoning FOIL R .25 .60
162 Impassioned Orator FOIL C .50 1.25
163 Intangible Virtue FOIL U .25 .60
164 Keeper of the Accord FOIL R .30 .75
165 Mantle of the Ancients FOIL R .50 1.25
166 Marshal's Anthem FOIL R .10 .25
167 Martial Coup FOIL R .20 .50
168 Open the Vaults FOIL R .40 1.00
169 Path to Exile FOIL U 1.50 4.00
170 Puresteel Paladin FOIL R 1.00 2.50
171 Secure the Wastes FOIL R .60 1.50
172 Single Combat FOIL R .12 .30
173 Swords to Plowshares FOIL U 2.00 5.00
174 Valorous Stance FOIL U .12 .30
175 Fraying Sanity FOIL R .12 .30

176 Glimmer of Genius FOIL U .20 .50
177 Inexorable Tide FOIL R 1.25 3.00
178 Mechanized Production FOIL M 1.50 4.00
179 One with the Machine FOIL R .15 .40
180 Thirst for Knowledge FOIL U .25 .60
181 Whirler Rogue FOIL U .15 .40
182 Bastion of Remembrance FOIL U 2.00 5.00
183 Black Market FOIL R 2.50 6.00
184 Deadly Dispute FOIL C 2.00 5.00
185 Lethal Scheme FOIL R .15 .40
186 Morbid Opportunist FOIL U 1.00 2.50
187 Pitiless Plunderer FOIL U 5.00 12.00
188 Blasphemous Act FOIL R 2.50 6.00
189 Chaos Warp FOIL R .75 2.00
190 Loyal Apprentice FOIL U 1.25 3.00
191 Sticky Fingers FOIL C .60 1.50
192 Stolen Strategy FOIL R .30 .75
193 Unexpected Windfall FOIL C 1.00 2.50
194 Abundant Growth FOIL C .25 .60
195 Branching Evolution FOIL R 3.00 8.00
196 Cultivate FOIL U 1.00 2.50
197 Farseek FOIL C 1.25 3.00
198 Fertile Ground FOIL C .25 .60
199 Guardian Project FOIL R 3.00 8.00
200 Hardened Scales FOIL R 1.25 3.00
201 Harmonize FOIL U .75 2.00
202 Heroic Intervention FOIL R 5.00 12.00
203 Inspiring Call FOIL U 2.50 6.00
204 Rampant Growth FOIL C 1.00 2.50
205 Rancor FOIL U 1.00 2.50
206 Squirrel Nest FOIL U .20 .50
207 Tireless Tracker FOIL R 1.00 2.50
208 Wild Growth FOIL C 1.00 2.50
209 Anguished Unmaking FOIL R 1.00 2.50
210 Assemble the Legion FOIL R .15 .40
211 Behemoth Sledge FOIL U .25 .60
212 Biomass Mutation FOIL R .10 .25
213 Casualties of War FOIL R .20 .50
214 Corpsejack Menace FOIL U .60 1.50
215 Fervent Charge FOIL R .30 .75
216 Find // Finality FOIL R .15 .40
217 General's Enforcer FOIL U .50 1.25
218 Heroic Reinforcements FOIL U .15 .40
219 Putrefy FOIL U .50 1.25
220 Ruinous Ultimatum FOIL R 1.00 2.50
221 Wake the Past FOIL R .20 .50
222 Wear // Tear FOIL U 1.00 2.50
223 Winding Constrictor FOIL U .50 1.25
224 Arcane Signet FOIL U 1.25 3.00
225 Basilisk Collar FOIL R 1.25 3.00
226 Bloodforged Battle-Axe FOIL R .25 .60
227 Brass Knuckles FOIL U .15 .40
228 Champion's Helm FOIL R 1.00 2.50
229 Contagion Clasp FOIL U .60 1.50
230 Everflowing Chalice FOIL U .50 1.25
231 Explorer's Scope FOIL C .25 .60
232 Fireshrieker FOIL U .60 1.50
233 Lightning Greaves FOIL U 4.00 10.00
234 Masterwork of Ingenuity FOIL R .20 .50
235 Mind Stone FOIL U .60 1.50
236 Mystic Forge FOIL R .60 1.50
237 Panharmonicon FOIL R 25.00 60.00
238 Skullclamp FOIL U 6.00 15.00
239 Sol Ring FOIL U 2.00 5.00
240 Solemn Simulacrum FOIL R 1.25 3.00
241 Steel Overseer FOIL R 2.00 5.00
242 Swiftfoot Boots FOIL U 2.50 6.00
243 Talisman of Conviction FOIL U .50 1.25
244 Talisman of Creativity FOIL U 1.50 4.00
245 Talisman of Curiosity FOIL U .75 2.00
246 Talisman of Dominance FOIL U 1.50 4.00
247 Talisman of Hierarchy FOIL U 1.00 2.50
248 Talisman of Indulgence FOIL U 2.00 5.00
249 Talisman of Progress FOIL U 1.25 3.00
250 Talisman of Resilience FOIL U .75 2.00
251 Thought Vessel FOIL C 1.25 3.00
252 Wayfarer's Bauble FOIL C 1.00 2.50
253 Ash Barrens FOIL C .10 .25
254 Buried Ruin FOIL U 1.25 3.00
255 Canopy Vista FOIL R .20 .50
256 Canyon Slough FOIL R .25 .60
257 Cinder Glade FOIL R .30 .75
258 Clifftop Retreat FOIL R 1.50 4.00
259 Command Tower FOIL C 2.00 5.00
260 Darkwater Catacombs FOIL R .50 1.25
261 Dragonskull Summit FOIL R 1.00 2.50
262 Drowned Catacomb FOIL R 1.00 2.50
263 Evolving Wilds FOIL C .12 .30
264 Exotic Orchard FOIL R 4.00 10.00
265 Fetid Pools FOIL R .20 .50
266 Glacial Fortress FOIL R 1.50 4.00
267 Hinterland Harbor FOIL R 1.25 3.00
268 Irrigated Farmland FOIL R .12 .30
269 Isolated Chapel FOIL R 1.00 2.50
270 Jungle Shrine FOIL U 1.25 3.00
271 Memorial to Glory FOIL U .25 .60
272 Mortuary Mire FOIL C 2.50 6.00
273 Mossfire Valley FOIL R .25 .60
274 Myriad Landscape FOIL U .40 1.00
275 Mystic Monastery FOIL U .50 1.25
276 Nesting Grounds FOIL R 1.25 3.00
277 Nomad Outpost FOIL U 2.50 6.00
278 Opulent Palace FOIL U 1.25 3.00
279 Path of Ancestry FOIL C .25 .60
280 Prairie Stream FOIL R .20 .50
281 Razortide Bridge FOIL C 1.50 4.00
282 Roadside Reliquary FOIL U .25 .60
283 Rogue's Passage FOIL U 25.00 60.00
284 Rootbound Crag FOIL R 2.00 5.00
285 Rustvale Bridge FOIL C 2.00 5.00
286 Scattered Groves FOIL R .20 .50
287 Scavenger Grounds FOIL R .30 .75
288 Shadowblood Ridge FOIL R .20 .50
289 Sheltered Thicket FOIL R .15 .40
290 Silverbluff Bridge FOIL C .60 1.50
291 Skycloud Expanse FOIL R .20 .50
292 Smoldering Marsh FOIL R .25 .60
293 Spire of Industry FOIL R .50 1.25
294 Sulfur Falls FOIL R 1.25 3.00
295 Sungrass Prairie FOIL R .10 .25
296 Sunken Hollow FOIL R .30 .75
297 Sunpetal Grove FOIL R 2.50 6.00
298 Tainted Field FOIL U 1.00 2.50
299 Tainted Isle FOIL U 1.25 3.00
300 Tainted Peak FOIL U 1.00 2.50
301 Tainted Wood FOIL U 1.25 3.00
302 Temple of Abandon FOIL R .20 .50
303 Temple of Deceit FOIL R .20 .50
304 Temple of Enlightenment FOIL R .12 .30
305 Temple of Epiphany FOIL R .12 .30
306 Temple of Malady FOIL R .20 .50
307 Temple of Malice FOIL R .40 1.00
308 Temple of Mystery FOIL R .15 .40
309 Temple of Plenty FOIL R .12 .30
310 Temple of Silence FOIL R .15 .40
311 Temple of the False God FOIL U .20 .50
312 Temple of Triumph FOIL R .15 .40
313 Terramorphic Expanse FOIL C .25 .60
314 Treasure Vault FOIL R 2.00 5.00
315 Windbrisk Heights FOIL R .20 .50
316 Woodland Cemetery FOIL R 2.50 6.00
317 Plains FULL ART FOIL C 1.50 4.00
318 Plains FULL ART FOIL C .50 1.25
319 Island FULL ART FOIL C 1.00 2.50
320 Island FULL ART FOIL C .40 1.00
321 Swamp FULL ART FOIL C 1.50 4.00
322 Swamp FULL ART FOIL C 1.25 3.00
323 Mountain FULL ART FOIL C 2.00 5.00
324 Mountain FULL ART FOIL C .40 1.00
325 Forest FULL ART FOIL C 1.25 3.00
326 Forest FULL ART FOIL C .60 1.50
327 Idolized PIP-BOY SHOWCASER 1.50 4.00
327 Idolized PIP-BOY SHOWCASE FOIL R 2.50 6.00
328 Securitron Squadron
PIP-BOY SHOWCASE FOIL R .75 2.00
328 Securitron Squadron PIP-BOY SHOWCASE R1.00 2.50
329 Radstorm PIP-BOY SHOWCASE R 3.00 8.00
329 Radstorm PIP-BOY SHOWCASE FOIL R 4.00 10.00
330 Synth Infiltrator PIP-BOY SHOWCASE FOIL R.20 .50
330 Synth Infiltrator PIP-BOY SHOWCASE R .20 .50
331 Nuclear Fallout PIP-BOY SHOWCASE R 2.50 6.00
331 Nuclear Fallout PIP-BOY SHOWCASE FOIL R4.00 10.00
332 Screeching Scorchbeast
PIP-BOY SHOWCASE FOIL R .50 1.25
332 Screeching Scorchbeast
PIP-BOY SHOWCASE R .50 1.25
333 V.A.T.S. PIP-BOY SHOWCASE R 1.50 4.00
333 V.A.T.S. PIP-BOY SHOWCASE FOIL R 2.00 5.00
334 Mysterious Stranger
PIP-BOY SHOWCASE FOIL R .60 1.50
334 Mysterious Stranger PIP-BOY SHOWCASE R.40 1.00
335 Watchful Radstag PIP-BOY SHOWCASE R .60 1.50
335 Watchful Radstag
PIP-BOY SHOWCASE FOIL R .75 2.00
336 Alpha Deathclaw
PIP-BOY SHOWCASE FOIL R 1.50 4.00
336 Alpha Deathclaw PIP-BOY SHOWCASE R 1.50 4.00
337 Armory Paladin PIP-BOY SHOWCASE R .30 .75
337 Armory Paladin PIP-BOY SHOWCASE FOIL R.40 1.00
338 Atomize PIP-BOY SHOWCASE FOIL R 2.00 5.00
338 Atomize PIP-BOY SHOWCASE R 2.00 5.00
339 Caesar, Legion's Emperor
PIP-BOY SHOWCASE M 1.00 2.50
339 Caesar, Legion's Emperor
PIP-BOY SHOWCASE FOIL M 1.50 4.00
340 Dogmeat, Ever Loyal
PIP-BOY SHOWCASE FOIL M 2.50 6.00
340 Dogmeat, Ever Loyal PIP-BOY SHOWCASE M2.50 6.00
341 Dr. Madison Li PIP-BOY SHOWCASE M 1.00 2.50
341 Dr. Madison Li PIP-BOY SHOWCASE FOIL M1.00 2.50
342 Inventory Management
PIP-BOY SHOWCASE FOIL R 1.50 4.00
342 Inventory Management
PIP-BOY SHOWCASE R 1.00 2.50
343 The Wise Mothman PIP-BOY SHOWCASE M4.00 10.00
343 The Wise Mothman
PIP-BOY SHOWCASE FOIL M 5.00 12.00
344 Prime Mirelurk Queen
PIP-BOY SHOWCASE FOIL R
(Hullbreaker Horror) 4.00 10.00
344 Prime Mirelurk Queen PIP-BOY SHOWCASE R
(Hullbreaker Horror) 3.00 8.00
345 Centurion of the Marked PIP-BOY SHOWCASE R
(Lord of the Undead) 2.00 5.00
345 Centurion of the Marked PIP-BOY SHOWCASE FOIL R
(Lord of the Undead) 2.50 6.00
346 West Tek Tyrant PIP-BOY SHOWCASE FOIL M
(Grave Titan) 1.25 3.00
346 West Tek Tyrant PIP-BOY SHOWCASE M
(Grave Titan) 1.00 2.50
347 Fog Crawler PIP-BOY SHOWCASE R/(Vigor)4.00 10.00
347 Fog Crawler PIP-BOY SHOWCASE FOIL R
(Vigor) 4.00 10.00
348 Ruzka, Terror of Point Lookout PIP-BOY SHOWCASE
FOIL R/(Ayula, Queen Among Bears) .40 1.00
348 Ruzka, Terror of Point Lookout PIP-BOY SHOWCASE R
(Ayula, Queen Among Bears) .30 .75
349 Scrounging Deathclaw PIP-BOY SHOWCASE FOIL M
(Tarmogoyf) 10.00 25.00
349 Scrounging Deathclaw PIP-BOY SHOWCASE M
(Tarmogoyf) 8.00 20.00
350 Specimen 73 PIP-BOY SHOWCASE FOIL R
(Hornet Queen) 1.25 3.00
350 Specimen 73 PIP-BOY SHOWCASE R
(Hornet Queen) 1.00 2.50
351 Toxic Sheepsquatch PIP-BOY SHOWCASE FOIL R
(Gemrazer) .40 1.00
351 Toxic Sheepsquatch PIP-BOY SHOWCASE R
(Gemrazer) .30 .75
352 Assaultron Invader PIP-BOY SHOWCASE FOIL R
(Walking Ballista) 8.00 20.00
352 Assaultron Invader PIP-BOY SHOWCASE R
(Walking Ballista) 8.00 20.00
353 Farewell VAULT BOY BORDERLESS R 8.00 20.00
353 Farewell VAULT BOY BORDERLESS FOIL R10.00 25.00
354 Ravages of War
VAULT BOY BORDERLESS FOIL M 10.00 25.00
354 Ravages of War VAULT BOY BORDERLESS M10.00 25.00
355 Vandalblast VAULT BOY BORDERLESS U 2.50 6.00
355 Vandalblast
VAULT BOY BORDERLESS FOIL U 2.50 6.00
356 Arcane Signet
VAULT BOY BORDERLESS FOIL U 8.00 20.00
356 Arcane Signet VAULT BOY BORDERLESS U6.00 15.00
357 Crucible of Worlds
VAULT BOY BORDERLESS M 12.00 30.00
357 Crucible of Worlds
VAULT BOY BORDERLESS FOIL M 12.00 30.00
358 Nuka-Cola Vending Machine
VAULT BOY BORDERLESS FOIL U 10.00 25.00
358 Nuka-Cola Vending Machine
VAULT BOY BORDERLESS U 10.00 25.00
359 Sol Ring VAULT BOY BORDERLESS M 12.00 30.00
359 Sol Ring VAULT BOY BORDERLESS FOIL M20.00 50.00
360 Command Tower
VAULT BOY BORDERLESS FOIL U 6.00 15.00
360 Command Tower VAULT BOY BORDERLESS U6.00 15.00
361 Wasteland VAULT BOY BORDERLESS R 12.00 30.00
361 Wasteland VAULT BOY BORDERLESS FOIL R12.00 30.00
362 Aradesh, the Founder EXT ART FOIL R .15 .40
362 Aradesh, the Founder EXT ART R .10 .25
363 Automated Assembly Line EXT ART R .20 .50
363 Automated Assembly Line EXT ART FOIL R.30 .75
364 Battle of Hoover Dam EXT ART FOIL R .25 .60
364 Battle of Hoover Dam EXT ART R .20 .50
365 Brotherhood Scribe EXT ART R .20 .50
365 Brotherhood Scribe EXT ART FOIL R .25 .60
366 Codsworth, Handy Helper EXT ART FOIL R4.00 10.00
366 Codsworth, Handy Helper EXT ART R 5.00 12.00
367 Overencumbered EXT ART R .25 .60
367 Overencumbered EXT ART FOIL R .25 .60
368 Overseer of Vault 76 EXT ART FOIL R .12 .30
368 Overseer of Vault 76 EXT ART R .12 .30
369 Pre-War Formalwear EXT ART R 1.25 3.00
369 Pre-War Formalwear EXT ART FOIL R 1.25 3.00
370 The Prydwen, Steel Flagship EXT ART FOIL R.25 .60
370 The Prydwen, Steel Flagship EXT ART R .25 .60
371 Sentry Bot EXT ART R .15 .40
371 Sentry Bot EXT ART FOIL R .25 .60
372 Sierra, Nuka's Biggest Fan EXT ART FOIL R.20 .50
372 Sierra, Nuka's Biggest Fan EXT ART R .30 .75
373 Yes Man, Personal Securitron EXT ART R .60 1.50
373 Yes Man, Personal Securitron
EXT ART FOIL R .50 1.25
374 Curie, Emergent Intelligence EXT ART FOIL R.25 .60
374 Curie, Emergent Intelligence EXT ART R .20 .50
375 James, Wandering Dad // Follow Him
EXT ART R .25 .60
375 James, Wandering Dad // Follow Him
EXT ART FOIL R .30 .75
376 Jason Bright, Glowing Prophet
EXT ART FOIL R .25 .60
376 Jason Bright, Glowing Prophet EXT ART R .20 .50
377 Mirelurk Queen EXT ART R .20 .50
377 Mirelurk Queen EXT ART FOIL R .25 .60
378 Nick Valentine, Private Eye EXT ART FOIL R.40 1.00
378 Nick Valentine, Private Eye EXT ART R .30 .75
379 Piper Wright, Publick Reporter EXT ART R .75 2.00
379 Piper Wright, Publick Reporter
EXT ART FOIL R 1.00 2.50
380 Struggle for Project Purity EXT ART FOIL R2.50 6.00
380 Struggle for Project Purity EXT ART R 2.00 5.00
381 Feral Ghoul EXT ART R 1.25 3.00
381 Feral Ghoul EXT ART FOIL R 1.25 3.00
382 Hancock, Ghoulish Mayor EXT ART R .40 1.00
382 Hancock, Ghoulish Mayor EXT ART FOIL R.50 1.25
383 Wasteland Raider EXT ART R .25 .60
383 Wasteland Raider EXT ART FOIL R .30 .75
384 Assaultron Dominator EXT ART R .15 .40
384 Assaultron Dominator EXT ART FOIL R .20 .50
385 Duchess, Wayward Tavernkeep EXT ART R .10 .25
385 Duchess, Wayward Tavernkeep
EXT ART FOIL R .15 .40
386 Grim Reaper's Sprint EXT ART R 1.25 3.00
386 Grim Reaper's Sprint EXT ART FOIL R 1.50 4.00
387 Junk Jet EXT ART R .12 .30
387 Junk Jet EXT ART FOIL R .15 .40
388 Megaton's Fate EXT ART FOIL R .25 .60
388 Megaton's Fate EXT ART R .25 .60
389 The Motherlode, Excavator EXT ART R .10 .25
389 The Motherlode, Excavator EXT ART FOIL R.20 .50
390 Plasma Caster EXT ART FOIL R .25 .60
390 Plasma Caster EXT ART R .25 .60
391 Powder Ganger EXT ART R .12 .30
391 Powder Ganger EXT ART FOIL R .20 .50
392 Rose, Cutthroat Raider EXT ART FOIL R 1.50 4.00
392 Rose, Cutthroat Raider EXT ART R 1.25 3.00
393 Synth Eradicator EXT ART R .15 .40
393 Synth Eradicator EXT ART FOIL R .12 .30
394 Thrill-Kill Disciple EXT ART FOIL R .10 .25
394 Thrill-Kill Disciple EXT ART R .10 .25
395 Veronica, Dissident Scribe EXT ART R .20 .50
395 Veronica, Dissident Scribe EXT ART FOIL R.25 .60
396 Wild Wasteland EXT ART FOIL R 1.00 2.50
396 Wild Wasteland EXT ART R 1.00 2.50
397 Animal Friend EXT ART R .25 .60
397 Animal Friend EXT ART FOIL R .25 .60
398 Harold and Bob, First Numens
EXT ART FOIL R .25 .60
398 Harold and Bob, First Numens EXT ART R .20 .50
399 Lily Bowen, Raging Grandma EXT ART R .25 .60
399 Lily Bowen, Raging Grandma EXT ART FOIL R.30 .75
400 Power Fist EXT ART FOIL R 6.00 15.00
400 Power Fist EXT ART R 5.00 12.00
401 Rampaging Yao Guai EXT ART R 1.25 3.00
401 Rampaging Yao Guai EXT ART FOIL R 1.25 3.00
402 Strong Back EXT ART FOIL R 2.00 5.00
402 Strong Back EXT ART R 2.00 5.00
403 Strong, the Brutish Thespian EXT ART R .30 .75
403 Strong, the Brutish Thespian EXT ART FOIL R.25 .60
404 Tato Farmer EXT ART FOIL R .40 1.00
404 Tato Farmer EXT ART R .30 .75
405 Agent Frank Horrigan EXT ART R .75 2.00
405 Agent Frank Horrigan EXT ART FOIL R 1.00 2.50
406 Almost Perfect EXT ART FOIL R .50 1.25
406 Almost Perfect EXT ART R .60 1.50
407 Arcade Gannon EXT ART R .15 .40
407 Arcade Gannon EXT ART FOIL R .15 .40
408 Boomer Scrapper EXT ART FOIL R .15 .40
408 Boomer Scrapper EXT ART R .10 .25
409 Cait, Cage Brawler EXT ART R .12 .30
409 Cait, Cage Brawler EXT ART FOIL R .20 .50
410 Cass, Hand of Vengeance EXT ART FOIL R .30 .75
410 Cass, Hand of Vengeance EXT ART R .15 .40
411 Colonel Autumn EXT ART R .20 .50
411 Colonel Autumn EXT ART FOIL R .20 .50
412 Desdemona, Freedom's Edge EXT ART FOIL R.12 .30
412 Desdemona, Freedom's Edge EXT ART R .10 .25
413 Elder Arthur Maxson EXT ART R .25 .60
413 Elder Arthur Maxson EXT ART FOIL R .25 .60
414 Electrosiphon EXT ART FOIL R .40 1.00
414 Electrosiphon EXT ART R .25 .60
415 Kellogg, Dangerous Mind EXT ART R 3.00 8.00
415 Kellogg, Dangerous Mind EXT ART FOIL R4.00 10.00
416 Liberty Prime, Recharged EXT ART FOIL M1.50 4.00
416 Liberty Prime, Recharged EXT ART M 2.50 6.00
417 MacCready, Lamplight Mayor
EXT ART FOIL R .40 1.00
417 MacCready, Lamplight Mayor EXT ART R .40 1.00
418 Marcus, Mutant Mayor EXT ART FOIL R .30 .75
418 Marcus, Mutant Mayor EXT ART R .25 .60
419 The Master, Transcendent EXT ART FOIL M1.00 2.50
419 The Master, Transcendent EXT ART M .75 2.00
420 Moira Brown, Guide Author EXT ART FOIL R.12 .30
420 Moira Brown, Guide Author EXT ART R .10 .25
421 Mr. House, President and CEO
EXT ART FOIL M 2.00 5.00
421 Mr. House, President and CEO EXT ART M2.00 5.00
422 Mutational Advantage EXT ART R 1.50 4.00
422 Mutational Advantage EXT ART FOIL R 1.25 3.00
423 The Nipton Lottery EXT ART FOIL R .40 1.00
423 The Nipton Lottery EXT ART R .25 .60
424 Paladin Elizabeth Taggerdy EXT ART R .25 .60
424 Paladin Elizabeth Taggerdy EXT ART FOIL R.30 .75
425 Preston Garvey, Minuteman EXT ART FOIL M.30 .75
425 Preston Garvey, Minuteman EXT ART M .30 .75
426 Red Death, Shipwrecker EXT ART R .40 1.00
426 Red Death, Shipwrecker EXT ART FOIL R .40 1.00
427 Rex, Cyber-Hound EXT ART FOIL R .40 1.00
427 Rex, Cyber-Hound EXT ART R .20 .50
428 Sentinel Sarah Lyons EXT ART R .20 .50
428 Sentinel Sarah Lyons EXT ART FOIL R .20 .50
429 Shaun, Father of Synths EXT ART FOIL R .50 1.25
429 Shaun, Father of Synths EXT ART R .40 1.00
430 Three Dog, Galaxy News DJ EXT ART R .30 .75
430 Three Dog, Galaxy News DJ EXT ART FOIL R.40 1.00
431 Brotherhood Vertibird EXT ART FOIL R .30 .75
431 Brotherhood Vertibird EXT ART R .30 .75
432 ED-E, Lonesome Eyebot EXT ART R .20 .50
432 ED-E, Lonesome Eyebot EXT ART FOIL R .30 .75
433 Mister Gutsy EXT ART FOIL R .30 .75
433 Mister Gutsy EXT ART R .30 .75
434 Nuka-Nuke Launcher EXT ART R .15 .40
434 Nuka-Nuke Launcher EXT ART FOIL R .20 .50
435 Pip-Boy 3000 EXT ART FOIL R 5.00 12.00
435 Pip-Boy 3000 EXT ART R 4.00 10.00
436 Recon Craft Theta EXT ART R .15 .40
436 Recon Craft Theta EXT ART FOIL R .25 .60
437 T-45 Power Armor EXT ART FOIL R .30 .75
437 T-45 Power Armor EXT ART R .25 .60
438 Desolate Mire EXT ART R .60 1.50
438 Desolate Mire EXT ART FOIL R .60 1.50
439 Diamond City EXT ART FOIL R 1.00 2.50
439 Diamond City EXT ART R 1.00 2.50
440 Ferrous Lake EXT ART R .50 1.25
440 Ferrous Lake EXT ART FOIL R .50 1.25
441 HELIOS One EXT ART FOIL R .40 1.00
441 HELIOS One EXT ART R 1.00 2.50
442 Junktown EXT ART R .30 .75
442 Junktown EXT ART FOIL R .30 .75
443 Mariposa Military Base EXT ART FOIL R .20 .50
443 Mariposa Military Base EXT ART R .20 .50
444 Overflowing Basin EXT ART R .50 1.25
444 Overflowing Basin EXT ART FOIL R .75 2.00
445 Sunscorched Divide EXT ART FOIL R .75 2.00
445 Sunscorched Divide EXT ART R .50 1.25
446 Viridescent Bog EXT ART R .40 1.00
446 Viridescent Bog EXT ART FOIL R .50 1.25
447 Austere Command EXT ART FOIL R .50 1.25
447 Austere Command EXT ART R .40 1.00
448 Captain of the Watch EXT ART R .20 .50
448 Captain of the Watch EXT ART FOIL R .12 .30
449 Entrapment Maneuver EXT ART FOIL R .15 .40
449 Entrapment Maneuver EXT ART R .12 .30
450 Hour of Reckoning EXT ART R .20 .50
450 Hour of Reckoning EXT ART FOIL R .15 .40
451 Keeper of the Accord EXT ART R .20 .50
451 Keeper of the Accord EXT ART FOIL R .20 .50
452 Mantle of the Ancients EXT ART R .20 .50
452 Mantle of the Ancients EXT ART FOIL R .40 1.00
453 Marshal's Anthem EXT ART R .15 .40
453 Marshal's Anthem EXT ART FOIL R .20 .50
454 Martial Coup EXT ART R .15 .40
454 Martial Coup EXT ART FOIL R .30 .75
455 Open the Vaults EXT ART R .20 .50
455 Open the Vaults EXT ART FOIL R .20 .50
456 Puresteel Paladin EXT ART R 1.00 2.50
456 Puresteel Paladin EXT ART FOIL R 1.00 2.50
457 Secure the Wastes EXT ART FOIL R .40 1.00
457 Secure the Wastes EXT ART R .30 .75
458 Single Combat EXT ART R .20 .50
458 Single Combat EXT ART FOIL R .20 .50
459 Fraying Sanity EXT ART FOIL R .15 .40
459 Fraying Sanity EXT ART R .12 .30
460 Inexorable Tide EXT ART R 2.50 6.00
460 Inexorable Tide EXT ART FOIL R 2.00 5.00
461 Mechanized Production EXT ART FOIL M .50 1.25
461 Mechanized Production EXT ART M .60 1.50
462 One with the Machine EXT ART R .20 .50
462 One with the Machine EXT ART FOIL R .20 .50
463 Black Market EXT ART FOIL R 1.00 2.50
463 Black Market EXT ART R .75 2.00
464 Lethal Scheme EXT ART R .20 .50
464 Lethal Scheme EXT ART FOIL R .20 .50
465 Blasphemous Act EXT ART FOIL R 2.00 5.00
465 Blasphemous Act EXT ART R 2.50 6.00
466 Chaos Warp EXT ART R .50 1.25
466 Chaos Warp EXT ART FOIL R .60 1.50
467 Stolen Strategy EXT ART FOIL R .20 .50
467 Stolen Strategy EXT ART R .12 .30
468 Branching Evolution EXT ART R 2.50 6.00
468 Branching Evolution EXT ART FOIL R 2.50 6.00
469 Guardian Project EXT ART FOIL R 3.00 8.00
469 Guardian Project EXT ART R 2.50 6.00
470 Hardened Scales EXT ART R 1.00 2.50
470 Hardened Scales EXT ART FOIL R .75 2.00
471 Heroic Intervention EXT ART FOIL R 5.00 12.00
471 Heroic Intervention EXT ART R 5.00 12.00
472 Tireless Tracker EXT ART R .30 .75
472 Tireless Tracker EXT ART FOIL R .25 .60
473 Anguished Unmaking EXT ART FOIL R .60 1.50
473 Anguished Unmaking EXT ART R .50 1.25
474 Assemble the Legion EXT ART R .12 .30
474 Assemble the Legion EXT ART FOIL R .20 .50
475 Biomass Mutation EXT ART FOIL R .12 .30
475 Biomass Mutation EXT ART R .10 .25
476 Casualties of War EXT ART R .50 1.25
476 Casualties of War EXT ART FOIL R .50 1.25
477 Fervent Charge EXT ART FOIL R .30 .75
477 Fervent Charge EXT ART R .25 .60

478 Ruinous Ultimatum EXT ART R 1.25 3.00
478 Ruinous Ultimatum EXT ART FOIL R 1.25 3.00
479 Wake the Past EXT ART FOIL R .30 .75
479 Wake the Past EXT ART R .20 .50
480 Basilisk Collar EXT ART R 1.00 2.50
480 Basilisk Collar EXT ART FOIL R .75 2.00
481 Bloodforged Battle-Axe EXT ART FOIL R .20 .50
481 Bloodforged Battle-Axe EXT ART R .25 .60
482 Champion's Helm EXT ART R .50 1.25
482 Champion's Helm EXT ART FOIL R .30 .75
483 Masterwork of Ingenuity EXT ART FOIL R .30 .75
483 Masterwork of Ingenuity EXT ART R .20 .50
484 Mystic Forge EXT ART R .50 1.25
484 Mystic Forge EXT ART FOIL R .50 1.25
485 Panharmonicon EXT ART FOIL R 2.00 5.00
485 Panharmonicon EXT ART R 2.50 6.00
486 Solemn Simulacrum EXT ART FOIL R .50 1.25
486 Solemn Simulacrum EXT ART R .50 1.25
487 Steel Overseer EXT ART FOIL R .50 1.25
487 Steel Overseer EXT ART R .60 1.50
488 Canopy Vista EXT ART FOIL R .30 .75
488 Canopy Vista EXT ART R .30 .75
489 Canyon Slough EXT ART FOIL R .15 .40
489 Canyon Slough EXT ART R .15 .40
490 Cinder Glade EXT ART FOIL R .40 1.00
490 Cinder Glade EXT ART R .60 1.50
491 Clifftop Retreat EXT ART R 1.25 3.00
491 Clifftop Retreat EXT ART FOIL R 1.00 2.50
492 Darkwater Catacombs EXT ART FOIL R .20 .50
492 Darkwater Catacombs EXT ART R .20 .50
493 Dragonskull Summit EXT ART R 1.25 3.00
493 Dragonskull Summit EXT ART FOIL R 1.50 4.00
494 Drowned Catacomb EXT ART FOIL R 1.25 3.00
494 Drowned Catacomb EXT ART R 1.50 4.00
495 Exotic Orchard EXT ART R 1.00 2.50
495 Exotic Orchard EXT ART FOIL R 1.25 3.00
496 Fetid Pools EXT ART FOIL R .20 .50
496 Fetid Pools EXT ART R .15 .40
497 Glacial Fortress EXT ART R 1.25 3.00
497 Glacial Fortress EXT ART FOIL R 1.00 2.50
498 Hinterland Harbor EXT ART FOIL R 1.00 2.50
498 Hinterland Harbor EXT ART R 1.25 3.00
499 Irrigated Farmland EXT ART R .20 .50
499 Irrigated Farmland EXT ART FOIL R .20 .50
500 Isolated Chapel EXT ART FOIL R 1.25 3.00
500 Isolated Chapel EXT ART R 1.25 3.00
501 Mossfire Valley EXT ART R .20 .50
501 Mossfire Valley EXT ART FOIL R .20 .50
502 Nesting Grounds EXT ART FOIL R .60 1.50
502 Nesting Grounds EXT ART R 1.00 2.50
503 Prairie Stream EXT ART R .20 .50
503 Prairie Stream EXT ART FOIL R .40 1.00
504 Rootbound Crag EXT ART FOIL R 1.25 3.00
504 Rootbound Crag EXT ART R 1.50 4.00
505 Scattered Groves EXT ART R .15 .40
505 Scattered Groves EXT ART FOIL R .12 .30
506 Scavenger Grounds EXT ART FOIL R .50 1.25
506 Scavenger Grounds EXT ART R .50 1.25
507 Shadowblood Ridge EXT ART R .20 .50
507 Shadowblood Ridge EXT ART FOIL R .25 .60
508 Sheltered Thicket EXT ART FOIL R .15 .40
508 Sheltered Thicket EXT ART R .12 .30
509 Skycloud Expanse EXT ART R .12 .30
509 Skycloud Expanse EXT ART FOIL R .15 .40
510 Smoldering Marsh EXT ART FOIL R .30 .75
510 Smoldering Marsh EXT ART R .40 1.00
511 Spire of Industry EXT ART R .30 .75
511 Spire of Industry EXT ART FOIL R 1.00 2.50
512 Sulfur Falls EXT ART FOIL R 1.00 2.50
512 Sulfur Falls EXT ART R 1.00 2.50
513 Sungrass Prairie EXT ART R .12 .30
513 Sungrass Prairie EXT ART FOIL R .15 .40
514 Sunken Hollow EXT ART FOIL R .40 1.00
514 Sunken Hollow EXT ART R .40 1.00
515 Sunpetal Grove EXT ART R 1.50 4.00
515 Sunpetal Grove EXT ART FOIL R 1.25 3.00
516 Temple of Abandon EXT ART FOIL R .15 .40
516 Temple of Abandon EXT ART R .10 .25
517 Temple of Deceit EXT ART R .20 .50
517 Temple of Deceit EXT ART FOIL R .20 .50
518 Temple of Enlightenment EXT ART FOIL R .15 .40
518 Temple of Enlightenment EXT ART R .10 .25
519 Temple of Epiphany EXT ART R .12 .30
519 Temple of Epiphany EXT ART FOIL R .20 .50
520 Temple of Malady EXT ART R .15 .40
520 Temple of Malady EXT ART FOIL R .20 .50
521 Temple of Malice EXT ART R .15 .40
521 Temple of Malice EXT ART FOIL R .20 .50
522 Temple of Mystery EXT ART R .15 .40
522 Temple of Mystery EXT ART FOIL R .20 .50
523 Temple of Plenty EXT ART R .10 .25
523 Temple of Plenty EXT ART FOIL R .15 .40
524 Temple of Silence EXT ART R .20 .50
524 Temple of Silence EXT ART FOIL R .20 .50
525 Temple of Triumph EXT ART R .25 .60
525 Temple of Triumph EXT ART FOIL R .20 .50
526 Treasure Vault EXT ART FOIL R 1.25 3.00
526 Treasure Vault EXT ART R 2.00 5.00
527 Windbrisk Heights EXT ART R .20 .50
527 Windbrisk Heights EXT ART FOIL R .30 .75
528 Woodland Cemetery EXT ART FOIL R 1.00 2.50
528 Woodland Cemetery EXT ART R 1.25 3.00
529 Caesar, Legion's Emperor SURGE FOIL M 6.00 15.00
530 Dogmeat, Ever Loyal SURGE FOIL M 10.00 25.00
531 Dr. Madison Li SURGE FOIL M 3.00 8.00
532 The Wise Mothman SURGE FOIL M 8.00 20.00
533 Liberty Prime, Recharged SURGE FOIL M 2.00 5.00
534 The Master, Transcendent SURGE FOIL M 2.50 6.00
535 Mr. House, President and
CEO SURGE FOIL M 2.50 6.00
536 Preston Garvey, Minuteman SURGE FOIL M .50 1.25
537 Aradesh, the Founder SURGE FOIL R .50 1.25
538 Automated Assembly Line SURGE FOIL R .60 1.50
539 Battle of Hoover Dam SURGE FOIL R 1.00 2.50
540 Brotherhood Outcast SURGE FOIL U 4.00 10.00
541 Brotherhood Scribe SURGE FOIL R 1.25 3.00
542 Codsworth, Handy Helper SURGE FOIL R 3.00 8.00
543 Commander Sofia Daguerre SURGE FOIL U 3.00 8.00
544 Gary Clone SURGE FOIL U 4.00 10.00
545 Idolized SURGE FOIL R 5.00 12.00
546 Overencumbered SURGE FOIL R 2.00 5.00
547 Overseer of Vault 76 SURGE FOIL R 1.25 3.00
548 Paladin Danse, Steel Maverick SURGE FOIL U 10.00 25.00
549 Pre-War Formalwear SURGE FOIL R 2.50 6.00
550 The Prydwen, Steel Flagship SURGE FOIL R .60 1.50
551 Securitron Squadron SURGE FOIL R 4.00 10.00
552 Sentry Bot SURGE FOIL R .60 1.50
553 Sierra, Nuka's Biggest Fan SURGE FOIL R 3.00 8.00
554 Vault 13: Dweller's Journey SURGE FOIL R 1.50 4.00
555 Vault 75: Middle School SURGE FOIL R 3.00 8.00
556 Vault 101: Birthday Party SURGE FOIL R 1.50 4.00
557 Yes Man, Personal Securitron SURGE FOIL R 2.00 5.00
558 Curie, Emergent Intelligence SURGE FOIL R 1.00 2.50
559 James, Wandering Dad //
Follow Him SURGE FOIL R .60 1.50
560 Jason Bright, Glowing Prophet SURGE FOIL R 1.50 4.00
561 Mirelurk Queen SURGE FOIL R 1.00 2.50
562 Nerd Rage SURGE FOIL U 12.00 30.00
563 Nick Valentine, Private Eye SURGE FOIL R 1.25 3.00
564 Piper Wright, Publick Reporter SURGE FOIL R 1.25 3.00
565 Radstorm SURGE FOIL R 10.00 25.00
566 Robobrain War Mind SURGE FOIL U 4.00 10.00
567 Struggle for Project Purity SURGE FOIL R 2.50 6.00
568 Synth Infiltrator SURGE FOIL R 1.50 4.00
569 Vexing Radgull SURGE FOIL U 5.00 12.00
570 Bloatfly Swarm SURGE FOIL U 3.00 8.00
571 Butch DeLoria, Tunnel Snake SURGE FOIL U 5.00 12.00
572 Feral Ghoul SURGE FOIL R 2.50 6.00
573 Hancock, Ghoulish Mayor SURGE FOIL R 1.50 4.00
574 Infesting Radroach SURGE FOIL U 4.00 10.00
575 Nuclear Fallout SURGE FOIL R 8.00 20.00
576 Ruthless Radrat SURGE FOIL U 2.00 5.00
577 Screeching Scorchbeast SURGE FOIL R 2.50 6.00
578 V.A.T.S. SURGE FOIL R 6.00 15.00
579 Vault 12: The Necropolis SURGE FOIL R 4.00 10.00
580 Wasteland Raider SURGE FOIL R 1.00 2.50
581 Acquired Mutation SURGE FOIL U 1.25 3.00
582 Assaultron Dominator SURGE FOIL R .40 1.00
583 Bottle-Cap Blast SURGE FOIL U 10.00 25.00
584 Crimson Caravaneer SURGE FOIL U 1.25 3.00
585 Duchess, Wayward Tavernkeep SURGE FOIL R .25 .60
586 Grim Reaper's Sprint SURGE FOIL R 3.00 8.00
587 Ian the Reckless SURGE FOIL U 1.25 3.00
588 Junk Jet SURGE FOIL R .30 .75
589 Megaton's Fate SURGE FOIL R 1.25 3.00
590 The Motherlode, Excavator SURGE FOIL R .50 1.25
591 Mysterious Stranger SURGE FOIL R 1.25 3.00
592 Plasma Caster SURGE FOIL R 1.00 2.50
593 Powder Ganger SURGE FOIL R .60 1.50
594 Rose, Cutthroat Raider SURGE FOIL R 4.00 10.00
595 Synth Eradicator SURGE FOIL R 1.00 2.50
596 Thrill-Kill Disciple SURGE FOIL R .75 2.00
597 Vault 21: House Gambit SURGE FOIL R 2.50 6.00
598 Veronica, Dissident Scribe SURGE FOIL R .60 1.50
599 Wild Wasteland SURGE FOIL R 3.00 8.00
600 Animal Friend SURGE FOIL R 1.25 3.00
601 Bighorner Rancher SURGE FOIL U 4.00 10.00
602 Break Down SURGE FOIL U 1.25 3.00
603 Cathedral Acolyte SURGE FOIL U 5.00 12.00
604 Glowing One SURGE FOIL U 5.00 12.00
605 Gunner Conscript SURGE FOIL U 2.00 5.00
606 Harold and Bob, First Numens SURGE FOIL R .50 1.25
607 Lily Bowen, Raging Grandma SURGE FOIL R 1.25 3.00
608 Lumbering Megasloth SURGE FOIL U 15.00 40.00
609 Power Fist SURGE FOIL R 10.00 25.00
610 Rampaging Yao Guai SURGE FOIL R 2.00 5.00
611 Strong Back SURGE FOIL R 2.50 6.00
612 Strong, the Brutish Thespian SURGE FOIL R .60 1.50
613 Super Mutant Scavenger SURGE FOIL U .60 1.50
614 Tato Farmer SURGE FOIL R 1.25 3.00
615 Watchful Radstag SURGE FOIL R 3.00 8.00
616 Well Rested SURGE FOIL U 10.00 25.00
617 Agent Frank Horrigan SURGE FOIL R 3.00 8.00
618 Almost Perfect SURGE FOIL R 2.00 5.00
619 Alpha Deathclaw SURGE FOIL R 4.00 10.00
620 Arcade Gannon SURGE FOIL R .50 1.25
621 Armory Paladin SURGE FOIL R 1.25 3.00
622 Atomize SURGE FOIL R 4.00 10.00
623 Boomer Scrapper SURGE FOIL R 1.00 2.50
624 Cait, Cage Brawler SURGE FOIL R .50 1.25
625 Cass, Hand of Vengeance SURGE FOIL R .75 2.00
626 Colonel Autumn SURGE FOIL R 1.50 4.00
627 Contaminated Drink SURGE FOIL U 4.00 10.00
628 Craig Boone, Novac Guard SURGE FOIL U 10.00 25.00
629 Desdemona, Freedom's Edge SURGE FOIL R .50 1.25
630 Elder Arthur Maxson SURGE FOIL R 1.00 2.50
631 Elder Owyn Lyons SURGE FOIL U 1.50 4.00
632 Electrosiphon SURGE FOIL R .75 2.00
633 Inventory Management SURGE FOIL R 4.00 10.00
634 Kellogg, Dangerous Mind SURGE FOIL R 3.00 8.00
635 Legate Lanius, Caesar's Ace SURGE FOIL U 6.00 15.00
636 MacCready, Lamplight Mayor SURGE FOIL R 2.00 5.00
637 Marcus, Mutant Mayor SURGE FOIL R 1.50 4.00
638 Moira Brown, Guide Author SURGE FOIL R .50 1.25
639 Mutational Advantage SURGE FOIL R 2.00 5.00
640 Nightkin Ambusher SURGE FOIL U 3.00 8.00
641 The Nipton Lottery SURGE FOIL R 1.50 4.00
642 Paladin Elizabeth Taggerdy SURGE FOIL R 1.50 4.00
643 Raul, Trouble Shooter SURGE FOIL U 12.00 30.00
644 Red Death, Shipwrecker SURGE FOIL R .75 2.00
645 Rex, Cyber-Hound SURGE FOIL R 1.00 2.50
646 Sentinel Sarah Lyons SURGE FOIL R 1.00 2.50
647 Shaun, Father of Synths SURGE FOIL R .75 2.00
648 Three Dog, Galaxy News DJ SURGE FOIL R 1.00 2.50
649 Vault 11: Voter's Dilemma SURGE FOIL R 1.50 4.00
650 Vault 87: Forced Evolution SURGE FOIL R 2.00 5.00
651 Vault 112: Sadistic Simulation SURGE FOIL R 1.50 4.00
652 White Glove Gourmand SURGE FOIL U 2.00 5.00
653 Young Deathclaws SURGE FOIL U 2.00 5.00
654 Agility Bobblehead SURGE FOIL U 15.00 40.00
655 Behemoth of Vault 0 SURGE FOIL U 3.00 8.00
656 Brotherhood Vertibird SURGE FOIL R 1.25 3.00
657 C.A.M.P. SURGE FOIL U 2.50 6.00
658 Charisma Bobblehead SURGE FOIL U 12.00 30.00
659 ED-E, Lonesome Eyebot SURGE FOIL R 2.00 5.00
660 Endurance Bobblehead SURGE FOIL U 15.00 40.00
661 Expert-Level Safe SURGE FOIL U 2.00 5.00
662 Intelligence Bobblehead SURGE FOIL U 12.00 30.00
663 Luck Bobblehead SURGE FOIL U 20.00 50.00
664 Mister Gutsy SURGE FOIL R .50 1.25
665 Nuka-Cola Vending Machine SURGE FOIL U 20.00 50.00
666 Nuka-Nuke Launcher SURGE FOIL R 1.25 3.00
667 Perception Bobblehead SURGE FOIL U 12.00 30.00
668 Pip-Boy 3000 SURGE FOIL R 6.00 15.00
669 Recon Craft Theta SURGE FOIL R 1.00 2.50
670 Silver Shroud Costume SURGE FOIL U 30.00 80.00
671 Strength Bobblehead SURGE FOIL U 15.00 40.00
672 Survivor's Med Kit SURGE FOIL U 1.50 4.00
673 T-45 Power Armor SURGE FOIL R 1.50 4.00
674 Desolate Mire SURGE FOIL R 1.50 4.00
675 Diamond City SURGE FOIL R 3.00 8.00
676 Ferrous Lake SURGE FOIL R 1.50 4.00
677 HELIOS One SURGE FOIL R 1.50 4.00
678 Junktown SURGE FOIL R 2.00 5.00
679 Mariposa Military Base SURGE FOIL R 1.00 2.50
680 Overflowing Basin SURGE FOIL R 1.50 4.00
681 Sunscorched Divide SURGE FOIL R 1.50 4.00
682 Viridescent Bog SURGE FOIL R 2.00 5.00
683 All That Glitters SURGE FOIL C 4.00 10.00
684 Austere Command SURGE FOIL R 1.50 4.00
685 Captain of the Watch SURGE FOIL R .60 1.50
686 Crush Contraband SURGE FOIL U 2.00 5.00
687 Dispatch SURGE FOIL U 6.00 15.00
688 Entrapment Maneuver SURGE FOIL R 1.25 3.00
689 Hour of Reckoning SURGE FOIL R .40 1.00
690 Impassioned Orator SURGE FOIL C .75 2.00
691 Intangible Virtue SURGE FOIL U 1.50 4.00
692 Keeper of the Accord SURGE FOIL R .50 1.25
693 Mantle of the Ancients SURGE FOIL R 1.00 2.50
694 Marshal's Anthem SURGE FOIL R 2.00 5.00
695 Martial Coup SURGE FOIL R .50 1.25
696 Open the Vaults SURGE FOIL R .50 1.25
697 Path to Exile SURGE FOIL U 6.00 15.00
698 Puresteel Paladin SURGE FOIL R 2.00 5.00
699 Secure the Wastes SURGE FOIL R 1.25 3.00
700 Single Combat SURGE FOIL R .50 1.25
701 Swords to Plowshares SURGE FOIL U 8.00 20.00
702 Valorous Stance SURGE FOIL U .75 2.00
703 Fraying Sanity SURGE FOIL R .60 1.50
704 Glimmer of Genius SURGE FOIL U 2.00 5.00
705 Inexorable Tide SURGE FOIL R 2.50 6.00
706 Mechanized Production SURGE FOIL M 1.50 4.00
707 One with the Machine SURGE FOIL R .50 1.25
708 Thirst for Knowledge SURGE FOIL U .75 2.00
709 Whirler Rogue SURGE FOIL U 1.50 4.00
710 Bastion of Remembrance SURGE FOIL U 5.00 12.00
711 Black Market SURGE FOIL R 1.25 3.00
712 Deadly Dispute SURGE FOIL C 6.00 15.00
713 Lethal Scheme SURGE FOIL R .75 2.00
714 Morbid Opportunist SURGE FOIL U 4.00 10.00
715 Pitiless Plunderer SURGE FOIL U 10.00 25.00
716 Blasphemous Act SURGE FOIL R 2.50 6.00
717 Chaos Warp SURGE FOIL R .75 2.00
718 Loyal Apprentice SURGE FOIL U 3.00 8.00
719 Sticky Fingers SURGE FOIL C 1.50 4.00
720 Stolen Strategy SURGE FOIL R .60 1.50
721 Unexpected Windfall SURGE FOIL C 5.00 12.00
722 Abundant Growth SURGE FOIL C 1.25 3.00
723 Branching Evolution SURGE FOIL R 2.50 6.00
724 Cultivate SURGE FOIL U 3.00 8.00
725 Farseek SURGE FOIL C 2.50 6.00
726 Fertile Ground SURGE FOIL C 4.00 10.00
727 Guardian Project SURGE FOIL R 3.00 8.00
728 Hardened Scales SURGE FOIL R .75 2.00
729 Harmonize SURGE FOIL U 2.50 6.00
730 Heroic Intervention SURGE FOIL R 5.00 12.00
731 Inspiring Call SURGE FOIL U 5.00 12.00
732 Rampant Growth SURGE FOIL C 2.00 5.00
733 Rancor SURGE FOIL U 3.00 8.00
734 Squirrel Nest SURGE FOIL U 4.00 10.00
735 Tireless Tracker SURGE FOIL R .50 1.25
736 Wild Growth SURGE FOIL C 4.00 10.00
737 Anguished Unmaking SURGE FOIL R 1.25 3.00
738 Assemble the Legion SURGE FOIL R .30 .75
739 Behemoth Sledge SURGE FOIL U 1.25 3.00
740 Biomass Mutation SURGE FOIL R .40 1.00
741 Casualties of War SURGE FOIL R 1.25 3.00
742 Corpsejack Menace SURGE FOIL U 4.00 10.00
743 Fervent Charge SURGE FOIL R 1.00 2.50
744 Find // Finality SURGE FOIL R .50 1.25
745 General's Enforcer SURGE FOIL U 5.00 12.00
746 Heroic Reinforcements SURGE FOIL U .60 1.50
747 Putrefy SURGE FOIL U 4.00 10.00
748 Ruinous Ultimatum SURGE FOIL R 2.00 5.00
749 Wake the Past SURGE FOIL R 1.00 2.50
750 Wear // Tear SURGE FOIL U 4.00 10.00
751 Winding Constrictor SURGE FOIL U 8.00 20.00
752 Arcane Signet SURGE FOIL U 2.00 5.00
753 Basilisk Collar SURGE FOIL R 2.00 5.00
754 Bloodforged Battle-Axe SURGE FOIL R .50 1.25
755 Brass Knuckles SURGE FOIL U .60 1.50
756 Champion's Helm SURGE FOIL R .75 2.00
757 Contagion Clasp SURGE FOIL U 2.00 5.00
758 Everflowing Chalice SURGE FOIL U 3.00 8.00
759 Explorer's Scope SURGE FOIL C 1.50 4.00
760 Fireshrieker SURGE FOIL U 4.00 10.00
761 Lightning Greaves SURGE FOIL U 6.00 15.00
762 Masterwork of Ingenuity SURGE FOIL R .60 1.50
763 Mind Stone SURGE FOIL U 2.50 6.00
764 Mystic Forge SURGE FOIL R 2.50 6.00
765 Panharmonicon SURGE FOIL R 2.50 6.00
766 Skullclamp SURGE FOIL U 8.00 20.00
767 Sol Ring SURGE FOIL U 5.00 12.00
768 Solemn Simulacrum SURGE FOIL R .50 1.25
769 Steel Overseer SURGE FOIL R 1.00 2.50
770 Swiftfoot Boots SURGE FOIL U 6.00 15.00
771 Talisman of Conviction SURGE FOIL U 2.50 6.00
772 Talisman of Creativity SURGE FOIL U 3.00 8.00
773 Talisman of Curiosity SURGE FOIL U 3.00 8.00
774 Talisman of Dominance SURGE FOIL U 4.00 10.00
775 Talisman of Hierarchy SURGE FOIL U 2.50 6.00
776 Talisman of Indulgence SURGE FOIL U 4.00 10.00
777 Talisman of Progress SURGE FOIL U 4.00 10.00
778 Talisman of Resilience SURGE FOIL U 3.00 8.00
779 Thought Vessel SURGE FOIL C 5.00 12.00
780 Wayfarer's Bauble SURGE FOIL C 2.00 5.00
781 Ash Barrens SURGE FOIL C .50 1.25
782 Buried Ruin SURGE FOIL U 3.00 8.00
783 Canopy Vista SURGE FOIL R .30 .75
784 Canyon Slough SURGE FOIL R .50 1.25
785 Cinder Glade SURGE FOIL R .50 1.25
786 Clifftop Retreat SURGE FOIL R 1.00 2.50
787 Command Tower SURGE FOIL C 5.00 12.00
788 Darkwater Catacombs SURGE FOIL R .75 2.00
789 Dragonskull Summit SURGE FOIL R 1.50 4.00
790 Drowned Catacomb SURGE FOIL R 1.00 2.50
791 Evolving Wilds SURGE FOIL C .75 2.00
792 Exotic Orchard SURGE FOIL R 1.00 2.50
793 Fetid Pools SURGE FOIL R .50 1.25
794 Glacial Fortress SURGE FOIL R .50 1.25
795 Hinterland Harbor SURGE FOIL R 1.25 3.00
796 Irrigated Farmland SURGE FOIL R 1.25 3.00
797 Isolated Chapel SURGE FOIL R 1.50 4.00
798 Jungle Shrine SURGE FOIL U 4.00 10.00
799 Memorial to Glory SURGE FOIL U 2.00 5.00
800 Mortuary Mire SURGE FOIL C 2.00 5.00
801 Mossfire Valley SURGE FOIL R .60 1.50
802 Myriad Landscape SURGE FOIL U .75 2.00
803 Mystic Monastery SURGE FOIL U 2.00 5.00
804 Nesting Grounds SURGE FOIL R 1.00 2.50
805 Nomad Outpost SURGE FOIL U 2.00 5.00
806 Opulent Palace SURGE FOIL U 4.00 10.00
807 Path of Ancestry SURGE FOIL C 1.00 2.50
808 Prairie Stream SURGE FOIL R .60 1.50
809 Razortide Bridge SURGE FOIL C 2.50 6.00
810 Roadside Reliquary SURGE FOIL U 1.00 2.50
811 Rogue's Passage SURGE FOIL U 4.00 10.00
812 Rootbound Crag SURGE FOIL R 2.00 5.00
813 Rustvale Bridge SURGE FOIL C 3.00 8.00
814 Scattered Groves SURGE FOIL R .40 1.00
815 Scavenger Grounds SURGE FOIL R 1.50 4.00
816 Shadowblood Ridge SURGE FOIL R 1.00 2.50
817 Sheltered Thicket SURGE FOIL R .30 .75
818 Silverbluff Bridge SURGE FOIL C 1.50 4.00
819 Skycloud Expanse SURGE FOIL R .40 1.00
820 Smoldering Marsh SURGE FOIL R .25 .60
821 Spire of Industry SURGE FOIL R .75 2.00
822 Sulfur Falls SURGE FOIL R 1.00 2.50
823 Sungrass Prairie SURGE FOIL R .60 1.50
824 Sunken Hollow SURGE FOIL R .50 1.25
825 Sunpetal Grove SURGE FOIL R 1.50 4.00
826 Tainted Field SURGE FOIL U 4.00 10.00
827 Tainted Isle SURGE FOIL U 4.00 10.00
828 Tainted Peak SURGE FOIL U 2.00 5.00
829 Tainted Wood SURGE FOIL U 5.00 12.00
830 Temple of Abandon SURGE FOIL R .40 1.00
831 Temple of Deceit SURGE FOIL R .50 1.25
832 Temple of Enlightenment SURGE FOIL R .75 2.00
833 Temple of Epiphany SURGE FOIL R .40 1.00
834 Temple of Malady SURGE FOIL R .60 1.50
835 Temple of Malice SURGE FOIL R .75 2.00
836 Temple of Mystery SURGE FOIL R .40 1.00
837 Temple of Plenty SURGE FOIL R .50 1.25
838 Temple of Silence SURGE FOIL R .50 1.25
839 Temple of the False God SURGE FOIL U 1.25 3.00
840 Temple of Triumph SURGE FOIL R .50 1.25
841 Terramorphic Expanse SURGE FOIL C .75 2.00
842 Treasure Vault SURGE FOIL R 2.50 6.00
843 Windbrisk Heights SURGE FOIL R .40 1.00
844 Woodland Cemetery SURGE FOIL R .60 1.50
845 Plains FULL ART SURGE FOIL C 2.50 6.00
846 Plains FULL ART SURGE FOIL C 1.00 2.50
847 Island FULL ART SURGE FOIL C 2.50 6.00
848 Island FULL ART SURGE FOIL C .75 2.00
849 Swamp FULL ART SURGE FOIL C 2.50 6.00
850 Swamp FULL ART SURGE FOIL C 2.00 5.00
851 Mountain FULL ART SURGE FOIL C 2.50 6.00
852 Mountain FULL ART SURGE FOIL C 1.00 2.50
853 Forest FULL ART SURGE FOIL C 2.00 5.00
854 Forest FULL ART SURGE FOIL C .75 2.00
855 Idolized SURGE FOIL R 15.00 40.00
856 Securitron Squadron SURGE FOIL R 10.00 25.00
857 Radstorm SURGE FOIL R 20.00 50.00
858 Synth Infiltrator SURGE FOIL R 6.00 15.00
859 Nuclear Fallout SURGE FOIL R 25.00 60.00
860 Screeching Scorchbeast SURGE FOIL R 6.00 15.00
861 V.A.T.S. SURGE FOIL R 20.00 50.00
862 Mysterious Stranger SURGE FOIL R 8.00 20.00
863 Watchful Radstag SURGE FOIL R 6.00 15.00
864 Alpha Deathclaw SURGE FOIL R 10.00 25.00
865 Armory Paladin SURGE FOIL R 5.00 12.00
866 Atomize SURGE FOIL R 12.00 30.00
867 Caesar, Legion's Emperor SURGE FOIL M 20.00 50.00
868 Dogmeat, Ever Loyal SURGE FOIL M 25.00 60.00
869 Dr. Madison Li SURGE FOIL M 15.00 40.00
870 Inventory Management SURGE FOIL R 12.00 30.00
871 The Wise Mothman SURGE FOIL M 50.00 120.00
872 Hullbreaker Horror SURGE FOIL R 15.00 40.00
873 Lord of the Undead SURGE FOIL R 5.00 12.00
874 Grave Titan SURGE FOIL M 8.00 20.00
875 Vigor SURGE FOIL R 15.00 40.00
876 Ayula, Queen Among Bears SURGE FOIL R 4.00 10.00
877 Tarmogoyf SURGE FOIL M 12.00 30.00
878 Hornet Queen SURGE FOIL R 6.00 15.00
879 Gemrazer SURGE FOIL R 3.00 8.00
880 Walking Ballista SURGE FOIL R 25.00 60.00
881 Farewell SURGE FOIL R 30.00 80.00
882 Ravages of War SURGE FOIL M 30.00 80.00
883 Vandalblast SURGE FOIL U 25.00 60.00
884 Arcane Signet SURGE FOIL U 40.00 100.00
885 Crucible of Worlds SURGE FOIL M 25.00 60.00
886 Nuka-Cola Vending Machine SURGE FOIL U 40.00 100.00
887 Sol Ring SURGE FOIL M 100.00 250.00
888 Command Tower SURGE FOIL U 30.00 80.00
889 Wasteland SURGE FOIL R 40.00 100.00
890 Aradesh, the Founder SURGE FOIL R .20 .50
891 Automated Assembly Line SURGE FOIL R .50 1.25
892 Battle of Hoover Dam SURGE FOIL R .50 1.25
893 Brotherhood Scribe SURGE FOIL R 1.50 4.00
894 Codsworth, Handy Helper SURGE FOIL R 6.00 15.00
895 Overencumbered SURGE FOIL R .60 1.50
896 Overseer of Vault 76 SURGE FOIL R .20 .50
897 Pre-War Formalwear SURGE FOIL R 3.00 8.00
898 The Prydwen, Steel Flagship SURGE FOIL R 1.25 3.00
899 Sentry Bot SURGE FOIL R .40 1.00
900 Sierra, Nuka's Biggest Fan SURGE FOIL R 1.00 2.50
901 Yes Man, Personal Securitron SURGE FOIL R 2.00 5.00
902 Curie, Emergent Intelligence SURGE FOIL R 1.25 3.00
903 James, Wandering Dad //
Follow Him SURGE FOIL R .50 1.25
904 Jason Bright, Glowing Prophet SURGE FOIL R .75 2.00
905 Mirelurk Queen SURGE FOIL R .60 1.50
906 Nick Valentine, Private Eye SURGE FOIL R 1.00 2.50
907 Piper Wright, Publick Reporter SURGE FOIL R 1.25 3.00
908 Struggle for Project Purity SURGE FOIL R 4.00 10.00
909 Feral Ghoul SURGE FOIL R 3.00 8.00
910 Hancock, Ghoulish Mayor SURGE FOIL R 1.00 2.50
911 Wasteland Raider SURGE FOIL R .50 1.25
912 Assaultron Dominator SURGE FOIL R .60 1.50
913 Duchess, Wayward Tavernkeep SURGE FOIL R .25 .60
914 Grim Reaper's Sprint SURGE FOIL R 4.00 10.00
915 Junk Jet SURGE FOIL R .50 1.25
916 Megaton's Fate SURGE FOIL R .25 .60
917 The Motherlode, Excavator SURGE FOIL R .40 1.00
918 Plasma Caster SURGE FOIL R .40 1.00
919 Powder Ganger SURGE FOIL R .15 .40
920 Rose, Cutthroat Raider SURGE FOIL R 2.50 6.00
921 Synth Eradicator SURGE FOIL R .40 1.00
922 Thrill-Kill Disciple SURGE FOIL R .20 .50
923 Veronica, Dissident Scribe SURGE FOIL R .40 1.00

924 Wild Wasteland SURGE FOIL R 2.50 6.00
925 Animal Friend SURGE FOIL R .75 2.00
926 Harold and Bob, First Numens SURGE FOIL R .40 1.00
927 Lily Bowen, Raging Grandma SURGE FOIL R .60 1.50
928 Power Fist SURGE FOIL R 8.00 20.00
929 Rampaging Yao Guai SURGE FOIL R 2.50 6.00
930 Strong Back SURGE FOIL R 3.00 8.00
931 Strong, the Brutish Thespian SURGE FOIL R .50 1.25
932 Tato Farmer SURGE FOIL R 1.25 3.00
933 Agent Frank Horrigan SURGE FOIL R 5.00 12.00
934 Almost Perfect SURGE FOIL R .50 1.25
935 Arcade Gannon SURGE FOIL R .40 1.00
936 Boomer Scrapper SURGE FOIL R .25 .60
937 Cait, Cage Brawler SURGE FOIL R .50 1.25
938 Cass, Hand of Vengeance SURGE FOIL R .40 1.00
939 Colonel Autumn SURGE FOIL R .60 1.50
940 Desdemona, Freedom's Edge SURGE FOIL R .15 .40
941 Elder Arthur Maxson SURGE FOIL R .50 1.25
942 Electrosiphon SURGE FOIL R 1.00 2.50
943 Kellogg, Dangerous Mind SURGE FOIL R 5.00 12.00
944 Liberty Prime, Recharged SURGE FOIL M 5.00 12.00
945 MacCready, Lamplight Mayor SURGE FOIL R 1.00 2.50
946 Marcus, Mutant Mayor SURGE FOIL R .50 1.25
947 The Master, Transcendent SURGE FOIL M 3.00 8.00
948 Moira Brown, Guide Author SURGE FOIL R .20 .50
949 Mr. House, President and
CEO SURGE FOIL M 5.00 12.00
950 Mutational Advantage SURGE FOIL R 2.00 5.00
951 The Nipton Lottery SURGE FOIL R .50 1.25
952 Paladin Elizabeth Taggerdy SURGE FOIL R 2.00 5.00
953 Preston Garvey, Minuteman SURGE FOIL M .75 2.00
954 Red Death, Shipwrecker SURGE FOIL R 1.25 3.00
955 Rex, Cyber-Hound SURGE FOIL R 1.00 2.50
956 Sentinel Sarah Lyons SURGE FOIL R .60 1.50
957 Shaun, Father of Synths SURGE FOIL R 1.00 2.50
958 Three Dog, Galaxy News DJ SURGE FOIL R 1.00 2.50
959 Brotherhood Vertibird SURGE FOIL R .50 1.25
960 ED-E, Lonesome Eyebot SURGE FOIL R .50 1.25
961 Mister Gutsy SURGE FOIL R .50 1.25
962 Nuka-Nuke Launcher SURGE FOIL R .30 .75
963 Pip-Boy 3000 SURGE FOIL R 8.00 20.00
964 Recon Craft Theta SURGE FOIL R .50 1.25
965 T-45 Power Armor SURGE FOIL R 1.00 2.50
966 Desolate Mire SURGE FOIL R 1.25 3.00
967 Diamond City SURGE FOIL R 2.50 6.00
968 Ferrous Lake SURGE FOIL R 1.25 3.00
969 HELIOS One SURGE FOIL R 3.00 8.00
970 Junktown SURGE FOIL R .40 1.00
971 Mariposa Military Base SURGE FOIL R .50 1.25
972 Overflowing Basin SURGE FOIL R 1.25 3.00
973 Sunscorched Divide SURGE FOIL R 1.00 2.50
974 Viridescent Bog SURGE FOIL R 1.00 2.50
975 Austere Command SURGE FOIL R 1.00 2.50
976 Captain of the Watch SURGE FOIL R .25 .60
977 Entrapment Maneuver SURGE FOIL R .25 .60
978 Hour of Reckoning SURGE FOIL R .30 .75
979 Keeper of the Accord SURGE FOIL R .50 1.25
980 Mantle of the Ancients SURGE FOIL R .60 1.50
981 Marshal's Anthem SURGE FOIL R .25 .60
982 Martial Coup SURGE FOIL R .30 .75
983 Open the Vaults SURGE FOIL R .40 1.00
984 Puresteel Paladin SURGE FOIL R 2.50 6.00
985 Secure the Wastes SURGE FOIL R .60 1.50
986 Single Combat SURGE FOIL R .20 .50
987 Fraying Sanity SURGE FOIL R .25 .60
988 Inexorable Tide SURGE FOIL R 2.50 6.00
989 Mechanized Production SURGE FOIL M 1.50 4.00
990 One with the Machine SURGE FOIL R .20 .50
991 Black Market SURGE FOIL R 1.00 2.50
992 Lethal Scheme SURGE FOIL R .60 1.50
993 Blasphemous Act SURGE FOIL R 2.50 6.00
994 Chaos Warp SURGE FOIL R 1.00 2.50
995 Stolen Strategy SURGE FOIL R .40 1.00
996 Branching Evolution SURGE FOIL R 5.00 12.00
997 Guardian Project SURGE FOIL R 4.00 10.00
998 Hardened Scales SURGE FOIL R 2.00 5.00
999 Heroic Intervention SURGE FOIL R 5.00 12.00
1000 Tireless Tracker SURGE FOIL R .60 1.50
1001 Anguished Unmaking SURGE FOIL R .60 1.50
1002 Assemble the Legion SURGE FOIL R .30 .75
1003 Biomass Mutation SURGE FOIL R .20 .50
1004 Casualties of War SURGE FOIL R 1.50 4.00
1005 Fervent Charge SURGE FOIL R .50 1.25
1006 Ruinous Ultimatum SURGE FOIL R 2.00 5.00
1007 Wake the Past SURGE FOIL R .40 1.00
1008 Basilisk Collar SURGE FOIL R 2.00 5.00
1009 Bloodforged Battle-Axe SURGE FOIL R .40 1.00
1010 Champion's Helm SURGE FOIL R .50 1.25
1011 Masterwork of Ingenuity SURGE FOIL R .50 1.25
1012 Mystic Forge SURGE FOIL R .75 2.00
1013 Panharmonicon SURGE FOIL R 2.00 5.00
1014 Solemn Simulacrum SURGE FOIL R .75 2.00
1015 Steel Overseer SURGE FOIL R 1.50 4.00
1016 Canopy Vista SURGE FOIL R .75 2.00
1017 Canyon Slough SURGE FOIL R .25 .60
1018 Cinder Glade SURGE FOIL R 1.00 2.50
1019 Clifftop Retreat SURGE FOIL R 2.50 6.00
1020 Darkwater Catacombs SURGE FOIL R .30 .75
1021 Dragonskull Summit SURGE FOIL R 2.50 6.00
1022 Drowned Catacomb SURGE FOIL R 2.50 6.00
1023 Exotic Orchard SURGE FOIL R 3.00 8.00
1024 Fetid Pools SURGE FOIL R .30 .75
1025 Glacial Fortress SURGE FOIL R 1.00 2.50
1026 Hinterland Harbor SURGE FOIL R 2.00 5.00
1027 Irrigated Farmland SURGE FOIL R .25 .60
1028 Isolated Chapel SURGE FOIL R 2.00 5.00
1029 Mossfire Valley SURGE FOIL R .50 1.25
1030 Nesting Grounds SURGE FOIL R 2.00 5.00
1031 Prairie Stream SURGE FOIL R .50 1.25
1032 Rootbound Crag SURGE FOIL R 1.25 3.00
1033 Scattered Groves SURGE FOIL R .20 .50
1034 Scavenger Grounds SURGE FOIL R 1.00 2.50
1035 Shadowblood Ridge SURGE FOIL R .50 1.25
1036 Sheltered Thicket SURGE FOIL R .30 .75
1037 Skycloud Expanse SURGE FOIL R .40 1.00
1038 Smoldering Marsh SURGE FOIL R .60 1.50
1039 Spire of Industry SURGE FOIL R 2.50 6.00
1040 Sulfur Falls SURGE FOIL R 2.50 6.00
1041 Sungrass Prairie SURGE FOIL R .40 1.00
1042 Sunken Hollow SURGE FOIL R .60 1.50
1043 Sunpetal Grove SURGE FOIL R 1.50 4.00
1044 Temple of Abandon SURGE FOIL R .30 .75
1045 Temple of Deceit SURGE FOIL R .30 .75
1046 Temple of Enlightenment SURGE FOIL R .25 .60
1047 Temple of Epiphany SURGE FOIL R .25 .60
1048 Temple of Malady SURGE FOIL R 2.50 6.00
1049 Temple of Malice SURGE FOIL R .25 .60
1050 Temple of Mystery SURGE FOIL R .25 .60
1051 Temple of Plenty SURGE FOIL R .25 .60
1052 Temple of Silence SURGE FOIL R .40 1.00
1053 Temple of Triumph SURGE FOIL R .25 .60
1054 Treasure Vault SURGE FOIL R 3.00 8.00
1055 Windbrisk Heights SURGE FOIL R .40 1.00
1056 Woodland Cemetery SURGE FOIL R 1.50 4.00
1057 Strength Bobblehead
SERIAL DOUBLE RAINBOW FOIL U 250.00 600.00
1058 Perception Bobblehead
SERIAL DOUBLE RAINBOW FOIL U 250.00 600.00
1059 Endurance Bobblehead
SERIAL DOUBLE RAINBOW FOIL U 250.00 600.00
1060 Charisma Bobblehead
SERIAL DOUBLE RAINBOW FOIL U 250.00 600.00
1061 Intelligence Bobblehead
SERIAL DOUBLE RAINBOW FOIL U 300.00 800.00
1062 Agility Bobblehead
SERIAL DOUBLE RAINBOW FOIL U 300.00 800.00
1063 Luck Bobblehead
SERIAL DOUBLE RAINBOW FOIL U 300.00 800.00
1064 Caesar, Legion's Emperor
THICK STOCK SURGE FOIL M .10 .25
1065 Dogmeat, Ever Loyal
THICK STOCK SURGE FOIL M .10 .25
1066 Dr. Madison Li
THICK STOCK SURGE FOIL M .10 .25
1067 The Wise Mothman
THICK STOCK SURGE FOIL M .10 .25

2024 Magic The Gathering Universes Beyond Fallout Commander

1 Caesar, Legion's Emperor FOIL M .60 1.50
2 Dogmeat, Ever Loyal FOIL M .25 .60
3 Dr. Madison Li FOIL M .20 .50
4 The Wise Mothman FOIL M .40 1.00
5 Liberty Prime, Recharged FOIL M 1.00 2.50
6 The Master, Transcendent FOIL M 2.00 5.00
8 Preston Garvey, Minuteman FOIL M 5.00 12.00
9 Aradesh, the Founder R .08 .20
10 Automated Assembly Line R .10 .25
11 Battle of Hoover Dam R .08 .20
12 Brotherhood Outcast U .10 .25
13 Brotherhood Scribe R .10 .25
14 Codsworth, Handy Helper R 3.00 8.00
15 Commander Sofia Daguerre U .10 .25
16 Gary Clone U .10 .25
17 Idolized R 1.00 2.50
18 Overencumbered R .10 .25
19 Overseer of Vault 76 R .10 .25
20 Paladin Danse, Steel Maverick U .20 .50
21 Pre-War Formalwear R .30 .75
22 The Prydwen, Steel Flagship R .10 .25
23 Securitron Squadron R .60 1.50
24 Sentry Bot R .10 .25
25 Sierra, Nuka's Biggest Fan R .10 .25
26 Vault 13: Dweller's Journey R .04 .10
27 Vault 75: Middle School R .10 .25
28 Vault 101: Birthday Party R .05 .12
29 Yes Man, Personal Securitron R .20 .50
30 Curie, Emergent Intelligence R .10 .25
31 James, Wandering Dad // Follow Him R .10 .25
32 Jason Bright, Glowing Prophet R .05 .12
33 Mirelurk Queen R .12 .30
34 Nerd Rage U 2.00 5.00
35 Nick Valentine, Private Eye R .08 .20
36 Piper Wright, Publick Reporter R .15 .40
37 Radstorm R 3.00 8.00
38 Robobrain War Mind U .10 .25
39 Struggle for Project Purity R 1.25 3.00
40 Synth Infiltrator R .08 .20
41 Vexing Radgull U .12 .30
42 Bloatfly Swarm U .10 .25
43 Butch DeLoria, Tunnel Snake U .12 .30
44 Feral Ghoul R .60 1.50
45 Hancock, Ghoulish Mayor R .10 .25
46 Infesting Radroach U .10 .25
47 Nuclear Fallout R 1.50 4.00
48 Ruthless Radrat U .08 .20
49 Screeching Scorchbeast R .10 .25
50 V.A.T.S. R .40 1.00
51 Vault 12: The Necropolis R .08 .20
52 Wasteland Raider R .10 .25
53 Acquired Mutation U .08 .20
54 Assaultron Dominator R .10 .25
55 Bottle-Cap Blast U .75 2.00
56 Crimson Caravaneer U .10 .25
57 Duchess, Wayward Tavernkeep R .04 .10
58 Grim Reaper's Sprint R 1.00 2.50
59 Ian the Reckless U .10 .25
60 Junk Jet R .08 .20
61 Megaton's Fate R .10 .25
62 The Motherlode, Excavator R .10 .25
63 Mysterious Stranger R .10 .25
64 Plasma Caster R .10 .25
65 Powder Ganger R .08 .20
66 Rose, Cutthroat Raider R .75 2.00
67 Synth Eradicator R .10 .25
68 Thrill-Kill Disciple R .05 .12
69 Vault 21: House Gambit R .08 .20
70 Veronica, Dissident Scribe R .08 .20
71 Wild Wasteland R .50 1.25
72 Animal Friend R .10 .25
73 Bighorner Rancher U .25 .60
74 Break Down U .05 .12
75 Cathedral Acolyte U .15 .40
76 Glowing One U .10 .25
77 Gunner Conscript U .05 .12
78 Harold and Bob, First Numens R .10 .25
79 Lily Bowen, Raging Grandma R .10 .25
80 Lumbering Megasloth U .50 1.25
81 Power Fist R 3.00 8.00
82 Rampaging Yao Guai R 1.25 3.00
83 Strong Back R 1.50 4.00
84 Strong, the Brutish Thespian R .08 .20
85 Super Mutant Scavenger U .05 .12
86 Tato Farmer R .12 .30
87 Watchful Radstag R .40 1.00
88 Well Rested U 3.00 8.00
89 Agent Frank Horrigan R .25 .60
90 Almost Perfect R .10 .25
91 Alpha Deathclaw R .60 1.50
92 Arcade Gannon R .05 .12
93 Armory Paladin R .10 .25
94 Atomize R 1.00 2.50
95 Boomer Scrapper R .04 .10
96 Cait, Cage Brawler R .10 .25
97 Cass, Hand of Vengeance R .05 .12
98 Colonel Autumn R .10 .25
99 Contaminated Drink U .05 .12
100 Craig Boone, Novac Guard U .10 .25
101 Desdemona, Freedom's Edge R .08 .20
102 Elder Arthur Maxson R .10 .25
103 Elder Owyn Lyons U .10 .25
104 Electrosiphon R .15 .40
105 Inventory Management R .50 1.25
106 Kellogg, Dangerous Mind R 2.00 5.00
107 Legate Lanius, Caesar's Ace U .10 .25
108 MacCready, Lamplight Mayor R .12 .30
109 Marcus, Mutant Mayor R .10 .25
110 Moira Brown, Guide Author R .10 .25
111 Mutational Advantage R 1.25 3.00
112 Nightkin Ambusher U .04 .10
113 The Nipton Lottery R .08 .20
114 Paladin Elizabeth Taggerdy R .12 .30
115 Raul, Trouble Shooter U .20 .50
116 Red Death, Shipwrecker R .10 .25
117 Rex, Cyber-Hound R .10 .25
118 Sentinel Sarah Lyons R .10 .25
119 Shaun, Father of Synths R .10 .25
120 Three Dog, Galaxy News DJ R .10 .25
121 Vault 11: Voter's Dilemma R .04 .10
122 Vault 87: Forced Evolution R .08 .20
123 Vault 112: Sadistic Simulation R .10 .25
124 White Glove Gourmand U .08 .20
125 Young Deathclaws U .10 .25
126 Agility Bobblehead U 1.25 3.00
127 Behemoth of Vault 0 U .10 .25
128 Brotherhood Vertibird R .12 .30
129 C.A.M.P. U .10 .25
130 Charisma Bobblehead U .75 2.00
131 ED-E, Lonesome Eyebot R .10 .25
132 Endurance Bobblehead U .60 1.50
133 Expert-Level Safe U .05 .12
134 Intelligence Bobblehead U .75 2.00
135 Luck Bobblehead U 2.50 6.00
136 Mister Gutsy R .10 .25
137 Nuka Cola Vending Machine U 8.00 20.00
138 Nuka-Nuke Launcher R .05 .12
139 Perception Bobblehead U 1.00 2.50
140 Pip-Boy 3000 R 2.50 6.00
141 Recon Craft Theta R .10 .25
142 Silver Shroud Costume U 5.00 12.00
143 Strength Bobblehead U 1.00 2.50
144 Survivor's Med Kit U .08 .20
145 T-45 Power Armor R .10 .25
146 Desolate Mire R .50 1.25
147 Diamond City R .75 2.00
148 Ferrous Lake R .40 1.00
149 HELIOS One R .30 .75
150 Junktown R .10 .25
151 Mariposa Military Base R .10 .25
152 Overflowing Basin R .25 .60
153 Sunscorched Divide R .40 1.00
154 Viridescent Bog R .20 .50
155 All That Glitters C .40 1.00
156 Austere Command R .20 .50
157 Captain of the Watch R .10 .25
158 Crush Contraband U .05 .12
159 Dispatch U .60 1.50
160 Entrapment Maneuver R .08 .20
161 Hour of Reckoning R .10 .25
162 Impassioned Orator C .05 .12
163 Intangible Virtue U .10 .25
164 Keeper of the Accord R .10 .25
165 Mantle of the Ancients R .20 .50
166 Marshal's Anthem R .08 .20
167 Martial Coup R .10 .25
168 Open the Vaults R .10 .25
169 Path to Exile U .50 1.25
170 Puresteel Paladin R .60 1.50
171 Secure the Wastes R .20 .50
172 Single Combat R .10 .25
173 Swords to Plowshares U .60 1.50
174 Valorous Stance U .04 .10
175 Fraying Sanity R .10 .25
176 Glimmer of Genius U .04 .10
177 Inexorable Tide R 1.25 3.00
178 Mechanized Production M .30 .75
179 One with the Machine R .05 .12
180 Thirst for Knowledge U .08 .20
181 Whirler Rogue U .04 .10
182 Bastion of Remembrance U .40 1.00
183 Black Market R 1.00 2.50
184 Deadly Dispute C .60 1.50
185 Lethal Scheme R .10 .25
186 Morbid Opportunist U .40 1.00
187 Pitiless Plunderer U 3.00 8.00
188 Blasphemous Act R 1.25 3.00
189 Chaos Warp R .25 .60
190 Loyal Apprentice U .12 .30
191 Sticky Fingers C .10 .25
192 Stolen Strategy R .10 .25
193 Unexpected Windfall C .50 1.25
194 Abundant Growth C .08 .20
195 Branching Evolution R 2.00 5.00
196 Cultivate U .40 1.00
197 Farseek C .60 1.50
198 Fertile Ground C .12 .30
199 Guardian Project R 3.00 8.00
200 Hardened Scales R .60 1.50
201 Harmonize U .12 .30
202 Heroic Intervention R 5.00 12.00
203 Inspiring Call U .25 .60
204 Rampant Growth C .25 .60
205 Rancor U .50 1.25
206 Squirrel Nest U .05 .12
207 Tireless Tracker R .20 .50
208 Wild Growth C .15 .40
209 Anguished Unmaking R .60 1.50
210 Assemble the Legion R .10 .25
211 Behemoth Sledge U .08 .20
212 Biomass Mutation R .08 .20
213 Casualties of War R .12 .30
214 Corpsejack Menace U .10 .25
215 Fervent Charge R .10 .25
216 Find // Finality R .08 .20
217 General's Enforcer U .08 .20
218 Heroic Reinforcements U .04 .10
219 Putrefy U .10 .25
220 Ruinous Ultimatum R 1.00 2.50
221 Wake the Past R .08 .20
222 Wear // Tear U .60 1.50
223 Winding Constrictor U .10 .25
224 Arcane Signet U .20 .50
225 Basilisk Collar R .60 1.50
226 Bloodforged Battle-Axe R .15 .40
227 Brass Knuckles U .04 .10
228 Champion's Helm R .50 1.25
229 Contagion Clasp U .15 .40
230 Everflowing Chalice U .12 .30
231 Explorer's Scope C .10 .25
232 Fireshrieker U .10 .25
233 Lightning Greaves U 3.00 8.00
234 Masterwork of Ingenuity R .15 .40
235 Mind Stone U .10 .25
236 Mystic Forge R .25 .60
237 Panharmonicon R 1.50 4.00
238 Skullclamp U 4.00 10.00
239 Sol Ring U .60 1.50
240 Solemn Simulacrum R .30 .75
241 Steel Overseer R .20 .50
242 Swiftfoot Boots U 1.00 2.50
243 Talisman of Conviction U .10 .25
244 Talisman of Creativity U .50 1.25
245 Talisman of Curiosity U .12 .30
246 Talisman of Dominance U .40 1.00
247 Talisman of Hierarchy U .60 1.50
248 Talisman of Indulgence U 1.00 2.50
249 Talisman of Progress U .20 .50
250 Talisman of Resilience U .20 .50
251 Thought Vessel C .60 1.50
252 Wayfarer's Bauble C .10 .25
253 Ash Barrens C .04 .10
254 Buried Ruin U .10 .25
255 Canopy Vista R .10 .25
256 Canyon Slough R .10 .25
257 Cinder Glade R .12 .30
258 Clifftop Retreat R .25 .60
259 Command Tower C .10 .25
260 Darkwater Catacombs R .10 .25
261 Dragonskull Summit R .60 1.50
262 Drowned Catacomb R 1.00 2.50
263 Evolving Wilds C .05 .12
264 Exotic Orchard R .10 .25
265 Fetid Pools R .08 .20
266 Glacial Fortress R .50 1.25
267 Hinterland Harbor R .60 1.50
268 Irrigated Farmland R .05 .12
269 Isolated Chapel R .75 2.00
270 Jungle Shrine U .10 .25
271 Memorial to Glory U .04 .10
272 Mortuary Mire C .10 .25
273 Mossfire Valley R .10 .25
274 Myriad Landscape U .10 .25
275 Mystic Monastery U .10 .25
276 Nesting Grounds R .25 .60
277 Nomad Outpost U .12 .30
278 Opulent Palace U .15 .40
279 Path of Ancestry C .10 .25
280 Prairie Stream R .10 .25
281 Razortide Bridge C .10 .25
282 Roadside Reliquary U .04 .10
283 Rogue's Passage U .12 .30
284 Rootbound Crag R 1.00 2.50
285 Rustvale Bridge C .12 .30
286 Scattered Groves R .10 .25
287 Scavenger Grounds R .15 .40
288 Shadowblood Ridge R .10 .25
289 Sheltered Thicket R .08 .20
290 Silverbluff Bridge C .10 .25
291 Skycloud Expanse R .05 .12
292 Smoldering Marsh R .10 .25
293 Spire of Industry R .10 .25
294 Sulfur Falls R .50 1.25
295 Sungrass Prairie R .08 .20
296 Sunken Hollow R .10 .25
297 Sunpetal Grove R 1.25 3.00
298 Tainted Field U .10 .25
299 Tainted Isle U .12 .30
300 Tainted Peak U .12 .30
301 Tainted Wood U .20 .50
302 Temple of Abandon R .05 .12
303 Temple of Deceit R .10 .25
304 Temple of Enlightenment R .08 .20
305 Temple of Epiphany R .08 .20
306 Temple of Malady R .10 .25
307 Temple of Malice R .10 .25
308 Temple of Mystery R .08 .20
309 Temple of Plenty R .08 .20
310 Temple of Silence R .10 .25
311 Temple of the False God U .08 .20
312 Temple of Triumph R .05 .12
313 Terramorphic Expanse C .08 .20
314 Treasure Vault R 1.25 3.00
315 Windbrisk Heights R .10 .25
316 Woodland Cemetery R .75 2.00
317 Plains FULL ART C .10 .25
318 Plains FULL ART C .10 .25
319 Island FULL ART C .15 .40
320 Island FULL ART C .10 .25
321 Swamp FULL ART C .20 .50
322 Swamp FULL ART C .15 .40
323 Mountain FULL ART C .12 .30
324 Mountain FULL ART C .10 .25
325 Forest FULL ART C .20 .50
326 Forest FULL ART C .10 .25

2024 Magic The Gathering Universes Beyond Fallout Promos

1068 War Room P 2.00 5.00

Pokemon

1999 Pokemon Base 1st Edition

1 Alakazam HOLO R/Thin Stamp	25.00	50.00
3 Chansey HOLO R/Thin Stamp	3.00	6.00
4 Charizard HOLO R/Thin Stamp	40.00	100.00
5 Clefairy HOLO R/Thin Stamp	12.00	30.00
7 Hitmonchan HOLO R/Thin Stamp	7.50	15.00
9 Magneton HOLO R/Thin Stamp	7.50	15.00
10 Mewtwo HOLO R/Thin Stamp	6.00	12.00
11 Nidoking HOLO R/Thin Stamp	4.00	8.00
12 Ninetales HOLO R/Thin Stamp	5.00	10.00
13 Poliwrath HOLO R/Thin Stamp	3.00	6.00
14 Raichu HOLO R/Thin Stamp	100.00	250.00
16 Zapdos HOLO R/Thin Stamp	25.00	60.00
17 Beedrill R/Thick Stamp	15.00	30.00
18 Dragonair R/Thick Stamp	40.00	80.00
19 Dugtrio R/Thick Stamp	7.50	15.00
20 Electabuzz R/Thick Stamp	250.00	600.00
21 Electrode R/Thick Stamp	6.00	12.00
22 Pidgeotto R/Thick Stamp	25.00	60.00
23 Arcanine U/Thick Stamp	30.00	75.00
24 Charmeleon U/Thick Stamp	6.00	12.00
25 Dewgong U/Thick Stamp	6.00	12.00
26 Dratini U/Thick Stamp	5.00	10.00
27 Farfetch'd U/Thick Stamp	3.00	6.00
28 Growlithe U/Thick Stamp	6.00	12.00
29 Haunter U/Thick Stamp	2.50	5.00
30 Ivysaur U/Thick Stamp	7.50	15.00
31 Jynx U/Thick Stamp	7.50	15.00
32 Kadabra U/Thick Stamp	5.00	10.00
33 Kakuna UER U/Thick Stamp	6.00	12.00
34 Machoke U/Thick Stamp	10.00	20.00
35 Magikarp U/Thick Stamp	7.50	15.00
36 Magmar U/Thick Stamp	6.00	12.00
37 Nidorino U/Thick Stamp	2.50	5.00
38 Poliwhirl U/Thick Stamp	1.00	2.00
39 Porygon U/Thick Stamp	1.50	3.00
40 Raticate U/Thick Stamp	5.00	10.00
41 Seel U/Thick Stamp	1.50	3.00
42 Wartortle U/Thick Stamp	1.50	3.00
43 Abra C/Thick Stamp	.75	1.50
44 Bulbasaur UER C/Thick Stamp	.75	1.50
45 Caterpie UER C/Thick Stamp	1.50	3.00
46 Charmander C/Thick Stamp	.50	1.00
47 Diglett C/Thick Stamp	.75	1.50
48 Doduo C/Thick Stamp	125.00	300.00
49 Drowzee C/Thick Stamp	100.00	250.00
50 Gastly C/Thick Stamp	4.00	8.00
51 Koffing C/Thick Stamp	3.00	6.00
52 Machop C/Thick Stamp	.50	1.00
53 Magnemite C/Thick Stamp	.30	.75
54 Metapod UER C/Thick Stamp	1.25	2.50
55 Nidoran C/Thick Stamp	4.00	10.00
56 Onix C/Thick Stamp	2.50	5.00
57 Pidgey C/Thick Stamp	1.00	2.00
58 Pikachu (Red cheeks) ERR C/Thick Stamp	.15	.30
58 Pikachu (Yellow cheeks) COR C/Thick Stamp	.75	1.50
59 Poliwag C/Thick Stamp	.04	.10
60 Ponyta C/Thick Stamp	.10	.25
61 Rattata C/Thick Stamp	.75	1.50
62 Sandshrew C/Thick Stamp	.75	1.50
63 Squirtle C/Thick Stamp	1.00	2.00
64 Starmie C/Thick Stamp	.60	1.25
65 Staryu C/Thick Stamp	.75	1.50
66 Tangela C/Thick Stamp	.60	1.25
67 Voltorb UER C/Thick Stamp	.75	1.50
68 Vulpix UER C/Thick Stamp	.75	1.50
69 Weedle C/Thick Stamp	.50	1.00
70 Clefairy Doll R/Thick Stamp	3.00	6.00
71 Computer Search R/Thick Stamp	1.25	2.50
72 Devolution Spray R/Thick Stamp	10.00	20.00
73 Impostor Professor Oak R/Thick Stamp	5.00	12.00
74 Item Finder R/Thick Stamp	2.00	4.00
75 Lass R/Thick Stamp	.50	1.00
76 Pokemon Breeder R/Thick Stamp	.25	.50
77 Pokemon Trader R/Thick Stamp	1.00	2.00
78 Scoop Up R/Thick Stamp	10.00	25.00
79 Super Energy Removal R/Thick Stamp	10.00	25.00
80 Defender U/Thick Stamp	25.00	60.00
81 Energy Retrieval U/Thick Stamp	4.00	8.00
82 Full Heal U/Thick Stamp	40.00	100.00
83 Maintenance U/Thick Stamp	25.00	50.00
84 Plus Power U/Thick Stamp	5.00	10.00
85 Pokemon Center U/Thick Stamp	6.00	12.00
86 Pokemon Flute U/Thick Stamp	.75	1.50
87 Pokedex U/Thick Stamp	2.00	4.00
88 Professor Oak U/Thick Stamp	.50	1.00
89 Revive U/Thick Stamp	30.00	75.00
90 Super Potion U/Thick Stamp	.75	1.50
91 Bill C#(Thick Stamp	.75	1.50
92 Energy Removal C/Thick Stamp	.75	1.50
93 Gust of Wind C/Thick Stamp	1.00	2.00
94 Potion C/Thick Stamp	.75	1.50
95 Switch C/Thick Stamp	2.00	4.00
96 Double Colorless Energy U/Thick Stamp	2.00	4.00
97 Fighting Energy C/Thick Stamp	7.50	15.00
98 Fire Energy C/Thick Stamp	1.00	2.00
99 Grass Energy C/Thick Stamp	.12	.25
100 Lightning Energy C/Thick Stamp	.75	1.50
101 Psychic Energy C/Thick Stamp	.07	.15
102 Water Energy/Thick Stamp	4.00	8.00

1999 Pokemon Base Shadowless

1 Alakazam HOLO R	.12	.25
2 Blastoise HOLO R	.50	1.00
3 Chansey HOLO R	.07	.15
4 Charizard HOLO R	.08	.20
5 Clefairy HOLO R	.07	.15
6 Gyarados HOLO R	.15	.40
7 Hitmonchan HOLO R	1.25	2.50
9 Magneton HOLO R	.75	1.50
10 Mewtwo HOLO R	.30	.75
11 Nidoking HOLO R	2.50	5.00
12 Ninetales HOLO R	.07	.15
13 Poliwrath HOLO R	.01	.08
14 Raichu HOLO R	.04	.10
15 Venusaur HOLO R	.60	1.25
16 Zapdos HOLO R	.60	1.25
17 Beedrill R	1.00	2.00
18 Dragonair R	2.50	5.00
19 Dugtrio R	.04	.10
20 Electabuzz R	.08	.20
21 Electrode R	2.50	5.00
22 Pidgeotto R	.75	1.50
23 Arcanine U	.75	1.50
24 Charmeleon U	.07	.15
25 Dewgong U	1.25	2.50
26 Dratini U	1.25	2.50
27 Farfetch'd U	1.50	4.00
28 Growlithe U	5.00	12.00
29 Haunter U	.25	.50
30 Ivysaur U	.08	.20
31 Jynx U	.04	.10
32 Kadabra U	1.00	2.00
33 Kakuna (Length/Length) ERR U	.50	1.00
33 Kakuna (Length/Weight) COR U	.75	1.50
34 Machoke U	.04	.10
35 Magikarp U	.01	.08
36 Magmar U	7.50	15.00
37 Nidorino U	.60	1.25
38 Poliwhirl U	.75	1.50
39 Porygon U	.75	1.50
40 Raticate U	.07	.15
41 Seel U	2.50	5.00
42 Wartortle U	2.50	5.00
43 Abra C	3.00	6.00
44 Bulbasaur (Length/Length) ERR C	2.50	5.00
44 Bulbasaur (Length/Weight) COR C	1.50	3.00
45 Caterpie (HP 40) ERR C	1.00	2.00
45 Caterpie (40 HP) COR C	.75	1.50
46 Charmander C	.60	1.25
47 Diglett C	.60	1.25
48 Doduo C	.75	1.50
49 Drowzee C	.60	1.25
50 Gastly C	.60	1.25
51 Koffing C	.10	.20
52 Machop C	.60	1.25
53 Magnemite C	.60	1.25
54 Metapod (HP 70) ERR C	6.00	12.00
54 Metapod (70 HP) COR C	7.50	15.00
55 Nidoran C	10.00	20.00
56 Onix C	2.00	4.00
57 Pidgey C	10.00	20.00
58 Pikachu (Red Cheeks) ERR C	4.00	8.00
58 Pikachu (Yellow Cheeks) COR C	2.50	5.00
59 Poliwag C	30.00	60.00
60 Ponyta C	12.50	25.00
61 Rattata C	4.00	8.00
62 Sandshrew C	75.00	200.00
63 Squirtle C	20.00	50.00
64 Starmie C	6.00	12.00
65 Staryu C	25.00	60.00
66 Tangela C	3.00	6.00
67 Voltorb (Monster Ball) ERR C	1.50	3.00
67 Voltorb (Poke Ball) COR C	.75	1.50
68 Vulpix UER C	5.00	10.00
69 Weedle C	4.00	8.00
70 Clefairy Doll R	300.00	800.00
71 Computer Search R	100.00	250.00
72 Devolution Spray R	75.00	200.00
73 Impostor Professor Oak R	25.00	50.00
74 Item Finder R	20.00	40.00
75 Lass R	10.00	20.00
76 Pokemon Breeder R	10.00	20.00
77 Pokemon Trader R	4.00	8.00
78 Scoop Up R	7.50	15.00
79 Super Energy Removal R	30.00	60.00
80 Defender U	.12	.25
81 Energy Retrieval U	40.00	100.00
82 Full Heal U	.30	.75
83 Maintenance U	7.50	15.00
84 Plus Power U	2.50	5.00
85 Pokemon Center U	7.50	15.00
86 Pokemon Flute U	.50	1.00
87 Pokedex U	2.50	6.00
88 Professor Oak U	1.50	3.00
89 Revive U	1.00	2.00
90 Super Potion U	4.00	8.00
91 Bill C	3.00	6.00
92 Energy Removal C	3.00	6.00
93 Gust of Wind C	2.00	4.00
94 Potion C	4.00	8.00
95 Switch C	12.50	25.00
96 Double Colorless Energy U	20.00	50.00
97 Fighting Energy C	30.00	75.00
98 Fire Energy C	7.50	15.00
99 Grass Energy C	5.00	10.00
100 Lightning Energy C	1.00	2.00
101 Psychic Energy C	12.50	25.00
102 Water Energy C	4.00	8.00

1999 Pokemon Base Unlimited

1 Alakazam HOLO R	1.25	2.50
2 Blastoise HOLO R	10.00	25.00
3 Chansey HOLO R	10.00	25.00
4 Charizard HOLO R	25.00	60.00
5 Clefairy HOLO R	3.00	6.00
6 Gyarados HOLO R	6.00	10.00
7 Hitmonchan HOLO R	.75	1.50
9 Magneton HOLO R	1.25	2.50
10 Mewtwo HOLO R	.75	1.50
11 Nidoking HOLO R	7.50	15.00
12 Ninetales HOLO R	.12	.25
13 Poliwrath HOLO R	.20	.50
14 Raichu HOLO R	7.50	15.00
15 Venusaur HOLO R	2.50	5.00
16 Zapdos HOLO R	1.00	2.50
17 Beedrill (D.efending) ERR R	4.00	8.00
17 Beedrill (Defending) COR R	.08	.20
18 Dragonair R	1.25	2.50
19 Dugtrio R	.10	.20
20 Electabuzz R	.10	.20
21 Electrode R	.12	.30
22 Pidgeotto R	1.25	2.50
23 Arcanine U	1.25	2.50
24 Charmeleon U	.10	.20
25 Dewgong U	.75	1.50
26 Dratini U	.75	1.50
27 Farfetch'd U	1.25	2.50
28 Growlithe U	.75	1.50
29 Haunter U	.25	.50
30 Ivysaur U	3.00	8.00
31 Jynx U	1.25	2.50
32 Kadabra U	4.00	8.00
33 Kakuna (Length/Length) ERR U	.75	1.50
33 Kakuna (Length/Weight) COR U	.04	.10
34 Machoke U	.10	.25
35 Magikarp U	.50	1.00
36 Magmar U	.50	1.00
37 Nidorino U	.75	1.50
38 Poliwhirl U	.75	1.50
39 Porygon U	.75	1.50
40 Raticate U	.75	1.50
41 Seel U	1.00	2.00
42 Wartortle (Evo Box Squirtle) COR U	2.50	5.00
42 Wartortle (Evo Box Wartortle) ERR U	1.00	2.00
43 Abra C	5.00	10.00
44 Bulbasaur (Length/Length) ERR C	.50	1.00
44 Bulbasaur (Length/Weight) COR C	7.50	15.00
45 Caterpie (HP 40) ERR C	1.00	2.00
45 Caterpie (40 HP) COR C	6.00	12.00
46 Charmander C	4.00	8.00
47 Diglett (Energy Sideways) ERR C	2.00	4.00
47 Diglett (Energy Upright) COR C	.25	.50
48 Doduo C	2.00	4.00
49 Drowzee C	.75	1.50
50 Gastly C	.08	.20
51 Koffing C	.08	.20
52 Machop C	4.00	8.00
53 Magnemite C	.50	1.00
54 Metapod (HP 70) ERR C	1.00	2.00
54 Metapod (70 HP) COR C	.75	1.50
55 Nidoran C	.60	1.25
56 Onix C	.75	1.50
57 Pidgey C	.60	1.25
58 Pikachu (Yellow Cheeks) COR C	.75	1.50
59 Poliwag C	1.00	2.00
60 Ponyta C	1.25	2.50
61 Rattata C	.60	1.25
62 Sandshrew C	3.00	6.00
63 Squirtle C	.75	1.50
64 Starmie C	.50	1.00
65 Staryu C	.01	.08
66 Tangela C	.04	.10
67 Voltorb (Monster Ball) ERR C	.12	.25
67 Voltorb (Poke Ball) COR C	.60	1.25
68 Vulpix UER C	.60	1.25
69 Weedle C	.25	.50
70 Clefairy Doll R	.60	1.25
71 Computer Search R	1.00	2.00
72 Devolution Spray R	.10	.20
73 Impostor Professor Oak R	1.25	2.50
74 Item Finder R	.75	1.50
75 Lass R	.04	.10
76 Pokemon Breeder R	.04	.10
77 Pokemon Trader R	.75	1.50
78 Scoop Up R	.75	1.50
79 Super Energy Removal R	.75	1.50
80 Defender U	7.50	15.00
81 Energy Retrieval U	.75	1.50
82 Full Heal U	1.00	2.00
83 Maintenance U	.10	.20
84 Plus Power U	2.00	5.00
85 Pokemon Center U	.75	1.50
86 Pokemon Flute U	.30	.75
87 Pokedex U	1.50	3.00
88 Professor Oak U	.75	1.50
89 Revive U	.60	1.25
90 Super Potion U	2.50	5.00
91 Bill C	1.00	2.00
92 Energy Removal C	.75	1.50
93 Gust of Wind C	1.00	2.00
94 Potion C	.75	1.50
95 Switch C	.60	1.25
96 Double Colorless Energy U	1.00	2.00
97 Fighting Energy C	2.00	4.00
98 Fire Energy C	20.00	40.00
99 Grass Energy C	20.00	40.00
100 Lightning Energy C	4.00	8.00
101 Psychic Energy C	4.00	8.00
102 Water Energy C	1.50	3.00

1999 Pokemon Burger King

1 Bulbasaur	1.50	3.00
2 Ivysaur	1.25	2.50
3 Venusaur	1.00	2.00
4 Charmander	.75	1.50
5 Charmeleon	.75	1.50
6 Charizard	.75	1.50
7 Squirtle	20.00	50.00
8 Wartortle	4.00	8.00
9 Blastoise	.12	.25
10 Caterpie	.15	.40
11 Metapod	.08	.20
12 Butterfree	30.00	80.00
13 Weedle	12.50	25.00
14 Kakuna	3.00	6.00
15 Beedrill	7.50	15.00
16 Pidgey	50.00	120.00
17 Pidegotto	1.25	2.50
18 Pidgeot	.75	1.50
19 Rattata	1.00	2.00
20 Raticate	.75	1.50
21 Spearow	.75	1.50
22 Fearow	1.00	2.00
23 Ekans	.75	1.50
24 Arbok	.75	1.50
25 Pikachu	2.50	5.00
26 Raichu	1.00	2.00
27 Sandshrew	1.00	2.00
28 Sandslash	60.00	125.00
29 Nidoran-F	3.00	6.00
30 Nidorina	.75	1.50
31 Nidoqueen	1.00	2.00
32 Nidoran-M	25.00	60.00
33 Nidorino	15.00	40.00
34 Nidoking	12.50	25.00
35 Clefairy	200.00	500.00
36 Clefable	60.00	150.00
37 Vulpix	30.00	65.00
38 Ninetales	30.00	75.00
39 Jigglypuff	6.00	12.00
40 Wigglytuff	3.00	6.00
41 Zubat	4.00	8.00
42 Golbat	3.00	6.00
43 Oddish	2.00	4.00
44 Gloom	4.00	8.00
45 Vileplume	125.00	300.00
46 Paras	10.00	20.00
47 Parasect	25.00	50.00
48 Venonat	4.00	8.00
49 Venomoth	5.00	10.00
50 Diglett	3.00	6.00
51 Dugtrio	12.50	25.00
52 Meowth	5.00	10.00

53 Persian	6.00	12.00
54 Psyduck	40.00	100.00
55 Golduck	12.00	30.00
56 Mankey	1.25	2.50
57 Primeape	12.50	25.00
58 Growlithe	3.00	6.00
59 Arcanine	4.00	8.00
60 Poliwag	.25	.50
61 Poliwhirl	1.50	3.00
62 Poliwrath	30.00	80.00
63 Abra	6.00	12.00
64 Kadabra	.12	.25
65 Alakazam	25.00	60.00
66 Machop	25.00	60.00
67 Machoke	75.00	200.00
68 Machamp	1.50	3.00
69 Bellsprout	.30	.75
70 Weepinbell	4.00	8.00
71 Victreebel	.75	1.50
72 Tentacool	.50	1.00
73 Tentacruel	.75	1.50
74 Geodude	4.00	8.00
75 Graveler	2.00	4.00
76 Golem	2.00	4.00
77 Ponyta	20.00	40.00
78 Rapidash	.75	1.50
79 Slowpoke	3.00	6.00
80 Slowbro	.25	.50
81 Magnemite	.12	.25
82 Magneton	.60	1.25
83 Farfetch'd	.75	1.50
84 Doduo	.75	1.50
85 Dodrio	.12	.25
86 Seel	2.50	5.00
87 Dewgong	1.50	3.00
88 Grimer	.10	.20
89 Muk	.75	1.50
90 Shellder	4.00	8.00
91 Cloyster	2.50	5.00
92 Gastly	.01	.08
93 Haunter	.04	.10
94 Gengar	1.50	3.00
95 Onix	.60	1.25
96 Drowzee	5.00	10.00
97 Hypno	1.00	2.00
98 Krabby	.12	.25
99 Kingler	.30	.60
100 Voltorb	.75	1.50
101 Electrode	.01	.08
102 Exeggcute	.01	.08
103 Exeggutor	1.00	2.00
104 Cubone	1.00	2.50
105 Marowak	.50	1.00
106 Hitmonlee	.50	1.00
107 Hitmonchan	.50	1.00
108 Lickitung	.60	1.25
109 Koffing	1.50	3.00
110 Weezing	.04	.10
111 Rhyhorn	.08	.20
112 Rhydon	1.00	2.00
113 Chansey	.75	1.50
114 Tangela	.30	.60
115 Kangaskhan	.60	1.25
116 Horsea	.07	.15
117 Seadra	1.25	2.50
118 Goldeen	1.25	2.50
119 Seaking	1.00	2.00
120 Staryu	2.00	4.00
121 Starmie	.07	.15
122 Mr. Mime	5.00	10.00
123 Scyther	.30	.75
124 Jynx	2.00	4.00
125 Electabuzz	1.50	3.00
126 Magmar	.75	1.50
127 Pinsir	.50	1.00
128 Tauros	25.00	60.00
129 Magikarp	.75	2.00
130 Gyarados	4.00	8.00
131 Lapras	1.00	2.00
132 Ditto	2.00	4.00
133 Eevee	1.50	3.00
134 Vaporeon	1.50	3.00
135 Jolteon	1.00	2.00
136 Flareon	.75	1.50
137 Porygon	.50	1.00
138 Omanyte	2.00	4.00
139 Omastar	.12	.25
140 Kabuto	1.25	2.50
141 Kabutops	.75	1.50
142 Aerodactyl	.75	1.50
143 Snorlax	.75	1.50
144 Articuno	.50	1.00
145 Zapdos	.75	1.50
146 Moltres	1.00	2.00
147 Dratini	.75	1.50
148 Dragonair	.60	1.25
149 Dragonite	.12	.25
150 Mewtwo	20.00	40.00
151 Mew	2.50	5.00

1999 Pokemon Fossil 1st Edition

1 Aerodactyl HOLO R	6.00	12.00
2 Articuno HOLO R	2.50	5.00
3 Ditto HOLO R	.75	1.50
4 Dragonite HOLO R	.75	1.50
5 Gengar HOLO R	1.50	3.00
6 Haunter HOLO R	1.00	2.00
7 Hitmonlee HOLO R STAIN ERR	60.00	125.00
7 Hitmonlee HOLO R	.75	1.50
8 Hypno HOLO R	.75	1.50
9 Kabutops HOLO R	.10	.20
10 Lapras HOLO R	.75	1.50
11 Magneton HOLO R	.75	1.50
12 Moltres HOLO R	.75	1.50
13 Muk HOLO R	.75	1.50
14 Raichu HOLO R	4.00	8.00
15 Zapdos HOLO R	.50	1.00
16 Aerodactyl R	3.00	6.00
17 Articuno R	2.50	5.00
18 Ditto R	1.25	2.50
19 Dragonite R	.08	.20
20 Gengar R	250.00	600.00
21 Haunter R	200.00	500.00
22 Hitmonlee R	60.00	120.00
23 Hypno R	75.00	150.00
24 Kabutops R	50.00	100.00
25 Lapras R	250.00	600.00
26 Magneton R	.25	.50
27 Moltres R	.12	.25
28 Muk R	.04	.10
29 Raichu R	.10	.25
30 Zapdos R	1.25	2.50
31 Arbok U	1.25	2.50
32 Cloyster U	1.25	2.50
33 Gastly U	25.00	50.00
34 Golbat U	7.50	15.00
35 Golduck U	6.00	12.00
36 Golem U	250.00	600.00
37 Graveler U	10.00	20.00
38 Kingler U	150.00	300.00
39 Magmar U	3.00	6.00
40 Omastar U	3.00	6.00
41 Sandslash U	2.50	5.00
42 Seadra U	6.00	12.00
43 Slowbro U	5.00	10.00
44 Tentacruel U	7.50	15.00
45 Weezing U	.50	1.00
46 Ekans C	4.00	8.00
47 Geodude C	200.00	500.00
48 Grimer C	40.00	100.00
49 Horsea C	2.50	5.00
50 Kabuto C	10.00	20.00
51 Krabby C	2.50	5.00
52 Omanyte C	2.50	5.00
53 Psyduck C	7.50	15.00
54 Shellder C	100.00	250.00
55 Slowpoke C	100.00	250.00
56 Tentacool C	20.00	40.00
57 Zubat C	12.50	25.00
58 Mr. Fuji U	.75	1.50
59 Energy Search C	.75	1.50
60 Gambler C	.75	1.50
61 Recycle C	3.00	6.00
62 Mysterious Fossil C	125.00	300.00

1999 Pokemon Fossil Unlimited

1 Aerodactyl HOLO R	10.00	20.00
2 Articuno HOLO R	3.00	6.00
3 Ditto HOLO R	7.50	15.00
4 Dragonite HOLO R	6.00	12.00
5 Gengar HOLO R	1.00	2.00
6 Haunter HOLO R	2.50	5.00
7 Hitmonlee HOLO R	2.50	5.00
8 Hypno HOLO R	.75	1.50
9 Kabutops HOLO R	4.00	8.00
10 Lapras HOLO R	2.50	5.00
11 Magneton HOLO R	30.00	60.00
12 Moltres HOLO R	25.00	60.00
13 Muk HOLO R	25.00	60.00
14 Raichu HOLO R	100.00	250.00
15 Zapdos HOLO R COR	1.00	2.00
15 Zapdos HOLO R ERR	1.00	2.00
16 Aerodactyl R	2.00	4.00
17 Articuno R	1.25	2.50
18 Ditto R	.75	1.50
19 Dragonite R	.75	1.50
20 Gengar R	2.50	5.00
21 Haunter R	2.00	4.00
22 Hitmonlee R	.75	1.50
23 Hypno R	.75	1.50
24 Kabutops R	.10	.20
25 Lapras R	2.00	4.00
26 Magneton R	10.00	20.00
27 Moltres R	1.50	3.00
28 Muk R	.75	1.50
29 Raichu R	1.25	2.50
30 Zapdos R	1.00	2.00
31 Arbok U	.04	.10
32 Cloyster U	.04	.10
33 Gastly U	.75	1.50
34 Golbat U	1.50	3.00
35 Golduck U	1.00	2.00
36 Golem U	.12	.25
37 Graveler U	.08	.20
38 Kingler U	.04	.10
39 Magmar U	.50	1.25
40 Omastar U	1.00	2.00
41 Sandslash U	.75	1.50
42 Seadra U	.07	.15
43 Slowbro U	.60	1.25
44 Tentacruel U	.75	1.50
45 Weezing U	.75	1.50
46 Ekans C	.60	1.25
47 Geodude C	4.00	8.00
48 Grimer C	.75	1.50
49 Horsea C	.07	.15
50 Kabuto C	.50	1.00
51 Krabby C	1.00	2.50
52 Omanyte C	4.00	8.00
53 Psyduck C	10.00	20.00
54 Shellder C	1.00	2.00
55 Slowpoke C	.75	1.50
56 Tentacool C	.75	1.50
57 Zubat C	.50	1.00
58 Mr. Fuji U	.75	1.50
59 Energy Search C	1.25	2.50
60 Gambler C	.60	1.25
61 Recycle C	.75	1.50
62 Mysterious Fossil C	.08	.20

1999 Pokemon Jungle 1st Edition

1 Clefable HOLO R	1.50	3.00
2 Electrode HOLO R	1.25	2.50
3 Flareon HOLO R	.60	1.25
4 Jolteon HOLO R	.50	1.00
5 Kangaskhan HOLO R	.60	1.25
6 Mr. Mime HOLO R	.60	1.25
7 Nidoqueen HOLO R	1.00	2.00
8 Pidgeot HOLO R	1.25	2.50
9 Pinsir HOLO R	1.25	2.50
10 Scyther HOLO R	.75	1.50
11 Snorlax HOLO R	.01	.08
12 Vaporeon HOLO R	.04	.10
13 Venomoth HOLO R	.50	1.25
14 Victreebel HOLO R	1.00	2.00
15 Vileplume HOLO R	.60	1.25
16 Wigglytuff HOLO R	.07	.15
17 Clefable R	.15	.40
18 Electrode UER R	6.00	12.00
19 Flareon R	.30	.60
20 Jolteon R	.01	.08
21 Kangaskhan R	.04	.10
22 Mr. Mime R	1.50	3.00
23 Nidoqueen R	1.00	2.00
24 Pidgeot R	.10	.20
25 Pinsir R	3.00	6.00
26 Scyther R	.75	1.50
27 Snorlax R	.75	1.50
28 Vaporeon R	1.00	2.00
29 Venomoth R	2.00	4.00
30 Victreebel R	.01	.08
31 Vileplume R	.04	.10
32 Wigglytuff R	1.25	2.50
33 Butterfree (""d"" Edition) ERR U	10.00	20.00
33 Butterfree (1 Edition) COR U	1.00	2.00
34 Dodrio U	.75	1.50
35 Exeggutor U	4.00	8.00
36 Fearow U	12.50	25.00
37 Gloom U	1.50	3.00
38 Lickitung U	.60	1.25
39 Marowak U	.25	.50
40 Nidorina U	1.00	2.00
41 Parasect U	15.00	30.00
42 Persian U	1.50	3.00
43 Primeape U	.75	1.50
44 Rapidash UER U	.07	.15
45 Rhydon U	.60	1.25
46 Seaking U	.60	1.25
47 Tauros U	.75	1.50
48 Weepinbell U	.50	1.00
49 Bellsprout C	.50	1.00
50 Cubone C	.75	1.50
51 Eevee C	.30	.75
52 Exeggcute C	3.00	6.00
53 Goldeen C	.25	.50
54 Jigglypuff C	.25	.50
55 Mankey C	.04	.10
56 Meowth C	.10	.25
57 Nidoran C	.75	1.50
58 Oddish C	2.00	4.00
59 Paras C	40.00	100.00
60 Pikachu C	12.00	30.00
61 Rhyhorn C	12.50	25.00
62 Spearow C	200.00	500.00
63 Venonat C	1.50	3.00
64 Trainer: Poke Ball C	.50	1.00

1999 Pokemon Jungle Unlimited

1 Clefable HOLO ERR R	100.00	250.00
1 Clefable HOLO COR R	4.00	8.00
2 Electrode HOLO COR R	75.00	150.00
2 Electrode HOLO ERR R	15.00	30.00
3 Flareon HOLO ERR R	4.00	8.00
3 Flareon HOLO COR R	25.00	50.00
4 Jolteon HOLO COR R	7.50	15.00
4 Jolteon HOLO ERR R	2.00	4.00
5 Kangaskhan HOLO COR R	2.00	4.00
5 Kangaskhan HOLO ERR R	7.50	15.00
6 Mr. Mime HOLO COR R	3.00	6.00
6 Mr. Mime HOLO ERR R	1.00	2.00
7 Nidoqueen HOLO COR R	4.00	8.00
7 Nidoqueen HOLO ERR R	40.00	100.00
8 Pidgeot HOLO COR R	4.00	8.00
8 Pidgeot HOLO ERR R	.50	1.00
9 Pinsir HOLO COR R	.75	1.50
9 Pinsir HOLO ERR R	1.25	2.50
10 Scyther HOLO COR R	75.00	200.00
10 Scyther HOLO ERR R	.12	.25
11 Snorlax HOLO COR R	20.00	40.00
11 Snorlax HOLO ERR R	15.00	30.00
12 Vaporeon HOLO COR R	10.00	20.00
12 Vaporeon HOLO ERR R	5.00	10.00
13 Venomoth HOLO COR R	3.00	6.00
13 Venomoth HOLO ERR R	.75	1.50
14 Victreebel HOLO COR R	1.50	3.00
14 Victreebel HOLO ERR R	7.50	15.00
15 Vileplume HOLO COR R	100.00	250.00
15 Vileplume HOLO ERR R	30.00	80.00
16 Wigglytuff HOLO COR R	10.00	20.00
16 Wigglytuff HOLO R ERR	75.00	200.00
17 Clefable R	.50	1.00
18 Electrode R	12.50	25.00
19 Flareon R	4.00	8.00
20 Jolteon R	.75	1.50
21 Kangaskhan R	7.50	15.00
22 Mr. Mime R	7.50	15.00
23 Nidoqueen R	1.50	3.00
24 Pidgeot R	6.00	10.00
25 Pinsir R	40.00	80.00
26 Scyther R	2.50	5.00
27 Snorlax R	.75	1.50
28 Vaporeon R	4.00	10.00
29 Venomoth R	4.00	10.00
30 Victreebel R	25.00	60.00
31 Vileplume R	.60	1.25
32 Wigglytuff R	.30	.60
33 Butterfree U	.60	1.25
34 Dodrio U	.75	1.50
35 Exeggutor U	1.25	2.50
36 Fearow U	2.00	4.00
37 Gloom U	1.50	3.00
38 Lickitung U	2.50	5.00
39 Marowak U	3.00	6.00
40 Nidorina U	7.50	15.00
41 Parasect U	2.00	4.00
42 Persian U	2.00	4.00
43 Primeape U	.75	1.50
44 Rapidash UER U	3.00	6.00
45 Rhydon U	.50	1.00
46 Seaking U	.60	1.50
47 Tauros U	.75	1.50
48 Weepinbell U	.12	.25
49 Bellsprout C	.30	.60
50 Cubone C	.50	1.00
51 Eevee C	1.00	2.50
52 Exeggcute C	.75	1.50
53 Goldeen C	5.00	10.00
54 Jigglypuff C	1.00	2.00
55 Mankey C	1.00	2.00
56 Meowth C	.20	.40
57 Nidoran C	.75	1.50
58 Oddish C	.75	1.50
59 Paras C	.75	1.50
60 Pikachu C	1.50	3.00
61 Rhyhorn C	.75	1.50
62 Spearow C	2.00	4.00
63 Venonat C	.75	1.50
64 Trainer: Poke Ball C	2.50	5.00

1999-00 Pokemon Base Fourth Print

1 Alakazam HOLO R	.04	.10
2 Blastoise HOLO R	.04	.10
3 Chansey HOLO R	.60	1.25
4 Charizard HOLO R	.08	.20
5 Clefairy HOLO R	.60	1.25
6 Gyarados HOLO R	.60	1.25
7 Hitmonchan HOLO R	.08	.20
9 Magneton HOLO R	.05	.12
10 Mewtwo HOLO R	1.50	3.00
11 Nidoking HOLO R	.75	1.50
12 Ninetales HOLO R	2.00	4.00
13 Poliwrath HOLO R	1.00	2.00
14 Raichu HOLO R	.60	1.50
15 Venusaur HOLO R	.07	.15
16 Zapdos HOLO R	.75	1.50
17 Beedrill R	.50	1.00
18 Dragonair R	1.25	2.50
19 Dugtrio R	.75	1.50
20 Electabuzz R	1.00	2.00
21 Electrode R	.12	.25
22 Pidgeotto R	.20	.50
23 Arcanine U	.50	1.00
24 Charmeleon U	10.00	20.00
25 Dewgong U	.75	1.50
26 Dratini U	.20	.50
27 Farfetch'd U	2.00	4.00
28 Growlithe U	.60	1.25
29 Haunter U	.75	1.50
30 Ivysaur U	.60	1.25
31 Jynx U	.75	1.50
32 Kadabra U	1.00	2.00
33 Kakuna (Length/Length Error) U	.60	1.25
33 Kakuna (Length/Weight Corr.) U	.60	1.25
34 Machoke U	2.00	4.00
35 Magikarp U	.50	1.00
36 Magmar U	.15	.30
37 Nidorino U	.50	1.00
38 Poliwhirl U	.75	1.50
39 Porygon U	.60	1.25
40 Raticate U	.60	1.25
41 Seel U	.25	.50
42 Wartortle U	.25	.50
43 Abra C	1.50	3.00
44 Bulbasaur (Length/Length Error) C	2.50	5.00
44 Bulbasaur (Length/Weight Corr.) C	2.00	4.00
45 Caterpie (HP 40 Error) C	1.00	2.00
45 Caterpie (40 HP Corr.) C	2.00	4.00
46 Charmander C	.25	.50
47 Diglett C	.75	1.50
48 Doduo C	.10	.20
49 Drowzee C	.60	1.25
50 Gastly C	.50	1.00
51 Koffing C	2.50	5.00
52 Machop C	2.50	5.00
53 Magnemite C	125.00	250.00
54 Metapod (HP 70 Error) C	75.00	150.00
54 Metapod (70 HP Corr.) C	.25	.50
55 Nidoran C	1.25	2.50
56 Onix C	.75	1.50
57 Pidgey C	.75	1.50
58 Pikachu (Red cheeks Error) C	3.00	6.00
58 Pikachu (Yellow cheeks Corr.)C	10.00	20.00
59 Poliwag C	20.00	50.00
60 Ponyta C	150.00	300.00
61 Rattata C	7.50	15.00
62 Sandshrew C	4.00	8.00
63 Squirtle C	.25	.50
64 Starmie C	12.50	25.00
65 Staryu C	2.50	5.00
66 Tangela C	.25	.50
67 Voltorb (Monster Ball Error) C	2.00	4.00
67 Voltorb (Poké Ball Corr.) C	.75	1.50
68 Vulpix (UER) C	.08	.20
69 Weedle C	.05	.12
70 Clefairy Doll R	3.00	6.00
71 Computer Search R	125.00	250.00
72 Devolution Spray R	.20	.50
73 Impostor Professor Oak R	4.00	8.00
74 Item Finder R	.12	.25
75 Lass R	.50	1.00
76 Pokémon Breeder R	4.00	8.00
77 Pokémon Trader R	3.00	6.00
78 Scoop Up R	3.00	6.00
79 Super Energy Removal R	10.00	20.00
80 Defender U	40.00	100.00
81 Energy Retrieval U	2.00	4.00
82 Full Heal U	2.50	5.00
83 Maintenance U	7.50	15.00

84 Plus Power U	50.00	120.00
85 Pokémon Center U	15.00	40.00
86 Pokémon Flute U	12.50	25.00
87 Pokédex U	40.00	100.00
88 Professor Oak U	12.00	30.00
89 Revive U	2.00	4.00
90 Super Potion U	.60	1.25
91 Bill C	.75	1.50
92 Energy Removal C	40.00	100.00
93 Gust of Wind C	.60	1.25
94 Potion C	1.00	2.00
95 Switch C	.10	.20
96 Double Colorless Energy U	12.50	25.00
97 Fighting Energy C	2.00	4.00
98 Fire Energy C	30.00	75.00
99 Grass Energy C	4.00	8.00
100 Lightning Energy C	.75	1.50
101 Psychic Energy C	4.00	8.00
102 Water Energy C	.30	.75

2000 Pokemon Gym Challenge 1st Edition

1 Blaine's Arcanine HOLO R	1.00	2.00
2 Blaine's Charizard HOLO R	.60	1.25
3 Brock's Ninetales HOLO R	10.00	20.00
4 Erika's Venusaur HOLO R	.20	.40
5 Giovanni's Gyarados HOLO R	1.00	2.00
6 Giovanni's Machamp HOLO R	2.50	5.00
7 Giovanni's Nidoking HOLO R	1.00	2.00
8 Giovanni's Persian HOLO R	40.00	100.00
9 Koga's Beedrill HOLO R	1.00	2.00
10 Koga's Ditto HOLO R	2.50	5.00
11 Lt. Surge's Raichu HOLO R	5.00	10.00
12 Misty's Golduck HOLO R	1.50	3.00
13 Misty's Gyarados HOLO R	2.50	6.00
14 Rocket's Mewtwo HOLO R	2.50	6.00
15 Rocket's Zapdos HOLO R	2.00	4.00
16 Sabrina's Alakazam HOLO R	2.00	4.00
17 Blaine HOLO R	1.25	2.50
18 Giovanni HOLO R	12.00	30.00
19 Koga HOLO R	12.00	30.00
20 Sabrina HOLO R	30.00	80.00
21 Blaine's Ninetales R	5.00	10.00
22 Brock's Dugtrio R	2.50	5.00
23 Giovanni's Nidoqueen R	.25	.50
24 Giovanni's Pinsir R	2.00	4.00
25 Koga's Arbok R	.75	1.50
26 Koga's Muk R	1.25	2.50
27 Koga's Pidgeotto R	.60	1.25
28 Lt. Surge's Jolteon R	.75	1.50
29 Sabrina's Gengar R	.60	1.25
30 Sabrina's Golduck R	.60	1.25
31 Blaine's Charmeleon U	1.00	2.00
32 Blaine's Dodrio U	3.00	8.00
33 Blaine's Rapidash U	1.00	2.00
34 Brock's Graveler U	.75	1.50
35 Brock's Primeape U	2.50	5.00
36 Brock's Sandslash U	.30	.75
37 Brock's Vulpix U	.75	1.50
38 Erika's Bellsprout U	.75	1.50
39 Erika's Bulbasaur U	2.00	5.00
40 Erika's Clefairy U	.07	.15
41 Erika's Ivysaur U	.12	.30
42 Giovanni's Machoke U	1.50	3.00
43 Giovanni's Meowth U	.75	1.50
44 Giovanni's Nidorina U	.75	1.50
45 Giovanni's Nidorino U	.07	.15
46 Koga's Golbat U	.75	1.50
47 Koga's Kakuna U	.01	.08
48 Koga's Koffing U	.04	.10
49 Koga's Pidgey U	1.00	2.00
50 Koga's Weezing U	.75	1.50
51 Lt. Surge's Eevee U	.50	1.00
52 Lt. Surge's Electrode U	.10	.20
53 Lt. Surge's Raticate U	.01	.08
54 Misty's Dewgong U	.01	.08
55 Sabrina's Haunter U	.08	.20
56 Sabrina's Hypno U	.75	1.50
57 Sabrina's Jynx U	.75	1.50
58 Sabrina's Kadabra U	1.25	2.50
59 Sabrina's Mr. Mime U	.75	1.50
60 Blaine's Charmander C	75.00	150.00
61 Blaine's Doduo C	3.00	6.00
62 Blaine's Growlithe C	2.00	4.00
63 Blaine's Mankey C	1.00	2.00
64 Blaine's Ponyta C	.60	1.25
65 Blaine's Rhyhorn C	1.00	2.00
66 Blaine's Vulpix C	1.50	3.00
67 Brock's Diglett C	.75	1.50
68 Brock's Geodude C	1.25	2.50
69 Erika's Jigglypuff C	1.00	2.00
70 Erika's Oddish C	1.50	3.00
71 Erika's Paras C	.75	1.50
72 Giovanni's Machop C	.75	1.50
73 Giovanni's Magikarp C	.30	.75
74 Giovanni's Meowth C	.75	1.50
75 Giovanni's Nidoran (Fem) C	.07	.15
76 Giovanni's Nidoran (Male) C	.75	1.50
77 Koga's Ekans C	.30	.75
78 Koga's Grimer C	.75	1.50
79 Koga's Koffing C	.30	.75
80 Koga's Pidgey C	1.25	2.50
81 Koga's Tangela C	.75	1.50
82 Koga's Weedle C	1.25	2.50
83 Koga's Zubat C	.75	1.50
84 Lt. Surge's Pikachu C	.01	.08
85 Lt. Surge's Rattata C	.05	.12
86 Lt. Surge's Voltorb C	.25	.50
87 Misty's Horsea C	3.00	6.00
88 Misty's Magikarp C	1.00	2.00
89 Misty's Poliwag C	1.00	2.00
90 Misty's Psyduck C	.04	.10
91 Misty's Seel C	.05	.12
92 Misty's Staryu C	1.00	2.00
93 Sabrina's Abra C	.60	1.25
94 Sabrina's Abra C	.75	1.50
95 Sabrina's Drowzee C	.75	1.50
96 Sabrina's Gastly C	20.00	40.00
97 Sabrina's Gastly C	.25	.50
98 Sabrina's Porygon C	2.00	4.00
99 Sabrina's Psyduck C	.25	.50
100 Blaine R	.08	.20
101 Brock's Protection R	.05	.12
102 Chaos Gym R	.75	1.50
103 Erika's Kindness R	20.00	50.00
104 Giovanni R	75.00	150.00
105 Giovanni's Last Resort R	5.00	10.00
106 Koga R	6.00	12.00
107 Lt. Surge's Secret Plan R	.60	1.25
108 Misty's Wish R	.75	1.50
109 Resistance Gym R	7.50	15.00
110 Sabrina R	7.50	15.00
111 Blaine's Quiz #2 U	7.50	15.00
112 Blaine's Quiz #3 U	3.00	6.00
113 Cinnabar City Gym U	1.00	2.00
114 Fuchsia City Gym U	.60	1.25
115 Koga's Ninja Trick U	.25	.50
116 Master Ball U	5.00	10.00
117 Max Revive U	1.00	2.00
118 Misty's Tears U	4.00	8.00
119 Rocket's Minefield Gym U	6.00	12.00
120 Rocket's Secret Experiment U	50.00	120.00
121 Sabrina's Psychic Control U	.75	1.50
122 Saffron City Gym U	.30	.60
123 Viridian City Gym U	.75	1.50
124 Fervor C	.25	.50
125 Transparent Walls C	1.25	2.50
126 Warp Point C	1.00	2.00
127 Fighting Energy C	2.50	6.00
128 Fire Energy C	7.50	15.00
129 Grass Energy C	3.00	6.00
130 Lightning Energy C	25.00	60.00
131 Psychic Energy C	6.00	15.00
132 Water Energy C	12.50	25.00

2000 Pokemon Gym Heroes 1st Edition

1 Blaine's Moltres HOLO R	150.00	400.00
2 Brock's Rhydon HOLO R	30.00	80.00
3 Erika's Clefable HOLO R	12.00	30.00
4 Erika's Dragonair HOLO R	30.00	80.00
5 Erika's Vileplume HOLO R	5.00	12.00
6 Lt. Surge's Electabuzz HOLO R	150.00	300.00
7 Lt. Surge's Fearow HOLO R	7.50	15.00
8 Lt. Surge's Magneton HOLO R	.25	.50
9 Misty's Seadra HOLO R	3.00	6.00
10 Misty's Tentacruel HOLO R	15.00	30.00
11 Rocket's Hitmonchan HOLO R	15.00	40.00
12 Rocket's Moltres HOLO R	10.00	20.00
13 Rocket's Scyther HOLO R	.60	1.25
14 Sabrina's Gengar HOLO R	3.00	6.00
15 Brock HOLO R	10.00	20.00
16 Erika HOLO R	2.00	4.00
17 Lt. Surge HOLO R	1.50	3.00
18 Misty HOLO R	1.25	2.50
19 The Rocket's Trap HOLO R	.75	1.50
20 Brock's Golem R	.75	1.50
21 Brock's Onix R	.10	.20
22 Brock's Rhyhorn R	.60	1.25
23 Brock's Sandslash R	.60	1.25
24 Brock's Zubat R	40.00	100.00
25 Erika's Clefairy R	15.00	30.00
26 Erika's Victreebel R	2.50	5.00
27 Lt. Surge's Electabuzz R	1.50	3.00
28 Lt. Surge's Raichu R	20.00	40.00
29 Misty's Cloyster R	3.00	6.00
30 Misty's Goldeen R	.60	1.25
31 Misty's Poliwrath R	4.00	8.00
32 Misty's Tentacool R	.25	.50
33 Rocket's Snorlax R	.08	.20
34 Sabrina's Venomoth R	.25	.50
35 Blaine's Growlithe U	2.50	5.00
36 Blaine's Kangaskhan U	10.00	20.00
37 Blaine's Magmar U	1.50	3.00
38 Brock's Geodude U	3.00	6.00
39 Brock's Golbat U	12.00	30.00
40 Brock's Graveler U	12.00	30.00
41 Brock's Lickitung U	40.00	100.00
42 Erika's Dratini U	6.00	12.00
43 Erika's Exeggcute U	.12	.25
44 Erika's Exeggutor U	7.50	15.00
45 Erika's Gloom U	.75	1.50
46 Erika's Gloom U	1.25	2.50
47 Erika's Oddish U	.60	1.25
48 Erika's Weepinbell U	1.00	2.00
49 Erika's Weepinbell U	.60	1.25
50 Lt. Surge's Magnemite U	.08	.20
51 Lt. Surge's Raticate U	.50	1.00
52 Lt. Surge's Spearow U	1.25	2.50
53 Misty's Poliwhirl U	.60	1.50
54 Misty's Psyduck U	3.00	6.00
55 Misty's Seaking U	3.00	6.00
56 Misty's Starmie U	1.25	2.50
57 Misty's Tentacool U	.20	.40
58 Sabrina's Haunter U	1.00	2.00
59 Sabrina's Jynx U	3.00	6.00
60 Sabrina's Slowbro U	.75	1.50
61 Blaine's Charmander C	2.50	5.00
62 Blaine's Growlithe C	7.50	15.00
63 Blaine's Ponyta C	1.50	3.00
64 Blaine's Tauros C	1.00	2.00
65 Blaine's Vulpix C	.50	1.00
66 Brock's Geodude C	1.00	2.00
67 Brock's Mankey C	.60	1.25
68 Brock's Mankey C	1.25	2.50
69 Brock's Onix C	.75	1.50
70 Brock's Rhyhorn C	.75	1.50
71 Brock's Sandshrew C	1.00	2.00
72 Brock's Sandshrew C	.60	1.25
73 Brock's Vulpix C	.10	.20
74 Brock's Zubat C	1.00	2.00
75 Erika's Bellsprout C	.75	1.50
76 Erika's Bellsprout C	.75	1.50
77 Erika's Exeggcute C	1.00	2.00
78 Erika's Oddish C	.30	.75
79 Erika's Tangela C	.04	.10
80 Lt. Surge's Magnemite C	.10	.25
81 Lt. Surge's Pikachu C	.01	.08
82 Lt. Surge's Rattata C	.04	.10
83 Lt. Surge's Spearow C	.60	1.25
84 Lt. Surge's Voltorb C	.07	.15
85 Misty's Goldeen C	.12	.30
86 Misty's Horsea C	1.00	2.00
87 Misty's Poliwag C	1.00	2.00
88 Misty's Seel C	1.50	3.00
89 Misty's Shellder C	5.00	10.00
90 Misty's Staryu C	1.50	3.00
91 Sabrina's Abra C	.75	1.50
92 Sabrina's Drowzee C	.07	.15
93 Sabrina's Gastly C	.07	.15
94 Sabrina's Mr. Mime C	1.25	2.50
95 Sabrina's Slowpoke C	3.00	6.00
96 Sabrina's Venonat C	.75	1.50
97 Blaine's Quiz #1 R	1.25	2.50
98 Brock R	2.50	5.00
99 Charity R	1.25	2.50
100 Erika R	1.00	2.00
101 Lt. Surge R	1.25	2.50
102 Misty R	.20	.40
103 No Removal Gym R	1.00	2.00
104 The Rocket's Training Gym R	.12	.25
105 Blaine's Last Resort U	1.25	2.50
106 Brock's Training Method U	.25	.50
107 Celadon City Gym U	.08	.20
108 Cerulean City Gym U	.04	.10
109 Erika's Maids U	2.00	4.00
110 Erika's Perfume U	1.00	2.00
111 Good Manners U	7.50	15.00
112 Lt. Surge's Treaty U	.04	.10
113 Minion of Team Rocket U	.10	.25
114 Misty's Wrath U	.75	1.50
115 Pewter City Gym U	2.00	4.00
116 Recall U	.50	1.00
117 Sabrina's ESP U	.12	.25
118 Secret Mission U	20.00	40.00
119 Tickling Machine U	.08	.20
120 Vermillion City Gym U	.07	.15
121 Blaine's Gamble C	1.00	2.00
122 Energy Flow C	40.00	100.00
123 Misty's Duel C	.50	1.00
124 Narrow Gym C	7.50	15.00
125 Sabrina's Gaze C	40.00	80.00
126 Trash Exchange C	4.00	8.00
127 Fighting Energy C	1.00	2.00
128 Fire Energy C	.60	1.25
129 Grass Energy C	.60	1.25
130 Lightning Energy C	.60	1.25
131 Psychic Energy C	3.00	6.00
132 Water Energy C	.25	.50

2000 Pokemon Neo Genesis 1st Edition

1 Ampharos HOLO R	4.00	8.00
2 Azumarill HOLO R	.75	1.50
3 Bellossom HOLO R	1.00	2.00
4 Feraligatr HOLO R	4.00	8.00
5 Feraligatr HOLO R	.50	1.00
6 Heracross HOLO R	2.50	5.00
7 Jumpluff HOLO R	.12	.25
8 Kingdra HOLO R	7.50	15.00
9 Lugia HOLO R	1.25	2.50
10 Meganium HOLO R	.25	.50
11 Meganium HOLO R	6.00	12.00
12 Pichu HOLO R	2.50	5.00
13 Skarmory HOLO R	40.00	100.00
14 Slowking HOLO R	.50	1.00
15 Steelix HOLO R	.60	1.25
16 Togetic HOLO R	12.50	25.00
17 Typhlosion HOLO R	17.50	35.00
18 Typhlosion HOLO R	3.00	6.00
19 Metal Energy HOLO R	.25	.50
20 Cleffa R	.30	.60
21 Donphan R	.60	1.25
22 Elekid R	.75	1.50
23 Magby R	.01	.08
24 Murkrow R	.01	.08
25 Sneasel R	2.50	5.00
26 Aipom U	100.00	200.00
27 Ariados U	25.00	60.00
28 Bayleef U	10.00	25.00
29 Bayleef U	1.00	2.00
30 Clefairy U	5.00	10.00
31 Croconaw U	10.00	20.00
32 Croconaw U	7.50	15.00
33 Electabuzz U	.75	1.50
34 Flaaffy U	.75	1.50
35 Furret U	.75	1.50
36 Gloom U	.08	.20
37 Granbull U	30.00	80.00
38 Lanturn U	5.00	10.00
39 Ledian U	.25	.50
40 Magmar U	3.00	8.00
41 Miltank U	7.50	15.00
42 Noctowl U	7.50	15.00
43 Phanpy U	3.00	6.00
44 Piloswine U	1.25	2.50
45 Quagsire U	.10	.20
46 Quilava U	1.00	2.00
47 Quilava U	.75	1.50
48 Seadra U	.75	1.50
49 Skiploom U	40.00	100.00
50 Sunflora U	4.00	8.00
51 Togepi U	7.50	15.00
52 Xatu U	.25	.50
53 Chikorita C	7.50	15.00
54 Chikorita C	4.00	8.00
55 Chinchou C	.20	.40
56 Cyndaquil C	1.50	3.00
57 Cyndaquil C	2.50	5.00
58 Girafarig C	3.00	6.00
59 Gligar C	.75	1.50
60 Hoothoot C	2.00	4.00
61 Hoppip C	3.00	6.00
62 Horsea C	.25	.50
63 Ledyba C	.25	.50
64 Mantine C	6.00	12.00
65 Mareep C	10.00	20.00
66 Marill C	2.50	5.00
67 Natu C	1.00	2.00
68 Oddish C	12.00	30.00
69 Onix C	12.00	30.00
70 Pikachu C	40.00	100.00
71 Sentret C	15.00	40.00
72 Shuckle C	.75	1.50
73 Slowpoke C	.60	1.25
74 Snubbull C	7.50	15.00
75 Spinarak C	30.00	75.00
76 Stantler C	3.00	6.00
77 Sudowoodo C	6.00	12.00
78 Sunkern C	10.00	20.00
79 Swinub C	1.25	2.50
80 Totodile C	.01	.08
81 Totodile C	.04	.10
82 Wooper C	2.00	4.00
83 Arcade Game R	2.50	5.00
84 Ecogym R	.75	1.50
85 Energy Charge R	1.00	2.50
86 Focus Band R	.07	.15
87 Mary R	7.50	15.00
88 PokeGear R	2.50	5.00
89 Super Energy Retrieval R	1.50	3.00
90 Time Capsule R	1.50	3.00
91 Bill's Teleporter U	.75	1.50
92 Card-Flip Game U	.75	1.50
93 Gold Berry U	5.00	10.00
94 Miracle Berry U	.75	1.50
95 New Pokedex U	.60	1.25
96 Professor Elm U	1.50	3.00
97 Sprout Tower U	.75	1.50
98 Super Scoop Up U	1.00	2.00
99 Berry C	3.00	6.00
100 Double Gust C	.75	1.50
101 Moo-Moo Milk C	.60	1.25
102 Pokemon March C	.75	1.50
103 Super Rod C	1.00	2.00
104 Darkness Energy R	3.00	6.00
105 Recycle Energy R	1.00	2.00
106 Fighting Energy C	1.00	2.00
107 Fire Energy C	7.50	15.00
108 Grass Energy C	.75	1.50
109 Lightning Energy C	.75	1.50
110 Psychic Energy C	.60	1.25
111 Water Energy C	1.25	2.50

2000 Pokemon Team Rocket 1st Edition

1 Dark Alakazam HOLO R	1.00	2.00
2 Dark Arbok HOLO R ERR	.75	1.50
3 Dark Blastoise HOLO R	.60	1.25
4 Dark Charizard HOLO R	.25	.50
5 Dark Dragonite HOLO R	.08	.20
6 Dark Dugtrio HOLO R	.10	.25
7 Dark Golbat HOLO R	1.25	2.50
8 Dark Gyarados HOLO R	.07	.15
9 Dark Hypno HOLO R	.12	.30
10 Dark Machamp HOLO R	1.25	2.50
11 Dark Magneton HOLO R	.75	1.50
12 Dark Slowbro HOLO R	.75	1.50
13 Dark Vileplume HOLO R	1.50	3.00
14 Dark Weezing HOLO R	4.00	10.00
15 Here Comes Team Rocket HOLO R	.50	1.00
16 Rocket's Sneak Attack HOLO R	1.25	3.00
17 Rainbow Energy HOLO R	.30	.60
18 Dark Alakazam R	.75	1.50
19 Dark Arbok R ERR	.75	1.50
20 Dark Blastoise R	1.50	3.00
21 Dark Charizard R	.60	1.25
22 Dark Dragonite R	1.00	2.00
23 Dark Dugtrio R	.10	.20
24 Dark Golbat R	3.00	6.00
25 Dark Gyarados R	3.00	6.00
26 Dark Hypno R	1.50	3.00
27 Dark Machamp R	1.00	2.00
28 Dark Magneton R	1.00	2.00
29 Dark Slowbro R	.75	1.50
30 Dark Vileplume R	1.50	3.00
31 Dark Weezing R	1.00	2.00
32 Dark Charmeleon U	1.25	2.50
33 Dark Dragonair U	25.00	60.00
34 Dark Electrode U	100.00	200.00
35 Dark Flareon U	12.50	25.00
36 Dark Gloom U	5.00	10.00
37 Dark Golduck U	1.25	2.50
38 Dark Jolteon U	.25	.50
39 Dark Kadabra U	1.00	2.00
40 Dark Machoke U	.75	1.50
41 Dark Muk U	60.00	125.00
42 Dark Persian U	1.00	2.00
43 Dark Primeape U	3.00	6.00
44 Dark Rapidash U ERR	.12	.25
45 Dark Vaporeon U	.12	.25
46 Dark Wartortle U	1.00	2.00
47 Magikarp U	.08	.20
48 Porygon U	.75	1.50
49 Abra C	.08	.20
50 Charmander C	4.00	8.00
51 Dark Raticate C	.25	.50
52 Diglett C	2.50	5.00
53 Dratini C	7.50	15.00
54 Drowzee C	2.50	5.00
55 Eevee C	4.00	8.00
56 Ekans C	1.00	2.00
57 Grimer C	2.00	4.00
58 Koffing C	2.00	4.00
59 Machop C	.75	1.50
60 Magnemite C	10.00	20.00
61 Mankey C	.75	1.50
62 Meowth C	15.00	30.00
63 Oddish C	25.00	50.00
64 Ponyta C	40.00	100.00

65 Psyduck C 10.00 25.00
66 Rattata C 7.50 15.00
67 Slowpoke C .30 .75
68 Squirtle C 40.00 100.00
69 Voltorb C .30 .60
70 Zubat C .60 1.25
71 Here Comes Team Rocket R 2.50 5.00
72 Rocket's Sneak Attack R 7.50 15.00
73 The Boss's Way U .75 1.50
74 Challenge U .60 1.25
75 Digger U .10 .20
76 Imposter Oak's Revenge U .25 .50
77 Nightly Garbage Run U .75 1.50
78 Goop Gas Attack C 1.25 2.50
79 Sleep C 500.00 1,200.00
80 Rainbow Energy R 6.00 12.00
81 Full Heal Energy U 7.50 15.00
82 Potion Energy U 4.00 8.00
83 Dark Raichu HOLO R UCE .01 .08

2001 Pokemon Neo Discovery 1st Edition

1 Espeon HOLO R .04 .10
2 Forretress HOLO R 40.00 100.00
3 Hitmontop HOLO R 10.00 25.00
4 Houndoom HOLO R 12.50 25.00
5 Houndour HOLO R 125.00 300.00
6 Kabutops HOLO R 2.00 4.00
7 Magnemite HOLO R 1.50 3.00
8 Politoed HOLO R 1.25 2.50
9 Poliwrath HOLO R 4.00 8.00
10 Scizor HOLO R 7.50 15.00
11 Smeargle HOLO R 2.50 5.00
12 Tyranitar HOLO R 7.50 15.00
13 Umbreon HOLO R 7.50 15.00
14 Unown A HOLO R 30.00 80.00
15 Ursaring HOLO R 1.50 3.00
16 Wobbuffet HOLO R .25 .50
17 Yanma HOLO R 7.50 15.00
18 Beedrill R .25 .50
19 Butterfree R 1.00 2.00
20 Espeon R .75 1.50
21 Forretress R .30 .60
22 Hitmontop R .75 1.50
23 Houndoom R .07 .15
24 Houndour R .25 .50
25 Kabutops R 10.00 25.00
26 Magnemite R 10.00 25.00
27 Politoed R 40.00 100.00
28 Poliwrath R 5.00 10.00
29 Scizor R 1.25 2.50
30 Smeargle R .60 1.25
31 Tyranitar R .25 .50
32 Umbreon R 30.00 75.00
33 Unown A R .25 .50
34 Ursaring R 2.50 5.00
35 Wobbuffet R 2.00 4.00
36 Yanma R 2.00 5.00
37 Corsola U 20.00 40.00
38 Eevee U 2.00 4.00
39 Houndour U 3.00 6.00
40 Igglybuff U 3.00 6.00
41 Kakuna U 1.00 2.00
42 Metapod U .01 .08
43 Omastar U .04 .10
44 Poliwhirl U 1.00 2.00
45 Pupitar U .75 2.00
46 Scyther U 2.00 4.00
47 Unown D U .50 1.00
48 Unown F U .75 1.50
49 Unown M U .75 1.50
50 Unown N U 1.25 2.50
51 Unown U U .75 1.50
52 Xatu U .75 1.50
53 Caterpie C 7.50 15.00
54 Dunsparce C .60 1.25
55 Hoppip C .75 1.50
56 Kabuto C 1.25 2.50
57 Larvitar C .60 1.25
58 Mareep C .50 1.00
59 Natu C 2.00 4.00
60 Omanyte C .07 .15
61 Pineco C .75 1.50
62 Poliwag C .25 .50
63 Sentret C .08 .20
64 Spinarak C .05 .12
65 Teddiursa C 2.50 5.00
66 Tyrogue C 1.00 2.00
67 Unown E C .60 1.25
68 Unown I C 1.50 3.00
69 Unown O C 3.00 6.00
70 Weedle C .30 .75
71 Wooper C 7.50 15.00
72 Trainer: Fossil Egg U .30 .60
73 Trainer: Hyper Devolution Spray U 2.50 5.00
74 Trainer: Ruin Wall U 1.50 3.00
75 Trainer: Energy Ark C .75 1.50

2001 Pokemon Neo Revelation 1st Edition

1 Ampharos HOLO R .10 .20
2 Blissey HOLO R 4.00 8.00
3 Celebi HOLO R .01 .08
4 Crobat HOLO R .04 .10
5 Delibird HOLO R .12 .25
6 Entei HOLO R .12 .30
7 Ho-oh HOLO R 1.50 3.00
8 Houndoom HOLO R 1.00 2.00
9 Jumpluff HOLO R 1.00 2.00
10 Magneton HOLO R .75 1.50
11 Misdreavus HOLO R .75 1.50
12 Porygon 2 HOLO R .25 .50
13 Raikou HOLO R .08 .20
14 Suicune HOLO R 1.25 2.50
15 Aerodactyl R .08 .20
16 Celebi R .04 .10
17 Entei R .75 1.50
18 Ho-oh R .25 .50
19 Kingdra R .01 .08
20 Lugia R .10 .25
21 Raichu R .60 1.25
22 Raikou R .75 1.50
23 Skarmory R 4.00 8.00
24 Sneasel R .10 .20
25 Starmie R 1.25 2.50
26 Sudowoodo R 1.00 2.00
27 Suicune R .50 1.00
28 Flaaffy U 1.25 2.50
29 Golbat U 30.00 80.00
30 Graveler U 12.50 25.00
31 Jynx U 100.00 200.00
32 Lanturn U 1.00 2.00
33 Magcargo U 1.25 2.50
34 Octillery U 1.50 3.00
35 Parasect U 15.00 30.00
36 Piloswine U .75 1.50
37 Seaking U .75 1.50
38 Stantler U .12 .25
39 Unown B U .75 1.50
40 Unown Y U 2.00 4.00
41 Aipom C 7.50 15.00
42 Chinchou C 1.00 2.00
43 Farfetch'd C .12 .25
44 Geodude C 5.00 10.00
45 Goldeen C 1.00 2.00
46 Murkrow C 40.00 80.00
47 Paras C 7.50 15.00
48 Quagsire C .75 1.50
49 Qwilfish C .75 1.50
50 Remoraid C 2.50 5.00
51 Shuckle C 1.00 2.00
52 Skiploom C 1.25 2.50
53 Slugma C .25 .50
54 Smoochum C .12 .25
55 Snubbull C .75 1.50
56 Staryu C 7.50 15.00
57 Swinub C 7.50 15.00
58 Unown K C .01 .08
59 Zubat C .01 .08
60 Balloon Berry U 7.50 15.00
61 Healing Field U 10.00 20.00
62 Pokemon Breeder Fields U 2.00 4.00
63 Rocket's Hideout U 30.00 80.00
64 Old Rod C .07 .15
65 Shining Gyarados HOLO R .20 .50
66 Shining Magikarp HOLO R .30 .60

2002 Pokemon-e Expedition

1 Alakazam HOLO R 1.25 2.50
2 Ampharos HOLO R 50.00 120.00
3 Arbok HOLO R 5.00 12.00
4 Blastoise HOLO R 2.00 4.00
5 Butterfree HOLO R 6.00 12.00
6 Charizard HOLO R 1.25 2.50
7 Clefable HOLO R .75 1.50
8 Cloyster HOLO R .10 .20
9 Dragonite HOLO R .75 1.50
10 Dugtrio HOLO R 1.50 3.00
11 Fearow HOLO R .60 1.25
12 Feraligatr HOLO R 1.25 2.50
13 Gengar HOLO R .75 1.50
14 Golem HOLO R 3.00 6.00
15 Kingler HOLO R 1.00 2.00
16 Machamp HOLO R 3.00 6.00
17 Magby HOLO R .01 .08
18 Meganium HOLO R .05 .12
19 Mew HOLO R 25.00 50.00
20 Mewtwo HOLO R 1.00 2.00
21 Ninetales HOLO R 5.00 10.00
22 Pichu HOLO R 3.00 6.00
23 Pidgeot HOLO R 75.00 200.00
24 Poliwrath HOLO R 2.00 4.00
25 Raichu HOLO R 17.50 35.00
26 Rapidash HOLO R 60.00 150.00
27 Skarmory HOLO R 20.00 50.00
28 Typhlosion HOLO R 15.00 30.00
29 Tyranitar HOLO R 400.00 1,000.00
30 Venusaur HOLO R 4.00 8.00
31 Vileplume HOLO R 4.00 8.00
32 Weezing HOLO R 2.50 5.00
33 Alakazam R 25.00 60.00
34 Ampharos R 7.50 15.00
35 Arbok R .75 1.50
36 Blastoise R 1.00 2.00
37 Blastoise R .75 1.50
38 Butterfree R 4.00 8.00
39 Charizard R .75 2.00
40 Charizard R .50 1.00
41 Clefable R 1.50 3.00
42 Cloyster R 2.50 5.00
43 Dragonite R .50 1.00
44 Dugtrio R .25 .50
45 Fearow R 1.00 2.00
46 Feraligatr R 6.00 12.00
47 Feraligatr R 2.00 4.00
48 Gengar R 2.50 5.00
49 Golem R 7.50 15.00
50 Kingler R 4.00 8.00
51 Machamp R 20.00 40.00
52 Magby R .08 .20
53 Meganium R 7.50 15.00
54 Meganium R 2.50 5.00
55 Mew R .75 1.50
56 Mewtwo R 60.00 125.00
57 Ninetales R 3.00 6.00
58 Pichu R .25 .50
59 Pidgeot R 15.00 40.00
60 Poliwrath R 15.00 40.00
61 Raichu R 50.00 120.00
62 Rapidash R .60 1.25
63 Skarmory R .60 1.25
64 Typhlosion R .75 1.50
65 Typhlosion R 2.00 4.00
66 Tyranitar R 1.00 2.00
67 Venusaur R .75 1.50
68 Venusaur R .75 1.50
69 Vileplume R 12.50 25.00
70 Weezing R .07 .15
71 Bayleef U 3.00 6.00
72 Chansey U .25 .50
73 Charmeleon U 5.00 12.00
74 Croconaw U .60 1.25
75 Dragonair U .30 .75
76 Electabuzz U 1.00 2.00
77 Flaafy U 1.00 2.00
78 Gloom U 1.25 2.50
79 Graveler U 3.00 6.00
80 Haunter U 1.50 3.00
81 Hitmonlee U .30 .60
82 Ivysaur U 15.00 30.00
83 Jynx U .25 .50
84 Kadabra U 2.50 5.00
85 Machoke U .04 .10
86 Magmar U .05 .12
87 Metapod U .12 .25
88 Pidgeotto U 7.50 15.00
89 Poliwhirl U .75 1.50
90 Pupitar U .75 1.50
91 Quilava U 1.00 2.00
92 Wartortle U .10 .20
93 Abra C .75 2.00
94 Bulbasaur C .75 1.50
95 Bulbasaur C .75 1.50
96 Caterpie C .25 .50
97 Charmander C .12 .25
98 Charmander C .12 .25
99 Chikorita C .75 1.50
100 Chikorita C 1.25 2.50
101 Clefairy C .10 .20
102 Corsola C .25 .50
103 Cubone C .75 1.50
104 Cyndaquil C .75 1.50
105 Cyndaquil C 10.00 20.00
106 Diglett C 7.50 15.00
107 Dratini C 30.00 60.00
108 Ekans C 1.25 2.50
109 Gastly C .50 1.00
110 Geodude C .07 .15
111 Goldeen C .12 .30
112 Hoppip C 1.50 3.00
113 Houndour C .25 .50
114 Koffing C .75 1.50
115 Krabby C 1.00 2.00
116 Larvitar C .75 1.50
117 Machop C .12 .25
118 Magikarp C 25.00 60.00
119 Mareep C 125.00 250.00
120 Marill C 1.25 2.50
121 Meowth C .75 1.50
122 Oddish C 1.00 2.00
123 Pidgey C 1.00 2.00
124 Pikachu C .08 .20
125 Poliwag C .04 .10
126 Ponyta C .50 1.25
127 Qwilfish C .75 1.50
128 Rattata C .60 1.25
129 Shellder C 2.50 6.00
130 Spearow C 10.00 20.00
131 Squirtle C 15.00 30.00
132 Squirtle C .75 1.50
133 Tauros C .12 .25
134 Totodile C .07 .15
135 Totodile C 5.00 10.00
136 Vulpix C 6.00 12.00
137 Bill's Maintenance C 1.00 2.00
138 Copycat C 1.25 2.50
139 Dual Ball C .75 1.50
140 Energy Removal 2 U .75 1.50
141 Energy Restore U .01 .08
142 Mary's Impulse U .04 .10
143 Master Ball U .75 1.50
144 Multi Technical U 30.00 75.00
145 Pokemon Nurse U 1.00 2.00
146 Pokemon Reversal U 1.25 3.00
147 Power Charge U 1.00 2.00
148 Professor Elm's U 5.00 10.00
149 Professor Oak's U 4.00 8.00
150 Strength Charm U 2.50 5.00
151 Super Scoop Up U 2.00 4.00
152 Warp Point U .40 1.00
153 Energy Search C .10 .20
154 Full Heal C 7.50 15.00
155 Moo-moo Milk C 7.50 15.00
156 Potion C .04 .10
157 Switch C .10 .25
158 Darkness Energy R 1.25 2.50
159 Metal Energy R 1.00 2.00
160 Fighting Energy C .10 .20
161 Fire Energy C .75 1.50
162 Grass Energy C .75 1.50
163 Lightning Energy C .75 1.50
164 Psychic Energy C .25 .50
165 Water Energy C 50.00 120.00

2002 Pokemon Legendary Collection

1 Alakazam HOLO R 2.50 5.00
2 Articuno HOLO R 10.00 20.00
3 Charizard HOLO R 1.00 2.00
4 Dark Blastoise HOLO R 20.00 50.00
5 Dark Dragonite HOLO R 6.00 15.00
6 Dark Persian HOLO R 2.00 4.00
7 Dark Raichu HOLO R 1.25 2.50
8 Dark Slowbro HOLO R 1.25 2.50
9 Dark Vaporeon HOLO R .60 1.25
10 Flareon HOLO R .60 1.25
11 Gengar HOLO R 75.00 200.00
12 Gyarados HOLO R .10 .20
13 Hitmonlee HOLO R 3.00 6.00
14 Jolteon HOLO R 10.00 20.00
15 Machamp HOLO R 7.50 15.00
16 Muk HOLO R .25 .50
17 Ninetales HOLO R .05 .12
18 Venusaur HOLO R .50 1.25
19 Zapdos HOLO R .30 .75
20 Beedrill R 7.50 15.00
21 Butterfree R 30.00 60.00
22 Electrode R .75 1.50
23 Exeggutor R .75 1.50
24 Golem R .30 .75
25 Hypno R 3.00 6.00
26 Jynx R 60.00 150.00
27 Kabutops R 12.00 30.00
28 Magneton R 12.50 25.00
29 Mewtwo R 200.00 500.00
30 Moltres R .75 1.50
31 Nidoking R .01 .08
32 Nidoqueen R .05 .12
33 Pidgeot R .75 1.50
34 Pidgeotto R .75 1.50
35 Rhydon R 1.50 3.00
36 Arcanine U 7.50 15.00
37 Charmeleon U .08 .20
38 Dark Dragonair U 2.00 4.00
39 Dark Wartortle U .25 .50
40 Dewgong U 3.00 6.00
41 Dodrio U .25 .50
42 Fearow U 3.00 6.00
43 Golduck U 6.00 12.00
44 Graveler U .75 1.50
45 Growlithe U 30.00 60.00
46 Haunter U 3.00 6.00
47 Ivysaur U 10.00 20.00
48 Kabuto U 3.00 6.00
49 Kadabra U 50.00 120.00
50 Kakuna U 2.00 4.00
51 Machoke U .50 1.00
52 Magikarp U .75 1.50
53 Meowth U .60 1.25
54 Metapod U .75 1.50
55 Nidorina U 7.50 15.00
56 Nidorino U 1.25 2.50
57 Omanyte U .07 .15
58 Omastar U 7.50 15.00
59 Primeape U 10.00 20.00
60 Rapidash U 1.25 2.50
61 Raticate U 1.50 3.00
62 Sandslash U 1.00 2.00
63 Seadra U 1.50 3.00
64 Snorlax U 1.00 2.00
65 Tauros U .07 .15
66 Tentacruel U 30.00 75.00
67 Abra C .50 1.00
68 Bulbasaur C 30.00 80.00
69 Caterpie C 30.00 80.00
70 Charmander C 125.00 300.00
71 Doduo C 2.50 5.00
72 Dratini C .75 1.50
73 Drowzee C 2.00 4.00
74 Eevee C 7.50 15.00
75 Exeggcute C .60 1.25
76 Gastly C 7.50 15.00
77 Geodude C 5.00 10.00
78 Grimer C 5.00 10.00
79 Machop C 1.25 2.50
80 Magnemite C .75 1.50
81 Mankey C 3.00 6.00
82 Nidoran (F) C .75 1.50
83 Nidoran (M) C .25 .50
84 Onix C 1.50 3.00
85 Pidgey C .75 1.50
86 Pikachu C 1.00 2.00
87 Ponyta C .75 1.50
88 Psyduck C 2.00 4.00
89 Rattata C 1.00 2.00
90 Rhyhorn C 1.50 3.00
91 Sandshrew C 1.25 2.50
92 Seel C 1.00 2.00
93 Slowpoke C 1.25 2.50
94 Spearow C .12 .25
95 Squirtle C 1.50 3.00
96 Tentacool C 1.25 2.50
97 Voltorb C .75 1.50
98 Vulpix C 3.00 6.00
99 Weedle C 1.50 3.00
100 Full Heal Energy U .12 .25
101 Potion Energy U .08 .20
102 Pokemon Breeder R .75 1.50
103 Pokemon Trader R .10 .20
104 Scoop Up R .10 .20
105 The Boss's Way U .25 .50
106 Challenge! U .10 .20
107 Energy Retrieval U .30 .75
108 Bill C .01 .08
109 Mysterious Fossil C .05 .12
110 Potion C .01 .08

2002 Pokemon Neo Destiny 1st Edition

1 Dark Ampharos HOLO R .08 .20
2 Dark Crobat HOLO R .50 1.00
3 Dark Donphan HOLO R .10 .20
4 Dark Espeon HOLO R .12 .30
5 Dark Feraligatr HOLO R 7.50 15.00
6 Dark Gengar HOLO R 7.50 15.00
7 Dark Houndoom HOLO R 1.00 2.00
8 Dark Porygon2 HOLO R .30 .60
9 Dark Scizor HOLO R .75 1.50
10 Dark Typhlosion HOLO R 1.50 3.00
11 Dark Tyranitar HOLO R .75 1.50
12 Light Arcanine HOLO R .75 1.50
13 Light Azumarill HOLO R .10 .20
14 Light Dragonite HOLO R 2.50 5.00
15 Light Togetic HOLO R .30 .60
16 Miracle Energy HOLO R 1.00 2.00
17 Dark Ariados R 25.00 60.00
18 Dark Magcargo R .50 1.00
19 Dark Omastar R 1.50 3.00
20 Dark Slowking R 1.50 3.00
21 Dark Ursaring R .10 .20
22 Light Dragonair R .75 1.50

23 Light Lanturn R 3.00 6.00
24 Light Ledian R 50.00 100.00
25 Light Machamp R .12 .25
26 Light Piloswine R 2.50 5.00
27 Unown G R 2.00 4.00
28 Unown H R .75 1.50
29 Unown W R .75 1.50
30 Unown X R .07 .15
31 Chansey U 4.00 8.00
32 Dark Croconaw U 1.25 3.00
33 Dark Exeggutor U 1.00 2.00
34 Dark Flaaffy U 15.00 30.00
35 Dark Forretress U .50 1.25
36 Dark Haunter U .60 1.25
37 Dark Omanyte U 7.50 15.00
38 Dark Pupitar U 3.00 6.00
39 Dark Quilava U .75 1.50
40 Dark Wigglytuff U .75 1.50
41 Heracross U .60 1.25
42 Hitmonlee U 6.00 12.00
43 Houndour U 1.50 3.00
44 Jigglypuff U 2.50 5.00
45 Light Dewgong U 200.00 400.00
46 Light Flareon U .10 .20
47 Light Golduck U .75 1.50
48 Light Jolteon U 1.25 2.50
49 Light Machoke U 2.00 4.00
50 Light Ninetales U .75 1.50
51 Light Slowbro U 1.25 2.50
52 Light Vaporeon U 1.25 2.50
53 Light Venomoth U 20.00 40.00
54 Light Wigglytuff U 20.00 40.00
55 Scyther U 2.00 4.00
56 Togepi U 7.50 15.00
57 Unown C U 7.50 15.00
58 Unown P U .25 .50
59 Unown Q U 40.00 100.00
60 Unown Z U 50.00 120.00
61 Cyndaquil C 20.00 50.00
62 Dark Octillery C 1.00 2.00
63 Dratini C 30.00 80.00
64 Exeggcute C 10.00 25.00
65 Gastly C 15.00 30.00
66 Girafarig C 250.00 600.00
67 Gligar C 1.00 2.00
68 Growlithe C .10 .20
69 Hitmonchan C .08 .20
70 Larvitar C .10 .25
71 Ledyba C 4.00 8.00
72 Light Sunflora C .60 1.25
73 Machop C .01 .08
74 Mantine C .04 .10
75 Mareep C 2.00 4.00
76 Phanpy C 75.00 200.00
77 Pineco C .10 .20
78 Porygon C .50 1.00
79 Psyduck C 5.00 10.00
80 Remoraid C 3.00 6.00
81 Seel C 30.00 60.00
82 Slugma C 6.00 12.00
83 Sunkern C .75 1.50
84 Swinub C 10.00 20.00
85 Totodile C 7.50 15.00
86 Unown L C 1.50 3.00
87 Unown S C 60.00 150.00
88 Unown T C .30 .75
89 Unown V C 2.50 5.00
90 Venonat C .60 1.25
91 Vulpix C 1.25 2.50
92 Broken Ground Gym R .75 1.50
93 EXP.ALL R 1.00 2.00
94 Impostor Professor Oak's Invention R .75 1.50
95 Radio Tower R .75 1.50
96 Thought Wave Machine R 7.50 15.00
97 Counterattack Claws U 7.50 15.00
98 Energy Amplifier U .50 1.00
99 Energy Stadium U .75 1.50
100 Lucky Stadium U 4.00 8.00
101 Magnifier U 2.50 5.00
102 Pokemon Personality Test U .75 1.50
103 Team Rocket's Evil Deeds U .60 1.25
104 Heal Powder C .60 1.25
105 Mail from Bill C .75 1.50
106 Shining Celebi HOLO R .60 1.25
107 Shining Charizard HOLO R .07 .15
108 Shining Kabutops HOLO R 3.00 6.00
109 Shining Mewtwo HOLO R 2.50 5.00
110 Shining Noctowl HOLO R .50 1.00
111 Shining Raichu HOLO R 7.50 15.00
112 Shining Steelix HOLO R .60 1.25
113 Shining Tyranitar HOLO R .75 1.50

2003 Pokemon-e Aquapolis

1 Ampharos R .75 1.50
2 Arcanine R .75 1.50
3 Ariados R 7.50 15.00
4 Azumarill R .30 .75
5 Bellossom R .08 .20
6 Blissey R 1.00 2.00
7 Donphan R .75 1.50
8 Electrode R .25 .50
9 Elekid R 7.50 15.00
10 Entei R 100.00 200.00
11 Espeon R 10.00 25.00
12 Exeggutor R 10.00 25.00
13 Exeggutor R 75.00 200.00
14 Houndoom R 1.50 3.00
15 Houndoom R .30 .75
16 Hypno R .75 1.50
17 Jumpluff R 2.50 5.00
18 Jynx R 1.25 2.50
19 Kingdra R 1.25 2.50
20 Lanturn R .12 .25
21 Lanturn R 1.50 4.00
22 Magneton R 2.00 4.00
23 Muk R 1.50 3.00
24 Nidoking R 1.25 2.50
25 Ninetales R 2.00 4.00
26 Octillery R 1.25 2.50
27 Parasect R 1.25 2.50
28 Porygon2 R .75 1.50
29 Primeape R 2.00 4.00
30 Quagsire R 2.00 4.00
31 Rapidash R .75 1.50
32 Scizor R 1.50 3.00
33 Slowbro R .75 1.50
34 Slowking R 7.50 15.00
35 Steelix R .75 1.50
36 Sudowoodo R .50 1.00
37 Suicune R .75 1.50
38 Tentacruel R .10 .20
39 Togetic R .75 1.50
40 Tyranitar R 1.00 2.00
41 Umbreon R .75 1.50
42 Victreebel R .10 .20
43 Vileplume R .25 .50
44 Zapdos R 1.50 4.00
45 Bellsprout U 2.50 5.00
46 Dodrio U .10 .20
47 Flaaffy U .12 .25
48 Furret U 1.00 2.00
49 Gloom U .10 .20
51 Growlithe U 20.00 50.00
52 Magnemite U .75 1.50
53 Marill U 1.25 2.50
54 Marowak U 1.00 2.00
55 Nidorino U 1.50 3.00
56 Pupitar U .30 .75
57 Scyther U .07 .15
58 Seadra U .75 1.50
59 Seaking U .10 .20
60 Skiploom U 5.00 10.00
61 Smoochum U 3.00 6.00
62 Spinarak U 1.25 2.50
63 Tyrogue U .75 1.50
64 Voltorb U 1.25 2.50
65 Weepinbell U 60.00 125.00
66 Wooper U 1.00 2.00
67 Aipom C .75 1.50
68 Bellsprout C .60 1.50
69 Chansey C .10 .25
70 Chinchou C 2.50 5.00
71 Chinchou C .75 1.50
72 Cubone C 4.00 8.00
73 Doduo C .10 .20
75 Eevee C 10.00 20.00
76 Exeggcute C .75 1.50
77 Exeggcute C .60 1.25
78 Goldeen C 2.50 5.00
79 Grimer C 7.50 15.00
80 Growlithe C .60 1.25
81 Hitmonchan C .75 1.50
82 Hitmontop C .60 1.25
83 Hoppip C 25.00 50.00
84 Horsea C 3.00 6.00
85 Horsea C 12.50 25.00
86 Houndour C .25 .50
87 Houndour C 12.50 25.00
88 Kangaskhan C 4.00 8.00
89 Larvitar C 100.00 250.00
90 Lickitung C 5.00 12.00
91 Magnemite C 20.00 50.00
92 Mankey C 2.50 6.00
93 Mareep C .60 1.25
94 Miltank C .75 1.50
96 Nidoran C 3.00 6.00
97 Oddish C 3.00 6.00
98 Onix C .75 1.50
99 Paras C .50 1.00
H1 Ampharos HOLO R .60 1.25
H2 Arcanine HOLO R .08 .20
H3 Ariados HOLO R .04 .10
H4 Azumarill HOLO R 5.00 10.00
H5 Bellossom HOLO R .12 .25
H6 Blissey HOLO R .75 1.50
H7 Electrode HOLO R .50 1.00
H8 Entei HOLO R 4.00 8.00
H9 Espeon HOLO R 4.00 8.00
100 Phanpy C .25 .50
101 Pinsir C 30.00 80.00
102 Ponyta C 10.00 25.00
104 Psyduck C 12.50 25.00
105 Remoraid C 200.00 500.00
106 Scyther C 1.50 3.00
107 Sentret C .60 1.25
108 Slowpoke C 2.00 4.00
109 Smeargle C 150.00 300.00
110 Sneasel C 3.00 6.00
111 Spinarak C 7.50 15.00
112 Tangela C 20.00 40.00
113 Tentacool C 1.00 2.00
114 Togepi C .75 1.50
115 Voltorb C 75.00 200.00
116 Vulpix C 1.00 2.00
117 Wooper C .75 1.50
118 Apricorn Forest R 3.00 6.00
119 Darkness Cube U .08 .20
120 Energy Switch U .60 1.25
121 Fighting Cube 01 U .50 1.00
122 Fire Cube 01 U 2.50 5.00
123 Forest Guardian U .01 .08
124 Grass Cube 01 U .08 .20
125 Healing Berry U 1.00 2.00
126 Juggler U 1.25 2.50
127 Lightning Cube 01 U .30 .60
128 Memory Berry U 2.50 5.00
129 Metal Cube 01 U .12 .25
130 Pokemon Fan Club U 1.50 3.00
131 Pokemon Park U 20.00 50.00
132 Psychic Cube 01 U .60 1.25
133 Seer U 2.50 5.00
134 Super Energy Removal 2 U 4.00 8.00
135 Time Shard U 10.00 20.00
136 Town Volunteers U .07 .15
137 Traveling Salesman U .07 .15
138 Undersea Ruins U .75 1.50
139 Power Plant U .60 1.25
140 Water Cube 1 U 7.50 15.00
141 Weakness Guard U .08 .20
142 Darkness Energy R .50 1.00
143 Metal Energy R 1.00 2.00
144 Rainbow Energy R .60 1.25
145 Boost Energy U .01 .08
146 Crystal Energy U .04 .10
147 Warp Energy U 1.00 2.00
148 Kingdra HOLO R 250.00 500.00
149 Lugia HOLO R 10.00 25.00
150 Nidoking HOLO R 10.00 25.00
50A Golduck U 30.00 80.00
50B Golduck U 6.00 12.00
74A Drowzee C .25 .50
74B Drowzee C 3.00 6.00
95A Mr. Mime C 2.00 4.00
95B Mr. Mime C .60 1.25
H10 Exeggutor HOLO R .50 1.00
H11 Houndoom HOLO R 1.25 2.50
H12 Hypno HOLO R .75 1.50
H13 Jumpluff HOLO R .15 .30
H14 Kingdra HOLO R 1.25 2.50
H15 Lanturn HOLO R .25 .50
H16 Magneton HOLO R .01 .08
H17 Muk HOLO R .08 .20
H18 Nidoking HOLO R 3.00 6.00
H19 Ninetales HOLO R 2.00 4.00
H20 Octillery HOLO R 1.00 2.00
H21 Scizor HOLO R .75 1.50
H22 Slowking HOLO R 1.50 3.00
H23 Steelix HOLO R .75 1.50
H24 Sudowoodo HOLO R 6.00 12.00
H25 Suicune HOLO R 1.25 2.50
H26 Tentacruel HOLO R 3.00 6.00
H27 Togetic HOLO R 1.50 3.00
H28 Tyranitar HOLO R .60 1.25
H29 Umbreon HOLO R 1.00 2.00
H30 Victreebel HOLO R .60 1.25
H31 Vileplume HOLO R 1.25 2.50
H32 Zapdos HOLO R .75 1.50
103A Porygon C .75 1.50
103B Porygon C .01 .08

2003 Pokemon EX Dragon

1 Absol HOLO R .04 .10
2 Altaria HOLO R 7.50 15.00
3 Crawdaunt HOLO R 1.50 3.00
4 Flygon HOLO R 1.25 2.50
5 Golem HOLO R 1.50 4.00
6 Grumpig HOLO R 2.50 5.00
7 Minun HOLO R .12 .25
8 Plusle HOLO R .30 .75
9 Roselia HOLO R .01 .08
10 Salamence HOLO R .04 .10
11 Shedinja HOLO R 2.00 4.00
12 Torkoal HOLO R 2.00 4.00
13 Crawdaunt R .08 .20
14 Dragonair R 12.00 30.00
15 Flygon R .08 .20
16 Girafarig R 1.25 2.50
17 Magneton R .60 1.25
18 Ninjask R .50 1.25
19 Salamence R 1.50 3.00
20 Shelgon R .12 .25
21 Skarmory R 1.00 2.00
22 Vibrava R .30 .60
23 Bagon U 2.00 4.00
24 Camerupt U 1.50 3.00
25 Combusken U 1.00 2.00
26 Dratini U 1.00 2.00
27 Flaaffy U .60 1.25
28 Forretress U .10 .20
29 Graveler U .10 .20
30 Graveler U .75 1.50
31 Grovyle U .60 1.25
32 Gyarados U 1.00 2.00
33 Horsea U 1.00 2.00
34 Houndoom U .25 .50
35 Magneton U 15.00 30.00
36 Marshtomp U .60 1.25
37 Meditite U .60 1.25
38 Ninjask U .01 .08
39 Seadra U .05 .12
40 Seadra U 2.50 5.00
41 Shelgon U .10 .20
42 Shelgon U .60 1.25
43 Shuppet U 7.50 15.00
44 Snorunt U .10 .20
45 Swellow U .12 .25
46 Vibrava U 6.00 12.00
47 Vibrava U 1.50 3.00
48 Whiscash U 7.50 15.00
49 Bagon C .25 .50
50 Bagon C .05 .12
51 Barboach C .50 1.25
52 Corphish C .75 1.50
53 Corphish C .75 1.50
54 Corphish C .75 1.50
55 Geodude C 1.25 2.50
56 Geodude C 150.00 300.00
57 Grimer C .75 1.50
58 Horsea C .60 1.25
59 Houndour C 2.50 5.00
60 Magikarp C 12.50 25.00
61 Magnemite C .10 .20
62 Magnemite C .07 .15
63 Magnemite C .25 .50
64 Mareep C .75 1.50
65 Mudkip C 3.00 6.00
66 Nincada C 8.00 20.00
67 Nincada C 2.50 5.00
68 Nincada C 2.00 4.00
69 Numel C .60 1.25
70 Numel C .75 1.50
71 Pineco C 1.25 2.50
72 Slugma C .08 .20
73 Spoink C .04 .10
74 Spoink C 1.00 2.00
75 Swablu C .10 .20
76 Taillow C 3.00 6.00
77 Torchic C .60 1.25
78 Trapinch C .75 1.50
79 Trapinch C 7.50 15.00
80 Treecko C .75 1.50
81 Wurmple C 2.50 5.00
82 Balloon Berry C 100.00 250.00
83 Buffer Piece C 25.00 60.00
84 Energy Recycle System C 40.00 100.00
85 High Pressure System C 12.00 30.00
86 Low Pressure System C 15.00 30.00
87 Mr. Briney's Compassion C 200.00 500.00
88 TV Reporter U 6.00 12.00
89 Ampharos EX HOLO R 1.25 2.50
90 Dragonite EX HOLO R .75 1.50
91 Golem EX HOLO R 100.00 250.00
92 Kingdra EX HOLO R .07 .15
93 Latias EX HOLO R 1.00 2.00
94 Latios EX HOLO R 250.00 600.00
95 Magcargo EX HOLO R 7.50 15.00
96 Muk EX HOLO R 1.25 2.50
97 Rayquaza EX HOLO R 1.00 2.00
98 Charmander HOLO R 4.00 8.00
99 Charmeleon HOLO R .60 1.25
100 Charizard HOLO R 1.00 2.00

2003 Pokemon EX Ruby and Sapphire

1 Aggron HOLO R 2.00 4.00
2 Beautifly HOLO R 6.00 12.00
3 Blaziken HOLO R 1.50 3.00
4 Camerupt HOLO R 5.00 10.00
5 Delcatty HOLO R .75 1.50
6 Dustox HOLO R .07 .15
7 Gardevoir HOLO R 7.50 15.00
8 Hariyama HOLO R 40.00 100.00
9 Manectric HOLO R 6.00 12.00
10 Mightyena HOLO R 1.25 2.50
11 Sceptile HOLO R .10 .20
12 Slaking HOLO R 2.00 4.00
13 Swampert HOLO R .75 1.50
14 Wailord HOLO R .75 1.50
15 Blaziken R .75 1.50
16 Breloom R 100.00 200.00
17 Donphan R .25 .50
18 Nosepass R 2.00 4.00
19 Pelipper R 1.25 2.50
20 Sceptile R 10.00 20.00
21 Seaking R 1.00 2.00
22 Sharpedo R 1.25 2.50
23 Swampert R 30.00 60.00
24 Weezing R 1.50 3.00
25 Aron U 12.00 30.00
26 Cascoon U 12.00 30.00
27 Combusken U 30.00 80.00
28 Combusken U .12 .25
29 Delcatty U 1.00 2.00
30 Electrike U 4.00 8.00
31 Grovyle U 6.00 12.00
32 Grovyle U .60 1.25
33 Hariyama U 1.50 3.00
34 Kirlia U 7.50 15.00
35 Kirlia U 6.00 12.00
36 Lairon U 4.00 8.00
37 Lairon U 7.50 15.00
38 Linoone U 2.00 4.00
39 Manectric U 1.00 2.00
40 Marshtomp U 2.50 5.00
41 Marshtomp U 3.00 6.00
42 Mightyena U 1.50 3.00
43 Silcoon U .04 .10
44 Skitty U .10 .25
45 Slakoth U .25 .50
46 Swellow U 1.50 3.00
47 Vigoroth U .05 .12
48 Wailmer U .25 .60
49 Aron C 2.50 5.00
50 Aron C .12 .25
51 Carvanha C 40.00 100.00
52 Electrike C 1.50 3.00
53 Electrike C 1.50 3.00
54 Koffing C .12 .25
55 Goldeen C 3.00 8.00
56 Makuhita C 1.00 2.00
57 Makuhita C .50 1.00
58 Makuhita C 1.00 2.00
59 Mudkip C 1.50 3.00
60 Mudkip C .20 .40
61 Numel C 12.50 25.00
62 Phanpy C 1.00 2.50
63 Poochyena C 1.00 2.00
64 Poochyena C .75 1.50
65 Poochyena C 2.50 5.00
66 Ralts C .60 1.25
67 Ralts C 2.00 4.00
68 Ralts C .75 2.00
69 Shroomish C 1.00 2.00
70 Skitty C 1.00 2.00
71 Skitty C 2.00 4.00
72 Taillow C 1.25 2.50
73 Torchic C 1.00 2.00
74 Torchic C 2.00 4.00
75 Treecko C .75 1.50
76 Treecko C .75 1.50
77 Wingull C .60 1.25
78 Wurmple C .75 1.50
79 Zigzagoon C .07 .15
80 Trainer: Energy Removal 2 U .15 .40
81 Trainer: Energy Restore U .75 1.50
82 Trainer: Energy Switch U 15.00 40.00
83 Trainer: Lady Outing U .20 .40
84 Trainer: Lum Berry U .75 1.50

85 Trainer: Oran Berry U	1.00	2.00
86 Trainer: Poke Ball U	10.00	20.00
87 Trainer: Pokemon Reversal U	.75	1.50
88 Trainer: PokeNav U	.75	1.50
89 Trainer: Professor Birch U	15.00	30.00
90 Trainer: Energy Search C	.08	.20
91 Trainer: Potion C	15.00	30.00
92 Trainer: Switch C	.75	1.50
93 Darkness Energy R	.75	1.50
94 Metal Energy R	7.50	15.00
95 Rainbow Energy R	40.00	80.00
96 Chansey EX HOLO R	1.25	2.50
97 Electabuzz EX HOLO R	.75	1.50
98 Hitmonchan EX HOLO R	1.25	3.00
99 Lapras EX HOLO R	15.00	30.00
100 Magmar EX HOLO R	.12	.25
101 Mewtwo EX HOLO R	1.25	2.50
102 Scyther EX HOLO R	.75	1.50
103 Sneasel EX HOLO R	.30	.60
104 Grass Energy C	3.00	6.00
105 Fighting Energy C	1.25	2.50
106 Water Energy C	.10	.20
107 Psychic Energy C	1.50	3.00
108 Fire Energy C	.12	.25
109 Lightning Energy C	12.50	25.00

2003 Pokemon EX Sandstorm

1 Armaldo HOLO R	2.50	5.00
2 Cacturne HOLO R	1.25	2.50
3 Cradily HOLO R	.30	.75
4 Dusclops HOLO R	.60	1.25
5 Flareon HOLO R	.10	.20
6 Jolteon HOLO R	.50	1.00
7 Ludicolo HOLO R	.60	1.25
8 Lunatone HOLO R	.10	.20
9 Mawile HOLO R	.75	1.50
10 Sableye HOLO R	7.50	15.00
11 Seviper HOLO R	3.00	6.00
12 Shiftry HOLO R	.25	.50
13 Solrock HOLO R	1.25	2.50
14 Zangoose HOLO R	.75	1.50
15 Arcanine R	4.00	8.00
16 Espeon R	1.00	2.00
17 Golduck R	75.00	200.00
18 Kecleon R	.30	.75
19 Omastar R	.75	1.50
20 Pichu R	.10	.20
21 Sandslash R	1.00	2.00
22 Shiftry R	.60	1.25
23 Steelix R	.60	1.25
24 Umbreon R	2.50	5.00
25 Vaporeon R	1.25	2.50
26 Wobbuffet R	1.25	2.50
27 Anorith U	1.00	2.00
28 Anorith U	.75	1.50
29 Arbok U	.75	1.50
30 Azumarill U	2.00	4.00
31 Azurill U	.75	1.50
32 Baltoy U	10.00	20.00
33 Breloom U	.12	.25
34 Delcatty U	.50	1.00
35 Electabuzz U	4.00	8.00
36 Elekid U	.60	1.25
37 Fearow U	40.00	100.00
38 Illumise U	.60	1.25
39 Kabuto U	.75	1.50
40 Kirlia U	6.00	12.00
41 Lairon U	.75	1.50
42 Lileep U	.10	.20
43 Lileep U	.50	1.00
44 Linoone U	1.50	3.00
45 Lombre U	60.00	125.00
46 Lombre U	.50	1.00
47 Murkrow U	.05	.12
48 Nuzleaf U	.10	.25
49 Nuzleaf U	.08	.20
50 Pelipper U	.08	.20
51 Quilava U	.60	1.25
52 Vigoroth U	.75	1.50
53 Volbeat U	.10	.20
54 Wynaut U	.07	.15
55 Xatu U	1.25	2.50
56 Aron C	1.00	2.00
57 Cacnea C	.75	1.50
58 Cacnea C	.75	1.50
59 Cyndaquil C	30.00	75.00
60 Dunsparce C	250.00	600.00
61 Duskull C	50.00	120.00
62 Duskull C	25.00	50.00
63 Eevee C	3.00	6.00
64 Ekans C	2.00	4.00
65 Growlithe C	.75	1.50
66 Lotad C	12.00	30.00
67 Lotad C	12.00	30.00
68 Marill C	30.00	80.00
69 Natu C	1.50	3.00
70 Omanyte C	.75	1.50
71 Onix C	.30	.75
72 Pikachu C	.75	1.50
73 Psyduck C	1.25	2.50
74 Ralts C	.60	1.25
75 Sandshrew C	4.00	8.00
76 Seedot C	1.50	3.00
77 Seedot C	.60	1.25
78 Shroomish C	.04	.10
79 Skitty C	.05	.12
80 Slakoth C	.10	.20
81 Spearow C	3.00	6.00
82 Trapinch C	40.00	100.00
83 Wailmer C	10.00	25.00
84 Wingull C	10.00	25.00
85 Zigzagoon C	6.00	15.00
86 Double Full Heal U	2.00	5.00
87 Lanette's Net Search U	5.00	10.00
88 Rare Candy U	3.00	6.00
89 Wally's Training U	2.00	4.00
90 Claw Fossil C	1.50	3.00
91 Mysterious Fossil C	2.50	5.00
92 Root Fossil C	.60	1.25
93 Multi Energy R	.12	.25
94 Aerodactyl EX HOLO R	.08	.20
95 Aggron EX HOLO R	1.00	2.00
96 Gardevoir EX HOLO R	2.00	4.00
97 Kabutops EX HOLO R	1.00	2.00
98 Raichu EX HOLO R	1.00	2.00
99 Typhlosion EX HOLO R	.75	1.50
100 Wailord EX HOLO R	1.25	2.50

2003 Pokemon-e Skyridge

1 Aerodactyl R	1.50	3.00
2 Alakazam R	4.00	8.00
3 Arcanine R	1.25	2.50
4 Articuno R	1.50	3.00
5 Beedrill R	.50	1.00
6 Crobat R	.75	1.50
7 Dewgong R	2.00	4.00
8 Flareon R	.04	.10
9 Forretress R	.08	.20
10 Gengar R	3.00	6.00
11 Gyarados R	1.00	2.00
12 Houndoom R	1.00	2.00
13 Jolteon R	2.50	5.00
14 Kabutops R	1.50	3.00
15 Ledian R	1.00	2.00
16 Machamp R	1.00	2.00
17 Magcargo R	40.00	100.00
18 Magcargo R	250.00	500.00
19 Magneton R	3.00	6.00
20 Magneton R	.12	.25
21 Moltres R	1.00	2.00
22 Nidoqueen R	1.25	2.50
23 Omastar R	1.25	2.50
24 Piloswine R	.60	1.25
25 Politoed R	1.25	2.50
26 Poliwrath R	3.00	6.00
27 Raichu R	2.00	4.00
28 Raikou R	2.50	5.00
29 Rhydon R	2.50	5.00
30 Starmie R	1.00	2.00
31 Steelix R	.75	1.50
32 Umbreon R	.30	.75
33 Vaporeon R	1.00	2.00
34 Wigglytuff R	1.00	2.00
35 Xatu R	2.50	5.00
36 Electrode U	1.00	2.00
37 Kabuto U	1.00	2.00
38 Machoke U	.75	1.50
39 Misdreavus U	1.00	2.00
40 Noctowl U	7.50	15.00
41 Omanyte U	.01	.08
42 Persian U	.04	.10
43 Piloswine U	1.00	2.00
44 Starmie U	.12	.25
45 Wobbuffet U	1.25	3.00
46 Abra C	.75	1.50
47 Buried Fossil C	15.00	30.00
48 Cleffa C	10.00	20.00
49 Delibird C	1.00	2.00
50 Diglett C	3.00	6.00
51 Ditto C	.75	1.50
52 Dugtrio C	10.00	20.00
53 Dunsparce C	.25	.50
54 Eevee C	1.50	3.00
55 Farfetch'd C	15.00	30.00
56 Forretress C	.50	1.00
57 Gastly C	.75	1.50
58 Girafarig C	2.50	5.00
59 Gligar C	2.00	4.00
60 Golbat C	2.00	4.00
61 Granbull C	.60	1.25
62 Growlithe C	.30	.75
63 Haunter C	.07	.15
64 Heracross C	1.25	2.50
65 Hoothoot C	1.25	2.50
66 Houndour C	.07	.15
67 Igglybuff C	2.00	4.00
68 Jigglypuff C	.25	.50
69 Kadabra C	.10	.25
70 Kakuna C	.12	.30
71 Lapras C	.25	.50
72 Ledyba C	.25	.50
73 Ledyba C	1.25	2.50
74 Machop C	.75	1.50
75 Magikarp C	.75	1.50
76 Magnemite C	.50	1.00
77 Mantine C	6.00	12.00
78 Meowth C	20.00	40.00
79 Murkrow C	.01	.08
80 Natu C	.04	.10
81 Nidoran F C	.10	.20
82 Nidoran F C	12.00	30.00
83 Nidorina C	100.00	250.00
84 Pikachu C	.75	1.50
85 Pineco C	1.25	2.50
86 Pineco C	1.25	2.50
87 Poliwag C	1.25	2.50
88 Poliwhirl C	.25	.50
89 Raticate C	.60	1.25
90 Rattata C	1.25	2.50
91 Rhyhorn C	1.00	2.00
92 Sandshrew C	2.00	4.00
93 Sandslash C	3.00	8.00
94 Seel C	.75	1.50
95 Seel C	2.50	5.00
96 Shuckle C	.40	1.00
97 Skarmory C	2.00	4.00
98 Slugma C	.10	.20
99 Slugma C	1.25	2.50
H1 Alakazam HOLO R	4.00	8.00
H2 Arcanine HOLO R	.75	1.50
H3 Articuno HOLO R	.75	1.50
H4 Beedrill HOLO R	.50	1.00
H5 Crobat HOLO R	.07	.15
H6 Dewgong HOLO R	.07	.15
H7 Flareon HOLO R	1.25	2.50
H8 Forretress HOLO R	.40	.80
H9 Gengar HOLO R	2.50	5.00
100 Snorlax C	1.50	3.00
101 Snubbull C	.08	.20
102 Stantler C	.04	.10
103 Staryu C	40.00	100.00
104 Staryu C	.75	1.50
105 Sunflora C	1.00	2.00
106 Sunkern C	.75	1.50
107 Swinub C	.75	1.50
108 Swinub C	3.00	6.00
109 Teddiursa C	15.00	30.00
110 Ursaring C	1.50	3.00
111 Venomoth C	12.00	30.00
112 Venonat C	40.00	100.00
113 Voltorb C	12.00	30.00
114 Weedle C	.75	1.50
115 Weedle C	25.00	50.00
116 Yanma C	.75	1.50
117 Zubat C	50.00	120.00
118 Zubat C	20.00	50.00
119 Ancient Ruins U	15.00	30.00
120 Relic Hunter U	500.00	1,200.00
121 Apricorn Maker U	.20	.40
122 Crystal Shard U	.75	1.50
123 Desert Shaman U	.75	1.50
124 Fast Ball U	.15	.40
125 Fisherman U	1.25	2.50
126 Friend Ball U	.60	1.25
127 Hyper Potion U	.75	1.50
128 Lure Ball U	.04	.10
129 Miracle Sphere (Alpha) U	.05	.12
130 Miracle Sphere (Beta) U	1.50	3.00
131 Miracle Sphere (Gamma) U	10.00	25.00
132 Mirage Stadium U	3.00	8.00
133 Mystery Plate (Alpha) U	2.00	4.00
134 Mystery Plate (Beta) U	1.25	3.00
135 Mystery Plate (Gamma) U	1.25	3.00
136 Mystery Plate (Delta) U	5.00	12.00
137 Mystery Zone U	4.00	8.00
138 Oracle U	75.00	200.00
139 Star Piece U	30.00	80.00
140 Underground Expedition U	3.00	6.00
141 Underground Lake U	2.00	4.00
142 Bounce Energy U	3.00	6.00
143 Cyclone Energy U	.60	1.25
144 Retro Energy U	.30	.60
145 Celebi HOLO R	1.25	2.50
146 Charizard HOLO R	.75	1.50
147 Crobat HOLO R	2.00	4.00
148 Golem HOLO R	.20	.40
149 Ho-Oh HOLO R	.20	.50
150 Kabutops HOLO R	4.00	8.00
H10 Gyarados HOLO R	5.00	10.00
H11 Houndoom HOLO R	1.25	2.50
H12 Jolteon HOLO R	1.25	2.50
H13 Kabutops HOLO R	5.00	12.00
H14 Ledian HOLO R	1.50	4.00
H15 Machamp HOLO R	3.00	6.00
H16 Magcargo HOLO R	6.00	12.00
H17 Magcargo HOLO R	2.50	5.00
H18 Magneton HOLO R	.60	1.25
H19 Magneton HOLO R	1.25	2.50
H20 Moltres HOLO R	2.50	5.00
H21 Nidoqueen HOLO R	1.00	2.00
H22 Piloswine HOLO R	1.25	2.50
H23 Politoed HOLO R	2.50	5.00
H24 Poliwrath HOLO R	1.00	2.00
H25 Raichu HOLO R	1.50	3.00
H26 Raikou HOLO R	1.25	2.50
H27 Rhydon HOLO R	1.50	3.00
H28 Starmie HOLO R	.60	1.25
H29 Steelix HOLO R	1.50	3.00
H30 Umbreon HOLO R	12.50	25.00
H31 Vaporeon HOLO R	1.25	2.50
H32 Xatu HOLO R	1.50	3.00

2004 Pokemon EX FireRed and LeafGreen

1 Beedrill HOLO R	1.00	2.00
2 Butterfree HOLO R	.60	1.25
3 Dewgong HOLO R	.04	.10
4 Ditto HOLO R	.10	.25
5 Exeggutor HOLO R	3.00	6.00
6 Kangaskhan HOLO R	3.00	6.00
7 Marowak HOLO R	1.00	2.00
8 Nidoking HOLO R	2.00	4.00
9 Nidoqueen HOLO R	.75	1.50
10 Pidgeot HOLO R	1.25	2.50
11 Poliwrath HOLO R	1.25	2.50
12 Raichu HOLO R	.12	.25
13 Rapidash HOLO R	.75	1.50
14 Slowbro HOLO R	1.00	2.00
15 Snorlax HOLO R	1.00	2.00
16 Tauros HOLO R	2.50	5.00
17 Victreebel HOLO R	3.00	6.00
18 Arcanine R	1.50	3.00
19 Chansey R	.60	1.50
20 Cloyster R	.60	1.25
21 Dodrio R	.75	1.50
22 Dugtrio R	2.00	4.00
23 Farfetch'd R	12.50	25.00
24 Fearow R	.10	.20
25 Hypno R	1.25	2.50
26 Kingler R	20.00	50.00
27 Magneton R	4.00	10.00
28 Primeape R	25.00	50.00
29 Scyther R	7.50	15.00
30 Tangela R	.75	1.50
31 Charmeleon U	1.00	2.00
32 Drowzee U	.75	1.50
33 Exeggcute U	.60	1.50
34 Haunter U	4.00	8.00
35 Ivysaur U	7.50	15.00
36 Kakuna U	7.50	15.00
37 Lickitung U	.75	1.50
38 Mankey U	.25	.50
39 Metapod U	.08	.20
40 Nidorina U	.50	1.25
41 Nidorino U	1.25	2.50
42 Onix U	1.25	2.50
43 Parasect U	.60	1.25
44 Persian U	20.00	50.00
45 Pidgeotto U	.75	1.50
46 Poliwhirl U	1.50	3.00
47 Porygon U	2.00	4.00
48 Raticate U	1.50	3.00
49 Venomoth U	2.00	4.00
50 Wartortle U	.75	1.50
51 Weepinbell U	.01	.08
52 Wigglytuff U	.05	.12
53 Bellsprout C	1.00	2.00
54 Bulbasaur C	1.00	2.00
55 Bulbasaur C	2.00	4.00
56 Caterpie C	.75	1.50
57 Charmander C	.07	.15
58 Charmander C	.75	1.50
59 Clefairy C	.50	1.00
60 Cubone C	.25	.50
61 Diglett C	1.25	2.50
62 Doduo C	.08	.20
63 Gastly C	.60	1.25
64 Growlithe C	.07	.15
65 Jigglypuff C	.07	.15
66 Krabby C	1.25	2.50
67 Magikarp C	.50	1.00
68 Magnemite C	.75	1.50
69 Meowth C	.75	1.50
70 Nidoran F C	.08	.20
71 Nidoran M C	.10	.25
72 Paras C	2.50	5.00
73 Pidgey C	.12	.25
74 Pikachu C	1.00	2.00
75 Poliwag C	1.25	2.50
76 Ponyta C	1.00	2.00
77 Rattata C	.10	.20
78 Seel C	.10	.20
79 Shellder C	.25	.50
80 Slowpoke C	200.00	500.00
81 Spearow C	6.00	12.00
82 Squirtle C	5.00	10.00
83 Squirtle C	5.00	10.00
84 Venonat C	250.00	500.00
85 Voltorb C	30.00	75.00
86 Weedle C	12.50	25.00
87 Bill's Maintenance U	6.00	12.00
88 Celio's Network U	4.00	8.00
89 Energy Removal 2 U	2.50	5.00
90 Energy Switch U	1.50	3.00
91 EXP.ALL U	.75	1.50
92 Great Ball U	.75	1.50
93 Life Herb U	1.00	2.00
94 Mt. Moon U	.07	.15
95 Poke Ball U	2.00	4.00
96 PokeDEX HANDY 909 U	.30	.75
97 Pokemon Reversal U	.60	1.25
98 Professor Oak's Research U	40.00	80.00
99 Super Scoop Up U	2.50	5.00
100 VS Seeker U	2.50	5.00
101 Potion C	1.25	2.50
102 Switch C	1.00	2.00
103 Multi Energy HOLO R	1.00	2.00
104 Blastoise EX HOLO R	2.00	4.00
105 Charizard EX HOLO R	1.50	3.00
106 Clefable EX HOLO R	6.00	12.00
107 Electrode EX HOLO R	.40	1.00
108 Gengar EX HOLO R	.40	1.00
109 Gyarados EX HOLO R	.30	.75
110 Mr. Mime EX HOLO R	.07	.15
111 Mr. Mime EX HOLO R	.75	1.50
112 Venusaur EX HOLO R	1.00	2.00
113 Charmander HOLO R	2.00	4.00
114 Articuno EX HOLO R	12.50	25.00
115 Moltres EX HOLO R	1.25	2.50
116 Zapdos EX HOLO R	1.00	2.00

2004 Pokemon EX Hidden Legends

1 Banette HOLO R	2.00	4.00
2 Claydol HOLO R	.75	1.50
3 Crobat HOLO R	1.00	2.00
4 Dark Celebi HOLO R	1.25	2.50
5 Electrode HOLO R	10.00	25.00
6 Exploud HOLO R	5.00	10.00
7 Heracross HOLO R	2.50	5.00
8 Jirachi HOLO R	2.00	4.00
9 Machamp HOLO R	.08	.20
10 Medicham HOLO R	.05	.12
11 Metagross HOLO R	5.00	12.00
12 Milotic HOLO R	2.00	5.00
13 Pinsir HOLO R	.50	1.00
14 Shiftry HOLO R	15.00	40.00
15 Walrein HOLO R	4.00	10.00
16 Bellossom R	4.00	8.00
17 Chimecho R	125.00	300.00
18 Gorebyss R	2.50	5.00
19 Huntail R	1.50	4.00
20 Masquerain R	10.00	25.00
21 Metang R	2.50	5.00
22 Ninetales R	3.00	6.00
23 Rain Castform R	.75	1.50
24 Relicanth R	1.00	2.00
25 Snow-cloud Castform R	1.25	2.50
26 Sunny Castform R	.75	1.50
27 Tropius R	1.50	3.00
28 Beldum U	4.00	8.00
29 Beldum U	6.00	12.00
30 Castform U	30.00	80.00
31 Claydol U	.75	1.50
32 Corsola U	.75	1.50
33 Dodrio U	.75	1.50
34 Glalie U	2.00	4.00
35 Gloom U	.75	1.50
36 Golbat U	1.00	2.00
37 Igglybuff U	2.50	5.00

38 Lanturn U	.75	1.50
39 Loudred U	.50	1.00
40 Luvdisc U	.75	1.50
41 Machoke U	.01	.08
42 Medicham U	.04	.10
43 Metang U	3.00	6.00
44 Metang U	.07	.15
45 Nuzleaf U	.75	1.50
46 Rhydon U	.75	1.50
47 Sealeo U	1.00	2.00
48 Spinda U	.75	1.50
49 Starmie U	2.50	5.00
50 Swalot U	10.00	20.00
51 Tentacruel U	.75	1.50
52 Baltoy C	1.25	2.50
53 Baltoy C	2.00	4.00
54 Beldum C	1.00	2.00
55 Chikorita C	1.00	2.00
56 Chinchou C	3.00	6.00
57 Chinchou C	2.00	4.00
58 Clamperl C	2.50	5.00
59 Cyndaquil C	.75	1.50
60 Doduo C	2.50	5.00
61 Feebas C	.75	1.50
62 Gulpin C	1.00	2.00
63 Jigglypuff C	.60	1.25
64 Machop C	7.50	15.00
65 Meditite C	.75	1.50
66 Meditite C	7.50	15.00
67 Minun C	25.00	50.00
68 Oddish C	1.00	2.00
69 Plusle C	.75	1.50
70 Rhyhorn C	40.00	100.00
71 Seedot C	.10	.20
72 Shuppet C	1.50	3.00
73 Snorunt C	1.00	2.00
74 Spheal C	1.25	2.50
75 Staryu C	2.50	5.00
76 Surskit C	.75	1.50
77 Tentacool C	.25	.50
78 Togepi C	.04	.10
79 Totodile C	.08	.20
80 Voltorb C	1.00	2.00
81 Vulpix C	.04	.10
82 Whismur C	.04	.10
83 Zubat C	1.50	3.00
84 Ancient Technical Machine [Ice] U	.07	.15
85 Ancient Technical Machine [Rock] U	10.00	20.00
86 Ancient Technical Machine [Steel] U	.75	1.50
87 Ancient Tomb U	3.00	6.00
88 Desert Ruins U	.60	1.25
89 Island Cave U	1.00	2.00
90 Life Herb U	1.00	2.00
91 Magnetic Storm U	1.50	3.00
92 Steven's Advice U	.75	1.50
93 Groudon EX HOLO R	7.50	15.00
94 Kyogre EX HOLO R	.75	1.50
95 Metagross EX HOLO R	.30	.75
96 Ninetales EX HOLO R	.10	.20
97 Regice EX HOLO R	.75	1.50
98 Regirock EX HOLO R	.07	.15
99 Registeel EX HOLO R	.75	1.50
100 Vileplume EX HOLO R	.60	1.25
101 Wigglytuff EX HOLO R	.75	1.50
102 Groudon HOLO R	1.25	2.50

2004 Pokemon EX Team Magma vs. Team Aqua

1 Team Aqua's Cacturne HOLO R	1.25	2.50
2 Team Aqua's Crawdaunt HOLO R	.08	.20
3 Team Aqua's Kyogre HOLO R	1.25	2.50
4 Team Aqua's Manectric HOLO R	100.00	250.00
5 Team Aqua's Sharpedo HOLO R	4.00	8.00
6 Team Aqua's Walrein HOLO R	3.00	6.00
7 Team Magma's Aggron HOLO R	15.00	30.00
8 Team Magma's Claydol HOLO R	2.00	4.00
9 Team Magma's Groudon HOLO R	7.50	15.00
10 Team Magma's Houndoom HOLO R	4.00	8.00
11 Team Magma's Rhydon HOLO R	1.25	2.50
12 Team Magma's Torkoal HOLO R	.15	.30
13 Raichu R	.75	1.50
14 Team Aqua's Crawdaunt R	.60	1.25
15 Team Aqua's Mightyena R	.08	.20
16 Team Aqua's Sealeo R	.12	.30
17 Team Aqua's Seviper R	.30	.75
18 Team Aqua's Sharpedo R	1.50	3.00
19 Team Magma's Camerupt R	.75	1.50
20 Team Magma's Lairon R	1.50	3.00
21 Team Magma's Mightyena R	4.00	8.00
22 Team Magma's Rhydon R	.75	1.50
23 Team Magma's Zangoose R	1.50	3.00
24 Team Aqua's Cacnea U	2.50	5.00
25 Team Aqua's Carvanha U	.60	1.50
26 Team Aqua's Corphish U	.40	1.00
27 Team Aqua's Electrike U	.50	1.25
28 Team Aqua's Lanturn U	5.00	10.00
29 Team Aqua's Manectric U	1.50	3.00
30 Team Aqua's Mightyena U	.60	1.25
31 Team Aqua's Sealeo U	1.50	3.00
32 Team Magma's Baltoy U	1.00	2.00
33 Team Magma's Claydol U	12.50	25.00
34 Team Magma's Houndoom U	3.00	6.00
35 Team Magma's Houndour U	3.00	6.00
36 Team Magma's Lairon U	1.00	2.00
37 Team Magma's Mightyena U	1.25	2.50
38 Team Magma's Rhyhorn U	.75	1.50
39 Bulbasaur C	2.00	4.00
40 Cubone C	.60	1.25
41 Jigglypuff C	3.00	8.00
42 Meowth C	7.50	15.00
43 Pikachu C	7.50	15.00
44 Psyduck C	.75	1.50
45 Slowpoke C	.60	1.25
46 Squirtle C	2.00	4.00
47 Team Aqua's Carvanha C	.30	.60
48 Team Aqua's Carvanha C	.75	1.50
49 Team Aqua's Chinchou C	.01	.08
50 Team Aqua's Corphish C	.04	.10
51 Team Aqua's Corphish C	.10	.20
52 Team Aqua's Electrike C	20.00	50.00
53 Team Aqua's Electrike C	6.00	15.00
54 Team Aqua's Poochyena C	12.00	30.00
55 Team Aqua's Poochyena C	2.50	6.00
56 Team Aqua's Spheal C	4.00	8.00
57 Team Aqua's Spheal C	1.50	3.00
58 Team Magma's Aron C	40.00	100.00
59 Team Magma's Aron C	.75	1.50
60 Team Magma's Baltoy C	2.50	5.00
61 Team Magma's Baltoy C	1.00	2.00
62 Team Magma's Houndour C	1.25	2.50
63 Team Magma's Houndour C	1.25	2.50
64 Team Magma's Numel C	.40	.80
65 Team Magma's Poochyena C	1.50	3.00
66 Team Magma's Poochyena C	12.00	30.00
67 Team Magma's Rhyhorn C	3.00	8.00
68 Team Magma's Rhyhorn C	2.50	5.00
69 Team Aqua Schemer U	1.50	3.00
70 Team Magma Schemer U	3.00	6.00
71 Archie U	1.25	2.50
72 Dual Ball U	.60	1.25
73 Maxie U	1.25	2.50
74 Strength Charm U	.07	.15
75 Team Aqua Ball U	2.00	4.00
76 Team Aqua Belt U	.75	1.50
77 Team Aqua Conspirator U	.75	1.50
78 Team Aqua Hideout U	1.00	2.00
79 Team Aqua Technical Machine 01 U	1.00	2.00
80 Team Magma Ball U	1.50	3.00
81 Team Magma Belt U	.05	.12
82 Team Magma Conspirator U	.10	.25
83 Team Magma Hideout U	1.00	2.00
84 Team Magma Tech. Machine 01 U	7.50	15.00
85 Warp Point U	3.00	6.00
86 Aqua Energy U	25.00	60.00
87 Magma Energy U	.75	1.50
88 Double Rainbow Energy R	1.50	3.00
89 Blaziken EX HOLO R	.07	.15
90 Cradily EX HOLO R	.25	.50
91 Entei EX HOLO R	1.50	3.00
92 Raikou EX HOLO R	.10	.20
93 Sceptile EX HOLO R	.75	1.50
94 Suicune EX HOLO R	1.50	3.00
95 Swampert EX HOLO R	1.25	2.50
96 Absol HOLO R	.75	1.50
97 Jirachi HOLO R	.08	.20

2004 Pokemon EX Team Rocket Returns

1 Azumarill HOLO R	.04	.10
2 Dark Ampharos HOLO R	1.50	3.00
3 Dark Crobat HOLO R	1.00	2.00
4 Dark Electrode HOLO R	.60	1.25
5 Dark Houndoom HOLO R	1.00	2.00
6 Dark Hypno HOLO R	1.25	2.50
7 Dark Marowak HOLO R	10.00	20.00
8 Dark Octillery HOLO R	12.00	30.00
9 Dark Slowking HOLO R	60.00	125.00
10 Dark Steelix HOLO R	1.50	3.00
11 Jumpluff HOLO R	3.00	6.00
12 Kingdra HOLO R	.75	1.50
13 Piloswine HOLO R	1.00	2.00
14 Togetic HOLO R	2.50	5.00
15 Dark Dragonite R	3.00	6.00
16 Dark Muk R	.07	.15
17 Dark Raticate R	.75	1.50
18 Dark Sandslash R	1.50	3.00
19 Dark Tyranitar R	.75	1.50
20 Dark Tyranitar R	.75	1.50
21 Delibird R	3.00	6.00
22 Furret R	1.00	2.00
23 Ledian R	.75	1.50
24 Magby R	.75	1.50
25 Misdreavus R	2.00	4.00
26 Quagsire R	.75	1.50
27 Qwilfish R	.75	1.50
28 Yanma R	1.00	2.00
29 Dark Arbok U	.05	.12
30 Dark Ariados U	.10	.25
31 Dark Dragonair U	.25	.50
32 Dark Dragonair U	.01	.08
33 Dark Flaaffy U	.04	.10
34 Dark Golbat U	5.00	10.00
35 Dark Golduck U	.30	.75
36 Dark Gyarados U	1.50	3.00
37 Dark Houndoom U	4.00	8.00
38 Dark Magcargo U	1.25	2.50
39 Dark Magneton U	1.00	2.00
40 Dark Pupitar U	.50	1.00
41 Dark Pupitar U	1.25	2.50
42 Dark Weezing U	.75	1.50
43 Heracross U	.08	.20
44 Magmar U	.60	1.25
45 Mantine U	1.00	2.00
46 Rocket's Meowth U	7.50	15.00
47 Rocket's Wobbuffet U	.75	1.50
48 Seadra U	1.25	2.50
49 Skiploom U	.75	1.50
50 Togepi U	15.00	40.00
51 Cubone C	2.00	4.00
52 Dratini C	.75	1.50
53 Dratini C	10.00	20.00
54 Drowzee C	.12	.25
55 Ekans C	6.00	12.00
56 Grimer C	.75	1.50
57 Hoppip C	1.00	2.00
58 Horsea C	2.00	4.00
59 Houndour C	.50	1.00
60 Houndour C	.75	1.50
61 Koffing C	1.00	2.00
62 Larvitar C	1.25	2.50
63 Larvitar C	.12	.25
64 Ledyba C	1.25	2.50
65 Magikarp C	2.50	5.00
66 Magnemite C	1.00	2.00
67 Mareep C	1.50	3.00
68 Marill C	1.25	2.50
69 Onix C	1.25	2.50
70 Psyduck C	2.00	4.00
71 Rattata C	1.25	2.50
72 Rattata C	.01	.08
73 Remoraid C	.04	.10
74 Sandshrew C	8.00	20.00
75 Sentret C	1.50	3.00
76 Slowpoke C	1.50	3.00
77 Slugma C	2.00	4.00
78 Spinarak C	7.50	15.00
79 Swinub C	12.50	25.00
80 Voltorb C	7.50	15.00
81 Wooper C	25.00	50.00
82 Zubat C	1.00	2.00
83 Copycat U	.01	.08
84 Pokemon Retriever U	.04	.10
85 Pow! Hand Extension U	8.00	20.00
86 Rocket's Admin. U	.30	.60
87 Rocket's Hideout U	7.50	15.00
88 Rocket's Mission U	1.00	2.00
89 Rocket's Poke Ball U	.60	1.50
90 Rocket's Tricky Gym U	.60	1.50
91 Surprise! Time Machine U	.50	1.25
92 Swoop! Teleporter U	15.00	40.00
93 Venture Bomb U	10.00	20.00
94 Dark Metal Energy U	7.50	15.00
95 R Energy U	.75	1.50
96 Rocket's Articuno EX HOLO R	1.25	2.50
97 Rocket's Entei EX HOLO R	.60	1.25
98 Rocket's Hitmonchan EX HOLO R	1.50	3.00
99 Rocket's Mewtwo EX HOLO R	.75	1.50
100 Rocket's Moltres EX HOLO R	.12	.25
101 Rocket's Scizor EX HOLO R	.08	.20
102 Rocket's Scyther EX HOLO R	10.00	25.00
103 Rocket's Sneasel EX HOLO R	3.00	8.00
104 Rocket's Snorlax EX HOLO R	4.00	8.00
105 Rocket's Suicune EX HOLO R	50.00	120.00
106 Rocket's Zapdos EX HOLO R	2.50	5.00
107 Mudkip Gold Star HOLO R	1.25	2.50
108 Torchic Gold Star HOLO R	1.00	2.00
109 Treecko Gold Star HOLO R	1.50	3.00
110 Charmeleon SCR	6.00	12.00
111 Here Comes Team Rocket! SCR	2.00	4.00

2004 Pokemon EX Trainer Kit

2 Latios HOLO R	2.00	4.00
4 Latias HOLO R	.12	.25

2004 Pokemon Organized Play Series 1

1 Blaziken R	.75	1.50
2 Metagross R	.75	1.50
3 Rayquaza R	20.00	50.00
4 Sceptile R	4.00	10.00
5 Swampert R	3.00	6.00
6 Beautifly U	6.00	12.00
7 Masquerain U	.60	1.25
8 Murkrow U	1.50	3.00
9 Pupitar U	2.00	4.00
10 Torkoal U	2.00	4.00
11 Larvitar C	1.25	2.50
12 Minun C	.50	1.00
13 Plusle C	1.00	2.00
14 Surskit C	.75	1.50
15 Swellow C	.75	1.50
16 Armaldo EX R	1.50	3.00
17 Tyranitar EX R	12.00	30.00

2005 Pokemon EX Delta Species

1 Beedrill HOLO R	5.00	12.00
2 Crobat HOLO R	2.00	4.00
3 Dragonite HOLO R	6.00	12.00
4 Espeon HOLO R	.75	1.50
5 Flareon HOLO R	.30	.75
6 Gardevoir HOLO R	.75	1.50
7 Jolteon HOLO R	5.00	10.00
8 Latias HOLO R	2.50	5.00
9 Latios HOLO R	1.50	3.00
10 Marowak HOLO R	2.00	4.00
11 Metagross HOLO R	.75	1.50
12 Mewtwo HOLO R	1.00	2.00
13 Rayquaza HOLO R	.75	1.50
14 Salamence HOLO R	1.25	2.50
15 Starmie HOLO R	10.00	20.00
16 Tyranitar HOLO R	1.50	3.00
17 Umbreon HOLO R	1.50	3.00
18 Vaporeon HOLO R	60.00	125.00
19 Azumarill R	2.00	4.00
20 Azurill R	.07	.15
21 Holon's Electrode R	.75	1.50
22 Holon's Magneton R	.12	.25
23 Hypno R	.75	1.50
24 Mightyena R	5.00	10.00
25 Porygon2 R	.08	.20
26 Rain Castform R	.04	.10
27 Sandslash R	3.00	6.00
28 Slowking R	1.50	3.00
29 Snow-cloud Castform R	.75	1.50
30 Starmie R	1.25	2.50
31 Sunny Castform R	.04	.10
32 Swellow R	.08	.20
33 Weezing R	1.00	2.00
34 Castform U	3.00	6.00
35 Ditto U	2.00	4.00
36 Ditto U	.25	.50
37 Ditto U	.04	.10
38 Ditto U	.08	.20
39 Ditto (U)	12.50	25.00
40 Ditto U	7.50	15.00
41 Dragonair U	2.00	4.00
42 Dragonair U	40.00	100.00
43 Golbat U	2.50	5.00
44 Hariyama U	2.00	4.00
45 Illumise U	7.50	15.00
46 Kakuna U	1.50	3.00
47 Kirlia U	.07	.15
48 Magneton U	1.00	2.00
49 Metang U	2.00	4.00
50 Persian U	1.00	2.00
51 Pupitar U	.30	.75
52 Rapidash U	.07	.15
53 Shelgon U	1.50	3.00
54 Shelgon U	7.50	15.00
55 Skarmory U	.75	1.50
56 Volbeat U	1.50	3.00
57 Bagon C	1.00	2.00
58 Bagon C	1.00	2.00
59 Beldum C	2.50	5.00
60 Cubone C	1.50	3.00
61 Ditto C	7.50	15.00
62 Ditto C	1.25	2.50
63 Ditto C	1.25	2.50
64 Ditto C	.75	1.50
65 Dratini C	.60	1.25
66 Dratini C	2.50	5.00
67 Drowzee C	1.50	3.00
68 Eevee C	.60	1.25
69 Eevee C	.60	1.25
70 Holon's Magnemite C	.08	.20
71 Holon's Voltorb C	1.25	2.50
72 Koffing C	1.25	2.50
73 Larvitar C	12.00	30.00
74 Magnemite C	2.50	5.00
75 Makuhita C	2.50	5.00
76 Marill C	.04	.10
77 Meowth C	.05	.12
78 Ponyta C	5.00	12.00
79 Poochyena C	1.50	3.00
80 Porygon C	1.25	2.50
81 Ralts C	1.25	2.50
82 Sandshrew C	1.00	2.00
83 Slowpoke C	.60	1.25
84 Staryu C	1.50	3.00
85 Staryu C	1.50	3.00
86 Taillow C	.75	1.50
87 Weedle C	40.00	100.00
88 Zubat C	7.50	15.00
89 Dual Ball U	1.00	2.00
90 Great Ball U	3.00	6.00
91 Holon Farmer U	1.25	2.50
92 Holon Lass U	2.50	6.00
93 Holon Mentor U	2.00	5.00
94 Holon Research Tower U	.75	1.50
95 Holon Researcher U	6.00	15.00
96 Holon Ruins U	3.00	8.00
97 Holon Scientist U	4.00	8.00
98 Holon Transceiver U	40.00	100.00
99 Master Ball U	1.50	3.00
100 Super Scoop Up U	.17	.35
101 Potion C	.15	.40
102 Switch C	3.00	6.00
103 Darkness Energy R	.60	1.25
104 Holon Energy FF R	1.50	3.00
105 Holon Energy GL R	1.25	2.50
106 Holon Energy WP R	.50	1.00
107 Metal Energy R	1.00	2.00
108 Flareon EX HOLO R	1.00	2.00
109 Jolteon EX HOLO R	.60	1.25
110 Vaporeon EX HOLO R	6.00	12.00
111 Groudon Gold Star HOLO R	5.00	12.00
112 Kyogre Gold Star HOLO R	2.50	6.00
113 Metagross Gold Star HOLO R	1.50	3.00
114 Azumarill SCR	3.00	6.00

2005 Pokemon EX Deoxys

1 Altaria HOLO R	2.50	5.00
2 Beautifly HOLO R	2.50	5.00
3 Breloom HOLO R	1.00	2.00
4 Camerupt HOLO R	3.00	6.00
5 Claydol HOLO R	.75	1.50
6 Crawdaunt HOLO R	5.00	12.00
7 Dusclops HOLO R	2.00	5.00
8 Gyarados HOLO R	.75	1.50
9 Jirachi HOLO R	1.25	2.50
10 Ludicolo HOLO R	50.00	100.00
11 Metagross HOLO R	10.00	20.00
12 Mightyena HOLO R	.01	.08
13 Ninjask HOLO R	.05	.12
14 Shedinja HOLO R	2.00	4.00
15 Slaking HOLO R	.60	1.25
16 Deoxys (Normal) R	.60	1.25
17 Deoxys (Attack) R	2.00	4.00
18 Deoxys (Defense) R	.10	.20
19 Ludicolo R	.75	1.50
20 Magcargo R	.12	.25
21 Pelipper R	1.25	2.50
22 Rayquaza R	1.25	2.50
23 Sableye R	.60	1.25
24 Seaking R	.75	1.50
25 Shiftry R	4.00	8.00
26 Skarmory R	1.50	3.00
27 Tropius R	1.50	3.00
28 Whiscash R	.75	1.50
29 Xatu R	2.00	4.00
30 Donphan U	.75	1.50
31 Golbat U	1.00	2.00
32 Grumpig U	12.50	25.00
33 Lombre U	30.00	60.00
34 Lombre U	1.25	2.50
35 Lotad U	1.50	3.00
36 Lunatone U	.60	1.25
37 Magcargo U	1.50	3.00
38 Manectric U	1.25	2.50
39 Masquerain U	.75	1.50
40 Metang U	2.00	4.00
41 Minun U	4.00	8.00
42 Nosepass U	.50	1.25
43 Nuzleaf U	.15	.40
44 Plusle U	1.25	2.50
45 Shelgon U	.04	.10
46 Silcoon U	.04	.10

47 Solrock U	.75	1.50
48 Starmie U	.60	1.25
49 Swellow U	.07	.15
50 Vigoroth U	1.00	2.00
51 Weezing U	.60	1.25
52 Bagon C	1.00	2.00
53 Baltoy C	7.50	15.00
54 Barboach C	1.25	2.50
55 Beldum C	1.50	3.00
56 Carvanha C	1.00	2.00
57 Corphish C	.10	.20
58 Duskull C	.08	.20
59 Electrike C	.08	.20
60 Electrike C	1.25	2.50
61 Goldeen C	1.25	2.50
62 Koffing C	1.00	2.00
63 Lotad C	.07	.15
64 Magikarp C	3.00	6.00
65 Makuhita C	.07	.15
66 Natu C	.75	1.50
67 Nincada C	.12	.25
68 Numel C	.25	.50
69 Phanpy C	.01	.08
70 Poochyena C	.25	.60
71 Seedot C	1.25	2.50
72 Shroomish C	1.00	2.00
73 Slakoth C	1.50	3.00
74 Slugma C	.75	1.50
75 Slugma C	1.00	2.00
76 Spoink C	1.25	2.50
77 Staryu C	1.50	3.00
78 Surskit C	.75	1.50
79 Swablu C	1.25	2.50
80 Taillow C	1.00	2.00
81 Wingull C	1.25	2.50
82 Wurmple C	.75	1.50
83 Zubat C	1.00	2.00
84 Balloon Berry U	7.50	15.00
85 Crystal Shard U	1.25	2.50
86 Energy Charge U	1.50	3.00
87 Lady Outing U	.75	1.50
88 Master Ball U	2.00	4.00
89 Meteor Falls U	2.00	4.00
90 Professor Cozmo's Discovery U	1.50	3.00
91 Space Center U	1.00	2.00
92 Strength Charm U	.75	1.50
93 Boost Energy U	1.50	3.00
94 Healing Energy U	.07	.15
95 Scramble Energy U	5.00	10.00
96 Crobat EX HOLO R	4.00	10.00
97 Deoxys EX (Normal) HOLO R	4.00	10.00
98 Deoxys EX (Attack) HOLO R	.60	1.25
99 Deoxys EX (Defense) HOLO R	.50	1.00
100 Hariyama EX HOLO R	.75	1.50
101 Manectric EX HOLO R	.75	1.50
102 Rayquaza EX HOLO R	.30	.75
103 Salamence EX HOLO R	.75	1.50
104 Sharpedo EX HOLO R	6.00	12.00
105 Latias Gold Star HOLO R	1.50	3.00
106 Latios Gold Star HOLO R	.50	1.00
107 Rayquaza Gold Star HOLO R	1.50	3.00
108 Rocket's Raikou EX HOLO R	.75	1.50

2005 Pokemon EX Emerald

1 Blaziken HOLO R	12.00	30.00
2 Deoxys HOLO R	.60	1.25
3 Exploud HOLO R	.07	.15
4 Gardevoir HOLO R	2.50	5.00
5 Groudon HOLO R	2.00	4.00
6 Kyogre HOLO R	1.25	2.50
7 Manectric HOLO R	.75	1.50
8 Milotic HOLO R	1.00	2.00
9 Rayquaza HOLO R	4.00	10.00
10 Sceptile HOLO R	1.50	3.00
11 Swampert HOLO R	.25	.50
12 Chimecho R	.04	.10
13 Glalie R	.10	.25
14 Groudon R	1.25	2.50
15 Kyogre R	.12	.25
16 Manectric R	.50	1.25
17 Nosepass R	1.25	2.50
18 Relicanth R	1.25	2.50
19 Rhydon R	1.25	2.50
20 Seviper R	.75	1.50
21 Zangoose R	4.00	8.00
22 Breloom U	.75	1.50
23 Camerupt U	1.00	2.00
24 Claydol U	1.00	2.00
25 Combusken U	1.25	2.50
26 Dodrio U	1.25	2.50
27 Electrode U	4.00	10.00
28 Grovyle U	2.50	6.00
29 Grumpig U	5.00	10.00
30 Grumpig U	2.50	5.00
31 Hariyama U	2.00	4.00
32 Illumise U	2.50	5.00
33 Kirlia U	.01	.08
34 Linoone U	.05	.12
35 Loudred U	3.00	6.00
36 Marshtomp U	.25	.50
37 Minun U	1.50	3.00
38 Ninetales U	7.50	15.00
39 Plusle U	20.00	40.00
40 Swalot U	.10	.20
41 Swellow U	1.00	2.00
42 Volbeat U	.75	1.50
43 Baltoy C	.75	1.50
44 Cacnea C	.12	.25
45 Doduo C	.12	.25
46 Duskull C	2.00	4.00
47 Electrike C	.75	1.50
48 Electrike C	3.00	6.00
49 Feebas C	2.50	5.00
50 Feebas C	1.00	2.00
51 Gulpin C	7.50	15.00
52 Larvitar C	3.00	6.00
53 Luvdisc C	3.00	6.00
54 Makuhita C	1.00	2.00
55 Meditite C	5.00	12.00
56 Mudkip C	2.50	6.00
57 Numel C	12.50	25.00
58 Numel C	2.50	5.00
59 Pichu C	.75	1.50
60 Pikachu C	.25	.50
61 Ralts C	.60	1.25
62 Rhyhorn C	30.00	75.00
63 Shroomish C	10.00	25.00
64 Snorunt C	4.00	10.00
65 Spoink C	4.00	8.00
66 Spoink C	40.00	100.00
67 Swablu C	.25	.60
68 Taillow C	.20	.50
69 Torchic C	1.25	2.50
70 Treecko C	.75	1.50
71 Voltorb C	12.50	25.00
72 Vulpix C	.12	.25
73 Whismur C	1.50	3.00
74 Zigzagoon C	.50	1.00
75 Battle Frontier U	1.00	2.00
76 Double Full Heal U	6.00	12.00
77 Lanette's Net Search U	.60	1.25
78 Lum Berry U	.75	1.50
79 Mr. Stone's Project U	1.25	2.50
80 Oran Berry U	.60	1.25
81 Pokenav U	2.00	4.00
82 Professor Birch U	.25	.60
83 Rare Candy U	1.00	2.00
84 Scott U	2.00	4.00
85 Wally's Training U	.75	1.50
86 Darkness Energy R	1.50	3.00
87 Double Rainbow Energy R	.75	1.50
88 Metal Energy R	.30	.75
89 Mutli Energy R	.04	.10
90 Altaria EX HOLO R	.10	.25
91 Cacturne EX HOLO R	.50	1.00
92 Camerupt EX HOLO R	1.25	2.50
93 Deoxys EX HOLO R	1.50	3.00
94 Dusclops EX HOLO R	.30	.75
95 Medicham EX HOLO R	.60	1.25
96 Milotic EX HOLO R	.75	1.50
97 Raichu EX HOLO R	1.25	2.50
98 Regice EX HOLO R	1.25	2.50
99 Regirock HOLO R	1.25	2.50
100 Registeel HOLO R	12.50	25.00
101 Grass Energy HOLO	2.50	5.00
102 Fire Energy HOLO	1.25	2.50
103 Water Energy HOLO	2.50	5.00
104 Lightning Energy HOLO	.08	.20
105 Psychic Energy HOLO	.10	.25
106 Fighting Energy HOLO	2.00	4.00
107 Farfetch'd SCR	.60	1.25

2005 Pokemon EX Unseen Forces

1 Ampharos HOLO R	1.00	2.00
2 Ariados HOLO R	2.50	5.00
3 Bellossom HOLO R	2.00	4.00
4 Feraligatr HOLO R	1.00	2.00
5 Flareon HOLO R	1.00	2.00
6 Forretress HOLO R	.25	.50
7 Houndoom HOLO R	.12	.25
8 Jolteon HOLO R	8.00	20.00
9 Meganium HOLO R	1.00	2.50
10 Octillery HOLO R	2.50	5.00
11 Poliwrath HOLO R	60.00	150.00
12 Porygon 2 HOLO R	.75	1.50
13 Slowbro HOLO R	1.00	2.00
14 Slowking HOLO R	1.00	2.00
15 Sudowoodo HOLO R	.07	.15
16 Sunflora HOLO R	5.00	12.00
17 Typhlosion HOLO R	7.50	15.00
18 Ursaring HOLO R	.08	.20
19 Vaporeon HOLO R	.60	1.25
20 Chansey R	1.50	3.00
21 Cleffa R	.50	1.00
22 Electabuzz R	.60	1.25
23 Elekid R	1.00	2.00
24 Hitmonchan R	1.50	3.00
25 Hitmonlee R	2.00	4.00
26 Hitmontop R	1.50	3.00
27 Ho-Oh R	.60	1.25
28 Jynx R	1.50	3.00
29 Lugia R	3.00	8.00
30 Murkrow R	1.25	2.50
31 Smoochum R	.75	1.50
32 Stantler R	1.50	3.00
33 Tyrogue R	5.00	10.00
34 Aipom U	1.00	2.00
35 Bayleef U	.25	.50
36 Clefable U	.04	.10
37 Corsola U	.05	.12
38 Croconaw U	2.50	5.00
39 Granbull U	.01	.08
40 Lanturn U	.01	.08
41 Magcargo U	1.25	2.50
42 Miltank U	1.50	3.00
43 Noctowl U	.60	1.25
44 Quagsire U	1.00	2.00
45 Quilava U	.60	1.25
46 Scyther U	.50	1.00
47 Shuckle U	.75	1.50
48 Smeargle U	.08	.20
49 Xatu U	.04	.10
50 Yanma U	8.00	20.00
51 Chikorita C	2.50	5.00
52 Chinchou C	.75	1.50
53 Clefairy C	1.25	2.50
54 Cyndaquil C	1.50	3.00
55 Eevee C	1.00	2.00
56 Flaaffy C	7.50	15.00
57 Gligar C	5.00	12.00
58 Gloom C	2.00	5.00
59 Hoothoot C	2.50	5.00
60 Houndour C	.75	1.50
61 Larvitar C	1.50	3.00
62 Mareep C	1.50	3.00
63 Natu C	2.00	4.00
64 Oddish C	1.25	2.50
65 Onix C	1.25	2.50
66 Pineco C	.75	1.50
67 Poliwag C	1.25	2.50
68 Poliwhirl C	1.00	2.00
69 Porygon C	7.50	15.00
70 Pupitar C	1.25	2.50
71 Remoraid C	3.00	8.00
72 Slowpoke C	2.00	4.00
73 Slugma C	1.00	2.00
74 Snubbull C	1.50	3.00
75 Spinarak C	2.50	5.00
76 Sunkern C	.75	1.50
77 Teddiursa C	.07	.15
78 Totodile C	4.00	8.00
79 Wooper C	6.00	15.00
80 Curse Powder U	2.50	6.00
81 EnergyRecycle System U	.12	.25
82 EnergyRemoval 2 U	1.25	2.50
83 EnergyRoot U	.60	1.25
84 Energy Switch U	.75	1.50
85 Fluffy Berry U	15.00	30.00
86 Mary'sRequest U	3.00	6.00
87 Poke Ball U	1.25	2.50
88 PokemonReversal U	1.00	2.00
89 Professor Elm's Training Method U	.30	.75
90 Protective Orb U	25.00	50.00
91 Sitrus Berry U	.30	.75
92 SolidRage U	2.00	5.00
93 Warp Point U	.75	1.50
94 Energy Search C	.75	1.50
95 Potion C	1.25	2.50
96 Darkness Energy R	.30	.75
97 Metal Energy R	.12	.25
98 Boost Energy U	1.25	2.50
99 Cyclone Energy U	.75	1.50
100 Warp Energy U	.75	1.50
101 Blissey EX UR HOLO	2.50	5.00
102 Espeon EX UR HOLO	1.50	3.00
103 Feraligatr EX UR HOLO	.01	.08
104 Ho-Oh EX UR HOLO	.05	.12
105 Lugia EX UR HOLO	2.50	5.00
106 Meganium EX UR HOLO	.60	1.25
107 Politoed EX UR HOLO	1.25	2.50
108 Scizor EX UR HOLO	2.00	4.00
109 Steelix EX UR HOLO	.75	1.50
110 Typhlosion EX UR HOLO	.75	1.50
111 Tyranitar EX UR HOLO	.75	1.50
112 Umbreon EX UR HOLO	.75	1.50
113 Entei Gold Star HOLO R	.50	1.00
114 Raikou Gold Star HOLO R	.75	1.50
115 Suicune Gold Star HOLO R	.20	.50
116 Rocket's Persian EX HOLO R	6.00	12.00
117 Celebi EX SCR	.75	1.50

2005 Pokemon EX Unseen Forces Unown

A Unown A HOLO R	.75	1.50
B Unown B HOLO R	1.25	2.50
C Unown C HOLO R	1.25	2.50
D Unown D HOLO R	1.50	3.00
E Unown E HOLO R	2.50	5.00
F Unown F HOLO R	3.00	6.00
G Unown G HOLO R	2.50	5.00
H Unown H HOLO R	.75	1.50
I Unown I HOLO R	.75	1.50
J Unown J HOLO R	1.00	2.00
K Unown K HOLO R	.60	1.25
L Unown L HOLO R	.75	1.50
M Unown N HOLO R	.10	.20
N Unown M HOLO R	2.00	4.00
O Unown O HOLO R	1.00	2.00
P Unown P HOLO R	2.00	4.00
Q Unown Q HOLO R	1.00	2.00
R Unown R HOLO R	.12	.25
S Unown S HOLO R	.75	1.50
T Unown T HOLO R	1.50	3.00
U Unown U HOLO R	4.00	8.00
V Unown V HOLO R	.25	.50
W Unown W HOLO R	.60	1.50
X Unown X HOLO R	1.25	2.50
Y Unown Y HOLO R	.75	1.50
Z Unown Z HOLO R	.75	1.50
QM Unown ? HOLO R	1.00	2.00
EP Unown ! HOLO R	.10	.20

2005 Pokemon Organized Play Series 2

1 Entei R	5.00	12.00
2 Pidgeot R	.75	1.50
3 Raikou R	1.25	2.50
4 Suicune R	.08	.20
5 Tauros R	3.00	8.00
6 Venusaur R	.50	1.25
7 Ivysaur U	2.50	5.00
8 Mr. Briney's Compassion U	.75	1.50
9 Multi Technical Machine 01 U	1.00	2.00
10 Pokémon Park U	50.00	120.00
11 TV Reporter U	.60	1.25
12 Bulbasaur C	1.00	2.00
13 Cacnea C	1.00	2.00
14 Luvdisc C	7.50	15.00
15 Phanpy C	1.50	3.00
16 Pikachu C	1.50	3.00
17 Celebi EX R	.75	1.50

2006 Pokemon EX Crystal Guardians

1 Banette HOLO R	.08	.20
2 Blastoise HOLO R	.08	.20
3 Camerupt HOLO R	3.00	8.00
4 Charizard HOLO R	.75	1.50
5 Dugtrio HOLO R	.30	.75
6 Ludicolo HOLO R	5.00	10.00
7 Luvdisc HOLO R	1.50	3.00
8 Manectric HOLO R	1.00	2.00
9 Mawile HOLO R	1.00	2.00
10 Sableye HOLO R	1.25	2.50
11 Swalot HOLO R	.30	.75
12 Tauros HOLO R	.75	1.50
13 Wigglytuff HOLO R	.04	.10
14 Blastoise R	.08	.20
15 Cacturne R	1.50	3.00
16 Combusken R	.60	1.25
17 Dusclops R	2.50	5.00
18 Fearow R	.12	.25
19 Grovyle R	5.00	12.00
20 Grumpig R	1.50	3.00
21 Igglybuff R	.75	1.50
22 Kingler R	1.25	2.50
23 Loudred R	7.50	15.00
24 Marshtomp R	2.50	5.00
25 Medicham R	1.25	2.50
26 Pelipper R	.60	1.25
27 Swampert R	.75	1.50
28 Venusaur R	2.00	4.00
29 Charmeleon U	15.00	30.00
30 Charmeleon U	5.00	12.00
31 Combusken U	2.00	5.00
32 Grovyle U	1.00	2.00
33 Gulpin U	1.25	2.50
34 Ivysaur U	.07	.15
35 Ivysaur U	.15	.40
36 Lairon U	3.00	6.00
37 Lombre U	10.00	20.00
38 Marshtomp U	.75	1.50
39 Nuzleaf U	.07	.15
40 Shuppet U	.60	1.25
41 Skitty U	.75	1.50
42 Wartortle U	2.00	4.00
43 Wartortle U	1.00	2.00
44 Aron C	1.25	2.50
45 Bulbasaur C	.25	.50
46 Bulbasaur C	.75	1.50
47 Cacnea C	1.00	2.00
48 Charmander C	2.00	4.00
49 Charmander C	2.00	4.00
50 Diglett C	10.00	20.00
51 Duskull C	3.00	6.00
52 Electrike C	3.00	6.00
53 Jigglypuff C	2.50	6.00
54 Krabby C	4.00	8.00
55 Lotad C	1.25	2.50
56 Meditite C	2.00	4.00
57 Mudkip C	5.00	12.00
58 Mudkip C	2.00	5.00
59 Numel C	1.50	3.00
60 Seedot C	.75	1.50
61 Spearow C	7.50	15.00
62 Spoink C	1.50	3.00
63 Squirtle C	.20	.50
64 Squirtle C	1.00	2.00
65 Torchic C	12.50	25.00
66 Torchic C	.25	.60
67 Treecko C	.75	1.50
68 Treecko C	1.00	2.00
69 Whismur C	1.00	2.00
70 Wingull C	1.00	2.00
71 Bill's Maintenance U	.30	.75
72 Castaway U	.60	1.25
73 Celio's Network U	.04	.10
74 Cessation Crystal U	.08	.20
75 Crystal Beach U	.75	1.50
76 Crystal Shard U	.60	1.50
77 Double Full Heal U	1.25	2.50
78 Dual Ball U	1.50	3.00
79 Holon Circle U	.75	1.50
80 Memory Berry U	.60	1.25
81 Mysterious Shard U	.75	1.50
82 Poke Ball U	1.25	2.50
83 PokeNav U	2.50	5.00
84 Warp Point U	1.00	2.00
85 Windstorm U	.10	.20
86 Energy Search C	.75	1.50
87 Potion C	.75	1.50
88 Double Rainbow Energy R	6.00	12.00
89 Aggron EX HOLO R	1.00	2.00
90 Blaziken EX HOLO R	.75	1.50
91 Delcatty EX HOLO R	2.00	4.00
92 Exploud EX HOLO R	1.25	2.50
93 Groudon EX HOLO R	2.00	4.00
94 Jirachi EX HOLO R	.04	.10
95 Kyogre EX HOLO R	.10	.25
96 Sceptile EX HOLO R	12.50	25.00
97 Shiftry EX HOLO R	.75	1.50
98 Swampert EX HOLO R	1.00	2.00
99 Alakazam GOLD STAR HOLO R	.07	.15
100 Celebi GOLD STAR HOLO R	.75	1.50

2006 Pokemon EX Dragon Frontiers

1 Ampharos HOLO R	.75	1.50
2 Feraligatr HOLO R	6.00	12.00
3 Heracross HOLO R	7.50	15.00
4 Meganium HOLO R	2.00	4.00
5 Milotic HOLO R	2.50	5.00
6 Nidoking HOLO R	2.00	4.00
7 Nidoqueen HOLO R	.75	1.50
8 Ninetales HOLO R	.75	1.50
9 Pinsir HOLO R	.75	1.50
10 Snorlax HOLO R	.75	1.50
11 Togetic HOLO R	.75	1.50
12 Typhlosion HOLO R	2.00	4.00
13 Arbok R	.40	.80
14 Cloyster R	.75	1.50
15 Dewgong R	1.50	3.00
16 Gligar R	3.00	6.00
17 Jynx R	1.00	2.00
18 Ledian R	1.25	2.50
19 Lickitung R	6.00	12.00
20 Mantine R	7.50	15.00
21 Quagsire R	.75	1.50
22 Seadra R	4.00	8.00
23 Tropius R	.50	1.00
24 Vibrava R	.08	.20
25 Xatu R	.04	.10

26 Bayleef U 2.50 5.00
27 Croconaw U 2.50 5.00
28 Dragonair U .75 1.50
29 Electabuzz U 1.25 2.50
30 Flaaffy U 10.00 20.00
31 Horsea U .75 1.50
32 Kirlia U 10.00 25.00
33 Kirlia U 5.00 10.00
34 Nidorina U 2.00 4.00
35 Nidorino U 2.50 6.00
36 Quilava U 1.00 2.50
37 Seadra U 2.50 5.00
38 Shelgon U 8.00 20.00
39 Smeargle U .75 1.50
40 Swellow U .75 1.50
41 Togepi U 1.00 2.00
42 Vibrava U 1.50 3.00
43 Bagon C .50 1.00
44 Chikorita C .60 1.25
45 Cyndaquil C 2.00 4.00
46 Dratini C 1.00 2.00
47 Ekans C .75 1.50
48 Elekid C .15 .30
49 Feebas C 5.00 12.00
50 Horsea C .75 1.50
51 Larvitar C .07 .15
52 Larvitar C 3.00 6.00
53 Ledyba C .75 1.50
54 Mareep C .75 1.50
55 Natu C 1.00 2.00
56 Nidoran C .75 1.50
57 Nidoran C 2.50 5.00
58 Pupitar C .75 1.50
59 Pupitar C .75 1.50
60 Ralts C 1.00 2.00
61 Ralts C .60 1.25
62 Seel C 5.00 10.00
63 Shellder C 1.25 2.50
64 Smoochum C 6.00 12.00
65 Swablu C .25 .60
66 Taillow C 6.00 12.00
67 Totodile C 5.00 12.00
68 Trapinch C 2.00 4.00
69 Trapinch C .10 .20
70 Vulpix C 5.00 12.00
71 Wooper C 2.00 5.00
72 Buffer Piece U 1.50 3.00
73 Copycat U 1.00 2.00
74 Holon Legacy U 12.50 25.00
75 Holon Mentor U 1.25 2.50
76 Island Hermit U .75 1.50
77 Mr. Stone's Project U .75 1.50
78 Old Rod U 1.00 2.00
79 Professor Elm's Training Method U .75 1.50
80 Professor Oak's Research U 2.50 5.00
81 Strength Charm U 20.00 40.00
82 TV Reporter U 1.50 3.00
83 Switch C 1.00 2.00
84 Holon Energy FF R 2.00 4.00
85 Holon Energy GL R .30 .60
86 Holon Energy WP R .60 1.25
87 Boost Energy U .01 .08
88 Rainbow Energy U .05 .12
89 Scramble Energy U 6.00 12.00
90 Altaria EX HOLO R 1.00 2.00
91 Dragonite EX HOLO R 1.25 2.50
92 Flygon EX HOLO R 2.00 4.00
93 Gardevoir EX HOLO R .75 1.50
94 Kingdra EX HOLO R .25 .50
95 Latias EX HOLO R 2.50 5.00
96 Latios EX HOLO R .60 1.25
97 Rayquaza EX HOLO R 1.00 2.00
98 Salamence EX HOLO R 2.50 5.00
99 Tyranitar EX HOLO R .04 .10
100 Charizard Gold Star HOLO R .10 .25
101 Mew Gold Star HOLO R 5.00 12.00

2006 Pokemon EX Holon Phantoms

1 Armaldo HOLO R 2.00 5.00
2 Cradily HOLO R .60 1.25
3 Deoxys Attack HOLO R 15.00 30.00
4 Deoxys Defense HOLO R 2.00 4.00
5 Deoxys Normal HOLO R 2.00 4.00
6 Deoxys Speed HOLO R .60 1.50
7 Flygon HOLO R 30.00 75.00
8 Gyarados HOLO R .60 1.50
9 Kabutops HOLO R .07 .15
10 Kingdra HOLO R .50 1.25
11 Latias HOLO R 1.25 2.50
12 Latios HOLO R 1.50 3.00
13 Omastar HOLO R 1.50 3.00
14 Pidgeot HOLO R .08 .20
15 Raichu HOLO R .75 1.50
16 Rayquaza HOLO R 1.25 2.50
17 Vileplume HOLO R .60 1.25
18 Absol R 4.00 10.00
19 Bellossom R .30 .75
20 Blaziken R 1.50 3.00
21 Latias R 1.50 3.00
22 Latios R 7.50 15.00
23 Mawile R 1.00 2.00
24 Mewtwo R 4.00 10.00
25 Nosepass R .30 .60
26 Rayquaza R 1.25 2.50
27 Regice R 1.25 2.50
28 Regirock R 1.25 2.50
29 Registeel R .07 .15
30 Relicanth R .75 1.50
31 Sableye R 1.50 3.00
32 Seviper R 1.25 2.50
33 Torkoal R .75 1.50
34 Zangoose R 3.00 6.00
35 Aerodactyl U 7.50 15.00
36 Camerupt U 1.25 2.50
37 Chimecho U 1.00 2.00
38 Claydol U 1.25 2.50
39 Combusken U .75 1.50
40 Donphan U 1.00 2.00
41 Exeggutor U 1.00 2.00
42 Gloom U .12 .25
43 Golduck U .15 .40
44 Holon's Castform U .75 1.50
45 Lairon U 2.00 4.00
46 Manectric U .50 1.00
47 Masquerain U .75 1.50
48 Persian U 3.00 6.00
49 Pidgeotto U .40 .80
50 Primeape U .10 .20
51 Raichu U 1.00 2.00
52 Seadra U 1.50 4.00
53 Sharpedo U .30 .75
54 Vibrava U 1.25 2.50
55 Whiscash U 1.50 3.00
56 Wobbuffet U 1.25 2.50
57 Anorith C 1.25 2.50
58 Aron C 1.00 2.00
59 Baltoy C .10 .20
60 Barboach C .10 .20
61 Carvanha C 1.50 3.00
62 Corphish C 1.50 3.00
63 Corphish C .12 .25
64 Electrike C .08 .20
65 Exeggcute C .05 .12
66 Horsea C .08 .20
67 Kabuto C 1.00 2.00
68 Lileep C .75 1.50
69 Magikarp C .75 1.50
70 Mankey C 4.00 10.00
71 Meowth C 2.00 4.00
72 Numel C 1.00 2.00
73 Oddish C 3.00 6.00
74 Omanyte C 7.50 15.00
75 Phanpy C 2.50 6.00
76 Pichu C .60 1.50
77 Pidgey C 2.50 5.00
78 Pikachu C 2.00 4.00
79 Pikachu C 30.00 80.00
80 Poochyena C .75 1.50
81 Psyduck C 1.25 2.50
82 Surskit C .75 1.50
83 Torchic C .75 1.50
84 Trapinch C 1.50 3.00
85 Holon Adventurer U 1.50 3.00
86 Holon Fossil U 6.00 15.00
87 Holon Lake U .60 1.25
88 Mr. Stone's Project U .12 .25
89 Professor Cozmo's Discovery U 1.25 2.50
90 Rare Candy U 1.00 2.00
91 Claw Fossil C 2.50 5.00
92 Mysterious Fossil C .75 1.50
93 Root Fossil C .50 1.00
94 Darkness Energy R 2.00 4.00
95 Metal Energy R 7.50 15.00
96 Multi Energy R 2.00 4.00
97 d Rainbow Energy U .75 1.50
98 Dark Metal Energy U .50 1.00
99 Crawdaunt EX HOLO R .75 1.50
100 Mew EX HOLO R 2.50 5.00
101 Mightyena EX HOLO R 3.00 6.00
102 Gyarados Gold Star HOLO R 1.00 2.00
103 Mewtwo Gold Star HOLO R .75 1.50
104 Pikachu Gold Star HOLO R 1.25 2.50
105 Grass Energy HOLO R 2.50 5.00
106 Fire Energy HOLO R 2.50 5.00
107 Water Energy HOLO R .75 1.50
108 Lightning Energy HOLO R 1.25 2.50
109 Psychic Energy HOLO R 1.25 2.50
110 Fighting Energy HOLO R 1.25 2.50
111 Mew HOLO R 5.00 12.00

2006 Pokemon EX Legend Maker

1 Aerodactyl HOLO R 6.00 12.00
2 Aggron HOLO R 1.50 3.00
3 Cradily HOLO R 6.00 12.00
4 Delcatty HOLO R .75 1.50
5 Gengar HOLO R 1.00 2.00
6 Golem HOLO R .60 1.25
7 Kabutops HOLO R 1.25 2.50
8 Lapras HOLO R 6.00 12.00
9 Machamp HOLO R 4.00 10.00
10 Mew HOLO R 1.50 4.00
11 Muk HOLO R 3.00 6.00
12 Shiftry HOLO R 1.50 3.00
13 Victreebel HOLO R 2.50 5.00
14 Wailord HOLO R 3.00 6.00
15 Absol R 1.00 2.00
16 Girafarig R 1.25 2.50
17 Gorebyss R 1.25 2.50
18 Huntail R .75 1.50
19 Lanturn R 2.50 5.00
20 Lunatone R 2.50 5.00
21 Magmar R 1.50 3.00
22 Magneton R 12.50 25.00
23 Omastar R .04 .10
24 Pinsir R .04 .10
25 Solrock R 1.25 2.50
26 Spinda R .75 1.50
27 Torkoal R 1.50 3.00
28 Wobbuffet R 1.50 3.00
29 Anorith U .50 1.00
30 Cascoon U .10 .25
31 Dunsparce U .30 .75
32 Electrode U .75 1.50
33 Furret U 15.00 30.00
34 Graveler U 1.00 2.50
35 Haunter U 15.00 30.00
36 Kabuto U .07 .15
37 Kecleon U 17.50 35.00
38 Lairon U .40 1.00
39 Machoke U 1.50 3.00
40 Misdreavus U .75 1.50
41 Nuzleaf U 1.25 2.50
42 Roselia U 2.00 5.00
43 Sealeo U 10.00 25.00
44 Tangela U 5.00 12.00
45 Tentacruel U 1.25 2.50
46 Vibrava U 1.50 3.00
47 Weepinbell U .75 1.50
48 Aron C 1.50 3.00
49 Bellsprout C .75 1.50
50 Chinchou C 2.00 4.00
51 Clamperl C 4.00 8.00
52 Gastly C 1.50 3.00
53 Geodude C .75 1.50
54 Grimer C .40 .80
55 Growlithe C 1.50 3.00
56 Lileep C 2.50 5.00
57 Machop C .60 1.25
58 Magby C 2.00 4.00
59 Magnemite C .10 .20
60 Omanyte C 1.25 2.50
61 Seedot C 1.50 3.00
62 Sentret C .75 1.50
63 Shuppet C 5.00 10.00
64 Skitty C .75 1.50
65 Spheal C 2.00 4.00
66 Tentacool C .17 .35
67 Trapinch C .12 .30
68 Voltorb C .01 .08
69 Wailmer C .04 .10
70 Wurmple C 2.00 4.00
71 Wynaut C 1.25 2.50
72 Cursed Stone U 1.25 2.50
73 Fieldworker U .08 .20
74 Full Flame U .10 .25
75 Giant Stump U .60 1.25
76 Power Tree U 1.00 2.00
77 Strange Cave U 2.50 5.00
78 Claw Fossil C 1.50 3.00
79 Mysterious Fossil C 1.00 2.00
80 Root Fossil C .75 2.00
81 Rainbow Energy R .40 1.00
82 React Energy U 1.50 3.00
83 Arcanine EX HOLO R .25 .50
84 Armaldo EX HOLO R .07 .15
85 Banette EX HOLO R 1.00 2.00
86 Dustox EX HOLO R 1.00 2.00
87 Flygon EX HOLO R .08 .20
88 Mew EX HOLO R 1.25 2.50
89 Walrein EX HOLO R .30 .75
90 Regice Gold Star HOLO R 1.50 3.00
91 Regirock Gold Star HOLO R 1.25 2.50
92 Registeel Gold Star HOLO R 1.50 3.00
93 Pikachu HOLO R 4.00 10.00

2006 Pokemon Organized Play Series 3

1A Blastoise R 1.00 2.00
1B Blastoise HOLO R .12 .25
2A Flareon R .60 1.25
2B Flareon HOLO R 3.00 6.00
3A Jolteon R .50 1.00
3B Jolteon HOLO R .75 1.50
4A Minun R 7.50 15.00
4B Minun HOLO R 2.50 5.00
5A Plusle R 2.50 5.00
5B Plusle HOLO R 3.00 8.00
6A Vaporeon R .40 1.00
6B Vaporeon HOLO R 2.50 5.00
7 Combusken U 20.00 50.00
8 Donphan U .60 1.25
9 Forretress U .75 1.50
10 High Pressure System U 1.25 2.50
11 Low Pressure System U 1.25 2.50
12 Ditto (Mr. Mime) C .75 1.50
13 Eevee C 4.00 8.00
14 Ivysaur C 1.25 2.50
15 Marshtomp C 1.00 2.00
16 Pichu Bros. C .75 1.50
17A Ho-oh EX R .75 1.50
17B Ho-oh EX HOLO R .60 1.25

2006 Pokemon Organized Play Series 4

1 Chimecho R .75 1.50
2A Deoxys R 4.00 8.00
2B Deoxys HOLO R 2.00 4.00
3A Flygon R 1.50 3.00
3B Flygon HOLO R .75 1.50
4A Mew R 5.00 12.00
4B Mew HOLO R 1.25 2.50
5 Sceptile R .10 .20
6A Combusken U .75 1.50
6B Combusken HOLO R .60 1.25
7 Grovyle U 5.00 12.00
8 Heal Energy U 1.50 3.00
9 Pokémon Fan Club U 1.00 2.00
10 Scramble Energy U 1.00 2.00
11A Mudkip C .75 1.50
11B Mudkip HOLO R .75 1.50
12 Pidgey C 3.00 6.00
13A Pikachu C .60 1.25
13B Pikachu HOLO R .75 1.50
14 Squirtle C 2.00 4.00
15 Treecko C 1.50 3.00
16A Wobbuffet C 1.00 2.00
16B Wobbuffet HOLO R 10.00 25.00
17 Deoxys EX R 3.00 8.00

2007 Pokemon Diamond and Pearl

1 Dialga HOLO R .25 .50
2 Dusknoir HOLO R .01 .08
3 Electivire HOLO R .01 .08
4 Empoleon HOLO R 1.00 2.00
5 Infernape HOLO R 4.00 8.00
6 Lucario HOLO R 1.25 2.50
7 Luxray HOLO R 1.50 3.00
8 Magnezone HOLO R 1.25 2.50
9 Manaphy HOLO R .75 1.50
10 Mismagius HOLO R 1.50 3.00
11 Palkia HOLO R 1.25 2.50
12 Rhyperior HOLO R 12.50 25.00
13 Roserade HOLO R 1.25 2.50
14 Shiftry HOLO R 2.00 4.00
15 Skuntank HOLO R .75 1.50
16 Staraptor HOLO R 1.25 2.50
17 Torterra HOLO R 1.25 2.50
18 Azumarill R 2.00 4.00
19 Beautifly R 12.50 25.00
20 Bibarel R 6.00 12.00
21 Carnivine R .04 .10
22 Clefable R .08 .20
23 Drapion R .01 .08
24 Drifblim R .05 .12
25 Dustox R 2.50 5.00
26 Floatzel R .40 1.00
27 Gengar R .60 1.25
28 Heracross R .50 1.00
29 Hippowdon R 1.00 2.00
30 Lopunny R .07 .15
31 Machamp R .12 .30
32 Medicham R .25 .50
33 Munchlax R .01 .08
34 Noctowl R .08 .20
35 Pachirisu R 3.00 6.00
36 Purugly R 5.00 10.00
37 Snorlax R .75 1.50
38 Steelix R .75 1.50
39 Vespiquen R .75 1.50
40 Weavile R 15.00 30.00
41 Wobbuffet R .75 1.50
42 Wynaut R .75 1.50
43 Budew U 12.00 30.00
44 Cascoon U 4.00 10.00
45 Cherrim U 1.25 2.50
46 Drifloon U 15.00 30.00
47 Dusclops U 1.50 4.00
48 Elekid U .75 2.00
49 Grotle U 3.00 6.00
50 Haunter U .75 1.50
51 Hippopotas U .60 1.25
52 Luxio U .50 1.00
53 Machoke U .50 1.00
54 Magneton U .75 1.50
55 Mantyke U .75 1.50
56 Monferno U 1.25 2.50
57 Nuzleaf U 2.00 4.00
58 Prinplup U 2.50 5.00
59 Rapidash U 1.00 2.00
60 Rhydon U 7.50 15.00
61 Riolu U 1.50 3.00
62 Seaking U .75 1.50
63 Silcoon U .50 1.00
64 Staravia U .15 .30
65 Unown A U .60 1.25
66 Unown B U 1.00 2.00
67 Unown C U .75 1.50
68 Unown D U 2.00 4.00
69 Azurill C .50 1.00
70 Bidoof C 1.50 3.00
71 Bonsly C 1.25 2.50
72 Buizel C 2.00 4.00
73 Buneary C 1.50 3.00
74 Chatot C 3.00 8.00
75 Cherubi C 1.25 2.50
76 Chimchar C 1.50 3.00
77 Clefairy C 1.50 3.00
78 Cleffa C .25 .50
79 Combee C .07 .15
80 Duskull C 1.50 3.00
81 Electabuzz C .75 1.50
82 Gastly C 1.00 2.00
83 Glameow C 1.25 2.50
84 Goldeen C 1.25 2.50
85 Hoothoot C 1.25 2.50
86 Machop C .30 .75
87 Magnemite C .75 1.50
88 Marill C .50 1.00
89 Meditite C 3.00 8.00
90 Mime Jr. C .75 1.50
91 Misdreavus C 2.50 5.00
92 Onix C 1.00 2.00
93 Piplup C 1.50 3.00
94 Ponyta C .75 1.50
95 Rhyhorn C 1.00 2.00
96 Roselia C 2.50 5.00
97 Seedot C .10 .20
98 Shinx C 1.00 2.00
99 Skorupi C 3.00 6.00
100 Sneasel C 1.25 2.50
101 Starly C 2.50 5.00
102 Stunky C 2.50 5.00
103 Turtwig C .75 1.50
104 Wurmple C 7.50 15.00
105 Double Full Heal U 1.50 4.00
106 Energy Restore U .50 1.25
107 Energy Switch U 2.50 5.00
108 Night Pokemon Center U 25.00 60.00
109 PlusPower U 1.50 3.00
110 Poke Ball U .75 1.50
111 Pokedex HANDY910s U 1.00 2.00
112 Professor Rowan U .10 .20
113 Rival U .08 .20
114 Speed Stadium U .10 .25
115 Super Scoop Up U 7.50 15.00
116 Warp Point U 1.50 3.00
117 Energy Search C 1.50 3.00
118 Potion C 1.00 2.00
119 Switch C .04 .10
120 Empoleon Lv.X HOLO R .08 .20
121 Infernape Lv.X HOLO R 1.00 2.00
122 Torterra Lv.X HOLO R 1.50 3.00
123 Grass Energy C .07 .15
124 Fire Energy C .60 1.25
125 Water Energy C 10.00 25.00
126 Lightning Energy C 12.00 30.00
127 Fighting Energy C .07 .15
128 Psychic Energy C 5.00 10.00

129 Darkness Energy C .75 1.50
130 Metal Energy C .60 1.25

2007 Pokemon Diamond and Pearl Mysterious Treasures

1 Aggron HOLO R 1.25 2.50
2 Alakazam HOLO R 1.25 2.50
3 Ambipom HOLO R .60 1.25
4 Azelf HOLO R 2.00 4.00
5 Blissey HOLO R 1.25 2.50
6 Bronzong HOLO R 1.50 3.00
7 Celebi HOLO R 4.00 10.00
8 Feraligatr HOLO R 2.00 5.00
9 Garchomp HOLO R 1.00 2.00
10 Honchkrow HOLO R 1.50 3.00
11 Lumineon HOLO R 1.50 3.00
12 Magmortar HOLO R .10 .20
13 Meganium HOLO R .60 1.25
14 Mesprit HOLO R 10.00 20.00
15 Raichu HOLO R 2.00 4.00
16 Typhlosion HOLO R 1.50 3.00
17 Tyranitar HOLO R 2.00 4.00
18 Uxie HOLO R 6.00 12.00
19 Abomasnow R 3.00 6.00
20 Ariados R .50 1.00
21 Bastiodon R .75 1.50
22 Chimecho R 1.00 2.00
23 Crobat R .30 .75
24 Exeggutor R 1.25 2.50
25 Glalie R 1.00 2.00
26 Gyarados R 10.00 20.00
27 Kricketune R 1.50 3.00
28 Manectric R 1.25 2.50
29 Mantine R 2.50 5.00
30 Mr. Mime R 3.00 6.00
31 Nidoqueen R .75 1.50
32 Ninetales R .50 1.00
33 Rampardos R .50 1.00
34 Slaking R .10 .20
35 Sudowoodo R .08 .20
36 Toxicroak R .25 .50
37 Unown R .04 .10
38 Ursaring R .05 .12
39 Walrein R .75 1.50
40 Whiscash R .75 1.50
41 Bayleef U .60 1.25
42 Chingling U .75 1.50
43 Cranidos U 3.00 6.00
44 Croconaw U .75 1.50
45 Dewgong U .01 .08
46 Dodrio U .04 .10
47 Dunsparce U .01 .08
48 Gabite U .01 .08
49 Girafarig U .75 1.50
50 Golbat U 1.50 3.00
51 Graveler U .50 1.25
52 Happiny U .60 1.50
53 Lairon U .50 1.25
54 Magmar U 1.50 3.00
55 Masquerain U .60 1.25
56 Nidorina U .50 1.00
57 Octillery U .75 1.50
58 Parasect U 30.00 75.00
59 Pupitar U 7.50 15.00
60 Quilava U .25 .50
61 Sandslash U .75 1.50
62 Sealeo U 10.00 25.00
63 Shieldon U 4.00 10.00
64 Tropius U 7.50 15.00
65 Unown E U 1.00 2.00
66 Unown M U .50 1.00
67 Unown T U .08 .20
68 Vigoroth U 1.00 2.00
69 Abra C .75 1.50
70 Aipom C 2.00 4.00
71 Aron C 1.50 3.00
72 Barboach C .50 1.00
73 Bidoof C .75 1.50
74 Bronzor C 1.00 2.00
75 Buizel C 2.00 4.00
76 Chansey C 1.50 3.00
77 Chikorita C 1.50 4.00
78 Croagunk C 2.50 5.00
79 Cyndaquil C 2.00 4.00
80 Doduo C 3.00 6.00
81 Electrike C 2.00 4.00
82 Exeggcute C 2.00 4.00
83 Finneon C .08 .20
84 Geodude C .08 .20
85 Gible C .30 .60
86 Kricketot C 1.25 2.50
87 Larvitar C .60 1.25
88 Magby C 2.00 4.00
89 Magikarp C 3.00 8.00
90 Murkrow C 1.50 3.00
91 Nidoran C .75 1.50
92 Paras C .75 1.50
93 Pichu C .75 1.50
94 Pikachu C 1.00 2.00
95 Remoraid C .75 1.50
96 Sandshrew C 3.00 6.00
97 Seel C 1.50 3.00
98 Shinx C .12 .25
99 Slakoth C .10 .20
100 Snorunt C 1.00 2.00
101 Snover C .20 .50
102 Spheal C 1.25 2.50
103 Spinarak C 3.00 6.00
104 Surskit C 1.50 3.00
105 Teddiursa C 1.00 2.00
106 Totodile C .75 1.50
107 Vulpix C 1.00 2.00
108 Zubat C 1.25 2.50
109 Bebe's Search U 1.25 2.50
110 Dusk Ball U .12 .25
111 Fossil Excavator U 2.50 5.00
112 Lake Boundary U 7.50 15.00
113 Night Maintenance U 3.00 6.00
114 Quick Ball U 2.50 6.00
115 Team Galactic's Wager U .40 1.00
116 Armor Fossil C 2.50 5.00
117 Skull Fossil C 25.00 60.00
118 Multi Energy R .75 1.50
119 Darkness Energy U .75 1.50
120 Metal Energy U .60 1.25
121 Electivire Lv.X HOLO R .75 1.50
122 Lucario Lv.X HOLO R 1.25 2.50
123 Magmortar Lv.X HOLO R 1.50 3.00
124 Time Space Distortion HOLO SCR 1.25 2.50

2007 Pokemon Diamond and Pearl Secret Wonders

1 Ampharos HOLO R .60 1.25
2 Blastoise HOLO R .60 1.25
3 Charizard HOLO R 1.00 2.00
4 Entei HOLO R .75 1.50
5 Flygon HOLO R .60 1.25
6 Gallade HOLO R .75 1.50
7 Gardevoir HOLO R 7.50 15.00
8 Gastrodon East Sea HOLO R .25 .60
9 Gastrodon West Sea HOLO R .01 .08
10 Ho-Oh HOLO R .10 .25
11 Jumpluff HOLO R .75 1.50
12 Lickilicky HOLO R .60 1.25
13 Ludicolo HOLO R .75 1.50
14 Lugia HOLO R 1.00 2.00
15 Mew HOLO R 2.50 5.00
16 Raikou HOLO R 3.00 6.00
17 Roserade HOLO R 2.50 5.00
18 Salamence HOLO R 6.00 15.00
19 Suicune HOLO R 1.00 2.00
20 Venusaur HOLO R 2.00 4.00
21 Absol R .05 .12
22 Arcanine R .60 1.50
23 Banette R .25 .50
24 Dugtrio R .75 1.50
25 Electivire R .08 .20
26 Electrode R 1.25 2.50
27 Furret R 7.50 15.00
28 Golduck R .12 .25
29 Golem R 2.50 5.00
30 Jynx R 8.00 20.00
31 Magmortar R 2.00 5.00
32 Minun R .60 1.25
33 Mothim R 2.00 4.00
34 Nidoking R 3.00 6.00
35 Pidgeot R 6.00 12.00
36 Plusle R .75 1.50
37 Sharpedo R .75 1.50
38 Sunflora R .75 1.50
39 Unown S R 50.00 120.00
40 Weavile R .60 1.25
41 Wormadam Plant Cloak R 12.50 25.00
42 Wormadam Sandy Cloak R 2.50 5.00
43 Wormadam Trash Cloak R .10 .20
44 Xatu R 1.50 3.00
45 Breloom U .07 .15
46 Charmeleon U .15 .40
47 Cloyster U .75 1.50
48 Donphan U 2.00 4.00
49 Farfetch'd U .60 1.25
50 Flaaffy U .60 1.25
51 Ivysaur U .75 1.50
52 Kecleon U .75 1.50
53 Kirlia U 3.00 6.00
54 Lombre U 1.00 2.00
55 Miltank U 2.00 4.00
56 Muk U 1.00 2.00
57 Nidorino U .60 1.50
58 Pidgeotto U .50 1.25
59 Pinsir U .75 2.00
60 Quagsire U .12 .25
61 Raticate U .75 1.50
62 Roselia U .75 1.50
63 Sableye U 1.50 3.00
64 Shelgon U .30 .75
65 Skiploom U .60 1.25
66 Smeargle U .60 1.25
67 Smoochum U .75 1.50
68 Unown K U 50.00 100.00
69 Unown N U 2.00 4.00
70 Unown O U 4.00 8.00
71 Unown X U 1.00 2.00
72 Unown Z U .75 1.50
73 Venomoth U 4.00 10.00
74 Vibrava U 1.25 3.00
75 Wartortle U 1.25 2.50
76 Bagon C .60 1.25
77 Bulbasaur C .75 1.50
78 Burmy Plant Cloak C .75 1.50
79 Burmy Sandy Cloak C 1.50 3.00
80 Burmy Trash Cloak C 1.25 2.50
81 Carvanha C 1.00 2.00
82 Charmander C 7.50 15.00
83 Clefairy C 1.00 2.00
84 Corsola C .60 1.25
85 Diglett C 1.50 3.00
86 Duskull C 1.00 2.00
87 Electabuzz C 1.50 3.00
88 Grimer C 1.00 2.00
89 Growlithe C .12 .25
90 Hoppip C 1.00 2.00
91 Lickitung C 1.50 3.00
92 Lotad C .12 .25
93 Magmar C 1.25 2.50
94 Mareep C .75 1.50
95 Murkrow C 1.00 2.00
96 Natu C 4.00 8.00
97 Nidoran C .01 .08
98 Phanpy C .04 .10
99 Pidgey C 1.50 4.00
100 Psyduck C .75 1.50
101 Qwilfish C 2.50 5.00
102 Ralts C 3.00 8.00
103 Rattata C .75 1.50
104 Sentret C 1.50 3.00
105 Shellder C 1.50 3.00
106 Shellos East Sea C 2.50 5.00
107 Shellos West Sea C .08 .20
108 Shroomish C .75 1.50
109 Shuckle C 1.25 2.50
110 Shuppet C .30 .75
111 Spinda C 1.00 2.00
112 Squirtle C .07 .15
113 Stantler C .12 .30
114 Sunkern C 1.50 3.00
115 Trapinch C .25 .50
116 Venonat C .60 1.25
117 Voltorb C 4.00 8.00
118 Wooper C 1.25 2.50
119 Bebe's Search U .07 .15
120 Night Maintenance U .75 1.50
121 PlusPower U 2.50 5.00
122 Professor Oak's Visit U 2.00 4.00
123 Professor Rowan U 1.25 2.50
124 Rival U .75 1.50
125 Roseanne's Research U .60 1.25
126 Team Galactic's Mars U .08 .20
127 Potion C .08 .20
128 Switch C 6.00 15.00
129 Darkness Energy U .75 2.00
130 Metal Energy U 2.50 5.00
131 Gardevoir LV.X HOLO R 40.00 100.00
132 Honchkrow LV.X HOLO R .75 1.50

2007 Pokemon EX Power Keepers

1 Aggron HOLO R 1.00 2.00
2 Altaria HOLO R 2.50 5.00
3 Armaldo HOLO R 2.00 4.00
4 Banette HOLO R .07 .15
5 Blaziken HOLO R 1.25 2.50
6 Charizard HOLO R 1.50 3.00
7 Cradily HOLO R .75 1.50
8 Delcatty HOLO R .75 1.50
9 Gardevoir HOLO R 3.00 6.00
10 Kabutops HOLO R 1.50 3.00
11 Machamp HOLO R 1.50 3.00
12 Raichu HOLO R 1.25 2.50
13 Slaking HOLO R 1.25 2.50
14 Dusclops R 3.00 6.00
15 Lanturn R 4.00 10.00
16 Magneton R 3.00 6.00
17 Mawile R 1.50 3.00
18 Mightyena R .75 1.50
19 Ninetales R 1.50 3.00
20 Omastar R .25 .50
21 Pichu R .04 .10
22 Sableye R .10 .25
23 Seviper R 1.00 2.00
24 Wobbuffet R 1.00 2.00
25 Zangoose R .60 1.25
26 Anorith U .75 1.50
27 Cacturne U .75 1.50
28 Charmeleon U .60 1.25
29 Combusken U 2.50 5.00
30 Glalie U 1.25 2.50
31 Kirlia U 1.00 2.00
32 Lairon U .07 .15
33 Machoke U 5.00 10.00
34 Medicham U 1.50 3.00
35 Metang U 5.00 12.00
36 Nuzleaf U .75 1.50
37 Sealeo U .75 1.50
38 Sharpedo U .75 1.50
39 Shelgon U .60 1.25
40 Vibrava U 1.00 2.00
41 Vigoroth U 1.25 2.50
42 Aron C 1.00 2.00
43 Bagon C 10.00 20.00
44 Baltoy C 2.50 5.00
45 Beldum C .60 1.25
46 Cacnea C .75 1.50
47 Carvanha C 1.00 2.00
48 Charmander C 7.50 15.00
49 Chinchou C 2.00 4.00
50 Duskull C .75 1.50
51 Kabuto C 1.25 2.50
52 Lileep C .75 1.50
53 Machop C .30 .60
54 Magnemite C .60 1.25
55 Meditite C 2.00 4.00
56 Omanyte C .10 .20
57 Pikachu C 1.25 2.50
58 Poochyena C 1.50 3.00
59 Ralts C .30 .75
60 Seedot C .01 .08
61 Shuppet C .04 .10
62 Skitty C 1.00 2.00
63 Slakoth C 3.00 6.00
64 Snorunt C 1.00 2.50
65 Spheal C .75 2.00
66 Swablu C 1.00 2.50
67 Torchic C .75 1.50
68 Trapinch C 12.50 25.00
69 Vulpix C 1.50 3.00
70 Wynaut C 1.25 2.50
71 Battle Frontier U 3.00 6.00
72 Drake's Stadium U 30.00 75.00
73 Energy Recycle System U .04 .10
74 Energy Removal 2 U .05 .12
75 Energy Switch U 1.25 2.50
76 Glacia's Stadium U 5.00 12.00
77 Great Ball U 2.50 6.00
78 Master Ball U .75 1.50
79 Phoebe's Stadium U 1.25 2.50
80 Professor Birch U .75 1.50
81 Scott U 2.00 4.00
82 Sidney's Stadium U 1.25 2.50
83 Steven's Advice U 1.25 2.50
84 Claw Fossil C 10.00 25.00
85 Mysterious Fossil C 2.50 6.00
86 Root Fossil C .75 1.50
87 Darkness Energy R 1.25 2.50
88 Metal Energy R 1.25 3.00
89 Multi Energy R .30 .75
90 Cyclone Energy U 1.50 3.00
91 Warp Energy U .60 1.25
92 Absol EX HOLO R 1.50 3.00
93 Claydol EX HOLO R 1.50 3.00
94 Flygon EX HOLO R .75 1.50
95 Metagross EX HOLO R 1.25 2.50
96 Salamence EX HOLO R 5.00 12.00
97 Shiftry EX HOLO R 2.00 4.00
98 Skarmory EX HOLO R 6.00 12.00
99 Walrein EX HOLO R 3.00 6.00
100 Flareon Gold Star HOLO R .01 .08
101 Jolteon Gold Star HOLO R .04 .10
102 Vaporeon Gold Star HOLO R 1.50 3.00
103 Grass Energy HOLO R 1.00 2.00
104 Fire Energy HOLO R 1.50 3.00
105 Water Energy HOLO R 2.00 5.00
106 Lightning Energy HOLO R 2.50 5.00
107 Psychic Energy HOLO R 2.50 6.00
108 Fighting Energy HOLO R .75 1.50

2007 Pokemon Organized Play Series 5

1 Ho-Oh R 1.50 3.00
1 Ho-Oh HOLO R .75 1.50
2 Lugia R .75 1.50
2 Lugia HOLO R .75 1.50
3 Mew R .60 1.25
3 Mew HOLO R 1.50 3.00
4 Double Rainbow Energy R 1.25 2.50
5 Charmeleon U .75 1.50
6 Bill's Maintenance U 2.00 4.00
7 Rare Candy U 1.25 2.50
8 Boost Energy U .07 .15
9 Delta Rainbow Energy U .75 1.50
10 Charmander C 1.25 2.50
11 Meowth C 3.00 6.00
12 Pikachu C .01 .08
12 Pikachu HOLO R .04 .10
13 Pikachu C .60 1.25
14 Pelipper C .60 1.25
14 Pelipper HOLO R .75 1.50
15 Zangoose C 1.50 3.00
15 Zangoose HOLO R 2.50 5.00
16 Espeon Gold Star R 2.00 4.00
17 Umbreon Gold Star R 1.50 4.00

2007 Pokemon Organized Play Series 6

1 Bastiodon R .40 1.00
2 Lucario R 2.50 5.00
3A Manaphy R 3.00 6.00
3B Manaphy HOLO R 20.00 50.00
4 Pachirisu R 1.50 3.00
5 Rampardos R .25 .50
6 Drifloon U 3.00 6.00
7A Gible U 1.00 2.00
7B Gible HOLO R .75 1.50
8A Riolu U .75 1.50
8B Riolu HOLO R .10 .20
9A Pikachu U .07 .15
9B Pikachu HOLO R .07 .15
10 Staravia U .60 1.25
11 Bidoof C .60 1.25
12 Buneary C 3.00 6.00
13 Cherubi C 1.25 2.50
14A Chimchar C 2.00 4.00
14B Chimchar HOLO R 1.50 3.00
15B Piplup HOLO R .75 1.50
15A Piplup C 7.50 15.00
16 Starly C .01 .08
17 Turtwig C .04 .10

2008 Pokemon Burger King

6 Lucario 10.00 25.00
9 Manaphy .60 1.25
35 Pachirisu 4.00 8.00
49 Grotle .25 .50
52 Happiny 1.00 2.00
56 Monferno .01 .08
58 Prinplup .10 .25
76 Chimchar 1.25 2.50
93 Piplup 1.00 2.00
94 Pikachu .08 .20
98 Shinx 2.00 4.00
103 Turtwig .75 1.50

2008 Pokemon Diamond and Pearl Great Encounters

1 Blaziken HOLO R .75 1.50
2 Cresselia HOLO R .75 1.50
3 Darkrai HOLO R .10 .20
4 Darkrai HOLO R 2.50 5.00
5 Pachirisu HOLO R 7.50 15.00
6 Porygon-Z HOLO R 1.00 2.00
7 Rotom HOLO R .75 1.50
8 Sceptile HOLO R 1.25 2.50
9 Swampert HOLO R 2.00 4.00
10 Tangrowth HOLO R .75 1.50
11 Togekiss HOLO R 1.25 2.50
12 Altaria R 1.25 2.50
13 Beedrill R .60 1.25
14 Butterfree R .08 .20
15 Claydol R .05 .12
16 Dialga R 1.25 2.50
17 Exploud R .60 1.25
18 Houndoom R .75 1.50
19 Hypno R .60 1.25
20 Kingler R 1.25 2.50
21 Lapras R 1.25 2.50
22 Latias R 1.00 2.00
23 Latios R .75 1.50
24 Mawile R 7.50 15.00
25 Milotic R 2.00 4.00
26 Palkia R .75 1.50
27 Primeape R 2.00 4.00

28 Slowking R .30 .75
29 Unown H R .30 .75
30 Wailord R 1.00 2.00
31 Weezing R .30 .75
32 Wigglytuff R .75 1.50
33 Arbok U .10 .20
34 Cacturne U 2.00 4.00
35 Combusken U .75 1.50
36 Delibird U .25 .50
37 Floatzel U 25.00 50.00
38 Gorebyss U 1.00 2.00
39 Granbull U .75 1.50
40 Grovyle U 12.50 25.00
41 Hariyama U 5.00 12.00
42 Huntail U 1.50 4.00
43 Linoone U 2.00 4.00
44 Loudred U 1.00 2.50
45 Magcargo U .75 2.00
46 Marshtomp U 1.00 2.50
47 Metapod U .15 .30
48 Pelipper U .60 1.25
49 Porygon2 U .75 1.50
50 Purugly U .07 .15
51 Relicanth U .08 .20
52 Seviper U 1.50 3.00
53 Skarmory U .60 1.25
54 Slowbro U .75 1.50
5.50E+01 Togetic U 1.25 2.50
5.60E+01 Unown F U .75 1.50
5.70E+01 Unown G U 1.00 2.00
5.80E+01 Wailmer U .75 1.50
5.90E+01 Zangoose U .75 1.50
6.00E+01 Baltoy C 1.00 2.00
6.10E+01 Buizel C 3.00 6.00
6.20E+01 Cacnea C 2.50 5.00
63 Caterpie C .60 1.25
64 Clamperl C 1.50 3.00
65 Drowzee C .75 1.50
66 Ekans C .75 1.50
67 Feebas C 1.50 3.00
68 Glameow C 1.50 4.00
69 Houndour C .75 1.50
70 Igglybuff C .08 .20
71 Illumise C .75 1.50
72 Jigglypuff C 3.00 6.00
73 Kakuna C 1.25 3.00
74 Koffing C .40 1.00
75 Krabby C .30 .60
76 Lunatone C .60 1.25
77 Luvdisc C 1.50 3.00
78 Makuhita C 1.50 4.00
79 Mankey C 1.25 2.50
80 Mudkip C 5.00 12.00
81 Porygon C 10.00 20.00
82 Slowpoke C 3.00 6.00
83 Slugma C 1.50 3.00
84 Snubbull C .75 1.50
85 Solrock C .75 1.50
86 Swablu C 1.50 4.00
87 Tangela C 1.00 2.50
88 Togepi C 1.00 2.50
89 Torchic C 1.25 2.50
90 Treecko C .75 1.50
91 Unown L C 1.25 2.50
92 Volbeat C 3.00 6.00
93 Weedle C .75 1.50
94 Whismur C .15 .30
95 Wingull C .12 .25
96 Zigzagoon C 1.25 2.50
97 Amulet Coin U .30 .75
98 Felicity's Drawing U .60 1.25
99 Leftovers U 1.00 2.00
100 Moonlight Stadium U 1.25 2.50
101 Premier Ball U 2.00 4.00
102 Rare Candy U 1.00 2.00
103 Cresselia LV.X HOLO R .75 1.50
104 Darkrai LV.X HOLO R .75 1.50
105 Dialga LV.X HOLO R 1.50 3.00
106 Palkia LV.X HOLO R 6.00 12.00

2008 Pokemon Diamond and Pearl Legends Awakened

1 Deoxys Normal Form HOLO R .12 .25
2 Dragonite HOLO R 4.00 10.00
3 Froslass HOLO R .60 1.50
4 Giratina HOLO R 2.50 5.00
5 Gliscor HOLO R 40.00 100.00
6 Heatran HOLO R 1.50 3.00
7 Kingdra HOLO R .08 .20
8 Luxray HOLO R .10 .25
9 Mamoswine HOLO R 1.50 3.00
10 Metagross HOLO R 1.25 2.50
11 Mewtwo HOLO R 2.50 5.00
12 Politoed HOLO R .20 .40
13 Probopass HOLO R .07 .15
14 Rayquaza HOLO R .60 1.25
15 Regigigas HOLO R .75 1.50
16 Spiritomb HOLO R 2.50 5.00
17 Yanmega HOLO R .01 .08
18 Armaldo R .05 .12
19 Azelf R .75 1.50
20 Bellossom R .75 1.50
21 Cradily R .75 1.50
22 Crawdaunt R .60 1.25
23 Delcatty R .75 1.50
24 Deoxy's Attack Form R 1.00 2.00
25 Deoxy's Defense Form R 2.00 4.00
26 Deoxy's Speed Form R .75 1.50
27 Ditto R 3.00 6.00
28 Forretress R .50 1.00
29 Groudon R 1.25 2.50
30 Heatran R 6.00 15.00
31 Jirachi R .01 .08
32 Kyogre R .04 .10
33 Lopunny R .75 1.50
34 Mesprit R .50 1.00
35 Poliwrath R 1.25 2.50
36 Regice R .10 .25
37 Regigigas R .60 1.50
38 Regirock R .25 .50
39 Registeel R 2.00 4.00
40 Shedinja R .75 1.50
41 Torkoal R .75 1.50
42 Unown ! R .30 .75
43 Uxie R .60 1.25
44 Victreebel R 1.00 2.00
45 Vileplume R 2.00 4.00
46 Anorith U .12 .25
47 Camerupt U 1.25 2.50
48 Castform U 1.50 3.00
49 Castform Rain Form U .10 .20
50 Castform Snow-Cloud Form U .75 1.50
51 Castform Sunny Form U 1.50 3.00
52 Dragonair U .50 1.00
53 Drifblim U .75 1.50
54 Exeggutor U 1.25 2.50
55 Gliscor U 1.00 2.00
56 Grumpig U 7.50 15.00
57 Houndoom U 1.00 2.00
58 Lanturn U 1.25 2.50
59 Lanturn U 1.50 3.00
60 Ledian U .75 1.50
61 Lucario U 2.00 4.00
62 Luxio U 2.50 5.00
63 Marowak U 1.50 3.00
64 Metang U .75 1.50
65 Metang U 1.25 2.50
66 Mightyena U 1.00 2.00
67 Ninjask U 2.50 5.00
68 Persian U .75 1.50
69 Piloswine U .75 1.50
70 Seadra U .75 1.50
71 Starmie U 1.50 3.00
72 Swalot U 2.00 4.00
73 Swellow U 1.25 2.50
74 Tauros U 4.00 8.00
75 Tentacruel U 40.00 80.00
76 Unown J U 30.00 75.00
77 Unown R U 7.50 15.00
78 Unown U U .60 1.25
79 Unown V U .60 1.25
80 Unown W U .75 1.50
81 Unown Y U 1.00 2.00
82 Unown ? U 1.00 2.00
83 Beldum C .12 .25
84 Beldum C .15 .40
85 Bellsprout C 20.00 40.00
86 Buneary C 5.00 12.00
87 Chinchou C 2.00 5.00
88 Chinchou C 1.00 2.00
89 Corphish C .01 .08
90 Cubone C .04 .10
91 Dratini C 5.00 10.00
92 Drifloon C .75 1.50
93 Exeggcute C .75 1.50
94 Gligar C .75 1.50
95 Gligar C 1.50 3.00
96 Gloom C 1.25 2.50
97 Gloom C .75 1.50
98 Gulpin C 2.00 5.00
99 Hitmonchan C 1.25 2.50
100 Hitmonlee C .60 1.25
101 Hitmontop C 3.00 6.00
102 Horsea C 3.00 8.00
103 Houndour C 3.00 8.00
104 Ledyba C .40 1.00
105 Lileep C 1.25 2.50
106 Meowth C 1.00 2.00
107 Misdreavus C 1.25 2.50
108 Nincada C .10 .20
109 Nosepass C .75 1.50
110 Numel C 1.00 2.00
111 Oddish C .75 1.50
112 Oddish C 1.00 2.00
113 Pineco C .07 .15
114 Poliwag C .15 .40
115 Poliwhirl C .30 .60
116 Poochyena C .75 1.50
117 Riolu C 1.00 2.00
118 Shinx C 1.50 3.00
119 Skitty C 3.00 8.00
120 Sneasel C 3.00 6.00
121 Spoink C 4.00 8.00
122 Staryu C 1.50 3.00
123 Swinub C 1.50 3.00
124 Taillow C .30 .75
125 Tentacool C 1.25 2.50
126 Tyrogue C .75 1.50
127 Weepinbell C .75 1.50
128 Yanma C 1.00 2.50
129 Bubble Coat U 2.00 4.00
130 Buck's Training U 1.50 3.00
131 Cynthia's Feelings U .50 1.00
132 Energy Pickup U 2.00 4.00
133 Poke Radar U 1.00 2.50
134 Snowpoint Temple U .50 1.00
135 Stark Mountain U 2.50 5.00
136 Technical Machine TS-1 U 1.00 2.00
137 Technical Machine TS-2 U 1.25 3.00
138 Claw Fossil C .40 1.00
139 Root Fossil C 2.00 4.00
140 Azelf LV.X HOLO R .60 1.50
141 Gliscor LV.X HOLO R .12 .25
142 Magnezone LV.X HOLO R 1.50 3.00
143 Mesprit LV.X HOLO R 2.00 4.00
144 Mewtwo LV.X HOLO R 1.25 2.50
145 Rhyperior LV.X HOLO R .10 .20
146 Uxie LV.X HOLO R .75 1.50

2008 Pokemon Diamond and Pearl Majestic Dawn

1 Articuno HOLO R .07 .15
2 Cresselia HOLO R 1.25 2.50
3 Darkrai HOLO R .04 .10
4 Dialga HOLO R .10 .25
5 Glaceon HOLO R .75 1.50
6 Kabutops HOLO R 2.50 5.00
7 Leafeon HOLO R 1.00 2.50
8 Manaphy HOLO R .50 1.25
9 Mewtwo HOLO R 2.50 5.00
10 Moltres HOLO R 1.00 2.50
11 Palkia HOLO R .50 1.25
12 Phione HOLO R 8.00 20.00
13 Rotom HOLO R 1.00 2.00
14 Zapdos HOLO R 1.00 2.00
15 Aerodactyl R 6.00 12.00
16 Bronzong R 1.50 3.00
17 Empoleon R .75 1.50
18 Espeon R 2.50 5.00
19 Flareon R .75 1.50
20 Glaceon R .75 1.50
21 Hippowdon R 1.25 2.50
22 Infernape R .75 1.50
23 Jolteon R .75 1.50
24 Leafeon R 1.00 2.00
25 Minun R .30 .60
26 Omastar R 1.50 3.00
27 Phione R .75 1.50
28 Plusle R .30 .60
29 Scizor R .75 1.50
30 Torterra R 1.50 3.00
31 Toxicroak R 2.00 4.00
32 Umbreon R 1.00 2.00
33 Unown P R 1.25 2.50
34 Vaporeon R 1.00 2.00
35 Ambipom U 2.50 5.00
36 Fearow U .25 .50
37 Grotle U .04 .10
38 Kangaskhan U .10 .25
39 Lickitung U 1.50 3.00
40 Manectric U .12 .25
41 Monferno U .75 1.50
42 Mothim U .60 1.25
43 Pachirisu U .60 1.25
44 Prinplup U 1.25 2.50
45 Raichu U 4.00 8.00
46 Scyther U .75 1.50
47 Staravia U .75 1.50
48 Sudowoodo U 1.25 2.50
49 Unown Q U 1.25 2.50
50 Aipom C .75 1.50
51 Aipom C 1.25 2.50
52 Bronzor C 2.00 4.00
53 Buneary C .08 .20
54 Burmy Sand Cloak C .04 .10
55 Chatot C 25.00 60.00
56 Chimchar C .60 1.25
57 Chimchar C .07 .15
58 Chingling C .50 1.00
59 Combee C 2.00 4.00
60 Croagunk C .75 1.50
61 Drifloon C 7.50 15.00
62 Eevee C 3.00 6.00
63 Eevee C 7.50 15.00
64 Electrike C .60 1.25
65 Glameow C 2.00 4.00
66 Hippopotas C .60 1.25
67 Kabuto C .01 .08
68 Munchlax C .04 .10
69 Omanyte C 1.25 2.50
70 Pikachu C .60 1.25
71 Piplup C 1.50 3.00
72 Piplup C .04 .10
73 Shellos East Sea C .04 .10
74 Spearow C .75 1.50
75 Starly C 2.50 5.00
76 Stunky C 1.25 2.50
77 Turtwig C 10.00 20.00
78 Turtwig C 1.50 3.00
79 Dawn Stadium U .75 1.50
80 Dusk Ball U 1.00 2.00
81 Energy Restore U 1.50 3.00
82 Fossil Excavator U 12.50 25.00
83 Mom's Kindness U .50 1.25
84 Old Amber U 1.00 2.50
85 Poke Ball U 1.00 2.00
86 Quick Ball U .75 1.50
87 Super Scoop Up U 2.50 5.00
88 Warp Point C .50 1.00
89 Dome Fossil C 2.00 4.00
90 Energy Search C 2.00 4.00
91 Helix Fossil C 6.00 12.00
92 Call Energy U .75 1.50
93 Darkness Energy U 1.25 2.50
94 Health Energy U 1.50 4.00
95 Metal Energy U .60 1.25
96 Recover Energy U .10 .20
97 Garchomp LV.X HOLO R .75 1.50
98 Glaceon LV.X HOLO R .75 1.50
99 Leafeon LV.X HOLO R .75 1.50
100 Porygon-Z LV.X HOLO R 2.00 4.00

2008 Pokemon Diamond and Pearl Stormfront

1 Dusknoir HOLO R 1.25 2.50
2 Empoleon HOLO R .75 1.50
3 Infernape HOLO R 1.25 2.50
4 Lumineon HOLO R .75 1.50
5 Magnezone HOLO R .01 .08
6 Magnezone HOLO R .04 .10
7 Mismagius HOLO R 1.25 3.00
8 Raichu HOLO R 3.00 6.00
9 Regigigas HOLO R 2.00 4.00
10 Sceptile HOLO R .08 .20
11 Torterra HOLO R .01 .08
12 Abomasnow R .01 .08
13 Bronzong R .75 1.50
14 Cherrim R .75 1.50
15 Drapion R .12 .25
16 Drifblim R .75 1.50
17 Dusknoir R .75 1.50
18 Gengar R 1.25 3.00
19 Gyarados R .40 1.00
20 Machamp R .25 .50
21 Mamoswine R .75 1.50
22 Rapidash R .75 1.50
23 Roserade R .50 1.00
24 Salamence R .75 1.50
25 Scizor R 1.25 2.50
26 Skuntank R 1.25 2.50
27 Staraptor R .60 1.50
28 Steelix R 2.50 6.00
29 Tangrowth R 1.25 2.50
30 Tyranitar R .07 .15
31 Vespiquen R .60 1.25
32 Bibarel U .75 1.50
33 Budew U 2.00 4.00
34 Dusclops U .75 1.50
35 Dusclops U 4.00 8.00
36 Electrode U 2.00 4.00
37 Electrode U 2.00 4.00
38 Farfetch'd U 1.25 3.00
39 Grovyle U .25 .60
40 Haunter U .30 .75
41 Machoke U .60 1.25
42 Magneton U 2.50 5.00
43 Magneton U .75 1.50
44 Miltank U 2.50 5.00
45 Pichu U 4.00 8.00
46 Piloswine U 1.25 2.50
47 Pupitar U .60 1.25
48 Sableye U .75 1.50
49 Scyther U .07 .15
50 Shelgon U 2.50 5.00
51 Skarmory U .30 .75
52 Staravia U 3.00 6.00
53 Bagon C 2.00 4.00
54 Bidoof C 1.00 2.00
55 Bronzor C 2.00 4.00
56 Cherubi C .75 1.50
57 Combee C 1.00 2.50
58 Drifloon C 5.00 10.00
59 Duskull C 1.25 2.50
60 Duskull C 1.25 2.50
61 Finneon C 1.25 2.50
62 Gastly C 1.50 3.00
63 Larvitar C 1.00 2.00
64 Machop C .75 1.50
65 Magikarp C .75 2.00
66 Magnemite C .30 .75
67 Magnemite C 2.50 5.00
68 Misdreavus C 20.00 50.00
69 Onix C .75 1.50
70 Pikachu C 1.25 2.50
71 Ponyta C .30 .60
72 Roselia C .50 1.00
73 Skorupi C .75 1.50
74 Snover C 1.50 3.00
75 Starly C .75 1.50
76 Stunky C 1.00 2.00
77 Swinub C .25 .50
78 Tangela C 5.00 10.00
79 Treecko C .60 1.25
80 Voltorb C .75 1.50
81 Voltorb C .25 .50
82 Conductive Quarry U 1.50 3.00
83 Energy Link U .10 .25
84 Energy Switch U .50 1.25
85 Great Ball U 2.50 5.00
86 Luxury Ball U 1.00 2.00
87 Marley's Request U .08 .20
88 Poke Blower U .05 .12
89 Poke Drawer U 3.00 6.00
90 Poke Healer U .75 1.50
91 Premier Ball U 2.00 4.00
92 Potion C .75 1.50
93 Switch C .75 2.00
94 Cyclone Energy U .60 1.25
95 Warp Energy U .75 1.50
96 Dusknoir LV.X HOLO R .75 1.50
97 Heatran LV.X HOLO R 6.00 15.00
98 Machamp LV.X HOLO R .75 1.50
99 Raichu LV.X HOLO R .75 1.50
100 Regigigas LV.X HOLO R 1.00 2.00
101 Charmander HOLO R 5.00 10.00
102 Charmeleon HOLO R .75 1.50
103 Charizard HOLO R 1.00 2.00
SH1 Drifloon UR .75 1.50
SH2 Duskull UR 1.00 2.00
SH3 Voltorb .07 .15

2008 Pokemon Organized Play Series 7

1 Ampharos R .12 .30
2 Gallade R 1.00 2.00
3 Latias R 1.50 3.00
4 Latios R 1.50 3.00
5 Mothim R .75 1.50
6 Delibird U 6.00 12.00
7 Flaaffy U .30 .75
8 Kirlia HOLO R 1.00 2.00
8 Kirlia U 2.50 5.00
9 Stantler U 3.00 6.00
10 Wormadam U 2.50 5.00
11 Burmy C 1.25 2.50
12 Burmy C 1.50 3.00
13 Corsola C 7.50 15.00
14 Mareep C 1.25 2.50
15 Ralts C .10 .20
16 Sentret C 3.00 6.00
17 Spinda C .50 1.00

2008 Pokemon Organized Play Series 8

1 Heatran R .75 1.50
2 Lucario R 4.00 8.00
3 Luxray HOLO R .60 1.25
4 Probopass HOLO R .75 1.50
5 Yanmega R 1.25 2.50
6 Cherrim U .75 1.50

7 Carnivine U 7.50 15.00
8 Luxio U .75 1.50
9 Night Maintenance U 3.00 8.00
10 Rare Candy U 3.00 6.00
11 Roseanne's Research U 1.00 2.00
12 Chimchar C#((Cracked Ice Reverse Holo) 1.50 4.00
13 Croagunk C .50 1.00
14 Happiny C .30 .60
15 Piplup C .75 1.50
16 Riolu C .75 1.50
17 Turtwig C .30 .75

2009 Pokemon Burger King Platinum

1 Chimchar 1.25 2.50
2 Dialga 1.00 2.00
3 Eevee 1.25 2.50
4 Giratina .30 .75
5 Glaceon .01 .08
6 Leafeon .08 .20
7 Meowth .60 1.25
8 Palkia 4.00 10.00
9 Pichu 4.00 8.00
10 Pikachu 2.00 4.00
11 Piplup .08 .20
12 Turtwig .01 .08

2009 Pokemon Organized Play Series 9

1 Garchomp R .04 .10
2 Manaphy R 6.00 12.00
3 Raichu R 1.00 2.00
4 Regigigas R .75 1.50
5 Rotom HOLO R .50 1.00
6 Buizel U .75 1.50
7 Croagunk U .60 1.25
8 Gabite U 2.00 4.00
9 Lopunny U .75 1.50
10 Pachirisu U 1.00 2.00
11 Pichu U 2.00 5.00
12 Buneary C .40 1.00
13 Chimchar C .08 .20
14 Gible C .04 .10
15 Pikachu C .12 .25
16 Piplup C .07 .15
17 Turtwig C 1.25 3.00

2009 Pokemon Platinum

1 Ampharos HOLO R .60 1.25
2 Blastoise HOLO R .75 1.50
3 Blaziken HOLO R 1.00 2.00
4 Delcatty HOLO R 1.00 2.00
5 Dialga HOLO R .07 .15
6 Dialga HOLO R .60 1.25
7 Dialga HOLO R .75 1.50
8 Gardevoir HOLO R 3.00 6.00
9 Giratina HOLO R 1.50 3.00
10 Giratina HOLO R .75 1.50
11 Manectric HOLO R 1.50 4.00
12 Palkia HOLO R .40 1.00
13 Rampardos HOLO R 1.00 2.00
14 Shaymin HOLO R 1.25 2.50
15 Shaymin HOLO R 2.00 4.00
16 Slaking HOLO R 1.25 2.50
17 Weavile HOLO R .07 .15
18 Altaria R 2.50 5.00
19 Banette R 2.00 4.00
20 Bastiodon R 1.00 2.00
21 Beautifly R 1.50 3.00
22 Blissey R 1.50 3.00
23 Dialga R 1.50 3.00
24 Dugtrio R .10 .20
25 Dustox R 1.25 2.50
26 Empoleon R 7.50 15.00
27 Giratina R .07 .15
28 Giratina R .12 .30
29 Golduck R 1.00 2.00
30 Gyarados R .75 1.50
31 Infernape R .75 1.50
32 Kricketune R 2.50 6.00
33 Lickilicky R 1.25 3.00
34 Ludicolo R 2.50 5.00
35 Luvdisc R 30.00 80.00
36 Ninetales R 1.00 2.00
37 Palkia R 1.00 2.00
38 Shaymin R 2.00 4.00
39 Torterra R 2.50 5.00
40 Toxicroak R 1.00 2.00
41 Bronzong U 12.50 25.00
42 Cacturne U 2.50 5.00
43 Carnivine U 1.50 3.00
44 Cascoon U .60 1.25
45 Combusken U 1.00 2.00
46 Cranidos U 2.00 4.00
47 Crobat U 1.00 2.00
48 Flaaffy U .50 1.00
49 Grotle U .50 1.00
50 Houndoom U 1.50 3.00
51 Kirlia U 1.00 2.00
52 Lombre U 2.50 5.00
53 Lucario U 2.00 4.00
54 Mightyena U 1.25 2.50
55 Mismagius U .60 1.25
56 Monferno U 1.00 2.00
57 Muk U 2.00 4.00
58 Octillery U 1.25 2.50
59 Prinplup U 1.25 2.50
60 Probopass U 1.00 2.00
61 Seviper U .75 1.50
62 Shieldon U 1.00 2.00
63 Silcoon U 1.00 2.00
64 Vigoroth U .60 1.25
65 Wartortle U 7.50 15.00
66 Zangoose U .75 1.50
67 Cacnea C .50 1.00
68 Carnivine C 6.00 12.00
69 Chansey C 1.25 2.50
70 Chimchar C .75 1.50
71 Combee C .75 1.50
72 Diglett C .50 1.00
73 Dunsparce C 2.00 4.00
74 Electrike C 1.50 3.00
75 Grimer C .10 .20
76 Happiny C .01 .08
77 Honchkrow C .05 .12
78 Kricketot C 3.00 6.00
79 Lapras C 1.25 2.50
80 Lickitung C .75 1.50
81 Lotad C 1.50 3.00
82 Mareep C 1.25 2.50
83 Misdreavus C .01 .08
84 Nosepass C .08 .20
85 Piplup C 6.00 12.00
86 Poochyena C 3.00 6.00
87 Psyduck C 1.50 3.00
88 Purugly C .75 1.50
89 Ralts C 1.00 2.00
90 Remoraid C 1.25 2.50
91 Riolu C .20 .40
92 Shuppet C .75 1.50
93 Skitty C 2.50 6.00
94 Skuntank C 12.50 25.00
95 Slakoth C 3.00 6.00
96 Squirtle C 1.50 4.00
97 Swablu C 2.50 5.00
98 Tauros C 2.00 4.00
99 Torchic C 2.00 4.00
100 Torkoal C .30 .75
101 Turtwig C 2.50 5.00
102 Vulpix C .01 .08
103 Wurmple C .05 .12
104 Broken Time-Space U .75 1.50
105 Cyrus's Conspiracy U 1.25 2.50
106 Galactic HQ U .10 .20
107 Level Max U 1.25 2.50
108 Life Herb U 1.00 2.50
109 Looker's Investigation U 7.50 15.00
110 Memory Berry U 7.50 15.00
111 Miasma Valley U .01 .08
112 Pluspower U .10 .25
113 Poke Ball U 1.00 2.00
114 Pokedex Handy 910s U .50 1.00
115 Pokemon Rescue U 6.00 12.00
116 Energy Gain U 2.50 5.00
117 Power Spray U .75 1.50
118 Poke Turn U .75 1.50
119 Armor Fossil C .60 1.25
120 Skull Fossil C 3.00 6.00
121 Rainbow Energy U .60 1.25
122 Dialga LV.X HOLO R 1.00 2.00
123 Drapion LV.X HOLO R 1.00 2.50
124 Giratina LV.X HOLO R .30 .75
125 Palkia LV.X HOLO R 1.00 2.00
126 Shaymin LV.X HOLO R .75 1.50
127 Shaymin LV.X HOLO R .75 1.50
128 Electabuzz HOLO R 1.00 2.00
129 Hitmonchan HOLO R .07 .15
130 Scyther HOLO R .75 1.50
SH4 Lotad HOLO R .07 .15
SH5 Swablu HOLO R .75 1.50
SH6 Vulpix HOLO R .50 1.00

2009 Pokemon Platinum Arceus

1 Charizard HOLO R 1.00 2.00
2 Froslass HOLO R 1.50 3.00
3 Heatran HOLO R .75 1.50
4 Kabutops HOLO R 1.25 2.50
5 Luxray HOLO R .25 .50
6 Mothim HOLO R 1.00 2.50
7 Probopass HOLO R 1.25 2.50
8 Salamence HOLO R 2.50 5.00
9 Swalot HOLO R 2.00 5.00
10 Tangrowth HOLO R .50 1.25
11 Toxicroak HOLO R .75 1.50
12 Zapdos HOLO R 2.50 5.00
13 Aerodactyl R 1.25 2.50
14 Bronzong R 1.00 2.00
15 Cherrim R 1.25 2.50
16 Gengar R 1.00 2.00
17 Gengar R .75 1.50
18 Glalie R 2.00 4.00
19 Golem R .30 .75
20 Hariyama R 1.00 2.00
21 Lopunny R 2.00 4.00
22 Manectric R .50 1.00
23 Omastar R 1.00 2.00
24 Pelipper R .07 .15
25 Pichu R .75 1.50
26 Porygon-Z R .08 .20
27 Raichu R .01 .08
28 Rapidash R .01 .08
29 Raticate R 1.00 2.00
30 Sceptile R 4.00 8.00
31 Sceptile R 2.00 5.00
32 Spiritomb R 1.00 2.50
33 Bronzong U 2.50 5.00
34 Bronzor U 12.00 30.00
35 Charmeleon U 1.00 2.00
36 Gastly U 1.00 2.00
37 Graveler U 1.50 3.00
38 Grovyle U 6.00 12.00
39 Grovyle U .08 .20
40 Gulpin U .10 .25
41 Haunter U 1.50 3.00
42 Haunter U .60 1.25
43 Luxio U 1.00 2.00
44 Manectric U 1.00 2.00
45 Pelipper U .30 .60
46 Ponyta U .50 1.00
47 Rapidash U 1.00 2.00
48 Shelgon U .60 1.25
49 Wormadam U 1.25 2.50
50 Wormadam U 3.00 6.00
51 Wormadam U .75 1.50
52 Bagon C 1.50 3.00
53 Beedrill C .75 1.50
54 Bronzor C .75 1.50
55 Buneary C .60 1.25
56 Burmy C .75 1.50
57 Burmy C .75 1.50
58 Burmy C 4.00 8.00
59 Charmander C 3.00 6.00
60 Cherubi C 2.00 4.00
61 Croagunk C .60 1.25
62 Electrike C .75 1.50
63 Electrike C 1.50 3.00
64 Gastly C .10 .20
65 Geodude C 1.25 2.50
66 Gulpin C .50 1.00
67 Kabuto C 1.00 2.00
68 Makuhita C .01 .08
69 Nosepass C .05 .12
70 Omanyte C 7.50 15.00
71 Pikachu C 3.00 6.00
72 Ponyta C 1.00 2.00
73 Rattata C .12 .25
74 Shinx C 1.00 2.00
75 Snorunt C 1.25 2.50
76 Tangela C 1.25 2.50
77 Tangela C .75 1.50
78 Treecko C 1.00 2.00
79 Treecko C 1.50 3.00
80 Wingull C .75 1.50
81 Wingull C 1.00 2.00
82 Beginning Door U .30 .75
83 Bench Shield U .75 1.50
84 Buffer Piece U .60 1.25
85 Department Store Girl U .75 1.50
86 Energy Restore U 7.50 15.00
87 Expert Belt U .75 1.50
88 Lucky Egg U .75 1.50
89 Old Amber U .60 1.25
90 Professor Oak's Visit U 1.00 2.00
91 Ultimate Zone U 1.00 2.00
92 Dome Fossil C 1.00 2.00
93 Helix Fossil C 1.00 2.00
94 Arceus LV.X HOLO R 2.00 5.00
95 Arceus LV.X HOLO R 15.00 30.00
96 Arceus LV.X HOLO R 5.00 12.00
97 Gengar LV.X HOLO R .01 .08
98 Salamence LV.X HOLO R .04 .10
99 Tangrowth LV.X HOLO R .75 1.50
SH10 Bagon HOLO R 1.50 3.00
SH11 Ponyta HOLO R 4.00 8.00
SH12 Shinx HOLO R 1.50 3.00
AR1 Arceus HOLO R .60 1.25
AR2 Arceus HOLO R .10 .20
AR3 Arceus HOLO R 1.25 2.50
AR4 Arceus HOLO R 1.50 4.00
AR5 Arceus HOLO R 4.00 8.00
AR6 Arceus HOLO R 5.00 10.00
AR7 Arceus HOLO R 7.50 15.00
AR8 Arceus HOLO R 6.00 12.00
AR9 Arceus HOLO R .60 1.25

2009 Pokemon Platinum Rising Rivals

1 Arcanine HOLO R 1.00 2.00
2 Bastiodon GL HOLO R .75 1.50
3 Darkrai G HOLO R 1.50 3.00
4 Floatzel GL HOLO R .15 .30
5 Flygon HOLO R 1.50 3.00
6 Froslass GL HOLO R .60 1.25
7 Jirachi HOLO R 1.25 2.50
8 Lucario GL HOLO R .75 1.50
9 Luxray GL HOLO R 1.50 3.00
10 Mismagius GL HOLO R .60 1.25
11 Rampardos GL HOLO R .75 1.50
12 Roserade GL HOLO R .75 1.50
13 Shiftry HOLO R .75 1.50
14 Aggron R .75 1.50
15 Beedrill R 1.00 2.50
16 Bronzong 4 R .20 .50
17 Drapion 4 R 1.00 2.50
18 Espeon 4 R 1.00 2.50
19 Flareon R .25 .60
20 Gallade 4 R 1.25 2.50
21 Gastrodon East Sea R .60 1.25
22 Gastrodon West Sea R 2.00 4.00
23 Golem 4 R 1.50 3.00
24 Heracross 4 R 1.25 2.50
25 Hippowdon R .50 1.00
26 Jolteon R 2.00 4.00
27 Mamoswine GL R 1.25 2.50
28 Mr. Mime 4 R .75 1.50
29 Nidoking R 4.00 8.00
30 Nidoqueen R 2.00 4.00
31 Raichu GL R .12 .25
32 Rhyperior 4 R .50 1.00
33 Snorlax R 1.00 2.00
34 Vaporeon R .75 1.50
35 Vespiquen 4 R .08 .20
36 Walrein R .01 .08
37 Yanmega 4 R .04 .10
38 Alakazam 4 U .50 1.00
39 Electrode G U 3.00 6.00
40 Gengar GL U 2.00 4.00
41 Glaceon U .75 1.50
42 Hippowdon 4 U 1.25 2.50
43 Infernape 4 U .07 .15
44 Lairon U 2.00 4.00
45 Leafeon U 2.50 5.00
46 Machamp GL U .60 1.25
47 Rapidash 4 U 1.00 2.00
48 Scizor 4 U 2.00 4.00
49 Sharpedo U 2.00 4.00
50 Starmie U 2.00 4.00
51 Steelix GL U .60 1.50
52 Tropius U .12 .30
53 Vibrava U 7.50 15.00
54 Whiscash 4 U 1.00 2.00
55 Aerodactyl GL C 1.00 2.00
56 Ambipom G C 3.00 8.00
57 Aron C 1.00 2.50
58 Carvanha C 2.50 5.00
59 Eevee C 10.00 25.00
60 Flareon 4 C .75 1.50
61 Forretress G C .75 1.50
62 Gliscor 4 C .75 1.50
63 Growlithe C .50 1.00
64 Hippopotas C 1.50 3.00
65 Houndoom 4 C 1.25 2.50
66 Kakuna C .75 1.50
67 Kecleon C .25 .50
68 Koffing C .75 1.50
69 Munchlax C .75 1.50
70 Munchlax C 1.00 2.00
71 Nidoran F C .75 1.50
72 Nidoran M C .75 1.50
73 Nidorina C .75 1.50
74 Nidorino C 1.50 3.00
75 Nuzleaf C 1.25 2.50
76 Quagsire GL C 3.00 6.00
77 Sealeo C .25 .50
78 Seedot C 1.50 3.00
79 Shellos East Sea C .60 1.25
80 Shellos West Sea C .60 1.25
81 Snorlax C .50 1.00
82 Spheal C 1.25 2.50
83 Staryu C 1.25 2.50
84 Trapinch C .60 1.25
85 Turtwig GL C .08 .20
86 Weedle C .05 .12
87 Weezing C .75 1.50
88 Aaron's Collection U .75 1.50
89 Bebe's Search U .75 1.50
90 Bertha's Warmth U 1.25 2.50
91 Flint's Willpower U 1.25 2.50
92 Lucian's Assignment U 7.50 15.00
93 Pokemon Contest Hall U .60 1.25
94 Sunyshore City Gym U 1.00 2.00
95 Technical Machine G U 1.50 3.00
96 SP-Radar U 1.50 3.00
97 Underground Expedition U 1.50 3.00
98 Volkner's Philosophy U .75 1.50
99 Darkness Energy U 1.50 3.00
100 Metal Energy U 1.25 2.50
101 SP Energy U .25 .50
102 Upper Energy U .01 .08
103 Alakazam 4 LV.X HOLO R .08 .20
104 Floatzel GL LV.X HOLO R .07 .15
105 Flygon LV.X HOLO R .60 1.25
106 Gallade 4 LV.X HOLO R 1.25 2.50
107 Hippowdon LV.X HOLO R .50 1.00
108 Infernape 4 LV.X HOLO R 1.00 2.00
109 Luxray GL LV.X HOLO R .75 1.50
110 Mismagius GL LV.X HOLO R .75 1.50
111 Snorlax LV.X HOLO R 1.50 3.00
112 Pikachu HOLO SCR 1.00 2.00
113 Flying Pikachu HOLO SCR 1.25 2.50
114 Surfing Pikachu HOLO SCR .25 .50
RT1 Fan Rotom HOLO R 7.50 15.00
RT2 Frost Rotom HOLO R 1.00 2.50
RT3 Heat Rotom HOLO R .75 1.50
RT4 Mow Rotom HOLO R .30 .60
RT5 Wash Rotom HOLO R .60 1.25
RT6 Charons Choice HOLO R 3.00 6.00

2009 Pokemon Platinum Supreme Victors

1 Absol HOLO R .01 .08
2 Blaziken HOLO R .05 .12
3 Drifblim HOLO R .08 .20
4 Electivire HOLO R .07 .15
5 Garchomp HOLO R .75 1.50
6 Magmortar HOLO R .75 1.50
7 Metagross HOLO R 2.50 5.00
8 Rayquaza HOLO R .75 1.50
9 Regigigas HOLO R .60 1.25
10 Rhyperior HOLO R .75 1.50
11 Staraptor HOLO R 2.00 4.00
12 Swampert HOLO R .60 1.25
13 Venusaur HOLO R .60 1.25
14 Yanmega HOLO R 6.00 15.00
15 Arcanine R 1.25 2.50
16 Articuno R 4.00 8.00
17 Butterfree R .75 1.50
18 Camerupt R .75 1.50
19 Camerupt R 1.00 2.00
20 Charizard R 4.00 8.00
21 Chimecho R 1.00 2.00
22 Claydol R 7.50 15.00
23 Crawdaunt R 1.50 3.00
24 Dewgong R 1.25 3.00
25 Dodrio R 1.50 3.00
26 Dusknoir R .60 1.25
27 Empoleon R .60 1.25
28 Exploud R .01 .08
29 Honchkrow R .04 .10
30 Lickilicky R .12 .25
31 Lucario R .75 1.50
32 Lunatone R .75 1.50
33 Mawile R 1.00 2.00
34 Medicham R 1.00 2.00
35 Milotic R .60 1.25
36 Moltres R .60 1.50
37 Mr. Mime R 2.00 4.00
38 Parasect R .60 1.25
39 Primeape R 1.50 3.00
40 Roserade R .60 1.25
41 Sableye R .75 1.50
42 Sandslash R .40 1.00
43 Seaking R .12 .25
44 Shedinja R .60 1.25
45 Solrock R .75 1.50
46 Spinda R 1.25 2.50
47 Wailord R .60 1.25
48 Zapdos R .75 1.50
49 Altaria U .75 1.50
50 Arcanine U 1.00 2.50

51 Bibarel U	.25	.60
52 Breloom U	3.00	6.00
53 Carnivine U	5.00	10.00
54 Chatot U	1.00	2.50
55 Cherrim U	2.00	4.00
56 Dragonite U	1.00	2.00
57 Drifblim U	1.50	4.00
58 Floatzel U	.40	1.00
59 Gabite U	1.00	2.00
60 Garchomp U	1.00	2.00
61 Hippopotas U	.07	.15
62 Ivysaur U	5.00	10.00
63 Lopunny U	1.50	3.00
64 Loudred U	7.50	15.00
65 Magmar U	3.00	6.00
66 Manectric U	.75	1.50
67 Marshtomp U	.75	1.50
68 Masquerain U	2.00	4.00
69 Metang U	.60	1.25
70 Milotic U	.75	1.50
71 Minun U	2.00	4.00
72 Murkrow U	2.00	4.00
73 Ninjask U	.25	.50
74 Numel U	.40	1.00
75 Pinsir U	7.50	15.00
76 Plusle U	1.00	2.00
77 Raichu U	.75	1.50
78 Raticate U	.75	1.50
79 Relicanth U	2.00	5.00
80 Rhydon U	.50	1.25
81 Roserade U	2.50	5.00
82 Rotom U	.75	1.50
83 Skarmory U	12.00	30.00
84 Spiritomb U	.75	1.50
85 Staravia U	.75	1.50
86 Togekiss U	4.00	8.00
87 Wailmer U	1.50	3.00
88 Yanma U	.75	1.50
89 Baltoy C	.75	1.50
90 Beldum C	.25	.50
91 Bidoof C	1.50	3.00
92 Buizel C	2.00	4.00
93 Bulbasaur C	1.25	2.50
94 Buneary C	.75	1.50
95 Chatot C	.60	1.25
96 Cherubi C	.60	1.25
97 Chimchar C	.12	.25
98 Chingling C	.75	1.50
99 Combee C	1.25	2.50
100 Corphish C	1.50	3.00
101 Croagunk C	2.50	5.00
102 Doduo C	2.00	4.00
103 Drifloon C	1.00	2.00
104 Feebas C	1.50	3.00
105 Geodude C	3.00	6.00
106 Gible C	2.50	5.00
107 Goldeen C	1.00	2.00
108 Growlithe C	1.25	2.50
109 Kricketot C	.75	1.50
110 Magikarp C	1.25	2.50
111 Magnemite C	.60	1.25
112 Mankey C	2.00	4.00
113 Meditite C	.10	.20
114 Meowth C	2.00	4.00
115 Mime Jr. C	.75	1.50
116 Mudkip C	1.00	2.00
117 Nincada C	.75	1.50
118 Pachirisu C	1.50	3.00
119 Paras C	1.00	2.00
120 Pikachu C	1.25	3.00
121 Piplup C	3.00	6.00
122 Rhyhorn C	1.00	2.00
123 Roselia C	1.00	2.00
124 Sandshrew C	.07	.15
125 Seel C	.07	.15
126 Shinx C	30.00	60.00
127 Shroomish C	.01	.08
128 Skorupi C	.04	.10
129 Starly C	.75	1.50
130 Surskit C	2.00	4.00
131 Turtwig C	.60	1.25
132 Whismur C	.75	1.50
133 Zubat C	.75	1.50
134 Battle Tower U	.01	.08
135 Champion Room U	.05	.12
136 Cynthia's Guidance U	2.00	5.00
137 Cyrus's Initiative U	1.50	3.00
138 Night Teleporter U	5.00	10.00
139 Palmer's Contribution U	.60	1.25
140 VS. Seeker U	.75	1.50
141 Absol LV.X HOLO R	7.50	15.00
142 Blaziken LV.X HOLO R	1.50	3.00
143 Charizard LV.X HOLO R	1.00	2.00
144 Electivire LV.X HOLO R	1.25	2.50
145 Garchomp LV.X HOLO R	.75	1.50
146 Rayquaza LV.X HOLO R	.75	1.50
147 Staraptor LV.X HOLO R	1.00	2.00
148 Articuno HOLO R	10.00	25.00
149 Moltres HOLO R	.07	.15
150 Zapdos HOLO R	.60	1.25
SH7 Milotic HOLO R	2.00	4.00
SH9 Yanma HOLO R	.75	1.50
SH8 Relicanth HOLO R	.30	.60

2010 Pokemon HeartGold and SoulSilver

1 Arcanine HOLO R	.60	1.25
2 Azumarill HOLO R	1.50	3.00
3 Clefable HOLO R	2.50	5.00
4 Gyarados HOLO R	1.25	2.50
5 Hitmontop HOLO R	2.50	5.00
6 Jumpluff HOLO R	.75	1.50
7 Ninetales HOLO R	1.25	2.50
8 Noctowl HOLO R	.60	1.25
9 Quagsire HOLO R	.75	1.50
10 Raichu HOLO R	.60	1.25
11 Shuckle HOLO R	.60	1.25
12 Slowking HOLO R	.08	.20
13 Wobbuffet HOLO R	4.00	8.00
14 Ampharos R	.75	1.50
15 Ariados R	.75	1.50
16 Butterfree R	.30	.75
17 Cleffa R	.04	.10
18 Exeggutor R	.05	.12
19 Farfetch'd R	1.25	2.50
20 Feraligatr R	1.50	3.00
21 Furret R	1.00	2.50
22 Granbull R	.75	1.50
23 Hypno R	.10	.20
24 Lapras R	1.50	3.00
25 Ledian R	1.00	2.00
26 Meganium R	1.00	2.00
27 Persian R	1.25	2.50
28 Pichu R	3.00	6.00
29 Sandslash R	.60	1.25
30 Smoochum R	2.00	4.00
31 Sunflora R	1.25	3.00
32 Typhlosion R	.30	.75
33 Tyrogue R	1.25	2.50
34 Weezing R	.08	.20
35 Bayleef U	.04	.10
36 Blissey U	.75	1.50
37 Corsola U	1.50	4.00
38 Croconaw U	.40	1.00
39 Delibird U	2.50	5.00
40 Donphan U	1.25	2.50
41 Dunsparce U	7.50	15.00
42 Flaaffy U	1.00	2.00
43 Heracross U	.75	1.50
44 Igglybuff U	.60	1.25
45 Mantine U	3.00	6.00
46 Metapod U	.50	1.00
47 Miltank U	.75	1.50
48 Parasect U	2.00	4.00
49 Quilava U	4.00	8.00
50 Qwilfish U	.75	1.50
51 Skiploom U	10.00	20.00
52 Slowbro U	.75	1.50
53 Starmie U	12.50	25.00
54 Unown U	.75	1.50
55 Unown U	.75	1.50
56 Wigglytuff U	2.00	5.00
57 Caterpie C	1.25	3.00
58 Chansey C	2.50	5.00
59 Chikorita C	10.00	25.00
60 Clefairy C	.75	1.50
61 Cyndaquil C	1.25	2.50
62 Drowzee C	.50	1.00
63 Exeggcute C	.75	1.50
64 Girafarig C	1.00	2.00
65 Growlithe C	1.50	3.00
66 Hoothoot C	2.00	4.00
67 Hoppip C	.75	1.50
68 Jigglypuff C	.30	.60
69 Jynx C	.07	.15
70 Koffing C	.07	.15
71 Ledyba C	.20	.50
72 Magikarp C	2.50	5.00
73 Mareep C	.75	1.50
74 Marill C	.60	1.25
75 Meowth C	2.00	4.00
76 Paras C	7.50	15.00
77 Phanpy C	1.50	3.00
78 Pikachu C	1.50	3.00
79 Sandshrew C	.04	.10
80 Sentret C	.08	.20
81 Slowpoke C	.15	.30
82 Snubbull C	.25	.50
83 Spinarak C	2.50	5.00
84 Staryu C	.60	1.25
85 Sunkern C	1.25	2.50
86 Totodile C	.75	1.50
87 Vulpix C	1.25	2.50
88 Wooper C	.75	1.50
89 Bill U	.60	1.25
90 Copycat U	.75	1.50
91 Energy Switch U	.75	1.50
92 Fisherman U	1.50	3.00
93 Full Heal U	1.50	3.00
94 Moo-moo Milk U	1.50	3.00
95 Poke Ball U	1.25	2.50
96 Pokegear 3.0 U	1.25	2.50
97 Pokemon Collector U	1.00	2.00
98 Pokemon Communication U	1.50	3.00
99 Pokemon Reversal U	2.00	4.00
100 Professor Elm's Training Method U	1.00	2.00
101 Professor Oak's New Theory U	1.25	2.50
102 Switch U	.30	.60
103 Double Colorless Energy U	.75	1.50
104 Rainbow Energy U	1.25	3.00
105 Ampharos Prime HOLO SR	.04	.10
106 Blissey Prime HOLO SR	.10	.25
107 Donphan Prime HOLO SR	2.00	4.00
108 Feraligatr Prime HOLO SR	.07	.15
109 Meganium Prime HOLO SR	30.00	60.00
110 Typhlosion Prime HOLO SR	.50	1.00
111 Ho-Oh LEGEND Top HOLO R	1.25	2.50
112 Ho-Oh LEGEND Bottom HOLO R	1.25	2.50
113 Lugia LEGEND Top HOLO R	.60	1.25
114 Lugia LEGEND Bottom HOLO R	1.00	2.00
115 Grass Energy C	.04	.10
116 Fire Energy C	.08	.20
117 Water Energy C	1.00	2.00
118 Lightning Energy C	2.00	4.00
119 Psychic Energy C	1.00	2.00
120 Fighting Energy C	1.50	4.00
121 Darkness Energy C	1.50	3.00
122 Metal Energy C	5.00	10.00
123 Gyarados HOLO R	.60	1.25
124 Alph Lithograph UR	1.25	2.50

2010 Pokemon HeartGold and SoulSilver Triumphant

1 Aggron HOLO R	6.00	12.00
2 Altaria HOLO R	1.50	3.00
3 Celebi HOLO R	5.00	10.00
4 Drapion HOLO R	.75	1.50
5 Mamoswine HOLO R	1.00	2.00
6 Nidoking HOLO R	.75	1.50
7 Porygon-Z HOLO R	1.50	3.00
8 Rapidash HOLO R	3.00	8.00
9 Solrock HOLO R	.07	.15
10 Spiritomb HOLO R	.75	1.50
11 Venomoth HOLO R	3.00	6.00
12 Victreebel HOLO R	1.25	2.50
13 Ambipom R	.75	1.50
14 Banette R	2.50	5.00
15 Bronzong R	.75	1.50
16 Carnivine R	.75	1.50
17 Ditto R	2.00	4.00
18 Dragonite R	1.50	3.00
19 Dugtrio R	.60	1.25
20 Electivire R	.20	.50
21 Elekid R	5.00	10.00
22 Golduck R	1.50	3.00
23 Grumpig R	.75	1.50
24 Kricketune R	.08	.20
25 Lunatone R	.60	1.25
26 Machamp R	.75	1.50
27 Magmortar R	.75	1.50
28 Nidoqueen R	.75	1.50
29 Pidgeot R	1.25	2.50
30 Sharpedo R	1.25	2.50
31 Wailord R	1.25	2.50
32 Dragonair U	1.00	2.00
33 Electabuzz U	1.00	2.50
34 Electrode U	.75	1.50
35 Haunter U	1.25	2.50
36 Kangaskhan U	7.50	15.00
37 Lairon U	.12	.25
38 Lickilicky U	.75	1.50
39 Luvdisc U	2.50	5.00
40 Machoke U	.75	1.50
41 Magby U	.75	1.50
42 Magmar U	1.25	2.50
43 Magneton U	1.00	2.00
44 Marowak U	1.00	2.50
45 Nidorina U	.20	.50
46 Nidorino U	4.00	8.00
47 Pidgeotto U	4.00	8.00
48 Piloswine U	1.25	3.00
49 Porygon2 U	.40	1.00
50 Tentacruel U	15.00	30.00
51 Unown U	.08	.20
52 Wailmer U	.10	.25
53 Weepinbell U	1.50	3.00
54 Yanmega U	.07	.15
55 Aipom C	.75	1.50
56 Aron C	2.50	5.00
57 Bellsprout C	3.00	8.00
58 Bronzor C	1.00	2.50
59 Carvanha C	2.50	5.00
60 Cubone C	10.00	25.00
61 Diglett C	1.00	2.00
62 Dratini C	.60	1.25
63 Gastly C	.50	1.00
64 Illumise C	1.00	2.00
65 Kricketot C	1.00	2.00
66 Lickitung C	1.25	2.50
67 Machop C	1.00	2.00
68 Magnemite C	.60	1.25
69 Nidoran F C	.75	1.50
70 Nidoran M C	.75	1.50
71 Pidgey C	20.00	40.00
72 Ponyta C	.07	.15
73 Porygon C	.20	.50
74 Psyduck C	1.50	3.00
75 Shuppet C	7.50	15.00
76 Skorupi C	1.50	3.00
77 Spoink C	.12	.25
78 Swablu C	1.00	2.00
79 Swinub C	1.00	2.00
80 Tentacool C	.60	1.25
81 Venonat C	1.25	2.50
82 Volbeat C	.75	1.50
83 Voltorb C	.75	1.50
84 Yanma C	1.25	2.50
85 Black Belt U	25.00	50.00
86 Indigo Plateau U	1.25	2.50
87 Junk Arm U	3.00	6.00
88 Seeker U	.25	.50
89 Twins U	1.00	2.00
90 Rescue Energy U	1.00	2.00
91 Absol Prime HOLO R	1.25	2.50
92 Celebi Prime HOLO R	1.00	2.00
93 Electrode Prime HOLO R	.75	1.50
94 Gengar Prime HOLO R	.75	1.50
95 Machamp Prime HOLO R	.30	.75
96 Magnezone Prime HOLO R	.50	1.25
97 Mew Prime HOLO R	2.00	4.00
98 Yanmega Prime HOLO R	1.50	3.00
99 Darkrai & Cresselia LEGEND HOLO R	.75	1.50
100 Darkrai & Cresselia LEGEND HOLO R	.50	1.00
101 Palkia & Dialga LEGEND HOLO R	2.50	5.00
102 Palkia & Dialga LEGEND HOLO R	.12	.25
SP Alph Lithograph UR	1.00	2.00

2010 Pokemon HeartGold and SoulSilver Undaunted

1 Bellossom HOLO R	.75	1.50
2 Espeon HOLO R	1.25	2.50
3 Forretress HOLO R	.60	1.25
4 Gliscor HOLO R	.75	1.50
5 Houndoom HOLO R	1.50	4.00
6 Magcargo HOLO R	.60	1.25
7 Scizor HOLO R	1.50	3.00
8 Smeargle HOLO R	2.50	5.00
9 Togekiss HOLO R	.75	1.50
10 Umbreon HOLO R	1.50	3.00
11 Dodrio R	1.25	3.00
12 Drifblim R	4.00	8.00
13 Forretress R	.60	1.25
14 Hariyama R	2.50	5.00
15 Honchkrow R	.75	1.50
16 Honchkrow R	1.25	2.50
17 Leafeon R	1.00	2.00
18 Metagross R	1.00	2.00
19 Mismagius R	8.00	20.00
20 Rotom R	4.00	8.00
21 Skarmory R	.05	.12
22 Tropius R	.10	.25
23 Vespiquen R	.01	.08
24 Vileplume R	.04	.10
25 Weavile R	.60	1.25
26 Flareon U	.75	1.50
27 Gloom U	1.00	2.00
28 Jolteon U	2.00	4.00
29 Lairon U	3.00	6.00
30 Metang U	.75	1.50
31 Muk U	.60	1.25
32 Pinsir U	1.25	2.50
33 Raichu U	3.00	6.00
34 Raticate U	2.00	4.00
35 Sableye U	.60	1.25
36 Scyther U	1.00	2.00
37 Skuntank U	1.25	2.50
38 Slowbro U	.75	1.50
39 Togetic U	5.00	10.00
40 Unown U	.10	.20
41 Vaporeon U	.75	1.50
42 Aron C	2.50	5.00
43 Beldum C	1.25	2.50
44 Combee C	.75	1.50
45 Doduo C	.75	1.50
46 Drifloon C	3.00	6.00
47 Eevee C	.75	1.50
48 Eevee C	.75	1.50
49 Gligar C	1.50	3.00
50 Grimer C	1.00	2.00
51 Hitmonchan C	1.25	2.50
52 Hitmonlee C	.75	1.50
53 Houndour C	.10	.20
54 Houndour C	.10	.20
55 Makuhita C	.15	.40
56 Mawile C	1.25	2.50
57 Misdreavus C	.75	1.50
58 Murkrow C	.75	1.50
59 Murkrow C	2.50	5.00
60 Oddish C	.75	1.50
61 Pikachu C	.75	1.50
62 Pineco C	1.00	2.00
63 Pineco C	1.25	2.50
64 Rattata C	1.25	2.50
65 Scyther C	2.00	5.00
66 Slowpoke C	2.00	4.00
67 Slugma C	1.50	3.00
68 Sneasel C	1.25	2.50
69 Stunky C	2.50	5.00
70 Togepi C	1.50	3.00
71 Burned Tower U	4.00	8.00
72 Defender U	.30	.60
73 Energy Exchanger U	1.25	2.50
74 Flower Shop Lady U	.10	.20
75 Legend Box U	.30	.75
76 Ruins of Alph U	.75	1.50
77 Sage's Training U	.60	1.25
78 Team Rocket's Trickery U	.60	1.25
79 Darkness Energy U	.08	.20
80 Metal Energy U	.04	.10
81 Espeon Prime HOLO R	1.00	2.50
82 Houndoom Prime HOLO R	.25	.60
83 Raichu Prime HOLO R	.01	.08
84 Scizor Prime HOLO R	.05	.12
85 Slowking Prime HOLO R	1.25	2.50
86 Umbreon Prime HOLO R	1.25	2.50
87 Kyogre & Groudon LEGEND HOLO R	1.25	2.50
88 Kyogre & Groudon LEGEND HOLO R	.60	1.25
89 Rayquaza & Deoxys LEGEND HOLO R	2.00	4.00
90 Rayquaza & Deoxys LEGEND HOLO R	1.25	3.00
SP Alph Lithograph UR	.40	1.00

2010 Pokemon HeartGold and SoulSilver Unleashed

1 Jirachi HOLO R	.75	1.50
2 Magmortar HOLO R	.75	1.50
3 Manaphy HOLO R	1.50	4.00
4 Metagross HOLO R	.50	1.25
5 Mismagius HOLO R	2.50	5.00
6 Octillery HOLO R	10.00	25.00
7 Politoed HOLO R	.75	1.50
8 Shaymin HOLO R	.07	.15
9 Sudowoodo HOLO R	1.00	2.00
10 Torterra HOLO R	.75	1.50
11 Xatu HOLO R	1.25	2.50
12 Beedrill R	.07	.15
13 Blastoise R	.60	1.25
14 Crobat R	1.00	2.00
15 Fearow R	1.00	2.00
16 Floatzel R	.75	1.50
17 Kingdra R	4.00	8.00
18 Lanturn R	1.25	2.50
19 Lucario R	.75	1.50
20 Ninetales R	1.25	2.50
21 Poliwrath R	2.00	4.00
22 Primeape R	2.00	4.00
23 Roserade R	25.00	50.00
24 Steelix R	1.00	2.00
25 Torkoal R	2.00	4.00
26 Tyranitar R	.75	1.50
27 Ursaring R	.08	.20
28 Cherrim U	1.00	2.00
29 Dunsparce U	.60	1.25
30 Golbat U	.30	.75
31 Grotle U	1.25	2.50
32 Kakuna U	.75	1.50
33 Metang U	2.50	5.00

34 Minun U	.25	.50
35 Numel U	.01	.08
36 Plusle U	.10	.25
37 Poliwhirl U	.50	1.00
38 Pupitar U	1.50	3.00
39 Pupitar U	.50	1.00
40 Seadra U	.25	.50
41 Tauros U	1.00	2.00
42 Wartortle U	1.25	2.50
43 Aipom C	.60	1.25
44 Beldum C	1.25	2.50
45 Buizel C	.75	1.50
46 Carnivine C	.01	.08
47 Cherubi C	.04	.10
48 Chinchou C	1.50	3.00
49 Horsea C	2.00	4.00
50 Larvitar C	3.00	6.00
51 Larvitar C	.50	1.00
52 Magmar C	.30	.60
53 Mankey C	.75	1.50
54 Misdreavus C	1.25	3.00
55 Natu C	1.25	2.50
56 Onix C	.25	.50
57 Onix C	.75	1.50
58 Poliwag C	.75	1.50
59 Remoraid C	2.50	5.00
60 Riolu C	.60	1.25
61 Roselia C	1.25	2.50
62 Spearow C	1.00	2.00
63 Squirtle C	.50	1.25
64 Stantler C	.75	1.50
65 Teddiursa C	1.00	2.00
66 Tropius C	.25	.50
67 Turtwig C	4.00	10.00
68 Vulpix C	.50	1.00
69 Weedle C	.60	1.25
70 Zubat C	.75	1.50
71 Cheerleader's Cheer U	.60	1.25
72 Dual Ball U	.75	1.50
73 Emcee's Chatter U	.50	1.00
74 Energy Returner U	1.00	2.00
75 Engineer's Adjustments U	2.50	6.00
76 Good Rod U	.10	.20
77 Interviewer's Questions U	2.50	5.00
78 Judge U	.25	.50
79 Life Herb U	.01	.08
80 Plus Power U	.10	.25
81 Pokemon Circulator U	.75	1.50
82 Rare Candy U	.01	.08
83 Super Scoop Up U	.04	.10
84 Crobat Prime HOLO R	.75	1.50
85 Kingdra Prime HOLO R	1.50	3.00
86 Lanturn Prime HOLO R	.60	1.25
87 Steelix Prime HOLO R	4.00	8.00
88 Tyranitar Prime HOLO R	.10	.20
89 Ursaring Prime HOLO R	.75	1.50
90 Entei & Raikou LEGEND HOLO R	.75	1.50
91 Entei & Raikou LEGEND HOLO R	.30	.60
92 Raikou & Suicune LEGEND HOLO R	.75	1.50
93 Raikou & Suicune LEGEND HOLO R	2.50	5.00
94 Suicune & Entei LEGEND HOLO R	1.00	2.00
95 Suicune & Entei LEGEND HOLO R	.60	1.25
96 Alph Lithograph R	.75	1.50

2011 Pokemon Black and White

1 Snivy C	1.00	2.00
2 Snivy C	.10	.20
3 Servine U	.12	.30
4 Servine U	2.00	4.00
5 Serperior HOLO R	.07	.15
6 Serperior HOLO R	1.00	2.00
7 Pansage C	.75	1.50
8 Simisage U	.75	1.50
9 Petilil C	1.25	2.50
10 Lilligant R	1.00	2.00
11 Maractus U	3.00	6.00
12 Maractus R	.75	1.50
13 Deerling C	3.00	6.00
14 Sawsbuck R	1.00	2.00
15 Tepig C	1.50	3.00
16 Tepig C	2.50	5.00
17 Pignite U	1.25	2.50
18 Pignite U	2.50	6.00
19 Emboar HOLO R	.75	1.50
20 Emboar HOLO R	3.00	6.00
21 Pansear C	.60	1.25
22 Simisear U	1.25	2.50
23 Darumaka C	.60	1.25
24 Darumaka U	.60	1.25
25 Darmanitan R	1.50	4.00
26 Reshiram HOLO R	.30	.75
27 Oshawott C	2.50	5.00
28 Oshawott C	2.50	5.00
29 Dewott U	.01	.08
30 Dewott U	.04	.10
31 Samurott HOLO R	.07	.15
32 Samurott HOLO R	1.50	3.00
33 Panpour C	.75	1.50
34 Simipour U	1.25	2.50
35 Basculin U	1.50	3.00
36 Ducklett C	.75	1.50
37 Swanna R	.75	1.50
38 Alomomola U	1.25	3.00
39 Alomomola R	.25	.60
40 Blitzle C	.60	1.25
41 Blitzle C	1.50	3.00
42 Zebstrika U	10.00	20.00
43 Zebstrika R	1.50	3.00
44 Joltik C	.75	1.50
45 Joltik C	.75	1.50
46 Galvantula R	.60	1.25
47 Zekrom HOLO R	.75	1.50
48 Munna U	.08	.20
49 Musharna R	.05	.12
50 Woobat C	.75	1.50
51 Swoobat U	.07	.15
52 Venipede C	.07	.15
53 Whirlipede U	1.00	2.00
54 Scolipede R	.60	1.25
55 Solosis C	2.00	4.00
56 Duosion U	.75	1.50
57 Reuniclus HOLO R	4.00	8.00
58 Timburr C	2.50	5.00
59 Timburr C	2.50	5.00
60 Gurdurr U	.75	1.50
61 Throh R	1.50	3.00
62 Sawk R	3.00	6.00
63 Sandile C	4.00	8.00
64 Krokorok U	1.25	3.00
65 Krookodile HOLO R	1.25	3.00
66 Purrloin C	6.00	15.00
67 Liepard R	4.00	8.00
68 Scraggy C	2.50	5.00
69 Scrafty R	2.00	4.00
70 Zorua C	50.00	120.00
71 Zoroark HOLO R	1.25	2.50
72 Vullaby C	2.00	4.00
73 Mandibuzz R	1.25	2.50
74 Klink C	2.00	4.00
75 Klang U	.30	.60
76 Klinklang HOLO R	.10	.20
77 Patrat C	1.00	2.50
78 Patrat C	.25	.60
79 Watchog U	2.00	4.00
80 Lillipup C	12.00	30.00
81 Lillipup C	.75	1.50
82 Herdier U	3.00	6.00
83 Stoutland R	.75	1.50
84 Pidove C	1.25	2.50
85 Tranquill U	.15	.30
86 Unfezant R	6.00	12.00
87 Audino U	.75	1.50
88 Minccino C	.30	.60
89 Cinccino R	.60	1.25
90 Bouffalant U	1.00	2.00
91 Bouffalant R	.30	.60
92 Energy Retrieval U	.60	1.25
93 Energy Search C	2.00	4.00
94 Energy Switch U	.60	1.25
95 Full Heal U	1.25	2.50
96 PlusPower U	.08	.20
97 Poke Ball U	.75	1.50
98 Pokedex U	1.25	2.50
99 Pokemon Communication U	.50	1.00
100 Potion C	.75	1.50
101 Professor Juniper U	1.00	2.00
102 Revive U	.75	1.50
103 Super Scoop Up U	1.25	3.00
104 Switch U	12.50	25.00
105 Grass Energy C	.75	1.50
106 Fire Energy C	.30	.75
107 Water Energy C	1.00	2.00
108 Lightning Energy C	1.25	2.50
109 Psychic Energy C	1.25	3.00
110 Fighting Energy C	2.50	5.00
111 Darkness Energy C	1.00	2.00
112 Metal Energy C	.75	1.50
113 Reshiram FULL ART UR	.12	.25
114 Zekrom FULL ART UR	.60	1.25
115 Pikachu UR	1.50	3.00

2011 Pokemon Black and White Emerging Powers

1 Pansage C	1.00	2.00
2 Simisage R	2.00	4.00
3 Sewaddle C	2.50	6.00
4 Sewaddle C	1.00	2.00
5 Swadloon U	.60	1.25
6 Swadloon U	2.00	4.00
7 Leavanny R	.60	1.25
8 Leavanny R	1.00	2.00
9 Cottonee C	1.00	2.00
10 Cottonee C	.75	1.50
11 Whimsicott U	.12	.25
12 Whimsicott R	.12	.25
13 Petilil C	.75	1.50
14 Lilligant U	2.50	5.00
15 Deerling C	.75	1.50
16 Sawsbuck R	.30	.60
17 Virizion HOLO R	.50	1.00
18 Pansear C	3.00	6.00
19 Simisear R	.01	.08
20 Darumaka C	.05	.12
21 Darmanitan R	.50	1.00
22 Panpour C	2.00	4.00
23 Simipour R	2.00	4.00
24 Basculin C	.60	1.25
25 Basculin U	2.50	5.00
26 Ducklett C	.10	.20
27 Swanna R	1.00	2.00
28 Cubchoo C	.60	1.25
29 Cubchoo C	.75	1.50
30 Beartic HOLO R	.12	.25
31 Beartic R	.15	.40
32 Emolga C	5.00	10.00
33 Joltik C	.75	1.50
34 Galvantula U	.75	1.50
35 Thundurus HOLO R	1.00	2.00
36 Woobat C	1.25	2.50
37 Swoobat R	1.25	2.50
38 Venipede C	.60	1.25
39 Whirlipede U	1.25	2.50
40 Scolipede R	1.25	2.50
41 Sigilyph U	1.00	2.00
42 Sigilyph U	.75	1.50
43 Gothita C	.30	.75
44 Gothita C	1.00	2.00
45 Gothorita U	1.50	3.00
46 Gothorita U	.25	.50
47 Gothitelle HOLO R	.04	.10
48 Gothitelle R	.10	.25
49 Roggenrola C	5.00	10.00
50 Roggenrola C	1.50	3.00
51 Boldore U	2.00	4.00
52 Boldore U	1.00	2.50
53 Gigalith R	4.00	8.00
54 Drilbur U	1.50	3.00
55 Drilbur C	3.00	6.00
56 Excadrill HOLO R	.01	.08
57 Excadrill R	.04	.10
58 Throh U	1.25	3.00
59 Sawk U	.30	.75
60 Sandile C	2.00	4.00
61 Krokorok U	2.00	4.00
62 Krookodile R	1.00	2.00
63 Terrakion HOLO R	2.50	5.00
64 Purrloin C	.01	.08
65 Liepard R	.04	.10
66 Zorua U	1.50	3.00
67 Zoroark HOLO R	.75	1.50
68 Vullaby C	1.50	3.00
69 Mandibuzz R	1.25	2.50
70 Ferroseed C	1.25	2.50
71 Ferroseed C	.12	.25
72 Ferrothorn R	2.00	5.00
73 Ferrothorn U	.50	1.25
74 Klink C	.75	1.50
75 Klang U	.75	1.50
76 Klinklang R	.60	1.25
77 Cobalion HOLO R	.60	1.25
78 Patrat C	1.00	2.00
79 Watchog U	.75	1.50
80 Pidove C	.75	1.50
81 Tranquill U	.75	1.50
82 Unfezant R	1.00	2.00
83 Audino U	2.50	5.00
84 Minccino C	.60	1.25
85 Cinccino U	.08	.20
86 Rufflet C	.04	.10
87 Rufflet C	7.50	15.00
88 Braviary HOLO R	5.00	10.00
89 Tornadus HOLO R	2.50	5.00
90 Bianca U	.75	1.50
91 Cheren U	1.25	2.50
92 Crushing Hammer U	.08	.20
93 Great Ball U	1.00	2.00
94 Max Potion U	.20	.40
95 Pokemon Catcher U	.75	1.50
96 Recycle U	.30	.75
97 Thundurus FULL ART UR	.50	1.00
98 Tornadus FULL ART UR	.50	1.00

2011 Pokemon Black and White Noble Victories

1 Sewaddle C	.25	.50
2 Swadloon U	2.00	4.00
3 Leavanny HOLO R	8.00	20.00
4 Petilil C	1.00	2.50
5 Lilligant R	2.00	4.00
6 Dwebble C	8.00	20.00
7 Crustle U	1.00	2.50
8 Karrablast C	100.00	250.00
9 Foongus C	3.00	6.00
10 Amoonguss U	1.50	3.00
11 Shelmet C	.60	1.25
12 Accelgor R	1.50	3.00
13 Virizion HOLO R	1.00	2.00
14 Victini HOLO R	1.00	2.00
15 Victini HOLO R	1.00	2.00
16 Pansear C	.75	1.50
17 Simisear U	1.50	4.00
18 Heatmor U	3.00	6.00
19 Larvesta C	.60	1.25
20 Larvesta C	1.25	2.50
21 Volcarona R	.50	1.00
22 Tympole C	1.00	2.00
23 Palpitoad U	1.00	2.00
24 Seismitoad R	2.00	5.00
25 Tirtouga U	1.00	2.00
26 Carracosta R	2.00	4.00
27 Vanillite C	.75	1.50
28 Vanillish U	.75	1.50
29 Vanilluxe R	.75	1.50
30 Frillish C	1.50	3.00
31 Jellicent R	.01	.08
32 Cryogonal U	.05	.12
33 Cryogonal R	1.25	3.00
34 Kyurem HOLO R	.25	.50
35 Blitzle C	.01	.08
36 Zebstrika R	.10	.25
37 Emolga U	.01	.08
38 Tynamo C	.04	.10
39 Tynamo C	.75	1.50
40 Eelektrik U	.60	1.25
41 Eelektross HOLO R	.60	1.25
42 Stunfisk C	1.00	2.00
43 Victini R	1.00	2.00
44 Yamask C	1.50	3.00
45 Yamask C	2.00	4.00
46 Cofagrigus R	.75	1.50
47 Cofagrigus R	.07	.15
48 Trubbish C	1.25	2.50
49 Garbodor U	1.50	3.00
50 Solosis C	.30	.75
51 Duosion U	1.25	2.50
52 Reuniclus R	6.00	12.00
53 Reuniclus R	.75	1.50
54 Elgyem C	.01	.08
55 Elgyem C	.01	.08
56 Beheeyem R	.75	1.50
57 Litwick C	2.50	5.00
58 Litwick C	.75	1.50
59 Lampent U	.75	1.50
60 Chandelure R	.60	1.25
61 Gigalith R	1.25	2.50
62 Timburr C	.75	1.50
63 Gurdurr U	.12	.25
64 Conkeldurr HOLO R	.15	.40
65 Conkeldurr R	.75	1.50
66 Archen U	2.00	4.00
67 Archeops R	.07	.15
68 Stunfisk U	1.50	3.00
69 Mienfoo C	.75	1.50
70 Mienshao U	.75	1.50
71 Golett C	.60	1.25
72 Golurk R	.07	.15
73 Terrakion HOLO R	2.50	5.00
74 Landorus HOLO R	3.00	6.00
75 Pawniard C	1.25	2.50
76 Bisharp U	.75	1.50
77 Deino C	1.25	2.50
78 Zweilous U	.75	1.50
79 Hydreigon HOLO R	1.00	2.00
80 Escavalier R	1.00	2.00
81 Pawniard C	1.50	3.00
82 Bisharp HOLO R	4.00	8.00
83 Durant U	1.25	3.00
84 Cobalion HOLO R	2.50	5.00
85 Audino U	3.00	6.00
86 Axew C	.75	1.50
87 Fraxure U	1.50	3.00
88 Haxorus HOLO R	.30	.75
89 Druddigon R	.75	1.50
90 Cover Fossil U	1.00	2.00
91 Eviolite U	.50	1.00
92 N U	1.25	2.50
93 Plume Fossil U	2.00	5.00
94 Rocky Helmet U	.40	1.00
95 Super Rod U	.07	.15
96 Xtransceiver U	1.00	2.00
97 Virizion FULL ART UR	1.00	2.00
98 Victini FULL ART UR	4.00	8.00
99 Terrakion FULL ART UR	.60	1.25
100 Cobalion FULL ART UR	1.25	2.50
101 N FULL ART UR	.75	1.50
102 Meowth UR	1.25	2.50

2011 Pokemon Call of Legends

1 Clefable HOLO R	1.50	3.00
2 Deoxys HOLO R	1.50	3.00
3 Dialga HOLO R	6.00	12.00
4 Espeon HOLO R	.75	1.50
5 Forretress HOLO R	3.00	6.00
6 Groudon HOLO R	1.00	2.50
7 Gyarados HOLO R	.40	1.00
8 Hitmontop HOLO R	.75	1.50
9 Ho-Oh HOLO R	.75	1.50
10 Houndoom HOLO R	.60	1.25
11 Jirachi HOLO R	.75	1.50
12 Kyogre HOLO R	1.25	2.50
13 Leafeon HOLO R	.75	1.50
14 Lucario HOLO R	.08	.20
15 Lugia HOLO R	.04	.10
16 Magmortar HOLO R	1.00	2.00
17 Ninetales HOLO R	.60	1.25
18 Pachirisu HOLO R	.15	.30
19 Palkia HOLO R	.75	1.50
20 Rayquaza HOLO R	.75	1.50
21 Smeargle HOLO R	.75	1.50
22 Umbreon HOLO R	.75	1.50
23 Ampharos R	.75	1.50
24 Cleffa R	.75	1.50
25 Feraligatr R	10.00	20.00
26 Granbull R	.60	1.25
27 Meganium R	.60	1.25
28 Mismagius R	.10	.20
29 Mr. Mime R	.25	.50
30 Pidgeot R	3.00	6.00
31 Skarmory R	.60	1.25
32 Slowking R	1.00	2.00
33 Snorlax R	1.50	3.00
34 Tangrowth R	.75	1.50
35 Typhlosion R	2.00	4.00
36 Tyrogue R	1.50	4.00
37 Ursaring R	.50	1.25
38 Weezing R	2.00	4.00
39 Zangoose R	1.50	4.00
40 Bayleef U	.50	1.25
41 Croconaw U	25.00	60.00
42 Donphan (U)	1.00	2.00
43 Flaaffy U	2.50	5.00
44 Flareon U	.60	1.25
45 Jolteon U	1.25	2.50
46 Magby U	1.50	3.00
47 Mime Jr. U	5.00	12.00
48 Pidgeotto U	1.00	2.00
49 Quilava U	.75	1.50
50 Riolu U	.75	1.50
51 Seviper U	3.00	6.00
52 Vaporeon U	1.25	2.50
53 Chikorita C	1.50	3.00
54 Clefairy C	.75	1.50
55 Cyndaquil C	.75	1.50
56 Eevee C	.75	1.50
57 Hitmonchan C	.75	1.50
58 Hitmonlee C	.75	1.50
59 Houndour C	1.25	3.00
60 Koffing C	3.00	6.00
61 Magikarp C	2.50	5.00
62 Magmar C	.75	1.50
63 Mareep C	1.50	4.00
64 Mawile C	1.50	3.00
65 Misdreavus C	.60	1.25
66 Phanpy C	1.25	2.50
67 Pidgey C	.60	1.25
68 Pineco C	.75	1.50
69 Relicanth C	1.25	2.50
70 Slowpoke C	.75	1.50

71 Snubbull C	.50	1.00
72 Tangela C	.60	1.25
73 Teddiursa C	1.00	2.00
74 Totodile C	.12	.25
75 Vulpix C	.75	1.50
76 Cheerleader's Cheer U	1.25	2.50
77 Copycat U	.75	1.50
78 Dual Ball U	1.00	2.00
79 Interviewer's Questions U	1.00	2.00
80 Lost Remover U	1.25	2.50
81 Lost World U	.75	1.50
82 Professor Elm's Training Method U	2.00	4.00
83 Professor Oak's New Theory U	.75	1.50
84 Research Record U	.75	1.50
85 Sage's Training U	.75	1.50
86 Darkness Energy U	.08	.20
87 Metal Energy U	2.00	4.00
88 Grass Energy C	5.00	10.00
89 Fire Energy C	.75	1.50
90 Water Energy C	.75	1.50
91 Lightning Energy C	1.00	2.00
92 Psychic Energy C	.75	1.50
93 Fighting Energy C	.75	1.50
94 Darkness Energy C	.30	.75
95 Metal Energy C	.75	1.50

2011 Pokemon Call of Legends Shiny

SL1 Deoxys HOLO R	.50	1.00
SL2 Dialga HOLO R	.01	.08
SL3 Entei HOLO R	.04	.10
SL4 Groudon HOLO R	1.25	2.50
SL5 Ho-Oh HOLO R	.60	1.25
SL6 Kyogre HOLO R	1.00	2.00
SL7 Lugia HOLO R	.50	1.00
SL8 Palkia HOLO R	.75	1.50
SL9 Raikou HOLO R	2.50	5.00
SL10 Rayquaza HOLO R	1.25	2.50
SL11 Suicune HOLO R	.75	1.50

2011 Pokemon McDonald's Collection

1 Snivy	2.00	4.00
2 Maractus	.60	1.25
3 Tepig	.75	1.50
4 Oshawott	.75	1.50
5 Alomomola	.12	.25
6 Blitzle	1.50	3.00
7 Munna	2.00	4.00
8 Sandile	2.50	5.00
9 Zorua	2.00	5.00
10 Klink	3.00	6.00
11 Pidove	2.00	4.00
12 Audino	1.50	3.00

2012 Pokemon Black and White Boundaries Crossed

1 Oddish C	.75	1.50
2 Gloom U	2.00	5.00
3 Vileplume HOLO R	.25	.60
4 Bellossom R	1.00	2.00
5 Tangela C	.50	1.00
6 Tangrowth HOLO R	.01	.08
7 Scyther C	.01	.08
8 Heracross U	2.50	5.00
9 Celebi EX UR	.07	.15
10 Shaymin R	.75	1.50
11 Snivy C	2.50	5.00
12 Servine U	1.25	2.50
13 Serperior HOLO R	.04	.10
14 Cottonee C	.05	.12
15 Whimsicott R	1.25	2.50
16 Petilil U	.12	.25
17 Lilligant R	.75	1.50
18 Charmander C	1.25	2.50
19 Charmeleon U	1.50	3.00
20 Charizard HOLO R	.75	1.50
21 Numel C	1.00	2.00
22 Camerupt R	.60	1.25
23 Victini R	.75	1.50
24 Tepig C	.75	1.50
25 Pignite U	.08	.20
26 Emboar HOLO R	.10	.25
27 Darumaka C	2.00	4.00
28 Darmanitan U	.25	.50
29 Squirtle C	1.50	3.00
30 Wartortle U	.10	.25
31 Blastoise HOLO R	.40	1.00
32 Psyduck C	.75	1.50
33 Psyduck C	.75	1.50
34 Golduck U	.75	1.50
35 Golduck R	1.00	2.50
36 Marill C	.40	1.00
37 Azumarill U	4.00	8.00
38 Delibird U	1.00	2.00
39 Oshawott C	.75	1.50
40 Dewott U	4.00	8.00
41 Samurott HOLO R	1.00	2.00
42 Ducklett C	.75	1.50
43 Swanna U	.10	.20
44 Frillish C	.07	.15
45 Jellicent R	1.50	3.00
46 Cryogonal U	.15	.30
47 Keldeo HOLO R	.75	1.50
48 Keldeo R	.08	.20
49 Keldeo EX UR	1.00	2.00
50 Pikachu C	3.00	8.00
51 Voltorb C	.75	2.00
52 Electrode U	2.00	4.00
53 Electabuzz C	50.00	120.00
54 Electivire HOLO R	1.25	2.50
55 Chinchou C	1.25	2.50
56 Blitzle C	.75	1.50
57 Zebstrika HOLO R	.75	1.50
58 Wobbuffet U	.60	1.25
59 Spoink C	2.50	6.00
60 Grumpig R	.07	.15
61 Duskull C	3.00	6.00
62 Dusclops U	.75	1.50
63 Dusknoir HOLO R	1.50	3.00
64 Croagunk C	1.00	2.00
65 Croagunk U	.75	1.50
66 Toxicroak R	7.50	15.00
67 Cresselia EX UR	.07	.15
68 Munna U	5.00	10.00
69 Musharna R	.30	.75
70 Woobat C	1.00	2.00
71 Swoobat R	.50	1.25
72 Venipede C	.15	.40
73 Whirlipede U	.60	1.25
74 Scolipede HOLO R	.75	1.50
75 Gothita C	.60	1.25
76 Gothorita U	.75	1.50
77 Meloetta HOLO R	.75	1.50
78 Sandshrew C	1.25	2.50
79 Sandslash U	2.50	6.00
80 Gligar C	6.00	12.00
81 Gliscor HOLO R	.75	1.50
82 Makuhita C	.01	.08
83 Trapinch C	.04	.10
84 Dwebble C	1.00	2.00
85 Crustle HOLO R	.60	1.25
86 Mienfoo C	.60	1.25
87 Mienfoo U	2.00	4.00
88 Mienshao U	1.25	2.50
89 Landorus EX UR	.50	1.00
90 Purrloin C	.50	1.00
91 Liepard HOLO R	.60	1.25
92 Vullaby C	1.00	2.00
93 Mandibuzz U	1.50	3.00
94 Scizor HOLO R	2.00	4.00
95 Skarmory U	.04	.10
96 Skarmory U	.01	.08
97 Klink U	1.25	2.50
98 Vibrava U	.12	.25
99 Flygon HOLO R	1.25	3.00
100 Black Kyurem R	.60	1.25
101 Black Kyurem EX UR	1.00	2.00
102 White Kyurem R	.07	.15
103 White Kyurem EX UR	20.00	40.00
104 Rattata C	.75	1.50
105 Raticate U	1.50	3.00
106 Meowth C	1.50	3.00
107 Farfetch'd U	.75	1.50
108 Ditto HOLO R	1.50	3.00
109 Snorlax U	1.50	3.00
110 Togepi C	1.50	3.00
111 Dunsparce C	.75	1.50
112 Taillow C	.75	1.50
113 Skitty C	2.00	4.00
114 Delcatty U	.50	1.00
115 Spinda C	1.00	2.00
116 Buneary C	7.50	15.00
117 Lopunny U	.75	1.50
118 Patrat C	2.50	5.00
119 Watchog U	.75	1.50
120 Lillipup C	.75	1.50
121 Herdier U	2.00	4.00
122 Stoutland HOLO R	.75	1.50
123 Pidove C	.60	1.25
124 Tranquill U	.25	.50
125 Unfezant R	.01	.08
126 Audino R	.08	.20
127 Aspertia City Gym U	3.00	6.00
128 Energy Search C	2.00	4.00
129 Great Ball U	.60	1.25
130 Hugh U	.01	.08
131 Poke Ball C	.05	.12
132 Potion C	2.00	5.00
133 Rocky Helmet U	2.50	5.00
134 Skyla U	5.00	10.00
135 Switch C	1.50	3.00
136 Town Map U	1.00	2.00
137 Computer Search HOLO R	2.50	5.00
138 Crystal Edge HOLO R	.75	1.50
139 Crystal Wall HOLO R	.75	1.50
140 Gold Potion HOLO R	5.00	10.00
141 Celebi EX FULL ART UR	7.50	15.00
142 Keldeo EX FULL ART UR	1.50	3.00
143 Cresselia EX FULL ART UR	1.25	3.00
144 Landorus EX FULL ART UR	.25	.60
145 Black Kyurem EX FULL ART UR	.60	1.25
146 White Kyurem EX FULL ART UR	1.00	2.00
147 Bianca FULL ART UR	1.00	2.00
148 Cheren FULL ART UR	1.00	2.00
149 Skyla FULL ART UR	.75	1.50
150 Golurk SCR	1.50	3.00
151 Terrakion SCR	1.50	3.00
152 Altaria SCR	1.00	2.00
153 Rocky Helmet SCR	.75	1.50

2012 Pokemon Black and White Dark Explorers

1 Bulbasaur C	.75	1.50
2 Ivysaur U	3.00	6.00
3 Venusaur HOLO R	.60	1.25
4 Scyther U	.75	1.50
5 Carnivine R	1.50	3.00
6 Leafeon R	.60	1.50
7 Dwebble C	.30	.60
8 Crustle U	1.25	2.50
9 Karrablast C	.75	1.50
10 Shelmet C	1.25	2.50
11 Accelgor R	.75	1.50
12 Flareon U	1.00	2.00
13 Entei EX HOLO R	.75	1.50
14 Torchic C	1.25	2.50
15 Torchic C	2.50	5.00
16 Combusken U	1.25	2.50
17 Blaziken HOLO R	.04	.10
18 Torkoal U	.10	.25
19 Heatmor R	.75	1.50
20 Larvesta C	.25	.50
21 Larvesta C	.50	1.00
22 Volcarona HOLO R	.60	1.25
23 Slowpoke C	.10	.20
24 Slowbro U	7.50	15.00
25 Vaporeon U	.60	1.25
26 Kyogre EX HOLO R	1.25	2.50
27 Piplup C	.75	1.50
28 Prinplup U	.15	.30
29 Empoleon HOLO R	1.00	2.00
30 Glaceon R	.60	1.25
31 Tympole C	1.50	3.00
32 Palpitoad U	.01	.08
33 Vanillite C	.01	.08
34 Vanillish U	1.25	2.50
35 Ducklett C	.07	.15
36 Swanna R	.25	.60
37 Jolteon U	.25	.60
38 Raikou EX HOLO R	1.00	2.50
39 Plusle C	2.00	4.00
40 Minun C	8.00	20.00
41 Joltik C	.75	1.50
42 Joltik C	.75	1.50
43 Galvantula R	1.50	3.00
44 Tynamo C	.60	1.25
45 Tynamo C	1.25	2.50
46 Eelektrik U	1.25	2.50
47 Eelektross HOLO R	1.50	3.00
48 Espeon R	1.25	2.50
49 Slowking R	1.00	2.00
50 Woobat C	1.25	2.50
51 Yamask U	.75	1.50
52 Cofagrigus R	.75	1.50
53 Aerodactyl R	1.25	2.50
54 Groudon EX HOLO R	3.00	6.00
55 Drilbur C	.07	.15
56 Excadrill R	.12	.30
57 Excadrill R	1.25	2.50
58 Timburr C	2.00	5.00
59 Gurdurr U	6.00	12.00
60 Umbreon U	2.00	4.00
61 Umbreon U	.10	.20
62 Sableye U	.75	1.50
63 Darkrai EX HOLO R	.60	1.25
64 Sandile C	.60	1.25
65 Krokorok U	.75	1.50
66 Krookodile HOLO R	.60	1.50
67 Scraggy C	.20	.50
68 Scrafty R	1.00	2.00
69 Zorua C	1.25	2.50
70 Zorua C	3.00	6.00
71 Zoroark R	1.25	2.50
72 Bisharp R	.75	1.50
73 Vullaby C	1.00	2.00
74 Escavalier R	.60	1.25
75 Klink C	.75	1.50
76 Klang U	1.00	2.00
77 Klinklang HOLO R	.75	1.50
78 Pawniard C	1.25	2.50
79 Bisharp R	2.00	4.00
80 Chansey C	2.00	4.00
81 Chansey C	.75	1.50
82 Blissey HOLO R	2.00	4.00
83 Eevee C	1.25	3.00
84 Eevee C	1.50	3.00
85 Chatot U	4.00	8.00
86 Lillipup C	1.00	2.00
87 Herdier U	.07	.15
88 Stoutland R	1.00	2.00
89 Haxorus HOLO R	.60	1.25
90 Tornadus EX HOLO R	.75	1.50
91 Cheren U	.07	.15
92 Dark Claw U	2.00	4.00
93 Dark Patch U	1.50	3.00
94 Enhanced Hammer U	1.50	4.00
95 Hooligans Jim & Cas U	.75	1.50
96 N U	.60	1.25
97 Old Amber Aerodactyl U	.75	1.50
98 Professor Juniper U	1.00	2.00
99 Random Receiver U	.75	1.50
100 Rare Candy U	.60	1.25
101 Twist Mountain U	.60	1.25
102 Ultra Ball U	1.25	2.50
103 Entei EX FULL ART UR	.75	1.50
104 Kyogre EX FULL ART UR	1.25	2.50
105 Raikou EX FULL ART UR	.75	1.50
106 Groudon EX FULL ART UR	.60	1.25
107 Darkrai EX FULL ART UR	3.00	6.00
108 Tornadus EX FULL ART UR	.25	.50
109 Gardevoir SCR	.01	.08
110 Archeops SCR	.10	.25
111 Pokemon Catcher SCR	1.25	2.50

2012 Pokemon Black and White Dragons Exalted

1 Hoppip C	.25	.50
2 Skiploom U	1.50	3.00
3 Jumpluff R	1.25	2.50
4 Yanma C	.60	1.25
5 Yanmega R	3.00	8.00
6 Wurmple C	2.00	4.00
7 Silcoon U	1.00	2.00
8 Beautifly R	2.50	5.00
9 Cascoon U	1.00	2.00
10 Nincada C	.75	1.50
11 Ninjask U	1.50	3.00
12 Roselia U	1.25	2.50
13 Roselia C	.08	.20
14 Roserade U	2.00	4.00
15 Roserade R	.50	1.00
16 Maractus U	.60	1.25
17 Foongus C	.75	1.50
18 Vulpix C	2.00	4.00
19 Ninetales HOLO R	.60	1.25
20 Magmar C	.60	1.25
21 Magmortar R	.10	.20
22 Ho-Oh EX UR	2.00	4.00
23 Magikarp C	1.25	3.00
24 Gyarados R	.25	.60
25 Wailmer U	.75	1.50
26 Wailord HOLO R	.75	1.50
27 Feebas C	3.00	6.00
28 Milotic HOLO R	.75	1.50
29 Spheal C	.75	1.50
30 Sealeo U	.75	1.50
31 Walrein R	1.25	2.50
32 Buizel C	2.00	4.00
33 Floatzel U	.75	1.50
34 Tympole C	1.25	2.50
35 Palpitoad U	.01	.08
36 Seismitoad R	.04	.10
37 Alomomola R	.08	.20
38 Mareep C	.04	.10
39 Flaaffy U	30.00	60.00
40 Ampharos HOLO R	.07	.15
41 Electrike C	.10	.20
42 Electrike C	1.00	2.00
43 Manectric R	1.00	2.00
44 Manectric R	1.50	3.00
45 Emolga U	.75	1.50
46 Mew EX UR	1.25	2.50
47 Dustox R	.30	.75
48 Shedinja R	.08	.20
49 Drifloon C	.60	1.25
50 Drifloon C	.75	1.50
51 Drifblim R	1.00	2.00
52 Sigilyph HOLO R	2.50	5.00
53 Trubbish C	.75	1.50
54 Garbodor HOLO R	.60	1.25
55 Gothita C	2.50	5.00
56 Gothorita U	.01	.08
57 Gothitelle R	.05	.12
58 Golett C	.60	1.25
59 Golurk HOLO R	.75	1.50
60 Cubone C	.60	1.25
61 Marowak R	1.00	2.50
62 Nosepass C	.50	1.25
63 Baltoy C	2.00	4.00
64 Claydol R	8.00	20.00
65 Roggenrola C	1.25	2.50
66 Boldore U	.75	1.50
67 Gigalith HOLO R	.10	.20
68 Throh U	.12	.30
69 Sawk U	1.25	2.50
70 Stunfisk U	1.00	2.00
71 Terrakion EX UR	.10	.20
72 Murkrow C	2.00	4.00
73 Honchkrow R	.60	1.25
74 Houndour C	1.50	3.00
75 Houndoom R	1.25	2.50
76 Stunky C	3.00	8.00
77 Skuntank U	2.50	5.00
78 Aron C	2.00	4.00
79 Lairon U	.01	.08
80 Aggron HOLO R	.05	.12
81 Registeel EX UR	1.00	2.00
82 Probopass R	.60	1.25
83 Durant U	.75	1.50
84 Altaria HOLO R	4.00	8.00
85 Rayquaza EX UR	2.50	5.00
86 Gible C	.75	1.50
87 Gible C	1.50	3.00
88 Gabite U	.75	1.50
89 Gabite U	12.50	25.00
90 Garchomp HOLO R	.75	1.50
91 Garchomp R	.75	1.50
92 Giratina EX UR	.50	1.00
93 Deino C	.12	.25
94 Deino C	.50	1.25
95 Zweilous U	.15	.40
96 Zweilous U	1.00	2.00
97 Hydreigon HOLO R	1.25	2.50
98 Hydreigon R	1.00	2.00
99 Aipom C	.20	.40
100 Ambipom R	.75	1.50
101 Slakoth C	1.25	2.50
102 Vigoroth U	.60	1.25
103 Slaking HOLO R	.60	1.25
104 Swablu U	.75	1.50
105 Swablu C	1.25	2.50
106 Bidoof C	1.25	3.00
107 Bibarel U	.60	1.25
108 Audino U	1.00	2.00
109 Minccino C	25.00	50.00
110 Bouffalant U	.10	.20
111 Rufflet C	1.00	2.00
112 Braviary R	1.50	3.00
113 Devolution Spray U	1.50	3.00
114 Giant Cape U	.50	1.00
115 Rescue Scarf U	.75	1.50
116 Tool Scrapper U	2.50	5.00
117 Blend Energy GFPD U	1.00	2.00
118 Blend Energy WLFM U	1.00	2.00
119 Ho-Oh EX FULL ART UR	.75	1.50
120 Mew EX FULL ART UR	.60	1.25
121 Terrakion EX FULL ART UR	1.00	2.00
122 Registeel EX FULL ART UR	1.00	2.00
123 Rayquaza EX FULL ART UR	.60	1.25
124 Giratina EX FULL ART UR	.75	1.50
125 Serperior UR	3.00	6.00
126 Reuniclus UR	.01	.08
127 Krookodile UR	.04	.10
128 Rayquaza UR	1.00	2.00

2012 Pokemon Black and White Next Destinies

1 Pinsir R	1.50	3.00
2 Seedot C	1.25	2.50
3 Kricketot C	1.00	2.50
4 Kricketune U	.75	1.50
5 Shaymin EX UR	2.50	5.00
6 Pansage C	1.50	3.00
7 Simisage R	2.00	4.00
8 Foongus C	.75	1.50
9 Amoonguss R	1.00	2.00
10 Growlithe C	.60	1.25
11 Growlithe C	1.00	2.50
12 Arcanine R	2.50	5.00
13 Arcanine U	.60	1.25
14 Moltres HOLO R	.75	1.50
15 Pansear C	1.00	2.00
16 Simisear R	1.00	2.00

17 Darumaka C .75 1.50
18 Litwick C 2.00 4.00
19 Lampent U 2.00 4.00
20 Chandelure HOLO R 1.50 3.00
21 Reshiram HOLO R .60 1.25
22 Reshiram EX UR .75 1.50
23 Staryu C .60 1.25
24 Starmie U .60 1.25
25 Lapras R .75 1.50
26 Lapras U .75 1.50
27 Articuno HOLO R 4.00 8.00
28 Panpour C .25 .50
29 Simipour R .04 .10
30 Basculin U .08 .20
31 Vanillite C 1.25 2.50
32 Vanillish U 1.25 2.50
33 Vanilluxe HOLO R 1.00 2.50
34 Frillish U .20 .50
35 Jellicent R 1.25 2.50
36 Cubchoo C 2.50 5.00
37 Beartic R .08 .20
38 Kyurem EX UR .04 .10
39 Pikachu C 3.00 6.00
40 Raichu U .75 1.50
41 Zapdos HOLO R 1.25 2.50
42 Shinx C 2.50 5.00
43 Shinx C 2.00 4.00
44 Luxio U .60 1.50
45 Luxio U .75 1.50
46 Luxray HOLO R .75 1.50
47 Blitzle C .75 1.50
48 Zebstrika R .75 1.50
49 Emolga U .50 1.00
50 Zekrom HOLO R 1.00 2.00
51 Zekrom EX UR .75 1.50
52 Grimer C .60 1.25
53 Muk R 1.00 2.00
54 Mewtwo EX UR .75 1.50
55 Ralts C 1.00 2.00
56 Kirlia U 1.25 2.50
57 Gardevoir HOLO R 1.25 2.50
58 Munna C .50 1.25
59 Musharna R .12 .30
60 Darmanitan R 2.00 4.00
61 Elgyem C .75 1.50
62 Beheeyem R 1.00 2.00
63 Riolu C 1.25 2.50
64 Lucario HOLO R .75 1.50
65 Hippopotas C 1.00 2.00
66 Hippowdon U 2.00 4.00
67 Mienfoo C .15 .30
68 Mienshao U .60 1.25
69 Sneasel C .60 1.25
70 Weavile R 1.00 2.00
71 Nuzleaf U .07 .15
72 Shiftry R .50 1.00
73 Scraggy U .75 1.50
74 Scrafty HOLO R 3.00 6.00
75 Bronzor C .01 .08
76 Bronzong R .05 .12
77 Ferroseed C 2.00 4.00
78 Jigglypuff U .60 1.25
79 Wigglytuff R .75 1.50
80 Meowth C .50 1.25
81 Persian R .30 .75
82 Regigigas EX UR 2.00 4.00
83 Pidove C .75 1.50
84 Minccino U 5.00 12.00
85 Cinccino HOLO R 2.00 4.00
86 Cilan U .75 1.50
87 Exp. Share U .75 1.50
88 Heavy Ball U 1.25 3.00
89 Level Ball U .75 1.50
90 Pokemon Center U 7.50 15.00
91 Skyarrow Bridge U 1.50 3.00
92 Double Colorless Energy U .01 .08
93 Prism Energy U .04 .10
94 Shaymin EX FULL ART UR .08 .20
95 Reshiram EX FULL ART UR 1.25 2.50
96 Kyurem EX FULL ART UR .25 .50
97 Zekrom EX FULL ART UR .60 1.25
98 Mewtwo EX FULL ART UR 1.00 2.00
99 Regigigas EX FULL ART UR 3.00 6.00
100 Emboar UR 1.50 3.00
101 Chandelure UR .08 .20
102 Zoroark UR .10 .25
103 Hydreigon UR .12 .25

2012 Pokemon Black and White Dragon Vault

1 Dratini 2.00 4.00
2 Dratini .60 1.25
3 Dragonair .75 1.50
4 Dragonair .60 1.25
5 Dragonite .07 .15
6 Bagon .12 .30
7 Shelgon .75 1.50
8 Salamence .40 1.00
9 Latias .15 .40
10 Latios 1.00 2.00
11 Rayquaza 1.25 2.50
12 Axew 1.25 2.50
13 Axew 1.25 2.50
14 Fraxure 2.00 5.00
15 Fraxure 1.50 3.00
16 Haxorus .75 1.50
17 Druddigon 1.50 3.00
18 Exp. Share .75 1.50
19 First Ticket 7.50 15.00
20 Super Rod 2.00 4.00
21 Kyurem 1.00 2.00

2012 Pokemon McDonald's Collection

1 Servine 12.50 25.00
2 Pansage 1.25 2.50
3 Dwebble 1.50 3.00
4 Pignite 1.00 2.00
5 Dewott .60 1.25
6 Emolga .75 1.50
7 Woobat 1.25 2.50
8 Drilbur .01 .08
9 Purrloin .05 .12
10 Scraggy 1.50 3.00
11 Klang .20 .40
12 Axew .75 1.50

2013 Pokemon Black and White Legendary Treasures

1 Tangela C 2.00 4.00
2 Tangrowth R .07 .15
3 Shuckle U .10 .20
4 Cherubi U 1.25 2.50
5 Carnivine U 1.25 2.50
6 Snivy C .07 .15
7 Servine U .75 1.50
8 Serperior HOLO R 1.50 3.00
9 Sewaddle C 2.00 4.00
10 Sewaddle C 2.00 4.00
11 Swadloon U 1.00 2.00
12 Leavanny HOLO R .75 1.50
13 Dwebble C 1.25 2.50
14 Crustle U 1.00 2.00
15 Virizion HOLO R 2.50 5.00
16 Genesect HOLO R .75 1.50
17 Charmander C .75 1.50
18 Charmeleon U .75 1.50
19 Charizard HOLO R .75 1.50
20 Vulpix C .60 1.50
21 Ninetales R 7.50 15.00
22 Moltres HOLO R 1.25 2.50
23 Victini HOLO R .75 1.50
24 Victini EX HOLO R .75 1.50
25 Tepig C .60 1.25
26 Pignite U 1.50 3.00
27 Emboar HOLO R 2.00 4.00
28 Reshiram HOLO R .60 1.25
29 Reshiram EX HOLO R 3.00 6.00
30 Magikarp C 2.50 5.00
31 Gyarados R .25 .50
32 Articuno HOLO R 1.25 2.50
33 Piplup C .04 .10
34 Prinplup U .10 .25
35 Empoleon R 1.50 3.00
36 Phione R .60 1.25
37 Oshawott C 1.25 2.50
38 Dewott U 1.25 2.50
39 Samurott HOLO R 1.00 2.00
40 Tympole C 1.25 2.50
41 Palpitoad U .75 1.50
42 Seismitoad R 1.25 2.50
43 Kyurem HOLO R 1.00 2.00
44 Kyurem EX HOLO R 3.00 6.00
45 Keldeo EX HOLO R .01 .08
46 Zapdos HOLO R .04 .10
47 Pluslе U 1.00 2.00
48 Minun U .75 1.50
49 Emolga U .25 .50
50 Thundurus HOLO R .75 1.50
51 Zekrom HOLO R .60 1.25
52 Zekrom EX HOLO R 1.00 2.00
53 Mewtwo HOLO R .75 1.50
54 Mewtwo EX HOLO R .75 1.50
55 Natu C 1.25 2.50
56 Xatu R 2.00 5.00
57 Misdreavus C 1.50 3.00
58 Mismagius R .07 .15
59 Ralts C 2.50 5.00
60 Kirlia U .12 .25
61 Sableye U 1.25 3.00
62 Croagunk C .20 .50
63 Toxicroak R .25 .50
64 Woobat C 4.00 8.00
65 Swoobat U .60 1.25
66 Sigilyph HOLO R .04 .10
67 Trubbish C .08 .20
68 Garbodor HOLO R 1.00 2.00
69 Gothita C 1.25 2.50
70 Gothita C 3.00 6.00
71 Gothorita U .75 1.50
72 Gothitelle HOLO R .75 1.50
73 Solosis C .15 .30
74 Solosis C 5.00 10.00
75 Duosion U 1.00 2.00
76 Reuniclus R 1.25 3.00
77 Chandelure EX HOLO R .25 .60
78 Meloetta HOLO R 2.00 4.00
79 Riolu U 10.00 25.00
80 Lucario HOLO R .60 1.25
81 Gallade R .75 1.50
82 Excadrill EX HOLO R .30 .75
83 Stunfisk U 1.00 2.00
84 Terrakion HOLO R .60 1.25
85 Landorus HOLO R 1.00 2.00
86 Meloetta R .12 .25
87 Spiritomb U .12 .30
88 Darkrai EX HOLO R .75 1.50
89 Zorua C 1.25 2.50
90 Zoroark HOLO R 1.25 2.50
91 Cobalion HOLO R 1.25 2.50
92 Altaria U .75 1.50
93 Rayquaza HOLO R 2.00 4.00
94 Gible C .60 1.25
95 Gabite U .50 1.25
96 Garchomp HOLO R .15 .40
97 Deino C .60 1.25
98 Zweilous U 3.00 6.00
99 Hydreigon HOLO R .75 1.50
100 Black Kyurem EX HOLO R 1.25 3.00
101 White Kyurem EX HOLO R 1.00 2.00
102 Lugia EX HOLO R .75 1.50
103 Swablu C 1.00 2.00
104 Minccino C 2.50 5.00
105 Cinccino HOLO R 1.00 2.00
106 Druddigon U 10.00 20.00
107 Bouffalant U .75 1.50
108 Tornadus HOLO R 1.50 4.00
109 Bianca U .30 .60
110 Cedric Juniper U .75 1.50
111 Crushing Hammer U 1.00 2.00
112 Energy Switch U 1.50 3.00
113 Double Colorless Energy U .75 1.50
114 Reshiram FULL ART SCR 1.50 3.00
115 Zekrom FULL ART SCR .01 .08

2013 Pokemon Black and White Legendary Treasures Radiant Collection

RC1 Snivy C .10 .25
RC2 Servine C 1.00 2.00
RC3 Serperior U 7.50 15.00
RC4 Growlithe U 1.25 2.50
RC5 Torchic C 3.00 6.00
RC6 Piplup U .75 1.50
RC7 Pikachu U .07 .15
RC8 Ralts C .75 1.50
RC9 Kirlia C 2.50 5.00
RC10 Gardevoir U 1.25 2.50
RC11 Meloetta EX R 1.25 2.50
RC12 Stunfisk U .10 .20
RC13 Purrloin U 1.50 3.00
RC14 Eevee U 1.50 3.00
RC15 Teddiursa C .75 1.50
RC16 Ursaring C .75 1.50
RC17 Audino C .75 1.50
RC18 Minccino C .60 1.25
RC19 Cinccino U .75 1.50
RC20 Elesa C .10 .20
RC21 Shaymin EX FULL ART UR .10 .20
RC22 Reshiram FULL ART UR 2.50 5.00
RC23 Emolga FULL ART UR .50 1.00
RC24 Mew EX FULL ART UR 1.00 2.00
RC25 Meloetta EX FULL ART UR 1.25 2.50

2013 Pokemon Black and White Plasma Blast

1 Surskit C 1.00 2.00
2 Masquerain R .75 1.50
3 Lileep U .60 1.25
4 Cradily R 1.00 2.00
5 Tropius U 1.50 4.00
6 Karrablast C 1.50 3.00
7 Shelmet C 1.25 2.50
8 Accelgor R 1.25 2.50
9 Virizion EX HOLO R 1.25 2.50
10 Genesect R 1.50 3.00
11 Genesect EX HOLO R 4.00 8.00
12 Larvesta C .75 1.50
13 Volcarona R .75 1.50
14 Squirtle C .08 .20
15 Wartortle U 2.50 5.00
16 Blastoise HOLO R 1.00 2.00
17 Lapras C .30 .75
18 Remoraid C 10.00 20.00
19 Octillery U .50 1.00
20 Suicune R .60 1.25
21 Snorunt C .60 1.25
22 Glalie U 1.00 2.00
23 Froslass R 1.00 2.00
24 Relicanth U 1.25 2.50
25 Snover C .75 1.50
26 Abomasnow U .75 1.50
27 Tirtouga U .75 1.50
28 Carracosta R 1.00 2.00
29 Ducklett C .75 1.50
30 Kyurem EX HOLO R 1.25 2.50
31 Tynamo C .75 1.50
32 Eelektrik U .07 .15
33 Eelektross HOLO R 1.50 3.00
34 Drifloon C 1.50 3.00
35 Drifblim R 1.50 3.00
36 Uxie R .12 .25
37 Mesprit HOLO R .75 1.50
38 Azelf R .60 1.25
39 Munna C 1.00 2.00
40 Musharna U .07 .15
41 Sigilyph HOLO R 1.00 2.00
42 Solosis C 1.25 2.50
43 Duosion U .01 .08
44 Reuniclus R .04 .10
45 Golett C .75 1.50
46 Golurk HOLO R 1.00 2.00
47 Machop C .60 1.25
48 Machoke U 1.00 2.00
49 Machamp HOLO R 1.25 2.50
50 Machamp R .50 1.25
51 Throh C 7.50 15.00
52 Sawk C 2.50 5.00
53 Archen U 1.50 3.00
54 Archeops HOLO R .75 1.50
55 Houndour C .75 1.50
56 Houndoom HOLO R 1.00 2.00
57 Aron C .25 .50
58 Lairon U .01 .08
59 Aggron R .05 .12
60 Jirachi EX HOLO R .75 1.50
61 Escavalier R 1.25 2.50
62 Bagon C .60 1.25
63 Shelgon U 2.00 5.00
64 Salamence HOLO R .25 .60
65 Dialga EX HOLO R 1.00 2.00
66 Palkia EX HOLO R .60 1.25
67 Axew C .75 1.50
68 Fraxure U .75 1.50
69 Haxorus HOLO R .75 1.50
70 Druddigon C 1.00 2.00
71 Kangaskhan C .75 1.50
72 Porygon C 1.50 3.00
73 Porygon2 U .12 .25
74 Porygon-Z HOLO R .75 1.50
75 Teddiursa C 1.00 2.00
76 Ursaring U 1.00 2.00
77 Chatot U 7.50 15.00
78 Caitlin U 5.00 10.00
79 Cover Fossil U .75 1.50
80 Energy Retrieval U .75 1.50
81 Iris U 1.25 2.50
82 Plume Fossil U 1.50 3.00
83 Pokémon Catcher U 2.00 4.00
84 Professor Juniper U 3.00 6.00
85 Rare Candy U .25 .50
86 Reversal Trigger U 1.00 2.00
87 Root Fossil Lileep U .75 2.00
88 Silver Bangle U .25 .60
89 Silver Mirror U 2.00 4.00
90 Ultra Ball U 8.00 20.00
91 Plasma Energy U .50 1.25
92 G Booster HOLO R .15 .40
93 G Scope HOLO R 1.00 2.00
94 Master Ball HOLO R 1.25 2.50
95 Scoop Up Cyclone HOLO R 7.50 15.00
96 Virizion EX FULL ART UR 8.00 20.00
97 Genesect EX FULL ART UR 1.00 2.50
98 Jirachi EX FULL ART UR .75 1.50
99 Dialga EX FULL ART UR .75 1.50
100 Palkia EX FULL ART UR 3.00 6.00
101 Iris FULL ART UR .60 1.25
102 Exeggcute SCR 1.00 2.00
103 Virizion SCR .75 1.50
104 Dusknoir SCR 1.50 3.00
105 Rare Candy SCR .60 1.25

2013 Pokemon Black and White Plasma Freeze

1 Weedle C .75 1.50
2 Kakuna U .25 .50
3 Beedrill R 2.00 4.00
4 Exeggcute U .75 1.50
5 Exeggutor R .08 .20
6 Treecko C .08 .20
7 Grovyle U .10 .25
8 Sceptile HOLO R 1.00 2.00
9 Cacnea C 1.00 2.00
10 Cacturne R 1.50 3.00
11 Leafeon R .10 .20
12 Flareon U 2.00 4.00
13 Heatran EX HOLO R .60 1.25
14 Litwick C .20 .40
15 Lampent U 1.25 2.50
16 Chandelure HOLO R .75 1.50
17 Reshiram HOLO R 1.00 2.00
18 Horsea C .75 1.50
19 Seadra U .60 1.25
20 Vaporeon U .75 1.50
21 Wooper C .60 1.25
22 Quagsire R 1.25 2.50
23 Glaceon R 2.50 5.00
24 Tympole C 1.50 3.00
25 Palpitoad U .60 1.25
26 Seismitoad R .75 1.50
27 Vanillite C .04 .10
28 Vanillish U .10 .25
29 Vanilluxe R .12 .25
30 Cryogonal U 1.25 2.50
31 Kyurem HOLO R 1.25 2.50
32 Voltorb C 1.50 3.00
33 Electrode HOLO R 2.00 4.00
34 Jolteon U .75 1.50
35 Chinchou C .50 1.00
36 Lanturn U 1.00 2.00
37 Pachirisu C 6.00 15.00
38 Thundurus EX HOLO R 1.00 2.00
39 Zekrom HOLO R 4.00 8.00
40 Nidoran F C 1.00 2.00
41 Nidorina U 1.00 2.00
42 Nidoqueen R .50 1.00
43 Nidoran M C 2.50 5.00
44 Nidorino U .08 .20
45 Grimer C .04 .10
46 Muk R 1.25 2.50
47 Mr. Mime R .60 1.25
48 Espeon U .60 1.25
49 Sableye R .75 1.50
50 Beldum C 7.50 15.00
51 Metang U 2.00 4.00
52 Metagross HOLO R .60 1.25
53 Deoxys EX HOLO R .75 1.50
54 Yamask C 1.00 2.00
55 Yamask C .75 1.50
56 Cofagrigus HOLO R .75 1.50
57 Cofagrigus R 2.50 5.00
58 Nidoking R 1.25 2.50
59 Mankey C 1.25 2.50
60 Primeape C .75 1.50
61 Onix U .60 1.25
62 Makuhita C 1.00 2.00
63 Hariyama R 1.00 2.00
64 Umbreon HOLO R 1.25 2.50
65 Sneasel C .60 1.25
66 Weavile R .75 1.50
67 Absol HOLO R 1.00 2.00
68 Sandile C .60 1.25
69 Krokorok U .50 1.25
70 Krookodile R 2.50 5.00
71 Pawniard C 2.50 5.00
72 Pawniard C .75 1.50
73 Bisharp R .75 1.50
74 Bisharp U 5.00 10.00
75 Deino C .60 1.25
76 Deino C .75 1.50
77 Zweilous U 1.00 2.00
78 Hydreigon HOLO R 1.00 2.00
79 Steelix R 1.50 3.00
80 Mawile U .75 1.50
81 Dratini C 4.00 8.00
82 Dragonair U .60 1.50
83 Dragonite HOLO R .20 .50
84 Kingdra HOLO R .75 1.50
85 Latias EX HOLO R 2.00 4.00
86 Latios EX HOLO R .01 .08
87 Rattata C .04 .10
88 Raticate R 1.00 2.00

89 Eevee C	.75	1.50
90 Eevee C	.01	.08
91 Hoothoot C	.10	.25
92 Noctowl U	1.00	2.00
93 Miltank U	1.25	2.50
94 Kecleon R	1.50	3.00
95 Starly C	.50	1.00
96 Staravia U	1.50	3.00
97 Staraptor R	.75	1.50
99 Float Stone U	2.00	4.00
100 Frozen City U	1.25	2.50
101 Ghetsis HOLO R	.75	1.50
102 Shadow Triad U	.75	1.50
103 Superior Energy Retrieval U	.10	.20
104 Team Plasma Badge U	.75	1.50
105 Team Plasma Ball U	1.00	2.00
106 Plasma Energy U	.10	.20
107 Life Dew AR	3.00	6.00
108 Rock Guard AR	1.50	3.00
109 Heatran EX UR	15.00	30.00
110 Thundurus EX UR	.15	.30
111 Deoxys EX UR	1.00	2.00
112 Latias EX UR	1.50	4.00
113 Latios EX UR	1.00	2.50
114 Tornadus EX UR	2.00	4.00
115 Ghetsis UR	.40	1.00
116 Professor Juniper UR	.20	.50
117 Empoleon SCR	2.00	4.00
118 Sigilyph SCR	8.00	20.00
119 Garbodor SCR	3.00	6.00
120 Garchomp SCR	.60	1.25
121 Max Potion SCR	2.00	4.00
122 Ultra Ball SCR	.75	1.50

2013 Pokemon Black and White Plasma Storm

1 Turtwig C	4.00	8.00
2 Grotle U	.60	1.25
3 Torterra R	.60	1.25
4 Combee C	1.00	2.00
5 Vespiquen R	.75	1.50
6 Cherubi C	.75	1.50
7 Cherrim R	.30	.75
8 Sewaddle C	.01	.08
9 Swadloon U	.08	.20
10 Leavanny R	1.50	3.00
11 Maractus U	3.00	6.00
12 Foongus C	1.25	2.50
13 Amoonguss U	.50	1.25
14 Moltres EX HOLO R	.15	.40
15 Chimchar C	.30	.60
16 Monferno U	.75	1.50
17 Infernape HOLO R	.07	.15
18 Victini EX HOLO R	.75	1.50
19 Pansear C	.50	1.00
20 Simisear U	.07	.15
21 Litwick C	.04	.10
22 Lampent U	.10	.25
23 Heatmor U	1.00	2.00
24 Squirtle C	2.00	4.00
25 Articuno EX HOLO R	.75	1.50
26 Swinub C	.75	1.50
27 Piloswine U	2.00	4.00
28 Mamoswine R	.08	.20
29 Lotad C	.75	1.50
30 Lombre U	2.00	4.00
31 Ludicolo R	2.50	5.00
32 Carvanha C	2.00	4.00
33 Sharpedo R	.60	1.25
34 Manaphy HOLO R	1.50	3.00
35 Vanillite C	.75	1.50
36 Vanillish U	1.25	2.50
37 Vanilluxe R	.12	.25
38 Frillish C	1.25	2.50
39 Jellicent R	1.00	2.00
40 Cubchoo C	1.25	2.50
41 Beartic R	.60	1.25
42 Magnemite C	.75	1.50
43 Magnemite C	6.00	12.00
44 Magneton U	1.50	3.00
45 Magneton U	1.00	2.00
46 Magnezone HOLO R	2.00	4.00
47 Magnezone R	1.00	2.00
48 Zapdos EX HOLO R	1.00	2.00
49 Rotom U	.75	1.50
50 Joltik C	.75	1.50
51 Galvantula U	.30	.60
52 Zubat C	3.00	6.00
53 Zubat C	.08	.20
54 Golbat U	.04	.10
55 Crobat HOLO R	1.00	2.50
56 Koffing C	2.50	5.00
57 Koffing U	.75	1.50
58 Weezing HOLO R	1.25	2.50
59 Ralts C	2.50	5.00
60 Kirlia U	2.00	4.00
61 Gallade HOLO R	.12	.25
62 Giratina R	.15	.40
63 Trubbish U	.50	1.00
64 Trubbish C	.75	1.50
65 Trubbish C	.60	1.25
66 Garbodor HOLO R	.75	1.50
67 Garbodor R	1.25	2.50
68 Elgyem C	.75	1.50
69 Elgyem U	.75	1.50
70 Beheeyem R	.75	1.50
71 Phanpy C	.50	1.00
72 Donphan U	2.50	5.00
73 Lunatone U	.60	1.25
74 Solrock U	.75	1.50
75 Riolu C	.75	1.50
76 Riolu C	.60	1.25
77 Lucario U	.50	1.00
78 Lucario HOLO R	.75	1.50
79 Timburr C	.30	.75
80 Gurdurr U	.60	1.25
81 Conkeldurr R	1.00	2.00
82 Purrloin C	.75	1.50
83 Purrloin C	3.00	6.00
84 Liepard R	1.00	2.00
85 Scraggy C	.07	.15
86 Scrafty R	1.25	3.00
87 Skarmory R	1.00	2.00
88 Klink C	2.00	4.00
89 Klang U	.75	1.50
90 Klinklang HOLO R	.75	1.50
91 Durant U	1.00	2.00
92 Durant U	.08	.20
93 Cobalion EX HOLO R	5.00	10.00
94 Druddigon R	4.00	8.00
95 Black Kyurem EX HOLO R	1.25	2.50
96 White Kyurem EX HOLO R	1.00	2.00
97 Clefairy C	1.00	2.00
98 Clefable R	.60	1.50
99 Doduo C	2.50	5.00
100 Dodrio R	.75	1.50
101 Snorlax R	3.00	6.00
102 Togepi C	1.00	2.00
103 Togetic U	1.00	2.00
104 Togekiss HOLO R	.01	.08
105 Whismur C	.04	.10
106 Loudred U	1.00	2.00
107 Exploud R	.08	.20
108 Lugia EX HOLO R	.15	.40
109 Skitty C	12.50	25.00
110 Patrat C	1.00	2.00
111 Patrat C	5.00	10.00
112 Watchog U	.50	1.25
113 Watchog R	.15	.40
114 Bouffalant R	.75	1.50
115 Rufflet C	.20	.50
116 Braviary R	1.25	2.50
117 Bicycle U	1.25	2.50
118 Colress U	1.25	2.50
119 Colress Machine U	1.25	2.50
120 Escape Rope U	.75	1.50
121 Ether U	1.00	2.00
122 Eviolite U	2.00	4.00
123 Hypnotoxic Laser U	1.25	2.50
124 Plasma Frigate U	10.00	20.00
125 Team Plasma Grunt U	.75	1.50
126 Virbank City Gym U	1.50	3.00
127 Plasma Energy U	1.25	2.50
128 Dowsing Machine AR	1.00	2.00
129 Scramble Switch AR	1.25	2.50
130 Victory Piece AR	.75	1.50
131 Victini EX FULL ART UR	1.00	2.00
132 Articuno EX FULL ART UR	7.50	15.00
133 Cobalion EX FULL ART UR	1.00	2.50
134 Lugia EX FULL ART UR	7.50	15.00
135 Colress FULL ART UR	7.50	15.00
136 Charizard SCR	.07	.15
137 Blastoise SCR	.75	1.50

2014 Pokemon XY

1 Venusaur EX HOLO R	.25	.50
2 M Venusaur EX HOLO R	.50	1.25
3 Weedle C	.25	.60
4 Kakuna U	2.00	4.00
5 Beedrill R	6.00	15.00
6 Ledyba C	1.00	2.00
7 Ledian U	.75	1.50
8 Volbeat U	3.00	6.00
9 Illumise U	3.00	6.00
10 Pansage C	2.50	5.00
11 Simisage R	.60	1.25
12 Chespin C	6.00	12.00
13 Quilladin U	6.00	12.00
14 Chesnaught HOLO R	2.00	5.00
15 Scatterbug C	1.50	3.00
16 Spewpa U	.25	.50
17 Vivillon HOLO R	.04	.10
18 Skiddo C	.08	.20
19 Gogoat HOLO R	1.00	2.00
20 Slugma C	.75	1.50
21 Magcargo R	.75	1.50
22 Pansear C	1.00	2.50
23 Simisear R	.15	.40
24 Fennekin C	.75	1.50
25 Braixen U	.10	.20
26 Delphox HOLO R	.12	.25
27 Fletchinder U	1.00	2.00
28 Talonflame HOLO R	1.00	2.00
29 Blastoise EX HOLO R	.07	.15
30 M Blastoise EX HOLO R	1.00	2.00
31 Shellder C	1.50	3.00
32 Cloyster R	3.00	6.00
33 Staryu C	.75	1.50
34 Starmie R	.50	1.00
35 Lapras HOLO R	2.00	4.00
36 Corsola U	.75	1.50
37 Panpour C	1.25	2.50
38 Simipour R	1.00	2.00
39 Froakie C	.60	1.25
40 Frogadier U	.60	1.25
41 Greninja HOLO R	.75	1.50
42 Pikachu C	1.25	2.50
43 Raichu HOLO R	1.00	2.00
44 Voltorb C	.75	1.50
45 Electrode U	.75	1.50
46 Emolga EX HOLO R	.75	1.50
47 Ekans C	.10	.20
48 Arbok R	.75	1.50
49 Spoink C	1.25	2.50
50 Grumpig R	1.00	2.00
51 Venipede C	.08	.20
52 Whirlipede U	.08	.20
53 Scolipede R	1.25	2.50
54 Phantump C	.50	1.00
55 Trevenant HOLO R	2.00	4.00
56 Pumpkaboo C	.75	1.50
57 Gourgeist HOLO R	1.00	2.00
58 Diglett C	1.25	2.50
59 Dugtrio R	.75	1.50
60 Rhyhorn C	1.00	2.00
61 Rhydon R	1.00	2.00
62 Rhyperior HOLO R	1.50	3.00
63 Lunatone U	.08	.20
64 Solrock U	.60	1.25
65 Timburr C	1.00	2.00
66 Gurdurr U	.75	1.50
67 Conkeldurr R	.60	1.25
68 Sableye U	3.00	6.00
69 Sandile C	.60	1.25
70 Krokorok U	.07	.15
71 Krookodile R	1.50	4.00
72 Zorua C	.75	1.50
73 Zoroark HOLO R	2.00	5.00
74 Inkay U	1.00	2.00
75 Inkay C	.75	1.50
76 Malamar R	1.00	2.00
77 Malamar R	1.00	2.00
78 Yveltal R	1.00	2.00
79 Yveltal EX HOLO R	1.00	2.00
80 Skarmory EX HOLO R	1.50	3.00
81 Pawniard C	1.25	2.50
82 Bisharp R	.60	1.25
83 Honedge C	.50	1.25
84 Doublade U	2.00	4.00
85 Aegislash R	.75	1.50
86 Aegislash HOLO R	7.50	15.00
87 Jigglypuff C	.50	1.00
88 Jigglypuff C	.75	1.50
89 Wigglytuff R	1.25	2.50
90 Wigglytuff R	1.50	3.00
91 Mr. Mime U	.01	.08
92 Spritzee C	.04	.10
93 Aromatisse HOLO R	.07	.15
94 Swirlix C	.75	1.50
95 Slurpuff HOLO R	.07	.15
96 Xerneas R	.60	1.25
97 Xerneas EX HOLO R	.75	1.50
98 Doduo C	.75	1.50
99 Dodrio U	.30	.60
100 Tauros R	1.00	2.00
101 Dunsparce U	2.00	4.00
102 Taillow C	1.50	3.00
103 Swellow R	.75	1.50
104 Skitty C	.05	.12
105 Delcatty U	.12	.30
106 Bidoof C	1.00	2.00
107 Bibarel R	.75	1.50
108 Lillipup C	1.25	2.50
109 Herdier U	7.50	15.00
110 Stoutland R	4.00	8.00
111 Bunnelby C	1.00	2.00
112 Diggersby U	.10	.20
113 Fletchling C	1.25	2.50
114 Furfrou HOLO R	.75	1.50
115 Cassius U	.75	1.50
116 Evosoda U	1.25	3.00
117 Fairy Garden U	.20	.50
118 Great Ball U	.75	1.50
119 Hard Charm U	1.50	3.00
120 Max Revive U	2.00	4.00
121 Muscle Band U	2.50	5.00
122 Professor Sycamore U	1.25	2.50
123 Professor's Letter U	.75	1.50
124 Red Card U	6.00	12.00
125 Roller Skates U	1.00	2.00
126 Shadow Circle U	4.00	8.00
127 Shauna U	.75	1.50
128 Super Potion U	.20	.40
129 Team Flare Grunt U	1.00	2.00
130 Double Colorless Energy U	1.25	2.50
131 Rainbow Energy U	5.00	10.00
132 Grass Energy C	1.50	3.00
133 Fire Energy C	.75	1.50
134 Water Energy C	1.25	2.50
135 Lightning Energy C	4.00	8.00
136 Psychic Energy C	5.00	10.00
137 Fighting Energy C	2.00	4.00
138 Darkness Energy C	1.00	2.50
139 Metal Energy C	.30	.75
140 Fairy Energy C	2.00	4.00
141 Venusaur EX FULL ART UR	1.00	2.50
142 Blastoise EX FULL ART UR	.30	.75
143 Emolga EX FULL ART UR	.60	1.25
144 Yveltal EX FULL ART UR	8.00	20.00
145 Skarmory EX FULL ART UR	7.50	15.00
146 Xerneas EX FULL ART UR	.75	1.50

2014 Pokemon XY Flashfire

1 Caterpie C	3.00	6.00
2 Metapod U	.60	1.25
3 Butterfree R	1.25	2.50
4 Pineco C	1.00	2.00
5 Seedot C	1.25	2.50
6 Nuzleaf U	3.00	8.00
7 Shiftry HOLO R	2.50	6.00
8 Roselia C	.60	1.25
9 Roserade U	.75	1.50
10 Maractus U	1.25	2.50
11 Charizard EX HOLO R	.75	1.50
12 Charizard EX HOLO R	1.50	3.00
13 M Charizard EX HOLO R	.75	1.50
14 Ponyta C	.10	.20
15 Rapidash U	.25	.50
16 Torkoal U	.04	.10
17 Fletchinder U	.10	.25
18 Litleo C	.12	.25
19 Litleo C	3.00	6.00
20 Pyroar HOLO R	.60	1.25
21 Qwilfish R	1.25	2.50
22 Feebas C	2.50	5.00
23 Milotic HOLO R	.40	1.00
24 Spheal C	.15	.40
25 Sealeo U	.75	1.50
26 Walrein R	1.00	2.00
27 Luvdisc U	.75	1.50
28 Buizel C	2.50	5.00
29 Floatzel R	.75	1.50
30 Bergmite C	.25	.50
31 Avalugg U	1.00	2.00
32 Shinx C	1.25	2.50
33 Luxio U	.08	.20
34 Luxray R	.08	.20
35 Magnezone EX HOLO R	3.00	6.00
36 Helioptile C	.60	1.25
37 Heliolisk R	1.00	2.00
38 Duskull C	.50	1.00
39 Dusclops U	.75	1.50
40 Dusknoir HOLO R	1.00	2.00
41 Toxicroak EX HOLO R	.75	1.50
42 Espurr C	1.00	2.00
43 Meowstic R	1.25	2.50
44 Skrelp C	.75	1.50
45 Geodude C	2.00	4.00
46 Graveler U	1.25	2.50
47 Golem R	1.00	2.00
48 Binacle C	.75	1.50
49 Barbaracle R	1.50	3.00
50 Sneasel U	.12	.25
51 Sneasel C	.75	1.50
52 Weavile R	1.50	3.00
53 Stunky C	2.00	4.00
54 Stunky C	.60	1.25
55 Skuntank R	.10	.20
56 Sandile C	.01	.08
57 Krokorok U	.05	.12
58 Scraggy C	.75	1.50
59 Scrafty R	.60	1.25
60 Forretress R	1.25	2.50
61 Durant R	.50	1.25
62 Flabebe C	.30	.75
63 Flabebe C	.75	1.50
64 Floette R	.75	1.50
65 Floette U	2.00	4.00
66 Florges HOLO R	.08	.20
67 Spritzee C	1.00	2.00
68 Carbink HOLO R	.60	1.25
69 M Charizard EX HOLO R	1.00	2.00
70 Druddigon HOLO R	.08	.20
71 Dragalge R	.08	.20
72 Goomy C	.75	1.50
73 Sliggoo U	.60	1.25
74 Goodra HOLO R	.75	1.50
75 Pidgey C	1.50	4.00
76 Pidgeotto U	2.00	4.00
77 Pidgeot R	.75	1.50
78 Kangaskhan EX HOLO R	.75	1.50
79 M Kangaskhan EX HOLO R	.75	1.50
80 Snorlax R	10.00	20.00
81 Sentret C	.75	1.50
82 Furret R	1.25	2.50
83 Miltank U	.10	.20
84 Buneary C	.75	1.50
85 Lopunny R	.75	1.50
86 Fletchling C	.01	.08
87 Furfrou U	.08	.20
88 Blacksmith U	1.25	2.50
89 Fiery Torch U	.75	1.50
90 Lysandre U	.75	1.50
91 Magnetic Storm U	1.00	2.00
92 Pal Pad U	.25	.50
93 Pokemon Center Lady U	.01	.08
94 Pokemon Fan Club U	.05	.12
95 Protection Cube U	.75	1.50
96 Sacred Ash U	.12	.25
97 Startling Megaphone U	2.50	5.00
98 Trick Shovel U	1.25	2.50
99 Ultra Ball U	1.50	3.00
100 Charizard EX FULL ART UR	.75	1.50
101 Magnezone EX FULL ART UR	.60	1.25
102 Toxicroak EX FULL ART UR	.75	1.50
103 Kangaskhan EX FULL ART UR	.75	1.50
104 Lysandre FULL ART UR	1.00	2.00
105 Pokemon Center Lady FULL ART UR	.75	1.50
106 Pokemon Fan Club FULL ART UR	1.00	2.00
107 M Charizard EX UR	.60	1.25
108 M Charizard EX UR	.12	.25
109 M Kangaskhan UR	.50	1.25

2014 Pokemon XY Furious Fists

1 Bellsprout C	.12	.30
2 Weepinbell U	7.50	15.00
3 Victreebel HOLO R	.75	1.50
4 Heracross EX HOLO R	.75	1.50
5 MHeracross EX HOLO R	.75	1.50
6 Shroomish C	2.50	5.00
7 Leafeon R	.30	.60
8 Shelmet C	12.50	25.00
9 Accelgor U	1.25	2.50
10 Magmar C	.60	1.25
11 Magmortar R	1.50	4.00
12 Torchic C	7.50	15.00
13 Combusken U	1.25	2.50
14 Blaziken HOLO R	1.00	2.00
15 Poliwag C	.75	1.50
16 Poliwhirl U	1.00	2.50
17 Poliwrath HOLO R	.25	.60
18 Politoed R	2.00	4.00
19 Glaceon R	6.00	15.00
20 Seismitoad EX HOLO R	.60	1.25
21 Cubchoo C	.75	1.50
22 Beartic R	2.50	5.00
23 Clauncher C	1.00	2.00
24 Clawitzer HOLO R	1.00	2.00
25 Amaura U	.01	.08
26 Aurorus R	.04	.10
27 Pikachu C	.75	1.50
28 Raichu U	1.00	2.00
29 Electabuzz C	10.00	20.00
30 Electivire R	.75	1.50
31 Plusle C	.75	1.50
32 Minun C	.75	1.50
33 Thundurus R	2.00	4.00
34 Dedenne U	1.00	2.00
35 Drowzee C	8.00	20.00

36 Hypno R	7.50	15.00
37 Jynx R	.75	1.50
38 Skorupi C	2.00	4.00
39 Gothita C	1.25	2.50
40 Gothorita U	1.50	3.00
41 Gothitelle R	.75	2.00
42 Golett C	.15	.40
43 Golurk R	1.25	2.50
44 Machop C	2.00	4.00
45 Machoke U	.60	1.25
46 Machamp HOLO R	.60	1.25
47 Hitmonlee U	.75	1.50
48 Hitmonchan U	.60	1.25
49 Hitmontop U	.75	1.50
50 Breloom R	.75	1.50
51 Makuhita C	.75	1.50
52 Hariyama R	.75	1.50
53 Trapinch C	.07	.15
54 Lucario EX HOLO R	1.00	2.00
55 MLucario EX HOLO R	1.50	3.00
56 Mienfoo C	.75	1.50
57 Mienshao U	.75	1.50
58 Landorus HOLO R	1.25	2.50
59 Pancham U	.75	1.50
60 Pancham C	.75	1.50
61 Tyrunt U	2.50	5.00
62 Tyrantrum R	7.50	15.00
63 Hawlucha HOLO R	.60	1.25
64 Hawlucha EX HOLO R	1.50	3.00
65 Drapion R	.07	.15
66 Scraggy C	1.50	3.00
67 Scrafty U	.75	1.50
68 Pangoro R	1.25	2.50
69 Clefairy C	.50	1.00
70 Clefairy C	.60	1.25
71 Clefable U	1.00	2.00
72 Sylveon R	1.00	2.00
73 Klefki U	.75	1.50
74 Dragonite EX HOLO R	1.25	2.50
75 Vibrava U	1.00	2.00
76 Flygon R	.75	1.50
77 Noivern HOLO R	1.25	2.50
78 Lickitung C	.25	.50
79 Lickilicky U	1.00	2.00
80 Eevee C	1.25	2.50
81 Slakoth C	.75	1.50
82 Vigoroth U	.75	1.50
83 Slaking HOLO R	.75	1.50
84 Patrat C	.50	1.00
85 Watchog U	2.50	5.00
86 Tornadus R	.50	1.00
87 Noibat C	1.25	2.50
88 Battle Reporter U	1.00	2.00
89 Energy Switch U	1.50	3.00
90 Fighting Stadium U	2.00	5.00
91 Focus Sash U	1.25	2.50
92 Fossil Researcher U	3.00	6.00
93 Full Heal U	3.00	6.00
94 Jaw Fossil U	.75	1.50
95 Korrina U	.75	1.50
96 Maintenance U	1.50	3.00
97 Mountain Ring U	.50	1.25
98 Sail Fossil U	.75	1.50
99 Sparkling Robe U	2.50	5.00
100 Super Scoop Up U	1.25	2.50
101 Tool Retriever U	1.00	2.00
102 Training Center U	.50	1.00
103 Herbal Energy U	1.00	2.00
104 Strong Energy U	1.25	2.50
105 Heracross EX HOLO UR	3.00	6.00
106 Seismitoad EX HOLO UR	.08	.20
107 Lucario EX HOLO UR	.04	.10
108 Dragonite EX HOLO UR	.05	.12
109 Battle Reporter HOLO UR	.75	1.50
110 Fossil Researcher HOLO UR	.60	1.25
111 Korrina HOLO UR	1.25	2.50
112 MHeracross EX SCR	1.25	2.50
113 MLucario EX SCR	1.00	2.00

2014 Pokemon XY Phantom Forces

1 Venonat C	1.00	2.00
2 Venomoth R	.50	1.00
3 Yanma C	.75	1.50
4 Yanmega R	.15	.30
5 Sewaddle C	.04	.10
6 Swadloon U	.10	.25
7 Leavanny R	.75	1.50
8 Karrablast C	1.25	2.50
9 Fletchinder U	1.25	2.50
10 Talonflame R	.75	1.50
11 Litleo C	.60	1.25
12 Pyroar HOLO R	.08	.20
13 Krabby C	.15	.40
14 Kingler U	1.50	3.00
15 Totodile C	1.25	2.50
16 Croconaw U	1.00	2.00
17 Feraligatr HOLO R	1.50	3.00
18 Finneon C	1.25	2.50
19 Lumineon U	.60	1.25
20 Frillish C	1.00	2.00
21 Jellicent R	1.25	2.50
22 Alomomola C	.25	.50
23 Manectric EX HOLO R	.04	.10
24 MManectric EX HOLO R	.05	.12
25 Pachirisu R	.75	1.50
26 Joltik C	.75	1.50
27 Galvantula R	1.25	2.50
28 Helioptile C	1.25	2.50
29 Helioptile C	.75	2.00
30 Heliolisk HOLO R	.15	.40
31 Zubat C	.20	.40
32 Golbat U	12.50	25.00
33 Crobat R	1.25	2.50
34 Gengar EX HOLO R	1.50	3.00
35 MGengar EX HOLO R	.75	1.50
36 Wobbuffet U	2.50	6.00
37 Gulpin C	.50	1.00
38 Swalot R	1.50	3.00
39 Munna C	.75	1.50
40 Musharna R	2.00	4.00
41 Litwick C	3.00	6.00
42 Lampent U	1.00	2.00
43 Chandelure HOLO R	2.00	4.00
44 Pumpkaboo C	1.00	2.00
45 Gourgeist HOLO R	1.00	2.00
46 Gligar C	.60	1.25
47 Gliscor R	.60	1.25
48 Roggenrola C	.30	.60
49 Boldore U	.75	2.00
50 Gigalith HOLO R	.30	.75
51 Murkrow C	2.00	4.00
52 Honchkrow R	1.50	3.00
53 Poochyena C	8.00	20.00
54 Mightyena R	1.00	2.00
55 Spiritomb R	1.50	3.00
56 Purrloin C	.10	.20
57 Liepard U	.12	.30
58 Malamar EX HOLO R	7.50	15.00
59 Skarmory C	4.00	8.00
60 Bronzor C	.75	1.50
61 Bronzong R	2.50	6.00
62 Dialga EX HOLO R	.50	1.00
63 Heatran HOLO R	1.00	2.00
64 Escavalier R	20.00	40.00
65 Aegislash EX HOLO R	.07	.15
66 Klefki U	2.00	4.00
67 Florges EX HOLO R	.60	1.25
68 Swirlix C	.75	1.50
69 Slurpuff HOLO R	1.00	2.00
70 Dedenne C	.75	1.50
71 Diancie HOLO R	.40	1.00
72 Deino C	.15	.40
73 Zweilous U	7.50	15.00
74 Hydreigon HOLO R	.30	.75
75 Goomy C	.75	1.50
76 Sliggoo U	.75	1.50
77 Goodra HOLO R	1.00	2.00
78 Spearow C	.75	1.50
79 Fearow U	.12	.25
80 Chansey C	.60	1.25
81 Blissey R	.04	.10
82 Girafarig U	.04	.10
83 Whismur C	.75	1.50
84 Loudred U	.60	1.25
85 Exploud R	.75	1.50
86 Regigigas HOLO R	.60	1.25
87 Bunnelby C	1.25	2.50
88 Diggersby R	.07	.15
89 Fletchling C	1.00	2.00
90 Furfrou U	.75	1.50
91 AZ U	.10	.20
92 Battle Compressor U	.12	.25
93 Dimension Valley U	.75	1.50
94 Enhanced Hammer U	1.25	2.50
95 Gengar Spirit Link U	.50	1.00
96 Hand Scope U	1.25	2.50
97 Head Ringer HOLO R	1.00	2.00
98 Jamming Net HOLO R	.75	1.50
99 Lysandre's Trump Card U	.75	1.50
100 Manectric Spirit Link U	1.00	2.00
101 Professor Sycamore U	.75	1.50
102 Robo Substitute U	1.25	2.50
103 Roller Skates U	.75	1.50
104 Shauna U	.75	1.50
105 Steel Shelter U	.50	1.00
106 Target Whistle U	.75	1.50
107 Tierno U	1.00	2.00
108 Trick Coin U	1.25	2.50
109 VS Seeker U	2.00	4.00
110 Xerosic U	1.25	2.50
111 Double Colorless Energy U	1.00	2.00
112 Mystery Energy U	3.00	6.00
113 Manectric EX UR	.08	.20
114 Gengar EX UR	.10	.25
115 Malamar EX UR	2.00	4.00
116 Florges EX UR	.60	1.25
117 AZ UR	.30	.75
118 Lysandre's Trump Card UR	1.25	2.50
119 Xerosic UR	7.50	15.00
120 MManectric EX HOLO SCR	.75	1.50
121 MGengar EX HOLO SCR	1.25	2.50
122 Dialga EX HOLO SCR	1.00	2.50

2015 Pokemon XY Ancient Origins

1 Oddish C	2.50	5.00
2 Gloom U	.75	1.50
3 Vileplume R	.75	1.50
4 Bellossom U	.60	1.25
5 Spinarak C	.75	1.50
6 Ariados U	.75	1.50
7 Sceptile EX HOLO R	.75	1.50
8 M Sceptile EX HOLO R	.30	.75
9 Combee C	.75	1.50
10 Vespiquen U	.75	1.50
11 Vespiquen Double R	1.50	3.00
12 Virizion HOLO R	.07	.15
13 Flareon U	.12	.30
14 Entei R	1.00	2.00
15 Entei HOLO R	1.00	2.00
16 Larvesta C	.07	.15
17 Volcarona HOLO R	.04	.10
18 Volcarona Stop R	.10	.25
19 Magikarp C	.08	.20
20 Gyarados R	.75	1.50
21 Gyarados HOLO R	4.00	8.00
22 Vaporeon U	7.50	15.00
23 Relicanth C	.20	.40
24 Regice R	1.50	3.00
25 Kyurem EX HOLO R	1.25	2.50
26 Jolteon HOLO R	.04	.10
27 Ampharos EX HOLO R	.12	.30
28 M Ampharos EX HOLO R	1.25	2.50
29 Rotom U	7.50	15.00
30 Unown C	1.50	3.00
31 Baltoy C	1.00	2.00
32 Baltoy Stop C	20.00	40.00
33 Claydol R	.75	1.50
34 Golett C	.12	.25
35 Golurk Stop R	.50	1.25
36 Hoopa EX HOLO R	.75	1.50
37 Machamp EX HOLO R	.75	1.50
38 Wooper C	1.00	2.00
39 Quagsire C	.10	.20
40 Regirock R	6.00	12.00
41 Golurk C	.60	1.25
42 Tyranitar EX HOLO R	.60	1.25
43 M Tyranitar EX HOLO R	1.25	2.50
44 Sableye U	1.50	3.00
45 Inkay C	.75	1.50
46 Malamar C	.75	1.50
47 Beldum C	2.00	4.00
48 Metang U	7.50	15.00
49 Metagross R	1.25	2.50
50 Metagross R	1.00	2.00
51 Registeel R	.30	.75
52 Ralts C	1.25	2.50
53 Kirlia U	.75	1.50
54 Gardevoir HOLO R	1.00	2.00
55 Cottonee C	.75	1.50
56 Whimsicott U	2.00	5.00
57 Giratina EX HOLO R	2.50	5.00
58 Goomy C	1.25	2.50
59 Sliggoo U	.50	1.25
60 Goodra HOLO R	.15	.40
61 Meowth C	.75	1.50
62 Persian C	.60	1.25
63 Eevee C	1.25	2.50
64 Porygon C	6.00	12.00
65 Porygon2 U	10.00	20.00
66 Porygon-Z R	1.25	2.50
67 Porygon-Z HOLO R	.75	1.50
68 Lugia EX HOLO R	.60	1.25
69 Ace Trainer U	1.25	2.50
70 Ampharos Spirit Link U	1.50	3.00
71 Eco Arm U	2.00	5.00
72 Energy Recycler U	.30	.75
73 Faded Town U	2.00	4.00
74 Forest of Giant Plants U	8.00	20.00
75 Hex Maniac U	1.25	2.50
76 Level Ball U	.25	.50
77 Lucky Helmet U	.01	.08
78 Lysandre U	.05	.12
79 Paint Roller U	.60	1.25
80 Sceptile Spirit Link U	1.50	3.00
81 Tyranitar Spirit Link U	2.00	5.00
82 Dangerous Energy U	1.25	2.50
83 Flash Energy U	7.50	15.00
84 Sceptile EX UR FULL ART	12.50	25.00
85 M Sceptile EX UR FULL ART	1.00	2.00
86 Kyurem EX UR FULL ART	3.00	6.00
87 Ampharos EX UR FULL ART	1.25	2.50
88 M Ampharos EX UR FULL ART	1.25	2.50
89 Hoopa EX UR FULL ART	.75	1.50
90 Machamp EX UR FULL ART	.75	1.50
91 Tyranitar EX UR FULL ART	1.25	2.50
92 M Tyranitar EX UR FULL ART	1.00	2.00
93 Giratina EX UR FULL ART	.60	1.25
94 Lugia EX UR FULL ART	.75	1.50
95 Steven UR FULL ART	4.00	8.00
96 Primal Kyogre EX UR FULL ART	1.50	3.00
97 Primal Groudon EX UR FULL ART	.30	.75
98 M Rayquaza EX UR FULL ART	.60	1.25
99 Energy Retrieval SCR	.10	.20
100 Trainers' Mail SCR	1.25	2.50

2015 Pokemon XY Breakthrough

1 Paras C	.01	.08
2 Parasect R	.08	.20
3 Pinsir U	.50	1.25
4 Cacnea C	.12	.30
5 Pansage C	1.25	2.50
6 Simisage R	1.50	3.00
7 Chespin (Nosh) C	2.50	5.00
8 Chespin (Work) C	.75	1.50
9 Chespin (Tree Climb) C	.75	1.50
10 Quilladin U	1.25	2.50
11 Chesnaught HOLO R	.75	1.50
12 Chesnaught BREAK	1.00	2.00
13 Scatterbug C	.60	1.25
14 Spewpa U	1.50	3.00
15 Vivillon HOLO R	1.25	2.50
16 Skiddo C	.75	1.50
17 Gogoat U	.07	.15
18 Cyndaquil C	1.00	2.00
19 Quilava U	.50	1.00
20 Typhlosion HOLO R	1.50	3.00
21 Houndoom EX HOLO R	.75	1.50
22 MHoundoom EX HOLO R	.75	1.50
23 Pansear C	1.00	2.00
24 Simisear R	.60	1.25
25 Fennekin C	.01	.08
26 Braixen U	.05	.12
27 Goldeen C	.75	1.50
28 Seaking U	1.00	2.00
29 Staryu C	1.00	2.00
30 Starmie U	1.25	2.50
31 Remoraid (Wild River) C	2.50	5.00
32 Remoraid (Ion Pool) C	2.00	4.00
33 Octillery HOLO R	.60	1.25
34 Glalie EX HOLO R	.75	1.50
35 MGlalie EX HOLO R	.75	1.50
36 Piplup C	.75	1.50
37 Prinplup U	.60	1.25
38 Empoleon HOLO R	.60	1.25
39 Snover C	.75	1.50
40 Abomasnow R	.12	.25
41 Panpour C	.15	.40
42 Simipour R	.75	1.50
43 Vanillite C	.07	.15
44 Vanillish U	1.50	3.00
45 Vanilluxe R	1.00	2.00
46 Froakie C	.60	1.50
47 Frogadier U	3.00	6.00
48 Pikachu C	2.50	5.00
49 Raichu R	.75	1.50
50 Raichu BREAK R	1.00	2.00
51 Magnemite (Glittering Guidance) C	.60	1.25
52 Magnemite (Sparking Generator) C	.25	.50
53 Magneton U	.01	.08
54 Magnezone HOLO R	.08	.20
55 Raikou HOLO R	1.00	2.00
56 Stunfisk U	1.25	2.50
57 Dedenne U	.75	1.50
58 Gastly C	.60	1.25
59 Haunter U	1.50	3.00
60 Gengar HOLO R	.75	1.50
61 Mewtwo EX (Photon Wave) EX HOLO R	.40	1.00
62 Mewtwo EX (Shatter Shot) EX HOLO R	.75	1.50
63 M Mewtwo EX (Vanishing Strike) EX HOLO R	1.25	2.50
64 M Mewtwo EX (Psychic Infinity) EX HOLO R	.60	1.25
65 Misdreavus C	.30	.75
66 Mismagius HOLO R	2.50	5.00
67 Wobbuffet U	.75	1.50
68 Ralts C	.75	1.50
69 Kirlia U	1.25	2.50
70 Cresselia R	.75	1.50
71 Woobat C	1.00	2.00
72 Swoobat U	2.00	4.00
73 Elgyem C	1.00	2.00
74 Beheeyem U	.75	1.50
75 Sandshrew C	1.50	3.00
76 Sandslash U	1.25	2.50
77 Cubone C	1.25	2.50
78 Marowak R	.75	2.00
79 Marowak BREAK R	1.00	2.00
80 Swinub C	.10	.20
81 Piloswine U	.50	1.00
82 Mamoswine HOLO R	.60	1.25
83 Hippopotas C	1.25	2.50
84 Gallade HOLO R	.60	1.50
85 Meloetta HOLO R	.20	.50
86 Pancham C	2.50	5.00
87 Hawlucha R	1.25	2.50
88 Cacturne U	1.00	2.00
89 Zorua (Moonlight Madness) C	1.50	3.00
90 Zorua (Whiny Voice) C	.75	1.50
91 Zoroark HOLO R	4.00	8.00
92 Zoroark BREAK R	.75	1.50
93 Inkay C	.50	1.25
94 Yveltal HOLO R	.15	.40
95 Bronzor C	.60	1.25
96 Bronzong R	.01	.08
97 Mr. Mime R	.04	.10
98 Snubbull C	1.25	2.50
99 Granbull U	7.50	15.00
100 Ralts (Magical Shot) C	1.25	2.50
101 Flabebe C	.50	1.00
102 Floette U	.60	1.25
103 Florges R	2.00	4.00
104 Florges BREAK R	15.00	40.00
105 Spritzee C	125.00	300.00
106 Aromatisse R	2.00	4.00
107 Xerneas HOLO R	10.00	25.00
108 Axew (Brat Snack) C	2.00	5.00
109 Axew (Extra Chop) C	75.00	200.00
110 Fraxure U	10.00	20.00
111 Haxorus HOLO R	.15	.30
112 Noivern R	.50	1.00
113 Noivern BREAK R	1.50	3.00
114 Meowth C	1.25	2.50
115 Doduo (Simultaneous Peck) C	2.50	5.00
116 Doduo (Double Stab) C	.50	1.00
117 Dodrio R	5.00	12.00
118 Snorlax U	5.00	12.00
119 Hoothoot C	1.25	2.50
120 Noctowl R	1.00	2.00
121 Teddiursa C	2.00	4.00
122 Ursaring U	1.25	2.50
123 Smeargle R	1.25	2.50
124 Swablu C	.75	1.50
125 Starly C	.12	.25
126 Staravia U	.60	1.25
127 Staraptor R	1.25	2.50
128 Chatot R	.75	1.50
129 Rufflet C	.75	1.50
130 Braviary R	.75	1.50
131 Noibat C	.75	1.50
132 Noibat (Mysterious Beam) C	1.50	3.00
133 Assault Vest U	3.00	6.00
134 Brigette U	1.00	2.00
135 Buddy-Buddy Rescue U	1.50	3.00
136 Fisherman U	.08	.20
137 Float Stone U	.60	1.25
138 Giovanni's Scheme U	.10	.20
139 Glalie Spirit Link U	.01	.08
140 Heavy Ball U	.04	.10
141 Heavy Boots U	1.25	2.50
142 Houndoom Spirit Link U	.25	.50
143 Judge U	.04	.10
144 Mewtwo Spirit Link U	.10	.25
145 Parallel City U	.10	.20
146 Professor's Letter U	.75	1.50
147 Reserved Ticket U	1.25	2.50
148 Skyla U	1.50	3.00
149 Super Rod U	1.25	2.50
150 Town Map U	2.00	4.00
151 Burning Energy U	.01	.08
152 Rainbow Energy U	.05	.12
153 Houndoom EX UR FULL ART	.75	1.50
154 MHoundoom EX UR FULL ART	.07	.15
155 Glalie EX UR FULL ART	1.50	3.00
156 MGlalie EX UR FULL ART	.60	1.25
157 Mewtwo EX (Photon Wave) UR FULL ART	.75	1.50

158 Mewtwo EX (Shatter Shot) UR FULL ART	.60	1.25
159 Mewtwo EX (Vanishing Strike) UR FULL ART	.75	1.50
160 Mewtwo EX (Psychic Infinity) UR FULL ART	.75	1.50
161 Brigette UR FULL ART	1.50	3.00
162 Giovanni's Scheme UR FULL ART	1.25	2.50
163 Mewtwo EX (Photon Wave) SCR	1.50	3.00
164 Mewtwo EX (Shatter Shot) SCR	1.00	2.00

2015 Pokemon XY Double Crisis

1 Team Magma's Numel C	1.25	2.50
2 Team Magma's Camerupt HOLO R	1.25	2.50
3 Team Aqua's Spheal C	1.00	2.00
4 Team Aqua's Sealeo C	1.50	3.00
5 Team Aqua's Walrein HOLO R	1.00	2.00
6 Team Aqua's Kyogre EX HOLO R	1.25	2.50
7 Team Aqua's Grimer C	.75	1.50
8 Team Aqua's Muk HOLO R	.75	1.50
9 Team Aqua's Seviper C	.60	1.25
10 Team Magma's Baltoy C	.75	1.50
11 Team Magma's Claydol HOLO R	.75	1.50
12 Team Magma's Aron C	1.25	2.50
13 Team Magma's Lairon C	.75	1.50
14 Team Magma's Aggron HOLO R	1.50	3.00
15 Team Magma's Groudon EX HOLO R	2.50	5.00
16 Team Aqua's Poochyena C	.75	1.50
17 Team Magma's Poochyena C	.08	.20
18 Team Aqua's Mightyena C	.05	.12
19 Team Magma's Mightyena C	1.00	2.00
20 Team Aqua's Carvanha C	.30	.75
21 Team Aqua's Sharpedo HOLO R	.12	.30
22 Team Magma's Zangoose C	.60	1.25
23 Aqua Diffuser U	.01	.08
24 Magma Pointer U	.05	.12
25 Team Aqua Admin U	1.25	2.50
26 Team Aqua Grunt U	.75	2.00
27 Team Aqua's Great Ball U	3.00	6.00
28 Team Aqua's Secret Base U	1.00	2.00
29 Team Magma Admin U	.75	1.50
30 Team Magma Grunt U	.30	.75
31 Team Magma's Great Ball U	.75	1.50
32 Team Magma's Secret Base U	1.00	2.00
33 Double Aqua Energy U	.75	1.50
34 Double Magma Energy U	1.25	2.50

2015 Pokemon XY Primal Clash

1 Weedle C	1.25	2.50
2 Kakuna U	10.00	20.00
3 Beedrill R	.75	1.50
4 Tangela C	1.50	3.00
5 Tangrowth R	1.50	3.00
6 Treecko C	1.50	3.00
7 Grovyle U	.60	1.25
8 Sceptile R	.75	1.50
9 Sceptile HOLO R	2.50	5.00
10 Lotad C	.50	1.25
11 Lombre U	1.50	3.00
12 Ludicolo HOLO R	.75	1.50
13 Surskit C	.75	1.50
14 Masquerain U	.75	1.50
15 Shroomish C	.75	1.50
16 Breloom R	3.00	6.00
17 Volbeat C	.75	1.50
18 Illumise C	.30	.60
19 Trevenant EX HOLO R	.25	.60
20 Vulpix C	.10	.20
21 Ninetales R	.75	1.50
22 Slugma C	.75	1.50
23 Magcargo U	1.25	2.50
24 Magcargo R	.75	1.50
25 Torchic C	2.00	4.00
26 Torchic U	1.00	2.00
27 Combusken U	1.50	3.00
28 Blaziken HOLO R	1.50	3.00
29 Camerupt EX HOLO R	.20	.50
30 Horsea C	1.00	2.00
31 Seadra U	.50	1.25
32 Staryu C	.15	.40
33 Mudkip C	5.00	10.00
34 Marshtomp U	4.00	8.00
35 Swampert R	1.50	3.00
36 Swampert HOLO R	.60	1.25
37 Ludicolo R	.75	1.50
38 Wailord EX HOLO R	.75	2.00
39 Barboach C	.25	.60
40 Whiscash U	2.00	4.00
41 Whiscash R	6.00	15.00
42 Corphish C	.60	1.25
43 Feebas C	.75	1.50
44 Milotic HOLO R	.75	1.50
45 Spheal C	.75	1.50
46 Spheal C	1.00	2.00
47 Sealeo U	.25	.50
48 Walrein R	.75	1.50
49 Clamperl C	1.00	2.00
50 Huntail HOLO R	.60	1.25
51 Gorebyss U	.75	1.50
52 Gorebyss R	2.00	4.00
53 Kyogre R	.60	1.25
54 Kyogre EX HOLO R	1.50	4.00
55 Primal Kyogre EX HOLO R	3.00	8.00
56 Manaphy HOLO R	.75	1.50
57 Chinchou C	1.00	2.00
58 Lanturn U	3.00	6.00
59 Electrike C	.10	.20
60 Electrike U	.10	.20
61 Manectric HOLO R	.75	1.50
62 Tynamo C	.75	1.50
63 Eelektrik U	.75	1.50
64 Eelektrik R	1.00	2.00
65 Eelektross HOLO R	6.00	12.00
66 Nidoran C	2.00	4.00
67 Nidorina U	.75	1.50
68 Nidoqueen U	1.00	2.00
69 Nidoqueen R	.07	.15
70 Tentacool C	3.00	6.00
71 Tentacool U	1.25	2.50
72 Tentacruel R	.60	1.25
73 Starmie R	.08	.20
74 Rhyhorn C	1.50	3.00
75 Rhydon U	2.50	5.00
76 Rhyperior R	2.50	5.00
77 Rhyperior HOLO R	1.50	3.00
78 Nosepass C	1.25	2.50
79 Meditite C	.20	.40
80 Medicham HOLO R	.50	1.00
81 Medicham R	4.00	10.00
82 Trapinch C	.75	1.50
83 Solrock C	.75	1.50
84 Groudon R	.10	.20
85 Groudon EX HOLO R	5.00	10.00
86 Primal Groudon EX HOLO R	.75	1.50
87 Hippopotas C	.60	1.25
88 Hippowdon HOLO R	.60	1.25
89 Drilbur C	.60	1.25
90 Diggersby R	1.00	2.00
91 Sharpedo EX HOLO R	.60	1.25
92 Crawdaunt HOLO R	1.25	2.50
93 Aggron EX HOLO R	1.25	2.50
94 MegaAggron EX HOLO R	4.00	8.00
95 Probopass R	2.00	4.00
96 Excadrill R	2.50	5.00
97 Excadrill HOLO R	1.50	3.00
98 Honedge C	.75	1.50
99 Doublade U	.75	1.50
100 Aegislash HOLO R	.07	.15
101 Mr. Mime U	1.00	2.00
102 Marill C	.10	.20
103 Azumarill R	1.50	3.00
104 Azumarill HOLO R	.30	.60
105 Gardevoir EX HOLO R	1.25	2.50
106 MegaGardevoir EX HOLO R	.10	.20
107 Kingdra R	.75	1.50
108 Kingdra HOLO R	1.00	2.00
109 Vibrava U	.75	1.50
110 Flygon HOLO R	.75	1.50
111 Zigzagoon C	1.50	3.00
112 Linoone U	.08	.20
113 Skitty C	2.50	5.00
114 Delcatty R	1.00	2.00
115 Spinda C	.60	1.50
116 Bidoof C	.12	.30
117 Bidoof U	2.50	5.00
118 Bibarel U	3.00	6.00
119 Bouffalant U	.75	1.50
120 Bunnelby C	10.00	20.00
121 Bunnelby U	1.25	2.50
122 Acro Bike U	.75	1.50
123 Aggron Spirit Link U	1.00	2.00
124 Archie's Ace in the Hole U	.60	1.25
125 Dive Ball U	1.00	2.00
126 Energy Retrieval U	.75	1.50
127 Escape Rope U	.75	2.00
128 Exp. Share U	6.00	12.00
129 Fresh Water Set U	1.25	2.50
130 Gardevoir Spirit Link U	1.00	2.00
131 Groudon Spirit Link U	4.00	8.00
132 Kyogre Spirit Link U	.75	1.50
133 Maxie's Hidden Ball Trick U	.75	1.50
134 Professor Birch's Observations U	.75	1.50
135 Rare Candy U	.75	1.50
136 Repeat Ball U	1.00	2.00
137 Rough Seas U	1.00	2.00
138 Scorched Earth U	1.00	2.00
139 Shrine of Memories U	2.00	4.00
140 Silent Lab U	1.50	3.00
141 Teammates U	.50	1.25
142 Weakness Policy U	1.00	2.00
143 Shield Energy U	.75	1.50
144 Wonder Energy U	1.25	2.50
145 Trevenant EX FULL ART UR	1.25	2.50
146 Camerupt EX FULL ART UR	1.25	2.50
147 Wailord EX FULL ART UR	2.00	4.00
148 Kyogre EX FULL ART UR	2.50	5.00
149 Primal Kyogre EX FULL ART UR	.04	.10
150 Groudon EX FULL ART UR	.04	.10
151 Primal Groudon EX FULL ART UR	.75	1.50
152 Sharpedo EX FULL ART UR	4.00	10.00
153 Aggron EX FULL ART UR	.50	1.25
154 MegaAggron EX FULL ART UR	10.00	20.00
155 Gardevoir EX FULL ART UR	1.00	2.00
156 MegaGardevoir EX FULL ART UR	.08	.20
157 Archie's Ace in the Hole FULL ART UR	.04	.10
158 Maxie's Hidden Ball Trick FULL ART UR	.75	1.50
159 Professor Birch's Observations FULL ART UR	.60	1.25
160 Teammates FULL ART UR	.25	.50
161 Dive Ball SCR	.01	.08
162 Enhanced Hammer SCR	.05	.12
163 Switch SCR	3.00	6.00
164 Weakness Policy SCR	.60	1.50

2015 Pokemon XY Roaring Skies

1 Exeggcute C	.25	.60
2 Exeggutor U	2.00	4.00
3 Wurmple C	8.00	20.00
4 Silcoon U	1.00	2.00
5 Beautifly HOLO R	1.25	2.50
6 Cascoon C	1.25	2.50
7 Dustox U	1.00	2.00
8 Dustox R	1.25	2.50
9 Nincada C	1.25	2.50
10 Ninjask U	1.00	2.00
11 Shedinja R	.75	1.50
12 Tropius U	1.50	3.00
13 Victini R	1.25	2.50
14 Fletchinder U	.30	.75
15 Talonflame R	.60	1.25
16 Articuno R	4.00	8.00
17 Articuno R	1.25	2.50
18 Wingull C	1.25	2.50
19 Pelipper U	1.50	3.00
20 Pikachu C	.75	1.50
21 Voltorb C	1.25	2.50
22 Electrode U	3.00	8.00
23 Zapdos R	3.00	6.00
24 Electrike C	.01	.08
25 Manectric U	.04	.10
26 Thundurus EX HOLO R	.75	1.50
27 Natu C	.15	.30
28 Natu C	.75	1.50
29 Xatu R	.75	1.50
30 Shuppet C	3.00	6.00
31 Banette R	.75	1.50
32 Banette R	4.00	8.00
33 Deoxys HOLO R	.75	1.50
34 Gallade EX HOLO R	3.00	6.00
35 Mega Gallade EX HOLO R	2.50	5.00
36 Gligar C	1.50	3.00
37 Gliscor U	.60	1.25
38 Binacle C	5.00	10.00
39 Hawlucha C	2.50	5.00
40 Absol HOLO R	.75	1.50
41 Inkay C	.20	.50
42 Jirachi HOLO R	1.00	2.00
43 Togepi C	1.00	2.00
44 Togetic U	1.50	3.00
45 Togekiss R	1.25	2.50
46 Togekiss HOLO R	3.00	8.00
47 Carbink R	.60	1.50
48 Klefki R	.75	1.50
49 Dratini C	1.00	2.00
50 Dragonair U	.75	1.50
51 Dragonite R	.75	1.50
52 Dragonite HOLO R	6.00	12.00
53 Altaria U	1.25	2.50
54 Bagon C	.75	1.50
55 Bagon C	.75	1.50
56 Shelgon U	1.25	2.50
57 Salamence HOLO R	1.00	2.00
58 Latios EX HOLO R	1.00	2.00
59 Mega Latios EX HOLO R	.75	1.50
60 Rayquaza EX HOLO R	5.00	10.00
61 Mega Rayquaza EX HOLO R	.12	.25
62 Hydreigon EX HOLO R	.75	1.50
63 Reshiram HOLO R	.75	1.50
64 Zekrom HOLO R	.75	1.50
65 Spearow C	.60	1.25
66 Fearow U	.75	1.50
67 Meowth C	1.25	2.50
68 Dunsparce C	.10	.20
69 Skarmory R	.30	.60
70 Taillow C	.60	1.25
71 Swellow R	1.25	2.50
72 Swellow HOLO R	.25	.50
73 Swablu C	.12	.25
74 Altaria R	.60	1.25
75 Rayquaza EX HOLO R	1.00	2.00
76 Mega Rayquaza EX HOLO R	.75	1.50
77 Shaymin EX HOLO R	1.50	3.00
78 Pidove C	2.50	5.00
79 Tranquill U	.08	.20
80 Unfezant U	1.50	3.00
81 Unfezant R	1.00	2.00
82 Fletchling C	.75	1.50
83 Gallade Spirit Link U	1.00	2.00
84 Healing Scarf U	1.25	2.50
85 Latios Spirit Link U	1.00	2.00
86 Mega Turbo U	.60	1.25
87 Rayquaza Spirit Link U	.10	.20
88 Revive U	.12	.30
89 Sky Field U	.75	1.50
90 Steven U	3.00	6.00
91 Switch U	.75	1.50
92 Trainers' Mail U	3.00	6.00
93 Ultra Ball U	1.00	2.00
94 Wally U	.50	1.25
95 Wide Lens U	.10	.20
96 Winona U	.01	.08
97 Double Dragon Energy U	.08	.20
98 Thundurus EX UR	.60	1.25
99 Gallade EX UR	.75	1.50
100 Mega Gallade EX UR	1.25	2.50
101 Latios EX UR	.75	1.50
102 Mega Latios EX UR FULL ART	.75	1.50
103 Hydreigon EX UR FULL ART	2.00	4.00
104 Rayquaza EX UR FULL ART	1.00	2.00
105 Mega Rayquaza EX UR FULL ART	1.25	2.50
106 Shaymin EX UR FULL ART	.75	1.50
107 Wally UR	.75	1.50
108 Winona UR	.75	1.50
109 Energy Switch UR	.50	1.00
110 VS Seeker UR	1.00	2.00

2016 Pokemon XY Evolutions

1 Venusaur EX UR	.75	1.50
2 Mega Venusaur EX UR	.75	1.50
3 Caterpie C	.50	1.25
4 Metapod U	.25	.50
5 Weedle C	1.50	3.00
6 Kakuna U	.75	1.50
7 Beedrill R	12.50	25.00
8 Tangela C	1.25	2.50
9 Charmander C	.75	1.50
10 Charmeleon U	.60	1.25
11 Charizard HOLO R	4.00	8.00
12 Charizard EX UR	.08	.20
13 Mega Charizard EX UR	.04	.10
14 Vulpix C	.75	1.50
15 Ninetales HOLO R	3.00	6.00
16 Ninetales BREAK HOLO BREAK	.75	1.50
17 Growlithe C	.75	1.50
18 Arcanine R	.75	1.50
19 Ponyta C	.25	.60
20 Magmar U	.60	1.25
21 Blastoise EX UR	2.00	4.00
22 Mega Blastoise EX UR	1.50	3.00
23 Poliwag C	.25	.50
24 Poliwhirl U	.04	.10
25 Poliwrath HOLO R	.40	1.00
26 Slowbro EX UR	1.50	3.00
27 Mega Slowbro EX UR	.75	1.50
28 Seel C	4.00	8.00
29 Dewgong R	25.00	50.00
30 Staryu C	1.50	3.00
31 Starmie R	.60	1.25
32 Starmie BREAK HOLO BREAK	1.50	3.00
33 Magikarp C	.50	1.25
34 Gyarados HOLO R	.30	.75
35 Pikachu C	2.00	4.00
36 Raichu HOLO R	6.00	15.00
37 Magnemite C	.20	.50
38 Magneton HOLO R	.10	.25
39 Voltorb C	.60	1.25
40 Electrode R	.60	1.50
41 Electabuzz C	.15	.40
42 Zapdos HOLO R	2.00	4.00
43 Nidoran C	1.00	2.00
44 Nidorino U	.60	1.25
45 Nidoking HOLO R	.75	1.50
46 Nidoking BREAK HOLO BREAK	2.00	4.00
47 Gastly C	1.25	2.50
48 Haunter U	.75	1.50
49 Drowzee C	.01	.08
50 Koffing U	.08	.20
51 Mewtwo R	1.50	3.00
52 Mewtwo EX UR	.75	1.50
53 Mew HOLO R	.15	.30
54 Sandshrew C	4.00	8.00
55 Diglett C	1.00	2.00
56 Dugtrio R	.75	1.50
57 Machop C	.75	1.50
58 Machoke U	1.00	2.00
59 Machamp HOLO R	.60	1.25
60 Machamp BREAK HOLO BREAK	.60	1.25
61 Onix C	1.50	3.00
62 Hitmonchan HOLO R	3.00	6.00
63 Clefairy HOLO R	.75	1.50
64 Pidgeot EX UR	.75	1.50
65 Mega Pidgeot EX UR	1.00	2.00
66 Rattata C	.75	1.50
67 Raticate R	1.25	2.50
68 Farfetch'd R	1.00	2.00
69 Doduo C	1.25	2.50
70 Chansey HOLO R	2.50	5.00
71 Porygon U	2.00	5.00
72 Dragonite EX UR	1.25	3.00
73 Blastoise Spirit Link U	.08	.20
74 Brocks Grit U	.04	.10
75 Charizard Spirit Link U	1.25	2.50
76 Devolution Spray U	1.00	2.00
77 Energy Retrieval U	.07	.15
78 Full Heal U	1.00	2.00
79 Maintenance U	.75	1.50
80 Misty's Determination U	.75	1.50
81 Pidgeot Spirit Link U	4.00	8.00
82 Pokedex U	3.00	6.00
83 Potion U	3.00	6.00
84 Professor Oak's Hint U	1.00	2.00
85 Revive U	1.25	2.50
86 Slowbro Spirit Link U	.75	1.50
87 Super Potion U	1.25	2.50
88 Switch U	.10	.20
89 Venusaur Spirit Link U	.60	1.25
90 Double Colorless Energy U	.75	1.50
91 Grass Energy C	1.25	2.50
92 Fire Energy C	1.50	3.00
93 Water Energy C	.75	1.50
94 Lightning Energy C	.75	1.50
95 Psychic Energy C	1.25	2.50
96 Fighting Energy C	.75	1.50
97 Darkness Energy C	1.00	2.00
98 Metal Energy C	.75	1.50
99 Fairy Energy C	.60	1.25
100 Mega Venusaur EX FULL ART UR	1.25	2.50
101 Mega Charizard EX FULL ART UR	1.50	3.00
102 Mega Blastoise EX FULL ART UR	2.00	4.00
103 Mewtwo EX FULL ART UR	1.50	3.00
104 Pidgeot EX FULL ART UR	1.50	3.00
105 Mega Pidgeot EX FULL ART UR	3.00	6.00
106 Dragonite EX FULL ART UR	1.50	3.00
107 Brocks Grit FULL ART UR	1.50	3.00
108 Misty's Determination FULL ART SR	.60	1.50
109 Exeggutor SCR	2.00	4.00
110 Flying Pikachu SCR	2.00	4.00
111 Surfing Pikachu SCR	.30	.60
112 Imakuni's Doduo SCR	.60	1.25

2016 Pokemon Generations

1 Venusaur EX HOLO R	.01	.08
2 M Venusaur EX HOLO R	.10	.25
3 Caterpie C	.04	.10
4 Metapod U	.10	.25
5 Butterfree HOLO R	1.50	3.00
6 Paras C	.10	.20
7 Parasect R	1.25	2.50
8 Tangela C	1.50	3.00
9 Pinsir R	1.25	2.50
10 Leafeon EX HOLO R	1.00	2.00
11 Charizard EX HOLO R	2.50	5.00
12 MCharizard EX HOLO R	.10	.20
13 Ninetales EX HOLO R	.12	.30
14 Ponyta C	.75	1.50
15 Rapidash R	1.00	2.00
16 Magmar C	.75	1.50
17 Blastoise EX HOLO R	.60	1.25
18 MBlastoise EX HOLO R	1.00	2.00
19 Shellder C	.75	1.50
20 Cloyster U	.30	.75
21 Krabby C	1.00	2.00
22 Magikarp C	1.00	2.00
23 Gyarados R	.01	.08
24 Vaporeon EX HOLO R	.04	.10
25 Articuno HOLO R FULL ART	.50	1.25
26 Pikachu C	5.00	10.00
27 Raichu HOLO R	1.25	2.50
28 Jolteon EX HOLO R	.75	1.50

29 Zapdos HOLO R FULL ART .75 1.50
30 Zubat C 1.25 2.50
31 Golbat U .20 .50
32 Slowpoke C .15 .40
33 Gastly C .30 .75
34 Haunter U .08 .20
35 Gengar HOLO R .75 1.50
36 Jynx R .75 1.50
37 Meowstic EX HOLO R 1.00 2.00
38 Diglett C .07 .15
39 Dugtrio R 1.00 2.00
40 Machop C .75 1.50
41 Machoke U 1.00 2.00
42 Machamp HOLO R 3.00 6.00
43 Geodude C 1.50 3.00
44 Graveler U .25 .50
45 Golem HOLO R .04 .10
46 Golem EX HOLO R .05 .12
47 Hitmonlee R .60 1.25
48 Hitmonchan R .75 1.50
49 Rhyhorn C 4.00 8.00
50 Clefairy C 3.00 6.00
51 Clefable U 1.50 3.00
52 Mr. Mime U .75 1.50
53 Meowth C .75 1.50
54 Persian U .75 1.50
55 Doduo C 1.00 2.00
56 Dodrio R 1.00 2.50
57 Tauros R .40 1.00
58 Snorlax R 2.00 4.00
59 Clemont U 10.00 25.00
60 Crushing Hammer U .60 1.25
61 Energy Switch U .75 1.50
62 Evosoda U 6.00 12.00
63 Imakuni? U 1.00 2.00
64 Maintenance U 1.50 3.00
65 Max Revive U 1.25 2.50
66 Olympia U .60 1.25
67 Poke Ball U .50 1.00
68 Pokemon Center Lady U 1.00 2.00
69 Pokemon Fan Club U .30 .60
70 Revitalizer U .75 1.50
71 Red Card U .50 1.25
72 Shauna U .12 .30
73 Team Flare Grunt U 1.00 2.00
74 Double Colorless Energy U 2.50 5.00
75 Grass Energy C .60 1.25
76 Fire Energy C .75 1.50
77 Water Energy C .60 1.25
78 Lightning Energy C .10 .20
79 Psychic Energy C .75 1.50
80 Fighting Energy C .75 1.50
81 Darkness Energy C .50 1.00
82 Metal Energy C .75 1.50
83 Fairy Energy C .75 1.50

2016 Pokemon Generations Radiant Collection

RC1 Chikorita C .75 1.50
RC2 Shroomish C 2.00 4.00
RC3 Charmander C 1.25 2.50
RC4 Charmeleon C .25 .50
RC5 Charizard U .01 .08
RC6 Flareon EX HOLO R .10 .25
RC7 Snorunt C 1.00 2.00
RC8 Froslass U .30 .75
RC9 Raichu C .75 1.50
RC10 Dedenne U 1.00 2.00
RC11 Wobbuffet C .60 1.50
RC12 Gulpin C .75 2.00
RC13 Jirachi U 1.00 2.00
RC14 Espurr C .30 .60
RC15 Meowstic U .75 1.50
RC16 Yveltal U .12 .25
RC17 Flabebe C .75 1.50
RC18 Floette U .75 1.50
RC19 Swirlix U 2.00 4.00
RC20 Slurpuff U 1.00 2.00
RC21 Sylveon EX HOLO R .75 1.50
RC22 Diancie U 2.50 5.00
RC23 Swablu C 2.00 4.00
RC24 Altaria U 7.50 15.00
RC25 Fletchling C 6.00 12.00
RC26 Floral Crown C .30 .60
RC27 Wally U 1.00 2.00
RC28 Flareon EX UR FULL ART .10 .20
RC29 Pikachu FULL ART UR .12 .30
RC30 Gardevoir EX UR FULL ART 1.50 3.00
RC31 M Gardevoir EX FULL ART UR 1.00 2.00
RC32 Sylveon EX FULL ART UR 3.00 6.00

2016 Pokemon XY Breakpoint

1 Chikorita C 2.00 4.00
2 Bayleef U 1.25 2.50
3 Meganium HOLO R .60 1.25
4 Seedot C 1.00 2.00
5 Kricketot C .75 1.50
6 Kricketune U 1.25 2.50
7 Petilil C 1.25 2.50
8 Lilligant R 1.50 3.00
9 Durant U 1.50 3.00
10 Growlithe C 1.00 2.00
11 Arcanine U 1.00 2.00
12 Numel C 2.00 4.00
13 Camerupt R .75 1.50
14 Emboar EX HOLO R 7.50 15.00
15 Heatmor U .75 1.50
16 Psyduck C 1.25 2.50
17 Golduck R .60 1.25
18 Golduck BREAK R .60 1.25
19 Slowpoke C 1.50 3.00
20 Slowbro U 2.00 4.00
21 Slowking HOLO R 1.00 2.00
22 Shellder/Razor Shell C 4.00 8.00
23 Shellder/Clamp C .60 1.50
24 Cloyster U 1.50 3.00
25 Staryu C 1.25 2.50
26 Gyarados EX HOLO R 1.25 2.50
27 M Gyarados EX HOLO R .60 1.25
28 Lapras U 7.50 15.00
29 Corsola C .04 .10
30 Suicune HOLO R .05 .12
31 Palkia EX HOLO R .60 1.25
32 Manaphy EX HOLO R .75 1.50
33 Tympole C .07 .15
34 Palpitoad U .08 .20
35 Seismitoad R .75 1.50
36 Ducklett C 1.50 3.00
37 Swanna U .75 1.50
38 Froakie C .60 1.25
39 Frogadier U .07 .15
40 Greninja R 1.25 2.50
41 Greninja BREAK R .04 .10
42 Electabuzz C .08 .20
43 Electivire U .75 1.50
44 Shinx C 1.50 3.00
45 Luxio U 2.00 4.00
46 Luxray R 1.25 2.50
47 Luxray BREAK R .50 1.25
48 Blitzle C .50 1.00
49 Zebstrika R .75 1.50
50 Drowzee C .75 1.50
51 Hypno R 1.25 2.50
52 Espeon EX HOLO R .75 1.50
53 Skorupi C 1.50 3.00
54 Drapion R 2.00 4.00
55 Sigilyph U 4.00 8.00
56 Trubbish C .75 1.50
57 Garbodor HOLO R .75 1.50
58 Espurr C 1.25 2.50
59 Meowstic R 1.50 3.00
60 Honedge C .60 1.25
61 Doublade U 1.50 3.00
62 Aegislash HOLO R 1.25 2.50
63 Skrelp C .75 1.50
64 Phantump C 1.00 2.00
65 Trevenant R 4.00 8.00
66 Trevenant BREAK R 1.50 3.00
67 Sudowoodo U .75 1.50
68 Gible C 2.50 5.00
69 Gabite U .75 1.50
70 Garchomp HOLO R 2.50 5.00
71 Pancham C .75 1.50
72 Nuzleaf U .30 .60
73 Shiftry R .75 1.50
74 Darkrai EX HOLO R 6.00 15.00
75 Pangoro R 1.25 3.00
76 Scizor EX HOLO R 2.00 4.00
77 M Scizor EX HOLO R 6.00 12.00
78 Mawile U 2.50 5.00
79 Ferroseed C 50.00 120.00
80 Ferrothorn R 2.00 4.00
81 Clefairy C .30 .75
82 Clefable R .75 1.50
83 Togekiss EX HOLO R 1.50 3.00
84 Spritzee C 1.00 2.00
85 Aromatisse U 1.25 2.50
86 Dragalge HOLO R .75 1.50
87 Rattata C .75 1.50
88 Raticate R 1.25 2.50
89 Raticate BREAK R .60 1.25
90 Dunsparce U 4.00 8.00
91 Stantler U .75 1.50
92 Ho-Oh EX HOLO R .50 1.25
93 Glameow C .15 .40
94 Purugly U .10 .25
95 Furfrou C .12 .30
96 All-Night Party U 1.25 2.50
97 Bursting Balloon U 1.50 3.00
98 Delinquent U 1.00 2.00
99 Fighting Fury Belt U .08 .20
100 Great Ball U .05 .12
101 Gyarados Spirit Link U 2.00 4.00
102 Max Elixir U 1.00 2.00
103 Max Potion U 1.25 2.50
104 Misty's Determination U 1.00 2.50
105 Pokemon Catcher U .75 2.00
106 Potion U .75 1.50
107 Professor Sycamore U .75 1.50
108 Psychic's Third Eye U 1.25 2.50
109 Puzzle of Time U .75 1.50
110 Reverse Valley U 1.25 2.50
111 Scizor Spirit Link U 1.50 3.00
112 Tierno U 2.00 4.00
113 Splash Energy U 1.00 2.00
114 Gyarados EX UR .75 1.50
115 M Gyarados EX UR 1.25 2.50
116 Manaphy EX UR 1.00 2.00
117 Espeon EX UR .50 1.00
118 Darkrai EX UR 5.00 10.00
119 Scizor EX UR .75 1.50
120 M Scizor EX UR .60 1.25
121 Ho-Oh EX UR .25 .50
122 Skyla UR 1.50 3.00
123 Gyarados EX SCR 1.00 2.00

2016 Pokemon XY Fates Collide

1 Shuckle U 1.00 2.00
2 Burmy C 1.00 2.00
3 Wormadam (Solar Ray) U 1.00 2.00
4 Mothim R .75 1.50
5 Snivy C 1.50 3.00
6 Servine U 2.50 5.00
7 Serperior R 1.25 2.50
8 Deerling C 1.50 3.00
9 Moltres R 1.25 2.50
10 Fennekin (Will-O-) C .07 .15
11 Fennekin (Invite Out) C 2.00 4.00
12 Braixen U 1.50 3.00
13 Delphox HOLO R 1.25 2.50
14 Delphox BREAK R 3.00 6.00
15 Seel C .60 1.25
16 Dewgong U .75 1.50
17 Omanyte U 4.00 8.00
18 Omastar R 1.00 2.00
19 Omastar BREAK R 1.00 2.00
20 Glaceon EX HOLO R .08 .20
21 White Kyurem HOLO R .05 .12
22 Binacle C .25 .50
23 Barbaracle R .04 .10
24 Rotom R .08 .20
25 Alakazam EX HOLO R 1.25 2.50
26 MAlakazam EX HOLO R 1.25 2.50
27 Koffing C .60 1.25
28 Weezing U 4.00 8.00
29 Mew HOLO R 5.00 10.00
30 Spoink C 2.50 5.00
31 Grumpig R 1.00 2.00
32 Gothita C 1.50 3.00
33 Solosis C 3.00 6.00
34 Duosion U 1.50 3.00
35 Reuniclus R .07 .15
36 Diglett C .08 .20
37 Marowak R 1.25 2.50
38 Kabuto U .60 1.50
39 Kabutops R 1.25 2.50
40 Larvitar C .01 .08
41 Larvitar C .05 .12
42 Pupitar U .75 1.50
43 Regirock EX HOLO R .75 1.50
44 Wormadam (Sand Spray) U .75 1.50
45 Riolu C .12 .25
46 Riolu C 1.25 2.50
47 Lucario (Beatdown) R 2.50 5.00
48 Hawlucha U 1.00 2.00
49 Carbink R 1.50 3.00
50 Carbink (Safeguard) C 1.25 2.50
51 CarbinkBREAK R .75 1.50
52 Zygarde (Lookout) U .60 1.25
53 Zygarde (Rumble) R 2.00 4.00
54 Zygarde EX HOLO R .50 1.25
55 Umbreon EX HOLO R .75 1.50
56 Tyranitar HOLO R 1.00 2.00
57 Vullaby C 1.25 2.50
58 Mandibuzz R .75 1.50
59 Wormadam (Return Attack) U .10 .20
60 Bronzor C .75 1.50
61 Bronzong R .75 1.50
62 BronzongBREAK R .75 1.50
63 Lucario (Vacuum Wave) HOLO R 2.50 5.00
64 Genesect EX HOLO R 1.00 2.00
65 Jigglypuff C .60 1.25
66 Wigglytuff U 1.50 3.00
67 Mr. Mime R 2.00 4.00
68 Snubbull C 1.00 2.00
69 MAltaria EX HOLO R .60 1.25
70 Cottonee C 3.00 6.00
71 Whimsicott U .15 .30
72 Diancie EX HOLO R 1.50 3.00
73 Kingdra EX HOLO R 2.00 4.00
74 Meowth C 2.00 4.00
75 Kangaskhan U 1.00 2.00
76 Aerodactyl R 1.25 2.50
77 Snorlax R .60 1.50
78 Lugia R .25 .60
79 LugiaBREAK R 2.00 4.00
80 Whismur C 15.00 40.00
81 Loudred U 1.00 2.00
82 Exploud R 1.25 2.50
83 Altaria EX HOLO R .20 .40
84 Audino EX HOLO R .20 .50
85 MAudino EX HOLO R .75 1.50
86 Minccino (Cleaning Up) C .75 1.50
87 Minccino (Tail Smack) C .40 1.00
88 Cinccino (Sweeping Cure) U .12 .30
89 Cinccino (Sweeping Cure) U 1.00 2.00
90 Alakazam Spirit Link U 1.00 2.00
91 Altaria Spirit Link U .60 1.25
92 Audino Spirit Link U 6.00 12.00
93 Bent Spoon U 10.00 20.00
94 Chaos Tower U .01 .08
95 Devolution Spray U .05 .12
96 Dome Fossil Kabuto U 1.00 2.00
97 Energy Pouch U 3.00 6.00
98 Energy Reset U .30 .75
99 Fairy Drop U 1.25 2.50
100 Fairy Garden U 1.00 2.00
101 Fossil Excavation Kit U 1.50 3.00
102 Helix Fossil Omanyte U 1.25 2.50
103 Lass's Special U .75 1.50
104 MCatcher U 2.00 4.00
105 N U .25 .50
106 Old Amber Aerodactyl U .50 1.25
107 Pokémon Fan Club U .50 1.00
108 Power Memory U .75 1.50
109 Random Receiver U .01 .08
110 Scorched Earth U .05 .12
111 Shauna U 1.50 3.00
112 Team Rocket's Handiwork U .75 1.50
113 Ultra Ball U .60 1.50
114 Double Colorless Energy U 1.25 3.00
115 Strong Energy U .75 1.50
116 Glaceon EX UR .60 1.25
117 Alakazam EX UR 1.00 2.00
118 MAlakazam EX UR .60 1.25
119 Umbreon EX UR 1.25 2.50
120 Genesect EX UR .60 1.25
121 MAltaria EX UR .75 1.50
122 Kingdra EX UR .25 .50
123 Altaria EX UR 4.00 8.00
124 Team Rocket's Handiwork UR .75 1.50
125 Alakazam EX SR .75 1.50

2016 Pokemon XY Steam Siege

1 Tangela C .75 1.50
2 Tangrowth U 1.25 2.50
3 Hoppip C .75 1.50
4 Skiploom U .75 1.50
5 Jumpluff R 1.25 2.50
6 Yanma C 4.00 8.00
7 Yanmega R 1.50 3.00
8 Yanmega BREAK HOLO R .75 1.50
9 Seedot C .08 .20
10 Nuzleaf U .05 .12
11 Shiftry HOLO R 4.00 8.00
12 Foongus C .75 1.50
13 Amoonguss R .75 1.50
14 Larvesta C .75 1.50
15 Volcarona R .60 1.25
16 Ponyta C .75 1.50
17 Rapidash U .75 1.50
18 Chimchar C 1.25 2.50
19 Monferno U 1.25 2.50
20 Infernape HOLO R 1.50 3.00
21 Talonflame BREAK HOLO R .60 1.25
22 Litleo C .10 .20
23 Pyroar R 1.00 2.00
24 Pyroar BREAK HOLO R 4.00 8.00
25 Volcanion R .60 1.25
26 Volcanion EX HOLO R 2.50 5.00
27 Mantine C 1.00 2.00
28 Shellos C .75 1.50
29 Gastrodon R .25 .50
30 Oshawott C 1.50 3.00
31 Dewott U .75 1.50
32 Samurott R 1.00 2.00
33 Clauncher C 3.00 6.00
34 Clawitzer R 1.25 2.50
35 Clawitzer BREAK HOLO R .60 1.25
36 Bergmite C .07 .15
37 Avalugg R .75 1.50
38 Mareep C .08 .20
39 Flaaffy U 1.50 3.00
40 Ampharos HOLO R .60 1.50
41 Joltik C 1.25 2.50
42 Galvantula R .75 1.50
43 Nidoran C 1.50 3.00
44 Nidorino U .75 1.50
45 Nidoking R .50 1.00
46 Drifloon C .75 1.50
47 Drifblim U 1.50 3.00
48 Litwick C 2.00 4.00
49 Lampent U .60 1.25
50 Chandelure HOLO R .75 1.50
51 Hoopa R .75 1.50
52 Mankey C .75 1.50
53 Primeape R .75 1.50
54 Nosepass C .75 1.50
55 Probopass R 1.00 2.00
56 Anorith U .60 1.50
57 Armaldo R 1.50 3.00
58 Croagunk C 7.50 15.00
59 Toxicroak R .04 .10
60 Sneasel C .05 .12
61 Weavile R .60 1.25
62 Spiritomb R .60 1.25
63 Pawniard C 1.00 2.00
64 Bisharp HOLO R 1.25 2.50
65 Yveltal HOLO R 125.00 250.00
66 Yveltal BREAK HOLO R .60 1.25
67 Steelix EX HOLO R 1.00 2.00
68 Mega Steelix EX HOLO R .75 1.50
69 Shieldon U .60 1.25
70 Bastiodon R .50 1.00
71 Klink C 1.00 2.00
72 Klang U 2.00 4.00
73 Klinklang HOLO R .20 .40
74 Cobalion R 3.00 6.00
75 Magearna EX HOLO R .75 1.50
76 Marill C .50 1.25
77 Azumarill U .25 .60
78 Gardevoir EX HOLO R 2.00 4.00
79 Mega Gardevoir EX HOLO R 6.00 15.00
80 Klefki U 1.00 2.00
81 Xerneas HOLO R .25 .50
82 Xerneas BREAK HOLO R .60 1.25
83 Druddigon R 1.25 2.50
84 Deino C 2.00 4.00
85 Zweilous U .75 1.50
86 Hydreigon HOLO R 1.00 2.00
87 Hydreigon BREAK HOLO R 2.50 5.00
88 Meowth C 1.25 2.50
89 Persian U 2.00 4.00
90 Aipom C 6.00 12.00
91 Ambipom U .75 1.50
92 Rufflet C .75 1.50
93 Braviary U .50 1.00
94 Fletchling C .75 1.50
95 Fletchinder U 1.50 3.00
96 Talonflame R 2.00 4.00
97 Hawlucha U 4.00 8.00
98 Armor Fossil Shieldon U 1.50 3.00
99 Captivating Poke Puff U 1.25 2.50
100 Claw Fossil Anorith U .04 .10
101 Gardevoir Spirit Link U .10 .25
102 Greedy Dice U 1.25 2.50
103 Ninja Boy U 1.00 2.00
104 Pokemon Ranger U 1.00 2.00
105 Special Charge U 1.00 2.00
106 Steelix Spirit Link U 1.00 2.00
107 Volcanion EX FULL ART UR 2.00 4.00
108 Steelix EX FULL ART UR 1.25 3.00
109 Mega Steelix EX UR FULL ART .50 1.00
110 Magearna EX UR FULL ART 1.00 2.00
111 Gardevoir EX UR FULL ART .75 2.00
112 Mega Gardevoir EX UR FULL ART .75 1.50
113 Pokemon Ranger UR FULL ART 1.50 3.00
114 Professor Sycamore UR FULL ART .75 1.50
115 Volcanion EX SCR .75 1.50
116 Gardevoir EX SCR 1.00 2.00

2017 Pokemon Sun and Moon

1 Caterpie C .60 1.25
2 Metapod U .75 1.50
3 Butterfree R 1.00 2.00
4 Paras C .50 1.00
5 Parasect R 2.50 5.00
6 Pinsir U .01 .08
7 Surskit C .04 .10
8 Masquerain R .75 1.50

9 Rowlet C .75 1.50
10 Dartrix U 1.25 2.50
11 Decidueye R 1.25 2.50
12 Decidueye GX UR 1.00 2.00
13 Grubbin C .75 1.50
14 Fomantis C .60 1.25
15 Lurantis GX UR 1.50 3.00
16 Morelull C .75 1.50
17 Shiinotic HOLO R 4.00 8.00
18 Bounsweet C 1.25 2.50
19 Steenee U 1.00 2.00
20 Tsareena HOLO R .20 .50
21 Growlithe C .60 1.25
22 Arcanine HOLO R 5.00 10.00
23 Torkoal C 1.00 2.00
24 Litten C 2.00 4.00
25 Torracat U 2.00 4.00
26 Incineroar R .60 1.25
27 Incineroar GX UR 1.25 2.50
28 Psyduck C 1.00 2.00
29 Golduck R 1.50 3.00
30 Poliwag C .25 .50
31 Poliwhirl U .01 .08
32 Poliwrath HOLO R .08 .20
33 Shellder C 1.25 2.50
34 Cloyster R 1.50 3.00
35 Lapras GX UR 1.50 3.00
36 Corsola U .50 1.00
37 Wingull C .60 1.25
38 Pelipper U .07 .15
39 Popplio C .60 1.50
40 Brionne U 1.00 2.00
41 Primarina R 1.00 2.00
42 Primarina GX UR .75 1.50
43 Crabominable R .60 1.25
44 Wishiwashi U 1.50 3.00
45 Dewpider C 4.00 8.00
46 Araquanid U .75 1.50
47 Pyukumuku U 1.25 2.50
48 Bruxish R .75 1.50
49 Chinchou C .75 1.50
50 Lanturn R 1.50 3.00
51 Charjabug U 2.50 5.00
52 Vikavolt HOLO R .75 1.50
53 Togedemaru C .75 1.50
54 Zubat C .75 1.50
55 Golbat U 1.00 2.00
56 Crobat HOLO R .50 1.00
57 Alolan Grimer C 1.00 2.00
58 Alolan Muk HOLO R 1.00 2.00
59 Drowzee C .50 1.25
60 Hypno U .75 1.50
61 Espeon GX UR 1.00 2.00
62 Mareanie C 1.25 2.50
63 Toxapex HOLO R .60 1.25
64 Cosmog C .60 1.25
65 Cosmoem R 1.25 2.50
66 Lunala GX UR 200.00 400.00
67 Makuhita C 7.50 15.00
68 Hariyama R .01 .08
69 Roggenrola C .04 .10
70 Boldore U 1.25 2.50
71 Gigalith HOLO R .30 .60
72 Crabrawler C .75 1.50
73 Passimian U 2.00 4.00
74 Sandygast C 1.00 2.00
75 Palossand R 7.50 15.00
76 Alolan Rattata C .75 1.50
77 Alolan Raticate U 1.00 2.00
78 Alolan Meowth C .75 1.50
79 Alolan Persian U .75 1.50
80 Umbreon GX UR .20 .40
81 Carvanha C 2.00 4.00
82 Sharpedo HOLO R .60 1.50
83 Sandile C .40 1.00
84 Krokorok U 2.00 4.00
85 Krookodile HOLO R 8.00 20.00
86 Alolan Diglett C 2.50 5.00
87 Alolan Dugtrio HOLO R 2.00 4.00
88 Skarmory C .60 1.25
89 Solgaleo GX UR 1.50 3.00
90 Snubbull C .75 1.50
91 Granbull U 1.50 3.00
92 Cutiefly C 1.00 2.00
93 Ribombee HOLO R 1.50 4.00
94 Dratini C 10.00 20.00
95 Dragonair U 2.50 5.00
96 Dragonite HOLO R 1.50 3.00
97 Spearow C .75 1.50
98 Fearow C 1.00 2.00
99 Kangaskhan HOLO R 1.00 2.00
100 Tauros GX UR 1.25 2.50
101 Eevee C .07 .15
102 Spinda U 1.50 3.00
103 Lillipup C 1.00 2.00
104 Herdier U 1.25 2.50
105 Stoutland R .50 1.00
106 Pikipek C 7.50 15.00
107 Trumbeak U 2.00 4.00
108 Toucannon R .75 1.50
109 Yungoos C .08 .20
110 Gumshoos GX UR .10 .25
111 Stufful C 1.00 2.00
112 Bewear U .30 .60
113 Oranguru HOLO R 2.50 5.00
114 Big Malasada U 1.00 2.00
115 Crushing Hammer U 2.00 4.00
116 Energy Retrieval U 1.50 3.00
117 Energy Switch U 1.00 2.00
118 Exp. Share U .20 .40
119 Great Ball U .60 1.25
120 Hau U .75 1.50
121 Ilima U 1.25 2.50
122 Lillie U .75 2.00
123 Nest Ball U .75 2.00
124 Poison Barb U .75 1.50
125 Poke Ball U 1.25 2.50
126 Pokemon Catcher U 1.00 2.00
127 Potion U .60 1.25
128 Professor Kukui U 3.00 6.00
129 Rare Candy U .30 .75
130 Repel U .75 1.50
131 Rotom Dex U 1.50 3.00
132 Switch U 10.00 20.00
133 Team Skull Grunt U 2.50 5.00
134 Timer Ball U .10 .20
135 Ultra Ball U .12 .25
136 Double Colorless Energy U .15 .40
137 Rainbow Energy U .75 1.50
138 Lurantis GX FULL ART UR .10 .20
139 Lapras GX FULL ART UR 1.50 3.00
140 Espeon GX FULL ART UR 1.50 3.00
141 Lunala GX FULL ART UR .75 1.50
142 Umbreon GX FULL ART UR .04 .10
143 Solgaleo GX FULL ART UR .10 .25
144 Tauros GX FULL ART UR 1.50 3.00
145 Gumshoos GX FULL ART UR 2.00 4.00
146 Ilima FULL ART UR 2.00 4.00
147 Lillie FULL ART UR .60 1.25
148 Professor Kukui FULL ART UR .75 1.50
149 Team Skull Grunt FULL ART UR 1.00 2.00
150 Lurantis GX SCR .60 1.25
151 Lapras GX SCR 10.00 20.00
152 Espeon GX SCR .75 1.50
153 Lunala GX SCR 1.25 2.50
154 Umbreon GX SCR 1.00 2.00
155 Solgaleo GX SCR .60 1.25
156 Tauros GX SCR .75 1.50
157 Gumshoos GX SCR .60 1.25
158 Nest Ball SCR .01 .08
159 Rotom Dex SCR .04 .10
160 Switch SCR 2.00 4.00
161 Ultra Ball SCR 1.00 2.00
162 Psychic Energy SCR 1.50 3.00
163 Metal Energy SCR .60 1.25

2017 Pokemon Sun and Moon Burning Shadows

1 Caterpie C .01 .08
2 Metapod U .04 .10
3 Butterfree R .25 .50
4 Oddish C .04 .10
5 Gloom U .10 .25
6 Vileplume HOLO R .75 1.50
7 Tangela C 4.00 8.00
8 Tangrowth R 1.25 2.50
9 Ledyba C .30 .75
10 Ledian R 1.00 2.00
11 Heracross R 1.00 2.00
12 Pansage C .30 .75
13 Simisage U 1.00 2.00
14 Dewpider C 2.50 5.00
15 Araquanid R 2.50 5.00
16 Wimpod C 1.25 2.50
17 Golisopod GX UR .12 .25
18 Charmander C .60 1.50
19 Charmeleon U 1.25 2.50
20 Charizard GX UR .75 1.50
21 Ho Oh GX UR 1.25 2.50
22 Pansear C 1.00 2.00
23 Simisear U .08 .20
24 Heatmor U .04 .10
25 Salazzle GX UR 1.50 3.00
26 Turtonator R .25 .50
27 Alolan Vulpix C 2.50 5.00
28 Alolan Ninetales R 1.25 2.50
29 Horsea C 1.00 2.00
30 Seadra U .75 1.50
31 Kingdra HOLO R .30 .75
32 Magikarp C 1.00 2.00
33 Gyarados HOLO R 1.00 2.00
34 Marill C .07 .15
35 Azumarill R .75 1.50
36 Panpour C 1.50 3.00
37 Simipour U .30 .60
38 Bruxish R .60 1.25
39 Tapu Fini GX UR .75 1.50
40 Pikachu C 1.00 2.00
41 Raichu HOLO R .75 1.50
42 Electabuzz U 1.00 2.00
43 Electivire R .50 1.25
44 Tynamo C .75 1.50
45 Eelektrik U 1.00 2.00
46 Eelektross R .75 1.50
47 Togedemaru C 1.25 2.50
48 Slowking R .60 1.25
49 Wobbuffet U 1.25 2.50
50 Seviper U 5.00 10.00
51 Duskull C .60 1.25
52 Dusclops U .75 1.50
53 Dusknoir HOLO R .75 1.50
54 Croagunk C 1.25 2.50
55 Toxicroak R 1.00 2.00
56 Venipede C .30 .75
57 Whirlipede U .15 .30
58 Scolipede R 1.25 2.50
59 Espurr C 2.00 4.00
60 Meowstic R 2.00 4.00
61 Sandygast C .75 1.50
62 Palossand HOLO R 1.00 2.00
63 Necrozma GX UR .08 .20
64 Machamp GX UR .60 1.25
65 Rhyhorn C 1.50 3.00
66 Rhydon U .75 1.50
67 Rhyperior HOLO R 10.00 20.00
68 Lunatone U 2.00 4.00
69 Solrock U 1.50 4.00
70 Riolu C .60 1.50
71 Lucario HOLO R 2.00 4.00
72 Sawk C 1.50 4.00
73 Crabrawler C .60 1.50
74 Crabominable R 6.00 15.00
75 Lycanroc HOLO R 1.50 3.00
76 Lycanroc R 1.50 3.00
77 Mudbray C 1.00 2.00
78 Mudsdale R 1.25 2.50
79 Passimian R 2.50 5.00
80 Marshadow GX UR 1.00 2.50
81 Alolan Rattata C .60 1.50
82 Alolan Raticate R .01 .08
83 Alolan Grimer C .04 .10
84 Alolan Muk GX UR .30 .60
85 Sneasel C .75 1.50
86 Weavile R .60 1.25
87 Darkrai HOLO R .75 1.50
88 Darkrai GX UR 1.50 3.00
89 Inkay C 1.00 2.00
90 Malamar R 1.50 3.00
91 Ralts C .75 1.50
92 Kirlia U .08 .20
93 Gardevoir GX UR 2.00 4.00
94 Diancie HOLO R .75 1.50
95 Cutiefly C 1.00 2.00
96 Ribombee U .75 1.50
97 Morelull C 1.25 2.50
98 Shiinotic R .75 1.50
99 Noivern GX UR 1.00 2.00
100 Zygarde HOLO R .75 1.50
101 Meowth C 1.00 2.00
102 Persian R .10 .20
103 Porygon C .12 .30
104 Porygon2 U 3.00 6.00
105 Porygon Z HOLO R 2.00 4.00
106 Hoothoot C .75 1.50
107 Noctowl U .75 1.50
108 Bouffalant U 5.00 10.00
109 Noibat C 5.00 10.00
110 Stufful C .60 1.25
111 Bewear R .07 .15
112 Acerola U 1.25 2.50
113 Bodybuilding Dumbbells U .10 .20
114 Escape Rope U .75 1.50
115 Guzma U 2.50 5.00
116 Kiawe U 4.00 8.00
117 Lana U .75 1.50
118 Mount Lanakila U .25 .60
119 Olivia U .25 .50
120 Plumeria U .10 .25
121 Po Town U .25 .60
122 Rotom Dex Poke Finder Mode U .60 1.25
123 Sophocles U 1.00 2.00
124 Super Scoop Up U .75 1.50
125 Tormenting Spray U .60 1.25
126 Weakness Policy U .60 1.25
127 Wicke U 1.00 2.00
128 Wishful Baton U .75 1.50
129 Golisopod GX FULL ART UR 1.00 2.00
130 Tapu Bulu GX FULL ART UR 3.00 6.00
131 Ho Oh GX FULL ART UR 1.00 2.00
132 Salazzle GX FULL ART UR 1.25 2.50
133 Tapu Fini GX FULL ART UR 1.50 3.00
134 Necrozma GX FULL ART UR 1.50 3.00
135 Machamp GX FULL ART UR .75 1.50
136 Lycanroc GX FULL ART UR 1.50 3.00
137 Marshadow GX FULL ART UR .75 1.50
138 Alolan Muk GX FULL ART UR .01 .08
139 Darkrai GX FULL ART UR .04 .10
140 Gardevoir GX FULL ART UR 1.00 2.00
141 Noivern GX FULL ART UR .50 1.25
142 Acerola FULL ART UR 2.50 5.00
143 Guzma FULL ART UR 1.25 2.50
144 Kiawe FULL ART UR .75 1.50
145 Plumeria FULL ART UR .10 .20
146 Sophocles FULL ART UR 1.25 2.50
147 Wicke FULL ART UR .25 .50
148 Golisopod GX SCR 1.00 2.00
149 Tapu Bulu GX SCR .60 1.25
150 Charizard GX SCR 1.25 2.50
151 Salazzle GX SCR .75 1.50
152 Tapu Fini GX SCR .75 1.50
153 Necrozma GX SCR 3.00 6.00
154 Machamp GX SCR 1.00 2.00
155 Lycanroc GX SCR 1.00 2.00
156 Marshadow GX SCR 1.25 2.50
157 Alolan Muk GX SCR 1.00 2.00
158 Darkrai GX SCR 1.00 2.00
159 Gardevoir GX SCR .30 .75
160 Noivern GX SCR .60 1.25
161 Bodybuilding Dumbbells SCR .07 .15
162 Choice Band SCR .75 1.50
163 Escape Rope SCR .75 1.50
164 Multi Switch SCR 2.00 4.00
165 Rescue Stretcher SCR .75 1.50
166 Super Scoop Up SCR 2.00 5.00
167 Fire Energy SCR .60 1.25
168 Darkness Energy SCR 1.25 2.50
169 Fairy Energy SCR 5.00 10.00

2017 Pokemon Sun and Moon Crimson Invasion

1 Weedle C .40 1.00
2 Kakuna U 1.25 2.50
3 Beedrill R 2.00 4.00
4 Exeggcute C .75 1.50
5 Cacnea C .75 1.50
6 Cacturne R .75 1.50
7 Karrablast C .75 1.50
8 Shelmet C .15 .30
9 Accelgor U 1.50 3.00
10 Skiddo C .60 1.25
11 Gogoat HOLO R .75 1.50
12 Alolan Marowak HOLO R 1.00 2.00
13 Numel C .75 1.50
14 Camerupt R 1.50 3.00
15 Staryu C 1.50 3.00
16 Starmie R .75 1.50
17 Magikarp C 7.50 15.00
18 Gyarados GX UR .75 1.50
19 Swinub C 1.50 3.00
20 Piloswine U .75 1.50
21 Mamoswine R 2.00 4.00
22 Remoraid C 1.50 3.00
23 Octillery R 1.00 2.50
24 Corphish C .30 .75
25 Crawdaunt R 12.00 30.00
26 Feebas C 1.00 2.00
27 Milotic HOLO R .75 1.50
28 Regice HOLO R .30 .75
29 Shellos C .75 1.50
30 Pikachu C 1.50 3.00
31 Alolan Raichu HOLO R 1.00 2.00
32 Alolan Geodude C .60 1.25
33 Alolan Graveler U .25 .50
34 Alolan Golem GX UR .01 .08
35 Emolga U .10 .25
36 Gastly C 7.50 15.00
37 Haunter U 1.00 2.50
38 Gengar HOLO R .01 .08
39 Misdreavus C .04 .10
40 Mismagius R .30 .60
41 Spoink C 2.50 5.00
42 Grumpig U 1.25 2.50
43 Chimecho C .50 1.00
44 Pumpkaboo C .50 1.00
45 Gourgeist R .10 .20
46 Salandit C 1.00 2.00
47 Salazzle HOLO R 1.25 2.50
48 Oranguru R 1.25 2.50
49 Nihilego GX UR .60 1.25
50 Mankey C 1.50 3.00
51 Primeape R 1.25 2.50
52 Cubone C .75 1.50
53 Regirock R .75 1.50
54 Gastrodon U .08 .20
55 Stufful C 3.00 6.00
56 Bewear HOLO R 1.00 2.00
57 Buzzwole GX UR .01 .08
58 Houndour C .01 .08
59 Houndoom R 1.00 2.50
60 Deino C .75 1.50
61 Zweilous U .75 1.50
62 Hydreigon R .12 .25
63 Guzzlord GX UR .75 1.50
64 Mawile U .75 1.50
65 Aron C 1.50 3.00
66 Lairon U 1.50 3.00
67 Aggron HOLO R 4.00 8.00
68 Registeel R 1.25 2.50
69 Escavalier R .60 1.25
70 Kartana GX UR .75 1.50
71 Jigglypuff C 1.25 2.50
72 Wigglytuff R 7.50 15.00
73 Xerneas HOLO R .75 1.50
74 Alolan Exeggutor GX UR 1.25 2.50
75 Jangmo o C .75 1.50
76 Hakamo o U 25.00 50.00
77 Kommo o R 3.00 6.00
78 Miltank U 1.50 3.00
79 Swablu C 2.50 5.00
80 Altaria R .75 1.50
81 Starly C 1.50 3.00
82 Staravia U .50 1.00
83 Staraptor R 2.00 4.00
84 Regigigas HOLO R 1.00 2.00
85 Minccino C 1.50 3.00
86 Cinccino U 7.50 15.00
87 Bunnelby C 1.50 3.00
88 Diggersby U 1.50 3.00
89 Type Null HOLO R .75 1.50
90 Silvally GX UR 1.25 2.50
91 Counter Catcher U .30 .75
92 Dashing Pouch U .20 .50
93 Devoured Field U .60 1.25
94 Fighting Memory U .60 1.25
95 Gladion U 1.00 2.00
96 Lusamine U 1.00 2.00
97 Peeking Red Card U .75 2.00
98 Psychic Memory U 2.50 5.00
99 Sea of Nothingness U 1.50 3.00
100 Counter Energy U 1.25 2.50
101 Gyarados GX FULL ART UR 2.50 5.00
102 Alolan Golem GX FULL ART UR .60 1.25
103 Nihilego GX FULL ART UR 3.00 6.00
104 Buzzwole GX FULL ART UR 1.00 2.00
105 Guzzlord GX FULL ART UR 1.25 2.50
106 Kartana GX FULL ART UR .30 .75
107 Alolan Exeggutor GX FULL ART UR 1.00 2.00
108 Silvally GX FULL ART UR 1.00 2.00
109 Gladion FULL ART UR .75 1.50
110 Lusamine FULL ART UR .07 .15
111 Olivia FULL ART UR 1.25 2.50
112 Gyarados GX SCR 1.00 2.00
113 Alolan Golem GX SCR 1.00 2.00
114 Nihilego GX SCR .75 1.50
115 Buzzwole GX SCR .07 .15
116 Guzzlord GX SCR 1.00 2.00
117 Kartana GX SCR .25 .50
118 Alolan Exeggutor GX SCR .60 1.25
119 Silvally GX SCR .75 1.50
120 Counter Catcher SCR 1.25 2.50
121 Wishful Baton SCR .25 .50
122 Counter Energy SCR 1.25 2.50
123 Warp Energy SCR .10 .20
124 Water Energy SCR .12 .30

2017 Pokemon Sun and Moon Guardians Rising

1 Bellsprout C .75 1.50
2 Weepinbell U .75 1.50
3 Victreebel R .60 1.25
4 Petilil C 1.25 2.50
5 Lilligant R .50 1.00
6 Phantump C 5.00 10.00
7 Trevenant R .75 1.50
8 Wimpod C .08 .20
9 Golisopod HOLO R .05 .12
10 Victini HOLO R .75 1.50
11 Litwick C .75 1.50
12 Lampent U 1.50 3.00
13 Chandelure HOLO R 2.00 4.00

14 Oricorio R .75 1.50
15 Salandit C 2.50 5.00
16 Salazzle R 2.00 4.00
17 Turtonator R .50 1.25
18 Turtonator GX UR .30 .60
19 Alolan Sandshrew C 2.00 4.00
20 Alolan Sandslash U .60 1.50
21 Alolan Vulpix C .25 .60
22 Alolan Ninetales GX UR 2.00 4.00
23 Tentacool C 1.00 2.00
24 Tentacruel U 15.00 40.00
25 Politoed HOLO R .75 1.50
26 Delibird C .75 1.50
27 Carvanha C 1.00 2.00
28 Sharpedo R .75 1.50
29 Wailmer C 1.00 2.00
30 Wailord R 1.25 2.50
31 Snorunt C .07 .15
32 Glalie U .12 .30
33 Vanillite C .60 1.25
34 Vanillish U 1.25 2.50
35 Vanilluxe R 1.00 2.00
36 Alomomola U 1.00 2.00
37 Wishiwashi C 1.25 2.50
38 Wishiwashi GX UR 2.50 5.00
39 Mareanie C .60 1.25
40 Alolan Geodude C .75 2.00
41 Alolan Graveler U .75 1.50
42 Alolan Golem HOLO R 3.00 6.00
43 Helioptile C .30 .60
44 Heliolisk R 1.50 3.00
45 Vikavolt GX UR 2.00 4.00
46 Oricorio R .75 1.50
47 Tapu Koko GX UR 3.00 8.00
48 Slowpoke C 2.50 6.00
49 Slowbro U 2.00 4.00
50 Trubbish C 20.00 50.00
51 Garbodor R .50 1.00
52 Gothita C .60 1.25
53 Gothorita U 1.00 2.00
54 Gothitelle R .75 2.00
55 Oricorio R .10 .25
56 Oricorio R .75 1.50
57 Toxapex GX UR 1.25 2.50
58 Mimikyu HOLO R .75 1.50
59 Dhelmise HOLO R .75 1.50
60 Tapu Lele GX-UR .50 1.00
61 Lunala R 1.00 2.50
62 Machop C .75 1.50
63 Machop C 1.50 3.00
64 Machoke U 2.50 5.00
65 Machamp HOLO R 1.50 3.00
66 Sudowoodo U 1.50 3.00
67 Gligar C .75 1.50
68 Gliscor U .75 1.50
69 Nosepass C .01 .08
70 Barboach C .01 .08
71 Whiscash R .60 1.25
72 Pancham C 2.00 4.00
73 Rockruff C 1.25 2.50
74 Lycanroc GX UR .75 1.50
75 Mudbray C 4.00 10.00
76 Mudsdale HOLO R .75 1.50
77 Minior HOLO R .60 1.25
78 Murkrow C 2.50 5.00
79 Honchkrow R 2.50 5.00
80 Sableye U .60 1.25
81 Absol HOLO R .60 1.25
82 Pangoro R 1.50 3.00
83 Beldum C 2.50 5.00
84 Metang U 1.00 2.00
85 Metagross GX UR .10 .20
86 Probopass R .75 1.50
87 Solgaleo R 1.00 2.00
88 Clefairy C 1.00 2.00
89 Clefable U .50 1.00
90 Cottonee C .50 1.00
91 Whimsicott U .50 1.00
92 Sylveon GX UR 1.25 2.50
93 Comfey HOLO R .75 1.50
94 Goomy C .75 1.50
95 Sliggoo U 7.50 15.00
96 Goodra HOLO R 1.50 3.00
97 Drampa HOLO R .50 1.00
98 Jangmo o C .30 .75
99 Hakamo o U 1.00 2.00
100 Kommo-O GX UR 1.25 2.50
101 Chansey C 1.50 3.00
102 Blissey HOLO R 1.00 2.00
103 Taillow C 5.00 12.00
104 Swellow R 1.50 3.00
105 Castform C 1.25 2.50
106 Rayquaza R 3.00 6.00
107 Patrat C .75 1.50
108 Watchog U 6.00 12.00
109 Fletchling C 1.00 2.00
110 Fletchinder U .75 1.50
111 Talonflame R 1.25 2.50
112 Stufful C 1.00 2.00
113 Bewear U .07 .15
114 Komala U 2.50 5.00
115 Drampa GX UR 1.25 2.50
116 Aether Paradise Conservation Area U 1.00 2.00
117 Altar of the Moone U 1.50 3.00
118 Altar of the Sunne U .75 1.50
119 Aqua Patch U .75 1.50
120 Brooklet Hill U .01 .08
121 Choice Band U .04 .10
122 Energy Loto U .75 1.50
123 Energy Recycler U .30 .75
124 Enhanced Hammer U .30 .75
125 Field Blower U 1.25 2.50
126 Hala U 1.00 2.00
127 Mallow U .08 .20
128 Max Potion U 1.50 3.00
129 Multi Switch U 1.25 2.50
130 Rescue Stretcher U 7.50 15.00
131 Turtonator GX FULL ART UR .60 1.25
132 Alolan Ninetales GX FULL ART UR 1.50 3.00
133 Wishiwashi GX FULL ART UR 1.00 2.00
134 Vikavolt GX FULL ART UR 2.00 4.00
135 Tapu Koko GX FULL ART UR 2.00 4.00
136 Toxapex GX FULL ART UR .25 .50
137 Tapu Lele GX FULL ART UR .08 .20
138 Lycanroc GX FULL ART UR .50 1.25
139 Metagross GX FULL ART UR 2.00 4.00
140 Sylveon GX FULL ART UR 1.25 2.50
141 Kommo-O GX FULL ART UR .30 .75
142 Drampa GX FULL ART UR 1.25 2.50
143 Hala FULL ART UR .30 .75
144 Hau FULL ART UR .75 1.50
145 Mallow FULL ART UR 30.00 60.00
146 Decidueye GX FULL ART SCR 1.50 3.00
147 Incineroar GX FULL ART SCR 1.25 2.50
148 Turtonator GX FULL ART SCR .50 1.25
149 Primarina GX FULL ART SCR 1.25 2.50
150 Alolan Ninetales GX FULL ART SCR .75 1.50
151 Wishiwashi GX FULL ART SCR .75 1.50
152 Vikavolt GX FULL ART SCR 6.00 12.00
153 Tapu Koko GX FULL ART SCR .75 1.50
154 Toxapex GX FULL ART SCR .75 1.50
155 Tapu Lele GX FULL ART SCR 1.25 2.50
156 Lycanroc GX FULL ART SCR 3.00 6.00
157 Metagross GX FULL ART SCR 2.00 4.00
158 Sylveon GX FULL ART SCR 1.50 3.00
159 Kommo-O GX FULL ART SCR .60 1.50
160 Drampa GX FULL ART SCR 1.00 2.00
161 Aqua Patch FULL ART SCR .60 1.25
162 Enhanced Hammer FULL ART SCR 2.00 4.00
163 Field Blower FULL ART SCR .50 1.00
164 Max Potion FULL ART SCR .75 1.50
165 Rare Candy FULL ART SCR .75 1.50
166 Double Colorless Energy FULL ART SCR 2.50 6.00
167 Grass Energy FULL ART SCR 1.50 4.00
168 Lightning Energy FULL ART SCR 2.00 4.00
169 Fighting Energy FULL ART SCR 50.00 120.00

2017 Pokemon Sun and Moon Shining Legends

1 Bulbasaur C 1.00 2.00
2 Ivysaur C .30 .60
3 Venusaur U 1.50 3.00
4 Shroomish C .75 1.50
5 Breloom C .01 .08
6 Carnivine U .04 .10
7 Shaymin HOLO R 1.00 2.00
8 Virizion HOLO R .75 1.50
9 Shining Genesect HOLO R 1.00 2.00
10 Entei GX UR .75 1.50
11 Torkoal C 3.00 6.00
12 Larvesta C .60 1.50
13 Volcarona U .75 1.50
14 Reshiram HOLO R .75 1.50
15 Litten C .50 1.00
16 Torracat C 1.50 3.00
17 Incineroar U .25 .50
18 Totodile C .75 1.50
19 Croconaw C .60 1.25
20 Feraligatr U 1.00 2.00
21 Qwilfish C .60 1.25
22 Buizel C .60 1.25
23 Floatzel U .75 1.50
24 Palkia HOLO R .25 .50
25 Manaphy HOLO R .75 1.50
26 Keldeo HOLO R 1.25 2.50
27 Shining Volcanion HOLO R .60 1.25
28 Pikachu C .60 1.25
29 Raichu GX UR .01 .08
30 Voltorb C .04 .10
31 Electrode U 4.00 10.00
32 Raikou HOLO R 1.00 2.00
33 Plusle C 1.25 2.50
34 Minun C 1.50 3.00
35 Zekrom HOLO R .60 1.25
36 Ekans C .75 1.50
37 Arbok U .75 1.50
38 Jynx C .75 1.50
39 Mewtwo GX UR 1.25 2.50
40 Shining Mew HOLO R 5.00 10.00
41 Latios HOLO R .01 .08
42 Shining Jirachi HOLO R .04 .10
43 Golett C 3.00 6.00
44 Golurk U .75 1.50
45 Marshadow HOLO R 1.50 3.00
46 Stunfisk C .12 .25
47 Spiritomb U .60 1.25
48 Purrloin C .07 .15
49 Liepard U .75 1.50
50 Scraggy C 2.00 4.00
51 Scrafty U 12.50 25.00
52 Zorua C 1.25 2.50
53 Zoroark GX UR 1.00 2.00
54 Yveltal HOLO R .08 .20
55 Hoopa HOLO R .08 .20
56 Shining Rayquaza HOLO R .50 1.00
57 Shining Arceus HOLO R .60 1.25
58 Damage Mover U 1.25 2.50
59 Energy Retrieval U 1.25 2.50
60 Great Ball U 1.50 3.00
61 Hau U .75 1.50
62 Lillie U .75 1.50
63 Pokemon Breeder U 1.00 2.00
64 Pokemon Catcher U 1.00 2.00
65 Sophocles U 1.25 2.50
66 Super Scoop Up U .75 1.50
67 Switch U 2.00 4.00
68 Ultra Ball U 5.00 10.00
69 Double Colorless Energy U 1.00 2.00
70 Warp Energy U 5.00 10.00
71 Entei GX FULL ART UR 1.00 2.00
72 Mewtwo GX FULL ART UR 4.00 8.00
73 Pokemon Breeder FULL ART UR 25.00 50.00
74 Entei GX SCR .07 .15
75 Raichu GX SCR .15 .40
76 Mewtwo GX SCR 1.50 3.00
77 Zoroark GX SCR 1.25 2.50
78 Mewtwo GX SCR 1.50 3.00

2018 Pokemon Dragon Majesty

1 Charmander C .75 2.00
2 Charmeleon U 1.00 2.00
3 Charizard HOLO R .75 1.50
4 Torchic C 1.50 3.00
5 Combusken U .25 .50
6 Blaziken HOLO R .60 1.25
7 Victini Prism Star HOLO R .50 1.00
8 Darumaka C 2.50 5.00
9 Darmanitan U .07 .15
10 Heatmor U .08 .20
11 Reshiram GX UR 1.50 3.00
12 Litten C 1.25 2.50
13 Salandit C .25 .50
14 Salazzle U .01 .08
15 Horsea C .10 .25
16 Horsea C 7.50 15.00
17 Seadra U .50 1.00
18 Kingdra GX UR .75 1.50
19 Magikarp C .60 1.25
20 Gyarados HOLO R 2.00 4.00
21 Lapras U 2.00 4.00
22 Totodile C .75 1.50
23 Croconaw U 1.50 3.00
24 Feraligatr HOLO R 1.50 3.00
25 Wooper C 1.00 2.00
26 Quagsire U 7.50 15.00
27 Corsola C .75 1.50
28 Feebas C .75 1.50
29 Milotic U 1.25 3.00
30 Phione U 1.00 2.00
31 Wishiwashi C 2.00 4.00
32 Trapinch C 1.50 3.00
33 Hydreigon HOLO R 1.25 2.50
34 Dratini C .75 1.50
35 Dratini C .60 1.25
36 Dragonair U .50 1.00
37 Dragonite GX UR 2.50 5.00
38 Vibrava C 1.50 3.00
39 Flygon U 1.00 2.00
40 Altaria HOLO R .75 1.50
41 Altaria GX UR 2.50 6.00
42 Bagon C 1.25 3.00
43 Shelgon U 2.00 4.00
44 Salamence GX UR 25.00 60.00
45 Druddigon U 2.00 4.00
46 Zekrom HOLO R .75 1.50
47 Kyurem HOLO R .75 1.50
48 White Kyurem GX UR 3.00 6.00
49 Zygarde U .60 1.25
50 Turtonator U .30 .60
51 Drampa U 1.50 3.00
52 Jangmo-o C 1.25 2.50
53 Hakamo-o C 1.00 2.00
54 Kommo-o HOLO R 1.00 2.00
55 Kangaskhan C 5.00 10.00
56 Swablu C .75 1.50
57 Swablu C .30 .60
58 Blaine's Last Stand HOLO R .75 1.50
59 Dragon Talon U .75 1.50
60 Fiery Flint U 1.25 2.50
61 Lance Prism Star HOLO R 1.25 3.00
62 Switch Raft U .60 1.25
63 Wela Volcano Park U 1.00 2.00
64 Zinnia U .75 1.50
65 Reshiram GX FULL ART UR .75 1.50
66 Kingdra GX FULL ART UR 1.25 2.50
67 Dragonite GX FULL ART UR 1.25 2.50
69 Blaine's Last Stand FULL ART UR .07 .15
70 Zinnia FULL ART UR .30 .75
71 Reshiram GX SCR .75 1.50
72 Altaria GX SCR 1.50 3.00
73 Salamence GX SCR .75 1.50
74 White Kyurem GX SCR .60 1.25
75 Dragon Talon SCR 1.00 2.00
76 Fiery Flint SCR 2.50 5.00
77 Switch Raft SCR 1.00 2.00
78 Ultra Necrozma GX SCR 1.00 2.00

2018 Pokemon Sun and Moon Celestial Storm

1 Bellsprout C .75 1.50
2 Weepinbell U 3.00 6.00
3 Victreebel HOLO R 1.50 3.00
4 Scyther U .75 1.50
5 Spinarak C .75 1.50
6 Ariados HOLO R 2.00 4.00
7 Treecko C 1.25 2.50
8 Treecko C .07 .15
9 Grovyle U 7.50 15.00
10 Sceptile R 40.00 80.00
11 Seedot C .01 .08
12 Seedot C .04 .10
13 Nuzleaf U .75 1.50
14 Shiftry GX UR .75 1.50
15 Surskit C .30 .75
16 Masquerain U 1.25 2.50
17 Volbeat U 1.00 2.00
18 Illumise U .01 .08
19 Cacnea C .08 .20
20 Cacturne U .75 1.50
21 Tropius U .07 .15
22 Dhelmise R .12 .30
23 Slugma C 1.00 2.00
24 Magcargo R .75 1.50
25 Torchic C .75 1.50
26 Torchic C 2.50 5.00
27 Combusken U .07 .15
28 Blaziken GX UR 1.25 2.50
29 Torkoal U 2.00 4.00
30 Oricorio U 1.00 2.00
31 Articuno GX UR .75 1.50
32 Mudkip C 1.00 2.00
33 Mudkip C .60 1.25
34 Marshtomp U 4.00 8.00
35 Swampert R .04 .10
36 Lotad C .05 .12
37 Lombre U 3.00 8.00
38 Ludicolo HOLO R 1.50 3.00
39 Wailmer C .75 1.50
40 Wailord R .75 1.50
41 Clamperl C .75 1.50
42 Huntail U 1.50 3.00
43 Gorebyss U .75 2.00
44 Luvdisc C .75 1.50
45 Regice R .07 .15
46 Kyogre HOLO R 7.50 15.00
47 Voltorb C 2.00 4.00
48 Electrode GX UR 1.00 2.00
49 Chinchou C 1.25 2.50
50 Lanturn U 1.50 3.00
51 Electrike C .30 .75
52 Manectric R 5.00 10.00
53 Plusle U .75 1.50
54 Minun U 1.25 2.50
55 Oricorio U 1.50 3.00
56 Mr. Mime GX UR .25 .50
57 Gulpin C .01 .08
58 Swalot U .04 .10
59 Spoink C 1.00 2.00
60 Grumpig R .08 .20
61 Lunatone HOLO R .10 .20
62 Solrock U 2.50 5.00
63 Shuppet C .75 1.50
64 Shuppet C .60 1.25
65 Banette R .75 1.50
66 Banette GX UR 7.50 15.00
67 Deoxys HOLO R 1.25 2.50
68 Deoxys R .08 .20
69 Deoxys R .10 .25
70 Lunala HOLO R .60 1.25
71 Onix C .75 1.50
72 Phanpy C 2.50 5.00
73 Donphan U .12 .25
74 Larvitar C 1.00 2.00
75 Pupitar U .75 1.50
76 Meditite C 1.00 2.00
77 Medicham R 1.25 3.00
78 Baltoy C 1.00 2.00
79 Claydol R .75 1.50
80 Regirock R 5.00 10.00
81 Groudon HOLO R .60 1.25
82 Palossand GX UR 3.00 6.00
83 Minior U 1.50 3.00
84 Alolan Rattata C .60 1.25
85 Alolan Raticate GX UR 2.00 4.00
86 Sneasel C .75 1.50
87 Tyranitar HOLO R .30 .60
88 Sableye U .75 1.50
89 Steelix HOLO R .75 1.50
90 Scizor GX UR .01 .08
91 Mawile U .04 .10
92 Beldum C 1.25 2.50
93 Beldum C 1.00 2.00
94 Metang U .50 1.00
95 Metagross HOLO R .60 1.25
96 Registeel R .75 1.50
97 Jirachi Prism Star HOLO R .75 1.50
98 Heatran HOLO R 1.50 3.00
99 Solgaleo HOLO R 1.00 2.00
100 Celesteela HOLO R 1.25 2.50
101 Kartana R 2.00 5.00
102 Stakataka GX UR .75 1.50
103 Bagon C .75 1.50
104 Bagon C 1.50 3.00
105 Shelgon U .07 .15
106 Salamence HOLO R 1.25 2.50
107 Latias Prism Star HOLO R .75 1.50
108 Latios Prism Star HOLO R 1.00 2.00
109 Rayquaza GX UR .60 1.25
110 Dunsparce U 2.00 4.00
111 Wingull C .20 .40
112 Pelipper U 6.00 15.00
113 Slakoth C 2.00 5.00
114 Vigoroth U 2.00 4.00
115 Slaking HOLO R 30.00 80.00
116 Whismur C 1.00 2.00
117 Whismur C 1.25 2.50
118 Loudred U 1.00 2.00
119 Exploud R 1.00 2.00
120 Skitty C .75 1.50
121 Delcatty HOLO R 2.00 4.00
122 Kecleon U .08 .20
123 Acro Bike U .10 .25
124 Apricorn Maker U 3.00 6.00
125 Beast Ball U .60 1.25
126 Bill's Maintenance U 2.50 5.00
127 Copycat U 4.00 8.00
128 Energy Recycle System U 1.50 3.00
129 Energy Switch U .60 1.25
130 Fisherman U 4.00 8.00
131 Friend Ball U .12 .25
132 Hau U .60 1.25
133 Hiker U .75 1.50
134 Hustle Belt U .60 1.25
135 Last Chance Potion U .60 1.25
136 Life Herb U .30 .60
137 Lisia U .75 1.50
138 Lure Ball U 1.00 2.00
139 The Masked Royal U 1.00 2.00
140 PokéNav U .07 .15
141 Rainbow Brush U .75 2.00
142 Rare Candy U 1.25 2.50
144 Sky Pillar U .10 .20
145 Steven's Resolve HOLO R 3.00 6.00
146 Super Scoop Up U 1.25 2.50
147 Switch U 1.00 2.00
148 Tate & Liza U 2.00 4.00

149 TV Reporter U	.60	1.25
150 Underground Expedition U	.75	1.50
151 Rainbow Energy U	.75	1.50
152 Shiftry GX FULL ART UR	.07	.15
153 Blaziken GX FULL ART UR	.15	.40
154 Articuno GX FULL ART UR	20.00	40.00
155 Electrode GX FULL ART UR	1.00	2.00
156 Mr. Mime GX FULL ART UR	1.00	2.00
157 Banette GX FULL ART UR	.75	1.50
158 Scizor GX FULL ART UR	.60	1.25
159 Stakataka GX FULL ART UR	1.50	3.00
160 Rayquaza GX FULL ART UR	1.00	2.00
161 Apricorn Maker FULL ART UR	1.00	2.50
162 Bill's Maintenance FULL ART UR	2.00	4.00
163 Copycat FULL ART UR	.75	1.50
164 Lisia FULL ART UR	1.00	2.00
165 Steven's Resolve FULL ART UR	.25	.50
166 Tate & Liza FULL ART UR	.75	1.50
167 TV Reporter FULL ART UR	1.00	2.00
168 Underground Expedition FULL ART UR	.60	1.25
169 Shiftry GX SCR	1.00	2.00
170 Blaziken GX SCR	.01	.08
171 Articuno GX SCR	.01	.08
172 Electrode GX SCR	.01	.08
173 Mr. Mime GX SCR	.04	.10
174 Banette GX SCR	1.25	2.50
175 Scizor GX SCR	1.50	3.00
176 Stakataka GX SCR	.25	.50
177 Rayquaza GX SCR	.01	.08
178 Acro Bike SCR	.10	.25
179 Hustle Belt SCR	2.50	5.00
180 Life Herb SCR	.75	2.00
181 PokéNav SCR	.75	1.50
182 Rainbow Brush SCR	1.25	2.50
183 Rainbow Energy SCR	.75	1.50

2018 Pokemon Sun and Moon Forbidden Light

1 Exeggcute C	1.00	2.00
2 Alolan Exeggutor R	3.00	6.00
3 Snover C	1.25	2.50
4 Abomasnow R	.60	1.25
5 Scatterbug C	.30	.75
6 Scatterbug C	4.00	8.00
7 Spewpa U	.75	1.50
8 Vivillon R	.75	1.50
9 Skiddo C	1.25	2.50
10 Gogoat U	.75	1.50
11 Pheromosa HOLO R	1.00	2.00
12 Alolan Marowak R	.60	1.25
13 Heatran R	.75	1.50
14 Fennekin C	2.00	4.00
15 Fennekin C	1.25	2.50
16 Braixen U	1.00	2.00
17 Delphox HOLO R	.01	.08
18 Litleo C	.04	.10
19 Pyroar HOLO R	.01	.08
20 Palkia GX UR	.01	.08
21 Froakie C	.75	1.50
22 Froakie C	.75	1.50
23 Frogadier U	.60	1.50
24 Greninja GX UR	.75	1.50
25 Clauncher C	3.00	6.00
26 Clawitzer R	1.00	2.50
27 Amaura U	125.00	250.00
28 Aurorus HOLO R	1.00	2.00
29 Bergmite C	.07	.15
30 Avalugg R	.60	1.25
31 Volcanion Prism Star HOLO R	.50	1.00
32 Dewpider C	.60	1.25
33 Araquanid U	.75	1.50
34 Magnemite C	1.00	2.00
35 Magneton U	10.00	20.00
36 Magnezone HOLO R	1.00	2.00
37 Helioptile C	2.50	5.00
38 Heliolisk U	2.50	5.00
39 Xurkitree R	2.00	4.00
40 Rotom R	.08	.20
41 Uxie U	.10	.25
42 Mesprit U	3.00	6.00
43 Azelf U	1.25	2.50
44 Espurr C	2.00	4.00
45 Meowstic R	.30	.60
46 Honedge C	.75	1.50
47 Honedge C	.20	.40
48 Doublade U	1.50	3.00
49 Aegislash R	12.50	25.00
50 Inkay C	1.00	2.00
51 Malamar R	.75	1.50
52 Skrelp C	1.50	3.00
53 Dragalge R	1.25	2.50
54 Hoopa U	1.50	3.00
55 Poipole U	.25	.50
56 Naganadel GX UR	.04	.10
57 Cubone C	.08	.20
58 Torterra R	1.00	2.50
59 Infernape HOLO R	1.25	2.50
60 Gible C	.75	1.50
61 Gabite U	.75	1.50
62 Garchomp HOLO R	.30	.75
63 Croagunk C	.75	1.50
64 Toxicroak R	1.25	2.50
65 Pancham C	1.50	3.00
66 Binacle C	.75	1.50
67 Barbaracle R	1.00	2.00
68 Tyrunt U	.25	.50
69 Tyrantrum HOLO R	5.00	12.00
70 Hawlucha U	4.00	10.00
71 Zygarde U	2.00	4.00
72 Zygarde R	20.00	50.00
73 Zygarde GX UR	1.25	2.50
74 Diancie Prism Star HOLO R	.75	1.50
75 Rockruff C	1.25	2.50
76 Lycanroc R	2.50	5.00
77 Buzzwole R	.75	1.50
78 Pangoro R	1.00	2.00
79 Yveltal GX UR	2.50	5.00
80 Guzzlord HOLO R	.12	.25
81 Empoleon HOLO R	.15	.40
82 Dialga GX UR	3.00	6.00
83 Flabebe C	.75	1.50
84 Flabebe C	2.50	5.00
85 Floette U	1.50	3.00
86 Florges R	.01	.08
87 Sylveon R	.08	.20
88 Dedenne U	.75	1.50
89 Klefki U	1.00	2.00
90 Xerneas GX UR	1.25	2.50
91 Goomy C	.75	1.50
92 Goomy C	.07	.15
93 Sliggoo U	.07	.15
94 Goodra HOLO R	2.50	5.00
95 Ultra Necrozma GX UR	1.50	3.00
96 Arceus Prism Star HOLO R	2.50	5.00
97 Bunnelby C	1.00	2.00
98 Diggersby U	1.00	2.00
99 Furfrou C	5.00	10.00
100 Noibat C	.75	1.50
101 Noivern R	1.50	3.00
102 Beast Ring R	1.25	2.50
103 Bonnie U	.75	1.50
104 Crasher Wake U	.75	1.50
105 Diantha HOLO R	1.50	3.00
106 Eneporter U	.60	1.25
107 Fossil Excavation Map U	.60	1.50
108 Judge U	1.00	2.00
109 Lady U	.75	1.50
110 Lysandre Prism Star HOLO R	.25	.50
111 Lysandre Labs U	.75	1.50
112 Metal Frying Pan U	1.50	3.00
113 Mysterious Treasure U	1.25	2.50
114 Ultra Recon Squad U	1.50	3.00
115 Ultra Space U	.30	.75
116 Unidentified Fossil U	1.50	3.00
117 Beast Energy Prism Star HOLO R	.75	1.50
118 Unit Energy FDF U	.60	1.25
119 Palkia GX UR Full Art	1.50	3.00
120 Greninja GX UR Full Art	.08	.20
121 Naganadel GX UR Full Art	1.00	2.00
122 Lucario GX UR Full Art	.75	1.50
123 Zygarde GX UR Full Art	1.00	2.00
124 Yveltal GX UR Full Art	1.00	2.00
125 Dialga GX UR Full Art	3.00	6.00
126 Xerneas GX UR Full Art	1.25	2.50
127 Ultra Necrozma GX UR Full Art	.75	1.50
128 Bonnie UR Full Art	1.25	2.50
129 Crasher Wake UR Full Art	1.50	3.00
130 Diantha UR Full Art	1.25	2.50
131 Ultra Recon Squad UR Full Art	15.00	30.00
132 Palkia GX SCR	.75	1.50
133 Greninja GX SCR	2.00	4.00
134 Naganadel GX SCR	.75	1.50
135 Lucario GX SCR	5.00	10.00
136 Zygarde GX SCR	.75	1.50
137 Yveltal GX SCR	.75	1.50
138 Dialga GX SCR	.60	1.25
139 Xerneas GX SCR	.75	1.50
140 Ultra Necrozma GX SCR	1.50	3.00
141 Beast Ring SCR	.60	1.25
142 Eneporter SCR	1.00	2.00
143 Energy Recycler SCR	.75	1.50
144 Metal Frying Pan SCR	1.00	2.00
145 Mysterious Treasure SCR	1.00	2.00
146 Unit Energy FDF SCR	.30	.75

2018 Pokemon Sun and Moon Lost Thunder

1 Tangela C	1.00	2.00
2 Tangrowth R	.60	1.25
3 Scyther C	2.00	4.00
4 Pinsir U	.01	.08
5 Chikorita C	.04	.10
6 Chikorita C	.75	1.50
7 Bayleef U	.40	1.00
8 Meganium HOLO R	7.50	15.00
9 Spinarak C	3.00	6.00
10 Ariados U	6.00	12.00
11 Hoppip C	.25	.50
12 Hoppip C	7.50	15.00
13 Skiploom U	.30	.75
14 Jumpluff HOLO R	.75	1.50
15 Pineco C	.60	1.50
16 Shuckle U	.30	.60
17 Shuckle GX UR	1.00	2.00
18 Heracross U	.75	2.00
19 Celebi PRISM HOLO R	.75	1.50
20 Treecko C	.60	1.25
21 Grovyle U	.75	1.50
22 Sceptile GX UR	.75	1.50
23 Wurmple C	1.00	2.00
24 Wurmple C	.25	.50
25 Silcoon U	.01	.08
26 Beautifly R	.10	.25
27 Cascoon U	2.00	4.00
28 Dustox R	1.00	2.00
29 Nincada C	.07	.15
30 Ninjask U	2.00	4.00
31 Combee C	1.50	3.00
32 Vespiquen U	.75	1.50
33 Shaymin HOLO R	1.00	2.00
34 Virizion GX UR	.60	1.25
35 Skiddo C	1.00	2.00
36 Gogoat U	.75	1.50
37 Tapu Bulu HOLO R	.75	1.50
38 Moltres R	.07	.15
39 Cyndaquil C	.15	.40
40 Cyndaquil C	.75	1.50
41 Quilava U	2.50	6.00
42 Typhlosion HOLO R	1.25	3.00
43 Slugma C	2.00	4.00
44 Magcargo GX UR	50.00	120.00
45 Houndour C	.75	1.50
46 Houndoom R	1.00	2.00
47 Entei R	1.50	3.00
48 Heatran HOLO R	7.50	15.00
49 Victini R	.75	1.50
50 Litleo C	4.00	8.00
51 Pyroar R	1.50	3.00
52 Blacephalon GX UR	2.50	5.00
53 Alolan Vulpix C	1.25	2.50
54 Slowpoke C	2.50	5.00
55 Slowking R	.75	1.50
56 Lapras R	.50	1.00
57 Delibird U	.75	1.50
58 Mantine U	1.00	2.00
59 Suicune HOLO R	.75	1.50
60 Suicune GX UR	.07	.15
61 Cubchoo C	.10	.20
62 Beartic R	.60	1.25
63 White Kyurem HOLO R	3.00	6.00
64 Popplio C	1.00	2.00
65 Popplio C	1.00	2.00
66 Brionne U	3.00	6.00
67 Primarina R	.75	1.50
68 Mareanie C	15.00	30.00
69 Toxapex R	4.00	8.00
70 Bruxish C	.75	1.50
71 Electabuzz U	1.50	3.00
72 Electivire R	1.25	2.50
73 Chinchou C	2.00	4.00
74 Lanturn R	2.50	5.00
75 Mareep C	1.25	2.50
76 Mareep C	1.50	3.00
77 Flaaffy U	.75	1.50
78 Ampharos HOLO R	1.50	3.00
79 Raikou R	.75	1.50
80 Pachirisu C	.10	.20
81 Blitzle C	1.00	2.00
82 Zebstrika R	.60	1.25
83 Stunfisk C	5.00	10.00
84 Dedenne C	.60	1.50
85 Tapu Koko HOLO R	1.00	2.00
86 Zeraora GX UR	.25	.60
87 Natu C	.75	1.50
88 Xatu U	1.50	3.00
89 Espeon R	1.50	3.00
90 Unown R	.75	1.50
91 Unown R	1.25	2.50
92 Unown R	2.50	5.00
93 Wobbuffet R	.08	.20
94 Girafarig U	1.25	2.50
95 Shedinja R	.60	1.25
96 Sableye U	.60	1.25
97 Giratina HOLO R	1.25	2.50
98 Sigilyph GX UR	1.25	2.50
99 Yamask C	.75	1.50
100 Cofagrigus R	.75	1.50
101 Litwick C	.75	1.50
102 Lampent U	2.00	4.00
103 Chandelure HOLO R	1.25	2.50
104 Meloetta R	.01	.08
105 Mareanie C	.01	.08
106 Nihilego HOLO R	.08	.20
107 Poipole C	.05	.12
108 Naganadel HOLO R	.15	.30
109 Onix C	.20	.50
110 Sudowoodo U	2.00	4.00
111 Phanpy C	.60	1.25
112 Donphan R	.04	.10
113 Hitmontop U	.12	.30
114 Larvitar C	.75	1.50
115 Larvitar C	.25	.50
116 Pupitar U	.75	1.50
117 Carbink C	.60	1.25
118 Alolan Meowth C	.60	1.25
119 Alolan Persian R	1.00	2.00
120 Umbreon R	.50	1.00
121 Tyranitar GX UR	1.00	2.00
122 Alolan Diglett C	.30	.75
123 Alolan Dugtrio U	.75	1.50
124 Forretress R	.25	.50
125 Steelix R	2.00	4.00
126 Scizor HOLO R	1.25	2.50
127 Dialga HOLO R	.75	1.50
128 Durant C	1.25	2.50
129 Cobalion HOLO R	1.25	2.50
130 Genesect GX UR	.75	1.50
131 Magearna U	12.50	25.00
132 Alolan Ninetales GX UR	7.50	15.00
133 Jigglypuff C	1.50	3.00
134 Wigglytuff R	.60	1.50
135 Marill C	1.25	2.50
136 Azumarill R	7.50	15.00
137 Snubbull C	.75	1.50
138 Granbull R	1.00	2.00
139 Ralts C	.60	1.25
140 Kirlia U	.75	1.50
141 Gardevoir HOLO R	7.50	15.00
142 Dedenne U	.30	.60
143 Carbink U	1.00	2.50
144 Xerneas PRISM HOLO R	1.25	2.50
145 Cutiefly C	.25	.50
146 Ribombee R	.40	1.00
147 Morelull C	.30	.60
148 Shiinotic U	.75	1.50
149 Mimikyu GX UR	.75	1.50
150 Tapu Lele HOLO R	.75	1.50
151 Tapu Fini HOLO R	.75	1.50
152 Chansey C	.60	1.25
153 Blissey HOLO R	.15	.30
154 Ditto PRISM HOLO R	1.00	2.50
155 Eevee C	1.00	2.00
156 Stantler U	.75	1.50
157 Smeargle R	.01	.08
158 Miltank R	.01	.08
159 Lugia GX UR	.30	.75
160 Ho-Oh R	1.25	2.50
161 Kecleon U	.75	1.50
162 Kecleon U	.75	1.50
163 Pikipek C	.75	1.50
164 Pikipek C	.60	1.25
165 Trumbeak U	1.25	2.50
166 Toucannon R	1.00	2.00
167 Adventure Bag U	7.50	15.00
168 Aether Foundation Employee U	3.00	6.00
169 Choice Helmet U	.75	1.50
170 Counter Gain U	.60	1.25
171 Custom Catcher U	1.50	3.00
172 Electropower U	.75	1.50
173 Faba U	1.50	3.00
174 Fairy Charm G U	10.00	20.00
175 Fairy Charm P U	2.50	5.00
176 Fairy Charm F U	30.00	60.00
177 Fairy Charm D U	1.50	3.00
178 Heat Factory PRISM HOLO R	.60	1.25
179 Kahili U	1.25	2.50
180 Life Forest PRISM HOLO R	.75	1.50
181 Lost Blender U	.50	1.00
182 Lusamine PRISM HOLO R	1.50	3.00
183 Mina U	.60	1.25
184 Mixed Herbs U	.12	.25
185 Moomoo Milk U	.12	.25
186 Morty U	1.50	3.00
187 Net Ball U	2.50	5.00
188 Professor Elm's Lecture U	.60	1.25
189 Sightseer U	1.50	3.00
190 Spell Tag U	8.00	20.00
191 Thunder Mountain PRISM HOLO R	3.00	8.00
192 Wait and See U	2.00	4.00
193 Whitney U	25.00	60.00
194 Memoray Energy U	2.50	5.00
195 Shuckle GX FULL ART UR	1.00	2.00
196 Sceptile GX FULL ART UR	.15	.30
197 Virizion GX FULL ART UR	.75	1.50
198 Magcargo GX FULL ART UR	.75	1.50
199 Blacephalon GX FULL ART UR	.75	1.50
200 Suicune GX UR	1.00	2.00
201 Zeraora GX FULL ART UR	1.00	2.00
202 Sigilyph GX FULL ART UR	.04	.10
203 Tyranitar GX FULL ART UR	.04	.10
204 Genesect GX FULL ART UR	.60	1.25
205 Alolan Ninetales GX FULL ART UR	1.25	2.50
206 Mimikyu GX FULL ART UR	1.25	2.50
207 Lugia GX FULL ART UR	2.00	4.00
208 Faba FULL ART UR	1.00	2.00
209 Judge FULL ART UR	1.25	2.50
210 Kahili FULL ART UR	1.00	2.00
211 Mina FULL ART UR	.75	1.50
212 Morty FULL ART UR	1.50	3.00
213 Professor Elm's Lecture FULL ART UR	.07	.15
214 Whitney FULL ART UR	.75	1.50
215 Shuckle GX SCR	.60	1.50
216 Sceptile GX SCR	.60	1.25
217 Virizion GX SCR	.60	1.25
218 Magcargo GX SCR	1.00	2.00
219 Blacephalon GX SCR	1.25	2.50
220 Suicune GX SCR	1.50	3.00
221 Zeraora GX SCR	.08	.20
222 Sigilyph GX SCR	.75	1.50
223 Tyranitar GX SCR	.75	1.50
224 Genesect GX SCR	1.25	2.50
225 Alolan Ninetales GX SCR	1.25	2.50
226 Mimikyu GX SCR	.75	1.50
227 Lugia GX SCR	1.50	3.00
228 Adventure Bag SCR	.60	1.25
229 Choice Helmet SCR	1.00	2.00
230 Counter Gain SCR	1.00	2.00
231 Custom Catcher SCR	.04	.10
232 Electropower SCR	.10	.25
233 Lost Blender SCR	.75	1.50
234 Net Ball SCR	.08	.20
235 Spell Tag SCR	2.50	5.00
236 Wait and See Hammer SCR	1.00	2.00

2018 Pokemon Sun and Moon Ultra Prism

1 Exeggcute C	2.50	5.00
2 Yanma C	.75	1.50
3 Yanmega U	.75	1.50
4 Roselia C	1.50	3.00
5 Roserade R	1.50	3.00
6 Turtwig C	3.00	6.00
7 Turtwig C	1.25	2.50
8 Grotle U	2.50	5.00
9 Torterra HOLO R	.60	1.25
10 Cherubi C	.50	1.00
11 Cherrim U	.60	1.25
12 Carnivine C	1.50	3.00
13 Leafeon GX UR	.60	1.25
14 Mow Rotom R	.50	1.00
15 Shaymin HOLO R	.10	.20
16 Dewpider C	1.00	2.00
17 Araquanid R	.60	1.50
18 Magmar C	2.00	4.00
19 Magmortar HOLO R	1.50	3.00
20 Chimchar C	1.00	2.00
21 Chimchar C	2.00	4.00
22 Monferno U	.30	.60
23 Infernape HOLO R	.75	1.50
24 Heat Rotom R	1.25	2.50
25 Salandit C	1.25	2.50
26 Salazzle R	.10	.20
27 Turtonator U	.75	1.50
28 Alolan Sandshrew C	1.25	2.50
29 Alolan Sandslash R	.75	1.50
30 Alolan Vulpix C	1.25	2.50
31 Piplup C	.07	.15
32 Piplup C	1.25	2.50
33 Prinplup U	.60	1.50
34 Empoleon R	3.00	6.00
35 Buizel C	.75	1.50
36 Floatzel U	.75	1.50
37 Snover C	.60	1.50
38 Abomasnow R	1.25	2.50

39 Glaceon GX UR	2.50	5.00
40 Wash Rotom R	2.50	5.00
41 Frost Rotom R	1.00	2.00
42 Manaphy U	.60	1.25
43 Electabuzz C	3.00	6.00
44 Electivire R	.50	1.00
45 Shinx C	3.00	6.00
46 Shinx C	.50	1.00
47 Luxio U	2.00	4.00
48 Luxray HOLO R	1.00	2.00
49 Pachirisu C	.75	1.50
50 Rotom U	.75	1.50
51 Drifloon C	1.00	2.00
52 Drifblim U	.75	1.50
53 Spiritomb U	2.50	5.00
54 Skorupi C	.60	1.25
55 Drapion R	1.00	2.50
56 Croagunk C	1.25	2.50
57 Toxicroak R	.75	1.50
58 Giratina Prism HOLO R	.75	1.50
59 Cresselia HOLO R	1.25	2.50
60 Cosmog C	2.00	4.00
61 Cosmoem U	.60	1.25
62 Lunala Prism HOLO R	2.50	5.00
63 Dawn Wings Necrozma GX UR	4.00	10.00
64 Cranidos U	2.50	6.00
65 Rampardos HOLO R	2.00	4.00
66 Riolu C	30.00	80.00
67 Lucario HOLO R	.25	.50
68 Hippopotas C	.01	.08
69 Hippowdon R	.10	.25
70 Passimian C	.08	.20
71 Murkrow C	.05	.12
72 Honchkrow U	.07	.15
73 Sneasel C	.20	.50
74 Weavile HOLO R	1.00	2.00
75 Stunky C	.60	1.25
76 Skuntank U	2.50	5.00
77 Darkrai Prism HOLO R	.75	1.50
78 Alolan Diglett C	1.00	2.00
79 Alolan Dugtrio U	1.00	2.00
80 Magnemite C	1.50	3.00
81 Magnemite C	1.00	2.00
82 Magneton U	.04	.10
83 Magnezone HOLO R	.05	.12
84 Shieldon U	.75	1.50
85 Bastiodon HOLO R	1.00	2.00
86 Bronzor C	3.00	6.00
87 Bronzong U	1.25	2.50
88 Heatran HOLO R	4.00	8.00
89 Solgaleo Prism HOLO R	4.00	8.00
90 Dusk Mane Necrozma GX UR	2.00	4.00
91 Magearna R	1.25	2.50
92 Morelull C	1.25	2.50
93 Shiinotic R	1.50	3.00
94 Tapu Lele R	.75	2.00
95 Alolan Exeggutor R	1.25	2.50
96 Gible C	10.00	20.00
97 Gible C	.07	.15
98 Gabite U	.75	1.50
99 Garchomp R	1.25	2.50
100 Dialga GX UR	2.50	5.00
101 Palkia GX UR	1.25	2.50
102 Lickitung C	1.50	3.00
103 Lickilicky R	.75	1.50
104 Eevee C	1.50	3.00
105 Eevee C	1.25	2.50
106 Buneary C	.07	.15
107 Lopunny U	1.25	2.50
108 Glameow C	.75	1.50
109 Purugly U	.60	1.25
110 Fan Rotom R	.75	1.50
111 Shaymin R	.75	1.50
112 Yungoos C	.60	1.25
113 Gumshoos U	.60	1.25
114 Oranguru U	10.00	20.00
115 Type: Null R	1.25	2.50
116 Silvally GX UR	1.00	2.00
117 Drampa HOLO R	.75	1.50
118 Ancient Crystal U	1.50	3.00
119 Cynthia U	.30	.75
120 Cyrus Prism HOLO R	.75	1.50
121 Electric Memory U	.08	.20
122 Escape Board U	.60	1.25
123 Fire Memory U	2.00	4.00
124 Gardenia U	.75	1.50
125 Lillie U	.04	.10
126 Looker U	.01	.08
127 Looker Whistle U	1.25	2.50
128 Mars U	.01	.08
129 Missing Clover U	.10	.25
130 Mt. Coronet U	.75	1.50
131 Order Pad U	.75	1.50
132 Pal Pad U	.75	1.50
133 Pokemon Fan Club U	.75	1.50
134 Unidentified Fossil U	1.25	2.50
135 Volkner U	.75	1.50
136 Super Boost Energy Prism HOLO R	1.50	3.00
137 Unit Energy GFW U	.60	1.50
138 Unit Energy LPM U	.12	.30
139 Leafeon GX UR	.25	.60
140 Pheromosa GX UR	1.00	2.00
141 Glaceon GX UR	.75	1.50
142 Xurkitree GX UR	.75	1.50
143 Dawn Wings Necrozma GX UR	.30	.75
144 Celesteela GX UR	.75	1.50
145 Dusk Mane Necrozma GX UR	2.00	4.00
146 Dialga GX UR	1.25	2.50
147 Palkia GX UR	1.50	3.00
148 Cynthia UR	.25	.60
149 Gardenia UR	.08	.20
150 Lana UR	.08	.20
151 Lillie UR	.30	.60
152 Looker UR	2.00	4.00
153 Lusamine UR	1.25	2.50
154 Mars UR	2.50	5.00
155 Pokemon Fan Club UR	1.50	3.00
156 Volkner UR	1.00	2.00
157 Leafeon GX SCR	1.50	3.00
158 Pheromosa GX SCR	1.00	2.50
159 Glaceon GX SCR	.75	1.50
160 Xurkitree GX SCR	2.50	5.00
161 Dawn Wings Necrozma GX SCR	.75	1.50
162 Celesteela GX SCR	.12	.25
163 Dusk Mane Necrozma GX SCR	.15	.40
164 Dialga GX SCR	1.25	2.50
165 Palkia GX SCR	2.50	5.00
166 Crushing Hammer SCR	1.25	2.50
167 Escape Board SCR	2.00	4.00
168 Missing Clover SCR	10.00	20.00
169 Peeking Red Card SCR	1.00	2.00
170 Unit Energy GFW SCR	.60	1.25
171 Unit Energy LPM SCR	.12	.25
172 Lunala GX SCR	.75	1.50
173 Solgaleo GX SCR	.50	1.00

2019 Pokemon Detective Pikachu

1 Bulbasaur C	1.50	3.00
2 Ludicolo R	2.50	5.00
3 Morelull C	10.00	20.00
4 Charmander C	40.00	80.00
5 Charizard HOLO R	.75	1.50
6 Arcanine R	.75	1.50
7 Psyduck C	.75	1.50
8 Magikarp C	1.00	2.00
9 Greninja HOLO R	.60	1.25
10 Detective Pikachu R	.75	1.50
11 Mr. Mime R	.30	.75
12 Mewtwo HOLO R	1.25	2.50
13 Machamp R	1.00	2.00
14 Jigglypuff C	.50	1.00
15 Snubbull C	1.00	2.00
16 Lickitung C	1.00	2.00
17 Ditto HOLO R	.60	1.25
18 Slaking R	4.00	8.00

2019 Pokemon Sun and Moon Cosmic Eclipse

1 Venusaur & Snivy GX URR	1.50	3.00
2 Oddish C	2.00	4.00
3 Gloom U	1.00	2.00
4 Vileplume GX URR	3.00	6.00
5 Tangela C	6.00	12.00
6 Tangrowth U	.25	.50
7 Sunkern C	.04	.10
8 Sunflora R	.08	.20
9 Heracross U	.75	1.50
10 Lileep U	.12	.25
11 Cradily R	.30	.75
12 Tropius U	.75	1.50
13 Kricketot C	1.25	2.50
14 Kricketune U	.75	1.50
15 Deerling C	.60	1.25
16 Sawsbuck HOLO R	4.00	10.00
17 Rowlet C	3.00	8.00
18 Rowlet C	2.00	4.00
19 Dartrix U	30.00	80.00
20 Decidueye HOLO R	.60	1.25
21 Buzzwole HOLO R	1.00	2.00
22 Charizard & Braixen GX URR	1.00	2.00
23 Ponyta C	.75	1.50
24 Rapidash U	.75	1.50
25 Flareon U	.50	1.25
26 Slugma C	1.50	3.00
27 Magcargo R	1.25	2.50
28 Entei R	.07	.15
29 Torkoal U	1.25	2.50
30 Victini HOLO R	.50	1.00
31 Tepig C	.60	1.25
32 Pignite U	2.00	4.00
33 Emboar R	1.25	2.50
34 Larvesta U	1.00	2.00
35 Volcarona GX URR	.75	1.50
36 Litleo C	.75	1.50
37 Pyroar U	25.00	50.00
38 Blastoise & Piplup GX URR	1.25	2.50
39 Alolan Vulpix C	.07	.15
40 Psyduck C	1.00	2.00
41 Golduck U	1.00	2.00
42 Vaporeon U	1.00	2.00
43 Sneasel C	1.25	2.50
44 Weavile R	1.00	2.00
45 Wailmer C	1.25	2.50
46 Wailord R	.75	1.50
47 Snorunt C	.30	.75
48 Glalie R	.75	1.50
49 Spheal C	.60	1.25
50 Spheal C	1.25	2.50
51 Sealeo U	.75	1.50
52 Walrein R	100.00	200.00
53 Kyogre R	1.00	2.00
54 Piplup C	.04	.10
55 Prinplup U	.08	.20
56 Empoleon R	1.50	3.00
57 Phione R	.12	.25
58 Tympole C	.75	1.50
59 Ducklett C	1.50	3.00
60 Swanna R	2.00	4.00
61 Black Kyurem HOLO R	2.00	4.00
62 Wishiwashi HOLO R	1.00	2.00
63 Wishiwashi GX URR	.75	1.50
64 Dewpider C	.04	.10
65 Araquanid U	.08	.20
66 Pikachu C	.07	.15
67 Raichu R	.60	1.50
68 Magnemite C	.75	1.50
69 Magneton HOLO R	.75	1.50
70 Jolteon U	.75	1.50
71 Chinchou C	.08	.20
72 Lanturn R	.04	.10
73 Togedemaru U	1.25	2.50
74 Togedemaru C	1.00	2.00
75 Solgaleo & Lunala GX URR	.60	1.25
76 Koffing C	.75	1.50
77 Weezing R	2.00	4.00
78 Natu C	2.00	4.00
79 Xatu R	.30	.60
80 Ralts C	.60	1.25
81 Kirlia U	2.50	5.00
82 Gallade HOLO R	.75	1.50
83 Duskull C	3.00	6.00
84 Dusclops U	2.50	5.00
85 Dusknoir HOLO R	2.00	4.00
86 Rotom U	.01	.08
87 Woobat C	.05	.12
88 Swoobat R	2.50	5.00
89 Golett C	.10	.20
90 Golurk R	.60	1.50
91 Skrelp C	.10	.20
92 Dragalge R	.12	.30
93 Phantump C	.25	.50
94 Trevenant R	1.25	2.50
95 Oricorio GX URR	.60	1.25
96 Mimikyu U	.75	1.50
97 Mimikyu R	.75	1.50
98 Dhelmise U	.50	1.00
99 Cosmog C	1.00	2.00
100 Cosmog C	5.00	10.00
101 Cosmoem U	2.50	5.00
102 Lunala HOLO R	.30	.60
103 Marshadow R	1.00	2.00
104 Blacephalon HOLO R	.75	1.50
105 Onix C	2.00	4.00
106 Nosepass C	.75	1.50
107 Trapinch C	2.50	5.00
108 Trapinch C	30.00	75.00
109 Vibrava U	.75	2.00
110 Flygon GX URR	.50	1.00
111 Anorith U	1.25	2.50
112 Armaldo R	.75	1.50
113 Groudon R	7.50	15.00
114 Drilbur C	5.00	10.00
115 Excadrill HOLO R	1.50	3.00
116 Palpitoad C	1.25	2.50
117 Seismitoad R	.60	1.25
118 Throh U	.30	.75
119 Pancham C	3.00	6.00
120 Pangoro U	1.50	3.00
121 Crabrawler C	1.25	2.50
122 Crabominable R	2.00	4.00
123 Rockruff C	4.00	8.00
124 Lycanroc HOLO R	2.00	4.00
125 Passimian C	.60	1.25
126 Sandygast C	1.25	2.50
127 Palossand R	.60	1.25
128 Alolan Meowth C	2.00	4.00
129 Alolan Persian GX URR	.75	1.50
130 Alolan Grimer C	1.25	2.50
131 Alolan Muk R	.60	1.25
132 Carvanha C	.75	1.50
133 Absol U	1.25	2.50
134 Pawniard C	.25	.60
135 Bisharp U	.25	.50
136 Guzzlord HOLO R	.04	.10
137 Alolan Sandshrew C	.10	.25
138 Alolan Sandslash R	.75	1.50
139 Steelix HOLO R	2.00	5.00
140 Mawile U	2.00	5.00
141 Probopass U	2.00	4.00
142 Solgaleo HOLO R	100.00	250.00
143 Togepi & Cleffa & Igglybuff GX URR	1.50	3.00
144 Clefairy U	.75	1.50
145 Alolan Ninetales HOLO R	.50	1.25
146 Azurill C	3.00	6.00
147 Cottonee C	1.00	2.00
148 Whimsicott R	3.00	6.00
149 Flabébé C	.75	1.50
150 Flabébé C	3.00	6.00
151 Floette U	1.00	2.00
152 Florges HOLO R	1.00	2.00
153 Swirlix C	2.50	5.00
154 Slurpuff R	.75	1.50
155 Sylveon R	1.50	3.00
156 Arceus & Dialga & Palkia GX URR	1.25	2.50
157 Reshiram & Zekrom GX URR	.60	1.25
158 Naganadel & Guzzlord GX URR	2.00	4.00
159 Drampa R	1.25	2.50
160 Jangmo-o C	.75	1.50
161 Jangmo-o C	2.50	5.00
162 Hakamo-o U	1.00	2.00
163 Kommo-o HOLO R	1.00	2.00
164 Ultra Necrozma HOLO R	.04	.10
165 Mega Lopunny & Jigglypuff GX URR	.10	.25
166 Eevee C	1.50	3.00
167 Eevee C	.75	1.50
168 Igglybuff U	.10	.20
169 Aipom C	.75	1.50
170 Ambipom U	1.00	2.00
171 Teddiursa C	.75	1.50
172 Ursaring R	1.25	2.50
173 Zangoose U	2.00	4.00
174 Lillipup C	.08	.20
175 Herdier U	1.25	2.50
176 Stoutland HOLO R	.30	.75
177 Rufflet C	1.25	2.50
178 Braviary R	1.00	2.50
179 Helioptile C	.50	1.25
180 Heliolisk R	2.00	4.00
181 Stufful C	8.00	20.00
182 Bewear R	.60	1.25
183 Type: Null U	.60	1.25
184 Silvally GX URR	.75	1.50
185 Beastite U	.75	1.50
186 Bellelba & Brycen-Man U	1.25	2.50
187 Chaotic Swell U	.75	1.50
188 Clay U	1.50	3.00
189 Cynthia & Caitlin U	.75	1.50
190 Dragonium Z: Dragon Claw U	.75	1.50
191 Erika U	.08	.20
192 Great Catcher U	.04	.10
193 Guzma & Hala U	1.25	2.50
194 Island Challenge Amulet U	.30	.75
195 Lana's Fishing Rod U	2.50	5.00
196 Lillie's Full Force U	1.50	3.00
197 Lillie's Poké Doll U	2.50	5.00
198 Mallow & Lana U	2.50	5.00
199 Misty & Lorelei U	.30	.60
200 N's Resolve U	.10	.25
201 Professor Oak's Setup U	.20	.50
202 Red & Blue U	.04	.10
203 Roller Skater U	.12	.30
204 Rosa HOLO R	.75	1.50
205 Roxie U	.75	2.00
206 Tag Call U	.75	1.50
207 Unidentified Fossil U	.30	.75
208 Will U	1.50	3.00
209 Draw Energy U	.75	2.00
210 Venusaur & Snivy GX UR FULL ART	3.00	6.00
211 Vileplume GX UR FULL ART	.30	.60
212 Charizard & Braixen GX UR FULL ART	1.25	2.50
213 Volcarona GX UR FULL ART	2.00	4.00
214 Blastoise & Piplup GX UR FULL ART	1.25	2.50
215 Blastoise & Piplup GX UR ALT ART	1.25	2.50
216 Solgaleo & Lunala GX UR FULL ART	1.25	2.50
217 Oricorio GX UR FULL ART	1.25	2.50
218 Flygon GX UR FULL ART	10.00	20.00
219 Alolan Persian GX UR FULL ART	.75	1.50
220 Arceus & Dialga & Palkia GX UR FULL ART	.75	1.50
221 Arceus & Dialga & Palkia GX UR ALT ART	1.50	3.00
222 Reshiram & Zekrom GX UR FULL ART	.75	1.50
223 Naganadel & Guzzlord GX UR FULL ART	1.00	2.00
224 Naganadel & Guzzlord GX UR ALT ART	.75	1.50
225 Mega Lopunny & Jigglypuff GX UR FULL ART	.12	.25
226 Mega Lopunny & Jigglypuff GX UR ALT ART	.12	.25
227 Silvally GX UR FULL ART	1.25	2.50
228 Cynthia & Caitlin UR FULL ART	2.00	4.00
229 Guzma & Hala UR FULL ART	1.25	2.50
230 Lillie's Full Force UR FULL ART	2.00	4.00
231 Mallow & Lana UR FULL ART	3.00	6.00
232 N's Resolve UR FULL ART	1.25	2.50
233 Professor Oak's Setup UR FULL ART	.12	.25
234 Red & Blue UR FULL ART	.15	.40
235 Roller Skater UR FULL ART	1.00	2.00
236 Rosa UR FULL ART	1.25	2.50
237 Torkoal SCR	.75	1.50
238 Weavile SCR	1.50	3.00
239 Piplup SCR	.30	.75
240 Wishiwashi SCR	1.25	2.50
241 Pikachu SCR	.60	1.25
242 Magnemite SCR	3.00	8.00
243 Koffing SCR	.75	1.50
244 Gallade SCR	.75	1.50
245 Mimikyu SCR	2.50	5.00
246 Excadrill SCR	.60	1.25
247 Steelix SCR	.75	1.50
248 Stoutland SCR	.60	1.25
249 Venusaur & Snivy GX SCR	1.00	2.00
250 Vileplume GX SCR	.60	1.25
251 Charizard & Braixen GX SCR	.60	1.25
252 Volcarona GX SCR	.75	1.50
253 Blastoise & Piplup GX SCR	.75	1.50
254 Solgaleo & Lunala GX SCR	.75	1.50
255 Oricorio GX SCR	.75	1.50
256 Flygon GX SCR	2.00	4.00
257 Alolan Persian GX SCR	1.25	2.50
258 Arceus & Dialga & Palkia GX SCR	.25	.50
259 Reshiram & Zekrom GX SCR	.04	.10
260 Naganadel & Guzzlord GX SCR	.05	.12
261 Mega Lopunny & Jigglypuff GX SCR	3.00	6.00
262 Silvally GX SCR	1.25	2.50
263 Giant Hearth SCR	2.50	5.00
264 Great Catcher SCR	.75	1.50
265 Island Challenge Amulet SCR	1.25	2.50
266 Lana's Fishing Rod SCR	1.00	2.00
267 Lillie's Poké Doll SCR	.75	1.50
268 Martial Arts Dojo SCR	.30	.60
269 Power Plant SCR	.75	1.50
270 Tag Call SCR	1.25	3.00
271 Draw Energy SCR	1.25	2.50

2019 Pokemon Sun and Moon Hidden Fates

1 Caterpie C	1.50	3.00
2 Metapod U	3.00	6.00
3 Butterfree R	.60	1.25
4 Paras C	1.25	2.50
5 Scyther U	1.50	3.00
6 Pinsir GX URR	2.00	4.00
7 Charmander C	1.50	3.00
8 Charmeleon U	.07	.15
9 Charizard GX URR	.75	1.50
10 Magmar U	1.25	2.50
11 Psyduck C	1.50	3.00
12 Slowpoke C	1.00	2.00
13 Staryu C	1.00	2.00
14 Starmie GX URR	.60	1.25
15 Magikarp C	1.25	2.50
16 Gyarados GX URR	.60	1.25
17 Lapras R	.60	1.25
18 Vaporeon HOLO R	.75	1.50
19 Pikachu C	.75	1.50
20 Raichu GX URR	1.00	2.00
21 Voltorb C	.08	.20
22 Electrode R	1.25	2.50
23 Jolteon R	2.00	4.00
24 Zapdos HOLO R	25.00	50.00
25 Ekans C	2.50	5.00
26 Ekans C	1.25	2.50
27 Arbok R	.75	1.50
28 Koffing C	.75	1.50
29 Weezing R	1.50	3.00
30 Jynx U	.75	1.50
31 Mewtwo GX URR	1.00	2.00
32 Mew R	.60	1.25
33 Geodude C	.30	.75
34 Graveler U	.20	.50

35 Golem R 2.00 4.00
36 Onix GX URR 8.00 20.00
37 Cubone C .75 1.50
38 Clefairy C .08 .20
39 Clefairy C .10 .25
40 Clefable R 20.00 40.00
41 Jigglypuff C .07 .15
42 Wigglytuff GX URR .50 1.25
43 Mr. Mime R .75 1.50
44 Moltres & Zapdos & Articuno GX URR .75 1.50
45 Farfetch'd U .60 1.25
46 Chansey U .75 1.50
47 Kangaskhan R 1.00 2.00
48 Eevee HOLO R 1.50 3.00
49 Eevee C 3.00 6.00
50 Snorlax R .75 1.50
51 Bill's Analysis R .75 1.50
52 Blaine's Last Stand R 3.00 6.00
53 Brock's Grit U 1.00 2.00
54 Brock's Pewter City Gym U .60 1.50
55 Brock's Training HOLO R .04 .10
56 Erika's Hospitality R .08 .20
57 Giovanni's Exile U .60 1.25
58 Jessie & James HOLO R .60 1.50
59 Koga's Trap U 1.25 2.50
60 Lt. Surge's Strategy U 1.50 3.00
61 Misty's Cerulean City Gym U 1.50 3.00
62 Misty's Determination U .75 1.50
63 Misty's Water Command HOLO R 5.00 12.00
64 Pokémon Center Lady U .25 .50
65 Sabrina's Suggestion U .75 1.50
66 Moltres & Zapdos & Articuno GX UR FULL ART .01 .08
67 Giovanni's Exile UR FULL ART .08 .20
68 Jessie & James UR FULL ART .30 .60
69 Moltres & Zapdos & Articuno GX SCR 1.50 3.00

2019 Pokemon Sun and Moon Hidden Fates Shiny Vault

SV1 Scyther SHR .75 1.50
SV2 Rowlet SHR .15 .30
SV3 Dartrix SHR 1.00 2.00
SV4 Wimpod SHR .75 1.50
SV5 Pheromosa SHR 1.00 2.00
SV6 Charmander SHR .04 .10
SV7 Charmeleon SHR .10 .25
SV8 Alolan Vulpix SHR 2.00 4.00
SV9 Wooper SHR 6.00 12.00
SV10 Quagsire SHR .60 1.25
SV11 Froakie SHR .75 1.50
SV12 Frogadier SHR 1.25 2.50
SV13 Voltorb SHR .60 1.25
SV14 Xurkitree SHR 1.00 2.00
SV15 Seviper SHR .50 1.00
SV16 Shuppet SHR .75 1.50
SV17 Inkay SHR 1.50 3.00
SV18 Malamar SHR .75 1.50
SV19 Poipole SHR 1.25 2.50
SV20 Sudowoodo SHR 1.00 2.00
SV21 Riolu SHR 1.50 3.00
SV22 Lucario SHR 3.00 6.00
SV23 Rockruff SHR 2.00 4.00
SV24 Buzzwole SHR 3.00 6.00
SV25 Zorua SHR .75 1.50
SV26 Guzzlord SHR .60 1.25
SV27 Magnemite SHR .75 1.50
SV28 Magneton SHR .30 .60
SV29 Magnezone SHR .75 1.50
SV30 Beldum SHR 1.50 3.00
SV31 Metang SHR 2.50 5.00
SV32 Celesteela SHR 1.00 2.00
SV33 Kartana SHR .75 1.50
SV34 Ralts SHR .75 1.50
SV35 Kirlia SHR .07 .15
SV36 Diancie SHR .15 .40
SV37 Altaria SHR .75 1.50
SV38 Gible SHR 1.25 2.50
SV39 Gabite SHR 2.00 4.00
SV40 Garchomp SHR .75 1.50
SV41 Eevee SHR .75 1.50
SV42 Swablu SHR .30 .60
SV43 Noibat SHR .60 1.25
SV44 Oranguru SHR 1.25 2.50
SV45 Type: Null SHR .60 1.25
SV46 Leafeon GX UR 1.25 3.00
SV47 Decidueye GX UR .75 1.50
SV48 Golisopod GX UR .75 1.50
SV49 Charizard GX UR 1.25 2.50
SV50 Ho-Oh GX UR 1.25 2.50
SV51 Reshiram GX UR 1.00 2.00
SV52 Turtonator GX UR .75 1.50
SV53 Alolan Ninetales GX UR 1.50 3.00
SV54 Articuno GX UR 2.50 5.00
SV55 Glaceon GX UR .07 .15
SV56 Greninja GX UR 2.00 4.00
SV57 Electrode GX UR .60 1.25
SV58 Xurkitree GX UR 1.25 2.50
SV59 Mewtwo GX UR 1.25 2.50
SV60 Espeon GX UR 1.25 2.50
SV61 Banette GX UR .08 .20
SV62 Nihilego GX UR .10 .25
SV63 Naganadel GX UR .75 1.50
SV64 Lucario GX UR .50 1.00
SV65 Zygarde GX UR 1.00 2.00
SV66 Lycanroc GX UR .75 1.50
SV67 Lycanroc GX UR .75 1.50
SV68 Buzzwole GX UR 1.50 3.00
SV69 Umbreon GX UR 1.25 2.50
SV70 Darkrai GX UR 7.50 15.00
SV71 Guzzlord GX UR 1.25 2.50
SV72 Scizor GX UR 2.00 4.00
SV73 Kartana GX UR 1.25 3.00
SV74 Stakataka GX UR 1.00 2.00
SV75 Gardevoir GX UR 2.50 5.00
SV76 Sylveon GX UR 1.00 2.00
SV77 Altaria GX UR .75 1.50
SV78 Noivern GX UR .12 .25
SV79 Silvally GX UR .12 .30
SV80 Drampa GX UR 3.00 6.00
SV81 Aether Foundation Employee UR .07 .15
SV82 Cynthia UR .50 1.00
SV83 Fisherman UR .75 1.50
SV84 Guzma UR 2.50 5.00
SV85 Hiker UR 1.25 2.50
SV86 Lady UR .75 1.50
SV87 Aether Paradise Conservation Area SCR .60 1.25
SV88 Brooklet Hill SCR 1.00 2.00
SV89 Mt. Coronet SCR .75 2.00
SV90 Shrine of Punishment SCR .30 .75
SV91 Tapu Bulu GX SCR 2.00 4.00
SV92 Tapu Fini GX SCR 3.00 8.00
SV93 Tapu Koko GX SCR 1.25 2.50
SV94 Tapu Lele GX SCR 1.00 2.00

2019 Pokemon Sun and Moon Team Up

1 Celebi & Venusaur GX URR .30 .60
2 Weedle C .75 1.50
3 Weedle C 1.50 3.00
4 Kakuna U 1.25 2.50
5 Beedrill R 1.25 2.50
6 Paras C 2.50 5.00
7 Parasect R .75 1.50
8 Exeggcute C .30 .60
9 Pinsir R .75 1.50
10 Shaymin HOLO R 1.25 2.50
11 Charmander C 1.25 2.50
12 Charmander C 1.25 2.50
13 Charmeleon U 2.50 5.00
14 Charizard R 7.50 15.00
15 Vulpix C 4.00 8.00
16 Ninetales R .10 .20
17 Ponyta C .75 2.00
18 Rapidash U .60 1.50
19 Moltres HOLO R 2.50 5.00
20 Litten C .25 .50
21 Torracat U .75 1.50
22 Squirtle C .01 .08
23 Squirtle C .05 .12
24 Wartortle U .25 .50
25 Blastoise R 1.50 3.00
26 Psyduck C 1.25 2.50
27 Golduck U 3.00 6.00
28 Staryu C .01 .08
29 Magikarp C .04 .10
30 Gyarados HOLO R .10 .20
31 Lapras R .75 1.50
32 Articuno HOLO R .01 .08
33 Pikachu & Zekrom GX URR .04 .10
34 Alolan Geodude C .30 .60
35 Alolan Geodude C 6.00 12.00
36 Alolan Graveler U 3.00 6.00
37 Alolan Golem R .60 1.25
38 Voltorb C .75 1.50
39 Electrode HOLO R 1.00 2.00
40 Zapdos HOLO R .60 1.25
41 Mareep C 2.00 4.00
42 Flaaffy U .75 1.50
43 Ampharos GX URR .50 1.25
44 Blitzle C 1.25 2.50
45 Zebstrika R 3.00 6.00
46 Emolga C 1.25 2.50
47 Joltik C .50 1.00
48 Galvantula R 2.00 4.00
49 Helioptile C 2.00 4.00
50 Heliolisk U .60 1.25
51 Tapu Koko HOLO R 1.25 2.50
52 Zeraora HOLO R 1.50 3.00
53 Gengar & Mimikyu GX URR 1.25 2.50
54 Nidoran C 1.50 3.00
55 Nidorina U 1.25 2.50
56 Nidoqueen R .25 .50
57 Nidoran C .07 .15
58 Nidorino U .60 1.25
59 Nidoking R .75 1.50
60 Tentacool C .60 1.25
61 Tentacruel U 1.25 2.50
62 Grimer C 2.50 5.00
63 Muk R .75 1.50
64 Alolan Marowak R 1.00 2.00
65 Starmie R 7.50 15.00
66 Mr. Mime R .75 1.50
67 Mr. Mime GX URR 1.50 3.00
68 Jynx U 1.50 3.00
69 Cosmog C .08 .20
70 Cosmoem U .04 .10
71 Mankey C .75 1.50
72 Primeape R 1.00 2.00
73 Hitmonlee U .75 1.50
74 Hitmonchan U .75 1.50
75 Omanyte U .75 1.50
76 Omastar HOLO R 1.50 3.00
77 Kabuto U .75 1.50
78 Kabutops R 1.25 2.50
79 Larvitar C 1.00 2.00
80 Pupitar U 1.00 2.50
81 Pancham C 1.25 2.50
82 Lycanroc GX URR 2.50 5.00
83 Alolan Grimer C 1.50 3.00
84 Alolan Muk R 1.25 2.50
85 Tyranitar HOLO R 5.00 10.00
86 Poochyena C .60 1.25
87 Mightyena R .50 1.00
88 Absol HOLO R 1.50 3.00
89 Spiritomb U 1.50 4.00
90 Zorua C 50.00 100.00
91 Zoroark HOLO R 1.50 3.00
92 Vullaby C .75 1.50
93 Mandibuzz R 1.00 2.00
94 Pangoro R .75 1.50
95 Yveltal HOLO R .30 .75
96 Hoopa GX URR .60 1.25
97 Incineroar GX URR .75 1.50
98 Skarmory R 10.00 20.00
99 Jirachi HOLO R .75 1.50
100 Bronzor C 4.00 8.00
101 Bronzong R 75.00 200.00
102 Ferroseed C 2.50 5.00
103 Ferrothorn R 1.00 2.00
104 Pawniard C .75 1.50
105 Bisharp R .30 .75
106 Cobalion GX URR .75 1.50
107 Honedge C 1.25 2.50
108 Doublade U .60 1.25
109 Aegislash HOLO R 1.50 3.00
110 Klefki C 2.00 4.00
111 Alolan Ninetales HOLO R .60 1.25
112 Mimikyu R .60 1.25
113 Latias & Latios GX URR .25 .50
114 Alolan Exeggutor R .01 .08
115 Alolan Exeggutor R .08 .20
116 Dratini C 1.00 2.00
117 Dratini C 3.00 6.00
118 Dragonair U 1.00 2.00
119 Dragonite HOLO R 1.00 2.00
120 Eevee & Snorlax GX URR 1.00 2.00
121 Pidgey C 1.00 2.00
122 Pidgey C .75 1.50
123 Pidgeotto C .01 .08
124 Pidgeot R .04 .10
125 Meowth C 1.50 3.00
126 Persian U .75 1.50
127 Farfetch'd U .75 1.50
128 Kangaskhan U .60 1.25
129 Tauros U .75 1.50
130 Aerodactyl R 1.00 2.00
131 Lugia HOLO R 1.25 2.50
132 Zangoose HOLO R .07 .15
133 Bill's Analysis HOLO R .75 1.50
134 Black Market HOLO R .15 .30
135 Brock's Grit U .20 .50
136 Buff Padding U 2.00 4.00
137 Dana U .10 .20
138 Dangerous Drill U .07 .15
139 Electrocharger U 2.50 5.00
140 Erika's Hospitality HOLO R .75 2.00
141 Evelyn U .60 1.50
142 Fairy Charm UB U 1.00 2.00
143 Grass Memory U 1.50 4.00
144 Ingo & Emmet U .60 1.50
145 Jasmine U 2.00 4.00
146 Judge Whistle U 4.00 10.00
147 Lavender Town U .01 .08
148 Metal Goggles U .04 .10
149 Morgan U .75 1.50
150 Nanu U 1.00 2.00
151 Nita U 1.50 3.00
152 Pokemon Communication U .75 1.50
153 Return Label U 1.00 2.00
154 Sabrina's Suggestion U .01 .08
155 Unidentified Fossil U .10 .25
156 Viridian Forest U .30 .60
157 Water Memory U 3.00 6.00
159 Celebi & Venusaur GX UR FULL ART .75 1.50
160 Magikarp & Wailord GX UR FULL ART 1.50 3.00
161 Magikarp & Wailord GX UR ALT FULL ART 1.25 2.50
162 Pikachu & Zekrom GX UR FULL ART .07 .15
163 Ampharos GX UR FULL ART 1.00 2.00
164 Gengar & Mimikyu GX UR FULL ART .75 1.50
165 Gengar & Mimikyu GX UR ALT FULL ART .75 1.50
166 Hoopa GX UR FULL ART 1.50 3.00
167 Incineroar GX UR FULL ART .50 1.00
168 Cobalion GX UR FULL ART 10.00 20.00
169 Latias & Latios GX UR FULL ART 75.00 150.00
170 Latias & Latios GX UR ALT FULL ART .60 1.25
171 Eevee & Snorlax GX UR FULL ART .75 1.50
172 Brock's Grit UR FULL ART 1.50 3.00
173 Dana UR FULL ART 1.25 2.50
174 Erika's Hospitality UR FULL ART 2.00 4.00
175 Evelyn UR FULL ART 1.00 2.00
176 Ingo & Emmet UR FULL ART .75 1.50
177 Jasmine UR FULL ART .60 1.25
178 Morgan UR FULL ART 7.50 15.00
179 Nanu UR FULL ART 1.00 2.00
180 Nita UR FULL ART 1.00 2.00
181 Sabrina's Suggestion UR FULL ART 2.00 4.00
182 Celebi & Venusaur GX SCR 1.00 2.00
183 Magikarp & Wailord GX SCR 1.50 3.00
184 Pikachu & Zekrom GX SCR 3.00 6.00
185 Ampharos GX SCR 2.50 5.00
186 Gengar & Mimikyu GX SCR .75 1.50
187 Hoopa GX SCR .07 .15
188 Incineroar GX SCR 1.50 3.00
189 Cobalion GX SCR .50 1.00
190 Latias & Latios GX SCR .08 .20
191 Eevee & Snorlax GX SCR .01 .08
192 Dangerous Drill SCR 1.50 3.00
193 Electrocharger SCR .08 .20
194 Judge Whistle SCR 2.00 4.00
195 Metal Goggles SCR 1.00 2.00
196 Pokemon Communication SCR 1.00 2.00

2019 Pokemon Sun and Moon Unbroken Bonds

1 Pheromosa & Buzzwole GX URR 1.00 2.00
2 Caterpie C .75 1.50
3 Metapod U 1.00 2.00
4 Butterfree R 1.00 2.00
5 Oddish C .75 1.50
6 Oddish C .75 1.50
7 Gloom U 1.00 2.00
8 Vileplume HOLO R 1.00 2.00
9 Venonat C 2.00 4.00
10 Venonat C .75 1.50
11 Venomoth R 1.00 2.00
12 Venomoth GX URR 2.00 4.00
13 Bellsprout C 1.25 2.50
14 Weepinbell U 17.50 35.00
15 Victreebel R 2.00 4.00
16 Tangela C 1.00 2.00
17 Tangrowth R .60 1.25
18 Grubbin C .75 1.50
19 Kartana HOLO R .75 1.50
20 Reshiram & Charizard GX URR .15 .30
21 Growlithe C 1.50 3.00
22 Arcanine HOLO R .60 1.25
23 Darumaka C .60 1.25
24 Darmanitan R .75 1.50
25 Volcanion HOLO R 7.50 15.00
26 Litten C .75 1.50
27 Litten C .75 1.50
28 Torracat U .60 1.25
29 Incineroar R 1.00 2.00
30 Salandit C .25 .50
31 Salazzle R .01 .08
32 Blacephalon R .10 .25
33 Squirtle C .75 1.50
34 Wartortle U .50 1.00
35 Blastoise GX URR 1.50 3.00
36 Poliwag C 1.50 4.00
37 Poliwag C 5.00 10.00
38 Poliwhirl U .75 1.50
39 Poliwrath R .75 1.50
40 Tentacool C .75 1.50
41 Tentacruel U .01 .08
42 Slowpoke C .05 .12
43 Slowbro HOLO R 1.00 2.00
44 Seel C .07 .15
45 Dewgong R .12 .30
46 Krabby C 1.50 3.00
47 Kingler R .75 1.50
48 Goldeen C 1.50 3.00
49 Seaking R .30 .60
50 Kyurem HOLO R .60 1.25
51 Froakie C 1.50 3.00
52 Frogadier U .60 1.25
53 Pyukumuku U .75 1.50
54 Pikachu C .60 1.25
55 Raichu R .75 1.50
56 Stunfisk R .30 .60
57 Dedenne GX URR .75 1.50
58 Charjabug U .12 .25
59 Vikavolt HOLO R 2.50 5.00
60 Zeraora R .75 1.50
61 Muk & Alolan Muk GX URR 2.50 5.00
62 Ekans C 2.00 4.00
63 Arbok R 1.50 3.00
64 Zubat C .75 1.50
65 Golbat U 1.25 2.50
66 Crobat HOLO R .30 .75
67 Gastly C 5.00 12.00
68 Gastly C .75 2.00
69 Haunter U .75 1.50
70 Gengar R .60 1.25
71 Drowzee C .75 1.50
72 Hypno R 1.25 2.50
73 Koffing C .12 .30
74 Weezing R .25 .60
75 Mewtwo R .60 1.25
76 Mew HOLO R .75 1.50
77 Misdreavus C .30 .60
78 Mismagius R .60 1.25
79 Espurr C .75 1.50
80 Meowstic R 15.00 30.00
81 Marshadow HOLO R .60 1.50
82 Marshadow & Machamp GX URR .25 .60
83 Sandshrew C 2.00 4.00
84 Sandslash R 6.00 15.00
85 Diglett C 1.25 2.50
86 Dugtrio R .75 1.50
87 Geodude C .60 1.25
88 Graveler U 10.00 20.00
89 Golem HOLO R 1.00 2.00
90 Cubone C .75 1.50
91 Marowak R .07 .15
92 Rhyhorn C 2.00 4.00
93 Rhyhorn C .05 .12
94 Rhydon U .10 .25
95 Rhyperior R .50 1.00
96 Wooper C .75 1.50
97 Quagsire R 7.50 15.00
98 Gligar C 7.50 15.00
99 Gliscor U 2.00 4.00
100 Tyrogue U 1.50 3.00
101 Hitmontop U .10 .20
102 Riolu C .75 1.50
103 Landorus HOLO R .75 1.50
104 Crabrawler C .75 1.50
105 Crabominable R 1.25 2.50
106 Stakataka HOLO R .75 1.50
107 Greninja & Zoroark GX URR 2.00 4.00
108 Murkrow C .60 1.25
109 Honchkrow GX URR .75 1.50
110 Carvanha C .75 1.50
111 Sharpedo R 2.50 5.00
112 Spiritomb HOLO R 1.50 3.00
113 Sandile C 1.50 3.00
114 Sandile C .08 .20
115 Krokorok U .04 .10
116 Krookodile R .08 .20
117 Greninja HOLO R .75 1.50
118 Inkay C 1.00 2.00
119 Malamar HOLO R .75 1.50
120 Lucario & Melmetal GX URR 1.25 2.50
121 Alolan Diglett C 2.00 4.00
122 Alolan Dugtrio R .12 .25
123 Aron C .60 1.25
124 Lairon U .75 1.50
125 Aggron R 2.00 4.00
126 Lucario HOLO R 1.00 2.00
127 Genesect R .60 1.25
128 Meltan C 1.00 2.00
129 Melmetal HOLO R 1.25 2.50
130 Gardevoir & Sylveon GX URR .75 1.50
131 Cleffa U 17.50 35.00
132 Clefairy C 1.25 2.50
133 Clefable R .60 1.25
134 Jigglypuff C .75 1.50

135 Wigglytuff R 1.25 2.50
136 Togepi C .01 .08
137 Togetic U .01 .08
138 Togekiss HOLO R 1.50 3.00
139 Cottonee C .75 1.50
140 Whimsicott GX URR .60 1.25
141 Spritzee C 1.00 2.00
142 Aromatisse R 1.50 3.00
143 Rattata C .75 1.50
144 Raticate U .10 .20
145 Spearow C .60 1.25
146 Fearow U 1.00 2.00
147 Meowth C .75 1.50
148 Persian R .25 .50
149 Persian GX URR .10 .25
150 Doduo C .25 .60
151 Dodrio U .01 .08
152 Lickitung C .05 .12
153 Lickilicky R .75 1.50
154 Porygon C .75 1.50
155 Porygon C 1.00 2.00
156 Porygon2 U 1.25 3.00
157 Porygon-Z HOLO R .75 1.50
158 Snorlax HOLO R .75 1.50
159 Glameow C 1.25 2.50
160 Purugly R .75 1.50
161 Happiny U 1.25 2.50
162 Chatot U .12 .25
163 Celesteela GX URR .12 .30
164 Beast Bringer U 1.25 2.50
165 Chip-Chip Ice Axe U 1.00 2.00
166 Devolution Spray Z U 1.50 3.00
167 Dusk Stone U 3.00 6.00
168 Dust Island U .75 1.50
169 Electromagnetic Radar U 1.50 3.00
170 Energy Spinner U .75 1.50
171 Fairy Charm Ability U .75 1.50
172 Fairy Charm L U .75 1.50
173 Fire Crystal U 2.50 5.00
174 Giovanni's Exile U 1.00 2.00
175 Green's Exploration U 1.00 2.00
176 Janine U 2.50 5.00
177 Koga's Trap U 10.00 20.00
178 Lt. Surge's Strategy U .07 .15
179 Martial Arts Dojo U 1.25 2.50
180 Metal Core Barrier U 1.00 2.00
181 Molayne U 1.00 2.00
182 Pokegear 3.0 U 2.50 5.00
183 Power Plant U 5.00 10.00
184 Red's Challenge HOLO R .75 1.50
185 Samson Oak U 1.25 2.50
186 Stealthy Hood U .75 2.00
187 Surprise Box U 10.00 20.00
188 Ultra Forest Kartenvoy U 2.00 4.00
189 Welder U 2.00 4.00
190 Triple Acceleration Energy U 1.50 3.00
191 Pheromosa & Buzzwole GX UR FULL ART 2.00 4.00
192 Pheromosa & Buzzwole GX UR ALT FULL ART.75 1.50
193 Venomoth GX UR FULL ART .75 2.00
194 Reshiram & Charizard GX UR FULL ART .60 1.25
195 Dedenne GX UR FULL ART .75 1.50
196 Muk & Alolan Muk GX UR FULL ART .25 .50
197 Muk & Alolan Muk GX UR FULL ART .01 .08
198 Marshadow & Machamp GX UR FULL ART .04 .10
199 Marshadow & Machamp GX UR FULL ART .30 .60
200 Greninja & Zoroark GX UR FULL ART 2.50 5.00
201 Greninja & Zoroark GX UR FULL ART .75 1.50
202 Honchkrow GX UR FULL ART 1.00 2.00
203 Lucario & Melmetal GX UR FULL ART 2.00 5.00
204 Gardevoir & Sylveon GX UR FULL ART .60 1.50
205 Gardevoir & Sylveon GX UR FULL ART 2.00 4.00
206 Whimsicott GX UR FULL ART 3.00 8.00
207 Persian GX UR FULL ART .12 .25
208 Celesteela GX UR FULL ART 5.00 10.00
209 Green's Exploration UR FULL ART 1.25 2.50
210 Janine UR FULL ART 4.00 8.00
211 Koga's Trap UR FULL ART 1.00 2.00
212 Molayne UR FULL ART 1.00 2.00
213 Red's Challenge UR FULL ART .50 1.00
214 Welder UR FULL ART .75 1.50
215 Pheromosa & Buzzwole GX SCR .75 1.50
216 Venomoth GX SCR 1.50 3.00
217 Reshiram & Charizard GX SCR 7.50 15.00
218 Blastoise GX SCR .07 .15
219 Dedenne GX SCR .75 1.50
220 Muk & Alolan Muk GX SCR .75 1.50
221 Marshadow & Machamp GX SCR 7.50 15.00
222 Greninja & Zoroark GX SCR 1.00 2.00
223 Honchkrow GX SCR 2.50 5.00
224 Lucario & Melmetal GX SCR .60 1.25
225 Gardevoir & Sylveon GX SCR 1.50 3.00
226 Whimsicott GX SCR .08 .20
227 Persian GX SCR .08 .20
228 Celesteela GX SCR .08 .20
229 Beast Bringer SCR 3.00 6.00
230 Electromagnetic Radar SCR 3.00 6.00
231 Fire Crystal SCR 1.50 3.00
232 Metal Core Barrier SCR .60 1.25
233 Pokegear 3.0 SCR 2.50 5.00
234 Triple Acceleration Energy SCR 2.50 5.00

2019 Pokemon Sun and Moon Unified Minds

1 Rowlet & Alolan Exeggutor GX URR 2.50 5.00
2 Yanma C .75 1.50
3 Yanmega U .75 1.50
4 Celebi HOLO R 1.25 2.50
5 Shroomish C 1.00 2.00
6 Sewaddle C .75 1.50
7 Sewaddle C 1.25 2.50
8 Swadloon U 1.25 2.50
9 Leavanny R 1.50 3.00
10 Dwebble C 2.50 5.00
11 Crustle R .75 1.50
12 Karrablast C 1.00 2.00
13 Foongus C 1.00 2.00
14 Amoonguss R 1.50 3.00
15 Fomantis C .60 1.25
16 Lurantis U 1.50 3.00
17 Bounsweet C 1.50 3.00
18 Steenee U .75 1.50
19 Tsareena HOLO R 1.25 2.50
20 Dhelmise U 1.00 2.00
21 Magmar C 1.50 3.00
22 Magmortar R 12.50 25.00
23 Numel C .75 1.50
24 Camerupt R .60 1.25
25 Heatran GX URR .60 1.25
26 Victini HOLO R .08 .20
27 Litwick C .01 .08
28 Litwick C .04 .10
29 Lampent U .01 .08
30 Chandelure HOLO R .01 .08
31 Fletchinder C .60 1.25
32 Talonflame R .75 1.50
33 Salandit C 6.00 15.00
34 Salazzle R 2.00 4.00
35 Slowpoke & Psyduck GX URR 1.00 2.00
36 Lapras U 2.00 4.00
37 Snorunt C .75 1.50
38 Froslass HOLO R .75 1.50
39 Finneon C 1.50 3.00
40 Lumineon U 1.25 2.50
41 Snover C .07 .15
42 Abomasnow R 1.25 2.50
43 Basculin U 1.25 2.50
44 Tirtouga U 1.25 2.50
45 Carracosta U .60 1.25
46 Cryogonal C 6.00 12.00
47 Keldeo GX URR 5.00 10.00
48 Dewpider C .75 1.50
49 Araquanid R .75 1.50
50 Wimpod C 5.00 10.00
51 Golisopod HOLO R .60 1.25
52 Pyukumuku U 1.25 2.50
53 Tapu Fini R .75 2.00
54 Raichu & Alolan Raichu GX URR 1.50 3.00
55 Pikachu C 1.25 2.50
56 Pikachu C .07 .15
57 Alolan Raichu HOLO R 2.00 4.00
58 Magnemite C 2.50 5.00
59 Magneton U 1.00 2.00
60 Magnezone HOLO R 2.00 4.00
61 Joltik C 30.00 60.00
62 Galvantula R .30 .75
63 Tynamo C .60 1.25
64 Tynamo C .75 1.50
65 Eelektrik U .75 1.50
66 Eelektross HOLO R .60 1.50
67 Stunfisk C .01 .08
68 Thundurus U .04 .10
69 Tapu Koko HOLO R 1.25 2.50
70 Xurkitree R .75 1.50
71 Mewtwo & Mew GX URR 1.00 2.00
72 Espeon & Deoxys GX URR .30 .60
73 Exeggcute C 2.00 4.00
74 Exeggutor R 2.50 5.00
75 Alolan Marowak R 1.50 4.00
76 Jynx U 1.00 2.50
77 Wynaut U 2.00 4.00
78 Latios GX URR 8.00 20.00
79 Jirachi GX URR .75 1.50
80 Drifloon C .75 1.50
81 Drifblim R 7.50 15.00
82 Skorupi C .75 1.50
83 Uxie HOLO R 2.50 5.00
84 Mesprit U 1.25 2.50
85 Azelf U .75 1.50
86 Giratina HOLO R 7.50 15.00
87 Cresselia U .20 .40
88 Munna C 1.00 2.00
89 Musharna U .75 1.50
90 Elgyem U .60 1.25
91 Beheeyem R .50 1.00
92 Honedge C .20 .40
93 Honedge C .75 1.50
94 Doublade U .75 1.50
95 Aegislash HOLO R .12 .25
96 Mareanie C .20 .50
97 Toxapex R 1.25 2.50
98 Salandit C .08 .20
99 Salazzle R .15 .40
100 Cosmog C .25 .50
101 Necrozma R .04 .10
102 Poipole C .10 .25
103 Onix C 2.00 4.00
104 Steelix R 1.25 2.50
105 Cubone C .60 1.25
106 Aerodactyl GX URR .60 1.25
107 Heracross U .30 .60
108 Breloom U .75 1.50
109 Meditite C .60 1.25
110 Medicham R 1.50 3.00
111 Relicanth U 1.25 2.50
112 Gible C 1.25 2.50
113 Gabite U .75 1.50
114 Garchomp HOLO R 1.50 3.00
115 Riolu C 25.00 50.00
116 Riolu C .75 1.50
117 Lucario R 2.00 4.00
118 Drilbur C .75 1.50
119 Excadrill R 1.25 2.50
120 Archen U .75 1.50
121 Archeops R 1.00 2.00
122 Terrakion HOLO R 7.50 15.00
123 Meloetta R .75 1.50
124 Zygarde R .75 1.50
125 Umbreon & Darkrai GX URR 1.25 2.50
126 Mega Sableye & Tyranitar GX URR 6.00 12.00
127 Alolan Grimer C 1.50 3.00
128 Murkrow C .07 .15
129 Murkrow C .08 .20
130 Honchkrow R .75 1.50
131 Sneasel C 1.00 2.00
132 Weavile GX URR .30 .60
133 Sableye U .60 1.25
134 Drapion R 1.00 2.00
135 Purrloin C 1.00 2.00
136 Liepard R 1.00 2.00
137 Scraggy C 1.25 2.50
138 Scrafty R .60 1.25
139 Yveltal HOLO R .75 1.50
140 Hoopa HOLO R .60 1.25
141 Mawile GX URR 1.50 3.00
142 Escavalier R .25 .50
143 Cottonee C .01 .08
144 Whimsicott R .10 .25
145 Dedenne U .75 1.50
146 Garchomp & Giratina GX URR 1.00 2.00
147 Dratini C 2.00 4.00
148 Dratini C .07 .15
149 Dragonair U 7.50 15.00
150 Dragonair U 1.25 2.50
151 Dragonite R .75 1.50
152 Dragonite GX URR .60 1.25
153 Latias R .01 .08
154 Axew C .04 .10
155 Fraxure U 20.00 40.00
156 Haxorus HOLO R 1.00 2.00
157 Druddigon C .25 .50
158 Noibat C .75 1.50
159 Noivern R 1.00 2.00
160 Naganadel GX URR .08 .20
161 Lickitung C .05 .12
162 Lickilicky R .01 .08
163 Kangaskhan HOLO R .04 .10
164 Tauros U 1.00 2.00
165 Hoothoot C .25 .50
166 Noctowl U 1.25 2.50
167 Slakoth C 1.25 2.50
168 Slakoth C 2.50 5.00
169 Vigoroth U 1.50 3.00
170 Slaking HOLO R .75 1.50
171 Bidoof C 2.00 4.00
172 Bibarel U 1.25 2.50
173 Munchlax U 15.00 30.00
174 Pidove C 1.50 3.00
175 Tranquill U 1.00 2.00
176 Unfezant R .75 1.50
177 Audino U .75 1.50
178 Tornadus U .75 1.50
179 Fletchling C .10 .20
180 Yungoos C 1.50 3.00
181 Gumshoos R 1.25 2.50
182 Oranguru U 2.50 5.00
183 Type: Null U 3.00 8.00
184 Silvally HOLO R 1.50 3.00
185 Komala U 2.50 5.00
186 Blaine's Quiz Show U 1.50 3.00
187 Blizzard Town U 1.00 2.00
188 Blue's Tactics U .75 1.50
189 Bug Catcher U .07 .15
190 Channeler U .75 2.00
191 Cherish Ball U .75 2.00
192 Coach Trainer U 1.50 3.00
193 Dark City U .60 1.25
194 Ear-Ringing Bell U .75 1.50
195 Flyinium Z: Air Slash U .75 1.50
196 Giant Bomb U 4.00 8.00
197 Giant Hearth U 1.00 2.50
198 Great Potion U .25 .60
199 Grimsley U 2.00 4.00
200 Hapu U 12.00 30.00
201 Karate Belt U 3.00 6.00
202 Misty's Favor U .30 .60
203 Normalium Z: Tackle U .60 1.25
204 Poke Maniac U .60 1.50
205 Pokemon Research Lab U .10 .25
206 Reset Stamp U 1.50 3.00
207 Slumbering Forest U .75 1.50
208 Stadium Nav U .75 1.50
209 Tag Switch U 1.50 3.00
210 Unidentified Fossil U .75 1.50
211 U-Turn Board U .75 1.50
212 Recycle Energy U .75 1.50
213 Weakness Guard Energy U 3.00 6.00
214 Rowlet & Alolan Exeggutor GX UR FULL ART1.50 3.00
215 Rowlet & Alolan Exeggutor GX UR ALT FULL ART .60 1.25
216 Heatran GX UR .07 .15
217 Slowpoke & Psyduck GX UR FULL ART .30 .75
218 Slowpoke & Psyduck GX UR ALT FULL ART .08 .20
219 Keldeo GX UR FULL ART .75 1.50
220 Raichu & Alolan Raichu GX UR FULL ART .25 .50
221 Raichu & Alolan Raichu GX UR ALT FULL ART7.50 15.00
222 Mewtwo & Mew GX UR FULL ART .75 1.50
223 Latios GX UR FULL ART 1.50 3.00
224 Aerodactyl GX UR FULL ART 1.25 2.50
225 Mega Sableye & Tyranitar GX UR FULL ART .75 1.50
226 Mega Sableye & Tyranitar GX UR ALT ART .75 1.50
227 Mawile GX UR FULL ART .75 1.50
228 Garchomp & Giratina GX UR 1.50 3.00
229 Dragonite GX UR FULL ART .30 .60
230 Naganadel GX UR FULL ART .75 1.50
231 Blue's Tactics UR FULL ART .60 1.25
232 Channeler UR FULL ART 1.00 2.00
233 Coach Trainer UR FULL ART .30 .60
234 Grimsley UR FULL ART .75 1.50
235 Misty's Favor UR FULL ART .75 1.50
236 Poke Maniac UR FULL ART .75 1.50
237 Rowlet & Alolan Exeggutor GX SCR .75 1.50
238 Heatran GX SCR 1.00 2.00
239 Slowpoke & Psyduck GX SCR 2.00 4.00
240 Keldeo GX SCR .50 1.00
241 Raichu & Alolan Raichu GX SCR .75 1.50
242 Mewtwo & Mew GX SCR 2.00 4.00
243 Latios GX SCR 1.25 2.50
244 Aerodactyl GX SCR 1.00 2.00
245 Mega Sableye & Tyranitar GX SCR 1.50 3.00
246 Mawile GX SCR .75 1.50
247 Garchomp & Giratina GX SCR .75 1.50
248 Dragonite GX SCR 1.00 2.00
249 Naganadel GX SCR 3.00 6.00
250 Cherish Ball SCR 2.00 4.00
251 Giant Bomb SCR 2.50 5.00
252 Karate Belt SCR 1.25 2.50
253 Reset Stamp SCR .75 1.50
254 Tag Switch SCR .75 1.50
255 U-Turn Board SCR 2.00 4.00
256 Viridian Forest SCR 2.50 5.00
257 Recycle Energy SCR .10 .20
258 Weakness Guard Energy SCR 1.00 2.00

2020 Pokemon Sword and Shield

1 Celebi V URR .75 1.50
2 Roselia C .01 .08
3 Roselia C .10 .25
4 Roserade R 1.25 2.50
5 Cottonee C .50 1.00
6 Whimsicott R .75 1.50
7 Maractus C .08 .20
8 Durant R .05 .12
9 Dhelmise V URR .01 .08
10 Grookey C .04 .10
11 Grookey C .08 .20
12 Thwackey U 7.50 15.00
13 Thwackey U .75 1.50
14 Rillaboom HOLO R .25 .50
15 Rillaboom R .60 1.25
16 Blipbug C .01 .08
17 Blipbug C .05 .12
18 Dottler U 1.50 3.00
19 Orbeetle R 1.50 3.00
20 Gossifleur C 1.00 2.00
21 Eldegoss U 1.50 3.00
22 Vulpix C .75 1.50
23 Ninetales R 1.25 2.50
24 Torkoal V URR .50 1.00
25 Victini V URR .75 1.50
26 Heatmor U 1.00 2.00
27 Salandit C .75 1.50
28 Salazzle U .75 1.50
29 Turtonator R 1.00 2.00
30 Scorbunny C 3.00 6.00
31 Scorbunny C .60 1.25
32 Raboot U 30.00 75.00
33 Raboot U .10 .20
34 Cinderace HOLO R .12 .30
35 Cinderace HOLO R .75 1.50
36 Cinderace R 7.50 15.00
37 Sizzlipede C 5.00 10.00
38 Sizzlipede C .20 .40
39 Centiskorch R 2.00 4.00
40 Shellder C 1.00 2.00
41 Cloyster R 1.25 2.50
42 Krabby C .75 1.50
43 Krabby C 7.50 15.00
44 Kingler U .50 1.00
45 Goldeen C 25.00 50.00
46 Goldeen C 2.50 5.00
47 Seaking U 1.25 2.50
48 Lapras R 1.25 2.50
49 Lapras V URR .10 .20
50 Lapras VMAX URR 1.50 4.00
51 Qwilfish U .75 2.00
52 Mantine U 2.00 4.00
53 Keldeo V URR .75 1.50
54 Sobble C .75 1.50
55 Sobble C .75 1.50
56 Drizzile U .60 1.25
57 Drizzile U 3.00 6.00
58 Inteleon HOLO R 1.50 3.00
59 Inteleon R 1.25 3.00
60 Chewtle C .75 1.50
61 Drednaw R 4.00 8.00
62 Cramorant R 2.00 5.00
63 Snom C .50 1.25
64 Frosmoth HOLO R 2.00 4.00
65 Pikachu C 15.00 40.00
66 Raichu R .60 1.50
67 Chinchou C .08 .20
68 Chinchou C .30 .60
69 Lanturn R .75 1.50
70 Joltik C 1.50 3.00
71 Galvantula U 2.00 4.00
72 Tapu Koko V URR 2.50 5.00
73 Yamper C .60 1.25
74 Yamper C .75 1.50
75 Boltund HOLO R .75 1.50
76 Boltund HOLO R 1.50 3.00
77 Pincurchin C 2.00 4.00
78 Morpeko R 2.50 5.00
79 Morpeko V URR .60 1.25
80 Morpeko VMAX URR 1.00 2.00
81 Galarian Ponyta C .75 1.50
82 Galarian Rapidash R 1.00 2.00
83 Gastly C .50 1.00
84 Haunter U 1.00 2.00
85 Gengar HOLO R 1.25 2.50
86 Wobbuffet V URR 1.25 2.50
87 Munna C 1.00 2.00
88 Musharna R 1.25 2.50
89 Sinistea C 10.00 20.00
90 Polteageist R 1.50 3.00
91 Indeedee V URR .75 1.50
92 Diglett C .75 1.50
93 Dugtrio U .60 1.25
94 Hitmonlee U .75 1.50
95 Hitmonchan U 1.25 2.50
96 Rhyhorn C 15.00 30.00
97 Rhyhorn C .15 .30
98 Rhydon U .20 .50
99 Rhyperior HOLO R 25.00 50.00

100 Sudowoodo U .60 1.25
101 Baltoy C 1.00 2.00
102 Baltoy C .60 1.25
103 Claydol R 50.00 100.00
104 Regirock V URR .75 1.50
105 Mudbray C 1.25 2.50
106 Mudsdale R 1.00 2.00
107 Silicobra C .75 1.50
108 Silicobra C .75 1.50
109 Sandaconda R .12 .25
110 Sandaconda HOLO R .60 1.25
111 Clobbopus C .50 1.00
112 Clobbopus C .07 .15
113 Grapploct R .75 1.50
114 Stonjourner R 1.50 3.00
115 Stonjourner V URR .75 1.50
116 Stonjourner VMAX URR 4.00 8.00
117 Galarian Zigzagoon C 1.00 2.00
118 Galarian Linoone U .75 1.50
119 Galarian Obstagoon HOLO R 1.50 3.00
120 Sableye V URR 1.25 2.50
121 Skorupi C 10.00 20.00
122 Drapion R .60 1.25
123 Croagunk C 5.00 10.00
124 Toxicroak HOLO R .75 1.50
125 Nickit C .75 1.50
126 Thievul R 1.25 2.50
127 Galarian Meowth C 1.25 2.50
128 Galarian Perrserker HOLO R .30 .60
129 Mawile C 1.50 3.00
130 Ferroseed C 6.00 12.00
131 Ferrothorn U .50 1.00
132 Galarian Stunfisk U 1.25 3.00
133 Pawniard C 1.00 2.00
134 Bisharp U .75 1.50
135 Corviknight R 1.00 2.00
136 Cufant C 3.00 6.00
137 Copperajah HOLO R 2.00 4.00
138 Zacian V URR .60 1.25
139 Zamazenta V URR 1.50 3.00
140 Snorlax R .08 .20
141 Snorlax V URR 1.00 2.00
142 Snorlax VMAX URR 1.50 3.00
143 Hoothoot C 1.00 2.50
144 Noctowl R .75 2.00
145 Minccino C .25 .50
146 Minccino C .04 .10
147 Cinccino R .08 .20
148 Oranguru HOLO R 1.25 2.50
149 Drampa R .75 1.50
150 Rookidee C 2.00 4.00
151 Corvisquire U .60 1.25
152 Wooloo C .30 .60
153 Wooloo C .75 1.50
154 Dubwool U 1.00 2.00
155 Cramorant V URR 1.00 2.00
156 Air Balloon U 1.25 2.50
157 Bede U 2.00 4.00
158 Big Charm U 2.00 4.00
159 Crushing Hammer U 2.00 4.00
160 Energy Retrieval U 1.25 2.50
161 Energy Search U .75 1.50
162 Energy Switch U .08 .20
163 Evolution Incense U .10 .25
164 Great Ball U 1.00 2.00
165 Hop U 2.50 5.00
166 Hyper Potion U .30 .60
167 Lucky Egg U 20.00 40.00
168 Lum Berry U .75 1.50
169 Marnie HOLO R .75 1.50
170 Metal Saucer U 2.50 6.00
171 Ordinary Rod U 1.00 2.50
172 Pal Pad U 2.00 4.00
173 Poké Kid U 8.00 20.00
174 Pokégear 3.0 U .07 .15
175 Pokémon Catcher U 1.50 3.00
176 Pokémon Center Lady U .01 .08
177 Potion U .05 .12
178 Professor's Research HOLO R 1.00 2.00
179 Quick Ball U 2.00 4.00
180 Rare Candy U 1.25 2.50
181 Rotom Bike U .60 1.25
182 Sitrus Berry U 1.50 3.00
183 Switch U 2.50 5.00
184 Team Yell Grunt U 2.50 5.00
185 Vitality Band U .30 .60
186 Aurora Energy U .75 1.50
187 Dhelmise V FULL ART UR .12 .25
188 Torkoal V FULL ART UR .75 1.50
189 Lapras V FULL ART UR 1.50 3.00
190 Morpeko V FULL ART UR 1.50 4.00
191 Wobbuffet V FULL ART UR .01 .08
192 Indeedee V FULL ART UR .01 .08
193 Stonjourner V FULL ART UR .60 1.25
194 Sableye V FULL ART UR 1.50 3.00
195 Zacian V FULL ART UR 1.25 2.50
196 Zamazenta V FULL ART UR .75 1.50
197 Snorlax V FULL ART UR .75 1.50
198 Cramorant V FULL ART UR 1.25 2.50
199 Bede FULL ART UR 1.00 2.00
200 Marnie FULL ART UR 2.00 4.00
201 Professor's Research FULL ART UR 6.00 12.00
202 Team Yell Grunt FULL ART UR .75 1.50
203 Lapras VMAX SCR 1.00 2.00
204 Morpeko VMAX SCR 10.00 20.00
205 Stonjourner VMAX SCR .75 1.50
206 Snorlax VMAX SCR .75 1.50
207 Bede SCR 1.25 2.50
208 Marnie SCR .07 .15
209 Professor's Research SCR .75 1.50
210 Team Yell Grunt SCR 1.00 2.00
211 Zacian V SCR .75 1.50
212 Zamazenta V SCR .75 1.50
213 Air Balloon SCR 30.00 75.00
214 Metal Saucer SCR 12.50 25.00
215 Ordinary Rod SCR .60 1.25
216 Quick Ball SCR .60 1.25

2020 Pokemon Sword and Shield Champion's Path

1 Venusaur V URR 1.25 2.50
2 Weedle C 17.50 35.00
3 Kakuna C 1.25 2.50
4 Beedrill U 1.00 2.00
5 Eldegoss V URR 1.50 3.00
6 Vulpix C .60 1.25
7 Victini U .75 1.50
8 Incineroar V URR 17.50 35.00
9 Sizzlipede C 1.50 3.00
10 Centiskorch HOLO R .75 1.50
11 Carvanha C .60 1.25
12 Sharpedo U .75 1.50
13 Wailord V URR 1.00 2.00
14 Drednaw V URR 60.00 125.00
15 Drednaw VMAX URR .60 1.25
16 Gardevoir V URR .75 1.50
17 Gardevoir VMAX URR .10 .20
18 Hatenna C 1.00 2.00
19 Hattrem U 2.50 5.00
20 Hatterene HOLO R 3.00 6.00
21 Galarian Cursola V URR .75 1.50
22 Alcremie V URR .60 1.25
23 Alcremie VMAX URR .75 1.50
24 Machop C 12.50 25.00
25 Machoke U .75 1.50
26 Machamp HOLO R .75 1.50
27 Lucario V URR 1.50 3.00
28 Zygarde HOLO R .75 1.50
29 Rockruff C 1.25 2.50
30 Lycanroc HOLO R .75 1.50
31 Rolycoly C .07 .15
32 Grapploct V URR .75 1.50
33 Ekans C .60 1.25
34 Arbok U .60 1.25
35 Galarian Zigzagoon C 2.00 4.00
36 Galarian Linoone C .75 1.50
37 Galarian Obstagoon HOLO R 1.25 2.50
38 Absol U 3.00 6.00
39 Purrloin C 1.00 2.00
40 Liepard U .01 .08
41 Scraggy C .04 .10
42 Scrafty HOLO R 1.25 2.50
43 Trubbish C 7.50 15.00
44 Inkay C .75 1.50
45 Malamar U .10 .20
46 Nickit C .12 .30
47 Duraludon V URR .75 1.50
48 Swablu C .25 .50
49 Altaria HOLO R .60 1.25
50 Bede U 3.00 8.00
51 Full Heal C .75 2.00
52 Great Ball U .75 1.50
53 Hop U .08 .20
54 Hyper Potion U .04 .10
55 Kabu U 3.00 6.00
56 Marnie HOLO R .75 1.50
57 Milo U .75 1.50
58 Piers U .75 1.50
59 Poké Ball C .75 1.50
60 Pokémon Center Lady U .75 1.50
61 Potion C 3.00 6.00
62 Professor's Research HOLO R 1.25 2.50
63 Rotom Bike U .75 1.50
64 Rotom Phone U 1.00 2.00
65 Sonia U 1.50 3.00
66 Suspicious Food Tin U 3.00 6.00
67 Team Yell Grunt U 20.00 40.00
68 Turffield Stadium U 150.00 300.00
69 Drednaw V UR FULL ART .75 1.50
70 Gardevoir V UR FULL ART .75 1.50
71 Galarian Cursola V UR FULL ART .10 .20
72 Grapploct V UR FULL ART .30 .60
73 Hop UR FULL ART .75 1.50
74 Charizard VMAX SCR .75 1.50
75 Drednaw VMAX SCR 2.00 4.00
76 Gardevoir VMAX SCR 2.00 4.00
77 Kabu SCR 1.50 3.00
78 Piers SCR .60 1.25
79 Charizard V SCR 1.00 2.00
80 Suspicious Food Tin SCR .25 .50

2020 Pokemon Sword and Shield Darkness Ablaze

1 Butterfree V URR 12.50 25.00
2 Butterfree VMAX URR 1.25 2.50
3 Paras C 1.00 2.00
4 Parasect U 30.00 75.00
5 Carnivine U 1.50 3.00
6 Pansage C .75 1.50
7 Simisage U .50 1.00
8 Karrablast C 1.25 2.50
9 Shelmet C 1.25 2.50
10 Accelgor R 15.00 30.00
11 Rowlet C 40.00 80.00
12 Dartrix U 1.25 2.50
13 Decidueye HOLO R 3.00 6.00
14 Bounsweet C .07 .15
15 Steenee U 1.00 2.00
16 Tsareena R .75 1.50
17 Wimpod C 1.50 3.00
18 Golisopod HOLO R 1.25 2.50
19 Charizard V URR 2.00 4.00
20 Charizard VMAX URR .08 .20
21 Houndoom V URR .05 .12
22 Torchic C 15.00 30.00
23 Combusken U 3.00 6.00
24 Blaziken HOLO R .07 .15
25 Heatran HOLO R .75 1.50
26 Pansear C 1.25 2.50
27 Simisear U .08 .20
28 Galarian Darmanitan R .75 1.50
29 Larvesta C 1.25 2.50
30 Volcarona R .60 1.25
31 Fletchinder U 1.00 2.00
32 Talonflame R 1.25 2.50
33 Centiskorch V URR .75 1.50
34 Centiskorch VMAX URR .75 1.50
35 Galarian Mr. Mime C 1.50 3.00
36 Galarian Mr. Rime R .60 1.25
37 Suicune HOLO R .75 1.50
38 Feebas C 10.00 20.00
39 Milotic HOLO R 1.25 2.50
40 Relicanth U 1.00 2.00
41 Panpour C 2.50 5.00
42 Simipour U 2.00 4.00
43 Galarian Darumaka C 1.00 2.00
44 Galarian Darmanitan R .75 1.50
45 Vanillite C 1.50 3.00
46 Vanillish U 2.00 4.00
47 Vanilluxe R 1.00 2.50
48 Cubchoo C .75 1.50
49 Beartic R .01 .08
50 Wishiwashi C .04 .10
51 Mareanie C 1.00 2.00
52 Toxapex U 3.00 6.00
53 Dracovish HOLO R .07 .15
54 Arctovish R .12 .30
55 Mareep C .07 .15
56 Flaaffy U 1.50 3.00
57 Ampharos R .60 1.25
58 Electrike C 2.00 4.00
59 Manectric R .75 1.50
60 Vikavolt V URR 150.00 300.00
61 Tapu Koko HOLO R 3.00 6.00
62 Toxel C .12 .25
63 Toxtricity HOLO R 2.00 4.00
64 Pincurchin HOLO R 1.25 3.00
65 Dracozolt R .30 .60
66 Arctozolt HOLO R .01 .08
67 Jigglypuff C .04 .10
68 Wigglytuff R 2.50 5.00
69 Mew V URR 1.00 2.00
70 Snubbull C .75 1.50
71 Granbull R 1.50 3.00
72 Lunatone U .75 1.50
73 Gothita C .60 1.25
74 Gothorita U 7.50 15.00
75 Gothitelle R 1.00 2.00
76 Golett C 2.50 5.00
77 Golurk R .75 1.50
78 Dedenne U .75 1.50
79 Morelull C 15.00 30.00
80 Shiinotic U 1.25 2.50
81 Mimikyu R .08 .20
82 Sinistea C .15 .40
8.30E+01 Polteageist U .75 1.50
8.40E+01 Diglett C 1.50 3.00
8.50E+01 Dugtrio U 4.00 8.00
8.60E+01 Larvitar C .75 1.50
8.70E+01 Pupitar U .60 1.25
8.80E+01 Tyranitar HOLO R 1.25 2.50
8.90E+01 Trapinch C 1.25 2.50
9.00E+01 Vibrava U 30.00 75.00
91 Flygon R .60 1.25
92 Solrock U 2.50 5.00
93 Hippopotas C .75 1.50
94 Hippowdon R 2.00 4.00
95 Rhyperior V URR 1.00 2.00
96 Diggersby R 7.50 15.00
97 Passimian C .75 1.50
98 Galarian Sirfetch'd R 7.50 15.00
99 Galarian Slowbro V URR 20.00 40.00
100 Grimer C .75 2.00
101 Muk R 7.50 15.00
102 Spinarak C 1.50 3.00
103 Ariados U 1.25 2.50
104 Crobat V URR .75 1.50
105 Darkrai HOLO R 1.00 2.00
106 Purrloin C .60 1.25
107 Liepard R .75 1.50
108 Deino C .75 1.50
109 Zweilous U .10 .20
110 Hydreigon R 1.00 2.00
111 Hoopa HOLO R .75 1.50
112 Nickit C 1.25 2.50
113 Thievul R .60 1.25
114 Grimmsnarl V URR .50 1.00
115 Grimmsnarl VMAX URR .50 1.25
116 Eternatus V URR .20 .50
117 Eternatus VMAX URR 2.00 4.00
118 Scizor V URR 8.00 20.00
119 Scizor VMAX URR .75 1.50
120 Skarmory C 12.50 25.00
121 Aron C 1.00 2.00
122 Lairon U 1.00 2.00
123 Aggron HOLO R .07 .15
124 Escavalier R 12.50 25.00
125 Klink C 1.25 2.50
126 Klang U 2.50 5.00
127 Klinklang R .75 1.50
128 Galarian Stunfisk V URR .30 .60
129 Meltan C .25 .50
130 Melmetal R .01 .08
131 Cufant C .08 .20
132 Copperajah HOLO R 4.00 8.00
133 Kangaskhan HOLO R .08 .20
134 Tauros C .08 .20
135 Sentret C .75 1.50
136 Furret U .10 .20
137 Dunsparce C .75 1.50
138 Teddiursa C .75 1.50
139 Ursaring U 3.00 6.00
140 Lugia R .30 .60
141 Skitty C 1.50 3.00
142 Delcatty R 2.00 4.00
143 Salamence V URR .75 1.50
144 Salamence VMAX URR 2.50 5.00
145 Starly C .30 .60
146 Staravia U .50 1.00
147 Staraptor R 20.00 40.00
148 Ducklett C 1.00 2.00
149 Swanna R .75 1.50
150 Bunnelby C 1.00 2.00
151 Fletchling C .08 .20
152 Skwovet C 1.25 2.50
153 Greedent R 1.00 2.00
154 Rookidee C 2.50 5.00
155 Corvisquire U 10.00 20.00
156 Corviknight HOLO R 3.00 6.00
157 Big Parasol U .75 2.00
158 Billowing Smoke U 1.25 2.50
159 Bird Keeper U .01 .08
160 Cape of Toughness U .04 .10
161 Familiar Bell U .75 1.50
162 Glimwood Tangle U 1.25 2.50
163 Kabu U 1.25 2.50
164 Old PC U 3.00 8.00
165 Piers U 2.00 4.00
166 Pokemon Breeder's Nurturing U 1.00 2.00
167 Rare Fossil U .01 .08
168 Rose U .04 .10
169 Rose Tower U 1.00 2.00
170 Spikemuth U .07 .15
171 Struggle Gloves U .20 .50
172 Turbo Patch U 2.50 5.00
173 Yell Horn U 12.50 25.00
174 Heat Energy U 20.00 40.00
175 Hiding Energy U 25.00 50.00
176 Powerful Energy U 200.00 400.00
177 Butterfree V UR FULL ART .75 1.50
178 Houndoom V UR FULL ART .75 1.50
179 Centiskorch V UR FULL ART .75 1.50
180 Vikavolt V UR FULL ART .60 1.50
181 Rhyperior V UR FULL ART 3.00 6.00
182 Crobat V UR FULL ART .30 .60
183 Scizor V UR FULL ART .75 1.50
184 Galarian Stunfisk V UR FULL ART 2.00 4.00
185 Salamence V UR FULL ART .75 1.50
186 Kabu UR FULL ART .75 1.50
187 Piers UR FULL ART 1.25 2.50
188 Pokemon Breeder's Nurturing UR FULL ART1.25 2.50
189 Rose UR FULL ART 1.25 2.50
190 Butterfree VMAX SCR 5.00 10.00
191 Centiskorch VMAX SCR 3.00 6.00
192 Eternatus VMAX SCR .60 1.25
193 Scizor VMAX SCR .75 1.50
194 Salamence VMAX SCR .75 1.50
195 Pokemon Breeder's Nurturing SCR 1.50 3.00
196 Rose SCR 1.25 2.50
197 Rillaboom SCR .60 1.25
198 Coalossal SCR .75 1.50
199 Big Parasol SCR .75 1.50
200 Turbo Patch SCR 6.00 12.00
201 Capture Energy SCR 2.00 4.00

2020 Pokemon Sword and Shield Rebel Clash

1 Caterpie C .75 1.50
2 Metapod U .75 1.50
3 Butterfree R .75 1.50
4 Scyther C 1.25 2.50
5 Shuckle U .60 1.25
6 Heracross U 1.00 2.00
7 Lotad C .75 1.50
8 Lombre U 1.25 2.50
9 Ludicolo R .75 1.50
10 Surskit C 1.50 3.00
11 Masquerain U .75 1.50
12 Snover C .60 1.25
13 Abomasnow R 4.00 8.00
14 Phantump C .75 1.50
15 Trevenant R 17.50 35.00
16 Grubbin C 1.50 3.00
17 Rillaboom V URR 10.00 20.00
18 Rillaboom VMAX URR 1.00 2.00
19 Eldegoss V URR .75 1.50
20 Applin C 20.00 40.00
21 Applin C 50.00 100.00
22 Flapple HOLO R 1.00 2.00
23 Appletun HOLO R 25.00 50.00
24 Vulpix C 1.00 2.00
25 Ninetales R 7.50 15.00
26 Ninetales V URR .60 1.25
27 Growlithe C 3.00 6.00
28 Arcanine R 3.00 6.00
29 Magmar C 1.00 2.00
30 Magmortar R 2.00 4.00
31 Litwick C .50 1.25
32 Lampent U .60 1.25
33 Chandelure HOLO R 2.00 4.00
34 Heatmor U .10 .20
35 Cinderace V URR .75 1.50
36 Cinderace VMAX URR 1.00 2.00
37 Galarian Mr. Mime C 2.00 4.00
38 Galarian Mr. Rime R .60 1.25
39 Magikarp C 1.50 3.00
40 Gyarados HOLO R .25 .60
41 Wingull C .15 .40
42 Pelipper U 2.00 4.00
43 Milotic V URR 6.00 15.00
44 Tympole C 1.00 2.00
45 Palpitoad U .75 1.50
46 Seismitoad R .60 1.25
47 Galarian Darumaka C .75 1.50
48 Galarian Darmanitan R 1.50 3.00
49 Inteleon V URR 1.25 2.50
50 Inteleon VMAX URR .60 1.25
51 Cramorant R 2.00 5.00
52 Arrokuda C 1.00 2.50
53 Barraskewda R 4.00 8.00
54 Eiscue HOLO R .20 .50
55 Eiscue V URR 7.50 15.00
56 Voltorb C 7.50 15.00
57 Electrode U .60 1.25
58 Electabuzz C .30 .60
59 Electivire R .07 .15

60 Shinx C 12.50 25.00
61 Luxio U 75.00 150.00
62 Luxray HOLO R .60 1.25
63 Helioptile C .60 1.25
64 Heliolisk U 1.50 3.00
65 Charjabug U .75 1.50
66 Vikavolt HOLO R 2.00 4.00
67 Boltund V URR 2.50 6.00
68 Toxel C .75 1.50
69 Toxtricity R .75 1.50
70 Toxtricity V URR 1.50 3.00
71 Toxtricity VMAX URR .20 .40
72 Pincurchin V URR .15 .40
73 Morpeko U 1.25 2.50
74 Clefairy C 20.00 40.00
75 Clefable HOLO R .75 1.50
76 Natu C .10 .20
77 Xatu U 7.50 15.00
78 Galarian Corsola C 2.00 4.00
79 Galarian Cursola HOLO R .30 .75
80 Sigilyph R 7.50 15.00
81 Sandygast C .75 1.50
82 Palossand U .08 .20
83 Hatenna C .04 .10
84 Hattrem U .04 .10
85 Hatterene HOLO R .60 1.25
86 Milcery C .07 .15
87 Alcremie R 1.00 2.00
88 Indeedee U 1.00 2.00
89 Dreepy C 1.25 2.50
90 Drakloak U .75 1.50
91 Dragapult HOLO R 1.00 2.00
92 Dragapult V URR .08 .20
93 Dragapult VMAX URR .04 .10
94 Galarian Farfetch'd C .60 1.25
95 Galarian Sirfetch'd HOLO R .75 1.50
96 Nosepass C 1.00 2.00
97 Meditite C 1.50 3.00
98 Medicham U .75 1.50
99 Barboach C .60 1.25
100 Whiscash R .07 .15
101 Galarian Yamask C .75 1.50
102 Galarian Runerigus R 1.50 3.00
103 Binacle C .75 1.50
104 Barbaracle R 1.00 2.00
105 Rolycoly C 1.25 2.50
106 Carkol U 1.25 2.50
107 Coalossal HOLO R 15.00 30.00
108 Sandaconda V URR 15.00 30.00
109 Falinks U .60 1.25
110 Falinks V URR .75 1.50
111 Stonjourner HOLO R 7.50 15.00
112 Koffing C 15.00 30.00
113 Galarian Weezing HOLO R 15.00 30.00
114 Stunky C 20.00 40.00
115 Skuntank U 30.00 60.00
116 Spiritomb R .75 1.50
117 Trubbish C 10.00 20.00
118 Garbodor R 1.50 3.00
119 Vullaby C 1.50 3.00
120 Mandibuzz R 1.00 2.00
121 Malamar V URR .12 .30
122 Malamar VMAX URR .25 .60
123 Impidimp C 1.50 3.00
124 Morgrem U .50 1.25
125 Grimmsnarl HOLO R .25 .50
126 Galarian Meowth C .01 .08
127 Galarian Perrserker R .40 1.00
128 Scizor R 1.50 3.00
129 Bronzor C .50 1.00
130 Bronzong U .60 1.25
131 Probopass R .75 1.50
132 Durant U .50 1.00
133 Honedge C .75 1.50
134 Doublade U 1.00 2.00
135 Aegislash R .75 1.50
136 Copperajah V URR .60 1.25
137 Copperajah VMAX URR 1.25 2.50
138 Duraludon HOLO R 3.00 6.00
139 Zacian R 5.00 10.00
140 Zamazenta R 1.50 3.00
141 Snorlax R 1.00 2.00
142 Chatot U 10.00 20.00
143 Pidove C 2.50 5.00
144 Tranquill U .75 1.50
145 Unfezant R 1.00 2.00
146 Bunnelby C 1.00 2.50
147 Diggersby R 1.00 2.50
148 Hawlucha U .07 .15
149 Stufful C 3.00 6.00
150 Bewear U 2.00 4.00
151 Skwovet C 4.00 10.00
152 Greedent R 5.00 10.00
153 Dubwool V URR .75 1.50
154 Boss's Orders HOLO R 1.25 2.50
155 Burning Scarf U .60 1.25
156 Capacious Bucket U .75 1.50
157 Cursed Shovel U .75 1.50
158 Dan U .30 .60
159 Full Heal U 1.00 2.00
160 Galar Mine U 7.50 15.00
161 Milo U 30.00 75.00
162 Nugget U 1.25 2.50
163 Oleana U 30.00 60.00
164 Poke Ball U .50 1.25
165 Scoop Up Net U .20 .50
166 Skyla U 2.00 4.00
167 Sonia U 10.00 25.00
168 Tool Scrapper U .75 1.50
169 Training Court U .60 1.25
170 Turffield Stadium U .60 1.25
171 Capture Energy U 1.00 2.00
172 Horror P Energy U 7.50 15.00
173 Speed L Energy U .75 1.50
174 Twin Energy U 1.00 2.00
175 Rillaboom V UR FULL ART .60 1.25
176 Eldegoss V UR FULL ART 1.25 2.50
177 Ninetales V UR FULL ART .60 1.25
178 Cinderace V UR FULL ART 2.00 4.00
179 Milotic V UR FULL ART .50 1.00
180 Inteleon V UR FULL ART 1.00 2.00
181 Boltund V UR FULL ART 75.00 150.00
182 Toxtricity V UR FULL ART 1.00 2.00
183 Dragapult V UR FULL ART .75 1.50
184 Sandaconda V UR FULL ART 15.00 30.00
185 Falinks V UR FULL ART 15.00 30.00
186 Malamar V UR FULL ART 3.00 6.00
187 Copperajah V UR FULL ART .12 .25
188 Dubwool V UR FULL ART .75 1.50
189 Boss's Orders UR FULL ART 1.50 3.00
190 Milo UR FULL ART 12.50 25.00
191 Oleana UR FULL ART .60 1.25
192 Sonia UR FULL ART 15.00 30.00
193 Rillaboom VMAX SCR 3.00 6.00
194 Cinderace VMAX SCR .30 .75
195 Inteleon VMAX SCR .75 1.50
196 Toxtricity VMAX SCR 1.00 2.00
197 Dragapult VMAX SCR 4.00 10.00
198 Malamar VMAX SCR 2.50 6.00
199 Copperajah VMAX SCR 2.00 4.00
200 Boss's Orders SCR 10.00 25.00
201 Milo SCR 1.25 2.50
202 Oleana SCR .25 .50
203 Sonia SCR .01 .08
204 Frosmoth SCR .10 .25
205 Galarian Perrserker SCR .75 1.50
206 Big Charm SCR .60 1.25
207 Scoop Up Net SCR 1.00 2.00
208 Tool Scrapper SCR 1.00 2.00
209 Twin Energy SCR .05 .12

2020 Pokemon Sword and Shield Vivid Voltage

1 Weedle C 2.00 4.00
2 Kakuna U .50 1.00
3 Beedrill R 20.00 40.00
4 Exeggcute C .60 1.25
5 Exeggutor R 25.00 50.00
6 Yanma C 30.00 75.00
7 Yanmega R 60.00 125.00
8 Pineco C 25.00 50.00
9 Celebi AR .75 1.50
10 Seedot C 60.00 125.00
11 Nuzleaf U 4.00 10.00
12 Shiftry R .01 .08
13 Nincada C .01 .08
14 Ninjask R 1.25 2.50
15 Shaymin HOLO R .75 1.50
16 Genesect HOLO R 12.50 25.00
17 Skiddo C 20.00 40.00
18 Gogoat U .60 1.25
19 Dhelmise U .60 1.25
20 Orbeetle V URR .08 .20
21 Orbeetle VMAX URR 4.00 8.00
22 Zarude V URR 1.25 3.00
23 Charmander C .75 1.50
24 Charmeleon U .75 2.00
25 Charizard R .75 1.50
26 Flareon R .75 1.50
27 Slugma C 1.00 2.00
28 Magcargo U .12 .25
29 Talonflame V URR 2.50 5.00
30 Vaporeon R 1.00 2.00
31 Wailmer C 1.50 3.00
32 Wailord HOLO R 1.00 2.00
33 Oshawott C 6.00 12.00
34 Dewott U .30 .60
35 Samurott R 3.00 6.00
36 Galarian Darmanitan V URR 1.50 3.00
37 Galarian Darmanitan VMAX URR .30 .75
38 Chewtle C .20 .50
39 Drednaw R 25.00 50.00
40 Cramorant U 1.25 2.50
41 Arrokuda C 1.50 3.00
42 Barraskewda R 5.00 12.00
43 Pikachu V URR .12 .25
44 Pikachu VMAX URR 4.00 8.00
45 Voltorb C 50.00 100.00
46 Electrode HOLO R 1.50 3.00
47 Jolteon R .75 1.50
48 Zapdos HOLO R .75 1.50
49 Ampharos V URR 2.00 4.00
50 Raikou AR 2.00 4.00
51 Electrike C .75 1.50
52 Manectric R 20.00 40.00
53 Blitzle C .50 1.00
54 Zebstrika U .60 1.25
55 Joltik C .20 .40
56 Galvantula U 3.00 6.00
57 Tynamo C 1.00 2.00
58 Eelektrik U .60 1.25
59 Eelektross R .60 1.25
60 Zekrom HOLO R .07 .15
61 Zeraora HOLO R .40 1.00
62 Pincurchin U .20 .50
63 Clefairy C .75 1.50
64 Clefable R 3.00 8.00
65 Girafarig U .75 1.50
66 Shedinja R 1.25 2.50
67 Shuppet C 1.25 2.50
68 Banette R .75 1.50
69 Duskull C 1.00 2.00
70 Dusclops U 75.00 150.00
71 Dusknoir HOLO R .50 1.00
72 Chimecho C .75 1.50
73 Woobat C .10 .20
74 Swoobat U .07 .15
75 Cottonee C 2.50 5.00
76 Whimsicott R 1.25 2.50
77 Dedenne C 1.25 2.50
78 Xerneas HOLO R 15.00 30.00
79 Diancie HOLO R 7.50 15.00
80 Milcery C .75 1.50
81 Alcremie R .50 1.25
82 Zacian AR 1.25 2.50
83 Wooper C 2.00 4.00
84 Quagsire R .75 1.50
85 Shuckle U 15.00 30.00
86 Phanpy C .75 2.00
87 Donphan R .25 .50
88 Hitmontop U .01 .08
89 Regirock HOLO R .05 .12
90 Riolu C 40.00 80.00
91 Drilbur C 7.50 15.00
92 Terrakion HOLO R .60 1.25
93 Zygarde HOLO R .75 1.50
94 Rockruff C 1.50 3.00
95 Lycanroc R 20.00 40.00
96 Mudbray C 1.00 2.00
97 Mudsdale R .60 1.25
98 Coalossal V URR 3.00 6.00
99 Coalossal VMAX URR .60 1.25
100 Clobbopus C 1.25 2.50
101 Grapploct R .75 1.50
102 Zamazenta AR .08 .20
103 Poochyena C .75 1.50
104 Mightyena U .75 1.50
105 Sableye U .60 1.25
106 Drapion V URR 25.00 50.00
107 Sandile C 30.00 75.00
108 Krokorok U 25.00 50.00
109 Krookodile R .75 1.50
110 Trubbish C 60.00 125.00
111 Garbodor R 1.00 2.50
112 Galarian Meowth C .75 1.50
113 Galarian Perrserker R 20.00 40.00
114 Forretress R 10.00 20.00
115 Steelix V URR .75 1.50
116 Beldum C .01 .08
117 Metang U .10 .25
118 Metagross R .01 .08
119 Jirachi AR .12 .30
120 Lucario R .30 .75
121 Dialga HOLO R .60 1.25
122 Excadrill U 1.00 2.00
123 Ferroseed C .50 1.00
124 Ferrothorn U 1.25 2.50
125 Galarian Stunfisk U 1.25 2.50
126 Aegislash V URR 1.50 3.00
127 Aegislash VMAX URR 20.00 40.00
128 Magearna HOLO R .75 1.50
129 Duraludon HOLO R 4.00 8.00
130 Eevee C .75 1.50
131 Snorlax HOLO R 1.00 2.50
132 Lugia HOLO R 25.00 50.00
133 Taillow C .60 1.25
134 Swellow U 2.50 5.00
135 Whismur C 3.00 6.00
136 Loudred U .75 1.50
137 Exploud R .60 1.25
138 Rayquaza AR 12.50 25.00
139 Chatot C 1.25 2.50
140 Togekiss V URR .30 .60
141 Togekiss VMAX URR .75 1.50
142 Tornadus HOLO R .75 1.50
143 Pikipek C 7.50 15.00
144 Trumbeak U .50 1.00
145 Toucannon R 1.00 2.00
146 Allister U 1.00 2.00
147 Bea U 125.00 250.00
148 Beauty U .60 1.25
149 Cara Liss U .30 .75
150 Circhester Bath U .30 .75
151 Drone Rotom U .50 1.00
152 Hero's Medal U 4.00 10.00
153 League Staff U 30.00 60.00
154 Leon HOLO R 2.00 4.00
155 Memory Capsule U 1.25 2.50
156 Moomoo Cheese U .50 1.00
157 Nessa U .75 1.50
158 Opal U 7.50 15.00
159 Rocky Helmet U .75 1.50
160 Telescopic Sight U .10 .20
161 Wyndon Stadium U .75 1.50
162 Aromatic Grass Energy U 20.00 40.00
163 Coating Metal Energy U 7.50 15.00
164 Stone Fighting Energy U 15.00 30.00
165 Wash Water Energy U 20.00 40.00
166 Orbeetle V UR FULL ART .20 .40
167 Zarude V UR FULL ART .50 1.00
168 Talonflame V UR FULL ART 1.00 2.00
169 Galarian Darmanitan V UR FULL ART 3.00 6.00
170 Pikachu V UR FULL ART 5.00 10.00
171 Ampharos V UR FULL ART 1.00 2.00
172 Alakazam V UR FULL ART 1.25 2.50
173 Coalossal V UR FULL ART 1.25 2.50
174 Galarian Sirfetch'd V UR FULL ART 1.25 2.50
175 Drapion V UR FULL ART 2.50 5.00
176 Steelix V UR FULL ART .60 1.25
177 Aegislash V UR FULL ART 1.25 2.50
178 Togekiss V UR FULL ART 1.25 2.50
179 Allister UR FULL ART 3.00 6.00
180 Bea UR FULL ART 1.50 3.00
181 Beauty UR FULL ART .50 1.00
182 Leon UR FULL ART 1.00 2.00
183 Nessa UR FULL ART .50 1.25
184 Opal UR FULL ART .20 .50
185 Pokemon Center Lady UR FULL ART .75 1.50
186 Orbeetle VMAX SCR 4.00 10.00
187 Galarian Darmanitan VMAX SCR .08 .20
188 Pikachu VMAX SCR .75 1.50
189 Coalossal VMAX SCR .75 1.50
190 Aegislash VMAX SCR 1.25 2.50
191 Togekiss VMAX SCR .01 .08
192 Allister SCR .04 .10
193 Bea SCR 1.00 2.00
194 Beauty SCR 1.25 2.50
195 Leon SCR .30 .75
196 Nessa SCR 2.00 4.00
197 Opal SCR 1.00 2.00
198 Galarian Obstagoon SCR .25 .50
199 Oranguru SCR .08 .20
200 Cape of Toughness SCR .50 1.25
201 Hero's Medal SCR 20.00 40.00
202 Memory Capsule SCR 75.00 150.00
203 Telescopic Sight SCR 1.25 2.50

2021 Pokemon Celebrations

1 Ho-Oh R .08 .20
2 Reshiram R 1.50 3.00
3 Kyogre R 30.00 60.00
4 Palkia R .75 1.50
5 Pikachu HOLO R .60 1.25
6 Flying Pikachu V URR .75 1.50
7 Flying Pikachu VMAX R 1.50 3.00
8 Surfing Pikachu V URR 2.00 5.00
9 Surfing Pikachu VMAX R .04 .10
10 Zekrom R .05 .12
11 Mew HOLO R .25 .50
12 Xerneas R 2.00 4.00
13 Cosmog R 15.00 30.00
14 Cosmoem R 3.00 8.00
15 Lunala HOLO R .75 1.50
16 Zacian V URR .75 1.50
17 Groudon R .75 1.50
18 Zamazenta V URR 25.00 50.00
19 Yveltal R .75 1.50
20 Dialga R 15.00 30.00
21 Solgaleo HOLO R 1.25 2.50
22 Lugia R 1.00 2.00
23 Professor's Research HOLO R .60 1.25
24 Professor's Research UR .50 1.00
25 Mew SCR 2.00 4.00

2021 Pokemon Celebrations Classic Collection Confetti Holofoil

2 Blastoise HOLO R .25 .50
4 Charizard HOLO R .08 .20
8 Dark Gyarados HOLO R .75 2.00
9 Team Magma's Groudon HOLO R .75 1.50
15 Venusaur HOLO R .75 1.50
15 Here Comes Team Rocket! HOLO R .75 1.50
15 Rocket's Zapdos HOLO R .07 .15
15 Claydol R .75 1.50
17 Umbreon Star R .75 1.50
20 Cleffa R .75 1.50
24 ____'s Pikachu 1.25 2.50
54 Mewtwo EX URR 1.00 2.00
60 Tapu Lele GX URR 1.00 2.00
66 Shining Magikarp HOLO R .75 1.50
73 Imposter Professor Oak R 1.00 2.00
76 M Rayquaza EX URR 3.00 6.00
86 Rocket's Admin. U 7.50 15.00
88 Mew EX HOLO R .75 1.50
93 Gardevoir EX D HOLO R 2.00 4.00
97 Xerneas EX URR .60 1.25
107 Donphan HOLO SR .75 1.50
109 Luxray GL LV.X HOLO R .08 .20
113 Reshiram UR 30.00 60.00
114 Zekrom UR 250.00 500.00
145 Garchomp C LV.X HOLO R 1.25 2.50

2021 Pokemon McDonald's Collection

1 Bulbasaur 7.50 15.00
2 Chikorita .75 1.50
3 Treecko 4.00 10.00
4 Turtwig 5.00 10.00
5 Snivy 3.00 6.00
6 Chespin 12.50 25.00
7 Rowlet 25.00 50.00
8 Grookey .60 1.25
9 Charmander 200.00 400.00
10 Cyndaquil 30.00 75.00
11 Torchic 12.50 25.00
12 Chimchar .40 1.00
13 Tepig 1.50 3.00
14 Fennekin .75 1.50
15 Litten 1.25 2.50
16 Scorbunny 30.00 60.00
17 Squirtle .08 .20
18 Totodile .04 .10
19 Mudkip 1.00 2.00
20 Piplup 1.00 2.00
21 Oshawott .01 .08
22 Froakie .01 .08
23 Popplio 12.50 25.00
24 Sobble 2.50 5.00
25 Pikachu 2.50 5.00

2021 Pokemon Sword and Shield Battle Styles

1 Bellsprout C .75 1.50
2 Weepinbell U .75 1.50
3 Victreebel R .60 1.25
4 Cacnea C 1.00 2.00
5 Cacturne U 1.50 3.00
6 Kricketune V URR 1.00 2.00
7 Cherubi C 1.00 2.00
8 Cherrim R .50 1.25
9 Carnivine U .20 .50
10 Durant U .75 1.50
11 Scatterbug C 4.00 10.00
12 Spewpa U 1.00 2.00
13 Vivillon R .60 1.25
14 Fomantis C .75 1.50
15 Lurantis R 1.25 2.50
16 Tapu Bulu HOLO R .10 .20
17 Blipbug C 75.00 150.00
18 Flapple V URR 1.00 2.00
19 Flapple VMAX R 5.00 10.00
20 Entei HOLO R 1.25 2.50
21 Victini V URR 2.50 5.00
22 Victini VMAX R .75 1.50
23 Tepig C .75 1.50
24 Pignite U .10 .20
25 Emboar HOLO R .07 .15
26 Heatmor U 1.50 3.00

27 Salandit C .75 1.50
28 Salazzle R .75 1.50
29 Sizzlipede C .60 1.25
30 Centiskorch R 1.00 2.00
31 Horsea C 2.50 5.00
32 Seadra U 12.50 25.00
33 Kingdra HOLO R 3.00 6.00
34 Galarian Mr. Mime C .60 1.25
35 Galarian Mr. Rime R 1.00 2.00
36 Remoraid C .75 1.50
37 Octillery HOLO R 1.50 3.00
38 Corphish C 1.00 2.00
39 Crawdaunt U 4.00 10.00
40 Empoleon V URR 30.00 60.00
41 Frillish C 1.25 2.50
42 Jellicent R .60 1.25
43 Bruxish U 75.00 150.00
44 Electabuzz C .25 .50
45 Electivire R .01 .08
46 Shinx C .05 .12
47 Luxio U 30.00 75.00
48 Luxray HOLO R .50 1.00
49 Pachirisu C 7.50 15.00
50 Tapu Koko V URR .07 .15
51 Tapu Koko VMAX R 1.00 2.00
52 Yamper C .75 1.50
53 Boltund R 1.25 2.50
54 Galarian Slowpoke C .01 .08
55 Spoink C .10 .25
56 Grumpig U .10 .20
57 Baltoy C 1.25 2.50
58 Claydol R 17.50 35.00
59 Chimecho C 250.00 500.00
60 Espurr C .75 1.50
61 Meowstic HOLO R 3.00 6.00
62 Mimikyu V URR .60 1.25
63 Necrozma V URR .75 2.00
64 Dottler U .60 1.25
65 Orbeetle HOLO R .75 1.50
66 Mankey C 1.25 2.50
67 Primeape R .75 1.50
68 Onix C 4.00 8.00
69 Cubone C 1.25 2.50
70 Marowak R .75 1.50
71 Gligar C 2.00 4.00
72 Gliscor U 10.00 20.00
73 Timburr C 7.50 15.00
74 Gurdurr U 15.00 30.00
75 Conkeldurr R 5.00 12.00
76 Mienfoo C .08 .20
77 Mienshao R .05 .12
78 Rolycoly C 12.50 25.00
79 Carkol U .60 1.25
80 Coalossal HOLO R .75 1.50
81 Silicobra C 2.50 5.00
82 Sandaconda HOLO R .40 1.00
83 Falinks R 5.00 10.00
84 Stonjourner R 2.00 4.00
85 Single Strike Urshifu V URR .01 .08
86 Single Strike Urshifu VMAX R .05 .12
87 Rapid Strike Urshifu V URR .75 1.50
88 Rapid Strike Urshifu VMAX R 2.50 5.00
89 Zubat C 50.00 100.00
90 Golbat U 1.25 2.50
91 Crobat HOLO R .75 1.50
92 Galarian Slowbro R .75 1.50
93 Murkrow C .75 1.50
94 Honchkrow U 75.00 150.00
95 Houndour C 12.50 25.00
96 Houndoom HOLO R .75 1.50
97 Tyranitar V URR 1.00 2.00
98 Morpeko U .75 1.50
99 Steelix HOLO R 1.50 4.00
100 Mawile C 1.00 2.00
101 Bronzor C .07 .15
102 Bronzong HOLO R .60 1.25
103 Pawniard C .75 1.50
104 Bisharp U 1.00 2.00
105 Honedge C .60 1.25
106 Doublade U 3.00 6.00
107 Aegislash HOLO R 1.00 2.00
108 Aegislash R .60 1.25
109 Corviknight V URR 1.00 2.00
110 Corviknight VMAX R 1.50 3.00
111 Spearow C .60 1.25
112 Fearow U .07 .15
113 Lickitung C 1.25 2.50
114 Lickilicky R 7.50 15.00
115 Glameow C .75 1.50
116 Purugly U 1.00 2.00
117 Stoutland V URR .75 1.50
118 Bouffalant U .50 1.00
119 Drampa R 250.00 500.00
120 Indeedee U .30 .75
121 Bruno U 2.50 5.00
122 Camping Gear U .50 1.25
123 Cheryl U .20 .50
124 Energy Recycler U .75 1.50
125 Escape Rope U 5.00 12.00
126 Exp. Share U .75 1.50
127 Fan of Waves U 2.00 4.00
128 Korrina's Focus U .75 1.50
129 Level Ball U 1.25 2.50
130 Phoebe U 30.00 75.00
131 Rapid Strike Scroll of Swirls U .75 1.50
132 Rapid Strike Style Mustard U .75 1.50
133 Single Strike Scroll of Scorn U 25.00 50.00
134 Single Strike Style Mustard U .10 .20
135 Sordward and Shielbert U .60 1.25
136 Tool Jammer U .60 1.25
137 Tower of Darkness U 1.00 2.00
138 Tower of Waters U 2.00 4.00
139 Urn of Vitality U .60 1.25
140 Rapid Strike Energy U .75 1.50
141 Single Strike Energy U 1.00 2.00
142 Kricketune V UR FULL ART 1.25 2.50
143 Flapple V UR FULL ART 1.50 3.00
144 Victini V UR FULL ART 17.50 35.00
145 Empoleon V UR FULL ART .60 1.25
146 Empoleon V UR ALT FULL ART 7.50 15.00
147 Tapu Koko V UR FULL ART 2.50 5.00
148 Mimikyu V UR FULL ART 2.00 4.00
149 Necrozma V UR FULL ART .08 .20
150 Single Strike Urshifu V UR FULL ART 1.00 2.50
151 Single Strike Urshifu V UR ALT FULL ART 1.50 3.00
152 Rapid Strike Urshifu V UR FULL ART .60 1.25
153 Rapid Strike Urshifu V UR ALT ART .60 1.25
154 Tyranitar V UR FULL ART 30.00 60.00
155 Tyranitar V UR ALT FULL ART 8.00 20.00
156 Corviknight V UR FULL ART .10 .20
157 Stoutland V UR FULL ART .25 .50
158 Bruno UR FULL ART .04 .10
159 Cheryl UR FULL ART .40 1.00
160 Korrina's Focus UR FULL ART 20.00 40.00
161 Phoebe UR FULL ART .75 1.50
162 Rapid Strike Style Mustard UR FULL ART 1.25 2.50
163 Single Strike Style Mustard UR FULL ART 3.00 6.00
164 Flapple VMAX RAINBOW R .04 .10
165 Victini VMAX RAINBOW R .05 .12
166 Tapu Koko VMAX RAINBOW R 1.25 2.50
167 Single Strike Urshifu VMAX RAINBOW R .75 1.50
168 Single Strike Urshifu VMAX SCR ALT ART 6.00 12.00
169 Rapid Strike Urshifu VMAX RAINBOW R 30.00 60.00
170 Rapid Strike Urshifu VMAX SCR 5.00 10.00
171 Corviknight VMAX RAINBOW R .60 1.25
172 Bruno RAINBOW R .75 1.50
173 Cheryl RAINBOW R 1.25 2.50
174 Korrina's Focus RAINBOW R 1.00 2.00
175 Phoebe RAINBOW R 1.00 2.00
176 Rapid Strike Style Mustard RAINBOW R .75 1.50
177 Single Strike Style Mustard RAINBOW R 1.25 2.50
178 Octillery SCR 1.00 2.00
179 Houndoom SCR 7.50 15.00
180 Exp. Share SCR 250.00 500.00
181 Level Ball SCR .07 .15
182 Rapid Strike Energy SCR 2.50 5.00
183 Single Strike Energy SCR .08 .20

2021 Pokemon Sword and Shield Chilling Reign

1 Weedle C .75 1.50
2 Kakuna U .75 1.50
3 Beedrill HOLO R .60 1.25
4 Ledyba C 5.00 12.00
5 Ledian U .75 1.50
6 Heracross C .75 1.50
7 Celebi V URR .10 .20
8 Celebi VMAX R 1.25 2.50
9 Snover C 1.25 2.50
10 Abomasnow R 4.00 8.00
11 Deerling C .75 1.50
12 Sawsbuck R .75 2.00
13 Bounsweet C .50 1.00
14 Steenee U 300.00 600.00
15 Tsareena R 4.00 8.00
16 Grookey C .01 .08
17 Thwackey U .10 .25
18 Rillaboom HOLO R .75 1.50
19 Zarude HOLO R .12 .25
20 Blaziken V URR .75 1.50
21 Blaziken VMAX R 2.50 5.00
22 Castform Sunny Form C 2.00 4.00
23 Larvesta C .15 .30
24 Volcarona R .75 1.50
25 Volcanion V URR 1.25 2.50
26 Scorbunny C .60 1.25
27 Raboot U 30.00 75.00
28 Cinderace HOLO R 1.00 2.00
29 Lapras C .75 1.50
30 Sneasel C 1.50 3.00
31 Weavile HOLO R .75 1.50
32 Delibird C 17.50 35.00
33 Castform Rainy Form C 2.00 4.00
34 Castform Snowy Form C 1.00 2.00
35 Snorunt C 4.00 10.00
36 Froslass HOLO R 1.25 2.50
37 Spheal C 2.50 5.00
38 Sealeo U .07 .15
39 Walrein R 2.50 5.00
40 Tapu Fini HOLO R 6.00 12.00
41 Sobble C .75 1.50
42 Drizzile U 1.00 2.00
43 Inteleon HOLO R .75 1.50
44 Rapid Strike Urshifu HOLO R .08 .20
45 Ice Rider Calyrex V URR .10 .25
46 Ice Rider Calyrex VMAX R .12 .25
47 Mareep C .08 .20
48 Flaaffy U 200.00 400.00
49 Ampharos R .60 1.25
50 Blitzle C 150.00 300.00
51 Zebstrika R .75 1.50
52 Thundurus HOLO R .75 1.50
53 Zeraora V URR 1.50 3.00
54 Galarian Slowpoke C .60 1.25
55 Gastly C .25 .50
56 Haunter U .05 .12
57 Gengar HOLO R .25 .60
58 Galarian Articuno V URR 4.00 8.00
59 Ralts C 17.50 35.00
60 Kirlia U .75 1.50
61 Gardevoir HOLO R 2.00 4.00
62 Shuppet C .75 1.50
63 Banette R 1.00 2.00
64 Cresselia HOLO R 12.50 25.00
65 Golett C .01 .08
66 Golurk R .04 .10
67 Swirlix C 1.25 2.50
68 Slurpuff R 5.00 10.00
69 Inkay C .50 1.00
70 Malamar R 25.00 50.00
71 Hatenna C 12.50 25.00
72 Hattrem U 3.00 6.00
73 Hatterene HOLO R 3.00 8.00
74 Shadow Rider Calyrex V URR 2.00 4.00
75 Shadow Rider Calyrex VMAX R 125.00 250.00
76 Diglett C 1.00 2.00
77 Dugtrio R .60 1.25
78 Galarian Farfetch'd C .75 1.50
79 Galarian Sirfetch'd R 1.00 2.00
80 Galarian Zapdos V URR .75 1.50
81 Gallade R .60 1.25
82 Galarian Yamask C .75 1.50
83 Galarian Runerigus HOLO R .75 1.50
84 Crabrawler C .75 1.50
85 Crabominable U .75 1.50
86 Rockruff C 3.00 6.00
87 Lycanroc HOLO R 1.00 2.00
88 Passimian R 1.25 2.50
89 Sandaconda V URR .60 1.25
90 Sandaconda VMAX R .60 1.25
91 Clobbopus C .50 1.00
92 Grapploct HOLO R 1.25 2.50
93 Kubfu C .12 .25
94 Koffing C 1.50 4.00
95 Weezing R 1.00 2.00
96 Galarian Weezing R .75 1.50
97 Galarian Moltres V URR 1.00 2.00
98 Galarian Slowking HOLO R .50 1.00
99 Galarian Slowking V URR 5.00 10.00
100 Galarian Slowking VMAX R 1.00 2.00
101 Qwilfish C 1.50 3.00
102 Seviper R 2.00 4.00
103 Spiritomb R 1.00 2.00
104 Liepard V URR .75 1.50
105 Venipede C 1.50 3.00
106 Whirlipede U 1.00 2.00
107 Scolipede R .60 1.25
108 Single Strike Urshifu HOLO R .07 .15
109 Aron C 7.50 15.00
110 Lairon U .60 1.50
111 Aggron R .75 1.50
112 Metagross V URR 1.50 4.00
113 Metagross VMAX R .75 1.50
114 Cobalion HOLO R .75 1.50
115 Tauros HOLO R .60 1.25
116 Porygon C 12.50 25.00
117 Porygon2 U 2.00 4.00
118 Porygon-Z HOLO R 1.50 3.00
119 Blissey V URR .60 1.25
120 Zangoose R 1.50 3.00
121 Castform C 7.50 15.00
122 Kecleon R .60 1.25
123 Shaymin HOLO R .25 .50
124 Tornadus V URR 1.50 3.00
125 Tornadus VMAX R 2.50 5.00
126 Furfrou C .60 1.50
127 Skwovet C 2.50 5.00
128 Greedent HOLO R 1.25 2.50
129 Agatha U 2.50 5.00
130 Avery U .08 .20
131 Brawly U .04 .10
132 Caitlin U 1.00 2.00
133 Crushing Gloves U .75 1.50
134 Doctor U 10.00 20.00
135 Dyna Tree Hill U 1.25 2.50
136 Echoing Horn U .60 1.50
137 Expedition Uniform U 30.00 60.00
138 Fire-Resistant Gloves U .30 .75
139 Flannery U .04 .10
140 Fog Crystal U .25 .60
141 Galarian Chestplate U 1.50 3.00
142 Honey U .75 1.50
143 Justified Gloves U .12 .25
144 Karen's Conviction U 2.00 4.00
145 Klara U 3.00 8.00
146 Melony U 200.00 400.00
147 Old Cemetery U 4.00 8.00
148 Path to the Peak U 1.25 2.50
149 Peonia U .75 1.50
150 Peony U .75 1.50
151 Rapid Strike Scroll of the Skies U .07 .15
152 Rugged Helmet U 3.00 6.00
153 Siebold U 15.00 30.00
154 Single Strike Scroll of Piercing U 1.00 2.00
155 Weeding Gloves U .60 1.25
156 Welcoming Lantern U .01 .08
157 Impact Energy U .04 .10
158 Lucky Energy U .75 1.50
159 Spiral Energy U .07 .15
160 Celebi V UR FULL ART 1.50 3.00
161 Blaziken V UR FULL ART .75 1.50
162 Volcanion V UR FULL ART .60 1.25
163 Ice Rider Calyrex V UR FULL ART 12.50 25.00
164 Ice Rider Calyrex V UR ALT FULL ART .75 1.50
165 Zeraora V UR FULL ART 2.00 4.00
166 Zeraora V UR ALT FULL ART 7.50 15.00
167 Galarian Rapidash V UR FULL ART 1.00 2.00
168 Galarian Rapidash V UR ALT FULL ART .08 .20
169 Galarian Articuno V UR FULL ART .75 1.50
170 Galarian Articuno V UR ALT FULL ART .75 1.50
171 Shadow Rider Calyrex V UR FULL ART 1.50 3.00
172 Shadow Rider Calyrex V UR ALT FULL ART 60.00 125.00
173 Galarian Zapdos V UR FULL ART 1.00 2.00
174 Galarian Zapdos V UR ALT FULL ART 5.00 10.00
175 Sandaconda V UR FULL ART 3.00 6.00
176 Galarian Moltres V UR FULL ART 7.50 15.00
177 Galarian Moltres V UR ALT FULL ART 1.00 2.00
178 Galarian Slowking V UR FULL ART 200.00 400.00
179 Galarian Slowking V UR ALT FULL ART 1.25 2.50
180 Liepard V UR FULL ART .75 1.50
181 Metagross V UR FULL ART 3.00 6.00
182 Blissey V UR FULL ART 1.25 2.50
183 Blissey V UR ALT FULL ART .12 .25
184 Tornadus V UR FULL ART .12 .30
185 Tornadus V UR ALT FULL ART 1.25 2.50
186 Agatha UR FULL ART .60 1.25
187 Avery UR FULL ART .75 1.50
188 Brawly UR FULL ART 1.00 2.00
189 Caitlin UR FULL ART .75 1.50
190 Doctor UR FULL ART .75 1.50
191 Flannery UR FULL ART 1.25 2.50
192 Honey UR FULL ART 1.25 2.50
193 Karen's Conviction UR FULL ART 3.00 6.00
194 Klara UR FULL ART 1.25 2.50
195 Melony UR FULL ART .75 1.50
196 Peonia UR FULL ART .12 .25
197 Peony UR FULL ART .75 1.50
198 Siebold UR FULL ART .25 .50
199 Celebi VMAX SCR .50 1.00
200 Blaziken VMAX SCR 3.00 6.00
201 Blaziken VMAX SCR ALT ART .75 2.00
202 Ice Rider Calyrex VMAX SCR 1.25 2.50
203 Ice Rider Calyrex VMAX SCR ALT ART 2.50 5.00
204 Shadow Rider Calyrex VMAX SCR 60.00 125.00
205 Shadow Rider Calyrex VMAX SCR ALT ART .50 1.00
206 Sandaconda VMAX SCR .30 .75
207 Galarian Slowking VMAX SCR .50 1.00
208 Metagross VMAX SCR 2.50 5.00
209 Tornadus VMAX SCR 2.50 5.00
210 Agatha SCR 15.00 30.00
211 Avery SCR .60 1.25
212 Brawly SCR 1.25 2.50
213 Caitlin SCR .75 1.50
214 Doctor SCR 12.50 25.00
215 Flannery SCR 1.25 2.50
216 Karen's Conviction SCR .60 1.50
217 Klara SCR .75 1.50
218 Melony SCR .60 1.25
219 Peonia SCR .75 1.50
220 Peony SCR .50 1.00
221 Siebold SCR 5.00 10.00
222 Electrode SCR .01 .08
223 Bronzong SCR .04 .10
224 Snorlax SCR .75 1.50
225 Echoing Horn SCR 12.50 25.00
226 Fan of Waves SCR .30 .75
227 Fog Crystal SCR .04 .10
228 Rugged Helmet SCR .50 1.25
229 Urn of Vitality SCR .10 .20
230 Welcoming Lantern SCR .60 1.25
231 Water Energy SCR 1.25 2.50
232 Psychic Energy SCR 1.50 3.00
233 Fighting Energy SCR .75 1.50

2021 Pokemon Sword and Shield Evolving Skies

1 Pinsir R 1.00 2.00
2 Hoppip C .75 1.50
3 Skiploom U 1.25 2.50
4 Jumpluff HOLO R 4.00 8.00
5 Seedot C 1.25 2.50
6 Tropius R 1.00 2.00
7 Leafeon V URR 12.00 30.00
8 Leafeon VMAX R 1.50 3.00
9 Petilil C .07 .15
10 Lilligant R 5.00 10.00
11 Dwebble C 1.25 3.00
12 Crustle U 1.25 2.50
13 Trevenant V URR .60 1.25
14 Trevenant VMAX R .75 1.50
15 Gossifleur C .60 1.25
16 Eldegoss HOLO R .75 1.50
17 Applin C 1.25 2.50
18 Flareon VMAX R 125.00 250.00
19 Entei HOLO R 1.00 2.00
20 Victini HOLO R 5.00 10.00
21 Volcarona V URR .01 .08
22 Litleo C .10 .25
23 Pyroar U 25.00 50.00
24 Psyduck C 10.00 20.00
25 Golduck U .75 1.50
26 Tentacool C 1.25 2.50
27 Tentacruel U 30.00 75.00
28 Gyarados V URR .25 .50
29 Gyarados VMAX R .01 .08
30 Vaporeon VMAX R .08 .20
31 Suicune V URR 1.50 3.00
32 Lotad C 1.00 2.00
33 Lombre U 1.00 2.00
34 Ludicolo HOLO R 1.50 3.00
35 Carvanha C .60 1.50
36 Sharpedo R .75 1.50
37 Feebas C .60 1.25
38 Milotic R 60.00 125.00
39 Luvdisc C 1.00 2.00
40 Glaceon V URR 4.00 8.00
41 Glaceon VMAX R .60 1.25
42 Tympole C 5.00 10.00
43 Cryogonal C 6.00 12.00
44 Bergmite C .60 1.25
45 Avalugg U .60 1.25
46 Wishiwashi R 1.00 2.00
47 Eiscue U .30 .60
48 Arctovish V URR .60 1.25
49 Pikachu C .60 1.25
50 Raichu HOLO R .60 1.25
51 Jolteon VMAX R 1.00 2.00
52 Chinchou C 1.25 2.50
53 Lanturn U 3.00 6.00
54 Mareep C 1.00 2.00
55 Flaaffy U 1.00 2.00
56 Ampharos R .25 .50
57 Emolga C .75 1.50
58 Dracozolt V URR 4.00 10.00
59 Dracozolt VMAX R .12 .30
60 Regieleki HOLO R .25 .60
61 Drowzee C .07 .15
62 Hypno U 1.25 2.50
63 Galarian Articuno HOLO R 2.00 4.00
64 Espeon V URR .75 1.50
65 Espeon VMAX R .60 1.25
66 Wobbuffet C .75 1.50
67 Sableye C 600.00 1,200.00
68 Woobat C 1.25 2.50
69 Swoobat U 1.25 2.50
70 Golurk V URR 2.50 5.00
71 Flabébé C .12 .25
72 Floette U .20 .50
73 Florges HOLO R 1.25 2.50
74 Sylveon V URR 20.00 40.00

75 Sylveon VMAX R	.10	.20
76 Pumpkaboo C	3.00	6.00
77 Gourgeist R	.08	.20
78 Cutiefly C	.10	.25
79 Ribombee U	200.00	400.00
80 Marshadow HOLO R	.75	1.50
81 Hitmonchan C	.75	1.50
82 Galarian Zapdos HOLO R	1.50	3.00
83 Medicham V URR	.08	.20
84 Hippopotas C	.75	1.50
85 Hippowdon U	.75	1.50
86 Roggenrola C	.75	1.50
87 Boldore U	30.00	60.00
88 Gigalith R	.60	1.25
89 Palpitoad U	.75	1.50
90 Seismitoad R	.75	1.50
91 Lycanroc V URR	.75	1.50
92 Lycanroc VMAX R	.08	.20
93 Galarian Moltres HOLO R	1.25	2.50
94 Umbreon V URR	.50	1.00
95 Umbreon VMAX R	1.25	2.50
96 Nuzleaf U	17.50	35.00
97 Shiftry R	10.00	25.00
98 Scraggy C	2.00	4.00
99 Scrafty U	1.00	2.00
100 Garbodor V URR	.75	1.50
101 Garbodor VMAX R	1.00	2.50
102 Zorua C	.07	.15
103 Zoroark HOLO R	1.25	2.50
104 Nickit C	1.25	2.50
105 Thievul R	.75	1.50
106 Altaria R	3.00	6.00
107 Bagon C	1.00	2.00
108 Shelgon U	1.25	2.50
109 Salamence HOLO R	1.50	3.00
110 Rayquaza V URR	1.25	2.50
111 Rayquaza VMAX R	.01	.08
112 Dialga HOLO R	.04	.10
113 Deino C	7.50	15.00
114 Zweilous U	1.50	3.00
115 Hydreigon HOLO R	1.25	2.50
116 Kyurem HOLO R	1.25	2.50
117 Noivern V URR	.75	1.50
118 Zygarde HOLO R	1.00	2.00
119 Drampa R	.75	1.50
120 Flapple R	1.00	2.00
121 Appletun R	.75	1.50
122 Duraludon V URR	.50	1.00
123 Duraludon VMAX R	.75	1.50
124 Regidrago HOLO R	.07	.15
125 Eevee C	12.50	25.00
126 Teddiursa C	1.00	2.00
127 Ursaring U	2.50	5.00
128 Smeargle R	2.00	4.00
129 Slakoth C	.75	1.50
130 Vigoroth U	.07	.15
131 Slaking HOLO R	.75	1.50
132 Swablu C	6.00	12.00
133 Lillipup C	12.50	25.00
134 Herdier U	1.00	2.00
135 Stoutland R	1.25	2.50
136 Rufflet C	.50	1.00
137 Braviary U	.30	.60
138 Fletchling C	.60	1.50
139 Fletchinder U	1.25	2.50
140 Talonflame R	1.00	2.00
141 Aroma Lady U	5.00	12.00
142 Boost Shake U	1.00	2.00
143 Copycat U	1.00	2.00
144 Crystal Cave U	250.00	500.00
145 Digging Gloves U	.60	1.25
146 Dream Ball U	2.50	5.00
147 Elemental Badge U	.07	.15
148 Full Face Guard U	.15	.40
149 Gordie U	.75	1.50
150 Lucky Ice Pop U	2.50	5.00
151 Moon & Sun Badge U	.60	1.25
152 Raihan U	10.00	20.00
153 Rapid Strike Scroll of the Flying Dragon U	.04	.10
154 Rescue Carrier U	.05	.12
155 Ribbon Badge U	1.50	3.00
156 Rubber Gloves U	.10	.20
157 Shopping Center U	.60	1.25
158 Single Strike Scroll of the Fanged Dragon U	.75	1.50
159 Snow Leaf Badge U	12.50	25.00
160 Spirit Mask U	7.50	15.00
161 Stormy Mountains U	4.00	8.00
162 Switching Cups U	20.00	40.00
163 Toy Catcher U	7.50	15.00
164 Zinnia's Resolve U	.25	.50
165 Treasure Energy U	.08	.20
166 Leafeon V UR	.25	.60
167 Leafeon V UR	1.00	2.00
168 Trevenant V UR	.08	.20
169 Flareon V UR	.04	.10
170 Volcarona V UR	.75	1.50
171 Gyarados V UR	1.25	2.50
172 Vaporeon V UR	2.50	5.00
173 Suicune V UR	1.00	2.00
174 Glaceon V UR	1.00	2.00
175 Glaceon V UR	.07	.15
176 Arctovish V UR	.25	.60
177 Jolteon V UR	2.00	5.00
178 Dracozolt V UR	.75	1.50
179 Espeon V UR	.75	1.50
180 Espeon V UR	.20	.40
181 Golurk V UR	.60	1.25
182 Golurk V UR	1.25	2.50
183 Sylveon V UR	2.00	4.00
184 Sylveon V UR	25.00	50.00
185 Medicham V UR	1.50	3.00
186 Medicham V UR	.08	.20
187 Lycanroc V UR	1.00	2.00
188 Umbreon V UR	.75	1.50
189 Umbreon V UR	.60	1.25
190 Garbodor V UR	.75	1.50
191 Dragonite V UR	.75	1.50
192 Dragonite V UR	1.00	2.00
193 Rayquaza V UR	3.00	6.00
194 Rayquaza V UR	.08	.20
195 Noivern V UR	.04	.10
196 Noivern V UR	1.00	2.00
197 Duraludon V UR	3.00	8.00
198 Duraludon V UR	150.00	300.00
199 Aroma Lady UR	2.50	5.00
200 Copycat UR	60.00	125.00
201 Gordie UR	15.00	30.00
202 Raihan UR	1.00	2.00
203 Zinnia's Resolve UR	.75	1.50
204 Leafeon VMAX SCR	12.50	25.00
205 Leafeon VMAX SCR ALT ART	1.25	2.50
206 Trevenant VMAX SCR	.75	1.50
207 Gyarados VMAX SCR	.10	.20
208 Glaceon VMAX SCR	15.00	30.00
209 Glaceon VMAX SCR ALT ART	1.00	2.00
210 Dracozolt VMAX SCR	12.50	25.00
211 Sylveon VMAX SCR	.75	1.50
212 Sylveon VMAX SCR ALT ART	.05	.12
213 Lycanroc VMAX SCR	.10	.25
214 Umbreon VMAX SCR	10.00	20.00
215 Umbreon VMAX SCR ALT ART	1.25	3.00
216 Garbodor VMAX SCR	.30	.75
217 Rayquaza VMAX SCR	.75	1.50
218 Rayquaza VMAX SCR ALT ART	.75	1.50
219 Duraludon VMAX SCR	20.00	40.00
220 Duraludon VMAX SCR ALT ART	.10	.20
221 Aroma Lady SCR	5.00	10.00
222 Copycat SCR	.60	1.25
223 Gordie SCR	.25	.50
224 Raihan SCR	.01	.08
225 Zinnia's Resolve SCR	.08	.20
226 Froslass SCR	1.00	2.00
227 Inteleon SCR	.07	.15
228 Cresselia SCR	.30	.75
229 Boost Shake SCR	.75	1.50
230 Crystal Cave SCR	.75	1.50
231 Full Face Guard SCR	1.00	2.00
232 Stormy Mountains SCR	.75	1.50
233 Toy Catcher SCR	250.00	500.00
234 Turffield Stadium SCR	17.50	35.00
235 Lightning Energy SCR	.60	1.25
236 Darkness Energy SCR	.60	1.25
237 Metal Energy SCR	1.25	2.50

2021 Pokemon Sword and Shield Fusion Strike

1 Caterpie C	3.00	6.00
2 Metapod U	.75	1.50
3 Butterfree HOLO R	200.00	400.00
4 Shroomish C	2.50	5.00
5 Breloom U	3.00	6.00
6 Breloom V UR	4.00	10.00
7 Pansage C	10.00	20.00
8 Simisage U	1.00	2.00
9 Sewaddle C	.60	1.25
10 Swadloon U	1.50	3.00
11 Leavanny R	1.00	2.00
12 Maractus R	1.00	2.50
13 Shelmet C	2.00	4.00
14 Accelgor R	.75	1.50
15 Virizion R	1.25	2.50
16 Phantump C	2.50	5.00
17 Trevenant U	.01	.08
18 Grubbin C	.04	.10
19 Dewpider C	.50	1.00
20 Araquanid R	10.00	20.00
21 Tsareena V UR	2.00	4.00
22 Rillaboom V UR	.07	.15
23 Rillaboom VMAX UR	1.25	2.50
24 Gossifleur C	.75	1.50
25 Eldegoss U	400.00	800.00
26 Appletun V UR	.75	1.50
27 Zarude U	1.00	2.00
28 Vulpix (28) C	.75	1.50
29 Vulpix (29) C	1.00	2.00
30 Ninetales U	.75	1.50
31 Ninetales U	2.00	4.00
32 Growlithe C	.75	1.50
33 Arcanine R	.60	1.25
34 Slugma C	.75	1.50
35 Magcargo U	2.50	5.00
36 Victini U	1.50	3.00
37 Pansear C	1.00	2.00
38 Simisear C	50.00	100.00
39 Chandelure V UR	12.50	25.00
40 Chandelure VMAX UR	.75	1.50
41 Heatmor U	.75	1.50
42 Oricorio R	2.50	6.00
43 Cinderace V UR	1.00	2.00
44 Cinderace V UR	1.25	2.50
45 Cinderace VMAX UR	.08	.20
46 Sizzlipede C	.07	.15
47 Sizzlipede C	.75	1.50
48 Centiskorch R	1.00	2.00
49 Centiskorch R	1.25	2.50
50 Shellder C	.75	1.50
51 Cloyster R	.75	1.50
52 Staryu C	1.00	2.00
53 Starmie HOLO R	.75	1.50
54 Lapras U	1.00	2.00
55 Totodile C	.75	2.00
56 Croconaw U	.75	1.50
57 Feraligatr HOLO R	1.50	3.00
58 Marill C	25.00	50.00
59 Azumarill R	.75	1.50
60 Qwilfish C	1.25	2.50
61 Mantine C	10.00	20.00
62 Mudkip C	1.25	2.50
63 Marshtomp U	.75	1.50
64 Swampert HOLO R	1.00	2.00
65 Clamperl C	1.25	2.50
66 Huntail R	1.25	2.50
67 Gorebyss R	.10	.20
68 Panpour C	25.00	50.00
69 Simipour U	.07	.15
70 Basculin C	1.25	2.50
71 Galarian Darumaka C	.75	1.50
72 Galarian Darmanitan U	.10	.25
73 Greninja V UR	.10	.25
74 Clauncher C	15.00	30.00
75 Clawitzer U	.04	.10
76 Crabominable V UR	.05	.12
77 Pyukumuku U	2.50	6.00
78 Inteleon V UR	.07	.15
79 Inteleon VMAX UR	4.00	8.00
80 Chewtle C	.60	1.25
81 Dreadnaw U	7.50	15.00
82 Arrokuda C	.50	1.00
83 Barraskewda U	.60	1.25
84 Snom U	3.00	6.00
85 Frosmoth U	.08	.20
86 Pikachu V UR	.04	.10
87 Voltorb C	3.00	6.00
88 Electrode R	200.00	400.00
89 Plusle C	.75	1.50
90 Minun C	40.00	80.00
91 Shinx C	.60	1.25
92 Luxio U	.60	1.25
93 Luxray R	.75	1.50
94 Rotom C	.60	1.25
95 Tynamo C	.75	1.50
96 Eelektrik U	1.00	2.00
97 Eelektross R	30.00	75.00
98 Helioptile C	.25	.50
99 Heliolisk U	.01	.08
100 Charjabug U	.10	.25
101 Vikavolt R	6.00	12.00
102 Zeraora R	7.50	15.00
103 Boltund V UR	2.00	4.00
104 Boltund VMAX UR	.60	1.25
105 Toxel C	6.00	12.00
106 Toxel C	7.50	15.00
107 Toxtricity HOLO R	1.50	3.00
108 Toxtricity HOLO R	.75	1.50
109 Morpeko C	.75	1.50
110 Jigglypuff C	.50	1.00
111 Wigglytuff U	2.00	5.00
112 Jynx C	5.00	10.00
113 Mew V UR	.75	1.50
114 Mew VMAX UR	.08	.20
115 Snubbull C	.60	1.25
116 Granbull R	.50	1.00
117 Galarian Corsola C	2.00	4.00
118 Galarian Cursola R	1.25	2.50
119 Mawile C	.75	1.50
120 Deoxys HOLO R	.75	1.50
121 Munna C	10.00	20.00
122 Musharna U	.75	1.50
123 Sigilyph C	.75	1.50
124 Meloetta R	4.00	8.00
125 Sandygast C	2.00	4.00
126 Palossand R	1.25	2.50
127 Indeedee C	.12	.25
128 Dreepy C	1.25	2.50
129 Drakloak U	1.00	2.00
130 Dragapult HOLO R	.25	.50
131 Sandshrew C	.50	1.25
132 Sandslash U	1.00	2.50
133 Mankey C	1.50	3.00
134 Primeape U	.75	1.50
135 Geodude C	1.50	3.00
137 Golem R	.08	.20
138 Onix C	.05	.12
139 Steelix HOLO R	12.50	25.00
140 Gligar C	3.00	6.00
141 Gliscor U	.01	.08
142 Makuhita C	.04	.10
143 Hariyama U	1.50	3.00
144 Baltoy C	20.00	40.00
145 Claydol R	.75	1.50
146 Lucario V UR	.30	.60
147 Drillbur C	.75	2.00
148 Landorus HOLO R	12.50	25.00
149 Pancham C	.60	1.25
150 Stufful C	.60	1.25
151 Bewear U	1.00	2.00
152 Clobbopus C	.60	1.25
153 Grapploct U	1.25	2.50
154 Falinks U	.07	.15
155 Falinks C	.10	.20
156 Gengar V UR	.12	.30
157 Gengar VMAX UR	.60	1.25
158 Tyranitar V UR	.75	1.50
159 Galarian Zigzagoon C	1.50	3.00
160 Galarian Linoone U	.75	1.50
161 Galarian Obstagoon HOLO R	.75	1.50
162 Carvanha C	.75	1.50
163 Sharpedo U	.75	1.50
164 Absol R	.75	1.50
165 Croagunk C	.75	1.50
166 Toxicroak R	1.50	3.00
167 Darkrai U	125.00	250.00
168 Trubbish C	.60	1.25
169 Garbodor U	.75	1.50
170 Zorua C	.75	1.50
171 Zoroark U	1.25	2.50
172 Vullaby C	.10	.20
173 Mandibuzz U	.10	.20
174 Pangoro U	1.00	2.00
175 Yveltal R	1.50	3.00
176 Impidimp C	.60	1.25
177 Morgrem U	.01	.08
178 Grimmsnarl HOLO R	.04	.10
179 Morpeko C	5.00	10.00
180 Galarian Meowth C	2.00	4.00
181 Galarian Perrserker U	6.00	12.00
182 Skarmory C	50.00	100.00
183 Excadrill U	.50	1.00
184 Durant C	.75	1.50
185 Genesect V UR	.50	1.00
186 Klefki C	.75	1.50
187 Togedemaru U	1.00	2.00
188 Meltan C	.75	1.50
189 Melmetal HOLO R	.75	1.50
190 Corviknight R	.75	1.50
191 Cufant C	1.00	2.00
192 Copperajah U	.75	1.50
193 Latias R	.75	1.50
194 Latios R	.75	1.50
195 Goomy C	.75	1.50
196 Sliggoo U	2.00	4.00
197 Goodra R	1.00	2.00
198 Turtonator U	1.25	2.50
199 Meowth C	1.50	3.00
200 Persian U	2.50	5.00
201 Dodrio V UR	2.50	5.00
202 Chansey C	10.00	20.00
203 Blissey R	7.50	15.00
204 Kangaskhan R	1.25	2.50
205 Eevee C	.75	1.50
206 Snorlax C	5.00	10.00
207 Dunsparce U	.25	.50
208 Stantler U	.01	.08
209 Smeargle C	.08	.20
210 Skitty C	1.00	2.00
211 Delcatty U	.07	.15
212 Buneary C	.75	1.50
213 Lopunny U	.75	1.50
214 Bunnelby C	1.00	2.00
215 Diggersby U	2.00	4.00
216 Hawlucha U	3.00	6.00
217 Greedent V UR	2.00	5.00
218 Greedent VMAX UR	.01	.08
219 Rookidee C	.01	.08
220 Corvisquire U	.10	.20
221 Wooloo C	1.00	2.00
222 Wooloo C	.60	1.25
223 Dubwool U	.60	1.25
224 Adventurer's Discovery U	.60	1.25
225 Battle VIP Pass U	.75	1.50
226 Bug Catcher U	40.00	80.00
227 Chili & Cilan & Cress U	1.50	3.00
228 Cook U	.75	1.50
229 Cram-o-matic U	.75	1.50
230 Cross Switcher U	3.00	8.00
231 Crossceiver U	.60	1.25
232 Dancer U	25.00	50.00
233 Elesa's Sparkle U	.08	.20
234 Farewell Bell U	.07	.15
235 Judge U	.10	.20
236 Power Tablet U	2.50	5.00
237 Quick Ball U	2.00	5.00
238 Schoolboy U	.75	1.50
239 Schoolgirl U	1.25	2.50
240 Shauna U	2.00	4.00
241 Sidney U	.50	1.00
242 Skaters' Park U	.60	1.25
243 Spongy Gloves U	.08	.20
244 Fusion Strike Energy U	.01	.08
245 Celebi V FULL ART UR	.75	1.50
246 Tsareena V FULL ART UR	.75	1.50
247 Chandelure V FULL ART UR	2.50	5.00
248 Crabominable V FULL ART UR	2.50	5.00
249 Boltund V FULL ART UR	.01	.08
250 Mew V FULL ART UR	.01	.08
251 Mew V ALT ART UR	.75	1.50
252 Sandaconda V FULL ART UR	2.50	5.00
253 Hoopa V FULL ART UR	30.00	75.00
254 Genesect V FULL ART UR	5.00	10.00
255 Genesect V ALT ART UR	.75	1.50
256 Greedent V FULL ART UR	6.00	12.00
257 Greedent V ALT ART UR	.75	1.50
258 Chili & Cilan & Cress FULL ART UR	.07	.15
259 Dancer FULL ART UR	.60	1.25
260 Elesa's Sparkle FULL ART UR	1.25	2.50
261 Schoolboy FULL ART UR	.75	1.50
262 Schoolgirl FULL ART UR	.60	1.25
263 Shauna FULL ART UR	100.00	200.00
264 Sidney FULL ART UR	.75	1.50
265 Chandelure VMAX SCR	1.25	2.50
266 Inteleon VMAX ALT ART SCR	.75	1.50
267 Boltund VMAX SCR	75.00	150.00
268 Mew VMAX SCR	2.50	5.00
269 Mew VMAX ALT ART SCR	1.00	2.00
270 Espeon VMAX ALT ART SCR	12.50	25.00
271 Gengar VMAX ALT ART SCR	3.00	6.00
272 Greedent VMAX SCR	2.50	5.00
273 Chili & Cilan & Cress SCR	.75	1.50
274 Dancer SCR	.75	1.50
275 Elesa's Sparkle SCR	.75	1.50
276 Schoolboy SCR	.08	.20
277 Schoolgirl SCR	.10	.25
278 Shauna SCR	1.50	3.00
279 Sidney SCR	1.50	3.00
280 Flaaffy SCR	6.00	12.00
281 Power Tablet SCR	.10	.20
282 Training Court SCR	1.00	2.00
283 Grass Energy SCR	1.25	2.50
284 Fire Energy SCR	.75	1.50

2021 Pokemon Sword and Shield Shining Fates

1 Yanma C	1.25	2.50
2 Yanmega R	2.00	5.00
3 Celebi R	.75	1.50
4 Cacnea C	2.50	5.00
5 Tropius U	.75	1.50
6 Rowlet C	.50	1.00
7 Dartrix U	5.00	10.00
8 Decidueye HOLO R	2.50	6.00
9 Dhelmise V URR	1.25	2.50
10 Dhelmise VMAX R	.10	.20
11 Grookey C	.60	1.25
12 Thwackey U	.75	1.50
13 Rillaboom HOLO R	1.00	2.00
14 Gossifleur C	1.25	2.50
15 Eldegoss U	.60	1.25
16 Zarude R	.25	.50
17 Reshiram AR	.01	.08
18 Cinderace V URR	.05	.12

19 Cinderace VMAX R	.08	.20
20 Horsea C	.05	.12
21 Kyogre AR	3.00	6.00
22 Buizel C	1.00	2.50
23 Floatzel U	.75	1.50
24 Manaphy R	1.00	2.00
25 Volcanion R	.75	1.50
26 Chewtle C	.75	1.50
27 Drednaw R	1.25	2.50
28 Cramorant U	4.00	8.00
29 Snom C	1.25	2.50
30 Frosmoth HOLO R	.75	1.50
31 Shinx C	.75	1.50
32 Luxio U	.75	1.50
33 Luxray HOLO R	1.25	2.50
34 Rotom U	.50	1.25
35 Morpeko C	.75	1.50
36 Morpeko C	.75	1.50
37 Morpeko V URR	.75	1.50
38 Morpeko VMAX R	1.00	2.00
39 Indeedee V URR	.75	1.50
40 Trapinch C	1.25	2.50
41 Koffing C	.75	1.50
42 Galarian Weezing HOLO R	7.50	15.00
43 Spinarak C	1.00	2.00
44 Crobat V URR	1.00	2.00
45 Crobat VMAX R	1.25	2.50
46 Yveltal AR	7.50	15.00
47 Nickit C	.60	1.25
48 Thievul HOLO R	.75	1.50
49 Cufant C	.07	.15
50 Ditto V URR	2.00	4.00
51 Ditto VMAX R	.08	.20
52 Eevee C	.60	1.25
53 Greedent V URR	10.00	20.00
54 Cramorant V URR	.60	1.25
55 Cramorant VMAX R	6.00	12.00
56 Indeedee HOLO R	.07	.15
57 Ball Guy U	.01	.08
58 Boss's Orders R	.01	.08
59 Gym Trainer U	1.25	2.50
60 Professor's Research R	3.00	6.00
61 Rusted Shield U	10.00	20.00
62 Rusted Sword U	2.00	4.00
63 Team Yell Towel U	20.00	40.00
64 Alcremie V UR FULL ART	.08	.20
65 Ball Guy UR FULL ART	.12	.30
66 Bird Keeper UR FULL ART	.08	.20
67 Cara Liss UR FULL ART	.10	.25
68 Gym Trainer UR FULL ART	.75	1.50
69 Piers UR FULL ART	.60	1.25
70 Poke Kid UR FULL ART	2.50	5.00
71 Rose UR FULL ART	.07	.15
72 Skyla UR FULL ART	3.00	6.00
73 Alcremie VMAX RAINBOW R	.75	1.50

2021 Pokemon Sword and Shield Shining Fates Shiny Vault

SV001 Rowlet SHR	.75	1.50
SV002 Dartrix SHR	.75	1.50
SV003 Decidueye SHR	1.00	2.00
SV004 Grookey SHR	4.00	8.00
SV005 Thwackey SHR	.12	.25
SV006 Rillaboom SHR	.60	1.25
SV007 Blipbug SHR	.75	1.50
SV008 Dottler SHR	.75	1.50
SV009 Orbeetle SHR	.08	.20
SV010 Gossifleur SHR	.08	.20
SV011 Eldegoss SHR	10.00	20.00
SV012 Applin SHR	15.00	30.00
SV013 Flapple SHR	3.00	6.00
SV014 Appletun SHR	4.00	8.00
SV015 Scorbunny SHR	.40	1.00
SV016 Raboot SHR	.30	.75
SV017 Cinderace SHR	.05	.12
SV018 Sizzlipede SHR	.20	.50
SV019 Centiskorch SHR	1.00	2.00
SV020 Galarian Mr. Mime SHR	.75	1.50
SV021 Galarian Mr. Rime SHR	.10	.20
SV022 Suicune SHR	1.50	3.00
SV023 Galarian Darumaka SHR	.50	1.00
SV024 Galarian Darmanitan SHR	.60	1.25
SV025 Sobble SHR	.75	1.50
SV026 Drizzile SHR	15.00	30.00
SV027 Inteleon SHR	.50	1.00
SV028 Chewtle SHR	1.00	2.00
SV029 Drednaw SHR	1.00	2.50
SV030 Cramorant SHR	15.00	30.00
SV031 Arrokuda SHR	.75	1.50
SV032 Barraskewda SHR	2.00	4.00
SV033 Snom SHR	.75	1.50
SV034 Frosmoth SHR	.75	1.50
SV035 Eiscue SHR	.60	1.25
SV036 Dracovish SHR	7.50	15.00
SV037 Arctovish SHR	100.00	200.00
SV038 Rotom SHR	1.50	3.00
SV039 Yamper SHR	1.25	3.00
SV040 Boltund SHR	.75	1.50
SV041 Toxel SHR	.75	1.50
SV042 Toxtricity SHR	.75	1.50
SV043 Pincurchin SHR	1.00	2.00
SV044 Morpeko SHR	.75	1.50
SV045 Dracozolt SHR	3.00	6.00
SV046 Arctozolt SHR	10.00	20.00
SV047 Galarian Ponyta SHR	.50	1.00
SV048 Galarian Rapidash SHR	.12	.25
SV049 Galarian Corsola SHR	.15	.40
SV050 Galarian Cursola SHR	.08	.20
SV051 Dedenne SHR	.12	.30
SV052 Sinistea SHR	.75	1.50
SV053 Polteageist SHR	1.00	2.00
SV054 Hatenna SHR	.75	1.50
SV055 Hattrem SHR	12.50	25.00
SV057 Milcery SHR	7.50	15.00
SV058 Alcremie SHR	2.50	5.00
SV059 Indeedee SHR	1.25	2.50
SV060 Dreepy SHR	.60	1.25
SV061 Drakloak SHR	.60	1.25
SV062 Dragapult SHR	2.50	6.00
SV063 Galarian Farfetch'd SHR	.75	1.50
SV064 Galarian Sirfetch'd SHR	1.25	2.50
SV065 Galarian Yamask SHR	.12	.25
SV066 Galarian Runerigus SHR	.75	2.00
SV067 Rolycoly SHR	5.00	10.00
SV068 Carkol SHR	.50	1.00
SV069 Coalossal SHR	15.00	30.00
SV070 Silicobra SHR	20.00	40.00
SV071 Sandaconda SHR	.04	.10
SV072 Clobbopus SHR	.10	.25
SV073 Grapploct SHR	3.00	6.00
SV074 Falinks SHR	.60	1.25
SV075 Stonjourner SHR	.60	1.25
SV076 Koffing SHR	.07	.15
SV077 Galarian Weezing SHR	10.00	20.00
SV078 Galarian Zigzagoon SHR	1.00	2.00
SV079 Galarian Linoone SHR	1.00	2.50
SV080 Galarian Obstagoon SHR	1.50	3.00
SV081 Nickit SHR	.75	1.50
SV082 Thievul SHR	2.00	4.00
SV083 Impidimp SHR	.75	1.50
SV084 Morgrem SHR	1.00	2.00
SV085 Grimmsnarl SHR	1.00	2.00
SV086 Galarian Meowth SHR	.30	.75
SV087 Galarian Perrserker SHR	2.50	6.00
SV088 Galarian Stunfisk SHR	50.00	100.00
SV089 Corviknight SHR	.75	1.50
SV090 Cufant SHR	.75	1.50
SV091 Copperajah SHR	.30	.75
SV092 Duraludon SHR	.05	.12
SV093 Minccino SHR	.75	2.00
SV094 Cinccino SHR	1.00	2.00
SV095 Ducklett SHR	1.25	2.50
SV096 Swanna SHR	.60	1.25
SV097 Bunnelby SHR	.75	1.50
SV098 Oranguru SHR	1.00	2.00
SV099 Skwovet SHR	1.00	2.00
SV100 Greedent SHR	1.25	2.50
SV101 Rookidee SHR	.75	1.50
SV102 Corvisquire SHR	.75	1.50
SV103 Wooloo SHR	.75	2.00
SV104 Dubwool SHR	3.00	6.00
SV105 Rillaboom V SHR	5.00	10.00
SV106 Rillaboom VMAX SHR	12.50	25.00
SV107 Charizard VMAX SHR	.75	1.50
SV108 Centiskorch V SHR	1.25	2.50
SV109 Centiskorch VMAX SHR	.12	.25
SV110 Lapras V SHR	.12	.30
SV111 Lapras VMAX SHR	1.00	2.00
SV112 Toxtricity V SHR	1.00	2.00
SV113 Toxtricity VMAX SHR	1.00	2.00
SV114 Indeedee V SHR	.75	1.50
SV115 Falinks V SHR	.75	1.50
SV116 Grimmsnarl V SHR	3.00	6.00
SV117 Grimmsnarl VMAX SHR	1.25	2.50
SV118 Ditto V SHR	.60	1.25
SV119 Ditto VMAX SHR	.60	1.50
SV120 Dubwool V SHR	2.50	5.00
SV121 Eternatus V SCR	1.50	3.00
SV122 Eternatus VMAX SCR	.75	1.50

2022 Pokemon Battle Academy 2022 Cinderace Deck

1 Sizzlipede	25.00	50.00
2 Fire Energy	15.00	30.00
3 Fire Energy	.07	.15
4 Victini	4.00	8.00
5 Fire Energy	.25	.50
6 Fire Energy	.50	1.25
7 Ninetales	.10	.20
8 Fire Energy	.75	2.00
9 Fire Energy	.12	.25
10 Fire Energy	.75	1.50
11 Fire Energy	.01	.08
12 Fire Energy	.04	.10
13 Vulpix	1.00	2.00
14 Sizzlipede	.75	1.50
15 Centiskorch	1.25	2.50
16 Fire Energy	.50	1.00
17 Sizzlipede	.75	1.50
18 Vulpix	.75	1.50
19 Larvesta	.75	1.50
20 Fire Energy	.75	2.00
21 Shauna	1.00	2.50
22 Fire Energy	.75	1.50
23 Ninetales	3.00	6.00
24 Fire Energy	.50	1.00
25 Energy Retrieval	1.25	2.50
26 Fire Energy	.30	.75
27 Volcarona	.75	1.50
28 Hop	1.00	2.00
29 Fire Energy	.75	1.50
30 Centiskorch	.60	1.25
31 Vulpix	3.00	8.00
32 Fire Energy	.60	1.25
33 Great Ball	1.00	2.00
34 Bug Catcher	1.00	2.00
35 Fire Energy	1.00	2.00
36 Larvesta	4.00	8.00
37 Energy Retrieval	20.00	40.00
38 Fire Energy	1.00	2.00
39 Turtonator	1.25	2.50
40 Switch	.25	.50
41 Hop	.60	1.25
42 Potion	.75	1.50
43 Great Ball	.01	.08
44 Volcarona	.01	.08
45 Sonia	12.50	25.00
46 Larvesta	7.50	15.00
47 Bug Catcher	.75	1.50
48 Great Ball	.75	1.50
49 Pokemon Catcher	12.50	25.00
50 Shauna	.60	1.25
51 Centiskorch	.07	.15
52 Hop	15.00	40.00
53 Victini	.60	1.25
54 Pokemon Catcher	.75	1.50
55 Great Ball	.10	.20
56 Sizzlipede	.08	.20
57 Hop	10.00	20.00
58 Switch	1.50	3.00
59 Shauna	.75	1.50
60 Cinderace V	1.25	2.50

2022 Pokemon Battle Academy 2022 Eevee Deck

35 Galarian Zigzagoon	.25	.50
36 Galarian Linoone	.04	.10
162 Carvanha	.20	.50
163 Sharpedo	.75	1.50
164 Great Ball	1.00	2.00
165 Hop	1.50	3.00
165 Piers	3.00	6.00
167 Darkrai	.60	1.25
167 Sonia	.30	.60
170 Zorua	.07	.15
171 Zoroark	.75	1.50
183 Switch	1.00	2.00
226 Bug Catcher	2.50	5.00
228 Cook	.60	1.25
240 Shauna	.60	1.25
NNO Darkness Energy	.12	.25
SWSH065 Eevee V	.75	1.50
SWSH193 Galarian Obstagoon	.01	.08

2022 Pokemon Battle Academy 2022 Pikachu Deck

1 Yamper	.04	.10
2 Blitzle	.60	1.25
3 Lightning Energy	.60	1.25
4 Lightning Energy	.60	1.25
5 Zeraora	7.50	15.00
6 Shinx	.75	1.50
7 Lightning Energy	.75	1.50
8 Lightning Energy	1.50	3.00
9 Lightning Energy	.01	.08
10 Lightning Energy	.10	.25
11 Lightning Energy	.25	.50
12 Lightning Energy	2.00	4.00
13 Hop	.75	2.00
14 Luxio	1.00	2.00
15 Blitzle	1.00	2.00
16 Boltund	.60	1.25
17 Lightning Energy	30.00	75.00
18 Potion	.75	1.50
19 Lightning Energy	.75	1.50
20 Shinx	1.00	2.00
21 Lightning Energy	1.25	2.50
22 Lightning Energy	.08	.20
23 Morpeko	.08	.20
24 Shauna	.60	1.25
25 Zebstrika	1.00	2.00
26 Bug Catcher	.75	1.50
27 Lightning Energy	2.00	4.00
28 Luxray	.60	1.50
29 Great Ball	7.50	15.00
30 Blitzle	.75	1.50
31 Lightning Energy	1.25	3.00
32 Energy Recycler	.60	1.25
33 Hop	.75	1.50
34 Zebstrika	.01	.08
35 Lightning Energy	.04	.10
36 Switch	.75	1.50
37 Luxio	.75	1.50
38 Great Ball	.10	.20
39 Lightning Energy	.12	.25
40 Potion	.10	.20
41 Shinx	.12	.30
42 Hop	1.50	4.00
43 Lightning Energy	1.00	2.00
44 Boss's Orders	.75	1.50
45 Shinx	1.25	2.50
46 Bug Catcher	4.00	8.00
47 Luxray	.75	1.50
48 Lightning Energy	.75	1.50
49 Great Ball	.75	1.50
50 Shauna	.75	1.50
51 Sonia	.12	.25
52 Switch	.07	.15
53 Luxio	1.00	2.00
54 Hop	.01	.08
55 Blitzle	.04	.10
56 Zebstrika	.12	.30
57 Great Ball	.12	.30
58 Yamper	1.25	2.50
59 Shauna	.60	1.25
60 Pikachu V	.75	1.50

2022 Pokemon GO

1 Bulbasaur C	6.00	12.00
2 Ivysaur U	.75	1.50
3 Venusaur HOLO R	1.00	2.00
4 Radiant Venusaur RDR	.25	.50
5 Alolan Exeggutor V URR	.01	.08
6 Spinarak C	.40	1.00
7 Ariados U	5.00	10.00
8 Charmander C	1.25	2.50
9 Charmeleon U	1.25	2.50
10 Charizard HOLO R	.08	.20
11 Radiant Charizard RDR	.60	1.25
12 Moltres HOLO R	1.00	2.00
13 Numel C	1.00	2.00
14 Camerupt U	.75	1.50
15 Squirtle C	2.00	4.00
16 Wartortle U	25.00	50.00
17 Blastoise HOLO R	.75	1.50
18 Radiant Blastoise RDR	2.00	4.00
19 Slowpoke C	.75	1.50
20 Slowbro U	15.00	30.00
21 Magikarp C	.75	1.50
22 Gyarados HOLO R	.25	.50
23 Lapras HOLO R	.60	1.25
24 Articuno HOLO R	.75	1.50
25 Wimpod C	.75	1.50
26 Golisopod HOLO R	.75	1.50
27 Pikachu C	.75	1.50
28 Pikachu HOLO R	.75	1.50
29 Zapdos HOLO R	.75	2.00
30 Mewtwo V URR	1.25	2.50
31 Mewtwo VSTAR R	2.50	5.00
32 Natu C	.75	2.00
33 Xatu U	1.00	2.00
34 Lunatone U	7.50	15.00
35 Sylveon HOLO R	1.50	3.00
36 Onix C	.60	1.25
37 Larvitar C	.75	1.50
38 Pupitar U	3.00	6.00
39 Solrock U	1.50	3.00
40 Conkeldurr V URR	.01	.08
41 Alolan Rattata C	.05	.12
42 Alolan Raticate C	.07	.15
43 Tyranitar HOLO R	.12	.30
44 Steelix U	.30	.75
45 Meltan C	1.00	2.00
46 Melmetal HOLO R	1.00	2.00
47 Melmetal V URR	.75	1.50
48 Melmetal VMAX R	.08	.20
49 Dragonite V URR	.04	.10
50 Dragonite VSTAR R	.60	1.50
51 Chansey C	1.00	2.50
52 Blissey HOLO R	1.50	3.00
53 Ditto HOLO R	.75	1.50
54 Eevee C	.75	1.50
55 Snorlax HOLO R	1.00	2.00
56 Aipom C	.10	.20
57 Ambipom C	.75	1.50
58 Slaking V URR	1.00	2.00
59 Bidoof C	.75	1.50
60 Bibarel C	.30	.60
61 Pidove C	.75	1.50
62 Tranquill C	3.00	6.00
63 Unfezant U	.60	1.25
64 Blanche U	.60	1.25
65 Candela U	.75	1.50
66 Egg Incubator U	.75	1.50
67 Lure Module U	30.00	60.00
68 PokeStop U	2.50	5.00
69 Rare Candy U	1.00	2.00
70 Spark U	1.00	2.00
71 Alolan Exeggutor V UR	.10	.20
72 Mewtwo V UR	.01	.08
73 Conkeldurr V UR	.05	.12
74 Conkeldurr V UR	.08	.20
75 Melmetal V UR	.75	1.50
76 Dragonite V UR	.25	.50
77 Slaking V UR	.04	.10
78 Professor's Research UR	.50	1.25
79 Mewtwo VSTAR RBWR	1.00	2.00
80 Melmetal VSTAR RBWR	.75	1.50
81 Dragonite VSTAR RBWR	.75	1.50
82 Blanche RBWR	1.50	3.00
83 Candela RBWR	1.00	2.00
84 Professor's Research RBWR	7.50	15.00
85 Spark RBWR	1.00	2.00
86 Mewtwo VSTAR SCR	.75	1.50
87 Egg Incubator SCR	.75	1.50
88 Lure Module SCR	1.25	2.50

2022 Pokemon McDonald's Collection

1 Ledyba	1.25	3.00
2 Rowlet	1.25	2.50
3 Gossifleur	.07	.15
4 Growlithe	7.50	15.00
5 Victini	.75	1.50
6 Lapras	1.00	2.00
7 Pikachu	1.25	2.50
8 Chinchou	1.25	2.50
9 Flaaffy	.75	1.50
10 Tynamo	10.00	20.00
11 Cutiefly	.50	1.00
12 Bewear	7.50	15.00
13 Pangoro	.75	1.50
14 Drampa	.75	1.50
15 Smeargle	1.25	2.50

2022 Pokemon Sword and Shield Astral Radiance

1 Beedrill V URR	.05	.12
2 Hisuian Voltorb C	.20	.50
3 Hisuian Electrode U	.08	.20
4 Scyther C	.10	.25
5 Scyther C	.75	1.50
6 Yanma C	7.50	15.00
7 Yanmega U	1.00	2.00
8 Heracross C	.60	1.25
9 Kricketot C	.07	.15
10 Kricketune U	.12	.30
11 Combee C	1.50	3.00
12 Vespiquen R	.08	.20
13 Leafeon R	.10	.25
14 Shaymin R	.60	1.50
15 Petilil C	.75	2.00
16 Hisuian Lilligant HOLO R	4.00	10.00
17 Hisuian Lilligant V URR	1.00	2.00
18 Hisuian Lilligant VSTAR R	.75	1.50
19 Rowlet C	1.00	2.00
20 Dartrix U	1.00	2.00
21 Ponyta C	.75	1.50
22 Rapidash R	.75	1.50
23 Cyndaquil C	1.50	3.00
24 Quilava U	4.00	8.00
25 Heatran V URR	1.00	2.00
26 Heatran VMAX R	1.00	2.00
27 Radiant Heatran RADIANT R	.12	.25
28 Psyduck C	.50	1.00
29 Golduck U	.60	1.25
30 Starmie V URR	1.00	2.00
31 Swinub C	.75	1.50
32 Piloswine U	3.00	6.00
33 Mamoswine R	.75	1.50
34 Mantine C	.08	.20

35 Barboach C	.07	.15
36 Whiscash U	1.00	2.00
37 Regice R	.60	1.25
38 Glaceon R	.75	1.50
39 Origin Forme Palkia V URR	.75	1.50
40 Origin Forme Palkia VSTAR R	1.25	2.50
41 Oshawott C	125.00	250.00
42 Dewott U	1.00	2.00
43 Hisuian Basculin C	1.25	2.50
44 Hisuian Basculegion R	.07	.15
45 Keldeo HOLO R	.75	1.50
46 Radiant Greninja RADIANT R	1.25	2.50
47 Bergmite C	1.25	2.50
48 Hisuian Avalugg R	.75	1.50
49 Galarian Mr. Rime V URR	.60	1.25
50 Luxray V URR	.25	.50
51 Regieleki R	.04	.10
52 Hisuian Typhlosion HOLO R	.30	.75
53 Hisuian Typhlosion V URR	1.50	3.00
54 Hisuian Typhlosion VSTAR R	1.00	2.00
55 Togepi C	.75	1.50
56 Togetic U	.75	1.50
57 Togekiss HOLO R	1.00	2.00
58 Misdreavus C	.75	1.50
59 Mismagius R	1.25	2.50
60 Ralts C	1.50	4.00
61 Kirlia U	.60	1.25
62 Gallade HOLO R	.75	1.50
63 Drifloon C	.60	1.25
64 Drifblim U	.75	1.50
65 Uxie U	.75	1.50
66 Mesprit HOLO R	1.50	3.00
67 Azelf U	5.00	10.00
68 Diancie HOLO R	.75	1.50
69 Wyrdeer HOLO R	1.50	3.00
70 Hisuian Growlithe C	.10	.25
71 Hisuian Arcanine R	.30	.75
72 Machamp V URR	1.25	2.50
73 Machamp VMAX R	1.00	2.00
74 Sudowoodo C	.07	.15
75 Regirock R	.10	.25
76 Cranidos U	.12	.30
77 Rampardos HOLO R	1.25	2.50
78 Lucario V URR	1.25	2.50
79 Hippopotas C	.08	.20
80 Hippowdon U	.08	.20
81 Radiant Hawlucha RADIANT R	1.00	2.00
82 Hisuian Decidueye HOLO R	.10	.20
83 Hisuian Decidueye V URR	.08	.20
84 Hisuian Decidueye VSTAR R	1.00	2.00
85 Kleavor R	.30	.75
86 Kleavor HOLO R	2.50	5.00
87 Kleavor V URR	.60	1.50
88 Hisuian Qwilfish C	.60	1.50
89 Hisuian Qwilfish C	1.00	2.00
90 Hisuian Overqwil U	7.50	15.00
91 Hisuian Overqwil R	1.00	2.00
92 Hisuian Sneasel C	1.25	2.50
93 Hisuian Sneasler HOLO R	.25	.50
94 Hisuian Sneasler V URR	.01	.08
95 Poochyena C	.08	.20
96 Mightyena R	.75	1.50
97 Absol HOLO R	1.25	2.50
98 Darkrai V URR	.75	1.50
99 Darkrai VSTAR R	.75	1.50
100 Hisuian Samurott HOLO R	2.50	5.00
101 Hisuian Samurott V URR	2.00	4.00
102 Hisuian Samurott VSTAR R	1.00	2.00
103 Nickit C	1.00	2.00
104 Thievul R	.60	1.25
105 Magnemite C	.08	.20
106 Magneton U	.07	.15
107 Magnezone HOLO R	.75	1.50
108 Registeel R	1.00	2.00
109 Shieldon U	6.00	12.00
110 Bastiodon HOLO R	1.50	3.00
111 Bronzor C	.75	1.50
112 Bronzong U	.75	1.50
113 Origin Forme Dialga V URR	.10	.20
114 Origin Forme Dialga VSTAR R	1.00	2.00
115 Pawniard C	.75	1.50
116 Bisharp U	.75	1.50
117 Garchomp V URR	1.50	3.00
118 Regidrago R	.75	1.50
119 Eevee C	1.00	2.00
120 Hoothoot C	1.00	2.00
121 Noctowl U	.60	1.25
122 Teddiursa C	.75	1.50
123 Ursaring U	3.00	8.00
124 Ursaluna R	1.00	2.00
125 Stantler C	.60	1.25
126 Miltank HOLO R	.60	1.25
127 Glameow C	3.00	6.00
128 Purugly U	.07	.15
129 Chatot C	12.50	25.00
130 Regigigas HOLO R	1.25	2.50
131 Rufflet C	2.00	5.00
132 Hisuian Braviary R	1.00	2.00
133 Oranguru V URR	.75	1.50
134 Wyrdeer V URR	.10	.20
135 Adaman HOLO R	.75	1.50
136 Canceling Cologne U	1.25	2.50
137 Choy U	.60	1.25
138 Cyllene U	.75	1.50
139 Dark Patch U	.10	.20
140 Energy Loto U	.12	.30
141 Feather Ball U	7.50	15.00
142 Gapejaw Bog U	1.00	2.00
143 Gardenia's Vigor U	2.00	4.00
144 Grant U	1.00	2.00
145 Gutsy Pickaxe U	.25	.50
146 Hisuian Heavy Ball U	.10	.25
147 Irida HOLO R	.40	1.00
148 Jubilife Village U	.75	1.50
149 Kamado U	.08	.20
150 Roxanne U	.04	.10
151 Spicy Seasoned Curry U	.75	1.50
152 Supereffective Glasses U	1.00	2.50
153 Sweet Honey U	.75	2.00
154 Switch Cart U	1.00	2.00
155 Temple of Sinnoh U	1.25	2.50
156 Trekking Shoes U	1.00	2.00
157 Unidentified Fossil U	.75	1.50
158 Wait and See Turbo U	2.00	4.00
159 Zisu U	.75	1.50
160 Beedrill V FULL ART UR	.60	1.25
161 Beedrill V ALT ART UR	.75	1.50
162 Hisuian Lilligant V UR	1.00	2.00
163 Hisuian Lilligant V UR	2.50	5.00
164 Virizion V UR	1.25	2.50
165 Heatran V UR	1.25	2.50
166 Starmie V UR	1.00	2.00
167 Origin Forme Palkia V UR	.75	1.50
168 Luxray V UR	10.00	20.00
169 Hisuian Typhlosion V UR	.01	.08
170 Jirachi V UR	.04	.10
171 Machamp V UR	2.00	4.00
172 Machamp V UR	1.00	2.00
173 Hisuian Decidueye V UR	3.00	6.00
174 Hisuian Sneasler V UR	.08	.20
175 Hisuian Sneasler V UR	1.50	3.00
176 Hisuian Samurott V UR	.60	1.25
177 Origin Forme Dialga V UR	.75	1.50
178 Garchomp V UR	.50	1.00
179 Oranguru V UR	.60	1.25
180 Wyrdeer V UR	.75	1.50
181 Adaman FULL ART UR	.75	1.50
182 Choy FULL ART UR	1.00	2.00
183 Cyllene FULL ART UR	.75	1.50
184 Gardenia's Vigor UR	.30	.75
185 Grant UR	.75	1.50
186 Irida UR	4.00	8.00
187 Kamado UR	.04	.10
188 Roxanne UR	.08	.20
189 Zisu UR	.25	.50
190 Hisuian Lilligant VSTAR RAINBOW R	.60	1.25
191 Heatran VMAX RAINBOW R	1.00	2.00
192 Origin Forme Palkia VSTAR RAINBOW R	.10	.20
193 Hisuian Typhlosion VSTAR RAINBOW R	.12	.30
194 Machamp VMAX RAINBOW R	12.50	25.00
195 Hisuian Decidueye VSTAR RAINBOW R	5.00	10.00
196 Kleavor VSTAR RAINBOW R	1.00	2.00
197 Hisuian Samurott VSTAR RAINBOW R	6.00	12.00
198 Origin Forme Dialga VSTAR RAINBOW R	.08	.20
199 Adaman RAINBOW R	.04	.10
200 Choy RBW R	.08	.20
201 Cyllene RBW R	.30	.75
202 Gardenia's Vigor RAINBOW R	.04	.10
203 Grant RAINBOW R	.40	1.00
204 Irida RAINBOW R	4.00	8.00
205 Kamado RAINBOW R	1.50	3.00
206 Roxanne RAINBOW R	2.00	4.00
207 Zisu RAINBOW R	.07	.15
208 Origin Form Palkia VSTAR SCR	.75	1.50
209 Hisuian Samurott VSTAR SCR	1.00	2.00
210 Origin Form Dialga VSTAR SCR	20.00	50.00
211 Choice Belt SCR	.75	1.50
212 Jubilife Village SCR	4.00	8.00
213 Path to the Peak SCR	.60	1.25
214 Temple of Sinnoh SCR	1.25	2.50
215 Trekking Shoes SCR	.75	2.00
216 Double Turbo Energy SCR	.75	2.00

2022 Pokemon Sword and Shield Astral Radiance Trainer Gallery

TG01 Abomasnow HOLO R	.07	.15
TG02 Flapple HOLO R	.60	1.25
TG03 Kingdra HOLO R	.60	1.25
TG04 Frosmoth HOLO R	2.50	5.00
TG05 Gardevoir HOLO R	3.00	6.00
TG06 Wyrdeer HOLO R	1.00	2.00
TG07 Falinks HOLO R	1.50	4.00
TG08 Kleavor HOLO R	3.00	6.00
TG09 Mightyena HOLO R	1.00	2.00
TG10 Galarian Obstagoon HOLO R	.08	.20
TG11 Bronzing HOLO R	.08	.20
TG12 Hoothoot HOLO R	1.25	2.50
TG13 Starmie V HOLO R	.75	1.50
TG14 Ice Rider Calyrex V URR	2.50	5.00
TG15 Ice Rider Calyrex VMAX URR	.25	.60
TG16 Galarian Articuno V URR	2.00	4.00
TG17 Shadow Rider Calyrex V URR	.75	1.50
TG18 Shadow Rider Calyrex VMAX URR	.75	1.50
TG19 Galarian Zapdos V URR	.75	1.50
TG20 Galarian Moltres V URR	.75	1.50
TG21 Zacian V URR	.60	1.25
TG22 Zamazenta V URR	.60	1.25
TG23 Garchomp V URR	.40	1.00
TG24 Allister UR	1.50	4.00
TG25 Bea UR	.75	1.50
TG26 Melony UR	.75	1.50
TG27 Milo UR	.12	.25
TG28 Piers UR	.75	2.00
TG29 Ice Rider Calyrex VMAX SCR	.75	1.50
TG30 Shadow Rider Calyrex VMAX SCR	.75	1.50

2022 Pokemon Sword and Shield Brilliant Stars

1 Exeggcute C	.12	.25
2 Exeggutor U	.20	.40
3 Shroomish C	.20	.50
4 Breloom R	40.00	80.00
5 Tropius U	2.00	4.00
6 Turtwig C	12.50	25.00
7 Grotle U	3.00	6.00
8 Torterra HOLO R	.60	1.25
9 Burmy C	.75	1.50
10 Wormadam R	.75	1.50
11 Mothim R	1.50	3.00
12 Cherubi C	1.00	2.00
13 Shaymin V URR	1.00	2.00
14 Shaymin VSTAR R	2.00	4.00
15 Karrablast C	1.25	2.50
16 Zarude V URR	3.00	6.00
17 Charizard V URR	.75	1.50
18 Charizard VSTAR R	.60	1.25
19 Magmar C	.75	1.50
20 Magmortar R	.75	1.50
21 Moltres HOLO R	.75	1.50
22 Entei V URR	3.00	6.00
23 Torkoal U	.01	.08
24 Chimchar C	.04	.10
25 Monferno U	.60	1.25
26 Infernape HOLO R	.30	.75
27 Simisear V URR	.10	.25
28 Kingler V URR	.40	1.00
29 Kingler VMAX R	2.50	5.00
30 Staryu C	.25	.50
31 Lapras R	.12	.25
32 Corphish C	.75	1.50
33 Crawdaunt U	1.25	2.50
34 Snorunt C	.12	.25
35 Piplup C	.75	2.00
36 Prinplup U	.75	1.50
37 Empoleon HOLO R	.75	1.50
38 Buizel C	.75	1.50
39 Floatzel U	1.25	2.50
40 Lumineon V URR	.40	1.00
41 Manaphy R	.75	1.50
42 Cubchoo C	.75	1.50
43 Beartic U	1.00	2.00
44 Eiscue R	.60	1.25
45 Raichu V URR	.75	1.50
46 Electabuzz C	.75	1.50
47 Electivire R	25.00	50.00
48 Raikou V URR	.75	1.50
49 Shinx C	.75	1.50
50 Luxio U	.75	1.50
51 Luxray R	.04	.10
52 Pachirisu U	.10	.25
53 Clefairy C	1.00	2.00
54 Clefable R	.60	1.25
55 Starmie U	.60	1.25
56 Mewtwo R	.30	.75
57 Granbull V URR	.10	.25
58 Baltoy C	.50	1.25
59 Claydol U	.60	1.25
60 Duskull C	.75	1.50
61 Dusclops U	.10	.20
62 Dusknoir HOLO R	.20	.50
63 Chimecho C	25.00	50.00
64 Whimsicott V URR	4.00	8.00
65 Whimsicott VSTAR R	1.00	2.00
66 Sigilyph U	.07	.15
67 Dedenne C	2.00	4.00
68 Mimikyu V URR	.60	1.25
69 Mimikyu VMAX R	1.25	2.50
70 Milcery C	.75	1.50
71 Alcremie R	.75	1.50
72 Hitmontop U	.60	1.25
73 Nosepass C	2.50	6.00
74 Trapinch C	.75	1.50
75 Vibrava U	.75	1.50
76 Flygon R	.75	1.50
77 Wormadam R	.75	1.50
78 Riolu C	1.25	2.50
79 Lucario HOLO R	1.25	2.50
80 Throh C	4.00	8.00
81 Sawk C	2.50	5.00
82 Golett C	3.00	6.00
83 Golurk R	.12	.25
84 Grimer C	.75	1.50
85 Muk R	.04	.10
86 Sneasel C	.10	.25
87 Weavile U	1.00	2.00
88 Honchkrow V URR	.60	1.25
89 Spiritomb C	.60	1.25
90 Purrloin C	1.00	2.00
91 Liepard R	1.50	3.00
92 Impidimp C	.75	1.50
93 Morgrem U	.75	1.50
94 Grimmsnarl R	.75	1.50
95 Morpeko V URR	250.00	500.00
96 Aggron V URR	.60	1.25
97 Aggron VMAX R	.75	1.50
98 Wormadam R	1.25	2.50
99 Probopass U	.60	1.25
100 Heatran R	1.25	2.50
101 Escavalier R	.08	.20
102 Klink C	1.00	2.00
103 Klang U	.75	1.50
104 Klinklang R	.75	1.50
105 Zamazenta V URR	1.00	2.00
106 Flygon V URR	.25	.50
107 Gible C	.10	.25
108 Gabite U	.40	1.00
109 Garchomp HOLO R	.75	1.50
110 Axew C	.75	1.50
111 Fraxure U	1.50	3.00
112 Haxorus R	1.25	2.50
113 Druddigon R	.75	1.50
114 Dracovish V URR	.75	1.50
115 Farfetch'd C	.60	1.25
116 Castform C	1.00	2.00
117 Starly C	1.50	4.00
118 Staravia U	2.00	4.00
119 Staraptor R	.07	.15
120 Bidoof C	.04	.10
121 Bibarel HOLO R	.08	.20
122 Arceus V URR	2.00	4.00
123 Arceus VSTAR R	.20	.40
124 Minccino C	.15	.40
125 Cinccino U	.60	1.25
126 Tornadus R	1.25	2.50
127 Hawlucha C	1.25	2.50
128 Drampa V URR	.75	1.50
129 Acerola's Premonition U	.75	1.50
130 Barry U	.12	.25
131 Blunder Policy U	.01	.08
132 Boss's Orders HOLO R	.08	.20
133 Café Master U	2.00	4.00
134 Cheren's Care U	.60	1.25
135 Choice Belt U	.60	1.25
136 Cleansing Gloves U	.75	1.50
137 Collapsed Stadium U	.75	1.50
138 Cynthia's Ambition U	1.50	3.00
139 Fresh Water Set U	2.50	5.00
140 Friends in Galar U	2.50	5.00
141 Gloria U	3.00	6.00
142 Hunting Gloves U	.08	.20
143 Kindler U	.08	.20
144 Magma Basin U	10.00	20.00
145 Marnie's Pride U	.01	.08
146 Pot Helmet U	.01	.08
147 Professor's Research HOLO R	.75	1.50
148 Roseanne's Backup U	1.25	2.50
149 Team Yell's Cheer U	75.00	150.00
150 Ultra Ball U	.75	1.50
151 Double Turbo Energy U	.50	1.00
152 Shaymin V UR	1.00	2.00
153 Charizard V UR	.75	1.50
154 Charizard V UR	.10	.25
155 Lumineon V UR	.15	.40
156 Lumineon V UR	.75	1.50
157 Pikachu V UR	.75	1.50
158 Raichu V UR	20.00	40.00
159 Granbull V UR	2.00	4.00
160 Whimsicott V UR	3.00	6.00
161 Honchkrow V UR	.75	1.50
162 Honchkrow V UR	.75	1.50
163 Zamazenta V UR	.75	1.50
164 Flygon V UR	.75	1.50
165 Arceus V UR	.60	1.25
166 Arceus V UR	.75	1.50
167 Barry UR	.75	1.50
168 Cheren's Care UR	1.00	2.00
169 Cynthia's Ambition UR	.20	.40
170 Kindler UR	2.00	4.00
171 Marnie's Pride UR	1.00	2.00
172 Roseanne's Backup UR	1.25	2.50
173 Shaymin VSTAR RBW R	.08	.20
174 Charizard VSTAR RBW R	1.00	2.00
175 Whimsicott VSTAR RBW R	3.00	8.00
176 Arceus VSTAR RBW R	.10	.20
177 Cheren's Care RBW R	2.50	5.00
178 Cynthia's Ambition RBW R	3.00	6.00
179 Kindler RBW R	.50	1.00
180 Roseanne's Backup RBW R	.12	.30
181 Galarian Articuno V SCR	.07	.15
182 Galarian Zapdos V SCR	.25	.50
183 Galarian Moltres V SCR	.01	.08
184 Arceus VSTAR SCR	.08	.20
185 Magma Basin SCR	.75	1.50
186 Ultra Ball SCR	1.00	2.00

2022 Pokemon Sword and Shield Brilliant Stars Trainers Gallery

TG01 Flareon HOLO R	.05	.12
TG02 Vaporeon HOLO R	.10	.25
TG03 Octillery HOLO R	15.00	30.00
TG04 Jolteon HOLO R	.30	.60
TG05 Zekrom HOLO R	.75	1.50
TG06 Dusknoir HOLO R	1.25	2.50
TG07 Dedenne HOLO R	1.25	2.50
TG08 Alcremie HOLO R	7.50	15.00
TG09 Ariados HOLO R	.25	.50
TG10 Houndoom HOLO R	1.00	2.00
TG11 Eevee HOLO R	1.25	2.50
TG12 Oranguru HOLO R	.75	1.50
TG13 Boltund V URR	.75	1.50
TG14 Sylveon V URR	3.00	6.00
TG15 Sylveon VMAX URR	.60	1.25
TG16 Mimikyu V URR	.75	1.50
TG17 Mimikyu VMAX URR	5.00	10.00
TG18 Single Strike Urshifu V URR	.50	1.00
TG19 Single Strike Urshifu VMAX URR	1.00	2.00
TG20 Rapid Strike Urshifu V URR	1.25	2.50
TG21 Rapid Strike Urshifu VMAX URR	.12	.25
TG22 Umbreon V URR	.25	.50
TG23 Umbreon VMAX URR	.04	.10
TG25 Café Master UR	.40	1.00
TG26 Gloria UR	1.00	2.00
TG27 Mustard (Rapid Strike) UR	.75	1.50
TG28 Mustard (Single Strike) UR	1.50	3.00
TG29 Single Strike Urshifu VMAX SCR	.75	1.50
TG30 Rapid Strike Urshifu VMAX SCR	4.00	8.00

2022 Pokemon Sword and Shield Lost Origin

1 Oddish C	1.00	2.00
2 Gloom U	.07	.15
3 Vileplume HOLO R	.25	.50
4 Paras C	.20	.50
5 Parasect R	.75	1.50
6 Wurmple C	1.50	3.00
7 Silcoon U	.08	.20
8 Beautifly HOLO R	1.50	3.00
9 Cascoon U	1.25	2.50
10 Dustox R	.01	.08
11 Seedot C	.05	.12
12 Nuzleaf U	10.00	20.00
13 Shiftry HOLO R	.75	1.50
14 Roselia C	1.25	2.50
15 Roserade U	.75	1.50
16 Phantump C	1.00	2.50
17 Trevenant HOLO R	7.50	15.00
18 Blipbug C	7.50	15.00
19 Dottler U	.07	.15
20 Orbeetle HOLO R	2.00	4.00
21 Slugma C	2.00	4.00
22 Magcargo R	2.00	4.00
23 Torkoal U	1.25	2.50
24 Litwick C	1.25	2.50
25 Lampent U	10.00	20.00
26 Chandelure HOLO R	.75	1.50
27 Delphox V UR	1.00	2.00
28 Litleo C	2.50	6.00
29 Pyroar HOLO R	6.00	12.00
30 Poliwag C	.60	1.50
31 Poliwhirl U	10.00	20.00
32 Politoed R	1.00	2.00
33 Seel C	1.00	2.00

34 Dewgong R	.75	1.50
35 Horsea C	.75	1.50
36 Seadra U	.60	1.25
37 Kingdra HOLO R	.60	1.25
38 Luvdisc C	1.25	2.50
39 Shellos C	10.00	20.00
40 Finneon C	10.00	20.00
41 Lumineon U	.75	1.50
42 Snover C	.75	1.50
43 Abomasnow U	.75	1.50
44 Hisuian Basculin C	.75	1.50
45 Hisuian Basculegion HOLO R	.75	1.50
46 Ducklett C	.25	.50
47 Swanna U	.10	.25
48 Kyurem V UR	.25	.60
49 Kyurem VMAX UR	3.00	6.00
50 Cramorant R	3.00	6.00
51 Glastrier HOLO R	.07	.15
52 Pikachu C	2.00	4.00
53 Raichu R	2.50	5.00
54 Electrike C	.10	.20
55 Manectric R	.60	1.25
56 Magnezone V UR	1.50	3.00
57 Magnezone VSTAR UR	.10	.20
58 Rotom V UR	.15	.40
59 Tynamo C	.08	.20
60 Eelektrik U	.75	1.50
61 Eelektross R	1.50	3.00
62 Clefairy C	.75	1.50
63 Clefable R	.75	1.50
64 Gastly C	.75	1.50
65 Haunter U	2.00	4.00
66 Gengar HOLO R	2.00	4.00
67 Mr. Mime R	.07	.15
68 Jynx C	.75	1.50
69 Radiant Gardevoir UR	.08	.20
70 Sableye HOLO R	.08	.20
71 Mawile C	1.00	2.00
72 Shuppet C	1.50	3.00
73 Banette R	1.00	2.50
74 Cresselia HOLO R	2.50	5.00
75 Hisuian Zorua C	.07	.15
76 Hisuian Zoroark HOLO R	12.50	25.00
77 Inkay C	3.00	6.00
78 Malamar R	.04	.10
79 Comfey R	.10	.25
80 Mimikyu R	15.00	30.00
81 Spectrier HOLO R	.30	.75
82 Enamorus V UR	.10	.25
83 Hisuian Growlithe C	.25	.60
84 Hisuian Arcanine HOLO R	1.00	2.00
85 Poliwrath R	.04	.10
86 Machop C	.10	.25
87 Machoke U	12.50	25.00
88 Machamp HOLO R	15.00	30.00
89 Rhyhorn C	1.00	2.00
90 Rhydon U	1.25	2.50
91 Rhyperior R	2.00	4.00
92 Aerodactyl V UR	.75	1.50
93 Aerodactyl VSTAR UR	.75	1.50
94 Sudowoodo C	4.00	8.00
95 Gligar C	1.00	2.00
96 Gliscor R	.75	1.50
97 Makuhita C	1.00	2.00
98 Hariyama U	3.00	6.00
99 Meditite C	5.00	10.00
100 Medicham U	.75	1.50
101 Relicanth U	.75	1.50
102 Gastrodon U	1.25	2.50
103 Mienfoo C	.75	1.50
104 Mienshao U	.75	1.50
105 Landorus R	.75	1.50
106 Binacle C	1.00	2.00
107 Barbaracle HOLO R	.60	1.25
108 Carbink U	.75	1.50
109 Rockruff C	12.50	25.00
110 Falinks C	2.50	5.00
111 Stonjourner R	12.50	25.00
112 Spinarak C	.60	1.25
113 Ariados R	.75	1.50
114 Murkrow C	1.50	3.00
115 Honchkrow R	.07	.15
116 Seviper U	1.25	3.00
117 Spiritomb R	.08	.20
118 Drapion V UR	.08	.20
119 Drapion VSTAR UR	.12	.25
120 Darkrai HOLO R	1.00	2.00
121 Inkay C	.10	.20
122 Hoopa R	.12	.30
123 Radiant Hisuian Sneasler UR	.12	.25
124 Radiant Steelix UR	.08	.20
125 Bronzor C	7.50	15.00
126 Bronzong U	1.25	2.50
127 Galarian Stunfisk U	.07	.15
128 Magearna R	.75	1.50
129 Galarian Perrserker V UR	1.00	2.00
130 Giratina V UR	7.50	15.00
131 Giratina VSTAR UR	1.00	2.00
132 Goomy C	4.00	8.00
133 Hisuian Sliggoo U	.10	.20
134 Hisuian Goodra HOLO R	.04	.10
135 Hisuian Goodra V UR	.10	.25
136 Hisuian Goodra VSTAR UR	.10	.25
137 Pidgeot V UR	.50	1.25
138 Lickitung C	.75	1.50
139 Lickilicky U	75.00	150.00
140 Porygon C	1.00	2.00
141 Porygon2 U	1.00	2.00
142 Porygon-Z R	.75	1.50
143 Snorlax HOLO R	15.00	30.00
144 Aipom C	4.00	8.00
145 Ambipom U	7.50	15.00
146 Hisuian Zoroark V UR	4.00	8.00
147 Hisuian Zoroark VSTAR UR	15.00	25.00
148 Bouffalant R	2.00	4.00
149 Komala U	1.00	2.00
150 Skwovet C	.75	1.50
151 Greedent R	.75	1.50
152 Arc Phone U	7.50	15.00
153 Arezu U	4.00	8.00
154 Box of Disaster U	1.25	2.50
155 Colress's Experiment U	.75	1.50
156 Damage Pump U	.75	1.50
157 Fantina U	.30	.75
158 Iscan U	1.00	2.00
159 Lady U	.75	1.50
160 Lake Acuity U	.75	1.50
161 Lost City U	.75	1.50
162 Lost Vacuum U	.75	1.50
163 Mirage Gate U	.10	.20
164 Miss Fortune Sisters U	2.00	4.00
165 Panic Mask U	.08	.20
166 Riley U	15.00	30.00
167 Thorton U	3.00	6.00
168 Tool Box U	1.25	3.00
169 Volo HOLO R	.60	1.25
170 Windup Arm U	.75	1.50
171 Gift Energy U	.75	1.50
172 Hisuian Electrode V UR FULL ART	.75	1.50
173 Delphox V UR FULL ART	.08	.20
174 Kyurem V UR FULL ART	.05	.12
175 Magnezone V UR FULL ART	.75	1.50
176 Rotom V UR FULL ART	1.25	2.50
177 Rotom V UR ALT ART	1.50	3.00
178 Enamorus V UR FULL ART	.75	1.50
179 Aerodactyl V UR FULL ART	.25	.50
180 Aerodactyl V UR ALT ART	.75	1.50
181 Gallade V UR FULL ART	.04	.10
182 Drapion V UR FULL ART	.75	2.00
183 Galarian Perrserker V UR FULL ART	3.00	6.00
184 Galarian Perrserker V UR ALT ART	4.00	8.00
185 Giratina V UR FULL ART	.07	.15
186 Giratina V UR ALT ART	.30	.75
187 Hisuian Goodra V UR FULL ART	.10	.25
188 Pidgeot V UR FULL ART	.30	.75
189 Arezu UR FULL ART	.50	1.00
190 Colress's Experiment UR FULL ART	.60	1.25
191 Fantina UR FULL ART	.08	.20
192 Iscan UR FULL ART	1.00	2.50
193 Lady UR FULL ART	1.50	4.00
194 Miss Fortune Sisters UR FULL ART	.07	.15
195 Thorton UR FULL ART	.01	.08
196 Volo UR FULL ART	.01	.08
197 Kyurem VMAX SCR	2.50	5.00
198 Magnezone VSTAR SCR	.07	.15
199 Aerodactyl VSTAR SCR	.50	1.00
200 Drapion VSTAR SCR	.75	1.50
201 Giratina VSTAR SCR	1.25	2.50
202 Hisuian Goodra VSTAR SCR	7.50	15.00
203 Hisuian Zoroark VSTAR SCR	.60	1.25
204 Arezu SCR	.75	1.50
205 Colress's Experiment SCR	7.50	15.00
206 Fantina SCR	.75	1.50
207 Iscan SCR	.75	1.50
208 Lady SCR	1.00	2.00
209 Miss Fortune Sisters SCR	4.00	8.00
210 Thorton SCR	10.00	20.00
211 Volo SCR	.75	1.50
212 Giratina VSTAR SCR	1.25	2.50
213 Hisuian Zoroark VSTAR SCR	7.50	15.00
214 Box of Disaster SCR	25.00	50.00
215 Collapsed Stadium SCR	1.25	2.50
216 Dark Patch SCR	2.00	4.00
217 Lost Vacuum SCR	.75	1.50

2022 Pokemon Sword and Shield Lost Origin Trainer Gallery

TG01 Parasect UR	1.50	4.00
TG02 Roserade UR	.08	.20
TG03 Charizard UR	.10	.25
TG04 Chandelure UR	6.00	12.00
TG05 Pikachu UR	.75	1.50
TG06 Gengar UR	2.50	5.00
TG07 Banette UR	3.00	6.00
TG08 Hisuian Arcanine UR	.07	.15
TG09 Spiritomb UR	.75	1.50
TG10 Snorlax UR	.07	.15
TG11 Castform UR	.08	.20
TG12 Orbeetle V UR	2.50	5.00
TG13 Orbeetle VMAX UR	.60	1.25
TG14 Centiskorch V UR	.75	1.50
TG15 Centiskorch VMAX UR	.60	1.25
TG16 Pikachu V UR	.60	1.25
TG17 Pikachu VMAX UR	5.00	10.00
TG18 Enamorus V UR	.75	1.50
TG19 Gallade V UR	1.00	2.00
TG20 Crobat V UR	1.50	3.00
TG21 Eternatus V UR	10.00	20.00
TG22 Eternatus VMAX UR	.08	.20
TG23 Adventurer's Discovery UR	.04	.10
TG24 Boss's Orders UR	1.50	3.00
TG25 Cook UR	.10	.20
TG26 Kabu UR	20.00	40.00
TG27 Nessa UR	.10	.20
TG28 Opal UR	2.50	5.00
TG29 Pikachu VMAX UR	.08	.20
TG30 Mew VMAX UR	.08	.20

2022 Pokemon Sword and Shield Silver Tempest

1 Venonat C	.30	.75
2 Venomoth U	300.00	750.00
3 Spinarak C	.08	.20
4 Ariados HOLO R	.12	.30
5 Sunkern C	.75	1.50
6 Sunflora U	1.00	2.00
7 Serperior V UR	.60	1.25
8 Serperior VSTAR UR	.75	1.50
9 Petilil C	.75	1.50
10 Hisuian Lilligant R	.75	1.50
11 Foongus C	7.50	15.00
12 Amoonguss R	4.00	8.00
13 Durant C	1.00	2.00
14 Virizion R	15.00	30.00
15 Chesnaught V UR	2.00	4.00
16 Radiant Tsareena RAR	1.25	2.50
17 Vulpix C	.75	1.50
18 Ninetales U	.75	1.50
19 Growlithe C	1.00	2.00
20 Arcanine R	1.00	2.00
21 Ponyta C	.10	.20
22 Rapidash HOLO R	12.50	25.00
23 Victini R	.75	1.50
24 Reshiram V UR	1.25	2.50
25 Fennekin C	.75	1.50
26 Braixen U	10.00	20.00
27 Delphox R	1.00	2.00
28 Fletchinder U	3.00	6.00
29 Talonflame R	2.50	5.00
30 Litten C	7.50	15.00
31 Torracat U	.07	.15
32 Incineroar R	3.00	6.00
33 Alolan Vulpix V UR	1.00	2.00
34 Alolan Vulpix VSTAR UR	.75	1.50
35 Omastar V UR	.75	1.50
36 Articuno HOLO R	3.00	6.00
37 Wailmer C	1.00	2.00
38 Wailord U	1.00	2.00
39 Feebas C	.10	.20
40 Milotic R	.15	.40
41 Snorunt C	3.00	6.00
42 Glalie U	.75	1.50
43 Froslass R	1.00	2.00
44 Relicanth C	2.00	5.00
45 Phione R	.30	.75
46 Keldeo R	.50	1.25
47 Dewpider C	.75	1.50
48 Araquanid U	1.00	2.00
49 Pikachu C	.08	.20
50 Raichu U	.05	.12
51 Chinchou C	.10	.20
52 Lanturn U	.75	1.50
53 Rotom C	.75	1.50
54 Emolga C	.75	1.50
55 Stunfisk C	3.00	6.00
56 Zeraora R	1,000.00	2,000.00
57 Regieleki V UR	.01	.08
58 Regieleki VMAX UR	.05	.12
59 Radiant Alakazam RAR	3.00	6.00
60 Drowzee C	10.00	20.00
61 Hypno U	7.50	15.00
62 Jynx U	.75	1.50
63 Misdreavus C	.75	1.50
64 Mismagius R	20.00	40.00
65 Unown V UR	.10	.25
66 Unown VSTAR UR	.15	.40
67 Ralts C	.50	1.00
68 Kirlia U	4.00	8.00
69 Gardevoir R	.10	.20
70 Mawile V UR	.75	1.50
71 Mawile VSTAR UR	1.25	2.50
72 Meditite C	.50	1.00
73 Medicham HOLO R	2.50	5.00
74 Chimecho C	.75	1.50
75 Sigilyph U	1.25	3.00
76 Solosis C	1.50	3.00
77 Duosion U	.75	1.50
78 Reuniclus HOLO R	.75	1.50
79 Elgyem C	.75	1.50
80 Beheeyem U	.25	.50
81 Espurr C	.10	.25
82 Meowstic U	.40	1.00
83 Swirlix C	2.00	4.00
84 Slurpuff U	.75	1.50
85 Dedenne U	.75	1.50
86 Indeedee C	.08	.20
87 Dreepy C	1.00	2.00
88 Drakloak U	15.00	30.00
89 Dragapult HOLO R	1.25	2.50
90 Hisuian Arcanine V UR	2.50	5.00
91 Phanpy C	.50	1.00
92 Donphan U	.60	1.25
93 Baltoy C	.75	1.50
94 Claydol U	.10	.20
95 Anorith U	.20	.50
96 Armaldo R	20.00	40.00
97 Terrakion HOLO R	15.00	30.00
98 Hawlucha C	20.00	40.00
99 Sandygast C	7.50	15.00
100 Palossand U	.07	.15
101 Stonjourner U	.30	.60
102 Ursaluna V UR	.75	1.50
103 Zubat C	1.00	2.00
104 Golbat U	60.00	125.00
105 Crobat HOLO R	.10	.20
106 Murkrow C	2.00	4.00
107 Honchkrow U	.01	.08
108 Skuntank V UR	.08	.20
109 Croagunk C	.75	1.50
110 Toxicroak U	250.00	500.00
111 Sandile C	.75	1.50
112 Krokorok U	1.25	2.50
113 Krookodile HOLO R	.25	.50
114 Mareanie C	.60	1.25
115 Toxapex U	.04	.10
116 Morpeko U	.10	.25
117 Beldum C	.75	1.50
118 Metang U	.75	1.50
119 Metagross HOLO R	.75	1.50
120 Radiant Jirachi RAR	1.25	2.50
121 Ferroseed C	17.50	35.00
122 Ferrothorn U	.08	.20
123 Klink C	.10	.25
124 Klang U	.20	.50
125 Klinklang R	.75	1.50
126 Cobalion R	10.00	20.00
127 Togedemaru C	1.50	3.00
128 Magearna V UR	1.50	3.00
129 Dratini C	.75	1.50
130 Dragonair U	10.00	20.00
131 Dragonite HOLO R	.75	1.50
132 Noibat C	.08	.20
133 Noivern R	.08	.20
134 Zygarde R	.25	.50
135 Regidrago V UR	1.00	2.00
136 Regidrago VSTAR UR	1.25	2.50
137 Smeargle C	7.50	15.00
138 Lugia V UR	2.00	4.00
139 Lugia VSTAR UR	.75	1.50
140 Ho-Oh V UR	.75	1.50
141 Spinda C	.75	1.50
142 Swablu C	7.50	15.00
143 Altaria U	.75	1.50
144 Buneary C	1.00	2.00
145 Lopunny U	.50	1.00
146 Archen U	2.50	5.00
147 Archeops HOLO R	5.00	10.00
148 Rufflet C	4.00	8.00
149 Hisuian Braviary R	12.50	25.00
150 Fletchling C	1.25	3.00
151 Brandon U	.10	.20
152 Candice U	2.50	6.00
153 Captivating Aroma U	30.00	75.00
154 Earthen Seal Stone HOLO R	.75	1.50
155 Emergency Jelly U	.75	1.50
156 Forest Seal Stone HOLO R	.12	.25
157 Furisode Girl U	15.00	30.00
158 Gym Trainer U	.10	.20
159 Lance U	40.00	80.00
160 Leafy Camo Poncho U	.30	.75
161 Primordial Altar U	.04	.10
162 Professor Laventon U	.60	1.50
163 Quad Stone U	.75	1.50
164 Serena U	.60	1.25
165 Unidentified Fossil U	.75	1.50
166 Wallace U	.05	.12
167 Worker U	.12	.30
168 Regenerative Energy U	6.00	12.00
169 V Guard Energy U	.30	.75
170 Serperior V UR FULL ART	1.00	2.00
171 Chesnaught V UR FULL ART	.04	.10
172 Reshiram V UR FULL ART	.10	.25
173 Alolan Vulpix V UR FULL ART	125.00	250.00
174 Omastar V UR FULL ART	5.00	10.00
175 Regieleki V UR FULL ART	.75	1.50
176 Unown V UR FULL ART	.75	1.50
177 Unown V UR ALT ART	.30	.60
178 Mawile V UR FULL ART	.75	1.50
179 Hisuian Arcanine V UR FULL ART	100.00	200.00
180 Skuntank V UR FULL ART	15.00	30.00
181 Skuntank V UR ALT ART	.75	1.50
182 Magearna V UR FULL ART	1.00	2.00
183 Regidrago V UR FULL ART	1.00	2.00
184 Regidrago V UR ALT ART	7.50	15.00
185 Lugia V UR FULL ART	1.25	2.50
186 Lugia V UR ALT ART	1.25	2.50
187 Ho-Oh V UR FULL ART	1.25	2.50
188 Brandon UR FULL ART	.08	.20
189 Candice UR FULL ART	.75	1.50
190 Furisode Girl UR FULL ART	1.50	3.00
191 Gym Trainer UR FULL ART	2.00	4.00
192 Lance UR FULL ART	1.00	2.00
193 Serena UR FULL ART	.75	1.50
194 Wallace UR FULL ART	.07	.15
195 Worker UR FULL ART	.75	1.50
196 Serperior VSTAR SCR	1.00	2.00
197 Alolan Vulpix VSTAR SCR	.07	.15
198 Regieleki VMAX SCR	1.50	3.00
199 Unown VSTAR SCR	7.50	15.00
200 Mawile VSTAR SCR	.75	1.50
201 Regidrago VSTAR SCR	.08	.20
202 Lugia VSTAR SCR	.08	.20
203 Brandon SCR	.08	.20
204 Candice SCR	.75	1.50
205 Furisode Girl SCR	.75	1.50
206 Lance SCR	.07	.15
207 Serena SCR	.75	1.50
208 Wallace SCR	.30	.75
209 Worker SCR	.10	.25
210 Serperior VSTAR SCR	.50	1.25
211 Lugia VSTAR SCR	.75	1.50
212 Energy Switch SCR	.05	.12
213 Gapejaw Bog SCR	.15	.40
214 Leafy Camo Poncho SCR	.75	1.50
215 V Guard Energy SCR	6.00	12.00

2022 Pokemon Sword and Shield Silver Tempest Trainer Gallery

TG01 Braixen HOLO R	.04	.10
TG02 Milotic HOLO R	.12	.30
TG03 Flaaffy HOLO R	25.00	50.00
TG04 Jynx HOLO R	.75	1.50
TG05 Gardevoir HOLO R	1.25	2.50
TG06 Malamar HOLO R	.12	.25
TG07 Rockruff HOLO R	250.00	500.00
TG08 Passimian HOLO R	2.00	5.00
TG09 Druddigon HOLO R	1.00	2.00
TG10 Smeargle HOLO R	.75	1.50
TG11 Altaria HOLO R	.10	.20
TG12 Kricketune V URR	.08	.20
TG13 Serperior V URR	.08	.20
TG14 Blaziken V URR	300.00	750.00
TG15 Blaziken VMAX URR	3.00	6.00
TG16 Zeraora V URR	30.00	60.00
TG17 Mawile V URR	1.25	2.50
TG18 Corviknight V URR	2.50	5.00
TG19 Corviknight VMAX URR	1.00	2.00
TG20 Rayquaza VMAX URR	.75	1.50
TG21 Duraludon VMAX URR	.60	1.25
TG22 Blissey V URR	.75	1.50
TG23 Friends in Galar UR	2.00	4.00
TG24 Gordie UR	12.50	25.00
TG25 Judge UR	7.50	15.00
TG26 Professor Burnet UR	2.00	4.00
TG27 Raihan UR	100.00	200.00
TG28 Sordward & Shielbert UR	.07	.15
TG29 Rayquaza VMAX SCR	.75	1.50
TG30 Duraludon VMAX SCR	.60	1.25

2022 Pokemon Trick or Trade

15 Trevenant	1.25	2.50
16 Phantump	.60	1.25

18 Hatenna	1.00	2.00
31 Litwick	7.50	15.00
32 Lampent	3.00	6.00
33 Chandelure	.60	1.25
49 Pikachu	.75	1.50
55 Gastly	.75	1.50
56 Haunter	10.00	20.00
56 Mewtwo	.60	1.25
57 Gengar	.75	1.50
58 Misdreavus	.75	1.50
59 Mismagius	.75	1.50
60 Duskull	150.00	300.00
61 Dusclops	.75	1.50
62 Dusknoir	1.00	2.00
69 Cubone	.75	2.00
72 Hattrem	.50	1.00
73 Hatterene	.75	1.50
76 Pumpkaboo	.75	1.50
77 Gourgeist	.08	.20
81 Mimikyu	.10	.25
82 Sinistea	.60	1.25
83 Polteageist	.07	.15
89 Zubat	30.00	60.00
93 Murkrow	12.50	25.00
102 Spinarak	.04	.10
103 Ariados	.10	.25
103 Nickit	.01	.08
105 Darkrai	.10	.25

2023 Pokemon McDonald's Collection

1 Sprigatito P	150.00	300.00
2 Fuecoco P	.08	.20
3 Quaxly P	17.50	35.00
4 Cetoddle P	.75	1.50
5 Cetitan P	.75	1.50
6 Pikachu P	4.00	8.00
7 Pawmi P	.50	1.00
8 Kilowattrel P	.15	.40
9 Flittle P	.60	1.50
10 Sandaconda P	.75	1.50
11 Klawf P	200.00	400.00
12 Blissey P	1.00	2.00
13 Tandemaus P	.75	1.50
14 Cyclizar P	2.00	4.00
15 Kirlia P	.60	1.25

2023 Pokemon Scarlet and Violet

1 Pineco C	2.00	4.00
2 Heracross U	.75	1.50
3 Shroomish C	3.00	6.00
4 Breloom U	.07	.15
5 Cacnea C	.10	.20
6 Cacturne U	1.50	3.00
7 Tropius C	.75	1.50
8 Scatterbug C	.75	1.50
9 Spewpa C	1.50	3.00
10 Vivillon U	3.00	6.00
11 Skiddo C	.75	1.50
12 Gogoat C	.75	1.50
13 Sprigatito C	1.25	2.50
14 Floragato U	20.00	40.00
15 Meowscarada R	.60	1.25
16 Tarountula C	1.00	2.00
17 Tarountula C	.10	.20
18 Tarountula C	2.50	5.00
19 Spidops EX RR	.75	1.50
20 Smoliv C	.50	1.00
21 Smoliv C	1.25	2.50
22 Dolliv C	.75	1.50
23 Arboliva R	2.50	5.00
24 Toedscool C	.60	1.25
25 Toedscool C	.75	1.50
26 Toedscruel U	.60	1.25
27 Capsakid C	.75	1.50
28 Capsakid C	.75	1.50
29 Scovillain U	.12	.25
30 Growlithe C	.04	.10
31 Growlithe C	.10	.25
32 Arcanine EX RR	.05	.12
33 Houndour C	.10	.25
34 Houndoom C	7.50	15.00
35 Torkoal U	125.00	250.00
36 Fuecoco C	1.50	3.00
37 Crocalor U	2.50	6.00
38 Skeledirge R	1.00	2.00
39 Charcadet C	.75	1.50
40 Charcadet C	3.00	8.00
41 Armarouge R	.75	1.50
42 Slowpoke C	.12	.25
43 Slowbro R	20.00	40.00
44 Magikarp C	2.50	5.00
45 Gyarados EX RR	1.00	2.00
46 Buizel C	.30	.60
47 Floatzel U	3.00	6.00
48 Alomomola C	7.50	15.00
49 Clauncher C	.75	1.50
50 Clawitzer C	.75	1.50
51 Bruxish C	.07	.15
52 Quaxly C	.30	.75
53 Quaxwell U	.75	1.50
54 Quaquaval R	.08	.20
55 Wiglett C	.04	.10
56 Wiglett C	2.50	5.00
57 Wugtrio U	1.50	3.00
58 Cetoddle C	25.00	50.00
59 Cetoddle C	.08	.20
60 Cetitan U	1.50	3.00
61 Dondozo R	7.50	15.00
62 Tatsugiri U	40.00	80.00
63 Magnemite C	.04	.10
64 Magneton C	.30	.75
65 Magnezone EX RR	.10	.20
66 Mareep C	.10	.20
67 Flaaffy U	.75	1.50
68 Pachirisu U	.75	1.50
69 Rotom C	.60	1.25
70 Rotom C	3.00	6.00
71 Toxel C	15.00	30.00
72 Toxtricity U	1.00	2.00
73 Pawmi C	1.50	3.00
74 Pawmi C	.75	1.50
75 Pawmo C	1.00	2.00
76 Pawmot R	.10	.20
77 Wattrel C	2.50	6.00
78 Wattrel C	.75	1.50
79 Kilowattrel U	.60	1.25
80 Miraidon R	.75	2.00
81 Miraidon EX RR	.75	1.50
82 Drowzee C	7.50	15.00
83 Hypno U	.08	.20
84 Ralts C	.07	.15
85 Kirlia C	.75	1.50
86 Gardevoir EX RR	.75	1.50
87 Shuppet C	1.25	2.50
88 Banette EX RR	1.00	2.00
89 Drifloon C	4.00	8.00
90 Drifblim U	.75	1.50
91 Flabebe C	.75	1.50
92 Floette C	7.50	15.00
93 Florges U	3.00	6.00
94 Dedenne C	10.00	20.00
95 Dedenne C	.60	1.25
96 Klefki R	.75	1.50
97 Fidough C	.75	1.50
98 Fidough C	.75	1.50
99 Dachsbun U	.08	.20
100 Flittle C	.04	.10
101 Flittle C	7.50	15.00
102 Flittle C	4.00	8.00
103 Espathra U	2.00	4.00
104 Greavard C	.75	1.50
105 Greavard C	2.50	6.00
106 Houndstone R	7.50	15.00
107 Mankey C	.04	.10
108 Primeape C	.30	.75
109 Annihilape R	.10	.20
110 Meditite C	7.50	15.00
111 Medicham U	1.00	2.00
112 Riolu C	.10	.20
113 Riolu C	25.00	50.00
114 Lucario U	1.50	3.00
115 Sandile C	1.25	2.50
116 Krokorok C	1.50	3.00
117 Krookodile U	.75	1.50
118 Hawlucha R	.75	1.50
119 Silicobra C	1.00	2.00
120 Sandaconda U	.75	1.50
121 Stonjourner U	6.00	12.00
122 Klawf R	.12	.25
123 Great Tusk EX RR	.05	.12
124 Koraidon R	.20	.50
125 Koraidon EX RR	1.00	2.00
126 Grimer C	.60	1.25
127 Muk U	.75	1.50
128 Seviper C	.75	1.50
129 Spiritomb U	7.50	15.00
130 Croagunk C	30.00	60.00
131 Toxicroak EX RR	1.00	2.50
132 Pawniard C	.60	1.50
133 Bisharp C	7.50	15.00
134 Kingambit R	.60	1.25
135 Maschiff C	3.00	8.00
136 Maschiff C	.60	1.25
137 Mabosstiff U	1.00	2.00
138 Bombirdier U	10.00	20.00
139 Forretress U	.75	1.50
140 Varoom C	7.50	15.00
141 Varoom C	.75	1.50
142 Revavroom R	1.00	2.00
143 Iron Treads EX RR	.30	.75
144 Chansey C	.75	1.50
145 Blissey U	.75	1.50
146 Zangoose C	.08	.20
147 Zangoose U	.05	.12
148 Starly C	7.50	15.00
149 Staravia C	.75	1.50
150 Staraptor U	.04	.10
151 Skwovet C	.30	.75
152 Greedent U	3.00	6.00
153 Indeedee R	.75	1.50
154 Lechonk C	2.00	4.00
155 Lechonk C	1.25	2.50
156 Lechonk C	.10	.20
157 Oinkologne U	125.00	250.00
158 Oinkologne EX RR	2.50	5.00
159 Tandemaus C	.75	1.50
160 Tandemaus C	.17	.35
161 Maushold U	.75	1.50
162 Squawkabilly C	1.25	2.50
163 Cyclizar U	1.50	3.00
164 Cyclizar R	.07	.15
165 Flamigo U	.05	.12
166 Arven U	.20	.50
167 Beach Court U	2.00	5.00
168 Crushing Hammer C	.07	.15
169 Defiance Band U	1.25	2.50
170 Electric Generator U	1.50	3.00
171 Energy Retrieval C	10.00	20.00
172 Energy Search C	20.00	40.00
173 Energy Switch C	2.00	5.00
174 Exp. Share U	7.50	15.00
175 Jacq U	7.50	15.00
176 Judge U	.75	1.50
177 Katy U	.75	1.50
178 Mesagoza U	.75	1.50
179 Miriam U	.75	1.50
180 Nemona C	.60	1.25
181 Nest Ball U	.75	1.50
182 Pal Pad C	1.00	2.00
183 Penny U	.75	1.50
184 Picnic Basket U	.75	1.50
185 Poké Ball C	.75	1.50
186 Pokégear 3.0 C	.60	1.25
187 Pokémon Catcher C	.08	.20
188 Potion C	.05	.12
189 Professor's Research [Professor Sada] R	6.00	12.00
190 Professor's Research [Professor Turo] R	7.50	15.00
191 Rare Candy C	20.00	40.00
192 Rock Chestplate U	.08	.20
193 Rocky Helmet U	4.00	8.00
194 Switch C	.04	.10
195 Team Star Grunt U	.20	.50
196 Ultra Ball U	.60	1.25
197 Vitality Band U	.75	1.50
198 Youngster U	.15	.30
199 Tarountula IR	.75	1.50
200 Dolliv IR	.75	1.50
201 Toedscool IR	1.00	2.00
202 Scovillain IR	5.00	12.00
203 Armarouge IR	2.00	4.00
204 Slowpoke IR	7.50	15.00
205 Clauncher IR	.10	.20
206 Wiglett IR	.75	1.50
207 Dondozo IR	1.00	2.00
208 Pachirisu IR	.10	.20
209 Pawmot IR	.75	1.50
210 Drowzee IR	7.50	15.00
211 Ralts IR	3.00	6.00
212 Kirlia IR	.05	.12
213 Fidough IR	.10	.25
214 Greavard IR	.07	.15
215 Riolu IR	2.00	4.00
216 Sandile IR	4.00	8.00
217 Klawf IR	7.50	15.00
218 Mabosstiff IR	.40	1.00
219 Bombirdier IR	.75	1.50
220 Kingambit IR	1.00	2.00
221 Starly IR	2.00	4.00
222 Skwovet IR	.01	.08
223 Spidops EX UR	.10	.25
224 Arcanine EX UR	7.50	15.00
225 Gyarados EX UR	1.00	2.00
226 Magnezone EX UR	1.00	2.00
227 Miraidon EX UR	1.00	2.00
228 Gardevoir EX UR	7.50	15.00
229 Banette EX UR	1.50	3.00
230 Great Tusk EX UR	7.50	15.00
231 Koraidon EX UR	1.25	2.50
232 Toxicroak EX UR	.75	1.50
233 Iron Treads EX UR	30.00	75.00
234 Oinkologne EX UR	.75	1.50
235 Arven UR	.08	.20
236 Jacq UR	1.00	2.00
237 Katy UR	1.00	2.00
238 Miriam UR	.75	1.50
239 Penny UR	7.50	15.00
240 Professor's Research [Professor Sada] UR	.04	.10
241 Professor's Research [Professor Turo] UR	.20	.50
242 Team Star Grunt UR	.40	1.00
243 Spidops EX SIR	.75	1.50
244 Miraidon EX SIR	1.50	3.00
245 Gardevoir EX SIR	1.25	2.50
246 Great Tusk EX SIR	.75	1.50
247 Koraidon EX SIR	2.50	5.00
248 Iron Treads EX SIR	.10	.20
249 Arven SIR	1.25	3.00
250 Jacq SIR	.07	.15
251 Miriam SIR	7.50	15.00
252 Penny SIR	2.50	5.00
253 Miraidon EX HR	2.00	4.00
254 Koraidon EX HR	.07	.15
255 Nest Ball HR	.05	.12
256 Rare Candy HR	.10	.25
257 Basic Lightning Energy HR	12.50	25.00
258 Basic Fighting Energy HR	7.50	15.00

2023 Pokemon Scarlet and Violet 151

1 Bulbasaur C	7.50	15.00
2 Ivysaur U	7.50	15.00
3 Venusaur ex RR	5.00	10.00
4 Charmander C	.75	1.50
5 Charmeleon U	.75	1.50
6 Charizard ex RR	4.00	8.00
7 Squirtle C	.04	.10
8 Wartortle U	.12	.30
9 Blastoise ex RR	.75	1.50
10 Caterpie C	1.25	2.50
11 Metapod C	4.00	8.00
12 Butterfree U	.30	.75
13 Weedle C	.75	1.50
14 Kakuna C	1.00	2.00
15 Beedrill R	1.00	2.00
16 Pidgey C	7.50	15.00
17 Pidgeotto C	.75	1.50
18 Pidgeot U	1.25	2.50
19 Rattata C	1.50	3.00
20 Raticate U	10.00	20.00
21 Spearow C	.60	1.25
22 Fearow U	.75	1.50
23 Ekans C	7.50	15.00
24 Arbok ex RR	6.00	12.00
25 Pikachu C	7.50	15.00
26 Raichu R	.75	1.50
27 Sandshrew C	.75	1.50
28 Sandslash U	.75	1.50
29 Nidoran C	.75	1.50
30 Nidorina U	.75	1.50
31 Nidoqueen U	.04	.10
32 Nidoran C	.20	.50
33 Nidorino U	.08	.20
34 Nidoking R	.10	.25
35 Clefairy C	.08	.20
36 Clefable U	.75	1.50
37 Vulpix C	.10	.20
38 Ninetales ex RR	.10	.20
39 Jigglypuff C	1.50	3.00
40 Wigglytuff ex RR	.10	.20
41 Zubat C	7.50	15.00
42 Golbat U	3.00	6.00
43 Oddish C	1.25	2.50
44 Gloom U	.75	1.50
45 Vileplume R	20.00	40.00
46 Paras C	.01	.08
47 Parasect U	.05	.12
48 Venonat C	7.50	15.00
49 Venomoth U	10.00	20.00
50 Diglett C	1.50	4.00
51 Dugtrio U	.75	1.50
52 Meowth C	1.00	2.00
53 Persian U	.10	.20
54 Psyduck C	7.50	15.00
55 Golduck U	1.50	3.00
56 Mankey C	20.00	50.00
57 Primeape U	7.50	15.00
58 Growlithe C	.60	1.25
59 Arcanine U	.75	1.50
60 Poliwag C	1.25	2.50
61 Poliwhirl C	2.00	4.00
62 Poliwrath U	1.50	3.00
63 Abra C	.75	1.50
64 Kadabra U	.75	1.50
65 Alakazam ex RR	.75	1.50
66 Machop C	.60	1.25
67 Machoke U	.75	1.50
68 Machamp R	.75	1.50
69 Bellsprout C	2.00	4.00
70 Weepinbell C	.04	.10
71 Victreebel U	.20	.50
72 Tentacool C	.75	1.50
73 Tentacruel U	.75	1.50
74 Geodude C	3.00	6.00
75 Graveler U	2.00	4.00
76 Golem ex RR	10.00	20.00
77 Ponyta C	.08	.20
78 Rapidash U	.10	.20
79 Slowpoke C	.08	.20
80 Slowbro U	.10	.25
81 Magnemite C	.10	.20
82 Magneton U	1.00	2.00
83 Farfetch'd C	.75	1.50
84 Doduo C	.04	.10
85 Dodrio R	.08	.20
86 Seel C	3.00	6.00
87 Dewgong U	7.50	15.00
88 Grimer C	1.00	2.00
89 Muk U	2.50	5.00
90 Shellder C	7.50	15.00
91 Cloyster U	.75	1.50
92 Gastly C	.50	1.00
93 Haunter U	.75	1.50
94 Gengar R	.75	1.50
95 Onix U	4.00	8.00
96 Drowzee C	4.00	8.00
97 Hypno U	1.50	4.00
98 Krabby C	3.00	6.00
99 Kingler U	.75	1.50
100 Voltorb C	.75	1.50
101 Electrode R	4.00	8.00
102 Exeggcute C	3.00	8.00
103 Exeggutor U	20.00	40.00
104 Cubone C	1.50	3.00
105 Marowak R	.30	.75
106 Hitmonlee U	.30	.75
107 Hitmonchan U	.07	.15
108 Lickitung C	.08	.20
109 Koffing C	.10	.25
110 Weezing R	.75	1.50
111 Rhyhorn C	1.25	2.50
112 Rhydon U	10.00	20.00
113 Chansey R	5.00	10.00
114 Tangela C	1.25	2.50
115 Kangaskhan ex RR	.08	.20
116 Horsea C	.75	1.50
117 Seadra U	.10	.25
118 Goldeen C	.40	1.00
119 Seaking U	.75	1.50
120 Staryu C	.60	1.25
121 Starmie R	.75	1.50
122 Mr. Mime R	1.00	2.00
123 Scyther U	7.50	15.00
124 Jynx ex RR	15.00	30.00
125 Electabuzz C	.75	1.50
126 Magmar C	1.50	3.00
127 Pinsir U	2.50	6.00
128 Tauros U	7.50	15.00
129 Magikarp C	.10	.20
130 Gyarados R	.10	.20
131 Lapras U	10.00	20.00
132 Ditto R	4.00	8.00
133 Eevee C	1.50	3.00
134 Vaporeon R	12.50	25.00
135 Jolteon R	.75	1.50
136 Flareon R	.01	.08
137 Porygon C	.10	.25
138 Omanyte U	.10	.20
139 Omastar R	2.50	5.00
140 Kabuto U	.10	.25
141 Kabutops R	.20	.50
142 Aerodactyl R	.75	1.50
143 Snorlax U	.75	1.50
144 Articuno R	3.00	6.00
145 Zapdos ex RR	.60	1.25
146 Moltres R	1.00	2.00
147 Dratini C	.75	1.50
148 Dragonair U	1.00	2.00
149 Dragonite R	20.00	40.00
150 Mewtwo R	.07	.15
151 Mew ex RR	.75	1.50
152 Antique Dome Fossil C	.75	1.50
153 Antique Helix Fossil C	1.00	2.50
154 Antique Old Amber C	4.00	8.00
155 Big Balloon U	.75	1.50
156 Bill's Transfer U	1.25	2.50
157 Cycling Road U	3.00	6.00
158 Daisy's Help U	.30	.75
159 Energy Sticker U	1.50	4.00
160 Erika's Invitation U	6.00	12.00
161 Giovanni's Charisma U	.75	1.50

162 Grabber U .04 .10
163 Leftovers U .40 1.00
164 Protective Goggles U 1.00 2.00
165 Rigid Band U .75 1.50
166 Bulbasaur IR 1.25 2.50
167 Ivysaur IR .75 1.50
168 Charmander IR .75 1.50
169 Charmeleon IR 1.50 3.00
170 Squirtle IR .60 1.25
171 Wartortle IR 4.00 8.00
172 Caterpie IR .10 .20
173 Pikachu IR .10 .20
174 Nidoking IR 10.00 20.00
175 Psyduck IR 10.00 20.00
176 Poliwhirl IR 6.00 15.00
177 Machoke IR 1.50 3.00
178 Tangela IR 6.00 12.00
179 Mr. Mime IR .01 .08
180 Omanyte IR .10 .25
181 Dragonair IR 10.00 20.00
182 Venusaur ex UR .75 1.50
183 Charizard ex UR 7.50 15.00
184 Blastoise ex UR .04 .10
185 Arbok ex UR .10 .25
186 Ninetales ex UR .07 .15
187 Wigglytuff ex UR 1.25 2.50
188 Alakazam ex UR 1.25 2.50
189 Golem ex UR 15.00 30.00
190 Kangaskhan ex UR .07 .15
191 Jynx ex UR 10.00 20.00
192 Zapdos ex UR 1.00 2.00
193 Mew ex UR 1.00 2.00
194 Bill's Transfer UR 1.50 3.00
195 Daisy's Help UR 7.50 15.00
196 Erika's Invitation UR 7.50 15.00
197 Giovanni's Charisma UR 3.00 6.00
198 Venusaur ex SIR 20.00 40.00
199 Charizard ex SIR 4.00 8.00
200 Blastoise ex SIR 4.00 8.00
201 Alakazam ex SIR 10.00 20.00
202 Zapdos ex SIR .08 .20
203 Erika's Invitation SIR .08 .20
204 Giovanni's Charisma SIR 1.25 3.00
205 Mew ex HR 7.50 15.00
206 Switch HR 7.50 15.00
207 Basic Psychic Energy HR .08 .20

2023 Pokemon Scarlet and Violet Obsidian Flames

1 Oddish C .75 1.50
2 Gloom C .10 .20
3 Bellossom U .60 1.25
4 Scyther C .75 1.50
5 Shuckle C 3.00 8.00
6 Surskit C .10 .20
7 Masquerain U 50.00 100.00
8 Combee C 4.00 8.00
9 Foongus C .75 1.50
10 Amoonguss U .10 .20
11 Phantump C .75 1.50
12 Trevenant U .08 .20
13 Rowlet C .08 .20
14 Dartrix U .10 .25
15 Decidueye EX RR 2.50 5.00
16 Bounsweet C 15.00 30.00
17 Steenee C .10 .20
18 Tsareena U .12 .25
19 Smoliv C .75 1.50
20 Dolliv C .75 1.50
21 Arboliva U 12.50 25.00
23 Capsakid C 4.00 8.00
24 Capsakid C .08 .20
25 Scovillain R .25 .60
26 Charmander C .75 1.50
27 Charmeleon U 2.00 4.00
28 Vulpix C 12.50 25.00
29 Ninetales U 1.50 4.00
30 Entei R 1.25 2.50
31 Numel C 1.00 2.00
32 Camerupt U 2.00 4.00
33 Victini EX RR 3.00 8.00
34 Darumaka C .10 .20
35 Darmanitan U 7.50 15.00
36 Litwick C .75 1.50
37 Lampent C 1.25 2.50
38 Chandelure U 1.50 3.00
39 Heatmor C 7.50 15.00
40 Larvesta C 25.00 50.00
41 Volcarona U .10 .20
42 Eiscue EX RR .04 .10
43 Charcadet C .10 .25
44 Armarouge U 12.00 30.00
45 Lapras U 30.00 60.00
46 Carvanha C .50 1.00
47 Sharpedo U 15.00 30.00
48 Buizel C 1.25 2.50
49 Floatzel U .08 .20
50 Tympole C 3.00 6.00
51 Palpitoad C .75 1.50
52 Seismitoad U 10.00 20.00
53 Cubchoo C .08 .20
54 Beartic U .12 .30
55 Cryogonal C .60 1.25
56 Froakie C 3.00 6.00
57 Frogadier U .75 1.50
58 Wiglett C 1.00 2.00
59 Wugtrio U .10 .20
60 Finizen C 4.00 10.00
61 Finizen C .75 1.50
62 Palafin R 1.25 2.50
63 Magnemite C 4.00 8.00
64 Magneton C 3.00 6.00
65 Magnezone U .07 .15
66 Tyranitar EX RR 7.50 15.00
67 Tynamo C 17.50 35.00
68 Eelektrik C 1.50 4.00
69 Eelektross U .60 1.25
70 Thundurus R .75 1.50
71 Toxel C 1.00 2.00
72 Toxtricity R .10 .20
73 Pawmot EX RR 25.00 50.00
74 Tadbulb C 1.00 2.00
75 Tadbulb C 1.50 3.00
76 Tadbulb C .10 .20
77 Bellibolt U .10 .20
78 Bellibolt U 1.00 2.00
79 Miraidon EX RR .75 1.50
80 Cleffa C .75 1.50
81 Clefairy C .75 1.50
82 Clefable EX RR 7.50 15.00
83 Togepi C 15.00 30.00
84 Togetic U 7.50 15.00
85 Togekiss R 12.50 25.00
86 Espeon U 5.00 10.00
87 Snubbull C 10.00 25.00
88 Granbull U 30.00 60.00
89 Mawile C .60 1.50
90 Spoink C 3.00 8.00
91 Grumpig U .60 1.25
92 Lunatone U .08 .20
93 Solrock U .10 .25
94 Baltoy C 30.00 75.00
95 Claydol R .75 1.50
96 Vespiquen EX RR 1.00 2.00
97 Sinistea C 10.00 20.00
98 Polteageist U .75 1.50
99 Greavard C .12 .25
100 Greavard C .75 1.50
101 Houndstone U 1.25 2.50
102 Houndstone EX RR .07 .15
103 Diglett C .10 .20
104 Dugtrio U 3.00 8.00
105 Larvitar C 20.00 40.00
106 Pupitar U .10 .20
107 Nosepass C 3.00 6.00
108 Barboach C .08 .20
109 Whiscash U .75 1.50
110 Bonsly C 15.00 40.00
111 Drilbur C 2.50 5.00
112 Stunfisk U 3.00 6.00
113 Diggersby U .07 .15
114 Crabrawler C 20.00 40.00
115 Crabominable U .75 1.50
116 Rockruff C 20.00 40.00
117 Lycanroc U .75 2.00
118 Toedscool C 1.25 2.50
119 Toedscruel U 15.00 30.00
120 Klawf EX RR .08 .20
121 Glimmet C .75 1.50
122 Glimmet C 4.00 8.00
123 Glimmora EX RR .10 .20
124 Koraidon EX RR 5.00 10.00
125 Charizard EX RR .08 .20
126 Paldean Wooper C .05 .12
127 Paldean Wooper C 4.00 10.00
128 Paldean Clodsire U .10 .20
129 Paldean Clodsire U .75 1.50
130 Umbreon U 1.50 3.00
131 Houndour C 17.50 35.00
132 Houndour C .60 1.25
133 Houndoom U 1.25 3.00
134 Houndoom EX RR 3.00 6.00
135 Absol EX RR .10 .20
136 Darkrai R .75 1.50
137 Inkay C 1.25 2.50
138 Malamar U 3.00 6.00
139 Salandit C .60 1.25
140 Salazzle U 1.00 2.00
141 Scizor R 5.00 10.00
142 Skarmory U 1.25 2.50
143 Mawile U 1.25 3.00
144 Bronzor C 12.00 30.00
145 Bronzong U .75 1.50
146 Probopass U 7.50 15.00
147 Excadrill U .10 .20
148 Pawniard C .75 1.50
149 Bisharp C 30.00 60.00
150 Kingambit U 10.00 20.00
151 Togedemaru C 10.00 20.00
152 Meltan C 7.50 15.00
153 Melmetal EX RR 2.00 4.00
154 Varoom C 1.00 2.00
155 Varoom C .75 1.50
156 Revavroom EX RR 7.50 15.00
157 Dratini C 15.00 30.00
158 Dragonair U 1.25 3.00
159 Dragonite EX RR 1.25 2.50
160 Altaria U .08 .20
161 Drampa U .05 .12
162 Pidgey C 5.00 10.00
163 Pidgeotto U 12.50 25.00
164 Pidgeot EX RR .75 1.50
165 Kangaskhan U .75 1.50
166 Eevee C 15.00 30.00
167 Zigzagoon C 1.50 3.00
168 Linoone U 1.25 3.00
169 Swablu C .08 .20
170 Lillipup C .75 1.50
171 Herdier C 1.25 2.50
172 Stoutland U .10 .20
173 Audino C 1.00 2.00
174 Bouffalant U .12 .25
175 Bunnelby C .75 1.50
176 Yungoos C 12.50 25.00
177 Gumshoos U 1.00 2.50
178 Skwovet C 1.00 2.00
179 Greedent EX RR 2.00 5.00
180 Lechonk C .10 .20
181 Lechonk C .75 1.50
182 Lechonk C .10 .20
183 Oinkologne U 25.00 50.00
184 Oinkologne U 7.50 15.00
185 Flamigo U 2.00 4.00
186 Arven U 150.00 300.00
187 Brassius U .08 .20
188 Geeta R .75 1.50
189 Letter of Encouragement U 12.50 25.00
190 Ortega U 1.50 4.00
191 Patrol Cap U .08 .20
192 Pokémon League Headquarters U .50 1.25
193 Poppy U 30.00 60.00
194 Ryme C 1.50 3.00
195 Team Star Grunt U .75 1.50
196 Town Store C .60 1.25
197 Vengeful Punch U 1.25 2.50
198 Gloom IR 15.00 40.00
199 Ninetales IR .75 1.50
200 Palafin IR .75 1.50
201 Bellibolt IR 7.50 15.00
202 Cleffa IR 4.00 8.00
203 Larvitar IR .10 .20
204 Houndour IR .07 .15
205 Scizor IR .75 1.50
206 Varoom IR .50 1.00
207 Pidgey IR 2.50 5.00
208 Pidgeotto IR 1.50 4.00
209 Lechonk IR .10 .20
210 Eiscue EX UR 7.50 15.00
211 Tyranitar EX UR .60 1.25
212 Vespiquen EX UR 2.50 5.00
213 Glimmora EX UR 3.00 6.00
214 Absol EX UR 1.25 2.50
215 Charizard EX UR 10.00 20.00
216 Revavroom EX UR 1.00 2.00
217 Pidgeot EX UR 20.00 40.00
218 Geeta UR .07 .15
219 Ortega UR .75 1.50
220 Poppy UR .10 .20
221 Ryme UR 10.00 20.00
222 Eiscue EX SIR .08 .20
223 Charizard EX SIR 10.00 20.00
224 Revavroom EX SIR 12.50 25.00
225 Pidgeot EX SIR .75 1.50
226 Geeta SIR 1.00 2.50
227 Poppy SIR .08 .20
228 Charizard EX HR .30 .75
229 Artazon HR 2.00 5.00
230 Basic Fire Energy HR 7.50 15.00

2023 Pokemon Scarlet and Violet Paldea Evolved

1 Hoppip C .75 1.50
2 Skiploom U 1.00 2.00
3 Jumpluff R .75 1.50
4 Pineco C 10.00 20.00
5 Forretress EX RR 10.00 25.00
6 Heracross U .07 .15
7 Tropius C .75 1.50
8 Combee C .75 1.50
9 Vespiquen U 2.50 5.00
10 Snover C .75 1.50
11 Abomasnow R .12 .25
12 Sprigatito C 12.50 25.00
13 Sprigatito C 5.00 10.00
14 Floragato U 5.00 12.00
15 Meowscarada EX RR 1.25 3.00
16 Tarountula C 15.00 30.00
17 Tarountula C 1.00 2.00
18 Spidops U .07 .15
19 Nymble C .75 1.50
20 Nymble C 1.25 2.50
21 Lokix R 1.25 2.50
22 Bramblin C 2.00 4.00
23 Bramblin C 7.50 15.00
24 Brambleghast U 75.00 150.00
25 Rellor C .75 1.50
26 Rellor C 1.50 4.00
27 Wo-Chien EX RR 3.00 6.00
28 Paldean Tauros U .08 .20
29 Fletchinder U .10 .25
30 Talonflame U 4.00 8.00
31 Litleo C 12.50 25.00
32 Pyroar U .08 .20
33 Oricorio R 1.00 2.50
34 Fuecoco C .75 1.50
35 Fuecoco C 1.25 2.50
36 Crocalor U .75 1.50
37 Skeledirge EX RR 10.00 20.00
38 Charcadet C .60 1.25
39 Charcadet C .75 1.50
40 Chi-Yu EX RR 4.00 8.00
41 Paldean Tauros U .08 .20
42 Magikarp C .25 .50
43 Gyarados R 10.00 20.00
44 Marill C 3.00 6.00
45 Azumarill U 20.00 40.00
46 Delibird C 1.50 3.00
47 Luvdisc C .07 .15
48 Eiscue U .75 1.50
49 Quaxly C 1.00 2.00
50 Quaxly C 10.00 20.00
51 Quaxwell U 3.00 6.00
52 Quaquaval EX RR 6.00 15.00
53 Cetoddle C 1.25 2.50
54 Cetoddle C .75 1.50
55 Cetitan U 10.00 20.00
56 Veluza R 1.00 2.00
57 Frigibax C 10.00 25.00
58 Frigibax C .75 1.50
59 Arctibax U 2.00 5.00
60 Baxcalibur R 2.00 5.00
61 Chien-Pao EX RR .08 .20
62 Pikachu C .10 .25
63 Pikachu EX RR 6.00 12.00
64 Raichu U 12.50 25.00
65 Magnemite C 1.00 2.00
66 Voltorb C 2.00 4.00
67 Electrode U 7.50 15.00
68 Shinx C .75 1.50
69 Shinx C .75 1.50
70 Luxio U .75 1.50
71 Luxray R 15.00 30.00
72 Pincurchin C .08 .20
73 Pincurchin U .10 .20
74 Pawmi C 75.00 150.00
75 Pawmo U 30.00 60.00
76 Pawmot R 1.50 4.00
77 Tadbulb C .10 .20
78 Tadbulb C .75 1.50
79 Bellibolt EX RR 2.50 6.00
80 Wattrel C 1.00 2.00
81 Wattrel C 25.00 50.00
82 Kilowattrel U .75 1.50
83 Jigglypuff C 10.00 20.00
84 Wigglytuff R .75 1.50
85 Slowpoke C 1.25 2.50
86 Slowking EX RR 7.50 15.00
87 Misdreavus C 5.00 10.00
88 Mismagius U 2.00 4.00
89 Spiritomb R .60 1.25
90 Gothita C 3.00 8.00
91 Gothorita C 4.00 10.00
92 Gothitelle U 1.50 3.00
93 Dedenne EX RR .75 1.50
94 Oranguru U 1.25 2.50
95 Sandygast C .60 1.25
96 Palossand U .60 1.25
97 Mimikyu R .08 .20
98 Ceruledge R .05 .12
99 Rabsca R 1.00 2.00
100 Tinkatink C 1.50 3.00
101 Tinkatink C .08 .20
102 Tinkatink C .10 .20
103 Tinkatuff U 2.50 5.00
104 Tinkatuff U 15.00 30.00
105 Tinkaton R .75 1.50
106 Mankey C 30.00 60.00
107 Primeape U .75 1.50
108 Paldean Tauros U 1.25 3.00
109 Sudowoodo U .60 1.25
110 Larvitar C .75 1.50
111 Pupitar U 1.50 3.00
112 Makuhita C 30.00 60.00
113 Hariyama R .10 .20
114 Croagunk C 1.50 3.00
115 Toxicroak U 1.25 3.00
116 Rockruff C 1.50 4.00
117 Lycanroc EX RR 7.50 15.00
118 Passimian U .60 1.25
119 Falinks C 6.00 15.00
120 Nacli C 3.00 6.00
121 Nacli C 2.50 5.00
122 Naclstack U 2.50 5.00
123 Garganacl R 7.50 15.00
124 Glimmet C .08 .20
125 Glimmet C .10 .25
126 Glimmora R .75 1.50
127 Ting-Lu EX RR 5.00 10.00
128 Paldean Wooper C .75 1.50
129 Paldean Wooper C 1.00 2.00
130 Paldean Clodsire EX RR 4.00 10.00
131 Murkrow C 15.00 30.00
132 Honchkrow U 2.50 5.00
133 Sneasel C .10 .20
134 Weavile R 1.00 2.50
135 Tyranitar R 3.00 6.00
136 Sableye R .60 1.25
137 Seviper U 10.00 20.00
138 Deino C 6.00 12.00
139 Zweilous U .75 1.50
140 Hydreigon R 1.00 2.00
141 Maschiff C 25.00 50.00
142 Maschiff C .75 1.50
143 Mabosstiff U .10 .20
144 Shroodle C 1.00 2.50
145 Shroodle C .75 1.50
146 Grafaiai U 6.00 15.00
147 Bombirdier U .75 1.50
148 Corviknight U 1.00 2.00
149 Cufant C 5.00 10.00
150 Copperajah EX RR 1.50 3.00
151 Orthworm R 60.00 125.00
152 Noibat C 3.00 6.00
153 Noivern EX RR 1.25 2.50
154 Girafarig C .08 .20
155 Farigiraf U .10 .25
156 Dunsparce C .75 1.50
157 Dudunsparce U 2.00 4.00
158 Wingull C .08 .20
159 Pelipper U 2.50 5.00
160 Slakoth C .75 1.50
161 Vigoroth U 2.50 5.00
162 Slaking R 4.00 8.00
163 Fletchling C .07 .15
164 Rookidee C .60 1.25
165 Corvisquire U 60.00 125.00
166 Tandemaus C 12.00 30.00
167 Tandemaus C .08 .20
168 Maushold U 1.00 2.50
169 Squawkabilly EX RR 25.00 50.00
170 Flamigo U 12.50 25.00
171 Artazon U .10 .20
172 Boss's Orders [Ghetsis] R .75 1.50
173 Bravery Charm U 4.00 10.00
174 Calamitous Snowy Mountain U 1.00 2.00
175 Calamitous Wasteland U .75 1.50
176 Choice Belt U 1.25 3.00
177 Clavell C 12.50 25.00
178 Delivery Drone U 40.00 80.00
179 Dendra U .75 1.50
180 Falkner U 25.00 50.00
181 Fighting Au Lait U 25.00 50.00
182 Giacomo U .60 1.25
183 Great Ball C 7.50 15.00
184 Grusha U .08 .20
185 Iono U .20 .50
186 Practice Studio U 17.50 35.00
187 Saguaro U 7.50 15.00
188 Super Rod C .75 1.50
189 Superior Energy Retrieval U 4.00 8.00

190 Jet Energy U 6.00 12.00
191 Luminous Energy U .10 .20
192 Reversal Energy U 3.00 6.00
193 Therapeutic Energy U 1.00 2.00
194 Heracross IR 3.00 6.00
195 Tropius IR 3.00 6.00
196 Sprigatito IR 1.00 2.50
197 Floragato IR .75 1.50
198 Bramblin IR 1.00 2.00
199 Fletchinder IR 1.50 3.00
200 Pyroar IR 3.00 6.00
201 Fuecoco IR 1.00 2.00
202 Crocalor IR 1.50 3.00
203 Magikarp IR .10 .20
204 Marill IR 5.00 12.00
205 Eiscue IR 12.50 25.00
206 Quaxly IR 7.50 15.00
207 Quaxwell IR .75 1.50
208 Frigibax IR .08 .20
209 Arctibax IR 3.00 8.00
210 Baxcalibur IR .08 .20
211 Raichu IR .75 2.00
212 Mismagius IR 3.00 6.00
213 Gothorita IR .75 1.50
214 Sandygast IR .75 2.00
215 Rabsca IR 2.50 5.00
216 Tinkatink IR 4.00 8.00
217 Tinkatuff IR 1.50 3.00
218 Paldean Tauros IR 1.00 2.50
219 Sudowoodo IR .10 .20
220 Nacli IR 10.00 20.00
221 Paldean Wooper IR .50 1.00
222 Tyranitar IR 17.50 35.00
223 Grafaiai IR 1.50 4.00
224 Orthworm IR .40 1.00
225 Rookidee IR .60 1.25
226 Maushold IR 2.50 5.00
227 Flamigo IR 12.50 25.00
228 Farigiraf IR 4.00 8.00
229 Dudunsparce IR .75 1.50
230 Forretress EX URR 2.50 5.00
231 Meowscarada EX URR .75 1.50
232 Wo-Chien EX URR 1.00 2.50
233 Skeledirge EX URR 6.00 12.00
234 Chi-Yu EX URR .10 .20
235 Quaquaval EX URR .75 1.50
236 Chien-Pao EX URR 1.00 2.00
237 Bellibolt EX URR 2.00 5.00
238 Slowking EX URR 6.00 12.00
239 Dedenne EX URR 3.00 6.00
240 Tinkaton EX URR .75 1.50
241 Lycanroc EX URR .08 .20
242 Annihilape EX URR .10 .25
243 Ting-Lu EX URR 75.00 150.00
244 Paldean Clodsire EX URR 7.50 15.00
245 Copperajah EX URR 1.00 2.50
246 Noivern EX URR 30.00 75.00
247 Squawkabilly EX URR 3.00 6.00
248 Boss's Orders [Ghetsis] URR .10 .20
249 Clavell URR 1.00 2.00
250 Dendra URR .75 1.50
251 Falkner URR .75 1.50
252 Giacomo URR 4.00 8.00
253 Grusha URR .08 .20
254 Iono URR 2.00 5.00
255 Saguaro URR 2.00 4.00
256 Meowscarada EX SIR 1.50 3.00
257 Wo-Chien EX SIR 5.00 10.00
258 Skeledirge EX SIR .75 1.50
259 Chi-Yu EX SIR .07 .15
260 Quaquaval EX SIR 12.50 25.00
261 Chien-Pao EX SIR 3.00 8.00
262 Tinkaton EX SIR 1.50 4.00
263 Ting-Lu EX SIR 1.00 2.00
264 Squawkabilly EX SIR 4.00 8.00
265 Boss's Orders [Ghetsis] SIR 1.25 2.50
266 Dendra SIR .08 .20
267 Giacomo SIR .50 1.25
268 Grusha SIR 2.50 5.00
269 Iono SIR 2.50 5.00
270 Saguaro SIR .60 1.25
271 Meowscarada EX HR 7.50 15.00
272 Skeledirge EX HR 2.50 5.00
273 Quaquaval EX HR 5.00 10.00
274 Chien-Pao EX HR 1.25 3.00
275 Ting-Lu EX HR 10.00 25.00
276 Super Rod HR .10 .20
277 Superior Energy Retrieval HR 12.50 25.00
278 Basic Grass Energy HR .60 1.25
279 Basic Water Energy HR 1.00 2.00

2023 Pokemon Scarlet and Violet Paradox Rift

1 Surskit C 1.00 2.00
2 Masquerain U 5.00 10.00
3 Froslass ex RR HOLO 1.25 2.50
4 Pansage C 5.00 12.00
5 Simisage U .08 .20
6 Dwebble C 10.00 20.00
7 Crustle C 1.25 2.50
8 Bounsweet C 3.00 6.00
9 Steenee U .75 1.50
10 Blipbug C 2.00 5.00
11 Dottler C .60 1.25
12 Orbeetle U 4.00 8.00
13 Nymble C 2.50 5.00
14 Nymble C .75 1.50
15 Toedscool C 30.00 75.00
16 Toedscool C 7.50 15.00
17 Toedscruel U .75 1.50
18 Wo-Chien R .08 .20
19 Magby C .12 .30
20 Pansear C .75 1.50
21 Simisear U 6.00 12.00
22 Volcanion R 20.00 40.00
23 Fuecoco C 2.50 5.00
24 Crocalor U 2.50 5.00
25 Charcadet C 2.50 5.00
26 Charcadet C 12.50 25.00
27 Armarouge ex RR HOLO .10 .20
28 Iron Moth R 12.50 25.00
29 Chi-Yu R .08 .20
30 Horsea C 6.00 12.00
31 Seadra C 1.50 3.00
32 Kingdra R 1.25 2.50
33 Remoraid C .08 .20
34 Octillery C .08 .20
35 Feebas C 3.00 8.00
36 Milotic R .60 1.25
37 Snorunt C .07 .15
38 Garchomp ex RR HOLO .50 1.00
39 Mantyke C .75 2.00
40 Palkia R 7.50 15.00
41 Panpour C 6.00 12.00
42 Simipour U .75 1.50
43 Vanillite C .60 1.25
44 Vanillish C 1.00 2.00
45 Vanilluxe U 1.25 3.00
46 Tsareena ex RR HOLO 3.00 6.00
47 Wimpod C 8.00 20.00
48 Wimpod C 12.50 25.00
49 Golisopod R 20.00 50.00
50 Golisopod ex RR HOLO 5.00 12.00
51 Wiglett C .12 .30
52 Wiglett C 4.00 8.00
53 Wugtrio U 5.00 10.00
54 Veluza U .60 1.25
55 Dondozo U .75 1.50
56 Iron Bundle U 20.00 40.00
57 Chien-Pao R 1.25 2.50
58 Mewtwo ex RR HOLO .07 .15
59 Elekid C 12.50 25.00
60 Plusle C 1.00 2.00
61 Minun C 7.50 15.00
62 Blitzle C .08 .20
63 Zebstrika U .10 .20
64 Joltik C 1.25 2.50
65 Galvantula C 17.50 35.00
66 Zekrom R 2.00 4.00
67 Oricorio C 3.00 6.00
68 Tapu Kokoex RR HOLO 5.00 10.00
69 Toxel C .12 .25
70 Iron Hands ex RR HOLO .75 1.50
71 Natu C 12.50 25.00
72 Xatu R 1.00 2.50
73 Latios R .60 1.25
74 Deoxys R .75 1.50
75 Yamask C 1.25 3.00
76 Cofagrigus ex RR HOLO 25.00 50.00
77 Pumpkaboo C 10.00 25.00
78 Gourgeist U 1.00 2.50
79 Flittle C 2.50 6.00
80 Flittle C .75 1.50
81 Espathra R .75 1.50
82 Tinkatink C 20.00 40.00
83 Tinkatink C 3.00 6.00
84 Tinkatuff C 7.50 15.00
85 Tinkaton U .10 .20
86 Scream Tail U 1.00 2.50
87 Gimmighoul C 2.00 4.00
88 Gimmighoul C .08 .20
89 Iron Valiant ex RR HOLO 2.00 4.00
90 Onix C .10 .20
91 Gligar C 50.00 100.00
92 Gliscor U 2.00 4.00
93 Groudon R 15.00 30.00
94 Gible C 2.00 5.00
95 Gabite C 2.50 5.00
96 Mienfoo C 2.00 4.00
97 Mienshao U 1.00 2.00
98 Hoopa ex RR HOLO 30.00 60.00
99 Minior U .75 1.50
100 Toxtricity ex RR HOLO 3.00 6.00
101 Nacli C 10.00 20.00
102 Nacli C 1.50 4.00
103 Naclstack C 5.00 12.00
104 Garganacl R 1.25 2.50
105 Klawf U 4.00 8.00
106 Flamigo C .08 .20
107 Slither Wing U 2.50 5.00
108 Sandy Shocks ex RR HOLO 6.00 12.00
109 Ting-Lu R 4.00 8.00
110 Zubat C .75 1.50
111 Golbat C .75 1.50
112 Crobat U 7.50 15.00
113 Absol U 2.50 5.00
114 Purrloin C 2.50 5.00
115 Liepard C 1.00 2.00
116 Trubbish C 1.00 2.50
117 Garbodor U .07 .15
118 Yveltal R 7.50 15.00
119 Nickit C 3.00 6.00
120 Thievul R .75 1.50
121 Morpeko R 2.00 5.00
122 Lokix R 12.50 25.00
123 Brute Bonnet R 1.00 2.50
124 Roaring Moon Ex RR HOLO .75 1.50
125 Steelix R 3.00 6.00
126 Jirachi C .12 .30
127 Ferroseed C .75 1.50
128 Ferrothorn U .75 1.50
129 Durant U 1.00 2.50
130 Honedge C .75 1.50
131 Honedge C 30.00 75.00
132 Doublade C 200.00 400.00
133 Doublade C 20.00 40.00
134 Aegislash R .75 2.00
135 Aegislashex RR HOLO 2.00 4.00
136 Zacian R .75 1.50
137 Skeledirgeex RR HOLO .75 1.50
138 Orthworm U 125.00 250.00
139 Gholdengoex RR HOLO 4.00 10.00
140 Altariaex RR HOLO 4.00 8.00
141 Tatsugiri U 10.00 20.00
142 Porygon C .75 1.50
143 Porygon2 C 6.00 15.00
144 Porygon-Z R 6.00 12.00
145 Aipom C .07 .15
146 Ambipom U .10 .20
147 Miltank C .75 1.50
148 Whismur C 5.00 12.00
149 Loudred C 12.50 25.00
150 Exploud U 4.00 8.00
151 Spinda C .75 1.50
152 Swablu C .08 .20
153 Tandemaus C 10.00 25.00
154 Tandemaus C .75 1.50
155 Mausholdex RR HOLO 2.50 5.00
156 Bombirdierex RR HOLO 2.50 5.00
157 Cyclizar U 4.00 8.00
158 Iron Jugulis R 1.50 3.00
159 Ancient Booster Energy Capsule U 3.00 6.00
160 Counter Catcher U 12.50 25.00
161 Cursed Duster U 1.00 2.50
162 Defiance Vest U 2.50 6.00
163 Earthen Vessel U 3.00 6.00
164 Future Booster Energy Capsule U 1.25 3.00
165 Larry C 4.00 8.00
166 Luxurious Cape U 1.00 2.00
167 Mela U 2.00 4.00
168 Norman U .07 .15
169 Parasol Lady C .10 .20
170 Professor Sada's Vitality U .75 1.50
171 Professor Turo's Scenario U .75 1.50
172 Rika U .75 1.50
173 Roark U 5.00 12.00
174 Shauntal U 5.00 12.00
175 Snorlax Doll U .75 1.50
176 Technical Machine: Blindside U 6.00 12.00
177 Technical Machine: Devolution U 2.50 5.00
178 Technical Machine: Evolution U 1.00 2.00
179 Technical Machine: Turbo Energize U 2.00 4.00
180 Techno Radar U 40.00 100.00
181 Tulip U .08 .20
182 Medical Energy U 1.25 3.00
183 Crustle IR HOLO 10.00 20.00
184 Dottler IR HOLO 1.00 2.50
185 Toedscruel IR HOLO .75 1.50
186 Magby IR HOLO .75 1.50
187 Iron Moth IR HOLO 1.25 2.50
188 Snorunt IR HOLO 75.00 150.00
189 Mantyke IR HOLO 1.50 3.00
190 Vanillish IR HOLO .07 .15
191 Wimpod IR HOLO 1.00 2.00
192 Veluza IR HOLO 15.00 30.00
193 Plusle IR HOLO 2.00 5.00
194 Minun IR HOLO .12 .25
195 Blitzle IR HOLO 2.50 5.00
196 Joltik IR HOLO .75 1.50
197 Espathra IR HOLO 15.00 30.00
198 Gimmighoul IR HOLO 4.00 8.00
199 Groudon IR HOLO 15.00 30.00
200 Mienshao IR HOLO .75 1.50
201 Minior IR HOLO 12.50 25.00
202 Garganacl IR HOLO 7.50 15.00
203 Slither Wing IR HOLO 6.00 12.00
204 Garbodor IR HOLO 7.50 15.00
205 Yveltal IR HOLO 1.00 2.00
206 Morpeko IR HOLO 4.00 10.00
207 Brute Bonnet IR HOLO 3.00 6.00
208 Steelix IR HOLO .08 .20
209 Ferrothorn IR HOLO 2.00 5.00
210 Aegislash IR HOLO 1.25 2.50
211 Aipom IR HOLO 1.00 2.00
212 Loudred IR HOLO .12 .25
213 Swablu IR HOLO 2.00 4.00
214 Porygon-Z IR HOLO .75 2.00
215 Cyclizar IR HOLO .75 1.50
216 Iron Jugulis IR HOLO .60 1.50
217 Froslass ex UR HOLO .15 .30
218 Armarouge ex UR HOLO 50.00 100.00
219 Garchomp ex UR HOLO 1.00 2.50
220 Tsareena ex UR HOLO 1.25 2.50
221 Golisopod ex UR HOLO 2.50 5.00
222 Tapu Koko ex UR HOLO 5.00 10.00
223 Iron Hands ex UR HOLO 7.50 15.00
224 Cofagrigus ex UR HOLO .60 1.25
225 Iron Valiant ex UR HOLO 6.00 12.00
226 Hoopa ex UR HOLO .75 1.50
227 Toxtricity ex UR HOLO 1.25 2.50
228 Sandy Shocks ex UR HOLO 7.50 15.00
229 Roaring Moon ex UR HOLO .75 1.50
230 Aegislash ex UR HOLO 6.00 12.00
231 Gholdengo ex UR HOLO 3.00 6.00
232 Altaria ex UR HOLO 1.00 2.50
233 Maushold ex UR HOLO 6.00 12.00
234 Bombirdier ex UR HOLO .50 1.00
235 Larry UR HOLO 5.00 12.00
236 Mela UR HOLO 30.00 60.00
237 Norman UR HOLO 3.00 6.00
238 Parasol Lady UR HOLO 3.00 6.00
239 Professor Sada's Vitality UR HOLO .08 .20
240 Professor Turo's Scenario UR HOLO .12 .25
241 Rika UR HOLO 1.00 2.00
242 Roark UR HOLO 6.00 15.00
243 Shauntal UR HOLO 1.00 2.00
244 Tulip UR HOLO 3.00 8.00
245 Garchomp ex SIR HOLO .50 1.25
246 Golisopod ex SIR HOLO 4.00 8.00
247 Tapu Koko ex SIR HOLO 1.50 3.00
248 Iron Hands ex SIR HOLO .60 1.25
249 Iron Valiant ex SIR HOLO .75 1.50
250 Sandy Shocks ex SIR HOLO 10.00 20.00
251 Roaring Moon ex SIR HOLO 30.00 75.00
252 Gholdengo ex SIR HOLO .75 1.50
253 Altaria ex SIR HOLO 2.00 4.00
254 Mela SIR HOLO 12.50 25.00
255 Parasol Lady SIR HOLO 1.25 2.50
256 Professor Sada's Vitality SIR HOLO 7.50 15.00
257 Professor Turo's Scenario SIR HOLO 1.50 4.00
258 Rika SIR HOLO 4.00 10.00
259 Tulip SIR HOLO .20 .40
260 Garchomp ex HR HOLO .50 1.25
261 Iron Valiant ex HR HOLO 6.00 12.00
262 Roaring Moon ex HR HOLO .08 .20
263 Beach Court HR HOLO 5.00 10.00
264 Counter Catcher HR HOLO .07 .15
265 Luxurious Cape HR HOLO 2.50 6.00
266 Reversal Energy HR HOLO 3.00 6.00

2023 Pokemon Sword and Shield Crown Zenith

1 Oddish C 15.00 30.00
2 Gloom U 6.00 12.00
3 Bellossom R 5.00 10.00
4 Tangela C 1.00 2.00
5 Tangrowth R .50 1.00
6 Scyther C 25.00 60.00
7 Sunkern C .10 .20
8 Yanma C 7.50 15.00
9 Yanmega R 7.50 15.00
10 Kricketot C 10.00 20.00
11 Cherubi C 2.50 5.00
12 Carnivine U 2.50 5.00
13 Leafeon V URR 5.00 10.00
14 Leafeon VSTAR R 10.00 20.00
15 Grubbin C 75.00 200.00
16 Zarude HOLO R 7.50 15.00
17 Calyrex HOLO R 1.50 4.00
18 Charizard V URR 1.50 4.00
19 Charizard VSTAR R 2.50 6.00
20 Radiant Charizard RAR 2.50 5.00
21 Entei HOLO R .75 1.50
22 Simisear V URR 15.00 40.00
23 Simisear VSTAR R 15.00 30.00
24 Larvesta C .30 .75
25 Volcarona R .60 1.25
26 Volcanion HOLO R .75 1.50
27 Salandit C 5.00 12.00
28 Salazzle U 6.00 12.00
29 Seel C 3.00 6.00
30 Galarian Mr. Mime C 6.00 12.00
31 Wailmer C 25.00 60.00
32 Wailord R 10.00 20.00
33 Corphish C 15.00 30.00
34 Snorunt C 3.00 6.00
35 Luvdisc C 6.00 12.00
36 Kyogre HOLO R 2.00 4.00
37 Kyogre V URR 2.00 5.00
38 Glaceon V URR 2.50 5.00
39 Shinx C 5.00 12.00
40 Shinx C 3.00 6.00
41 Luxio U 2.00 5.00
42 Luxio U 7.50 15.00
43 Luxray R .75 1.50
44 Luxray R 25.00 50.00
45 Rotom V URR 4.00 8.00
46 Rotom VSTAR R 2.00 5.00
47 Emolga C .75 1.50
48 Eelektrik U 1.00 2.50
49 Helioptile C 1.00 2.00
50 Heliolisk R 1.00 2.00
51 Radiant Charjabug RAR 2.00 4.00
52 Zeraora R 10.00 20.00
53 Zeraora V URR 3.00 6.00
54 Zeraora VMAX R 20.00 50.00
55 Zeraora VSTAR R .75 2.00
56 Pincurchin U 75.00 150.00
57 Exeggcute C 1.00 2.50
58 Exeggutor R 5.00 10.00
59 Mewtwo HOLO R 7.50 15.00
60 Mew V URR 5.00 12.00
61 Girafarig U 1.00 2.00
62 Lunatone U 6.00 12.00
63 Dusclops U 12.50 25.00
64 Tapu Lele HOLO R 4.00 8.00
65 Hatterene V URR 20.00 40.00
66 Hatterene VMAX R 2.50 5.00
67 Enamorus R .75 1.50
68 Graveler U 4.00 8.00
69 Solrock U 4.00 10.00
70 Baltoy C 1.00 2.50
71 Riolu C .75 1.50
72 Pancham C 3.00 6.00
73 Rockruff C 5.00 10.00
74 Lycanroc R 2.50 5.00
75 Koffing C 10.00 20.00
76 Absol HOLO R 1.50 4.00
77 Purrloin C .60 1.25
78 Liepard R .75 1.50
79 Krokorok U 3.00 8.00
80 Pangoro R 3.00 6.00
81 Skrelp C 7.50 15.00
82 Dragalge R 1.25 3.00
83 Hoopa HOLO R 6.00 12.00
84 Galarian Meowth C 3.00 6.00
85 Galarian Perrserker R 10.00 20.00
86 Scizor R 17.50 35.00
87 Aron C 3.00 6.00
88 Lairon U 1.25 2.50
89 Aggron HOLO R 7.50 15.00
90 Metang U 7.50 15.00
91 Pawniard C .75 1.50
92 Pawniard C .50 1.25
93 Bisharp U 2.50 5.00
94 Zacian HOLO R 2.50 5.00
95 Zacian V URR 8.00 20.00
96 Zacian VSTAR R 2.00 4.00
97 Zamazenta HOLO R 20.00 50.00
98 Zamazenta V URR 4.00 8.00
99 Zamazenta VSTAR R 1.25 2.50
100 Rayquaza V URR 1.00 2.00
101 Rayquaza VMAX R 3.00 6.00
102 Rayquaza VMAX R .50 1.25
103 Duraludon V URR 10.00 25.00
104 Duraludon VMAX R 6.00 12.00
105 Radiant Eternatus RAR 4.00 8.00
106 Tauros R 25.00 50.00
107 Ditto HOLO R 20.00 50.00
109 Snorlax R 10.00 20.00

110 Starly C 1.00 2.50
111 Bidoof C 7.50 15.00
112 Chatot C 30.00 75.00
113 Regigigas V URR .75 1.50
114 Regigigas VSTAR R .75 1.50
115 Shaymin U 2.00 5.00
116 Stoutland V URR 7.50 15.00
117 Yungoos C 2.50 5.00
118 Gumshoos R 7.50 15.00
119 Oranguru R 1.00 2.50
120 Greedent V URR 4.00 8.00
121 Wooloo C 3.00 6.00
122 Dubwool R 4.00 8.00
123 Bea HOLO R 3.00 8.00
124 Bede HOLO R 7.50 15.00
125 Crushing Hammer U 4.00 10.00
126 Digging Duo U 10.00 20.00
127 Energy Retrieval C 3.00 6.00
128 Energy Search C 6.00 15.00
129 Energy Switch U 20.00 50.00
130 Friends in Hisui U 1.25 3.00
131 Friends in Sinnoh U 15.00 30.00
132 Great Ball U 1.25 2.50
133 Hop HOLO R .75 1.50
134 Leon HOLO R 12.50 25.00
135 Lost Vacuum U 4.00 8.00
136 Nessa HOLO R 7.50 15.00
137 Poké Ball C 1.00 2.50
138 Pokémon Catcher U .75 1.50
139 Potion C 2.00 4.00
140 Raihan HOLO R 7.50 15.00
141 Rare Candy U 6.00 12.00
142 Rescue Carrier U 10.00 20.00
143 Sky Seal Stone HOLO R 2.50 5.00
144 Switch C 5.00 10.00
145 Trekking Shoes U 1.00 2.00
146 Ultra Ball U 1.00 2.00
147 Elesa's Sparkle FULL ART UR 3.00 6.00
148 Friends in Hisui FULL ART UR 4.00 8.00
149 Friends in Sinnoh FULL ART UR 7.50 15.00
150 Professor's Research [Professor Rowan] FULL ART UR 30.00 75.00
151 Volo FULL ART UR .75 2.00
152 Grass Energy TXT FULL ART UR 6.00 12.00
153 Fire Energy TXT FULL ART UR 75.00 150.00
154 Water Energy TXT FULL ART UR 4.00 10.00
155 Lightning Energy TXT FULL ART UR .75 1.50
156 Psychic Energy TXT FULL ART UR .75 1.50
157 Fighting Energy TXT FULL ART UR 2.50 6.00
158 Darkness Energy TXT FULL ART UR 30.00 60.00
159 Metal Energy TXT FULL ART UR 2.00 5.00
160 Pikachu SCR 5.00 10.00

2023 Pokemon Sword and Shield Crown Zenith Galarian Gallery

GG01 Hisuian Voltorb GGH 25.00 60.00
GG02 Kricketune GGH 4.00 10.00
GG03 Magmortar GGH 7.50 15.00
GG04 Oricorio GGH 2.50 5.00
GG05 Lapras GGH .75 2.00
GG06 Manaphy GGH 40.00 100.00
GG07 Keldeo GGH 2.00 5.00
GG08 Electivire GGH 3.00 6.00
GG09 Toxtricity GGH 12.50 25.00
GG10 Mew GGH 8.00 20.00
GG11 Lunatone GGH 2.50 5.00
GG12 Deoxys GGH 1.00 2.00
GG13 Diancie GGH 10.00 20.00
GG14 Comfey GGH 5.00 10.00
GG15 Solrock GGH .75 1.50
GG16 Absol GGH 1.00 2.00
GG17 Thievul GGH 20.00 40.00
GG18 Magnezone GGH 2.00 5.00
GG19 Altaria GGH 1.00 2.00
GG20 Latias GGH 7.50 15.00
GG21 Hisuian Goodra GGH .60 1.50
GG22 Ditto GGH 3.00 6.00
GG23 Dunsparce GGH 3.00 6.00
GG24 Miltank GGH 3.00 8.00
GG25 Bibarel GGH 4.00 8.00
GG26 Riolu GGH 2.50 6.00
GG27 Swablu GGH 3.00 6.00
GG28 Duskull GGH 1.00 2.00
GG29 Bidoof GGH 1.00 2.00
GG30 Pikachu GGH 7.50 15.00
GG31 Turtwig GGH 12.50 25.00
GG32 Paras GGH 10.00 25.00
GG33 Poochyena GGH 2.50 5.00
GG34 Mareep GGH 2.00 5.00
GG35 Leafeon VSTAR GGV 2.50 6.00
GG36 Entei V GGV 20.00 40.00
GG37 Simisear VSTAR GGV 2.50 5.00
GG38 Suicune V GGV 2.50 6.00
GG39 Lumineon V GGV 2.00 4.00
GG40 Glaceon VSTAR GGV 7.50 15.00
GG41 Raikou V GGV 7.50 15.00
GG42 Zeraora VMAX GGV .75 1.50
GG43 Zeraora VSTAR GGV .75 1.50
GG44 Mewtwo VSTAR GGV 4.00 8.00
GG45 Deoxys VMAX GGV 2.50 5.00
GG46 Deoxys VSTAR GGV 4.00 8.00
GG47 Hatterene VMAX GGV 6.00 12.00
GG48 Zacian V GGV 12.50 25.00
GG49 Drapion V GGV 4.00 8.00
GG50 Darkrai VSTAR GGV .60 1.50
GG51 Hisuian Samurott V GGV 12.50 25.00
GG52 Hisuian Samurott VSTAR GGV 10.00 20.00
GG53 Hoopa V GGV 1.00 2.50
GG54 Zamazenta V GGV 25.00 50.00
GG55 Regigigas VSTAR GGV 3.00 6.00
GG56 Hisuian Zoroark VSTAR GGV 1.25 3.00
GG57 Adaman GGU 50.00 120.00
GG58 Cheren's Care GGU .75 1.50
GG59 Colress's Experiment GGU .60 1.25
GG60 Cynthia's Ambition GGU .75 1.50
GG61 Gardenia's Vigor GGU 6.00 15.00
GG62 Grant GGU 4.00 8.00
GG63 Irida GGU 3.00 6.00
GG64 Melony GGU .75 1.50
GG65 Raihan GGU 2.50 5.00
GG66 Roxanne GGU 15.00 40.00
GG67 Origin Forme Palkia VSTAR GGS .75 1.50
GG68 Origin Forme Dialga VSTAR GGS 1.50 4.00
GG69 Giratina VSTAR GGS 75.00 150.00
GG70 Arceus VSTAR GGS 30.00 60.00

2023 Pokemon Trading Card Game Classic Blastoise and Suicune ex Deck

1 Squirtle 6.00 12.00
2 Wartortle 10.00 25.00
3 Blastoise 1.25 3.00
4 Staryu .75 1.50
5 Starmie .75 1.50
6 Magikarp 7.50 15.00
7 Gyarados 4.00 8.00
8 Lapras 4.00 8.00
9 Articuno 2.00 4.00
10 Suicuneex 6.00 12.00
11 Drowzee 15.00 30.00
12 Hypno 15.00 30.00
13 Mr. Mime 10.00 20.00
14 Mewtwo 200.00 400.00
15 Lt. Surge's Rattata 3.00 6.00
16 Lt. Surge's Raticate 10.00 25.00
17 Kangaskhan 25.00 60.00
18 Bill 3.00 6.00
19 Boss's Orders [Giovanni] 10.00 20.00
20 Computer Search 5.00 10.00
21 Drops in the Ocean .60 1.25
22 Fisherman .75 1.50
23 Poké Ball 4.00 8.00
24 Pokémon Fan Club 8.00 20.00
25 Professor Oak 2.50 6.00
26 Rare Candy 7.50 15.00
27 Rocket's Admin. 4.00 10.00
28 Super Rod 20.00 40.00
29 Switch .75 2.00
30 Ultra Ball 2.50 5.00
31 VS Seeker 12.50 25.00
32 Double Colorless Energy 30.00 60.00
33 Water Energy 3.00 6.00
34 Psychic Energy 7.50 15.00

2023 Pokemon Trading Card Game Classic Charizard and Ho-Oh ex Deck

1 Charmander 60.00 150.00
2 Charmeleon 1.00 2.50
3 Charizard 1.50 4.00
4 Ponyta 1.00 2.00
5 Rapidash 5.00 12.00
6 Magmar 7.50 15.00
7 Ho-Oh ex 1.50 3.00
8 Pikachu 6.00 12.00
9 Raichu 3.00 6.00
10 Voltorb 3.00 8.00
11 Electrode 25.00 50.00
12 Zapdos 75.00 150.00
13 Clefairy 10.00 20.00
14 Clefable 5.00 10.00
15 Dunsparce 7.50 15.00
16 Stantler 1.50 4.00
17 Miltank 30.00 75.00
18 Bill 5.00 10.00
19 Boss's Orders [Giovanni] 1.25 3.00
20 Computer Search .40 1.00
21 Poké Ball 2.00 4.00
22 Pokémon Fan Club 30.00 80.00
23 Professor Oak 2.50 5.00
24 Rare Candy 7.50 15.00
25 Rocket's Admin. 7.50 15.00
26 Scorching Charcoal 3.00 6.00
27 Super Rod 10.00 25.00
28 Super Scoop Up 125.00 250.00
29 Switch 20.00 40.00
30 Ultra Ball 3.00 6.00
31 VS Seeker 7.50 15.00
32 Double Colorless Energy 1.50 3.00
33 Fire Energy 7.50 15.00
34 Lightning Energy 7.50 15.00

2023 Pokemon Trading Card Game Classic Venusaur and Lugia ex Deck

1 Bulbasaur 3.00 8.00
2 Ivysaur 2.50 5.00
3 Venusaur 20.00 50.00
4 Paras 1.25 3.00
5 Parasect .50 1.25
6 Scyther 7.50 15.00
7 Pinsir .75 1.50
8 Sandshrew 1.00 2.00
9 Sandslash 3.00 6.00
10 Onix 12.50 25.00
11 Hitmonlee 1.00 2.00
12 Hitmonchan .75 1.50
13 Doduo 12.50 25.00
14 Dodrio 4.00 8.00
15 Chansey 7.50 15.00
16 Snorlax 2.00 4.00
17 Lugia ex 1.00 2.50
18 Bill 7.50 15.00
19 Boss's Orders [Giovanni] 40.00 100.00
20 Computer Search 1.50 4.00
21 Poké Ball 7.50 15.00
22 Pokémon Fan Club 50.00 100.00
23 Pokémon Nurse 2.00 5.00
24 Professor Oak 60.00 125.00
25 Rare Candy 7.50 15.00
26 Rocket's Admin. 1.00 2.50
27 Sun Seed 12.50 25.00
28 Super Rod 2.50 5.00
29 Switch 4.00 10.00
30 Ultra Ball 30.00 60.00
31 VS Seeker .75 2.00
32 Double Colorless Energy 4.00 8.00
33 Grass Energy 2.50 5.00
34 Fighting Energy 10.00 25.00

2024 Pokemon Scarlet and Violet Paldean Fates

1 Pineco C 1.25 2.50
2 Forretress EX RR 1.00 2.00
3 Maractus C 15.00 30.00
4 Toedscool C 8.00 20.00
5 Toedscruel EX RR 6.00 12.00
6 Espathra EX RR 1.50 4.00
7 Charmander C 12.50 25.00
8 Charmeleon U 17.50 35.00
9 Magmar C 25.00 50.00
10 Magmortar R 25.00 50.00
11 Numel C 5.00 10.00
12 Camerupt U 3.00 6.00
13 Heat Rotom R 1.25 3.00
14 Charcadet C 15.00 30.00
15 Armarouge R .50 1.25
16 Lapras C .75 1.50
17 Frigibax C 1.00 2.00
18 Pikachu C 7.50 15.00
19 Raichu R 20.00 50.00
20 Chinchou C 4.00 100.00
21 Lanturn U 1.00 2.00
22 Kilowattrel U .60 1.25
23 Exeggcute C 3.00 6.00
24 Exeggutor R 2.50 5.00
25 Natu C 5.00 10.00
26 Xatu R 6.00 15.00
27 Ralts C 6.00 12.00
28 Kirlia C 5.00 10.00
29 Gardevoir EX RR 2.00 4.00
30 Chimecho C .50 1.25
31 Mime Jr. C 25.00 50.00
32 Woobat C 1.25 2.50
33 Swoobat U 1.50 3.00
34 Cottonee C 5.00 10.00
35 Whimsicott U 10.00 20.00
36 Dedenne C 1.00 2.50
37 Mimikyu R 5.00 12.00
38 Fidough C 7.50 15.00
39 Dachsbun U 10.00 20.00
40 Ceruledge R 12.50 25.00
41 Flittle C 2.50 5.00
42 Greavard C 6.00 12.00
43 Houndstone R 1.50 4.00
44 Gimmighoul C 50.00 100.00
45 Mankey C .25 .60
46 Primeape U 15.00 30.00
47 Annihilape R 1.00 2.00
48 Phanpy C 1.50 3.00
49 Donphan U 4.00 8.00
50 Barboach C 15.00 30.00
51 Clobbopus C 10.00 20.00
52 Grapploct U 4.00 10.00
53 Great Tusk EX RR 5.00 10.00
54 Charizard EX RR 7.50 15.00
55 Gastly C .20 .50
56 Haunter C 6.00 15.00
57 Gengar U 6.00 15.00
58 Paldean Wooper C 2.00 4.00
59 Paldean Clodsire EX RR 5.00 10.00
60 Scraggy C .10 .20
61 Scrafty U 1.00 2.00
62 Maschiff C .75 1.50
63 Mabosstiff R 5.00 10.00
64 Varoom C 10.00 20.00
65 Revavroom R 3.00 8.00
66 Iron Treads EX RR 1.50 4.00
67 Gholdengo R 4.00 10.00
68 Noibat C 1.50 3.00
69 Noivern EX RR 6.00 12.00
70 Cyclizar R 15.00 30.00
71 Lechonk C 20.00 40.00
72 Oinkologne U 30.00 75.00
73 Tandemaus C .20 .50
74 Maushold U 6.00 12.00
75 Squawkabilly EX .75 1.50
76 Artazon U .75 1.50
77 Atticus U .20 .50
78 Clive U 3.00 6.00
79 Electric Generator U 7.50 15.00
80 Iono U 12.50 25.00
81 Moonlit Hill U 75.00 150.00
82 Nemona C 3.00 6.00
83 Nemona's Backpack U 4.00 8.00
84 Nest Ball U 5.00 10.00
85 Paldean Student C 2.00 5.00
86 Paldean Student C 10.00 20.00
87 Professor's Research [Professor Sada] R 1.50 4.00
88 Professor's Research [Professor Turo] R 5.00 10.00
89 Rare Candy C 6.00 12.00
90 Technical Machine: Crisis Punch U 15.00 40.00
91 Ultra Ball U .07 .15
92 Oddish SR 1.00 2.00
93 Gloom SR .60 1.25
94 Vileplume SR 10.00 20.00
95 Scyther SR 30.00 75.00
96 Hoppip SR 3.00 6.00
97 Skiploom SR 6.00 12.00
98 Jumpluff SR 5.00 10.00
99 Pineco SR .30 .75
100 Snover SR 3.00 6.00
101 Abomasnow SR 2.00 5.00
102 Smoliv SR 1.25 3.00
103 Dolliv SR 2.00 4.00
104 Arboliva SR 3.00 6.00
105 Toedscool SR 3.00 6.00
106 Capsakid SR 3.00 6.00
107 Scovillain SR 1.00 2.00
108 Rellor SR 1.25 2.50
109 Charmander SR 10.00 20.00
110 Charmeleon SR 2.50 5.00
111 Paldean Tauros SR 7.50 15.00
112 Entei SR .40 1.00
113 Oricorio SR 6.00 15.00
114 Charcadet SR 7.50 15.00
115 Armarouge SR 1.00 2.50
116 Slowpoke SR 3.00 8.00
117 Slowbro SR 4.00 8.00
118 Staryu SR 1.00 2.00
119 Starmie SR .75 1.50
120 Paldean Tauros SR 7.50 15.00
121 Wiglett SR 3.00 6.00
122 Wugtrio SR 2.50 5.00
123 Finizen SR 1.50 3.00
124 Palafin SR 30.00 75.00
125 Veluza SR 3.00 6.00
126 Dondozo SR .20 .50
127 Tatsugiri SR 3.00 6.00
128 Frigibax SR 12.50 25.00
129 Arctibax SR 1.00 2.00
130 Baxcalibur SR .75 1.50
131 Pikachu SR 5.00 10.00
132 Raichu SR 5.00 10.00
133 Voltorb SR 6.00 12.00
134 Electrode SR 4.00 10.00
135 Shinx SR 2.00 4.00
136 Luxio SR 20.00 40.00
137 Luxray SR 2.50 5.00
138 Pachirisu SR .25 .60
139 Thundurus SR 12.50 25.00
140 Toxel SR 1.00 2.50
141 Toxtricity SR 6.00 12.00
142 Pawmi SR 1.00 2.00
143 Pawmo SR .60 1.25
144 Pawmot SR 7.50 15.00
145 Wattrel SR 3.00 6.00
146 Kilowattrel SR 50.00 120.00
147 Wigglytuff SR 15.00 30.00
148 Abra SR 10.00 20.00
149 Kadabra SR 4.00 8.00
150 Cleffa SR 1.50 3.00
151 Natu SR 2.00 4.00
152 Xatu SR 7.50 15.00
153 Ralts SR .50 1.00
154 Kirlia SR .75 1.50
155 Drifloon SR 7.50 15.00
156 Drifblim SR 25.00 60.00
157 Mime Jr. SR 1.25 2.50
158 Spiritomb SR 7.50 15.00
159 Klefki SR 1.50 4.00
160 Mimikyu SR 5.00 10.00
161 Dachsbun SR 10.00 20.00
162 Ceruledge SR 2.00 4.00
163 Rabsca SR 4.00 8.00
164 Flittle SR 1.25 3.00
165 Tinkatink SR 60.00 150.00
166 Tinkatuff SR 2.00 4.00
167 Tinkaton SR .75 1.50
168 Houndstone SR 1.00 2.00
169 Mankey SR 5.00 10.00
170 Primeape SR 10.00 20.00
171 Annihilape SR 1.50 3.00
172 Paldean Tauros SR 30.00 60.00
173 Riolu SR 7.50 15.00
174 Lucario SR 6.00 12.00
175 Hawlucha SR 8.00 20.00
176 Nacli SR 3.00 6.00
177 Naclstack SR 1.00 2.00
178 Garganacl SR 1.25 2.50
179 Glimmet SR 1.25 3.00
180 Paldean Wooper SR 12.50 25.00
181 Murkrow SR 50.00 100.00
182 Sneasel SR 2.00 4.00
183 Weavile SR 7.50 15.00
184 Sableye SR 4.00 8.00
185 Pawniard SR 7.50 15.00
186 Bisharp SR 5.00 12.00
187 Kingambit SR 12.50 25.00
188 Mabosstiff SR 1.50 3.00
189 Shroodle SR 2.00 5.00
190 Grafaiai SR 6.00 12.00
191 Scizor SR 1.00 2.00
192 Varoom SR 1.25 2.50
193 Revavroom SR 75.00 150.00
194 Noibat SR 6.00 12.00
195 Cyclizar SR 2.00 4.00
196 Pidgey SR 15.00 40.00
197 Pidgeotto SR 3.00 6.00
198 Jigglypuff SR 10.00 20.00
199 Doduo SR .75 2.00
200 Dodrio SR 1.00 2.00
201 Ditto SR 1.25 2.50
202 Snorlax SR 7.50 15.00
203 Wingull SR 4.00 8.00
204 Pelipper SR 7.50 15.00
205 Skwovet SR 12.50 25.00
206 Greedent SR 5.00 12.00
207 Lechonk SR 4.00 10.00
208 Oinkologne SR 1.00 2.00
209 Tandemaus SR 1.00 2.00
210 Maushold SR 3.00 6.00
211 Flamigo SR 3.00 6.00
212 Forretress EX SUR 3.00 6.00
213 Toedscruel EX SUR 8.00 20.00
214 Espathra EX SUR 6.00 12.00
215 Alakazam EX SUR 10.00 20.00
216 Mew EX SUR 5.00 12.00
217 Gardevoir EX SUR 1.00 2.00
218 Glimmora EX SUR .60 1.25
219 Paldean Clodsire EX SUR 15.00 30.00
220 Noivern EX SUR 7.50 15.00
221 Pidgeot EX SUR 2.00 5.00
222 Wigglytuff EX SUR 6.00 12.00
223 Squawkabilly EX SUR .10 .20
224 Wugtrio IR .60 1.25
225 Palafin IR 1.00 2.00
226 Pawmi IR 5.00 10.00
227 Clive UR 3.00 6.00
228 Judge UR 4.00 10.00
229 Nemona UR 5.00 12.00

230 Paldean Student UR 1.25 2.50
231 Paldean Student UR 20.00 40.00
232 Mew EX SIR 2.50 5.00
233 Gardevoir EX SIR 20.00 40.00
234 Charizard EX SIR 1.50 4.00
235 Arven SIR 1.00 2.00
236 Clive SIR 1.00 2.00
237 Iono SIR 2.50 5.00
238 Nemona SIR 5.00 12.00
239 Penny SIR 2.50 5.00
240 Wo-Chien EX HR 60.00 125.00
241 Chi-Yu EX HR .75 2.00
242 Chien-Pao EX HR .75 1.50
243 Miraidon EX HR 1.00 2.00
244 Ting-Lu EX HR 2.00 4.00
245 Koraidon EX HR 5.00 10.00

2024 Pokemon Scarlet and Violet Temporal Forces

1 Scyther C 3.00 6.00
2 Pineco C 10.00 20.00
3 Seedot C 3.00 6.00
4 Nuzleaf C 12.50 25.00
5 Shiftry U 15.00 40.00
6 Shroomish C 7.50 15.00
7 Breloom C 15.00 30.00
8 Roselia C 5.00 10.00
9 Roserade U 4.00 8.00
10 Turtwig C 10.00 20.00
11 Grotle C 8.00 20.00
12 Torterra ex RR 5.00 10.00
13 Shaymin U 7.50 15.00
14 Cottonee C 25.00 50.00
15 Whimsicott R 4.00 8.00
16 Deerling C 2.50 5.00
17 Sawsbuck U 6.00 15.00
18 Grubbin C 10.00 20.00
19 Dhelmise U 7.50 15.00
20 Bramblin C 15.00 30.00
21 Brambleghast R 2.50 5.00
22 Scovillain ex RR 12.50 25.00
23 Rellor C 6.00 15.00
24 Rabsca U 6.00 12.00
25 Iron Leaves ex RR 6.00 15.00
26 Ponyta C 7.50 15.00
27 Rapidash U 5.00 10.00
28 Slugma C 25.00 50.00
29 Magcargo R 5.00 12.00
30 Victini C 7.50 15.00
31 Heatmor C 2.50 5.00
32 Litten C 6.00 15.00
33 Torracat C 3.00 6.00
34 Incineroar ex RR 7.50 15.00
35 Turtonator C 10.00 20.00
36 Sizzlipede C 4.00 10.00
37 Centiskorch U 7.50 15.00
38 Gouging Fire ex RR 3.00 6.00
39 Totodile C 7.50 15.00
40 Croconaw C 8.00 20.00
41 Feraligatr R 5.00 10.00
42 Carvanha C 2.00 4.00
43 Sharpedo U 7.50 15.00
44 Keldeo U 10.00 20.00
45 Snom C 7.50 15.00
46 Frosmoth C 3.00 6.00
47 Wiglett C 3.00 8.00
48 Finizen C 12.50 25.00
49 Palafin U 17.50 35.00
50 Walking Wake ex RR 4.00 8.00
51 Pikachu C 4.00 10.00
52 Raichu C 7.50 15.00
53 Electabuzz C 4.00 8.00
54 Electivire U 7.50 15.00
55 Charjabug C 12.50 25.00
56 Vikavolt U 6.00 12.00
57 Zeraora U 30.00 75.00
58 Yamper C 75.00 150.00
59 Boltund U 40.00 80.00
60 Wugtrio ex RR 6.00 12.00
61 Iron Hands U 75.00 150.00
62 Iron Thorns R 5.00 10.00
63 Mr. Mime C 2.50 5.00
64 Marill C 3.00 6.00
65 Azumarill C 60.00 125.00
66 Girafarig C 4.00 8.00
67 Latias U 7.50 15.00
68 Bronzor C 4.00 8.00
69 Bronzong U 4.00 8.00
70 Solosis C 3.00 6.00
71 Duosion C 10.00 20.00
72 Reuniclus U 3.00 6.00
73 Elgyem C 7.50 15.00
74 Beheeyem U 3.00 6.00
75 Cutiefly C 4.00 8.00
76 Ribombee U 7.50 15.00
77 Scream Tail U 5.00 10.00
78 Flutter Mane R 6.00 12.00
79 Iron Valiant U 3.00 6.00
80 Iron Valiant R 10.00 20.00
81 Iron Crown ex RR 6.00 12.00
82 Meditite C 5.00 10.00
83 Medicham C 7.50 15.00
84 Relicanth R 2.50 5.00
85 Drilbur C 7.50 15.00
86 Excadrill U 10.00 20.00
87 Golett C 7.50 15.00
88 Golurk U .75 1.50
89 Rockruff C .75 1.50
90 Lycanroc U .10 .20
91 Mudbray C 4.00 7.00
92 Mudsdale U .50 1.00
93 Rolycoly C 5.00 10.00
94 Carkol C .10 .20
95 Coalossal U 4.00 8.00
96 Great Tusk U .10 .20
97 Great Tusk U 5.00 10.00
98 Sandy Shocks U .10 .20
99 Iron Boulder ex RR 3.00 6.00
100 Ekans C 1.00 2.00
101 Arbok C 6.00 12.00
102 Gastly C 1.00 2.00
103 Haunter C 10.00 20.00
104 Gengar ex RR 1.00 2.00
105 Poochyena C 1.00 2.00
106 Mightyena C 5.00 10.00
107 Sableye U 5.00 10.00
108 Farigiraf ex RR 1.00 2.00
109 Roaring Moon R .50 1.00
110 Forretress U .50 1.00
111 Scizor ex RR 3.00 6.00
112 Mawile C 5.00 10.00
113 Beldum C 3.00 6.00
114 Metang C 1.00 2.00
115 Metagross U 1.00 2.00
116 Meltan C 5.00 10.00
117 Melmetal R 5.00 10.00
118 Iron Treads U 4.00 8.00
119 Koraidon R 3.00 6.00
120 Koraidon ex RR 1.00 2.00
121 Miraidon R 5.00 10.00
122 Miraidon ex RR .25 .50
123 Raging Bolt ex RR 1.00 2.00
124 Lickitung C 3.00 6.00
125 Lickilicky C 5.00 10.00
126 Hoothoot C 2.00 4.00
127 Noctowl C 2.00 4.00
128 Dunsparce C .25 .50
129 Dudunsparce R 3.00 6.00
130 Skitty C .25 .50
131 Delcatty U 3.00 6.00
132 Chatot C 1.00 2.00
133 Pidove C 1.00 2.00
134 Tranquill C .25 .50
135 Unfezant U 5.00 10.00
136 Minccino C 4.00 8.00
137 Cinccino U 7.50 15.00
138 Drampa R 6.00 12.00
139 Iron Jugulis U 2.00 4.00
140 Ancient Booster Energy Capsule U 7.50 15.00
141 Awakening Drum ACE 3.00 6.00
142 Bianca's Devotion U 3.00 6.00
143 Boxed Order U 30.00 60.00
144 Buddy-Buddy Poffin U 40.00 80.00
145 Ciphermaniac's Codebreaking U 40.00 80.00
146 Eri U 7.50 15.00
147 Explorer's Guidance U 7.50 15.00
148 Full Metal Lab U 6.00 12.00
149 Future Booster Energy Capsule U 4.00 8.00
150 Hand Trimmer U 6.00 12.00
151 Heavy Baton U 6.00 12.00
152 Hero's Cape ACE 10.00 20.00
153 Master Ball ACE .30 .75
154 Maximum Belt ACE 1.00 2.00
155 Morty's Conviction U 1.00 2.00
156 Perilous Jungle U .50 1.00
157 Prime Catcher ACE 1.50 3.00
158 Reboot Pod ACE 2.50 5.00
159 Rescue Board U 1.50 3.00
160 Salvatore U 1.00 2.00
161 Mist Energy U .50 1.00
162 Neo Upper Energy ACE 5.00 10.00
163 Shiftry IR 1.00 2.00
164 Grotle IR 1.50 3.00
165 Deerling IR .75 1.50
166 Sawsbuck IR 1.50 3.00
167 Litten IR 1.25 2.50
168 Snom IR 1.00 2.00
169 Charjabug IR .60 1.25
170 Bronzor IR 1.25 2.50
171 Reuniclus IR .75 1.50
172 Cutiefly IR 1.25 2.50
173 Relicanth IR .60 1.25
174 Excadrill IR 1.25 2.50
175 Mudsdale IR .60 1.25
176 Arbok IR 1.25 2.50
177 Gastly IR 2.00 4.00
178 Metagross IR .75 1.50
179 Meltan IR .60 1.25
180 Lickitung IR .60 1.25
181 Chatot IR 2.00 4.00
182 Minccino IR 3.00 6.00
183 Cinccino IR .75 1.50
184 Drampa IR .60 1.25
185 Torterra ex UR .60 1.25
186 Iron Leaves ex 1.25 2.50
187 Incineroar ex UR 15.00 30.00
188 Gouging Fire ex UR 7.50 15.00
189 Walking Wake ex UR 7.50 15.00
190 Wugtrio ex UR 10.00 20.00
191 Iron Crown ex UR 7.50 15.00
192 Iron Boulder ex UR 12.50 25.00
193 Gengar ex UR 12.50 25.00
194 Farigiraf ex UR 6.00 12.00
195 Scizor ex UR 6.00 12.00
196 Raging Bolt ex UR 30.00 75.00
197 Bianca's Devotion UR 7.50 15.00
198 Ciphermaniac's Codebreaking UR 7.50 15.00
199 Eri UR 2.50 5.00
200 Explorer's Guidance UR 10.00 20.00
201 Morty's Conviction UR 5.00 10.00
202 Salvatore UR 10.00 20.00
203 Iron Leaves ex SIR 5.00 10.00
204 Gouging Fire ex SIR 4.00 8.00
205 Walking Wake ex SIR 3.00 6.00
206 Iron Crown ex SIR 5.00 10.00
207 Iron Boulder ex SIR 5.00 10.00
208 Raging Bolt ex SIR 10.00 20.00
209 Bianca's Devotion SIR 2.50 5.00
210 Eri SIR 2.50 5.00
211 Morty's Conviction SIR 7.50 15.00
212 Salvatore SIR 7.50 15.00
213 Iron Leaves ex HR 6.00 12.00
214 Gouging Fire ex HR 1.50 3.00
215 Walking Wake ex HR 12.50 25.00
216 Iron Crown ex HR 5.00 10.00
217 Iron Boulder ex HR 3.00 6.00
218 Raging Bolt ex HR 6.00 12.00

2024 Pokemon Scarlet and Violet Twilight Masquerade

1 Tangela C 7.50 15.00
2 Tangrowth C 6.00 12.00
3 Pinsir C 2.00 4.00
4 Spinarak C 2.00 4.00
5 Ariados U 5.00 10.00
6 Sunkern C 125.00 250.00
7 Sunflora U 6.00 12.00
8 Heracross U 3.00 6.00
9 Volbeat C 2.00 4.00
10 Illumise C 20.00 40.00
11 Leafeon U 12.50 25.00
12 Phantump C 15.00 30.00
13 Trevenant C 7.50 15.00
14 Grookey C 25.00 50.00
15 Thwackey C 30.00 75.00
16 Rillaboom U 12.50 25.00
17 Applin C 15.00 30.00
18 Dipplin U 4.00 8.00
19 Iron Leaves R 7.50 15.00
20 Poltchageist C 5.00 10.00
21 Poltchageist C 5.00 10.00
22 Sinistcha R 4.00 8.00
23 Sinistcha ex RR 5.00 10.00
24 Teal Mask Ogerpon R 7.50 15.00
25 Teal Mask Ogerpon ex RR 5.00 10.00
26 Vulpix C 6.00 12.00
27 Ninetales C 4.00 8.00
28 Slugma C 4.00 8.00
29 Magcargo ex RR 10.00 20.00
30 Torkoal C 10.00 20.00
31 Chimchar C 1.50 3.00
32 Monferno C 3.00 6.00
33 Infernape R 5.00 10.00
34 Darumaka C 1.50 3.00
35 Darmanitan U 3.00 6.00
36 Litwick C 4.00 8.00
37 Lampent C 2.00 4.00
38 Chandelure R 2.50 5.00
39 Chi-Yu U 2.00 4.00
40 Hearthflame Mask Ogerpon ex RR 2.50 5.00
41 Poliwag C 2.50 5.00
42 Poliwhirl C 3.00 6.00
43 Poliwrath U 2.50 5.00
44 Goldeen C 2.50 5.00
45 Seaking C 1.50 3.00
46 Jynx C 4.00 8.00
47 Corphish C 4.00 8.00
48 Crawdaunt C 2.50 5.00
49 Feebas C 3.00 6.00
50 Milotic U 2.50 5.00
51 Snorunt C 1.25 2.50
52 Glalie U 10.00 20.00
53 Froslass R 2.50 5.00
54 Glaceon U 2.50 5.00
55 Phione C 2.00 4.00
56 Froakie C 7.50 15.00
57 Frogadier C 7.50 15.00
58 Cramorant U 2.50 5.00
59 Finizen C 2.00 4.00
60 Palafin U 1.25 2.50
61 Palafin ex RR 2.50 5.00
62 Iron Bundle U 2.00 4.00
63 Walking Wake R 1.50 3.00
64 Wellspring Mask Ogerpon ex RR 3.00 6.00
65 Zapdos R 2.50 5.00
66 Shinx C 3.00 6.00
67 Luxio C 2.00 4.00
68 Luxray ex RR 2.50 5.00
69 Emolga C 3.00 6.00
70 Helioptile C 2.50 5.00
71 Heliolisk C 3.00 6.00
72 Morpeko U 2.00 4.00
73 Tadbulb C 2.00 4.00
74 Bellibolt U 3.00 6.00
75 Wattrel C 2.50 5.00
76 Kilowattrel U 2.50 5.00
77 Iron Thorns ex RR 5.00 10.00
78 Clefairy C 3.00 6.00
79 Clefable U 2.50 5.00
80 Abra C 2.50 5.00
81 Kadabra C 1.25 2.50
82 Alakazam R 2.50 5.00
83 Girafarig C 1.50 3.00
84 Farigiraf U 2.00 4.00
85 Chimecho C 2.50 5.00
86 Flabebe C 2.00 4.00
87 Floette C 2.50 5.00
88 Florges U 2.00 4.00
89 Swirlix C 3.00 6.00
90 Slurpuff U 3.00 6.00
91 Sandygast C 1.25 2.50
92 Palossand C 2.50 5.00
93 Enamorus R 2.00 4.00
94 Scream Tail ex RR 2.00 4.00
95 Munkidori R 2.00 4.00
96 Fezandipiti R 2.50 5.00
97 Sandshrew C 2.50 5.00
98 Sandslash U 2.50 5.00
99 Hisuian Growlithe C 1.50 3.00
100 Hisuian Arcanine R 2.50 5.00
101 Nosepass C 2.50 5.00
102 Probopass U 2.50 5.00
103 Timburr C 1.00 2.00
104 Gurdurr C 2.00 4.00
105 Conkeldurr U 5.00 10.00
106 Greninja ex RR 3.00 6.00
107 Hawlucha C 2.00 4.00
108 Glimmet C 2.50 5.00
109 Glimmora U 2.50 5.00
110 Ting-Lu R 2.00 4.00
111 Okidogi R 2.50 5.00
112 Cornerstone Mask Ogerpon ex RR 5.00 10.00
113 Poochyena C 3.00 6.00
114 Mightyena U 2.50 5.00
115 Venipede C 3.00 6.00
116 Whirlipede C 2.00 4.00
117 Scolipede U 2.50 5.00
118 Brute Bonnet U 2.00 4.00
119 Skarmory C 1.50 3.00
120 Aron C 2.00 4.00
121 Lairon C 2.50 5.00
122 Aggron U 4.00 8.00
123 Heatran R 4.00 8.00
124 Varoom C 2.50 5.00
125 Revavroom U 2.00 4.00
126 Applin C 1.00 2.00
127 Dipplin U 2.50 5.00
128 Dreepy C 2.50 5.00
129 Drakloak C 5.00 10.00
130 Dragapult ex RR 2.50 5.00
131 Tatsugiri U 2.00 4.00
132 Farfetch'd C 2.50 5.00
133 Chansey C 2.50 5.00
134 Blissey ex RR 1.50 3.00
135 Eevee C 2.50 5.00
136 Snorlax U 1.50 3.00
137 Aipom C 2.50 5.00
138 Ambipom U 75.00 150.00
139 Ducklett C 1.25 2.50
140 Swanna U 2.00 4.00
141 Bloodmoon Ursaluna ex RR 2.50 5.00
142 Accompanying Flute U 2.50 5.00
143 Bug Catching Set U 3.00 6.00
144 Caretaker C 1.25 2.50
145 Carmine U 3.00 6.00
146 Community Center U 1.25 2.50
147 Cook U 1.25 2.50
148 Enhanced Hammer U 1.50 3.00
149 Festival Grounds U 3.00 6.00
150 Handheld Fan U 2.50 5.00
151 Hassel U 2.00 4.00
152 Hyper Aroma ACE 2.00 4.00
153 Jamming Tower U 1.25 2.50
154 Kieran U 3.00 6.00
155 Lana's Aid U 7.50 15.00
156 Love Ball U 2.50 5.00
157 Lucian U 1.50 3.00
158 Lucky Helmet U 1.50 3.00
159 Ogre's Mask U 2.00 4.00
160 Perrin U 1.25 2.50
161 Raifort U 1.50 3.00
162 Scoop Up Cyclone ACE 2.00 4.00
163 Secret Box ACE 1.50 3.00
164 Survival Brace ACE 2.00 4.00
165 Unfair Stamp ACE 4.00 8.00
166 Boomerang Energy U 6.00 12.00
167 Legacy Energy ACE 2.50 5.00
168 Pinsir IR 2.00 4.00
169 Sunflora IR 2.50 5.00
170 Dipplin IR 2.00 4.00
171 Poltchageist IR 2.00 4.00
172 Torkoal IR 2.00 4.00
173 Infernape IR 2.00 4.00
174 Froslass IR 2.00 4.00
175 Phione IR 1.50 3.00
176 Cramorant IR 2.00 4.00
177 Heliolisk IR 1.50 3.00
178 Wattrel IR 2.00 4.00
179 Chimecho IR 2.00 4.00
180 Enamorus IR 2.50 5.00
181 Hisuian Growlithe IR 2.00 4.00
182 Probopass IR 2.50 5.00
183 Timburr IR 2.00 4.00
184 Lairon IR 2.00 4.00
185 Applin IR 2.00 4.00
186 Tatsugiri IR 3.00 6.00
187 Chansey IR 12.50 25.00
188 Eevee IR 2.00 4.00
189 Sinistcha ex UR 2.00 4.00
190 Teal Mask Ogerpon ex UR 1.50 3.00
191 Magcargo ex UR 1.50 3.00
192 Hearthflame Mask Ogerpon ex UR 20.00 40.00
193 Palafin ex UR 7.50 15.00
194 Wellspring Mask Ogerpon ex UR 5.00 10.00
195 Luxray ex UR 250.00 500.00
196 Iron Thorns ex UR 1.50 3.00
197 Scream Tail ex UR 10.00 20.00
198 Greninja ex UR 10.00 20.00
199 Cornerstone Mask Ogerpon ex UR 5.00 10.00
200 Dragapult ex UR 7.50 15.00
201 Blissey ex UR 10.00 20.00
202 Bloodmoon Ursaluna ex UR 12.50 25.00
203 Caretaker UR 12.50 25.00
204 Carmine UR 7.50 15.00
205 Hassel UR 5.00 10.00
206 Kieran UR 30.00 60.00
207 Lana's Aid UR 15.00 30.00
208 Lucian UR 25.00 50.00
209 Perrin UR 4.00 8.00
210 Sinistcha ex SIR 6.00 12.00
211 Teal Mask Ogerpon ex SIR 4.00 8.00
212 Hearthflame Mask Ogerpon ex SIR 12.50 25.00
213 Wellspring Mask Ogerpon ex SIR 7.50 15.00
214 Greninja ex SIR 7.50 15.00
215 Cornerstone Mask Ogerpon ex SIR 7.50 15.00
216 Bloodmoon Ursaluna ex SIR 3.00 6.00
217 Carmine SIR 40.00 80.00
218 Kieran SIR 12.50 25.00
219 Lana's Aid SIR 12.50 25.00
220 Perrin SIR 5.00 10.00
221 Teal Mask Ogerpon ex HR 15.00 30.00
222 Bloodmoon Ursaluna ex HR 2.50 5.00
223 Buddy-Buddy Poffin HR 4.00 8.00
224 Enhanced Hammer HR 12.50 25.00
225 Rescue Board HR 30.00 75.00
226 Luminous Energy HR 7.50 15.00

YU-GI-OH!

2002 Yu-Gi-Oh Collector Tins

BPT001 Dark Magician SCR	3.00	6.00
BPT002 Summoned Skull SCR	2.50	5.00
BPT003 Blue Eyes White Dragon SCR	2.00	4.00
BPT004 Lord of D SCR	1.00	2.00
BPT005 Red Eyes B Dragon SCR	1.50	3.00
BPT006 B. Skull Dragon SCR	2.50	5.00

2002 Yu-Gi-Oh God Cards

GBI001 Slifer The Sky Dragon UR	15.00	30.00
GBI001 Slifer The Sky Dragon SCR	50.00	100.00
GBI002 Obelisk The Tormentor UR	20.00	40.00
GBI002 Obelisk The Tormentor SCR	50.00	100.00
GBI003 The Winged Dragon of Ra UR	20.00	40.00
GBI003 The Winged Dragon of Ra SCR	25.00	50.00

2002 Yu-Gi-Oh Legend of Blue Eyes White Dragon 1st Edition

LOB000 Tri-Horned Dragon SCR	75.00	150.00
LOB001 Blue-Eyes White Dragon UR	750.00	1,500.00
LOB002 Hitotsu-Me Giant C	4.00	8.00
LOB003 Flame Swordsman SR	100.00	200.00
LOB004 Skull Servant C	7.50	15.00
LOB005 Dark Magician UR	250.00	500.00
LOB006 Gaia the Fierce Knight UR	150.00	300.00
LOB007 Celtic Guardian SR	60.00	125.00
LOB008 Basic Insect C	5.00	10.00
LOB009 Mammoth Graveyard C	4.00	8.00
LOB010 Silver Fang C	4.00	8.00
LOB011 Dark Gray C	50.00	100.00
LOB012 Trial of Nightmare C	12.50	25.00
LOB013 Nemuriko C	4.00	8.00
LOB014 The 13th Grave C	4.00	8.00
LOB015 Charubin the Fire Knight R	7.50	15.00
LOB016 Flame Manipulator C	4.00	8.00
LOB017 Monster Egg C	4.00	8.00
LOB018 Firegrass C	5.00	10.00
LOB019 Darkfire Dragon R	10.00	20.00
LOB020 Dark King of the Abyss C	2.50	5.00
LOB021 Fiend Reflection #2 C	4.00	8.00
LOB022 Fusionist R	7.50	15.00
LOB023 Turtle Tiger C	3.00	6.00
LOB024 Petit Dragon C	2.00	4.00
LOB025 Petit Angel C	4.00	8.00
LOB026 Hinotama Soul C	1.00	2.00
LOB027 Aqua Madoor R	6.00	12.00
LOB028 Kagemusha of the Blue Flame C	3.00	6.00
LOB029 Flame Ghost R	2.00	4.00
LOB030 Two-Mouth Darkruler C	2.50	5.00
LOB031 Dissolverock C	2.00	4.00
LOB032 Root Water C	1.50	3.00
LOB033 The Furious Sea King C	.75	1.50
LOB034 Green Phantom King C	5.00	10.00
LOB035 Ray & Temperature C	3.00	6.00
LOB036 King Fog C	2.00	4.00
LOB037 Mystical Sheep #2 C	1.50	3.00
LOB038 Masaki the Legendary Swordsman C	2.00	4.00
LOB039 Kurama C	1.25	2.50
LOB040 Legendary Sword SP	10.00	20.00
LOB041 Beast Fangs SP	7.50	15.00
LOB042 Violet Crystal SP	10.00	20.00
LOB043 Book of Secret Arts SP	6.00	12.00
LOB044 Power of Kaishin SP	4.00	8.00
LOB045 Dragon Capture Jar R	6.00	12.00
LOB046 Forest C	1.25	2.50
LOB047 Wasteland C	2.50	5.00
LOB048 Mountain C	4.00	8.00
LOB049 Sogen C	2.50	5.00
LOB050 Umi C	6.00	12.00
LOB051 Yami C	4.00	8.00
LOB052 Dark Hole SR	50.00	100.00
LOB053 Raigeki SR	30.00	75.00
LOB054 Red Medicine C	4.00	10.00
LOB055 Sparks C	10.00	20.00
LOB056 Hinotama C	6.00	12.00
LOB057 Fissure R	7.50	15.00
LOB058 Trap Hole SR	12.50	25.00
LOB059 Polymerization SR	75.00	150.00
LOB060 Remove Trap C	2.50	5.00
LOB061 Two-Pronged Attack R	6.00	12.00
LOB062 Mystical Elf SR	30.00	75.00
LOB063 Tyhone C	5.00	10.00
LOB064 Beaver Warrior C	3.00	6.00
LOB065 Gravedigger Ghoul R	6.00	12.00
LOB066 Curse of Dragon SR	60.00	125.00
LOB067 Karbonala Warrior R	4.00	8.00
LOB068 Giant Soldier of Stone R	7.50	15.00
LOB069 Uraby C	3.00	6.00
LOB070 Red-Eyes Black Dragon UR	250.00	500.00
LOB071 Reaper of the Cards R	10.00	20.00
LOB072 Witty Phantom C	2.00	4.00
LOB073 Larvas C	2.50	5.00
LOB074 Hard Armor C	2.00	4.00
LOB075 Man Eater C	1.50	3.00
LOB076 M-Warrior #1 C	3.00	6.00
LOB077 M-Warrior #2 C	4.00	8.00
LOB078 Spirit of the Harp R	15.00	30.00
LOB079 Armaill C	2.00	4.00
LOB080 Terra the Terrible C	2.00	4.00
LOB081 Frenzied Panda C	1.50	3.00
LOB082 Kumootoko C	2.00	4.00
LOB083 Meda Bat C	2.00	4.00
LOB084 Enchanting Mermaid C	3.00	6.00
LOB085 Fireyarou C	3.00	6.00
LOB086 Dragoness the Wicked Knight R	10.00	20.00
LOB087 One-Eyed Shield Dragon C	2.50	5.00
LOB088 Dark Energy SP	12.50	25.00
LOB089 Laser Cannon Armor SP	4.00	8.00
LOB090 Vile Germs SP	3.00	6.00
LOB091 Silver Bow and Arrow SP	6.00	12.00
LOB093 Electro-Whip	3.00	6.00
LOB094 Mystical Moon SP	12.50	25.00
LOB095 Stop Defense R	12.50	25.00
LOB096 Machine Conversion Factory SP	5.00	10.00
LOB097 Raise Body Heat SP	10.00	20.00
LOB098 Follow Wind SP	12.50	25.00
LOB099 Goblin's Secret Remedy R	4.00	8.00
LOB100 Final Flame R	7.50	15.00
LOB101 Swords of Revealing Light SR	15.00	30.00
LOB102 Metal Dragon R	7.50	15.00
LOB103 Spike Seadra C	.60	1.25
LOB104 Tripwire Beast C	3.00	6.00
LOB105 Skull Red Bird C	2.50	5.00
LOB106 Armed Ninja R	5.00	10.00
LOB107 Flower Wolf R	7.50	15.00
LOB108 Man-Eater Bug SR	7.50	15.00
LOB109 Sand Stone C	4.00	8.00
LOB110 Hane-Hane R	5.00	10.00
LOB111 Misairuzame C	2.50	5.00
LOB112 Steel Ogre Grotto #1 C	5.00	10.00
LOB113 Lesser Dragon C	2.00	4.00
LOB114 Darkworld Thorns C	1.00	2.00
LOB115 Drooling Lizard C	5.00	10.00
LOB116 Armored Starfish C	1.00	2.00
LOB117 Succubus Knight C	3.00	6.00
LOB118 Monster Reborn UR	50.00	100.00
LOB119 Pot of Greed R	12.50	25.00
LOB120 Right Leg of the Forbidden One UR	125.00	250.00
LOB121 Left Leg of the Forbidden One UR	100.00	200.00
LOB122 Right Arm of the Forbidden One UR	100.00	200.00
LOB123 Left Arm of the Forbidden One UR	60.00	125.00
LOB124 Exodia the Forbidden One UR	200.00	400.00
LOB125 Gaia the Dragon Champion SCR	50.00	100.00

2002 Yu-Gi-Oh Magic Ruler 1st Edition North American English

MRL000 Blue-Eyes Toon Dragon SCR	200.00	400.00
MRL001 Penguin Knight C	.60	1.25
MRL002 Axe of Despair UR	12.50	25.00
MRL003 Black Pendant SR	2.00	4.00
MRL004 Horn of Light C	.75	1.50
MRL005 Malevolent Nuzzler C	.75	1.50
MRL006 Spellbinding Circle UR	20.00	40.00
MRL007 Metal Fish C	.50	1.00
MRL008 Electric Snake C	2.50	5.00
MRL009 Queen Bird C	.50	1.00
MRL010 Ameba R	3.00	6.00
MRL011 Peacock C	.50	1.00
MRL012 Maha Vailo SR	6.00	12.00
MRL013 Guardian of the Throne Room C	.75	1.50
MRL014 Fire Kraken C	.50	1.00
MRL015 Minar C	1.25	2.50
MRL016 Griggle C	.50	1.00
MRL017 Tyhone #2 C	.50	1.00
MRL018 Ancient One of the Deep Forest C	.50	1.00
MRL019 Dark Witch C	.75	1.50
MRL020 Weather Report C	1.00	2.00
MRL021 Mechanical Snail C	.50	1.00
MRL022 Giant Turtle Who Feeds on Flames C	.75	1.50
MRL023 Liquid Beast C	.50	1.00
MRL024 Hiro's Shadow Scout R	3.00	6.00
MRL025 High Tide Gyojin C	.50	1.00
MRL026 Invader of the Throne SR	4.00	8.00
MRL027 Whiptail Crow C	.60	1.25
MRL028 Slot Machine C	1.00	2.00
MRL029 Relinquished UR	30.00	75.00
MRL030 Red Archery Girl C	.50	1.00
MRL031 Gravekeeper's Servant C	1.50	3.00
MRL032 Curse of Fiend C	1.50	3.00
MRL033 Upstart Goblin C	1.00	2.00
MRL034 Toll C	1.00	2.00
MRL035 Final Destiny C	.75	1.50
MRL036 Snatch Steal UR	25.00	50.00
MRL037 Chorus of Sanctuary C	.75	1.50
MRL038 Confiscation SR	7.50	15.00
MRL039 Delinquent Duo UR	30.00	60.00
MRL040 Darkness Approaches C	1.00	2.00
MRL041 Fairy's Hand Mirror C	1.00	2.00
MRL042 Tailor of the Fickle C	1.00	2.00
MRL043 Rush Recklessly R	1.50	3.00
MRL044 The Reliable Guardian C	1.50	3.00
MRL045 The Forceful Sentry UR	7.50	15.00
MRL046 Chain Energy C	.75	1.50
MRL047 Mystical Space Typhoon UR	30.00	60.00
MRL048 Giant Trunade SR	10.00	20.00
MRL049 Painful Choice SR	6.00	12.00
MRL050 Snake Fang C	1.00	2.00
MRL051 Black Illusion Ritual SR	7.50	15.00
MRL052 Octoberser C	.50	1.00
MRL053 Psychic Kappa C	.50	1.00
MRL054 Horn of the Unicorn R	1.50	3.00
MRL055 Labyrinth Wall C	2.00	4.00
MRL056 Wall Shadow C	.60	1.25
MRL057 Twin Long Rods #2 C	.50	1.00
MRL058 Stone Ogre Grotto C	.50	1.00
MRL059 Magical Labyrinth C	.50	1.00
MRL060 Eternal Rest C	2.00	4.00
MRL061 Megamorph UR	12.50	25.00
MRL062 Commencement Dance C	.50	1.00
MRL063 Hamburger Recipe C	1.00	2.00
MRL064 House of Adhesive Tape C	.50	1.00
MRL065 Eatgaboon C	.50	1.00
MRL066 Turtle Oath C	.50	1.00
MRL067 Performance of Sword C	.50	1.00
MRL068 Hungry Burger C	1.50	3.00
MRL069 Crab Turtle C	.50	1.00
MRL070 Ryu-Ran C	1.25	2.50
MRL071 Manga Ryu-Ran R	2.00	4.00
MRL072 Toon Mermaid UR	20.00	40.00
MRL073 Toon Summoned Skull UR	30.00	75.00
MRL074 Jigen Bakudan C	1.00	2.00
MRL075 Hyozanryu R	2.00	4.00
MRL076 Toon World SR	12.50	25.00
MRL077 Cyber Jar R	6.00	12.00
MRL078 Banisher of the Light SR	2.50	5.00
MRL079 Giant Rat R	2.00	4.00
MRL080 Senju of the Thousand Hands R	1.50	3.00
MRL081 UFO Turtle R	.60	1.25
MRL082 Flash Assailant C	.50	1.00
MRL083 Karate Man R	1.50	3.00
MRL084 Dark Zebra C	1.50	3.00
MRL085 Giant Germ R	2.00	4.00
MRL086 Nimble Momonga R	2.00	4.00
MRL087 Spear Cretin C	.50	1.00
MRL088 Shining Angel R	2.00	4.00
MRL089 Boar Soldier C	.50	1.00
MRL090 Mother Grizzly R	1.50	3.00
MRL091 Flying Kamakiri #1 R	.75	1.50
MRL092 Ceremonial Bell C	.50	1.00
MRL093 Sonic Bird C	.50	1.00
MRL094 Mystic Tomato R	1.50	3.00
MRL095 Kotodama C	.50	1.00
MRL096 Gaia Power C	1.00	2.00
MRL097 Umiiruka C	.50	1.00
MRL098 Molten Destruction C	.50	1.00
MRL099 Rising Air Current C	.50	1.00
MRL100 Luminous Spark C	1.00	2.00
MRL101 Mystic Plasma Zone C	2.00	4.00
MRL102 Messenger of Peace SR	3.00	6.00
MRL103 Serpent Night Dragon SCR	30.00	60.00

2002 Yu-Gi-Oh Metal Raiders 1st Edition

MRD0 Gate Guardian SCR	75.00	150.00
MRD1 Feral Imp C	1.25	2.50
MRD2 Winged Dragon, Guardian of the Fortress 1 C	2.50	5.00
MRD3 Summoned Skull UR	100.00	200.00
MRD4 Rock Ogre Grotto 1 C	.60	1.25
MRD5 Armored Lizard C	1.00	2.00
MRD6 Killer Needle C	2.00	4.00
MRD7 Larvæ Moth C	1.00	2.00
MRD8 Harpie Lady C	1.50	3.00
MRD9 Harpie Lady Sisters SR	30.00	60.00
MRD10 Kojikocy C	1.00	2.00
MRD11 Cocoon of Evolution SP	2.50	5.00
MRD12 Crawling Dragon #2 C	1.00	2.00
MRD13 Armored Zombie C	1.50	3.00
MRD14 Mask of Darkness R	4.00	8.00
MRD15 Doma the Angel of Silence C	.75	1.50
MRD16 White Magical Hat R	3.00	6.00
MRD17 Big Eye C	.75	1.50
MRD18 Black Skull Dragon UR	40.00	80.00
MRD19 Masked Sorcerer R	.75	1.50
MRD20 Roaring Ocean Snake C	3.00	6.00
MRD21 Water Omotics C	5.00	10.00
MRD22 Ground Attacker Bugroth C	1.00	2.00
MRD23 Petit Moth C	1.50	3.00
MRD24 Elegant Egotist R	3.00	6.00
MRD25 Sanga of the Thunder SR	25.00	50.00
MRD26 Kazejin SR	20.00	40.00
MRD27 Suijin SR	15.00	30.00
MRD28 Mystic Lamp SP	4.00	8.00
MRD29 Steel Scorpion C	.75	1.50
MRD30 Ocubeam C	.50	1.00
MRD31 Leghul SP	1.50	3.00
MRD32 Ooguchi C	2.50	5.00
MRD33 Leogun C	2.00	4.00
MRD34 Blast Juggler C	1.50	3.00
MRD35 Jinzo #7 SP	1.50	3.00
MRD36 Magician of Faith R	10.00	20.00
MRD37 Ancient Elf C	1.00	2.00
MRD38 Deepsea Shark C	2.00	4.00
MRD39 Bottom Dweller C	.75	1.50
MRD40 Destroyer Golem C	.75	1.50
MRD41 Kaminari Attack C	.75	1.50
MRD42 Rainbow Flower SP	7.50	15.00
MRD43 Morinphen C	.50	1.00
MRD44 Mega Thunderball C	.50	1.00
MRD45 Tongyo C	.50	1.00
MRD46 Empress Judge C	1.00	2.00
MRD47 Pale Beast C	.50	1.00
MRD48 Electric Lizard C	1.00	2.00
MRD49 Hunter Spider C	.30	.75
MRD50 Ancient Lizard Warrior C	1.00	2.00
MRD51 Queen's Double SP	.75	1.50
MRD52 Trent C	1.50	3.00
MRD53 Disk Magician C	2.00	4.00
MRD54 Hyosube C	.50	1.00
MRD55 Hibikime C	.75	1.50
MRD56 Fake Trap R	2.50	5.00
MRD57 Tribute to the Doomed SR	1.00	2.00
MRD58 Soul Release C	2.50	5.00
MRD59 The Cheerful Coffin C	.50	1.00
MRD60 Change of Heart UR	30.00	60.00
MRD61 Baby Dragon SP	6.00	12.00
MRD62 Blackland Fire Dragon C	2.00	4.00
MRD63 Swamp Battleguard C	1.50	3.00
MRD64 Battle Steer C	1.50	3.00
MRD65 Time Wizard UR	100.00	200.00
MRD66 Saggi the Dark Clown C	7.50	15.00
MRD67 Dragon Piper C	.75	1.50
MRD68 Illusionist Faceless Mage C	1.50	3.00
MRD69 Sangan R	6.00	12.00
MRD70 Great Moth R	2.50	5.00
MRD71 Kuriboh SR	30.00	60.00
MRD72 Jellyfish C	.75	1.50
MRD73 Castle of Dark Illusions C	1.50	3.00
MRD74 King of Yamimakai C	1.50	3.00
MRD75 Catapult Turtle SR	6.00	12.00
MRD76 Mystic Horseman C	.50	1.00
MRD77 Rabid Horseman C	1.25	2.50
MRD78 Crass Clown SP	2.00	4.00
MRD79 Pumpking the King of Ghosts C	3.00	6.00
MRD80 Dream Clown SP	2.00	4.00
MRD81 Tainted Wisdom C	.50	1.00
MRD82 Ancient Brain C	1.50	3.00
MRD83 Guardian of the Labyrinth C	2.00	4.00
MRD84 Prevent Rat C	.50	1.00
MRD85 The Little Swordsman of Aile C	.50	1.00
MRD86 Princess of Tsurugi R	.75	1.50
MRD87 Protector of the Throne C	2.00	4.00
MRD88 Tremendous Fire C	3.00	6.00
MRD89 Jirai Gumo C	.75	1.50
MRD90 Shadow Ghoul R	6.00	12.00
MRD91 Labyrinth Tank C	7.50	15.00
MRD92 Ryu-Kishin Powered C	1.50	3.00
MRD93 Bickuribox C	2.00	4.00
MRD94 Giltia the D. Knight C	.75	1.50
MRD95 Launcher Spider C	.75	1.50
MRD96 Giga-Tech Wolf C	.75	1.50
MRD97 Thunder Dragon C	1.50	3.00
MRD98 7 Colored Fish C	1.00	2.00
MRD99 The Immortal of Thunder C	1.00	2.00
MRD100 Punished Eagle C	2.00	4.00
MRD101 Insect Soldiers of the Sky C	.50	1.00
MRD102 Hoshiningen R	1.50	3.00
MRD103 Musician King C	1.00	2.00
MRD104 Yado Karu C	.75	1.50
MRD105 Cyber Saurus C	.75	1.50
MRD106 Cannon Soldier R	3.00	6.00
MRD107 Muka Muka R	2.00	4.00
MRD108 The Bistro Butcher C	1.00	2.00
MRD109 Star Boy R	1.25	2.50
MRD110 Milus Radiant R	1.50	3.00
MRD111 Flame Cerebus C	.75	1.50
MRD112 Niwatori C	1.00	2.00
MRD113 Dark Elf R	3.00	6.00
MRD114 Mushroom Man #2 C	.60	1.25
MRD115 Lava Battleguard C	1.50	3.00
MRD116 Witch of the Black Forest R	7.50	15.00
MRD117 Little Chimera R	1.25	2.50
MRD118 Bladefly R	4.00	8.00
MRD119 Lady of Faith C	1.50	3.00
MRD120 Twin-Headed Thunder Dragon SR	20.00	40.00
MRD121 Witch's Apprentice R	1.50	3.00
MRD122 Blue-Winged Crown C	1.50	3.00
MRD123 Skull Knight C	1.25	2.50
MRD124 Gazelle the King of Mythical Beasts SP	2.00	4.00
MRD125 Garnecia Elefantis SR	5.00	10.00
MRD126 Barrel Dragon UR	12.50	25.00
MRD127 Solemn Judgment UR	150.00	300.00
MRD128 Magic Jammer UR	15.00	30.00
MRD129 Seven Tools of the Bandit UR	20.00	40.00
MRD130 Horn of Heaven UR	30.00	60.00
MRD131 Shield & Sword R	7.50	15.00
MRD132 Sword of Deep-Seated C	.75	1.50
MRD133 Block Attack C	1.00	2.00
MRD134 The Unhappy Maiden SP	1.50	3.00
MRD135 Robbin Goblin R	2.50	5.00
MRD136 Germ Infection C	.75	1.50
MRD137 Paralyzing Potion C	.50	1.00
MRD138 Mirror Force UR	75.00	150.00
MRD139 Ring of Magnetism C	.50	1.00

MRD140 Share the Pain C	1.50	3.00
MRD141 Stim-pack SP	6.00	12.00
MRD142 Heavy Storm SR	30.00	60.00
MRD143 Thousand Dragon SCR	60.00	125.00

2002 Yu-Gi-Oh Pharaoh's Servant 1st Edition

PSV0 Jinzo SCR	150.00	300.00
PSV1 Steel Ogre Grotto #2 C	.50	1.00
PSV2 Three-Headed Geedo C	.50	1.00
PSV3 Parasite Paracide SR	6.00	12.00
PSV4 7 Completed C	1.00	2.50
PSV5 Lightforce Sword R	1.25	2.50
PSV6 Chain Destruction UR	7.50	15.00
PSV7 Time Seal SP	3.00	6.00
PSV8 Graverobber SR	7.50	15.00
PSV9 Gift of the Mystical Elf SP	2.00	4.00
PSV10 The Eye of Truth SP	6.00	12.00
PSV11 Dust Tornado SR	7.50	15.00
PSV12 Call of the Haunted UR	25.00	50.00
PSV13 Solomon's Lawbook C	.75	1.50
PSV14 Earthshaker C	.50	1.00
PSV15 Enchanted Javelin C	.75	1.50
PSV16 Mirror Wall SR	5.00	10.00
PSV17 Gust C	.75	1.50
PSV18 Driving Snow C	.75	1.50
PSV19 Armored Glass C	.50	1.00
PSV20 World Suppression C	.60	1.25
PSV21 Mystic Probe C	.60	1.25
PSV22 Metal Detector C	.50	1.00
PSV23 Numinous Healer SP	2.00	4.00
PSV24 Appropriate R	1.00	2.00
PSV25 Forced Requisition R	.50	1.00
PSV26 DNA Surgery SP	1.50	3.00
PSV27 The Regulation of Tribe C	1.25	2.50
PSV28 Backup Soldier SR	2.00	4.00
PSV29 Major Riot SP	1.25	2.50
PSV30 Ceasefire UR	6.00	12.00
PSV31 Light of Intervention C	.50	1.00
PSV32 Respect Play C	.75	1.50
PSV33 Magical Hats SR	7.50	15.00
PSV34 Nobleman of Crossout SR	7.50	15.00
PSV35 Nobleman of Extermination R	1.50	3.00
PSV36 The Shallow Grave R	1.25	2.50
PSV37 Premature Burial UR	12.50	25.00
PSV38 Inspection SP	.50	1.00
PSV39 Prohibition R	3.00	6.00
PSV40 Morphing Jar #2 R	1.50	3.00
PSV41 Flame Champion C	.75	1.50
PSV42 Twin-Headed Fire Dragon C	.50	1.00
PSV43 Darkfire Soldier C	1.00	2.00
PSV44 Mr.Volcano C	.75	1.50
PSV45 Darkfire Soldier #2 C	1.00	2.00
PSV46 Kiseitai SP	.75	1.50
PSV47 Cyber Falcon C	1.00	2.00
PSV48 Flying Kamakiri #2 C	1.00	2.00
PSV49 Harpie's Brother C	.50	1.00
PSV50 Buster Blader UR	30.00	75.00
PSV51 Michizure R	1.50	3.00
PSV52 Minor Goblin Official SP	1.00	2.00
PSV53 Gamble C	.75	1.50
PSV54 Attack and Receive C	.50	1.00
PSV55 Solemn Wishes SP	1.50	3.00
PSV56 Skull Invitation R	1.50	3.00
PSV57 Bubonic Vermin C	.50	1.00
PSV58 Dark Bat C	.75	1.50
PSV59 Oni Tank T-34 C	.60	1.25
PSV60 Overdrive C	.60	1.25
PSV61 Burning Land C	.50	1.00
PSV62 Cold Wave C	1.00	2.00
PSV63 Fairy Meteor Crush SR	2.50	5.00
PSV64 Limiter Removal SR	4.00	8.00
PSV65 Rain of Mercy C	.50	1.00
PSV66 Monster Recovery R	.50	1.00
PSV67 Shift R	.75	1.50
PSV68 Insect Imitation C	.50	1.00
PSV69 Dimensionhole R	1.50	3.00
PSV70 Ground Collapse C	.75	1.50
PSV71 Magic Drain R	1.25	2.50
PSV72 Infinite Dismissal C	.50	1.00
PSV73 Gravity Bind R	.75	1.50
PSV74 Type Zero Magic Crusher C	.50	1.00
PSV75 Shadow of Eyes C	.75	1.50
PSV76 The Legendary Fisherman UR	12.50	25.00
PSV77 Sword Hunter SP	1.00	2.00
PSV78 Drill Bug C	.30	.75
PSV79 Deepsea Warrior C	.75	1.50
PSV80 Bite Shoes C	.50	1.00
PSV81 Spikebot C	.50	1.00
PSV82 Invitation to a Dark Sleep C	1.00	2.00
PSV83 Thousand-Eyes Idol SP	2.50	5.00
PSV84 Thousand-Eyes Restrict UR	30.00	60.00
PSV85 Girochin Kuwagata C	1.25	2.50
PSV86 Hayabusa Knight R	3.00	6.00
PSV87 Bombardment Beetle SP	.50	1.00
PSV88 4-Starred Ladybug of Doom SP	1.00	2.00
PSV89 Gradius SP	2.00	4.00
PSV90 Red-Moon Baby R	1.00	2.00
PSV91 Mad Sword Beast R	1.00	2.00
PSV92 Skull Mariner C	.50	1.00
PSV93 The All-Seeing White Tiger C	.50	1.00
PSV94 Goblin Attack Force UR	10.00	20.00
PSV95 Island Turtle SP	.50	1.00
PSV96 Wingweaver C	.75	1.50
PSV97 Science Soldier C	.50	1.00
PSV98 Souls of the Forbidden C	.50	1.00
PSV99 Dokuroyaiba C	.50	1.00
PSV100 The Fiend Megacyber UR	5.00	10.00
PSV101 Gearfried the Iron Knight SR	4.00	8.00
PSV102 Insect Barrier C	.50	1.00
PSV103 Beast of Talwar UR	7.50	15.00
PSV104 Imperial Order SCR	12.50	25.00

2002 Yu-Gi-Oh Pharaonic Guardian

PH1 Magma Giant	.10	.20
PH2 Shapesnatch	.10	.20
PH3 Soul-eater	.10	.20
PH4 Wan-fu Tiger King R	2.00	4.00
PH5 Birdface	.10	.20
PH6 Cruel	.10	.20
PH7 Armored Fly	.10	.20
PH8 Mermaid Princess SP	3.00	6.00
PH9 Xeno	.10	.20
PH10 Time Eater	.10	.20
PH11 Gurrage	.10	.20
PH12 Mysterious Sevant	.10	.20
PH13 Moist Alien SR	4.00	8.00
PH14 Gora-Turtle	.10	.20
PH15 Super Slash Samurai SR	5.00	10.00
PH16 Poison Mummy	.10	.20
PH17 Sandstorm Poltergeist	.10	.20
PH18 Pharoah's Guardian	.10	.20
PH19 Wandering Mummy R	2.00	4.00
PH20 De-zard the Great Priest UR	10.00	20.00
PH20 De-Zard Great Priest PR	15.00	30.00
PH21 Scarab Swarm	.10	.20
PH22 Locust Swarm	.10	.20
PH23 Fat Mummy	.10	.20
PH24 Octo-Pion	.10	.20
PH25 Guardian Sphynx UR	10.00	20.00
PH25 Guardian Sphynx PR	20.00	40.00
PH26 Pyramurtle	.10	.20
PH27 Dice Pot	.10	.20
PH28 Black Scorpion Gang	.10	.20
PH29 Don Zaruug UR	10.00	20.00
PH29 Don Zaruug PR	20.00	40.00
PH30 Camel Mummy	.10	.20
PH31 Suksy Serpent Man R	1.00	2.00
PH32 Book of Life SR	10.00	20.00
PH33 Book of Sun	.20	.40
PH34 Book of Moon	.20	.40
PH35 Nightmare Shimmer	.10	.20
PH36 Secret Door	.10	.20
PH37 Call of the Mummy	.10	.20
PH38 Scaredy Cat	.10	.20
PH39 Pyramid Power	.10	.20
PH40 Pharoah's Mask	.10	.20
PH41 Traveller's Ordeal R	2.00	4.00
PH42 Bottomless Quicksand	.10	.20
PH43 Curse of Pharoah R	2.00	4.00
PH44 Spiked Ceiling Trap	.10	.20
PH45 Golden Statue of Evil SR	4.00	8.00
PH46 Cursed Sarcophagus	.10	.20
PH47 Spiked Wall Trap	.10	.20
PH48 Dust Chute	.10	.20
PH49 Sundial of Destiny	.10	.20
PH50 Greedy Fool	.10	.20
PH51 Treasure Chest R	2.00	4.00
PHOO Lich Undead King SCR	10.00	20.00

2002 Yu-Gi-Oh Starter Deck Kaiba 1st Edition

SDK001 Blue-Eyes White Dragon UR	25.00	50.00
SDK002 Hitotsu-Me Giant C	2.50	5.00
SDK003 Ryu-Kishin C	.75	1.50
SDK004 The Wicked Worm Beast C	2.50	5.00
SDK005 Battle Ox C	2.50	5.00
SDK006 Koumori Dragon C	2.00	4.00
SDK007 Judge Man C	.50	1.00
SDK008 Rogue Doll C	1.50	3.00
SDK009 Kojikocy C	1.25	2.50
SDK010 Uraby C	.75	1.50
SDK011 Gyakutenno Megami C	3.00	6.00
SDK012 Mystic Horseman C	1.50	3.00
SDK013 Terra the Terrible C	.60	1.25
SDK014 Dark Titan of Terror C	1.00	2.00
SDK015 Dark Assassin C	3.00	6.00
SDK016 Master & Expert C	2.00	4.00
SDK17 Unknown Warrior of Fiend C	1.50	3.00
SDK018 Mystic Clown C	2.00	4.00
SDK019 Ogre of the Black Shadow C	2.00	4.00
SDK020 Dark Energy C	1.00	2.00
SDK021 Invigoration C	2.00	4.00
SDK022 Dark Hole C	1.50	3.00
SDK023 Ookazi C	.75	1.50
SDK024 Ryu-Kishin Powered C	.50	1.00
SDK025 Swordstalker C	1.00	2.00
SDK026 La Jinn the Mystical Genie of the Lamp C	7.50	15.00
SDK027 Rude Kaiser C	1.00	2.00
SDK028 Destroyer Golem C	1.50	3.00
SDK029 Skull Red Bird C	1.50	3.00
SDK030 D. Human C	1.50	3.00
SDK031 Pale Beast C	1.50	3.00
SDK032 Fissure C	.75	1.50
SDK033 Trap Hole C	1.50	3.00
SDK034 Two-Pronged Attack C	.75	1.50
SDK035 De-Spell C	1.25	2.50
SDK036 Monster Reborn C	2.50	5.00
SDK037 The Inexperienced Spy C	.50	1.00
SDK038 Reinforcements C	.50	1.00
SDK039 Ancient Telescope C	2.50	5.00
SDK040 Just Desserts C	1.50	3.00
SDK041 Lord of D. SR	10.00	20.00
SDK042 The Flute of Summoning Dragon SR	6.00	12.00
SDK043 Mysterious Puppeteer C	.75	1.50
SDK044 Trap Master C	1.25	2.50
SDK045 Sogen C	1.00	2.00
SDK046 Hane-Hane C	1.50	3.00
SDK047 Reverse Trap C	.50	1.00
SDK048 Reverse Trap C	.50	1.00
SDK049 Castle Walls C	2.50	5.00
SDK050 Ultimate Offering C	1.00	2.00

2002 Yu-Gi-Oh Starter Deck Yugi 1st Edition

SDY001 Mystical Elf C	10.00	20.00
SDY002 Feral Imp C	4.00	8.00
SDY003 Winged Dragon, Guardian of the Fortress 1 C	2.00	4.00
SDY004 Summoned Skull C	4.00	8.00
SDY005 Beaver Warrior C	3.00	6.00
SDY006 Dark Magician UR	60.00	125.00
SDY007 Gaia The Fierce Knight C	7.50	15.00
SDY008 Curse of Dragon C	4.00	8.00
SDY009 Celtic Guardian C	2.50	5.00
SDY010 Mammoth Graveyard C	2.00	4.00
SDY011 Great White C	2.50	5.00
SDY012 Silver Fang C	1.50	3.00
SDY013 Giant Soldier of Stone C	2.00	4.00
SDY014 Dragon Zombie C	3.00	6.00
SDY015 Doma the Angel of Silence C	1.50	3.00
SDY016 Ansatsu C	7.50	15.00
SDY017 Witty Phantom C	2.50	5.00
SDY018 Claw Reacher C	1.00	2.00
SDY019 Mystic Clown C	1.25	2.50
SDY020 Sword of Dark Destruction C	1.25	2.50
SDY021 Book of Secret Arts C	4.00	8.00
SDY022 Dark Hole C	.60	1.25
SDY023 Dian Keto the Cure Master C	1.25	2.50
SDY024 Ancient Elf C	5.00	10.00
SDY025 Magical Ghost C	2.00	4.00
SDY026 Fissure C	2.50	5.00
SDY027 Trap Hole C	1.25	2.50
SDY028 Two-Pronged Attack C	1.50	3.00
SDY029 De-Spell C	1.00	2.00
SDY030 Monster Reborn C	4.00	8.00
SDY031 Reinforcements C	1.25	2.50
SDY032 Change of Heart C	2.50	5.00
SDY033 The Stern Mystic C	1.00	2.00
SDY034 Wall of Illusion C	.75	1.50
SDY035 Neo the Magic Swordsman C	1.50	3.00
SDY036 Baron of the Fiend Sword C	2.00	4.00
SDY037 Man-Eating Treasure Chest C	2.50	5.00
SDY038 Sorcerer of the Doomed C	1.50	3.00
SDY039 Last Will C	3.00	6.00
SDY040 Waboku C	1.50	3.00
SDY041 Soul Exchange SR	3.00	6.00
SDY042 Card Destruction SR	3.00	6.00
SDY043 Trap Master C	1.50	3.00
SDY044 Dragon Capture Jar C	2.50	5.00
SDY045 Yami C	6.00	12.00
SDY046 Man-Eater Bug C	1.00	2.00
SDY047 Reverse Trap C	1.00	2.00
SDY048 Remove Trap C	.75	1.50
SDY049 Castle Walls C	1.25	2.50
SDY050 Ultimate Offering C	1.00	2.00

2002 Yu-Gi-Oh Tournament Pack 1

TP1001 Mechanicalchaser UR	400.00	800.00
TP1002 Axe Raider SR	125.00	250.00
TP1003 Kwagar Hercules SR	100.00	200.00
TP1004 Patrol Robo SR	30.00	60.00
TP1005 White Hole SR	30.00	75.00
TP1006 Elf's Light R	50.00	100.00
TP1007 Steel Shell R	7.50	15.00
TP1008 Blue Medicine R	20.00	40.00
TP1009 Raimei R	12.50	25.00
TP1010 Burning Spear R	20.00	40.00
TP1011 Gust Fan R	30.00	75.00
TP1012 Tiger Axe R	20.00	40.00
TP1013 Goddess with the Third Eye R	25.00	50.00
TP1014 Beastking of Swamps R	15.00	30.00
TP1015 Versago the Destroyer R	20.00	40.00
TP1016 Oscillo Hero #2 C	10.00	20.00
TP1017 Giant Flea C	3.00	6.00
TP1018 Bean Soldier C	5.00	10.00
TP1019 The Statue of Easter Island C	2.00	4.00
TP1020 Corroding Shark C	5.00	10.00
TP1021 WOW Warrior C	2.50	5.00
TP1022 Winged Dragon, Guardian of the Fortress C	12.50	25.00
TP1023 Oscillo Hero C	3.00	6.00
TP1024 Shining Friendship C	3.00	6.00
TP1025 Hercules Beetle C	10.00	20.00
TP1026 The Judgement Hand C	4.00	8.00
TP1027 Wodan the Resident of the Forest C	4.00	8.00
TP1028 Cyber Soldier of Darkworld C	5.00	10.00
TP1029 Cockroach Knight C	7.50	15.00
TP1030 Kuwagata Alpha C	6.00	12.00

2002 Yu-Gi-Oh Tournament Pack 2

TP2001 Morphing Jar UR	1,000.00	2,000.00
TP2002 Dragon Seeker SR	100.00	200.00
TP2003 Giant Red Seasnake SR	40.00	80.00
TP2004 Exile of the Wicked SR	25.00	50.00
TP2005 Call of the Grave SR	30.00	75.00
TP2006 Mikazukinoyaiba R	40.00	80.00
TP2007 Skull Guardian R	75.00	150.00
TP2008 Novox's Prayer R	40.00	80.00
TP2009 Dokurorider R	30.00	60.00
TP2010 Revival of Dokurorider R	30.00	60.00
TP2011 Beautiful Headhuntress R	60.00	125.00
TP2012 Sonic Maid R	30.00	60.00
TP2013 Mystical Sheep #1 R	10.00	20.00
TP2014 Warrior of Tradition R	60.00	125.00
TP2015 Soul of the Pure R	25.00	50.00
TP2016 Dancing Elf C	10.00	20.00
TP2017 Turu-Purun C	5.00	10.00
TP2018 Dharma Cannon C	3.00	6.00
TP2019 Stuffed Animal C	2.50	5.00
TP2020 Spirit of the Books C	3.00	6.00
TP2021 Faith Bird C	3.00	6.00
TP2022 Takuhee C	5.00	10.00
TP2023 Maiden of the Moonlight C	12.50	25.00
TP2024 Queen of Autumn Leaves C	12.50	25.00
TP2025 Two-Headed King Rex C	5.00	10.00
TP2026 Garoozis C	5.00	10.00
TP2027 Crawling Dragon C	3.00	6.00
TP2028 Parrot Dragon C	6.00	12.00
TP2029 Sky Dragon C	4.00	8.00
TP2030 Water Magician C	2.00	4.00

2003 Yu-Gi-Oh Collector Tins

BPT007 Dark Magician SCR	2.00	4.00
BPT008 Buster Blader SCR	3.00	6.00
BPT009 Blue-Eyes White Dragon SCR	5.00	10.00
BPT010 XYZ-Dragon Cannon SCR	1.00	2.00
BPT011 Jinzo SCR	2.50	5.00
BPT012 Gearfried the Iron Knight SCR	.75	1.50

2003 Yu-Gi-Oh Dark Crisis 1st Edition

DCR0 Vampire Lord SCR	6.00	12.00
DCR1 Battle Footballer C	.30	.75
DCR2 Nin-Ken Dog C	1.00	2.00
DCR3 Acrobat Monkey C	.30	.75
DCR4 Arsenal Summoner C	.30	.75
DCR5 Guardian Elma C	.30	.75
DCR6 Guardian Ceal UR	.60	1.25
DCR7 Guardian Grarl UR	1.25	2.50
DCR8 Guardian Baou R	.50	1.00
DCR9 Guardian Kay'est C	.30	.75
DCR10 Guardian Tryce R	.50	1.00
DCR11 Cyber Raider SP	.30	.75
DCR12 Reflect Bounder UR	3.00	6.00
DCR13 Little-Winguard SP	.30	.75
DCR14 Des Feral Imp R	.50	1.00
DCR15 Different Dimension Dragon SR	.60	1.25
DCR16 Shinato, King of a Higher Plane UR	2.50	5.00
DCR17 Dark Flare Knight SR	1.25	2.50
DCR18 Mirage Knight SR	1.25	2.50
DCR19 Berserk Dragon SR	1.50	3.00
DCR20 Exodia Necross UR	20.00	40.00
DCR21 Gyaku-Gire Panda SP	.30	.75
DCR22 Blindly Loyal Goblin C	.30	.75
DCR23 Despair from the Dark SP	.30	.75
DCR24 Maju Garzett SP	.30	.75
DCR25 Fear from the Dark R	.50	1.00
DCR26 Dark Scorpion - Chick the Yellow C	.30	.75
DCR27 D. D. Warrior Lady SR	1.00	2.00
DCR28 Thousand Needles C	.30	.75
DCR29 Shinato's Ark SP	.50	1.00
DCR30 A Deal with Dark Ruler SP	.50	1.00
DCR31 Contract with Exodia SP	.75	1.50
DCR32 Butterfly Dagger - Elma SR	.60	1.25
DCR33 Shooting Star Bow - Ceal C	.20	.40
DCR34 Gravity Axe - Grarl C	.20	.40
DCR35 Wicked-Breaking Flamberge R	.50	1.00
DCR36 Rod of Silence - Kay'est C	.30	.75
DCR37 Twin Swords of Flashing Light C	.30	.75
DCR38 Precious Cards from Beyond C	.30	.75
DCR39 Rod of the Mind's Eye C	.30	.75
DCR40 Fairy of the Spring C	.30	.75
DCR41 Token Thanksgiving C	.30	.75
DCR42 Morale Boost C	.30	.75
DCR43 Non-Spellcasting Area C	.30	.75
DCR44 Different Dimension Gate R	.50	1.00
DCR45 Final Attack Orders C	.30	.75
DCR46 Staunch Defender C	.30	.75
DCR47 Ojama Trio SP	1.00	2.00
DCR48 Arsenal Robber C	.30	.75
DCR49 Skill Drain R	2.00	4.00
DCR50 Really Eternal Rest C	.30	.75
DCR51 Kaiser Glider UR	1.25	2.50
DCR52 Interdimensional Matter Trans. UR	1.25	2.50
DCR53 Cost Down UR	1.50	3.00
DCR54 Gagagigo C	.30	.75
DCR55 D. D. Trainer C	.30	.75
DCR56 Ojama Green C	.30	.75
DCR57 Archfiend Soldier R	1.25	2.50
DCR58 Pandemonium Watchbear C	.30	.75
DCR59 Sasuke Samurai #2 C	.30	.75
DCR60 Dark Scorpion - Gorg C	.30	.75
DCR61 Dark Scorpion - Meanae C	.30	.75
DCR62 Outstanding Dog Marron SP	.30	.75
DCR63 Great Maju Garzett R	1.50	3.00
DCR64 Iron Blacksmith Kotetsu C	.30	.75
DCR65 Goblin of Greed C	.30	.75
DCR66 Mefist the Infernal General R	.50	1.00
DCR67 Vilepawn Archfiend C	.30	.75
DCR68 Shadowknight Archfiend C	.30	.75
DCR69 Darkbishop Archfiend R	.50	1.00
DCR70 Desrook Archfiend C	.30	.75
DCR71 Infernalqueen Archfiend R	.50	1.00
DCR72 Terrorking Archfiend SR	1.50	3.00
DCR73 Skull Archfiend of Lightning UR	1.50	3.00
DCR74 Metallizing Parasite - Lunalite R	.50	1.00
DCR75 Tsukuyomi R	1.50	3.00
DCR76 Mudora SR	.50	1.00
DCR77 Keldo C	.30	.75
DCR78 Kelbek C	.30	.75
DCR79 Zolga C	.30	.75
DCR80 Agido C	.30	.75
DCR81 Legendary Flame Lord R	.50	1.00
DCR82 Dark Master - Zorc SR	.60	1.25
DCR83 Spell Reproduction C	.30	.75
DCR84 Dragged Down into the Grave C	1.25	2.50
DCR85 Incandescent Ordeal SP	.30	.75
DCR86 Contract with the Abyss R	.50	1.00
DCR87 Contract with the Dark Master SP	.30	.75
DCR88 Falling Down SP	.50	1.00
DCR89 Checkmate C	.30	.75
DCR90 Cestus of Dagla C	.30	.75
DCR91 Final Countdown SP	.75	1.50
DCR92 Archfiend's Oath C	.30	.75
DCR93 Mustering of Dark Scorpions C	.30	.75
DCR94 Pandemonium SP	.60	1.25
DCR95 Altar for Tribute C	.30	.75
DCR96 Frozen soul C	.30	.75
DCR97 Battle-Scarred C	.30	.75
DCR98 Dark Scorpion Combination R	.50	1.00
DCR99 Archfiend's Roar C	.75	1.50
DCR100 Dice Re-Roll SP	.50	1.00
DCR101 Spell Vanishing SR	.30	.75
DCR102 Sakuretsu Armor C	.50	1.00
DCR103 Ray of Hope C	.30	.75
DCR104 Blast Held by a Tribute UR	2.00	4.00
DCR105 Judgment of Anubis SCR	1.50	3.00

2003 Yu-Gi-Oh Labyrinth of Nightmare 1st Edition

LON000 Gemini Elf SCR	10.00	20.00
LON001 The Masked Beast UR	3.00	6.00
LON002 Swordsman of Landstar C	.30	.75
LON003 Humanoid Slime SP	.50	1.00
LON004 Worm Drake C	.30	.75
LON005 Humanoid Worm Drake C	.30	.75
LON006 Revival Jam SR	2.00	4.00
LON007 Flying Fish C	.30	.75
LON008 Amphibian Beast R	.50	1.00
LON009 Shining Abyss C	.30	.75
LON010 Gadget Soldier C	.30	.75
LON011 Grand Tiki Elder C	.30	.75
LON012 Melchid the Four-Face Beast C	.30	.75
LON013 Nuvia the Wicked R	.50	1.00
LON014 Chosen One C	.30	.75

LON015 Mask of Weakness C	.30	.75
LON016 Curse of the Masked Beast C	.50	1.00
LON017 Mask of Dispel SR	.75	1.50
LON018 Mask of Restrict UR	10.00	20.00
LON019 Mask of the Accursed SR	1.00	2.00
LON020 Mask of Brutality R	.50	1.00
LON021 Return of the Doomed R	.30	.75
LON022 Lightning Blade C	.30	.75
LON023 Tornado Wall C	.50	1.00
LON024 Fairy Box C	.50	1.00
LON025 Torrential Tribute UR	6.00	12.00
LON026 Jam Breeding Machine R	.50	1.00
LON027 Infinite Cards R	.75	1.50
LON028 Jam Defender SP	.30	.75
LON029 Card of Safe Return UR	3.00	6.00
LON030 Lady Panther C	.30	.75
LON031 The Unfriendly Amazon C	.30	.75
LON032 Amazon Archer C	.30	.75
LON033 Crimson Sentry C	.30	.75
LON034 Fire Princess SR	.75	1.50
LON035 Lady Assailant of Flames C	.30	.75
LON036 Fire Sorcerer C	.30	.75
LON037 Spirit of the Breeze R	.50	1.00
LON038 Dancing Fairy C	.30	.75
LON039 Fairy Guardian C	.30	.75
LON040 Empress Mantis C	.30	.75
LON041 Cure Mermaid C	.30	.75
LON042 Hysteric Fairy C	.30	.75
LON043 Bio-Mage C	.30	.75
LON044 The Forgiving Maiden C	.30	.75
LON045 St. Joan C	.30	.75
LON046 Marie the Fallen One R	.50	1.00
LON047 Jar of Greed SR	1.25	2.50
LON048 Scroll of Bewitchment C	.30	.75
LON049 United We Stand UR	6.00	12.00
LON050 Mage Power UR	4.00	8.00
LON051 Offerings to the Doomed C	.30	.75
LON052 The Portrait's Secret C	.30	.75
LON053 The Gross Ghost of Fled Dreams C	.30	.75
LON054 Headless Knight C	.30	.75
LON055 Earthbound Spirit C	.30	.75
LON056 The Earl of Demise C	.30	.75
LON057 Boneheimer C	.30	.75
LON058 Flame Dancer C	.30	.75
LON059 Spherous Lady C	.30	.75
LON060 Lightning Conger C	.30	.75
LON061 Jowgen the Spiritualist R	1.50	3.00
LON062 Kycoo the Ghost Destroyer SR	1.50	3.00
LON063 Summoner of Illusions C	.30	.75
LON064 Bazoo the Soul-Eater SR	.75	1.50
LON065 Dark Necrofear UR	2.00	4.00
LON066 Soul of Purity and Light C	.30	.75
LON067 Spirit of Flames C	.30	.75
LON068 Aqua Spirit C	.30	.75
LON069 The Rock Spirit C	.30	.75
LON070 Garuda the Wind Spirit C	.30	.75
LON071 Gilasaurus R	.50	1.00
LON072 Tornado Bird R	.50	1.00
LON073 Dreamsprite C	.30	.75
LON074 Zombyra the Dark C	.50	1.00
LON075 Supply C	.30	.75
LON076 Maryokutai C	.30	.75
LON077 Last Warrior from Another Planet UR	1.50	3.00
LON078 Collected Power C	.30	.75
LON079 Dark Spirit of the Silent SR	.60	1.25
LON080 Royal Command UR	.75	1.50
LON081 Riryoku Field SR	.75	1.50
LON082 Skull Lair C	.60	1.25
LON083 Graverobber's Retribution C	.30	.75
LON084 Deal of Phantom C	.50	1.00
LON085 Destruction Punch R	.50	1.00
LON086 Blind Destruction C	.30	.75
LON087 The Emperor's Holiday C	.30	.75
LON088 Destiny Board UR	6.00	12.00
LON089 Spirit Message I R	.50	1.00
LON090 Spirit Message N R	.50	1.00
LON091 Spirit Message A R	.50	1.00
LON092 Spirit Message L R	.50	1.00
LON093 The Dark Door C	.30	.75
LON094 Spiritualism R	.50	1.00
LON095 Cyclon Laser C	.30	.75
LON096 Bait Doll C	.30	.75
LON097 De-Fusion SR	.75	1.50
LON098 Fusion Gate C	3.00	6.00
LON099 Ekibyo Drakmord C	.30	.75
LON100 Miracle Dig C	.30	.75
LON101 Dragonic Attack C	.30	.75
LON102 Spirit Elimination C	.30	.75
LON103 Vengeful Bog Spirit SP	.50	1.00
LON104 Magic Cylinder SCR	5.00	10.00

2003 Yu-Gi-Oh Legacy of Darkness 1st Edition

LOD0 Yata-Garasu SCR	10.00	20.00
LOD2 Dark Balter the Terrible SR	1.50	3.00
LOD3 Lesser Fiend R	.50	1.00
LOD4 Possessed Dark Soul C	.30	.75
LOD5 Winged Minion C	.30	.75
LOD6 Skull Knight #2 C	.30	.75
LOD7 Ryu-Kishin Clown C	.30	.75
LOD8 Twin-Headed Wolf C	.30	.75
LOD9 Opticlops R	.50	1.00
LOD1 Dark Ruler Ha Des UR	2.00	4.00
LOD10 Bark of Dark Ruler C	.30	.75
LOD11 Fatal Abacus R	.50	1.00
LOD12 Life Absorbing Machine C	.30	.75
LOD13 The Puppet Magic of Dark Ruler C	.30	.75
LOD14 Soul Demolition C	.30	.75
LOD15 Double Snare C	.30	.75
LOD16 Freed the Matchless General UR	.75	1.50
LOD17 Throwstone Unit C	.30	.75
LOD18 Marauding Captain UR	2.50	5.00
LOD19 Ryu Senshi SR	.60	1.25
LOD20 Warrior Dai Grepher C	.30	.75
LOD21 Mysterious Guard C	.30	.75
LOD22 Frontier Wiseman C	.30	.75
LOD23 Exiled Force SR	.60	1.25
LOD24 The Hunter with 7 Weapons C	.30	.75
LOD25 Shadow Tamer R	.50	1.00
LOD26 Dragon Manipulator C	.30	.75
LOD27 The A Forces R	.75	1.50
LOD28 Reinforcements of the Army SR	2.50	5.00
LOD29 Array of Revealing Light R	.50	1.00
LOD30 The Warrior Returning Alive R	.60	1.25
LOD31 Ready for Intercepting C	.30	.75
LOD32 A Feint Plan C	.30	.75
LOD33 Emergency Provisions C	.50	1.00
LOD34 Tyrant Dragon UR	6.00	12.00
LOD35 Spear Dragon SR	1.50	3.00
LOD36 Spirit Ryu C	.30	.75
LOD37 The Dragon Dwelling in the Cave C	.30	.75
LOD38 Lizard Soldier C	.30	.75
LOD39 Fiend Skull Dragon SR	.75	1.50
LOD40 Cave Dragon SP	.60	1.25
LOD41 Gray Wing C	.30	.75
LOD42 Troop Dragon C	.30	.75
LOD43 The Dragon's Bead R	.50	1.00
LOD44 A Wingbeat of Giant Dragon C	.50	1.00
LOD45 Dragon's Gunfire C	.30	.75
LOD46 Stamping Destruction C	.30	.75
LOD47 Super Rejuvenation C	.50	1.00
LOD48 Dragon's Rage C	.50	1.00
LOD49 Burst Breath C	.30	.75
LOD50 Luster Dragon SR	.75	1.50
LOD51 Robotic Knight C	.30	.75
LOD52 Wolf Axwielder C	.30	.75
LOD53 The Illusory Gentleman C	.30	.75
LOD54 Robolady C	.30	.75
LOD55 Roboyarou C	.30	.75
LOD56 Fiber Jar UR	3.00	6.00
LOD57 Serpentine Princess C	.30	.75
LOD58 Patrician of Darkness C	.30	.75
LOD59 Thunder Nyan Nyan R	.50	1.00
LOD60 Gradius Option C	.30	.75
LOD61 Woodland Sprite C	.30	.75
LOD62 Airknight Parshath UR	2.00	4.00
LOD63 Twin-Headed Behemoth SR	.60	1.25
LOD64 Maharaghi SP	.30	.75
LOD65 Inaba White Rabbit SP	.60	1.25
LOD66 Susa Soldier R	.50	1.00
LOD67 Yamata Dragon UR	5.00	10.00
LOD68 Great Long Nose SP	.30	.75
LOD69 Otohime SP	.50	1.00
LOD70 Hino-Kagu-Tsuchi UR	4.00	8.00
LOD71 Asura Priest SR	1.25	2.50
LOD72 Fushi No Tori C	.30	.75
LOD73 Super Robolady C	.30	.75
LOD74 Super Roboyarou C	.30	.75
LOD75 Fengsheng Mirror C	.30	.75
LOD76 Spring of Rebirth C	.30	.75
LOD77 Heart of Clear Water C	.50	1.00
LOD78 A Legendary Ocean C	.30	.75
LOD79 Fusion Sword Murasame Blade R	.50	1.00
LOD80 Smoke Grenade of the Thief SP	.60	1.25
LOD81 Creature Swap UR	3.00	6.00
LOD82 Spiritual Energy Settle Machine C	.30	.75
LOD83 Second Coin Toss R	.60	1.25
LOD84 Convulsion of Nature C	.30	.75
LOD85 The Secret of the Bandit C	.30	.75
LOD86 After Genocide R	.50	1.00
LOD87 Magic Reflector R	.50	1.00
LOD88 Blast with Chain R	.50	1.00
LOD89 Disppear SP	.30	.75
LOD90 Bubble Crash C	.30	.75
LOD91 Royal Oppression R	.75	1.50
LOD92 Bottomless Trap Hole R	1.50	3.00
LOD93 Bad Reaction to Simochi C	.60	1.25
LOD94 Omnious Fortunetelling C	.30	.75
LOD95 Spirit's Invitation C	.30	.75
LOD96 Nutrient Z C	.50	1.00
LOD97 Drop Off SR	.75	1.50
LOD98 Fiend Comedian C	.30	.75
LOD99 Last Turn UR	2.50	5.00
LOD100 Injection Fairy Lily SCR	5.00	10.00

2003 Yu-Gi-Oh Magician's Force 1st Edition

MFC000 Dark Magician Girl SCR	100.00	200.00
MFC001 People Running About C	.30	.75
MFC002 Oppressed People C	.50	1.00
MFC003 United Resistance C	.30	.75
MFC004 X-Head Cannon SR	2.00	4.00
MFC005 Y-Dragon Head SR	2.00	4.00
MFC006 Z-Metal Tank SR	2.00	4.00
MFC007 Dark Blade R	.60	1.25
MFC008 Pitch-Dark Dragon C	.30	.75
MFC009 Kiryu C	.30	.75
MFC010 Decayed Commander C	.30	.75
MFC011 Zombie Tiger C	.30	.75
MFC012 Giant Orc C	.30	.75
MFC013 Second Goblin C	.30	.75
MFC014 Vampire Orchis C	.30	.75
MFC015 Des Dendle C	.30	.75
MFC016 Burning Beast C	.30	.75
MFC017 Freezing Beast C	.30	.75
MFC018 Union Rider C	.30	.75
MFC019 D.D. Crazy Beast R	.50	1.00
MFC020 Spell Canceller UR	4.00	8.00
MFC021 Neko Mane King C	.50	1.00
MFC022 Helping Robo For Combat R	.50	1.00
MFC023 Dimension Jar SP	.30	.75
MFC024 Great Phantom Thief R	.50	1.00
MFC025 Roulette Barrel C	.30	.75
MFC026 Paladin of White Dragon UR	2.00	4.00
MFC027 White Dragon Ritual C	.30	.75
MFC028 Frontline Base C	.30	.75
MFC029 Demotion SP	.30	.75
MFC030 Combination Attack R	.50	1.00
MFC031 Kaiser Colosseum C	.50	1.00
MFC032 Autonomous Action Unit C	.30	.75
MFC033 Poison of the Old Man C	.30	.75
MFC034 Ante R	.50	1.00
MFC035 Dark Core R	1.00	2.00
MFC036 Raregold Armor C	.50	1.00
MFC037 Metalsilver Armor C	.30	.75
MFC038 Kishido Spirit C	.30	.75
MFC039 Tribute Doll R	.50	1.00
MFC040 Wave-Motion Cannon SP	4.00	8.00
MFC041 Huge Revolution C	.30	.75
MFC042 Thunder of Ruler C	.50	1.00
MFC043 Spell Shield Type-8 SR	.75	1.50
MFC044 Meteorain C	.30	.75
MFC045 Pineapple Blast C	.30	.75
MFC046 Secret Barrel SP	1.25	2.50
MFC047 Physical Double C	.30	.75
MFC048 Rivalry of Warlords C	.50	1.00
MFC049 Formation Union C	.30	.75
MFC050 Adhesion Trap Hole C	.50	1.00
MFC051 XY-Dragon Cannon UR	7.50	15.00
MFC052 XYZ-Dragon Cannon UR	10.00	20.00
MFC053 XZ-Tank Cannon SR	5.00	10.00
MFC054 YZ-Tank Dragon SR	2.00	4.00
MFC055 Great Angus C	.30	.75
MFC056 Aitsu C	.30	.75
MFC057 Sonic Duck C	.30	.75
MFC058 Luster Dragon UR	6.00	12.00
MFC059 Amazoness Paladin C	.30	.75
MFC060 Amazoness Fighter SP	.50	1.00
MFC061 Amazoness Swords Woman UR	3.00	6.00
MFC062 Amazoness Blowpiper C	.30	.75
MFC063 Amazoness Tiger R	.50	1.00
MFC064 Skilled White Magician SR	2.00	4.00
MFC065 Skilled Dark Magician SR	2.00	4.00
MFC066 Apprentice Magician R	.50	1.00
MFC067 Old Vindictive Magician C	.30	.75
MFC068 Chaos Command Magician UR	6.00	12.00
MFC069 Magical Marionette C	.30	.75
MFC070 Pixie Knight C	.30	.75
MFC071 Breaker the Magical Warrior UR	6.00	12.00
MFC072 Magical Plant Mandragola C	.30	.75
MFC073 Magical Scientist C	.30	.75
MFC074 Royal Magical Library C	.30	.75
MFC075 Armor Exe R	.50	1.00
MFC076 Tribe-Infecting Virus SR	1.50	3.00
MFC077 Des Koala R	.60	1.25
MFC078 Cliff the Trap Remover SP	.50	1.00
MFC079 Magical Merchant C	.60	1.25
MFC080 Koitsu C	.30	.75
MFC081 Cat's Ear Tribe R	.50	1.00
MFC082 Ultimate Obedient Fiend SP	.75	1.50
MFC083 Dark Cat with White Tail C	.30	.75
MFC084 Amazoness Spellcaster C	.30	.75
MFC085 Continuous Destruction Punch R	.50	1.00
MFC086 Big Bang Shot R	.50	1.00
MFC087 Gather Your Mind C	.30	.75
MFC088 Mass Driver C	.30	.75
MFC089 Senri Eye SP	.30	.75
MFC090 Emblem of Dragon Destroyer C	.50	1.00
MFC091 Jar Robber C	.30	.75
MFC092 My Body as a Shield C	.30	.75
MFC093 Pigeonholing Books of Spell SP	.30	.75
MFC094 Mega Ton Magical Cannon R	.50	1.00
MFC095 Pitch-Black Power Stone SP	.50	1.00
MFC096 Amazoness Archers SR	.75	1.50
MFC097 Dramatic Rescue R	.50	1.00
MFC098 Exhausting Spell C	.30	.75
MFC099 Hidden Book of Spell C	.30	.75
MFC100 Miracle Restoring C	.30	.75
MFC101 Remove Brainwashing C	.50	1.00
MFC102 Disarmament C	.30	.75
MFC103 Anti-Spell C	.30	.75
MFC104 The Spell Absorbing Life C	.30	.75
MFC105 Dark Paladin Misprint UR	50.00	100.00
MFC105 Dark Paladin Correct Art UR	50.00	100.00
MFC106 Double Spell UR	2.00	4.00
MFC107 Diffussion Wave-Motion SCR	.60	1.25

2003 Yu-Gi-Oh Pharaonic Guardian 1st Edition

PGD0 Ring of Destruction SCR	3.00	6.00
PGD1 Molten Behemoth C	.30	.75
PGD2 Shapesnatch C	.30	.75
PGD3 Souleater C	.30	.75
PGD4 King Tiger Wanghu R	.60	1.25
PGD5 Birdface C	.30	.75
PGD6 Kryuel C	.30	.75
PGD7 Arsenal Bug C	.30	.75
PGD8 Maiden of the Aqua C	.50	1.00
PGD9 Jowl of Dark Demise R	.50	1.00
PGD10 Timeater C	.30	.75
PGD11 Mucus Yolk C	.30	.75
PGD12 Servant of Catabolism C	.30	.75
PGD13 Moisture Creature R	.50	1.00
PGD14 Gora Turtle R	.50	1.00
PGD15 Sasuke Samurai SR	.60	1.25
PGD16 Poison Mummy C	.30	.75
PGD17 Dark Dust Spirit C	.30	.75
PGD18 Royal Keeper C	.30	.75
PGD19 Wandering Mummy R	.50	1.00
PGD20 Great Dezard UR	.60	1.25
PGD21 Swarm of Scarabs C	.30	.75
PGD22 Swarm of Locusts C	.30	.75
PGD23 Giant Axe Mummy C	.30	.75
PGD24 8-Claws Scorpion C	.30	.75
PGD25 Guardian Sphinx UR	.60	1.25
PGD26 Pyramid Turtle R	.50	1.00
PGD27 Dice Jar C	.75	1.50
PGD28 Dark Scorpion Burglars C	.30	.75
PGD29 Don Zaloog UR	1.00	2.00
PGD30 Des Lacooda C	.30	.75
PGD31 Fushioh Richie UR	.60	1.25
PGD32 Cobraman Sakuzy C	.30	.75
PGD33 Book of Life SR	1.25	2.50
PGD34 Book of Taiyou C	.75	1.50
PGD35 Book of Moon R	1.25	2.50
PGD36 Mirage of Nightmare SR	.60	1.25
PGD37 Secret Pass to the Treasure C	.30	.75
PGD38 Call of the Mummy C	.30	.75
PGD39 Timidity C	.30	.75
PGD40 Pyramid Energy C	.30	.75
PGD41 Tutan Mask C	.30	.75
PGD42 Ordeal of a Traveler SP	.60	1.25
PGD43 Bottomless Shifting Sand C	.30	.75
PGD44 Curse of Royal R	.50	1.00
PGD45 Needle Ceiling C	.30	.75
PGD46 Statue of the Wicked SR	.60	1.25
PGD47 Dark Coffin C	.30	.75
PGD48 Needle Wall C	.30	.75
PGD49 Trap Dustshoot C	.50	1.00
PGD50 Pyro Clock of Destiny C	.30	.75
PGD51 Reckless Greed R	.60	1.25
PGD52 Pharaoh's Treasure R	.50	1.00
PGD53 Master Kyonshee C	.30	.75
PGD54 Kabazauls C	1.00	2.00
PGD55 Inpachi C	.30	.75
PGD56 Dark Jeroid R	.50	1.00
PGD57 Newdoria R	.50	1.00
PGD58 Helpoemer UR	4.00	8.00
PGD59 Gravekeeper's Spy C	.30	.75
PGD60 Gravekeeper's Curse C	.30	.75
PGD61 Gravekeeper's Guard C	.30	.75
PGD62 Gravekeeper's Spear Soldier C	.30	.75
PGD63 Gravekeeper's Vassal C	.60	1.25
PGD64 Gravekeeper's Watcher R	.50	1.00
PGD65 Gravekeeper's Chief SR	.60	1.25
PGD66 Gravekeeper's Cannonholder C	.30	.75
PGD67 Gravekeeper's Assailant C	.30	.75
PGD68 A Man with Wdjat C	.30	.75
PGD69 Mystical Knight of Jackal UR	1.50	3.00
PGD70 A Cat of Ill Omen C	.30	.75
PGD71 Yomi Ship C	.50	1.00
PGD72 Winged Sage Falcos R	.50	1.00
PGD73 An Owl of Luck C	.30	.75
PGD74 Charm of Shabti C	.30	.75
PGD75 Cobra Jar SP	.30	.75
PGD76 Spirit Reaper R	1.25	2.50
PGD77 Nightmare Horse SP	.50	1.00
PGD78 Reaper on the Nightmare SR	1.25	2.50
PGD79 Dark Designator R	.50	1.00
PGD80 Card Shuffle C	.30	.75
PGD81 Reasoning C	.30	.75
PGD82 Dark Room of Nightmare SR	.60	1.25
PGD83 Different Dimension Capsule C	.30	.75
PGD84 Necrovalley SR	.75	1.50
PGD85 Buster Rancher C	.30	.75
PGD86 Hieroglyph Lithograph C	.30	.75
PGD87 Dark Snake Syndrome C	.30	.75
PGD88 Terraforming C	.50	1.00
PGD89 Banner of Courage C	.30	.75
PGD90 Metamorphosis C	.30	.75
PGD91 Royal Tribute C	.60	1.25
PGD92 Reversal Quiz SP	.60	1.25
PGD93 Coffin Seller R	.50	1.00
PGD94 Curse of Aging C	.30	.75
PGD95 Barrel Behind the Door SR	.60	1.25
PGD96 Raigeki Break C	.50	1.00
PGD97 Narrow Pass C	.30	.75
PGD98 Disturbance Strategy C	.30	.75
PGD99 Trap of Board Eraser SR	.60	1.25
PGD100 Rite of Spirit C	.30	.75
PGD101 Non Aggression Area C	.30	.75
PGD102 D. Tribe C	.30	.75
PGD103 Byser Shock UR	.60	1.25
PGD104 Question UR	1.25	2.50
PGD105 Rope of Life UR	.60	1.25
PGD106 Nightmare Wheel UR	2.00	4.00
PGD107 Lava Golem SCR	2.50	5.00

2003 Yu-Gi-Oh Starter Deck Joey 1st Edition

SDJ1 Red-Eyes Black Dragon UR	7.50	15.00
SDJ2 Swordsman of Landstar C	.60	1.25
SDJ3 Baby Dragon C	.60	1.25
SDJ4 Spirit of the Harp C	.60	1.25
SDJ5 Island Turtle C	.60	1.25
SDJ6 Flame Manipulator C	.60	1.25
SDJ7 Masaki the Legendary Swordsman C	.60	1.25
SDJ8 7 Colored Fish C	.60	1.25
SDJ9 Armored Lizard C	.60	1.25
SDJ10 Darkfire Soldier #1 C	.60	1.25
SDJ11 Harpie's Brother C	.60	1.25
SDJ12 Gearfried the Iron Knight C	.60	1.25
SDJ13 Karate Man C	.60	1.25
SDJ14 Milus Radiant C	.60	1.25
SDJ15 Time Wizard C	.60	1.25
SDJ16 Maha Vailo C	.60	1.25
SDJ17 Magician of Faith C	.60	1.25
SDJ18 Big Eye C	.60	1.25
SDJ19 Sangan C	.60	1.25
SDJ20 Princess of Tsurugi C	.60	1.25
SDJ21 White Magical Hat C	.60	1.25
SDJ22 Penguin Soldier SR	.60	1.25
SDJ23 Thousand Dragon C	.60	1.25
SDJ24 Flame Swordsman C	.60	1.25
SDJ25 Malevolent Nuzzler C	.60	1.25
SDJ26 Dark Hole C	.60	1.25
SDJ27 Dian Keto C	.60	1.25
SDJ28 Fissure C	.60	1.25
SDJ29 De-Spell C	.60	1.25
SDJ30 Change of Heart C	.60	1.25
SDJ31 Block Attack C	.60	1.25
SDJ32 Giant Trunade C	.60	1.25
SDJ33 The Reliable Guardian C	.60	1.25
SDJ34 Remove Trap C	.60	1.25
SDJ35 Monster Reborn C	.60	1.25
SDJ36 Polymerization C	.60	1.25
SDJ37 Mountain C	.60	1.25
SDJ38 Dragon Treasure C	.60	1.25
SDJ39 Eternal Rest C	.60	1.25
SDJ40 Shield & Sword C	.60	1.25
SDJ41 Scapegoat SR	.60	1.25
SDJ42 Just Desserts C	.60	1.25
SDJ43 Trap Hole C	.60	1.25
SDJ44 Reinforcements C	.60	1.25
SDJ45 Castle Walls C	.60	1.25
SDJ46 Waboku C	.60	1.25
SDJ47 Ultimate Offering C	.60	1.25
SDJ48 Seven Tools of the Bandit C	.60	1.25
SDJ49 Fake Trap C	.60	1.25
SDJ50 Reverse Trap C	.60	1.25

2003 Yu-Gi-Oh Starter Deck Pegasus 1st Edition

SDP1 Relinquished UR	3.00	6.00
SDP2 Red Archery Girl C	.20	.40
SDP3 Ryu-Ran C	.20	.40
SDP4 Illusionist Faceless Mage C	.20	.40
SDP5 Rogue Doll C	.20	.40
SDP6 Uraby C	.20	.40
SDP7 Giant Soldier of Stone C	.20	.40
SDP8 Aqua Madoor C	.20	.40
SDP9 Toon Alligator C	.75	1.50
SDP10 Hane-Hane C	.20	.40
SDP11 Sonic Bird C	.20	.40
SDP12 Jigen Bakudan C	.20	.40
SDP13 Mask of Darkness C	.20	.40
SDP14 Witch of the Black Forest C	.20	.40
SDP15 Man-Eater Bug C	.20	.40
SDP16 Muka Muka C	.20	.40
SDP17 Dream Clown C	.20	.40
SDP18 Armed Ninja C	.20	.40
SDP19 Hiro's Shadow C	.20	.40
SDP20 Blue-Eyes Toon Dragon C	.50	1.00
SDP21 Toon Summoned Skull C	.20	.40
SDP22 Manga Ryu-Ran C	.20	.40
SDP23 Toon Mermaid C	.20	.40
SDP24 Toon World C	1.00	2.00
SDP25 Black Pendant C	.20	.40
SDP26 Dark Hole C	.20	.40
SDP27 Dian Keto The Cure Master C	.20	.40
SDP28 Fissure C	.20	.40
SDP29 De-Spell C	.20	.40
SDP30 Change of Heart C	.20	.40
SDP31 Stop Defense C	.20	.40
SDP32 Mystical Space Typhoon C	.20	.40
SDP33 Rush Recklessly C	.20	.40
SDP34 Remove Trap C	.20	.40
SDP35 Monster Reborn C	.50	1.00
SDP36 Soul Release C	.20	.40
SDP37 Yami C	.20	.40
SDP38 Black Illusion Ritual C	.20	.40
SDP39 Ring of Magnetism C	.20	.40
SDP40 Graceful Charity SR	1.50	3.00
SDP41 Trap Hole C	.20	.40
SDP42 Reinforcements C	.20	.40
SDP43 Castle Walls C	.20	.40
SDP44 Waboku C	.20	.40
SDP45 Seven Tools of the Bandit C	.20	.40
SDP46 Ultimate Offering C	.20	.40
SDP47 Robbin' Goblin C	.20	.40
SDP48 Magic Jammer C	.20	.40
SDP49 Enchanted Javelin C	.20	.40
SDP50 Gryphon Wing SR	.50	1.00

2003 Yu-Gi-Oh The Duelists of the Roses

DOR001 Alpha The Magnet Warrior SCR	2.00	4.00
DOR002 Beta The Magnet Warrior SCR	2.00	4.00
DOR003 Gamma The Magnet Warrior SCR	2.00	4.00

2003 Yu-Gi-Oh Tournament Pack 3

TP3001 Needle Worm UR	30.00	75.00
TP3002 Anti Raigeki SR	20.00	40.00
TP3003 Mechanicalchaser SR	3.00	6.00
TP3004 B.Skull Dragon SR	15.00	30.00
TP3005 Horn of Heaven SR	15.00	30.00
TP3006 Axe Raider R	2.00	4.00
TP3007 Kwagar Hercules R	2.00	4.00
TP3008 Patrol Robo R	1.50	3.00
TP3009 White Hole R	2.00	4.00
TP3010 Dragon Capture Jar C	.75	1.50
TP3011 Goblin's Secret Remedy C	.75	1.50
TP3012 Final Flame C	.75	1.50
TP3013 Spirit of the Harp C	.75	1.50
TP3014 Pot of Greed C	.75	1.50
TP3015 Karbonala Warrior C	.75	1.50
TP3016 Darkfire Dragon C	.75	1.50
TP3017 Elegant Egotist C	.75	1.50
TP3018 Dark Elf C	.75	1.50
TP3019 Little Chimera C	.75	1.50
TP3020 Bladefly C	.75	1.50

2003 Yu-Gi-Oh Tournament Pack 4

TP4001 Royal Decree UR	50.00	100.00
TP4002 Morphing Jar SR	10.00	20.00
TP4003 Megamorph SR	2.00	4.00
TP4004 Chain Destruction SR	2.00	4.00
TP4005 The Fiend Megacyber SR	1.50	3.00
TP4006 Dragon Seeker R	1.25	2.50
TP4007 Giant Red Seasnake R	1.25	2.50
TP4008 Exile of the Wicked R	1.25	2.50
TP4009 Call of the Grave R	2.00	4.00
TP4010 Rush Recklessly C	.75	1.50
TP4011 Giant Rat C	.75	1.50
TP4012 Senju of Thousand Hands C	.75	1.50
TP4013 Karate Man C	.75	1.50
TP4014 Nimble Momonga C	.75	1.50
TP4015 Mystic Tomato C	.75	1.50
TP4016 Nobleman of Extermination C	.75	1.50
TP4017 Magic Drain C	.75	1.50
TP4018 Gravity Bird C	.75	1.50
TP4019 Hayabusa Knight C	.75	1.50
TP4020 Mad Sword Beast C	.75	1.50

2004 Yu-Gi-Oh Ancient Sanctuary 1st Edition

AST0 The End of Anubis SCR	3.00	6.00
AST1 Gogiga Gagagigo C	.20	.40
AST2 Warrior of Zera C	.30	.75
AST3 Sealmaster Meisei R	.30	.75
AST4 Mystical Shine Ball C	.50	1.00
AST5 Metal Armored Bug C	.20	.40
AST6 The Agent of Judgment Saturn UR	.75	1.50
AST7 The Agent of Wisdom Mercury R	.30	.75
AST8 The Agent of Creation Venus R	.75	1.50
AST9 The Agent of Force Mars SR	.50	1.00
AST10 The Unhappy Girl C	.20	.40
AST11 Soul-Absorbing Bone Tower R	1.00	2.00
AST12 The Kick Man C	.20	.40
AST13 Vampire Lady C	.20	.40
AST14 Stone Statue of the Aztecs SR	.50	1.00
AST15 Rocket Jumper C	.20	.40
AST16 Avatar of the Pot R	.30	.75
AST17 Legendary Jujitsu Master C	.30	.75
AST18 Gear Golem the Moving Fortress UR	.75	1.50
AST19 KA-2 Des Scissors C	.20	.40
AST20 Needle Burrower SR	.30	.75
AST21 Sonic Jammer C	.20	.40
AST22 Blowback Dragon UR	1.50	3.00
AST23 Zaborg the Thunder Monarch SR	1.50	3.00
AST24 Atomic Firefly C	.20	.40
AST25 Mermaid Knight C	.20	.40
AST26 Piranha Army C	.20	.40
AST27 Two Thousand Needles C	.20	.40
AST28 Disc Fighter C	.20	.40
AST29 Arcane Archer of the Forest C	.20	.40
AST30 Lady Ninja Yae C	.60	1.25
AST31 Goblin King C	.20	.40
AST32 Solar Flare Dragon C	.20	.40
AST33 White Magician Pikeru C	.20	.40
AST34 Archlord Zerato UR	2.00	4.00
AST35 Opti-Camouflage Armor C	1.50	3.00
AST36 Mystik Wok C	.20	.40
AST37 Enemy Controller UR	3.00	6.00
AST38 Burst Stream of Destruction UR	7.50	15.00
AST39 Monster Gate C	.20	.40
AST40 Amplifier SR	2.50	5.00
AST41 Weapon Change C	.20	.40
AST42 The Sanctuary in the Sky SR	1.50	3.00
AST43 Earthquake C	.20	.40
AST44 Talisman of Trap Sealing R	.30	.75
AST45 Goblin Thief C	.20	.40
AST46 Backfire C	.20	.40
AST47 Micro Ray C	.20	.40
AST48 Light of Judgment C	.20	.40
AST49 Talisman of Spell Sealing R	.30	.75
AST50 Wall of Revealing Light C	.50	1.00
AST51 Solar Ray C	.20	.40
AST52 Ninjitsu Art of Transformation C	.50	1.00
AST53 Beckoning Light C	.20	.40
AST54 Draining Shield R	.75	1.50
AST55 Armor Break C	.20	.40
AST56 Gigobyte C	.20	.40
AST57 Mokey Mokey C	1.00	2.00
AST58 Kozaky C	.20	.40
AST59 Fiend Scorpion C	.20	.40
AST60 Pharaoh's Servant C	.20	.40
AST61 Pharaonic Protector C	.20	.40
AST62 Spirit of the Pharaoh UR	.75	1.50
AST63 Theban Nightmare R	.30	.75
AST64 Aswan Apparition C	.20	.40
AST65 Protector of the Sanctuary C	.20	.40
AST66 Nubian Guard C	.20	.40
AST67 Legacy Hunter SR	.50	1.00
AST68 Desertapir C	.20	.40
AST69 Sand Gambler C	.20	.40
AST70 3-Hump Lacooda C	.20	.40
AST71 Ghost Knight of Jackal UR	.50	1.00
AST72 Absorbing Kid from the Sky C	.20	.40
AST73 Elephant Statue of Blessing C	.20	.40
AST74 Elephant Statue of Disaster C	.20	.40
AST75 Spirit Caller C	.20	.40
AST76 Emissary of the Afterlife SR	1.00	2.00
AST77 Grave Protector R	.30	.75
AST78 Double Coston R	.30	.75
AST79 Regenerating Mummy C	.20	.40
AST80 Night Assailant C	.50	1.00
AST81 Man-Thro' Tro' C	.20	.40
AST82 King of the Swamp R	4.00	8.00
AST83 Emissary of the Oasis C	.20	.40
AST84 Special Hurricane R	.30	.75
AST85 Order to Charge C	.20	.40
AST86 Sword of the Soul-Eater C	.20	.40
AST87 Dust Barrier C	.20	.40
AST88 Soul Reversal C	.20	.40
AST89 Spell Economics R	.30	.75
AST90 Blessings of the Nile C	.20	.40
AST91 7 C	.20	.40
AST92 Level Limit - Area B SP	2.00	4.00
AST93 Enchanting Fitting Room C	.20	.40
AST94 The Law of the Normal C	.20	.40
AST95 Dark Magic Attack UR	15.00	30.00
AST96 Delta Attacker C	.20	.40
AST97 Thousand Energy R	.30	.75
AST98 Triangle Power R	.30	.75
AST99 The Third Sarcophagus C	.20	.40
AST100 The Second Sarcophagus C	.20	.40
AST101 The First Sarcophagus SR	.50	1.00
AST102 Dora of Fate C	.20	.40
AST103 Judgment of the Desert C	.20	.40
AST104 Human-Wave Tactics C	.20	.40
AST105 Curse of Anubis UR	.75	1.50
AST106 Desert Sunlight C	.20	.40
AST107 Des Counterblow SR	.30	.75
AST108 Labyrinth of Nightmare C	.20	.40
AST109 Soul Resurrection R	.30	.75
AST110 Order to Smash C	.20	.40
AST111 Mazera Deville SCR	1.50	3.00

2004 Yu-Gi-Oh Capsule Monster Coliseum

CMCEN001 Abyss Soldier SR	4.00	8.00
CMCEN002 Inferno Hammer SR	1.00	2.00
CMCEN003 Teva SR	1.00	2.00

2004 Yu-Gi-Oh Collector Tins

CT1EN001 Total Defense Shogun SCR	1.25	2.50
CT1EN002 Blade Knight SCR	1.25	2.50
CT1EN003 Command Knight SCR	1.25	2.50
CT1EN004 Swift Gaia The Fierce Knight SCR	1.25	2.50
CT1EN005 Insect Queen SCR	1.25	2.50
CT1EN006 Obnoxious Celtic Guardian SCR	1.00	2.00

2004 Yu-Gi-Oh Dark Beginnings 1

DB1EN001 Penguin Knight C	.12	.25
DB1EN002 Axe of Despair R	.50	1.00
DB1EN003 Black Pendant R	.30	.60
DB1EN004 Horn of Light C	.12	.25
DB1EN005 Malevolent Nuzzler C	.12	.25
DB1EN006 Spellbinding Circle R	.30	.60
DB1EN007 Electric Snake C	.12	.25
DB1EN008 Ameba C	.12	.25
DB1EN009 Maha Vailo C	.12	.25
DB1EN010 Minar C	.12	.25
DB1EN011 Griggle C	.12	.25
DB1EN012 Hiro's Shadow Scout C	.12	.25
DB1EN013 Invader of the Throne C	.12	.25
DB1EN014 Slot Machine C	.12	.25
DB1EN015 Relinquished SR	.50	1.00
DB1EN016 Red Archery Girl C	.12	.25
DB1EN017 Gravekeeper's Servant C	.75	1.50
DB1EN018 Upstart Goblin C	3.00	6.00
DB1EN019 Toll C	.12	.25
DB1EN020 Final Destiny C	.12	.25
DB1EN021 Snatch Steal UR	2.00	4.00
DB1EN022 Chorus of Sanctuary C	.12	.25
DB1EN023 Confiscation C	.12	.25
DB1EN024 Delinquent Duo SR	6.00	12.00
DB1EN025 Fairy's Hand Mirror C	.12	.25
DB1EN026 Tailor of the Fickle C	.12	.25
DB1EN027 Rush Recklessly C	.12	.25
DB1EN028 The Reliable Guardian C	.12	.25
DB1EN029 The Forceful Sentry R	.30	.60
DB1EN030 Chain Energy C	.12	.25
DB1EN031 Mystical Space Typhoon SR	4.00	8.00
DB1EN032 Giant Trunade R	.30	.60
DB1EN033 Painful Choice C	.12	.25
DB1EN034 Horn of the Unicorn C	.12	.25
DB1EN035 Labyrinth Wall C	.12	.25
DB1EN036 Eternal Rest C	.12	.25
DB1EN037 Megamorph SR	1.00	2.00
DB1EN038 Manga Ryu-Ran C	.12	.25
DB1EN039 Toon Mermaid C	2.00	4.00
DB1EN040 Toon Summoned Skull R	.50	1.00
DB1EN041 Hyozanryu C	.12	.25
DB1EN042 Toon World C	.12	.25
DB1EN043 Cyber Jar R	.50	1.00
DB1EN044 Banisher of the Light C	.30	.60
DB1EN045 Giant Rat R	.30	.60
DB1EN046 Senju of the Thousand Hands C	.30	.60
DB1EN047 UFO Turtle C	.12	.25
DB1EN048 Flash Assailant C	.12	.25
DB1EN049 Karate Man C	.12	.25
DB1EN050 Giant Germ C	.50	1.00
DB1EN051 Nimble Momonga R	.50	1.00
DB1EN052 Shining Angel C	.12	.25
DB1EN053 Mother Grizzly C	.12	.25
DB1EN054 Flying Kamakiri #1 C	.12	.25
DB1EN055 Ceremonial Bell C	.12	.25
DB1EN056 Sonic Bird C	.12	.25
DB1EN057 Mystic Tomato R	.50	1.00
DB1EN058 Kotodama C	.12	.25
DB1EN059 Gaia Power C	.12	.25
DB1EN060 Umiiruka C	.12	.25
DB1EN061 Molten Destruction C	.12	.25
DB1EN062 Rising Air Current C	.25	.50
DB1EN063 Luminous Spark C	.30	.60
DB1EN064 Mystic Plasma Zone C	.12	.25
DB1EN065 Messenger of Peace C	1.00	2.00
DB1EN066 Blue-Eyes Toon Dragon SR	2.50	5.00
DB1EN067 Jinzo UR	4.00	8.00
DB1EN068 Parasite Paracide C	.12	.25
DB1EN069 Lightforce Sword C	.12	.25
DB1EN070 Chain Destruction C	.50	1.00
DB1EN071 Time Seal C	.12	.25
DB1EN072 Graverobber C	.12	.25
DB1EN073 Gift of the Mystical Elf C	.12	.25
DB1EN074 The Eye of Truth C	.12	.25
DB1EN075 Dust Tornado R	.30	.60
DB1EN076 Call Of The Haunted SR	1.50	3.00
DB1EN077 Enchanted Javelin C	.12	.25
DB1EN078 Mirror Wall C	.12	.25
DB1EN079 Numinous Healer C	.12	.25
DB1EN080 Forced Requisition C	.30	.60
DB1EN081 DNA Surgery C	1.50	3.00
DB1EN082 Backup Soldier C	.12	.25
DB1EN083 Ceasefire SR	.30	.60
DB1EN084 Light of Intervention C	.12	.25
DB1EN085 Respect Play C	.12	.25
DB1EN086 Imperial Order UR	.75	1.50
DB1EN087 Magical Hats R	.60	1.25
DB1EN088 Nobleman of Crossout SR	1.00	2.00
DB1EN089 Nobleman of Extermination C	.12	.25
DB1EN090 The Shallow Grave C	.50	1.00
DB1EN091 Premature Burial SR	.50	1.00
DB1EN092 Morphing Jar #2 R	1.00	2.00
DB1EN093 Kiseitai C	.12	.25
DB1EN094 Harpie's Brother C	.12	.25
DB1EN095 Buster Blader SR	1.50	3.00
DB1EN096 Dark Sage UR	5.00	10.00
DB1EN097 Big Shield Gardna UR	1.50	3.00
DB1EN098 Blue-Eyes White Dragon UR	2.00	4.00
DB1EN099 Hitotsu-Me Giant C	.12	.25
DB1EN100 Flame Swordsman R	.30	.60
DB1EN101 Skull Servant C	.50	1.00
DB1EN102 Dark Magician UR	1.25	2.50
DB1EN103 Gaia The Fierce Knight R	.30	.60
DB1EN104 Celtic Guardian C	.12	.25
DB1EN105 Mammoth Graveyard C	.12	.25
DB1EN106 Silver Fang C	.12	.25
DB1EN107 Flame Manipulator C	.12	.25
DB1EN108 Dark King of the Abyss C	.12	.25
DB1EN109 Aqua Madoor C	.12	.25
DB1EN110 Masaki the Legendary Swordsman C	.12	.25
DB1EN111 Dragon Capture Jar C	.12	.25
DB1EN112 Umi C	.12	.25
DB1EN113 Dark Hole SR	1.50	3.00
DB1EN114 Raigeki UR	20.00	40.00
DB1EN115 Red Medicine C	.12	.25
DB1EN116 Hinotama C	.12	.25
DB1EN117 Fissure R	.30	.60
DB1EN118 Trap Hole R	.30	.60
DB1EN119 Polymerization C	3.00	6.00
DB1EN120 Mystical Elf C	.12	.25
DB1EN121 Beaver Warrior C	.12	.25
DB1EN122 Gaia the Dragon Champion R	.50	1.00
DB1EN123 Curse of Dragon C	.12	.25
DB1EN124 Giant Soldier of Stone C	.12	.25
DB1EN125 Uraby C	.12	.25
DB1EN126 Red-Eyes B. Dragon SR	1.00	2.00
DB1EN127 Reaper of the Cards C	.12	.25
DB1EN128 Stop Defense C	.12	.25
DB1EN129 Swords of Revealing Light SR	1.50	3.00
DB1EN130 Armed Ninja C	.12	.25
DB1EN131 Man-Eater Bug R	.50	1.00
DB1EN132 Hane-Hane C	.12	.25
DB1EN133 Monster Reborn UR	7.50	15.00
DB1EN134 Pot of Greed SR	4.00	8.00
DB1EN135 Right Leg of the Forbidden One C	3.00	6.00
DB1EN136 Left Leg of the Forbidden One C	2.50	5.00
DB1EN137 Right Arm of the Forbidden One C	2.50	5.00
DB1EN138 Left Arm of the Forbidden One C	2.50	5.00
DB1EN139 Exodia the Forbidden One UR	4.00	8.00
DB1EN140 Feral Imp C	.12	.25
DB1EN141 Winged Dragon, Guardian of the Fortress #1 C	.12	.25
DB1EN142 Summoned Skull SR	1.00	2.00
DB1EN143 Armored Lizard C	.12	.25
DB1EN144 Larvae Moth C	.12	.25
DB1EN145 Harpie Lady C	.12	.25
DB1EN146 Harpie Lady Sisters C	.12	.25
DB1EN147 Kojikocy C	.12	.25
DB1EN148 Cocoon of Evolution C	.30	.60
DB1EN149 Armored Zombie C	.12	.25
DB1EN150 Mask of Darkness C	.12	.25
DB1EN151 White Magical Hat C	.12	.25
DB1EN152 Big Eye C	.12	.25
DB1EN153 B. Skull Dragon SR	5.00	10.00
DB1EN154 Masked Sorcerer C	.12	.25
DB1EN155 Petit Moth C	.12	.25
DB1EN156 Elegant Egotist C	.50	1.00
DB1EN157 Sanga of the Thunder C	1.00	2.00
DB1EN158 Kazejin C	.12	.25
DB1EN159 Suijin C	.30	.60
DB1EN160 Mystic Lamp C	.12	.25
DB1EN161 Blast Juggler C	.12	.25
DB1EN162 Jinzo #7 C	.12	.25
DB1EN163 Magician of Faith R	.50	1.00
DB1EN164 Fake Trap C	.12	.25
DB1EN165 Tribute to The Doomed R	.30	.60
DB1EN166 Soul Release C	.30	.60
DB1EN167 The Cheerful Coffin C	.50	1.00
DB1EN168 Change of Heart UR	2.00	4.00
DB1EN169 Makyura the Destructor SR	1.50	3.00
DB1EN170 Exchange SR	1.00	2.00
DB1EN171 Minor Goblin Official C	.12	.25
DB1EN172 Gamble C	.12	.25
DB1EN173 Attack and Receive C	.12	.25
DB1EN174 Solemn Wishes C	2.50	5.00
DB1EN175 Skull Invitation C	.12	.25
DB1EN176 Bubonic Vermin C	.12	.25
DB1EN177 Burning Land C	.12	.25
DB1EN178 Fairy Meteor Crush R	.30	.60
DB1EN179 Limiter Removal R	.30	.60
DB1EN180 Rain of Mercy C	.12	.25
DB1EN181 Monster Recovery C	.12	.25
DB1EN182 Shift C	.12	.25
DB1EN183 Dimensionhole C	.12	.25
DB1EN184 Ground Collapse C	.12	.25
DB1EN185 Magic Drain R	.30	.60
DB1EN186 Infinite Dismissal C	.12	.25
DB1EN187 Gravity Bind C	.12	.25
DB1EN188 Type Zero Magic Crusher C	.12	.25
DB1EN189 Shadow of Eyes R	.30	.60
DB1EN190 The Legendary Fisherman R	2.00	4.00
DB1EN191 Sword Hunter C	.12	.25
DB1EN192 Drill Bug C	.12	.25
DB1EN193 Deepsea Warrior C	.12	.25
DB1EN194 Thousand-Eyes Idol C	.12	.25
DB1EN195 Thousand-Eyes Restrict UR	7.50	15.00
DB1EN196 Hayabusa Knight R	.30	.60
DB1EN197 Bombardment Beetle C	.12	.25
DB1EN198 4-Starred Ladybug of Doom C	.12	.25
DB1EN199 Gradius C	.12	.25
DB1EN200 Red-Moon Baby C	.12	.25
DB1EN201 Mad Sword Beast R	.30	.60
DB1EN202 Goblin Attack Force SR	.50	1.00
DB1EN203 The Fiend Megacyber R	1.00	2.00
DB1EN204 Gearfried the Iron Knight R	.30	.60
DB1EN205 Insect Barrier C	.12	.25
DB1EN206 Swordsman of Landstar C	.12	.25
DB1EN207 Humanoid Slime C	.12	.25
DB1EN208 Worm Drake C	.12	.25
DB1EN209 Humanoid Worm Drake C	.12	.25
DB1EN210 Revival Jam C	1.00	2.00
DB1EN211 Amphibian Beast C	.12	.25
DB1EN212 Shining Abyss C	.12	.25
DB1EN213 Grand Tiki Elder C	.12	.25
DB1EN214 The Masked Beast SR	.50	1.00
DB1EN215 Melchid the Four-Face Beast C	.12	.25
DB1EN216 Nuvia the Wicked C	.12	.25
DB1EN217 Chosen One C	.12	.25
DB1EN218 Mask of Weakness C	.12	.25
DB1EN219 Curse of the Masked Beast C	.12	.25
DB1EN220 Mask of Dispel C	.12	.25
DB1EN221 Mask of Restrict C	.60	1.25
DB1EN222 Mask of the Accursed C	.12	.25
DB1EN223 Mask of Brutality C	.12	.25
DB1EN224 Return of the Doomed C	.12	.25
DB1EN225 Lightning Blade C	.12	.25
DB1EN226 Tornado Wall C	.12	.25
DB1EN227 Fairy Box C	.12	.25
DB1EN228 Torrential Tribute UR	2.50	5.00
DB1EN229 Jam Breeding Machine C	.12	.25
DB1EN230 Infinite Cards C	1.50	3.00
DB1EN231 Jam Defender C	.12	.25
DB1EN232 Card of Safe Return C	.30	.60
DB1EN233 Amazoness Archer C	.12	.25
DB1EN234 Fire Princess C	.12	.25
DB1EN235 Spirit of the Breeze C	.12	.25
DB1EN236 Dancing Fairy C	.12	.25
DB1EN237 Cure Mermaid C	.12	.25
DB1EN238 Hysteric Fairy C	.12	.25
DB1EN239 The Forgiving Maiden C	.12	.25

DB1EN240 St. Joan C .12 .25
DB1EN241 Marie the Fallen One C .12 .25
DB1EN242 Jar of Greed R .75 1.50
DB1EN243 Scroll of Bewitchment C .30 .60
DB1EN244 United We Stand UR 3.00 6.00
DB1EN245 Mage Power UR 2.50 5.00
DB1EN246 The Portrait's Secret C .12 .25
DB1EN247 The Gross Ghost of Fled Dreams C .12 .25
DB1EN248 Headless Knight C .12 .25
DB1EN249 Earthbound Spirit C .12 .25
DB1EN250 The Earl of Demise C .12 .25

2004 Yu-Gi-Oh Exclusive Pack

EP1EN001 Theinen The Great Sphinx UR 1.25 2.50
EP1EN002 Andro Sphinx UR 1.25 2.50
EP1EN003 Sphinx Teleia UR 1.25 2.50
EP1EN004 Rare Metal Dragon C .75 1.50
EP1EN005 Peten The Dark Clown C .75 1.50
EP1EN006 Familiar Knight C .75 1.50
EP1EN007 Inferno Tempest C .75 1.50
EP1EN008 Return From The Different Dimension C .25 .50

2004 Yu-Gi-Oh Invasion of Chaos 1st Edition

IOC0 Chaos Emperor Dragon Envoy End SCR 100.00 200.00
IOC1 Ojama Yellow C .20 .40
IOC2 Ojama Black C .20 .40
IOC3 Soul Tiger C .20 .40
IOC4 Big Koala C .20 .40
IOC5 Des Kangaroo C .20 .40
IOC6 Crimson Ninja C .20 .40
IOC7 Strike Ninja UR 2.50 5.00
IOC8 Gale Lizard C .20 .40
IOC9 Spirit of the Pot of Greed SP .20 .40
IOC10 Chopman the Desperate Outlaw C .20 .40
IOC11 Sasuke Samurai #3 R .30 .75
IOC12 D.D. Scout Plane SR .60 1.25
IOC13 Beserk Gorilla R .50 1.00
IOC14 Freed the Brave Wanderer SR .50 1.00
IOC15 Coach Goblin C .20 .40
IOC16 Witch Doctor of Chaos SP .20 .40
IOC17 Chaos Necromancer SP .30 .75
IOC18 Chaosrider Gustaph SR .60 1.25
IOC19 Inferno C .20 .40
IOC20 Fenrir C .20 .40
IOC21 Gigantes C .20 .40
IOC22 Silpheed C .20 .40
IOC23 Chaos Sorcerer C .30 .75
IOC24 Gren Maju Da Eiza C .50 1.00
IOC25 Black Luster Soldier Envoy Beginning UR 100.00 200.00
IOC26 Drillago R .30 .75
IOC27 Lekunga R .30 .75
IOC28 Lord Poison SP .50 1.00
IOC29 Bowganian SP .20 .40
IOC30 Granadora SP .20 .40
IOC31 Fuhma Shuriken R .30 .75
IOC32 Heart of the Underdog SP 1.50 3.00
IOC33 Wild Nature's Release SR .30 .75
IOC34 Ojama Delta Hurricane SP .20 .40
IOC35 Stumbling SP .60 1.25
IOC36 Chaos End C .20 .40
IOC37 Yellow Luster Shield C .20 .40
IOC38 Chaos Greed C .20 .40
IOC39 D.D. Designator SR .60 1.25
IOC40 D.D. Borderline C .20 .40
IOC41 Recycle C .20 .40
IOC42 Primal Seed C .20 .40
IOC43 Thunder Crash SP .20 .40
IOC44 Dimension Distortion SP .20 .40
IOC45 Reload SR .50 1.00
IOC46 Soul Absorption C .60 1.25
IOC47 Big Burn SR .50 1.00
IOC48 Blasting the Ruins C .20 .40
IOC49 Cursed Seal of Forbidden Spell C .75 1.50
IOC50 Tower of Babel C .20 .40
IOC51 Spatial Collapse C .20 .40
IOC52 Chain Disappearance R .75 1.50
IOC53 Zero Gravity C .20 .40
IOC54 Dark Mirror Force UR 2.00 4.00
IOC55 Energy Drain C .20 .40
IOC56 Giga Gagagigo SP 1.25 2.50
IOC57 Mad Dog of Darkness R .30 .75
IOC58 Neo Bug C .20 .40
IOC59 Sea Serpent Warrior of Darkness C .20 .40
IOC60 Terrorking Salmon C .20 .40
IOC61 Blazing Inpachi C .20 .40
IOC62 Burning Algae C .20 .40
IOC63 The Thing in the Crater C .20 .40
IOC64 Molten Zombie C .20 .40
IOC65 Dark Magician of Chaos UR 50.00 100.00
IOC66 Gora Turtle of Illusion C .20 .40
IOC67 Manticore of Darkness UR 1.25 2.50
IOC68 Stealth Bird SP .30 .75
IOC69 Sacred Crane C .50 1.00
IOC70 Enraged Battle Ox R .30 .75
IOC71 Don Turtle SP .20 .40
IOC72 Balloon Lizard C .20 .40
IOC73 Dark Dricreratops R .30 .75
IOC74 Hyper Hammerhead SP .20 .40
IOC75 Black Tyranno UR 1.00 2.00
IOC76 Anti-Aircraft Flower SP .20 .40
IOC77 Prickle Fairy C .20 .40
IOC78 Pinch Hopper SP 1.25 2.50
IOC79 Skull-Mark Ladybug SP .20 .40
IOC80 Insect Princess UR .60 1.25
IOC81 Amphibious Bugroth MK-3 C .20 .40
IOC82 Torpedo Fish SP .20 .40
IOC83 Levia-Dragon Daedalus UR 2.00 4.00
IOC84 Orca Mega-Fortress of Darkness SR .50 1.00
IOC85 Cannonball Spear Shellfish SP .30 .75
IOC86 Mataza the Zapper R .30 .75
IOC87 Guardian Angel Joan UR 1.50 3.00
IOC88 Manju of Ten Thousand Hands SP 7.50 15.00
IOC89 Getsu Fuhma R .30 .75
IOC90 Ryu Kokki C .20 .40
IOC91 Gryphon's Feather Duster C .20 .40
IOC92 Stray Lambs R .20 .40
IOC93 Smashing Ground SP .60 1.25
IOC94 Dimension Fusion UR 10.00 20.00
IOC95 Dedication Through Light & Darkness SR 2.00 4.00
IOC96 Salvage C .50 1.00
IOC97 Ultra Evolution Pill R .30 .75
IOC98 Multiplication of Ants C .20 .40
IOC99 Earth Chant SP .20 .40
IOC100 Jade Insect Whistle C .20 .40
IOC101 Destruction Ring R .30 .75
IOC102 Fiend's Hand Mirror C .20 .40
IOC103 Compulsory Evacuation Device R 2.00 4.00
IOC104 A Hero Emerges C .20 .40
IOC105 Self-Destruct Button SP .50 1.00
IOC106 Curse of Darkness R 2.00 4.00
IOC107 Begone, Knave! C .20 .40
IOC108 DNA Transplant C .20 .40
IOC109 Robbin' Zombie R .30 .75
IOC110 Trap Jammer SR .75 1.50
IOC111 Invader of Darkness SCR 2.00 4.00

2004 Yu-Gi-Oh Rise of Destiny 1st Edition

RDSEN01 Woodborg Inpachi .20 .40
RDSEN02 Mighty Guard .20 .40
RDSEN03 Bokoichi the Freightening Car .20 .40
RDSEN04 Harpie Girl .20 .40
RDSEN05 The Creator UR 1.25 2.50
RDSEN05 The Creator UTR 2.00 4.00
RDSEN06 The Creator Incarnate .20 .40
RDSEN07 Ultimate Insect LV3 R .30 .75
RDSEN07 Ultimate Insect LV3 UTR .60 1.25
RDSEN08 Mystic Swordsman LV6 UTR 3.00 6.00
RDSEN08 Mystic Swordsman LV6 UR 2.50 5.00
RDSEN09 Silent Swordsman LV3 UR 1.50 3.00
RDSEN09 Silent Swordsman LV3 UTR 2.00 4.00
RDSEN10 Nightmare Penguin .20 .40
RDSEN11 Heavy Mech Support Platform .20 .40
RDSEN12 Perfect Machine King UTR 3.00 6.00
RDSEN12 Perfect Machine King UR 2.50 5.00
RDSEN13 Element Magician C .20 .40
RDSEN14 Element Saurus C .20 .40
RDSEN15 Roc from the Valley of Haze C .20 .40
RDSEN16 Sasuke Samurai #4 UTR .60 1.25
RDSEN16 Sasuke Samurai #4 R .30 .75
RDSEN17 Harpie Lady 1 C .50 1.00
RDSEN18 Harpie Lady 2 C .20 .40
RDSEN19 Harpie Lady 3 C .20 .40
RDSEN20 Raging Flame Sprite C .20 .40
RDSEN21 Thestalos Firestorm Monarch UTR 5.00 10.00
RDSEN21 Thestalos Firestorm Monarch SR .50 1.00
RDSEN22 Eagle Eye C .20 .40
RDSEN23 Tactical Espionage Expert C .20 .40
RDSEN24 Invasion of Flames C .20 .40
RDSEN25 Creeping Doom Manta C .20 .40
RDSEN26 Pitch-Black Warwolf C .20 .40
RDSEN27 Mirage Dragon C .30 .75
RDSEN28 Gaia Soul the Combustible Collective UTR .60 1.25
RDSEN28 Gaia Soul the Combustible Collective R .30 .75
RDSEN29 Fox Fire C .20 .40
RDSEN30 Big Core UTR .60 1.25
RDSEN30 Big Core SR .30 .75
RDSEN31 Fusilier Dragon, the Duel Mode Beast UTR 1.25 2.50
RDSEN31 Fusilier Dragon, the Duel Mode Beast R .50 1.00
RDSEN32 Dekoichi the Battlechanted Locomotive UTR 1.50 3.00
RDSEN32 Dekoichi the Battlechanted Locomotive R .30 .75
RDSEN33 A-Team: Trap Disposal Unit UTR .60 1.25
RDSEN33 A-Team: Trap Disposal Unit R .30 .75
RDSEN34 Homunculus the Alchemic Being C .20 .40
RDSEN35 Dark Blade the Dragon Knight UTR 1.00 2.00
RDSEN35 Dark Blade the Dragon Knight R .30 .75
RDSEN36 Mokey Mokey King C .20 .40
RDSEN37 Serial Spell UTR .60 1.25
RDSEN37 Serial Spell R .30 .75
RDSEN38 Harpies' Hunting Ground C .20 .40
RDSEN39 Triangle Ecstasy Spark UTR 2.00 4.00
RDSEN39 Triangle Ecstasy Spark UR .50 1.00
RDSEN40 Necklace of Command UTR .60 1.25
RDSEN40 Necklace of Command R .30 .75
RDSEN41 Machine Duplication UTR 1.25 2.50
RDSEN41 Machine Duplication R .30 .75
RDSEN42 Flint UTR .60 1.25
RDSEN42 Flint R .30 .75
RDSEN43 Mokey Mokey Smackdown C .20 .40
RDSEN44 Back to Square One C .20 .40
RDSEN45 Monster Reincarnation UTR 6.00 12.00
RDSEN45 Monster Reincarnation SR .75 1.50
RDSEN46 Ballista of Rampart Smashing C .20 .40
RDSEN47 Lighten the Load C .20 .40
RDSEN48 Malice Dispersion C .20 .40
RDSEN49 Tragedy UTR .60 1.25
RDSEN49 Tragedy SR .30 .75
RDSEN50 Divine Wrath SR .60 1.25
RDSEN50 Divine Wrath UTR 3.00 6.00
RDSEN51 Xing Zhen Hu C .20 .40
RDSEN52 Rare Metalmorph R .30 .75
RDSEN52 Rare Metalmorph UTR .60 1.25
RDSEN53 Fruits of Kozaky's Studies C .20 .40
RDSEN54 Mind Haxorz C .20 .40
RDSEN55 Fuh-Rin-Ka-Zan C .20 .40
RDSEN56 Chain Burst R .30 .75
RDSEN56 Chain Burst UTR .60 1.25
RDSEN57 Pikeru's Circle of Enchantment UTR .75 1.50
RDSEN57 Pikeru's Circle of Enchantment SR .30 .75
RDSEN58 Spell Purification C .20 .40
RDSEN59 Astral Barrier C .20 .40
RDSEN60 Covering Fire R .30 .75
RDSEN60 Covering Fire UTR .60 1.25

2004 Yu-Gi-Oh Soul of the Duelist 1st Edition

SODEN01 Charcoal Inpachi R .30 .75
SODEN01 Charcoal Inpachi UTR 1.25 2.50
SODEN02 Neo Aqua Madoor C .20 .40
SODEN03 Skull Dog Marron C .20 .40
SODEN04 Goblin Calligrapher C .20 .40
SODEN05 Ultimate Insect LV1 R .30 .75
SODEN05 Ultimate Insect LV1 UTR .75 1.50
SODEN06 Horus Black Flame/Dragon LV4 UTR 3.00 6.00
SODEN06 Horus Black Flame/Dragon LV4 R 1.50 3.00
SODEN07 Horus Black Flame/Dragon LV6 SR 3.00 6.00
SODEN07 Horus Black Flame/Dragon LV6 UTR 3.00 6.00
SODEN08 Horus Black Flame/Dragon LV8 UTR 25.00 50.00
SODEN08 Horus Black Flame/Dragon LV8 UR 7.50 15.00
SODEN09 Dark Mimic LV1 C .20 .40
SODEN10 Dark Mimic LV3 R .30 .75
SODEN10 Dark Mimic LV3 UTR 2.00 4.00
SODEN11 Mystic Swordsman LV2 UTR 1.50 3.00
SODEN11 Mystic Swordsman LV2 R .30 .75
SODEN12 Mystic Swordsman LV4 UTR 2.50 5.00
SODEN12 Mystic Swordsman LV4 UR .75 1.50
SODEN13 Armed Dragon LV3 C .20 .40
SODEN14 Armed Dragon LV5 R .30 .75
SODEN14 Armed Dragon LV5 UTR 4.00 8.00
SODEN15 Armed Dragon LV7 UTR 10.00 20.00
SODEN15 Armed Dragon LV7 UR 4.00 8.00
SODEN16 Horus' Servant C .20 .40
SODEN17 Red-Eyes B. Chick C .30 .75
SODEN18 Malice Doll of Demise C .20 .40
SODEN19 Ninja Grandmaster Sasuke UTR 3.00 6.00
SODEN19 Ninja Grandmaster Sasuke R .50 1.00
SODEN20 Rafflesia Seduction R .30 .75
SODEN20 Rafflesia Seduction UTR .75 1.50
SODEN21 Ultimate Baseball Kid C .20 .40
SODEN22 Mobius the Frost Monarch UTR 7.50 15.00
SODEN22 Mobius the Frost Monarch SR .75 1.50
SODEN23 Element Dragon C .20 .40
SODEN24 Element Soldier C .20 .40
SODEN25 Howling Insect C .20 .40
SODEN26 Masked Dragon C .30 .75
SODEN27 Mind on Air UTR 1.00 2.00
SODEN27 Mind on Air R .30 .75
SODEN28 Unshaven Angler C .20 .40
SODEN29 The Trojan Horse C .20 .40
SODEN30 Nobleman-Eater Bug C .20 .40
SODEN31 Enraged Muka Muka C .20 .40
SODEN32 Hade-Hane C .20 .40
SODEN33 Penumbral Soldier Lady UTR .75 1.50
SODEN33 Penumbral Soldier Lady SR .50 1.00
SODEN34 Ojama King UTR 2.00 4.00
SODEN34 Ojama King R .50 1.00
SODEN35 Master of Oz UTR 6.00 12.00
SODEN35 Master of Oz R .30 .75
SODEN36 Sanwitch C .20 .40
SODEN37 Dark Factory of Mass Production C .60 1.25
SODEN38 Hammer Shot UTR 2.50 5.00
SODEN38 Hammer Shot R .30 .75
SODEN39 Mind Wipe C .20 .40
SODEN40 Abyssal Designator C .20 .40
SODEN41 Level Up! .30 .75
SODEN42 Inferno Fire Blast UTR 10.00 20.00
SODEN42 Inferno Fire Blast UR 3.00 6.00
SODEN43 Ectoplasmer UTR .60 1.25
SODEN43 Ectoplasmer SR .50 1.00
SODEN44 Graveyard in 4th Dimension C .20 .40
SODEN45 Two-Man Cell Battle C .20 .40
SODEN46 Big Wave Small Wave C .20 .40
SODEN47 Fusion Weapon C .20 .40
SODEN48 Ritual Weapon C .20 .40
SODEN49 Taunt C .20 .40
SODEN50 Absolute End C .20 .40
SODEN51 Spirit Barrier R 1.50 3.00
SODEN51 Spirit Barrier UTR 4.00 8.00
SODEN52 Ninjitsu Art of Decoy C .20 .40
SODEN53 Enervating Mist R .30 .75
SODEN53 Enervating Mist UTR 2.50 5.00
SODEN54 Heavy Slump C .30 .75
SODEN55 Greed SR .50 1.00
SODEN55 Greed UTR .60 1.25
SODEN56 Mind Crush C .60 1.25
SODEN57 Null and Void SR .50 1.00
SODEN57 Null and Void UTR .60 1.25
SODEN58 Gorgon's Eye C .20 .40
SODEN59 Cemetary Bomb C .20 .40
SODEN60 Hallowed Life Barrier SR .50 1.00
SODEN60 Hallowed Life Barrier UTR .75 1.50

2004 Yu-Gi-Oh The Movie

MOV-EN1 Blue-Eyes Shining Dragon SR 4.00 8.00
MOV-EN2 Sorcerer of Dark Magic C 2.50 5.00
MOV-EN3 Watapon C .75 1.50
MOV-EN4 Pyramid of Light C 2.00 4.00

2004 Yu-Gi-Oh Tournament Pack 5

TP5EN001 Luminous Soldier UR 2.50 5.00
TP5EN002 Big Shield Gardna SR 2.00 4.00
TP5EN003 Magical Thorn SR 2.00 4.00
TP5EN004 Luster Dragon SR 2.50 5.00
TP5EN005 Needle Worm SR 6.00 12.00
TP5EN006 Kycoo the Ghost Destroyer R 1.00 2.00
TP5EN007 Bazoo the Soul-Eater R 1.00 2.00
TP5EN008 Book of Life R 1.00 2.00
TP5EN009 Trap Board Eraser R 1.00 2.00
TP5EN010 Goddess with the Third Eye C 1.00 2.00
TP5EN011 Jowgen the Spiritualist C .25 .50
TP5EN012 Tornado Bird C .25 .50
TP5EN013 Destruction Punch C .25 .50
TP5EN014 Beastking of the Swamps C .25 .50
TP5EN015 Versago the Destroyer C .25 .50
TP5EN016 Mysticak Sheep #1 C .25 .50
TP5EN017 Pyramid Turtle C .25 .50
TP5EN018 Curse of Royal C .25 .50
TP5EN019 Winged Sage Falcos C .25 .50
TP5EN020 Dark Designator C .25 .50

2005 Yu-Gi-Oh Collector Tins

CT2EN001 Gilford the Lightning SCR 1.00 2.00
CT2EN002 Exarion Universe SCR 2.50 5.00
CT2EN003 Vorse Raider SCR 5.00 10.00
CT2EN004 Dark Magician Girl SCR 6.00 12.00
CT2EN005 Rocket Warrior SCR 4.00 8.00
CT2EN006 Panther Warrior SCR 3.00 6.00

2005 Yu-Gi-Oh Cybernetic Revolution 1st Edition

CRV1 Cycloid C .10 .20
CRV2 Soitsu C .10 .20
CRV3 Mad Lobster C .10 .20
CRV4 Jerry Beans Man C .10 .20
CRV5 Winged Kuriboh LV 10 UR 3.00 6.00
CRV5 Winged Kuriboh LV 10 UTR 10.00 20.00
CRV6 Patroid C .10 .20
CRV7 Gyroid C .10 .20
CRV8 Steamroid C .10 .20
CRV9 Drillroid C .10 .20
CRV11 Jetroid C .10 .20
CRV17 Cybernetic Cyclops C .10 .20
CRV18 Mechanical Hound C .10 .20
CRV19 Cyber Archfiend C .10 .20
CRV22 Giant Kozaky C .10 .20
CRV23 Indomitable Fighter Lei Lei C .10 .20
CRV24 Protective Soul Ailin C .10 .20
CRV25 Doitsu C .10 .20
CRV26 Des Frog C .10 .20
CRV27 T.A.D.P.O.L.E. C .10 .20
CRV28 Poison Draw Frog C .10 .20
CRV29 Tyranno Infinity C .10 .20
CRV30 Batteryman C .10 .20
CRV31 Ebon Magician Curran C .10 .20
CRV33 Steam Gyroid C .10 .20
CRV38 Fusion Recovery C .10 .20
CRV40 Dragon's Mirror C .10 .20
CRV42 Des Croaking C .10 .20
CRV43 Pot of Generosity C .10 .20
CRV44 Shien's Spy C .10 .20
CRV50 Spiritual Earth Art - Kurogane C .10 .20
CRV51 Spiritual Water Art - Aoi C .10 .20
CRV52 Spiritual Fire Art - Kurenai C .10 .20
CRV53 Spiritual Wind Art - Miyabi C .10 .20
CRV54 A Rival Appears! C .10 .20
CRV55 Magical Explosion R .50 1.00
CRV55 Magical Explosion UTR 3.00 6.00
CRV58 Conscription C .10 .20
CRV60 Prepare to Strike Back C .10 .20
CRV10A UFOroid SR .75 1.50
CRV10B UFOroid UTR .75 1.50
CRV12A Wroughtweiler R .50 1.00
CRV12B Wroughtweiler UTR 1.50 3.00
CRV13B Dark Catapulter UTR .50 1.00
CRV13B Dark Catapulter UTR .75 1.50
CRV14A Elemental Hero Bubbleman R .50 1.00
CRV14B Elemental Hero Bubbleman UTR 15.00 30.00
CRV15A Cyber Dragon SR 3.00 6.00
CRV15B Cyber Dragon UTR 30.00 75.00
CRV16A Cybernetic Magician SR .75 1.50
CRV16B Cybernetic Magician UTR .75 1.50
CRV20A Goblin Elite Attack Force SR .75 1.50
CRV20B Goblin Elite Attack Force UTR 1.50 3.00
CRV21A B.E.S. Crystal Core SR .75 1.50
CRV21B B.E.S. Crystal Core UTR 1.00 2.00
CRV32A D.D.M. Different Dimension (R) .50 1.00
CRV32B D.D.M. Different Dimension UTR 1.00 2.00
CRV34A UFOroid Fighter UR 1.00 2.00
CRV34B UFOroid Fighter UTR 2.50 5.00
CRV35A Cyber Twin Dragon SR 2.50 5.00
CRV35B Cyber Twin Dragon UTR 10.00 20.00
CRV36A Cyber End Dragon UR 6.00 12.00
CRV36B Cyber End Dragon UTR 25.00 50.00
CRV37A Power Bond UR 3.00 6.00
CRV37B Power Bond UTR 15.00 30.00
CRV39A Miracle Fusion R .50 1.00
CRV39B Miracle Fusion UTR 7.50 15.00
CRV41A System Down R .50 1.00
CRV41B System Down UTR 10.00 20.00
CRV45A Transcendant Wings R .50 1.00
CRV45B Transcendent Wings UTR 3.00 6.00
CRV46A Bubble Shuffle R .50 1.00
CRV46B Bubble Shuffle UTR .75 1.50
CRV47A Spark Blaster R .50 1.00
CRV47B Spark Blaster UTR .75 1.50
CRV48A Skyscraper SR 1.00 2.00
CRV48B Skyscraper UTR 3.00 6.00
CRV49A Fire Darts R .50 1.00
CRV49B Fire Darts UTR .75 1.50
CRV56A Rising Energy R .50 1.00
CRV56B Rising Energy UTR 1.00 2.00
CRV57A D.D. Trap Hole R .50 1.00
CRV57B D.D. Trap Hole UTR .75 1.50
CRV59A Dimension Wall R .50 1.00
CRV59B Dimension Wall UTR 2.50 5.00

2005 Yu-Gi-Oh Dark Beginnings 2

DB2001 Jowgen the Spiritualist R .50 1.00
DB2002 Kycoo the Ghost Destroyer R .50 1.00
DB2003 Bazoo the Soul-Eater R .50 1.00
DB2004 Dark Necrofear UR 1.00 2.00
DB2005 Soul of Purity and Light C .15 .30
DB2006 Aqua Spirit C 1.00 2.00
DB2007 The Rock Spirit C .15 .30
DB2008 Gilasaurus C .15 .30
DB2009 Tornado Bird C .15 .30
DB2010 Zombyra the Dark C .15 .30
DB2011 Maryokutai C .15 .30
DB2012 The Last Warrior SR 1.25 2.50
DB2013 Dark Spirit of the Silent C .15 .30
DB2014 Royal Command R .50 1.00
DB2015 Riryoku Field R .50 1.00
DB2016 Skull Lair C .15 .30
DB2017 Graverobber's Retribution C .15 .30
DB2018 Destruction Punch C .15 .30
DB2019 Blind Destruction C .15 .30
DB2020 The Emperor's Holiday C .15 .30
DB2021 Destiny Board C 1.50 3.00
DB2022 Spirit Message 'I' C .15 .30
DB2023 Spirit Message 'N' C .15 .30
DB2024 Spirit Message 'A' C .15 .30
DB2025 Spirit Message 'L' C .15 .30
DB2026 The Dark Door C .15 .30
DB2027 Spiritualism R .50 1.00
DB2028 Cyclon Laser C .15 .30
DB2029 De-Fusion C 1.00 2.00
DB2030 Fusion Gate R 2.50 5.00
DB2031 Ekibyo Drakmord C .15 .30
DB2032 Miracle Dig C 1.50 3.00

DB2033 Vengeful Bog Spirit C	.15	.30
DB2034 Blade Knight UR	1.25	2.50
DB2035 Baby Dragon C	.15	.30
DB2036 Blackland Fire Dragon C	.15	.30
DB2037 Battle Steer C	.15	.30
DB2038 Time Wizard SR	4.00	8.00
DB2039 Saggi the Dark Clown C	.15	.30
DB2040 Dragon Piper C	.15	.30
DB2041 Illusionist Faceless Mage C	.15	.30
DB2042 Sangan R	.50	1.00
DB2043 Great Moth C	.15	.30
DB2044 Kuriboh R	.50	1.00
DB2045 Thousand Dragon C	.15	.30
DB2046 King of Yamimakai C	.15	.30
DB2047 Catapult Turtle SR	1.00	2.00
DB2048 Mystic Horseman C	.15	.30
DB2049 Rabid Horseman C	.15	.30
DB2050 Crass Clown C	.15	.30
DB2051 Dream Clown C	.15	.30
DB2052 Princess of Tsurugi C	.15	.30
DB2053 Tremendous Fire C	.15	.30
DB2054 Jirai Gumo C	.15	.30
DB2055 Shadow Ghoul C	.15	.30
DB2056 Ryu-Kishin Powered C	.15	.30
DB2057 Launcher Spider C	.25	.50
DB2058 Thunder Dragon C	1.50	3.00
DB2059 The Immortal of Thunder C	.15	.30
DB2060 Hoshiningen C	.15	.30
DB2061 Cannon Soldier SR	1.00	2.00
DB2062 Muka Muka C	.15	.30
DB2063 The Bistro Butcher C	.15	.30
DB2064 Star Boy C	.15	.30
DB2065 Milus Radiant C	.15	.30
DB2066 Witch of the Black Forest R	.50	1.00
DB2067 Little Chimera C	.15	.30
DB2068 Bladefly C	.15	.30
DB2069 Twin-Headed Thunder Dragon C	.25	.50
DB2070 Witch's Apprentice C	.15	.30
DB2071 Gazelle the King of Mythical Beasts C	.15	.30
DB2072 Barrel Dragon UR	1.25	2.50
DB2073 Solemn Judgment SR	1.50	3.00
DB2074 Magic Jammer SR	1.25	2.50
DB2075 Seven Tools of the Bandit SR	1.00	2.00
DB2076 Horn of Heaven R	1.50	3.00
DB2077 Shield & Sword C	.15	.30
DB2078 Block Attack C	.15	.30
DB2079 The Unhappy Maiden C	.15	.30
DB2080 Robbin' Goblin C	.15	.30
DB2081 Mirror Force SR	4.00	8.00
DB2082 Ring of Magnetism R	.50	1.00
DB2083 Share the Pain C	.15	.30
DB2084 Heavy Storm SR	1.25	2.50
DB2085 Oscillo Hero #2 C	.15	.30
DB2086 Soul of the Pure C	.15	.30
DB2087 Dark-Piercing Light C	.15	.30
DB2088 The Statue of Easter Island C	.15	.30
DB2089 Shining Friendship C	.15	.30
DB2090 The Wicked Worm Beast C	.15	.30
DB2091 Tiger Axe C	.15	.30
DB2092 Axe Raider C	.15	.30
DB2093 Mechanicalchaser C	.15	.30
DB2094 Gemini Elf C	.15	.30
DB2095 Graceful Charity R	.50	1.00
DB2096 Two-Headed King Rex C	.15	.30
DB2097 Goddess with the Third Eye C	.15	.30
DB2098 Lord of the Lamp C	.15	.30
DB2099 Machine King C	.15	.30
DB2100 Cyber-Stein R	7.50	15.00
DB2101 Dragon Seeker C	.15	.30
DB2102 Needle Worm C	1.50	3.00
DB2103 Greenkappa C	.15	.30
DB2104 Morphing Jar R	1.50	3.00
DB2105 Penguin Soldier C	.15	.30
DB2106 Royal Decree SR	3.00	6.00
DB2107 Magical Thorn C	.50	1.00
DB2108 Restructer Revolution C	.15	.30
DB2109 Fusion Sage C	1.50	3.00
DB2110 Total Defense Shogun SR	1.25	2.50
DB2111 Swift Gaia the Fierce Knight UR	1.00	2.00
DB2112 Obnoxious Celtic Guard UR	1.25	2.50
DB2113 Luminous Soldier C	.15	.30
DB2114 Command Knight SR	1.25	2.50
DB2115 Kaiser Sea Horse C	.15	.30
DB2116 Vampire Lord UR	2.00	4.00
DB2117 Toon Goblin Attack Force C	2.00	4.00
DB2118 Toon Cannon Soldier C	.15	.30
DB2119 Toon Gemini Elf C	2.00	4.00
DB2120 Toon Masked Sorcerer C	2.00	4.00
DB2121 Toon Table of Contents C	1.50	3.00
DB2122 Toon Defense C	1.00	2.00
DB2123 Insect Queen UR	2.00	4.00
DB2124 Dark Ruler Ha Des UR	1.00	2.00
DB2125 Dark Balter the Terrible R	.50	1.00
DB2126 Lesser Fiend C	.15	.30
DB2127 Possessed Dark Soul C	.15	.30
DB2128 Winged Minion C	.15	.30
DB2129 Skull Knight #2 C	.15	.30
DB2130 Twin-Headed Wolf C	.15	.30
DB2131 Opticlops C	.15	.30
DB2132 Bark of Dark Ruler C	.15	.30
DB2133 Fatal Abacus C	.15	.30
DB2134 The Puppet Magic of Dark Ruler C	.25	.50
DB2135 Soul Demolition C	.15	.30
DB2136 Double Snare C	.15	.30
DB2137 Freed the Matchless General UR	1.25	2.50
DB2138 Marauding Captain R	.50	1.00
DB2139 Ryu Senshi R	.50	1.00
DB2140 Warrior Dai Grepher C	.15	.30
DB2141 Mysterious Guard C	.15	.30
DB2142 Frontier Wiseman C	.15	.30
DB2143 Exiled Force C	.15	.30
DB2144 Shadow Tamer C	.15	.30
DB2145 Dragon Manipulator C	.15	.30
DB2146 The A. Forces C	.15	.30
DB2147 Reinforcement of the Army R	.75	1.50
DB2148 Array of Revealing Light C	.15	.30
DB2149 The Warrior Returning Alive C	.15	.30
DB2150 Emergency Provisions R	.50	1.00
DB2151 Tyrant Dragon UR	3.00	6.00
DB2152 Spear Dragon SR	1.00	2.00
DB2153 Spirit Ryu C	.15	.30
DB2154 Fiend Skull Dragon R	.50	1.00
DB2155 Cave Dragon C	.15	.30
DB2156 Gray Wing C	.15	.30
DB2157 Troop Dragon C	.25	.50
DB2158 The Dragon's Bead C	.15	.30
DB2159 A Wingbeat of Giant Dragon C	.15	.30
DB2160 Dragon's Gunfire C	.15	.30
DB2161 Stamping Destruction C	.15	.30
DB2162 Super Rejuvenation C	.15	.30
DB2163 Dragon's Rage C	.15	.30
DB2164 Burst Breath C	.15	.30
DB2165 Luster Dragon #2 C	.15	.30
DB2166 Fiber Jar R	2.00	4.00
DB2167 Serpentine Princess C	.15	.30
DB2168 Patrician of Darkness C	.15	.30
DB2169 Thunder Nyan Nyan R	.50	1.00
DB2170 Gradius' Option C	.15	.30
DB2171 Injection Fairy Lily UR	3.00	6.00
DB2172 Woodland Sprite C	.15	.30
DB2173 Airknight Parshath SR	1.50	3.00
DB2174 Twin-Headed Behemoth C	.25	.50
DB2175 Maharaghi C	.15	.30
DB2176 Inaba White Rabbit C	.15	.30
DB2177 Yata-Garasu C	.60	1.25
DB2178 Susa Soldier SR	1.00	2.00
DB2179 Yamata Dragon SR	2.50	5.00
DB2180 Great Long Nose C	.15	.30
DB2181 Otohime C	.15	.30
DB2182 Hino-Kagu-Tsuchi UR	1.50	3.00
DB2183 Asura Priest C	.15	.30
DB2184 Fushi No Tori C	.15	.30
DB2185 Spring of Rebirth C	.15	.30
DB2186 Heart of Clear Water C	.15	.30
DB2187 A Legendary Ocean C	.15	.30
DB2188 Fusion Sword Murasame Blade C	.15	.30
DB2189 Smoke Grenade of the Thief C	.15	.30
DB2190 Creature Swap SR	1.00	2.00
DB2191 Spiritual Energy Settle Machine C	.15	.30
DB2192 Second Coin Toss C	.15	.30
DB2193 Convulsion of Nature C	.15	.30
DB2194 The Secret of the Bandit C	.15	.30
DB2195 After the Struggle C	.15	.30
DB2196 Magic Reflector C	1.50	3.00
DB2197 Blast with Chain R	.50	1.00
DB2198 Disappear C	.15	.30
DB2199 Bubble Crash C	.15	.30
DB2200 Royal Oppression R	.50	1.00
DB2201 Bottomless Trap Hole C	1.50	3.00
DB2202 Bad Reaction to Simochi C	1.50	3.00
DB2203 Ominous Fortunetelling C	.15	.30
DB2204 Spirit's Invitation C	.15	.30
DB2205 Drop Off C	.15	.30
DB2206 Last Turn R	.75	1.50
DB2207 King Tiger Wanghu C	.15	.30
DB2208 Birdface C	.15	.30
DB2209 Kryuel C	.15	.30
DB2210 Arsenal Bug C	.15	.30
DB2211 Maiden of the Aqua C	.15	.30
DB2212 Jowls of Dark Demise C	.15	.30
DB2213 Mucus Yolk C	.15	.30
DB2214 Moisture Creature C	.15	.30
DB2215 Gora Turtle C	.15	.30
DB2216 Sasuke Samurai R	.50	1.00
DB2217 Dark Dust Spirit C	.15	.30
DB2218 Royal Keeper C	.15	.30
DB2219 Wandering Mummy C	.15	.30
DB2220 Great Dezard SR	1.00	2.00
DB2221 Swarm of Scarabs C	.15	.30
DB2222 Swarm of Locusts C	.15	.30
DB2223 Giant Axe Mummy C	.15	.30
DB2224 Guardian Sphinx UR	1.00	2.00
DB2225 Pyramid Turtle R	.50	1.00
DB2226 Dice Jar C	.15	.30
DB2227 Dark Scorpion Burglars C	.15	.30
DB2228 Don Zaloog SR	1.25	2.50
DB2229 Fushioh Richie UR	1.25	2.50
DB2230 Book of Life SR	2.00	4.00
DB2231 Book of Taiyou C	.15	.30
DB2232 Book of Moon C	.15	.30
DB2233 Mirage of Nightmare C	.15	.30
DB2234 Secret Pass to the Treasures C	.15	.30
DB2235 Call of the Mummy C	.15	.30
DB2236 Timidity C	.15	.30
DB2237 Pyramid Energy C	.15	.30
DB2238 Tutan Mask C	.15	.30
DB2239 Ordeal of a Traveler C	.15	.30
DB2240 Bottomless Shifting Sand C	.15	.30
DB2241 Curse of Royal C	.15	.30
DB2242 Needle Ceiling C	.15	.30
DB2243 Statue of the Wicked R	.50	1.00
DB2244 Dark Coffin C	.15	.30
DB2245 Needle Wall C	.15	.30
DB2246 Trap Dustshoot C	.15	.30
DB2247 Reckless Greed C	.15	.30
DB2248 Pharaoh's Treasure C	.15	.30
DB2249 Perfectly Ultimate Great Moth UR	2.50	5.00
DB2250 Black Illusion Ritual C	.15	.30

2005 Yu-Gi-Oh Dark Revelation 1

DR1001 Master Kyonshee C	.30	.75
DR1002 Kabazauls C	.30	.75
DR1003 Inpachi C	.30	.75
DR1004 Dark Jeroid R	.50	1.00
DR1005 Newdoria R	.50	1.00
DR1006 Helpoemer SR	1.00	2.00
DR1007 Gravekeeper's Spy C	.30	.75
DR1008 Gravekeeper's Curse C	.30	.75
DR1009 Gravekeeper's Guard C	.30	.75
DR1010 Gravekeeper's Spear Soldier C	.30	.75
DR1011 Gravekeeper's Vassal C	.30	.75
DR1012 Gravekeeper's Watcher C	.30	.75
DR1013 Gravekeeper's Chief R	.50	1.00
DR1014 Gravekeeper's Cannonholder C	.30	.75
DR1015 Gravekeeper's Assailant C	.30	.75
DR1016 A Man with Wdjat C	.30	.75
DR1017 Mystical Knight of Jackal SR	1.00	2.00
DR1018 A Cat of Ill Omen C	2.00	4.00
DR1019 Yomi Ship C	.30	.75
DR1020 Winged Sage Falcos C	.30	.75
DR1021 An Owl of Luck C	.30	.75
DR1022 Charm of Shabti C	.30	.75
DR1023 Cobra Jar C	.30	.75
DR1024 Spirit Reaper R	.50	1.00
DR1025 Nightmare Horse C	.30	.75
DR1026 Reaper on the Nightmare R	1.25	2.50
DR1027 Dark Designator C	.30	.75
DR1028 Card Shuffle C	.30	.75
DR1029 Reasoning C	1.00	2.00
DR1030 Dark Room of Nightmare C	.30	.75
DR1031 Different Dimension Capsule C	.30	.75
DR1032 Necrovalley SR	1.00	2.00
DR1033 Buster Rancher C	.30	.75
DR1034 Hieroglyph Lithograph C	.30	.75
DR1035 Dark Snake Syndrome C	.30	.75
DR1036 Terraforming C	1.00	2.00
DR1037 Banner of Courage C	.30	.75
DR1038 Metamorphosis C	1.00	2.00
DR1039 Roayl Tribute C	.30	.75
DR1040 Reversal Quiz C	.30	.75
DR1041 Coffin Seller SR	1.00	2.00
DR1042 Curse of Aging C	.30	.75
DR1043 Barrel Behind the Door R	.50	1.00
DR1044 Raigeki Break C	.30	.75
DR1045 Narrow Pass C	.30	.75
DR1046 Disturbance Strategy C	.30	.75
DR1047 Trap of Board C	.30	.75
DR1048 Rite of Spirit C	.30	.75
DR1049 Non Aggression Area C	.30	.75
DR1050 D. Tribe C	.30	.75
DR1051 Lava Golem UR	2.00	4.00
DR1052 Byser Shock UR	1.00	2.00
DR1053 Question SR	1.00	2.00
DR1054 Rope of Life R	.50	1.00
DR1055 Nightmare Wheel UR	1.50	3.00
DR1056 People Running About C	.30	.75
DR1057 Oppressed People C	.30	.75
DR1058 United Resistance C	.30	.75
DR1059 X-Head Cannon R	.50	1.00
DR1060 Y-Dragon Head R	.50	1.00
DR1061 Z-Metal Tank R	.50	1.00
DR1062 Dark Blade C	.30	.75
DR1063 Pitch-Dark Dragon C	.30	.75
DR1064 Kiryu C	.30	.75
DR1065 Decayed Commander C	.30	.75
DR1066 Zombie Tiger C	.30	.75
DR1067 Giant Orc C	.30	.75
DR1068 Second Goblin C	.30	.75
DR1069 Vampire Orchis C	.30	.75
DR1070 Des Dendle C	.30	.75
DR1071 Burning Beast C	.30	.75
DR1072 Freezing Beast C	.30	.75
DR1073 Union Rider C	.30	.75
DR1074 D.D. Crazy Beast C	.30	.75
DR1075 Spell Canceller UR	5.00	10.00
DR1076 Neko Mane King C	.30	.75
DR1077 Helping Robo For Combat C	.30	.75
DR1078 Dimension Jar C	.30	.75
DR1079 Great Phantom Thief C	.30	.75
DR1080 Roulette Barrel C	.30	.75
DR1081 Paladin of White Dragon SR	1.00	2.00
DR1082 White Dragon Ritual C	.30	.75
DR1083 Frontline Base C	.30	.75
DR1084 Demotion C	.30	.75
DR1085 Combination Attack C	.30	.75
DR1086 Kaiser Colosseum C	3.00	6.00
DR1087 Autonomous Action Unit C	.30	.75
DR1088 Poison of the Old Man C	.30	.75
DR1089 Ante C	.30	.75
DR1090 Dark Core C	.30	.75
DR1091 Raregold Armor C	.30	.75
DR1092 Metalsilver C	.30	.75
DR1093 Kishido Spirit C	.30	.75
DR1094 Tribute Doll C	.30	.75
DR1095 Wave-Motion Cannon C	3.00	6.00
DR1096 Huge Revolution C	.30	.75
DR1097 Thunder of Ruler C	.30	.75
DR1098 Spell Shield Type-8 SR	1.00	2.00
DR1099 Meteorain C	.30	.75
DR1100 Pineapple Blast C	.30	.75
DR1101 Secret Barrel C	.30	.75
DR1102 Physical Double C	.30	.75
DR1103 Rivalry of Warlords C	.60	1.25
DR1104 Formation Union C	.30	.75
DR1105 Adhesion Trap Hole C	.30	.75
DR1106 XY-Dragon Cannon R	3.00	6.00
DR1107 XYZ-Dragon Cannon UR	1.00	2.00
DR1108 XZ-Tank Cannon R	2.00	4.00
DR1109 YZ-Tank Cannon R	1.25	2.50
DR1110 Great Angus C	.30	.75
DR1111 Aitsu C	.30	.75
DR1112 Sonic Duck C	.30	.75
DR1113 Luster Dragon C	.30	.75
DR1114 Amazoness Paladin C	.30	.75
DR1115 Amazoness Fighter C	.30	.75
DR1116 Amazoness Swords Woman SR	1.50	3.00
DR1117 Amazoness Blowpiper C	.30	.75
DR1118 Amazoness Tiger C	.30	.75
DR1119 Skilled White Magician R	.50	1.00
DR1120 Skilled Dark Magician R	1.25	2.50
DR1121 Apprentice Magician C	.30	.75
DR1122 Old Vindictive Magician C	.30	.75
DR1123 Chaos Command Magician SR	2.50	5.00
DR1124 Magical Marionette C	.30	.75
DR1125 Pixie Knight C	.30	.75
DR1126 Breaker the Magical Warrior UR	1.50	3.00
DR1127 Magical Plant Mandragola C	.30	.75
DR1128 Magical Scientist R	.50	1.00
DR1129 Royal Magical Library C	1.00	2.00
DR1130 Armor Exe C	.30	.75
DR1131 Tribe-Infecting Virus R	1.50	3.00
DR1132 Des Koala R	1.00	2.00
DR1133 Cliff the Trap Remover C	.30	.75
DR1134 Magical Merchant C	.30	.75
DR1135 Koitsu C	.30	.75
DR1136 Cat's Ear Tribe C	.30	.75
DR1137 Ultimate Obedient Fiend C	.30	.75
DR1138 Dark Cat with White Tail C	.30	.75
DR1139 Amazoness Spellcaster C	.30	.75
DR1140 Continuous Destruction Punch C	.30	.75
DR1141 Big Bang Shot R	.50	1.00
DR1142 Gather Your Mind C	.30	.75
DR1143 Mass Driver C	.30	.75
DR1144 Senri Eye C	.30	.75
DR1145 Emblem of Dragon Destroyer C	2.50	5.00
DR1146 Jar Robber C	.30	.75
DR1147 My Body as a Shield C	.30	.75
DR1148 Pigeonholing Books of Spell C	.30	.75
DR1149 Mega Ton Magical Cannon C	.30	.75
DR1150 Pitch-Black Power Stone C	.30	.75
DR1151 Amazoness Archers SR	1.00	2.00
DR1152 Dramatic Rescue R	.50	1.00
DR1153 Exhausting Spell C	.30	.75
DR1154 Hidden Book of Spell C	.30	.75
DR1155 Miracle Restoring C	.30	.75
DR1156 Remove Brainwashing C	3.00	6.00
DR1157 Disarmament C	.30	.75
DR1158 Anti-Spell C	.30	.75
DR1159 The Spell Absorbing Life C	.30	.75
DR1160 Dark Paladin UR	10.00	20.00
DR1161 Double Spell UR	1.50	3.00
DR1162 Diffusion Wave-Motion C	.30	.75
DR1163 Battle Footballer C	.30	.75
DR1164 Nin-Ken Dog C	.30	.75
DR1165 Acrobat Monkey C	.30	.75
DR1166 Arsenal Summoner C	.30	.75
DR1167 Guardian Elma C	.30	.75
DR1168 Guardian Ceal R	.50	1.00
DR1169 Guardian Grarl R	.60	1.25
DR1170 Guardian Baou C	.30	.75
DR1171 Guardian Kay'est C	.30	.75
DR1172 Guardian Tryce C	.30	.75
DR1173 Cyber Raider C	.30	.75
DR1174 Reflect Bounder SR	1.00	2.00
DR1175 Little-Winguard C	.30	.75
DR1176 Des Feral Imp C	.30	.75
DR1177 Different Dimension Dragon SR	1.00	2.00
DR1178 Shinato, King of a Higher Plane SR	2.50	5.00
DR1179 Dark Flare Knight SR	1.00	2.00
DR1180 Mirage Knight SR	1.00	2.00
DR1181 Berserk Dragon SR	1.00	2.00
DR1182 Exodia Necross SR	12.50	25.00
DR1183 Gyaku-Gire Panda C	.30	.75
DR1184 Blindly Loyal Goblin C	.30	.75
DR1185 Despair from the Dark C	.30	.75
DR1186 Maju Garzett C	.30	.75
DR1187 Fear from the Dark R	.50	1.00
DR1188 Dark Scorpion Chick the Yellow C	.30	.75
DR1189 D.D. Warrior Lady SR	1.50	3.00
DR1190 Thousand Needles C	.30	.75
DR1191 Shinato's Ark C	.30	.75
DR1192 A Deal with Dark Ruler C	.30	.75
DR1193 Contract with Exodia C	2.00	4.00
DR1194 Butterfly Dagger - Elma R	.50	1.00
DR1195 Shooting Star Bow - Ceal C	.30	.75
DR1196 Gravity Axe - Grarl C	.30	.75
DR1197 Wicked-Breaking Flamberge Baou C	.30	.75
DR1198 Rod of Silence - Kay'est C	.30	.75
DR1199 Twin Swords of Flashing Light - Tryce C	.30	.75
DR1200 Precious Cards from Beyond C	1.50	3.00
DR1201 Rod of the Mind's Eye C	.30	.75
DR1202 Fairy of the Spring C	.30	.75
DR1203 Token Thanksgiving C	.30	.75
DR1204 Morale Boost C	.30	.75
DR1205 Non-Spellcasting Area C	.30	.75
DR1206 Different Dimension Gate R	.50	1.00
DR1207 Final Attack Orders C	.30	.75
DR1208 Staunch Defender C	.30	.75
DR1209 Ojama Trio C	1.00	2.00
DR1210 Arsenal Robber C	.30	.75
DR1211 Skill Drain R	2.00	4.00
DR1212 Really Eternal Rest C	.30	.75
DR1213 Kaiser Glider UR	1.00	2.00
DR1214 Interdimensional Matter UR	1.00	2.00
DR1215 Cost Down UR	2.00	4.00
DR1216 Gagagigo C	.30	.75
DR1217 D.D. Trainer C	.30	.75
DR1218 Ojama Green C	.30	.75
DR1219 Archfiend Soldier C	.30	.75
DR1220 Pandemonium Watchbear C	.30	.75
DR1221 Sasuke Samurai #2 C	.30	.75
DR1222 Dark Scorpion Gorg the Strong C	.30	.75
DR1223 Dark Scorpion Meanae the Thorn C	.30	.75
DR1224 Outstanding Dog Marron C	1.00	2.00
DR1225 Great Maju Garzett C	2.00	4.00
DR1226 Iron Blacksmith Kotetsu C	.30	.75
DR1227 Goblin of Greed C	.30	.75
DR1228 Mefist the Infernal General C	.30	.75
DR1229 Vilepawn Archfiend C	.30	.75
DR1230 Shadowknight Archfiend C	.30	.75
DR1231 Darkbishop Archfiend C	.30	.75
DR1232 Desrook Archfiend C	.30	.75
DR1233 Infernalqueen Archfiend C	.30	.75
DR1234 Terrorking Archfiend SR	1.50	3.00
DR1235 Skull Archfiend of Lightning UR	1.00	2.00
DR1236 Metallizing Parasite Lunatite C	.30	.75
DR1237 Tsukuyomi C	1.00	2.00
DR1238 Mudora R	.50	1.00
DR1239 Keldo C	.30	.75
DR1240 Kelbek C	.30	.75
DR1241 Zolga C	.30	.75
DR1242 Agido C	.30	.75
DR1243 Legendary Flame Lord R	.50	1.00
DR1244 Dark Master Zorc SR	1.00	2.00
DR1245 Spell Reproduction C	.30	.75
DR1246 Dragged Down into the Grave C	1.00	2.00
DR1247 Incandescent Ordeal C	.30	.75
DR1248 Contract with the Abyss C	.30	.75
DR1249 Contract with the Dark Master C	.30	.75
DR1250 Falling Down C	.30	.75
DR1251 Checkmate C	.30	.75
DR1252 Cestus of Dagla C	.30	.75
DR1253 Final Countdown C	1.00	2.00
DR1254 Archfiend's Oath C	.30	.75

DR1255 Mustering of the Dark Scorpions C	.30	.75
DR1256 Pandemonium R	.50	1.00
DR1257 Altar for Tribute C	.30	.75
DR1258 Frozen Soul C	.30	.75
DR1259 Battle-Scarred C	.30	.75
DR1260 Dark Scorpion Combination C	.30	.75
DR1261 Archfiend's Roar C	.30	.75
DR1262 Dice Re-Roll C	.30	.75
DR1263 Spell Vanishing R	.50	1.00
DR1264 Sakuretsu Armor C	.30	.75
DR1265 Ray of Hope C	.30	.75
DR1266 Blast Held by a Tribute UR	1.00	2.00
DR1267 Judgment of Anubis UR	1.50	3.00

2005 Yu-Gi-Oh Dark Revelation 2

DR2001 Ojama Yellow C	.30	.75
DR2002 Ojama Black C	.30	.75
DR2003 Soul Tiger C	.30	.75
DR2004 Big Koala C	.30	.75
DR2005 Des Kangaroo C	.30	.75
DR2006 Crimson Ninja C	.30	.75
DR2007 Strike Ninja UR	3.00	6.00
DR2008 Gale Lizard C	.30	.75
DR2009 Spirit of the Pot of Greed C	.30	.75
DR2010 Chopman the Desperate Outlaw C	.30	.75
DR2011 Sasuke Samurai #3 C	.30	.75
DR2012 D.D. Scout Plane R	.50	1.00
DR2013 Berserk Gorilla R	.50	1.00
DR2014 Freed the Brave Wanderer SR	1.00	2.00
DR2015 Coach Goblin C	.30	.75
DR2016 Witch Doctor of Chaos C	.30	.75
DR2017 Chaos Necromancer C	.30	.75
DR2018 Chaosrider Gustaph SR	1.00	2.00
DR2019 Inferno C	.30	.75
DR2020 Fenrir R	.30	.75
DR2021 Gigantes C	.30	.75
DR2022 Silpheed C	.30	.75
DR2023 Chaos Sorcerer C	.30	.75
DR2024 Gren Maju Da Eiza C	.30	.75
DR2025 Black Luster Soldier - EOB UR	20.00	40.00
DR2026 Drillago R	.50	1.00
DR2027 Lekunga R	.50	1.00
DR2028 Lord Poison C	.30	.75
DR2029 Bowganian C	.30	.75
DR2030 Granadora C	.30	.75
DR2031 Fuhma Shuriken C	.30	.75
DR2032 Heart of the Underdog C	3.00	6.00
DR2033 Wild Nature's Release R	.50	1.00
DR2034 Ojama Delta Hurricane!! C	.30	.75
DR2035 Stumbling C	.30	.75
DR2036 Chaos End C	.30	.75
DR2037 Yellow Luster Shield C	.30	.75
DR2038 Chaos Greed C	.30	.75
DR2039 D.D. Designator SR	1.00	2.00
DR2040 D.D. Borderline C	.30	.75
DR2041 Recycle C	.30	.75
DR2042 Primal Seed C	.30	.75
DR2043 Thunder Crash C	.30	.75
DR2044 Dimension Distortion C	.30	.75
DR2045 Reload SR	.30	.75
DR2046 Soul Absorption C	.30	.75
DR2047 Big Burn SR	1.50	3.00
DR2048 Blasting the Ruins C	.30	.75
DR2049 Cursed Seal of the Forbidden Spell C	.30	.75
DR2050 Tower of Babel C	.30	.75
DR2051 Spatial Collapse C	.30	.75
DR2052 Chain Disappearance R	.50	1.00
DR2053 Zero Gravity C	.30	.75
DR2054 Dark Mirror Force SR	3.00	6.00
DR2055 Energy Drain C	.30	.75
DR2056 Chaos Emperor Dragon - EOE UR	20.00	40.00
DR2057 Giga Gagagigo C	.30	.75
DR2058 Mad Dog of Darkness C	.30	.75
DR2059 Neo Bug C	.30	.75
DR2060 Sea Serpent Warrior of Darkness C	.30	.75
DR2061 Terrorking Salmon C	.30	.75
DR2062 Blazing Inpachi C	.30	.75
DR2063 Burning Algae C	.30	.75
DR2064 The Thing in the Crater C	.30	.75
DR2065 Molten Zombie C	.30	.75
DR2066 Dark Magician of Chaos UR	20.00	40.00
DR2067 Gora Turtle of Illusion C	.30	.75
DR2068 Manticore of Darkness SR	1.00	2.00
DR2069 Stealth Bird R	.50	1.00
DR2070 Sacred Crane C	.30	.75
DR2071 Enraged Battle Ox C	.30	.75
DR2072 Don Turtle C	.30	.75
DR2073 Balloon Lizard C	.30	.75
DR2074 Dark Driceratops C	.30	.75
DR2075 Hyper Hammerhead C	.30	.75
DR2076 Black Tyranno UR	1.50	3.00
DR2077 Anti-Aircraft Flower C	.30	.75
DR2078 Prickle Fairy C	.30	.75
DR2079 Pinch Hopper C	.30	.75
DR2080 Skull-Mark Ladybug C	.30	.75
DR2081 Insect Princess UR	.30	.75
DR2082 Amphibious Bugroth MK-3 R	.50	1.00
DR2083 Torpedo Fish C	.30	.75
DR2084 Levia-Dragon - Daedalus UR	2.50	5.00
DR2085 Orca Mega-Fortress of Drknss R	.50	1.00
DR2086 Cannonball Spear Shellfish C	.30	.75
DR2087 Mataza the Zapper R	.50	1.00
DR2088 Guardian Angel Joan SR	1.00	2.00
DR2089 Manju of the Ten Thousand Hands C	.30	.75
DR2090 Getsu Fuhma C	.30	.75
DR2091 Ryu Kokki SR	2.00	4.00
DR2092 Gryphon's Feather Duster C	.30	.75
DR2093 Stray Lambs R	.50	1.00
DR2094 Smashing Ground C	.30	.75
DR2095 Dimension Fusion SR	5.00	10.00
DR2096 Dedication Light and Darkness SR	2.50	5.00
DR2097 Salvage C	.30	.75
DR2098 Ultra Evolution Pill C	.30	.75
DR2099 Multiplication of Ants C	.30	.75
DR2100 Earth Chant C	.30	.75
DR2101 Jade Insect Whistle C	.30	.75
DR2102 Destruction Ring C	.30	.75
DR2103 Fiend's Hand Mirror C	.30	.75
DR2104 Compulsory Evacuation Device R	2.00	4.00
DR2105 A Hero Emerges C	.30	.75
DR2106 Self-Destruct Button C	.30	.75
DR2107 Curse of Darkness R	.50	1.00
DR2108 Begone, Knave! C	.30	.75
DR2109 DNA Transplant C	.30	.75
DR2110 Robbin' Zombie R	.50	1.00
DR2111 Trap Jammer R	.50	1.00
DR2112 Invader of Darkness UR	1.00	2.00
DR2113 Gogiga Gagagigo C	.30	.75
DR2114 Warrior of Zera C	.30	.75
DR2115 Sealmaster Meisei C	.30	.75
DR2116 Mystic Shine Ball C	.30	.75
DR2117 Metal Armored Bug C	.30	.75
DR2118 The Agent of Judgment - Saturn SR	1.00	2.00
DR2119 The Agent of Wisdom - Mercury C	.30	.75
DR2120 The Agent of Creation - Venus C	.30	.75
DR2121 The Agent of Force - Mars C	.30	.75
DR2122 The Unhappy Girl C	.30	.75
DR2123 Soul-Absorbing Bone Tower C	.30	.75
DR2124 The Kick Man C	.30	.75
DR2125 Vampire Lady C	.30	.75
DR2126 Stone Statue of the Aztecs R	.50	1.00
DR2127 Rocket Jumper C	.30	.75
DR2128 Avatar of the Pot C	.30	.75
DR2129 Legendary Jujitsu Master C	.30	.75
DR2130 Gear Golem the Moving Fortress SR	1.00	2.00
DR2131 KA-2 Des Scissors C	.30	.75
DR2132 Needle Burrower R	.50	1.00
DR2133 Sonic Jammer C	.30	.75
DR2134 Blowback Dragon UR	2.00	4.00
DR2135 Zaborg the Thunder Monarch SR	1.50	3.00
DR2136 Atomic Firefly C	.30	.75
DR2137 Mermaid Knight R	.50	1.00
DR2138 Piranha Army C	.30	.75
DR2139 Two Thousand Needles C	.30	.75
DR2140 Disc Fighter C	.30	.75
DR2141 Arcane Archer of the Forest C	.30	.75
DR2142 Lady Ninja Yae C	.30	.75
DR2143 Goblin King C	.30	.75
DR2144 Solar Flare Dragon C	.30	.75
DR2145 White Magician Pikeru C	.30	.75
DR2146 Archlord Zerato UR	2.50	5.00
DR2147 Opti-Camouflage Armor C	2.50	5.00
DR2148 Mystik Wok C	.30	.75
DR2149 Enemy Controller SR	2.50	5.00
DR2150 Burst Stream of Destruction SR	7.50	15.00
DR2151 Monster Gate C	.30	.75
DR2152 Amplifier R	2.50	5.00
DR2153 Weapon Change C	.30	.75
DR2154 The Sanctuary in the Sky C	.30	.75
DR2155 Earthquake C	.30	.75
DR2156 Talisman of Trap Sealing C	.30	.75
DR2157 Goblin Thief C	.30	.75
DR2158 Backfire C	.30	.75
DR2159 Micro Ray C	.30	.75
DR2160 Light of Judgment C	.30	.75
DR2161 Talisman of Spell Sealing C	.30	.75
DR2162 Wall of Revealing Light C	.30	.75
DR2163 Solar Ray C	.30	.75
DR2164 Ninjitsu Art of Transformation C	.30	.75
DR2165 Beckoning Light C	.30	.75
DR2166 Draining Shield R	.50	1.00
DR2167 Armor Break C	.30	.75
DR2168 Mazera DeVille UR	1.00	2.00
DR2169 Gigobyte C	.30	.75
DR2170 Mokey Mokey C	.30	.75
DR2171 Kozaky C	.30	.75
DR2172 Fiend Scorpion C	.30	.75
DR2173 Pharaoh's Servant C	.30	.75
DR2174 Pharaonic Protector C	.30	.75
DR2175 Spirit of the Pharaoh UR	1.50	3.00
DR2176 Theban Nightmare R	.50	1.00
DR2177 Aswan Apparition C	.30	.75
DR2178 Protector of the Sanctuary R	.50	1.00
DR2179 Nubian Guard C	.30	.75
DR2180 Legacy Hunter SR	1.00	2.00
DR2181 Desertapir C	.30	.75
DR2182 Sand Gambler C	.30	.75
DR2183 3-Hump Lacooda C	.30	.75
DR2184 Ghost Knight of Jackal UR	1.00	2.00
DR2185 Absorbing Kid from the Sky C	.30	.75
DR2186 Elephant Statue of Blessing C	.30	.75
DR2187 Elephant Statue of Disaster C	.30	.75
DR2188 Spirit Caller C	.30	.75
DR2189 Emissary of the Afterlife SR	1.50	3.00
DR2190 Grave Protector C	.30	.75
DR2191 Double Coston R	.50	1.00
DR2192 Regenerating Mummy C	.30	.75
DR2193 Night Assailant R	2.00	4.00
DR2194 Man-Thro' Tro' C	.30	.75
DR2195 King of the Swamp C	7.50	15.00
DR2196 Emissary of the Oasis C	.30	.75
DR2197 Special Hurricane R	.50	1.00
DR2198 Order to Charge C	.30	.75
DR2199 Sword of the Soul-Eater C	.30	.75
DR2200 Dust Barrier C	.30	.75
DR2201 Soul Reversal C	.30	.75
DR2202 Spell Economics R	.50	1.00
DR2203 Blessings of the Nile C	.30	.75
DR2204 7 C	.30	.75
DR2205 Level Limit - Area B R	1.50	3.00
DR2206 Enchanting Fitting Room C	.30	.75
DR2207 The Law of the Normal C	.30	.75
DR2208 Dark Magic Attack UR	4.00	8.00
DR2209 Delta Attacker C	.30	.75
DR2210 Thousand Energy C	.30	.75
DR2211 Triangle Power C	.30	.75
DR2212 The Third Sarcophagus C	.30	.75
DR2213 The Second Sarcophagus C	.30	.75
DR2214 The First Sarcophagus SR	1.00	2.00
DR2215 Dora of Fate C	.30	.75
DR2216 Judgment of the Desert C	.30	.75
DR2217 Human-Wave Tactics C	.30	.75
DR2218 Curse of Anubis SR	1.00	2.00
DR2219 Desert Sunlight C	.30	.75
DR2220 Des Counterblow R	.50	1.00
DR2221 Labyrinth of Nightmare C	.30	.75
DR2222 Soul Resurrection R	.50	1.00
DR2223 Order to Smash C	.30	.75
DR2224 The End of Anubis UR	2.00	4.00

2005 Yu-Gi-Oh Elemental Energy 1st Edition

EEN1 Zure, Knight of Dark World C	.20	.40
EEN2 V-Tiger Jet C	.20	.40
EEN3 Blade Skater C	.20	.40
EEN4 Queen's Knight R	.50	1.00
EEN4 Queen's Knight UTR	3.00	6.00
EEN5 Jack's Knight R	.50	1.00
EEN5 Jack's Knight UTR	15.00	30.00
EEN6 King's Knight R	.50	1.00
EEN6 King's Knight UTR	3.00	6.00
EEN7 Elemental Hero Bladedge SR	.75	1.50
EEN7 Elemental Hero Bladedge UTR	4.00	8.00
EEN8 Elemental Hero Wildheart C	.20	.40
EEN9 Reborn Zombie C	.20	.40
EEN10 Chthonian Soldier R	.50	1.00
EEN10 Chthonian Soldier UTR	.75	1.50
EEN11 W-Wing Catapult C	.20	.40
EEN12 Infernal Incinerator C	.20	.40
EEN13 Hydrogeddon C	.20	.40
EEN14 Oxygeddon C	.20	.40
EEN15 Water Dragon SR	.75	1.50
EEN15 Water Dragon UTR	2.50	5.00
EEN16 Etoile Cyber C	.20	.40
EEN17 B.E.S. Tetran SR	.75	1.50
EEN17 B.E.S. Tetran UTR	.75	1.50
EEN18 Nanobreaker C	.20	.40
EEN19 Rapid-Fire Magician R	.50	1.00
EEN19 Rapid-Fire Magician UTR	.75	1.50
EEN20 Beiige, Vanguard of Dark World C	.20	.40
EEN21 Broww, Huntsman of Dark World R	.50	1.00
EEN21 Broww, Huntsman of Dark World UTR	5.00	10.00
EEN22 Brron, Mad King of Dark World R	.50	1.00
EEN22 Brron, Mad King of Dark World UTR	.75	1.50
EEN23 Sillva, Warlord of Dark World R	.50	1.00
EEN23 Sillva, Warlord of Dark World UTR	2.50	5.00
EEN24 Goldd, Wu-Lord of Dark World SR	.75	1.50
EEN24 Goldd, Wu-Lord of Dark World UTR	2.50	5.00
EEN25 Scarr, Scout of Dark World C	.20	.40
EEN26 Familiar-Possessed - Aussa C	.20	.40
EEN27 Familiar-Possessed - Eria C	.20	.40
EEN28 Familiar-Possessed - Hiita C	.20	.40
EEN29 Familiar-Possessed - Wynn C	.20	.40
EEN30 VW-Tiger Catapult C	.20	.40
EEN31 VWXYZ-Dragon Catapult Cannon SR	.75	1.50
EEN31 VWXYZ-Dragon Catapult Cannon UTR	3.00	6.00
EEN32 Cyber Blader UTR	1.50	3.00
EEN32 Cyber Blader SR	.75	1.50
EEN33 Elem.Hero Rampart Blast. UTR	7.50	15.00
EEN33 Elemental Hero Rampart Blaster UR	2.00	4.00
EEN34 Elemental Hero Tempest UTR	20.00	40.00
EEN34 Elemental Hero Tempest UR	2.50	5.00
EEN35 Elemental Hero Wildedge UTR	50.00	100.00
EEN35 Elemental Hero Wildedge UR	2.50	5.00
EEN36 Elem. Hero Shining Flare UTR	60.00	120.00
EEN36 Elem. Hero Shining Flare UR	6.00	12.00
EEN37 Pot of Avarice UTR	15.00	30.00
EEN37 Pot of Avarice SR	.75	1.50
EEN38 Dark World Lightning C	.20	.40
EEN39 Level Modulation C	.20	.40
EEN40 Ojamagic C	.20	.40
EEN41 Ojamuscle C	.20	.40
EEN42 Feather Shot UTR	.75	1.50
EEN42 Feather Shot R	.50	1.00
EEN43 Bonding - H2O C	.20	.40
EEN44 Chthonian Alliance UTR	.75	1.50
EEN44 Chthonian Alliance R	.50	1.00
EEN45 Armed Changer UTR	.75	1.50
EEN45 Armed Changer R	.50	1.00
EEN46 Branch! C	.20	.40
EEN47 Boss Rush C	.20	.40
EEN48 Gateway to Dark World C	.20	.40
EEN49 Hero Barrier UTR	.75	1.50
EEN49 Hero Barrier R	.50	1.00
EEN50 Chthonian Blast UTR	.75	1.50
EEN50 Chthonian Blast R	.50	1.00
EEN51 The Forces of Darkness C	.20	.40
EEN52 Dark Deal C	.20	.40
EEN53 Simultaneous Loss C	.20	.40
EEN54 Weed Out C	.20	.40
EEN55 The League of Uniform Nomenclature C	.20	.40
EEN56 Roll Out! C	.20	.40
EEN57 Chthonian Polymer C	.20	.40
EEN58 Feather Wind C	.20	.40
EEN59 Non-Fusion Area C	.20	.40
EEN60 Level Limit - Area A UTR	.75	1.50
EEN60 Level Limit - Area A R	.50	1.00

2005 Yu-Gi-Oh Flaming Eternity 1st Edition

FETEN1 Space Mambo C	.10	.20
FETEN2 Divine Dragon Ragnarok C	.75	1.50
FETEN3 Chu-Ske The Mouse Fighter C	.10	.20
FETEN4 Insect Knight C	.10	.20
FETEN5 Sacred Phoenix of Nephthys UR	1.50	3.00
FETEN5 Sacred Phoenix of Nephthys UTR	4.00	8.00
FETEN6 Hand of Nephthys C	.10	.20
FETEN7 Ultimate Insect LV5 UTR	3.00	6.00
FETEN7 Ultimate Insect LV5 R	.50	1.00
FETEN8 Silent Swordsman LV5 UTR	3.00	6.00
FETEN8 Silent Swordsman LV5 UR	1.25	2.50
FETEN9 Granmarg the Rock Monarch UTR	6.00	12.00
FETEN9 Granmarg the Rock Monarch SR	.75	1.50
FETEN10 Element Valkyrie C	.10	.20
FETEN11 Element Doom C	.10	.20
FETEN12 Maji-Gire Panda C	.10	.20
FETEN13 Catnipped Kitty C	.10	.20
FETEN14 Behemoth the King of all Animals UTR	1.25	2.50
FETEN14 Behemoth the King of all Animals SR	.75	1.50
FETEN15 Big-Tusked Mammoth R	.50	1.00
FETEN15 Big-Tusked Mammoth UTR	1.25	2.50
FETEN16 Kangaroo Champ C	.10	.20
FETEN17 Hyena C	.10	.20
FETEN18 Blade Rabbit C	.10	.20
FETEN19 Mecha-Dog Marron C	.10	.20
FETEN20 Blast Magician SR	.75	1.50
FETEN20 Blast Magician UTR	2.00	4.00
FETEN21 Chiron the Mage UTR	1.50	3.00
FETEN21 Chiron the Mage R	.50	1.00
FETEN22 Gearfried the Swordsmaster UR	2.00	4.00
FETEN22 Gearfried the Swordsmaster UTR	4.00	8.00
FETEN23 Armed Samurai - Ben Kei C	.10	.20
FETEN24 Shadowslayer R	.50	1.00
FETEN24 Shadowslayer UTR	1.25	2.50
FETEN25 Golem Sentry C	.10	.20
FETEN26 Abare Ushioni C	.10	.20
FETEN27 The Light - Hex-Sealed Fusion C	.10	.20
FETEN28 The Dark - Hex-Sealed Fusion C	.10	.20
FETEN29 The Earth - Hex-Sealed Fusion C	.10	.20
FETEN30 Whirlwind Prodigy C	.10	.20
FETEN31 Flame Ruler C	.10	.20
FETEN32 Firebird C	.10	.20
FETEN33 Rescue Cat C	.10	.20
FETEN34 Brain Jacker R	.50	1.00
FETEN34 Brain Jacker UTR	1.25	2.50
FETEN35 Gatling Dragon UTR	6.00	12.00
FETEN35 Gatling Dragon UR	2.00	4.00
FETEN36 King Dragun SR	4.00	8.00
FETEN36 King Dragun UTR	7.50	15.00
FETEN37 A Feather of the Phoenix UTR	6.00	12.00
FETEN37 A Feather of the Phoenix SR	.75	1.50
FETEN38 Poison Fangs C	.10	.20
FETEN39 Spell Absorption R	1.25	2.50
FETEN39 Spell Absorption UTR	4.00	8.00
FETEN40 Lightning Vortex UTR	10.00	20.00
FETEN40 Lightning Vortex SR	1.50	3.00
FETEN41 Meteor of Destruction R	.50	1.00
FETEN41 Meteor of Destruction UTR	1.25	2.50
FETEN42 Swords of Concealing Light UTR	10.00	20.00
FETEN42 Swords of Concealing Light R	.50	1.00
FETEN43 Spiral Spear Strike R	.50	1.00
FETEN43 Spiral Spear Strike UTR	3.00	6.00
FETEN44 Release Restraint C	.10	.20
FETEN45 Centrifugal Field C	.10	.20
FETEN46 Fulfillment of the Contract C	.10	.20
FETEN47 Re-Fusion C	.75	1.50
FETEN48 The Big March of Animals C	.10	.20
FETEN49 Cross Counter UTR	1.25	2.50
FETEN49 Cross Counter R	.50	1.00
FETEN50 Pole Position C	.10	.20
FETEN51 Penalty Game! UTR	2.00	4.00
FETEN51 Penalty Game! R	.50	1.00
FETEN52 Threatening Roar C	.25	.50
FETEN53 Phoenix Wing Wind Blast R	.50	1.00
FETEN53 Phoenix Wing Wind Blast UTR	15.00	30.00
FETEN54 Good Goblin Housekeeping C	.10	.20
FETEN55 Beast Soul Swap C	.10	.20
FETEN56 Assault on GHQ R	.50	1.00
FETEN56 Assault on GHQ UTR	1.25	2.50
FETEN57 D.D. Dynamite C	.25	.50
FETEN58 Deck Devastation Virus UTR	20.00	40.00
FETEN58 Deck Devastation Virus SR	2.50	5.00
FETEN59 Elemental Burst C	.10	.20
FETEN60 Forced Ceasefire R	.50	1.00
FETEN60 Forced Ceasefire UTR	1.25	2.50

2005 Yu-Gi-Oh Structure Deck Blaze of Destruction 1st Edition

SD3EN001 Infernal Flame Emperor UR	.50	1.00
SD3EN002 Great Angus C	.25	.50
SD3EN003 Blazing Inpachi C	.25	.50
SD3EN004 UFO Turtle- C	.25	.50
SD3EN005 Little Chimera C	.25	.50
SD3EN006 Inferno C	.25	.50
SD3EN007 Molten Zombie C	.25	.50
SD3EN008 Solar Flare Dragon C	.25	.50
SD3EN009 Ultimate Baseball Kid C	.25	.50
SD3EN010 Raging Flame Sprite C	.25	.50
SD3EN011 Thestalos the Firestorm Monarch C	.25	.50
SD3EN012 Gaia Soul the Combustible Collective C	.25	.50
SD3EN013 Fox Fire C	.25	.50
SD3EN014 Snatch Steal C	.25	.50
SD3EN015 Mystical Space Typhoon C	.25	.50
SD3EN016 Molten Destruction C	.25	.50
SD3EN017 Nobleman of Crossout C	.25	.50
SD3EN018 Premature Burial C	.25	.50
SD3EN019 Pot of Greed C	.25	.50
SD3EN020 Tribute to the Doomed C	.25	.50
SD3EN021 Heavy Storm C	.25	.50
SD3EN022 Dark Room of Nightmare C	.25	.50
SD3EN023 Reload C	.25	.50
SD3EN024 Level Limit - Area B C	.25	.50
SD3EN025 Necklace of Command C	.25	.50
SD3EN026 Meteor of Destruction C	.25	.50
SD3EN027 Dust Tornado C	.25	.50
SD3EN028 Call of the Haunted C	.25	.50
SD3EN029 Jar of Greed C	.25	.50
SD3EN030 Spell Shield Type-8 C	.25	.50
SD3EN031 Backfire C	.25	.50

2005 Yu-Gi-Oh Structure Deck Dragon's Roar 1st Edition

SD1EN001 Red-Eyes Darkness Dragon UR	2.00	4.00
SD1EN002 Red-Eyes B. Dragon C	.50	1.00
SD1EN003 Luster Dragon C	.20	.40
SD1EN004 Twin-Headed Behemoth C	.20	.40
SD1EN005 Armed Dragon LV3 C	.20	.40
SD1EN006 Armed Dragon LV5 C	.20	.40
SD1EN007 Red-Eyes B. Chick C	.20	.40
SD1EN008 Element Dragon C	.20	.40
SD1EN009 Masked Dragon C	.20	.40
SD1EN010 Snatch Steal C	.20	.40
SD1EN011 Mystical Space Typhoon C	.50	1.00
SD1EN012 Nobleman of Crossout C	.20	.40
SD1EN013 Premature Burial C	.20	.40
SD1EN014 Swords of Revealing Light C	.20	.40
SD1EN015 Pot of Greed C	.50	1.00
SD1EN016 Heavy Storm C	.20	.40
SD1EN017 Stamping Destruction C	.20	.40
SD1EN018 Creature Swap C	.20	.40
SD1EN019 Reload C	.20	.40
SD1EN020 The Graveyard in the Fourth Dimension C	.20	.40

SD1EN021 Call of the Haunted C .20 .40
SD1EN022 Ceasefire C .20 .40
SD1EN023 The Dragon's Bead C .20 .40
SD1EN024 Dragon's Rage C .20 .40
SD1EN025 Reckless Greed C .50 1.00
SD1EN026 Interdimensional Matter C .20 .40
SD1EN027 Trap Jammer C .20 .40
SD1EN028 Curse of Anubis C .20 .40

2005 Yu-Gi-Oh Structure Deck Fury from the Deep 1st Edition

SD4EN001 Ocean Dragon Lord - Neo- Daedalus UR.75 1.50
SD4EN002 7 Colored Fish C .20 .40
SD4EN003 Sea Serpent Warrior of Darkness C .20 .40
SD4EN004 Space Mambo C .20 .40
SD4EN005 Mother Grizzly C .20 .40
SD4EN006 Star Boy C .20 .40
SD4EN007 Tribe-Infecting Virus C .75 1.50
SD4EN008 Fenrir C .20 .40
SD4EN009 Amphibious Bugroth MK-3 C .20 .40
SD4EN010 Levia-Dragon - Daedalus C .50 1.00
SD4EN011 Mermaid Knight C .20 .40
SD4EN012 Mobius the Frost Monarch C .20 .40
SD4EN013 Unshaven Angler C .20 .40
SD4EN014 Creeping Doom Manta C .20 .40
SD4EN015 Snatch Steal C .20 .40
SD4EN016 Mystical Space Typhoon C .50 1.00
SD4EN017 Premature Burial C .20 .40
SD4EN018 Pot of Greed C .50 1.00
SD4EN019 Heavy Storm C .20 .40
SD4EN020 A Legendary Ocean C .20 .40
SD4EN021 Creature Swap C .20 .40
SD4EN022 Reload C .20 .40
SD4EN023 Salvage C .25 .50
SD4EN024 Hammer Shot C .20 .40
SD4EN025 Big Wave Small Wave C .20 .40
SD4EN026 Dust Tornado C .20 .40
SD4EN027 Call of the Haunted C .20 .40
SD4EN028 Gravity Bind C .20 .40
SD4EN029 Tornado Wall C .20 .40
SD4EN030 Torrential Tribute C .60 1.25
SD4EN031 Spell Shield Type-8 C .20 .40
SD4EN032 Xing Zhen Hu C .20 .40

2005 Yu-Gi-Oh Structure Deck Warrior's Triumph 1st Edition

SD5EN001 Gilford the Legend UR .75 1.50
SD5EN002 Warrior Lady of the Wasteland C .25 .50
SD5EN003 Dark Blade C .25 .50
SD5EN004 Goblin Attack Force C .25 .50
SD5EN005 Gearfried the Iron Knight C .25 .50
SD5EN006 Swift Gaia the Fierce Knight C .25 .50
SD5EN007 Obnoxious Celtic Guard C .25 .50
SD5EN008 Command Knight C .50 1.00
SD5EN009 Marauding Captain C .25 .50
SD5EN010 Exiled Force C .25 .50
SD5EN011 D.D. Warrior Lady C .25 .50
SD5EN012 Malaza the Zapper C .25 .50
SD5EN013 Mystic Swordsman LV2 C .25 .50
SD5EN014 Mystic Swordsman LV4 C .25 .50
SD5EN015 Ninja Grandmaster Sasuke C .25 .50
SD5EN016 Gearfried the Swordmaster C .25 .50
SD5EN017 Armed Samurai - Ben Kei C .25 .50
SD5EN018 Divine Sword - Phoenix Blade C .25 .50
SD5EN019 Snatch Steal C .25 .50
SD5EN020 Mystical Space Typhoon C .50 1.00
SD5EN021 Giant Trunade C .25 .50
SD5EN022 Lightning Blade C .25 .50
SD5EN023 Heavy Storm C .25 .50
SD5EN024 Reinforcement of the Army C .25 .50
SD5EN025 The Warrior Returning Alive C .25 .50
SD5EN026 Fusion Sword Murasame Blade C .25 .50
SD5EN027 Wicked-Breaking Flamberge - Baou C.25 .50
SD5EN028 Fairy of the Spring C .25 .50
SD5EN029 Reload C .25 .50
SD5EN030 Lightning Vortex C .25 .50
SD5EN031 Swords of Concealing Light C .75 1.50
SD5EN032 Release Restraint C .25 .50
SD5EN033 Call of the Haunted C .25 .50
SD5EN034 Magic Jammer C .25 .50
SD5EN035 Royal Decree C 1.25 2.50
SD5EN036 Blast with Chain C .25 .50

2005 Yu-Gi-Oh Structure Deck Zombie Madness 1st Edition

SD2EN001 Vampire Genesis UR 1.50 3.00
SD2EN002 Master Kyonshee C .20 .40
SD2EN003 Vampire Lord C .20 .40
SD2EN004 Dark Dust Spirit C .20 .40
SD2EN005 Pyramid Turtle C .20 .40
SD2EN006 Spirit Reaper C .20 .40
SD2EN007 Despair From The Dark C .20 .40
SD2EN008 Ryu Kokki C .20 .40
SD2EN009 Soul-Absorbing Bone Tower C .20 .40
SD2EN010 Vampire Lady C .20 .40
SD2EN011 Double Coston C .20 .40
SD2EN012 Regenerating Mummy C .20 .40
SD2EN013 Snatch Steal C .50 1.00
SD2EN014 Mystical Space Typhoon C .75 1.50
SD2EN015 Giant Trunade C .20 .40
SD2EN016 Nobleman of Crossout C .20 .40
SD2EN017 Pot of Greed C .50 1.00
SD2EN018 Card of Safe Return C .20 .40
SD2EN019 Heavy Storm C .20 .40
SD2EN020 Creature Swap C .20 .40
SD2EN021 Book of Life C .20 .40
SD2EN022 Call of the Mummy C .20 .40
SD2EN023 Reload C .20 .40
SD2EN024 Dust Tornado C .20 .40
SD2EN025 Torrential Tribute C .75 1.50
SD2EN026 Magic Jammer C .20 .40
SD2EN027 Reckless Greed C .50 1.00
SD2EN028 Compulsory Evacuation Device C .20 .40

2005 Yu-Gi-Oh The Lost Millennium 1st Edition

TLM1 Elemental Hero Avian C .50 1.00
TLM2 Elemental Hero Burstinatrix C .50 1.00
TLM3 Elemental Hero Clayman C .50 1.00
TLM4 Elemental Hero Sparkman C .50 1.00
TLM5 Winged Kuriboh SR 1.50 3.00
TLM6 Ancient Gear Golem UR 3.00 6.00
TLM6 Ancient Gear Golem UTR 10.00 20.00
TLM7 Ancient Gear Beast UTR 1.50 3.00
TLM7 Ancient Gear Beast R .50 1.00
TLM8 Ancient Gear Soldier C .20 .40
TLM9 Millennium Scorpion R .50 1.00
TLM9 Millennium Scorpion UTR 1.50 3.00
TLM-5 Winged Kuriboh UTR 5.00 10.00
TLM10 Ultimate Insect LV7 UTR 3.00 6.00
TLM10 Ultimate Insect LV7 SR .75 1.50
TLM11 Lost Guardian C .20 .40
TLM12 Hieracosphinx SR .75 1.50
TLM12 Hieracosphinx UTR 1.50 3.00
TLM13 Criosphinx UTR 1.50 3.00
TLM13 Criosphinx R .50 1.00
TLM14 Moai Interceptor Cannons C .20 .40
TLM15 Megarock Dragon SR .75 1.50
TLM15 Megarock Dragon UTR 3.00 6.00
TLM16 Dummy Golem C .20 .40
TLM17 Grave Ohja R .50 1.00
TLM17 Grave Ohja UTR 1.50 3.00
TLM18 Mine Golem C .20 .40
TLM19 Monk Fighter C .20 .40
TLM20 Master Monk SR .75 1.50
TLM20 Master Monk UTR 1.50 3.00
TLM21 Guardian Statue C .20 .40
TLM22 Medusa Worm C .20 .40
TLM23 D.D. Survivor R .50 1.00
TLM23 D.D. Survivor UTR 3.00 6.00
TLM24 Mid Shield Gardna UTR 1.50 3.00
TLM24 Mid Shield Gardna R .50 1.00
TLM25 White Ninja C .20 .40
TLM26 Aussa the Earth Charmer C .20 .40
TLM27 Eria the Water Charmer C .20 .40
TLM28 Hiita the Fire Charmer C .20 .40
TLM29 Wynn the Wind Charmer C .20 .40
TLM30 Batteryman AA C .20 .40
TLM31 Des Wombat C .20 .40
TLM32 King of the Skull Servants C .50 1.00
TLM33 Reshef the Dark Being UTR 5.00 10.00
TLM33 Reshef the Dark Being UR 2.00 4.00
TLM34 Elemental Mistress Doriado UTR 1.50 3.00
TLM34 Elemental Mistress Doriado R .50 1.00
TLM35 Elemental Hero Flame Wingman UTR 5.00 10.00
TLM35 Elemental Hero Flame Wingman UR 3.00 6.00
TLM36 Elemental Hero Thunder Giant UTR 5.00 10.00
TLM36 Elemental Hero Thunder Giant UR 2.50 5.00
TLM37 Card of Sanctity UTR 1.50 3.00
TLM37 Card of Sanctity SR .75 1.50
TLM38 Brain Control UTR 10.00 20.00
TLM38 Brain Control SR .75 1.50
TLM39 Gift of the Martyr C .20 .40
TLM40 Double Attack C .20 .40
TLM41 Battery Charger C .20 .40
TLM42 Kapinote Blow C .20 .40
TLM43 Doriado's Blessing C .20 .40
TLM44 Final Ritual of the Ancients C .20 .40
TLM45 Legendary Black Belt UTR 1.50 3.00
TLM45 Legendary Black Belt R .50 1.00
TLM46 Nitro Unit UTR 1.50 3.00
TLM46 Nitro Unit R .50 1.00
TLM47 Shifting Shadows C .20 .40
TLM48 Impenetrable Formation C .20 .40
TLM49 Hero Signal R .50 1.00
TLM49 Hero Signal UTR 1.50 3.00
TLM50 Pikeru's Second Sight C .20 .40
TLM51 Minefield Eruption C .20 .40
TLM52 Kozaky's Self-Destruct Button R .50 1.00
TLM52 Kozaky's Self-Destruct Button UTR 1.50 3.00
TLM53 Mispolymerization C .20 .40
TLM54 Level Conversion Lab C .20 .40
TLM55 Rock Bombardment C .20 .40
TLM56 Grave Lure C .20 .40
TLM57 Token Feastevil R .50 1.00
TLM57 Token Feastevil UTR 1.50 3.00
TLM58 Spell-Stopping Statute UTR 1.50 3.00
TLM58 Spell-Stopping Statute R .50 1.00
TLM59 Royal Surrender R .50 1.00
TLM59 Royal Surrender UTR 1.50 3.00
TLM60 Lone Wolf C .20 .40

2005 Yu-Gi-Oh Tournament Pack 6

TP6EN001 Toon Cannon Soldier UR 15.00 30.00
TP6EN002 Toon Table of Contents SR 10.00 20.00
TP6EN003 Fusion Sage SR 3.00 6.00
TP6EN004 Royal Decree SR 3.00 6.00
TP6EN005 Restructer Revolution SR 1.00 2.00
TP6EN006 Spear Dragon R .75 1.50
TP6EN007 Airknight Parshath R .75 1.50
TP6EN008 Susa Soldier R .75 1.50
TP6EN009 Yamata Dragon R .75 1.50
TP6EN010 Dark Balter the Terrible C .60 1.25
TP6EN011 Ryu Senshi C .60 1.25
TP6EN012 Emergency Provisions C .60 1.25
TP6EN013 Fiend Skull Dragon C .60 1.25
TP6EN014 Thunder Nyan Nyan C .60 1.25
TP6EN015 Last Turn C .60 1.25
TP6EN016 Archfiend Marmot of Nefariousness C .60 1.25
TP6EN017 Sleeping Lion C .60 1.25
TP6EN018 Nekogal #1 C .60 1.25
TP6EN019 Burglar C .60 1.25
TP6EN020 Clown Zombie C .60 1.25

2006 Yu-Gi-Oh Champion Pack Game One

CP01EN001 Satellite Cannon UR 15.00 30.00
CP01EN002 Book of Moon SR 125.00 250.00
CP01EN003 Metamorphosis SR 50.00 100.00
CP01EN004 Sakuretsu Armor SR 10.00 20.00
CP01EN005 Night Assailant SR 10.00 20.00
CP01EN006 Big Shield Gardna R .75 1.50
CP01EN007 Limiter Removal R .75 1.50
CP01EN008 Solemn Judgment R .75 1.50
CP01EN009 Reflect Bounder R .75 1.50
CP01EN010 Enemy Controller R .75 1.50
CP01EN011 Pot of Avarice R .75 1.50
CP01EN012 Thunder Kid C .60 1.25
CP01EN013 Mysterious Guard C .60 1.25
CP01EN014 King Tiger Wanghu C .60 1.25
CP01EN015 My Body as a Shield C .60 1.25
CP01EN016 Final Countdown C .60 1.25
CP01EN017 Mudora C .60 1.25
CP01EN018 Stealth Bird C .60 1.25
CP01EN019 Emissary of the Afterlife C .60 1.25
CP01EN020 Threatening Roar C .60 1.25

2006 Yu-Gi-Oh Collector Tins

CT03EN001 Elemental HERO Neos SCR 2.00 4.00
CT03EN002 Cyber Dragon SCR 2.50 5.00
CT03EN003 Raviel, Lord of Phantasms SCR 1.50 3.00
CT03EN004 Elemental HERO Shining Flare... SCR2.50 5.00
CT03EN005 Uria, Lord of Searing Flames SCR 2.50 5.00
CT03EN006 Hamon, Lord of Striking Thunder SCR2.00 4.00

2006 Yu-Gi-Oh Cyberdark Impact 1st Edition

CDIP1A Cyberdark Horn SR 1.25 2.50
CDIP1B Cyberdark Horn ULT 2.50 5.00
CDIP2A Cyberdark Edge SR 1.50 3.00
CDIP2B Cyberdark Edge ULT 4.00 8.00
CDIP3A Cyberdark Keel SR 1.25 2.50
CDIP3B Cyberdark Keel ULT 2.00 4.00
CDIP4 Cyber Ogre C .10 .20
CDIP5A Cyber Esper SR 1.00 2.00
CDIP5B Cyber Esper ULT 1.00 2.00
CDIP6 Allure Queen LV3 C .10 .20
CDIP7A Allure Queen LV5 R .50 1.00
CDIP7B Allure Queen LV5 ULT 2.00 4.00
CDIP8A Allure Queen LV7 UR 2.00 4.00
CDIP8B Allure Queen LV7 ULT 6.00 12.00
CDIP9 Dark Lucius LV4 C .10 .20
CDIP10A Dark Lucius LV6 R .50 1.00
CDIP10B Dark Lucius LV6 ULT 1.00 2.00
CDIP11A Dark Lucius LV8 UR 1.00 2.00
CDIP11B Dark Lucius LV8 ULT 2.50 5.00
CDIP12 Stray Asmodian C .10 .20
CDIP13 Abaki C .10 .20
CDIP14 Flame Ogre C .10 .20
CDIP15 Snipe Hunter C .50 1.00
CDIP16 Blast Asmodian C .10 .20
CDIP17 Vanity's Fiend R .50 1.00
CDIP17 Vanity's Fiend ULT 25.00 50.00
CDIP18 Barrier Statue of the Abyss C .10 .20
CDIP19 Barrier Statue of the Torrent C .10 .20
CDIP20 Barrier Statue of the Inferno C .10 .20
CDIP21 Barrier Statue of the Stormwinds C .10 .20
CDIP22 Barrier Statue of the Drought C .10 .20
CDIP23 Barrier Statue of the Heavens C .10 .20
CDIP24A Vanity's Ruler R 3.00 6.00
CDIP24B Vanity's Ruler ULT 6.00 12.00
CDIP25A Iris, the Earth Mother R .50 1.00
CDIP25B Iris, the Earth Mother ULT 1.00 2.00
CDIP26A Lightning Punisher R .50 1.00
CDIP26B Lightning Punisher ULT 1.00 2.00
CDIP27 Queen's Bodyguard C .10 .20
CDIP28 Combo Fighter C .10 .20
CDIP29A Combo Master R .50 1.00
CDIP29B Combo Master ULT 1.00 2.00
CDIP30 Man Beast of Ares C .10 .20
CDIP31A Rampaging Rhynos R .50 1.00
CDIP31B Rampaging Rhynos ULT 1.00 2.00
CDIP32A Storm Shooter SR .60 1.25
CDIP32B Storm Shooter ULT 1.00 2.00
CDIP33 Alien Infiltrator C .10 .20
CDIP34 Alien Mars C .10 .20
CDIP35A Cyberdark Dragon UR 2.00 4.00
CDIP35B Cyberdark Dragon ULT 15.00 30.00
CDIP36A Cyber Ogre 2 UR 1.25 2.50
CDIP36B Cyber Ogre 2 ULT 3.00 6.00
CDIP37 Corruption Cell A C .10 .20
CDIP38A Flash of the Forbidden Spell R .50 1.00
CDIP38B Flash of the Forbidden Spell ULT 1.00 2.00
CDIP39 Ritual Foregone C .10 .20
CDIP40 Instant Fusion C 2.50 5.00
CDIP41 Counter Cleaner C .10 .20
CDIP42 Linear Accelerator Cannon C .10 .20
CDIP43 Chain Strike C .10 .20
CDIP44A Miraculous Rebirth R .50 1.00
CDIP44B Miraculous Rebirth ULT 1.00 2.00
CDIP45 Mystical Wind Typhoon C .10 .20
CDIP46 Level Down!? C .10 .20
CDIP47A Degenerate Circuit R .50 1.00
CDIP47B Degenerate Circuit ULT 1.00 2.00
CDIP48 Senet Switch C .10 .20
CDIP49A Blasting Fuse R .50 1.00
CDIP49B Blasting Fuse ULT 1.00 2.00
CDIP50 Straight Flush C .10 .20
CDIP51 Justi-Break C .10 .20
CDIP52A Dimensional Inversion R .50 1.00
CDIP52B Dimensional Inversion ULT 1.00 2.00
CDIP53 Chain Healing C .10 .20
CDIP54 Chain Detonation C .10 .20
CDIP55 Byroad Sacrifice C .10 .20
CDIP56A Trojan Blast SR .60 1.25
CDIP56B Trojan Blast ULT 1.00 2.00
CDIP57 Accumulated Fortune C .10 .20
CDIP58A Cyber Shadow Gardna SR 1.00 2.00
CDIP58B Cyber Shadow Gardna ULT 3.00 6.00
CDIP59 Vanity's Call C .10 .20
CDIP60A Black Horn of Heaven R .50 1.00
CDIP60B Black Horn of Heaven ULT 5.00 10.00

2006 Yu-Gi-Oh Dark Revelation 3

DR3001 Charcoal Inpachi R .50 1.00
DR3002 Neo Aqua Madoor C .15 .30
DR3003 Skull Dog Marron C .15 .30
DR3004 Goblin Calligrapher C .15 .30
DR3005 Ultimate Insect LV1 R .50 1.00
DR3006 Horus the Black Flame Dragon LV4 R 1.50 3.00
DR3007 Horus the Black Flame Dragon LV6 SR 3.00 6.00
DR3008 Horus the Black Flame Dragon LV8 UR 5.00 10.00
DR3009 Dark Mimic LV1 C .15 .30
DR3010 Dark Mimic LV3 R .50 1.00
DR3011 Mystic Swordsman LV2 R 2.00 4.00
DR3012 Mystic Swordsman LV4 UR 2.50 5.00
DR3013 Armed Dragon LV3 C .15 .30
DR3014 Armed Dragon LV5 R .50 1.00
DR3015 Armed Dragon LV7 UR 5.00 10.00
DR3016 Horus' Servant C .15 .30
DR3017 Red-Eyes B. Chick C 1.00 2.00
DR3018 Malice Doll of Demise C .15 .30
DR3019 Ninja Grandmaster Sasuke R 1.50 3.00
DR3020 Rafflesia Seduction R .50 1.00
DR3021 Ultimate Baseball Kid .15 .30
DR3022 Mobius the Frost Monarch SR 6.00 12.00
DR3023 Element Dragon C .15 .30
DR3024 Element Soldier C .15 .30
DR3025 Howling Insect C .15 .30
DR3026 Masked Dragon C .15 .30
DR3027 Mind on Air R .50 1.00
DR3028 Unshaven Angler C .15 .30
DR3029 The Trojan Horse C .15 .30
DR3030 Nobleman-Eater Bug C .15 .30
DR3031 Enraged Muka Muka C .15 .30
DR3032 Hade-Hane C .15 .30
DR3033 Penumbral Soldier Lady SR 1.25 2.50
DR3034 Ojama King R .50 1.00
DR3035 Master of OZ R 1.50 3.00
DR3036 Sanwitch C .15 .30
DR3037 Dark Factory of Mass Production C 1.00 2.00
DR3038 Hammer Shot R .50 1.00
DR3039 Mind Wipe C .15 .30
DR3040 Abyssal Designator C .15 .30
DR3041 Level Up! C 1.00 2.00
DR3042 Inferno Fire Blast UR 5.00 10.00
DR3043 Ectoplasmer SR 1.25 2.50
DR3044 The Graveyard in the Fourth Dimension C.15 .30
DR3045 Two-Man Cell Battle C .15 .30
DR3046 Big Wave Small Wave C .15 .30
DR3047 Fusion Weapon C .15 .30
DR3048 Ritual Weapon C .15 .30
DR3049 Taunt C .15 .30
DR3050 Absolute End C .15 .30
DR3051 Spirit Barrier R 1.50 3.00
DR3052 Ninjitsu Art of Decoy C .15 .30
DR3053 Enervating Mist R .50 1.00
DR3054 Heavy Slump C .15 .30
DR3055 Greed SR 1.25 2.50
DR3056 Mind Crush C 1.50 3.00
DR3057 Null and Void SR 1.25 2.50
DR3058 Gorgon's Eye C .15 .30
DR3059 Cemetery Bomb C .15 .30
DR3060 Hallowed Life Barrier SR 1.25 2.50
DR3061 Woodborg Inpachi C .15 .30
DR3062 Mighty Guard C .15 .30
DR3063 Bokoichi the Freightening Car C .15 .30
DR3064 Harpie Girl C .15 .30
DR3065 The Creator UR 3.00 6.00
DR3066 The Creator Incarnate C .15 .30
DR3067 Ultimate Insect LV3 R .50 1.00
DR3068 Mystic Swordsman LV6 UR 5.00 10.00
DR3069 Silent Swordsman LV3 UR 1.25 2.50
DR3070 Nightmare Penguin C .15 .30
DR3071 Heavy Mech Support Platform C .15 .30
DR3072 Perfect Machine King UR 5.00 10.00
DR3073 Element Magician C .15 .30
DR3074 Element Saurus C .15 .30
DR3075 Roc from the Valley of Haze C .15 .30
DR3076 Sasuke Samurai #4 R .50 1.00
DR3077 Harpie Lady 1 C .15 .30
DR3078 Harpie Lady 2 C .15 .30
DR3079 Harpie Lady 3 C .15 .30
DR3080 Raging Flame Sprite C .15 .30
DR3081 Thestalos the Firestorm Monarch SR 2.50 5.00
DR3082 Eagle Eye C .15 .30
DR3083 Tactical Espionage Expert C .15 .30
DR3084 Invasion of Flames C .15 .30
DR3085 Creeping Doom Manta C .15 .30
DR3086 Pitch-Black Warwolf C .15 .30
DR3087 Mirage Dragon C .15 .30
DR3088 Gaia Soul the Combustible Collective R .50 1.00
DR3089 Fox Fire C .15 .30
DR3090 Big Core SR 1.25 2.50
DR3091 Fusilier Dragon, the Dual-Mode Beast R1.50 3.00
DR3092 Dekoichi the Battlechanted Locomotive R.50 1.00
DR3093 A-Team: Trap Disposal Unit R .50 1.00
DR3094 Homunculus the Alchemic Being C .15 .30
DR3095 Dark Blade the Dragon Knight R 1.50 3.00
DR3096 Mokey Mokey King C .15 .30
DR3097 Serial Spell R .50 1.00
DR3098 Harpies' Hunting Ground C .15 .30
DR3099 Triangle Ecstasy Spark SR 1.25 2.50
DR3100 Necklace of Command R .50 1.00
DR3101 Machine Duplication R 3.00 6.00
DR3102 Flint R .50 1.00
DR3103 Mokey Mokey Smackdown C .15 .30
DR3104 Back to Square One C .15 .30
DR3105 Monster Reincarnation SR 4.00 8.00
DR3106 Ballista of Rampart Smashing C .15 .30
DR3107 Lighten the Load C .15 .30
DR3108 Malice Dispersion C .15 .30
DR3109 Tragedy SR 1.25 2.50
DR3110 Divine Wrath SR 3.00 6.00
DR3111 Xing Zhen Hu C .15 .30
DR3112 Rare Metalmorph R .50 1.00
DR3113 Fruits of Kozaky's Studies C .15 .30
DR3114 Mind Haxorz C .15 .30
DR3115 Fuh-Rin-Ka-Zan C .15 .30
DR3116 Chain Burst R .50 1.00
DR3117 Pikeru's Circle of Enchantment SR 1.25 2.50
DR3118 Spell Purification C .15 .30
DR3119 Astral Barrier C .15 .30
DR3120 Covering Fire R .50 1.00
DR3121 Space Mambo C .15 .30
DR3122 Divine Dragon Ragnarok C 1.50 3.00
DR3123 Chu-Ske the Mouse Fighter C .15 .30
DR3124 Insect Knight C .15 .30
DR3125 Sacred Phoenix of Nephthys UR 2.50 5.00
DR3126 Hand of Nephthys C .15 .30
DR3127 Ultimate Insect LV5 R .50 1.00
DR3128 Silent Swordsman LV5 UR 2.50 5.00
DR3129 Granmarg the Rock Monarch SR 4.00 8.00
DR3130 Element Valkyrie C .15 .30
DR3131 Element Doom C .15 .30

DR3132 Maji-Gire Panda C .15 .30
DR3133 Catnipped Kitty C .15 .30
DR3134 Behemoth the King of All Animals SR 1.25 2.50
DR3135 Big-Tusked Mammoth R .50 1.00
DR3136 Kangaroo Champ C .15 .30
DR3137 Hyena C .15 .30
DR3138 Blade Rabbit C .15 .30
DR3139 Mecha-Dog Marron C .15 .30
DR3140 Blast Magician SR 1.25 2.50
DR3141 Chiron the Mage R .50 1.00
DR3142 Gearfried the Swordmaster UR 3.00 6.00
DR3143 Armed Samurai - Ben Kei C .15 .30
DR3144 Shadowslayer R .50 1.00
DR3145 Golem Sentry C .15 .30
DR3146 Abare Ushioni C .15 .30
DR3147 The Light - Hex-Sealed Fusion C .15 .30
DR3148 The Dark - Hex-Sealed Fusion C .15 .30
DR3149 The Earth - Hex-Sealed Fusion C .15 .30
DR3150 Whirlwind Prodigy C .15 .30
DR3151 Flame Ruler C .15 .30
DR3152 Firebird C .15 .30
DR3153 Rescue Cat C .15 .30
DR3154 Brain Jacker R .50 1.00
DR3155 Gatling Dragon UR 3.00 6.00
DR3156 King Dragun SR 6.00 12.00
DR3157 A Feather of the Phoenix SR 2.50 5.00
DR3158 Poison Fangs C .15 .30
DR3159 Spell Absorption R 5.00 10.00
DR3160 Lightning Vortex SR 3.00 6.00
DR3161 Meteor of Destruction R .50 1.00
DR3162 Swords of Concealing Light R 2.00 4.00
DR3163 Spiral Spear Strike R .50 1.00
DR3164 Release Restraint C .15 .30
DR3165 Centrifugal Field C .15 .30
DR3166 Fulfillment of the Contract C .15 .30
DR3167 Re-Fusion C 1.50 3.00
DR3168 The Big March of Animals C .15 .30
DR3169 Cross Counter R .50 1.00
DR3170 Pole Position C .15 .30
DR3171 Penalty Game! R .50 1.00
DR3172 Threatening Roar C 1.00 2.00
DR3173 Phoenix Wing Wind Blast R 1.50 3.00
DR3174 Good Goblin Housekeeping C .15 .30
DR3175 Beast Soul Swap C .15 .30
DR3176 Assault on GHQ R .50 1.00
DR3177 D.D. Dynamite C .15 .30
DR3178 Deck Devastation Virus SR 5.00 10.00
DR3179 Elemental Burst C .15 .30
DR3180 Forced Ceasefire R .50 1.00
DR3181 Elemental Hero Avian C .15 .30
DR3182 Elemental Hero Burstinatrix C .15 .30
DR3183 Elemental Hero Clayman C .15 .30
DR3184 Elemental Hero Sparkman C .15 .30
DR3185 Winged Kuriboh SR 3.00 6.00
DR3186 Ancient Gear Golem UR 4.00 8.00
DR3187 Ancient Gear Beast R .50 1.00
DR3188 Ancient Gear Soldier C .15 .30
DR3189 Millennium Scorpion R .50 1.00
DR3190 Ultimate Insect LV7 SR 3.00 6.00
DR3191 Lost Guardian C .15 .30
DR3192 Hieracosphinx SR 1.25 2.50
DR3193 Criosphinx R .50 1.00
DR3194 Moai Interceptor Cannons C .15 .30
DR3195 Megarock Dragon SR 1.25 2.50
DR3196 Dummy Golem C .15 .30
DR3197 Grave Ohja R .50 1.00
DR3198 Mine Golem C .15 .30
DR3199 Monk Fighter C .15 .30
DR3200 Master Monk SR 1.25 2.50
DR3201 Guardian Statue C .15 .30
DR3202 Medusa Worm C .15 .30
DR3203 D.D. Survivor R .50 1.00
DR3204 Mid Shield Gardna R .50 1.00
DR3205 White Ninja C .15 .30
DR3206 Aussa the Earth Charmer C .15 .30
DR3207 Eria the Water Charmer C .15 .30
DR3208 Hiita the Fire Charmer C .15 .30
DR3209 Wynn the Wind Charmer C .15 .30
DR3210 Batteryman AA C 1.00 2.00
DR3211 Des Wombat C .15 .30
DR3212 King of the Skull Servants C .15 .30
DR3213 Reshef the Dark Being UR 3.00 6.00
DR3214 Elemental Mistress Doriado R .50 1.00
DR3215 Elemental Hero Flame Wingman UR 4.00 8.00
DR3216 Elemental Hero Thunder Giant UR 3.00 6.00
DR3217 Card of Sanctity SR 1.25 2.50
DR3218 Brain Control SR 3.00 6.00
DR3219 Gift of the Martyr C .15 .30
DR3220 Double Attack C .15 .30
DR3221 Battery Charger C 1.00 2.00
DR3222 Kaminote Blow C .15 .30
DR3223 Doriado's Blessing C .15 .30
DR3224 Final Ritual of the Ancients C .15 .30
DR3225 Legendary Black Bel R .50 1.00
DR3226 Nitro Unit R .50 1.00
DR3227 Shifting Shadows C .15 .30
DR3228 Impenetrable Formation C .15 .30
DR3229 Hero Signal R .50 1.00
DR3230 Pikeru's Second Sight C .15 .30
DR3231 Minefield Eruption C .15 .30
DR3232 Kozaky's Self-Destruct Button R .50 1.00
DR3233 Mispolymerization C .15 .30
DR3234 Level Conversion Lab .15 .30
DR3235 Rock Bombardment C .15 .30
DR3236 Grave Lure C .15 .30
DR3237 Token Feastevil R .50 1.00
DR3238 Spell-Stopping StatuteRare R .50 1.00
DR3239 Royal Surrender R .50 1.00
DR3240 Lone Wolf C .15 .30

2006 Yu-Gi-Oh Duelist Pack Chazz Princeton 1st Edition

DP2EN001 V-Tiger Jet C .25 .50
DP2EN002 Ojama Green C .25 .50
DP2EN003 Ojama Yellow C .25 .50
DP2EN004 Ojama Black C .25 .50
DP2EN005 X-Head Cannon C .25 .50
DP2EN006 Y-Dragon Head C .25 .50
DP2EN007 Z-Metal Tank C .25 .50
DP2EN008 W-Wing Catapult C .25 .50
DP2EN009 Infernal Incinerator R .25 .50
DP2EN010 Armed Dragon LV3 C .25 .50
DP2EN011 Armed Dragon LV5 C .25 .50
DP2EN012 Armed Dragon LV7 SR 2.50 5.00
DP2EN013 Armed Dragon LV10 UR 15.00 30.00
DP2EN014 XYZ-Dragon Cannon R .25 .50
DP2EN015 Ojama King C .25 .50
DP2EN016 VW-Tiger Catapult R .25 .50
DP2EN017 VWXYZ-Dragon Catapult Cannon R .25 .50
DP2EN018 Ojama Delta Hurricane!! C .25 .50
DP2EN019 Level Modulation R .25 .50
DP2EN020 Ojamagic R .25 .50
DP2EN021 Ojamuscle R .25 .50
DP2EN022 Chthonian Alliance C .25 .50
DP2EN023 Armed Changer C .25 .50
DP2EN024 Magical Mallet SR 1.25 2.50
DP2EN025 Inferno Reckless Summon SR 3.00 6.00
DP2EN026 Ring of Defense UR 3.00 6.00
DP2EN027 Ojama Trio C .50 1.00
DP2EN028 Chtonian Blast C .25 .50
DP2EN029 Chthonian Polymer C .25 .50
DP2EN030 The Grave of Enkindling SR .25 .50

2006 Yu-Gi-Oh Duelist Pack Jaden Yuki 1st Edition

DP1EN001 Elemental HERO Avian C .25 .50
DP1EN002 Elemental HERO Burstinatrix C .25 .50
DP1EN003 Elemental HERO Clayman C .25 .50
DP1EN004 Elemental HERO Sparkman C .25 .50
DP1EN005 Winged Kuriboh R .75 1.50
DP1EN006 Winged Kuriboh LV10 R 1.25 2.50
DP1EN007 Wroughtweiler C .25 .50
DP1EN008 Dark Catapulter C .25 .50
DP1EN009 Elemental HERO Bubbleman C .25 .50
DP1EN010 Elemental HERO Flame Wingman SR 2.00 4.00
DP1EN011 Elemental HERO Thunder Giant R .75 1.50
DP1EN012 Elemental HERO Rampart Blaster R .75 1.50
DP1EN013 Elemental HERO Steam Healer UR 3.00 6.00
DP1EN014 Polymerization C .75 1.50
DP1EN015 Fusion Sage C .75 1.50
DP1EN016 The Warrior Returning Alive C .25 .50
DP1EN017 Feather Shot C .25 .50
DP1EN018 Transcendent Wings C .25 .50
DP1EN019 Bubble Shuffle C .25 .50
DP1EN020 Spark Blaster C .25 .50
DP1EN021 Skyscraper R 1.50 3.00
DP1EN022 Burst Return SR .25 .50
DP1EN023 Bubble Blaster SR .25 .50
DP1EN024 Bubble Illusion UR 1.50 3.00
DP1EN025 A Hero Emerges C .25 .50
DP1EN026 Draining Shield C .25 .50
DP1EN027 Negate Attack R .25 .50
DP1EN028 Hero Signal C .25 .50
DP1EN029 Feather Wind R .25 .50
DP1EN030 Clacy Charge SR .25 .50

2006 Yu-Gi-Oh Enemy of Justice 1st Edition

EOJ1 Destiny Hero - Doom Lord C .10 .20
EOJ2 Destiny Hero - Captain Tenacious C .10 .20
EOJ3A Destiny Hero - Diamond Dude R .50 1.00
EOJ3B Destiny Hero - Diamond Dude UTR 7.50 15.00
EOJ4A Destiny Hero - Dreadmaster UR 1.00 2.00
EOJ4B Destiny Hero - Dreadmaster UTR 5.00 10.00
EOJ5 Cyber Tutu C .10 .20
EOJ6 Cyber Gymnast C .10 .20
EOJ7A Cyber Prima SR .60 1.25
EOJ7B Cyber Prima UTR 1.00 2.00
EOJ8 Cyber Kirin C .10 .20
EOJ9A Cyber Phoenix SR .75 1.50
EOJ9B Cyber Phoenix UTR 3.00 6.00
EOJ10 Searchlightman C .10 .20
EOJ11A Victory Viper XX03 SR .60 1.25
EOJ11B Victory Viper XX03 UTR 1.25 2.50
EOJ12 Swift Birdman Joe C .10 .20
EOJ13A Harpie's Pet Baby Dragon R .50 1.00
EOJ13B Harpie's Pet Baby Dragon UTR 4.00 8.00
EOJ14 Majestic Mech - Senku C .10 .20
EOJ15A Majestic Mech - Ohka R .50 1.00
EOJ15B Majestic Mech - Ohka UTR 1.00 2.00
EOJ16A Majestic Mech - Goryu SR .60 1.25
EOJ16B Majestic Mech - Goryu UTR 1.00 2.00
EOJ17 Royal Knight C .10 .20
EOJ18A Herald of Green Light R .50 1.00
EOJ18B Herald of Green Light UTR 1.50 3.00
EOJ19A Herald of Purple Light R .50 1.00
EOJ19B Herald of Purple Light UTR 1.50 3.00
EOJ20 Bountiful Artemis C .10 .20
EOJ21 Layard the Liberator C .10 .20
EOJ22A Banisher of the Radiance R .60 1.25
EOJ22B Banisher of Radiance UTR 4.00 8.00
EOJ23A Voltanis the Adjudicator UR 1.50 3.00
EOJ23B Voltanis the Adjudicator UTR 2.50 5.00
EOJ24 Guard Dog C .10 .20
EOJ25 Whirlwind Weasel C .10 .20
EOJ26 Avalanching Aussa C .10 .20
EOJ27 Raging Eria C .10 .20
EOJ28 Blazing Hiita C .10 .20
EOJ29 Storming Wynn C .10 .20
EOJ30 Batteryman D C .10 .20
EOJ31A Super-Electromagnetic SR .60 1.25
EOJ31B Super-Electromagnetic UTR 1.25 2.50
EOJ32A Elem. Hero Phoenix UR 2.00 4.00
EOJ32B Elem. Hero Phoenix UTR 20.00 40.00
EOJ33A Elem. Hero Shining Phoenix UR 2.00 4.00
EOJ33B Elem. Hero Shining Phoenix UTR 20.00 40.00
EOJ34 Elemental Hero Mariner C .10 .20
EOJ35A Elemental Hero Wild Wingman SR .60 1.25
EOJ35B Elemental Hero Wild Wingman UTR 1.50 3.00
EOJ36 Elemental Hero Necroid Shaman C .10 .20
EOJ37 Misfortune C .10 .20
EOJ38 H - Heated Heart C .10 .20
EOJ39 E - Emergency Call C .10 .20
EOJ40 R - Righteous Justice C .10 .20
EOJ41 O - Oversoul C .10 .20
EOJ42A HERO Flash!! R .50 1.00
EOJ42B HERO Flash! UTR 1.00 2.00
EOJ43 Power Capsule C .10 .20
EOJ44 Celestial Transformation C .10 .20
EOJ45A Guard Penalty R .50 1.00
EOJ45B Guard Penalty UTR 1.00 2.00
EOJ46 Grand Convergence C .10 .20
EOJ47 Dimensional Fissure C .10 .20
EOJ48A Clock Tower Prison SR .60 1.25
EOJ48B Clock Tower Prison UTR 1.50 3.00
EOJ49A Life Equalizer R .75 1.50
EOJ49B Life Equilizer UTR 4.00 8.00
EOJ50 Elemental Recharge C .10 .20
EOJ51A Destruction of Destiny R .50 1.00
EOJ51B Destruction of Destiny UTR 1.00 2.00
EOJ52 Destiny Signal C .10 .20
EOJ53A D - Time R .50 1.00
EOJ53B D - Time UTR 1.00 2.00
EOJ54 D - Shield C .10 .20
EOJ55 Icarus Attack C .50 1.00
EOJ56A Elemental Absorber R .50 1.00
EOJ56B Elemental Absorber UTR 1.00 2.00
EOJ57 Macro Cosmos C .50 1.00
EOJ58A Miraculous Descent R .50 1.00
EOJ58B Miraculous Descent UTR 1.25 2.50
EOJ59 Shattered Axe C .10 .20
EOJ60A Forced Back R 1.50 3.00
EOJ60B Forced Back UTR 4.00 8.00

2006 Yu-Gi-Oh Power of the Duelist 1st Edition

POTD1 Elemental Hero Neos C .10 .20
POTD2 Sabersaurus C .10 .20
POTD3 Neo-Spacian Aqua Dolphin UTR 1.50 3.00
POTD3 Neo-Spacian Aqua Dolphin SR 2.50 5.00
POTD4 Neo Spacian Flare Scarab UTR 2.50 5.00
POTD4 Neo-Spacian Flare Scarab SR .60 1.25
POTD5 Neo-Spacian Dark Panther UTR 3.00 6.00
POTD5 Neo-Spacian Dark Panther SR .60 1.25
POTD6 Chryalis Dolphin C .10 .20
POTD7 Rallis The Star Bird C .10 .20
POTD8 Submarineroid UTR 1.50 3.00
POTD8 Submarineroid R .50 1.00
POTD9 Ambulanceroid C .10 .20
POTD10 Decoyroid C .10 .20
POTD11 Rescueroid C .10 .20
POTD12 Destiny Hero-Double Dude UTR 1.50 3.00
POTD12 Destiny Hero-Double Dude SR .60 1.25
POTD13 Destiny Hero-Defender C .10 .20
POTD14 Destiny Hero-Dogma UTR 4.00 8.00
POTD14 Destiny Hero-Dogma SR .60 1.25
POTD15 Destiny Hero-Blade Master C .10 .20
POTD16 Destiny Hero-Fear Monger C .10 .20
POTD17 Destiny Hero Dasher UTR 1.50 3.00
POTD17 Destiny Hero-Dasher R .50 1.00
POTD18 Black Ptera C .10 .20
POTD19 Black Stego C .10 .20
POTD20 Ultimate Tyranno UTR 2.00 4.00
POTD20 Ultimate Tyranno SR .60 1.25
POTD21 Miracle Jurassic Egg C .10 .20
POTD22 Babycerasaurus C .10 .20
POTD23 Bitelon C .10 .20
POTD24 Alien Grey C .10 .20
POTD25 Alien Skull C .10 .20
POTD26 Alien Hunter C .10 .20
POTD27 Alien Warrior UTR 2.00 4.00
POTD27 Alien Warrior R .50 1.00
POTD28 Alien Mother UTR 1.50 3.00
POTD28 Alien Mother R .50 1.00
POTD29 Cosmic Horror Gangi'el R .50 1.00
POTD29 Cosmic Horror Gangi'el UTR 1.50 3.00
POTD30 Flying Saucer Muusik'I C .10 .20
POTD31 Elemental Hero Aqua Neos UR 1.50 3.00
POTD31 Elemental Hero Aqua Neos UTR 1.50 3.00
POTD32 Elemental Hero Flare Neos UR 1.50 3.00
POTD32 Elemental Hero Flare Neos UTR 4.00 8.00
POTD33 Elemental Hero Dark Neos UR 1.50 3.00
POTD33 Elemental Hero Dark Neos UTR 5.00 10.00
POTD34 Chimeratech Overdragon UR 1.50 3.00
POTD34 Chimeratech Overdragon UTR 7.50 15.00
POTD35 Ambulance Rescueroid C .10 .20
POTD36 Super Vehicroid Jumbo Drill SR .60 1.25
POTD36 Super Vehicroid Jumbo Drill UTR 1.50 3.00
POTD37 Contact C .10 .20
POTD38 Fake Hero C .10 .20
POTD39 Spell Calling R .50 1.00
POTD39 Spell Calling UTR 1.50 3.00
POTD40 Vehicroid Connection Zone C .10 .20
POTD41 D-Spirit C .10 .20
POTD42 Overload Fusion R .60 1.25
POTD42 Overload Fusion UTR 5.00 10.00
POTD43 Cyclone Blade R .50 1.00
POTD43 Cyclone Blade UTR 1.50 3.00
POTD44 Future Fusion R .75 1.50
POTD44 Future Fusion UTR 5.00 10.00
POTD45 Common Soul C .10 .20
POTD46 Neo Space R .50 1.00
POTD46 Neo Space UTR 3.00 6.00
POTD47 Mausoleum of the Emperor C .10 .20
POTD48 Dark City R .50 1.00
POTD48 Dark City UTR 1.50 3.00
POTD49 Destiny Mirage C .10 .20
POTD50 D-Chain R .50 1.00
POTD50 D-Chain UTR 1.50 3.00
POTD51 Crop Circles C .10 .20
POTD52 The Paths of Destiny C .50 1.00
POTD53 Orbital Bombardment C .10 .20
POTD54 Royal Writ of Taxation C .10 .20
POTD55 Wonder Garage C .10 .20
POTD56 Supercharge R .50 1.00
POTD56 Supercharge UTR 1.50 3.00
POTD57 Cyber Summon Blaster R .50 1.00
POTD57 Cyber Summon Blaster UTR 1.50 3.00
POTD58 Fossil Excavation C .10 .20
POTD59 Synthetic Seraphim C .10 .20
POTD60 Brainwashing Beam C .10 .20

2006 Yu-Gi-Oh Shadow of Infinity 1st Edition

SOI1 Uria, Lord of Searing Flames UR 3.00 6.00
SOI1 Uria, Lord of Searing Flames UTR 75.00 150.00
SOI2 Hamon, Lord of Striking Thunder UTR 50.00 100.00
SOI2 Hamon, Lord of Striking Thunder UR 3.00 6.00
SOI3 Raviel, Lord of Phantasms UR 3.00 6.00
SOI3 Raviel, Lord of Phantasms UTR 30.00 75.00
SOI4 Elemental Hero Neo Bubbleman C .10 .20
SOI5 Hero Kid C .10 .20
SOI6 Cyber Barrier Dragon SR .60 1.25
SOI6 Cyber Barrier Dragon UTR 2.50 5.00
SOI7 Cyber Laser Dragon UTR 7.50 15.00
SOI7 Cyber Laser Dragon UR 3.00 6.00
SOI8 Ancient Gear C .10 .20
SOI9 Ancient Gear Cannon C .10 .20
SOI10 Proto-Cyber Dragon R .50 1.00
SOI10 Proto-Cyber Dragon UTR 3.00 6.00
SOI11 Adhesive Explosive UTR 1.00 2.00
SOI11 Adhesive Explosive R .50 1.00
SOI12 Machine King Prototype C .10 .20
SOI13 B.E.S. Covered Core SR .60 1.25
SOI13 B.E.S. Covered Core UTR 1.25 2.50
SOI14 D.D. Guide C .10 .20
SOI15 Chain Thrasher C .10 .20
SOI16 Disciple of the Forbidden Spell C .10 .20
SOI17 Tenkabito Shien C .10 .20
SOI18 Parasitic Ticky C .10 .20
SOI19 Gokipon C .10 .20
SOI20 Silent Insect C .10 .20
SOI21 Chainsaw Insect R .50 1.00
SOI21 Chainsaw Insect UTR 2.50 5.00
SOI22 Anteatereatingant C .10 .20
SOI23 Saber Beetle C .10 .20
SOI24 Doom Dozer R .60 1.25
SOI24 Doom Dozer UTR 3.00 6.00
SOI25 Treeborn Frog R .60 1.25
SOI25 Treeborn Frog UTR 7.50 15.00
SOI26 Beelze Frog C .10 .20
SOI27 Princess Pikeru R .50 1.00
SOI27 Princess Pikeru UTR 2.50 5.00
SOI28 Princess Curran R .50 1.00
SOI28 Princess Curran UTR 2.50 5.00
SOI29 Memory Crusher R .50 1.00
SOI29 Memory Crusher UTR .75 1.50
SOI30 Malice Ascendant C .10 .20
SOI31 Grass Phantom C .10 .20
SOI32 Sand Moth C .10 .20
SOI33 Divine Dragon - Excelion SR .60 1.25
SOI33 Divine Dragon-Excelion UTR 1.00 2.00
SOI34 Ruin, Queen of Oblivion SR .60 1.25
SOI34 Ruin, Queen of Oblivion UTR 3.00 6.00
SOI35 Demise, King of Armageddon SR 3.00 6.00
SOI35 Demise, King of Armageddon UTR 4.00 8.00
SOI36 D.3.S. Frog C .10 .20
SOI37 Hero Heart C .10 .20
SOI38 Magnet Circle LV2 C .10 .20
SOI39 Ancient Gear Factory C .10 .20
SOI40 Ancient Gear Drill C .10 .20
SOI41 Phantasmal Martyrs R .50 1.00
SOI41 Phantasmal Martyrs UTR 1.00 2.00
SOI42 Cyclone Boomerang R .50 1.00
SOI42 Cyclone Bommerang UTR 1.00 2.00
SOI43 Symbol of Heritage C .10 .20
SOI44 Trial of the Princesses C .10 .20
SOI45 Photon Generator Unit C .10 .20
SOI46 End of the World C .10 .20
SOI47 Ancient Gear Castle SR .60 1.25
SOI47 Ancient Gear Castle UTR 1.00 2.00
SOI48 Samsara C .10 .20
SOI49 Super Junior Confrontation C .10 .20
SOI50 Miracle Kids C .10 .20
SOI51 Attack Reflector Unit C .10 .20
SOI52 Damage Condenser SR .60 1.25
SOI52 Damage Condenser UTR 2.00 4.00
SOI53 Karma Cut UTR 6.00 12.00
SOI53 Karma Cut R .75 1.50
SOI54 Next to be Lost C .10 .20
SOI55 Generation Shift C .10 .20
SOI56 Full Salvo C .10 .20
SOI57 Success Probability 0% C .10 .20
SOI58 Option Hunter R .50 1.00
SOI58 Option Hunter UTR 1.00 2.00
SOI59 Goblin Out of the Frying Pan UTR 1.00 2.00
SOI59 Goblin Out of the Frying Pan R .50 1.00
SOI60 Malfunction UTR 1.00 2.00
SOI60 Malfunction R .50 1.00

2006 Yu-Gi-Oh Starter Deck 2006 1st Edition

YSDEN001 Gazelle the King of Mythical Beasts C .12 .25
YSDEN002 Warrior Dai Grepher C .15 .30
YSDEN003 Luster Dragon #2 C .10 .20
YSDEN004 Dark Blade C .12 .25
YSDEN005 Luster Dragon C .30 .60
YSDEN006 Warrior of Zera C .30 .60
YSDEN007 Elemental HERO Avian C .15 .30
YSDEN008 Elemental HERO Burstinatrix C .50 1.00
YSDEN009 Elemental HERO Clayman C .30 .75
YSDEN010 Elemental HERO Sparkman C .40 .80
YSDEN011 Skelengel C .12 .25
YSDEN012 Magician of Faith C .75 1.50
YSDEN013 Kuriboh C .20 .40
YSDEN014 Princess of Tsurugi C .20 .40
YSDEN015 Spear Dragon C .30 .75
YSDEN016 Spirit Caller C .20 .40
YSDEN017 The Trojan Horse C .12 .25
YSDEN018 Mirage Dragon C .15 .30
YSDEN019 Elemental HERO Bladedge UR .40 .80
YSDEN020 Ookazi C .30 .75
YSDEN021 Black Pendant C .15 .30
YSDEN022 Gaia Power C .30 .60
YSDEN023 Premature Burial C .30 .60
YSDEN024 Red Medicine C .30 .75
YSDEN025 Fissure C .10 .20
YSDEN026 Tribute to The Doomed C .30 .60
YSDEN027 Heavy Storm C 1.00 2.00
YSDEN028 The Warrior Returning Alive C .10 .20
YSDEN029 Dark Factory of Mass Production C .30 .75
YSDEN030 Monster Reincarnation C .10 .20
YSDEN031 Brain Control C .30 .75
YSDEN032 Reinforcements C .15 .30
YSDEN033 Castle Walls C .12 .25
YSDEN034 Ready for Intercepting C .15 .30

YSDEN035 Dust Tornado C .50 1.00
YSDEN036 Jar of Greed C .75 1.50
YSDEN037 Sakuretsu Armor C .75 1.50
YSDEN038 Compulsory Evacuation Device C .60 1.25
YSDEN039 Cemetery Bomb C .15 .30
YSDEN040 Magic Cylinder C .50 1.00
YSDENS01 Elemental HERO Sparkman UR 2.00 4.00

2006 Yu-Gi-Oh Dinosaur's Rage

SD9EN001 Super Conductor Tyranno UR .60 1.25
SD9EN002 Kabazauls C .20 .40
SD9EN003 Sabersaurus C .20 .40
SD9EN004 Mad Sword Beast C .20 .40
SD9EN005 Gilasaurus C .20 .40
SD9EN006 Dark Driceratops C .20 .40
SD9EN007 Hyper Hammerhead C .20 .40
SD9EN008 Black Tyranno C .20 .40
SD9EN009 Tyranno Infinity C .20 .40
SD9EN010 Hydrogeddon C .20 .40
SD9EN011 Oxygeddon C .20 .40
SD9EN012 Black Ptera C .20 .40
SD9EN013 Black Stego C .20 .40
SD9EN014 Ultimate Tyranno C .20 .40
SD9EN015 Miracle Jurassic Egg C .20 .40
SD9EN016 Babycerasaurus C .20 .40
SD9EN017 Big Evolution Pill C .20 .40
SD9EN018 Tail Swipe C .20 .40
SD9EN019 Jurassic World C .20 .40
SD9EN020 Sebek's Blessing C .20 .40
SD9EN021 Riryoku C .20 .40
SD9EN022 Mesmeric Control C .20 .40
SD9EN023 Mystical Space Typhoon C .60 1.25
SD9EN024 Megamorph C .20 .40
SD9EN025 Heavy Storm C .20 .40
SD9EN026 Lightning Vortex C .25 .50
SD9EN027 Magical Mallet C .75 1.50
SD9EN028 Hunting Instinct C .20 .40
SD9EN029 Survival Instinct C .20 .40
SD9EN030 Volcanic Eruption C .20 .40
SD9EN031 Seismic Shockwave C .20 .40
SD9EN032 Magical Arm Shield C .20 .40
SD9EN033 Negate Attack C .20 .40
SD9EN034 Goblin Out of the Frying Pan C .20 .40
SD9EN035 Malfunction C .20 .40
SD9EN036 Fossil Excavation C .20 .40
SD9ENSS1 Five-Headed Dragon UR .75 1.50

2006 Yu-Gi-Oh Structure Deck Invincible Fortress 1st Edition

SD7EN001 Exxod, Master of the Guard UR .60 1.25
SD7EN002 Great Spirit C .20 .40
SD7EN003 Giant Rat C .20 .40
SD7EN004 Maharaghi C .20 .40
SD7EN005 Guardian Sphinx C .20 .40
SD7EN006 Gigantes C .20 .40
SD7EN007 Stone Statue of the Aztecs C .25 .50
SD7EN008 Golem Sentry C .20 .40
SD7EN009 Hieracosphinx C .20 .40
SD7EN010 Criosphinx C .20 .40
SD7EN011 Moai Interceptor Cannons C .20 .40
SD7EN012 Megarock Dragon C .20 .40
SD7EN013 Guardian Statue C .20 .40
SD7EN014 Medusa Worm C .20 .40
SD7EN015 Sand Moth C .20 .40
SD7EN016 Canyon C .50 1.00
SD7EN017 Mystical Space Typhoon C .60 1.25
SD7EN018 Premature Burial C .20 .40
SD7EN019 Swords of Revealing Light C .20 .40
SD7EN020 Shield & Sword C .20 .40
SD7EN021 Magical Mallet C .75 1.50
SD7EN022 Hammer Shot C .20 .40
SD7EN023 Ectoplasmer C .20 .40
SD7EN024 Brain Control C .20 .40
SD7EN025 Shifting Shadows C .20 .40
SD7EN026 Waboku C .20 .40
SD7EN027 Ultimate Offering C .20 .40
SD7EN028 Magic Drain C .20 .40
SD7EN029 Robbin' Goblin C .20 .40
SD7EN030 Ordeal of a Traveler C .25 .50
SD7EN031 Reckless Greed C .50 1.00
SD7EN032 Compulsory Evacuation Device C .20 .40

2006 Yu-Gi-Oh Structure Deck Lord of the Storm 1st Edition

SD8EN001 Simorgh, Bird of Divinity UR .20 .40
SD8EN002 Sonic Shooter C .20 .40
SD8EN003 Sonic Duck C .20 .40
SD8EN004 Harpie Girl C .20 .40
SD8EN005 Slate Warrior C .20 .40
SD8EN006 Flying Kamakiri #1 C .20 .40
SD8EN007 Harpie Lady Sisters C .20 .40
SD8EN008 Bladefly C .20 .40
SD8EN009 Birdface C .20 .40
SD8EN010 Silpheed C .20 .40
SD8EN011 Lady Ninja Yae C .50 1.00
SD8EN012 Roc from the Valley of Haze C .20 .40
SD8EN013 Harpie Lady 1 C .20 .40
SD8EN014 Harpie Lady 2 C .20 .40
SD8EN015 Harpie Lady 3 C .20 .40
SD8EN016 Swift Birdman Joe C .20 .40
SD8EN017 Harpie's Pet Baby Dragon C .50 1.00
SD8EN018 Card Destruction C .20 .40
SD8EN019 Mystical Space Typhoon C .50 1.00
SD8EN020 Nobleman of Crossout C .20 .40
SD8EN021 Elegant Egotist C .20 .40
SD8EN022 Heavy Storm C .20 .40
SD8EN023 Reload C .20 .40
SD8EN024 Harpies' Hunting Ground C .20 .40
SD8EN025 Triangle Ecstasy Spark C .20 .40
SD8EN026 Lightning Vortex C .20 .40
SD8EN027 Hysteric Party C .50 1.00
SD8EN028 Aqua Chorus C .20 .40
SD8EN029 Dust Tornado C .20 .40
SD8EN030 Call of the Haunted C .20 .40
SD8EN031 Magic Jammer C .20 .40
SD8EN032 Dark Coffin C .20 .40
SD8EN033 Reckless Greed C .50 1.00
SD8EN034 Sakuretsu Armor C .20 .40
SD8EN035 Ninjitsu Art of Transformation C .50 1.00
SD8EN036 Icarus Attack C .60 1.25

2006 Yu-Gi-Oh Structure Deck Spellcaster's Judgment 1st Edition

SDEN6001 Dark Eradicator Warlock UR 2.00 4.00
SDEN6002 Mythical Beast Cerberus C .25 .50
SD6EN003 Dark Magician C .25 .50
SD6EN004 Gemini Elf C .25 .50
SD6EN005 Magician of Faith C .25 .50
SD6EN006 Skilled Dark Magician C .25 .50
SD6EN007 Apprentice Magician C .25 .50
SD6EN008 Chaos Command Magician C 1.25 2.50
SD6EN009 Breaker the Magical Warrior C .25 .50
SD6EN010 Royal Magical Library C .60 1.25
SD6EN011 Tsukuyomi C .60 1.25
SD6EN012 Chaos Sorcerer C .25 .50
SD6EN013 White Magician Pikeru C .25 .50
SD6EN014 Blast Magician C .25 .50
SD6EN015 Ebon Magician Curran C .25 .50
SD6EN016 Rapid-Fire Magician C .25 .50
SD6EN017 Magical Blast C .25 .50
SD6EN018 Mystical Space Typhoon C .60 1.25
SD6EN019 Nobleman of Crossout C .25 .50
SD6EN020 Premature Burial C .25 .50
SD6EN021 Swords of Revealing Light C .25 .50
SD6EN022 Mage Power C .25 .50
SD6EN023 Heavy Storm C .25 .50
SD6EN024 Diffusion Wave-Motion C .25 .50
SD6EN025 Reload C .25 .50
SD6EN026 Dark Magic Attack C .25 .50
SD6EN027 Spell Absorption C .75 1.50
SD6EN028 Lightning Vortex C .25 .50
SD6EN029 Magical Dimension C .25 .50
SD6EN030 Mystic Box C .50 1.00
SD6EN031 Nightmare's Steelcage C .25 .50
SD6EN032 Call of the Haunted C .25 .50
SD6EN033 Spell Shield Type-8 C .25 .50
SD6EN034 Pitch-Black Power Stone C .25 .50
SD6EN035 Divine Wrath C .25 .50
SD6EN036 Magic Cylinder C .50 1.00

2006 Yu-Gi-Oh Tournament Pack 7

TP7EN001 D.D. Warrior UR 6.00 12.00
TP7EN002 Warrior Eliminator SR 3.00 6.00
TP7EN003 Fortress Whale SR 50.00 100.00
TP7EN004 Luminous Soldier SR 2.00 4.00
TP7EN005 Breaker the Magical Warrior SR 10.00 20.00
TP7EN006 Goblin Attack Force R 1.00 2.00
TP7EN007 Amazoness Swords Woman R 2.00 4.00
TP7EN008 Chaos Command Magician R 2.00 4.00
TP7EN009 Scapegoat R .75 1.50
TP7EN010 Soul Exchange C .75 1.50
TP7EN011 Fortress Whale's Oath C .75 1.50
TP7EN012 Skilled Dark Magician C .75 1.50
TP7EN013 Skilled White Magician C .75 1.50
TP7EN014 Wall of Illusion C .75 1.50
TP7EN015 Last Will C .75 1.50
TP7EN016 Haniwa C .75 1.50
TP7EN017 Prisman C .75 1.50
TP7EN018 Millennium Golem C .75 1.50
TP7EN019 Dig Break C .75 1.50
TP7EN020 Nekogal #2 C .75 1.50

2006 Yu-Gi-Oh Tournament Pack 8

TP8EN001 Magical Arm Shield UR 10.00 20.00
TP8EN002 Harpies Feather Duster SR 100.00 200.00
TP8EN003 Slate Warrior SR 25.00 50.00
TP8EN004 Dunames Dark Witch SR 10.00 20.00
TP8EN005 Garma Sword SR 25.00 50.00
TP8EN006 Zaborg the Thunder Monarch R .75 1.50
TP8EN007 Granmarg the Rock Monarch R .75 1.50
TP8EN008 Mobius Frost Monarch R .75 1.50
TP8EN009 Thestalos the Firestorm Monarch R .75 1.50
TP8EN010 Garma Sword Oath C .75 1.50
TP8EN011 Berserk Gorilla C .75 1.50
TP8EN012 Ultimate Offering C .75 1.50
TP8EN013 Gatekeeper C .75 1.50
TP8EN014 Behegon C .75 1.50
TP8EN015 Violent Rain C .75 1.50
TP8EN016 Temple of Skulls C .75 1.50
TP8EN017 Blocker C .75 1.50
TP8EN018 Wretched Ghost of the Attic C .75 1.50
TP8EN019 Sectarian of Secrets C .75 1.50
TP8EN020 Necrolancer the Timelord C .75 1.50

2007 Yu-Gi-Oh Champion Pack Game Four

CP04EN001 Germa UR 4.00 8.00
CP04EN002 Ultimate Offering SR 7.50 15.00
CP04EN003 Bottomless Trap Hole SR 100.00 200.00
CP04EN004 Apprentice Magician SR 4.00 8.00
CP04EN005 Hydrogeddon SR 2.50 5.00
CP04EN006 Confiscation R .75 1.50
CP04EN007 Freed the Brave Wanderer R .75 1.50
CP04EN008 Divine Sword - Phoenix Blade R .75 1.50
CP04EN009 Return from the Different Dimension R .75 1.50
CP04EN010 Kinetic Soldier R .75 1.50
CP04EN011 Magician's Circle R .75 1.50
CP04EN012 Soul Exchange C .50 1.00
CP04EN013 Mother Grizzly C .50 1.00
CP04EN014 Grand Tiki Elder C .50 1.00
CP04EN015 Gigantes C .50 1.00
CP04EN016 Robbin' Goblin C .50 1.00
CP04EN017 Manju of the Ten Thousand Hands C .50 1.00
CP04EN018 Hand of Nephthys C .50 1.00
CP04EN019 D.D. Survivor C .50 1.00
CP04EN020 Treeborn Frog C .50 1.00

2007 Yu-Gi-Oh Champion Pack Game Three

CP03EN001 Magicians Unite UR 4.00 8.00
CP03EN002 Spirit Reaper SR 7.50 15.00
CP03EN003 Gravekeeper's Spy SR 15.00 30.00
CP03EN004 Sniper Hunter SR 5.00 10.00
CP03EN005 Dark World Lightning SR 2.50 5.00
CP03EN006 D.D. Assailant R .50 1.00
CP03EN007 Goldd Wu-Lord of Dark World R .50 1.00
CP03EN008 Manticore of Darkness R .50 1.00
CP03EN009 The Agent of Judgment - Saturn R .50 1.00
CP03EN010 Pikeru's Circle of Enchantment R .50 1.00
CP03EN011 Widespread Ruin R .50 1.00
CP03EN012 Fairy Dragon C .50 1.00
CP03EN013 Chiron the Mage C .50 1.00
CP03EN014 Kaibaman C .50 1.00
CP03EN015 B.E.S. Crystal Core C .50 1.00
CP03EN016 Gravekeeper's Chief C .50 1.00
CP03EN017 Wild Nature's Release C .50 1.00
CP03EN018 A Feather of the Phoenix C .50 1.00
CP03EN019 Contract with the Abyss C .50 1.00
CP03EN020 Necrovalley C .50 1.00

2007 Yu-Gi-Oh Champion Pack Game Two

CP02EN001 Magical Stone Excavation UR 10.00 20.00
CP02EN002 Nimble Momonga SR 5.00 10.00
CP02EN003 Magician of Faith SR 25.00 50.00
CP02EN004 Pyramid Turtle SR 3.00 6.00
CP02EN005 Smashing Ground SR 5.00 10.00
CP02EN006 Kuriboh R 2.00 4.00
CP02EN007 Abyss Soldier R 1.00 2.00
CP02EN008 Ring of Destruction R 2.00 4.00
CP02EN009 Morphing Jar R 4.00 8.00
CP02EN010 Dark Master - Zorc R 1.00 2.00
CP02EN011 Magical Dimension R 1.00 2.00
CP02EN012 Happy Lover C 3.00 6.00
CP02EN013 Rush Recklessly C .20 .40
CP02EN014 Ceasefire C .75 1.50
CP02EN015 Thunder Dragon C .75 1.50
CP02EN016 Twin-Headed Behemoth C .75 1.50
CP02EN017 Book of Taiyou C .75 1.50
CP02EN018 Terraforming C .75 1.50
CP02EN019 Big Bang Shot C .20 .40
CP02EN020 Stray Lambs C .20 .40

2007 Yu-Gi-Oh Collector Tins

CT04EN001 Elemental HERO Grand Neos SCR .75 1.50
CT04EN002 Crystal Beast Sapphire Pegasus SCR 2.00 4.00
CT04EN003 Destiny HERO - Plasma SCR 1.25 2.50
CT04EN004 Volcanic Doomfire SCR 1.25 2.50
CT04EN005 Rainbow Dragon SCR 2.50 5.00
CT04EN006 Elemental HERO Plasma Vice SCR 2.00 4.00

2007 Yu-Gi-Oh Dark Revelation 4

DR041 Cycroid C .25 .50
DR042 Soitsu C .25 .50
DR043 Mad Lobster C .25 .50
DR044 Jerry Beans Man C .25 .50
DR045 Winged Kuriboh LV10 UR 3.00 6.00
DR046 Patroid C .25 .50
DR047 Gyroid R .25 .50
DR048 Steamroid R .50 1.00
DR049 Drillroid SR 1.50 3.00
DR0410 UFOroid C .50 1.00
DR0411 Jetroid C .25 .50
DR0412 Wroughtweiler C .25 .50
DR0413 Dark Catapulter C .25 .50
DR0414 Elemental Hero Bubbleman C 1.00 2.00
DR0415 Cyber Dragon UR 10.00 20.00
DR0416 Cybernetic Magician R .50 1.00
DR0417 Cybernetic Cyclopean C .25 .50
DR0418 Mechanical Hound C 3.00 6.00
DR0419 Cyber Archfiend C .25 .50
DR0420 Goblin Elite Attack Force SR 1.50 3.00
DR0421 B.E.S. Crystal Core SR 1.50 3.00
DR0422 Giant Kozaky C .25 .50
DR0423 Indomitable Fighter Lei Lei C .25 .50
DR0424 Protective Soul Ailin C .25 .50
DR0425 Doitsu C .25 .50
DR0426 Des Frog C .50 1.00
DR0427 T.A.D.P.O.L.E. C .25 .50
DR0428 Poison Draw Frog C .25 .50
DR0429 Tyranno Infinity R .50 1.00
DR0430 Batteryman C C .25 .50
DR0431 Ebon Magician Curran C .25 .50
DR0432 D.D.M. Different Dimension R 2.50 5.00
DR0433 Steam Gyroid C .25 .50
DR0434 UFOroid Fighter R 1.50 3.00
DR0435 Cyber Twin Dragon UR 3.00 6.00
DR0436 Cyber End Dragon UR 5.00 10.00
DR0437 Power Bond SR 3.00 6.00
DR0438 Fusion Recovery C .25 .50
DR0439 Miracle Fusion SR 5.00 10.00
DR0440 Dragon's Mirror SR 25.00 50.00
DR0441 System Down R 2.50 5.00
DR0442 Des Croaking C .25 .50
DR0443 Pot of Generosity C .25 .50
DR0444 Shien's Spy C .25 .50
DR0445 Transcendent Wings C .60 1.25
DR0446 Bubble Shuffle C .25 .50
DR0447 Spark Blaster C .25 .50
DR0448 Skyscraper R .50 1.00
DR0449 Fire Darts C .25 .50
DR0450 Spiritual Earth Art - Kurogane C .25 .50
DR0451 Spiritual Water Art - Aoi C .25 .50
DR0452 Spiritual Fire Art - Kurenai C .25 .50
DR0453 Spiritual Wind Art - Miyabi C .25 .50
DR0454 A Rival Appears! C .25 .50
DR0455 Magical Explosion C .25 .50
DR0456 Rising Energy R .50 1.00
DR0457 D.D. Trap Hole C .25 .50
DR0458 Conscription C .25 .50
DR0459 Dimension Wall R 3.00 6.00
DR0460 Prepare to Strike Back C .25 .50
DR0461 Zure, Knight of Dark World C .25 .50
DR0462 V-Tiger Jet C .25 .50
DR0463 Blade Skater C .25 .50
DR0464 Queen's Knight R 2.50 5.00
DR0465 Jack's Knight R 2.50 5.00
DR0466 King's Knight R 2.50 5.00
DR0467 Elemental Hero Bladedge SR 1.50 3.00
DR0468 Elemental Hero Wildheart SR 3.00 6.00
DR0469 Reborn Zombie C .25 .50
DR0470 Chthonian Soldier C .25 .50
DR0471 W-Wing Catapult C .25 .50
DR0472 Infernal Incinerator C .25 .50
DR0473 Hydrogeddon SR 1.50 3.00
DR0474 Oxygeddon C .25 .50
DR0475 Water Dragon R 1.50 3.00
DR0476 Etoile Cyber C .25 .50
DR0477 B.E.S. Tetran SR 1.50 3.00
DR0478 Nanobreaker C .25 .50
DR0479 Rapid-Fire Magician R 1.50 3.00
DR0480 Beiige, Vanguard of Dark World C .25 .50
DR0481 Broww, Huntsman of Dark World R 1.50 3.00
DR0482 Brron, Mad King of Dark World R 2.50 5.00
DR0483 Sillva, Warlord of Dark World UR 3.00 6.00
DR0484 Goldd, Wu-Lord of Dark World UR 3.00 6.00
DR0485 Scarr, Scout of Dark World C .25 .50
DR0486 Familiar-Possessed - Aussa C .25 .50
DR0487 Familiar-Possessed - Eria C .25 .50
DR0488 Familiar-Possessed - Hiita C .25 .50
DR0489 Familiar-Possessed - Wynn C .25 .50
DR0490 VW-Tiger Catapult C .25 .50
DR0491 VWXYZ-Dragon Catapult Cannon R .50 1.00
DR0492 Cyber Blader R 1.00 2.00
DR0493 Elemental Hero Rampart Blaster R 5.00 10.00
DR0494 Elemental Hero Tempest SR 1.50 3.00
DR0495 Elemental Hero Wildedge R .50 1.00
DR0496 Elem. Hero Shining Flare UR 6.00 12.00
DR0497 Pot of Avarice UR 7.50 15.00
DR0498 Dark World Lightning R .50 1.00
DR0499 Level Modulation C .25 .50
DR04100 Ojamagic R .50 1.00
DR04101 Ojamuscle C .25 .50
DR04102 Feather Shot C .25 .50
DR04103 Bonding - H2O C .25 .50
DR04104 Chthonian Alliance C .25 .50
DR04105 Armed Changer C .25 .50
DR04106 Branch! C .25 .50
DR04107 Boss Rush C .25 .50
DR04108 Gateway to Dark World C .25 .50
DR04109 Hero Barrier C .25 .50
DR04110 Chthonian Blast C .25 .50
DR04111 The Forces of Darkness C .25 .50
DR04112 Dark Deal R 1.50 3.00
DR04113 Simultaneous Loss C .25 .50
DR04114 Weed Out C .25 .50
DR04115 The League of Uniform Nomenclature C .25 .50
DR04116 Roll Out! C .25 .50
DR04117 Chthonian Polymer C .25 .50
DR04118 Feather Wind C .25 .50
DR04119 Non-Fusion Area C 1.00 2.00
DR04120 Level Limit - Area A R .50 1.00
DR04121 Uria, Lord of Searing Flames UR 4.00 8.00
DR04122 Hamon, Lord of Striking Thunder UR 4.00 8.00
DR04123 Raviel, Lord of Phantasms UR 4.00 8.00
DR04124 Elemental Hero Neo Bubbleman C .25 .50
DR04125 Hero Kid R .50 1.00
DR04126 Cyber Barrier Dragon R .50 1.00
DR04127 Cyber Laser Dragon R .50 1.00
DR04128 Ancient Gear C .25 .50
DR04129 Ancient Gear Cannon C .25 .50
DR04130 Proto-Cyber Dragon SR 1.50 3.00
DR04131 Adhesive Explosive C .25 .50
DR04132 Machine King Prototype C .25 .50
DR04133 B.E.S. Covered Core SR 1.50 3.00
DR04134 D.D. Guide C .25 .50
DR04135 Chain Thrasher C .25 .50
DR04136 Disciple of the Forbidden Spell C .25 .50
DR04137 Tenkabito Shien R 2.50 5.00
DR04138 Parasitic Ticky C .25 .50
DR04139 Gokipon C .25 .50
DR04140 Silent Insect C .25 .50
DR04141 Chainsaw Insect R .50 1.00
DR04142 Anteatereatingant R .50 1.00
DR04143 Saber Beetle R .50 1.00
DR04144 Doom Dozer R 4.00 8.00
DR04145 Treeborn Frog UR 10.00 20.00
DR04146 Beelze Frog C .25 .50
DR04147 Princess Pikeru R 1.50 3.00
DR04148 Princess Curran R .50 1.00
DR04149 Memory Crusher C .25 .50
DR04150 Malice Ascendant C .25 .50
DR04151 Grass Phantom C .25 .50
DR04152 Sand Moth R .50 1.00
DR04153 Divine Dragon - Excelion SR 1.50 3.00
DR04154 Ruin, Queen of Oblivion SR 1.50 3.00
DR04155 Demise, King of Armageddon SR 2.50 5.00
DR04156 D.3.S. Frog C .25 .50
DR04157 Hero Heart C .25 .50
DR04158 Magnet Circle LV2 C .25 .50
DR04159 Ancient Gear Factory C .25 .50
DR04160 Ancient Gear Drill R .50 1.00
DR04161 Phantasmal Martyrs C .25 .50
DR04162 Cyclone Boomerang C .25 .50
DR04163 Symbol of Heritage C .25 .50
DR04164 Trial of the Princesses C .25 .50
DR04165 Photon Generator Unit C .25 .50
DR04166 End of the World C 1.00 2.00
DR04167 Ancient Gear Castle SR 1.50 3.00
DR04168 Samsara C .25 .50
DR04169 Super Junior Confrontation C .25 .50
DR04170 Miracle Kids C .25 .50
DR04171 Attack Reflector Unit C .25 .50
DR04172 Damage Condenser SR 1.50 3.00
DR04173 Karma Cut SR 7.50 15.00
DR04174 Next to be Lost C .25 .50
DR04175 Generation Shift C 1.00 2.00
DR04176 Full Salvo C .25 .50
DR04177 Success Probability 0 C .25 .50
DR04178 Option Hunter C .25 .50
DR04179 Goblin Out of the Frying Pan R .50 1.00
DR04180 Malfunction R .50 1.00
DR04181 Destiny Hero - Doom Lord R 7.50 15.00
DR04182 Destiny Hero - Captain Tenacious C .25 .50
DR04183 Destiny Hero - Diamond Dude SR 4.00 8.00
DR04184 Destiny Hero - Dreadmaster R 1.00 2.00
DR04185 Cyber Tutu C .50 1.00
DR04186 Cyber Gymnast R .50 1.00
DR04187 Cyber Prima R 1.50 3.00
DR04188 Cyber Kirin C .25 .50

DR04189 Cyber Phoenix UR 3.00 6.00
DR04190 Searchlightman C .25 .50
DR04191 Victory Viper XX03 SR 1.50 3.00
DR04192 Swift Birdman Joe C .25 .50
DR04193 Harpie's Pet Baby Dragon R 1.50 3.00
DR04194 Majestic Mech - Senku C .25 .50
DR04195 Majestic Mech - Ohka SR 1.50 3.00
DR04196 Majestic Mech - Goryu SR 1.50 3.00
DR04197 Royal Knight C .25 .50
DR04198 Herald of Green Light R 1.50 3.00
DR04199 Herald of Purple Light R 1.50 3.00
DR04200 Bountiful Artemis SR 60.00 125.00
DR04201 Layard the Liberator C .25 .50
DR04202 Banisher of the Radiance SR 5.00 10.00
DR04203 Voltanis the Adjudicator UR 3.00 6.00
DR04204 Guard Dog C .25 .50
DR04205 Whirlwind Weasel C .25 .50
DR04206 Avalanching Aussa C .25 .50
DR04207 Raging Eria C .25 .50
DR04208 Blazing Hiita C .25 .50
DR04209 Storming Wynn C .25 .50
DR04210 Batteryman D C .25 .50
DR04211 Super-Electromagnetic UR 3.00 6.00
DR04212 Elemental Hero Phoenix Enforcer R .50 1.00
DR04213 Elem. Hero Shining Phoenix UR 3.00 6.00
DR04214 Elemental Hero Mariner C .25 .50
DR04215 Elemental Hero Wild Wingman R 3.00 6.00
DR04216 Elemental Hero Necroid Shaman C .25 .50
DR04217 Misfortune C .25 .50
DR04218 H - Heated Heart C .25 .50
DR04219 E - Emergency Call C .60 1.25
DR04220 R - Righteous Justice C .25 .50
DR04221 O - Oversoul C .25 .50
DR04222 HERO Flash!! C .25 .50
DR04223 Power Capsule C .25 .50
DR04224 Celestial Transformation R .50 1.00
DR04225 Guard Penalty R .50 1.00
DR04226 Grand Convergence R .50 1.00
DR04227 Dimensional Fissure R 2.50 5.00
DR04228 Clock Tower Prison R .50 1.00
DR04229 Life Equalizer R 1.50 3.00
DR04230 Elemental Recharge C .25 .50
DR04231 Destruction of Destiny C .25 .50
DR04232 Destiny Signal R .50 1.00
DR04233 D - Time C .25 .50
DR04234 D - Shield C .25 .50
DR04235 Icarus Attack SR 20.00 40.00
DR04236 Elemental Absorber C .25 .50
DR04237 Macro Cosmos SR 15.00 30.00
DR04238 Miraculous Descent SR 1.50 3.00
DR04239 Shattered Axe C .25 .50
DR04240 Forced Back R 3.00 6.00
DR04241 Satellite Cannon SCR 10.00 20.00
DR04242 Gilford the Lightning SCR 5.00 10.00
DR04243 Exarion Universe SCR 25.00 50.00
DR04244 D.D. Assailant SCR 10.00 20.00
DR04245 Kaibaman SCR 15.00 30.00

2007 Yu-Gi-Oh Duelist Pack Aster Phoenix 1st Edition

DP05EN001 Destiny HERO - Doom Lord C .25 .50
DP05EN002 Destiny HERO - Captain Tenacious C .25 .50
DP05EN003 Destiny HERO - Diamond Dude C .25 .50
DP05EN004 Destiny HERO - Dreadmaster R .25 .50
DP05EN005 Destiny HERO - Double Dude R .25 .50
DP05EN006 Destiny HERO - Defender R .25 .50
DP05EN007 Destiny HERO - Dogma R .25 .50
DP05EN008 Destiny HERO - Blade Master C .25 .50
DP05EN009 Destiny HERO - Fear Monger R .25 .50
DP05EN010 Destiny HERO - Dasher C .25 .50
DP05EN011 Destiny HERO - Malicious UR 4.00 8.00
DP05EN012 Elemental HERO Phoenix Enforcer R .75 1.50
DP05EN013 Elemental HERO
Shining Phoenix Enforcer SR 1.50 3.00
DP05EN014 Misfortune C .25 .50
DP05EN015 Guard Penalty C .25 .50
DP05EN016 Clock Tower Prison R .25 .50
DP05EN017 D - Spirit C .25 .50
DP05EN018 Cyclone Blade C .25 .50
DP05EN019 Dark City C .25 .50
DP05EN020 Destiny Draw UR 4.00 8.00
DP05EN021 Over Destiny SR .25 .50
DP05EN022 Elemental Recharge C .25 .50
DP05EN023 Destruction of Destiny C .25 .50
DP05EN024 Destiny Signal C .25 .50
DP05EN025 D - Time C .25 .50
DP05EN026 D - Shield C .25 .50
DP05EN027 Destiny Mirage C .25 .50
DP05EN028 D - Chain C .25 .50
DP05EN029 D - Counter SR .25 .50
DP05EN030 Eternal Dread SR .25 .50

2007 Yu-Gi-Oh Duelist Pack Jaden Yuki 2 1st Edition

DP03EN001 Elemental HERO Neos C .25 .50
DP03EN002 Elemental HERO Bladedge R .25 .50
DP03EN003 Elemental HERO Wildheart C .25 .50
DP03EN004 Hero Kid C .25 .50
DP03EN005 Neo-Spacian Aqua Dolphin R .50 1.00
DP03EN006 Neo-Spacian Flare Scarab R .50 1.00
DP03EN007 Neo-Spacian Dark Panther R .50 1.00
DP03EN008 Chrysallis Dolphin C .25 .50
DP03EN009 Card Trooper UR 3.00 6.00
DP03EN010 Elemental HERO Wildedge R 1.25 2.50
DP03EN011 Elemental HERO Wild Wingman C .25 .50
DP03EN012 Elemental HERO Aqua Neos R .25 .50
DP03EN013 Elemental HERO Flare Neos R .25 .50
DP03EN014 Elemental HERO Dark Neos SR .75 1.50
DP03EN015 Cyclone Boomerang C .25 .50
DP03EN016 H - Heated Heart C .25 .50
DP03EN017 E - Emergency Call C .25 .50
DP03EN018 R - Righteous Justice C .25 .50
DP03EN019 O - Oversoul C .25 .50
DP03EN020 Hero Flash!! C .25 .50
DP03EN021 Contact C .25 .50
DP03EN022 Fake Hero C .25 .50
DP03EN023 Common Soul C .25 .50
DP03EN024 Neo Space C .25 .50
DP03EN025 Light Laser SR .25 .50
DP03EN026 Burial from a Different Dimension UR 3.00 6.00
DP03EN027 Hero Barrier C .25 .50
DP03EN028 Miracle Kids C .25 .50
DP03EN029 Edge Hammer SR .25 .50
DP03EN030 Kid Guard SR .25 .50

2007 Yu-Gi-Oh Duelist Pack Zane Truesdale 1st Edition

DP04EN001 Cyber Dragon R 1.25 2.50
DP04EN002 Cyber Barrier Dragon R .25 .50
DP04EN003 Cyber Laser Dragon R 1.25 2.50
DP04EN004 Prot-Cyber Dragon C .25 .50
DP04EN005 Cyber Kirin C .25 .50
DP04EN006 Cyber Phoenix C .25 .50
DP04EN007 Cyberdark Horn C 1.25 2.50
DP04EN008 Cyberdark Edge C .75 1.50
DP04EN009 Cyberdark Keel C .75 1.50
DP04EN010 Infernal Dragon UR 2.50 5.00
DP04EN011 Cyber Twin Dragon R .25 .50
DP04EN012 Cyber End Dragon R 2.00 4.00
DP04EN013 Chimeratech Overdragon R .60 1.25
DP04EN014 Cyberdark Dragon SR .75 1.50
DP04EN015 Mystical Space Typhoon C .50 1.00
DP04EN016 Limiter Removal C .25 .50
DP04EN017 De-Fusion C .75 1.50
DP04EN018 Creature Swap C .25 .50
DP04EN019 Different Dimension Capsule C .50 1.00
DP04EN020 Power Bond R .25 .50
DP04EN021 Photon Generator Unit C .25 .50
DP04EN022 Overload Fusion C .25 .50
DP04EN023 Future Fusion C .60 1.25
DP04EN024 Ruthless Denial SR .25 .50
DP04EN025 Call of the Haunted C .25 .50
DP04EN026 Trap Jammer C .50 1.00
DP04EN027 Attack Reflector Unit C .25 .50
DP04EN028 Return Soul SR .25 .50
DP04EN029 Damage Polarizer UR 1.25 2.50
DP04EN030 Fusion Guard SR .25 .50

2007 Yu-Gi-Oh Force of the Breaker 1st Edition

FOTB00 Volcanic Rocket SCR 15.00 30.00
FOTB01 Crystal Beast Ruby Carbuncle C .20 .40
FOTB02 Crystal Beast Amethyst Cat C .20 .40
FOTB03 Crystal Beast Emerald Tortoise C .20 .40
FOTB04 Crystal Beast Topaz Tiger UTR 7.50 15.00
FOTB04 Crystal Beast Topaz Tiger R .60 1.25
FOTB05 Crystal Beast Amber Mammoth C .20 .40
FOTB06 Crystal Beast Cobalt Eagle C .20 .40
FOTB07 Crystal Beast Sapphire Pegasus UTR 15.00 30.00
FOTB07 Crystal Beast Sapphire Pegasus UR 2.00 4.00
FOTB08 Volcanic Doomfire UTR 2.50 5.00
FOTB08 Volcanic Doomfire UR 1.25 2.50
FOTB09 Volcanic Shell UTR 5.00 10.00
FOTB09 Volcanic Shell R 1.50 3.00
FOTB10 Volcanic Scattershot C .20 .40
FOTB11 Volcanic Blaster C .20 .40
FOTB12 Volcanic Slicer UTR 2.50 5.00
FOTB12 Volcanic Slicer R .60 1.25
FOTB13 Volcanic Hammerer C .20 .40
FOTB14 Elemental Hero Captain Gold UTR 2.00 4.00
FOTB14 Elemental Hero Captain Gold UR .75 1.50
FOTB15 Gravekeeper's Commandant UTR 3.00 6.00
FOTB15 Gravekeeper's Commandant R .75 1.50
FOTB16 Warrior of Atlantis UTR 1.25 2.50
FOTB16 Warrior of Atlantis R .50 1.00
FOTB17 Destroyersaurus UTR .75 1.50
FOTB17 Destroyersaurus R .60 1.25
FOTB18 Zeradias, Herald of Heaven UTR 5.00 10.00
FOTB18 Zeradias, Herald of Heaven R .60 1.25
FOTB19 Archfiend General UTR 1.50 3.00
FOTB19 Archfiend General R .75 1.50
FOTB20 Harpie Queen UTR 20.00 40.00
FOTB20 Harpie Queen R 1.50 3.00
FOTB21 Sky Scourge Enrise UTR 1.00 2.00
FOTB21 Sky Scourge Enrise SR .60 1.25
FOTB22 Sky Scourge Norleras UTR 7.50 15.00
FOTB22 Sky Scourge Norleras SR .60 1.25
FOTB23 Sky Scourge Invicil UTR 1.25 2.50
FOTB23 Sky Scourge Invicil SR .60 1.25
FOTB24 Goe Goe the Gallant Ninja R .50 1.00
FOTB24 Goe Goe the Gallant Ninja UTR .75 1.50
FOTB25 Mei-Kou, Master of Barriers C .20 .40
FOTB26 Raiza the Storm Monarch SR 1.25 2.50
FOTB26 Raiza the Storm Monarch UTR 6.00 12.00
FOTB27 Seismic Crasher C .20 .40
FOTB28 Dweller in the Depths C .20 .40
FOTB29 Magna-Slash Dragon C .20 .40
FOTB30 Gravi-Crush Dragon C .20 .40
FOTB31 Soul of Fire SR .60 1.25
FOTB31 Soul of Fire UTR .75 1.50
FOTB32 Crystal Beacon C .20 .40
FOTB33 Rare Value UR .75 1.50
FOTB33 Rare Value UTR 3.00 6.00
FOTB34 Crystal Blessing C .20 .40
FOTB35 Crystal Abundance C .20 .40
FOTB36 Crystal Promise C .20 .40
FOTB37 Lucky Iron Axe R .50 1.00
FOTB37 Lucky Iron Axe UTR 1.00 2.00
FOTB38 Tornado C .20 .40
FOTB39 Wild Fire C .20 .40
FOTB40 Blaze Accelerator C .20 .40
FOTB41 Tri-Blaze Accelerator SR 1.00 2.00
FOTB41 Tri-Blaze Accelerator UTR 2.00 4.00
FOTB42 Field Barrier C .20 .40
FOTB43 A Cell Breeding Device C .20 .40
FOTB44 Otherworld - The A Zone C .20 .40
FOTB45 Ancient City - Rainbow Ruins R .50 1.00
FOTB45 Ancient City - Rainbow Ruins UTR 7.50 15.00
FOTB46 Triggered Summon R .50 1.00
FOTB46 Triggered Summon UTR 1.00 2.00
FOTB47 Last Resort C .20 .40
FOTB48 Crystal Raigeki C .20 .40
FOTB49 Volcanic Recharge C .20 .40
FOTB50 Terrible Deal C .20 .40
FOTB51 Breakthrough! C .20 .40
FOTB52 Backs to the Wall C .20 .40
FOTB53 Introduction to Gallantry C .20 .40
FOTB54 Secrets of the Gallant C .20 .40
FOTB55 Radiant Mirror Force SR .75 1.50
FOTB55 Radiant Mirror Force UTR 3.00 6.00
FOTB56 Hard-sellin' Goblin C .20 .40
FOTB57 Hard-sellin' Zombie C .20 .40
FOTB58 Mass Hypnosis C .20 .40
FOTB59 Gem Flash Energy C .20 .40
FOTB60 Firewall R .50 1.00
FOTB60 Firewall UTR 1.00 2.00
FOTB61 Diabolos, King of the Abyss SCR 3.00 6.00
FOTB62 Lich Lord, King SCR 1.25 2.50
FOTB63 Prometheus, King of the Shadows SCR 1.50 3.00
FOTB64 Mist Archfield SCR 2.00 4.00
FOTB65 Plague Wolf SCR 1.00 2.00
FOTB66 Recurring Nightmare SCR 5.00 10.00
FOTB67 Sword of Dark Rites SCR 1.25 2.50
FOTB68 Eradicator Epidemic SCR 7.50 15.00

2007 Yu-Gi-Oh Gladiator's Assault 1st Edition

GLAS0 Gladiator Beast Octavius SCR 1.50 3.00
GLAS1 Chamberlain of Six Samurai C .20 .40
GLAS2 Cloudian Smoke Ball C .20 .40
GLAS3 Evil Hero Malicious Edge SR .60 1.25
GLAS3 Evil Hero Malicious Edge UTR 2.00 4.00
GLAS4 Evil Hero Infernal Gainer R .50 1.00
GLAS5 Cloudian Eye of Typhoon SR .60 1.25
GLAS5 Cloudian Eye of Typhoon UTR 1.00 2.00
GLAS6 Cloudian Ghost Fog C .20 .40
GLAS7 Cloudian Nimbusman C .20 .40
GLAS8 Cloudian Sheep Cloud SR .60 1.25
GLAS8 Cloudian Sheep Cloud UTR 1.00 2.00
GLAS9 Cloudian Poison Cloud C .20 .40
GLAS10 Cloudian Acid Cloud R .50 1.00
GLAS11 Cloudian Cirrostratus R .75 1.50
GLAS12 Cloudian Altus R .50 1.00
GLAS13 Cloudian Turbulence C .20 .40
GLAS14 Truckroid C .20 .40
GLAS15 Stealthroid C .20 .40
GLAS16 Expressroid R .50 1.00
GLAS17 Gladiator Beast Alexander SR .60 1.25
GLAS17 Gladiator Beast Alexander UTR 1.00 2.00
GLAS18 Gladiator Beast Spartacus R .50 1.00
GLAS19 Gladiator Beast Murmillo R .50 1.00
GLAS20 Gladiator Beast Bestiari C .20 .40
GLAS21 Gladiator Beast Laquari R .60 1.25
GLAS22 Gladiator Beast Hoplomus C .20 .40
GLAS23 Gladiator Beast Dimacari C .20 .40
GLAS24 Gladiator Beast Secutor C .20 .40
GLAS25 Test Ape C .20 .40
GLAS26 Witch Doctor of Sparta C .20 .40
GLAS27 Infinity Dark C .20 .40
GLAS28 Magical Reflect Slime C .20 .40
GLAS29 Ancient Gear Knight C .20 .40
GLAS30 Goblin Black Ops R .50 1.00
GLAS31 Gambler of Legend C .20 .40
GLAS32 Enishi, Shiens Chancellor UR .75 1.50
GLAS32 Enishi, Shiens Chancellor UTR 1.50 3.00
GLAS33 Spirit of the Six Samurai C .20 .40
GLAS34 Alien Telepath R .50 1.00
GLAS35 Alien Hypno C .20 .40
GLAS36 Elemental Hero Chaos
Neos GR/Rainbow ERR 100.00 200.00
GLAS36 Elemental Hero Chaos Neos SCR 2.00 4.00
GLAS36 Elemental Hero Chaos Neos GR 7.50 15.00
GLAS37 Elemental Hero Plasma Vice SCR 2.50 5.00
GLAS38 Evil Hero Inferno Wing UR .75 1.50
GLAS38 Evil Hero Inferno Wing UTR 2.00 4.00
GLAS39 Evil Hero Lightning Golem UR .75 1.50
GLAS39 Evil Hero Lightning Golem UTR 1.25 2.50
GLAS40 Evil Hero Dark Gaia R .50 1.00
GLAS41 Super Vehicroid Stealth Union SCR 4.00 8.00
GLAS42 Superalloy Beast Raptinus C .20 .40
GLAS43 Gladiator Beast Galodiaz R .50 1.00
GLAS44 Gladiator Beast Heraklinos SCR 4.00 8.00
GLAS45 Contact Out C .20 .40
GLAS46 Swing of Memories C .20 .40
GLAS47 Dark Fusion R 1.50 3.00
GLAS48 Diamond-Dust Cyclone R .50 1.00
GLAS49 Summon Cloud C .20 .40
GLAS50 Lucky Cloud C .20 .40
GLAS51 Fog Control C .20 .40
GLAS52 Cloudian Squall C .20 .40
GLAS53 Super Double Summon C .20 .40
GLAS54 Colosseum Cage Gladiatr Beasts R 1.25 2.50
GLAS55 Glad.Beasts Bttle Halberd C .20 .40
GLAS56 Glad. Beasts Battle Gladius C .20 .40
GLAS57 Glad.Beasts Battle Manica R .50 1.00
GLAS58 Gladiator Beasts Respite R .50 1.00
GLAS59 Gladiators Return C .20 .40
GLAS60 Soul Devouring Bamboo Sword C .20 .40
GLAS61 Cunning of the Six Samurai SR .60 1.25
GLAS61 Cunning of the Six Samurai UTR 1.50 3.00
GLAS62 A Cell Incubator C .20 .40
GLAS63 Over Limit C .20 .40
GLAS64 No Entry!! C .20 .40
GLAS65 Natural Disaster C .20 .40
GLAS66 Rain Storm C .20 .40
GLAS67 Updraft SR .60 1.25
GLAS67 Updraft UTR 1.00 2.00
GLAS68 Release from Stone C .20 .40
GLAS69 Light-Imprisoning Mirror C .60 1.25
GLAS70 Shadow-Imprisoning Mirror C .60 1.25
GLAS71 Disarm C .20 .40
GLAS72 Parry C .20 .40
GLAS73 Swiftstrike Armor C .20 .40
GLAS74 DoubleEdged Sword Tech C .20 .40
GLAS75 Energy-Absorbing Monolith SR .60 1.25
GLAS75 Energy-Absorbing Monolith UTR 1.00 2.00
GLAS76 Cell Explosion Virus R .50 1.00
GLAS77 Detonator Circle A C .20 .40
GLAS78 Interdimensional Warp C .20 .40
GLAS79 Foolish Revival C .20 .40
GLAS80 An Unfortunate Report C .20 .40
GLAS81 Gladiator Beast Torax SR .60 1.25
GLAS81 Gladiator Beast Torax UTR 1.00 2.00
GLAS82 Test Tiger UR .75 1.50
GLAS82 Test Tiger UTR 4.00 8.00
GLAS83 Defensive Tactics SR .60 1.25
GLAS83 Defensive Tactics UTR 1.00 2.00
GLAS84 Dragon Ice SCR 4.00 8.00
GLAS85 Tongue Twister SCR 4.00 8.00
GLAS86 Skreech SCR 1.50 3.00
GLAS87 Royal Firestorm Guards SCR 15.00 30.00
GLAS88 Veil of Darkness SCR 2.00 4.00
GLAS89 Security Orb UR .75 1.50
GLAS89 Security Orb UTR 25.00 50.00
GLAS90 Necroface SCR 50.00 100.00
GLAS91 Gil Garth SCR 7.50 15.00
GLAS92 Soul Taker SCR 20.00 40.00
GLAS93 Magic Formula SCR 50.00 100.00
GLAS94 Silent Doom SCR 15.00 30.00

2007 Yu-Gi-Oh Premium Pack 1

PP01EN001 Magician of Black Chaos SCR 5.00 10.00
PP01EN002 Black Magic Ritual SCR .75 1.50
PP01EN003 Marshmallon SCR 3.00 6.00
PP01EN004 Marshmallon Glasses SCR .40 .80
PP01EN005 Gemini Imps SCR .50 1.00
PP01EN006 Return Zombie SCR .25 .50
PP01EN007 Shield Crush SCR .20 .40
PP01EN008 Dark Magic Curtain SCR .75 1.50
PP01EN009 Legacy of Yata-Garasu SCR 15.00 30.00
PP01EN009 Legacy of Yata-Garasu SR .75 1.50
PP01EN010 Zera Ritual SCR 4.00 8.00
PP01EN010 Zera Ritual SR .20 .40
PP01EN011 Zera the Mant SCR 25.00 50.00
PP01EN011 Zera the Mant SR .30 .60
PP01EN012 Javelin Beetle Pact SCR 3.00 6.00
PP01EN012 Javelin Beetle Pact SR .15 .30
PP01EN013 Javelin Beetle SCR 7.50 15.00
PP01EN013 Javelin Beetle SR .12 .25
PP01EN014 Metalmorph SCR 6.00 12.00
PP01EN014 Metalmorph SR .25 .50
PP01EN015 Red-Eyes Black Metal Dragon SCR 25.00 50.00
PP01EN015 Red-Eyes Black Metal Dragon SR .60 1.25

2007 Yu-Gi-Oh Starter Deck Jaden Yuki 1st Edition

YSDJEN000 Elemental HERO Necroshade UR 2.00 4.00
YSDJEN001 Cyber-Tech Alligator C .75 1.50
YSDJEN002 Gemini Elf C .30 .60
YSDJEN003 Dark Blade C .15 .30
YSDJEN004 Sonic Duck C .15 .30
YSDJEN005 Elemental HERO Avian C .60 1.25
YSDJEN006 Elemental HERO Burstinatrix C 1.25 2.50
YSDJEN007 Elemental HERO Clayman C .75 1.50
YSDJEN008 Elemental HERO Sparkman C .50 1.00
YSDJEN009 Poison Mummy C .15 .30
YSDJEN010 Mask of Darkness C .25 .50
YSDJEN011 Exiled Force C .30 .60
YSDJEN012 Little-Winguard C .25 .50
YSDJEN013 Mataza the Zapper C .20 .40
YSDJEN014 Ninja Grandmaster Sasuke C 1.00 2.00
YSDJEN015 Chiron the Mage C .12 .25
YSDJEN016 Shadowslayer C .30 .75
YSDJEN017 Elemental HERO Bubbleman SR .75 1.50
YSDJEN018 Elemental HERO Bladedge C .40 .80
YSDJEN019 Elemental HERO Wildheart C .60 1.25
YSDJEN020 Cybernetic Cyclopean C .12 .25
YSDJEN021 Rush Recklessly C .30 .60
YSDJEN022 Giant Trunade C .75 1.50
YSDJEN023 Lightning Blade C .75 1.50
YSDJEN024 Heavy Storm C 1.50 3.00
YSDJEN025 Banner of Courage C .15 .30
YSDJEN026 Smashing Ground C 1.00 2.00
YSDJEN027 Necklace of Command C .30 .60
YSDJEN028 Monster Reincarnation C .15 .30
YSDJEN029 Lightning Vortex C .75 1.50
YSDJEN030 Brain Control C .75 1.50
YSDJEN031 R - Righteous Justice C .15 .30
YSDJEN032 Lucky Iron Axe C .12 .25
YSDJEN033 Dust Tornado C .60 1.25
YSDJEN034 Trap Hole C .12 .25
YSDJEN035 Magic Jammer C .50 1.00
YSDJEN036 Sakuretsu Armor C .60 1.25
YSDJEN037 Compulsory Evacuation Device C .40 .80
YSDJEN038 Draining Shield C 2.50 5.00
YSDJEN039 Negate Attack C .30 .75
YSDJEN040 Magic Cylinder C .12 .25

2007 Yu-Gi-Oh Starter Deck Syrus Truesdale 1st Edition

YSDSEN000 Expressroid UR .75 1.50
YSDSEN001 Cyber-Tech Alligator C .60 1.25
YSDSEN002 Robotic Knight C .50 1.00
YSDSEN003 Dark Blade C .15 .30
YSDSEN004 Acrobat Monkey C .15 .30
YSDSEN005 Archfiend Soldier C 1.00 2.00
YSDSEN006 Cycroid C .40 .80
YSDSEN007 Jerry Beans Man C .50 1.00
YSDSEN008 Zure, Knight of Dark World C .20 .40
YSDSEN009 Poison Mummy C .30 .75
YSDSEN010 Mask of Darkness C .40 .80
YSDSEN011 Dekoichi the
Battlechanted Locomotive C 1.50 3.00
YSDSEN012 Chiron the Mage C .50 1.00
YSDSEN013 Patroid C .30 .75
YSDSEN014 Gyroid C .40 .80
YSDSEN015 Steamroid C .50 1.00
YSDSEN016 Drillroid SR .75 1.50
YSDSEN017 Submarineroid C .60 1.25
YSDSEN020 Abaki C .15 .30
YSDSEN021 Black Pendant C .15 .30
YSDSEN023 Giant Trunade C .75 1.50
YSDSEN024 Heavy Storm C 2.50 5.00
YSDSEN025 Book of Moon C .50 1.00
YSDSEN026 Smashing Ground C .30 .75
YSDSEN027 Enemy Controller C .30 .75
YSDSEN028 Earthquake C .15 .30
YSDSEN029 A Feather of the Phoenix C .25 .50
YSDSEN030 Lightning Vortex C 1.25 2.50
YSDSEN031 Brain Control C .50 1.00
YSDSEN032 Trap Hole C .15 .30
YSDSEN033 Magic Jammer C .50 1.00

YSDSEN034 Seven Tools of the Bandit C	.15	.30
YSDSEN035 Sakuretsu Armor C	.75	1.50
YSDSEN036 Threatening Roar C	.75	1.50
YSDSEN037 Negate Attack C	.75	1.50
YSDSEN038 Magic Cylinder C	1.25	2.50
YSDSEN039 Rising Energy C	.20	.40
YSDSEN040 Supercharge C	.15	.30

2007 Yu-Gi-Oh Strike of Neos 1st Edition

STON1A Gene-Warped Warwolf SR	.75	1.50
STON1B Gene-Warped Warwolf UTR	1.50	3.00
STON2A Frostosaurus R	.50	1.00
STON2B Frostosaurus UTR	2.00	4.00
STON3A Spiral Serpent R	.50	1.00
STON3B Spiral Serpent UTR	1.00	2.00
STON4A Neo-Spacian Air Hummingbird SR	.75	1.50
STON4B Neo-Spacian Air Hummingbird UTR	2.50	5.00
STON5A Neo-Spacian Grand Mole R	.75	1.50
STON5B Neo-Spacian Grand Mole UTR	6.00	12.00
STON6 Neo-Spacian Glow Moss C	.10	.20
STON7 The Six Samurai - Yaichi C	.10	.20
STON8 The Six Samurai - Kamon C	.10	.20
STON9 The Six Samurai - Yariza C	.10	.20
STON10 The Six Samurai - Nisashi C	.10	.20
STON11 The Six Samurai - Zanji C	.10	.20
STON12 The Six Samurai - Irou C	.10	.20
STON13A Great Shogun Shien SR	.60	1.25
STON13B Great Shogun Shien UTR	3.00	6.00
STON14 Shien's Footsoldier C	.10	.20
STON15A Sage of Silence R	.50	1.00
STON15B Sage of Silence UTR	1.25	2.50
STON16 Sage of Stillness C	.10	.20
STON17A Reign-Beaux, Overlord of Dark World UR	1.00	2.00
STON17B Reign-Beaux, Overlord of Dark World UTR	2.00	4.00
STON18 Kahkki, Guerilla of Dark World C	.10	.20
STON19 Gren, Tactician of Dark World C	.10	.20
STON20A Fusion Devourer R	.50	1.00
STON20B Fusion Devourer UTR	1.00	2.00
STON21 Electric Virus C	.10	.20
STON22 Puppet Plant C	.10	.20
STON23 Marionette Mite C	.10	.20
STON24A D.D. Crow R	.50	1.00
STON24B D.D. Crow UTR	6.00	12.00
STON25 Silent Abyss C	.10	.20
STON26 Firestorm Prominence C	.10	.20
STON27 Raging Earth C	.10	.20
STON28 Destruction Cyclone C	.10	.20
STON29 Radiant Spirit C	.10	.20
STON30 Umbral Soul C	.10	.20
STON31 Alien Psychic C	.10	.20
STON32 Lycanthrope C	.10	.20
STON33 Cú Chulainn the Awakened C	.10	.20
STON34A Elemental Hero Air Neos UR	7.50	15.00
STON34B Elemental Hero Air Neos UTR	15.00	30.00
STON35A Elemental Hero Grand Neos UR	1.00	2.00
STON35B Elemental Hero Grand Neos UTR	5.00	10.00
STON36A Elemental Hero Glow Neos UR	1.50	3.00
STON36B Elemental Hero Glow Neos UTR	3.00	6.00
STON37A Ancient Rules R	2.00	4.00
STON37B Ancient Rules UTR	6.00	12.00
STON38A Dark World Dealings SR	2.00	4.00
STON38B Dark World Dealings UTR	7.50	15.00
STON39A Neos Force R	.50	1.00
STON39B Neos Force UTR	1.00	2.00
STON40 Legendary Ebon Steed C	.10	.20
STON41 A Cell Scatter Burst C	.10	.20
STON42A Twister R	.50	1.00
STON42B Twister UTR	2.50	5.00
STON43 Synthesis Spell C	.10	.20
STON44 Emblem of the Awakening C	.10	.20
STON45 Advanced Ritual Art C	.10	.20
STON46A Card Trader SR	.60	1.25
STON46B Card Trader UTR	1.25	2.50
STON47 Shien's Castle of Mist C	.10	.20
STON48A Skyscraper 2 - Hero City SR	1.25	2.50
STON48B Skyscraper 2 - Hero City UTR	2.00	4.00
STON49 Change of Hero - Reflector Ray C	.10	.20
STON50A Hero Medal R	.50	1.00
STON50B Hero Medal UTR	1.00	2.00
STON51 Return of the Six Samurai C	.10	.20
STON52A Eliminating the League R	.50	1.00
STON52B Eliminating the League UTR	1.00	2.00
STON53 Flashbang C	.10	.20
STON54A The Transmigration Prophecy R	.50	1.00
STON54B The Transmigration Prophecy UTR	2.00	4.00
STON55 Anti-Fusion Device C	.10	.20
STON56 Ritual Sealing C	.10	.20
STON57A Birthright SR	.60	1.25
STON57B Birthright UTR	1.00	2.00
STON58 Swift Samurai Storm!	.10	.20
STON59A Cloak and Dagger R	.50	1.00
STON59B Cloak and Dagger UTR	1.50	3.00
STON60A Pulling the Rug R	.50	1.00
STON60B Pulling the Rug UTR	2.00	4.00
STON61 Neo-Parshath, Sky Paladin SCR	2.00	4.00
STON62 Meltiel, Sage of the Sky SCR	4.00	8.00
STON63 Harvest Angel of Wisdom SCR	2.00	4.00
STON64 Freya, Spirit of Victory SCR	6.00	12.00
STON65 Nova Summoner SCR	2.50	5.00
STON66 Radiant Jeral SCR	1.50	3.00
STON67 Gellenduo SCR	5.00	10.00
STON68 Aegis of Gaia SCR	1.25	2.50
STON0 Grandmaster of Six Samurai SCR	7.50	15.00

2007 Yu-Gi-Oh Structure Deck Machine Re-Volt 1st Edition

SD10EN001 Ancient Gear Dragon Gadjiltron UR	.50	1.00
SD10EN002 Ancient Gear Gadjiltron Chimera C	.25	.50
SD10EN003 Ancient Gear Engineer C	.60	1.25
SD10EN004 Boot-Up Soldier - Dread Dynamo C	.25	.50
SD10EN005 Mechanicalchaser C	.25	.50
SD10EN006 Green Gadget C	.25	.50
SD10EN007 Red Gadget C	.25	.50
SD10EN008 Yellow Gadget C	.25	.50
SD10EN009 Cannon Soldier C	.25	.50
SD10EN010 Gear Golem the Moving Fortress C	.25	.50
SD10EN011 Heavy Mech Support Platform C	.25	.50
SD10EN012 Ancient Gear Golem C	.25	.50
SD10EN013 Ancient Gear Beast C	.25	.50
SD10EN014 Ancient Gear Soldier C	.25	.50
SD10EN015 Ancient Gear C	.25	.50
SD10EN016 Ancient Gear Cannon C	.25	.50
SD10EN017 Ancient Gear Workshop C	.50	1.00
SD10EN018 Ancient Gear Tank C	.25	.50
SD10EN019 Ancient Gear Explosive C	.25	.50
SD10EN020 Ancient Gear Fist C	.25	.50
SD10EN021 Ancient Gear Factory C	.25	.50
SD10EN022 Ancient Gear Drill C	.25	.50
SD10EN023 Ancient Gear Castle C	.25	.50
SD10EN024 Mystical Space Typhoon C	.50	1.00
SD10EN025 Limiter Removal C	.25	.50
SD10EN026 Heavy Storm C	.25	.50
SD10EN027 Enemy Controller C	.25	.50
SD10EN028 Weapon Change C	.25	.50
SD10EN029 Machine Duplication C	1.25	2.50
SD10EN030 Pot of Avarice C	.25	.50
SD10EN031 Stronghold the Moving Fortress C	.25	.50
SD10EN032 Ultimate Offering C	.25	.50
SD10EN033 Sakuretsu Armor C	.25	.50
SD10EN034 Micro Ray C	.25	.50
SD10EN035 Rare Metalmorph C	.25	.50
SD10EN036 Covering Fire C	.25	.50
SD10EN037 Roll Out! C	.25	.50

2007 Yu-Gi-Oh Structure Deck Rise of the Dragon Lords 1st Edition

SDRLEN001 Felgrand Dragon UR	.60	1.25
SDRLEN002 Darkblaze Dragon C	.20	.40
SDRLEN003 Herald of Creation C	.20	.40
SDRLEN004 Decoy Dragon C	.40	.80
SDRLEN005 Spear Cretin C	.20	.40
SDRLEN006 Gilford the Lightning C	.30	.60
SDRLEN007 Morphing Jar C	2.00	4.00
SDRLEN008 Kaiser Sea Horse C	.15	.30
SDRLEN009 Tyrant Dragon C	.50	1.00
SDRLEN010 Twin-Headed Behemoth C	.15	.30
SDRLEN011 Guardian Angel Joan C	.50	1.00
SDRLEN012 Horus the Black Flame Dragon LV6 C	.25	.50
SDRLEN013 Masked Dragon C	.30	.75
SDRLEN014 The Creator C	.25	.50
SDRLEN015 The Creator Incarnate C	.20	.40
SDRLEN016 Flame Ruler C	.15	.30
SDRLEN017 Majestic Mech - Goryu C	.15	.30
SDRLEN018 Snipe Hunter C	.40	.80
SDRLEN019 Trade-In C	.60	1.25
SDRLEN020 Foolish Burial C	.75	1.50
SDRLEN021 Soul Exchange C	.15	.30
SDRLEN022 Giant Trunade C	.50	1.00
SDRLEN023 The Shallow Grave C	.60	1.25
SDRLEN024 Premature Burial C	.25	.50
SDRLEN025 A Wingbeat of Giant Dragon C	.30	.60
SDRLEN026 Terraforming C	.25	.50
SDRLEN027 Big Bang Shot C	.15	.30
SDRLEN028 Mystik Wok C	2.50	5.00
SDRLEN029 Lightning Vortex C	.50	1.00
SDRLEN030 Brain Control C	.25	.50
SDRLEN031 Mausoleum of the Emperor C	.20	.40
SDRLEN032 Malevolent Catastrophe C	.20	.40
SDRLEN033 Dust Tornado C	.30	.75
SDRLEN034 Call of the Haunted C	.20	.40
SDRLEN035 Magic Jammer C	.75	1.50
SDRLEN036 Sakuretsu Armor C	.50	1.00
SDRLEN037 Draining Shield C	.25	.50

2007 Yu-Gi-Oh Tactical Evolution 1st Edition

TAEV01 Alien Shocktrooper C	.10	.20
TAEV02 Volcanic Rat C	.10	.20
TAEV03 Renge Gatekeeper Dark World C	.10	.20
TAEV04 Hunter Dragon R	.50	1.00
TAEV05 Venom Cobra C	.10	.20
TAEV06 Rainbow Dragon SCR	6.00	12.00
TAEV06 Rainbow Dragon GR	50.00	100.00
TAEV07 Chrysalis Pantail C	.10	.20
TAEV08 Chrysalis Chicky C	.10	.20
TAEV09 Chrysalis Pinny C	.10	.20
TAEV10 Chrysalis Larva C	.10	.20
TAEV11 Chrysalis Mole C	.10	.20
TAEV12 Necro Gardna SR	.75	1.50
TAEV12 Necro Gardna UTR	2.50	5.00
TAEV13 Vennominaga Deity of Pois.Snakes SCR	30.00	75.00
TAEV14 Vennominon King of Pois.Snakes UR	.75	1.50
TAEV14 Vennominon King of Pois. Snakes UTR	2.00	4.00
TAEV15 Venom Snake C	.10	.20
TAEV16 Venom Boa C	.10	.20
TAEV17 Venom Serpent C	.10	.20
TAEV18 Elemental Hero Neos Alius SR	1.00	2.00
TAEV18 Elemental Hero Neos Alius UTR	4.00	8.00
TAEV19 Chthonian Emperor Dragon UTR	1.50	3.00
TAEV19 Chthonian Emperor Dragon UR	1.25	2.50
TAEV20 Aquarian Alessa SR	.60	1.25
TAEV20 Aquarian Alessa UTR	1.00	2.00
TAEV21 Lucky Pied Piper UTR	1.00	2.00
TAEV21 Lucky Pied Piper SR	1.50	3.00
TAEV22 Grasschopper R	.50	1.00
TAEV23 Goggle Golem C	.10	.20
TAEV24 Dawnbreak Gardna C	.10	.20
TAEV25 Doom Shaman SR	.60	1.25
TAEV25 Doom Shaman UTR	1.00	2.00
TAEV26 King Pyron C	.10	.20
TAEV27 Shadow Delver C	.10	.20
TAEV28 Flint Lock C	.10	.20
TAEV29 Gravitic Orb C	.10	.20
TAEV30 Phantom Cricket C	.10	.20
TAEV31 Crystal Seer UR	.75	1.50
TAEV31 Crystal Seer UTR	.75	1.50
TAEV32 Neo Space Pathfinder R	.60	1.25
TAEV33 Frost and Flame Dragon SCR	2.00	4.00
TAEV34 Desert Twister UR	.75	1.50
TAEV34 Desert Twister UTR	.75	1.50
TAEV35 Ritual Raven C	.10	.20
TAEV36 Razor Lizard C	.10	.20
TAEV37 Light Effigy C	.10	.20
TAEV38 Dark Effigy C	.10	.20
TAEV39 Zombie Master SR	1.25	2.50
TAEV39 Zombie Master UTR	15.00	30.00
TAEV40 Neo-Spacian Marine Dolphin C	.10	.20
TAEV41 Elemental Hero Marine Neos R	.50	1.00
TAEV42 Elemental Hero Darkbright UR	1.25	2.50
TAEV42 Elemental Hero Darkbright UTR	4.00	8.00
TAEV43 Elemental Hero Magma Neos SCR	7.50	15.00
TAEV44 Ojama Knight C	.10	.20
TAEV45 Fifth Hope SR	.75	1.50
TAEV45 Fifth Hope UTR	1.50	3.00
TAEV46 Reverse of Neos C	.10	.20
TAEV47 Convert Contract C	.10	.20
TAEV48 Cocoon Party C	.10	.20
TAEV49 NEX C	.10	.20
TAEV50 Cocoon Rebirth C	.10	.20
TAEV52 Snake Rain R	.75	1.50
TAEV53 Venom Shot C	.10	.20
TAEV54 Cyberdark Impact! SCR	15.00	30.00
TAEV55 Flint Missile C	.10	.20
TAEV56 Double Summon R	1.25	2.50
TAEV57 Summoner's Art R	.50	1.00
TAEV58 Creature Seizure C	.10	.20
TAEV59 Phalanx Pike R	1.25	2.50
TAEV60 Symbols of Duty R	.50	1.00
TAEV61 Amulet of Ambition C	.10	.20
TAEV62 Broken Bamboo Sword C	1.25	2.50
TAEV63 Mirror Gate SR	.60	1.25
TAEV63 Mirror Gate UTR	1.00	2.00
TAEV64 Hero Counterattack C	.10	.20
TAEV65 Cocoon Veil C	.10	.20
TAEV66 Snake Whistle C	.10	.20
TAEV67 Damage = Reptile R	.50	1.00
TAEV68 Snake Deity's Command R	.50	1.00
TAEV69 Rise of the Snake Deity C	.10	.20
TAEV70 Ambush Fangs C	.10	.20
TAEV71 Venom Burn C	.10	.20
TAEV72 Common Charity R	.50	1.00
TAEV73 Destructive Draw C	.10	.20
TAEV74 Shield Spear C	.10	.20
TAEV75 Strike Slash C	.10	.20
TAEV76 Spell Reclamation R	.50	1.00
TAEV77 Trap Reclamation R	.50	1.00
TAEV78 Gift Card C	1.50	3.00
TAEV79 The Gift of Greed C	.10	.20
TAEV80 Counter Counter C	.10	.20
TAEV81 Ocean's Keeper R	.50	1.00
TAEV82 Thousand-Eyes Jellyfish R	.50	1.00
TAEV83 Cranium Fish SCR	1.50	3.00
TAEV84 Abyssal Kingshark SCR	1.25	2.50
TAEV85 Mormolith SCR	.75	1.50
TAEV86 Fossil Tusker R	.50	1.00
TAEV87 Phantom Dragonray Bronto R	.50	1.00
TAEV88 Il Blud SCR	4.00	8.00
TAEV89 Blazewing Butterfly SR	.60	1.25
TAEV89 Blazewing Butterfly UTR	1.00	2.00
TAEV000 Gemini Summoner SCR	1.25	2.50
TAEV000 Gemini Summoner SR	2.00	4.00

2008 Yu-Gi-Oh 5D's Anniversary Pack

YAP1EN001 Blue-Eyes White Dragon UR	15.00	30.00
YAP1EN002 Red-Eyes B. Dragon UR	7.50	15.00
YAP1EN003 Summoned Skull UR	3.00	6.00
YAP1EN004 Celtic Guardian UR	2.00	4.00
YAP1EN005 Gyakutenno Megami UR	1.50	3.00
YAP1EN006 Buster Blader UR	5.00	10.00
YAP1EN007 Jinzo UR	3.00	6.00
YAP1EN008 Shiba-Warrior Taro UR	2.00	4.00

2008 Yu-Gi-Oh Champion Pack Game Five

CP51 Fiend's Sanctuary UR	10.00	20.00
CP520 Spirit Barrier C	.75	1.50
CP05EN002 Giant Germ SR	4.00	8.00
CP05EN003 Magical Merchant SR	6.00	12.00
CP05EN004 Wave Motion Cannon SR	7.50	15.00
CP05EN005 Trap Dustshoot SR	7.50	15.00
CP05EN006 Dark Necrofear R	.75	1.50
CP05EN007 Blowback Dragon R	.50	1.00
CP05EN008 Dark RUler Ha Des R	.75	1.50
CP05EN009 Deck Devastation Virus R	.75	1.50
CP05EN010 Pulling the Rug R	.75	1.50
CP05EN011 Anti Spell Fragrance R	10.00	20.00
CP05EN012 Amazon of the Seas C	.75	1.50
CP05EN013 Protector of the Sanctuary C	.75	1.50
CP05EN014 Double Coston C	.75	1.50
CP05EN015 Rescue Cat C	.50	1.00
CP05EN016 D.D. Crow C	.75	1.50
CP05EN017 Hammer Shot C	.20	.40
CP05EN018 Thousand Knives C	.75	1.50
CP05EN019 Cursed Seal of the Forbidden Spell C	.75	1.50

2008 Yu-Gi-Oh Champion Pack Game Seven

CP71 Voltic Kong UR	1.50	3.00
CP07EN002 Legendary Jujitsu Master SR	1.50	3.00
CP07EN003 Threatening Roar SR	5.00	10.00
CP07EN004 Gladiator Beast Bestiari SR	6.00	12.00
CP07EN005 Lonefire Blossom SR	30.00	75.00
CP07EN006 Elemental Hero Ocean R	4.00	8.00
CP07EN007 Fairy King Truesdale R	1.50	3.00
CP07EN008 Spell Striker R	1.25	2.50
CP07EN009 Vanity's Fiend R	6.00	12.00
CP07EN010 Dark World Dealings R	1.50	3.00
CP07EN011 Doom Shaman R	1.25	2.50
CP07EN012 Shovel Crusher C	.75	1.50
CP07EN013 Life Absorbing Machine C	.75	1.50
CP07EN014 Fusilier Dragon, the DualMode Beast C	.75	1.50
CP07EN015 Homunculus the Alchemic Being C	.75	1.50
CP07EN016 Memory Crusher C	.75	1.50
CP07EN017 Instant Fusion C	3.00	6.00
CP07EN018 Dimensional Inversion C	.75	1.50
CP07EN019 Ancient Rules C	4.00	8.00
CP07EN020 Counter Counter C	.75	1.50

2008 Yu-Gi-Oh Champion Pack Game Six

CP06EN001 Rigorous Reaver UR	1.50	3.00
CP06EN002 Destiny Hero - Fear Monger SR	4.00	8.00
CP06EN003 Old Vindictive Magician SR	4.00	8.00
CP06EN004 Phoenix Wing Wind Blast SR	10.00	20.00
CP06EN005 Blaze Accelerator SR	4.00	8.00
CP06EN006 Call of Darkness R	.75	1.50
CP06EN007 Blade Knight R	.75	1.50
CP06EN008 Super-Electromagnetic Voltech Dragon R	.75	1.50
CP06EN009 Elemental Hero Stratos R	1.25	2.50
CP06EN010 Helios Duo Megistus R	.75	1.50
CP06EN011 Mage Power R	2.00	4.00
CP06EN012 Sentinel of the Seas C	.75	1.50
CP06EN013 Batteryman AA C	.75	1.50
CP06EN014 Theban Nightmare C	.75	1.50
CP06EN015 Majestic Mech - Ohka C	.75	1.50
CP06EN016 Soul of Purity and Light C	.75	1.50
CP06EN017 Amplifier C	2.00	4.00
CP06EN018 Cold Wave C	.75	1.50
CP06EN019 Magical Hats C	.75	1.50
CP06EN020 Dimension Wall C	2.00	4.00

2008 Yu-Gi-Oh Collector Tins

CT05EN001 Stardust Dragon SCR	1.50	3.00
CT05EN002 Red Dragon Archfiend SCR	1.25	2.50
CT05EN003 Black Rose Dragon SCR	1.50	3.00
CT05EN004 Turbo Warrior SCR	.75	1.50

2008 Yu-Gi-Oh Crossroads of Chaos 1st Edition

CSOC0 Rose, Warrior of Revenge UR	2.00	4.00
CSOC0 Rose, Warrior of Revenge UTR	2.50	5.00
CSOC1 Healing Wave Generator C	.15	.30
CSOC2 Turbo Synchron R	1.00	2.00
CSOC3 Mad Archfiend R	.75	1.50
CSOC4 Wall of Ivy C	.15	.30
CSOC5 Copy Plant C	.15	.30
CSOC6 Morphtronic Celfon C	.15	.30
CSOC7 Morphtronic Magnen C	.15	.30
CSOC8 Morphtronic Datatron C	.15	.30
CSOC9 Morphtronic Boomboxen R	.60	1.25
CSOC10 Morphtronic Cameran C	.15	.30
CSOC11 Morphtronic Radion R	.75	1.50
CSOC12 Morphtronic Clocken C	.15	.30
CSOC13 Gadget Hauler C	.15	.30
CSOC14 Gadget Driver C	.15	.30
CSOC15 Search Striker R	.75	1.50
CSOC16 Pursuit Chaser C	.15	.30
CSOC17 Iron Chain Repairman R	.60	1.25
CSOC18 Iron Chain Snake C	.15	.30
CSOC19 Iron Chain Blaster C	.15	.30
CSOC20 Iron Chain Coil C	.15	.30
CSOC21 Power Injector C	.15	.30
CSOC22 Storm Caller R	.75	1.50
CSOC23 Psychic Jumper C	.15	.30
CSOC24 Nettles C	.15	.30
CSOC25 Gigantic Cephalotus C	.15	.30
CSOC26 Horseytail C	.15	.30
CSOC27 Botanical Girl C	.15	.30
CSOC28 Cursed Fig C	.15	.30
CSOC29 Tytannial, Princess of Camellias UR	4.00	8.00
CSOC29 Tytannial, Princess of Camellias UTR	1.50	3.00
CSOC30 Zombie Mammoth C	.15	.30
CSOC31 Plaguespreader Zombie UR	2.00	4.00
CSOC31 Plaguespreader Zombie UTR	10.00	20.00
CSOC32 Goblin Decoy Squad C	.15	.30
CSOC33 Comrade Swordsman of Landstar C	.15	.30
CSOC34 Hanewata SR	1.25	2.50
CSOC35 The White Stone of Legend C	.15	.30
CSOC36 Tiger Dragon R	1.25	2.50
CSOC37 Jade Knight C	.15	.30
CSOC38 Turbo Warrior UR	3.00	6.00
CSOC38 Turbo Warrior UTR	1.00	2.00
CSOC39 Black Rose Dragon UR	4.00	8.00
CSOC39 Black Rose Dragon UTR	15.00	30.00
CSOC39 Black Rose Dragon GR	75.00	150.00
CSOC40 Iron Chain Dragon R	1.50	3.00
CSOC41 Psychic Lifetrancer R	1.50	3.00
CSOC42 Queen of Thorns SR	2.00	4.00
CSOC43 Doomkaiser Dragon UR	1.50	3.00
CSOC43 Doomkaiser Dragon UTR	2.50	5.00
CSOC44 Revived King Ha Des UR	2.00	4.00
CSOC44 Revived King Ha Des UTR	3.00	6.00
CSOC45 Card Rotator C	.15	.30
CSOC46 Seed of Deception C	.15	.30
CSOC47 Mark of the Rose UR	1.50	3.00
CSOC47 Mark of the Rose UTR	1.50	3.00
CSOC48 Black Garden SR	1.25	2.50
CSOC49 Factory of 100 Machines C	.15	.30
CSOC50 Morphtronic Accelerator R	.60	1.25
CSOC51 Morphtronic Cord C	.15	.30
CSOC52 Morphtronic Engine C	.15	.30
CSOC53 Poison Chain C	.15	.30
CSOC54 Paralyzing Chain R	.60	1.25
CSOC55 Teleport C	.15	.30
CSOC56 Psychokinesis UR	1.50	3.00
CSOC56 Psychokinesis UTR	1.00	2.00
CSOC57 Miracle Fertilizer R	.75	1.50
CSOC58 Fragrance Storm C	.15	.30
CSOC59 The World Tree R	.75	1.50
CSOC60 Everliving Underworld Cannon C	.15	.30
CSOC61 Secret Village of the Spellcasters SR	10.00	20.00
CSOC62 Omega Goggles C	.15	.30
CSOC63 Battle Mania SR	.75	1.50
CSOC64 Confusion Chaff C	.15	.30
CSOC65 Urgent Tuning SR	1.25	2.50
CSOC66 Synchro Strike C	.15	.30
CSOC67 Prideful Roar R	.75	1.50
CSOC68 Revival Gift C	.15	.30
CSOC69 Lineage of Destruction C	.15	.30
CSOC70 Doppelganger C	.15	.30
CSOC71 Morphtransition C	.15	.30
CSOC72 Morphtronic Monitron C	.15	.30
CSOC73 Psychic Trigger SR	1.00	2.00
CSOC74 Pollinosis R	.50	1.00
CSOC75 Bamboo Scrap C	.15	.30
CSOC76 Plant Food Chain C	.15	.30

CSOC77 Trap of the Imperial Tomb R .50 1.00
CSOC78 DNA Checkup C .15 .30
CSOC79 Gozen Match C .15 .30
CSOC80 Giant Trap Hole C .15 .30
CSOC81 Seed of Flame UR 1.50 3.00
CSOC81 Seed of Flame UTR 3.00 6.00
CSOC82 Cactus Fighter R .60 1.25
CSOC83 Overdrive Teleporter SCR 10.00 20.00
CSOC84 Rai-Jin SR .75 1.50
CSOC85 Rai-Mei SR 2.00 4.00
CSOC86 Gladiator Beast Retiari SCR 2.50 5.00
CSOC87 Night's End Sorcerer SR 2.50 5.00
CSOC88 Tempest Magician SCR 3.00 6.00
CSOC89 Treacherous Trap Hole SCR 10.00 20.00
CSOC90 Puppet Master SR .75 1.50
CSOC91 Time Machine SCR 1.50 3.00
CSOC92 Virus Cannon R .60 1.25
CSOC93 Machine Lord Ur SCR 1.50 3.00
CSOC94 Mosaic Manticore R .50 1.00
CSOC95 Goka, the Pyre of Malice SR .75 1.50
CSOC96 Red Ogre SR .15 .30
CSOC97 Neos Wiseman SCR 2.50 5.00
CSOC98 Elem. Hero Divine SCR 2.00 4.00
CSOC99 Botanical Lion SR 3.00 6.00

2008 Yu-Gi-Oh Dark Legends

DLG1EN000 Gorz the Emissary of Darkness SCT1.00 2.00
DLG1EN001 Blue-Eyes Ultimate Dragon SR 12.50 25.00
DLG1EN002 Blue-Eyes White Dragon SR 3.00 6.00
DLG1EN003 Flame Swordsman C .30 .75
DLG1EN004 Dark Magician R 1.00 2.00
DLG1EN005 Gaia the Fierce Knight C .30 .75
DLG1EN006 Raigeki SR 15.00 30.00
DLG1EN007 Fissure R .50 1.00
DLG1EN008 Trap Hole C .30 .75
DLG1EN009 Polymerization C 1.50 3.00
DLG1EN010 Curse of Dragon C .30 .75
DLG1EN011 Giant Soldier of Stone C .30 .75
DLG1EN012 Red-Eyes B. Dragon R 4.00 8.00
DLG1EN013 Swords of Revealing Light R .50 1.00
DLG1EN014 Armed Ninja C .30 .75
DLG1EN015 Man-Eater Bug C .30 .75
DLG1EN016 Hane-Hane C .30 .75
DLG1EN017 Monster Reborn SR 2.50 5.00
DLG1EN018 Right Leg of the Forbidden One C 2.00 4.00
DLG1EN019 Left Leg of the Forbidden one C 2.00 4.00
DLG1EN020 Right Arm of the Forbidden one C 2.00 4.00
DLG1EN021 Left Arm of the Forbidden one C 2.00 4.00
DLG1EN022 Exodia the Forbidden One UR 7.50 15.00
DLG1EN023 Gaia the Dragon Champion C .50 1.00
DLG1EN024 Gate Guardian R 2.00 4.00
DLG1EN025 Summoned Skull C .30 .75
DLG1EN026 Harpie Lady C .30 .75
DLG1EN027 Harpie Lady Sisters C .30 .75
DLG1EN028 Mask of Darkness R .50 1.00
DLG1EN029 B. Skull Dragon R 2.50 5.00
DLG1EN030 Elegant Egotist C .30 .75
DLG1EN031 Sanga of the Thunder R .75 1.50
DLG1EN032 Kazejin R .50 1.00
DLG1EN033 Suijin R .50 1.00
DLG1EN034 Magician of Faith R .50 1.00
DLG1EN035 Baby Dragon C .30 .75
DLG1EN036 Time Wizard R 2.50 5.00
DLG1EN037 Sangan SR 3.00 6.00
DLG1EN038 Kuriboh C .30 .75
DLG1EN039 Catapult Turtle R .50 1.00
DLG1EN040 Jirai Gumo C .30 .75
DLG1EN041 Thunder Dragon C 1.00 2.00
DLG1EN042 Cannon Soldier C .30 .75
DLG1EN043 Twin-Headed Thunder Dragon C .30 .75
DLG1EN044 Gazelle the King of Mythical Beasts C.30 .75
DLG1EN045 Barrel Dragon R .50 1.00
DLG1EN046 Solemn Judgment SR 4.00 8.00
DLG1EN047 Magic Jammer C .30 .75
DLG1EN048 Seven Tools of the Bandit C .30 .75
DLG1EN049 Heavy Storm R .50 1.00
DLG1EN050 Thousand Dragon C .30 .75
DLG1EN051 Blue-Eyes Toon Dragon C 1.00 2.00
DLG1EN052 Axe of Despair C .30 .75
DLG1EN053 Black Pendant C .30 .75
DLG1EN054 Maha Vailo C .30 .75
DLG1EN055 Relinquished SR 1.00 2.00
DLG1EN056 Gravekeeper's Servant C .75 1.50
DLG1EN057 Upstart Goblin C 2.50 5.00
DLG1EN058 Mystical Space Typhoon C .60 1.25
DLG1EN059 Giant Trunade C .30 .75
DLG1EN060 Painful Choice C .30 .75
DLG1EN061 Black Illusion Ritual C .30 .75
DLG1EN062 Megamorph R .50 1.00
DLG1EN063 Manga Ryu-Ran C .30 .75
DLG1EN064 Toon Mermaid C 2.00 4.00
DLG1EN065 Toon Summoned Skull C .30 .75
DLG1EN066 Hyozanryu C .30 .75
DLG1EN067 Toon World C .30 .75
DLG1EN068 Giant Rat C .30 .75
DLG1EN069 Senju of the Thousand Hands C 1.00 2.00
DLG1EN070 UFO Turtle C .30 .75
DLG1EN071 Giant Germ C .30 .75
DLG1EN072 Nimble Momonga C .75 1.50
DLG1EN073 Shining Angel C .30 .75
DLG1EN074 Mother Grizzly C .30 .75
DLG1EN075 Flying Kamakiri #1 C .30 .75
DLG1EN076 Sonic Bird C .30 .75
DLG1EN077 Mystic Tomato C .30 .75
DLG1EN078 Gaia Power C .30 .75
DLG1EN079 Umiiruka C .30 .75
DLG1EN080 Molten Destruction C .30 .75
DLG1EN081 Rising Air Current C .30 .75
DLG1EN082 Luminous Spark C .30 .75
DLG1EN083 Messenger of Peace R 1.00 2.00
DLG1EN084 Wall of Illusion R .50 1.00
DLG1EN085 Card Destruction SR 1.00 2.00
DLG1EN086 La Jinn the
Mystical Genie of the Lamp C .30 .75
DLG1EN087 Lord of D. C .60 1.25
DLG1EN088 The Flute of Summoning Dragon R .50 1.00
DLG1EN089 Graceful Charity SR 2.00 4.00
DLG1EN090 Penguin Soldier R .50 1.00
DLG1EN091 Scapegoat SR 2.00 4.00
DLG1EN092 Blast Sphere UR 2.00 4.00
DLG1EN093 Copycat R 1.50 3.00
DLG1EN094 Relieve Monster UR 1.00 2.00
DLG1EN095 Cloning SR 1.00 2.00
DLG1EN096 Kaibaman R .50 1.00
DLG1EN097 Cyber Harpie Lady SR 5.00 10.00
DLG1EN098 Amazoness Chain Master R .50 1.00
DLG1EN099 Embodiment of Apophis SR 1.00 2.00
DLG1EN100 Exchange of the Spirit UR 5.00 10.00
DLG1EN101 Blizzard Dragon R .50 1.00
DLG1EN102 Metal Shooter R .50 1.00
DLG1EN103 Des Mosquito R .50 1.00
DLG1EN104 Green Baboon,
Defender of the Forest UR 1.00 2.00
DLG1EN105 Ancient Lamp SR 1.00 2.00
DLG1EN106 Dark Bribe UR 7.50 15.00
DLG1EN107 Card Trooper UR 2.00 4.00
DLG1EN108 Destiny Hero - Malicious SR 2.50 5.00
DLG1EN109 Destiny Draw SR 1.50 3.00
DLG1EN110 Meltiel, Sage of the Sky UR 3.00 6.00
DLG1EN111 Nova Summoner UR 1.50 3.00
DLG1EN112 Gellenduo UR 6.00 12.00

2008 Yu-Gi-Oh Duel Terminal Previews

DTP1EN001 Blue-Eyes White Dragon PR 100.00 200.00
DTP1EN002 Dark Magician SR 75.00 150.00
DTP1EN003 Red-Eyes B. Dragon DRPR 100.00 200.00
DTP1EN004 Ojama Yellow DNPR 20.00 40.00
DTP1EN005 Elemental Hero Neos DNPR 7.50 15.00
DTP1EN006 Buster Blader DNPR 20.00 40.00
DTP1EN007 Kuriboh DNPR 4.00 8.00
DTP1EN008 Winged Kuriboh DNPR 6.00 12.00
DTP1EN009 Cyber Dragon DRPR 50.00 100.00
DTP1EN010 Soul Exchange DNPR 3.00 6.00
DTP1EN011 Malevolent Nuzzler DNPR 3.00 6.00
DTP1EN012 Nobleman of Extermination DNPR 3.00 6.00
DTP1EN013 Burst Stream of Destruction DNPR20.00 40.00
DTP1EN014 Dark Magic Attack DNPR 20.00 40.00
DTP1EN015 Inferno Fire Blast DRPR 7.50 15.00
DTP1EN016 Dust Tornado DNPR 3.00 6.00
DTP1EN017 Mask of Weakness DNPR 3.00 6.00
DTP1EN018 Magic Jammer DNPR 5.00 10.00
DTP1EN019 Reinforcements DNPR 4.00 8.00
DTP1EN020 Negate Attack DNPR 5.00 10.00
DTP1EN021 Nitro Synchron DRPR 5.00 10.00
DTP1EN022 Ghost Gardna DNPR 3.00 6.00
DTP1EN023 Big Piece Golem DRPR 3.00 6.00
DTP1EN024 Dark Resonator DNPR 7.50 15.00
DTP1EN025 Handcuffs Dragon DNPR 3.00 6.00
DTP1EN026 Swift Gaia the Fierce Knight DNPR 7.50 15.00
DTP1EN027 Harpie Lady 1 DNPR 7.50 15.00
DTP1EN028 Crystal Beast Sapphire Pegasus DNPR3.00 6.00
DTP1EN029 Nitro Warrior DSPR 20.00 40.00
DTP1EN030 Goyo Guardian DSPR 100.00 200.00
DTP1EN031 Ally of Justice Catastor DRPR 30.00 75.00

2008 Yu-Gi-Oh The Duelist Genesis 1st Edition

TDGS000 Avenging Knight Parshath SCR 1.50 3.00
TDGS001 Turbo Booster C .10 .20
TDGS002 Nitro Synchron SR .50 1.00
TDGS003 Quillbolt Hedgehog C .10 .20
TDGS004 Ghost Gardna C .10 .20
TDGS005 Shield Warrior R .50 1.00
TDGS006 Small Piece Golem C .10 .20
TDGS007 Medium Piece Golem C .10 .20
TDGS008 Big Piece Golem R .50 1.00
TDGS009 Sinister Sprocket SR .30 .75
TDGS010 Dark Resonator R .50 1.00
TDGS011 Twin-Shield Defender C .10 .20
TDGS012 Jutte Fighter C .10 .20
TDGS013 Handcuffs Dragon R .50 1.00
TDGS014 Montage Dragon UR 1.50 3.00
TDGS014 Montage Dragon UTR 2.50 5.00
TDGS015 Gonogo C .10 .20
TDGS016 Mind Master R .50 1.00
TDGS017 Doctor Cranium C .10 .20
TDGS018 Krebons C .10 .20
TDGS019 Mind Protector C .10 .20
TDGS020 Psychic Commander C .50 1.00
TDGS021 Psychic Snail C .10 .20
TDGS022 Telekinetic Shocker C .10 .20
TDGS023 Destructotron C .10 .20
TDGS024 Gladiator Beast Equeste C .10 .20
TDGS025 Jenis, Lightsworn Mender C .50 1.00
TDGS026 Dharc the Dark Charmer C .10 .20
TDGS027 Mecha Bunny C .10 .20
TDGS028 Oyster Meister C .10 .20
TDGS029 Twin-Barrel Dragon SR .30 .75
TDGS030 Izanagi SR .30 .75
TDGS031 Kunoichi C .10 .20
TDGS032 Beast of the Pharaoh C .10 .20
TDGS033 Dark Hunter UR .50 1.00
TDGS033 Dark Hunter UTR .75 1.50
TDGS034 Kinka-byo SR 2.50 5.00
TDGS035 Yamato-no-Kami R .50 1.00
TDGS036 Silent Strider C .10 .20
TDGS037 Noisy Gnat C .10 .20
TDGS038 Multiple Piece Golem UR .50 1.00
TDGS038 Multiple Piece Golem UTR .75 1.50
TDGS039 Nitro Warrior UR .50 1.00
TDGS039 Nitro Warrior UTR 1.00 2.00
TDGS040 Stardust Dragon UR 3.00 6.00
TDGS040 Stardust Dragon UTR 15.00 30.00
TDGS040 Stardust Dragon GR 75.00 150.00
TDGS041 Red Dragon Archfiend UR 3.00 6.00
TDGS041 Red Dragon Archfiend UTR 4.00 8.00
TDGS042 Goyo Guardian UR 2.50 5.00
TDGS042 Goyo Guardian UTR 6.00 12.00
TDGS043 Magical Android SR 1.25 2.50
TDGS044 Thought Ruler Archfiend UR 2.00 4.00
TDGS044 Thought Ruler Archfiend UTR 4.00 8.00
TDGS045 Fighting Spirit R .50 1.00
TDGS046 Domino Effect C .10 .20
TDGS047 Junk Barrage C .10 .20
TDGS048 Battle Tuned C .10 .20
TDGS049 De-Synchro R .50 1.00
TDGS050 Lightwave Tuning C .10 .20
TDGS051 Psi-Station C .10 .20
TDGS052 Psi-Impulse C .10 .20
TDGS053 Emergency Teleport UR 5.00 10.00
TDGS053 Emergency Teleport UTR 20.00 40.00
TDGS054 Sword of Kusanagi C .10 .20
TDGS055 Orb of Yasaka C .50 1.00
TDGS056 Mirror of Yata C .10 .20
TDGS057 Geartown C .10 .20
TDGS058 Power Filter SR .50 1.00
TDGS059 Lightsworn Sabre SR 1.00 2.00
TDGS060 Unstable Evolution SR .30 .75
TDGS061 Recycling Batteries .50 1.00
TDGS062 Book of Eclipse C .50 1.00
TDGS063 Equip Shot C .10 .20
TDGS064 Graceful Revival R .50 1.00
TDGS065 Defense Draw R .50 1.00
TDGS066 Remote Revenge C .10 .20
TDGS067 Spacegate C .10 .20
TDGS068 Synchro Deflector C .10 .20
TDGS069 Broken Blocker SR .30 .75
TDGS070 Psychic Overload UTR 1.50 3.00
TDGS070 Psychic Overload UR .50 1.00
TDGS071 Psychic Rejuvenation C .10 .20
TDGS072 Telepathic Power C .10 .20
TDGS073 Mind Over Matter R .50 1.00
TDGS074 Gladiator Beast War Chariot SR .75 1.50
TDGS075 Lightsworn Barrier C .10 .20
TDGS076 Intercept SR 2.50 5.00
TDGS077 Judgment of Thunder C .10 .20
TDGS078 Fish Depth Charge C .10 .20
TDGS079 Needlebug Nest C .60 1.25
TDGS080 Overworked C .10 .20
TDGS081 Counselor Lily SR .50 1.00
TDGS082 Herald of Orange Light R .50 1.00
TDGS083 Izanami R .50 1.00
TDGS084 Maiden of Macabre R .50 1.00
TDGS085 Hand of the Six Samurai SCR 1.25 2.50
TDGS086 Cyber Shark SCR 1.25 2.50
TDGS087 Grapple Blocker R .50 1.00
TDGS088 Telekinetic Charging Cell R .50 1.00
TDGS089 Charge of the Light Brigade SCR 20.00 40.00
TDGS090 The Tricky R .50 1.00
TDGS091 Tricky Spell 4 C .10 .20
TDGS092 Trap of Darkness R .50 1.00
TDGS093 The Selection R .50 1.00
TDGS094 Splendid Venus SCR 1.25 2.50
TDGS095 Fiendish Engine W SCR .50 1.00
TDGS096 Cold Enchanter R .50 1.00
TDGS097 Ice Master SCR 1.50 3.00
TDGS098 Kunai with Chain SR .50 1.00
TDGS099 Toy Magician SCR 1.50 3.00
TDGSSE2 Gladiator Beast Heraklinos SR .30 .75
TDGSSP1 Avenging Knight Parshath SR 2.00 4.00

2008 Yu-Gi-Oh Duelist Pack Jaden Yuki 3 1st Edition

DP06EN001 Neo-Spacian Air Hummingbird C .50 1.00
DP06EN002 Neo-Spacian Grand Mole R .50 1.00
DP06EN003 Neo-Spacian Glow Moss C .10 .20
DP06EN004 Elemental Hero Captain Gold R .50 1.00
DP06EN005 Elemental Hero Neos Alius C .10 .20
DP06EN006 Evil Hero Malicious Edge SR 1.50 3.00
DP06EN007 Evil Hero Infernal Gainer C .10 .20
DP06EN008 Evil Hero Infernal Prodigy SR .75 1.50
DP06EN009 Armor Breaker R .50 1.00
DP06EN010 Evil Hero Dark Gaia C .10 .20
DP06EN011 Evil Hero Wild Cyclone UR .75 1.50
DP06EN012 Evil Hero Infernal Sniper SR .25 .50
DP06EN013 Evil Hero Malicious Fiend UR 2.00 4.00
DP06EN014 Skyscraper 2 - Hero City SR 1.50 3.00
DP06EN015 Reverse of Neos C .10 .20
DP06EN016 Convert Contact C .10 .20
DP06EN017 Swing of Memories C .50 1.00
DP06EN018 Dark Fusion C .75 1.50
DP06EN019 Dark Calling R .75 1.50
DP06EN020 Revoke Fusion R .60 1.25
DP06EN021 Hero Medal C .10 .20
DP06EN022 Mirror Gate C .10 .20
DP06EN023 Over Limit C .10 .20
DP06EN024 Hero Counterattack C .10 .20
DP06EN025 Hero's Rule 2 R .20 .40

2008 Yu-Gi-Oh Duelist Pack Jesse Anderson 1st Edition

DP71 Crystal Beast Ruby Carbuncle C .10 .20
DP72 Crystal Beast Amethyst Cat R .50 1.00
DP73 Crystal Beast Emerald Tortoise C .10 .20
DP74 Crystal Beast Topaz Tiger R .50 1.00
DP75 Crystal Beast Amber Mammoth C .10 .20
DP76 Crystal Beast Cobalt Eagle C .10 .20
DP77 Phantom Skyblaster UR .50 1.00
DP78 Grave Squirmer SR .60 1.25
DP79 Grinder Golem SR 2.00 4.00
DP710 Magna-Slash Dragon C .10 .20
DP711 Gravi-Crush Dragon C .10 .20
DP712 Twister C .20 .40
DP713 Crystal Beacon C .10 .20
DP714 Crystal Blessing C .10 .20
DP715 Crystal Abundance R .50 1.00
DP716 Crystal Promise C .10 .20
DP717 Ancient City - Rainbow Ruins R .50 1.00
DP718 Hand Destruction R 1.25 2.50
DP719 Crystal Release SR .60 1.25
DP720 Crystal Tree SR 1.25 2.50
DP721 Triggered Summon C .10 .20
DP722 Last Resort C .10 .20
DP723 Crystal Raigeki C .10 .20
DP724 Crystal Counter UR 2.50 5.00
DP725 Crystal Pair R .50 1.00

2008 Yu-Gi-Oh Gold Series

GLD1EN001 7 Colored Fish C .10 .20
GLD1EN002 Sonic Bird C .10 .20
GLD1EN003 Jinzo GUR 1.50 3.00
GLD1EN004 Summoner Of Illusions C .10 .20
GLD1EN005 Fire Princess C .10 .20
GLD1EN006 Needle Worm C 1.25 2.50
GLD1EN007 8-Claws Scorpion C .10 .20
GLD1EN008 Swarm Of Scarabs C .20 .40
GLD1EN009 Swarm Of Locusts C .10 .20
GLD1EN010 Des Lacooda C .20 .40
GLD1EN011 Newdoria C .10 .20
GLD1EN012 Don Zaloog GUR .50 1.00
GLD1EN013 Old Vindictive Magician C .10 .20
GLD1EN014 Breaker the Magical Warrior GUR 1.00 2.00
GLD1EN015 D.D. Warrior Lady GUR 1.00 2.00
GLD1EN016 Dark Magician of Chaos GUR 7.50 15.00
GLD1EN017 Stealth Bird C .60 1.25
GLD1EN018 Regenerating Mummy C .10 .20
GLD1EN019 Solar Flare Dragon C .10 .20
GLD1EN020 Rare Metal Dragon C .10 .20
GLD1EN021 Nightmare Penguin C .10 .20
GLD1EN022 Cyber Dragon GUR 1.25 2.50
GLD1EN023 Sillva, Warlord Of Dark World C .50 1.00
GLD1EN024 Goldd, Wu-Lord Of Dark World GUR.50 1.00
GLD1EN025 Doom Dozer C .10 .20
GLD1EN026 Grandmaster of the Six Samurai GUR1.25 2.50
GLD1EN027 Prometheus, King Of Shadows GUR .50 1.00
GLD1EN028 Blue-Eyes Ultimate Dragon GUR 10.00 20.00
GLD1EN029 Chimeratech Overdragon GUR .75 1.50
GLD1EN030 Swords of Revealing Light GUR 1.00 2.00
GLD1EN031 Heavy Storm GUR .75 1.50
GLD1EN032 Reinforcement of the Army GUR 1.25 2.50
GLD1EN033 Brain Control GUR .75 1.50
GLD1EN034 Offerings To The Doomed C .10 .20
GLD1EN035 Non-Spellcasting Area C .10 .20
GLD1EN036 Mist Body C .75 1.50
GLD1EN037 Pandemonium C .50 1.00
GLD1EN038 Crush Card Virus GUR 7.50 15.00
GLD1EN039 Mirror Force GUR 4.00 8.00
GLD1EN040 Torrential Tribute GUR 1.25 2.50
GLD1EN041 Needle Ceiling C .50 1.00
GLD1EN042 Royal Command C .10 .20
GLD1EN043 Rivalry Of Warlords C 1.00 2.00
GLD1EN044 Skill Drain C 1.50 3.00
GLD1EN045 Spell Shield Type-8 C .10 .20

2008 Yu-Gi-Oh Light of Destruction 1st Edition

LODT1 Honest SCR 10.00 20.00
LODT1 Honest GR 30.00 75.00
LODT2 Cross Porter C .15 .30
LODT3 Miracle Flipper C .15 .30
LODT4 Destiny Hero - Dread Servant C .15 .30
LODT5 Volcanic Queen C .15 .30
LODT6 Jinzo - Returner R 1.50 3.00
LODT7 Jinzo - Lord SR 1.50 3.00
LODT8 Arcana Force 0 - The Fool C .15 .30
LODT9 Arcana Force I - The Magician C .15 .30
LODT00 Guardian of Order SCR 4.00 8.00
LODT10 Arcana Force III - The Empress C .15 .30
LODT11 Arcana Force IV - The Emperor C .15 .30
LODT12 Arcana Force VI - The Lovers C .15 .30
LODT13 Arcana Force VII - The Chariot C .15 .30
LODT14 Arcana Force XIV - Temperance R .50 1.00
LODT15 Arcana Force XVIII - The Moon C .15 .30
LODT16 Arcana Force XXI - The World UR 1.50 3.00
LODT16 Arcana Force XXI - The World UTR 2.50 5.00
LODT17 Arcana Force EX - The Dark Ruler SCR2.00 4.00
LODT19 Lyla, Lightsworn Sorceress UR 3.00 6.00
LODT19 Lyla, Lightsworn Sorceress UTR 7.50 15.00
LODT20 Garoth, Lightsworn Warrior C .15 .30
LODT21 Lumina, Lightsworn Summoner R .50 1.00
LODT22 Ryko, Lightsworn Hunter SR .50 1.00
LODT23 Wulf, Lightsworn Beast SR .50 1.00
LODT24 Celestia, Lightsworn Angel UR .75 1.50
LODT24 Celestia, Lightsworn Angel UTR 1.50 3.00
LODT25 Gragonith, Lightsworn Dragon C .15 .30
LODT26 Judgment Dragon SCR 15.00 30.00
LODT27 Dark Valkyria R .50 1.00
LODT28 Substitoad R .15 .30
LODT29 Unifrog C .15 .30
LODT30 Batteryman Charger C .15 .30
LODT31 Batteryman Industrial Strength R .50 1.00
LODT32 Batteryman Micro-Cell C .15 .30
LODT33 Goblin Recon Squad C .15 .30
LODT34 Interplanetary Invader A C .15 .30
LODT35 Diskblade Rider R .50 1.00
LODT36 Golden Ladybug R 1.25 2.50
LODT37 DUCKER Mobile Cannon SR .75 1.50
LODT38 The Lady in Wight C .15 .30
LODT39 Simorgh, Bird of Ancestry R .50 1.00
LODT40 Cloudian - Storm Dragon C .15 .30
LODT41 Phantom Dragon UR .50 1.00
LODT41 Phantom Dragon UTR .50 1.00
LODT42 Destiny End Dragoon UTR 2.50 5.00
LODT42 Destiny End Dragoon UR 1.25 2.50
LODT43 Ultimate Ancient Gear Golem UR 5.00 10.00
LODT43 Ultimate Ancient Gear Golem UTR 5.00 10.00
LODT44 Gladiator Beast Gyzarus SR .50 1.00
LODT45 Hero Mask C .15 .30
LODT46 Space Gift C .15 .30
LODT47 Demise of the Land C .15 .30
LODT48 D - Formation C .15 .30
LODT49 Spell Gear C .15 .30
LODT50 Cup of Ace C .15 .30
LODT51 Light Barrier R .15 .30
LODT52 Solar Recharge UR 2.00 4.00
LODT52 Solar Recharge UTR 7.50 15.00
LODT53 Realm of Light C .15 .30
LODT54 Wetlands C .15 .30
LODT55 Quick Charger C .15 .30
LODT56 Short Circuit C .15 .30
LODT57 Light of Redemption SR .50 1.00
LODT58 Mystical Cards of Light C .15 .30
LODT59 Level Tuning C .15 .30
LODT60 Deck Lockdown R .75 1.50
LODT61 Ribbon of Rebirth R .20 .40
LODT62 Golden Bamboo Sword C .15 .30
LODT63 Limit Reverse C .15 .30
LODT64 Hero Blast R .20 .40
LODT65 Rainbow Gravity C .15 .30
LODT66 D - Fortune C .15 .30
LODT67 Reversal of Fate C .15 .30
LODT68 Tour of Doom C .15 .30
LODT69 Arcana Call C .15 .30
LODT70 Light Spiral C .15 .30
LODT71 Glorious Illusion R .20 .40

LODT72 Destruction Jammer R 1.25 2.50
LODT73 Froggy Forcefield R .20 .40
LODT74 Portable Battery Pack C .15 .30
LODT75 Gladiator Lash C .15 .30
LODT76 Raging Cloudian C .15 .30
LODT77 Sanguine Swamp C .15 .30
LODT78 Lucky Chance C .15 .30
LODT79 Summon Limit C .15 .30
LODT80 Dice Try! C .15 .30
LODT81 Aurkus, Lightsworn Druid SR .75 1.50
LODT82 Ehren, Lightsworn Monk SCR 4.00 8.00
LODT83 Dark General Freed SCR 1.25 2.50
LODT84 Magical Exemplar SR 1.25 2.50
LODT85 Maniacal Servant R .20 .40
LODT86 Nimble Musasabi R .20 .40
LODT87 Flame Spirit Ignis R .20 .40
LODT88 Super-Ancient Dinobeast UR 1.25 2.50
LODT88 Super-Ancient Dinobeast UTR 1.25 2.50
LODT89 Vanquishing Light SR .60 1.25
LODT90 Tualatin SCR 2.00 4.00
LODT91 Divine Knight Ishzark SR .50 1.00
LODT92 Angel 07 SCR 2.00 4.00
LODT93 Union Attack SR .60 1.25
LODT94 Owner's Seal R 4.00 8.00
LODT95 Helios Trice Megistus SR .60 1.25
LODT96 Dangerous Machine Type-6 UR .50 1.00
LODT96 Dangerous Machine Type-6 UTR .50 1.00
LODT97 Maximum Six UR .50 1.00
LODT97 Maximum Six UTR .50 1.00
LODT98 Fog King SCR 10.00 20.00
LODT99 Fossil Dyna Pachycephalo SCR 6.00 12.00

2008 Yu-Gi-Oh Premium Pack 2

PP02EN001 Super War Lion SCR 75.00 150.00
PP02EN001 Super War Lion SR .20 .40
PP02EN002 War-Lion Ritual SCR 30.00 60.00
PP02EN002 War-Lion Ritual SR .15 .30
PP02EN003 Sengenjin SCR 175.00 350.00
PP02EN003 Sengenjin SR 2.00 4.00
PP02EN004 Elemental HERO Woodsman SCR 1.00 2.00
PP02EN005 Elemental HERO Knospe SCR 100.00 200.00
PP02EN005 Elemental HERO Knospe SR 1.25 2.50
PP02EN006 Elemental HERO Poison Rose SCR75.00 150.00
PP02EN006 Elemental HERO Poison Rose SR .25 .50
PP02EN007 Elemental HERO Heat SCR 200.00 400.00
PP02EN007 Elemental HERO Heat SR 1.00 2.00
PP02EN008 Elemental HERO Lady Heat SCR 75.00 150.00
PP02EN008 Elemental HERO Lady Heat SR .75 1.50
PP02EN009 Elemental HERO Terra Firma SCR 1.75 3.50
PP02EN010 Elemental HERO Inferno SCR .60 1.25
PP02EN011 Rose Bud SR .20 .40
PP02EN011 Rose Bud SCR 7.50 15.00
PP02EN012 Hero's Bond SCR .75 1.50
PP02EN013 Terra Firma Gravity SCR 7.50 15.00
PP02EN013 Terra Firma Gravity SR .15 .30
PP02EN014 Elemental HERO Voltic SCR 3.00 6.00
PP02EN015 Carrierroid SCR .30 .75
PP02EN016 Mezuki SCR 12.50 25.00
PP02EN017 Evil Dragon Ananta SCR 2.00 4.00
PP02EN018 Athena SCR 1.00 2.00
PP02EN019 Hecatrice SCR 75.00 150.00
PP02EN019 Hecatrice SR .25 .50
PP02EN020 Valhalla, Hall of the Fallen SCR .75 1.50

2008 Yu-Gi-Oh Retro Pack 1

RP010 Blue-Eyes Ultimate Dragon SCR 15.00 30.00
RP011 Blue-Eyes White Dragon UR 30.00 75.00
RP013 Dark Magician UR 15.00 30.00
RP015 Raigeki UR 125.00 250.00
RP016 Fissure R 1.50 3.00
RP0111 Red-Eyes B. Dragon UR 7.50 15.00
RP0112 Swords of Revealing Light SR 2.50 5.00
RP0116 Monster Reborn SR 6.00 12.00
RP0117 Right Leg of the Forbidden One R 5.00 10.00
RP0118 Left Leg of the Forbidden One R 5.00 10.00
RP0119 Right Arm of the Forbidden One R 5.00 10.00
RP0120 Left Arm of the Forbidden One R 5.00 10.00
RP0121 Exodia the Forbidden One UR 10.00 20.00
RP0122 Gaia the Dragon Champion SR 2.00 4.00
RP0123 Gate Guardian UR 10.00 20.00
RP0124 Summoned Skull SR 2.50 5.00
RP0126 Harpie Lady Sisters R 1.00 2.00
RP0128 B. Skull Dragon R 5.00 10.00
RP0130 Sanga of the Thunder R 2.00 4.00
RP0131 Kazejin R 1.50 3.00
RP0132 Suijin R 1.50 3.00
RP0133 Magician of Faith R 1.50 3.00
RP0135 Time Wizard SR 5.00 10.00
RP0136 Sangan SR 7.50 15.00
RP0137 Kuriboh SR 2.00 4.00
RP0138 Catapult Turtle SR 2.00 4.00
RP0144 Barrel Dragon R 2.50 5.00
RP0145 Solemn Judgment SR 7.50 15.00
RP0148 Heavy Storm R 1.25 2.50
RP0150 Blue-Eyes Toon Dragon R 4.00 8.00
RP0151 Axe of Despair R 1.25 2.50
RP0154 Relinquished UR 3.00 6.00
RP0159 Painful Choice R 4.00 8.00
RP0161 Megamorph R 1.00 2.00
RP0182 Messenger of Peace R 2.00 4.00
RP0184 Card Destruction R 2.50 5.00
RP0185 La Jinn the Mystical Genie of the Lamp SR20.0040.00
RP0186 Lord of D. R 1.00 2.00
RP0187 The Flute of Summoning Dragon R 1.50 3.00
RP0188 Graceful Charity R 2.00 4.00
RP0190 Scapegoat UR 50.00 100.00
RP0191 Blast Sphere SCR 20.00 40.00
RP0192 Copycat SCR 50.00 100.00
RP0193 Relieve Monster SCR 10.00 20.00
RP0194 Cloning SCR 15.00 30.00
RP0195 Kaibaman SCR 20.00 40.00
RP0196 Cyber Harpie Lady SCR 150.00 300.00
RP0197 Amazoness Chain Master SCR 50.00 100.00
RP0198 Embodiment of Apophis SCR 20.00 40.00
RP0199 Exchange of the Spirit SCR 50.00 100.00
RP01100 Ancient Lamp SCR 25.00 50.00

2008 Yu-Gi-Oh Starter Deck 5D's 1st Edition

5DS1-EN001 Tune Warrior C .20 .40
5DS1-EN002 Water Spirit C .20 .40
5DS1-EN003 Axe Raider C .20 .40
5DS1-EN004 Dark Blade C .20 .40
5DS1-EN005 Charcoal Inpachi C .20 .40
5DS1-EN006 Woodborg Inpachi C .20 .40
5DS1-EN007 Spiral Serpent C .20 .40
5DS1-EN008 Renge, Gatekeeper of Dark World C.20 .40
5DS1-EN009 Atlantean Pikeman C .20 .40
5DS1-EN010 Sonic Chick C .20 .40
5DS1-EN011 Junk Synchron C .20 .40
5DS1-EN012 Speed Warrior C .20 .40
5DS1-EN013 Magna Drago C .20 .40
5DS1-EN014 Frequency Magician C .20 .40
5DS1-EN015 Copycat C .20 .40
5DS1-EN016 UFO Turtle C .20 .40
5DS1-EN017 Mystic Tomato C .20 .40
5DS1-EN018 Marauding Captain C .20 .40
5DS1-EN019 Exiled Force C .20 .40
5DS1-EN020 Synchro Boost C .20 .40
5DS1-EN021 Synchro Blast Wave C .20 .40
5DS1-EN022 Synchronized Realm C .20 .40
5DS1-EN023 The Warrior Returning Alive C .20 .40
5DS1-EN024 Smashing Ground C .20 .40
5DS1-EN025 Rush Recklessly C .20 .40
5DS1-EN026 Monster Reincarnation C .20 .40
5DS1-EN027 Lightning Vortex C .20 .40
5DS1-EN028 Twister C .20 .40
5DS1-EN029 Double Summon C .75 1.50
5DS1-EN030 Symbols of Duty C .20 .40
5DS1-EN031 Threatening Roar C .20 .40
5DS1-EN032 Scrap-Iron Scarecrow C .20 .40
5DS1-EN033 Miniaturize C .20 .40
5DS1-EN034 Spellbinding Circle C .20 .40
5DS1-EN035 Backup Soldier C .20 .40
5DS1-EN036 Trap Hole C .20 .40
5DS1-EN037 Sakuretsu Armor C .20 .40
5DS1-EN038 Divine Wrath C .20 .40
5DS1-EN039 Seven Tools of the Bandit C .20 .40
5DS1-EN040 Birthright C .20 .40
5DS1-EN041 Junk Warrior UR .20 .40
5DS1-EN042 Gaia Knight, the Force of Earth SR .20 .40
5DS1-EN043 Colossal Fighter SR .20 .40

2008 Yu-Gi-Oh Structure Deck Zombie World 1st Edition

SDZWEN001 Red-Eyes Zombie Dragon UR .75 1.50
SDZWEN002 Malevolent Mech - Goku En C .25 .50
SDZWEN003 Paladin of the Cursed Dragon C .25 .50
SDZWEN004 Gernia C .25 .50
SDZWEN005 Patrician of Darkness C .25 .50
SDZWEN006 Royal Keeper C .25 .50
SDZWEN007 Pyramid Turtle C .25 .50
SDZWEN008 Master Kyonshee C .25 .50
SDZWEN009 Spirit Reaper C .25 .50
SDZWEN010 Getsu Fuhma C .25 .50
SDZWEN011 Ryu Kokki C .25 .50
SDZWEN012 Regenerating Mummy C .25 .50
SDZWEN013 Des Lacooda C .25 .50
SDZWEN014 Marionette Mite C .25 .50
SDZWEN015 Plague Wolf C .25 .50
SDZWEN016 Zombie Master C .25 .50
SDZWEN017 Zombie World C 1.00 2.00
SDZWEN018 Spell Shattering Arrow C .50 1.00
SDZWEN019 Cold Wave C .25 .50
SDZWEN020 Magical Stone Excavation C .25 .50
SDZWEN021 Card of Safe Return C .25 .50
SDZWEN022 Creature Swap C .25 .50
SDZWEN023 Book of Life C .25 .50
SDZWEN024 Call of the Mummy C .25 .50
SDZWEN025 Terraforming C .60 1.25
SDZWEN026 Pot of Avarice C .25 .50
SDZWEN027 Shrink C .25 .50
SDZWEN028 Field Barrier C .25 .50
SDZWEN029 Soul Taker C .25 .50
SDZWEN030 Ribbon of Rebirth C .25 .50
SDZWEN031 Card Destruction C .25 .50
SDZWEN032 Imperial Iron Wall C .75 1.50
SDZWEN033 Dust Tornado C .25 .50
SDZWEN034 Bottomless Trap Hole C 1.00 2.00
SDZWEN035 Tutan Mask C .25 .50
SDZWEN036 Waboku C .25 .50
SDZWEN037 Magical Arm Shield C .25 .50

2009 Yu-Gi-Oh Ancient Prophecy 1st Edition

ANPR0 XX-Saber Gardestrike SCR 1.50 3.00
ANPR1 Kuribon R .50 1.00
ANPR2 Sunny Pixie C .15 .30
ANPR3 Sunlight Unicorn C .15 .30
ANPR4 Blackwing - Mistral the Silver Shield C .15 .30
ANPR5 Blackwing - Vayu UR .75 1.50
ANPR5 Blackwing - Vayu UTR 1.50 3.00
ANPR6 Blackwing - Fane the Steel Chain C .15 .30
ANPR7 Morphtronic Magnen Bar C .15 .30
ANPR8 Jester Lord R .50 1.00
ANPR9 Jester Confit SR 1.50 3.00
ANPR10 Fortune Lady Light R .50 1.00
ANPR11 Fortune Lady Fire R .50 1.00
ANPR12 Infernity Beast C .15 .30
ANPR13 Darksea Rescue R .50 1.00
ANPR14 Darksea Float C .15 .30
ANPR15 Turbo Rocket R .50 1.00
ANPR16 Earthbound Immortal Cusillu UR 1.00 2.00
ANPR16 Earthbound Immortal Cusillu UTR 1.50 3.00
ANPR17 Earthbound Immortal Chacu UR 1.50 3.00
ANPR17 Earthboudn Immortal Chacu UTR 3.00 6.00
ANPR18 Koa'ki Meiru Boulder C .15 .30
ANPR19 Koa'ki Meiru Crusader SR 1.00 2.00
ANPR20 Koa'ki Meiru Speeder R .50 1.00
ANPR21 Koa'ki Meiru Tornado R .50 1.00
ANPR22 Koa'ki Meiru Hydro Barrier C .15 .30
ANPR23 Scary Moth C .15 .30
ANPR24 Shiny Black C C .15 .30
ANPR25 Armed Sea Hunter C .15 .30
ANPR26 Divine Dragon Aquabizarre C .15 .30
ANPR27 Fishborg Blaster C .15 .30
ANPR28 Shark Cruiser C .15 .30
ANPR29 Armored Axon Kicker C .15 .30
ANPR30 Genetic Woman C .15 .30
ANPR31 Magicat R .50 1.00
ANPR32 Cyborg Doctor C .15 .30
ANPR33 White Potan C .15 .30
ANPR34 Minefieldriller SR .60 1.25
ANPR35 XX-Saber Faultroll SR 1.50 3.00
ANPR36 XX-Saber Ragigura C .15 .30
ANPR37 Flamvell Firedog R .50 1.00
ANPR38 Ancient Crimson Ape C .15 .30
ANPR39 Falchion R .50 1.00
ANPR40 Ancient Fairy Dragon UR 2.00 4.00
ANPR40 Ancient Fairy Dragon UTR 6.00 12.00
ANPR40 Ancient Fairy Dragon GR 15.00 30.00
ANPR41 Turbo Cannon SR .75 1.50
ANPR42 Archfiend Zombie-Skull SR 7.50 15.00
ANPR43 Ancient Sacred Wyvern UR 3.00 6.00
ANPR43 Ancient Sacred Wyvern UTR 6.00 12.00
ANPR44 XX-Saber Gottoms UR .75 1.50
ANPR44 XX-Saber Gottoms UTR 1.50 3.00
ANPR45 Release Restraint Wave C .15 .30
ANPR46 Silver Wing C .15 .30
ANPR47 Advance Draw C .15 .30
ANPR48 Ancient Forest SR .75 1.50
ANPR49 Emergency Assistance C .15 .30
ANPR50 Spirit Burner C .15 .30
ANPR51 Future Visions SR 3.00 6.00
ANPR52 Core Compression SR 1.00 2.00
ANPR53 Core Blaster C .15 .30
ANPR54 Solidarity R 1.25 2.50
ANPR55 Hydro Pressure Cannon C .15 .30
ANPR56 Water Hazard C .15 .30
ANPR57 Brain Research Lab C .15 .30
ANPR58 Saber Slash SR .75 1.50
ANPR59 Sword of Sparkles C .15 .30
ANPR60 Rekindling C .15 .30
ANPR61 Ancient Leaf C .15 .30
ANPR62 Fossil Dig C .15 .30
ANPR63 Skill Successor SR .75 1.50
ANPR64 Reinforce Truth R .50 1.00
ANPR65 Pixie Ring C .15 .30
ANPR66 Fairy Wind C .15 .30
ANPR67 Imperial Custom C .15 .30
ANPR68 Discord SR .50 1.00
ANPR69 Slip of Fortune C .15 .30
ANPR70 Depth Amulet C .15 .30
ANPR71 Damage Translation C .15 .30
ANPR72 Battle Teleportation C .15 .30
ANPR73 Core Reinforcement R .50 1.00
ANPR74 Iron Core Luster C .15 .30
ANPR75 Battle of the Elements C .15 .30
ANPR76 Aegis of the Ocean Dragon Lord C .15 .30
ANPR77 Psychic Soul C .15 .30
ANPR78 Flamvell Counter C .15 .30
ANPR79 At One With the Sword C .15 .30
ANPR80 A Major Upset C .15 .30
ANPR81 XX-Saber Fulhelmknight R .50 1.00
ANPR82 Koa'ki Meiru Ghoulungulate UR .75 1.50
ANPR82 Koa'ki Meiru Ghoulungulate UTR .50 1.00
ANPR83 Koa'ki Meiru Gravirose UR .75 1.50
ANPR83 Koa'ki Meiru Gravirose UTR .75 1.50
ANPR84 Psychic Emperor R .50 1.00
ANPR85 Card Guard SCR 4.00 8.00
ANPR86 Flamvell Commando UR .75 1.50
ANPR86 Flamvell Commando UTR .75 1.50
ANPR87 Pseudo Space R 3.00 6.00
ANPR88 Greed Grado SCR 1.50 3.00
ANPR89 Revival of the Immortals SR .60 1.25
ANPR90 Arcana Knight Joker R 1.50 3.00
ANPR91 Armityle the Chaos Phantom SCR 10.00 20.00
ANPR92 White Night Dragon SCR 3.00 6.00
ANPR93 Card Blocker SCR .50 1.00
ANPR94 Gaia Plate the Earth Giant UR 1.50 3.00
ANPR94 Gaia Plate the Earth Giant UTR 3.00 6.00
ANPR95 Sauropod Brachion R .50 1.00
ANPR96 Gaap the Divine Soldier R .50 1.00
ANPR97 Beast Machine King Barbaros Ur SR .75 1.50
ANPR98 Kasha SCR 1.00 2.00
ANPR99 Elemental Hero Gaia SCR 4.00 8.00

2009 Yu-Gi-Oh Champion Pack Game Eight

CP08EN002 Prohibition SR 4.00 8.00
CP08EN003 Mind Crush SR 20.00 40.00
CP08EN004 Dimensional Fissure SR 6.00 12.00
CP08EN005 Lumina, Lightsworn Summoner SR30.00 75.00
CP08EN006 Magician's Valkyria R 4.00 8.00
CP08EN007 Silent Magician LV4 R 2.00 4.00
CP08EN008 Great Shogun Shien R .50 1.00
CP08EN009 Herald of Creation R .50 1.00
CP08EN010 Burial from a Different Dimension R1.25 2.50
CP08EN011 Necro Gardna R .50 1.00
CP08EN012 Mushroom Man C .75 1.50
CP08EN013 Royal Oppression C 3.00 6.00
CP08EN014 Beckoning Light C .30 .75
CP08EN015 Neo-Spacian Dark Panther C .30 .75
CP08EN016 Alien Warrior C .30 .75
CP08EN017 Alien Mother C .30 .75
CP08EN018 Vanity's Ruler C .75 1.50
CP08EN019 Miraculous Rebirth C .30 .75
CP08EN020 Cell Explosion Virus C .30 .75
CP08EN001 Gravity Behemoth UR 1.50 3.00

2009 Yu-Gi-Oh Collector Tins

CT06EN001 Power Tool Dragon SCR .75 1.50
CT06EN002 Ancient Fairy Dragon SCR 1.25 2.50
CT06EN003 Majestic Star Dragon SCR .50 1.00
CT06EN004 Earthbound Immorta
l Wiraqocha Rasca SCR .50 1.00

2009 Yu-Gi-Oh Crimson Crisis 1st Edition

CRMS0 Colossal Fighter/Assault Mode SCR 1.25 2.50
CRMS1 Turret Warrior SR .75 1.50
CRMS2 Debris Dragon R .50 1.00
CRMS3 Hyper Synchron R .50 1.00
CRMS4 Red Dragon Archfiend UR 2.50 5.00
CRMS4 Red Dragon Archfiend UTR 3.00 6.00
CRMS4 Red Dragon Archfiend GR 6.00 12.00
CRMS5 Trap Eater C .15 .30
CRMS6 Twin-Sword Marauder C .15 .30
CRMS7 Dark Tinker C .15 .30
CRMS8 Blackwing - Gale the Whirlwind R .50 1.00
CRMS9 Blackwing - Bora the Spear C .15 .30
CRMS10 Blackwing - Sirocco the Dawn C .15 .30
CRMS11 Twilight Rose Knight SR 1.00 2.00
CRMS12 Summon Reactor-SK C .15 .30
CRMS13 Trap Reactor-Y Fi C .15 .30
CRMS14 Spell Reactor-RE C .15 .30
CRMS15 Black Salvo SR .75 1.50
CRMS16 Flying Fortress SKY FIRE R .50 1.00
CRMS17 Morphtronic Boarden C .15 .30
CRMS18 Morphtronic Slingen C .15 .30
CRMS19 Doomkaiser Dragon UR .75 1.50
CRMS19 Doomkaiser Dragon UTR .75 1.50
CRMS20 Hyper Psychic Blaster UR .75 1.50
CRMS20 Hyper Psychic Blaster UTR 1.00 2.00
CRMS21 Arcanite Magician UR 2.00 4.00
CRMS21 Arcanite Magician UTR 2.00 4.00
CRMS22 Arcane Apprentice R .50 1.00
CRMS23 Assault Mercenary C .15 .30
CRMS24 Assault Beast R .60 1.25
CRMS25 Night Wing Sorceress C .15 .30
CRMS26 Lifeforce Harmonizer UR .75 1.50
CRMS26 Lifeforce Harmonizer UTR .75 1.50
CRMS27 Gladiator Beast Samnite R .50 1.00
CRMS28 Dupe Frog C .15 .30
CRMS29 Flip Flop Frog C .15 .30
CRMS30 B.E.S. Big Core MK-2 R .50 1.00
CRMS31 Inmato R .50 1.00
CRMS32 Scanner SR .75 1.50
CRMS33 Dimension Fortress Weapon SR .75 1.50
CRMS34 Desert Protector C .15 .30
CRMS35 Cross-Sword Beetle C .15 .30
CRMS36 Bee List Soldier C .15 .30
CRMS37 Hydra Viper C .15 .30
CRMS38 Alien Overlord R .50 1.00
CRMS39 Alien Ammonite R .50 1.00
CRMS40 Dark Strike Fighter SR .75 1.50
CRMS41 Blackwing Armor Master UR 1.00 2.00
CRMS41 Blackwing Armor Master UTR 2.50 5.00
CRMS42 Hyper Psychic Blaster UR 2.50 5.00
CRMS42 Hyper Psychic Blaster UTR 1.50 3.00
CRMS43 Arcanite Magician SR .75 1.50
CRMS44 Cosmic Fortress Gol'gar UR 3.00 6.00
CRMS44 Cosmic Fortress Gol'gar UTR 4.00 8.00
CRMS45 Prevention Star C .15 .30
CRMS46 Vengeful Servant C .15 .30
CRMS47 Star Blast R .50 1.00
CRMS48 Raptor Wing Strike C .15 .30
CRMS49 Morphtronic Rusty Engine C .15 .30
CRMS50 Morphtronic Map C .15 .30
CRMS51 Assault Overload C .15 .30
CRMS52 Assault Teleport C .15 .30
CRMS53 Assault Revival C .15 .30
CRMS54 Psychic Sword C .15 .30
CRMS55 Telekinetic Power Well C .15 .30
CRMS56 Indomitable Gladiator Beast C .15 .30
CRMS57 Seed Cannon C .15 .30
CRMS58 Super Solar Nutrient C .15 .30
CRMS59 Six Scrolls of the Samurai C .15 .30
CRMS60 Verdant Sanctuary C .15 .30
CRMS61 Arcane Barrier R .50 1.00
CRMS62 Mysterious Triangle C .15 .30
CRMS63 Assault Mode Activate C .15 .30
CRMS64 Spirit Force SR .75 1.50
CRMS65 Descending Lost Star C .15 .30
CRMS66 Shining Silver Force R .50 1.00
CRMS67 Half or Nothing C .15 .30
CRMS68 Nightmare Archfiends C .15 .30
CRMS69 Ebon Arrow C .15 .30
CRMS70 Ivy Shackles C .15 .30
CRMS71 Fake Explosion C .15 .30
CRMS72 Morphtronic Forcefield C .15 .30
CRMS73 Morphtronic Mix-up C .15 .30
CRMS74 Assault Slash C .15 .30
CRMS75 Assault Counter C .15 .30
CRMS76 Psychic Tuning R .50 1.00
CRMS77 Metaphysical Regeneration C .15 .30
CRMS78 Trojan Gladiator Beast C .15 .30
CRMS79 Wall of Thorns R .50 1.00
CRMS80 Planet Pollutant Virus R .50 1.00
CRMS81 Dark Voltanis SCR 3.00 6.00
CRMS82 Prime Material Falcon SCR .50 1.00
CRMS83 Bone Crusher UTR .75 1.50
CRMS83 Bone Crusher UR .75 1.50
CRMS84 Alien Kid SR .75 1.50
CRMS85 Totem Dragon SR 2.00 4.00
CRMS86 Royal Swamp Eel SR .75 1.50
CRMS87 Submarine Frog C .15 .30
CRMS88 Code A Ancient Ruins SR 1.25 2.50
CRMS89 Synchro Change R .50 1.00
CRMS90 Multiply SR 1.50 3.00
CRMS91 Makiu, the Magical Mist R .50 1.00
CRMS92 Assault Armor R .50 1.00
CRMS93 Puppet King SCR .50 1.00
CRMS94 Zeta Reticulant SCR .50 1.00
CRMS95 Tethys, Goddess of Light SCR 2.00 4.00
CRMS96 Ido the Supreme Magical Force SCR .50 1.00
CRMS97 Violet Witch UR .75 1.50
CRMS97 Violet Witch UTR .50 1.00
CRMS98 Greed Quasar SCR 1.25 2.50
CRMS99 Armoroid SR .75 1.50

2009 Yu-Gi-Oh Duelist Pack Yugi 1st Edition

DPYG1 Dark Magician R .50 1.00
DPYG2 Summoned Skull SR 2.00 4.00
DPYG3 Queen's Knight C .15 .30
DPYG4 Jack's Knight C .15 .30
DPYG5 Kuriboh C .15 .30
DPYG6 Catapult Turtle C .15 .30
DPYG7 Buster Blader C .15 .30
DPYG8 Dark Magician Girl SR 2.50 5.00
DPYG9 Big Shield Gardna C .15 .30
DPYG10 Sorcerer of Dark Magic SR 3.00 6.00
DPYG11 King's Knight C .15 .30
DPYG12 Green Gadget C .15 .30
DPYG13 Red Gadget C .15 .30
DPYG14 Yellow Gadget C .15 .30
DPYG15 Marshmallon R 1.25 2.50

DPYG16 Dark Paladin UR 7.50 15.00
DPYG17 Black Luster Soldier R .50 1.00
DPYG18 Swords of Revealing Light C .15 .30
DPYG19 Monster Reborn R .50 1.00
DPYG20 Polymerization SR 7.50 15.00
DPYG21 Exchange R .50 1.00
DPYG22 Black Luster Ritual C .15 .30
DPYG23 Diffusion Wave-Motion C .15 .30
DPYG24 Brain Control C .15 .30
DPYG25 Card of Sanctity R .50 1.00
DPYG26 Spellbinding Circle C .15 .30
DPYG27 Mirror Force UR 2.00 4.00
DPYG28 Magical Hats R .75 1.50
DPYG29 Lightforce Sword C .15 .30
DPYG30 Stronghold the Moving Fortress C .15 .30

2009 Yu-Gi-Oh Duelist Pack Yusei 1st Edition

DP08EN001 Junk Synchron C .10 .20
DP08EN002 Speed Warrior C .10 .20
DP08EN003 Turbo Booster C .10 .20
DP08EN004 Nitro Synchron R .50 1.00
DP08EN005 Quillbolt Hedgehog C .10 .20
DP08EN006 Ghost Gardna C .10 .20
DP08EN007 Shield Warrior C .10 .20
DP08EN008 Healing Wave Generator C .10 .20
DP08EN009 Turbo Synchron R .50 1.00
DP08EN010 Fortress Warrior SR .25 .50
DP08EN011 Tuningware UR 1.00 2.00
DP08EN012 Junk Warrior R .50 1.00
DP08EN013 Nitro Warrior R .50 1.00
DP08EN014 Stardust Dragon SR 2.00 4.00
DP08EN015 Turbo Warrior R .50 1.00
DP08EN016 Armory Arm UR 2.00 4.00
DP08EN017 Fighting SPirit C .10 .20
DP08EN018 Domino Effect C .10 .20
DP08EN019 Junk Barrage C .10 .20
DP08EN020 Card Rotator C .10 .20
DP08EN021 Equip Shot C .10 .20
DP08EN022 Graceful Revival C .10 .20
DP08EN023 Defense Draw C .25 .50
DP08EN024 Remote Revenge C .10 .20
DP08EN025 Battle Mania R .50 1.00
DP08EN026 Confusion Chaff C .10 .20
DP08EN027 Urgent Tuning R .50 1.00
DP08EN028 Synchro Strike C .10 .20
DP08EN029 Give and Take SR .25 .50
DP08EN030 Limiter Overload SR .25 .50

2009 Yu-Gi-Oh Gold Series 2

GLD2EN001 Sangan GUR .75 1.50
GLD2EN002 Des Volstgalph GUR .75 1.50
GLD2EN003 Lekunga C .20 .40
GLD2EN004 Lord Poison C .20 .40
GLD2EN005 Rigorous Reaver C .20 .40
GLD2EN006 Zaborg the Thunder Monarch C .20 .40
GLD2EN007 Mobius the Frost Monarch C .20 .40
GLD2EN008 Thestalos the Firestorm Monarch C .20 .40
GLD2EN009 Granmarg the Rock Monarch C .20 .40
GLD2EN010 Treeborn Frog C .20 .40
GLD2EN011 Phantom Beast Cross-Wing C .20 .40
GLD2EN012 Phantom Beast Wild-Horn C .20 .40
GLD2EN013 Phantom Beast Thunder-Pegasus C .20 .40
GLD2EN014 Phantom Beast Rock-Lizard C .20 .40
GLD2EN015 Winged Rhynos C .20 .40
GLD2EN016 Snipe Hunter C .20 .40
GLD2EN017 The Six Samurai - Yaichi C .20 .40
GLD2EN018 The Six Samurai - Kamon C .20 .40
GLD2EN019 The Six Samurai - Yariza C .20 .40
GLD2EN020 The Six Samurai - Nisashi C .20 .40
GLD2EN021 The Six Samurai - Zanji C .20 .40
GLD2EN022 The Six Samurai - Irou C .20 .40
GLD2EN023 Volcanic Rocket GUR 1.00 2.00
GLD2EN024 Volcanic Shell C 1.25 2.50
GLD2EN025 Elemental Hero Captain Gold GUR 1.00 2.00
GLD2EN026 Raiza the Storm Monarch GUR 1.00 2.00
GLD2EN027 Necro Gardna GUR .75 1.50
GLD2EN028 Elemental Hero Neos Alius C .20 .40
GLD2EN029 Test Tiger GUR 1.00 2.00
GLD2EN030 Royal Firestorm Guards GUR 1.00 2.00
GLD2EN031 Dark Armed Dragon GUR 2.00 4.00
GLD2EN032 Prime Material Dragon GUR .75 1.50
GLD2EN033 Caius the Shadow Monarch GUR 1.25 2.50
GLD2EN034 Exile of the Wicked C .20 .40
GLD2EN035 Warrior Elimination C .20 .40
GLD2EN036 Giant Trunade C .20 .40
GLD2EN037 Mind Control GUR 1.00 2.00
GLD2EN038 Skyscraper C 1.25 2.50
GLD2EN039 Future Fusion GUR 1.00 2.00
GLD2EN040 Gold Sarcophagus GUR 1.50 3.00
GLD2EN041 Shien's Castle of Mist C .20 .40
GLD2EN042 Six Samurai United C .20 .40
GLD2EN043 Veil of Darkness GUR .75 1.50
GLD2EN044 Solemn Judgment GUR 1.00 2.00
GLD2EN045 Bottomless Trap Hole GUR 1.25 2.50
GLD2EN046 Compulsory Evacuation Device C .20 .40
GLD2EN047 Begone, Knave! C .20 .40
GLD2EN048 Phoenix Wing Wind Blast GUR 1.00 2.00
GLD2EN049 Return of the Six Samurai C .20 .40
GLD2EN050 Double-Edged Sword Technique C .20 .40

2009 Yu-Gi-Oh Raging Battle 1st Edition

RGBT00 Battlestorm SCR 1.50 3.00
RGBT01 Rockstone Warrior SR .75 1.50
RGBT02 Level Warrior SR 1.00 2.00
RGBT03 Strong Wind Dragon UR 2.00 4.00
RGBT03 Strong Wind Dragon UTR 2.00 4.00
RGBT04 Dark Verger R .50 1.00
RGBT05 Phoenixian Seed C .15 .30
RGBT06 Phoenixian Cluster Amaryllis SR .50 1.00
RGBT07 Rose Tentacles C .15 .30
RGBT08 Hedge Guard C .15 .30
RGBT09 Evil Thorn C .15 .30
RGBT10 Blackwing - Blizzard the Far North R .75 1.50
RGBT11 Blackwing - Shura the Blue Flame C .15 .30
RGBT12 Blackwing - Kalut the Moon Shadow C .15 .30
RGBT13 Blackwing - Elphin the Raven UR .50 1.00
RGBT13 Blackwing - Elphin the Raven UTR .75 1.50
RGBT14 Morphtronic Remoten R 1.00 2.00
RGBT15 Morphtronic Videon C .15 .30
RGBT16 Morphtronic Scopen C .15 .30
RGBT17 Gadget Arms C .15 .30
RGBT18 Torapart R .50 1.00
RGBT19 Earthbound Immortal Aslla Piscu UR 1.50 3.00
RGBT19 Earthbound Immortal Aslla Piscu UTR 1.50 3.00
RGBT20 Earthbound Immortal Ccapac UR 6.00 12.00
RGBT20 Earthbound Immortal Ccapac UTR 3.00 6.00
RGBT21 Koa'ki Meiru Valafar SR .75 1.50
RGBT22 Koa'ki Meiru Powerhand SR .50 1.00
RGBT23 Koa'ki Meiru Guardian C .15 .30
RGBT24 Koa'ki Meiru Drago UR 7.50 15.00
RGBT24 Koa'ki Meiru Drago UTR 20.00 40.00
RGBT25 Koa'ki Meiru Ice R .50 1.00
RGBT26 Koa'ki Meiru Doom C .15 .30
RGBT27 Brain Golem R .50 1.00
RGBT28 Minoan Centaur C .15 .30
RGBT29 Reinforced Human Psychic Borg SR .75 1.50
RGBT30 Master Gig C .15 .30
RGBT31 Emissary from Pandemonium C .15 .30
RGBT32 Gigastone Omega C .15 .30
RGBT33 Alien Dog C .15 .30
RGBT34 Spined Gillman C .15 .30
RGBT35 Deep Sea Diva R .50 1.00
RGBT36 Mermaid Archer C .15 .30
RGBT37 Lava Dragon C .15 .30
RGBT38 Vanguard of the Dragon C .15 .30
RGBT39 G.B. Hunter C .15 .30
RGBT40 Exploder Dragonwing UR 2.00 4.00
RGBT40 Exploder Dragonwing UTR 2.00 4.00
RGBT41 Blackwing Armed Wing SR .50 1.00
RGBT42 Power Tool Dragon UR 2.00 4.00
RGBT42 Power Tool Dragon UTR 2.50 5.00
RGBT42 Power Tool Dragon GR 6.00 12.00
RGBT43 Trident Dragion UR 1.25 2.50
RGBT43 Trident Dragion UTR 2.00 4.00
RGBT44 Sea Dragon Lord Gishilnodon SR 1.25 2.50
RGBT45 One for One R .75 1.50
RGBT46 Mind Trust C .15 .30
RGBT47 Thorn of Malice C .15 .30
RGBT48 Magic Planter SR 4.00 8.00
RGBT49 Wonder Clover C .15 .30
RGBT50 Against the Wind R .50 1.00
RGBT51 Black Whirlwind C .15 .30
RGBT52 Junk Box C .15 .30
RGBT53 Double Tool C&D C .15 .30
RGBT54 Morphtronic Repair Unit C .15 .30
RGBT55 Iron Core of Koa'ki Meiru R .50 1.00
RGBT56 Iron Core Immediate Disposal C .15 .30
RGBT57 Urgent Synthesis C .15 .30
RGBT58 Psychic Path C .15 .30
RGBT59 Natural Tune C .15 .30
RGBT60 Supremacy Berry C .15 .30
RGBT61 Forbidden Chalice UR 3.00 6.00
RGBT61 Forbidden Chalice UTR 10.00 20.00
RGBT62 Calming Magic R .50 1.00
RGBT63 Miracle Locus C .15 .30
RGBT64 Crimson Fire C .15 .30
RGBT65 Tuner Capture C .15 .30
RGBT66 Overdoom Line C .15 .30
RGBT67 Wicked Rebirth C .15 .30
RGBT68 Delta Crow - Anti Reverse SR 1.25 2.50
RGBT69 Level Retuner C .15 .30
RGBT70 Fake Feather C .15 .30
RGBT71 Trap Stun C .15 .30
RGBT72 Morphtronic Bind C .15 .30
RGBT73 Reckoned Power C .15 .30
RGBT74 Automatic Laser C .15 .30
RGBT75 Attack of the Cornered Rat C .15 .30
RGBT76 Proof of Powerlessness C .15 .30
RGBT77 Bone Temple Block C .15 .30
RGBT78 Grave of the Super UR 6.00 12.00
RGBT78 Grave of the Super UTR 6.00 12.00
RGBT79 Swallow Flip SR .50 1.00
RGBT80 Mirror of Oaths C .15 .30
RGBT81 Koa'ki Meiru War Arms SR .75 1.50
RGBT82 Immortal Ruler SCR 4.00 8.00
RGBT83 Hardened Armed Dragon SCR 3.00 6.00
RGBT84 Moja R .50 1.00
RGBT85 Beast Striker SR .50 1.00
RGBT86 King of the Beasts SCR 1.50 3.00
RGBT87 Swallow's Nest SR 5.00 10.00
RGBT88 Overwhelm SCR 3.00 6.00
RGBT89 Berserking R .50 1.00
RGBT90 Spell of Pain R .50 1.00
RGBT91 Light End Dragon SCR 1.50 3.00
RGBT92 Chaos-End Master SCR 4.00 8.00
RGBT93 Sphere of Chaos SCR 7.50 15.00
RGBT94 Snowman Eater R .50 1.00
RGBT95 Tree Otter R .50 1.00
RGBT96 Ojama Red R 1.00 2.00
RGBT97 Ojama Blue R 1.50 3.00
RGBT98 Ojama Country R 1.50 3.00
RGBT99 Emperor Sem R .50 1.00

2009 Yu-Gi-Oh Retro Pack 2

RP02EN000 Gorz the Emissary of Darkness SCR1.25 2.50
RP02EN001 Jinzo UR 2.50 5.00
RP02EN002 Parasite Paracide C .10 .20
RP02EN003 Lightforce Sword C .10 .20
RP02EN004 Chain Destruction R .75 1.50
RP02EN005 Dust Tornado C .10 .20
RP02EN006 Call of the Haunted C .10 .20
RP02EN007 Mirror Wall UR 1.25 2.50
RP02EN008 Appropriate C .10 .20
RP02EN009 Ceasefire R .75 1.50
RP02EN010 Magical Hats R 1.25 2.50
RP02EN011 Nobleman of Crossout C .10 .20
RP02EN012 Premature Burial C .10 .20
RP02EN013 Buster Blader SR 1.25 2.50
RP02EN014 Skull Invitation C .10 .20
RP02EN015 Limiter Removal SR 1.50 3.00
RP02EN016 Insect Imitation C .10 .20
RP02EN017 Magic Drain C .10 .20
RP02EN018 Gravity Bind C .10 .20
RP02EN019 The Legendary Fisherman R .60 1.25
RP02EN020 Thousand-Eyes Idol C .10 .20
RP02EN021 Thousand-Eyes Restrict UR 7.50 15.00
RP02EN022 4 Starred Ladybug of Doom C .10 .20
RP02EN023 Mad Sword Beast C .10 .20
RP02EN024 Goblin Attack Force C .10 .20
RP02EN025 Gearfried the Iron Knight R .60 1.25
RP02EN026 Gemini Elf C .10 .20
RP02EN027 The Masked Beast SR .50 1.00
RP02EN028 Revival Jam R 1.00 2.00
RP02EN029 Melchid the Four-Face Beast C .10 .20
RP02EN030 Curse of the Masked Beast C .10 .20
RP02EN031 Mask of Restrict C 7.50 15.00
RP02EN032 Lightning Blade C .10 .20
RP02EN033 Tornado Wall C .10 .20
RP02EN034 Torrential Tribute C .10 .20
RP02EN035 Infinite Cards R 2.00 4.00
RP02EN036 Jam Defender SR .60 1.25
RP02EN037 Card of Safe Return C .10 .20
RP02EN038 United We Stand UR 2.50 5.00
RP02EN039 Mage Power R .75 1.50
RP02EN040 Kycoo the Ghost Destroyer C .10 .20
RP02EN041 Bazoo the Soul-Eater C .10 .20
RP02EN042 Dark Necrofear SR .50 1.00
RP02EN043 Gilasaurus C .10 .20
RP02EN044 Dark Spirit of the Silent C .10 .20
RP02EN045 Destiny Board SR 2.00 4.00
RP02EN046 Spirit Message I C .10 .20
RP02EN047 Spirit Message N C .10 .20
RP02EN048 Spirit Message A C .10 .20
RP02EN049 Spirit Message L C .10 .20
RP02EN050 Magic Cylinder R .60 1.25
RP02EN051 Yata-Garasu C .10 .20
RP02EN052 Dark Ruler Ha Des UR .75 1.50
RP02EN053 Opticlops C .10 .20
RP02EN054 Freed the Matchless General R .60 1.25
RP02EN055 Emergency Provisions C .10 .20
RP02EN056 Tyrant Dragon SR 1.00 2.00
RP02EN057 Spear Dragon C .10 .20
RP02EN058 Airknight Parshath R 1.25 2.50
RP02EN059 Yamata Dragon R .50 1.00
RP02EN060 Hino-Kagu-Tsuchi SR 2.50 5.00
RP02EN061 Asura Priest C .10 .20
RP02EN062 A Legendary Ocean C .10 .20
RP02EN063 Creature Swap C .10 .20
RP02EN064 Bottomless Trap Hole C .50 1.00
RP02EN065 Injection Fairy Lily UR 1.25 2.50
RP02EN066 Ring of Destruction SCR 6.00 12.00
RP02EN067 Guardian Sphinx C .10 .20
RP02EN068 Don Zaloog R 1.25 2.50
RP02EN069 Book of Taiyou C .10 .20
RP02EN070 Book of Moon C .10 .20
RP02EN071 Reckless Greed C .10 .20
RP02EN072 Dark Jeroid R .50 1.00
RP02EN073 Newdoria R .60 1.25
RP02EN074 Helpoemer UR 1.25 2.50
RP02EN075 Gravekeeper's Spy C .10 .20
RP02EN076 Gravekeeper's Chief C .10 .20
RP02EN077 Gravekeeper's Assailant C .10 .20
RP02EN078 Dark Room of Nightmare C .10 .20
RP02EN079 Necrovalley R 1.50 3.00
RP02EN080 Barrel Behind the Door C .10 .20
RP02EN081 Nightmare Wheel R 1.50 3.00
RP02EN082 Lava Golem SR .75 1.50
RP02EN083 Morphing Jar R 2.50 5.00
RP02EN084 Royal Decree R 1.25 2.50
RP02EN085 Swift Gaia the Fierce Knight UR 1.00 2.00
RP02EN086 Obnoxious Celtic Guardian R .50 1.00
RP02EN087 Kaiser Sea Horse R .50 1.00
RP02EN088 Insect Queen SR .60 1.25
RP02EN089 Alpha The Magnet Warrior R .60 1.25
RP02EN090 Beta The Magnet Warrior R .60 1.25
RP02EN091 Gamma The Magnet Warrior R .60 1.25
RP02EN092 Valkyrion the Magna Warrior SCR10.00 20.00
RP02EN093 Harpie's Pet Dragon SCR 20.00 40.00
RP02EN094 Archfiend of Gilfer SCR 3.00 6.00
RP02EN095 Light and Darkness Dragon SCR 20.00 40.00
RP02EN096 Blue-Eyes Shining Dragon SCR 150.00 300.00
RP02EN097 Dragon Master Knight SCR 50.00 100.00
RP02EN098 Victory Dragon SCR 7.50 15.00
RP02EN099 Green Baboon,
Defender of the Forest SCR 4.00 8.00
RP02EN100 Dreadscythe Harvester SCR 1.00 2.00

2009 Yu-Gi-Oh Stardust Overdrive 1st Edition

SOVR0 Koa'ki Meiru Beetle SR .75 1.50
SOVR1 Majestic Dragon SR 1.25 2.50
SOVR2 Stardust Xiaolong R .60 1.25
SOVR3 Max Warrior SR .75 1.50
SOVR4 Quickdraw Synchron C .15 .30
SOVR5 Level Eater C .15 .30
SOVR6 Zero Gardna R .60 1.25
SOVR7 Regulus C .15 .30
SOVR8 Infernity Necromancer C .15 .30
SOVR9 Fortune Lady Wind R .75 1.50
SOVR10 Fortune Lady Water R .75 1.50
SOVR11 Fortune Lady Dark R 1.00 2.00
SOVR12 Fortune Lady Earth R .75 1.50
SOVR13 Solitaire Magician C .15 .30
SOVR14 Catoblepas and the Witch of Fate R .50 1.00
SOVR15 Dark Spider C .15 .30
SOVR16 Ground Spider C .15 .30
SOVR17 Relinquished Spider C .15 .30
SOVR18 Spyder Spider C .15 .30
SOVR19 Mother Spider R .50 1.00
SOVR20 Reptilianne Gorgon C .15 .30
SOVR21 Reptilianne Medusa C .15 .30
SOVR22 Reptilianne Scylla C .15 .30
SOVR23 Reptilianne Viper C .15 .30
SOVR24 Earthbound Immortal Ccarayhua UR 1.50 3.00
SOVR24 Earthbound Immortal Ccarayhua UTR 3.00 6.00
SOVR25 Earthbound Immortal Uru UR 2.50 5.00
SOVR25 Earthbound Immortal Uru UTR 3.00 6.00
SOVR26 Earth. Immortal Wiraqocha UR 1.50 3.00
SOVR26 Earth. Immortal Wiraqocha UTR 1.25 2.50
SOVR27 Koa'ki Meiru Sea Panther C .15 .30
SOVR28 Koa'ki Meiru Rooklord SR .75 1.50
SOVR29 Tuned Magician C .15 .30
SOVR30 Crusader of Endymion UR 1.50 3.00
SOVR30 Crusader of Endymion UTR 6.00 12.00
SOVR31 Woodland Archer C .15 .30
SOVR32 Knight of the Red Lotus SR 2.50 5.00
SOVR33 Energy Bravery C .15 .30
SOVR34 Swap Frog C .15 .30
SOVR35 Lord British Space Fighter R .60 1.25
SOVR36 Oshaleon C .15 .30
SOVR37 Djinn Releaser of Rituals R .60 1.25
SOVR38 Djinn Presider of Rituals R .50 1.00
SOVR39 Divine Grace - Northwemko UR 1.50 3.00
SOVR39 Divine Grace - Northwemko UTR 2.00 4.00
SOVR40 Majestic Star Dragon UR 1.50 3.00
SOVR40 Majestic Star Dragon UTR 2.00 4.00
SOVR40 Majestic Star Dragon GR 7.50 15.00
SOVR41 Blackwing - Silverwind UR 1.50 3.00
SOVR41 Blackwing - Silverwind UTR 1.25 2.50
SOVR42 Reptilianne Hydra SR .75 1.50
SOVR43 Black Brutdrago SR .75 1.50
SOVR44 Explosive Magician UR 2.00 4.00
SOVR44 Explosive Magician UTR 3.00 6.00
SOVR45 Spider Web C .15 .30
SOVR46 Earthbound Whirlwind SR .60 1.25
SOVR47 Savage Colosseum C .15 .30
SOVR48 Attack Pheromones C .15 .30
SOVR49 Molting Escape C .15 .30
SOVR50 Reptilianne Spawn C .15 .30
SOVR51 Fortune's Future SR 2.00 4.00
SOVR52 Time Passage C .15 .30
SOVR53 Iron Core Armor C .15 .30
SOVR54 Herculean Power C .15 .30
SOVR55 Gemini Spark C .15 .30
SOVR56 Ritual of Grace C .15 .30
SOVR57 Preparation of Rites SR 1.25 2.50
SOVR58 Moray of Greed C .15 .30
SOVR59 Spiritual Forest C .15 .30
SOVR60 Raging Mad Plants R .50 1.00
SOVR61 Insect Neglect C .15 .30
SOVR62 Faustian Bargain C .15 .30
SOVR63 Slip Summon C .15 .30
SOVR64 Synchro Barrier C .15 .30
SOVR65 Enlightenment C .15 .30
SOVR66 Bending Destiny C .15 .30
SOVR67 Inherited Fortune R .50 1.00
SOVR68 Spider Egg C .15 .30
SOVR69 Wolf in Sheep's Clothing C .15 .30
SOVR70 Earthbound Wave C .15 .30
SOVR71 Roar of the Earthbound C .15 .30
SOVR72 Limit Impulse C .15 .30
SOVR73 Infernity Force C .15 .30
SOVR74 Nega-Ton Corepanel R .50 1.00
SOVR75 Gemini Counter C .15 .30
SOVR76 Gemini Booster C .15 .30
SOVR77 Ritual Buster C .15 .30
SOVR78 Stygian Dirge C .15 .30
SOVR79 Seal of Wickedness SR .75 1.50
SOVR80 Appointer of the Red Lotus C .15 .30
SOVR81 Koa'ki Meiru Maximus UR 1.50 3.00
SOVR81 Koa'ki Meiru Maximus UTR 1.25 2.50
SOVR82 Shire, Lightsworn Spirit SR .75 1.50
SOVR83 Rinyan, Lightsworn Rogue R .60 1.25
SOVR84 Yellow Baboon, Archer UR 1.50 3.00
SOVR84 Yellow Baboon, Archer UTR 1.25 2.50
SOVR85 Gemini Scorpion R .50 1.00
SOVR86 Metabo-Shark SR .75 1.50
SOVR87 Earthbound Revival R .50 1.00
SOVR88 Reptilianne Poison R .50 1.00
SOVR89 Gateway of the Six SR 2.50 5.00
SOVR90 Dark Rabbit R .50 1.00
SOVR91 Shine Palace R .60 1.25
SOVR92 Dark Simorgh SCR 15.00 30.00
SOVR93 Victoria SCR 10.00 20.00
SOVR94 Ice Queen SCR 1.50 3.00
SOVR95 Shutendoji SCR 4.00 8.00
SOVR96 Archlord Kristya SCR 20.00 40.00
SOVR97 Guardian Eatos SCR 50.00 100.00
SOVR98 Clear Vice Dragon SCR 1.50 3.00
SOVR99 Clear World SCR 1.00 2.00

2009 Yu-Gi-Oh Starter Deck 5D's 1st Edition

5DS2EN001 Gogiga Gagagigo C 2.00 4.00
5DS2EN002 Sabersaurus C .12 .25
5DS2EN003 CyberTech Alligator C .30 .75
5DS2EN004 XSaber Anu Piranha C .30 .75
5DS2EN005 The Dragon Dwelling in the Cave C .12 .25
5DS2EN006 Road Synchron SR .30 .60
5DS2EN007 Powered Tuner C .20 .40
5DS2EN008 Goblin Attack Force C .25 .50
5DS2EN009 Penguin Soldier C .75 1.50
5DS2EN010 Sasuke Samurai C .17 .35
5DS2EN011 Des Koala C 1.00 2.00
5DS2EN012 Saber Beetle C .20 .40
5DS2EN013 Quillbolt Hedgehog C .20 .40
5DS2EN014 Junk Synchron C 1.00 2.00
5DS2EN015 Speed Warrior C .12 .25
5DS2EN016 Skelengel C .25 .50
5DS2EN017 Sonic Chick C .20 .40
5DS2EN018 Magna Drago C .12 .25
5DS2EN019 XSaber Airbellum C .25 .50
5DS2EN020 XSaber Galahad C .17 .35
5DS2EN021 Pride of the Weak C .20 .40
5DS2EN022 Rush Recklessly C .17 .35
5DS2EN023 Giant Trunade C .40 .80
5DS2EN024 Tribute to the Doomed C .25 .50
5DS2EN025 The Warrior Returning Alive C .30 .75
5DS2EN026 Emergency Provisions C .30 .60
5DS2EN027 Creature Swap C .30 .60
5DS2EN028 Twister C .12 .25
5DS2EN029 DeSynchro C .40 .80
5DS2EN030 Unstable Evolution C .17 .35
5DS2EN031 Ookazi C .07 .15
5DS2EN032 Synchro Boost C .40 .80
5DS2EN033 Gottoms Emergency Call C 1.75 3.50
5DS2EN034 Dust Tornado C .50 1.00
5DS2EN035 Magic Drain C .25 .50
5DS2EN036 Raigeki Break C .75 1.50
5DS2EN037 Limit Reverse C .25 .50
5DS2EN038 Scraplron Scarecrow C .75 1.50

5DS2EN039 Miniaturize C	.07	.15
5DS2EN040 Widespread Ruin C	.25	.50
5DS2EN041 Road Warrior UR	1.00	2.00
5DS2EN042 Junk Warrior C	.75	1.50
5DS2EN043 XSaber Urbellum SR	.17	.35

2009 Yu-Gi-Oh Structure Deck Spellcaster's Command 1st Edition

SDSC1 Endymion, the Master Magician UR	1.25	2.50
SDSC2 Disenchanter	.15	.30
SDSC3 Defender, the Magical Knight	.15	.30
SDSC4 Hannibal Necromancer	.15	.30
SDSC5 Summoner Monk	.15	.30
SDSC6 Dark Red Enchanter	.15	.30
SDSC7 Skilled Dark Magician	.15	.30
SDSC8 Apprentice Magician	.15	.30
SDSC9 Old Vindictive Magician	.15	.30
SDSC10 Magical Marionette	.15	.30
SDSC11 Breaker the Magical Warrior	.15	.30
SDSC12 Magical Plant Mandragola	.15	.30
SDSC13 Royal Magical Library	.15	.30
SDSC14 Blast Magician	.15	.30
SDSC15 Mythical Beast Cerberus	.15	.30
SDSC16 Mei-Kou, Master of Barriers	.15	.30
SDSC17 Crystal Seer	.15	.30
SDSC18 Magical Exemplar	.15	.30
SDSC19 Magical Citadel of Endymion	.15	.30
SDSC20 Spell Power Grasp	.15	.30
SDSC21 Magicians Unite	.15	.30
SDSC22 Mist Body	.15	.30
SDSC23 Malevolent Nuzzler	.15	.30
SDSC24 Giant Trunade	.15	.30
SDSC25 Fissure	.15	.30
SDSC26 Swords of Revealing Light	.15	.30
SDSC27 Mage Power	.15	.30
SDSC28 Terraforming	.15	.30
SDSC29 Enemy Controller	.15	.30
SDSC30 Book of Moon	.15	.30
SDSC31 Magical Blast	.15	.30
SDSC32 Magical Dimension	.15	.30
SDSC33 Twister	.15	.30
SDSC34 Field Barrier	.15	.30
SDSC35 Magician's Circle	.15	.30
SDSC36 Pitch-Black Power Stone	.15	.30
SDSC37 Tower of Babel	.15	.30
SDSC38 Magic Cylinder	.15	.30

2009 Yu-Gi-Oh Structure Deck Warriors' Strike 1st Edition

SDWS1 Phoenix Gearfried UR	.50	1.00
SDWS2 Evocator Chevalier SR	.10	.20
SDWS3 Featherizer SR	.10	.20
SDWS4 Gemini Soldier C	.10	.20
SDWS5 Spell Striker C	.50	1.00
SDWS6 Freed the Matchless General C	.10	.20
SDWS7 Marauding Captain C	.10	.20
SDWS8 Exiled Force C	.10	.20
SDWS9 D.D. Warrior Lady C	.60	1.25
SDWS10 Card Trooper C	.10	.20
SDWS11 Gemini Summoner C	.10	.20
SDWS12 Blazewing Butterfly C	.10	.20
SDWS13 D.D. Warrior C	.10	.20
SDWS14 Future Samurai C	.10	.20
SDWS15 Field-Commander Rahz C	.10	.20
SDWS16 Dark Valkyria C	.10	.20
SDWS17 Supervise C	.50	1.00
SDWS18 Mind Control C	.10	.20
SDWS19 Burden of the Mighty C	.75	1.50
SDWS20 Silent Doom C	.10	.20
SDWS21 Hidden Armory C	.60	1.25
SDWS22 Nightmare's Steelcage C	.10	.20
SDWS23 Mystical Space Typhoon C	.10	.20
SDWS24 Ekibyo Drakmord C	.10	.20
SDWS25 Reinforcement of the Army C	.10	.20
SDWS26 Big Bang Shot C	.10	.20
SDWS27 Divine Sword - Phoenix Blade C	.10	.20
SDWS28 Double Summon C	1.25	2.50
SDWS29 Symbols of Duty C	.10	.20
SDWS30 Swing of Memories C	.10	.20
SDWS31 Unleash Your Power! C	.10	.20
SDWS32 Dark Bribe C	.75	1.50
SDWS33 Kunai with Chain C	.10	.20
SDWS34 Sakuretsu Armor C	.60	1.25
SDWS35 Soul Resurrection C	.10	.20
SDWS36 Justi-Break C	.10	.20
SDWS37 Birthright C	.10	.20
SDWS38 Gemini Trap Hole C	.10	.20

2009 Yu-Gi-Oh Turbo Pack 1

TU01EN000 Judgment Dragon UTR	20.00	40.00
TU01EN001 Doomcaliber Knight UR	2.50	5.00
TU01EN002 Garoth, Lightsworn Warrior SR	1.25	2.50
TU01EN003 Krebons SR	2.50	5.00
TU01EN004 Gladiator Beast Samnite SR	.75	1.50
TU01EN005 Black Whirlwind SR	5.00	10.00
TU01EN006 Crush Card Virus R	1.25	2.50
TU01EN007 Satellite Cannon R	.60	1.25
TU01EN008 Rescue Cat R	.60	1.25
TU01EN009 Grandmaster of the Six Samurai R	.60	1.25
TU01EN010 TradeIn R	1.50	3.00
TU01EN011 Armageddon Knight R	.75	1.50
TU01EN012 Book of Moon C	.50	1.00
TU01EN013 Terraforming C	.75	1.50
TU01EN014 Hand Destruction C	1.00	2.00
TU01EN015 Gladiator Beast Murmillo C	.50	1.00
TU01EN016 Gladiator Beast Bestiari C	.50	1.00
TU01EN017 Gladiator Beast Laquari C	.50	1.00
TU01EN018 Golden Flying Fish C	.50	1.00
TU01EN019 Ryko, Lightsworn Hunter C	.50	1.00
TU01EN020 D.D.R. Different Dimension Reincarnation C	.50	1.00

2010 Yu-Gi-Oh Absolute Powerforce 1st Edition

ABPF0 Grvkpr's Prstss SR	.75	1.50
ABPF1 Unicycular C	.15	.30
ABPF2 Bicular C	.15	.30
ABPF3 Tricular C	.15	.30
ABPF4 Drill Synchron R	.50	1.00
ABPF5 Ogre of the Scarlet Sorrow SR	.75	1.50
ABPF6 Battle Fader UR	2.00	4.00
ABPF6 Battle Fader UTR	7.50	15.00
ABPF7 Power Supplier C	.15	.30
ABPF8 Magic Hole Golem C	.15	.30
ABPF9 Power Invader C	.15	.30
ABPF10 Dark Bug R	.50	1.00
ABPF11 Sword Master	.15	.30
ABPF12 Witch of the Black Rose UR	1.50	3.00
ABPF12 Witch of the Black Rose UTR	2.00	4.00
ABPF13 Rose Fairy C	.15	.30
ABPF14 Dragon Queen of Tragic Endings SR	.75	1.50
ABPF15 Reptilianne Servant C	.15	.30
ABPF16 Reptilianne Gardna C	.15	.30
ABPF17 Reptilianne Naga C	.15	.30
ABPF18 Reptilianne Vaskii R	.50	1.00
ABPF19 Oracle of the Sun SR	.75	1.50
ABPF20 Fire Ant Ascator C	.15	.30
ABPF21 Weeping Idol C	.15	.30
ABPF22 Apocatequil C	.15	.30
ABPF23 Supay C	.15	.30
ABPF24 Informer Spider C	.15	.30
ABPF25 Koa'ki Meiru Urnight UR	1.50	3.00
ABPF25 Koa'ki Meiru Urnight UTR	1.50	3.00
ABPF26 XX-Saber Garsem R	.50	1.00
ABPF27 Gravekeeper's Visionary SR	.75	1.50
ABPF28 Gravekeeper's Descendant R	.50	1.00
ABPF29 Black Potan C	.15	.30
ABPF30 Shreddder C	.15	.30
ABPF31 Pandaborg C	.15	.30
ABPF32 Codarus C	.15	.30
ABPF33 Consecrated Light C	.15	.30
ABPF34 Gundari C	.15	.30
ABPF35 Cyber Dragon Zwei R	.50	1.00
ABPF36 Oilman C	.15	.30
ABPF37 Djinn Cursenchanter of Rituals R	.50	1.00
ABPF38 Djinn Prognosticator of Rituals R	.50	1.00
ABPF39 Garlandolf, King of Destruction UR	1.50	3.00
ABPF39 Garlandolf, King of Destruction UTR	1.50	3.00
ABPF40 Majestic Red Dragon UR	1.50	3.00
ABPF40 Majestic Red Dragon UTR	1.50	3.00
ABPF40 Majestic Red Dragon GR	5.00	10.00
ABPF41 Drill Warrior UR	1.50	3.00
ABPF41 Drill Warrior UTR	1.50	3.00
ABPF42 Sun Dragon Inti UR	1.50	3.00
ABPF42 Sun Dragon Inti UTR	1.50	3.00
ABPF43 Moon Dragon Quilla UR	1.50	3.00
ABPF43 Moon Dragon Quilla UTR	1.50	3.00
ABPF44 XX-Saber Hyunlei UR	2.50	5.00
ABPF44 XX-Saber Hyunlei UTR	3.00	6.00
ABPF45 Cards of Consonance SR	2.50	5.00
ABPF46 Variety Comes Out C	.15	.30
ABPF47 Reptilianne Rage C	.15	.30
ABPF48 Advance Force C	.15	.30
ABPF49 Viper's Rebirth C	.15	.30
ABPF50 Temple of the Sun C	.15	.30
ABPF51 Rocket Pilder C	.15	.30
ABPF52 Break! Draw! C	.15	.30
ABPF53 Power Pickaxe R	.50	1.00
ABPF54 Spider's Lair C	.15	.30
ABPF55 Iron Core Specimen Lab SR	.75	1.50
ABPF56 Gravekeeper's Stele C	.15	.30
ABPF57 Machine Assembly Line C	.15	.30
ABPF58 Ritual of Destruction C	.15	.30
ABPF59 Ascending Soul R	.50	1.00
ABPF60 Ritual Cage R	.50	1.00
ABPF61 Pot of Benevolence C	.15	.30
ABPF62 Synchro Control SR	.75	1.50
ABPF63 Changing Destiny C	.15	.30
ABPF64 Fiendish Chain SR	3.00	6.00
ABPF65 Nature's Reflection C	.15	.30
ABPF66 Serpent Suppression C	.15	.30
ABPF67 Meteor Flare C	.15	.30
ABPF68 Offering to the Immortals R	.50	1.00
ABPF69 Destruct Potion C	.15	.30
ABPF70 Call of the Reaper C	.15	.30
ABPF71 Lair Wire C	.15	.30
ABPF72 Core Blast R	.50	1.00
ABPF73 Saber Hole SR	1.50	3.00
ABPF74 Machine King - 3000 B.C. C	.15	.30
ABPF75 Alien Brain C	.15	.30
ABPF76 Forgotten Temple of the Deep C	.15	.30
ABPF77 Tuner's Scheme SR	.75	1.50
ABPF78 Psi-Curse C	.15	.30
ABPF79 Widespread Dud C	.15	.30
ABPF80 Inverse Universe C	.15	.30
ABPF81 XX-Saber Emmersblade SCR	2.00	4.00
ABPF82 Alchemist of Black Spells UR	1.50	3.00
ABPF82 Alchemist of Black Spells UTR	2.00	4.00
ABPF83 Super-Nimble Mega Hamster SR	.75	1.50
ABPF84 Cactus Bouncer SCR	7.50	15.00
ABPF85 Dragonic Guard SR	.75	1.50
ABPF86 The Dragon Dwelling in the Deep SR	.75	1.50
ABPF87 Djinn Disserere of Rituals SCR	1.50	3.00
ABPF88 Earthbound Linewalker SCR	2.00	4.00
ABPF89 Core Transport Unit SCR	1.50	3.00
ABPF90 Gale Dogra R	.50	1.00
ABPF91 Berfomet R	.50	1.00
ABPF92 Chimera the Flying Mythical Beast R	.50	1.00
ABPF93 Viser Des R	.50	1.00
ABPF94 Evil Blast R	.50	1.00
ABPF95 Shield Wing SCR	1.50	3.00
ABPF96 Underground Arachnid SCR	1.50	3.00
ABPF97 Zeman the Ape King SCR	1.50	3.00
ABPF98 Skull Conductor R	.50	1.00
ABPF99 Shield Worm R	.50	1.00

2010 Yu-Gi-Oh Collector Tins

CT07EN001 Majestic Red Dragon SCR	.75	1.50
CT07EN002 Black-Winged Dragon SCR	.75	1.50
CT07EN003 Dragon Knight Draco-Equiste SCR	.75	1.50
CT07EN004 Shooting Star Dragon SCR	2.50	5.00
CT07EN005 Red Nova Dragon SCR	2.00	4.00
CT07EN006 Elemental HERO Stratos SR	.75	1.50
CT07EN007 Van'Dalgyon the Dark Dragon Lord SR	.75	1.50
CT07EN008 Cyber Dinosaur SR	.75	1.50
CT07EN009 Battle Fader SR	.75	1.50
CT07EN010 Green Baboon, Defender of the Forest SR	.75	1.50
CT07EN011 The Wicked Eraser SR	.75	1.50
CT07EN012 Blackwing - Vayu the Emblem of Honor SR	.75	1.50
CT07EN013 Chimeratech Fortress Dragon SR	4.00	8.00
CT07EN014 Archfiend of Gilfer SR	.75	1.50
CT07EN015 The Wicked Dreadroot SR	.75	1.50
CT07EN016 Dark Armed Dragon SR	.75	1.50
CT07EN017 Dragonic Knight SR	.75	1.50
CT07EN018 Elemental HERO Ocean SR	.75	1.50
CT07EN019 Dreadscythe Harvester SR	.75	1.50
CT07EN020 Gandora the Dragon of Destruction SR	.75	1.50
CT07EN021 Stardust Dragon SR	1.50	3.00
CT07EN022 Magician's Valkyria SR	2.50	5.00
CT07EN023 The Wicked Avatar SR	1.50	3.00
CT07EN024 Exodius the Ultimate Forbidden Lord SR	.75	1.50
CT07EN025 Red Dragon Archfiend SR	.75	1.50

2010 Yu-Gi-Oh Duelist Pack Collection Tins

DPCTEN004 Starlight Road SCR	4.00	8.00
DPCTENY01 Junk Synchron UR	3.00	6.00
DPCTENY02 Quillbolt Hedgehog SR	1.50	3.00
DPCTENY03 Synchro Blast Wave SR	1.50	3.00
DPCTENY04 Drill Synchron UR	2.50	5.00
DPCTENY05 Speed Warrior SR	1.25	2.50
DPCTENY06 Advance Draw SR	1.25	2.50
DPCTENY07 Scrap-Iron Scarecrow UR	2.50	5.00
DPCTENY08 Level Eater SR	1.25	2.50
DPCTENY09 One for One SR	1.25	2.50

2010 Yu-Gi-Oh Duelist Pack Yusei 2 1st Edition

DP09EN001 Stardust Dragon/Assault Mode SR	.50	1.00
DP09EN002 Road Synchron R	.25	.50
DP09EN003 Turret Warrior R	.25	.50
DP09EN004 Debris Dragon	.10	.20
DP09EN005 Hyper Synchron	.10	.20
DP09EN006 Rockstone Warrior R	.25	.50
DP09EN007 Level Warrior	.10	.20
DP09EN008 Majestic Dragon	.75	1.50
DP09EN009 Max Warrior R	.25	.50
DP09EN010 Quickdraw Synchron	.10	.20
DP09EN011 Level Eater	.10	.20
DP09EN012 Zero Gardna	.10	.20
DP09EN013 Gauntlet Warrior UR	.50	1.00
DP09EN014 Eccentric Boy SR	.50	1.00
DP09EN015 Road Warrior R	.75	1.50
DP09EN016 Junk Archer UR	2.50	5.00
DP09EN017 Prevention Star	.10	.20
DP09EN018 One for One R	.25	.50
DP09EN019 Release Restraint Wave	.10	.20
DP09EN020 Silver Wing	.10	.20
DP09EN021 Advance Draw	.10	.20
DP09EN022 Assault Mode Activate	.10	.20
DP09EN023 Spirit Force	.10	.20
DP09EN024 Descending Lost Star	.10	.20
DP09EN025 Miracle Locus	.10	.20
DP09EN026 Skill Successor R	.25	.50
DP09EN027 Reinforce Truth	.10	.20
DP09EN028 Slip Summon	.10	.20
DP09EN029 Scrubbed Raid SR	.50	1.00
DP09EN030 Tuner's Barrier SR	.50	1.00

2010 Yu-Gi-Oh Duelist Revolution 1st Edition

DREV0 Scrap Archfiend SR	1.25	2.50
DREV1 Earthquake Giant	.15	.30
DREV2 Effect Veiler UR	7.50	15.00
DREV2 Effect Veiler UTR	50.00	100.00
DREV3 Dash Warrior	.15	.30
DREV4 Damage Eater	.15	.30
DREV5 A/D Changer	.15	.30
DREV6 Stronghold Guardian	.15	.30
DREV7 Playful Possum R	.50	1.00
DREV8 Egotistical Ape R	.50	1.00
DREV9 Uni-Horned Familiar	.15	.30
DREV10 Monoceros	.15	.30
DREV11 D.D. Unicorn Knight R	.50	1.00
DREV12 Unibird SR	.50	1.00
DREV13 Bicorn Re'em	.15	.30
DREV14 Mine Mole	.15	.30
DREV15 Trident Warrior SR	.50	1.00
DREV16 Delta Flyer R	2.00	4.00
DREV17 Rhinotaurus	.15	.30
DREV18 Hypnocorn R	.50	1.00
DREV19 Scrap Chimera SR	.50	1.00
DREV20 Scrap Goblin	.15	.30
DREV21 Scrap Beast R	.50	1.00
DREV22 Scrap Hunter R	.50	1.00
DREV23 Scrap Golem R	.50	1.00
DREV24 Wattbetta	.15	.30
DREV25 Wattlemur	.15	.30
DREV26 Wattpheasant	.15	.30
DREV27 Naturia Mosquito	.15	.30
DREV28 Naturia Beans	.15	.30
DREV29 Naturia Bamboo Shoot UR	2.00	4.00
DREV29 Naturia Bamboo Shoot UTR	2.50	5.00
DREV30 Amazoness Sage	.15	.30
DREV31 Amazoness Trainee	.15	.30
DREV32 Amazoness Queen SR	3.00	6.00
DREV33 Lock Cat	.15	.30
DREV34 Elephun	.15	.30
DREV35 Synchro Fusionist R	.50	1.00
DREV36 Ambitious Gofer R	.50	1.00
DREV37 Final Psychic Ogre	.15	.30
DREV38 Dragon Knight Draco-Equiste UR	.50	1.00
DREV38 Dragon Knight Draco-Equiste UTR	.75	1.50
DREV38 Dragon Knight Draco-Equiste GR	2.50	5.00
DREV39 Ultimate Axon Kicker SR	1.25	2.50
DREV40 Thunder Unicorn UR	.50	1.00
DREV40 Thunder Unicorn UTR	.75	1.50
DREV41 Voltic Bicorn UR	.50	1.00
DREV41 Voltic Bicorn UTR	.75	1.50
DREV42 Lightning Tricorn UR	.50	1.00
DREV42 Lightning Tricorn UTR	.75	1.50
DREV43 Scrap Dragon UR	2.00	4.00
DREV43 Scrap Dragon UTR	5.00	10.00
DREV44 Watchimera UR	.50	1.00
DREV44 Watchimera UTR	.75	1.50
DREV45 Blind Spot Strike	.15	.30
DREV46 Double Cyclone	.15	.30
DREV47 Scrapyard SR	.50	1.00
DREV48 Scrapstorm SR	.50	1.00
DREV49 Scrap Sheen	.15	.30
DREV50 Wattcine	.15	.30
DREV51 Naturia Forest	.15	.30
DREV52 Landoise's Luminous Moss R	.50	1.00
DREV53 Amazoness Village R	.50	1.00
DREV54 Amazoness Fighting Spirit	.15	.30
DREV55 Unicorn Beacon SR	.50	1.00
DREV56 Beast Rage	.15	.30
DREV57 Miracle Synchro Fusion	.15	.30
DREV58 Pestilence	.15	.30
DREV59 Cursed Armaments	.15	.30
DREV60 Wiseman's Chalice SR	.50	1.00
DREV61 Summoning Curse	.15	.30
DREV62 Pot of Duality SCR	7.50	15.00
DREV63 Desperate Tag	.15	.30
DREV64 Battle Instinct	.15	.30
DREV65 Howl of the Wild	.15	.30
DREV66 Parallel Selection R	.50	1.00
DREV67 Reanimation Wave R	.50	1.00
DREV68 Barrier Wave	.15	.30
DREV69 Chain Whirlwind	.15	.30
DREV70 Scrap Rage	.15	.30
DREV71 Wattcannon	.15	.30
DREV72 Amazoness Willpower R	.50	1.00
DREV73 Queen's Pawn	.15	.30
DREV74 Beast Rising	.15	.30
DREV75 Horn of the Phantom Beast R	.50	1.00
DREV76 Paradox Fusion SR	1.00	2.00
DREV77 Solemn Warning UR	6.00	12.00
DREV77 Solemn Warning UTR	50.00	100.00
DREV78 Anti-Magic Prism	.15	.30
DREV79 Chivalry UR	1.00	2.00
DREV79 Chivalry UTR	2.00	4.00
DREV80 Light of Destruction	.15	.30
DREV81 Amazoness Scouts R	.50	1.00
DREV82 Naturia Pineapple SCR	.75	1.50
DREV83 D.D. Destroyer R	.50	1.00
DREV84 Dark Desertapir R	.50	1.00
DREV85 Psychic Nightmare SCR	1.50	3.00
DREV86 Guts of Steel R	.50	1.00
DREV87 Amazoness Heirloom SR	1.00	2.00
DREV88 Amazoness Shamanism SR	.50	1.00
DREV89 Super Rush Recklessly SR	.50	1.00
DREV90 Mystical Refpanel SCR	7.50	15.00
DREV91 Fabled Raven SCR	2.50	5.00
DREV92 Ally of Justice Cyclone Creator SCR	.75	1.50
DREV93 Miracle's Wake SCR	.75	1.50
DREV94 Flamvell Poun	.15	.30
DREV95 Flamvell Archer	.15	.30
DREV96 Flamvell Fiend	.15	.30
DREV97 Genex Worker	.15	.30
DREV98 Genex Power Planner	.15	.30
DREV99 Stygian Street Patrol SCR	2.00	4.00

2010 Yu-Gi-Oh Gold Series 3

GLD3EN001 Mist Valley Watcher C	.10	.20
GLD3EN002 Amazoness Archer C	.10	.20
GLD3EN003 Amazoness Paladin C	.10	.20
GLD3EN004 Amazoness Fighter C	.10	.20
GLD3EN005 Amazoness Swords Woman C	.20	.40
GLD3EN006 Amazoness Blowpiper C	.10	.20
GLD3EN007 Amazoness Tiger C	.10	.20
GLD3EN008 Destiny Hero - Malicious	1.25	2.50
GLD3EN009 Freya, Spirit of Victory C	.20	.40
GLD3EN010 Nova Summoner C	.20	.40
GLD3EN011 Exploder Dragon GUR	1.00	2.00
GLD3EN012 Goblin Zombie C	.75	1.50
GLD3EN013 Elemental Hero Prisma GUR	2.50	5.00
GLD3EN014 Dimensional Alchemist GUR	1.00	2.00
GLD3EN015 Judgment Dragon GUR	1.50	3.00
GLD3EN016 Amazoness Chain Master C	.10	.20
GLD3EN017 Mezuki GUR	1.00	2.00
GLD3EN018 Plaguespreader Zombie GUR	1.00	2.00
GLD3EN019 Vice Dragon GUR	1.00	2.00
GLD3EN020 Thunder King Rai-Oh GUR	1.25	2.50
GLD3EN021 Blackwing - Gale GUR	1.00	2.00
GLD3EN022 Blackwing - Bora the Spear C	.50	1.00
GLD3EN023 Blackwing - Sirocco the Dawn C	.50	1.00
GLD3EN024 Blackwing - Blizzard the Far North C	.50	1.00
GLD3EN025 Blackwing - Shura the Blue Flame C	.50	1.00
GLD3EN026 Blackwing - Kalut	.50	1.00
GLD3EN027 Infernity Archfiend GUR	1.00	2.00
GLD3EN028 Infernity Dwarf C	.10	.20
GLD3EN029 Infernity Guardian C	.10	.20
GLD3EN030 Reese the Ice Mistress C	.20	.40
GLD3EN031 Numbing Grub in the Ice Barrier C	.10	.20
GLD3EN032 Mist Condor C	.10	.20
GLD3EN033 Mist Valley Windmaster C	.10	.20
GLD3EN034 Worm Falco C	.10	.20
GLD3EN035 Worm Gulse C	.10	.20
GLD3EN036 Worm Hope C	.10	.20
GLD3EN037 Stardust Dragon GUR	2.50	5.00
GLD3EN038 Blackwing Armor Master GUR	1.00	2.00
GLD3EN039 Blackwing Armed Wing GUR	1.00	2.00
GLD3EN040 Mystical Space Typhoon GUR	1.50	3.00
GLD3EN041 My Body as a Shield GUR	1.00	2.00
GLD3EN042 Smashing Ground GUR	1.00	2.00
GLD3EN043 Enemy Controller GUR	1.00	2.00
GLD3EN044 Destiny Draw C	.30	.75
GLD3EN045 Black Whirlwind C	1.25	2.50
GLD3EN046 Amazoness Archers C	.10	.20
GLD3EN047 Dramatic Rescue C	.10	.20
GLD3EN048 Magical Arm Shield C	.10	.20
GLD3EN049 Icarus Attack GUR	1.00	2.00
GLD3EN050 Aegis of Gaia C	.10	.20

2010 Yu-Gi-Oh Hidden Arsenal 2 1st Edition

HA02EN001 Naturia Beetle SR	.50	1.00
HA02EN002 Naturia Rock SR	.50	1.00
HA02EN003 Naturia Guardian SCR	.60	1.25
HA02EN004 Naturia Vein SR	.50	1.00
HA02EN005 Genex Furnace SR	.50	1.00
HA02EN006 Genex Gaia SR	.50	1.00
HA02EN007 Genex Spare SR	.50	1.00

HA02EN008 Genex Turbine SR .50 1.00
HA02EN009 Genex Doctor SR .50 1.00
HA02EN010 Genex Solar SCR .60 1.25
HA02EN011 Dai-sojo of the Ice Barrier SCR .60 1.25
HA02EN012 Medium of the Ice Barrier SR .60 1.25
HA02EN013 Mist Valley Baby Roc SR .50 1.00
HA02EN014 Mist Valley Executor SR .50 1.00
HA02EN015 Flamvell Grunika SR .50 1.00
HA02EN016 Flamvell Baby SR .50 1.00
HA02EN017 Ally Mind SR .50 1.00
HA02EN018 Ally of Justice Nullfier SR .50 1.00
HA02EN019 Ally of Justice Searcher SR .50 1.00
HA02EN020 Ally of Justice Enemy Catcher SR .50 1.00
HA02EN021 Ally of Justice Thunder Armor SR .50 1.00
HA02EN022 Ally of Justice Cosmic SCR .60 1.25
HA02EN023 Worm Linx SR .50 1.00
HA02EN024 Worm Millidith SR .50 1.00
HA02EN025 Worm Noble SR .50 1.00
HA02EN026 Naturia Beast SCR 3.00 6.00
HA02EN027 Dewloren, Tiger King SCR 3.00 6.00
HA02EN028 Thermal Genex SCR .60 1.25
HA02EN029 Geo Genex SCR .60 1.25
HA02EN030 Ally of Justice Field Marshal SCR .75 1.50
HA02EN031 Fabled Lurrie SR .50 1.00
HA02EN032 Fabled Grimro SCR .50 1.00
HA02EN033 Fabled Gallabas SCR .60 1.25
HA02EN034 Fabled Kushano SR .60 1.25
HA02EN035 Jurrac Protops SR .50 1.00
HA02EN036 Jurrac Velo SR 1.00 2.00
HA02EN037 Jurrac Monoloph SR .50 1.00
HA02EN038 Jurrac Tyrannus SCR .75 1.50
HA02EN039 Naturia Antjaw SR .50 1.00
HA02EN040 Naturia Spiderfang SR .50 1.00
HA02EN041 Naturia Rosewhip SR .60 1.25
HA02EN042 Naturia Cosmobeet SR .50 1.00
HA02EN043 Genex Blastfan SR .50 1.00
HA02EN044 Genex Recycled SR .50 1.00
HA02EN045 Genex Army SCR .60 1.25
HA02EN046 Pilgrim of the Ice Barrier SR .50 1.00
HA02EN047 Geomancer of the Ice Barrier SR .50 1.00
HA02EN048 Mist Valley Falcon SR .60 1.25
HA02EN049 Mist Valley Apex Avian SCR 5.00 10.00
HA02EN050 Ally of Justice Reverse Break SR .50 1.00
HA02EN051 Ally of Justice Unlimiter SR .50 1.00
HA02EN052 Worm Opera SR .50 1.00
HA02EN053 Worm Prince SR .50 1.00
HA02EN054 Worm Queen SCR .60 1.25
HA02EN055 Worm Rakuyeh SR .50 1.00
HA02EN056 Fabled Valkyrus SCR 2.00 4.00
HA02EN057 Jurrac Giganoto SCR 1.50 3.00
HA02EN058 Naturia Leodrake SCR .60 1.25
HA02EN059 Windmill Genex SCR .60 1.25
HA02EN060 Mist Valley Thunder Lord SCR .60 1.25

2010 Yu-Gi-Oh Hidden Arsenal 3 1st Edition

HA03EN001 Fabled Urustos SR .25 .50
HA03EN002 Fabled Krus SCR 2.00 4.00
HA03EN003 Fabled Topi SR .25 .50
HA03EN004 Fabled Soulkius SCR .50 1.00
HA03EN005 Fabled Miztoji SR .25 .50
HA03EN006 Jurrac Ptera SR .25 .50
HA03EN007 Jurrac Iguanon SR .25 .50
HA03EN008 Jurrac Brachis SR .25 .50
HA03EN009 Jurrac Spinos SR .25 .50
HA03EN010 Naturia Dragonfly SR .25 .50
HA03EN011 Naturia Sunflower SR .25 .50
HA03EN012 Naturia Cliff SCR 1.50 3.00
HA03EN013 Naturia Tulip SR .25 .50
HA03EN014 R-Genex Turbo SR .25 .50
HA03EN015 R-Genex Overseer SR .25 .50
HA03EN016 R-Genex Crusher SR .25 .50
HA03EN017 R-Genex Magma SR .25 .50
HA03EN018 Shock Troops SR .30 .75
HA03EN019 Samurai of the Ice Barrier SR .25 .50
HA03EN020 Dewdark of the Ice Barrier SR .50 1.00
HA03EN021 Caravan of the Ice Barrier SR .25 .50
HA03EN022 Worm Solid SR .25 .50
HA03EN023 Worm Tentacles SR .25 .50
HA03EN024 Worm Ugly SR .25 .50
HA03EN025 Worm Victory SCR .50 1.00
HA03EN026 Fabled Leviathan SCR .60 1.25
HA03EN027 Jurrac Velphito SCR 1.00 2.00
HA03EN028 Naturia Barkion SCR 10.00 20.00
HA03EN029 Locomotion R-Genex SCR .50 1.00
HA03EN030 Gungnir, Dragon of the Ice Barrier SCR 6.00 12.00
HA03EN031 Dragunity Dux SCR 1.00 2.00
HA03EN032 Dragunity Legionnaire SR .25 .50
HA03EN033 Dragunity Tribus SR .25 .50
HA03EN034 Dragunity Darkspear SR .30 .75
HA03EN035 Dragunity Phalanx SCR 5.00 10.00
HA03EN036 Fabled Dyf SR .25 .50
HA03EN037 Fabled Ashenveil SCR .60 1.25
HA03EN038 Fabled Oltro SR .25 .50
HA03EN039 Jurrac Titano SCR .50 1.00
HA03EN040 Jurrac Guaiba SR .25 .50
HA03EN041 Jurrac Stauriko SR .25 .50
HA03EN042 Naturia Horneedle SR .25 .50
HA03EN043 Naturia Fruitfly SR .25 .50
HA03EN044 Naturia Hydrangea SR .25 .50
HA03EN045 R-Genex Accelerator SR .25 .50
HA03EN046 R-Genex Oracle SR .25 .50
HA03EN047 R-Genex Ultimum SR .25 .50
HA03EN048 Spellbreaker of the Ice Barrier SR .25 .50
HA03EN049 General Grunard SCR 1.25 2.50
HA03EN050 Ally of Justice Omni-Weapon SCR .50 1.00
HA03EN051 Ally of Justice Quarantine SR .25 .50
HA03EN052 Ally of Justice Cycle Reader SR .25 .50
HA03EN053 Worm Warlord SR .25 .50
HA03EN054 Worm Xex SR .25 .50
HA03EN055 Worm Yagan SR .25 .50
HA03EN056 Worm Zero SCR .60 1.25
HA03EN057 Dragunity Knight - Gae Bulg SCR 1.00 2.00
HA03EN058 Fabled Ragin SCR 1.50 3.00
HA03EN059 Vindikite R-Genex SCR .50 1.00
HA03EN060 Ally of Justice Decisive SCR 4.00 8.00

2010 Yu-Gi-Oh The Shining Darkness 1st Edition

TSHD0 XX-Saber Boggart Knight SR .75 1.50
TSHD1 Blackwing - Ghibli the Searing Wind .15 .30
TSHD2 Blackwing - Gust the Backblast R .50 1.00
TSHD3 Blackwing - Breeze the Zephyr UR 1.00 2.00
TSHD3 Blackwing - Breeze the Zephyr UTR 1.50 3.00
TSHD4 Changer Synchron .15 .30
TSHD5 Card Breaker .15 .30
TSHD6 Second Booster .15 .30
TSHD7 Archfiend Interceptor .15 .30
TSHD8 Dread Dragon R .50 1.00
TSHD9 Trust Guardian SR .50 1.00
TSHD10 Flare Resonator .15 .30
TSHD11 Synchro Magnet .15 .30
TSHD12 Infernity Mirage SR 1.25 2.50
TSHD13 Infernity Randomizer .15 .30
TSHD14 Infernity Beetle R .75 1.50
TSHD15 Infernity Avenger (R) .50 1.00
TSHD16 Revival Rose R .50 1.00
TSHD17 Morphtronic Vacuumen .15 .30
TSHD18 Bird of Roses SR .75 1.50
TSHD19 Spore .15 .30
TSHD20 Fairy Archer .15 .30
TSHD21 Biofalcon .15 .30
TSHD22 Cherry Inmato R .50 1.00
TSHD23 Magidog R .50 1.00
TSHD24 Lyna the Light Charmer .15 .30
TSHD25 Wattgiraffe SR 4.00 8.00
TSHD26 Wattfox .15 .30
TSHD27 Wattwoodpecker .15 .30
TSHD28 Koa'ki Meiru Sandman .15 .30
TSHD29 Memory Crush King .15 .30
TSHD30 Delta Tri R .50 1.00
TSHD31 Trigon .15 .30
TSHD32 Testudo Erat Numen SP 1.00 2.00
TSHD33 Ronintoadin .15 .30
TSHD34 Batteryman AAA .15 .30
TSHD35 Batteryman Fuel Cell R 1.25 2.50
TSHD36 Key Mouse .15 .30
TSHD37 Ally of Justice Core Destroyer R .50 1.00
TSHD38 Hunter of Black Feathers SP .20 .40
TSHD39 Herald of Perfection UR .75 1.50
TSHD39 Herald of Perfection UTR 5.00 10.00
TSHD40 Black-Winged Dragon UR 1.00 2.00
TSHD40 Black-Winged Dragon UTR 1.00 2.00
TSHD40 Black-Winged Dragon GR 6.00 12.00
TSHD41 Chaos King Archfiend UR 1.25 2.50
TSHD41 Chaos King Archfiend UTR 1.00 2.00
TSHD42 Infernity Doom Dragon UR 1.50 3.00
TSHD42 Infernity Doom Dragon UTR 2.00 4.00
TSHD43 Splendid Rose UR .50 1.00
TSHD43 Splendid Rose UTR .75 1.50
TSHD44 Chaos Goddess SCR 3.00 6.00
TSHD45 Black-Winged Strafe .15 .30
TSHD46 Cards for Black Feathers UR 1.00 2.00
TSHD46 Cards for Black Feathers UTR .75 1.50
TSHD47 ZERO-MAX SR .50 1.00
TSHD48 Infernity Launcher SR 1.00 2.00
TSHD49 Into The Void UR 20.00 40.00
TSHD49 Into The Void UTR 25.00 50.00
TSHD50 Intercept Wave UR .75 1.50
TSHD50 Intercept Wave UTR .50 1.00
TSHD51 Pyramid of Wonders R .50 1.00
TSHD52 The Fountain in the Sky R .50 1.00
TSHD53 Dragon Laser .15 .30
TSHD54 Wattcube .15 .30
TSHD55 Electromagnetic Shield R .50 1.00
TSHD56 Worm Call .15 .30
TSHD57 Magic Triangle of the Ice Barrier .15 .30
TSHD58 Koa'ki Meiru Initialize .15 .30
TSHD59 Dawn of the Herald .15 .30
TSHD60 Forbidden Graveyard .15 .30
TSHD61 Leeching the Light .15 .30
TSHD62 Corridor of Agony SP .20 .40
TSHD63 Power Frame SR .50 1.00
TSHD64 Blackwing - Backlash R .50 1.00
TSHD65 Blackwing - Bombardment .15 .30
TSHD66 Black Thunder .15 .30
TSHD67 Guard Mines R .50 1.00
TSHD68 Infernity Reflector .15 .30
TSHD69 Infernity Break .15 .30
TSHD70 Damage Gate SR .50 1.00
TSHD71 Infernity Inferno R .50 1.00
TSHD72 Phantom Hand .15 .30
TSHD73 Assault Spirits .15 .30
TSHD74 Blossom Bombardment .15 .30
TSHD75 Morphtronics, Scramble! .15 .30
TSHD76 Power Break .15 .30
TSHD77 Koa'ki Meiru Shield R .50 1.00
TSHD78 Crevice into the Different Dimension .15 .30
TSHD79 Synchro Ejection SR .50 1.00
TSHD80 Chaos Trap Hole SP 4.00 8.00
TSHD81 XX-Saber Darksoul UR .50 1.00
TSHD81 XX-Saber Darksoul UTR 2.50 5.00
TSHD82 Koa'ki Meiru Prototype R .50 1.00
TSHD83 Snyffus SCR .50 1.00
TSHD84 Nimble Sunfish SR .50 1.00
TSHD85 Akz, the Pumer R .50 1.00
TSHD86 Saber Vault SCR .50 1.00
TSHD87 Core Overclock SR .50 1.00
TSHD88 Wave-Motion Inferno SCR .50 1.00
TSHD89 Infernity Barrier SCR 2.50 5.00
TSHD90 Genex Controller .15 .30
TSHD91 Genex Undine .15 .30
TSHD92 Genex Searcher R .50 1.00
TSHD93 X-Saber Palomuro .15 .30
TSHD94 X-Saber Pashuul .15 .30
TSHD95 Hydro Genex SR .50 1.00
TSHD96 Ally of Justice Light Gazer SR .50 1.00
TSHD97 Genex Neutron SCR .50 1.00
TSHD98 Infernity Destroyer SCR .50 1.00
TSHD99 Koa'ki Meiru Bergzak SCR 1.50 3.00

2010 Yu-Gi-Oh Starstrike Blast 1st Edition

STBLEN000 Archfiend Empress SR .75 1.50
STBLEN001 Swift Scarecrow .15 .30
STBLEN002 Mirror Ladybug .15 .30
STBLEN003 Reed Butterfly .15 .30
STBLEN004 Needle Soldier .15 .30
STBLEN005 Necro Linker .15 .30
STBLEN006 Rescue Warrior .15 .30
STBLEN007 Power Giant UTR 1.50 3.00
STBLEN007 Power Giant UR .75 1.50
STBLEN008 Vice Berserker .15 .30
STBLEN009 Lancer Archfiend R .50 1.00
STBLEN010 Power Breaker SR 1.00 2.00
STBLEN011 Extra Veiler .15 .30
STBLEN012 Synchro Soldier .15 .30
STBLEN013 Creation Resonator R .50 1.00
STBLEN014 Attack Gainer .15 .30
STBLEN015 Blackwing - Elesian of Two Swords .15 .30
STBLEN016 Blackwing - Aurora the Northern Lights R .50 1.00
STBLEN017 Blackwing - Abrolhos the Megaquake R .50 1.00
STBLEN018 Glow-Up Bulb UTR 10.00 20.00
STBLEN018 Glow Up Bulb UR 3.00 6.00
STBLEN019 Karakuri Soldier mdl 236 Nisamu .15 .30
STBLEN020 Karakuri Merchant mdl 177 Inashichi R .50 1.00
STBLEN021 Karakuri Strategist mdl 248 Nishipachi .15 .30
STBLEN022 Karakuri Ninja mdl 339 Sazank SR .50 1.00
STBLEN023 Karakuri Bushi mdl 6318 Muzanichiha R .50 1.00
STBLEN024 Scrap Soldier R .50 1.00
STBLEN025 Scrap Searcher .15 .30
STBLEN026 Wattkiwi .15 .30
STBLEN027 Watthopper .15 .30
STBLEN028 Wattdragonfly .15 .30
STBLEN029 Wattsquirrel R .50 1.00
STBLEN030 Naturia Cherries SR 5.00 10.00
STBLEN031 Naturia Pumpkin .15 .30
STBLEN032 Naturia Stag Beetle .15 .30
STBLEN033 Dance Princess of the Ice Barrier SR 3.00 6.00
STBLEN034 Chain Dog R .50 1.00
STBLEN035 Wightmare .15 .30
STBLEN036 Anarchist Monk Ranshin SR 1.00 2.00
STBLEN037 Delg the Dark Monarch SR 3.00 6.00
STBLEN038 Supreme Arcanite Magician UR 3.00 6.00
STBLEN038 Supreme Arcanite Magician UTR 3.00 6.00
STBLEN039 Gaia Drake the Universal Force UR 5.00 10.00
STBLEN039 Gaia Drake, the Universal Force UTR 6.00 12.00
STBLEN040 Shooting Star Dragon UTR 4.00 8.00
STBLEN040 Shooting Star Dragon UR 3.00 6.00
STBLEN040 Shooting Star Dragon GR 10.00 20.00
STBLEN041 Formula Synchron R 2.00 4.00
STBLEN042 Red Nova Dragon UR 1.50 3.00
STBLEN042 Red Nova Dragon UTR 3.00 6.00
STBLEN043 Karakuri Shogun mdl 00 Burei UTR 2.00 4.00
STBLEN043 Karakuri Shogun mdl 00 Burei UR .75 1.50
STBLEN044 Scrap Twin Dragon UR 1.50 3.00
STBLEN044 Scrap Twin Dragon UTR 2.00 4.00
STBLEN045 Tuning UR 2.00 4.00
STBLEN045 Tuning UTR 5.00 10.00
STBLEN046 Karakuri Showdown Castle R .50 1.00
STBLEN047 Golden Gearbox .15 .30
STBLEN048 Karakuri Anatomy .15 .30
STBLEN049 Scrap Lube .15 .30
STBLEN050 Wattcastle R .50 1.00
STBLEN051 Wattjustment .15 .30
STBLEN052 Barkion's Bark .15 .30
STBLEN053 Leodrake's Mane .15 .30
STBLEN054 Medallion of the Ice Barrier .15 .30
STBLEN055 Mirror of the Ice Barrier .15 .30
STBLEN056 Koa'ki Ring .15 .30
STBLEN057 Darkworld Shackles .15 .30
STBLEN058 Axe of Fools .15 .30
STBLEN059 Cursed Bill .15 .30
STBLEN060 Tokkosho of Ghost Destroying R .50 1.00
STBLEN061 Heat Wave R .50 1.00
STBLEN062 White Elephant's Gift .15 .30
STBLEN063 D2 Shield SR .75 1.50
STBLEN064 Red Screen .15 .30
STBLEN065 Blackback SR .75 1.50
STBLEN066 Defenders Intersect .15 .30
STBLEN067 Gravity Collapse R .50 1.00
STBLEN068 Blackwing - Boobytrap .15 .30
STBLEN069 Star Siphon .15 .30
STBLEN070 Half Counter .15 .30
STBLEN071 Karakuri Trick House .15 .30
STBLEN072 Karakuri Klock SR .50 1.00
STBLEN073 Scrap Crash .15 .30
STBLEN074 Wattkeeper .15 .30
STBLEN075 Exterio's Fang .15 .30
STBLEN076 Vanity's Emptiness .15 .30
STBLEN077 Different Dimension Ground SR 1.25 2.50
STBLEN078 Powersink Stone .15 .30
STBLEN079 Tyrant's Temper SR 1.50 3.00
STBLEN080 Dark Trap Hole .15 .30
STBLEN081 Skull Meister SCR 7.50 15.00
STBLEN082 Droll & Lock Bird R 1.00 2.00
STBLEN083 Spellstone Sorcerer Karood SCR 1.00 2.00
STBLEN084 Scrap Mind Reader SCR .50 1.00
STBLEN085 Gravekeeper's Recruiter R 2.50 5.00
STBLEN086 Psi-Blocker SCR 2.50 5.00
STBLEN087 Koa'ki Meiru Wall R .50 1.00
STBLEN088 Karakuri Barrel mdl 96 Shinkuro R .50 1.00
STBLEN089 Mischief of the Yokai UTR 1.50 3.00
STBLEN089 Mischief of the Yokai UR 1.00 2.00
STBLEN090 Karakuri Spider .15 .30
STBLEN091 Royal Knight of the Ice Barrier SR .75 1.50
STBLEN092 Ally Salvo R .50 1.00
STBLEN093 Ally of Justice Thousand Arms .15 .30
STBLEN094 Ally of Justice Unknown Crusher .15 .30
STBLEN095 Genex Ally Duradark SCR .75 1.50
STBLEN096 The Fabled Rubyruda SCR 1.00 2.00
STBLEN097 Dragunity Knight - Vajrayana SR 2.00 4.00
STBLEN098 Dragunity Knight - Gae Dearg SCR 25.00 50.00
STBLEN099 Genex Ally Axel SCR 1.00 2.00

2010 Yu-Gi-Oh Starter Deck Duelist Toolbox 1st Edition

5DS3EN001 Battle Footballer C .20 .40
5DS3EN002 Blazing Inpachi C .25 .50
5DS3EN003 Tune Warrior C .25 .50
5DS3EN004 Rapid Warrior SR .17 .35
5DS3EN005 Synchron Explorer SR .17 .35
5DS3EN006 ManEater Bug C .30 .75
5DS3EN007 Hayabusa Knight C .12 .25
5DS3EN008 Chainsaw Insect C .25 .50
5DS3EN009 Worm Apocalypse C .12 .25
5DS3EN010 Junk Synchron C .75 1.50
5DS3EN011 Speed Warrior C .17 .35
5DS3EN012 Quillbolt Hedgehog C .12 .25
5DS3EN013 XSaber Galahad C .12 .25
5DS3EN014 Fortress Warrior C .25 .50
5DS3EN015 Turret Warrior C .30 .60
5DS3EN016 TwinSword Marauder C .17 .35
5DS3EN017 Dark Tinker C .25 .50
5DS3EN018 Quickdraw Synchron C .20 .40
5DS3EN019 Half Shut C .20 .40
5DS3EN020 Giant Trunade C .60 1.25
5DS3EN021 Card Destruction C .20 .40
5DS3EN022 Reinforcement of the Army C .12 .25
5DS3EN023 The Warrior Returning Alive C .12 .25
5DS3EN024 Banner of Courage C .12 .25
5DS3EN025 Enemy Controller C .25 .50
5DS3EN026 Hammer Shot C .30 .60
5DS3EN027 Monster Reincarnation C .12 .25
5DS3EN028 Synchro Boost C .12 .25
5DS3EN029 Wild Tornado C .17 .35
5DS3EN030 Trap Hole C .40 .80
5DS3EN031 Dust Tornado C .30 .75
5DS3EN032 Raigeki Break C .60 1.25
5DS3EN033 Rope of Life C .25 .50
5DS3EN034 Secret Barrel C 1.25 2.50
5DS3EN035 Sakuretsu Armor C .40 .80
5DS3EN036 Threatening Roar C .40 .80
5DS3EN037 Rising Energy C .12 .25
5DS3EN038 Defense Draw C .25 .50
5DS3EN039 Junk Destroyer UR .30 .75
5DS3EN040 XSaber Urbellum C .17 .35
5DS3EN041 Gaia Knight the Force of Earth C .75 1.50
5DS3EN042 XSaber Wayne SR .25 .50

2010 Yu-Gi-Oh Structure Deck Machina Mayhem 1st Edition

SDMMEN001 Machina Fortress UR 1.00 2.00
SDMMEN002 Machina Gearframe SR .75 1.50
SDMMEN003 Machina Peacekeeper SR .75 1.50
SDMMEN004 Scrap Recycler .12 .25
SDMMEN005 Commander Covington .12 .25
SDMMEN006 Machina Soldier .50 1.00
SDMMEN007 Machina Sniper .12 .25
SDMMEN008 Machina Defender .12 .25
SDMMEN009 Machina Force .12 .25
SDMMEN010 Kinetic Soldier .12 .25
SDMMEN011 Blast Sphere .12 .25
SDMMEN012 Heavy Mech Support Platform .12 .25
SDMMEN013 Cyber Dragon .12 .25
SDMMEN014 Proto-Cyber Dragon .12 .25
SDMMEN015 Green Gadget .12 .25
SDMMEN016 Red Gadget .12 .25
SDMMEN017 Yellow Gadget .12 .25
SDMMEN018 Armored Cybern .12 .25
SDMMEN019 Cyber Valley 1.50 3.00
SDMMEN020 The Big Saturn .12 .25
SDMMEN021 Machina Armored Unit .12 .25
SDMMEN022 Prohibition .12 .25
SDMMEN023 Swords of Revealing Light .12 .25
SDMMEN024 Shrink .12 .25
SDMMEN025 Frontline Base .12 .25
SDMMEN026 Machine Duplication .12 .25
SDMMEN027 Inferno Reckless Summon .12 .25
SDMMEN028 Hand Destruction 1.00 2.00
SDMMEN029 Card Trader .12 .25
SDMMEN030 Solidarity .50 1.00
SDMMEN031 Time Machine .12 .25
SDMMEN032 Dimensional Prison 3.00 6.00
SDMMEN033 Metalmorph .12 .25
SDMMEN034 Rare Metalmorph .12 .25
SDMMEN035 Ceasefire .12 .25
SDMMEN036 Compulsory Evacuation Device .12 .25
SDMMEN037 Roll Out! .12 .25

2010 Yu-Gi-Oh Structure Deck Marik 1st Edition

SDMAEN001 Gil Garth C .15 .30
SDMAEN002 Mystic Tomato C .15 .30
SDMAEN003 Viser Des C .15 .30
SDMAEN004 Legendary Fiend C .15 .30
SDMAEN005 Dark Jeroid C .15 .30
SDMAEN006 Newdoria C .15 .30
SDMAEN007 Gravekeeper's Spy C .75 1.50
SDMAEN008 Gravekeeper's Curse C .15 .30
SDMAEN009 Gravekeeper's Guard C .75 1.50
SDMAEN010 Gravekeeper's Spear Soldier C .25 .50
SDMAEN011 Gravekeeper's Chief C .25 .50
SDMAEN012 Gravekeeper's Cannonholder C .25 .50
SDMAEN013 Gravekeeper's Assailant C .25 .50
SDMAEN014 Lava Golem UR .75 1.50
SDMAEN015 Drillago C .15 .30
SDMAEN016 Bowganian C .15 .30
SDMAEN017 Gravekeeper's Commandant C .25 .50
SDMAEN018 Gravekeeper's Visionary C .25 .50
SDMAEN019 Gravekeeper's Descendant C .25 .50
SDMAEN020 Mystical Space Typhoon C .75 1.50
SDMAEN021 Nightmare's Steelcage C .25 .50
SDMAEN022 Creature Swap C .25 .50
SDMAEN023 Book of Moon C 2.00 4.00
SDMAEN024 Dark Room of Nightmare C .15 .30
SDMAEN025 Necrovalley C .50 1.00
SDMAEN026 Foolish Burial C .50 1.00
SDMAEN027 Magical Stone Excavation C .25 .50
SDMAEN028 Allure of Darkness C 1.50 3.00
SDMAEN029 Acid Trap Hole C .15 .30
SDMAEN030 Mirror Force C 2.50 5.00
SDMAEN031 Skull Invitation C .15 .30
SDMAEN032 Coffin Seller C .15 .30
SDMAEN033 Nightmare Wheel C .30 .75
SDMAEN034 Metal Reflect Slime C .30 .75
SDMAEN035 Malevolent Catastrophe C .25 .50
SDMAEN036 Dark Illusion C .25 .50
SDMAEN037 Mystical Beast of Serket UR .50 1.00
SDMAEN038 Tele of the Kings UR .50 1.00

2010 Yu-Gi-Oh Turbo Pack 2

TU02EN000 Gladiator Beast Heraklinos UTR	2.00	4.00
TU02EN001 Chaos Sorcerer UR	7.50	15.00
TU02EN002 Gravekeeper's Assailant SR	1.25	2.50
TU02EN003 Magical Dimension SR	20.00	40.00
TU02EN004 Foolish Burial SR	20.00	40.00
TU02EN005 Beckoning Light SR	1.25	2.50
TU02EN006 Gravekeeper's Spear Soldier R	.75	1.50
TU02EN007 My Body as a Shield R	.50	1.00
TU02EN008 Magical Stone Excavation R	.60	1.25
TU02EN009 Mist Archfiend R	.60	1.25
TU02EN010 Light-Imprisoning Mirror R	1.00	2.00
TU02EN011 Shadow-Imprisoning Mirror R	1.00	2.00
TU02EN012 Anti-Spell Fragrance C	.50	1.00
TU02EN013 Gravekeeper's Cannonholder C	.50	1.00
TU02EN014 Necrovalley C	.50	1.00
TU02EN015 Autonomous Action Unit C	.50	1.00
TU02EN016 Anti-Spell Fragrance C	6.00	12.00
TU02EN017 Reflect Bounder C	.50	1.00
TU02EN018 Mausoleum of the Emperor C	.50	1.00
TU02EN019 Gravekeeper's Commandant C	.75	1.50
TU02EN020 Iron Core of Koa'ki Meiru C	.50	1.00

2010 Yu-Gi-Oh Turbo Pack 3

TU03EN000 Caius the Shadow Monarch UTR	15.00	30.00
TU03EN001 Dark Grepher UR	3.00	6.00
TU03EN002 Rescue Cat SR	7.50	15.00
TU03EN003 Morphtronic Celfon SR	2.50	5.00
TU03EN004 Rekindling SR	3.00	6.00
TU03EN005 Treacherous Trap Hole SR	6.00	12.00
TU03EN006 Gladiator Beast Retiari R	1.25	2.50
TU03EN007 XX-Saber Faultroll R	.50	1.00
TU03EN008 XX-Saber Ragigura R	.50	1.00
TU03EN009 Magical Android R	.50	1.00
TU03EN010 Dark Eruption R	.50	1.00
TU03EN011 Saber Slash R	.50	1.00
TU03EN012 Destiny Hero - Diamond Dude C	.10	.20
TU03EN013 D.D. Crow C	.20	.40
TU03EN014 Superancient Deepsea King Coelacanth C	.10	.20
TU03EN015 Koa'ki Meiru Drago C	1.50	3.00
TU03EN016 Kycoo the Ghost Destroyer C	.10	.20
TU03EN017 Nobleman of Crossout C	.10	.20
TU03EN018 Cloak and Dagger C	.10	.20
TU03EN019 Gladiator Beast War Chariot C	.50	1.00
TU03EN020 Pollinosis C	.10	.20

2010 Yu-Gi-Oh Turbo Pack 4

TU04EN000 Tragoedia UTR	15.00	30.00
TU04EN001 Gottoms' Emergency Call UR	3.00	6.00
TU04EN002 Debris Dragon SR	2.50	5.00
TU04EN003 Blackwing - Sirocco the Dawn SR	1.50	3.00
TU04EN004 Deep Sea Diva SR	15.00	30.00
TU04EN005 Compulsory Evacuation Device SR	7.50	15.00
TU04EN006 Dunames Dark Witch R	.50	1.00
TU04EN007 The End of Anubis R	.60	1.25
TU04EN008 Psychic Commander R	.75	1.50
TU04EN009 Advanced Ritual Art R	.50	1.00
TU04EN010 Bark of Dark Ruler R	.50	1.00
TU04EN011 Swallow Flip R	.50	1.00
TU04EN012 Wattkid C	.25	.50
TU04EN013 Oscillo Hero C	.25	.50
TU04EN014 Mokey Mokey C	.25	.50
TU04EN015 Key Mace C	.25	.50
TU04EN016 King of the Skull Servants C	.50	1.00
TU04EN017 Dark Hole C	.50	1.00
TU04EN018 Amazoness Spellcaster C	.25	.50
TU04EN019 Gladiator Proving Ground C	.25	.50
TU04EN020 White Hole C	.60	1.25

2011 Yu-Gi-Oh 3-D Bonds Beyond Time Movie

YMP1EN001 Malefic Red-Eyes B. Dragon SCR	.75	1.50
YMP1EN002 Malefic Blue-Eyes White Dragon SCR	.75	1.50
YMP1EN003 Malefic Parallel Gear SCR	.75	1.50
YMP1EN004 Malefic Cyber End Dragon SCR	2.00	4.00
YMP1EN005 Malefic Rainbow Dragon SCR	.75	1.50
YMP1EN006 Junk Gardna SCR	.75	1.50
YMP1EN007 Malefic Paradox Dragon SCR	.75	1.50
YMP1EN008 Malefic World SCR	.75	1.50
YMP1EN009 Malefic Claw Stream SCR	.10	.20

2011 Yu-Gi-Oh Collector Tins

CT08EN001 Number 17: Leviathan Dragon SCR	.50	1.00
CT08EN002 Wind-Up Zenmaister SCR	.50	1.00
CT08EN003 Galaxy-Eyes Photon Dragon SCR	1.50	3.00
CT08EN004 Number 10: Illumiknight SCR	.50	1.00
CT08EN005 Beast King Barbaros SR	.50	1.00
CT08EN006 Dark Simorgh SR	.50	1.00
CT08EN007 Stygian Street Patrol SR	.50	1.00
CT08EN008 Pot of Duality SR	.75	1.50
CT08EN009 Neo-Parshath, the Sky Paladin SR	.50	1.00
CT08EN010 Archlord Kristya SR	1.00	2.00
CT08EN011 Elemental HERO Gaia SR	.50	1.00
CT08EN012 Fossil Dyna Pachycephalo SR	.50	1.00
CT08EN013 Guardian Eatos SR	.50	1.00
CT08EN014 Malefic Stardust Dragon SR	.50	1.00
CT08EN015 Solemn Warning SR	1.25	2.50
CT08EN016 Ehren, Lightsworn Monk SR	.50	1.00
CT08EN017 XX-Saber Darksoul SR	.50	1.00
CT08EN018 The Tyrant Neptune SR	.50	1.00

2011 Yu-Gi-Oh Duelist Pack Crow 1st Edition

DP11EN001 Blackwing - Gale the Whirlwind R	.60	1.25
DP11EN002 Blackwing - Bora the Spear R	.50	1.00
DP11EN003 Blackwing - Blizzard the Far North C	.60	1.25
DP11EN004 Blackwing - Shura the Blue Flame R	.50	1.00
DP11EN005 Blackwing - Elphin the Raven R	.50	1.00
DP11EN006 Blackwing - Mistral the Silver Shield C	.10	.20
DP11EN007 Blackwing - Fane the Steel Chain C	.10	.20
DP11EN008 Blackwing - Ghibli the Searing Wind C	.10	.20
DP11EN009 Blackwing - Gust the Backblast C	.10	.20
DP11EN010 Blackwing - Kochi the Daybreak R	.50	1.00
DP11EN011 Blackwing - Jetstream the Blue Sky UR	.75	1.50
DP11EN012 Blackwing - Zephyros the Elite UR	4.00	8.00
DP11EN013 Blackwing Armor Master SR	.50	1.00
DP11EN014 Blackwing Armed Wing R	.50	1.00
DP11EN015 Blackwing - Silverwind the Ascendant R	.50	1.00
DP11EN016 Black-Winged Dragon SR	.50	1.00
DP11EN017 Raptor Wing Strike C	.10	.20
DP11EN018 Against the Wind C	.10	.20
DP11EN019 Black-Winged Strafe C	.10	.20
DP11EN020 Cards for Black Feathers C	.10	.20
DP11EN021 Ebon Arrow C	.10	.20
DP11EN022 Delta Crow - Anti Reverse C	.75	1.50
DP11EN023 Level Retuner C	.10	.20
DP11EN024 Fake Feather C	.10	.20
DP11EN025 Blackwing - Backlash C	.10	.20
DP11EN026 Blackwing - Bombardment C	.10	.20
DP11EN027 Black Thunder C	.10	.20
DP11EN028 Guard Mines C	.10	.20
DP11EN029 Black Feather Beacon SR	.50	1.00
DP11EN030 Black Return SR	.50	1.00

2011 Yu-Gi-Oh Duelist Pack Yusei 3 1st Edition

DP10EN001 Sonic Chick C	.10	.20
DP10EN002 Shield Wing C	.10	.20
DP10EN003 Stardust Xiaolong C	.10	.20
DP10EN004 Drill Synchron C	.10	.20
DP10EN005 Card Breaker C	.10	.20
DP10EN006 Second Booster C	.10	.20
DP10EN007 Effect Veiler R	2.50	5.00
DP10EN008 Dash Warrior C	.10	.20
DP10EN009 Damage Eater C	.10	.20
DP10EN010 A/D Changer C	.10	.20
DP10EN011 Stronghold Guardian C	.10	.20
DP10EN012 Boost Warrior SR	.60	1.25
DP10EN013 Justice Bringer UR	.50	1.00
DP10EN014 Bri Synchron UR	.50	1.00
DP10EN015 Big One Warrior SR	.50	1.00
DP10EN016 Dragon Knight Draco-Equiste SR	.50	1.00
DP10EN017 Majestic Star Dragon R	.50	1.00
DP10EN018 Drill Warrior R	.50	1.00
DP10EN019 Cards of Consonance C	.50	1.00
DP10EN020 Variety Comes Out C	.10	.20
DP10EN021 Blind Spot Strike C	.10	.20
DP10EN022 Double Cyclone C	.10	.20
DP10EN023 Battle Waltz R	.50	1.00
DP10EN024 Synchro Gift R	.50	1.00
DP10EN025 Starlight Road R	.50	1.00
DP10EN026 Synchro Barrier C	.10	.20
DP10EN027 Power Frame C	.10	.20
DP10EN028 Desperate Tag C	.10	.20
DP10EN029 Cards of Sacrifice R	.50	1.00
DP10EN030 Synchro Material SR	.50	1.00

2011 Yu-Gi-Oh Extreme Victory 1st Edition

EXVC000 Reborn Tengu SR	1.00	2.00
EXVC001 Junk Servant R	.50	1.00
EXVC002 Unknown Synchron	.15	.30
EXVC003 Salvage Warrior R	.30	.75
EXVC004 Necro Defender R	.30	.75
EXVC005 Mystic Piper SCR	7.50	15.00
EXVC006 Force Resonator	.15	.30
EXVC007 Clock Resonator	.15	.30
EXVC008 Hiiten Tengu SR	.50	1.00
EXVC009 Kogarashi UR	.75	1.50
EXVC009 Kogarashi UTR	1.50	3.00
EXVC010 Morphtronic Lantron	.15	.30
EXVC011 Morphtronic Staplen	.15	.30
EXVC012 Meklord Army of Wisel	.15	.30
EXVC013 Meklord Army of Skiel	.15	.30
EXVC014 Meklord Army Granel R	.30	.75
EXVC015 Dragon Asterisk SR	.50	1.00
EXVC016 Cyber Magician SR	.50	1.00
EXVC017 T.G. Striker R	.50	1.00
EXVC018 T.G. Jet Falcon	.15	.30
EXVC019 T.G. Catapult Dragon	.15	.30
EXVC020 T.G. Warwolf	.15	.30
EXVC021 T.G. Rush Rhino R	.50	1.00
EXVC022 Buster Blaster R	.50	1.00
EXVC023 Esper Girl	.15	.30
EXVC024 Mental Seeker	.15	.30
EXVC025 Silent Psych Wiz SR	.50	1.00
EXVC026 Serene Psychic Witch	.15	.30
EXVC027 Hushed Psych Cleric R	.75	1.50
EXVC028 Elder of Six Samurai	.15	.30
EXVC029 Shien's Advisor SR	.50	1.00
EXVC030 Karakuri Komachi	.15	.30
EXVC031 Karakuri Ninja	.15	.30
EXVC032 Scrap Kong	.15	.30
EXVC033 Tradetoad R	.30	.75
EXVC034 Gladiator Tygerius	.15	.30
EXVC035 Jar Turtle	.15	.30
EXVC036 Aurora Paragon	.15	.30
EXVC037 Junk Berserker UTR	2.00	4.00
EXVC037 Junk Berserker GR	2.50	5.00
EXVC037 Junk Berserker UR	1.00	2.00
EXVC038 Life Strm Dragon UR	1.50	3.00
EXVC038 Life Strm Dragon UTR	2.00	4.00
EXVC039 Recipro Dragonfly R	.75	1.50
EXVC040 Wonder Magician UR	.75	1.50
EXVC040 Wonder Magician UTR	1.25	2.50
EXVC041 Power Gladiator SR	.50	1.00
EXVC042 Blade Blaster UR	.75	1.50
EXVC042 Blade Blaster UTR	1.00	2.00
EXVC043 Halberd Cannon UR	.75	1.50
EXVC043 Halberd Cannon UTR	1.00	2.00
EXVC044 Ovrmnd Archfnd UR	1.50	3.00
EXVC044 Ovrmnd Archfnd UTR	1.25	2.50
EXVC045 Scarlet Security	.15	.30
EXVC046 Red Dragon Vase	.15	.30
EXVC047 Resonator Call R	.60	1.25
EXVC048 Resonant Destruction	.15	.30
EXVC049 Fortissimo the Mobile	.15	.30
EXVC050 Boon of the Meklord	.15	.30
EXVC051 Resolute Meklord Army	.15	.30
EXVC052 Reboot	.15	.30
EXVC053 TGX1-HL	.15	.30
EXVC054 TGX300	.15	.30
EXVC055 ESP Amplifier	.15	.30
EXVC056 Psychic Feel Zone R	1.25	2.50
EXVC057 Shien's Dojo SR	.50	1.00
EXVC058 Runaway Karakuri	.15	.30
EXVC059 Contact Aquamirror	.15	.30
EXVC060 Soundproofed R	.30	.75
EXVC061 Out of the Blue	.15	.30
EXVC062 Self-Mummification	.15	.30
EXVC063 Red Carpet	.15	.30
EXVC064 Power-Up Adapter	.15	.30
EXVC065 Chaos Infinity R	.50	1.00
EXVC066 Mektimed Blast	.15	.30
EXVC067 Meklord Factory	.15	.30
EXVC068 TGX3-DX2 R	.50	1.00
EXVC069 TG-SX1	.15	.30
EXVC070 TG1-EM1	.15	.30
EXVC071 Psychic Reactor	.15	.30
EXVC072 Brain Hazard R	.50	1.00
EXVC073 Six Style - Dual Wield	.15	.30
EXVC074 Karakuri Cash SR	.50	1.00
EXVC075 Tyrant's Tantrum	.15	.30
EXVC076 Debunk SR	1.00	2.00
EXVC077 Sealing Ceremony	.15	.30
EXVC078 Safe Zone SR	1.50	3.00
EXVC079 Localized Tornado	.15	.30
EXVC080 W Nebula Meteorite	.15	.30
EXVC081 Vampire Dragon SCR	1.25	2.50
EXVC082 Dodger Dragon SR	1.50	3.00
EXVC083 Mara Alfar UR	.75	1.50
EXVC083 Mara Alfar UTR	1.25	2.50
EXVC084 Tour Guide Undrwrld SCR	7.50	15.00
EXVC085 Psi-Beast R	.60	1.25
EXVC086 Gladiator Beast UR	1.25	2.50
EXVC086 Gladiator Beast UTR	1.50	3.00
EXVC087 Gladiator Taming SCR	.50	1.00
EXVC088 Full House R	.50	1.00
EXVC089 Psych Shckwve SCR	3.00	6.00
EXVC090 Axe Dragonute	.15	.30
EXVC091 Lancer Dragonute SR	.50	1.00
EXVC092 Lancer Lindwurm	.15	.30
EXVC093 EH Neos Knight UR	3.00	6.00
EXVC093 EH Neos Knight UTR	3.00	6.00
EXVC094 Meklord Emperor SCR	1.50	3.00
EXVC095 Meklord Fortress R	.50	1.00
EXVC096 Blackwing Rain Shadow R	.60	1.25
EXVC097 Scrap Orthros SCR	1.25	2.50
EXVC098 Naturia Eggplant SR	.50	1.00
EXVC099 Blue Rose SCR	1.50	3.00

2011 Yu-Gi-Oh Generation Force 1st Edition

GENFEN000 Xyz Veil SR	.25	.50
GENFEN001 Gagaga Magician SR	.20	.40
GENFEN002 Gogogo Golem	.15	.30
GENFEN003 Achacha Archer	.15	.30
GENFEN004 Goblindbergh	.15	.30
GENFEN005 Big Jaws R	.20	.40
GENFEN006 Skull Kraken	.15	.30
GENFEN007 Drill Barnacle	.15	.30
GENFEN008 Jawsman R	.20	.40
GENFEN009 Crashbug X	.15	.30
GENFEN010 Crashbug Y	.15	.30
GENFEN011 Crashbug Z	.15	.30
GENFEN012 Super Crashbug SR	.20	.40
GENFEN013 Wind-Up Soldier	.15	.30
GENFEN014 Wind-Up Magician R	.20	.40
GENFEN015 Wind-Up Juggler SR	.20	.40
GENFEN016 Wind-Up Dog	.15	.30
GENFEN017 Wind-Up Snail R	.20	.40
GENFEN018 Spearfish Soldier	.15	.30
GENFEN019 Flyfang	.15	.30
GENFEN020 Skystarray R	.20	.40
GENFEN021 Airorca R	.20	.40
GENFEN022 Wingtortoise R	.20	.40
GENFEN023 Space-Time Police UR	.20	.40
GENFEN023 Space-Time Police UTR	.50	1.00
GENFEN024 Time Escaper SR	.20	.40
GENFEN025 Gem-Elephant	.15	.30
GENFEN026 Laval Magma Cannoneer	.15	.30
GENFEN027 Gishki Diviner R	.20	.40
GENFEN028 Gusto Codor	.15	.30
GENFEN029 Saambell the Summoner	.15	.30
GENFEN030 Geargiano	.15	.30
GENFEN031 Poki Draco	.15	.30
GENFEN032 Master of the Flaming Dragonswords	.15	.30
GENFEN033 Perditious Puppeteer	.15	.30
GENFEN034 Blue-Blooded Oni SR	.25	.50
GENFEN035 Ghost Ship R	.20	.40
GENFEN036 Absolute Crusader SR	.20	.40
GENFEN037 Big Emperor Penguin	.15	.30
GENFEN038 Milla the Temporal Magician	.15	.30
GENFEN039 17: Leviathan Dragon UR	.50	1.00
GENFEN039 17: Leviathan Dragon UTR	.75	1.50
GENFEN039 17: Leviathan Dragon GR	3.00	6.00
GENFEN040 Submersible Carrier SR	.20	.40
GENFEN041 Number 34: Terror-Byte UR	.20	.40
GENFEN041 Number 34: Terror-Byte UTR	.50	1.00
GENFEN042 Wind-Up Zenmaister UR	.20	.40
GENFEN042 Wind-Up Zenmaister UTR	.50	1.00
GENFEN043 Leviair the Sea Dragon UR	6.00	12.00
GENFEN043 Leviair the Sea Dragon UTR	15.00	30.00
GENFEN044 Tiras, Keeper of Genesis SCR	4.00	8.00
GENFEN045 Wonder Wand UR	2.50	5.00
GENFEN045 Wonder Wand UTR	4.00	8.00
GENFEN046 Double Up Chance	.15	.30
GENFEN047 Thunder Short	.15	.30
GENFEN048 Aqua Jet	.15	.30
GENFEN049 Surface SR	1.25	2.50
GENFEN050 Crashbug Road	.15	.30
GENFEN051 Infected Mail SR	.20	.40
GENFEN052 Cracking	.15	.30
GENFEN053 Legendary Wind-Up	.15	.30
GENFEN054 Wind-Up Factory SR	1.00	2.00
GENFEN055 Fish and Kicks	.15	.30
GENFEN056 Future Glow	.15	.30
GENFEN057 Vylon Filament	.15	.30
GENFEN058 Quill Pen of Gulldos SR	1.25	2.50
GENFEN059 Star Changer R	.20	.40
GENFEN060 Oni-Gami Combo	.15	.30
GENFEN061 Resonance Device R	.20	.40
GENFEN062 Peeking Goblin	.15	.30
GENFEN063 Asleep at the Switch	.15	.30
GENFEN064 Poseidon Waves	.15	.30
GENFEN065 Explosive Urchin	.15	.30
GENFEN066 Damage Vaccine MAX	.15	.30
GENFEN067 Overwind	.15	.30
GENFEN068 Underworld Egg Clutch	.15	.30
GENFEN069 Oh F!sh! R	.20	.40
GENFEN070 Bright Future R	.20	.40
GENFEN071 Past Image	.15	.30
GENFEN072 Burgeoning Whirlflame	.15	.30
GENFEN073 Treaty on Uniform Nomenclature	.15	.30
GENFEN074 Utopian Aura	.15	.30
GENFEN075 United Front R	.20	.40
GENFEN076 Curse of the Circle R	.20	.40
GENFEN077 Tyrant's Tummyache	.15	.30
GENFEN078 Attention! R	.20	.40
GENFEN079 Raigeki Bottle UR	.20	.40
GENFEN079 Raigeki Bottle UTR	.50	1.00
GENFEN080 Gravelstorm	.15	.30
GENFEN081 Sea Lancer R	.20	.40
GENFEN082 Piercing Moray UR	.20	.40
GENFEN082 Piercing Moray UTR	.50	1.00
GENFEN083 Lost Blue Breaker SCR	.50	1.00
GENFEN084 Pain Painter SCR	3.00	6.00
GENFEN085 Orient Dragon SCR	.75	1.50
GENFEN086 Adreus, Keeper SCR	15.00	30.00
GENFEN087 Fish and Swaps R	.20	.40
GENFEN088 Painful Return R	.20	.40
GENFEN089 Smashing Horn SCR	1.50	3.00
GENFEN090 Elemental HERO Flash	.15	.30
GENFEN091 Vision HERO Trinity SR	2.50	5.00
GENFEN092 Phantom Magician	.15	.30
GENFEN093 Elemental HERO Nova UR	7.50	15.00
GENFEN093 Elemental HERO Nova UTR	7.50	15.00
GENFEN094 Masked HERO Goka R	1.00	2.00
GENFEN095 Masked HERO Vapor SR	3.00	6.00
GENFEN096 Vision HERO Adoration SCR	7.50	15.00
GENFEN097 Mask Change	.15	.30
GENFEN098 A Hero Lives UR	3.00	6.00
GENFEN098 A Hero Lives UTR	7.50	15.00
GENFEN099 Steelswarm Roach SCR	2.50	5.00

2011 Yu-Gi-Oh Gold Series 4

GLD4EN001 Millennium Shield	.25	.50
GLD4EN002 Pendulum Machine	.25	.50
GLD4EN003 The Wicked Worm Beast	.25	.50
GLD4EN004 Goddess with the Third Eye	.25	.50
GLD4EN005 Beastking of the Swamps	.25	.50
GLD4EN006 Versago the Destroyer	.25	.50
GLD4EN007 Morphing Jar GUR	.50	1.00
GLD4EN008 Goddess of Whim	.25	.50
GLD4EN009 Injection Fairy Lily	.25	.50
GLD4EN010 Gravekeeper's Spy GUR	.50	1.00
GLD4EN011 Spirit Reaper GUR	.50	1.00
GLD4EN012 Chaos Sorcerer GUR	1.25	2.50
GLD4EN013 Black Luster Soldier Envoy of the Beginning GUR	4.00	8.00
GLD4EN014 White-Horned Dragon	.25	.50
GLD4EN015 Toon Dark Magician Girl	.50	1.00
GLD4EN016 Meltiel, Sage of the Sky	.25	.50
GLD4EN017 Radiant Jeral	.25	.50
GLD4EN018 Diabolos, King of the Abyss	.25	.50
GLD4EN019 Lich Lord, King of the Underworld	.25	.50
GLD4EN020 Prometheus, King of the Shadows	.25	.50
GLD4EN021 Mormolith	.25	.50
GLD4EN022 Darklord Zerato GUR	.25	.50
GLD4EN023 Doomcaliber Knight GUR	.50	1.00
GLD4EN024 Ryko, Lightsworn Hunter GUR	.50	1.00
GLD4EN025 Celestia, Lightsworn Angel GUR	.25	.50
GLD4EN026 Tytannial, Princess of Camellias GUR	.25	.50
GLD4EN027 Summoner Monk GUR	1.25	2.50
GLD4EN028 Genesis Dragon	1.00	2.00
GLD4EN029 Orichalcos Shunoros	.25	.50
GLD4EN030 Obelisk the Tormentor GUR	6.00	12.00
GLD4EN031 Five-Headed Dragon GUR	1.25	2.50
GLD4EN032 Gladiator Beast Gyzarus GUR	.50	1.00
GLD4EN033 Eternal Drought	.25	.50
GLD4EN034 Eradicating Aerosol	.25	.50
GLD4EN035 Soul Exchange	.25	.50
GLD4EN036 Toon World	.25	.50
GLD4EN037 Graceful Dice	.25	.50
GLD4EN038 Sage's Stone	1.25	2.50
GLD4EN039 Toon Table of Contents GUR	2.50	5.00
GLD4EN040 Pot of Avarice GUR	.50	1.00
GLD4EN041 Recurring Nightmare	1.00	2.00
GLD4EN042 Sword of Dark Rites	.25	.50
GLD4EN043 Trade-In	1.25	2.50
GLD4EN044 Magic Formula	.25	.50
GLD4EN045 Robbin' Goblin	.25	.50
GLD4EN046 Skull Dice	.25	.50
GLD4EN047 Royal Oppression GUR	.50	1.00
GLD4EN048 Xing Zhen Hu	.25	.50
GLD4EN049 Deck Devastation Virus	1.00	2.00
GLD4EN050 Trap Stun GUR	1.25	2.50

2011 Yu-Gi-Oh Hidden Arsenal 4 1st Edition

HA04EN001 Genex Ally Remote SR	.15	.30
HA04EN002 Genex Ally Powercell SCR	.25	.50
HA04EN003 Genex Ally Changer SR	.15	.30
HA04EN004 Genex Ally Volcannon SR	.15	.30
HA04EN005 Genex Ally Solid SR	.15	.30
HA04EN006 The Fabled Chawa SR	.15	.30
HA04EN007 The Fabled Catsith SR	.50	1.00
HA04EN008 The Fabled Cerburrel SCR	.25	.50
HA04EN009 The Fabled Ganashia SR	.15	.30
HA04EN010 The Fabled Nozoochee SR	.15	.30
HA04EN011 Dragunity Militum SR	.15	.30
HA04EN012 Dragunity Primus Pilus SCR	.25	.50
HA04EN013 Dragunity Brandistock SR	.15	.30
HA04EN014 Dragunity Javelin SR	.15	.30
HA04EN015 Jurrac Dino SR	.15	.30
HA04EN016 Jurrac Gallim SR	.15	.30
HA04EN017 Jurrac Aeolo SR	.15	.30
HA04EN018 Jurrac Herra SR	.25	.50
HA04EN019 Naturia Butterfly SR	.15	.30
HA04EN020 Naturia Ladybug SR	.15	.30
HA04EN021 Naturia Strawberry SR	.15	.30
HA04EN022 Defender of the Ice Barrier SR	.25	.50
HA04EN023 Warlock of the Ice Barrier SR	.15	.30
HA04EN024 Sacred Spirit of the Ice Barrier SR	.15	.30
HA04EN025 General Raiho of the Ice Barrier SCR	.25	.50
HA04EN026 Genex Ally Triarm SCR	.25	.50

HA04EN027 The Fabled Unicore SCR .50 1.00
HA04EN028 Dragunity Knight - Trident SCR .75 1.50
HA04EN029 Jurrac Meteor SCR .25 .50
HA04EN030 Naturia Landoise SCR .25 .50
HA04EN031 Neo Flamvell Origin SR .15 .30
HA04EN032 Neo Flamvell Hedgehog SR .15 .30
HA04EN033 Neo Flamvell Shaman SR .15 .30
HA04EN034 Neo Flamvell Garuda SR .15 .30
HA04EN035 Neo Flamvell Sabre SCR .25 .50
HA04EN036 Genex Ally Chemistrer SR .15 .30
HA04EN037 Genex Ally Birdman•SR .50 1.00
HA04EN038 Genex Ally Bellflame SR .15 .30
HA04EN039 Genex Ally Crusher SR .15 .30
HA04EN040 Genex Ally Reliever SCR .25 .50
HA04EN041 The Fabled Peggulsus SR .15 .30
HA04EN042 The Fabled Kokkator SR .15 .30
HA04EN043 Fabled Dianaira SCR .25 .50
HA04EN044 Dragunity Corsesca SR .15 .30
HA04EN045 Dragunity Partisan SR .15 .30
HA04EN046 Dragunity Pilum SR .15 .30
HA04EN047 Dragunity Angusticlavii SR .15 .30
HA04EN048 Naturia Stinkbug SR .15 .30
HA04EN049 Naturia Mantis SR .15 .30
HA04EN050 Naturia Ragweed SR .15 .30
HA04EN051 Naturia White Oak SCR .25 .50
HA04EN052 Strategist of the Ice Barrier SR .15 .30
HA04EN053 Secret Guards of the Ice Barrier SR .15 .30
HA04EN054 General Gantala of the Ice Barrier SCR.25 .50
HA04EN055 Naturia Exterio SCR .25 .50
HA04EN056 Ancient Flamvell Deity SCR .25 .50
HA04EN057 Genex Ally Triforce SCR .25 .50
HA04EN058 The Fabled Kudabbi SCR .25 .50
HA04EN059 Dragunity Knight - Barcha SCR .75 1.50
HA04EN060 Trishula, Dragon of the Ice Barrier SCR15.0030.00

2011 Yu-Gi-Oh Hidden Arsenal 5 1st Edition

HA05EN001 Gem Garnet SR 2.00 4.00
HA05EN002 Gem-Knight Sapphire SR .50 1.00
HA05EN003 Gem-Knight Tourmaline SR .50 1.00
HA05EN004 Gem-Knight Alexandrite SCR .75 1.50
HA05EN005 Gem-Armadillo SCR 2.00 4.00
HA05EN006 Gem-Merchant SR .10 .20
HA05EN007 Laval Miller SR .10 .20
HA05EN008 Soaring Eagle
Above the Searing Land SR .10 .20
HA05EN009 Laval Warrior SR .10 .20
HA05EN010 Prominence, Molten Swordsman SR.10 .20
HA05EN011 Laval Forest Sprite SR .10 .20
HA05EN012 Kayenn, the Master
Magma Blacksmith SR .10 .20
HA05EN013 Laval Burner SR .10 .20
HA05EN014 Laval Judgment Lord SCR .25 .50
HA05EN015 Vylon Cube SR .50 1.00
HA05EN016 Vylon Vanguard SR .10 .20
HA05EN017 Vylon Charger SR .10 .20
HA05EN018 Vylon Soldier SR .10 .20
HA05EN019 Gem-Knight Ruby SCR .75 1.50
HA05EN020 Gem-Knight Aquamarine SCR .25 .50
HA05EN021 Gem-Knight Topaz SCR .50 1.00
HA05EN022 Lavalval Dragon SCR .25 .50
HA05EN023 Laval the Greater SCR .25 .50
HA05EN024 Vylon Sigma SCR .25 .50
HA05EN025 Vylon Epsilon SCR 1.50 3.00
HA05EN026 Gem-Knight Fusion SR .50 1.00
HA05EN027 Searing Fire Wall SR .10 .20
HA05EN028 Vylon Material SR .10 .20
HA05EN029 Gem-Enhancement SR .10 .20
HA05EN030 Molten Whirlwind Wall SR .10 .20
HA05EN031 Gishki Abyss SR 1.00 2.00
HA05EN032 Gishki Vanity SR .10 .20
HA05EN033 Gishki Marker SR .10 .20
HA05EN034 Gishki Chain SCR .25 .50
HA05EN035 Gishki Ariel SR .25 .50
HA05EN036 Gishki Shadow SR .50 1.00
HA05EN037 Gusto Gulldo SR .50 1.00
HA05EN038 Gusto Egul SR .50 1.00
HA05EN039 Gusto Thunbolt SR .10 .20
HA05EN040 Winda, Priestess of Gusto SR .50 1.00
HA05EN041 Caam, Serenity of Gusto SCR 2.50 5.00
HA05EN042 Windaar, Sage of Gusto SR .10 .20
HA05EN043 Steelswarm Cell SR .10 .20
HA05EN044 Steelswarm Scout SR .10 .20
HA05EN045 Steelswarm Gatekeeper SR .10 .20
HA05EN046 Steelswarm Caller SR .10 .20
HA05EN047 Steelswarm Mantis SCR .25 .50
HA05EN048 Steelswarm Moth SR .10 .20
HA05EN049 Steelswarm Girastag SCR .25 .50
HA05EN050 Steelswarm Caucastag SCR .50 1.00
HA05EN051 Evigishki Mind Augus SCR .25 .50
HA05EN052 Evigishki Soul Ogre SCR .50 1.00
HA05EN053 Daigusto Gulldos SCR .50 1.00
HA05EN054 Daigusto Eguls SCR .25 .50
HA05EN055 Gishki Aquamirror SR 1.50 3.00
HA05EN056 Contact with Gusto SCR .60 1.25
HA05EN057 First Step Towards Infestation SR .10 .20
HA05EN058 Aquamirror Meditation SR .10 .20
HA05EN059 Blessings for Gusto SR .10 .20
HA05EN060 Infestation Wave SR .10 .20

2011 Yu-Gi-Oh Legendary Collection 2 1st Edition

LCGX001 Elemental HERO Avian .20 .40
LCGX002 HERO Avian (alt) SCR 1.50 3.00
LCGX003 Elemental HERO Burstinatrix .50 1.00
LCGX004 HERO Burstin (alt) SCR 1.25 2.50
LCGX005 Elemental HERO Clayman 1.25 2.50
LCGX006 Elemental HERO Sparkman .20 .40
LCGX007 HERO Spark (alt) SCR 1.25 2.50
LCGX008 Elemental HERO Neos 1.00 2.00
LCGX009 Winged Kuriboh .75 1.50
LCGX010 Winged Kuriboh LV10 1.50 3.00
LCGX011 Wroughtweiler .20 .40
LCGX012 Elemental HERO Bubbleman .50 1.00
LCGX013 Elemental HERO Bladedge .20 .40
LCGX014 Elemental HERO Wildheart .20 .40
LCGX015 HERO Necroshade R .50 1.00
LCGX016 Hero Kid .20 .40
LCGX017 Neo-Spacian Aqua Dolphin 1.00 2.00
LCGX018 Neo-Spacian Flare Scarab .50 1.00
LCGX019 Neo-Spacian Dark Panther .20 .40
LCGX020 Card Trooper .20 .40
LCGX021 Neo-Spacian Air Hummingbird .60 1.25
LCGX022 Neo-Spacian Grand Mole .20 .40
LCGX023 Neo-Spacian Glow Moss .20 .40
LCGX024 Elemental HERO Stratos .75 1.50
LCGX025 Elemental HERO Ocean R .50 1.00
LCGX026 Elemental HERO Captain Gold .75 1.50
LCGX027 Necro Gardna SCR .75 1.50
LCGX028 HERO Neos Alius SCR .75 1.50
LCGX029 HERO Malicious SCR .75 1.50
LCGX030 Evil HERO Infernal Gainer .20 .40
LCGX031 HERO Infernal Prodigy R .50 1.00
LCGX032 Card Ejector SR .75 1.50
LCGX033 Elemental Hero Prisma 2.50 5.00
LCGX034 HERO Woodsman SR .75 1.50
LCGX035 Elemental HERO Knospe R .50 1.00
LCGX036 Elemental HERO Poison Rose R .20 .40
LCGX037 Elemental HERO Heat .50 1.00
LCGX038 HERO Lady Heat .75 1.50
LCGX039 Elemental HERO Voltic .50 1.00
LCGX040 Neos Wiseman UR 1.00 2.00
LCGX041 Gallis Star Beast SCR .75 1.50
LCGX042 Dandylion SCR .75 1.50
LCGX043 Winged Kuriboh LV9 SCR .75 1.50
LCGX044 Card Blocker UR .50 1.00
LCGX045 HERO Flame SCR 2.50 5.00
LCGX046 HERO Thunder Giant 1.25 2.50
LCGX047 HERO Rampart Blaster SR .75 1.50
LCGX048 HERO Tempest SR 2.50 5.00
LCGX049 HERO Wildedge 1.50 3.00
LCGX050 HERO Shining SCR 4.00 8.00
LCGX051 HERO Steam Healer R 1.50 3.00
LCGX052 HERO Electrum UR .75 1.50
LCGX053 HERO Mudballman SR .75 1.50
LCGX054 Elemental HERO Mariner .20 .40
LCGX055 HERO Wild Wingman .20 .40
LCGX056 HERO Necroid Shaman .20 .40
LCGX057 HERO Aqua Neos SR .75 1.50
LCGX058 HERO Flare Neos .20 .40
LCGX059 HERO Dark Neos SCR .75 1.50
LCGX060 HERO Grand Neos SR .75 1.50
LCGX061 HERO Glow Neos R 1.25 2.50
LCGX062 HERO Marine Neos .20 .40
LCGX063 HERO Darkbright SR 1.50 3.00
LCGX064 HERO Magma Neos SR 2.50 5.00
LCGX065 HERO Chaos Neos UR 1.25 2.50
LCGX066 HERO Plasma Vice 2.00 4.00
LCGX067 HERO Inferno Wing SR .75 1.50
LCGX068 HERO Lightning SR .75 1.50
LCGX069 HERO Dark Gaia SR .75 1.50
LCGX070 HERO Wild Cyclone SR .75 1.50
LCGX071 HERO Infernal Sniper UR .50 1.00
LCGX072 HERO Malicious Fiend SR 1.25 2.50
LCGX073 HERO Storm Neos .60 1.25
LCGX074 Rainbow Neos SR .75 1.50
LCGX075 HERO Terra Firma SR .75 1.50
LCGX076 HERO Inferno SR .75 1.50
LCGX077 HERO Divine Neos UR .50 1.00
LCGX078 Miracle Fusion UR .75 1.50
LCGX079 Transcendent Wings .50 1.00
LCGX080 Bubble Shuffle R .20 .40
LCGX081 Spark Blaster .20 .40
LCGX082 Skyscraper 1.50 3.00
LCGX083 Feather Shot R .20 .40
LCGX084 Burst Return R .20 .40
LCGX085 Hero Heart .20 .40
LCGX086 Cyclone Boomerang .20 .40
LCGX087 Flute of Summoning UR .50 1.00
LCGX088 H - Heated Heart .20 .40
LCGX089 E - Emergency Call .20 .40
LCGX090 R - Righteous Justice .20 .40
LCGX091 O - Oversoul .20 .40
LCGX092 Hero Flash!! R .20 .40
LCGX093 Fake Hero R .20 .40
LCGX094 Neo Space R .50 1.00
LCGX095 Instant Fusion UR 5.00 10.00
LCGX096 Neos Force .20 .40
LCGX097 Skyscraper 2 SCR 1.25 2.50
LCGX098 Fifth Hope SCR 1.50 3.00
LCGX099 Dark Fusion UR 2.50 5.00
LCGX100 Dark Calling R .75 1.50
LCGX101 Super Polymer. SCR .75 1.50
LCGX102 Instant Neo Space .20 .40
LCGX103 Hero Mask .20 .40
LCGX104 Space Gift .20 .40
LCGX105 Rose Bud R .20 .40
LCGX106 HERO's Bond .20 .40
LCGX107 Hero Signal .20 .40
LCGX108 Hero Barrier .20 .40
LCGX109 Feather Wind .20 .40
LCGX110 Hero Ring SR .75 1.50
LCGX111 Clay Charge .20 .40
LCGX112 Miracle Kids .20 .40
LCGX113 Edge Hammer .20 .40
LCGX114 Kid Guard UR .50 1.00
LCGX115 Elemental Recharge .20 .40
LCGX116 Change of Hero - Reflector Ray .20 .40
LCGX117 Hero Spirit .20 .40
LCGX118 Hero Counterattack .20 .40
LCGX119 Mirror Gate UR .50 1.00
LCGX120 Hero Blast .20 .40
LCGX121 Terra Firma Gravity R .20 .40
LCGX122 HERO - Doom Lord .20 .40
LCGX123 HERO - Captain Tenacious .20 .40
LCGX124 HERO - Diamond SR .75 1.50
LCGX125 HERO - Dreadmaster SR .75 1.50
LCGX126 HERO - Double Dude .20 .40
LCGX127 HERO - Defender R .60 1.25
LCGX128 HERO - Dogma SR .75 1.50
LCGX129 HERO - Blade Master .20 .40
LCGX130 HERO - Fear Monger .20 .40
LCGX131 HERO - Dasher .20 .40
LCGX132 HERO - Malicious 1.50 3.00
LCGX133 HERO - Disk SCR .75 1.50
LCGX134 HERO - Plasma SR .75 1.50
LCGX135 HERO - Dunker .20 .40
LCGX136 HERO - Departed .20 .40
LCGX137 HERO - Dread Servant .20 .40
LCGX138 HERO Phoenix SR .75 1.50
LCGX139 HERO Shining SCR 1.25 2.50
LCGX140 Destiny End Dragoon SR 1.50 3.00
LCGX141 Clock Tower Prison .20 .40
LCGX142 D - Spirit .20 .40
LCGX143 Cyclone Blade .20 .40
LCGX144 Dark City .20 .40
LCGX145 Destiny Draw SCR .75 1.50
LCGX146 Over Destiny R .50 1.00
LCGX147 D - Formation .20 .40
LCGX148 Destiny Signal .20 .40
LCGX149 D-Time R .20 .40
LCGX150 D - Shield .20 .40
LCGX151 Destiny Mirage R .20 .40
LCGX152 D - Chain .20 .40
LCGX153 D - Counter .20 .40
LCGX154 D - Fortune .20 .40
LCGX155 Crystal Beast Ruby Carbuncle .20 .40
LCGX156 Crystal Beast Amethyst Cat .20 .40
LCGX157 Crystal Beast Emerald Tortoise .20 .40
LCGX158 Crystal Beast Topaz Tiger .20 .40
LCGX159 Crystal Beast Amber Mammoth .50 1.00
LCGX160 Crystal Beast Cobalt Eagle .20 .40
LCGX161 Crystal Beast Saph SR 2.00 4.00
LCGX162 Rainbow Dragon UR 2.50 5.00
LCGX163 Crystal Beacon R .20 .40
LCGX164 Rare Value SR .75 1.50
LCGX165 Crystal Blessing R .20 .40
LCGX166 Crystal Abundance R .20 .40
LCGX167 Crystal Promise R .20 .40
LCGX168 Ancient City - Rainbow .20 .40
LCGX169 Crystal Release UR .75 1.50
LCGX170 Crystal Tree UR 1.25 2.50
LCGX171 Crystal Raigeki .20 .40
LCGX172 Crystal Pair .75 1.50
LCGX173 Rainbow Path .20 .40
LCGX174 Rainbow Gravity .20 .40
LCGX175 Cyber Dragon UR 1.00 2.00
LCGX176 Cyber Dragon (alt) SCR 2.00 4.00
LCGX177 Proto-Cyber Dragon UR .50 1.00
LCGX178 Cyber Phoenix UR .50 1.00
LCGX179 Cyber Valley UR 1.00 2.00
LCGX180 Cyber Twin Dragon SCR .75 1.50
LCGX181 Cyber End Dragon SCR 3.00 6.00
LCGX182 Cyber Dragon (alt) SCR 3.00 6.00
LCGX183 Chimera Over SCR 1.25 2.50
LCGX184 Power Bond SCR 4.00 8.00
LCGX185 Overload Fusion R .60 1.25
LCGX186 Future Fusion UR 1.00 2.00
LCGX187 Magical Mallet UR 2.00 4.00
LCGX188 Dark End Dragon SCR .75 1.50
LCGX189 Light End Dragon UR .50 1.00
LCGX190 Hydrogeddon UR .50 1.00
LCGX191 Vennominaga Deity UR .50 1.00
LCGX192 Vennominon the King SR .75 1.50
LCGX193 Phantom of Chaos SCR 2.00 4.00
LCGX194 Phantom Skyblaster SCR .75 1.50
LCGX195 Grave Squirmer .20 .40
LCGX196 Grinder Golem 1.00 2.00
LCGX197 Yubel SCR 2.00 4.00
LCGX198 Yubel - Terror Inc SCR .75 1.50
LCGX199 Yubel - The Ultimate SCR 2.00 4.00
LCGX200 Mezuki .50 1.00
LCGX201 Cold Enchanter .20 .40
LCGX202 Ice Master .20 .40
LCGX203 Thunder King Rai-Oh 1.00 2.00
LCGX204 Darkness Destroy SCR .75 1.50
LCGX205 White Night Dragon UR .50 1.00
LCGX206 Kasha UR .50 1.00
LCGX207 Ice Queen UR .50 1.00
LCGX208 Shutendoji UR .50 1.00
LCGX209 Clear Vice Dragon SR .75 1.50
LCGX210 Darklord Desire SR .75 1.50
LCGX211 Armityle the Chaos UR 7.50 15.00
LCGX212 Fusion Recovery 2.50 5.00
LCGX213 System Down 2.00 4.00
LCGX214 Grand Convergence R .20 .40
LCGX215 Dim Fissure SCR 1.25 2.50
LCGX216 Venom Swamp .20 .40
LCGX217 Clear World SR .75 1.50
LCGX218 Macro Cosmos UR 1.25 2.50
LCGX219 Rise of the Snake Deity .20 .40
LCGX220 Dim Prison UR 1.25 2.50
LCGX221 Offering to the Snake .20 .40
LCGX222 Chamberlain of the Six .20 .40
LCGX223 Gladiator Beast Andal .20 .40
LCGX224 D.D. Survivor .20 .40
LCGX225 Banisher of Radiance SCR .75 1.50
LCGX226 Grandmaster of Samurai .20 .40
LCGX227 Six Samurai - Yaichi .20 .40
LCGX228 Six Samurai - Kamon .20 .40
LCGX229 Six Samurai - Yariza .20 .40
LCGX230 Six Samurai - Nisashi .20 .40
LCGX231 Six Samurai - Zanji .20 .40
LCGX232 Six Samurai - Irou .20 .40
LCGX233 Great Shogun Shien SCR 1.25 2.50
LCGX234 D.D. Crow SR .75 1.50
LCGX235 Beast Octavius UR .50 1.00
LCGX236 Beast Murmillo SCR .75 1.50
LCGX237 Beast Bestiari SCR 2.00 4.00
LCGX238 Beast Laquari SCR .75 1.50
LCGX239 Beast Hoplomus SCR .75 1.50
LCGX240 Beast Secutor SCR .75 1.50
LCGX241 Enishi, Chancellor SR .75 1.50
LCGX242 Test Tiger SCR .75 1.50
LCGX243 Rainbow Dark Dragon UR 1.25 2.50
LCGX244 Beast Darius SCR 1.25 2.50
LCGX245 Jain, Paladin UR .50 1.00
LCGX246 Garoth, Warrior UR 1.00 2.00
LCGX247 Lumina, Summoner UR 1.25 2.50
LCGX248 Wulf, Beast UR .50 1.00
LCGX249 Judgment Dragon .20 .40
LCGX250 Aurkus, Druid UR .50 1.00
LCGX251 Beast Equeste SCR 1.00 2.00
LCGX252 Beast Lanista UR .50 1.00
LCGX253 Beast Heraklinos SR .75 1.50
LCGX254 Beast's Respite R .20 .40
LCGX255 Gladiator's Return R .20 .40
LCGX256 Cunning of the Six Samurai .20 .40
LCGX257 Gladiator Ground R .20 .40
LCGX258 Light of Redemption .20 .40
LCGX259 Gateway of the Six .20 .40
LCGX260 Non-Fusion Area .60 1.25
LCGX261 Success Probability 0 .20 .40
LCGX262 Return of the Six Samurai .20 .40
LCGX263 Swiftstrike Armor R .20 .40
LCGX264 Double-Edged Sword .20 .40
LCGX265 Defensive Tactics UR .50 1.00
LCGX266 Beast War Chariot SCR 1.25 2.50

2011 Yu-Gi-Oh Photon Shockwave 1st Edition

PHSW000 Alexandrite Dragon SR .75 1.50
PHSW001 Bunilla C .15 .30
PHSW002 Rabidragon C .15 .30
PHSW003 Rai Rider C .15 .30
PHSW004 Stinging Swordsman C .15 .30
PHSW005 Kagetokage R .25 .50
PHSW006 Acorno C .15 .30
PHSW007 Pinecono C .15 .30
PHSW008 Friller Rabca SR .20 .40
PHSW009 Shark Stickers C .15 .30
PHSW010 Needle Sunfish C .15 .30
PHSW011 Galaxy-Eyes Photon Dragon UR 2.50 5.00
PHSW011 Galaxy-Eyes Photon Dragon UTR 3.00 6.00
PHSW011 Galaxy-Eyes Photon Dragon GR 7.50 15.00
PHSW012 Daybreaker R .25 .50
PHSW013 Lightserpent SR .20 .40
PHSW014 Plasma Ball C .15 .30
PHSW015 Photon Cerberus R .25 .50
PHSW016 Evoltile Gephyro C .15 .30
PHSW017 Evoltile Westlo SR .75 1.50
PHSW018 Evoltile Odonto C .15 .30
PHSW019 Evolsaur Vulcano R .25 .50
PHSW020 Evolsaur Cerato UR .60 1.25
PHSW020 Evolsaur Cerato UTR 1.00 2.00
PHSW021 Evolsaur Diplo R .25 .50
PHSW022 Wind-Up Warrior C .15 .30
PHSW023 Wind-Up Knight R .25 .50
PHSW024 Wind-Up Hunter SR .20 .40
PHSW025 Wind-Up Bat C .15 .30
PHSW026 Wind-Up Kitten (UR) 1.25 2.50
PHSW026 Wind-Up Kitten UTR 1.50 3.00
PHSW027 D.D. Telepon R .25 .50
PHSW028 Wattcobra C .15 .30
PHSW029 Naturia Marron C .15 .30
PHSW030 Prior of the Ice Barrier C .15 .30
PHSW031 Senior Silver Ninja C .15 .30
PHSW032 Rodenut C .15 .30
PHSW033 Fenghuang SR .20 .40
PHSW034 Tribe-Shocking Virus R .25 .50
PHSW035 Goblin Pothole Squad C .15 .30
PHSW036 Creepy Coney C .15 .30
PHSW037 Rescue Rabbit SCR 6.00 12.00
PHSW038 Baby Tiragon R .50 1.00
PHSW039 Number 83: Galaxy Queen SR .50 1.00
PHSW040 Black Ray Lancer SR .20 .40
PHSW041 Number 10: Illumiknight UR .50 1.00
PHSW041 Number 10: Illumiknight UTR .60 1.25
PHSW042 Number 20: Giga-Brilliant SR .20 .40
PHSW043 Evolzar Laggia UR .50 1.00
PHSW043 Evolzar Laggia UTR 1.50 3.00
PHSW044 Thunder End Dragon UR 4.00 8.00
PHSW044 Thunder End Dragon UTR 5.00 10.00
PHSW045 Altraffic Control C .15 .30
PHSW046 Ego Boost C .15 .30
PHSW047 Monster Slots C .15 .30
PHSW048 Cross Attack C .15 .30
PHSW049 Xyz Gift UR .20 .40
PHSW049 Xyz Gift UTR .50 1.00
PHSW050 Photon Veil UR .50 1.00
PHSW050 Photon Veil UTR 1.50 3.00
PHSW051 Photon Lead C .15 .30
PHSW052 Photon Booster R .25 .50
PHSW053 Evo-Karma C .15 .30
PHSW054 Evo-Miracle C .15 .30
PHSW055 Zenmailfunction C .15 .30
PHSW056 Extra Gate SR .20 .40
PHSW057 Shard of Greed SCR .75 1.50
PHSW058 Murmur of the Forest R .25 .50
PHSW059 Tri-Wight C .15 .30
PHSW060 One Day of Peace C .15 .30
PHSW061 Space Cyclone C .15 .30
PHSW062 Poisonous Winds C .15 .30
PHSW063 Heartfelt Appeal C .15 .30
PHSW064 Fiery Fervor C .15 .30
PHSW065 Damage Diet C .15 .30
PHSW066 Copy Knight R .25 .50
PHSW067 Mirror Mail C .15 .30
PHSW068 Fish Rain C .15 .30
PHSW069 Icy Crevasse C .15 .30
PHSW070 Lumenize C .15 .30
PHSW071 Evolutionary Bridge C .15 .30
PHSW072 Zenmairch C .15 .30
PHSW073 Wattcancel C .15 .30
PHSW074 Champion's Vigilance C .15 .30
PHSW075 Darklight SR .20 .40
PHSW076 Tyrant's Throes R .75 1.50
PHSW077 Sound the Retreat! C .15 .30
PHSW078 Deep Dark Trap Hole R .50 1.00
PHSW079 Eisbahn R .50 1.00
PHSW080 Sealing Ceremony of Suiton C .15 .30
PHSW081 Photon Sabre Tiger SR .50 1.00
PHSW082 Evolsaur Pelta R .25 .50
PHSW083 Wind-Up Rabbit SCR .75 1.50
PHSW084 D-Boyz SCR .75 1.50
PHSW085 Latinum, Exarch of Dark World UTR .60 1.25
PHSW085 Latinum, Exarch of Dark World UR .20 .40
PHSW086 Evolzar Dolkka SCR .75 1.50
PHSW087 Wind-Up Zenmaines SCR .75 1.50
PHSW088 Xyz Territory R .25 .50
PHSW089 Dark Smog SCR .75 1.50
PHSW090 Sergeant Electro UR .20 .40
PHSW090 Sergeant Electro UTR .50 1.00
PHSW091 Vylon Ohm C .15 .30
PHSW092 Laval Dual Slasher C .15 .30

PHSW093 Gem-Turtle SR .50 1.00
PHSW094 Laval Lancelord C .15 .30
PHSW095 Gishki Beast R .25 .50
PHSW096 Gem-Knight Emerald R .25 .50
PHSW097 Junk Defender R .25 .50
PHSW098 Metaion, the Timelord SCR .75 1.50
PHSW099 Infernity Knight SR .20 .40

2011 Yu-Gi-Oh Storm of Ragnarok 1st Edition

STOR000 Vortex Whrlwnd SR .20 .40
STOR001 Cosmic Compass C .15 .30
STOR002 Doppelwarrior R .20 .40
STOR003 Stardust Phantom R .20 .40
STOR004 D.D. Sprite SR .20 .40
STOR005 Top Runner C .15 .30
STOR006 Barrier Resonator C .15 .30
STOR007 Blackwing - Boreas the Sharp R .20 .40
STOR008 Blackwing - Brisote the Tailwind C .15 .30
STOR009 Blackwing - Calima the Haze C .15 .30
STOR010 Tanngrisnir of the Nordic Beasts SR .20 .40
STOR011 Guldfaxe of the Nordic Beasts R .20 .40
STOR012 Garmr of the Nordic Beasts C .15 .30
STOR013 Tanngnjostr of the Nordic Beasts R .20 .40
STOR014 Ljosalf of the Nordic Alfar C .15 .30
STOR015 Svartalf of the Nordic Alfar SR .20 .40
STOR016 Dverg of the Nordic Alfar R .20 .40
STOR017 Valkyrie of the Nordic Ascendant SR .75 1.50
STOR018 Mimir of the Nordic Ascendant C .15 .30
STOR019 Tyr of the Nordic Champions R .20 .40
STOR020 Legendary Six Samurai - Kizan SR 2.50 5.00
STOR021 Legendary Six Samurai - Enishi UR .50 1.00
STOR021 Legendary Six Samurai - Enishi UTR 2.00 4.00
STOR022 Legendary Six Samurai - Kageki R .20 .40
STOR023 Legendary Six Samurai - Shinai C .15 .30
STOR024 Legendary Six Samurai - Mizuho C .15 .30
STOR025 Kagemusha of the Six Samurai C .15 .30
STOR026 Shien's Squire C .15 .30
STOR027 Karakuri Watchdog mdl 313 Saizan C .15 .30
STOR028 Karakuri Ninja mdl 919 Kuick C .15 .30
STOR029 Scrap Worm R .20 .40
STOR030 Scrap Shark C .15 .30
STOR031 Wattberyx R .20 .40
STOR032 Wattmole C .15 .30
STOR033 Symphonic Warrior Basses SR .20 .40
STOR034 Symphonic Warrior Drumss SR .20 .40
STOR035 Symphonic Warrior Piaano R .20 .40
STOR036 Majioshaleon C .15 .30
STOR037 Yaksha C .15 .30
STOR038 Thor, Lord of the Aesir UR 1.00 2.00
STOR038 Thor, Lord of the Aesir UTR 2.00 4.00
STOR039 Loki, Lord of the Aesir UR 1.00 2.00
STOR039 Loki, Lord of the Aesir UTR 1.25 2.50
STOR040 Odin, Father of the Aesir UR 1.00 2.00
STOR040 Odin, Father of the Aesir UTR 1.00 2.00
STOR040 Odin, Father of the Aesir GR 3.00 6.00
STOR041 Legendary Six Samurai - Shi En UR 4.00 8.00
STOR041 Legendary Six Samurai - Shi En UTR 7.50 15.00
STOR042 Karakuri Steel Shogun mdl 00X Bureido UR .75 1.50
STOR042 Karakuri Steel Shogun mdl 00X Bureido UTR 2.00 4.00
STOR043 Atomic Scrap Dragon UR .50 1.00
STOR043 Atomic Scrap Dragon UTR .50 1.00
STOR044 Watthydra SR .20 .40
STOR045 Nordic Relic Draupnir C .15 .30
STOR046 Gotterdammerung C .15 .30
STOR047 March Towards Ragnarok R .20 .40
STOR048 Shien's Smoke Signal R .20 .40
STOR049 Six Strike - Triple Impact C .15 .30
STOR050 Asceticism of the Six Samurai R 2.50 5.00
STOR051 Temple of the Six SR .20 .40
STOR052 Karakuri Cash Cache C .15 .30
STOR053 Karakuri Gold Dust C .15 .30
STOR054 Wattkey C .15 .30
STOR055 Stardust Shimmer SR 1.50 3.00
STOR056 Resonator Engine C .15 .30
STOR057 Token Sundae C .15 .30
STOR058 Foolish Return R .20 .40
STOR059 Divine Wind of Mist Valley C .15 .30
STOR060 Vylon Matter C .15 .30
STOR061 Forbidden Lance SR 1.50 3.00
STOR062 Terminal World C .15 .30
STOR063 Hope for Escape R .60 1.25
STOR064 Zero Force C .15 .30
STOR065 Blackboost C .15 .30
STOR066 Divine Relic Mjollnir C .15 .30
STOR067 Solemn Authority C .15 .30
STOR068 Nordic Relic Brisingamen C .15 .30
STOR069 Nordic Relic Laevateinn C .15 .30
STOR070 Nordic Relic Gungnir R .20 .40
STOR071 The Golden Apples SCR .75 1.50
STOR072 Odin's Eye C .15 .30
STOR073 Gleipnir, the Fetters of Fenrir UR .75 1.50
STOR073 Gleipnir, the Fetters of Fenrir UTR 1.25 2.50
STOR074 Musakani Magatama R .20 .40
STOR075 Shien's Scheme C .15 .30
STOR076 Token Stampede C .15 .30
STOR077 Xing Zhen Hu Replica C .15 .30
STOR078 Tyrant's Tirade C .15 .30
STOR079 Tiki Curse C .15 .30
STOR080 Tiki Soul C .15 .30
STOR081 Vanadis of the Nordic Ascendant SCR 3.00 6.00
STOR082 Shien's Daredevil R .20 .40
STOR083 Karakuri Muso mdl 818 Haipa UR .50 1.00
STOR083 Karakuri Muso mdl 818 Haipa UTR .50 1.00
STOR084 Scrap Breaker SCR .50 1.00
STOR085 Chaos Hunter SCR 5.00 10.00
STOR086 Maxx C SCR 20.00 40.00
STOR087 The Nordic Lights UR .50 1.00
STOR087 The Nordic Lights UTR .50 1.00
STOR088 Nordic Relic Megingjord SCR .50 1.00
STOR089 Six Strike - Thunder Blast SCR .50 1.00
STOR090 Cyber Shield C .15 .30
STOR091 Hourglass of Courage C .15 .30
STOR092 Needle Ball C .15 .30
STOR093 Blood Sucker C .15 .30
STOR094 Overpowering Eye R .20 .40
STOR095 Worm Illidan C .15 .30
STOR096 Worm Jetelikpse C .15 .30
STOR097 Worm King SR .20 .40
STOR098 Elemental Hero Ice Edge SR .75 1.50
STOR099 Vylon Delta SCR 1.50 3.00

2011 Yu-Gi-Oh Structure Deck Dragunity Legion 1st Edition

SDDL01 Dragunity Arma Leyvaten UTR .50 1.00
SDDL02 Dragunity Arma Mystletainn SR .50 1.00
SDDL03 Dragunity Aklys SR .50 1.00
SDDL04 Dragunity Dux .25 .50
SDDL05 Dragunity Legionnaire .15 .30
SDDL06 Dragunity Tribus .15 .30
SDDL07 Dragunity Darkspear .15 .30
SDDL08 Dragunity Militum .15 .30
SDDL09 Dragunity Primus Pilus .15 .30
SDDL10 Dragunity Brandistock .15 .30
SDDL11 Dragunity Javelin .15 .30
SDDL12 Mist Valley Falcon .15 .30
SDDL13 Hunter Owl .15 .30
SDDL14 Garuda the Wind Spirit .15 .30
SDDL15 Flying Kamakiri #1 .15 .30
SDDL16 Spear Dragon .15 .30
SDDL17 Twin-Headed Behemoth .15 .30
SDDL18 Armed Dragon LV3 .15 .30
SDDL19 Armed Dragon LV5 .15 .30
SDDL20 Masked Dragon .25 .50
SDDL21 Dragon Ravine .75 1.50
SDDL22 Dragon Mastery .25 .50
SDDL23 United We Stand 1.25 2.50
SDDL24 Mage Power .50 1.00
SDDL25 Dragon's Gunfire .15 .30
SDDL26 Stamping Destruction .15 .30
SDDL27 Creature Swap .25 .50
SDDL28 Monster Reincarnation .25 .50
SDDL29 Foolish Burial .50 1.00
SDDL30 Card Destruction .15 .30
SDDL31 Windstorm of Etaqua .15 .30
SDDL32 Relieve Monster .25 .50
SDDL33 Legacy of Yata-Garasu .15 .30
SDDL34 Final Attack Orders .15 .30
SDDL35 Mirror Force .75 1.50
SDDL36 Dragon's Rage .15 .30
SDDL37 Bottomless Trap Hole .75 1.50
SDDL38 Spiritual Wind Art - Miyabi .15 .30
SDDL39 Icarus Attack .75 1.50

2011 Yu-Gi-Oh Structure Deck Gates of the Underworld 1st Edition

SDGUEN001 Grapha Dragon Lord of Dark World UR 1.25 2.50
SDGUEN002 Snoww Unlight of Dark World SR 1.25 2.50
SDGUEN003 Ceruli Guru of Dark World SR .75 1.50
SDGUEN004 Zure Knight of Dark World C .10 .20
SDGUEN005 Renge Gatekeeper of Dark World C .07 .15
SDGUEN006 Scarr Scout of Dark World C .12 .25
SDGUEN007 Kahkki Guerilla of Dark World C .10 .20
SDGUEN008 Gren Tactician of Dark World C .15 .30
SDGUEN009 Broww Huntsman of Dark World C .50 1.00
SDGUEN010 Beiige Vanguard of Dark World C .15 .30
SDGUEN011 Brron Mad King of Dark World C .07 .15
SDGUEN012 Sillva Warlord of Dark World C .20 .40
SDGUEN013 Goldd WuLord of Dark World C .12 .25
SDGUEN014 ReignBeaux Overlord of Dark World C .12 .25
SDGUEN015 Belial Marquis of Darkness C .12 .25
SDGUEN016 Tragoedia C .17 .35
SDGUEN017 Sangan C .40 .80
SDGUEN018 Newdoria C .25 .50
SDGUEN019 Goblin King C .20 .40
SDGUEN020 Grave Squirmer C .12 .25
SDGUEN021 Card Guard C .07 .15
SDGUEN022 Battle Fader C .50 1.00
SDGUEN023 The Gates of Dark World C .30 .60
SDGUEN024 Dark World Lightning C .10 .20
SDGUEN025 Gateway to Dark World C .07 .15
SDGUEN026 Dark World Dealings C .40 .80
SDGUEN027 Allure of Darkness C 1.50 3.00
SDGUEN028 Card Destruction C .30 .60
SDGUEN029 Terraforming C .25 .50
SDGUEN030 Dark Eruption C .07 .15
SDGUEN031 Dark Scheme C .12 .25
SDGUEN032 The Forces of Darkness C .07 .15
SDGUEN033 Deck Devastation Virus C .30 .75
SDGUEN034 Eradicator Epidemic Virus C 2.00 4.00
SDGUEN035 Mind Crush C .17 .35
SDGUEN036 Dark Deal C .12 .25
SDGUEN037 The Transmigration Prophecy C .20 .40
SDGUEN038 Escape from the Dark Dimension C .12 .25
SDGUEN039 Dark Bribe C .60 1.25

2011 Yu-Gi-Oh Structure Deck Lost Sanctuary 1st Edition

SDLS01 Master Hyperion UR 2.00 4.00
SDLS02 The Agent of Mystery - Earth SR 1.00 2.00
SDLS03 The Agent of Miracles - Jupiter SR .75 1.50
SDLS04 The Agent of Judgement - Saturn .30 .75
SDLS05 The Agent of Wisdom - Mercury .30 .75
SDLS06 The Agent of Creation - Venus .30 .75
SDLS07 The Agent of Force - Mars .30 .75
SDLS08 Mystical Shine Ball .30 .75
SDLS09 Splendid Venus .50 1.00
SDLS10 Tethys, Goddess of Light .75 1.50
SDLS11 Victoria .60 1.25
SDLS12 Athena .50 1.00
SDLS13 Marshmallon 1.00 2.00
SDLS14 Hecatrice .50 1.00
SDLS15 Shining Angel .60 1.25
SDLS16 Soul of Purity and Light .60 1.25
SDLS17 Airknight Parshath .30 .75
SDLS18 Nova Summoner .60 1.25
SDLS19 Zeradias, Herald of Heaven .30 .75
SDLS20 Honest .75 1.50
SDLS21 Hanewata .30 .75
SDLS22 Consecrated Light .60 1.25
SDLS23 Cards from the Sky 1.00 2.00
SDLS24 Valhalla, Hall of the Fallen .50 1.00
SDLS25 Terraforming .60 1.25
SDLS26 Smashing Ground 1.00 2.00
SDLS27 The Sanctuary in the Sky .75 1.50
SDLS28 Celestial Transformation .30 .75
SDLS29 Burial from a Different Dimension 1.50 3.00
SDLS30 Mausoleum of the Emperor .60 1.25
SDLS31 Solidarity 1.50 3.00
SDLS32 The Fountain in the Sky .30 .75
SDLS33 Divine Punishment .60 1.25
SDLS34 Return from the Different Dimension .60 1.25
SDLS35 Torrential Tribute 1.50 3.00
SDLS36 Beckoning Light .50 1.00
SDLS37 Miraculous Descent .30 .75
SDLS38 Solemn Judgment 4.00 8.00

2011 Yu-Gi-Oh Turbo Pack 5

TU05EN000 Colossal Fighter UTR 4.00 8.00
TU05EN001 Dark Hole UR 2.50 5.00
TU05EN002 Gladiator Beast Laquari SR 1.00 2.00
TU05EN003 Snowman Eater SR 1.50 3.00
TU05EN004 Six Samurai United SR 15.00 30.00
TU05EN005 Spell Shattering Arrow SR 2.50 5.00
TU05EN006 Puppet Plant R .50 1.00
TU05EN007 Wulf, Lightsworn Beast R .25 .50
TU05EN008 Cyber Eltanin R .20 .40
TU05EN009 Torrential Tribute R .75 1.50
TU05EN010 Escape from the Dark Dimension R .75 1.50
TU05EN011 Zoma the Spirit R .50 1.00
TU05EN012 Manju of the Ten Thousand Hands C 1.25 2.50
TU05EN013 Abyssal Kingshark C .15 .30
TU05EN014 Spirit of the Six Samurai C .15 .30
TU05EN015 Black Salvo C .15 .30
TU05EN016 Darkness Neosphere C 1.25 2.50
TU05EN017 Miracle Fusion C .75 1.50
TU05EN018 Shield Crush C .15 .30
TU05EN019 Seven Tools of the Bandit C .15 .30
TU05EN020 Royal Command C .15 .30

2011 Yu-Gi-Oh Turbo Pack 6

TU06EN000 Dark Armed Dragon UTR 25.00 50.00
TU06EN001 Sangan UR 5.00 10.00
TU06EN002 Chain Disappearance SR 5.00 10.00
TU06EN003 Masked Dragon SR 3.00 6.00
TU06EN004 Fishborg Blaster SR 2.00 4.00
TU06EN005 Quickdraw Synchron SR 10.00 20.00
TU06EN006 Zombie Master R .50 1.00
TU06EN007 Stardust Dragon R 2.00 4.00
TU06EN008 Red Dragon Archfiend R 1.00 2.00
TU06EN009 Black Garden R .50 1.00
TU06EN010 Armory Arm R 1.25 2.50
TU06EN011 Alector, Sovereign of Birds C .15 .30
TU06EN012 Fusion Gate C 1.25 2.50
TU06EN013 Kinetic Soldier C .10 .20
TU06EN014 Greenkappa C .10 .20
TU06EN015 Creature Swap C .15 .30
TU06EN016 Magical Dimension C .20 .40
TU06EN017 Bountiful Artemis C .50 1.00
TU06EN018 Gemini Spark C .20 .40
TU06EN019 Golem Dragon C .75 1.50
TU06EN020 Transforming Sphere C .10 .20

2012 Yu-Gi-Oh Abyss Rising 1st Edition

ABYR000 Ignoble Knight SR .25 .50
ABYR001 Gagaga Caesar R .25 .50
ABYR002 Bull Blader C .15 .30
ABYR003 Achacha Chanbara C .15 .30
ABYR004 Mogmole C .15 .30
ABYR005 Grandram C .15 .30
ABYR006 Tripod Fish C .15 .30
ABYR007 Deep Sweeper C .15 .30
ABYR008 Heroic Challenger - Extra Sword C .15 .30
ABYR009 Heroic Challenger - Night Watchman C .15 .30
ABYR010 Planet Pathfinder C .15 .30
ABYR011 Solar Wind Jammer C .15 .30
ABYR012 Heraldic Beast Aberconway C .15 .30
ABYR013 Heraldic Beast Berners Falcon C .15 .30
ABYR014 Mermail Abysslinde UR 2.50 5.00
ABYR014 Mermail Abysslinde UTR 2.50 5.00
ABYR015 Mermail Abyssgunde R .25 .50
ABYR016 Mermail Abysshilde C .15 .30
ABYR017 Mermail Abyssturge R .25 .50
ABYR018 Mermail Abysspike R .50 1.00
ABYR019 Mermail Abysslung C .15 .30
ABYR020 Mermail Abyssmegalo SCR 6.00 12.00
ABYR021 Stoic of Prophecy C .15 .30
ABYR022 Hermit of Prophecy C .15 .30
ABYR023 Justice of Prophecy R .60 1.25
ABYR024 Emperor of Prophecy R .25 .50
ABYR025 Madolche Croiwanssant C .15 .30
ABYR026 Madolche Marmalmaid C .15 .30
ABYR027 Madolche Messengelato R 1.00 2.00
ABYR028 Abyss Warrior C .15 .30
ABYR029 Snowman Creator C .15 .30
ABYR030 Fishborg Planter C .15 .30
ABYR031 Nimble Angler C .15 .30
ABYR032 Shore Knight R .25 .50
ABYR033 Mecha Sea Dragon Plesion C .15 .30
ABYR034 Metallizing Parasite - Soltite C .15 .30
ABYR035 Moulinglacia SCR 5.00 10.00
ABYR036 House Duston C .15 .30
ABYR037 Puny Penguin SP .10 .20
ABYR038 Missing Force SP .10 .20
ABYR039 No.32 Shark Drake UR .75 1.50
ABYR039 No.32 Shark Drake UTR 1.00 2.00
ABYR039 No.32 Shark Drake GR 2.00 4.00
ABYR040 One-Eyed Skill Gainer SR .50 1.00
ABYR041 Gagaga Cowboy SR .75 1.50
ABYR042 Heroic Champion - Gandiva UR 1.00 2.00
ABYR042 Heroic Champion - Gandiva UTR 1.50 3.00
ABYR043 Heroic Champion - Kusanagi SR 1.25 2.50
ABYR044 Number 9: Dyson Sphere UR 1.50 3.00
ABYR044 Number 9: Dyson Sphere UTR 1.50 3.00
ABYR045 No.8 Heraldic King SR .60 1.25
ABYR046 Mermail Abyssgaios UR 1.00 2.00
ABYR046 Mermail Abyssgaios UTR 1.50 3.00
ABYR047 Empress of Prophecy UR .25 .50
ABYR047 Empress of Prophecy UTR .50 1.00
ABYR048 Madolche Queen Tiaramisu UR 1.00 2.00
ABYR048 Madolche Queen Tiaramisu UTR 2.50 5.00
ABYR049 Snowdust Giant R .25 .50
ABYR050 Gagagigo the Risen R .25 .50
ABYR051 One-Shot Wand C .15 .30
ABYR052 Different Dimension Deepsea Trench C .15 .30
ABYR053 Tannhauser Gate SR .25 .50
ABYR054 Gravity Blaster C .15 .30
ABYR055 Advanced Heraldry Art R .25 .50
ABYR056 Abyss-scale of the Kraken C .15 .30
ABYR057 Lemuria, the Forgotten City C .15 .30
ABYR058 Spellbook of Eternity R .25 .50
ABYR059 Spellbook of Fate UR 2.00 4.00
ABYR059 Spellbook of Fate UTR 2.50 5.00
ABYR060 The Grand Spellbook Tower SCR 2.00 4.00
ABYR061 Madolche Ticket C .15 .30
ABYR062 Forbidden Dress SR .25 .50
ABYR063 Final Gesture C .15 .30
ABYR064 Mind Pollutant R .25 .50
ABYR065 The Humble Sentry SP .10 .20
ABYR066 Battle Break C .15 .30
ABYR067 Bubble Bringer SR .25 .50
ABYR068 Heroic Gift C .15 .30
ABYR069 Heroic Advance C .15 .30
ABYR070 Xyz Xtreme !! C .15 .30
ABYR071 Abyss-squall SR .25 .50
ABYR072 Abyss-sphere UR 2.00 4.00
ABYR072 Abyss-sphere UTR 2.00 4.00
ABYR073 Abyss-strom R .25 .50
ABYR074 Madolchepalooza SR 1.00 2.00
ABYR075 Memory of an Adversary SR .25 .50
ABYR076 Magic Deflector C .15 .30
ABYR077 That Wacky Alchemy! UR .15 .30
ABYR077 That Wacky Alchemy! UTR .25 .50
ABYR078 Cash Back SP .75 1.50
ABYR079 Unification C .15 .30
ABYR080 Retort SCR 1.25 2.50
ABYR081 Mermail Abyssmander R .25 .50
ABYR082 Red Dragon Ninja SR .25 .50
ABYR083 Slushy R .25 .50
ABYR084 Abyss Dweller SR 1.00 2.00
ABYR085 Giant Soldier of Steel SCR .50 1.00
ABYR086 Noble Arms - Arfeudutyr R .25 .50
ABYR087 Spellbook Library SCR .50 1.00
ABYR088 Spellbook Star Hall R .25 .50
ABYR089 Attack the Moon! SR .25 .50
ABYR090 Electromagnetic Bagworm C .15 .30
ABYR091 Rage of the Deep Sea C .15 .30
ABYR092 Ape Magician C .15 .30
ABYR093 Snowdust Dragon C .15 .30
ABYR094 Snow Dragon C .15 .30
ABYR095 Uminotaurus R .25 .50
ABYR096 Fishborg Launcher C .15 .30
ABYR097 Papa-Corn R .25 .50
ABYR098 Thunder Sea Horse SCR 1.00 2.00
ABYR099 Bahamut Shark SCR 2.00 4.00

2012 Yu-Gi-Oh Astral Pack 1

AP01EN001 Tsukuyomi UTR 7.50 15.00
AP01EN002 Debris Dragon UTR 7.50 15.00
AP01EN003 Photon Thrasher UTR 7.50 15.00
AP01EN004 Flamvell Firedog SR .50 1.00
AP01EN005 Genex Undine SR .75 1.50
AP01EN006 Kagemusha of the Six Samurai SR 3.00 6.00
AP01EN007 Inzektor Centipede SR .75 1.50
AP01EN008 Hieratic Dragon of Tefnuit SR 2.00 4.00
AP01EN009 Terraforming SR 7.50 15.00
AP01EN010 Moray of Greed SR 1.50 3.00
AP01EN011 Mask Change SR 1.50 3.00
AP01EN012 Hidden Armory SR 1.25 2.50
AP01EN013 The Gates of Dark World SR .50 1.00
AP01EN014 Hyena C .25 .50
AP01EN015 Dragon Ice C .25 .50
AP01EN016 Cyber Shark C .75 1.50
AP01EN017 Swift Scarecrow C .50 1.00
AP01EN018 Elemental HERO Ice Edge C .75 1.50
AP01EN019 Mystical Sand C 1.50 3.00
AP01EN020 Spiritual Forest C .15 .30
AP01EN021 Closed Forest C .20 .40
AP01EN022 Shrine of Mist Valley C .15 .30
AP01EN023 Thunder of Ruler C .15 .30
AP01EN024 Fuh-Rin-Ka-Zan C .15 .30
AP01EN025 Astral Barrier C .15 .30

2012 Yu-Gi-Oh Battle Pack Epic Dawn 1st Edition

BP01EN001 Witch of the Black R .25 .50
BP01EN002 Cyber Jar R .25 .50
BP01EN003 Jinzo R .50 1.00
BP01EN004 Injection Fairy Lily R .25 .50
BP01EN005 Dark Dust Spirit R .25 .50
BP01EN006 Skull Archfiend R .25 .50
BP01EN007 Dark Magician R .75 1.50
BP01EN008 Blowback Dragon R .25 .50
BP01EN009 Mobius the Frost R .25 .50
BP01EN010 Fox Fire R .25 .50
BP01EN011 Ancient Gear Golem R .25 .50
BP01EN012 Treeborn Frog R .25 .50
BP01EN013 Super Conductor R .25 .50
BP01EN014 Gorz the Emissary R .75 1.50
BP01EN015 Raiza the Storm R .25 .50
BP01EN016 White Night Dragon R .25 .50
BP01EN017 Deep Diver R .25 .50
BP01EN018 Caius the Shadow R .50 1.00
BP01EN019 Krebons R .25 .50
BP01EN020 Tragoedia R .50 1.00
BP01EN021 Obelisk the Tormentor R 5.00 10.00
BP01EN022 Machina Fortress R .75 1.50
BP01EN023 Tour Guide R 1.25 2.50
BP01EN024 Number 39: Utopia R .50 1.00
BP01EN025 Gachi Gachi Gantetsu R .25 .50
BP01EN026 Grenosaurus R .25 .50
BP01EN027 Num. 17: Leviathan R .25 .50
BP01EN028 Wind-Up Zenmaister R .25 .50
BP01EN029 Tiras, Keeper R 2.00 4.00
BP01EN030 Adreus, Keeper R 2.50 5.00
BP01EN031 Gem-Knight Pearl R .25 .50
BP01EN032 Raigeki R 10.00 20.00
BP01EN033 Swords of Revealing R .25 .50
BP01EN034 Pot of Greed R .60 1.25
BP01EN035 Harpie's Feather R 2.50 5.00
BP01EN036 Graceful Charity R .25 .50
BP01EN037 Change of Heart R .75 1.50
BP01EN038 Heavy Storm R .25 .50

BP01EN039 Snatch Steal R .25 .50
BP01EN040 Premature Burial R .25 .50
BP01EN041 Soul Exchange R .25 .50
BP01EN042 Scapegoat R .25 .50
BP01EN043 United We Stand R 1.50 3.00
BP01EN044 Creature Swap R .25 .50
BP01EN045 Burden of Mighty R .25 .50
BP01EN046 Pot of Duality R .60 1.25
BP01EN047 Solemn Judgment R .25 .50
BP01EN048 Mirror Force R 1.00 2.00
BP01EN049 Call of the Haunted R .25 .50
BP01EN050 Ring of Destruction R .75 1.50
BP01EN051 Torrential Tribute R .75 1.50
BP01EN052 Metal Reflect Slime R .50 1.00
BP01EN053 Skill Drain R 2.00 4.00
BP01EN054 Divine Wrath R .25 .50
BP01EN055 Dark Bribe R .75 1.50
BP01EN056 Greenkappa C .10 .20
BP01EN057 Penguin Soldier C .10 .20
BP01EN058 Mysterious Guard C .10 .20
BP01EN059 Exiled Force C .10 .20
BP01EN060 Old Vindictive Magician C .10 .20
BP01EN061 Breaker of the Magical .10 .20
BP01EN062 Grave Squirmer C .10 .20
BP01EN063 Ryko, Lightsworn Hunter C .10 .20
BP01EN064 Snowman Eater C .10 .20
BP01EN065 Fissure C .10 .20
BP01EN066 Tribute to the Doomed C .10 .20
BP01EN067 Axe of Despair C .10 .20
BP01EN068 Mystical Space Typhoon C .50 1.00
BP01EN069 Horn of the Unicorn C .10 .20
BP01EN070 Offerings to the Doomed C .10 .20
BP01EN071 Bait Doll C .10 .20
BP01EN072 Book of Moon C .10 .20
BP01EN073 Autonomous Action Unit C .10 .20
BP01EN074 Ante C .10 .20
BP01EN075 Big Bang Shot C .10 .20
BP01EN076 Fiend's Sanctuary C .10 .20
BP01EN077 Different Dimension Gate C .10 .20
BP01EN078 Enemy Controller C .10 .20
BP01EN079 Monster Gate C .10 .20
BP01EN080 Shield Crush C .10 .20
BP01EN081 Fighting Spirit C .10 .20
BP01EN082 Forbidden Chalice C .10 .20
BP01EN083 Darkworld Shackles C .10 .20
BP01EN084 Forbidden Lance C .75 1.50
BP01EN085 Infected Mail C .10 .20
BP01EN086 Ego Boost C .10 .20
BP01EN087 Kunai with Chain C .10 .20
BP01EN088 Dust Tornado C .10 .20
BP01EN089 Windstorm of Etaqua C .10 .20
BP01EN090 Magic Drain C .10 .20
BP01EN091 Magic Cylinder C .10 .20
BP01EN092 Shadow Spell C .10 .20
BP01EN093 Blast with Chain C .10 .20
BP01EN094 Needle Ceiling C .10 .20
BP01EN095 Reckless Greed C .50 1.00
BP01EN096 Nightmare Wheel C .10 .20
BP01EN097 Spell Shield Type-8 C .10 .20
BP01EN098 Interdimensional Matter Transporter C .10 .20
BP01EN099 Compulsory Evacuation .10 .20
BP01EN100 Prideful Roar C .10 .20
BP01EN101 Half or Nothing C .10 .20
BP01EN102 Skill Successor C .10 .20
BP01EN103 Pixie Ring C .10 .20
BP01EN104 Changing Destiny C .10 .20
BP01EN105 Fiendish Chain C 1.00 2.00
BP01EN106 Inverse Universe C .10 .20
BP01EN107 Miracle's Wake C .10 .20
BP01EN108 Power Frame C .10 .20
BP01EN109 Damage Gate C .10 .20
BP01EN110 Liberty at Last! C .10 .20
BP01EN111 Luster Dragon C .10 .20
BP01EN112 Archfiend Soldier C .10 .20
BP01EN113 Mad Dog of Darkness C .10 .20
BP01EN114 Charcoal Inpachi C .10 .20
BP01EN115 Insect Knight C .10 .20
BP01EN116 Gene-Warped Warwolf C .10 .20
BP01EN117 Buster Blader C .10 .20
BP01EN118 Goblin Attack Force C .10 .20
BP01EN119 Bazoo the Soul-Eater C .10 .20
BP01EN120 Zombyra the Dark C .10 .20
BP01EN121 Slate Warrior C .10 .20
BP01EN122 Dark Ruler Ha Des C .10 .20
BP01EN123 Freed the Matchless General C .10 .20
BP01EN124 Airknight Parshath C .10 .20
BP01EN125 Asura Priest C .10 .20
BP01EN126 Exarion Universe C .10 .20
BP01EN127 Vampire Lord C .10 .20
BP01EN128 Toon Gemini Elf C .10 .20
BP01EN129 King Tiger Wanghu C .10 .20
BP01EN130 Guardian Sphinx C .10 .20
BP01EN131 Skilled White Magician C .10 .20
BP01EN132 Zaborg the Thunder Monarch C .10 .20
BP01EN133 D.D. Assailant C .10 .20
BP01EN134 Theban Nightmare C .10 .20
BP01EN135 The Tricky C .10 .20
BP01EN136 Raging Flame Sprite C .10 .20
BP01EN137 Chiron the Mage C .10 .20
BP01EN138 Cyber Dragon C .10 .20
BP01EN139 Cybernetic Magician C .10 .20
BP01EN140 Goblin Elite Attack Force C .10 .20
BP01EN141 Doomcaliber Knight C .10 .20
BP01EN142 Chainsaw Insect C .10 .20
BP01EN143 Card Trooper C .10 .20
BP01EN144 Voltic Kong C .10 .20
BP01EN145 Botanical Lion C .10 .20
BP01EN146 Ancient Gear Knight C .10 .20
BP01EN147 Blizzard Dragon C .50 1.00
BP01EN148 Beast King Barbaros C .10 .20
BP01EN149 The Calculator C .10 .20
BP01EN150 Gaap the Divine Soldier C .10 .20
BP01EN151 Arcana Force XIV - Temperance C .10 .20
BP01EN152 Dark Valkyria C .10 .20
BP01EN153 Alector, Sovereign of Birds C .10 .20
BP01EN154 Twin-Barrel Dragon C .10 .20
BP01EN155 Abyssal Kingshark C .10 .20
BP01EN156 Jurrac Protops C .10 .20
BP01EN157 Hedge Guard C .10 .20
BP01EN158 Fabled Ashenveil C .10 .20
BP01EN159 Backup Warrior C .10 .20
BP01EN160 Ambitious Gofer C .10 .20
BP01EN161 Power Giant C .10 .20
BP01EN162 Card Guard C .10 .20
BP01EN163 Yaksha C .10 .20
BP01EN164 Gogogo Golem C .10 .20
BP01EN165 Big Jaws C .10 .20
BP01EN166 Wind-Up Soldier C .10 .20
BP01EN167 Wind-Up Dog C .10 .20
BP01EN168 Milla the Temporal Magician C .10 .20
BP01EN169 Ape Fighter C .10 .20
BP01EN170 Wind-Up Warrior C .10 .20
BP01EN171 Giant Soldier of Stone C .10 .20
BP01EN172 Mask of Darkness C .10 .20
BP01EN173 Morphing Jar C .10 .20
BP01EN174 Muka Muka C .10 .20
BP01EN175 Blast Sphere C .10 .20
BP01EN176 Big Shield Gardna C .10 .20
BP01EN177 Gilasaurus C .10 .20
BP01EN178 Possessed Dark Soul C .10 .20
BP01EN179 Twin-Headed Behemoth C .10 .20
BP01EN180 Makyura the Destructor C .10 .20
BP01EN181 Helping Robo for Combat C .10 .20
BP01EN182 Zolga C .10 .20
BP01EN183 Chaos Necromancer C .10 .20
BP01EN184 Stealth Bird C .50 1.00
BP01EN185 Hyper Hammerhead C .10 .20
BP01EN186 Grave Protector C .10 .20
BP01EN187 Night Assailant C .10 .20
BP01EN188 Pitch-Black Warwolf C .10 .20
BP01EN189 Dekoichi .10 .20
BP01EN190 Gyroid C .10 .20
BP01EN191 Drillroid C .10 .20
BP01EN192 Gravitic Orb C .10 .20
BP01EN193 Cloudian - Poison Cloud C .10 .20
BP01EN194 Des Mosquito C .10 .20
BP01EN195 Mad Reloader C .10 .20
BP01EN196 Phantom of Chaos C .50 1.00
BP01EN197 Cyber Valley C .10 .20
BP01EN198 Blue Thunder T-45 C .10 .20
BP01EN199 Vortex Trooper C .10 .20
BP01EN200 DUCKER Mobile Cannon C .10 .20
BP01EN201 Worm Barses C .10 .20
BP01EN202 Shield Warrior C .10 .20
BP01EN203 Dark Resonator C .10 .20
BP01EN204 Noisy Gnat C .10 .20
BP01EN205 Fabled Raven C .10 .20
BP01EN206 Fortress Warrior C .10 .20
BP01EN207 Twin-Sword Marauder C .10 .20
BP01EN208 Level Warrior C .10 .20
BP01EN209 Level Eater C .10 .20
BP01EN210 Naturia Strawberry C .10 .20
BP01EN211 Battle Fader C .50 1.00
BP01EN212 Amazoness Sage C .10 .20
BP01EN213 Amazoness Trainee C .10 .20
BP01EN214 Hardened Armed Dragon C 1.00 2.00
BP01EN215 Blackwing - Zephyros .10 .20
BP01EN216 Tanngrisnir of the Nordic Beasts C .10 .20
BP01EN217 Shine Knight C .10 .20
BP01EN218 Gagaga Magician C .10 .20
BP01EN219 Goblindbergh C .10 .20
BP01EN220 Psi-Blocker C .50 1.00

2012 Yu-Gi-Oh Collector Tins

CT09EN001 Evolzar Dolkka SCR .25 .50
CT09EN002 Heroic Champion - Excalibur SCR 1.25 2.50
CT09EN003 Ninja Grandmaster Hanzo SCR .25 .50
CT09EN004 Hieratic Sun Dragon... SCR 2.00 4.00
CT09EN005 Genex Neutron SR .25 .50
CT09EN006 Scrap Dragon SR .75 1.50
CT09EN007 Dark Highlander SR .25 .50
CT09EN008 Wind-Up Zenmaines SR .25 .50
CT09EN009 Blizzard Princess SR .25 .50
CT09EN010 Wind-Up Rabbit SR .25 .50
CT09EN011 Evolzar Laggia SR .25 .50
CT09EN012 Maxx C SR 5.00 10.00
CT09EN013 Tour Guide From the Underworld SR 1.50 3.00
CT09EN014 Number 16: Shock Master SR .75 1.50
CT09EN015 Rescue Rabbit SR .50 1.00
CT09EN016 Malefic Truth Dragon SR .25 .50
CT09EN017 X-Saber Souza SR .25 .50
CT09EN018 Leviair the Sea Dragon SR 3.00 6.00
CT09EN019 Prophecy Destroyer SCR .25 .50
CT09EN020 Endless Decay SR .25 .50
CT09EN021 Steelswarm Roach SR 1.00 2.00
CT09EN022 Photon Strike Bounzer SR .50 1.00
CT09EN023 Infernity Barrier SR .25 .50

2012 Yu-Gi-Oh Galactic Overlord 1st Edition

GAOV000 Noble Knight SR .20 .40
GAOV001 Wattaildragon .15 .30
GAOV002 Hieratic Seal of the Sun Dragon Overlord .15 .30
GAOV003 Overlay Owl .15 .30
GAOV004 Tasuke Knight SR .20 .40
GAOV005 Gagaga Gardna R .25 .50
GAOV006 Cardcar D SCR 2.50 5.00
GAOV007 Overlay Eater .15 .30
GAOV008 Hammer Shark R .25 .50
GAOV009 Hammer Bounzer SR .20 .40
GAOV010 Blade Bounzer .15 .30
GAOV011 Phantom Bounzer .15 .30
GAOV012 Morpho Butterspy .15 .30
GAOV013 Swallowtail Butterspy .15 .30
GAOV014 Moonlit Papillon .15 .30
GAOV015 Jumbo Drill SR .20 .40
GAOV016 Rocket Arrow Express R .25 .50
GAOV017 Cameraclops .15 .30
GAOV018 Hieratic Dragon of Nuit .15 .30
GAOV019 Dragon of Gebeb SR 1.00 2.00
GAOV020 Hieratic Dragon of Eset .15 .30
GAOV021 Hieratic Dragon of Nebthet .15 .30
GAOV022 Dragon of Tefnuit R .25 .50
GAOV023 Hieratic Dragon of Su .15 .30
GAOV024 Hieratic Dragon of Asar R .25 .50
GAOV025 Dragon of Sutekh UR .60 1.25
GAOV025 Dragon of Sutekh UTR .60 1.25
GAOV026 Evoltile Lagosucho .15 .30
GAOV027 Evolsaur Darwino .15 .30
GAOV028 Inzektor Firefly .15 .30
GAOV029 Inzektor Ladybug .15 .30
GAOV030 Inzektor Earwig .15 .30
GAOV031 Inzektor Giga-Cricket R .25 .50
GAOV032 Lightray Sorcerer R .25 .50
GAOV033 Lightray Daedalus .15 .30
GAOV034 Lightray Gearfried R .25 .50
GAOV035 Lightray Diabolos R .25 .50
GAOV036 Lady of D. .15 .30
GAOV037 Absorbing Jar R .25 .50
GAOV038 Red-Headed Oni .15 .30
GAOV039 Flame Tiger .15 .30
GAOV040 Nomadic Force .15 .30
GAOV041 Neo Galaxy-Eyes UR 5.00 10.00
GAOV041 Neo Galaxy-Eyes UTR 5.00 10.00
GAOV041 Neo Galaxy-Eyes (GR) 7.50 15.00
GAOV042 Shark Drake UR 1.00 2.00
GAOV042 Shark Drake UTR .60 1.25
GAOV043 Photon Strike SCR 1.50 3.00
GAOV044 Photon Papilloperative R .25 .50
GAOV045 Force Focus UR .60 1.25
GAOV045 Force Focus UTR .60 1.25
GAOV046 Gaia Dragon SR 7.50 15.00
GAOV047 Dragon King of Atum SR 3.00 6.00
GAOV048 Dragon Overlord SCR 4.00 8.00
GAOV049 Dragun Djinn SR 5.00 10.00
GAOV050 Inzektor Exa-Stag UR .60 1.25
GAOV050 Inzektor Exa-Stag UTR .60 1.25
GAOV051 Bound Wand (SR) .75 1.50
GAOV052 Mini-Guts .15 .30
GAOV053 Falling Current .15 .30
GAOV054 Berserk Scales .15 .30
GAOV055 Night Beam UR 1.25 2.50
GAOV055 Night Beam UTR 2.00 4.00
GAOV056 Seal of Convocation R 1.00 2.00
GAOV057 Hieratic Seal of Supremacy .15 .30
GAOV058 Evo-Diversity R .25 .50
GAOV059 Evo-Price R .25 .50
GAOV060 Final Inzektion R .25 .50
GAOV061 Crossbow - Zektarrow R .25 .50
GAOV062 Xyz Unit UR .60 1.25
GAOV062 Xyz Unit UTR .60 1.25
GAOV063 That Wacky Magic .15 .30
GAOV064 Constellar Belt .15 .30
GAOV065 Storm .15 .30
GAOV066 Nitwit Outwit .15 .30
GAOV067 Gamushara .15 .30
GAOV068 Commander of Swords .15 .30
GAOV069 Bounzer Guard .15 .30
GAOV070 Butterflyoke .15 .30
GAOV071 Hieratic Seal of Banishment .15 .30
GAOV072 Seal of Reflection SR .50 1.00
GAOV073 Zekt Conversion UR .60 1.25
GAOV073 Zekt Conversion UTR .60 1.25
GAOV074 Inzektor Gauntlet .15 .30
GAOV075 Return .15 .30
GAOV076 Dimension Slice R .25 .50
GAOV077 Light Art - Hijiri SR .20 .40
GAOV078 Sealing Ceremony of Raiton .15 .30
GAOV079 Aquamirror Cycle .15 .30
GAOV080 Double Payback .15 .30
GAOV081 Ancient Dragon R .25 .50
GAOV082 Hieratic Seal of the Dragon King .15 .30
GAOV083 Evoltile Elginero SR .20 .40
GAOV084 Lightray Grepher R .25 .50
GAOV085 Tardy Orc SCR .50 1.00
GAOV086 Draconnection UR 3.00 6.00
GAOV086 Draconnection UTR 5.00 10.00
GAOV087 Trial and Tribulation SCR 1.50 3.00
GAOV088 Seal From Ashes SCR 1.50 3.00
GAOV089 Xyz Wrath .15 .30
GAOV090 Big Eye SCR 5.00 10.00
GAOV091 Lucky Straight SCR 1.50 3.00
GAOV092 Beetron UR .60 1.25
GAOV092 Beetron UTR .60 1.25
GAOV093 Influence Dragon .15 .30
GAOV094 Bright Star Dragon .15 .30
GAOV095 Buten .15 .30
GAOV096 Doom Donuts .15 .30
GAOV097 Nimble Manta .15 .30
GAOV098 Shining Elf SR .20 .40
GAOV099 Flelf SR .20 .40

2012 Yu-Gi-Oh Gold Series Haunted Mine

GLD5EN001 Blue-Eyes White GGR 7.50 15.00
GLD5EN002 Patrician of Darkness C .10 .20
GLD5EN003 Pyramid Turtle C .10 .20
GLD5EN004 Dark Scorpion Burglars C .10 .20
GLD5EN005 Don Zaloog C .20 .40
GLD5EN006 Helpoemer C .10 .20
GLD5EN007 Dark Scorpion - Cliff the Trap Remover C .10 .20
GLD5EN008 Despair from the Dark C .10 .20
GLD5EN009 Fear from the Dark C .10 .20
GLD5EN010 Dark Scorpion - Chick the Yellow C .10 .20
GLD5EN011 Dark Scorpion - Gorg the Strong C .10 .20
GLD5EN012 Dark Scorpion - Meanae the Thorn C .10 .20
GLD5EN013 Ryu Kokki C .10 .20
GLD5EN014 Vampire Lady C .10 .20
GLD5EN015 Double Coston C .10 .20
GLD5EN016 Regenerating Mummy C .10 .20
GLD5EN017 Dark Mimic LV1 C .10 .20
GLD5EN018 Dark Mimic LV3 C .10 .20
GLD5EN019 Zombie Master C .50 1.00
GLD5EN020 Gernia C .10 .20
GLD5EN021 Goblin Zombie C .75 1.50
GLD5EN022 The Lady in Wight C .50 1.00
GLD5EN023 Red Ogre C .10 .20
GLD5EN024 Gorz the Emissary of Darkness GGR 2.50 5.00
GLD5EN025 Bone Crusher C .10 .20
GLD5EN026 Fabled Grimro GLD .50 1.00
GLD5EN027 Master Hyperion GLD .50 1.00
GLD5EN028 Grapha, Dragon Lord GR .50 1.00
GLD5EN029 Sephylon, the Ultimate GR .50 1.00
GLD5EN030 Herald of Perfection GGR 2.50 5.00
GLD5EN031 Brionac, Dragon GR 2.50 5.00
GLD5EN032 Naturia Beast GLD 1.50 3.00
GLD5EN033 Naturia Barkion GGR 2.00 4.00
GLD5EN034 Formula Synchron GLD 2.00 4.00
GLD5EN035 Karakuri Steel Shogun GR .75 1.50
GLD5EN036 Number 39: Utopia GLD 1.50 3.00
GLD5EN037 Dark Hole GLD 1.25 2.50
GLD5EN038 Mystical Space GGR 4.00 8.00
GLD5EN039 Book of Life C .25 .50
GLD5EN040 Call of the Mummy C .10 .20
GLD5EN041 Spellbook Organization C .20 .40
GLD5EN042 Mustering of the Dark Scorpions C .10 .20
GLD5EN043 Pyramid of Wonders C .10 .20
GLD5EN044 Dawn of the Herald C .20 .40
GLD5EN045 Solemn Judgment GGR 2.00 4.00
GLD5EN046 Call of the Haunted GLD 1.25 2.50
GLD5EN047 Physical Double C .10 .20
GLD5EN048 Hidden Spellbook C .10 .20
GLD5EN049 Zoma the Spirit C .50 1.00
GLD5EN050 Embodiment of Apophis C .10 .20
GLD5EN051 Machine King - 3000 B.C. C .10 .20
GLD5EN052 Starlight Road GLD .50 1.00
GLD5EN053 Tiki Curse C .10 .20
GLD5EN054 Tiki Soul C .10 .20
GLD5EN055 Copy Knight C .10 .20

2012 Yu-Gi-Oh Hidden Arsenal 6 1st Edition

HA06EN001 Gem-Knight Crystal SR .20 .40
HA06EN002 Laval Volcano Handmaiden SR .10 .20
HA06EN003 Laval Cannon SCR .25 .50
HA06EN004 Vylon Sphere SR .10 .20
HA06EN005 Vylon Tetra SR .10 .20
HA06EN006 Vylon Stella SR .10 .20
HA06EN007 Vylon Prism SR .15 .30
HA06EN008 Vylon Hept SR .10 .20
HA06EN009 Gishki Reliever SR .10 .20
HA06EN010 Gishki Noellia SR .10 .20
HA06EN011 Gusto Squirro SR .10 .20
HA06EN012 Reeze, Whirlwind of Gusto SR .10 .20
HA06EN013 Steelswarm Genome SR .10 .20
HA06EN014 Steelswarm Sentinel SR .10 .20
HA06EN015 Steelswarm Sting SR .10 .20
HA06EN016 Steelswarm Longhorn SCR .25 .50
HA06EN017 Steelswarm Hercules SCR .25 .50
HA06EN018 Evigishki Tetrogre SCR .25 .50
HA06EN019 Gem-Knight Citrine SCR .75 1.50
HA06EN020 Gem-Knight Prismaura SCR .75 1.50
HA06EN021 Laval Stennon SCR .25 .50
HA06EN022 Vylon Alpha SCR .25 .50
HA06EN023 Vylon Omega SCR .25 .50
HA06EN024 Daigusto Sphreez SCR .75 1.50
HA06EN025 Vylon Component SR .10 .20
HA06EN026 Vylon Element SR .10 .20
HA06EN027 Forbidden Arts of the Gishki SR .10 .20
HA06EN028 Pyroxene Fusion SR .10 .20
HA06EN029 Infestation Ripples SR .10 .20
HA06EN030 Infestation Tool SR .10 .20
HA06EN031 Gem-Knight Obsidian SR .50 1.00
HA06EN032 Gem-Knight Iolite SR .20 .40
HA06EN033 Gem-Knight Amber SR .20 .40
HA06EN034 Laval Lakeside Lady SCR .50 1.00
HA06EN035 Laval Coatl SR .10 .20
HA06EN036 Laval Blaster SR .10 .20
HA06EN037 Vylon Pentachloro SR .10 .20
HA06EN038 Vylon Tesseract SR .10 .20
HA06EN039 Vylon Stigma SR .10 .20
HA06EN040 Gishki Vision SR .25 .50
HA06EN041 Gishki Emilia SR .10 .20
HA06EN042 Gishki Mollusk SR .10 .20
HA06EN043 Gusto Falco SR .10 .20
HA06EN044 Kamui, Hope of Gusto SR .20 .40
HA06EN045 Musto, Oracle of Gusto SR .10 .20
HA06EN046 Evigishki Gustkraken SCR .25 .50
HA06EN047 Gem-Knight Amethyst SCR .50 1.00
HA06EN048 Lavalval Dragun SCR .25 .50
HA06EN049 Daigusto Falcos SCR .25 .50
HA06EN050 Gem-Knight Pearl SCR .50 1.00
HA06EN051 Lavalval Ignis SCR .25 .50
HA06EN052 Vylon Disigma SCR 1.50 3.00
HA06EN053 Evigishki Merrowgeist SCR .25 .50
HA06EN054 Daigusto Phoenix SCR 2.00 4.00
HA06EN055 Particle Fusion SR .10 .20
HA06EN056 Vylon Polytope SR .10 .20
HA06EN057 Vylon Segment SR .10 .20
HA06EN058 Dustflame Blast SR .10 .20
HA06EN059 Aquamirror Illusion SR .10 .20
HA06EN060 Whirlwind of Gusto SR .10 .20

2012 Yu-Gi-Oh Legendary Collection 3 Yugi's World 1st Edition

LCYWEN001 Dark Magician SCR 1.25 2.50
LCYWEN002 Gaia The Fierce Knight SR .60 1.25
LCYWEN003 Celtic Guardian SR .60 1.25
LCYWEN004 Silver Fang UR .50 1.00
LCYWEN005 Mystical Elf C .15 .30
LCYWEN006 Curse of Dragon R .25 .50
LCYWEN007 Giant Soldier of Stone C .15 .30
LCYWEN008 Feral Imp C .15 .30
LCYWEN009 Winged Dragon, Guardian... UR .50 1.00
LCYWEN010 Summoned Skull SR 1.00 2.00
LCYWEN011 Gazelle the King of Mythical Beasts UR .75 1.50
LCYWEN012 Alpha the Magnet Warrior C .15 .30
LCYWEN013 Beta the Magnet Warrior C .20 .40
LCYWEN014 Gamma the Magnet Warrior C .15 .30
LCYWEN015 Queen's Knight UR 1.00 2.00
LCYWEN016 Jack's Knight UR 1.25 2.50
LCYWEN017 King's Knight UR .75 1.50
LCYWEN018 Kuriboh SR .60 1.25
LCYWEN019 Catapult Turtle R .25 .50
LCYWEN020 Buster Blader SCR 2.50 5.00
LCYWEN021 Valkyrion the Magna Warrior SR .60 1.25
LCYWEN022 Dark Magician Girl SCR 4.00 8.00
LCYWEN023 Breaker the Magical Warrior UR .75 1.50
LCYWEN024 Mirage Knight C .15 .30
LCYWEN025 Black Luster Soldier Envoy... SCR 4.00 8.00
LCYWEN026 Dark Magician of Chaos SCR 5.00 10.00
LCYWEN027 Dark Sage C 1.25 2.50
LCYWEN028 Dark Magician Knight C 1.50 3.00

LCYWEN029 Sorcerer of Dark Magic C 1.50 3.00
LCYWEN030 Watapon C .15 .30
LCYWEN031 Swift Gaia the Fierce Knight C .15 .30
LCYWEN032 Big Shield Gardna SCR 1.25 2.50
LCYWEN033 Silent Swordsman LV3 C .15 .30
LCYWEN034 Silent Swordsman LV5 C .15 .30
LCYWEN035 Silent Swordsman LV7 C .50 1.00
LCYWEN036 Obnoxious Celtic Guard C .15 .30
LCYWEN037 Silent Magician LV4 C .50 1.00
LCYWEN038 Silent Magician LV8 C .50 1.00
LCYWEN039 Green Gadget UR .50 1.00
LCYWEN040 Red Gadget UR .50 1.00
LCYWEN041 Yellow Gadget UR .50 1.00
LCYWEN042 Archfiend of Gilfer R .25 .50
LCYWEN043 The Tricky C .15 .30
LCYWEN044 Gorz the Emissary of Darkness UR1.00 2.00
LCYWEN045 Berfomet SR .60 1.25
LCYWEN046 Black Luster Soldier C .50 1.00
LCYWEN047 Magician of Black Chaos C 1.50 3.00
LCYWEN048 Dark Paladin SCR 7.50 15.00
LCYWEN049 Dark Flare Knight C .50 1.00
LCYWEN050 Dragon Master Knight SR 2.50 5.00
LCYWEN051 Arcana Knight Joker SCR 2.50 5.00
LCYWEN052 Chimera the Flying Mythical Beast SR.60 1.25
LCYWEN053 Dark Hole SCR 1.00 2.00
LCYWEN054 Raigeki SCR 10.00 20.00
LCYWEN055 Fissure SR .60 1.25
LCYWEN056 Polymerization SR 1.25 2.50
LCYWEN057 Swords of Revealing Light UR .50 1.00
LCYWEN058 Monster Reborn UR 1.00 2.00
LCYWEN059 Pot of Greed SCR 1.50 3.00
LCYWEN060 Card Destruction SCR .60 1.25
LCYWEN061 Heavy Storm UR .50 1.00
LCYWEN062 Mystical Space Typhoon SCR 1.50 3.00
LCYWEN063 De-Fusion C .50 1.00
LCYWEN064 Graceful Charity SCR 2.00 4.00
LCYWEN065 Double Spell SR .60 1.25
LCYWEN066 Diffusion Wave-Motion SR .60 1.25
LCYWEN067 Thousand Knives C .15 .30
LCYWEN068 Heart of the Underdog C .15 .30
LCYWEN069 Dedication Through Light... SCR 3.00 6.00
LCYWEN070 Black Luster Ritual C 1.50 3.00
LCYWEN071 Dark Magic Attack C .50 1.00
LCYWEN072 Knight's Title C .15 .30
LCYWEN073 Sage's Stone R 1.50 3.00
LCYWEN074 Brain Control SCR .75 1.50
LCYWEN075 Magical Dimension C .15 .30
LCYWEN076 Mystic Box C .15 .30
LCYWEN077 Magicians Unite C .15 .30
LCYWEN078 Black Magic Ritual C 1.00 2.00
LCYWEN079 Dark Magic Curtain R 1.00 2.00
LCYWEN080 Gold Sarcophagus C 1.00 2.00
LCYWEN081 Soul Taker C .15 .30
LCYWEN082 Magic Formula C .50 1.00
LCYWEN083 Union Attack C .15 .30
LCYWEN084 Tricky Spell 4 C .15 .30
LCYWEN085 Spell Shattering Arrow C .50 1.00
LCYWEN086 Multiply R .75 1.50
LCYWEN087 Makiu, the Magical Mist C .15 .30
LCYWEN088 Detonate C .15 .30
LCYWEN089 Seven Tools of the Bandit SCR .60 1.25
LCYWEN090 Horn of Heaven SCR .60 1.25
LCYWEN091 Mirror Force SCR 1.25 2.50
LCYWEN092 Spellbinding Circle C .15 .30
LCYWEN093 Lightforce Sword SR .60 1.25
LCYWEN094 Chain Destruction C .15 .30
LCYWEN095 Dust Tornado UR .50 1.00
LCYWEN096 Magical Hats C .50 1.00
LCYWEN097 Shift SR .60 1.25
LCYWEN098 Collected Power C .15 .30
LCYWEN099 Magic Cylinder SR .60 1.25
LCYWEN100 Magician's Circle SR 1.00 2.00
LCYWEN101 Stronghold the Moving Fortress UR.50 1.00
LCYWEN102 Soul Rope C .15 .30
LCYWEN103 Blue-Eyes Toon Dragon R .75 1.50
LCYWEN104 Manga Ryu-Ran R .25 .50
LCYWEN105 Toon Mermaid R 1.25 2.50
LCYWEN106 Toon Summoned Skull R .25 .50
LCYWEN107 Toon Gemini Elf R .25 .50
LCYWEN108 Toon Goblin Attack Force R 2.00 4.00
LCYWEN109 Toon Cannon Soldier R 2.00 4.00
LCYWEN110 Toon Masked Sorcerer R 2.00 4.00
LCYWEN111 Toon Dark Magician Girl R .75 1.50
LCYWEN112 Dark-Eyes Illusionist R .25 .50
LCYWEN113 Relinquished R .50 1.00
LCYWEN114 Black Illusion Ritual R .25 .50
LCYWEN115 Toon World R .50 1.00
LCYWEN116 Toon Table of Contents R 1.25 2.50
LCYWEN117 Dragon Capture Jar R .25 .50
LCYWEN118 Toon Defense R .75 1.50
LCYWEN119 Man-Eater Bug C .15 .30
LCYWEN120 Sangan SCR 1.50 3.00
LCYWEN121 Morphing Jar UR .50 1.00
LCYWEN122 Puppet Master C .15 .30
LCYWEN123 Dark Master - Zorc C .15 .30
LCYWEN124 Change of Heart SCR 2.00 4.00
LCYWEN125 Exchange SCR .60 1.25
LCYWEN126 The Dark Door R .25 .50
LCYWEN127 Spiritualism C .15 .30
LCYWEN128 Contract with the Dark Master C .15 .30
LCYWEN129 Guardian Elma C .15 .30
LCYWEN130 Guardian Ceal C .15 .30
LCYWEN131 Guardian Grarl C .50 1.00
LCYWEN132 Guardian Baou C .15 .30
LCYWEN133 Guardian Kay'est C .15 .30
LCYWEN134 Guardian Tryce C .15 .30
LCYWEN135 My Body as a Shield C .15 .30
LCYWEN136 Butterfly Dagger - Elma C .50 1.00
LCYWEN137 Shooting Star Bow - Ceal C .50 1.00
LCYWEN138 Gravity Axe - Grarl C .15 .30
LCYWEN139 Wicked-Breaking Flamberge - Baou C.15 .30
LCYWEN140 Rod of Silence - Kay'est C .50 1.00
LCYWEN141 Twin Swords
of Flashing Light - Tryce C .75 1.50
LCYWEN142 Monster Reincarnation R .25 .50
LCYWEN143 Gil Garth UR .50 1.00
LCYWEN144 Bowganian SR .60 1.25
LCYWEN145 Machine Duplication SR 1.50 3.00
LCYWEN146 Hidden Soldiers R .25 .50
LCYWEN147 Rope of Life SCR .60 1.25
LCYWEN148 Malevolent Catastrophe SR .60 1.25
LCYWEN149 Harpie's Feather Duster SCR 4.00 8.00
LCYWEN150 Gravity Bind SR .60 1.25
LCYWEN151 Mechanicalchaser UR .50 1.00
LCYWEN152 Solemn Judgment SCR .60 1.25
LCYWEN153 Magic Jammer SCR .75 1.50
LCYWEN154 Sinister Serpent SCR .60 1.25
LCYWEN155 Mirage of Nightmare SCR .60 1.25
LCYWEN156 Ordeal of a Traveler C .50 1.00
LCYWEN157 Tri-Horned Dragon SR .60 1.25
LCYWEN158 Two-Headed King Rex SCR .75 1.50
LCYWEN159 Millennium Shield SR .60 1.25
LCYWEN160 Cosmo Queen UR .75 1.50
LCYWEN161 Fire Princess UR .50 1.00
LCYWEN162 Command Knight C .50 1.00
LCYWEN163 Malice Doll of Demise R .25 .50
LCYWEN164 White-Horned Dragon SR .60 1.25
LCYWEN165 Green Baboon,
Defender of the Forest C .15 .30
LCYWEN166 Summoner Monk UR 1.50 3.00
LCYWEN167 Commander Covington SCR .60 1.25
LCYWEN168 Machina Soldier SCR .60 1.25
LCYWEN169 Machina Sniper SCR .60 1.25
LCYWEN170 Machina Defender SCR .60 1.25
LCYWEN171 Machina Force SCR .60 1.25
LCYWEN172 Limiter Removal UR .75 1.50
LCYWEN173 Reinforcement of the Army SR .60 1.25
LCYWEN174 Dragged Down into the Grave SR 1.00 2.00
LCYWEN175 Ectoplasmer R .25 .50
LCYWEN176 Mind Control UR .50 1.00
LCYWEN177 Trap Hole UR .50 1.00
LCYWEN178 Imperial Order SCR .75 1.50
LCYWEN179 Mask of Restrict C 6.00 12.00
LCYWEN180 Torrential Tribute SCR 1.00 2.00
LCYWEN181 Bottomless Trap Hole UR 1.00 2.00
LCYWEN182 Royal Decree UR 1.00 2.00
LCYWEN183 Gravekeeper's Spy UR .50 1.00
LCYWEN184 Gravekeeper's Guard UR .50 1.00
LCYWEN185 Gravekeeper's Spear Soldier UR .50 1.00
LCYWEN186 Gravekeeper's Watcher C .15 .30
LCYWEN187 Gravekeeper's Chief UR .50 1.00
LCYWEN188 Gravekeeper's Cannonholder UR .50 1.00
LCYWEN189 Gravekeeper's Assailant UR .50 1.00
LCYWEN190 Charm of Shabti C .15 .30
LCYWEN191 Gravekeeper's Commandant UR 1.25 2.50
LCYWEN192 Gravekeeper's Descendant UR 1.00 2.00
LCYWEN193 Gravekeeper's Recruiter UR 3.00 6.00
LCYWEN194 Necrovalley UR 1.50 3.00
LCYWEN195 Royal Tribute UR .75 1.50
LCYWEN196 Rite of Spirit C .50 1.00
LCYWEN197 Horus the Black Flame Dragon LV4 C.15 .30
LCYWEN198 Horus the Black Flame Dragon LV6 C.25 .50
LCYWEN199 Horus the Black Flame Dragon LV8 C1.50 3.00
LCYWEN200 Mystic Swordsman LV2 C .15 .30
LCYWEN201 Mystic Swordsman LV4 C .15 .30
LCYWEN202 Mystic Swordsman LV6 C .50 1.00
LCYWEN203 Armed Dragon LV3 C .15 .30
LCYWEN204 Armed Dragon LV5 C .15 .30
LCYWEN205 Armed Dragon LV7 C 1.50 3.00
LCYWEN206 Horus' Servant C .15 .30
LCYWEN207 Level Up! C .60 1.25
LCYWEN208 Dark Grepher C 1.50 3.00
LCYWEN209 Dark Horus C .15 .30
LCYWEN210 The Dark Creator C .15 .30
LCYWEN211 Dark Nephthys C .15 .30
LCYWEN212 Darklord Zerato C .15 .30
LCYWEN213 Darknight Parshath C .15 .30
LCYWEN214 Dark General Freed C .15 .30
LCYWEN215 D.D. Warrior Lady R .25 .50
LCYWEN216 D.D. Scout Plane R .25 .50
LCYWEN217 D.D. Assailant R .25 .50
LCYWEN218 D.D. Warrior R .25 .50
LCYWEN219 Skull Servant UR 2.00 4.00
LCYWEN220 Dark King of the Abyss SCR .60 1.25
LCYWEN221 Aqua Madoor SCR .60 1.25
LCYWEN222 Yaranzo SR .60 1.25
LCYWEN223 Takriminos SR .60 1.25
LCYWEN224 Megasonic Eye SR .60 1.25
LCYWEN225 Yamadron SR .60 1.25
LCYWEN226 Three-Legged Zombie SR .60 1.25
LCYWEN227 Fairy's Gift SR .60 1.25
LCYWEN228 Kanan the Swordmistress UR .50 1.00
LCYWEN229 Mystical Shine Ball SR .60 1.25
LCYWEN230 Big Eye R .25 .50
LCYWEN231 Banisher of the Light C .15 .30
LCYWEN232 Giant Rat SCR .60 1.25
LCYWEN233 UFO Turtle SCR .60 1.25
LCYWEN234 Giant Germ C .50 1.00
LCYWEN235 Nimble Momonga C .75 1.50
LCYWEN236 Shining Angel SCR .60 1.25
LCYWEN237 Mother Grizzly SCR .60 1.25
LCYWEN238 Flying Kamakiri #1 SCR .60 1.25
LCYWEN239 Mystic Tomato SCR .60 1.25
LCYWEN240 Morphing Jar #2 SR .60 1.25
LCYWEN241 Goddess of Whim C .15 .30
LCYWEN242 Kycoo the Ghost Destroyer SCR .75 1.50
LCYWEN243 Summoner of Illusions C .15 .30
LCYWEN244 Needle Worm UR 1.25 2.50
LCYWEN245 Pyramid Turtle SCR .60 1.25
LCYWEN246 Spirit Reaper UR .50 1.00
LCYWEN247 Arsenal Summoner C .15 .30
LCYWEN248 Chaos Sorcerer SR .60 1.25
LCYWEN249 Levia-Dragon - Daedalus SCR .60 1.25
LCYWEN250 Manju of the Ten Thousand Hands C1.25 2.50
LCYWEN251 Invader of Darkness C .15 .30
LCYWEN252 The Agent of Wisdom - Mercury SR.60 1.25
LCYWEN253 The Agent of Creation - Venus SR .60 1.25
LCYWEN254 Solar Flare Dragon SR .60 1.25
LCYWEN255 Emissary of the Afterlife C .50 1.00
LCYWEN256 King of the Swamp C 4.00 8.00
LCYWEN257 The Creator C .15 .30
LCYWEN258 The Creator Incarnate C .15 .30
LCYWEN259 Sacred Phoenix of Nephthys SR .60 1.25
LCYWEN260 Hand of Nephthys R .25 .50
LCYWEN261 Armed Samurai - Ben Kei C .15 .30
LCYWEN262 The Light - Hex-Sealed Fusion C .15 .30
LCYWEN263 The Dark - Hex-Sealed Fusion C .15 .30
LCYWEN264 The Earth - Hex-Sealed Fusion C .15 .30
LCYWEN265 Upstart Goblin UR 4.00 8.00
LCYWEN266 Messenger of Peace C 1.00 2.00
LCYWEN267 Prohibition SCR .60 1.25
LCYWEN268 Fusion Gate SR 1.50 3.00
LCYWEN269 Creature Swap UR .50 1.00
LCYWEN270 Book of Moon SCR .60 1.25
LCYWEN271 Dark Snake Syndrome R .25 .50
LCYWEN272 Non-Spellcasting Area C .15 .30
LCYWEN273 Contract with the Abyss C .15 .30
LCYWEN274 Stray Lambs C .15 .30
LCYWEN275 Smashing Ground UR .50 1.00
LCYWEN276 Salvage SR 1.00 2.00
LCYWEN277 Earth Chant C .15 .30
LCYWEN278 Spell Economics C .15 .30
LCYWEN279 Level Limit - Area B C .75 1.50
LCYWEN280 A Feather of the Phoenix SCR .60 1.25
LCYWEN281 Swords of Concealing Light UR 4.00 8.00
LCYWEN282 Centrifugal Field C .15 .30
LCYWEN283 Acid Trap Hole R .25 .50
LCYWEN284 DNA Surgery C 1.25 2.50
LCYWEN285 Reckless Greed SR 1.25 2.50
LCYWEN286 Raigeki Break SR .60 1.25
LCYWEN287 Goblin Fan C .15 .30
LCYWEN288 Sakuretsu Armor SR 1.00 2.00
LCYWEN289 Chain Disappearance C .50 1.00
LCYWEN290 Dark Mirror Force R 1.00 2.00
LCYWEN291 Compulsory Evacuation Device SCR.60 1.25
LCYWEN292 DNA Transplant C .15 .30
LCYWEN293 Beckoning Light UR .50 1.00
LCYWEN294 Draining Shield C .50 1.00
LCYWEN295 Mind Crush UR 1.00 2.00
LCYWEN296 Penalty Game! C .15 .30
LCYWEN297 Threatening Roar SCR .75 1.50
LCYWEN298 Phoenix Wing Wind Blast SCR .60 1.25
LCYWEN299 Level Limit - Area A C .15 .30
LCYWEN300 Black Horn of Heaven SCR .60 1.25
LCYWEN301 Solemn Warning C 1.50 3.00
LCYWEN302 Right Leg of the Forbidden One SCR2.50 5.00
LCYWEN303 Left Leg of the Forbidden One SCR2.50 5.00
LCYWEN304 Right Arm of the Forbidden One SCR2.50 5.00
LCYWEN305 Left Arm of the Forbidden One SCR2.50 5.00
LCYWEN306 Exodia the Forbidden One SCR 2.50 5.00

2012 Yu-Gi-Oh Legendary Collection 3 Yugi's World Box Bonus

LC03001 The Seal of Orichalcos UR .60 1.25
LC03002 Dark Necrofear UR .50 1.00
LC03003 Guardian Eatos UR .50 1.00
LC03004 Five-Headed Dragon UR .50 1.00
LC03005 Emissary of Darkness Token UR .50 1.00
LC03006 Pink Kuriboh Token UR .50 1.00
LC03007 Orange Kuriboh Token UR .50 1.00

2012 Yu-Gi-Oh Order of Chaos 1st Edition

ORCS000 Inzektor Axe - Zektahawk SR .25 .50
ORCS000 Inzektor Axe - Zektahawk UR .50 1.00
ORCS001 Kurivolt C .15 .30
ORCS002 Darklon C .15 .30
ORCS003 Gagaga Girl SCR 2.00 4.00
ORCS004 Gogogo Giant R .10 .20
ORCS005 ZW - Unicorn Spear R .10 .20
ORCS006 Shocktopus C .15 .30
ORCS007 Photon Lizard R .10 .20
ORCS008 Photon Thrasher R .50 1.00
ORCS009 Photon Crusher C .15 .30
ORCS010 Photon Leo C .15 .30
ORCS011 Photon Circle C .15 .30
ORCS012 Reverse Buster R .10 .20
ORCS013 Flame Armor Ninja C .15 .30
ORCS014 Air Armor Ninja C .15 .30
ORCS015 Aqua Armor Ninja C .15 .30
ORCS016 Earth Armor Ninja C .15 .30
ORCS017 Inzektor Hornet SR 1.50 3.00
ORCS018 Inzektor Ant C .15 .30
ORCS019 Inzektor Centipede C .15 .30
ORCS020 Inzektor Dragonfly R .10 .20
ORCS021 Inzektor Giga-Mantis UR .50 1.00
ORCS021 Inzektor Giga-Mantis UTR .50 1.00
ORCS022 Inzektor Giga-Weevil C .15 .30
ORCS023 Wind-Up Rat SR .50 1.00
ORCS024 Wind-Up Honeybee C .15 .30
ORCS025 Evoltile Pleuro C .15 .30
ORCS026 Evoltile Casinerio R .10 .20
ORCS027 Evolsaur Elias C .15 .30
ORCS028 Evolsaur Terias C .15 .30
ORCS029 Ninja Grandmaster Hanzo UR .50 1.00
ORCS029 Ninja Grandmaster Hanzo UTR 1.50 3.00
ORCS030 Masked Ninja Ebisu C .15 .30
ORCS031 Upstart Golden Ninja C .15 .30
ORCS032 Chow Len the Prophet C .15 .30
ORCS033 Familiar-Possessed - Dharc C .15 .30
ORCS034 Dark Blade the
Captain of the Evil World R .10 .20
ORCS035 Trance Archfiend SP .10 .20
ORCS036 Divine Dragon Apocralyph C .15 .30
ORCS037 Darkstorm Dragon SR .25 .50
ORCS038 Numen erat Testudo C .15 .30
ORCS039 Twin Photon Lizard UR .50 1.00
ORCS039 Twin Photon Lizard UTR .50 1.00
ORCS040 Number C39: Utopia Ray UR .50 1.00
ORCS040 Number C39: Utopia Ray UTR .75 1.50
ORCS040 Number C39: Utopia Ray GR 2.50 5.00
ORCS041 Blade Armor Ninja SR .75 1.50
ORCS042 #12 Crimson Shadow Armor Ninja UR .50 1.00
ORCS042 #12 Crimson Shadow Armor Ninja UTR.50 1.00
ORCS043 Number 96: Dark Mist UR .75 1.50
ORCS043 Number 96: Dark Mist UTR .75 1.50
ORCS044 Wind-Up Carrier Zenmaity UR 2.50 5.00
ORCS044 Wind-Up Carrier Zenmaity UTR 2.50 5.00
ORCS045 Evolzar Solda UR 1.25 2.50
ORCS045 Evolzar Solda UTR .50 1.00
ORCS046 Inzektor Exa-Beetle SCR 1.50 3.00
ORCS047 Full-Force Strike C .15 .30
ORCS048 Gagagabolt R .10 .20
ORCS049 Double Defender C .15 .30
ORCS050 Galaxy Storm C .15 .30
ORCS051 Armor Ninjitsu Art of Alchemy SR .25 .50
ORCS052 Star Light, Star Bright C .15 .30
ORCS053 Armor Blast SR .25 .50
ORCS054 Inzektor Sword - Zektkaliber UR 1.00 2.00
ORCS054 Inzektor Sword - Zektkaliber UTR .50 1.00
ORCS055 Weights & Zenmaisures R .10 .20
ORCS056 Primordial Soup C .15 .30
ORCS057 Evo-Force SR .25 .50
ORCS058 Dark Mambele C .15 .30
ORCS059 Creeping Darkness SR .25 .50
ORCS060 Shrine of Mist Valley R .10 .20
ORCS061 Xyz Burst C .15 .30
ORCS062 Galaxy Wave C .15 .30
ORCS063 Dicephoon C .15 .30
ORCS064 Counterforce C .15 .30
ORCS065 Gagagaguard R .10 .20
ORCS066 Xyz Reflect UR .50 1.00
ORCS066 Xyz Reflect UTR .50 1.00
ORCS067 Splash Capture C .15 .30
ORCS068 Armor Ninjitsu Art of Freezing C .15 .30
ORCS069 Armor Ninjitsu Art of Rust Mist SR .25 .50
ORCS070 Inzektor Orb R .10 .20
ORCS071 Variable Form C .15 .30
ORCS072 Zenmailstrom C .15 .30
ORCS073 Degen-Force C .15 .30
ORCS074 Evo-Branch C .15 .30
ORCS075 Ninjitsu Art of Super Transformation SR1.00 2.00
ORCS076 Xyz Reborn SCR 2.50 5.00
ORCS077 Over Capacity R .10 .20
ORCS078 The Huge Revolution is Over C .15 .30
ORCS079 Royal Prison R .10 .20
ORCS080 Sealing Ceremony of Katon C .15 .30
ORCS081 Inzektor Hopper R .10 .20
ORCS082 Wind-Up Shark SR .25 .50
ORCS083 Evoltile Najasho SR .25 .50
ORCS084 White Dragon Ninja SCR 3.00 6.00
ORCS085 Interplanetarypurplythorny Dragon C .15 .30
ORCS086 Tour Bus From the Underworld SCR 1.25 2.50
ORCS087 Photon Trident C .15 .30
ORCS088 Evo-Instant R .10 .20
ORCS089 Ninjitsu Art of Duplication R .10 .20
ORCS090 White Night Queen R .10 .20
ORCS091 Danipon C .15 .30
ORCS092 Sweet Corn C .15 .30
ORCS093 Vampire Koala C .15 .30
ORCS094 Koalo-Koala C .15 .30
ORCS095 Dark Diviner SR .25 .50
ORCS096 Dark Flattop R .10 .20
ORCS097 Driven Daredevil SCR .60 1.25
ORCS098 Wind-Up Arsenal Zenmaioh SCR 10.00 20.00
ORCS099 M-X-Saber Invoker SCR 5.00 10.00
ORCSSP1 Inzektor Axe - Zektahawk UR .10 .20

2012 Yu-Gi-Oh Ra Yellow Mega Pack 1st Edition

RYMPEN001 Elemental HERO Avian ALT C .20 .40
RYMPEN002 Elemental HERO Burstinatrix ALT C .50 1.00
RYMPEN003 Elemental HERO Sparkman ALT C .25 .50
RYMPEN004 Elemental HERO Neos C .20 .40
RYMPEN005 Elemental HERO Necroshade C .20 .40
RYMPEN006 Card Trooper C .15 .30
RYMPEN007 Neo-Spacian Grand Mole SR .25 .50
RYMPEN008 Elemental HERO Stratos C .60 1.25
RYMPEN009 Necro Gardna SCR .25 .50
RYMPEN010 Elemental HERO Neos Alius SCR .50 1.00
RYMPEN011 Card Ejector C .15 .30
RYMPEN012 Elemental HERO Prisma C 1.50 3.00
RYMPEN013 Gallis the Star Beast C .15 .30
RYMPEN014 Winged Kuriboh LV9 R .25 .50
RYMPEN015 Card Blocker C .15 .30
RYMPEN016 Elemental HERO Flame Wingman R1.25 2.50
RYMPEN017 Elemental HERO Electrum C .50 1.00
RYMPEN018 Elemental HERO Mudballman C .50 1.00
RYMPEN019 Rainbow Neos C .20 .40
RYMPEN020 Elemental HERO Divine Neos C .25 .50
RYMPEN021 Miracle Fusion UR .60 1.25
RYMPEN022 The Flute of Summoning Kuriboh C.20 .40
RYMPEN023 H - Heated Heart SCR .25 .50
RYMPEN024 E - Emergency Call SCR 1.25 2.50
RYMPEN025 R - Righteous Justice SCR .25 .50
RYMPEN026 O - Oversoul SCR .25 .50
RYMPEN027 Hero Flash!! SCR .25 .50
RYMPEN028 Instant Fusion UR 4.00 8.00
RYMPEN029 Super Polymerization SCR .75 1.50
RYMPEN030 Hero Mask C .15 .30
RYMPEN031 Hero Signal SR .25 .50
RYMPEN032 Hero Blast SR .25 .50
RYMPEN033 Destiny HERO - Diamond Dude C .20 .40
RYMPEN034 Destiny HERO - Malicious SCR 2.50 5.00
RYMPEN035 Destiny HERO - Disk Commander R.25 .50
RYMPEN036 Destiny HERO - Plasma C .75 1.50
RYMPEN037 Destiny Draw SCR 1.25 2.50
RYMPEN038 Destiny Signal SR .25 .50
RYMPEN039 Destiny Mirage C .15 .30
RYMPEN040 Crystal Beast Ruby Carbuncle SR .50 1.00
RYMPEN041 Crystal Beast Amethyst Cat SR .25 .50
RYMPEN042 Crystal Beast Emerald Tortoise SR .25 .50
RYMPEN043 Crystal Beast Topaz Tiger SR .60 1.25
RYMPEN044 Crystal Beast Amber Mammoth SR .50 1.00
RYMPEN045 Crystal Beast Cobalt Eagle SR .50 1.00
RYMPEN046 Crystal Beast Sapphire Pegasus C1.50 3.00
RYMPEN047 Rainbow Dragon C 1.50 3.00
RYMPEN048 Crystal Beacon SCR .25 .50
RYMPEN049 Rare Value C .50 1.00
RYMPEN050 Crystal Blessing SCR .25 .50
RYMPEN051 Crystal Abundance SCR .25 .50
RYMPEN052 Crystal Promise SCR .25 .50
RYMPEN053 Ancient City - Rainbow Ruins C .15 .30
RYMPEN054 Crystal Release C .50 1.00
RYMPEN055 Crystal Raigeki SR .25 .50
RYMPEN056 Rainbow Path C .15 .30
RYMPEN057 Rainbow Gravity C .15 .30
RYMPEN058 Cyber Dragon C 1.25 2.50
RYMPEN059 Cyber Dragon ALT SCR 1.50 3.00
RYMPEN060 Cyber End Dragon ALT R 1.25 2.50
RYMPEN061 Chimeratech Overdragon R .50 1.00
RYMPEN062 Power Bond C .50 1.00
RYMPEN063 Overload Fusion C .75 1.50
RYMPEN064 Future Fusion UR .75 1.50
RYMPEN065 Magical Mallet C .75 1.50
RYMPEN066 Dark End Dragon SR .25 .50

RYMPEN067 Light End Dragon SR .25 .50
RYMPEN068 Vennominaga the Deity... R .25 .50
RYMPEN069 Vennominon the King... C .15 .30
RYMPEN070 Yubel R 1.25 2.50
RYMPEN071 Yubel - Terror Incarnate R .60 1.25
RYMPEN072 Yubel - The Ultimate Nightmare R .75 1.50
RYMPEN073 Mezuki C .60 1.25
RYMPEN074 Thunder King Rai-Oh C .75 1.50
RYMPEN075 Kasha C .15 .30
RYMPEN076 Shutendoji C .15 .30
RYMPEN077 Darklord Desire C .15 .30
RYMPEN078 Fusion Recovery C 2.50 5.00
RYMPEN079 System Down C 1.50 3.00
RYMPEN080 Grand Convergence C .15 .30
RYMPEN081 Dimensional Fissure SCR .60 1.25
RYMPEN082 Macro Cosmos UR .75 1.50
RYMPEN083 Rise of the Snake Deity C .15 .30
RYMPEN084 Dimensional Prison UR .75 1.50
RYMPEN085 Offering to the Snake Deity C .15 .30
RYMPEN086 D.D. Survivor C .15 .30
RYMPEN087 Grandmaster of the Six Samurai C .15 .30
RYMPEN088 The Six Samurai - Yaichi UR .25 .50
RYMPEN089 The Six Samurai - Kamon UR .25 .50
RYMPEN090 The Six Samurai - Yariza UR .25 .50
RYMPEN091 The Six Samurai - Nisashi UR .25 .50
RYMPEN092 The Six Samurai - Zanji UR .25 .50
RYMPEN093 The Six Samurai - Irou UR .25 .50
RYMPEN094 Great Shogun Shien C .15 .30
RYMPEN095 D.D. Crow SR .25 .50
RYMPEN096 Gladiator Beast Laquari SCR .25 .50
RYMPEN097 Enishi, Shien's Chancellor C .15 .30
RYMPEN098 Test Tiger C .25 .50
RYMPEN099 Rainbow Dark Dragon C .50 1.00
RYMPEN100 Jain, Lightsworn Paladin UR .25 .50
RYMPEN101 Garoth, Lightsworn Warrior R .25 .50
RYMPEN102 Lumina, Lightsworn Summoner UR .75 1.50
RYMPEN103 Wulf, Lightsworn Beast UR .50 1.00
RYMPEN104 Judgement Dragon C .15 .30
RYMPEN105 Aurkus, Lightsworn Druid C .15 .30
RYMPEN106 Gladiator Beast Lanista C .15 .30
RYMPEN107 Gladiator Beast's Respite C .15 .30
RYMPEN108 Gladiator's Return C .15 .30
RYMPEN109 Cunning of the Six Samurai C .15 .30
RYMPEN110 Gladiator Proving Ground UR .25 .50
RYMPEN111 Gateway of the Six C .15 .30
RYMPEN112 Double-Edged Sword Technique UR .50 1.00
RYMPEN113 Gladiator Beast War Chariot R .50 1.00

2012 Yu-Gi-Oh Return of the Duelist 1st Edition

REDU000 Noble Knight Gawayn SR .25 .50
REDU001 Trance the Magic Swordsman C .15 .30
REDU002 Damage Mage C .15 .30
REDU003 ZW - Phoenix Bow R .15 .30
REDU004 Photon Caesar C .15 .30
REDU005 Heroic Challenger - Spartan C .15 .30
REDU006 Heroic Challenger - War Hammer C .15 .30
REDU007 Heroic Challenger - Swordshield C .15 .30
REDU008 Heroic Challenger - Double Lance R .15 .30
REDU009 Chronomaly Mayan Machine C .15 .30
REDU010 Chronomaly Colossal Head R .15 .30
REDU011 Chronomaly Golden Jet C .15 .30
REDU012 Chronomaly Crystal Bones R .15 .30
REDU013 Chronomaly Crystal Skull R .15 .30
REDU014 Chronomaly Moai C .15 .30
REDU015 Spellbook Magician of Prophecy UR 4.00 8.00
REDU015 Spellbook Magician of Prophecy UTR 5.00 10.00
REDU016 Amores of Prophecy C .15 .30
REDU017 Temperance of Prophecy SR 1.50 3.00
REDU018 Strength of Prophecy C .15 .30
REDU019 Charioteer of Prophecy C .15 .30
REDU020 High Priestess of Prophecy SCR 6.00 12.00
REDU021 Madolche Mewfeuille C .15 .30
REDU022 Madolche Baaple C .15 .30
REDU023 Madolche Chouxvalier R .15 .30
REDU024 Madolche Magileine SR 6.00 12.00
REDU025 Madolche Butlerusk C .15 .30
REDU026 Madolche Puddingcess UR 2.00 4.00
REDU026 Madolche Puddingcess UTR 2.50 5.00
REDU027 Geargiano Mk-II R .15 .30
REDU028 Geargiaccelerator C .15 .30
REDU029 Geargiarsenal R .15 .30
REDU030 Geargiarmor SR .60 1.25
REDU031 Uniflora, Mystical Beast of the Forest C .15 .30
REDU032 Little Trooper C .15 .30
REDU033 Silver Sentinel UR .20 .40
REDU033 Silver Sentinel UTR .50 1.00
REDU034 Dust Knight R .15 .30
REDU035 Block Golem C .15 .30
REDU036 Atlantean Attack Squad C .15 .30
REDU037 Illusory Snatcher SR .25 .50
REDU038 Grandsoil the Elemental Lord SCR 1.25 2.50
REDU039 Three Thousand Needles SP .15 .30
REDU040 Goblin Marauding Squad SP .15 .30
REDU041 Heroic Champion - Excalibur UR 1.25 2.50
REDU041 Heroic Champion - Excalibur UTR 1.50 3.00
REDU041 Heroic Champion - Excalibur GR 3.00 6.00
REDU042 Chronomaly Crystal Chrononaut SR .75 1.50
REDU043 #33 Chronomaly Machu Mech UR 2.00 4.00
REDU043 #33 Chronomaly Machu Mech UTR 2.00 4.00
REDU044 Superdimensional Robot Galaxy... UR .75 1.50
REDU044 Superdimensional Robot Galaxy... UTR .60 1.25
REDU045 Hierophant of Prophecy UR .60 1.25
REDU045 Hierophant of Prophecy UTR .60 1.25
REDU046 Gear Gigant X SCR 3.00 6.00
REDU047 Alchemic Magician SR 1.25 2.50
REDU048 Soul of Silvermountain SR .25 .50
REDU049 Fairy King Albverdich R .15 .30
REDU050 Sword Breaker SR .25 .50
REDU051 Gagagarevenge SR .50 1.00
REDU052 Overlay Regen C .15 .30
REDU053 Heroic Chance C .15 .30
REDU054 Chronomaly Technology C .15 .30
REDU055 Chronomaly Pyramid Eye Tablet C .15 .30
REDU056 Galaxy Queen's Light C .15 .30
REDU057 Spellbook of Secrets UR 5.00 10.00
REDU057 Spellbook of Secrets UTR 6.00 12.00
REDU058 Spellbook of Power C .15 .30
REDU059 Spellbook of Life SR 1.25 2.50
REDU060 Spellbook of Wisdom R .15 .30
REDU061 Madolche Chateau C .15 .30
REDU062 Where Arf Thou? C .15 .30
REDU063 Generation Force C .15 .30
REDU064 Catapult Zone C .15 .30
REDU065 Cold Feet SP .15 .30
REDU066 Impenetrable Attack C .15 .30
REDU067 Gagagarush C .15 .30
REDU068 Heroic Retribution Sword C .15 .30
REDU069 Stonehenge Methods C .15 .30
REDU070 Madolche Lesson C .15 .30
REDU071 Madolche Waltz C .15 .30
REDU072 Madolche Tea Break R .15 .30
REDU073 Xyz Soul C .15 .30
REDU074 Compulsory Escape Device C .15 .30
REDU075 Turnabout C .15 .30
REDU076 Void Trap Hole SR 1.25 2.50
REDU077 Three of a Kind C .15 .30
REDU078 Soul Drain R .15 .30
REDU079 Rebound SR .25 .50
REDU080 Lucky Punch SP .15 .30
REDU081 Prophecy Destroyer UR .20 .40
REDU081 Prophecy Destroyer UTR .50 1.00
REDU082 Lightray Madoor C .15 .30
REDU083 Blue Dragon Ninja SR .25 .50
REDU084 Imairuka R .15 .30
REDU085 Revival Golem R .15 .30
REDU086 Noble Arms - Gallatin C .15 .30
REDU087 Spellbook Library of the Crescent R .15 .30
REDU088 Advance Zone SCR 1.00 2.00
REDU089 Ninjitsu Art of Shadow Sealing C .15 .30
REDU090 Chewbone C .15 .30
REDU091 Eco, Mystical Spirit of the Forest R .15 .30
REDU092 Number 6: Chronomaly Atlandis SCR .75 1.50
REDU093 Miracle Contact SCR 6.00 12.00
REDU094 Advanced Dark SCR 1.50 3.00
REDU095 Pahunder R .15 .30
REDU096 Mahunder R .15 .30
REDU097 Sishunder R .15 .30
REDU098 Number 91: Thunder Spark Dragon UR 1.25 2.50
REDU098 Number 91: Thunder Spark Dragon UTR 1.25 2.50
REDU099 Spirit Converter SCR .50 1.00

2012 Yu-Gi-Oh Starter Deck Xyz Symphony 1st Edition

YS12001 Alexandrite Dragon .10 .20
YS12002 Spirit of the Harp C .10 .20
YS12003 Frostosaurus C .10 .20
YS12004 Zubaba Knight C .10 .20
YS12005 Ganbara Knight C .10 .20
YS12006 Gogogo Golem C .10 .20
YS12007 Gogogo Giant C .10 .20
YS12008 Goblindbergh C .50 1.00
YS12009 Feedback Warrior C .10 .20
YS12010 Shine Knight C .10 .20
YS12011 Cyber Dragon C .20 .40
YS12012 Trident Warrior C .10 .20
YS12013 Chiron the Mage .10 .20
YS12014 Marauding Captain C .10 .20
YS12015 Penguin Soldier C .10 .20
YS12016 Sangan C .20 .40
YS12017 Giant Rat C .10 .20
YS12018 Shining Angel C .10 .20
YS12019 Blustering Winds C .10 .20
YS12020 Ego Boost C .10 .20
YS12021 Xyz Energy C .10 .20
YS12022 Star Changer C .10 .20
YS12023 Swords of Revealing Light C .10 .20
YS12024 Mystical Space Typhoon C .50 1.00
YS12025 Fissure C .10 .20
YS12026 Gravity Axe - Grarl C .10 .20
YS12027 Reinforcement of the Army C .20 .40
YS12028 Burden of the Mighty C .10 .20
YS12029 Heartfelt Appeal C .10 .20
YS12030 Xyz Effect C .10 .20
YS12031 Raigeki Break C .10 .20
YS12032 Trap Hole C .10 .20
YS12033 Dust Tornado C .10 .20
YS12034 Magic Cylinder C .50 1.00
YS12035 Draining Shield C .50 1.00
YS12036 Call of the Haunted C .10 .20
YS12037 Limit Reverse C .10 .20
YS12038 Seven Tools of the Bandit C .10 .20
YS12039 Number 39: Utopia UR .75 1.50
YS12040 Muzurhythm the String Djinn SR .10 .20
YS12041 Temtempo the Percussion Djinn SR .10 .20
YS12042 Melomelody the Brass Djinn SR .10 .20
YS12043 Maestroke the Symphony Djinn SR .50 1.00

2012 Yu-Gi-Oh Structure Deck Dragons Collide 1st Edition

SDDCEN001 Lightpulsar Dragon UR .30 .60
SDDCEN002 Darkflare Dragon UR .20 .40
SDDCEN003 Eclipse Wyvern SR .30 .75
SDDCEN004 BlueEyes White Dragon C .60 1.25
SDDCEN005 RedEyes B Dragon C .30 .75
SDDCEN006 The White Stone of Legend C .20 .40
SDDCEN007 RedEyes B Chick C .20 .40
SDDCEN008 Axe Dragonute C .12 .25
SDDCEN009 Vice Dragon C .12 .25
SDDCEN010 Gragonith Lightsworn Dragon C .12 .25
SDDCEN011 Prime Material Dragon C .30 .60
SDDCEN012 Dark Armed Dragon C .25 .50
SDDCEN013 RedEyes Darkness Metal Dragon C .20 .40
SDDCEN014 Chaos Sorcerer C .20 .40
SDDCEN015 Lord of D C .20 .40
SDDCEN016 Mystic Tomato C .60 1.25
SDDCEN017 Summoner Monk C .15 .30
SDDCEN018 Snipe Hunter C .30 .75
SDDCEN019 Herald of Creation C .12 .25
SDDCEN020 Jain Lightsworn Paladin C .10 .20
SDDCEN021 Lyla Lightsworn Sorceress C .25 .50
SDDCEN022 Kaibaman C .07 .15
SDDCEN023 Ryko Lightsworn Hunter C .50 1.00
SDDCEN024 Chaos Zone C .07 .15
SDDCEN025 Burst Stream of Destruction C .07 .15
SDDCEN026 Inferno Fire Blast C .10 .20
SDDCEN027 The Flute of Summoning Dragon C .10 .20
SDDCEN028 A Wingbeat of Giant Dragon C .12 .25
SDDCEN029 Book of Moon C .50 1.00
SDDCEN030 Magical Stone Excavation C .12 .25
SDDCEN031 Reasoning C .60 1.25
SDDCEN032 Monster Gate C .25 .50
SDDCEN033 Card Trader C .12 .25
SDDCEN034 DDR Different
Dimension Reincarnation C .25 .50
SDDCEN035 Charge of the Light Brigade C .75 1.50
SDDCEN036 Dragons Rebirth C .12 .25
SDDCEN037 Burst Breath C .12 .25
SDDCEN038 Call of the Haunted C .25 .50
SDDCEN039 Interdimensional Matter Transporter C .07 .15
SDDCEN040 Escape from the Dark Dimension C .07 .15

2012 Yu-Gi-Oh Structure Deck Realm of the Sea Emperor 1st Edition

SDRE001 Poseidra, the Atlantean UR .10 .20
SDRE002 Atlantean Dragoons SR .50 1.00
SDRE003 Atlantean Marksman .15 .30
SDRE004 Atlantean Heavy Infantry .15 .30
SDRE005 Atlantean Pikeman .15 .30
SDRE006 Atlantean Attack Squad .15 .30
SDRE007 Lost Blue Breaker .15 .30
SDRE008 Armed Sea Hunter .15 .30
SDRE009 Spined Gillman .15 .30
SDRE010 Deep Sea Diva .15 .30
SDRE011 Mermaid Archer .15 .30
SDRE012 Codarus .15 .30
SDRE013 Warrior of Atlantis .15 .30
SDRE014 Abyss Soldier .15 .30
SDRE015 Skreech .15 .30
SDRE016 Snowman Eater .15 .30
SDRE017 Nightmare Penguin .15 .30
SDRE018 Penguin Soldier .15 .30
SDRE019 Deep Diver .15 .30
SDRE020 Reese the Ice Mistress .15 .30
SDRE021 Mother Grizzly .15 .30
SDRE022 Friller Rabca .15 .30
SDRE023 Call of the Atlanteans SR .15 .30
SDRE024 A Legendary Ocean .15 .30
SDRE025 Terraforming .15 .30
SDRE026 Water Hazard .15 .30
SDRE027 Aqua Jet .15 .30
SDRE028 Surface .15 .30
SDRE029 Moray of Greed .15 .30
SDRE030 Salvage .15 .30
SDRE031 Dark Hole .15 .30
SDRE032 Big Wave Small Wave .15 .30
SDRE033 Aegis of the Ocean Dragon Lord .15 .30
SDRE034 Forgotten Temple of the Deep .15 .30
SDRE035 Tornado Wall .15 .30
SDRE036 Torrential Tribute .15 .30
SDRE037 Spiritual Water Art - Aoi .15 .30
SDRE038 Gravity Bind .15 .30
SDRE039 Poseidon Wave .15 .30

2012 Yu-Gi-Oh Structure Deck Samurai Warlords 1st Edition

SDWAEN001 Chamberlain of the Six Samurai C .10 .20
SDWAEN002 Grandmaster of the Six Samurai C .10 .20
SDWAEN003 The Six Samurai - Yariza C .10 .20
SDWAEN004 The Six Samurai - Zanji C .10 .20
SDWAEN005 The Six Samurai - Nisashi C .10 .20
SDWAEN006 The Six Samurai - Yaichi C .10 .20
SDWAEN007 The Six Samurai - Kamon C .10 .20
SDWAEN008 The Six Samurai - Irou C .10 .20
SDWAEN009 Great Shogun Shien C .10 .20
SDWAEN010 Shien's Footsoldier C .10 .20
SDWAEN011 Enishi, Shien's Chancellor C .10 .20
SDWAEN012 Spirit of the Six Samurai C .10 .20
SDWAEN013 Future Samurai C .10 .20
SDWAEN014 The Immortal Bushi C .10 .20
SDWAEN015 Hand of the Six Samurai C .10 .20
SDWAEN016 Legendary Six Samurai - Kizan C 1.25 2.50
SDWAEN017 Legendary Six Samurai - Enishi C 15.00 30.00
SDWAEN018 Legendary Six Samurai - Kageki SR .20 .40
SDWAEN019 Shien's Squire C .10 .20
SDWAEN020 Shien's Daredevil C .10 .20
SDWAEN021 Elder of the Six Samurai C .10 .20
SDWAEN022 Shien's Advisor C .10 .20
SDWAEN023 Dark Hole C .50 1.00
SDWAEN024 The A. Forces C .10 .20
SDWAEN025 Reinforcement of the Army C .20 .40
SDWAEN026 The Warrior Returning Alive C .10 .20
SDWAEN027 Cunning of the Six Samurai C .10 .20
SDWAEN028 Six Samurai United C .50 1.00
SDWAEN029 Gateway of the Six C .10 .20
SDWAEN030 Shien's Smoke Signal SR .25 .50
SDWAEN031 Temple of the Six C .10 .20
SDWAEN032 Shien's Dojo C .20 .40
SDWAEN033 Rivalry of Warlords C 1.25 2.50
SDWAEN034 Return of the Six Samurai C .10 .20
SDWAEN035 Double-Edged Sword Technique C .10 .20
SDWAEN036 Fiendish Chain C 1.25 2.50
SDWAEN037 Musakani Magatama C .15 .30
SDWAEN038 Shien's Scheme C .10 .20
SDWAEN039 Six Strike - Thunder Blast C .10 .20
SDWAEN040 Six Style - Dual Wield C .10 .20
SDWAEN041 Shadow of the
Six Samurai - Shien UR .10 .20

2012 Yu-Gi-Oh Turbo Pack 7

TU07EN000 Ally of Justice Catastor UTR 4.00 8.00
TU07EN001 Book of Moon UR 5.00 10.00
TU07EN002 Ninja Grandmaster Sasuke SR .50 1.00
TU07EN003 Yellow Gadget SR 2.00 4.00
TU07EN004 X-Saber Pashuul SR 2.00 4.00
TU07EN005 Horn of the Phantom Beast SR 2.50 5.00
TU07EN006 Dark Horus R .20 .40
TU07EN007 Lightning Warrior R .60 1.25
TU07EN008 Primal Seed R .25 .50
TU07EN009 Big Evolution Pill R .25 .50
TU07EN010 Tail Swipe R .25 .50
TU07EN011 Geartown R .50 1.00
TU07EN012 Seiyaryu C .25 .50
TU07EN013 Serpent Night Dragon C .25 .50
TU07EN014 Kotodama C .10 .20
TU07EN015 Gokipon C .25 .50
TU07EN016 Goe Goe the Gallant Ninja C .25 .50
TU07EN017 Herald of Orange Light C .25 .50
TU07EN018 Blackwing - Sirocco the Dawn C .25 .50
TU07EN019 Ninjitsu Art of Transformation C .25 .50
TU07EN020 Ninjitsu Art of Decoy C .25 .50

2012 Yu-Gi-Oh Turbo Pack 8

TU08EN000 Thunder King Rai-Oh UTR 15.00 30.00
TU08EN001 Skill Drain UR 15.00 30.00
TU08EN002 Green Gadget SR 2.00 4.00
TU08EN003 Red Gadget SR 2.00 4.00
TU08EN004 Upstart Goblin SR 15.00 30.00
TU08EN005 Mirror of Oaths SR 1.00 2.00
TU08EN006 Alligator's Sword R .50 1.00
TU08EN007 Lost Guardian R .10 .20
TU08EN008 Alligator's Sword Dragon R .20 .40
TU08EN009 Magicians Unite R .10 .20
TU08EN010 Ready for Intercepting R .10 .20
TU08EN011 Gozen Match R 1.50 3.00
TU08EN012 Elephant Statue of Blessing C .10 .20
TU08EN013 Elephant Statue of Disaster C .10 .20
TU08EN014 Gemini Imps C .10 .20
TU08EN015 Flamvell Firedog C .10 .20
TU08EN016 Wind-Up Factory C .50 1.00
TU08EN017 The Emperor's Holiday C .10 .20
TU08EN018 Really Eternal Rest C .10 .20
TU08EN019 Rock Bombardment C .10 .20
TU08EN020 Magician's Circle C .75 1.50

2013 Yu-Gi-Oh Astral Pack 2

AP02EN001 Atlantean Dragoons UTR 30.00 75.00
AP02EN002 Photon Papilloperative UTR 4.00 8.00
AP02EN003 Spellbook of Power UTR 25.00 50.00
AP02EN004 Interplanetarypurplythorny Dragon SR .50 1.00
AP02EN005 Geargiaccelerator SR 1.00 2.00
AP02EN006 Atlantean Heavy Infantry SR 2.50 5.00
AP02EN007 Slushy SR .20 .40
AP02EN008 Brotherhood of the Fire Fist - Hawk SR .20 .40
AP02EN009 Brotherhood of the Fire Fist - Raven SR .20 .40
AP02EN010 Harpies' Hunting Ground SR .50 1.00
AP02EN011 Gemini Spark SR 3.00 6.00
AP02EN012 Spiritual Water Art - Aoi SR .50 1.00
AP02EN013 Trap Stun SR .75 1.50
AP02EN014 Sky Scout C .20 .40
AP02EN015 Cyber Phoenix C .20 .40
AP02EN016 Light and Darkness Dragon C .75 1.50
AP02EN017 Justice of Prophecy C .50 1.00
AP02EN018 Barox C 1.25 2.50
AP02EN019 Pot of Avarice C .50 1.00
AP02EN020 Instant Fusion C 3.00 6.00
AP02EN021 Recycling Batteries C .20 .40
AP02EN022 Machina Armored Unit C .20 .40
AP02EN023 Photon Veil C .75 1.50
AP02EN024 Hysteric Party C .50 1.00
AP02EN025 Token Stampede C .20 .40

2013 Yu-Gi-Oh Astral Pack 3

AP03EN001 Atlantean Marksman UTR 20.00 40.00
AP03EN002 Maestroke the Symphony Djinn UTR 3.00 6.00
AP03EN003 Fire Formation - Tenki UTR 20.00 40.00
AP03EN004 Serene Psychic Witch SR .25 .50
AP03EN005 Mermail Abyssgunde SR 1.50 3.00
AP03EN006 Falling Down SR .25 .50
AP03EN007 Miracle Fertilizer SR 1.00 2.00
AP03EN008 Noble Arms - Gallatin SR .25 .50
AP03EN009 Spellbook Library of the Crescent SR 1.00 2.00
AP03EN010 Noble Arms - Arfeudutyr SR .25 .50
AP03EN011 Spellbook Star Hall SR .50 1.00
AP03EN012 Pollinosis SR .25 .50
AP03EN013 Wall of Thorns SR .25 .50
AP03EN014 Curtain of the Dark Ones C 1.00 2.00
AP03EN015 Jowgen the Spiritualist C .50 1.00
AP03EN016 Swarm of Scarabs C .25 .50
AP03EN017 Swarm of Locusts C .25 .50
AP03EN018 Des Lacooda C .25 .50
AP03EN019 Imprisoned Queen Archfiend C .25 .50
AP03EN020 Vampire Dragon C .50 1.00
AP03EN021 Kamionwizard C 2.50 5.00
AP03EN022 Gladiator Beast's
Battle Archfiend Shield C .25 .50
AP03EN023 Deck Lockdown C .50 1.00
AP03EN024 Super Solar Nutrient C .25 .50
AP03EN025 Archfiend's Roar C .25 .50
AP03EN026 Heavy Slump C .25 .50

2013 Yu-Gi-Oh Battle Pack 2 War of the Giants 1st Edition

BP02EN001 Luster Dragon C .25 .50
BP02EN002 Gene-Warped Warwolf C .10 .20
BP02EN003 Frostosaurus R .25 .50
BP02EN004 Alexandrite Dragon C .20 .40
BP02EN005 Magician of Faith R .50 1.00
BP02EN006 Maha Vailo C .10 .20
BP02EN007 Cyber Jar R .25 .50
BP02EN008 Goblin Attack Force C .10 .20
BP02EN009 The Fiend Megacyber R .25 .50
BP02EN010 Revival Jam C .10 .20
BP02EN011 Kycoo the Ghost Destroyer C .10 .20
BP02EN012 Bazoo the Soul-Eater C .10 .20
BP02EN013 Gilasaurus C .10 .20
BP02EN014 Zombyra the Dark C .10 .20
BP02EN015 Sinister Serpent C .20 .40
BP02EN016 Airknight Parshath R .25 .50
BP02EN017 Twin-Headed Behemoth C .10 .20
BP02EN018 Injection Fairy Lily R .25 .50
BP02EN019 Helping Robo for Combat C .10 .20
BP02EN020 Little-Winguard C .10 .20
BP02EN021 D.D. Warrior Lady R .25 .50
BP02EN022 Zolga C .10 .20
BP02EN023 Dark Magician of Chaos R .75 1.50
BP02EN024 Hyper Hammerhead C .10 .20
BP02EN025 Mataza the Zapper C .10 .20
BP02EN026 Guardian Angel Joan R .25 .50
BP02EN027 Slate Warrior R .25 .50
BP02EN028 D.D. Assailant R .25 .50
BP02EN029 Ninja Grandmaster Sasuke C .10 .20
BP02EN030 Pitch-Black Warwolf C .10 .20
BP02EN031 Mirage Dragon C .10 .20
BP02EN032 Big Shield Gardna C .10 .20
BP02EN033 Toon Gemini Elf C .10 .20

BP02EN034 Chiron the Mage C .10 .20
BP02EN035 Ancient Gear Golem R .25 .50
BP02EN036 Gyroid C .10 .20
BP02EN037 Steamroid C .10 .20
BP02EN038 Drillroid C .10 .20
BP02EN039 Cyber Dragon C .25 .50
BP02EN040 Goblin Elite Attack Force C .10 .20
BP02EN041 Exarion Universe C .10 .20
BP02EN042 Mythical Beast Cerberus C .10 .20
BP02EN043 Treeborn Frog C .20 .40
BP02EN044 Submarineroid C .10 .20
BP02EN045 Ultimate Tyranno R .25 .50
BP02EN046 Super Conductor Tyranno R .25 .50
BP02EN047 Brain Crusher R .25 .50
BP02EN048 Card Trooper C .10 .20
BP02EN049 Blockman C .10 .20
BP02EN050 Spell Striker C .50 1.00
BP02EN051 Winged Rhynos C .10 .20
BP02EN052 Necro Gardna C .10 .20
BP02EN053 Herald of Creation C .10 .20
BP02EN054 Evil HERO Malicious Edge R .25 .50
BP02EN055 Truckroid R .25 .50
BP02EN056 Ancient Gear Knight C .10 .20
BP02EN057 Dragon Ice C .10 .20
BP02EN058 Copycat C .50 1.00
BP02EN059 Cyber Valley R .25 .50
BP02EN060 Darklord Zerato R .25 .50
BP02EN061 Belial - Marquis of Darkness R .25 .50
BP02EN062 Doomcaliber Knight C .10 .20
BP02EN063 Exodius the Ultimate Forbidden Lord C.25 .50
BP02EN064 Dark Valkyria R .25 .50
BP02EN065 Phantom Dragon R .25 .50
BP02EN066 Shield Warrior C .10 .20
BP02EN067 Dark Resonator C .10 .20
BP02EN068 Krebons R .25 .50
BP02EN069 The Tricky C .10 .20
BP02EN070 Splendid Venus R .25 .50
BP02EN071 Plaguespreader Zombie C .50 1.00
BP02EN072 Machine Lord Ür C .10 .20
BP02EN073 Mosaic Manticore R .25 .50
BP02EN074 Botanical Lion C .10 .20
BP02EN075 Blizzard Dragon C .20 .40
BP02EN076 Des Mosquito C .10 .20
BP02EN077 Dandylion C .25 .50
BP02EN078 Fortress Warrior C .10 .20
BP02EN079 Twin-Sword Marauder C .10 .20
BP02EN080 Beast King Barbaros R .25 .50
BP02EN081 Hedge Guard C .10 .20
BP02EN082 Card Guard C .10 .20
BP02EN083 White Night Dragon R .25 .50
BP02EN084 Beast Machine King Barbaros Ür R .25 .50
BP02EN085 Evocator Chevalier C .10 .20
BP02EN086 Battle Fader C .60 1.25
BP02EN087 Oracle of the Sun C .10 .20
BP02EN088 Samurai of the Ice Barrier C .10 .20
BP02EN089 Jurrac Titano R .25 .50
BP02EN090 Darklord Desire R .25 .50
BP02EN091 Power Giant C .10 .20
BP02EN092 Anarchist Monk Ranshin C .10 .20
BP02EN093 Ape Fighter C .10 .20
BP02EN094 Tanngrisnir of the Nordic Beasts C .10 .20
BP02EN095 Chaos Hunter R .25 .50
BP02EN096 Axe Dragonute C .10 .20
BP02EN097 Vylon Soldier C .10 .20
BP02EN098 Blackwing - Zephyros the Elite C .20 .40
BP02EN099 Zubaba Knight C .10 .20
BP02EN100 Gogogo Golem C .10 .20
BP02EN101 Needle Sunfish C .10 .20
BP02EN102 Shocktopus C .10 .20
BP02EN103 Photon Thrasher C .60 1.25
BP02EN104 Interplanetarypurplythorny Dragon C.10 .20
BP02EN105 Tour Bus From the Underworld C .10 .20
BP02EN106 Vylon Tetra C .10 .20
BP02EN107 Vylon Stella C .10 .20
BP02EN108 Vylon Prism C .10 .20
BP02EN109 Photon Wyvern R .25 .50
BP02EN110 Tasuke Knight C .10 .20
BP02EN111 Gagaga Gardna C .10 .20
BP02EN112 Cardcar D R .25 .50
BP02EN113 Flame Tiger C .10 .20
BP02EN114 Tardy Orc C .10 .20
BP02EN115 Bull Blader R .25 .50
BP02EN116 Solar Wind Jammer C .10 .20
BP02EN117 Mermail Abyssmegalo R 3.00 6.00
BP02EN118 Dododo Bot C .10 .20
BP02EN119 Bacon Saver C .10 .20
BP02EN120 Amarylease C .10 .20
BP02EN121 Hyper-Ancient Shark Megalodon R .25 .50
BP02EN122 Pyrotech Mech - Shiryu R .25 .50
BP02EN123 Aye-Iron C .10 .20
BP02EN124 Mecha Phantom Beast Hamstrat C .10 .20
BP02EN125 Obelisk the Tormentor R 6.00 12.00
BP02EN126 The Winged Dragon of Ra R 5.00 10.00
BP02EN127 Slifer the Sky Dragon R 7.50 15.00
BP02EN128 Monster Reborn R .50 1.00

BP02EN129 Pot of Greed R .75 1.50
BP02EN130 Shield & Sword C .10 .20
BP02EN131 Axe of Despair C .10 .20
BP02EN132 Malevolent Nuzzler C .10 .20
BP02EN133 Rush Recklessly C .10 .20
BP02EN134 Horn of the Unicorn C .10 .20
BP02EN135 Premature Burial R .25 .50
BP02EN136 Scapegoat C .20 .40
BP02EN137 Graceful Charity R .25 .50
BP02EN138 Book of Moon C .25 .50
BP02EN139 Reasoning C .75 1.50
BP02EN140 Autonomous Action Unit C .10 .20
BP02EN141 Big Bang Shot C .10 .20
BP02EN142 Riryoku C .10 .20
BP02EN143 Gravity Axe - Grarl C .10 .20
BP02EN144 Enemy Controller C .10 .20
BP02EN145 Earthquake C .10 .20
BP02EN146 Shrink C .10 .20
BP02EN147 Swords of Concealing Light C 1.00 2.00
BP02EN148 Nightmare's Steelcage C .10 .20
BP02EN149 Mausoleum of the Emperor C .10 .20
BP02EN150 Card Trader R .25 .50
BP02EN151 Fiend's Sanctuary C .10 .20
BP02EN152 Union Attack C .10 .20
BP02EN153 Fighting Spirit C .10 .20
BP02EN154 Star Blast C .10 .20
BP02EN155 Forbidden Chalice C .25 .50
BP02EN156 Reptilianne Rage C .10 .20
BP02EN157 Rocket Pilder C .10 .20
BP02EN158 Half Shut C .10 .20
BP02EN159 Cursed Armaments C .10 .20
BP02EN160 Pot of Duality R .75 1.50
BP02EN161 Axe of Fools C .10 .20
BP02EN162 Forbidden Lance C .75 1.50
BP02EN163 Blustering Winds C .10 .20
BP02EN164 Ego Boost C .10 .20
BP02EN165 Shard of Greed R .25 .50
BP02EN166 Full-Force Strike R .25 .50
BP02EN167 Photon Sanctuary C .50 1.00
BP02EN168 Forbidden Dress C .10 .20
BP02EN169 Reverse Trap C .10 .20
BP02EN170 Waboku C .20 .40
BP02EN171 Call of the Haunted R .50 1.00
BP02EN172 Mirror Wall C .10 .20
BP02EN173 Metalmorph C .10 .20
BP02EN174 Mask of Weakness C .10 .20
BP02EN175 Reckless Greed R .25 .50
BP02EN176 Rope of Life C .10 .20
BP02EN177 Windstorm of Etaqua C .10 .20
BP02EN178 Zero Gravity C .10 .20
BP02EN179 A Hero Emerges C .10 .20
BP02EN180 Embodiment of Apophis C .10 .20
BP02EN181 Draining Shield C .50 1.00
BP02EN182 Curse of Anubis C .10 .20
BP02EN183 Labyrinth of Nightmare C .10 .20
BP02EN184 Threatening Roar C .25 .50
BP02EN185 Rising Energy C .10 .20
BP02EN186 Magical Arm Shield C .10 .20
BP02EN187 Shattered Axe C .10 .20
BP02EN188 Stronghold the Moving Fortress C .10 .20
BP02EN189 Strike Slash C .10 .20
BP02EN190 No Entry!! C .10 .20
BP02EN191 Cloning C .10 .20
BP02EN192 Sinister Seeds C .10 .20
BP02EN193 Metal Reflect Slime C .50 1.00
BP02EN194 Zoma the Spirit C .10 .20
BP02EN195 Miniaturize C .10 .20
BP02EN196 Spacegate C .10 .20
BP02EN197 Overworked C .10 .20
BP02EN198 Kunai with Chain C .10 .20
BP02EN199 Prideful Roar C .10 .20
BP02EN200 Time Machine C .25 .50
BP02EN201 Half or Nothing C .10 .20
BP02EN202 Miracle Locus C .10 .20
BP02EN203 Skill Successor C .10 .20
BP02EN204 Power Frame C .10 .20
BP02EN205 Damage Gate C .10 .20
BP02EN206 Miracle's Wake C .10 .20
BP02EN207 Half Counter C .10 .20
BP02EN208 The Golden Apples R .25 .50
BP02EN209 Tiki Curse C .10 .20
BP02EN210 Tiki Soul C .10 .20
BP02EN211 Impenetrable Attack C .10 .20
BP02EN212 Memory of an Adversary R .25 .50
BP02EN213 Dimension Gate C .10 .20
BP02EN214 Spikeshield with Chain R .25 .50
BP02EN215 Breakthrough Skill C .75 1.50

2013 Yu-Gi-Oh Collector Tins

CT10EN001 Tidal, Dragon Ruler of Waterfalls SCR.50 1.00
CT10EN002 Blaster, Dragon Ruler of Infernos SCR.75 1.50
CT10EN003 Redox, Dragon Ruler of Boulders SCR.50 1.00
CT10EN004 Tempest, Dragon Ruler of Storms SCR.50 1.00
CT10EN005 Black Luster Soldier... SR 2.00 4.00
CT10EN006 Ally of Justice Catastor SR 1.00 2.00
CT10EN007 Superdreadnought Rail Cannon... SR.25 .50
CT10EN008 Brotherhood of the Fire Fist Bear SR.25 .50
CT10EN009 Karakuri Shogun mdl 00 Burei SR .25 .50
CT10EN010 Gagaga Cowboy SR .75 1.50
CT10EN011 Number 40: Gimmick
Puppet of Strings SR .25 .50
CT10EN012 Diamond Dire Wolf SR 1.25 2.50
CT10EN013 Number 88: Gimmick Puppet of Leo SR.25 .50
CT10EN014 Spellbook of the Master SR .25 .50
CT10EN015 Rank-Up-Magic Barian's Force SR .25 .50
CT10EN016 Thunder Sea Horse SR .25 .50
CT10EN017 Gear Gigant X SR .50 1.00
CT10EN018 Number 50: Blackship of Corn SR 1.00 2.00

2013 Yu-Gi-Oh Cosmo Blazer 1st Edition

CBLZ000 Noble Arms - Caliburn SR .25 .50
CBLZ001 Dododo Bot C .15 .30
CBLZ002 Gogogo Ghost C .15 .30
CBLZ003 Bacon Saver C .15 .30
CBLZ004 Amarylease C .15 .30
CBLZ005 ZW - Lightning Blade R .15 .30
CBLZ006 ZW - Tornado Bringer R .15 .30
CBLZ007 ZW - Ultimate Shield C .15 .30
CBLZ008 Gagaga Clerk SR 1.00 2.00
CBLZ009 Spear Shark C .15 .30
CBLZ010 Double Shark C .15 .30
CBLZ011 Xyz Remora C .15 .30
CBLZ012 Hyper-Ancient Shark Megalodon R .15 .30
CBLZ013 Heraldic Beast Basilisk C .15 .30
CBLZ014 Heraldic Beast Eale C .10 .20
CBLZ015 Heraldic Beast Twin-Headed Eagle R .15 .30
CBLZ016 Heraldic Beast Unicorn C .15 .30
CBLZ017 Heraldic Beast Leo R .15 .30
CBLZ018 Garbage Ogre C .15 .30
CBLZ019 Garbage Lord C .15 .30
CBLZ020 Orbital 7 SR .25 .50
CBLZ021 Brotherhood of the Fire Fist - Hawk C .15 .30
CBLZ022 Brotherhood of the Fire Fist - Raven C .15 .30
CBLZ023 Brotherhood of the Fire Fist - Gorilla R .15 .30
CBLZ024 Brotherhood of the Fire Fist - Bear UR .60 1.25
CBLZ024 Brotherhood of the Fire Fist - Bear UTR1.50 3.00
CBLZ025 Brotherhood of the Fire Fist - Dragon SR1.00 2.00
CBLZ026 Brotherhood of the Fire Fist - Snake SR.25 .50
CBLZ027 Brotherhood of the Fire Fist - Swallow SR.25 .50
CBLZ028 Hazy Flame Cerbereus C .15 .30
CBLZ029 Hazy Flame Griffin C .15 .30
CBLZ030 Hazy Flame Sphynx C .15 .30
CBLZ031 Hazy Flame Peryton R .15 .30
CBLZ032 Mermail Abyssdine SR .25 .50
CBLZ033 Mermail Abyssnose C .15 .30
CBLZ034 Mermail Abyssleed SCR 2.50 5.00
CBLZ035 Fool of Prophecy SR .25 .50
CBLZ036 Reaper of Prophecy SR .25 .50
CBLZ037 Brushfire Knight R .15 .30
CBLZ038 Inari Fire C .15 .30
CBLZ039 Valkyrian Knight SR 1.00 2.00
CBLZ040 Pyrorex the Elemental SCR .50 1.00
CBLZ041 Pyrotech Mech - Shiryu C .15 .30
CBLZ042 Leotaur C .15 .30
CBLZ043 Star Drawing SP .50 1.00
CBLZ044 Red Duston SP .10 .20
CBLZ045 Heart-eartH Dragon UR 1.25 2.50
CBLZ045 Heart-eartH Dragon UTR 1.50 3.00
CBLZ045 Heart-eartH Dragon GR 2.50 5.00
CBLZ046 No. 53: Heart-eartH UR .60 1.25
CBLZ046 No. 53: Heart-eartH UTR 1.00 2.00
CBLZ047 ZW - Leo Arms UR .60 1.25
CBLZ047 ZW - Leo Arms UTR .60 1.25
CBLZ048 Brohood - Tiger King UR .60 1.25
CBLZ048 Brohood - Tiger King UTR 1.25 2.50
CBLZ049 Hazy Flame Basiltrice R .15 .30
CBLZ050 Mermail Abysstrite SR .60 1.25
CBLZ051 Diamond Dire Wolf SCR 4.00 8.00
CBLZ052 Lightning Chidori UR 2.50 5.00
CBLZ052 Lightning Chidori UTR 4.00 8.00
CBLZ053 Slacker Magician R .50 1.00
CBLZ054 Zerozerock C .15 .30
CBLZ055 Gagagadraw SR .25 .50
CBLZ056 Xyz Double Back C .15 .30
CBLZ057 Heraldry Reborn R .15 .30
CBLZ058 Fire Formation - Tensu C .15 .30
CBLZ059 Fire Formation - Tenki C .15 .30
CBLZ060 Hazy Pillar C .15 .30
CBLZ061 Abyss-scale of Cetus C .15 .30
CBLZ062 Spellbook of Master SCR 1.50 3.00
CBLZ063 The Big Cattle Drive C .15 .30
CBLZ064 March of the Monarchs C .15 .30
CBLZ065 Quick Booster UR .60 1.25
CBLZ065 Quick Booster UTR .60 1.25
CBLZ066 After the Storm C .15 .30
CBLZ067 Goblin Circus SP .10 .20
CBLZ068 Dimension Gate C .15 .30
CBLZ069 Xyz Dimension Splash C .15 .30
CBLZ070 Heraldry Change C .15 .30

CBLZ071 Fire Formation - Tensen C .15 .30
CBLZ072 Fire Formation - Tenken C .15 .30
CBLZ073 Ultimate Fire Formation - Seito R .15 .30
CBLZ074 Hazy Glory C .15 .30
CBLZ075 Abyss-scorn C .15 .30
CBLZ076 Spikeshield with Chain C .15 .30
CBLZ077 Xyz Tribalrivals C .15 .30
CBLZ078 Breakthrough Skill UR 2.50 5.00
CBLZ078 Breakthrough Skill UTR 7.50 15.00
CBLZ079 Jurrac Impact C .15 .30
CBLZ080 Dice-nied SP .10 .20
CBLZ081 Knight Medraut SCR 3.00 6.00
CBLZ082 Hazy Flame Mantikor R .15 .30
CBLZ083 Mermail Abysseus UR 7.50 15.00
CBLZ083 Mermail Abysseus UTR 15.00 30.00
CBLZ084 Bonfire Colossus SCR .20 .40
CBLZ085 Fairy Elfuria SCR 1.25 2.50
CBLZ086 Artorigus, King UR .60 1.25
CBLZ086 Artorigus, King UTR .60 1.25
CBLZ087 Infernal Flame Vixen R .15 .30
CBLZ088 Spell Wall C .15 .30
CBLZ089 Kickfire SCR .75 1.50
CBLZ090 Crimson Sunbird C .15 .30
CBLZ091 Ignition Beast Volcannon C .15 .30
CBLZ092 Noble Knight Joan R .15 .30
CBLZ093 Crimson Blader R .60 1.25
CBLZ094 Infernity Archer R .25 .50
CBLZ095 Blackwing - Gladius the Midnight Sun R.15 .30
CBLZ096 Blackwing - Damascus the Polar Night R.15 .30
CBLZ097 Brohood - Horse Prince SR 1.25 2.50
CBLZ098 Brohood - Spirit R .15 .30
CBLZ099 Brohood - Lion Emperor SR .75 1.50

2013 Yu-Gi-Oh Hidden Arsenal 7 1st Edition

HA07EN001 Gem-Knight Sardonyx SR .25 .50
HA07EN002 Laval Phlogis SR .15 .30
HA07EN003 Gishki Avance SR .15 .30
HA07EN004 Gusto Griffin SR .15 .30
HA07EN005 Constellar Sheratan SR .15 .30
HA07EN006 Constellar Aldebaran SR .15 .30
HA07EN007 Constellar Algiedi SR .30 .75
HA07EN008 Constellar Pollux SR .30 .75
HA07EN009 Constellar Zubeneschamali SCR .50 1.00
HA07EN010 Constellar Virgo SR .15 .30
HA07EN011 Evilswarm Heliotrope SR .25 .50
HA07EN012 Evilswarm Zahak SR .15 .30
HA07EN013 Evilswarm Ketos SR .15 .30
HA07EN014 Evilswarm O'lantern SR .15 .30
HA07EN015 Evilswarm Mandragora SR .30 .75
HA07EN016 Evilswarm Hraesvelg SR .15 .30
HA07EN017 Evilswarm Levianima SCR .20 .40
HA07EN018 Gem-Knight Zirconia SR .75 1.50
HA07EN019 Lavalval Chain SCR 4.00 8.00
HA07EN020 Daigusto Emeral SCR 15.00 30.00
HA07EN021 Constellar Hyades SCR .50 1.00
HA07EN022 Constellar Pleiades SCR .60 1.25
HA07EN023 Evilswarm Nightmare SR .50 1.00
HA07EN024 Evilswarm Bahamut SCR .60 1.25
HA07EN025 Molten Conduction Field SCR .20 .40
HA07EN026 Gishki Photomirror SR .15 .30
HA07EN027 Constellar Star Chart SCR .30 .75
HA07EN028 Fragment Fusion SR .15 .30
HA07EN029 Dust Storm of Gusto SR .15 .30
HA07EN030 Infestation Infection SCR .30 .75
HA07EN031 D.D. Esper Star Sparrow SCR .30 .75
HA07EN032 Beast-Warrior Puma SR .15 .30
HA07EN033 Phoenix Beast Gairuda SR .15 .30
HA07EN034 Ironhammer the Giant SR .15 .30
HA07EN035 D.D. Jet Iron SR .15 .30
HA07EN036 Aye-Iron SR .15 .30
HA07EN037 Tin Goldfish SR 7.50 15.00
HA07EN038 Gearspring Spirit SR .50 1.00
HA07EN039 Gem-Knight Lazuli SR 1.50 3.00
HA07EN040 Gishki Natalia SR .15 .30
HA07EN041 Constellar Sial SR .15 .30
HA07EN042 Constellar Rasalhague SR .15 .30
HA07EN043 Constellar Leonis SR .15 .30
HA07EN044 Constellar Acubens SR .15 .30
HA07EN045 Constellar Kaus SCR .25 .50
HA07EN046 Constellar Alrescha SR .15 .30
HA07EN047 Constellar Antares SR .15 .30
HA07EN048 Evilswarm Castor SR 1.00 2.00
HA07EN049 Evilswarm Obliviwisp SR .15 .30
HA07EN050 Evilswarm Azzathoth SR .15 .30
HA07EN051 Evilswarm Thunderbird SCR .60 1.25
HA07EN052 Evilswarm Salamandra SR .15 .30
HA07EN053 Evilswarm Golem SR .15 .30
HA07EN054 Evilswarm Coppelia SR .15 .30
HA07EN055 Sophia, Goddess of Rebirth SCR 1.00 2.00
HA07EN056 Gishki Psychelone SR .15 .30
HA07EN057 Gishki Zielgigas SCR 1.50 3.00
HA07EN058 Gem-Knight Seraphinite SR 15.00 30.00
HA07EN059 Gem-Knight Master Diamond SCR .50 1.00
HA07EN060 Tin Archduke SCR .20 .40

HA07EN061 Constellar Praesepe SCR .60 1.25
HA07EN062 Constellar Ptolemy M7 SCR 4.00 8.00
HA07EN063 Evilswarm Thanatos SCR .60 1.25
HA07EN064 Evilswarm Ophion SCR 7.50 15.00
HA07EN065 Evilswarm Ouroboros SCR 4.00 8.00
HA07EN066 Iron Call SCR 2.50 5.00
HA07EN067 Constellar Star Cradle SR .15 .30
HA07EN068 Infestation Pandemic SCR 2.00 4.00
HA07EN069 Constellar Meteor SR .15 .30
HA07EN070 Infestation Terminus SR .15 .30

2013 Yu-Gi-Oh Judgment of the Light 1st Edition

JOTL000 Galaxy Serpent SR .50 1.00
JOTL001 DZW - Chimera Clad R .10 .20
JOTL002 V Salamander R .10 .20
JOTL003 Interceptomato C .15 .30
JOTL004 Spell Recycler C .15 .30
JOTL005 Xyz Agent C .15 .30
JOTL006 Super Defense Robot Lio C .15 .30
JOTL007 Super Defense Robot Elephan C .15 .30
JOTL008 Super Defense Robot Monki C .15 .30
JOTL009 Star Seraph Scout C .15 .30
JOTL010 Star Seraph Sage C .15 .30
JOTL011 Star Seraph Sword C .15 .30
JOTL012 Umbral Horror Ghoul C .15 .30
JOTL013 Umbral Horror Unform C .15 .30
JOTL014 Umbral Horror Will o' the Wisp C .15 .30
JOTL015 Schwarzschild Limit Dragon C .15 .30
JOTL016 Bujin Yamato UR .60 1.25
JOTL017 Bujingi Quilin SR .25 .50
JOTL018 Bujingi Turtle C .15 .30
JOTL019 Bujingi Wolf C .15 .30
JOTL020 Bujingi Crane R .10 .20
JOTL021 Bujingi Ophidian C .15 .30
JOTL022 Mecha Phantom Beast Warbluran R .10 .20
JOTL023 Mecha Phantom Beast Blue Impala UR .25 .50
JOTL024 Mecha Phantom Beast Coltwing C .15 .30
JOTL025 Mecha Phantom Beast Harrliard C .15 .30
JOTL026 Brotherhood of the Fire Fist - Boar R .10 .20
JOTL027 Brotherhood of the Fire Fist - Caribou C.15 .30
JOTL028 World of Prophecy SCR .50 1.00
JOTL029 Archfiend Heiress R .10 .20
JOTL030 Archfiend Cavalry R .10 .20
JOTL031 Archfiend Emperor,
the First Lord of Horror R .10 .20
JOTL032 Traptrix Atrax R .10 .20
JOTL033 Traptrix Myrmeleo R .50 1.00
JOTL034 Traptrix Nepenthes C .15 .30
JOTL035 The Calibrator C .15 .30
JOTL036 Talaya, Princess of Cherry Blossoms SR.50 1.00
JOTL037 Cheepcheepcheep C .15 .30
JOTL038 Masked Chameleon UR 1.50 3.00
JOTL039 Flying C SP .50 1.00
JOTL040 Yellow Duston SP .10 .20
JOTL041 Mecha Phantom Beast Concoruda SR .25 .50
JOTL042 Brotherhood of the Fire Fist - Kirin R .10 .20
JOTL043 Mist Bird Clausolas SR .75 1.50
JOTL044 Underworld Fighter Balmung R .10 .20
JOTL045 Armades, Keeper of Boundaries SCR 2.00 4.00
JOTL046 HTS Psyhemuth SR .25 .50
JOTL047 Star Eater GR 7.50 15.00
JOTL047 Star Eater SCR .50 1.00
JOTL047 Star Eater UTR 4.00 8.00
JOTL048 Number C39: Utopia Ray Victory SR 2.50 5.00
JOTL048 Number C39: Utopia Ray Victory UTR 2.50 5.00
JOTL049 Shark Caesar C .15 .30
JOTL050 Starliege Lord Galaxion SR .25 .50
JOTL051 Googly-Eyes Drum Dragon C .15 .30
JOTL052 Ice Princess Zereort C .15 .30
JOTL053 Number 102: Star Seraph Sentry R .10 .20
JOTL054 Number 66: Master Key Beetle SR .75 1.50
JOTL055 Number 104: Masquerade R .50 1.00
JOTL056 Number C104: Umbral Horror SR .50 1.00
JOTL056 Number C104: Umbral Horror UTR .75 1.50
JOTL057 Bujintei Susanowo UR .25 .50
JOTL057 Bujintei Susanowo UTR .75 1.50
JOTL058 Herald of Pure Light SR 2.50 5.00
JOTL059 Rank-Up-Magic Numeron Force UR .25 .50
JOTL059 Rank-Up-Magic Numeron Force UTR .50 1.00
JOTL060 Xyz Reception C .15 .30
JOTL061 Sargasso the D.D. Battlefield C .15 .30
JOTL062 Sargasso Lighthouse C .15 .30
JOTL063 Bujincarnation R .10 .20
JOTL064 Vertical Landing C .15 .30
JOTL065 Fire Formation - Yoko SR .25 .50
JOTL066 Archfiend Palabyrinth R .10 .20
JOTL067 Transmodify SCR 10.00 20.00
JOTL068 Black and White Wave C .15 .30
JOTL069 Single Purchase SP .10 .20
JOTL070 Reverse Glasses C .15 .30
JOTL071 Xyz Revenge Shuffle C .15 .30
JOTL072 Corrupted Keys R .10 .20
JOTL073 Vain Betrayer C .15 .30
JOTL074 Bujin Regalia - The Sword C .15 .30

JOTL075 Bujinfidel C	.15	.30
JOTL076 Sonic Boom C	.15	.30
JOTL077 Traptrix Trap Hole Nightmare SR	.60	1.25
JOTL078 Xyz Reversal C	.15	.30
JOTL079 Shapesister UR	.25	.50
JOTL080 Armageddon Designator SP	.10	.20
JOTL081 Bujingi Warg C	.15	.30
JOTL082 Mecha Phantom Beast Aerosguin UR	.25	.50
JOTL083 Cockadoodledoo UR	2.50	5.00
JOTL084 Noble Knight Drystan SCR	.50	1.00
JOTL085 Tour Bus To Forbidden Realms R	.10	.20
JOTL086 Confronting the C R	.10	.20
JOTL087 Angel of Zera SCR	.50	1.00
JOTL088 Xyz Encore UR	.60	1.25
JOTL089 Moon Dance Ritual R	.10	.20
JOTL090 The Atmosphere C	.15	.30
JOTL091 Junk Blader C	.15	.30
JOTL092 Coach Captain Bearman UR	.25	.50
JOTL093 Coach Soldier Wolfbark SCR	2.00	4.00
JOTL094 Brotherhood Fire Fist - Rooster SCR	1.00	2.00
JOTL095 Fire King Avatar Yaksha SR	1.50	3.00
JOTL096 Fishborg Archer C	.15	.30
JOTL097 Fencing Fire Ferret C	.15	.30
JOTL098 Kujakujaku C	.15	.30
JOTL099 Madolche Chickolates C	.15	.30

2013 Yu-Gi-Oh Legendary Collection 4 Joey's World 1st Edition

LCJW001 Flame Manipulator C	.30	.75
LCJW002 Masaki the Legendary Swordsman C	.30	.75
LCJW003 Red-Eyes B. Dragon UR	.60	1.25
LCJW004 Rude Kaiser C	.30	.75
LCJW005 Rock Ogre Grotto 1 C	.30	.75
LCJW006 Baby Dragon SR	.15	.30
LCJW007 Axe Raider C	.30	.75
LCJW008 Tiger Axe C	.30	.75
LCJW009 Garoozis C	.30	.75
LCJW010 Swordsman of Landstar C	.30	.75
LCJW011 Cyber-Tech Alligator C	.30	.75
LCJW012 Alligator's Sword C	.30	.75
LCJW013 Meotoko C	.30	.75
LCJW014 Kageningen C	.30	.75
LCJW015 Stone Armadiller C	.30	.75
LCJW016 Anthrosaurus C	.30	.75
LCJW017 Skull Stalker C	.30	.75
LCJW018 Wolf C	.30	.75
LCJW019 Hero of the East C	.30	.75
LCJW020 Swamp Battleguard C	.30	.75
LCJW021 Time Wizard C	.30	.75
LCJW022 Lava Battleguard C	.30	.75
LCJW023 Jinzo R	.50	1.00
LCJW024 The Legendary Fisherman C	.30	.75
LCJW025 Sword Hunter C	.30	.75
LCJW026 Hayabusa Knight C	.30	.75
LCJW027 Mad Sword Beast C	.30	.75
LCJW028 Goblin Attack Force C	.30	.75
LCJW029 The Fiend Megacyber C	.30	.75
LCJW030 Gearfried the Iron Knight C	.30	.75
LCJW031 Red-Eyes Black Metal Dragon C	.30	.75
LCJW032 Marauding Captain C	.30	.75
LCJW033 Fiber Jar C	.30	.75
LCJW034 Sasuke Samurai C	.30	.75
LCJW035 Neko Mane King C	.30	.75
LCJW036 Little-Winguard C	.30	.75
LCJW037 Insect Queen C	.30	.75
LCJW038 Red-Eyes B. Chick SR	.50	1.00
LCJW039 Red-Eyes Darkness Dragon C	.30	.75
LCJW040 Gearfried the Swordmaster C	.30	.75
LCJW041 Gilford the Lightning C	.30	.75
LCJW042 Rocket Warrior C	.30	.75
LCJW043 Panther Warrior C	.30	.75
LCJW044 Gilford the Legend C	.30	.75
LCJW045 Copycat C	.30	.75
LCJW046 Divine Knight Ishzark C	.30	.75
LCJW047 Maximum Six C	.30	.75
LCJW048 Comrade Swordsman of Landstar C	.30	.75
LCJW049 Red-Eyes Wyvern C	.30	.75
LCJW050 Red-Eyes Darkness Metal Dragon SCR	6.00	12.00
LCJW051 Phoenix Gearfried C	.30	.75
LCJW052 Lightray Gearfried C	.30	.75
LCJW053 Flame Swordsman C	.30	.75
LCJW054 B. Skull Dragon R	.75	1.50
LCJW055 Thousand Dragon C	.30	.75
LCJW056 Alligator's Sword Dragon C	.30	.75
LCJW057 Raigeki SCR	10.00	20.00
LCJW058 Hinotama C	.30	.75
LCJW059 Polymerization SR	1.25	2.50
LCJW060 Monster Reborn UR	1.00	2.00
LCJW061 Pot of Greed SCR	1.00	2.00
LCJW062 Salamandra C	.30	.75
LCJW063 Giant Trunade C	.30	.75
LCJW064 Premature Burial C	.30	.75
LCJW065 Graceful Dice C	.30	.75
LCJW066 Scapegoat SCR	.60	1.25
LCJW067 The Warrior Returning Alive C	.30	.75
LCJW068 Meteor of Destruction C	.30	.75
LCJW069 Release Restraint C	.30	.75
LCJW070 Foolish Burial SCR	2.50	5.00
LCJW071 Silent Doom SR	.15	.30
LCJW072 Dangerous Machine Type-6 C	.30	.75
LCJW073 Trap Hole C	.30	.75
LCJW074 Skull Dice C	.30	.75
LCJW075 Metalmorph C	.30	.75
LCJW076 Fairy Box C	.30	.75
LCJW077 Collected Power C	.30	.75
LCJW078 Bottomless Trap Hole SCR	1.50	3.00
LCJW079 Drop Off C	.30	.75
LCJW080 Magical Arm Shield C	.30	.75
LCJW081 Kunai with Chain C	.30	.75
LCJW082 Harpie Lady SR	.15	.30
LCJW083 Harpie Girl C	.30	.75
LCJW084 Dunames Dark Witch UR	.15	.30
LCJW085 Harpie Lady Sisters C	.30	.75
LCJW086 Harpie's Pet Dragon UR	2.00	4.00
LCJW087 Amazoness Paladin SR	.15	.30
LCJW088 Amazoness Fighter C	.30	.75
LCJW089 Amazoness Tiger UR	.10	.20
LCJW090 Harpie Lady 1 SR	.50	1.00
LCJW091 Harpie Lady 2 SR	.15	.30
LCJW092 Harpie Lady 3 SR	.15	.30
LCJW093 Harpie's Pet Baby Dragon C	.30	.75
LCJW094 Harpie Queen UR	1.50	3.00
LCJW095 Amazoness Scouts C	.30	.75
LCJW096 Cyber Harpie Lady C	.30	.75
LCJW097 Harpie Dancer UR	3.00	6.00
LCJW098 Elegant Egotist SR	.15	.30
LCJW099 Harpie's Feather Duster SCR	3.00	6.00
LCJW100 Amazoness Spellcaster C	.30	.75
LCJW101 Spell Reproduction C	.30	.75
LCJW102 Harpies' Hunting Ground SR	.15	.30
LCJW103 Triangle Ecstasy Spark C	.30	.75
LCJW104 Amazoness Village C	.30	.75
LCJW105 Cyber Shield C	.30	.75
LCJW106 Fairy's Hand Mirror C	.30	.75
LCJW107 Mirror Wall C	.30	.75
LCJW108 Gravity Bind C	.30	.75
LCJW109 Shadow of Eyes C	.30	.75
LCJW110 Gryphon Wing C	.30	.75
LCJW111 Trap Jammer SCR	.75	1.50
LCJW112 Hysteric Party SR	.50	1.00
LCJW113 Revival Jam C	.30	.75
LCJW114 Dark Jeroid C	.30	.75
LCJW115 Newdoria C	.30	.75
LCJW116 Helpoemer C	.30	.75
LCJW117 Lava Golem R	.10	.20
LCJW118 Drillago C	.30	.75
LCJW119 Lekunga C	.30	.75
LCJW120 Lord Poison C	.30	.75
LCJW121 Makyura the Destructor C	.30	.75
LCJW122 Legendary Fiend C	.30	.75
LCJW123 Black Pendant C	.30	.75
LCJW124 Jam Breeding Machine C	.30	.75
LCJW125 Vengeful Bog Spirit C	.30	.75
LCJW126 Card of Sanctity C	.30	.75
LCJW127 Magical Stone Excavation C	.30	.75
LCJW128 Spell of Pain C	.30	.75
LCJW129 Magic Jammer C	.30	.75
LCJW130 Mirror Force SCR	1.00	2.00
LCJW131 Jam Defender C	.30	.75
LCJW132 Coffin Seller C	.30	.75
LCJW133 Rope of Life C	.30	.75
LCJW134 Nightmare Wheel C	.30	.75
LCJW135 Judgment of Anubis C	.30	.75
LCJW136 Malevolent Catastrophe C	.30	.75
LCJW137 Relieve Monster C	.30	.75
LCJW138 Metal Reflect Slime C	.30	.75
LCJW139 Serpent Night Dragon C	.30	.75
LCJW140 Two-Headed King Rex C	.30	.75
LCJW141 Crawling Dragon C	.30	.75
LCJW142 Kabazauls SCR	.25	.50
LCJW143 Sabersaurus SCR	.25	.50
LCJW144 Tomozaurus C	.30	.75
LCJW145 Little D C	.30	.75
LCJW146 Sword Arm of Dragon C	.30	.75
LCJW147 Megazowler C	.30	.75
LCJW148 Gilasaurus C	.30	.75
LCJW149 Tyrant Dragon C	.30	.75
LCJW150 Dark Driceratops C	.30	.75
LCJW151 Hyper Hammerhead C	.30	.75
LCJW152 Black Tyranno C	.30	.75
LCJW153 Tyranno Infinity C	.30	.75
LCJW154 Black Ptera C	.30	.75
LCJW155 Black Stego C	.30	.75
LCJW156 Miracle Jurassic Egg C	.30	.75
LCJW157 Babycerasaurus C	.30	.75
LCJW158 Destroyersaurus SCR	.25	.50
LCJW159 Bracchio-Raidus C	.30	.75
LCJW160 Ultra Evolution Pill C	.30	.75
LCJW161 Big Evolution Pill C	.30	.75
LCJW162 Tail Swipe C	.30	.75
LCJW163 Jurassic World C	.30	.75
LCJW164 Fossil Dig C	.30	.75
LCJW165 Fossil Excavation C	.30	.75
LCJW166 Hunting Instinct C	.30	.75
LCJW167 Survival Instinct C	.30	.75
LCJW168 Volcanic Eruption C	.30	.75
LCJW169 Seismic Shockwave C	.30	.75
LCJW170 Seiyaryu C	.30	.75
LCJW171 Launcher Spider C	.30	.75
LCJW172 Slot Machine C	.30	.75
LCJW173 Zoa C	.30	.75
LCJW174 Ancient Tool C	.30	.75
LCJW175 Giganto C	.30	.75
LCJW176 Sword Slasher C	.30	.75
LCJW177 Barrel Dragon C	.30	.75
LCJW178 Metalzoa C	.30	.75
LCJW179 Machine King C	.30	.75
LCJW180 Blast Sphere C	.30	.75
LCJW181 Fiendish Engine Ω C	.30	.75
LCJW182 Solemn Judgment SCR	.60	1.25
LCJW183 Dragon Zombie C	.30	.75
LCJW184 Armored Zombie C	.30	.75
LCJW185 The Snake Hair C	.30	.75
LCJW186 Vampire Baby C	.30	.75
LCJW187 Patrician of Darkness C	.30	.75
LCJW188 Dark Dust Spirit C	.30	.75
LCJW189 Pyramid Turtle SR	.15	.30
LCJW190 Spirit Reaper UR	.60	1.25
LCJW191 Vampire Lord C	.30	.75
LCJW192 Despair from the Dark C	.30	.75
LCJW193 Fear from the Dark C	.30	.75
LCJW194 Ryu Kokki C	.30	.75
LCJW195 Soul-Absorbing Bone Tower C	.30	.75
LCJW196 Vampire Lady C	.30	.75
LCJW197 Regenerating Mummy C	.30	.75
LCJW198 Vampire Genesis C	.30	.75
LCJW199 Reborn Zombie C	.30	.75
LCJW200 Plague Wolf C	.30	.75
LCJW201 Return Zombie C	.30	.75
LCJW202 Zombie Master C	.30	.75
LCJW203 Il Blud C	.30	.75
LCJW204 Vampire's Curse C	.30	.75
LCJW205 Goblin Zombie C	.30	.75
LCJW206 Red-Eyes Zombie Dragon R	.10	.20
LCJW207 Malevolent Mech - Goku En C	.30	.75
LCJW208 Paladin of the Cursed Dragon C	.30	.75
LCJW209 Skull Conductor C	.30	.75
LCJW210 Great Mammoth of Goldfine C	.30	.75
LCJW211 Book of Life UR	.60	1.25
LCJW212 Call of the Mummy SR	.15	.30
LCJW213 Zombie World UR	1.25	2.50
LCJW214 Everliving Underworld Cannon C	.30	.75
LCJW215 Pyramid of Wonders C	.30	.75
LCJW216 Overpowering Eye C	.30	.75
LCJW217 Call of the Haunted SR	1.00	2.00
LCJW218 Tutan Mask C	.30	.75
LCJW219 Trap of the Imperial Tomb C	.30	.75
LCJW220 Labyrinth Wall C	.30	.75
LCJW221 Dungeon Worm C	.30	.75
LCJW222 Monster Tamer C	.30	.75
LCJW223 Gate Guardian C	.30	.75
LCJW224 Sanga of the Thunder C	.30	.75
LCJW225 Kazejin C	.30	.75
LCJW226 Suijin C	.30	.75
LCJW227 Jirai Gumo C	.30	.75
LCJW228 Shadow Ghoul C	.30	.75
LCJW229 Wall Shadow C	.30	.75
LCJW230 Labyrinth Tank C	.30	.75
LCJW231 Magical Labyrinth C	.30	.75
LCJW232 Fairy Meteor Crush C	.30	.75
LCJW233 Tribute Doll C	.30	.75
LCJW234 Riryoku C	.30	.75
LCJW235 Summoned Skull R	.50	1.00
LCJW236 Beast of Talwar R	.10	.20
LCJW237 Toon Summoned Skull R	.10	.20
LCJW238 Lesser Fiend R	.10	.20
LCJW239 Shadow Tamer R	.10	.20
LCJW240 Fiend Skull Dragon R	.10	.20
LCJW241 A Deal with Dark Ruler R	.10	.20
LCJW242 Beiige, Vanguard of Dark World UR	.60	1.25
LCJW243 Broww, Huntsman of Dark World SCR	.75	1.50
LCJW244 Brron, Mad King of Dark World UR	.60	1.25
LCJW245 Sillva, Warlord of Dark World SCR	.25	.50
LCJW246 Goldd, Wu-Lord of Dark World SCR	.25	.50
LCJW247 Scarr, Scout of Dark World C	.30	.75
LCJW248 Snoww, Unlight of Dark World SCR	.50	1.00
LCJW249 Dark World Lightning SCR	.25	.50
LCJW250 Gateway to Dark World SCR	.25	.50
LCJW251 Dark World Dealings SR	1.25	2.50
LCJW252 Dark World Grimoire C	.30	.75
LCJW253 The Gates of Dark World UR	.60	1.25
LCJW254 The Forces of Darkness C	.30	.75
LCJW255 Gravekeeper's Spy SCR	.25	.50
LCJW256 Gravekeeper's Curse C	.30	.75
LCJW257 Gravekeeper's Vassal C	.30	.75
LCJW258 Gravekeeper's Priestess R	.10	.20
LCJW259 Gravekeeper's Visionary R	.10	.20
LCJW260 Necrovalley C	.30	.75
LCJW261 Gravekeeper's Stele UR	.60	1.25
LCJW262 Dice Jar C	.30	.75
LCJW263 Roulette Barrel C	.30	.75
LCJW264 Blowback Dragon C	.30	.75
LCJW265 Snipe Hunter C	.30	.75
LCJW266 Twin-Barrel Dragon C	.30	.75
LCJW267 Gatling Dragon C	.30	.75
LCJW268 Second Coin Toss C	.30	.75
LCJW269 Blind Destruction C	.30	.75
LCJW270 Needle Wall C	.30	.75
LCJW271 Dice Re-Roll C	.30	.75
LCJW272 Dice Try C	.30	.75
LCJW273 Sixth Sense C	.30	.75
LCJW274 Adhesion Trap Hole C	.30	.75
LCJW275 D.D. Trap Hole C	.30	.75
LCJW276 Giant Trap Hole C	.30	.75
LCJW277 Treacherous Trap Hole C	.30	.75
LCJW278 Chaos Trap Hole C	.30	.75
LCJW279 Cave Dragon C	.30	.75
LCJW280 Injection Fairy Lily C	.30	.75
LCJW281 Berserk Dragon C	.30	.75
LCJW282 Strike Ninja C	.30	.75
LCJW283 Dark Hole SCR	.75	1.50
LCJW284 Heavy Storm UR	.60	1.25
LCJW285 Mystical Space Typhoon SCR	1.50	3.00
LCJW286 Reinforcement of the Army UR	.60	1.25
LCJW287 Super Rejuvenation SR	.15	.30
LCJW288 Book of Moon SCR	.75	1.50
LCJW289 Stray Lambs UR	.10	.20
LCJW290 Pot of Avarice SCR	.50	1.00
LCJW291 Trade-In UR	4.00	8.00
LCJW292 Horn of Heaven UR	.60	1.25
LCJW293 Chain Destruction R	.10	.20
LCJW294 Torrential Tribute SCR	1.25	2.50
LCJW295 Compulsory Evacuation Device SCR	.50	1.00
LCJW296 Spirit Barrier C	.30	.75
LCJW297 Black Horn of Heaven UR	.60	1.25
LCJW298 Imperial Iron Wall UR	1.00	2.00

2013 Yu-Gi-Oh Legendary Collection 4 Joey's World Box Bonus

LC04001 Blue Flame Swordsman UR	.10	.20
LC04002 Harpie Lady Phoenix Formation UR	.10	.20
LC04003 Card of Last Will UR	.10	.20
LC04004 Blue Sheep Token UR	.10	.20
LC04005 Orange Sheep Token UR	.10	.20
LC04006 Pink Sheep Token UR	.10	.20
LC04007 Yellow Sheep Token UR	.10	.20
LC04008 White Lamb Token UR	.10	.20
LC04009 Pink Lamb Token UR	.10	.20

2013 Yu-Gi-Oh Lord of the Tachyon Galaxy 1st Edition

LTGY000 Mecha Phantom Beast Turtletracer SR	.20	.40
LTGY001 Bachibachibachi C	.15	.30
LTGY002 Gogogo Gigas R	.15	.30
LTGY003 Mimimic C	.15	.30
LTGY004 Dotedotengu C	.15	.30
LTGY005 Tatakawa Knight C	.15	.30
LTGY006 Little Fairy C	.15	.30
LTGY007 Sharkraken C	.15	.30
LTGY008 Big Whale R	.15	.30
LTGY009 Starfish C	.15	.30
LTGY010 Panther Shark C	.15	.30
LTGY011 Eagle Shark C	.15	.30
LTGY012 Blizzard Falcon C	.15	.30
LTGY013 Aurora Wing C	.15	.30
LTGY014 Radius, the Half-Moon Dragon C	.15	.30
LTGY015 Parsec, the Interstellar Dragon C	.15	.30
LTGY016 Battlin' Boxer Headgeared C	.15	.30
LTGY017 Battlin' Boxer Glassjaw C	.15	.30
LTGY018 Battlin' Boxer Sparrer C	.15	.30
LTGY019 Battlin' Boxer Switchitter C	.15	.30
LTGY020 Battlin' Boxer Counterpunch C	.15	.30
LTGY021 Mecha Phantom Beast Megaraptor SR	.20	.40
LTGY022 Mecha Phantom Beast Tetherwolf R	.15	.30
LTGY023 Mecha Phantom Beast Blackfalcon C	.15	.30
LTGY024 Mecha Phantom Beast Stealthray C	.15	.30
LTGY025 Mecha Phantom Beast Hamstrat UR	.20	.40
LTGY025 Mecha Phantom Beast Hamstrat UTR	.60	1.25
LTGY026 Brotherhood of the Fire Fist - Wolf C	.15	.30
LTGY027 Brotherhood of the Fire Fist - Leopard C	.15	.30
LTGY028 Brotherhood of the Fire Fist - Rhino R	.15	.30
LTGY029 Brotherhood of the Fire Fist - Buffalo R	.15	.30
LTGY030 Mermail Abyssocea C	.15	.30
LTGY031 Wheel of Prophecy R	.15	.30
LTGY032 Madolche Hootcake SR	.75	1.50
LTGY033 Legendary Atlantean Tridon C	.15	.30
LTGY034 Fire King Avatar Garunix C	.15	.30
LTGY035 Harpie Channeler UR	2.00	4.00
LTGY035 Harpie Channeler UTR	2.50	5.00
LTGY036 Altitude Knight R	.15	.30
LTGY037 Windrose the Elemental Lord SCR	.50	1.00
LTGY038 Redox, Dragon Ruler of Boulders R	.25	.50
LTGY039 Tidal, Dragon Ruler of Waterfalls R	.25	.50
LTGY040 Blaster, Dragon Ruler of Infernos R	.50	1.00
LTGY041 Tempest, Dragon Ruler of Storms R	.25	.50
LTGY042 Risebell the Star Adjuster SP	.10	.20
LTGY043 Green Duston SP	.10	.20
LTGY044 #107 Galaxy-Eyes Tachyon Dragon GR	20.00	40.00
LTGY044 #107 Galaxy-Eyes Tachyon Dragon UR	7.50	15.00
LTGY044 #107 Galaxy-Eyes Tachyon Dragon UTR	15.00	30.00
LTGY045 Gauntlet Launcher UR	.20	.40
LTGY045 Gauntlet Launcher UTR	.60	1.25
LTGY046 Fairy Cheer Girl R	.15	.30
LTGY047 CXyz Dark Fairy Cheer Girl R	.15	.30
LTGY048 Shark Fortress C	.15	.30
LTGY049 Ice Beast Zerofyne R	1.25	2.50
LTGY050 Battlin' Boxer Lead Yoke R	.15	.30
LTGY051 #105 Battlin' Boxer Star Cestus SR	.60	1.25
LTGY052 #C105 Battlin' Boxer Comet Cestus UR	.20	.40
LTGY052 #C105 Battlin' Boxer Comet Cestus UTR	.60	1.25
LTGY053 Mecha Phantom Beast Dracossack SCR	5.00	10.00
LTGY054 Brotherhood of the Fire Fist - Cardinal SCR	.50	1.00
LTGY055 Harpie's Pet Phantasmal Dragon R	.20	.40
LTGY056 King of the Feral Imps C	.15	.30
LTGY057 Gagagawind C	.15	.30
LTGY058 Magnum Shield C	.15	.30
LTGY059 Xyz Revenge R	.15	.30
LTGY060 Rank-Up-Magic Barian's Force UR	.20	.40
LTGY060 Rank-Up-Magic Barian's Force UTR	.60	1.25
LTGY061 Scramble!! Scramble!! UR	.20	.40
LTGY061 Scramble!! Scramble!! UTR	.60	1.25
LTGY062 Fire Formation - Gyokkou SR	.50	1.00
LTGY063 Spellbook of Judgment SCR	1.25	2.50
LTGY064 Abyss-scale of the Mizuchi C	.15	.30
LTGY065 Hysteric Sign SR	1.50	3.00
LTGY066 Sacred Sword of Seven Stars SR	.75	1.50
LTGY067 Jewels of the Valiant C	.15	.30
LTGY068 Summon Breaker SP	.10	.20
LTGY069 Pinpoint Guard SCR	1.00	2.00
LTGY070 Memory Loss C	.15	.30
LTGY071 Torrential Reborn SCR	.50	1.00
LTGY072 Xyz Block C	.15	.30
LTGY073 Aerial Recharge C	.15	.30
LTGY074 Do a Barrel Roll R	.15	.30
LTGY075 Fire Formation - Kaiyo C	.15	.30
LTGY076 Madolche Nights SR	.20	.40
LTGY077 Geargiagear SR	.20	.40
LTGY078 High Tide on Fire Island C	.15	.30
LTGY079 Mind Drain C	.15	.30
LTGY080 Dragoncarnation SP	.20	.40
LTGY081 Noble Knight Gwalchavad UR	.20	.40
LTGY081 Noble Knight Gwalchavad UTR	.60	1.25
LTGY082 Brotherhood of the Fire Fist - Coyote SCR	.50	1.00
LTGY083 Mermail Abyssbalaen UR	.20	.40
LTGY083 Mermail Abyssbalaen UTR	.60	1.25
LTGY084 Trifortressops R	.15	.30
LTGY085 Ghost Fairy Elfobia SR	.20	.40
LTGY086 Totem Bird SCR	.75	1.50
LTGY087 Noble Arms of Destiny SR	.20	.40
LTGY088 Spellbook of Miracles C	.15	.30
LTGY089 Five Brothers Explosion C	.15	.30
LTGY090 Sonic Warrior C	.15	.30
LTGY091 Constellar Omega UR	.50	1.00
LTGY091 Constellar Omega UTR	.60	1.25
LTGY092 Number 69: Heraldry Crest R	.15	.30
LTGY093 Constellar Sombre SR	.20	.40
LTGY094 Evilswarm Kerykeion SR	.75	1.50
LTGY095 Reactan, Dragon Ruler of Pebbles C	.15	.30
LTGY096 Stream, Dragon Ruler of Droplets C	.15	.30
LTGY097 Burner, Dragon Ruler of Sparks C	.15	.30
LTGY098 Lightning, Dragon Ruler of Drafts C	.15	.30
LTGY099 Duck Fighter SR	.20	.40

2013 Yu-Gi-Oh Number Hunters 1st Edition

NUMH001 Chronomaly Aztec Mask Golem SR	.10	.20
NUMH002 Chronomaly Cabrera Trebuchet SR	.10	.20
NUMH003 Chronomaly Mud Golem SR	.10	.20
NUMH004 Chronomaly Sol Monolith SR	.10	.20
NUMH005 Gimmick Puppet Egg Head SR	.50	1.00
NUMH006 Gimmick Puppet Gear Changer SR	.20	.40
NUMH007 Gimmick Puppet Twilight Joker SR	.10	.20
NUMH008 Gimmick Puppet Scissor Arms SR	.20	.40
NUMH009 Gimmick Puppet Nightmare SR	.10	.20
NUMH010 Heroic Challenger - Ambush Soldier SCR	.20	.40
NUMH011 Heroic Challenger - Clasp Sword SR	.10	.20
NUMH012 Blue Mountain Butterspy SR	.50	1.00
NUMH013 Box of Friends SCR	1.25	2.50
NUMH014 Zombowwow SR	.10	.20
NUMH015 Gash the Dust Lord SR	.10	.20
NUMH016 Zubaba Knight SR	.10	.20
NUMH017 Gogogo Golem SR	.10	.20
NUMH018 Kagetokage SR	.25	.50

NUMH019 Kurivolt SR .10 .20
NUMH020 Gogogo Giant SR .10 .20
NUMH021 Gagaga Gardna SR .10 .20
NUMH022 Photon Cerberus SR .10 .20
NUMH023 Photon Lizard SR .10 .20
NUMH024 Rocket Arrow Express SR .10 .20
NUMH025 Battle Warrior SR .10 .20
NUMH026 Number 54: Lion Heart SCR 1.50 3.00
NUMH027 #15 Gimmick Puppet Giant Grinder SCR2.50 5.00
NUMH028 Number 44: Sky Pegasus SCR 1.00 2.00
NUMH029 Number 49: Fortune Tune SCR 1.50 3.00
NUMH030 Number 57: Tri-Head Dust Dragon SCR.60 1.25
NUMH031 Number 63: Shamoji Soldier SR .10 .20
NUMH032 Number 74: Master of Blades SCR 1.50 3.00
NUMH033 Number 85: Crazy Box SR .50 1.00
NUMH034 Number 87: Queen of the Night SR .60 1.25
NUMH035 Mechquipped Angineer SR .50 1.00
NUMH036 CXyz Mechquipped Djinn Angeneral SR.10 .20
NUMH037 Coach King Giantrainer SCR .20 .40
NUMH038 CXyz Coach Lord Ultimatrainer SCR 1.50 3.00
NUMH039 Norito the Moral Leader SCR 1.50 3.00
NUMH040 CXyz Simon the Great Moral Leader SCR.20 .40
NUMH041 Comics Hero King Arthur SCR 1.50 3.00
NUMH042 CXyz Comics Hero Legend Arthur SCR.20 .40
NUMH043 Battlecruiser Dianthus SR .10 .20
NUMH044 CXyz Battleship Cherry Blossom SCR .20 .40
NUMH045 Skypalace Gangaridai SCR .50 1.00
NUMH046 CXyz Skypalace Babylon SCR .20 .40
NUMH047 Photon Alexandra Queen SCR .20 .40
NUMH048 Night Papilloperative SR .10 .20
NUMH049 Unformed Void SR .10 .20
NUMH050 Princess Cologne SCR .20 .40
NUMH051 Baby Tiragon SR .10 .20
NUMH052 Chakra SR .10 .20
NUMH053 Resurrection of Chakra SR .10 .20
NUMH054 Gimmick Puppet Ritual SR .10 .20
NUMH055 Stoic Challenge SR .10 .20
NUMH056 Overlay Capture SR .10 .20
NUMH057 Insect Armor with Laser Cannon SR .10 .20
NUMH058 Number Wall SCR .60 1.25
NUMH059 Heraldry Record SR .10 .20
NUMH060 Butterspy Protection SR .10 .20

2013 Yu-Gi-Oh Shadow Specters 1st Edition

SHSP000 Ghostrick Ghoul SR .20 .40
SHSP001 Labradorite Dragon SR 2.50 5.00
SHSP002 Chow Chow Chan C .15 .30
SHSP003 Malicevorous Spoon C .15 .30
SHSP004 Malicevorous Fork C .15 .30
SHSP005 Malicevorous Knife C .15 .30
SHSP006 Battlin' Boxer Rib Gardna C .15 .30
SHSP007 Battlin' Boxer Rabbit Puncher C .15 .30
SHSP008 Secret Sect Druid Wid C .15 .30
SHSP009 Secret Sect Druid Dru C .15 .30
SHSP010 Mythic Tree Dragon C .15 .30
SHSP011 Mythic Water Dragon C .15 .30
SHSP012 Armed Protector Dragon C .15 .30
SHSP013 Soul Drain Dragon C .15 .30
SHSP014 Baby Raccoon Ponpoko C .15 .30
SHSP015 Baby Raccoon Tantan C .15 .30
SHSP016 Ghostrick Lantern SR 2.50 5.00
SHSP017 Ghostrick Specter C .15 .30
SHSP018 Ghostrick Witch C .15 .30
SHSP019 Ghostrick Yuki-onna C .15 .30
SHSP020 Ghostrick Jiangshi C .15 .30
SHSP021 Ghostrick Stein C .15 .30
SHSP022 Bujin Mikazuchi UR 1.00 2.00
SHSP023 Bujingi Crow R .10 .20
SHSP024 Bujingi Ibis C .15 .30
SHSP025 Bujingi Boar C .15 .30
SHSP026 Bujingi Centipede C .15 .30
SHSP027 Mecha Phantom Beast Sabre Hawk C .15 .30
SHSP028 Mecha Phantom Beast Kalgriffin R .10 .20
SHSP029 Vampire Sorcerer UR 2.00 4.00
SHSP030 Shadow Vampire SCR .50 1.00
SHSP031 Vampire Grace C .15 .30
SHSP032 Pumprincess the Princess of Ghosts C .15 .30
SHSP033 Yellow-Bellied Oni C .15 .30
SHSP034 Vampire Hunter SR .20 .40
SHSP035 Aratama R .10 .20
SHSP036 Rasetsu C .15 .30
SHSP037 Skelesaurus C .15 .30
SHSP038 Knight Day Grepher C .15 .30
SHSP039 Genomix Fighter UR .15 .30
SHSP040 Marina, Princess of Sunflowers SR .20 .40
SHSP041 Granmarg the Mega Monarch SCR .50 1.00
SHSP042 Swarm of Crows R .10 .20
SHSP043 Terrene Toothed Tsuchinoko C .15 .30
SHSP044 Risebell the Star Psycher SP .10 .20
SHSP045 Blue Duston SP .10 .20
SHSP046 Number C96: Dark Storm SR .20 .40
SHSP046 Number C96: Dark Storm UTR .50 1.00
SHSP047 Number 65: Djinn Buster R .10 .20
SHSP048 Number C65: King Overfiend R .10 .20
SHSP049 Battlin' Boxer Cheat Commissioner R .10 .20
SHSP050 Number 46: Dragluon SR 2.50 5.00
SHSP050 Number 46: Dragluon UTR 5.00 10.00
SHSP051 Number 64: Ronin Raccoon Sandayu R.50 1.00
SHSP052 Ghostrick Alucard UR 1.50 3.00
SHSP052 Ghostrick Alucard UTR 2.50 5.00
SHSP053 Bujintei Kagutsuchi UR .60 1.25
SHSP053 Bujintei Kagutsuchi UTR .75 1.50
SHSP054 Crimson Knight Vampire Bram UR 1.25 2.50
SHSP055 Meliae of the Trees SCR .50 1.00
SHSP056 Divine Dragon Knight Felgrand GR 7.50 15.00
SHSP056 Divine Dragon Knight Felgrand SCR 6.00 12.00
SHSP056 Divine Dragon Knight Felgrand UTR 6.00 12.00
SHSP057 Puralis, the Purple Pyrotile R .10 .20
SHSP058 Giganticastle R .10 .20
SHSP059 Gagagatag C .15 .30
SHSP060 Battlin' Boxing Spirits SR .60 1.25
SHSP061 Dragon Shield C .15 .30
SHSP062 Ghostrick Mansion C .15 .30
SHSP063 Bujin Regalia - The Mirror R .10 .20
SHSP064 Vampire Kingdom C .15 .30
SHSP065 Pot of Dichotomy SCR 1.00 2.00
SHSP066 Swords at Dawn R .10 .20
SHSP067 Return of the Monarchs UR 2.50 5.00
SHSP068 Sacred Serpent's Wake C .15 .30
SHSP069 Magicalized Duston Mop SP .10 .20
SHSP070 Burst Rebirth R .10 .20
SHSP071 Numbers Overlay Boost C .15 .30
SHSP072 Intrigue Shield C .15 .30
SHSP073 Ghostrick Vanish C .15 .30
SHSP074 Ghostrick Scare C .15 .30
SHSP075 Vampire Takeover SR .20 .40
SHSP076 Mistake SCR 1.00 2.00
SHSP077 Chain Ignition C .15 .30
SHSP078 Grisaille Prison R .50 1.00
SHSP079 Survival of the Fittest C .15 .30
SHSP080 BIG Win!! SP .10 .20
SHSP081 Bujingi Raven R .10 .20
SHSP082 Vampire Duke R .10 .20
SHSP083 Archfiend Giant R .10 .20
SHSP084 Lady of the Lake SCR .50 1.00
SHSP085 Noble Knight Borz SR .20 .40
SHSP086 Ignoble Knight of High Laundsallyn SCR.50 1.00
SHSP087 Sacred Noble Knight of King Artorigus UR.75 1.50
SHSP088 Noble Arms - Excaliburn SR .20 .40
SHSP089 Sinister Yorishiro UR .60 1.25
SHSP090 Celestial Wolf Lord, Blue Sirius UR .60 1.25
SHSP091 Mira the Star-Bearer C .15 .30
SHSP092 Dragard SR .60 1.25
SHSP093 White Dragon Wyverburster C .15 .30
SHSP094 Kidmodo Dragon SR 1.50 3.00
SHSP095 Secret Sanctuary of the Spellcasters R .10 .20
SHSP096 Black Dragon Collapserpent C .15 .30
SHSP097 Armored Kappa SR .20 .40
SHSP098 Oh Tokenbaum! R .10 .20
SHSP099 Vivid Knight R .10 .20
SHSPSP1 Ghostrick Ghoul UR .60 1.25

2013 Yu-Gi-Oh Star Pack 2013 1st Edition

SP13001 Zubaba Knight C .25 .50
SP13002 Gagaga Magician C .25 .50
SP13003 Gogogo Golem C .25 .50
SP13004 Achacha Archer C .25 .50
SP13005 Goblindbergh C .60 1.25
SP13006 Big Jaws C .25 .50
SP13007 Skull Kraken C .25 .50
SP13008 Galaxy-Eyes Photon Dragon C 1.50 3.00
SP13009 Kagetokage C 1.25 2.50
SP13010 Friller Rabca C .75 1.50
SP13011 Needle Sunfish C .25 .50
SP13012 Photon Cerberus C .25 .50
SP13013 Kurivolt C .25 .50
SP13014 Darklon C .25 .50
SP13015 Flame Armor Ninja C .25 .50
SP13016 Air Armor Ninja C .25 .50
SP13017 Aqua Armor Ninja C .25 .50
SP13018 Earth Armor Ninja C .25 .50
SP13019 Flelf C .50 1.00
SP13020 Chewbone C .50 1.00
SP13021 Number 39: Utopia C .50 1.00
SP13022 Grenosaurus C .25 .50
SP13023 No. 17: Leviathan Dragon .50 1.00
SP13024 Submersible Aero Shark .25 .50
SP13025 Number 34: Terror-Byte C .75 1.50
SP13026 Number 10: Illumiknight C .75 1.50
SP13027 Baby Tiragon C .25 .50
SP13028 Number 83: Galaxy Queen C .50 1.00
SP13029 Black Ray Lancer C .60 1.25
SP13030 Number 12: Crimson
Shadow Armor Ninja C .25 .50
SP13031 Number 96: Dark Mist C .75 1.50
SP13032 Wonder Wand C .50 1.00
SP13033 Infected Mail C .25 .50
SP13034 Ego Boost C .25 .50
SP13035 Monster Slots C .25 .50
SP13036 Heartfelt Appeal C .25 .50
SP13037 Icy Crevasse C .25 .50
SP13038 Nitwit Outwit C .25 .50
SP13039 Faith Bird C .25 .50
SP13040 Gilford the Lightning C .25 .50
SP13041 Gandora the Dragon .25 .50
SP13042 Metalmorph C .25 .50
SP13043 Arcana - Dark Ruler .25 .50
SP13044 Arcana - Light Ruler .60 1.25
SP13045 Barbaroid, Battle Machine 6.00 12.00
SP13046 Elemental HERO Escuridao C 2.00 4.00
SP13047 Meklord Emperor Wisel C .25 .50
SP13048 Seven Swords Warrior C .25 .50
SP13049 Catapult Warrior C .75 1.50
SP13050 One for One C .25 .50

2013 Yu-Gi-Oh Starter Deck Kaiba Reloaded 1st Edition

YSKREN001 Blue Eyes White Dragon UTR 2.00 4.00
YSKREN001 Blue Eyes White Dragon C .50 1.00
YSKREN002 Aqua Madoor C .15 .30
YSKREN003 La Jinn the Mystical
Genie of the Lamp C .15 .30
YSKREN004 Battle Ox C .15 .30
YSKREN005 Opticlops C .15 .30
YSKREN006 The Dragon Dwelling in the Cave C .15 .30
YSKREN007 Luster Dragon C .15 .30
YSKREN008 X Head Cannon C .15 .30
YSKREN009 Mad Dog of Darkness C .15 .30
YSKREN010 Vorse Raider C .15 .30
YSKREN011 Alexandrite Dragon C .15 .30
YSKREN012 Wattaildragon C .15 .30
YSKREN013 Twin Headed Behemoth C .15 .30
YSKREN014 Yomi Ship C .15 .30
YSKREN015 Des Feral Imp C .15 .30
YSKREN016 Kaiser Sea Horse C .15 .30
YSKREN017 Chaos Necromancer C .15 .30
YSKREN018 Blade Knight C .15 .30
YSKREN019 Horus the Black Flame Dragon LV4 C.50 1.00
YSKREN020 Horus the Black Flame Dragon LV6 C.50 1.00
YSKREN021 Cybernetic Cyclopean C .15 .30
YSKREN022 Puppet Plant C .15 .30
YSKREN023 Des Mosquito C .15 .30
YSKREN024 Tiger Dragon C .15 .30
YSKREN025 Vanguard of the Dragon C .15 .30
YSKREN026 Divine Dragon Apocralyph C .15 .30
YSKREN027 Interplanetarypurplythorny Dragon C.15 .30
YSKREN028 Dark Hole C .75 1.50
YSKREN029 Soul Exchange C .15 .30
YSKREN030 Tribute to The Doomed C .15 .30
YSKREN031 Rush Recklessly C .15 .30
YSKREN032 Mystical Space Typhoon C .15 .30
YSKREN033 Offerings to the Doomed C .15 .30
YSKREN034 Stamping Destruction C .15 .30
YSKREN035 Enemy Controller C .15 .30
YSKREN036 Burst Stream of Destruction C .15 .30
YSKREN037 Shrink C .15 .30
YSKREN038 Shield Crush C .15 .30
YSKREN039 Silent Doom C .15 .30
YSKREN040 Dragonic Tactics C .15 .30
YSKREN041 Shard of Greed C .15 .30
YSKREN042 Trap Hole C .15 .30
YSKREN043 Sakuretsu Armor C .15 .30
YSKREN044 Shadow Spell C .15 .30
YSKREN045 Widespread Ruin C .15 .30
YSKREN046 Threatening Roar C .15 .30
YSKREN047 Birthright C .15 .30
YSKREN048 Damage Gate C .15 .30

2013 Yu-Gi-Oh Starter Deck Yugi Reloaded 1st Edition

YSYREN001 Dark Magician UTR 1.25 2.50
YSYREN001 Dark Magician C .15 .30
YSYREN002 Mystical Elf C .15 .30
YSYREN003 Giant Soldier of Stone C .15 .30
YSYREN004 Summoned Skull C .15 .30
YSYREN005 Neo the Magic Swordsman C .15 .30
YSYREN006 Gemini Elf C .15 .30
YSYREN007 Dark Blade C .15 .30
YSYREN008 Kuriboh C .15 .30
YSYREN009 Buster Blader C .15 .30
YSYREN010 4-Starred Ladybug of Doom C .15 .30
YSYREN011 Dark Magician Girl C .15 .30
YSYREN012 Skilled White Magician C .15 .30
YSYREN013 Skilled Dark Magician C .15 .30
YSYREN014 Old Vindictive Magician C .15 .30
YSYREN015 Breaker the Magical Warrior C .15 .30
YSYREN016 Double Coston C .15 .30
YSYREN017 Silent Swordsman LV3 C .15 .30
YSYREN018 Silent Swordsman LV5 C .15 .30
YSYREN019 Green Gadget C .15 .30
YSYREN020 Red Gadget C .15 .30
YSYREN021 Yellow Gadget C .15 .30
YSYREN022 Electric Virus C .15 .30
YSYREN023 Magician's Valkyria C .60 1.25
YSYREN024 The Tricky C .15 .30
YSYREN025 Dark Hole C .15 .30
YSYREN026 Swords of Revealing Light C .15 .30
YSYREN027 Black Pendant C .15 .30
YSYREN028 Mystical Space Typhoon C .15 .30
YSYREN029 Mage Power C .15 .30
YSYREN030 Book of Moon C .15 .30
YSYREN031 Thousand Knives C .15 .30
YSYREN032 Dark Magic Attack C .15 .30
YSYREN033 Magical Dimension C .15 .30
YSYREN034 Ancient Rules C .15 .30
YSYREN035 Magicians Unite C .15 .30
YSYREN036 Soul Taker C .15 .30
YSYREN037 Shard of Greed C .15 .30
YSYREN038 Trap Hole C .15 .30
YSYREN039 Waboku C .15 .30
YSYREN040 Mirror Force C .15 .30
YSYREN041 Spellbinding Circle C .15 .30
YSYREN042 Call of the Haunted C .15 .30
YSYREN043 Magic Cylinder C .15 .30
YSYREN044 Miracle Restoring C .15 .30
YSYREN045 Zero Gravity C .15 .30
YSYREN046 Rising Energy C .15 .30

2013 Yu-Gi-Oh Structure Deck Onslaught of the Fire Kings 1st Edition

SDOKEN001 Fire King High Avatar Garunix UR .75 1.50
SDOKEN002 Fire King Avatar Barong C 1.00 2.00
SDOKEN003 Fire King Avatar Kirin C .10 .20
SDOKEN004 Sacred Phoenix of Nephthys C .10 .20
SDOKEN005 Manticore of Darkness C .10 .20
SDOKEN006 Goka, the Pyre of Malice C .10 .20
SDOKEN007 Hazy Flame Hyppogrif C .10 .20
SDOKEN008 Laval Lancelord C .10 .20
SDOKEN009 Flamvell Firedog C .10 .20
SDOKEN010 Flamvell Poun C .10 .20
SDOKEN011 Neo Flamvell Sabre C .10 .20
SDOKEN012 Royal Firestorm Guards C .10 .20
SDOKEN013 Volcanic Rocket C .50 1.00
SDOKEN014 Volcanic Counter C .10 .20
SDOKEN015 Molten Zombie C .10 .20
SDOKEN016 Spirit of Flames C .10 .20
SDOKEN017 Raging Flame Sprite C .10 .20
SDOKEN018 Fox Fire C .10 .20
SDOKEN019 Flame Tiger C .10 .20
SDOKEN020 Little Chimera C .10 .20
SDOKEN021 UFO Turtle C .10 .20
SDOKEN022 Onslaught of the Fire Kings SR 1.00 2.00
SDOKEN023 Circle of the Fire Kings SR .60 1.25
SDOKEN024 Rekindling C .10 .20
SDOKEN025 Blaze Accelerator C .10 .20
SDOKEN026 Wild Nature's Release C .10 .20
SDOKEN027 Pot of Duality C .75 1.50
SDOKEN028 Hand Destruction C 1.00 2.00
SDOKEN029 Creature Swap C .10 .20
SDOKEN030 Burden of the Mighty C .10 .20
SDOKEN031 Backfire C .10 .20
SDOKEN032 Flamvell Counter C .10 .20
SDOKEN033 Phoenix Wing Wind Blast C .50 1.00
SDOKEN034 Horn of the Phantom Beast C .50 1.00
SDOKEN035 Blast with Chain C .10 .20
SDOKEN036 Spiritual Fire Art - Kurenai C .10 .20
SDOKEN037 Regretful Rebirth C .10 .20
SDOKEN038 Nightmare Wheel C .10 .20
SDOKEN039 Call of the Haunted C .10 .20

2013 Yu-Gi-Oh Structure Deck Saga of Blue-Eyes White Dragon 1st Edition

SDBE040 Azure-Eyes Silver Dragon UR 1.25 2.50
SDBEEN001 Blue-Eyes White Dragon UR 1.25 2.50
SDBEEN002 Rabidragon C .15 .30
SDBEEN003 Alexandrite Dragon C .30 .75
SDBEEN004 Luster Dragon C .15 .30
SDBEEN005 Flamvell Guard C .15 .30
SDBEEN006 Maiden with Eyes of Blue SR 2.00 4.00
SDBEEN007 Rider of the Storm Winds C .15 .30
SDBEEN008 Darkstorm Dragon C .15 .30
SDBEEN009 Kaiser Glider C .15 .30
SDBEEN010 Hieratic Dragon of Tefnuit C .15 .30
SDBEEN011 Mirage Dragon C .15 .30
SDBEEN012 Divine Dragon Apocralyph C .15 .30
SDBEEN013 The White Stone of Legend C .50 1.00
SDBEEN014 Kaibaman C .15 .30
SDBEEN015 Herald of Creation C .15 .30
SDBEEN016 Kaiser Sea Horse C .15 .30
SDBEEN017 Honest C .15 .30
SDBEEN018 Shining Angel C .15 .30
SDBEEN019 Dragon Shrine SR 1.25 2.50
SDBEEN020 Silver's Cry C 2.00 4.00
SDBEEN021 Burst Stream of Destruction C .15 .30
SDBEEN022 Stamping Destruction C .15 .30
SDBEEN023 A Wingbeat of Giant Dragon C .15 .30
SDBEEN024 Trade-In C 1.25 2.50
SDBEEN025 Cards of Consonance C .50 1.00
SDBEEN026 White Elephant's Gift C .15 .30
SDBEEN027 One for One C .15 .30
SDBEEN028 Monster Reborn C .50 1.00
SDBEEN029 Dragonic Tactics C .15 .30
SDBEEN030 Soul Exchange C .15 .30
SDBEEN031 Swords of Revealing Light C .15 .30
SDBEEN032 Enemy Controller C .15 .30
SDBEEN033 Castle of Dragon Souls C .15 .30
SDBEEN034 Fiendish Chain C 1.00 2.00
SDBEEN035 Kunai with Chain C .15 .30
SDBEEN036 Damage Condenser C .15 .30
SDBEEN037 Call of the Haunted C .15 .30
SDBEEN038 Compulsory Evacuation Device C .30 .75
SDBEEN039 Champion's Vigilance C .15 .30

2013 Yu-Gi-Oh Super Starter Deck V For Victory 1st Edition

YS13001 Cosmo Queen C .10 .20
YS13002 Trance the Magic Swordsman C .10 .20
YS13003 Neo the Magic Swordsman C .10 .20
YS13004 Mystical Elf C .10 .20
YS13005 Chamberlain of the Six Samurai C .10 .20
YS13006 Gagaga Child C .50 1.00
YS13007 Magical Undertaker C .10 .20
YS13008 Caligo Claw Crow C .10 .20
YS13009 Gagaga Magician C .10 .20
YS13010 Gagaga Girl C .10 .20
YS13011 Gagaga Gardna C .10 .20
YS13012 Zubaba Knight C .10 .20
YS13013 Ganbara Knight C .10 .20
YS13014 Achacha Archer C .10 .20
YS13015 Goblindbergh C .10 .20
YS13016 Kagetokage C .20 .40
YS13017 Tasuke Knight C .10 .20
YS13018 ZW - Unicorn Spear C .10 .20
YS13019 Marauding Captain C .10 .20
YS13020 Old Vindictive Magician C .10 .20
YS13021 Swords of Burning Light C .10 .20
YS13022 Blustering Winds C .10 .20
YS13023 Wonder Wand C .20 .40
YS13024 Double or Nothing C .10 .20
YS13025 Ego Boost C .10 .20
YS13026 Gagagarevenge C .20 .40
YS13027 Xyz Unit C .10 .20
YS13028 The A. Forces C .10 .20
YS13029 Reinforcement of the Army C .10 .20
YS13030 The Warrior Returning Alive C .10 .20
YS13031 Puzzle Reborn C .10 .20
YS13032 Gagagashield C .10 .20
YS13033 Copy Knight C .10 .20
YS13034 Impenetrable Attack C .10 .20
YS13035 Utopian Aura C .10 .20
YS13036 Xyz Effect C .10 .20
YS13037 Shadow Spell C .10 .20
YS13038 Dust Tornado C .10 .20
YS13039 Call of the Haunted C .10 .20
YS13040 Dark Bribe C .75 1.50
YS13041 Number 39: Utopia SR .60 1.25
YS13042 Number C39: Utopia Ray UR .25 .50

2013 Yu-Gi-Oh Super Starter Deck V For Victory 1st Edition Power-Up Pack

YS13V01 Number C39: Utopia Ray V UR .10 .20
YS13V02 Rank-Up-Magic Limited
Barian's Force UR .10 .20
YS13V03 ZW - Eagle Claw C .10 .20
YS13V04 Ganbara Lancer C .10 .20
YS13V05 Bite Bug C .10 .20
YS13V06 Crane Crane C .10 .20
YS13V07 Gentlemander C .10 .20
YS13V08 Grenosaurus C .10 .20
YS13V09 Number 30: Acid Golem of Destruction C.50 1.00
YS13V10 Shining Elf C .10 .20
YS13V11 Number 6: Chronomaly Atlandis C .20 .40
YS13V12 Mystical Space Typhoon SR 1.00 2.00
YS13V13 Swords of Revealing Light SR .50 1.00
YS13V14 Mirror Force SR 1.00 2.00
YS13V15 Magic Cylinder SR .50 1.00

2013 Yu-Gi-Oh Zexal Collection Tins 1st Edition

ZTINEN001 Dododo Warrior SR .12 .25
ZTINEN002 Number 61: Volcasaurus UR 1.00 2.00
ZTINEN003 Number 19: Freezadon UR .60 1.25
ZTINEN004 Gagagaback SR .12 .25
ZTINEN005 Gagagashield UR .30 .60
ZTINEN006 Photon Pirate SR .25 .50
ZTINEN007 Photon Satellite SR .20 .40
ZTINEN008 Photon Slasher SR .30 .75
ZTINEN009 Kuriphoton UR .30 .60
ZTINEN010 Dimension Wanderer SR .12 .25
ZTINEN011 Galaxy Wizard UR 2.50 5.00
ZTINEN012 Galaxy Knight UR .30 .75
ZTINEN013 Number 56: Gold Rat SR .25 .50
ZTINEN014 Starliege Paladynamo UR .50 1.00

ZTINEN015 Message in a Bottle SR .20 .40
ZTINEN016 Accellight UR .25 .50
ZTINEN017 Galaxy Expedition UR 3.00 6.00
ZTINEN018 Galaxy Zero SR .30 .60
ZTINEN019 Triple Star Trion SR .12 .25
ZTINEN020 Zubaba Buster SR .12 .25
ZTINEN021 Chachaka Archer SR .12 .25
ZTINENV01 Gagaga Magician UTR .75 1.50
ZTINENV02 Number 20: Giga-Brilliant UTR .50 1.00
ZTINENV03 Gagagabolt UTR .25 .50

2014 Yu-Gi-Oh Astral Pack 4

AP04EN001 Dandylion UTR 10.00 20.00
AP04EN002 Maxx "C" UTR 75.00 150.00
AP04EN003 Necrovalley UTR 20.00 40.00
AP04EN004 Blackwing - Gale the Whirlwind SR1.00 2.00
AP04EN005 Blackwing - Kalut the Moon Shadow SR 1.00 2.00
AP04EN006 Consecrated Light SR .75 1.50
AP04EN007 Swift Scarecrow SR 1.50 3.00
AP04EN008 Crimson Blader SR 1.50 3.00
AP04EN009 Break! Draw! SR .20 .40
AP04EN010 Spellbook of Wisdom SR 2.00 4.00
AP04EN011 Spellbook of Eternity SR 1.25 2.50
AP04EN012 Fire Formation - Tensu SR 2.00 4.00
AP04EN013 Soul Drain SR 1.00 2.00
AP04EN014 Wings of Wicked Flame C .50 1.00
AP04EN015 Morphing Jar #2 C .20 .40
AP04EN016 Magical Merchant C .50 1.00
AP04EN017 Lonefire Blossom C .60 1.25
AP04EN018 Fossil Dyna Pachycephalo C 1.00 2.00
AP04EN019 Tytannial, Princess of Camellias C .15 .30
AP04EN020 Scrap Beast C .30 .75
AP04EN021 Ma'at C .10 .20
AP04EN022 Mavelus C 10.00 20.00
AP04EN023 Reasoning C .25 .50
AP04EN024 Archfiend's Oath C .20 .40
AP04EN025 Black Garden C 1.00 2.00
AP04EN026 Scrapstorm C .20 .40

2014 Yu-Gi-Oh Astral Pack 5

AP05EN001 Bujin Yamato UTR 7.50 15.00
AP05EN002 Gagaga Cowboy UTR 10.00 20.00
AP05EN003 Pot of Duality UTR 50.00 100.00
AP05EN004 Card Trooper SR .20 .40
AP05EN005 Jenis, Lightsworn Mender SR .50 1.00
AP05EN006 Geargiarsenal SR .30 .75
AP05EN007 Mermail Abysspike SR .75 1.50
AP05EN008 Star Drawing SR 1.00 2.00
AP05EN009 Bujingi Turtle SR .20 .40
AP05EN010 Advanced Ritual Art SR .75 1.50
AP05EN011 Charge of the Light Brigade SR 2.00 4.00
AP05EN012 Overworked SR .50 1.00
AP05EN013 Full House SR .75 1.50
AP05EN014 Blackland Fire Dragon C .30 .75
AP05EN015 Copy Plant C .15 .30
AP05EN016 Hanewata C .15 .30
AP05EN017 Rinyan, Lightsworn Rogue C .15 .30
AP05EN018 Skelgon C 1.50 3.00
AP05EN019 Queen of Thorns C 1.00 2.00
AP05EN020 Empress of Prophecy C .15 .30
AP05EN021 Soul Exchange C .15 .30
AP05EN022 Book of Moon C .50 1.00
AP05EN023 Lightsworn Sabre C .60 1.25
AP05EN024 Spiritual Forest C .15 .30
AP05EN025 Spellbook Library of the Heliosphere C.50 1.00
AP05EN026 Jurrac Impact C .15 .30

2014 Yu-Gi-Oh Astral Pack 6

AP06EN001 Tour Guide From the Underworld UTR25.00 50.00
AP06EN002 Number 11: Big Eye UTR 15.00 30.00
AP06EN003 Traptrix Trap Hole Nightmare UTR 7.50 15.00
AP06EN004 Traptrix Myrmeleo SR .75 1.50
AP06EN005 White Dragon Wyverburster SR .75 1.50
AP06EN006 Black Dragon Collapserpent SR .75 1.50
AP06EN007 Superheavy Samurai Big Benkei SR .50 1.00
AP06EN008 Shaddoll Beast SR 2.00 4.00
AP06EN009 Underworld Fighter Balmung SR .30 .75
AP06EN010 Number 80: Rhapsody in Berserk SR1.50 3.00
AP06EN011 Summoner's Art SR 5.00 10.00
AP06EN012 Bujincarnation SR .75 1.50
AP06EN013 Infernity Break SR .50 1.00
AP06EN014 Sea Kamen C .50 1.00
AP06EN015 Gruesome Goo C .60 1.25
AP06EN016 Amazon of the Seas C .50 1.00
AP06EN017 King of the Skull Servants C .50 1.00
AP06EN018 Vanity's Fiend C 2.50 5.00
AP06EN019 Van'Dalgyon the Dark Dragon Lord C.20 .40
AP06EN020 Machina Fortress C 1.00 2.00
AP06EN021 Man-eating Black Shark C 1.00 2.00
AP06EN022 Madolche Queen Tiaramisu C .50 1.00
AP06EN023 Nobleman of Crossout C .20 .40
AP06EN024 Thunder Crash C .20 .40
AP06EN025 The Monarchs Stormforth C .25 .50
AP06EN026 Ceasefire C .20 .40
AP06EN027 Royal Command C .20 .40
AP06EN028 Cursed Seal of the Forbidden Spell C.75 1.50

2014 Yu-Gi-Oh Battle Pack 2 War of the Giants Round 2

BPR2001 Evilswarm Heliotrope C .10 .20
BPR2002 Wall of Illusion SR .25 .50
BPR2003 Big Eye C .10 .20
BPR2004 Kazejin SR .25 .50
BPR2005 Otohime C .10 .20
BPR2006 Yomi Ship SR .25 .50
BPR2007 Winged Sage Falcos C .10 .20
BPR2008 Cyber Raider C .10 .20
BPR2009 Berserk Gorilla C .10 .20
BPR2010 Invader of Darkness C .10 .20
BPR2011 Legendary Jujitsu Master SR .25 .50
BPR2012 Blade Knight C .10 .20
BPR2013 Big-Tusked Mammoth SR .25 .50
BPR2014 Golem Sentry SR .25 .50
BPR2015 Adhesive Explosive SR .25 .50
BPR2016 Cyber Gymnast SR .25 .50
BPR2017 Cyber Prima (SR) .25 .50
BPR2019 Destiny HERO - Defender C .50 1.00
BPR2020 Archfiend of Gilfer SR .25 .50
BPR2021 Legendary Fiend SR .25 .50
BPR2022 Lyla, Lightsworn Sorceress SR 1.00 2.00
BPR2023 Montage Dragon C .75 1.50
BPR2024 Cursed Fig SR .25 .50
BPR2025 Red Ogre SR .25 .50
BPR2026 Blackwing - Elphin the Raven SR .25 .50
BPR2027 Sauropod Brachion C .10 .20
BPR2028 Worm Apocalypse C .10 .20
BPR2029 Worm Jetelikpse C .10 .20
BPR2030 Infernity Destroyer SR .25 .50
BPR2031 Medium of the Ice Barrier C .10 .20
BPR2032 A/D Changer C .10 .20
BPR2033 Playful Possum C .10 .20
BPR2034 Hypnocorn SR .25 .50
BPR2035 Wattlemur C .10 .20
BPR2036 Fabled Soulkius SR .25 .50
BPR2037 Power Breaker C .10 .20
BPR2038 Jurrac Gallim C .10 .20
BPR2039 General Raiho of the Ice Barrier SR .25 .50
BPR2040 Meklord Army of Granel SR .25 .50
BPR2041 Skull Kraken C .10 .20
BPR2042 Skystarray C .10 .20
BPR2043 Sergeant Electro SR .25 .50
BPR2044 Chow Len the Prophet SR .25 .50
BPR2045 White Night Queen C .10 .20
BPR2046 Junk Forward C .10 .20
BPR2047 Swallowtail Butterspy C .10 .20
BPR2048 Cameraclops SR .25 .50
BPR2049 Madolche Baaple SR .25 .50
BPR2050 Evilswarm Ketos SR .25 .50
BPR2051 Evilswarm Mandrago C .20 .40
BPR2052 Mogmole C .10 .20
BPR2053 Deep Sweeper C .10 .20
BPR2054 Heroic Challenger - Night Watchman C.10 .20
BPR2055 Garbage Lord C .10 .20
BPR2056 D.D. Esper Star Sparrow C .10 .20
BPR2057 Evilswarm Obliviwisp C .10 .20
BPR2058 Evilswarm Salamandra C .10 .20
BPR2059 Dododo Warrior SR .25 .50
BPR2060 Mecha Phantom Beast Tetherwolf C .10 .20
BPR2061 Mecha Phantom Beast Blackfalcon C .10 .20
BPR2062 Mecha Phantom Beast Stealthray SR .25 .50
BPR2063 Gentlemander C .10 .20
BPR2064 Schwarzschild Limit Dragon C .10 .20
BPR2065 Tribute to The Doomed SR .25 .50
BPR2066 Share the Pain SR .25 .50
BPR2067 Stim-Pack C .10 .20
BPR2068 Black Pendant C .10 .20
BPR2069 Megamorph SR .25 .50
BPR2070 Dark Core SR .50 1.00
BPR2071 Different Dimension Gate SR .25 .50
BPR2072 Back to Square One SR .25 .50
BPR2073 Mystic Box SR .25 .50
BPR2074 Lucky Iron Axe C .10 .20
BPR2075 Double Summon C 1.00 2.00
BPR2076 Ribbon of Rebirth C .10 .20
BPR2077 Release Restraint Wave SR .25 .50
BPR2078 Berserk Scales C .10 .20
BPR2079 Shift SR .25 .50
BPR2080 Riryoku Field C .10 .20
BPR2081 Needle Ceiling C .10 .20
BPR2082 Pineapple Blast C .10 .20
BPR2083 Adhesion Trap Hole SR .25 .50
BPR2084 Covering Fire C .10 .20
BPR2085 Conscription C .10 .20
BPR2086 Chthonian Blast C .10 .20
BPR2087 Dark Bribe SR 1.25 2.50
BPR2088 Nordic Relic Laevateinn SR .25 .50
BPR2089 Nordic Relic Brisingamen SR .25 .50
BPR2090 Attention! C .10 .20
BPR2091 Raigeki Bottle SR .25 .50
BPR2092 Nitwit Outwit C .10 .20
BPR2093 Butterflyoke SR .25 .50
BPR2094 Dimension Slice C .20 .40
BPR2095 Magical Explosion SR .25 .50
BPR2096 Memory Loss C .10 .20
BPR2097 Butterspy Protection C .10 .20
BPR2098 Reverse Glasses C .10 .20
BPR2099 Fog King UR 6.00 12.00
BPR2100 High Priestess of Prophecy UR 2.50 5.00
BPR2101 Dragunity Knight - Vajrayana UR 2.00 4.00
BPR2102 Number 11: Big Eye UR 2.50 5.00
BPR2103 Safe Zone UR 1.25 2.50

2014 Yu-Gi-Oh Battle Pack 3 Monster League

BP03EN001 Jerry Beans Man C .15 .30
BP03EN002 Bazoo the Soul-Eater C .15 .30
BP03EN003 Frontier Wiseman C .15 .30
BP03EN004 Arsenal Bug R .15 .30
BP03EN005 Breaker the Magical Warrior R .20 .40
BP03EN006 Mudora R .15 .30
BP03EN007 Gale Lizard C .15 .30
BP03EN008 Berserk Gorilla R .15 .30
BP03EN009 Lord Poison C .15 .30
BP03EN010 Sacred Crane C .15 .30
BP03EN011 Enraged Battle Ox C .15 .30
BP03EN012 Hyper Hammerhead C .15 .30
BP03EN013 Slate Warrior R .15 .30
BP03EN014 Toon Gemini Elf R .15 .30
BP03EN015 Chiron the Mage R .15 .30
BP03EN016 Gyroid C .15 .30
BP03EN017 Goblin Elite Attack Force R .15 .30
BP03EN018 Mythical Beast Cerberus C .15 .30
BP03EN019 Machine King Prototype R .15 .30
BP03EN020 Cyber Phoenix C .15 .30
BP03EN021 Victory Viper XX03 C .15 .30
BP03EN022 Herald of Green Light C .15 .30
BP03EN023 Herald of Purple Light C .15 .30
BP03EN024 Submarineroid C .15 .30
BP03EN025 Black Stego C .15 .30
BP03EN026 Card Trooper R .15 .30
BP03EN027 Freya, Spirit of Victory C .15 .30
BP03EN028 Exploder Dragon C .30 .75
BP03EN029 Dweller in the Depths C .15 .30
BP03EN030 Winged Rhynos R .15 .30
BP03EN031 Blizzard Dragon R .20 .40
BP03EN032 Evil HERO Infernal Gainer C .15 .30
BP03EN033 Ancient Gear Knight R .15 .30
BP03EN034 Royal Firestorm Guards R .25 .50
BP03EN035 Dark Crusader C .15 .30
BP03EN036 The Immortal Bushi C .15 .30
BP03EN037 Black Veloci R .15 .30
BP03EN038 Sea Koala C .15 .30
BP03EN039 Blue Thunder T-45 R .15 .30
BP03EN040 Golden Flying Fish R .15 .30
BP03EN041 Aztekipede, the Worm Warrior R .15 .30
BP03EN042 Jain, Lightsworn Paladin R .15 .30
BP03EN043 Diskblade Rider R .15 .30
BP03EN044 Magical Exemplar R .20 .40
BP03EN045 Rigorous Reaver C .15 .30
BP03EN046 Mezuki R .60 1.25
BP03EN047 Gonogo C .15 .30
BP03EN048 Telekinetic Shocker R .15 .30
BP03EN049 Destructotron C .15 .30
BP03EN050 Herald of Orange Light R .50 1.00
BP03EN051 Psychic Jumper C .15 .30
BP03EN052 Seed of Flame C .15 .30
BP03EN053 Cross-Sword Beetle R .60 1.25
BP03EN054 Defender, the Magical Knight C .15 .30
BP03EN055 Battlestorm R .15 .30
BP03EN056 Koa'ki Meiru Guardian R .15 .30
BP03EN057 Koa'ki Meiru Drago R .75 1.50
BP03EN058 Koa'ki Meiru Doom R .15 .30
BP03EN059 Spined Gillman R .15 .30
BP03EN060 Vanguard of the Dragon R .15 .30
BP03EN061 Koa'ki Meiru War Arms C .15 .30
BP03EN062 Tree Otter C .25 .50
BP03EN063 X-Saber Airbellum C .15 .30
BP03EN064 Sunlight Unicorn R .15 .30
BP03EN065 Card Guard R .15 .30
BP03EN066 Koa'ki Meiru Beetle R .15 .30
BP03EN067 Reptilianne Gorgon C .15 .30
BP03EN068 Metabo-Shark R .15 .30
BP03EN069 Shutendoji C .30 .75
BP03EN070 Gauntlet Warrior C .15 .30
BP03EN071 Shredder C .15 .30
BP03EN072 Koa'ki Meiru Sandman R .15 .30
BP03EN073 Jurrac Protops C .15 .30
BP03EN074 Mist Valley Falcon R .15 .30
BP03EN075 Trident Warrior R .15 .30
BP03EN076 Rhinotaurus R .15 .30
BP03EN077 Hypnocorn C .15 .30
BP03EN078 Stygian Street Patrol C .50 1.00
BP03EN079 Fabled Ashenveil C .15 .30
BP03EN080 Chain Dog C .15 .30
BP03EN081 Koa'ki Meiru Wall R .15 .30
BP03EN082 Genex Ally Bellflame R .15 .30
BP03EN083 Meklord Army of Granel C .15 .30
BP03EN084 Silent Psychic Wizard R .15 .30
BP03EN085 Dodger Dragon R .50 1.00
BP03EN086 Wind-Up Juggler R .15 .30
BP03EN087 Airorca C .15 .30
BP03EN088 Time Escaper C .15 .30
BP03EN089 Lion Alligator R .15 .30
BP03EN090 Friller Rabca C .15 .30
BP03EN091 Vylon Ohm C .15 .30
BP03EN092 Shocktopus C .15 .30
BP03EN093 Chow Len the Prophet R .15 .30
BP03EN094 Vampire Koala R .15 .30
BP03EN095 Flame Tiger R .15 .30
BP03EN096 Tardy Orc R .15 .30
BP03EN097 Madolche Baaple C .15 .30
BP03EN098 Evilswarm Ketos R .15 .30
BP03EN099 Evilswarm O'lantern C .15 .30
BP03EN100 Electromagnetic Bagworm C .15 .30
BP03EN101 Uminotaurus C .15 .30
BP03EN102 Leotaur R .15 .30
BP03EN103 Aye-Iron R .15 .30
BP03EN104 Evilswarm Thunderbird C .30 .75
BP03EN105 Magical Undertaker C .15 .30
BP03EN106 Gentlemander C .15 .30
BP03EN107 Fencing Fire Ferret R .15 .30
BP03EN108 Skelesaurus R .15 .30
BP03EN109 Knight Day Grepher R .15 .30
BP03EN110 Gorgonic Golem C .15 .30
BP03EN111 Ghostrick Jackfrost C .15 .30
BP03EN112 Black Brachios R .15 .30
BP03EN113 Tackle Crusader C .15 .30
BP03EN114 Stegocyber C .15 .30
BP03EN115 Master Craftsman Gamil C .15 .30
BP03EN133 Swords of Revealing Light C .15 .30
BP03EN134 Rush Recklessly C .15 .30
BP03EN135 7 Completed C .15 .30
BP03EN136 Premature Burial C .15 .30
BP03EN137 Mask of Brutality C .15 .30
BP03EN138 Offerings to the Doomed C .15 .30
BP03EN139 Scapegoat C .30 .75
BP03EN140 The Warrior Returning Alive C .15 .30
BP03EN141 Dragon's Gunfire C .15 .30
BP03EN142 Stamping Destruction C .15 .30
BP03EN143 Fusion Sword Murasame Blade C .15 .30
BP03EN144 Creature Swap C .15 .30
BP03EN145 Book of Life C .25 .50
BP03EN146 Call of the Mummy C .15 .30
BP03EN147 Banner of Courage C .15 .30
BP03EN148 Cestus of Dagla C .15 .30
BP03EN149 Enemy Controller C .15 .30
BP03EN150 Earthquake C .15 .30
BP03EN151 Swords of Concealing Light C 4.00 8.00
BP03EN152 Magicians Unite C .15 .30
BP03EN153 Ribbon of Rebirth C .15 .30
BP03EN154 Valhalla, Hall of the Fallen C 2.00 4.00
BP03EN155 Fighting Spirit C .15 .30
BP03EN156 Psi-Station C .15 .30
BP03EN157 Unstable Evolution C .15 .30
BP03EN158 Recycling Batteries C .20 .40
BP03EN159 Book of Eclipse C .60 1.25
BP03EN160 Mark of the Rose C .30 .75
BP03EN161 Psychokinesis C .15 .30
BP03EN162 Miracle Fertilizer C .75 1.50
BP03EN163 Psychic Sword C .15 .30
BP03EN164 Forbidden Chalice C .30 .75
BP03EN165 Raging Mad Plants C .15 .30
BP03EN166 Reptilianne Rage C .15 .30
BP03EN167 Machine Assembly Line C .15 .30
BP03EN168 Pyramid of Wonders C .15 .30
BP03EN169 Cursed Armaments C .15 .30
BP03EN170 Wattjustment C .15 .30
BP03EN171 Closed Forest C .15 .30
BP03EN172 Forbidden Lance C 1.00 2.00
BP03EN173 Wonder Wand C .30 .75
BP03EN174 Murmur of the Forest C .15 .30
BP03EN175 Bound Wand C .15 .30
BP03EN176 Night Beam C .30 .75
BP03EN177 Spellbook of Wisdom C .50 1.00
BP03EN178 Call of the Atlanteans C .15 .30
BP03EN179 One-Shot Wand C .15 .30
BP03EN180 Forbidden Dress C .15 .30
BP03EN181 Noble Arms - Arfeudutyr C .15 .30
BP03EN182 Noble Arms - Caliburn C .15 .30
BP03EN183 Ayers Rock Sunrise C .15 .30
BP03EN184 Forbidden Scripture C .15 .30
BP03EN185 Card Advance C 5.00 10.00
BP03EN186 Bashing Shield C .20 .40
BP03EN187 Call of the Haunted C .15 .30
BP03EN188 Mirror Wall C .15 .30
BP03EN189 Metalmorph C .15 .30
BP03EN190 Mask of Weakness C .15 .30
BP03EN191 Bark of Dark Ruler C .15 .30
BP03EN192 Ready for Intercepting C .15 .30
BP03EN193 Burst Breath C .15 .30
BP03EN194 Blast with Chain C .15 .30
BP03EN195 Tutan Mask C .15 .30
BP03EN196 Windstorm of Etaqua C .15 .30
BP03EN197 Zero Gravity C .15 .30
BP03EN198 Shadow Spell C .15 .30
BP03EN199 Curse of Anubis C .15 .30
BP03EN200 Rare Metalmorph C .15 .30
BP03EN201 Magical Arm Shield C .15 .30
BP03EN202 Dark Bribe C 1.00 2.00
BP03EN203 Chaos Burst C .15 .30
BP03EN204 No Entry!! C .15 .30
BP03EN205 Hate Buster C .15 .30
BP03EN206 Miniaturize C .15 .30
BP03EN207 Psychic Overload C .15 .30
BP03EN208 Telepathic Power C .15 .30
BP03EN209 Mind Over Matter C .20 .40
BP03EN210 Kunai with Chain C .15 .30
BP03EN211 Pollinosis C .15 .30
BP03EN212 Plant Food Chain C .15 .30
BP03EN213 Miracle Locus C .15 .30
BP03EN214 Skill Successor C .15 .30
BP03EN215 Alien Brain C .15 .30
BP03EN216 Forgotten Temple of the Deep C .15 .30
BP03EN217 Psi-Curse C .15 .30
BP03EN218 Damage Gate C .15 .30
BP03EN219 Super Rush Recklessly C .15 .30
BP03EN220 Miracle's Wake C .15 .30
BP03EN221 Nordic Relic Laevateinn C .15 .30
BP03EN222 Psychic Reactor C .15 .30
BP03EN223 Poseidon Wave C .15 .30
BP03EN224 Raigeki Bottle C .15 .30
BP03EN225 Butterflyoke C .15 .30
BP03EN226 Dimension Gate C .15 .30
BP03EN227 Breakthrough Skill C 1.00 2.00
BP03EN228 Pinpoint Guard C .25 .50
BP03EN229 Memory Loss C .15 .30
BP03EN230 Butterspy Protection C .15 .30
BP03EN231 Intrigue Shield C .15 .30
BP03EN232 Inspiration C .15 .30
BP03EN233 Ghosts From the Past C .15 .30
BP03EN234 Unbreakable Spirit C .15 .30
BP03EN235 Typhoon C .75 1.50
BP03EN236 Swamp Mirrorer C .25 .50
BP03EN237 Quantum Cat C .50 1.00

2014 Yu-Gi-Oh Dragons of Legend 1st Edition

DRLGEN001 Legendary Knight Timaeus SCR 4.00 8.00
DRLGEN002 Kuribandit SCR .75 1.50
DRLGEN003 Amulet Dragon SCR 6.00 12.00
DRLGEN004 Dark Magician Girl the Dragon Knight SCR 10.00 20.00
DRLGEN005 The Eye of Timaeus SCR 10.00 20.00
DRLGEN006 Legend of Heart SCR 1.50 3.00
DRLGEN007 Berserker Soul SCR .20 .40
DRLGEN008 Relay Soul SR .25 .50
DRLGEN009 Guardian Eatos SR .25 .50
DRLGEN010 Guardian Dreadscythe SCR 1.00 2.00
DRLGEN011 Celestial Sword Eatos SR .25 .50
DRLGEN012 Reaper Scythe Dreadscythe SR .25 .50
DRLGEN013 Guarded Treasure SCR .50 1.00
DRLGEN014 Soul Charge SR 2.00 4.00
DRLGEN015 Sabatiel The Philosopher's Stone SR.25 .50
DRLGEN016 Flash Fusion SR .25 .50
DRLGEN017 Battle Fusion SR .25 .50
DRLGEN018 Final Fusion SR .25 .50
DRLGEN019 Pair Cycroid SR .25 .50
DRLGEN020 Ayers Rock Sunrise SR .25 .50
DRLGEN021 Doble Passe SCR .60 1.25
DRLGEN022 Carboneddon SR .25 .50
DRLGEN023 Mathematician SCR 1.00 2.00
DRLGEN024 Ra's Disciple SCR 2.00 4.00
DRLGEN025 Mound of the Bound Creator SCR 1.00 2.00
DRLGEN026 Shooting Star SCR .20 .40
DRLGEN027 Blackwing Oroshi the Squall SR .25 .50
DRLGEN028 Blackwing Steam the Cloak SR .25 .50
DRLGEN029 Blackwing Hurricane the Tornado SR.25 .50
DRLGEN030 Black Sonic SCR 4.00 8.00
DRLGEN031 Black Wing Revenge SR .25 .50
DRLGEN032 Shadow Impulse SR .25 .50
DRLGEN033 Assault Dog SR .25 .50
DRLGEN034 Gate Blocker SCR .10 .20
DRLGEN035 Wiretap SR .25 .50
DRLGEN036 Lionhearted Locomotive SR .25 .50
DRLGEN037 Express Train Trolley Olley SCR .20 .40
DRLGEN038 Construction Train Signal Red SR .25 .50
DRLGEN039 Train Connection SR .25 .50
DRLGEN040 Abyss Splash SR .25 .50
DRLGEN041 Abyss Supra Splash SR .25 .50
DRLGEN042 Rank Up Magic Quick Chaos SCR 1.00 2.00
DRLGEN043 Chaos Chimera Dragon SR .25 .50
DRLGEN044 Rank Up Magic

Admiration of the 1000s SCR .20 .40
DRLGEN045 Magic Hand SR .25 .50
DRLGEN046 Fire Hand SCR .75 1.50
DRLGEN047 Ice Hand SCR .75 1.50
DRLGEN048 Prominence Hand SR .25 .50
DRLGEN049 Giant Red Hand SR .25 .50
DRLGEN050 Lillybot SR .25 .50
DRLGEN051 Rising Sun Slash SR .25 .50

2014 Yu-Gi-Oh Duelist Alliance 1st Edition

DUEAEN000 Dragon Horn Hunter SR .60 1.25
DUEAEN001 Flash Knight R .30 .75
DUEAEN002 Foucault's Cannon SR .30 .75
DUEAEN003 Metaphys Armed Dragon C .10 .20
DUEAEN004 Odd-Eyes Pendulum Dragon SCR 5.00 10.00
DUEAEN004u Odd-Eyes Pendulum Dragon UTR7.50 15.00
DUEAEN005 Performapal Skeeter Skimmer C .10 .20
DUEAEN006 Performapal Whip Snake R .30 .75
DUEAEN007 Performapal Sword Fish C .10 .20
DUEAEN008 Performapal Hip Hippo C .10 .20
DUEAEN009 Performapal Kaleidoscorp R .30 .75
DUEAEN010 Performapal Turn Toad R .30 .75
DUEAEN011 Superheavy Samurai Blue Brawler C.10 .20
DUEAEN012 Superheavy Samurai Swordsman C .10 .20
DUEAEN013 Superheavy Samurai Big Benkei R .30 .75
DUEAEN014 Aria the Melodious Diva C .10 .20
DUEAEN015 Sonata the Melodious Diva C .10 .20
DUEAEN016 Mozarta the Melodious Maestra R .30 .75
DUEAEN017 Battleguard King C .10 .20
DUEAEN018 Satellarknight Deneb UR 3.00 6.00
DUEAEN019 Satellarknight Altair R .30 .75
DUEAEN020 Satellarknight Vega C .10 .20
DUEAEN021 Satellarknight Alsahm SR 1.25 2.50
DUEAEN022 Satellarknight Unukalhai C .10 .20
DUEAEN023 Shaddoll Falco R .30 .75
DUEAEN024 Shaddoll Hedgehog C .10 .20
DUEAEN025 Shaddoll Squamata C .10 .20
DUEAEN026 Shaddoll Dragon R .30 .75
DUEAEN027 Shaddoll Beast R .30 .75
DUEAEN028 Suanni, Fire of the Yang Zing SR 4.00 8.00
DUEAEN029 Bi'an, Earth of the Yang Zing SR 1.50 3.00
DUEAEN030 Bixi, Water of the Yang Zing SR .60 1.25
DUEAEN031 Pulao, Wind of the Yang Zing SR .20 .40
DUEAEN032 Chiwen, Light of the Yang Zing UR7.50 15.00
DUEAEN033 Artifact Chakram C .10 .20
DUEAEN034 Artifact Lancea C .10 .20
DUEAEN035 Nefarious Archfiend Eater... C .10 .20
DUEAEN036 The Agent of Entropy - Uranus C .10 .20
DUEAEN037 Djinn Demolisher of Rituals C .10 .20
DUEAEN038 Batteryman 9-Volt C .10 .20
DUEAEN039 Resonance Insect C .10 .20
DUEAEN040 Breaker the Dark Magical Warrior C .10 .20
DUEAEN041 Raiza the Mega Monarch SCR .75 1.50
DUEAEN042 Dogu C .10 .20
DUEAEN043 Hypnosister SR .30 .75
DUEAEN044 Re-Cover C .10 .20
DUEAEN045 Deskbot 001 C .10 .20
DUEAEN046 Spy-C-Spy C .10 .20
DUEAEN047 Wightprince C .10 .20
DUEAEN048 El Shaddoll Winda UR 3.00 6.00
DUEAEN049 El Shaddoll Construct UR 2.50 5.00
DUEAEN049u El Shaddoll Construct UTR 15.00 30.00
DUEAEN050 Saffira, Queen of Dragons UTR 2.50 5.00
DUEAEN050 Saffira, Queen of Dragons UR 1.50 3.00
DUEAEN051 Baxia, Brightness of the Yang Zing SCR 1.25 2.50
DUEAEN051u Baxia, Brightness of the Yang Zing UTR 3.00 6.00
DUEAEN052 Samsara, Dragon of Rebirth SR 1.00 2.00
DUEAEN053 Stellarknight Delteros SCR 1.00 2.00
DUEAEN053g Stellarknight Delteros GR 6.00 12.00
DUEAEN053u Stellarknight Delteros UTR 1.50 3.00
DUEAEN054 Castel, the Skyblaster Musketeer SR2.00 4.00
DUEAEN055 Hippo Carnival C .10 .20
DUEAEN056 Feast of the Wild LV5 C .10 .20
DUEAEN057 Stellarknight Alpha C .10 .20
DUEAEN058 Satellarknight Skybridge R .30 .75
DUEAEN059 Shaddoll Fusion SR 5.00 10.00
DUEAEN060 Curse of the Shadow Prison C .10 .20
DUEAEN061 Yang Zing Path SCR 2.00 4.00
DUEAEN062 Yang Zing Prana C .10 .20
DUEAEN063 Hymn of Light C .10 .20
DUEAEN064 Dracocension C .10 .20
DUEAEN065 Magical Spring SCR .75 1.50
DUEAEN066 The Monarchs Stormforth C .10 .20
DUEAEN067 Pop-Up C .10 .20
DUEAEN068 Battleguard Rage C .10 .20
DUEAEN069 Battleguard Howling C .10 .20
DUEAEN070 Stellarnova Wave C .10 .20
DUEAEN071 Stellarnova Alpha UR 1.50 3.00
DUEAEN072 Sinister Shadow Games UR .75 1.50
DUEAEN073 Shaddoll Core SR .60 1.25
DUEAEN074 Yang Zing Creation UR .60 1.25
DUEAEN075 Yang Zing Unleashed C .10 .20
DUEAEN076 Chain Dispel C .10 .20
DUEAEN077 Face-Off R .30 .75
DUEAEN078 Pendulum Back SR .30 .75
DUEAEN079 Time-Space Trap Hole SCR 1.00 2.00
DUEAEN080 That Six C .10 .20
DUEAEN081 Doomstar Magician UR .50 1.00
DUEAEN082 Scarm... R .30 .75
DUEAEN083 Graff... R .30 .75
DUEAEN084 Cir... R .30 .75
DUEAEN085 Dante... SCR 4.00 8.00
DUEAEN086 Traveler and Burning Abyss SR .30 .75
DUEAEN087 U.A. Mighty Slugger R .30 .75
DUEAEN088 U.A. Perfect Ace R .30 .75
DUEAEN089 U.A. Stadium C .10 .20
DUEAEN090 Gaia, the Polar Knight C .10 .20
DUEAEN091 Gaia, the Mid-Knight Sun C .10 .20
DUEAEN092 Chaos Seed C .10 .20
DUEAEN093 Exchange of Night and Day C .10 .20
DUEAEN094 Number 58: Burner Visor C .10 .20
DUEAEN095 Felis, Lightsworn Archer UR 3.00 6.00
DUEAEN096 Fishborg Doctor C .10 .20
DUEAEN097 Panzer Dragon R .30 .75
DUEAEN098 Cloudcastle C .10 .20
DUEAEN099 Pilgrim Reaper C .10 .20

2014 Yu-Gi-Oh Legacy of the Valiant 1st Edition

LVAL000 Sylvan Bladefender SR .15 .30
LVAL001 White Duston SP .10 .20
LVAL002 ZW - Asura Strike R .10 .20
LVAL003 Gillagillancer C .15 .30
LVAL004 Rainbow Kuriboh SCR 1.25 2.50
LVAL005 Overlay Sentinel C .15 .30
LVAL006 Overlay Booster C .15 .30
LVAL007 Photon Chargeman C .15 .30
LVAL008 Chronomaly Moai Carrier C .15 .30
LVAL009 Chronomaly Winged Sphinx C .15 .30
LVAL010 Deep-Space Cruiser IX C .15 .30
LVAL011 Gorgonic Golem C .15 .30
LVAL012 Gorgonic Gargoyle C .15 .30
LVAL013 Gorgonic Ghoul C .15 .30
LVAL014 Gorgonic Cerberus C .15 .30
LVAL015 Sylvan Peaskeeper R .10 .20
LVAL016 Sylvan Komushroomo R .20 .40
LVAL017 Sylvan Marshalleaf UR .50 1.00
LVAL018 Sylvan Flowerknight SR .25 .50
LVAL019 Sylvan Guardioak C .15 .30
LVAL020 Sylvan Hermitree UR 1.25 2.50
LVAL021 Ghostrick Jackfrost C .15 .30
LVAL022 Ghostrick Mary SR 4.00 8.00
LVAL023 Ghostrick Nekomusume C .15 .30
LVAL024 Ghostrick Skeleton C .15 .30
LVAL025 Ghostrick Mummy C .15 .30
LVAL026 Bujin Arasuda UR .50 1.00
LVAL027 Bujingi Peacock R .10 .20
LVAL028 Bujingi Swallow C .15 .30
LVAL029 Bujingi Fox R .10 .20
LVAL030 Bujingi Hare SR 1.00 2.00
LVAL031 Gravekeeper's Nobleman UR 2.50 5.00
LVAL032 Gravekeeper's Ambusher C .15 .30
LVAL033 Gravekeeper's Shaman SR .50 1.00
LVAL034 Gravekeeper's Oracle UR 1.00 2.00
LVAL035 Mystic Macrocarpa Seed C .15 .30
LVAL036 Kalantosa, Mystical Beast of the Forest C.15 .30
LVAL037 Nikitama R .20 .40
LVAL038 Black Brachios C .15 .30
LVAL039 Chirubimé, Princess of Autumn Leaves SR.30 .75
LVAL040 Mobius the Mega Monarch GR 4.00 8.00
LVAL040 Mobius the Mega Monarch SCR 1.25 2.50
LVAL041 Sirenorca C .15 .30
LVAL042 Xyz Avenger C .15 .30
LVAL043 Tackle Crusader C .15 .30
LVAL044 Majiosheldon SP .10 .20
LVAL045 Paladin of Photon Dragon R .10 .20
LVAL046 Number C101: Silent Honor DARK UR2.00 4.00
LVAL046 Number C101: Silent Honor DARK UTR2.00 4.00
LVAL047 Number 101: Silent Honor ARK UR 2.50 5.00
LVAL047 Number 101: Silent Honor ARK UTR 7.50 15.00
LVAL048 Number 39: Utopia Roots R .50 1.00
LVAL048 Number 39: Utopia Roots UTR 2.50 5.00
LVAL049 Number C69: Heraldry Crest of Horror R.30 .75
LVAL050 Number C92: Heart-eartH Chaos Dragon R.10 .20
LVAL051 Gorgonic Guardian C .15 .30
LVAL052 Alsei, the Sylvan High Protector UR 4.00 8.00
LVAL053 Ghostrick Dullahan R 2.50 5.00
LVAL054 Bujintei Tsukuyomi UR 7.50 15.00
LVAL054 Bujintei Tsukuyomi UTR 20.00 40.00
LVAL055 Fairy Knight Ingunar SR .30 .75
LVAL056 Evilswarm Exciton Knight SCR 10.00 20.00
LVAL057 Downerd Magician SCR 1.25 2.50
LVAL058 Leo, the Keeper of the Sacred Tree R .75 1.50
LVAL059 Rank-Up-Magic Astral Force UR .75 1.50
LVAL059 Rank-Up-Magic Astral Force UTR 4.00 8.00
LVAL060 Rank-Down-Magic Numeron Fall R .10 .20
LVAL061 Xyz Shift C .15 .30
LVAL062 Luminous Dragon Ritual C .15 .30
LVAL063 Mount Sylvania SR .30 .75
LVAL064 Ghostrick Museum C .15 .30
LVAL065 Bujinunity R .10 .20
LVAL066 Hidden Temples of Necrovalley R .10 .20
LVAL067 Onomatopaira R .60 1.25
LVAL068 Xyz Override C .15 .30
LVAL069 Stand-Off SP .10 .20
LVAL070 Shared Ride SCR .60 1.25
LVAL071 Release, Reverse, Burst C .15 .30
LVAL072 Purge Ray C .15 .30
LVAL073 Sylvan Blessing C .15 .30
LVAL074 Ghostrick-Go-Round R .75 1.50
LVAL075 Bujin Regalia - The Jewel C .15 .30
LVAL076 Imperial Tombs of Necrovalley SCR 2.00 4.00
LVAL077 The Monarchs Awaken C .15 .30
LVAL078 Skill Prisoner SR .30 .75
LVAL079 Oath of Companionship R .10 .20
LVAL080 Duston Roller SP .10 .20
LVAL081 Sylvan Mikorange R .10 .20
LVAL082 Ghostrick Yeti C .15 .30
LVAL083 Bujingi Pavo SR .20 .40
LVAL084 Gravekeeper's Heretic R .20 .40
LVAL085 Noble Knight Peredur SR .20 .40
LVAL086 Gwenhwyfar, Queen of Noble Arms SCR1.00 2.00
LVAL087 Powered Inzektron SR .50 1.00
LVAL088 Obedience Schooled SR .60 1.25
LVAL089 The First Monarch SCR .60 1.25
LVAL090 Dark Artist C .15 .30
LVAL091 Swordsman from a Distant Land C .15 .30
LVAL092 Queen Angel of Roses SR .20 .40
LVAL093 Rose Witch C .15 .30
LVAL094 Snapdragon C .15 .30
LVAL095 Alpacaribou, Mystical Beast of the Forest C .15 .30
LVAL096 Mighty Warrior C .15 .30
LVAL097 Dododo Buster C .15 .30
LVAL098 Interplanetarypurplythorny Beast C .15 .30
LVAL099 Starship Spy Plane C .15 .30
LVALSP1 Sylvan Bladefender UR .60 1.25

2014 Yu-Gi-Oh Legendary Collection 5D's

LC05EN001 Jormungardr the Nordic Serpent UR .50 1.00
LC05EN002 Fenrir the Nordic Wolf UR .75 1.50
LC05EN003 Stardust Flash UR 1.50 3.00
LC05EN004 Black Rose Dragon UR 1.50 3.00
LC05EN005 Shooting Quasar Dragon UR 1.50 3.00
LC5DEN001 Sonic Chick C .10 .20
LC5DEN002 Junk Synchron SCR 1.25 2.50
LC5DEN003 Speed Warrior C .10 .20
LC5DEN004 Nitro Synchron C .10 .20
LC5DEN005 Quillbolt Hedgehog SCR .75 1.50
LC5DEN006 Turbo Synchron C .10 .20
LC5DEN007 Tuningware SCR 2.00 4.00
LC5DEN008 Turret Warrior R .25 .50
LC5DEN009 Debris Dragon SCR 2.50 5.00
LC5DEN010 Hyper Synchron C .10 .20
LC5DEN011 Road Synchron C .10 .20
LC5DEN012 Majestic Dragon C 2.00 4.00
LC5DEN013 Quickdraw Synchron UR 1.50 3.00
LC5DEN014 Level Eater R .25 .50
LC5DEN015 Drill Synchron SR .50 1.00
LC5DEN016 Shield Wing R .25 .50
LC5DEN017 Synchron Explorer UR 1.25 2.50
LC5DEN018 Effect Veiler C 4.00 8.00
LC5DEN019 Bri Synchron C .10 .20
LC5DEN020 Doppelwarrior SR 1.50 3.00
LC5DEN021 Junk Servant C .10 .20
LC5DEN022 Unknown Synchron SCR 1.25 2.50
LC5DEN023 Junk Defender C .10 .20
LC5DEN024 Junk Forward C .10 .20
LC5DEN025 Junk Blader C .10 .20
LC5DEN026 Mono Synchron R 1.25 2.50
LC5DEN027 Steam Synchron R 1.25 2.50
LC5DEN028 Dragon Knight Draco-Equiste R .25 .50
LC5DEN029 Junk Warrior SR .50 1.00
LC5DEN030 Colossal Fighter SCR .50 1.00
LC5DEN031 Stardust Dragon C 3.00 6.00
LC5DEN031u Stardust Dragon UR 1.25 2.50
LC5DEN032 Nitro Warrior C .10 .20
LC5DEN033 Turbo Warrior C .10 .20
LC5DEN034 Armory Arm SCR 3.00 6.00
LC5DEN035 Road Warrior C 1.25 2.50
LC5DEN036 Majestic Star Dragon SR .25 .50
LC5DEN037 Junk Archer SR .75 1.50
LC5DEN038 Drill Warrior SCR .50 1.00
LC5DEN039 Junk Destroyer SR .50 1.00
LC5DEN040 Shooting Star Dragon SR 2.50 5.00
LC5DEN041 Formula Synchron SCR 3.00 6.00
LC5DEN042 Lightning Warrior UR .60 1.25
LC5DEN043 Junk Berserker SR .50 1.00
LC5DEN044 Junk Barrage C .10 .20
LC5DEN045 One for One UR .60 1.25
LC5DEN046 Silver Wing C .10 .20
LC5DEN047 Advance Draw UR 1.25 2.50
LC5DEN048 Cards of Consonance UR .60 1.25
LC5DEN049 Tuning C .10 .20
LC5DEN050 Battle Waltz C .10 .20
LC5DEN051 Scrap-Iron Scarecrow UR 2.00 4.00
LC5DEN052 Graceful Revival C .10 .20
LC5DEN053 Urgent Tuning C .10 .20
LC5DEN054 Spirit Force C .10 .20
LC5DEN055 Descending Lost Star C .10 .20
LC5DEN056 Starlight Road UR .75 1.50
LC5DEN057 Dark Resonator C .10 .20
LC5DEN058 Trap Eater UR .50 1.00
LC5DEN059 Vice Dragon C .10 .20
LC5DEN060 Strong Wind Dragon R .75 1.50
LC5DEN061 Battle Fader SCR 1.50 3.00
LC5DEN062 Flare Resonator C .10 .20
LC5DEN063 Power Breaker R .25 .50
LC5DEN064 Extra Veiler C .10 .20
LC5DEN065 Creation Resonator C 2.00 4.00
LC5DEN066 Barrier Resonator C .10 .20
LC5DEN067 Force Resonator C .10 .20
LC5DEN068 Clock Resonator C .10 .20
LC5DEN069 Red Dragon Archfiend C .10 .20
LC5DEN069u Red Dragon Archfiend UR 2.00 4.00
LC5DEN070 Exploder Dragonwing R .50 1.00
LC5DEN071 Majestic Red Dragon SR .50 1.00
LC5DEN072 Chaos King Archfiend SR .50 1.00
LC5DEN073 Red Nova Dragon SR 1.25 2.50
LC5DEN074 Crimson Blader SCR 2.00 4.00
LC5DEN075 Resonator Engine C .10 .20
LC5DEN076 Scarlet Security SR .50 1.00
LC5DEN077 Red Dragon Vase R .25 .50
LC5DEN078 Resonator Call C .10 .20
LC5DEN079 Resonant Destruction C .10 .20
LC5DEN080 Crimson Fire R .25 .50
LC5DEN081 Changing Destiny C .10 .20
LC5DEN082 Fiendish Chain SCR 5.00 10.00
LC5DEN083 Red Screen C .10 .20
LC5DEN084 Red Carpet C .10 .20
LC5DEN085 Twilight Rose Knight C 1.00 2.00
LC5DEN086 Violet Witch R .25 .50
LC5DEN087 Dark Verger C .10 .20
LC5DEN088 Rose Tentacles R .25 .50
LC5DEN089 Hedge Guard UR .75 1.50
LC5DEN090 Evil Thorn C .10 .20
LC5DEN091 Rose Fairy C .10 .20
LC5DEN092 Glow-Up Bulb SCR 5.00 10.00
LC5DEN093 Blue Rose Dragon SR .50 1.00
LC5DEN094 Fallen Angel of Roses UR .60 1.25
LC5DEN095 Rosaria, the Stately Fallen Angel UR.60 1.25
LC5DEN096 Queen Angel of Roses UR .60 1.25
LC5DEN097 Rose Witch C .10 .20
LC5DEN098 Rose Archer SR .50 1.00
LC5DEN099 Black Rose Dragon C 1.00 2.00
LC5DEN100 Splendid Rose R .25 .50
LC5DEN101 Black Garden SCR .75 1.50
LC5DEN102 Fragrance Storm UR .50 1.00
LC5DEN103 Thorn of Malice C .10 .20
LC5DEN104 Magic Planter UR 4.00 8.00
LC5DEN105 Ivy Shackles C .10 .20
LC5DEN106 Overdoom Line C .10 .20
LC5DEN107 Wicked Rebirth C .10 .20
LC5DEN108 Blossom Bombardment C .10 .20
LC5DEN109 Star Siphon C .10 .20
LC5DEN110 Blackwing - Gale the Whirlwind UR .50 1.00
LC5DEN111 Blackwing - Bora the Spear UR 1.25 2.50
LC5DEN112 Blackwing - Sirocco the Dawn UR .50 1.00
LC5DEN113 Blackwing - Blizzard the Far North UR.75 1.50
LC5DEN114 Blackwing - Shura the Blue Flame UR.50 1.00
LC5DEN115 Blackwing - Kalut the Moon Shadow UR .50 1.00
LC5DEN116 Blackwing - Elphin the Raven C .10 .20
LC5DEN117 Blackwing - Mistral the Silver Shield C.10 .20
LC5DEN118 Blackwing - Vayu the Emblem of Honor SCR .50 1.00
LC5DEN119 Blackwing - Fane the Steel Chain C .10 .20
LC5DEN120 Blackwing - Ghibli the Searing Wind C.10 .20
LC5DEN121 Blackwing - Gust the Backblast C .10 .20
LC5DEN122 Blackwing - Breeze the Zephyr C .10 .20
LC5DEN123 Blackwing - Etesian of Two Swords C.10 .20
LC5DEN124 Blackwing - Aurora the Northern Lights C .10 .20
LC5DEN125 Blackwing - Abrolhos the Megaquake C .10 .20
LC5DEN126 Blackwing - Boreas the Sharp C .10 .20
LC5DEN127 Blackwing - Brisote the Tailwind C .10 .20
LC5DEN128 Blackwing - Calima the Haze C .10 .20
LC5DEN129 Blackwing - Kogarashi the Wanderer C.10 .20
LC5DEN130 Blackwing - Kochi the Daybreak C .10 .20
LC5DEN131 Blackwing - Gladius the Midnight Sun UR .75 1.50
LC5DEN132 Blackwing Armor Master SCR .50 1.00
LC5DEN133 Blackwing Armed Wing UR .50 1.00
LC5DEN134 Blackwing - Silverwind the Ascendant SR .50 1.00
LC5DEN135 Black-Winged Dragon C 2.00 4.00
LC5DEN135u Black-Winged Dragon UR .50 1.00
LC5DEN136 De-Synchro SR 1.25 2.50
LC5DEN137 Raptor Wing Strike C .10 .20
LC5DEN138 Black Whirlwind UR 2.50 5.00
LC5DEN139 Cards for Black Feathers R .25 .50
LC5DEN140 Delta Crow - Anti Reverse SCR 1.50 3.00
LC5DEN141 Trap Stun SCR 2.50 5.00
LC5DEN142 Blackwing - Backlash C .10 .20
LC5DEN143 Blackback C .10 .20
LC5DEN144 Blackboost C .10 .20
LC5DEN145 Black Return C .10 .20
LC5DEN146 Earthbound Immortal Aslla Piscu SR.50 1.00
LC5DEN147 Earthbound Immortal Ccapac Apu SR.50 1.00
LC5DEN148 Earthbound Immortal Cusillu SR .50 1.00
LC5DEN149 E.I. Chacu Challhua SR .50 1.00
LC5DEN150 E.I. Wiraqocha Rasca SR .50 1.00
LC5DEN151 Earthbound Immortal Ccarayhua SR .50 1.00
LC5DEN152 Earthbound Immortal Uru SR .50 1.00
LC5DEN153 Earthbound Immortal Linewalker SR .50 1.00
LC5DEN154 Hundred Eyes Dragon SR .50 1.00
LC5DEN155 Earthbound Whirlwind R .25 .50
LC5DEN156 Earthbound Revival C .10 .20
LC5DEN157 Revival of the Immortals C .10 .20
LC5DEN158 Earthbound Wave R .25 .50
LC5DEN159 Roar of the Earthbound C .10 .20
LC5DEN160 Offering to the Immortals C .10 .20
LC5DEN161 Meklord Astro Mekanikle SCR .75 1.50
LC5DEN162 Meklord Emperor Granel SR .50 1.00
LC5DEN163 Meklord Army of Wisel R .25 .50
LC5DEN164 Meklord Army of Skiel R .25 .50
LC5DEN165 Meklord Army of Granel C .10 .20
LC5DEN166 Meklord Astro Dragon Asterisk SCR.50 1.00
LC5DEN167 Meklord Emperor Skiel SR 2.00 4.00
LC5DEN168 Meklord Emperor Wisel SR .50 1.00
LC5DEN169 Fortissimo the Mobile Fortress C .10 .20
LC5DEN170 Boon of the Meklord Emperor C .10 .20
LC5DEN171 The Resolute Meklord Army C .10 .20
LC5DEN172 Reboot C .10 .20
LC5DEN173 Meklord Fortress SR .50 1.00
LC5DEN174 Chaos Infinity SR .60 1.25
LC5DEN175 Mektimed Blast C .10 .20
LC5DEN176 Meklord Factory SR .50 1.00
LC5DEN177 Tanngrisnir of the Nordic Beasts SCR.50 1.00
LC5DEN178 Guldfaxe of the Nordic Beasts SCR .50 1.00
LC5DEN179 Garmr of the Nordic Beasts C .10 .20
LC5DEN180 Tanngnjostr of the Nordic Beasts SCR1.50 3.00
LC5DEN181 Ljosalf of the Nordic Alfar C .10 .20
LC5DEN182 Svartalf of the Nordic Alfar UR 3.00 6.00
LC5DEN183 Dverg of the Nordic Alfar SCR .50 1.00
LC5DEN184 Valkyrie of the Nordic Ascendant SCR.75 1.50
LC5DEN185 Mimir of the Nordic Ascendant C .10 .20
LC5DEN186 Tyr of the Nordic Champions C .10 .20
LC5DEN187 Vanadis of the Nordic Ascendant UR1.25 2.50
LC5DEN188 Mara of the Nordic Alfar C .10 .20
LC5DEN189 Thor, Lord of the Aesir SCR .75 1.50
LC5DEN190 Loki, Lord of the Aesir SCR .50 1.00
LC5DEN191 Odin, Father of the Aesir SCR .50 1.00
LC5DEN192 Nordic Relic Draupnir R .25 .50
LC5DEN193 Gotterdammerung C .10 .20
LC5DEN194 March Towards Ragnarok C .10 .20
LC5DEN195 The Nordic Lights C .10 .20
LC5DEN196 Divine Relic Mjollnir R .25 .50
LC5DEN197 Solemn Authority C .10 .20
LC5DEN198 Nordic Relic Brisingamen R .25 .50
LC5DEN199 Nordic Relic Laevateinn R .25 .50
LC5DEN200 Nordic Relic Gungnir UR .50 1.00
LC5DEN201 The Golden Apples R .25 .50
LC5DEN202 Odin's Eye C .10 .20
LC5DEN203 Gleipnir, the Fetters of Fenrir SCR .75 1.50
LC5DEN204 Nordic Relic Megingjord R .25 .50
LC5DEN205 T.G. Cyber Magician SCR 2.00 4.00
LC5DEN206 T.G. Striker UR 1.25 2.50
LC5DEN207 T.G. Jet Falcon C .10 .20
LC5DEN208 T.G. Catapult Dragon C .10 .20
LC5DEN209 T.G. Warwolf SCR 1.25 2.50
LC5DEN210 T.G. Rush Rhino UR .50 1.00
LC5DEN211 T.G. Hyper Librarian SCR .50 1.00
LC5DEN212 T.G. Recipro Dragonfly C .10 .20
LC5DEN213 T.G. Wonder Magician SCR 5.00 10.00
LC5DEN214 T.G. Power Gladiator C .10 .20
LC5DEN215 T.G. Blade Blaster SR .50 1.00
LC5DEN216 T.G. Halberd Cannon SR .50 1.00
LC5DEN217 TGX1-HL UR .75 1.50
LC5DEN218 TGX300 C .10 .20
LC5DEN219 TGX3-DX2 UR .50 1.00
LC5DEN220 TG-SX1 C .10 .20
LC5DEN221 TG1-EM1 SCR .75 1.50
LC5DEN222 Black Salvo C .10 .20
LC5DEN223 Oracle of the Sun C .10 .20
LC5DEN224 Fire Ant Ascator R .25 .50
LC5DEN225 Supay R .25 .50
LC5DEN226 Super-Nimble Mega Hamster SCR .75 1.50
LC5DEN227 Maxx "C" UR 3.00 6.00
LC5DEN228 Metaion, the Timelord SR .75 1.50

LC5DEN229 Sephylon, the Ultimate Timelord SR	.50	1.00
LC5DEN230 Avenging Knight Parshath C	.10	.20
LC5DEN231 Goyo Guardian SR	4.00	8.00
LC5DEN232 Magical Android UR	.75	1.50
LC5DEN233 Thought Ruler Archfiend SCR	1.00	2.00
LC5DEN234 Dark Strike Fighter C	.10	.20
LC5DEN235 Hyper Psychic Blaster R	.25	.50
LC5DEN236 Power Tool Dragon C	.60	1.25
LC5DEN237 Trident Dragion SCR	1.25	2.50
LC5DEN238 Ancient Fairy Dragon C	1.25	2.50
LC5DEN238u Ancient Fairy Dragon UR	1.25	2.50
LC5DEN239 Ancient Sacred Wyvern SCR	2.00	4.00
LC5DEN240 Mist Wurm UR	2.00	4.00
LC5DEN241 Sun Dragon Inti C	.10	.20
LC5DEN242 Moon Dragon Quilla C	.10	.20
LC5DEN243 Stygian Sergeants SCR	.50	1.00
LC5DEN244 Naturia Beast UR	2.00	4.00
LC5DEN245 Naturia Barkion UR	2.50	5.00
LC5DEN246 Life Stream Dragon C	.50	1.00
LC5DEN247 Orient Dragon UR	.60	1.25
LC5DEN248 Driven Daredevil R	.25	.50
LC5DEN249 Vulcan the Divine SCR	3.00	6.00
LC5DEN250 Synchro Blast Wave C	.10	.20
LC5DEN251 Emergency Teleport SCR	10.00	20.00
LC5DEN252 Savage Colosseum C	.10	.20
LC5DEN253 Vanity's Emptiness SCR	15.00	30.00
LC5DEN254 Roaring Earth C	.10	.20
LC5DEN255 Debunk SCR	2.50	5.00
LC5DEN256 Full House SCR	.75	1.50

2014 Yu-Gi-Oh The New Challengers 1st Edition

NECHEN000 Lancephorhynchus SR	.15	.30
NECHEN001 Performapal Cheermole R	.10	.20
NECHEN002 Performapal Trampolynx R	.10	.20
NECHEN003 Block Spider C	.15	.30
NECHEN004 Canon the Melodious Diva C	.15	.30
NECHEN005 Serenade the Melodious Diva C	.15	.30
NECHEN006 Elegy the Melodious Diva C	.15	.30
NECHEN007 Shopina the Melodious Maestra R	.10	.20
NECHEN008 Superheavy Samurai Kabuto C	.15	.30
NECHEN009 Superheavy Samurai Scales R	.10	.20
NECHEN010 Superheavy Samurai Soulfire Suit C	.15	.30
NECHEN011 Superheavy Samurai Soulshield Wall C	.15	.30
NECHEN012 Superheavy Samurai Soulbreaker Armor C	.15	.30
NECHEN013 Superheavy Samurai Soulbang Cannon C	.15	.30
NECHEN014 Edge Imp Sabres SR	2.00	4.00
NECHEN015 Fluffal Leo C	.15	.30
NECHEN016 Fluffal Bear C	.15	.30
NECHEN017 Fluffal Dog R	.50	1.00
NECHEN018 Fluffal Owl R	.50	1.00
NECHEN019 Fluffal Cat C	.15	.30
NECHEN020 Fluffal Rabbit C	.15	.30
NECHEN021 Qliphort Scout UR	.50	1.00
NECHEN022 Qliphort Carrier SR	.50	1.00
NECHEN023 Qliphort Helix SR	1.25	2.50
NECHEN024 Qliphort Disk SCR	.75	1.50
NECHEN025 Qliphort Shell R	.10	.20
NECHEN026 Apoqliphort Towers R	.10	.20
NECHEN027 Satellarknight Sirius R	.10	.20
NECHEN028 Satellarknight Procyon C	.15	.30
NECHEN029 Satellarknight Betelgeuse C	.15	.30
NECHEN030 Shaddoll Hound C	.15	.30
NECHEN031 Taotie, Shadow of the Yang Zing SR	.15	.30
NECHEN032 Jiaotu, Darkness of the Yang Zing UR	6.00	12.00
NECHEN033 Lindbloom C	.15	.30
NECHEN034 Night Dragolich UR	.60	1.25
NECHEN035 Unmasked Dragon R	.10	.20
NECHEN036 Machina Megaform SR	.15	.30
NECHEN037 Zaborg the Mega Monarch UR	1.00	2.00
NECHEN038 Valerifawn, Mystical Beast of the Forest C	.15	.30
NECHEN039 Rescue Hamster SR	1.50	3.00
NECHEN040 Watch Dog C	.15	.30
NECHEN041 Denko Sekka UR	3.00	6.00
NECHEN042 Deskbot 002 C	.15	.30
NECHEN043 Ms. Judge NR	.10	.20
NECHEN044 Scrounging Goblin NR	.10	.20
NECHEN045 Herald of Ultimateness UR	.50	1.00
NECHEN046 Frightfur Bear R	.10	.20
NECHEN046u Frightfur Bear UTR	.75	1.50
NECHEN047 Frightfur Wolf R	.50	1.00
NECHEN048 El Shaddoll Grysta SCR	.75	1.50
NECHEN049 El Shaddoll Shekhinaga SCR	.75	1.50
NECHEN049u El Shaddoll Shekhinaga UTR	2.00	4.00
NECHEN050 First of the Dragons SR	1.00	2.00
NECHEN051 Yazi, Evil of the Yang Zing SCR	.75	1.50
NECHEN051u Yazi, Evil of the Yang Zing UTR	1.50	3.00
NECHEN052 Herald of the Arc Light SR	.75	1.50
NECHEN053 Dark Rebellion Xyz Dragon SCR	2.00	4.00
NECHEN053u Dark Rebellion Xyz Dragon UTR	3.00	6.00
NECHEN054 Stellarknight Triverr UR	.15	.30
NECHEN054u Stellarknight Triverr UTR	.60	1.25
NECHEN055 Wonder Balloons C	.15	.30
NECHEN056 Mimiclay C	.15	.30
NECHEN057 Draw Muscle R	.10	.20
NECHEN058 Magical Star Illusion C	.15	.30
NECHEN059 1st Movement Solo SR	.60	1.25
NECHEN060 Toy Vendor C	.15	.30
NECHEN061 Saqlifice UR	.20	.40
NECHEN062 Laser Qlip C	.15	.30
NECHEN063 Hexatellarknight C	.15	.30
NECHEN064 El Shaddoll Fusion SR	.50	1.00
NECHEN065 Celestia C	.15	.30
NECHEN066 Oracle of the Herald C	.15	.30
NECHEN067 Strike of the Monarchs C	.15	.30
NECHEN068 Cursed Bamboo Sword C	.15	.30
NECHEN069 Command Performance C	.15	.30
NECHEN070 Performapal Revival C	.15	.30
NECHEN071 Punch-in-the-Box C	.15	.30
NECHEN072 The Phantom Knights of Shadow Veil C	.15	.30
NECHEN073 Qlimate Change C	.15	.30
NECHEN074 Qlipper Launch C	.15	.30
NECHEN075 Yang Zing Brutality C	.15	.30
NECHEN076 Naturia Sacred Tree R	.10	.20
NECHEN077 Oasis of Dragon Souls R	.75	1.50
NECHEN078 Fusion Reserve UR	2.50	5.00
NECHEN079 Solemn Scolding SCR	3.00	6.00
NECHEN080 Different Dimension Encounter C	.15	.30
NECHEN081 Fusion Substitute C	.15	.30
NECHEN082 Rubic... UR	1.25	2.50
NECHEN083 Alich... R	.10	.20
NECHEN084 Calcab... R	.10	.20
NECHEN085 Virgil... SCR	.75	1.50
NECHEN086 Fire Lake of the Burning Abyss SR	.50	1.00
NECHEN087 U.A. Midfielder R	.50	1.00
NECHEN088 U.A. Goalkeeper R	.10	.20
NECHEN089 U.A. Powered Jersey C	.15	.30
NECHEN090 Ruffian Railcar C	.15	.30
NECHEN091 SZW - Fenrir Sword C	.15	.30
NECHEN092 Gogogo Goram C	.15	.30
NECHEN093 Dododo Driver C	.15	.30
NECHEN094 Xyz Change Tactics R	.10	.20
NECHEN095 Number 39: Utopia Beyond SR	1.25	2.50
NECHEN096 CXyz Barian Hope SR	.15	.30
NECHEN097 Shogi Lance C	.15	.30
NECHEN098 Guiding Light C	.15	.30
NECHEN099 Number 99: Utopic Dragon SCR	2.00	4.00
NECHENS01 Lancephorhynchus SR	.15	.30
NECHENS02 Edge Imp Sabres SR	2.00	4.00
NECHENS03 Qliphort Carrier SR	.50	1.00
NECHENS04 Qliphort Helix SR	1.25	2.50
NECHENS05 Taotie, Shadow of the Yang Zing SR	.15	.30
NECHENS06 Machina Megaform SR	.15	.30
NECHENS07 Rescue Hamster SR	1.50	3.00
NECHENS08 First of the Dragons SR	1.00	2.00
NECHENS09 Herald of the Arc Light SR	.75	1.50
NECHENS10 1st Movement Solo SR	.50	1.00
NECHENS11 El Shaddoll Fusion SR	.50	1.00
NECHENS12 Fire Lake of the Burning Abyss SR	.50	1.00
NECHENS13 Number 39: Utopia Beyond SR	1.25	2.50
NECHENS14 CXyz Barian Hope SR	.15	.30

2014 Yu-Gi-Oh Noble Knights of the Round Table Boxed Set

NKRTEN001 Merlin PR	.75	1.50
NKRTEN002 Noble Knight Bedwyr PR	.75	1.50
NKRTEN003 Noble Knight Artorigus PR	.40	.80
NKRTEN004 Noble Knight Gawayn PR	.75	1.50
NKRTEN005 Ignoble Knight of Black Laundsallyn PR	.30	.60
NKRTEN006 Noble Knight Medraut PR	1.00	2.00
NKRTEN007 Noble Knight Gwalchavad PR	.25	.50
NKRTEN008 Noble Knight Drystan PR	.30	.75
NKRTEN009 Noble Knight Borz PR	.30	.60
NKRTEN010 Noble Knight Peredur PR	.30	.60
NKRTEN011 Noble Knight Eachtar PR	.20	.40
NKRTEN012 Gwenhwyfar, Queen of Noble Arms PR	1.25	2.50
NKRTEN013 Lady of the Lake PR	1.00	2.00
NKRTEN014 Honest PR	1.25	2.50
NKRTEN015 Knight Day Grepher PR	.20	.40
NKRTEN016 Dawn Knight PR	.30	.60
NKRTEN017 Last Chapter of the Noble Knights PR	1.00	2.00
NKRTEN018 Noble Knights of the Round Table PR	.15	.30
NKRTEN019 Noble Arms - Gallatin PR	.20	.40
NKRTEN020 Noble Arms - Arfeudutyr PR	.40	.80
NKRTEN021 Noble Arms - Caliburn PR	.25	.50
NKRTEN022 Noble Arms of Destiny PR	.30	.75
NKRTEN023 Noble Arms - Excaliburn PR	1.25	2.50
NKRTEN024 Dark Hole PR	2.50	5.00
NKRTEN025 Swords of Revealing Light PR	1.00	2.00
NKRTEN026 Reinforcement of the Army PR	2.50	5.00
NKRTEN027 Book of Moon PR	4.00	8.00
NKRTEN028 Foolish Burial PR	3.00	6.00
NKRTEN029 Release Restraint Wave PR	.15	.30
NKRTEN030 Swords at Dawn PR	.20	.40
NKRTEN031 Avalon PR	.20	.40
NKRTEN032 Call of the Haunted PR	1.00	2.00
NKRTEN033 Malevolent Catastrophe PR	.40	.80
NKRTEN034 Dimensional Prison PR	3.00	6.00
NKRTEN035 Solemn Warning PR	1.25	2.50
NKRTEN036 Ignoble Knight of High Laundsallyn PR	.75	1.50
NKRTEN037 Artorigus, King of the Noble Knights PR	6.00	12.00
NKRTEN038 Sacred Noble Knight of King Artorigus PR	2.00	4.00
NKRTEN039 Effect Veiler PR	7.50	15.00
NKRTEN040 Mystical Space Typhoon PR	4.00	8.00
NKRTEN041 Gold Sarcophagus PR	2.00	4.00
NKRTEN042 Forbidden Lance PR	4.00	8.00
NKRTEN043 Torrential Tribute PR	3.00	6.00
NKRTEN044 Compulsory Evacuation Device PR	3.00	6.00

2014 Yu-Gi-Oh Premium Gold 1st Edition

PGLD001 Gimmick Puppet Dreary Doll SCR	.60	1.25
PGLD002 Gimmick Puppet Magnet Doll SCR	.50	1.00
PGLD003 Chronomaly Tula Guardian SCR	.20	.40
PGLD004 Big Belly Knight SCR	.20	.40
PGLD005 Power Tool Mecha Dragon SCR	.20	.40
PGLD006 Ancient Pixie Dragon SCR	.75	1.50
PGLD007 Junk Puppet SCR	.20	.40
PGLD008 Chronomaly City Babylon SCR	.20	.40
PGLD009 Utopia Buster SCR	.20	.40
PGLD010 Chronomaly Gordian Knot SCR	.20	.40
PGLD011 Gimmick Puppet Humpty Dumpty SCR	.20	.40
PGLD012 Gimmick Puppet Shadow Feeler SCR	.20	.40
PGLD013 Silent Wobby SCR	.20	.40
PGLD014 Dynatherium SCR	.20	.40
PGLD015 Dragonecro Nethersoul Dragon SCR	1.00	2.00
PGLD016 Beelze of the Diabolic Dragons SCR	7.50	15.00
PGLD017 Blackfeather Darkrage Dragon SCR	.75	1.50
PGLD018 #C6 Chronomaly Chaos Atlandis SCR	.20	.40
PGLD019 #C15 Gimmick Puppet Giant Hunter SCR	.20	.40
PGLD020 #C40 Gimmick Puppet of Dark Strings SCR	.50	1.00
PGLD021 #C88 Gimmick Puppet Disaster Leo SCR	.50	1.00
PGLD022 Number C9: Chaos Dyson Sphere SCR	.20	.40
PGLD023 Number 13: Embodiment of Crime SCR	.20	.40
PGLD024 #31 Embodiment of Punishment SCR	.20	.40
PGLD025 Number 82: Heartlandraco SCR	2.50	5.00
PGLD026 Tri-Edge Levia SCR	.50	1.00
PGLD027 Rank-Up-Magic Argent Chaos Force SCR	1.25	2.50
PGLD028 Gagaga Academy Emergency Network SCR	1.00	2.00
PGLD029 Ghost of a Grudge SCR	1.00	2.00
PGLD030 Obelisk the Tormentor SCR	7.50	15.00
PGLD031 The Winged Dragon of Ra SCR	7.50	15.00
PGLD032 Slifer the Sky Dragon SCR	7.50	15.00
PGLD033 Dark Magician Girl GR	2.00	4.00
PGLD034 Lonefire Blossom GR	1.50	3.00
PGLD035 Honest GR	1.00	2.00
PGLD036 Effect Veiler GR	3.00	6.00
PGLD037 Gagaga Magician GR	.50	1.00
PGLD038 Galaxy-Eyes Photon Dragon GR	2.00	4.00
PGLD039 Lightpulsar Dragon GR	.75	1.50
PGLD040 Darkflare Dragon GR	.50	1.00
PGLD041 Eclipse Wyvern GR	.50	1.00
PGLD042 Crane Crane GR	.50	1.00
PGLD043 Colossal Fighter GR	.20	.40
PGLD044 Number 32: Shark Drake GR	.50	1.00
PGLD045 Brotherhood of the Fire Fist - Tiger King GR	.50	1.00
PGLD046 Solar Recharge GR	.50	1.00
PGLD047 Forbidden Chalice GR	1.00	2.00
PGLD048 Forbidden Lance GR	1.00	2.00
PGLD049 Forbidden Dress GR	.50	1.00
PGLD050 Fire Formation - Tenki GR	.50	1.00
PGLD051 Jinzo GR	1.00	2.00
PGLD052 Breaker the Magical Warrior GR	.50	1.00
PGLD053 Cyber Dragon GR	1.00	2.00
PGLD054 Goldd, Wu-Lord of Dark World GR	.15	.30
PGLD055 Blue-Eyes Ultimate Dragon GR	7.50	15.00
PGLD056 Chimeratech Overdragon GR	.75	1.50
PGLD057 Swords of Revealing Light GR	.50	1.00
PGLD058 Reinforcement of the Army GR	.50	1.00
PGLD059 Mirror Force GR	1.25	2.50
PGLD060 Torrential Tribute GR	1.00	2.00
PGLD061 Des Volstgalph GR	.50	1.00
PGLD062 Raiza the Storm Monarch GR	.50	1.00
PGLD063 Necro Gardna GR	.15	.30
PGLD064 Dark Armed Dragon GR	1.50	3.00
PGLD065 Prime Material Dragon GR	.50	1.00
PGLD066 Caius the Shadow Monarch GR	.50	1.00
PGLD067 Mind Control GR	.50	1.00
PGLD068 Gold Sarcophagus GR	1.00	2.00
PGLD069 Bottomless Trap Hole GR	1.00	2.00
PGLD070 Phoenix Wing Wind Blast GR	.50	1.00
PGLD071 Exploder Dragon GR	.50	1.00
PGLD072 Judgment Dragon GR	1.50	3.00
PGLD073 Mezuki GR	.75	1.50
PGLD074 Plaguespreader Zombie GR	.75	1.50
PGLD075 Thunder King Rai-Oh GR	1.00	2.00
PGLD076 Stardust Dragon GR	2.00	4.00
PGLD077 Blackwing Armor Master GR	.50	1.00
PGLD078 Blackwing Armed Wing GR	.15	.30
PGLD079 Mystical Space Typhoon GR	1.25	2.50
PGLD080 Icarus Attack GR	.75	1.50
PGLD081 Morphing Jar GR	.50	1.00
PGLD082 Gravekeeper's Spy GR	.15	.30
PGLD083 Spirit Reaper GR	.50	1.00
PGLD084 Chaos Sorcerer GR	.75	1.50
PGLD085 Black Luster Soldier... GR	3.00	6.00
PGLD086 Ryko, Lightsworn Hunter GR	.20	.40
PGLD087 Celestia, Lightsworn Angel GR	.15	.30
PGLD088 Tytannial, Princess of Camellias GR	.15	.30
PGLD089 Summoner Monk GR	1.25	2.50
PGLD090 Trap Stun GR	.75	1.50

2014 Yu-Gi-Oh Primal Origin 1st Edition

PRIOEN000A Artifact Scythe SR	.50	1.00
PRIOEN000B Artifact Scythe UR	1.25	2.50
PRIOEN001 ZS - Vanish Sage C	.15	.30
PRIOEN002 Galaxy Mirror Sage C	.15	.30
PRIOEN003 Galaxy Tyranno R	.15	.30
PRIOEN004 Heliosphere Dragon C	.15	.30
PRIOEN005 Mermaid Shark R	.15	.30
PRIOEN006 Gazer Shark C	.15	.30
PRIOEN007 Blizzard Thunderbird C	.15	.30
PRIOEN008 Battlin' Boxer Big Bandage C	.15	.30
PRIOEN009 Battlin' Boxer Veil C	.15	.30
PRIOEN010 Umbral Horror Ghost C	.15	.30
PRIOEN011 Artifact Moralltach SR	.75	1.50
PRIOEN012 Artifact Beagalltach C	.15	.30
PRIOEN013 Artifact Failnaught C	.15	.30
PRIOEN014 Artifact Aegis C	.15	.30
PRIOEN015 Artifact Achilleshield C	.15	.30
PRIOEN016 Artifact Labrys C	.15	.30
PRIOEN017 Artifact Caduceus R	.15	.30
PRIOEN018 Sylvan Cherubsprout C	.15	.30
PRIOEN019A Sylvan Snapdrassinagon R	.15	.30
PRIOEN019B Sylvan Snapdrassinagon UR	.20	.40
PRIOEN020 Sylvan Lotuswain C	.15	.30
PRIOEN021 Sylvan Sagequoia UR	.50	1.00
PRIOEN022 Ghostrick Doll C	.15	.30
PRIOEN023 Ghostrick Warwolf C	.15	.30
PRIOEN024 Bujin Hirume UR	1.00	2.00
PRIOEN025 Traptrix Dionaea R	.15	.30
PRIOEN026 Mecha Phantom Beast O-Lion R	.15	.30
PRIOEN027 Hazy Flame Hydra C	.15	.30
PRIOEN028 Madolche Anjelly UR	3.00	6.00
PRIOEN029 Pilica, Descendant of Gusto SR	1.50	3.00
PRIOEN030 Gladiator Beast Augustus R	.15	.30
PRIOEN031 Lucent, Netherlord of Dark World SR	2.00	4.00
PRIOEN032 Ancient Gear Box C	.15	.30
PRIOEN033 Dawn Knight R	.15	.30
PRIOEN034 Majesty's Fiend SCR	5.00	10.00
PRIOEN035 Thestalos the Mega Monarch SCR	5.00	10.00
PRIOEN036 Beautunaful Princess R	.15	.30
PRIOEN037 Nopenguin C	.15	.30
PRIOEN038 Condemned Maiden C	.15	.30
PRIOEN039 Starduston C	.15	.30
PRIOEN040A #62 Galaxy-Eyes Prime Photon Dragon UR	5.00	10.00
PRIOEN040B #62 Galaxy-Eyes Prime Photon Dragon UTR	7.50	15.00
PRIOEN041 #C107 Neo Galaxy Eyes Tachyon Dragon SR	.75	1.50
PRIOEN041 #C107 Neo Galaxy Eyes Tachyon Dragon UTR	1.25	2.50
PRIOEN042 Number 103: Ragnazero R	.75	1.50
PRIOEN043 Number C103: Ragnafinity R	.15	.30
PRIOEN044A Number C102: Archfiend Seraph SR	.50	1.00
PRIOEN044B Number C102: Archfiend Seraph UTR	.50	1.00
PRIOEN045 Number 80: Rhapsody in Berserk R	.50	1.00
PRIOEN046 Number C80: Requiem in Berserk R	.15	.30
PRIOEN047 Number 43: Manipulator of Souls C	.15	.30
PRIOEN048 #C43 High Manipulator of Chaos R	.15	.30
PRIOEN049 Artifact Durendal UR	2.00	4.00
PRIOEN049 Artifact Durendal UTR	3.00	6.00
PRIOEN050 Orea, the Sylvan High Arbiter SCR	.75	1.50
PRIOEN051 Ghostrick Socuteboss R	.60	1.25
PRIOEN052A Bujinki Amaterasu SCR	.75	1.50
PRIOEN052B Bujinki Amaterasu GR	2.00	4.00
PRIOEN052C Bujinki Amaterasu UTR	1.00	2.00
PRIOEN053 Phantom Fortress Enterblathnir R	.15	.30
PRIOEN054 Cairngorgon, Antiluminescent Knight SR	.50	1.00
PRIOEN055 Phonon Pulse Dragon R	.15	.30
PRIOEN056 Reverse Breaker C	.15	.30
PRIOEN057 Galactic Charity C	.15	.30
PRIOEN058 Rank-Up Magic - The Seventh One SCR	.75	1.50
PRIOEN059 Don Thousand's Throne R	.15	.30
PRIOEN060 Artifact Ignition UR	2.00	4.00
PRIOEN061 Artifacts Unleashed C	.15	.30
PRIOEN062 Sylvan Charity UR	.20	.40
PRIOEN063 Ghostrick Parade C	.15	.30
PRIOEN064 Bujintervention C	.15	.30
PRIOEN065 Diamond Core of Koa'ki Meiru C	.15	.30
PRIOEN066 Scrap Factory C	.15	.30
PRIOEN067 Forbidden Scripture SCR	.75	1.50
PRIOEN068 Jackpot 7 C	.15	.30
PRIOEN069 Double Dragon Descent C	.15	.30
PRIOEN070 Tachyon Chaos Hole SR	.50	1.00
PRIOEN071 Last Counter UR	.20	.40
PRIOEN072 Artifact Sanctum UR	3.00	6.00
PRIOEN073 Sylvan Waterslide C	.15	.30
PRIOEN074 Ghostrick Night C	.15	.30
PRIOEN075 Bujincident C	.15	.30
PRIOEN076 The Monarchs Erupt SR	.50	1.00
PRIOEN077 Evo-Singularity C	.15	.30
PRIOEN078 Xyz Universe R	.50	1.00
PRIOEN079A And the Band Played On C	.15	.30
PRIOEN079B And the Band Played On UR	.20	.40
PRIOEN080 Tri-and-Guess C	.15	.30
PRIOEN081 Noble Knight Brothers SCR	2.00	4.00
PRIOEN082 Noble Knight Eachtar SR	.50	1.00
PRIOEN083 Sylvan Princessprout SR	.50	1.00
PRIOEN084 Bujingi Sinyou UR	.20	.40
PRIOEN085 Vampire Vamp SR	.75	1.50
PRIOEN086 Gladiator Beast Nerokius SCR	1.25	2.50
PRIOEN087 Noble Knights of the Round Table UR	.20	.40
PRIOEN088 Avalon SR	.50	1.00
PRIOEN089 Escalation of the Monarchs SR	.60	1.25
PRIOEN090 Bolt Penguin C	.15	.30
PRIOEN091 Phantom King Hydride C	.15	.30
PRIOEN092 Number 42: Galaxy Tomahawk C	.15	.30
PRIOEN093 Rose Archer R	.15	.30
PRIOEN094 Shogi Knight C	.15	.30
PRIOEN095 Gimmick Puppet Des Troy C	.15	.30
PRIOEN096 ZW - Sleipnir Mail C	.15	.30
PRIOEN097 Number 48: Shadow Lich C	.15	.30
PRIOEN098 Galaxy Dragon C	.15	.30
PRIOEN099 Hundred-Footed Horror C	.15	.30
PRIOENDE3 Agent of Entropy - Uranus R	.50	1.00
PRIOENDE4 Re-Cover R	.15	.30

2014 Yu-Gi-Oh Star Pack 2014 1st Edition

SP14001 Gogogo Golem C	.10	.20
SP14002 Daybreaker C	.10	.20
SP14003 Gogogo Giant C	.10	.20
SP14004 ZW - Unicorn Spear C	.10	.20
SP14005 Shocktopus C	.10	.20
SP14006 Photon Lizard C	.10	.20
SP14007 Photon Thrasher C	.75	1.50
SP14008 Photon Crusher C	.10	.20
SP14009 Reverse Breaker C	.10	.20
SP14010 Tasuke Knight C	.10	.20
SP14011 Gagaga Gardna C	.10	.20
SP14012 Cardcar D C	.50	1.00
SP14013 Hammer Shark C	.10	.20
SP14014 Jumbo Drill C	.10	.20
SP14015 Rocket Arrow Express C	.10	.20
SP14016 Aye-Iron C	.10	.20
SP14017 Tin Goldfish C	1.25	2.50
SP14018 Dododo Warrior C	.10	.20
SP14019 Zubaba Buster C	.10	.20
SP14020 Twin Photon Lizard C	.10	.20
SP14021 Thunder End Dragon C	2.00	4.00
SP14022 Number C39: Utopia Ray C	.10	.20
SP14023 Number 32: Shark Drake C	.50	1.00
SP14024 Photon Strike Bounzer C	.75	1.50
SP14025 Photon Papilloperative C	.50	1.00
SP14026 Number 25: Force Focus C	.50	1.00
SP14027 Number 7: Lucky Straight C	.50	1.00
SP14028 Muzurhythm the String Djinn C	.10	.20
SP14029 Temtempo the Percussion Djinn C	.10	.20
SP14030 Melomelody the Brass Djinn C	.10	.20
SP14031 Maestroke the Symphony Djinn C	.50	1.00
SP14032 Cross Attack C	.10	.20
SP14033 Gagagabolt C	.10	.20
SP14034 Star Light, Star Bright C	.10	.20
SP14035 Bound Wand C	.10	.20
SP14036 Mini-Guts C	.10	.20
SP14037 Xyz Effect C	.10	.20
SP14038 Xyz Reflect C	.20	.40
SP14039 Morphing Jar #2 C	.10	.20
SP14040 Magical Merchant C	.50	1.00
SP14041 Reasoning C	1.00	2.00
SP14042 Ma'at C	.10	.20
SP14043 Chimeratech Overdragon C	.10	.20
SP14044 Malefic Truth Dragon C	.10	.20
SP14045 Guldfaxe of the Nordic Beasts C	.50	1.00
SP14046 Svartalf of the Nordic Altar C	.10	.20
SP14047 Valkyrie of the Nordic Ascendant C	1.00	2.00
SP14048 Thor, Lord of the Aesir C	.60	1.25
SP14049 Loki, Lord of the Aesir C	.10	.20
SP14050 Odin, Father of the Aesir C	.50	1.00

2014 Yu-Gi-Oh Structure Deck Cybor Dragon Revolution 1st Edition

SDCR001 Cyber Dragon Core SR	2.00	4.00
SDCR002 Cyber Dragon Drei SR	2.50	5.00
SDCR004 Cyber Dragon Zwei	.15	.30
SDCR005 Proto-Cyber Dragon	.15	.30
SDCR006 Cyber Valley	.15	.30
SDCR007 Cyber Larva	.15	.30
SDCR008 Cyber Phoenix	.15	.30
SDCR009 Cyber Dinosaur	.15	.30
SDCR010 Cyber Eltanin	.15	.30
SDCR011 Armored Cybern	.15	.30
SDCR012 Satellite Cannon	.15	.30
SDCR013 Solar Wind Jammer	.15	.30
SDCR014 Jade Knight	.15	.30
SDCR015 FalchionB	.15	.30
SDCR016 Reflect Bounder	.15	.30
SDCR017 The Light - Hex-Sealed Fusion	.15	.30
SDCR018 Shining Angel	.15	.30
SDCR019 Cyber Repair Plant	4.00	8.00
SDCR020 Evolution Burst	.15	.30
SDCR021 Super Polymerization	1.00	2.00
SDCR022 Power Bond	.50	1.00
SDCR023 Limiter Removal	.20	.40
SDCR024 Megamorph	.15	.30
SDCR025 D.D.R. - Different Dimension Reincarnation	.30	.75
SDCR026 Mystical Space Typhoon	.60	1.25
SDCR027 Light of Redemption	.15	.30
SDCR028 Machina Armored Unit	.15	.30
SDCR029 Cyber Network	.25	.50
SDCR030 Cybernetic Hidden Technology	.15	.30
SDCR031 Three of a Kind	.15	.30
SDCR032 Trap Stun	1.00	2.00
SDCR033 Dimensional Prison	1.00	2.00
SDCR034 Malevolent Catastrophe	.15	.30
SDCR035 Waboku	.30	.75
SDCR036 Call of the Haunted	.15	.30
SDCR037 Cyber Twin Dragon UR	.30	.75
SDCR038 Cyber Dragon Nova UR	2.50	5.00
SDCR003a Cyber Dragon (black)	.20	.40
SDCR003b Cyber Dragon (white)	.50	1.00

2014 Yu-Gi-Oh Structure Deck Geargia Rampage 1st Edition

SDGREN001 Geargiano Mk-III SR	.15	.30
SDGREN002 Geargiattacker SR	.10	.20
SDGREN003 Geargiauger UR	.50	1.00
SDGREN004 Geargiano C	.10	.20
SDGREN005 Geargiano MK-II C	.10	.20
SDGREN006 Geargiaccelerator C	.20	.40
SDGREN007 Geargiarsenal C	.20	.40
SDGREN008 Geargiarmor C	.20	.40
SDGREN009 Green Gadget C	.10	.20
SDGREN010 Red Gadget C	.10	.20
SDGREN011 Yellow Gadget C	.10	.20
SDGREN012 Ancient Gear Gadjiltron Chimera C	.10	.20
SDGREN013 Ancient Gear Gadjiltron Dragon C	.20	.40
SDGREN014 Jumbo Drill C	.10	.20
SDGREN015 Minefieldriller C	.10	.20
SDGREN016 Card Trooper C	.10	.20
SDGREN017 Swift Scarecrow C	.30	.75
SDGREN018 Oilman C	.10	.20
SDGREN019 Heavy Mech Support Platform C	.10	.20
SDGREN020 Giant Rat C	.10	.20
SDGREN021 Geartown C	.10	.20
SDGREN022 Limiter Removal C	.10	.20
SDGREN023 Machine Assembly Line C	.10	.20
SDGREN024 Fissure C	.10	.20
SDGREN025 Smashing Ground C	.20	.40
SDGREN026 Double Summon C	1.25	2.50
SDGREN027 Creature Swap C	.10	.20
SDGREN028 Terraforming C	.60	1.25
SDGREN029 Geargiagear C	.20	.40
SDGREN030 Stronghold the Moving Fortress C	.10	.20
SDGREN031 Metalmorph C	.10	.20
SDGREN032 Rare Metalmorph C	.10	.20
SDGREN033 Roll Out! C	.10	.20
SDGREN034 Geargiagear Gigant XG UR	.20	.40
SDGREN035 Gear Gigant X C	2.50	5.00

2014 Yu-Gi-Oh Structure Deck Realm of Light 1st Edition

SDLIEN001 Alexandrite Dragon C	.10	.20
SDLIEN002 Minerva, Lightsworn Maiden SR	.50	1.00
SDLIEN003 Raiden, Hand of the Lightsworn SR	1.50	3.00
SDLIEN004 Judgment Dragon C	.20	.40
SDLIEN005 Gragonith, Lightsworn Dragon C	.10	.20
SDLIEN006 Celestia, Lightsworn Angel C	.10	.20
SDLIEN007 Jain, Lightsworn Paladin C	.10	.20
SDLIEN008 Lyla, Lightsworn Sorceress C	.10	.20
SDLIEN009 Garoth, Lightsworn Warrior C	.10	.20
SDLIEN010 Wulf, Lightsworn Beast C	.10	.20
SDLIEN011 Ehren, Lightsworn Monk C	.10	.20
SDLIEN012 Lumina, Lightsworn Summoner C	.10	.20
SDLIEN013 Aurkus, Lightsworn Druid C	.10	.20
SDLIEN014 Shire, Lightsworn Spirit C	.10	.20
SDLIEN015 Ryko, Lightsworn Hunter C	.10	.20
SDLIEN016 Honest C	.20	.40
SDLIEN017 Lightray Diabolos C	.10	.20
SDLIEN018 Lightray Daedalus C	.10	.20
SDLIEN019 Vylon Prism C	.10	.20
SDLIEN020 Fabled Raven C	.10	.20
SDLIEN021 The Fabled Cerburrel C	.10	.20
SDLIEN022 Blackwing - Zephyros the Elite C	.10	.20
SDLIEN023 Necro Gardna C	.10	.20
SDLIEN024 Lightsworn Sanctuary UR	.50	1.00
SDLIEN025 Realm of Light C	.10	.20
SDLIEN026 Solar Recharge C	.20	.40
SDLIEN027 Charge of the Light Brigade C	.10	.20
SDLIEN028 Monster Reincarnation C	.10	.20
SDLIEN029 Foolish Burial C	.25	.50
SDLIEN030 Glorious Illusion C	.10	.20
SDLIEN031 Lightsworn Barrier C	.10	.20
SDLIEN032 Vanquishing Light C	.10	.20
SDLIEN033 Beckoning Light C	.10	.20
SDLIEN034 Skill Successor C	.10	.20
SDLIEN035 Breakthrough Skill C	.60	1.25
SDLIEN036 Michael, the Arch-Lightsworn UR	.50	1.00

2014 Yu-Gi-Oh Super Starter Deck Space-Time Showdown 1st Edition

YS14EN001 Wattaildragon C	.15	.30
YS14EN002 Luster Dragon C	.15	.30
YS14EN003 Hunter Dragon C	.20	.40
YS14EN004 Millennium Shield C	.15	.30
YS14EN005 Dark Blade C	.15	.30
YS14EN006 Warrior Dai Grepher C	.15	.30
YS14EN007 Chamberlain of the Six Samurai C	.15	.30
YS14EN008 Mystical Elf C	.15	.30
YS14EN009 Stargazer Magician SR	.25	.50
YS14EN010 Timegazer Magician SR	.50	1.00
YS14EN011 Aether, the Empowering Dragon C	.15	.30
YS14EN012 Ventdra, the Empowered Warrior C	.15	.30
YS14EN013 Arnis, the Empowered Warrior C	.15	.30
YS14EN014 Terratiger, the Empowered Warrior C	.15	.30
YS14EN015 Hydrotortoise, the Empowered Warrior C	.15	.30
YS14EN016 Golden Dragon Summoner C	.15	.30
YS14EN017 Blue Dragon Summoner C	1.00	2.00
YS14EN018 Red Sparrow Summoner C	.15	.30
YS14EN019 White Tiger Summoner C	.15	.30
YS14EN020 Green Turtle Summoner C	.15	.30
YS14EN021 Sorcerous Spell Wall C	.15	.30
YS14EN022 Supply Squad C	.30	.75
YS14EN023 Lightning Vortex C	.60	1.25
YS14EN024 Mystical Space Typhoon C	.20	.40
YS14EN025 Ego Boost C	.15	.30
YS14EN026 Axe of Despair C	.50	1.00
YS14EN027 Lucky Iron Axe C	.15	.30
YS14EN028 Monster Reincarnation C	.15	.30
YS14EN029 Dark Factory of Mass Production C	.30	.75
YS14EN030 Poison of the Old Man C	.30	.75
YS14EN031 Trap Hole C	.15	.30
YS14EN032 Sakuretsu Armor C	.25	.50
YS14EN033 Raigeki Break C	.15	.30
YS14EN034 Dust Tornado C	.15	.30
YS14EN035 Shadow Spell C	.15	.30
YS14EN036 A Hero Emerges C	.15	.30
YS14EN037 Soul Resurrection C	.15	.30
YS14EN038 Jar of Greed C	.30	.75
YS14EN039 Magic Jammer C	.20	.40
YS14EN040 Seven Tools of the Bandit C	.15	.30

2014 Yu-Gi-Oh Super Starter Deck Space-Time Showdown 1st Edition Power-Up Pack

YS14ENA01 Odd-Eyes Dragon UR	.25	.50
YS14ENA02 Des Volstgalph C	.15	.30
YS14ENA03 Kaiser the Light Monarch C	3.00	6.00
YS14ENA04 D.D. Warrior Lady C	.20	.40
YS14ENA05 Sacred Crane C	.15	.30
YS14ENA06 Amazoness Sage C	.15	.30
YS14ENA07 Injection Fairy Lily C	.15	.30
YS14ENA08 The A. Forces C	.15	.30
YS14ENA09 Reinforcement of the Army C	.15	.30
YS14ENA10 Dark Hole UR	.50	1.00
YS14ENA11 Swords of Revealing Light C	.15	.30
YS14ENA12 Mirror Force C	.50	1.00
YS14ENA13 Call of the Haunted C	.15	.30
YS14ENA14 Magic Cylinder C	.60	1.25
YS14ENA15 Divine Wrath C	.25	.50

2015 Yu-Gi-Oh Astral Pack 7

AP07EN001 Gaia Dragon, the Thunder Charger UR	10.00	20.00
AP07EN002 Castel, the Skyblaster Musketeer UR	25.00	50.00
AP07EN003 Spell Shattering Arrow UR	5.00	10.00
AP07EN004 Satellarknight Altair SR	1.00	2.00
AP07EN005 Satellarknight Unukalhai SR	.75	1.50
AP07EN006 Djinn Demolisher of Rituals SR	.50	1.00
AP07EN007 Scarm... SR	.50	1.00
AP07EN008 Leo, the Keeper of the Sacred Tree SR	3.00	6.00
AP07EN009 Number 103: Ragnazero SR	3.00	6.00
AP07EN010 Level Limit - Area B SR	1.50	3.00
AP07EN011 Twister SR	.15	.30
AP07EN012 Dragon Ravine SR	1.50	3.00
AP07EN013 Level Limit - Area A SR	.20	.40
AP07EN014 Invader from Another Dimension C	.60	1.25
AP07EN015 Lord of the Lamp C	.50	1.00
AP07EN016 Senju of the Thousand Hands C	1.00	2.00
AP07EN017 Volcanic Scattershot C	.60	1.25
AP07EN018 Gladiator Beast Bestiari C	.50	1.00
AP07EN019 Madolche Puddingcess C	1.50	3.00
AP07EN020 Brotherhood of the Fire Fist - Spirit C	.60	1.25
AP07EN021 Soul Hunter C	1.50	3.00
AP07EN022 Dawn of the Herald C	1.50	3.00
AP07EN023 Storm C	.50	1.00
AP07EN024 Spiritual Wind Art - Miyabi C	.50	1.00
AP07EN025 Light-Imprisoning Mirror C	.60	1.25
AP07EN026 Shadow-Imprisoning Mirror C	.60	1.25
AP07EN027 Fairy Wind C	.10	.20

2015 Yu-Gi-Oh Astral Pack 8

AP08EN001 Trishula, Dragon of the Ice Barrier UTR	30.00	75.00
AP08EN002 Mystical Space Typhoon UTR	25.00	50.00
AP08EN003 Fiendish Chain UTR	10.00	20.00
AP08EN004 Igknight Margrave SR	.20	.40
AP08EN005 Igknight Gallant SR	.50	1.00
AP08EN006 Toon Masked Sorcerer SR	3.00	6.00
AP08EN007 Graff... SR	.30	.75
AP08EN008 Black Luster Soldier... SR	1.00	2.00
AP08EN009 Spiritual Beast Rampengu SR	1.50	3.00
AP08EN010 Instant Fusion SR	1.50	3.00
AP08EN011 Kozmotown SR	.75	1.50
AP08EN012 Book of Eclipse SR	2.50	5.00
AP08EN013 Lose 1 Turn SR	1.50	3.00
AP08EN014 Rhaimundos of the Red Sword C	.75	1.50
AP08EN015 Fireyarou C	.50	1.00
AP08EN016 Twin-Headed Behemoth C	.20	.40
AP08EN017 Swift Gaia the Fierce Knight C	.20	.40
AP08EN018 Kinka-byo C	4.00	8.00
AP08EN019 Red-Eyes Wyvern C	.60	1.25
AP08EN020 Gem-Knight Obsidian C	1.25	2.50
AP08EN021 Vermillion Sparrow C	1.25	2.50
AP08EN022 Masked HERO Koga C	.20	.40
AP08EN023 Machine Duplication C	1.25	2.50
AP08EN024 U.A. Stadium C	.20	.40
AP08EN025 Black Horn of Heaven C	.50	1.00
AP08EN026 Safe Zone C	1.00	2.00
AP08EN027 Unpossessed C	.30	.75

2015 Yu-Gi-Oh Clash of Rebellions 1st Edition

COREEN000 Sky Dragoons of Draconia R	.20	.40
COREEN001 Mystery Shell Dragon C	.10	.20
COREEN002 Risebell the Summoner C	.10	.20
COREEN003 Xiangke Magician SR	1.00	2.00
COREEN004 Xiangsheng Magician SR	.50	1.00
COREEN005 Performapal Camelump C	.10	.20
COREEN006 Performapal Drummerilla C	.10	.20
COREEN007 Superheavy Samurai Blowtorch C	.10	.20
COREEN008 Opera the Melodious Diva C	.10	.20
COREEN009 Tamtam the Melodious Diva C	.10	.20
COREEN010 Fluffal Mouse SR	1.00	2.00
COREEN011 D/D Pandora C	.10	.20
COREEN012 Crystal Rose R	.20	.40
COREEN013 Raidraptor - Fuzzy Lanius C	.10	.20
COREEN014 Raidraptor - Singing Lanius C	.10	.20
COREEN015 Performage Damage Juggler C	.10	.20
COREEN016 Performage Flame Eater C	.10	.20
COREEN017 Performage Hat Tricker C	.10	.20
COREEN018 Performage Trick Clown C	.10	.20
COREEN019 Performage Stilts Launcher C	.10	.20
COREEN020 Red-Eyes Black Flare Dragon SR	6.00	12.00
COREEN021 The Black Stone of Legend SCR	10.00	20.00
COREEN022 Black Metal Dragon C	.10	.20
COREEN023 Red-Eyes Archfiend of Lightning SR	1.50	3.00
COREEN024 Keeper of the Shrine C	.10	.20
COREEN025 Luster Pendulum, the Dracoslayer SR	1.00	2.00
COREEN026 Igknight Squire C	.10	.20
COREEN027 Igknight Crusader SR	2.00	4.00
COREEN028 Igknight Templar UR	.50	1.00
COREEN029 Igknight Paladin C	.10	.20
COREEN030 Igknight Margrave C	.10	.20
COREEN031 Igknight Gallant C	.10	.20
COREEN032 Igknight Lancer R	.20	.40
COREEN033 Igknight Champion R	.20	.40
COREEN034 Aromage Jasmine SCR	7.50	15.00
COREEN035 Aromage Cananga C	.10	.20
COREEN036 Aromage Rosemary UR	3.00	6.00
COREEN037 Aromage Bergamot R	.20	.40
COREEN038 Aroma Jar C	.10	.20
COREEN039 Infernoid Decatron SR	1.00	2.00
COREEN040 Bird of Paradise Lost C	.10	.20
COREEN041 Magical Abductor R	.20	.40
COREEN042 Archfiend Eccentrick SCR	5.00	10.00
COREEN043 Toon Cyber Dragon R	.75	1.50
COREEN044 Deskbot 005 C	.10	.20
COREEN045 Retaliating C NR	.10	.20
COREEN046 D/D/D Oracle King d'Arc R	.60	1.25
COREEN047 Gem-Knight Lady Brilliant Diamond UR	1.00	2.00
COREEN048 Archfiend Black Skull Dragon UR	3.00	6.00
COREEN048u Archfiend Black Skull Dragon UTR	4.00	8.00
COREEN049 Infernoid Tierra UR	.75	1.50
COREEN049u Infernoid Tierra UTR	1.00	2.00
COREEN050 Ignister Prominence... UR	1.00	2.00
COREEN050u Ignister Prominence... UTR	3.00	6.00
COREEN051 Odd-Eyes Rebellion Dragon SCR	1.50	3.00
COREEN051u Odd-Eyes Rebellion Dragon UTR	3.00	6.00
COREEN052 D/D/D Marksman King Tell R	.20	.40
COREEN053 Performage Trapeze Magician R	.20	.40
COREEN054 Red-Eyes Flare Metal Dragon SCR	3.00	6.00
COREEN054 Red Eyes Flare Metal Dragn GR	10.00	20.00
COREEN054u Red-Eyes Flare Metal Dragon UTR	5.00	10.00
COREEN055 Pianissimo C	.10	.20
COREEN056 Brilliant Fusion SR	5.00	10.00
COREEN057 Rank-Up-Magic Raptor's Force C	.10	.20
COREEN058 Bubble Barrier C	.10	.20
COREEN059 Red-Eyes Fusion SR	3.00	6.00
COREEN060 Cards of the Red Stone UR	3.00	6.00
COREEN061 Ignition Phoenix C	.10	.20
COREEN062 Aroma Garden C	.10	.20
COREEN063 Void Imagination SR	.30	.75
COREEN064 Back-Up Rider C	.10	.20
COREEN065 Mistaken Arrest SCR	1.00	2.00
COREEN066 Wavering Eyes C	.10	.20
COREEN067 Chicken Game C	.10	.20
COREEN068 Brilliant Spark C	.10	.20
COREEN069 Raidraptor - Return C	.10	.20
COREEN070 Raptor's Gust C	.10	.20
COREEN071 Trick Box C	.10	.20
COREEN072 Return of the Red-Eyes C	.10	.20
COREEN073 Igknight Burst R	.20	.40
COREEN074 Humid Winds C	.10	.20
COREEN075 Dried Winds SR	.25	.50
COREEN076 Storming Mirror Force SCR	7.50	15.00
COREEN077 Ferret Flames C	.10	.20
COREEN078 Balance of Judgment C	.10	.20
COREEN079 Extra Buck R	.20	.40
COREEN080 Side Effects? NR	.10	.20
COREEN081 Extinction on Schedule C	.10	.20
COREEN082 Kozmo Farmgirl UR	2.00	4.00
COREEN083 Kozmo Goodwitch SR	.50	1.00
COREEN084 Kozmo Sliprider R	.20	.40
COREEN085 Kozmo Forerunner R	.20	.40
COREEN086 Kozmotown R	.20	.40
COREEN087 Dogoran, the Mad Flame Kaiju R	1.50	3.00
COREEN088 Kumongous, the Sticky String Kaiju R	.60	1.25
COREEN089 Kyoutou Waterfront C	.10	.20
COREEN090 Performapal Silver Claw C	.10	.20
COREEN091 Escher the Frost Vassal C	.10	.20
COREEN092 Absorb Fusion UR	1.50	3.00
COREEN093 Performapal Salutiger C	.10	.20
COREEN094 Superheavy Samurai Ogre Shutendoji SR	.75	1.50
COREEN095 Hi-Speedroid Kendama UR	.25	.50
COREEN096 Dragong R	.20	.40
COREEN097 Mandragon R	.20	.40
COREEN098 Tatsunoko SCR	1.00	2.00
COREEN099 Secret Blast C	.10	.20
COREENSE1 Ultimaya Tzolkin SR	2.50	5.00
COREENSE2 Frightfur Tiger SR	.30	.75
COREENSE3 Engraver of the Mark SR	.10	.20
COREENSE4 Destruction Sword Flash SR	.10	.20

2015 Yu-Gi-Oh Crossed Souls 1st Edition

CROSEN000 Sea Dragoons of Draconia R	.15	.30
CROSEN001 Phantom Gryphon C	.10	.20
CROSEN002 Performapal Elephammer R	.10	.20
CROSEN003 Performapal Bowhopper C	.10	.20
CROSEN004 Performapal Lizardraw C	.10	.20
CROSEN005 Performapal Springoose C	.10	.20
CROSEN006 Superheavy Samurai Big Waraji C	.10	.20
CROSEN007 Superheavy Samurai Gigagloves C	.10	.20
CROSEN008 Superheavy Samurai Battleball SR	1.00	2.00
CROSEN009 Superheavy Samurai Soulbuster Gauntlet C	.10	.20
CROSEN010 Soprano the Melodious Songstress C	.10	.20
CROSEN011 Fluffal Sheep C	.10	.20
CROSEN012 Edge Imp Saw C	.10	.20
CROSEN013 Edge Imp Chain C	.10	.20
CROSEN014 Edge Imp Tomahawk R	.10	.20
CROSEN015 Edge Imp Frightfuloid C	.10	.20
CROSEN016 Raidraptor - Sharp Lanius C	.10	.20
CROSEN017 Raidraptor - Mimicry Lanius C	.10	.20
CROSEN018 Yosenju Kodam C	.10	.20
CROSEN019 Yosenju Oyam R	.10	.20
CROSEN020 Satellarknight Zefrathuban UR	1.50	3.00
CROSEN021 Stellarknight Zefraxciton R	.10	.20
CROSEN022 Shaddoll Zefranaga C	.10	.20
CROSEN023 Shaddoll Zefracore C	.10	.20
CROSEN024 Zefraxi, Treasure of the Yang Zing UR	2.50	5.00
CROSEN025 Zefraniu, Secret of the Yang Zing R	.50	1.00
CROSEN026 Zefrasaber, Swordmaster of the Nekroz C	.10	.20
CROSEN027 Zefraxa, Flame Beast of the Nekroz C	.10	.20
CROSEN028 Ritual Beast Tamer Zeframpilica C	.10	.20
CROSEN029 Ritual Beast Tamer Zefrawendi R	.10	.20
CROSEN030 Infernoid Pirmais UR	.75	1.50
CROSEN031 Infernoid Sjette C	.10	.20
CROSEN032 Infernoid Devyaty UR	3.00	6.00
CROSEN033 Ghost Ogre & Snow Rabbit SCR	30.00	75.00
CROSEN034 Magma Dragon C	.10	.20
CROSEN035 Deskbot 004 C	.10	.20
CROSEN036 Doomdog Octhros C	.10	.20
CROSEN037 Putrid Pudding Body Buddies C	.10	.20
CROSEN038 Nekroz of Sophia SCR	1.50	3.00
CROSEN038u Nekroz of Sophia UTR	1.50	3.00
CROSEN039 Schuberta the Melodious Maestra R	.15	.30
CROSEN040 Bloom Diva the Melodious Choir UR	.20	.40
CROSEN041 Frightfur Leo SR	1.50	3.00
CROSEN042 Frightfur Sheep SR	.50	1.00
CROSEN043 Frightfur Chimera R	.10	.20
CROSEN043u Frightfur Chimera UTR	1.50	3.00
CROSEN044 El Shaddoll Anoyatyllis SCR	4.00	8.00
CROSEN045 Ritual Beast Ulti-Gaiapelio UR	3.00	6.00
CROSEN045u Ritual Beast Ulti-Gaiapelio UTR	3.00	6.00
CROSEN046 Clear Wing Synchro Dragon GR	10.00	20.00
CROSEN046 Clear Wing Synchro Dragon SCR	5.00	10.00
CROSEN046u Clear Wing Synchro Dragon UTR	5.00	10.00
CROSEN047 Chaofeng, Phantom of the Yang Zing SR	4.00	8.00
CROSEN048 Raidraptor - Blaze Falcon R	.30	.75
CROSEN049 Raidraptor - Revolution Falcon R	.10	.20
CROSEN050 Tellarknight Ptolemaeus UR	1.00	2.00
CROSEN050u Tellarknight Ptolemaeus UTR	2.00	4.00
CROSEN051 Madolche Puddingcess... UR	3.00	6.00
CROSEN052 Performapal Recasting C	.10	.20
CROSEN053 Fusion Conscription R	.30	.75
CROSEN054 Frightfur Factory C	.10	.20
CROSEN055 Suture Rebirth R	.10	.20
CROSEN056 Frightfur Fusion R	.50	1.00
CROSEN057 Rank-Up-Magic Revolution Force R	.10	.20
CROSEN058 Yosen Whirlwind C	.10	.20
CROSEN059 Zefra Path C	.10	.20
CROSEN060 Oracle of Zefra SCR	4.00	8.00
CROSEN061 Void Vanishment SR	1.50	3.00
CROSEN062 Galaxy Cyclone SCR	2.00	4.00
CROSEN063 Harmonic Oscillation C	.10	.20
CROSEN064 Pendulum Rising C	.10	.20
CROSEN065 Unexpected Dai SR	2.50	5.00
CROSEN066 Performapal Pinch Helper C	.10	.20
CROSEN067 Melodious Illusion R	.20	.40
CROSEN068 Fluffal Crane C	.10	.20
CROSEN069 Designer Frightfur C	.10	.20
CROSEN070 Dizzying Winds of Yosen Village C	.10	.20
CROSEN071 Chosen of Zefra C	.10	.20
CROSEN072 Zefra Divine Strike SR	.50	1.00
CROSEN073 Void Purification R	.10	.20
CROSEN074 Jar of Avarice SCR	2.00	4.00
CROSEN075 Lose 1 Turn UR	1.50	3.00
CROSEN076 Fiend Griefing C	.10	.20
CROSEN077 Abyss Stungray C	.10	.20
CROSEN078 Statue of Anguish Pattern C	.10	.20
CROSEN079 Monster Rebone SR	.10	.20
CROSEN080 Diceversity C	.10	.20
CROSEN081 Moon Mirror Shield R	1.00	2.00
CROSEN082 Draghig... SR	.15	.30
CROSEN083 Barbar, Malebranche of the Burning Abyss R	.10	.20
CROSEN084 Dante, Pilgrim of the Burning Abyss SCR	1.50	3.00
CROSEN085 The Terminus of the Burning Abyss UR	.20	.40
CROSEN086 U.A. Dreadnought Dunker C	.10	.20
CROSEN087 U.A. Rival Rebounder C	.10	.20
CROSEN088 U.A. Signing Deal C	.10	.20
CROSEN089 U.A. Penalty Box C	.10	.20
CROSEN090 Half Unbreak C	.10	.20
CROSEN091 The Melody of Awakening Dragon SR	1.25	2.50
CROSEN092 Cybernetic Fusion Support C	.10	.20
CROSEN093 Powerful Rebirth SR	.50	1.00
CROSEN094 Number S39: Utopia Prime SR	.75	1.50
CROSEN095 Galaxy-Eyes Full Armor... SR	2.00	4.00
CROSEN096 Performapal Thunderhino C	.10	.20
CROSEN097 Primitive Butterfly C	.10	.20
CROSEN098 Junk Anchor R	.10	.20
CROSEN099 Harpie Harpist SR	1.00	2.00

2015 Yu-Gi-Oh Dimension of Chaos 1st Edition

DOCSEN000 Samurai Cavalry of Reptier R	.20	.40
DOCSEN001 Performapal Secondonkey R	.50	1.00
DOCSEN002 Performapal Splashmammoth R	.20	.40
DOCSEN003 Performapal Helpprincess R	.20	.40

DOCSEN004 Superheavy Samurai Thief C .15 .30
DOCSEN005 Superheavy Samurai Transporter C .15 .30
DOCSEN006 Superheavy Samurai Drum C .15 .30
DOCSEN007 Superheavy Samurai Soulhorns C .15 .30
DOCSEN088 Gameciel, the Sea Turtle Kaiju R 4.00 8.00
DOCSEN008 Superheavy Samurai Soulclaw C .15 .30
DOCSEN009 Fluffal Wings C .15 .30
DOCSEN010 D/D Berfomet R .60 1.25
DOCSEN011 D/D Swirl Slime C .15 .30
DOCSEN012 D/D Necro Slime C .15 .30
DOCSEN013 Raidraptor - Wild Vulture C .15 .30
DOCSEN014 Raidraptor - Skull Eagle C .15 .30
DOCSEN015 Performage Mirror Conductor C .15 .30
DOCSEN016 Performage Plushfire C .15 .30
DOCSEN017 The Legendary Fisherman III SR .50 1.00
DOCSEN018 Assault Blackwing - Kunai the Drizzle R .15 .30
DOCSEN019 Charging Gaia the Fierce Knight UR4.00 8.00
DOCSEN020 Sphere Kuriboh R .25 .50
DOCSEN021 Super Soldier Soul C .15 .30
DOCSEN022 Beginning Knight SR 1.00 2.00
DOCSEN023 Evening Twilight Knight SR 2.50 5.00
DOCSEN024 Vector Pendulum, the Dracoverlord SR1.50 3.00
DOCSEN025 Majespecter Cat - Nekomata SR 1.25 2.50
DOCSEN026 Majespecter Raccoon - Bunbuku UR15.00 30.00
DOCSEN027 Majespecter Crow - Yata C .15 .30
DOCSEN028 Majespecter Fox - Kyubi C .15 .30
DOCSEN029 Majespecter Unicorn - Kirin R 2.00 4.00
DOCSEN030 Igknight Cavalier C .15 .30
DOCSEN031 Igknight Veteran C .15 .30
DOCSEN032 Graydle Slime R .30 .75
DOCSEN033 Graydle Alligator C .15 .30
DOCSEN034 Graydle Cobra C .15 .30
DOCSEN035 Graydle Eagle C .15 .30
DOCSEN036 Skilled Red Magician R .10 .20
DOCSEN037 Giant Pairfish R .10 .20
DOCSEN038 Toon Barrel Dragon R .25 .50
DOCSEN039 Deskbot 006 C .15 .30
DOCSEN040 Pot of The Forbidden SP 1.25 2.50
DOCSEN041 Dr. Frankenderp SP .10 .20
DOCSEN042 Black Luster Soldier - Super Soldier UR 7.50 15.00
DOCSEN042 Black Luster Soldier - Super Soldier UTR 7.50 15.00
DOCSEN043 Frightfur Sabre-Tooth UR 10.00 20.00
DOCSEN044 D/D/D Wave Oblivion King Caesar... SR 4.00 8.00
DOCSEN045 Odd-Eyes Vortex Dragon SCR 10.00 20.00
DOCSEN045 Odd-Eyes Vortex Dragon UTR 15.00 30.00
DOCSEN046 Scarlight Red Dragon Archfiend SCR20.00 40.00
DOCSEN046 Scarlight Red Dragon Archfiend UTR20.00 40.00
DOCSEN046 Scarlight Red Dragon Archfiend GR25.00 50.00
DOCSEN047 Assault Blackwing Raikiri... UR 7.50 15.00
DOCSEN047 Assault Blackwing Raikiri... UTR 7.50 15.00
DOCSEN048 Graydle Dragon SR 2.50 5.00
DOCSEN049 Deskbot Jet C .15 .30
DOCSEN050 D/D/D Duo-Dawn King Kali Yuga SR2.50 5.00
DOCSEN051 Raidraptor - Fiend Eagle R .15 .30
DOCSEN052 Majester Paladin... UR 1.25 2.50
DOCSEN052 Majester Paladin... UTR 2.50 5.00
DOCSEN053 Shuffle Reborn C .15 .30
DOCSEN054 Rank-Up-Magic Raid Force R .25 .50
DOCSEN055 Raptor's Ultimate Mace C .15 .30
DOCSEN056 Super Soldier Ritual R .30 .75
DOCSEN057 Gateway to Chaos SR 2.00 4.00
DOCSEN058 Majesty's Pegasus SR .75 1.50
DOCSEN059 Majespecter Storm C .15 .30
DOCSEN060 Majespecter Cyclone SR .50 1.00
DOCSEN061 Igknight Reload UR 5.00 10.00
DOCSEN062 Graydle Impact C .15 .30
DOCSEN063 Odd-Eyes Fusion SCR 15.00 30.00
DOCSEN064 Psychic Blade C .15 .30
DOCSEN065 Painful Decision SCR 10.00 20.00
DOCSEN066 Super Rush Headlong SP .10 .20
DOCSEN067 Frightfur March C .15 .30
DOCSEN068 D/D/D Contract Change C .15 .30
DOCSEN069 Dark Contract with Errors C .15 .30
DOCSEN070 Super Soldier Rebirth C .15 .30
DOCSEN071 Super Soldier Shield UR 1.25 2.50
DOCSEN072 Majespecter Tornado UR 2.50 5.00
DOCSEN073 Majespecter Tempest C .15 .30
DOCSEN074 Graydle Parasite SR 1.25 2.50
DOCSEN075 Graydle Split C .15 .30
DOCSEN076 Blazing Mirror Force SCR 2.00 4.00
DOCSEN077 Pendulum Area R .10 .20
DOCSEN078 Urgent Ritual Art SCR 1.25 2.50
DOCSEN079 Grand Horn of Heaven C .15 .30
DOCSEN080 First-Aid Squad SP .10 .20
DOCSEN081 Painful Escape SCR 1.25 2.50
DOCSEN082 Kozmo Strawman UR 2.50 5.00
DOCSEN083 Kozmoll Wickedwitch C .15 .30
DOCSEN084 Kozmo DOG Fighter SR .30 .75
DOCSEN085 Kozmo Dark Destroyer SCR 7.50 15.00
DOCSEN086 Kozmo Lightsword C .15 .30
DOCSEN087 Radian, the Multidimensional Kaiju R1.25 2.50
DOCSEN089 Kaiju Capture Mission C .15 .30
DOCSEN090 D/D/D Wave King Caesar R .30 .75
DOCSEN091 D/D Savant Galilei C .15 .30
DOCSEN092 D/D Savant Kepler C .15 .30
DOCSEN093 Dark Contract with the Gate C .15 .30
DOCSEN094 Dark Contract with the Swamp King C.15 .30
DOCSEN095 Dark Contract with the Witch C .15 .30
DOCSEN096 Contract Laundering C .15 .30
DOCSEN097 D/D/D Human Resources C .15 .30
DOCSEN098 D/D/D Rebel King Leonidas SR 5.00 10.00
DOCSEN099 D/D/D Oblivion King Abyss Ragnarok R 4.00 8.00

2015 Yu-Gi-Oh Dragons of Legend 2 1st Edition

DRL2EN001 Timaeus the Knight of Destiny SCR .20 .40
DRL2EN002 Legendary Knight Critias SCR .10 .20
DRL2EN003 Doom Virus Dragon SCR 2.50 5.00
DRL2EN004 Tyrant Burst Dragon SCR .20 .40
DRL2EN005 Mirror Force Dragon SCR 4.00 8.00
DRL2EN006 The Fang of Critias SCR 3.00 6.00
DRL2EN007 Tyrant Wing SR .10 .20
DRL2EN008 Legendary Knight Hermos SCR .10 .20
DRL2EN009 Time Magic Hammer SCR .15 .30
DRL2EN010 Rocket Hermos Cannon SCR .10 .20
DRL2EN011 Goddess Bow SCR .15 .30
DRL2EN012 Red-Eyes Black Dragon Sword SCR .60 1.25
DRL2EN013 The Claw of Hermos SCR 2.50 5.00
DRL2EN014 Roulette Spider SR .10 .20
DRL2EN015 Double Magical Arm Bind SR .10 .20
DRL2EN016 Lord of the Red SCR .60 1.25
DRL2EN017 Red-Eyes Transmigration SR .10 .20
DRL2EN018 Paladin of Dark Dragon SCR 1.50 3.00
DRL2EN019 Dark Dragon Ritual SR .30 .75
DRL2EN020 Red-Eyes Spirit SR .10 .20
DRL2EN021 Red-Eyes Burn SR .50 1.00
DRL2EN022 Toon Ancient Gear Golem SR .60 1.25
DRL2EN023 Toon Kingdom SCR 25.00 50.00
DRL2EN024 Toon Rollback SR .30 .75
DRL2EN025 Shadow Toon SR .60 1.25
DRL2EN026 Comic Hand SCR 1.50 3.00
DRL2EN027 Mimicat SCR 15.00 30.00
DRL2EN028 Toon Mask SCR 1.00 2.00
DRL2EN029 Toon Briefcase SR .60 1.25
DRL2EN030 Prediction Princess Coinorma SR .10 .20
DRL2EN031 Prediction Princess Petalelf SR .10 .20
DRL2EN032 Prediction Princess Astromorrigan SR .10 .20
DRL2EN033 Prediction Princess Arrowsylph SR .10 .20
DRL2EN034 Prediction Princess Crystaldine SR .10 .20
DRL2EN035 Prediction Princess Tarotrei SCR .60 1.25
DRL2EN036 Prediction Ritual SR .10 .20
DRL2EN037 Black Cat-astrophe SR .10 .20
DRL2EN038 Reverse Reuse SR .10 .20
DRL2EN039 Aquaactress Tetra SR .10 .20
DRL2EN040 Aquaactress Guppy SR .10 .20
DRL2EN041 Aquaactress Arowana SR .10 .20
DRL2EN042 Aquarium Stage SR .10 .20
DRL2EN043 Aquarium Set SR .10 .20
DRL2EN044 Aquarium Lighting SR .10 .20
DRL2EN045 Aqua Story - Urashima SR .10 .20

2015 Yu-Gi-Oh Duelist Pack Battle City

DPBCEN001 The Winged Dragon of Ra - Sphere Mode UR 20.00 40.00
DPBCEN002 Juragedo SR 4.00 8.00
DPBCEN003 Legion the Fiend Jester SR 3.00 6.00
DPBCEN004 Anti-Magic Arrows UR 3.00 6.00
DPBCEN005 Multiple Destruction UR .50 1.00
DPBCEN006 Black Luster Soldier SR 1.50 3.00
DPBCEN007 Black Luster Ritual C .10 .20
DPBCEN008 Dark Magician SR .60 1.25
DPBCEN009 Dark Magician Girl SR 2.00 4.00
DPBCEN010 Buster Blader R .15 .30
DPBCEN011 Archfiend of Gilfer C .10 .20
DPBCEN012 Jack's Knight C .10 .20
DPBCEN013 Queen's Knight C .10 .20
DPBCEN014 King's Knight C .10 .20
DPBCEN015 Kuriboh C .10 .20
DPBCEN016 Blue-Eyes White Dragon UR 2.50 5.00
DPBCEN017 Lord of D. C .10 .20
DPBCEN018 The Flute of Summoning Dragon C .10 .20
DPBCEN019 Enemy Controller C .10 .20
DPBCEN020 Crush Card Virus R .75 1.50
DPBCEN021 Red-Eyes B. Dragon SR 1.25 2.50
DPBCEN022 Gearfried the Iron Knight C .10 .20
DPBCEN023 Rocket Warrior C .10 .20
DPBCEN024 Time Wizard C .10 .20
DPBCEN025 Foolish Burial R .20 .40
DPBCEN026 Insect Queen C .10 .20
DPBCEN027 Jinzo R .15 .30
DPBCEN028 The Legendary Fisherman C .10 .20
DPBCEN029 Dragged Down into the Grave C .10 .20
DPBCEN030 Embodiment of Apophis R .10 .20
DPBCEN031 The Masked Beast R .10 .20
DPBCEN032 Curse of the Masked Beast C .10 .20
DPBCEN033 Dark Necrofear R .10 .20
DPBCEN034 Lava Golem R .50 1.00
DPBCEN035 Magical Stone Excavation C .10 .20
DPBCEN036 Malevolent Catastrophe C .10 .20
DPBCEN037 Harpie Lady C .10 .20
DPBCEN038 Harpie Lady Sisters C .10 .20
DPBCEN039 Elegant Egotist C .10 .20
DPBCEN040 Hysteric Party C .10 .20
DPBCEN041 Barrel Dragon R .15 .30
DPBCEN042 Blast Sphere C .10 .20
DPBCEN043 Blue-Eyes Toon Dragon C .75 1.50
DPBCEN044 Toon Dark Magician Girl C .30 .75
DPBCEN045 Toon Gemini Elf C .10 .20
DPBCEN046 Toon World C .50 1.00
DPBCEN047 Toon Table of Contents R 3.00 6.00

2015 Yu-Gi-Oh High-Speed Riders 1st Edition

HSRDEN001 Speedroid Terrortop SR 10.00 20.00
HSRDEN002 Speedroid Tri-Eyed Dice C .10 .20
HSRDEN003 Speedroid Double Yoyo C .10 .20
HSRDEN004 Speedroid Razorang R .20 .40
HSRDEN005 Speedroid Menko C .10 .20
HSRDEN006 Speedroid Taketomborg SR .75 1.50
HSRDEN007 Speedroid Ohajikid R .20 .40
HSRDEN008 Speedroid Red-Eyed Dice SR .25 .50
HSRDEN009 Hi-Speedroid Kendama R .20 .40
HSRDEN010 Hi-Speedroid Chanbara SCR 15.00 30.00
HSRDEN011 Speed Recovery SR .20 .40
HSRDEN012 Shock Surprise R .20 .40
HSRDEN013 Synchro Cracker C .10 .20
HSRDEN014 Dice Roll Battle R .20 .40
HSRDEN015 Red Sprinter SR .50 1.00
HSRDEN016 Red Resonator C .10 .20
HSRDEN017 Synkron Resonator C .10 .20
HSRDEN018 Chain Resonator C .10 .20
HSRDEN019 Mirror Resonator SR .10 .20
HSRDEN020 Dark Resonator C .10 .20
HSRDEN021 Vice Dragon C .10 .20
HSRDEN022 Red Wyvern SCR 4.00 8.00
HSRDEN023 Red Dragon Archfiend C .10 .20
HSRDEN024 Red Nova Dragon R .20 .40
HSRDEN025 Resonator Call C .10 .20
HSRDEN026 Red Cocoon C .10 .20
HSRDEN027 Red Carpet R .20 .40
HSRDEN028 PSY-Frame Driver R .20 .40
HSRDEN029 PSY-Framegear Alpha C .10 .20
HSRDEN030 PSY-Framegear Beta UR 1.00 2.00
HSRDEN031 PSY-Framegear Gamma UR 10.00 20.00
HSRDEN032 PSY-Framegear Delta R .20 .40
HSRDEN033 PSY-Framegear Epsilon C .10 .20
HSRDEN034 PSY-Framelord Zeta SR .20 .40
HSRDEN035 PSY-Framelord Omega SCR 10.00 20.00
HSRDEN036 PSY-Frame Circuit R .50 1.00
HSRDEN037 PSY-Frame Overload R .20 .40
HSRDEN038 Goyo Chaser UR .15 .30
HSRDEN039 Goyo Predator UR .25 .50
HSRDEN040 Hot Red Dragon Archfiend SR 1.00 2.00
HSRDEN041 Hot Red Dragon Archfiend Abyss UR10.00 20.00
HSRDEN042 Hot Red Dragon Archfiend Bane SCR10.00 20.00
HSRDEN043 Stardust Spark Dragon SR 3.00 6.00
HSRDEN044 Black Rose Moonlight Dragon SR 4.00 8.00
HSRDEN045 Expressroid C .10 .20
HSRDEN046 Krebons C .10 .20
HSRDEN047 Armoroid C .10 .20
HSRDEN048 Silent Psychic Wizard C .10 .20
HSRDEN049 Serene Psychic Witch C .10 .20
HSRDEN050 Hushed Psychic Cleric C .10 .20
HSRDEN051 Cardcar D C .10 .20
HSRDEN052 Trishula, Dragon of the Ice Barrier SCR 25.00 50.00
HSRDEN053 Mystical Space Typhoon C .50 1.00
HSRDEN054 Emergency Teleport UR .75 1.50
HSRDEN055 Psychokinesis C .10 .20
HSRDEN056 Pot of Duality R 1.50 3.00
HSRDEN057 Future Glow C .10 .20
HSRDEN058 Compulsory Evacuation Device C .10 .20
HSRDEN059 Supercharge C .10 .20
HSRDEN060 Psychic Overload C .10 .20

2015 Yu-Gi-Oh Mega Tin Mega Pack 1st Edition

MP15EN001 Artifact Scythe SR .50 1.00
MP15EN002 Galaxy Mirror Sage C .15 .30
MP15EN003 Galaxy Tyranno R .25 .50
MP15EN004 Heliosphere Dragon C .12 .25
MP15EN005 Blizzard Thunderbird C .12 .25
MP15EN006 Artifact Moralltach SR 1.25 2.50
MP15EN007 Artifact Beagalltach C .15 .30
MP15EN008 Artifact Failnaught C .12 .25
MP15EN009 Artifact Aegis C .12 .25
MP15EN010 Artifact Achilleshield C .12 .25
MP15EN011 Artifact Labrys C .12 .25
MP15EN012 Artifact Caduceus R .25 .50
MP15EN013 Sylvan Cherubsprout C .12 .25
MP15EN014 Sylvan Snapdrassinagon R .12 .25
MP15EN015 Sylvan Lotuswain C .12 .25
MP15EN016 Sylvan Sagequoia UR .40 .80
MP15EN017 Bujin Hirume UR 1.00 2.00
MP15EN018 Traptrix Dionaea R .60 1.25
MP15EN019 Madolche Anjelly UR 3.00 6.00
MP15EN020 Gladiator Beast Augustus R 1.00 2.00
MP15EN021 Thestalos the Mega Monarch SCR .75 1.50
MP15EN022 Number 62: Galaxy-Eyes Prime Photon Dragon UR 2.00 4.00
MP15EN023 Number C107: Neo Galaxy-Eyes Tachyon Dragon SR 1.00 2.00
MP15EN024 Number C102: Archfiend Seraph SR.30 .75
MP15EN025 Number 43: Manipulator of Souls C.15 .30
MP15EN026 Number C43: High Manipulator of Chaos R .25 .50
MP15EN027 Artifact Durendal UR .25 .50
MP15EN028 Orea, the Sylvan High Arbiter SCR1.50 3.00
MP15EN029 Bujinki Amaterasu SCR .30 .75
MP15EN030 Cairngorgon, Antiluminescent Knight SR .50 1.00
MP15EN031 Phonon Pulse Dragon R .40 .80
MP15EN032 Galactic Charity C .12 .25
MP15EN033 Rank-Up-Magic - The Seventh One SCR .50 1.00
MP15EN034 Artifact Ignition UR .50 1.00
MP15EN035 Artifacts Unleashed C .07 .15
MP15EN036 Sylvan Charity UR .75 1.50
MP15EN038 Forbidden Scripture SCR .30 .60
MP15EN039 Double Dragon Descent C .15 .30
MP15EN040 Tachyon Chaos Hole SR .75 1.50
MP15EN041 Artifact Sanctum UR 1.25 2.50
MP15EN042 Sylvan Waterslide C .12 .25
MP15EN043 Bujincident C .20 .40
MP15EN044 The Monarchs Erupt SR .30 .75
MP15EN045 And the Band Played On C .30 .60
MP15EN046 Noble Knight Brothers SCR .75 1.50
MP15EN047 Noble Knight Eachtar SR .15 .30
MP15EN048 Sylvan Princessprout SR 1.00 2.00
MP15EN049 Bujingi Sinyou UR .30 .60
MP15EN050 Vampire Vamp SR .50 1.00
MP15EN051 Gladiator Beast Nerokius SCR .75 1.50
MP15EN052 Noble Knights of the Round Table UR.25 .50
MP15EN053 Avalon SR .15 .30
MP15EN054 Escalation of the Monarchs SR .60 1.25
MP15EN055 Number 42: Galaxy Tomahawk C .30 .60
MP15EN056 Number 48: Shadow Lich C .30 .75
MP15EN057 Galaxy Dragon C .30 .60
MP15EN058 Flash Knight R .20 .40
MP15EN059 Foucault's Cannon SR .10 .20
MP15EN060 Metaphys Armed Dragon C .12 .25
MP15EN061 Performapal Skeeter Skimmer C .07 .15
MP15EN062 Performapal Whip Snake R .30 .60
MP15EN063 Performapal Sword Fish C .12 .25
MP15EN064 Performapal Hip Hippo C .12 .25
MP15EN066 Performapal Turn Toad R .12 .25
MP15EN067 Superheavy Samurai Blue Brawler C.12 .25
MP15EN068 Superheavy Samurai Swordsman C .12 .25
MP15EN069 Superheavy Samurai Big Benkei R .75 1.50
MP15EN070 Aria the Melodious Diva C .30 .60
MP15EN071 Sonata the Melodious Diva C .25 .50
MP15EN072 Mozarta the Melodious Maestra R .75 1.50
MP15EN073 Battleguard King C .12 .25
MP15EN074 Satellarknight Deneb UR 7.50 15.00
MP15EN075 Satellarknight Altair R .30 .60
MP15EN076 Satellarknight Vega C .25 .50
MP15EN077 Satellarknight Unukalhai C .20 .40
MP15EN078 Shaddoll Falco R .25 .50
MP15EN079 Shaddoll Hedgehog C .15 .30
MP15EN080 Shaddoll Squamata C .30 .75
MP15EN081 Shaddoll Dragon R .75 1.50
MP15EN082 Shaddoll Beast R .40 .80
MP15EN083 Suanni, Fire of the Yang Zing SR 2.00 4.00
MP15EN084 Bi'an, Earth of the Yang Zing SR 1.50 3.00
MP15EN085 Bixi, Water of the Yang Zing SR .30 .60
MP15EN086 Pulao, Wind of the Yang Zing SR .20 .40
MP15EN087 Chiwen, Light of the Yang Zing UR12.50 25.00
MP15EN088 Artifact Chakram C .12 .25
MP15EN089 Artifact Lancea C 1.00 2.00
MP15EN090 Djinn Demolisher of Rituals C .12 .25
MP15EN091 Raiza the Mega Monarch SCR 1.50 3.00
MP15EN092 Deskbot 001 C .07 .15
MP15EN093 El Shaddoll Winda UR 2.50 5.00
MP15EN094 El Shaddoll Construct UR .75 1.50
MP15EN095 Saffira, Queen of Dragons UR 1.00 2.00
MP15EN096 Baxia, Brightness of the Yang Zing SCR 2.50 5.00
MP15EN097 Samsara, Dragon of Rebirth SR .75 1.50
MP15EN098 Stellarknight Delteros SCR 2.00 4.00
MP15EN099 Hippo Carnival C .20 .40
MP15EN100 Feast of the Wild LV5 C .12 .25
MP15EN101 Stellarknight Alpha C .15 .30
MP15EN102 Satellarknight Skybridge R 1.00 2.00
MP15EN103 Shaddoll Fusion SR 1.25 2.50
MP15EN104 Curse of the Shadow Prison C .12 .25
MP15EN105 Yang Zing Path SCR 1.25 2.50
MP15EN106 Yang Zing Prana C .10 .20
MP15EN107 Hymn of Light C .15 .30
MP15EN108 Magical Spring SCR .40 .80
MP15EN109 The Monarchs Stormforth C .20 .40
MP15EN110 Battleguard Rage C .12 .25
MP15EN111 Battleguard Howling C .07 .15
MP15EN112 Stellarnova Wave C .12 .25
MP15EN113 Stellarnova Alpha UR 2.00 4.00
MP15EN114 Sinister Shadow Games UR .40 .80
MP15EN115 Shaddoll Core SR .50 1.00
MP15EN116 Yang Zing Creation UR .60 1.25
MP15EN117 Yang Zing Unleashed C .07 .15
MP15EN118 Chain Dispel C .20 .40
MP15EN119 Time-Space Trap Hole SCR 1.25 2.50
MP15EN120 Doomstar Magician UR .25 .50
MP15EN121 Dante, Traveler of the Burning Abyss SCR 2.50 5.00
MP15EN122 Number 58: Burner Visor C .30 .60
MP15EN123 Felis, Lightsworn Archer UR .60 1.25
MP15EN124 Panzer Dragon R .40 .80
MP15EN125 Cloudcastle C .20 .40
MP15EN126 Performapal Cheermole R .20 .40
MP15EN127 Performapal Trampolynx R .30 .60
MP15EN128 Canon the Melodious Diva C .40 .80
MP15EN129 Serenade the Melodious Diva C .20 .40
MP15EN130 Elegy the Melodious Diva C .30 .60
MP15EN131 Shopina the Melodious Maestra R .60 1.25
MP15EN132 Superheavy Samurai Kabuto C .12 .25
MP15EN133 Superheavy Samurai Scales R 6.00 12.00
MP15EN134 Superheavy Samurai Soulfire Suit C.12 .25
MP15EN135 Superheavy Samurai Soulshield Wall C .15 .30
MP15EN136 Superheavy Samurai Soulbreaker Armor C .20 .40
MP15EN137 Superheavy Samurai Soulbang Cannon C .15 .30
MP15EN138 Fluffal Leo C .15 .30
MP15EN139 Fluffal Bear C .75 1.50
MP15EN140 Fluffal Dog R .75 1.50
MP15EN141 Fluffal Owl R .25 .50
MP15EN142 Fluffal Cat C .30 .60
MP15EN143 Fluffal Rabbit C .25 .50
MP15EN144 Qliphort Scout UR .60 1.25
MP15EN145 Qliphort Disk SCR .75 1.50
MP15EN146 Satellarknight Sirius R .25 .50
MP15EN147 Satellarknight Procyon C .15 .30
MP15EN148 Satellarknight Betelgeuse C .25 .50
MP15EN149 Shaddoll Hound C .12 .25
MP15EN150 Taotie, Shadow of the Yang Zing SR.15 .30
MP15EN151 Jiaotu, Darkness of the Yang Zing UR4.00 8.00
MP15EN152 Lindbloom C .12 .25
MP15EN153 Night Dragolich UR .30 .60
MP15EN154 Zaborg the Mega Monarch UR 1.00 2.00
MP15EN155 Denko Sekka UR .75 1.50
MP15EN156 Deskbot 002 C .20 .40
MP15EN157 Herald of Ultimateness UR .75 1.50
MP15EN158 Frightfur Bear R .30 .60
MP15EN159 Frightfur Wolf R .25 .50
MP15EN160 El Shaddoll Grysta SCR .60 1.25
MP15EN161 El Shaddoll Shekhinaga SCR 1.00 2.00
MP15EN162 First of the Dragons SR 1.00 2.00
MP15EN163 Yazi, Evil of the Yang Zing SCR 2.00 4.00
MP15EN164 Herald of the Arc Light SR 4.00 8.00
MP15EN165 Stellarknight Triverr UR 1.25 2.50
MP15EN166 Wonder Balloons C .12 .25
MP15EN167 Mimiclay C .12 .25
MP15EN168 Draw Muscle R .25 .50
MP15EN169 1st Movement Solo SR .75 1.50
MP15EN170 Toy Vendor C .30 .60
MP15EN171 Saqlifice UR 1.00 2.00
MP15EN172 Laser Qlip C .12 .25
MP15EN173 Hexatellarknight C .07 .15
MP15EN174 El Shaddoll Fusion SR .50 1.00
MP15EN175 Celestia C .15 .30
MP15EN176 Oracle of the Herald C .20 .40
MP15EN177 Strike of the Monarchs C .12 .25
MP15EN178 Command Performance C .12 .25
MP15EN179 Performapal Revival C .07 .15
MP15EN180 Punch-in-the-Box C .15 .30
MP15EN181 The Phantom Knights of Shadow Veil C .20 .40
MP15EN182 Qlimate Change C .12 .25
MP15EN183 Qlipper Launch C .12 .25
MP15EN184 Yang Zing Brutality C .12 .25
MP15EN185 Fusion Reserve UR .30 .75
MP15EN186 Solemn Scolding SCR 2.50 5.00
MP15EN187 Virgil, Rock Star of the Burning Abyss SCR .30 .75
MP15EN188 Number 39: Utopia Beyond SR 1.25 2.50
MP15EN189 CXyz Barian Hope SR .30 .60
MP15EN190 Number 90: Utopic Dragon SCR 3.00 6.00
MP15EN191 Performapal Fire Mufflerlion C .12 .25
MP15EN192 Performapal Partnaga C .12 .25

MP15EN193 Performapal Friendonkey C .12 .25
MP15EN194 Performapal Spikeagle C .07 .15
MP15EN195 Performapal Stamp Turtle C .12 .25
MP15EN196 Performapal Trump Witch R .12 .25
MP15EN197 Superheavy Samurai Flutist SR 1.50 3.00
MP15EN198 Superheavy Samurai Trumpeter SR1.50 3.00
MP15EN199 Superheavy Samurai Soulpiercer C1.00 2.00
MP15EN200 Superheavy Samurai Soulbeads C .15 .30
MP15EN201 Raidraptor - Vanishing Lanius C .30 .60
MP15EN202 Gem-Knight Lapis C .30 .60
MP15EN203 Infernoid Antra SR .40 .80
MP15EN204 Infernoid Harmadik UR 1.00 2.00
MP15EN205 Infernoid Patrulea R .30 .60
MP15EN206 Infernoid Piaty C .12 .25
MP15EN207 Infernoid Seitsemas C .15 .30
MP15EN208 Infernoid Attondel C .15 .30
MP15EN209 Infernoid Onuncu SCR .75 1.50
MP15EN210 Qliphort Stealth UR 1.25 2.50
MP15EN211 Apoqliphort Skybase UR .25 .50
MP15EN212 Satellarknight Capella C .15 .30
MP15EN213 Dance Princess of the Nekroz R .40 .80
MP15EN214 Jinzo - Jector SR .40 .80
MP15EN215 Caius the Mega Monarch UR 1.50 3.00
MP15EN216 Lightning Rod Lord SR .12 .25
MP15EN217 Uni-Zombie C .50 1.00
MP15EN218 Deskbot 003 C .20 .40
MP15EN219 Nekroz of Gungnir SCR .50 1.00
MP15EN220 Rune-Eyes Pendulum Dragon UR .60 1.25
MP15EN221 El Shaddoll Wendigo SR .40 .80
MP15EN222 Metaphys Horus UR .30 .75
MP15EN223 Raidraptor - Rise Falcon C .25 .50
MP15EN224 Stellarknight Constellar Diamond UR3.00 6.00
MP15EN225 Sky Cavalry Centaurea UR .50 1.00
MP15EN226 Illusion Balloons C .12 .25
MP15EN227 Raidraptor - Nest R .30 .60
MP15EN228 Void Seer SR .25 .50
MP15EN229 Void Expansion R .15 .30
MP15EN230 Nephe Shaddoll Fusion SCR .30 .75
MP15EN231 Nekroz Cycle R .30 .75
MP15EN232 Tenacity of the Monarchs R .75 1.50
MP15EN233 Pot of Riches SCR .30 .75
MP15EN234 A Wild Monster Appears! SCR .25 .50
MP15EN235 Pendulum Shift C .12 .25
MP15EN236 Performapal Call C .12 .25
MP15EN237 Wall of Disruption C .60 1.25
MP15EN238 Last Minute Cancel C .07 .15
MP15EN239 Raidraptor - Readiness C .15 .30
MP15EN240 Eye of the Void UR .15 .30
MP15EN241 Void Launch SR .12 .25
MP15EN242 Re-qliate C .12 .25
MP15EN243 Echo Oscillation C .12 .25
MP15EN244 Toy Knight C .07 .15
MP15EN245 Swordsman of Revealing Light UR .75 1.50
MP15EN246 Level Lifter C .12 .25
MP15EN247 Soul Strike C .15 .30

2015 Yu-Gi-Oh Premium Gold Return of the Bling 1st Edition

PGL2EN001 Junk Giant GSR .10 .20
PGL2EN002 Absolute King Back Jack GSR .20 .40
PGL2EN003 Rose Lover GSR .50 1.00
PGL2EN004 Rose Paladin GSR .20 .40
PGL2EN005 Ghost Charon... GSR .10 .20
PGL2EN006 Blackwing Kris the Crack of Dawn GSR4.00 8.00
PGL2EN007 Blackwing Pinaki
the Waxing Moon GSR .50 1.00
PGL2EN008 Peropero Cerperus GSR .15 .30
PGL2EN009 Tristan, Knight of Underworld GSR .50 1.00
PGL2EN010 Isolde, Belle of Underworld GSR .30 .75
PGL2EN011 Masked HERO Anki GSR 1.00 2.00
PGL2EN012 Blackwing Tamer... GSR .50 1.00
PGL2EN013 Blackwing Nothung Starlight GSR 1.25 2.50
PGL2EN014 Dragocytos
Corrupted Nethersoul... GSR .60 1.25
PGL2EN015 #95 Galaxy-Eyes Dark Matter... GSR4.00 8.00
PGL2EN016 Cat Shark GSR .50 1.00
PGL2EN017 Number 14: Greedy Sarameya GSR .30 .75
PGL2EN018 Number 21: Frozen Lady Justice GSR.30 .75
PGL2EN019 Parallel Twister GSR .20 .40
PGL2EN020 Stardust Re-Spark GSR .20 .40
PGL2EN021 Santa Claws GSR .30 .75
PGL2EN022 Right Leg of the Forbidden One GDR1.00 2.00
PGL2EN023 Left Leg of the Forbidden One GDR .75 1.50
PGL2EN024 Right Arm of the Forbidden One GDR1.00 2.00
PGL2EN025 Left Arm of the Forbidden One GDR .75 1.50
PGL2EN026 Exodia the Forbidden One GDR 2.00 4.00
PGL2EN027 Sinister Serpent GDR .15 .30
PGL2EN028 Card Trooper GDR .20 .40
PGL2EN029 Elemental HERO Neos Alius GDR .25 .50
PGL2EN030 Dandylion GDR .50 1.00
PGL2EN031 Debris Dragon GDR .60 1.25
PGL2EN032 Mystical Beast of Serket GDR .10 .20
PGL2EN033 Glow-Up Bulb GDR 10.00 20.00
PGL2EN034 Metaion, the Timelord GDR 2.50 5.00
PGL2EN035 Bujin Yamato GDR .50 1.00
PGL2EN036 Traptrix Atrax GDR .30 .75
PGL2EN037 Traptrix Myrmeleo GDR .75 1.50
PGL2EN038 Traptrix Nepenthes GDR .30 .75
PGL2EN039 Mathematician GDR .30 .75
PGL2EN040 Sylvan Sagequoia GDR .20 .40
PGL2EN041 Traptrix Dionaea GDR .30 .75
PGL2EN042 Goyo Guardian GDR 1.00 2.00
PGL2EN043 Armades, Keeper of Boundaries GDR1.00 2.00
PGL2EN044 Lavalval Chain GDR 2.00 4.00
PGL2EN045 Madolche Queen Tiaramisu GDR .50 1.00
PGL2EN046 Number 101: Silent Honor ARK GDR3.00 6.00
PGL2EN047 Downerd Magician GDR 1.50 3.00
PGL2EN048 Raigeki GDR 20.00 40.00
PGL2EN049 Book of Moon GDR .60 1.25
PGL2EN050 Advanced Ritual Art GDR 1.00 2.00
PGL2EN051 Foolish Burial GDR 1.25 2.50
PGL2EN052 Charge of the Light Brigade GDR .60 1.25
PGL2EN053 Rekindling GDR .20 .40
PGL2EN054 Preparation of Rites GDR .25 .50
PGL2EN055 Pot of Duality GDR 1.50 3.00
PGL2EN056 Temple of the Kings GDR .20 .40
PGL2EN057 The Grand Spellbook Tower GDR .75 1.50
PGL2EN058 Rank-Up-Magic Barian's Force GDR.15 .30
PGL2EN059 Rank-Up-Magic Numeron Force GDR.20 .40
PGL2EN060 Rank-Up-Magic Astral Force GDR .25 .50
PGL2EN061 Sylvan Charity GDR .15 .30
PGL2EN062 Ceasefire GDR .20 .40
PGL2EN063 Ring of Destruction GDR .50 1.00
PGL2EN064 Chain Disappearance GDR .75 1.50
PGL2EN065 Compulsory Evacuation Device GDR.30 .75
PGL2EN066 Exchange of the Spirit GDR .15 .30
PGL2EN067 Karma Cut GDR .75 1.50
PGL2EN068 Solemn Warning GDR 2.50 5.00
PGL2EN069 Traptrix Trap Hole Nightmare GDR .50 1.00
PGL2EN070 Crush Card Virus GDR 1.00 2.00
PGL2EN071 Veil of Darkness GDR .20 .40
PGL2EN072 Elemental HERO Prisma GDR 1.00 2.00
PGL2EN073 Blackwing - Gale the Whirlwind GDR1.00 2.00
PGL2EN074 My Body as a Shield GDR 2.00 4.00
PGL2EN075 Smashing Ground GDR .15 .30
PGL2EN076 Enemy Controller GDR .20 .40
PGL2EN077 Doomcaliber Knight GDR .20 .40
PGL2EN078 Five-Headed Dragon GDR 1.00 2.00
PGL2EN079 Gladiator Beast Gyzarus GDR .20 .40
PGL2EN080 Blue-Eyes White Dragon GDR 1.00 2.00
PGL2EN081 Gorz the Emissary of Darkness GDR .75 1.50
PGL2EN082 Master Hyperion GDR .20 .40
PGL2EN083 Grapha, Dragon
Lord of Dark World GDR .60 1.25
PGL2EN084 Sephylon, the Ultimate Timelord GDR.50 1.00
PGL2EN085 Herald of Perfection GDR 1.25 2.50
PGL2EN086 Naturia Beast GDR 3.00 6.00
PGL2EN087 Naturia Barkion GDR 1.00 2.00
PGL2EN088 Formula Synchron GDR 1.50 3.00
PGL2EN089 Dark Hole GDR 1.00 2.00
PGL2EN090 Call of the Haunted GDR 1.00 2.00
PGL2EN091 Starlight Road GDR 1.00 2.00

2015 Yu-Gi-Oh The Secret Forces 1st Edition

THSFEN001 Mayosenju Daibak SCR 4.00 8.00
THSFEN002 Yosenju Misak SCR .15 .30
THSFEN003 Yosenju Kama 1 SCR .75 1.50
THSFEN004 Yosenju Kama 2 SCR 1.00 2.00
THSFEN005 Yosenju Kama 3 SCR .75 1.50
THSFEN006 Yosenju Shinchu L SR .10 .20
THSFEN007 Yosenju Shinchu R SR .15 .30
THSFEN008 Yosen Training Grounds SR .10 .20
THSFEN009 Yosenjus' Secret Move SR .15 .30
THSFEN010 Shurit, Strategist of the Nekroz SR .15 .30
THSFEN011 Great Sorcerer of the Nekroz SR .10 .20
THSFEN012 Exa, Enforcer of the Nekroz SR .10 .20
THSFEN013 Nekroz of Clausolas SCR .50 1.00
THSFEN014 Nekroz of Brionac SCR 10.00 20.00
THSFEN015 Nekroz of Trishula SCR 15.00 30.00
THSFEN016 Nekroz of Unicore SCR .50 1.00
THSFEN017 Nekroz of Valkyrus SCR 25.00 50.00
THSFEN018 Nekroz of Catastor SCR .20 .40
THSFEN019 Nekroz of Decisive Armor SCR .20 .40
THSFEN020 Nekroz Mirror SCR .30 .75
THSFEN021 Nekroz Kaleidoscope SCR 1.00 2.00
THSFEN022 Ritual Beast Tamer Lara SCR .50 1.00
THSFEN023 Ritual Beast Tamer Elder SCR 1.25 2.50
THSFEN024 Ritual Beast Tamer Wen SCR .30 .75
THSFEN025 Spiritual Beast Apelio SR .60 1.25
THSFEN026 Spiritual Beast Pettlephin SR .10 .20
THSFEN027 Spiritual Beast Cannahawk SR .20 .40
THSFEN028 Ritual Beast Ulti-Apelio SCR 2.00 4.00
THSFEN029 Ritual Beast Ulti-Pettlephin SCR .75 1.50
THSFEN030 Ritual Beast Ulti-Cannahawk SCR .30 .75
THSFEN031 Ritual Beast's Bond SR .10 .20
THSFEN032 Ritual Beast Steeds SR .25 .50
THSFEN033 Manju of the Ten Thousand Hands SR 5.00 10.00
THSFEN034 Necro Gardna SR .10 .20
THSFEN035 Armageddon Knight SR .60 1.25
THSFEN036 Djinn Releaser of Rituals SR .10 .20
THSFEN037 Djinn Presider of Rituals SR .10 .20
THSFEN038 Djinn Cursenchanter of Rituals SR .10 .20
THSFEN039 Djinn Prognosticator of Rituals SR .10 .20
THSFEN040 Djinn Disserere of Rituals SR .15 .30
THSFEN041 Gishki Chain SR .10 .20
THSFEN042 Gishki Shadow SR .10 .20
THSFEN043 Gishki Noellia SR .10 .20
THSFEN044 Cardcar D SR .20 .40
THSFEN045 Gishki Vision SR .10 .20
THSFEN046 Altitude Knight SR .10 .20
THSFEN047 Abyss Dweller SR 1.00 2.00
THSFEN048 Soul Release SR .20 .40
THSFEN049 Soul Absorption SR .10 .20
THSFEN050 Ritual Weapon SR .10 .20
THSFEN051 Burial from a Different Dimension SR .75 1.50
THSFEN052 Advanced Ritual Art SR .60 1.25
THSFEN053 Preparation of Rites SR .20 .40
THSFEN054 Ascending Soul SR .10 .20
THSFEN055 Ritual Cage SR .10 .20
THSFEN056 Divine Wind of Mist Valley SR .10 .20
THSFEN057 Fire Formation - Tenki SR 1.25 2.50
THSFEN058 Royal Decree SR 1.00 2.00
THSFEN059 Vanity's Emptiness SR 2.00 4.00
THSFEN060 Aquamirror Cycle SR .10 .20

2015 Yu-Gi-Oh Secrets of Eternity 1st Edition

SECEEN000 Dragoons of Draconia R .30 .75
SECEEN001 Performapal Fire Mufflerlion C .10 .20
SECEEN002 Performapal Partnaga C .10 .20
SECEEN003 Performapal Friendonkey C .10 .20
SECEEN004 Performapal Spikeagle C .10 .20
SECEEN005 Performapal Stamp Turtle C .10 .20
SECEEN006 Performapal Trump Witch R .10 .20
SECEEN007 Superheavy Samurai Flutist SR 2.00 4.00
SECEEN008 Superheavy Samurai Trumpeter SR .75 1.50
SECEEN009 Superheavy Samurai Soulpiercer C .10 .20
SECEEN010 Superheavy Samurai Soulbeads C .10 .20
SECEEN011 Raidraptor - Vanishing Lanius C .10 .20
SECEEN012 Gem-Knight Lapis C .10 .20
SECEEN013 Infernoid Antra SR .30 .75
SECEEN014 Infernoid Harmadik UR 1.25 2.50
SECEEN015 Infernoid Patrulea R .20 .40
SECEEN016 Infernoid Piaty C .10 .20
SECEEN017 Infernoid Seitsemas C .10 .20
SECEEN018 Infernoid Attondel C .10 .20
SECEEN019 Infernoid Onuncu SCR .60 1.25
SECEEN019u Infernoid Onuncu UTR 1.50 3.00
SECEEN020 Qliphort Monolith SCR 5.00 10.00
SECEEN021 Qliphort Cephalopod SR .30 .75
SECEEN022 Qliphort Stealth UR .30 .75
SECEEN023 Apoqliphort Skybase UR .75 1.50
SECEEN024 Satellarknight Capella C .10 .20
SECEEN025 Satellarknight Rigel SR .30 .75
SECEEN026 Yosenju Magat C .10 .20
SECEEN027 Yosenju Tsujik C .10 .20
SECEEN028 Dance Princess of the Nekroz R .15 .30
SECEEN029 Spiritual Beast Rampengu C .10 .20
SECEEN030 Morphtronic Smartfon C .10 .20
SECEEN031 Jinzo - Jector SR .75 1.50
SECEEN032 Skilled Blue Magician SR .50 1.00
SECEEN033 Koa'ki Meiru Overload R .25 .50
SECEEN034 Jigabyte C .10 .20
SECEEN035 Caius the Mega Monarch UR 5.00 10.00
SECEEN036 Thunderclap Skywolf SR .10 .20
SECEEN037 Lightning Rod Lord SR .10 .20
SECEEN038 Dragon Dowser R .10 .20
SECEEN039 Frontline Observer R .15 .30
SECEEN040 Uni-Zombie C .50 1.00
SECEEN041 Deskbot 003 C .60 1.25
SECEEN042 Legendary Maju Garzett C .10 .20
SECEEN043 Marmiting Captain C .10 .20
SECEEN044 Nekroz of Gungnir SCR 1.00 2.00
SECEEN044u Nekroz of Gungnir UTR 2.00 4.00
SECEEN045 Rune-Eyes Pendulum Dragon UR 1.00 2.00
SECEEN046 Gem-Knight Lady Lapis Lazuli R .15 .30
SECEEN047 El Shaddoll Wendigo SR .30 .75
SECEEN048 Superheavy Samurai Warlord... SR 2.00 4.00
SECEEN048u Superheavy Samurai Warlord... UTR2.50 5.00
SECEEN049 Metaphys Horus UR 1.00 2.00
SECEEN049u Metaphys Horus UTR 3.00 6.00
SECEEN050 Raidraptor - Rise Falcon C .10 .20
SECEEN051 Stellarknight Constellar Diamond UR.60 1.25
SECEEN051u Stellarknight Constellar Diamond UTR2.00 4.00
SECEEN052 Sky Cavalry Centaurea UR 5.00 10.00
SECEEN053 Illusion Balloons C .10 .20
SECEEN054 Raidraptor - Nest R .10 .20
SECEEN055 Constellar Twinkle C .10 .20
SECEEN056 Gottoms' Second Call R .15 .30
SECEEN057 Void Seer SR .50 1.00
SECEEN058 Void Expansion R .10 .20
SECEEN059 Nephe Shaddoll Fusion SCR .75 1.50
SECEEN060 Nekroz Cycle R .15 .30
SECEEN061 Tenacity of the Monarchs R .50 1.00
SECEEN062 Dragunity Divine Lance C .10 .20
SECEEN063 Pot of Riches SCR 2.00 4.00
SECEEN064 A Wild Monster Appears! SCR 1.00 2.00
SECEEN065 Pendulum Shift C .10 .20
SECEEN066 Extra Net C .10 .20
SECEEN067 Performapal Call C .10 .20
SECEEN068 Wall of Disruption C .10 .20
SECEEN069 Last Minute Cancel C .10 .20
SECEEN070 Raidraptor - Readiness C .10 .20
SECEEN071 Eye of the Void UR .25 .50
SECEEN072 Void Launch SR .10 .20
SECEEN073 Re-qliate C .10 .20
SECEEN074 Ritual Beast Ambush C .10 .20
SECEEN075 Zenmaiday C .10 .20
SECEEN076 Unpossessed C .10 .20
SECEEN077 Blaze Accelerator Reload C .10 .20
SECEEN078 Soul Transition SCR 1.25 2.50
SECEEN079 Echo Oscillation C .10 .20
SECEEN080 Double Trap Hole C .10 .20
SECEEN081 Mischief of the Gnomes C .10 .20
SECEEN082 Farfa... R .75 1.50
SECEEN083 Libic... R .10 .20
SECEEN084 Cagna... R .10 .20
SECEEN085 Malacoda... SCR 3.00 6.00
SECEEN085 Malacoda... GR 5.00 10.00
SECEEN086 Good & Evil in the Burning Abyss SR.75 1.50
SECEEN087 U.A. Playmaker R .10 .20
SECEEN088 U.A. Blockbacker R .10 .20
SECEEN089 U.A. Turnover Tactics R .10 .20
SECEEN090 Gogogo Golem - Golden Form C .10 .20
SECEEN091 Dododo Witch C .10 .20
SECEEN092 Dododo Swordsman C .10 .20
SECEEN093 Toy Knight C .10 .20
SECEEN094 Explossum C .10 .20
SECEEN095 Swordsman of Revealing Light UR 1.50 3.00
SECEEN096 Doggy Diver R .10 .20
SECEEN097 Level Lifter C .10 .20
SECEEN098 Gogogo Talisman C .10 .20
SECEEN099 Soul Strike C .10 .20

2015 Yu-Gi-Oh Star Pack ARC-V

SP15EN001 Gem-Knight Tourmaline C .60 1.25
SP15EN002 Swamp Battleguard C .10 .20
SP15EN003 Lava Battleguard C .10 .20
SP15EN004 Mobius the Frost Monarch C .20 .40
SP15EN005 XX-Saber Fulhelmknight C .10 .20
SP15EN006 XX-Saber Boggart Knight C .50 1.00
SP15EN007 Constellar Algiedi C .10 .20
SP15EN008 Constellar Kaus C .20 .40
SP15EN009 Mobius the Mega Monarch C 2.00 4.00
SP15EN010 Stargazer Magician C .25 .50
SP15EN011 Timegazer Magician C .50 1.00
SP15EN012 Odd-Eyes Pendulum Dragon C .10 .20
SP15EN013 Performapal Whip Snake C .10 .20
SP15EN014 Performapal Sword Fish C .10 .20
SP15EN015 Performapal Hip Hippo C .10 .20
SP15EN016 Performapal Kaleidoscorp C .10 .20
SP15EN017 Superheavy Samurai Big Benkei C .75 1.50
SP15EN018 Aria the Melodious Diva C .10 .20
SP15EN019 Mozarta the Melodious Maestra C .20 .40
SP15EN020 Battleguard King C .10 .20
SP15EN021 Performapal Trampolynx C .10 .20
SP15EN022 Edge Imp Sabres C 4.00 8.00
SP15EN023 Fluffal Bear C .10 .20
SP15EN024 Performapal Fire Mufflerlion C .10 .20
SP15EN025 Performapal Partnaga C .10 .20
SP15EN026 Performapal Friendonkey C .10 .20
SP15EN027 Performapal Trump Witch C .10 .20
SP15EN028 Superheavy Samurai Trumpeter C .75 1.50
SP15EN029 Raidraptor - Vanishing Lanius C .50 1.00
SP15EN030 Gem-Knight Master Diamond C .20 .40
SP15EN031 Frightfur Bear C .10 .20
SP15EN032 Rune-Eyes Pendulum Dragon C .50 1.00
SP15EN033 X-Saber Souza C .10 .20
SP15EN034 Superheavy Samurai
Warlord Susanowo C 2.50 5.00
SP15EN035 Constellar Pleiades C .75 1.50
SP15EN036 Dark Rebellion Xyz Dragon C 2.00 4.00
SP15EN037 Raidraptor - Rise Falcon C .10 .20
SP15EN038 Polymerization C 4.00 8.00
SP15EN039 Gem-Knight Fusion C .75 1.50
SP15EN040 Hippo Carnival C .10 .20
SP15EN041 Feast of the Wild LV5 C .10 .20
SP15EN042 Wonder Balloons C .10 .20
SP15EN043 Toy Vendor C .50 1.00
SP15EN044 Illusion Balloons C .10 .20
SP15EN045 Raidraptor - Nest C .25 .50
SP15EN046 Command Performance C .10 .20
SP15EN047 Performapal Revival C .10 .20
SP15EN048 The Phantom Knights of Shadow Veil C.10 .20
SP15EN049 Wall of Disruption C .10 .20
SP15EN050 Raidraptor - Readiness C .10 .20

2015 Yu-Gi-Oh Starter Deck Dark Legion 1st Edition

YS15ENL00 D/D/D Dragon King Pendragon SCR.75 1.50
YS15ENL01 Beast of Talwar C .12 .25
YS15ENL02 Archfiend Soldier C .50 1.00
YS15ENL03 The Dragon Dwelling in the Cave C .20 .40
YS15ENL04 Gravi-Crush Dragon C .15 .30
YS15ENL05 Goblin Elite Attack Force C .12 .25
YS15ENL06 Axe Dragonute C .12 .25
YS15ENL07 Lancer Lindwurm C .15 .30
YS15ENL08 Mad Archfiend C .20 .40
YS15ENL09 Fabled Ashenveil C .07 .15
YS15ENL10 Lancer Dragonute C .12 .25
YS15ENL11 Theban Nightmare C .07 .15
YS15ENL12 Exploder Dragon SHR .30 .60
YS15ENL13 Grave Squirmer C .10 .20
YS15ENL14 Dark Hole SHR .50 1.00
YS15ENL15 Smashing Ground SHR .60 1.25
YS15ENL16 Monster Reincarnation C .20 .40
YS15ENL17 Mystical Space Typhoon C .30 .60
YS15ENL18 Rush Recklessly C .12 .25
YS15ENL19 Axe of Despair C 1.50 3.00
YS15ENL20 Malevolent Nuzzler C .12 .25
YS15ENL21 Banner of Courage C .10 .20
YS15ENL22 Mirror Force SHR .60 1.25
YS15ENL23 Magic Cylinder SHR .40 .80
YS15ENL24 Trap Hole C .12 .25
YS15ENL25 Dust Tornado C .30 .75
YS15ENL26 Mask of Weakness C .07 .15
YS15ENL27 Call of the Haunted C .12 .25
YS15ENL28 Negate Attack C .50 1.00

2015 Yu-Gi-Oh Starter Deck Saber Force 1st Edition

YS15ENF00 Odd-Eyes Saber Dragon SCR 1.00 2.00
YS15ENF01 Alexandrite Dragon C .15 .30
YS15ENF02 Mystical Elf C .07 .15
YS15ENF03 Odd-Eyes Dragon SHR .20 .40
YS15ENF04 Kaiser Glider C .12 .25
YS15ENF05 Cyber Dragon C .12 .25
YS15ENF06 Herald of Creation C .07 .15
YS15ENF07 Blade Knight C .40 .80
YS15ENF08 Mirage Dragon C .12 .25
YS15ENF09 Maha Vailo C .15 .30
YS15ENF10 DUCKER Mobile Cannon C .12 .25
YS15ENF11 Skelengel C .15 .30
YS15ENF12 The Calculator C .20 .40
YS15ENF13 Dark Hole SHR .40 .80
YS15ENF14 Smashing Ground SHR .75 1.50
YS15ENF15 Monster Reincarnation C .20 .40
YS15ENF16 Mystical Space Typhoon C .30 .60
YS15ENF17 Rush Recklessly C .12 .25
YS15ENF18 Poison of the Old Man C .30 .75
YS15ENF19 Black Pendant C .25 .50
YS15ENF20 Malevolent Nuzzler C .25 .50
YS15ENF21 Mirror Force SHR .50 1.00
YS15ENF22 Magic Cylinder SHR .40 .80
YS15ENF23 Pinpoint Guard C .15 .30
YS15ENF24 Trap Hole C .25 .50
YS15ENF25 Dust Tornado C .30 .75
YS15ENF26 Call of the Haunted C .15 .30
YS15ENF27 Negate Attack C .30 .75

2015 Yu-Gi-Oh Structure Deck Hero Strike 1st Edition

SDHSEN001 Elemental HERO Shadow Mist SR 4.00 8.00
SDHSEN002 Elemental HERO Ocean C .20 .40
SDHSEN003 Elemental HERO Woodsman C .20 .40
SDHSEN004 Elemental HERO Voltic C .10 .20
SDHSEN005 Elemental HERO Heat C .10 .20
SDHSEN006 Elemental HERO Avian C .10 .20
SDHSEN007 Elemental HERO Neos C .20 .40
SDHSEN008 Elemental HERO Neos Alius C .15 .30
SDHSEN009 Elemental HERO Bladedge C .10 .20
SDHSEN010 Elemental HERO Necroshade C .15 .30
SDHSEN011 Elemental HERO Wildheart C .20 .40
SDHSEN012 Elemental HERO Bubbleman C .60 1.25
SDHSEN013 Neo-Spacian Grand Mole C .20 .40
SDHSEN014 Honest C .50 1.00
SDHSEN015 Card Trooper C .10 .20
SDHSEN016 Winged Kuriboh C .30 .75
SDHSEN017 Summoner Monk C 1.25 2.50
SDHSEN018 Homunculus the Alchemic Being C .10 .20
SDHSEN019 Mask Change II C .50 1.00
SDHSEN020 Form Change C .25 .50
SDHSEN021 Mask Charge C 1.00 2.00
SDHSEN022 Mask Change C .25 .50
SDHSEN023 Polymerization C 1.25 2.50
SDHSEN024 Miracle Fusion C .60 1.25
SDHSEN025 Parallel World Fusion C .10 .20
SDHSEN026 A Hero Lives C 3.00 6.00
SDHSEN027 Hero Mask C .10 .20
SDHSEN028 H - Heated Heart C .10 .20
SDHSEN029 E - Emergency Call C .10 .20
SDHSEN030 R - Righteous Justice C .10 .20

SDHSEN031 0 - Oversoul C .10 .20
SDHSEN032 Reinforcement of the Army C .20 .40
SDHSEN033 The Warrior Returning Alive C .10 .20
SDHSEN034 Pot of Duality C 2.00 4.00
SDHSEN035 Hero Signal C .10 .20
SDHSEN036 Hero Blast C .10 .20
SDHSEN037 Call of the Haunted C .15 .30
SDHSEN038 Bottomless Trap Hole C .50 1.00
SDHSEN039 Compulsory Evacuation Device C .25 .50
SDHSEN040 Battleguard Howling C .10 .20
SDHSEN041 Contrast HERO Chaos UR .15 .30
SDHSEN042 Masked HERO Koga SR .20 .40
SDHSEN043 Masked HERO Divine Wind SR .20 .40
SDHSEN044 Masked HERO Dark Law SR 3.00 6.00
SDHSEN045 Elemental HERO Great Tornado C .10 .20

2015 Yu-Gi-Oh Structure Deck Master of Pendulum 1st Edition

SDMPEN001 Dragonpulse Magician C .15 .30
SDMPEN009 Odd-Eyes Pendulum Dragon C .15 .30
SDMPEN017 Fencing Fire Ferret C .15 .30
SDMPEN025 Sky Iris C .15 .30
SDMPEN033 Forbidden Dress C .15 .30
SDMPEN041 Odd-Eyes Meteorburst Dragon UR .75 1.50
SDMPEN002 Dragonpit Magician C .15 .30
SDMPEN003 Nobledragon Magician SR .15 .30
SDMPEN004 Oafdragon Magician SR .50 1.00
SDMPEN005 Wisdom-Eye Magician SR .25 .50
SDMPEN006 Performapal Skullcrobat Joker C .15 .30
SDMPEN007 Stargazer Magician C .15 .30
SDMPEN008 Timegazer Magician C .15 .30
SDMPEN010 Performapal Silver Claw C .15 .30
SDMPEN011 Performapal Salutiger C .15 .30
SDMPEN012 Performapal Trump Witch C .15 .30
SDMPEN013 Metaphys Armed Dragon C .15 .30
SDMPEN014 Chaos Hunter C .15 .30
SDMPEN015 Fusilier Dragon,
the Dual-Mode Beast C .15 .30
SDMPEN016 Lyla, Lightsworn Sorceress C .15 .30
SDMPEN018 Inari Fire C .15 .30
SDMPEN019 Nefarious Archfiend... C .15 .30
SDMPEN020 Jigabyte C .15 .30
SDMPEN021 Goblindbergh C .15 .30
SDMPEN022 X-Saber Airbellum C .15 .30
SDMPEN023 Magna Drago C .15 .30
SDMPEN024 Re-Cover C .15 .30
SDMPEN026 Pendulum Call C .15 .30
SDMPEN027 Pendulum Shift C .15 .30
SDMPEN028 Pendulum Rising C .15 .30
SDMPEN029 Sacred Sword of Seven Stars C .15 .30
SDMPEN030 Summoner's Art C .15 .30
SDMPEN031 Mystical Space Typhoon C .15 .30
SDMPEN032 Scapegoat C .15 .30
SDMPEN034 Polymerization C .15 .30
SDMPEN035 Terraforming C .15 .30
SDMPEN036 Pendulum Back C .15 .30
SDMPEN037 Powerful Rebirth C .15 .30
SDMPEN038 Traptrix Trap Hole Nightmare C .15 .30
SDMPEN039 Torrential Tribute C .15 .30
SDMPEN040 Eradicator Epidemic Virus C .15 .30
SDMPEN042 Odd-Eyes Absolute Dragon UR .50 1.00
SDMPEN043 Rune-Eyes Pendulum Dragon C .15 .30

2015 Yu-Gi-Oh Structure Deck Synchron Extreme 1st Edition

SDSEEN001 Jet Synchron SR .60 1.25
SDSEEN002 Rush Warrior C .15 .30
SDSEEN003 Synchron Carrier C .15 .30
SDSEEN004 Junk Synchron C .15 .30
SDSEEN005 Quickdraw Synchron C .15 .30
SDSEEN006 Drill Synchron C .15 .30
SDSEEN007 Turbo Synchron C .15 .30
SDSEEN008 Unknown Synchron C .15 .30
SDSEEN009 Fleur Synchron C .15 .30
SDSEEN010 Synchron Explorer C .15 .30
SDSEEN011 Speed Warrior C .15 .30
SDSEEN012 Sonic Warrior C .15 .30
SDSEEN013 Doppelwarrior C .15 .30
SDSEEN014 Quillbolt Hedgehog C .15 .30
SDSEEN015 Tuningware C .15 .30
SDSEEN016 Swift Scarecrow C .15 .30
SDSEEN017 Level Eater C .15 .30
SDSEEN018 Effect Veiler C .15 .30
SDSEEN019 Genex Neutron C .15 .30
SDSEEN020 Genex Ally Birdman C .15 .30
SDSEEN021 Plaguespreader Zombie C .15 .30
SDSEEN022 White Dragon Wyverburster C .15 .30
SDSEEN023 Black Dragon Collapserpent C .15 .30
SDSEEN024 Scrap Fist SR .10 .20
SDSEEN025 Limit Overdrive C .15 .30
SDSEEN026 Starlight Junktion C .15 .30
SDSEEN027 Tuning C .15 .30
SDSEEN028 Reinforcement of the Army C .15 .30
SDSEEN029 The Warrior Returning Alive C .15 .30
SDSEEN030 Dark Eruption C .15 .30
SDSEEN031 One for One C .15 .30
SDSEEN032 Night Beam C .15 .30
SDSEEN033 Double Cyclone C .15 .30
SDSEEN034 Scrap-Iron Statue C .15 .30
SDSEEN035 Scrap-Iron Scarecrow C .15 .30
SDSEEN036 Limiter Overload C .15 .30
SDSEEN037 Call of the Haunted C .15 .30
SDSEEN038 Imperial Iron Wall C .15 .30
SDSEEN039 Solemn Warning C .15 .30
SDSEEN040 Stardust Warrior UR .30 .75
SDSEEN041 Jet Warrior UR .20 .40
SDSEEN042 Accel Synchron SR .60 1.25
SDSEEN043 Junk Warrior C .15 .30

2015 Yu-Gi-Oh World Superstars

WSUPEN001 Chronomaly Nebra Disk SCR .15 .30
WSUPEN002 #36 Chronomaly Chateau Huyuk SR .20 .40
WSUPEN003 Heraldic Beast Amphisbaena SR .20 .40
WSUPEN004 Number 18: Heraldry Patriarch SR .20 .40
WSUPEN005 Augmented Heraldry SR .20 .40
WSUPEN006 Gagaga Sister SCR .50 1.00
WSUPEN007 Number 55: Gogogo Goliath SR .20 .40
WSUPEN008 Dodododraw SR .20 .40
WSUPEN009 Galaxy-Eyes Cloudragon SR .50 1.00
WSUPEN010 Galaxy Soldier SCR 10.00 20.00
WSUPEN011 Photon Stream of Destruction SR .20 .40
WSUPEN012 Tachyon Transmigration SCR .75 1.50
WSUPEN013 Battlin' Boxer Shadow SR .20 .40
WSUPEN014 #79 Battlin' Boxer Nova Kaiser SR .20 .40
WSUPEN015 Jolt Counter SR .20 .40
WSUPEN016 Heroic Challenger -
Assault Halberd SR .20 .40
WSUPEN017 Heroic Challenger -
Thousand Blades SR .20 .40
WSUPEN018 Star Seraph Scepter SCR .50 1.00
WSUPEN019 Star Seraph Scale SR .20 .40
WSUPEN020 Star Seraph Sovereignty SCR 5.00 10.00
WSUPEN021 Numeral Hunter SCR .10 .20
WSUPEN022 #86 Heroic Champion
Rhongomyniad SCR 1.50 3.00
WSUPEN023 Humhumming the Key Djinn SR .20 .40
WSUPEN024 Onomatopia SCR .10 .20
WSUPEN025 Marshalling Field SCR .15 .30
WSUPEN026 Number F0: Utopic Future SCR 3.00 6.00
WSUPEN027 Gagaga Samurai SR .75 1.50
WSUPEN028 Gagaga Mancer SR .20 .40
WSUPEN029 Guard Go! SR .20 .40
WSUPEN030 Hi-Five the Sky SCR .10 .20
WSUPEN031 The Door of Destiny SCR .10 .20
WSUPEN032 Elemental HERO Blazeman SCR 3.00 6.00
WSUPEN033 Naturia Gaiastrio SR .20 .40
WSUPEN034 Mecha Phantom Beast Jaculuslan SR .20 .40
WSUPEN035 Ghostrick Angel of Mischief SR 1.25 2.50
WSUPEN036 Flowerbot SR .20 .40
WSUPEN037 Humpty Grumpty SR .20 .40
WSUPEN038 Dragoroar SR .20 .40
WSUPEN039 Planckton SR .20 .40
WSUPEN040 Guerilla Kite SR .20 .40
WSUPEN041 Wattsychic Fighter SR .20 .40
WSUPEN042 Earthshattering Event SCR .10 .20
WSUPEN043 Ghostrick Break SR .20 .40
WSUPEN044 P.M. Captor SR .10 .20
WSUPEN045 Spiritual Whisper SR .20 .40
WSUPEN046 Xyz-Raypierce SR .20 .40
WSUPEN047 Heavy Knight of the Flame SR .20 .40
WSUPEN048 BOXer SR .20 .40
WSUPEN049 Kabuki Dragon SR .20 .40
WSUPEN050 Pendulum Impenetrable SCR .10 .20
WSUPEN051 Legendary Dragon of White SCR 6.00 12.00
WSUPEN052 Legendary Magician of Dark SCR 6.00 12.00

2015 Yu-Gi-Oh Yugi's Legendary Decks

YGLDENA00 Electromagnetic Turtle SCR 1.00 2.00
YGLDENA01 Black Luster Soldier C .15 .30
YGLDENA02 Black Luster Soldier... C .15 .30
YGLDENA03 Dark Magician C .15 .30
YGLDENA04 Dark Magician Girl C .15 .30
YGLDENA05 Gaia The Fierce Knight C .15 .30
YGLDENA06 Summoned Skull C .15 .30
YGLDENA07 Curse of Dragon C .15 .30
YGLDENA08 Catapult Turtle C .15 .30
YGLDENA09 Celtic Guardian C .15 .30
YGLDENA10 Winged Dragon... C .15 .30
YGLDENA11 Feral Imp C .15 .30
YGLDENA12 Beaver Warrior C .15 .30
YGLDENA13 Griffore C .15 .30
YGLDENA14 Mystical Elf C .15 .30
YGLDENA15 Giant Soldier of Stone C .15 .30
YGLDENA16 Mammoth Graveyard C .15 .30
YGLDENA17 Exodia the Forbidden One UR 2.50 5.00
YGLDENA18 Right Leg of the Forbidden One UR 1.50 3.00
YGLDENA19 Left Leg of the Forbidden One UR 1.50 3.00
YGLDENA20 Right Arm of the Forbidden One UR 1.50 3.00
YGLDENA21 Left Arm of the Forbidden One UR 1.50 3.00
YGLDENA22 Kuriboh C .15 .30
YGLDENA23 Monster Reborn C .15 .30
YGLDENA24 Swords of Revealing Light C .15 .30
YGLDENA25 Mystic Box C .15 .30
YGLDENA26 Brain Control C .15 .30
YGLDENA27 Monster Recovery C .15 .30
YGLDENA28 Spell Shattering Arrow C .15 .30
YGLDENA29 Horn of the Unicorn C .15 .30
YGLDENA30 Mystical Moon C .15 .30
YGLDENA31 Burning Land C .15 .30
YGLDENA32 Multiply C .15 .30
YGLDENA33 Detonate C .15 .30
YGLDENA34 Makiu, the Magical Mist C .15 .30
YGLDENA35 Polymerization C .15 .30
YGLDENA36 Black Luster Ritual C .15 .30
YGLDENA37 Mirror Force C .15 .30
YGLDENA38 Magical Hats C .15 .30
YGLDENA39 The Eye of Truth C .15 .30
YGLDENA40 Shift C .15 .30
YGLDENA41 Gaia the Dragon Champion C .15 .30
YGLDENB00 Dark Renewal SCR 10.00 20.00
YGLDENB01 Valkyrion the Magna Warrior UR .30 .75
YGLDENB02 Dark Magician UR 3.00 6.00
YGLDENB03 Dark Magician Girl UR 2.50 5.00
YGLDENB04 Buster Blader C .15 .30
YGLDENB05 Archfiend of Gilfer C .15 .30
YGLDENB06 Jack's Knight C .15 .30
YGLDENB07 Queen's Knight C .15 .30
YGLDENB08 King's Knight C .15 .30
YGLDENB09 Berfomet C .15 .30
YGLDENB10 Gazelle the King of Mythical Beasts C .15 .30
YGLDENB11 Alpha The Magnet Warrior C .15 .30
YGLDENB12 Beta The Magnet Warrior C .15 .30
YGLDENB13 Gamma The Magnet Warrior C .15 .30
YGLDENB14 Big Shield Gardna C .15 .30
YGLDENB15 Kuriboh C .15 .30
YGLDENB16 Monster Reborn C .15 .30
YGLDENB17 Swords of Revealing Light UR .20 .40
YGLDENB18 Dark Magic Curtain C .15 .30
YGLDENB19 Thousand Knives C .15 .30
YGLDENB20 Magic Formula C .15 .30
YGLDENB21 Magical Dimension C .15 .30
YGLDENB22 Diffusion Wave-Motion C .15 .30
YGLDENB23 Double Spell C .15 .30
YGLDENB24 Ectoplasmer C .15 .30
YGLDENB25 Soul Taker C .15 .30
YGLDENB26 Pot of Greed C .15 .30
YGLDENB27 Card Destruction C .15 .30
YGLDENB28 Exchange C .15 .30
YGLDENB29 Monster Recovery C .15 .30
YGLDENB30 Polymerization C .15 .30
YGLDENB31 De-Fusion C .15 .30
YGLDENB32 Multiply C .15 .30
YGLDENB33 Mirror Force UR 2.00 4.00
YGLDENB34 Magical Hats C .15 .30
YGLDENB35 Magic Cylinder C .15 .30
YGLDENB36 Spellbinding Circle C .15 .30
YGLDENB37 Lightforce Sword C .15 .30
YGLDENB38 Chain Destruction C .15 .30
YGLDENB39 Soul Rope C .15 .30
YGLDENB40 Tragedy C .15 .30
YGLDENB41 Chimera the Flying Mythical Beast C .15 .30
YGLDENC00 Black Illusion SCR 1.25 2.50
YGLDENC01 Magician of Black Chaos UR .75 1.50
YGLDENC02 Dark Magician of Chaos UR 3.00 6.00
YGLDENC03 Gandora the Dragon of Destruction C .15 .30
YGLDENC04 Silent Magician LV8 UR .50 1.00
YGLDENC05 Silent Magician LV4 C .15 .30
YGLDENC06 Silent Swordsman LV7 C .15 .30
YGLDENC07 Silent Swordsman LV5 C .15 .30
YGLDENC08 Silent Swordsman LV3 C .15 .30
YGLDENC09 Dark Magician UR .75 1.50
YGLDENC10 Dark Magician Girl C .15 .30
YGLDENC11 Buster Blader C .15 .30
YGLDENC12 The Tricky C .15 .30
YGLDENC13 Jack's Knight C .15 .30
YGLDENC14 Queen's Knight C .15 .30
YGLDENC15 King's Knight C .15 .30
YGLDENC16 Green Gadget C .15 .30
YGLDENC17 Red Gadget C .15 .30
YGLDENC18 Yellow Gadget C .15 .30
YGLDENC19 Skilled Dark Magician C .15 .30
YGLDENC20 Skilled White Magician C .15 .30
YGLDENC21 Blockman C .15 .30
YGLDENC22 Marshmallon C .15 .30
YGLDENC23 Kuriboh C .15 .30
YGLDENC24 Monster Reborn C .15 .30
YGLDENC25 Swords of Revealing Light C .15 .30
YGLDENC26 Gold Sarcophagus UR 4.00 8.00
YGLDENC27 Card of Sanctity C .15 .30
YGLDENC28 Polymerization C .15 .30
YGLDENC29 Dark Magic Attack C .15 .30
YGLDENC30 Magicians Unite C .15 .30
YGLDENC31 Dedication through
Light and Darkness C .15 .30
YGLDENC32 Black Magic Ritual C .15 .30
YGLDENC33 Tricky Spell 4 C .15 .30
YGLDENC34 Emblem of Dragon Destroyer C .15 .30
YGLDENC35 Marshmallon Glasses C .15 .30
YGLDENC36 Mirror Force C .15 .30
YGLDENC37 Magician's Circle C .15 .30
YGLDENC38 Shattered Axe C .15 .30
YGLDENC39 Stronghold the Moving Fortress C .15 .30
YGLDENC40 Miracle Restoring C .15 .30
YGLDENC41 Dark Paladin C .15 .30
YGLDENG01 Slifer the Sky Dragon UR 2.50 5.00
YGLDENG02 Obelisk the Tormentor UR 2.50 5.00
YGLDENG03 The Winged Dragon of Ra UR 2.50 5.00
YGLDENTKN Token UR .50 1.00
NNO1 Duelist Kingdom UR .30 .75
NNO2 Glory of the King's Hand UR .30 .75
NNO3 Set Sail for the Kingdom UR .25 .50

2016 Yu-Gi-Oh Breakers of Shadow 1st Edition

BOSHEN000 Steel Cavalry of Dinon R .10 .20
BOSHEN001 Tuning Magician SR .10 .20
BOSHEN002 Timebreaker Magician R .10 .20
BOSHEN003 Performapal Monkeyboard C .15 .30
BOSHEN004 Performapal Guitartle R .10 .20
BOSHEN005 Performapal Bit Bite Turtle C .15 .30
BOSHEN006 Performapal Rain Goat C .15 .30
BOSHEN007 Performapal Trump Girl C .15 .30
BOSHEN008 Superheavy Samurai Magnet C .15 .30
BOSHEN009 Superheavy
Samurai Prepped Defense C .15 .30
BOSHEN010 Superheavy Samurai General Jade C .15 .30
BOSHEN011 Superheavy Samurai General Coral C .15 .30
BOSHEN012 Solo the Melodious Songstress C .15 .30
BOSHEN013 Score the Melodious Diva C .15 .30
BOSHEN014 Blackwing - Harmattan the Dust C .15 .30
BOSHEN015 Twilight Ninja Shingetsu C .15 .30
BOSHEN016 Twilight Ninja Nichirin, the Chunin C .15 .30
BOSHEN017 Twilight Ninja Getsuga, the Shogun R .10 .20
BOSHEN018 Buster Blader... UR 1.25 2.50
BOSHEN019 Buster Whelp... SR .20 .40
BOSHEN020 Dragon Buster Destruction Sword C .15 .30
BOSHEN021 Wizard Buster Destruction Sword C .15 .30
BOSHEN022 Robot Buster Destruction Sword C .15 .30
BOSHEN023 Master Pendulum, the Dracoslayer SR .60 1.25
BOSHEN024 Dinomist Stegosaur C .15 .30
BOSHEN025 Dinomist Plesios C .15 .30
BOSHEN026 Dinomist Pteran R .10 .20
BOSHEN027 Dinomist Brachion C .15 .30
BOSHEN028 Dinomist Ceratops C .15 .30
BOSHEN029 Dinomist Rex SR .20 .40
BOSHEN030 Majespecter Toad - Ogama SR .10 .20
BOSHEN031 Shiranui Spectralsword UR 1.00 2.00
BOSHEN032 Shiranui Smith C .15 .30
BOSHEN033 Shiranui Spiritmaster R .10 .20
BOSHEN034 Shiranui Samurai C .15 .30
BOSHEN035 Dark Doriado C .15 .30
BOSHEN036 Guiding Ariadne SR .15 .30
BOSHEN037 Al-Lumi'raj C .15 .30
BOSHEN038 Toon Buster Blader R .10 .20
BOSHEN039 Deskbot 007 C .15 .30
BOSHEN040 Deskbot 008 C .15 .30
BOSHEN041 Engraver of the Mark SP .10 .20
BOSHEN042 Zany Zebra SP .10 .20
BOSHEN043 Odd-Eyes Gravity Dragon UR .75 1.50
BOSHEN044 Goyo Emperor R .10 .20
BOSHEN045 Buster Blader... SCR 5.00 10.00
BOSHEN045 Buster Blader... R .10 .20
BOSHEN046 Dinoster Power,
the Mighty Dracoslayer R .30 .75
BOSHEN047 Enlightenment Paladin UR .60 1.25
BOSHEN048 Superheavy Samurai Beast Kyubi R .10 .20
BOSHEN049 Hi-Speedroid Hagoita R .10 .20
BOSHEN050 Goyo Defender R .10 .20
BOSHEN051 Goyo King R .10 .20
BOSHEN052 Buster Dragon UR 2.50 5.00
BOSHEN053 Shiranui Samuraisaga C .15 .30
BOSHEN054 Shiranui Shogunsaga UR .60 1.25
BOSHEN055 Aegaion the Sea Castrum C .15 .30
BOSHEN056 Performance Hurricane C .15 .30
BOSHEN057 Pendulum Storm SR .10 .20
BOSHEN058 Hi-Speed Re-Level C .15 .30
BOSHEN059 Destruction Swordsman Fusion C .15 .30
BOSHEN060 Karma of the
Destruction Swordsman C .15 .30
BOSHEN061 Draco Face-Off C .15 .30
BOSHEN062 Dinomic Powerload C .15 .30
BOSHEN063 Dinomist Charge C .15 .30
BOSHEN064 Majespecter Sonics C .15 .30
BOSHEN065 Shiranui Style Synthesis C .15 .30
BOSHEN066 Odd-Eyes Advent R .10 .20
BOSHEN067 Twin Twisters SR 10.00 20.00
BOSHEN068 Mistaken Accusation SP .10 .20
BOSHEN069 Dragon's Bind C .15 .30
BOSHEN070 Follow Wing C .15 .30
BOSHEN071 Reject Reborn R .10 .20
BOSHEN072 Destruction Sword Flash C .15 .30
BOSHEN073 Dinomist Rush C .15 .30
BOSHEN074 Majespecter Supercell SR .10 .20
BOSHEN075 Shiranui Style Swallow's Slash C .15 .30
BOSHEN076 Quaking Mirror Force UR 10.00 20.00
BOSHEN077 Pendulum Reborn R .10 .20
BOSHEN078 Forbidden Apocrypha C .15 .30
BOSHEN079 Solemn Strike SCR 30.00 75.00
BOSHEN080 Bad Luck Blast SP .10 .20
BOSHEN081 Ultimate Providence SCR 2.00 4.00
BOSHEN082 Kozmo Tincan UR 5.00 10.00
BOSHEN083 Kozmo Soartroopers SR .20 .40
BOSHEN084 Kozmo Delta Shuttle C .15 .30
BOSHEN085 Kozmo Dark Eclipser SCR 2.50 5.00
BOSHEN086 Kozmojo SCR 10.00 20.00
BOSHEN087 Gadarla, the Mystery Dust Kaiju R .10 .20
BOSHEN088 Jizukiru, the Star Destroying Kaiju R 1.00 2.00
BOSHEN089 Interrupted Kaiju Slumber SR .60 1.25
BOSHEN090 Performapal Pendulum Sorcerer SCR 7.50 15.00
BOSHEN091 Fiendish Rhino Warrior R .50 1.00
BOSHEN092 Neptabyss, the Atlantean Prince UR 1.00 2.00
BOSHEN093 Chimeratech Rampage Dragon SR .20 .40
BOSHEN094 Cyber Dragon Infinity SCR 15.00 30.00
BOSHEN095 Red-Eyes Retro Dragon SR .20 .40
BOSHEN096 Dharma-Eye Magician SR .10 .20
BOSHEN097 Black Luster Soldier -
Sacred Soldier UR .75 1.50
BOSHEN098 Arisen Gaia the Fierce Knight R .10 .20
BOSHEN099 Traptrix Rafflesia SCR 4.00 8.00

2016 Yu-Gi-Oh The Dark Illusion 1st Edition

TDILEN000 Magical Something R .20 .40
TDILEN001 Performapal BotEyes Lizard C .15 .30
TDILEN002 Performapal Gongato C .15 .30
TDILEN003 Performapal Extra Slinger C .15 .30
TDILEN004 Performapal Inflater Tapir C .15 .30
TDILEN005 Performapal Gumgumouton R .20 .40
TDILEN006 Performapal Bubblebowwow C .15 .30
TDILEN007 Performapal Radish Horse C .15 .30
TDILEN008 Performapal Life Swordsman C .15 .30
TDILEN009 Acrobatic Magician R .20 .40
TDILEN010 DD Savant Thomas R .60 1.25
TDILEN011 DD Savant Nikola C .15 .30
TDILEN012 Blackwing Tornado the Reverse Wind C .15 .30
TDILEN013 Blackwing Gofu the Vague Shadow C .15 .30
TDILEN014 Red Warg C .15 .30
TDILEN015 Red Gardna C .15 .30
TDILEN016 Red Mirror C .15 .30
TDILEN017 Magician of Dark Illusion SR 1.00 2.00
TDILEN018 Magicians Robe C .15 .30
TDILEN019 Magicians Rod SR 1.50 3.00
TDILEN020 Master Peace the True Dracoslayer UR .50 1.00
TDILEN021 Metalfoes Steelen C .15 .30
TDILEN022 Metalfoes Silverd C .15 .30
TDILEN023 Metalfoes Goldriver R .20 .40
TDILEN024 Metalfoes Volflame R .20 .40
TDILEN025 True King Agnimazud the Vanisher UR 7.50 15.00
TDILEN026 Dinomist Ankylos C .15 .30
TDILEN027 Triamid monster C .15 .30
TDILEN028 Triamid Hunter R .20 .40
TDILEN029 Triamid Master R .20 .40
TDILEN030 Triamid Sphinx SR .10 .20
TDILEN031 Shiranui Solitaire UR 3.00 6.00
TDILEN032 Toon Dark Magician SR .75 1.50
TDILEN033 Scapeghost C .15 .30
TDILEN034 Block Dragon UR .75 1.50
TDILEN035 Amaterasu SR .10 .20
TDILEN036 Dragon Ninja monster C .15 .30
TDILEN037 Spell Strider SR .10 .20
TDILEN038 Zap Mustung C .15 .30
TDILEN039 Totem Five C .15 .30
TDILEN040 Tuning Gum R .20 .40
TDILEN041 Wrecker Panda SP .15 .30
TDILEN042 Fairy Tail Snow SP .15 .30
TDILEN043 Metalfoes Adamante R .20 .40
TDILEN044 Metalfoes Orichalc C .15 .30
TDILEN045 Metalfoes Crimsonite R .20 .40
TDILEN046 Nirvana High Paladin SCR 4.00 8.00
TDILEN047 Assault Blackwing... R .20 .40
TDILEN048 Assault Blackwing... C .15 .30
TDILEN049 Assault Blackwing... SR .20 .40
TDILEN050 Tyrant Red Dragon Archfiend UR 1.25 2.50
TDILEN051 Coral Dragon SCR 7.50 15.00
TDILEN052 Ebon High Magician SR .10 .20
TDILEN053 Super Hippo Carnival C .15 .30
TDILEN054 Luna Light Perfume SR .20 .40
TDILEN055 Frightfur Sanctuary C .15 .30
TDILEN056 Forbidden Dark Contract... C .15 .30
TDILEN057 Dark Magical Circle SCR 30.00 75.00
TDILEN058 Illusion Magic R .20 .40
TDILEN059 Dark Magic Expanded C .15 .30

TDILEN060 Metamorformation SR .10 .20
TDILEN061 Metalfoes Fusion SR .15 .30
TDILEN062 Triamid Fortress C .15 .30
TDILEN063 Triamid Cruiser R .20 .40
TDILEN064 Triamid Kingolem R .20 .40
TDILEN065 Cosmic Cyclone SCR 20.00 40.00
TDILEN066 Pot of Desires SCR 30.00 75.00
TDILEN067 Magical MidBreaker Field C .15 .30
TDILEN068 Card of the Soul SP .15 .30
TDILEN069 Fusion Fright Waltz C .15 .30
TDILEN070 King Scarlet C .15 .30
TDILEN071 Magician Navigation SCR 25.00 50.00
TDILEN072 Metalfoes Counter C .15 .30
TDILEN073 Metalfoes Combination SR .30 .75
TDILEN074 Triamid Pulse R .20 .40
TDILEN075 Destruction Sword Memories C .15 .30
TDILEN076 Floodgate Trap Hole UR 4.00 8.00
TDILEN077 Premature Return UR .50 1.00
TDILEN078 Unified Front C .15 .30
TDILEN079 Pendulum Hole C .15 .30
TDILEN080 The Forceful Checkpoint SCR 1.00 2.00
TDILEN081 Ninjitsu Art Notebook C .15 .30
TDILEN082 Subterror Nemesis Warrior R .20 .40
TDILEN083 Subterror Behemoth Umastryx UR 2.00 4.00
TDILEN084 Subterror Behemoth Stalagmo UR 1.50 3.00
TDILEN085 The Hidden City SCR 7.50 15.00
TDILEN086 SPYRAL Super Agent UR 2.50 5.00
TDILEN087 SPYRAL QuikFix R .20 .40
TDILEN088 SPYRAL GEAR Drone R .20 .40
TDILEN089 SPYRAL GEAR Big Red R .20 .40
TDILEN090 Heavy Freight Train Derricrane C .15 .30
TDILEN091 #81 Superdreadnought Rail Cannon... SR .25 .50
TDILEN092 Revolving Switchyard C .15 .30
TDILEN093 Dragodies the Empowered Warrior C .15 .30
TDILEN094 Empowerment C .15 .30
TDILEN095 Paleozoic Olenoides C .15 .30
TDILEN096 Paleozoic Hallucigenia C .15 .30
TDILEN097 Paleozoic Canadia C .15 .30
TDILEN098 Paleozoic Pikaia C .15 .30
TDILEN099 Paleozoic Anomalocaris SR .30 .75

2016 Yu-Gi-Oh The Dark Side of Dimensions Movie Pack 1st Edition

MVP1EN001 Neo Blue Eyes Ultimate Dragon UR 1.50 3.00
MVP1EN002 Kaiser Vorse Raider UR .15 .30
MVP1EN003 Assault Wyvern UR .15 .30
MVP1EN004 Blue Eyes Chaos MAX Dragon UR 3.00 6.00
MVP1EN005 Deep Eyes White Dragon UR 1.00 2.00
MVP1EN006 Pandemic Dragon UR .15 .30
MVP1EN007 Dragons Fighting Spirit UR .15 .30
MVP1EN008 Chaos Form UR 4.00 8.00
MVP1EN009 Induced Explosion UR .15 .30
MVP1EN010 Counter Gate UR .15 .30
MVP1EN011 Krystal Avatar UR .15 .30
MVP1EN012 Sentry Soldier of Stone UR .15 .30
MVP1EN013 Marshmacaron UR .15 .30
MVP1EN014 Berry Magician Girl UR 1.00 2.00
MVP1EN015 Apple Magician Girl UR .60 1.25
MVP1EN016 Kiwi Magician Girl UR .75 1.50
MVP1EN017 Silver Gadget UR 2.00 4.00
MVP1EN018 Gold Gadget UR 2.00 4.00
MVP1EN019 Dark Magic Veil UR 1.00 2.00
MVP1EN020 Magical Contract Door UR .15 .30
MVP1EN021 Dimension Reflector UR .15 .30
MVP1EN022 Dig of Destiny UR .15 .30
MVP1EN023 Dimension Sphinx UR .15 .30
MVP1EN024 Dimension Guardian UR .75 1.50
MVP1EN025 Dimension Mirage UR .15 .30
MVP1EN026 Dark Horizon UR .15 .30
MVP1EN027 Metamorphortress UR .15 .30
MVP1EN028 Magicians Defense UR .60 1.25
MVP1EN029 Final Geas UR .15 .30
MVP1EN030 Metalhold the Moving Blockade UR .15 .30
MVP1EN031 Spiritual Swords of Revealing Light UR .15 .30
MVP1EN032 Vijam the Cubic Seed UR .50 1.00
MVP1EN033 Dark Garnex the Cubic Beast UR .15 .30
MVP1EN034 Blade Garoodia the Cubic Beast UR .15 .30
MVP1EN035 Buster Gundil the Cubic Behemoth UR .15 .30
MVP1EN036 Geira Guile the Cubic King UR .15 .30
MVP1EN037 Vulcan Dragni the Cubic King UR .15 .30
MVP1EN038 Indiora Doom Volt the Cubic Emperor UR .15 .30
MVP1EN039 Crimson Nova the Dark Cubic Lord UR .50 1.00
MVP1EN040 Crimson Nova Trinity Dark Cubic Lord UR .50 1.00
MVP1EN041 Cubic Karma UR .75 1.50
MVP1EN042 Cubic Wave UR .15 .30
MVP1EN043 Cubic Rebirth UR .15 .30
MVP1EN044 Cubic Mandala UR .15 .30
MVP1EN045 Unification of the Cubic Lords UR .15 .30
MVP1EN046 Blue Eyes Alternative White Dragon UR 10.00 20.00
MVP1EN047 Clear Kuriboh UR .15 .30
MVP1EN048 Celtic Guard of Noble Arms UR .15 .30
MVP1EN049 GandoraX the Dragon of Demolition UR .50 1.00
MVP1EN050 Lord Gaia the Fierce Knight UR .15 .30
MVP1EN051 Lemon Magician Girl UR .15 .30
MVP1EN052 Chocolate Magician Girl UR 2.00 4.00
MVP1EN053 Palladium Oracle Mahad UR 1.50 3.00
MVP1EN054 Dark Magician UR .75 1.50
MVP1EN055 BlueEyes White Dragon UR .75 1.50
MVP1EN056 Dark Magician Girl UR 1.50 3.00
MVP1EN057 Slifer the Sky Dragon UR .75 1.50

2016 Yu-Gi-Oh Destiny Soldiers 1st Edition

DESOEN001 Destiny HERO Drilldark SR .15 .30
DESOEN002 Destiny HERO Dynatag SR .15 .30
DESOEN003 Destiny HERO Decider SCR .50 1.00
DESOEN004 Destiny HERO Dystopia SCR .50 1.00
DESOEN005 Destiny HERO Dark Angel SCR .50 1.00
DESOEN006 Destiny HERO Celestial SCR 4.00 8.00
DESOEN007 D Cubed SCR .50 1.00
DESOEN008 DFusion SCR .50 1.00
DESOEN009 Destiny HERO Diamond Dude SR .15 .30
DESOEN010 Destiny HERO Malicious SR .50 1.00
DESOEN011 Destiny HERO Dogma SR .15 .30
DESOEN012 Destiny HERO Plasma SR .15 .30
DESOEN013 Destiny End Dragoon SR .15 .30
DESOEN014 Destiny Draw SR .15 .30
DESOEN015 Over Destiny SR .15 .30
DESOEN016 Abyss Actor Evil Heel SCR .50 1.00
DESOEN017 Abyss Actor Funky Comedian SR .15 .30
DESOEN018 Abyss Actor Superstar SCR .50 1.00
DESOEN019 Abyss Actor Sassy Rookie SR .15 .30
DESOEN020 Abyss Actor Extras SR .15 .30
DESOEN021 Abyss Actor Leading Lady SCR .50 1.00
DESOEN022 Abyss Actor Wild Hope SCR .50 1.00
DESOEN023 Abyss Script Fantasy Magic SR .15 .30
DESOEN024 Abyss Script Opening Ceremony SR .15 .30
DESOEN025 Abyss Script Fire Dragon's Lair SR .15 .30
DESOEN026 Abyss Prop Wild Wagon SR .15 .30
DESOEN027 Abyss Script Rise of the Abyss King SCR .50 1.00
DESOEN028 Abyss Actors Back Stage SR .15 .30
DESOEN029 Darklord Morningstar SCR .50 1.00
DESOEN030 Darklord Ixchel SCR 20.00 40.00
DESOEN031 Darklord Tezcatlipoca SCR .50 1.00
DESOEN032 Darklord Nasten SCR 6.00 12.00
DESOEN033 Darklord Amdusc SCR .50 1.00
DESOEN034 Banishment of the Darklords SCR 1.50 3.00
DESOEN035 Darklord Contact SCR .50 1.00
DESOEN036 Darklord Rebellion SCR .50 1.00
DESOEN037 Darklord Enchantment SCR .50 1.00
DESOEN038 Darklord Asmodeus SR .15 .30
DESOEN039 Darklord Superbia SR .15 .30
DESOEN040 Darklord Edeh Arae SR .15 .30
DESOEN041 Darklord Zerato SR .15 .30
DESOEN042 Dark Hole SR 1.00 2.00
DESOEN043 Fires of Doomsday SR .15 .30
DESOEN044 Allure of Darkness SR 3.00 6.00
DESOEN045 Escape from the Dark Dimension SR .15 .30
DESOEN046 Darklord Marie SR .15 .30
DESOEN047 Prometheus, King of the Shadows SR .15 .30
DESOEN048 Darklord Nurse Reficule SR .15 .30
DESOEN049 Doomsday Horror SR .15 .30
DESOEN050 Archlord Kristya SR .15 .30
DESOEN051 Trade In SR 1.50 3.00
DESOEN052 Veil of Darkness SR .15 .30
DESOEN053 The Beginning of the End SR .15 .30
DESOEN054 Dark Eruption SR .15 .30
DESOEN055 Valhalla, Hall of the Fallen SR .15 .30
DESOEN056 Advance Draw SR .15 .30
DESOEN057 Dark Mambele SR .15 .30
DESOEN058 Creeping Darkness SR .15 .30
DESOEN059 Destiny Signal SR .15 .30
DESOEN060 Dark Illusion SR .15 .30

2016 Yu-Gi-Oh Dragons of Legend Unleashed 1st Edition

DRL3EN001 OddEyes Mirage Dragon SCR 2.00 4.00
DRL3EN002 Performapal Uni UR .10 .20
DRL3EN003 Performapal Corn UR .10 .20
DRL3EN004 Raidraptor Napalm Dragonius UR .10 .20
DRL3EN005 Raidraptor Blade Burner Falcon UR .10 .20
DRL3EN006 The Tripper Mercury SCR .20 .40
DRL3EN007 The Blazing Mars SCR .20 .40
DRL3EN008 The Grand Jupiter SCR .20 .40
DRL3EN009 The Despair Uranus SCR .20 .40
DRL3EN010 The Suppression Pluto SCR .20 .40
DRL3EN011 Cyber Petit Angel UR .50 1.00
DRL3EN012 Cyber Angel Benten SCR 7.50 15.00
DRL3EN013 Cyber Angel Idaten SCR 2.50 5.00
DRL3EN014 Cyber Angel Dakini SCR 1.00 2.00
DRL3EN015 Machine Angel Ritual UR .50 1.00
DRL3EN016 Ritual Sanctuary SCR 10.00 20.00
DRL3EN017 Red Nova SCR .25 .50
DRL3EN018 Zushin the Sleeping Giant UR .10 .20
DRL3EN019 HandHolding Genie UR .10 .20
DRL3EN020 Scrum Force UR .10 .20
DRL3EN021 #100 Numeron Dragon SCR .75 1.50
DRL3EN022 #24 Dragulas the Vampiric Dragon SCR .75 1.50
DRL3EN023 #45 Crumble Logos the Prophet of Demolition SCR 1.00 2.00
DRL3EN024 #51 Finisher the Strong Arm SCR .20 .40
DRL3EN025 Number 59 Crooked Cook UR .30 .75
DRL3EN026 Number 78 Number Archive UR .10 .20
DRL3EN027 Number 98 Antitopian SCR .60 1.25
DRL3EN028 Cipher Wing UR .10 .20
DRL3EN029 GalaxyEyes Cipher Dragon SCR 7.50 15.00
DRL3EN030 Galaxy Stealth Dragon SCR .60 1.25
DRL3EN031 Flower Cardian Pine SCR .50 1.00
DRL3EN032 Flower Cardian Zebra Grass UR .10 .20
DRL3EN033 Flower Cardian Willow UR .10 .20
DRL3EN034 Flower Cardian Paulownia UR .10 .20
DRL3EN035 Flower Cardian Pine with Crane UR .10 .20
DRL3EN036 Flower Cardian Zebra Grass... UR .10 .20
DRL3EN037 Flower Cardian Willow... UR .10 .20
DRL3EN038 Flower Cardian Paulownia... UR .10 .20
DRL3EN039 Flower Cardian Lightshower SCR .50 1.00
DRL3EN040 Flower Gathering UR .10 .20
DRL3EN041 Legendary Knight Timaeus UR .30 .75
DRL3EN042 Kuribandit UR .50 1.00
DRL3EN043 Amulet Dragon UR 1.25 2.50
DRL3EN044 Dark Magician Girl the Dragon Knight UR 2.50 5.00
DRL3EN045 The Eye of Timaeus UR 4.00 8.00
DRL3EN046 Legend of Heart UR .50 1.00
DRL3EN047 Berserker Soul UR .10 .20
DRL3EN048 Relay Soul UR .10 .20
DRL3EN049 Guardian Dreadscythe UR .10 .20
DRL3EN050 Reaper Scythe Dreadscythe UR .10 .20
DRL3EN051 Soul Charge UR 1.50 3.00
DRL3EN052 Ras Disciple UR .60 1.25
DRL3EN053 Mound of the Bound Creator UR .10 .20
DRL3EN054 Wiretap UR .10 .20
DRL3EN055 Timaeus the Knight of Destiny UR .30 .75
DRL3EN056 Legendary Knight Critias UR .10 .20
DRL3EN057 Doom Virus Dragon UR .60 1.25
DRL3EN058 Tyrant Burst Dragon UR 2.00 4.00
DRL3EN059 Mirror Force Dragon UR .75 1.50
DRL3EN060 The Fang of Critias UR .75 1.50
DRL3EN061 Tyrant Wing UR .10 .20
DRL3EN062 Legendary Knight Hermos UR .10 .20
DRL3EN063 Time Magic Hammer UR .10 .20
DRL3EN064 Rocket Hermos Cannon UR .10 .20
DRL3EN065 Goddess Bow UR .10 .20
DRL3EN066 RedEyes Black Dragon Sword UR .10 .20
DRL3EN067 The Claw of Hermos UR .50 1.00
DRL3EN068 Lord of the Red UR .10 .20
DRL3EN069 RedEyes Transmigration UR .10 .20
DRL3EN070 The Seal of Orichalcos UR .25 .50
DRL3EN071 Snow Plow Hustle Rustle UR .10 .20
DRL3EN072 Night Express Knight UR 2.50 5.00
DRL3EN073 Special Schedule UR .50 1.00

2016 Yu-Gi-Oh Duelist Pack Rivals of the Pharaoh 1st Edition

DPRPEN001 Silent Swordsman UR 10.00 20.00
DPRPEN002 Silent Magician UR 10.00 20.00
DPRPEN003 Silent Paladin UR 7.50 15.00
DPRPEN004 Silent Sword Slash SR 2.50 5.00
DPRPEN005 Silent Burning SR 2.50 5.00
DPRPEN006 Magnet Reverse SR .75 1.50
DPRPEN007 Magnet Force SR .75 1.50
DPRPEN008 Neutron Blast UR 6.00 12.00
DPRPEN009 Lullaby of Obedience UR 15.00 30.00
DPRPEN010 Tribute Burial SR 3.00 6.00
DPRPEN011 Dark Sanctuary UR 7.50 15.00
DPRPEN012 Dragon Master Knight R 1.00 2.00
DPRPEN013 Dark Magician of Chaos R 1.25 2.50
DPRPEN014 Dedication through Light and Darkness C .15 .30
DPRPEN015 Fiends Sanctuary R .75 1.50
DPRPEN016 Silent Swordsman LV3 C .15 .30
DPRPEN017 Silent Swordsman LV5 C .15 .30
DPRPEN018 Silent Swordsman LV7 C .15 .30
DPRPEN019 Silent Magician LV4 C .15 .30
DPRPEN020 Silent Magician LV8 C .15 .30
DPRPEN021 Green Gadget C .15 .30
DPRPEN022 Red Gadget C .15 .30
DPRPEN023 Yellow Gadget C .15 .30
DPRPEN024 Stronghold the Moving Fortress C .15 .30
DPRPEN025 BlueEyes Ultimate Dragon R 1.00 2.00
DPRPEN026 BlueEyes Shining Dragon C .15 .30
DPRPEN027 YZTank Dragon R .75 1.50
DPRPEN028 Dragons Mirror R 2.00 4.00
DPRPEN029 Dragon Shrine R 1.25 2.50
DPRPEN030 Silvers Cry SR 4.00 8.00
DPRPEN031 Castle of Dragon Souls R .75 1.50
DPRPEN032 Helpoemer C .15 .30
DPRPEN033 Metal Reflect Slime R .75 1.50
DPRPEN034 Blast Held by a Tribute C .15 .30
DPRPEN035 Exchange of the Spirit C .15 .30
DPRPEN036 Mystical Beast of Serket C .15 .30
DPRPEN037 Temple of the Kings C .15 .30
DPRPEN038 Sangan C .15 .30
DPRPEN039 Necroface C .15 .30
DPRPEN040 Dark Necrofear C .15 .30
DPRPEN041 Destiny Board C .15 .30
DPRPEN042 Spirit Message I C .15 .30
DPRPEN043 Spirit Message N C .15 .30
DPRPEN044 Spirit Message A C .15 .30
DPRPEN045 Spirit Message L C .15 .30
DPRPEN046 ThousandEyes Restrict R 1.25 2.50

2016 Yu-Gi-Oh Infinite Gold 1st Edition

PGL3EN001 Angmarl the Fiendish Monarch GSCR .30 .75
PGL3EN002 Junk Changer GSCR .30 .75
PGL3EN003 Junkuriboh GSCR .30 .75
PGL3EN004 Magical King Moonstar GSCR .30 .75
PGL3EN005 Stardust Charge Warrior GSCR 2.00 4.00
PGL3EN006 Phantasmal Lord Ultimitl... GSCR .30 .75
PGL3EN007 #37 Hope Woven Dragon Spider Shark GSCR .75 1.50
PGL3EN008 #38 Hope Harbinger Dragon Titanic Galaxy GSCR 10.00 20.00
PGL3EN009 Number 35: Ravenous Tarantula GSCR .75 1.50
PGL3EN010 Number 84: Pain Gainer GSCR .75 1.50
PGL3EN011 Number 77: The Seven Sins GSCR 2.00 4.00
PGL3EN012 Frost Blast of the Monarchs GSCR .30 .75
PGL3EN013 Tsukumo Slash GSCR .30 .75
PGL3EN014 Shining Hope Road GSCR .30 .75
PGL3EN015 Phantom Knights of Shade Brigandine GSCR .30 .75
PGL3EN016 Phantom Knights of Dark Gauntlets GSCR .30 .75
PGL3EN017 Phantom Knights of Tomb Shield GSCR .30 .75
PGL3EN018 Dark Advance GSCR .30 .75
PGL3EN019 King's Consonance GSCR .30 .75
PGL3EN020 Red Supremacy GSCR .30 .75
PGL3EN021 Beatrice, Lady of the Eternal GSCR 1.25 2.50
PGL3EN022 Fire Hand GSCR .30 .75
PGL3EN023 Ice Hand GSCR .30 .75
PGL3EN024 Kozmo Farmgirl GSCR 1.50 3.00
PGL3EN025 Kozmo Goodwitch GSCR .30 .75
PGL3EN026 Kozmo Sliprider GSCR .75 1.50
PGL3EN027 Kozmo Forerunner GSCR .30 .75
PGL3EN028 Kozmo Strawman GSCR 2.00 4.00
PGL3EN029 Kozmoll Wickedwitch GSCR .30 .75
PGL3EN030 Kozmo DOG Fighter GSCR .30 .75
PGL3EN031 Kozmo Dark Destroyer GSCR .75 1.50
PGL3EN032 Kozmotown GSCR .75 1.50
PGL3EN033 Kozmo Lightsword GSCR .30 .75
PGL3EN034 Horn of Heaven GSCR .30 .75
PGL3EN035 Black Horn of Heaven GSCR .60 1.25
PGL3EN036 Treacherous Trap Hole GSCR .30 .75
PGL3EN037 Deep Dark Trap Hole GSCR .30 .75
PGL3EN038 Void Trap Hole GSCR .30 .75
PGL3EN039 Time-Space Trap Hole GSCR .75 1.50
PGL3EN040 Grand Horn of Heaven GSCR .30 .75
PGL3EN041 Vector Pendulum, the Dracoverlord GLDR .30 .75
PGL3EN042 Maxx "C" GLDR 4.00 8.00
PGL3EN043 Scarm... GLDR .75 1.50
PGL3EN044 Graff... GLDR .30 .75
PGL3EN045 Cir... GLDR .30 .75
PGL3EN046 Rubic... GLDR .30 .75
PGL3EN047 Alich... GLDR .30 .75
PGL3EN048 Calcab... GLDR .30 .75
PGL3EN049 Farfa... GLDR .75 1.50
PGL3EN050 Libic... GLDR .30 .75
PGL3EN051 Cagna... GLDR .30 .75
PGL3EN052 Ghost Ogre & Snow Rabbit GLDR 6.00 12.00
PGL3EN053 Draghig... GLDR .30 .75
PGL3EN054 Barbar... GLDR .30 .75
PGL3EN055 Luster Pendulum, the Dracoslayer GLDR 1.00 2.00
PGL3EN056 Archfiend Eccentrick GLDR 3.00 6.00
PGL3EN057 Chimeratech Fortress Dragon GLDR .75 1.50
PGL3EN058 Dante... GLDR 3.00 6.00
PGL3EN059 Black Rose Dragon GLDR .75 1.50
PGL3EN060 Arcanite Magician GLDR .30 .75
PGL3EN061 Virgil... GLDR .30 .75
PGL3EN062 Ignister Prominence... GLDR .30 .75
PGL3EN063 Number 11: Big Eye GLDR 5.00 10.00
PGL3EN064 Digvorzhak, King of Heavy Industry GLDR .30 .75
PGL3EN065 Daigusto Emeral GLDR 25.00 50.00
PGL3EN066 Constellar Pleiades GLDR .50 1.00
PGL3EN067 Gagaga Cowboy GLDR .75 1.50
PGL3EN068 Abyss Dweller GLDR 1.25 2.50
PGL3EN069 Bahamut Shark GLDR 1.00 2.00
PGL3EN070 Lightning Chidori GLDR .75 1.50
PGL3EN071 Constellar Ptolemy M7 GLDR .30 .75
PGL3EN072 Evilswarm Ouroboros GLDR .30 .75
PGL3EN073 Number 61: Volcasaurus GLDR .75 1.50
PGL3EN074 Norito the Moral Leader GLDR .30 .75
PGL3EN075 Number 106: Giant Hand GLDR 4.00 8.00
PGL3EN076 Castel, the Skyblaster Musketeer GLDR 2.50 5.00
PGL3EN077 Dante... GLDR 3.00 6.00
PGL3EN078 Red-Eyes Flare Metal Dragon GLDR 1.50 3.00
PGL3EN079 Majester Paladin... GLDR .30 .75
PGL3EN080 Reasoning GLDR .30 .75
PGL3EN081 Emergency Teleport GLDR .75 1.50
PGL3EN082 Spell Shattering Arrow GLDR .30 .75
PGL3EN083 Mask Change GLDR .60 1.25
PGL3EN084 Shared Ride GLDR .30 .75
PGL3EN085 The Monarchs Stormforth GLDR .75 1.50
PGL3EN086 Mask Change II GLDR .75 1.50
PGL3EN087 Galaxy Cyclone GLDR 1.25 2.50
PGL3EN088 The Terminus of the Burning Abyss GLDR .30 .75
PGL3EN089 Mistaken Arrest GLDR .30 .75
PGL3EN090 Draco Face-Off GLDR .30 .75
PGL3EN091 Remove Brainwashing GLDR .30 .75
PGL3EN092 Dark Mirror Force GLDR .30 .75
PGL3EN093 Radiant Mirror Force GLDR .30 .75
PGL3EN094 Fairy Wind GLDR .30 .75
PGL3EN095 Breakthrough Skill GLDR 1.00 2.00
PGL3EN096 Mistake GLDR .30 .75
PGL3EN097 The Traveler and the Burning Abyss GLDR .30 .75
PGL3EN098 Fire Lake of the Burning Abyss GLDR .30 .75
PGL3EN099 Storming Mirror Force GLDR 6.00 12.00
PGL3EN100 Blazing Mirror Force GLDR 1.00 2.00

2016 Yu-Gi-Oh Invasion Vengeance 1st Edition

INOVEN000 Space Dragster R .20 .40
INOVEN001 Dragon Core Hexer R .20 .40
INOVEN002 Performapal Whim Witch R .20 .40
INOVEN003 Performapal Flip Hippo C .15 .30
INOVEN004 Performapal Seal Eel C .15 .30
INOVEN005 Performapal Changeraffe C .15 .30
INOVEN006 Predaplant Flytrap R .20 .40
INOVEN007 Predaplant Moray Nepenthes C .15 .30
INOVEN008 Predaplant Squid Drosera C .15 .30
INOVEN009 Superheavy Samurai Soulpeacemaker R .20 .40
INOVEN010 Cipher Twin Raptor C .15 .30
INOVEN011 Cipher Mirror Knight C .15 .30
INOVEN012 Flower Cardian Clover with Boar C .15 .30
INOVEN013 Flower Cardian Maple with Deer C .15 .30
INOVEN014 Flower Cardian Peony with Butterfly C .15 .30
INOVEN015 Crystron Quan SR .20 .40
INOVEN016 Crystron Citree UR 1.25 2.50
INOVEN017 Crystron Prasiortle C .15 .30
INOVEN018 Crystron Smiger C .15 .30
INOVEN019 Crystron Thystvern C .15 .30
INOVEN020 Crystron Rosenix C .15 .30
INOVEN021 True King Bahrastos the Fathomer UR 1.25 2.50
INOVEN022 Raremetalfoes Bismugear C .15 .30
INOVEN023 Chemicritter Hydron Hawk C .15 .30
INOVEN024 Chemicritter Carbo Crab C .15 .30
INOVEN025 Chemicritter Oxy Ox C .15 .30
INOVEN026 PolyChemicritter Dioxogre R .20 .40
INOVEN027 PolyChemicritter Hydragon C .15 .30
INOVEN028 Meteor Dragon RedEyes Impact R .20 .40
INOVEN029 PSYFrame MultiThreader C .15 .30
INOVEN030 Graydle Slime Jr C .15 .30
INOVEN031 Aromaseraphy Angelica C .15 .30
INOVEN032 Doki Doki C .15 .30
INOVEN033 Torque Tune Gear SR .15 .30
INOVEN034 Pandoras Jewelry Box SP .15 .30
INOVEN035 Fairy Tail Sleeper SP .15 .30
INOVEN036 Cyber Angel Vrash SR .20 .40
INOVEN037 Sauravis the Ancient and Ascended SCR 1.25 2.50
INOVEN038 Starving Venom Fusion Dragon SCR 10.00 20.00
INOVEN039 Fullmetalfoes Alkahest SCR 1.50 3.00
INOVEN040 Metalfoes Mithrilium UR 1.25 2.50
INOVEN041 Meteor Black Comet Dragon UR 3.00 6.00
INOVEN042 Superheavy Samurai Ninja Sarutobi R .20 .40
INOVEN043 Flower Cardian Boardefly R .20 .40
INOVEN044 Crystron Quandax UR .60 1.25
INOVEN045 Crystron Ametrix SR .20 .40
INOVEN046 Crystron Phoenix UR .60 1.25
INOVEN047 Aromaseraphy Rosemary R .20 .40
INOVEN048 Denglong First of the Yang Zing UR 3.00 6.00
INOVEN049 Dark Requiem Xyz Dragon SCR 1.50 3.00
INOVEN050 VolaChemicritter Methydraco SR .20 .40
INOVEN051 Darktellarknight Batlamyus UR .30 .75
INOVEN052 Toadally Awesome SCR 15.00 30.00
INOVEN053 Amazing Pendulum C .15 .30
INOVEN054 Phantom Knights RankUpMagic Launch SR .20 .40
INOVEN055 Flower Stacking C .15 .30
INOVEN056 Super Koi Koi R .20 .40

INOVEN057 Crystolic Potential C .15 .30
INOVEN058 Fullmetalfoes Fusion SR .20 .40
INOVEN059 Catalyst Field UR .60 1.25
INOVEN060 RedEyes Insight R .20 .40
INOVEN061 Igknights Unite C .15 .30
INOVEN062 Tellarknight Genesis SR .20 .40
INOVEN063 A Cell Recombination Device C .15 .30
INOVEN064 Sprites Blessing C .15 .30
INOVEN065 Pot of Acquisitiveness SR .20 .40
INOVEN066 Quarantine SP .15 .30
INOVEN067 Kings Synchro SR .20 .40
INOVEN068 Double Cipher C .15 .30
INOVEN069 Cipher Bit C .15 .30
INOVEN070 Fraud Freeze C .15 .30
INOVEN071 Crystron Entry C .15 .30
INOVEN072 Crystron Impact C .15 .30
INOVEN073 Burnout R .15 .30
INOVEN074 PSYFrame Accelerator C .15 .30
INOVEN075 Graydle Combat C .15 .30
INOVEN076 Qlifes End R .20 .40
INOVEN077 Nine Pillars of Yang Zing R .20 .40
INOVEN078 Dimensional Barrier SCR 25.00 50.00
INOVEN079 Summon Gate C .15 .30
INOVEN080 Present Card SP .15 .30
INOVEN081 Vermillion Dragon Mech SCR 2.00 4.00
INOVEN082 Subterror Nemesis Archer SCR 4.00 8.00
INOVEN083 Subterror Behemoth Stygokraken SR .20 .40
INOVEN084 Subterror Behemoth Ultramafus UR 1.25 2.50
INOVEN085 Subterror Behemoth Burrowing R .20 .40
INOVEN086 Charming Resort Staff R .20 .40
INOVEN087 SPYRAL Master Plan SR .20 .40
INOVEN088 SPYRAL MISSION Assault R .20 .40
INOVEN089 SPYRAL Resort SR .20 .40
INOVEN090 Saber Reflection R .20 .40
INOVEN091 Constellar Tempest R .20 .40
INOVEN092 Caninetaur C .15 .30
INOVEN093 DinoSewing C .15 .30
INOVEN094 Mare Mare C .15 .30
INOVEN095 Paleozoic Eldonia C .15 .30
INOVEN096 Paleozoic Dinomischus C .15 .30
INOVEN097 Paleozoic Marrella C .15 .30
INOVEN098 Paleozoic Leanchoilia C .15 .30
INOVEN099 Paleozoic Opabinia SR .20 .40

2016 Yu-Gi-Oh Legendary Decks II

LDK2ENJ01 RedEyes B Dragon C .25 .50
LDK2ENJ02 RedEyes Black Flare Dragon C 2.00 4.00
LDK2ENJ03 RedEyes Archfiend of Lightning C .25 .50
LDK2ENJ04 RedEyes Retro Dragon C .25 .50
LDK2ENJ05 The Black Stone of Legend UR 3.00 6.00
LDK2ENJ06 Black Metal Dragon C .25 .50
LDK2ENJ07 Axe Raider C .25 .50
LDK2ENJ08 Alligators Sword C .25 .50
LDK2ENJ09 Baby Dragon C .25 .50
LDK2ENJ10 Jinzo C .25 .50
LDK2ENJ11 Goblin Attack Force C .25 .50
LDK2ENJ12 Gearfried the Iron Knight C .25 .50
LDK2ENJ13 Rocket Warrior C .25 .50
LDK2ENJ14 Blue Flame Swordsman C .25 .50
LDK2ENJ15 Time Wizard C .25 .50
LDK2ENJ16 Phoenix Gearfried C .25 .50
LDK2ENJ17 Gemini Summoner C .25 .50
LDK2ENJ18 Blazewing Butterfly C .25 .50
LDK2ENJ19 Dark Valkyria C .25 .50
LDK2ENJ20 Command Knight C .25 .50
LDK2ENJ21 Valkyrian Knight C .25 .50
LDK2ENJ22 Keeper of the Shrine C .25 .50
LDK2ENJ23 Inferno Fire Blast C .25 .50
LDK2ENJ24 RedEyes Fusion C 1.25 2.50
LDK2ENJ25 Cards of the Red Stone C .60 1.25
LDK2ENJ26 Polymerization C 1.00 2.00
LDK2ENJ27 Salamandra C .25 .50
LDK2ENJ28 Scapegoat C .25 .50
LDK2ENJ29 Foolish Burial C .25 .50
LDK2ENJ30 Roulette Spider C .25 .50
LDK2ENJ31 Supervise C .25 .50
LDK2ENJ32 Mystical Space Typhoon C .60 1.25
LDK2ENJ33 Symbols of Duty C .25 .50
LDK2ENJ34 Return of the RedEyes UR .75 1.50
LDK2ENJ35 RedEyes Spirit C .25 .50
LDK2ENJ36 Kunai with Chain C .25 .50
LDK2ENJ37 Call of the Haunted C .25 .50
LDK2ENJ38 Torrential Tribute C .75 1.50
LDK2ENJ39 Burst Breath C .25 .50
LDK2ENJ40 Curse of Anubis C .25 .50
LDK2ENJ41 RedEyes Flare Metal Dragon UR 1.25 2.50
LDK2ENJ42 Archfiend Black Skull Dragon C .25 .50
LDK2ENJ43 Alligators Sword Dragon C .25 .50
LDK2ENK01 BlueEyes White Dragon (LOB) C 1.00 2.00
LDK2ENK01 BlueEyes White Dragon (Tablet) C 1.00 2.00
LDK2ENK01 BlueEyes White Dragon (Starter) C 1.00 2.00
LDK2ENK02 Dragon Spirit of White C 1.50 3.00
LDK2ENK03 Kaibaman C .25 .50
LDK2ENK04 The White Stone of Legend C .25 .50
LDK2ENK05 The White Stone of Ancients C 5.00 10.00
LDK2ENK06 Maiden with Eyes of Blue UR 1.25 2.50
LDK2ENK07 Protector with Eyes of Blue C .25 .50
LDK2ENK08 Master with Eyes of Blue C .25 .50
LDK2ENK09 Battle Ox C .25 .50
LDK2ENK10 La Jinn the Mystical Genie of the Lamp C .25 .50
LDK2ENK11 Vorse Raider C .25 .50
LDK2ENK12 Alexandrite Dragon C .25 .50
LDK2ENK13 Blade Knight C .25 .50
LDK2ENK14 Ancient Lamp C .25 .50
LDK2ENK15 Tiger Dragon C .25 .50
LDK2ENK16 Kidmodo Dragon C .25 .50
LDK2ENK17 King of the Swamp C .75 1.50
LDK2ENK18 Rider of the Storm Winds C .25 .50
LDK2ENK19 Burst Stream of Destruction C .25 .50
LDK2ENK20 Beacon of White C .25 .50
LDK2ENK21 Mausoleum of White C .25 .50
LDK2ENK22 Polymerization C 1.00 2.00
LDK2ENK23 Enemy Controller C .25 .50
LDK2ENK24 Shrink C .25 .50
LDK2ENK25 Silent Doom C .25 .50
LDK2ENK26 The Melody of Awakening Dragon UR 1.25 2.50
LDK2ENK27 Ancient Rules C .50 1.00
LDK2ENK28 Tradeln C .60 1.25
LDK2ENK29 Where Arf Thou C .60 1.25
LDK2ENK30 Pot of Dichotomy C .25 .50
LDK2ENK31 Fusion Substitute C .25 .50
LDK2ENK32 Unexpected Dai C .60 1.25
LDK2ENK33 Negate Attack C .25 .50
LDK2ENK34 Final Attack Orders C .25 .50
LDK2ENK35 Shadow Spell C .25 .50
LDK2ENK36 Cloning C .25 .50
LDK2ENK37 Fusion Reserve C .25 .50
LDK2ENK38 Jar of Avarice C .25 .50
LDK2ENK39 AzureEyes Silver Dragon C .50 1.00
LDK2ENK40 BlueEyes Ultimate Dragon UR .75 1.50
LDK2ENK41 First of the Dragons C .25 .50
LDK2ENS01 Slifer the Sky Dragon UR .75 1.50
LDK2ENS02 Obelisk the Tormentor UR .75 1.50
LDK2ENS03 The Winged Dragon of Ra UR 2.50 5.00
LDK2ENS04 Dark Burning Attack SCR .75 1.50
LDK2ENS05 Dark Burning Magic SCR .75 1.50
LDK2ENS06 Eternal Soul SCR 3.00 6.00
LDK2ENT01 Token (Yugi) UR .75 1.50
LDK2ENT02 Token (Kaiba) UR .75 1.50
LDK2ENT03 Token (Joey) UR .75 1.50
LDK2ENY01 The Legendary Exodia Incarnate UR 2.00 4.00
LDK2ENY02 Ties of the Brethren UR 3.00 6.00
LDK2ENY03 Obliterate UR .75 1.50
LDK2ENY04 Exodia the Forbidden One C 1.00 2.00
LDK2ENY05 Left Arm of the Forbidden One C .60 1.25
LDK2ENY06 Right Arm of the Forbidden One C .60 1.25
LDK2ENY07 Left Leg of the Forbidden One C .60 1.25
LDK2ENY08 Right Leg of the Forbidden One C .60 1.25
LDK2ENY09 Exodia Necross C .25 .50
LDK2ENY10 Dark Magician C .25 .50
LDK2ENY11 Dark Magician Girl C .25 .50
LDK2ENY12 Buster Blader C .25 .50
LDK2ENY13 Silent Magician LV8 C .25 .50
LDK2ENY14 Silent Magician LV4 C .25 .50
LDK2ENY15 The Tricky C .25 .50
LDK2ENY16 Big Shield Gardna C .25 .50
LDK2ENY17 Magician's Valkyria C .25 .50
LDK2ENY18 Blast Magician C .25 .50
LDK2ENY19 Blockman C .25 .50
LDK2ENY20 Marshmallon C .25 .50
LDK2ENY21 Sangan C .25 .50
LDK2ENY22 Gold Sarcophagus C .75 1.50
LDK2ENY23 Swords of Revealing Light C .25 .50
LDK2ENY24 Magical Dimension C .25 .50
LDK2ENY25 Magicians Unite C .25 .50
LDK2ENY26 Tricky Spell 4 C .25 .50
LDK2ENY27 Thousand Knives C .25 .50
LDK2ENY28 Dark Magic Attack C .25 .50
LDK2ENY29 Contract with Exodia C .25 .50
LDK2ENY30 Messenger of Peace C .25 .50
LDK2ENY31 Dark Factory of Mass Production C .25 .50
LDK2ENY32 Monster Reincarnation C .25 .50
LDK2ENY33 Secret Village of the Spellcasters C 1.50 3.00
LDK2ENY34 Pot of Duality C 1.25 2.50
LDK2ENY35 Mirror Force C 1.00 2.00
LDK2ENY36 Magical Hats C .25 .50
LDK2ENY37 Magic Cylinder C .25 .50
LDK2ENY38 Magician's Circle C .25 .50
LDK2ENY39 Backup Soldier C .25 .50
LDK2ENY40 Gravity Bind C .25 .50

2016 Yu-Gi-Oh Mega Tin Mega Pack 1st Edition

MP16EN001 Phantom Gryphon C .15 .30
MP16EN002 Performapal Elephammer R .30 .75
MP16EN003 Performapal Bowhopper C .15 .30
MP16EN004 Performapal Lizardraw C .15 .30
MP16EN005 Performapal Springoose C .15 .30
MP16EN006 Superheavy Samurai Big Waraji C .15 .30
MP16EN007 Superheavy Samurai Gigagloves C .15 .30
MP16EN008 Superheavy Samurai Soulbuster Gauntlet C .15 .30
MP16EN009 Soprano the Melodious Songstress C .15 .30
MP16EN010 Fluffal Sheep C .15 .30
MP16EN011 Edge Imp Saw C .15 .30
MP16EN012 Edge Imp Chain C .15 .30
MP16EN013 Edge Imp Frightfuloid C .15 .30
MP16EN014 Raidraptor Sharp Lanius C .15 .30
MP16EN015 Raidraptor Mimicry Lanius C .15 .30
MP16EN016 Magma Dragon C .15 .30
MP16EN017 Deskbot 004 C .15 .30
MP16EN018 Doomdog Octhros C .15 .30
MP16EN019 Putrid Pudding Body Buddies C .15 .30
MP16EN020 Bloom Diva the Melodious Choir UR .50 1.00
MP16EN021 Frightfur Chimera R .30 .75
MP16EN022 Clear Wing Synchro Dragon SCR 1.00 2.00
MP16EN023 Performapal Recasting C .15 .30
MP16EN024 Fusion Conscription R .30 .75
MP16EN025 Frightfur Factory C .15 .30
MP16EN026 Frightfur Fusion R .30 .75
MP16EN027 Galaxy Cyclone SCR 1.00 2.00
MP16EN028 Harmonic Oscillation C .15 .30
MP16EN029 Pendulum Rising C .15 .30
MP16EN030 Performapal Pinch Helper C .15 .30
MP16EN031 Fluffal Crane C .15 .30
MP16EN032 Designer Frightfur C .15 .30
MP16EN033 Jar of Avarice SCR .30 .75
MP16EN034 Lose 1 Turn UR .75 1.50
MP16EN035 Fiend Griefing C .15 .30
MP16EN036 Abyss Stungray C .15 .30
MP16EN037 Statue of Anguish Pattern C .15 .30
MP16EN038 Diceversity C .15 .30
MP16EN039 Moon Mirror Shield R .75 1.50
MP16EN040 Half Unbreak C .15 .30
MP16EN041 The Melody of Awakening Dragon SR 4.00 8.00
MP16EN042 Cybernetic Fusion Support C .15 .30
MP16EN043 Number S39: Utopia Prime SR .60 1.25
MP16EN044 GalaxyEyes Full Armor Photon Dragon SR 2.00 4.00
MP16EN045 Performapal Thunderhino C .15 .30
MP16EN046 Primitive Butterfly C .15 .30
MP16EN047 Mystery Shell Dragon C .15 .30
MP16EN048 Risebell the Summoner C .15 .30
MP16EN049 Xiangke Magician SR .60 1.25
MP16EN050 Xiangsheng Magician SR .50 1.00
MP16EN051 Performapal Camelump C .15 .30
MP16EN052 Performapal Drummerrilla C .15 .30
MP16EN053 Superheavy Samurai Blowtorch C .15 .30
MP16EN054 Opera the Melodious Diva C .15 .30
MP16EN055 Tamtam the Melodious Diva C .15 .30
MP16EN056 Fluffal Mouse SR .30 .75
MP16EN057 DD Pandora C .15 .30
MP16EN058 Raidraptor Fuzzy Lanius C .15 .30
MP16EN059 Raidraptor Singing Lanius C .15 .30
MP16EN060 Performage Flame Eater C .15 .30
MP16EN061 Performage Hat Tricker C .15 .30
MP16EN062 Performage Trick Clown C .15 .30
MP16EN063 Performage Stilts Launcher C .15 .30
MP16EN064 Keeper of the Shrine C .15 .30
MP16EN065 Igknight Squire C .15 .30
MP16EN066 Igknight Templar UR 1.50 3.00
MP16EN067 Igknight Paladin C .15 .30
MP16EN068 Igknight Margrave C .15 .30
MP16EN069 Igknight Gallant C .15 .30
MP16EN070 Aromage Cananga C .15 .30
MP16EN071 Aroma Jar C .15 .30
MP16EN072 Bird of Paradise Lost C .15 .30
MP16EN073 Magical Abductor R .30 .75
MP16EN074 Toon Cyber Dragon R 1.25 2.50
MP16EN075 Deskbot 005 C .15 .30
MP16EN076 Retaliating "C" C .15 .30
MP16EN077 DDD Oracle King dArc R 1.00 2.00
MP16EN078 OddEyes Rebellion Dragon SCR .50 1.00
MP16EN079 DDD Marksman King Tell R .30 .75
MP16EN080 Performage Trapeze Magician R 2.00 4.00
MP16EN081 Pianissimo C .15 .30
MP16EN082 Brilliant Fusion SR 10.00 20.00
MP16EN083 RankUpMagic Raptors Force C .15 .30
MP16EN084 Bubble Barrier C .15 .30
MP16EN085 Ignition Phoenix C .15 .30
MP16EN086 Aroma Garden C .15 .30
MP16EN087 BackUp Rider C .15 .30
MP16EN088 Brilliant Spark C .15 .30
MP16EN089 Raidraptor Return C .15 .30
MP16EN090 Raptors Gust C .15 .30
MP16EN091 Trick Box C .15 .30
MP16EN092 Humid Winds C .15 .30
MP16EN093 Ferret Flames C .15 .30
MP16EN094 Balance of Judgment C .15 .30
MP16EN095 Extra Buck R .30 .75
MP16EN096 Side Effects? C .15 .30
MP16EN097 Extinction on Schedule C .15 .30
MP16EN098 Dogoran the Mad Flame Kaiju R .60 1.25
MP16EN099 Kumongous the Sticky String Kaiju R 1.50 3.00
MP16EN100 Kyoutou Waterfront C .15 .30
MP16EN101 Performapal Silver Claw C .15 .30
MP16EN102 Performapal Salutiger C .15 .30
MP16EN103 Tatsunoko SCR .20 .40
MP16EN104 Secret Blast C .15 .30
MP16EN105 Performapal Secondonkey R .30 .75
MP16EN106 Performapal Splashmammoth R .30 .75
MP16EN107 Performapal Helpprincess R .30 .75
MP16EN108 Superheavy Samurai Thief C .15 .30
MP16EN109 Superheavy Samurai Transporter C .15 .30
MP16EN110 Superheavy Samurai Drum C .15 .30
MP16EN111 Superheavy Samurai Soulhorns C .15 .30
MP16EN112 Superheavy Samurai Soulclaw C .15 .30
MP16EN113 DD Berfomet R .30 .75
MP16EN114 DD Swirl Slime C .15 .30
MP16EN115 DD Necro Slime C .15 .30
MP16EN116 Raidraptor Wild Vulture C .15 .30
MP16EN117 Raidraptor Skull Eagle C .15 .30
MP16EN118 Performapal Mirror Conductor C .15 .30
MP16EN119 Assault Blackwing Kunai the Drizzle R .30 .75
MP16EN120 Charging Gaia the Fierce Knight UR .75 1.50
MP16EN121 Sphere Kuriboh R .60 1.25
MP16EN122 Super Soldier Soul C .15 .30
MP16EN123 Beginning Knight SR 1.25 2.50
MP16EN124 Evening Twilight Knight SR 1.25 2.50
MP16EN125 Majespecter Cat Nekomata SR .30 .75
MP16EN126 Majespecter Raccoon Bunbuku UR .50 1.00
MP16EN127 Majespecter Crow Yata C .15 .30
MP16EN128 Majespecter Fox Kyubi C .15 .30
MP16EN129 Majespecter Unicorn Kirin R .30 .75
MP16EN130 Igknight Cavalier C .15 .30
MP16EN131 Igknight Veteran C .15 .30
MP16EN132 Toon Barrel Dragon R .30 .75
MP16EN133 Deskbot 006 C .15 .30
MP16EN134 Pot of The Forbidden C .15 .30
MP16EN135 Dr Frankenderp C .15 .30
MP16EN136 Black Luster Soldier Super Soldier UR 1.00 2.00
MP16EN137 Frightfur SabreTooth UR 1.50 3.00
MP16EN138 DDD Wave Oblivion King Caesar... SR .75 1.50
MP16EN139 OddEyes Vortex Dragon SCR .50 1.00
MP16EN140 Scarlight Red Dragon Archfiend SCR 2.00 4.00
MP16EN141 Assault Blackwing... UR 1.25 2.50
MP16EN142 Deskbot Jet C .15 .30
MP16EN143 DDD DuoDawn King Kali Yuga SR .60 1.25
MP16EN144 Shuffle Reborn C .15 .30
MP16EN145 Raptors Ultimate Mace C .15 .30
MP16EN146 Super Soldier Ritual R 1.00 2.00
MP16EN147 Majespecter Storm C .15 .30
MP16EN148 Igknight Reload UR .75 1.50
MP16EN149 OddEyes Fusion SCR .20 .40
MP16EN150 Psychic Blade C .15 .30
MP16EN151 Painful Decision SCR .30 .75
MP16EN152 Super Rush Headlong C .15 .30
MP16EN153 Frightfur March C .15 .30
MP16EN154 DDD Contract Change C .15 .30
MP16EN155 Dark Contract with Errors C .15 .30
MP16EN156 Super Soldier Rebirth C .15 .30
MP16EN157 Super Soldier Shield UR .30 .75
MP16EN158 Majespecter Tornado UR .50 1.00
MP16EN159 Majespecter Tempest C .15 .30
MP16EN160 Grand Horn of Heaven C .15 .30
MP16EN161 FirstAid Squad C .15 .30
MP16EN162 Painful Escape SCR .10 .20
MP16EN163 Radian the Multidimensional Kaiju R 1.50 3.00
MP16EN164 Gameciel the Sea Turtle Kaiju R 10.00 20.00
MP16EN165 Kaiju Capture Mission C .15 .30
MP16EN166 DD Savant Galilei C .15 .30
MP16EN167 DD Savant Kepler C .15 .30
MP16EN168 Dark Contract with the Gate C .15 .30
MP16EN169 Dark Contract with the Swamp King C .15 .30
MP16EN170 Dark Contract with the Witch C .15 .30
MP16EN171 Contract Laundering C .15 .30
MP16EN172 DDD Human Resources C .15 .30
MP16EN173 DDD Rebel King Leonidas SR 1.00 2.00
MP16EN174 Timebreaker Magician R .30 .75
MP16EN175 Performapal Guitartle R .30 .75
MP16EN176 Performapal Bit Bite Turtle C .15 .30
MP16EN177 Performapal Rain Goat C .15 .30
MP16EN178 Performapal Trump Girl C .15 .30
MP16EN179 Superheavy Samurai Magnet C .15 .30
MP16EN180 Superheavy Samurai Prepped Defense C .15 .30
MP16EN181 Superheavy Samurai General Jade C .15 .30
MP16EN182 Superheavy Samurai General Coral C .15 .30
MP16EN183 Solo the Melodious Songstress C .15 .30
MP16EN184 Score the Melodious Diva C .15 .30
MP16EN185 Blackwing Harmattan the Dust C .15 .30
MP16EN186 Twilight Ninja Shingetsu C .15 .30
MP16EN187 Twilight Ninja Nichirin the Chunin C .15 .30
MP16EN188 Twilight Ninja Getsuga the Shogun R .30 .75
MP16EN189 Buster Blader... UR .50 1.00
MP16EN190 Dragon Buster Destruction Sword C .15 .30
MP16EN191 Wizard Buster Destruction Sword C .15 .30
MP16EN192 Robot Buster Destruction Sword C .15 .30
MP16EN193 Dinomist Stegosaur C .15 .30
MP16EN194 Dinomist Plesios C .15 .30
MP16EN195 Dinomist Pteran R .30 .75
MP16EN196 Dinomist Brachion C .15 .30
MP16EN197 Dinomist Ceratops C .15 .30
MP16EN198 Dinomist Rex SR .20 .40
MP16EN199 Shiranui Spectralsword UR .30 .75
MP16EN200 Shiranui Smith C .15 .30
MP16EN201 Shiranui Spiritmaster R 1.25 2.50
MP16EN202 Shiranui Samurai C .15 .30
MP16EN203 Dark Doriado C .15 .30
MP16EN204 AlLumiraj C .15 .30
MP16EN205 Toon Buster Blader R .30 .75
MP16EN206 Deskbot 007 C .15 .30
MP16EN207 Deskbot 008 C .15 .30
MP16EN208 Engraver of the Mark C .15 .30
MP16EN209 Zany Zebra C .15 .30
MP16EN210 Buster Blader... SCR .50 1.00
MP16EN211 Shiranui Samuraisaga C .15 .30
MP16EN212 Shiranui Shogunsaga UR .25 .50
MP16EN213 Aegaion the Sea Castrum C .15 .30
MP16EN214 Performance Hurricane C .15 .30
MP16EN215 Destruction Swordsman Fusion C .15 .30
MP16EN216 Karma of the Destruction Swordsman C .15 .30
MP16EN217 Dinomic Powerload C .15 .30
MP16EN218 Dinomist Charge C .15 .30
MP16EN219 Majespecter Sonics C .15 .30
MP16EN220 Shiranui Style Synthesis C .15 .30
MP16EN221 Twin Twisters SR 6.00 12.00
MP16EN222 Mistaken Accusation C .15 .30
MP16EN223 Dragons Bind C .15 .30
MP16EN224 Follow Wing C .15 .30
MP16EN225 Reject Reborn R .30 .75
MP16EN226 Destruction Sword Flash C .15 .30
MP16EN227 Dinomist Rush C .15 .30
MP16EN228 Shiranui Style Swallows Slash C .15 .30
MP16EN229 Pendulum Reborn R .30 .75
MP16EN230 Forbidden Apocrypha C .15 .30
MP16EN231 Solemn Strike SCR 7.50 15.00
MP16EN232 Bad Luck Blast C .15 .30
MP16EN233 Ultimate Providence SCR .50 1.00
MP16EN234 Gadarla the Mystery Dust Kaiju R 1.00 2.00
MP16EN235 Jizukiru the Star Destroying Kaiju R 3.00 6.00
MP16EN236 Neptabyss the Atlantean Prince UR .50 1.00
MP16EN237 Cyber Dragon Infinity SCR 1.50 3.00
MP16EN238 Arisen Gaia the Fierce Knight R .30 .75
MP16EN239 Traptrix Rafflesia SCR 1.00 2.00

2016 Yu-Gi-Oh Millennium Pack 1st Edition

MIL1EN001 The Winged Dragon of Ra - Immortal Phoenix UR 3.00 6.00
MIL1EN002 Curse of Dragonfire UR .20 .40
MIL1EN003 Holding Arms SR .25 .50
MIL1EN004 Holding Legs SR .75 1.50
MIL1EN005 Gandora the Dragon of Destruction C .10 .20
MIL1EN006 Gilford the Lightning C .10 .20
MIL1EN007 Exodius the Ultimate Forbidden Lord C .10 .20
MIL1EN008 Relinquished C .10 .20
MIL1EN009 Dark Master - Zorc C .10 .20
MIL1EN010 Sky Galloping Gaia the Dragon Champion SR .30 .75
MIL1EN011 B. Skull Dragon C .10 .20
MIL1EN012 Five-Headed Dragon C .10 .20
MIL1EN013 Rebellion UR .25 .50
MIL1EN014 Card of Demise UR 30.00 75.00
MIL1EN015 Left Arm Offering SR 5.00 10.00
MIL1EN016 The True Name SR 1.25 2.50
MIL1EN017 Symbol of Friendship R .20 .40
MIL1EN018 Shrink C .10 .20
MIL1EN019 Scapegoat C .10 .20
MIL1EN020 Black Illusion Ritual C .10 .20
MIL1EN021 Contract with the Dark Master C .10 .20
MIL1EN022 Trap Hole of Spikes SR .75 1.50
MIL1EN023 Ring of Destruction C .10 .20
MIL1EN024 Nightmare Wheel C .10 .20
MIL1EN025 Celtic Guardian R .20 .40
MIL1EN026 Gaia The Fierce Knight R .20 .40
MIL1EN027 Red-Eyes B. Dragon C .10 .20
MIL1EN028 Summoned Skull C .10 .20
MIL1EN029 La Jinn the Mystical Genie of the Lamp C .10 .20
MIL1EN030 Launcher Spider C .10 .20
MIL1EN031 Tiger Axe C .10 .20
MIL1EN032 Vorse Raider C .10 .20
MIL1EN033 Pendulum Machine C .10 .20
MIL1EN034 Kuriboh C .10 .20
MIL1EN035 Red-Eyes Black Metal Dragon C .10 .20
MIL1EN036 Panther Warrior R .20 .40
MIL1EN037 Viser Des C .10 .20
MIL1EN038 Flame Swordsman R .20 .40
MIL1EN039 Thousand Dragon R .20 .40
MIL1EN040 XYZ-Dragon Cannon R .20 .40
MIL1EN041 Dark Paladin C .10 .20

MIL1EN042 Toon World C .10 .20
MIL1EN043 Spiral Spear Strike C .10 .20
MIL1EN044 Acid Trap Hole R .20 .40
MIL1EN045 Metalmorph C .10 .20
MIL1EN046 Widespread Ruin R .20 .40
MIL1EN047 Crush Card Virus C .10 .20
MIL1EN048 Kunai with Chain R .20 .40

2016 Yu-Gi-Oh OTS Tournament Pack 1

OP01EN001 Bountiful Artemis UTR 15.00 30.00
OP01EN002 Vanity's Fiend UTR 20.00 40.00
OP01EN003 Masked HERO Dark Law UTR 20.00 40.00
OP01EN004 Droll & Lock Bird SR 7.50 15.00
OP01EN005 Infernoid Patrulea SR .75 1.50
OP01EN006 Performapal Lizardraw SR .75 1.50
OP01EN007 Performapal Skullcrobat Joker SR 5.00 10.00
OP01EN008 Performapal Monkeyboard SR .50 1.00
OP01EN009 Performapal Guitartle SR .60 1.25
OP01EN010 Dinoster Power Mighty Dracoslayer SR1.25 2.50
OP01EN011 Anti-Spell Fragrance SR 10.00 20.00
OP01EN012 Imperial Iron Wall SR 1.25 2.50
OP01EN013 Typhoon SR 2.00 4.00
OP01EN014 Skull Servant C 2.00 4.00
OP01EN015 Battle Warrior C .60 1.25
OP01EN016 Mezuki C 1.25 2.50
OP01EN017 The White Stone of Legend C .75 1.50
OP01EN018 Flying "C" C .75 1.50
OP01EN019 Zombie Warrior C 2.00 4.00
OP01EN020 Michael, the Arch-Lightsworn C 1.25 2.50
OP01EN021 Cyber Dragon Nova C 2.50 5.00
OP01EN022 Mage Power C 1.25 2.50
OP01EN023 Offerings to the Doomed C .15 .30
OP01EN024 Monster Gate C .30 .75
OP01EN025 Allure of Darkness C 3.00 6.00
OP01EN026 Summoning Curse C .50 1.00
OP01EN027 Advance Zone C .50 1.00

2016 Yu-Gi-Oh OTS Tournament Pack 2

OP02EN001 Fog King UTR 6.00 12.00
OP02EN002 Kuraz the Light Monarch UTR 10.00 20.00
OP02EN003 Raigeki UTR 50.00 100.00
OP02EN004 Gameciel the Sea Turtle Kaiju SR 7.50 15.00
OP02EN005 Fiendish Rhino Warrior SR .75 1.50
OP02EN006 Mithra the Thunder Vassal SR .75 1.50
OP02EN007 Phantom Knights of Ragged Gloves SR.60 1.25
OP02EN008 Super Quantum Blue Layer SR .60 1.25
OP02EN009 System Down SR 1.00 2.00
OP02EN010 Mask of Restrict SR 4.00 8.00
OP02EN011 Ninjitsu Art of Transformation SR .50 1.00
OP02EN012 Armor Ninjitsu Art of Freezing SR .50 1.00
OP02EN013 The Prime Monarch SR 2.00 4.00
OP02EN014 Takuhee C .75 1.50
OP02EN015 Temple of Skulls C .60 1.25
OP02EN016 Dark Eradicator Warlock C .60 1.25
OP02EN017 Infernity Archfiend C .30 .75
OP02EN018 Cyber Dragon Core C 1.50 3.00
OP02EN019 Galaxy Dragon C .25 .50
OP02EN020 Prediction Princess Coinorma C .50 1.00
OP02EN021 Prediction Princess Tarotrei C .60 1.25
OP02EN022 Skullbird C 1.00 2.00
OP02EN023 United We Stand C 2.00 4.00
OP02EN024 The Melody of Awakening Dragon C1.00 2.00
OP02EN025 Prediction Ritual C .50 1.00
OP02EN026 Ninjitsu Art of SuperTransformation C.50 1.00
OP02EN027 Wiretap C .50 1.00

2016 Yu-Gi-Oh OTS Tournament Pack 3

OP03EN001 Swap Frog UTR 75.00 150.00
OP03EN002 Speedroid Terrortop UTR 30.00 60.00
OP03EN003 Super Quantal Mech
Beast Grampulse UTR 12.50 25.00
OP03EN004 Metalfoes Goldriver SR .25 .50
OP03EN005 Dupe Frog SR 7.50 15.00
OP03EN006 Ally of Justice Cycle Reader SR .50 1.00
OP03EN007 Paladin of Felgrand SR .30 .60
OP03EN008 Igknight Reload SR .20 .40
OP03EN009 Sky Iris SR 2.50 5.00
OP03EN010 Domain of the True Monarchs SR .50 1.00
OP03EN011 Magic Deflector SR 3.00 6.00
OP03EN012 Chaos Trap Hole SR .50 1.00
OP03EN013 Oasis of Dragon Souls SR .30 .75
OP03EN014 Enchanting Mermaid SP .30 .60
OP03EN015 Slime Toad C .17 .35
OP03EN016 Cipher Soldier C 2.00 4.00
OP03EN017 Black Dragon's Chick C .25 .50
OP03EN018 D.D. Crow C 1.00 2.00
OP03EN019 Doom Shaman C .15 .30
OP03EN020 Hecatrice C .20 .40
OP03EN021 Oyster Meister C .25 .50
OP03EN022 Beast of the Pharaoh C .25 .50
OP03EN023 Night's End Sorcerer C .17 .35
OP03EN024 Darkstorm Dragon C .15 .30
OP03EN025 Uni-Zombie C .50 1.00
OP03EN026 Rare Fish SP .50 1.00
OP03EN027 Fusionist SP .75 1.50

2016 Yu-Gi-Oh Shining Victories 1st Edition

SHVIEN000 Magical Cavalry of Cxulub R .20 .40
SHVIEN001 Angel Trumpeter C .10 .20
SHVIEN002 Performapal Sellshell Crab C .10 .20
SHVIEN003 Performapal Odd-Eyes Light Phoenix R.20 .40
SHVIEN004 Performapal Odd-Eyes Unicorn R .20 .40
SHVIEN005 Performapal Fireflux C .10 .20
SHVIEN006 Speedroid Den-Den Daiko Duke R .20 .40
SHVIEN007 Speedroid Pachingo-Kart R .20 .40
SHVIEN008 Lunalight Blue Cat R .20 .40
SHVIEN009 Lunalight Purple Butterfly C .10 .20
SHVIEN010 Lunalight White Rabbit C .10 .20
SHVIEN011 Lunalight Black Sheep C .10 .20
SHVIEN012 Lunalight Wolf C .10 .20
SHVIEN013 Lunalight Tiger C .10 .20
SHVIEN014 Raidraptor - Avenge Vulture C .10 .20
SHVIEN015 Raidraptor - Pain Lanius C .10 .20
SHVIEN016 Raidraptor - Booster Strix C .10 .20
SHVIEN017 Blackwing - Decay the Ill Wind C .10 .20
SHVIEN018 Dragon Spirit of White UR .10 .20
SHVIEN019 Protector with Eyes of Blue C .10 .20
SHVIEN020 Sage with Eyes of Blue UR .10 .20
SHVIEN021 Master with Eyes of Blue C .10 .20
SHVIEN022 The White Stone of Ancients UR .10 .20
SHVIEN023 Lector Pendulum, the Dracoverlord UR.10 .20
SHVIEN024 Amorphage Gluttony R .20 .40
SHVIEN025 Amorphage Lechery UR .10 .20
SHVIEN026 Amorphage Greed R .20 .40
SHVIEN027 Amorphage Envy R .20 .40
SHVIEN028 Amorphage Wrath C .10 .20
SHVIEN029 Amorphage Pride C .10 .20
SHVIEN030 Amorphage Sloth SCT 4.00 8.00
SHVIEN031 Amorphage Goliath SR .10 .20
SHVIEN032 Dinomist Spinos C .10 .20
SHVIEN033 Digital Bug Cocoondenser C .10 .20
SHVIEN034 Digital Bug Centibit C .10 .20
SHVIEN035 Digital Bug Websolder C .10 .20
SHVIEN036 Red-Eyes Toon Dragon SR .10 .20
SHVIEN037 Ryu Okami C .10 .20
SHVIEN038 Tenmataitei R .20 .40
SHVIEN039 Spirit of the Fall Wind R .10 .20
SHVIEN040 Ghost Reaper & Winter Cherries SCT25.00 50.00
SHVIEN041 Gendo the Ascetic Monk C .10 .20
SHVIEN042 Deskbot 009 C .10 .20
SHVIEN043 Dicelops C .10 .20
SHVIEN044 Amorphactor Pain... SR .10 .20
SHVIEN045 Bloom Prima the Melodious Choir R .20 .40
SHVIEN046 Lunalight Cat Dancer R .20 .40
SHVIEN047 Lunalight Panther Dancer UR .10 .20
SHVIEN048 Lunalight Leo Dancer SR .10 .20
SHVIEN049 Crystal Wing Synchro Dragon SCT60.00 125.00
SHVIEN050 Hi-Speedroid Puzzle R .20 .40
SHVIEN051 Assault Blackwing... SR .10 .20
SHVIEN052 Blue-Eyes Spirit Dragon SCT 15.00 30.00
SHVIEN053 Raidraptor - Ultimate Falcon SR .10 .20
SHVIEN054 Digital Bug Scaradiator C .10 .20
SHVIEN055 Digital Bug Corebage C .10 .20
SHVIEN056 Digital Bug Rhinosebus SR .10 .20
SHVIEN057 Fortissimo C .10 .20
SHVIEN058 Rank-Up-Magic Skip Force R .20 .40
SHVIEN059 Mausoleum of White R .20 .40
SHVIEN060 Beacon of White C .10 .20
SHVIEN061 Forge of the True Dracos C .10 .20
SHVIEN062 Amorphous Persona UR .10 .20
SHVIEN063 Amorphage Infection SR .10 .20
SHVIEN064 Bug Matrix C .10 .20
SHVIEN065 Pre-Preparation of Rites SR .10 .20
SHVIEN066 Fusion Tag R .20 .40
SHVIEN067 Tuner's High SR .10 .20
SHVIEN068 Deskbot Base C .10 .20
SHVIEN069 Finite Cards C .10 .20
SHVIEN070 Re-dyce-cle C .10 .20
SHVIEN071 Lunalight Reincarnation Dance C .10 .20
SHVIEN072 Amorphage Lysis R .20 .40
SHVIEN073 Dinomist Eruption C .10 .20
SHVIEN074 Bug Emergency C .10 .20
SHVIEN075 Drowning Mirror Force SCT 10.00 20.00
SHVIEN076 Wonder Xyz C .10 .20
SHVIEN077 Rise to Full Height C .10 .20
SHVIEN078 Bad Aim C .10 .20
SHVIEN079 Unwavering Bond UR .10 .20
SHVIEN080 Graceful Tear C .10 .20
SHVIEN081 Cattle Call SR .10 .20
SHVIEN082 Kozmo Scaredy Lion SR .10 .20
SHVIEN083 Kozmoll Dark Lady SCT 7.50 15.00
SHVIEN084 Kozmo Landwalker SR .10 .20
SHVIEN085 Kozmo Dark Planet SCT 4.00 8.00
SHVIEN086 Kozmourning C .10 .20
SHVIEN087 Thunder King,
the Lightningstrike Kaiju R .20 .40
SHVIEN088 Super Anti-Kaiju War Machine... R .20 .40
SHVIEN089 The Kaiju Files C .10 .20
SHVIEN090 Cuben C .10 .20
SHVIEN091 World Carrotweight Champion C .10 .20
SHVIEN092 Fire King Island C .10 .20
SHVIEN093 Dwarf Star Dragon Planeter C .10 .20
SHVIEN094 Geargiarichor C .10 .20
SHVIEN095 Geargia Change C .10 .20
SHVIEN096 Stardust Sifr Divine Dragon UR .10 .20
SHVIEN097 Hot Red Dragon Archfiend... UR .10 .20
SHVIEN098 Priestess with Eyes of Blue SR .10 .20
SHVIEN099 Blue-Eyes Twin Burst Dragon SCT10.00 20.00
SHVIENSE1 Ebon Illusion Magician SR .10 .20
SHVIENSE2 Elemental HERO Core SR .10 .20
SHVIENSE3 Magician's Rob SR .10 .20
SHVIENSE4 Scapeghost SR .10 .20

2016 Yu-Gi-Oh Starter Deck Yuya 1st Edition

YS16EN001 Performapal Sleight Hand Magician UR.30 .75
YS16EN002 Performapal King Bear UR .30 .75
YS16EN003 Performapal Swincobra C .10 .20
YS16EN004 Performapal Momoncarpet SR .20 .40
YS16EN005 Performapal Parrotrio SR .30 .75
YS16EN006 Performapal Longphone Bull SR .20 .40
YS16EN007 Performapal Teeter Totter Hopper C .10 .20
YS16EN008 Odd-Eyes Pendulum Dragon C .10 .20
YS16EN009 Stargazer Magician C .10 .20
YS16EN010 Timegazer Magician C .10 .20
YS16EN011 Performapal Drummerilla C .10 .20
YS16EN012 Performapal Secondonkey C .10 .20
YS16EN013 Performapal Hip Hippo C .10 .20
YS16EN014 Foucault's Cannon C .10 .20
YS16EN015 Archfiend Eccentrick C 3.00 6.00
YS16EN016 Gene-Warped Warwolf C .10 .20
YS16EN017 Beast King Barbaros C .10 .20
YS16EN018 Pitch-Black Warwolf C .10 .20
YS16EN019 Dragon Dowser C .10 .20
YS16EN020 Giant Rat C .10 .20
YS16EN021 Performapal Dramatic Theater C .10 .20
YS16EN022 Smile World C .10 .20
YS16EN023 Hippo Carnival C .10 .20
YS16EN024 Draw Muscle C .10 .20
YS16EN025 Mystical Space Typhoon C .50 1.00
YS16EN026 Lightning Vortex C .10 .20
YS16EN027 Book of Moon C .10 .20
YS16EN028 Lucky Iron Axe C .10 .20
YS16EN029 Burden of the Mighty C .10 .20
YS16EN030 Back-Up Rider C .10 .20
YS16EN031 Performapal Show Down C .10 .20
YS16EN032 Performapal Pinch Helper C .10 .20
YS16EN033 Wall of Disruption C .10 .20
YS16EN034 Ceasefire C .10 .20
YS16EN035 Raigeki Break C .10 .20
YS16EN036 Draining Shield C .10 .20
YS16EN037 Threatening Roar C .10 .20
YS16EN038 Dark Bribe C 1.25 2.50
YS16EN039 Chaos Burst C .10 .20
YS16EN040 Pendulum Reborn C .10 .20
YS16ENT01 Hippo Token Orange T .10 .20
YS16ENT02 Hippo Token Yellow T .10 .20
YS16ENT03 Hippo Token Blue T .10 .20

2016 Yu-Gi-Oh Structure Deck Emperor of Darkness 1st Edition

SR01EN000 Ehther the Heavenly Monarch UR .50 1.00
SR01EN001 Erebus the Underworld Monarch UR .50 1.00
SR01EN002 Eidos the Underworld Squire SR .50 1.00
SR01EN003 Edea the Heavenly Squire SR .50 1.00
SR01EN004 Caius the Shadow Monarch C .20 .40
SR01EN005 Zaborg the Thunder Monarch C .10 .20
SR01EN006 Granmarg the Rock Monarch C .10 .20
SR01EN007 Mobius the Frost Monarch C .10 .20
SR01EN008 Thestalos the Firestorm Monarch C .10 .20
SR01EN009 Raiza the Storm Monarch C .10 .20
SR01EN010 Lucius the Shadow Vassal C .10 .20
SR01EN011 Mithra the Thunder Vassal C .10 .20
SR01EN012 Landrobe the Rock Vassal C .10 .20
SR01EN013 Escher the Frost Vassal C .10 .20
SR01EN014 Berlineth the Firestorm Vassal C .10 .20
SR01EN015 Garum the Storm Vassal C .10 .20
SR01EN016 Illusory Snatcher C .10 .20
SR01EN017 Tragoedia C .15 .30
SR01EN018 Dandylion C .10 .20
SR01EN019 Mathematician C .20 .40
SR01EN020 Level Eater C .10 .20
SR01EN021 Battle Fader C .20 .40
SR01EN022 Rainbow Kuriboh C .10 .20
SR01EN023 Pantheism of the Monarchs SR .60 1.25
SR01EN024 Domain of the True Monarchs C .75 1.50
SR01EN025 March of the Monarchs C .10 .20
SR01EN026 Return of the Monarchs C .20 .40
SR01EN027 The Monarchs Stormforth C .20 .40
SR01EN028 Strike of the Monarchs C .10 .20
SR01EN029 Tenacity of the Monarchs C .10 .20
SR01EN030 Soul Exchange C .10 .20
SR01EN031 Enemy Controller C .10 .20
SR01EN032 Dicephoon C .10 .20
SR01EN033 Soul Charge C 2.00 4.00
SR01EN034 The Prime Monarch C .60 1.25
SR01EN035 The First Monarch C .10 .20
SR01EN036 Escalation of the Monarchs C .10 .20
SR01EN037 The Monarchs Awaken C .10 .20
SR01EN038 The Monarchs Erupt C .10 .20
SR01EN039 By Order of the Emperor C .10 .20
SR01EN040 Pinpoint Guard C .10 .20
SR01ENTKN Token C .20 .40

2016 Yu-Gi-Oh Structure Deck Rise of the True Dragons 1st Edition

SR02EN000 Arkbrave Dragon UR .30 .75
SR02EN001 Divine Dragon Lord Felgrand UR .25 .50
SR02EN002 Dragon Knight of Creation SR .20 .40
SR02EN003 Paladin of Felgrand C .20 .40
SR02EN004 Guardian of Felgrand C .20 .40
SR02EN005 Felgrand Dragon C .20 .40
SR02EN006 Darkblaze Dragon C .20 .40
SR02EN007 Herald of Creation C .20 .40
SR02EN008 Decoy Dragon C .20 .40
SR02EN009 Red-Eyes Darkness Metal Dragon C .60 1.25
SR02EN010 Red-Eyes Wyvern C .20 .40
SR02EN011 White Night Dragon C .20 .40
SR02EN012 Darkstorm Dragon C .20 .40
SR02EN013 Armed Protector Dragon C .20 .40
SR02EN014 Evilswarm Zahak C .20 .40
SR02EN015 Eclipse Wyvern C .20 .40
SR02EN016 White Dragon Wyverburster C .20 .40
SR02EN017 Black Dragon Collapserpent C .20 .40
SR02EN018 Keeper of the Shrine C .20 .40
SR02EN019 Kidmodo Dragon C .20 .40
SR02EN020 Jain, Lightsworn Paladin C .20 .40
SR02EN021 Ehren, Lightsworn Monk C .20 .40
SR02EN022 Raiden, Hand of the Lightsworn C .50 1.00
SR02EN023 Card Trooper C .20 .40
SR02EN024 Ruins of the Divine Dragon Lords SR.10 .20
SR02EN025 Return of the Dragon Lords SR 7.50 15.00
SR02EN026 Dragon Ravine C .20 .40
SR02EN027 A Wingbeat of Giant Dragon C .20 .40
SR02EN028 Trade-In C .75 1.50
SR02EN029 Foolish Burial C .20 .40
SR02EN030 Hand Destruction C .60 1.25
SR02EN031 Reinforcement of the Army C .20 .40
SR02EN032 The Warrior Returning Alive C .20 .40
SR02EN033 Charge of the Light Brigade C .20 .40
SR02EN034 Terraforming C 1.00 2.00
SR02EN035 Dragon's Rebirth C .20 .40
SR02EN036 Burst Breath C .20 .40
SR02EN037 Needlebug Nest C .20 .40
SR02EN038 Breakthrough Skill C .60 1.25
SR02EN039 Call of the Haunted C .20 .40
SR02EN040 Oasis of Dragon Souls C .20 .40
SR02ENTKN Dragon Lord Token C .20 .40

2016 Yu-Gi-Oh Structure Deck Seto Kaiba 1st Edition

SDKSEN001 AAssault Core SR 2.00 4.00
SDKSEN002 BBuster Drake SR 2.00 4.00
SDKSEN003 CCrush Wyvern SR 2.00 4.00
SDKSEN004 Heavy Mech Support Armor C .15 .30
SDKSEN005 XHead Cannon C .15 .30
SDKSEN006 YDragon Head C .15 .30
SDKSEN007 ZMetal Tank C .15 .30
SDKSEN008 Heavy Mech Support Platform C .15 .30
SDKSEN009 BlueEyes White Dragon C .15 .30
SDKSEN010 Kaiser Glider C .15 .30
SDKSEN011 Lord of D C .15 .30
SDKSEN012 Vampire Lord C .15 .30
SDKSEN013 Enraged Battle Ox C .15 .30
SDKSEN014 Des Feral Imp C .15 .30
SDKSEN015 Peten the Dark Clown C .15 .30
SDKSEN016 Interplanetarypurplythorny Dragon C.15 .30
SDKSEN017 Blizzard Dragon C .15 .30
SDKSEN018 Keeper of the Shrine C .15 .30
SDKSEN019 Luster Dragon C .15 .30
SDKSEN020 Union Hangar C .15 .30
SDKSEN021 Majesty with Eyes of Blue C .15 .30
SDKSEN022 Burst Stream of Destruction C .15 .30
SDKSEN023 The Flute of Summoning Dragon C .15 .30
SDKSEN024 Silent Doom C .15 .30
SDKSEN025 Shrink C .15 .30
SDKSEN026 Enemy Controller C .15 .30
SDKSEN027 Megamorph C .15 .30
SDKSEN028 Limiter Removal C .15 .30
SDKSEN029 Frontline Base C .15 .30
SDKSEN030 Union Scramble C .15 .30
SDKSEN031 Crush Card Virus C .15 .30
SDKSEN032 Negate Attack C .15 .30
SDKSEN033 Ring of Destruction C .15 .30
SDKSEN034 Interdimensional Matter Transporter C.15 .30
SDKSEN035 Cloning C .15 .30
SDKSEN036 Final Attack Orders C .15 .30
SDKSEN037 Call of the Haunted C .15 .30
SDKSEN038 Roll Out! C .15 .30
SDKSEN039 Fiendish Chain C .15 .30
SDKSEN040 AtoZDragon Buster Cannon UR 2.50 5.00
SDKSEN041 ABCDragon Buster UR 2.50 5.00
SDKSEN042 XYZDragon Cannon C .15 .30
SDKSEN043 XYDragon Cannon C .15 .30
SDKSEN044 XZTank Cannon C .15 .30

2016 Yu-Gi-Oh Structure Deck Yugi Moto 1st Edition

SDMYEN001 Alpha The Electromagnet Warrior SR1.50 3.00
SDMYEN002 Beta The Electromagnet Warrior SR1.50 3.00
SDMYEN003 Gamma The Electromagnet Warrior SR1.50 3.00
SDMYEN004 Berserkion the
Electromagna Warrior UR 2.50 5.00
SDMYEN005 Kuribohrn C .15 .30
SDMYEN006 Valkyrion the Magna Warrior C .15 .30
SDMYEN007 Alpha The Magnet Warrior C .15 .30
SDMYEN008 Beta The Magnet Warrior C .15 .30
SDMYEN009 Gamma The Magnet Warrior C .15 .30
SDMYEN010 Dark Magician C .15 .30
SDMYEN011 Dark Magician Girl C .15 .30
SDMYEN012 Buster Blader C .15 .30
SDMYEN013 Jacks Knight C .15 .30
SDMYEN014 Queens Knight C .15 .30
SDMYEN015 Kings Knight C .15 .30
SDMYEN016 Berfomet C .15 .30
SDMYEN017 Gazelle the King of Mythical Beasts C.15 .30
SDMYEN018 Obnoxious Celtic Guard C .15 .30
SDMYEN019 Giant Soldier of Stone C .15 .30
SDMYEN020 Kuriboh C .15 .30
SDMYEN021 Skilled Dark Magician C .15 .30
SDMYEN022 Skilled White Magician C .15 .30
SDMYEN023 TwinHeaded Behemoth C .15 .30
SDMYEN024 Magnetic Field C .15 .30
SDMYEN025 Dark Magic Inheritance C .15 .30
SDMYEN026 Dark Magic Attack C .15 .30
SDMYEN027 Dark Magic Curtain C .15 .30
SDMYEN028 Mystic Box C .15 .30
SDMYEN029 Swords of Revealing Light C .15 .30
SDMYEN030 Spell Shattering Arrow C .15 .30
SDMYEN031 Polymerization C .15 .30
SDMYEN032 DeFusion C .15 .30
SDMYEN033 Swords of Concealing Light C .15 .30
SDMYEN034 Attack the Moon! C .15 .30
SDMYEN035 Magnet Conversion C .15 .30
SDMYEN036 Magicians Circle C .15 .30
SDMYEN037 Mirror Force C .15 .30
SDMYEN038 Magic Cylinder C .15 .30
SDMYEN039 Soul Rope C .15 .30
SDMYEN040 Rock Bombardment C .15 .30
SDMYEN041 Imperion Magnum... UR 2.50 5.00
SDMYEN042 Arcana Knight Joker C .15 .30
SDMYEN043 Dark Paladin C .15 .30
SDMYEN044 Chimera the Flying Mythical Beast C.15 .30
SDMYEN045 Buster Blader... C .15 .30

2016 Yu-Gi-Oh Wing Raiders 1st Edition

WIRAEN001 Phantom Knights of Ancient Cloak UR7.50 15.00
WIRAEN002 Phantom Knights of Silent Boots SR.50 1.00
WIRAEN003 Phantom Knights of Ragged Gloves C.10 .20
WIRAEN004 Phantom Knights of Cloven Helm R .10 .20
WIRAEN005 Phantom Knights of Fragile Armor SR.10 .20
WIRAEN006 Phantom
Knights of Break Sword SCR 50.00 100.00
WIRAEN007 Dark Rebellion Xyz Dragon R 1.00 2.00
WIRAEN008 Phantom Knights' Spear R .10 .20
WIRAEN009 Phantom Knights' Fog Blade UR 10.00 20.00
WIRAEN010 Phantom Knights' Sword R .10 .20
WIRAEN011 Phantom Knights' Wing C .10 .20
WIRAEN012 The Phantom Knights of Shadow Veil C.10 .20
WIRAEN013 Booby Trap E SR .20 .40
WIRAEN014 Raidraptor - Necro Vulture SR .10 .20
WIRAEN015 Raidraptor - Last Strix C .10 .20
WIRAEN016 Raidraptor - Vanishing Lanius C .10 .20
WIRAEN017 Raidraptor - Fuzzy Lanius C .10 .20
WIRAEN018 Raidraptor - Singing Lanius C .10 .20
WIRAEN019 Raidraptor - Sharp Lanius C .10 .20
WIRAEN020 Raidraptor - Mimicry Lanius C .10 .20
WIRAEN021 Raidraptor - Tribute Lanius UR 3.00 6.00
WIRAEN022 Raidraptor - Force Strix SCR 15.00 30.00
WIRAEN023 Raidraptor - Revolution Falcon C .10 .20
WIRAEN024 Raidraptor -
Satellite Cannon Falcon SCR 7.50 15.00
WIRAEN025 Raidraptor - Call UR 1.00 2.00
WIRAEN026 Raidraptor - Nest C .10 .20
WIRAEN027 Rank-Up-Magic Doom Double Force R.10 .20
WIRAEN028 Rank-Up-Magic Soul Shave Force SR.20 .40
WIRAEN029 Raidraptor - Readiness C .10 .20
WIRAEN030 Super Quantum Red Layer UR 7.50 15.00
WIRAEN031 Super Quantum Green Layer SR .20 .40
WIRAEN032 Super Quantum Blue Layer R .30 .75

WIRAEN033 Super Quantal Fairy Alphan C .10 .20
WIRAEN034 Super Quantal...Grampulse R .60 1.25
WIRAEN035 Super Quantal...Aeroboros SR .20 .40
WIRAEN036 Super Quantal...Magnaliger UR 1.00 2.00
WIRAEN037 Super Quantal...Great Magnus SCR2.00 4.00
WIRAEN038 Super Quantal...Magnacarrier R .10 .20
WIRAEN039 Super Quantal...Magnaslayer C .10 .20
WIRAEN040 Crane Crane C .10 .20
WIRAEN041 Harpie Harpist R .10 .20
WIRAEN042 Gem-Knight Pearl C .10 .20
WIRAEN043 Gagaga Cowboy R .30 .75
WIRAEN044 Zubaba General C .10 .20
WIRAEN045 Number 66: Master Key Beetle C .10 .20
WIRAEN046 Ghostrick Alucard R .30 .75
WIRAEN047 Number 101: Silent Honor ARK SR2.00 4.00
WIRAEN048 Bujinki Amaterasu C .10 .20
WIRAEN049 Cairngorgon, Antiluminescent Knight C.10 .20
WIRAEN050 Number 52: Diamond Crab King SCR2.00 4.00
WIRAEN051 Mystical Space Typhoon C .30 .75
WIRAEN052 Reinforcement of the Army C .10 .20
WIRAEN053 Forbidden Chalice C .10 .20
WIRAEN054 Swallow's Nest R .10 .20
WIRAEN055 Rank-Up-Magic Astral Force C .10 .20
WIRAEN056 Bottomless Trap Hole C .50 1.00
WIRAEN057 Call of the Haunted C .10 .20
WIRAEN058 Icarus Attack SR .20 .40
WIRAEN059 Needlebug Nest C .10 .20
WIRAEN060 Xyz Reborn SR .50 1.00

2017 Yu-Gi-Oh Battles of Legend Light's Revenge 1st Edition

BLLREN001 Odd Eyes Lancer Dragon UR .15 .30
BLLREN002 Performapal Odd Eyes Minitaurus UR.15 .30
BLLREN003 Performapal Odd Eyes Dissolver UR .15 .30
BLLREN004 Performapal Odd Eyes Synchron SCR.50 1.00
BLLREN005 Performapal Five Rainbow Magician UR.15 .30
BLLREN006 Odd Eyes Venom Dragon SCR 1.25 2.50
BLLREN007 DDD Super...Bright Armageddon UR .15 .30
BLLREN008 DDD Super...Dark Armageddon UR .15 .30
BLLREN009 Superheavy Samurai Helper UR .15 .30
BLLREN010 Superheavy Samurai Fist UR .15 .30
BLLREN011 Superheavy
Samurai Steam Train King UR .15 .30
BLLREN012 Abyss Actor Curtain Raiser UR .15 .30
BLLREN013 Abyss Script Abysstainment UR .15 .30
BLLREN014 Raidraptor Rudder Strix UR .15 .30
BLLREN015 Raidraptor Final Fortress Falcon UR .15 .30
BLLREN016 Twilight Ninja Jogen UR .15 .30
BLLREN017 Twilight Ninja Kagen UR .15 .30
BLLREN018 White Moray UR .15 .30
BLLREN019 White Aura Dolphin SCR .50 1.00
BLLREN020 White Aura Whale SCR .50 1.00
BLLREN021 Gladiator Beast Noxious SCR 1.00 2.00
BLLREN022 Gladiator Beast Andabata UR .15 .30
BLLREN023 Gladiator Beast Tamer Editor SCR .50 1.00
BLLREN024 Destiny HERO Dreamer UR .15 .30
BLLREN025 Destiny HERO Dusktopia SCR .50 1.00
BLLREN026 Vision HERO Witch Raider SCR .25 .50
BLLREN027 Giant Rex UR .15 .30
BLLREN028 Double Evolution Pill SCR 1.50 3.00
BLLREN029 Spacetime Transcendence UR .15 .30
BLLREN030 Jurassic Impact UR .15 .30
BLLREN031 Lazion the Timelord UR .20 .40
BLLREN032 Zaphion the Timelord UR .50 1.00
BLLREN033 Sadion the Timelord UR .20 .40
BLLREN034 Kamion the Timelord UR .20 .40
BLLREN035 Time Maiden SCR .75 1.50
BLLREN036 Lyla Lightsworn Sorceress UR .20 .40
BLLREN037 Garoth Lightsworn Warrior UR .15 .30
BLLREN038 Lumina Lightsworn Summoner UR .20 .40
BLLREN039 Wulf Lightsworn Beast UR .15 .30
BLLREN040 Celestia Lightsworn Angel UR .15 .30
BLLREN041 Judgment Dragon UR .50 1.00
BLLREN042 Raiden Hand of the Lightsworn UR .20 .40
BLLREN043 Felis Lightsworn Archer UR .60 1.25
BLLREN044 Minerva the Exalted Lightsworn SCR15.00 30.00
BLLREN045 Solar Recharge UR .20 .40
BLLREN046 Witch of the Black Forest UR .15 .30
BLLREN047 Vanitys Fiend UR 2.00 4.00
BLLREN048 Crusader of Endymion UR .15 .30
BLLREN049 Cactus Bouncer UR .15 .30
BLLREN050 Spellbook Magician of Prophecy UR1.00 2.00
BLLREN051 Mermail Abyssteus SCR 2.50 5.00
BLLREN052 Denko Sekka SCR 3.00 6.00
BLLREN053 Galaxy Soldier UR 3.00 6.00
BLLREN054 Infernoid Devyaty UR .15 .30
BLLREN055 Sage with Eyes of Blue SCR 5.00 10.00
BLLREN056 Elemental HERO Nova Master UR .50 1.00
BLLREN057 Vision HERO Adoration UR .75 1.50
BLLREN058 Archfiend Zombie Skull UR .20 .40
BLLREN059 Dragunity Knight Gae Dearg UR 1.50 3.00
BLLREN060 Trishula Dragon of the Ice Barrier SCR3.00 6.00
BLLREN061 PSY Framelord Omega SCR 5.00 10.00
BLLREN062 Crystal Wing Synchro Dragon SCR5.00 10.00
BLLREN063 M X Saber Invoker SCR 1.50 3.00
BLLREN064 Neo Galaxy Eyes Photon Dragon UR1.00 2.00
BLLREN065 Gaia Dragon the Thunder Charger UR.60 1.25
BLLREN066 Number 11 Big Eye UR .75 1.50
BLLREN067 #107 Galaxy Eyes Tachyon Dragon UR1.50 3.00
BLLREN068 Evilswarm Exciton Knight UR 1.50 3.00
BLLREN069 Bujintei Tsukuyomi UR .60 1.25
BLLREN070 #62 Galaxy Eyes
Prime Photon Dragon UR .75 1.50
BLLREN071 Phantom Knights of Break Sword SCR3.00 6.00
BLLREN072 Raidraptor Force Strix UR 1.50 3.00
BLLREN073 Raidraptor Satellite Cannon Falcon UR.15 .30
BLLREN074 Into the Void UR 1.25 2.50
BLLREN075 Spellbook of Secrets UR 1.00 2.00
BLLREN076 Miracle Contact UR 1.00 2.00
BLLREN077 Transmodify UR .20 .40
BLLREN078 Anti Spell Fragrance UR 2.00 4.00
BLLREN079 Different Dimension Ground UR 1.50 3.00
BLLREN080 Artifact Sanctum SCR 3.00 6.00

2017 Yu-Gi-Oh Circuit Break 1st Edition

CIBREN000 Hallohallo R .20 .40
CIBREN001 Defect Compiler C .15 .30
CIBREN002 Capacitor Stalker C .15 .30
CIBREN003 Link Infra Flier C .15 .30
CIBREN004 Trickstar Narkissus R .20 .40
CIBREN005 Dark Angel C .15 .30
CIBREN006 Gouki Headbatt C .15 .30
CIBREN007 Gateway Dragon SR .60 1.25
CIBREN008 Sniffer Dragon C .15 .30
CIBREN009 Anesthrokket Dragon C .15 .30
CIBREN010 Autorokket Dragon SR .60 1.25
CIBREN011 Magnarokket Dragon UR 2.00 4.00
CIBREN012 Altergeist Marionetter UR 1.25 2.50
CIBREN013 Altergeist Silquitous SR .60 1.25
CIBREN014 Altergeist Meluseek UR 1.25 2.50
CIBREN015 Altergeist Kunquery C .15 .30
CIBREN016 Krawler Spine C .15 .30
CIBREN017 Krawler Axon C .15 .30
CIBREN018 Krawler Glial C .15 .30
CIBREN019 Krawler Receptor C .15 .30
CIBREN020 Krawler Ranvier C .15 .30
CIBREN021 Krawler Dendrite C .15 .30
CIBREN022 World Legacy World Armor R .20 .40
CIBREN023 Metaphys Ragnarok SR .60 1.25
CIBREN024 Metaphys Daedalus R .20 .40
CIBREN025 Metaphys Nephthys SR .60 1.25
CIBREN026 Metaphys Tyrant Dragon R .20 .40
CIBREN027 Metaphys Executor SR .60 1.25
CIBREN028 Mermail Abyssnerei C .15 .30
CIBREN029 Fire King Avatar Arvata R .20 .40
CIBREN030 Mecha Phantom Beast Raiten C .15 .30
CIBREN031 The Accumulator C .15 .30
CIBREN032 Soldier Dragons C .15 .30
CIBREN033 Duck Dummy C .15 .30
CIBREN034 Leng Ling C .15 .30
CIBREN035 Self Destruct Ant C .15 .30
CIBREN036 Amano Iwato C .15 .30
CIBREN037 Fantastic Striborg R .20 .40
CIBREN038 Destrudo the Lost Dragons Frisson R.20 .40
CIBREN039 Elemental Grace Doriado R .20 .40
CIBREN040 Nimble Beaver SP .12 .25
CIBREN041 Muscle Medic SP .12 .25
CIBREN042 Borreload Dragon SCR 15.00 30.00
CIBREN043 Link Bumper SR .60 1.25
CIBREN044 Trickstar Black Catbat UR 1.25 2.50
CIBREN045 Gouki Thunder Ogre UR 1.25 2.50
CIBREN046 Twin Triangle Dragon R .20 .40
CIBREN047 Altergeist Primebanshee UR 1.00 2.00
CIBREN048 X Krawler Synaphysis C .15 .30
CIBREN049 X Krawler Neurogos C .15 .30
CIBREN050 X Krawler Qualiark SR .60 1.25
CIBREN051 Akashic Magician SCR 15.00 30.00
CIBREN052 Mistar Boy C .15 .30
CIBREN053 Security Block R .20 .40
CIBREN054 Dragonoid Generator R .20 .40
CIBREN055 Squib Draw SCR 5.00 10.00
CIBREN056 Quick Launch SCR 5.00 10.00
CIBREN057 World Legacy in Shadow C .15 .30
CIBREN058 World Legacy Clash C .15 .30
CIBREN059 Metaphys Factor C .15 .30
CIBREN060 Asymmetaphys UR 3.00 6.00
CIBREN061 One Time Passcode R .20 .40
CIBREN062 Arrivalrivals UR 2.00 4.00
CIBREN063 Overdone Burial SCR 4.00 8.00
CIBREN064 Temple of the Minds Eye C .15 .30
CIBREN065 Backup Squad R .20 .40
CIBREN066 Burning Bamboo Sword SP .12 .25
CIBREN067 Cyberse Beacon C .15 .30
CIBREN068 Link Restart C .15 .30
CIBREN069 Remote Rebirth?? C .15 .30
CIBREN070 Altergeist Camouflage R .20 .40
CIBREN071 Altergeist Protocol SR .60 1.25
CIBREN072 Personal Spoofing R .20 .40
CIBREN073 World Legacy Pawns C .15 .30
CIBREN074 World Legacy Trap Globe SR .60 1.25
CIBREN075 Metaphys Dimension R .20 .40
CIBREN076 Metaverse R .20 .40
CIBREN077 Evenly Matched SCR 50.00 100.00
CIBREN078 Fuse Line SCR 2.00 4.00
CIBREN079 Broken Line UR 2.00 4.00
CIBREN080 Ojama Duo SP .12 .25
CIBREN081 Samurai Destroyer R .20 .40
CIBREN082 Vendread Chimera SCR 6.00 12.00
CIBREN083 Vendread Striges C .15 .30
CIBREN084 Vendread Nights SR .60 1.25
CIBREN085 Vendread Reunion R .20 .40
CIBREN086 FA Whip Crosser C .15 .30
CIBREN087 FA Turbo Charger C .15 .30
CIBREN088 FA Off Road Grand Prix C .15 .30
CIBREN089 FA Pit Stop C .15 .30
CIBREN090 Lunalight Crimson Fox C .15 .30
CIBREN091 Lunalight Kaleido Chick C .15 .30
CIBREN092 Lyrilusc Recital Starling C .15 .30
CIBREN093 Amazoness Spy C .15 .30
CIBREN094 Amazoness Pet Liger C .15 .30
CIBREN095 Amazoness Empress C .15 .30
CIBREN096 Quiet Life SR .60 1.25
CIBREN097 #41 Bagooska the
Terribly Tired Tapir SR 2.50 5.00
CIBREN098 Subterror Behemoth Fiendess SR .60 1.25
CIBREN099 SPYRAL Double Helix UR 25.00 50.00

2017 Yu-Gi-Oh Code of the Duelist 1st Edition

COTDEN000 Vendread Houndhorde UR PR 3.00 6.00
COTDEN000 Vendread Houndhorde R .25 .50
COTDEN001 Cyberse Wizard SR .50 1.00
COTDEN002 Backup Secretary C .12 .25
COTDEN003 Stack Reviver C .12 .25
COTDEN004 Launcher Commander C .12 .25
COTDEN005 Salvagent Driver UR 1.00 2.00
COTDEN006 Trickstar Lilybell R .25 .50
COTDEN007 Trickstar Lycoris SR .50 1.00
COTDEN008 Trickstar Candina UR 4.00 8.00
COTDEN009 Gouki Twistcobra SR .30 .75
COTDEN010 Gouki Suprex R .25 .50
COTDEN011 Gouki Riscorpio R .25 .50
COTDEN012 Hack Worm C .12 .25
COTDEN013 Jack Wyvern C .12 .25
COTDEN014 Cracking Dragon SR .30 .75
COTDEN015 Supreme King Dragon Odd-Eyes R .25 .50
COTDEN016 Predaplant Banksiogre C .12 .25
COTDEN017 D/D Vice Typhon C .12 .25
COTDEN018 Crowned by the World Chalice C .12 .25
COTDEN019 Chosen by the World Chalice C .12 .25
COTDEN020 Beckoned by the World Chalice C .12 .25
COTDEN021 World Chalice Guardragon UR 6.00 12.00
COTDEN022 Lee the World Chalice Fairy UR 7.50 15.00
COTDEN023 World Legacy - World Chalice R .25 .50
COTDEN024 Jain, Twilightsworn General C .12 .25
COTDEN025 Lyla, Twilightsworn Enchantress SR .50 1.00
COTDEN026 Lumina, Twilightsworn Shaman SCR6.00 12.00
COTDEN027 Ryko, Twilightsworn Fighter R .25 .50
COTDEN028 Punishment Dragon UR 2.50 5.00
COTDEN029 Rescue Ferret SCR 6.00 12.00
COTDEN030 Traptrix Mantis SR 1.25 2.50
COTDEN031 Motivating Captain R .25 .50
COTDEN032 Treasure Panda C .12 .25
COTDEN033 Zombina C .12 .25
COTDEN034 Re: EX R .25 .50
COTDEN035 Orbital Hydralander C .12 .25
COTDEN036 The Ascended of Thunder SP .12 .25
COTDEN037 Parry Knights SP .12 .25
COTDEN038 Supreme King
Dragon Starving Venom R .25 .50
COTDEN039 Supreme King Dragon Clear Wing R.25 .50
COTDEN040 D/D/D Gust High King Alexander R .25 .50
COTDEN041 Supreme King
Dragon Dark Rebellion R .25 .50
COTDEN042 D/D/D Wave High King Caesar SR .50 1.00
COTDEN043 Firewall Dragon SCR 25.00 50.00
COTDEN044 Trickstar Holly Angel UR 2.50 5.00
COTDEN045 Gouki The Great Ogre SR .30 .75
COTDEN046 Topologic Bomber Dragon SCR 10.00 20.00
COTDEN047 Imduk the World Chalice Dragon R .25 .50
COTDEN048 Ib the World Chalice Priestess SR .50 1.00
COTDEN049 Auram the World
Chalice Blademaster SR .30 .75
COTDEN050 Ningirsu the World
Chalice Warrior SCR 10.00 20.00
COTDEN051 Gaia Saber, the Lightning Shadow SCR6.00 12.00
COTDEN052 Missus Radiant SR 1.25 2.50
COTDEN053 Trickstar Light Stage UR 4.00 8.00
COTDEN054 Gouki Re-Match SR .30 .75
COTDEN055 Air Cracking Storm C .12 .25
COTDEN056 Smile Universe C .12 .25
COTDEN057 World Legacy Discovery R .25 .50
COTDEN058 World Legacy's Heart C .12 .25
COTDEN059 March of the Dark Brigade UR 2.00 4.00
COTDEN060 Twilight Twin Dragons C .12 .25
COTDEN061 Emerging Emergency
Rescute Rescue C .12 .25
COTDEN062 Spellbook of Knowledge UR 15.00 30.00
COTDEN063 Gravity Lash C .12 .25
COTDEN064 Boogie Trap C .12 .25
COTDEN065 Castle Link UR .60 1.25
COTDEN066 Defense Zone SP .12 .25
COTDEN067 Three Strikes Barrier C .12 .25
COTDEN068 Trickstar Reincarnation SCR 15.00 30.00
COTDEN069 Pulse Mines C .12 .25
COTDEN070 Supreme Rage C .12 .25
COTDEN071 World Legacy Landmark C .12 .25
COTDEN072 Twilight Eraser R .25 .50
COTDEN073 Twilight Cloth C .12 .25
COTDEN074 Dark World Brainwashing C .12 .25
COTDEN075 Break Off Trap Hole SR .30 .75
COTDEN076 Heavy Storm Duster SR 1.50 3.00
COTDEN077 Back to the Front R 1.00 2.00
COTDEN078 Recall R .25 .50
COTDEN079 Blind Obliteration R .25 .50
COTDEN080 Transmission Gear SP .12 .25
COTDEN081 Samurai Skull C .12 .25
COTDEN082 Revendread Slayer R .25 .50
COTDEN083 Vendread Revenants C .12 .25
COTDEN084 Revendread Origin C .12 .25
COTDEN085 Vendread Reorigin SCR 6.00 12.00
COTDEN086 F.A. Sonic Meister C .12 .25
COTDEN087 F.A. Hang On Mach C .12 .25
COTDEN088 F.A. Circuit Grand Prix C .12 .25
COTDEN089 F.A. Downforce C .12 .25
COTDEN090 Junk Breaker C .12 .25
COTDEN091 Infernity Patriarch C .12 .25
COTDEN092 Gogogo Aristera & Dexia C .12 .25
COTDEN093 Wicked Acolyte Chilam Sabak C .12 .25
COTDEN094 Galaxy Worm C .12 .25
COTDEN095 Performapal Trumpanda C .12 .25
COTDEN096 Destiny HERO - Dangerous C .12 .25
COTDEN097 Abyss Actor - Trendy Understudy C .12 .25
COTDEN098 Speedroid Passinglider C .12 .25
COTDEN099 Ancient Gear
Golem - Ultimate Pound C .12 .25

2017 Yu-Gi-Oh The Dark Side of Dimensions Movie Pack Gold Edition

MVP1ENG01 Neo Blue Eyes Ultimate Dragon GR2.00 4.00
MVP1ENG02 Kaiser Vorse Raider GR .30 .75
MVP1ENG03 Assault Wyvern GR .30 .75
MVP1ENG04 Blue Eyes Chaos MAX Dragon GR2.00 4.00
MVP1ENG05 Deep Eyes White Dragon GR .30 .75
MVP1ENG06 Pandemic Dragon GR .30 .75
MVP1ENG07 Dragon's Fighting Spirit GR .30 .75
MVP1ENG08 Chaos Form GR 2.00 4.00
MVP1ENG09 Induced Explosion GR .30 .75
MVP1ENG10 Counter Gate GR .30 .75
MVP1ENG11 Krystal Avatar GR .30 .75
MVP1ENG12 Sentry Soldier of Stone GR .30 .75
MVP1ENG13 Marshmacaron GR .30 .75
MVP1ENG14 Berry Magician Girl GR .50 1.00
MVP1ENG15 Apple Magician Girl GR .50 1.00
MVP1ENG16 Kiwi Magician Girl GR .60 1.25
MVP1ENG17 Silver Gadget GR 1.00 2.00
MVP1ENG18 Gold Gadget GR 1.00 2.00
MVP1ENG19 Dark Magic Veil GR 1.25 2.50
MVP1ENG20 Magical Contract Door GR .30 .75
MVP1ENG21 Dimension Reflector GR .30 .75
MVP1ENG22 Dig of Destiny GR .30 .75
MVP1ENG23 Dimension Sphinx GR .30 .75
MVP1ENG24 Dimension Guardian GR .30 .75
MVP1ENG25 Dimension Mirage GR .30 .75
MVP1ENG26 Dark Horizon GR .30 .75
MVP1ENG27 Metamorphortress GR .30 .75
MVP1ENG28 Magicians' Defense GR .30 .75
MVP1ENG29 Final Geas GR .30 .75
MVP1ENG30 Metalhold the Moving Blockade GR.30 .75
MVP1ENG31 Spiritual Swords
of Revealing Light GR .30 .75
MVP1ENG32 Vijam the Cubic Seed GR .30 .75
MVP1ENG33 Dark Garnex the Cubic Beast GR .30 .75
MVP1ENG34 Blade Garoodia the Cubic Beast GR.30 .75
MVP1ENG35 Buster Gundil the Cubic Behemoth GR.30 .75
MVP1ENG36 Geira Guile the Cubic King GR .30 .75
MVP1ENG37 Vulcan Dragni the Cubic King GR .30 .75
MVP1ENG38 Indiora Doom Volt Cubic Emperor GR.30 .75
MVP1ENG39 Crimson Nova Dark Cubic Lord GR.30 .75
MVP1ENG40 Crimson Nova
Trinity Dark Cubic Lord GR .30 .75
MVP1ENG41 Cubic Karma GR .30 .75
MVP1ENG42 Cubic Wave GR .30 .75
MVP1ENG43 Cubic Rebirth GR .30 .75
MVP1ENG44 Cubic Mandala GR .30 .75
MVP1ENG45 Unification of the Cubic Lords GR .30 .75
MVP1ENG46 Blue Eyes
Alternative White Dragon GR 10.00 20.00
MVP1ENG47 Clear Kuriboh GR .30 .75
MVP1ENG48 Celtic Guard of Noble Arms GR .30 .75
MVP1ENG49 GandoraX the
Dragon of Demolition GR .30 .75
MVP1ENG50 Lord Gaia the Fierce Knight GR .30 .75
MVP1ENG51 Lemon Magician Girl GR .50 1.00
MVP1ENG52 Chocolate Magician Girl GR .30 .75
MVP1ENG53 Palladium Oracle Mahad GR .75 1.50
MVP1ENG54 Dark Magician GR .60 1.25
MVP1ENG55 BlueEyes White Dragon GR .60 1.25
MVP1ENG56 Dark Magician Girl GR .75 1.50
MVP1ENG57 Slifer the Sky Dragon GR .60 1.25
MVP1ENGV1 Duza the Meteor Cubic Vessel GSR1.25 2.50
MVP1ENGV2 Krystal Dragon GSR .75 1.50
MVP1ENGV3 Dark Magician GSR 2.00 4.00
MVP1ENGV4 Blue Eyes White Dragon GSR 2.00 4.00

2017 Yu-Gi-Oh Duelist Pack Dimensional Guardians 1st Edition

DPDGEN001 Spiral Flame Strike UR 5.00 10.00
DPDGEN002 Performapal Ballad SR .60 1.25
DPDGEN003 Performapal Barracuda SR .60 1.25
DPDGEN004 Speedroid Dominobutterfly UR 2.00 4.00
DPDGEN005 Pendulum Fusion SR 5.00 10.00
DPDGEN006 Frightfur Daredevil SR 2.00 4.00
DPDGEN007 Frightfur Reborn UR 4.00 8.00
DPDGEN008 Raidraptor Replica UR 2.00 4.00
DPDGEN009 Cyber Prima C .12 .25
DPDGEN010 Cyber Tutubon C .12 .25
DPDGEN011 Etoile Cyber C .12 .25
DPDGEN012 Cyber Petit Angel R .20 .40
DPDGEN013 Cyber Angel Vrash C .12 .25
DPDGEN014 Cyber Angel Dakini R .20 .40
DPDGEN015 Cyber Angel Benten SR .60 1.25
DPDGEN016 Cyber Angel Idaten C .12 .25
DPDGEN017 Machine Angel Ritual C .12 .25
DPDGEN018 Machine Angel Absolute Ritual R .20 .40
DPDGEN019 Ritual Sanctuary UR 1.25 2.50
DPDGEN020 Dark Resonator C .12 .25
DPDGEN021 Synkron Resonator C .12 .25
DPDGEN022 Chain Resonator C .12 .25
DPDGEN023 Mirror Resonator C .12 .25
DPDGEN024 Red Resonator R .20 .40
DPDGEN025 Red Warg C .12 .25
DPDGEN026 Red Gardna C .12 .25
DPDGEN027 Red Sprinter C .12 .25
DPDGEN028 Red Mirror C .12 .25
DPDGEN029 Resonator Call R .20 .40
DPDGEN030 Tyrant Red Dragon Archfiend UR .60 1.25
DPDGEN031 Scarlight Red Dragon Archfiend R .50 1.00
DPDGEN032 Red Wyvern C .12 .25
DPDGEN033 Reject Reborn C .12 .25
DPDGEN034 Kings Synchro R .20 .40
DPDGEN035 Cipher Wing C .12 .25
DPDGEN036 Cipher Twin Raptor R .20 .40
DPDGEN037 Cipher Mirror Knight C .12 .25
DPDGEN038 Cipher Etranger R .20 .40
DPDGEN039 Neo Galaxy Eyes Cipher Dragon UR.30 .75
DPDGEN040 GalaxyEyes Cipher Dragon SR 3.00 6.00
DPDGEN041 Starliege Paladynamo R .20 .40
DPDGEN042 Rank Up Magic Cipher Ascension C.12 .25
DPDGEN043 Double Cipher C .12 .25
DPDGEN044 Cipher Bit C .12 .25
DPDGEN045 Cipher Spectrum C .12 .25

2017 Yu-Gi-Oh Duelist Saga 1st Edition

DUSAEN001 Double Fin Shark UR .15 .30
DUSAEN002 Silent Angler UR .15 .30
DUSAEN003 Depth Shark UR .15 .30
DUSAEN004 Saber Shark UR .15 .30
DUSAEN005 Guard Penguin UR .15 .30
DUSAEN006 Number 94 Crystalzero UR .15 .30
DUSAEN007 Full Armored Crystalzero Lancer UR.15 .30
DUSAEN008 Full Armored Black Ray Lancer UR .15 .30
DUSAEN009 Sea Lords Amulet UR .15 .30
DUSAEN010 Diamond Dust UR .15 .30
DUSAEN011 Chain Summon UR .15 .30
DUSAEN012 Brohunder UR .15 .30
DUSAEN013 Number 28 Titanic Moth UR .15 .30
DUSAEN014 Number 70 Malevolent Sin UR .15 .30
DUSAEN015 Necroid Synchro UR .15 .30
DUSAEN016 Wandering King Wildwind UR .15 .30
DUSAEN017 Synchro Call UR .15 .30
DUSAEN018 Celestial Double Star Shaman UR .15 .30
DUSAEN019 Legacy of a HERO UR .50 1.00
DUSAEN020 Gozuki UR 1.00 2.00
DUSAEN021 Vision HERO Vyon UR 2.00 4.00
DUSAEN022 Darklord Ukoback UR .15 .30
DUSAEN023 Darklord Descent UR .15 .30
DUSAEN024 Legacy of the Duelist UR .50 1.00
DUSAEN025 Chaos Scepter Blast UR .50 1.00
DUSAEN026 Diabound Kernel UR .15 .30

DUSAEN027 Harpies Feather Storm UR .50 1.00
DUSAEN028 Elemental HERO Honest Neos UR 5.00 10.00
DUSAEN029 Skydive Scorcher UR .15 .30
DUSAEN030 Dark Summoning Beast UR .50 1.00
DUSAEN031 Fallen Paradise UR .15 .30
DUSAEN032 White Veil UR .15 .30
DUSAEN033 Power Wall UR .15 .30
DUSAEN034 Cosmic Blazar Dragon UR 1.25 2.50
DUSAEN035 Clear Effector UR .15 .30
DUSAEN036 Cosmic Flare UR .15 .30
DUSAEN037 Converging Wishes UR .15 .30
DUSAEN038 Clashing Souls UR .15 .30
DUSAEN039 Light Wing Shield UR .15 .30
DUSAEN040 Halfway to Forever UR .15 .30
DUSAEN041 Contract with Don Thousand UR .15 .30
DUSAEN042 Dueltaining UR .15 .30
DUSAEN043 BlueEyes White Dragon UR 2.50 5.00
DUSAEN044 Magician of Faith UR 1.50 3.00
DUSAEN045 Jinzo UR 1.00 2.00
DUSAEN046 Brain Control UR .20 .40
DUSAEN047 Royal Decree UR 1.00 2.00
DUSAEN048 Mirror Force UR 1.00 2.00
DUSAEN049 Imperial Order UR 2.50 5.00
DUSAEN050 Necrovalley UR .50 1.00
DUSAEN051 DD Warrior Lady UR .15 .30
DUSAEN052 Tsukuyomi UR .50 1.00
DUSAEN053 Black Luster Soldier... UR 5.00 10.00
DUSAEN054 Dark Magician of Chaos UR .75 1.50
DUSAEN055 Monster Gate UR .30 .75
DUSAEN056 Doomcaliber Knight UR .15 .30
DUSAEN057 Cyber Dragon UR 1.00 2.00
DUSAEN058 Treeborn Frog UR .20 .40
DUSAEN059 Dandylion UR .20 .40
DUSAEN060 Dimensional Fissure UR .60 1.25
DUSAEN061 NeoSpacian Grand Mole UR .15 .30
DUSAEN062 Future Fusion UR .60 1.25
DUSAEN063 Advanced Ritual Art UR 2.00 4.00
DUSAEN064 Mezuki UR 2.50 5.00
DUSAEN065 Chimeratech Fortress Dragon UR .25 .50
DUSAEN066 Fossil Dyna Pachycephalo UR .50 1.00
DUSAEN067 Dark Armed Dragon UR .50 1.00
DUSAEN068 RedEyes Darkness Metal Dragon UR1.50 3.00
DUSAEN069 Honest UR 2.00 4.00
DUSAEN070 Judgment Dragon UR 1.00 2.00
DUSAEN071 Gladiator Beast Gyzarus UR .15 .30
DUSAEN072 Rescue Cat UR 1.50 3.00
DUSAEN073 Brionac Dragon of the Ice Barrier UR3.00 6.00
DUSAEN074 Junk Synchron UR .30 .75
DUSAEN075 Goyo Guardian UR .50 1.00
DUSAEN076 Plaguespreader Zombie UR .50 1.00
DUSAEN077 Black Rose Dragon UR 1.00 2.00
DUSAEN078 Blackwing Gale the Whirlwind UR .15 .30
DUSAEN079 Deep Sea Diva UR .30 .75
DUSAEN080 Battle Fader UR .60 1.25
DUSAEN081 Trishula Dragon of the Ice Barrier UR2.00 4.00
DUSAEN082 Infernity Launcher UR .30 .75
DUSAEN083 Effect Veiler UR 2.00 4.00
DUSAEN084 Pot of Duality UR 3.00 6.00
DUSAEN085 Solemn Warning UR 4.00 8.00
DUSAEN086 Formula Synchron UR 1.00 2.00
DUSAEN087 A Hero Lives UR 1.00 2.00
DUSAEN088 Evolzar Laggia UR 1.00 2.00
DUSAEN089 Constellar Ptolemy M7 UR .25 .50
DUSAEN090 Evilswarm Ophion UR .15 .30
DUSAEN091 Tour Guide From the Underworld UR1.00 2.00
DUSAEN092 Soul Charge UR 2.50 5.00
DUSAEN093 Castel the Skyblaster Musketeer UR2.50 5.00
DUSAEN094 Masked HERO Dark Law UR 4.00 8.00
DUSAEN095 MXSaber Invoker UR .50 1.00
DUSAEN096 Uria Lord of Searing Flames UR 1.25 2.50
DUSAEN097 Hamon Lord of Striking Thunder UR1.50 3.00
DUSAEN098 Raviel Lord of Phantasms UR .75 1.50
DUSAEN099 Armityle the Chaos Phantom UR 1.50 3.00
DUSAEN100 Dark Magician UR .75 1.50

2017 Yu-Gi-Oh Fusion Enforcers 1st Edition

FUENEN001 Predaplant Sarraceniant SR .15 .30
FUENEN002 Predaplant Drosophyllum Hydra SCR.15 .30
FUENEN003 Predaplant Pterapenthes SR .15 .30
FUENEN004 Predaplant Spinodionaea SCR .30 .75
FUENEN005 Predaplant Chlamydosundew SCR 1.00 2.00
FUENEN006 Predaplant Flytrap SR .15 .30
FUENEN007 Predaplant Moray Nepenthes SR .15 .30
FUENEN008 Predaplant Squid Drosera SR .15 .30
FUENEN009 Predaplant Chimerafflesia SCR 1.00 2.00
FUENEN010 Greedy Venom Fusion Dragon SCR .50 1.00
FUENEN011 Predaponics SCR .15 .30
FUENEN012 Predapruning SR .15 .30
FUENEN013 Predaplanet SR .15 .30
FUENEN014 Fluffal Octopus SCR .50 1.00
FUENEN015 Fluffal Penguin SR 1.00 2.00
FUENEN016 Fluffal Dog SR .15 .30
FUENEN017 Fluffal Owl SR .15 .30
FUENEN018 Edge Imp Sabres SR .15 .30
FUENEN019 Edge Imp Chain SR .15 .30
FUENEN020 Frightfur Kraken SCR 3.00 6.00
FUENEN021 Frightfur Wolf SR .15 .30
FUENEN022 Frightfur Tiger SCR .50 1.00
FUENEN023 Frightfur Sheep SR .15 .30
FUENEN024 Toy Vendor SR .15 .30
FUENEN025 Frightfur Fusion SR .15 .30
FUENEN026 Aleister the Invoker SR .50 1.00
FUENEN027 Invoked Caliga SCR .15 .30
FUENEN028 Invoked Raidjin SCR 1.25 2.50
FUENEN029 Invoked Cocytus SCR .15 .30
FUENEN030 Invoked Purgatrio SCR .15 .30
FUENEN031 Invoked Magellanica SCR .30 .75
FUENEN032 Invoked Mechaba SCR 15.00 30.00
FUENEN033 Invoked Elysium SCR .15 .30
FUENEN034 Magical Meltdown SCR 1.25 2.50
FUENEN035 Invocation SCR 15.00 30.00
FUENEN036 The Book of the Law SCR .15 .30
FUENEN037 Omega Summon SCR .30 .75
FUENEN038 Summoner of Illusions SR .15 .30
FUENEN039 Summoner Monk SR .15 .30
FUENEN040 King of the Swamp SR .75 1.50
FUENEN041 Fusion Substitute SR .15 .30
FUENEN042 Instant Fusion SR 1.50 3.00
FUENEN043 Fusion Recovery SR .50 1.00
FUENEN044 Phoenix Wing Wind Blast SR .15 .30
FUENEN045 Homunculus the Alchemic Being SR.15 .30
FUENEN046 Lonefire Blossom SR 1.00 2.00
FUENEN047 Elemental HERO Prisma SR .75 1.50
FUENEN048 Performapal Trump Witch SR .15 .30
FUENEN049 Polymerization SR 1.50 3.00
FUENEN050 Fusion Gate SR .15 .30
FUENEN051 ReFusion SR .15 .30
FUENEN052 Branch! SR .15 .30
FUENEN053 Miracle Fertilizer SR .15 .30
FUENEN054 Mark of the Rose SR .15 .30
FUENEN055 Super Solar Nutrient SR .15 .30
FUENEN056 Battle Fusion SR .15 .30
FUENEN057 Fusion Conscription SR .15 .30
FUENEN058 Paradox Fusion SR .15 .30
FUENEN059 Grisaille Prison SR .15 .30
FUENEN060 Fusion Reserve SR .15 .30

2017 Yu-Gi-Oh Legendary Dragon Decks Cyber Dragon Deck 1st Edition

LEDDENB00 Chimeratech Megafleet Dragon UR1.25 2.50
LEDDENB01 Cyber Dragon C .15 .30
LEDDENB02 Cyber Dragon Zwei C .15 .30
LEDDENB03 Cyber Dragon Drei C .15 .30
LEDDENB04 Cyber Dragon Core C .15 .30
LEDDENB05 Proto Cyber Dragon C .15 .30
LEDDENB06 Cyber Valley C .15 .30
LEDDENB07 Cyber Phoenix C .15 .30
LEDDENB08 Cyber Dinosaur C .15 .30
LEDDENB09 Cyber Eltanin C .15 .30
LEDDENB10 Armored Cybern C .15 .30
LEDDENB11 Machina Fortress C .15 .30
LEDDENB12 Cyber Repair Plant C .15 .30
LEDDENB12 Cyber Repair Plant UR 1.25 2.50
LEDDENB13 Cybernetic Fusion Support C .15 .30
LEDDENB14 Evolution Burst C .15 .30
LEDDENB15 Power Bond C .15 .30
LEDDENB16 Overload Fusion C .15 .30
LEDDENB17 Future Fusion C .15 .30
LEDDENB18 Limiter Removal C .15 .30
LEDDENB19 Machina Armored Unit C .15 .30
LEDDENB20 Cyber Network C .15 .30
LEDDENB20 Cyber Network UR 1.25 2.50
LEDDENB21 Cyber Shadow Gardna C .15 .30
LEDDENB22 Storming Mirror Force C .15 .30
LEDDENB23 Quaking Mirror Force C .15 .30
LEDDENB24 Drowning Mirror Force C .15 .30
LEDDENB25 Cyber End Dragon C .15 .30
LEDDENB26 Cyber Twin Dragon C .15 .30
LEDDENB27 Chimeratech Overdragon C .15 .30
LEDDENB28 Chimeratech Fortress Dragon C .15 .30
LEDDENB29 Chimeratech Rampage Dragon C .15 .30
LEDDENB29 Chimeratech Rampage Dragon UR 1.25 2.50
LEDDENB30 Cyber Dragon Nova C .15 .30
LEDDENB31 Cyber Dragon Infinity UR 1.25 2.50

2017 Yu-Gi-Oh Legendary Dragon Decks Dimensional Dragons Deck 1st Edition

LEDDENC00 Odd Eyes Arc Pendulum Dragon UR1.25 2.50
LEDDENC01 Odd Eyes Pendulum Dragon C .15 .30
LEDDENC01 Odd Eyes Pendulum Dragon UR 1.25 2.50
LEDDENC02 Supreme King Dragon Odd Eyes C .15 .30
LEDDENC03 Odd Eyes Phantom Dragon C .15 .30
LEDDENC04 Odd Eyes Persona Dragon C .15 .30
LEDDENC05 Odd Eyes Mirage Dragon C .15 .30
LEDDENC06 Performapal Odd Eyes Light Phoenix C.15 .30
LEDDENC07 Performapal Odd Eyes Unicorn C .15 .30
LEDDENC08 Performapal Skullcrobat Joker C .15 .30
LEDDENC09 Performapal Rain Goat C .15 .30
LEDDENC10 Performapal U Go Golem C .15 .30
LEDDENC11 Nobledragon Magician C .15 .30
LEDDENC12 Odd Eyes Gravity Dragon C .15 .30
LEDDENC13 Sky Iris C .15 .30
LEDDENC14 Odd Eyes Fusion C .15 .30
LEDDENC15 Odd Eyes Advent C .15 .30
LEDDENC16 Spiral Flame Strike C .15 .30
LEDDENC17 Duelist Alliance C .15 .30
LEDDENC18 Pendulum Impenetrable C .15 .30
LEDDENC19 Pendulum Storm C .15 .30
LEDDENC20 Pot of Riches C .15 .30
LEDDENC21 Terraforming C .15 .30
LEDDENC22 Echo Oscillation C .15 .30
LEDDENC23 Pendulum Reborn C .15 .30
LEDDENC24 Pendulum Switch C .15 .30
LEDDENC25 Starving Venom Fusion Dragon UR1.25 2.50
LEDDENC26 Supreme King
Dragon Starving Venom C .15 .30
LEDDENC27 Odd Eyes Vortex Dragon C .15 .30
LEDDENC28 Performapal Gatlinghoul C .15 .30
LEDDENC29 Clear Wing Synchro Dragon UR 1.25 2.50
LEDDENC30 Supreme King Dragon Clear Wing C.15 .30
LEDDENC31 Odd Eyes Meteorburst Dragon C .15 .30
LEDDENC32 Dark Rebellion Xyz Dragon UR 1.25 2.50
LEDDENC33 Supreme
King Dragon Dark Rebellion C .15 .30
LEDDENC34 Odd Eyes Absolute Dragon C .15 .30

2017 Yu-Gi-Oh Legendary Dragon Decks Dragons of Atlantis Deck 1st Edition

LEDDENA00 Dark Magician the Dragon Knight UR1.25 2.50
LEDDENA01 Dark Magician C .15 .30
LEDDENA02 Dark Magician Girl C .15 .30
LEDDENA03 Apprentice Illusion Magician UR 1.25 2.50
LEDDENA04 Magicians Robe C .15 .30
LEDDENA05 Magicians Rod C .15 .30
LEDDENA06 Skilled Dark Magician C .15 .30
LEDDENA07 Legendary Knight Timaeus C .15 .30
LEDDENA08 Legendary Knight Critias C .15 .30
LEDDENA09 Legendary Knight Hermos C .15 .30
LEDDENA10 Breaker the Magical Warrior C .15 .30
LEDDENA11 Magical Exemplar C .15 .30
LEDDENA12 Big Shield Gardna C .15 .30
LEDDENA13 Absolute Crusader C .15 .30
LEDDENA14 Dark Magic Curtain C .15 .30
LEDDENA15 Dark Magical Circle UR 1.25 2.50
LEDDENA16 Illusion Magic C .15 .30
LEDDENA17 Dark Magic Expanded C .15 .30
LEDDENA19 Dark Magic Inheritance C .15 .30
LEDDENA19 Thousand Knives C .15 .30
LEDDENA20 Dark Magic Attack C .15 .30
LEDDENA21 The Eye of Timaeus C .15 .30
LEDDENA22 The Fang of Critias C .15 .30
LEDDENA23 The Claw of Hermos C .15 .30
LEDDENA24 Legend of Heart C .15 .30
LEDDENA25 Swords of Revealing Light C .15 .30
LEDDENA26 Pot of Duality C .15 .30
LEDDENA27 Reinforcement of the Army C .15 .30
LEDDENA28 Eternal Soul UR 1.25 2.50
LEDDENA29 Magician Navigation UR 1.25 2.50
LEDDENA30 Dark Renewal C .15 .30
LEDDENA31 Crush Card Virus C .15 .30
LEDDENA32 Mirror Force C .15 .30
LEDDENA33 Tyrant Wing C .15 .30
LEDDENA34 Dark Paladin C .15 .30
LEDDENA35 Amulet Dragon C .15 .30
LEDDENA36 Dark Magician
Girl the Dragon Knight C .15 .30
LEDDENA37 Doom Virus Dragon C .15 .30
LEDDENA38 Tyrant Burst Dragon C .15 .30
LEDDENA39 Mirror Force Dragon C .15 .30
LEDDENA40 Time Magic Hammer C .15 .30
LEDDENA41 Rocket Hermos Cannon C .15 .30
LEDDENA42 Goddess Bow C .15 .30
LEDDENA43 Red Eyes Black Dragon Sword C .15 .30

2017 Yu-Gi-Oh Legendary Duelists 1st Edition

LEDUEN000 Red Eyes B Dragon C .15 .30
LEDUEN001 Red Eyes Baby Dragon UR 6.00 12.00
LEDUEN002 Gearfried the Red Eyes Iron Knight UR5.00 10.00
LEDUEN003 Red Eyes Slash Dragon UR 6.00 12.00
LEDUEN004 Red Eyes Fang with Chain UR 4.00 8.00
LEDUEN005 Red Eyes Retro Dragon C .15 .30
LEDUEN006 Red Eyes Fusion C .15 .30
LEDUEN007 Inferno Fire Blast C .15 .30
LEDUEN008 Amazoness Princess SR 2.00 4.00
LEDUEN009 Amazoness Baby Tiger UR 3.00 6.00
LEDUEN010 Amazoness Call R .30 .75
LEDUEN011 Amazoness Onslaught R .30 .75
LEDUEN012 Amazoness Archer C .15 .30
LEDUEN013 Amazoness Swords Woman C .15 .30
LEDUEN014 Amazoness Village C .15 .30
LEDUEN015 The Legendary Fisherman II SR .50 1.00
LEDUEN016 Citadel Whale UR 2.00 4.00
LEDUEN017 Rage of Kairyu Shin R .30 .75
LEDUEN018 Sea Stealth Attack R .30 .75
LEDUEN019 The Legendary Fisherman C .15 .30
LEDUEN020 The Legendary Fisherman III C .15 .30
LEDUEN021 A Legendary Ocean C .15 .30
LEDUEN022 Cyberdark Cannon R .30 .75
LEDUEN023 Cyberdark Claw R .30 .75
LEDUEN024 Cyberdarkness Dragon SR 1.50 3.00
LEDUEN025 Cyberdark Inferno SR 2.00 4.00
LEDUEN026 Cyberdark Horn C .15 .30
LEDUEN027 Cyberdark Edge C .15 .30
LEDUEN028 Cyberdark Keel C .15 .30
LEDUEN029 Mixeroid R .30 .75
LEDUEN030 Super Vehicroid Mobile Base SR .30 .75
LEDUEN031 Megaroid City R .30 .75
LEDUEN032 Emergeroid Call UR 2.00 4.00
LEDUEN033 Expressroid C .15 .30
LEDUEN034 Armoroid C .15 .30
LEDUEN035 Vehicroid Connection Zone C .15 .30
LEDUEN036 Water Dragon Cluster SR .75 1.50
LEDUEN037 Duoterion SR .60 1.25
LEDUEN038 Bonding D2O R .30 .75
LEDUEN039 Bonding DHO R .30 .75
LEDUEN040 Hydrogeddon C .15 .30
LEDUEN041 Oxygeddon C .15 .30
LEDUEN042 Water Dragon C .15 .30
LEDUEN043 Sphere Kuriboh C .15 .30
LEDUEN044 Yomi Ship C .15 .30
LEDUEN045 Leotaur C .15 .30
LEDUEN046 Sergeant Electro C .15 .30
LEDUEN047 Riryoku C .15 .30
LEDUEN048 Monster Reincarnation C .15 .30
LEDUEN049 Wonder Balloons C .15 .30
LEDUEN050 The Golden Apples C .15 .30
LEDUEN051 Bonding H2O C .15 .30

2017 Yu-Gi-Oh Maximum Crisis 1st Edition

MACREN000 Pendulum Switch R .20 .40
MACREN001 Performapal Sky Magician R .20 .40
MACREN002 Performapal Sky Pupil R .20 .40
MACREN003 Performapal Revue Dancer C .15 .30
MACREN004 Performapal U Go Golem R .20 .40
MACREN005 Performapal Coin Dragon R .20 .40
MACREN006 Speedroid Skull Marbles C .15 .30
MACREN007 Speedroid Maliciousmagnet C .15 .30
MACREN008 Speedroid Rubberband Plane R .20 .40
MACREN009 Predaplant Ophrys Scorpio R 1.50 3.00
MACREN010 Predaplant Darlingtonia Cobra C .15 .30
MACREN011 Predaplant Cordyceps C .15 .30
MACREN012 Lyrilusc Cobalt Sparrow C .15 .30
MACREN013 Lyrilusc Sapphire Swallow C .15 .30
MACREN014 Lyrilusc Turquoise Warbler C .15 .30
MACREN015 DD Ghost C .15 .30
MACREN016 Double Resonator C .15 .30
MACREN017 Supreme King Gate Zero SR .50 1.00
MACREN018 Supreme King Gate Infinity SR .50 1.00
MACREN019 Supreme King Dragon Darkwurm C.15 .30
MACREN020 Majesty Maiden
the True Dracocaster UR 2.00 4.00
MACREN021 Ignis Heat the True Dracowarrior UR1.00 2.00
MACREN022 Dinomight Knight
True Dracofighter UR 5.00 10.00
MACREN023 Dreiath III True
Dracocavalry General UR .75 1.50
MACREN024 Master Peace True
Dracoslaying King SCR 20.00 40.00
MACREN025 Metaltron XII the
True Dracombatant SR .50 1.00
MACREN026 Mariamne the True Dracophoenix UR2.00 4.00
MACREN027 Zoodiac Kataroost C .15 .30
MACREN028 Phantasm Spiral Dragon R .20 .40
MACREN029 Digital Bug LEDybug C .15 .30
MACREN030 Zefraath SR .50 1.00
MACREN031 Ariel Priestess of the Nekroz R .20 .40
MACREN032 BES Big Core MK 3 R .20 .40
MACREN033 Pendulumucho SR .50 1.00
MACREN034 Baobaboon C .15 .30
MACREN035 Fire Cracker C .15 .30
MACREN036 Ash Blossom and
Joyous Spring SCR 60.00 120.00
MACREN037 Familiar Possessed Lyna SP .15 .30
MACREN038 Fairy Tail Luna SR .50 1.00
MACREN039 Supreme King Z ARC SCR 3.00 6.00
MACREN040 Performapal Gatlinghoul UR .60 1.25
MACREN041 Lyrilusc Independent Nightingale SR.50 1.00
MACREN042 Phantom Knights
of Cursed Javelin SR .50 1.00
MACREN043 Lyrilusc Assembled Nightingale SR.50 1.00
MACREN044 Raidraptor Stranger Falcon R .20 .40
MACREN045 DDD Stone King Darius R .20 .40
MACREN046 True King of All Calamities SR 1.00 2.00
MACREN047 Zoodiac Hammerkong C .15 .30
MACREN048 Zoodiac Chakanine UR 3.00 6.00
MACREN049 Magicians Right Hand C .15 .30
MACREN050 Magicians Left Hand C .15 .30
MACREN051 Magicians Restage R .20 .40
MACREN052 Ultra Polymerization SCR 5.00 10.00
MACREN053 Dragonic Diagram SCR 60.00 125.00
MACREN054 True Draco Heritage UR 5.00 10.00
MACREN055 Disciples of the True Dracophoenix C.15 .30
MACREN056 Pacifis the Phantasm City R .20 .40
MACREN057 Phantasm Spiral Crash C .15 .30
MACREN058 Phantasm Spiral Grip C .15 .30
MACREN059 Phantasm Spiral Wave C .15 .30
MACREN060 Bug Signal C .15 .30
MACREN061 Zefra Providence R .20 .40
MACREN062 BEF Zelos C .15 .30
MACREN063 Duelist Alliance SCR 4.00 8.00
MACREN064 Set Rotation SP .15 .30
MACREN065 Break Away C .15 .30
MACREN066 Phantom Knights of Lost Vambrace C.15 .30
MACREN067 Phantom Knights
of Wrong Magnetring C .15 .30
MACREN068 Dark Contract
with the Eternal Darkness R .20 .40
MACREN069 True Kings Return UR 4.00 8.00
MACREN070 True Draco Apocalypse C .15 .30
MACREN071 Zoodiac Gathering C .15 .30
MACREN072 Phantasm Spiral Battle R .20 .40
MACREN073 Phantasm Spiral Power C .15 .30
MACREN074 Phantasm Spiral Assault C .15 .30
MACREN075 Prologue of the
Destruction Swordsman C .15 .30
MACREN076 Dinomists Howling C .15 .30
MACREN077 Zefra War C .15 .30
MACREN078 Waterfall of Dragon Souls SR .50 1.00
MACREN079 Unending Nightmare SCR 10.00 20.00
MACREN080 Diamond Duston SP .15 .30
MACREN081 Tornado Dragon SCR 10.00 20.00
MACREN082 Subterror Fiendess SR .50 1.00
MACREN083 Subterror
Behemoth Phospheroglacier C .15 .30
MACREN084 Subterror Behemoth Speleogeist C .15 .30
MACREN085 Subterror Final Battle R .20 .40
MACREN086 SPYRAL Sleeper SR .50 1.00
MACREN087 SPYRAL GEAR Last Resort R .20 .40
MACREN088 SPYRAL GEAR Fully Armed UR 1.50 3.00
MACREN089 SPYRAL MISSION Rescue C .15 .30
MACREN090 Gift Exchange C .15 .30
MACREN091 Kaiser Sea Snake C .15 .30
MACREN092 Bujin Hiruko R .20 .40
MACREN093 Sylvan Princessprite SR .50 1.00
MACREN094 Artifact Vajra C .15 .30
MACREN095 Mild Turkey C .15 .30
MACREN096 Ghost Beef C .15 .30
MACREN097 Vennu Bright Bird of Divinity C .15 .30
MACREN098 Primal Cry C .15 .30
MACREN099 Onikuji C .15 .30

2017 Yu-Gi-Oh Mega Tin Mega Pack 1st Edition

MP17DE001 Angel Trumpeter C .10 .20
MP17DE002 Performapal Sellshell Crab C .10 .20
MP17DE003 Performapal Fireflux C .10 .20
MP17DE004 Speedroid Den Den Daiko Duke R .15 .30
MP17DE005 Speedroid Pachingo Kart R .15 .30
MP17DE006 Raidraptor Avenge Vulture C .10 .20
MP17DE007 Raidraptor Pain Lanius C .10 .20
MP17DE008 Raidraptor Booster Strix C .10 .20
MP17DE009 Blackwing Decay the Ill Wind C .10 .20
MP17DE010 Dragon Spirit of White UR 1.25 2.50
MP17DE011 Protector with Eyes of Blue C .10 .20
MP17DE012 Master with Eyes of Blue C .10 .20
MP17DE013 The White Stone of Ancients UR 2.00 4.00
MP17DE014 Lector Pendulum the Dracoverlord UR.10 .20
MP17DE015 Dinomist Spinos C .10 .20
MP17DE016 Digital Bug Cocoondenser C .10 .20
MP17DE017 Digital Bug Centibit C .10 .20
MP17DE018 Digital Bug Websolder C .10 .20
MP17DE019 Ryu Okami C .10 .20
MP17DE020 Tenmataitei R .15 .30
MP17DE021 Spirit of the Fall Wind R .15 .30
MP17DE022 Ghost Reaper and
Winter Cherries SCR 4.00 8.00
MP17DE023 Gendo the Ascetic Monk C .10 .20
MP17DE024 Deskbot 009 C .10 .20
MP17DE025 Dicelops C .10 .20
MP17DE026 Hi Speedroid Puzzle R .15 .30
MP17DE027 Digital Bug Scaradiator C .10 .20
MP17DE028 Digital Bug Corebage C .10 .20
MP17DE029 Rank Up Magic Skip Force R .15 .30
MP17DE030 Mausoleum of White R .15 .30
MP17DE031 Beacon of White C .10 .20
MP17DE032 Forge of the True Dracos C .10 .20
MP17DE033 Bug Matrix C .10 .20
MP17DE034 Pre Preparation of Rites SR .15 .30
MP17DE035 Fusion Tag R .15 .30

MP17DE036 Deskbot Base C	.10	.20
MP17DE037 Finite Cards C	.10	.20
MP17DE038 Re dyce cle C	.10	.20
MP17DE039 Dinomist Eruption C	.10	.20
MP17DE040 Bug Emergency C	.10	.20
MP17DE041 Drowning Mirror Force SCR	1.25	2.50
MP17DE042 Wonder Xyz C	.10	.20
MP17DE043 Rise to Full Height C	.10	.20
MP17DE044 Bad Aim C	.10	.20
MP17DE045 Graceful Tear C	.10	.20
MP17DE046 Thunder King the Lightningstrike Kaiju R	.15	.30
MP17DE047 Super Anti Kaiju War Machine... R	.15	.30
MP17DE048 The Kaiju Files C	.10	.20
MP17DE049 Cuben C	.10	.20
MP17DE050 World Carrotweight Champion C	.10	.20
MP17DE051 Dwarf Star Dragon Planeter C	.10	.20
MP17DE052 Geargianchor C	.10	.20
MP17DE053 Geargia Change C	.10	.20
MP17DE054 Stardust Sifr Divine Dragon UR	.10	.20
MP17DE055 Priestess with Eyes of Blue SR	.15	.30
MP17DE056 Blue Eyes Twin Burst Dragon SCR	3.00	6.00
MP17DE057 Magical Something R	.15	.30
MP17DE058 Performapal Bot Eyes Lizard C	.10	.20
MP17DE059 Performapal Gongato C	.10	.20
MP17DE060 Performapal Extra Slinger C	.10	.20
MP17DE061 Performapal Inflater Tapir C	.10	.20
MP17DE062 Performapal Bubblebowwow C	.10	.20
MP17DE063 Performapal Radish Horse C	.10	.20
MP17DE064 Performapal Life Swordsman C	.10	.20
MP17DE065 DD Savant Thomas R	.15	.30
MP17DE066 DD Savant Nikola C	.10	.20
MP17DE067 Blackwing Tornado the Reverse Wind C	.10	.20
MP17DE068 Blackwing Gofu the Vague Shadow C	.10	.20
MP17DE069 Red Warg C	.10	.20
MP17DE070 Red Gardna C	.10	.20
MP17DE071 Red Mirror C	.10	.20
MP17DE072 Magician of Dark Illusion SR	.15	.30
MP17DE073 Magicians Robe C	.10	.20
MP17DE074 Magicians Rod SR	.15	.30
MP17DE075 Master Peace the True Dracoslayer UR	.10	.20
MP17DE076 Metalfoes Steelen C	.10	.20
MP17DE077 Metalfoes Silverd C	.10	.20
MP17DE078 Metalfoes Goldriver R	.15	.30
MP17DE079 Metalfoes Vollfame R	.15	.30
MP17DE080 True King Agnimazud the Vanisher UR	1.00	2.00
MP17DE081 Dinomist Ankylos C	.10	.20
MP17DE082 Shiranui Solitaire UR	2.50	5.00
MP17DE083 Toon Dark Magician SR	.15	.30
MP17DE084 Scapeghost C	.10	.20
MP17DE085 Block Dragon UR	.25	.50
MP17DE086 Black Dragon Ninja C	.10	.20
MP17DE087 Zap Mustung C	.10	.20
MP17DE088 Totem Five C	.10	.20
MP17DE089 Tuning Gum R	.15	.30
MP17DE090 Wrecker Panda C	.10	.20
MP17DE091 Fairy Tail Snow C	.10	.20
MP17DE092 Metalfoes Adamante R	.15	.30
MP17DE093 Metalfoes Orichalc C	.10	.20
MP17DE094 Metalfoes Crimsonite R	.15	.30
MP17DE095 Assault Blackwing Sayo... R	.15	.30
MP17DE096 Assault Blackwing Sohaya... C	.10	.20
MP17DE097 Super Hippo Carnival C	.10	.20
MP17DE098 Frightfur Sanctuary C	.10	.20
MP17DE099 Forbidden Dark Contract/Swamp King C	.10	.20
MP17DE100 Dark Magical Circle SCR	5.00	10.00
MP17DE101 Illusion Magic R	.15	.30
MP17DE102 Dark Magic Expanded C	.10	.20
MP17DE103 Metamorformation SR	.15	.30
MP17DE104 Metalfoes Fusion SR	.15	.30
MP17DE105 Cosmic Cyclone SCR	5.00	10.00
MP17DE106 Magical Mid Breaker Field C	.10	.20
MP17DE107 Card of the Soul C	.10	.20
MP17DE108 Fusion Fright Waltz C	.10	.20
MP17DE109 King Scarlet C	.10	.20
MP17DE110 Magician Navigation SCR	5.00	10.00
MP17DE111 Metalfoes Counter C	.10	.20
MP17DE112 Metalfoes Combination SR	.15	.30
MP17DE113 Destruction Sword Memories C	.10	.20
MP17DE114 Floodgate Trap Hole UR	1.25	2.50
MP17DE115 Unified Front C	.10	.20
MP17DE116 Pendulum Hole C	.10	.20
MP17DE117 Ninjitsu Art Notebook C	.10	.20
MP17DE118 Heavy Freight Train Derricrane C	.10	.20
MP17DE119 Revolving Switchyard C	.10	.20
MP17DE120 Dragodies the Empowered Warrior C	.10	.20
MP17DE121 Empowerment C	.10	.20
MP17DE122 Paleozoic Olenoides C	.10	.20
MP17DE123 Paleozoic Hallucigenia C	.10	.20
MP17DE124 Paleozoic Canadia C	.10	.20
MP17DE125 Paleozoic Pikaia C	.10	.20
MP17DE126 Paleozoic Anomalocaris SR	.15	.30
MP17DE127 Dragon Core Hexer R	.15	.30
MP17DE128 Performapal Flip Hippo C	.10	.20
MP17DE129 Performapal Seal Eel C	.10	.20
MP17DE130 Performapal Changeraffe C	.10	.20
MP17DE131 Predaplant Flytrap R	.15	.30
MP17DE132 Predaplant Moray Nepenthes C	.10	.20
MP17DE133 Predaplant Squid Drosera C	.10	.20
MP17DE134 Superheavy Samurai Soulpeacemaker R	.15	.30
MP17DE135 Cipher Twin Raptor C	.10	.20
MP17DE136 Cipher Mirror Knight C	.10	.20
MP17DE137 Crystron Prasiortle C	.10	.20
MP17DE138 Crystron Smiger C	.10	.20
MP17DE139 Crystron Thystvern C	.10	.20
MP17DE140 Crystron Rosenix C	.10	.20
MP17DE141 True King Bahrastos the Fathomer UR	.50	1.00
MP17DE142 Raremetalfoes Bismugear C	.10	.20
MP17DE143 PSY Frame Multi Threader C	.10	.20
MP17DE144 Doki Doki C	.10	.20
MP17DE145 Pandoras Jewelry Box C	.10	.20
MP17DE146 Fairy Tail Sleeper C	.10	.20
MP17DE147 Starving Venom Fusion Dragon SCR	1.00	2.00
MP17DE148 Metalfoes Mithrilium UR	.20	.40
MP17DE149 Superheavy Samurai Ninja Sarutobi R	.15	.30
MP17DE150 Toadally Awesome SCR	2.50	5.00
MP17DE151 Amazing Pendulum C	.10	.20
MP17DE152 Phantom Knights Rank Up Magic Launch SR	.15	.30
MP17DE153 Crystolic Potential C	.10	.20
MP17DE154 Fullmetalfoes Fusion SR	.15	.30
MP17DE155 Igknights Unite C	.10	.20
MP17DE156 Sprites Blessing C	.10	.20
MP17DE157 Quarantine C	.10	.20
MP17DE158 Double Cipher C	.10	.20
MP17DE159 Cipher Bit C	.10	.20
MP17DE160 Crystron Entry C	.10	.20
MP17DE161 Crystron Impact C	.10	.20
MP17DE162 PSY Frame Accelerator C	.10	.20
MP17DE163 Dimensional Barrier SCR	5.00	10.00
MP17DE164 Summon Gate C	.10	.20
MP17DE165 Caninetaur C	.10	.20
MP17DE166 Dino Sewing C	.10	.20
MP17DE167 Mare Mare C	.10	.20
MP17DE168 Paleozoic Eldonia C	.10	.20
MP17DE169 Paleozoic Dinomischus C	.10	.20
MP17DE170 Paleozoic Marrella C	.10	.20
MP17DE171 Paleozoic Leanchoilia C	.10	.20
MP17DE172 Paleozoic Opabinia SR	.15	.30
MP17DE173 Fusion Recycling Plant R	.15	.30
MP17DE174 Performapal Handstandaccoon C	.10	.20
MP17DE175 Speedroid Gum Prize C	.10	.20
MP17DE176 Speedroid Horse Stilts C	.10	.20
MP17DE177 Fusion Parasite R	.15	.30
MP17DE178 Cyber Tutubon C	.10	.20
MP17DE179 Cipher Etranger C	.10	.20
MP17DE180 Ancient Gear Hunting Hound C	.10	.20
MP17DE181 Zoodiac Ratpier SR	.15	.30
MP17DE182 Zoodiac Bunnyblast C	.10	.20
MP17DE183 Zoodiac Whiptail SR	.15	.30
MP17DE184 Zoodiac Thoroughblade UR	.20	.40
MP17DE185 Zoodiac Ramram C	.10	.20
MP17DE186 True King Lithosagym the Disaster SR	.15	.30
MP17DE187 Crystron Rion C	.10	.20
MP17DE188 Shinobird Crow C	.10	.20
MP17DE189 Shinobird Crane C	.10	.20
MP17DE190 Shinobird Pigeon C	.10	.20
MP17DE191 Envoy of Chaos R	.15	.30
MP17DE192 Spiritual Beast Tamer Winda R	.15	.30
MP17DE193 Miscellaneousaurus C	.10	.20
MP17DE194 Apprentice Piper C	.10	.20
MP17DE195 Hebo Lord of the River C	.10	.20
MP17DE196 Eater of Millions C	.10	.20
MP17DE197 Wightprincess C	.10	.20
MP17DE198 Metrognome C	.10	.20
MP17DE199 Fairy Tail Rella C	.10	.20
MP17DE200 Shinobaroness Peacock R	.15	.30
MP17DE201 Shinobaron Peacock R	.15	.30
MP17DE202 Ancient Gear Howitzer C	.10	.20
MP17DE203 Superheavy Samurai Stealth Ninja R	.15	.30
MP17DE204 Shiranui Sunsaga R	.15	.30
MP17DE205 Odd Eyes Raging Dragon UR	.30	.75
MP17DE206 Zoodiac Broadbull SCR	1.50	3.00
MP17DE207 Zoodiac Tigermortar UR	.20	.40
MP17DE208 Zoodiac Drident SCR	1.00	2.00
MP17DE209 Zoodiac Boarbow R	.15	.30
MP17DE210 Rank Up Magic Cipher Ascension C	.10	.20
MP17DE211 Zodiac Sign C	.10	.20
MP17DE212 Zoodiac Barrage SCR	2.00	4.00
MP17DE213 Shinobirds Calling C	.10	.20
MP17DE214 Shinobird Power Spot C	.10	.20
MP17DE215 Super Soldier Synthesis C	.10	.20
MP17DE216 Super Quantal Alphan Spike C	.10	.20
MP17DE217 Ritual Beast Return C	.10	.20
MP17DE218 Foolish Burial Goods SCR	2.00	4.00
MP17DE219 Terminal World NEXT C	.10	.20
MP17DE220 Lost Wind R	.15	.30
MP17DE221 Cipher Spectrum C	.10	.20
MP17DE222 Ancient Gear Reborn R	.15	.30
MP17DE223 Zoodiac Combo C	.10	.20
MP17DE224 Shinobird Salvation C	.10	.20
MP17DE225 Beginning of Heaven and Earth C	.10	.20
MP17DE226 Shiranui Style Samsara C	.10	.20
MP17DE227 Purushaddoll Aeon C	.10	.20
MP17DE228 Full Force Virus SCR	.60	1.25
MP17DE229 Switcheroroo R	.15	.30
MP17DE230 Massivemorph C	.10	.20
MP17DE231 Sea Monster of Theseus SCR	.75	1.50
MP17DE232 Symphonic Warrior Guitaar C	.10	.20
MP17DE233 Symphonic Warrior Synthess C	.10	.20
MP17DE234 Symph Amplifire C	.10	.20
MP17DE235 Rocket Hand C	.10	.20
MP17DE236 Mekanikal Arkfiend C	.10	.20
MP17DE237 Lightsworn Judgment C	.10	.20
MP17DE238 Symphonic Warrior Miccs C	.10	.20
MP17DE239 Dark Contract with the Entities UR	.20	.40

2017 Yu-Gi-Oh OTS Tournament Pack 4

OP04EN001 Number S39: Utopia the Lightning UTR	30.00	60.00
OP04EN002 Instant Fusion UTR	75.00	150.00
OP04EN003 Solemn Strike UTR	100.00	200.00
OP04EN004 Metalfoes Vollfame SR	.20	.40
OP04EN005 Ronintoadin SR	2.50	5.00
OP04EN006 Photon Thrasher SR	.50	1.00
OP04EN007 Retaliating C**** SR	1.50	3.00
OP04EN008 Kumongous, the Sticky String Kaiju SR	7.50	15.00
OP04EN009 D/D Swirl Slime SR	.75	1.50
OP04EN010 D/D/D Oblivion King Abyss Ragnarok SR	6.00	12.00
OP04EN011 Blackwing - Gofu the Vague Shadow SR	1.25	2.50
OP04EN012 One Day of Peace SR	4.00	8.00
OP04EN013 Union Hangar SR	1.00	2.00
OP04EN014 Water Magician SP	1.25	2.50
OP04EN015 Behegon SP	.40	.80
OP04EN016 B.E.S. Big Core C	.20	.40
OP04EN017 Barrier Statue of the Torrent C	.30	.75
OP04EN018 Barrier Statue of the Inferno C	.20	.40
OP04EN019 Coach Captain Bearman C	.12	.25
OP04EN020 Artifact Lancea C	.75	1.50
OP04EN021 Super Anti-Kaiju War Machine Mecha-Dogoran C	.15	.30
OP04EN022 Marine Beast SP	1.25	2.50
OP04EN023 Superdreadnought Rail Cannon Gustav Max C	.75	1.50
OP04EN024 Coach King Giantrainer C	7.50	15.00
OP04EN025 Seismic Shockwave C	.20	.40
OP04EN026 Inverse Universe C	.15	.30
OP04EN027 Horn of the Phantom Beast C	.15	.30

2017 Yu-Gi-Oh OTS Tournament Pack 5

OP05EN001 Ghost Ogre & Snow Rabbit UTR	125.00	250.00
OP05EN002 Zoodiac Whiptail UTR	20.00	40.00
OP05EN003 Terraforming UTR	75.00	150.00
OP05EN004 Dogoran, the Mad Flame Kaiju SR	5.00	10.00
OP05EN005 Fairy Tail - Snow SR	4.00	8.00
OP05EN006 SPYRAL Quik-Fix SR	1.00	2.00
OP05EN007 Fairy Tail - Sleeper SR	.30	.75
OP05EN008 Zoodiac Ramram SR	1.25	2.50
OP05EN009 Ultimate Ancient Gear Golem SR	.75	1.50
OP05EN010 Swing of Memories SR	.30	.75
OP05EN011 Disciples of the True Dracophoenix SR	1.50	3.00
OP05EN012 Lost Wind SR	.75	1.50
OP05EN013 True Draco Apocalypse SR	2.00	4.00
OP05EN014 Snakeyashi SP	.50	1.00
OP05EN015 Feral Imp SP	.30	.60
OP05EN016 Mystical Shine Ball C	.50	1.00
OP05EN017 The Agent of Creation - Venus C	.30	.75
OP05EN018 Kagetokage C	.60	1.25
OP05EN019 Tin Goldfish C	.75	1.50
OP05EN020 Scapeghost C	.25	.50
OP05EN021 Fairy Tail - Luna C	.20	.40
OP05EN022 Rose Spectre of Dunn SP	.75	1.50
OP05EN023 Elemental HERO Absolute Zero C	10.00	20.00
OP05EN024 Scapegoat C	.20	.40
OP05EN025 Chain Summoning C	.50	1.00
OP05EN026 Secret Village of the Spellcasters C	.40	.80
OP05EN027 Grave of the Super Ancient Organism C	2.00	4.00

2017 Yu-Gi-Oh OTS Tournament Pack 6

OP06EN001 Decode Talker UTR	12.50	25.00
OP06EN002 Brilliant Fusion UTR	25.00	50.00
OP06EN003 Invocation UTR	60.00	125.00
OP06EN004 Revendread Slayer SR	1.25	2.50
OP06EN005 Fairy Tail - Rella SR	.40	.80
OP06EN006 Paleozoic Canadia SR	1.00	2.00
OP06EN007 Paleozoic Eldonia SR	.30	.60
OP06EN008 Paleozoic Hallucigenia SR	.60	1.25
OP06EN009 Set Rotation SR	2.50	5.00
OP06EN010 Black Metal Dragon SR	12.50	25.00
OP06EN011 Windwitch - Winter Bell SR	.75	1.50
OP06EN012 Trickstar Lilybell SR	1.50	3.00
OP06EN013 Overload Fusion SR	2.00	4.00
OP06EN014 Gem-Knight Garnet C	.40	.80
OP06EN015 Shiranui Spiritmaster C	.25	.50
OP06EN016 Predaplant Ophrys Scorpio C	.50	1.00
OP06EN017 Gozuki C	2.00	4.00
OP06EN018 Lightray Grepher C	.12	.25
OP06EN019 Recurring Nightmare C	.17	.35
OP06EN020 Dragon Shrine C	.30	.60
OP06EN021 Phantom Skyblaster C	.17	.35
OP06EN022 Ojama Blue C	.75	1.50
OP06EN023 Disturbance Strategy C	.20	.40
OP06EN024 Enishi, Shien's Chancellor C	.12	.25
OP06EN025 Amazoness Queen C	4.00	8.00
OP06EN026 Gem-Knight Seraphinite C	.15	.30

2017 Yu-Gi-Oh Pendulum Evolution 1st Edition

PEVOEN001 Astrograph Sorcerer UR	3.00	6.00
PEVOEN002 Chronograph Sorcerer UR	3.00	6.00
PEVOEN003 Double Iris Magician UR	3.00	6.00
PEVOEN004 Black Fang Magician UR	3.00	6.00
PEVOEN005 White Wing Magician UR	3.00	6.00
PEVOEN006 Purple Poison Magician UR	3.00	6.00
PEVOEN007 Star Pendulumgraph UR	3.00	6.00
PEVOEN008 Time Pendulumgraph UR	3.00	6.00
PEVOEN009 Timestar Magician UR	3.00	6.00
PEVOEN010 Harmonizing Magician UR	3.00	6.00
PEVOEN011 Stargazer Magician SR	.50	1.00
PEVOEN012 Timegazer Magician SR	.50	1.00
PEVOEN013 Dragonpulse Magician SR	.50	1.00
PEVOEN014 Dragonpit Magician SR	.50	1.00
PEVOEN015 Nobledragon Magician SR	.50	1.00
PEVOEN016 Oafdragon Magician SR	.50	1.00
PEVOEN017 Wisdom Eye Magician SR	.50	1.00
PEVOEN018 Dharma Eye Magician SR	.50	1.00
PEVOEN019 Timebreaker Magician SR	.50	1.00
PEVOEN020 Tuning Magician SR	.50	1.00
PEVOEN021 Doomstar Magician SR	.50	1.00
PEVOEN022 Performapal Skullcrobat Joker SR	.50	1.00
PEVOEN023 Odd Eyes Pendulum Dragon SR	.50	1.00
PEVOEN024 Foucaults Cannon SR	.50	1.00
PEVOEN025 Hypnosister SR	.50	1.00
PEVOEN026 Archfiend Eccentrick SR	.50	1.00
PEVOEN027 Guiding Ariadne SR	.50	1.00
PEVOEN028 Rescue Hamster SR	.50	1.00
PEVOEN029 Magical Abductor SR	.50	1.00
PEVOEN030 Odd Eyes Vortex Dragon SR	.50	1.00
PEVOEN031 Enlightenment Paladin SR	.50	1.00
PEVOEN032 Odd Eyes Meteorburst Dragon SR	.50	1.00
PEVOEN033 Odd Eyes Absolute Dragon SR	.50	1.00
PEVOEN034 Amazing Pendulum SR	.50	1.00
PEVOEN035 Pendulum Storm SR	.50	1.00
PEVOEN036 Pendulum Call SR	.50	1.00
PEVOEN037 Pendulum Shift SR	.50	1.00
PEVOEN038 Odd Eyes Fusion SR	.50	1.00
PEVOEN039 Dragons Mirror SR	.50	1.00
PEVOEN040 Summoners Art SR	.50	1.00
PEVOEN041 Pendulum Reborn SR	.50	1.00
PEVOEN042 Echo Oscillation SR	.50	1.00
PEVOEN043 Unwavering Bond SR	.50	1.00
PEVOEN044 Satellarknight Zefrathuban SR	.50	1.00
PEVOEN045 Stellarknight Zefraxciton SR	.50	1.00
PEVOEN046 Zefraxi Treasure of the Yang Zing SR	.50	1.00
PEVOEN047 Zefraniu Secret of the Yang Zing SR	.50	1.00
PEVOEN048 Ritual Beast Tamer Zeframpilica SR	.50	1.00
PEVOEN049 Ritual Beast Tamer Zefrawendi SR	.50	1.00
PEVOEN050 Oracle of Zefra SR	.50	1.00
PEVOEN051 Zefra Divine Strike SR	.50	1.00
PEVOEN052 Raremetalfoes Bismugear SR	.50	1.00
PEVOEN053 Metalfoes Crimsonite SR	.50	1.00
PEVOEN054 Metalfoes Orichalc SR	.50	1.00
PEVOEN055 Metalfoes Adamante SR	.50	1.00
PEVOEN056 Metalfoes Counter SR	.50	1.00
PEVOEN057 Qliphort Scout SR	.50	1.00
PEVOEN058 Qliphort Monolith SR	.50	1.00
PEVOEN059 Master Pendulum the Dracoslayer SR	.50	1.00
PEVOEN060 Lector Pendulum the Dracoverlord SR	.50	1.00

2017 Yu-Gi-Oh Raging Tempest 1st Edition

RATEEN000 Fusion Recycling Plant R	.10	.20
RATEEN001 Dragoncaller Magician SR	.15	.30
RATEEN002 Performapal Handstandaccoon C	.10	.20
RATEEN003 Performapal Dag Daggerman UR	.15	.30
RATEEN004 Performapal Laugh Maker R	.10	.20
RATEEN005 Speedroid Gum Prize C	.10	.20
RATEEN006 Speedroid Horse Stilts C	.10	.20
RATEEN007 Windwitch Ice Bell UR	7.50	15.00
RATEEN008 Windwitch Snow Bell UR	.50	1.00
RATEEN009 Fusion Parasite R	.10	.20
RATEEN010 Cyber Tutubon C	.10	.20
RATEEN011 Cipher Etranger C	.10	.20
RATEEN012 Flower Cardian Cherry Blossom... C	.10	.20
RATEEN013 Ancient Gear Hunting Hound C	.10	.20
RATEEN014 Zoodiac Ratpier SR	.15	.30
RATEEN015 Zoodiac Bunnyblast C	.10	.20
RATEEN016 Zoodiac Whiptail SR	.15	.30
RATEEN017 Zoodiac Thoroughblade UR	.15	.30
RATEEN018 Zoodiac Ramram C	.10	.20
RATEEN019 True King Lithosagym the Disaster SR	.15	.30
RATEEN020 Crystron Rion C	.10	.20
RATEEN021 Crystron Sulfefnir SR	.15	.30
RATEEN022 Shinobird Crow C	.10	.20
RATEEN023 Shinobird Crane C	.10	.20
RATEEN024 Shinobird Pigeon C	.10	.20
RATEEN025 Envoy of Chaos R	.10	.20
RATEEN026 Spiritual Beast Tamer Winda R	.10	.20
RATEEN027 Tierra Source of Destruction SR	.15	.30
RATEEN028 Miscellaneousaurus C	.10	.20
RATEEN029 Apprentice Piper C	.10	.20
RATEEN030 Hebo Lord of the River C	.10	.20
RATEEN031 Yokotuner C	.10	.20
RATEEN032 Eater of Millions C	.10	.20
RATEEN033 Wightprincess C	.10	.20
RATEEN034 Metrognome SR	.15	.30
RATEEN035 Fairy Tail Rella SP	.15	.30
RATEEN036 Cyber Angel Natasha SR	.15	.30
RATEEN037 Shinobaroness Peacock R	.10	.20
RATEEN038 Shinobaron Peacock R	.10	.20
RATEEN039 Brave Eyes Pendulum Dragon SCR	.50	1.00
RATEEN040 Windwitch Crystal Bell R	.10	.20
RATEEN041 Chaos Ancient Gear Giant SR	1.00	2.00
RATEEN042 Ancient Gear Howitzer C	.10	.20
RATEEN043 Windwitch Winter Bell R	.10	.20
RATEEN044 Superheavy Samurai Stealth Ninja R	.10	.20
RATEEN045 Flower Cardian Lightflare R	.10	.20
RATEEN046 Crystron Quariongandrax UR	.15	.30
RATEEN047 Shiranui Sunsaga R	.10	.20
RATEEN048 OddEyes Raging Dragon UR	.50	1.00
RATEEN049 Neo Galaxy Eyes Cipher Dragon SR	.15	.30
RATEEN050 Heavy Armored Train Ironwolf SR	.15	.30
RATEEN051 Zoodiac Broadbull SCR	.50	1.00
RATEEN052 Zoodiac Tigermortar UR	.15	.30
RATEEN053 Zoodiac Drident SCR	.50	1.00
RATEEN054 Zoodiac Boarbow R	.10	.20
RATEEN055 Machine Angel Absolute Ritual C	.10	.20
RATEEN056 RankUpMagic Cipher Ascension C	.10	.20
RATEEN057 Recardination C	.10	.20
RATEEN058 Zodiac Sign C	.10	.20
RATEEN059 Zoodiac Barrage SCR	1.50	3.00
RATEEN060 Shinobirds Calling C	.10	.20
RATEEN061 Shinobird Power Spot C	.10	.20
RATEEN062 Super Soldier Synthesis C	.10	.20
RATEEN063 Super Quantal Alphan Spike C	.10	.20
RATEEN064 Ritual Beast Return C	.10	.20
RATEEN065 Foolish Burial Goods SCR	3.00	6.00
RATEEN066 That Grass Looks Greener SCR	6.00	12.00
RATEEN067 Terminal World NEXT SP	.15	.30
RATEEN068 Lost Wind R	1.00	2.00
RATEEN069 Cipher Spectrum C	.10	.20
RATEEN070 Ancient Gear Reborn R	.10	.20
RATEEN071 Zoodiac Combo C	.10	.20
RATEEN072 Shinobird Salvation C	.10	.20
RATEEN073 Beginning of Heaven and Earth C	.10	.20
RATEEN074 Shiranui Style Samsara C	.10	.20
RATEEN075 Majespecter Gust C	.10	.20
RATEEN076 Void Feast C	.10	.20
RATEEN077 Purushaddoll Aeon C	.10	.20
RATEEN078 Full Force Virus SCR	1.50	3.00
RATEEN079 Switcheroroo R	.10	.20
RATEEN080 Massivemorph SP	.15	.30
RATEEN081 Sea Monster of Theseus SCR	.60	1.25
RATEEN082 Subterror Nemesis Defender R	.10	.20
RATEEN083 Subterror Behemoth Dragossuary SR	.15	.30
RATEEN084 Subterror Behemoth Voltelluric R	.50	1.00
RATEEN085 Subterror Cave Clash SR	.15	.30
RATEEN086 SPYGAL Misty UR	.15	.30
RATEEN087 SPYRAL Tough R	.10	.20
RATEEN088 SPYRAL GEAR Utility Wire SR	.15	.30
RATEEN089 SPYRAL MISSION Recapture R	.10	.20
RATEEN090 Symphonic Warrior Guitaar C	.10	.20
RATEEN091 Symphonic Warrior Synthess C	.10	.20
RATEEN092 Symph Amplifire C	.10	.20
RATEEN093 Rocket Hand C	.10	.20
RATEEN094 Mekanikal Arkfiend C	.10	.20
RATEEN095 Lightsworn Judgment C	.10	.20
RATEEN096 Symphonic Warrior Miccs C	.10	.20
RATEEN097 Delta The Magnet Warrior SR	.15	.30
RATEEN098 Windwitch Glass Bell UR	.15	.30
RATEEN099 Dark Contract with the Entities UR	.15	.30

2017 Yu-Gi-Oh Spirit Warriors 1st Edition

SPWAEN001 Secret Six Samurai - Fuma SCR	1.25	2.50
SPWAEN002 Secret Six Samurai - Genba SR	.50	1.00
SPWAEN003 Secret Six Samurai - Hatsume SCR	1.25	2.50
SPWAEN004 Secret Six Samurai - Doji SCR	1.25	2.50

SPWAEN005 Secret Six Samurai - Kizaru SCR 1.25 2.50
SPWAEN006 Secret Six Samurai - Rihan SCR 1.25 2.50
SPWAEN007 Secret Skills of the Six Samurai SCR1.25 2.50
SPWAEN008 The Six Shinobi SR .50 1.00
SPWAEN009 Grandmaster of the Six Samurai SR.50 1.00
SPWAEN010 Legendary Six Samurai - Kizan SR .50 1.00
SPWAEN011 Legendary Six Samurai - Shi En SCR1.25 2.50
SPWAEN012 Shadow of the Six Samurai - Shien SR.50 1.00
SPWAEN013 Six Samurai United SR .50 1.00
SPWAEN014 Gateway of the Six SR .50 1.00
SPWAEN015 Shien's Smoke Signal SR .50 1.00
SPWAEN016 Magical Musketeer Caspar SCR 25.00 50.00
SPWAEN017 Magical Musketeer Doc SR .50 1.00
SPWAEN018 Magical Musketeer Kidbrave SR .50 1.00
SPWAEN019 Magical Musketeer Starfire SCR 15.00 30.00
SPWAEN020 Magical Musketeer Calamity SR .50 1.00
SPWAEN021 Magical Musketeer Wild SR .50 1.00
SPWAEN022 Magical Musket Mastermind Zakiel SCR 1.25 2.50
SPWAEN023 Magical Musket - Steady Hands SR.50 1.00
SPWAEN024 Magical Musket - Cross-Domination SCR 1.25 2.50
SPWAEN025 Magical Musket - Desperado SR .50 1.00
SPWAEN026 Magical Musket - Dancing Needle SCR 1.25 2.50
SPWAEN027 Magical Musket - Fiendish Deal SR.50 1.00
SPWAEN028 Magical Musket - Last Stand SCR 1.25 2.50
SPWAEN029 The Weather Painter Snow SCR 10.00 20.00
SPWAEN030 The Weather Painter Rain SR .50 1.00
SPWAEN031 The Weather Painter Cloud SCR 1.25 2.50
SPWAEN032 The Weather Painter Sun SCR 1.25 2.50
SPWAEN033 The Weather Painter Thunder SCR1.25 2.50
SPWAEN034 The Weather Painter Aurora SCR 1.25 2.50
SPWAEN035 The Weather Painter Rainbow SCR1.25 2.50
SPWAEN036 The Weather Snowy Canvas SR .50 1.00
SPWAEN037 The Weather Rainy Canvas SR .50 1.00
SPWAEN038 The Weather Cloudy Canvas SR .50 1.00
SPWAEN039 The Weather Sunny Canvas SR .50 1.00
SPWAEN040 The Weather Thundery Canvas SCR1.25 2.50
SPWAEN041 The Weather Auroral Canvas SR .50 1.00
SPWAEN042 Hand of the Six Samurai SR .50 1.00
SPWAEN043 Legendary Six Samurai - Kageki SR.50 1.00
SPWAEN044 Legendary Six Samurai - Shinai SR.50 1.00
SPWAEN045 Legendary Six Samurai - Mizuho SR.50 1.00
SPWAEN046 Shien's Advisor SR .50 1.00
SPWAEN047 Honest SR .50 1.00
SPWAEN048 Asceticism of the Six Samurai SR .50 1.00
SPWAEN049 Shien's Dojo SR .50 1.00
SPWAEN050 Photon Veil SR .50 1.00
SPWAEN051 Constellar Belt SR .50 1.00
SPWAEN052 Return of the Six Samurai SR .50 1.00
SPWAEN053 Backs to the Wall SR .50 1.00
SPWAEN054 Double-Edged Sword Technique SR.50 1.00
SPWAEN055 Musakani Magatama SR .50 1.00
SPWAEN056 Battleguard Howling SR .50 1.00
SPWAEN057 Beckoning Light SR .50 1.00
SPWAEN058 Scrap-Iron Scarecrow SR .50 1.00
SPWAEN059 Scrap-Iron Statue SR .50 1.00
SPWAEN060 Miraculous Descent SR .50 1.00

2017 Yu-Gi-Oh Star Pack Battle Royal 1st Edition

SP17EN001 The Legendary Fisherman C .10 .20
SP17EN002 Fluffal Leo C .10 .20
SP17EN003 Mayosenju Daibak C .10 .20
SP17EN004 Yosenju Kama 1 C .10 .20
SP17EN005 Yosenju Kama 2 C .10 .20
SP17EN006 Yosenju Kama 3 C .10 .20
SP17EN007 Yosenju Shinchu L C .10 .20
SP17EN008 Yosenju Shinchu R C .10 .20
SP17EN009 Superheavy Samurai Big Waraji C .10 .20
SP17EN010 Superheavy Samurai Gigagloves C .10 .20
SP17EN011 Superheavy Samurai Battleball C .10 .20
SP17EN012 Superheavy Samurai Soulbuster Gauntlet C .10 .20
SP17EN013 Soprano the Melodious Songstress C.10 .20
SP17EN014 Fluffal Sheep C .10 .20
SP17EN015 Edge Imp Saw C .10 .20
SP17EN016 Performapal Thunderhino C .10 .20
SP17EN017 Xiangke Magician C .10 .20
SP17EN018 Xiangsheng Magician C .10 .20
SP17EN019 Performapal Drummerilla C .10 .20
SP17EN020 Opera the Melodious Diva C .10 .20
SP17EN021 Crystal Rose C .10 .20
SP17EN022 Speedroid Terrortop C .10 .20
SP17EN023 Speedroid TriEyed Dice C .10 .20
SP17EN024 Speedroid Double Yoyo C .10 .20
SP17EN025 Performapal Secondonkey C .10 .20
SP17EN026 DD Swirl Slime C .10 .20
SP17EN027 DD Necro Slime C .10 .20
SP17EN028 The Legendary Fisherman III C .10 .20
SP17EN029 DDD Oblivion King Abyss Ragnarok C.10 .20
SP17EN030 Solo the Melodious Songstress C .10 .20
SP17EN031 Score the Melodious Diva C .10 .20
SP17EN032 Performapal OddEyes Light Phoenix C.10 .20
SP17EN033 Performapal OddEyes Unicorn C .10 .20
SP17EN034 Performapal Fireflux C .10 .20
SP17EN035 Schuberta the Melodious Maestra C .10 .20
SP17EN036 Bloom Diva the Melodious Choir C .10 .20
SP17EN037 Frightfur Leo C .10 .20
SP17EN038 Frightfur Sheep C .10 .20
SP17EN039 Frightfur Chimera C .10 .20
SP17EN040 DDD Oracle King dArc C .10 .20
SP17EN041 Bloom Prima the Melodious Choir C.10 .20
SP17EN042 Superheavy Samurai Ogre Shutendoji C.10 .20
SP17EN043 HiSpeedroid Kendama C .10 .20
SP17EN045 DDD DuoDawn King Kali Yuga C .10 .20
SP17EN046 Frightfur Fusion C .10 .20
SP17EN047 Pianissimo C .10 .20
SP17EN048 Speed Recovery C .10 .20
SP17EN049 Urgent Tuning C .10 .20
SP17EN050 Yosenjus Secret Move C .10 .20

2017 Yu-Gi-Oh Starter Deck Link Strike 1st Edition

YS17EN001 Bitron C .50 1.00
YS17EN002 Draconnet C .50 1.00
YS17EN003 RAM Clouder SR 2.00 4.00
YS17EN004 Linkslayer UR 2.00 4.00
YS17EN005 Galaxy Serpent C .50 1.00
YS17EN006 Mystery Shell Dragon C .50 1.00
YS17EN007 Beast King Barbaros C .50 1.00
YS17EN008 Cyber Dragon C .50 1.00
YS17EN009 Photon Thrasher C .50 1.00
YS17EN010 Exarion Universe C .50 1.00
YS17EN011 Evilswarm Mandragora C .50 1.00
YS17EN012 Marauding Captain C .50 1.00
YS17EN013 Sangan C .50 1.00
YS17EN014 Kuribandit C .50 1.00
YS17EN015 Marshmallon C .50 1.00
YS17EN016 Cardcar D C .50 1.00
YS17EN017 Ryko Lightsworn Hunter C .50 1.00
YS17EN018 Battle Fader C .50 1.00
YS17EN019 Swift Scarecrow C .50 1.00
YS17EN020 Effect Veiler C .50 1.00
YS17EN021 Cynet Universe C .50 1.00
YS17EN022 Monster Reincarnation C .50 1.00
YS17EN023 Dark Hole C .50 1.00
YS17EN024 Mystical Space Typhoon C .50 1.00
YS17EN025 Book of Moon C .50 1.00
YS17EN026 Forbidden Lance C .50 1.00
YS17EN027 United We Stand C .50 1.00
YS17EN028 Pot of Duality C .50 1.00
YS17EN029 Burden of the Mighty C .50 1.00
YS17EN030 Supply Squad C .50 1.00
YS17EN031 Terraforming C .50 1.00
YS17EN032 Jar of Avarice C .50 1.00
YS17EN033 Call of the Haunted C .50 1.00
YS17EN034 Mirror Force C .50 1.00
YS17EN035 Torrential Tribute C .50 1.00
YS17EN036 Ring of Destruction C .50 1.00
YS17EN037 Bottomless Trap Hole C .50 1.00
YS17EN038 Compulsory Evacuation Device C .50 1.00
YS17EN039 Fiendish Chain C .50 1.00
YS17EN040 Dark Bribe C .50 1.00
YS17EN041 Decode Talker UR 3.00 6.00
YS17EN042 Honeybot SR 2.50 5.00
YS17EN043 Link Spider SR 3.00 6.00

2017 Yu-Gi-Oh Structure Deck Cyberse Link 1st Edition

SDCLEN001 Digitron C .15 .30
SDCLEN002 Dotscaper C .15 .30
SDCLEN003 Cliant C .15 .30
SDCLEN004 Backlinker C .15 .30
SDCLEN005 Balancer Lord C .15 .30
SDCLEN006 ROM Cloudia C .15 .30
SDCLEN007 Boot Staggered C .15 .30
SDCLEN008 Dual Assembwurm SR .50 1.00
SDCLEN009 Cyberse Wizard C .15 .30
SDCLEN010 Backup Secretary C .15 .30
SDCLEN011 Stack Reviver C .15 .30
SDCLEN012 Launcher Commander C .15 .30
SDCLEN013 Tragoedia C .15 .30
SDCLEN014 Summoner Monk C .15 .30
SDCLEN015 Card Trooper C .15 .30
SDCLEN016 Debris Dragon C .15 .30
SDCLEN017 Mathematician C .15 .30
SDCLEN018 Crane Crane C .15 .30
SDCLEN019 Magician of Faith C .15 .30
SDCLEN020 Jester Confit C .15 .30
SDCLEN021 Glow Up Bulb C .50 1.00
SDCLEN022 Kinka byo C .15 .30
SDCLEN023 Cynet Backdoor SR .50 1.00
SDCLEN024 Soul Charge C .50 1.00
SDCLEN025 Shuffle Reborn C .15 .30
SDCLEN026 DDR Different Dimension Reincarnation C .15 .30
SDCLEN027 Gold Sarcophagus C .50 1.00
SDCLEN028 Mind Control C .15 .30
SDCLEN029 Cosmic Cyclone C 2.50 5.00
SDCLEN030 Moon Mirror Shield C .15 .30
SDCLEN031 Where Arf Thou C .15 .30
SDCLEN032 Recoded Alive C .15 .30
SDCLEN033 Miracle's Wake C .15 .30
SDCLEN034 Powerful Rebirth C .15 .30
SDCLEN035 Premature Return C .15 .30
SDCLEN036 Swamp Mirrorer C .15 .30
SDCLEN037 Quantum Cat C .15 .30
SDCLEN038 Storming Mirror Force C .75 1.50
SDCLEN039 Dimensional Barrier C 2.00 4.00
SDCLEN040 Ghosts From the Past C .15 .30
SDCLEN041 Encode Talker UR 1.00 2.00
SDCLEN042 Tri Gate Wizard UR 2.00 4.00
SDCLEN043 Binary Sorceress SR .20 .40

2017 Yu-Gi-Oh Structure Deck Dinosmashers Fury 1st Edition

SR04EN000 Petiteranodon UR 2.00 4.00
SR04EN001 Ultimate Conductor Tyranno UR 1.50 3.00
SR04EN002 Souleating Oviraptor SR 4.00 8.00
SR04EN003 Megalosmasher X C .15 .30
SR04EN004 Sabersaurus C .15 .30
SR04EN005 Super Conductor Tyranno C .15 .30
SR04EN006 Ultimate Tyranno C .15 .30
SR04EN007 SuperAncient Dinobeast C .15 .30
SR04EN008 Sauropod Brachion C .15 .30
SR04EN009 Tyranno Infinity C .15 .30
SR04EN010 Black Brachios C .15 .30
SR04EN011 Miracle Jurassic Egg C .15 .30
SR04EN012 Gilasaurus C .15 .30
SR04EN013 Babycerasaurus C .15 .30
SR04EN014 Miscellaneousaurus C .15 .30
SR04EN015 Evilswarm Salamandra C .15 .30
SR04EN016 Stegocyber C .15 .30
SR04EN017 Trifortressops C .15 .30
SR04EN018 Skelesaurus C .15 .30
SR04EN019 Chewbone C .15 .30
SR04EN020 Rescue Rabbit C .15 .30
SR04EN021 Lost World SR 1.50 3.00
SR04EN022 Fossil Dig C .15 .30
SR04EN023 Big Evolution Pill C .15 .30
SR04EN024 Twin Twisters C .15 .30
SR04EN025 Burial from a Different Dimension C .15 .30
SR04EN026 Swords of Concealing Light C .15 .30
SR04EN027 Painful Decision C .15 .30
SR04EN028 Unexpected Dai C .15 .30
SR04EN029 Terraforming C .15 .30
SR04EN030 Survivals End SR .30 .75
SR04EN031 Survival of the Fittest C .15 .30
SR04EN032 Fossil Excavation C .15 .30
SR04EN033 Extinction on Schedule C .15 .30
SR04EN034 Ojama Trio C .15 .30
SR04EN035 Nightmare Archfiends C .15 .30
SR04EN036 Quaking Mirror Force C .15 .30
SR04EN037 Grand Horn of Heaven C .15 .30
SR04EN038 Secret Blast C .15 .30
SR04ENTKN Jurraegg Token C .15 .30

2017 Yu-Gi-Oh Structure Deck Machine Reactor 1st Edition

SR03EN000 Ancient Gear Gadget UR 1.25 2.50
SR03EN001 Ancient Gear Reactor Dragon UR 1.00 2.00
SR03EN002 Ancient Gear Hydra SR .75 1.50
SR03EN003 Ancient Gear Wyvern SR 1.50 3.00
SR03EN004 Ancient Gear Gadjiltron Dragon C .15 .30
SR03EN005 Ancient Gear Golem C .15 .30
SR03EN006 Ancient Gear Gadjiltron Chimera C .15 .30
SR03EN007 Ancient Gear Beast C .15 .30
SR03EN008 Ancient Gear Engineer C .15 .30
SR03EN009 Ancient Gear Knight C .15 .30
SR03EN010 Ancient Gear Soldier C .15 .30
SR03EN011 Ancient Gear Box C .15 .30
SR03EN012 Geargiauger C .15 .30
SR03EN013 Planet Pathfinder C .15 .30
SR03EN014 Minefieldriller C .15 .30
SR03EN015 Card Trooper C .15 .30
SR03EN016 Gigantes C .15 .30
SR03EN017 BOXer C .15 .30
SR03EN018 Hardened Armed Dragon C .15 .30
SR03EN019 Spell Striker C .15 .30
SR03EN020 Maxx C C .15 .30
SR03EN021 Ancient Gear Catapult SR 1.25 2.50
SR03EN022 Ancient Gear Fortress C .15 .30
SR03EN023 Ancient Gear Castle C .15 .30
SR03EN024 Ancient Gear Workshop C .15 .30
SR03EN025 Geartown C .15 .30
SR03EN026 Mausoleum of the Emperor C .15 .30
SR03EN027 Pseudo Space C .15 .30
SR03EN028 Limiter Removal C .15 .30
SR03EN029 Machine Duplication C .15 .30
SR03EN030 Inferno Reckless Summon C .15 .30
SR03EN031 Galaxy Cyclone C .15 .30
SR03EN032 Terraforming C .15 .30
SR03EN033 Jar of Avarice C .15 .30
SR03EN034 Mischief of the Gnomes C .15 .30
SR03EN035 Machine King 3000 BC C .15 .30
SR03EN036 Fiendish Chain C .15 .30
SR03EN037 Call of the Haunted C .15 .30
SR03EN038 The Huge Revolution is Over C .15 .30
SR03ENTKN Ancient Gear Token C .15 .30

2017 Yu-Gi-Oh Structure Deck Pendulum Domination 1st Edition

SDPDEN001 DDD Chaos King Apocalypse UR 1.50 3.00
SDPDEN002 DD Savant Newton C .15 .30
SDPDEN003 DD Savant Copernicus C .15 .30
SDPDEN004 DD Orthros SR 1.00 2.00
SDPDEN005 DD Lamia SR 3.00 6.00
SDPDEN006 DDD Doom King Armageddon C .15 .30
SDPDEN007 DD Cerberus C .15 .30
SDPDEN008 DD Lilith C .15 .30
SDPDEN009 DD Nighthowl C .15 .30
SDPDEN010 DD Savant Galilei C .15 .30
SDPDEN011 DD Savant Kepler C .15 .30
SDPDEN012 DDD Oblivion King Abyss Ragnarok C.15 .30
SDPDEN013 DDD Supreme King Kaiser C .15 .30
SDPDEN014 DD Proud Ogre C .15 .30
SDPDEN015 DD Proud Chevalier C .15 .30
SDPDEN016 Dark Armed Dragon C .15 .30
SDPDEN017 Dark Grepher C .15 .30
SDPDEN018 Armageddon Knight C .15 .30
SDPDEN019 Trance Archfiend C .15 .30
SDPDEN020 Kuribandit C .15 .30
SDPDEN021 Stygian Street Patrol C .15 .30
SDPDEN022 Stygian Security C .15 .30
SDPDEN023 Dark Contract with the Yamimakai C.15 .30
SDPDEN024 Dark Contract with the Gate C .15 .30
SDPDEN025 Dark Contract with the Swamp King C.15 .30
SDPDEN026 Forbidden Dark Contract/Swamp King C .15 .30
SDPDEN027 Foolish Burial C .15 .30
SDPDEN028 One for One C .15 .30
SDPDEN029 Allure of Darkness C .15 .30
SDPDEN030 Dark Eruption C .15 .30
SDPDEN031 Emergency Provisions C .15 .30
SDPDEN032 DD Reroll C .15 .30
SDPDEN033 DD Recruits C .15 .30
SDPDEN034 DDD Human Resources C .15 .30
SDPDEN035 Dark Contract with the Witch C .15 .30
SDPDEN036 Dark Contract with Errors C .15 .30
SDPDEN037 Contract Laundering C .15 .30
SDPDEN038 Sinister Yorishiro C .15 .30
SDPDEN039 Escape from the Dark Dimension C .15 .30
SDPDEN040 Hope for Escape C .15 .30
SDPDEN041 DDD Dragonbane King Beowulf UR3.00 6.00
SDPDEN042 DDD Cursed King Siegfried SR 3.00 6.00
SDPDEN043 DDD Wave King Caesar C .15 .30

2018 Yu-Gi-Oh Battles of Legend Relentless Revenge 1st Edition

BLR-EN001 Orgoth the Relentless SCR 2.50 5.00
BLRREN002 Summon Dice UR .60 1.25
BLRREN003 Flying Elephant SCR 2.50 5.00
BLRREN004 Prinzessin SCR 2.50 5.00
BLRREN005 Pumpkin Carriage UR .60 1.25
BLRREN006 Iron Hans UR .60 1.25
BLRREN007 Iron Knight UR .60 1.25
BLRREN008 Glife the Phantom Bird SCR 2.50 5.00
BLRREN009 Hexe Trude SCR 2.50 5.00
BLRREN010 Golden Castle of Stromberg SCR 30.00 75.00
BLRREN011 Glass Slippers SCR 2.50 5.00
BLRREN012 Iron Cage UR .60 1.25
BLRREN013 Litmus Doom Swordsman UR .60 1.25
BLRREN014 Litmus Doom Ritual UR .60 1.25
BLRREN015 Living Fossil SCR 2.50 5.00
BLRREN016 Cyber Emergency SCR 5.00 10.00
BLRREN017 Born from Draconis UR .60 1.25
BLRREN018 Cyber Eltanin UR .60 1.25
BLRREN019 Cyber Larva UR .60 1.25
BLRREN020 Slash Draw UR .60 1.25
BLRREN021 Michion, the Timelord UR .60 1.25
BLRREN022 Hailon, the Timelord UR .60 1.25
BLRREN023 Raphion, the Timelord UR .60 1.25
BLRREN024 Gabrion, the Timelord UR .60 1.25
BLRREN025 Sandaion, the Timelord UR .60 1.25
BLRREN026 Metaion, the Timelord UR .60 1.25
BLRREN027 Empty Machine SCR 2.50 5.00
BLRREN028 Infinite Machine SCR 2.50 5.00
BLRREN029 Infinite Light SCR 2.50 5.00
BLRREN030 #27 Dreadnought Dreadnoid SCR 7.50 15.00
BLRREN031 #67 Pair-a-Dice Smasher SCR 2.50 5.00
BLRREN032 #75 Bamboozling Gossip Shadow SCR 10.00 20.00
BLRREN033 #90 Galaxy-Eyes Photon Lord SCR4.00 8.00
BLRREN034 Iron Draw SCR 2.50 5.00
BLRREN035 Glorious Numbers SCR 2.50 5.00
BLRREN036 Hayate the Earth Star UR .60 1.25
BLRREN037 Tenma the Sky Star UR .60 1.25
BLRREN038 Kaiki the Unity Star UR .60 1.25
BLRREN039 Idaten the Conqueror Star UR .60 1.25
BLRREN040 Shura the Combat Star UR .60 1.25
BLRREN041 Hibernation Dragon SCR 2.50 5.00
BLRREN042 Triggering Wurm SCR 2.50 5.00
BLRREN043 Topologic Gumblar Dragon SCR 10.00 20.00
BLRREN044 Borrelguard Dragon SCR 7.50 15.00
BLRREN045 Flash Charge Dragon SCR 2.50 5.00
BLRREN046 Monster Reborn SCR 2.50 5.00
BLRREN047 Torrential Tribute UR .60 1.25
BLRREN048 Cyber Dragon UR .60 1.25
BLRREN049 Neo-Spacian Aqua Dolphin UR .60 1.25
BLRREN050 Neo-Spacian Air Hummingbird UR .60 1.25
BLRREN051 Neo-Spacian Grand Mole UR .60 1.25
BLRREN052 Neo-Spacian Dark Panther UR .60 1.25
BLRREN053 Card Trooper SCR 2.50 5.00
BLRREN054 Rainbow Dark Dragon UR .60 1.25
BLRREN055 Convert Contact UR .60 1.25
BLRREN056 Sephylon, the Ultimate Timelord UR .60 1.25
BLRREN057 T.G. Wonder Magician UR .60 1.25
BLRREN058 Norito the Moral Leader UR .60 1.25
BLRREN059 Performage Damage Juggler UR .60 1.25
BLRREN060 Performage Trick Clown UR .60 1.25
BLRREN061 Phantom Knights of Ancient Cloak SCR2.50 5.00
BLRREN062 Phantom Knights of Silent Boots SCR2.50 5.00
BLRREN063 Supreme King Dragon Darkwurm SCR2.50 5.00
BLRREN064 Brilliant Fusion SCR 2.50 5.00
BLRREN065 Phantom Knights' Fog Blade SCR 2.50 5.00
BLRREN066 Altergeist Hexstia UR .60 1.25
BLRREN067 Altergeist Manifestation UR .60 1.25
BLRREN068 PSY-Frame Driver UR .60 1.25
BLRREN069 Pyrorex the Elemental Lord UR .60 1.25
BLRREN070 Windrose the Elemental Lord UR .60 1.25
BLRREN071 Noble Knight Medraut UR .60 1.25
BLRREN072 Noble Knight Brothers UR .60 1.25
BLRREN073 Merlin SCR 2.50 5.00
BLRREN074 Uni-Zombie UR .60 1.25
BLRREN075 Gameciel, the Sea Turtle Kaiju SCR5.00 10.00
BLRREN076 Darklord Ixchel SCR 2.50 5.00
BLRREN077 Darklord Nasten UR .60 1.25
BLRREN078 Eater of Millions UR .60 1.25
BLRREN079 Elemental HERO Honest Neos SCR2.50 5.00
BLRREN080 Trickstar Narkissus UR .60 1.25
BLRREN081 Fullmetalfoes Alkahest UR .60 1.25
BLRREN082 Metalfoes Mithrilium SCR 2.50 5.00
BLRREN083 Crystron Quandax SCR 2.50 5.00
BLRREN084 Tornado Dragon SCR 2.50 5.00
BLRREN085 #41 Bagooska the Terribly Tired Tapir UR .60 1.25
BLRREN086 Imduk the World Chalice Dragon UR.60 1.25
BLRREN087 Gaia Saber, the Lightning Shadow UR.60 1.25
BLRREN088 Preparation of Rites UR .60 1.25
BLRREN089 Kyoutou Waterfront UR .60 1.25
BLRREN090 Pre-Preparation of Rites UR .60 1.25
BLRREN091 The Kaiju Files UR .60 1.25
BLRREN092 Union Hangar SCR 2.50 5.00
BLRREN093 Banishment of the Darklords UR .60 1.25
BLRREN094 Darklord Contact UR .60 1.25
BLRREN095 Foolish Burial Goods UR .60 1.25
BLRREN096 Dragonic Diagram SCR 5.00 10.00
BLRREN097 Duelist Alliance UR .60 1.25
BLRREN098 World Legacy Discovery UR .60 1.25
BLRREN099 World Legacy's Heart UR .60 1.25
BLRREN100 Solemn Judgment UR .60 1.25
BLRREN101 Bottomless Trap Hole UR .60 1.25
BLRREN102 Solemn Strike UR 2.50 5.00
BLRREN103 Darklord Enchantment UR .60 1.25
BLRREN104 Unending Nightmare UR .60 1.25
BLRREN105 Trickstar Reincarnation SCR 6.00 12.00

2018 Yu-Gi-Oh Cybernetic Horizon 1st Edition

CYHOEN000 Contact Gate C .15 .30
CYHOEN001 SIMM Tablir R .20 .40
CYHOEN002 Cluster Congester C .15 .30
CYHOEN003 Gouki Moonsault C .15 .30
CYHOEN004 Gouki Tagpartner C .15 .30
CYHOEN005 Gouki Ringtrainer C .15 .30
CYHOEN006 Crusadia Reclusia C .15 .30
CYHOEN007 Crusadia Arboria C .15 .30
CYHOEN008 Crusadia Leonis C .15 .30
CYHOEN009 Crusadia Draco C .15 .30
CYHOEN010 Crusadia Maximus SR .60 1.25
CYHOEN011 World Legacy - World Crown R .20 .40
CYHOEN012 Impcantation Candoll R .20 .40
CYHOEN013 Impcantation Talismandra R .20 .40
CYHOEN014 Cyber Dragon Vier C .15 .30
CYHOEN015 Cyber Dragon Herz UR 7.50 15.00
CYHOEN016 Dragunity Senatus SR .60 1.25
CYHOEN017 Dragunity Couse C .15 .30
CYHOEN018 Metaphys Decoy Dragon C .15 .30
CYHOEN019 Umbramirage the Elemental Lord SR.60 1.25
CYHOEN020 Cosmo Brain C .15 .30
CYHOEN021 Mana Dragon Zirnitron SR .60 1.25
CYHOEN022 Terrifying Toddler of Torment C .15 .30
CYHOEN023 Psychic Ace C .15 .30

CYHOEN024 Cupid Volley C .15 .30
CYHOEN025 Centerfrog C .15 .30
CYHOEN026 Cyberse Magician UR 1.00 2.00
CYHOEN027 Ruin, Angel of Oblivion C .15 .30
CYHOEN028 Demise, Agent of Armageddon C .15 .30
CYHOEN029 Ruin, Supreme Queen of Oblivion R .20 .40
CYHOEN030 Demise, Supreme
King of Armageddon R .20 .40
CYHOEN031 Paladin of Storm Dragon R .20 .40
CYHOEN032 Dragunity Knight - Luin R .20 .40
CYHOEN033 Dragunity Knight - Ascalon UR .50 1.00
CYHOEN034 Borrelsword Dragon SCR 50.00 100.00
CYHOEN035 Cyberse Witch R .20 .40
CYHOEN036 Link Devotee C .15 .30
CYHOEN037 Restoration Point Guard C .15 .30
CYHOEN038 Gouki Heel Ogre C .15 .30
CYHOEN039 Gouki The Giant Ogre R .20 .40
CYHOEN040 Miniborrel Dragon C .15 .30
CYHOEN041 Vorticular Drumgon SR .60 1.25
CYHOEN042 Crusadia Magius SR .60 1.25
CYHOEN043 Crusadia Regulex C .15 .30
CYHOEN044 Crusadia Equimax UR 7.50 15.00
CYHOEN045 Mekk-Knight of the Morning Star SCR5.00 10.00
CYHOEN046 Cyber Dragon Zieger UR 7.50 15.00
CYHOEN047 Sky Striker Ace - Hayate SR .60 1.25
CYHOEN048 Reprodocus R .20 .40
CYHOEN049 Wee Witch's Apprentice SR .60 1.25
CYHOEN050 Hip Hoshiningen SR .60 1.25
CYHOEN051 Cynet Ritual R .20 .40
CYHOEN052 Zero Extra Link C .15 .30
CYHOEN053 Borrel Regenerator C .15 .30
CYHOEN054 Crusadia Revival SR .60 1.25
CYHOEN055 Crusadia Power C .15 .30
CYHOEN056 Cycle of the World C .15 .30
CYHOEN057 Breaking of the World C .15 .30
CYHOEN058 Turning of the World C .15 .30
CYHOEN059 Cyber Revsystem SCR 15.00 30.00
CYHOEN060 World Legacy Survivor SR .60 1.25
CYHOEN061 World Legacy's Memory C .15 .30
CYHOEN062 Mythical Institution C .15 .30
CYHOEN063 Beast Magic Attack C .15 .30
CYHOEN064 Celestial Observatory SCR 3.00 6.00
CYHOEN065 Solitary Sword of Poison C .15 .30
CYHOEN066 Cross Breed R .20 .40
CYHOEN067 Ledger of Legerdemain SCR 3.00 6.00
CYHOEN068 Shield Handler C .15 .30
CYHOEN069 Mirror Force Launcher SR .60 1.25
CYHOEN070 Link Turret C .15 .30
CYHOEN071 Crusadia Vanguard C .15 .30
CYHOEN072 Renewal of the World R .20 .40
CYHOEN073 Cybernetic Overflow C .15 .30
CYHOEN074 Dragunity Legion C .15 .30
CYHOEN075 World Legacy's Mind Meld C .15 .30
CYHOEN076 Metaphys Ascension C .15 .30
CYHOEN077 Ballista Squad C .15 .30
CYHOEN078 The Deep Grave R .20 .40
CYHOEN079 Universal Adapter C .15 .30
CYHOEN080 Dealer's Choice SP .15 .30
CYHOEN081 Pinpoint Landing SCR 6.00 12.00
CYHOEN082 Danger! Bigfoot! SCR 30.00 75.00
CYHOEN083 Danger! Nessie! SCR 50.00 100.00
CYHOEN084 Danger! Chupacabra! UR 6.00 12.00
CYHOEN085 Danger!? Jackalope? UR 7.50 15.00
CYHOEN086 Realm of Danger! UR .30 .75
CYHOEN087 Danger! Zone UR 1.00 2.00
CYHOEN088 Noble Knight Custennin SR .60 1.25
CYHOEN089 Sacred Noble Knight
of King Custennin UR 1.00 2.00
CYHOEN090 Noble Knight Pellinore SR .60 1.25
CYHOEN091 Noble Arms - Clarent SR .60 1.25
CYHOEN092 Divine Serpent Geh C .15 .30
CYHOEN093 Performapal Handsamuraiger C .15 .30
CYHOEN094 Performapal Lebellman C .15 .30
CYHOEN095 Performapal Gold Fang R .20 .40
CYHOEN096 White Stingray R .20 .40
CYHOEN097 Interrupt Resistor R .20 .40
CYHOEN098 Link Disciple R .20 .40
CYHOEN099 Gladiator Beast Dragacius R .20 .40

2018 Yu-Gi-Oh Dark Saviors 1st Edition

DASAEN001 Vampire Familiar SR .20 .40
DASAEN002 Vampire Retainer SR .20 .40
DASAEN003 Vampire Fräulein SCR .50 1.00
DASAEN004 Vampire Grimson SR .20 .40
DASAEN005 Vampire Scarlet Scourge SCR .50 1.00
DASAEN006 Vampire Red Baron SR .10 .20
DASAEN007 Dhampir Vampire Sheridan SCR 2.00 4.00
DASAEN008 Vampire Desire SCR .50 1.00
DASAEN009 Vampire's Domain SCR .50 1.00
DASAEN010 Vampire Awakening SR .20 .40
DASAEN011 Vampire Domination SCR .50 1.00
DASAEN012 Shadow Vampire SR .20 .40
DASAEN013 Crimson Knight Vampire Bram SR .15 .30
DASAEN014 Donpa, Marksman Fur Hire SR .10 .20
DASAEN015 Recon, Scout Fur Hire SR .10 .20
DASAEN016 Helmer, Helmsman Fur Hire SR .20 .40
DASAEN017 Beat, Bladesman Fur Hire SCR 5.00 10.00
DASAEN018 Seal, Strategist Fur Hire SR .10 .20
DASAEN019 Bravo, Fighter Fur Hire SR .15 .30
DASAEN020 Sagitta, Maverick Fur Hire SCR .10 .20
DASAEN021 Dyna, Hero Fur Hire SCR .50 1.00
DASAEN022 Wiz, Sage Fur Hire SCR .50 1.00
DASAEN023 Rafale, Champion Fur Hire SCR .50 1.00
DASAEN024 Fandora, the Flying Furtress SR .10 .20
DASAEN025 Mayhem Fur Hire SCR .60 1.25
DASAEN026 Training Fur Hire... SCR .15 .30
DASAEN027 Sky Striker Ace - Kagari SR 1.00 2.00
DASAEN028 Sky Striker Ace - Shizuku SR .60 1.25
DASAEN029 Sky Striker Ace - Raye SR 1.00 2.00
DASAEN030 Sky Striker Mobilize - Engage! SCR100.00200.00
DASAEN031 Sky Striker...Afterburners! SCR 7.50 15.00
DASAEN032 Sky Striker...Jamming Waves! SCR1.50 3.00
DASAEN033 Sky Striker Mecha - Hornet Drones SR.60 1.25
DASAEN034 Sky Striker Mecha -
Widow Anchor SCR 30.00 75.00
DASAEN035 Sky Striker Mecha - Eagle Booster SR.50 1.00
DASAEN036 Sky Striker Mecha -
Shark Cannon SCR 1.50 3.00
DASAEN037 Sky Striker...Hercules Base SR .60 1.25
DASAEN038 Sky Striker...Multirole SCR 7.50 15.00
DASAEN039 Sky Striker Airspace - Area Zero SR .50 1.00
DASAEN040 Armageddon Knight SR .15 .30
DASAEN041 Plaguespreader Zombie SR .10 .20
DASAEN042 Dark Grepher SR .15 .30
DASAEN043 Toon Table of Contents SR .60 1.25
DASAEN044 The Monarchs Stormforth SR .10 .20
DASAEN045 Drowning Mirror Force SR .10 .20
DASAEN046 Mystic Tomato SR .10 .20
DASAEN047 Vampiric Orchis SR .10 .20
DASAEN048 Vampiric Koala SR .10 .20
DASAEN049 Vampire Sorcerer SR .20 .40
DASAEN050 Vampire Vamp SR .10 .20
DASAEN051 Kuribandit SR .10 .20
DASAEN052 Scapegoat SR .60 1.25
DASAEN053 Reinforcement of the Army SR .10 .20
DASAEN054 Allure of Darkness SR 1.50 3.00
DASAEN055 Magical Citadel of Endymion SCR .60 1.25
DASAEN056 Spell Power Grasp SR .10 .20
DASAEN057 Quick Booster SR .10 .20
DASAEN058 Foolish Burial Goods SR .60 1.25
DASAEN059 Mirror Force SR .50 1.00
DASAEN060 Horn of the Phantom Beast SR .10 .20

2018 Yu-Gi-Oh Extreme Force 1st Edition

EXFOEN000 Yoko-Zuna Sumo Spirit C .10 .20
EXFOEN001 Zombino C .10 .20
EXFOEN002 Lockout Gardna C .10 .20
EXFOEN003 Striping Partner C .10 .20
EXFOEN004 Flick Clown C .10 .20
EXFOEN005 Bitrooper C .10 .20
EXFOEN006 Beltlink Wall Dragon C .10 .20
EXFOEN007 Shelrokket Dragon R .30 .75
EXFOEN008 Metalrokket Dragon R .30 .75
EXFOEN009 Tindangle Angel C .10 .20
EXFOEN010 Tindangle Base Gardna C .10 .20
EXFOEN011 Tindangle Hound C .10 .20
EXFOEN012 Tindangle Protector C .10 .20
EXFOEN013 Tindangle Intruder C .10 .20
EXFOEN014 Mekk-Knight Blue Sky SCR 10.00 20.00
EXFOEN015 Mekk-Knight Green Horizon C .10 .20
EXFOEN016 Mekk-Knight Orange Sunset C .10 .20
EXFOEN017 Mekk-Knight Yellow Star R .30 .75
EXFOEN018 Mekk-Knight Red Moon R .30 .75
EXFOEN019 Mekk-Knight Indigo Eclipse SR .60 1.25
EXFOEN020 Mekk-Knight Purple Nightfall SCR10.00 20.00
EXFOEN021 World Legacy - World Shield C .10 .20
EXFOEN022 Mythical Beast Jackal R .30 .75
EXFOEN023 Mythical Beast Garuda UR 1.50 3.00
EXFOEN024 Mythical Beast Medusa SR .60 1.25
EXFOEN025 Mythical Beast Basilisk R .30 .75
EXFOEN026 Mythical Beast Jackal King UR 1.50 3.00
EXFOEN027 Mythical Beast Master Cerberus SCR7.50 15.00
EXFOEN028 Artifact Mjollnir C .10 .20
EXFOEN029 Grappler Angler C .10 .20
EXFOEN030 Mahjong Munia Maidens C .10 .20
EXFOEN031 D.D. Seeker C .10 .20
EXFOEN032 Ghost Bird of Bewitchment R .30 .75
EXFOEN033 Desmanian Devil R .30 .75
EXFOEN034 Wattkinetic Puppeteer C .10 .20
EXFOEN035 Inspector Boarder SCR 10.00 20.00
EXFOEN036 Overtyx Qoatlus SR .60 1.25
EXFOEN037 Contact C C .10 .20
EXFOEN038 Excode Talker UR 3.00 6.00
EXFOEN039 Underclock Taker C .10 .20
EXFOEN040 Vector Scare Archfiend R .30 .75
EXFOEN041 Flame Administrator C .10 .20
EXFOEN042 Recovery Sorcerer C .10 .20
EXFOEN043 Secure Gardna C .10 .20
EXFOEN044 Three Burst Dragon UR 1.50 3.00
EXFOEN045 Tindangle Acute Cerberus C .10 .20
EXFOEN046 Altergeist Hexstia SR .60 1.25
EXFOEN047 Mekk-Knight Spectrum Supreme UR2.50 5.00
EXFOEN048 Saryuja Skull Dread SCR 50.00 100.00
EXFOEN049 Clara & Rushka, the Ventriloduo UR3.00 6.00
EXFOEN050 Duelittle Chimera R .30 .75
EXFOEN051 Link Hole C .10 .20
EXFOEN052 Fire Prison C .10 .20
EXFOEN053 Boot Sector Launch UR 1.50 3.00
EXFOEN054 Nagel's Protection C .10 .20
EXFOEN055 Euler's Circuit C .10 .20
EXFOEN056 World Legacy Scars R .30 .75
EXFOEN057 World Legacy Key R .30 .75
EXFOEN058 Mythical Bestiary UR 1.50 3.00
EXFOEN059 Glory of the Noble Knights R .30 .75
EXFOEN060 Power of the Guardians SR .60 1.25
EXFOEN061 Pendulum Paradox SCR 4.00 8.00
EXFOEN062 Hey, Trunade! SCR 15.00 30.00
EXFOEN063 Downbeat SR .60 1.25
EXFOEN064 Column Switch C .10 .20
EXFOEN065 Trading Places C .10 .20
EXFOEN066 Parallel Port Armor C .10 .20
EXFOEN067 Cynet Refresh C .10 .20
EXFOEN068 Borrel Cooling C .10 .20
EXFOEN069 Tindangle Delaunay C .10 .20
EXFOEN070 Altergeist Manifestation SR .60 1.25
EXFOEN071 World Legacy Whispers R .30 .75
EXFOEN072 World Legacy's Secret UR 1.50 3.00
EXFOEN073 Mythical Bestiamorph R .30 .75
EXFOEN074 Ghostrick Renovation C .10 .20
EXFOEN075 Call of the Archfiend C .10 .20
EXFOEN076 There Can Only Be One SR .60 1.25
EXFOEN077 Dai Dance C .10 .20
EXFOEN078 Showdown/Secret
Sense Scroll Techniques C .10 .20
EXFOEN079 Parthian Shot C .10 .20
EXFOEN080 Oops! C .10 .20
EXFOEN081 Kuro-Obi Karate Spirit C .10 .20
EXFOEN082 Vendread Battlelord SR .60 1.25
EXFOEN083 Vendread Core SR .60 1.25
EXFOEN084 Vendread Charge R .30 .75
EXFOEN085 Vendread Revolution SR .60 1.25
EXFOEN086 F.A. Auto Navigator C .10 .20
EXFOEN087 F.A. Motorhome Transport C .10 .20
EXFOEN088 F.A. City Grand Prix C .10 .20
EXFOEN089 F.A. Test Run C .10 .20
EXFOEN090 Masterking Archfiend R .30 .75
EXFOEN091 Curious, the Lightsworn Dominion SR2.00 4.00
EXFOEN092 Gem-Knight Phantom Quartz SR .60 1.25
EXFOEN093 Steelswarm Origin R .30 .75
EXFOEN094 Isolde, Two Tales
of the Noble Knights UR 7.50 15.00
EXFOEN095 Qliphort Genius R .30 .75
EXFOEN096 Ritual Beast Ulti-Kimunfalcos R .30 .75
EXFOEN097 Zefra Metaltron SR .60 1.25
EXFOEN098 Heavymetalfoes Electrumite SCR 75.00 150.00
EXFOEN099 Scramble Egg C .10 .20

2018 Yu-Gi-Oh Flames of Destruction 1st Edition

FLODEN000 Kai-Den Kendo Spirit C .10 .20
FLODEN001 Protron C .10 .20
FLODEN002 Prompthorn C .10 .20
FLODEN003 Backup Operator R .25 .50
FLODEN004 Link Streamer C .10 .20
FLODEN005 Degrade Buster SR .60 1.25
FLODEN006 Trickstar Nightshade C .10 .20
FLODEN007 Trickstar Mandrake C .10 .20
FLODEN008 Trickstar Rhodode SR .60 1.25
FLODEN009 Gouki Octostretch C .10 .20
FLODEN010 Gouki Bearhug C .10 .20
FLODEN011 Defrag Dragon C .10 .20
FLODEN012 Background Dragon C .10 .20
FLODEN013 Tindangle Trinity C .10 .20
FLODEN014 Altergeist Multifaker UR 15.00 30.00
FLODEN015 Altergeist Pixiel C .10 .20
FLODEN016 Mekk-Knight Avram C .10 .20
FLODEN017 Knightmare Corruptor Iblee SCR 50.00 100.00
FLODEN018 World Legacy - World Lance R .25 .50
FLODEN019 Elementsaber Aina C .10 .20
FLODEN020 Elementsaber Makani UR 2.00 4.00
FLODEN021 Elementsaber Nalu SR .60 1.25
FLODEN022 Elementsaber Malo C .10 .20
FLODEN023 Elementsaber Lapauila SR .60 1.25
FLODEN024 Elementsaber Molehu UR 2.00 4.00
FLODEN025 Elementsaber Lapauila Mana SR .60 1.25
FLODEN026 Forceaurage the Elemental Lord SR .60 1.25
FLODEN027 Solar Batteryman C .10 .20
FLODEN028 Watch Cat C .10 .20
FLODEN029 Trancefamiliar C .10 .20
FLODEN030 Three Trolling Trolls C .10 .20
FLODEN031 Yajiro Invader C .10 .20
FLODEN032 Iron Dragon Tiamaton UR 2.00 4.00
FLODEN033 Ghost Belle & Haunted Mansion SCR50.00100.00
FLODEN034 Red Hared Hasty Horse SP .25 .50
FLODEN035 Boycotton SP .25 .50
FLODEN036 Topologic Trisbaena SCR 7.50 15.00
FLODEN037 Space Insulator C .10 .20
FLODEN038 Trickstar Bella Madonna UR 2.00 4.00
FLODEN039 Trickstar Bloom C .10 .20
FLODEN040 Trickstar Delfiendium R .25 .50
FLODEN041 Gouki The Master Ogre SR .60 1.25
FLODEN042 Altergeist Kidolga C .10 .20
FLODEN043 Knightmare Mermaid R .25 .50
FLODEN044 Knightmare Goblin UR 7.50 15.00
FLODEN045 Knightmare Cerberus SR .60 1.25
FLODEN046 Knightmare Phoenix SR .60 1.25
FLODEN047 Knightmare Unicorn SCR 25.00 50.00
FLODEN048 Knightmare Gryphon SCR 25.00 50.00
FLODEN049 Wind-Up Maintenance Zenmaicon SR.60 1.25
FLODEN050 Vampire Sucker SCR 6.00 12.00
FLODEN051 Fire Fighting Daruma Doll R .25 .50
FLODEN052 Greatfly R .25 .50
FLODEN053 Cybersal Cyclone C .10 .20
FLODEN054 Trickstar Light Arena R .25 .50
FLODEN055 Trickstar Bouquet R .25 .50
FLODEN056 Gouki Face Turn R .25 .50
FLODEN057 World Legacy's Corruption C .10 .20
FLODEN058 World Legacy Succession UR 2.00 4.00
FLODEN059 World Legacy's Nightmare C .10 .20
FLODEN060 Palace of the Elemental Lords UR 2.00 4.00
FLODEN061 Restoration of the Monarchs C .10 .20
FLODEN062 Sekka's Light R .25 .50
FLODEN063 Link Bound SR .60 1.25
FLODEN064 Staring Contest C .10 .20
FLODEN065 Called by the Grave C .50 1.00
FLODEN066 Monster Reborn Reborn C .10 .20
FLODEN067 Limit Code C .10 .20
FLODEN068 Red Reboot SR .60 1.25
FLODEN069 Gergonne's End C .10 .20
FLODEN070 Altergeist Emulatelf C .10 .20
FLODEN071 World Legacy Awakens R .25 .50
FLODEN072 World Legacy Struggle R .25 .50
FLODEN073 World Legacy's Sorrow SR .60 1.25
FLODEN074 Elemental Training UR 2.00 4.00
FLODEN075 The Sanctified Darklord R .25 .50
FLODEN076 Network Trap Hole UR 2.00 4.00
FLODEN077 Infinite Impermanence SCR 75.00 150.00
FLODEN078 Heartless Drop Off R .25 .50
FLODEN079 Mamemaki SP .25 .50
FLODEN080 Waking the Dragon SP 1.50 3.00
FLODEN081 Super Team Buddy Force Unite! SCR2.00 4.00
FLODEN082 Revendread Executor R .25 .50
FLODEN083 Vendread Anima R .25 .50
FLODEN084 Revendread Evolution C .10 .20
FLODEN085 Vendread Nightmare C .10 .20
FLODEN086 Vendread Daybreak C .10 .20
FLODEN087 F.A. Dark Dragster R .25 .50
FLODEN088 F.A. Dawn Dragster R .25 .50
FLODEN089 F.A. Winners R .25 .50
FLODEN090 F.A. Dead Heat C .10 .20
FLODEN091 F.A. Overheat R .25 .50
FLODEN092 Crystal Master C .10 .20
FLODEN093 Crystal Keeper C .10 .20
FLODEN094 Flower Cardian Moonflowerviewing C.10 .20
FLODEN095 Shaddoll Construct C .10 .20
FLODEN096 Inzektor Picofalena C .10 .20
FLODEN097 Madolche Fresh Sistart C .10 .20
FLODEN098 Rainbow Refraction SR .60 1.25
FLODEN099 Crystal Conclave C .10 .20

2018 Yu-Gi-Oh Hidden Summoners 1st Edition

HISUEN001 Matriarch of Nephthys SR .12 .25
HISUEN002 Disciple of Nephthys SCR .50 1.00
HISUEN003 Chronicler of Nephthys SR .12 .25
HISUEN004 Defender of Nephthys SR .12 .25
HISUEN005 Devotee of Nephthys SCR .30 .75
HISUEN006 Cerulean Sacred
Phoenix of Nephthys SCR 1.25 2.50
HISUEN007 Nephthys, the Sacred Preserver SCR1.25 2.50
HISUEN008 Nephthys, the Sacred Flame SCR .50 1.00
HISUEN009 Rebirth of Nephthys SR .12 .25
HISUEN010 Last Hope of Nephthys SR .12 .25
HISUEN011 Awakening of Nephthys SR .12 .25
HISUEN012 Sacred Phoenix of Nephthys SR .12 .25
HISUEN013 Hand of Nephthys SR .12 .25
HISUEN014 Prank-Kids Fansies SR .25 .50
HISUEN015 Prank-Kids Lampsies SR .25 .50
HISUEN016 Prank-Kids Dropsies SR .25 .50
HISUEN017 Prank-Kids Rocket Ride SR .25 .50
HISUEN018 Prank-Kids Weather Washer SR .20 .40
HISUEN019 Prank-Kids Battle Butler SCR 1.25 2.50
HISUEN020 Prank-Kids Dodo-Doodle-Doo SCR5.00 10.00
HISUEN021 Prank-Kids Bow-Wow-Bark SR .30 .75
HISUEN022 Prank-Kids Rip-Roarin-Roaster SCR2.50 5.00
HISUEN023 Prank-Kids Place SCR 15.00 30.00
HISUEN024 Prank-Kids Pranks SR .75 1.50
HISUEN025 Prank-Kids Pandemonium SR .25 .50
HISUEN026 Prank-Kids Plan SR .20 .40
HISUEN027 Dakki, the Graceful Mayakashi SCR1.25 2.50
HISUEN028 Tsukahagi, the
Poisonous Mayakashi SR .12 .25
HISUEN029 Hajun, the Winged Mayakashi SCR 1.25 2.50
HISUEN030 Shafu, the Wheeled Mayakashi SCR .50 1.00
HISUEN031 Yasha, the Skeletal Mayakashi SR .12 .25
HISUEN032 Oboro-Guruma,
the Wheeled Mayakashi SCR .30 .75
HISUEN033 Tsuchigumo, the
Poisonous Mayakashi SCR .30 .75
HISUEN034 Tengu, the Winged Mayakashi SCR .50 1.00
HISUEN035 Yoko, the Graceful Mayakashi SCR 1.00 2.00
HISUEN036 Gashadokuro,
the Skeletal Mayakashi SCR 1.50 3.00
HISUEN037 Yuki-Onna, the Ice Mayakashi SCR 1.25 2.50
HISUEN038 Mayakashi Return SCR 1.25 2.50
HISUEN039 Mayakashi Metamorphosis SR .12 .25
HISUEN040 Night's End Sorcerer SR .12 .25
HISUEN041 Shiranui Spectralsword SR .12 .25
HISUEN042 Preparation of Rites SR .12 .25
HISUEN043 Ultra Polymerization SR .12 .25
HISUEN044 De-Synchro SR .12 .25
HISUEN045 Phoenix Wing Wind Blast SR .12 .25
HISUEN046 Thunder Dragon SR .20 .40
HISUEN047 Manju of the Ten Thousand Hands SR2.00 4.00
HISUEN048 Shiranui Spiritmaster SR .20 .40
HISUEN049 Shiranui Samurai SR .12 .25
HISUEN050 Tatsunoko SR .12 .25
HISUEN051 Gold Sarcophagus SCR 2.00 4.00
HISUEN052 Fulfillment of the Contract SR .12 .25
HISUEN053 Re-Fusion SR .12 .25
HISUEN054 Ritual Foregone SR .12 .25
HISUEN055 Onslaught of the Fire Kings SR .12 .25
HISUEN056 Circle of the Fire Kings SR .12 .25
HISUEN057 Flash Fusion SR .12 .25
HISUEN058 Fusion Recycling Plant SR .20 .40
HISUEN059 Rivalry of Warlords SR 2.50 5.00
HISUEN060 Gozen Match SR 2.50 5.00

2018 Yu-Gi-Oh Legendary Collection Kaiba Mega Pack 1st Edition

LCKC-EN001 Blue-Eyes Wt.Dragon LOB ART UR2.00 4.00
LCKC-EN001 Blue-Eyes Wt.Dragon SDK ART UR2.00 4.00
LCKC-EN001 Blue-Eyes Wt.
Dragon WORLD ART UR 2.00 4.00
LCKC-EN001 Blue-Eyes Wt.Dragon TABLE ART UR2.00 4.00
LCKC-EN002 La Jinn Mystical
Genie of the Lamp UR 2.00 4.00
LCKC-EN003 Vorse Raider UR 2.00 4.00
LCKC-EN004 Judge Man UR 2.00 4.00
LCKC-EN005 X-Head Cannon UR 2.00 4.00
LCKC-EN006 Y-Dragon Head UR 2.00 4.00
LCKC-EN007 Z-Metal Tank UR 2.00 4.00
LCKC-EN008 Blue-Eyes Shining Dragon SCR 3.00 6.00
LCKC-EN009 Kaibaman UR 2.00 4.00
LCKC-EN010 The White Stone of Legend SCR 3.00 6.00
LCKC-EN011 The White Stone of Ancients SCR 3.00 6.00
LCKC-EN012 Maiden with Eyes of Blue SCR 3.00 6.00
LCKC-EN013 Protector with Eyes of Blue UR 2.00 4.00
LCKC-EN014 Master with Eyes of Blue UR 2.00 4.00
LCKC-EN015 Sage with Eyes of Blue SCR 3.00 6.00
LCKC-EN016 Priestess with Eyes of Blue SCR 3.00 6.00
LCKC-EN017 Rider of the Storm Winds UR 2.00 4.00
LCKC-EN018 Dragon Spirit of White SCR 3.00 6.00
LCKC-EN019 A-Assault Core SCR 3.00 6.00
LCKC-EN020 B-Buster Drake SCR 3.00 6.00
LCKC-EN021 C-Crush Wyvern SCR 3.00 6.00
LCKC-EN022 Heavy Mech Support Platform UR2.00 4.00
LCKC-EN023 Heavy Mech Support Armor UR 2.00 4.00
LCKC-EN024 Vampire Lord UR 2.00 4.00
LCKC-EN025 Burst Stream of Destruction SCR 3.00 6.00
LCKC-EN026 Polymerization SCR 3.00 6.00
LCKC-EN027 The Flute of Summoning Dragon UR2.00 4.00
LCKC-EN028 The Melody
of Awakening Dragon SCR 3.00 6.00
LCKC-EN029 Card of Demise SCR 15.00 30.00
LCKC-EN030 Fiend's Sanctuary SCR 3.00 6.00
LCKC-EN031 Majesty with Eyes of Blue SCR 3.00 6.00
LCKC-EN032 Enemy Controller SCR 3.00 6.00
LCKC-EN033 Ring of Defense UR 2.00 4.00
LCKC-EN034 Silver's Cry SCR 3.00 6.00
LCKC-EN035 Beacon of White SCR 3.00 6.00
LCKC-EN036 Mausoleum of White UR 2.00 4.00
LCKC-EN037 The Fang of Critias UR 2.00 4.00
LCKC-EN038 Soul Exchange UR 2.00 4.00
LCKC-EN039 Ancient Rules SCR 3.00 6.00
LCKC-EN040 Cost Down SCR 3.00 6.00
LCKC-EN041 Neutron Blast SCR 3.00 6.00
LCKC-EN042 Lullaby of Obedience SCR 3.00 6.00
LCKC-EN043 Shrink UR 2.00 4.00
LCKC-EN044 De-Fusion SCR 3.00 6.00
LCKC-EN045 Spell Reproduction UR 2.00 4.00
LCKC-EN046 Crush Card Virus (Original Art) UR4.00 8.00

LCKC-EN046 Crush Card Virus (Alt Art) UR 4.00 8.00
LCKC-EN047 Deck Devastation Virus UR 2.00 4.00
LCKC-EN048 Eradicator Epidemic Virus UR 4.00 8.00
LCKC-EN049 Full Force Virus UR 2.00 4.00
LCKC-EN050 Ring of Destruction UR 2.00 4.00
LCKC-EN051 Castle of Dragon Souls UR 2.00 4.00
LCKC-EN052 Interdimensional
Matter Transporter SCR 3.00 6.00
LCKC-EN053 Mirror Force UR 2.00 4.00
LCKC-EN054 Tyrant Wing UR 2.00 4.00
LCKC-EN055 Cloning UR 2.00 4.00
LCKC-EN056 Virus Cannon UR 2.00 4.00
LCKC-EN057 Blue-Eyes Ultimate Dragon SCR 3.00 6.00
LCKC-EN058 Blue-Eyes Twin Burst Dragon UR 2.00 4.00
LCKC-EN059 ABC-Dragon Buster SCR 3.00 6.00
LCKC-EN060 VW-Tiger Catapult UR 2.00 4.00
LCKC-EN061 XYZ-Dragon Cannon UR 2.00 4.00
LCKC-EN062 Mirror Force Dragon UR 2.00 4.00
LCKC-EN063 Tyrant Burst Dragon UR 2.00 4.00
LCKC-EN064 Doom Virus Dragon UR 2.00 4.00
LCKC-EN065 Dragon Master Knight SCR 3.00 6.00
LCKC-EN066 Azure-Eyes Silver Dragon SCR 3.00 6.00
LCKC-EN067 Thunder Dragon UR 2.00 4.00
LCKC-EN068 Dark Armed Dragon SCR 3.00 6.00
LCKC-EN069 Tiger Dragon UR 2.00 4.00
LCKC-EN070 Ancient Fairy Dragon UR 4.00 8.00
LCKC-EN071 Beelze of the Diabolic Dragons SCR10.00 20.00
LCKC-EN072 Dragon Ravine SCR 3.00 6.00
LCKC-EN073 Dragonic Tactics SCR 3.00 6.00
LCKC-EN074 Return of the Dragon Lords SCR 3.00 6.00
LCKC-EN075 Dragon Shrine SCR 3.00 6.00
LCKC-EN076 Trade-In SCR 3.00 6.00
LCKC-EN077 Droll & Lock Bird UR 10.00 20.00
LCKC-EN078 Ghost Ogre & Snow Rabbit UR 10.00 20.00
LCKC-EN079 Ghost Reaper & Winter Cherries UR4.00 8.00
LCKC-EN080 Ash Blossom & Joyous Spring UR50.00 100.00
LCKC-EN081 D.D. Crow UR 2.00 4.00
LCKC-EN082 V-Tiger Jet UR 2.00 4.00
LCKC-EN083 W-Wing Catapult UR 2.00 4.00
LCKC-EN084 Dragunity Dux UR 2.00 4.00
LCKC-EN085 Dragunity Legionnaire UR 2.00 4.00
LCKC-EN086 Dragunity Phalanx UR 2.00 4.00
LCKC-EN087 Number S39:
Utopia the Lightning SCR 10.00 20.00
LCKC-EN088 Raigeki UR 20.00 40.00
LCKC-EN089 Fusion Sage UR 2.00 4.00
LCKC-EN090 Terraforming SCR 7.50 15.00
LCKC-EN091 Double Summon UR 6.00 12.00
LCKC-EN092 Cards of Consonance SCR 3.00 6.00
LCKC-EN093 The Monarchs Stormforth UR 2.00 4.00
LCKC-EN094 Chain Disappearance SCR 3.00 6.00
LCKC-EN095 Fiendish Chain UR 2.00 4.00
LCKC-EN096 Parrot Dragon UR 2.00 4.00
LCKC-EN097 Giant Red Seasnake UR 2.00 4.00
LCKC-EN098 Mikazukinoyaiba UR 2.00 4.00
LCKC-EN099 Warrior Elimination UR 2.00 4.00
LCKC-EN100 Exile of the Wicked UR 2.00 4.00
LCKC-EN101 Delinquent Duo SCR 3.00 6.00
LCKC-EN102 White Hole SCR 3.00 6.00
LCKC-EN103 Call of the Grave SCR 3.00 6.00
LCKC-EN104 Anti Raigeki SCR 3.00 6.00
LCKC-EN105 Just Desserts UR 2.00 4.00
LCKC-EN106 Goddess of Sweet Revenge SCR 3.00 6.00
LCKC-EN107 The King of D. SCR 3.00 6.00
LCKC-EN108 Destruction Dragon SCR 3.00 6.00
LCKC-EN109 Dragon Revival Rhapsody SCR 3.00 6.00
LCKC-EN110 Loop of Destruction SCR 3.00 6.00

2018 Yu-Gi-Oh Legendary Duelists Ancient Millennium 1st Edition

LED2-EN000 Relinquished C .15 .30
LED2-EN001 Millennium-Eyes Illusionist UR 15.00 30.00
LED2-EN002 Illusionist Faceless Magician R .30 .75
LED2-EN003 Millennium-Eyes Restrict UR 15.00 30.00
LED2-EN004 Relinquished Fusion UR 15.00 30.00
LED2-EN005 Thousand-Eyes Restrict C .15 .30
LED2-EN006 Black Illusion Ritual C .15 .30
LED2-EN007 Parasite Paranoid R .30 .75
LED2-EN008 Metamorphosed Insect Queen SR 2.50 5.00
LED2-EN009 Cocoon of Ultra Evolution UR 15.00 30.00
LED2-EN010 Corrosive Scales R .30 .75
LED2-EN011 Pinch Hopper C .15 .30
LED2-EN012 Insect Queen C .15 .30
LED2-EN013 Perfectly Ultimate Great Moth C .15 .30
LED2-EN014 BM-4 Blast Spider R .30 .75
LED2-EN015 Desperado Barrel Dragon UR 15.00 30.00
LED2-EN016 Heavy Metal Raiders SR .15 .30
LED2-EN017 Proton Blast SR 2.50 5.00
LED2-EN018 Blast Sphere C .15 .30
LED2-EN019 Barrel Dragon C .15 .30
LED2-EN020 Time Machine C .15 .30
LED2-EN021 Armed Dragon Catapult Cannon SR2.50 5.00
LED2-EN022 Ojamassimilation R .30 .75
LED2-EN023 Ojamatch R .30 .75
LED2-EN024 Ojama Pajama R .30 .75
LED2-EN025 Armed Dragon LV3 C .15 .30
LED2-EN026 Armed Dragon LV5 C .15 .30
LED2-EN027 Armed Dragon LV7 C .15 .30
LED2-EN028 VWXYZ-Dragon Catapult Cannon C.15 .30
LED2-EN029 Ojamagic C .15 .30
LED2-EN030 Ancient Gear Frame R .30 .75
LED2-EN031 Ancient Gear Megaton Golem SR 2.50 5.00
LED2-EN032 Ancient Gear Fusion UR 15.00 30.00
LED2-EN033 Corss-Dimensional Duel SR 2.50 5.00
LED2-EN034 Ancient Gear Golem C .15 .30
LED2-EN035 Ancient Gear Golem-Ultimate Pound C.15 .30
LED2-EN036 Ultimate Ancient Gear Golem C .15 .30
LED2-EN037 Rainbow Overdragon SR 2.50 5.00
LED2-EN038 Rainbow Bridge UR 15.00 30.00
LED2-EN039 Crystal Bond UR 15.00 30.00
LED2-EN040 Ultimate Crystal Magic SR .15 .30
LED2-EN041 Crystal Beast Ruby Carbuncle C .15 .30
LED2-EN042 Crystal Beast Sapphire Pegasus C .15 .30
LED2-EN043 Rainbow Dragon C .15 .30
LED2-EN044 Crystal Release C .15 .30
LED2-EN045 Crystal Tree C .15 .30
LED2-EN046 Vortex Trooper C .15 .30
LED2-EN047 Panzer Dragon C .15 .30
LED2-EN048 Instant Fusion C .15 .30
LED2-EN049 Limiter Removal C .15 .30
LED2-EN050 Worm Bait C .15 .30
LED2-EN051 Mimicat R .30 .75
LED2-EN052 Toon Kingdom R .30 .75

2018 Yu-Gi-Oh Legendary Duelists White Dragon Abyss 1st Edition

LED3EN000 Blue-Eyes Chaos MAX Dragon UR 4.00 8.00
LED3EN001 Blue-Eyes Chaos Dragon UR 7.50 15.00
LED3EN002 Blue-Eyes Solid Dragon UR 1.25 2.50
LED3EN003 Bingo Machine, Go!!! UR 15.00 30.00
LED3EN004 Rage with Eyes of Blue SR 1.00 2.00
LED3EN005 The Ultimate
Creature of Destruction SR 3.00 6.00
LED3EN006 Blue-Eyes White Dragon C .60 1.25
LED3EN007 The White Stone of Legend C .30 .60
LED3EN008 Maiden with Eyes of Blue C .20 .40
LED3EN009 The Melody of Awakening Dragon C .75 1.50
LED3EN010 Dragon Shrine C .12 .25
LED3EN011 Chaos Form C .30 .75
LED3EN012 Cyber Eternity Dragon UR 2.50 5.00
LED3EN013 Cyber Pharos R .15 .30
LED3EN014 Cyberload Fusion SR .40 .80
LED3EN015 Super Strident Blaze R .12 .25
LED3EN016 Cybernetic Revolution SR .40 .80
LED3EN017 Cyber End Dragon C .10 .20
LED3EN018 Cyber Twin Dragon C .25 .50
LED3EN019 Chimeratech Rampage Dragon C .20 .40
LED3EN020 Cyber Dragon Drei C .12 .25
LED3EN021 Cyber Repair Plant C .10 .20
LED3EN022 Power Bond C .15 .30
LED3EN023 Blackwing Full Armor Master UR 1.50 3.00
LED3EN024 Blackwing -
Simoon the Poison Wind SR .50 1.00
LED3EN025 Blackwing - Auster the South Wind R.30 .75
LED3EN026 Glowing Crossbow R .10 .20
LED3EN027 Blackbird Close R .15 .30
LED3EN028 Black-Winged Dragon C .40 .80
LED3EN029 Blackwing - Bora the Spear C .30 .60
LED3EN030 Blackwing - Oroshi the Squall C .12 .25
LED3EN031 Blackwing - Zephyros the Elite C .15 .30
LED3EN032 Black Whirlwind C .40 .80
LED3EN033 Delta Crow - Anti Reverse C .12 .25
LED3EN034 Starliege Photon Blast Dragon UR .75 1.50
LED3EN035 Photon Vanisher R 1.25 2.50
LED3EN036 Photon Orbital UR 12.50 25.00
LED3EN037 Photon Hand UR .50 1.00
LED3EN038 Photon Change R .12 .25
LED3EN039 Galaxy-Eyes Photon Dragon SR 2.50 5.00
LED3EN040 Galaxy Knight SR .40 .80
LED3EN041 Photon Thrasher C .25 .50
LED3EN042 Photon Crusher C .12 .25
LED3EN043 Kuriphoton C .10 .20
LED3EN044 Accellight C .15 .30
LED3EN045 Abyss Actor - Mellow Madonna SR2.00 4.00
LED3EN046 Abyss Actor - Comic Relief R .12 .25
LED3EN047 Abyss Script - Romantic Terror R .12 .25
LED3EN048 Abyss Playhouse - Fantastic Theater R.12 .25
LED3EN049 Abyss Actors' Curtain Call C .07 .15
LED3EN050 Abyss Actor - Superstar C .12 .25
LED3EN051 Abyss Actor - Leading Lady C .10 .20
LED3EN052 Abyss Actor - Trendy Understudy C .07 .15
LED3EN053 Abyss Script - Opening Ceremony C.12 .25
LED3EN054 Abyss Script -
Rise of the Abyss King C .12 .25
LED3EN055 Abyss Actors Back Stage C .07 .15

2018 Yu-Gi-Oh Legendary Hero Aesir Deck

LEHDENB00 Gullveig of the Nordic Ascendant UR.30 .60
LEHDENB01 Tanngrisnir of the Nordic Beasts C .10 .20
LEHDENB01 Tanngrisnir of the Nordic Beasts UR.10 .20
LEHDENB02 Tanngnjostr of the Nordic Beasts C .10 .20
LEHDENB03 Garmr of the Nordic Beasts C .07 .15
LEHDENB04 Guldfaxe of the Nordic Beasts C .07 .15
LEHDENB05 Dverg of the Nordic Alfar C .07 .15
LEHDENB06 Ljosalf of the Nordic Alfar C .07 .15
LEHDENB07 Svartalf of the Nordic Alfar C .07 .15
LEHDENB08 Mara of the Nordic Alfar C .12 .25
LEHDENB09 Mimir of the Nordic Ascendant C .12 .25
LEHDENB10 Valkyrie of the Nordic Ascendant C .20 .40
LEHDENB11 Vanadis of the Nordic Ascendant C .40 .80
LEHDENB12 Tyr of the Nordic Champions C .07 .15
LEHDENB13 The Nordic Lights C .07 .15
LEHDENB14 Nordic Relic Draupnir C .07 .15
LEHDENB15 March Towards Ragnarok C .07 .15
LEHDENB16 Forbidden Chalice C .30 .75
LEHDENB17 Forbidden Lance C .30 .60
LEHDENB18 Forbidden Dress C .12 .25
LEHDENB19 Monster Reborn C .25 .50
LEHDENB20 Soul Charge C .17 .35
LEHDENB21 Dark Hole UR .50 1.00
LEHDENB22 Hey, Trunade! C .25 .50
LEHDENB23 Mystical Space Typhoon C 1.00 2.00
LEHDENB24 Gleipnir, the Fetters of Fenrir C .07 .15
LEHDENB25 Nordic Relic Brisingamen C .07 .15
LEHDENB26 Nordic Relic Laevateinn C .07 .15
LEHDENB27 Nordic Relic Gungnir C .07 .15
LEHDENB28 Nordic Relic Megingjord C .07 .15
LEHDENB29 Solemn Authority C .07 .15
LEHDENB30 Thor, Lord of the Aesir C .25 .50
LEHDENB31 Loki, Lord of the Aesir C .17 .35
LEHDENB32 Odin, Father of the Aesir C .30 .60
LEHDENB33 Leo, the Keeper of the Sacred Tree C.12 .25
LEHDENB34 Ascension Sky Dragon UR .17 .35
LEHDENB35 Beelzeus of the Diabolic Dragons C .12 .25
LEHDENB36 Beelze of the Diabolic Dragons C .60 1.25
LEHDENB37 Scrap Dragon C .12 .25
LEHDENB38 Coral Dragon UR 2.00 4.00

2018 Yu-Gi-Oh Legendary Hero Destiny Deck

LEHDENA00 Xtra HERO Dread Decimator UR 1.25 2.50
LEHDENA01 Destiny HERO - Dogma C .12 .25
LEHDENA02 Destiny HERO - Plasma C .17 .35
LEHDENA03 Destiny HERO - Dreadmaster C .12 .25
LEHDENA04 Destiny HERO - Malicious C .75 1.50
LEHDENA04 Destiny HERO - Malicious UR 1.50 3.00
LEHDENA05 Destiny HERO - Celestial C .25 .50
LEHDENA06 Destiny HERO - Diamond Dude C .10 .20
LEHDENA07 Destiny HERO - Dread Servant C .12 .25
LEHDENA08 Destiny HERO - Disk Commander UR.12 .25
LEHDENA09 Destiny HERO - Dark Angel C .30 .60
LEHDENA10 Destiny HERO - Dynatag C .30 .60
LEHDENA11 Destiny HERO - Drilldark C .12 .25
LEHDENA12 Destiny HERO - Decider C .20 .40
LEHDENA13 Destiny HERO - Dreamer C .07 .15
LEHDENA14 D-Cubed C .07 .15
LEHDENA15 Elemental HERO Shadow Mist C 2.00 4.00
LEHDENA16 Elemental HERO Blazeman C .40 .80
LEHDENA17 Destiny Draw C .12 .25
LEHDENA17 Destiny Draw UR .25 .50
LEHDENA18 Over Destiny C .07 .15
LEHDENA19 Clock Tower Prison C .12 .25
LEHDENA20 Dark City C .07 .15
LEHDENA21 Mask Change C .25 .50
LEHDENA22 Polymerization C .75 1.50
LEHDENA23 Monster Reborn C .25 .50
LEHDENA24 Magical Stone Excavation C .12 .25
LEHDENA25 Terraforming C .20 .40
LEHDENA26 A Feather of the Phoenix C .12 .25
LEHDENA27 Destiny Signal C .07 .15
LEHDENA28 D-Time C .10 .20
LEHDENA29 Eternal Dread C .12 .25
LEHDENA30 D-Fusion C .07 .15
LEHDENA31 Destiny End Dragoon C .10 .20
LEHDENA32 Destiny HERO - Dusktopia C .10 .20
LEHDENA33 Destiny HERO - Dystopia C .20 .40
LEHDENA34 Destiny HERO - Dangerous C .12 .25
LEHDENA35 Masked HERO Dark Law C .75 1.50
LEHDENA36 Masked HERO Anki C .20 .40
LEHDENA37 Xtra HERO Wonder Driver UR 3.00 6.00

2018 Yu-Gi-Oh Legendary Hero Phantom Knights Deck

LEHDENC00 The Phantom Knights
of Rusty Bardiche UR .30 .75
LEHDENC01 The Phantom Knights
of Ancient Cloak C .12 .25
LEHDENC02 The Phantom Knights
of Silent Boots C .12 .25
LEHDENC03 The Phantom Knights
of Ragged Gloves C .07 .15
LEHDENC04 The Phantom Knights
of Cloven Helm C .07 .15
LEHDENC05 The Phantom
Knights of Fragile Armor C .07 .15
LEHDENC06 Armageddon Knight C .12 .25
LEHDENC07 Blue Mountain Butterspy C .12 .25
LEHDENC08 Rescue Ferret C .12 .25
LEHDENC09 Junk Forward C .30 .75
LEHDENC10 Kagemucha Knight C .10 .20
LEHDENC11 Cockadoodledoo C .07 .15
LEHDENC12 Effect Veiler C 1.25 2.50
LEHDENC13 The Phantom
Knights' Rank-Up-Magic Launch C .12 .25
LEHDENC14 Phantom Knights' Spear C .07 .15
LEHDENC15 Dark Hole C .40 .80
LEHDENC16 Monster Reborn C .20 .40
LEHDENC17 Foolish Burial C .75 1.50
LEHDENC18 Reinforcement of the Army C .20 .40
LEHDENC19 Dark Eruption C .07 .15
LEHDENC20 Twin Twisters UR .60 1.25
LEHDENC21 Phantom Knights' Fog Blade C .75 1.50
LEHDENC22 Phantom Knights' Sword C .12 .25
LEHDENC23 Phantom Knights' Wing C .12 .25
LEHDENC24 The Phantom Knights
of Shadow Veil C .07 .15
LEHDENC25 The Phantom Knights
of Shade Brigandine C .40 .80
LEHDENC26 The Phantom Knights
of Dark Gauntlets C .07 .15
LEHDENC27 The Phantom Knights
of Tomb Shield C .07 .15
LEHDENC28 The Phantom Knights
of Lost Vambrace C .07 .15
LEHDENC29 The Phantom Knights
of Wrong Magnetring C .07 .15
LEHDENC30 The Phantom Knights
of Mist Claws UR .12 .25
LEHDENC31 The Phantom Knights
of Break Sword UR .20 .40
LEHDENC32 The Phantom Knights
of Cursed Javelin C .12 .25
LEHDENC33 Dark Rebellion Xyz Dragon C .30 .75
LEHDENC34 Dark Requiem Xyz Dragon C .20 .40
LEHDENC35 Evilswarm Nightmare C .40 .80
LEHDENC36 Evilswarm Thanatos C .07 .15
LEHDENC37 Number 86: Heroic Champion -
Rhongomyniad UR .25 .50
LEHDENC38 Leviair the Sea Dragon C .75 1.50
LEHDENC39 Dante, Traveler of the Burning Abyss C.40 .80

2018 Yu-Gi-Oh Mega Tin Mega Pack 1st Edition

MP18-EN001 Speedroid Skull Marbles C .10 .20
MP18-EN002 Speedroid Maliciousmagnet C .10 .20
MP18-EN003 Double Resonator C .10 .20
MP18-EN004 Majesty Maiden True Dracocaster UR.60 1.25
MP18-EN005 Mariamne, the True Dracophoenix UR.10 .20
MP18-EN006 Digital Bug LEDybug C .10 .20
MP18-EN007 Ariel, Priestess of the Nekroz R .10 .20
MP18-EN008 Pendulumucho SR .10 .20
MP18-EN009 Baobaboon C .10 .20
MP18-EN010 Familiar-Possessed - Lyna C .10 .20
MP18-EN011 Supreme King Z-ARC SCR 1.00 2.00
MP18-EN012 Magician's Right Hand C .10 .20
MP18-EN013 Magician's Left Hand C .10 .20
MP18-EN014 Ultra Polymerization SCR .50 1.00
MP18-EN015 Dragonic Diagram SCR 2.00 4.00
MP18-EN016 True Draco Heritage UR 1.50 3.00
MP18-EN017 Disciples of the True Dracophoenix C.10 .20
MP18-EN018 Bug Signal C .10 .20
MP18-EN019 Set Rotation C .10 .20
MP18-EN020 Break Away C .10 .20
MP18-EN021 Phantom Knights of Lost Vambrace C.10 .20
MP18-EN022 Phantom Knights
of Wrong Magnetring C .10 .20
MP18-EN023 True Draco Apocalypse C .10 .20
MP18-EN024 Waterfall of Dragon Souls SR .10 .20
MP18-EN025 Kaiser Sea Snake C .10 .20
MP18-EN026 Sylvan Princessprite SR .10 .20
MP18-EN027 Artifact Vajra C .10 .20
MP18-EN028 Mild Turkey C .10 .20
MP18-EN029 Ghost Beef C .10 .20
MP18-EN030 Onikuji C .10 .20
MP18-EN031 Backup Secretary C .10 .20
MP18-EN032 Stack Reviver C .10 .20
MP18-EN033 Launcher Commander C .10 .20
MP18-EN034 Salvagent Driver UR .10 .20
MP18-EN035 Trickstar Lilybell R .10 .20
MP18-EN036 Trickstar Lycoris SR .10 .20
MP18-EN037 Trickstar Candina UR 1.50 3.00
MP18-EN038 Gouki Twistcobra SR .10 .20
MP18-EN039 Gouki Suprex R .10 .20
MP18-EN040 Gouki Riscorpio R .10 .20
MP18-EN041 Hack Worm C .10 .20
MP18-EN042 Jack Wyvern C .10 .20
MP18-EN043 Cracking Dragon SR .10 .20
MP18-EN044 Crowned by the World Chalice C .10 .20
MP18-EN045 Chosen by the World Chalice C .10 .20
MP18-EN046 Beckoned by the World Chalice C .10 .20
MP18-EN047 World Chalice Guardragon UR .25 .50
MP18-EN048 Lee the World Chalice Fairy UR .25 .50
MP18-EN049 World Legacy - World Chalice R .10 .20
MP18-EN050 Jain, Twilightsworn General C .10 .20
MP18-EN051 Lyla, Twilightsworn Enchantress SR.10 .20
MP18-EN052 Lumina, Twilightsworn Shaman SCR.60 1.25
MP18-EN053 Ryko, Twilightsworn Fighter R .10 .20
MP18-EN054 Rescue Ferret SCR .60 1.25
MP18-EN055 Motivating Captain R .10 .20
MP18-EN056 Treasure Panda C .10 .20
MP18-EN057 Zombina C .10 .20
MP18-EN058 Re: EX R .10 .20
MP18-EN059 Orbital Hydralander C .10 .20
MP18-EN060 The Ascended of Thunder C .10 .20
MP18-EN061 Parry Knights C .10 .20
MP18-EN062 Firewall Dragon SCR 10.00 20.00
MP18-EN063 Trickstar Holly Angel UR .10 .20
MP18-EN064 Gouki The Great Ogre SR .10 .20
MP18-EN065 Topologic Bomber Dragon SCR 7.50 15.00
MP18-EN066 Imduk the World Chalice Dragon R.10 .20
MP18-EN067 Ib the World Chalice Priestess SR .10 .20
MP18-EN068 Ningirsu the
World Chalice Warrior SCR 1.50 3.00
MP18-EN069 Trickstar Light Stage UR 1.50 3.00
MP18-EN070 Gouki Re-Match SR .10 .20
MP18-EN071 Air Cracking Storm C .10 .20
MP18-EN072 Smile Universe C .10 .20
MP18-EN073 World Legacy Discovery R .10 .20
MP18-EN074 World Legacy's Heart C .10 .20
MP18-EN075 Emerging
Emergency Rescute Rescue C .10 .20
MP18-EN076 Spellbook of Knowledge UR 5.00 10.00
MP18-EN077 Gravity Lash C .10 .20
MP18-EN078 Defense Zone C .10 .20
MP18-EN079 Three Strikes Barrier C .10 .20
MP18-EN080 Pulse Mines C .10 .20
MP18-EN081 World Legacy Landmark C .10 .20
MP18-EN082 Twilight Eraser R .10 .20
MP18-EN083 Twilight Cloth C .10 .20
MP18-EN084 Dark World Brainwashing C .10 .20
MP18-EN085 Break Off Trap Hole SR .10 .20
MP18-EN086 Heavy Storm Duster SR .20 .40
MP18-EN087 Back to the Front R .60 1.25
MP18-EN088 Recall R .10 .20
MP18-EN089 Samurai Skull C .10 .20
MP18-EN090 Vendread Reorigin SCR .25 .50
MP18-EN091 F.A. Sonic Meister C .10 .20
MP18-EN092 F.A. Hang On Mach C .10 .20
MP18-EN093 F.A. Circuit Grand Prix C .10 .20
MP18-EN094 F.A. Downforce C .10 .20
MP18-EN095 Junk Breaker C .10 .20
MP18-EN096 Infernity Patriarch C .10 .20
MP18-EN097 Gogogo Aristera & Dexia C .10 .20
MP18-EN098 Wicked Acolyte Chilam Sabak C .10 .20
MP18-EN099 Galaxy Worm C .10 .20
MP18-EN100 Destiny HERO - Dangerous C .10 .20
MP18-EN101 Abyss Actor - Trendy Understudy C.10 .20
MP18-EN102 Speedroid Passinglider C .10 .20
MP18-EN103 Ancient Gear Golem -
Ultimate Pound C .10 .20
MP18-EN104 Defect Compiler C .10 .20
MP18-EN105 Capacitor Stalker C .10 .20
MP18-EN106 Link Infra-Flier C .10 .20
MP18-EN107 Trickstar Narkissus R .10 .20
MP18-EN108 Gouki Headbatt C .10 .20
MP18-EN109 Sniffer Dragon C .10 .20
MP18-EN110 Anesthrokket Dragon C .10 .20
MP18-EN111 Autorokket Dragon SR .10 .20
MP18-EN112 Magnarokket Dragon UR .25 .50
MP18-EN113 Altergeist Marionetter UR .60 1.25
MP18-EN114 Altergeist Silquitous SR .10 .20
MP18-EN115 Altergeist Meluseek UR 1.50 3.00
MP18-EN116 Altergeist Kunquery C .10 .20
MP18-EN117 World Legacy - World Armor R .10 .20
MP18-EN118 Mermail Abyssnerei C .10 .20
MP18-EN119 Mecha Phantom Beast Raiten C .10 .20
MP18-EN120 The Accumulator C .10 .20
MP18-EN121 Soldier Dragons C .10 .20
MP18-EN122 Duck Dummy C .10 .20
MP18-EN123 Leng Ling C .10 .20
MP18-EN124 Self-Destruct Ant C .10 .20
MP18-EN125 Amano-Iwato C .10 .20
MP18-EN126 Fantastic Striborg R .10 .20
MP18-EN127 Destrudo the Lost Dragon's Frisson R.30 .75
MP18-EN128 Elemental Grace Doriado R .10 .20
MP18-EN129 Nimble Beaver C .10 .20
MP18-EN130 Muscle Medic C .10 .20
MP18-EN131 Borreload Dragon SCR 15.00 30.00
MP18-EN132 Trickstar Black Catbat UR .10 .20
MP18-EN133 Gouki Thunder Ogre UR .10 .20

MP18-EN134 Twin Triangle Dragon R .10 .20
MP18-EN135 Altergeist Primebanshee UR .10 .20
MP18-EN136 Security Block R .10 .20
MP18-EN137 Dragonoid Generator R .10 .20
MP18-EN138 Squib Draw SCR .10 .20
MP18-EN139 Quick Launch SCR .50 1.00
MP18-EN140 World Legacy Clash C .10 .20
MP18-EN141 One-Time Passcode R .10 .20
MP18-EN142 Arrivalrivals UR .15 .30
MP18-EN143 Overdone Burial SCR .10 .20
MP18-EN144 Temple of the Mind's Eye C .10 .20
MP18-EN145 Backup Squad R .10 .20
MP18-EN146 Burning Bamboo Sword C .10 .20
MP18-EN147 Cyberse Beacon C .10 .20
MP18-EN148 Link Restart C .10 .20
MP18-EN149 Remote Rebirth C .10 .20
MP18-EN150 Altergeist Camouflage R .10 .20
MP18-EN151 Altergeist Protocol SR .10 .20
MP18-EN152 Personal Spoofing R .10 .20
MP18-EN153 World Legacy Pawns C .10 .20
MP18-EN154 Evenly Matched SCR 20.00 40.00
MP18-EN155 Fuse Line SCR .10 .20
MP18-EN156 Broken Line UR .10 .20
MP18-EN157 Ojama Duo C .10 .20
MP18-EN158 Vendread Chimera SCR .25 .50
MP18-EN159 F.A. Whip Crosser C .10 .20
MP18-EN160 F.A. Turbo Charger C .10 .20
MP18-EN161 F.A. Off-Road Grand Prix C .10 .20
MP18-EN162 F.A. Pit Stop C .10 .20
MP18-EN163 Lunalight Crimson Fox C .10 .20
MP18-EN164 Lunalight Kaleido Chick C .10 .20
MP18-EN165 Amazoness Spy C .10 .20
MP18-EN166 Amazoness Pet Liger C .10 .20
MP18-EN167 Amazoness Empress C .10 .20
MP18-EN168 Yoko-Zuna Sumo Spirit C .10 .20
MP18-EN169 Zombino C .10 .20
MP18-EN170 Lockout Gardna C .10 .20
MP18-EN171 Striping Partner C .10 .20
MP18-EN172 Flick Clown C .10 .20
MP18-EN173 Bitrooper C .10 .20
MP18-EN174 Linkbelt Wall Dragon C .10 .20
MP18-EN175 Shelrokket Dragon R .10 .20
MP18-EN176 Metalrokket Dragon R .10 .20
MP18-EN177 Mekk-Knight Blue Sky SCR 6.00 12.00
MP18-EN178 Mekk-Knight Green Horizon C .10 .20
MP18-EN179 Mekk-Knight Orange Sunset C .10 .20
MP18-EN180 Mekk-Knight Yellow Star R .10 .20
MP18-EN181 Mekk-Knight Red Moon R .10 .20
MP18-EN182 Mekk-Knight Indigo Eclipse SR .10 .20
MP18-EN183 Mekk-Knight Purple Nightfall SCR 6.00 12.00
MP18-EN184 World Legacy - World Shield C .10 .20
MP18-EN185 Mythical Beast Master Cerberus SCR 3.00 6.00
MP18-EN186 Artifact Mjollnir C .10 .20
MP18-EN187 Grappler Angler C .10 .20
MP18-EN188 Mahjong Munia Maidens C .10 .20
MP18-EN189 D.D. Seeker C .10 .20
MP18-EN190 Ghost Bird of Bewitchment R .10 .20
MP18-EN191 Desmanian Devil R .10 .20
MP18-EN192 Wattkinetic Puppeteer C .10 .20
MP18-EN193 Inspector Boarder SCR 2.00 4.00
MP18-EN194 Overtex Qoatlus SR .10 .20
MP18-EN195 Contact C C .10 .20
MP18-EN196 Underclock Taker C .10 .20
MP18-EN197 Flame Administrator C .10 .20
MP18-EN198 Recovery Sorcerer C .10 .20
MP18-EN199 Security Block C .10 .20
MP18-EN200 Altergeist Hexstia SR .10 .20
MP18-EN201 Mekk-Knight Spectrum Supreme UR .10 .20
MP18-EN202 Saryuja Skull Dread SCR 15.00 30.00
MP18-EN203 Link Hole C .10 .20
MP18-EN204 Fire Prison C .10 .20
MP18-EN205 World Legacy Scars R .10 .20
MP18-EN206 World Legacy Key R .10 .20
MP18-EN207 Glory of the Noble Knights R .10 .20
MP18-EN208 Power of the Guardians SR .10 .20
MP18-EN209 Pendulum Paradox SCR .10 .20
MP18-EN210 Hey, Trunade! SCR 1.50 3.00
MP18-EN211 Column Switch C .10 .20
MP18-EN212 Trading Places C .10 .20
MP18-EN213 Parallel Port Armor C .10 .20
MP18-EN214 Cynet Refresh C .10 .20
MP18-EN215 Borrel Cooling C .10 .20
MP18-EN216 Altergeist Manifestation SR .10 .20
MP18-EN217 World Legacy Whispers R .10 .20
MP18-EN218 World Legacy's Secret UR .60 1.25
MP18-EN219 Call of the Archfiend C .10 .20
MP18-EN220 Dai Dance C .10 .20
MP18-EN221 Showdown...
Secret Sense Scroll Techniques C .10 .20
MP18-EN222 Parthian Shot C .10 .20
MP18-EN223 Oops! C .10 .20
MP18-EN224 Kuro-Obi Karate Spirit C .10 .20
MP18-EN225 F.A. Auto Navigator C .10 .20
MP18-EN226 F.A. Motorhome Transport C .10 .20
MP18-EN227 F.A. City Grand Prix C .10 .20
MP18-EN228 F.A. Test Run C .10 .20
MP18-EN229 Heavymetalfoes Electrumite SCR 6.00 12.00
MP18-EN230 Scramble Egg C .10 .20
MP18-EN231 Ruin, Queen of Oblivion C .75 1.50
MP18-EN232 Demise, King of Armageddon C .10 .20
MP18-EN233 End of the World C .10 .20

2018 Yu-Gi-Oh OTS Tournament Pack 7

OP07EN001 Herald of Orange Light UTR 60.00 125.00
OP07EN002 Link Spider UTR 25.00 50.00
OP07EN003 Cosmic Cyclone UTR 60.00 125.00
OP07EN004 Royal Magical Library SR 1.25 2.50
OP07EN005 SPYRAL Tough SR .60 1.25
OP07EN006 World Legacy - World Chalice**** SR .75 1.50
OP07EN007 Destrudo the Lost Dragon's Frisson SR 5.00 10.00
OP07EN008 Magical Citadel of Endymion SR .25 .50
OP07EN009 Fossil Dig SR 1.50 3.00
OP07EN010 Divine Punishment SR .75 1.50
OP07EN011 Paleozoic Dinomischus SR .60 1.25
OP07EN012 Paleozoic Marrella SR .75 1.50
OP07EN013 Paleozoic Leanchoilia SR .75 1.50
OP07EN014 Prickle Fairy C .15 .30
OP07EN015 Insect Princess C .12 .25
OP07EN016 Zeradias, Herald of Heaven C .50 1.00
OP07EN017 Book of Life C .75 1.50
OP07EN018 Rare Value C .12 .25
OP07EN019 Zombie World C 1.25 2.50
OP07EN020 Spell Power Grasp C .15 .30
OP07EN021 Wavering Eyes C .10 .20
OP07EN022 Pitch-Black Power Stone C .12 .25
OP07EN023 Token Feastevil C .10 .20
OP07EN024 Lucky Chance C .12 .25
OP07EN025 Blowback Dragon C .75 1.50
OP07EN026 Gatling Dragon C 7.50 15.00

2018 Yu-Gi-Oh OTS Tournament Pack 8

OP08EN001 Droll & Lock Bird UTR 125.00 250.00
OP08EN002 Sky Striker Ace - Kagari UTR 125.00 250.00
OP08EN003 Scapegoat UTR 30.00 75.00
OP08EN004 Ruin, Supreme Queen of Oblivion SR .75 1.50
OP08EN005 Demise, Supreme
King of Armageddon SR .75 1.50
OP08EN006 Twin Triangle Dragon SR .30 .75
OP08EN007 Underclock Taker SR .25 .50
OP08EN008 Machine Duplication SR 3.00 6.00
OP08EN009 Broken Bamboo Sword SR 1.00 2.00
OP08EN010 Space Gift SR .30 .75
OP08EN011 Secret Village of the Spellcasters SR .75 1.50
OP08EN012 Waking the Dragon SR .75 1.50
OP08EN013 Invader of Darkness C .10 .20
OP08EN014 Ritual Raven C .20 .40
OP08EN015 Ojama Red C .30 .75
OP08EN016 Artifact Moralltach C 1.00 2.00
OP08EN017 Twilight Ninja Getsuga, the Shogun C 1.00 2.00
OP08EN018 Windwitch - Snow Bell C 1.00 2.00
OP08EN019 Windwitch - Glass Bell C 1.50 3.00
OP08EN020 Divine Sword - Phoenix Blade C 1.50 3.00
OP08EN021 Neo Space C .75 1.50
OP08EN022 Axe of Fools C .20 .40
OP08EN023 Ninjitsu Art Notebook C .25 .50
OP08EN024 Nutrient Z C .20 .40
OP08EN025 Cursed Seal of the Forbidden Spell C .75 1.50
OP08EN026 Sky Striker Ace Token SR 1.50 3.00

2018 Yu-Gi-Oh OTS Tournament Pack 9

OP09EN001 Elemental HERO Stratos UTR 75.00 150.00
OP09EN002 Trickstar Lycoris UTR 20.00 40.00
OP09EN003 Sky Striker Ace - Shizuku UTR 100.00 200.00
OP09EN004 Morphing Jar SR 2.50 5.00
OP09EN005 Galaxy Wizard SR .75 1.50
OP09EN006 Thunder Dragonmatrix SR 1.50 3.00
OP09EN007 Reprodocus SR .30 .75
OP09EN008 Card Destruction SR .75 1.50
OP09EN009 Super Polymerization SR 3.00 6.00
OP09EN010 Galaxy Expedition SR 2.50 5.00
OP09EN011 Sekka's Light SR .40 .80
OP09EN012 Personal Spoofing SR 2.00 4.00
OP09EN013 Elemental HERO Neos Alius C .15 .30
OP09EN014 T.G. Cyber Magician C .17 .35
OP09EN015 T.G. Striker C .75 1.50
OP09EN016 T.G. Warwolf C .30 .75
OP09EN017 T.G. Rush Rhino C .15 .30
OP09EN018 Jet Synchron C .30 .75
OP09EN019 Number 107: Galaxy
Eyes Tachyon Dragon C .40 .80
OP09EN020 Instant Neo Space C .20 .40
OP09EN021 Silent Graveyard C .50 1.00
OP09EN022 Fusion Substitute C .17 .35
OP09EN023 Imperial Order C .60 1.25
OP09EN024 Imperial Tombs of Necrovalley C .15 .30
OP09EN025 Tachyon Transmigration C .25 .50
OP09EN026A Mecha Phantom
Beast Token Dracossack SR 7.50 15.00
OP09EN026B Mecha Phantom
Beast Token Harrliard SR 2.50 5.00
OP09EN026C Mecha Phantom
Beast Token Megaraptor SR 3.00 6.00

2018 Yu-Gi-Oh OTS Tournament Pack 10

OP10EN001 Thunder Dragon Colossus UTR 50.00 100.00
OP10EN002 Galatea, the Orcust Automaton UTR 30.00 60.00
OP10EN003 Sky Striker Ace - Hayate UTR 40.00 80.00
OP10EN004 Breaker the Dark Magical Warrior SR .25 .50
OP10EN005 Batteryman Solar SR 1.00 2.00
OP10EN006 Salamangreat Mole SR .25 .50
OP10EN007 Jizukiru, the Star Destroying Kaiju SR 3.00 6.00
OP10EN008 Shiranui Sunsaga SR .50 1.00
OP10EN009 Salamangreat Sunlight Wolf SR .25 .50
OP10EN010 Hiita the Fire Charmer, Ablaze SR 2.50 5.00
OP10EN011 Revolving Switchyard SR 1.00 2.00
OP10EN012 Orcustrated Babel SR .50 1.00
OP10EN013 Breaker the Magical Warrior C .30 .75
OP10EN014 Assault Beast C .75 1.50
OP10EN015 Stardust Dragon/Assault Mode C .12 .25
OP10EN016 Super Quantum Red Layer C .75 1.50
OP10EN017 Explosive Magician C .12 .25
OP10EN018 T.G. Hyper Librarian C .75 1.50
OP10EN019 Number 81: Superdreadnought
Rail Cannon Super Dora C .17 .35
OP10EN020 Super Quantal Mech
Beast Magnaliger C .30 .60
OP10EN021 My Body as a Shield C .50 1.00
OP10EN022 Dragon's Mirror C .17 .35
OP10EN023 Super Quantal Mech
Ship Magnacarrier C .40 .80
OP10EN024 Mythical Bestiary C .12 .25
OP10EN025 Assault Mode Activate C .30 .75
OP10EN026 Trickstar Token SR .75 1.50

2018 Yu-Gi-Oh Shadows in Valhalla 1st Edition

SHVA-EN001 Valkyrie Dritte SR .10 .20
SHVA-EN002 Valkyrie Zweite SR .10 .20
SHVA-EN003 Valkyrie Erste SR .10 .20
SHVA-EN004 Valkyrie Brunhilde SCR 6.00 12.00
SHVA-EN005 Fortune Chariot SR .10 .20
SHVA-EN006 Ride of the Valkyries SCR 7.50 15.00
SHVA-EN007 Mischief of the Time Goddess SCR 10.00 20.00
SHVA-EN008 Goddess Skuld's Oracle SR .10 .20
SHVA-EN009 Goddess Verdande's Guidance SR .10 .20
SHVA-EN010 Goddess Urd's Verdict SR .10 .20
SHVA-EN011 Ninja Grandmaster Saizo SCR 2.50 5.00
SHVA-EN012 Yellow Ninja SR .10 .20
SHVA-EN013 Yellow Dragon Ninja SCR 2.00 4.00
SHVA-EN014 Hidden Village of Ninjitsu Arts SCR 1.50 3.00
SHVA-EN015 Ninjitsu Art
Mirage-Transformation SCR 1.00 2.00
SHVA-EN016 Old Entity Chthugua SCR 1.00 2.00
SHVA-EN017 Outer Entity Nyarla SCR 2.00 4.00
SHVA-EN018 Outer Entity Azzathoth SCR 2.00 4.00
SHVA-EN019 Forbidden Trapezohedron SCR 1.00 2.00
SHVA-EN020 Aleister the Meltdown Invoker SCR 25.00 50.00
SHVA-EN021 Strike Ninja SR .10 .20
SHVA-EN022 Ninja Grandmaster Hanzo SR .10 .20
SHVA-EN023 Upstart Golden Ninja SR .10 .20
SHVA-EN024 White Dragon Ninja SR .10 .20
SHVA-EN025 Red Dragon Ninja SR .10 .20
SHVA-EN026 Twilight Ninja Jogen SR .10 .20
SHVA-EN027 Armor Ninjitsu Art of Alchemy SR .10 .20
SHVA-EN028 Ninjitsu Art of Transformation SR .10 .20
SHVA-EN029 Ninjitsu Art of
Super-Transformation SR .10 .20
SHVA-EN030 Armor Ninjitsu Art of Rust Mist SR .10 .20
SHVA-EN031 Elemental HERO Neos SR .10 .20
SHVA-EN032 Neo-Spacian Glow Moss SR .10 .20
SHVA-EN033 Neo-Spacian Flare Scarab SR .10 .20
SHVA-EN034 Elemental HERO Magma Neos SR .10 .20
SHVA-EN035 Elemental HERO Chaos Neos SR .10 .20
SHVA-EN036 Vision HERO Trinity SR .10 .20
SHVA-EN037 Mermail Abyssmegalo SR 1.00 2.00
SHVA-EN038 Mermail Abyssleed SR .30 .75
SHVA-EN039 Mermail Abyssteus SR .10 .20
SHVA-EN040 Aleister the Invoker SCR 2.00 4.00
SHVA-EN041 Invoked Mechaba SR 2.50 5.00
SHVA-EN042 Magical Meltdown SR .10 .20
SHVA-EN043 Invocation SR 2.50 5.00
SHVA-EN044 Omega Summon SR .10 .20
SHVA-EN045 Mist Valley Apex Avian SR .10 .20
SHVA-EN046 Windwitch - Ice Bell SCR 2.50 5.00
SHVA-EN047 Ash Blossom & Joyous Spring SR 15.00 30.00
SHVA-EN048 Gem-Knight Seraphinite SCR 2.00 4.00
SHVA-EN049 El Shaddoll Winda SCR 1.00 2.00
SHVA-EN050 Dragunity Knight - Vajrayana SCR .60 1.25
SHVA-EN051 Hi-Speedroid Chanbara SR .60 1.25
SHVA-EN052 Akashic Magician SR .10 .20
SHVA-EN053 Cyberdark Impact! SR .60 1.25
SHVA-EN054 Golden Bamboo Sword SR .60 1.25
SHVA-EN055 Magic Planter SR .10 .20
SHVA-EN056 Advanced Dark SR .10 .20
SHVA-EN057 Shaddoll Fusion SCR 2.00 4.00
SHVA-EN058 Gateway to Chaos SCR 1.00 2.00
SHVA-EN059 Twin Twisters SCR 2.50 5.00
SHVA-EN060 Urgent Ritual Art SR .10 .20

2018 Yu-Gi-Oh Soul Fusion 1st Edition

SOFUEN000 Alviss of the Nordic Alfar C .15 .30
SOFUEN001 Clock Wyvern R .20 .40
SOFUEN002 Salamangreat Meer C .15 .30
SOFUEN003 Salamangreat Foxy C .15 .30
SOFUEN004 Salamangreat Falco C .15 .30
SOFUEN005 Salamangreat Jack Jaguar C .15 .30
SOFUEN006 Dinowrestler Capoeiraptor C .15 .30
SOFUEN007 Dinowrestler Capaptera C .15 .30
SOFUEN008 Dinowrestler Systegosaur C .15 .30
SOFUEN009 Dinowrestler Pankratops C .15 .30
SOFUEN010 Galaxy Cleric C .15 .30
SOFUEN011 Galaxy Brave C .15 .30
SOFUEN012 Gravekeeper's Headman R .20 .40
SOFUEN013 Gravekeeper's Spiritualist C .15 .30
SOFUEN014 Orcust Bass Bombard R .20 .40
SOFUEN015 Orcust Cymbal Skeleton R .20 .40
SOFUEN016 Orcust Harp Horror R .20 .40
SOFUEN017 World Legacy - World Wand C .15 .30
SOFUEN018 Thunder Dragonmatrix R .20 .40
SOFUEN019 Thunder Dragondark UR 15.00 30.00
SOFUEN020 Thunder Dragonhawk UR 2.50 5.00
SOFUEN021 Thunder Dragonroar UR 10.00 20.00
SOFUEN022 Thunder Dragonduo SR .30 .75
SOFUEN023 Impcantation Penciplume C .15 .30
SOFUEN024 Impcantation Bookstone C .15 .30
SOFUEN025 Chaos Dragon Levianeer SCR 6.00 12.00
SOFUEN026 Mystrick Hulder SR .30 .75
SOFUEN027 Diana the Light Spirit C .15 .30
SOFUEN028 Condemned Witch SCR 4.00 8.00
SOFUEN029 Bearblocker C .15 .30
SOFUEN030 Gokipole R .20 .40
SOFUEN031 Token Collector R .20 .40
SOFUEN032 Two-for-One Team C .15 .30
SOFUEN033 Salamangreat Emerald Eagle C .15 .30
SOFUEN034 Cyberse Clock Dragon UR .60 1.25
SOFUEN035 Gravekeeper's Supernaturalist R .20 .40
SOFUEN036 Thunder Dragon Colossus SCR 60.00 125.00
SOFUEN037 Thunder Dragon Titan SCR 5.00 10.00
SOFUEN038 Diplexer Chimera C .15 .30
SOFUEN039 Clock Spartoi R .20 .40
SOFUEN040 Salamangreat Heatleo R .20 .40
SOFUEN041 Dinowrestler King T Wrextle C .15 .30
SOFUEN042 Galaxy-Eyes Solflare Dragon UR .60 1.25
SOFUEN043 Galatea, the Orcust Automaton SR .30 .75
SOFUEN044 Longirsu, the Orcust Orchestrator SR .30 .75
SOFUEN045 Orcustrion UR .75 1.50
SOFUEN046 Crusadia Soatha C .15 .30
SOFUEN047 Folgo, Justice Fur Hire SR .30 .75
SOFUEN048 Agave Dragon C .15 .30
SOFUEN049 Some Summer Summoner SR .30 .75
SOFUEN050 Cynet Fusion R .20 .40
SOFUEN051 Salamangreat Sanctuary C .15 .30
SOFUEN052 Rise of the Salamangreat C .15 .30
SOFUEN053 Will of the Salamangreat C .15 .30
SOFUEN054 World Dino Wrestling C .15 .30
SOFUEN055 Necrovalley Throne SR .30 .75
SOFUEN056 Galaxy Trance R .20 .40
SOFUEN057 Orcustrated Babel R .20 .40
SOFUEN058 Orcustrated Return SCR 5.00 10.00
SOFUEN059 Orcustrated Einsatz C .15 .30
SOFUEN060 Thunder Dragon Fusion UR .50 1.00
SOFUEN061 Sky Striker Maneuver - Vector Blast SR .30 .75
SOFUEN062 Giant Ballpark C .15 .30
SOFUEN063 Herald of the Abyss SR .30 .75
SOFUEN064 Concentrating Current C .15 .30
SOFUEN065 Extra-Foolish Burial SR .30 .75
SOFUEN066 Parallel Panzer C .15 .30
SOFUEN067 Salamangreat Gift C .15 .30
SOFUEN068 Necrovalley Temple R .20 .40
SOFUEN069 Eternal Galaxy C .15 .30
SOFUEN070 Orcustrated Attack C .15 .30
SOFUEN071 Orcustrated Core C .15 .30
SOFUEN072 Thunder Dragons'
Hundred Thunders R .20 .40
SOFUEN073 Thunder Dragon Discharge R .20 .40
SOFUEN074 Crusadia Krawler C .15 .30
SOFUEN075 Necro Fusion C .15 .30
SOFUEN076 Invicibility Barrier C .15 .30
SOFUEN077 Toll Hike R .20 .40
SOFUEN078 Trap Trick SCR 25.00 50.00
SOFUEN079 The Revenge of the Normal C .15 .30
SOFUEN080 Subsurface Stage Divers C .15 .30
SOFUEN081 Consolation Prize R .20 .40
SOFUEN082 Danger! Thunderbird! SCR 4.00 8.00
SOFUEN083 Danger! Dogman! SR .30 .75
SOFUEN084 Danger! Mothman! SR .30 .75
SOFUEN085 Danger!? Tsuchinoko? SCR 50.00 100.00
SOFUEN086 Danger! Response Team UR .60 1.25
SOFUEN087 Second Expedition into Danger! SR .30 .75
SOFUEN088 Noble Knight Iyvanne SR .30 .75
SOFUEN089 Morgan, the Enchantress of Avalon UR 1.25 2.50
SOFUEN090 Heritage of the Chalice UR 2.00 4.00
SOFUEN091 Until Noble Arms Are Needed... C .15 .30
SOFUEN092 Fluffal Patchwork C .15 .30
SOFUEN093 Edge Imp Cotton Eater C .15 .30
SOFUEN094 Predaplant Dragostapelia C .15 .30
SOFUEN095 D/D/D Flame High King Genghis C .15 .30
SOFUEN096 DDD...Purple Armageddon C .15 .30
SOFUEN097 Predaplast C .15 .30
SOFUEN098 Ostinato C .15 .30
SOFUEN099 Frightfur Patchwork R .20 .40

2018 Yu-Gi-Oh Star Pack VRAINS 1st Edition

SP18EN001 Bitron C .20 .40
SP18EN002 Backup Secretary C .20 .40
SP18EN003 Cyberse Wizard C .15 .30
SP18EN004 Salvagent Driver C .10 .20
SP18EN005 Stack Reviver C .15 .30
SP18EN006 Draconnet C .50 1.00
SP18EN007 Capacitor Stalker C .10 .20
SP18EN008 Defect Compiler C .10 .20
SP18EN009 Linkslayer C .60 1.25
SP18EN010 Backlinker C .12 .25
SP18EN011 Dotscaper C .25 .50
SP18EN012 Dual Assembwurm C .12 .25
SP18EN013 Flick Clown C .07 .15
SP18EN014 Cracking Dragon C .10 .20
SP18EN015 Hack Worm C .30 .75
SP18EN016 Jack Wyvern C .12 .25
SP18EN017 Gouki Riscorpio C .50 1.00
SP18EN018 Gouki Suprex C 1.50 3.00
SP18EN019 Gouki Twistcobra C 1.00 2.00
SP18EN020 Trickstar Candina C 1.25 2.50
SP18EN021 Trickstar Lilybell C .30 .60
SP18EN022 Trickstar Lycoris C .50 1.00
SP18EN023 Trickstar Narkissus C .20 .40
SP18EN024 Dark Angel C .20 .40
SP18EN025 Gateway Dragon C .15 .30
SP18EN026 Sniffer Dragon C .07 .15
SP18EN027 Linkbelt Wall Dragon C .15 .30
SP18EN028 Altergeist Marionetter C .40 .80
SP18EN029 Altergeist Kunquery C .25 .50
SP18EN030 Altergeist Silquitous C .25 .50
SP18EN031 Decode Talker SFR .25 .50
SP18EN032 Link Bumper C .12 .25
SP18EN033 Honeybot C .15 .30
SP18EN034 Gouki The Great Ogre C .15 .30
SP18EN035 Gouki Thunder Ogre C .30 .75
SP18EN036 Twin Triangle Dragon C .17 .35
SP18EN037 Altergeist Primebanshee C .75 1.50
SP18EN038 Security Block C .12 .25
SP18EN039 Gouki Rematch C .75 1.50
SP18EN040 Trickstar Light Stage C 2.00 4.00
SP18EN041 Dragonoid Generator C .20 .40
SP18EN042 Air Cracking Storm C .07 .15
SP18EN043 Fire Prison C .07 .15
SP18EN044 Cyberse Beacon C .07 .15
SP18EN045 Three Strikes Barrier C .10 .20
SP18EN046 Pulse Mines C .12 .25
SP18EN047 Altergeist Camouflage C .17 .35
SP18EN048 Altergeist Protocol C .75 1.50
SP18EN049 Personal Spoofing C .40 .80
SP18EN050 Link Restart C .07 .15

2018 Yu-Gi-Oh Starter Deck Codebreaker 1st Edition

YS18-EN001 Leotron C .15 .30
YS18-EN002 Texchanger C .15 .30
YS18-EN003 Widget Kid SR .60 1.25
YS18-EN004 Cyberse White Hat UR .60 1.25
YS18-EN005 Bitron C .15 .30
YS18-EN006 RAM Clouder C .15 .30
YS18-EN007 Linkslayer C .15 .30
YS18-EN008 Backup Secretary C .15 .30
YS18-EN009 Launcher Commander C .15 .30
YS18-EN010 Cliant C .15 .30
YS18-EN011 Bitrooper C .15 .30
YS18-EN012 Flamvell Guard C .15 .30
YS18-EN013 Beast King Barbaros C .15 .30
YS18-EN014 Cyber Dragon C .15 .30
YS18-EN015 Exarion Universe C .15 .30
YS18-EN016 Evilswarm Mandragora C .15 .30
YS18-EN017 Marshmallon C .15 .30
YS18-EN018 Ryko, Lightsworn Hunter C .15 .30
YS18-EN019 Battle Fader C .15 .30
YS18-EN020 Swift Scarecrow C .15 .30
YS18-EN021 Cynet Recovery SR .60 1.25
YS18-EN022 Cynet Universe C .15 .30
YS18-EN023 Scapegoat C .15 .30
YS18-EN024 Monster Reborn C .15 .30

YS18-EN025 Dark Hole C .15 .30
YS18-EN026 Mystical Space Typhoon C .15 .30
YS18-EN027 Book of Moon C .15 .30
YS18-EN028 United We Stand C .15 .30
YS18-EN029 Card Trader C .15 .30
YS18-EN030 Burden of the Mighty C .15 .30
YS18-EN031 Ego Boost C .15 .30
YS18-EN032 Supply Squad C .15 .30
YS18-EN033 Cynet Regression C .15 .30
YS18-EN034 Shadow Spell C .15 .30
YS18-EN035 Call of the Haunted C .15 .30
YS18-EN036 Mirror Force C .15 .30
YS18-EN037 Torrential Tribute C .15 .30
YS18-EN038 Bottomless Trap Hole C .15 .30
YS18-EN039 Zero Gravity C .15 .30
YS18-EN040 Compulsory Evacuation Device C .15 .30
YS18-EN041 Transcode Talker UR .60 1.25
YS18-EN042 Pentestag SR .60 1.25
YS18-EN043 Decode Talker C .15 .30
YS18-EN044 Link Spider C .15 .30
YS18-EN045 Linkuriboh C 3.00 6.00

2018 Yu-Gi-Oh Structure Deck Lair of Darkness 1st Edition

SR06-EN000 Lilith, Lady of Lament UR 1.50 3.00
SR06-EN001 Darkest Diabolos, Lord of the Lair UR1.50 3.00
SR06-EN002 Ahrima, the Wicked Warden SR .60 1.25
SR06-EN003 Duke Shade, the Sinister Shadow Lord C .15 .30
SR06-EN004 Diabolos, King of the Abyss C .15 .30
SR06-EN005 Lich Lord, King of the Underworld C.15 .30
SR06-EN006 Prometheus, King of the Shadows C.15 .30
SR06-EN007 Archfiend Emperor First Lord of Horror C .15 .30
SR06-EN008 Caius the Mega Monarch C .15 .30
SR06-EN009 Legendary Maju Garzett C .15 .30
SR06-EN010 Vanity's Fiend C .15 .30
SR06-EN011 Mist Archfiend C .15 .30
SR06-EN012 Infernal Dragon C .15 .30
SR06-EN013 Archfiend Cavalry C .15 .30
SR06-EN014 Stygian Street Patrol C .15 .30
SR06-EN015 Phantom of Chaos C .15 .30
SR06-EN016 Plague Wolf C .15 .30
SR06-EN017 Fiendish Rhino Warrior C .15 .30
SR06-EN018 Kuribandit C .15 .30
SR06-EN019 Tour Guide From the Underworld C.15 .30
SR06-EN020 Absolute King Back Jack C .15 .30
SR06-EN021 Relinkuriboh C .15 .30
SR06-EN022 Lair of Darkness SR .60 1.25
SR06-EN023 Recurring Nightmare C .15 .30
SR06-EN024 Allure of Darkness C .15 .30
SR06-EN025 Hand Destruction C .15 .30
SR06-EN026 Foolish Burial Goods C .15 .30
SR06-EN027 Boogie Trap C .15 .30
SR06-EN028 Fires of Doomsday C .15 .30
SR06-EN029 Veil of Darkness C .15 .30
SR06-EN030 Grinning Grave Virus SR .60 1.25
SR06-EN031 Crush Card Virus C .15 .30
SR06-EN032 Deck Devastation Virus C .15 .30
SR06-EN033 Eradicator Epidemic Virus C .15 .30
SR06-EN034 Full Force Virus C .15 .30
SR06-EN035 Darklight C .15 .30
SR06-EN036 Trap of Darkness C .15 .30
SR06-EN037 Mind Crush C .15 .30
SR06-EN038 Rise to Full Height C .15 .30
SR06-EN039 Curse of Darkness C .15 .30
SR06-EN040 Sinister Yorishiro C .15 .30
SR06-ENTKN Shadow Token C .15 .30

2018 Yu-Gi-Oh Structure Deck Powercode Link 1st Edition

SDPL-EN001 Datacorn C .10 .20
SDPL-EN002 Garbage Collector C .10 .20
SDPL-EN003 Sea Archiver SR .10 .20
SDPL-EN004 Flame Bufferlo SR .50 1.00
SDPL-EN005 Lady Debug SR 1.00 2.00
SDPL-EN006 Antialian C .10 .20
SDPL-EN007 Storm Cipher C .10 .20
SDPL-EN008 Segmental Dragon UR .10 .20
SDPL-EN009 Cyberse Gadget C .10 .20
SDPL-EN010 Juragedo C 1.50 3.00
SDPL-EN011 Mecha Phantom Beast Tetherwolf C.10 .20
SDPL-EN012 Reborn Tengu C .20 .40
SDPL-EN013 Skull Meister C .10 .20
SDPL-EN014 Goblindbergh C .10 .20
SDPL-EN015 Phantom Skyblaster C .20 .40
SDPL-EN016 Genex Ally Birdman C .10 .20
SDPL-EN017 Effect Veiler C 1.00 2.00
SDPL-EN018 Magical Merchant C .10 .20
SDPL-EN019 Cosmic Compass C .10 .20
SDPL-EN020 Launcher Commander C .10 .20
SDPL-EN021 Cynet Storm C .10 .20
SDPL-EN022 Night Beam C .10 .20
SDPL-EN023 Offerings to the Doomed C .10 .20
SDPL-EN024 Forbidden Chalice C .10 .20
SDPL-EN025 Scapegoat C .10 .20
SDPL-EN026 Swords of Revealing Light C .10 .20
SDPL-EN027 Reasoning C .10 .20
SDPL-EN028 Fires of Doomsday C .10 .20
SDPL-EN029 One for One C .10 .20
SDPL-EN030 Terraforming C .50 1.00
SDPL-EN031 Packet Link C .10 .20
SDPL-EN032 Wild Tornado C .10 .20
SDPL-EN033 Traptrix Trap Hole Nightmare C .10 .20
SDPL-EN034 Blazing Mirror Force C .10 .20
SDPL-EN035 Trap Stun C .10 .20
SDPL-EN036 Safe Zone C .10 .20
SDPL-EN037 Call of the Haunted C .10 .20
SDPL-EN038 Reckless Greed C .10 .20
SDPL-EN039 Debunk C .10 .20
SDPL-EN040 Powercode Talker UR .10 .20
SDPL-EN041 Traffic Ghost C .20 .40
SDPL-EN042 LANphorhynchus C 1.00 2.00

2018 Yu-Gi-Oh Structure Deck Wave of Light 1st Edition

SR05-EN000 Eva UR .60 1.25
SR05-EN001 Sacred Arch-Airknight Parshath UR .50 1.00
SR05-EN002 Minerva, Scholar of the Sky C .10 .20
SR05-EN003 Power Angel Valkyria SR .75 1.50
SR05-EN004 Neo-Parshath, the Sky Paladin C .10 .20
SR05-EN005 Airknight Parshath C .10 .20
SR05-EN006 Meltiel, Sage of the Sky C .10 .20
SR05-EN007 Harvest Angel of Wisdom C .10 .20
SR05-EN008 Bountiful Artemis C .10 .20
SR05-EN009 Layard the Liberator C .10 .20
SR05-EN010 Guiding Ariadne C .10 .20
SR05-EN011 Archlord Kristya C .10 .20
SR05-EN012 Splendid Venus C .10 .20
SR05-EN013 Athena C .10 .20
SR05-EN014 Tethys, Goddess of Light C .10 .20
SR05-EN015 Hecatrice C .10 .20
SR05-EN016 Gellenduo C .10 .20
SR05-EN017 Nova Summoner C .10 .20
SR05-EN018 Honest C .10 .20
SR05-EN019 Herald of Orange Light C .10 .20
SR05-EN020 Herald of Green Light C .10 .20
SR05-EN021 Herald of Purple Light C .10 .20
SR05-EN022 Guiding Light C .10 .20
SR05-EN023 D.D. Sprite C .10 .20
SR05-EN024 Hanewata C .10 .20
SR05-EN025 The Sanctum of Parshath SR .75 1.50
SR05-EN026 The Sanctuary in the Sky C .10 .20
SR05-EN027 Cards from the Sky C .10 .20
SR05-EN028 Celestial Transformation C .10 .20
SR05-EN029 Valhalla, Hall of the Fallen C .10 .20
SR05-EN030 Ties of the Brethren C 2.00 4.00
SR05-EN031 Rebirth of Parshath SR .75 1.50
SR05-EN032 Light of Judgment C .10 .20
SR05-EN033 Miraculous Descent C .10 .20
SR05-EN034 Synthetic Seraphim C .10 .20
SR05-EN035 Divine Punishment C .10 .20
SR05-EN036 Dark Bribe C .10 .20
SR05-EN037 Solemn Warning C .75 1.50
SR05-EN038 Ultimate Providence C .10 .20
SR05-EN039 Drastic Drop Off C .10 .20
SR05-EN040 Recall C .10 .20
SR05-ENTKN Synthetic Seraphim Token C .10 .20

2018 Yu-Gi-Oh Structure Deck Zombie Horde 1st Edition

SR07EN000 Tatsunecro SR .12 .25
SR07EN001 Doomking Balerdroch UR .30 .75
SR07EN002 Necroworld Banshee SR .50 1.00
SR07EN003 Glow-Up Bloom SR .75 1.50
SR07EN004 Kasha C .10 .20
SR07EN005 Red-Eyes Zombie Dragon C .50 1.00
SR07EN006 Malevolent Mech - Goku En C .12 .25
SR07EN007 Endless Decay C .12 .25
SR07EN008 Paladin of the Cursed Dragon C .15 .30
SR07EN009 Immortal Ruler C .12 .25
SR07EN010 Zombie Master C 1.25 2.50
SR07EN011 Tristan, Knight of the Underworld C .10 .20
SR07EN012 Mezuki C 1.25 2.50
SR07EN013 Gozuki C 3.00 6.00
SR07EN014 Shutendoji C .12 .25
SR07EN015 Pyramid Turtle C .25 .50
SR07EN016 Goblin Zombie C .30 .75
SR07EN017 Isolde, Belle of the Underworld C .12 .25
SR07EN018 Shiranui Solitaire C 1.25 2.50
SR07EN019 Uni-Zombie C .60 1.25
SR07EN020 Marionette Mite C .10 .20
SR07EN021 Beast of the Pharaoh C .15 .30
SR07EN022 Scapeghost C .25 .50
SR07EN023 Zombie Necronize C 2.00 4.00
SR07EN024 Zombie Power Struggle C .30 .75
SR07EN025 Zombie World C 1.50 3.00
SR07EN026 Overpowering Eye C .12 .25
SR07EN027 Book of Life C 1.50 3.00
SR07EN028 Call of the Mummy C .12 .25
SR07EN029 Foolish Burial C .75 1.50
SR07EN030 Monster Gate C .15 .30
SR07EN031 Dragged Down into the Grave C .60 1.25
SR07EN032 Burial from a Different Dimension C .50 1.00
SR07EN033 Shared Ride C .40 .80
SR07EN034 Return of the Zombies C .30 .75
SR07EN035 Haunted Shrine C .17 .35
SR07EN036 Trap of the Imperial Tomb C .10 .20
SR07EN037 Needlebug Nest C .12 .25
SR07EN038 Metaverse C .25 .50
SR07EN039 Anti-Spell Fragrance C .75 1.50
SR07EN040 Mask of Restrict C 1.25 2.50
SR07EN041 Red-Eyes Zombie Necro Dragon UR .75 1.50

2019 Yu-Gi-Oh Battles of Legend Hero's Revenge 1st Edition

BLHREN000 Five-Headed Dragon SCR .75 1.50
BLHREN001 Ipiria SCR .30 .75
BLHREN002 Water of Life UR .15 .30
BLHREN003 Gold Moon Coin UR .15 .30
BLHREN004 Gingerbread House UR .25 .50
BLHREN005 Vision HERO Minimum Ray UR .12 .25
BLHREN006 Vision HERO Multiply Guy UR .12 .25
BLHREN007 Vision HERO Increase SCR 5.00 10.00
BLHREN008 Vision HERO Poisoner UR .10 .20
BLHREN009 Vision HERO Gravito UR .15 .30
BLHREN010 Vision HERO Faris SCR .20 .40
BLHREN011 Vision Release UR .15 .30
BLHREN012 Vision Fusion SCR .15 .30
BLHREN013 Apparition UR .10 .20
BLHREN014 Fortune Fairy Hikari SCR .30 .75
BLHREN015 Fortune Fairy En UR .15 .30
BLHREN016 Fortune Fairy Hu UR .15 .30
BLHREN017 Fortune Fairy Swee UR .15 .30
BLHREN018 Fortune Fairy Ann UR .15 .30
BLHREN019 Fortune Fairy Chee UR .15 .30
BLHREN020 Unacceptable Result UR .15 .30
BLHREN021 Miracle Stone UR .15 .30
BLHREN022 Lucky Loan UR .15 .30
BLHREN023 T.G. Gear Zombie SCR .15 .30
BLHREN024 T.G. Drill Fish UR .12 .25
BLHREN025 T.G. Metal Skeleton UR .15 .30
BLHREN026 Sonic Stun UR .12 .25
BLHREN027 Number 26: Spaceway Octobypass UR.15 .30
BLHREN028 Number 60: Dugares the Timeless UR.75 1.50
BLHREN029 Number 76: Harmonizer Gradielle UR.50 1.00
BLHREN030 Number 97: Draglubion SCR .60 1.25
BLHREN031 Battlewasp - Pin the Bullseye UR .10 .20
BLHREN032 Battlewasp - Dart the Hunter UR .10 .20
BLHREN033 Battlewasp - Sting the Poison UR .10 .20
BLHREN034 Battlewasp - Twinbow the Attacker UR.10 .20
BLHREN035 Battlewasp - Arbalest the Rapidfire UR.10 .20
BLHREN036 Battlewasp - Azusa the Ghost Bow UR.10 .20
BLHREN037 Battlewasp - Halberd the Charge UR.10 .20
BLHREN038 Battlewasp... SCR .30 .75
BLHREN039 Battlewasp - Ballista the Armageddon UR .10 .20
BLHREN040 Summoning Swarm UR .10 .20
BLHREN041 Revival Swarm UR .10 .20
BLHREN042 Battlewasp - Nest UR .10 .20
BLHREN043 All-Eyes Phantom Dragon SCR .30 .75
BLHREN044 Hi-Speedroid Kitedrake SCR .60 1.25
BLHREN045 Avendread Savior SCR .50 1.00
BLHREN046 Black Luster Soldier... SCR 50.00 100.00
BLHREN047 Harpie Conductor SCR .50 1.00
BLHREN048 Double Headed Anger Knuckle SCR .25 .50
BLHREN049 Traptrix Sera SCR 3.00 6.00
BLHREN050 Hi-Speedroid Rubber Band Shooter SCR .25 .50
BLHREN051 PSY-Framelord Lambda SCR 5.00 10.00
BLHREN052 Magical Musketeer Max UR .50 1.00
BLHREN053 Gimmick Puppet Chimera Doll UR .10 .20
BLHREN054 Salamangreat Almiraj SCR .10 .20
BLHREN055 Stardust Mirage SCR .12 .25
BLHREN056 Dark Sacrifice SCR .50 1.00
BLHREN057 Foolish Burial UR 1.00 2.00
BLHREN058 Symbol of Friendship UR .10 .20
BLHREN059 Vision HERO Vyon SCR .60 1.25
BLHREN060 Vision HERO Witch Raider UR .10 .20
BLHREN061 Elemental HERO Stratos UR .50 1.00
BLHREN062 Vision HERO Trinity UR .12 .25
BLHREN063 Destiny HERO - Dangerous UR .15 .30
BLHREN064 Elemental HERO Neos Knight SCR .12 .25
BLHREN065 Elemental HERO Absolute Zero UR .25 .50
BLHREN066 Dragonecro Nethersoul Dragon UR .30 .75
BLHREN067 Lunalight Crimson Fox UR .12 .25
BLHREN068 Lunalight Kaleido Chick UR .12 .25
BLHREN069 Predaplast UR .12 .25
BLHREN070 Dinowrestler Pankratops SCR 4.00 8.00
BLHREN071 Borrelsword Dragon SCR 50.00 100.00
BLHREN072 Salamangreat Sanctuary UR .15 .30
BLHREN073 Will of the Salamangreat UR .15 .30
BLHREN074 Cyber-Stein SCR .60 1.25
BLHREN075 Guardian of Order UR .10 .20
BLHREN076 White Dragon Wyverburster UR .25 .50
BLHREN077 Black Dragon Collapserpent UR .25 .50
BLHREN078 Artifact Scythe UR .50 1.00
BLHREN079 Artifact Lancea SCR 3.00 6.00
BLHREN080 Shaddoll Falco UR .20 .40
BLHREN081 Shaddoll Hedgehog UR .20 .40
BLHREN082 Shaddoll Squamata UR .25 .50
BLHREN083 Shaddoll Beast UR .15 .30
BLHREN084 Subterror Guru UR .30 .75
BLHREN085 Herald of the Arc Light UR .50 1.00
BLHREN086 Nekroz Cycle SCR .50 1.00
BLHREN087 Interrupted Kaiju Slumber SCR 1.00 2.00
BLHREN088 Summon Limit UR 2.50 5.00
BLHREN089 Sky Striker Ace - Raye SCR .60 1.25
BLHREN090 Sky Striker Mobilize - Engage! SCR10.00 20.00
BLHREN091 Sky Striker Maneuver - Afterburners! UR .30 .75
BLHREN092 Sky Striker Mecha - Widow Anchor SCR 5.00 10.00
BLHREN093 Number 93: Utopia Kaiser SCR 2.00 4.00

2019 Yu-Gi-Oh Chaos Impact 1st Edition

CHIMEN000 Monster Express R .15 .30
CHIMEN001 Suppression Collider C .10 .20
CHIMEN002 Marincess Mandarin R .15 .30
CHIMEN003 Marincess Crown Tail C .10 .20
CHIMEN004 Marincess Blue Tang SCR 5.00 10.00
CHIMEN005 Chobham Armor Dragon C .10 .20
CHIMEN006 Dinowrestler Martial Ampelo C .10 .20
CHIMEN007 Dinowrestler Valeonyx C .10 .20
CHIMEN008 Unchained Twins - Aruha R .15 .30
CHIMEN008 Unchained Twins - Aruha SLR 75.00 150.00
CHIMEN009 Unchained Twins - Rakea R .15 .30
CHIMEN010 Unchained Soul of Disaster SCR 2.50 5.00
CHIMEN011 Gladiator Beast Sagittarii R .15 .30
CHIMEN012 Gladiator Beast Attorix R .15 .30
CHIMEN013 Gladiator Beast Vespasius R .15 .30
CHIMEN014 Starliege Seyfert SCR 25.00 50.00
CHIMEN015 Nebula Dragon R .15 .30
CHIMEN016 Galactic Spiral Dragon C .10 .20
CHIMEN017 Aromage Laurel C .10 .20
CHIMEN018 Aromage Marjoram C .10 .20
CHIMEN019 Tenyi Spirit - Ashuna C .10 .20
CHIMEN020 Evoltile Megachirella C .10 .20
CHIMEN021 World Legacy - World Key"" C .10 .20
CHIMEN022 Infinitrack Brutal Dozer C .10 .20
CHIMEN023 Gizmek Yata, the Gleaming Vanguard SR .50 1.00
CHIMEN024 Primineral Kongreat SR .20 .40
CHIMEN025 Prometeor, the Burning Star C .10 .20
CHIMEN026 Brinegir C .10 .20
CHIMEN027 Luna the Dark Spirit C .10 .20
CHIMEN028 D.D. Patrol Plane C .10 .20
CHIMEN029 Hop Ear Squadron R .15 .30
CHIMEN030 Bayonater, the Baneful Barrel C .10 .20
CHIMEN031 Mimikuril C .10 .20
CHIMEN032 Bonze Alone C .10 .20
CHIMEN033 Gladiator Beast Domitianus SR .75 1.50
CHIMEN034 Aromaseraphy Sweet Marjoram SR .20 .40
CHIMEN035 Draco Berserker of the Tenyi UR 4.00 8.00
CHIMEN036 Gallant Granite UR 2.00 4.00
CHIMEN037 Firewall Dragon Darkfluid SCR 3.00 6.00
CHIMEN038 Protocol Gardna C .10 .20
CHIMEN039 Salamangreat Pyro Phoenix SLR 60.00 125.00
CHIMEN039 Salamangreat Pyro Phoenix SCR 10.00 20.00
CHIMEN040 Marincess Crystal Heart SR .20 .40
CHIMEN041 Marincess Wonder Heart C .10 .20
CHIMEN042 Marincess Sea Angel C .10 .20
CHIMEN043 Unchained Soul of Rage SCR 5.00 10.00
CHIMEN044 Unchained Soul of Anguish SCR 2.00 4.00
CHIMEN045 Unchained Abomination UR 6.00 12.00
CHIMEN046 Test Panther UR .75 1.50
CHIMEN047 Galaxy Satellite Dragon SR .60 1.25
CHIMEN048 Gorgon, Empress of the Evil Eyed SLR 50.00 100.00
CHIMEN048 Gorgon, Empress of the Evil Eyed SR.20 .40
CHIMEN049 I:P Masquerena UR 30.00 75.00
CHIMEN049 I:P Masquerena SLR 300.00 600.00
CHIMEN050 Seraphim Papillion C .10 .20
CHIMEN051 Salamangreat Burning Shell C .10 .20
CHIMEN052 Salamangreat Transcendence R .15 .30
CHIMEN053 Marincess Battle Ocean C .10 .20
CHIMEN054 Abomination's Prison SCR 10.00 20.00
CHIMEN055 Wailing of the Unchained Souls UR1.00 2.00
CHIMEN056 Gladiator Beast's Comeback C .10 .20
CHIMEN057 Gladiator Beast United R .15 .30
CHIMEN058 Gladiator Rejection UR 1.25 2.50
CHIMEN059 Aroma Gardening C .10 .20
CHIMEN060 Wattrain C .10 .20
CHIMEN061 The World Legacy C .10 .20
CHIMEN062 Evil Eye of Gorgoneio SR .20 .40
CHIMEN063 Bownty UR .25 .50
CHIMEN064 Cauldron of the Old Man C .10 .20
CHIMEN065 Spiritual Entanglement R .15 .30
CHIMEN066 Old Mind C .10 .20
CHIMEN067 Marincess Snow C .10 .20
CHIMEN068 Marincess Cascade C .10 .20
CHIMEN069 Escape of the Unchained C .10 .20
CHIMEN070 Abominable Chamber of the Unchained C .10 .20
CHIMEN071 Gladiator Beast Charge C .10 .20
CHIMEN072 Gladiator Naumachia C .10 .20
CHIMEN073 Tachyon Spiral Galaxy C .10 .20
CHIMEN074 Blessed Winds R .15 .30
CHIMEN075 World Reassembly C .10 .20
CHIMEN076 Crusher Run C .10 .20
CHIMEN077 Peaceful Burial SR .20 .40
CHIMEN078 Jelly Cannon R .15 .30
CHIMEN079 Soul Levy C .10 .20
CHIMEN080 Boompoline!! C .10 .20
CHIMEN081 Primineral Mandstrong C .10 .20
CHIMEN082 Desert Locusts C .10 .20
CHIMEN083 Tyrant Farm R .15 .30
CHIMEN084 Brutal Beast Battle R .15 .30
CHIMEN085 Phantasos, the Dream Mirror Friend SR .20 .40
CHIMEN086 Phantasos, the Dream Mirror Foe SR.20 .40
CHIMEN087 Oneiros, the Dream Mirror Erlking SR.20 .40
CHIMEN088 Dream Mirror Phantasms SR .20 .40
CHIMEN089 Dream Mirror of Chaos C .10 .20
CHIMEN090 Dream Mirror Hypnagogia SR .20 .40
CHIMEN091 Dream Mirror Oneiromancy R .15 .30
CHIMEN092 Overburst Dragon R .15 .30
CHIMEN093 Action Magic - Full Turn C .10 .20
CHIMEN094 Action Magic - Double Banking C .10 .20
CHIMEN095 Astra Ghouls C .10 .20
CHIMEN096 Bye Bye Damage C .10 .20
CHIMEN097 Dances with Beasts C .10 .20
CHIMEN098 Striker Dragon UR 15.00 30.00
CHIMEN099 Draco Masters of the Tenyi UR 1.25 2.50

2019 Yu-Gi-Oh Dark Neostorm 1st Edition

DANEEN000 Gnomaterial SCR 25.00 50.00
DANEEN001 Firewall Guardian C .15 .30
DANEEN002 Grid Sweeper C .15 .30
DANEEN003 Salamangreat Fennec C .15 .30
DANEEN004 Overflow Dragon C .15 .30
DANEEN005 Altergeist Fifinellag C .15 .30
DANEEN006 Dinowrestler Eskrimamenchi C .15 .30
DANEEN007 Dinowrestler Coelasilat C .15 .30
DANEEN008 Dinowrestler Martial Anga C .15 .30
DANEEN009 Destiny HERO - Drawhand C .15 .30
DANEEN010 Psi-Reflector R .25 .50
DANEEN011 Assault Sentinel C .15 .30
DANEEN012 T.G. Halberd Cannon/Assault Mode R.25 .50
DANEEN013 Super Quantum White Layer C .15 .30
DANEEN014 Neo Flamvell Lady C .15 .30
DANEEN015 Filo, Messenger Fur Hire R .25 .50
DANEEN016 Yuki-Musume, the Ice Mayakashi C .15 .30
DANEEN017 Knightmare Incarnation Idlee SCR 4.00 8.00
DANEEN018 World Legacy Guardragon Mardark R.25 .50
DANEEN019 Deus X-Krawler C .15 .30
DANEEN020 Omni Dragon Brotaur SCR 15.00 30.00
DANEEN021 Chaos Betrayer R .25 .50
DANEEN022 Loud Cloud the Storm Serpent C .15 .30
DANEEN023 Xyz Slidolphin C .15 .30
DANEEN024 Star Staring Starling R .25 .50
DANEEN025 Ghost Sister & Spooky Dogwood SCR10.0020.00
DANEEN026 Handigallop C .15 .30
DANEEN027 Emperor Maju Garzett C .15 .30
DANEEN028 Cupid Dunk C .15 .30
DANEEN029 Crealtar, the Impcantation Originator C.15 .30
DANEEN030 Dinowrestler Chimera T Wrextle C .15 .30
DANEEN031 Destiny HERO - Dominance SR .30 .75
DANEEN032 World Chalice Guardragon Almarduke R .25 .50
DANEEN033 Altergeist Dragvirion C .15 .30
DANEEN034 Dinowrestler Giga Spinosavate R .25 .50
DANEEN035 Ib the World Chalice Justiciar SCR15.00 30.00
DANEEN036 Firewall eXceed Dragon UR .50 1.00
DANEEN037 Super Quantal Mech Beast Lusterrex SR .30 .75
DANEEN038 Dingirsu Orcust Evening Star UR15.00 30.00
DANEEN039 Madolche Teacher Glassoufle R .25 .50
DANEEN040 Cyberse Reminder C .15 .30
DANEEN041 Dilingerous Dragon C .15 .30
DANEEN042 Dinowrestler Terra Parkourio C .15 .30
DANEEN043 Gouki The Blade Ogre C .15 .30
DANEEN044 Gouki The Solid Ogre C .15 .30
DANEEN045 Xtra HERO Cross Crusader R 1.50 3.00
DANEEN046 Neo Super...Blaster Magna SR .30 .75
DANEEN047 Mekk-Knight Crusadia Avramax SCR10.00 20.00
DANEEN048 World Gears of Theurlogical Demiurgy UR .50 1.00
DANEEN049 Puzzlomino, the Drop-n-Deleter C .15 .30
DANEEN050 Amphibious Swarmship Amblowhale R.25 .50
DANEEN051 Cynet Mining SCR 30.00 75.00
DANEEN052 Salamangreat Recureance UR .50 1.00
DANEEN053 Tyrant Dino Fusion C .15 .30
DANEEN054 Fusion Destiny SR 2.00 4.00

DANEEN055 Assault Mode Zero C .15 .30
DANEEN056 Super Quantal Alphancall Appeal C .15 .30
DANEEN057 Mayakashi Winter SR .30 .75
DANEEN058 Cloudian Aerosol C .15 .30
DANEEN059 World Legacy Monstrosity UR 2.50 5.00
DANEEN060 Guardragon Reincarnation C .15 .30
DANEEN061 Crusadia Testament C .15 .30
DANEEN062 Impcantation Thanatosis C .15 .30
DANEEN063 Dirge of the Lost Dragon SR .30 .75
DANEEN064 Mystic Mine SR 2.00 4.00
DANEEN065 Mordschlag C .15 .30
DANEEN066 Stand In C .15 .30
DANEEN067 Packet Swap C .15 .30
DANEEN068 Altergeist Haunted Rock C .15 .30
DANEEN069 D - Tactics R .25 .50
DANEEN070 Assault Reboot R .25 .50
DANEEN071 Super Quantal
Union - Magnaformation C .15 .30
DANEEN072 Magical Musket - Crooked Crown C .15 .30
DANEEN073 The Weather Rainbowed Canvas R .25 .50
DANEEN074 Orcust Crescendo SR .30 .75
DANEEN075 World Legacy Collapse C .15 .30
DANEEN076 World Legacy Cliffhanger C .15 .30
DANEEN077 Chain Hole SR .30 .75
DANEEN078 Crackdown SR 2.50 5.00
DANEEN079 Snowman Effect C .15 .30
DANEEN080 Dice It C .15 .30
DANEEN081 Muddy Mudragon R .25 .50
DANEEN082 Saryuja's Shackles C .15 .30
DANEEN083 Danger! Excitement! Mystery! UR .50 1.00
DANEEN084 Danger! Feets of Strength! R .25 .50
DANEEN085 You're in Danger! R .25 .50
DANEEN086 Valkyrie Funfte R .25 .50
DANEEN087 Valkyrie Erda UR .50 1.00
DANEEN088 Valkyrie Chariot C .15 .30
DANEEN089 Valkyrie's Embrace UR .50 1.00
DANEEN090 Pegasus Wing C .15 .30
DANEEN091 Loge's Flame SR .30 .75
DANEEN092 Number 5: Doom Chimera Dragon SR .30 .75
DANEEN093 Number XX: Utopic Dark Infinity UR .50 1.00
DANEEN094 Mermail Abyssalacia UR .50 1.00
DANEEN095 Cherubini... SCR 10.00 20.00
DANEEN096 Speedlift C .15 .30
DANEEN097 Pendulum Halt SR .30 .75
DANEEN098 Whitefish Salvage R .25 .50
DANEEN099 Memories of Hope SR .30 .75

2019 Yu-Gi-Oh Fists of the Gadgets 1st Edition

FIGAEN001 Boot-Up Corporal
Command Dynamo SR .15 .30
FIGAEN002 Boot-Up Admiral
Destroyer Dynamo SCR .20 .40
FIGAEN003 Boot-Up Order - Gear Charge SR .15 .30
FIGAEN004 Boot-Up Order - Gear Force SCR .20 .40
FIGAEN005 Powerhold the Moving Battery SR .15 .30
FIGAEN006 Green Gadget SR .15 .30
FIGAEN007 Red Gadget SR .15 .30
FIGAEN008 Yellow Gadget SR .15 .30
FIGAEN009 Gold Gadget SR .15 .30
FIGAEN010 Silver Gadget SR .15 .30
FIGAEN011 BOTFF Ram SCR .20 .40
FIGAEN012 BOTFF Elephant SCR 15.00 30.00
FIGAEN013 BOTFF Panda SCR 10.00 20.00
FIGAEN014 BOTFF Eland SCR 3.00 6.00
FIGAEN015 BOTFF Swan SCR .25 .50
FIGAEN016 BOTFF Eagle SCR 10.00 20.00
FIGAEN017 BOTFF Peacock SCR .75 1.50
FIGAEN018 Fire Fortress atop Liang Peak SCR .20 .40
FIGAEN019 Fire Formation - Domei SCR .20 .40
FIGAEN020 Fire Formation - Ingen SCR .20 .40
FIGAEN021 Ultimate Fire Formation - Sinto SCR .20 .40
FIGAEN022 BOTFF Gorilla SR .15 .30
FIGAEN023 BOTFF Bear SR .15 .30
FIGAEN024 BOTFF Spirit SR .15 .30
FIGAEN025 BOTFF Rooster SR .15 .30
FIGAEN026 BOTFF Cardinal SR .15 .30
FIGAEN027 BOTFF Tiger King SR .15 .30
FIGAEN028 Fire Formation - Tenki SCR 1.00 2.00
FIGAEN029 Fire Formation - Tensu SR .15 .30
FIGAEN030 Fire Formation - Yoko SR .15 .30
FIGAEN031 Archfiend's Awakening SCR .20 .40
FIGAEN032 Archfiend's Call SCR .20 .40
FIGAEN033 Archfiend's Ascent SCR .20 .40
FIGAEN034 Archfiend's Manifestation SCR .20 .40
FIGAEN035 Latency SR .15 .30
FIGAEN036 Swap Cleric SR .15 .30
FIGAEN037 Defcon Bird SR .15 .30
FIGAEN038 Prohibit Snake SR .15 .30
FIGAEN039 Code Radiator SCR 7.50 15.00
FIGAEN040 Spool Code? SR .15 .30
FIGAEN041 Cynet Optimization SR .15 .30
FIGAEN042 Cynet Conflict SR .15 .30
FIGAEN043 Code Talker SR .15 .30
FIGAEN044 Shootingcode Talker SR .15 .30
FIGAEN045 Elphase SR .15 .30
FIGAEN046 Talkback Lancer SR .15 .30
FIGAEN047 Rasterliger SR .15 .30
FIGAEN048 Subterror Fiendess SR .15 .30
FIGAEN049 The Hidden City SR 2.50 5.00
FIGAEN050 Subterror Final Battle SR .15 .30
FIGAEN051 Scrap Recycler SR 4.00 8.00
FIGAEN052 Majesty Maiden,
the True Dracocaster SR .15 .30
FIGAEN053 Ignis Heat, the True Dracowarrior SCR 2.00 4.00
FIGAEN054 Dinomight Knight True Dracofighter SR .15 .30
FIGAEN055 Amorphage Lechery SR .15 .30
FIGAEN056 Amorphage Sloth SR .60 1.25
FIGAEN057 Amorphage Goliath SR .15 .30
FIGAEN058 Chronograph Sorcerer SR .15 .30
FIGAEN059 Mythical Beast Master Cerberus SR 1.00 2.00
FIGAEN060 Starving Venom Fusion Dragon SR .50 1.00

2019 Yu-Gi-Oh The Infinity Chasers 1st Edition

INCHEN001 Infinitrack Harvester SCR 5.00 10.00
INCHEN002 Infinitrack Anchor Drill SCR 6.00 12.00
INCHEN003 Infinitrack Crab Crane SR .10 .20
INCHEN004 Infinitrack Drag Shovel SR .10 .20
INCHEN005 Infinitrack Trencher SCR .30 .75
INCHEN006 Infinitrack Tunneller SR .10 .20
INCHEN007 Infinitrack River Stormer SCR .20 .40
INCHEN008 Infinitrack Mountain Smasher SR .10 .20
INCHEN009 Infinitrack Earth Slicer SCR .30 .75
INCHEN010 Infinitrack Goliath SR .10 .20
INCHEN011 Infinitrack Fortress Megaclops SCR .30 .75
INCHEN012 Outrigger Extension SR .50 1.00
INCHEN013 Spin Turn SR .10 .20
INCHEN014 Witchcrafter Potterie SR .20 .40
INCHEN015 Witchcrafter Pittore SCR .60 1.25
INCHEN016 Witchcrafter Schmietta SR .15 .30
INCHEN017 Witchcrafter Edel SR 1.25 2.50
INCHEN018 Witchcrafter Haine SR 2.50 5.00
INCHEN019 Witchcrafter Madame Verre SCR 10.00 20.00
INCHEN020 Witchcrafter Creation SCR 25.00 50.00
INCHEN021 Witchcrafter Holiday SCR .60 1.25
INCHEN022 Witchcrafter Collaboration SR .12 .25
INCHEN023 Witchcrafter Draping SR .10 .20
INCHEN024 Witchcrafter Bystreet SCR .50 1.00
INCHEN025 Witchcrafter Scroll SCR .30 .75
INCHEN026 Witchcrafter Masterpiece SR .10 .20
INCHEN027 Serziel, Watcher of the Evil Eye SCR 20.00 40.00
INCHEN028 Medusa, Watcher of the Evil Eye SR .60 1.25
INCHEN029 Catoblepas, Familiar of the Evil Eye SR .10 .20
INCHEN030 Basilius, Familiar of the Evil Eye SR .10 .20
INCHEN031 Zerrziel, Ruler of the Evil Eyed SCR .30 .75
INCHEN032 Evil Eye of Selene SCR .30 .75
INCHEN033 Evil Eye Domain - Pareidolia SCR .50 1.00
INCHEN034 Evil Eye Awakening SCR .20 .40
INCHEN035 Evil Eye Confrontation SR .12 .25
INCHEN036 Evil Eye Repose SCR .25 .50
INCHEN037 Evil Eye Defeat SR .25 .50
INCHEN038 Evil Eye Mesmerism SCR .20 .40
INCHEN039 Evil Eye Retribution SCR .25 .50
INCHEN040 Confronting the "C" SR .10 .20
INCHEN041 Juragedo SR .15 .30
INCHEN042 Hidden Armory SR .20 .40
INCHEN043 Secret Village of the Spellcasters SR .60 1.25
INCHEN044 Rank-Up-Magic Astral Force SR .10 .20
INCHEN045 Marshalling Field SR .10 .20
INCHEN046 Heavy Freight Train Derricrane SR .15 .30
INCHEN047 Performapal Sky Magician SR .10 .20
INCHEN048 Mythical Beast Jackal King SR 2.50 5.00
INCHEN049 Arcanite Magician SR .12 .25
INCHEN050 Digvorzhak, King of Heavy Industry SR .12 .25
INCHEN051 Mecha Phantom Beast Dracossack SR .50 1.00
INCHEN052 Phantom Fortress Enterblathnir SR .15 .30
INCHEN053 Spell Absorption SR .15 .30
INCHEN054 Wonder Wand SR .15 .30
INCHEN055 Bound Wand SR .10 .20
INCHEN056 Tannhauser Gate SR .10 .20
INCHEN057 Magician's Right Hand SR .15 .30
INCHEN058 Magician's Left Hand SR .15 .30
INCHEN059 Spellbook of Knowledge SR .60 1.25
INCHEN060 Magic Cylinder SR .15 .30

2019 Yu-Gi-Oh Legendary Duelists Immortal Destiny 1st Edition

LED5EN000 Earthbound Immortal Ccapac Apu R .12 .25
LED5EN001 Curse Necrofear UR 10.00 20.00
LED5EN002 Dark Spirit of Banishment SR 2.00 4.00
LED5EN003 Dark Spirit of Malice SR 2.50 5.00
LED5EN004 Dark Spirit's Mastery UR 2.00 4.00
LED5EN005 Sentence of Doom SR .30 .75
LED5EN006 Dark Necrofear C .10 .20
LED5EN007 Doomcaliber Knight C .10 .20
LED5EN008 Diabound Kernel C .10 .20
LED5EN009 Dark Sanctuary R .12 .25
LED5EN010 Zoma the Spirit C .10 .20
LED5EN011 Call of the Earthbound C .10 .20
LED5EN012 Evil HERO Malicious Bane UR 60.00 125.00
LED5EN013 Evil HERO Adusted Gold UR 75.00 150.00
LED5EN014 Evil HERO Sinister Necrom UR .60 1.25
LED5EN015 Supreme King's Castle R .12 .25
LED5EN016 Evil Mind R .12 .25
LED5EN017 Evil HERO Malicious Edge C .10 .20
LED5EN018 Evil HERO Infernal Gainer C .10 .20
LED5EN019 Evil HERO Infernal Prodigy C .10 .20
LED5EN020 Evil HERO Malicious Fiend C .10 .20
LED5EN021 Dark Fusion C .10 .20
LED5EN022 Dark Calling C .10 .20
LED5EN023 Earthbound Greater Linewalker UR .60 1.25
LED5EN024 Ascator, Dawnwalker UR 1.25 2.50
LED5EN025 Supay, Duskwalker UR 1.25 2.50
LED5EN026 Earthbound Geoglyph SR .30 .75
LED5EN027 Ultimate Earthbound Immortal R .12 .25
LED5EN028 Earthbound Immortal
Wiraqocha Rasca C .10 .20
LED5EN029 Oracle of the Sun C .10 .20
LED5EN030 Fire Ant Ascator C .10 .20
LED5EN031 Supay C .10 .20
LED5EN032 Sun Dragon Inti C .10 .20
LED5EN033 Moon Dragon Quilla C .10 .20
LED5EN034 Gimmick Puppet Gigantes Doll SR .25 .50
LED5EN035 Gimmick Puppet Terror Baby R .12 .25
LED5EN036 Gimmick Puppet Bisque Doll SR .75 1.50
LED5EN037 Perform Puppet R .12 .25
LED5EN038 Puppet Parade C .10 .20
LED5EN039 Gimmick Puppet Dreary Doll C .10 .20
LED5EN040 Gimmick Puppet Magnet Doll C .10 .20
LED5EN041 Gimmick Puppet Des Troy C .10 .20
LED5EN042 Gimmick Puppet Humpty Dumpty C .10 .20
LED5EN043 Number 40:
Gimmick Puppet of Strings C .10 .20
LED5EN044 Junk Puppet C .10 .20
LED5EN045 Predaplant Triphyoverutum SR 5.00 10.00
LED5EN046 Predaplant Heliamphorhynchus SR .60 1.25
LED5EN047 Predapractice UR 1.25 2.50
LED5EN048 Predaprime Fusion R .12 .25
LED5EN049 Predaplanning R .12 .25
LED5EN050 Predaplant Drosophyllum Hydra C .10 .20
LED5EN051 Predaplant Chlamydosundew C .10 .20
LED5EN052 Starving Venom Fusion Dragon R .75 1.50
LED5EN053 Predaplant Dragostapelia C .10 .20
LED5EN054 Predaponics C .10 .20
LED5EN055 Predaplast C .10 .20
LED5EN056 Earthbound Immortal Revival C .10 .20
LED5EN057 Roar of the Earthbound Immortal C .10 .20

2019 Yu-Gi-Oh Legendary Duelists Sisters of the Rose 1st Edition

LED4EN000 Harpie's Feather Storm SR .60 1.25
LED4EN001 Harpie Perfumer UR 10.00 20.00
LED4EN002 Harpie Oracle SR 1.25 2.50
LED4EN003 Alluring Mirror Split UR 4.00 8.00
LED4EN004 Harpie's Feather Rest UR 4.00 8.00
LED4EN005 Harpie Lady Elegance R .25 .50
LED4EN006 Harpie Lady Sisters C .15 .30
LED4EN007 Harpie Queen C .15 .30
LED4EN008 Elegant Egotist C .15 .30
LED4EN009 Harpies' Hunting Ground C .15 .30
LED4EN010 Harpie Lady Phoenix Formation C .15 .30
LED4EN011 Triangle Ecstasy Spark C .15 .30
LED4EN012 Cyber Angel Izana SR .60 1.25
LED4EN013 Cyber Egg Angel R .25 .50
LED4EN014 Merciful Machine Angel SR .60 1.25
LED4EN015 Incarnated Machine Angel R .25 .50
LED4EN016 Magnificent Machine Angel R .25 .50
LED4EN017 Cyber Petit Angel C .15 .30
LED4EN018 Cyber Angel Benten C .15 .30
LED4EN019 Cyber Angel Idaten C .15 .30
LED4EN020 Cyber Angel Dakini C .15 .30
LED4EN021 Machine Angel Ritual C .15 .30
LED4EN022 Ritual Sanctuary C .15 .30
LED4EN023 Garden Rose Maiden UR 4.00 8.00
LED4EN024 Dark Rose Fairy R .25 .50
LED4EN025 Red Rose Dragon R .25 .50
LED4EN026 Frozen Rose UR 4.00 8.00
LED4EN027 Blooming of the Darkest Rose R .25 .50
LED4EN028 Black Rose Dragon C .15 .30
LED4EN029 Twilight Rose Knight C .15 .30
LED4EN030 Witch of the Black Rose C .15 .30
LED4EN031 Blue Rose Dragon C .15 .30
LED4EN032 Black Garden C .15 .30
LED4EN033 Mark of the Rose C .15 .30
LED4EN034 Superdreadnought...
Juggernaut Liebe UR 10.00 20.00
LED4EN035 Super Express Bullet Train UR 5.00 10.00
LED4EN036 Flying Pegasus Railroad Stampede SR 1.50 3.00
LED4EN037 Urgent Schedule UR 15.00 30.00
LED4EN038 Barrage Blast UR .60 1.25
LED4EN039 Superdreadnought...Gustav Max R .25 .50
LED4EN040 Night Express Knight C .15 .30
LED4EN041 Snow Plow Hustle Rustle C .15 .30
LED4EN042 Ruffian Railcar C .15 .30
LED4EN043 Construction Train Signal Red C .15 .30
LED4EN044 Special Schedule C .15 .30
LED4EN045 Lunalight Sabre Dancer SR 2.50 5.00
LED4EN046 Lunalight Emerald Bird R .25 .50
LED4EN047 Lunalight Yellow Marten R .25 .50
LED4EN048 Lunalight Fusion SR 4.00 8.00
LED4EN049 Lunalight Serenade Dance SR 4.00 8.00
LED4EN050 Lunalight Blue Cat C .15 .30
LED4EN051 Lunalight Kaleido Chick C .15 .30
LED4EN052 Lunalight Cat Dancer C .15 .30
LED4EN053 Lunalight Panther Dancer C .15 .30
LED4EN054 Lunalight Leo Dancer C .15 .30
LED4EN055 Luna Light Perfume C .15 .30

2019 Yu-Gi-Oh Mystic Fighters 1st Edition

MYFIEN001 Mathmech Sigma SR .15 .30
MYFIEN002 Mathmech Nabla SR .15 .30
MYFIEN003 Mathmech Addition SR 2.50 5.00
MYFIEN004 Mathmech Subtraction SR .15 .30
MYFIEN005 Mathmech Multiplication SR .15 .30
MYFIEN006 Mathmech Division SR .15 .30
MYFIEN007 Geomathmech Magma SCR .30 .75
MYFIEN008 Geomathmech Final Sigma SCR 1.00 2.00
MYFIEN009 Primathmech Laplacian SCR 2.50 5.00
MYFIEN010 Mathmech Equation SCR .30 .75
MYFIEN011 Mathmech Billionblade Nayuta SR .15 .30
MYFIEN012 Mathmech Superfactorial SCR .20 .40
MYFIEN013 Mathmech Induction SCR .20 .40
MYFIEN014 Nurse Dragonmaid SCR 20.00 40.00
MYFIEN015 Dragonmaid Ernus SR .15 .30
MYFIEN016 Laundry Dragonmaid SR 2.00 4.00
MYFIEN017 Dragonmaid Nudyarl SCR .50 1.00
MYFIEN018 Kitchen Dragonmaid SCR 50.00 100.00
MYFIEN019 Dragonmaid Tinkhec SR .15 .30
MYFIEN020 Parlor Dragonmaid SR 4.00 8.00
MYFIEN021 Dragonmaid Lorpar SCR .50 1.00
MYFIEN022 House Dragonmaid SCR .75 1.50
MYFIEN023 Dragonmaid Hospitality SR 4.00 8.00
MYFIEN024 Dragonmaid Welcome SCR .50 1.00
MYFIEN025 Dragonmaid Changeover SR .15 .30
MYFIEN026 Dragonmaid Downtime SR .15 .30
MYFIEN027 Mardel, Generaider Boss of Light SCR 10.00 20.00
MYFIEN028 Frodi, Generaider Boss of Swords SR .15 .30
MYFIEN029 Dovelgus, Generaider Boss of Iron SCR .20 .40
MYFIEN030 Naglfar, Generaider Boss of Fire SCR .25 .50
MYFIEN031 Nidhogg, Generaider Boss of Ice SCR .50 1.00
MYFIEN032 Hela, Generaider Boss of Doom SR 4.00 8.00
MYFIEN032 Jormungandr, Generaider
Boss of Eternity SCR .50 1.00
MYFIEN034 Generaider Boss Stage SCR 15.00 30.00
MYFIEN035 Generaider Boss Quest SCR .50 1.00
MYFIEN036 Generaider Boss Loot SR .15 .30
MYFIEN037 Generaider Boss Fight SR .15 .30
MYFIEN038 Generaider Boss Room SR .15 .30
MYFIEN039 Generaider Boss Bite SR .15 .30
MYFIEN040 Primathmech Alembertian SCR 15.00 30.00
MYFIEN041 Jinzo SR .50 1.00
MYFIEN042 Lonefire Blossom SR .15 .30
MYFIEN043 Debris Dragon SR .15 .30
MYFIEN044 Brotherhood of the
Fire Fist - Dragon SR .15 .30
MYFIEN045 Tempest, Dragon Ruler of Storms SR .30 .75
MYFIEN046 Lightning, Dragon Ruler of Drafts SR .15 .30
MYFIEN047 Balancer Lord SR .50 1.00
MYFIEN048 World Legacy Guardragon Mardark SR .15 .30
MYFIEN049 True King of All Calamities SR 1.00 2.00
MYFIEN050 Dragon's Gunfire SR .15 .30
MYFIEN051 Stamping Destruction SR .15 .30
MYFIEN052 Super Rejuvenation SR .15 .30
MYFIEN053 Monster Gate SR .15 .30
MYFIEN054 Dark World Dealings SR .75 1.50
MYFIEN055 Rekindling SR .15 .30
MYFIEN056 Dragon Ravine SR .50 1.00
MYFIEN057 Cynet Backdoor SR .15 .30
MYFIEN058 Appropriate SR .15 .30
MYFIEN059 Heavy Slump SR .15 .30
MYFIEN060 Waking the Dragon SR .50 1.00

2019 Yu-Gi-Oh OTS Tournament Pack 11

OP11EN001 Dingirsu, the Orcust
of the Evening Star UR 30.00 75.00
OP11EN002 Sky Striker Ace - Kaina UR 15.00 30.00
OP11EN003 Pot of Desires UR 50.00 100.00
OP11EN004 Fortune Lady Light SR .50 1.00
OP11EN005 Subterror Nemesis Archer SR .40 .80
OP11EN006 Altergeist Kunquery SR .60 1.25
OP11EN007 Orcust Harp Horror SR 3.00 6.00
OP11EN008 Orcust Knightmare SR 1.25 2.50
OP11EN009 Aloof Lupine SR .75 1.50
OP11EN010 Salamangreat Violet Chimera SR .40 .80
OP11EN011 Fortune's Future SR .25 .50
OP11EN012 Metaverse SR 1.00 2.00
OP11EN013 Cyber Dragon C .12 .25
OP11EN014 Boot-Up Soldier - Dread Dynamo C .12 .25
OP11EN015 Fortune Lady Fire C .12 .25
OP11EN016 Fortune Lady Water C .25 .50
OP11EN017 Limiter Removal C .15 .30
OP11EN018 Future Visions C .30 .75
OP11EN019 Moray of Greed C .75 1.50
OP11EN020 True Draco Heritage C .40 .80
OP11EN021 Stronghold the Moving Fortress C .07 .15
OP11EN022 All-Out Attacks C .12 .25
OP11EN023 Synchro Material C .10 .20
OP11EN024 Eisbahn C .10 .20
OP11EN025 True King's Return C .75 1.50
OP11EN026 Duel Dragon Token SR .30 .75

2019 Yu-Gi-Oh OTS Tournament Pack 12

OP12EN001 Chaos Dragon Levianeer UR 25.00 50.00
OP12EN002 Twin Twisters UR 30.00 75.00
OP12EN003 Solemn Judgment UR 75.00 150.00
OP12EN004 Gren Maju Da Eiza SR 2.50 5.00
OP12EN005 Crusadia Leonis SR .40 .80
OP12EN006 Salamangreat Jack Jaguar SR 1.50 3.00
OP12EN007 Orcust Cymbal Skeleton SR 1.00 2.00
OP12EN008 Servant of Endymion SR 1.25 2.50
OP12EN009 Tenyi Spirit - Adhara SR .60 1.25
OP12EN010 Tenyi Spirit - Vishuda SR .75 1.50
OP12EN011 Time Thief Redoer SR .75 1.50
OP12EN012 Salamangreat Rage SR .75 1.50
OP12EN013 Gigantes C .15 .30
OP12EN014 Brotherhood of the Fire Fist - Raven C .12 .25
OP12EN015 Magician's Robe C .30 .60
OP12EN016 Sea Archiver C .40 .80
OP12EN017 Flame Bufferlo C .30 .60
OP12EN018 Salamangreat Fowl C .15 .30
OP12EN019 Kaminari Attack C .17 .35
OP12EN020 Brotherhood of the
Fire Fist - Horse Prince C .30 .60
OP12EN021 Hi-Speedroid Chanbara C .07 .15
OP12EN022 Dark Hole C .50 1.00
OP12EN023 Makiu, the Magical Mist C .07 .15
OP12EN024 Contract with the Abyss C .20 .40
OP12EN025 Fire Formation - Tenki C .50 1.00
OP12EN026 Primal Being Token SR 3.00 6.00

2019 Yu-Gi-Oh Rising Rampage 1st Edition

RIRAEN000 Capshell SCR 1.25 2.50
RIRAEN001 Rescue Interlacer C .15 .30
RIRAEN002 Cross Debug C .15 .30
RIRAEN003 Marincess Sea Horse PRISM SCR 150.00 300.00
RIRAEN003 Marincess Sea Horse UR 7.50 15.00
RIRAEN004 Marincess Sea Star C .15 .30
RIRAEN005 DMZ Dragon C .15 .30
RIRAEN006 Dinowrestler Martial Ankylo C .15 .30
RIRAEN007 Dinowrestler Rambrachio C .15 .30
RIRAEN008 Fortune Lady Past R .25 .50
RIRAEN009 Yosenju Sabu C .15 .30
RIRAEN010 Yosenju Izna C .15 .30
RIRAEN011 Mayosenju Hitot SR .30 .75
RIRAEN012 Tenyi Spirit - Adhara R 1.50 3.00
RIRAEN013 Tenyi Spirit - Shthana R 1.25 2.50
RIRAEN014 Tenyi Spirit - Mapura R .25 .50
RIRAEN015 Tenyi Spirit - Nahata R .25 .50
RIRAEN016 Tenyi Spirit - Vishuda R .60 1.25
RIRAEN017 Simorgh, Bird of Beginning C .15 .30
RIRAEN018 Simorgh, Bird of Bringing R .25 .50
RIRAEN019 Simorgh, Bird of Calamity C .15 .30
RIRAEN020 Simorgh, Bird of Protection C .15 .30
RIRAEN021 Simorgh, Lord of the Storm SR .30 .75
RIRAEN022 Simorgh of Darkness SR .30 .75
RIRAEN023 B.E.S. Blaster Cannon Core SR .30 .75
RIRAEN024 Vic Viper T301 R .25 .50
RIRAEN025 Reptilianne Lamia C .15 .30
RIRAEN026 Ranryu C .15 .30
RIRAEN027 Avida, Rebuilder of Worlds SR .30 .75
RIRAEN028 Witchcrafter Golem Aruru SCR 3.00 6.00
RIRAEN029 Gizmek Orochi/Serpentron
Sky Slasher SCR 15.00 30.00
RIRAEN030 Cataclysmic Cryonic Coldo C .15 .30
RIRAEN031 Voltester C .15 .30
RIRAEN032 Tlakalel, His Malevolent Majesty R .25 .50
RIRAEN033 Beatraptor C .15 .30
RIRAEN034 Spirit Sculptor SR .30 .75
RIRAEN035 Reversible Beetle C .15 .30
RIRAEN036 Megistric Maginician C .15 .30
RIRAEN037 Magicalibra C .15 .30
RIRAEN038 Fortune Lady Every SCR 5.00 10.00
RIRAEN039 Borreload eXcharge Dragon UR 1.00 2.00
RIRAEN040 Marincess Blue Slug UR 5.00 10.00
RIRAEN041 Marincess Coral Anemone SCR 25.00 50.00
RIRAEN042 Marincess Marbled Rock SCR 6.00 12.00
RIRAEN043 Monk of the Tenyi R .25 .50
RIRAEN044 Shaman of the Tenyi UR 4.00 8.00

RIRAEN045 Berserker of the Tenyi R .25 .50
RIRAEN046 Wynn the Wind Charmer, Verdant R .50 1.00
RIRAEN046 Wynn Wind Charmer
Verdant PRISM SCR 150.00 300.00
RIRAEN047 Linkmail Archfiend SR .30 .75
RIRAEN048 Apollousa, Bow of the Goddess SCR50.00 100.00
RIRAEN048 Apollousa Bow
of Goddess PRISM SCR 300.00 600.00
RIRAEN049 Defender of the Labyrinth C .15 .30
RIRAEN050 Baba Barber C .15 .30
RIRAEN051 Link Back C .15 .30
RIRAEN052 Grid Rod C .15 .30
RIRAEN053 Rising Fire R .25 .50
RIRAEN054 Fury of Fire C .15 .30
RIRAEN055 Fortune Vision R .25 .50
RIRAEN056 Fortune Lady Calling UR .50 1.00
RIRAEN057 Yosenju Wind Worship C .15 .30
RIRAEN058 Flawless Perfection of the Tenyi R .25 .50
RIRAEN059 Vessel for the Dragon Cycle R .25 .50
RIRAEN060 Elborz, the Sacred Lands of Simorgh C.15 .30
RIRAEN061 Simorgh Onslaught C .15 .30
RIRAEN062 Simorgh Repulsion C .15 .30
RIRAEN063 Hypernova Burst SR .30 .75
RIRAEN064 Psychic Fervor C .15 .30
RIRAEN065 Blockout Curtain C .15 .30
RIRAEN066 Sextet Summon C .15 .30
RIRAEN067 Draw Discharge C .15 .30
RIRAEN068 Marincess Wave UR .60 1.25
RIRAEN069 Marincess Current C .15 .30
RIRAEN070 Fortune Lady Rewind R .25 .50
RIRAEN071 Yosenjus' Sword Sting C .15 .30
RIRAEN072 Fists of the Unrivaled Tenyi R .25 .50
RIRAEN073 Simorgh Sky Battle C .15 .30
RIRAEN074 World Legacy Bestowal C .15 .30
RIRAEN075 The Return to the Normal C .15 .30
RIRAEN076 Get Out! SCR 7.50 15.00
RIRAEN077 Storm Dragon's Return PRISM SCR60.00 125.00
RIRAEN077 Storm Dragon's Return SR 1.00 2.00
RIRAEN078 Setuppercut C .15 .30
RIRAEN079 Dwimmered Glimmer C .15 .30
RIRAEN080 Fighting Dirty C .15 .30
RIRAEN081 Barricadeborg Blocker C .15 .30
RIRAEN082 Hraesvelgr, the
Desperate Doom Eagle R .25 .50
RIRAEN083 Star Power!! R .25 .50
RIRAEN084 Fuhma Wave C .15 .30
RIRAEN085 Ikelos, the Dream Mirror Sprite UR .30 .75
RIRAEN086 Ikelos, the Dream Mirror Mara SR 1.00 2.00
RIRAEN087 Morpheus, the
Dream Mirror White Knight SR 1.00 2.00
RIRAEN088 Morpheus, the Dream
Mirror Black Knight UR .30 .75
RIRAEN089 Dream Mirror of Joy SR .30 .75
RIRAEN090 Dream Mirror of Terror SR .30 .75
RIRAEN091 Dream Mirror Fantasy C .15 .30
RIRAEN092 Yosenju Oroshi Channeling C .15 .30
RIRAEN093 Number 29: Mannequin Cat C .15 .30
RIRAEN094 Kikinagashi Fucho C .15 .30
RIRAEN095 White Aura Monoceros SR .30 .75
RIRAEN096 White Howling SR .50 1.00
RIRAEN097 F.A. Shining Star GT C .15 .30
RIRAEN098 Dragunity Knight - Romulus UR 5.00 10.00
RIRAEN099 Rogue of Endymion C .15 .30

2019 Yu-Gi-Oh Savage Strike 1st Edition

SASTEN000 Danger! Ogopogo! UR 2.00 4.00
SASTEN001 Catche Eve L2 C .15 .30
SASTEN002 Cyberse Synchron R .20 .40
SASTEN003 Salamangreat Wolvie C .15 .30
SASTEN004 Salamangreat Parro C .15 .30
SASTEN005 Salamangreat Foxer C .15 .30
SASTEN006 Speedburst Dragon R .20 .40
SASTEN007 Rokket Synchron R .20 .40
SASTEN008 Neo Space Connector C .15 .30
SASTEN009 T.G. Screw Serpent R .20 .40
SASTEN010 T.G. Booster Raptor C .15 .30
SASTEN011 T.G. Tank Grub C .15 .30
SASTEN012 Guardragon Justicia C .15 .30
SASTEN013 Guardragon Garmides C .15 .30
SASTEN014 Guardragon Promineses C .15 .30
SASTEN015 Guardragon Andrako R .20 .40
SASTEN016 World Legacy - World Ark"" R .20 .40
SASTEN017 Shiranui Spectralsword Shade SR .30 .75
SASTEN018 Shiranui Swordmaster C .15 .30
SASTEN019 Shiranui Squire SR .30 .75
SASTEN020 Fantastical Dragon Phantazmay SCR60.00 125.00
SASTEN021 Orcust Knightmare C .15 .30
SASTEN022 Prank-Kids Rocksies C .15 .30
SASTEN023 Madolche Petingcessoeur R .20 .40
SASTEN024 Psychic Wheeleder SCR 20.00 40.00
SASTEN025 Psychic Tracker C .15 .30
SASTEN026 Thunderclap Monk SR .30 .75
SASTEN027 Lappis Dragon R .20 .40
SASTEN028 Cataclysmic Scorching Sunburner C.15 .30
SASTEN029 Squirt Squid C .15 .30
SASTEN030 Aloof Lupine C .15 .30
SASTEN031 Extraceratops C .15 .30
SASTEN032 Impcantation Chalislime R .20 .40
SASTEN033 Trickstar Band Sweet Guitar SR .30 .75
SASTEN034 Salamangreat Violet Chimera R .20 .40
SASTEN035 Elemental HERO Brave Neos SR .30 .75
SASTEN036 Elemental HERO Cosmo Neos SR .30 .75
SASTEN037 Borreload Savage Dragon UR 20.00 40.00
SASTEN038 Cyberse Quantum Dragon UR .60 1.25
SASTEN039 T.G. Star Guardian UR .60 1.25
SASTEN040 Shiranui Swordsaga C .15 .30
SASTEN041 Shiranui Squiresaga C .15 .30
SASTEN042 Hyper Psychic Riser R .20 .40
SASTEN043 Cyberse Integrator C .15 .30
SASTEN044 Cyberse Wicckid C .15 .30
SASTEN045 Update Jammer C .15 .30
SASTEN046 Detonate Deleter R .20 .40
SASTEN047 Clock Lizard C .15 .30
SASTEN048 Salamangreat Sunlight Wolf R 6.00 12.00
SASTEN049 Trickstar Divaridis UR .60 1.25
SASTEN050 T.G. Trident Launcher SCR 1.50 3.00
SASTEN051 Guardragon Elpy SR .30 .75
SASTEN052 Guardragon Pisty SR .30 .75
SASTEN053 Guardragon Agarpain SR .30 .75
SASTEN054 Shiranui Skillsaga Supremacy UR 1.50 3.00
SASTEN055 Sky Striker Ace - Kaina SR .30 .75
SASTEN056 Hiita the Fire Charmer, Ablaze R .20 .40
SASTEN057 Fusion of Fire R 1.50 3.00
SASTEN058 Trickstar Live Stage SCR 2.50 5.00
SASTEN059 Trickstar Fusion R .20 .40
SASTEN060 Neos Fusion SR .30 .75
SASTEN061 Guardragon Shield R .20 .40
SASTEN062 World Legacy Guardragon UR 5.00 10.00
SASTEN063 Ghost Meets Girl -
A Shiranui's Story UR .60 1.25
SASTEN064 Shiranui Style Solemnity C .15 .30
SASTEN065 Impcantation Inception C .15 .30
SASTEN066 Uni-Song Tuning C .15 .30
SASTEN067 Pot of Extravagance SCR 50.00 100.00
SASTEN068 Edge of the Ring C .15 .30
SASTEN069 Child's Play C .15 .30
SASTEN070 Summon Over C .15 .30
SASTEN071 NEXT SR .30 .75
SASTEN072 Guardragon Corewakening C .15 .30
SASTEN073 Guardragon Cataclysm R .20 .40
SASTEN074 Shiranui Style Success C .15 .30
SASTEN075 Fateful Hour SR .30 .75
SASTEN076 Orcustrated Release C .15 .30
SASTEN077 Subterror Succession C .15 .30
SASTEN078 Dark Factory of More Production R .20 .40
SASTEN079 Witch's Strike SCR 10.00 20.00
SASTEN080 Loss Time C .15 .30
SASTEN081 Super...Mecha-Thunder-King SCR 5.00 10.00
SASTEN082 Time Thief Winder C .15 .30
SASTEN083 Time Thief Bezel Ship C .15 .30
SASTEN084 Time Thief Regulator C .15 .30
SASTEN085 Time Thief Redoer C .15 .30
SASTEN086 Time Thief Hack C .15 .30
SASTEN087 Time Thief Flyback C .15 .30
SASTEN088 Valkyrie Sechste SCR 3.00 6.00
SASTEN089 Valkyrie Vierte? SR .30 .75
SASTEN090 Final Light UR .60 1.25
SASTEN091 Apple of Enlightenment?? R .20 .40
SASTEN092 Cyberse Converter C .15 .30
SASTEN093 Legendary Secret of the Six Samurai C.15 .30
SASTEN094 Subterror Guru C .15 .30
SASTEN095 Trickstar Corobane UR 7.50 15.00
SASTEN096 Performapal Clay Breaker C .15 .30
SASTEN097 Super Armored
Robot Armed Black Iron C .15 .30
SASTEN098 Shinobi Necro C .15 .30
SASTEN099 Red Rising Dragon C .15 .30

2019 Yu-Gi-Oh Structure Deck Order of the Spellcasters 1st Edition

SR08EN001 Endymion, the
Mighty Master of Magic UR .60 1.25
SR08EN002 Reflection of Endymion SR .30 .75
SR08EN003 Magister of Endymion C .15 .30
SR08EN004 Servant of Endymion C 2.50 5.00
SR08EN005 Endymion, the Master Magician C .15 .30
SR08EN006 Crusader of Endymion C .15 .30
SR08EN007 Defender, the Magical Knight C .15 .30
SR08EN008 Mythical Beast Cerberus C .15 .30
SR08EN009 Mythical Beast Medusa C .15 .30
SR08EN010 Magical Something C .15 .30
SR08EN011 Magical Exemplar C .15 .30
SR08EN012 Magical Abductor C .15 .30
SR08EN013 Disenchanter C .15 .30
SR08EN014 Apprentice Magician C .15 .30
SR08EN015 Dark Magician of Chaos C .30 .75
SR08EN016 Fairy Tail - Luna C .15 .30
SR08EN017 Summoner Monk C .15 .40
SR08EN018 Spellbook Magician of Prophecy C .25 .50
SR08EN019 Magical Undertaker C .15 .30
SR08EN020 Magician of Faith C .15 .30
SR08EN021 Droll & Lock Bird C 2.00 4.00
SR08EN022 Spell Power Mastery SR 1.50 3.00
SR08EN023 Endymion's Lab C .15 .30
SR08EN024 Magical Citadel of Endymion C .15 .30
SR08EN025 Spell Power Grasp C .15 .30
SR08EN026 Arcane Barrier C .15 .30
SR08EN027 Spellbook of Secrets C .25 .50
SR08EN028 Spellbook of Power C .15 .30
SR08EN029 Spellbook of Wisdom C .15 .30
SR08EN030 Magical Blast C .15 .30
SR08EN031 Magical Dimension C .15 .30
SR08EN032 Terraforming C .20 .40
SR08EN033 Left Arm Offering C .30 .75
SR08EN034 Pot of Desires C 1.50 3.00
SR08EN035 Mythical Bestiamorph C .15 .30
SR08EN036 Pitch-Black Power Stone C .15 .30
SR08EN037 Extra Buck C .15 .30
SR08EN038 Gagagashield C .15 .30
SR08EN039 Magician's Circle C .15 .30
SR08EN040 Day-Breaker the
Shining Magical Warrior UR .30 .75
SR08EN041 Dwimmered Path SR .30 .75

2019 Yu-Gi-Oh Structure Deck Rokket Revolt 1st Edition

SDRREN001 Silverrokket Dragon SR .25 .50
SDRREN002 Rokket Tracer SR .60 1.25
SDRREN003 Rokket Recharger C .15 .30
SDRREN004 Exploderokket Dragon C .15 .30
SDRREN005 Absorouter Dragon SR .60 1.25
SDRREN006 Checksum Dragon C .15 .30
SDRREN007 Anesthrokket Dragon C .15 .30
SDRREN008 Autorokket Dragon C .15 .30
SDRREN009 Magnarokket Dragon C .15 .30
SDRREN010 Shelrokket Dragon C .15 .30
SDRREN011 Metalrokket Dragon C .15 .30
SDRREN012 Rokket Synchron C .15 .30
SDRREN013 Gateway Dragon C .15 .30
SDRREN014 Defrag Dragon C .15 .30
SDRREN015 Background Dragon C .15 .30
SDRREN016 Labradorite Dragon C .15 .30
SDRREN017 Paladin of Felgrand C .15 .40
SDRREN018 Dragon Knight of Creation C .15 .30
SDRREN019 Keeper of the Shrine C .15 .30
SDRREN020 World Chalice Guardragon C .15 .30
SDRREN021 Raiden, Hand of the Lightsworn C .15 .30
SDRREN022 Borrel Supplier C .15 .30
SDRREN023 Rapid Trigger C .15 .30
SDRREN024 Squib Draw C .15 .30
SDRREN025 Quick Launch C .30 .75
SDRREN026 Boot Sector Launch C .15 .30
SDRREN027 Borrel Regenerator C .15 .30
SDRREN028 Dragon Shrine C .15 .30
SDRREN029 Ruins of the Divine Dragon Lords C.15 .30
SDRREN030 Return of the Dragon Lords C .60 1.25
SDRREN031 Polymerization C .50 1.00
SDRREN032 Twin Twisters C 1.50 3.00
SDRREN033 Zero-Day Blaster SR .25 .50
SDRREN034 Execute Protocols C .15 .30
SDRREN035 Red Reboot C .30 .75
SDRREN036 Link Turret C .15 .30
SDRREN037 Mirror Force Launcher C .15 .30
SDRREN038 Mirror Force C .15 .30
SDRREN039 Magic Cylinder C .15 .30
SDRREN040 Imperial Order C .50 1.00
SDRREN041 Topologic Zeroboros UR .30 .75
SDRREN042 Borreload Furious Dragon UR .30 .75
SDRREN043 Quadborrel Dragon UR .30 .75
SDRREN044 Borreload Dragon C .75 1.50
SDRREN045 Triple Burst Dragon C .60 1.25
SDRREN046 Booster Dragon C .15 .30

2019 Yu-Gi-Oh Structure Deck Soulburner 1st Edition

SDSBEN001 Salamangreat Raccoon C .15 .30
SDSBEN002 Salamangreat Mole C .15 .30
SDSBEN003 Salamangreat Gazelle SR .20 .40
SDSBEN004 Salamangreat Spinny SR .30 .75
SDSBEN005 Salamangreat Fowl C .15 .30
SDSBEN006 Salamangreat Beat Bison C .15 .30
SDSBEN007 Salamangreat Meer C .15 .30
SDSBEN008 Salamangreat Foxy C .15 .30
SDSBEN009 Salamangreat Falco C .15 .30
SDSBEN010 Salamangreat Jack Jaguar C .15 .30
SDSBEN011 Salamangreat Wolvie C .15 .30
SDSBEN012 Salamangreat Parro C .15 .30
SDSBEN013 Salamangreat Foxer C .15 .30
SDSBEN014 True King Agnimazud, the Vanisher C.25 .50
SDSBEN015 Dogoran, the Mad Flame Kaiju C .50 1.00
SDSBEN016 Flamvell Firedog C .15 .30
SDSBEN017 Fencing Fire Ferret C .15 .30
SDSBEN018 Inferno C .15 .30
SDSBEN019 Ash Blossom & Joyous Spring C 6.00 12.00
SDSBEN020 Red Resonator C .15 .30
SDSBEN021 Volcanic Shell C .15 .30
SDSBEN022 Formud Skipper C .15 .30
SDSBEN023 Salamangreat Circle SR .20 .40
SDSBEN024 Salamangreat Claw C .15 .30
SDSBEN025 Salamangreat Sanctuary C .15 .30
SDSBEN026 Will of the Salamangreat C .15 .30
SDSBEN027 Monster Reincarnation C .15 .30
SDSBEN028 Circle of the Fire Kings C .15 .30
SDSBEN029 Transmodify C .15 .30
SDSBEN030 Link Bound C .15 .30
SDSBEN031 Magic Planter C .15 .30
SDSBEN032 Salamangreat Rage C .15 .30
SDSBEN033 Salamangreat Roar SR .20 .40
SDSBEN034 Salamangreat Gift C .15 .30
SDSBEN035 The Transmigration Prophecy C .15 .30
SDSBEN036 Threatening Roar C .15 .30
SDSBEN037 Break Off Trap Hole C .15 .30
SDSBEN038 Backfire C .15 .30
SDSBEN039 Gozen Match C .25 .50
SDSBEN040 Salamangreat Heatleo
(alternate artwork) UR .25 .50
SDSBEN041 Salamangreat Heatleo C .15 .30
SDSBEN042 Salamangreat Miragestallio UR .25 .50
SDSBEN043 Salamangreat Balelynx UR .25 .50
SDSBEN044 Flame Administrator C .15 .30
SDSBEN045 Duelittle Chimera C .15 .30

2020 Yu-Gi-Oh Battles of Legend Armageddon 1st Edition

BLAREN000 Number 39: Utopia SLR 200.00 400.00
BLAREN001 Dark Spell Regeneration SCR .75 1.50
BLAREN002 Powered Crawler SCR .75 1.50
BLAREN003 Intruder Alarm - Yellow Alert UR .75 1.50
BLAREN004 Penguin Torpedo UR .75 1.50
BLAREN005 Weathering Soldier SCR 2.50 5.00
BLAREN006 Fossil Warrior Skull King SCR 2.00 4.00
BLAREN007 Fossil Warrior Skull Knight SCR 7.50 15.00
BLAREN008 Fossil Warrior Skull Bone SCR 1.00 2.00
BLAREN009 Fossil Dragon Skullgios SCR 1.50 3.00
BLAREN010 Fossil Dragon Skullgar SCR 1.25 2.50
BLAREN011 Fossil Fusion SCR 1.50 3.00
BLAREN012 Time Stream SCR 2.50 5.00
BLAREN013 Specimen Inspection SCR .75 1.50
BLAREN014 Miracle Rupture SCR 5.00 10.00
BLAREN015 Psychic Wave UR .75 1.50
BLAREN016 Armored White Bear SCR .75 1.50
BLAREN017 Afterglow UR 1.00 2.00
BLAREN018 High Rate Draw SCR .75 1.50
BLAREN019 Malefic Paradigm Dragon UR .75 1.50
BLAREN020 Numeron Wall UR 1.00 2.00
BLAREN021 Number C1: Numeron
Chaos Gate Sunya SCR 1.25 2.50
BLAREN022 Number 1: Numeron Gate Ekam UR1.00 2.00
BLAREN023 Number 2: Numeron Gate Dve UR 1.00 2.00
BLAREN024 Number 3: Numeron Gate Trini UR .75 1.50
BLAREN025 Number 4: Numeron Gate Catvari UR1.00 2.00
BLAREN026 Numeron Network SCR 2.50 10.00
BLAREN027 Numeron Calling SCR 1.50 3.00
BLAREN028 Number 3: Cicada King UR 1.25 2.50
BLAREN029 Flower Cardian Cherry Blossom UR .75 1.50
BLAREN030 Super All In! UR .75 1.50
BLAREN031 Glacial Beast Blizzard Wolf SCR 1.00 2.00
BLAREN032 Glacial Beast Polar Penguin SCR 1.50 3.00
BLAREN033 Glacial Beast Iceberg Narwhal SCR .75 1.50
BLAREN034 Fire Flint Lady UR 1.25 2.50
BLAREN035 Appliancer Socketroll UR .75 1.50
BLAREN036 Appliancer Breakerbuncle UR .75 1.50
BLAREN037 Appliancer Copybokkle UR .75 1.50
BLAREN038 Appliancer Celtopus UR .75 1.50
BLAREN039 Appliancer Kappa Scale UR .75 1.50
BLAREN040 Appliancer Vacculephant UR .75 1.50
BLAREN041 Appliancer Laundry Dragon UR .75 1.50
BLAREN042 Appliancer Dryer Drake UR .75 1.50
BLAREN043 Appliancer Reuse UR .75 1.50
BLAREN044 Appliancer Test UR .75 1.50
BLAREN045 Appliancer Electrilyrical World UR .75 1.50
BLAREN046 Number F0: Utopic Future Slash SCR1.00 2.00
BLAREN047 Darkness Metal... SCR 3.00 6.00
BLAREN048 Trishula... SCR 2.50 5.00
BLAREN049 Judgment, the Dragon of Heaven SCR1.50 3.00
BLAREN050 Dark Armed... SCR 2.00 4.00
BLAREN051 Chaos Emperor... SCR 40.00 80.00
BLAREN052 Book of Moon UR 1.50 3.00
BLAREN053 Elemental HERO Neos Alius UR .75 1.50
BLAREN054 Elemental HERO
Shining Flare Wingman UR 1.50 3.00
BLAREN055 Elemental HERO Chaos Neos UR .60 1.25
BLAREN056 Elemental HERO Escuridao SCR 1.50 3.00
BLAREN057 Goyo Guardian UR .75 1.50
BLAREN058 Goyo Defender UR .75 1.50
BLAREN059 Koa'ki Meiru Drago UR 1.25 2.50
BLAREN060 Black Whirlwind UR 1.00 2.00
BLAREN061 Blackwing - Kris the Crack of Dawn UR2.00 4.00
BLAREN062 Assault Blackwing -
Sohaya the Rain Storm UR .75 1.50
BLAREN063 Boost Warrior UR 1.25 2.50
BLAREN064 Steam Synchron UR 1.00 2.00
BLAREN065 Junk Anchor UR .75 1.50
BLAREN066 BOTFF Lion Emperor UR .75 1.50
BLAREN067 Kalantosa... UR 1.50 3.00
BLAREN068 Valerifawn... UR .75 1.50
BLAREN069 #C92 Heart-eartH Chaos Dragon SCR1.00 2.00
BLAREN070 Number S39: Utopia the Lightning UR1.50 3.00
BLAREN071 Obedience Schooled UR 1.25 2.50
BLAREN072 Mecha Phantom Beast O-Lion UR 1.00 2.00
BLAREN073 Madolche Anjelly SCR 2.50 5.00
BLAREN074 Artifact Ignition SCR 1.50 3.00
BLAREN075 Artifact Sanctum UR 3.00 6.00
BLAREN076 Ra's Disciple UR .75 1.50
BLAREN077 Nekroz of Gungnir UR 1.00 2.00
BLAREN078 Galaxy Worm UR .75 1.50
BLAREN079 Dragon Buster Destruction Sword UR1.00 2.00
BLAREN080 Invoked Caliga UR 1.00 2.00
BLAREN081 Invoked Raidjin UR 1.50 3.00
BLAREN082 Invoked Purgatrio UR .75 1.50
BLAREN083 Invoked Elysium UR .75 1.50
BLAREN084 Invocation SCR 20.00 25.00
BLAREN085 Chimeratech Megafleet Dragon SCR4.00 8.00
BLAREN086 Secure Gardna UR 1.25 2.50
BLAREN087 Formud Skipper UR 1.00 2.00
BLAREN088 Danger!? Jackalope? SCR 1.50 3.00
BLAREN089 Salamangreat Sunlight Wolf UR 1.25 2.50
BLAREN090 Salamangreat Gazelle UR .75 1.50
BLAREN091 Topologic Zeroboros UR .75 1.50
BLAREN092 Cross-Sheep UR 2.00 4.00
BLAREN10K Ten Thousand Dragon 10K SCR 750.00 1,500.00

2020 Yu-Gi-Oh The Dark Side of Dimensions Movie Pack Secret Edition

MVP1ENS01 Neo Blue-Eyes Ultimate Dragon SCR2.50 5.00
MVP1ENS02 Kaiser Vorse Raider SCR .25 .50
MVP1ENS03 Assault Wyvern SCR .30 .75
MVP1ENS04 Blue-Eyes Chaos MAX Dragon SCR2.50 5.00
MVP1ENS05 Deep-Eyes White Dragon SCR 1.00 2.00
MVP1ENS06 Pandemic Dragon SCR .15 .30
MVP1ENS07 Dragon's Fighting Spirit SCR .15 .30
MVP1ENS08 Chaos Form SCR 1.25 2.50
MVP1ENS09 Induced Explosion SCR .12 .25
MVP1ENS10 Counter Gate SCR .20 .40
MVP1ENS11 Krystal Avatar SCR .12 .25
MVP1ENS12 Sentry Soldier of Stone SCR .25 .50
MVP1ENS13 Marshmacaron SCR .40 .80
MVP1ENS14 Berry Magician Girl SCR 1.25 2.50
MVP1ENS15 Apple Magician Girl SCR 1.00 2.00
MVP1ENS16 Kiwi Magician Girl SCR 1.25 2.50
MVP1ENS17 Silver Gadget SCR .30 .60
MVP1ENS18 Gold Gadget SCR .30 .75
MVP1ENS19 Dark Magic Veil SCR .75 1.50
MVP1ENS20 Magical Contract Door SCR .17 .35
MVP1ENS21 Dimension Reflector SCR .12 .25
MVP1ENS22 Dig of Destiny SCR .12 .25
MVP1ENS23 Dimension Sphinx SCR .12 .25
MVP1ENS24 Dimension Guardian SCR .25 .50
MVP1ENS25 Dimension Mirage SCR .12 .25
MVP1ENS26 Dark Horizon SCR .17 .35
MVP1ENS27 Metamorphortress SCR .15 .30
MVP1ENS28 Magicians' Defense SCR .60 1.25
MVP1ENS29 Final Geas SCR .12 .25
MVP1ENS30 Metalhold the Moving Blockade SCR.17 .35
MVP1ENS31 Spiritual Swords
of Revealing Light SCR .25 .50
MVP1ENS32 Vijam the Cubic Seed SCR 1.25 2.50
MVP1ENS33 Dark Garnex the Cubic Beast SCR .12 .25
MVP1ENS34 Blade Garoodia the Cubic Beast SCR.20 .40
MVP1ENS35 Buster Gundil
the Cubic Behemoth SCR .25 .50
MVP1ENS36 Geira Guile the Cubic King SCR .25 .50
MVP1ENS37 Vulcan Dragni the Cubic King SCR .15 .30
MVP1ENS38 Indiora Doom Volt
the Cubic Emperor SCR .20 .40
MVP1ENS39 Crimson Nova
the Dark Cubic Lord SCR .75 1.50
MVP1ENS40 Crimson Nova
Trinity the Dark Cubic Lord SCR .30 .60
MVP1ENS41 Cubic Karma SCR .40 .80
MVP1ENS42 Cubic Wave SCR .40 .80
MVP1ENS43 Cubic Rebirth SCR .20 .40
MVP1ENS44 Cubic Mandala SCR .17 .35
MVP1ENS45 Unification of the Cubic Lords SCR.40 .80
MVP1ENS46 Blue-Eyes Alternative
White Dragon SCR 7.50 15.00
MVP1ENS47 Clear Kuriboh SCR .25 .50
MVP1ENS48 Celtic Guard of Noble Arms SCR .25 .50
MVP1ENS49 Gandora-X the
Dragon of Demolition SCR .30 .60
MVP1ENS50 Lord Gaia the Fierce Knight SCR .40 .80
MVP1ENS51 Lemon Magician Girl SCR 1.50 3.00

MVP1ENS52 Chocolate Magician Girl SCR 2.50 5.00
MVP1ENS53 Palladium Oracle Mahad SCR 6.00 12.00
MVP1ENS54 Dark Magician SCR 4.00 8.00
MVP1ENS55 Blue-Eyes White Dragon SCR 7.50 15.00
MVP1ENS56 Dark Magician Girl SCR 7.50 15.00
MVP1ENS57 Slifer the Sky Dragon SCR 1.50 3.00
MVP1ENSV1 Duza the Meteor Cubic Vessel UR .20 .40
MVP1ENSV2 Krystal Dragon UR .12 .25
MVP1ENSV3 Dark Magician UR .75 1.50
MVP1ENSV4 Blue-Eyes White Dragon UR 1.00 2.00
MVP1ENSV5 Obelisk the Tormentor UR .75 1.50
MVP1ENSV6 Slifer the Sky Dragon UR .40 .80

2020 Yu-Gi-Oh Duel Overload 1st Edition

DUOVEN001 Crystron Halqifibrax UR 7.50 15.00
DUOVEN002 Celestial Knightlord Parshath UR 3.00 6.00
DUOVEN003 Alien Shocktrooper M-Frame UR .75 1.50
DUOVEN004 D/D/D Abyss King Gilgamesh UR 2.00 4.00
DUOVEN005 Raidraptor - Wise Strix UR 1.50 3.00
DUOVEN006 Condemned Darklord UR 3.00 6.00
DUOVEN007 Five-Headed Link Dragon UR 1.50 3.00
DUOVEN008 Protector Whelp... UR 1.50 3.00
DUOVEN009 Union Carrier UR 5.00 10.00
DUOVEN010 Ancient Gear Ballista UR 3.00 6.00
DUOVEN011 Herald of Mirage Lights UR .75 1.50
DUOVEN012 Simorgh, Bird of Sovereignty UR 1.00 2.00
DUOVEN013 Xtra HERO Infernal Devicer UR 1.50 3.00
DUOVEN014 Selene... UR 25.00 50.00
DUOVEN015 Crossrose Dragon UR 1.25 2.50
DUOVEN016 Reptilianne Echidna UR .75 1.50
DUOVEN017 Mecha Phantom Beast Auroradon UR3.00 6.00
DUOVEN018 Bujinki Ahashima UR 3.00 6.00
DUOVEN019 Artifact Dagda UR 12.50 25.00
DUOVEN020 Bloom Harmonist... UR .75 1.50
DUOVEN021 Predaplant Verte Anaconda UR 10.00 20.00
DUOVEN022 Abyss Actor - Hyper Director UR .75 1.50
DUOVEN023 Lib the World Key Blademaster UR2.00 4.00
DUOVEN024 Sky Striker Ace - Zeke UR 6.00 12.00
DUOVEN025 Yuki-Onna... UR 3.00 6.00
DUOVEN026 Tenyi Spirit - Sahasrara UR 1.00 2.00
DUOVEN027 Angraecum Umbrella UR .75 1.50
DUOVEN028 Firebrand Hymnist UR .75 1.50
DUOVEN029 Armillyre, the Starleader Dragon UR.75 1.50
DUOVEN030 Awakening of the Possessed UR 1.00 2.00
DUOVEN031 Kingyo Sukui UR .60 1.25
DUOVEN032 Ferocious Flame Swordsman UR .75 1.50
DUOVEN033 Ojama Emperor UR .75 1.50
DUOVEN034 Speedroid Marble Machine UR .75 1.50
DUOVEN035 Speedroid Hexasaucer UR .75 1.50
DUOVEN036 Dark Anthelion Dragon UR .75 1.50
DUOVEN037 Starving Venemy
Lethal Dose Dragon UR .75 1.50
DUOVEN038 Dangerous Frightfur Nightmary UR .75 1.50
DUOVEN039 Phantasm Emperor Trilojig UR .75 1.50
DUOVEN040 Rose Bell of Revelation UR 1.00 2.00
DUOVEN041 Synchro Transcend UR .75 1.50
DUOVEN042 Enma's Judgment UR .75 1.50
DUOVEN043 Graveyard of Wandering Souls UR .75 1.50
DUOVEN044 Malefic Divide UR .75 1.50
DUOVEN045 Malefic Selector UR .75 1.50
DUOVEN046 Malefic Tune UR .75 1.50
DUOVEN047 Cubic Ascension UR .75 1.50
DUOVEN048 Malefic Paradox Gear UR .75 1.50
DUOVEN049 Malefic Territory UR .75 1.50
DUOVEN050 Cubic Dharma UR .75 1.50
DUOVEN051 Cubic Causality UR .75 1.50
DUOVEN052 Card of Fate UR .75 1.50
DUOVEN053 Relinquished Anima UR 2.00 4.00
DUOVEN054 Traptrix Genlisea UR 1.50 3.00
DUOVEN055 Hollow Giants UR .75 1.50
DUOVEN056 Mayakashi Mayhem UR .75 1.50
DUOVEN061 Vanity's Ruler UR .75 1.50
DUOVEN062 Gigaplant UR .75 1.50
DUOVEN063 Swap Frog UR 3.00 6.00
DUOVEN064 Wattgiraffe UR .75 1.50
DUOVEN065 Wightmare UR .75 1.50
DUOVEN066 Blackwing - Zephyros the Elite UR .75 1.50
DUOVEN067 Scrap Orthros UR .75 1.50
DUOVEN068 Madolche Magileine UR 2.50 5.00
DUOVEN069 Destiny HERO - Celestial UR 1.25 2.50
DUOVEN070 Secret Six Samurai - Fuma UR .75 1.50
DUOVEN071 Magical Musketeer Caspar UR .75 1.50
DUOVEN072 Magical Musketeer Starfire UR .75 1.50
DUOVEN073 Witchcrafter Madame Verre UR .75 1.50
DUOVEN074 Fantastical Dragon Phantazmay UR3.00 6.00
DUOVEN075 Sauravis, the
Ancient and Ascended UR 2.00 4.00
DUOVEN076 The Last Warrior
from Another Planet UR 2.00 4.00
DUOVEN077 King Dragun UR .75 1.50
DUOVEN078 Super Vehicroid - Stealth Union UR.75 1.50
DUOVEN079 Chaos Goddess UR .75 1.50
DUOVEN080 PSY-Framelord Omega UR 2.00 4.00
DUOVEN081 Daigusto Emeral UR .75 1.50
DUOVEN082 Madolche Puddingcess... UR 2.00 4.00
DUOVEN083 Number 27:
Dreadnought Dreadnoid UR 1.00 2.00
DUOVEN084 Dingirsu... UR 7.50 15.00
DUOVEN085 Salamangreat Almiraj UR 2.00 4.00
DUOVEN086 Mystical Space Typhoon UR 1.50 3.00
DUOVEN087 Magic Formula UR .60 1.25
DUOVEN088 Terraforming UR 2.50 5.00
DUOVEN089 Double Evolution Pill UR 2.00 4.00
DUOVEN090 Deck Lockdown UR .75 1.50
DUOVEN091 Zombie World UR 3.00 6.00
DUOVEN092 Cyber Emergency UR 2.00 4.00
DUOVEN093 Hysteric Sign UR .75 1.50
DUOVEN094 Golden Castle of Stromberg UR .75 1.50
DUOVEN095 Cynet Mining UR 4.00 8.00
DUOVEN096 Witchcrafter Creation UR 1.00 2.00
DUOVEN097 Compulsory Evacuation Device UR1.00 2.00
DUOVEN098 Paleozoic Dinomischus UR 2.00 4.00
DUOVEN099 Infinite Impermanence UR 7.50 15.00
DUOVEN100 Cybernetic Overflow UR 1.00 2.00

2020 Yu-Gi-Oh Eternity Code 1st Edition

ETCOEN000 Piwraithe the Ghost Pirate C .10 .20
ETCOEN001 Parallel eXceed C .50 1.00
ETCOEN002 Codebreaker Zero Day C .10 .20
ETCOEN003 Salamangreat Zebroid X C .10 .20
ETCOEN004 Gouki Iron Claw C .10 .20
ETCOEN005 Gouki Guts C .10 .20
ETCOEN006 Marincess Basilalima C .10 .20
ETCOEN007 Noctovision Dragon C .20 .40
ETCOEN008 Archnemeses Protos UR 1.25 2.50
ETCOEN009 Archnemeses Eschatos UR 2.00 4.00
ETCOEN010 Nemeses Flag SR .30 .75
ETCOEN011 Nemeses Umbrella SR .30 .75
ETCOEN012 Nemeses Corridor SR .30 .75
ETCOEN013 Deep Sea Artisan C .10 .20
ETCOEN014 Deep Sea Sentry C .10 .20
ETCOEN015 Deep Sea Minstrel C .10 .20
ETCOEN016 Red Familiar C .10 .20
ETCOEN017 Crimson Resonator C .10 .20
ETCOEN018 Lantern Shark C .10 .20
ETCOEN019 Buzzsaw Shark C .10 .20
ETCOEN020 Ancient Warriors -
Ambitious Cao De SR .20 .40
ETCOEN021 Ancient Warriors -
Fearsome Zhang Yuan C .10 .20
ETCOEN022 Ancient Warriors -
Deceptive Jia Wen C .10 .20
ETCOEN023 Ancient Warriors -
Ingenious Zhuge Kong SR .25 .50
ETCOEN024 Girsu, the Orcust Mekk-Knight SCR20.00 40.00
ETCOEN025 Thunder Dragonlord C .10 .20
ETCOEN026 Chamber Dragonmaid SCR 7.50 15.00
ETCOEN026 Chamber Dragonmaid SLR 200.00 400.00
ETCOEN027 Harr, Generaider Boss of Storms SR .25 .50
ETCOEN028 Loptr, Shadow of
the Generaider Bosses UR 1.00 2.00
ETCOEN029 Unchained Twins - Sarama C .10 .20
ETCOEN030 King Beast Barbaros C .10 .20
ETCOEN031 Gizmek Uka, the
Festive Fox of Fecundity SCR 5.00 10.00
ETCOEN032 Trias Hierarchia C .10 .20
ETCOEN033 Cataclysmic Circumpolar Chilblainia C.10 .20
ETCOEN034 Union Driver UR .75 1.50
ETCOEN035 Malice, Lady of Lament SR .20 .40
ETCOEN036 Ghost Mourner & Moonlit Chill SCR20.00 40.00
ETCOEN036 Ghost Mourner &
Moonlit Chill SLR 400.00 800.00
ETCOEN037 Animadorned Archosaur SCR 25.00 50.00
ETCOEN038 Goldilocks the Battle Landscaper C .10 .20
ETCOEN039 Magical Hound C .10 .20
ETCOEN040 Invoked Augoeides SR .30 .75
ETCOEN041 Dragonmaid Sheou UR 1.25 2.50
ETCOEN042 Deep Sea Prima Donna UR .50 1.00
ETCOEN043 Ravenous Crocodragon Archethys UR1.50 3.00
ETCOEN044 Valiant Shark Lancer SR .20 .40
ETCOEN045 Traptrix Allomerus SLR 200.00 400.00
ETCOEN045 Traptrix Allomerus UR 1.00 2.00
ETCOEN046 Accesscode Talker SCR 50.00 100.00
ETCOEN047 Proxy F Magician C .10 .20
ETCOEN048 Splash Mage C .10 .20
ETCOEN049 Linkross UR 10.00 20.00
ETCOEN050 The Arrival Cyberse @Ignister SR .20 .40
ETCOEN051 Codebreaker Virus Berserker C .10 .20
ETCOEN052 Codebreaker Virus Swordsman C .10 .20
ETCOEN053 Gouki The Powerload Ogre C .10 .20
ETCOEN054 Marincess Great Bubble Reef SR .20 .40
ETCOEN055 Eria the Water Charmer, Gentle SLR300.00 750.00
ETCOEN055 Eria the Water Charmer, Gentle SR .20 .40
ETCOEN056 A.I. Contact SR .20 .40
ETCOEN057 Burning Draw SR .20 .40
ETCOEN058 Link Burst C .10 .20
ETCOEN059 Stairs of Mail C .10 .20
ETCOEN060 Nemeses Adrastea C .10 .20
ETCOEN061 Deep Sea Aria SCR 3.00 6.00
ETCOEN062 Resonator Command C .10 .20
ETCOEN063 Torpedo Takedown C .10 .20
ETCOEN064 Madolche Salon UR 4.00 8.00
ETCOEN065 Void Apocalypse SR .20 .40
ETCOEN066 Heavy Forward UR .50 1.00
ETCOEN067 Witchcrafter Unveiling SR .25 .50
ETCOEN068 Evil Eye Reemergence C .10 .20
ETCOEN069 Ancient Warriors Saga... C .10 .20
ETCOEN070 Megalith Unformed C .10 .20
ETCOEN071 Fusion Deployment UR 4.00 8.00
ETCOEN072 Flourishing Frolic C .10 .20
ETCOEN073 A.I.Q C .10 .20
ETCOEN074 Red Reign SR .20 .40
ETCOEN075 Xyz Revive Splash C .10 .20
ETCOEN076 Madolche Promenade SR .20 .40
ETCOEN077 Witchcrafter Patronus SR .20 .40
ETCOEN078 Gravedigger's Trap Hole SCR 10.00 20.00
ETCOEN079 Titanocider SCR 4.00 8.00
ETCOEN080 Pinpoint Dash C .10 .20
ETCOEN081 Rose Girl SR .20 .40
ETCOEN082 Scrypton SR .20 .40
ETCOEN083 Taotie Dragon C .10 .20
ETCOEN084 Necroquip Prism C .10 .20
ETCOEN085 Bluebeard, the Plunder
Patroll Shipwright C .10 .20
ETCOEN086 Goldenhair, the Newest
Plunder Patroll C .10 .20
ETCOEN087 Plunder Patrollship Lys SCR 2.00 4.00
ETCOEN088 Plunder Patroll
Shipshape Ships Shipping SR .20 .40
ETCOEN089 Emblem of the Plunder Patroll UR 1.50 3.00
ETCOEN090 Pride of the Plunder Patroll C .10 .20
ETCOEN091 Plunder Patroll Parrrty SR .20 .40
ETCOEN092 Superheavy Samurai Wagon C .10 .20
ETCOEN093 Rain Bozu C .10 .20
ETCOEN094 Performapal Turn Trooper C .10 .20
ETCOEN095 Armored Bitron SR .20 .40
ETCOEN096 Gussari @Ignister SR .20 .40
ETCOEN097 Gatchiri @Ignister SR .20 .40
ETCOEN098 Machina Metalcruncher UR 2.50 5.00
ETCOEN099 Superheavy Samurai
Swordmaster Musashi C .10 .20
ETCOEN100 Effect Veiler SLR 500.00 1,000.00

2020 Yu-Gi-Oh Genesis Impact 1st Edition

GEIMEN001 Crowley, the Magistus of Grimoires SR.15 .30
GEIMEN002 Zoroa, the Magistus of Flames UR 1.50 3.00
GEIMEN003 Rilliona, the Magistus of Verre CR25.00 50.00
GEIMEN003 Rilliona, the Magistus of Verre UR 4.00 8.00
GEIMEN004 Endymion, the Magistus of Mastery R.10 .20
GEIMEN005 Aiwass, the Magistus Spell Spirit SR.15 .30
GEIMEN006 Vahram, the Magistus
Divinity Dragon SR .12 .25
GEIMEN007 Ninaruru, the Magistus
Glass Goddess CR 12.50 25.00
GEIMEN007 Ninaruru, the
Magistus Glass Goddess SR .12 .25
GEIMEN008 Artemis, the Magistus
Moon Maiden CR 40.00 80.00
GEIMEN008 Artemis, the Magistus
Moon Maiden UR 10.00 20.00
GEIMEN009 Trismagistus SR .12 .25
GEIMEN010 Magistus Theurgy R .10 .20
GEIMEN011 Magistus Invocation R .10 .20
GEIMEN012 Magistus Vritra R .10 .20
GEIMEN013 Live Twin Ki-sikil CR 50.00 100.00
GEIMEN013 Live Twin Ki-sikil SR .50 1.00
GEIMEN014 Live Twin Lil-la CR 60.00 120.00
GEIMEN014 Live Twin Lil-la SR .30 .75
GEIMEN015 Evil Twin Ki-sikil CR 75.00 150.00
GEIMEN015 Evil Twin Ki-sikil UR 15.00 30.00
GEIMEN016 Evil Twin Lil-la CR 60.00 120.00
GEIMEN016 Evil Twin Lil-la UR 10.00 20.00
GEIMEN017 Evil Twins Ki-sikil & Lil-la CR 30.00 60.00
GEIMEN017 Evil Twins Ki-sikil & Lil-la UR 2.00 4.00
GEIMEN018 Live Twin Home SR .15 .30
GEIMEN019 Live Twin Channel R .10 .20
GEIMEN020 Secret Password SR .20 .40
GEIMEN021 Evil Twin Challenge R .10 .20
GEIMEN022 Evil Twin GG EZ R .10 .20
GEIMEN023 Evil Twin Present R .12 .25
GEIMEN024 Drytron Alpha Thuban SR .30 .75
GEIMEN025 Drytron Beta Rastaban R .12 .25
GEIMEN026 Drytron Gamma Eltanin R .12 .25
GEIMEN027 Drytron Delta Altais R .10 .20
GEIMEN028 Drytron Zeta Aldhibah R .10 .20
GEIMEN029 Drytron Meteonis Draconids CR 25.00 50.00
GEIMEN029 Drytron Meteonis Draconids UR 2.00 4.00
GEIMEN030 Drytron Meteonis Quadrantids CR15.00 30.00
GEIMEN030 Drytron Meteonis Quadrantids SR .20 .40
GEIMEN031 Drytron Fafnir SR .20 .40
GEIMEN032 Meteonis Drytron CR 40.00 80.00
GEIMEN032 Meteonis Drytron UR 5.00 10.00
GEIMEN033 Drytron Nova UR 15.00 30.00
GEIMEN034 Drytron Eclipse R .10 .20
GEIMEN035 Drytron Asterism R .10 .20
GEIMEN036 Drytron Meteor Shower R .10 .20
GEIMEN037 Cyberse Gadget R .12 .25
GEIMEN038 Performage Hat Tricker R .10 .20
GEIMEN039 Star Drawing R .10 .20
GEIMEN040 Cyber Angel Benten R .10 .20
GEIMEN041 Knightmare Gryphon R .10 .20
GEIMEN042 Cyber Emergency SR .75 1.50
GEIMEN043 Extra-Foolish Burial R .12 .25
GEIMEN044 Born from Draconis R .10 .20
GEIMEN045 Bottomless Trap Hole R .15 .30
GEIMEN046 Herald of Ultimateness R .10 .20
GEIMEN047 Impcantation Chalislime SR .30 .60
GEIMEN048 Beat Cop from the Underworld CR17.50 35.00
GEIMEN048 Beat Cop from the Underworld SR .20 .40
GEIMEN049 Backup Secretary R .12 .25
GEIMEN050 Knightmare Unicorn CR 50.00 100.00
GEIMEN050 Knightmare Unicorn R .50 1.00
GEIMEN051 Knightmare Phoenix CR 60.00 120.00
GEIMEN051 Knightmare Phoenix R .30 .75
GEIMEN052 Number 96: Dark Mist R .10 .20
GEIMEN053 Aleister the Invoker of Madness CR20.00 40.00
GEIMEN053 Aleister the Invoker of Madness UR .60 1.25
GEIMEN054 The Book of the Law R .10 .20
GEIMEN055 Invoked Cocytus R .12 .25
GEIMEN056 Invoked Magellanica R .10 .20
GEIMEN057 Cynet Regression R .10 .20
GEIMEN058 World Legacy - World Lance R .10 .20
GEIMEN059 Engraver of the Mark R .10 .20
GEIMEN060 Performage Damage Juggler R .10 .20

2020 Yu-Gi-Oh Ignition Assault 1st Edition

IGASEN000 Annihilator Archfiend R .75 1.50
IGASEN001 Pikari @Ignister SCR 4.00 8.00
IGASEN002 Bururu @Ignister R 4.00 8.00
IGASEN003 Doyon @Ignister UR 1.25 2.50
IGASEN004 Achichi @Ignister SCR 5.00 10.00
IGASEN005 Hiyari @Ignister C .75 1.50
IGASEN006 Doshin @Ignister C .75 1.50
IGASEN007 Donyoribo @Ignister C .75 1.50
IGASEN008 Ancient Warriors -
Masterful Sun Mou UR 5.00 10.00
IGASEN009 Ancient Warriors -
Graceful Zhou Gong R 1.25 2.50
IGASEN010 Ancient Warriors - Eccentric Lu Jing R.75 1.50
IGASEN011 Ancient Warriors -
Virtuous Liu Xuan UR 3.00 6.00
IGASEN012 Ancient Warriors - Loyal Guan Yun SR.75 1.50
IGASEN013 Ancient Warriors - Valiant Zhang De R.60 1.25
IGASEN014 Karakuri Bonze mdl 9763 Kunamzan C.75 1.50
IGASEN015 Karakuri Gama
mdl 4624 Shirokunishi C .50 1.00
IGASEN016 Chronomaly Tuspa Rocket C .60 1.25
IGASEN017 Arcjet Lightcraft R .60 1.25
IGASEN018 Time Thief Chronocorder C .10 .20
IGASEN019 Abominable Unchained Soul SR 1.50 3.00
IGASEN020 Sky Striker Ace - Roze UR 5.00 10.00
IGASEN020 Sky Striker Ace - Roze SLR 150.00 300.00
IGASEN021 Witchcrafter Genni SR .25 .50
IGASEN022 Utgarda, Generaider
Boss of Delusion SR .25 .50
IGASEN023 Ghostrick Fairy C .75 1.50
IGASEN024 Gizmek Kaku... SCR 3.00 6.00
IGASEN025 Cataclysmic Crusted Calcifida C .60 1.25
IGASEN026 Jack-o-Bolan SR 1.25 2.50
IGASEN027 Ibicella Lutea R .30 .75
IGASEN028 Obsessive Uvualoop C .10 .20
IGASEN029 Daruma Dropper C .30 .75
IGASEN030 Transcicada C .10 .20
IGASEN031 Squeaknight C .10 .20
IGASEN032 Battle Survivor C .60 1.25
IGASEN033 Cupid Serve C .60 1.25
IGASEN034 Water Leviathan @Ignister C .10 .20
IGASEN035 Megalith Ophiel SR 1.00 2.00
IGASEN036 Megalith Hagith C .75 1.50
IGASEN037 Megalith Och C .75 1.50
IGASEN038 Megalith Phaleg C .75 1.50
IGASEN039 Megalith Bethor C .75 1.50
IGASEN040 Megalith Aratron SR .60 1.25
IGASEN041 Earth Golem @Ignister R 1.25 2.50
IGASEN042 Wind Pegasus @Ignister SR .25 .50
IGASEN043 Karakuri Super
Shogun mdl 00N Bureibu SR .50 1.00
IGASEN044 Light Dragon @Ignister SR .75 1.50
IGASEN045 Dark Templar @Ignister UR 1.25 2.50
IGASEN046 Fire Phoenix @Ignister R 1.25 2.50
IGASEN047 Cross-Sheep R 3.00 6.00
IGASEN048 Aussa the Earth
Charmer, Immovable SLR 125.00 250.00
IGASEN048 Aussa the Earth Charmer, Immovable R3.00 6.00
IGASEN049 Gravity Controller C 1.00 2.00
IGASEN050 Ignister A.I.Land SCR 3.00 6.00
IGASEN051 TA.I. Strike C .10 .20
IGASEN052 A.I.dle Reborn R .60 1.25
IGASEN053 A.I. Love Fusion R 1.50 3.00
IGASEN054 A.I.'s Ritual C .75 1.50
IGASEN055 Ancient Warriors Saga -
Three Visits UR 1.50 3.00
IGASEN056 Ancient Warriors Saga -
Sun-Liu Alliance R .50 1.00
IGASEN057 Megalith Portal C .75 1.50
IGASEN058 Karakuri Gama Oil C .50 1.00
IGASEN059 Condolence Puppet C .60 1.25
IGASEN060 Charged-Up Heraldry C .30 .75
IGASEN061 Time Thief Startup C .10 .20
IGASEN062 Sky Striker Maneuver -
Scissors Cross R .20 .40
IGASEN063 Ghost Meets Girl... C .50 1.00
IGASEN064 Dragonmaid Send-Off C .75 1.50
IGASEN065 Disposable Learner Device C .60 1.25
IGASEN066 Kuji-Kiri Curse SR .75 1.50
IGASEN067 Lightning Storm SLR 200.00 400.00
IGASEN067 Lightning Storm SCR 100.00 200.00
IGASEN068 Double-Edged Sword C .75 1.50
IGASEN069 A.I. Shadow C .75 1.50
IGASEN070 Ancient Warriors Saga... R 1.00 2.00
IGASEN071 Megalith Promotion R 2.50 5.00
IGASEN072 Megalith Emergence C .60 1.25
IGASEN073 Karakuri Cash Inn C .60 1.25
IGASEN074 Resurgam Xyz C .10 .20
IGASEN075 Time Thief Retrograde C .10 .20
IGASEN076 Sales Pitch SCR 2.00 4.00
IGASEN077 Armory Call C .75 1.50
IGASEN078 Mutually Affured Destruction C .60 1.25
IGASEN079 Fiendish Portrait R 6.00 12.00
IGASEN080 Head Judging C .75 1.50
IGASEN081 Guard Ghost C .60 1.25
IGASEN082 Feedran, the Winds of Mischief C .75 1.50
IGASEN083 Nine-Lives Cat C .75 1.50
IGASEN084 Execution of the Contract C .60 1.25
IGASEN085 Whitebeard, the
Plunder Patroll Helm UR 6.00 12.00
IGASEN086 Redbeard, the Plunder Patroll Matey UR7.50 15.00
IGASEN087 Plunder Patrollship Brann SCR 2.50 5.00
IGASEN088 Plunder Patrollship Moerk SCR 2.50 5.00
IGASEN089 Blackbeard, the
Plunder Patroll Captain UR 7.50 15.00
IGASEN090 Plunder Patroll Shipyarrrd R .20 .40
IGASEN091 Plunder Patroll Booty R .20 .40
IGASEN092 Shiny Black C** Squadder** C .10 .20
IGASEN093 Marincess Pascalus SR 4.00 8.00
IGASEN094 Time Thief Perpetua SLR 125.00 250.00
IGASEN094 Time Thief Perpetua SR .25 .50
IGASEN095 Bellcat Fighter C .75 1.50
IGASEN096 Code Talker Inverted SR .75 1.50
IGASEN097 Linguriboh UR 2.50 5.00
IGASEN098 Link Party C .50 1.00
IGASEN099 Matching Outfits C .30 .75

2020 Yu-Gi-Oh Legendary Duelists Magical Hero 1st Edition

LED6EN000 Dark Magician Girl C .25 .50
LED6EN001 The Dark Magicians UR 20.00 40.00
LED6EN002 Magicians' Souls UR 60.00 120.00
LED6EN003 Soul Servant UR 6.00 12.00
LED6EN004 Secrets of Dark Magic R .50 1.00
LED6EN005 Magicians' Combination UR 2.50 5.00
LED6EN006 Magician of Dark Illusion R .30 .75
LED6EN007 Apprentice Illusion Magician SR 4.00 8.00
LED6EN008 Magician's Rod C .25 .50
LED6EN009 Dark Magical Circle C .25 .50
LED6EN010 Illusion Magic C .12 .25
LED6EN011 Magician Navigation R .25 .50
LED6EN012 Elemental HERO Sunrise UR 4.00 8.00
LED6EN013 Elemental HERO Liquid Soldier UR30.00 75.00
LED6EN014 Generation Next SR .50 1.00
LED6EN015 Favorite Hero UR .75 1.50
LED6EN016 Magistery Alchemist SR .25 .50
LED6EN017 Winged Kuriboh C .12 .25
LED6EN018 Neo-Spacian Aqua Dolphin C .12 .25
LED6EN019 Elemental HERO Honest Neos SR .75 1.50
LED6EN020 Miracle Fusion C .12 .25
LED6EN021 Skyscraper C .12 .25
LED6EN022 A Hero Lives C .12 .25
LED6EN023 Satellite Warrior UR .75 1.50
LED6EN024 Junk Converter SR 2.00 4.00
LED6EN025 Satellite Synchron SR 1.00 2.00
LED6EN026 Synchro Chase UR .75 1.50
LED6EN027 Scrap-Iron Signal R .25 .50
LED6EN028 Accel Synchron C .12 .25
LED6EN029 Cosmic Blazar Dragon C .12 .25
LED6EN030 Jet Synchron C .25 .50
LED6EN031 Doppelwarrior C .12 .25
LED6EN032 Quickdraw Synchron C .12 .25
LED6EN033 Tuning C .12 .25
LED6EN034 Gagagaga Magician SR .60 1.25

LED6EN035 Zubababancho Gagagacoat R	.25	.50
LED6EN036 Dododowarf Gogogoglove R	.25	.50
LED6EN037 Onomatopickup R	.25	.50
LED6EN038 Future Drive R	.25	.50
LED6EN039 Number F0: Utopic Future C	.12	.25
LED6EN040 Gagaga Samurai C	.12	.25
LED6EN041 Gogogo Giant C	.12	.25
LED6EN042 Dododo Buster C	.12	.25
LED6EN043 Onomatopaira C	.12	.25
LED6EN044 Halfway to Forever C	.12	.25
LED6EN045 Performapal Celestial Magician SR	2.00	4.00
LED6EN046 Odd-Eyes Wizard Dragon R	.25	.50
LED6EN047 Performapal Popperup R	1.00	2.00
LED6EN048 Smile Action C	.25	.50
LED6EN049 Pendulum Dimension C	.12	.25
LED6EN050 Timegazer Magician C	.12	.25
LED6EN051 Performapal Pendulum Sorcerer C	.12	.25
LED6EN052 Chronograph Sorcerer C	.12	.25
LED6EN053 Harmonizing Magician C	.12	.25
LED6EN054 Supreme King Z-ARC C	.12	.25
LED6EN055 Spiral Flame Strike C	.12	.25

2020 Yu-Gi-Oh Legendary Duelists Rage of Ra 1st Edition

LED7EN000 The Winged Dragon of Ra GR	200.00	400.00
LED7EN000 The Winged Dragon of Ra UR ALT ART	12.50	25.00
LED7EN001 Egyptian God Slime UR	30.00	60.00
LED7EN002 Reactor Slime R	.20	.40
LED7EN003 Guardian Slime UR	3.00	6.00
LED7EN004 Ancient Chant UR	20.00	40.00
LED7EN005 Blaze Cannon UR	1.50	3.00
LED7EN006 Millennium Revelation SR	1.25	2.50
LED7EN007 Sun God Unification SR	.15	.30
LED7EN008 Makyura the Destructor (erratum) R	.12	.25
LED7EN009 Juragedo C	.10	.20
LED7EN010 Holding Arms C	.10	.20
LED7EN011 Holding Legs C	.10	.20
LED7EN012 Monster Reborn C	.10	.20
LED7EN013 Left Arm Offering C	.10	.20
LED7EN014 The True Name UR	.75	1.50
LED7EN015 Metal Reflect Slime C	.10	.20
LED7EN016 Meklord Astro Dragon Triskelion UR	.50	1.00
LED7EN017 Meklord Emperor Wisel... SR	.15	.30
LED7EN018 Meklord Nucleus Infinity Core SR	.30	.60
LED7EN019 Meklord Army Deployer Obbligato SR	1.00	2.00
LED7EN020 Meklord Assembly SR	.30	.60
LED7EN021 Meklord Deflection R	.12	.25
LED7EN022 Meklord Astro the Eradicator R	.12	.25
LED7EN023 Meklord Emperor Wisel C	.10	.20
LED7EN024 Meklord Emperor Granel C	.10	.20
LED7EN025 Meklord Emperor Skiel C	.10	.20
LED7EN026 Meklord Astro Mekanikle C	.10	.20
LED7EN027 Meklord Astro Dragon Asterisk C	.10	.20
LED7EN028 Meklord Army of Wisel C	.10	.20
LED7EN029 Meklord Fortress C	.10	.20
LED7EN030 Chaos Infinity C	.10	.20
LED7EN031 Jinzo the Machine Menace UR	1.00	2.00
LED7EN032 Psychic Bounder SR	1.25	2.50
LED7EN033 Psychic Megacyber R	.12	.25
LED7EN034 Cyber Energy Shock R	.12	.25
LED7EN035 Law of the Cosmos SR	.15	.30
LED7EN036 Cosmos Channelling R	.12	.25
LED7EN037 Everlasting Alloy R	.12	.25
LED7EN038 Jinzo C	.10	.20
LED7EN039 Jinzo - Returner C	.10	.20
LED7EN040 Jinzo - Lord C	.10	.20
LED7EN041 Jinzo - Jector C	.10	.20
LED7EN042 Brain Control C	.10	.20
LED7EN043 Amplifier C	.10	.20
LED7EN044 Mind Control C	.10	.20
LED7EN045 Psychic Shockwave C	.10	.20
LED7EN046 Ra's Disciple C	.10	.20
LED7EN047 Meklord Army of Skiel C	.10	.20
LED7EN048 Meklord Army of Granel C	.10	.20
LED7EN049 Boon of the Meklord Emperor C	.10	.20
LED7EN050 The Resolute Meklord Army C	.10	.20
LED7EN051 Reboot C	.10	.20
LED7EN052 A Wild Monster Appears! R	.12	.25
LED7EN053 Mound of the Bound Creator R	.12	.25
LED7EN054 Token Sundae C	.10	.20
LED7EN055 Token Stampede C	.10	.20
LED7EN056 White Aura Bihamut UR	.30	.75

2020 Yu-Gi-Oh Legendary Duelists Season 1 1st Edition

LDS1EN001 Red-Eyes Black Dragon UR/green	2.00	4.00
LDS1EN001 Red-Eyes Black Dragon UR/blue	2.00	4.00
LDS1EN001 Red-Eyes Black Dragon UR/purple	2.00	4.00
LDS1EN002 Black Dragon's Chick C	.15	.30
LDS1EN003 Red-Eyes Darkness Dragon C	.15	.30
LDS1EN004 Red-Eyes Darkness Metal Dragon ALT ART C	.15	.30
LDS1EN005 Red-Eyes Wyvern C	.15	.30
LDS1EN006 Malefic Red-Eyes Black Dragon C	.15	.30
LDS1EN007 The Black Stone of Legend C	.15	.30
LDS1EN008 Black Metal Dragon C	.15	.30
LDS1EN009 Red-Eyes Retro Dragon C	.15	.30
LDS1EN010 Red-Eyes Baby Dragon SCR	6.00	12.00
LDS1EN011 Gearfried the Red-Eyes Iron Knight SCR	3.00	6.00
LDS1EN012 Black Skull Dragon C	.15	.30
LDS1EN013 Meteor Black Dragon C	.15	.30
LDS1EN014 Red-Eyes Slash Dragon SCR	3.00	6.00
LDS1EN015 Red-Eyes Flare Metal Dragon UR/green	1.50	3.00
LDS1EN015 Red-Eyes Flare Metal Dragon UR/purple	1.50	3.00
LDS1EN015 Red-Eyes Flare Metal Dragon UR/blue	1.50	3.00
LDS1EN016 Inferno Fire Blast C	.15	.30
LDS1EN017 Red-Eyes Fusion C	.15	.30
LDS1EN018 Cards of the Red Stone C	.15	.30
LDS1EN019 Red-Eyes Insight C	.15	.30
LDS1EN020 Return of the Red-Eyes C	.15	.30
LDS1EN021 Red-Eyes Fang with Chain SCR	3.00	6.00
LDS1EN022 Amazoness Princess C	.15	.30
LDS1EN023 Amazoness Baby Tiger UR/green	.50	1.00
LDS1EN023 Amazoness Baby Tiger UR/purple	.50	1.00
LDS1EN023 Amazoness Baby Tiger UR/blue	.50	1.00
LDS1EN024 Amazoness Call UR/green	.30	.75
LDS1EN024 Amazoness Call UR/purple	.30	.75
LDS1EN024 Amazoness Call UR/blue	.30	.75
LDS1EN025 Amazoness Onslaught C	.15	.30
LDS1EN026 The Legendary Fisherman II C	.15	.30
LDS1EN027 Citadel Whale UR/green	.30	.60
LDS1EN027 Citadel Whale UR/purple	.30	.60
LDS1EN027 Citadel Whale UR/blue	.30	.60
LDS1EN028 Rage of Kairyu-Shin C	.15	.30
LDS1EN029 A Legendary Ocean C	.15	.30
LDS1EN030 Sea Stealth Attack C	.15	.30
LDS1EN031 Cyberdark Horn C	.15	.30
LDS1EN032 Cyberdark Edge C	.15	.30
LDS1EN033 Cyberdark Keel C	.15	.30
LDS1EN034 Cyberdark Cannon C	.15	.30
LDS1EN035 Cyberdark Claw C	.15	.30
LDS1EN036 Cyberdark Dragon C	.15	.30
LDS1EN037 Cyberdarkness Dragon C	.15	.30
LDS1EN038 Cyberdark Impact! C	.15	.30
LDS1EN039 Cyberdark Inferno C	.15	.30
LDS1EN040 Mixeroid C	.15	.30
LDS1EN041 Super Vehicroid - Mobile Base C	.15	.30
LDS1EN042 Vehicroid Connection Zone C	.15	.30
LDS1EN043 Megaroid City C	.15	.30
LDS1EN044 Emergeroid Call C	.15	.30
LDS1EN045 Millennium-Eyes Illusionist UR/green	.30	.75
LDS1EN045 Millennium-Eyes Illusionist UR/purple	.30	.75
LDS1EN045 Millennium-Eyes Illusionist UR/blue	.30	.75
LDS1EN046 Illusionist Faceless Magician C	.15	.30
LDS1EN047 Relinquished C	.15	.30
LDS1EN048 Black Illusion Ritual C	.15	.30
LDS1EN049 Relinquished Fusion UR/green	.50	1.00
LDS1EN049 Relinquished Fusion UR/blue	.50	1.00
LDS1EN049 Relinquished Fusion UR/purple	.50	1.00
LDS1EN050 Thousand-Eyes Restrict C	.15	.30
LDS1EN051 Millennium-Eyes Restrict SCR	6.00	12.00
LDS1EN052 Toon Alligator C	.15	.30
LDS1EN053 Manga Ryu-Ran C	.15	.30
LDS1EN054 Toon Mermaid C	.15	.30
LDS1EN055 Toon Summoned Skull C	.15	.30
LDS1EN056 Blue-Eyes Toon Dragon C	.15	.30
LDS1EN057 Toon Dark Magician Girl C	.15	.30
LDS1EN058 Toon Masked Sorcerer C	.15	.30
LDS1EN059 Toon Gemini Elf C	.15	.30
LDS1EN060 Toon Cannon Soldier C	.15	.30
LDS1EN061 Toon Goblin Attack Force C	.15	.30
LDS1EN062 Toon Cyber Dragon C	.15	.30
LDS1EN063 Toon Ancient Gear Golem C	.15	.30
LDS1EN064 Toon Barrel Dragon C	.15	.30
LDS1EN065 Toon Buster Blader C	.15	.30
LDS1EN066 Red-Eyes Toon Dragon C	.15	.30
LDS1EN067 Toon Dark Magician C	.15	.30
LDS1EN068 Toon World UR/green	.30	.75
LDS1EN068 Toon World UR/blue	.30	.75
LDS1EN068 Toon World UR/purple	.30	.75
LDS1EN069 Toon Table of Contents UR/green	1.25	2.50
LDS1EN069 Toon Table of Contents UR/purple	1.25	2.50
LDS1EN070 Toon Defense C	.15	.30
LDS1EN071 Parasite Paranoid C	.15	.30
LDS1EN072 Metamorphosed Insect Queen C	.15	.30
LDS1EN073 Cocoon of Ultra Evolution SCR	1.00	2.00
LDS1EN074 Corrosive Scales C	.15	.30
LDS1EN075 Barrel Dragon C	.15	.30
LDS1EN076 Desperado Barrel Dragon UR/green	.50	1.00
LDS1EN076 Desperado Barrel Dragon UR/blue	.50	1.00
LDS1EN076 Desperado Barrel Dragon UR/purple	.50	1.00
LDS1EN077 Heavy Metal Raiders UR/green	.30	.60
LDS1EN077 Heavy Metal Raiders UR/blue	.30	.60
LDS1EN077 Heavy Metal Raiders UR/purple	.30	.60
LDS1EN078 Time Machine C	.15	.30
LDS1EN079 Proton Blast C	.15	.30
LDS1EN080 Ancient Gear Golem C	.15	.30
LDS1EN081 Ancient Gear Gadget C	.15	.30
LDS1EN082 Ancient Gear Reactor Dragon C	.15	.30
LDS1EN083 Ancient Gear Hydra C	.15	.30
LDS1EN084 Ancient Gear Wyvern C	.15	.30
LDS1EN085 Ancient Gear Golem - Ultimate Pound C	.15	.30
LDS1EN086 Ancient Gear Frame C	.15	.30
LDS1EN087 Ultimate Ancient Gear Golem C	.15	.30
LDS1EN088 Ancient Gear Megaton Golem UR/green	.50	1.00
LDS1EN088 Ancient Gear Megaton Golem UR/purple	.50	1.00
LDS1EN088 Ancient Gear Megaton Golem UR/blue	.50	1.00
LDS1EN089 Ancient Gear Catapult C	.15	.30
LDS1EN090 Ancient Gear Fusion SCR	5.00	10.00
LDS1EN091 Cross-Dimensional Duel C	.15	.30
LDS1EN092 Crystal Beast Ruby Carbuncle C	.15	.30
LDS1EN093 Crystal Beast Amethyst Cat C	.15	.30
LDS1EN094 Crystal Beast Amber Mammoth C	.15	.30
LDS1EN095 Crystal Beast Emerald Tortoise C	.15	.30
LDS1EN096 Crystal Beast Topaz Tiger C	.15	.30
LDS1EN097 Crystal Beast Cobalt Eagle C	.15	.30
LDS1EN098 Crystal Beast Sapphire Pegasus C	.15	.30
LDS1EN099 Rainbow Dragon C	.15	.30
LDS1EN100 Rainbow Dark Dragon C	.15	.30
LDS1EN101 Rainbow Overdragon UR/green	1.00	2.00
LDS1EN101 Rainbow Overdragon UR/purple	1.00	2.00
LDS1EN101 Rainbow Overdragon UR/blue	1.00	2.00
LDS1EN102 Crystal Beacon C	.15	.30
LDS1EN103 Ancient City - Rainbow Ruins C	.15	.30
LDS1EN104 Rare Value C	.15	.30
LDS1EN105 Crystal Blessing C	.15	.30
LDS1EN106 Crystal Abundance C	.15	.30
LDS1EN107 Crystal Release C	.15	.30
LDS1EN108 Crystal Tree C	.15	.30
LDS1EN109 Advanced Dark C	.15	.30
LDS1EN110 Rainbow Refraction C	.15	.30
LDS1EN111 Rainbow Bridge UR/green	1.00	2.00
LDS1EN111 Rainbow Bridge UR/purple	1.00	2.00
LDS1EN111 Rainbow Bridge UR/blue	1.00	2.00
LDS1EN112 Crystal Bond UR/green	2.00	4.00
LDS1EN112 Crystal Bond UR/purple	2.00	4.00
LDS1EN112 Crystal Bond UR/blue	2.00	4.00
LDS1EN113 Counter Gem C	.15	.30
LDS1EN114 Rainbow Path C	.15	.30
LDS1EN115 Rainbow Gravity C	.15	.30
LDS1EN116 Crystal Conclave C	.15	.30
LDS1EN117 Ultimate Crystal Magic UR/purple	.30	.75
LDS1EN117 Ultimate Crystal Magic UR/green	.30	.75
LDS1EN117 Ultimate Crystal Magic UR/blue	.30	.75
LDS1EN118 Curse of Dragon, the Cursed Dragon UR	.30	.60
LDS1EN119 Machina Resavenger UR	.30	.60
LDS1EN120 Fury of Kairyu-Shin UR	.30	.60
LDS1EN121 Melffy Rabby UR	.30	.60

2020 Yu-Gi-Oh Maximum Gold 1st Edition

MAGOEN001 Blue-Eyes White Dragon PGR	12.50	25.00
MAGOEN002 Dark Magician PGR	6.00	12.00
MAGOEN003 Red-Eyes Black Dragon PGR	2.50	5.00
MAGOEN004 Elemental HERO Stratos PGR ALT ART	1.50	3.00
MAGOEN005 Infernity Mirage PGR	.20	.40
MAGOEN006 Droll & Lock Bird PGR ALT ART	7.50	15.00
MAGOEN007 Tour Guide/Underworld PGR ALT ART	1.25	2.50
MAGOEN007 Tour Guide From the Underworld PGR	1.25	2.50
MAGOEN008 Artifact Lancea PGR	1.00	2.00
MAGOEN009 Ghost Ogre & Snow Rabbit PGR ALT ART	2.00	4.00
MAGOEN009 Ghost Ogre & Snow Rabbit PGR	2.00	4.00
MAGOEN010 Gh.Reaper/Wi.Cherries PGR ALT ART	.30	.60
MAGOEN010 Ghost Reaper & Winter Cherries PGR	.30	.60
MAGOEN011 Ash Blossom & Joyous Spring PGR ALT ART	12.50	25.00
MAGOEN011 Ash Blossom & Joyous Spring PGR ALT ART	12.50	25.00
MAGOEN012 Gh.Belle/Hau.Mansion PGR ALT ART	4.00	8.00
MAGOEN012 Ghost Belle & Haunted Mansion PGR	4.00	8.00
MAGOEN013 Gh.Sister/Sp.Dogwood PGR ALT ART	.50	1.00
MAGOEN013 Ghost Sister & Spooky Dogwood PGR	.50	1.00
MAGOEN014 Kozmo Dark Destroyer PGR	.30	.60
MAGOEN015 Miscellaneousaurus PGR	.50	1.00
MAGOEN016 Aleister the Invoker PGR ALT ART	1.00	2.00
MAGOEN017 Chaos Dragon Levianeer PGR ALT ART	1.50	3.00
MAGOEN017 Chaos Dragon Levianeer PGR	1.50	3.00
MAGOEN018 Fantastical Dragon Phantazmay PGR ALT ART	3.00	6.00
MAGOEN019 Nibiru, the Primal Being PGR	10.00	20.00
MAGOEN020 Nurse Dragonmaid PGR	.75	1.50
MAGOEN021 Laundry Dragonmaid PGR	.50	1.00
MAGOEN022 Kitchen Dragonmaid PGR	1.50	3.00
MAGOEN023 Parlor Dragonmaid PGR	.75	1.50
MAGOEN024 Eldlich the Golden Lord PGR	3.00	6.00
MAGOEN025 Gaia the Dragon Champion PGR	.30	.60
MAGOEN026 Elder Entity N'tss PGR	2.00	4.00
MAGOEN027 House Dragonmaid PGR	.60	1.25
MAGOEN028 Herald of the Arc Light PGR	1.00	2.00
MAGOEN029 Stardust Charge Warrior PGR	.75	1.50
MAGOEN030 Martial Metal Marcher PGR	.20	.40
MAGOEN031 Constellar Pleiades PGR	.30	.60
MAGOEN032 Dark Rebellion Xyz Dragon PGR	.50	1.00
MAGOEN033 Cyber Dragon Infinity PGR	2.00	4.00
MAGOEN034 Number S39: Utopia the Lightning PGR	1.00	2.00
MAGOEN035 Beatrice, Lady of the Eternal PGR	1.00	2.00
MAGOEN036 Zoodiac Drident PGR	.20	.40
MAGOEN037 Zoodiac Chakanine PGR	.30	.75
MAGOEN038 Sky Striker Ace - Kagari PGR ALT ART	.50	1.00
MAGOEN038 Sky Striker Ace - Kagari PGR	.50	1.00
MAGOEN039 Borrelsword Dragon PGR ALT ART	4.00	8.00
MAGOEN040 The Phantom Knights of Rusty Bardiche PGR	.30	.75
MAGOEN041 Apollousa, Bow of the Goddess PGR ALT ART	6.00	12.00
MAGOEN042 Harpie's Feather Duster PGR	3.00	6.00
MAGOEN043 Anti-Magic Arrows PGR	.30	.60
MAGOEN044 Polymerization PGR	1.00	2.00
MAGOEN045 Monster Reborn PGR	1.00	2.00
MAGOEN046 Reinforcement of the Army PGR	.50	1.00
MAGOEN047 Super Polymerization PGR	2.50	5.00
MAGOEN048 Forbidden Chalice PGR	.60	1.25
MAGOEN049 Rank-Up-Magic - The Seventh One PGR	.20	.40
MAGOEN050 Kozmotown PGR	.20	.40
MAGOEN051 Solemn Judgment PGR	2.50	5.00
MAGOEN052 Infinite Impermanence PGR	17.50	35.00
MAGOEN053 Foolish Burial R	.50	1.00
MAGOEN054 Foolish Burial Goods R	1.50	3.00
MAGOEN055 Extra-Foolish Burial R	.15	.30
MAGOEN056 Number 15: Gimmick Puppet Giant Grinder R	.15	.30
MAGOEN057 Number 39: Utopia Beyond R	.50	1.00
MAGOEN058 Number 74: Master of Blades R	.15	.30
MAGOEN059 Number 87: Queen of the Night R	.15	.30
MAGOEN060 Number 101: Silent Honor ARK R	.20	.40
MAGOEN061 Number C101: Silent Honor DARK R	.15	.30
MAGOEN062 Number 107: Galaxy-Eyes Tachyon Dragon R	1.00	2.00
MAGOEN063 #C107 Neo Galaxy Eyes Tachyon Dragon R	.20	.40
MAGOEN064 Mecha Phantom Beast Blue Impala R	.15	.30
MAGOEN065 Mecha Phantom Beast Coltwing R	.15	.30
MAGOEN066 Mecha Phantom Beast Jaculuslan R	.15	.30
MAGOEN067 Mecha Phantom Beast Dracossack R	.15	.30
MAGOEN068 Madolche Hootcake R	.30	.75
MAGOEN069 Madolche Chateau R	.15	.30
MAGOEN070 Madolche Nights R	.15	.30
MAGOEN071 Brotherhood of the Fire Fist - Buffalo R	.15	.30
MAGOEN072 Brotherhood of the Fire Fist - Coyote R	.15	.30
MAGOEN073 Fire Formation - Gyokkou R	.15	.30
MAGOEN074 Traptrix Myrmeleo R	.30	.60
MAGOEN075 Traptrix Dionaea R	.30	.60
MAGOEN076 Traptrix Mantis R	.30	.60
MAGOEN077 Mistake R	.15	.30
MAGOEN078 Tour Bus To Forbidden Realms R	.15	.30
MAGOEN079 Shared Ride R	.60	1.25
MAGOEN080 Mistaken Arrest R	.15	.30
MAGOEN081 Mistaken Accusation R	.15	.30
MAGOEN082 Noble Knight Drystan R	.15	.30
MAGOEN083 Noble Knight Brothers R	.15	.30
MAGOEN084 Noble Knight Eachtar R	.15	.30
MAGOEN085 Noble Knight Pellinore R	.15	.30
MAGOEN086 Noble Knights of the Round Table R	.15	.30
MAGOEN087 Hidden Temples of Necrovalley R	.15	.30
MAGOEN088 Necrovalley Throne R	.15	.30
MAGOEN089 Imperial Tombs of Necrovalley R	.15	.30
MAGOEN090 Domain of the True Monarchs R	.30	.60
MAGOEN091 The First Monarch R	.15	.30
MAGOEN092 The Monarchs Erupt R	.15	.30
MAGOEN093 The Prime Monarch R	.15	.30
MAGOEN094 Synchron Carrier R	.15	.30
MAGOEN095 Starlight Junktion R	.15	.30
MAGOEN096 Storming Mirror Force R	.75	1.50
MAGOEN097 Drowning Mirror Force R	.30	.60
MAGOEN098 Speedroid Taketomborg R	.15	.30
MAGOEN099 Speedroid Red-Eyed Dice R	.15	.30
MAGOEN100 Buster Blader, the Destruction Swordmaster R	.30	.60
MAGOEN101 Buster Blader/Dragon Destroyer Swordsman R	.60	1.25
MAGOEN102 Caligo Claw Crow R	.15	.30
MAGOEN103 Union Hangar R	.15	.30
MAGOEN104 Union Scramble R	.15	.30
MAGOEN105 Darklord Morningstar R	.15	.30
MAGOEN106 Darklord Ixchel R	.15	.30
MAGOEN107 Darklord Nasten R	.15	.30
MAGOEN108 Darklord Contact R	.15	.30
MAGOEN109 Darklord Rebellion R	.15	.30
MAGOEN110 D.D. Warrior Lady R	.15	.30
MAGOEN111 Barrier Statue of the Abyss R	.15	.30
MAGOEN112 Barrier Statue of the Torrent R	.15	.30
MAGOEN113 Barrier Statue of the Inferno R	.15	.30
MAGOEN114 Barrier Statue of the Stormwinds R	.60	1.25
MAGOEN115 Barrier Statue of the Drought R	.15	.30
MAGOEN116 Barrier Statue of the Heavens R	.15	.30
MAGOEN117 Scrap Recycler R	.30	.60
MAGOEN118 Grapha, Dragon Lord of Dark World R	.15	.30
MAGOEN119 Planet Pathfinder R	.30	.60
MAGOEN120 Coach Soldier Wolfbark R	.15	.30
MAGOEN121 Gogogo Gigas R	.15	.30
MAGOEN122 Silent Angler R	.15	.30
MAGOEN123 Cyber Dragon Core R	.30	.60
MAGOEN124 Wightprince R	.30	.60
MAGOEN125 The White Stone of Ancients R	.50	1.00
MAGOEN126 Eater of Millions R	.20	.40
MAGOEN127 Flame Bufferlo R	.30	.60
MAGOEN128 Lady Debug R	1.00	2.00
MAGOEN129 Condemned Witch R	.15	.30
MAGOEN130 Superdimensional Robot Galaxy Destroyer R	.15	.30
MAGOEN131 Gear Gigant X R	.15	.30
MAGOEN132 Harpie's Pet Phantasmal Dragon R	.30	.60
MAGOEN133 Skypalace Gangaridai R	.15	.30
MAGOEN134 Toadally Awesome R	4.00	8.00
MAGOEN135 Linkuriboh R	1.25	2.50
MAGOEN136 Transcode Talker R	.30	.60
MAGOEN137 Mekk-Knight of the Morning Star R	.15	.30
MAGOEN138 Mind Control R	.15	.30
MAGOEN139 Mage Power R	.15	.30
MAGOEN140 Machine Duplication R	1.25	2.50
MAGOEN141 Terraforming R	.30	.60
MAGOEN142 Dragon's Mirror R	.30	.75
MAGOEN143 Trade-In R	.30	.75
MAGOEN144 Preparation of Rites R	.50	1.00
MAGOEN145 Tuning R	.15	.30
MAGOEN146 Temple of the Six R	.15	.30
MAGOEN147 Night Beam R	.15	.30
MAGOEN148 Miracle Contact R	.15	.30
MAGOEN149 Circle of the Fire Kings R	.15	.30
MAGOEN150 Sacred Sword of Seven Stars R	.15	.30
MAGOEN151 Unexpected Dai R	.50	1.00
MAGOEN152 Magical Meltdown R	.30	.75
MAGOEN153 Set Rotation R	.15	.30
MAGOEN154 Lost World R	.15	.30
MAGOEN155 Hey, Trunade! R	.15	.30
MAGOEN156 Called by the Grave R	2.00	4.00
MAGOEN157 Lair of Darkness R	.30	.60
MAGOEN158 Dimensional Prison R	.30	.60
MAGOEN159 Tachyon Transmigration R	.15	.30
MAGOEN160 Lose 1 Turn R	.15	.30
MAGOEN161 Trickstar Reincarnation R	.60	1.25
MAGOEN162 There Can Be Only One R	.60	1.25

2020 Yu-Gi-Oh OTS Tournament Pack 13

OP13EN001 Book of Moon UTR	50.00	100.00
OP13EN002 Abyss Dweller UTR	60.00	120.00
OP13EN003 Traptrix Rafflesia UTR	30.00	75.00
OP13EN004 Deep Sea Diva SR	.75	1.50
OP13EN005 Scrap Golem SR	1.00	2.00
OP13EN006 ABC-Dragon Buster SR	.30	.60
OP13EN007 Junk Speeder SR	.30	.75
OP13EN008 Crystal Wing Synchro Dragon SR	.60	1.25
OP13EN009 Bahamut Shark SR	1.00	2.00
OP13EN010 Where Arf Thou? SR	1.50	3.00
OP13EN011 SPYRAL GEAR - Drone SR	.30	.75
OP13EN012 SPYRAL MISSION - Rescue SR	.30	.75
OP13EN013 Goblin King C	.30	.75
OP13EN014 The Lady in Wight C	.30	.75
OP13EN015 Dimension Fortress Weapon C	.20	.40
OP13EN016 Spore C	.30	.75
OP13EN017 Formula Synchron C	.75	1.50
OP13EN018 Ultimaya Tzolkin C	.50	1.00
OP13EN019 Goyo Defender C	.20	.40
OP13EN020 Muddy Mudragon C	.20	.40
OP13EN021 Xyz Unit C	.30	.75
OP13EN022 Bottomless Trap Hole C	.20	.40
OP13EN023 Dimensional Prison C	.30	.75
OP13EN024 Gravity Collapse C	.20	.40
OP13EN025 Floodgate Trap Hole C	.20	.40
OP13EN026 Generaider Token SR	2.00	4.00

2020 Yu-Gi-Oh OTS Tournament Pack 14

OP14EN001 Super Polymerization UTR	75.00	150.00
OP14EN002 Toon Kingdom UTR	30.00	75.00
OP14EN003 Nibiru, the Primal Being UTR	125.00	250.00
OP14EN004 Madolche Messengelato SR	3.00	6.00
OP14EN005 Infernity General SR	.30	.60
OP14EN006 Super Quantum Red Layer SR	1.00	2.00
OP14EN007 Parallel eXceed SR	6.00	12.00
OP14EN008 Raidraptor - Force Strix SR	2.00	4.00
OP14EN009 Smoke Grenade of the Thief SR	1.00	2.00
OP14EN010 U.A. Signing Deal SR	.50	1.00
OP14EN011 Appointer of the Red Lotus SR	2.00	4.00
OP14EN012 Unpossessed SR	.50	1.00

OP14EN013 Atlantean Dragoons C .75 1.50
OP14EN014 Weeping Idol C .20 .40
OP14EN015 Evil Thorn C .50 1.00
OP14EN016 Raidraptor - Singing Lanius C .20 .40
OP14EN017 The Phantom Knights
of Ancient Cloak C .30 .75
OP14EN018 Void Ogre Dragon C .50 1.00
OP14EN019 Demise of the Land C 1.00 2.00
OP14EN020 Cattle Call C .20 .40
OP14EN021 Phantom Knights'
Rank-Up-Magic Launch C .20 .40
OP14EN022 Shien's Spy C .30 .75
OP14EN023 Raidraptor - Nest C .20 .40
OP14EN024 Icarus Attack C .30 .75
OP14EN025 Phantom Knights
of Shade Brigandine C 2.50 5.00
OP14EN026 Dual Avatar Spirit Token SR 1.25 2.50

2020 Yu-Gi-Oh Phantom Rage 1st Edition

PHRAEN000 Myutant Cry C .10 .20
PHRAEN001 Raider's Wing UR 2.00 4.00
PHRAEN002 The Phantom Knights
of Stained Greaves C .10 .20
PHRAEN003 The Phantom Knights
of Torn Scales SCR 15.00 30.00
PHRAEN003 The Phantom Knights
of Torn Scales SLR 125.00 250.00
PHRAEN004 Raidraptor - Heel Eagle C .10 .20
PHRAEN005 Raidraptor - Strangle Lanius SR .50 1.00
PHRAEN006 Tri-Brigade Nervall C .10 .20
PHRAEN007 Tri-Brigade Kerass SR .75 1.50
PHRAEN008 Tri-Brigade Fraktall UR 12.50 25.00
PHRAEN009 Dogmatika Ashiyan UR .20 .40
PHRAEN010 Virtual World Mai-Hime - Lulu UR12.50 25.00
PHRAEN011 Virtual World Roshi - Laolao SR .75 1.50
PHRAEN012 Virtual World Xiezhi - Jiji C .10 .20
PHRAEN013 Virtual World Kirin - Lili C .10 .20
PHRAEN014 Dual Avatar Fists - Yuhi SR .12 .25
PHRAEN015 Dual Avatar Feet - Kokoku SR .12 .25
PHRAEN016 Infernity Conjurer C .10 .20
PHRAEN017 Infernity Wildcat C .10 .20
PHRAEN018 U.A. Libero Spiker C .10 .20
PHRAEN019 U.A. Player Manager C .10 .20
PHRAEN020 Awakening
of the Possessed - Gagigobyte C .10 .20
PHRAEN021 Awakening
of the Possessed - Rasenryu C .10 .20
PHRAEN022 Gizmek Makami... SR .15 .30
PHRAEN023 Alpha, the Master of Beasts SCR 12.50 25.00
PHRAEN023 Alpha, the Master of Beasts SLR150.00 300.00
PHRAEN024 Prufinesse, the Tactical Trapper C .10 .20
PHRAEN026 Magical Broker C .10 .20
PHRAEN027 Gluttonous Reptolphin Greethys C .10 .20
PHRAEN028 Cupid Fore C .10 .20
PHRAEN029 Hinezumi Hanabi C .10 .20
PHRAEN031 Brigrand the Glory Dragon UR .50 1.00
PHRAEN032 Dual Avatar Fists -
Armored Ah-Gyo SR .12 .25
PHRAEN033 Dual Avatar Feet - Armored Un-Gyo SR.12 .25
PHRAEN034 Dual Avatar - Empowered Kon-Gyo UR.30 .60
PHRAEN035 Armityle the Chaos Phantasm... UR .50 1.00
PHRAEN036 Virtual World Kyubi - Shenshen SCR6.00 12.00
PHRAEN037 Infernity Doom Archfiend SR .12 .25
PHRAEN038 Infernoble Knight Captain Oliver SR .20 .40
PHRAEN039 Penguin Brave C .10 .20
PHRAEN040 Raider's Knight UR 1.50 3.00
PHRAEN041 Arc Rebellion Xyz Dragon SCR 4.00 8.00
PHRAEN042 Virtual World Shell - Jaja C .10 .20
PHRAEN043 Virtual World Phoenix - Fanfan UR .75 1.50
PHRAEN044 Joyous Melffys SR .15 .30
PHRAEN045 Divine Arsenal AA-ZEUS... SCR 30.00 75.00
PHRAEN045 Divine Arsenal AA-ZEUS... SLR 300.00 600.00
PHRAEN046 Tri-Brigade Ferrijit
Barren Blossom SLR 200.00 400.00
PHRAEN046 Tri-Brigade Ferrijit/Barren Blossom UR3.00 6.00
PHRAEN047 Tri-Brigade Rugal the Silver Sheller C.10 .20
PHRAEN048 Tri-Brigade Shuraig
Ominous Omen SCR 12.50 25.00
PHRAEN049 Prank-Kids Meow-Meow-Mu SR .50 1.00
PHRAEN050 Geonator Transverser C .10 .20
PHRAEN051 Phantom Knights'
Rank-Up-Magic Force UR 4.00 8.00
PHRAEN052 Tri-Brigade Stand-Off C .10 .20
PHRAEN053 Tri-Brigade Airborne Assault SCR 1.00 2.00
PHRAEN054 Dogmatikacism C .10 .20
PHRAEN055 Virtual World City - Kauwloon SR .50 1.00
PHRAEN056 Virtual World Gate - Qinglong C .10 .20
PHRAEN057 Dual Avatar Invitation SCR .60 1.25
PHRAEN059 Dual Avatar Defeating Evil C .10 .20
PHRAEN060 Infernity Paranoia C .10 .20
PHRAEN061 U.A. Hyper Stadium SR .15 .30
PHRAEN062 U.A. Locker Room C .10 .20
PHRAEN063 Charge Into a Dark World C .10 .20
PHRAEN064 Arcana Reading C .10 .20
PHRAEN065 Rookie Fur Hire C .10 .20
PHRAEN066 Xyz Import C .10 .20
PHRAEN067 Jack-In-The-Hand C .10 .20
PHRAEN068 Raider's Unbreakable Mind C .10 .20
PHRAEN070 Tri-Brigade Revolt C .10 .20
PHRAEN071 Tri-Brigade Oath C .10 .20
PHRAEN072 Virtual World Gate - Chuche SR .50 1.00
PHRAEN073 Dual Avatar Return C .10 .20
PHRAEN074 Dual Avatar Compact C .10 .20
PHRAEN075 Infernity Suppression C .10 .20
PHRAEN076 U.A. Man of the Match C .10 .20
PHRAEN077 Free-Range Monsters C .10 .20
PHRAEN078 Warning Point SCR 3.00 6.00
PHRAEN079 Banquet of Millions C .10 .20
PHRAEN080 One or Eight C .10 .20
PHRAEN081 Mahaama the Fairy Dragon C .10 .20
PHRAEN082 Jabbing Panda C .10 .20
PHRAEN083 Periallis, Empress of Blossoms C .10 .20
PHRAEN084 Myutant M-05 UR .75 1.50
PHRAEN085 Myutant ST-46 UR .75 1.50
PHRAEN086 Myutant GB-88 C .10 .20
PHRAEN087 Myutant Beast SR .12 .25
PHRAEN088 Myutant Mist SR .15 .30
PHRAEN089 Myutant Arsenal SR .12 .25
PHRAEN090 Myutant Synthesis SR .20 .40
PHRAEN091 Myutant Ultimus SCR 1.50 3.00
PHRAEN092 Myutant Evolution Lab UR .75 1.50
PHRAEN093 Myutant Fusion C .10 .20
PHRAEN094 Myutant Blast C .10 .20
PHRAEN095 Myutant Clash C .10 .20
PHRAEN096 Myutant Expansion C .10 .20
PHRAEN097 Virtual World Beast - Jiujiu SR .20 .40
PHRAEN098 Virtual World Dragon - Longlong SR.15 .30
PHRAEN099 Virtual World Hime - Nyannyan SR .60 1.25
PHRAEN100 Hiita the Fire Charmer, Ablaze SLR150.00 300.00

2020 Yu-Gi-Oh Rise of the Duelist 1st Edition

ROTDEN000 Gaia the Fierce Knight Origin SR .50 1.00
ROTDEN001 Gaia the Magical Knight SR .20 .40
ROTDEN002 Curse of Dragon, the Cursed Dragon C.12 .25
ROTDEN003 Artillery Catapult Turtle UR 1.25 2.50
ROTDEN004 Soldier Gaia The Fierce Knight SR .20 .40
ROTDEN005 Dogmatika Ecclesia... PRISM SCR500.001,000.00
ROTDEN005 Dogmatika Ecclesia, the Virtuous UR15.00 30.00
ROTDEN006 Dogmatika Theo, the Iron Punch C .12 .25
ROTDEN007 Dogmatika Adin, the Enlightened SR.20 .40
ROTDEN008 Dogmatika Fleurdelis,
the Knighted SCR 15.00 30.00
ROTDEN009 Dogmatika Maximus SCR 15.00 30.00
ROTDEN010 Dogmatika Nexus C .12 .25
ROTDEN011 Fallen of Albaz SCR 4.00 8.00
ROTDEN012 Infernoble Knight Astolfo C .12 .25
ROTDEN013 Infernoble Knight Ogier SR .20 .40
ROTDEN014 Infernoble Knight Oliver SR .20 .40
ROTDEN015 Infernoble Knight Maugis C .12 .25
ROTDEN016 Melffy Rabby C .12 .25
ROTDEN017 Melffy Fenny C .12 .25
ROTDEN018 Melffy Catty SR .20 .40
ROTDEN019 Melffy Puppy SR .20 .40
ROTDEN020 Melffy Pony C .12 .25
ROTDEN021 Fluffal Dolphin C .20 .40
ROTDEN022 Edge Imp Scythe C .20 .40
ROTDEN023 Capricious Darklord C .12 .25
ROTDEN024 Indulged Darklord C .12 .25
ROTDEN025 Darklord Nergal C .12 .25
ROTDEN026 Machina Resavenger C .12 .25
ROTDEN027 Unauthorized Bootup Device C .12 .25
ROTDEN028 Mathmech Diameter C .12 .25
ROTDEN029 Nemeses Keystone SR .30 .60
ROTDEN030 Koa'ki Meiru Supplier UR .60 1.25
ROTDEN031 Thunder Hand C .12 .25
ROTDEN032 Gizmek Okami... UR .75 1.50
ROTDEN033 Lifeless Leaffish UR .50 1.00
ROTDEN034 Red Potan C .12 .25
ROTDEN035 Dracoon Lamp C .12 .25
ROTDEN036 Megalith Phul C .12 .25
ROTDEN037 Gaia the Magical
Knight... PRISM SCR 150.00 300.00
ROTDEN037 Gaia the Magical Knight of Dragons SR.20 .40
ROTDEN038 Titaniklad the Ash Dragon SCR 7.50 15.00
ROTDEN039 Frightfur Cruel Whale C .12 .25
ROTDEN040 The First Darklord SR .20 .40
ROTDEN041 Infernoble Knight Captain Roland C .12 .25
ROTDEN042 Infernoble Knight Emperor Charles UR1.25 2.50
ROTDEN043 Chaos Ruler,
the Chaotic Magical Dragon SCR 6.00 12.00
ROTDEN044 Melffy of the Forest UR 3.00 6.00
ROTDEN045 Melffy Mommy C .12 .25
ROTDEN046 Rikka Queen Strenna UR .50 1.00
ROTDEN047 Drill Driver Vespenato C .12 .25
ROTDEN048 Ancient Warriors Oath... SR .20 .40
ROTDEN049 Galloping Gaia C .12 .25
ROTDEN050 Spiral Fusion C .12 .25
ROTDEN051 Dogmatika Nation C .12 .25
ROTDEN052 Nadir Servant SCR 50.00 100.00
ROTDEN053 Infernoble Arms - Durendal** UR 4.00 8.00
ROTDEN054 Infernoble Arms - Hauteclere** C .12 .25
ROTDEN055 Infernoble Arms - Joyeuse** SR .30 .60
ROTDEN056 Melffy Tag C .12 .25
ROTDEN057 Melffy Hide-and-Seek C .12 .25
ROTDEN058 Frightfur Repair C .12 .25
ROTDEN059 Magellanica, the Deep Sea City SR .20 .40
ROTDEN060 Ancient Warriors Saga... C .12 .25
ROTDEN061 Adamancipator Friends SCR 1.50 3.00
ROTDEN062 Triple Tactics Talent PRISM SCR400.00 800.00
ROTDEN062 Triple Tactics Talent SCR 50.00 100.00
ROTDEN063 Blizzard SR .30 .75
ROTDEN064 Fury of Kairyu-Shin C .12 .25
ROTDEN065 Forbidden Droplet SCR 50.00 100.00
ROTDEN066 Heavenly Dragon Circle C .12 .25
ROTDEN067 Diced Dice C .12 .25
ROTDEN068 Spiral Discharge C .12 .25
ROTDEN069 Spiral Reborn C .12 .25
ROTDEN070 Dogmatika Punishment C .12 .25
ROTDEN071 Dogmatika Encounter C .12 .25
ROTDEN072 Horn of Olifant C .12 .25
ROTDEN073 Melffy Playhouse C .12 .25
ROTDEN074 Frightfur Jar C .12 .25
ROTDEN075 Darklord Uprising C .12 .25
ROTDEN076 Shaddoll Schism UR 5.00 10.00
ROTDEN077 Dragonmaid Tidying SR .30 .60
ROTDEN078 Redeemable Jar SR .20 .40
ROTDEN079 Ice Dragon's Prison UR 6.00 12.00
ROTDEN080 Junk Sleep C .12 .25
ROTDEN081 Abyss Actor - Twinkle Little Star C .12 .25
ROTDEN082 Performapal Card Gardna C .12 .25
ROTDEN083 Odd-Eyes Revolution Dragon SCR 7.50 15.00
ROTDEN084 D/D Ark C .12 .25
ROTDEN085 D/D Evil C .12 .25
ROTDEN086 Wynn the Wind
Channeler PRISM SCR 250.00 500.00
ROTDEN086 Wynn the Wind Channeler UR 1.50 3.00
ROTDEN087 Selegiare the Luminous
Lunar Dragon UR .50 1.00
ROTDEN088 Ret-time Reviver Emit-ter SR .30 .75
ROTDEN089 Speedroid Block-n-Roll SR .20 .40
ROTDEN090 Speedroid CarTurbo UR .50 1.00
ROTDEN091 D/D Dog SR .20 .40
ROTDEN092 Performapal Odd-Eyes Metal Claw SR.20 .40
ROTDEN093 Rampaging Smashtank Rhynosaber SR.20 .40
ROTDEN094 Raidraptor - Arsenal Falcon SR .30 .75
ROTDEN095 Raidraptor -
Revolution Falcon - Air Raid SR .30 .75
ROTDEN096 Linkerbell C .12 .25
ROTDEN097 Superheavy Samurai Scarecrow C .12 .25
ROTDEN098 Yaminabe Party SR .20 .40
ROTDEN099 Revenge Rally SR .20 .40
ROTDEN100 D.D. Crow PRISM SCR 300.00 600.00

2020 Yu-Gi-Oh Secret Slayers 1st Edition

SESLEN001 Adamancipator Seeker SCR .75 1.50
SESLEN002 Adamancipator Researcher SCR 30.00 75.00
SESLEN003 Adamancipator Analyzer SCR .50 1.00
SESLEN004 Adamancipator Crystal - Leonite SR .15 .30
SESLEN005 Adamancipator Crystal - Raptite SR .15 .30
SESLEN006 Adamancipator Crystal - Dragite SR .15 .30
SESLEN007 Adamancipator Risen - Leonite SCR2.50 5.00
SESLEN008 Adamancipator Risen - Raptite SR .15 .30
SESLEN009 Adamancipator Risen - Dragite SCR .75 1.50
SESLEN010 Adamancipator Laputite SR .50 1.00
SESLEN011 Adamancipator Signs SR 2.00 4.00
SESLEN012 Adamancipator Relief SCR .15 .30
SESLEN013 Adamancipator Resonance SR .15 .30
SESLEN014 Rikka Petal SR 1.25 2.50
SESLEN015 Primula the Rikka Fairy SCR .30 .75
SESLEN016 Cyclamen the Rikka Fairy SR .15 .30
SESLEN017 Mudan the Rikka Fairy SCR .50 1.00
SESLEN018 Erica the Rikka Fairy SR .15 .30
SESLEN019 Snowdrop the Rikka Fairy SR 1.00 2.00
SESLEN020 Hellebore the Rikka Fairy SR .15 .30
SESLEN021 Kanzashi the Rikka Queen SR .15 .30
SESLEN022 Teardrop the Rikka Queen SCR 6.00 12.00
SESLEN023 Rikka Glamour SCR 2.50 5.00
SESLEN024 Rikka Flurries SCR .25 .50
SESLEN025 Rikka Tranquility SR .20 .40
SESLEN026 Rikka Sheet SCR .50 1.00
SESLEN027 Eldlich the Golden Lord SCR 100.00 200.00
SESLEN028 Cursed Eldland SR 1.50 3.00
SESLEN029 Eldlixir of Black Awakening SCR 4.00 8.00
SESLEN030 Eldlixir of White Destiny SCR .20 .40
SESLEN031 Eldlixir of Scarlet Sanguine SCR .50 1.00
SESLEN032 Guardian of the Golden Land SCR .20 .40
SESLEN033 Huaquero of the Golden Land SCR .30 .75
SESLEN034 Conquistador of the Golden Land SCR.30 .75
SESLEN035 Golden Land Forever! SR .50 1.00
SESLEN036 El Dorado Adelantado SCR .20 .40
SESLEN037 Doki Doki SR .15 .30
SESLEN038 Block Dragon SR .25 .50
SESLEN039 Rose Lover SR .15 .30
SESLEN040 Lonefire Blossom SR .30 .75
SESLEN041 Tytannial, Princess of Camellias SR .15 .30
SESLEN042 Uni-Zombie SR .20 .40
SESLEN043 Upstart Goblin SR 1.00 2.00
SESLEN044 Galaxy Cyclone SR .30 .75
SESLEN045 Solemn Judgment SR 2.00 4.00
SESLEN046 Il Blud SR .15 .30
SESLEN047 Nine-Tailed Fox SR .15 .30
SESLEN048 Koa'ki Meiru Guardian SR .25 .50
SESLEN049 Koa'ki Meiru Sandman SR .15 .30
SESLEN050 Koa'ki Meiru Wall SR .15 .30
SESLEN051 Koa'ki Meiru Overload SR .15 .30
SESLEN052 Talaya, Princess of
Cherry Blossoms SR .15 .30
SESLEN053 Mariña, Princess of Sunflowers SR .15 .30
SESLEN054 Chirubimé, Princess
of Autumn Leaves SR .15 .30
SESLEN055 D.D. Borderline SR .15 .30
SESLEN056 Miracle Fertilizer SR .15 .30
SESLEN057 Pyramid of Wonders SR .15 .30
SESLEN058 Rock Bombardment SR .15 .30
SESLEN059 Pollinosis SR .15 .30
SESLEN060 Trap Trick SR .60 1.25

2020 Yu-Gi-Oh Speed Duel Battle City Box 1st Edition

SBCBEN001 Dark Magician C .30 .75
SBCBEN001 Dark Magician SCR 2.00 4.00
SBCBEN002 Aqua Madoor C .12 .25
SBCBEN003 Buster Blader C .17 .35
SBCBEN003 Buster Blader SCR 4.00 8.00
SBCBEN004 Archfiend of Gilfer C .12 .25
SBCBEN005 Swift Gaia the Fierce Knight C .20 .40
SBCBEN005 Swift Gaia the Fierce Knight SCR 1.00 2.00
SBCBEN006 Kycoo the Ghost Destroyer C 2.00 4.00
SBCBEN007 Skilled White Magician C .12 .25
SBCBEN008 Breaker the Magical Warrior C 1.00 2.00
SBCBEN008 Breaker the Magical Warrior SCR 7.50 15.00
SBCBEN009 Skilled Red Magician C .12 .25
SBCBEN010 Dark Magic Curtain C .12 .25
SBCBEN011 Polymerization C .75 1.50
SBCBEN012 De-Fusion C .40 .80
SBCBEN013 Book of Moon C .50 1.00
SBCBEN014 Emblem of Dragon Destroyer C .30 .60
SBCBEN015 Destruction Swordsman Fusion C .30 .60
SBCBEN016 Fusion Recycling Plant C .15 .30
SBCBEN017 Magical Hats C .20 .40
SBCBEN018 Fairy Wind C .12 .25
SBCBEN019 Darklight C .12 .25
SBCBEN020 Metaverse C .50 1.00
SBCBEN020 Metaverse SCR 5.00 10.00
SBCBEN021 Dark Paladin C .30 .60
SBCBEN021 Dark Paladin SCR 5.00 10.00
SBCBEN022 Valkyrion the Magna Warrior C .25 .50
SBCBEN022 Valkyrion the Magna Warrior SCR 1.00 2.00
SBCBEN023 Alpha The Magnet Warrior C .25 .50
SBCBEN024 Beta The Magnet Warrior C .30 .75
SBCBEN025 Gamma The Magnet Warrior C .30 .60
SBCBEN026 Delta The Magnet Warrior C .30 .75
SBCBEN027 Giant Soldier of Stone C .12 .25
SBCBEN028 Destroyer Golem C .10 .20
SBCBEN029 The Rock Spirit C .12 .25
SBCBEN030 Granmarg the Rock Monarch C .17 .35
SBCBEN031 Absorbing Jar C .12 .25
SBCBEN032 Block Golem C .15 .30
SBCBEN033 Attack the Moon! C .12 .25
SBCBEN034 Magnetic Field C .50 1.00
SBCBEN035 Zero Gravity C .15 .30
SBCBEN036 Mind Crush C .60 1.25
SBCBEN037 Rock Bombardment C .07 .15
SBCBEN038 Sealing Ceremony of Mokuton C .10 .20
SBCBEN039 Unbreakable Spirit C .12 .25
SBCBEN040 Magnet Force C .25 .50
SBCBEN041 Magnet Conversion C .25 .50
SBCBEN042 Gazelle the King of Mythical Beasts C.12 .25
SBCBEN043 Berfomet C .12 .25
SBCBEN044 Phantom Beast Cross-Wing C .07 .15
SBCBEN045 Phantom Beast Wild-Horn C .07 .15
SBCBEN046 Phantom Beast Thunder-Pegasus C .07 .15
SBCBEN047 Giant Rat C .15 .30
SBCBEN048 Bazoo the Soul-Eater C .12 .25
SBCBEN049 Manticore of Darkness C .12 .25
SBCBEN050 Enraged Battle Ox C .20 .40
SBCBEN051 Ghost Knight of Jackal C .12 .25
SBCBEN052 Behemoth the King of All Animals C.15 .30
SBCBEN053 Green Baboon,
Defender of the Forest C .12 .25
SBCBEN054 Wild Nature's Release C .12 .25
SBCBEN055 The Big March of Animals C .12 .25
SBCBEN056 Spiritual Forest C .12 .25
SBCBEN057 Fire Formation - Tenki C .30 .60
SBCBEN057 Fire Formation - Tenki SCR 3.00 6.00
SBCBEN058 The Big Cattle Drive C .15 .30
SBCBEN059 Riryoku Field C .12 .25
SBCBEN060 Howl of the Wild C .07 .15
SBCBEN061 Horn of the Phantom Beast C .15 .30
SBCBEN062 Chimera the Flying Mythical Beast C.15 .30
SBCBEN063 X-Head Cannon C .30 .75
SBCBEN064 Y-Dragon Head C .40 .80
SBCBEN065 Z-Metal Tank C .40 .80
SBCBEN066 Heavy Mech Support Platform C .17 .35
SBCBEN067 Victory Viper XX03 C .17 .35
SBCBEN068 DUCKER Mobile Cannon C .12 .25
SBCBEN069 Jade Knight C .20 .40
SBCBEN070 Falchionß C .17 .35
SBCBEN071 Machina Gearframe C 1.00 2.00
SBCBEN072 Machina Peacekeeper C .17 .35
SBCBEN073 Delta Tri C .12 .25
SBCBEN074 United We Stand C .40 .80
SBCBEN075 Frontline Base C .20 .40
SBCBEN076 Machine Assembly Line C .15 .30
SBCBEN077 Union Hangar C .30 .75
SBCBEN077 Union Hangar SCR 1.25 2.50
SBCBEN078 Solitary Sword of Poison C .20 .40
SBCBEN079 Formation Union C .07 .15
SBCBEN080 Rare Metalmorph C .15 .30
SBCBEN081 Roll Out! C .12 .25
SBCBEN082 Union Scramble C .25 .50
SBCBEN083 XY-Dragon Cannon C .30 .75
SBCBEN084 XYZ-Dragon Cannon C .30 .60
SBCBEN085 XZ-Tank Cannon C .40 .80
SBCBEN086 YZ-Tank Dragon C .40 .80
SBCBEN087 Blue-Eyes White Dragon C .60 1.25
SBCBEN087 Blue-Eyes White Dragon SCR 4.00 8.00
SBCBEN088 Saggi the Dark Clown C .15 .30
SBCBEN089 Swordstalker C .12 .25
SBCBEN090 La Jinn the Mystical
Genie of the Lamp C .17 .35
SBCBEN091 Vorse Raider C .25 .50
SBCBEN092 Dark Blade C .10 .20
SBCBEN093 Maha Vailo C .15 .30
SBCBEN094 Zombyra the Dark C .20 .40
SBCBEN095 Spear Dragon C .25 .50
SBCBEN096 Kaiser Glider C .12 .25
SBCBEN097 Fiend's Sanctuary C .15 .30
SBCBEN098 Soul Exchange C .30 .60
SBCBEN099 Shrink C 2.50 5.00
SBCBEN100 Mage Power C .30 .60
SBCBEN101 Silent Doom C .12 .25
SBCBEN102 Acid Trap Hole C .12 .25
SBCBEN103 Negate Attack C .20 .40
SBCBEN104 Magic Drain C .20 .40
SBCBEN105 Final Attack Orders C .12 .25
SBCBEN106 Inspiration C .12 .25
SBCBEN107 Masked Beast Des Gardius C .75 1.50
SBCBEN107 Masked Beast Des Gardius SCR .20 .40
SBCBEN108 Shining Abyss C .12 .25
SBCBEN109 Grand Tiki Elder C .12 .25
SBCBEN110 Melchid the Four-Face Beast C .12 .25
SBCBEN111 Beast of Talwar C .15 .30
SBCBEN112 Opticlops C .10 .20
SBCBEN113 Wall of Illusion C .30 .75
SBCBEN114 Night Assailant C .30 .75
SBCBEN115 Ritual Raven C .12 .25
SBCBEN116 The Masked Beast C .12 .25
SBCBEN117 Nobleman of Extermination C .75 1.50
SBCBEN118 Mask of Brutality C .07 .15
SBCBEN119 The Mask of Remnants C .15 .30
SBCBEN120 Curse of the Masked Beast C .15 .30
SBCBEN121 Pre-Preparation of Rites C 3.00 6.00
SBCBEN122 Widespread Ruin C 1.50 3.00
SBCBEN123 Mask of Weakness C .07 .15
SBCBEN124 Bark of Dark Ruler C .07 .15
SBCBEN125 Soul Demolition C .07 .15
SBCBEN126 Dark Smog C .10 .20
SBCBEN127 Keldo C .12 .25
SBCBEN128 Mudora C .12 .25
SBCBEN129 Zolga C .10 .20
SBCBEN130 Kelbek C .12 .25
SBCBEN131 Skelengel C .15 .30
SBCBEN132 Airknight Parshath C 3.00 6.00
SBCBEN132 Airknight Parshath SCR .25 .50
SBCBEN133 Moisture Creature C .07 .15
SBCBEN134 Guardian Angel Joan C .12 .25
SBCBEN135 Angel 07 C .17 .35
SBCBEN136 Dimensional Alchemist C 2.50 5.00
SBCBEN137 Bonze Alone C .07 .15
SBCBEN138 Nobleman of Crossout C 7.50 15.00
SBCBEN138 Nobleman of Crossout SCR .75 1.50
SBCBEN139 Foolish Burial C 6.00 12.00
SBCBEN139 Foolish Burial SCR .75 1.50
SBCBEN140 Cestus of Dagla C .12 .25
SBCBEN141 Valhalla, Hall of the Fallen C .75 1.50
SBCBEN141 Valhalla, Hall of the Fallen SCR .25 .50
SBCBEN142 Cosmic Cyclone C 5.00 10.00
SBCBEN142 Cosmic Cyclone SCR .40 .80
SBCBEN143 Waboku C 1.25 2.50
SBCBEN144 Rope of Life C .12 .25
SBCBEN145 Drop Off C .20 .40

SBCBEN146 Lost Wind C .50 1.00
SBCBEN146 Lost Wind SCR 3.00 6.00
SBCBEN147 Jinzo C 7.50 15.00
SBCBEN147 Jinzo SCR .40 .80
SBCBEN148 The Fiend Megacyber C .15 .30
SBCBEN149 Freed the Matchless General C .12 .25
SBCBEN150 Mysterious Guard C .12 .25
SBCBEN151 Exiled Force C .30 .75
SBCBEN152 Swarm of Scarabs C .15 .30
SBCBEN153 Swarm of Locusts C .20 .40
SBCBEN154 Des Lacooda C .17 .35
SBCBEN155 Dark Scorpion - Gorg the Strong C .17 .35
SBCBEN156 Dark Scorpion - Meanae the Thorn C .17 .35
SBCBEN157 Amplifier C .15 .30
SBCBEN158 Lightning Blade C .17 .35
SBCBEN159 Creature Swap C .75 1.50
SBCBEN160 Reinforcements of the Army C .25 .50
SBCBEN160 Reinforcements of the Army SCR 10.00 20.00
SBCBEN161 The Warrior Returning Alive C .17 .35
SBCBEN162 Hammer Shot C 1.00 2.00
SBCBEN163 Hidden Armory C .12 .25
SBCBEN164 Draining Shield C .30 .75
SBCBEN165 Psychic Shockwave C .17 .35
SBCBEN166 Battleguard Rage C .12 .25
SBCBEN167 Red-Eyes Black Dragon C .50 1.00
SBCBEN167 Red-Eyes Black Dragon SCR 4.00 8.00
SBCBEN168 Dunames Dark Witch C .12 .25
SBCBEN169 Ally of Justice Clausolas C .15 .30
SBCBEN170 Hannibal Necromancer C .12 .25
SBCBEN171 Banisher of the Light C .12 .25
SBCBEN172 Rocket Warrior C .12 .25
SBCBEN173 Cyber Harpie Lady C .25 .50
SBCBEN174 Spell Canceller C .20 .40
SBCBEN174 Spell Canceller SCR 3.00 6.00
SBCBEN175 Strike Ninja C .10 .20
SBCBEN176 Blowback Dragon C .60 1.25
SBCBEN177 Regenerating Mummy C .12 .25
SBCBEN178 Pitch-Black Warwolf C .12 .25
SBCBEN179 Banisher of the Radiance C .40 .80
SBCBEN180 Twin-Barrel Dragon C .40 .80
SBCBEN181 Skilled Blue Magician C .15 .30
SBCBEN182 Buster Blader, the
Destruction Swordmaster C .17 .35
SBCBEN183 Performance of Sword C .12 .25
SBCBEN184 Dokurorider C .17 .35
SBCBEN185 Paladin of White Dragon C .17 .35
SBCBEN186 Commencement Dance C .07 .15
SBCBEN187 Revival of Dokurorider C .10 .20
SBCBEN188 Magic Formula C .25 .50
SBCBEN189 White Dragon Ritual C .15 .30
SBCBEN190 Archfiend's Oath C .15 .30
SBCBEN191 Storm C .10 .20
SBCBEN192 The Puppet Magic of Dark Ruler C .10 .20
SBCBEN193 Mirror Wall C .30 .75
SBCBEN194 Judgment of Anubis C .25 .50
SBCBEN195 Embodiment of Apophis C .20 .40
SBCBEN196 Spell Purification C .12 .25
SBCBEN197 Machine King - 3000 B.C. C .12 .25
SBCBEN198 Copy Knight C .10 .20
SBCBEN199 Swamp Mirrorer C .15 .30
SBCBEN200 Quantum Cat C .12 .25
SBCBEN201 Slifer the Sky Dragon SCR .75 1.50
SBCBEN202 Obelisk the Tormentor SCR 1.00 2.00
SBCBEN203 The Winged Dragon of Ra SCR 4.00 8.00

2020 Yu-Gi-Oh Speed Duel Battle City Box 1st Edition Skill Cards

SBCBENS01 Fury of Thunder C .07 .15
SBCBENS02 It's No Monster, It's a God! C .12 .25
SBCBENS03 Hieratic Chant C .12 .25
SBCBENS04 It's Jinzo! C .10 .20
SBCBENS05 The Psychic Duelist C .07 .15
SBCBENS06 Guardians of the Tomb C .12 .25
SBCBENS07 Union Combination C .17 .35
SBCBENS08 Spell of Mask C .15 .30
SBCBENS09 Magician's Act C .12 .25
SBCBENS10 Endless Traps C .12 .25
SBCBENS11 No More Mrs. Nice Mai! C .12 .25
SBCBENS12 I'm Just Gonna Attack! C .20 .40
SBCBENS13 Rise of the Fallen C .12 .25
SBCBENS14 Beasts of Phantom C .12 .25
SBCBENS15 Magnetic Attraction C .20 .40
SBCBENS16 Power of Friendship C .12 .25
SBCBENS17 Fusion Party! C .20 .40
SBCBENS18 Ritual Ceremony C .17 .35
SBCBENS19 Low Blow C .07 .15
SBCBENS20 Digging for Gold C .12 .25

2020 Yu-Gi-Oh Structure Deck Mechanized Madness 1st Edition

SR10EN001 Machina Citadel UR .50 1.00
SR10EN002 Machina Air Raider SR .30 .75
SR10EN003 Machina Irradiator C .12 .25
SR10EN004 Machina Fortress C .12 .25
SR10EN005 Machina Gearframe C .12 .25
SR10EN006 Machina Peacekeeper C .12 .25
SR10EN007 Machina Force C .12 .25
SR10EN008 Machina Megaform C .12 .25
SR10EN009 Machina Cannon C .12 .25
SR10EN010 Machina Soldier C .12 .25
SR10EN011 Machina Sniper C .12 .25
SR10EN012 Machina Defender C .12 .25
SR10EN013 Commander Covington C .12 .25
SR10EN014 Jizukiru, the Star Destroying Kaiju C .60 1.25
SR10EN015 Snow Plow Hustle Rustle C .12 .25
SR10EN016 Genex Ally Birdman C .12 .25
SR10EN017 Scrap Recycler C 1.00 2.00
SR10EN018 Torque Tune Gear C .12 .25
SR10EN019 Righty Driver C .12 .25
SR10EN020 Lefty Driver C .12 .25
SR10EN021 Deskbot 001 C .50 1.00
SR10EN022 Deskbot 003 C .12 .25
SR10EN023 Machina Redeployment SR 1.00 2.00
SR10EN024 Machina Defense Perimeter C .12 .25
SR10EN025 Machina Armored Unit C .12 .25
SR10EN026 Iron Call C .12 .25
SR10EN027 Iron Draw C .12 .25
SR10EN028 Magnet Reverse C .50 1.00
SR10EN029 Limiter Removal C .20 .40
SR10EN030 Ties of the Brethren C .30 .75
SR10EN031 Pot of Avarice C 1.00 2.00
SR10EN032 Cosmic Cyclone C 1.00 2.00
SR10EN033 Supply Squad C .12 .25
SR10EN034 Machina Overdrive C .12 .25
SR10EN035 Cyber Summon Blaster C .12 .25
SR10EN036 Back to the Front C .12 .25
SR10EN037 Trap Trick C .60 1.25
SR10EN038 Begone, Knave! C .12 .25
SR10EN039 Solemn Strike C 1.00 2.00
SR10EN040 Machina Possesstorage UR .25 .50
SR10EN041 Unauthorized Reactivation SR .75 1.50

2020 Yu-Gi-Oh Structure Deck Sacred Beasts 1st Edition

SDSAEN001 Raviel, Lord of Phantasms... UR .75 1.50
SDSAEN002 Chaos Core C .12 .25
SDSAEN003 Dark Beckoning Beast C 1.00 2.00
SDSAEN004 Chaos Summoning Beast C .75 1.50
SDSAEN005 Dark Summoning Beast C .30 .60
SDSAEN006 Phantom of Chaos C .12 .25
SDSAEN007 Phantom Skyblaster C .12 .25
SDSAEN008 Mad Reloader C .12 .25
SDSAEN009 Grave Squirmer C .12 .25
SDSAEN010 Rainbow Dark Dragon C .12 .25
SDSAEN011 Tragoedia C .12 .25
SDSAEN012 Radian, the Multidimensional Kaiju C 1.25 2.50
SDSAEN013 Chaos Hunter C .12 .25
SDSAEN014 Puppet Master C .12 .25
SDSAEN015 Stygian Street Patrol C .12 .25
SDSAEN016 Farfa, Malebranche
of the Burning Abyss C .12 .25
SDSAEN017 The Fabled Cerburrel C .12 .25
SDSAEN018 Danger! Chupacabra! C .30 .60
SDSAEN019 Cerulean Skyfire SR .30 .60
SDSAEN020 Opening of the Spirit Gates C 1.00 2.00
SDSAEN021 Fallen Paradise C .12 .25
SDSAEN022 Phantasmal Martyrs C .12 .25
SDSAEN023 Spell Chronicle C .12 .25
SDSAEN024 Terraforming C .12 .25
SDSAEN025 Set Rotation C .12 .25
SDSAEN026 Mound of the Bound Creator C .50 1.00
SDSAEN027 One for One C .50 1.00
SDSAEN028 The Beginning of the End C .12 .25
SDSAEN029 Pot of Desires C 1.00 2.00
SDSAEN030 Owner's Seal C .12 .25
SDSAEN031 Field Barrier C .30 .60
SDSAEN032 Swords of Concealing Light C .12 .25
SDSAEN033 Mystical Space Typhoon C .30 .60
SDSAEN034 Hyper Blaze SR .30 .75
SDSAEN035 Awakening of the Sacred Beasts C .30 .75
SDSAEN036 Escape from the Dark Dimension C .12 .25
SDSAEN037 Shapesister C .12 .25
SDSAEN038 Imperial Custom C .12 .25
SDSAEN039 Mistake C .12 .25
SDSAEN040 Dark Factory of More Production C .12 .25
SDSAEN041 Phantasm Emperor Trilojig C .12 .25
SDSAEN042 Uria, Lord of Searing Flames UR .50 1.00
SDSAEN043 Hamon, Lord of Striking Thunder UR .50 1.00
SDSAEN044 Raviel, Lord of Phantasms UR .50 1.00
SDSAEN045 Armityle the Chaos Phantasm UR .60 1.25
SDSAEN046 Dimension Fusion Destruction SR .60 1.25
SDSAEN047 Phantasmal Martyr Token C .12 .25
SDSAEN048 Phantasm Token C .12 .25

2020 Yu-Gi-Oh Structure Deck Shaddoll Showdown 1st Edition

SDSHEN001 Qadshaddoll Keios SR .25 .50
SDSHEN002 Reeshaddoll Wendi SR 2.00 4.00
SDSHEN003 Naelshaddoll Ariel SR .25 .50
SDSHEN004 Shaddoll Falco C .15 .30
SDSHEN005 Shaddoll Hedgehog C .15 .30
SDSHEN006 Shaddoll Squamata C .15 .30
SDSHEN007 Shaddoll Dragon C .25 .50
SDSHEN008 Shaddoll Beast C .15 .30
SDSHEN009 Shaddoll Hound C .15 .30
SDSHEN010 Shaddoll Zefranaga C .15 .30
SDSHEN011 Shaddoll Zefracore C .15 .30
SDSHEN012 Black Luster Soldier... C .50 1.00
SDSHEN013 Lava Golem C .15 .30
SDSHEN014 Dark Armed Dragon C .15 .30
SDSHEN015 Fairy Tail - Sleeper C .15 .30
SDSHEN016 Performage Trick Clown C .15 .30
SDSHEN017 Armageddon Knight C .15 .30
SDSHEN018 Felis, Lightsworn Archer C .15 .30
SDSHEN019 Electromagnetic Turtle C .15 .30
SDSHEN020 Mathematician C .15 .30
SDSHEN021 Kuribandit C .15 .30
SDSHEN022 Peropero Cerperus C .15 .30
SDSHEN023 Curse of the Shadow Prison C .15 .30
SDSHEN024 El Shaddoll Fusion C .15 .30
SDSHEN025 Nephe Shaddoll Fusion C .15 .30
SDSHEN026 Super Polymerization C 2.50 5.00
SDSHEN027 Instant Fusion C .60 1.25
SDSHEN028 Allure of Darkness C 2.50 5.00
SDSHEN029 Foolish Burial C .50 1.00
SDSHEN030 Living Fossil C .15 .30
SDSHEN031 Pot of Avarice C 1.00 2.00
SDSHEN032 Twin Twisters C 1.00 2.00
SDSHEN033 Resh Shaddoll Incarnation SR .50 1.00
SDSHEN034 Shaddoll Core C .15 .30
SDSHEN035 Sinister Shadow Games C .15 .30
SDSHEN036 Purushaddoll Aeon C .15 .30
SDSHEN037 Lost Wind C .30 .75
SDSHEN038 Unending Nightmare C .15 .30
SDSHEN039 Necro Fusion C .15 .30
SDSHEN040 Subterror Succession C .15 .30
SDSHEN041 El Shaddoll Grysta UR .20 .40
SDSHEN042 El Shaddoll Wendigo C .15 .30
SDSHEN043 El Shaddoll Anoyatyllis C .15 .30
SDSHEN044 Shaddoll Construct C .15 .30
SDSHEN045 El Shaddoll Apkallone UR .75 1.50
SDSHEN046 El Shaddoll Construct ALT ART UR .50 1.00
SDSHEN047 El Shaddoll Winda ALT ART SR .25 .50
SDSHEN048 El Shaddoll Shekhinaga SR .25 .50
SDSHEN049 Shaddoll Fusion SR .50 1.00

2020 Yu-Gi-Oh Structure Deck Spirit Charmers 1st Edition

SDCHEN001 Aussa the Earth Charmer C .10 .20
SDCHEN002 Eria the Water Charmer C .10 .20
SDCHEN003 Hiita the Fire Charmer C .10 .20
SDCHEN004 Wynn the Wind Charmer C .10 .20
SDCHEN005 Awakening of the Possessed... UR .12 .25
SDCHEN006 Awakening of the Possessed... UR .12 .25
SDCHEN007 Nefarious Archfiend
Eater of Nefariousness C .10 .20
SDCHEN008 Jigabyte C .10 .20
SDCHEN009 Inari Fire C .10 .20
SDCHEN010 Ranryu C .10 .20
SDCHEN011 Fairy Tail - Sleeper C .10 .20
SDCHEN012 Fairy Tail - Rella C .10 .20
SDCHEN013 Fairy Tail - Luna C .15 .30
SDCHEN014 Witchcrafter Golem Aruru C .10 .20
SDCHEN015 Dark Doriado C .10 .20
SDCHEN016 Witch of the Black Forest C .10 .20
SDCHEN017 Effect Veiler C 1.25 2.50
SDCHEN018 Denko Sekka C .12 .25
SDCHEN019 Grand Spiritual Art - Ichirin UR .15 .30
SDCHEN020 Awakening of the Possessed C .10 .20
SDCHEN021 Raigeki SR 1.00 2.00
SDCHEN022 Secret Village of the Spellcasters C .20 .40
SDCHEN023 Spellbook of Knowledge C .20 .40
SDCHEN024 Terraforming C .12 .25
SDCHEN025 Book of Eclipse C .10 .20
SDCHEN026 Twin Twisters C .60 1.25
SDCHEN027 Dark Ruler No More C 4.00 8.00
SDCHEN028 Possessed Partnerships SR .15 .30
SDCHEN029 Unpossessed C .10 .20
SDCHEN030 Spiritual Earth Art - Kurogane C .10 .20
SDCHEN031 Spiritual Water Art - Aoi C .10 .20
SDCHEN032 Spiritual Fire Art - Kurenai C .10 .20
SDCHEN033 Spiritual Wind Art - Miyabi C .10 .20
SDCHEN034 Metaverse C .15 .30
SDCHEN035 Dimensional Barrier C .12 .25
SDCHEN036 Solemn Warning C .20 .40
SDCHEN037 Familiar-Possessed -
Aussa UR ALT ART 1.00 2.00
SDCHEN037 Familiar-Possessed - Aussa C .10 .20
SDCHEN038 Familiar-Possessed - Eria UR ALT ART 1.00 2.00
SDCHEN038 Familiar-Possessed - Eria C .10 .20
SDCHEN039 Familiar-Possessed -
Hiita UR ALT ART .60 1.25
SDCHEN039 Familiar-Possessed - Hiita C .10 .20
SDCHEN040 Familiar-Possessed -
Wynn UR ALT ART .75 1.50
SDCHEN040 Familiar-Possessed - Wynn C .10 .20
SDCHEN041 Spirit Charmers UR .20 .40

2020 Yu-Gi-Oh Structure Deck Spirit Charmers 1st Edition Tokens

SDCHENT01 Token Aussa and Wynn SR .40 .80
SDCHENT02 Token Hiita and Eria SR .40 .80
SDCHENT03 Token Hiita and Aussa SR .30 .75
SDCHENT04 Token Eria and Wynn SR .75 1.50
SDCHENT05 Token Charmers and
Their Familiars SR .75 1.50

2020 Yu-Gi-Oh Tin of Lost Memories 1st Edition

MP20EN001 Danger! Ogopogo! PRISM SCR .60 1.25
MP20EN002 Salamangreat Wolvie C .07 .15
MP20EN003 Salamangreat Parro C .07 .15
MP20EN004 Salamangreat Foxer C .07 .15
MP20EN005 Speedburst Dragon C .07 .15
MP20EN006 Rokket Synchron C .20 .40
MP20EN007 Neo Space Connector C .17 .35
MP20EN008 Guardragon Justicia C .07 .15
MP20EN009 Guardragon Garmides C .07 .15
MP20EN010 Guardragon Promineses C .07 .15
MP20EN011 Guardragon Andrake C .07 .15
MP20EN012 Fantastical Dragon Phantazmay SR 1.75 3.50
MP20EN013 Madolche Petingcessoeur C .12 .25
MP20EN014 Psychic Wheeleder UR .40 .80
MP20EN015 Aloof Lupine R .20 .40
MP20EN016 Salamangreat Violet Chimera C .10 .20
MP20EN017 Borreload Savage Dragon PRISM SCR 7.50 15.00
MP20EN018 Cyberse Quantum Dragon PRISM SCR 1.00 2.00
MP20EN019 Hyper Psychic Riser C .07 .15
MP20EN020 Salamangreat Sunlight Wolf C .15 .30
MP20EN021 Guardragon Elpy PRISM SCR .30 .75
MP20EN022 Guardragon Pisty PRISM SCR 1.50 3.00
MP20EN023 Sky Striker Ace - Kaina PRISM SCR 2.00 4.00
MP20EN024 Hiita the Fire Charmer, Ablaze C .17 .35
MP20EN025 Fusion of Fire C .07 .15
MP20EN026 Trickstar Fusion C .07 .15
MP20EN027 Neos Fusion PRISM SCR 3.00 6.00
MP20EN028 Guardragon Shield C .07 .15
MP20EN029 World Legacy Guardragon PRISM SCR .75 1.50
MP20EN030 Pot of Extravagance PRISM SCR 6.00 12.00
MP20EN031 Guardragon Corewakening C .07 .15
MP20EN032 Guardragon Cataclysm C .12 .25
MP20EN033 Subterror Succession C .07 .15
MP20EN034 Dark Factory of More Production C .07 .15
MP20EN035 Witch's Strike UR 3.00 6.00
MP20EN036 Super Anti-Kaiju War Machine Mecha-
Thunder-King UR .15 .30
MP20EN037 Time Thief Winder SR .12 .25
MP20EN038 Time Thief Bezel Ship C .07 .15
MP20EN039 Time Thief Regulator R .17 .35
MP20EN040 Time Thief Redoer PRISM SCR 3.00 6.00
MP20EN041 Time Thief Hack C .07 .15
MP20EN042 Time Thief Flyback C .07 .15
MP20EN043 Valkyrie Sechste UR .17 .35
MP20EN044 Valkyrie Vierte R .10 .20
MP20EN045 Final Light R .12 .25
MP20EN046 Apple of Enlightenment C .07 .15
MP20EN047 Subterror Guru R .12 .25
MP20EN048 Trickstar Corobane PRISM SCR .75 1.50
MP20EN049 Shinobi Necro SR .30 .75
MP20EN050 Gnomaterial UR .75 1.50
MP20EN051 Salamangreat Fennec C .07 .15
MP20EN052 Dinowrestler Eskrimamenchi C .07 .15
MP20EN053 Dinowrestler Coelasilat C .10 .20
MP20EN054 Dinowrestler Martial Anga C .07 .15
MP20EN055 Destiny HERO - Drawhand C .15 .30
MP20EN056 Neo Flamvell Lady C .10 .20
MP20EN057 Knightmare Incarnation Idlee SR .10 .20
MP20EN058 World Legacy Guardragon Mardark C .07 .15
MP20EN059 Omni Dragon Brotaur UR .75 1.50
MP20EN060 Chaos Betrayer C .07 .15
MP20EN061 Xyz Slidolphin C .07 .15
MP20EN062 Emperor Maju Garzett R .07 .15
MP20EN063 Dinowrestler Chimera T Wrextle C .07 .15
MP20EN064 Destiny HERO -
Dominance PRISM SCR .50 1.00
MP20EN065 World Chalice
Guardragon Almarduke C .15 .30
MP20EN066 Dinowrestler Giga Spinosavate C .12 .25
MP20EN067 Firewall eXceed Dragon SR .12 .25
MP20EN068 Madolche Teacher Glassouffle C .12 .25
MP20EN069 Dinowrestler Terra Parkourio C .07 .15
MP20EN070 Xtra HERO Cross Crusader C .60 1.25
MP20EN071 Mekk-Knight Crusadia Avramax UR 1.25 2.50
MP20EN072 Cynet Mining SR 1.75 3.50
MP20EN073 Salamangreat Recureance C .07 .15
MP20EN074 Tyrant Dino Fusion C .10 .20
MP20EN075 Fusion Destiny UR 1.25 2.50
MP20EN076 World Legacy Monstrosity PRISM SCR 1.25 2.50
MP20EN077 Guardragon Reincarnation C .07 .15
MP20EN078 Crusadia Testament R .10 .20
MP20EN079 Dirge of the Lost Dragon UR .12 .25
MP20EN080 Mystic Mine PRISM SCR 1.25 2.50
MP20EN081 Mordschlag C .07 .15
MP20EN082 World Legacy Cliffhanger C .07 .15
MP20EN083 Chain Hole R .12 .25
MP20EN084 Crackdown PRISM SCR .75 1.50
MP20EN085 Danger! Excitement! Mystery! R .12 .25
MP20EN086 Danger! Feets of Strength! C .07 .15
MP20EN087 You're in Danger! C .10 .20
MP20EN088 Valkyrie Funfte C .07 .15
MP20EN089 Valkyrie Erda SR .12 .25
MP20EN090 Valkyrie Chariot C .07 .15
MP20EN091 Valkyrie's Embrace R .12 .25
MP20EN092 Pegasus Wing C .07 .15
MP20EN093 Loge's Flame R .07 .15
MP20EN094 Number XX: Utopic Dark Infinity SR .12 .25
MP20EN095 Mermail Abyssalacia SR .12 .25
MP20EN096 Cherubini, Ebon
Angel of the Burning Abyss UR 7.50 15.00
MP20EN097 Speedlift SR .10 .20
MP20EN098 Pendulum Halt SR .10 .20
MP20EN099 Whitefish Salvage SR .12 .25
MP20EN100 Memories of Hope UR .30 .75
MP20EN101 Capshell R .20 .40
MP20EN102 Marincess Sea Horse SR .25 .50
MP20EN103 Marincess Sea Star C .07 .15
MP20EN104 Dinowrestler Martial Ankylo C .07 .15
MP20EN105 Dinowrestler Rambrachio C .07 .15
MP20EN106 Tenyi Spirit - Adhara C .40 .80
MP20EN107 Tenyi Spirit - Shthana C .20 .40
MP20EN108 Tenyi Spirit - Mapura C .07 .15
MP20EN109 Tenyi Spirit - Nahata C .07 .15
MP20EN110 Tenyi Spirit - Vishuda C .25 .50
MP20EN111 B.E.S. Blaster Cannon Core C .07 .15
MP20EN112 Ranryu C .07 .15
MP20EN113 Witchcrafter Golem Aruru UR .60 1.25
MP20EN114 Gizmek Orochi, the
Serpentron Sky Slasher UR .30 .75
MP20EN115 Beatraptor SR .07 .15
MP20EN116 Spirit Sculptor R .07 .15
MP20EN117 Borreload eXcharge Dragon SR .12 .25
MP20EN118 Marincess Blue Slug SR 2.50 5.00
MP20EN119 Marincess Coral Anemone UR .75 1.50
MP20EN120 Marincess Marbled Rock UR .12 .25
MP20EN121 Monk of the Tenyi C 1.00 2.00
MP20EN122 Shaman of the Tenyi PRISM SCR 2.00 4.00
MP20EN123 Berserker of the Tenyi C .10 .20
MP20EN124 Wynn the Wind Charmer, Verdant UR .75 1.50
MP20EN125 Linkmail Archfiend R .10 .20
MP20EN126 Apollousa, Bow of the Goddess UR 6.00 12.00
MP20EN127 Defender of the Labyrinth C .07 .15
MP20EN128 Rising Fire C .07 .15
MP20EN129 Fury of Fire C .07 .15
MP20EN130 Flawless Perfection of the Tenyi C .12 .25
MP20EN131 Vessel for the Dragon Cycle C 1.00 2.00
MP20EN132 Draw Discharge C .07 .15
MP20EN133 Marincess Wave R .30 .60
MP20EN134 Marincess Current C .07 .15
MP20EN135 Fists of the Unrivaled Tenyi C .12 .25
MP20EN136 The Return to the Normal C .07 .15
MP20EN137 Get Out! UR .50 1.00
MP20EN138 Storm Dragon's Return UR .25 .50
MP20EN139 Dwimmered Glimmer C .07 .15
MP20EN140 Barricadeborg Blocker R .12 .25
MP20EN141 Hraesvelgr, the
Desperate Doom Eagle C .12 .25
MP20EN142 White Aura Monoceros R .12 .25
MP20EN143 White Howling R .12 .25
MP20EN144 F.A. Shining Star GT SR .10 .20
MP20EN145 Dragunity Knight -
Romulus PRISM SCR 1.25 2.50
MP20EN146 Rogue of Endymion SR .10 .20
MP20EN147 Marincess Mandarin C .50 1.00
MP20EN148 Marincess Crown Tail C .07 .15
MP20EN149 Marincess Blue Tang SR .30 .60
MP20EN150 Dinowrestler Martial Ampelo C .07 .15
MP20EN151 Dinowrestler Valeonyx C .07 .15
MP20EN152 Unchained Twins - Aruha C .50 1.00
MP20EN153 Unchained Twins - Rakea C .25 .50
MP20EN154 Unchained Soul of Disaster SR .20 .40
MP20EN155 Gladiator Beast Sagittarii C .07 .15
MP20EN156 Gladiator Beast Attorix C .07 .15
MP20EN157 Gladiator Beast Vespasius C .07 .15
MP20EN158 Starliege Seyfert UR 4.00 8.00
MP20EN159 Nebula Dragon C .30 .75
MP20EN160 Galactic Spiral Dragon C .12 .25
MP20EN161 Tenyi Spirit - Ashuna C .50 1.00
MP20EN162 Infinitrack Brutal Dozer C .12 .25
MP20EN163 Gizmek Yata, the Gleaming
Vanguard PRISM SCR .20 .40
MP20EN164 Hop Ear Squadron C 1.00 2.00
MP20EN165 Gladiator Beast Domitianus UR .12 .25
MP20EN166 Draco Berserker
of the Tenyi PRISM SCR 2.00 4.00

MP20EN167 Gallant Granite PRISM SCR	1.25	2.50
MP20EN168 Firewall Dragon Darkfluid SR	.30	.60
MP20EN169 Salamangreat Pyro Phoenix UR	.40	.80
MP20EN170 Marincess Crystal Heart R	.12	.25
MP20EN171 Marincess Wonder Heart C	.07	.15
MP20EN172 Marincess Sea Angel C	.07	.15
MP20EN173 Unchained Soul of Rage UR	7.50	15.00
MP20EN174 Unchained Soul of Anguish SR	.30	.60
MP20EN175 Unchained Abomination PRISM SCR	6.00	12.00
MP20EN176 Test Panther SR	.12	.25
MP20EN177 Gorgon, Empress of the Evil Eyed R	.12	.25
MP20EN178 I:P Masquerena PRISM SCR	4.00	8.00
MP20EN179 Salamangreat Burning Shell C	.07	.15
MP20EN180 Salamangreat Transcendence C	.07	.15
MP20EN181 Marincess Battle Ocean C	.07	.15
MP20EN182 Abomination's Prison UR	10.00	20.00
MP20EN183 Wailing of the Unchained Souls SR	.25	.50
MP20EN184 Gladiator Beast's Comeback C	.12	.25
MP20EN185 Gladiator Beast United C	.07	.15
MP20EN186 Gladiator Rejection SR	.15	.30
MP20EN187 Evil Eye of Gorgoneio C	.10	.20
MP20EN188 Spiritual Entanglement C	.12	.25
MP20EN189 Marincess Snow C	.10	.20
MP20EN190 Marincess Cascade C	.07	.15
MP20EN191 Escape of the Unchained C	.20	.40
MP20EN192 Abominable Chamber of the Unchained C	.17	.35
MP20EN193 Gladiator Beast Charge C	.07	.15
MP20EN194 Gladiator Naumachia C	.07	.15
MP20EN195 Crusher Run C	.07	.15
MP20EN196 Peaceful Burial UR	.12	.25
MP20EN197 Jelly Cannon C	.12	.25
MP20EN198 Desert Locusts C	.10	.20
MP20EN199 Tyrant Farm C	.07	.15
MP20EN200 Overburst Dragon SR	.07	.15
MP20EN201 Astra Ghouls SR	.07	.15
MP20EN202 Bye Bye Damage SR	.12	.25
MP20EN203 Dances with Beasts SR	.07	.15
MP20EN204 Striker Dragon PRISM SCR	2.00	4.00
MP20EN205 Draco Masters of the Tenyi PRISM SCR	.30	.75
MP20EN206 Infinitrack Harvester UR	2.50	5.00
MP20EN207 Infinitrack Anchor Drill UR	1.50	3.00
MP20EN208 Infinitrack Crab Crane C	.07	.15
MP20EN209 Infinitrack Drag Shovel C	.07	.15
MP20EN210 Infinitrack Trencher SR	.15	.30
MP20EN211 Infinitrack Tunneller C	.75	1.50
MP20EN212 Infinitrack River Stormer UR	.25	.50
MP20EN213 Infinitrack Mountain Smasher UR	.17	.35
MP20EN214 Infinitrack Earth Slicer UR	.30	.75
MP20EN215 Infinitrack Goliath UR	1.00	2.00
MP20EN216 Infinitrack Fortress Megaclops UR	.50	1.00
MP20EN217 Outrigger Extension UR	.10	.20
MP20EN218 Spin Turn UR	.10	.20
MP20EN219 Witchcrafter Potterie UR	.25	.50
MP20EN220 Witchcrafter Pittore UR	.75	1.50
MP20EN221 Witchcrafter Schmietta UR	.75	1.50
MP20EN222 Witchcrafter Edel PRISM SCR	.75	1.50
MP20EN223 Witchcrafter Haine PRISM SCR	.60	1.25
MP20EN224 Witchcrafter Madame Verre SR	.40	.80
MP20EN225 Witchcrafter Creation SR	.20	.40
MP20EN226 Witchcrafter Holiday UR	1.50	3.00
MP20EN227 Witchcrafter Collaboration R	.20	.40
MP20EN228 Witchcrafter Draping C	.12	.25
MP20EN229 Witchcrafter Bystreet UR	.75	1.50
MP20EN230 Witchcrafter Scroll SR	.15	.30
MP20EN231 Witchcrafter Masterpiece UR	.30	.75
MP20EN232 Serziel, Watcher of the Evil Eye UR	1.25	2.50
MP20EN233 Medusa, Watcher of the Evil Eye UR	.30	.75
MP20EN234 Catoblepas, Familiar of the Evil Eye C	.10	.20
MP20EN235 Basilius, Familiar of the Evil Eye C	.07	.15
MP20EN236 Zerziel, Ruler of the Evil Eyed SR	.12	.25
MP20EN237 Evil Eye of Selene UR	.20	.40
MP20EN238 Evil Eye Domain - Pareidolia UR	.30	.60
MP20EN239 Evil Eye Awakening UR	.17	.35
MP20EN240 Evil Eye Confrontation C	.10	.20
MP20EN241 Evil Eye Repose SR	.10	.20
MP20EN242 Evil Eye Defeat UR	.25	.50
MP20EN243 Evil Eye Mesmerism SR	.10	.20
MP20EN244 Evil Eye Retribution SR	.10	.20
MP20EN245 Magicalized Fusion PRISM SCR	2.00	4.00
MP20EN246 Successor Soul UR	.50	1.00
MP20EN247 Strength in Unity UR	.30	.60
MP20EN248 Destined Rivals UR	1.25	2.50
MP20EN249 Red-Eyes Dark Dragoon UR	12.50	25.00

2020 Yu-Gi-Oh Toon Chaos 1st Edition

TOCHEN001 Toon Black Luster Soldier CR	200.00	400.00
TOCHEN001 Toon Black Luster Soldier UR	10.00	20.00
TOCHEN002 Toon Harpie Lady CR	75.00	150.00
TOCHEN002 Toon Harpie Lady SR	.15	.30
TOCHEN003 Toon Bookmark CR	50.00	100.00
TOCHEN003 Toon Bookmark UR	10.00	20.00
TOCHEN004 Toon Page-Flip CR	50.00	100.00
TOCHEN004 Toon Page-Flip UR	10.00	20.00
TOCHEN005 Toon Terror SR	.15	.30
TOCHEN006 The Chaos Creator CR	60.00	120.00
TOCHEN006 The Chaos Creator UR	10.00	20.00
TOCHEN007 Chaos Daedalus CR	50.00	100.00
TOCHEN007 Chaos Daedalus UR	1.50	3.00
TOCHEN008 Chaos Valkyria CR	60.00	120.00
TOCHEN008 Chaos Valkyria SR	.15	.30
TOCHEN009 Chaos Space CR	100.00	200.00
TOCHEN009 Chaos Space SR	.15	.30
TOCHEN010 Eternal Chaos SR	.15	.30
TOCHEN011 Infernoble Knight - Renaud UR	20.00	40.00
TOCHEN012 Immortal Phoenix Gearfried CR	100.00	200.00
TOCHEN012 Immortal Phoenix Gearfried UR	20.00	40.00
TOCHEN013 Sublimation Knight SR	.15	.30
TOCHEN014 Infernoble Knight - Roland UR	2.50	5.00
TOCHEN015 Evocator Eveque R	.12	.25
TOCHEN016 Gearbreed SR	.50	1.00
TOCHEN017 Supermagic Sword of Raptinus SR	.50	1.00
TOCHEN018 Cross Over R	.20	.40
TOCHEN019 Gemini Ablation SR	.15	.30
TOCHEN020 Fluffal Angel SR	.25	.50
TOCHEN021 Frightfur Meister SR	.30	.75
TOCHEN022 Code Generator R	.25	.50
TOCHEN023 Valkyrie Sigrun SR	.15	.30
TOCHEN024 Magician of Hope SR	.20	.40
TOCHEN025 PSY-Frame Driver R	.50	1.00
TOCHEN026 Sangan R	.12	.25
TOCHEN027 Witch of the Black Forest R	.12	.25
TOCHEN028 Chaos Sorcerer R	.12	.25
TOCHEN029 Black Luster Soldier... CR	300.00	600.00
TOCHEN029 Black Luster Soldier... R	.12	.25
TOCHEN030 Chaos Emperor Dragon... CR	125.00	250.00
TOCHEN030 Chaos Emperor Dragon... R	.12	.25
TOCHEN031 Lightpulsar Dragon R	.12	.25
TOCHEN032 Darkflare Dragon R	.12	.25
TOCHEN033 Black Luster Soldier - Envoy of the Evening Twilight R	.30	.75
TOCHEN034 Dwarf Star Dragon Planeter R	.12	.25
TOCHEN035 Black Luster Soldier - Sacred Soldier R	.20	.40
TOCHEN036 PSY-Framegear Gamma CR	75.00	150.00
TOCHEN036 PSY-Framegear Gamma R	.75	1.50
TOCHEN037 Curse of Dragonfire R	.12	.25
TOCHEN038 True King Lithosagym, the Disaster R	.12	.25
TOCHEN039 Envoy of Chaos R	.25	.50
TOCHEN040 Elemental HERO Solid Soldier R	.12	.25
TOCHEN041 Keeper of Dragon Magic R	.12	.25
TOCHEN042 Micro Coder SR	.30	.75
TOCHEN043 Masked HERO Goka R	.12	.25
TOCHEN044 Masked HERO Vapor R	.12	.25
TOCHEN045 Masked HERO Acid R	.12	.25
TOCHEN046 Masked HERO Dian R	.12	.25
TOCHEN047 Masked HERO Blast R	.12	.25
TOCHEN048 Frightfur Sabre-Tooth SR	.15	.30
TOCHEN049 Mudragon of the Swamp R	.12	.25
TOCHEN050 Stardust Dragon CR	200.00	400.00
TOCHEN050 Stardust Dragon R	.12	.25
TOCHEN051 Number 68: Sanaphond the Sky Prison R	.12	.25
TOCHEN052 Number 75: Bamboozling Gossip Shadow R	.12	.25
TOCHEN053 Progleo R	.12	.25
TOCHEN054 Toon World R	.12	.25
TOCHEN055 Supervise R	.12	.25
TOCHEN056 Chaos Zone R	.12	.25
TOCHEN057 Pot of Desires R	.12	.25
TOCHEN058 Cynet Codec R	.12	.25
TOCHEN059 Pot of Extravagance CR	125.00	250.00
TOCHEN059 Pot of Extravagance UR	20.00	40.00
TOCHEN060 Starlight Road R	.12	.25

2021 Yu-Gi-Oh Ancient Guardians 1st Edition

ANGUEN001 Nunu, the Ogdoadic Remnant SR	.30	.75
ANGUEN002 Nauya, the Ogdoadic Remnant SR	.60	1.25
ANGUEN003 Flogos, the Ogdoadic Boundless R	.12	.25
ANGUEN004 Zohah, the Ogdoadic Boundless R	.12	.25
ANGUEN005 Keurse, the Ogdoadic Light SR	.20	.40
ANGUEN006 Aleirtt, the Ogdoadic Dark SR	.20	.40
ANGUEN007 Aron, the Ogdoadic King CR	20.00	40.00
ANGUEN007 Aron, the Ogdoadic King UR	2.50	5.00
ANGUEN008 Amunessia, the Ogdoadic Queen CR	25.00	50.00
ANGUEN008 Amunessia, the Ogdoadic Queen UR	3.00	6.00
ANGUEN009 Ogdoabyss, the Ogdoadic Overlord CR	30.00	60.00
ANGUEN009 Ogdoabyss, the Ogdoadic Overlord UR	4.00	8.00
ANGUEN010 Ogdoadic Water Lily SR	1.00	2.00
ANGUEN011 Ogdoadic Origin R	.12	.25
ANGUEN012 Ogdoadic Hollow R	.12	.25
ANGUEN013 Ogdoadic Calling R	.12	.25
ANGUEN014 DoSolfachord Cutia SR	.20	.40
ANGUEN015 ReSolfachord Dreamia R	.12	.25
ANGUEN016 MiSolfachord Eliteia R	.12	.25
ANGUEN017 FaSolfachord Fancia CR	30.00	75.00
ANGUEN017 FaSolfachord Fancia UR	6.00	12.00
ANGUEN018 SolSolfachord Gracia CR	20.00	40.00
ANGUEN018 SolSolfachord Gracia SR	.20	.40
ANGUEN019 LaSolfachord Angelia SR	.20	.40
ANGUEN020 TiSolfachord Beautia CR	20.00	40.00
ANGUEN020 TiSolfachord Beautia UR	2.50	5.00
ANGUEN021 DoSolfachord Coolia CR	25.00	50.00
ANGUEN021 DoSolfachord Coolia UR	4.00	8.00
ANGUEN022 Solfachord Elegance SR	.20	.40
ANGUEN023 Solfachord Scale R	.12	.25
ANGUEN024 Solfachord Harmonia SR	.20	.40
ANGUEN025 Solfachord Musica R	.12	.25
ANGUEN026 Solfachord Formal R	.12	.25
ANGUEN027 Ursarctic Mikpolar SR	.20	.40
ANGUEN028 Ursarctic Miktanus SR	.20	.40
ANGUEN029 Ursarctic Mikbilis SR	.20	.40
ANGUEN030 Ursarctic Megapolar R	.12	.25
ANGUEN031 Ursarctic Megatanus R	.12	.25
ANGUEN032 Ursarctic Megabilis R	.12	.25
ANGUEN033 Ursarctic Polari CR	20.00	40.00
ANGUEN033 Ursarctic Polari UR	4.00	8.00
ANGUEN034 Ursarctic Septentrion CR	15.00	30.00
ANGUEN034 Ursarctic Septentrion UR	2.00	4.00
ANGUEN035 Ursarctic Grand Chariot CR	15.00	30.00
ANGUEN035 Ursarctic Grand Chariot UR	1.25	2.50
ANGUEN036 Ursarctic Departure SR	.20	.40
ANGUEN037 Ursarctic Slider SR	.20	.40
ANGUEN038 Ursarctic Big Dipper UR	2.50	5.00
ANGUEN039 Ursarctic Quint Charge R	.12	.25
ANGUEN040 Vennominon the King of Poisonous Snakes R	.12	.25
ANGUEN041 Vennominaga Deity... CR	20.00	40.00
ANGUEN041 Vennominaga Deity... R	.12	.25
ANGUEN042 Evil Dragon Ananta R	.12	.25
ANGUEN043 Skull Meister CR	75.00	150.00
ANGUEN043 Skull Meister R	.12	.25
ANGUEN044 Lightserpent R	.12	.25
ANGUEN045 Luster Pendulum, the Dracoslayer R	.12	.25
ANGUEN046 Dinowrestler Pankratops CR	75.00	150.00
ANGUEN046 Dinowrestler Pankratops R	.12	.25
ANGUEN047 Dinoster Power, the Mighty Dracoslayer R	.12	.25
ANGUEN048 Ignister Prominence... R	.12	.25
ANGUEN049 King of the Feral Imps R	.12	.25
ANGUEN050 Majester Paladin... R	.12	.25
ANGUEN051 Snake Rain CR	30.00	75.00
ANGUEN051 Snake Rain R	.12	.25
ANGUEN052 Trade-In CR	50.00	100.00
ANGUEN052 Trade-In R	.30	.60
ANGUEN053 Viper's Rebirth R	.12	.25
ANGUEN054 Ayers Rock Sunrise R	.12	.25
ANGUEN055 Pot of Riches R	.12	.25
ANGUEN056 Wavering Eyes R	.12	.25
ANGUEN057 Igknight Reload R	.12	.25
ANGUEN058 Damage = Reptile R	.12	.25
ANGUEN059 Rise of the Snake Deity R	.12	.25
ANGUEN060 Offering to the Snake Deity R	.12	.25

2021 Yu-Gi-Oh Blazing Vortex 1st Edition

BLVOEN000 War Rock Mountain SCR	2.50	5.00
BLVOEN001 Armed Dragon Thunder LV10 SCR	5.00	10.00
BLVOEN001 Armed Dragon Thunder LV10 SLR	125.00	250.00
BLVOEN002 Armed Dragon Thunder LV7 UR	3.00	6.00
BLVOEN003 Armed Dragon Thunder LV5 SR	.30	.75
BLVOEN004 Armed Dragon Thunder LV3 SR	.50	1.00
BLVOEN005 Armed Dragon LV10 White UR	1.25	2.50
BLVOEN006 Springans Rockey C	.10	.20
BLVOEN007 Springans Pedor C	.10	.20
BLVOEN008 Springans Branga C	.10	.20
BLVOEN009 Springans Captain Sargas C	.10	.20
BLVOEN010 Tri-Brigade Kitt SR	1.00	2.00
BLVOEN011 S-Force Rappa Chiyomaru SCR	4.00	8.00
BLVOEN012 S-Force Professor DiGamma C	.10	.20
BLVOEN013 S-Force Orrafist SR	.15	.30
BLVOEN014 S-Force Gravitino UR	.50	1.00
BLVOEN015 S-Force Pla-Tina UR	1.00	2.00
BLVOEN016 Windwitch - Blizzard Bell C	.10	.20
BLVOEN017 Windwitch - Freeze Bell UR	.75	1.50
BLVOEN018 Fabled Marcosia C	.10	.20
BLVOEN019 The Fabled Abanc C	.10	.20
BLVOEN020 Parametalfoes Melcaster C	.10	.20
BLVOEN021 Metalfoes Vanisher SR	.15	.30
BLVOEN022 Constellar Caduceus SR	.15	.30
BLVOEN023 Digital Bug Registrider C	.10	.20
BLVOEN024 Maha Vailo, Light of the Heavens SR	.15	.30
BLVOEN025 Ancient Warriors - Rebellious Lu Feng SR	.15	.30
BLVOEN026 Neiroy, the Dream Mirror Disciple C	.10	.20
BLVOEN027 Machina Unclaspare C	.10	.20
BLVOEN028 Live Twin Lil-la Treat SLR	125.00	250.00
BLVOEN028 Live Twin Lil-la Treat UR	2.00	4.00
BLVOEN029 Heavenly Zephyr - Miradora SCR	7.50	15.00
BLVOEN029 Heavenly Zephyr - Miradora SLR	125.00	250.00
BLVOEN030 Fairy Archer Ingunar C	.10	.20
BLVOEN031 Radiant Vouirescence C	.10	.20
BLVOEN032 Gigathunder Giclops C	.10	.20
BLVOEN033 Amanokujaki C	.10	.20
BLVOEN034 Guitar Gurnards Duonigis C	.10	.20
BLVOEN035 Wightbaking SR	.50	1.00
BLVOEN036 Ojama Pink C	.10	.20
BLVOEN037 Knight of Armor Dragon C	.10	.20
BLVOEN038 Sprind the Irondash Dragon C	.10	.20
BLVOEN039 Parametalfoes Azortless SR	.15	.30
BLVOEN040 Eldlich the Mad Golden Lord SCR	2.50	5.00
BLVOEN041 Dual Avatar - Empowered Mitsu-Jaku UR	.30	.75
BLVOEN042 Oneiros, the Dream Mirror Tormentor SR	.15	.30
BLVOEN043 Windwitch - Diamond Bell UR	.30	.60
BLVOEN044 Fabled Andwraith SR	.15	.30
BLVOEN045 Dragunity Knight - Gormfaobhar SR	.15	.30
BLVOEN046 Springans Ship - Exblowrer UR	1.25	2.50
BLVOEN047 Sacred Tree Beast, Hyperyton SR	.50	1.00
BLVOEN048 S-Force Justify UR	1.00	2.00
BLVOEN049 Heavymetalfoes Amalgam C	.10	.20
BLVOEN050 Underworld Goddess of the Closed World SCR	15.00	30.00
BLVOEN051 Armed Dragon Flash SCR	5.00	10.00
BLVOEN052 Armed Dragon Blitz C	.10	.20
BLVOEN053 Armed Dragon Lightning C	.10	.20
BLVOEN054 Springans Watch SR	.20	.40
BLVOEN055 Great Sand Sea - Gold Golgonda SR	.15	.30
BLVOEN056 Tri-Brigade Rendezvous C	.10	.20
BLVOEN057 S-Force Bridgehead SCR	3.00	6.00
BLVOEN058 S-Force Showdown C	.10	.20
BLVOEN059 Windwitch Chimes SR	.20	.40
BLVOEN060 Stairway to a Fabled Realm C	.10	.20
BLVOEN061 Parametalfoes Fusion C	.10	.20
BLVOEN062 Seven Cities of the Golden Land UR	.60	1.25
BLVOEN063 Archfiend's Staff of Despair C	.10	.20
BLVOEN064 Armor Dragon Ritual C	.10	.20
BLVOEN065 Pot of Prosperity SCR	75.00	150.00
BLVOEN065 Pot of Prosperity SLR	300.00	600.00
BLVOEN066 Tilted Try C	.10	.20
BLVOEN067 Armed Dragon Thunderbolt SR	.15	.30
BLVOEN068 Springans Call! C	.10	.20
BLVOEN069 Springans Blast! C	.10	.20
BLVOEN070 Dogmatika Genesis C	.10	.20
BLVOEN071 S-Force Specimen C	.10	.20
BLVOEN072 Icy Breeze Refrain C	.10	.20
BLVOEN073 Fabled Treason C	.10	.20
BLVOEN074 Ancient Warriors Saga - Chivalrous Path C	.10	.20
BLVOEN075 Virtual World Gate - Xuanwu C	.10	.20
BLVOEN076 Dual Avatar Ascendance C	.10	.20
BLVOEN077 Dream Mirror Recap C	.10	.20
BLVOEN078 E.M.R. SR	.15	.30
BLVOEN079 Angel Statue - Azurune SR	.50	1.00
BLVOEN080 Linear Equation Cannon C	.10	.20
BLVOEN081 Materiactor Gigadra SR	.15	.30
BLVOEN082 Raging Storm Dragon - Beaufort IX C	.10	.20
BLVOEN083 Coordius the Triphasic Dealmon UR	.60	1.25
BLVOEN084 Materiactor Gigaboros SR	.15	.30
BLVOEN085 Steel Star Regulator C	.10	.20
BLVOEN086 Breath of Acclamation C	.10	.20
BLVOEN087 Greater Polymerization UR	1.50	3.00
BLVOEN088 Reinforcement of the Army's Troops C	.10	.20
BLVOEN089 Psychic Eraser Laser SR	.75	1.50
BLVOEN090 Synchro Transmission C	.10	.20
BLVOEN091 Pendulum Encore C	.10	.20
BLVOEN092 Underdog SCR	2.00	4.00
BLVOEN093 War Rock Fortia SR	.15	.30
BLVOEN094 War Rock Gactos SR	.20	.40
BLVOEN095 War Rock Orpis C	.10	.20
BLVOEN096 War Rock Skyler C	.10	.20
BLVOEN097 War Rock Bashileos UR	.60	1.25
BLVOEN098 War Rock Ordeal C	.10	.20
BLVOEN099 Virtual World Oto-Hime - Toutou SR	.30	.60
BLVOEN100 Trishula, Dragon of the Ice Barrier SLR	250.00	500.00

2021 Yu-Gi-Oh Brothers of Legend 1st Edition

BROLEN000 #17 Leviathan Dragon (Astral Text) SLR	50.00	100.00
BROLEN001 Kuribah UR	.30	.75
BROLEN002 Kuribee UR	.30	.75
BROLEN003 Kuriboo UR	.30	.75
BROLEN004 Kuribeh UR	.30	.75
BROLEN005 Kuribabylon UR	.30	.75
BROLEN006 Five Star Twilight UR	.30	.60
BROLEN007 Yowie SCR	.20	.40
BROLEN008 Penguin Sword UR	.12	.25
BROLEN009 D - Force SCR	.50	1.00
BROLEN010 Doctor D UR	.12	.25
BROLEN011 Dragonroid SCR	.20	.40
BROLEN012 Rebirth Judgment SCR	.20	.40
BROLEN013 Ice Barrier UR	.15	.30
BROLEN014 Ice Knight UR	.15	.30
BROLEN015 Summon Storm UR	.15	.30
BROLEN016 Wing Requital SCR	.75	1.50
BROLEN017 Noble Knight's Shield-Bearer SCR	.20	.40
BROLEN018 Horse of the Floral Knights UR	.12	.25
BROLEN019 Noble Knight's Spearholder UR	.12	.25
BROLEN020 Centaur Mina SCR	.20	.40
BROLEN021 Ecole de Zone SCR	.20	.40
BROLEN022 Soul Binding Gate UR	.12	.25
BROLEN023 Piri Reis Map SCR	1.25	2.50
BROLEN024 Ice Mirror UR	.12	.25
BROLEN025 ZW - Sylphid Wing UR	.12	.25
BROLEN026 ZS - Ouroboros Sage UR	.12	.25
BROLEN027 Ultimate Leo Utopia Ray SCR	.20	.40
BROLEN028 Zexal Catapult UR	.12	.25
BROLEN029 Silent Sea Nettle UR	.30	.75
BROLEN030 Number 4: Stealth Kragen SCR	1.25	2.50
BROLEN031 Stealth Kragen Spawn SCR	1.00	2.00
BROLEN032 Grandpa Demetto SCR	.20	.40
BROLEN033 Doll House UR	.12	.25
BROLEN034 Starving Venemy Dragon SCR	.20	.40
BROLEN035 Speedroid Scratch SCR	.20	.40
BROLEN036 Lyrilusc - Bird Strike SCR	.20	.40
BROLEN037 Toy Parade SCR	.20	.40
BROLEN038 Cipher Biplane SCR	.20	.40
BROLEN039 Cipher Interference UR	.12	.25
BROLEN040 Double Exposure SCR	.20	.40
BROLEN041 FA.I.ghting Spirit UR	.12	.25
BROLEN042 A.I.'s Show UR	.12	.25
BROLEN043 Appliancer Propelion UR	.12	.25
BROLEN044 Appliancer Conversion UR	.12	.25
BROLEN045 Altergeist Memorygant SCR	.50	1.00
BROLEN046 Altergeist Pookuery SCR	.40	.80
BROLEN047 Altergeist Fijialert SCR	.20	.40
BROLEN048 Right-Hand Shark UR	.12	.25
BROLEN049 Left-Hand Shark UR	.12	.25
BROLEN050 Hidden Fangs of Revenge UR	.12	.25
BROLEN051 White Mirror UR	.12	.25
BROLEN052 The Ice-Bound God UR	.12	.25
BROLEN053 Astraltopia UR	.12	.25
BROLEN054 Zexal Field UR	.12	.25
BROLEN055 The Deal of Destiny UR	.12	.25
BROLEN056 Numbers Protection UR	.12	.25
BROLEN057 Number 99: Utopia Dragonar SCR	.30	.75
BROLEN058 ZS - Utopic Sage SCR	.20	.40
BROLEN059 Number 39: Utopia (New Artwork) UR	.12	.25
BROLEN060 Hyper Rank-Up-Magic Utopiforce UR	.20	.40
BROLEN061 Astral Kuriboh SCR	.20	.40
BROLEN062 Kuriboh (alternate artwork) UR	.15	.30
BROLEN063 Kuribohrn UR	.12	.25
BROLEN064 Performapal Kuribohble SCR	.20	.40
BROLEN065 Detonate UR	.12	.25
BROLEN066 Magician's Souls SCR	25.00	50.00
BROLEN067 Red-Eyes Fusion UR	.30	.75
BROLEN068 Evil HERO Adusted Gold SCR	4.00	8.00
BROLEN069 Evil HERO Malicious Bane SCR	3.00	6.00
BROLEN070 Thought Ruler Archfiend UR	.15	.30
BROLEN071 Shooting Star Dragon UR	.20	.40
BROLEN072 Starlight Road UR	.12	.25
BROLEN073 Number 89: Diablosis the Mind Hacker SCR	.75	1.50
BROLEN074 Gadarla, the Mystery Dust Kaiju UR	.30	.75
BROLEN075 Interrupted Kaiju Slumber UR	.30	.75
BROLEN076 Kaiju Capture Mission UR	.12	.25
BROLEN077 Eidos the Underworld Squire UR	.12	.25
BROLEN078 Edea the Heavenly Squire UR	.12	.25
BROLEN079 The Phantom Knights of Ragged Gloves UR	.12	.25
BROLEN080 Nibiru, the Primal Being SCR	10.00	20.00
BROLEN081 Infernoid Decatron UR	.12	.25
BROLEN082 Infernoid Tierra SCR	.20	.40
BROLEN083 Wind-Up Arsenal Zenmaioh UR	.12	.25
BROLEN084 Inzektor Exa-Beetle UR	.12	.25
BROLEN085 Downerd Magician UR	.50	1.00
BROLEN086 Beatrice, Lady of the Eternal UR	.12	.25
BROLEN087 Relinquished Anima SCR	1.50	3.00
BROLEN088 Allure of Darkness UR	1.50	3.00
BROLEN089 Fossil Dig UR	.30	.60
BROLEN090 Forbidden Droplet SCR	40.00	80.00
BROLEN091 Rank-Up-Magic Argent Chaos Force UR	.12	.25
BROLEN092 Resurgam Xyz UR	.12	.25
BROLEN093 Void Feast UR	.12	.25
BROLEN094 Red-Eyes Dark Dragoon SLR	200.00	400.00

2021 Yu-Gi-Oh Burst of Destiny 1st Edition

BODEEN000 Heritage of the Light C	.10	.20
BODEEN001 Rokket Caliber UR	1.00	2.00
BODEEN002 Double Disrupter Dragon SR	.12	.25
BODEEN003 Swordsoul of Mo Ye SCR	15.00	30.00
BODEEN004 Swordsoul of Taia SR	.50	1.00
BODEEN005 Swordsoul Strategist Longyuan UR	1.00	2.00
BODEEN006 Swordsoul Auspice Chunjun SR	.12	.25

BODEEN007 Incredible Ecclesia, the Virtuous SCR25.00 50.00
BODEEN007 Incredible Ecclesia,
the Virtuous SLR 200.00 400.00
BODEEN008 Icejade Acti C .10 .20
BODEEN009 Icejade Tinola C .10 .20
BODEEN010 Icejade Tremora SCR 2.50 5.00
BODEEN011 Ad Libitum of Despia SR .75 1.50
BODEEN012 Floowandereeze & Snowl SCR 1.00 2.00
BODEEN012 Floowandereeze & Snowl SLR 40.00 80.00
BODEEN013 Floowandereeze & Robina SR .60 1.25
BODEEN014 Floowandereeze & Eglen SR .75 1.50
BODEEN015 Floowandereeze & Stri C .15 .30
BODEEN016 Floowandereeze & Toccan C .10 .20
BODEEN017 Floowandereeze & Empen SCR 10.00 20.00
BODEEN018 Destiny HERO - Denier SR .30 .75
BODEEN019 Reptilianne Nyami C .10 .20
BODEEN020 Reptilianne Coatl C .10 .20
BODEEN021 Magnificent Magikey Mafteal C .10 .20
BODEEN022 Gunkan Suship Uni C .10 .20
BODEEN023 Gunkan Suship Shirauo C .10 .20
BODEEN024 Penguin Squire C .10 .20
BODEEN025 Penguin Ninja C .10 .20
BODEEN026 Penguin Cleric C .10 .20
BODEEN027 Starry Knight Orbitael C .10 .20
BODEEN028 Machina Ruinforce UR 1.00 2.00
BODEEN029 Mimicking Man-Eater Bug C .10 .20
BODEEN030 King of the Heavenly Prison SCR 15.00 30.00
BODEEN031 Fengli the Soldrapom C .10 .20
BODEEN032 Geminize Lord Golknight C .10 .20
BODEEN033 Undaunted Bumpkin Beast C .10 .20
BODEEN034 Meowseclick SR .12 .25
BODEEN035 Outstanding Dog Mary C .10 .20
BODEEN036 Borreload Riot Dragon UR .40 .80
BODEEN037 Transonic Bird C .10 .20
BODEEN038 Masquerade the Blazing Dragon UR12.50 25.00
BODEEN039 Destiny HERO... SCR 30.00 60.00
BODEEN040 Ultimate Flagship Ursatron SR .12 .25
BODEEN041 Swordsoul Grandmaster - Chixiao SCR4.00 8.00
BODEEN041 Swordsoul Grandmaster -
Chixiao SLR 125.00 250.00
BODEEN042 Swordsoul Supreme Sovereign... UR3.00 6.00
BODEEN043 Reptilianne Melusine SR .12 .25
BODEEN044 Magikey Fiend - Transfurlmine SR .12 .25
BODEEN045 Zoroa, the Magistus
Conflagrant Calamity SCR .75 1.50
BODEEN046 Cupid Pitch C .10 .20
BODEEN047 Magikey Spirit - Vepartu SR .15 .30
BODEEN048 Gunkan Suship Uni-class... SR .30 .60
BODEEN049 Gunkan Suship
Shirauo-class Carrier C .10 .20
BODEEN050 Borrelcode Dragon UR .75 1.50
BODEEN051 Evil Twin's Trouble Sunny UR 7.50 15.00
BODEEN051 Evil Twin's Trouble Sunny SLR 200.00 400.00
BODEEN052 Heavy Interlock SR .15 .30
BODEEN053 Swordsoul Emergence UR 5.00 10.00
BODEEN054 Swordsoul Sacred Summit SR .12 .25
BODEEN055 Branded in High Spirits SR .30 .75
BODEEN056 Icejade Cradle SR .25 .50
BODEEN057 Branded in Red SR 2.00 4.00
BODEEN058 Floowandereeze and the
Magnificent Map UR 3.00 6.00
BODEEN059 Floowandereeze and the
Unexplored Wind SR .30 .75
BODEEN060 Reptilianne Ramifications SR .20 .40
BODEEN061 Reptilianne Recoil C .10 .20
BODEEN062 Magikey Battle C .10 .20
BODEEN063 Royal Penguins Garden C .10 .20
BODEEN064 Sonic Tracker C .10 .20
BODEEN065 Sunvine Sowing SR .15 .30
BODEEN066 Ursarctic Drytron C .10 .20
BODEEN067 Supernatural Danger Zone SR .12 .25
BODEEN068 Night Flight C .10 .20
BODEEN069 Small World SCR 12.50 25.00
BODEEN070 Magical Cylinders C .10 .20
BODEEN071 Detonation Code C .10 .20
BODEEN072 Swordsoul Assessment C .10 .20
BODEEN073 Swordsoul Blackout C .10 .20
BODEEN074 Floowandereeze and
the Dreaming Town SR .20 .40
BODEEN075 Floowandereeze and the Scary Sea SR.15 .30
BODEEN076 Break the Destiny C .10 .20
BODEEN077 Magikey Locking C .10 .20
BODEEN078 Stained Glass of Light and Dark SR .15 .30
BODEEN079 Giant Starfall C .10 .20
BODEEN080 Laundry Trap C .10 .20
BODEEN081 Night Sword Serpent C .10 .20
BODEEN082 D.D. Assault Carrier C .10 .20
BODEEN083 Abyss Keeper C .10 .20
BODEEN084 Apex Predation C .10 .20
BODEEN085 Beetrooper Assault Roller C .10 .20
BODEEN086 Beetrooper Light Flapper UR .15 .30
BODEEN087 Heavy Beetrooper Mighty Neptune UR.20 .40
BODEEN088 Ultra Beetrooper Absolute Hercules UR.25 .50
BODEEN089 Beetrooper Descent UR .75 1.50
BODEEN090 Beetrooper Landing C .10 .20
BODEEN091 Beetrooper Squad C .10 .20
BODEEN092 Flip Frozen C .10 .20
BODEEN093 Bravedrive C .10 .20
BODEEN094 Rebuilder C .10 .20
BODEEN095 Threshold Borg C .10 .20
BODEEN096 Cynet Crosswipe C .10 .20
BODEEN097 Danger! Disturbance! Disorder! C .10 .20
BODEEN098 Bayonet Punisher SR .12 .25
BODEEN099 Cynet Cascade C .10 .20
BODEEN100 Elemental HERO Stratos SLR 150.00 300.00
BODEENSP1 Floowandereeze & Empen UR 12.50 25.00

2021 Yu-Gi-Oh Dawn of Majesty 1st Edition

DAMAEN000 Beetrooper Scout Buggy SCR 10.00 20.00
DAMAEN001 Converging Wills Dragon C .10 .20
DAMAEN002 Stardust Synchron SCR 12.50 25.00
DAMAEN003 Stardust Trail C .10 .20
DAMAEN004 Despian Comedy SR .15 .30
DAMAEN005 Despian Tragedy C .10 .20
DAMAEN006 Aluber the Jester of Despia SCR 30.00 60.00
DAMAEN007 Dramaturge of Despia UR 6.00 12.00
DAMAEN008 Albion the Shrouded Dragon SR .30 .60
DAMAEN009 The Iris Swordsoul SLR 200.00 400.00
DAMAEN009 The Iris Swordsoul SCR 17.50 35.00
DAMAEN010 Clavkiys, the Magikey Skyblaster C .10 .20
DAMAEN011 Gunkan Suship Shari C .10 .20
DAMAEN012 Gunkan Suship Ikura C .10 .20
DAMAEN013 Chronomaly Magella Globe SR .15 .30
DAMAEN014 Chronomaly Acambaro Figures C .10 .20
DAMAEN015 Gizmek Inaba, the
Hopping Hare of Hakuto SR .15 .30
DAMAEN016 Gizmek Naganaki,
the Sunrise Signaler UR .50 1.00
DAMAEN017 Gizmek Taniguku,
the Immobile Intellect UR .30 .75
DAMAEN018 Gizmek Arakami,
the Hailbringer Hog SR .15 .30
DAMAEN019 Gusto Vedir C .10 .20
DAMAEN020 Amazement Assistant Delia SR .20 .40
DAMAEN021 Alien Stealthbuster C .10 .20
DAMAEN022 Carpiponica, Mystical
Beast of the Forest C .10 .20
DAMAEN023 Glacier Aqua Madoor C .10 .20
DAMAEN024 Antihuman Intelligence
ME-PSY-YA SLR 75.00 150.00
DAMAEN024 Antihuman Intelligence
ME-PSY-YA SCR 3.00 6.00
DAMAEN025 Protecting Spirit Loagaeth SLR 100.00 200.00
DAMAEN025 Protecting Spirit Loagaeth UR 2.00 4.00
DAMAEN026 Master's Diploman C .10 .20
DAMAEN027 Konohanasakuya C .10 .20
DAMAEN028 Doombearer Psychopompos C .10 .20
DAMAEN029 Slower Swallow C .10 .20
DAMAEN030 Saambell the Star Bonder C .10 .20
DAMAEN031 Aeropixthree C .10 .20
DAMAEN032 Magikey
Mechmusket - Batosbuster SR .20 .40
DAMAEN033 Magikey
Mechmortar - Garesglasser SR .20 .40
DAMAEN034 Despian Quaeritis UR 4.00 8.00
DAMAEN035 Despian Proskenion SR .20 .40
DAMAEN036 Magikey Beast - Ansyalabolas SR .20 .40
DAMAEN037 Magikey Dragon - Andrabime SR .20 .40
DAMAEN038 Allvain the Essence of Vanity C .10 .20
DAMAEN039 Shooting Majestic
Star Dragon SLR 125.00 250.00
DAMAEN039 Shooting Majestic Star Dragon SCR6.00 12.00
DAMAEN040 Daigusto Laplampilica SR .15 .30
DAMAEN041 Stellar Wind Wolfrayet UR 2.50 5.00
DAMAEN042 Gaiarmor Dragonshell C .10 .20
DAMAEN043 Gunkan Suship
Ikura-class Dreadnought C .10 .20
DAMAEN044 Chronomaly Vimana UR 1.25 2.50
DAMAEN045 Vololeniges... SR .20 .40
DAMAEN046 Dragonlark Pairen C .10 .20
DAMAEN047 Cosmic Slicer Zer'oll C .10 .20
DAMAEN048 GranSolfachord Musecia UR .50 1.00
DAMAEN049 Dispatchparazzi C .10 .20
DAMAEN050 Arrive in Light SCR 3.00 6.00
DAMAEN051 Stardust Illumination UR 1.00 2.00
DAMAEN052 Majestic Absorption C .10 .20
DAMAEN053 Despia, Theater of the Branded C .10 .20
DAMAEN054 Branded Opening SR .50 1.00
DAMAEN055 Branded Bond C .10 .20
DAMAEN056 Magikey Maftea UR 2.50 5.00
DAMAEN057 Magikey World UR 2.50 5.00
DAMAEN058 Gunkan Sushipyard
Seaside Supper Spot C .10 .20
DAMAEN059 Chronomaly Temple - Trilithon C .10 .20
DAMAEN060 Sacred Scrolls of the
Gizmek Legend SCR 1.25 2.50
DAMAEN061 Tailwind of Gusto C .10 .20
DAMAEN062 Live Twin Sunny's Snitch SR .75 1.50
DAMAEN063 Triamid Loading C .10 .20
DAMAEN064 Dimer Synthesis C .10 .20
DAMAEN065 High Ritual Art UR 1.00 2.00
DAMAEN066 Ready Fusion SCR 15.00 30.00
DAMAEN067 Synchro Overtake SCR 7.50 15.00
DAMAEN068 Pendulum Treasure SR .20 .40
DAMAEN069 Margin Trading C .10 .20
DAMAEN070 Majestic Mirage SR .15 .30
DAMAEN071 Springans Interluder C .10 .20
DAMAEN072 Magikey Duo C .10 .20
DAMAEN073 Magikey Unlocking C .10 .20
DAMAEN074 Gunkan Suship Daily Special C .10 .20
DAMAEN075 Chronomaly Esperanza Glyph C .10 .20
DAMAEN076 Amaze Attraction Viking Vortex C .10 .20
DAMAEN077 Monster Assortment C .10 .20
DAMAEN078 Beast King Unleashed C .10 .20
DAMAEN079 Stall Turn SR .15 .30
DAMAEN080 Jar of Generosity C .10 .20
DAMAEN081 Baby Mudragon C .10 .20
DAMAEN082 Pazuzule C .10 .20
DAMAEN083 Night's End Administrator SR .20 .40
DAMAEN084 Ra'ten, the Heavenly General C .10 .20
DAMAEN085 D.D.D. - Different Dimension Derby C.10 .20
DAMAEN086 Beetrooper Scale Bomber SR .20 .40
DAMAEN087 Beetrooper Sting Lancer UR 2.50 5.00
DAMAEN088 Beetrooper Armor Horn SR .20 .40
DAMAEN089 Giant Beetrooper Invincible Atlas UR1.25 2.50
DAMAEN090 Beetrooper Formation SR .15 .30
DAMAEN091 Beetrooper Fly & Sting C .10 .20
DAMAEN092 Link Apple SR .15 .30
DAMAEN093 Flying Red Carp C .10 .20
DAMAEN094 Dinowrestler Iguanodraka SR .15 .30
DAMAEN095 Tindangle Jhrelth SR .20 .40
DAMAEN096 Shinobi Insect Hagakuremino C .10 .20
DAMAEN097 Two Toads with One Sting C .10 .20
DAMAEN098 Trickstar Festival SR .15 .30
DAMAEN099 Gouki Finishing Move C .10 .20
DAMAEN100 Stardust Dragon SLR 400.00 800.00
DAMAENSP1 Beetrooper Scout Buggy UR 12.50 25.00

2021 Yu-Gi-Oh Ghosts from the Past 1st Edition

GFTPEN001 Vampire Voivode UR .75 1.50
GFTPEN002 Laval Archer UR .20 .40
GFTPEN003 Lavalval Salamander UR .30 .60
GFTPEN004 Hieratic Sky Dragon
Overlord of Heliopolis UR 1.00 2.00
GFTPEN005 Hieratic Seal of Creation UR .50 1.00
GFTPEN006 Nehshaddoll Genius UR 2.00 4.00
GFTPEN007 Helshaddoll Hollow UR .75 1.50
GFTPEN008 Nekroz of Areadbhair UR .75 1.50
GFTPEN009 Fairy Tail - Rochka UR .30 .60
GFTPEN010 Fairy Tail Tales UR .30 .60
GFTPEN011 Galaxy-Eyes Cipher X Dragon UR 1.00 2.00
GFTPEN012 Time Thief Adjuster UR 3.00 6.00
GFTPEN013 Time Thief Double Barrel UR 1.00 2.00
GFTPEN014 Sunseed Genius Loci UR .20 .40
GFTPEN015 Sunvine Maiden UR .50 1.00
GFTPEN016 Sunseed Shadow UR .75 1.50
GFTPEN017 Sunseed Twin UR .60 1.25
GFTPEN018 Sunavalon Dryas UR .75 1.50
GFTPEN019 Sunavalon Dryades UR .30 .75
GFTPEN020 Sunavalon Dryanome UR .60 1.25
GFTPEN021 Sunavalon Dryatrentiay UR .75 1.50
GFTPEN022 Sunvine Gardna UR .30 .60
GFTPEN023 Sunvine Healer UR .20 .40
GFTPEN024 Sunvine Thrasher UR .75 1.50
GFTPEN025 Sunvine Shrine UR .50 1.00
GFTPEN026 Sunavalon Bloom UR .50 1.00
GFTPEN027 Starry Night, Starry Dragon UR 1.00 2.00
GFTPEN028 Starry Knight Rayel UR .75 1.50
GFTPEN029 Starry Knight Astel UR .30 .75
GFTPEN030 Starry Knight Flamel UR .75 1.50
GFTPEN031 Starry Knight Balefire UR .75 1.50
GFTPEN032 Starry Knight Sky UR .60 1.25
GFTPEN033 Starry Knight Ceremony UR .75 1.50
GFTPEN034 Starry Knight Arrival UR .75 1.50
GFTPEN035 Starry Knight Blast UR .30 .75
GFTPEN036 Dragunity Arma Gram UR .60 1.25
GFTPEN037 Dragunity Legatus UR 2.00 4.00
GFTPEN038 Dragunity Remus UR 4.00 8.00
GFTPEN039 Dragunity Draft UR .20 .40
GFTPEN040 Dragunity Whirlwind UR .60 1.25
GFTPEN041 Dragunity Glow UR 1.50 3.00
GFTPEN042 Dragunity Oubliette UR .30 .60
GFTPEN043 Dragunity Knight - Areadbhair UR .50 1.00
GFTPEN044 Shooting Star Dragon T.G. EX UR 1.00 2.00
GFTPEN045 Red Supernova Dragon UR 2.50 5.00
GFTPEN046 Laval Volcano Handmaiden UR .20 .40
GFTPEN047 Lavalval Dragon UR .20 .40
GFTPEN048 Molten Conduction Field UR .20 .40
GFTPEN049 Hieratic Dragon of Eset UR .30 .75
GFTPEN050 Hieratic Dragon of Tefnuit UR .20 .40
GFTPEN051 Hieratic Dragon King of Atum UR .20 .40
GFTPEN052 Hieratic Sun Dragon
Overlord of Heliopolis UR .20 .40
GFTPEN053 Hieratic Seal of the
Heavenly Spheres UR 2.50 5.00
GFTPEN054 Hieratic Seal of Convocation UR .50 1.00
GFTPEN055 Hieratic Seal of Supremacy UR .20 .40
GFTPEN056 Hieratic Seal of Banishment UR .20 .40
GFTPEN057 Hieratic Seal of Reflection UR .20 .40
GFTPEN058 Hieratic Seal from the Ashes UR .20 .40
GFTPEN059 Galaxy-Eyes Cipher Blade Dragon UR.20 .40
GFTPEN060 Time Thief Winder UR .75 1.50
GFTPEN061 Time Thief Bezel Ship UR .50 1.00
GFTPEN062 Time Thief Regulator UR .75 1.50
GFTPEN063 Time Thief Chronocorder UR .50 1.00
GFTPEN064 Time Thief Redoer UR .30 .75
GFTPEN065 Time Thief Perpetua UR .30 .60
GFTPEN066 Time Thief Hack UR .30 .60
GFTPEN067 Time Thief Startup UR .50 1.00
GFTPEN068 Time Thief Flyback UR .20 .40
GFTPEN069 Time Thief Retrograde UR .30 .60
GFTPEN070 Seiyaryu UR .30 .75
GFTPEN071 Hyozanryu UR .20 .40
GFTPEN072 Arkbrave Dragon UR .20 .40
GFTPEN073 Dragunity Phalanx UR .30 .60
GFTPEN074 Gigantes UR .20 .40
GFTPEN075 Armed Dragon LV10 UR .75 1.50
GFTPEN076 Mist Valley Baby Roc UR .20 .40
GFTPEN077 Evil Thorn UR .60 1.25
GFTPEN078 Mine Mole UR .20 .40
GFTPEN079 Photon Thrasher UR .60 1.25
GFTPEN080 Madolche Puddingcess UR .50 1.00
GFTPEN081 Tackle Crusader UR .20 .40
GFTPEN082 Thestalos the Mega Monarch UR .30 .75
GFTPEN083 Re-Cover UR .20 .40
GFTPEN084 Raidraptor - Tribute Lanius UR .75 1.50
GFTPEN085 Kozmo Tincan UR .50 1.00
GFTPEN086 Kozmoll Dark Lady UR .30 .75
GFTPEN087 Raremetalfoes Bismugear UR .20 .40
GFTPEN088 Backup Secretary UR .30 .75
GFTPEN089 Salamangreat Falco UR .30 .75
GFTPEN090 Danger! Thunderbird! UR 1.00 2.00
GFTPEN091 Madolche Petingcessoeur UR .75 1.50
GFTPEN092 Salamangreat Fowl UR .30 .60
GFTPEN093 Dragon Knight Draco-Equiste UR .20 .40
GFTPEN094 Metalfoes Orichalc UR .20 .40
GFTPEN095 Metalfoes Mithrilium UR .20 .40
GFTPEN096 Meteor Black Comet Dragon UR 1.00 2.00
GFTPEN097 Buster Dragon UR .75 1.50
GFTPEN098 Artifact Durandal UR .20 .40
GFTPEN099 Dark Requiem Xyz Dragon UR .30 .75
GFTPEN100 Metalfoes Steelen UR .30 .60
GFTPEN101 Metalfoes Silverd UR .30 .60
GFTPEN102 Metalfoes Goldriver UR .30 .60
GFTPEN103 Metalfoes Volflame UR .20 .40
GFTPEN104 Fresh Madolche Sistart UR .20 .40
GFTPEN105 Update Jammer UR .50 1.00
GFTPEN106 Splash Mage UR .60 1.25
GFTPEN107 Salvage UR .50 1.00
GFTPEN108 Geartown UR .20 .40
GFTPEN109 Emergency Teleport UR 2.00 4.00
GFTPEN110 Ojama Country UR .30 .75
GFTPEN111 Miracle Synchro Fusion UR .20 .40
GFTPEN112 Mask Change UR .50 1.00
GFTPEN113 Mask Change II UR .50 1.00
GFTPEN114 Resonator Engine UR .20 .40
GFTPEN115 Resonator Call UR .50 1.00
GFTPEN116 Xyz Burst UR .20 .40
GFTPEN117 Madolche Chateau UR .50 1.00
GFTPEN118 Metalfoes Fusion UR .20 .40
GFTPEN119 Orcustrated Return UR .75 1.50
GFTPEN120 Royal Prison UR .20 .40
GFTPEN121 The Monarchs Erupt UR .50 1.00
GFTPEN122 Phantom Knights' Fog Blade UR 1.50 3.00
GFTPEN123 Kozmojo UR .20 .40
GFTPEN124 Metalfoes Counter UR .20 .40
GFTPEN125 Metalfoes Combination UR .20 .40
GFTPEN126 Evenly Matched UR 10.00 20.00
GFTPEN127 Terror of Trishula UR .20 .40
GFTPEN128 Dark Magician GR 500.00 1,000.00
GFTPEN129 Blue-Eyes Alternative
White Dragon GR 200.00 400.00
GFTPEN130 Crystal Wing Synchro Dragon GR125.00 250.00
GFTPEN131 Firewall Dragon GR 100.00 200.00
GFTPEN132 Black Luster Soldier -
Soldier of Chaos GR 200.00 400.00

2021 Yu-Gi-Oh King's Court 1st Edition

KICOEN001 Arcana Triumph Joker UR 2.50 5.00
KICOEN001 Arcana Triumph Joker CR 30.00 75.00
KICOEN002 Joker's Knight UR 7.50 15.00
KICOEN002 Joker's Knight CR 30.00 60.00
KICOEN003 Imperial Bower UR 4.00 8.00
KICOEN003 Imperial Bower CR 15.00 30.00
KICOEN004 Joker's Straight UR 5.00 10.00
KICOEN004 Joker's Straight CR 15.00 30.00
KICOEN005 Face Card Fusion SR .15 .30
KICOEN006 Thunderspeed Summon SR .20 .40
KICOEN007 Joker's Wild SR .15 .30
KICOEN008 Court of Cards SR .15 .30
KICOEN009 Magnet Induction SR .15 .30
KICOEN010 XYZ Hyper Cannon SR .15 .30
KICOEN011 Golden-Eyes Idol R .12 .25
KICOEN012 Zolga the Prophet R .12 .25
KICOEN013 Number F0: Utopic Draco Future UR10.00 20.00
KICOEN013 Number F0: Utopic Draco Future CR60.00 120.00
KICOEN014 Gilti-Gearfried the
Magical Steel Knight UR 1.25 2.50
KICOEN014 Gilti-Gearfried the
Magical Steel Knight CR 12.50 25.00
KICOEN015 Crystal Girl SR .15 .30
KICOEN016 Tindangle Dholes SR .15 .30
KICOEN017 Rose Princess SR .30 .60
KICOEN018 Morph King Stygi-Gel UR .30 .60
KICOEN019 White Rose Cloister SR .30 .60
KICOEN020 Burning Soul UR .75 1.50
KICOEN021 Hyper Galaxy SR .15 .30
KICOEN021 Hyper Galaxy CR 12.50 25.00
KICOEN022 Pendulum Transfer R .12 .25
KICOEN023 Pendulum Xyz R .12 .25
KICOEN024 Dowsing Fusion R .12 .25
KICOEN025 Eternal Bond R .12 .25
KICOEN026 Queen's Knight R .12 .25
KICOEN026 Queen's Knight CR 25.00 50.00
KICOEN027 King's Knight R .12 .25
KICOEN027 King's Knight CR 25.00 50.00
KICOEN028 Jack's Knight R .12 .25
KICOEN028 Jack's Knight CR 20.00 40.00
KICOEN029 Arcana Knight Joker R .12 .25
KICOEN030 Arcana Extra Joker R .12 .25
KICOEN031 Gravekeeper's Spy R .12 .25
KICOEN032 Majestic Dragon R .12 .25
KICOEN033 Stardust Xiaolong R .12 .25
KICOEN034 Rescue Rabbit CR 30.00 75.00
KICOEN034 Rescue Rabbit R .12 .25
KICOEN035 ZW - Tornado Bringer R .12 .25
KICOEN036 ZW - Ultimate Shield R .12 .25
KICOEN037 ZW - Eagle Claw R .12 .25
KICOEN038 Scrap Twin Dragon SR .15 .30
KICOEN039 Cloudcastle R .12 .25
KICOEN040 Baxia, Brightness of the Yang Zing R.12 .25
KICOEN041 Chaofeng, Phantom
of the Yang Zing SR .15 .30
KICOEN042 Number 39: Utopia R .12 .25
KICOEN042 Number 39: Utopia CR 30.00 75.00
KICOEN043 Evolzar Dolkka UR .75 1.50
KICOEN044 Wind-Up Arsenal Zenmaioh R .12 .25
KICOEN045 Number C39: Utopia Ray R .12 .25
KICOEN046 Constellar Ptolemy M7 R .12 .25
KICOEN047 ZW - Leo Arms R .12 .25
KICOEN048 Number 49: Fortune Tune SR .20 .40
KICOEN049 Number F0: Utopic Future R .12 .25
KICOEN050 Infinite Cards R .12 .25
KICOEN051 Reinforcement of the Army R .12 .25
KICOEN051 Reinforcement of the Army CR 60.00 120.00
KICOEN052 The Warrior Returning Alive R .12 .25
KICOEN053 Ties of the Brethren R .12 .25
KICOEN054 Pot of Duality R .20 .40
KICOEN055 Unexpected Dai R .12 .25
KICOEN056 World Legacy Guardragon SR .30 .60
KICOEN057 Lightning Storm UR 25.00 50.00
KICOEN057 Lightning Storm CR 60.00 120.00
KICOEN058 Rivalry of Warlords R .12 .25
KICOEN058 Rivalry of Warlords CR 30.00 75.00
KICOEN059 Converging Wishes R .12 .25
KICOEN060 The Wicked Dreadroot R .12 .25
KICOEN061 The Wicked Avatar R .12 .25
KICOEN062 The Wicked Eraser R .12 .25
KICOEN063 Slifer the Sky Dragon UPR 50.00 100.00
KICOEN063 Slifer the Sky Dragon SCPR 300.00 750.00
KICOEN064 Obelisk the Tormentor UPR 40.00 80.00
KICOEN064 Obelisk the Tormentor SCPR 250.00 500.00
KICOEN065 The Winged Dragon of Ra UPR 40.00 80.00
KICOEN065 The Winged Dragon of Ra SCPR 200.00 400.00

2021 Yu-Gi-Oh Legendary Duelists Season 2 1st Edition

LDS2EN001 Blue-Eyes White Dragon UR (blue) 2.00 4.00
LDS2EN001 Blue-Eyes White Dragon UR (green) 2.00 4.00
LDS2EN001 Blue-Eyes White Dragon UR (purple) 2.00 4.00
LDS2EN001 Blue-Eyes White Dragon UR 2.00 4.00

LDS2EN002 Kaibaman C .12 .25
LDS2EN003 Decoy Dragon C .12 .25
LDS2EN004 The White Stone of Legend C .30 .60
LDS2EN005 Malefic Blue-Eyes White Dragon C .12 .25
LDS2EN006 Maiden with Eyes of Blue C .12 .25
LDS2EN007 Priestess with Eyes of Blue C .12 .25
LDS2EN008 Blue-Eyes Alternative White Dragon UR6.00 12.00
LDS2EN008 Blue-Eyes Alt.White Dragon UR (blue)6.00 12.00
LDS2EN008 Blue-Eyes Alt.White Dragon UR (green)6.00 12.00
LDS2EN008 Blue-Eyes Alt.White Dragon UR (purple) 6.00 12.00
LDS2EN009 Dragon Spirit of White C .12 .25
LDS2EN010 Protector with Eyes of Blue C .12 .25
LDS2EN011 Sage with Eyes of Blue UR 3.00 6.00
LDS2EN011 Sage with Eyes of Blue UR (blue) 2.50 5.00
LDS2EN011 Sage with Eyes of Blue UR (green) 2.50 5.00
LDS2EN011 Sage with Eyes of Blue UR (purple)2.50 5.00
LDS2EN012 Master with Eyes of Blue C .12 .25
LDS2EN013 The White Stone of Ancients UR 1.50 3.00
LDS2EN013 The White Stone of Ancients UR (blue).75 1.50
LDS2EN013 The White Stone of Ancients UR (green) .75 1.50
LDS2EN013 The White Stone of Ancients UR (purple) .75 1.50
LDS2EN014 Blue-Eyes Solid Dragon UR .75 1.50
LDS2EN014 Blue-Eyes Solid Dragon UR (blue) .75 1.50
LDS2EN014 Blue-Eyes Solid Dragon UR (green) .50 1.00
LDS2EN014 Blue-Eyes Solid Dragon UR (purple).50 1.00
LDS2EN015 Blue-Eyes Abyss Dragon SCR 12.50 25.00
LDS2EN016 Blue-Eyes Chaos MAX Dragon UR 1.00 2.00
LDS2EN016 Blue-Eyes Chaos MAX Dragon UR (blue) 1.00 2.00
LDS2EN016 Blue-Eyes Chaos MAX Dragon UR (green) 1.00 2.00
LDS2EN016 Blue-Eyes Chaos MAX Dragon UR (purple) 1.00 2.00
LDS2EN017 Blue-Eyes Chaos Dragon SCR 6.00 12.00
LDS2EN018 Blue-Eyes Ultimate Dragon UR 1.00 2.00
LDS2EN018 Blue-Eyes Ultimate Dragon UR (blue)1.00 2.00
LDS2EN018 Blue-Eyes Ultimate Dragon UR (green)1.00 2.00
LDS2EN018 Blue-Eyes Ultimate Dragon UR (purple)1.00 2.00
LDS2EN019 Blue-Eyes Twin Burst Dragon UR 1.50 3.00
LDS2EN019 Blue-Eyes Twin Burst Dragon UR (blue)1.50 3.00
LDS2EN019 Blue-Eyes Twin Burst Dragon UR (green) 1.50 3.00
LDS2EN019 Blue-Eyes Twin Burst Dragon UR (purple) 1.50 3.00
LDS2EN020 Blue-Eyes Spirit Dragon UR 1.25 2.50
LDS2EN020 Blue-Eyes Spirit Dragon UR (blue) 1.25 2.50
LDS2EN020 Blue-Eyes Spirit Dragon UR (green)1.25 2.50
LDS2EN020 Blue-Eyes Spirit Dragon UR (purple)1.25 2.50
LDS2EN021 Burst Stream of Destruction C .12 .25
LDS2EN022 Dragon Shrine C .12 .25
LDS2EN023 Mausoleum of White C .12 .25
LDS2EN024 Beacon of White C .12 .25
LDS2EN025 Chaos Form C .12 .25
LDS2EN026 Neutron Blast C .12 .25
LDS2EN027 Majesty with Eyes of Blue C .12 .25
LDS2EN028 Bingo Machine, Go!!! SCR 7.50 15.00
LDS2EN029 Rage with Eyes of Blue UR .75 1.50
LDS2EN029 Rage with Eyes of Blue UR (blue) .30 .75
LDS2EN029 Rage with Eyes of Blue UR (green) .30 .75
LDS2EN029 Rage with Eyes of Blue UR (purple) .30 .75
LDS2EN030 The Ultimate Creature of Destruction UR 2.00 4.00
LDS2EN030 The Ultimate Creature of Destruction UR (blue) 1.00 2.00
LDS2EN030 Ult. Creature of Destruction UR (green)1.00 2.00
LDS2EN030 Ult. Creature of Destruction UR (purple) 1.00 2.00
LDS2EN031 Cyber Pharos C .12 .25
LDS2EN032 Cyber Dragon Nachster UR (green)1.50 3.00
LDS2EN032 Cyber Dragon Nachster UR (purple)1.50 3.00
LDS2EN032 Cyber Dragon Nachster UR 1.50 3.00
LDS2EN032 Cyber Dragon Nachster UR (blue) 1.50 3.00
LDS2EN033 Cyber Eternity Dragon UR (blue) .75 1.50
LDS2EN033 Cyber Eternity Dragon UR (green) .75 1.50
LDS2EN033 Cyber Eternity Dragon UR (purple) .75 1.50
LDS2EN033 Cyber Eternity Dragon UR .75 1.50
LDS2EN034 Cyber Dragon Sieger C .12 .25
LDS2EN035 Cyberload Fusion UR (blue) 1.00 2.00
LDS2EN035 Cyberload Fusion UR (green) 1.00 2.00
LDS2EN035 Cyberload Fusion UR (purple) 1.00 2.00
LDS2EN035 Cyberload Fusion UR 1.00 2.00
LDS2EN036 Super Strident Blaze C .12 .25
LDS2EN037 Cybernetic Revolution C .12 .25
LDS2EN038 Blackwing - Gust the Backblast C .12 .25
LDS2EN039 Blackwing - Pinaki the Waxing Moon C.12 .25
LDS2EN040 Blackwing... UR (blue) 1.00 2.00
LDS2EN040 Blackwing... UR (green) 1.00 2.00
LDS2EN040 Blackwing... UR (purple) 1.00 2.00
LDS2EN040 Blackwing - Simoon the Poison Wind UR 1.00 2.00
LDS2EN041 Blackwing - Auster the South Wind C.12 .25
LDS2EN042 Blackwing Tamer -
Obsidian Hawk Joe C .12 .25
LDS2EN043 Blackwing - Nothung the Starlight C.12 .25
LDS2EN044 Blackwing Full Armor Master SCR 1.25 2.50
LDS2EN045 Glowing Crossbow C .12 .25
LDS2EN046 Blackbird Close C .12 .25
LDS2EN047 Galaxy-Eyes Photon Dragon UR (blue)1.00 2.00
LDS2EN047 Galaxy-Eyes Photon Dragon UR (green)1.00 2.00
LDS2EN047 Galaxy-Eyes Photon Dragon UR (purple) 1.00 2.00
LDS2EN047 Galaxy-Eyes Photon Dragon UR 1.50 3.00
LDS2EN048 Galaxy Wizard C .12 .25
LDS2EN049 Galaxy Knight UR (blue) .30 .75
LDS2EN049 Galaxy Knight UR (green) .30 .75
LDS2EN049 Galaxy Knight UR (purple) .30 .75
LDS2EN049 Galaxy Knight UR .50 1.00
LDS2EN050 Photon Vanisher C .30 .60
LDS2EN051 Photon Orbital SCR 4.00 8.00
LDS2EN052 Galaxy-Eyes Afterglow Dragon SCR7.50 15.00
LDS2EN053 #62 Galaxy-Eyes Prime Photon Dragon C .60 1.25
LDS2EN054 Starliege Photon Blast Dragon UR (blue) .50 1.00
LDS2EN054 Starliege Photon Blast Dragon UR (green) .50 1.00
LDS2EN054 Starliege Photon Blast Dragon UR (purple) .50 1.00
LDS2EN054 Starliege Photon Blast Dragon UR .50 1.00
LDS2EN055 Galaxy Zero C .12 .25
LDS2EN056 Photon Hand C .12 .25
LDS2EN057 Photon Change C .12 .25
LDS2EN058 Abyss Actor - Extras C .12 .25
LDS2EN059 Abyss Actor - Wild Hope C .12 .25
LDS2EN060 Abyss Actor - Mellow Madonna C .12 .25
LDS2EN061 Abyss Actor - Comic Relief C .12 .25
LDS2EN062 Abyss Script - Romantic Terror C .12 .25
LDS2EN063 Abyss Playhouse - Fantastic Theater C.12 .25
LDS2EN064 Abyss Actors' Curtain Call C .12 .25
LDS2EN065 Harpie Lady Sisters UR (blue) .30 .75
LDS2EN065 Harpie Lady Sisters UR (green) .30 .75
LDS2EN065 Harpie Lady Sisters UR (purple) .30 .75
LDS2EN065 Harpie Lady Sisters UR .60 1.25
LDS2EN066 Harpie's Pet Dragon UR (blue) .50 1.00
LDS2EN066 Harpie's Pet Dragon UR (green) .50 1.00
LDS2EN066 Harpie's Pet Dragon UR (purple) .50 1.00
LDS2EN066 Harpie's Pet Dragon UR .75 1.50
LDS2EN067 Cyber Harpie Lady C .12 .25
LDS2EN068 Harpie Lady 1 C .12 .25
LDS2EN069 Harpie Lady 2 C .12 .25
LDS2EN070 Harpie Lady 3 C .12 .25
LDS2EN071 Harpie's Pet Baby Dragon C .12 .25
LDS2EN072 Harpie Queen C .12 .25
LDS2EN073 Harpie Channeler UR (blue) 1.00 2.00
LDS2EN073 Harpie Channeler UR (green) 1.00 2.00
LDS2EN073 Harpie Channeler UR (purple) 1.00 2.00
LDS2EN073 Harpie Channeler UR 1.00 2.00
LDS2EN074 Harpie Dancer C .12 .25
LDS2EN075 Harpie Harpist C .30 .75
LDS2EN076 Harpie Perfumer SCR 7.50 15.00
LDS2EN077 Harpie Oracle UR (blue) 1.00 2.00
LDS2EN077 Harpie Oracle UR (green) 1.00 2.00
LDS2EN077 Harpie Oracle UR (purple) 1.00 2.00
LDS2EN077 Harpie Oracle UR 1.00 2.00
LDS2EN078 Harpie Conductor C .50 1.00
LDS2EN079 Cyber Shield C .12 .25
LDS2EN080 Elegant Egotist C .12 .25
LDS2EN081 Harpies' Hunting Ground C .12 .25
LDS2EN082 Triangle Ecstasy Spark C .12 .25
LDS2EN083 Hysteric Sign C .12 .25
LDS2EN084 Harpie Lady Phoenix Formation C .12 .25
LDS2EN085 Alluring Mirror Split C .30 .60
LDS2EN086 Harpie's Feather Rest C .12 .25
LDS2EN087 Hysteric Party C .12 .25
LDS2EN088 Harpie's Feather Storm C .75 1.50
LDS2EN089 Harpie Lady Elegance C .12 .25
LDS2EN090 Cyber Egg Angel C .12 .25
LDS2EN091 Cyber Angel Izana C .12 .25
LDS2EN092 Merciful Machine Angel C .12 .25
LDS2EN093 Incarnated Machine Angel C .12 .25
LDS2EN094 Magnificent Machine Angel C .12 .25
LDS2EN095 Rose Tentacles C .12 .25
LDS2EN096 Twilight Rose Knight C .12 .25
LDS2EN097 Witch of the Black Rose C .20 .40
LDS2EN098 Revival Rose C .12 .25
LDS2EN099 Bird of Roses C .12 .25
LDS2EN100 Rose Witch C .12 .25
LDS2EN101 Queen Angel of Roses C .12 .25
LDS2EN102 Rose Lover C .12 .25
LDS2EN103 Fallen Angel of Roses C .12 .25
LDS2EN104 Blue Rose Dragon UR (blue) .50 1.00
LDS2EN104 Blue Rose Dragon UR (green) .50 1.00
LDS2EN104 Blue Rose Dragon UR .50 1.00
LDS2EN104 Blue Rose Dragon UR (purple) .50 1.00
LDS2EN105 Rose Archer C .12 .25
LDS2EN106 Rose Paladin C .12 .25
LDS2EN107 Dark Rose Fairy C .12 .25
LDS2EN108 Red Rose Dragon UR 1.50 3.00
LDS2EN108 Red Rose Dragon UR (blue) .60 1.25
LDS2EN108 Red Rose Dragon UR (purple) .60 1.25
LDS2EN108 Red Rose Dragon UR (green) .60 1.25
LDS2EN109 White Rose Dragon UR 1.00 2.00
LDS2EN109 White Rose Dragon UR (blue) 1.00 2.00
LDS2EN109 White Rose Dragon UR (green) 1.00 2.00
LDS2EN109 White Rose Dragon UR (purple) 1.00 2.00
LDS2EN110 Black Rose Dragon UR .60 1.25
LDS2EN110 Black Rose Dragon UR (blue) .60 1.25
LDS2EN110 Black Rose Dragon UR (green) .60 1.25
LDS2EN110 Black Rose Dragon UR (purple) .60 1.25
LDS2EN111 Splendid Rose C .12 .25
LDS2EN112 Black Rose Moonlight Dragon UR 1.50 3.00
LDS2EN112 Black Rose Moonlight Dragon UR (blue) 1.50 3.00
LDS2EN112 Black Rose Moonlight Dragon UR (green) 1.50 3.00
LDS2EN112 Black Rose Moonlight Dragon UR (purple) 1.50 3.00
LDS2EN113 Garden Rose Maiden SCR 5.00 10.00
LDS2EN114 Crossrose Dragon UR .50 1.00
LDS2EN114 Crossrose Dragon UR (blue) .50 1.00
LDS2EN114 Crossrose Dragon UR (green) .50 1.00
LDS2EN114 Crossrose Dragon UR (purple) .50 1.00
LDS2EN115 Mark of the Rose C .12 .25
LDS2EN116 Black Garden C .30 .60
LDS2EN117 Thorn of Malice C .12 .25
LDS2EN118 Rose Bell of Revelation C .12 .25
LDS2EN119 Frozen Rose UR .75 1.50
LDS2EN119 Frozen Rose UR (blue) .75 1.50
LDS2EN119 Frozen Rose UR (green) .75 1.50
LDS2EN119 Frozen Rose UR (purple) .75 1.50
LDS2EN120 Blooming of the Darkest Rose C .12 .25
LDS2EN121 Super Express Bullet Train UR 1.50 3.00
LDS2EN121 Super Express Bullet Train UR (blue)1.00 2.00
LDS2EN121 Super Express Bullet Train UR (green)1.00 2.00
LDS2EN121 Super Express Bullet Train UR (purple)1.00 2.00
LDS2EN122 Flying Pegasus Railroad Stampede C.12 .25
LDS2EN123 #81 Superdreadnought Rail Cannon... C .30 .75
LDS2EN124 Superdreadnought Rail Cannon... SCR7.50 15.00
LDS2EN125 Urgent Schedule SCR 7.50 15.00
LDS2EN126 Barrage Blast C .12 .25
LDS2EN127 Lunalight Emerald Bird C .12 .25
LDS2EN128 Lunalight Yellow Marten C .12 .25
LDS2EN129 Lunalight Sabre Dancer C .12 .25
LDS2EN130 Lunalight Fusion C .12 .25
LDS2EN131 Lunalight Serenade Dance C .12 .25

2021 Yu-Gi-Oh Legendary Duelists Synchro Storm 1st Edition

LED8EN001 Clear Wing Synchro Dragon SR .50 1.00
LED8EN002 Speedroid Fuki-Modoshi Piper SR .15 .30
LED8EN003 Speedroid Ultra Hound SR .40 .80
LED8EN004 Hi-Speedroid Cork Shooter UR 2.00 4.00
LED8EN005 Crystal Clear Wing Synchro Dragon GR 20.00 40.00
LED8EN005 Crystal Clear Wing Synchro Dragon UR2.00 4.00
LED8EN006 Hi-Speedroid Clear Wing Rider UR .15 .30
LED8EN007 Speedroid Wheel SR .40 .80
LED8EN008 Speedroid Dupligate R .10 .20
LED8EN009 Speedroid Terrortop C .07 .15
LED8EN010 Speedroid Double Yoyo C .07 .15
LED8EN011 Speedroid Taketomborg C .07 .15
LED8EN012 Speedroid Red-Eyed Dice C .07 .15
LED8EN013 Speedroid Den-Den Daiko Duke C .07 .15
LED8EN014 Speedroid Horse Stilts C .07 .15
LED8EN015 Speedroid Marble Machine C .07 .15
LED8EN016 Speedroid CarTurbo C .07 .15
LED8EN017 Hi-Speedroid Chanbara C .07 .15
LED8EN018 Hi-Speedroid Kitedrake R .10 .20
LED8EN019 Speed Recovery C .07 .15
LED8EN020 Speedlift C .07 .15
LED8EN021 Sauge de Fleur UR .50 1.00
LED8EN022 White Steed of the Floral Knights SR.12 .25
LED8EN023 Necro Synchron UR .30 .75
LED8EN024 Baronne de Fleur UR 75.00 150.00
LED8EN025 Fleuret de Fleur SR .12 .25
LED8EN026 Synchro Dilemma R .10 .20
LED8EN027 Pennant of Revolution R .10 .20
LED8EN028 Sorciere de Fleur C .07 .15
LED8EN029 Necro Fleur C .07 .15
LED8EN030 Noble Knight Joan C .07 .15
LED8EN031 Fleur Synchron R .10 .20
LED8EN032 Chevalier de Fleur R .10 .20
LED8EN033 Z-ONE C .07 .15
LED8EN034 Liberty at Last! C .07 .15
LED8EN035 Lyrilusc - Beryl Canary R .12 .25
LED8EN036 Lyrilusc - Celestine Wagtail UR .75 1.50
LED8EN037 Lyrilusc - Ensemblue Robin UR .60 1.25
LED8EN038 Lyrilusc - Promenade Thrush SR .50 1.00
LED8EN039 Lyrilusc - Bird Call UR 1.50 3.00
LED8EN040 Lyrilusc - Bird Sanctuary SR .30 .60
LED8EN041 Lyrilusc - Phantom Feathers R .10 .20
LED8EN042 Lyrilusc - Cobalt Sparrow C .07 .15
LED8EN043 Lyrilusc - Sapphire Swallow C .07 .15
LED8EN044 Lyrilusc - Turquoise Warbler C .07 .15
LED8EN045 Lyrilusc - Assembled Nightingale R .15 .30
LED8EN046 Lyrilusc - Recital Starling C .07 .15
LED8EN047 Quillbolt Hedgehog C .07 .15
LED8EN048 Synchron Explorer C .07 .15
LED8EN049 Unknown Synchron C .07 .15
LED8EN050 Rush Warrior C .07 .15
LED8EN051 Mariamne, the True Dracophoenix C .07 .15
LED8EN052 Stardust Warrior C .07 .15
LED8EN053 Stardust Assault Warrior C .07 .15
LED8EN054 Totem Bird R .10 .20
LED8EN055 Tornado Dragon C .07 .15
LED8EN056 Quill Pen of Gulldos C .07 .15

2021 Yu-Gi-Oh Lightning Overdrive 1st Edition

LIOVEN000 Diviner of the Herald SCR 30.00 75.00
LIOVEN001 ZW - Pegasus Twin Saber C .10 .20
LIOVEN002 ZS - Armed Sage C .10 .20
LIOVEN003 ZS - Ascended Sage UR 3.00 6.00
LIOVEN004 Supreme Sovereign Serpent of Golgonda SR .15 .30
LIOVEN005 Springans Brothers C .10 .20
LIOVEN006 Amazement Administrator Arlekino SCR 10.00 20.00
LIOVEN007 Amazement Ambassador Bufo C .10 .20
LIOVEN008 Amazement Attendant Comica UR 1.50 3.00
LIOVEN009 Roxrose Dragon SR .30 .75
LIOVEN010 Ruddy Rose Witch SR .30 .60
LIOVEN011 Danmari @Ignister C .10 .20
LIOVEN012 Bujin Mahitotsu C .10 .20
LIOVEN013 Bujin Torifune SR .15 .30
LIOVEN014 S-Force Dog Tag C .10 .20
LIOVEN015 S-Force Edge Razor C .10 .20
LIOVEN016 Traptrix Vesiculo UR .75 1.50
LIOVEN017 Live Twin Ki-sikil Frost SLR 150.00 300.00
LIOVEN017 Live Twin Ki-sikil Frost UR 6.00 12.00
LIOVEN018 Blackeyes, the Plunder Patroll Seaguide C .10 .20
LIOVEN019 Starry Knight Ciel C .10 .20
LIOVEN020 Judge of the Ice Barrier C .10 .20
LIOVEN021 Scrap Raptor C .10 .20
LIOVEN022 Dark Honest SCR 6.00 12.00
LIOVEN023 Bahalutiya, the Grand Radiance SCR2.00 4.00
LIOVEN023 Bahalutiya, the Grand Radiance SLR60.00 120.00
LIOVEN024 Pharaonic Guardian Sphinx C .10 .20
LIOVEN025 Sky Scourge Cidhels C .10 .20
LIOVEN026 Anchamoufrite C .10 .20
LIOVEN027 Dark Eye Nightmare C .10 .20
LIOVEN028 World Soul - Carbon C .10 .20
LIOVEN029 Yamorimori C .10 .20
LIOVEN030 Clock Arc C .10 .20
LIOVEN031 Otoshidamashi C .10 .20
LIOVEN032 White Knight of Dogmatika UR .50 1.00
LIOVEN033 Albion the Branded Dragon UR 6.00 12.00
LIOVEN034 Mysterion the Dragon Crown UR 1.00 2.00
LIOVEN035 Ruddy Rose Dragon SCR 12.50 25.00
LIOVEN036 Garden Rose Flora SR .60 1.25
LIOVEN037 Lavalval Exlord SR .15 .30
LIOVEN038 Star Mine C .10 .20
LIOVEN039 Ultimate Dragonic Utopia Ray UR .50 1.00
LIOVEN040 ZW - Dragonic Halberd SR .15 .30
LIOVEN041 Springans Merrymaker SR .15 .30
LIOVEN042 Rilliona... UR .50 1.00
LIOVEN043 Drytron Mu Beta Fafnir SCR 7.50 15.00
LIOVEN044 Tri-Brigade Bearbrumm... SR .30 .75
LIOVEN045 Dark Infant @Ignister SR .30 .60
LIOVEN046 Traptrix Cularia UR 1.25 2.50
LIOVEN047 Paleozoic Cambroraster C .10 .20
LIOVEN048 Benghalancer the Resurgent SCR 1.00 2.00
LIOVEN049 Lyna the Light Charmer, Lustrous SLR 250.00 500.00
LIOVEN049 Lyna the Light Charmer, Lustrous SR.60 1.25
LIOVEN050 Rank-Up-Magic Zexal Force SR .30 .60
LIOVEN051 Zexal Construction SR .30 .60
LIOVEN052 Zexal Entrust C .10 .20
LIOVEN053 Dogmatikalamity C .10 .20
LIOVEN054 Springans Booty C .10 .20
LIOVEN055 Branded in White SR .20 .40
LIOVEN056 Amazing Time Ticket SCR 6.00 12.00
LIOVEN057 Amazement Special Show C .10 .20
LIOVEN058 Amazement Precious Park SR .15 .30
LIOVEN059 Basal Rose Shoot C .10 .20
LIOVEN060 A.I. Meet You C .10 .20
LIOVEN061 You and A.I. C .10 .20
LIOVEN062 Bujincandescence C .10 .20
LIOVEN063 Birth of the Prominence Flame C .10 .20
LIOVEN064 Book of Lunar Eclipse SCR 4.00 8.00
LIOVEN064 Book of Lunar Eclipse SLR 75.00 150.00
LIOVEN065 One-Kuri-Way C .10 .20
LIOVEN066 Hidden Springs of the Far East C .10 .20
LIOVEN067 Zexal Alliance C .10 .20
LIOVEN068 Screams of the Branded C .10 .20
LIOVEN069 Judgment of the Branded C .10 .20
LIOVEN070 Amazement Family Faces SR .15 .30
LIOVEN071 Amaze Attraction Cyclo-Coaster UR 1.25 2.50
LIOVEN072 Amaze Attraction Wonder Wheel C .10 .20
LIOVEN073 Amaze Attraction Majestic Merry-Go-Round C .10 .20
LIOVEN074 Amaze Attraction Rapid Racing C .10 .20
LIOVEN075 Amaze Attraction Horror House UR 2.50 5.00
LIOVEN076 A.I. Challenge You C .10 .20
LIOVEN077 S-Force Chase UR .50 1.00
LIOVEN078 One by One C .10 .20
LIOVEN079 Boo-Boo Game C .10 .20
LIOVEN080 Fukubiki C .10 .20
LIOVEN081 Proof of Pruflas SR .15 .30
LIOVEN082 Thron the Disciplined Angel SR .15 .30
LIOVEN083 Pendransaction SR .15 .30
LIOVEN084 Expendable Dai SR .15 .30
LIOVEN085 Terrors of the Underroot C .10 .20
LIOVEN086 War Rock Wento SR .15 .30
LIOVEN087 War Rock Mammud C .10 .20
LIOVEN088 War Rock Meteoragon C 1.00 2.00
LIOVEN089 War Rock Dignity UR .50 1.00
LIOVEN090 War Rock Spirit SR .15 .30
LIOVEN091 War Rock Generations C .10 .20
LIOVEN092 War Rock Big Blow C .10 .20
LIOVEN093 Eda the Sun Magician SR .20 .40
LIOVEN094 Staysailor Romarin SR .30 .60
LIOVEN095 D/D/D Supersight King Zero Maxwell C.10 .20
LIOVEN096 Binary Blader C .10 .20
LIOVEN097 Sunavalon Daphne C .10 .20
LIOVEN098 Sunavalon Melias SR .15 .30
LIOVEN099 Sunvine Cross Breed C .10 .20
LIOVEN100 Black Rose Dragon SLR 300.00 600.00

2021 Yu-Gi-Oh Maximum Gold El Dorado 1st Edition

MGEDEN001 Blue-Eyes White Dragon PGR LOB ART 2.50 5.00
MGEDEN002 Dark Magician PGR LOB ART .75 1.50
MGEDEN003 Red-Eyes Black Dragon PGR 2.50 5.00
MGEDEN004 Elemental HERO Neos PGR .30 .60
MGEDEN005 Exodia the Forbidden One PGR .75 1.50
MGEDEN006 Rescue Cat PGR 3.00 6.00
MGEDEN006 Rescue Cat PGR ALT ART 3.00 6.00
MGEDEN007 Destiny HERO - Plasma PGR ALT ART.30 .60
MGEDEN008 Fossil Dyna Pachycephalo PGR .20 .40
MGEDEN009 Red-Eyes Drk. Metal Dragon PGR ALT ART 1.00 2.00
MGEDEN009 Red-Eyes Darkness Metal Dragon PGR .75 1.50
MGEDEN010 Scrap Chimera PGR .40 .80
MGEDEN011 Tempest, Dragon Ruler of Storms PGR.12 .25
MGEDEN012 PSY-Framegear Gamma PGR 3.00 6.00
MGEDEN013 Familiar-Possessed - Lyna PGR ALT ART .25 .50
MGEDEN014 Ultimate Conductor Tyranno PGR .75 1.50
MGEDEN015 Souleating Oviraptor PGR .75 1.50
MGEDEN016 The Weather Painter Snow PGR .25 .50
MGEDEN017 Sky Striker Ace - Raye PGR .40 .80
MGEDEN018 Danger! Bigfoot! PGR 1.00 2.00
MGEDEN018 Danger! Bigfoot! PGR ALT ART 1.00 2.00
MGEDEN019 Danger! Nessie! PGR 1.25 2.50
MGEDEN020 Rokket Tracer PGR .30 .60
MGEDEN021 Sky Striker Ace - Roze PGR .50 1.00
MGEDEN022 Chamber Dragonmaid PGR 7.50 15.00
MGEDEN023 Ghost Mourner & Moonlit Chill PGR1.50 3.00
MGEDEN023 Ghost Mourner & Moonlit Chill PGR ALT ART 1.50 3.00
MGEDEN024 Eldlich the Golden Lord PGR ALT ART3.00 6.00
MGEDEN025 Invoked Mechaba PGR .75 1.50
MGEDEN026 Black Rose Dragon PGR .30 .75
MGEDEN026 Black Rose Dragon PGR ALT ART .75 1.50
MGEDEN027 Trishula, Dragon of the Ice Barrier PGR .15 .30
MGEDEN028 Evolzar Laggia PGR .75 1.50
MGEDEN029 Evolzar Dolkka PGR .60 1.25
MGEDEN030 Primathmech Alembertian PGR .50 1.00
MGEDEN031 Number C1000: Numerounius PGR.25 .50
MGEDEN032 #iC1000: Numerounius Numerounia PGR .20 .40
MGEDEN033 The Weather Painter Rainbow PGR .25 .50
MGEDEN034 Knightmare Unicorn PGR 1.50 3.00
MGEDEN034 Knightmare Unicorn PGR ALT ART2.50 5.00
MGEDEN035 I:P Masquerena PGR 4.00 8.00
MGEDEN035 I:P Masquerena PGR ALT ART 6.00 12.00
MGEDEN036 Predaplant Verte Anaconda PGR 1.50 3.00
MGEDEN037 Accesscode Talker PGR 30.00 75.00
MGEDEN038 Raigeki PGR 2.50 5.00
MGEDEN039 Book of Moon PGR .50 1.00
MGEDEN040 Magical Dimension PGR .12 .25
MGEDEN041 Gold Sarcophagus PGR .30 .75
MGEDEN042 Fire Formation - Tenki PGR .50 1.00
MGEDEN044 Invocation PGR 1.50 3.00
MGEDEN045 Prank-Kids Place PGR .30 .75

MGEDEN046 Pot of Extravagance PGR 2.50 5.00
MGEDEN047 Mystic Mine PGR 2.50 5.00
MGEDEN048 Cursed Eldland PGR 3.00 6.00
MGEDEN049 Eldlixir of Black Awakening PGR .60 1.25
MGEDEN050 Numeron Chaos Ritual PGR .15 .30
MGEDEN051 Numeron Storm PGR .12 .25
MGEDEN052 Torrential Tribute PGR .60 1.25
MGEDEN053 Starlight Road PGR .15 .30
MGEDEN054 Conquistador of the Golden Land PGR2.50 5.00
MGEDEN055 Giant Rex R .17 .35
MGEDEN056 Babycerasaurus R .17 .35
MGEDEN057 Fossil Dig R .17 .35
MGEDEN058 Lost World R .17 .35
MGEDEN059 Scrap Golem R .12 .25
MGEDEN060 Scrap Dragon R .12 .25
MGEDEN061 Scrap Wyvern R .12 .25
MGEDEN062 Super Express Bullet Train R .15 .30
MGEDEN063 Urgent Schedule R .60 1.25
MGEDEN064 Superdreadnought
Rail Cannon Gustav Max R .75 1.50
MGEDEN065 #81 Superdreadnought
Rail Cannon... R .15 .30
MGEDEN066 Superdreadnought Rail Cannon... R1.00 2.00
MGEDEN067 Hot Red Dragon Archfiend R .12 .25
MGEDEN068 Hot Red Dragon Archfiend Abyss R .15 .30
MGEDEN069 Hot Red Dragon Archfiend Bane R .12 .25
MGEDEN070 Hot Red Dragon
Archfiend King Calamity R .12 .25
MGEDEN071 Zefraxi, Treasure of the Yang Zing R .12 .25
MGEDEN072 Zefraniu, Secret of the Yang Zing R .12 .25
MGEDEN073 Oracle of Zefra R .12 .25
MGEDEN074 PSY-Frame Driver R .15 .30
MGEDEN075 PSY-Framelord Zeta R .12 .25
MGEDEN076 PSY-Framelord Omega R .50 1.00
MGEDEN077 PSY-Framelord Lambda R .20 .40
MGEDEN078 The Phantom Knights
of Ancient Cloak R .15 .30
MGEDEN079 The Phantom Knights
of Silent Boots R .15 .30
MGEDEN080 The Phantom Knights
of Break Sword R .20 .40
MGEDEN081 Numeron Wall R .12 .25
MGEDEN082 Number C1: Numeron
Chaos Gate Sunya R .12 .25
MGEDEN083 Number 1: Numeron Gate Ekam R .15 .30
MGEDEN084 Number 2: Numeron Gate Dve R .15 .30
MGEDEN085 Number 3: Numeron Gate Trini R .15 .30
MGEDEN086 Number 4: Numeron Gate Catvari R .15 .30
MGEDEN087 Numeron Network R .15 .30
MGEDEN088 Numeron Calling R .20 .40
MGEDEN089 Number 9: Dyson Sphere R .12 .25
MGEDEN090 #41 Bagooska the
Terribly Tired Tapir R .50 1.00
MGEDEN091 Altergeist Marionetter R .12 .25
MGEDEN092 Altergeist Silquitous R .12 .25
MGEDEN093 Altergeist Meluseek R .12 .25
MGEDEN094 Altergeist Kunquery R .12 .25
MGEDEN095 Altergeist Multifaker R .12 .25
MGEDEN096 The Weather Painter Rain R .12 .25
MGEDEN097 The Weather Painter Thunder R .12 .25
MGEDEN098 The Weather Snowy Canvas R .12 .25
MGEDEN099 The Weather Cloudy Canvas R .12 .25
MGEDEN100 The Weather Thundery Canvas R .12 .25
MGEDEN101 The Weather Rainbowed Canvas R .12 .25
MGEDEN102 Micro Coder R .15 .30
MGEDEN103 Excode Talker R .12 .25
MGEDEN104 Code Talker R .12 .25
MGEDEN105 Shootingcode Talker R .12 .25
MGEDEN106 Code Talker Inverted R .12 .25
MGEDEN107 Prank-Kids Lampsies R .20 .40
MGEDEN108 Prank-Kids Dropsies R .20 .40
MGEDEN109 Prank-Kids Fansies R .20 .40
MGEDEN110 Prank-Kids Rocksies R .12 .25
MGEDEN111 Prank-Kids Rocket Ride R .12 .25
MGEDEN112 Prank-Kids Weather Washer R .12 .25
MGEDEN113 Prank-Kids Battle Butler R .12 .25
MGEDEN114 Prank-Kids Dodo-Doodle-Doo R .25 .50
MGEDEN115 Prank-Kids Bow-Wow-Bark R .12 .25
MGEDEN116 Prank-Kids Meow-Meow-Mu R .12 .25
MGEDEN117 Prank-Kids Pranks R .12 .25
MGEDEN118 Prank-Kids Pandemonium R .15 .30
MGEDEN119 Hiita the Fire Charmer, Ablaze R .15 .30
MGEDEN120 Wynn the Wind Charmer, Verdant R .15 .30
MGEDEN121 Aussa the Earth
Charmer, Immovable R .12 .25
MGEDEN122 Eria the Water Charmer, Gentle R .12 .25
MGEDEN123 Eldlich the Mad Golden Lord R .12 .25
MGEDEN124 Eldlixir of White Destiny R .20 .40
MGEDEN125 Eldlixir of Scarlet Sanguine R 1.00 2.00
MGEDEN126 Guardian of the Golden Land R .12 .25
MGEDEN127 Huaquero of the Golden Land R .75 1.50
MGEDEN128 Golden Land Forever! R .20 .40
MGEDEN129 El Dorado Adelantado R .12 .25
MGEDEN130 Deep Sea Diva R 2.00 4.00
MGEDEN131 Kagemucha Knight R .12 .25
MGEDEN132 White Dragon Wyverburster R .12 .25
MGEDEN133 Black Dragon Collapserpent R .12 .25
MGEDEN134 Majesty's Fiend R .12 .25
MGEDEN135 Cyberse Gadget R .12 .25
MGEDEN136 Eva R .12 .25
MGEDEN137 Rainbow Neos R .15 .30
MGEDEN138 Ultimaya Tzolkin R .12 .25
MGEDEN139 Constellar Ptolemy M7 R .12 .25
MGEDEN140 Raidraptor - Ultimate Falcon R .15 .30
MGEDEN141 Firewall Dragon (red) R ALT ART .25 .50
MGEDEN141 Firewall Dragon (purple) R ALT ART.25 .50
MGEDEN142 Dragunity Knight - Romulus R .25 .50
MGEDEN143 Battle Shogun of the Six Samurai R.12 .25
MGEDEN144 Salamangreat Almiraj R .75 1.50
MGEDEN145 Striker Dragon R .50 1.00
MGEDEN146 Upstart Goblin R .75 1.50
MGEDEN147 Ancient Gear Fusion R .12 .25
MGEDEN148 Cynet Mining R 3.00 6.00
MGEDEN149 Dragonmaid Hospitality R .75 1.50
MGEDEN150 Summon Limit R 1.25 2.50
MGEDEN151 Broken Line R .12 .25
MGEDEN152 Trap Trick R .75 1.50

2021 Yu-Gi-Oh OTS Tournament Pack 15

OP15EN001 Armed Dragon LV10 UTR 50.00 100.00
OP15EN002 Dark Requiem Xyz Dragon UTR 30.00 75.00
OP15EN003 Crystron Halqifibrax UTR 60.00 120.00
OP15EN004 Shaddoll Dragon SR 3.00 6.00
OP15EN005 Zoodiac Boarbow SR 2.50 5.00
OP15EN006 Barricadeborg Blocker SR 1.00 2.00
OP15EN007 Cross Over SR .30 .60
OP15EN008 Noctovision Dragon SR 3.00 6.00
OP15EN009 Proxy F Magician SR .50 1.00
OP15EN010 Infernoble Knight Captain Roland SR.75 1.50
OP15EN011 Melffy Mommy SR .60 1.25
OP15EN012 Dogmatika Punishment SR 6.00 12.00
OP15EN013 Gryphon Wing C .30 .75
OP15EN014 Armed Dragon LV7 C .30 .75
OP15EN015 Armed Dragon LV5 C .15 .30
OP15EN016 Armed Dragon LV3 C .15 .30
OP15EN017 D.D.R. - Different
Dimension Reincarnation C .50 1.00
OP15EN018 Tri-Wight C .30 .75
OP15EN019 Shadow Vampire C .15 .30
OP15EN020 Rank-Up-Magic - The Seventh One C.15 .30
OP15EN021 Amorphactor Pain... C .30 .75
OP15EN022 Amorphous Persona C .30 .75
OP15EN023 Windwitch - Ice Bell C .30 .60
OP15EN024 Vampire's Domain C .30 .75
OP15EN025 Mahaama the Fairy Dragon C .15 .30
OP15EN026 World Legacy Token SR 2.00 4.00

2021 Yu-Gi-Oh OTS Tournament Pack 16

OP16EN001 Cyber Dragon UTR 125.00 250.00
OP16EN002 Firewall Dragon UTR 25.00 50.00
OP16EN003 Forbidden Droplet UTR 150.00 300.00
OP16EN004 Cyber-Stein SR .75 1.50
OP16EN005 King of the Skull Servants SR 1.50 3.00
OP16EN006 Mausoleum of the Emperor SR .30 .60
OP16EN007 Token Stampede SR .30 .60
OP16EN008 Phonon Pulse Dragon SR .30 .75
OP16EN009 Tri-Brigade Nervall SR 2.50 5.00
OP16EN010 Geonator Transverser SR .50 1.00
OP16EN011 Virtual World Gate - Qinglong SR 2.00 4.00
OP16EN012 Drytron Zeta Aldhibah SR 1.50 3.00
OP16EN013 Drytron Delta Altais SR 1.00 2.00
OP16EN014 Cyber Saurus C .30 .60
OP16EN015 Miracle Dig C .30 .75
OP16EN016 Royal Magical Library C .30 .60
OP16EN017 Peten the Dark Clown C .30 .75
OP16EN018 Power Filter C .20 .40
OP16EN019 Lord British Space Fighter C .30 .75
OP16EN020 Reptilianne Hydra C .60 1.25
OP16EN021 Alien Brain C .30 .75
OP16EN022 Lion Alligator C .30 .75
OP16EN023 Stardust Flash C .20 .40
OP16EN024 Cosmic Flare C .50 1.00
OP16EN025 Stardust Wish C .30 .75
OP16EN026 Breath of Acclamation C .30 .60

2021 Yu-Gi-Oh OTS Tournament Pack 17

OP17EN001 Number 39: Utopia UTR 12.50 25.00
OP17EN002 Infinite Impermanence UTR 125.00 250.00
OP17EN003 Black Luster Soldier -
Soldier of Chaos UTR 50.00 100.00
OP17EN004 Power Bond SR .50 1.00
OP17EN005 The Great Emperor Penguin SR .75 1.50
OP17EN006 Cyber Dragon Nova SR 1.50 3.00
OP17EN007 Resonance Insect SR .75 1.50
OP17EN008 Flawless Perfection of the Tenyi SR .30 .60
OP17EN009 Vessel for the Dragon Cycle SR 2.00 4.00
OP17EN010 Penguin Brave SR .30 .60
OP17EN011 Scrap Raptor SR 2.50 5.00
OP17EN012 Basal Rose Shoot SR 2.00 4.00
OP17EN013 Penguin Soldier C .30 .75
OP17EN014 Outstanding Dog Marron C .12 .25
OP17EN015 Junk Synchron C .30 .75
OP17EN016 Dark Simorgh C .40 .80
OP17EN017 T.G. Wonder Magician C .50 1.00
OP17EN018 Utopian Aura C .15 .30
OP17EN019 Inzektor Dragonfly C .10 .20
OP17EN020 Number C39: Utopia Ray V C .10 .20
OP17EN021 SZW - Fenrir Sword C .10 .20
OP17EN022 Yazi, Evil of the Yang Zing C .20 .40
OP17EN023 Painful Decision C .50 1.00
OP17EN024 Shaman of the Tenyi C .30 .60
OP17EN025 Tenyi Spirit - Sahasrara C .20 .40
OP17EN026 Ice Barrier Token SR .30 .75

2021 Yu-Gi-Oh Structure Deck Cyber Strike 1st Edition

SDCSEN001 Attachment Cybern C .10 .20
SDCSEN002 Cyberdark Chimera UR .25 .50
SDCSEN003 Cyber Dragon C .15 .30
SDCSEN004 Cyber Dragon Zwei C .10 .20
SDCSEN005 Cyber Dragon Drei C .10 .20
SDCSEN006 Cyber Dragon Vier C .10 .20
SDCSEN007 Cyber Dragon Nachster C .10 .20
SDCSEN008 Cyber Dragon Core C .10 .20
SDCSEN009 Cyber Dragon Herz SR .20 .40
SDCSEN010 Cyber Pharos C .10 .20
SDCSEN011 Cyber Valley C .10 .20
SDCSEN012 Cyber Phoenix C .10 .20
SDCSEN013 Cyberdark Horn C .10 .20
SDCSEN014 Cyberdark Edge C .10 .20
SDCSEN015 Cyberdark Keel C .10 .20
SDCSEN016 Cyberdark Cannon C .10 .20
SDCSEN017 Cyberdark Claw C .10 .20
SDCSEN018 Leng Ling C .10 .20
SDCSEN019 Jizukiru, the Star Destroying Kaiju C.12 .25
SDCSEN020 Gizmek Orochi,
the Serpentron Sky Slasher C .12 .25
SDCSEN021 Gale Dogra C .10 .20
SDCSEN022 Cyber Eternal C .10 .20
SDCSEN023 Cyberdark Realm UR .15 .30
SDCSEN024 Cyber Repair Plant C .10 .20
SDCSEN025 Cyber Emergency C .15 .30
SDCSEN026 Cyberload Fusion C .10 .20
SDCSEN027 Cyberdark Impact! C .10 .20
SDCSEN028 Cyberdark Inferno C .10 .20
SDCSEN029 Future Fusion C .10 .20
SDCSEN030 Fusion Deployment SR .20 .40
SDCSEN031 Fusion Tag C .10 .20
SDCSEN032 Machine Duplication C .30 .60
SDCSEN033 Limiter Removal C .10 .20
SDCSEN034 Cyberdark Invasion C .10 .20
SDCSEN035 Cybernetic Revolution C .10 .20
SDCSEN036 Infinite Impermanence SR 7.50 15.00
SDCSEN037 Power Wall C .10 .20
SDCSEN038 Call of the Haunted C .20 .40
SDCSEN039 Paleozoic Canadia C .10 .20
SDCSEN040 Cybernetic Overflow C .10 .20
SDCSEN041 Cyber End Dragon UR .30 .75
SDCSEN042 Chimeratech Overdragon C .10 .20
SDCSEN043 Cyberdarkness Dragon C .10 .20
SDCSEN044 Cyberdark End Dragon UR .15 .30
SDCSEN045 Cyberdark Dragon C .10 .20
SDCSEN046 Cybernetic Horizon UR .15 .30
SDCSEN047 Power Bond C .10 .20
SDCSEN048 Overload Fusion C .10 .20

2021 Yu-Gi-Oh Structure Deck Freezing Chains 1st Edition

SDFCEN001 General Wayne of the Ice Barrier C .15 .30
SDFCEN002 Revealer of the Ice Barrier UR .75 1.50
SDFCEN003 Speaker for the Ice Barriers UR .30 .60
SDFCEN004 Hexa Spirit of the Ice Barrier C .10 .20
SDFCEN005 Zuijin of the Ice Barrier UR .15 .30
SDFCEN006 Blizzed, Defender of the Ice Barrier C.10 .20
SDFCEN007 Cryomancer of the Ice Barrier C .10 .20
SDFCEN008 Prior of the Ice Barrier C .10 .20
SDFCEN009 Defender of the Ice Barrier C .10 .20
SDFCEN010 Warlock of the Ice Barrier C .10 .20
SDFCEN011 Spellbreaker of the Ice Barrier C .10 .20
SDFCEN012 Strategist of the Ice Barrier C .10 .20
SDFCEN013 Dance Princess of the Ice Barrier C .10 .20
SDFCEN014 Dai-sojo of the Ice Barrier C .10 .20
SDFCEN015 General Raiho of the Ice Barrier C .10 .20
SDFCEN016 Medium of the Ice Barrier C .10 .20
SDFCEN017 General Gantala of the Ice Barrier C .10 .20
SDFCEN018 General Grunard of the Ice Barrier C.10 .20
SDFCEN019 Genex Controller C .10 .20
SDFCEN020 Genex Undine C .10 .20
SDFCEN021 Aqua Spirit C .10 .20
SDFCEN022 Dupe Frog C 1.50 3.00
SDFCEN023 Ronintoadin C 3.00 6.00
SDFCEN024 Fishborg Launcher C .10 .20
SDFCEN025 Moulinglacia the Elemental Lord C .10 .20
SDFCEN026 Silent Angler C .25 .50
SDFCEN027 Winds Over the Ice Barrier UR .15 .30
SDFCEN028 Freezing Chains of the Ice Barrier C .25 .50
SDFCEN029 Magic Triangle of the Ice Barrier C .10 .20
SDFCEN030 Medallion of the Ice Barrier C .15 .30
SDFCEN031 Mirror of the Ice Barrier C .10 .20
SDFCEN032 Salvage C .20 .40
SDFCEN033 Surface C .20 .40
SDFCEN034 Where Arf Thou? C .30 .60
SDFCEN035 Appointer of the Red Lotus C .30 .60
SDFCEN036 Fiendish Chain C .25 .50
SDFCEN037 Eisbahn C .10 .20
SDFCEN038 Mind Drain C .15 .30
SDFCEN039 Heavy Storm Duster C .30 .60
SDFCEN040 Crackdown C .75 1.50
SDFCEN041 Trishula, Zero Dragon
of the Ice Barrier UR 1.00 2.00
SDFCEN042 Dewloren, Tiger King
of the Ice Barrier UR .15 .30
SDFCEN043 Brionac, Dragon of the Ice Barrier SR.20 .40
SDFCEN044 Gungnir, Dragon of the Ice Barrier SR.15 .30
SDFCEN045 Trishula, Dragon of the Ice Barrier SR.15 .30
SDFCEN046 Terror of Trishula C .10 .20

2021 Yu-Gi-Oh Tin of Ancient Battles 1st Edition

MP21EN001 Pikari @Ignister UR .30 .75
MP21EN002 Doyon @Ignister C .10 .20
MP21EN003 Achichi @Ignister UR .30 .75
MP21EN004 Arcjet Lightcraft C .10 .20
MP21EN005 Sky Striker Ace - Roze PRISM SCR .60 1.25
MP21EN006 Witchcrafter Genni C .10 .20
MP21EN007 Gizmek Kaku... UR .12 .25
MP21EN008 Jack-o-Bolan C .10 .20
MP21EN009 Ibicella Lutea C .10 .20
MP21EN010 Obsessive Uvualoop C .10 .20
MP21EN011 Daruma Dropper C .10 .20
MP21EN012 Transcicada C .10 .20
MP21EN013 Squeaknight C .10 .20
MP21EN014 Battle Survivor C .10 .20
MP21EN015 Wind Pegasus @Ignister C .15 .30
MP21EN016 Light Dragon @Ignister C .10 .20
MP21EN017 Dark Templar @Ignister C .10 .20
MP21EN018 Cross-Sheep PRISM SCR .50 1.00
MP21EN019 Aussa the Earth
Charmer, Immovable UR .20 .40
MP21EN020 Gravity Controller SR .12 .25
MP21EN021 Ignister A.I.Land UR .12 .25
MP21EN022 T.A.I. Strike C .10 .20
MP21EN023 A.I.dle Reborn C .10 .20
MP21EN024 A.I. Love Fusion C .10 .20
MP21EN025 A.I.'s Ritual C .10 .20
MP21EN026 Ghost Meets Girl... UR .12 .25
MP21EN027 Disposable Learner Device C .10 .20
MP21EN028 Kuji-Kiri Curse C .10 .20
MP21EN029 A.I. Shadow C .10 .20
MP21EN030 Sales Pitch R .15 .30
MP21EN031 Armory Call SR .12 .25
MP21EN032 Mutually Affured Destruction C .10 .20
MP21EN033 Fiendish Portrait SR .12 .25
MP21EN034 Feedran, the Winds of Mischief C .10 .20
MP21EN035 Nine-Lives Cat C .10 .20
MP21EN036 Execution of the Contract C .10 .20
MP21EN037 Shiny Black C"" Squadder"" SR .12 .25
MP21EN038 Marincess Pascalus R .20 .40
MP21EN039 Bellcat Fighter C .10 .20
MP21EN040 Code Talker Inverted C .10 .20
MP21EN041 Linguriboh SR .15 .30
MP21EN042 Link Party C .10 .20
MP21EN043 Parallel eXceed PRISM SCR 2.00 4.00
MP21EN044 Salamangreat Zebroid X C .10 .20
MP21EN045 Gouki Iron Claw C .10 .20
MP21EN046 Gouki Guts C .10 .20
MP21EN047 Marincess Basilalima C .10 .20
MP21EN048 Noctovision Dragon SR .20 .40
MP21EN049 Deep Sea Artisan C .10 .20
MP21EN050 Deep Sea Sentry C .10 .20
MP21EN051 Deep Sea Minstrel C .10 .20
MP21EN052 Red Familiar C .10 .20
MP21EN053 Crimson Resonator C .10 .20
MP21EN054 Lantern Shark C .20 .40
MP21EN055 Buzzsaw Shark C .12 .25
MP21EN056 Girsu, the Orcust Mekk-Knight UR .50 1.00
MP21EN057 King Beast Barbaros UR .12 .25
MP21EN058 Trias Hierarchia UR .15 .30
MP21EN059 Union Driver R .15 .30
MP21EN060 Malice, Lady of Lament PRISM SCR.25 .50
MP21EN061 Ghost Mourner & Moonlit Chill UR2.00 4.00
MP21EN062 Animadorned Archosaur UR 1.50 3.00
MP21EN063 Magical Hound SR .12 .25
MP21EN064 Invoked Augoeides PRISM SCR .50 1.00
MP21EN065 Dragonmaid Sheou PRISM SCR .75 1.50
MP21EN066 Deep Sea Prima Donna C .10 .20
MP21EN067 Ravenous Crocodragon Archethys C.10 .20
MP21EN068 Traptrix Allomerus SR .12 .25
MP21EN069 Proxy F Magician C .10 .20
MP21EN070 Gouki The Powerload Ogre C .10 .20
MP21EN071 Marincess Great Bubble Reef C .10 .20
MP21EN072 Eria the Water Charmer UR .25 .50
MP21EN073 A.I. Contact UR .12 .25
MP21EN074 Burning Draw UR .12 .25
MP21EN075 Link Burst C .10 .20
MP21EN076 Deep Sea Aria SR .12 .25
MP21EN077 Resonator Command C .10 .20
MP21EN078 Torpedo Takedown C .10 .20
MP21EN079 Heavy Forward SR .12 .25
MP21EN080 Witchcrafter Unveiling C .10 .20
MP21EN081 Fusion Deployment PRISM SCR 1.50 3.00
MP21EN082 Flourishing Frolic C .10 .20
MP21EN083 A.I.Q C .10 .20
MP21EN084 Red Reign C .10 .20
MP21EN085 Witchcrafter Patronus C .10 .20
MP21EN086 Gravedigger's Trap Hole UR 1.00 2.00
MP21EN087 Titanocider SR .12 .25
MP21EN088 Rose Girl C .10 .20
MP21EN089 Superheavy Samurai Wagon SR .12 .25
MP21EN090 Rain Bozu C .10 .20
MP21EN091 Performapal Turn Trooper SR .12 .25
MP21EN092 Gussari @Ignister C .10 .20
MP21EN093 Gatchiri @Ignister C .10 .20
MP21EN094 Machina Metalcruncher PRISM SCR.30 .75
MP21EN095 Superheavy
Samurai Swordmaster... SR .12 .25
MP21EN096 Gaia the Fierce Knight Origin R .15 .30
MP21EN097 Gaia the Magical Knight C .10 .20
MP21EN098 Curse of Dragon, the Cursed Dragon C.10 .20
MP21EN099 Artillery Catapult Turtle SR .12 .25
MP21EN100 Soldier Gaia The Fierce Knight C .10 .20
MP21EN101 Dogmatika Ecclesia,
the Virtuous PRISM SCR 4.00 8.00
MP21EN102 Dogmatika Theo, the Iron Punch UR.12 .25
MP21EN103 Dogmatika Adin, the Enlightened UR.12 .25
MP21EN104 Dogmatika Fleurdelis, the Knighted UR.30 .75
MP21EN105 Dogmatika Maximus UR .75 1.50
MP21EN106 Dogmatika Nexus UR .12 .25
MP21EN107 Fallen of Albaz UR 1.00 2.00
MP21EN108 Infernoble Knight Astolfo C .10 .20
MP21EN109 Infernoble Knight Ogier C .10 .20
MP21EN110 Infernoble Knight Oliver C .10 .20
MP21EN111 Infernoble Knight Maugis C .10 .20
MP21EN112 Melffy Rabby C .10 .20
MP21EN113 Melffy Fenny C .10 .20
MP21EN114 Melffy Catty C .20 .40
MP21EN115 Melffy Puppy C .15 .30
MP21EN116 Melffy Pony C .10 .20
MP21EN117 Capricious Darklord C .10 .20
MP21EN118 Indulged Darklord C .10 .20
MP21EN119 Darklord Nergal C .10 .20
MP21EN120 Thunder Hand SR .12 .25
MP21EN121 Gizmek Okami... SR .12 .25
MP21EN122 Lifeless Leaffish C .10 .20
MP21EN123 Dracoon Lamp C .10 .20
MP21EN124 Gaia the Magical Knight... PRISM SCR.30 .60
MP21EN125 Titaniklad the Ash Dragon UR .12 .25
MP21EN126 Infernoble Knight Captain Roland SR.12 .25
MP21EN127 Infernoble Knight Emperor Charles R.15 .30
MP21EN128 Chaos Ruler, the
Chaotic Magical Dragon UR 2.50 5.00
MP21EN129 Melffy of the Forest SR .12 .25
MP21EN130 Melffy Mommy C .10 .20
MP21EN131 Rikka Queen Strenna C .10 .20
MP21EN132 Drill Driver Vespenato C .10 .20
MP21EN133 Spiral Fusion R .15 .30
MP21EN134 Dogmatika Nation C .10 .20
MP21EN135 Nadir Servant UR 3.00 6.00
MP21EN136 Infernoble Arms - Durendal"""" SR .12 .25
MP21EN137 Infernoble Arms - Hauteclere"""" SR.12 .25
MP21EN138 Infernoble Arms - Joyeuse"""" SR .12 .25
MP21EN139 Melffy Tag C .10 .20
MP21EN140 Melffy Hide-and-Seek C .10 .20
MP21EN141 Magellanica, the Deep Sea City C .10 .20
MP21EN142 Adamancipator Friends UR .12 .25
MP21EN143 Triple Tactics Talent UR 15.00 30.00
MP21EN144 Blizzard C .10 .20
MP21EN145 Fury of Kairyu-Shin C .10 .20
MP21EN146 Diced Dice C .10 .20
MP21EN147 Dogmatika Punishment PRISM SCR2.00 4.00
MP21EN148 Dogmatika Encounter C .10 .20
MP21EN149 Horn of Olifant C .10 .20
MP21EN150 Melffy Playhouse C .10 .20
MP21EN151 Darklord Uprising C .10 .20
MP21EN152 Shaddoll Schism PRISM SCR .75 1.50
MP21EN153 Dragonmaid Tidying R .50 1.00
MP21EN154 Redeemable Jar C .10 .20
MP21EN155 Ice Dragon's Prison PRISM SCR 4.00 8.00
MP21EN156 Junk Sleep C .10 .20
MP21EN157 Odd-Eyes Revolution Dragon UR .75 1.50
MP21EN158 Wynn the Wind Channeler PRISM SCR.50 1.00
MP21EN159 Seleglare... PRISM SCR .20 .40
MP21EN160 Ret-time Reviver Emit-ter C .10 .20
MP21EN161 Speedroid Block-n-Roll C .10 .20

MP21EN162 Speedroid CarTurbo R .15 .30
MP21EN163 Rampaging Smashtank Rhynosaber C .10 .20
MP21EN164 Linkerbell C .10 .20
MP21EN165 Superheavy Samurai Scarecrow SR .12 .25
MP21EN166 Raider's Wing R .15 .30
MP21EN167 The Phantom Knights of Stained Greaves SR .12 .25
MP21EN168 The Phantom Knights of Torn Scales UR .50 1.00
MP21EN169 Tri-Brigade Nervall UR .20 .40
MP21EN170 Tri-Brigade Kerass UR .60 1.25
MP21EN171 Tri-Brigade Fraktall PRISM SCR 2.00 4.00
MP21EN172 Dogmatika Ashiyan PRISM SCR .20 .40
MP21EN173 Virtual World Mai-Hime - Lulu PRISM SCR .75 1.50
MP21EN174 Virtual World Roshi - Laolao PRISM SCR .75 1.50
MP21EN175 Virtual World Xiezhi - Jiji UR .15 .30
MP21EN176 Virtual World Kirin - Lili UR .15 .30
MP21EN177 Awakening of the Possessed - Gagigobyte C .10 .20
MP21EN178 Awakening of the Possessed - Rasenryu C .10 .20
MP21EN179 Alpha, the Master of Beasts UR 2.50 5.00
MP21EN180 Prufinesse, the Tactical Trapper C .10 .20
MP21EN181 Rock Band Xenoguitar C .10 .20
MP21EN182 Magical Broker C .10 .20
MP21EN183 Gluttonous Reptolphin Greethys C .10 .20
MP21EN184 Hinezumi Hanabi C .10 .20
MP21EN185 Brigrand the Glory Dragon R .15 .30
MP21EN186 Virtual World Kyubi - Shenshen SR .20 .40
MP21EN187 Infernity Doom Archfiend C .10 .20
MP21EN188 Infernoble Knight Captain Oliver C .10 .20
MP21EN189 Penguin Brave C .10 .20
MP21EN190 Raider's Knight R .25 .50
MP21EN191 Arc Rebellion Xyz Dragon SR .25 .50
MP21EN192 Virtual World Shell - Jaja R .15 .30
MP21EN193 Virtual World Phoenix - Fanfan R .15 .30
MP21EN194 Joyous Melffys C .10 .20
MP21EN195 Divine Arsenal AA-ZEUS - Sky Thunder UR 10.00 20.00
MP21EN196 Tri-Brigade Ferrijit... PRISM SCR 1.00 2.00
MP21EN197 Tri-Brigade Rugal the Silver Sheller SR .20 .40
MP21EN198 Tri-Brigade Shuraig the Ominous Omen UR 2.00 4.00
MP21EN199 Geonator Transverser SR .12 .25
MP21EN200 Phantom Knights' Rank-Up-Magic Force R .25 .50
MP21EN201 Tri-Brigade Stand-Off C .10 .20
MP21EN202 Tri-Brigade Airborne Assault R .15 .30
MP21EN203 Dogmatikacism C .10 .20
MP21EN204 Virtual World City - Kauwloon R .25 .50
MP21EN205 Virtual World Gate - Qinglong R .15 .30
MP21EN206 Charge Into a Dark World C .10 .20
MP21EN207 Rookie Fur Hire C .10 .20
MP21EN208 Xyz Import SR .12 .25
MP21EN209 Jack-In-The-Hand C .10 .20
MP21EN210 Raider's Unbreakable Mind C .10 .20
MP21EN211 Raidraptor's Phantom Knights Claw C .10 .20
MP21EN212 Tri-Brigade Revolt PRISM SCR .75 1.50
MP21EN213 Tri-Brigade Oath C .10 .20
MP21EN214 Virtual World Gate - Chuche R .30 .75
MP21EN215 Free-Range Monsters C .10 .20
MP21EN216 Warning Point SR .12 .25
MP21EN217 One or Eight C .10 .20
MP21EN218 Mahaama the Fairy Dragon UR .12 .25
MP21EN219 Jabbing Panda C .10 .20
MP21EN220 Periallis, Empress of Blossoms C .10 .20
MP21EN221 Virtual World Beast - Jiujiu R .15 .30
MP21EN222 Virtual World Dragon - Longlong R .15 .30
MP21EN223 Virtual World Hime - Nyannyan PRISM SCR .30 .60
MP21EN224 Adamancipator Seeker SR .12 .25
MP21EN225 Adamancipator Researcher UR .50 1.00
MP21EN226 Adamancipator Analyzer SR .12 .25
MP21EN227 Adamancipator Crystal - Leonite C .10 .20
MP21EN228 Adamancipator Crystal - Raptite C .10 .20
MP21EN229 Adamancipator Crystal - Dragite C .15 .30
MP21EN230 Adamancipator Risen - Leonite UR .12 .25
MP21EN231 Adamancipator Risen - Raptite UR .15 .30
MP21EN232 Adamancipator Risen - Dragite UR .50 1.00
MP21EN233 Adamancipator Laputite C .10 .20
MP21EN234 Adamancipator Signs PRISM SCR .30 .60
MP21EN235 Adamancipator Relief SR .12 .25
MP21EN236 Adamancipator Resonance C .10 .20
MP21EN237 Drytron Beta Rastaban SR .12 .25
MP21EN238 Drytron Gamma Eltanin SR .15 .30
MP21EN239 Drytron Delta Altais SR .12 .25
MP21EN240 Drytron Zeta Aldhibah PRISM SCR .20 .40
MP21EN241 Cyberse Accelerator C .10 .20
MP21EN242 Gouki Destroy Ogre C .10 .20
MP21EN243 Qadshaddoll Keios UR .12 .25
MP21EN244 Reeshaddoll Wendi UR .20 .40
MP21EN245 Naelshaddoll Ariel UR .12 .25
MP21EN246 El Shaddoll Apkallone PRISM SCR .60 1.25
MP21EN247 El Shaddoll Construct PRISM SCR ALT ART .50 1.00
MP21EN248 Raviel, Lord of Phantasms... PRISM SCR .20 .40
MP21EN249 Dark Beckoning Beast UR 1.00 2.00
MP21EN250 Chaos Summoning Beast SR .12 .25
MP21EN251 Opening of the Spirit Gates UR .30 .75
MP21EN252 Uria, Lord of Searing Flames PRISM SCR .50 1.00
MP21EN253 Hamon, Lord of Striking Thunder PRISM SCR .50 1.00
MP21EN254 Raviel, Lord of Phantasms PRISM SCR .40 .80
MP21EN255 True Light UR 1.25 2.50
MP21EN256 Magician's Salvation UR .75 1.50
MP21EN257 Piercing the Darkness UR .50 1.00
MP21EN258 Crossout Designator UR 20.00 40.00

2022 Yu-Gi-Oh Battle of Chaos 1st Edition

25THEN001 Dark Magician ALT ART UR 75.00 150.00
BACHEN000 Libromancer Geek Boy SCR 3.00 6.00
BACHEN001 Magikuriboh SR .75 1.50
BACHEN002 Dimension Conjurer C .10 .20
BACHEN003 Timaeus the United Dragon UR 3.00 6.00
BACHEN004 Blue-Eyes Jet Dragon SCR 7.50 15.00
BACHEN004 Blue-Eyes Jet Dragon SLR 75.00 150.00
BACHEN005 Dictator of D. SR .75 1.50
BACHEN006 Icejade Kosmochlor SCR .75 1.50
BACHEN007 Icejade Aegirine UR .50 1.00
BACHEN008 Icejade Creation Kingfisher SR .12 .25
BACHEN009 Dinomorphia Therizia SCR 7.50 15.00
BACHEN009 Dinomorphia Therizia SLR 75.00 150.00
BACHEN010 Dinomorphia Diplos C .10 .20
BACHEN011 Nordic Beast Gullinbursti SR .12 .25
BACHEN012 Nordic Smith Ivaldi SR .12 .25
BACHEN013 D/D Gryphon SR .75 1.50
BACHEN014 Ghostrick Siren C .10 .20
BACHEN015 Vampire Ghost UR .60 1.25
BACHEN016 S-Force Lapcewell C .10 .20
BACHEN017 S-Force Retroactive SR .12 .25
BACHEN018 Neiroy, the Dream Mirror Traitor C .10 .20
BACHEN019 Myutant Mutant C .10 .20
BACHEN020 Epsilon The Magnet Warrior C .10 .20
BACHEN021 The Agent of Destruction - Venus C .10 .20
BACHEN022 Kaiza the Hidden Star C .10 .20
BACHEN023 Simorgh, Bird of Perfection C .10 .20
BACHEN024 Skilled Brown Magician C .10 .20
BACHEN025 Chaos Nephthys UR .25 .50
BACHEN026 Epigonen, the Impersonation Invader SR .12 .25
BACHEN027 Submareed Tour Ride C .10 .20
BACHEN028 Alice, Lady of Lament SR .20 .40
BACHEN029 Leafplace Plaice C .10 .20
BACHEN030 Mad Hacker C .10 .20
BACHEN031 Silvervine Senri C .10 .20
BACHEN032 Shining Piecephilia C .10 .20
BACHEN033 Darton the Mechanical Monstrosity C .10 .20
BACHEN034 Illusion of Chaos SCR 20.00 40.00
BACHEN034 Illusion of Chaos SLR 125.00 250.00
BACHEN035 White Relic of Dogmatika SR .12 .25
BACHEN036 Master of Chaos UR 2.50 5.00
BACHEN037 Blue-Eyes Tyrant Dragon UR 3.00 6.00
BACHEN038 Dinomorphia Kentregina UR 7.50 1.50
BACHEN039 Dinomorphia Stealthbergia SR .30 .75
BACHEN040 Guardian Chimera SCR 25.00 50.00
BACHEN041 Swordsoul Sinister Sovereign... SCR 3.00 6.00
BACHEN042 Maple Maiden C .10 .20
BACHEN043 Dark Dimension Soldier SR .12 .25
BACHEN044 D/D/D Deviser King Deus Machinex UR 2.00 4.00
BACHEN045 The Zombie Vampire SCR 7.50 15.00
BACHEN046 Onibimaru Soul Sweeper C .10 .20
BACHEN047 Ghostrick Festival C .10 .20
BACHEN048 Vampire Fascinator SR .20 .40
BACHEN049 Dharc the Dark Charmer, Gloomy SLR 250.00 400.00
BACHEN049 Dharc the Dark Charmer, Gloomy SR 1.25 2.50
BACHEN050 Vision with Eyes of Blue SR .25 .50
BACHEN051 Ultimate Fusion SR .75 1.50
BACHEN052 Icejade Cenote Enion Cradle SR .12 .25
BACHEN053 Branded Disciple C .10 .20
BACHEN054 Dogmatikamacabre C .10 .20
BACHEN055 Nordic Relic Hlidskjalf SR .12 .25
BACHEN056 Dark Contract with Patent License SR .12 .25
BACHEN057 Ghostrick Shot C .10 .20
BACHEN058 Ogdoadic Serpent Strike C .10 .20
BACHEN059 Ursarctic Radiation UR .20 .40
BACHEN060 Floowandereeze Advent of Adventure UR 10.00 20.00
BACHEN061 XYZ Combine SR .12 .25
BACHEN062 Clear New World C .10 .20
BACHEN063 Sales Ban SCR 2.50 5.00
BACHEN064 Top Share C .10 .20
BACHEN065 Uradora of Fate C .10 .20
BACHEN066 Icejade Erosion C .10 .20
BACHEN067 Swordsoul Strife C .10 .20
BACHEN068 Dinomorphia Domain SCR 5.00 10.00
BACHEN069 Dinomorphia Alert C .10 .20
BACHEN070 Dinomorphia Brute C .10 .20
BACHEN071 Dinomorphia Shell C .10 .20
BACHEN072 Dinomorphia Sonic C .10 .20
BACHEN073 Dinomorphia Reversion SR .12 .25
BACHEN074 Nordic Relic Svalinn SR .12 .25
BACHEN075 D/D/D Headhunt C .10 .20
BACHEN076 Ghostrick or Treat C .10 .20
BACHEN077 Monster Rebirth C .10 .20
BACHEN078 Tribe Drive C .10 .20
BACHEN079 Imprudent Intrusion C .10 .20
BACHEN080 End of the Line C .10 .20
BACHEN081 Dragonbite UR .30 .75
BACHEN082 Flowerdino C .10 .20
BACHEN083 Rock Scales C .10 .20
BACHEN084 The Great Double Casted Caster C .10 .20
BACHEN085 Sol and Luna UR .25 .50
BACHEN086 Libromancer Magigirl SR .12 .25
BACHEN087 Libromancer Agent SR .12 .25
BACHEN088 Libromancer Firestarter SR .12 .25
BACHEN089 Libromancer Doombroker UR 1.00 2.00
BACHEN090 Libromancer First Appearance UR 1.50 3.00
BACHEN091 Libromancer Intervention SR .20 .40
BACHEN092 Fire Opal Head C .10 .20
BACHEN093 Doll Monster Miss Mädchen C .10 .20
BACHEN094 Doll Monster Bear-Bear C .10 .20
BACHEN095 Smoke Mosquito C .10 .20
BACHEN096 Nowru Aries the Vernal Dragon C .10 .20
BACHEN097 Groza, Tyrant of Thunder C .10 .20
BACHEN098 Doll Happiness C .10 .20
BACHEN099 Smile Potion C .10 .20
BACHEN100 The Dark Magicians SLR 150.00 300.00

2022 Yu-Gi-Oh Battles of Legend Crystal Revenge 1st Edition

BLCREN001 Royal Straight Slasher SCR .15 .30
BLCREN002 Royal Straight UR .15 .30
BLCREN003 Dragon Nails UR .15 .30
BLCREN004 Thunder Ball UR .15 .30
BLCREN005 Dice Dungeon UR .15 .30
BLCREN006 Dimension Dice UR .15 .30
BLCREN007 Clockwork Night SCR 4.00 8.00
BLCREN008 EN Shuffle SCR 1.25 2.50
BLCREN009 Battle of Sleeping Spirits UR .15 .30
BLCREN010 ACB Ruby Carbuncle SCR .30 .75
BLCREN011 ACB Amethyst Cat SCR .30 .75
BLCREN012 ACB Emerald Tortoise SCR .30 .75
BLCREN013 ACB Topaz Tiger SCR .30 .75
BLCREN014 ACB Amber Mammoth SCR .30 .75
BLCREN015 ACB Cobalt Eagle SCR .30 .75
BLCREN016 ACB Sapphire Pegasus SCR .30 .75
BLCREN017 Dyna Base UR .15 .30
BLCREN018 Dyna Tank UR .15 .30
BLCREN019 Gadget Box UR .15 .30
BLCREN020 Morphtronic Impact Return UR .15 .30
BLCREN021 Tool Box UR .15 .30
BLCREN022 Crystal Skull UR .15 .30
BLCREN023 Curse Reflection Doll UR .15 .30
BLCREN024 Stonehenge UR .15 .30
BLCREN025 Dream Shark UR .15 .30
BLCREN026 Heroic Call UR .15 .30
BLCREN027 Oily Cicada UR .15 .30
BLCREN028 Dream Cicada UR .15 .30
BLCREN029 Number 2: Ninja Shadow Mosquito SCR .50 1.00
BLCREN030 Ninjitsu Art of Mosquito Marching UR .15 .30
BLCREN031 Performapal Odd-Eyes Seer UR .15 .30
BLCREN032 Doodle Beast - Stego SCR .30 .75
BLCREN033 Doodle Beast - Tyranno SCR .30 .75
BLCREN034 Doodlebook - Uh uh uh! UR .15 .30
BLCREN035 Todoroki the Earthbolt Star UR .15 .30
BLCREN036 Senko the Skybolt Star UR .15 .30
BLCREN037 Raijin the Breakbolt Star UR .15 .30
BLCREN038 Amazoness Hall UR .15 .30
BLCREN039 Amazoness Hot Spring UR .15 .30
BLCREN040 G Golem Rock Hammer UR .15 .30
BLCREN041 G Golem Pebble Dog UR .15 .30
BLCREN042 G Golem Crystal Heart UR .15 .30
BLCREN043 G Golem Stubborn Menhir UR .15 .30
BLCREN044 G Golem Invalid Dolmen SCR .15 .30
BLCREN045 G Golem Dignified Trilithon SCR .15 .30
BLCREN046 Gravity Balance UR .15 .30
BLCREN047 Crystal Beast Ruby Carbuncle UR .15 .30
BLCREN048 Crystal Beast Amethyst Cat UR .15 .30
BLCREN049 Crystal Beast Emerald Tortoise UR .15 .30
BLCREN050 Crystal Beast Topaz Tiger UR .15 .30
BLCREN051 Crystal Beast Amber Mammoth UR .15 .30
BLCREN052 Crystal Beast Cobalt Eagle UR .15 .30
BLCREN053 Crystal Beast Sapphire Pegasus UR .15 .30
BLCREN054 Advanced Dark UR .15 .30
BLCREN055 Rainbow Bridge UR .15 .30
BLCREN056 Blackwing - Gale the Whirlwind UR .25 .50
BLCREN057 Blackwing - Bora the Spear UR .25 .50
BLCREN058 Blackwing - Sirocco the Dawn UR .25 .50
BLCREN059 Blackwing - Blizzard the Far North UR .25 .50
BLCREN060 Blackwing - Vayu the Emblem of Honor SCR .30 .75
BLCREN061 Blackwing - Breeze the Zephyr UR .25 .50
BLCREN062 Blackwing - Simoon the Poison Wind UR .25 .50
BLCREN063 Blackwing - Gram the Shining Star UR .25 .50
BLCREN064 Blackwing Full Armor Master UR .15 .30
BLCREN065 Toon Black Luster Soldier SCR 4.00 8.00
BLCREN066 Toon Harpie Lady UR .15 .30
BLCREN067 Toon Bookmark SCR .60 1.25
BLCREN068 Toon Page-Flip SCR .75 1.50
BLCREN069 Toon Terror UR .15 .30
BLCREN070 The Chaos Creator SCR .25 .50
BLCREN071 Chaos Daedalus UR .15 .30
BLCREN072 Chaos Valkyria UR .15 .30
BLCREN073 Chaos Space SCR 2.00 4.00
BLCREN074 Odd-Eyes Persona Dragon SCR .20 .40
BLCREN075 Odd-Eyes Phantasma Dragon SCR .20 .40
BLCREN076 Odd-Eyes Rebellion Dragon UR .15 .30
BLCREN077 D.D. Crow UR .60 1.25
BLCREN078 Edge Imp Chain UR .15 .30
BLCREN079 Token Collector UR .15 .30
BLCREN080 Koa'ki Meiru Supplier SCR .20 .40
BLCREN081 Doomkaiser Dragon SCR .15 .30
BLCREN082 Revived King Ha Des SCR .60 1.25
BLCREN083 Borreload Savage Dragon SCR 7.50 15.00
BLCREN083 Borreload Savage Dragon SLR 175.00 350.00
BLCREN084 Number 100: Numeron Dragon SCR .50 1.00
BLCREN085 Number F0: Utopic Draco Future SCR 4.00 8.00
BLCREN086 Frightfur Patchwork UR .15 .30
BLCREN087 Salamangreat Circle UR .15 .30
BLCREN088 Fusion Destiny SCR 1.25 2.50
BLCREN089 Emblem of the Plunder Patroll UR .15 .30
BLCREN090 Hieratic Seal of the Heavenly Spheres UR .15 .30
BLCREN091 Avendread Savior UR .15 .30
BLCREN092 Selene, Queen of the Master Magicians SCR 5.00 10.00
BLCREN093 Accesscode Talker SCR 20.00 40.00
BLCREN093 Accesscode Talker SLR 300.00 600.00
BLCREN094 Blackbeard, the Plunder Patroll Captain SCR .25 .50
BLCREN095 Artemis, the Magistus Moon Maiden SCR .30 .60
BLCREN096 Evil Twin Ki-sikil SCR 1.50 3.00
BLCREN097 Evil Twin Lil-la SCR .60 1.25
BLCREN098 Yata-Garasu SLR 75.00 150.00
BLCREN099 Blackwing Armor Master SLR 75.00 150.00
BLCREN100 Super Polymerization SLR 125.00 250.00
BLCREN101 Exodia the Forbidden One SLR 300.00 750.00
BLCREN102 Right Leg of the Forbidden One SLR 150.00 300.00
BLCREN103 Left Leg of the Forbidden One SLR 125.00 250.00
BLCREN104 Right Arm of the Forbidden One SLR 150.00 300.00
BLCREN105 Left Arm of the Forbidden One SLR 150.00 300.00

2022 Yu-Gi-Oh Darkwing Blast 1st Edition

DABLEN000 Spellbound SCR 3.00 6.00
DABLEN001 Blackwing - Vata the Emblem of Wandering SR .30 .60
DABLEN002 Blackwing - Shamal the Sandstorm SR .25 .50
DABLEN003 Blackwing - Chinook the Snow Blast SR .12 .25
DABLEN004 Blackwing - Sudri the Phantom Glimmer UR 4.00 8.00
DABLEN005 Blackwing - Zonda the Dusk C .07 .15
DABLEN006 Bystial Magnamhut SR 10.00 20.00
DABLEN007 Bystial Saronir SR 1.25 2.50
DABLEN008 Bystial Druiswurm SR 3.00 6.00
DABLEN009 The Bystial Lubellion SCR 50.00 100.00
DABLEN010 The Bystial Alba Los UR .25 .50
DABLEN011 Blazing Cartesia, the Virtuous SCR 30.00 75.00
DABLEN011 Blazing Cartesia, the Virtuous SLR 200.00 400.00
DABLEN012 Kashtira Fenrir UR 30.00 60.00
DABLEN013 Kashtira Unicorn UR 2.50 5.00
DABLEN014 Kashtira Ogre C .07 .15
DABLEN015 Tobari the Sky Ninja C .07 .15
DABLEN016 Mitsu the Insect Ninja SLR 60.00 125.00
DABLEN016 Mitsu the Insect Ninja UR 1.00 2.00
DABLEN017 Baku the Beast Ninja SR .12 .25
DABLEN018 Kagero the Cannon Ninja C .07 .15
DABLEN019 Prediction Princess Bibliomuse C .07 .15
DABLEN020 Naturia Mole Cricket C .07 .15
DABLEN021 Naturia Camellia C .07 .15
DABLEN022 Ignis Phoenix, the Dracoslayer SCR 1.50 3.00
DABLEN023 Majesty Pegasus, the Dracoslayer UR 1.00 2.00
DABLEN024 Dinomight Powerload, the Dracoslayer SR .20 .40
DABLEN025 Vera the Vernusylph Goddess UR .30 .75
DABLEN026 Vernusylph of the Misting Seedlings SR .50 1.00
DABLEN027 Rex, Freight Fur Hire SR 1.00 2.00
DABLEN028 Celestia Apparatus Tesea C .07 .15
DABLEN029 Soul Scissors C .07 .15
DABLEN030 Lady Labrynth of the Silver Castle SCR 20.00 40.00
DABLEN030 Lady Labrynth of the Silver Castle SLR 175.00 350.00
DABLEN031 Infernalqueen Salmon C .07 .15
DABLEN032 Han-Shi Kyudo Spirit C .07 .15
DABLEN033 Laughing Puffin C .07 .15
DABLEN034 Turbo-Tainted Hot Rod GT19 C .07 .15
DABLEN035 Psychic Rover C .07 .15
DABLEN036 Cucumber Horse C .07 .15
DABLEN037 Silent Wolf Calupo C .07 .15
DABLEN038 Prediction Princess Tarotreith SR .12 .25
DABLEN039 Tearlaments Rulkallos SCR 3.00 6.00
DABLEN039 Tearlaments Rulkallos SLR 100.00 200.00
DABLEN040 Meizen the Battle Ninja UR .60 1.25
DABLEN041 Freki the Runick Fangs C .07 .15
DABLEN042 Black-Winged Assault Dragon UR 2.50 5.00
DABLEN043 Blackwing - Boreastorm the Wicked Wind SR .12 .25
DABLEN044 Shamisen Samsara Sorrowcat SR .12 .25
DABLEN045 Kashtira Shangri-Ira SR .20 .40
DABLEN046 Mereologic Aggregator SR .25 .50
DABLEN047 Wollow, Founder of the Drudge Dragons SR .20 .40
DABLEN048 Spright Sprind SCR 7.50 15.00
DABLEN049 Donner, Dagger Fur Hire SR .60 1.25
DABLEN050 Worldsea Dragon Zealantis SCR 4.00 8.00
DABLEN051 Muckraker From the Underworld SCR 12.50 25.00
DABLEN052 Black Feather Whirlwind SR .12 .25
DABLEN053 Branded Regained SR .50 1.00
DABLEN054 Decisive Battle of Golgonda C .07 .15
DABLEN055 Tri-Brigade Showdown C .07 .15
DABLEN056 Tearlaments Grief C .07 .15
DABLEN057 Tearlaments Heartbeat C .07 .15
DABLEN058 Tearlaments Scream C .07 .15
DABLEN059 Scareclaw Decline C .07 .15
DABLEN060 Kashtira Birth SR .25 .50
DABLEN061 Ninjitsu Art Notebook of Mystery UR .75 1.50
DABLEN062 Ninjitsu Art Tool - Iron Digger C .07 .15
DABLEN063 Underworld Ritual of Prediction C .07 .15
DABLEN064 Naturia Blessing C .07 .15
DABLEN065 Dragonic Pendulum C .07 .15
DABLEN066 Vernusylph in Full Bloom C .07 .15
DABLEN067 Curse of Aramatir C .07 .15
DABLEN068 Vaylantz Wakening - Solo Activation UR .50 1.00
DABLEN069 Terrors in the Hidden City SR .12 .25
DABLEN070 Original Bamboo Sword C .07 .15
DABLEN071 Blackwing - Twin Shadow C .07 .15
DABLEN072 Black Shadow Squall C .07 .15
DABLEN073 Branded Beast SR .20 .40
DABLEN074 Spright Double Cross SR .20 .40
DABLEN075 Scareclaw Twinsaw C .07 .15
DABLEN076 Kashtira Preparations C .07 .15
DABLEN077 Ninjitsu Art of Dancing Leaves C .07 .15
DABLEN078 Simul Archfiends SR .12 .25
DABLEN079 Stars Align across the Milky Way C .07 .15
DABLEN080 The Great Noodle Inversion C .07 .15
DABLEN081 Bayerock Dragon C .07 .15
DABLEN082 Zalamander Catalyzer C .07 .15
DABLEN083 Tilting Entertainment C .07 .15
DABLEN084 Destructive Daruma Karma Cannon UR 3.00 6.00
DABLEN085 Zep, Ruby of the Ghoti UR 1.25 2.50
DABLEN086 Ixeep, Omen of the Ghoti C .07 .15
DABLEN087 Snopios, Shade of the Ghoti SR .12 .25
DABLEN088 Arionpos, Serpent of the Ghoti UR 1.50 3.00
DABLEN089 Guoglim, Spear of the Ghoti SCR .60 1.25
DABLEN090 Ghoti Cosmos C .07 .15
DABLEN091 Ghoti Fury SR .12 .25
DABLEN092 Yorishiro of the Aqua C .07 .15
DABLEN093 Amazoness Golden Whip Master C .07 .15
DABLEN094 Amazoness Silver Sword Master C .07 .15
DABLEN095 Amazoness War Chief C .07 .15
DABLEN096 Amazoness Spiritualist C .07 .15
DABLEN097 Amazoness Augusta C .07 .15
DABLEN098 Amazoness Pet Liger King C .07 .15
DABLEN099 Amazoness Secret Arts C .07 .15
DABLEN100 Black-Winged Dragon SLR 75.00 150.00

2022 Yu-Gi-Oh Dimension Force 1st Edition

DIFOEN000 Libromancer Fire SCR 4.00 8.00
DIFOEN001 Performapal Gentrude SR .12 .25
DIFOEN002 Performapal Ladyange SR .12 .25
DIFOEN003 Therion Bull Ain C .10 .20
DIFOEN004 Therion Reaper Fum C .10 .20
DIFOEN005 Therion Duke Yul C .10 .20
DIFOEN006 Therion Lily Borea SCR 7.50 15.00
DIFOEN007 Therion King Regulus SCR 30.00 60.00
DIFOEN007 Therion King Regulus SLR 150.00 300.00
DIFOEN008 Visas Starfrost SCR 7.50 15.00
DIFOEN009 Scareclaw Astra C .10 .20

DIFOEN010 Scareclaw Belone C .10 .20
DIFOEN011 Scareclaw Acro C .10 .20
DIFOEN012 Scareclaw Reichheart UR 1.25 2.50
DIFOEN013 Mad Mauler C .10 .20
DIFOEN014 Alghoul Mazera C .10 .20
DIFOEN015 Heroic Challenger - Knuckle Sword C .10 .20
DIFOEN016 Heroic Challenger - Morning Star C .10 .20
DIFOEN017 Predaplant Byblisp C .10 .20
DIFOEN018 Predaplant Bufolicula C .10 .20
DIFOEN019 Predaplant Triantis C .10 .20
DIFOEN020 Symphonic Warrior Guitariss C .10 .20
DIFOEN021 Symphonic Warrior DJJ C .10 .20
DIFOEN022 Noh-P.U.N.K. Deer Note UR 4.00 8.00
DIFOEN023 Illegal Knight SCR 2.50 5.00
DIFOEN024 Ancient Warriors - Savage Don Ying C .10 .20
DIFOEN025 Battleguard Cadet C .10 .20
DIFOEN026 Light Law Medium C .10 .20
DIFOEN027 Divine Dragon Titanomakhia C .10 .20
DIFOEN028 Sunlit Sentinel C .10 .20
DIFOEN029 Amphibious Bugroth MK-11 C .10 .20
DIFOEN030 Supreme Sea Mare C .10 .20
DIFOEN031 Reverse Jar C .10 .20
DIFOEN032 Yamatako Orochi C .10 .20
DIFOEN033 Devouring Sarcoughagus C .10 .20
DIFOEN034 Odd-Eyes Pendulumgraph Dragon SCR 1.25 2.50
DIFOEN035 Alba-Lenatus the Abyss Dragon SCR 7.50 15.00
DIFOEN035 Alba-Lenatus the Abyss Dragon SLR 75.00 150.00
DIFOEN036 Starving Venom Predapower Fusion Dragon UR 1.25 2.50
DIFOEN037 Predaplant Ambulomelides C .10 .20
DIFOEN038 Dinomorphia Rexterm UR 3.00 6.00
DIFOEN039 Red-Eyes Zombie Dragon Lord UR 2.00 4.00
DIFOEN040 Skeletal Dragon Felgrand UR .75 1.50
DIFOEN041 Immortal Dragon SR .50 1.00
DIFOEN042 Symphonic Warrior Rockks C .10 .20
DIFOEN043 Psychic End Punisher SCR 12.50 25.00
DIFOEN044 Heroic Champion - Claivesolish SR .12 .25
DIFOEN045 Heroic Champion - Jarngreipr C .10 .20
DIFOEN046 Exosisters Magnifica SLR 150.00 300.00
DIFOEN046 Exosisters Magnifica UR 6.00 12.00
DIFOEN047 Musical Sumo Dice Games C .10 .20
DIFOEN048 Beyond the Pendulum SCR 5.00 10.00
DIFOEN049 Scareclaw Tri-Heart SCR 4.00 8.00
DIFOEN050 The Weather Painter Moonbow UR .30 .75
DIFOEN051 Sylvan Dancepione SR .12 .25
DIFOEN052 Extra Pendulum SR .12 .25
DIFOEN053 Therion Discolosseum UR 5.00 10.00
DIFOEN054 Endless Engine Argyro System UR 1.25 2.50
DIFOEN055 Therion Charge SR .12 .25
DIFOEN056 Icejade Curse C .10 .20
DIFOEN057 Branded Loss C .10 .20
DIFOEN058 Primitive Planet Reichphobia UR 1.50 3.00
DIFOEN059 Scareclaw Arrival SR .20 .40
DIFOEN060 Zombie Reborn SR .50 1.00
DIFOEN061 Heroic Envoy SR .12 .25
DIFOEN062 Generalprobe C .10 .20
DIFOEN063 The Weather Forecast SR .12 .25
DIFOEN064 Ancient Warriors Saga... C .10 .20
DIFOEN065 War Rock Medium C .10 .20
DIFOEN066 Materiactor Annulus C .10 .20
DIFOEN067 Parasomnia Pillow C .10 .20
DIFOEN068 Surprise Chain C .10 .20
DIFOEN069 Pendulum Scale C .10 .20
DIFOEN070 Therion Cross SR .12 .25
DIFOEN071 Therion Stand Up! C .10 .20
DIFOEN072 Branded Banishment SR .75 1.50
DIFOEN073 Dogmatikaturgy C .10 .20
DIFOEN074 Scareclaw Sclash SR .12 .25
DIFOEN075 Scareclaw Alternative C .10 .20
DIFOEN076 Haunted Zombies C .10 .20
DIFOEN077 Dinomorphia Frenzy UR 2.00 4.00
DIFOEN078 Ichiroku's Ledger Book C .10 .20
DIFOEN079 XX-clusion C .10 .20
DIFOEN080 Vivid Tail C .10 .20
DIFOEN081 Colonel on C-String C .10 .20
DIFOEN082 Navy Dragon Mech SR .12 .25
DIFOEN083 Patissciel Couverture SLR 50.00 100.00
DIFOEN083 Patissciel Couverture SR .12 .25
DIFOEN084 Omega Judgment C .10 .20
DIFOEN085 Backup Team C .10 .20
DIFOEN086 Libromancer Mystigirl SR .12 .25
DIFOEN087 Libromancer Fireburst UR .30 .75
DIFOEN088 Libromancer Realized SR .12 .25
DIFOEN089 Libromancer Bonded SR .12 .25
DIFOEN090 Libromancer Displaced UR .30 .75
DIFOEN091 Libromancer Prevented SR .12 .25
DIFOEN092 Motor Frenzy SR .12 .25
DIFOEN093 Chow Sai the Ghost Stopper SR .12 .25
DIFOEN094 Crow Tengu C .10 .20
DIFOEN095 Yakusa, Lord of the Eight Thunders SR .12 .25
DIFOEN096 Changshi the Spiridao SR .30 .60
DIFOEN097 Curse of Dragon... SR .12 .25
DIFOEN098 Odd-Eyes Wing Dragon SR .12 .25
DIFOEN099 V-LAN Hydra C .10 .20
DIFOEN100 Ghost Belle & Haunted Mansion SLR 200.00 400.00

2022 Yu-Gi-Oh Ghosts from the Past The 2nd Haunting 1st Edition

GFP2EN001 Crystal Beast Rainbow Dragon UR .50 1.00
GFP2EN002 D/D/D Vice King Requiem UR .12 .25
GFP2EN003 Elemental HERO Neos Kluger UR .30 .60
GFP2EN004 Odd-Eyes Rebellion Dragon Overlord UR .12 .25
GFP2EN005 Decode Talker Heatsoul UR 1.00 2.00
GFP2EN006 Borrelend Dragon UR 1.00 2.00
GFP2EN007 Majesty Hyperion UR .12 .25
GFP2EN008 The Agent of Life - Neptune UR .60 1.25
GFP2EN009 The Executor of the Underworld - Pluto UR .12 .25
GFP2EN010 Masterflare Hyperion UR .30 .60
GFP2EN011 Protector of The Agents - Moon UR .30 .60
GFP2EN012 The Chorus in the Sky UR .12 .25
GFP2EN013 The Sacred Waters in the Sky UR .60 1.25
GFP2EN014 Fallen Sanctuary UR .20 .40
GFP2EN015 Flint Cragger UR .15 .30
GFP2EN016 Shell Knight UR .12 .25
GFP2EN017 Infernity Sage UR .12 .25
GFP2EN018 Infernity Pawn UR .12 .25
GFP2EN019 Fossil Machine Skull Convoy UR .12 .25
GFP2EN020 Fossil Machine Skull Wagon UR .12 .25
GFP2EN021 Fossil Machine Skull Buggy UR .12 .25
GFP2EN022 Contract with the Void UR .12 .25
GFP2EN023 Void Cauldron UR .12 .25
GFP2EN024 Code Exporter UR .12 .25
GFP2EN025 Salamangreat Blaze Dragon UR .25 .50
GFP2EN026 Brute Enforcer UR .12 .25
GFP2EN027 Altergeist Failover UR .12 .25
GFP2EN028 Trackblack UR .12 .25
GFP2EN029 Puppet Queen UR .12 .25
GFP2EN030 Motor Shell UR .12 .25
GFP2EN031 Leraje the God of Archery UR .12 .25
GFP2EN032 Onmoraki UR .12 .25
GFP2EN033 Dark Alligator UR .12 .25
GFP2EN034 Reptia Egg UR .12 .25
GFP2EN035 Performapal Miss Director UR .12 .25
GFP2EN036 Primal Dragon, the Primordial UR .12 .25
GFP2EN037 Samsara Dragon UR .12 .25
GFP2EN038 Cocatorium the Heavy Metal Avian UR .12 .25
GFP2EN039 Chaos Grepher UR .12 .25
GFP2EN040 Proxy Horse UR .20 .40
GFP2EN041 Outburst Dragon UR .20 .40
GFP2EN042 Victorica, Angel of Bravery UR .20 .40
GFP2EN043 Rookie Warrior Lady UR .12 .25
GFP2EN044 Time Thief Temporwhal UR .15 .30
GFP2EN045 Chronicle Magician UR .15 .30
GFP2EN046 Mystical Shine Ball UR .15 .30
GFP2EN047 Master Hyperion UR .15 .30
GFP2EN048 The Agent of Wisdom - Mercury UR .12 .25
GFP2EN049 The Agent of Creation - Venus UR .12 .25
GFP2EN050 The Agent of Mystery - Earth UR .12 .25
GFP2EN051 The Agent of Force - Mars UR .12 .25
GFP2EN052 The Agent of Miracles - Jupiter UR .12 .25
GFP2EN053 The Agent of Judgment - Saturn UR .12 .25
GFP2EN054 The Agent of Entropy - Uranus UR .12 .25
GFP2EN055 Vision HERO Minimum Ray UR .12 .25
GFP2EN056 Vision HERO Multiply Guy UR .12 .25
GFP2EN057 Vision HERO Increase UR .75 1.50
GFP2EN058 Vision HERO Poisoner UR .12 .25
GFP2EN059 Vision HERO Faris UR 1.50 3.00
GFP2EN060 Vision HERO Vyon UR .20 .40
GFP2EN061 Vision HERO Gravito UR .12 .25
GFP2EN062 Inzektor Hornet UR .12 .25
GFP2EN063 Inzektor Giga-Mantis UR .12 .25
GFP2EN064 Ghostrick Lantern UR .12 .25
GFP2EN065 Ghostrick Specter UR .12 .25
GFP2EN066 Ghostrick Jiangshi UR .12 .25
GFP2EN067 Ghostrick Stein UR .12 .25
GFP2EN068 Ghostrick Mary UR .12 .25
GFP2EN069 Ghostrick Mummy UR .12 .25
GFP2EN070 Vampire Sorcerer UR .12 .25
GFP2EN071 Shadow Vampire UR .12 .25
GFP2EN072 Vampire Grace UR .12 .25
GFP2EN073 Vampire Duke UR .12 .25
GFP2EN074 D/D Swirl Slime UR .12 .25
GFP2EN075 D/D Necro Slime UR .12 .25
GFP2EN076 D/D Savant Copernicus UR .12 .25
GFP2EN077 D/D Lamia UR .12 .25
GFP2EN078 D/D Savant Thomas UR .12 .25
GFP2EN079 D/D/D Destiny King Zero Laplace UR .12 .25
GFP2EN080 Go! - D/D/D Divine Zero King Rage UR .12 .25
GFP2EN081 Code Radiator UR .20 .40
GFP2EN082 Code Generator UR .12 .25
GFP2EN083 Tenyi Spirit - Adhara UR .30 .60
GFP2EN084 Tenyi Spirit - Shthana UR .20 .40
GFP2EN085 Tenyi Spirit - Mapura UR .12 .25
GFP2EN086 Tenyi Spirit - Nahata UR .12 .25
GFP2EN087 Tenyi Spirit - Vishuda UR 1.00 2.00
GFP2EN088 Tenyi Spirit - Ashuna UR .30 .75
GFP2EN089 Mardel, Generaider Boss of Light UR .20 .40
GFP2EN090 Hela, Generaider Boss of Doom UR .12 .25
GFP2EN091 Whitebeard, the Plunder Patroll Helm UR .25 .50
GFP2EN092 Redbeard, the Plunder Patroll Matey UR .30 .60
GFP2EN093 Bluebeard, the Plunder Patroll Shipwright UR .25 .50
GFP2EN094 Goldenhair, the Newest Plunder Patroll UR .25 .50
GFP2EN095 Despian Comedy UR .12 .25
GFP2EN096 Despian Tragedy UR .75 1.50
GFP2EN097 Aluber the Jester of Despia UR 4.00 8.00
GFP2EN098 Dramaturge of Despia UR .75 1.50
GFP2EN099 Manju of the Ten Thousand Hands UR .75 1.50
GFP2EN100 Alien Ammonite UR .12 .25
GFP2EN101 Malefic Cyber End Dragon UR .12 .25
GFP2EN102 Doppelwarrior UR .25 .50
GFP2EN103 Mecha Phantom Beast Coltwing UR .12 .25
GFP2EN104 Box of Friends UR .12 .25
GFP2EN105 Galaxy Soldier UR 1.25 2.50
GFP2EN106 Raiza the Mega Monarch UR .20 .40
GFP2EN107 Deskbot 001 UR .12 .25
GFP2EN108 Retaliating C UR .12 .25
GFP2EN109 Cipher Twin Raptor UR .12 .25
GFP2EN110 Wandering King Wildwind UR .30 .75
GFP2EN111 Dotscaper UR .15 .30
GFP2EN112 Tatsunecro UR .12 .25
GFP2EN113 Doomking Balerdroch UR .25 .50
GFP2EN114 Necroworld Banshee UR 1.25 2.50
GFP2EN115 Glow-Up Bloom UR .60 1.25
GFP2EN116 Reptilianne Lamia UR .12 .25
GFP2EN117 Mathmech Addition UR .15 .30
GFP2EN118 Rare Fish UR .20 .40
GFP2EN119 Mystical Sand UR .15 .30
GFP2EN120 Great Mammoth of Goldfine UR .12 .25
GFP2EN121 Rose Spectre of Dunn UR .12 .25
GFP2EN122 Sanwitch UR .12 .25
GFP2EN123 Chimeratech Fortress Dragon UR .30 .75
GFP2EN124 Chimeratech Rampage Dragon UR .12 .25
GFP2EN125 Dark Magician the Dragon Knight UR .60 1.25
GFP2EN126 Chimeratech Megafleet Dragon UR .12 .25
GFP2EN127 Quintet Magician UR .75 1.50
GFP2EN128 Plunder Patrollship Lys UR .15 .30
GFP2EN129 Fossil Warrior Skull Knight UR .15 .30
GFP2EN130 Baxia, Brightness of the Yang Zing UR .12 .25
GFP2EN131 Yazi, Evil of the Yang Zing UR .12 .25
GFP2EN132 Nirvana High Paladin UR .12 .25
GFP2EN133 Red-Eyes Zombie Necro Dragon UR .20 .40
GFP2EN134 Geomathmech Final Sigma UR .12 .25
GFP2EN135 Plunder Patrollship Brann UR .12 .25
GFP2EN136 Cupid Pitch UR .20 .40
GFP2EN137 Princess Cologne UR .12 .25
GFP2EN138 Crimson Knight Vampire Bram UR .12 .25
GFP2EN139 Ghostrick Dullahan UR .12 .25
GFP2EN140 Ghostrick Socuteboss UR .12 .25
GFP2EN141 Sky Cavalry Centaurea UR .50 1.00
GFP2EN142 D/D/D Duo-Dawn King Kali Yuga UR .12 .25
GFP2EN143 #38 Hope Harbinger Dragon Titanic Galaxy UR 1.25 2.50
GFP2EN144 Number 60: Dugares the Timeless UR .75 1.50
GFP2EN145 Number 97: Draglubion UR .30 .75
GFP2EN146 Primathmech Laplacian UR .12 .25
GFP2EN147 Jormungandr, Generaider Boss of Eternity UR .12 .25
GFP2EN148 Plunder Patrollship Moerk UR .12 .25
GFP2EN149 Crystron Halqifibrax UR 1.50 3.00
GFP2EN150 Vampire Sucker UR .30 .60
GFP2EN151 The Sanctuary in the Sky UR .25 .50
GFP2EN152 The Flute of Summoning Kuriboh UR .12 .25
GFP2EN153 Advanced Ritual Art UR .12 .25
GFP2EN154 Zombie World UR .75 1.50
GFP2EN155 Reptilianne Spawn UR .12 .25
GFP2EN156 Inzektor Sword - Zektkaliber UR .12 .25
GFP2EN157 Vampire Kingdom UR .12 .25
GFP2EN158 Yang Zing Prana UR .12 .25
GFP2EN159 Dark Contract with the Gate UR .50 1.00
GFP2EN160 Dark Contract with the Swamp King UR .12 .25
GFP2EN161 Domain of the True Monarchs UR .12 .25
GFP2EN162 The Sanctum of Parshath UR .12 .25
GFP2EN163 Generaider Boss Stage UR .12 .25
GFP2EN164 Plunder Patroll Shipyarrrd UR .30 .75
GFP2EN165 Heavenly Dragon Circle UR .12 .25
GFP2EN166 Fossil Fusion UR .12 .25
GFP2EN167 Despia, Theater of the Branded UR .20 .40
GFP2EN168 Vampire Takeover UR .12 .25
GFP2EN169 Yang Zing Brutality UR .12 .25
GFP2EN170 Pendulum Area UR .12 .25
GFP2EN171 Nine Pillars of Yang Zing UR .12 .25
GFP2EN172 Vampire Domination UR .12 .25
GFP2EN173 Cynet Conflict UR .12 .25
GFP2EN174 Fists of the Unrivaled Tenyi UR .12 .25
GFP2EN175 Blue-Eyes White Dragon GR 125.00 250.00
GFP2EN176 Red-Eyes Black Dragon GR 60.00 125.00
GFP2EN177 Dark Magician Girl GR 150.00 300.00
GFP2EN178 Cyber Dragon GR 40.00 80.00
GFP2EN179 Dark Armed Dragon GR 30.00 60.00
GFP2EN180 The Winged Dragon of Ra - Sphere Mode GR 40.00 80.00
GFP2EN181 Blue-Eyes Ultimate Dragon GR 30.00 75.00
GFP2EN182 Red Dragon Archfiend GR 30.00 60.00
GFP2EN183 The Eye of Timaeus GR 15.00 30.00

2022 Yu-Gi-Oh The Grand Creators 1st Edition

GRCREN001 Ukiyoe-P.U.N.K. Sharakusai R .15 .30
GRCREN002 Gagaku-P.U.N.K. Wa Gon SR .12 .25
GRCREN003 Joruri-P.U.N.K. Madame Spider SR .15 .30
GRCREN004 Noh-P.U.N.K. Ze Amin SR .30 .75
GRCREN005 Noh-P.U.N.K. Foxy Tune CR 50.00 100.00
GRCREN005 Noh-P.U.N.K. Foxy Tune UR 20.00 40.00
GRCREN006 Noh-P.U.N.K. Ogre Dance CR 25.00 50.00
GRCREN006 Noh-P.U.N.K. Ogre Dance UR 2.50 5.00
GRCREN007 Ukiyoe-P.U.N.K. Rising Carp R .15 .30
GRCREN008 Ukiyoe-P.U.N.K. Amazing Dragon UR 1.00 2.00
GRCREN008 Ukiyoe-P.U.N.K. Amazing Dragon CR 15.00 30.00
GRCREN009 Gagaku-P.U.N.K. Wild Picking R .12 .25
GRCREN010 Gagaku-P.U.N.K. Crash Beat R .12 .25
GRCREN011 Joruri-P.U.N.K. Dangerous Gabu SR .12 .25
GRCREN012 Joruri-P.U.N.K. Nashiwari Surprise R .12 .25
GRCREN013 Exosister Elis SR .50 1.00
GRCREN014 Exosister Stella SR .30 .75
GRCREN015 Exosister Irene R .15 .30
GRCREN016 Exosister Sophia UR 10.00 20.00
GRCREN016 Exosister Sophia CR 30.00 60.00
GRCREN017 Exosister Mikailis UR 10.00 20.00
GRCREN017 Exosister Mikailis CR 60.00 125.00
GRCREN018 Exosister Kaspitell R .12 .25
GRCREN019 Exosister Gibrine SR .12 .25
GRCREN020 Exosister Asophiel SR .12 .25
GRCREN021 Exosister Pax CR 40.00 80.00
GRCREN021 Exosister Pax UR 12.50 25.00
GRCREN022 Exosister Arment R .15 .30
GRCREN023 Exosister Carpedivem R .15 .30
GRCREN024 Exosister Vadis SR .12 .25
GRCREN025 Rite of Aramesir CR 75.00 150.00
GRCREN025 Rite of Aramesir UR 25.00 50.00
GRCREN026 Water Enchantress of the Temple CR 75.00 150.00
GRCREN026 Water Enchantress of the Temple UR 12.50 25.00
GRCREN027 Magicore Warrior of the Relics SR .12 .25
GRCREN028 Wandering Gryphon Rider SR .12 .25
GRCREN029 Fateful Adventure CR 25.00 50.00
GRCREN029 Fateful Adventure UR 1.50 3.00
GRCREN030 Dunnell, the Noble Arms of Light R .15 .30
GRCREN031 Starlit Papillon R .15 .30
GRCREN032 Dracoback, the Ridable Dragon R .15 .30
GRCREN033 Zaralaam the Dark Palace R .15 .30
GRCREN034 Forest of Lost Flowers R .15 .30
GRCREN035 Thunder Discharge R .15 .30
GRCREN036 Breath of Resurrection SR .12 .25
GRCREN037 Zektrike Kou-Ou CR 7.50 15.00
GRCREN037 Zektrike Kou-Ou UR .30 .75
GRCREN038 Inzektor Hornet CR 12.50 25.00
GRCREN038 Inzektor Hornet R .15 .30
GRCREN039 Inzektor Centipede R .15 .30
GRCREN040 Inzektor Dragonfly CR 12.50 25.00
GRCREN040 Inzektor Dragonfly SR .12 .25
GRCREN041 Inzektor Hopper R .15 .30
GRCREN042 Inzektor Ladybug R .15 .30
GRCREN043 Risebell the Star Adjuster R .15 .30
GRCREN044 Gokipole R .15 .30
GRCREN045 Psychic Wheeleder R .15 .30
GRCREN046 Psychic Tracker R .15 .30
GRCREN047 Virtual World Hime - Nyannyan R .15 .30
GRCREN048 Inzektor Exa-Beetle R .15 .30
GRCREN049 Inzektor Exa-Stag R .15 .30
GRCREN050 Castel, the Skyblaster Musketeer R .15 .30
GRCREN051 Inzektor Picofalena SR .12 .25
GRCREN052 Insect Imitation R .15 .30
GRCREN053 Ties of the Brethren R .15 .30
GRCREN054 Hidden Armory R .15 .30
GRCREN055 Emergency Teleport R .50 1.00
GRCREN055 Emergency Teleport CR 30.00 75.00
GRCREN056 Inzektor Sword - Zektkaliber R .15 .30
GRCREN057 Torrential Tribute CR 30.00 75.00
GRCREN057 Torrential Tribute R .15 .30
GRCREN058 Xyz Universe SR .12 .25
GRCREN059 Solemn Strike CR 30.00 60.00
GRCREN059 Solemn Strike R .30 .75
GRCREN060 Armory Call R .15 .30

2022 Yu-Gi-Oh Hidden Arsenal Chapter 1 1st Edition

HAC1EN001 Blue-Eyes White Dragon (tablet art) DTUPR .75 1.50
HAC1EN002 Dark Magician (tablet art) DTUPR .30 .75
HAC1EN003 Red-Eyes Black Dragon (DT01 artwork) DTUPR .60 1.25
HAC1EN004 Elemental HERO Neos C .07 .15
HAC1EN004 Elemental HERO Neos DTNPR 1.50 3.00
HAC1EN005 Kuriboh C .07 .15
HAC1EN005 Kuriboh DTNPR .60 1.25
HAC1EN006 Barrel Dragon DTUPR .20 .40
HAC1EN007 Buster Blader C .07 .15
HAC1EN007 Buster Blader DTNPR 1.50 3.00
HAC1EN008 Lava Golem DTUPR 2.50 5.00
HAC1EN009 Night Assailant DTUPR .75 1.50
HAC1EN010 Harpie Lady 1 C .07 .15
HAC1EN010 Harpie Lady 1 DTNPR .50 1.00
HAC1EN011 Harpie Lady 2 C .07 .15
HAC1EN011 Harpie Lady 2 DTNPR .60 1.25
HAC1EN012 Harpie Lady 3 C .07 .15
HAC1EN012 Harpie Lady 3 DTNPR .30 .60
HAC1EN013 Winged Kuriboh C .07 .15
HAC1EN013 Winged Kuriboh DTNPR 1.25 2.50
HAC1EN014 Cyber Dragon DTUPR .75 1.50
HAC1EN015 Elemental HERO Stratos C .07 .15
HAC1EN015 Elemental HERO Stratos DTNPR 3.00 6.00
HAC1EN016 Card Trooper DTUPR .25 .50
HAC1EN017 Red-Eyes Darkness Metal Dragon C .07 .15
HAC1EN017 Red-Eyes Darkness Metal Dragon DTNPR 2.00 4.00
HAC1EN018 Dark Paladin DTUPR .75 1.50
HAC1EN019 Elemental HERO Flame Wingman DTUPR .50 1.00
HAC1EN020 Elemental HERO Shining Flare Wingman C .07 .15
HAC1EN020 El.HERO Shining Flare Wingman DTNPR 2.00 4.00
HAC1EN021 Goyo Guardian C .07 .15
HAC1EN021 Goyo Guardian DTNPR 1.00 2.00
HAC1EN022 Polymerization DTUPR 3.00 6.00
HAC1EN023 Mystical Space Typhoon DTUPR .50 1.00
HAC1EN024 Book of Moon DTUPR .75 1.50
HAC1EN025 Enemy Controller C .07 .15
HAC1EN025 Enemy Controller DTNPR .75 1.50
HAC1EN026 Waboku C .07 .15
HAC1EN026 Waboku DTNPR 4.00 8.00
HAC1EN027 Dust Tornado C .07 .15
HAC1EN027 Dust Tornado DTNPR 1.25 2.50
HAC1EN028 Skill Drain DTUPR 10.00 20.00
HAC1EN029 Blizzed, Defender of the Ice Barrier C .07 .15
HAC1EN029 Blizzed, Defender of the Ice Barrier DTNPR .20 .40
HAC1EN030 Blizzard Warrior C .07 .15
HAC1EN030 Blizzard Warrior DTNPR .25 .50
HAC1EN031 Cryomancer of the Ice Barrier C .07 .15
HAC1EN031 Cryomancer of the Ice Barrier DTNPR .20 .40
HAC1EN032 Royal Knight of the Ice Barrier C .07 .15
HAC1EN032 Royal Knight of the Ice Barrier DTNPR .25 .50
HAC1EN033 Dai-sojo of the Ice Barrier C .07 .15
HAC1EN033 Dai-sojo of the Ice Barrier DTNPR .30 .60
HAC1EN034 Medium of the Ice Barrier C .07 .15
HAC1EN034 Medium of the Ice Barrier DTNPR .30 .60
HAC1EN035 Pilgrim of the Ice Barrier C .07 .15
HAC1EN035 Pilgrim of the Ice Barrier DTNPR .20 .40
HAC1EN036 Geomancer of the Ice Barrier C .07 .15
HAC1EN036 Geomancer of the Ice Barrier DTNPR .15 .30
HAC1EN037 Shock Troops of the Ice Barrier C .07 .15
HAC1EN037 Shock Troops of the Ice Barrier DTNPR .20 .40
HAC1EN038 Samurai of the Ice Barrier C .07 .15
HAC1EN038 Samurai of the Ice Barrier DTNPR .20 .40
HAC1EN039 Dewdark of the Ice Barrier C .07 .15
HAC1EN039 Dewdark of the Ice Barrier DTNPR .20 .40
HAC1EN040 Caravan of the Ice Barrier C .07 .15
HAC1EN040 Caravan of the Ice Barrier DTNPR .12 .25
HAC1EN041 Spellbreaker of the Ice Barrier C .07 .15
HAC1EN041 Spellbreaker of the Ice Barrier DTNPR .20 .40
HAC1EN042 General Grunard of the Ice Barrier DTNPR .25 .50
HAC1EN042 General Grunard of the Ice Barrier C .07 .15
HAC1EN043 Defender of the Ice Barrier C .07 .15
HAC1EN043 Defender of the Ice Barrier DTNPR .25 .50
HAC1EN044 Warlock of the Ice Barrier C .07 .15
HAC1EN044 Warlock of the Ice Barrier DTNPR .12 .25
HAC1EN045 Sacred Spirit of the Ice Barrier C .07 .15
HAC1EN045 Sacred Spirit of the Ice Barrier DTNPR .12 .25
HAC1EN046 General Raiho of the Ice Barrier C .07 .15
HAC1EN046 General Raiho of the Ice Barrier DTNPR .30 .75
HAC1EN047 Strategist of the Ice Barrier C .07 .15
HAC1EN047 Strategist of the Ice Barrier DTNPR .30 .60
HAC1EN048 Secret Guards of the Ice Barrier C .07 .15
HAC1EN048 Secret Guards of the Ice Barrier DTNPR .20 .40
HAC1EN049 General Gantala of the Ice Barrier C .07 .15
HAC1EN049 General Gantala of the Ice Barrier DTNPR .15 .30
HAC1EN050 Dance Princess of the Ice Barrier C .07 .15
HAC1EN050 Dance Princess of the Ice Barrier DTNPR .25 .50
HAC1EN051 Brionac, Dragon of the Ice Barrier DTUPR .25 .50
HAC1EN052 Dewloren, Tiger King of the Ice Barrier DTUPR .20 .40
HAC1EN053 Gungnir, Dragon of the Ice Barrier DTUPR .20 .40
HAC1EN054 Trishula, Dragon

of the Ice Barrier DTUPR	.30	.75
HAC1EN055 Medallion of the Ice Barrier C	.07	.15
HAC1EN055 Medallion of the Ice Barrier DTNPR	1.50	3.00
HAC1EN056 Mist Valley Thunderbird C	.07	.15
HAC1EN056 Mist Valley Thunderbird DTNPR	.20	.40
HAC1EN057 Mist Valley Shaman C	.07	.15
HAC1EN057 Mist Valley Shaman DTNPR	.30	.60
HAC1EN058 Mist Valley Soldier C	.07	.15
HAC1EN058 Mist Valley Soldier DTNPR	.25	.50
HAC1EN059 Mist Valley Baby Roc C	.07	.15
HAC1EN059 Mist Valley Baby Roc DTNPR	.30	.75
HAC1EN060 Mist Valley Executor C	.07	.15
HAC1EN060 Mist Valley Executor DTNPR	.20	.40
HAC1EN061 Mist Valley Falcon C	.07	.15
HAC1EN061 Mist Valley Falcon DTNPR	.20	.40
HAC1EN062 Mist Valley Apex Avian DTUPR	.50	1.00
HAC1EN063 Mist Valley Thunder Lord C	.07	.15
HAC1EN063 Mist Valley Thunder Lord DTNPR	.12	.25
HAC1EN064 Flamvell Guard C	.07	.15
HAC1EN064 Flamvell Guard DTNPR	.12	.25
HAC1EN065 Flamvell Dragnov C	.07	.15
HAC1EN065 Flamvell Dragnov DTNPR	.12	.25
HAC1EN066 Flamvell Magician C	.07	.15
HAC1EN066 Flamvell Magician DTNPR	.12	.25
HAC1EN067 Flamvell Grunika C	.07	.15
HAC1EN067 Flamvell Grunika DTNPR	.12	.25
HAC1EN068 Flamvell Baby C	.07	.15
HAC1EN068 Flamvell Baby DTNPR	.12	.25
HAC1EN069 Neo Flamvell Origin C	.07	.15
HAC1EN069 Neo Flamvell Origin DTNPR	.12	.25
HAC1EN070 Neo Flamvell Hedgehog C	.07	.15
HAC1EN070 Neo Flamvell Hedgehog DTNPR	.12	.25
HAC1EN071 Neo Flamvell Shaman C	.07	.15
HAC1EN071 Neo Flamvell Shaman DTNPR	.12	.25
HAC1EN072 Neo Flamvell Garuda C	.07	.15
HAC1EN072 Neo Flamvell Garuda DTNPR	.12	.25
HAC1EN073 Neo Flamvell Sabre C	.07	.15
HAC1EN073 Neo Flamvell Sabre DTNPR	.12	.25
HAC1EN074 Flamvell Urquizas C	.07	.15
HAC1EN074 Flamvell Urquizas DTNPR	.12	.25
HAC1EN075 Ancient Flamvell Deity C	.07	.15
HAC1EN075 Ancient Flamvell Deity DTNPR	.12	.25
HAC1EN076 Ally of Justice Clausolas C	.07	.15
HAC1EN076 Ally of Justice Clausolas DTNPR	.12	.25
HAC1EN077 Ally Mind C	.07	.15
HAC1EN077 Ally Mind DTNPR	.12	.25
HAC1EN078 Ally of Justice Garadholg C	.07	.15
HAC1EN078 Ally of Justice Garadholg DTNPR	.12	.25
HAC1EN079 Ally of Justice Rudra C	.07	.15
HAC1EN079 Ally of Justice Rudra DTNPR	.12	.25
HAC1EN080 Ally of Justice Nullfier C	.07	.15
HAC1EN080 Ally of Justice Nullfier DTNPR	.12	.25
HAC1EN081 Ally of Justice Searcher C	.07	.15
HAC1EN081 Ally of Justice Searcher DTNPR	.12	.25
HAC1EN082 Ally of Justice Enemy Catcher C	.07	.15
HAC1EN082 Ally of Justice Enemy Catcher DTNPR	.12	.25
HAC1EN083 Ally of Justice Thunder Armor C	.07	.15
HAC1EN083 Ally of Justice Thunder Armor DTNPR	.12	.25
HAC1EN084 Ally of Justice Cosmic Gateway C	.07	.15
HAC1EN084 Ally of Justice Cosmic Gateway DTNPR	.12	.25
HAC1EN085 Ally of Justice Reverse Break C	.07	.15
HAC1EN085 Ally of Justice Reverse Break DTNPR	.12	.25
HAC1EN086 Ally of Justice Unlimiter C	.07	.15
HAC1EN086 Ally of Justice Unlimiter DTNPR	.12	.25
HAC1EN087 Ally of Justice Omni-Weapon C	.07	.15
HAC1EN087 Ally of Justice Omni-Weapon DTNPR	.12	.25
HAC1EN088 Ally of Justice Quarantine C	.07	.15
HAC1EN088 Ally of Justice Quarantine DTNPR	.12	.25
HAC1EN089 Ally of Justice Cycle Reader C	.07	.15
HAC1EN089 Ally of Justice Cycle Reader DTNPR	.12	.25
HAC1EN090 Ally of Justice Catastor C	.07	.15
HAC1EN090 Ally of Justice Catastor DTNPR	.12	.25
HAC1EN091 Ally of Justice Field Marshall C	.07	.15
HAC1EN091 Ally of Justice Field Marshall DTNPR	.12	.25
HAC1EN092 Ally of Justice Decisive Armor DTUPR	.12	.25
HAC1EN093 Naturia Beetle C	.07	.15
HAC1EN093 Naturia Beetle DTNPR	.12	.25
HAC1EN094 Naturia Rock C	.07	.15
HAC1EN094 Naturia Rock DTNPR	.12	.25
HAC1EN095 Naturia Guardian C	.07	.15
HAC1EN095 Naturia Guardian DTNPR	.12	.25
HAC1EN096 Naturia Vein C	.07	.15
HAC1EN096 Naturia Vein DTNPR	.12	.25
HAC1EN097 Naturia Antjaw C	.07	.15
HAC1EN097 Naturia Antjaw DTNPR	.12	.25
HAC1EN098 Naturia Spiderfang C	.07	.15
HAC1EN098 Naturia Spiderfang DTNPR	.12	.25
HAC1EN099 Naturia Rosewhip C	.07	.15
HAC1EN099 Naturia Rosewhip DTNPR	.12	.25
HAC1EN100 Naturia Cosmobeet C	.07	.15
HAC1EN100 Naturia Cosmobeet DTNPR	.12	.25
HAC1EN101 Naturia Dragonfly C	.07	.15
HAC1EN101 Naturia Dragonfly DTNPR	.12	.25
HAC1EN102 Naturia Sunflower C	.07	.15
HAC1EN102 Naturia Sunflower DTNPR	.12	.25
HAC1EN103 Naturia Cliff C	.07	.15
HAC1EN103 Naturia Cliff DTNPR	.12	.25
HAC1EN104 Naturia Tulip C	.07	.15
HAC1EN104 Naturia Tulip DTNPR	.12	.25
HAC1EN105 Naturia Horneedle C	.07	.15
HAC1EN105 Naturia Horneedle DTNPR	.12	.25
HAC1EN106 Naturia Fruitfly C	.07	.15
HAC1EN106 Naturia Fruitfly DTNPR	.12	.25
HAC1EN107 Naturia Hydrangea C	.07	.15
HAC1EN107 Naturia Hydrangea DTNPR	.12	.25
HAC1EN108 Naturia Butterfly C	.07	.15
HAC1EN108 Naturia Butterfly DTNPR	.12	.25
HAC1EN109 Naturia Ladybug C	.07	.15
HAC1EN109 Naturia Ladybug DTNPR	.12	.25
HAC1EN110 Naturia Strawberry C	.07	.15
HAC1EN110 Naturia Strawberry DTNPR	.12	.25
HAC1EN111 Naturia Bamboo Shoot DTUPR	.12	.25
HAC1EN112 Naturia Stinkbug C	.07	.15
HAC1EN112 Naturia Stinkbug DTNPR	.12	.25
HAC1EN113 Naturia Mantis C	.07	.15
HAC1EN113 Naturia Mantis DTNPR	.12	.25
HAC1EN114 Naturia Ragweed C	.07	.15
HAC1EN114 Naturia Ragweed DTNPR	.12	.25
HAC1EN115 Naturia White Oak C	.07	.15
HAC1EN115 Naturia White Oak DTNPR	.12	.25
HAC1EN116 Naturia Cherries DTUPR	.12	.25
HAC1EN117 Naturia Pumpkin C	.07	.15
HAC1EN117 Naturia Pumpkin DTNPR	.12	.25
HAC1EN118 Naturia Pineapple C	.07	.15
HAC1EN118 Naturia Pineapple DTNPR	.12	.25
HAC1EN119 Naturia Exterio DTUPR	.12	.25
HAC1EN120 Naturia Beast DTUPR	.12	.25
HAC1EN121 Naturia Leodrake C	.07	.15
HAC1EN121 Naturia Leodrake DTNPR	.12	.25
HAC1EN122 Naturia Barkion DTUPR	.12	.25
HAC1EN123 Naturia Landoise C	.07	.15
HAC1EN123 Naturia Landoise DTNPR	.12	.25
HAC1EN124 Fabled Lurrie C	.07	.15
HAC1EN124 Fabled Lurrie DTNPR	.12	.25
HAC1EN125 Fabled Grimro DTUPR	.12	.25
HAC1EN126 Fabled Gallabas C	.07	.15
HAC1EN126 Fabled Gallabas DTNPR	.12	.25
HAC1EN127 Fabled Kushano C	.07	.15
HAC1EN127 Fabled Kushano DTNPR	.12	.25
HAC1EN128 Fabled Urustos C	.07	.15
HAC1EN128 Fabled Urustos DTNPR	.12	.25
HAC1EN129 Fabled Krus C	.07	.15
HAC1EN129 Fabled Krus DTNPR	.12	.25
HAC1EN130 Fabled Topi C	.07	.15
HAC1EN130 Fabled Topi DTNPR	.12	.25
HAC1EN131 Fabled Soulkius C	.07	.15
HAC1EN131 Fabled Soulkius DTNPR	.12	.25
HAC1EN132 Fabled Miztoji C	.07	.15
HAC1EN132 Fabled Miztoji DTNPR	.12	.25
HAC1EN133 Fabled Dyf C	.07	.15
HAC1EN133 Fabled Dyf DTNPR	.12	.25
HAC1EN134 Fabled Ashenveil C	.07	.15
HAC1EN134 Fabled Ashenveil DTNPR	.12	.25
HAC1EN135 Fabled Oltro C	.07	.15
HAC1EN135 Fabled Oltro DTNPR	.12	.25
HAC1EN136 The Fabled Chawa C	.07	.15
HAC1EN136 The Fabled Chawa DTNPR	.12	.25
HAC1EN137 The Fabled Catsith C	.07	.15
HAC1EN137 The Fabled Catsith DTNPR	.12	.25
HAC1EN138 The Fabled Cerburrel C	.07	.15
HAC1EN138 The Fabled Cerburrel DTNPR	.12	.25
HAC1EN139 The Fabled Ganashia C	.07	.15
HAC1EN139 The Fabled Ganashia DTNPR	.12	.25
HAC1EN140 The Fabled Nozoochee C	.07	.15
HAC1EN140 The Fabled Nozoochee DTNPR	.12	.25
HAC1EN141 The Fabled Peggulsus C	.07	.15
HAC1EN141 The Fabled Peggulsus DTNPR	.12	.25
HAC1EN142 The Fabled Kokkator C	.07	.15
HAC1EN142 The Fabled Kokkator DTNPR	.12	.25
HAC1EN143 Fabled Dianaira C	.07	.15
HAC1EN143 Fabled Dianaira DTNPR	.12	.25
HAC1EN144 Fabled Valkyrus C	.07	.15
HAC1EN144 Fabled Valkyrus DTNPR	.12	.25
HAC1EN145 Fabled Leviathan C	.07	.15
HAC1EN145 Fabled Leviathan DTNPR	.12	.25
HAC1EN146 Fabled Ragin DTUPR	.12	.25
HAC1EN147 The Fabled Unicore C	.07	.15
HAC1EN147 The Fabled Unicore DTNPR	.12	.25
HAC1EN148 The Fabled Kudabbi C	.07	.15
HAC1EN148 The Fabled Kudabbi DTNPR	.12	.25
HAC1EN149 Dragunity Dux DTUPR	.12	.25
HAC1EN150 Dragunity Legionnaire C	.07	.15
HAC1EN150 Dragunity Legionnaire DTNPR	.12	.25
HAC1EN151 Dragunity Tribus DTNPR	.12	.25
HAC1EN151 Dragunity Tribus C	.07	.15
HAC1EN152 Dragunity Darkspear C	.07	.15
HAC1EN152 Dragunity Darkspear DTNPR	.12	.25
HAC1EN153 Dragunity Phalanx DTNPR	.12	.25
HAC1EN154 Dragunity Militum C	.07	.15
HAC1EN154 Dragunity Militum DTNPR	.12	.25
HAC1EN155 Dragunity Primus Pilus C	.07	.15
HAC1EN155 Dragunity Primus Pilus DTNPR	.12	.25
HAC1EN156 Dragunity Brandistock C	.07	.15
HAC1EN156 Dragunity Brandistock DTNPR	.12	.25
HAC1EN157 Dragunity Javelin C	.07	.15
HAC1EN157 Dragunity Javelin DTNPR	.12	.25
HAC1EN158 Dragunity Corsesca C	.07	.15
HAC1EN158 Dragunity Corsesca DTNPR	.12	.25
HAC1EN159 Dragunity Partisan C	.07	.15
HAC1EN159 Dragunity Partisan DTNPR	.12	.25
HAC1EN160 Dragunity Pilum C	.07	.15
HAC1EN160 Dragunity Pilum DTNPR	.12	.25
HAC1EN161 Dragunity Angusticlavii C	.07	.15
HAC1EN161 Dragunity Angusticlavii DTNPR	.12	.25
HAC1EN162 Dragunity Knight - Gae Bulg DTUPR	.12	.25
HAC1EN163 Dragunity Knight - Gae Dearg C	.07	.15
HAC1EN163 Dragunity Knight - Gae Dearg DTNPR	.12	.25
HAC1EN164 Dragunity Knight - Trident C	.07	.15
HAC1EN164 Dragunity Knight - Trident DTNPR	.12	.25
HAC1EN165 Dragunity Knight - Barcha DTUPR	.12	.25
HAC1EN166 Mist Wurm DTUPR	.12	.25
HAC1EN167 Wrath of Neos C	.07	.15
HAC1EN167 Wrath of Neos DTNPR	.12	.25
HAC1EN168 Detonate C	.07	.15
HAC1EN168 Detonate DTNPR	.12	.25
HAC1EN169 Berserker Crush C	.07	.15
HAC1EN169 Berserker Crush DTNPR	.12	.25
HAC1EN170 Evolution Burst C	.07	.15
HAC1EN170 Evolution Burst DTNPR	.12	.25
HAC1EN171 Swallow's Nest C	.07	.15
HAC1EN171 Swallow's Nest DTNPR	.12	.25

2022 Yu-Gi-Oh Hidden Arsenal Chapter 1 Limited Edition

HAC1EN172 Dragunity Guisarme SCR	.30	.75
HAC1EN173 Armed Dragon, the Armored Dragon SCR	.60	1.25
HAC1EN174 Pile Armed Dragon SCR	1.50	3.00
HAC1EN175 Deep Sea Repetiteur SCR	.30	.60
HAC1EN176 Armory Arm SCR	2.00	4.00
HAC1EN177 Power Tool Dragon SCR	1.50	3.00
HAC1EN178 Formula Synchron SCR	.75	1.50

2022 Yu-Gi-Oh Legendary Duelists Duels from the Deep

LED9EN000 Number 101: Silent Honor ARK GR	20.00	40.00
LED9EN001 Abyss Shark UR	3.00	6.00
LED9EN002 Crystal Shark SR	.30	.60
LED9EN003 N.As.H. Knight SR	.15	.30
LED9EN004 CXyz N.As.Ch. Knight SR	.15	.30
LED9EN005 Barian's Chaos Draw SR	.12	.25
LED9EN006 Seventh Ascension UR	1.25	2.50
LED9EN007 Seventh Eternity R	.15	.30
LED9EN008 Silent Angler C	.10	.20
LED9EN009 Xyz Remora C	.10	.20
LED9EN010 Number C101: Silent Honor DARK C	.10	.20
LED9EN011 Bahamut Shark R	.15	.30
LED9EN012 Full Armored Black Ray Lancer C	.10	.20
LED9EN013 Number 71: Rebarian Shark C	.10	.20
LED9EN014 Rank-Up-Magic - The Seventh One C	.10	.20
LED9EN015 Rank-Up-Magic Quick Chaos C	.10	.20
LED9EN016 Mega Fortress Whale UR	.30	.60
LED9EN017 Ocean Dragon Lord - Kairyu-Shin UR	.75	1.50
LED9EN018 Doom Kraken SR	.30	.75
LED9EN019 Electric Jellyfish SR	.50	1.00
LED9EN020 Fish Sonar UR	7.50	15.00
LED9EN021 Sea Stealth II R	.15	.30
LED9EN022 Kairyu-Shin's Dark Reef R	.15	.30
LED9EN023 The Legendary Fisherman C	.10	.20
LED9EN024 The Legendary Fisherman II C	.10	.20
LED9EN025 The Legendary Fisherman III C	.10	.20
LED9EN026 Citadel Whale C	.10	.20
LED9EN027 Rage of Kairyu-Shin C	.10	.20
LED9EN028 Fury of Kairyu-Shin C	.10	.20
LED9EN029 Torrential Tribute C	.10	.20
LED9EN030 Sea Stealth Attack C	.10	.20
LED9EN031 Marincess Springirl SR	2.00	4.00
LED9EN032 Marincess Sleepy Maiden R	.15	.30
LED9EN033 Marincess Coral Triangle UR	.75	1.50
LED9EN034 Marincess Aqua Argonaut UR	.75	1.50
LED9EN035 Marincess Dive UR	7.50	15.00
LED9EN036 Marincess Circulation R	.15	.30
LED9EN037 Marincess Bubble Ring R	.15	.30
LED9EN038 Marincess Sea Horse C	.10	.20
LED9EN039 Marincess Pascalus C	.10	.20
LED9EN040 Marincess Sea Angel C	.10	.20
LED9EN041 Marincess Coral Anemone R	.15	.30
LED9EN042 Marincess Crystal Heart C	.10	.20
LED9EN043 Marincess Wonder Heart C	.10	.20
LED9EN044 Marincess Battle Ocean C	.10	.20
LED9EN045 Marincess Wave C	.10	.20
LED9EN046 Frostosaurus C	.10	.20
LED9EN047 Levia-Dragon - Daedalus R	.15	.30
LED9EN048 Cyber Shark C	.10	.20
LED9EN049 Double Fin Shark R	.15	.30
LED9EN050 Saber Shark C	.10	.20
LED9EN051 Marincess Blue Tang C	.10	.20
LED9EN052 Buzzsaw Shark C	.10	.20
LED9EN053 Number 106: Giant Hand SR	.30	.75
LED9EN054 Marincess Marbled Rock C	.10	.20
LED9EN055 Lemuria, the Forgotten City C	.10	.20
LED9EN056 Forbidden Droplet UR	30.00	75.00

2022 Yu-Gi-Oh Magnificent Mavens 1st Edition

MAMAEN001 Surgical Striker - H.A.M.P. UR	.20	.40
MAMAEN002 Aileron UR	.15	.30
MAMAEN003 Sky Striker Mobilize - Linkage! UR	4.00	8.00
MAMAEN004 Sky Striker Ace - Raye UR	.15	.30
MAMAEN005 Sky Striker Ace - Kagari UR	.25	.50
MAMAEN006 Sky Striker Ace - Shizuku UR	1.00	2.00
MAMAEN007 Sky Striker Ace - Hayate UR	.60	1.25
MAMAEN008 Sky Striker Ace - Zeke UR	.15	.30
MAMAEN009 Sky Striker Mobilize - Engage! UR	.50	1.00
MAMAEN010 Sky Striker Mecha - Widow Anchor UR	1.00	2.00
MAMAEN011 Sky Striker Mecha - Shark Cannon UR	.15	.30
MAMAEN012 Sky Striker Mecha Modules - Multirole UR	.75	1.50
MAMAEN013 Sky Striker Ace Token UR	.20	.40
MAMAEN014 Yuki-Onna, the Icicle Mayakashi UR	.15	.30
MAMAEN015 Ghost Meets Girl... UR	.15	.30
MAMAEN016 Dakki, the Graceful Mayakashi UR	.15	.30
MAMAEN017 Hajun, the Winged Mayakashi UR	.15	.30
MAMAEN018 Gashadokuro, the Skeletal Mayakashi UR	.15	.30
MAMAEN019 Mayakashi Return UR	.15	.30
MAMAEN020 Witchcrafter Vice-Madame UR	.20	.40
MAMAEN021 Witchcrafter Confusion Confession UR	.15	.30
MAMAEN022 Witchcrafter Haine UR	.15	.30
MAMAEN023 Witchcrafter Genni UR	.15	.30
MAMAEN024 Witchcrafter Creation UR	.15	.30
MAMAEN025 Keldo the Sacred Protector UR	.30	.75
MAMAEN026 Mudora the Sword Oracle UR	.30	.75
MAMAEN027 Kelbek the Ancient Vanguard UR	.50	1.00
MAMAEN028 Agido the Ancient Sentinel UR	.50	1.00
MAMAEN029 Gravekeeper's Trap PH SCR	30.00	60.00
MAMAEN029 Gravekeeper's Trap PH UR	30.00	75.00
MAMAEN029 Gravekeeper's Trap UR	.15	.30
MAMAEN030 Exchange of Despair and Hope UR	.15	.30
MAMAEN031 Blast Held by Destiny UR	.15	.30
MAMAEN032 Exchange of the Spirit UR	.20	.40
MAMAEN033 The Iris Swordsoul UR	.30	.60
MAMAEN034 Swordsoul of Mo Ye UR	4.00	8.00
MAMAEN035 Swordsoul of Taia UR	.30	.75
MAMAEN036 Swordsoul Strategist Longyuan UR	.50	1.00
MAMAEN037 Swordsoul Auspice Chunjun UR	.15	.30
MAMAEN038 Swordsoul Grandmaster - Chixiao UR	1.75	3.50
MAMAEN039 Supreme Sovereign - Chengying UR	.60	1.25
MAMAEN040 Sinister Sovereign - Qixing Longyuan UR	.15	.30
MAMAEN041 Swordsoul Emergence UR	3.00	6.00
MAMAEN042 Swordsoul Sacred Summit UR	.15	.30
MAMAEN043 Swordsoul Assessment UR	.15	.30
MAMAEN044 Swordsoul Blackout UR	.25	.50
MAMAEN045 Swordsoul Strife UR	.15	.30
MAMAEN046 Yata-Garasu UR	.25	.50
MAMAEN047 Black Luster Soldier... UR	.50	1.00
MAMAEN048 Vampire's Curse UR	.15	.30
MAMAEN049 Doom Dozer UR	.15	.30
MAMAEN050 Mezuki UR	.40	.80
MAMAEN051 Chaos Hunter UR	.50	1.00
MAMAEN052 Beautunaful Princess UR	.25	.50
MAMAEN053 D/D Savant Kepler UR	.15	.30
MAMAEN054 Shiranui Solitaire UR	.20	.40
MAMAEN055 Bururu @Ignister UR	.15	.30
MAMAEN056 Blue-Eyes Abyss Dragon UR	.50	1.00
MAMAEN057 Galaxy-Eyes Afterglow Dragon UR	.50	1.00
MAMAEN058 Rilliona, the Magistus of Verre UR	.15	.30
MAMAEN059 Incredible Ecclesia, the Virtuous UR	1.00	2.00
MAMAEN060 Therion Bull"" Ain"" UR	.15	.30
MAMAEN061 Therion Duke"" Yul"" UR	.15	.30
MAMAEN062 Dragonecro Nethersoul Dragon UR	.25	.50
MAMAEN063 Elder Entity N'tss UR	.75	1.50
MAMAEN064 Millennium-Eyes Restrict PH UR	75.00	150.00
MAMAEN064 Millennium-Eyes Restrict PH SCR	30.00	75.00
MAMAEN064 Millennium-Eyes Restrict UR	.50	1.00
MAMAEN065 Predaplant Ambulomelides UR	.15	.30
MAMAEN066 Cat Shark UR	.15	.30
MAMAEN067 Number 93: Utopia Kaiser UR	.15	.30
MAMAEN068 Toadally Awesome UR	1.25	2.50
MAMAEN069 Onibimaru Soul Sweeper UR	.15	.30
MAMAEN070 Knightmare Cerberus UR	.30	.60
MAMAEN071 Knightmare Phoenix UR	.30	.75
MAMAEN072 Borrelsword Dragon UR	.60	1.25
MAMAEN073 Black Luster Soldier... UR	2.50	5.00
MAMAEN073 Black Luster Soldier... PH SCR	40.00	80.00
MAMAEN073 Black Luster Soldier... PH UR	75.00	150.00
MAMAEN074 Traptrix Sera UR	.50	1.00
MAMAEN075 Apollousa, Bow of the Goddess UR	4.00	8.00
MAMAEN076 Harpie's Feather Duster UR	2.00	4.00
MAMAEN077 Scapegoat UR	.25	.50
MAMAEN078 Change of Heart PH SCR	75.00	150.00
MAMAEN078 Change of Heart PH UR	125.00	250.00
MAMAEN078 Change of Heart UR	1.25	2.50
MAMAEN079 A Legendary Ocean UR	.15	.30
MAMAEN080 Instant Fusion UR	.30	.75
MAMAEN081 A Hero Lives UR	.50	1.00
MAMAEN082 Dark Calling UR	.15	.30
MAMAEN083 Secret Village of the Spellcasters UR	.60	1.25
MAMAEN084 Foolish Return UR	.15	.30
MAMAEN085 Pendulum Call UR	.30	.60
MAMAEN086 Magician's Restage UR	.15	.30
MAMAEN087 Cyber Revsystem UR	.30	.60
MAMAEN088 Dragonmaid Changeover UR	.15	.30
MAMAEN089 Lightning Storm PH UR	75.00	150.00
MAMAEN089 Lightning Storm PH SCR	30.00	75.00
MAMAEN089 Lightning Storm UR	6.00	12.00
MAMAEN090 Triple Tactics Talent PH SCR	75.00	150.00
MAMAEN090 Triple Tactics Talent PH UR	100.00	200.00
MAMAEN090 Triple Tactics Talent UR	10.00	20.00
MAMAEN091 Dracoback, the Rideable Dragon UR	.15	.30
MAMAEN092 Anti-Spell Fragrance UR	.50	1.00
MAMAEN093 Metal Reflect Slime UR	.15	.30
MAMAEN094 Skill Drain UR	1.50	3.00
MAMAEN095 Non-Fusion Area UR	.15	.30
MAMAEN096 Light-Imprisoning Mirror UR	.30	.60
MAMAEN097 Shadow-Imprisoning Mirror UR	.30	.60
MAMAEN098 Gozen Match UR	1.50	3.00
MAMAEN099 Evenly Matched UR	4.00	8.00
MAMAEN100 Infinite Impermanence UR	7.50	15.00
MAMAEN101 Ice Dragon's Prison UR	.60	1.25
MAMAEN102 Dark Soul Token UR	.15	.30
MAMAEN103 G Golem Token UR	.15	.30
MAMAEN104 Blue-Eyes White Dragon PH SCR	125.00	250.00
MAMAEN104 Blue-Eyes White Dragon PH UR	125.00	250.00
MAMAEN105 Red-Eyes Black Dragon PH SCR	60.00	125.00
MAMAEN105 Red-Eyes Black Dragon PH UR	125.00	250.00
MAMAEN106 Elemental HERO Neos PH SCR	75.00	150.00
MAMAEN106 Elemental HERO Neos PH UR	100.00	200.00
MAMAEN107 Dark Magician Girl PH SCR	300.00	750.00
MAMAEN107 Dark Magician Girl PH UR	300.00	750.00
MAMAEN108 Reinforcement of the Army PH SCR	40.00	80.00
MAMAEN108 Reinforcement of the Army PH UR	100.00	200.00
MAMAEN109 Necrovalley PH SCR	75.00	150.00
MAMAEN109 Necrovalley PH UR	125.00	250.00
MAMAEN110 Gold Sarcophagus PH SCR	60.00	125.00
MAMAEN110 Gold Sarcophagus PH UR	125.00	250.00
MAMAEN111 The Seal of Orichalcos PH SCR	40.00	80.00
MAMAEN111 The Seal of Orichalcos PH UR	125.00	250.00
MAMAEN112 Toon Kingdom PH SCR	25.00	50.00
MAMAEN112 Toon Kingdom PH UR	75.00	150.00
MAMAEN113 The True Name PH SCR	25.00	50.00
MAMAEN113 The True Name PH UR	60.00	125.00
MAMAEN114 Crystal Bond PH SCR	25.00	50.00
MAMAEN114 Crystal Bond PH UR	60.00	125.00
MAMAEN115 Mirror Force PH SCR	50.00	100.00
MAMAEN115 Mirror Force PH UR	60.00	125.00

2022 Yu-Gi-Oh OTS Tournament Pack 18

OP18EN001 Dogmatika Ecclesia, the Virtuous UTR	25.00	50.00
OP18EN002 Divine Arsenal AA-ZEUS - Sky Thunder UTR	30.00	60.00
OP18EN003 Fusion Destiny UTR	30.00	60.00
OP18EN004 Destiny HERO - Dasher SR	.50	1.00
OP18EN005 Babycerasaurus SR	.75	1.50
OP18EN006 Kagemucha Knight SR	.25	.50
OP18EN007 Contact C SR	.75	1.50
OP18EN008 Token Collector SR	2.00	4.00
OP18EN009 Kwagar Hercules SR	.25	.50
OP18EN010 The Phantom Knights of Break Sword SR	.25	.50
OP18EN011 Inzektor Picofalena SR	.20	.40
OP18EN012 Monk of the Tenyi SR	1.00	2.00
OP18EN013 Manju of the Ten Thousand Hands C	.30	.60
OP18EN014 Tanngnjostr of the Nordic Beasts C	.20	.40
OP18EN015 Dverg of the Nordic Alfar C	.20	.40
OP18EN016 The Phantom Knights of Silent Boots C	.20	.40
OP18EN017 Destiny HERO - Celestial C	.20	.40
OP18EN018 Vampire Familiar C	.25	.50
OP18EN019 Vampire Retainer C	.20	.40
OP18EN020 Impcantation Talismandra C	.30	.75
OP18EN021 Impcantation Penciplume C	.12	.25
OP18EN022 Ghostrick Angel of Mischief C	.50	1.00
OP18EN023 Gullveig of the Nordic Ascendant C	.15	.30
OP18EN024 Dark Magical Circle C	.25	.50
OP18EN025 Ghostrick Break C	.15	.30
OP18EN026 Ogdoadic Token SR	.50	1.00

2022 Yu-Gi-Oh OTS Tournament Pack 19

OP19EN001 Fallen of Albaz UTR 30.00 75.00
OP19EN002 Water Enchantress of the Temple UTR30.00 60.00
OP19EN003 Skill Drain UTR 40.00 80.00
OP19EN004 Caius the Shadow Monarch SR .75 1.50
OP19EN005 Trap Eater SR .30 .60
OP19EN006 Pain Painter SR .30 .60
OP19EN007 D/D Berfomet SR .25 .50
OP19EN008 Performapal Odd-Eyes Dissolver SR .25 .50
OP19EN009 D/D/D Flame King Genghis SR .30 .75
OP19EN010 D/D/D Oracle King d'Arc SR .60 1.25
OP19EN011 Forbidden Chalice SR 2.00 4.00
OP19EN012 Hercules Beetle SR .50 1.00
OP19EN013 Kuwagata Alpha SR .50 1.00
OP19EN014 Swamp Battleguard C .10 .20
OP19EN015 Lava Battleguard C .20 .40
OP19EN016 Night Assailant C .20 .40
OP19EN017 Gorz the Emissary of Darkness C .30 .75
OP19EN018 Lonefire Blossom C .30 .60
OP19EN019 Heroic Challenger - Thousand Blades C .15 .30
OP19EN020 Wisdom-Eye Magician C .30 .75
OP19EN021 Performapal Skullcrobat Joker C .20 .40
OP19EN022 Fairy Tail - Snow C 1.00 2.00
OP19EN023 Destrudo the Lost Dragon's Frisson C .25 .50
OP19EN024 Heroic Champion - Excalibur C .30 .75
OP19EN025 Heroic Champion - Gandiva C .20 .40
OP19EN026 Symph Amplifire C .12 .25
OP19EN027 Red Reboot C .20 .40
OP19EN028 Mask Token SR .30 .60
OP19EN029 Slime Token SR .75 1.50

2022 Yu-Gi-Oh OTS Tournament Pack 20

OP20EN001 Ghost Reaper & Winter Cherries UTR20.00 40.00
OP20EN002 Sky Striker Ace - Raye UTR 25.00 50.00
OP20EN003 Aluber the Jester of Despia UTR 15.00 30.00
OP20EN004 Neko Mane King SR .30 .75
OP20EN005 Herald of Orange Light SR 1.25 2.50
OP20EN006 Nimble Beaver SR .75 1.50
OP20EN007 Anchamoufrite SR .30 .60
OP20EN008 Gadget Gamer SR .15 .30
OP20EN009 Morphtronic Earfon SR .20 .40
OP20EN010 Ninja Grandmaster Saizo SR .30 .75
OP20EN011 Ninjitsu Art Notebook SR .20 .40
OP20EN012 Grave of the Super Ancient Organism SR 2.00 4.00
OP20EN013 Elephant Statue of Disaster C .07 .15
OP20EN014 King of the Swamp C .60 1.25
OP20EN015 Naturia Marron C .12 .25
OP20EN016 Ninja Grandmaster Hanzo C .12 .25
OP20EN017 Blackwing - Tornado the Reverse Wind C .07 .15
OP20EN018 Blackwing Armed Wing C .20 .40
OP20EN019 Number 22: Zombiestein C .20 .40
OP20EN020 Abyss Dweller C .50 1.00
OP20EN021 Hidden Village of Ninjitsu Arts C .07 .15
OP20EN022 Amazoness Shamanism C .15 .30
OP20EN023 Ninjitsu Art of Duplication C .25 .50
OP20EN024 And the Band Played On C .15 .30
OP20EN025 Naturia Sacred Tree C .12 .25
OP20EN026 Mimesis Elephant C .07 .15
OP20EN027 Option Token SR .15 .30

2022 Yu-Gi-Oh Power of the Elements 1st Edition

POTEEN000 Ghoti of the Deep Beyond SCR 2.00 4.00
POTEEN001 Elemental HERO Spirit of Neos SR .30 .60
POTEEN002 Cross Keeper C .07 .15
POTEEN003 Spright Blue SCR 17.50 35.00
POTEEN004 Spright Jet SR .30 .75
POTEEN005 Spright Pixies C .07 .15
POTEEN006 Spright Red C .07 .15
POTEEN007 Spright Carrot C .07 .15
POTEEN008 Therion Empress" Alasia" SR .15 .30
POTEEN009 Therion Irregular UR .50 1.00
POTEEN010 Icejade Creation Aegirocassis C .07 .15
POTEEN011 Albaz the Ashen SR .15 .30
POTEEN012 Tearlaments Merrli C .07 .15
POTEEN013 Tearlaments Havnis C .07 .15
POTEEN014 Tearlaments Scheiren SR .30 .75
POTEEN015 Tearlaments Reinoheart UR 2.50 5.00
POTEEN016 Vernusylph of the Flourishing Hills UR2.00 4.00
POTEEN017 Vernusylph of the Awakening Forests SR .60 1.25
POTEEN018 Vernusylph of the Flowering Fields C.07 .15
POTEEN019 Vernusylph of the Thawing Mountains C .07 .15
POTEEN020 Gem-Knight Quartz SR .15 .30
POTEEN021 Brilliant Rose C .07 .15
POTEEN022 Melffy Wally C .07 .15
POTEEN023 Melffy Pinny C .07 .15
POTEEN024 Scar of the Vendread C .07 .15
POTEEN025 Exosister Martha SCR 4.00 8.00
POTEEN025 Exosister Martha SLR 75.00 150.00
POTEEN026 Gunkan Suship Shari Red C .07 .15
POTEEN027 Rikka Princess C .07 .15
POTEEN028 Mathmech Circular SR .50 1.00
POTEEN029 Krawler Soma C .07 .15
POTEEN030 Mokey Mokey Adrift C .07 .15
POTEEN031 Kurikara Divincarnate SCR 30.00 75.00
POTEEN031 Kurikara Divincarnate SLR 125.00 250.00
POTEEN032 Aussa the Earth Channeler SLR 40.00 80.00
POTEEN032 Aussa the Earth Channeler UR .20 .40
POTEEN033 Grandtusk Dragon SR .15 .30
POTEEN034 Eka the Flame Buddy SR .15 .30
POTEEN035 Propa Gandake C .07 .15
POTEEN036 Cartorhyn the Hidden Gem of the Seafront C .07 .15
POTEEN037 Emperor Tanuki's Critter Count SR .15 .30
POTEEN038 Nightmell the Dark Bonder C .07 .15
POTEEN039 Hydralander Orbit C .07 .15
POTEEN040 Vendread Scavenger SR .15 .30
POTEEN041 Elemental HERO Shining Neos Wingman UR .75 1.50
POTEEN042 Tearlaments Kitkallos UR 1.00 2.00
POTEEN043 Tearlaments Kaleido-Heart SCR 2.00 4.00
POTEEN044 Gem-Knight Lady Rose Diamond SR.15 .30
POTEEN045 Merry Melffys C .07 .15
POTEEN046 P.U.N.K. JAM Dragon Drive SR .25 .50
POTEEN047 Gigantic Spright UR 4.00 8.00
POTEEN048 Ashura King SCR .75 1.50
POTEEN049 Spright Elf UR 1.25 2.50
POTEEN050 Scareclaw Light-Heart UR 1.00 2.00
POTEEN051 EN - Engage Neo Space SR .20 .40
POTEEN052 Instant Contact SCR 2.00 4.00
POTEEN053 EN Wave SR .15 .30
POTEEN054 Over Fusion C .07 .15
POTEEN055 Spright Starter UR 4.00 8.00
POTEEN056 Spright Gamma Burst C .07 .15
POTEEN057 Spright Smashers C .07 .15
POTEEN058 Branded in Central Dogmatika C .07 .15
POTEEN059 Scareclaw Straddle SR .15 .30
POTEEN060 Primeval Planet Perlereino SCR 12.50 25.00
POTEEN061 Vernusylph Corolla SR .15 .30
POTEEN062 Scatter Fusion SR .15 .30
POTEEN063 Melffy Staring Contest SR .15 .30
POTEEN064 Ravenous Vendread C .07 .15
POTEEN065 P.U.N.K. JAM Extreme Session SR .30 .60
POTEEN066 Rikka Konkon SR .20 .40
POTEEN067 Ultimate Slayer SCR 10.00 20.00
POTEEN067 Ultimate Slayer SLR 75.00 150.00
POTEEN068 Digit Jamming C .07 .15
POTEEN069 Favorite Contact UR .60 1.25
POTEEN070 Branded Expulsion C .07 .15
POTEEN071 Tearlaments Metanoise C .07 .15
POTEEN072 Tearlaments Sulliek C .07 .15
POTEEN073 Tearlaments Cryme C .07 .15
POTEEN074 Vernusylph and the Changing Season C .07 .15
POTEEN075 Vernusylph and the Flower Buds C .07 .15
POTEEN076 Exosister Returnia SR .25 .50
POTEEN077 Amaze Attraction Thrill Train C .07 .15
POTEEN078 Terrors of the Overroot C .07 .15
POTEEN079 Draco-Utopian Aura SCR .75 1.50
POTEEN080 Double Dust Tornado Twins C .07 .15
POTEEN081 Vanguard of the Underground Emperor C .07 .15
POTEEN082 Garura, Wings of Resonant Life UR10.00 20.00
POTEEN083 Pitknight Earlie C .07 .15
POTEEN084 Moray of Avarice UR .30 .75
POTEEN085 Mimesis Elephant C .07 .15
POTEEN086 Paces, Light of the Ghoti UR .50 1.00
POTEEN087 Shif, Fairy of the Ghoti SR .25 .50
POTEEN088 Eanoc, Sentry of the Ghoti C .07 .15
POTEEN089 Askaan, the Bicorned Ghoti C .07 .15
POTEEN090 The Most Distant, Deepest Depths C.07 .15
POTEEN091 Ghoti Chain C .07 .15
POTEEN092 Loris, Lady of Lament SR .15 .30
POTEEN093 Morphtronic Telefon C .07 .15
POTEEN094 Gadget Gamer C .07 .15
POTEEN095 Morphtronic Scannen C .07 .15
POTEEN096 Morphtronic Earfon C .07 .15
POTEEN097 Power Tool Braver Dragon SR .20 .40
POTEEN098 Morphtronic Converter C .07 .15
POTEEN099 Life Extreme C .07 .15
POTEEN100 Destiny HERO - Destroyer Phoenix Enforcer SLR 175.00 350.00

2022 Yu-Gi-Oh Speed Duel GX Duel Academy Box 1st Edition

SGX1ENA01 Elemental HERO Avian C .15 .30
SGX1ENA02 Elemental HERO Burstinatrix C .15 .30
SGX1ENA03 Elemental HERO Clayman C .15 .30
SGX1ENA04 Elemental HERO Sparkman C .15 .30
SGX1ENA05 Goddess with the Third Eye C .75 1.50
SGX1ENA06 Winged Kuriboh SCR .75 1.50
SGX1ENA06 Winged Kuriboh C .10 .20
SGX1ENA07 Wroughtweiler C .10 .20
SGX1ENA08 Elemental HERO Bubbleman C .15 .30
SGX1ENA09 Elemental HERO Bladedge C .15 .30
SGX1ENA10 Elemental HERO Wildheart C .15 .30
SGX1ENA11 Elemental HERO Necroshade C .15 .30
SGX1ENA12 Polymerization SCR 3.00 6.00
SGX1ENA12 Polymerization C .25 .50
SGX1ENA13 Fusion Sage C .10 .20
SGX1ENA14 Reinforcement of the Army C .12 .25
SGX1ENA15 Skyscraper C .12 .25
SGX1ENA16 Fusion Recovery C .10 .20
SGX1ENA17 R - Righteous Justice C .10 .20
SGX1ENA18 Negate Attack C .10 .20
SGX1ENA19 A Hero Emerges C .10 .20
SGX1ENA20 Hero Signal C .10 .20
SGX1ENA21 Elemental HERO Flame Wingman C .15 .30
SGX1ENA21 Elemental HERO Flame Wingman SCR1.50 3.00
SGX1ENA22 Elemental HERO Thunder Giant C .15 .30
SGX1ENA23 Elemental HERO Rampart Blaster C .15 .30
SGX1ENA24 Elemental HERO Steam Healer C .15 .30
SGX1ENA25 Elemental HERO Darkbright C .15 .30
SGX1ENA26 Elemental HERO Plasma Vice C .15 .30
SGX1ENB01 Destiny HERO - Plasma C .10 .20
SGX1ENB01 Destiny HERO - Plasma SCR 1.25 2.50
SGX1ENB02 Destiny HERO - Doom Lord C .10 .20
SGX1ENB03 Destiny HERO - Diamond Dude C .10 .20
SGX1ENB04 Destiny HERO - Blade Master C .10 .20
SGX1ENB05 Destiny HERO - Dasher C .50 1.00
SGX1ENB05 Destiny HERO - Dasher SCR 2.50 5.00
SGX1ENB06 Destiny HERO - Fear Monger C .10 .20
SGX1ENB07 Destiny HERO - Dogma C .10 .20
SGX1ENB08 Destiny HERO - Malicious C .25 .50
SGX1ENB09 Destiny HERO - Dark Angel C .15 .30
SGX1ENB10 Polymerization C .25 .50
SGX1ENB11 Reinforcement of the Army C .12 .25
SGX1ENB12 Fusion Sword Murasame Blade C .10 .20
SGX1ENB13 Dark City C .10 .20
SGX1ENB14 D - Spirit C .10 .20
SGX1ENB15 Over Destiny C .10 .20
SGX1ENB16 Night Beam C .20 .40
SGX1ENB17 Destiny Signal C .10 .20
SGX1ENB18 D - Chain C .10 .20
SGX1ENB19 D - Counter C .10 .20
SGX1ENB20 Destiny End Dragoon C .10 .20
SGX1ENB21 Destiny HERO - Dangerous C .15 .30
SGX1ENC01 Ojama Yellow C .12 .25
SGX1ENC02 Ojama Green C .12 .25
SGX1ENC03 Ojama Black C .12 .25
SGX1ENC04 V-Tiger Jet C .10 .20
SGX1ENC05 Chiron the Mage C .10 .20
SGX1ENC06 Armed Dragon LV3 C .10 .20
SGX1ENC07 Armed Dragon LV5 C .10 .20
SGX1ENC08 Armed Dragon LV7 SCR .60 1.25
SGX1ENC08 Armed Dragon LV7 C .10 .20
SGX1ENC09 W-Wing Catapult C .10 .20
SGX1ENC10 Ojama Red C .12 .25
SGX1ENC11 Ojama Blue C .12 .25
SGX1ENC12 Polymerization C .25 .50
SGX1ENC13 Ojama Delta Hurricane! C .12 .25
SGX1ENC14 Ojamagic C .10 .20
SGX1ENC15 Tri-Wight C .10 .20
SGX1ENC16 Ojamatch C .10 .20
SGX1ENC17 The Grave of Enkindling C .10 .20
SGX1ENC18 Super Rush Recklessly C .10 .20
SGX1ENC19 Spikeshield with Chain C .12 .25
SGX1ENC20 Wall of Disruption C .75 1.50
SGX1ENC21 Ojama King SCR .50 1.00
SGX1ENC21 Ojama King C .12 .25
SGX1ENC22 VW-Tiger Catapult C .10 .20
SGX1ENC23 Ojama Knight C .12 .25
SGX1END01 Ancient Gear Golem C .10 .20
SGX1END01 Ancient Gear Golem SCR 1.50 3.00
SGX1END02 Mechanicalchaser C .10 .20
SGX1END03 Giant Rat C .10 .20
SGX1END04 The Trojan Horse C .10 .20
SGX1END05 Dekoichi the Battlechanted Locomotive SCR 2.50 5.00
SGX1END05 Dekoichi the Battlechanted Locomotive C .50 1.00
SGX1END06 Ancient Gear Beast C .10 .20
SGX1END07 Ancient Gear Soldier C .10 .20
SGX1END08 Ancient Gear C .10 .20
SGX1END09 Ancient Gear Engineer C .10 .20
SGX1END10 Ancient Gear Knight C .10 .20
SGX1END11 Ancient Gear Gadget C .10 .20
SGX1END12 Earthquake C .12 .25
SGX1END13 Ancient Gear Castle C .10 .20
SGX1END14 Geartown C .10 .20
SGX1END15 Double Cyclone C .10 .20
SGX1END16 Card Advance C .10 .20
SGX1END17 Metalmorph C .10 .20
SGX1END18 Statue of the Wicked C .10 .20
SGX1END19 Damage Condenser C .10 .20
SGX1END20 Miniaturize C .10 .20
SGX1END21 Ultimate Ancient Gear Golem C .10 .20
SGX1END21 Ultimate Ancient Gear Golem SCR .50 1.00
SGX1ENE01 Blade Skater C .10 .20
SGX1ENE02 Senju of the Thousand Hands C .12 .25
SGX1ENE03 Sonic Bird C .12 .25
SGX1ENE04 D.D. Warrior Lady C .15 .30
SGX1ENE04 D.D. Warrior Lady SCR 2.00 4.00
SGX1ENE05 Warrior Lady of the Wasteland C .10 .20
SGX1ENE06 Etoile Cyber C .10 .20
SGX1ENE07 Cyber Tutu C .10 .20
SGX1ENE08 Cyber Gymnast C .10 .20
SGX1ENE09 Cyber Prima C .10 .20
SGX1ENE10 Cyber Angel Benten C .10 .20
SGX1ENE11 Cyber Angel Idaten C .10 .20
SGX1ENE12 Cyber Angel Izana C .10 .20
SGX1ENE13 The Warrior Returning Alive C .10 .20
SGX1ENE14 Ritual Weapon C .12 .25
SGX1ENE15 Machine Angel Ritual C .10 .20
SGX1ENE16 Berserk Scales C .10 .20
SGX1ENE17 Cosmic Cyclone C 1.50 3.00
SGX1ENE18 Hallowed Life Barrier C .10 .20
SGX1ENE19 Doble Passe C .10 .20
SGX1ENE20 Jar of Avarice C .10 .20
SGX1ENE21 Cyber Blader C .10 .20
SGX1ENE21 Cyber Blader SCR .30 .75
SGX1ENF01 Rainbow Dragon C .10 .20
SGX1ENF01 Rainbow Dragon SCR 1.50 3.00
SGX1ENF02 Crystal Beast Amethyst Cat C .10 .20
SGX1ENF03 Crystal Beast Amber Mammoth C .10 .20
SGX1ENF04 Crystal Beast Ruby Carbuncle C .20 .40
SGX1ENF05 Crystal Beast Emerald Tortoise C .10 .20
SGX1ENF06 Crystal Beast Topaz Tiger C .10 .20
SGX1ENF07 Crystal Beast Cobalt Eagle C .10 .20
SGX1ENF08 Crystal Beast Sapphire Pegasus SCR1.50 3.00
SGX1ENF08 Crystal Beast Sapphire Pegasus C .10 .20
SGX1ENF09 Crystal Seer C .10 .20
SGX1ENF10 Ancient City - Rainbow Ruins C .10 .20
SGX1ENF11 Rare Value C .12 .25
SGX1ENF12 Crystal Blessing C .10 .20
SGX1ENF13 Crystal Promise C .10 .20
SGX1ENF14 Crystal Release C .10 .20
SGX1ENF15 Crystal Tree C .10 .20
SGX1ENF16 Crystal Raigeki C .10 .20
SGX1ENF17 Rainbow Life C .15 .30
SGX1ENF18 Rainbow Gravity C .10 .20
SGX1ENF19 Gravelstorm C .10 .20
SGX1ENF20 Crystal Conclave C .10 .20
SGX1ENF21 Rainbow Overdragon C .15 .30
SGX1ENG01 Cyber Dragon SCR 3.00 6.00
SGX1ENG01 Cyber Dragon C .10 .20
SGX1ENG02 Hunter Dragon C .10 .20
SGX1ENG03 Proto-Cyber Dragon C .10 .20
SGX1ENG04 Cyber Phoenix C .10 .20
SGX1ENG05 Cyberdark Horn C .10 .20
SGX1ENG06 Cyberdark Edge C .10 .20
SGX1ENG07 Cyberdark Keel C .10 .20
SGX1ENG08 Exploder Dragon C .10 .20
SGX1ENG09 Cyber Valley C .10 .20
SGX1ENG10 Cyberdark Claw C .10 .20
SGX1ENG11 Polymerization C .25 .50
SGX1ENG12 Different Dimension Capsule C .10 .20
SGX1ENG13 Future Fusion C .10 .20
SGX1ENG14 Overload Fusion C .10 .20
SGX1ENG15 Cyberdark Impact! C .10 .20
SGX1ENG16 Trap Jammer C .10 .20
SGX1ENG17 Cyber Shadow Gardna C .10 .20
SGX1ENG18 Straight Flush C .10 .20
SGX1ENG19 Memory Loss C .10 .20
SGX1ENG20 Cyber Network C .10 .20
SGX1ENG21 Cyber End Dragon C .10 .20
SGX1ENG21 Cyber End Dragon SCR 1.25 2.50
SGX1ENG22 Chimeratech Overdragon C .10 .20
SGX1ENG23 Cyberdark Dragon C .10 .20
SGX1ENH01 Volcanic Doomfire C .10 .20
SGX1ENH01 Volcanic Doomfire SCR .75 1.50
SGX1ENH02 Blazing Inpachi C .10 .20
SGX1ENH03 Charcoal Inpachi C .10 .20
SGX1ENH04 UFO Turtle C .10 .20
SGX1ENH05 Spirit of Flames C .10 .20
SGX1ENH06 Raging Flame Sprite C .10 .20
SGX1ENH07 Volcanic Shell C .10 .20
SGX1ENH08 Volcanic Blaster C .10 .20
SGX1ENH09 Volcanic Hammerer C .10 .20
SGX1ENH10 Volcanic Rocket C .20 .40
SGX1ENH10 Volcanic Rocket SCR 1.25 2.50
SGX1ENH11 Royal Firestorm Guards C .12 .25
SGX1ENH12 Salamandra C .12 .25
SGX1ENH13 Twin Twisters C .10 .20
SGX1ENH14 Blaze Accelerator C .10 .20
SGX1ENH15 Tri-Blaze Accelerator C .10 .20
SGX1ENH16 Wild Fire C .10 .20
SGX1ENH17 Michizure C .10 .20
SGX1ENH18 Covering Fire C .10 .20
SGX1ENH19 Firewall C .10 .20
SGX1ENI01 Hourglass of Life C .10 .20
SGX1ENI02 Big Koala C .10 .20
SGX1ENI03 Mokey Mokey C .30 .75
SGX1ENI04 Don Zaloog C .30 .60
SGX1ENI04 Don Zaloog SCR 2.00 4.00
SGX1ENI05 Apprentice Magician SCR 1.00 2.00
SGX1ENI05 Apprentice Magician C .10 .20
SGX1ENI06 Des Kangaroo C .10 .20
SGX1ENI07 Gyroid C .10 .20
SGX1ENI08 Hydrogeddon SCR .50 1.00
SGX1ENI08 Hydrogeddon C .10 .20
SGX1ENI09 Rainbow Dark Dragon C .10 .20
SGX1ENI10 Black Brachios C .10 .20
SGX1ENI11 Toon Ancient Gear Golem C .10 .20
SGX1ENI12 Sphere Kuriboh SCR .75 1.50
SGX1ENI12 Sphere Kuriboh C .12 .25
SGX1ENI13 Master of Oz C .10 .20
SGX1ENI14 VWXYZ-Dragon Catapult Cannon C .10 .20
SGX1ENI15 Book of Moon SCR 2.50 5.00
SGX1ENI15 Book of Moon C .60 1.25
SGX1ENI16 Fusion Weapon C .10 .20
SGX1ENI17 Mokey Mokey Smackdown C .10 .20
SGX1ENI18 Crystal Beacon C .10 .20
SGX1ENI19 Ojama Country C .12 .25
SGX1ENI20 Advanced Dark C .10 .20
SGX1ENI21 Rising Energy C .12 .25
SGX1ENI22 Justi-Break C .10 .20
SGX1ENI23 Floodgate Trap Hole SCR 1.25 2.50
SGX1ENI23 Floodgate Trap Hole C .50 1.00

2022 Yu-Gi-Oh Speed Duel GX Duel Academy Box 1st Edition Skill Cards

SGX1ENS01 Here Goes Something! .15 .30
SGX1ENS02 Powerful Group of Guys .15 .30
SGX1ENS03 Land of the Ojamas .15 .30
SGX1ENS04 Ancient Fusion .15 .30
SGX1ENS05 Cyber Blade Fusion .15 .30
SGX1ENS06 Crystal Transcendance .15 .30
SGX1ENS07 Forbidden Cyber Style Technique .15 .30
SGX1ENS08 Blaze Accelerator Deployment .15 .30
SGX1ENS09 The Right Hero for the Job .15 .30
SGX1ENS10 Looking into the Future .15 .30
SGX1ENS11 Armed and Ready! .15 .30
SGX1ENS12 Middle-Aged Mechs .15 .30
SGX1ENS13 Machine Angel Ascension .15 .30
SGX1ENS14 Rainbow Crystal Collection .15 .30
SGX1ENS15 Cyberdark Style .15 .30
SGX1ENS16 Volcanic Cannon .15 .30
SGX1ENS17 Energizing Elements .15 .30
SGX1ENS18 Room for Growth .15 .30
SGX1ENS19 I've Got Dino DNA! .15 .30
SGX1ENS20 Consumed By Darkness .15 .30

2022 Yu-Gi-Oh Structure Deck Albaz Strike 1st Edition

SDAZEN001 Tri-Brigade Mercourier UR .15 .30
SDAZEN002 Springans Kitt UR .12 .25
SDAZEN003 The Golden Swordsoul UR .12 .25
SDAZEN004 Fallen of Albaz C .12 .25
SDAZEN005 Albion the Shrouded Dragon C .10 .20
SDAZEN006 Dogmatika Fleurdelis, the Knighted C.10 .20
SDAZEN007 Red-Eyes Darkness Metal Dragon C .15 .30
SDAZEN008 Thunder King, the Lightningstrike Kaiju C .10 .20
SDAZEN009 Chaos Dragon Levianeer C .20 .40
SDAZEN010 Radian, the Multidimensional Kaiju C.15 .30
SDAZEN011 Artifact Scythe C .15 .30
SDAZEN012 White Dragon Wyverburster C .10 .20
SDAZEN013 Black Dragon Collapserpent C .10 .20
SDAZEN014 Starliege Seyfert C .12 .25
SDAZEN015 Keeper of Dragon Magic C .10 .20
SDAZEN016 Summoner Monk C .10 .20
SDAZEN017 Ghost Ogre & Snow Rabbit C 1.00 2.00
SDAZEN018 Effect Veiler C 1.00 2.00
SDAZEN019 Omni Dragon Brotaur C .10 .20
SDAZEN020 Branded Lost C .10 .20
SDAZEN021 Branded Fusion SR 1.00 2.00
SDAZEN022 Branded in White C .10 .20
SDAZEN023 Branded Bond C .10 .20
SDAZEN024 Fusion Gate C .10 .20
SDAZEN025 Fusion Recycling Plant C .10 .20
SDAZEN026 Fusion Substitute C .10 .20
SDAZEN027 Gold Sarcophagus C .12 .25
SDAZEN028 Pot of Extravagance C 1.25 2.50
SDAZEN029 Called by the Grave C .75 1.50
SDAZEN030 Dark Ruler No More C 2.00 4.00
SDAZEN031 Branded Sword SR .12 .25
SDAZEN032 Branded Retribution SR .12 .25
SDAZEN033 Screams of the Branded C .10 .20
SDAZEN034 Judgment of the Branded C .10 .20
SDAZEN035 Necro Fusion C .10 .20
SDAZEN036 Back to the Front C .10 .20
SDAZEN037 Warning Point C .10 .20
SDAZEN038 There Can Be Only One C .15 .30
SDAZEN039 Dimensional Barrier C .15 .30
SDAZEN040 Waking the Dragon C .10 .20
SDAZEN041 Mirrorjade the Iceblade Dragon UR .25 .50
SDAZEN042 Lubellion the Searing Dragon UR .20 .40
SDAZEN043 Titaniklad the Ash Dragon C .10 .20

SDAZEN044 Brigrand the Glory Dragon C .10 .20
SDAZEN045 Spring the Irondash Dragon C .10 .20
SDAZEN046 Albion the Branded Dragon C .15 .30
SDAZEN047 Albaz the Shrouded C .10 .20
SDAZEN048 Ecclesia the Exiled C .10 .20
SDAZEN049 Tri-Brigade C .10 .20
SDAZEN050 The Virtuous Vestals C .10 .20
SDAZEN051 Aluber the Dogmatic C .10 .20

2022 Yu-Gi-Oh Structure Deck Dark World 1st Edition

SR13EN001 Reign-Beaux,
Overking of Dark World UR .25 .50
SR13EN002 Genta, Gateman of Dark World SR .60 1.25
SR13EN003 Parl, Hermit of Dark World SR .15 .30
SR13EN004 Reign-Beaux, Overlord of Dark World C.12 .25
SR13EN005 Lucent, Netherlord of Dark World C .15 .30
SR13EN006 Latinum, Exarch of Dark World C .07 .15
SR13EN007 Goldd, Wu-Lord of Dark World C .07 .15
SR13EN008 Sillva, Warlord of Dark World C .07 .15
SR13EN009 Brron, Mad King of Dark World C .07 .15
SR13EN010 Beiige, Vanguard of Dark World C .07 .15
SR13EN011 Broww, Huntsman of Dark World C .15 .30
SR13EN012 Scarr, Scout of Dark World C .07 .15
SR13EN013 Kahkki, Guerilla of Dark World C .07 .15
SR13EN014 Gren, Tactician of Dark World C .07 .15
SR13EN015 Ceruli, Guru of Dark World C .07 .15
SR13EN016 Zure, Knight of Dark World C .07 .15
SR13EN017 Renge, Gatekeeper of Dark World C .07 .15
SR13EN018 Danger! Bigfoot! C .25 .50
SR13EN019 Danger! Thunderbird! C .20 .40
SR13EN020 Danger! Mothman! C .20 .40
SR13EN021 Danger!? Tsuchinoko? C .30 .75
SR13EN022 Lilith, Lady of Lament C .07 .15
SR13EN023 Fabled Raven C .07 .15
SR13EN024 Absolute King Back Jack C .07 .15
SR13EN025 Dark World Puppetry UR .20 .40
SR13EN026 Dark World Archives UR .20 .40
SR13EN027 Dark World Dealings C .15 .30
SR13EN028 Charge Into a Dark World C .07 .15
SR13EN029 Gateway to Dark World C .07 .15
SR13EN030 Dark World Lightning C .07 .15
SR13EN031 Dragged Down into the Grave C .07 .15
SR13EN032 Card Destruction C .15 .30
SR13EN033 Dark World Punishment SR .20 .40
SR13EN034 The Forces of Darkness C .07 .15
SR13EN035 Dark World Brainwashing C .07 .15
SR13EN036 Dark Smog C .07 .15
SR13EN037 Mind Crush C .15 .30
SR13EN038 Deck Devastation Virus C .20 .40
SR13EN039 Paleozoic Dinomischus C .15 .30
SR13EN040 Skill Drain C 1.00 2.00
SR13EN041 Grapha, Dragon
Overlord of Dark World UR .30 .75
SR13EN042 Dark World Accession UR .20 .40
SR13EN043 Grapha, Dragon Lord of Dark World C.12 .25
SR13EN044 Snoww, Unlight of Dark World C .20 .40
SR13EN045 The Gates of Dark World C .07 .15

2022 Yu-Gi-Oh Tactical Masters 1st Edition

TAMAEN001 Shinonome the Vaylantz Priestess UR.50 1.00
TAMAEN002 Saion the Vaylantz Archer R .12 .25
TAMAEN003 Nazuki the Vaylantz Ninja R .12 .25
TAMAEN004 Hojo the Vaylantz Warrior SR .15 .30
TAMAEN005 Vaylantz Buster Baron SR .15 .30
TAMAEN006 Vaylantz Voltage Viscount R .12 .25
TAMAEN007 Vaylantz Mad Marquess R .12 .25
TAMAEN008 Vaylantz Dominator Duke R .12 .25
TAMAEN009 Mamonaka the Vaylantz United CR7.50 15.00
TAMAEN009 Mamonaka the Vaylantz United UR .50 1.00
TAMAEN010 Vaylantz Genesis Grand Duke SR .15 .30
TAMAEN011 Vaylantz Wars -
The Place of Beginning UR .50 1.00
TAMAEN012 Vaylantz World - Shinra Bansho SR .15 .30
TAMAEN013 Vaylantz World - Konig Wissen SR .15 .30
TAMAEN014 Lovely Labrynth
of the Silver Castle UR .50 1.00
TAMAEN015 Labrynth Archfiend R .12 .25
TAMAEN016 Ariane the Labrynth Servant UR .50 1.00
TAMAEN016 Ariane the Labrynth Servant CR 17.50 35.00
TAMAEN017 Arianna the Labrynth Servant CR 50.00 100.00
TAMAEN017 Arianna the Labrynth Servant UR 12.50 25.00
TAMAEN018 Labrynth Chandraglier R .12 .25
TAMAEN019 Labrynth Stovie Torbie R .12 .25
TAMAEN020 Labrynth Cooclock R .12 .25
TAMAEN021 Labrynth Labyrinth CR 17.50 35.00
TAMAEN021 Labrynth Labyrinth SR .15 .30
TAMAEN022 Labrynth Set-Up SR .15 .30
TAMAEN023 Welcome Labrynth UR .50 1.00
TAMAEN024 Farewelcome Labrynth R .12 .25
TAMAEN025 Labrynth Barrage SR .15 .30
TAMAEN026 Archfiend's Ghastly Glitch SR .15 .30
TAMAEN027 Runick Fountain UR .50 1.00
TAMAEN028 Runick Allure R .12 .25
TAMAEN029 Runick Tip CR 40.00 80.00
TAMAEN029 Runick Tip UR .50 1.00
TAMAEN030 Runick Flashing Fire SR .15 .30
TAMAEN031 Runick Destruction SR .15 .30
TAMAEN032 Runick Dispelling R .12 .25
TAMAEN033 Runick Freezing Curses SR .15 .30
TAMAEN034 Runick Slumber R .12 .25
TAMAEN035 Runick Golden Droplet SR .15 .30
TAMAEN036 Runick Smiting Storm R .12 .25
TAMAEN037 Hugin the Runick Wings UR 7.50 15.00
TAMAEN038 Munin the Runick Wings SR .15 .30
TAMAEN039 Geri the Runick Fangs SR .15 .30
TAMAEN040 Astrograph Sorcerer R .12 .25
TAMAEN040 Astrograph Sorcerer CR 25.00 50.00
TAMAEN041 Book of Eclipse R .12 .25
TAMAEN042 Senet Switch R .12 .25
TAMAEN043 Scapegoat R .12 .25
TAMAEN044 Compulsory Evacuation Device R .12 .25
TAMAEN045 Trap Trick R .12 .25
TAMAEN046 Invader of Darkness R .12 .25
TAMAEN047 Droll & Lock Bird R 2.00 4.00
TAMAEN047 Droll & Lock Bird CR 60.00 125.00
TAMAEN048 Absolute King Back Jack R .12 .25
TAMAEN049 Lilith, Lady of Lament R .12 .25
TAMAEN050 Bearblocker R .12 .25
TAMAEN051 Malice, Lady of Lament R .12 .25
TAMAEN052 Quick Booster R .12 .25
TAMAEN053 Cosmic Cyclone R .12 .25
TAMAEN053 Cosmic Cyclone CR 25.00 50.00
TAMAEN054 Pendulum Fusion R .12 .25
TAMAEN055 Duelist Alliance R .12 .25
TAMAEN056 Anti-Spell Fragrance R .12 .25
TAMAEN056 Anti-Spell Fragrance CR 30.00 60.00
TAMAEN057 Reckless Greed R .12 .25
TAMAEN058 Imperial Iron Wall R .12 .25
TAMAEN059 Fiend Griefing R .12 .25
TAMAEN060 Pendulum Switch R .12 .25

2022 Yu-Gi-Oh Tin of the Pharoah's Gods 1st Edition

MP22EN001 Armed Dragon Thunder LV10 UR .15 .30
MP22EN002 Armed Dragon
Thunder LV7 PRISM SCR .25 .50
MP22EN003 Armed Dragon Thunder LV5 C .07 .15
MP22EN004 Armed Dragon Thunder LV3 C .07 .15
MP22EN005 Armed Dragon LV10 White R .12 .25
MP22EN006 Tri-Brigade Kitt PRISM SCR .30 .75
MP22EN007 Windwitch - Blizzard Bell C .07 .15
MP22EN008 Windwitch - Freeze Bell C .07 .15
MP22EN009 Fabled Marcosia C .07 .15
MP22EN010 The Fabled Abanc C .07 .15
MP22EN011 Metalfoes Vanisher C .07 .15
MP22EN012 Constellar Caduceus C .07 .15
MP22EN013 Maha Vailo, Light of the Heavens R .12 .25
MP22EN014 Machina Unclaspare UR .15 .30
MP22EN015 Live Twin Lil-la Treat SR .12 .25
MP22EN016 Heavenly Zephyr - Miradora UR .15 .30
MP22EN017 Fairy Archer Ingunar C .07 .15
MP22EN018 Radiant Vouirescence SR .12 .25
MP22EN019 Amanokujaki R .12 .25
MP22EN020 Guitar Gurnards Duonigis C .07 .15
MP22EN021 Wightbaking C .07 .15
MP22EN022 Parametalfoes Azortless C .07 .15
MP22EN023 Windwitch - Diamond Bell R .12 .25
MP22EN024 Fabled Andwraith C .07 .15
MP22EN025 Dragunity Knight - Gormfaobhar C .07 .15
MP22EN026 Sacred Tree Beast, Hyperyton C .07 .15
MP22EN027 Heavymetalfoes Amalgam R .12 .25
MP22EN028 Underworld Goddess... PRISM SCR2.00 4.00
MP22EN029 Armed Dragon Flash R .12 .25
MP22EN030 Armed Dragon Blitz C .07 .15
MP22EN031 Armed Dragon Lightning C .07 .15
MP22EN032 Tri-Brigade Rendezvous C .07 .15
MP22EN033 Windwitch Chimes C .07 .15
MP22EN034 Stairway to a Fabled Realm C .07 .15
MP22EN035 Parametalfoes Fusion R .12 .25
MP22EN036 Archfiend's Staff of Despair R .12 .25
MP22EN037 Pot of Prosperity PRISM SCR 25.00 50.00
MP22EN038 Armed Dragon Thunderbolt C .07 .15
MP22EN039 Dogmatika Genesis UR .15 .30
MP22EN040 Icy Breeze Refrain C .07 .15
MP22EN041 Fabled Treason C .07 .15
MP22EN042 Virtual World Gate - Xuanwu SR .12 .25
MP22EN043 E.M.R. C .07 .15
MP22EN044 Angel Statue - Azurune C .07 .15
MP22EN045 Materiactor Gigadra C .07 .15
MP22EN046 Coordius the Triphasic Dealmon C .07 .15
MP22EN047 Materiactor Gigaboros C .07 .15
MP22EN048 Steel Star Regulator C .07 .15
MP22EN049 Breath of Acclamation UR .15 .30
MP22EN050 Greater Polymerization PRISM SCR .25 .50
MP22EN051 Reinforcement
of the Army's Troops UR .15 .30
MP22EN052 Psychic Eraser Laser C .07 .15
MP22EN053 Synchro Transmission R .12 .25
MP22EN054 War Rock Skyler UR .15 .30
MP22EN055 Virtual World Oto-Hime - Toutou R .12 .25
MP22EN056 Diviner of the Herald PRISM SCR 5.00 10.00
MP22EN057 ZW - Pegasus Twin Saber SR .12 .25
MP22EN058 ZS - Armed Sage SR .12 .25
MP22EN059 ZS - Ascended Sage PRISM SCR .25 .50
MP22EN060 Roxrose Dragon PRISM SCR .25 .50
MP22EN061 Ruddy Rose Witch R .12 .25
MP22EN062 Danmari @Ignister SR .12 .25
MP22EN063 Traptrix Vesiculo SR .12 .25
MP22EN064 Live Twin Ki-sikil Frost SR .12 .25
MP22EN065 Blackeyes, the
Plunder Patroll Seaguide C .07 .15
MP22EN066 Judge of the Ice Barrier C .07 .15
MP22EN067 Scrap Raptor UR .30 .75
MP22EN068 Dark Honest UR .15 .30
MP22EN069 Bahalutiya, the Grand Radiance R .12 .25
MP22EN070 Pharaonic Guardian Sphinx UR .15 .30
MP22EN071 Anchamoufrite C .07 .15
MP22EN072 Dark Eye Nightmare UR .15 .30
MP22EN073 Yamorimori C .07 .15
MP22EN074 Otoshidamashi UR .15 .30
MP22EN075 White Knight of Dogmatika SR .12 .25
MP22EN076 Albion the Branded
Dragon PRISM SCR .60 1.25
MP22EN077 Ruddy Rose Dragon PRISM SCR .40 .80
MP22EN078 Garden Rose Flora R .12 .25
MP22EN079 Lavalval Exlord R .12 .25
MP22EN080 Star Mine C .07 .15
MP22EN081 Ultimate Dragonic
Utopia Ray PRISM SCR .25 .50
MP22EN082 ZW - Dragonic Halberd R .12 .25
MP22EN083 Rilliona... R .12 .25
MP22EN084 Drytron Mu Beta Fafnir PRISM SCR.25 .50
MP22EN085 Tri-Brigade Bearbrumm... UR .15 .30
MP22EN086 Dark Infant @Ignister UR .15 .30
MP22EN087 Traptrix Cularia SR .12 .25
MP22EN088 Paleozoic Cambroraster SR .12 .25
MP22EN089 Lyna the Light Charmer, Lustrous UR.20 .40
MP22EN090 Rank-Up-Magic Zexal Force R .12 .25
MP22EN091 Zexal Construction UR .15 .30
MP22EN092 Zexal Entrust C .07 .15
MP22EN093 Branded in White C .07 .15
MP22EN094 Basal Rose Shoot C .07 .15
MP22EN095 A.I. Meet You UR .15 .30
MP22EN096 You and A.I. C .07 .15
MP22EN097 Bujincandescence C .07 .15
MP22EN098 Birth of the Prominence Flame R .12 .25
MP22EN099 Book of Lunar Eclipse SR .12 .25
MP22EN100 One-Kuri-Way C .07 .15
MP22EN101 Hidden Springs of the Far East C .07 .15
MP22EN102 Zexal Alliance C .07 .15
MP22EN103 Screams of the Branded SR .12 .25
MP22EN104 Judgment of the Branded C .07 .15
MP22EN105 Proof of Pruflas R .12 .25
MP22EN106 Thron the Disciplined Angel R .12 .25
MP22EN107 Pendransaction R .12 .25
MP22EN108 Expendable Dai C .07 .15
MP22EN109 Terrors of the Underroot C .07 .15
MP22EN110 Eda the Sun Magician C .07 .15
MP22EN111 Staysailor Romarin C .07 .15
MP22EN112 D/D/D Supersight
King Zero Maxwell UR .15 .30
MP22EN113 Binary Blader SR .12 .25
MP22EN114 Sunavalon Daphne SR .12 .25
MP22EN115 Sunavalon Melias C .07 .15
MP22EN116 Sunvine Cross Breed SR .12 .25
MP22EN117 Beetrooper Scout Buggy R .20 .40
MP22EN118 Converging Wills Dragon C .07 .15
MP22EN119 Stardust Synchron UR .25 .50
MP22EN120 Stardust Trail UR .15 .30
MP22EN121 Despian Comedy C .07 .15
MP22EN122 Despian Tragedy C .07 .15
MP22EN123 Aluber the Jester
of Despia PRISM SCR 1.75 3.50
MP22EN124 Dramaturge of Despia PRISM SCR .25 .50
MP22EN125 Albion the Shrouded Dragon C .07 .15
MP22EN126 Clavkiys, the Magikey Skyblaster R .12 .25
MP22EN127 Gunkan Suship Shari SR .12 .25
MP22EN128 Gunkan Suship Ikura C .07 .15
MP22EN129 Chronomaly Magella Globe C .07 .15
MP22EN130 Gizmek Inaba,
the Hopping Hare of Hakuto C .07 .15
MP22EN131 Gizmek Naganaki,
the Sunrise Signaler C .07 .15
MP22EN132 Gizmek Taniguku,
the Immobile Intellect C .07 .15
MP22EN133 Gizmek Arakami,
the Hailbringer Hog C .07 .15
MP22EN134 Carpiponica,
Mystical Beast of the Forest C .07 .15
MP22EN135 Glacier Aqua Madoor R .12 .25
MP22EN136 Master's Diploman C .07 .15
MP22EN137 Slower Swallow SR .12 .25
MP22EN138 Aeropixthree C .07 .15
MP22EN139 Magikey Mechmusket - Batosbuster C.07 .15
MP22EN140 Magikey Mechmortar - Garesglasser C.07 .15
MP22EN141 Despian Quaeritis PRISM SCR .30 .75
MP22EN142 Despian Proskenion C .07 .15
MP22EN143 Magikey Beast - Ansyalabolas C .07 .15
MP22EN144 Magikey Dragon - Andrabime C .07 .15
MP22EN145 Allvain the Essence of Vanity UR .15 .30
MP22EN146 Stellar Wind Wolfrayet C .07 .15
MP22EN147 Gaiarmor Dragonshell UR .15 .30
MP22EN148 Gunkan Suship
Ikura-class Dreadnought C .07 .15
MP22EN149 Chronomaly Vimana R .12 .25
MP22EN150 Voloferniges, the
Darkest Dragon Doomrider R .12 .25
MP22EN151 Dragonlark Pairen UR .15 .30
MP22EN152 Stardust Illumination R .12 .25
MP22EN153 Majestic Absorption C .07 .15
MP22EN154 Despia, Theater of the Branded R .12 .25
MP22EN155 Branded Opening PRISM SCR 1.50 3.00
MP22EN156 Branded Bond UR .15 .30
MP22EN157 Magikey Maftea C .07 .15
MP22EN158 Magikey World R .12 .25
MP22EN159 Gunkan Sushipyard
Seaside Supper Spot C .07 .15
MP22EN160 Sacred Scrolls of the Gizmek Legend R.12 .25
MP22EN161 Live Twin Sunny's Snitch C .07 .15
MP22EN162 High Ritual Art SR .12 .25
MP22EN163 Ready Fusion PRISM SCR .75 1.50
MP22EN164 Synchro Overtake UR .15 .30
MP22EN165 Pendulum Treasure R .12 .25
MP22EN166 Majestic Mirage R .12 .25
MP22EN167 Magikey Duo C .07 .15
MP22EN168 Magikey Unlocking C .07 .15
MP22EN169 Gunkan Suship Daily Special C .07 .15
MP22EN170 Monster Assortment R .12 .25
MP22EN171 Beast King Unleashed SR .12 .25
MP22EN172 Baby Mudragon UR .15 .30
MP22EN173 Pazuzule C .07 .15
MP22EN174 Beetrooper Scale Bomber C .07 .15
MP22EN175 Beetrooper Sting Lancer C .07 .15
MP22EN176 Beetrooper Armor Horn C .07 .15
MP22EN177 Giant Beetrooper Invincible Atlas C .07 .15
MP22EN178 Beetrooper Formation C .07 .15
MP22EN179 Beetrooper Fly & Sting C .07 .15
MP22EN180 Link Apple C .07 .15
MP22EN181 Flying Red Carp C .07 .15
MP22EN182 Dinowrestler Iguanodraka C .07 .15
MP22EN183 Shinobi Insect Hagakuremino C .07 .15
MP22EN184 Trickstar Festival C .07 .15
MP22EN185 Gouki Finishing Move SR .12 .25
MP22EN186 Heritage of the Light UR .15 .30
MP22EN187 Rokket Caliber C .07 .15
MP22EN188 Incredible Ecclesia,
the Virtuous PRISM SCR 1.50 3.00
MP22EN189 Icejade Acti C .07 .15
MP22EN190 Icejade Tinola C .07 .15
MP22EN191 Icejade Tremora SR .12 .25
MP22EN192 Ad Libitum of Despia C .07 .15
MP22EN193 Flowandereeze & Snowl R .20 .40
MP22EN194 Flowandereeze & Robina R .30 .60
MP22EN195 Flowandereeze & Eglen R .30 .60
MP22EN196 Flowandereeze & Stri SR .12 .25
MP22EN197 Flowandereeze & Toccan UR .15 .30
MP22EN198 Flowandereeze & Empen SR .12 .25
MP22EN199 Destiny HERO - Denier C .07 .15
MP22EN200 Maginificent Magikey Mafteal C .07 .15
MP22EN201 Gunkan Suship Uni C .07 .15
MP22EN202 Gunkan Suship Shirauo C .07 .15
MP22EN203 Machina Ruinforce SR .12 .25
MP22EN204 Mimicking Man-Eater Bug UR .15 .30
MP22EN205 Lord of the
Heavenly Prison PRISM SCR 1.50 3.00
MP22EN206 Undaunted Bumpkin Beast C .07 .15
MP22EN207 Meowseclick C .07 .15
MP22EN208 Masquerade the Blazing Dragon SR .12 .25
MP22EN209 Destiny HERO... PRISM SCR 3.00 6.00
MP22EN210 Ultimate Flagship Ursatron R .12 .25
MP22EN211 Magikey Fiend - Transfurlmine R .12 .25
MP22EN212 Zoroa, the Magistus
Conflagrant Calamity C .07 .15
MP22EN213 Magikey Spirit - Vepartu R .12 .25
MP22EN214 Gunkan Suship Uni-class... C .07 .15
MP22EN215 Gunkan Suship
Shirauo-class Carrier C .07 .15
MP22EN216 Evil?Twin's Trouble Sunny PRISM SCR.30 .75
MP22EN217 Branded in High Spirits C .07 .15
MP22EN218 Icejade Cradle C .07 .15
MP22EN219 Branded in Red R .75 1.50
MP22EN220 Flowandereeze... PRISM SCR .30 .75
MP22EN221 Flowandereeze
and the Unexplored Wind C .20 .40
MP22EN222 Magikey Battle C .07 .15
MP22EN223 Sunvine Sowing C .07 .15
MP22EN224 Supernatural Danger Zone C .07 .15
MP22EN225 Small World PRISM SCR 4.00 8.00
MP22EN226 Magical Cylinders SR .12 .25
MP22EN227 Flowandereeze
and the Dreaming Town C .07 .15
MP22EN228 Flowandereeze and the Scary Sea C.07 .15
MP22EN229 Magikey Locking C .07 .15
MP22EN230 Stained Glass of Light & Dark R .12 .25
MP22EN231 Laundry Trap R .12 .25
MP22EN232 Night Sword Serpent C .07 .15
MP22EN233 D.D. Assault Carrier UR .15 .30
MP22EN234 Abyss Keeper UR .15 .30
MP22EN235 Apex Predation UR .15 .30
MP22EN236 Beetrooper Assault Roller C .07 .15
MP22EN237 Beetrooper Light Flapper C .07 .15
MP22EN238 Heavy Beetrooper Mighty Neptune C.07 .15
MP22EN239 Ultra Beetrooper Absolute Hercules C.07 .15
MP22EN240 Beetrooper Descent C .07 .15
MP22EN241 Beetrooper Landing C .07 .15
MP22EN242 Beetrooper Squad C .07 .15
MP22EN243 Flip Frozen C .07 .15
MP22EN244 Bravedrive C .07 .15
MP22EN245 Rebuildeer UR .15 .30
MP22EN246 Threshold Borg UR .15 .30
MP22EN247 Cynet Crosswipe C .07 .15
MP22EN248 Danger! Disturbance! Disorder! UR .15 .30
MP22EN249 Cynet Cascade C .07 .15
MP22EN250 Contract with the Abyss UR .15 .30
MP22EN251 Earth Chant UR .15 .30
MP22EN252 Sprite's Blessing UR .15 .30
MP22EN253 Lightning Storm PRISM SCR 6.00 12.00
MP22EN254 Forbidden Droplet PRISM SCR 7.50 15.00
MP22EN255 Ghost Ogre &
Snow Rabbit PRISM SCR 1.50 3.00
MP22EN256 Ghost Reaper & Winter Cherries SR.12 .25
MP22EN257 Ash Blossom &
Joyous Spring PRISM SCR 6.00 12.00
MP22EN258 Ghost Belle &
Haunted Mansion PRISM SCR 1.75 3.50
MP22EN259 Ghost Sister & Spooky Dogwood SR.12 .25
MP22EN260 Ghost Mourner & Moonlit Chill SR .12 .25
MP22EN261 Nibiru, the Primal Being UR 2.50 5.00
MP22EN262 Dark Ruler No More UR .15 .30
MP22EN263 Dimension Shifter UR .50 1.00
MP22EN264 Red-Eyes Dark Dragoon PRISM SCR10.00 20.00
MP22EN265 Crossout Designator PRISM SCR 7.50 15.00
MP22EN266 Blue-Eyes White Dragon PRISM SCR5.00 10.00
MP22EN267 Red-Eyes Black Dragon PRISM SCR3.00 6.00
MP22EN268 Dark Magician Girl PRISM SCR 7.50 15.00
MP22EN269 Duel Tower PRISM SCR .25 .50
MP22EN270 Rainbow Bridge
of Salvation PRISM SCR .30 .75
MP22EN271 Link into the VRAINS! PRISM SCR .30 .75
MP22EN272 Soul Energy MAX!!! UR .15 .30
MP22EN273 The Revived Sky God UR .30 .75
MP22EN274 The Breaking Ruin God UR .15 .30
MP22EN275 The True Sun God UR .15 .30

2023 Yu-Gi-Oh 25th Anniversary Rarity Collection

RA01EN001 Lava Golem SR .25 .60
RA01EN001 Lava Golem PCR 1.00 2.50
RA01EN001 Lava Golem PSR 1.25 3.00
RA01EN001 Lava Golem PUR 1.00 2.50
RA01EN001 Lava Golem QCSCR 10.00 25.00
RA01EN001 Lava Golem SEC 1.00 2.50
RA01EN001 Lava Golem UR .25 .60
RA01EN002 Lonefire Blossom SR .10 .25
RA01EN002 Lonefire Blossom PCR .60 1.50
RA01EN002 Lonefire Blossom PSR .50 1.25
RA01EN002 Lonefire Blossom PUR .75 2.00
RA01EN002 Lonefire Blossom QCSCR 6.00 15.00
RA01EN002 Lonefire Blossom SEC .40 1.00
RA01EN002 Lonefire Blossom UR .10 .25
RA01EN003 Effect Veiler SR 1.50 4.00
RA01EN003 Effect Veiler PCR 8.00 20.00
RA01EN003 Effect Veiler PSR 8.00 20.00
RA01EN003 Effect Veiler PUR 5.00 12.00
RA01EN003 Effect Veiler QCSCR 40.00 100.00
RA01EN003 Effect Veiler SEC 6.00 15.00
RA01EN003 Effect Veiler UR 1.50 4.00
RA01EN004 Vision HERO Faris SR .12 .30
RA01EN004 Vision HERO Faris PCR .40 1.00
RA01EN004 Vision HERO Faris PSR .50 1.25
RA01EN004 Vision HERO Faris PUR .40 1.00
RA01EN004 Vision HERO Faris QCSCR 6.00 15.00
RA01EN004 Vision HERO Faris SEC .20 .50
RA01EN004 Vision HERO Faris UR .12 .30
RA01EN005 Tour Guide From the
Underworld QCSCR 10.00 25.00
RA01EN005 Tour Guide From the Underworld SEC.50 1.25
RA01EN005 Tour Guide From the Underworld UR.15 .40
RA01EN005 Tour Guide From the Underworld SR.15 .40
RA01EN005 Tour Guide From the Underworld PCR.75 2.00
RA01EN005 Tour Guide From the Underworld PSR1.00 2.50
RA01EN005 Tour Guide From the Underworld PUR1.25 3.00
RA01EN006 Artifact Lancea SR .10 .25

RA01EN006 Artifact Lancea PCR	.25	.60
RA01EN006 Artifact Lancea PSR	8.00	20.00
RA01EN006 Artifact Lancea PUR	.50	1.25
RA01EN006 Artifact Lancea QCSCR	.50	1.25
RA01EN006 Artifact Lancea SEC	.60	1.50
RA01EN006 Artifact Lancea UR	.10	.25
RA01EN007 The Winged Dragon of Ra - Sphere Mode SR	.30	.75
RA01EN007 The Winged Dragon of Ra - Sphere Mode PCR	.50	1.25
RA01EN007 The Winged Dragon of Ra - Sphere Mode PSR	5.00	12.00
RA01EN007 The Winged Dragon of Ra - Sphere Mode PUR	1.00	2.50
RA01EN007 The Winged Dragon of Ra - Sphere Mode QCSCR	1.00	2.50
RA01EN007 The Winged Dragon of Ra - Sphere Mode SEC	.75	2.00
RA01EN007 The Winged Dragon of Ra - Sphere Mode UR	.25	.60
RA01EN008 Ash Blossom & Joyous Spring SR	3.00	8.00
RA01EN008 Ash Blossom & Joyous Spring PCR	5.00	12.00
RA01EN008 Ash Blossom & Joyous Spring PSR	100.00	250.00
RA01EN008 Ash Blossom & Joyous Spring PUR	8.00	20.00
RA01EN008 Ash Blossom & Joyous Spring QCSCR	6.00	15.00
RA01EN008 Ash Blossom & Joyous Spring SEC	10.00	25.00
RA01EN008 Ash Blossom & Joyous Spring UR	2.50	6.00
RA01EN009 Fairy Tail - Luna SR	.05	.12
RA01EN009 Fairy Tail - Luna PCR	.20	.50
RA01EN009 Fairy Tail - Luna PSR	.20	.50
RA01EN009 Fairy Tail - Luna PUR	.20	.50
RA01EN009 Fairy Tail - Luna QCSCR	1.50	4.00
RA01EN009 Fairy Tail - Luna SEC	.10	.25
RA01EN009 Fairy Tail - Luna UR	.08	.20
RA01EN010 Inspector Boarder SR	.10	.25
RA01EN010 Inspector Boarder PCR	.40	1.00
RA01EN010 Inspector Boarder PSR	.25	.60
RA01EN010 Inspector Boarder PUR	.30	.75
RA01EN010 Inspector Boarder QCSCR	3.00	8.00
RA01EN010 Inspector Boarder SEC	.15	.40
RA01EN010 Inspector Boarder UR	.05	.12
RA01EN011 Ghost Belle & Haunted Mansion SR	.25	.60
RA01EN011 Ghost Belle & Haunted Mansion PCR	3.00	8.00
RA01EN011 Ghost Belle & Haunted Mansion PSR	2.00	5.00
RA01EN011 Ghost Belle & Haunted Mansion PUR	2.00	5.00
RA01EN011 Ghost Belle & Haunted Mansion QCSCR	20.00	50.00
RA01EN011 Ghost Belle & Haunted Mansion SEC	1.00	2.50
RA01EN011 Ghost Belle & Haunted Mansion UR	.30	.75
RA01EN012 Blackwing - Simoon the Poison Wind SR	.15	.40
RA01EN012 Blackwing - Simoon the Poison Wind PCR	.20	.50
RA01EN012 Blackwing - Simoon the Poison Wind PSR	.25	.60
RA01EN012 Blackwing - Simoon the Poison Wind PUR	.25	.60
RA01EN012 Blackwing - Simoon the Poison Wind QCSCR	1.50	4.00
RA01EN012 Blackwing - Simoon the Poison Wind SEC	.12	.30
RA01EN012 Blackwing - Simoon the Poison Wind UR	.04	.10
RA01EN013 Danger!? Jackalope? SR	.10	.25
RA01EN013 Danger!? Jackalope? PCR	.20	.50
RA01EN013 Danger!? Jackalope? PSR	.40	1.00
RA01EN013 Danger!? Jackalope? PUR	.30	.75
RA01EN013 Danger!? Jackalope? QCSCR	2.00	5.00
RA01EN013 Danger!? Jackalope? SEC	.20	.50
RA01EN013 Danger!? Jackalope? UR	.10	.25
RA01EN014 Dimension Shifter SR	.15	.40
RA01EN014 Dimension Shifter PCR	2.50	6.00
RA01EN014 Dimension Shifter PSR	1.50	4.00
RA01EN014 Dimension Shifter PUR	2.00	5.00
RA01EN014 Dimension Shifter QCSCR	20.00	50.00
RA01EN014 Dimension Shifter SEC	.75	2.00
RA01EN014 Dimension Shifter UR	.12	.30
RA01EN015 Nibiru, the Primal Being PUR	4.00	10.00
RA01EN015 Nibiru, the Primal Being QCSCR	25.00	60.00
RA01EN015 Nibiru, the Primal Being SEC	1.25	3.00
RA01EN015 Nibiru, the Primal Being UR	1.00	2.50
RA01EN015 Nibiru, the Primal Being SR	1.50	4.00
RA01EN015 Nibiru, the Primal Being PCR	4.00	10.00
RA01EN015 Nibiru, the Primal Being PSR	2.50	6.00
RA01EN016 Blue-Eyes Abyss Dragon SR	.12	.30
RA01EN016 Blue-Eyes Abyss Dragon PCR	.40	1.00
RA01EN016 Blue-Eyes Abyss Dragon PSR	.50	1.25
RA01EN016 Blue-Eyes Abyss Dragon PUR	.40	1.00
RA01EN016 Blue-Eyes Abyss Dragon QCSCR	3.00	8.00
RA01EN016 Blue-Eyes Abyss Dragon SEC	.25	.60
RA01EN016 Blue-Eyes Abyss Dragon UR	.12	.30
RA01EN017 Galaxy-Eyes Afterglow Dragon SR	.08	.20
RA01EN017 Galaxy-Eyes Afterglow Dragon PCR	.25	.60
RA01EN017 Galaxy-Eyes Afterglow Dragon PSR	.30	.75
RA01EN017 Galaxy-Eyes Afterglow Dragon PUR	.30	.75
RA01EN017 Galaxy-Eyes Afterglow Dragon QCSCR	4.00	10.00
RA01EN017 Galaxy-Eyes Afterglow Dragon SEC	.20	.50
RA01EN017 Galaxy-Eyes Afterglow Dragon UR	.10	.25
RA01EN018 Wynn the Wind Channeler SR	.05	.12
RA01EN018 Wynn the Wind Channeler PCR	.20	.50
RA01EN018 Wynn the Wind Channeler PSR	.25	.60
RA01EN018 Wynn the Wind Channeler PUR	.20	.50
RA01EN018 Wynn the Wind Channeler QCSCR	1.50	4.00
RA01EN018 Wynn the Wind Channeler SEC	.10	.25
RA01EN018 Wynn the Wind Channeler UR	.10	.25
RA01EN019 Eldlich the Golden Lord SR	.05	.12
RA01EN019 Eldlich the Golden Lord ALT ART SR	.10	.25
RA01EN019 Eldlich the Golden Lord ALT ART PCR	.40	1.00
RA01EN019 Eldlich the Golden Lord ALT ART PSR	.30	.75
RA01EN019 Eldlich the Golden Lord ALT ART PUR	.40	1.00
RA01EN019 Eldlich the Golden Lord ALT ART QCSCR	5.00	12.00
RA01EN019 Eldlich the Golden Lord ALT ART SEC	.20	.50
RA01EN019 Eldlich the Golden Lord ALT ART UR	.10	.25
RA01EN019 Eldlich the Golden Lord PCR	.25	.60
RA01EN019 Eldlich the Golden Lord PSR	.30	.75
RA01EN019 Eldlich the Golden Lord PUR	.30	.75
RA01EN019 Eldlich the Golden Lord QCSCR	3.00	8.00
RA01EN019 Eldlich the Golden Lord SEC	.20	.50
RA01EN019 Eldlich the Golden Lord UR	.10	.25
RA01EN020 Dogmatika Ecclesia, the Virtuous SR	.10	.25
RA01EN020 Dogmatika Ecclesia, the Virtuous PCR	.75	2.00
RA01EN020 Dogmatika Ecclesia, the Virtuous PSR	.60	1.50
RA01EN020 Dogmatika Ecclesia, the Virtuous PUR	1.00	2.50
RA01EN020 Dogmatika Ecclesia, the Virtuous QCSCR	5.00	12.00
RA01EN020 Dogmatika Ecclesia, the Virtuous SEC	.25	.60
RA01EN020 Dogmatika Ecclesia, the Virtuous UR	.12	.30
RA01EN021 Fallen of Albaz SR	.10	.25
RA01EN021 Fallen of Albaz PCR	2.00	5.00
RA01EN021 Fallen of Albaz PSR	3.00	8.00
RA01EN021 Fallen of Albaz PUR	2.00	5.00
RA01EN021 Fallen of Albaz QCSCR	15.00	40.00
RA01EN021 Fallen of Albaz SEC	1.25	3.00
RA01EN021 Fallen of Albaz UR	.10	.25
RA01EN022 Alpha, the Master of Beasts SR	.10	.25
RA01EN022 Alpha, the Master of Beasts PCR	.25	.60
RA01EN022 Alpha, the Master of Beasts PSR	.25	.60
RA01EN022 Alpha, the Master of Beasts PUR	.25	.60
RA01EN022 Alpha, the Master of Beasts QCSCR	2.00	5.00
RA01EN022 Alpha, the Master of Beasts SEC	.12	.30
RA01EN022 Alpha, the Master of Beasts UR	.10	.25
RA01EN023 The Iris Swordsoul SR	.10	.25
RA01EN023 The Iris Swordsoul PCR	.20	.50
RA01EN023 The Iris Swordsoul PSR	.30	.75
RA01EN023 The Iris Swordsoul PUR	.25	.60
RA01EN023 The Iris Swordsoul QCSCR	3.00	8.00
RA01EN023 The Iris Swordsoul SEC	.15	.40
RA01EN023 The Iris Swordsoul UR	.05	.12
RA01EN024 Cyber Angel Benten PCR	.50	1.25
RA01EN024 Cyber Angel Benten PSR	.25	.60
RA01EN024 Cyber Angel Benten PUR	.30	.75
RA01EN024 Cyber Angel Benten QCSCR	4.00	10.00
RA01EN024 Cyber Angel Benten SEC	.10	.25
RA01EN024 Cyber Angel Benten UR	.08	.20
RA01EN024 Cyber Angel Benten SR	.10	.25
RA01EN025 Masked HERO Dark Law SR	.10	.25
RA01EN025 Masked HERO Dark Law PCR	.60	1.50
RA01EN025 Masked HERO Dark Law PSR	1.00	2.50
RA01EN025 Masked HERO Dark Law PUR	.75	2.00
RA01EN025 Masked HERO Dark Law QCSCR	10.00	25.00
RA01EN025 Masked HERO Dark Law SEC	.25	.60
RA01EN025 Masked HERO Dark Law UR	.12	.30
RA01EN026 Elder Entity N'tss SR	.12	.30
RA01EN026 Elder Entity N'tss PCR	.50	1.25
RA01EN026 Elder Entity N'tss PSR	.60	1.50
RA01EN026 Elder Entity N'tss PUR	.50	1.25
RA01EN026 Elder Entity N'tss QCSCR	6.00	15.00
RA01EN026 Elder Entity N'tss SEC	.30	.75
RA01EN026 Elder Entity N'tss UR	.10	.25
RA01EN027 Predaplant Dragostapelia SR	.10	.25
RA01EN027 Predaplant Dragostapelia PCR	.75	2.00
RA01EN027 Predaplant Dragostapelia PSR	.50	1.25
RA01EN027 Predaplant Dragostapelia PUR	.60	1.50
RA01EN027 Predaplant Dragostapelia QCSCR	10.00	25.00
RA01EN027 Predaplant Dragostapelia SEC	.25	.60
RA01EN027 Predaplant Dragostapelia UR	.10	.25
RA01EN028 Mudragon of the Swamp SR	.15	.40
RA01EN028 Mudragon of the Swamp PCR	.50	1.25
RA01EN028 Mudragon of the Swamp PSR	.60	1.50
RA01EN028 Mudragon of the Swamp PUR	.50	1.25
RA01EN028 Mudragon of the Swamp QCSCR	10.00	25.00
RA01EN028 Mudragon of the Swamp SEC	.25	.60
RA01EN028 Mudragon of the Swamp UR	.10	.25
RA01EN029 Egyptian God Slime SR	.12	.30
RA01EN029 Egyptian God Slime PCR	.50	1.25
RA01EN029 Egyptian God Slime PSR	.60	1.50
RA01EN029 Egyptian God Slime PUR	.60	1.50
RA01EN029 Egyptian God Slime QCSCR	3.00	8.00
RA01EN029 Egyptian God Slime SEC	.25	.60
RA01EN029 Egyptian God Slime UR	.12	.30
RA01EN030 Ancient Fairy Dragon SR	.10	.25
RA01EN030 Ancient Fairy Dragon PCR	.40	1.00
RA01EN030 Ancient Fairy Dragon PSR	.60	1.50
RA01EN030 Ancient Fairy Dragon PUR	.50	1.25
RA01EN030 Ancient Fairy Dragon QCSCR	8.00	20.00
RA01EN030 Ancient Fairy Dragon SEC	.30	.75
RA01EN030 Ancient Fairy Dragon UR	.12	.30
RA01EN031 Herald of the Arc Light SR	.12	.30
RA01EN031 Herald of the Arc Light PCR	.60	1.50
RA01EN031 Herald of the Arc Light PSR	.60	1.50
RA01EN031 Herald of the Arc Light PUR	.50	1.25
RA01EN031 Herald of the Arc Light QCSCR	8.00	20.00
RA01EN031 Herald of the Arc Light SEC	.50	1.25
RA01EN031 Herald of the Arc Light UR	.12	.30
RA01EN032 Junk Speeder SR	.05	.12
RA01EN032 Junk Speeder PCR	.20	.50
RA01EN032 Junk Speeder PSR	.15	.40
RA01EN032 Junk Speeder PUR	.20	.50
RA01EN032 Junk Speeder QCSCR	2.00	5.00
RA01EN032 Junk Speeder SEC	.12	.30
RA01EN032 Junk Speeder UR	.05	.12
RA01EN033 Borreload Savage Dragon SR	.15	.40
RA01EN033 Borreload Savage Dragon PCR	.60	1.50
RA01EN033 Borreload Savage Dragon PSR	.60	1.50
RA01EN033 Borreload Savage Dragon PUR	.75	2.00
RA01EN033 Borreload Savage Dragon QCSCR	4.00	10.00
RA01EN033 Borreload Savage Dragon SEC	.20	.50
RA01EN033 Borreload Savage Dragon UR	.12	.30
RA01EN034 Baronne de Fleur PCR	1.25	3.00
RA01EN034 Baronne de Fleur PSR	2.00	5.00
RA01EN034 Baronne de Fleur PUR	1.25	3.00
RA01EN034 Baronne de Fleur QCSCR	10.00	25.00
RA01EN034 Baronne de Fleur SEC	.60	1.50
RA01EN034 Baronne de Fleur UR	.25	.60
RA01EN034 Baronne de Fleur SR	.30	.75
RA01EN035 Downerd Magician SR	.10	.25
RA01EN035 Downerd Magician PCR	.40	1.00
RA01EN035 Downerd Magician PSR	.40	1.00
RA01EN035 Downerd Magician PUR	.25	.60
RA01EN035 Downerd Magician QCSCR	4.00	10.00
RA01EN035 Downerd Magician SEC	.25	.60
RA01EN035 Downerd Magician UR	.10	.25
RA01EN036 Ghostrick Angel of Mischief SR	.05	.12
RA01EN036 Ghostrick Angel of Mischief PCR	.30	.75
RA01EN036 Ghostrick Angel of Mischief PSR	.25	.60
RA01EN036 Ghostrick Angel of Mischief PUR	.30	.75
RA01EN036 Ghostrick Angel of Mischief QCSCR	2.50	6.00
RA01EN036 Ghostrick Angel of Mischief SEC	.12	.30
RA01EN036 Ghostrick Angel of Mischief UR	.08	.20
RA01EN037 Galaxy-Eyes Full Armor Photon Dragon SR	.10	.25
RA01EN037 Galaxy-Eyes Full Armor Photon Dragon PCR	.30	.75
RA01EN037 Galaxy-Eyes Full Armor Photon Dragon PSR	.25	.60
RA01EN037 Galaxy-Eyes Full Armor Photon Dragon PUR	.25	.60
RA01EN037 Galaxy-Eyes Full Armor Photon Dragon QCSCR	2.00	5.00
RA01EN037 Galaxy-Eyes Full Armor Photon Dragon SEC	.15	.40
RA01EN037 Galaxy-Eyes Full Armor Photon Dragon UR	.10	.25
RA01EN038 Red-Eyes Flare Metal Dragon SR	.12	.30
RA01EN038 Red-Eyes Flare Metal Dragon PCR	.60	1.50
RA01EN038 Red-Eyes Flare Metal Dragon PSR	.75	2.00
RA01EN038 Red-Eyes Flare Metal Dragon PUR	.60	1.50
RA01EN038 Red-Eyes Flare Metal Dragon QCSCR	5.00	12.00
RA01EN038 Red-Eyes Flare Metal Dragon SEC	.30	.75
RA01EN038 Red-Eyes Flare Metal Dragon UR	.12	.30
RA01EN039 Number 100: Numeron Dragon SR	.10	.25
RA01EN039 Number 100: Numeron Dragon PCR	.25	.60
RA01EN039 Number 100: Numeron Dragon PSR	.25	.60
RA01EN039 Number 100: Numeron Dragon PUR	.25	.60
RA01EN039 Number 100: Numeron Dragon QCSCR	2.50	6.00
RA01EN039 Number 100: Numeron Dragon SEC	.10	.25
RA01EN039 Number 100: Numeron Dragon UR	.08	.20
RA01EN040 Dingirsu, the Orcust of the Evening Star SR	.15	.40
RA01EN040 Dingirsu, the Orcust of the Evening Star PCR	.50	1.25
RA01EN040 Dingirsu, the Orcust of the Evening Star PSR	.50	1.25
RA01EN040 Dingirsu, the Orcust of the Evening Star PUR	.50	1.25
RA01EN040 Dingirsu, the Orcust of the Evening Star QCSCR	4.00	10.00
RA01EN040 Dingirsu, the Orcust of the Evening Star SEC	.20	.50
RA01EN040 Dingirsu, the Orcust of the Evening Star UR	.10	.25
RA01EN041 Time Thief Redoer SR	.10	.25
RA01EN041 Time Thief Redoer PCR	.50	1.25
RA01EN041 Time Thief Redoer PSR	.40	1.00
RA01EN041 Time Thief Redoer PUR	.30	.75
RA01EN041 Time Thief Redoer QCSCR	4.00	10.00
RA01EN041 Time Thief Redoer SEC	.20	.50
RA01EN041 Time Thief Redoer UR	.12	.30
RA01EN042 Cherubini, Ebon Angel of the Burning Abyss SR	.08	.20
RA01EN042 Cherubini, Ebon Angel of the Burning Abyss PCR	.20	.50
RA01EN042 Cherubini, Ebon Angel of the Burning Abyss PSR	.25	.60
RA01EN042 Cherubini, Ebon Angel of the Burning Abyss PUR	.30	.75
RA01EN042 Cherubini, Ebon Angel of the Burning Abyss QCSCR	3.00	8.00
RA01EN042 Cherubini, Ebon Angel of the Burning Abyss SEC	.12	.30
RA01EN042 Cherubini, Ebon Angel of the Burning Abyss UR	.10	.25
RA01EN043 Knightmare Unicorn ALT ART SEC	.25	.60
RA01EN043 Knightmare Unicorn ALT ART UR	.12	.30
RA01EN043 Knightmare Unicorn PCR	.50	1.25
RA01EN043 Knightmare Unicorn PSR	.40	1.00
RA01EN043 Knightmare Unicorn PUR	.40	1.00
RA01EN043 Knightmare Unicorn QCSCR	3.00	8.00
RA01EN043 Knightmare Unicorn SEC	.20	.50
RA01EN043 Knightmare Unicorn UR	.10	.25
RA01EN043 Knightmare Unicorn SR	.15	.40
RA01EN043 Knightmare Unicorn ALT ART SR	.12	.30
RA01EN043 Knightmare Unicorn ALT ART PCR	.60	1.50
RA01EN043 Knightmare Unicorn ALT ART PSR	.60	1.50
RA01EN043 Knightmare Unicorn ALT ART PUR	.60	1.50
RA01EN043 Knightmare Unicorn ALT ART QCSCR	6.00	15.00
RA01EN044 Mekk-Knight Crusadia Avramax SR	.10	.25
RA01EN044 Mekk-Knight Crusadia Avramax PCR	.50	1.25
RA01EN044 Mekk-Knight Crusadia Avramax PSR	.40	1.00
RA01EN044 Mekk-Knight Crusadia Avramax PUR	.50	1.25
RA01EN044 Mekk-Knight Crusadia Avramax QCSCR	3.00	8.00
RA01EN044 Mekk-Knight Crusadia Avramax SEC	.20	.50
RA01EN044 Mekk-Knight Crusadia Avramax UR	.10	.25
RA01EN045 Code Talker Inverted SR	.04	.10
RA01EN045 Code Talker Inverted PCR	.12	.30
RA01EN045 Code Talker Inverted PSR	.12	.30
RA01EN045 Code Talker Inverted PUR	.12	.30
RA01EN045 Code Talker Inverted QCSCR	.60	1.50
RA01EN045 Code Talker Inverted SEC	.10	.25
RA01EN045 Code Talker Inverted UR	.05	.12
RA01EN046 Striker Dragon SR	.10	.25
RA01EN046 Striker Dragon PCR	.25	.60
RA01EN046 Striker Dragon PSR	.25	.60
RA01EN046 Striker Dragon PUR	.30	.75
RA01EN046 Striker Dragon QCSCR	8.00	20.00
RA01EN046 Striker Dragon SEC	.20	.50
RA01EN046 Striker Dragon UR	.10	.25
RA01EN047 Selene, Queen of the Master Magicians SR	.15	.40
RA01EN047 Selene, Queen of the Master Magicians PCR	.60	1.50
RA01EN047 Selene, Queen of the Master Magicians PSR	.75	2.00
RA01EN047 Selene, Queen of the Master Magicians PUR	.60	1.50
RA01EN047 Selene, Queen of the Master Magicians QCSCR	8.00	20.00
RA01EN047 Selene, Queen of the Master Magicians SEC	.50	1.25
RA01EN047 Selene, Queen of the Master Magicians UR	.15	.40
RA01EN048 Decode Talker Heatsoul SR	.10	.25
RA01EN048 Decode Talker Heatsoul PCR	.25	.60
RA01EN048 Decode Talker Heatsoul PSR	.50	1.25
RA01EN048 Decode Talker Heatsoul PUR	.25	.60
RA01EN048 Decode Talker Heatsoul QCSCR	3.00	8.00
RA01EN048 Decode Talker Heatsoul SEC	.20	.50
RA01EN048 Decode Talker Heatsoul UR	.10	.25
RA01EN049 Artemis, the Magistus Moon Maiden SR	.10	.25
RA01EN049 Artemis, the Magistus Moon Maiden PCR	.25	.60
RA01EN049 Artemis, the Magistus Moon Maiden PSR	.25	.60
RA01EN049 Artemis, the Magistus Moon Maiden PUR	.25	.60
RA01EN049 Artemis, the Magistus Moon Maiden QCSCR	3.00	8.00
RA01EN049 Artemis, the Magistus Moon Maiden SEC	.15	.40
RA01EN049 Artemis, the Magistus Moon Maiden UR	.10	.25
RA01EN050 Change of Heart SR	.15	.40
RA01EN050 Change of Heart PCR	1.00	2.50
RA01EN050 Change of Heart PSR	1.00	2.50
RA01EN050 Change of Heart PUR	1.25	3.00
RA01EN050 Change of Heart QCSCR	10.00	25.00
RA01EN050 Change of Heart SEC	.60	1.50
RA01EN050 Change of Heart UR	.20	.50
RA01EN051 Reinforcement of the Army SR	.12	.30
RA01EN051 Reinforcement of the Army PCR	1.00	2.50
RA01EN051 Reinforcement of the Army PSR	1.00	2.50
RA01EN051 Reinforcement of the Army PUR	1.00	2.50
RA01EN051 Reinforcement of the Army QCSCR	10.00	25.00
RA01EN051 Reinforcement of the Army SEC	.60	1.50
RA01EN051 Reinforcement of the Army UR	.12	.30
RA01EN052 Reasoning UR	.10	.25
RA01EN052 Reasoning SR	.10	.25
RA01EN052 Reasoning PCR	.40	1.00
RA01EN052 Reasoning PSR	.30	.75
RA01EN052 Reasoning PUR	.50	1.25
RA01EN052 Reasoning QCSCR	4.00	10.00
RA01EN052 Reasoning SEC	.25	.60
RA01EN053 Fossil Dig SR	.10	.25
RA01EN053 Fossil Dig PCR	.40	1.00
RA01EN053 Fossil Dig PSR	.40	1.00
RA01EN053 Fossil Dig PUR	.50	1.25
RA01EN053 Fossil Dig QCSCR	4.00	10.00
RA01EN053 Fossil Dig SEC	.25	.60
RA01EN053 Fossil Dig UR	.08	.20
RA01EN054 Spellbook of Judgment SR	.10	.25
RA01EN054 Spellbook of Judgment PCR	.20	.50
RA01EN054 Spellbook of Judgment PSR	.20	.50
RA01EN054 Spellbook of Judgment PUR	.20	.50
RA01EN054 Spellbook of Judgment QCSCR	1.50	4.00
RA01EN054 Spellbook of Judgment SEC	.12	.30
RA01EN054 Spellbook of Judgment UR	.10	.25
RA01EN055 Pre-Preparation of Rites SR	.10	.25
RA01EN055 Pre-Preparation of Rites PCR	.75	2.00
RA01EN055 Pre-Preparation of Rites PSR	.60	1.50
RA01EN055 Pre-Preparation of Rites PUR	.75	2.00
RA01EN055 Pre-Preparation of Rites QCSCR	5.00	12.00
RA01EN055 Pre-Preparation of Rites SEC	.50	1.25
RA01EN055 Pre-Preparation of Rites UR	.10	.25
RA01EN056 Pot of Desires SR	.20	.50
RA01EN056 Pot of Desires PCR	1.00	2.50
RA01EN056 Pot of Desires PSR	1.00	2.50
RA01EN056 Pot of Desires PUR	1.00	2.50
RA01EN056 Pot of Desires QCSCR	10.00	25.00
RA01EN056 Pot of Desires SEC	1.00	2.50
RA01EN056 Pot of Desires UR	.20	.50
RA01EN057 Called by the Grave SR	.50	1.25
RA01EN057 Called by the Grave PCR	2.00	5.00
RA01EN057 Called by the Grave PSR	2.00	5.00
RA01EN057 Called by the Grave PUR	2.00	5.00
RA01EN057 Called by the Grave QCSCR	25.00	60.00
RA01EN057 Called by the Grave SEC	1.50	4.00
RA01EN057 Called by the Grave UR	.50	1.25
RA01EN058 Magicalized Fusion SR	.10	.25
RA01EN058 Magicalized Fusion PCR	.20	.50
RA01EN058 Magicalized Fusion PSR	.20	.50
RA01EN058 Magicalized Fusion PUR	.25	.60
RA01EN058 Magicalized Fusion QCSCR	1.50	4.00
RA01EN058 Magicalized Fusion SEC	.12	.30
RA01EN058 Magicalized Fusion UR	.10	.25
RA01EN059 Pot of Extravagance SR	.20	.50
RA01EN059 Pot of Extravagance PCR	1.00	2.50
RA01EN059 Pot of Extravagance PSR	.50	1.25
RA01EN059 Pot of Extravagance PUR	.75	2.00
RA01EN059 Pot of Extravagance QCSCR	5.00	12.00
RA01EN059 Pot of Extravagance SEC	.50	1.25
RA01EN059 Pot of Extravagance UR	.25	.60
RA01EN060 Dark Ruler No More SR	.20	.50
RA01EN060 Dark Ruler No More PCR	2.00	5.00
RA01EN060 Dark Ruler No More PSR	1.50	4.00
RA01EN060 Dark Ruler No More PUR	1.25	3.00
RA01EN060 Dark Ruler No More QCSCR	20.00	50.00
RA01EN060 Dark Ruler No More SEC	1.00	2.50
RA01EN060 Dark Ruler No More UR	.25	.60
RA01EN061 Lightning Storm SR	1.25	3.00
RA01EN061 Lightning Storm PCR	2.00	5.00
RA01EN061 Lightning Storm PSR	2.00	5.00
RA01EN061 Lightning Storm PUR	2.50	6.00
RA01EN061 Lightning Storm QCSCR	15.00	40.00
RA01EN061 Lightning Storm SEC	1.50	4.00
RA01EN061 Lightning Storm UR	1.00	2.50
RA01EN062 Nadir Servant SEC	.60	1.50
RA01EN062 Nadir Servant UR	.40	1.00
RA01EN062 Nadir Servant SR	.50	1.25
RA01EN062 Nadir Servant PCR	1.00	2.50
RA01EN062 Nadir Servant PSR	1.25	3.00
RA01EN062 Nadir Servant PUR	1.50	4.00
RA01EN062 Nadir Servant QCSCR	10.00	25.00
RA01EN063 Triple Tactics Talent SR	5.00	12.00
RA01EN063 Triple Tactics Talent PCR	6.00	15.00
RA01EN063 Triple Tactics Talent PSR	5.00	12.00
RA01EN063 Triple Tactics Talent PUR	6.00	15.00
RA01EN063 Triple Tactics Talent QCSCR	30.00	80.00
RA01EN063 Triple Tactics Talent SEC	4.00	10.00
RA01EN063 Triple Tactics Talent UR	4.00	10.00
RA01EN064 Forbidden Droplet SR	3.00	8.00
RA01EN064 Forbidden Droplet PCR	5.00	12.00
RA01EN064 Forbidden Droplet PSR	4.00	10.00

RA01EN064 Forbidden Droplet PUR 4.00 10.00
RA01EN064 Forbidden Droplet QCSCR 30.00 80.00
RA01EN064 Forbidden Droplet SEC 3.00 8.00
RA01EN064 Forbidden Droplet UR 2.50 6.00
RA01EN065 Chaos Space SR .10 .25
RA01EN065 Chaos Space PCR .25 .60
RA01EN065 Chaos Space PSR .25 .60
RA01EN065 Chaos Space PUR .40 1.00
RA01EN065 Chaos Space QCSCR 3.00 8.00
RA01EN065 Chaos Space SEC .15 .40
RA01EN065 Chaos Space UR .08 .20
RA01EN066 Pot of Prosperity SR 4.00 10.00
RA01EN066 Pot of Prosperity PCR 5.00 12.00
RA01EN066 Pot of Prosperity PSR 5.00 12.00
RA01EN066 Pot of Prosperity PUR 5.00 12.00
RA01EN066 Pot of Prosperity QCSCR 20.00 50.00
RA01EN066 Pot of Prosperity SEC 4.00 10.00
RA01EN066 Pot of Prosperity UR 3.00 8.00
RA01EN067 Small World SR .20 .50
RA01EN067 Small World PCR .40 1.00
RA01EN067 Small World PSR .40 1.00
RA01EN067 Small World PUR .60 1.50
RA01EN067 Small World QCSCR 4.00 10.00
RA01EN067 Small World SEC .30 .75
RA01EN067 Small World UR .20 .50
RA01EN068 Magician's Salvation SR .10 .25
RA01EN068 Magician's Salvation PCR .25 .60
RA01EN068 Magician's Salvation PSR .40 1.00
RA01EN068 Magician's Salvation PUR .30 .75
RA01EN068 Magician's Salvation QCSCR 2.50 6.00
RA01EN068 Magician's Salvation SEC .20 .50
RA01EN068 Magician's Salvation UR .10 .25
RA01EN069 Compulsory Evacuation Device SR .10 .25
RA01EN069 Compulsory Evacuation Device PCR .60 1.50
RA01EN069 Compulsory Evacuation Device PSR .50 1.25
RA01EN069 Compulsory Evacuation Device PUR .75 2.00
RA01EN069 Compulsory Evacuation Device QCSCR 4.00 10.00
RA01EN069 Compulsory Evacuation Device SEC .40 1.00
RA01EN069 Compulsory Evacuation Device UR .10 .25
RA01EN070 Summon Limit SR .10 .25
RA01EN070 Summon Limit PCR .75 2.00
RA01EN070 Summon Limit PSR .75 2.00
RA01EN070 Summon Limit PUR 1.00 2.50
RA01EN070 Summon Limit QCSCR 3.00 8.00
RA01EN070 Summon Limit SEC .25 .60
RA01EN070 Summon Limit UR .15 .40
RA01EN071 Ice Barrier SR .10 .25
RA01EN071 Ice Barrier PCR .20 .50
RA01EN071 Ice Barrier PSR .25 .60
RA01EN071 Ice Barrier PUR .25 .60
RA01EN071 Ice Barrier QCSCR 4.00 10.00
RA01EN071 Ice Barrier SEC .20 .50
RA01EN071 Ice Barrier UR .10 .25
RA01EN072 Dimensional Barrier QCSCR 15.00 40.00
RA01EN072 Dimensional Barrier SEC 1.25 3.00
RA01EN072 Dimensional Barrier UR .25 .60
RA01EN072 Dimensional Barrier SR .20 .50
RA01EN072 Dimensional Barrier PCR 2.00 5.00
RA01EN072 Dimensional Barrier PSR 2.00 5.00
RA01EN072 Dimensional Barrier PUR 1.50 4.00
RA01EN073 Harpie's Feather Storm SR .20 .50
RA01EN073 Harpie's Feather Storm PCR .50 1.25
RA01EN073 Harpie's Feather Storm PSR .50 1.25
RA01EN073 Harpie's Feather Storm PUR .50 1.25
RA01EN073 Harpie's Feather Storm QCSCR 4.00 10.00
RA01EN073 Harpie's Feather Storm SEC .25 .60
RA01EN073 Harpie's Feather Storm UR .10 .25
RA01EN074 Evenly Matched SR .75 2.00
RA01EN074 Evenly Matched PCR 3.00 8.00
RA01EN074 Evenly Matched PSR 2.50 6.00
RA01EN074 Evenly Matched PUR 2.50 6.00
RA01EN074 Evenly Matched QCSCR 25.00 60.00
RA01EN074 Evenly Matched SEC 2.00 5.00
RA01EN074 Evenly Matched UR .75 2.00
RA01EN075 Infinite Impermanence SR 4.00 10.00
RA01EN075 Infinite Impermanence PCR 8.00 20.00
RA01EN075 Infinite Impermanence PSR 10.00 25.00
RA01EN075 Infinite Impermanence PUR 8.00 20.00
RA01EN075 Infinite Impermanence QCSCR 40.00 100.00
RA01EN075 Infinite Impermanence SEC 4.00 10.00
RA01EN075 Infinite Impermanence UR 3.00 8.00
RA01EN076 Dogmatika Punishment SR .12 .30
RA01EN076 Dogmatika Punishment PCR .50 1.25
RA01EN076 Dogmatika Punishment PSR .50 1.25
RA01EN076 Dogmatika Punishment PUR .60 1.50
RA01EN076 Dogmatika Punishment QCSCR 8.00 20.00
RA01EN076 Dogmatika Punishment SEC .25 .60
RA01EN076 Dogmatika Punishment UR .12 .30
RA01EN077 Shaddoll Schism SR .10 .25
RA01EN077 Shaddoll Schism PCR .25 .60
RA01EN077 Shaddoll Schism PSR .20 .50
RA01EN077 Shaddoll Schism PUR .20 .50
RA01EN077 Shaddoll Schism QCSCR 1.25 3.00
RA01EN077 Shaddoll Schism SEC .10 .25
RA01EN077 Shaddoll Schism UR .10 .25
RA01EN078 Ice Dragon's Prison SR .12 .30
RA01EN078 Ice Dragon's Prison PCR .40 1.00
RA01EN078 Ice Dragon's Prison PSR .50 1.25
RA01EN078 Ice Dragon's Prison PUR .50 1.25
RA01EN078 Ice Dragon's Prison QCSCR 3.00 8.00
RA01EN078 Ice Dragon's Prison SEC .25 .60
RA01EN078 Ice Dragon's Prison UR .12 .30
RA01EN079 Tri-Brigade Revolt SR .05 .12
RA01EN079 Tri-Brigade Revolt PCR .20 .50
RA01EN079 Tri-Brigade Revolt PSR .20 .50
RA01EN079 Tri-Brigade Revolt PUR .25 .60
RA01EN079 Tri-Brigade Revolt QCSCR 1.50 4.00
RA01EN079 Tri-Brigade Revolt SEC .10 .25
RA01EN079 Tri-Brigade Revolt UR .05 .12

2023 Yu-Gi-Oh 25th Anniversary Tin Dueling Heroes

TN23EN001 Dark Magician QCSCR 6.00 15.00
TN23EN002 Exodia the Forbidden One QCSCR 1.50 4.00
TN23EN003 Red-Eyes Black Dragon QCSCR 3.00 8.00
TN23EN004 Rainbow Dragon QCSCR .75 2.00
TN23EN005 Cyber Dragon QCSCR 5.00 12.00
TN23EN006 Elemental HERO Neos QCSCR 1.00 2.50
TN23EN007 Salamangreat Blaze Dragon QCSCR .30 .75
TN23EN008 Firewall Dragon QCSCR .50 1.25
TN23EN009 Decode Talker QCSCR .40 1.00
TN23EN010 Enlightenment Paladin QCSCR .30 .75
TN23EN011 Odd-Eyes Pendulum Dragon QCSCR .30 .75
TN23EN012 Galaxy-Eyes Photon Dragon QCSCR 2.00 5.00
TN23EN013 Number 39: Utopia QCSCR .60 1.50
TN23EN014 Black Rose Dragon QCSCR 4.00 10.00
TN23EN015 Blackwing Armor Master QCSCR 2.50 6.00
TN23EN016 Stardust Dragon QCSCR 6.00 15.00

2023 Yu-Gi-Oh Age Of Overlord 1st Edition

AGOVEN000 Magicians of Bonds and Unity QCSCR 25.00 60.00
AGOVEN001 Supreme King Gate Magician SR .25 .60
AGOVEN002 Supreme King Dragon Lightwurm C .08 .20
AGOVEN003 T.G. Rocket Salamander SEC .60 1.50
AGOVEN003 T.G. Rocket Salamander QCSCR 10.00 25.00
AGOVEN004 Visas Samsara SR 2.00 5.00
AGOVEN004 Visas Samsara QCSCR 20.00 50.00
AGOVEN005 Veda Kalarcanum SR .08 .20
AGOVEN006 Diabellstar the Black Witch SEC 20.00 50.00
AGOVEN006 Diabellstar the Black Witch QCSCR 125.00 300.00
AGOVEN007 Snake-Eye Ash SR 2.00 5.00
AGOVEN008 Snake-Eye Oak SR .30 .75
AGOVEN009 Snake-Eye Birch SR .15 .40
AGOVEN010 Snake-Eyes Flamberge Dragon SEC 10.00 25.00
AGOVEN010 Snake-Eyes Flamberge Dragon QCSCR 50.00 120.00
AGOVEN011 Imsety, Glory of Horus SEC 40.00 100.00
AGOVEN011 Imsety, Glory of Horus QCSCR 75.00 200.00
AGOVEN012 Duamutef, Blessing of Horus SEC 1.25 3.00
AGOVEN012 Duamutef, Blessing of Horus QCSCR 25.00 60.00
AGOVEN013 Hapi, Guidance of Horus SR .12 .30
AGOVEN014 Qebehsenuef, Protection of Horus SR .12 .30
AGOVEN015 Wattuna C .08 .20
AGOVEN016 Nephilabyss, the Ogdoadic Overlord SR .08 .20
AGOVEN017 Arias the Labrynth Butler SEC 10.00 25.00
AGOVEN017 Arias the Labrynth Butler QCSCR 50.00 120.00
AGOVEN018 Vanquish Soul Jiaolong UR .40 1.00
AGOVEN018 Vanquish Soul Jiaolong QCSCR 20.00 50.00
AGOVEN019 Poissonniere de Nouvelles SR .12 .30
AGOVEN020 Dark Hole Dragon UR .75 2.00
AGOVEN020 Dark Hole Dragon QCSCR 12.00 30.00
AGOVEN021 UFOLight C .08 .20
AGOVEN022 Seed-Spitting Saplings SR .08 .20
AGOVEN023 I.A.S. -Invasive Alien Species- C .08 .20
AGOVEN024 Tarai C .08 .20
AGOVEN025 Master Tao the Chanter C .08 .20
AGOVEN026 Cursed Bride Doll C .08 .20
AGOVEN027 Origami Goddess C .08 .20
AGOVEN028 Shinobaroness Shade Peacock C .08 .20
AGOVEN029 Shinobaron Shade Peacock C .08 .20
AGOVEN030 Odd-Eyes Arcray Dragon UR .40 1.00
AGOVEN030 Odd-Eyes Arcray Dragon QCSCR 10.00 25.00
AGOVEN031 Earthbound Servant Geo Gremlina C .08 .20
AGOVEN032 Berfomet the Mythical King of Phantom Beasts SR .20 .50
AGOVEN033 Gaia Prominence, the Fierce Force C .08 .20
AGOVEN034 T.G. Mighty Striker SR .08 .20
AGOVEN035 T.G. Over Dragonar UR .20 .50
AGOVEN035 T.G. Over Dragonar QCSCR 5.00 12.00
AGOVEN036 T.G. Glaive Blaster UR .12 .30
AGOVEN036 T.G. Glaive Blaster QCSCR 5.00 12.00
AGOVEN037 Mannadium Trisukta UR .30 .75
AGOVEN037 Mannadium Trisukta QCSCR 12.00 30.00
AGOVEN038 Wattkyuki C .08 .20
AGOVEN039 Xyz Armor Torpedo SR .12 .30
AGOVEN040 Xyz Armor Fortress SR .12 .30
AGOVEN041 Full Armored Dark Knight Lancer UR .60 1.50
AGOVEN041 Full Armored Dark Knight Lancer QCSCR 15.00 40.00
AGOVEN042 Super Starslayer TY-PHON - Sky Crisis UR 20.00 50.00
AGOVEN042 Super Starslayer TY-PHON - Sky Crisis QCSCR 125.00 300.00
AGOVEN043 Infernal Flame Banshee UR 1.00 2.50
AGOVEN043 Infernal Flame Banshee QCSCR 20.00 50.00
AGOVEN044 Transcendosaurus Exaraptor C .08 .20
AGOVEN045 Exceed the Pendulum SR .25 .60
AGOVEN046 S:P Little Knight SEC 75.00 200.00
AGOVEN046 S:P Little Knight QCSCR 250.00 600.00
AGOVEN047 Pendulum Evolution C .08 .20
AGOVEN048 Wings of Light SR .15 .40
AGOVEN049 T.G. Limiter Removal SEC .40 1.00
AGOVEN049 T.G. Limiter Removal QCSCR 5.00 12.00
AGOVEN050 T.G. All Clear SR .08 .20
AGOVEN051 Xyz Entrust C .08 .20
AGOVEN052 Realm Elegy SR .08 .20
AGOVEN053 Realm Eulogy C .08 .20
AGOVEN054 WANTED: Seeker of Sinful Spoils SEC 50.00 120.00
AGOVEN054 WANTED: Seeker of Sinful Spoils QCSCR 150.00 400.00
AGOVEN055 Sinful Spoils of Doom - Rciela C .08 .20
AGOVEN056 Divine Temple of the Snake-Eye UR 1.25 3.00
AGOVEN056 Divine Temple of the Snake-Eye QCSCR 25.00 60.00
AGOVEN057 Original Sinful Spoils - Snake-Eye UR 4.00 10.00
AGOVEN057 Original Sinful Spoils - Snake-Eye QCSCR 40.00 100.00
AGOVEN058 King's Sarcophagus UR 5.00 12.00
AGOVEN058 King's Sarcophagus QCSCR 50.00 120.00
AGOVEN059 Fire Recovery SR .50 1.25
AGOVEN060 Synchro Rumble SR .12 .30
AGOVEN061 Stars Align Above the Shrine C .08 .20
AGOVEN062 Wattkingdom C .08 .20
AGOVEN063 Ogdoadic Daybreak C .08 .20
AGOVEN064 Concours de Cuisine C .08 .20
AGOVEN065 Angelica's Angelic Ring C .08 .20
AGOVEN066 Card Scanner C .08 .20
AGOVEN067 The Immortal Bushi Mourns the Mortal Body C .08 .20
AGOVEN068 Miracle of the Supreme King C .08 .20
AGOVEN069 Soul of the Supreme Celestial King C .08 .20
AGOVEN070 T.G. Close C .08 .20
AGOVEN071 Full-Armored Xyz C .08 .20
AGOVEN072 Sharv Sarga C .08 .20
AGOVEN073 Loka Samsara C .08 .20
AGOVEN074 Sinful Spoils of Betrayal - Silvera SR .12 .30
AGOVEN075 Startling Stare of the Snake-Eyes C .08 .20
AGOVEN076 Canopic Protector SR .08 .20
AGOVEN077 Nemleria Repeter C .08 .20
AGOVEN078 Vanquish Soul Snow Devil C .08 .20
AGOVEN079 Starry Dragon's Cycle SR .08 .20
AGOVEN080 Escapegoat C .08 .20
AGOVEN081 Ken the Warrior Dragon C .08 .20
AGOVEN082 Gen the Diamond Tiger C .08 .20
AGOVEN083 Asset Mountis C .08 .20
AGOVEN084 Pitknight Filly C .08 .20
AGOVEN085 Wattsychic Fighting Porter C .08 .20
AGOVEN086 Fallen of the Tistina C .08 .20
AGOVEN087 Returned of the Tistina C .08 .20
AGOVEN088 Tainted of the Tistina UR .12 .30
AGOVEN088 Tainted of the Tistina QCSCR 4.00 10.00
AGOVEN089 Tistina, the Divinity that Defies Darkness UR .15 .40
AGOVEN089 Tistina, the Divinity that Defies Darkness QCSCR 5.00 12.00
AGOVEN090 Play of the Tistina C .08 .20
AGOVEN091 Embrace of the Tistina SR .08 .20
AGOVEN092 Discordance of the Tistina C .08 .20
AGOVEN093 Rose Papillon C .08 .20
AGOVEN094 Burning Dragon SR .08 .20
AGOVEN095 Starring Knight C .08 .20
AGOVEN096 Red Arrows C .08 .20
AGOVEN097 Sweet Roommaid C .08 .20
AGOVEN098 Lil-la Rap C .08 .20
AGOVEN099 Switch Point SR .08 .20
AGOVEN100 Alpha Summon C .08 .20

2023 Yu-Gi-Oh Amazing Defenders 1st Edition

AMDEEN001 Rescue-ACE Impulse SR .25 .50
AMDEEN002 Rescue-ACE Air Lifter R .12 .25
AMDEEN003 Rescue-ACE Monitor SR .15 .30
AMDEEN004 Rescue-ACE Hydrant UR 12.50 25.00
AMDEEN004 Rescue-ACE Hydrant CR 40.00 80.00
AMDEEN005 Rescue-ACE Fire Attacker R .12 .25
AMDEEN006 Rescue-ACE Fire Engine SR .15 .30
AMDEEN007 Rescue-ACE Turbulence CR 25.00 50.00
AMDEEN007 Rescue-ACE Turbulence UR 7.50 15.00
AMDEEN008 Rescue-ACE HQ R .12 .25
AMDEEN009 RESCUE! UR 2.50 5.00
AMDEEN010 ALERT! UR 2.50 5.00
AMDEEN011 CONTAIN! R .12 .25
AMDEEN012 EXTINGUISH! R .12 .25
AMDEEN013 Purrely CR 75.00 150.00
AMDEEN013 Purrely UR 10.00 20.00
AMDEEN014 Epurrely Happiness R .12 .25
AMDEEN015 Epurrely Beauty SR .15 .30
AMDEEN016 Epurrely Plump SR .15 .30
AMDEEN017 Expurrely Happiness CR 15.00 30.00
AMDEEN017 Expurrely Happiness SR .20 .40
AMDEEN018 Expurrely Noir CR 40.00 80.00
AMDEEN018 Expurrely Noir SR .15 .30
AMDEEN019 Stray Purrely Street R .12 .25
AMDEEN020 My Friend Purrely CR 40.00 80.00
AMDEEN020 My Friend Purrely UR 7.50 15.00
AMDEEN021 Purrely Happy Memory R .12 .25
AMDEEN022 Purrely Pretty Memory CR 50.00 100.00
AMDEEN022 Purrely Pretty Memory UR .50 1.00
AMDEEN023 Purrely Delicious Memory R .12 .25
AMDEEN024 Purrelyeap!? R .12 .25
AMDEEN025 Ha-Re the Sword Mikanko CR 40.00 80.00
AMDEEN025 Ha-Re the Sword Mikanko SR .25 .50
AMDEEN026 Ni-Ni the Mirror Mikanko CR 30.00 60.00
AMDEEN026 Ni-Ni the Mirror Mikanko SR .20 .40
AMDEEN027 Ohime the Manifested Mikanko UR 15.00 30.00
AMDEEN028 Heavenly Gate of the Mikanko UR .75 1.50
AMDEEN029 The Great Mikanko Ceremony R .12 .25
AMDEEN030 Mikanko Fire Dance SR .20 .40
AMDEEN031 Mikanko Purification Dance R .12 .25
AMDEEN032 Mikanko Water Arabesque UR 10.00 20.00
AMDEEN033 Mikanko Reflection Rondo CR 20.00 40.00
AMDEEN033 Mikanko Reflection Rondo R .12 .25
AMDEEN034 Mikanko Kagura R .12 .25
AMDEEN035 Mikanko Promise R .12 .25
AMDEEN036 Mikanko Rivalry R .12 .25
AMDEEN037 Gizmek Naganaki, the Sunrise Signaler R .12 .25
AMDEEN038 Infernoble Knight - Renaud CR 30.00 60.00
AMDEEN038 Infernoble Knight - Renaud SR .15 .30
AMDEEN039 Reinforcement of the Army R .12 .25
AMDEEN040 One for One CR 30.00 60.00
AMDEEN040 One for One SR .50 1.00
AMDEEN041 Hidden Armory R .12 .25
AMDEEN042 Infernoble Arms - Durendal R .12 .25
AMDEEN043 Double-Edged Sword R .12 .25
AMDEEN044 Xyz Import R .12 .25
AMDEEN045 Xyz Tribalrivals R .12 .25
AMDEEN046 Card Trooper CR 15.00 30.00
AMDEEN046 Card Trooper R .12 .25
AMDEEN047 Armed Protector Dragon R .12 .25
AMDEEN048 Gizmek Orochi... CR 17.50 35.00
AMDEEN048 Gizmek Orochi, the Serpentron Sky Slasher R .12 .25
AMDEEN049 Immortal Phoenix Gearfried SR .20 .40
AMDEEN050 Infernoble Knight - Roland R .12 .25
AMDEEN051 Sauravis, the Ancient and Ascended R .12 .25
AMDEEN052 Isolde, Two Tales of the Noble Knights CR 40.00 80.00
AMDEEN052 Isolde, Two Tales of the Noble Knights SR .30 .75
AMDEEN053 Limiter Removal R .12 .25
AMDEEN054 Machine Duplication R .12 .25
AMDEEN055 Preparation of Rites R .20 .40
AMDEEN056 Overlay Regen SR .15 .30
AMDEEN057 Sprite's Blessing R .12 .25
AMDEEN058 Sacred Scrolls of the Gizmek Legend R .12 .25
AMDEEN059 Piri Reis Map R .12 .25
AMDEEN060 Xyz Reborn R .12 .25

2023 Yu-Gi-Oh Battles of Legend Monstrous Revenge 1st Edition

BLMREN001 Dark Magician Knight of Dr.Magic SCR .75 1.50
BLMREN001 Dark Magician Knight of Dr.Magic QCSCR 75.00 150.00
BLMREN002 Armed Neos QCSCR 40.00 80.00
BLMREN002 Armed Neos SCR 1.50 3.00
BLMREN003 Assault Synchron QCSCR 75.00 150.00
BLMREN003 Assault Synchron SCR 5.00 10.00
BLMREN004 Numbers Last Hope UR .15 .30
BLMREN005 Odd-Eyes Rebellion Xyz Dragon UR .15 .30
BLMREN006 Rokket Coder SCR .30 .60
BLMREN007 Extox Hydra QCSCR 20.00 40.00
BLMREN007 Extox Hydra SCR .75 1.50
BLMREN008 Tri-Edge Master SCR .25 .50
BLMREN008 Tri-Edge Master QCSCR 25.00 50.00
BLMREN009 Daidaratant the Ooze Giant SCR .15 .30
BLMREN010 Don't Slip, the Dog of War UR .15 .30
BLMREN011 RGB Rainbowlution SCR .12 .25
BLMREN012 Elemental HERO Flame Wingman... SCR .50 1.00
BLMREN013 Link Decoder UR .15 .30
BLMREN014 Courageous Crimson Chevalier... SCR .30 .60
BLMREN015 Puppet Pawn UR .15 .30
BLMREN016 Puppet Rook UR .15 .30
BLMREN017 Promotion UR .15 .30
BLMREN018 Battlefield Tragedy SCR .15 .30
BLMREN019 Black Mamba UR .15 .30
BLMREN020 Urubonus, the Avatar of Malice UR .15 .30
BLMREN021 Lamia UR .15 .30
BLMREN022 Viper's Grudge UR .15 .30
BLMREN023 Ghost Lancer, the Underworld Spearman UR .15 .30
BLMREN024 Ghost Sleeper, the Underworld Princess UR .15 .30
BLMREN025 Ghost Wyvern, the Underworld Dragon UR .15 .30
BLMREN026 Ghost Fusion UR .15 .30
BLMREN027 Xyz Bento UR .15 .30
BLMREN028 Performapal Odd-Eyes Butler UR .15 .30
BLMREN029 Performapal Odd-Eyes Valet UR .15 .30
BLMREN030 Performapal Barokuriboh UR .15 .30
BLMREN031 Performapal Classikuriboh UR .15 .30
BLMREN032 Arms Regeneration UR .15 .30
BLMREN033 Praying Mantis UR .15 .30
BLMREN034 Guard Mantis UR .15 .30
BLMREN035 Golden Rule SCR .60 1.25
BLMREN036 Duality SCR 7.50 15.00
BLMREN037 Shadow's Light SCR 1.00 2.00
BLMREN038 Protection of the Elements UR .15 .30
BLMREN039 Blackwing - Sharnga the Waning Moon UR .15 .30
BLMREN040 Rose Shaman UR .15 .30
BLMREN041 Final Cross UR .15 .30
BLMREN042 Cattycorn UR .15 .30
BLMREN043 Photon Jumper SCR .20 .40
BLMREN044 Mother Spider Splitter UR .15 .30
BLMREN045 Baby Spider UR .15 .30
BLMREN046 DDDD...Emperor Zero Paradox UR .15 .30
BLMREN047 Additional Mirror Level 7 UR .15 .30
BLMREN048 Synchro Zone SCR .15 .30
BLMREN049 Sage of Strength - Akash UR .15 .30
BLMREN050 Sage of Wisdom - Himmel UR .15 .30
BLMREN051 Sage of Benevolence - Ciela UR .15 .30
BLMREN052 Sky Striker Ace - Azalea SCR 12.50 25.00
BLMREN053 Volcanic Shell UR .15 .30
BLMREN053 Volcanic Shell QCSCR 30.00 60.00
BLMREN054 Dark Armed Dragon QCSCR 40.00 80.00
BLMREN054 Dark Armed Dragon UR .20 .40
BLMREN055 Aratama UR .15 .30
BLMREN056 SPYRAL Quik-Fix UR .15 .30
BLMREN056 SPYRAL Quik-Fix QCSCR 25.00 50.00
BLMREN057 Knightmare Corruptor Iblee SCR .75 1.50
BLMREN058 Photon Vanisher UR .15 .30
BLMREN059 Danger! Nessie! SCR .75 1.50
BLMREN059 Danger! Nessie! QCSCR 30.00 60.00
BLMREN060 Mathmech Sigma UR .15 .30
BLMREN061 Ukiyoe-P.U.N.K. Sharakusai UR .15 .30
BLMREN062 Noh-P.U.N.K. Ze Amin UR .15 .30
BLMREN063 Noh-P.U.N.K. Foxy Tune SCR 2.50 5.00
BLMREN063 Noh-P.U.N.K. Foxy Tune QCSCR 50.00 100.00
BLMREN064 Noh-P.U.N.K. Ogre Dance SCR .30 .60
BLMREN065 Water Enchantress of the Temple SCR 2.50 5.00
BLMREN065 Water Enchantress of the Temple QCSCR 30.00 75.00
BLMREN066 Noh-P.U.N.K. Deer Note UR .15 .30
BLMREN067 Spright Carrot UR .15 .30
BLMREN068 Celestial Apparatus Tesea UR .15 .30
BLMREN069 Bystial Baldrake UR .15 .30
BLMREN070 Sakitama UR .15 .30
BLMREN071 Mysterion the Dragon Crown SCR .15 .30
BLMREN072 Ukiyoe-P.U.N.K. Rising Carp UR .15 .30
BLMREN073 Junk Archer SCR .20 .40
BLMREN074 Draco Berserker of the Tenyi SCR .40 .80
BLMREN075 Ukiyoe-P.U.N.K. Amazing Dragon SCR .15 .30
BLMREN076 Madolche Queen Tiaramisu SCR .30 .75
BLMREN076 Madolche Queen Tiaramisu QCSCR 30.00 60.00
BLMREN077 Number 92: Heart-eartH Dragon SCR .75 1.50
BLMREN077 Number 92: Heart eartH Dragon QCSCR 25.00 50.00
BLMREN078 Herald of Pure Light SCR .20 .40
BLMREN079 Number 65: Djinn Buster UR .15 .30
BLMREN080 Number 72: Shogi Rook UR .15 .30
BLMREN081 Dante, Traveler of the Burning Abyss QCSCR 50.00 100.00
BLMREN081 Dante, Traveler of the Burning Abyss SCR .20 .40
BLMREN082 Stellarknight Constellar Diamond UR .15 .30
BLMREN083 Tellarknight Ptolemaeus QCSCR 30.00 75.00
BLMREN083 Tellarknight Ptolemaeus SCR .20 .40
BLMREN084 Divine Arsenal AA-ZEUS - Sky Thunder QCSCR 75.00 150.00
BLMREN084 Divine Arsenal AA-ZEUS - Sky Thunder SCR 7.50 15.00
BLMREN085 I:P Masquerena QCSCR 150.00 300.00
BLMREN085 I:P Masquerena SCR 2.50 5.00
BLMREN086 Dark Hole QCSCR 30.00 60.00
BLMREN086 Dark Hole SCR .75 1.50
BLMREN087 Terraforming SCR 1.00 2.00

BLMREN087 Terraforming QCSCR 50.00 100.00
BLMREN088 Dimensional Fissure UR .15 .30
BLMREN089 Super Polymerization SCR 2.00 4.00
BLMREN089 Super Polymerization QCSCR 50.00 100.00
BLMREN090 Book of Eclipse SCR .30 .75
BLMREN091 Sky Striker Mobilize -
Engage! QCSCR 125.00 250.00
BLMREN091 Sky Striker Mobilize - Engage! SCR3.00 6.00
BLMREN092 Mathmech Equation UR .15 .30
BLMREN093 Rite of Aramesir QCSCR 50.00 100.00
BLMREN093 Rite of Aramesir SCR 10.00 20.00
BLMREN094 Dunnell, the Noble Arms of Light UR.15 .30
BLMREN095 Starlit Papillon UR .15 .30
BLMREN096 Zaralaam the Dark Palace UR .15 .30
BLMREN097 Forest of Lost Flowers UR .15 .30
BLMREN098 Spright Smashers UR .15 .30
BLMREN099 Curse of Aramatir UR .15 .30
BLMREN100 Macro Cosmos UR .30 .60
BLMREN101 Thunder Discharge UR .15 .30
BLMREN102 Welcome Labrynth QCSCR 60.00 125.00
BLMREN102 Welcome Labrynth SCR 2.00 4.00
BLMREN103 The Bystial Lubellion QCSCR 150.00 300.00
BLMREN104 Lady Labrynth
of the Silver Castle QCSCR 75.00 150.00

2023 Yu-Gi-Oh Cyberstorm Access 1st Edition

CYACEN000 Numbers Eveil UR .30 .60
CYACEN001 Firewall Defenser UR 4.00 8.00
CYACEN002 Firewall Phantom C .07 .15
CYACEN003 Superheavy Samurai Motorbike C .07 .15
CYACEN004 Superheavy Samurai Stealthy C .07 .15
CYACEN005 Superheavy Samurai
Soulgaia Booster C .07 .15
CYACEN006 Superheavy
Samurai Prodigy Wakaushi SR .60 1.25
CYACEN007 Superheavy
Samurai Monk Big Benkei C .07 .15
CYACEN008 The Bystial Aluber SR .15 .30
CYACEN009 Fallen of Argyros C .07 .15
CYACEN010 Icejade Ran Aegerine UR 4.00 8.00
CYACEN011 Guiding Quem, the Virtuous SCR 15.00 30.00
CYACEN011 Guiding Quem, the Virtuous SLR175.00 350.00
CYACEN012 Mannadium Riumheart UR 5.00 10.00
CYACEN013 Mannadium Fearless SR .20 .40
CYACEN014 Mannadium Meek SR .25 .50
CYACEN015 Dreaming Nemleria SR .15 .30
CYACEN016 Nemleria Dream Defender - Oreiller C.07 .15
CYACEN017 Nemleria Dream Defender - Couette C.07 .15
CYACEN018 Purrelyly C .07 .15
CYACEN019 Hu-Li the Jewel Mikanko C .07 .15
CYACEN020 Tellarknight Altairan SR .15 .30
CYACEN021 Tellarknight Lyran SR .15 .30
CYACEN022 Infinitrack Road Roller UR .20 .40
CYACEN023 Amazement Abomination Arlekino C.07 .15
CYACEN024 Tsumuha-Kutsunagi
the Lord of Swords SCR .75 1.50
CYACEN025 Full Active Duplex C .07 .15
CYACEN026 Harvest Angel of Doom SR .15 .30
CYACEN027 Sakitama C .07 .15
CYACEN028 Kitsuni Kitsunebi C .07 .15
CYACEN029 Ringowurm... UR 10.00 20.00
CYACEN030 PenduLuMoon C .07 .15
CYACEN031 Wannabee! SR .75 1.50
CYACEN032 Bunny Ear Enthusiast C .07 .15
CYACEN033 Cyberse Sage C .07 .15
CYACEN034 Cyberse Desavewurm C .07 .15
CYACEN035 Albion the Sanctifire Dragon SCR 7.50 15.00
CYACEN036 Vicious Astraloud SCR 5.00 10.00
CYACEN037 Beetrooper Cruel Saturnas SR .15 .30
CYACEN038 Dual Avatar - Manifested A-Un C .07 .15
CYACEN039 Superheavy Samurai
Brave Masurawo UR .50 1.00
CYACEN040 Superheavy Samurai
Commander Shanawo SR .15 .30
CYACEN041 Bystial Dis Pater UR 7.50 15.00
CYACEN042 Despian Luluwalilith SCR 10.00 20.00
CYACEN042 Despian Luluwalilith SLR 150.00 300.00
CYACEN043 Mannadium Prime-Heart UR .30 .75
CYACEN044 Chaos Angel SCR 40.00 80.00
CYACEN045 Tellarknight Constellar Caduceus UR.50 1.00
CYACEN046 Virtual World Tiger - Fufu C .07 .15
CYACEN047 Firewall Dragon Singularity SCR 2.00 4.00
CYACEN047 Firewall Dragon Singularity SLR 60.00 125.00
CYACEN048 Protectcode Talker SR .15 .30
CYACEN049 GranSolfachord Coolia SR .15 .30
CYACEN050 S-Force Nightchaser SR .15 .30
CYACEN051 Cynet Rollback SR .15 .30
CYACEN052 Swordsoul Punishment C .07 .15
CYACEN053 Tri-Brigade Roar SR .20 .40
CYACEN054 New Frontier C .07 .15
CYACEN055 Kashtira Akstra C .07 .15
CYACEN056 Mannadium Imaginings C .07 .15
CYACEN057 Mannadium Abscission C .07 .15
CYACEN058 Peaceful Planet Calarium SCR 15.00 30.00
CYACEN059 Dream Tower of Princess Nemleria C.07 .15
CYACEN060 Sweet Dreams, Nemleria C .07 .15
CYACEN061 Purrely Sleepy Memory C .07 .15
CYACEN062 Mikanko Dance - Mayowashidori C .07 .15
CYACEN063 Libromancer Origin Story UR .30 .75
CYACEN064 Constellar Tellarknights SR .15 .30
CYACEN065 Solfachord Symphony C .07 .15
CYACEN066 Gunkan Suship Catch-of-the-Day C .07 .15
CYACEN067 Time-Tearing Morganite SR 2.50 5.00
CYACEN068 Pig Iron vs. Pen Peg C .07 .15
CYACEN069 Cynet Circuit C .07 .15
CYACEN070 Brightest, Blazing, Branded King C .07 .15
CYACEN071 Etude of the Branded C .07 .15
CYACEN072 Mannadium Breakheart C .07 .15
CYACEN073 Mannadium Reframing C .07 .15
CYACEN074 A Shattered, Colorless Realm C .07 .15
CYACEN075 REINFORCE! C .07 .15
CYACEN076 Dinomorphia Intact C .07 .15
CYACEN077 Fusion Duplication C .07 .15
CYACEN078 Trap Tracks C .07 .15
CYACEN079 Double Hooking C .07 .15
CYACEN080 Hatsugai C .07 .15
CYACEN081 Moissa Knight, the Comet General C.07 .15
CYACEN082 Golden Cloud Beast - Malong C .07 .15
CYACEN083 Imperial Princess Quinquery C .07 .15
CYACEN084 Pendulum Pendant C .07 .15
CYACEN085 How Did Dai Get Here? C .07 .15
CYACEN086 Gold Pride - Roller Baller SCR 5.00 10.00
CYACEN087 Gold Pride - Pin Baller UR .50 1.00
CYACEN088 Gold Pride - Chariot Carrie SLR 75.00 150.00
CYACEN088 Gold Pride - Chariot Carrie UR .75 1.50
CYACEN089 Gold Pride -
That Came Out of Nowhere! UR .30 .60
CYACEN090 Gold Pride - Pedal to the Metal! C .07 .15
CYACEN091 Gold Pride -
Better Luck Next Time! SCR 10.00 20.00
CYACEN092 Gold Pride - It's Neck and Neck! C .07 .15
CYACEN093 Wish Dragon SR .15 .30
CYACEN094 Votis SR .15 .30
CYACEN095 Adularia of the June Moon SR .15 .30
CYACEN096 Kittytail, Mystical
Beast of the Forest SR .15 .30
CYACEN097 Baromet the Sacred Sheep Shrub SR.15 .30
CYACEN098 Reincarnation
of the Seventh Emperors SR .15 .30
CYACEN099 Rebirth of the Seventh Emperors SR.15 .30
CYACEN100 Visas Starfrost SLR 150.00 300.00
CYACENSP1 Tsumuha-Kutsunagi
the Lord of Swords UR 4.00 8.00

2023 Yu-Gi-Oh Dark Crisis 25th Anniversary Edition

DCREN000 Vampire Lord SCR 2.50 5.00
DCREN001 Battle Footballer C .10 .20
DCREN002 Nin-Ken Dog C .10 .20
DCREN003 Acrobat Monkey C .10 .20
DCREN004 Arsenal Summoner C .10 .20
DCREN005 Guardian Elma C .12 .25
DCREN006 Guardian Ceal UR 3.00 6.00
DCREN007 Guardian Grarl UR 3.00 6.00
DCREN008 Guardian Baou R .15 .30
DCREN009 Guardian Kay'est C .12 .25
DCREN010 Guardian Tryce R .30 .60
DCREN011 Cyber Raider C .20 .40
DCREN012 Reflect Bounder UR 4.00 8.00
DCREN013 Little-Winguard C .10 .20
DCREN014 Des Feral Imp R .15 .30
DCREN015 Different Dimension Dragon SR .60 1.25
DCREN016 Shinato, King of a Higher Plane UR 7.50 15.00
DCREN017 Dark Flare Knight SR 2.50 5.00
DCREN018 Mirage Knight SR .75 1.50
DCREN019 Berserk Dragon SR .75 1.50
DCREN020 Exodia Necross UR 15.00 30.00
DCREN021 Gyaku-Gire Panda C .75 1.50
DCREN022 Blindly Loyal Goblin C .10 .20
DCREN023 Despair from the Dark C .12 .25
DCREN024 Maju Garzett C .10 .20
DCREN025 Fear from the Dark R .15 .30
DCREN026 Dark Scorpion - Chick the Yellow C .10 .20
DCREN027 D. D. Warrior Lady SR 2.00 4.00
DCREN028 Thousand Needles C .10 .20
DCREN029 Shinato's Ark C .20 .40
DCREN030 A Deal with Dark Ruler C .10 .20
DCREN031 Contract with Exodia C .20 .40
DCREN032 Butterfly Dagger - Elma SR .75 1.50
DCREN033 Shooting Star Bow - Ceal C .10 .20
DCREN034 Gravity Axe - Grarl C .10 .20
DCREN035 Wicked-Breaking Flamberge R .15 .30
DCREN036 Rod of Silence - Kay'est C .10 .20
DCREN037 Twin Swords of Flashing Light C .20 .40
DCREN038 Precious Cards from Beyond C .12 .25
DCREN039 Rod of the Mind's Eye C .10 .20
DCREN040 Fairy of the Spring C .10 .20
DCREN041 Token Thanksgiving C .15 .30
DCREN042 Morale Boost C .10 .20
DCREN043 Non-Spellcasting Area C .10 .20
DCREN044 Different Dimension Gate R .15 .30
DCREN045 Final Attack Orders C .10 .20
DCREN046 Staunch Defender C .10 .20
DCREN047 Ojama Trio C .50 1.00
DCREN048 Arsenal Robber C .10 .20
DCREN049 Skill Drain R 1.50 3.00
DCREN050 Really Eternal Rest C .10 .20
DCREN051 Kaiser Glider UR 3.00 6.00
DCREN052 Interdimensional Matter Trans. UR 1.50 3.00
DCREN053 Cost Down UR 2.00 4.00
DCREN054 Gagagigo C .10 .20
DCREN055 D. D. Trainer C .10 .20
DCREN056 Ojama Green C .20 .40
DCREN057 Archfiend Soldier R .50 1.00
DCREN058 Pandemonium Watchbear C .10 .20
DCREN059 Sasuke Samurai #2 C .10 .20
DCREN060 Dark Scorpion - Gorg C .10 .20
DCREN061 Dark Scorpion - Meanae C .10 .20
DCREN062 Outstanding Dog Marron C .10 .20
DCREN063 Great Maju Garzett R .30 .75
DCREN064 Iron Blacksmith Kotetsu C .10 .20
DCREN065 Goblin of Greed C .10 .20
DCREN066 Mefist the Infernal General R .20 .40
DCREN067 Vilepawn Archfiend C .10 .20
DCREN068 Shadowknight Archfiend C .10 .20
DCREN069 Darkbishop Archfiend R .15 .30
DCREN070 Desrook Archfiend C .12 .25
DCREN071 Infernalqueen Archfiend R .12 .25
DCREN072 Terrorking Archfiend SR .75 1.50
DCREN073 Skull Archfiend of Lightning UR 6.00 12.00
DCREN074 Metallizing Parasite - Lunatite R .20 .40
DCREN075 Tsukuyomi R 1.00 2.00
DCREN076 Mudora SR .50 1.00
DCREN077 Keldo C .12 .25
DCREN078 Kelbek C .12 .25
DCREN079 Zolga C .15 .30
DCREN080 Agido C .10 .20
DCREN081 Legendary Flame Lord R .12 .25
DCREN082 Dark Master - Zorc SR .60 1.25
DCREN083 Spell Reproduction C .10 .20
DCREN084 Dragged Down into the Grave C .15 .30
DCREN085 Incandescent Ordeal C .12 .25
DCREN086 Contract with the Abyss R .20 .40
DCREN087 Contract with the Dark Master C .20 .40
DCREN088 Falling Down C .25 .50
DCREN089 Checkmate C .10 .20
DCREN090 Cestus of Dagla C .10 .20
DCREN091 Final Countdown C .30 .75
DCREN092 Archfiend's Oath C .12 .25
DCREN093 Mustering of Dark Scorpions C .10 .20
DCREN094 Pandemonium C .25 .50
DCREN095 Altar for Tribute C .10 .20
DCREN096 Frozen Soul C .10 .20
DCREN097 Battle-Scarred C .10 .20
DCREN098 Dark Scorpion Combination R .15 .30
DCREN099 Archfiend's Roar C .10 .20
DCREN100 Dice Re-Roll C .15 .30
DCREN101 Spell Vanishing SR 1.25 2.50
DCREN102 Sakuretsu Armor C .30 .75
DCREN103 Ray of Hope C .10 .20
DCREN104 Blast Held by a Tribute UR 2.00 4.00
DCREN105 Judgment of Anubis SCR 1.00 2.00

2023 Yu-Gi-Oh Invasion of Chaos 25th Anniversary Edition

IOCEN000 Chaos Emperor
Dragon - Envoy of the End SCR 7.50 15.00
IOCEN001 Ojama Yellow C .20 .40
IOCEN002 Ojama Black C .25 .50
IOCEN003 Soul Tiger C .10 .20
IOCEN004 Big Koala C .12 .25
IOCEN005 Des Kangaroo C .10 .20
IOCEN006 Crimson Ninja C .10 .20
IOCEN007 Strike Ninja UR 3.00 6.00
IOCEN008 Gale Lizard C .10 .20
IOCEN009 Spirit of the Pot of Greed C .10 .20
IOCEN010 Chopman the Desperate Outlaw C .10 .20
IOCEN011 Sasuke Samurai #3 R .12 .25
IOCEN012 D.D. Scout Plane SR .75 1.50
IOCEN013 Beserk Gorilla R .15 .30
IOCEN014 Freed the Brave Wanderer SR .75 1.50
IOCEN015 Coach Goblin C .12 .25
IOCEN016 Witch Doctor of Chaos C .10 .20
IOCEN017 Chaos Necromancer C .20 .40
IOCEN018 Chaosrider Gustaph SR .50 1.00
IOCEN019 Inferno C .12 .25
IOCEN020 Fenrir C .10 .20
IOCEN021 Gigantes C .10 .20
IOCEN022 Silpheed C .10 .20
IOCEN023 Chaos Sorcerer C .20 .40
IOCEN024 Gren Maju Da Eiza C .30 .60
IOCEN025 Black Luster Soldier... UR 10.00 20.00
IOCEN026 Drillago R .20 .40
IOCEN027 Lekunga R .30 .75
IOCEN028 Lord Poison C .15 .30
IOCEN029 Bowganian C .10 .20
IOCEN030 Granadora C .10 .20
IOCEN031 Fuhma Shuriken R .15 .30
IOCEN032 Heart of the Underdog C .12 .25
IOCEN033 Wild Nature's Release SR 1.25 2.50
IOCEN034 Ojama Delta Hurricane C .10 .20
IOCEN035 Stumbling C .50 1.00
IOCEN036 Chaos End C .10 .20
IOCEN037 Yellow Luster Shield C .10 .20
IOCEN038 Chaos Greed C .10 .20
IOCEN039 D.D. Designator SR .75 1.50
IOCEN040 D.D. Borderline C .12 .25
IOCEN041 Recycle C .12 .25
IOCEN042 Primal Seed C .15 .30
IOCEN043 Thunder Crash C .10 .20
IOCEN044 Dimension Distortion C .10 .20
IOCEN045 Reload SR .60 1.25
IOCEN046 Soul Absorption C .10 .20
IOCEN047 Big Burn SR .50 1.00
IOCEN048 Blasting the Ruins C .10 .20
IOCEN049 Cursed Seal of Forbidden Spell C .12 .25
IOCEN050 Tower of Babel C .10 .20
IOCEN051 Spatial Collapse C .10 .20
IOCEN052 Chain Disappearance R .15 .30
IOCEN053 Zero Gravity C .10 .20
IOCEN054 Dark Mirror Force UR 4.00 8.00
IOCEN055 Energy Drain C .15 .30
IOCEN056 Giga Gagagigo C .10 .20
IOCEN057 Mad Dog of Darkness R .15 .30
IOCEN058 Neo Bug C .10 .20
IOCEN059 Sea Serpent Warrior of Darkness C .10 .20
IOCEN060 Terrorking Salmon C .12 .25
IOCEN061 Blazing Inpachi C .10 .20
IOCEN062 Burning Algae C .10 .20
IOCEN063 The Thing in the Crater C .12 .25
IOCEN064 Molten Zombie C .10 .20
IOCEN065 Dark Magician of Chaos UR 10.00 20.00
IOCEN066 Gora Turtle of Illusion C .15 .30
IOCEN067 Manticore of Darkness UR 2.50 5.00
IOCEN068 Stealth Bird C .10 .20
IOCEN069 Sacred Crane C .12 .25
IOCEN070 Enraged Battle Ox R .20 .40
IOCEN071 Don Turtle C .12 .25
IOCEN072 Balloon Lizard C .10 .20
IOCEN073 Dark Driceratops R .15 .30
IOCEN074 Hyper Hammerhead C .10 .20
IOCEN075 Black Tyranno UR 2.50 5.00
IOCEN076 Anti-Aircraft Flower C .12 .25
IOCEN077 Prickle Fairy C .10 .20
IOCEN078 Pinch Hopper C .30 .60
IOCEN079 Skull-Mark Ladybug C .12 .25
IOCEN080 Insect Princess UR 2.00 4.00
IOCEN081 Amphibious Bugroth MK-3 C .10 .20
IOCEN082 Torpedo Fish C .10 .20
IOCEN083 Levia-Dragon Daedalus UR 2.50 5.00
IOCEN084 Orca Mega-Fortress of Darkness SR 1.50 3.00
IOCEN085 Cannonball Spear Shellfish C .10 .20
IOCEN086 Mataza the Zapper R .25 .50
IOCEN087 Guardian Angel Joan UR 2.00 4.00
IOCEN088 Manju of Ten Thousand Hands C .30 .60
IOCEN089 Getsu Fuhma R .15 .30
IOCEN090 Ryu Kokki C .12 .25
IOCEN091 Gryphon's Feather Duster C .12 .25
IOCEN092 Stray Lambs R .15 .30
IOCEN093 Smashing Ground C .50 1.00
IOCEN094 Dimension Fusion UR 15.00 30.00
IOCEN095 Dedication Through
Light & Darkness SR .60 1.25
IOCEN096 Salvage C .12 .25
IOCEN097 Ultra Evolution Pill R .15 .30
IOCEN098 Multiplication of Ants C .15 .30
IOCEN099 Earth Chant C .10 .20
IOCEN100 Jade Insect Whistle C .10 .20
IOCEN101 Destruction Ring R .15 .30
IOCEN102 Fiend's Hand Mirror C .10 .20
IOCEN103 Compulsory Evacuation Device R .50 1.00
IOCEN104 A Hero Emerges C .20 .40
IOCEN105 Self-Destruct Button C .10 .20
IOCEN106 Curse of Darkness R .17 .35
IOCEN107 Begone, Knave! C .10 .20
IOCEN108 DNA Transplant C .12 .25
IOCEN109 Robbin' Zombie R .12 .25
IOCEN110 Trap Jammer SR .75 1.50
IOCEN111 Invader of Darkness SCR 2.00 4.00

2023 Yu-Gi-Oh Legend of Blue-Eyes White Dragon 25th Anniversary Edition

LOBEN000 Tri-Horned Dragon SCR 4.00 8.00
LOBEN001 Blue-Eyes White Dragon UR 30.00 75.00
LOBEN002 Hitotsu-Me Giant C .10 .20
LOBEN003 Flame Swordsman SR 1.50 3.00
LOBEN004 Skull Servant C 30.00 75.00
LOBEN005 Dark Magician UR 20.00 40.00
LOBEN006 Gaia the Fierce Knight UR 7.50 15.00
LOBEN007 Celtic Guardian SR 1.25 2.50
LOBEN008 Basic Insect C .10 .20
LOBEN009 Mammoth Graveyard C .10 .20
LOBEN010 Silver Fang C .10 .20
LOBEN011 Dark Gray C .10 .20
LOBEN012 Trial of Nightmare C .10 .20
LOBEN013 Nemuriko C .10 .20
LOBEN014 The 13th Grave C .10 .20
LOBEN015 Charubin the Fire Knight R .30 .60
LOBEN016 Flame Manipulator C .10 .20
LOBEN017 Monster Egg C .10 .20
LOBEN018 Firegrass C .10 .20
LOBEN019 Darkfire Dragon R .75 1.50
LOBEN020 Dark King of the Abyss C .10 .20
LOBEN021 Fiend Reflection #2 C .10 .20
LOBEN022 Fusionist R .30 .75
LOBEN023 Turtle Tiger C .10 .20
LOBEN024 Petit Dragon C .10 .20
LOBEN025 Petit Angel C .10 .20
LOBEN026 Hinotama Soul C .10 .20
LOBEN027 Aqua Madoor R .15 .30
LOBEN028 Kagemusha of the Blue Flame C .10 .20
LOBEN029 Flame Ghost R .50 1.00
LOBEN030 Two-Mouth Darkruler C .10 .20
LOBEN031 Dissolverock C .10 .20
LOBEN032 Root Water C .10 .20
LOBEN033 The Furious Sea King C .10 .20
LOBEN034 Green Phantom King C .10 .20
LOBEN035 Ray & Temperature C .10 .20
LOBEN036 King Fog C .10 .20
LOBEN037 Mystical Sheep #2 C .10 .20
LOBEN038 Masaki the Legendary Swordsman C .10 .20
LOBEN039 Kurama C .10 .20
LOBEN040 Legendary Sword C .10 .20
LOBEN041 Beast Fangs C .10 .20
LOBEN042 Violet Crystal C .10 .20
LOBEN043 Book of Secret Arts C .10 .20
LOBEN044 Power of Kaishin C .10 .20
LOBEN045 Dragon Capture Jar R .15 .30
LOBEN046 Forest C .10 .20
LOBEN047 Wasteland C .10 .20
LOBEN048 Mountain C .10 .20
LOBEN049 Sogen C .10 .20
LOBEN050 Umi C .10 .20
LOBEN051 Yami C .10 .20
LOBEN052 Dark Hole SR 1.50 3.00
LOBEN053 Raigeki SR 2.50 5.00
LOBEN054 Red Medicine C .10 .20
LOBEN055 Sparks C .10 .20
LOBEN056 Hinotama C .10 .20
LOBEN057 Fissure R .50 1.00
LOBEN058 Trap Hole SR 1.25 2.50
LOBEN059 Polymerization SR 2.00 4.00
LOBEN060 Remove Trap C .10 .20
LOBEN061 Two-Pronged Attack R .15 .30
LOBEN062 Mystical Elf SR 1.50 3.00
LOBEN063 Tyhone C .10 .20
LOBEN064 Beaver Warrior C .10 .20
LOBEN065 Gravedigger Ghoul R .30 .60
LOBEN066 Curse of Dragon SR 2.00 4.00
LOBEN067 Karbonala Warrior R .50 1.00
LOBEN068 Giant Soldier of Stone R .30 .60
LOBEN069 Uraby C .10 .20
LOBEN070 Red-Eyes Black Dragon UR 25.00 50.00
LOBEN071 Reaper of the Cards R .25 .50
LOBEN072 Witty Phantom C .10 .20
LOBEN073 Larvas C .10 .20
LOBEN074 Hard Armor C .10 .20
LOBEN075 Man Eater C .10 .20
LOBEN076 M-Warrior #1 C .10 .20
LOBEN077 M-Warrior #2 C .10 .20
LOBEN078 Spirit of the Harp R .20 .40
LOBEN079 Armaill C .10 .20
LOBEN080 Terra the Terrible C .10 .20
LOBEN081 Frenzied Panda C .10 .20
LOBEN082 Kumootoko C .10 .20
LOBEN083 Meda Bat C .10 .20
LOBEN084 Enchanting Mermaid C .10 .20
LOBEN085 Fireyarou C .10 .20
LOBEN086 Dragoness the Wicked Knight R .50 1.00
LOBEN087 One-Eyed Shield Dragon C .10 .20
LOBEN088 Dark Energy C .10 .20
LOBEN089 Laser Cannon Armor C .10 .20
LOBEN090 Vile Germs C .10 .20
LOBEN091 Silver Bow and Arrow C .10 .20
LOBEN092 Dragon Treasure C .10 .20
LOBEN093 Electro-Whip C .10 .20

LOBEN094 Mystical Moon C .10 .20
LOBEN095 Stop Defense R .30 .60
LOBEN096 Machine Conversion Factory C .10 .20
LOBEN097 Raise Body Heat C .10 .20
LOBEN098 Follow Wind C .10 .20
LOBEN099 Goblin's Secret Remedy R .15 .30
LOBEN100 Final Flame R .30 .60
LOBEN101 Swords of Revealing Light SR 1.50 3.00
LOBEN102 Metal Dragon R .30 .60
LOBEN103 Spike Seadra C .10 .20
LOBEN104 Tripwire Beast C .10 .20
LOBEN105 Skull Red Bird C .10 .20
LOBEN106 Armed Ninja R .15 .30
LOBEN107 Flower Wolf R .30 .60
LOBEN108 Man-Eater Bug SR 1.25 2.50
LOBEN109 Sand Stone C .10 .20
LOBEN110 Hane-Hane R .20 .40
LOBEN111 Misairuzame C .10 .20
LOBEN112 Steel Ogre Grotto #1 C .10 .20
LOBEN113 Lesser Dragon C .10 .20
LOBEN114 Darkworld Thorns C .10 .20
LOBEN115 Drooling Lizard C .10 .20
LOBEN116 Armored Starfish C .10 .20
LOBEN117 Succubus Knight C .10 .20
LOBEN118 Monster Reborn UR 7.50 15.00
LOBEN119 Pot of Greed R 2.50 5.00
LOBEN120 Right Leg of the Forbidden One UR10.00 20.00
LOBEN121 Left Leg of the Forbidden One UR 7.50 15.00
LOBEN122 Right Arm of the Forbidden One UR10.00 20.00
LOBEN123 Left Arm of the Forbidden One UR 7.50 15.00
LOBEN124 Exodia the Forbidden One UR 20.00 40.00
LOBEN125 Gaia the Dragon Champion SCR 4.00 8.00

2023 Yu-Gi-Oh Legendary Collection 25th Anniversary Edition

LC01EN001 Obelisk the Tormentor UR .30 .75
LC01EN001 Obelisk the Tormentor QSCR 6.00 12.00
LC01EN002 Slifer the Sky Dragon UR .30 .75
LC01EN002 Slifer the Sky Dragon QSCR 7.50 15.00
LC01EN003 The Winged Dragon of Ra UR .40 .80
LC01EN003 The Winged Dragon of Ra QSCR 6.00 12.00
LC01EN004 Blue-Eyes White Dragon UR .30 .75
LC01EN004 Blue-Eyes White Dragon QSCR 10.00 20.00
LC01EN005 Dark Magician UR .30 .60
LC01EN005 Dark Magician QSCR 6.00 12.00
LC01EN006 Red-Eyes Black Dragon UR .30 .60
LC01EN006 Red-Eyes Black Dragon QSCR 5.00 10.00

2023 Yu-Gi-Oh Maze of Memories 1st Edition

MAZEEN001 Labyrinth Heavy Tank SR .40 .80
MAZEEN002 Shadow Ghoul of the Labyrinth R .12 .25
MAZEEN003 Gate Guardians Combined SR .30 .75
MAZEEN004 Gate Guardian of
Thunder and Wind SR .25 .50
MAZEEN005 Gate Guardian of Wind and Water SR.40 .80
MAZEEN006 Gate Guardian
of Water and Thunder SR .25 .50
MAZEEN007 Labyrinth Wall Shadow R .12 .25
MAZEEN008 Double Attack! Wind and Thunder!! R.12 .25
MAZEEN009 Riryoku Guardian R .12 .25
MAZEEN010 Prey of the Jirai Gumo R .12 .25
MAZEEN011 Black Luster Soldier... CR 30.00 60.00
MAZEEN011 Black Luster Soldier... UR 2.50 5.00
MAZEEN012 Red-Eyes Soul R .25 .50
MAZEEN013 Duel Academy CR 7.50 15.00
MAZEEN013 Duel Academy UR .50 1.00
MAZEEN014 Wake Up Your Elemental HERO CR30.00 75.00
MAZEEN014 Wake Up Your Elemental HERO UR5.00 10.00
MAZEEN015 Evolution End Burst SR .15 .30
MAZEEN016 On Your Mark, Get Set, DUEL! CR15.00 30.00
MAZEEN016 On Your Mark, Get Set, DUEL! SR .20 .40
MAZEEN017 Time to Stand Up R .12 .25
MAZEEN018 This Creepy Little Punk R .12 .25
MAZEEN019 Accel Synchro Stardust Dragon CR100.00 200.00
MAZEEN019 Accel Synchro Stardust Dragon UR25.00 50.00
MAZEEN020 Overlay Network SR .20 .40
MAZEEN021 Number 39: Utopia Rising CR 10.00 20.00
MAZEEN021 Number 39: Utopia Rising SR .15 .30
MAZEEN022 Barian Untopia R .12 .25
MAZEEN023 Saga of the Dragon Emperor R .12 .25
MAZEEN024 Performapal Duelist Extraordinaire R.12 .25
MAZEEN025 Kahyoreigetsu R .12 .25
MAZEEN026 Battle Royal Mode - Joining R .12 .25
MAZEEN027 Soul of the Supreme King R .12 .25
MAZEEN028 Firewall Dragon Darkfluid... CR 25.00 50.00
MAZEEN028 Firewall Dragon Darkfluid... UR 2.50 5.00
MAZEEN029 Angel of Blue Tears R .12 .25
MAZEEN030 Forge a New Future R .12 .25
MAZEEN031 Labyrinth Wall R .12 .25
MAZEEN032 Sanga of the Thunder R .12 .25
MAZEEN033 Kazejin R .12 .25
MAZEEN034 Suijin R .12 .25
MAZEEN035 Gate Guardian CR 20.00 40.00
MAZEEN035 Gate Guardian R .12 .25
MAZEEN036 Superancient Deepsea
King Coelacanth SR .15 .30
MAZEEN037 Blackwing - Kalut the Moon Shadow R.12 .25
MAZEEN038 Blackwing - Elphin the Raven R .12 .25
MAZEEN039 Blackwing - Zephyros the Elite R .12 .25
MAZEEN040 Psi-Beast SR .15 .30
MAZEEN041 Wind-Up Kitten UR .50 1.00
MAZEEN042 Nimble Angler R .12 .25
MAZEEN043 Mekk-Knight Blue Sky R .12 .25
MAZEEN044 Mekk-Knight Yellow Star R .12 .25
MAZEEN045 Mekk-Knight Red Moon R .12 .25
MAZEEN046 Photon Orbital CR 12.50 25.00
MAZEEN046 Photon Orbital R .12 .25
MAZEEN047 Rikka Petal R .12 .25
MAZEEN048 Mudan the Rikka Fairy R .12 .25
MAZEEN049 Guardian Chimera UR .50 10.00
MAZEEN049 Guardian Chimera CR 30.00 75.00
MAZEEN050 Ancient Fairy Dragon R .12 .25
MAZEEN051 Baronne de Fleur CR 150.00 300.00
MAZEEN051 Baronne de Fleur UR 30.00 60.00
MAZEEN052 Alsei, the Sylvan High Protector SR .15 .30
MAZEEN053 Teardrop the Rikka Queen CR 25.00 50.00
MAZEEN053 Teardrop the Rikka Queen UR 1.25 2.50
MAZEEN054 Mekk-Knight Crusadia Avramax CR25.00 50.00
MAZEEN054 Mekk-Knight Crusadia Avramax SR .50 1.00
MAZEEN055 Cost Down R .12 .25
MAZEEN056 Overload Fusion R .12 .25
MAZEEN057 Burial from a Different Dimension R.12 .25
MAZEEN058 Court of Justice R .12 .25
MAZEEN059 Spellbook of Fate CR 7.50 15.00
MAZEEN059 Spellbook of Fate SR .15 .30
MAZEEN060 Super Soldier Ritual R .12 .25
MAZEEN061 Chaos Form R .12 .25
MAZEEN062 Rikka Glamour UR 2.50 5.00
MAZEEN063 Solemn Judgment CR 30.00 75.00
MAZEEN063 Solemn Judgment SR 2.50 5.00
MAZEEN064 Royal Decree R .12 .25
MAZEEN065 Imperial Iron Wall R .12 .25
MAZEEN066 Treacherous Trap Hole R .12 .25
MAZEEN067 Deep Dark Trap Hole R .12 .25

2023 Yu-Gi-Oh Metal Raiders 25th Anniversary Edition

MRDEN000 Gate Guardian SCR 4.00 8.00
MRDEN001 Feral Imp C .10 .20
MRDEN002 Winged Dragon,
Guardian of the Fortress 1 C .12 .25
MRDEN003 Summoned Skull UR 12.50 25.00
MRDEN004 Rock Ogre Grotto 1 C .10 .20
MRDEN005 Armored Lizard C .12 .25
MRDEN006 Killer Needle C .50 1.00
MRDEN007 Larvae Moth C .12 .25
MRDEN008 Harpie Lady C .30 .75
MRDEN009 Harpie Lady Sisters SR .75 1.50
MRDEN010 Kojikocy C .10 .20
MRDEN011 Cocoon of Evolution C .50 1.00
MRDEN012 Crawling Dragon #2 C .12 .25
MRDEN013 Armored Zombie C .10 .20
MRDEN014 Mask of Darkness R .25 .50
MRDEN015 Doma the Angel of Silence C .12 .25
MRDEN016 White Magical Hat R .20 .40
MRDEN017 Big Eye C .15 .30
MRDEN018 Black Skull Dragon UR 15.00 30.00
MRDEN019 Masked Sorcerer R .25 .50
MRDEN020 Roaring Ocean Snake C .12 .25
MRDEN021 Water Omotics C .12 .25
MRDEN022 Ground Attacker Bugroth C .12 .25
MRDEN023 Petit Moth C .12 .25
MRDEN024 Elegant Egotist R .15 .30
MRDEN025 Sanga of the Thunder SR 2.50 5.00
MRDEN026 Kazejin SR 2.50 5.00
MRDEN027 Suijin SR 2.00 4.00
MRDEN028 Mystic Lamp C .20 .40
MRDEN029 Steel Scorpion C .12 .25
MRDEN030 Ocubeam C .15 .30
MRDEN031 Leghul C .20 .40
MRDEN032 Ooguchi C .15 .30
MRDEN033 Leogun C .12 .25
MRDEN034 Blast Juggler C .12 .25
MRDEN035 Jinzo #7 C .12 .25
MRDEN036 Magician of Faith R .75 1.50
MRDEN037 Ancient Elf C .12 .25
MRDEN038 Deepsea Shark C .20 .40
MRDEN039 Bottom Dweller C .10 .20
MRDEN040 Destroyer Golem C .10 .20
MRDEN041 Kaminari Attack C .12 .25
MRDEN042 Rainbow Flower C .20 .40
MRDEN043 Morinphen C .10 .20
MRDEN044 Mega Thunderball C .10 .20
MRDEN045 Tongyo C .12 .25
MRDEN046 Empress Judge C .10 .20
MRDEN047 Pale Beast C .12 .25
MRDEN048 Electric Lizard C .12 .25
MRDEN049 Hunter Spider C .10 .20
MRDEN050 Ancient Lizard Warrior C .12 .25
MRDEN051 Queen's Double C .20 .40
MRDEN052 Trent C .12 .25
MRDEN053 Disk Magician C .15 .30
MRDEN054 Hyosube C .10 .20
MRDEN055 Hibikime C .12 .25
MRDEN056 Fake Trap R .15 .30
MRDEN057 Tribute to the Doomed SR .75 1.50
MRDEN058 Soul Release C .20 .40
MRDEN059 The Cheerful Coffin C .15 .30
MRDEN060 Change of Heart UR 5.00 10.00
MRDEN061 Baby Dragon C .15 .30
MRDEN062 Blackland Fire Dragon C .12 .25
MRDEN063 Swamp Battleguard C .10 .20
MRDEN064 Battle Steer C .10 .20
MRDEN065 Time Wizard UR 12.50 25.00
MRDEN066 Saggi the Dark Clown C .20 .40
MRDEN067 Dragon Piper C .12 .25
MRDEN068 Illusionist Faceless Mage C .10 .20
MRDEN069 Sangan R .50 1.00
MRDEN070 Great Moth R .60 1.25
MRDEN071 Kuriboh SR .75 1.50
MRDEN072 Jellyfish C .12 .25
MRDEN073 Castle of Dark Illusions C .50 1.00
MRDEN074 King of Yamimakai C .12 .25
MRDEN075 Catapult Turtle SR 1.00 2.00
MRDEN076 Mystic Horseman C .10 .20
MRDEN077 Rabid Horseman C .10 .20
MRDEN078 Crass Clown C .12 .25
MRDEN079 Pumpking the King of Ghosts C .25 .50
MRDEN080 Dream Clown C .17 .35
MRDEN081 Tainted Wisdom C .10 .20
MRDEN082 Ancient Brain C .10 .20
MRDEN083 Guardian of the Labyrinth C .12 .25
MRDEN084 Prevent Rat C .12 .25
MRDEN085 The Little Swordsman of Aile C .10 .20
MRDEN086 Princess of Tsurugi R .15 .30
MRDEN087 Protector of the Throne C .10 .20
MRDEN088 Tremendous Fire C .20 .40
MRDEN089 Jirai Gumo C .12 .25
MRDEN090 Shadow Ghoul R .30 .60
MRDEN091 Labyrinth Tank C .12 .25
MRDEN092 Ryu-Kishin Powered C .12 .25
MRDEN093 Bickuribox C .20 .40
MRDEN094 Gilti the D. Knight C .20 .40
MRDEN095 Launcher Spider C .10 .20
MRDEN096 Giga-Tech Wolf C .15 .30
MRDEN097 Thunder Dragon C 2.00 4.00
MRDEN098 7 Colored Fish C .20 .40
MRDEN099 The Immortal of Thunder C .10 .20
MRDEN100 Punished Eagle C .20 .40
MRDEN101 Insect Soldiers of the Sky C .15 .30
MRDEN102 Hoshiningen R .50 1.00
MRDEN103 Musician King C .20 .40
MRDEN104 Yado Karu C .10 .20
MRDEN105 Cyber Saurus C .12 .25
MRDEN106 Cannon Soldier R .30 .75
MRDEN107 Muka Muka R .20 .40
MRDEN108 The Bistro Butcher C .10 .20
MRDEN109 Star Boy R .20 .40
MRDEN110 Milus Radiant R .30 .75
MRDEN111 Flame Cerebus C .10 .20
MRDEN112 Niwatori C .10 .20
MRDEN113 Dark Elf R .30 .75
MRDEN114 Mushroom Man #2 C .20 .40
MRDEN115 Lava Battleguard C .10 .20
MRDEN116 Witch of the Black Forest R .25 .50
MRDEN117 Little Chimera R .20 .40
MRDEN118 Bladefly R .12 .25
MRDEN119 Lady of Faith C .12 .25
MRDEN120 Twin-Headed Thunder Dragon SR 1.50 3.00
MRDEN121 Witch's Apprentice R .12 .25
MRDEN122 Blue-Winged Crown C .10 .20
MRDEN123 Skull Knight C .15 .30
MRDEN124 Gazelle the King of Mythical Beasts C.10 .20
MRDEN125 Garnecia Elefantis SR .30 .75
MRDEN126 Barrel Dragon UR 6.00 12.00
MRDEN127 Solemn Judgment UR 7.50 15.00
MRDEN128 Magic Jammer UR 2.50 5.00
MRDEN129 Seven Tools of the Bandit UR 2.50 5.00
MRDEN130 Horn of Heaven UR 1.50 3.00
MRDEN131 Shield & Sword R .15 .30
MRDEN132 Sword of Deep-Seated C .10 .20
MRDEN133 Block Attack C .10 .20
MRDEN134 The Unhappy Maiden C .20 .40
MRDEN135 Robbin Goblin R .50 1.00
MRDEN136 Germ Infection C .10 .20
MRDEN137 Paralyzing Potion C .12 .25
MRDEN138 Mirror Force UR 10.00 20.00
MRDEN139 Ring of Magnetism C .12 .25
MRDEN140 Share the Pain C .10 .20
MRDEN141 Stim-pack C .12 .25
MRDEN142 Heavy Storm SR 3.00 6.00
MRDEN143 Thousand Dragon SCR 3.00 6.00

2023 Yu-Gi-Oh Pharaoh's Servant 25th Anniversary Edition

PSVEN000 Jinzo SCR 15.00 30.00
PSVEN001 Steel Ogre Grotto #2 C .15 .30
PSVEN002 Three-Headed Geedo C .10 .20
PSVEN003 Parasite Paracide SR 1.00 2.00
PSVEN004 7 Completed C .10 .20
PSVEN005 Lightforce Sword R .15 .30
PSVEN006 Chain Destruction UR 3.00 6.00
PSVEN007 Time Seal C .30 .60
PSVEN008 Graverobber SR .60 1.25
PSVEN009 Gift of the Mystical Elf C .10 .20
PSVEN010 The Eye of Truth C .20 .40
PSVEN011 Dust Tornado SR 2.50 5.00
PSVEN012 Call of the Haunted UR 4.00 8.00
PSVEN013 Solomon's Lawbook C .10 .20
PSVEN014 Earthshaker C .10 .20
PSVEN015 Enchanted Javelin C .10 .20
PSVEN016 Mirror Wall SR 1.00 2.00
PSVEN017 Gust C .10 .20
PSVEN018 Driving Snow C .10 .20
PSVEN019 Armored Glass C .10 .20
PSVEN020 World Suppression C .10 .20
PSVEN021 Mystic Probe C .10 .20
PSVEN022 Metal Detector C .10 .20
PSVEN023 Numinous Healer C .15 .30
PSVEN024 Appropriate R .15 .30
PSVEN025 Forced Requisition R .15 .30
PSVEN026 DNA Surgery C .75 1.50
PSVEN027 The Regulation of Tribe C .10 .20
PSVEN028 Backup Soldier SR .75 1.50
PSVEN029 Major Riot C .10 .20
PSVEN030 Ceasefire UR 2.50 5.00
PSVEN031 Light of Intervention C .10 .20
PSVEN032 Respect Play C .10 .20
PSVEN033 Magical Hats SR .75 1.50
PSVEN034 Nobleman of Crossout SR 3.00 6.00
PSVEN035 Nobleman of Extermination R .30 .75
PSVEN036 The Shallow Grave R .25 .50
PSVEN037 Premature Burial UR 5.00 10.00
PSVEN038 Inspection C .10 .20
PSVEN039 Prohibition R 1.50 3.00
PSVEN040 Morphing Jar #2 R .30 .60
PSVEN041 Flame Champion C .10 .20
PSVEN042 Twin-Headed Fire Dragon C .10 .20
PSVEN043 Darkfire Soldier C .10 .20
PSVEN044 Mr.Volcano C .10 .20
PSVEN045 Darkfire Soldier #2 C .10 .20
PSVEN046 Kiseitai C .15 .30
PSVEN047 Cyber Falcon C .10 .20
PSVEN048 Flying Kamakiri #2 C .10 .20
PSVEN049 Sky Scout C .12 .25
PSVEN050 Buster Blader UR 6.00 12.00
PSVEN051 Michizure R .15 .30
PSVEN052 Minor Goblin Official C .10 .20
PSVEN053 Gamble C .10 .20
PSVEN054 Attack and Receive C .10 .20
PSVEN055 Solemn Wishes C .50 1.00
PSVEN056 Skull Invitation R .20 .40
PSVEN057 Bubonic Vermin C .10 .20
PSVEN058 Dark Bat C .10 .20
PSVEN059 Oni Tank T-34 C .10 .20
PSVEN060 Overdrive C .10 .20
PSVEN061 Burning Land C .12 .25
PSVEN062 Cold Wave C .50 1.00
PSVEN063 Fairy Meteor Crush SR .50 1.00
PSVEN064 Limiter Removal SR 1.25 2.50
PSVEN065 Rain of Mercy C .10 .20
PSVEN066 Monster Recovery R .15 .30
PSVEN067 Shift R .15 .30
PSVEN068 Insect Imitation C .10 .20
PSVEN069 Dimensionhole R .15 .30
PSVEN070 Ground Collapse C .50 1.00
PSVEN071 Magic Drain R .15 .30
PSVEN072 Infinite Dismissal C .10 .20
PSVEN073 Gravity Bind R .30 .75
PSVEN074 Type Zero Magic Crusher C .10 .20
PSVEN075 Shadow of Eyes C .10 .20
PSVEN076 The Legendary Fisherman UR 3.00 6.00
PSVEN077 Sword Hunter C .20 .40
PSVEN078 Drill Bug C .10 .20
PSVEN079 Deepsea Warrior C .10 .20
PSVEN080 Bite Shoes C .10 .20
PSVEN081 Spikebot C .10 .20
PSVEN082 Invitation to a Dark Sleep C .10 .20
PSVEN083 Thousand-Eyes Idol C .50 1.00
PSVEN084 Thousand-Eyes Restrict UR 7.50 15.00
PSVEN085 Girochin Kuwagata C .10 .20
PSVEN086 Hayabusa Knight R .20 .40
PSVEN087 Bombardment Beetle C .10 .20
PSVEN088 4-Starred Ladybug of Doom C .10 .20
PSVEN089 Gradius C .10 .20
PSVEN090 Vampire Baby R .15 .30
PSVEN091 Mad Sword Beast R .25 .50
PSVEN092 Skull Mariner C .10 .20
PSVEN093 The All-Seeing White Tiger C .10 .20
PSVEN094 Goblin Attack Force UR 2.50 5.00
PSVEN095 Island Turtle C .12 .25
PSVEN096 Wingweaver C .10 .20
PSVEN097 Science Soldier C .10 .20
PSVEN098 Souls of the Forbidden C .10 .20
PSVEN099 Dokuroyaiba C .10 .20
PSVEN100 The Fiend Megacyber UR 2.50 5.00
PSVEN101 Gearfried the Iron Knight SR .75 1.50
PSVEN102 Insect Barrier C .12 .25
PSVEN103 Beast of Talwar UR 2.50 5.00
PSVEN104 Imperial Order SCR 1.50 3.00

2023 Yu-Gi-Oh Photon Hypernova 1st Edition

PHHYEN000 Gravekeeper's Inscription SCR 2.00 4.00
PHHYEN001 Photon Emperor C .07 .15
PHHYEN002 Galaxy Summoner C .07 .15
PHHYEN003 Galactikuriboh SR .20 .40
PHHYEN004 Bystial Baldrake C .07 .15
PHHYEN005 The Abyss Dragon Swordsoul SR .15 .30
PHHYEN006 Kashtira Riseheart UR 1.50 3.00
PHHYEN007 Scareclaw Kashtira C .07 .15
PHHYEN008 Tearlaments Kashtira UR 5.00 10.00
PHHYEN009 Chaos Witch SR .25 .50
PHHYEN010 Shell of Chaos C .07 .15
PHHYEN011 Core of Chaos C .07 .15
PHHYEN012 Mental Tuner C .07 .15
PHHYEN013 Chaos Mirage Dragon SR .30 .60
PHHYEN014 Bio Insect Armor C .07 .15
PHHYEN015 Infinite Antlion C .07 .15
PHHYEN016 Abyss Actor - Liberty Dramatist C .07 .15
PHHYEN017 Jio the Gravity Ninja C .07 .15
PHHYEN018 Gishki Grimness C .07 .15
PHHYEN019 Basiltrice, Familiar of the Evil Eye C.07 .15
PHHYEN020 Vala, Seidhr
of the Generaider Bosses C .07 .15
PHHYEN021 Beargram... UR .60 1.25
PHHYEN022 Manticore of Smashing C .07 .15
PHHYEN023 Choju of the Trillion Hands SR .15 .30
PHHYEN024 Fierce Tiger Monghu C .07 .15
PHHYEN025 Fairyant the Circular Sorcerer SR .15 .30
PHHYEN026 Sari of the Silverwing Axe C .07 .15
PHHYEN027 Couples of Aces C .07 .15
PHHYEN028 Dimensional Allotrope Varis SR .15 .30
PHHYEN029 Meteor Rush - Monochroid C .07 .15
PHHYEN030 Sneaky C SR .20 .40
PHHYEN031 Dogmatika Alba Zoa SR .20 .40
PHHYEN032 Evigishki Neremanas SR .15 .30
PHHYEN033 Granguignol the Dusk Dragon SLR150.00 300.00
PHHYEN033 Granguignol the Dusk Dragon UR 4.00 8.00
PHHYEN034 Rindbrumm the Striking Dragon UR2.00 4.00
PHHYEN035 Ultimate Great Insect SR .15 .30
PHHYEN036 Yaguramaru the Armor Ninja C .07 .15
PHHYEN037 Arktos XII - Chronochasm Vaylantz SR.15 .30
PHHYEN038 Icejade Gymir Aegirine UR 3.00 6.00
PHHYEN039 Chaos Archfiend UR 1.50 3.00
PHHYEN040 Chaos Beast C .07 .15
PHHYEN041 Plunder Patrollship Jord SR .15 .30
PHHYEN042 Circle of the Fairies C .07 .15
PHHYEN043 #C62Neo Galaxy
Eyes Prime Photon Dragon UR 1.50 3.00
PHHYEN044 Galaxy Photon Dragon SCR 2.00 4.00
PHHYEN045 Gigantic Champion Sargas SCR 3.00 6.00
PHHYEN046 Kashtira Arise-Heart SCR 3.00 6.00
PHHYEN046 Kashtira Arise-Heart SLR 125.00 250.00
PHHYEN047 Laevatein, Generaider
Boss of Shadows UR .50 1.00

PHHYEN048 Tri-Brigade Arms Bucephalus II SLR 60.00 125.00
PHHYEN048 Tri-Brigade Arms Bucephalus II SR .75 1.50
PHHYEN049 Abyss Actor - Super Producer C .07 .15
PHHYEN050 Dyna Mondo C .07 .15
PHHYEN051 Galaxy Hundred C .07 .15
PHHYEN052 Numeron Creation C .07 .15
PHHYEN053 Icejade Manifestation C .07 .15
PHHYEN054 Tally-Ho! Springans C .07 .15
PHHYEN055 Dogmatikamatrix SR .20 .40
PHHYEN056 Light of the Branded C .07 .15
PHHYEN057 Kashtira Overlap C .07 .15
PHHYEN058 Kashtiratheosis SCR 7.50 15.00
PHHYEN059 Pressured Planet Wraitsoth SCR 12.50 25.00
PHHYEN060 Scareclaw Defanging C .07 .15
PHHYEN061 Tearlaments Perlegia C .07 .15
PHHYEN062 Giant Ballgame C .07 .15
PHHYEN063 Abyss Actors' Dress Rehearsal SR .15 .30
PHHYEN064 Abyss Script - Dramatic Story C .07 .15
PHHYEN065 Tenchi Kaimei C .07 .15
PHHYEN066 Gishki Nekromirror C .07 .15
PHHYEN067 Focused Aquamirror C .07 .15
PHHYEN068 Evil Eyes Unleashed C .07 .15
PHHYEN069 Triple Tactic Thrust SCR 50.00 100.00
PHHYEN070 Land Flipping C .07 .15
PHHYEN071 Photon Timestop C .07 .15
PHHYEN072 Gigantic Thundercross C .07 .15
PHHYEN073 Branded Befallen C .07 .15
PHHYEN074 Trivikarma UR .75 1.50
PHHYEN075 Kashtira Big Bang C .07 .15
PHHYEN076 Chaos Phantasm C .07 .15
PHHYEN077 Big Welcome Labrynth UR 4.00 8.00
PHHYEN078 Weighbridge SCR 1.00 2.00
PHHYEN079 Sour Scheduling - Red Vinegar Vamoose C .07 .15
PHHYEN080 Intimidating Ore - Summonite C .07 .15
PHHYEN081 Minairuka C .07 .15
PHHYEN082 Orphebull the Harmonious Bullfighter Bard UR .50 1.00
PHHYEN083 Diabolantis the Menacing Mantis C .07 .15
PHHYEN084 Xyz Align C .07 .15
PHHYEN085 Made to Order Mermaid Outfit Outfitter SR .15 .30
PHHYEN086 Gold Pride - Leon SCR 7.50 15.00
PHHYEN087 Gold Pride - Nytro Head SR .20 .40
PHHYEN088 Gold Pride - Captain Carrie SLR 125.00 250.00
PHHYEN088 Gold Pride - Captain Carrie UR 2.50 5.00
PHHYEN089 Gold Pride - Star Leon UR .75 1.50
PHHYEN090 Gold Pride - Nytro Blaster SR .15 .30
PHHYEN091 Gold Pride - The Crowd Goes Wild! SCR 1.50 3.00
PHHYEN092 Gold Pride - Start Your Engines! SR .15 .30
PHHYEN093 Cassimolar C .07 .15
PHHYEN094 Queen Butterfly Danaus SR .15 .30
PHHYEN095 Qardan the Clear-Sighted SR .15 .30
PHHYEN096 Pharaonic Advent SR .15 .30
PHHYEN097 Aphophis the Swamp Deity SR .15 .30
PHHYEN098 Green Ninja SR .15 .30
PHHYEN099 Humongous Hive Hegemon - Zexstagger SR .15 .30
PHHYEN100 Mirrorjade the Iceblade Dragon SLR 225.00 450.00

2023 Yu-Gi-Oh Speed Duel Streets of Battle City

SBC1ENA01 Dark Magician SEC 4.00 10.00
SBC1ENA01 Dark Magician C .40 1.00
SBC1ENA02 Skilled Dark Magician C .15 .40
SBC1ENA03 Alchemist of Black Spells C .10 .25
SBC1ENA04 Blast Magician C .10 .25
SBC1ENA05 Dark Magician Girl SEC 10.00 25.00
SBC1ENA05 Dark Magician Girl C .25 .60
SBC1ENA06 Buster Blader C .12 .30
SBC1ENA07 Skilled White Magician C .12 .30
SBC1ENA08 Breaker the Magical Warrior C .25 .60
SBC1ENA09 Apprentice Magician C .10 .25
SBC1ENA10 Magician of Faith C .15 .40
SBC1ENA11 Old Vindictive Magician C .12 .30
SBC1ENA12 Malice Dispersion C .04 .10
SBC1ENA13 Mage Power C .15 .40
SBC1ENA14 Solitary Sword of Poison C .10 .25
SBC1ENA15 Spell Power Grasp C .10 .25
SBC1ENA16 Destruction Swordsman Fusion C .12 .30
SBC1ENA17 Miracle Restoring C .10 .25
SBC1ENA18 Pitch-Black Power Stone C .10 .25
SBC1ENA19 Ready for Intercepting C .05 .12
SBC1ENA20 Dark Paladin C .15 .40
SBC1ENB01 Gearfried the Iron Knight SEC .50 1.25
SBC1ENB01 Gearfried the Iron Knight C .10 .25
SBC1ENB02 Marauding Captain SEC .60 1.50
SBC1ENB02 Marauding Captain C .12 .30
SBC1ENB03 Time Wizard C .15 .40
SBC1ENB04 Rocket Warrior C .10 .25
SBC1ENB05 Little-Winguard C .05 .12
SBC1ENB06 Command Knight C .12 .30
SBC1ENB07 Freed the Matchless General C .10 .25
SBC1ENB08 Alligator's Sword C .10 .25
SBC1ENB09 Baby Dragon C .12 .30
SBC1ENB10 Roulette Spider C .10 .25
SBC1ENB11 Dicephoon C .10 .25
SBC1ENB12 Graceful Dice C .15 .40
SBC1ENB13 Polymerization C .25 .60
SBC1ENB14 Reinforcement of the Army C .12 .30
SBC1ENB15 Lightning Blade C .10 .25
SBC1ENB16 United We Stand C .25 .60
SBC1ENB17 Blast with Chain C .15 .40
SBC1ENB18 Skull Dice C .15 .40
SBC1ENB19 Kunai with Chain C .12 .30
SBC1ENB20 Karbonala Warrior C .12 .30
SBC1ENB21 Giltia the D. Knight C .12 .30
SBC1ENB22 Flame Swordsman C .40 1.00
SBC1ENB22 Flame Swordsman SEC 4.00 10.00
SBC1ENB23 Alligator's Sword Dragon C .10 .25
SBC1ENB24 Thousand Dragon C .15 .40
SBC1ENC01 The Legendary Fisherman C .10 .25
SBC1ENC01 The Legendary Fisherman SEC .40 1.00
SBC1ENC02 Airorca C .05 .12
SBC1ENC03 Flyfang C .10 .25
SBC1ENC04 Needle Sunfish C .10 .25
SBC1ENC05 Oyster Meister C .12 .30
SBC1ENC06 Piercing Moray C .10 .25
SBC1ENC07 Maiden of the Aqua C .15 .40
SBC1ENC08 Fiend Kraken C .15 .40
SBC1ENC09 7 Colored Fish C .10 .25
SBC1ENC10 The Legendary Fisherman II C .10 .25
SBC1ENC11 Fortress Whale C .12 .30
SBC1ENC12 Salvage C .12 .30
SBC1ENC13 Umi C .05 .12
SBC1ENC14 Water Hazard C .10 .25
SBC1ENC15 Big Wave Small Wave C .10 .25
SBC1ENC16 Surface C .10 .25
SBC1ENC17 Fortress Whale's Oath C .10 .25
SBC1ENC18 Tornado Wall C .12 .30
SBC1ENC19 Fish Depth Charge C .12 .30
SBC1ENC20 Paleozoic Eldonia C .10 .25
SBC1END01 Insect Queen SEC .30 .75
SBC1END01 Insect Queen C .10 .25
SBC1END02 Parasite Paracide SEC .25 .60
SBC1END02 Parasite Paracide C .10 .25
SBC1END03 Chainsaw Insect C .10 .25
SBC1END04 Magnetic Mosquito C .08 .20
SBC1END05 Prickle Fairy C .10 .25
SBC1END06 Howling Insect C .15 .40
SBC1END07 Resonance Insect C .10 .25
SBC1END08 Parasite Paranoid C .15 .40
SBC1END09 Pinch Hopper C .10 .25
SBC1END10 Insect Princess C .12 .30
SBC1END11 Gokibore C .10 .25
SBC1END12 Metal Armored Bug C .10 .25
SBC1END13 Multiplication of Ants C .12 .30
SBC1END14 Insect Barrier C .10 .25
SBC1END15 Verdant Sanctuary C .15 .40
SBC1END16 Eradicating Aerosol C .12 .30
SBC1END17 Spider Egg C .10 .25
SBC1END18 DNA Surgery C .20 .50
SBC1END19 Dust Tornado SEC 5.00 12.00
SBC1END19 Dust Tornado C .25 .60
SBC1END20 Widespread Ruin ALT ART SEC .50 1.25
SBC1END20 Widespread Ruin C .15 .40
SBC1ENE01 Jinzo C .12 .30
SBC1ENE02 Jinzo - Lord C .10 .25
SBC1ENE03 Jinzo - Returner C .12 .30
SBC1ENE04 Reflect Bounder SEC .40 1.00
SBC1ENE04 Reflect Bounder C .15 .40
SBC1ENE05 Destructotron C .10 .25
SBC1ENE06 Dr. Frankenderp C .10 .25
SBC1ENE07 The Fiend Megacyber C .10 .25
SBC1ENE08 Spell Canceller C .12 .30
SBC1ENE09 Cyber Raider C .12 .30
SBC1ENE10 Golgoil C .12 .30
SBC1ENE11 Cyber Energy Shock C .10 .25
SBC1ENE12 Cosmos Channelling C .10 .25
SBC1ENE13 Gift of the Martyr C .10 .25
SBC1ENE14 Amplifier C .08 .20
SBC1ENE15 Foolish Burial C .25 .60
SBC1ENE16 Cosmic Cyclone C .12 .30
SBC1ENE17 Creature Swap C .15 .40
SBC1ENE17 Creature Swap SEC 1.50 4.00
SBC1ENE18 Psychic Shockwave C .10 .25
SBC1ENE19 Mind Crush C .12 .30
SBC1ENE19 Mind Crush SEC 1.50 4.00
SBC1ENE20 Draining Shield C .12 .30
SBC1ENF01 Red-Eyes Black Dragon C .40 1.00
SBC1ENF01 Red-Eyes Black Dragon SEC 3.00 8.00
SBC1ENF02 Gear Golem the Moving Fortress C .12 .30
SBC1ENF03 Voltic Kong C .10 .25
SBC1ENF04 Airknight Parshath C .12 .30
SBC1ENF05 Dark Red Enchanter C .10 .25
SBC1ENF06 Twin-Barrel Dragon C .15 .40
SBC1ENF07 Hannibal Necromancer C .10 .25
SBC1ENF08 Magician of Faith C .12 .30
SBC1ENF09 Mask of Darkness C .12 .30
SBC1ENF10 Sphere Kuriboh C .12 .30
SBC1ENF11 Ledger of Legerdemain C .15 .40
SBC1ENF12 Allure of Darkness C .25 .60
SBC1ENF13 Twister C .10 .25
SBC1ENF14 Night Beam C .50 1.25
SBC1ENF14 Night Beam SEC .12 .30
SBC1ENF15 Nobleman of Crossout C .50 1.25
SBC1ENF16 Pineapple Blast C .10 .25
SBC1ENF17 Metalmorph C .12 .30
SBC1ENF18 Michizure C .12 .30
SBC1ENF19 The Forceful Checkpoint C .12 .30
SBC1ENF20 Floodgate Trap Hole C .12 .30
SBC1ENG01 Dark Magician SEC 1.00 2.50
SBC1ENG02 Chow Sai the Ghost Stopper C .12 .30
SBC1ENG03 Chow Len the Prophet C .10 .25
SBC1ENG04 Anarchist Monk Ranshin C .10 .25
SBC1ENG05 Mei-Kou, Master of Barriers C .10 .25
SBC1ENG06 Kycoo the Ghost Destroyer SEC 2.50 6.00
SBC1ENG06 Kycoo the Ghost Destroyer C .75 2.00
SBC1ENG07 Legion the Fiend Jester C .15 .40
SBC1ENG08 Double Coston C .12 .30
SBC1ENG09 Sealmaster Meisei C .10 .25
SBC1ENG10 Dark Magician C .20 .50
SBC1ENG11 Anti-Magic Arrows SEC 2.00 5.00
SBC1ENG11 Anti-Magic Arrows C .12 .30
SBC1ENG12 Talisman of Trap Sealing C .12 .30
SBC1ENG13 Dark Magic Curtain SEC .40 1.00
SBC1ENG13 Dark Magic Curtain C .12 .30
SBC1ENG14 Thousand Knives C .12 .30
SBC1ENG15 Dark Magic Attack C .20 .50
SBC1ENG16 Summoner's Art C .15 .40
SBC1ENG18 Birthright C .10 .25
SBC1ENG19 Dark Renewal SEC .30 .75
SBC1ENG19 Dark Renewal C .15 .40
SBC1ENH01 Slifer the Sky Dragon SEC .30 .75
SBC1ENH02 Revival Jam C .12 .30
SBC1ENH03 Humanoid Slime C .12 .30
SBC1ENH04 Worm Drake C .10 .25
SBC1ENH05 Reactor Slime C .10 .25
SBC1ENH06 Muka Muka C .10 .25
SBC1ENH07 Enraged Muka Muka C .08 .20
SBC1ENH08 Magical Reflect Slime C .12 .30
SBC1ENH09 Sinister Serpent C .20 .50
SBC1ENH10 Mother Grizzly C .15 .40
SBC1ENH11 Jam Breeding Machine C .12 .30
SBC1ENH12 Emergency Provisions C .15 .40
SBC1ENH13 Infinite Cards C .10 .25
SBC1ENH14 Token Sundae C .12 .30
SBC1ENH15 Polymerization C .25 .60
SBC1ENH16 Jam Defender C .12 .30
SBC1ENH17 Solemn Wishes C .20 .50
SBC1ENH18 Token Stampede C .10 .25
SBC1ENH19 Humanoid Worm Drake C .10 .25
SBC1ENI01 Summoned Skull C .12 .30
SBC1ENI01 Summoned Skull SEC 4.00 10.00
SBC1ENI02 Brain Crusher C .10 .25
SBC1ENI03 Chaos Command Magician C .10 .25
SBC1ENI04 Cross-Sword Beetle C .10 .25
SBC1ENI05 Gearfried the Red-Eyes Iron Knight C .40 1.00
SBC1ENI06 Goblin Attack Force C .15 .40
SBC1ENI06 Goblin Attack Force SEC .75 2.00
SBC1ENI07 Maiden of Macabre C .12 .30
SBC1ENI08 Magical Marionette C .12 .30
SBC1ENI09 Pumprincess the Princess of Ghosts C .08 .20
SBC1ENI10 Red-Eyes Baby Dragon C 1.00 2.50
SBC1ENI11 Reversible Beetle C .10 .25
SBC1ENI12 Warrior of Atlantis C .30 .75
SBC1ENI13 Zera the Mant C .15 .40
SBC1ENI14 Acid Rain C .10 .25
SBC1ENI15 Book of Taiyou C .20 .50
SBC1ENI16 Exchange C .10 .25
SBC1ENI16 Exchange SEC .40 1.00
SBC1ENI17 Last Day of Witch C .10 .25
SBC1ENI18 Mega Ton Magical Cannon C .10 .25
SBC1ENI19 Zera Ritual C .10 .25
SBC1ENI20 Barrel Behind the Door C .15 .40
SBC1ENI21 Exhausting Spell C .10 .25
SBC1ENI22 Magical Arm Shield C .12 .30
SBC1ENI23 Blowback Dragon C .15 .40
SBC1ENI24 Dark Scorpion - Meanae the Thorn C .10 .25
SBC1ENI25 Dark Scorpion - Gorg the Strong C .10 .25
SBC1ENI26 Skilled Red Magician C .10 .25
SBC1ENI27 A Legendary Ocean C .12 .30
SBC1ENI28 Book of Moon C .40 1.00
SBC1ENI29 Fusion Weapon C .10 .25
SBC1ENI30 Hammer Shot C .12 .30
SBC1ENI31 Lost Wind C .10 .25
SBC1ENI32 Metal Reflect Slime C .12 .30
SBC1ENI33 Wall of Disruption C .12 .30
SBC1ENS01 Ultimate Wizardry C .10 .25
SBC1ENS02 Iron Grit C .10 .25
SBC1ENS03 Whale of a Tale C .08 .20
SBC1ENS04 Insect Infestation C .10 .25
SBC1ENS05 Intel from the Cosmos C .10 .25
SBC1ENS06 Stalked by the Rare Hunters C .10 .25
SBC1ENS07 Now You See Them... C .10 .25
SBC1ENS08 Slimey Slimes C .10 .25
SBC1ENS09 The Dragon Hunting Swordsman C .10 .25
SBC1ENS10 Heart of a Warrior C .10 .25
SBC1ENS11 A Bountiful Ocean C .10 .25
SBC1ENS12 My Precious Queen! C .10 .25
SBC1ENS13 The Machine Menace C .10 .25
SBC1ENS14 Collector C .10 .25
SBC1ENS15 A Terrible Fate C .10 .25
SBC1ENS16 Slimey Disposition C .10 .25
SBC1ENS17 Malicious Motivation C .10 .25
SBC1ENS18 KaibaCorp Research C .10 .25
SBC1ENS19 Battle City Siren C .12 .30
SBC1ENS20 Premature Material C .08 .20

2023 Yu-Gi-Oh Spell Ruler 25th Anniversary Edition

SRLEN000 Blue-Eyes Toon Dragon SR 20.00 40.00
SRLEN001 Penguin Knight C .10 .20
SRLEN002 Axe of Despair UR 3.00 6.00
SRLEN003 Black Pendant SR .75 1.50
SRLEN004 Horn of Light C .10 .20
SRLEN005 Malevolent Nuzzler C .10 .20
SRLEN006 Spellbinding Circle UR 3.00 6.00
SRLEN007 Metal Fish C .10 .20
SRLEN008 Electric Snake C .10 .20
SRLEN009 Queen Bird C .10 .20
SRLEN010 Ameba R .15 .30
SRLEN011 Peacock C .10 .20
SRLEN012 Maha Vailo SR .50 1.00
SRLEN013 Guardian of the Throne Room C .10 .20
SRLEN014 Fire Kraken C .10 .20
SRLEN015 Minar C .10 .20
SRLEN016 Griggle C .10 .20
SRLEN017 Tyhone 2 C .10 .20
SRLEN018 Ancient One of the Deep Forest C .10 .20
SRLEN019 Dark Witch C .10 .20
SRLEN020 Weather Report C .10 .20
SRLEN021 Mechanical Snail C .10 .20
SRLEN022 Giant Turtle Who Feeds on Flames C .10 .20
SRLEN023 Liquid Beast C .10 .20
SRLEN024 Hiros Shadow Scout R .20 .40
SRLEN025 High Tide Gyojin C .10 .20
SRLEN026 Invader of the Throne SR .30 .75
SRLEN027 Whiptail Crow C .10 .20
SRLEN028 Slot Machine C .10 .20
SRLEN029 Relinquished UR 7.50 15.00
SRLEN030 Red Archery Girl C .10 .20
SRLEN031 Gravekeeper's Servant C .30 .60
SRLEN032 Curse of Fiend C .15 .30
SRLEN033 Upstart Goblin C .60 1.25
SRLEN034 Toll C .10 .20
SRLEN035 Final Destiny C .10 .20
SRLEN036 Snatch Steal UR 10.00 20.00
SRLEN037 Chorus of Sanctuary C .10 .20
SRLEN038 Confiscation SR .75 1.50
SRLEN039 Delinquent Duo UR 15.00 30.00
SRLEN040 Darkness Approaches C .10 .20
SRLEN041 Fairys Hand Mirror C .10 .20
SRLEN042 Tailor of the Fickle C .10 .20
SRLEN043 Rush Recklessly R .15 .30
SRLEN044 The Reliable Guardian C .10 .20
SRLEN045 The Forceful Sentry UR 4.00 8.00
SRLEN046 Chain Energy C .20 .40
SRLEN047 Mystical Space Typhoon UR 7.50 15.00
SRLEN048 Giant Trunade SR 6.00 12.00
SRLEN049 Painful Choice SR 1.50 3.00
SRLEN050 Snake Fang C .10 .20
SRLEN051 Black Illusion Ritual SR 2.00 4.00
SRLEN052 Octoberser C .10 .20
SRLEN053 Psychic Kappa C .10 .20
SRLEN054 Horn of the Unicorn R .15 .30
SRLEN055 Labyrinth Wall C .10 .20
SRLEN056 Wall Shadow C .10 .20
SRLEN057 Twin Long Rods 2 C .10 .20
SRLEN058 Stone Ogre Grotto C .10 .20
SRLEN059 Magical Labyrinth C .10 .20
SRLEN060 Eternal Rest C .10 .20
SRLEN061 Megamorph UR 2.50 5.00
SRLEN062 Commencement Dance C .10 .20
SRLEN063 Hamburger Recipe C .20 .40
SRLEN064 House of Adhesive Tape C .10 .20
SRLEN065 Eatgaboon C .10 .20
SRLEN066 Turtle Oath C .15 .30
SRLEN067 Performance of Sword C .10 .20
SRLEN068 Hungry Burger C .15 .30
SRLEN069 Crab Turtle C .15 .30
SRLEN070 RyuRan C .10 .20
SRLEN071 Manga Ryu-Ran R .15 .30
SRLEN072 Toon Mermaid UR 5.00 10.00
SRLEN073 Toon Summoned Skull UR 7.50 15.00
SRLEN074 Jigen Bakudan C .10 .20
SRLEN075 Hyozanryu R .15 .30
SRLEN076 Toon World SR 1.25 2.50
SRLEN077 Cyber Jar R 1.25 2.50
SRLEN078 Banisher of the Light SR .50 1.00
SRLEN079 Giant Rat R .15 .30
SRLEN080 Senju of the Thousand Hands R .30 .60
SRLEN081 UFO Turtle R .30 .75
SRLEN082 Flash Assailant C .10 .20
SRLEN083 Karate Man R .20 .40
SRLEN084 Dark Zebra C .20 .40
SRLEN085 Giant Germ R .50 1.00
SRLEN086 Nimble Momonga R .15 .30
SRLEN087 Spear Cretin C .10 .20
SRLEN088 Shining Angel R .30 .75
SRLEN089 Boar Soldier C .10 .20
SRLEN090 Mother Grizzly R .15 .30
SRLEN091 Flying Kamakiri 1 R .15 .30
SRLEN092 Ceremonial Bell C .10 .20
SRLEN093 Sonic Bird C .15 .30
SRLEN094 Mystic Tomato R .50 1.00
SRLEN095 Kotodama C .10 .20
SRLEN096 Gaia Power C .15 .30
SRLEN097 Umiiruka C .10 .20
SRLEN098 Molten Destruction C .10 .20
SRLEN099 Rising Air Current C .20 .40
SRLEN100 Luminous Spark C .10 .20
SRLEN101 Mystic Plasma Zone C .10 .20
SRLEN102 Messenger of Peace SR 2.50 5.00
SRLEN103 Serpent Night Dragon SCR 3.00 6.00

2023 Yu-Gi-Oh Structure Deck Beware of Traptrix 1st Edition

SDBTEN001 Traptrix Pudica UR .20 .40
SDBTEN002 Traptrix Arachnocampa SR .25 .50
SDBTEN003 Traptrix Atrax C .07 .15
SDBTEN004 Traptrix Myrmeleo C .07 .15
SDBTEN005 Traptrix Nepenthes C .07 .15
SDBTEN006 Traptrix Dionaea C .07 .15
SDBTEN007 Traptrix Genlisea C .07 .15
SDBTEN008 Traptrix Vesiculo C .07 .15
SDBTEN009 Gadarla, the Mystery Dust Kaiju C .07 .15
SDBTEN010 Kumongous, the Sticky String Kaiju C .07 .15
SDBTEN011 Retaliating C"""" C .07 .15
SDBTEN012 Resonance Insect C .07 .15
SDBTEN013 Lonefire Blossom C .07 .15
SDBTEN014 Ash Blossom & Joyous Spring C 3.00 6.00
SDBTEN015 Rose Lover C .07 .15
SDBTEN016 Sauge de Fleur C .07 .15
SDBTEN017 Mekk-Knight Purple Nightfall C .07 .15
SDBTEN018 Mekk-Knight Blue Sky C .07 .15
SDBTEN019 Artifact Moralltach C .07 .15
SDBTEN020 Fire Hand C .07 .15
SDBTEN021 Ice Hand C .07 .15
SDBTEN022 Thunder Hand C .07 .15
SDBTEN023 Traptrip Garden UR .20 .40
SDBTEN024 Traptantalizing Tune UR .20 .40
SDBTEN025 Raigeki C .75 1.50
SDBTEN026 Harpie's Feather Duster C .60 1.25
SDBTEN027 Terrifying Trap Hole Nightmare C .07 .15
SDBTEN028 Trap Hole C .07 .15
SDBTEN029 Bottomless Trap Hole C .07 .15
SDBTEN030 Void Trap Hole C .07 .15
SDBTEN031 Traptrix Trap Hole Nightmare C .07 .15
SDBTEN032 Floodgate Trap Hole C .07 .15
SDBTEN033 Gravedigger's Trap Hole C .07 .15
SDBTEN034 Trap Trick C .07 .15
SDBTEN035 The Phantom Knights of Shade Brigandine C .07 .15
SDBTEN036 Artifact Sanctum C .07 .15
SDBTEN037 Naturia Sacred Tree C .07 .15

SDBTEN038 Evenly Matched SR 3.00 6.00
SDBTEN039 Traptrix Rafflesia C .07 .15
SDBTEN040 Traptrix Allomerus C .07 .15
SDBTEN041 Traptrix Cularia C .07 .15
SDBTEN042 Traptrix Pinguicula UR .20 .40
SDBTEN043 Traptrix Atypus UR .15 .30
SDBTEN044 Traptrix Sera C .07 .15
SDBTEN045 Traptrix Mantis C .07 .15
SDBTEN046 Traptrix Holeutea SR .20 .40

2023 Yu-Gi-Oh The Pot Collection

TBC1-ENS01 Pot of Greed QCSR 60.00 150.00
TBC1EN001 Pot of Greed UR 15.00 40.00
TBC1EN002 Pot of Generosity UR 3.00 8.00
TBC1EN003 Pot of Avarice UR 15.00 40.00
TBC1EN004 Pot of Benevolence UR 2.00 5.00
TBC1EN005 Pot of Riches UR 2.50 6.00
TBC1EN006 Pot of Acquisitiveness UR 5.00 12.00
TBC1EN007 Pot of Duality UR 20.00 50.00
TBC1EN008 Pot of Dichotomy UR 1.50 4.00
TBC1EN009 Pot of Desires UR 10.00 25.00
TBC1EN010 Pot of Extravagance UR 6.00 15.00
TBC1EN011 Pot of Prosperity UR 20.00 50.00
TBC1EN012 Spirit of the Pot of Greed UR 2.00 5.00
TBC1EN013 Moray of Greed UR 10.00 25.00
TBC1EN014 Shard of Greed UR 2.00 5.00

2023 Yu-Gi-Oh Valiant Smashers

VASMEN001 Mementoal Tecuhtlica - Combined Creation UR 2.00 5.00
VASMEN001 Mementoal Tecuhtlica - Combined Creation CR 12.00 30.00
VASMEN001 Mementoal Tecuhtlica - Combined Creation QCSR 25.00 60.00
VASMEN002 Mementotlan-Horned Dragon R .10 .25
VASMEN003 Mementotlan Tatsunootoshigo SR .15 .40
VASMEN004 Mementotlan Dark Blade SR .25 .60
VASMEN004 Mementotlan Dark Blade CR 40.00 100.00
VASMEN005 Mementotlan Angwitch UR 15.00 40.00
VASMEN005 Mementotlan Angwitch CR 40.00 100.00
VASMEN006 Mementotlan Mace SR .12 .30
VASMEN007 Mementotlan Goblin R .10 .25
VASMEN008 Mementomictlan R .10 .25
VASMEN008 Mementomictlan CR 15.00 40.00
VASMEN009 Mementotlan Bone Party UR 15.00 40.00
VASMEN010 Mementotlan Bone Back R .10 .25
VASMEN011 Mementotlan Fracture Dance R .10 .25
VASMEN012 Mementotlan Cranium Burst R .10 .25
VASMEN013 Terraforming R .10 .25
VASMEN014 Supply Squad R .04 .10
VASMEN015 There Can Be Only One R .05 .12
VASMEN016 Centur-Ion Primera UR 15.00 40.00
VASMEN016 Centur-Ion Primera CR 40.00 100.00
VASMEN017 Centur-Ion Trudea UR 10.00 25.00
VASMEN017 Centur-Ion Trudea CR 40.00 100.00
VASMEN018 Centur-Ion Emeth VI UR .50 1.25
VASMEN018 Centur-Ion Emeth VI CR 10.00 25.00
VASMEN019 Centur-Ion Legatia UR 4.00 10.00
VASMEN019 Centur-Ion Legatia CR 10.00 25.00
VASMEN019 Centur-Ion Legatia QCSR 30.00 80.00
VASMEN020 Stand Up Centur-Ion! SR .30 .75
VASMEN020 Stand Up Centur-Ion! CR 40.00 100.00
VASMEN021 Emblema Oath UR 15.00 40.00
VASMEN022 Centur-Ion Bonds SR .10 .25
VASMEN023 Centur-Ion Phalanx SR .10 .25
VASMEN024 Centur-Ion True Awakening SR .10 .25
VASMEN025 Summoner Monk R .10 .25
VASMEN026 Draco Berserker of the Tenyi R .10 .25
VASMEN027 Angel of Zera R .04 .10
VASMEN028 Magic Planter R .10 .25
VASMEN029 Synchro Transmission R .04 .10
VASMEN030 Gravity Collapse R .10 .25
VASMEN031 Angello Vaalmonica SR .10 .25
VASMEN031 Angello Vaalmonica CR 20.00 50.00
VASMEN032 Dimonno Vaalmonica SR .10 .25
VASMEN032 Dimonno Vaalmonica CR 20.00 50.00
VASMEN033 Duralume, Vaalmonican Heathen Hallow SR .10 .25
VASMEN034 Zebufera, Vaalmonican Hallow Heathen SR .10 .25
VASMEN035 Vaalmonica, the Agathokakological Voice UR 6.00 15.00
VASMEN035 Vaalmonica, the Agathokakological Voice CR 25.00 60.00
VASMEN036 Vaalmonica Scelta UR 6.00 15.00
VASMEN036 Vaalmonica Scelta CR 20.00 50.00
VASMEN037 Vaalmonica Versare SR .10 .25
VASMEN038 Vaalmonica Intonare SR .12 .30
VASMEN039 Vaalmonica Followed Rhythm SR .10 .25
VASMEN040 Vaalmonica Chosen Melody SR .10 .25
VASMEN041 Protecting Spirit Loagaeth R .05 .12
VASMEN042 Performage Trick Clown R .05 .12
VASMEN043 Ghost Sister & Spooky Dogwood R .10 .25
VASMEN044 Number 41: Bagooska the Terribly Tired Tapir R .20 .50
VASMEN045 Stained Glass of Light & Dark R .05 .12
VASMEN046 Honest R .10 .25
VASMEN046 Honest CR 15.00 40.00
VASMEN047 Dark Honest R .10 .25
VASMEN047 Dark Honest CR 6.00 15.00
VASMEN048 Archlord Kristya R .12 .30
VASMEN048 Archlord Kristya QCSR 40.00 100.00
VASMEN049 Meklord Emperor Wisel R .04 .10
VASMEN050 Meklord Emperor Granel R .04 .10
VASMEN051 Abominable Unchained Soul R .05 .12
VASMEN052 Ibicella Lutea R .04 .10
VASMEN053 Archnemeses Eschatos R .05 .12
VASMEN054 Colossal Fighter R .10 .25
VASMEN055 Foolish Burial R .10 .25
VASMEN056 Valhalla, Hall of the Fallen R .08 .20
VASMEN057 Advance Draw R .05 .12
VASMEN058 Imperial Custom R .05 .12
VASMEN059 Call of the Haunted R .10 .25
VASMEN060 Apophis the Swamp Deity R .08 .20

2023 Yu-Gi-Oh Wild Survivors 1st Edition

WISUEN001 Xeno Meteorus CR 25.00 50.00
WISUEN001 Xeno Meteorus SR .60 1.25
WISUEN002 Transcendosaurus Meteorus SR .20 .40
WISUEN003 Transcendosaurus Gigantozowler SR .15 .30
WISUEN004 Transcendosaurus Glaciasaurus R .12 .25
WISUEN005 Transcendosaurus Drillygnathus R .12 .25
WISUEN006 Ground Xeno UR 20.00 40.00
WISUEN007 Supersoaring R .12 .25
WISUEN008 Frostosaurus R .12 .25
WISUEN009 Ultimate Conductor Tyranno CR 40.00 80.00
WISUEN009 Ultimate Conductor Tyranno R .12 .25
WISUEN010 Giant Rex R .12 .25
WISUEN011 Miscellaneousaurus R .12 .25
WISUEN012 Souleating Oviraptor CR 40.00 80.00
WISUEN012 Souleating Oviraptor R .12 .25
WISUEN013 Babycerasaurus R .12 .25
WISUEN014 Petiteranodon R .12 .25
WISUEN015 Evolzar Solda R .12 .25
WISUEN016 Vanquish Soul Razen CR 75.00 150.00
WISUEN016 Vanquish Soul Razen UR 15.00 30.00
WISUEN017 Vanquish Soul Pantera UR 1.25 2.50
WISUEN018 Vanquish Soul Heavy Borger CR 50.00 100.00
WISUEN018 Vanquish Soul Heavy Borger UR 10.00 20.00
WISUEN019 Vanquish Soul Dr. Mad Love CR 50.00 100.00
WISUEN019 Vanquish Soul Dr. Mad Love UR 10.00 20.00
WISUEN020 Vanquish Soul Pluton HG SR .15 .30
WISUEN021 Vanquish Soul Caesar Valius CR 60.00 125.00
WISUEN021 Vanquish Soul Caesar Valius UR 2.50 5.00
WISUEN022 Rock of the Vanquisher UR 10.00 20.00
WISUEN023 Stake Your Soul! CR 40.00 80.00
WISUEN023 Stake Your Soul! UR 10.00 20.00
WISUEN024 Vanquish Soul Dust Devil SR .15 .30
WISUEN025 Vanquish Soul - Continue? SR .15 .30
WISUEN026 Vanquish Soul Trinity Burst SR .15 .30
WISUEN027 Vanquish Soul Calamity Caesar R .12 .25
WISUEN028 Fire Formation - Tenki CR 20.00 40.00
WISUEN028 Fire Formation - Tenki R .12 .25
WISUEN029 Buerillabaisse de Nouvelles R .12 .25
WISUEN030 Confiras de Nouvelles SR .15 .30
WISUEN031 Poeltis de Nouvelles SR .20 .40
WISUEN032 Foie Glasya de Nouvelles SR .15 .30
WISUEN033 Balameuniere de Nouvelles SR .15 .30
WISUEN034 Baelgrill de Nouvelles SR .15 .30
WISUEN035 Nouvelles Restaurant At Table CR 20.00 40.00
WISUEN035 Nouvelles Restaurant At Table UR 4.00 8.00
WISUEN036 Voici la Carte UR 4.00 8.00
WISUEN037 Recette de Poisson SR .15 .30
WISUEN038 Recette de Viande SR .15 .30
WISUEN039 Recette de Personnel R .12 .25
WISUEN040 Chef's Special Recipe CR 12.50 25.00
WISUEN040 Chef's Special Recipe R .12 .25
WISUEN041 Hungry Burger CR 30.00 60.00
WISUEN041 Hungry Burger SR .15 .30
WISUEN042 Hamburger Recipe R .12 .25
WISUEN043 Impcantation Candoll R .12 .25
WISUEN044 Impcantation Talismandra R .12 .25
WISUEN045 Preparation of Rites R .20 .40
WISUEN046 Manju of the Ten Thousand Hands R .12 .25
WISUEN047 True King Lithosagym, the Disaster R .12 .25
WISUEN048 Impcantation Penciplume R .12 .25
WISUEN049 Impcantation Bookstone R .12 .25
WISUEN050 Animadorned Archosaur CR 25.00 50.00
WISUEN050 Animadorned Archosaur R .12 .25
WISUEN051 Impcantation Chalislime R .12 .25
WISUEN052 Enemy Controller R .12 .25
WISUEN053 Double Evolution Pill R .12 .25
WISUEN054 Allure of Darkness R .12 .25
WISUEN055 Fossil Dig CR 40.00 80.00
WISUEN055 Fossil Dig R .12 .25
WISUEN056 Pre-Preparation of Rites R .12 .25
WISUEN057 Lost World R .12 .25
WISUEN058 Deck Devastation Virus R .12 .25
WISUEN059 Eradicator Epidemic Virus R .12 .25
WISUEN060 There Can Be Only One CR 40.00 80.00
WISUEN060 There Can Be Only One R 40.00 80.00

2024 Yu-Gi-Oh 2-Player Starter Set

STASEN001 Elemental HERO Sparkman C .10 .25
STASEN002 Inpachi C .10 .25
STASEN003 Spirit of the Harp C .10 .25
STASEN004 Launcher Spider C .10 .25
STASEN005 Ryu-Ran C .08 .20
STASEN006 Ojama Green C .10 .25
STASEN007 Gil Garth C .12 .30
STASEN008 Ally of Justice Clausolas C .04 .10
STASEN009 Swords of Revealing Light C .10 .25
STASEN010 Back-Up Rider C .08 .20
STASEN011 Apprentice Piper C .10 .25
STASEN012 Storming Mirror Force C .20 .50
STASEN013 Scapegoat C .10 .25
STASEN014 Cardcar D C .10 .25
STASEN015 The Warrior Returning Alive C .10 .25
STASEN016 One-Time Passcode C .10 .25
STASEN017 D.D. Crow C .20 .50
STASEN018 Obsessive Uvualoop C .12 .30
STASEN019 Visas Starfrost C .10 .25
STASEN020 Mannadium Fearless C .10 .25
STASEN021 Barrier Resonator C .10 .25
STASEN022 Fissure C .10 .25
STASEN023 Mask of Darkness C .10 .25
STASEN024 Dark Hole C .10 .25
STASEN025 Kunai with Chain C .10 .25
STASEN026 Mask of the Accursed C .10 .25
STASEN027 Magic Cylinder C .20 .50
STASEN028 Mage Power C .10 .25
STASEN029 Mobius the Frost Monarch C .10 .25
STASEN030 Card Trooper C .10 .25
STASEN031 Quillbolt Hedgehog C .10 .25
STASEN032 Dark Resonator C .10 .25
STASEN033 Power Frame C .10 .25
STASEN034 White Elephant's Gift C .10 .25
STASEN035 Liberty at Last! C .10 .25
STASEN036 Phantom King Hydride C .10 .25
STASEN037 Supply Squad C .10 .25
STASEN038 Galaxy Cyclone C .10 .25
STASEN039 Mannadium Fearless C .10 .25
STASEN040 Back to the Front C .10 .25
STASEN041 Stygian Sergeants UR .12 .30
STASEN042 Coral Dragon UR .40 1.00
STASEN043 Rampaging Smashtank Rhynosaber UR .10 .25
STASEN044 Mannadium Prime-Heart UR .10 .25
STAXEN001 Queen's Knight C .08 .20
STAXEN002 Giant Soldier of Stone C .10 .25
STAXEN003 La Jinn the Mystical Genie of the Lamp C .08 .20
STAXEN004 Rabidragon C .12 .30
STAXEN005 Dark Magician C .12 .30
STAXEN006 Ojama Yellow C .12 .30
STAXEN007 Swordstalker C .10 .25
STAXEN008 Trade-In C .10 .25
STAXEN009 No Entry!! C .12 .30
STAXEN010 Draining Shield C .10 .25
STAXEN011 White Ninja C .12 .30
STAXEN012 Thousand Knives C .12 .30
STAXEN013 Cost Down C .10 .25
STAXEN014 Call of the Haunted C .10 .25
STAXEN015 Cyber Dragon C .10 .25
STAXEN016 Eldlich the Golden Lord C .10 .25
STAXEN017 Skill Successor C .12 .30
STAXEN018 Crane Crane C .08 .20
STAXEN019 Xyz Reborn C .10 .25
STAXEN020 Dark Magician Girl C .15 .40
STAXEN021 Chiron the Mage C .10 .25
STAXEN022 Magician of Faith C .10 .25
STAXEN023 Penguin Soldier C .10 .25
STAXEN024 Mystical Space Typhoon C .20 .50
STAXEN025 Book of Moon C .20 .50
STAXEN026 Needle Ceiling C .10 .25
STAXEN027 Gravity Axe - Grarl C .10 .25
STAXEN028 Dark Factory of Mass Production C .10 .25
STAXEN029 Gyroid C .01 .08
STAXEN030 Swing of Memories C .10 .25
STAXEN031 Beast King Barbaros C .10 .25
STAXEN032 Burden of the Mighty C .10 .25
STAXEN033 Fighting Spirit C .10 .25
STAXEN034 Gagaga Magician C .12 .30
STAXEN035 Star Changer C .10 .25
STAXEN036 Attraffic Control C .10 .25
STAXEN037 Night Beam C .10 .25
STAXEN038 Star Drawing C .10 .25
STAXEN039 Magical Broker C .08 .20
STAXEN040 Fierce Tiger Monghu C .10 .25
STAXEN041 Daigusto Emeral UR .10 .25
STAXEN042 Number 20: Giga-Brilliant UR .10 .25
STAXEN043 Castel, the Skyblaster Musketeer UR .10 .25
STAXEN044 Divine Arsenal AA-ZEUS - Sky Thunder UR 5.00 12.00

2024 Yu-Gi-Oh 25th Anniversary Ultimate Kaiba Set

KC01EN000 Blue-Eyes White Dragon QCSCR 125.00 300.00
KC01EN001 Attack Guidance Armor UR 50.00 120.00
KC01EN002 Life Shaver UR 25.00 60.00
KC01EN003 Magical Trick Mirror UR 30.00 80.00
KC01EN004 Blue-Eyes White Dragon UR 5.00 12.00
KC01EN005 Hyozanryu UR 2.00 5.00
KC01EN006 Judge Man UR 2.50 6.00
KC01EN007 Swordstalker UR 10.00 25.00
KC01EN008 Steel Ogre Grotto #2 UR 1.50 4.00
KC01EN009 Gyakutenno Megami UR 3.00 8.00
KC01EN010 Gadget Soldier UR 2.50 6.00
KC01EN011 Rude Kaiser UR 4.00 10.00
KC01EN012 Vorse Raider UR 2.50 6.00
KC01EN013 X-Head Cannon UR 5.00 12.00
KC01EN014 La Jinn the Mystical Genie of the Lamp UR 2.00 5.00
KC01EN015 Battle Ox UR 8.00 20.00
KC01EN016 Ryu-Kishin Powered UR 3.00 8.00
KC01EN017 Mystic Horseman UR 2.00 5.00
KC01EN018 Grappler UR 10.00 25.00
KC01EN019 Hitotsu-Me Giant UR 4.00 10.00
KC01EN020 Ryu-Kishin UR 3.00 8.00
KC01EN021 Saggi the Dark Clown UR 10.00 25.00
KC01EN022 Obelisk the Tormentor UR 6.00 15.00
KC01EN023 Masked Beast Des Gardius UR 2.50 6.00
KC01EN024 Kaiser Glider UR 1.50 4.00
KC01EN025 Invitation to a Dark Sleep UR 1.50 4.00
KC01EN026 Des Feral Imp UR 2.50 6.00
KC01EN027 Blade Knight UR 3.00 8.00
KC01EN028 Y-Dragon Head UR 2.50 6.00
KC01EN029 Z-Metal Tank UR 2.50 6.00
KC01EN030 Lord of D. UR 2.00 5.00
KC01EN031 The Wicked Worm Beast UR 6.00 15.00
KC01EN032 Ancient Lamp UR 2.50 6.00
KC01EN033 Blue-Eyes Ultimate Dragon UR 4.00 10.00
KC01EN034 XYZ-Dragon Cannon UR 5.00 12.00
KC01EN035 XY-Dragon Cannon UR 3.00 8.00
KC01EN036 Rabid Horseman UR 2.50 6.00
KC01EN037 Monster Reborn OCG ART UR 20.00 50.00
KC01EN038 Polymerization UR 8.00 20.00
KC01EN039 Stop Defense UR 3.00 8.00
KC01EN040 Mesmeric Control UR 2.50 6.00
KC01EN041 The Flute of Summoning Dragon UR 2.50 6.00
KC01EN042 Soul Exchange UR 2.50 6.00
KC01EN043 Silent Doom UR 2.50 6.00
KC01EN044 Lullaby of Obedience UR 4.00 10.00
KC01EN045 Cost Down UR 1.00 2.50
KC01EN046 Card of Demise UR 5.00 12.00
KC01EN047 Fiend's Sanctuary UR 2.50 6.00
KC01EN048 Shrink UR 2.50 6.00
KC01EN049 Enemy Controller UR 6.00 15.00
KC01EN050 Megamorph UR 2.00 5.00
KC01EN051 Dark Energy UR 1.50 4.00
KC01EN052 Spell Absorption UR 2.00 5.00
KC01EN053 Crush Card Virus UR 4.00 10.00
KC01EN054 Gift of The Mystical Elf UR 2.00 5.00
KC01EN055 Ring of Destruction OCG ART UR 4.00 10.00
KC01EN056 Virus Cannon UR 1.50 4.00
KC01EN057 Interdimensional Matter Transporter UR 1.50 4.00
KC01EN058 Cloning UR 1.50 4.00
KC01EN059 Shadow Spell UR 2.00 5.00
KC01EN060 Final Attack Orders UR 4.00 10.00
KC01EN061 Negate Attack UR 4.00 10.00

2024 Yu-Gi-Oh 25th Anniversary Ultimate Kaiba Set Promo

NNO Blue-Eyes White Dragon SEC 150.00 400.00

2024 Yu-Gi-Oh Battles of Legend: Terminal Revenge 1st Edition

BLTREN001 Winged Kuriboh LV6 SCR .25 .60
BLTREN001 Winged Kuriboh LV6 QCSCR 20.00 50.00
BLTREN002 Shining Star Dragon SCR .75 2.00
BLTREN002 Shining Star Dragon QCSCR 15.00 40.00
BLTREN003 Full Armored Utopic Ray Lancer SCR .10 .25
BLTREN004 Brionac, the Magical Ice Dragon SCR 1.50 4.00
BLTREN005 Lancea, Ancestral Dragon of the Ice Mountain SCR 6.00 15.00
BLTREN005 Lancea, Ancestral Dragon of the Ice Mountain QCSCR 25.00 60.00
BLTREN006 Georgius, Swordsman of the Ice Barrier SCR .30 .75
BLTREN007 Mirror Mage of the Ice Barrier SCR 2.00 5.00
BLTREN008 Frozen Domain of the Ice Barrier UR .10 .25
BLTREN009 Arms of Genex Return Zero SCR .10 .25
BLTREN010 Repair Genex Controller SCR .12 .30
BLTREN010 Repair Genex Controller QCSCR 8.00 20.00
BLTREN011 R-Genex Undine UR .05 .12
BLTREN012 R-Genex Turing UR .05 .12
BLTREN013 Infernoid Evil SCR 2.50 6.00
BLTREN013 Infernoid Evil QCSCR 20.00 50.00
BLTREN014 Infernoid Flood SCR 1.25 3.00
BLTREN015 Void Reignition UR .10 .25
BLTREN016 Void Breach UR .10 .25
BLTREN017 Spiritual Beast Tamer Lara SCR 10.00 25.00
BLTREN017 Spiritual Beast Tamer Lara QCSCR 50.00 120.00
BLTREN018 Ritual Beast Ulti-Nochiudrago SCR .15 .40
BLTREN019 Ritual Beast Ulti-Reirautari SCR .10 .25
BLTREN020 Ritual Beast Inheritance SCR .50 1.25
BLTREN021 Toy Soldier UR .10 .25
BLTREN022 Toy Tank UR .10 .25
BLTREN023 Toy Box UR .12 .30
BLTREN024 Electro Blaster UR .08 .20
BLTREN025 Division UR .04 .10
BLTREN026 Oil SCR 2.00 5.00
BLTREN027 Ebon Sun SCR .25 .60
BLTREN028 Red Lotus King, Flame Crime SCR 6.00 15.00
BLTREN028 Red Lotus King, Flame Crime QCSCR 25.00 60.00
BLTREN029 Synchro Creed SCR .08 .20
BLTREN030 Gathering Light UR .10 .25
BLTREN031 Earthbound Resonance UR .05 .12
BLTREN032 Electrode Beast Cation UR .04 .10
BLTREN033 Electrode Beast Anion UR .04 .10
BLTREN034 Sacrifice Level-Up UR .05 .12
BLTREN035 White Circle Reef UR .10 .25
BLTREN036 Arbitration of White UR .10 .25
BLTREN037 Synchro Panic UR .05 .12
BLTREN038 Mira Match UR .04 .10
BLTREN039 Ace Spades Speculation SCR .20 .50
BLTREN040 Wonky Quartet UR .10 .25
BLTREN041 Life Hack UR .10 .25
BLTREN042 Bunch of Beast Bodies UR .10 .25
BLTREN043 Pillar of the Future - Cyanos UR .10 .25
BLTREN044 Sky Striker Ace - Azalea Temperance SCR .40 1.00
BLTREN045 Blaze, Supreme Ruler of All Dragons SCR 1.25 3.00
BLTREN045 Blaze, Supreme Ruler of All Dragons QCSCR 12.00 30.00
BLTREN046 Archfiend's Advent SCR 1.25 3.00
BLTREN046 Archfiend's Advent QCSCR 12.00 30.00
BLTREN047 Phantom of Yubel SCR 25.00 60.00
BLTREN047 Phantom of Yubel QCSCR 125.00 300.00
BLTREN048 Ancient Gear Dragon SCR .15 .40
BLTREN049 Sengenjin UR .10 .25
BLTREN050 Genex Controller UR .10 .25
BLTREN051 The Legendary Exodia Incarnate SCR .25 .60
BLTREN051 The Legendary Exodia Incarnate QCSCR 20.00 50.00
BLTREN052 The End of Anubis SCR .20 .50

BLTREN053 Guard Dog UR	.12	.30
BLTREN054 Substitoad SCR	4.00	10.00
BLTREN055 Genex Power Planner UR	.08	.20
BLTREN056 Genex Ally Duradark UR	.08	.20
BLTREN057 Genex Ally Birdman UR	.05	.12
BLTREN058 Genex Ally Birdman UR	.10	.25
BLTREN059 Scrap Goblin UR	.05	.12
BLTREN060 Infernoid Harmadik SCR	.15	.40
BLTREN061 Infernoid Patrulea UR	.10	.25
BLTREN062 Infernoid Piaty UR	.05	.12
BLTREN063 Infernoid Seitsemas UR	.10	.25
BLTREN064 Infernoid Attondel UR	.08	.20
BLTREN065 Infernoid Onuncu UR	.08	.20
BLTREN066 Spiritual Beast Rampengu UR	.20	.50
BLTREN067 Infernoid Pirmais SCR	.12	.30
BLTREN068 Infernoid Sjette UR	.08	.20
BLTREN069 Infernoid Decatron SCR	.15	.40
BLTREN069 Infernoid Decatron QCSCR	20.00	50.00
BLTREN070 Spiritual Beast Tamer Winda UR	.10	.25
BLTREN071 Orcust Harp Horror UR	.10	.25
BLTREN071 Orcust Harp Horror QCSCR	15.00	40.00
BLTREN072 Diviner of the Herald UR	1.25	3.00
BLTREN072 Diviner of the Herald QCSCR	40.00	100.00
BLTREN073 General Wayne of the Ice Barrier UR	.10	.25
BLTREN074 Hexa Spirit of the Ice Barrier UR	.10	.25
BLTREN075 Spright Blue UR	2.00	5.00
BLTREN076 Spright Jet UR	.10	.25
BLTREN077 Spright Pixies UR	.08	.20
BLTREN078 Spright Red UR	.10	.25
BLTREN079 Kurikara Divincarnate SCR	4.00	10.00
BLTREN080 Blazing Cartesia, the Virtuous UR	.50	1.25
BLTREN081 Icejade Ran Aegirine SCR	.40	1.00
BLTREN082 Barox UR	.10	.25
BLTREN083 Skelgon UR	.10	.25
BLTREN084 Ritual Beast Ulti-Cannahawk UR	.10	.25
BLTREN085 Ritual Beast Ulti-Cannahawk UR	.10	.25
BLTREN086 Ritual Beast Ulti-Gaiapelio SCR	.10	.25
BLTREN087 Granguignol the Dusk Dragon SCR	3.00	8.00
BLTREN088 Genex Ally Axel UR	.05	.12
BLTREN089 Ib the World Chalice Justiciar UR	.15	.40
BLTREN089 Ib the World Chalice Justiciar QCSCR	10.00	25.00
BLTREN090 Icejade Gymir Aegirine SCR	.40	1.00
BLTREN091 Gigantic Spright SCR	.50	1.25
BLTREN091 Gigantic Spright QCSCR	30.00	80.00
BLTREN092 Ritual Beast Ulti-Kimunfalcos UR	.05	.12
BLTREN093 Aromaseraphy Jasmine SCR	1.25	3.00
BLTREN093 Aromaseraphy Jasmine QCSCR	20.00	50.00
BLTREN094 Proxy F Magician SCR	.12	.30
BLTREN094 Proxy F Magician QCSCR	10.00	25.00
BLTREN095 Spright Sprind UR	.50	1.25
BLTREN095 Spright Sprind QCSCR	25.00	60.00
BLTREN096 Snatch Steal SCR	.75	2.00
BLTREN096 Snatch Steal QCSCR	30.00	80.00
BLTREN097 Medallion of the Ice Barrier UR	.10	.25
BLTREN098 Medallion of the Ice Barrier UR	.50	1.25
BLTREN099 Spirit Converter UR	.04	.10
BLTREN100 Void Vanishment SCR	.30	.75
BLTREN101 Void Imagination SCR	.12	.30
BLTREN102 Void Imagination SCR	.20	.50
BLTREN103 Freezing Chains of the Ice Barrier UR	.10	.25
BLTREN104 Spright Starter SCR	2.50	6.00
BLTREN105 Spright Gamma Burst UR	.08	.20
BLTREN106 Ritual Beast Ambush UR	.10	.25
BLTREN107 Tri-Brigade Mercourier SCR	.10	.25
BLTREN108 Springans Kitt UR	.10	.25
BLTREN109 The Golden Swordsoul UR	.05	.12
BLTREN110 Branded Lost UR	.20	.50
BLTREN111 Branded Fusion SCR	1.00	2.50
BLTREN111 Branded Fusion QCSCR	60.00	150.00
BLTREN112 Branded Sword UR	.10	.25
BLTREN113 Branded Retribution UR	.12	.30
BLTREN114 Mirrorjade the Iceblade Dragon UR	.12	.30
BLTREN115 Lubellion the Searing Dragon UR	.12	.30
BLTREN115 Lubellion the Searing Dragon QCSCR	60.00	150.00
BLTREN116 Sky Striker Ace - Raye QCSCR	75.00	200.00
BLTREN117 Sky Striker Ace - Roze QCSCR	40.00	100.00
BLTREN118 Dragon Master Magia QCSCR	300.00	800.00

2024 Yu-Gi-Oh Battles of Legends Chapter 1 1st Edition

BLC1EN011 White Aura Whale UR	.50	1.25
BLC1EN011 White Aura Whale SILVER TEXT UR	.25	.60
BLC1EN012 Judgment Dragon UR	.75	2.00
BLC1EN012 Judgment Dragon SILVER TEXT UR	.40	1.00
BLC1EN013 Minerva, the Exalted Lightsworn UR	1.50	4.00
BLC1EN013 Minerva, the Exalted Lightsworn SILVER TEXT UR	.50	1.25
BLC1EN014 Sage with Eyes of Blue UR	2.50	6.00
BLC1EN014 Sage with Eyes of Blue SILVER TEXT UR	2.00	5.00
BLC1EN015 Evilswarm Exciton Knight UR	1.50	4.00
BLC1EN015 Evilswarm Exciton Knight SILVER TEXT UR	.60	1.50
BLC1EN016 Orgoth the Relentless UR	.20	.50
BLC1EN016 Orgoth the Relentless SILVER TEXT UR	.12	.30
BLC1EN017 Flying Elephant UR	.20	.50
BLC1EN017 Flying Elephant SILVER TEXT UR	.10	.25
BLC1EN018 Number 90: Galaxy Eyes Photon Lord UR	5.00	12.00
BLC1EN018 Number 90: Galaxy Eyes Photon Lord SILVER TEXT UR	4.00	10.00
BLC1EN019 Borrelguard Dragon UR	.15	.40
BLC1EN019 Borrelguard Dragon SILVER TEXT UR	.15	.40
BLC1EN020 Cyber Dragon UR	.40	1.00
BLC1EN020 Cyber Dragon SILVER TEXT UR	.25	.60
BLC1EN021 Cyber Dragon UR	.60	1.50
BLC1EN021 Cyber Dragon ALT ART SILVER TEXT UR	.30	.75
BLC1EN022 Elemental HERO Stratos UR	1.00	2.50
BLC1EN022 Elemental HERO Stratos ALT ART SILVER TEXT UR	.60	1.50
BLC1EN023 Borrelsword Dragon UR	.25	.60
BLC1EN023 Borrelsword Dragon ALT ART SILVER TEXT UR	.20	.50
BLC1EN024 Sky Striker Maneuver - Afterburners! UR	.75	2.00
BLC1EN024 Sky Striker Maneuver - Afterburners! SILVER TEXT UR	.40	1.00
BLC1EN025 Miracle Rupture SILVER TEXT UR	.10	.25
BLC1EN025 Miracle Rupture UR	.40	1.00
BLC1EN026 Chaos Emperor, the Dragon of Armageddon SILVER TEXT UR	1.00	2.50
BLC1EN026 Chaos Emperor, the Dragon of Armageddon UR	2.00	5.00
BLC1EN027 Yubel SILVER TEXT UR	4.00	10.00
BLC1EN027 Yubel UR	5.00	12.00
BLC1EN028 Yubel - Terror Incarnate SILVER TEXT UR	.60	1.50
BLC1EN028 Yubel - Terror Incarnate UR	1.50	4.00
BLC1EN029 Yubel - The Ultimate Nightmare SILVER TEXT UR	.40	1.00
BLC1EN029 Yubel - The Ultimate Nightmare UR	1.00	2.50
BLC1EN030 Destiny HERO - Malicious SILVER TEXT UR	1.00	2.50
BLC1EN030 Destiny HERO - Malicious UR	2.50	6.00
BLC1EN031 Xtra HERO Wonder Driver SILVER TEXT UR	.20	.50
BLC1EN031 Xtra HERO Wonder Driver UR	.50	1.25
BLC1EN032 E - Emergency Call SILVER TEXT UR	.50	1.25
BLC1EN032 E - Emergency Call UR	1.50	4.00
BLC1EN033 Dogoran, the Mad Flame Kaiju SILVER TEXT UR	.25	.60
BLC1EN033 Dogoran, the Mad Flame Kaiju UR	.75	2.00
BLC1EN034 Kumongous, the Sticky String Kaiju SILVER TEXT UR	.25	.60
BLC1EN034 Kumongous, the Sticky String Kaiju UR	.75	2.00
BLC1EN035 Radian, the Multidimensional Kaiju SILVER TEXT UR	.60	1.50
BLC1EN035 Radian, the Multidimensional Kaiju UR	1.50	4.00
BLC1EN036 Jizukiru, the Star Destroying Kaiju SILVER TEXT UR	.30	.75
BLC1EN036 Jizukiru, the Star Destroying Kaiju UR	.60	1.50
BLC1EN037 Number 54: Lion Heart SILVER TEXT UR	.15	.40
BLC1EN037 Number 54: Lion Heart UR	.25	.60
BLC1EN038 Number 77: The Seven Sins SILVER TEXT UR	.15	.40
BLC1EN038 Number 77: The Seven Sins UR	.40	1.00
BLC1EN039 Number 39: Utopia ALT ART SILVER TEXT UR	4.00	10.00
BLC1EN039 Number 39: Utopia UR	10.00	25.00
BLC1EN040 Gimmick Puppet Nightmare SILVER TEXT UR	.30	.75
BLC1EN040 Gimmick Puppet Nightmare UR	1.50	4.00
BLC1EN041 Harpie Perfumer SILVER TEXT UR	.30	.75
BLC1EN041 Harpie Perfumer UR	.50	1.25
BLC1EN042 Quick Launch UR	.50	1.25
BLC1EN042 Quick Launch SILVER TEXT UR	.40	1.00
BLC1EN043 Security Dragon UR	.25	.60
BLC1EN043 Security Dragon SILVER TEXT UR	.12	.30
BLC1EN044 Darkness Metal, the Dragon of Dark Steel UR	3.00	8.00
BLC1EN044 Darkness Metal, the Dragon of Dark Steel SILVER TEXT UR	2.00	5.00
BLC1EN045 Trishula, the Dragon of Icy Imprisonment UR	2.00	5.00
BLC1EN045 Trishula, the Dragon of Icy Imprisonment SILVER TEXT UR	1.00	2.50
BLC1EN046 Judgment, the Dragon of Heaven UR	2.00	5.00
BLC1EN046 Judgment, the Dragon of Heaven SILVER TEXT UR	1.25	3.00
BLC1EN047 Raidraptor - Rudder Strix C	.10	.25
BLC1EN048 Raidraptor - Final Fortress Falcon C	.08	.20
BLC1EN049 Twilight Ninja Jogen C	.08	.20
BLC1EN050 Twilight Ninja Kagen C	.08	.20
BLC1EN051 White Moray C	.05	.12
BLC1EN052 White Aura Dolphin C	.10	.25
BLC1EN053 Destiny HERO - Dreamer C	.08	.20
BLC1EN054 Destiny HERO - Dusktopia C	.10	.25
BLC1EN055 Lyla, Lightsworn Sorceress C	.15	.40
BLC1EN056 Garoth, Lightsworn Warrior C	.12	.30
BLC1EN057 Lumina, Lightsworn Summoner C	.12	.30
BLC1EN058 Wulf, Lightsworn Beast C	.60	1.50
BLC1EN059 Celestia, Lightsworn Angel C	.12	.30
BLC1EN060 Raiden, Hand of the Lightsworn C	.12	.30
BLC1EN061 Felis, Lightsworn Archer C	.15	.40
BLC1EN062 Solar Recharge C	.75	2.00
BLC1EN063 Vanity's Fiend C	.12	.30
BLC1EN064 Crusader of Endymion C	.08	.20
BLC1EN065 Cactus Bouncer C	.10	.25
BLC1EN066 Denko Sekka C	.10	.25
BLC1EN067 Galaxy Soldier C	.30	.75
BLC1EN068 Elemental HERO Nova Master C	.10	.25
BLC1EN069 Vision HERO Adoration C	.10	.25
BLC1EN070 Neo Galaxy-Eyes Photon Dragon C	.10	.25
BLC1EN071 Gaia Dragon, the Thunder Charger C	.10	.25
BLC1EN072 Number 107: Galaxy-Eyes Tachyon Dragon C	.15	.40
BLC1EN073 Raidraptor - Satellite Cannon Falcon C	.10	.25
BLC1EN074 Into the Void C	.12	.30
BLC1EN075 Miracle Contact C	.10	.25
BLC1EN076 Different Dimension Ground C	.15	.40
BLC1EN077 Water of Life C	.10	.25
BLC1EN078 Gold Moon Coin C	.10	.25
BLC1EN079 Gingerbread House C	.08	.20
BLC1EN080 Vision HERO Minimum Ray C	.10	.25
BLC1EN081 Vision HERO Multiply Guy C	.10	.25
BLC1EN082 Vision HERO Increase C	.25	.60
BLC1EN083 Vision HERO Poisoner C	.10	.25
BLC1EN084 Vision HERO Gravito C	.10	.25
BLC1EN085 Vision Release C	.10	.25
BLC1EN086 Vision Fusion C	.10	.25
BLC1EN087 Apparition C	.10	.25
BLC1EN088 T.G. Gear Zombie C	.10	.25
BLC1EN089 T.G. Drill Fish C	.10	.25
BLC1EN090 T.G. Metal Skeleton C	.10	.25
BLC1EN091 Sonic Stun C	.10	.25
BLC1EN092 Hi-Speedroid Kitedrake C	.10	.25
BLC1EN093 Harpie Conductor C	.10	.25
BLC1EN094 Hi-Speedroid Rubber Band Shooter C	.10	.25
BLC1EN095 PSY-Framelord Lambda C	.10	.25
BLC1EN096 Salamangreat Almiraj C	.15	.40
BLC1EN097 Vision HERO Vyon C	.12	.30
BLC1EN098 Vision HERO Witch Raider C	.10	.25
BLC1EN099 Vision HERO Trinity C	.10	.25
BLC1EN100 Destiny HERO - Dangerous C	.08	.20
BLC1EN101 Elemental HERO Neos Knight C	.10	.25
BLC1EN102 Dinowrestler Pankratops C	.12	.30
BLC1EN103 Interrupted Kaiju Slumber C	.12	.30
BLC1EN104 Living Fossil C	.10	.25
BLC1EN105 Cyber Emergency C	.10	.25
BLC1EN106 Born from Draconis C	.08	.20
BLC1EN107 Cyber Eltanin C	.08	.20
BLC1EN108 Cyber Larva C	.12	.30
BLC1EN109 Number 27: Dreadnought Dreadnoid C	.10	.25
BLC1EN110 Number 75: Bamboozling Gossip Shadow C	.12	.30
BLC1EN111 Iron Draw C	.10	.25
BLC1EN112 Glorious Numbers C	.10	.25
BLC1EN113 Hibernation Dragon C	.10	.25
BLC1EN114 Flash Charge Dragon C	.10	.25
BLC1EN115 The Phantom Knights of Ancient Cloak C	.10	.25
BLC1EN116 The Phantom Knights of Silent Boots C	.10	.25
BLC1EN117 Phantom Knights' Fog Blade C	.12	.30
BLC1EN118 Altergeist Manifestation C	.08	.20
BLC1EN119 PSY-Frame Driver C	.10	.25
BLC1EN120 Elemental HERO Honest Neos C	.12	.30
BLC1EN121 Preparation of Rites C	.10	.25
BLC1EN122 Kyoutou Waterfront C	.10	.25
BLC1EN123 The Kaiju Files C	.08	.20
BLC1EN124 Union Hangar C	.10	.25
BLC1EN125 Dragonic Diagram C	.12	.30
BLC1EN126 Dark Spell Regeneration C	.10	.25
BLC1EN127 Powered Crawler C	.10	.25
BLC1EN128 Weathering Soldier C	.10	.25
BLC1EN129 Fossil Warrior Skull King C	.10	.25
BLC1EN130 Fossil Warrior Skull Knight C	.12	.30
BLC1EN131 Fossil Warrior Skull Bone C	.10	.25
BLC1EN132 Fossil Dragon Skullgios C	.10	.25
BLC1EN133 Fossil Dragon Skullgar C	.10	.25
BLC1EN134 Fossil Fusion C	.10	.25
BLC1EN135 Time Stream C	.10	.25
BLC1EN136 Specimen Inspection C	.10	.25
BLC1EN137 High Rate Draw C	.10	.25
BLC1EN138 Elemental HERO Neos Alius C	.10	.25
BLC1EN139 Elemental HERO Shining Flare Wingman C	.10	.25
BLC1EN140 Elemental HERO Chaos Neos C	.08	.20
BLC1EN141 Elemental HERO Escuridao C	.12	.30
BLC1EN142 Black Whirlwind C	.15	.40
BLC1EN143 Blackwing - Kris the Crack of Dawn C	.10	.25
BLC1EN144 Assault Blackwing - Sohaya the Rain Storm C	.05	.12
BLC1EN145 Steam Synchron C	.10	.25
BLC1EN146 Junk Anchor C	.10	.25
BLC1EN147 Kalantosa, Mystical Beast of the Forest C	.08	.20
BLC1EN148 Valerifawn, Mystical Beast of the Forest C	.08	.20
BLC1EN149 Number C92: Heart-eartH Chaos Dragon C	.08	.20
BLC1EN150 Number S39: Utopia the Lightning C	.10	.25
BLC1EN151 Number 84: Pain Gainer C	.12	.30
BLC1EN152 Elemental HERO Prisma C	.40	1.00
BLC1EN153 Destiny HERO - Denier C	.10	.25
BLC1EN154 Elemental HERO Gaia C	.40	1.00
BLC1EN155 Elemental HERO Sunrise C	.15	.40
BLC1EN156 Xtra HERO Dread Decimator C	.12	.30
BLC1EN157 Xtra HERO Cross Crusader C	.25	.60
BLC1EN158 A Hero Lives C	.10	.25
BLC1EN159 Fusion Destiny C	.30	.75
BLC1EN160 Gren Maju Da Eiza C	.10	.25
BLC1EN161 Chronomaly Tuspa Rocket C	.08	.20
BLC1EN162 White Aura Bihamut C	.10	.25
BLC1EN163 SPYRAL Double Helix C	.10	.25

2024 Yu-Gi-Oh Battles of Legends Chapter 1 Limited Edition

BLC1EN001 Number 11: Big Eye SEC	1.50	4.00
BLC1EN002 Black Luster Soldier - Soldier of Chaos SEC	2.00	5.00
BLC1EN003 Elemental HERO Stratos SEC	3.00	8.00
BLC1EN004 Elemental HERO Absolute Zero SEC	5.00	12.00
BLC1EN005 Gameciel, the Sea Turtle Kaiju SEC	2.00	5.00
BLC1EN006 Dark Armed, the Dragon of Annihilation SEC	1.25	3.00
BLC1EN007 Neos Wiseman SEC	.60	1.50
BLC1EN008 Timelord Progenitor Vorpgate SEC	1.50	4.00
BLC1EN009 Xtra HERO Internal Devicer SEC	1.50	4.00
BLC1EN010 Cyber Slash Harpie Lady SEC	1.50	4.00

2024 Yu-Gi-Oh Legacy of Destruction 1st Edition

LEDEEN000 Magicians of Bonds and Unity QCSCR	40.00	100.00
LEDEEN001 Gandora-G the Dragon of Destruction SCR	3.00	8.00
LEDEEN001 Gandora-G the Dragon of Destruction QCSCR	20.00	50.00
LEDEEN002 Silent Swordsman Zero UR	.60	1.50
LEDEEN002 Silent Swordsman Zero QCSCR	15.00	40.00
LEDEEN003 Silent Magician Zero SCR	4.00	10.00
LEDEEN003 Silent Magician Zero QCSCR	20.00	50.00
LEDEEN004 Gadget Trio UR	2.00	5.00
LEDEEN004 Gadget Trio QCSCR	20.00	50.00
LEDEEN005 Moremarshmallon SR	.10	.25
LEDEEN006 Ancient Gear Dark Golem SR	.12	.30
LEDEEN007 Ancient Gear Tanker C	.05	.12
LEDEEN008 Ancient Gear Commander C	.05	.12
LEDEEN009 Refrain the Melodious Songstress C	.08	.20
LEDEEN010 Couplet the Melodious Songstress C	.05	.12
LEDEEN011 Snake-Eyes Diabellstar UR	.75	2.00
LEDEEN011 Snake-Eyes Diabellstar QCSCR	25.00	60.00
LEDEEN012 Diabellze the Original Sinkeeper SCR	5.00	12.00
LEDEEN012 Diabellze the Original Sinkeeper QCSCR	30.00	80.00
LEDEEN013 Ragnaraika the Evil Seed SCR	8.00	20.00
LEDEEN013 Ragnaraika the Evil Seed QCSCR	25.00	60.00
LEDEEN014 Ragnaraika Samurai Beetle C	.08	.20
LEDEEN015 Ragnaraika Armored Lizard C	.05	.12
LEDEEN016 Tenpai Dragon Paidra SR	5.00	12.00
LEDEEN017 Tenpai Dragon Fadra C	.10	.25
LEDEEN018 Tenpai Dragon Chundra C	.10	.25
LEDEEN019 Gruesome Grave Squirmer C	.10	.25
LEDEEN020 Gold Pride - Eliminator SR	.10	.25
LEDEEN021 Centur-Ion Gargoyle II C	.04	.10
LEDEEN022 Seletrice Vaalmonica UR	.75	2.00
LEDEEN022 Seletrice Vaalmonica QCSCR	25.00	60.00
LEDEEN023 Lightsworn Dragonling UR	60.00	150.00
LEDEEN023 Lightsworn Dragonling QCSCR	6.00	15.00
LEDEEN024 Weiss, Lightsworn Archfiend C	.10	.25
LEDEEN025 Wightlord C	.05	.12
LEDEEN026 Golgoil the Steel Seismic Smasher C	.04	.10
LEDEEN027 Mikazukinoyaiba, the Moon Fang Dragon C	.08	.20
LEDEEN028 Talons of Shurilane C	.04	.10
LEDEEN029 Nightmare Apprentice SCR	60.00	150.00
LEDEEN029 Nightmare Apprentice QCSCR	20.00	50.00
LEDEEN030 Dinovatus Docus C	.01	.08
LEDEEN031 Cyclos the Circular Sprite C	.04	.10
LEDEEN032 Fishborg Harpooner SR	.20	.50
LEDEEN033 Cooling Embers C	.05	.12
LEDEEN034 Saffira, Divine Dragon of the Voiceless Voice UR	10.00	25.00
LEDEEN034 Saffira, Divine Dragon of the Voiceless Voice QCSCR	.25	.60
LEDEEN035 Bacha the Melodious Maestra C	.08	.20
LEDEEN036 Flowering Etoile the Melodious Magnifical SR	.30	.75
LEDEEN037 Mementotlan Twin Dragon C	.08	.20
LEDEEN038 Enlightenment Dragon SR	.15	.40
LEDEEN039 Sangenpai Bident Dragion	.10	.25
LEDEEN040 Sangenpai Transcendent Dragion SR	.50	1.25
LEDEEN041 Gold Pride - Eradicator UR	8.00	20.00
LEDEEN041 Gold Pride - Eradicator QCSCR	.20	.50
LEDEEN042 Centur-Ion Auxila SCR	20.00	50.00
LEDEEN042 Centur-Ion Auxila QCSCR	2.50	6.00
LEDEEN043 Minerva, the Athenian Lightsworn UR	40.00	100.00
LEDEEN043 Minerva, the Athenian Lightsworn QCSCR	1.00	2.50
LEDEEN044 Goblin Biker Troika Griare SR	.10	.25
LEDEEN045 Varudras, the Final Bringer of the End Times SCR	50.00	120.00
LEDEEN045 Varudras, the Final Bringer of the End Times QCSCR	8.00	20.00
LEDEEN046 Tantrum Toddler C	.08	.20
LEDEEN047 Ragnaraika Skeletal Soldier C	.05	.12
LEDEEN048 Ragnaraika Mantis Monk C	.04	.10
LEDEEN049 Ragnaraika Chain Coils SR	.12	.30
LEDEEN050 Ragnaraika Stag Sovereign UR	15.00	40.00
LEDEEN050 Ragnaraika Stag Sovereign QCSCR	.25	.60
LEDEEN051 Shining Sarcophagus SCR	10.00	25.00
LEDEEN051 Shining Sarcophagus QCSCR	25.00	60.00
LEDEEN052 Turn Silence SR	.10	.25
LEDEEN053 Ties That Bind UR	.60	1.50
LEDEEN053 Ties That Bind QCSCR	10.00	25.00
LEDEEN054 Future Silence SCR	8.00	20.00
LEDEEN054 Future Silence QCSCR	25.00	60.00
LEDEEN055 Ancient Gear Advance C	.05	.12
LEDEEN056 Melodious Concerto C	.04	.10
LEDEEN057 Sinful Spoils Struggle C	.10	.25
LEDEEN058 Ragnaraika Bloom SCR	4.00	10.00
LEDEEN058 Ragnaraika Bloom QCSCR	20.00	50.00
LEDEEN059 Sangen Summoning C	.08	.20
LEDEEN060 Sangen Kaimen C	.10	.25
LEDEEN061 Nightmare Throne UR	20.00	50.00
LEDEEN061 Nightmare Throne QCSCR	100.00	250.00

LEDEEN062 Blessing of the Voiceless Voice SR .12 .30
LEDEEN063 Mementotlan Fusion C .04 .10
LEDEEN064 Wake Up Centur-Ion! UR .30 .75
LEDEEN064 Wake Up Centur-Ion! QCSCR 10.00 25.00
LEDEEN065 Vaalmonica Invitare C .05 .12
LEDEEN066 Vaalmonica Disarmonia C .04 .10
LEDEEN067 Way Where There's a Will SR .15 .40
LEDEEN068 Blink Out C .08 .20
LEDEEN069 Metaltronus SR .50 1.25
LEDEEN070 In Papa's Footsteps C .04 .10
LEDEEN071 Stronghold the Hidden Fortress C .04 .10
LEDEEN072 Ancient Gear Duel C .04 .10
LEDEEN073 Goblin Biker Grand Pileup C .05 .12
LEDEEN074 Sinful Spoils Subdual C .08 .20
LEDEEN075 Sinful Spoils of Slumber - Morrian C.10 .25
LEDEEN076 Ragnaraika Hunting Dance C .05 .12
LEDEEN077 Lightsworn Aegis C .08 .20
LEDEEN078 Mirage Mirror Force SR .10 .25
LEDEEN079 Zoma the Earthbound Spirit C .08 .20
LEDEEN080 Simultaneous Equation Cannons C .04 .10
LEDEEN081 Pyrite Knight SR .10 .25
LEDEEN082 Battleguard Echoes SR .08 .20
LEDEEN083 Double Dai C .08 .20
LEDEEN084 Krishnerd Witch C .10 .25
LEDEEN085 Jungle Dweller C .05 .12
LEDEEN086 Multi-Universe SR .10 .25
LEDEEN087 Vouiburial, the Dragon Undertaker UR.50 1.25
LEDEEN087 Vouiburial, the Dragon Undertaker QCSCR 10.00 25.00
LEDEEN088 Aiza the Dragoness of Deranged Devotion C .05 .12
LEDEEN089 Haggard Lizardose C .08 .20
LEDEEN090 Shaman of the Ashened City SR .10 .25
LEDEEN091 Spearhead of the Ashened City SR .10 .25
LEDEEN092 Veidos the Dragon of Endless Darkness UR .60 1.50
LEDEEN092 Veidos the Dragon of Endless Darkness QCSCR 15.00 40.00
LEDEEN093 Embers of the Ashened SR .10 .25
LEDEEN094 Rekindling the Ashened SR .10 .25
LEDEEN095 Extinguishing the Ashened C .04 .10
LEDEEN096 Ashened to Endlessness C .04 .10
LEDEEN097 Dandy Whitelion SR .10 .25
LEDEEN098 Pendulum Witch SR .12 .30
LEDEEN099 Code of Soul SR .12 .30
LEDEEN100 Supreme King Z-ARC - Synchro Universe SR .10 .25

2024 Yu-Gi-Oh Maze of Millennia 1st Edition

MZMIEN000 Junk Warrior QCSCR 10.00 25.00
MZMIEN001 Fighting Flame Swordsman UR 4.00 10.00
MZMIEN001 Fighting Flame Swordsman CR 10.00 25.00
MZMIEN002 Salamandra, the Flying Flame Dragon SR .20 .50
MZMIEN003 Mirage Swordsman R .10 .25
MZMIEN004 Ultimate Flame Swordsman SR .25 .60
MZMIEN004 Ultimate Flame Swordsman CR 12.00 30.00
MZMIEN005 Fighting Flame Dragon R .12 .30
MZMIEN006 Flame Swordsrealm SR .12 .30
MZMIEN007 Salamandra Fusion R .10 .25
MZMIEN008 Fighting Flame Sword UR 2.50 6.00
MZMIEN009 Salamandra with Chain R .12 .30
MZMIEN010 Flame Swordsdance R .10 .25
MZMIEN011 Eye of Illusion UR 1.25 3.00
MZMIEN011 Eye of Illusion CR 10.00 25.00
MZMIEN012 Kaitoptera SR .40 1.00
MZMIEN013 Horned Saurus R .15 .40
MZMIEN014 Clorless, Chaos King of Dark World SR .40 1.00
MZMIEN015 Arcana Force XV - The Fiend SR .12 .30
MZMIEN016 Bonfire UR 20.00 50.00
MZMIEN016 Bonfire CR 50.00 120.00
MZMIEN017 Combat Wheel R .05 .12
MZMIEN018 Ashoka Pillar SR .10 .25
MZMIEN019 Cabrera Stone R .04 .10
MZMIEN020 Triangle O R .04 .10
MZMIEN021 Totem Pole R .04 .10
MZMIEN022 Earthbound Release R .10 .25
MZMIEN023 Number 1: Infection Buzzking UR 1.25 3.00
MZMIEN023 Number 1: Infection Buzzking CR 12.00 30.00
MZMIEN024 Photon Delta Wing CR 10.00 25.00
MZMIEN024 Photon Delta Wing UR 2.00 5.00
MZMIEN025 Armored Xyz CR 10.00 25.00
MZMIEN025 Armored Xyz SR .25 .60
MZMIEN026 Ring Announcer R .08 .20
MZMIEN027 Earthbound Prisoner Ground Keeper R.20 .50
MZMIEN028 Earthbound Prisoner Stone Sweeper SR 2.50 6.00
MZMIEN029 Earthbound Prisoner Line Walker R .20 .50
MZMIEN030 Earthbound Servant Geo Kraken R .12 .30
MZMIEN031 Earthbound Servant Geo Grasha SR .10 .25
MZMIEN031 Earthbound Servant Geo Grasha CR4.00 10.00
MZMIEN032 Earthbound Servant Geo Gremlin R .10 .25
MZMIEN033 Earthbound Servant Geo Gryphon SR.12 .30
MZMIEN034 Earthbound Prison SR .20 .50
MZMIEN035 Harmonic Synchro Fusion CR 6.00 15.00
MZMIEN035 Harmonic Synchro Fusion UR 1.25 3.00
MZMIEN036 Phoenix Gearblade SR .10 .25
MZMIEN037 Drastic Draw UR .20 .50
MZMIEN037 Drastic Draw CR 2.00 5.00
MZMIEN038 Transaction Rollback UR 15.00 40.00
MZMIEN038 Transaction Rollback CR 40.00 100.00
MZMIEN039 Code Hack R .08 .20
MZMIEN040 Chimera the Flying Mythical Beast CR4.00 10.00
MZMIEN040 Chimera the Flying Mythical Beast R.08 .20
MZMIEN041 Gazelle the King of Mythical Beasts R.04 .10
MZMIEN042 Berfomet R .05 .12
MZMIEN043 Doppelwarrior R .05 .12
MZMIEN044 Jet Synchron CR 20.00 50.00
MZMIEN044 Jet Synchron R .10 .25
MZMIEN045 Satellite Synchron R .10 .25
MZMIEN046 De-Synchro R .10 .25
MZMIEN047 Synchro Chase R .04 .10
MZMIEN048 Earthbound Immortal Aslla piscu R .01 .08
MZMIEN049 Earthbound Linewalker R .04 .10
MZMIEN050 Earthbound Greater Linewalker R .04 .10
MZMIEN051 Hundred Eyes Dragon R .05 .12
MZMIEN052 Earthbound Geoglyph R .05 .12
MZMIEN053 Full Armored Crystalzero Lancer R .10 .25
MZMIEN054 Full Armored Black Ray Lancer R .05 .12
MZMIEN055 Supreme King Gate Zero R .10 .25
MZMIEN056 Supreme King Gate Infinity R .08 .20
MZMIEN057 Supreme King Dragon Darkwurm R .10 .25
MZMIEN058 Supreme King Dragon Odd-Eyes R .04 .10
MZMIEN059 Supreme King Dragon Clear Wing R.10 .25
MZMIEN060 Supreme King Dragon Dark Rebellion R .05 .12
MZMIEN061 Supreme Rage R .05 .12
MZMIEN062 Altergeist Marionetter R .04 .10
MZMIEN063 Altergeist Silquitous R .04 .10
MZMIEN064 Altergeist Meluseek R .05 .12
MZMIEN065 Altergeist Multifaker R .05 .12
MZMIEN065 Altergeist Multifaker CR 8.00 20.00
MZMIEN066 Altergeist Hexstia R .10 .25
MZMIEN067 Altergeist Primebanshee R .08 .20
MZMIEN068 Altergeist Protocol R .08 .20
MZMIEN069 Ancient Chant UR 2.00 5.00
MZMIEN069 Ancient Chant CR 6.00 15.00
MZMIEN070 Millennium Revelation R .08 .20
MZMIEN071 Sun God Unification R .04 .10
MZMIEN072 Majespecter Raccoon - Bunbuku SR.12 .30
MZMIEN072 Majespecter Raccoon - Bunbuku CR15.00 40.00
MZMIEN073 Majespecter Crow - Yata R .10 .25
MZMIEN074 Majespecter Toad - Ogama R .05 .12
MZMIEN075 Majespecter Cyclone R .10 .25
MZMIEN076 Rescue-ACE Hydrant SR 1.00 2.50
MZMIEN077 Rescue-ACE Turbulence SR .10 .25
MZMIEN078 RESCUE! R .10 .25
MZMIEN079 REINFORCE! R .10 .25
MZMIEN080 EXTINGUISH! R .08 .20
MZMIEN081 EMERGENCY! R .08 .20
MZMIEN082 CONTAIN! R .05 .12
MZMIEN083 ALERT! R .10 .25
MZMIEN084 Triple Tactics Thrust UR 30.00 80.00

2024 Yu-Gi-Oh Phantom Nightmare 1st Edition

PHNIEN000 Magicians of Bonds and Unity QCSCR 40.00 100.00
PHNIEN001 Spirit of Yubel SR 2.50 6.00
PHNIEN002 Geistgrinder Golem C .05 .12
PHNIEN003 Samsara D Lotus SR 1.25 3.00
PHNIEN004 Raidraptor - Noir Lanius C .05 .12
PHNIEN005 Raidraptor - Bloom Vulture SR .40 1.00
PHNIEN006 White Sunfish C .08 .20
PHNIEN007 White Sardine SR .40 1.00
PHNIEN008 Goblin Biker Dugg Charger UR 1.25 3.00
PHNIEN008 Goblin Biker Dugg Charger QCSCR15.00 40.00
PHNIEN009 Goblin Biker Clatter Sploder SR .15 .40
PHNIEN010 Goblin Biker Boom Mach C .10 .25
PHNIEN011 Goblin Biker Mean Merciless SR .20 .50
PHNIEN012 Snake-Eyes Poplar UR 3.00 8.00
PHNIEN012 Snake-Eyes Poplar QCSCR 40.00 100.00
PHNIEN013 Dark Guardian C .10 .25
PHNIEN014 Phantasmal Summoning Beast C .04 .10
PHNIEN015 Keaf, Murk of the Ghoti SR .10 .25
PHNIEN016 Psiics, Moonlight of the Ghoti SR .10 .25
PHNIEN017 Mementotlan Ghattic C .10 .25
PHNIEN018 Horus the Black Flame Deity SEC 1.25 3.00
PHNIEN018 Horus the Black Flame Deity QCSCR10.00 25.00
PHNIEN019 Lo, the Prayers of the Voiceless Voice SEC 10.00 25.00
PHNIEN019 Lo, the Prayers of the Voiceless Voice QCSCR 75.00 200.00
PHNIEN020 Saffira, Dragon Queen of the Voiceless Voice UR 2.50 6.00
PHNIEN020 Saffira, Dragon Queen of the Voiceless Voice QCSCR 60.00 150.00
PHNIEN021 Sauravis, Dragon Sage of the Voiceless Voice SR .12 .30
PHNIEN022 Aromalilith Rosalina SR 1.50 4.00
PHNIEN023 Majespecter Porcupine - Yamarashi SR.15 .40
PHNIEN024 Carnot the Eternal Machine UR .60 1.50
PHNIEN024 Carnot the Eternal Machine QCSCR8.00 20.00
PHNIEN025 Magmacho Dragon C .01 .08
PHNIEN026 Time Reloader C .04 .10
PHNIEN027 Berserk Archfiend C .01 .08
PHNIEN028 E Stranger Big Bang C .04 .10
PHNIEN029 Goblin Freefall Squad C .01 .08
PHNIEN030 Emissary from the House of Wax SR .20 .50
PHNIEN031 Procession of the Tea Jar C .05 .12
PHNIEN032 EM:P Meowmine UR 1.50 4.00
PHNIEN032 EM:P Meowmine QCSCR 20.00 50.00
PHNIEN033 Mokomoko C .04 .10
PHNIEN034 Principug C .04 .10
PHNIEN035 Jongleur-Ghoul Illusionist C .05 .12
PHNIEN036 Royal Rhino with Deceitful Dice C .05 .12
PHNIEN037 Skull Guardian, Protector of the Voiceless Voice UR .60 1.50
PHNIEN037 Skull Guardian, Protector of the Voiceless Voice QCSCR 50.00 120.00
PHNIEN038 Yubel - The Loving Defender Forever UR 4.00 10.00
PHNIEN038 Yubel - The Loving Defender Forever QCSCR 75.00 200.00
PHNIEN039 Aromalilith Magnolia SR .10 .25
PHNIEN040 Master of Ham C .10 .25
PHNIEN041 White Aura Porpoise C .05 .12
PHNIEN042 Enigmaster Packbit SEC 2.00 5.00
PHNIEN042 Enigmaster Packbit QCSCR 20.00 50.00
PHNIEN043 Vagnawa the Moon-Eating Dragon C.04 .10
PHNIEN044 Fish Lamp C .01 .08
PHNIEN045 Raidraptor - Rising Rebellion Falcon UR .60 1.50
PHNIEN045 Raidraptor - Rising Rebellion Falcon QCSCR 15.00 40.00
PHNIEN046 Raidraptor - Brave Strix SR .15 .40
PHNIEN047 Goblin Biker Big Gabonga SEC 1.00 2.50
PHNIEN047 Goblin Biker Big Gabonga QCSCR10.00 25.00
PHNIEN048 Goblin's Crazy Beast C .04 .10
PHNIEN049 Majespecter Draco - Ryu UR .30 .75
PHNIEN049 Majespecter Draco - Ryu QCSCR 10.00 25.00
PHNIEN050 Aromalilith Rosemary SR .12 .30
PHNIEN051 Majespecter Orthrus - Nue SEC .40 1.00
PHNIEN051 Majespecter Orthrus - Nue QCSCR20.00 50.00
PHNIEN052 Promethean Princess, Bestower of Flames UR 12.00 30.00
PHNIEN052 Promethean Princess, Bestower of Flames QCSCR 100.00 250.00
PHNIEN053 Sorcerer of Sebek C .10 .25
PHNIEN054 Nightmare Pain SR .75 2.00
PHNIEN055 Mature Chronicle C .10 .25
PHNIEN056 Rise Rank-Up-Magic Raidraptor's Force SR .15 .40
PHNIEN057 Raidraptor - Roost C .04 .10
PHNIEN058 White Reincarnation C .05 .12
PHNIEN059 Ages of Stars and Frost C .01 .08
PHNIEN060 Goblin Biker Grand Bash UR .25 .60
PHNIEN060 Goblin Biker Grand Bash QCSCR 6.00 15.00
PHNIEN061 Goblin Biker Grand Entrance SEC 2.00 5.00
PHNIEN061 Goblin Biker Grand Entrance QCSCR12.00 30.00
PHNIEN062 Dramatic Snake-Eye Chase C .10 .25
PHNIEN063 Dark Element C .08 .20
PHNIEN064 Earthbound Fusion C .08 .20
PHNIEN065 Walls of the Imperial Tomb SR .20 .50
PHNIEN066 Prayers of the Voiceless Voice C .10 .25
PHNIEN067 Barrier of the Voiceless Voice SR .20 .50
PHNIEN068 Aroma Blend C .05 .12
PHNIEN069 Majespecter Wind SR .15 .40
PHNIEN070 Mutamorphosis SEC .60 1.50
PHNIEN070 Mutamorphosis QCSCR 10.00 25.00
PHNIEN071 Materialization C .04 .10
PHNIEN072 Flock Together C .01 .08
PHNIEN073 Eternal Favorite C .10 .25
PHNIEN074 Raidraptor - Glorious Bright C .04 .10
PHNIEN075 Goblin Biker Grand Stampede C .05 .12
PHNIEN076 Radiance of the Voiceless Voice C .08 .20
PHNIEN077 Aroma Healing C .04 .10
PHNIEN078 The Black Goat Laughs SEC 10.00 25.00
PHNIEN078 The Black Goat Laughs QCSCR 50.00 120.00
PHNIEN079 Terrors of the Afterroot SR .08 .20
PHNIEN080 Iron Thunder SEC 3.00 8.00
PHNIEN080 Iron Thunder QCSCR 15.00 40.00
PHNIEN081 Psychic Processor UR .60 1.50
PHNIEN081 Psychic Processor QCSCR 10.00 25.00
PHNIEN082 Psychic Arsenal SR .10 .25
PHNIEN083 Emergency Apport C .01 .08
PHNIEN084 Conbirdable C .04 .10
PHNIEN085 Swarm of Centipedes C .04 .10
PHNIEN086 Sunset Beat SR .12 .30
PHNIEN087 Tricorn the Cacophonous Concert C .04 .10
PHNIEN088 Swallow's Cowrie C .12 .30
PHNIEN089 Xyz Force C .05 .12
PHNIEN090 Veidos the Eruption Dragon of Extinction SEC 10.00 25.00
PHNIEN090 Veidos the Eruption Dragon of Extinction QCSCR 40.00 100.00
PHNIEN091 King of the Ashened City SR .20 .50
PHNIEN092 Hero of the Ashened City SR .20 .50
PHNIEN093 Priestess of the Ashened City UR 2.00 5.00
PHNIEN093 Priestess of the Ashened City QCSCR20.00 50.00
PHNIEN094 Obsidim, the Ashened City SR .40 1.00
PHNIEN095 Awakening of Veidos UR 12.00 30.00
PHNIEN095 Awakening of Veidos QCSCR 2.00 5.00
PHNIEN096 Ashened for Eternity C .04 .10
PHNIEN097 Three-Eyed Ghost C .04 .10
PHNIEN098 Mystic Potato C .01 .08
PHNIEN099 Junk Dragonlet C .05 .12
PHNIEN100 Ultimeat Offering C .08 .20

2024 Yu-Gi-Oh The Infinite Forbidden

INFOEN000 Dragon of Pride and Soul QCSCR 30.00 80.00
INFOEN001 Sengenjin Wakes from a Millennium UR 20.00 50.00
INFOEN001 Sengenjin Wakes from a Millennium QCSCR 4.00 10.00
INFOEN002 Golem that Guards the Millennium Treasures C .10 .25
INFOEN003 Shield of the Millennium Dynasty UR20.00 50.00
INFOEN003 Shield of the Millennium Dynasty QCSCR 2.00 5.00
INFOEN004 Maiden of the Millennium Moon C .10 .25
INFOEN005 Fiend Reflection of the Millennium C.10 .25
INFOEN006 Dark Magician the Magician of Black Magic UR 2.00 5.00
INFOEN006 Dark Magician the Magician of Black Magic QCSCR 30.00 80.00
INFOEN007 Gimmick Puppet Little Soldiers C .08 .20
INFOEN008 Gimmick Puppet Rouge Doll C .08 .20
INFOEN009 Gimmick Puppet Cattle Scream C .05 .12
INFOEN010 Light End Sublimation Dragon C .10 .25
INFOEN011 Dark End Evaporation Dragon C .10 .25
INFOEN012 Knight Armed Dragon, the Armored Knight Dragon C .10 .25
INFOEN013 Astellar of the White Forest SCR 15.00 40.00
INFOEN013 Astellar of the White Forest QCSCR60.00 150.00
INFOEN014 Elzette of the White Forest SCR 10.00 25.00
INFOEN014 Elzette of the White Forest QCSCR40.00 100.00
INFOEN015 Silvy of the White Forest C .08 .20
INFOEN016 Rucia of the White Forest C .08 .20
INFOEN017 Fiendsmith Engraver SCR 50.00 120.00
INFOEN017 Fiendsmith Engraver QCSCR 150.00 400.00
INFOEN018 Ragnaraika Wicked Butterfly SR .10 .25
INFOEN019 Tenpai Dragon Genroku UR 4.00 10.00
INFOEN019 Tenpai Dragon Genroku QCSCR 40.00 100.00
INFOEN020 Mementotlan Shleepy C .05 .12
INFOEN021 Centur-Ion Atrii SR .10 .25
INFOEN022 Drytron Nu II C .08 .20
INFOEN023 Lord of the Missing Barrows SR .10 .25
INFOEN024 Cosmo Queen the Queen of Prayers C.08 .20
INFOEN025 Paralyzing Mushroom C .05 .12
INFOEN026 Disablaster the Negation Fortress UR.25 .60
INFOEN026 Disablaster the Negation Fortress QCSCR 10.00 25.00
INFOEN027 Mulcharmy Purulia SCR 30.00 80.00
INFOEN027 Mulcharmy Purulia QCSCR 75.00 200.00
INFOEN028 Dora Dora C .10 .25
INFOEN029 Broomy C .05 .12
INFOEN030 Bettan Bat C .04 .10
INFOEN031 Depresspard C .04 .10
INFOEN032 Drytron Meteonis DA Draconids SR .10 .25
INFOEN033 The Unstoppable Exodia Incarnate UR1.00 2.50
INFOEN033 The Unstoppable Exodia Incarnate QCSCR 25.00 60.00
INFOEN034 Light and Darkness Dragonlord UR .75 2.00
INFOEN034 Light and Darkness Dragonlord QCSCR 20.00 50.00
INFOEN035 Fiendsmith's Lacrima C .05 .12
INFOEN036 Fiendsmith's Desirae SR .10 .25
INFOEN037 Mementomictlan Tecuhtlica - Creation King SR .10 .25
INFOEN038 Silvera, Wolf Tamer of the White Forest UR .60 1.50
INFOEN038 Silvera, Wolf Tamer of the White Forest QCSCR 25.00 60.00
INFOEN039 Rciela, Sinister Soul of the White Forest UR .50 1.25
INFOEN039 Rciela, Sinister Soul of the White Forest QCSCR 30.00 80.00
INFOEN040 Diabell, Queen of the White Forest SCR2.50 6.00
INFOEN040 Diabell, Queen of the White Forest QCSCR 25.00 60.00
INFOEN041 DPH Gendamoore C .08 .20
INFOEN042 Gimmick Puppet Fantasix Machinix SR.10 .25
INFOEN043 CXyz Gimmick Puppet Fanatix Machinix SR .10 .25
INFOEN044 Madolche Queen Tiarafraise SR .10 .25
INFOEN045 Heretical Phobos Covos SR .10 .25
INFOEN046 Fiendsmith's Requiem SCR 2.50 6.00
INFOEN046 Fiendsmith's Requiem QCSCR 40.00 100.00
INFOEN047 Fiendsmith's Sequence C .08 .20
INFOEN048 Ragnaraika Selene Snapper C .05 .12
INFOEN049 Varar, Vaalmonican Concord SR .10 .25
INFOEN050 Madolche Mini Meowcaroons C .08 .20
INFOEN051 Cosmic Tree Irmistil C .04 .10
INFOEN052 Silhouhatte Rabbit SCR 4.00 10.00
INFOEN052 Silhouhatte Rabbit QCSCR 30.00 80.00
INFOEN053 Millennium Ankh SCR 4.00 10.00
INFOEN053 Millennium Ankh QCSCR 15.00 40.00
INFOEN054 Wedju Temple UR .60 1.50
INFOEN054 Wedju Temple QCSCR 10.00 25.00
INFOEN055 Obliterate!!! Blaze SR .10 .25
INFOEN056 Mansion of the Dreadful Dolls C .08 .20
INFOEN057 Dragon's Light and Darkness C .10 .25
INFOEN058 Tales of the White Forest UR 2.50 6.00
INFOEN058 Tales of the White Forest QCSCR 25.00 60.00
INFOEN059 Beware the White Forest SR .10 .25
INFOEN060 Susurrus of the Sinful Spoils SR .10 .25
INFOEN061 Fiendsmith's Tract SCR 8.00 20.00
INFOEN061 Fiendsmith's Tract QCSCR 40.00 100.00
INFOEN062 Fiendsmith's Sanct C .05 .12
INFOEN063 Emblema Salvation C .05 .12
INFOEN064 Vesper Girsu C .10 .25
INFOEN065 Trap Gatherer C .04 .10
INFOEN066 Interdimensional Matter Forwarder C.08 .20
INFOEN067 That's 10! C .05 .12
INFOEN068 Exxod Fires of Rage SR .10 .25
INFOEN069 Dark Magic Mirror Force SR .10 .25
INFOEN070 Service Puppet Play C .08 .20
INFOEN071 Woes of the White Forest C .08 .20
INFOEN072 Fiendsmith in Paradise SR .08 .20
INFOEN073 Sangen Kaiho C .08 .20
INFOEN074 Guardian of the Voiceless Voice C .04 .10
INFOEN075 Vaalmonica Creation C .08 .20
INFOEN076 Meteoroa Drytron C .04 .10
INFOEN077 Madolche Dessert C .08 .20
INFOEN078 Dominus Purge SCR 6.00 15.00
INFOEN078 Dominus Purge QCSCR 20.00 50.00
INFOEN079 Silhouhatte UR .25 .60
INFOEN079 Silhouhatte QCSCR 8.00 20.00
INFOEN080 Three in One C .05 .12
INFOEN081 Magicolloidal Sol SR .08 .20
INFOEN082 Vulmina, Statue of the Sacred Dragon C.05 .12
INFOEN083 Kuebiko SR .05 .12
INFOEN084 Dipsea Fiend C .04 .10
INFOEN085 Necroquip Princess C .05 .12
INFOEN086 The League of Uniform Nomenclature Strikes C .05 .12
INFOEN087 Kochobo's Hinamatsuri C .05 .12
INFOEN088 Zapper Shrimp C .10 .25
INFOEN089 Aerial Eater C .08 .20
INFOEN090 Mimighoul Master UR 3.00 8.00
INFOEN090 Mimighoul Master QCSCR 20.00 50.00
INFOEN091 Mimighoul Dragon SR .12 .30
INFOEN092 Mimighoul Cerberus SR .12 .30
INFOEN093 Mimighoul Archfiend SR .12 .30
INFOEN094 Mimighoul Dungeon UR 4.00 10.00
INFOEN094 Mimighoul Dungeon QCSCR 20.00 50.00
INFOEN095 Mimighoul Maker SR .25 .60
INFOEN096 Mimighoul Room SR .12 .30
INFOEN097 Blazing Bombardment Beast C .05 .12
INFOEN098 Moon of the Closed Heaven C .10 .25
INFOEN099 Spell Card Monster Reborn SR 1.00 2.50
INFOEN100 Spell Card Soul Exchange SR .15 .40